I give thanks to my God at every remembrance

of you, praying always with joy

in my every prayer for all of you.

Philippians 1, 3–4

Presented to

_____

By

_____

On

_____

PRAY IT!

This book can change your life. The Bible's essential message is this: God **LOVES** us and wants to be in a lifelong **friendship** with us. The Bible tells the story of God's love, revealed most perfectly in Jesus' **life**, **death**, and **RESURRECTION**. Through Christ, God offers us forgiveness, freedom, companionship, and **new** life. It is a wonderful gift, but we must choose to **ACCEPT** it. How will you **respond** to that invitation?

Lord God, here I am!

You created me and know me completely.

You know all about my life—my joys and my

sufferings, my questions and my dreams.

I know you love me, even when I feel my sins

and mistakes make me unlovable.

Help me to love you, God, with all my heart,

mind, and soul, and to love all people,

even as I love myself.

Jesus, thank you for showing me how to live.

I know you want only the best for my life,

and I believe following you is the way to a

full and abundant life.

Holy Spirit, give me the courage and wisdom

to be Jesus' follower, even when it isn't easy.

Fill me with the joy and peace that comes

from doing your will.

Amen.

THE Catholic Youth Bible
REVISED

For the text of the articles and introductions
Nihil Obstat: Rev. William M. Becker, S.T.D.
Censor Deputatus
October 20, 2004
Imprimatur: †Most Rev. Bernard J. Harrington, D.D.
Bishop of Winona
October 20, 2004

For the text of the New American Bible (NAB)
OLD TESTAMENT
Nihil Obstat: Stephen J. Hartdegen, O.F.M., L.S.S.
Christian P. Ceroke, O. Carm., S.T.D.
Imprimatur: †Patrick Cardinal O'Boyle, D.D.
Archbishop of Washington
July 27, 1970

NEW TESTAMENT
Nihil Obstat: Stephen J. Hartdegen, O.F.M., L.S.S.
Censor Deputatus
Imprimatur: †James A. Hickey, S.T.D., J.C.D.
Archbishop of Washington
August 27, 1986

PSALMS
Imprimatur: Most Rev. Daniel E. Pilarczyk
President, National Conference of Catholic Bishops
October 10, 1991

Revised edition article writers: Tony Tamberino; Victor Valenzuela; Larry Schatz, F.S.C.; Lisa-Marie Calderone-Stewart; and Vikki Shepp

Article and introduction writers: Eduardo Arnouil; Lisa-Marie Calderone-Stewart; Carmen María Cervantes; Catherine Cory; Gary Dreier; Karen Emmerich; Carole Goodwin; Ron Kenney; Edward P. Kunzman; Judi Lanciotti; Joseph A. Morris, C.M.; Daniel Ponsetto; Rosa Sanchez; Larry Schatz, F.S.C.; Valerie Shields; Brian Singer-Towns; and Michael Theisen

The acknowledgments continue on page 1727.

Produced with the assistance of The Livingstone Corporation. Project staff include: Christopher D. Hudson, Ashley Taylor, Joel Bartlett, Rosalie Krusemark, Thomas Ristow, Troy Ristow, Kathleen Ristow, and Katie Gieser.

The Catholic Youth Bible, Revised
Copyright © 2005 by Saint Mary's Press, Christian Brothers Publications, 702 Terrace Heights, Winona, MN 55987-1318, www.smp.org. All rights reserved. Except for the use of NAB verses as stipulated, no part of this book may be reproduced by any means without the written permission of the publisher.

Printed in the United States of America

Printing: 9 8 7 6 5 4 3

Year: 2013 12 11 10 09 08 07 06

ISBN 0-88489-794-X, paper
ISBN 0-88489-798-2, hardcover
ISBN 0-88489-799-0, leatherette
5067201

Library of Congress Cataloging-in-Publication Data

Bible. English. New American. 2005.
The Catholic youth Bible : New American Bible including the revised Psalms and the revised New Testament / translated from the original languages with critical use of all the ancient sources.—Rev. ed.
p. cm.
ISBN 0-88489-798-2 (hardcover)—ISBN 0-88489-794-X (pbk.)—ISBN 0-88489-799-0 (leatherette)
I. Title.
BS192.3.A12004 .W56
220.5′2054-dc22

2005001257

THE
Catholic
Youth
Bible

REVISED

New American Bible
Including the Revised Psalms and the Revised New Testament
Translated from the Original Languages with Critical Use of
All the Ancient Sources

Saint Mary's Press®

Contents

The New Testament

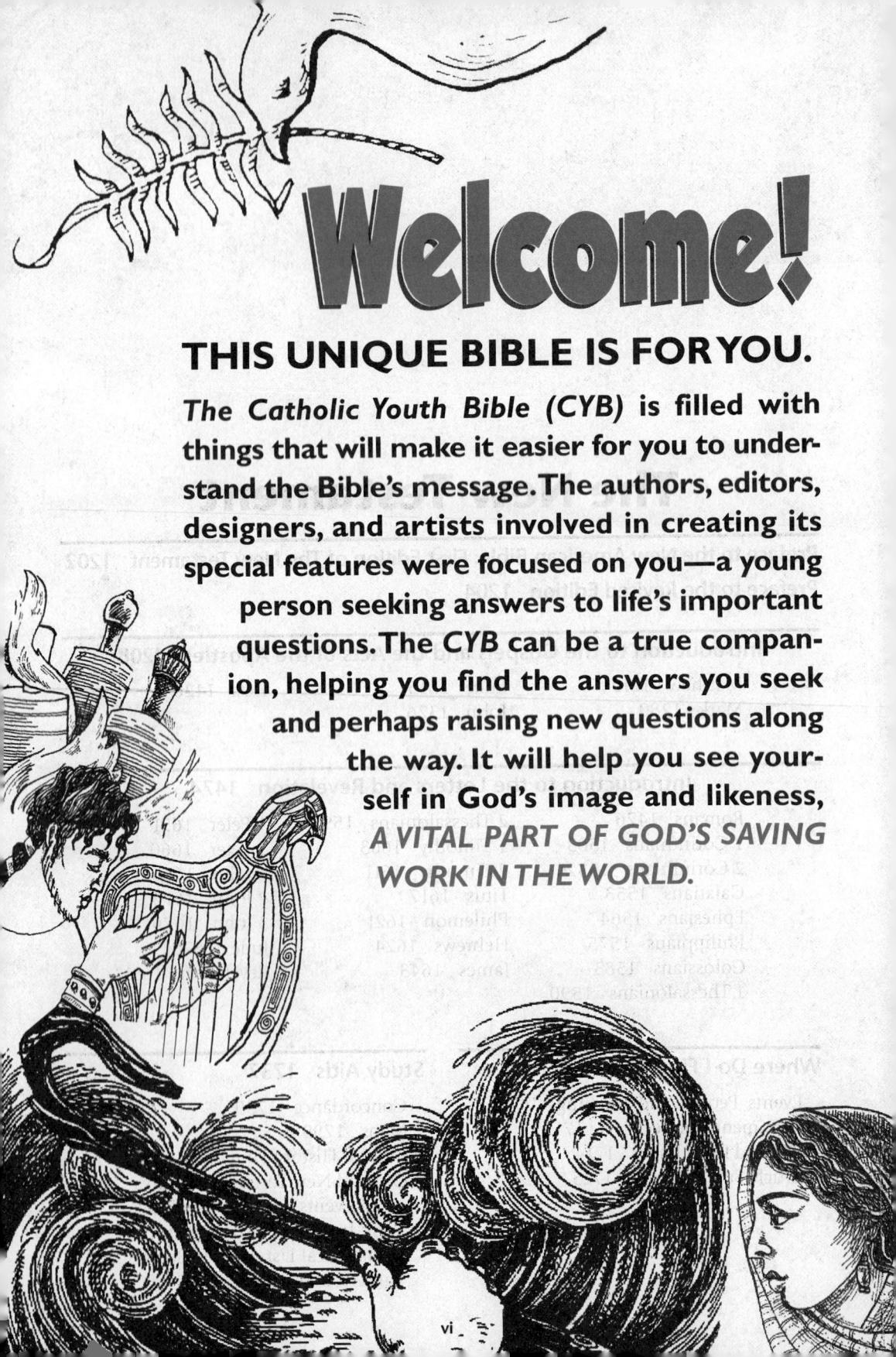

Welcome!

THIS UNIQUE BIBLE IS FOR YOU.

The Catholic Youth Bible (CYB) is filled with things that will make it easier for you to understand the Bible's message. The authors, editors, designers, and artists involved in creating its special features were focused on you—a young person seeking answers to life's important questions. The *CYB* can be a true companion, helping you find the answers you seek and perhaps raising new questions along the way. It will help you see yourself in God's image and likeness, *A VITAL PART OF GOD'S SAVING WORK IN THE WORLD.*

WHAT MAKES THIS YOUTH BIBLE *CATHOLIC?*

For starters, its introductions and articles reflect Catholic interpretation of the Bible and make connections to Catholic beliefs and traditions. In addition, this Bible contains all seventy-three books and letters that form a complete Catholic Bible, seven more than most other Bibles (see "The Case of the Missing Books," near Tb 1, 16). Does this mean that other Christians cannot use *The Catholic Youth Bible?* Not at all. When it comes to the Scriptures, Christians from all cultures and denominations have more in common than they have differences.

AS YOU USE THIS BIBLE, keep in mind two important points. The first is that the Bible is for everyone. Wherever you are in your relationship with God, *the Bible can speak to you.* The articles in the *CYB* invite you to consider what the church teaches about God's message in the Bible whether you are a committed Christian or a searcher with lots of questions.

The second point is that all the special features in *The Catholic Youth Bible* are designed to encourage you *to read the Bible itself.* It is the Bible's stories, poems, prophecies, and letters that carry this central message: *God desires a loving relationship with us.* The special features of this Bible can help you understand God's message. *BUT IT IS GOD'S WORD IN THE BIBLE THAT CAN CHANGE YOUR LIFE.*

Love one another

SPECIAL FEATURES

The Catholic Youth Bible is loaded with special features to help make it easier for you to read and understand the Bible. Here is a list of some of those features and where to find them.

HOW TO READ AND STUDY THE BIBLE

The chapter that follows this general introduction gives advice for interpreting the Bible and a process for studying the Bible alone or with a group.

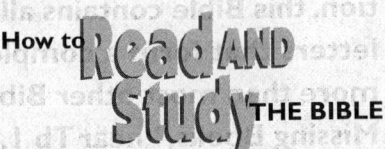

SUGGESTED READING PLANS

This chapter offers some great reading plans to get you started in studying the Bible.

SECTION INTRODUCTIONS

Each major section of the Bible (the Pentateuch, the historical books, the wisdom books, the prophetic books, the Gospels and the Acts of the Apostles, and the Letters and Revelation) begins with background on the books in that section.

BOOK INTRODUCTIONS

Introductions at the beginning of most books (sometimes two or three books share a single introduction) give insight into each book's central message and an overview of its contents. You can find more extensive book introductions in other editions of the New American Bible.

LIVE IT!

The "Live It!" articles apply the Bible's messages to situations you may be facing now or will face in the future.

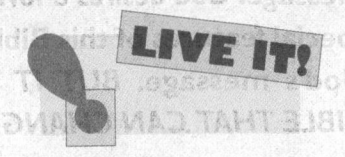

PRAY IT!

The "Pray It!" articles can help you use the Bible for personal prayer. They show the biblical basis for the prayer and sacramental life of the Catholic church.

DID YOU KNOW?

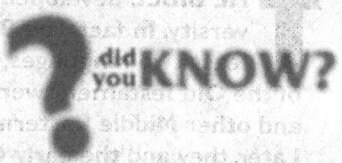

The "Did You Know?" articles provide background from biblical scholars to help you understand the culture and traditions of biblical times, or the church's interpretation of certain passages.

INTRODUCING . . .

The "Introducing . . ." articles give a quick introduction to the lives of important biblical people.

CATHOLIC CONNECTIONS

The "Catholic Connections" articles show the biblical basis for many Catholic Christian beliefs and practices.

CULTURAL CONNECTIONS

The "Cultural Connections" articles explain how people in different cultures have understood and lived out God's revelation in the Bible. The articles represent many of the diverse cultures that have found their home in the United States.

WHERE DO I FIND IT?

Several indexes are located at the back of the Bible. The first index helps you locate Bible passages on events, people, and teachings of Jesus. The second index helps you find Bible passages related to each sacrament. The third index helps you find Bible passages related to life and faith issues. The fourth index leads you to articles on specific topics.

STUDY AIDS

A concordance, color maps, a timeline, and pictures are found at the back of the Bible. The timeline and maps will help you locate where and when different biblical events occurred.

The Bible Is MULTICULTURAL

THE BIBLE developed in the midst of great cultural diversity. In fact, the Bible was originally written in at least two languages, Hebrew and Greek. The people of the Old Testament were influenced by Arabic, Egyptian, and other Middle Eastern cultures that surrounded them. Later, they and the early Christian church were influenced by the Greek and Roman cultures. In the Bible, God is revealed as the God of *all* nations and *all* cultures.

As the Word of God, the Bible's core message of God's love for human beings speaks to people of any culture. That is one reason the Bible has been translated into more languages than any other book in the world. Christians also believe that God is at work in the lives of people of every culture, whether or not they have been formally introduced to the Christian message. Listening to other cultures' experience of God can deepen Christian people's appreciation of God's message present in the Bible.

We also live in a multicultural world. *The Catholic Youth Bible* responds to this reality in two main ways. First, all the articles attempt to speak in a way that people of all cultures can appreciate and understand. Second, some articles have been specially written to represent distinct cultural perspectives. Most of these articles represent African American, Asian American, Hispanic and Latino, and Native American perspectives. The revised edition of *The Catholic Youth Bible* includes additional articles representing cultural perspectives from around the world.

All the articles share cultural experiences and traditions, religious symbols, prayers, and poetry, and they connect all these elements to the Bible. "Cultural Connections," an entry in the subject index at the back of the Bible, lists the locations of all these articles. If you would like to read articles from one of the four major cultural perspectives mentioned above, the subject index still contains entries for those.

The cultural perspectives represented in *The Catholic Youth Bible* are a small sampling of the many unique cultures in the world. Because of space restrictions, articles on many cultures could not be included. Despite these limitations, the multicultural articles can deepen your appreciation of the Bible's message and of the rich ways different cultures live that message.

NAVIGATING *The Catholic Youth Bible*

THE CATHOLIC YOUTH BIBLE has several aids to help you locate references to Bible books and the Bible's special features. The contents on pages iv–v will be your main guide in locating the different books and features. However, the last page in the color section (facing the back cover) lists all the Bible books alphabetically and gives their abbreviations and beginning page numbers. You will find this a useful and easy-to-locate guide. Also, the section "Where Do I Find It?" offers several types of indexes to help you locate specific passages and articles.

Throughout *The Catholic Youth Bible,* there are many references to specific Bible passages. These references are given in shorthand form, such as Jn 3, 16–17. The initial letters are the abbreviation for (or, in a few cases, the full name of) the Bible book. The number before the comma stands for the chapter, and the number(s) after the comma stands for the verse(s). So Jn 3, 16–17 refers to the Gospel According to John, chapter 3, verses 16 to 17.

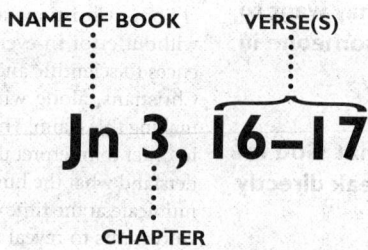

NAME OF BOOK   VERSE(S)

Jn 3, 16–17

CHAPTER

Most of the articles end with a citation identifying the Bible passage the article is based on. It is important to read the passage before reading the article.

In addition to the Bible text, you will find footnotes and Scripture cross-references printed along the bottom of each page. Every time you see an obelisk (†) in the Bible text, you will find a corresponding footnote labeled with the same chapter and verse numbers at the bottom of the page. The footnotes provide you with added information about words and phrases mentioned in the Bible. Every time you see an asterisk (*) in the Bible text, you will find a corresponding cross-reference labeled with the same chapter and verse numbers at the bottom of the page. The cross-references direct you to similar Scripture passages.

QUESTIONS AND ANSWERS About the Bible

THE BIBLE—which is also called the sacred Scriptures—tells the story of the loving relationship between God and humankind. It brings people to a deeper relationship with God, teaches important truths about Christian faith, and challenges how we live our life and relate with other people. However, studying the Bible raises questions for many people. This section gives some answers to key questions from Catholic Christian teaching. Because these are brief answers to important questions, you may want to talk more about them with someone in your family, church, or school.

What does it mean to say that God inspired the Bible? Did God speak directly to the Bible's authors?

Christians make a fantastic claim about the Bible: God is the author of the sacred Scriptures. They believe the Bible is God's word, containing the truths that God wishes to reveal to humankind for our salvation. Through the Holy Spirit, God inspired the human authors of the Bible's books to reveal these truths in their writings. These two concepts—God's **inspiration** of the biblical authors and God's **revelation** in their writings of the truths about God and God's will for us—are two important Christian beliefs about the Bible.

To say that biblical authors were inspired by God does not mean that they took dictation directly from God. They were true authors using creative literary forms to communicate the people's experience of God. In fact, many of the books had more than one author. Some books went through several decades of development in which the stories were told and retold, written down, combined, and edited. The church believes the Holy Spirit was guiding the many people involved throughout this whole process.

How do I know that what is in the Bible is true? Aren't there mistakes in the Bible?

Christians believe that the Bible is true and without errors when it teaches the things God wishes to reveal for the sake of our salvation. This is called the **inerrancy** of the Bible.

Some Christians also believe that the Bible is without error in every respect, including all references to scientific and historical facts. But Catholic Christians, along with others, are cautious about making this claim. The Catholic church teaches that in order to interpret the Bible correctly, we must understand what the human authors intended to communicate at the time of their writing. To know what God wants to reveal through their words, we must take into account "the conditions of their time and culture, the literary genres in use at that time, and the modes of feeling, speaking, and narrating then current" (*Catechism of the Catholic Church,* no. 110).

In other words, from our modern viewpoint, some statements in the Bible may seem like mistakes. But these "mistakes" may be due to the difference between a biblical author's cultural perspective and our cultural perspective. Or they may be due to our misunderstanding of a biblical author's use of literary devices such as metaphors, fiction, and poetry. Or perhaps they are due to a biblical author's different understanding of science or history. In its introductions and articles, *The Catholic Youth Bible* will help you understand the biblical authors' intentions and the church's teaching about what God is revealing through them.

Why do Catholics believe that the Bible alone isn't enough to teach all the truths about the Christian faith?

All Christians believe that God's complete revelation—all that people need to know about God and about their relation to God—is expressed in Jesus Christ. They believe that Jesus is the living Word of God, "the image of the invisible God" (Col 1, 15). All Christians believe that the Bible is a primary way of communicating God's revelation, which has its ultimate source in Christ.

But Catholic Christians believe that God's revelation is also communicated through **sacred Tradition**. Sacred Tradition, which is sometimes simply called Tradition, is all that the first Apostles learned from Jesus and the Holy Spirit. Under the guidance of the Holy Spirit, it is preserved, taught, and reinterpreted for each new generation by the Apostles' successors—the pope and bishops. Scripture and Tradition are closely related and support each other, having their common source in Jesus Christ. Some of the articles in *The Catholic Youth Bible* expand on the Bible's message with teaching from sacred Tradition.

Why does the Bible have two testaments?

The Bible reveals God's plan for humanity. It is divided into two parts. The Old Testament records the relationship between God and the descendants of Abraham, particularly the descendants of Abraham's grandson Jacob. At different times in their history, these descendants are called the Hebrews, the Israelites, and the Jews. The Old Testament contains their religious history, laws, and sacred stories. Because the Old Testament contains the sacred Scriptures of the Jewish people, many Christians also call the Old Testament the Hebrew Scriptures.

The New Testament presents Jesus as the full revelation of God. Jesus was a Jew, and he affirmed the core beliefs of the Jewish faith. He knew and cherished the Hebrew Scriptures. But he also revealed new insights into God's desired relationship with human beings. After his Resurrection, as his followers lived out the implications of his teachings, they eventually formed a new religious faith that came to

be called Christianity. The books and letters in the New Testament record their central teachings and beliefs about Jesus.

The church teaches that there is a profound unity to the Old and New Testaments in relation to God's revelation. "The Old Testament prepares for the New and the New Testament fulfills the Old; the two shed light on each other; both are true Word of God" (*Catechism*, no. 140). This is why both the Old and New Testaments are used in Catholic liturgy and catechism.

The Bible was written a long time ago. What does it have to do with my life today?

Christians believe the Bible's core message of God's desire to be in a loving relationship with human beings is greater than the difficulties caused by the passing of time and by cultural differences between the biblical era and our time. They believe that the more people read, reflect on, and study the Bible, the more they can discover what God is saying to people today. The Bible's message does not wear out or become obsolete. However, the Bible was originally written by and for people who lived in different historical circumstances. In order to make the Bible relevant to our time, people need to interpret it in its proper context (see the next chapter, "How to Read and Study the Bible," for help with this). This process of making the Bible's message current for our time is called **actualization**.

Each person, community, and culture brings its life experiences to interact with God's revelation in the Bible. God's word sheds light on our hopes and struggles and in so doing becomes a source of new life for us. Knowing that God forgives our sins, liberates us from the things that oppress and enslave us, and rejoices in our successes gives us the inner peace we all seek. The Bible tells us that we are entrusted with Jesus' mission to share God's peace, justice, and love—a mission that gives true meaning to our life.

Of course, the best way to discover what the Bible has to do with your life is to read and study it yourself. The same Holy Spirit who inspired the original authors will also be your companion as you spend time with the Bible—comforting, exciting, challenging, and encouraging you along your way.

How to Read AND Study THE BIBLE

MAKING SENSE OF THE BIBLE

> "And the Word became flesh and made his dwelling among us"
> (Jn 1, 14).

God's Word came to earth as a person, Jesus Christ. Jesus was fully human so that people could experience God's love firsthand. He was also fully God so that through him death is overcome and new life is breathed into sinful humanity.

The Bible is called God's word because it is closely linked to Jesus. Like Jesus, it can be said to be both human and divine. It is divine because it reveals to us God and God's plan. But it is also the work of human authors and reflects their knowledge, culture, and biases. It is through their words that the Bible reveals God's nature, God's saving work in the world (often called salvation history), and God's purpose for humanity—including our lives. It follows that an important part of understanding the Bible is understanding the human authors' intentions.

However, understanding the authors' intentions isn't enough either. We must also look at the message of any individual book or passage within the bigger picture of the entire Bible's message and the church's interpretation of it. Here are some suggestions for considering these different contexts when you read the Bible.

Consider the Book's Central Themes

The Bible's authors usually had a central theme or themes in mind when writing their particular book or letter. So when you are confused about the meaning of a particular verse or passage, it often helps to go back and read the whole chapter or even check out the introduction to the book. For example, you may wonder what Jesus is trying to teach us in the story of the prodigal son, Lk 15, 11–32. You might try reading from the beginning of chapter 15. You'll find that Jesus told the story in response to people who criticized him for welcoming sinners. This helps us understand that the prodigal son story teaches that we are supposed to welcome sinners too.

Consider the Historical Situation and the Audience

Certain Bible passages do not make sense unless we understand the historical situation the author was trying to address. The introductions to each of the books in *The Catholic Youth Bible* help you with this. For example, in Am 5, 21.23 God tells the people: "I hate, I spurn your feasts, I take no pleasure in your solemnities; . . . / Away with your noisy songs!" Doesn't God like worship? In the introduction to Amos, we learn that God sent Amos to speak against the rich people who exploited the poor and then attended elaborate religious festivals to worship God. The hypocrisy was what God hated.

Consider the Teaching of the Whole Bible

An old saying calls us to "use the Bible to interpret the Bible." Some people focus on a single verse from the Bible and ignore other passages on the same subject. For example, some churches will not allow women in any position of leadership. They base this on 1 Cor 14, 34, which says, "women should keep silent in the churches." But in doing this, they disregard other passages, such as those in which Paul pays respect to women who were ministers and leaders in the church.

Consider the Church's Interpretation

Most Christian churches have traditions and teachings for interpreting the Bible and applying its message. For Roman Catholics, bishops ultimately have the responsibility for properly interpreting God's revelation in the Bible. Many other people (Scripture scholars, priests, parish ministers, and teachers, for example) help us understand the bishops' interpretation of Scripture and how to apply it to our lives. *The Catholic Youth Bible* points out the Catholic church's established teaching for important passages, especially in the "Catholic Connections" articles. When in doubt, ask a priest, minister, parish leader, teacher, or parent for help in looking for the correct interpretation of a confusing passage.

HEAD AND HEART

Sometimes when you pick up the Bible, you want to study and learn. Maybe you want to learn some Bible history or understand more about Baptism. Maybe you want to know why the Gospel of John is so different from the other Gospels. These are things of the head, the intellect.

Sometimes when you pick up the Bible, you are hungry to grow closer to God. You want to experience God's presence in your life or receive guidance about a problem. These are things of the heart, the soul.

Ask God to touch both your head and heart when you read the Bible. It's important to be open to both because we were created to be whole people. *The Catholic Youth Bible* can help. Some of the articles, particularly the introductions to the books, the "Did You Know?" articles, and the "Catholic Connections" articles, give background to help your understanding for head reading. The "Live It!" and "Pray It!" articles are more for your heart reading.

THE PRIMA PROCESS

Prima is the Latin word for "first." In the PRIMA process, each letter of the word stands for a step in reading and studying the Bible individually or with a group. Using the PRIMA process helps you remember to keep God first in your life!

Pray. Begin with a prayer that your time with the Bible will draw you closer to God.

Read attentively, trusting that God will give you what you need to learn or grow.

Imagine what was going on when the passage was first written. What is its cultural and historical context? Try to put yourself into the story. What was the author trying to get across?

Meditate on what you have read. How does this fit in the context of the rest of the Bible's teaching? with the church's teaching? What do you think God is teaching you?

Apply what you have read to your life. God may be calling you to address a particular issue or relationship. Or you may find words of comfort and support you need at this particular time. Carry God's word into the rest of your day, the rest of your life!

PERSONAL AND GROUP STUDY

Personal Reading and Study

Faith is personal. Reading the Bible by yourself can help you grow in both your head and heart relationships with God. Choose a time that fits for you and make a commitment to read *The Catholic Youth Bible* regularly, at least once a week if not every day. The PRIMA process and the Bible reading plans in the next chapter will give you a structure for your personal reading.

Group Reading and Study

Your faith is personal, but it is not private. The Bible itself teaches that God calls us to be part of a Christian community. Reading and studying the Bible with a group can feed you and teach you in an exciting way. Consider starting a group Bible study by inviting some friends or family members to meet with you. Or check at your parish to see what Bible studies might already be going on.

Again, the PRIMA process and the Bible reading plans in this book can provide a structure for reading the Bible with a group. Check with your parish or school for other resources you can use with a group.

MAKING A PLAN

Note: All the reading plans described in this section are found in the next chapter, "Suggested Reading Plans."

The Catholic church has an excellent plan for reading and studying the Bible, called the lectionary. The lectionary includes a cycle of Scripture passages read at Sunday Eucharist in the liturgy of the word. It is inspiring to know that other Catholics all over the world are hearing and reflecting on the same Scriptures at the same time. Studying the Sunday lectionary readings can make a big difference in your appreciation of the Eucharist. You can use reading plan 1, "Reading the Bible with the Church," to help you do this for part of the year. It lists the Sunday lectionary readings for the entire year.

Reading whole books of the Bible is important to fully understanding the Bible in context. But it rarely works to say, "I'm going to read the whole Bible cover to cover." Most people quit when they hit the detailed laws in the Book of Exodus. So as a start, you can use reading plan 2, "A Walk Through the Bible," which gives a four-week overview of the important events in the Bible. After that you might read one of the four Gospels—Mark is good because it is short and filled with action. Then try the Acts of the Apostles. Follow this by one of the letters from the New Testament—1 Corinthians is a good one to start with. Eventually, move on to Genesis and Exodus from the Old Testament to see how their themes are connected to the New Testament books you have read.

You could also make a plan to study themes in the Bible. To get started, pick from reading plans 3 to 8, which cover topics such as sin and salvation, suffering, God's call, and women in the Bible. Or use the article subject index in the back of *The Catholic Youth Bible* to create your own reading plan on a topic that interests you.

The Church Year

THE FEAST DAYS AND HOLY DAYS celebrated by Catholics and other Christians follow a yearly pattern. This pattern is called the liturgical year; it is different from the calendar year. Here is a description of the major seasons in the liturgical year. It might help you if you also take a look at the circular diagram of the liturgical year, found on page xvii.

Advent begins the liturgical year four Sundays before Christmas. It is a time of preparation for the coming of Christ. The Advent season can be found on the liturgical year wheel in November and December. It is represented by the small graphic of an Advent wreath.

The **Christmas** season lasts twelve days, beginning with Christmas Day and concluding with the feast of the Baptism of the Lord. This season is found at the top part of the liturgical year wheel. The cross reminds us that the wood of the manger becomes the wood of the cross.

Lent begins with Ash Wednesday and lasts forty days. It is a solemn time of fasting, prayer, and almsgiving in preparation for Easter. The small picture of the palms and cross in the liturgical year wheel symbolizes all of Lent as a journey toward Palm Sunday, when the same crowd that waves palms and yells "Hosanna!" ends up waving angry fists and shouting "Crucify him!"

The **Easter Triduum** is the celebration of Holy Thursday, Good Friday, and the Easter Vigil on Holy Saturday. At this one, continuous, three-day liturgy, Christians remember the Lord's Supper, Christ's Passion and death, and his Resurrection. These feasts are at the heart of the liturgical year. They are represented by the picture of the Easter candle, which makes its appearance in the darkness of the Easter Vigil. The vestments and altar cloths seen are red on Good Friday and white on the other two days.

The **Easter** Season lasts fifty days, beginning with Easter Sunday and ending with the feast of Pentecost. The symbol of the lamb represents Jesus, the innocent sacrificial lamb of God. The symbol of the Holy Spirit reminds us that the Holy Spirit came to the disciples, in the rush of wind and tongues of fire. The altar cloths and vestments are white throughout the Easter season, and then red on Pentecost. Red is the color of the Holy Spirit (as in Confirmation Mass) and of the celebration of feast days associated with martyrs, people killed for their faith (such as the feast of Saints Peter and Paul).

The season of **Ordinary Time** is made up of the days between Christmas and Lent, and the days between Easter and Advent. The bread and wine show us that the main focus of Ordinary Time is the ministry of Jesus, represented by the grapes and bread of communion. There are some special feast days during Ordinary Time that are not celebrated with green vestments and altar cloths, such as Trinity Sunday and the Feast of the Body and Blood of Christ, the first two Sundays after Pentecost, and the Feast of Christ the King, the last Sunday before Advent. You'll see white on all three of those days. The particular dates and days these feasts fall upon vary from year to year.

Christmas is always December 25, so counting backwards four Sundays shows the four Sundays of Advent. Sometimes Advent includes Thanksgiving weekend, and sometimes it doesn't, depending on which day of the week Christmas is.

Easter is always the first Sunday after the first full moon in the spring. Counting backwards six Sundays and then one Wednesday shows when Ash Wednesday and Lent begin. Sometimes Easter is in March, and sometimes it is in April.

On page xviii, you will find a Bible reading plan that corresponds to the readings of the Bible heard on Sundays throughout these seasons. That is an excellent way to get to know the Bible and the liturgical year at the same time.

Suggested Reading Plans

READING PLAN 1: Reading the Bible with the Church

This reading plan lists the Sunday readings for the liturgical year.

ADVENT AND CHRISTMAS

Year A (2007, 2010, 2013)	Year B (2005, 2008, 2011)	Year C (2006, 2009, 2012)
The First Sunday of Advent		
Is 2, 1–5	Is 63, 16–17.19; 64, 2–7	Jer 33, 14–16
Rom 13, 11–14	1 Cor 1, 3–9	1 Thes 3, 12—4, 2
Mt 24, 37–44	Mk 13, 33–37	Lk 21, 25–28.34–36
The Second Sunday of Advent		
Is 11, 1–10	Is 40, 1–5.9–11	Bar 5, 1–9
Rom 15, 4–9	2 Pt 3, 8–14	Phil 1, 4–6.8–11
Mt 3, 1–12	Mk 1, 1–8	Lk 3, 1–6
The Third Sunday of Advent		
Is 35, 1–6.10	Is 61, 1–2.10–11	Zep 3, 14–18
Jas 5, 7–10	1 Thes 5, 16–24	Phil 4, 4–7
Mt 11, 2–11	Jn 1, 6–8.19–28	Lk 3, 10–18
The Fourth Sunday of Advent		
Is 7, 10–14	2 Sm 7, 1–5.8–11.14.16	Mi 5, 1–4
Rom 1, 1–7	Rom 16, 25–27	Heb 10, 5–10
Mt 1, 18–24	Lk 1, 26–38	Lk 1, 39–45
Midnight Mass *(25 December, every year, readings are the same for all cycles)*		
Is 9, 1–6	Is 9, 1–6	Is 9, 1–6
Ti 2, 11–14	Ti 2, 11–14	Ti 2, 11–14
Lk 2, 1–14	Lk 2, 1–14	Lk 2, 1–14
Feast of the Holy Family		
Sir 3, 2–7.12–14	Sir 3, 2–7.12–14	Sir 3, 2–7.12–14
Col 3, 12–21	Col 3, 12–21	Col 3, 12–21
Mt 2, 13–15.19–23	Lk 2, 22–40 or 2, 22.39–40	Lk 2, 41–52
Solemnity of Mary, Mother of God *(1 January, every year, readings are the same for all cycles)*		
Nm 6, 22–27	Nm 6, 22–27	Nm 6, 22–27
Gal 4, 4–7	Gal 4, 4–7	Gal 4, 4–7
Lk 2, 16–21	Lk 2, 16–21	Lk 2, 16–21
Epiphany *(readings are the same for all cycles)*		
Is 60, 1–6	Is 60, 1–6	Is 60, 1–6
Eph 3, 2–3.5–6	Eph 3, 2–3.5–6	Eph 3, 2–3.5–6
Mt 2, 1–12	Mt 2, 1–12	Mt 2, 1–12
Baptism of the Lord		
Is 42, 1–4.6–7	Is 42, 1–4.6–7	Is 42, 1–4.6–7
Acts 10, 34–38	Acts 10, 34–38	Acts 10, 34–38
Mt 3, 13–17	Mk 1, 7–11	Lk 3, 15–16.21–22

LENT AND EASTER

Year A (2008, 2011, 2014)	Year B (2006, 2009, 2012)	Year C (2007, 2010, 2013)
Ash Wednesday *(readings are the same for all cycles)*		
Jl 2, 12–18	Jl 2, 12–18	Jl 2, 12–18
2 Cor 5, 20—6, 2	2 Cor 5, 20—6, 2	2 Cor 5, 20—6, 2
Mt 6, 1–6.16–18	Mt 6, 1–6.16–18	Mt 6, 1–6.16–18
The First Sunday of Lent		
Gn 2, 7–9; 3, 1–7	Gn 9, 8–15	Dt 26, 4–10
Rom 5, 12–19	1 Pt 3, 18–22	Rom 10, 8–13
Mt 4, 1–11	Mk 1, 12–15	Lk 4, 1–13

LENT AND EASTER (*continued*)

Year A (2008, 2011, 2014)	Year B (2006, 2009, 2012)	Year C (2007, 2010, 2013)
The Second Sunday of Lent		
Gn. 12, 1–4	Gn 22, 1–2.9.10–13.15–18	Gn 15, 5–12.17–18
2 Tm 1, 8–10	Rom 8, 31–34	Phil 3, 17–4, 1
Mt 17, 1–9	Mk 9, 2–10	Lk 9, 28–36
The Third Sunday of Lent		
Ex 17, 3–7	Ex 20, 1–17	Ex 3, 1–8.13–15
Rom 5, 1–2.5–8	1 Cor 1, 22–25	1 Cor 10, 1–6.10–12
Jn 4, 5–42	Jn 2, 13–25	Lk 13, 1–9
The Fourth Sunday of Lent		
1 Sm 16, 1.6–7.10–13	2 Chr 36, 14–17.19–23	Jos 5, 9.10–12
Eph 5, 8–14	Eph 2, 4–10	2 Cor 5, 17–21
Jn 9, 1–41	Jn 3, 14–21	Lk 15, 1–3.11–32
The Fifth Sunday of Lent		
Ez 37, 12–14	Jer 31, 31–34	Is 43, 16–21
Rom 8, 8–11	Heb 5, 7–9	Phil 3, 8–14
Jn 11, 1–45	Jn 12, 20–33	Jn 8, 1–11
Passion Sunday (Palm Sunday)		
Is 50, 4–7	Is 50, 4–7	Is 50, 4–7
Phil 2, 6–11	Phil 2, 6–11	Phil 2, 6–11
Mt 26, 14—27, 66	Mk 14, 1—15, 47	Lk 22, 14—23, 56
Holy Thursday (*readings are the same for all cycles*)		
Ex 12, 1–8.11–14	Ex 12, 1–8.11–14	Ex 12, 1–8.11–14
1 Cor 11, 23–26	1 Cor 11, 23–26	1 Cor 11, 23–26
Jn 13, 1–15	Jn 13, 1–15	Jn 13, 1–15
Good Friday (*readings are the same for all cycles*)		
Is 52, 13—53, 12	Is 52, 13—53, 12	Is 52, 13—53, 12
Heb 4, 14–16; 5, 7–9	Heb 4, 14–16; 5, 7–9	Heb 4, 14–16; 5, 7–9
Jn 18, 1—19, 42	Jn 18, 1—19, 42	Jn 18, 1—19, 42
Easter Sunday (*readings are the same for all cycles*)		
Acts 10, 34.37–43	Acts 10, 34.37–43	Acts 10, 34.37–43
Col 3, 1–4 or 1 Cor 5, 6–8	Col 3, 1–4 or 1 Cor 5, 6–8	Col 3, 1–4 or 1 Cor 5, 6–8
Jn 20, 1–9	Jn 20, 1–9	Jn 20, 1–9
Second Sunday of Easter		
Acts 2, 42–47	Acts 4, 32–35	Acts 5, 12–16
1 Pt 1, 3–9	1 Jn 5, 1–6	Rv 1, 9–11.12–13.17–19
Jn 20, 19–31	Jn 20, 19–31	Jn 20, 19–31
Third Sunday of Easter		
Acts 2, 14.22–28	Acts 3, 13–15.17–19	Acts 5, 27–32.40–41
1 Pt 1, 17–21	1 Jn 2, 1–5	Rv 5, 11–14
Lk 24, 13–35	Lk 24, 35–48	Jn 21, 1–19 or 1–14
Fourth Sunday of Easter		
Acts 2, 14.36–41	Acts 4, 8–12	Acts 13, 14.43–52
1 Pt 2, 20–25	1 Jn 3, 1–2	Rv 7, 9.14–17
Jn 10, 1–10	Jn 10, 11–18	Jn 10, 27–30
Fifth Sunday of Easter		
Acts 6, 1–7	Acts 9, 26–31	Acts 14, 21–27
1 Pt 2, 4–9	1 Jn 3, 18–24	Rv 21, 1–5
Jn 14, 1–12	Jn 15, 1–8	Jn 13, 31–35
Sixth Sunday of Easter		
Acts 8, 5–8.14–17	Acts 10, 25–26.34–35.44–48	Acts 15, 1–2.22–29
1 Pt 3, 15–18	1 Jn 4, 7–10	Rv 21, 10–14.22–23
Jn 14, 15–21	Jn 15, 9–17	Jn 14, 23–29
Seventh Sunday of Easter		
Acts 1, 12–14	Acts 1, 15–17.20–26	Acts 7, 55–60
1 Pt 4, 13–16	1 Jn 4, 11–16	Rv 22, 12–14.16–17.20
Jn 17, 1–11	Jn 17, 11–19	Jn 17, 20–26
Pentecost Sunday (*readings are the same for all cycles*)		
Acts 2, 1–11	Acts 2, 1–11	Acts 2, 1–11
1 Cor 12, 3–7.12–13	1 Cor 12, 3–7.12–13	1 Cor 12, 3–7.12–13
Jn 20, 19–23	Jn 20, 19–23	Jn 20, 19–23

ORDINARY TIME

Year A (2008, 2011, 2014)	Year B (2006, 2009, 2012)	Year C (2007, 2010, 2013)

First Sunday in Ordinary Time *(see the Feast of the Baptism of the Lord under "Advent and Christmas")*

Second Sunday in Ordinary Time

Is 49, 3.5-6	1 Sm 3, 3b-10.19	Is 62, 1-5
1 Cor 1, 1-3	1 Cor 6, 13c-15a.17-20	1 Cor 12, 4-11
Jn 1, 29-34	Jn 1, 35-42	Jn 2, 1-11

Third Sunday in Ordinary Time

Is 8, 23-9, 3	Jon 3, 1-5.10	Neh 8, 2-4a.5-6.8-10
1 Cor 1, 10-13.17	1 Cor 7, 29-31	1 Cor 12, 12-30
Mt 4, 12-23	Mk 1, 14-20	Lk 1, 1-4; 4, 14-21

Fourth Sunday in Ordinary Time

Zep 2, 3; 3, 12-13	Dt 18, 15-20	Jer 1, 4-5.17-19
1 Cor 1, 26-31	1 Cor 7, 32-35	1 Cor 12, 31-13, 13
Mt 5, 1-12a	Mk 1, 21-28	Lk 4, 21-30

Fifth Sunday in Ordinary Time

Is 58, 7-10	Jb 7, 1-4.6-7	Is 6, 1-2a.3-8
1 Cor 2, 1-5	1 Cor 9, 16-19.22-23	1 Cor 15, 1-11
Mt 5, 13-16	Mk 1, 29-39	Lk 5, 1-11

Sixth Sunday in Ordinary Time

Sir 15, 15-20	Lv 13, 1-2.44-46	Jer 17, 5-8
1 Cor 2, 6-10	1 Cor 10, 31-11, 1	1 Cor 15, 12.16-20
Mt 5, 17-37	Mk 1, 40-45	Lk 6, 17.20-26

Seventh Sunday in Ordinary Time

Lv 19, 1-2.17-18	Is 43, 18-19.21-22.24b-25	1 Sm 26, 2.7-9.12-13.22-23
1 Cor 3, 16-23	2 Cor 1, 18-22	1 Cor 15, 45-49
Mt 5, 38-48	Mk 2, 1-12	Lk 6, 27-38

Eighth Sunday in Ordinary Time

Is 49, 14-15	Hos 2, 16b.17b.21-22	Sir 27, 4-7
1 Cor 4, 1-5	2 Cor 3, 1b-6	1 Cor 15, 54-58
Mt 6, 24-34	Mk 2, 18-22	Lk 6, 39-45

Ninth Sunday in Ordinary Time

Dt 11, 18.26-28.32	Dt 5, 12-15	1 Kgs 8, 41-43
Rom 3, 21-25a.28	2 Cor 4, 6-11	Gal 1, 1-2.6-10
Mt 7, 21-27	Mk 2, 23-3, 6	Lk 7, 1-10

Tenth Sunday in Ordinary Time

Hos 6, 3-6	Gn 3, 9-15	1 Kgs 17, 17-24
Rom 4, 18-25	2 Cor 4, 13-5, 1	Gal 1, 11-19
Mt 9, 9-13	Mk 3, 20-35	Lk 7, 11-17

Eleventh Sunday in Ordinary Time

Ex 19, 2-6a	Ez 17, 22-24	2 Sm 12, 7-10.13
Rom 5, 6-11	2 Cor 5, 6-10	Gal 2, 16.19-21
Mt 9, 36-10, 8	Mk 4, 26-34	Lk 7, 36-8, 3

Twelfth Sunday in Ordinary Time

Jer 20, 10-13	Jb 38, 1.8-11	Zec 12, 10-11; 13, 1
Rom 5, 12-15	2 Cor 5, 14-17	Gal 3, 26-29
Mt 10, 26-33	Mk 4, 35-41	Lk 9, 18-24

Thirteenth Sunday in Ordinary Time

2 Kgs 4, 8-11.14-16a	Wis 1, 13-15; 2, 23-24	1 Kgs 19, 16b.19-21
Rom 6, 3-4.8-11	2 Cor 8, 7.9.13-15	Gal 5, 1.13-18
Mt 10, 37-42	Mk 5, 21-43	Lk 9, 51-62

Fourteenth Sunday in Ordinary Time

Zec 9, 9-10	Ez 2, 2-5	Is 66, 10-14c
Rom 8, 9.11-13	2 Cor 12, 7-10	Gal 6, 14-18
Mt 11, 25-30	Mk 6, 1-6	Lk 10, 1-12.17-20

Fifteenth Sunday in Ordinary Time

Is 55, 10-11	Am 7, 12-15	Dt 30, 10-14
Rom 8, 18-23	Eph 1, 3-14	Col 1, 15-20
Mt 13, 1-23	Mk 6, 7-13	Lk 10, 25-37

Sixteenth Sunday in Ordinary Time

Wis 12, 13.16-19	Jer 23, 1-6	Gn 18, 1-10a
Rom 8, 26-27	Eph 2, 13-18	Col 1, 24-28
Mt 13, 24-43	Mk 6, 30-34	Lk 10, 38-42

Seventeenth Sunday in Ordinary Time

1 Kgs 3, 5.7-12	2 Kgs 4, 42-44	Gn 18, 20-32
Rom 8, 28-30	Eph 4, 1-6	Col 2, 12-14
Mt 13, 44-52	Jn 6, 1-15	Lk 11, 1-13

Year A (2008, 2011, 2014)	Year B (2006, 2009, 2012)	Year C (2007, 2010, 2013)
Eighteenth Sunday in Ordinary Time		
Is 55, 1-3	Ex 16, 2-4.12-15	Eccl 1, 2; 2, 21-23
Rom 8, 35.37-39	Eph 4, 17.20-24	Col 3, 1-5.9-11
Mt 14, 13-21	Jn 6, 24-35	Lk 12, 13-21
Nineteenth Sunday in Ordinary Time		
1 Kgs 19, 9a.11-13a	1 Kgs 19, 4-8	Wis 18, 6-9
Rom 9, 1-5	Eph 4, 30-5, 2	Heb 11, 1-2.8-19
Mt 14, 22-33	Jn 6, 41-51	Lk 12, 32-48
Twentieth Sunday in Ordinary Time		
Is 56, 1.6-7	Prv 9, 1-6	Jer 38, 4-6.8-10
Rom 11, 13-15.29-32	Eph 5, 15-20	Heb 12, 1-4
Mt 15, 21-28	Jn 6, 51-58	Lk 12, 49-53
Twenty-First Sunday in Ordinary Time		
Is 22, 19-23	Jos 24, 1-2a.15-17.18b	Is 66, 18-21
Rom 11, 33-36	Eph 5, 21-32	Heb 12, 5-7.11-13
Mt 16, 13-20	Jn 6, 60-69	Lk 13, 22-30
Twenty-Second Sunday in Ordinary Time		
Jer 20, 7-9	Dt 4, 1-2.6-8	Sir 3, 17-18.20.28-29
Rom 12, 1-2	Jas 1, 17-18.21b-22.27	Heb 12, 18-19.22-24a
Mt 16, 21-27	Mk 7, 1-8.14-15.21-23	Lk 14, 1.7-14
Twenty-Third Sunday in Ordinary Time		
Ez 33, 7-9	Is 35, 4-7a	Wis 9, 13-18b
Rom 13, 8-10	Jas 2, 1-5	Phlm 9-10.12-17
Mt 18, 15-20	Mk 7, 31-37	Lk 14, 25-33
Twenty-Fourth Sunday in Ordinary Time		
Sir 27, 30-28, 9	Is 50, 5-9a	Ex 32, 7-11.13-14
Rom 14, 7-9	Jas 2, 14-18	1 Tm 1, 12-17
Mt 18, 21-35	Mk 8, 27-35	Lk 15, 1-32
Twenty-Fifth Sunday in Ordinary Time		
Is 55, 6-9	Wis 2, 12.17-20	Am 8, 4-7
Phil 1, 20c-24.27a	Jas 3, 16-4, 3	1 Tm 2, 1-8
Mt 20, 1-16a	Mk 9, 30-37	Lk 16, 1-13
Twenty-Sixth Sunday in Ordinary Time		
Ez 18, 25-28	Nm 11, 25-29	Am 6, 1a.4-7
Phil 2, 1-11	Jas 5, 1-6	1 Tm 6, 11-16
Mt 21, 28-32	Mk 9, 38-43.45.47-48	Lk 16, 19-31
Twenty-Seventh Sunday in Ordinary Time		
Is 5, 1-7	Gn 2, 18-24	Hb 1, 2-3; 2, 2-4
Phil 4, 6-9	Heb 2, 9-11	2 Tm 1, 6-8.13-14
Mt 21, 33-43	Mk 10, 2-16	Lk 17, 5-10
Twenty-Eighth Sunday in Ordinary Time		
Is 25, 6-10a	Wis 7, 7-11	2 Kgs 5, 14-17
Phil 4, 12-14.19-20	Heb 4, 12-13	2 Tm 2, 8-13
Mt 22, 1-14	Mk 10, 17-30	Lk 17, 11-19
Twenty-Ninth Sunday in Ordinary Time		
Is 45, 1.4-6	Is 53, 10-11	Ex 17, 8-13
1 Thes 1, 1-5b	Heb 4, 14-16	2 Tm 3, 14-4, 2
Mt 22, 15-21	Mk 10, 35-45	Lk 18, 1-8
Thirtieth Sunday in Ordinary Time		
Ex 22, 20-26	Jer 31, 7-9	Sir 35, 12-14.16-18
1 Thes 1, 5c-10	Heb 5, 1-6	2 Tm 4, 6-8.16-183
Mt 22, 34-40	Mk 10, 46-52	Lk 18, 9-14
Thirty-First Sunday in Ordinary Time		
Mal 1, 14b-2, 2b.8-10	Dt 6, 2-6	Wis 11, 22-12, 2
1 Thes 2, 7b-9.13	Heb 7, 23-28	2 Thes 1, 11-2, 2
Mt 23, 1-12	Mk 12, 28b-34	Lk 19, 1-10
Thirty-Second Sunday in Ordinary Time		
Wis 6, 12-16	1 Kgs 17, 10-16	2 Mc 7, 1-2.9-14
1 Thes 4, 13-18	Heb 9, 24-28	2 Thes 2, 16-3, 5
Mt 25, 1-13	Mk 12, 38-44	Lk 20, 27-38
Thirty-Third Sunday in Ordinary Time		
Prv 31, 10-13.19-20.30-31	Dn 12, 1-3	Mal 3, 19-20a
1 Thes 5, 1-6	Heb 10, 11-14.18	2 Thes 3, 7-12
Mt 25, 14-30	Mk 13, 24-32	Lk 21, 5-19
Thirty-Fourth Sunday in Ordinary Time (*The Solemnity of Our Lord Jesus Christ the King*)		
Ez 34, 11-12.15-17	Dn 7, 13-14	2 Sm 5, 1-3
1 Cor 15, 20-26.28	Rv 1, 5-8	Col 1, 12-20
Mt 25, 31-46	Jn 18, 33b-37	Lk 23, 35-43

READING PLAN 2:
A Walk Through the Bible

In four weeks, you can visit some of the highlights of the Bible in chronological order.

Day	Bible Reading	Story
❏ 1	Gn, chs 1–2	Creation
❏ 2	Gn, ch 3	the first sin
❏ 3	Gn 6, 5—9, 17	the Flood
❏ 4	Gn 17, 1—18, 15	God's covenant with Abraham
❏ 5	Gn, chs 37. 42–45	Joseph and his brothers
❏ 6	Ex, chs 2–4	the birth and call of Moses
❏ 7	Ex, chs 12–14	God's victory over Pharaoh
❏ 8	Ex, chs 19–20	the Covenant at Sinai and the Ten Commandments
❏ 9	Jgs, chs 13–16	Sampson
❏ 10	1 Sm, ch 17	David and Goliath
❏ 11	2 Sm, chs 6–7	God's promise to David
❏ 12	2 Chr, chs 1–3	King Solomon
❏ 13	2 Chr, chs 34–36	from King Josiah to the fall of Jerusalem
❏ 14	Ps 51, 139	David's repentance and God's presence

Day	Bible Reading	Story
❏ 15	Wis, chs 7–9	God's wisdom
❏ 16	Mi, chs 1–3	the sins of Judah and Israel
❏ 17	Is, chs 11–12	promises of hope
❏ 18	Mal, ch 3	the day of the Lord
❏ 19	Lk, ch 2	the birth and childhood of Jesus
❏ 20	Mt, chs 5–7	Jesus' Sermon on the Mount
❏ 21	Lk, chs 15–16	Jesus' parables
❏ 22	Mk, ch 15	the death of Jesus
❏ 23	Jn, ch 20	the Resurrection of Jesus
❏ 24	Acts 9, 1–22	the conversion of Saul (Paul)
❏ 25	1 Cor, chs 12–14	Christian community
❏ 26	Gal, chs 1–3	faith and the Law
❏ 27	Jas	Christian living
❏ 28	Rv, chs 21.22. Epilogue	the new heaven and the new earth

READING PLAN 5:
The Justice of God

God, it seems, has a preference for the poor. Spend a week reading about God's justice in the Old Testament, and a week in the New Testament.

Day	Bible Reading	Theme
❏ 1	Gn 1, 1—2, 3	God's Creation is good.
❏ 2	Gn, ch 45	God sides with the youngest.
❏ 3	Ex 3, 7–10	God sides with the oppressed.
❏ 4	Lv, ch 25	the Jubilee year
❏ 5	Dt 24, 10–21	God is with the least.
❏ 6	Ps 82	justice to the needy
❏ 7	Am 5, 21–24; 8, 4–10	Let justice roll down.
❏ 8	Mt 5, 43–48	Love your enemies.
❏ 9	Mt 19, 13–15	Jesus welcomes little children.
❏ 10	Mt 25, 31–46	Jesus identifies with the least.
❏ 11	Lk 1, 46–55; 6, 20–26	God reverses the world's order.
❏ 12	Lk 16, 19–31	a rich man and poor Lazarus
❏ 13	Lk 22, 24–27	Who is the greatest?
❏ 14	Jas 2, 1–13	showing favorites?

READING PLAN 6:
Sin and Salvation

The truth is, none of us is perfect—we are all sinners. But God has a plan to save us. Take a two-week journey as you walk from sin to salvation.

Day	Bible Reading	Theme
❏ 1	Gn, ch 3	the first sin
❏ 2	Gn, ch 6	evil everywhere
❏ 3	Gn 12, 1–9	God starts a relationship.
❏ 4	Ex 6, 1–9	God rescues God's people.
❏ 5	Lv, ch 4	a sacrifice for sin
❏ 6	Jn 3, 1–21	for God so loved the world
❏ 7	Mk 8, 31–38	a new sacrifice
❏ 8	Rom 7, 13–25	the predicament
❏ 9	Rom 6, 1–8. 20–23	the promise
❏ 10	Gal 3, 23–29	children of God
❏ 11	Jl 2, 12–13; 1 Jn 1, 8—2, 2	return, repent, and confess
❏ 12	Ps 51	confession prayer
❏ 13	Heb 10, 8–15	the only sacrifice
❏ 14	Mt 26, 26–28	the Eucharist

READING PLAN 3:
Images of God

God has revealed the divine self to us in many wonderful ways. Enjoy two weeks of "seeing" the different pictures of our God.

Day	Bible Reading	Picture of God
❏ 1	Gn 1, 26—3, 24	Creator
❏ 2	Ex 3, 13–15; 6, 2–3	"I AM"
❏ 3	Lv 11, 44–45; Mt 25, 31–46	holy one and judge
❏ 4	Dt, ch 20	warrior and defender
❏ 5	Ps 12, 6	advocate of the poor
❏ 6	Ps 23	great shepherd
❏ 7	Jb 42, 1–6; Jer 18, 1–11	mysterious awesome one
❏ 8	Wis 6, 12–20	feminine, wise
❏ 9	Is 49, 14–15	faithful mother
❏ 10	Jon 1, 1–2; 3, 5–10	universal God of all
❏ 11	Lk 11, 1–4	father
❏ 12	Lk, ch 15	domestic God
❏ 13	Jn 1, 1–18; Col 1, 15–20	Jesus, the Word made flesh
❏ 14	1 Cor, ch 13; 1 Jn 4, 7–8	love

READING PLAN 4:
Called by God

Throughout the Bible, God calls people to serve. You too are called to be a disciple. Take two weeks and pray about your call.

Day	Bible Reading	The One Called
❏ 1	Gn 12, 1–9	Abram (Abraham)
❏ 2	Ex 3, 1—4, 17	Moses
❏ 3	Ru	Ruth
❏ 4	1 Sm, ch 3	Samuel
❏ 5	1 Sm, ch 16	David
❏ 6	Is 43, 1–7	Isiah
❏ 7	Jer 1, 4–10	Jeremiah
❏ 8	Mt 4, 18–22	the first disciples
❏ 9	Mk 8, 31–38	any disciple
❏ 10	Lk 9, 1–6	any disciple
❏ 11	Lk 18, 18–30	a rich ruler
❏ 12	Acts 9, 1–19	Saul (Paul)
❏ 13	Eph 5, 1–20	any disciple
❏ 14	1 Pt 2, 9–17	you!

READING PLAN 7:
Why Do We Suffer?

Why God allows suffering has been a question for many of the Bible's authors. During this two-week study, look for the growing awareness that God is with us in our suffering.

Day	Bible Reading	Theme or Article Title
❏ 1	introduction to Tb	God rescues the suffering?
❏ 2	Tb, ch 3	suffering and suicide
❏ 3	Jb 1, 13–21	suffering and faith
❏ 4	the article near Job 24, 1	"A Long Debate"
❏ 5	the article near Jb 38, 1—42, 6	"Why?"
❏ 6	Ps 6	praying for deliverance
❏ 7	the article near Lam 5, 22	"Growing Through Loss"
❏ 8	Is 52, 13—53, 12	the suffering servant
❏ 9	Jn 12, 24–26	the paschal mystery
❏ 10	the article near Mk 15, 16–20	"Facing the Hard Times"
❏ 11	the article near Mt 27, 27–44	"Suffering Prayer"
❏ 12	2 Cor 1, 3–11	God's presence
❏ 13	2 Cor 11, 16–29	Paul's suffering
❏ 14	1 Pt 3, 13—4, 19	suffering as a Christian

READING PLAN 8:
Women in the Bible

In the ancient world, many people considered women to be inferior to men. But throughout the Bible, God shows otherwise. Here is a two-week look at women who have served God and the church.

Day	Bible Reading	Woman or Women
❏ 1	Gn 2, 18—3, 20	Eve
❏ 2	Gn 17, 15–16; 21, 1–7	Sarai (Sarah)
❏ 3	Ex 15, 19–21	Miriam
❏ 4	Jgs, chs 4–5	Deborah
❏ 5	Ru	Ruth
❏ 6	1 Sm 1, 1—2, 10	Hannah
❏ 7	Est, ch 8	Esther
❏ 8	Lk 1, 5–25.57–66	Elizabeth
❏ 9	Lk 1, 26—2, 20	Mary, the mother of our Lord
❏ 10	Lk 2, 36–38	Anna
❏ 11	Jn 20, 1–18	Mary Magdalene
❏ 12	Jn 11, 1–44; 12, 1–8	Mary and Martha
❏ 13	Acts 16, 11–15; ch 18	Lydia and Priscilla
❏ 14	Rom 16, 1–7	Phoebe and Junia

Preface to the New American Bible: The Old Testament

On September 30, 1943, His Holiness Pope Pius XII issued his now famous encyclical on scripture studies, *Divino afflante Spiritu*. He wrote: "We ought to explain the original text which was written by the inspired author himself and has more authority and greater weight than any, even the very best, translation whether ancient or modern. This can be done all the more easily and fruitfully if to the knowledge of languages be joined a real skill in literary criticism of the same text."

Early in 1944, in conformity with the spirit of the encyclical, and with the encouragement of Archbishop Cicognani, Apostolic Delegate to the United States, the Bishops' Committee of the Confraternity of Christian Doctrine requested members of The Catholic Biblical Association of America to translate the sacred scriptures from the original languages or from the oldest extant form of the text, and to present the sense of the biblical text in as correct a form as possible.

The first English Catholic version of the Bible, the Douay-Rheims (1582-1609/10), and its revision by Bishop Challoner (1750) were based on the Latin Vulgate. In view of the relative certainties more recently attained by textual and higher criticism, it has become increasingly desirable that contemporary translations of the sacred books into English be prepared in which due reverence for the text and strict observance of the rules of criticism would be combined.

The New American Bible has accomplished this in response to the need of the church in America today. It is the achievement of some fifty biblical scholars, the greater number of whom, though not all, are Catholics. In particular, the editors-in-chief have devoted twenty-five years to this work. The collaboration of scholars who are not Catholic fulfills the directive of the Second Vatican Council, not only that "correct translations be made into different languages especially from the original texts of the sacred books," but that, "with the approval of the church authority, these translations be produced in cooperation with separated brothers" so that "all Christians may be able to use them."

The text of the books contained in *The New American Bible* is a completely new translation throughout. From the original and the oldest available texts of the sacred books, it aims to convey as directly as possible the thought and individual style of the inspired writers. The better understanding of Hebrew and Greek, and the steady development of the science of textual criticism, the fruit of patient study since the time of St. Jerome, have allowed the translators and editors in their use of all available materials to approach more closely than ever before the sense of what the sacred authors actually wrote.

Where the translation supposes the received text—Hebrew, Aramaic, or Greek, as the case may be—ordinarily contained in the best-known editions, as the original or the oldest extant form, no additional remarks are necessary. But for those who are happily able to study the original text of the scriptures at firsthand, a supplementary series of textual notes pertaining to the Old Testament was added originally in an appendix to the typical edition. (It is now obtainable in a separate booklet from The Catholic Biblical Association of America, The Catholic University of America, Washington, DC 20064.) These notes furnish a guide in those cases in which the editorial board judges that the manuscripts in the original languages, or the evidence of the ancient versions, or some similar source, furnish the correct reading of a passage, or at least a reading more true to the original than that customarily printed in the available editions.

The Massoretic text of 1 and 2 Samuel has in numerous instances been corrected by the more ancient manuscripts Samuel a, b, and c from Cave 4 of Qumran, with the aid of important evidence from the Septuagint in both its oldest form and its Lucianic recension. Fragments of the lost Book of Tobit in Aramaic and in Hebrew, recovered from Cave 4 of Qumran, are in substantial agreement with the Sinaiticus Greek recension used for the translation of this book. The lost original Hebrew text of 1 Maccabees is replaced by its oldest extant form in Greek. Judith, 2 Maccabees, and parts of Esther are also translated from the Greek.

The basic text for the Psalms is not the Massoretic but one which the editors considered closer to the original inspired form, namely the Hebrew text underlying the new Latin Psalter of the Church, the *Liber Psalmorum* (1944[1], 1945[2]). Nevertheless they retained full liberty to establish the reading of the original text on sound critical principles.

The translation of Sirach, based on the original Hebrew as far as it is preserved and corrected from the ancient versions, is often interpreted in the light of the traditional Greek text. In the Book of Baruch the basic text is the Greek of the Septuagint, with some readings derived from an underlying Hebrew form no longer extant. In the deuterocanonical sections of Daniel (3, 24–91, chapter 13 and chapter 14 [these are Azariah, Susanna, and Bel and the Dragon respectively in WORDsearch]), the basic text is the Greek text of Theodotion, occasionally revised according to the Greek text of the Septuagint.

In some instances in the Book of Job, in Proverbs, Sirach, Isaiah, Jeremiah, Ezekiel, Hosea, Amos, Micah, Nahum, Habakkuk, and Zechariah there is good reason to believe that the original order of lines was accidentally disturbed in the transmission of the text. The verse numbers given in such cases are always those of the current Hebrew text, though the arrangement differs. In these instances the textual notes advise the reader of the difficulty. Cases of exceptional dislocation are called to the reader's attention by footnotes.

The Books of *Genesis* to *Ruth* were first published in 1952; the Wisdom Books, *Job* to *Sirach*, in 1955; the Prophetic Books, *Isaiah* to *Malachi*, in 1961; and the Historical Books, *Samuel* to *Maccabees*, in 1969. In the present edition of *Genesis* to *Ruth* there are certain new features: a general introduction to the Pentateuch, a retranslation of the text of Genesis with an introduction, cross-references, and revised textual notes, besides new and expanded exegetical notes which take into consideration the various sources or literary traditions.

The revision of *Job* to *Sirach* includes changes in strophe division in Job and Proverbs and in titles of principal parts and sections of Wisdom and Ecclesiastes. Corrections in the text of Sirach are made in Sir 39, 27—44, 17 on the basis of the Masada text, and in 51, 13–30 on the basis of the occurrence of this canticle in the Psalms scroll from Qumran Cave 11. In this typical edition, new corrections are reflected in the textual notes of Job, Proverbs, Wisdom, and Sirach. In the Psalms, the enumeration found in the Hebrew text is followed instead of the double enumeration, according to both the Hebrew and the Latin Vulgate texts, contained in the previous edition of this book.

In the Prophetic Books *Isaiah* to *Malachi*, only minor revisions have been made in the structure and wording of the texts, and in the textual notes.

The spelling of proper names in *The New American Bible* follows the customary forms found in most English Bibles since the Authorized Version.

The work of translating the Bible has been characterized as "the sacred and apostolic work of interpreting the word of God and of presenting it to the laity in translations as clear as the difficulty of the matter and the limitations of human knowledge permit" (A. G. Cicognani, Apostolic Delegate, in *The Catholic Biblical Quarterly*, 6, [1944], 389–90). In the appraisal of the present work, it is hoped that the words of the encyclical *Divino afflante Spiritu* will serve as a guide: "Let all the sons of the church bear in mind that the efforts of these resolute laborers in the vineyard of the Lord should be judged not only with equity and justice but also with the greatest charity; all moreover should abhor that intemperate zeal which imagines that whatever is new should for that very reason be opposed or suspected."

Conscious of their personal limitations for the task thus defined, those who have prepared this text cannot expect that it will be considered perfect; but they can hope that it may deepen in its readers "the right understanding of the divinely given Scriptures," and awaken in them "that piety by which it behooves us to be grateful to the God of all providence, who from the throne of his majesty has sent these books as so many personal letters to his own children" *(Divino afflante Spiritu)*.

THE *Old Testament*

Introduction to the

Pentateuch

Did you ever get to a movie late? Did you end up bothering your friends who got there on time by asking: "What's happening? Why did he do that? What did she mean by that?" Like the first crucial minutes of a movie, the five books of the Pentateuch set the stage for much of what happens in the rest of the Bible. If you are not familiar with their wonderful stories, you might find yourself asking: "What's happening? Why is he doing that? Why did she say that?" when reading later books.

In-depth

THE NAME PENTATEUCH LITERALLY MEANS A "five-part writing." Thus, the Pentateuch is the first five books of the Old Testament: Genesis, Exodus, Leviticus, Numbers, and Deuteronomy. These books are special to Jewish and Christian believers because they tell of the origins of God's people and their unique relationship with God—sometimes called salvation history. They are the blueprint needed for properly understanding the rest of the Bible. The Pentateuch introduces the idea of a single God who is responsible for all creation. It also tells that this God is active in the world and in the lives of its people and that the Israelites have been called into a special relationship with this God.

One of the central elements of the special relationship between God and the Israelites described in the Pentateuch is the Sinai Covenant. A covenant is a solemn promise between two parties, where both parties agree to fulfill certain obligations. The Sinai Covenant is the most famous one between God and Israel, with Moses as the mediator, which you will read about in Exodus. In Genesis you will read about the covenants God makes with Noah, Abraham, and Jacob, which lead to the Sinai Covenant.

Reading the Pentateuch is like appreciating a fine tapestry. When you view a tapestry from the front, all the threads combine to make a beautiful, coherent image. In the same way, an overall look at the covenants, stories, and laws in the Pentateuch forms a picture of the love relationship between God and the people of Israel. A close look at the back of a tapestry shows a chaotic mix of colors and yarn. So too a closer look at the writings in the Pentateuch reveals not one story but many.

Biblical scholars speak of four primary sources for the stories and traditions in the Pentateuch. The sources reflect four different schools of thought about Israel's relationship with God. For convenience, each source is referred to as an individual author.

- The Yahwist used Yahweh as God's name. This writer focused on the southern kingdom of Judah, used lots of stories, emphasized God's closeness to humanity, and portrayed God acting as a human person.
- The Elohist referred to God as Elohim or Lord. The Elohist wrote about the northern kingdom of Israel and was concerned about idolatry and morality. The writings of the Elohist presented God speaking through symbols such as a burning bush.
- The Deuteronomist emphasized the Law as the foundation of the kingdom of Judah. The Deuteronomist emerged toward the end of the monarchy (the time of the Israelite kings), when the Covenant Law seemed to have been forgotten.
- Finally, the Priestly writer emphasized religious rituals and the role of the priesthood. This writer portrayed God as more distant and used a more formal style. This source was written after the Babylonian Exile.

Knowing that these four sources contributed to the final form of the Pentateuch can help us understand that the Pentateuch books are not simply records of events as they occurred but rather faith accounts about the Israelites' growing relationship with God, inspired by God and told from different perspectives.

In the Pentateuch, God reveals how much God loves the human race collectively and how much God loves us personally. God wishes to be in a relationship with us today just as much as God did back then. The Pentateuch reminds us that we are all children of God.

Other Background

- Some of the most familiar stories and people of the Old Testament are found in Genesis and Exodus. Genesis includes the stories of Creation, Adam and Eve, Noah and the Flood, Abraham and Sarah, and Joseph and his brothers. Exodus contains the stories of Moses and the burning bush, Pharaoh and the ten plagues, the parting of the Red Sea, and the Ten Commandments.

- The Jews also refer to the five books of the Pentateuch as the Torah, meaning "teaching" or "instruction."

- An ancient tradition named Moses as the author of the Pentateuch. This was no doubt due to Moses' importance in the Pentateuch itself. But evidence suggests that most of the Pentateuch was written hundreds of years after Moses' death.

- The two types of writing in the Pentateuch are stories and laws. Genesis is all stories, Leviticus and Deuteronomy are mostly laws, and Exodus and Numbers are about half stories and half laws.

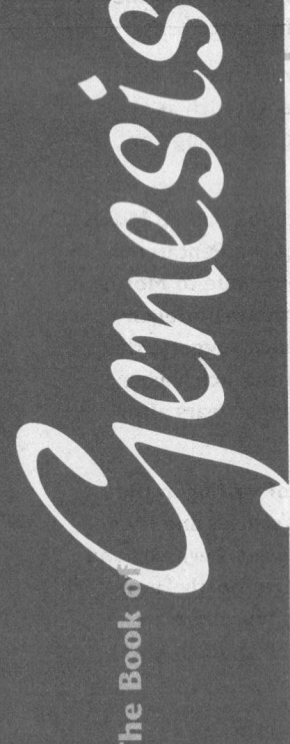

The Book of Genesis

Displays of awesome cosmic power, tender love stories, tearful family reunions, and tales of deceit, rape, murder, and worldwide destruction. Does this sound like the script for next summer's blockbuster movie? No, it's the Book of Genesis! It is the story of how a world created for love and harmony goes astray because of human sin. Through it all, God is at work, forming a people to restore what was lost.

At a Glance

I. The Primeval History (1, 1—11, 26).

II. The Patriarch Abraham (11, 27—25, 18).

III. The Patriarchs Isaac and Jacob (25, 19—36, 43).

IV. Joseph and His Brothers (37, 1—50, 26).

In-depth

Genesis gathers together inspired stories and traditions that reveal God's nature and purpose and the beginning of the Israelites' special relationship with God. Genesis has four main sections. The first section (1, 1—11, 26) contains some of the Bible's most memorable stories about Creation and the effect of sin. Chapters 1–2 tell two stories of Creation that portray the beauty and wonder of the natural world and emphasize the goodness and harmony that God intended in Creation. Creation culminates in human beings, made in God's own image. Those first human beings, Adam and Eve, live in a wonderful garden in harmony with God, Creation, and each other. But in chapter 3, sin enters the world, and as a result, Adam and Eve will experience separation, suffering, and ultimately death.

And sin spreads, first to the family (Cain and Abel in chapter 4), then to all society (Noah and the Flood in chapters 6–9). Even after the Flood and God's covenant with Noah, the story of the tower of Babel demonstrates that sin pits nation against nation. As you read these chapters, remember that they were written not as historical accounts or scientific explanations but as symbolic stories that shared faith experiences and taught important religious truths.

Sections two through four of Genesis (11, 27—50, 26) tell the story of the origins of the Israelite people. The story begins with Abraham and Sarah (originally called Abram and Sarai) and continues with Ishmael and Isaac and with Isaac and Rebekah's children, Esau and Jacob. Genesis ends with Joseph, one of Jacob's twelve sons, cleverly saving Egypt and Israel from famine. These sections introduce the covenant God makes with Abraham and remind the reader that God's plans will overcome human sin and weakness.

Quick Facts

Period Covered
The stories in the first eleven chapters are primeval history. Genesis 11, 27—50, 26 covers the period of the ancestors, or patriarchs and matriarchs (from 2000 to 1500 B.C.).

Author
An unknown author gathered oral traditions and stories from tribal peoples sometime from 1225 to 1000 B.C. (see Introduction to the Pentateuch).

Themes
the goodness of Creation, human responsibility, the effects of sin, covenant, God's bringing good out of evil

Genesis

I: The Primeval History

First Story of Creation

1 ¹*† In the beginning, when God created the heavens and the earth, ²*† the earth was a formless wasteland, and darkness covered the abyss, while a mighty wind swept over the waters.

³* Then God said, "Let there be light," and there was light. ⁴ God saw how good the light was. God then separated the light from the darkness. ⁵† God called the light "day," and the darkness he called "night." Thus evening came, and morning followed—the first day.

⁶ Then God said, "Let there be a dome in the middle of the waters, to separate one body of water from the other." And so it happened: ⁷* God made the dome, and it separated the water above the dome from the water below it. ⁸ God called the dome "the sky." Evening came, and morning followed—the second day.

⁹* Then God said, "Let the water under the sky be gathered into a single basin, so that the dry land may appear." And so it happened: the water under the sky was gathered into its basin, and the dry land appeared. ¹⁰ God called the dry land "the earth," and the basin of the water he called "the sea." God saw how good it was. ¹¹* Then God said, "Let the earth bring forth vegetation: every kind of plant that bears seed and every kind of fruit tree on earth that bears fruit with its seed in it." And so it happened: ¹² the earth brought forth every kind of plant that bears seed and every kind of fruit tree on earth that bears fruit with its seed in it. God saw how good it was. ¹³ Evening came, and morning followed—the third day.

¹⁴* Then God said: "Let there be lights in the dome of the sky, to separate day from night. Let them mark the fixed times, the days and the years, ¹⁵ and serve as luminaries in the dome of the sky, to shed light upon the earth." And so it happened: ¹⁶* God made the two great lights, the greater one to govern the day, and the lesser one to govern the night; and he made the stars. ¹⁷ God set them in the dome of the sky, to shed light upon the earth, ¹⁸ to govern the day and the night, and to separate the light from the darkness. God saw how good it was.

---

†

1, 1—2, 4a: This section introduces the whole Pentateuch. It shows how God brought an orderly universe out of primordial chaos.

1, 2: *The abyss:* the primordial ocean according to the ancient Semitic cosmogony. After God's creative activity, part of this vast body forms the salt-water seas (vv 9f); part of it is the fresh water under the earth (Ps 33, 7; Ez 31, 4), which wells forth on the earth as springs and fountains (Gn 7, 11; 8, 2; Prv 3, 20). Part of it, "the upper water" (Ps 148, 4; Dn 3, 60), is held up by the dome of the sky (Gn 1, 6f) from which rain descends on the earth (Gn 7, 11; 2 Kgs 7, 2.19; Ps 104, 13). *A mighty wind:* literally, "a wind of God," or "a spirit of God"; cf Gn 8, 1.

1, 5: In ancient Israel a day was considered to begin at sunset. Ac-cording to the highly artificial literary structure of Gn 1, 1—2, 4a, God's creative activity is divided into six days to teach the sacredness of the sabbath rest on the seventh day in the Israelite religion (Gn 2, 2f).

*

1, 1: Gn 2, 1.4; Pss 8, 4; 38—39; 90, 2; Wis 11, 17; Sir 16, 24; Jer 10, 12; 2 Mc 7, 28; Acts 14, 15; Col 1, 16f; Heb 1, 2f; 3, 4; 11, 3; Rv 4, 11.	**1, 7:** Prv 8, 27f; 2 Pt 3, 5. **1, 9:** Jb 38, 8; Ps 33, 7; Jer 5, 22. **1, 11:** Ps 104, 14. **1, 14:** Jb 26, 10; Ps 19, 1f; Bar 3, 33.
1, 2: Jer 4, 23. **1, 3:** 2 Cor 4, 6.	**1, 16:** Dt 4, 19; Ps 136, 7ff; Wis 13, 2ff; Jer 31, 35.

¹⁹ Evening came, and morning followed—the fourth day.

²⁰* Then God said, "Let the water teem with an abundance of living creatures, and on the earth let birds fly beneath the dome of the sky." And so it happened: ²¹ God created the great sea monsters and all kinds of swimming creatures with which the water teems, and all kinds of winged birds. God saw how good it was, ²²* and God blessed them, saying, "Be fertile, multiply, and fill the water of the seas; and let the birds multiply on the earth." ²³ Evening came, and morning followed—the fifth day.

did you KNOW?

Literary Genres

Some Christians believe that God actually created the world in seven twenty-four-hour days. Such a belief comes from a literal reading of the first chapter of Genesis, as though it were a scientific textbook. However, Genesis was written not as a science article but as symbolic stories, sometimes called mythic stories, that convey great moral and spiritual truths. We should not try to come to any scientific conclusions about the creation of the world from reading these stories.

Mythic stories are one literary type, or genre. You just have to look in a newspaper to see examples of different literary genres: news stories, advice columns, editorials, and comics. Each genre has different rules for interpreting its meaning. The Bible also contains many types of literary genres, including hero stories, poetry, laws, legends, fictional satire, debates, and letters. To properly understand the Bible, pay attention to the literary genre—otherwise, you might believe the Bible is saying something God doesn't intend.

▸ Gn 1, 1—2, 4

IN THE BEGINNING

"In the beginning, when God created the heavens and the earth . . ." (Gn 1, 1). This simple verse is one of the foundational beliefs of Christianity. We are not a random collection of atoms. The world is not a lucky combination of cosmic circumstances. The universe did not just accidentally happen.

The beginning of wisdom is acknowledging that a higher power is at work in our life, that the universe has purpose, and that everything was created by God. The ancient writers and editors of Genesis expressed these ideas in the Creation stories. The church affirms these beliefs. They are expressed in a prayer called the Apostles' Creed, which begins, "I believe in God the father almighty, creator of heaven and earth."

Genesis expresses another foundational belief: God created everything good! Read the story in chapter 1 and see how this belief is constantly repeated: And humankind is "very good," created in God's own image. This is God's message to you in the first chapter of the Bible: You carry God's image within you. You are very good! Don't let anyone ever convince you otherwise.

▸ Gn 1, 1—2, 4

²⁴* Then God said, "Let the earth bring forth all kinds of living creatures: cattle, creeping things, and wild animals of all kinds." And so it happened: ²⁵ God made all kinds of wild animals, all kinds of cattle, and all kinds of creeping things of the earth. God saw how good it was. ²⁶*† Then God said: "Let us make man in our image, after our likeness. Let them have dominion over the fish of the sea, the birds of the air, and the cattle, and over all the wild animals and all the creatures that crawl on the ground."

²⁷   God created man in his image;
        in the divine image he created him;
        male and female he created them.

1, 26: Man is here presented as the climax of God's creative activity; he resembles God primarily because of the dominion God gives him over the rest of creation.

1, 20: Jb 12, 7–10.
1, 22: Gn 8, 17.
1, 24: Sir 16, 27f; Bar 3, 32.
1, 26f: Gn 5, 1.3; 9, 6; Ps 8, 5f;

Wis 2, 23; 10, 2; Sir 17, 1.3f; Jas 3, 7; 1 Cor 11, 7; Eph 4, 24; Col 3, 10; Mt 19, 4; Mk 10, 6.

In God's Image

God does not make mistakes; people do. Some people might be tempted to deny their racial heritage, to even change their physical appearance in order to fit into the latest fad or the dominant cultural image of beauty. We must remember that physical features are not accidents. God planned for them—we are all made in God's image.

If we are to authentically love ourselves, we must love our whole selves. This includes a love for dark skin or light skin; straight hair or tight curly hair; wide nose or pug nose; and all the variation in between. Whatever our appearance, we are all blessed of God.

Dear God, I praise you for who I am on the inside and on the outside. Amen.

▸ Gn 1, 26–27

28* God blessed them, saying to them: "Be fertile and multiply; fill the earth and subdue it. Have dominion over the fish of the sea, the birds of the air, and all the living things that move on the earth." 29* God also said: "See, I give you every seed-bearing plant all over the earth and every tree that has seed-bearing fruit on it to be your food; 30 and to all the animals of the land, all the birds of the air, and all the living creatures that crawl on the ground, I give all the green plants for food." And so it happened. 31* God looked at everything he had made, and he found it very good. Evening came, and morning followed—the sixth day.

2 1* Thus the heavens and the earth and all their array were completed. 2* Since on the seventh day God was finished with the work he had been doing, he rested on the seventh day from all the work he had undertaken. 3* So God blessed the seventh day and made it holy, because

on it he rested from all the work he had done in creation.

4 Such is the story of the heavens and the earth at their creation.

Second Story of Creation

† At the time when the LORD God made the earth and the heavens— 5 while as yet there was no field shrub on earth and no grass of the field had sprouted, for the LORD God had sent no rain upon the earth and there was no man to till the soil, 6 but a stream was welling up out of the earth and was

The Sabbath

Even God needed to take a rest. The writer of Genesis makes this point to remind readers to set aside a day for rest and prayer, which Jewish people call the Sabbath. Honoring the Sabbath is an act of trust in God. It means we believe that the world will not fall apart if we stop our activity. The world is in God's hands. We can hear this truth echoed in Jesus' words:

Notice how the flowers grow. They do not toil or spin. But I tell you, not even Solomon in all his splendor was dressed like one of them. If God so clothes the grass in the field that grows today and is thrown into the oven tomorrow, will he not much more provide for you, O you of little faith? (Lk 12, 27–28)

Traditionally, Christians rest and pray on Sunday because it is the day Jesus was resurrected. In our culture today, it seems that many people are losing this practice. What could we gain if we recommitted ourselves to a day of rest, celebration, and prayer? What can you do personally to more fully honor the concept of "Sabbath" rest?

▸ Gn 2, 1–3

---

† **2, 4b–25:** This section is chiefly concerned with the creation of man. It is much older than the narrative of Gn 1, 1—2, 4a. Here God is depicted as creating man before the rest of his creatures, which are made for man's sake.

* 1, 28: Gn 8, 17; 9, 1; Pss 8,
     6–9; 115, 16; Wis 9, 2.
1, 29f: Gn 9, 3; Ps 104, 14f.
1, 31: 1 Tm 4, 4.
2, 1: Is 45, 12; Jn 1, 3.

2, 2: Ex 20, 9ff; 31, 17; Heb
     4, 4.10.
2, 3: Ex 20, 11; Dt 5, 14;
     Neh 9, 14.

Cultural Connections

GOD IS OUR CREATOR!

According to Genesis, chapters 1–2, God created the universe and is the source of order in all creation. Creation is good, and its goodness is reflected in the harmony, peace, and love between the Creator and his creatures, and among the creatures themselves. In Hispanic theological traditions, this ideal relationship—symbolized by the way God and Adam and Eve relate in the Garden of Eden—is considered the foundation in which salvation history is rooted.

- How are your relationships with God, your friends, your family, and nature characterized by harmony, peace, and love?
- Reflect on how you can improve some of your strained relationships, and ask God's help to do it.

Human beings are created in God's image and likeness and share God's attributes: freedom, love, knowledge, and the ability to create. With these gifts comes the responsibility of caring for all creation.

- Give thanks and praise to God for creation, especially for your own life and the lives of the people around you.
- Think of how you, your family, and your community can take better care of all creation. Pray that you fully develop your capacity to love, to know the truth, and to use your freedom wisely.

God established a covenant with us at the moment of our creation, and we keep this covenant by freely placing ourselves in God's hands and being responsive to God's invitation to live in communion with God and people.

- How do you use your freedom to respond to God's invitation?
- Think about the aspects of your life for which you most need God's wisdom to live in harmony and love. Put yourself in God's hands, and let God help and direct you.

▶ Genesis, chapters 1–2

---

watering all the surface of the ground— 7*† the LORD God formed man out of the clay of the ground and blew into his nostrils the breath of life, and so man became a living being.

8*† Then the LORD God planted a garden in Eden, in the east, and he placed there the man whom he had formed. 9* Out of the ground the LORD God made various trees grow that were delightful to look at and good for food, with the tree of life in the middle of the garden and the tree of the knowledge of good and bad.

10† A river rises in Eden to water the garden; beyond there it divides and becomes four branches. 11 The name of the first is the Pishon; it is the one that winds through the whole land of Havilah, where there is gold. 12 The gold of that land is excellent; bdellium and lapis lazuli are also there. 13* The name of the second river is the Gihon; it is the one that winds all through the land of Cush. 14 The name of the third river is the Tigris; it is the one that flows east of Asshur. The fourth river is the Euphrates.

15* The LORD God then took the man and settled

2, 7: God is portrayed as a potter molding man's body out of clay. There is a play on words in Hebrew between *adam* ("man") and *adama* ("ground"). *Being:* literally, "soul."

2, 8: *Eden:* used here as the name of a region in southern Mesopotamia; the term is derived from the Sumerian word *eden*, "fertile plain." A similar-sounding Hebrew word means "delight"; the *garden in Eden* could therefore be understood as the "garden of delight," so that, through the Greek version, it is now known also as "paradise," literally, a "pleasure park."

2, 10–14: *Rises:* in flood to overflow its banks. *Beyond there:* as one travels upstream. *Branches:* literally, "heads," i.e., upper courses.

Eden is near the head of the Persian Gulf, where the Tigris and the Euphrates join with two other streams to form a single river. *The land of Cush* here and in Gn 10, 8, is not Ethiopia (Nubia) as elsewhere, but the region of the Kassites east of Mesopotamia.

2, 7: Gn 3, 19; 18, 27; Tb 8, 6; Jb 34, 15; Pss 103, 14; 104, 29; Eccl 3, 20; 12, 7; Wis 7, 1; Sir 33, 10; 1 Cor 15, 45.
2, 8: Is 51, 3; Ez 31, 9.
2, 9: Gn 3, 22; Prv 3, 18; Rv 2, 7; 22, 2.14.
2, 13: Sir 24, 25.
2, 15: Sir 7, 15.

him in the garden of Eden, to cultivate and care for it. 16* The LORD God gave man this order: "You are free to eat from any of the trees of the garden 17* except the tree of knowledge of good and bad. From that tree you shall not eat; the moment you eat from it you are surely doomed to die."

18* The LORD God said: "It is not good for the man to be alone. I will make a suitable partner for him." 19 So the LORD God formed out of the ground various wild animals and various birds of the air, and he brought them to the man to see what he would call them; whatever the man called each of them would be its name. 20 The man gave names to all the cattle, all the birds of the air, and all the wild animals; but none proved to be the suitable partner for the man.

21* So the LORD God cast a deep sleep on the man, and while he was asleep, he took out one of his ribs and closed up its place with flesh. 22 The LORD God then built up into a woman the rib that he had taken from the man. When he brought her to the man, 23† the man said:

"This one, at last, is bone of my bones
　　and flesh of my flesh;
This one shall be called 'woman,'
　　for out of 'her man' this one has
　　　　been taken."

24*† That is why a man leaves his father and mother and clings to his wife, and the two of them become one body.

25 The man and his wife were both naked, yet they felt no shame.

The Fall of Man

3 1 Now the serpent was the most cunning of all the animals that the LORD God had made. The serpent asked the woman, "Did God really tell you not to eat from any of the trees in the garden?" 2 The woman answered the serpent: "We may eat of the fruit of the trees in the garden; 3* it is only about the fruit of the tree in the middle of the garden that God said, 'You shall not eat it or even touch it, lest you die.'" 4* But the serpent said to the woman: "You certainly will not die! 5† No, God knows well that the moment you eat of it your eyes will be opened and you will be like gods who know what is good and what is bad." 6* The woman saw that the tree was good for food, pleasing to the eyes, and desirable for gaining wisdom. So she took

Catholic Connections

ORIGINAL SIN BREAKS OUR RELATIONSHIP WITH GOD

The story of Adam and Eve is about the human weakness for sinning and disobeying God. The serpent tells Adam and Eve they can be like God, and know good and evil. After disobeying God, they recognize that they are naked and feel shame. Their relationship of trust with God is broken. This story teaches that soon after men and women were created, sin entered human history and led to pain and suffering.

Adam and Eve's disobedience has affected every human being except Jesus and his mother, Mary. At our birth, we are deprived of the original holiness and justice God intended us to have. This state is called original sin, but it is not a sin that we personally commit. Original sin is, in a sense, inherited. Our relationship with God is imperfect because of this and can be fully restored only through Baptism.

▶ Gn 3, 1–24

some of its fruit and ate it; and she also gave some to her husband, who was with her, and he ate it. 7 Then the eyes of both of them were opened, and they realized that they were naked; so they sewed fig leaves together and made loincloths for themselves.

8*† When they heard the sound of the LORD God moving about in the garden at the breezy time of the day, the man and his wife hid themselves from the LORD God among the trees of the garden. 9 The LORD God then called to the man and asked him, "Where are you?" 10 He answered, "I heard you in

---

† **2, 23:** There is a play on the similar-sounding Hebrew words *ishsha* ("woman") and *ishah* ("her man, her husband").
2, 24: *One body:* literally "one flesh"; classical Hebrew has no specific word for "body." The sacred writer stresses the fact that conjugal union is willed by God.
3, 5: *Like gods who know:* or "like God who knows."
3, 8: *The breezy time of the day:* literally "the wind of the day." On most days in Palestine a cooling breeze blows from the sea shortly before sunset.

2, 16: Ps 104, 14.
2, 17: Gn 3, 2f; Rom 6, 23.
2, 18: Tb 8, 6; Sir 36, 24;
　　1 Cor 11, 9; 1 Tm 2,
　　13.
2, 21: Sir 17, 1; 1 Cor 11, 8f;
　　1 Tm 2, 13.
2, 24: Mt 19, 5; Mk 10, 7;

1 Cor 7, 10f;
Eph 5, 31.
3, 3: Gn 2, 17; Rom 6, 23.
3, 4f: Wis 2, 24; Sir 25, 14;
　　Is 14, 14; Jn 8, 44;
　　2 Cor 11, 3.
3, 6: Gn 3, 22; 1 Tm 2, 14.
3, 8: Jer 23, 24.

the garden; but I was afraid, because I was naked, so I hid myself." 11 Then he asked, "Who told you that you were naked? You have eaten, then, from the tree of which I had forbidden you to eat!" 12 The man replied, "The woman whom you put here with me—she gave me fruit from the tree, and so I ate it." 13* The LORD God then asked the woman, "Why did you do such a thing?" The woman answered, "The serpent tricked me into it, so I ate it."

14* Then the LORD God said to the serpent:

"Because you have done this, you shall
    be banned
    from all the animals
    and from all the wild creatures;
On your belly shall you crawl,
    and dirt shall you eat
    all the days of your life.
15*†I will put enmity between you and
    the woman,
    and between your offspring and hers;
He will strike at your head,
    while you strike at his heel."

16* To the woman he said:

"I will intensify the pangs of
    your childbearing;
in pain shall you bring forth children.
Yet your urge shall be for your husband,
    and he shall be your master."

17* To the man he said: "Because you listened to your wife and ate from the tree of which I had forbidden you to eat,

"Cursed be the ground because of you!
In toil shall you eat its yield
    all the days of your life.
18 Thorns and thistles shall it bring forth to you,
    as you eat of the plants of the field.
19* By the sweat of your face
    shall you get bread to eat,

Until you return to the ground,
    from which you were taken;
For you are dirt,
    and to dirt you shall return."

20† The man called his wife Eve, because she became the mother of all the living.

21 For the man and his wife the LORD God made leather garments, with which he clothed them. 22* Then the LORD God said: "See! The man has become like one of us, knowing what is good and what is bad! Therefore, he must not be allowed to put out his hand to take fruit from the tree of life also, and thus eat of it and live forever." 23 The LORD God therefore banished him from the garden of Eden, to till the ground from which he had been taken. 24† When he expelled the man, he settled him east of the garden of Eden; and he stationed the cherubim and the fiery revolving sword, to guard the way to the tree of life.

Cain and Abel

4 1† The man had relations with his wife Eve, and she conceived and bore Cain, saying, "I have produced a man with the help of the LORD." 2 Next she bore his brother Abel. Abel became a keeper of flocks, and Cain a tiller of the soil. 3 In the course of time Cain brought an offering to the LORD from the fruit of the soil, 4* while Abel, for his part, brought one of the best firstlings of his flock. The LORD looked with favor on Abel and his offering, 5 but on Cain and his offering he did not. Cain greatly resented this and was crestfallen. 6 So the LORD said to Cain: "Why are you so resentful and crestfallen? 7*† If you do well, you can hold up your head; but if not, sin is a demon lurking at the door: his urge is toward you, yet you can be his master."

8* Cain said to his brother Abel, "Let us go out in the field." When they were in the field, Cain attacked his brother Abel and killed him. 9 Then the LORD asked Cain, "Where is your brother Abel?" He answered, "I do not know. Am I my brother's

---

3, 15: *He will strike . . . at his heel:* since the antecedent for *he* and *his* is the collective noun *offspring,* i.e., all the descendants of the woman, a more exact rendering of the sacred writer's words would be, "They will strike . . . at their heels." However, later theology saw in this passage more than unending hostility between snakes and men. The serpent was regarded as the devil (Wis 2, 24; Jn 8, 44; Rv 12, 9; 20, 2), whose eventual defeat seems implied in the contrast between *head* and *heel.* Because "the Son of God was revealed to destroy the works of the devil" (1 Jn 3, 8), the passage can be understood as the first promise of a Redeemer for fallen mankind. The woman's offspring then is primarily Jesus Christ.

3, 20: This verse seems to be out of place; it would fit better after v 24. The Hebrew name *hawwa* ("Eve") is related to the Hebrew word *hay* ("living").

3, 24: The above rendering is based on the ancient Greek version; that of the current Hebrew is, When he expelled the man, he settled east of the garden of Eden, the cherubim.

4, 1: The Hebrew name *qayin* ("Cain") and the term *qaniti* ("I have produced") present another play on words.

4, 7: *Demon lurking:* in Hebrew, *robes,* literally "croucher," is used here, like the similar Akkadian term *rabisu,* to designate a certain kind of evil spirit.

3, 13: 2 Cor 11, 3.
3, 14: Is 65, 25; Mi 7, 17; Rv 12, 9.
3, 15: Is 7, 14; 9, 5; Rom 16, 20; 1 Jn 3, 8; Rv 12, 17.
3, 16: 1 Cor 11, 3; Eph 5, 22f; 1 Tm 2, 12.
3, 17: Gn 5, 29; Rom 5, 12; 8, 20; Heb 6, 8.
3, 19: Gn 2, 7; Jb 10, 9; 34, 15; Pss 90, 3; 103, 14;

Eccl 3, 20; 12, 7; Wis 15, 8; Sir 10, 9; 17, 2; Rom 5, 12; 1 Cor 15, 21; Heb 9, 27.
3, 22: Gn 2, 9; Rv 22, 2.14.
4, 4: Ex 34, 19; Heb 11, 4.
4, 7: Sir 7, 1; Jude 11.
4, 8: Wis 10, 3; Mt 23, 35; Lk 11, 51; 1 Jn 3, 12; Jude 11.

Brothers and Sisters

"Am I my brother's keeper?" (Gn 4, 9). With that famous question, Cain pretends that he does not know where his brother is. God does not answer Cain's question directly, but each of us knows the response. We are—each of us and all of us—responsible for one another: family, friends, and strangers. We are brothers and sisters because God has created us that way. We cannot avoid our obligation to watch out for one another.

Are there people in your life who need you to be a brother or sister to them? If so, commit yourself right now to reach out to them.

▶ Gn 4, 9

keeper?" 10 The LORD then said: "What have you done! Listen: Your brother's blood cries out to me from the soil! 11* Therefore you shall be banned from the soil that opened its mouth to receive your brother's blood from your hand. 12 If you till the soil, it shall no longer give you its produce. You shall become a restless wanderer on the earth." 13 Cain said to the LORD: "My punishment is too great to bear. 14 Since you have now banished me from the soil, and I must avoid your presence and become a restless wanderer on the earth, anyone may kill me at sight." 15† "Not so!" the LORD said to him. "If anyone kills Cain, Cain shall be avenged sevenfold." So the LORD put a mark on Cain, lest anyone should kill him at sight. 16† Cain then left the LORD's presence and settled in the land of Nod, east of Eden.

Descendants of Cain and Seth

17† Cain had relations with his wife, and she conceived and bore Enoch. Cain also became the founder of a city, which he named after his son Enoch. 18 To Enoch was born Irad, and Irad became the father of Mehujael; Mehujael became the father of Methusael, and Methusael became the father of Lamech. 19 Lamech took two wives; the name of the first was Adah, and the name of the second Zillah. 20 Adah gave birth to Jabal, the ancestor of all who dwell in tents and keep cattle. 21 His brother's name was Jubal; he was the ancestor of all who play the lyre and the pipe. 22 Zillah, on her part, gave birth to Tubalcain, the ancestor of all who forge instruments of bronze and iron. The sister of Tubalcain was Naamah. 23 Lamech said to his wives:

"Adah and Zillah, hear my voice;
    wives of Lamech, listen to my utterance:
I have killed a man for wounding me,
    a boy for bruising me.
24. If Cain is avenged sevenfold,
    then Lamech seventy-sevenfold."

THE CYCLE OF VIOLENCE

Cain was a murderer. Some might say he deserved the death penalty. But in Gn 4, 15, God marks Cain so that he is protected from being killed. God seeks to stop the cycle of violence. Why kill someone to show that it is wrong to kill someone?

Think of a television show or movie with violent sequences that you have seen recently. What attitude did it portray toward violence? Often, violence in revenge is shown as justified, even satisfying. How does violence on television or in the movies affect your own attitude toward it? How might you respond to God's call to stop the cycle of violence?

▶ Gn 4, 15

---

† **4, 15:** *A mark:* probably a tattoo. The use of tattooing for tribal marks has always been common among the nomads of the Near Eastern deserts.

4, 16: *The land of Nod:* not a definite geographic region. The term merely means "the land of nomads."

4, 17–22: In vv 12–16 Cain was presented as the archetype of nomadic peoples. The sacred author in this section follows another ancient tradition that makes Cain the prototype of sedentary peoples with higher material culture.

4, 11: Dt 27, 24.

25† Adam again had relations with his wife, and she gave birth to a son whom she called Seth. "God has granted me more offspring in place of Abel," she said, "because Cain slew him." 26* To Seth, in turn, a son was born, and he named him Enosh.

At that time men began to invoke the LORD by name.

Generations: Adam to Noah

5 1*†This is the record of the descendants of Adam. When God created man, he made him in the likeness of God; 2 he created them male and female. When they were created, he blessed them and named them "man."

3* Adam was one hundred and thirty years old when he begot a son in his likeness, after his image; and he named him Seth.* 4 Adam lived eight hundred years after the birth of Seth, and he had other sons and daughters. 5 The whole lifetime of Adam was nine hundred and thirty years; then he died.

6 When Seth was one hundred and five years old, he became the father of Enosh. 7 Seth lived eight hundred and seven years after the birth of Enosh, and he had other sons and daughters. 8 The whole lifetime of Seth was nine hundred and twelve years; then he died.

9 When Enosh was ninety years old, he became the father of Kenan. 10 Enosh lived eight hundred and fifteen years after the birth of Kenan, and he had other sons and daughters. 11 The whole lifetime of Enosh was nine hundred and five years; then he died.

12 When Kenan was seventy years old, he became the father of Mahalalel. 13 Kenan lived eight hundred and forty years after the birth of Mahalalel, and he had other sons and daughters. 14 The whole lifetime of Kenan was nine hundred and ten years; then he died.

15 When Mahalalel was sixty-five years old, he became the father of Jared. 16 Mahalalel lived eight hundred and thirty years after the birth of Jared, and he had other sons and daughters. 17 The whole lifetime of Mahalalel was eight hundred and ninety-five years; then he died.

18 When Jared was one hundred and sixty-two years old, he became the father of Enoch. 19 Jared lived eight hundred years after the birth of Enoch, and he had other sons and daughters. 20 The whole lifetime of Jared was nine hundred and sixty-two years; then he died.

21 When Enoch was sixty-five years old, he became the father of Methuselah. 22 Enoch lived three hundred years after the birth of Methuselah, and he had other sons and daughters. 23 The whole lifetime of Enoch was three hundred and sixty-five years. 24*† Then Enoch walked with God, and he was no longer here, for God took him.

25 When Methuselah was one hundred and eighty-seven years old, he became the father of Lamech. 26 Methuselah lived seven hundred and eighty-two years after the birth of Lamech, and he had other sons and daughters. 27 The whole lifetime of Methuselah was nine hundred and sixty-nine years; then he died.

28 When Lamech was one hundred and eighty-two years old, he begot a son 29*† and named him Noah, saying, "Out of the very ground that the LORD has put under a curse, this one shall bring us relief from our work and the toil of our hands." 30 Lamech lived five hundred and ninety-five years after the birth of Noah, and he had other sons and daughters. 31 The whole lifetime of Lamech was seven hundred and seventy-seven years; then he died.

32* When Noah was five hundred years old, he became the father of Shem, Ham and Japheth.

Origin of the Nephilim

6 1† When men began to multiply on earth and daughters were born to them, 2*† the sons of

---

4, 25f: *Has granted:* Hebrew *shat,* a wordplay on the name *shet* ("Seth"). *Enosh:* in Hebrew, a synonym of *adam* ("man"). *At that time . . . name:* men began to call God by his personal name, Yahweh, rendered as "the Lord" in this version of the Bible. The ancient, so-called Yahwist source used here employs the name Yahweh long before the time of Moses. Another ancient source, the Elohist (from its use of the term *Elohim,* "God," instead of *Yahweh,* "Lord," for the pre-Mosaic period), makes Moses the first to use Yahweh as the proper name of Israel's God, previously known by other names as well; cf Ex 3, 13ff.

5, 1–32: Although this chapter, with its highly schematic form, belongs to the relatively late "Priestly document," it is based on very ancient traditions. Together with Gn 11, 10–26, its primary purpose is to bridge the genealogical gap between Adam and Abraham. Adam's line is traced through Seth, but several names in the series are the same as, or similar to, certain names in Cain's line (Gn 4, 17ff). The long lifespans attributed to these ten antediluvian patriarchs have a symbolic rather than a historical value. Babylonian tradition also recorded ten kings with fantastically high ages who reigned successively before the flood.

5, 24: In place of the usual formula, *Then he died,* the change to

Enoch walked with God clearly implies that he did not die, but like Elijah (2 Kgs 2, 11f) was taken alive to God's abode.

5, 29: There is a similarity in sound between the Hebrew word *noah,* "Noah," and the verbal phrase *yenahamenu,* "he will bring us relief"; this latter refers both to the curse put on the soil because of the fall of man (Gn 3, 17ff) and to Noah's success in agriculture, especially in raising grapes for wine (Gn 9, 20f).

6, 1–4: This is apparently a fragment of an old legend that had borrowed much from ancient mythology. The sacred author incorporates it here, not only in order to account for the prehistoric giants of Palestine, whom the Israelites called the *Nephilim,* but also to introduce the story of the flood with a moral orientation—the constantly increasing wickedness of mankind.

6, 2: *The sons of heaven:* literally "the sons of the gods" or "the sons of God," i.e., the celestial beings of mythology.

4, 26: 1 Chr 1, 1; Lk 3, 38.

5, 1: Gn 1, 27; Wis 2, 23; Sir 17, 1; 1 Cor 11, 7; Jas 3, 9.

5, 3: Gn 4, 25.

5, 3–32: 1 Chr 1, 1–4;

Lk 3, 36ff.

5, 24: Wis 4, 10f; Sir 44, 16; 49, 14; Heb 11, 5.

5, 29: Gn 3, 17ff.

5, 32: Gn 6, 10; 10, 1.

6, 2: Mt 24, 38; Lk 17, 26f.

heaven saw how beautiful the daughters of man were, and so they took for their wives as many of them as they chose. ³† Then the LORD said: "My spirit shall not remain in man forever, since he is but flesh. His days shall comprise one hundred and twenty years."

and the birds of the air, for I am sorry that I made them." ⁸ But Noah found favor with the LORD.

⁹* These are the descendants of Noah. Noah, a good man and blameless in that age, ¹⁰ for he walked with God, begot three sons: Shem, Ham and Japheth.

Sin Has Social Consequences

At the beginning of the Noah story, sin has continued to spread so that it has become an accepted part of society. The Great Flood, which wipes out a whole civilization, symbolizes the consequences of widespread sin. Later in Genesis, the story of the tower of Babel (11, 1–9) symbolizes another consequence of the institutionalized sin of disobedience and pride.

When sin becomes part of our social systems and our institutions, the church calls it social sin. Social sin is a result of personal sin, but it is bigger than any one person's choice. Examples of social sin are the unequal distribution of the world's wealth, the exploitation of workers by corporations, and discrimination based on race or gender. The good news is that God's saving power is greater than social sin! What are the effects of social sin in your community? in your country? in the world? How are Christians in your church or community organizing to stand against social sin?

▶ Gn 6, 1—9, 17

⁴*† At that time the Nephilim appeared on earth (as well as later), after the sons of heaven had intercourse with the daughters of man, who bore them sons. They were the heroes of old, the men of renown.

Warning of the Flood

⁵*† When the LORD saw how great was man's wickedness on earth, and how no desire that his heart conceived was ever anything but evil, ⁶ he regretted that he had made man on the earth, and his heart was grieved.

⁷ So the LORD said: "I will wipe out from the earth the men whom I have created, and not only the men, but also the beasts and the creeping things

¹¹* In the eyes of God the earth was corrupt and full of lawlessness. ¹²* When God saw how corrupt the earth had become, since all mortals led depraved lives on earth, ¹³* he said to Noah: "I have decided to put an end to all mortals on earth; the earth is full of lawlessness because of them. So I will destroy them and all life on earth.

Preparation for the Flood

¹⁴† "Make yourself an ark of gopherwood, put various compartments in it, and cover it inside and out with pitch. ¹⁵† This is how you shall build it: the length of the ark shall be three hundred cubits, its width fifty cubits, and its height thirty cubits.

---

† **6, 3:** *My spirit:* the breath of life referred to in Gn 2, 7. *His days . . . years:* probably the time God would still let men live on earth before destroying them with the flood, rather than the maximum span of life God would allot to individual men in the future.

6, 4: *As well as later:* According to Nm 13, 33, when the Israelites invaded Palestine and found there the tall aboriginal Anakim, they likened them to the Nephilim; cf Dt 2, 10f. Perhaps the huge megalithic structures in Palestine were thought to have been built by a race of giants, whose superhuman strength was attributed to semi-divine origin. *The heroes of old:* the legendary worthies of ancient mythology.

6, 5—8, 22: The story of the great flood here recorded is a composite narrative based on two separate sources interwoven into an intricate patchwork. To the Yahwist source, with some later editorial additions, are usually assigned 6, 5–8; 7, 1–5.7–10.12.16b.17b.22–23; 8, 2b–3a.6–12.13b.20–22. The other sections come from the "Priestly document." The combination of the two sources produced certain duplications (e.g., 6, 13–22 of the Yahwist source, beside 7, 1–5 of the Priestly source); also certain inconsistencies, such as the number of the various animals taken into the ark (6, 19f;

7, 14f of the Priestly source, beside 7, 2f of the Yahwist source), and the timetable of the flood (8, 3–5.13f of the Priestly source, beside 7, 4.10.12.17b; 8, 6.10.12 of the Yahwist source). Both biblical sources go back ultimately to an ancient Mesopotamian story of a great flood, preserved in the eleventh tablet of the Gilgamesh Epic. The latter account, in some respects remarkably similar to the biblical account, is in others very different from it.

6, 14: *Gopherwood:* an unidentified wood not mentioned elsewhere; *gopher* is merely the Hebrew word for it.

6, 15: The dimensions of Noah's ark were approximately 440 x 73 x 44 feet, a foot and a half to the cubit. The ark of the Babylonian flood story was an exact cube, 120 cubits in length, width, and height.

---

*
6, 4: Wis 14, 6; Bar 3, 26.   **6, 12:** Ps 14, 2.
6, 5: Ps 14, 2f.   **6, 13:** Sir 40, 9f; 44, 17; Mt
6, 9: Wis 10, 4; Sir 44, 17.   24, 37ff.
6, 11: Jb 22, 15ff.

GN

16† Make an opening for daylight in the ark, and finish the ark a cubit above it. Put an entrance in the side of the ark, which you shall make with bottom, second and third decks. 17* I, on my part, am about to bring the flood [waters] on the earth, to destroy everywhere all creatures in which there is the breath of life; everything on earth shall perish. 18* But with you I will establish my covenant; you and your sons, your wife and your sons' wives, shall go into the ark. 19 Of all other living creatures you shall bring two into the ark, one male and one female, that you may keep them alive with you. 20 Of all kinds of birds, of all kinds of beasts, and of all kinds of creeping things, two of each shall come into the ark with you, to stay alive. 21 Moreover, you are to provide yourself with all the food that is to be eaten, and store it away, that it may serve as provisions for you and for them." 22 This Noah did; he carried out all the commands that God gave him.

7 1* Then the LORD said to Noah: "Go into the ark, you and all your household, for you alone in this age have I found to be truly just. 2 Of every clean animal, take with you seven pairs, a male and its mate; and of the unclean animals, one pair, a male and its mate; 3 likewise, of every clean bird of the air, seven pairs, a male and a female, and of all the unclean birds, one pair, a male and a female. Thus you will keep their issue alive over all the earth. 4* Seven days from now I will bring rain down on the earth for forty days and forty nights, and so I will wipe out from the surface of the earth every moving creature that I have made." 5 Noah did just as the LORD had commanded him.

The Great Flood

6 Noah was six hundred years old when the flood waters came upon the earth. 7* Together with his sons, his wife, and his sons' wives, Noah went into the ark because of the waters of the flood. 8 Of the clean animals and the unclean, of the birds, and of everything that creeps on the ground, 9* [two by two] male and female entered the ark with Noah, just as the LORD had commanded him. 10 As soon as the seven days were over, the waters of the flood came upon the earth.

11† In the six hundredth year of Noah's life, in the second month, on the seventeenth day of the month: it was on that day that

All the fountains of the great abyss burst forth,
and the floodgates of the sky were opened.

?did you KNOW?

The Flood

The sin of Adam and Eve in the garden starts a disastrous trend in which each generation adds to sin in the world. This sin leads to the corruption of the world and the destruction of human beings. The Great Flood illustrates the ancient belief that God washed the world clean of this sinfulness and gave another chance to those who were faithful to God.

Other ancient cultures had stories about great floods. But in those stories, vindictive gods caused the floods for petty reasons. These gods had no real love for humanity. The Bible's Flood story is unique because it insists that God acted out of justice and in response to great evil.

God takes great care to save Noah and his family because they are faithful to God. After the Flood, God makes a covenant with Noah, promising never to destroy the earth by flood again—another unique element not found in the stories of other cultures.

▸ **Gn 6, 1—9, 17**

12 For forty days and forty nights heavy rain poured down on the earth.

13 On the precise day named, Noah and his sons Shem, Ham and Japheth, and Noah's wife, and the three wives of Noah's sons had entered the ark, 14 together with every kind of wild beast, every kind of domestic animal, every kind of creeping thing of the earth, and every kind of bird. 15 Pairs of all creatures in which there was the breath of life entered the ark with Noah. 16 Those that entered were male and female, and of all species they came, as God had commanded Noah. Then the LORD shut him in.

17 The flood continued upon the earth for forty days. As the waters increased, they lifted the ark, so that it rose above the earth. 18 The swelling waters increased greatly, but the ark floated on the surface of the waters. 19 Higher and higher above the earth

---

† **6, 16:** *Opening for daylight:* a conjectural rendering of the Hebrew word *sohar*, occurring only here. The reference is probably to an open space on all sides near the top of the ark to admit light and air. The ark also had a window or hatch, which could be opened and closed (Gn 8, 6).

7, 11: *Abyss:* the subterranean ocean; see note on Gn 1, 2.

6, 17: Gn 7, 4.21; 2 Pt 2, 5.
6, 18: Gn 9, 9; Wis 14, 6;
　Heb 11, 7; 1 Pt 3, 20.
7, 1: Wis 10, 4; Sir 44, 17;
　2 Pt 2, 5.
7, 4: Gn 6, 17; 2 Pt 2, 5.
7, 7: Wis 14, 6; 1 Pt 3, 20;
　2 Pt 2, 5.
7, 9: Gn 6, 19.

8, 11

from the earth. [8] Then he sent out a dove, to see if the waters had lessened on the earth. [9] But the dove could find no place to alight and perch, and it returned to him in the ark, for there was water all over the earth. Putting out his hand, he caught the dove and drew it back to him inside the ark. [10] He waited seven days more and again sent the dove out from the ark. [11] In the evening the dove came back to him, and there in its bill was a plucked-off olive leaf! So Noah knew that the waters had lessened on the earth. [12] He waited still another seven days and then released the dove once more; and this time it did not come back.

[13] In the six hundred and first year of Noah's life, in the first month, on the first day of the month, the water began to dry up on the earth. Noah then removed the covering of the ark and saw that the surface of the ground was drying up. [14] In the second month, on the twenty-seventh day of the month, the earth was dry.

rose the waters, until all the highest mountains everywhere were submerged, [20] the crest rising fifteen cubits higher than the submerged mountains. [21]* All creatures that stirred on earth perished: birds, cattle, wild animals, and all that swarmed on the earth, as well as all mankind. [22] Everything on dry land with the faintest breath of life in its nostrils died out. [23] The LORD wiped out every living thing on earth: man and cattle, the creeping things and the birds of the air; all were wiped out from the earth. Only Noah and those with him in the ark were left.

8 [7, 24]† The waters maintained their crest over the earth for one hundred and fifty days, [8, 1] and then God remembered Noah and all the animals, wild and tame, that were with him in the ark. So God made a wind sweep over the earth, and the waters began to subside. [2] The fountains of the abyss and the floodgates of the sky were closed, and the downpour from the sky was held back. [3] Gradually the waters receded from the earth. At the end of one hundred and fifty days, the waters had so diminished [4]† that, in the seventh month, on the seventeenth day of the month, the ark came to rest on the mountains of Ararat. [5] The waters continued to diminish until the tenth month, and on the first day of the tenth month the tops of the mountains appeared.

[6]† At the end of forty days Noah opened the hatch he had made in the ark, [7] and he sent out a raven, to see if the waters had lessened on the earth. It flew back and forth until the waters dried off

did you KNOW?

Water in the Bible

For the ancient Hebrews, although water often represented a source of life, it also represented forces of destruction over which God triumphs. In the story of Creation, God is portrayed as mastering the waters that represent chaos (Gn 1, 1–2) — God constructs the upper and lower firmaments to hold back the waters. At the time of the Great Flood, God releases the waters, and they destroy life on the earth. At the time of the Exodus, God will once again display the divine mastery of the waters, as will Jesus Christ later on.

[15] Then God said to Noah: [16] "Go out of the ark, together with your wife and your sons and your sons' wives. [17]* Bring out with you every living thing that is with you—all bodily creatures, be they birds or animals or creeping things of the earth—

7, 24: This verse belongs to chapter 7 but its contents properly introduce chapter 8.
8, 4: *Ararat:* ancient Urartu, north of the Mesopotamian plain, part of modern Armenia.
8, 6: In the original Yahwist source, from which this verse is taken, the forty days refer to the full period of the flood itself (cf Gn

7, 4.17); in the present context, however, they seem to refer to a period following the date just given in v 5 from the Priestly source.

7, 21ff: Jb 22, 16; Mt 24, 39; Lk 17, 27; 2 Pt 3, 6.   **8, 17:** Gn 1, 22.28.

and let them abound on the earth, breeding and multiplying on it." 18 So Noah came out, together with his wife and his sons and his sons' wives; 19 and all the animals, wild and tame, all the birds, and all the creeping creatures of the earth left the ark, one kind after another.

20 Then Noah built an altar to the LORD, and choosing from every clean animal and every clean bird, he offered holocausts on the altar. 21*† When the LORD smelled the sweet odor, he said to himself: "Never again will I doom the earth because of man, since the desires of man's heart are evil from the start; nor will I ever again strike down all living beings, as I have done.

22*   As long as the earth lasts,
            seedtime and harvest,
            cold and heat,
        Summer and winter,
            and day and night
        shall not cease."

Covenant with Noah

9 1* God blessed Noah and his sons and said to them: "Be fertile and multiply and fill the earth. 2 Dread fear of you shall come upon all the animals of the earth and all the birds of the air, upon all the creatures that move about on the ground and all the fishes of the sea; into your power they are delivered. 3*† Every creature that is alive shall be yours to eat; I give them all to you as I did the green plants. 4*† Only flesh with its lifeblood still in it you shall not eat. 5* For your own lifeblood, too, I will demand an accounting: from every animal I will demand it, and from man in regard to his fellow man I will demand an accounting for human life.

6*   If anyone sheds the blood of man,
            by man shall his blood be shed;
        For in the image of God
            has man been made.

7* Be fertile, then, and multiply; abound on earth and subdue it."

8 God said to Noah and to his sons with him: 9* "See, I am now establishing my covenant with you and your descendants after you 10 and with every living creature that was with you: all the birds, and the various tame and wild animals that were with you and came out of the ark. 11* I will establish my covenant with you, that never again shall all bodily creatures be destroyed by the waters of a

PRAY IT?
The Rainbow

What do you see when you see a rainbow? Do you see a multicolored arc caused by the refraction of sunlight through droplets of water? Or do you see a wonder of nature that causes you to stop and stare in awe? Something as remarkable as a rainbow can never be reduced to a scientific explanation. It's no wonder that the writer of Genesis used it as a symbol of God's covenant promise. When God and Israel see the rainbow in the clouds, they will recall their covenant together.

God of imagination and color, only you could come up with the idea of a rainbow! Rainstorm and sunshine, harmony and diversity, mercy and hope, promise and joy, wonder and awe. Are these inside me, the wondrous creation you delight in? Guide me to the rainbows in my life!

▶ Gn 9, 8–17

flood; there shall not be another flood to devastate the earth." 12 God added: "This is the sign that I am giving for all ages to come, of the covenant between me and you and every living creature with you: 13* I set my bow in the clouds to serve as a sign of the covenant between me and the earth. 14 When I bring clouds over the earth, and the bow appears in the clouds, 15* I will recall the covenant I have made between me and you and all living beings, so that the waters shall never again become a flood to destroy all mortal beings. 16 As the bow appears in

---

8, 21: *From the start:* literally "from his youth." It is uncertain whether this means from the beginning of the human race or from the early years of the individual.

9, 3: Antediluvian creatures, including man, are depicted as vegetarians (Gn 1, 29f), becoming carnivorous only after the flood.

9, 4: Because a living being dies when it loses most of its blood, the ancients regarded blood as the seat of life, and therefore as sacred. Although in itself the prohibition against eating meat with blood in it is comparable to the ritual laws of the Mosaic code, the Jews considered it binding on all men, because it was given by God to Noah, the new ancestor of all mankind; therefore the early Christian Church retained it for a time (Acts 15, 20.29).

8, 21: Sir 44, 18; Is 54, 9; Rom 7, 18.
8, 22: Jer 33, 20.25.
9, 1: Gn 1, 2.28; 8, 17; Jas 3, 7.
9, 3: Gn 1, 29f; Dt 12, 15.
9, 4: Lv 7, 26f; 17, 4; Dt 12, 16.23; 1 Sm 14, 33; Acts 15, 20.
9, 5: Gn 4, 10f; Ex 21, 12.
9, 6: Gn 1, 26f; Lv 24, 17; Nm 35, 33; Jas 3, 9.
9, 7: Gn 1, 28; 8, 17; 9, 2.
9, 9: Gn 6, 18.
9, 11: Sir 44, 18; Is 54, 9.
9, 13: Sir 43, 12.
9, 15: Is 54, 9.

the clouds, I will see it and recall the everlasting covenant that I have established between God and all living beings—all mortal creatures that are on earth." 17 God told Noah: "This is the sign of the covenant I have established between me and all mortal creatures that are on earth."

Noah and His Sons

18*† The sons of Noah who came out of the ark were Shem, Ham and Japheth. (Ham was the father of Canaan.) 19 These three were the sons of Noah, and from them the whole earth was peopled.

20 Now Noah, a man of the soil, was the first to plant a vineyard. 21* When he drank some of the wine, he became drunk and lay naked inside his tent. 22 Ham, the father of Canaan, saw his father's nakedness, and he told his two brothers outside about it. 23 Shem and Japheth, however, took a robe, and holding it on their backs, they walked backward and covered their father's nakedness; since their faces were turned the other way, they did not see their father's nakedness. 24 When Noah woke up from his drunkenness and learned what his youngest son had done to him, 25* he said:

> "Cursed be Canaan!
> The lowest of slaves
> shall he be to his brothers."

26† He also said:

> "Blessed be the LORD, the God of Shem!
> Let Canaan be his slave.
> 27† May God expand Japheth,
> so that he dwells among the tents
> of Shem;
> and let Canaan be his slave."

28 Noah lived three hundred and fifty years after the flood. 29 The whole lifetime of Noah was nine hundred and fifty years; then he died.

Table of the Nations

10 1† These are the descendants of Noah's sons, Shem, Ham and Japheth, to whom sons were born after the flood.

2*†The descendants of Japheth:
Gomer, Magog, Madai, Javan, Tubal,
Meshech and Tiras.*
3† The descendants of Gomer:
Ashkenaz, Riphath and Togarmah.
4† The descendants of Javan:
Elishah, Tarshish, the Kittim and
the Rodanim.

5 These are the descendants of Japheth, and from them sprang the maritime nations, in their respective lands—each with its own language—by their clans within their nations.

6† The descendants of Ham:
Cush, Mizraim, Put and Canaan.
7 The descendants of Cush:
Seba, Havilah, Sabtah, Raamah and Sabteca.
The descendants of Raamah:
Sheba and Dedan.

8† Cush became the father of Nimrod, who was the first potentate on earth. 9 He was a mighty hunter by the grace of the LORD; hence the saying, "Like Nimrod, a mighty hunter by the grace of the LORD." 10† The chief cities of his kingdom were Babylon, Erech and Accad, all of them in the land of Shinar. 11† From that land he went forth to Asshur, where he built Nineveh, Rehoboth-Ir and

---

† **9, 18–27:** This story seems to be a composite of two earlier accounts; in the one, Ham was guilty, whereas, in the other, it was Canaan. One purpose of the story is to justify the Israelites' enslavement of the Canaanites because of certain indecent sexual practices in the Canaanite religion. Obviously the story offers no justification for enslaving African Negroes, even though Canaan is presented as a "son" of Ham because the land of Canaan belonged to Hamitic Egypt at the time of the Israelite invasion.

9, 26: *Blessed . . . Shem:* perhaps the text read originally, "Blessed of the LORD be Shem," which would be expected in the context.

9, 27: In the Hebrew text there is a play on the words *yapt* ("expand") and *yepet* ("Japheth").

10, 1–32: This chapter presents a remarkably good classification of the various peoples known to the ancient Israelites; it is theologically important as stressing the basic family unity of all men on earth. The relationship between the various peoples is based partly on linguistic, partly on geographic, and partly on political grounds *according to their . . . languages, . . . lands and nations:* (v 31). In general, *the descendants of Japheth* (vv 2–5) are the peoples of the Indo-European languages to the north and west of Mesopotamia and Syria; *the descendants of Ham* (vv 6–20) are the Hamitic-speaking peoples of northern Africa; and *the descendants of Shem* (vv 21–31) are the Semitic-speaking peoples of Mesopotamia, Syria and Arabia.

But there are many exceptions to this rule; the Semitic-speaking peoples of Canaan, for instance, are considered descendants of Ham, because at the time they were subject to Hamitic Egypt (vv 6.15–19). This chapter is a composite from the Yahwist source (vv 8–19.21. 24–30) of about the ninth century B.C., and the Priestly source (vv 1–7.20.22f.31f) of a few centuries later. That is why certain tribes of Arabia are listed under both Ham (v 7) and Shem (vv 26ff).

10, 2: *Gomer:* the Cimmerians; *Madai:* the Medes; *Javan:* the Greeks.

10, 3: *Ashkenaz:* the Scythians.

10, 4: *Elishah:* Cyprus; *the Kittim:* certain inhabitants of Cyprus; *the Rodanim:* the inhabitants of Rhodes.

10, 6: *Cush:* Biblical Ethiopia, modern Nubia; *Mizraim:* Egypt; *Put:* either Punt in East Africa or Libya.

10, 8: *Cush:* here, the Kassites; see note on Gn 2, 10–14. *Nimrod:* probably Tukulti-Ninurta I (thirteenth century B.C.), the first Assyrian conqueror of Babylonia and a famous city-builder at home.

10, 10: *Shinar:* ancient Sumer in southern Mesopotamia, mentioned also in Gn 11, 2; 14, 1.

9, 18: Gn 5, 32; 10, 1.
9, 21: Lam 4, 21; Heb 2, 15.
9, 25: Dt 27, 16; Wis 12, 11.

10, 2–8: 1 Chr 1, 5–10.
10, 2: Ez 38, 2.

Calah, 12† as well as Resen, between Nineveh and Calah, the latter being the principal city.

13* Mizraim became the father of the Ludim, the Anamim, the Lehabim, the Naphtuhim, 14† the Pathrusim, the Casluhim, and the Caphtorim from whom the Philistines sprang.

15† Canaan became the father of Sidon, his firstborn, and of Heth; 16 also of the Jebusites, the Amorites, the Girgashites, 17 the Hivites, the Arkites, the Sinites, 18 the Arvadites, the Zemarites and the Hamathites. Afterward, the clans of the Canaanites spread out, 19† so that the Canaanite borders extended from Sidon all the way to Gerar, near Gaza, and all the way to Sodom, Gomorrah, Admah and Zeboiim, near Lasha.

20 These are the descendants of Ham, according to their clans and languages, by their lands and nations.

21 To Shem also, Japheth's oldest brother and the ancestor of all the children of Eber, sons were born.

22* The descendants of Shem:
Elam, Asshur, Arpachshad, Lud and Aram.
23   The descendants of Aram:
Uz, Hul, Gether and Mash.

24 Arpachshad became the father of Shelah, and Shelah became the father of Eber. 25† To Eber two sons were born: the name of the first was Peleg, for in his time the world was divided; and the name of his brother was Joktan.

26 Joktan became the father of Almodad, Sheleph, Hazarmaveth, Jerah, 27 Hadoram, Uzal, Diklah, 28 Obal, Abimael, Sheba 29 Ophir, Havilah and Jobab. All these were descendants of Joktan. 30 Their settlements extended all the way to Sephar, the eastern hill country.

31 These are the descendants of Shem, according to their clans and languages, by their lands and nations.

32 These are the groupings of Noah's sons, according to their origins and by their nations. From these the other nations of the earth branched out after the flood.

The Tower of Babel

11 1† The whole world spoke the same language, using the same words. 2† While men were migrating in the east, they came upon a valley in the land of Shinar and settled there. 3 They said to one another, "Come, let us mold bricks and harden them with fire." They used bricks for stone, and bitumen for mortar. 4† Then they said, "Come, let us build ourselves a city and a tower with its top in the sky, and so make a name for ourselves; otherwise we shall be scattered all over the earth."

5 The LORD came down to see the city and the tower that the men had built. 6 Then the LORD said: "If now, while they are one people, all speaking the same language, they have started to do this, nothing will later stop them from doing whatever they presume to do. 7 Let us then go down and there confuse their language, so that one will not understand what another says." 8 Thus the LORD scattered them from there all over the earth, and they stopped building the city. 9† That is why it was called Babel, because there the LORD confused the speech of all the world. It was from that place that he scattered them all over the earth.

The Line from Shem to Abraham

10*† This is the record of the descendants of Shem. When Shem was one hundred years old, he became the father of Arpachshad, two years after the flood. 11 Shem lived five hundred years after the birth of Arpachshad, and he had other sons and daughters.

12† When Arpachshad was thirty-five years old, he became the father of Shelah. 13 Arpachshad lived four hundred and three years after the birth of Shelah, and he had other sons and daughters.

14 When Shelah was thirty years old, he became the father of Eber. 15 Shelah lived four hundred and

---

10, 11: *Asshur:* Assyria. *Rehoboth-Ir:* literally "wide-streets city," was probably not the name of another city, but an epithet of Nineveh; cf Jon 3, 3.

10, 12: *Calah:* Assyrian Kalhu, the capital of Assyria in the ninth century B.C.

10, 14: *The Pathrusim:* the people of upper (southern) Egypt; cf Is 11, 11; Jer 44, 1; Ez 29, 14; 30, 14. *Caphtorim:* Crete; for Caphtor as the place of origin of the Philistines, cf Dt 2, 23; Am 9, 7; Jer 47, 4.

10, 15: *Heth:* the biblical Hittites; see note on Gn 23, 3.

10, 19: *Lasha:* the reading of this name is uncertain; perhaps it should be "Bela"; cf Gn 14, 2.

10, 25: In the Hebrew text there is a play on the name *Peleg* and the word *niplega,* "was divided."

11, 1–9: This story, based on traditions about the temple towers or ziggurats of Babylonia, is used by the sacred writer primarily to illustrate man's increasing wickedness, shown here in his presumptuous effort to create an urban culture apart from God. The secondary motive in the story is to present an imaginative origin of the diversity of the languages among the various peoples inhabiting the earth, as well as an artificial explanation of the name "Babylon."

11, 2: *Shinar:* see note on Gn 10, 10.

11, 4: *Tower with its top in the sky:* a direct reference to the chief ziggurat of Babylon, the *E-sag-ila,* signifying "the house that raises high its head." Babylonian ziggurats were the earliest skyscrapers.

11, 9: *Babel:* the Hebrew form of the name "Babylon"; the native name, *Bab-ili,* means "gate of the gods." The Hebrew word *balil,* "he confused," has a similar sound. Apparently the name referred originally only to a certain part of the city, the district near the gate that led to the temple area.

11, 10–26: This section is a continuation of the genealogical record given in Gn 5, 1–32; see note there. Although the ages of the patriarchs in this list are much lower than those of the antediluvian patriarchs, they are still artificial and devoid of historical value. The ages given here are from the current Hebrew text; the Samaritan and Greek texts have divergent sets of numbers in most cases.

11, 12: The Greek text has a certain Kenan (cf Gn 5, 9f) between Arpachshad and Shelah. The text is followed in Lk 3, 36.

10, 13–18: 1 Chr 1, 11–16.   11, 10–26: 1 Chr 1, 24–27; Lk
10, 22–29: 1 Chr 1, 17–23.   3, 34ff.

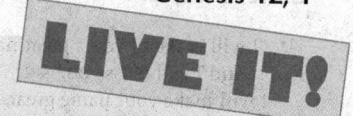

A Barrier or a Bridge?

Language can be either a barrier or a bridge. Through our speech, we connect with other people. And we often hear it expressed that love, music, and a smile are universal languages. Yet, languages also separate, symbolizing differences between cultures and nations that can erupt in wars and other atrocities.

The story of the tower of Babel is an ancient explanation of why the separation between people, symbolized by different languages, occurs. The people ignore God's command to "fill the earth" (Gn 1, 28). Instead, they gather in one place to try to build a tower reaching to heaven, a sin of pride and arrogance. God confuses their language to foil their plan. It is not language but pride that separates us.

In the Acts of the Apostles, chapter 2, language serves as a bridge. The Holy Spirit enables the people from many different lands to hear the Apostles speaking in their own languages. The Spirit serves to unify us, no matter what earthly language we speak. Anyone who has attended a World Youth Day knows that when we live by the Spirit, we can rise above the differences of language and culture. The Good News is universal and unites us!

▶ Gn 11, 1–9

three years after the birth of Eber, and he had other sons and daughters.

16† When Eber was thirty-four years old, he became the father of Peleg. 17 Eber lived four hundred and thirty years after the birth of Peleg, and he had other sons and daughters.

18 When Peleg was thirty years old, he became the father of Reu. 19 Peleg lived two hundred and nine years after the birth of Reu, and he had other sons and daughters.

20 When Reu was thirty-two years old, he became the father of Serug. 21 Reu lived two hundred and seven years after the birth of Serug, and he had other sons and daughters.

22 When Serug was thirty years old, he became the father of Nahor. 23 Serug lived two hundred years after the birth of Nahor, and he had other sons and daughters.

24 When Nahor was twenty-nine years old, he became the father of Terah. 25 Nahor lived one hundred and nineteen years after the birth of Terah, and he had other sons and daughters.

26* When Terah was seventy years old, he became the father of Abram, Nahor and Haran.

II: The Patriarch Abraham

Terah

27 This is the record of the descendants of Terah. Terah became the father of Abram, Nahor and Haran, and Haran became the father of Lot. 28† Haran died before his father Terah, in his native land, in Ur of the Chaldeans. 29* Abram and Nahor took wives; the name of Abram's wife was Sarai, and the name of Nahor's wife was Milcah, daughter of Haran, the father of Milcah and Iscah. 30 Sarai was barren; she had no child.

31*† Terah took his son Abram, his grandson Lot, son of Haran, and his daughter-in-law Sarai, the wife of his son Abram, and brought them out of Ur of the Chaldeans, to go to the land of Canaan. But when they reached Haran, they settled there. 32† The lifetime of Terah was two hundred and five years; then Terah died in Haran.

Abram's Call and Migration

12 1* The LORD said to Abram: "Go forth from the land of your kinsfolk and from your father's house to a land that I will show you.

---

† 11, 16: *Eber:* the eponymous ancestor of the Hebrews, "descendants of Eber" (Gn 10, 21.24–30); see note on Gn 14, 13.

11, 28: *Ur of the Chaldeans:* Ur was an extremely ancient city of the Sumerians (later, of the Babylonians) in southern Mesopotamia. The Greek text has "the land of the Chaldeans." In either case, the term *Chaldeans* is an anachronism, because the Chaldeans were not known to history until approximately a thousand years after Abraham's time.

11, 31: The Samaritan and Greek texts include Nahor and his wife in Terah's migration to Haran. Although this is probably due to scribal harmonization, Nahor's family actually did migrate to Haran; cf Gn 24, 10; 27, 43.

11, 32: Since Terah was seventy years old when his son Abraham was born (v 26), and Abraham was seventy-five when he left Haran (Gn 12, 4), Terah lived in Haran for sixty years after Abraham's departure. According to the tradition in the Samaritan text, Terah died when he was one hundred and forty-five years old, therefore, in the same year in which Abraham left Haran. This is the tradition followed in St. Stephen's speech: Abraham left Haran "after his father died" (Acts 7, 4).

* 11, 26: Jos 24, 2; 1 Chr 1, 27.   5, 6–9: Acts 7, 4.
11, 29: Gn 17, 15; 20, 12.   12, 1: Acts 7, 3; Heb 11, 8.
11, 31: Jos 24, 3; Neh 9, 7; Jdt

2* "I will make of you a great nation,
   and I will bless you;
I will make your name great,
   so that you will be a blessing.
3*†I will bless those who bless you
   and curse those who curse you.
All the communities of the earth
   shall find blessing in you."

7* The LORD appeared to Abram and said, "To your descendants I will give this land." So Abram built an altar there to the LORD who had appeared to him. 8 From there he moved on to the hill country east of Bethel, pitching his tent with Bethel to the west and Ai to the east. He built an altar there to the LORD and invoked the LORD by name. 9† Then Abram journeyed on by stages to the Negeb.

Introducing
▶ ABRAHAM AND SARAH

Abraham, whose name was originally Abram, is an important figure for three major world religions: Judaism, Christianity, and Islam. Abraham is regarded as the great example of faith in God. He first appears in Gn 11, 26. For many years, Abram lives in Haran in northern Mesopotamia (see map 1, "The World of the Patriarchs") with his wife, Sarai. God calls Abram and Sarai to leave their home, seals a covenant with them, and changes their names to Abraham and Sarah. God's covenant promises that they will be the parents "of a host of nations" (17, 5) and their descendants will be as numerous as the "stars of the sky" (22, 17).

Later, God requests that Abraham sacrifice his son Isaac. God stops him from going through with it, but Abraham's willingness to cooperate with God and his complete trust in God become the foundation for Israel's faith. Not surprisingly, in the Old Testament, when a prophet or teacher needed an example of someone with unwavering trust in God, Abraham was often cited.

In the New Testament, Abraham is revered as the first patriarch to enter into a covenant with God (see Mt 1, 1; Lk 16, 19–31) and the great pioneer of Israel's faith (Acts 7, 2–50; Rom 4, 1–25; Heb 7, 1–10).

▶ **Gn 12, 1—25, 11**

4* Abram went as the LORD directed him, and Lot went with him. Abram was seventy-five years old when he left Haran. 5† Abram took his wife Sarai, his brother's son Lot, all the possessions that they had accumulated, and the persons they had acquired in Haran, and they set out for the land of Canaan. When they came to the land of Canaan, 6 Abram passed through the land as far as the sacred place at Shechem, by the terebinth of Moreh. (The Canaanites were then in the land.)

Abram and Sarai in Egypt

10* There was famine in the land; so Abram went down to Egypt to sojourn there, since the famine in the land was severe. 11 When he was about to enter Egypt, he said to his wife Sarai: "I know well how beautiful a woman you are. 12 When the Egyptians see you, they will say, 'She is his wife'; then they will kill me, but let you live. 13*† Please say, therefore, that you are my sister, so that it may go well with me on your account and my life may be

---

12, 3: *Shall find blessing in you:* the sense of the Hebrew expression is probably reflexive, "shall bless themselves through you" (i.e., in giving a blessing they shall say, "May you be as blessed as Abraham"), rather than passive, "shall be blessed in you." Since the term is understood in a passive sense in the New Testament (Acts 3, 25; Gal 3, 8), it is rendered here by a neutral expression that admits of both meanings. So also in the blessings given by God to Isaac (Gn 26, 4) and Jacob (Gn 28, 14).

12, 5: *Persons:* slaves and retainers that formed the social aggregate under the leadership of Abraham; cf Gn 14, 14.

12, 9: *The Negeb:* the semidesert land of southern Palestine.

12, 13: *You are my sister:* although Abraham's deceit may not be

fully defensible, his statement was at least a half-truth; Sarah was indeed his relative, called "a sister" in Hebrew; cf Gn 20, 12. Moreover, the ancient traditions on which this story and the parallel ones in Gn 20, 1–18 and 26, 6–11 are based, probably come from the Hurrian custom of wife-sister marriage. Among the Hurrians, with whom Abraham's clan lived in close contact at Haran, a man could adopt his wife as his sister and thus give her higher status.

12, 2: Gn 17, 6; Sir 44, 20;
     Rom 4, 17–22.
12, 3: Gn 18, 18; 22, 18; Acts
     3, 25; Gal 3, 8.
12, 4f: Gn 11, 31; Jos 24, 3;

Acts 7, 4.
12, 7: Ex 33, 1; Dt 34, 4; Acts
     7, 5.
12, 10: Gn 26, 1.
12, 13: Gn 20, 12f; 26, 7.

spared for your sake." ¹⁴ When Abram came to Egypt, the Egyptians saw how beautiful the woman was; ¹⁵ and when Pharaoh's courtiers saw her, they praised her to Pharaoh. So she was taken into Pharaoh's palace. ¹⁶† On her account it went very well with Abram, and he received flocks and herds, male and female slaves, male and female asses, and camels.

¹⁷* But the LORD struck Pharaoh and his household with severe plagues because of Abram's wife Sarai. ¹⁸ Then Pharaoh summoned Abram and said to him: "How could you do this to me! Why didn't you tell me she was your wife? ¹⁹ Why did you say, 'She is my sister,' so that I took her for my wife? Here, then, is your wife. Take her and be gone!"

²⁰ Then Pharaoh gave men orders concerning him, and they sent him on his way, with his wife and all that belonged to him.

Abram and Lot Part

13 ¹* From Egypt Abram went up to the Negeb with his wife and all that belonged to him, and Lot accompanied him. ²* Now Abram was very rich in livestock, silver and gold. ³ From the Negeb he traveled by stages toward Bethel, to the place between Bethel and Ai where his tent had formerly stood, ⁴* the site where he had first built the altar; and there he invoked the LORD by name.

⁵ Lot, who went with Abram, also had flocks and herds and tents, ⁶ so that the land could not support them if they stayed together; their possessions were so great that they could not dwell together. ⁷ There were quarrels between the herdsmen of Abram's livestock and those of Lot's. (At this time the Canaanites and the Perizzites were occupying the land.)

⁸ So Abram said to Lot: "Let there be no strife between you and me, or between your herdsmen and mine, for we are kinsmen. ⁹ Is not the whole land at your disposal? Please separate from me. If you prefer the left, I will go to the right; if you prefer the right, I will go to the left." ¹⁰ Lot looked about and saw how well watered the whole Jordan Plain was as far as Zoar, like the LORD'S own garden, or like Egypt. (This was before the LORD had destroyed Sodom and Gomorrah.) ¹¹ Lot, therefore, chose for himself the whole Jordan Plain and set out eastward. Thus they

separated from each other; ¹² Abram stayed in the land of Canaan, while Lot settled among the cities of the Plain, pitching his tents near Sodom. ¹³* Now the inhabitants of Sodom were very wicked in the sins they committed against the LORD.

¹⁴* After Lot had left, the LORD said to Abram: "Look about you, and from where you are, gaze to the north and south, east and west; ¹⁵* all the land that you see I will give to you and your descendants forever. ¹⁶* I will make your descendants like the dust of the earth; if anyone could count the dust of the earth, your descendants too might be counted. ¹⁷ Set forth and walk about in the land, through its length and breadth, for to you I will give it." ¹⁸* Abram moved his tents and went on to settle near the terebinth of Mamre, which is at Hebron. There he built an altar to the LORD.

The Four Kings

14 ¹† In the days of . . . , Amraphel king of Shinar, Arioch king of Ellasar, Chedorlaomer king of Elam, and Tidal king of Goiim ² made war on Bera king of Sodom, Birsha king of Gomorrah, Shinab king of Admah, Shemeber king of Zeboiim, and the king of Bela (that is, Zoar). ³† All the latter kings joined forces in the Valley of Siddim (that is, the Salt Sea). ⁴ For twelve years they had been subject to Chedorlaomer, but in the thirteenth year they rebelled. ⁵† In the fourteenth year Chedorlaomer and the kings allied with him came and defeated the Rephaim in Ashteroth-karnaim, the Zuzim in Ham, the Emim in Shaveh-kiriathaim, ⁶* and the Horites in the hill country of Seir, as far as El-paran, close by the wilderness. ⁷ They then turned back and came to Enmishpat (that is, Kadesh), and they subdued the whole country both of the Amalekites and of the Amorites who dwelt in Hazazon-tamar. ⁸ Thereupon the king of Sodom, the king of Gomorrah, the king of Admah, the king of Zeboiim, and the king of Bela (that is, Zoar) marched out, and in the Valley of Siddim they went into battle against them: ⁹ against Chedorlaomer king of Elam, Tidal king of Goiim, Amraphel king of Shinar, and Arioch king of Ellasar—four kings against five. ¹⁰ Now the Valley of Siddim was full of bitumen pits; and as the kings of Sodom and Gomorrah fled, they fell into these, while the rest

---

12, 16: *Camels:* domesticated camels probably did not come into common use in the ancient Near East until the end of the 2nd millennium B.C. Thus the mention of camels at the time of the patriarchs (Gn 24, 11–64; 30, 43; 31, 17.34; 32, 8.16; 37, 25) is seemingly an anachronism.

14, 1: *In the days of . . . :* the personal name by which the event is dated has not been preserved.

14, 3: *The Salt Sea:* now known as the Dead Sea.

14, 5f: The five kings came from north to south through the land east of the Jordan.

12, 17: Ps 105, 14.
13, 1: Gn 12, 9.
13, 2: Ps 112, 1ff; Prv 10, 22.
13, 4: Gn 12, 8.
13, 13: Gn 18, 20; Ez 16, 49;
    2 Pt 2, 6ff; Jude 7.
13, 14: Gn 28, 14.

13, 15: Gn 12, 7; Mt 5, 4;
    Lk 1, 55; Acts 7, 5;
    Gal 3, 16.
13, 16: Gn 22, 17; Nm 23, 10.
13, 18: Gn 14, 13.
14, 6: Dt 2, 12.

fled to the mountains. ¹¹ The victors seized all the possessions and food supplies of Sodom and Gomorrah and then went their way, ¹²* taking with them Abram's nephew Lot, who had been living in Sodom, as well as his possessions.

¹³† A fugitive came and brought the news to Abram the Hebrew, who was camping at the terebinth of Mamre the Amorite, a kinsman of Eshcol and Aner; these were in league with Abram. ¹⁴ When Abram heard that his nephew had been captured, he mustered three hundred and eighteen of his retainers, born in his house, and went in pursuit as far as Dan. ¹⁵ He and his party deployed against them at night, defeated them, and pursued them as far as Hobah, which is north of Damascus.

¹⁶ He recovered all the possessions, besides bringing back his kinsman Lot and his possessions, along with the women and the other captives.

¹⁷ When Abram returned from his victory over Chedorlaomer and the kings who were allied with him, the king of Sodom went out to greet him in the Valley of Shaveh (that is, the King's Valley). ¹⁸*† Melchizedek, king of Salem, brought out bread and wine, and being a priest of God Most High, he blessed Abram with these words:

¹⁹† "Blessed be Abram by God Most High,
      the creator of heaven and earth;
²⁰† And blessed be God Most High,
      who delivered your foes into your hand."

Then Abram gave him a tenth of everything.

²¹ The king of Sodom said to Abram, "Give me the people; the goods you may keep." ²²† But Abram replied to the king of Sodom: "I have sworn to the LORD, God Most High, the creator of heaven and earth, ²³ that I would not take so much as a thread or a sandal strap from anything that is yours, lest you should say, 'I made Abram rich.' ²⁴ Nothing for me except what my servants have used up and the share that is due to the men who joined me— Aner, Eshcol and Mamre; let them take their share."

The Covenant with Abram

15 ¹ Some time after these events, this word of the LORD came to Abram in a vision:

"Fear not, Abram!
   I am your shield;
   I will make your reward very great."

² But Abram said, "O Lord GOD, what good will your gifts be, if I keep on being childless and have as my heir the steward of my house, Eliezer?" ³ Abram continued, "See, you have given me no offspring, and so one of my servants will be my heir." ⁴* Then the word of the LORD came to him: "No, that one shall not be your heir; your own issue shall be your heir." ⁵* He took him outside and said,

Catholic Connections

BREAD AND WINE

Melchizedek, a king and priest, uses bread and wine in a ritual to bless Abram. Bread and wine served as an ancient symbol of nourishment and celebration. The sacrament of the Eucharist has its roots in rituals such as this one. See Heb 7, 1–10 for a New Testament interpretation of Melchizedek's importance.

▶ Gn 14, 17–20

---

† **14, 13:** *Abram the Hebrew:* elsewhere in the Old Testament, until the last pre-Christian centuries, the term "Hebrew" is used only by non-Israelites, or by Israelites in speaking to foreigners, since it evidently had a disparaging connotation—something like "immigrant." The account in this chapter may, therefore, have been taken originally from a non-Israelite source, in which Abraham, a warlike sheik of Palestine, appears as a truly historical figure of profane history.

14, 18: *Salem:* traditionally identified with Jerusalem (Ps 76, 3), but the Hebrew text is not certain; instead of the present *melek shalem* ("king of Salem") the original may have been *melek shelomo* ("a king allied to him"). In Heb 7, 2, "king of Salem" is interpreted as "king of peace" (*shalom*).

14, 19: *God most High:* in Hebrew, *el-elyon.* In Canaanite texts, each element may occur separately as the name of a specific deity,

or they may be applied together to a single deity, as is done here by the Canaanite priest Melchizedek. For the Israelites, *el* became a poetic synonym for *elohim* ("God"); *elyon* ("Most High") became one of the titles of their God Yahweh.

14, 20: *Abram gave him:* literally "he gave him"; but *Abram* is to be understood as the subject of the sentence, for the tithes were the tenth part assigned to priests; cf Heb 7, 4–10.

14, 22: Abraham uses the name of the Canaanite god *el-elyon* ("God, the Most High") in apposition to the name of his God, *yahweh* ("the LORD").

* 14, 12: Gn 13, 10ff.   15, 5: Gn 22, 17; 28, 14;
14, 18: Ps 110, 4; Heb 5, 6.   Ex 32, 13; Dt 1, 10;
         10; 7, 1.   Sir 44, 21; Rom 4, 18;
15, 4: Gn 17, 16.   Heb 11, 12.

"Look up at the sky and count the stars, if you can. Just so," he added, "shall your descendants be." 6*† Abram put his faith in the LORD, who credited it to him as an act of righteousness.

7* He then said to him, "I am the LORD who brought you from Ur of the Chaldeans to give you this land as a possession." 8 "O Lord GOD," he asked, "how am I to know that I shall possess it?" 9*† He answered him, "Bring me a three-year-old heifer, a three-year-old she-goat, a three-year-old ram, a turtledove, and a young pigeon." 10 He brought him all these, split them in two, and placed each half opposite the other; but the birds he did not cut up. 11 Birds of prey swooped down on the carcasses, but Abram stayed with them. 12 As the sun was about to set, a trance fell upon Abram, and a deep, terrifying darkness enveloped him.

13* Then the LORD said to Abram: "Know for certain that your descendants shall be aliens in a land not their own, where they shall be enslaved and oppressed for four hundred years. 14* But I will bring judgment on the nation they must serve, and in the end they will depart with great wealth. 15 You, however, shall join your forefathers in peace; you shall be buried at a contented old age. 16*† In the fourth time-span the others shall come back here; the wickedness of the Amorites will not have reached its full measure until then."

17† When the sun had set and it was dark, there appeared a smoking brazier and a flaming torch, which passed between those pieces. 18*† It was on that occasion that the LORD made a covenant with Abram, saying: "To your descendants I give this land, from the Wadi of Egypt to the Great River [the Euphrates], 19* the land of the Kenites, the Kenizzites, the Kadmonites, 20 the Hittites, the Perizzites, the Rephaim, 21 the Amorites, the Canaanites, the Girgashites, and the Jebusites."

Birth of Ishmael

16 1*† Abram's wife Sarai had borne him no children. She had, however, an Egyptian maidservant named Hagar. 2* Sarai said to Abram: "The LORD has kept me from bearing children. Have

intercourse, then, with my maid; perhaps I shall have sons through her." Abram heeded Sarai's request. 3 Thus, after Abram had lived ten years in the land of Canaan, his wife Sarai took her maid, Hagar the Egyptian, and gave her to her husband Abram to be his concubine. 4* He had intercourse with her, and she became pregnant. When she became

did you KNOW?

Fire

Fire appears frequently throughout the Old Testament, symbolizing two aspects of God: presence and holiness. Fire symbolizes a special presence of God in the sealing of the covenant with Abraham (Gn 15, 17), in the burning bush (Ex 3, 2), and in the pillar of fire leading Israel through the desert (Ex 13, 21). Fire also symbolizes God's holiness appearing to purge and purify those who deviate from God's ways, as in Sodom and Gomorrah (Gn 19, 24) and the seventh plague against Egypt (Ex 9, 23).

▶ Gn 15, 17

aware of her pregnancy, she looked on her mistress with disdain. 5* So Sarai said to Abram: "You are responsible for this outrage against me. I myself gave my maid to your embrace; but ever since she became aware of her pregnancy, she has been looking on me with disdain. May the LORD decide between you and me!" 6 Abram told Sarai: "Your maid is in your power. Do to her whatever you please." Sarai then abused her so much that Hagar ran away from her.

7*† The LORD's messenger found her by a spring

---

† **15, 6:** Abraham's *faith* in God's promises was regarded as *an act of righteousness*, i.e., as expressing the "right" attitude of man toward God. In turn, God credited this to Abraham, i.e., gave him title to the fulfillment of God's promises. St. Paul (Rom 4, 1–25; Gal 3, 6–9) makes Abraham's faith a model for that of Christians.

15, 9: *Three-year-old:* ritually mature.

15, 16: *Time-span:* the Hebrew term *dor* is commonly rendered as "generation," but it may signify a period of varying length. Neither this passage nor the statement about the four hundred years has any value for determining how long the Israelites were in Egypt.

15, 17: *Brazier:* literally "oven"; a portable one is meant here. The smoke and fire represent God's presence. Although the text does not mention it, Abraham no doubt also walked between the split carcasses. For the meaning of this strange ceremony, see note on Jer 34, 18f.

15, 18: *Made a covenant:* literally "cut a covenant"; the expression derives from the ceremony of cutting the animals in two.

16, 1–6: Sarah's actions are all in keeping with the laws of the time, as known from ancient extra-biblical sources.

16, 7: *The LORD's messenger:* a manifestation of God in human form; therefore in v 13 the messenger is identified with the Lord himself.

---

*

15, 6: 1 Mc 2, 52; Rom 4, 3.9.22; Gal 3, 6f; Jas 2, 23.
15, 7: Gn 11, 31; 12, 1; Ex 32, 13; Neh 9, 7f; Acts 7, 2f.
15, 9: Lv 1, 14.
15, 13: Ex 12, 40; Nm 20, 15; Jdt 5, 9f; Is 52, 4; Acts 13, 20; Gal 3, 17.
15, 14: Ex 3, 8.21f.

15, 16: 1 Kgs 21, 26.
15, 18: Ex 32, 13; Neh 9, 8; Ps 105, 11; Sir 44, 21.
15, 19f: Dt 7, 1.
16, 1: Gn 11, 30.
16, 2: Gn 21, 8f; Gal 4, 22.
16, 4: 1 Sm 1, 6; Prv 30, 23.
16, 5–16: Gn 21, 10–19.
16, 7: Ex 15, 22.

Love and Jealousy

A love triangle in the Bible! The relationship between Abram, Sarai, and Hagar is shocking by Christian moral standards but would not have been unusual in their time. A patriarch like Abram would often have children by several wives, slaves, and concubines (something like mistresses who lived with the household). It's not surprising that such relationships would have fostered jealousy and tension. The conflict between Hagar and Sarai must have been fierce for Hagar to leave the security of Abram's household.

So, why does God's angel seek out Hagar and ask her to return to a place where she is likely to be mistreated? To answer this, we have to remember that the writer of Genesis was concerned more with explaining the rise of nations than with teaching a moral lesson. Hagar must return to bear her son, Ishmael, so that the Ishmaelites (descendants of Ishmael) have a clear connection to Abraham as their ancestor.

Today, we encourage victims of abuse and harassment to speak out and take action. When we encounter people who have been abused or harassed, we need to help them seek justice and set things right. Remember the larger message in Genesis—that every person is created in God's image and is to be treated with the utmost dignity and respect. Carrying out this message is our responsibility as brothers and sisters to one another.

▶ Gn 16, 1–16

---

in the wilderness, the spring on the road to Shur, 8 and he asked, "Hagar, maid of Sarai, where have you come from and where are you going?" She answered, "I am running away from my mistress, Sarai." 9 But the LORD's messenger told her: "Go back to your mistress and submit to her abusive treatment. 10* I will make your descendants so numerous," added the LORD's messenger, "that they will be too many to count. 11† Besides," the LORD's messenger said to her:

"You are now pregnant and shall
　　bear a son;
　you shall name him Ishmael,
　for the LORD has heard you,
　　God has answered you.

12* He shall be a wild ass of a man,
　　his hand against everyone,
　　and everyone's hand against him;
　in opposition to all his kin
　　shall he encamp."

13*† To the LORD who spoke to her she gave a name, saying, "You are the God of Vision"; she meant, "Have I really seen God and remained alive after my vision?" 14† That is why the well is called Beer-lahai-roi. It is between Kadesh and Bered.

15* Hagar bore Abram a son, and Abram named the son whom Hagar bore him Ishmael. 16 Abram was eighty-six years old when Hagar bore him Ishmael.

Covenant of Circumcision

17 1*† When Abram was ninety-nine years old, the LORD appeared to him and said: "I am God the Almighty. Walk in my presence and be blameless. 2* Between you and me I will establish my covenant, and I will multiply you exceedingly."

3 When Abram prostrated himself, God continued to speak to him: 4* "My covenant with you is this: you are to become the father of a host of nations. 5*† No longer shall you be called Abram; your name shall be Abraham, for I am making you the father of

---

†
16, 11: *Ishmael:* in Hebrew the name means "God has heard."

16, 13: *The God of Vision:* in Hebrew, *el-roi;* hence the name of the spring. *Remained alive:* for the ancient notion that a person died on seeing God, cf Gn 32, 31; Ex 20, 19; Dt 4, 33; Jgs 13, 22.

16, 14: *Beer-lahai-roi:* probably "the well of living sight," i.e., the well where one can see (God) and yet live.

17, 1: *The Almighty:* traditional but incorrect rendering of the divine title *shaddai,* of uncertain meaning.

17, 5: *Abram* and *Abraham* are merely two forms of the same

name, both meaning, "the father is exalted"; another variant form is Abiram (Nm 16, 1; 1 Kgs 16, 34). The additional *-ha-* in the form Abraham is explained by folk etymology as coming from *ab-hamon goyim,* "father of a host of nations."

*
16, 10: Gn 17, 20; 21, 13.18; 25, 12–18.	17, 1: Gn 35, 11; Ex 6, 3.
16, 12: Gn 21, 20; 25, 18.	17, 2: Gn 12, 2; 13, 16; Ex 32, 13.
16, 13: Gn 24, 62.	17, 4: Sir 44, 21; Rom 4, 17.
16, 15: Gn 16, 2; Gal 4, 22.	17, 5: Neh 9, 7.

a host of nations. ⁶ I will render you exceedingly fertile; I will make nations of you; kings shall stem from you. ⁷* I will maintain my covenant with you and your descendants after you throughout the ages as an everlasting pact, to be your God and the God of your descendants after you. ⁸* I will give to you and to your descendants after you the land in which you are now staying, the whole land of Canaan, as a permanent possession; and I will be their God."

⁹ God also said to Abraham: "On your part, you and your descendants after you must keep my covenant throughout the ages. ¹⁰* This is my covenant with you and your descendants after you that you must keep: every male among you shall be circumcised. ¹¹* Circumcise the flesh of your foreskin, and that shall be the mark of the covenant between you and me. ¹²* Throughout the ages, every male among you, when he is eight days old, shall be circumcised, including houseborn slaves and those acquired with money from any foreigner who is not of your blood. ¹³ Yes, both the houseborn slaves and those acquired with money must be circumcised. Thus my covenant shall be in your flesh as an everlasting pact. ¹⁴ If a male is uncircumcised, that is, if the flesh of his foreskin has not been cut away, such a one shall be cut off from his people; he has broken my covenant."

did you KNOW?

Circumcision

Circumcision, the removal of the foreskin of the penis, was practiced by many peoples in the ancient world. In Israel, circumcision was performed shortly after birth. It symbolized that this person belonged to the people of God, and was required by the covenant that God made first with Abraham, then with Moses and all Israel. Today, most Jews continue circumcision as a religious practice, and other people may be circumcised for personal reasons.

In the early church, circumcision became the center of a controversy about whether Gentiles who wanted to become Christians had to first become Jews (Acts of the Apostles, chapter 15; Phil 3, 2–9).

▶ Gn 17, 9–14

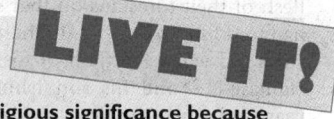

Covenant

Covenant is a powerful word in the Bible, with deep religious significance because it expresses the intimate relationship between God and God's people. At its most basic level, a covenant is a promise by both parties involved to do certain things.

In the covenant God makes with Noah, God promises never to destroy the earth again, and Noah's family promises to fill the earth and subdue it (Gn 9, 1–17). In the covenant with Abraham, God promises that Abram's descendants will be numerous and become a great nation. In return, Abram and all the male members of his household and their male descendants must practice circumcision to mark that they belong to God (17, 1–27). In the Covenant made at Mount Sinai with Moses (Ex 19, 1–9) and the Hebrew people, God promises to give them the Promised Land. In return, they promise to follow the laws God gives to them.

As told by the author of Genesis, these covenants are always initiated by God, who wants to lead the people to a better way of life. But the people must respond to God's offer as a sign of their faith in God. The New Testament tells of a new and lasting Covenant for all people and for all time (2 Cor 3, 3; Gal 4, 21–31).

And so we, each of us, are part of these ancient promises. Like the many faithful people who have gone before us, we too are the descendants of Abraham and Sarah, believers in the one God and members of God's family. We too are heirs to a special, intimate relationship with the Holy One of Israel.

▶ Gn 17, 1–27

17, 7: Ps 105, 42; Lk 1, 72f; Gal 3, 16.
17, 8: Ex 32, 13; Dt 1, 8; 14,

2; Lk 1, 55; Acts 7, 5.
17, 10: Jn 7, 22; Acts 7, 8; Rom 4, 11.

17, 11: Sir 44, 21.

17, 12: Lv 12, 3; Lk 1, 59; 2, 21.

15† God further said to Abraham: "As for your wife Sarai, do not call her Sarai; her name shall be Sarah. 16* I will bless her, and I will give you a son by her. Him also will I bless; he shall give rise to nations, and rulers of peoples shall issue from him." 17*† Abraham prostrated himself and laughed as he said to himself, "Can a child be born to a man who is a hundred years old? Or can Sarah give birth at ninety?" 18 Then Abraham said to God, "Let but Ishmael live on by your favor!" 19* God replied: "Nevertheless, your wife Sarah is to bear you a son, and you shall call him Isaac. I will maintain my covenant with him as an everlasting pact, to be his God and the God of his descendants after him. 20* As for Ishmael, I am heeding you: I hereby bless him. I will make him fertile and will multiply him exceedingly. He shall become the father of twelve chieftains, and I will make of him a great nation. 21* But my covenant I will maintain with Isaac, whom Sarah shall bear to you by this time next year." 22 When he had finished speaking with him, God departed from Abraham.

23 Then Abraham took his son Ishmael and all his slaves, whether born in his house or acquired with his money—every male among the members of Abraham's household—and he circumcised the flesh of their foreskins on that same day, as God had told him to do. 24* Abraham was ninety-nine years old when the flesh of his foreskin was circumcised, 25 and his son Ishmael was thirteen years old when the flesh of his foreskin was circumcised. 26 Thus, on that same day Abraham and his son Ishmael were circumcised; 27 and all the male members of his household, including the slaves born in his house or acquired with his money from foreigners, were circumcised with him.

Abraham's Visitors

18 1 The LORD appeared to Abraham by the terebinth of Mamre, as he sat in the entrance of his tent, while the day was growing hot. 2* Looking up, he saw three men standing nearby. When he saw them, he ran from the entrance of the tent to greet them; and bowing to the ground, 3† he said: "Sir, if I may ask you this favor, please do not go on past your servant. 4 Let some water be brought, that you may bathe your feet, and then rest yourselves under the tree. 5 Now that you have come this close to your servant, let me bring you a little food, that you may refresh yourselves; and afterward you may go on your way." "Very well," they replied, "do as you have said."

6† Abraham hastened into the tent and told Sarah, "Quick, three seahs of fine flour! Knead it and make rolls." 7 He ran to the herd, picked out a tender, choice steer, and gave it to a servant, who quickly prepared it. 8† Then he got some curds and milk, as well as the steer that had been prepared, and set these before them; and he waited on them under the tree while they ate.

9 "Where is your wife Sarah?" they asked him. "There in the tent," he replied. 10*† One of them said, "I will surely return to you about this time next year, and Sarah will then have a son." Sarah was listening at the entrance of the tent, just behind him. 11* Now Abraham and Sarah were old, advanced in years, and Sarah had stopped having her womanly periods. 12† So Sarah laughed to herself and said, "Now that I am so withered and my husband is so old, am I still to have sexual pleasure?" 13 But the LORD said to Abraham: "Why did Sarah laugh and say, 'Shall I really bear a child, old as I am?' 14* Is anything too marvelous for the LORD to do? At the appointed time, about this time next year, I will return to you, and Sarah will have a son." 15 Because she was afraid, Sarah dissembled, saying, "I didn't laugh." But he said, "Yes you did."

Abraham Intercedes for Sodom

16 The men set out from there and looked down toward Sodom; Abraham was walking with them, to see them on their way. 17 The LORD reflected: "Shall I hide from Abraham what I am about to do, 18* now that he is to become a great and populous nation, and all the nations of the earth are to find blessing in him? 19 Indeed, I have singled him out that he may direct his sons and his

---

17, 15: *Sarai* and *Sarah* are variant forms of the same name, both meaning "princess."

17, 17: *Laughed: yishaq,* which is the Hebrew form of the name "Isaac"; other similar explanations of the name are given in Gn 18, 12 and 21, 6.

18, 3: Abraham addresses the leader of the group, whom he does not yet recognize as Yahweh; in the next two verses he speaks to all three men. The other two are later (Gn 19, 1) identified as messengers.

18, 6: *Three seahs:* one ephah, about half a bushel.

18, 8: *Curds:* a type of soft cheese or yoghurt.

18, 10: *One of them:* i.e., the Lord. Abraham now realizes this for the first time when he hears the prediction of a miraculous birth. *About this time next year:* literally "when the time becomes alive,"

i.e., at the time when birth is due after the period of gestation; the conception is understood as taking place soon after the prediction.

18, 12: *Sarah laughed:* see note on Gn 17, 17.

17, 16: Gn 18, 18; Gal 4, 23.
17, 17: Rom 4, 19; Heb 11, 11f.
17, 19: Gn 11, 30; 21, 2; Ex 32, 13; Sir 44, 22.
17, 20: Gn 16, 10; 21, 13.18; 25, 12–16.
17, 21: Gn 18, 14; 21, 2; 26, 2–5; Rom 9, 7.
17, 24: Gn 17, 10; Rom 4, 11.
18, 2: Heb 13, 1f.
18, 10: Gn 17, 19; 21, 1; 2 Kgs 4, 16; Rom 9, 9.
18, 11: Gn 17, 17; Rom 4, 19; Heb 11, 11f.
18, 14: Mt 19, 26; Mk 10, 27; Lk 1, 37; 18, 27; Rom 4, 21.
18, 18: Lk 1, 55.

What's So Funny?

Laughter is not a word we usually associate with the Bible, and certainly not with the Old Testament. Most of the stories are serious, filled with accounts of sacrifice, battles, and the Covenant. But here is Sarah, an old woman, long past childbearing age. She overhears one of Abraham's mysterious guests tell him that in a year, he and Sarah will have a son (Gn 18, 10). How can she help but laugh? She and Abraham do produce, of course, a son called Isaac, whose Hebrew name, Yishaq, means "laughed." Sarah's cynical chuckles must have turned to joyful laughs at the birth of her beloved son. Laughter is a wonderful response to the gift of life and is a natural and often spontaneous response to God's presence within us and around us.

"Is anything too marvelous for the LORD to do?" (verse 14). We are all tempted to laugh at the notion that miracles can happen to us. As we grow in faith and open ourselves to God's goodness, our laughter will change from cynical laughter to joyful laughter.

▶ Gn 18, 9–15

Get Close to God

Our prayers reveal what we believe about God and what we value. Abraham's bargaining for the inhabitants of Sodom and Gomorrah shows his faith, his care for others, and his closeness with God. Although he is humble, he deals with God as a friend whom he is not afraid to be honest with.

We too must be honest with God in our prayer. Too many Christians simply do not trust God enough to be completely themselves with God. They are afraid to share their doubts, anger, grief, and frustrations. But God is big enough to handle it all. Find a way in your prayer to share your innermost thoughts and feelings with God. For some people, journaling helps; others yell and shout aloud at the Lord. Remember that God's healing touch cannot enter our life until we are willing to share our deepest feelings.

▶ Gn 18, 22–33

posterity to keep the way of the LORD by doing what is right and just, so that the LORD may carry into effect for Abraham the promises he made about him." 20*† Then the LORD said: "The outcry against Sodom and Gomorrah is so great, and their sin so grave, 21 that I must go down and see whether or not their actions fully correspond to the cry against them that comes to me. I mean to find out."

22 While the two men walked on farther toward Sodom, the LORD remained standing before Abraham. 23 Then Abraham drew nearer to him and said: "Will you sweep away the innocent with the guilty? 24 Suppose there were fifty innocent people in the city; would you wipe out the place, rather than spare it for the sake of the fifty innocent people within it? 25* Far be it from you to do such a thing, to make the innocent die with the guilty, so that the innocent and the guilty would be treated alike! Should not the judge of all the world act with justice?" 26 The LORD replied, "If I find fifty innocent people in the city of Sodom, I will spare the whole place for their sake." 27* Abraham spoke up again: "See how I am presuming to speak to my Lord, though I am but dust and ashes! 28 What if there are five less than fifty innocent people? Will you destroy the whole city because of those five?" "I will not destroy it," he answered, "if I find forty-five there." 29 But

---

18, 20: Israelite tradition was unanimous in ascribing the destruction of Sodom and Gomorrah to the wickedness of these cities, but tradition varied in regard to the nature of this wickedness. According to the present account of the Yahwist, the sin of Sodom was homosexuality (Gn 19, 4f), which is therefore also known as sodomy; but according to Isaiah (1, 9f; 3, 9), it was a lack of social

justice; Ezekiel (16, 46–51) described it as a disregard for the poor, whereas Jeremiah (23, 14) saw it as general immorality.

18, 20: Gn 19, 13; Is 3, 9; Lk 17, 28; Jude 7.
18, 25: Dt 32, 4; Jb 8, 3.20; Wis 12, 15.
18, 27: Sir 10, 9; 17, 27.

Abraham persisted, saying, "What if only forty are found there?" He replied, "I will forbear doing it for the sake of the forty." ³⁰ Then he said, "Let not my Lord grow impatient if I go on. What if only thirty are found there?" He replied, "I will forbear doing it if I can find but thirty there." ³¹ Still he went on, "Since I have thus dared to speak to my Lord, what if there are no more than twenty?" "I will not destroy it," he answered, "for the sake of the twenty." ³²* But he still persisted, "Please, let not my Lord grow angry if I speak up this last time. What if there are at least ten there?" "For the sake of those ten," he replied, "I will not destroy it."

³³ The LORD departed as soon as he had finished speaking with Abraham, and Abraham returned home.

⁴* Before they went to bed, all the townsmen of Sodom, both young and old—all the people to the last man—closed in on the house. ⁵ They called to Lot and said to him, "Where are the men who came to your house tonight? Bring them out to us that we may have intimacies with them." ⁶ Lot went out to meet them at the entrance. When he had shut the door behind him, ⁷ he said, "I beg you, my brothers, not to do this wicked thing. ⁸ I have two daughters who have never had intercourse with men. Let me bring them out to you, and you may do to them as you please. But don't do anything to these men, for you know they have come under the shelter of my roof." ⁹* They replied, "Stand back! This fellow," they sneered, "came here as an immigrant, and now he dares to give orders! We'll treat you worse than them!" With that, they pressed hard

Be Kind to Strangers

If our first gesture to outsiders were one of respect, kindness, and gracious hospitality, what might our world be like? The story of Sodom and Gomorrah shows us the results of disrespect, inhospitality, and the attempted sexual abuse of strangers. Like Abraham, Lot is a wonderful host. But the people of Sodom want Lot's visitors for their own sexual pleasure, which, in this story, amounts to homosexual rape. This horrendous crime calls for the most severe punishment.

As children of God, it is our responsibility to extend our kindness to stranger and friend alike. So how are visitors or new students treated in your school? How are visitors treated in your home?

▸ **Gn 19, 1–11**

Destruction of Sodom and Gomorrah

19 ¹ The two angels reached Sodom in the evening, as Lot was sitting at the gate of Sodom. When Lot saw them, he got up to greet them; and bowing down with his face to the ground, ²*† he said, "Please, gentlemen, come aside into your servant's house for the night, and bathe your feet; you can get up early to continue your journey." But they replied, "No, we shall pass the night in the town square." ³ He urged them so strongly, however, that they turned aside to his place and entered his house. He prepared a meal for them, baking cakes without leaven, and they dined.

against Lot, moving in closer to break down the door. ¹⁰ But his guests put out their hands, pulled Lot inside with them, and closed the door; ¹¹† at the same time they struck the men at the entrance of the house, one and all, with such a blinding light that they were utterly unable to reach the doorway.

¹²*† Then the angels said to Lot: "Who else belongs to you here? Your sons [sons-in-law] and your daughters and all who belong to you in the city— take them away from it! ¹³* We are about to destroy this place, for the outcry reaching the LORD against those in the city is so great that he has sent us to

---

† **19, 2:** *Gentlemen:* Lot does not yet know that the distinguished-looking men are God's messengers; cf Gn 18, 3.
19, 11: *Blinding light:* a preternatural flash that temporarily dazed the wicked men and revealed to Lot the true nature of his guests.
19, 12: Since Lot apparently had no *sons,* a glossator interpreted the term to mean *sons-in-law.*

* 18, 32: Jer 5, 1; Ez 22, 30.
19, 2: Wis 10, 6; Sir 16, 8; Ez 16, 50; Heb 13, 1f.
19, 4–9: Jgs 19, 22–25; Jude 7.
19, 9: Gn 13, 12; 2 Pt 2, 7f.
19, 12: 2 Pt 7, 9.
19, 13: Is 1, 7.9; Zep 2, 9; Lk 17, 29.

destroy it." ¹⁴† So Lot went out and spoke to his sons-in-law, who had contracted marriage with his daughters. "Get up and leave this place," he told them; "the LORD is about to destroy the city." But his sons-in-law thought he was joking.

¹⁵ As dawn was breaking, the angels urged Lot on, saying, "On your way! Take with you your wife and your two daughters who are here, or you will be swept away in the punishment of the city." ¹⁶ When he hesitated, the men, by the LORD's mercy, seized his hand and the hands of his wife and his two daughters and led them to safety outside the city. ¹⁷* As soon as they had been brought outside, he was told: "Flee for your life! Don't look back or stop anywhere on the Plain. Get off to the hills at once, or you will be swept away." ¹⁸ "Oh, no, my lord!" replied Lot. ¹⁹ "You have already thought enough of your servant to do me the great kindness of intervening to save my life. But I cannot flee to the hills to keep the disaster from overtaking me, and so I shall die. ²⁰† Look, this town ahead is near enough to escape to. It's only a small place. Let me flee there—it's a small place, isn't it?—that my life may be saved." ²¹ "Well, then," he replied, "I will also grant you the favor you now ask. I will not overthrow the town you speak of. ²²* Hurry, escape there! I cannot do anything until you arrive there." That is why the town is called Zoar.

²³* The sun was just rising over the earth as Lot arrived in Zoar; ²⁴* at the same time the LORD rained down sulphurous fire upon Sodom and Gomorrah [from the LORD out of heaven]. ²⁵*† He overthrew those cities and the whole Plain, together with the inhabitants of the cities and the produce of the soil. ²⁶* But Lot's wife looked back, and she was turned into a pillar of salt.

²⁷ Early the next morning Abraham went to the place where he had stood in the LORD'S presence. ²⁸*† As he looked down toward Sodom and Gomorrah and the whole region of the Plain, he saw dense smoke over the land rising like fumes from a furnace.

²⁹ Thus it came to pass: when God destroyed the Cities of the Plain, he was mindful of Abraham by sending Lot away from the upheaval by which God overthrew the cities where Lot had been living.

Moabites and Ammonites

³⁰† Since Lot was afraid to stay in Zoar, he and his two daughters went up from Zoar and settled in the hill country, where he lived with his two daughters in a cave. ³¹ The older one said to the younger: "Our father is getting old, and there is not a man on earth to unite with us as was the custom everywhere. ³² Come, let us ply our father with wine and then lie with him, that we may have offspring by our father." ³³ So that night they plied their father with wine, and the older one went in and lay with her father; but he was not aware of her lying down or her getting up. ³⁴ Next day the older one said to the younger: "Last night it was I who lay with my father. Let us ply him with wine again tonight, and then you go in and lie with him, that we may both have offspring by our father." ³⁵ So that night, too, they plied their father with wine, and then the younger one went in and lay with him; but again he was not aware of her lying down or her getting up.

³⁶ Thus both of Lot's daughters became pregnant by their father. ³⁷*† The older one gave birth to a son whom she named Moab, saying, "From my father." He is the ancestor of the Moabites of today. ³⁸*† The younger one, too, gave birth to a son, and she named him Ammon, saying, "The son of my kin." He is the ancestor of the Ammonites of today.

Abraham at Gerar

20 ¹† Abraham journeyed on to the region of the Negeb, where he settled between Kadesh and Shur. While he stayed in Gerar, ² he said of his wife Sarah, "She is my sister." So Abimelech, king of Gerar, sent and took Sarah. ³ But God came to Abimelech in a dream one night and said to him, "You are about to die because of the woman you have taken, for she has a husband." ⁴ Abimelech, who had not approached her, said: "O Lord, would you slay a man even though he is innocent? ⁵ He himself told me, 'She is my sister,' and she herself

---

19, 14: It is uncertain whether Lot's *sons-in-law* were fully married to his daughters or only "engaged" to them (Israelite "engagement" was the first part of the marriage ceremony), or even whether the daughters involved were the same as, or different from, the two daughters who were still in their father's house.

19, 20: *A small place:* the Hebrew word *misar*, literally "a little thing," has the same root consonants as the name of the town *Zoar* in v 22.

19, 25: *Overthrew:* the consistent use of this term, literally "turned upside down," to describe the destruction of the *Cities of the Plain* seems to imply that their upheaval (v 29) was caused primarily by an earthquake; this would naturally be accompanied by a disastrous fire, especially in a region containing bitumen (Gn 14, 10) and its accompanying gases.

19, 28f: From the height east of Hebron, Abraham could easily see the region at the southern end of the Dead Sea, where the *Cities of the Plain* were probably located.

19, 30–38: This Israelite tale about the origin of Israel's neighbors east of the Jordan and the Dead Sea was told partly to ridicule these racially related but rival nations and partly to give folk etymologies for their names.

19, 37: *From my father:* in Hebrew, *meabi,* similar in sound to the name "Moab."

19, 38: *The son of my kin:* in Hebrew, *ben-ammi,* similar in sound to the name "Ammonites."

20, 1–18: This story from the Elohist source (see note on Gn 4, 25) combines elements found in the two very similar but distinct stories of the Yahwist source in Gn 12, 10–20 and 26, 6–11.

19, 17: Wis 10, 6.
19, 22: Wis 10, 6.
19, 23: Pss 9, 6; 11, 6; 107, 34.
19, 24: Wis 10, 7; Is 1, 9; 13, 19;
    Lam 4, 6; 17, 29; 2 Pt 2, 6.
19, 25: Dt 29, 22; Jer 50, 40;

    Am 4, 11.
19, 28: Rv 9, 2; 14, 10f.
19, 37: Dt 2, 9.
19, 38: Dt 2, 19.

also stated, 'He is my brother.' I did it in good faith and with clean hands." 6 God answered him in the dream: "Yes, I know you did it in good faith. In fact, it was I who kept you from sinning against me; that is why I did not let you touch her. 7† Therefore, return the man's wife—as a spokesman he will intercede for you—that your life may be saved. If you do not return her, you can be sure that you and all who are yours will certainly die."

8 Early the next morning Abimelech called all his court officials and informed them of everything that had happened, and the men were horrified. 9 Then Abimelech summoned Abraham and said to him: "How could you do this to us! What wrong did I do to you that you should have brought such monstrous guilt on me and my kingdom? You have treated me in an intolerable way. 10 What were you afraid of," he asked him, "that you should have done such a thing?" 11 "I was afraid," answered Abraham, "because I thought there would surely be no fear of God in this place, and so they would kill me on account of my wife. 12* Besides, she is in truth my sister, but only my father's daughter, not my mother's; and so she became my wife. 13 When God sent me wandering from my father's house, I asked her: 'Would you do me this favor? In whatever place we come to, say that I am your brother.' "

14 Then Abimelech took flocks and herds and male and female slaves and gave them to Abraham; and after he restored his wife Sarah to him, 15 he said, "Here, my land lies at your disposal; settle wherever you please." 16† To Sarah he said: "See, I have given your brother a thousand shekels of silver. Let that serve you as a vindication before all who are with you; your honor has been preserved with everyone." 17 Abraham then interceded with God, and God restored health to Abimelech, that is, to his wife and his maidservants, so that they could bear children; 18 for God had tightly closed every womb in Abimelech's household on account of Abraham's wife Sarah.

Birth of Isaac

21 1* The LORD took note of Sarah as he had said he would; he did for her as he had promised. 2* Sarah became pregnant and bore Abraham a son in his old age, at the set time that God had stated. 3* Abraham gave the name Isaac to this son of his whom Sarah bore him. 4* When

Hagar's Rescue

Genesis 21, 9–21 is part 2 of the Hagar and Ishmael story begun in 16, 1–16. Once again, Hagar is the victim of Sarah's jealousy. But this time God does not send her back. Seemingly facing certain death, Hagar receives from God the ability to see the opportunity for life in front of her. This time the writer of Genesis makes the point that God rescues the abused and abandoned. Hagar and Ishmael survive, and from their descendants a great people emerges.

Hagar's story reminds us that God wants to rescue us from oppression, injustice, and abuse. Often, we want to ask God to magically take these things away. But because God has given human beings free will, we cannot always be spared from the abuse and injustice of others. In your prayer, you can always ask God to rescue you, to give you the vision to see the healthy choices you can make to improve your situation. Do that right now if you are in an unjust or abusive situation.

▶ Gn 21, 9–21

his son Isaac was eight days old, Abraham circumcised him, as God had commanded. 5 Abraham was a hundred years old when his son Isaac was born to him. 6* Sarah then said, "God has given me cause to laugh, and all who hear of it will laugh with me. 7 Who would have told Abraham," she added, "that Sarah would nurse children! Yet I have borne him a son in his old age." 8 Isaac grew, and on the day of the child's weaning Abraham held a great feast.

9† Sarah noticed the son whom Hagar the Egyptian had borne to Abraham playing with her son Isaac; 10* so she demanded of Abraham: "Drive out that slave and her son! No son of that slave is going

---

20, 7: *Spokesman:* the Hebrew term *nabi* used here is regularly translated as "prophet," but it simply means "one who speaks on behalf of another," whether the latter is God, as in almost all cases, or another man, as in Ex 4, 16.

20, 16: *A thousand shekels of silver:* not a gift distinct from that of the animals and the slaves (v 14), but the monetary value of these.

21, 9–19: This story of Hagar's expulsion, in the Elohist source, is in general a duplicate of the one from the Yahwist source in Gn 16, 5–14; but the two stories differ greatly in detail.

20, 12: Gn 12, 13.
21, 1: Gn 17, 19; 18, 10.
21, 2: Gal 4, 23; Heb 11, 11.
21, 3: Mt 1, 2; Lk 3, 34.
21, 4: Gn 17, 10ff; Acts 7, 8.
21, 6: Gn 17, 17.
21, 10: Jgs 11, 2; Gal 4, 30.

to share the inheritance with my son Isaac!" [11] Abraham was greatly distressed, especially on account of his son Ishmael. [12]* But God said to Abraham: "Do not be distressed about the boy or about your slave woman. Heed the demands of Sarah, no matter what she is asking of you; for it is through Isaac that descendants shall bear your name. [13] As for the son of the slave woman, I will make a great nation of him also, since he too is your offspring."

[14]† Early the next morning Abraham got some bread and a skin of water and gave them to Hagar. Then, placing the child on her back, he sent her away. As she roamed aimlessly in the wilderness of Beer-sheba, [15] the water in the skin was used up. So she put the child down under a shrub, [16] and then went and sat down opposite him, about a bowshot away; for she said to herself, "Let me not watch to see the child die." As she sat opposite him, he began to cry. [17]* God heard the boy's cry, and God's messenger called to Hagar from heaven: "What is the matter, Hagar? Don't be afraid; God has heard the boy's cry in this plight of his. [18] Arise, lift up the boy and hold him by the hand; for I will make of him a great nation." [19] Then God opened her eyes, and she saw a well of water. She went and filled the skin with water, and then let the boy drink.

[20] God was with the boy as he grew up. He lived in the wilderness and became an expert bowman, [21] with his home in the wilderness of Paran. His mother got a wife for him from the land of Egypt.

The Pact at Beer-sheba

[22]† About that time Abimelech, accompanied by Phicol, the commander of his army, said to Abraham: "God is with you in everything you do. [23]† Therefore, swear to me by God at this place that you will not deal falsely with me or with my progeny and posterity, but will act as loyally toward me and the land in which you stay as I have acted toward you." [24] To this Abraham replied, "I so swear."

[25] Abraham, however, reproached Abimelech about a well that Abimelech's men had seized by force. [26] "I have no idea who did that," Abimelech replied. "In fact, you never told me about it, nor did I ever hear of it until now."

[27] Then Abraham took sheep and cattle and gave them to Abimelech and the two made a pact. [28] Abraham also set apart seven ewe lambs of the flock, [29] and Abimelech asked him, "What is the purpose of these seven ewe lambs that you have set apart?" [30] Abraham answered, "The seven ewe lambs you shall accept from me that thus I may have your acknowledgment that the well was dug by me." [31]† This is why the place is called Beer-sheba; the two of them took an oath there. [32] When they had thus made the pact in Beer-sheba, Abimelech, along with Phicol, the commander of his army, left and returned to the land of the Philistines.

[33]† Abraham planted a tamarisk at Beer-sheba, and there he invoked by name the LORD, God the Eternal. [34] Abraham resided in the land of the Philistines for many years.

The Testing of Abraham

22 [1]*† Some time after these events, God put Abraham to the test. He called to him, "Abraham!" "Ready!" he replied. [2]*† Then God said: "Take your son Isaac, your only one, whom you love, and go to the land of Moriah. There you shall offer him up as a holocaust on a height that I will point out to you." [3] Early the next morning Abraham saddled his donkey, took with him his son Isaac, and two of his servants as well, and with the wood that he had cut for the holocaust, set out for the place of which God had told him.

[4] On the third day Abraham got sight of the place from afar. [5] Then he said to his servants: "Both of you stay here with the donkey, while the boy and I go on over yonder. We will worship and then come back to you." [6] Thereupon Abraham took the wood for the holocaust and laid it on his son Isaac's shoulders, while he himself carried the fire and the knife. [7] As the two walked on together, Isaac spoke to his father Abraham: "Father!" he said. "Yes, son," he replied. Isaac continued, "Here are the fire and

---

† **21, 14:** *Placing the child on her back:* the phrase is translated from an emended form of the Hebrew text. In the current faulty Hebrew text, Abraham put the bread and the waterskin on Hagar's back, while her son apparently walked beside her. This reading seems to be a scribal attempt at harmonizing the present passage with the data of the Priestly source, in which Ishmael would have been at least fourteen years old when Isaac was born; compare Gn 16, 16 with 21, 5; cf 17, 25. But in the present Elohist story Ishmael is obviously a little boy, not much older than Isaac; cf vv 15, 18.

21, 22: Here and in v 32 the Greek text has ". . . Abimelech, accompanied by Ahuzzath, his councilor, and Phicol . . ."; but this is probably a secondary harmonization with Gn 26, 26. Abimelech took Phicol with him in order to intimidate Abraham by a show of strength.

21, 23: *This place:* Beer-sheba (v 31). Abimelech had come from Gerar (Gn 20, 2), about thirty miles west of Beer-sheba.

21, 31: *Beer-sheba:* the Hebrew name really means "the well of the seven," i.e., the place where there are seven wells, alluded to in the episode of the *seven ewe lambs,* vv 28ff; but it can also be interpreted to mean "the well of the oath."

21, 33: *God the Eternal:* in Hebrew, *el olam,* perhaps the name of the deity of the pre-Israelite sanctuary at Beer-sheba, but used by Abraham merely as a title of Yahweh; cf Is 40, 28.

22, 1: *God put Abraham to the test:* to prove the firmness of Abraham's faith in God's promise that through Isaac all the nations of the earth would find blessing; cf Gn 18, 10.18; 21, 12.

22, 2: *Only one:* uniquely precious, especially loved; therefore the same term is rendered in vv 12.16 as "beloved."

*
21, 12: Rom 9, 7; Heb 11, 18.	22, 2: 2 Chr 3, 1; 1 Mc 2, 52;
21, 17: Gn 16, 7.	Heb 11, 17.
22, 1: Sir 44, 20.	

the wood, but where is the sheep for the holocaust?" 8 "Son," Abraham answered, "God himself will provide the sheep for the holocaust." Then the two continued going forward.

9* When they came to the place of which God had told him, Abraham built an altar there and arranged the wood on it. Next he tied up his son Isaac, and put him on top of the wood on the altar. 10* Then he reached out and took the knife to slaughter his son. 11 But the LORD'S messenger called to him from heaven, "Abraham, Abraham!" "Yes, Lord," he answered. 12* "Do not lay your hand on the boy," said the messenger. "Do not do the least thing to him. I know now how devoted you are to God, since you did not withhold from me your own beloved son." 13 As Abraham looked

about, he spied a ram caught by its horns in the thicket. So he went and took the ram and offered it up as a holocaust in place of his son. 14† Abraham named the site Yahweh-yireh; hence people now say, "On the mountain the LORD will see."

15 Again the LORD'S messenger called to Abraham from heaven 16* and said: "I swear by myself, declares the LORD, that because you acted as you did in not withholding from me your beloved son, 17* I

Chap. 22

Ultimate Trust in God!

To us it seems horrible that God would ask Abraham to sacrifice his son Isaac. But this story is meant to be a sign of Abraham's complete trust in God. Ultimately, God prevented the sacrifice because God wanted not Isaac's death but Abraham's faith. Because of his willingness to respond to God's demand, Abraham is recognized as the father of our faith. Our trust in God should be as total as Abraham's trust was.

We probably won't ever be faced with the test of Abraham, but the story shows us the power of faith. Because of Abraham's faith in God's promise, Isaac lived and became the father of Jacob, whose twelve sons became the twelve tribes of Israel. In your prayer, reflect or journal on the following questions:

■ Because of your beliefs, have you ever had to give up someone or something that was precious to you?
■ How has your life been enriched as a result of your trust in God in a difficult situation?

▸ Gn 22, 1–19

will bless you abundantly and make your descendants as countless as the stars of the sky and the sands of the seashore; your descendants shall take possession of the gates of their enemies, 18* and in your descendants all the nations of the earth shall find blessing—all this because you obeyed my command."

19 Abraham then returned to his servants, and they set out together for Beer-sheba, where Abraham made his home.

Nahor's Descendants

20† Some time afterward, the news came to Abraham: "Milcah too has borne sons, to your brother Nahor: 21 Uz, his first-born, his brother Buz, Kemuel (the father of Aram), 22 Chesed, Hazo, Pildash, Jidlaph and Bethuel." 23 Bethuel became the father of Rebekah. These eight Milcah bore to

---

† **22, 14:** *Yahweh-yireh:* a Hebrew expression meaning "the Lord will see"; the reference is to the words in v 8, "God himself will see to it."
22, 20–24: A list of Aramean tribes who lived to the east and northeast of Israel, twelve in number, like the twelve tribes of Israel (Gn 35, 23) and the twelve tribes of Ishmael (Gn 25, 12–16).

*
22, 9: Jas 2, 21.
22, 10: Wis 10, 5.
22, 12: Rom 8, 32; 1 Jn 4, 9.
22, 16f: Gn 15, 5; Ex 32, 13;
  Lk 1, 73; Rom 4, 13;
Heb 6, 13f; 11, 12.
22, 17: Gn 24, 60.
22, 18: Gn 12, 3; 18, 18; 26,
  4; Sir 44, 21; Acts 3,
  25; Gal 3, 16.

Abraham's brother Nahor. [24] His concubine, whose name was Reumah, also bore children: Tebah, Gaham, Tahash and Maacah.

Purchase of a Burial Place

23 [1] The span of Sarah's life was one hundred and twenty-seven years. [2] She died in Kiriath-arba (that is, Hebron) in the land of Canaan, and Abraham performed the customary mourning rites for her. [3]† Then he left the side of his dead one and addressed the Hittites: [4]*† "Although I am a resident alien among you, sell me from your holdings a piece of property for a burial ground, that I may bury my dead wife." [5] The Hittites answered Abraham: "Please, sir, [6] listen to us! You are an elect of God among us. Bury your dead in the choicest of our burial sites. None of us would deny you his burial ground for the burial of your dead." [7] Abraham, however, began to bow low before the local citizens, the Hittites, [8] while he appealed to them: "If you will allow me room for burial of my dead, listen to me! Intercede for me with Ephron, son of Zohar, asking him [9] to sell me the cave of Machpelah that he owns; it is at the edge of his field. Let him sell it to me in your presence, at its full price, for a burial place."

[10]† Now Ephron was present with the Hittites. So Ephron the Hittite replied to Abraham in the hearing of the Hittites who sat on his town council: [11] "Please, sir, listen to me! I give you both the field and the cave in it; in the presence of my kinsmen I make this gift. Bury your dead!" [12] But Abraham, after bowing low before the local citizens, addressed Ephron in the hearing of these men: [13] "Ah, if only you would please listen to me! I will pay you the price of the field. Accept it from me, that I may bury my dead there." [14] Ephron replied to Abraham, "Please, [15]† sir, listen to me! A piece of land worth four hundred shekels of silver—what is that between you and me, as long as you can bury your dead?" [16]*† Abraham accepted Ephron's terms; he weighed out to him the silver that Ephron had stipulated in the hearing of the Hittites, four hundred shekels of silver at the current market value.

[17]* Thus Ephron's field in Machpelah, facing Mamre, together with its cave and all the trees anywhere within its limits, was conveyed [18] to Abraham by purchase in the presence of all the Hittites who sat on Ephron's town council. [19] After this transaction, Abraham buried his wife Sarah in the cave of the field of Machpelah, facing Mamre (that is, Hebron) in the land of Canaan. [20] Thus the field with its cave was transferred from the Hittites to Abraham as a burial place.

Isaac and Rebekah

24 [1] Abraham had now reached a ripe old age, and the LORD had blessed him in every way. [2]*† Abraham said to the senior servant of his household, who had charge of all his possessions: "Put your hand under my thigh, [3]* and I will make you swear by the LORD, the God of heaven and the God of earth, that you will not procure a wife for my son from the daughters of the Canaanites among whom I live, [4] but that you will go to my own land and to my kindred to get a wife for my son Isaac." [5] The servant asked him: "What if the woman is unwilling to follow me to this land? Should I then take your son back to the land from which you migrated?" [6] "Never take my son back there for any reason," Abraham told him. [7]* "The LORD, the God of heaven, who took me from my father's house and the land of my kin, and who confirmed by oath the promise he then made to me, 'I will give this land to your descendants'— he will send his messenger before you, and you will obtain a wife for my son there. [8] If the woman is unwilling to follow you, you will be released from this oath. But never take my son back there!" [9] So the servant put his hand under the thigh of his master Abraham and swore to him in this undertaking.

[10]† The servant then took ten of his master's camels, and bearing all kinds of gifts from his master, he made his way to the city of Nahor in Aram Naharaim. [11] Near evening, at the time when women go out to draw water, he made the camels

---

23, 3: *The Hittites:* a non-Semitic people in Canaan; their relationship to the well-known Hittites of Asia Minor is uncertain.

23, 4: *A resident alien:* literally "a sojourner and a settler," i.e., a long-term resident alien. Such a one would normally not have the right to own property. The importance of Abraham's purchase of the field in Machpelah, which is worded in technical legal terms, lies in the fact that it gave his descendants their first, though small, land rights in the country that God had promised the patriarch they would one day inherit as their own. Abraham therefore insists on purchasing the field and not receiving it as a gift.

23, 10: *Who sat on his town council:* probable meaning of the literal translation, "who came in at the gate of his city"; so also in v 18.

23, 15: *Four hundred shekels:* probably an exorbitant sum; Jeremiah (32, 9) paid only seventeen shekels for his field in Anathoth, though the Babylonian invasion no doubt helped to reduce the price.

23, 16: *The current market value:* the standard weight called a shekel varied according to time and place.

24, 2: *Put your hand under my thigh:* the symbolism of this act was apparently connected with the Hebrew concept of children issuing from their father's "thigh" (Gn 46, 26; Ex 1, 5). Perhaps the man who took such an oath was thought to bring the curse of sterility on himself if he did not fulfill his sworn promise. Jacob made Joseph swear in the same way (Gn 47, 29). In both these instances, the oath was taken to carry out the last request of a man upon his death.

24, 10: *Nahor:* it is uncertain whether this is to be understood as the name of Abraham's brother (Gn 11, 27), Rebekah's grandfather (Gn 24, 15), or the city of the same name (as known from the Mari documents); *Aram Naharaim,* situated near Haran (Gn 11, 31) in northern Mesopotamia.

23, 4: Gn 33, 19; Acts 7, 16;
    Heb 11, 9.
23, 16: Acts 7, 16.
23, 17f: Gn 49, 29f.
24, 2f: Gn 47, 29.

24, 3: Gn 24, 37; 28, 1f; Jgs
    14, 3; Tb 4, 12.
24, 7: Gn 12, 7; Ex 6, 8; Tb
    5, 17; Gal 3, 16.

kneel by the well outside the city. 12† Then he prayed: "LORD, God of my master Abraham, let it turn out favorably for me today and thus deal graciously with my master Abraham. 13 While I stand here at the spring and the daughters of the townsmen are coming out to draw water, 14 if I say to a girl, 'Please lower your jug, that I may drink,' and she answers, 'Take a drink, and let me give water to your camels, too,' let her be the one whom you have decided upon for your servant Isaac. In this way I shall know that you have dealt graciously with my master."

15* He had scarcely finished these words when Rebekah (who was born to Bethuel, son of Milcah, the wife of Abraham's brother Nahor) came out with a jug on her shoulder. 16 The girl was very beautiful, a virgin, untouched by man. She went down to the spring and filled her jug. As she came up, 17 the servant ran toward her and said, "Please give me a sip of water from your jug." 18 "Take a drink, sir," she replied, and quickly lowering the jug onto her hand, she gave him a drink. 19 When she had let him drink his fill, she said, "I will draw water for your camels, too, until they have drunk their fill." 20 With that, she quickly emptied her jug into the drinking trough and ran back to the well to draw more water, until she had drawn enough for all the camels. 21 The man watched her the whole time, silently waiting to learn whether or not the LORD had made his errand successful. 22 When the camels had finished drinking, the man took out a gold ring weighing half a shekel, which he fastened on her nose, and two gold bracelets weighing ten shekels, which he put on her wrists. 23 Then he asked her: "Whose daughter are you? Tell me, please. And is there room in your father's house for us to spend the night?" 24 She answered: "I am the daughter of Bethuel the son of Milcah, whom she bore to Nahor. 25 There is plenty of straw and fodder at our place," she added, "and room to spend the night." 26 The man then bowed down in worship to the LORD, 27 saying: "Blessed be the LORD, the God of my master Abraham, who has not let his constant kindness toward my master fail. As for myself also, the LORD has led me straight to the house of my master's brother."

28 Then the girl ran off and told her mother's household about it. 29* Now Rebekah had a brother named Laban. 30 As soon as he saw the ring and the bracelets on his sister Rebekah and heard her words about what the man had said to her, Laban rushed outside to the man at the spring. When he reached him, he was still standing by the camels at the spring. 31 So he said to him: "Come, blessed of

the LORD! Why are you staying outside when I have made the house ready for you, as well as a place for the camels?" 32 The man then went inside; and while the camels were being unloaded and provided with straw and fodder, water was brought to bathe his feet and the feet of the men who were with him. 33 But when the table was set for him, he said, "I will not eat until I have told my tale." "Do so," they replied.

34 "I am Abraham's servant," he began. 35 "The LORD has blessed my master so abundantly that he has become a wealthy man; he has given him flocks and herds, silver and gold, male and female slaves, and camels and asses. 36 My master's wife Sarah bore a son to my master in her old age, and he has given him everything he owns. 37 My master put me under oath, saying: 'You shall not procure a wife for my son among the daughters of the Canaanites in whose land I live; 38 instead, you shall go to my father's house, to my own relatives, to get a wife for my son.' 39 When I asked my master, 'What if the woman will not follow me?' 40* he replied: 'The LORD, in whose presence I have always walked, will send his messenger with you and make your errand successful, and so you will get a wife for my son from my own kindred of my father's house. 41 Then you shall be released from my ban. If you visit my kindred and they refuse you, then, too, you shall be released from my ban.'

42 "When I came to the spring today, I prayed: 'LORD, God of my master Abraham, may it be your will to make successful the errand I am engaged on! 43 While I stand here at the spring, if I say to a young woman who comes out to draw water, Please give me a little water from your jug, 44 and she answers, Not only may you have a drink, but I will give water to your camels, too—let her be the woman whom the LORD has decided upon for my master's son.'

45 "I had scarcely finished saying this prayer to myself when Rebekah came out with a jug on her shoulder. After she went down to the spring and drew water, I said to her, 'Please let me have a drink.' 46 She quickly lowered the jug she was carrying and said, 'Take a drink, and let me bring water for your camels, too.' So I drank, and she watered the camels also. 47 When I asked her, 'Whose daughter are you?' she answered, 'The daughter of Bethuel, son of Nahor, born to Nahor by Milcah.' So I put the ring on her nose and the bracelets on her wrists. 48 Then I bowed down in worship to the LORD, blessing the LORD, the God of my master Abraham, who had led me on the right road to obtain the daughter of my master's kinsman for his son. 49 If, therefore, you have in mind to show true loyalty to

---

† **24, 12:** *Let it turn out favorably for me:* let me have a favorable omen; cf end of v 14.

24, 15: Gn 22, 23.   24, 40: Tb 5, 17; 10, 13.
24, 29: Gn 27, 43.

my master, let me know; but if not, let me know that, too. I can then proceed accordingly."

[50]* Laban and his household said in reply: "This thing comes from the LORD; we can say nothing to you either for or against it. [51] Here is Rebekah, ready for you; take her with you, that she may become the wife of your master's son, as the LORD has said." [52] When Abraham's servant heard their answer, he bowed to the ground before the LORD. [53] Then he brought out objects of silver and gold and articles of clothing and presented them to Rebekah; he also gave costly presents to her brother and mother. [54]* After he and the men with him had eaten and drunk, they spent the night there.

When they were up the next morning, he said, "Give me leave to return to my master." [55] Her brother and mother replied, "Let the girl stay with us a short while, say ten days; after that she may go." [56] But he said to them, "Do not detain me, now that the LORD has made my errand successful; let me go back to my master." [57] They answered, "Let us call the girl and see what she herself has to say about it." [58] So they called Rebekah and asked her, "Do you wish to go with this man?" She answered, "I do." [59] At this they allowed their sister Rebekah and her nurse to take leave, along with Abraham's servant and his men. [60]* Invoking a blessing on Rebekah, they said:

"Sister, may you grow
    into thousands of myriads;
And may your descendants gain possession
    of the gates of their enemies!"

[61] Then Rebekah and her maids started out; they mounted their camels and followed the man. So the servant took Rebekah and went on his way.

[62]* Meanwhile Isaac had gone from Beer-lahai-roi and was living in the region of the Negeb. [63]† One day toward evening he went out . . . in the field, and as he looked around, he noticed that camels were approaching. [64] Rebekah, too, was looking about, and when she saw him, she alighted from her camel [65] and asked the servant, "Who is the man out there, walking through the fields toward us?" "That is my master," replied the servant. Then she covered herself with her veil.

[66] The servant recounted to Isaac all the things he had done. [67] Then Isaac took Rebekah into his tent; he married her, and thus she became his wife. In his

? did you KNOW?

Abraham's Descendants

God promised Hagar that her son Ishmael would be made "a great nation" (Gn 21, 18). The Old Testament lists twelve princely tribes that descended from Abraham's older son (Gn 25, 13–16), tribes traditionally associated with the people of ancient Edom. A much later Islamic tradition identifies Muhammad and his descendants—the Muslims—as "children of Ishmael."

Abraham's younger son, Isaac, was the father of Jacob. The Jewish people trace their lineage to Jacob and his twelve sons. Because Jesus was a Jew, Christians ultimately trace their ancestry through Jacob to Abraham as well.

Thus, three major world religions—Judaism, Christianity, and Islam—all see Abraham as their "father in faith."

▶ Gn 25, 12–18

love for her Isaac found solace after the death of his mother Sarah.

Abraham's Sons by Keturah

25 [1]*† Abraham married another wife, whose name was Keturah. [2] She bore him Zimran, Jokshan, Medan, Midian, Ishbak and Shuah. [3]* Jokshan became the father of Sheba and Dedan. The descendants of Dedan were the Asshurim, the Letushim, and the Leummim. [4] The descendants of Midian were Ephah, Epher, Hanoch, Abida and Eldaah. All of these were descendants of Keturah.

[5] Abraham deeded everything that he owned to his son Isaac. [6]† To his sons by concubinage, however, he made grants while he was still living, as he sent them away eastward, to the land of Kedem, away from his son Isaac.

24, 63: *He went out:* the meaning of the Hebrew term that follows this is obscure.

25, 1–11: Though mentioned here, Abraham's marriage to a "concubine," or wife of secondary rank, and his death are not to be understood as happening chronologically after the events narrated in the preceding chapter.

25, 6: *The land of Kedem:* or "the country of the East," the region

inhabited by the Kedemites or Easterners (Gn 29, 1; Jgs 6, 3.33; Jb 1, 3; Is 11, 14). The names mentioned in vv 2ff, as far as they can be identified, are those of tribes in the Arabian desert.

24, 50f: Tb 7, 12.   24, 62: Gn 16, 13f; 25, 11.
24, 54: Tb 7, 14; 8, 20.   25, 1–4: 1 Chr 1, 32f.
24, 60: Gn 22, 17.   25, 3: Is 21, 13.

G
N

Death of Abraham

7 The whole span of Abraham's life was one hundred and seventy-five years. 8 Then he breathed his last, dying at a ripe old age, grown old after a full life; and he was taken to his kinsmen. 9* His sons Isaac and Ishmael buried him in the cave of Machpelah, in the field of Ephron, son of Zohar the Hittite, which faces Mamre, 10 the field that Abraham had bought from the Hittites; there he was buried next to his wife Sarah. 11 After the death of Abraham, God blessed his son Isaac, who made his home near Beer-lahai-roi.

Sibling Rivalry

It is common for siblings to have conflict in their relationship, but with Jacob and Esau, the conflict becomes extreme. Follow their story in Genesis, chapters 27–28, 33.

For another story of extreme sibling rivalry, see 37, 12–36. Joseph's brothers (all sons of Jacob) are so jealous of him that they plot to kill him. But instead, he gets sold as a slave—and that turns out to be a great career move for him.

The story of the prodigal son in Lk 15, 11–32 is yet another example of sibling rivalry.

Do you have any brothers or sisters? If so, how do you treat them? Do you ever pray for them? Do you ever tell them that you care about them—even if they drive you crazy at times?

If you don't have any brothers or sisters, how about cousins, neighbors, or friends? All relationships get better with prayer and care.

▶ Gn 25, 19–34

Descendants of Ishmael

12 These are the descendants of Abraham's son Ishmael, whom Hagar the Egyptian, Sarah's slave, bore to Abraham. 13* These are the names of Ishmael's sons, listed in the order of their birth: Nebaioth (Ishmael's first-born), Kedar, Adbeel, Mibsam,* 14 Mishma, Dumah, Massa, 15 Hadad, Tema, Jetur, Naphish and Kedemah. 16* These are the sons of Ishmael, their names by their villages and encampments; twelve chieftains of as many tribal groups.

17 The span of Ishmael's life was one hundred and thirty-seven years. After he had breathed his last and died, he was taken to his kinsmen. 18*† The Ishmaelites ranged from Havilah-by-Shur, which is on the border of Egypt, all the way to Asshur; and each of them pitched camp in opposition to his various kinsmen.

III: The Patriarchs Isaac and Jacob

Birth of Esau and Jacob

19 This is the family history of Isaac, son of Abraham; Abraham had begotten Isaac. 20* Isaac was forty years old when he married Rebekah, the daughter of Bethuel the Aramean of Paddan-aram and the sister of Laban the Aramean. 21 Isaac entreated the LORD on behalf of his wife, since she was sterile. The LORD heard his entreaty, and Rebekah became pregnant. 22 But the children in her womb jostled each other so much that she exclaimed, "If this is to be so, what good will it do me!" She went to consult the LORD, 23* and he answered her:

"Two nations are in your womb,
　　two peoples are quarreling while still
　　　　within you;
But one shall surpass the other,
　　and the older shall serve the younger."

24* When the time of her delivery came, there were twins in her womb. 25† The first to emerge was reddish, and his whole body was like a hairy mantle; so they named him Esau. 26*† His brother came out next, gripping Esau's heel; so they named him

---

† **25, 18:** *Pitched camp:* literally "fell"; the same Hebrew verb is used in Jgs 7, 12 in regard to the hostile encampment of Bedouin tribes. The present passage shows the fulfillment of the prediction contained in Gn 16, 12.

25, 25: *Reddish:* in Hebrew, *admoni,* a reference to Edom, another name for Esau (v 30; 36, 1). Edom, however, was really the name of the country south of Moab where the descendants of Esau lived. It was called the "red" country because of its reddish sandstone. *Hairy:* in Hebrew, *sear,* a reference to Seir, another name for Edom (Gn 36, 8). One might expect the text to say, "So they named him Seir"; but Esau (*esaw*) also means "hairy."

25, 26: *Esau's heel:* the Hebrew is *baaqeb esaw,* a reference to the name Jacob; cf Gn 27, 36. Probably, however, the name Jacob has no true etymological connection with the Hebrew word for "heel" (*aqeb*), but is instead a shortened form of some such name as *yaaqob-el* ("may God protect").

25, 9f: Gn 23, 3–20.　　　　　　　25, 20: Gn 24, 66.
25, 13–16: 1 Chr 1, 29ff.　　　　25, 23: Gn 27, 29; Nm 24, 18;
25, 13: Is 60, 7.　　　　　　　　　　Mal 1, 2–5; Rom 9, 11f.
25, 16: Gn 17, 20.　　　　　　　　25, 24: Hos 12, 3.
25, 18: Gn 16, 12.　　　　　　　　25, 26: Mt 1, 2

Jacob. Isaac was sixty years old when they were born.

27* As the boys grew up, Esau became a skillful hunter, a man who lived in the open; whereas Jacob was a simple man, who kept to his tents. 28 Isaac preferred Esau, because he was fond of game; but Rebekah preferred Jacob. 29 Once, when Jacob was cooking a stew, Esau came in from the open, famished. 30† He said to Jacob, "Let me gulp down some of that red stuff; I'm starving." (That is why he was called Edom.) 31*† But Jacob replied, "First give me your birthright in exchange for it." 32 "Look," said Esau, "I'm on the point of dying. What good will any birthright do me?" 33* But Jacob insisted, "Swear to me first!" So he sold Jacob his birthright under oath. 34 Jacob then gave him some bread and the lentil stew; and Esau ate, drank, got up, and went his way. Esau cared little for his birthright.

Isaac and Abimelech

26 1* There was a famine in the land (distinct from the earlier one that had occurred in the days of Abraham), and Isaac went down to Abimelech, king of the Philistines in Gerar.* 2 The LORD appeared to him and said: "Do not go down to Egypt, but continue to camp wherever in this land I tell you. 3* Stay in this land, and I will be with you and bless you; for to you and your descendants I will give all these lands, in fulfillment of the oath that I swore to your father Abraham. 4* I will make your descendants as numerous as the stars in the sky and give them all these lands, and in your descendants all the nations of the earth shall find blessing— 5 this because Abraham obeyed me, keeping my mandate (my commandments, my ordinances and my instructions)."

6† So Isaac settled in Gerar. 7 When the men of the place asked questions about his wife, he answered, "She is my sister." He was afraid, if he called her his wife, the men of the place would kill him on account of Rebekah, since she was very beautiful. 8 But when he had been there for a long time, Abimelech, king of the Philistines, happened to look out of a window and was surprised to see Isaac fondling his wife Rebekah. 9 He called Isaac and said: "She must certainly be your wife! How could you have said, 'She is my sister'?" Isaac replied, "I thought I might lose my life on her account." 10 "How could you do this to us!" exclaimed Abimelech. "It would have taken very little for one of the men to lie with your wife, and you would have thus brought guilt upon us!" 11 Abimelech therefore gave this warning to all his men: "Anyone who molests this man or his wife shall forthwith be put to death."

12† Isaac sowed a crop in that region and reaped a hundredfold the same year. Since the LORD blessed him, 13* he became richer and richer all the time, until he was very wealthy indeed. 14 He acquired such flocks and herds, and so many work animals, that the Philistines became envious of him. (15* The Philistines had stopped up and filled with dirt all the wells that his father's servants had dug back in the days of his father Abraham.) 16 So Abimelech said to Isaac, "Go away from us; you have become far too numerous for us." 17 Isaac left there and made the Wadi Gerar his regular campsite. (18 Isaac reopened the wells which his father's servants had dug back in the days of his father Abraham and which the Philistines had stopped up after Abraham's death; he gave them the same names that his father had given them.) 19 But when Isaac's servants dug in the wadi and reached spring water in their well, 20† the shepherds of Gerar quarreled with Isaac's servants, saying, "The water belongs to us!" So the well was called Esek, because they had challenged him there. 21† Then they dug another well, and they quarreled over that one too; so it was called Sitnah. 22 When he had moved on from there, he dug still another well; but over this one they did not quarrel. It was called Rehoboth, because he said, "The LORD has now given us ample room, and we shall flourish in the land."

23 From there Isaac went up to Beer-sheba. 24* The same night the LORD appeared to him and said: "I am the God of your father Abraham. You have no need to fear, since I am with you. I will bless you and multiply your descendants for the sake of my servant Abraham." 25 So he built an altar

---

25, 30: Red stuff: in Hebrew, adom; another play on the word "Edom," the "red" land.

25, 31: Birthright: the privilege that entitled the first-born son to a position of honor in the family and to a double share in the possessions inherited from the father.

26, 6–11: The Yahwist's version of the wife-sister episode at Gerar; the Elohist's version (Gn 20, 1–18) is connected with Abraham and Sarah.

26, 12–33: The Yahwist's version of the story about the wells at Beer-sheba; again, the Elohist's version (Gn 21, 22f) is connected with Abraham. A redactor joined the two accounts by means of the parenthetical verses 15 and 18.

26, 20: Esek: "challenge."

26, 21: Sitnah: "opposition"; one might expect the text to be continued by some such words as "because they were in opposition there."

25, 27: Gn 27, 6f.
25, 31: Dt 21, 17.
25, 33: Heb 12, 16.
26, 1–14: Gn 12, 10–20.
26, 1: Gn 12, 1.
26, 3: Gn 12, 7; 15, 18; Ex 32, 13; Ps 105, 9; Sir
44, 22; Heb 11, 9.
26, 4: Gn 12, 3; 22, 17f; 28, 14; Ex 32, 13.
26, 13f: Jb 1, 3.
26, 15–24: Gn 21, 25–31.
26, 24: Gn 46, 3.

Ge

...here and invoked the LORD by name. After he had pitched his tent there, his servants began to dig a well nearby.

26* Abimelech had meanwhile come to him from Gerar, accompanied by Ahuzzath, his councilor, and Phicol, the general of his army. 27 Isaac asked them, "Why have you come to me, seeing that you hate me and have driven me away from you?" 28 They answered: "We are convinced that the LORD is with you, so we propose that there be a sworn agreement between our two sides—between you and us. Let us make a pact with you: 29 you shall not act unkindly toward us, just as we have not molested you, but have always acted kindly toward you and have let you depart in peace. Henceforth, 'The LORD'S blessing be upon you!'" 30 Isaac then made a feast for

33† He called it Shibah; hence the name of the city, Beer-sheba, to this day.

34*† When Esau was forty years old, he married Judith, daughter of Beeri the Hittite, and Basemath, daughter of Elon the Hivite. 35 But they became a source of embitterment to Isaac and Rebekah.

Jacob's Deception

27 1† When Isaac was so old that his eyesight had failed him, he called his older son Esau and said to him, "Son!" "Yes, father!" he replied. 2 Isaac then said, "As you can see, I am so old that I may now die at any time. 3 Take your gear, therefore—your quiver and bow—and go out into the country to hunt some game for me. 4† With your catch prepare an appetizing dish for me, such

Introducing

▶ JACOB

According to the Bible, Abraham was the father of Isaac, and Isaac was the father of Jacob, and Jacob was the father of twelve sons who became the leaders of the twelve tribes of Israel. Jacob, like his ancestors, participated in the covenant with God that promised a great land and many descendants. He is portrayed as a very human character with a wide range of emotions and actions, both good and bad. Jacob is a repentant brother, a kind father, and a successful herder, but he is also a trickster who steals his brother Esau's birthright and his father's blessing (Gn 25, 29–34; 27, 1–29). It is no wonder that Jacob's name means "supplanter" or "heel grabber."

In a dream, God renews the covenant promises to Jacob (28, 10–17), and in another dream (35, 9–15), God changes Jacob's name to Israel (Gn 32, 23–33). Jacob's descendants become known as the Israelites. His story reveals that God's blessing continues to work even through flawed human beings.

▶ Gn 25, 19—50, 14

them, and they ate and drank. 31 Early the next morning they exchanged oaths. Then Isaac bade them farewell, and they departed from him in peace.

32 That same day Isaac's servants came and brought him news about the well they had been digging; they told him, "We have reached water!"

as I like, and bring it to me to eat, so that I may give you my special blessing before I die."

5* Rebekah had been listening while Isaac was speaking to his son Esau. So when Esau went out into the country to hunt some game for his father, 6 Rebekah said to her son Jacob, "Listen! I over-

---

† **26, 33:** *Shibah:* "seven," for the sake of a closer assonance with Beer-sheba; but the present version of the story says nothing about there being seven wells there as implied in Gn 21, 28–31. The Greek version understood the Hebrew text more logically as *shebua,* "oath," in keeping with the present story.

26, 34f: These verses from the Priestly source, which have no logical connection with the preceding stories, serve as an introduction to the following section on Esau's loss of his birthright by suggesting a motivation for this in Isaac's and Rebekah's dislike for Esau's Canaanite wives.

27, 1–45: What Jacob did in deceiving his father and thereby cheating Esau out of Isaac's deathbed blessing is condemned as blameworthy, not only by Hosea (12, 4) and Jeremiah (9, 3), but also,

indirectly, by the Yahwist narrator of the present story, who makes the reader sympathize with Esau as the innocent victim of a cruel plot, and shows that Jacob and his mother, the instigator of the plot, paid for it by a lifelong separation from each other. The story was told because it was part of the mystery of God's ways in salvation history—his use of weak, sinful men to achieve his own ultimate purpose.

27, 4: *My special blessing:* "the blessing of my soul." The same expression is used also in vv 19.25.31. In the context it must mean something like a solemn deathbed blessing, believed to be especially efficacious.

26, 26–33: Gn 21, 22–31;   26, 34f: Gn 27, 46.
Prv 16, 7.   27, 5: Gn 25, 28.

heard your father tell your brother Esau, 7 'Bring me some game and with it prepare an appetizing dish for me to eat, that I may give you my blessing with the LORD'S approval before I die.' 8 Now, son, listen carefully to what I tell you. 9 Go to the flock and get me two choice kids. With these I will prepare an appetizing dish for your father, such as he likes. 10 Then bring it to your father to eat, that he may bless you before he dies." 11* "But my brother Esau is a hairy man," said Jacob to his mother Rebekah, "and I am smooth-skinned! 12 Suppose my father feels me? He will think I am making sport of him, and I shall bring on myself a curse instead of a blessing." 13 His mother, however, replied: "Let any curse against you, son, fall on me! Just do as I say. Go and get me the kids."

did you KNOW?

God's Surprising Choice

In most ancient cultures, including Israel's, the oldest son of the family was expected to inherit his father's property (the birthright) and authority (the blessing). In the story of Esau and Jacob, Jacob tricks Esau (the oldest son) out of his birthright (Gn 25, 29–34) and deceives his blind father into giving him the blessing (27, 1–29).

It is surprising that Genesis makes no comment on the morality of Jacob's actions. However, the story is not about morality but about God's justice: God is not bound by human expectations. Again and again in the Old Testament, God defies human rules by choosing the "little ones" for big responsibilities: Jacob, Joseph, Ruth, David, and Esther, for example. Even the Israelites themselves were an unlikely choice on God's part. Why didn't God choose a nation of great wealth and power instead of a group that was enslaved?

The story of Jacob and Esau reminds us that God does not bow to human rules, expectations, or plans. God's ways are often surprising! (For more on God's surprising choices, see reading plan 5, "The Justice of God.")

▸ Gn 27, 1–40

14 So Jacob went and got them and brought them to his mother; and with them she prepared an appetizing dish, such as his father liked. 15 Rebekah then took the best clothes of her older son Esau that she had in the house, and gave them to her younger son Jacob to wear; 16 and with the skins of the kids she covered up his hands and the hairless parts of his neck. 17 Then she handed her son Jacob the appetizing dish and the bread she had prepared.

18 Bringing them to his father, Jacob said, "Father!" "Yes?" replied Isaac. "Which of my sons are you?" 19 Jacob answered his father: "I am Esau, your first-born. I did as you told me. Please sit up and eat some of my game, so that you may give me your special blessing." 20 But Isaac asked, "How did you succeed so quickly, son?" He answered, "The LORD, your God, let things turn out well with me." 21 Isaac then said to Jacob, "Come closer, son, that I may feel you, to learn whether you really are my son Esau or not." 22 So Jacob moved up closer to his father. When Isaac felt him, he said, "Although the voice is Jacob's, the hands are Esau's." 23 (He failed to identify him because his hands were hairy, like those of his brother Esau; so in the end he gave him his blessing.) 24 Again he asked him, "Are you really my son Esau?" "Certainly," he replied. 25 Then Isaac said, "Serve me your game, son, that I may eat of it and then give you my blessing." Jacob served it to him, and Isaac ate; he brought him wine, and he drank. 26 Finally his father Isaac said to him, "Come closer, son, and kiss me." 27* As Jacob went up and kissed him, Isaac smelled the fragrance of his clothes. With that, he blessed him, saying,

> "Ah, the fragrance of my son
> is like the fragrance of a field
> that the LORD has blessed!

28 "May God give to you
of the dew of the heavens
And of the fertility of the earth
abundance of grain and wine.

29* "Let peoples serve you,
and nations pay you homage;
Be master of your brothers,
and may your mother's sons bow down
to you.

"Cursed be those who curse you,
and blessed be those who bless you."

30 Jacob had scarcely left his father, just after Isaac

27, 11: Gn 25, 25.
27, 27: Gn 22, 17f; Heb 11, 20.

27, 29: Gn 25, 23; 49, 8; Nm 24, 9.

GN

had finished blessing him, when his brother Esau came back from his hunt. 31 Then he too prepared an appetizing dish with his game, and bringing it to his father, he said, "Please, father, eat some of your son's game, that you may then give me your special blessing." 32 "Who are you?" his father Isaac asked him. "I am Esau," he replied, "your first-born son." 33 With that, Isaac was seized with a fit of uncontrollable trembling. "Who was it, then," he asked, "that hunted game and brought it to me? I finished eating it just before you came, and I blessed him. Now he must remain blessed!" 34 On hearing his father's words, Esau burst into loud, bitter sobbing. "Father, bless me too!" he begged. 35 When Isaac explained, "Your brother came here by a ruse and carried off your blessing," 36*† Esau exclaimed, "He has been well named Jacob! He has now supplanted me twice! First he took away my birthright, and now he has taken away my blessing." Then he pleaded, "Haven't you saved a blessing for me?" 37 Isaac replied: "I have already appointed him your master, and I have assigned to him all his kinsmen as his slaves; besides, I have enriched him with grain and wine. What then can I do for you, son?" 38* But Esau urged his father, "Have you only that one blessing, father? Bless me too!" Isaac, however, made no reply; and Esau wept aloud. 39* Finally Isaac spoke again and said to him:

"Ah, far from the fertile earth
       shall be your dwelling;
   far from the dew of the heavens above!

40* "By your sword you shall live,
       and your brother you shall serve;
   But when you become restive,
       you shall throw off his yoke from
           your neck."

41* Esau bore Jacob a grudge because of the blessing his father had given him. He said to himself, "When the time of mourning for my father comes, I will kill my brother Jacob." 42 When Rebekah got news of what her older son Esau had in mind, she called her younger son Jacob and said to him: "Listen! Your brother Esau intends to settle

accounts with you by killing you. 43 Therefore, son, do what I tell you: flee at once to my brother Laban in Haran, 44 and stay with him a while until your brother's fury subsides 45 [until your brother's anger against you subsides] and he forgets what you did to him. Then I will send for you and bring you back. Must I lose both of you in a single day?"

Jacob Sent to Laban

46*† Rebekah said to Isaac: "I am disgusted with life because of the Hittite women. If Jacob also should marry a Hittite woman, a native of the land, like these women, what good would life be to me?"

28 1* Isaac therefore called Jacob, greeted him with a blessing, and charged him: "You shall not marry a Canaanite woman! 2* Go now to Paddan-aram, to the home of your mother's father Bethuel, and there choose a wife for yourself from among the daughters of your uncle Laban. 3 May God Almighty bless you and make you fertile, multiply you that you may become an assembly of peoples. 4* May he extend to you and your descendants the blessing he gave to Abraham, so that you may gain possession of the land where you are staying, which he assigned to Abraham." 5* Then Isaac sent Jacob on his way; he went to Paddan-aram, to Laban, son of Bethuel, the Aramean, and brother of Rebekah, the mother of Jacob and Esau.

6 Esau noted that Isaac had blessed Jacob when he sent him to Paddan-aram to get himself a wife there, charging him, as he gave him his blessing, not to marry a Canaanite woman, 7 and that Jacob had obeyed his father and mother and gone to Paddan-aram. 8 Esau realized how displeasing the Canaanite women were to his father Isaac, 9* so he went to Ishmael, and in addition to the wives he had, married Mahalath, the daughter of Abraham's son Ishmael and sister of Nebaioth.

Jacob's Dream at Bethel

10 Jacob departed from Beer-sheba and proceeded toward Haran. 11† When he came upon a certain shrine, as the sun had already set, he stopped there

---

27, 36: *He has now supplanted me:* in Hebrew, *wayyaqebeni,* a wordplay on the name Jacob, *yaaqob;* see Jer 9, 3 and note, as well as Gn 25, 26. There is also a play between the Hebrew words *bekora* ("birthright") and *beraka* ("blessing").

27, 46—28, 9: This section, which is from the Priestly source and a direct sequel of Gn 26, 34f, presents a different, though not contradictory, reason for Jacob's going to Paddan-aram: namely, to preserve racial purity among the chosen people. The account of Esau's marriages is given for the purpose of explaining the racial mixture of the Edomites, who were descended in part from tribes related to Israel, in part from older peoples in Edom called Hittites, Horites or Hivites, and in part from the Ishmaelite (Arabian) tribes who later invaded the region.

28, 11: *Shrine:* literally "place," often used specifically of a sacred site. Here the place was Bethel (v 19), a sacred site as early as the time of Abraham (Gn 12, 8).

27, 36: Gn 25, 26.29–34;
       Hos 12, 4.
27, 38: Heb 12, 17.
27, 39: Heb 11, 20.
27, 40: 2 Kgs 8, 20.22;
       2 Chr 21, 8.
27, 41: Wis 10, 10; Ob 10.

27, 46: Gn 26, 34f.
28, 1: Gn 24, 3f; 26, 35.
28, 2: Gn 22, 22; 17, 1f.4f.
28, 4: Ex 32, 13.
28, 5: Jdt 8, 26.
28, 9: Gn 36, 2f.

G
N

Friendship with God

Just as Jacob is leaving his home and everything he knows, God establishes a personal relationship with him through a dream. In this relationship, God and Jacob interact personally, are accountable to each other, and trust each other. Jacob will need this relationship to help him through the tough times ahead. See Gn 32, 23–33 for further developments in Jacob's relationship with God.

God, I want to know your presence. Use my dreams and my waking thoughts; use my family, friends, and neighbors; use your holy word. Use them all to reach me. For I know your presence will sustain me on my most difficult journeys, as it did Jacob.

▸ Gn 28, 10–22

for the night. Taking one of the stones at the shrine, he put it under his head and lay down to sleep at that spot. 12*† Then he had a dream: a stairway rested on the ground, with its top reaching to the heavens; and God's messengers were going up and down on it. 13* And there was the LORD standing beside him and saying: "I, the LORD, am the God of your forefather Abraham and the God of Isaac; the land on which you are lying I will give to you and your descendants. 14* These shall be as plentiful as the dust of the earth, and through them you shall spread out east and west, north and south. In you and your descendants all the nations of the earth shall find blessing. 15* Know that I am with you; I will protect you wherever you go, and bring you back to this land. I will never leave you until I have done what I promised you."

16 When Jacob awoke from his sleep, he exclaimed, "Truly, the LORD is in this spot, although I did not know it!" 17† In solemn wonder he cried

out: "How awesome is this shrine! This is nothing else but an abode of God, and that is the gateway to heaven!" 18*† Early the next morning Jacob took the stone that he had put under his head, set it up as a memorial stone, and poured oil on top of it. 19*† He called that site Bethel, whereas the former name of the town had been Luz.

20 Jacob then made this vow: "If God remains with me, to protect me on this journey I am making and to give me enough bread to eat and clothing to wear, 21 and I come back safe to my father's house, the LORD shall be my God. 22 This stone that I have set up as a memorial stone shall be God's abode. Of everything you give me, I will faithfully return a tenth part to you."

Arrival in Haran

29 1*† After Jacob resumed his journey, he came to the land of the Easterners. 2* Looking about, he saw a well in the open country, with three droves of sheep huddled near it, for droves were watered from that well. A large stone covered the mouth of the well. 3 Only when all the shepherds were assembled there could they roll the stone away from the mouth of the well and water the flocks. Then they would put the stone back again over the mouth of the well.

4 Jacob said to them, "Friends, where are you from?" "We are from Haran," they replied. 5* Then he asked them, "Do you know Laban, son of Nahor?" "We do," they answered. 6 He inquired further, "Is he well?" "He is," they answered; "and here comes his daughter Rachel with his flock." 7 Then he said: "There is still much daylight left; it is hardly the time to bring the animals home. Why don't you water the flocks now, and then continue pasturing them?" 8 "We cannot," they replied, "until all the shepherds are here to roll the stone away from the mouth of the well; only then can we water the flocks."

9 While he was still talking with them, Rachel arrived with her father's sheep; she was the one who tended them. 10 As soon as Jacob saw Rachel, the daughter of his uncle Laban, with the sheep of his uncle Laban, he went up, rolled the stone away from the mouth of the well, and watered his uncle's

---

† **28, 12:** *Stairway:* in Hebrew, *sullam,* traditionally but inaccurately, translated as "ladder." The corresponding verb, *salal,* means "to heap up" something, such as dirt for a highway or ramp. The imagery in Jacob's dream is derived from the Babylonian ziggurat or temple tower, "with its top in the sky" (Gn 11, 4), and with brick steps leading up to a small temple at the top.
28, 17: *This:* the stone Jacob used as a headrest; cf v 22. *That:* the stairway Jacob saw in his dream.
28, 18: *Memorial stone:* in Hebrew, *masseba,* a stone which might vary in shape and size, set upright and usually intended for some religious purpose. Since the custom of erecting such "sacred pillars" in Palestine went back to its pre-Israelite period, their pagan associations were often retained; therefore, later Israelite religion for-

bade their erection (Lv 26, 1; Dt 16, 22) and ordered the destruction of those that were associated with paganism (Ex 34, 31; Dt 12, 3).
28, 19: *Bethel:* i.e., "house of God"; the reference is to the abode of God in v 17.
29, 1: *Easterners:* see note on Gn 25, 6.

28, 12: Jn 1, 51.
28, 13: Dt 1, 8; Mi 7, 28.
28, 14: Gn 12, 3; 13, 14f; 15, 5f; 18, 18; 22, 17f; 26, 4; Dt 19, 8; Sir 44, 21.
28, 15: Gn 31, 3.
28, 18: Gn 31, 13; 35, 14f.
28, 19: Gn 35, 6; 48, 3; Jos 18, 13; Jgs 1, 23; Hos 12, 4.
29, 1: Wis 10, 10.
29, 2: Gn 24, 11f.
29, 5: Tb 7, 4.

GN

sheep. [11]† Then Jacob kissed Rachel and burst into tears. [12] He told her that he was her father's relative, Rebekah's son, and she ran to tell her father. [13] When Laban heard the news about his sister's son Jacob, he hurried out to meet him. After embracing and kissing him, he brought him to his house. Jacob then recounted to Laban all that had happened, [14]† and Laban said to him, "You are indeed my flesh and blood."

to Jacob, and Jacob consummated the marriage with her. [24] (Laban assigned his slave girl Zilpah to his daughter Leah as her maidservant.) [25]† In the morning Jacob was amazed: it was Leah! So he cried out to Laban: "How could you do this to me! Was it not for Rachel that I served you? Why did you dupe me?" [26] "It is not the custom in our country," Laban replied, "to marry off a younger daughter before an older one. [27]*† Finish the bridal week for

When Lies Boomerang

Predictably, Jacob becomes upset when he finds out that he has been deceived by Laban (Gn 29, 25). Yet, the very reason Jacob is working for his uncle Laban is that he has fled from his brother Esau, whom he deceived several years ago (27, 1–40). Jacob's lies and deceit have boomeranged, so now he is the victim.

Somehow, our lies, gossip, and manipulation of others often come back to haunt us. So it was with Jacob. So it will be with us if we follow his example.

▶ Gn 29, 15–30

Marriage to Leah and Rachel

After Jacob had stayed with him a full month, [15] Laban said to him: "Should you serve me for nothing just because you are a relative of mine? Tell me what your wages should be." [16] Now Laban had two daughters; the older was called Leah, the younger Rachel. [17]† Leah had lovely eyes, but Rachel was well formed and beautiful. [18]† Since Jacob had fallen in love with Rachel, he answered Laban, "I will serve you seven years for your younger daughter Rachel." [19] Laban replied, "I prefer to give her to you rather than to an outsider. Stay with me." [20]* So Jacob served seven years for Rachel, yet they seemed to him but a few days because of his love for her.

[21] Then Jacob said to Laban, "Give me my wife, that I may consummate my marriage with her, for my term is now completed." [22] So Laban invited all the local inhabitants and gave a feast. [23] At the nightfall he took his daughter Leah and brought her

this one, and then I will give you the other too, in return for another seven years of service with me." [28] Jacob agreed. He finished the bridal week for Leah, and then Laban gave him his daughter Rachel in marriage. [29] (Laban assigned his slave girl Bilhah to his daughter Rachel as her maidservant.) [30]* Jacob then consummated his marriage with Rachel also, and he loved her more than Leah. Thus he remained in Laban's service another seven years.

Jacob's Children

[31] When the LORD saw that Leah was unloved, he made her fruitful, while Rachel remained barren. [32]*† Leah conceived and bore a son, and she named him Reuben; for she said, "It means, 'The LORD saw my misery; now my husband will love me.'" [33]† She conceived again and bore a son, and said, "It means, 'The LORD heard that I was unloved,' and therefore he has given me this one also"; so she named him Simeon. [34]† Again she conceived and

---

29, 11: *Burst into tears:* literally "raised his voice and wept," i.e., for joy.

29, 14: *Flesh and blood:* literally "bone and flesh," i.e., a close relative; on the Hebrew idiom, see Gn 2, 23.

29, 17: *Lovely eyes:* The adjective modifying *eyes* is often translated as "weak," but "lovely" is the more probable word.

29, 18: Jacob offers to render service (Jos 15, 16f; 1 Sm 17, 25; 18, 17) in lieu of the customary bridal price (Ex 22, 16f; Dt 22, 29).

29, 25: *Jacob was amazed:* he had not recognized Leah because a bride was veiled when she was brought to her bridegroom; cf Gn 24, 65.

29, 27: *The bridal week:* an ancient wedding lasted for seven days of festivities; cf Jgs 14, 12.

29, 32: *Reuben:* The literal meaning of the Hebrew name is

"look, a son!" But in this case, as also with the names of all the other sons of Jacob, a symbolic rather than an etymological interpretation of the name is given, because the name and the persons were regarded as closely interrelated. The symbolic interpretation of Reuben's name, according to the Yahwist source, is based on the similar-sounding, *raa beonyi,* "he saw my misery." In the Elohist source, the name is explained by the similar-sounding *yeehabani,* "he will love me."

29, 33: *Simeon:* in popular etymology, related to *shama,* "he heard."

29, 34: *Levi:* related to *yillaweh,* "he will become attached."

29, 20: Hos 12, 13.   29, 30: Dt 21, 15ff.
29, 27: Hos 12, 13.   29, 32: Gn 49, 3.

bore a son, and she said, "Now at last my husband will become attached to me, since I have now borne him three sons"; that is why she named him Levi. ³⁵*† Once more she conceived and bore a son, and she said, "This time I will give grateful praise to the LORD"; therefore she named him Judah. Then she stopped bearing children.

30 ¹* When Rachel saw that she failed to bear children to Jacob, she became envious of her sister. She said to Jacob, "Give me children or I shall die!" ²* In anger Jacob retorted, "Can I take the place of God, who has denied you the fruit of the womb?" ³*† She replied, "Here is my maidservant Bilhah. Have intercourse with her, and let her give birth on my knees, so that I too may have offspring, at least through her." ⁴† So she gave him her maidservant Bilhah as a consort, and Jacob had intercourse with her. ⁵ When Bilhah conceived and bore a son, ⁶† Rachel said, "God has vindicated me; indeed he has heeded my plea and given me a son." Therefore she named him Dan. ⁷ Rachel's maidservant Bilhah conceived again and bore a second son, ⁸† and Rachel said, "I engaged in a fateful struggle with my sister, and I prevailed." So she named him Naphtali.

⁹ When Leah saw that she had ceased to bear children, she gave her maidservant Zilpah to Jacob as a consort. ¹⁰ So Jacob had intercourse with Zilpah, and she conceived and bore a son. ¹¹† Leah then said, "What good luck!" So she named him Gad. ¹² Then Leah's maidservant Zilpah bore a second son to Jacob; ¹³† and Leah said, "What good fortune!"—meaning, "Women call me fortunate." So she named him Asher.

¹⁴† One day, during the wheat harvest, when Reuben was out in the field, he came upon some mandrakes which he brought home to his mother Leah. Rachel asked Leah, "Please let me have some of your son's mandrakes." ¹⁵ Leah replied, "Was it not enough for you to take away my husband, that you must now take my son's mandrakes too?" "Very

well, then!" Rachel answered. "In exchange for your son's mandrakes, Jacob may lie with you tonight." ¹⁶ That evening, when Jacob came home from the fields, Leah went out to meet him. "You are now to come in with me," she told him, "because I have paid for you with my son's mandrakes." So that night he slept with her, ¹⁷ and God heard her prayer; she conceived and bore a fifth son to Jacob. ¹⁸† Leah then said, "God has given me my reward for having let my husband have my maidservant"; so she named him Issachar. ¹⁹ Leah conceived again and bore a sixth son to Jacob; ²⁰† and she said, "God has brought me a precious gift. This time my husband will offer me presents, now that I have borne him six sons"; so she named him Zebulun. ²¹ Finally, she gave birth to a daughter, and she named her Dinah.

²² Then God remembered Rachel; he heard her prayer and made her fruitful. ²³* She conceived and bore a son, and she said, "God has removed my disgrace." ²⁴† So she named him Joseph, meaning, "May the LORD add another son to this one for me!"

Jacob Outwits Laban

²⁵ After Rachel gave birth to Joseph, Jacob said to Laban: "Give me leave to go to my homeland. ²⁶ Let me have my wives, for whom I served you, and my children, too, that I may depart. You know very well the service that I have rendered you." ²⁷ Laban answered him: "If you will please. . . .

"I have learned through divination that it is because of you that God has blessed me. ²⁸ So," he continued, "state what wages you want from me, and I will pay them." ²⁹ Jacob replied: "You know what work I did for you and how well your livestock fared under my care; ³⁰ the little you had before I came has grown into very much, since the LORD's blessings came upon you in my company. Therefore I should now do something for my own household as well." ³¹ "What should I pay you?" Laban asked. Jacob answered: "You do not have to pay me anything outright. I will again pasture and tend your

---

29, 35: *Judah:* related to *odeh,* "I will give grateful praise."

30, 3: *On my knees:* in the ancient Near East, a father would take a newborn child in his lap to signify that he acknowledged it as his own; Rachel uses the ceremony in order to adopt the child and establish her legal rights to it.

30, 4: *Consort:* the Hebrew word normally means "wife," but here it refers to a wife of secondary rank, who did not have the full legal rights of an ordinary wife.

30, 6: *Dan:* explained by the term *dannanni,* "he has vindicated me."

30, 8: *Naphtali:* explained by the phrase *naptule elohim niptalti,* literally, "in a divine wrestling match I have wrestled," perhaps implying the concept of an ordeal; hence the above rendering, *I engaged in a fateful struggle.*

30, 11: *Gad:* explained by the Hebrew term *begad,* literally "in luck," i.e., *what good luck!*

30, 13: *Asher:* explained by the term *beoshri,* literally "in my good fortune," i.e., *what good fortune,* and by the term *ishsheruni,* "they call me fortunate."

30, 14: *Mandrakes:* an herb whose root was anciently thought to promote conception. The Hebrew word for mandrakes, *dudaim,* has erotic connotations, since it sounds like the words *daddayim* ("breasts") and *dodim* ("sexual pleasure").

30, 18: *Issachar:* explained by the terms, *sekari,* "my reward," and in v 16, *sakor sekartika,* literally "I have hired you," i.e., I have paid for you.

30, 20: *Zebulun:* related to the Akkadian word *zubullum,* "bridegroom's gift," is explained by the terms, *zebadani . . . zebed tob,* "he has brought me a precious gift," and *yizbeleni,* "he will offer me presents."

30, 24: *Joseph:* explained by the words *yosep,* "may he add," and in v 23, *asap,* "he has removed."

29, 35: Mt 1, 2; Lk 3, 33. 30, 3: Gn 16, 2ff.
30, 1: Prv 30, 16. 30, 23: Lk 1, 25.
30, 2: 2 Kgs 5, 7.

G
N

flock, if you do this one thing for me: [32]† go through your whole flock today and remove from it every dark animal among the sheep and every spotted or speckled one among the goats. Only such animals shall be my wages. [33] In the future, whenever you check on these wages of mine, let my honesty testify against me: any animal in my possession that is not a speckled or spotted goat, or a dark sheep, got there by theft!" [34] "Very well," agreed Laban. "Let it be as you say."

[35]† That same day Laban removed the streaked and spotted he-goats and all the speckled and spotted she-goats, all those with some white on them, as well as the fully dark-colored sheep; these he left . . . in charge of his sons. [36] Then he put a three days' journey between himself and Jacob, while Jacob continued to pasture the rest of Laban's flock.

[37] Jacob, however, got some fresh shoots of poplar, almond and plane trees, and he made white stripes in them by peeling off the bark down to the white core of the shoots. [38] The rods that he had thus peeled he then set upright in the watering troughs, so that they would be in front of the animals that drank from the troughs. When the animals were in heat as they came to drink, [39]† the goats mated by the rods, and so they brought forth streaked, speckled and spotted kids. [40] The sheep, on the other hand, Jacob kept apart, and he set these animals to face the streaked or fully dark-colored animals of Laban. Thus he produced special flocks of his own, which he did not put with Laban's flock. [41] Moreover, whenever the hardier animals were in heat, Jacob would set the rods in the troughs in full view of these animals, so that they mated by the rods; [42] but with the weaker animals he would not put the rods there. So the feeble animals would go to Laban, but the sturdy ones to Jacob. [43] Thus the man grew increasingly prosperous, and he came to own not only large flocks but also male and female servants and camels and asses.

Flight from Laban

31 [1] Jacob learned that Laban's sons were saying, "Jacob has taken everything that belonged to our father, and he has accumulated all this wealth of his by using our father's property." [2] Jacob perceived, too, that Laban's attitude toward him was not what it had previously been. [3]* Then the LORD said to Jacob, "Return to the land of your fathers, where you were born, and I will be with you."

[4] So Jacob sent for Rachel and Leah to meet him where he was in the field with his flock. [5] There he said to them: "I have noticed that your father's attitude toward me is not as it was in the past; but the God of my father has been with me. [6] You well know what effort I put into serving your father; [7]* yet your father cheated me and changed my wages time after time. God, however, did not let him do me any harm. [8]† Whenever your father said, 'The speckled animals shall be your wages,' the entire flock would bear speckled young; whenever he said, 'The streaked animals shall be your wages,' the entire flock would bear streaked young. [9] Thus God reclaimed your father's livestock and gave it to me. [10] Once, in the breeding season, I had a dream in which I saw mating he-goats that were streaked, speckled and mottled. [11] In the dream God's messenger called to me, 'Jacob!' 'Here!' I replied. [12] Then he said, 'Note well. All the he-goats in the flock, as they mate, are streaked, speckled and mottled, for I have seen all the things that Laban has been doing to you. [13]* I am the God who appeared to you in Bethel, where you anointed a memorial stone and made a vow to me. Up, then! Leave this land and return to the land of your birth.'"

[14] Rachel and Leah answered him: "Have we still an heir's portion in our father's house? [15]† Are we not regarded by him as outsiders? He not only sold us; he has even used up the money that he got for us! [16]* All the wealth that God reclaimed from our father really belongs to us and our children. Therefore, do just as God has told you." [17] Jacob proceeded to put his children and wives on camels, [18] and he drove off with all his livestock and all the property he had acquired in Paddan-aram, to go to his father Isaac in the land of Canaan.

[19]*† Now Laban had gone away to shear his sheep, and Rachel had meanwhile appropriated her

---

30, 32: *Dark . . . sheep . . . spotted or speckled . . . goats:* In the Near East the normal color of sheep is light gray, whereas that of goats is uniform dark brown or black. Ordinarily, therefore, Jacob would have received but few animals.

30, 35: By giving the abnormally colored animals to his sons, Laban not only deprived Jacob of his first small wages, but he also designed to prevent in this way the future breeding of such animals in the part of his flock entrusted to Jacob.

30, 39–42: Jacob's stratagem was based on the widespread notion among simple people that visual stimuli can have prenatal effects on the offspring of breeding animals. Thus, the rods on which Jacob had whittled stripes or bands or chevron marks were thought to cause the female goats that looked at them to bear kids with lighter-colored marks on their dark hair, while the gray ewes were

thought to bear lambs with dark marks on them simply by visual cross-breeding with the dark goats.

31, 8–12: This Elohist account of the miraculous increase in Jacob's flock differs somewhat from the Yahwist account given in Gn 30, 32–42.

31, 15: *Outsiders:* literally "foreign women"; they lacked the favored legal status of native women. *Used up:* literally "eaten, consumed"; the bridal price that a man received for giving his daughter in marriage was legally reserved as her inalienable dowry.

31, 19: *Household idols:* in Hebrew, *teraphim,* figurines used in divination (Ez 21, 26; Zec 10, 2). Laban calls them his "gods" (v 30).

31, 3: Gn 26, 3; 28, 15; 32, 10. **31, 16:** Wis 10, 10f.
31, 7: Jdt 8, 26. **31, 19:** Gn 19, 34; 1 Sm 19, 13.
31, 13: Gn 28, 18.

father's household idols. 20† Jacob had hood-winked Laban the Aramean by not telling him of his intended flight. 21 Thus he made his escape with all that he had. Once he was across the Euphrates, he headed for the highlands of Gilead.

22 On the third day, word came to Laban that Jacob had fled. 23† Taking his kinsmen with him, he pursued him for seven days until he caught up with him in the hill country of Gilead. 24* But that night God appeared to Laban the Aramean in a dream and warned him, "Take care not to threaten Jacob with any harm."

Jacob and Laban in Gilead

25 When Laban overtook Jacob, Jacob's tents were pitched in the highlands; Laban also pitched his tents there, on Mount Gilead. 26† "What do you mean," Laban demanded of Jacob, "by hoodwink-ing me and carrying off my daughters like war captives? 27 Why did you dupe me by stealing away secretly? You should have told me, and I would have sent you off with merry singing to the sound of tambourines and harps. 28 You did not even allow me a parting kiss to my daughters and grand-children! What you have now done is a senseless thing. 29 I have it in my power to harm all of you; but last night the God of your father said to me, 'Take care not to threaten Jacob with any harm!' 30 Granted that you had to leave because you were desperately homesick for your father's house, why did you steal my gods?" 31 "I was frightened," Jacob replied to Laban, "at the thought that you might take your daughters away from me by force. 32 But as for your gods, the one you find them with shall not remain alive! If, with my kinsmen looking on, you identify anything here as belonging to you, take it." Jacob, of course, had no idea that Rachel had stolen the idols.

33 Laban then went in and searched Jacob's tent and Leah's tent, as well as the tents of the two maidservants; but he did not find the idols. Leav-ing Leah's tent, he went into Rachel's. 34* Now Rachel had taken the idols, put them inside a camel cushion, and seated herself upon them.

When Laban had rummaged through the rest of her tent without finding them, 35 Rachel said to her father, "Let not my lord feel offended that I cannot rise in your presence; a woman's period is upon me." So, despite his search, he did not find his idols.

36 Jacob, now enraged, upbraided Laban. "What crime or offense have I committed," he demanded, "that you should hound me so fiercely? 37 Now that you have ransacked all my things, have you found a single object taken from your belongings? If so, produce it here before your kinsmen and mine, and let them decide between us two.

38 "In the twenty years that I was under you, no ewe or she-goat of yours ever miscarried, and I have never feasted on a ram of your flock. 39*† I never brought you an animal torn by wild beasts; I made good the loss myself. You held me responsible for anything stolen by day or night. 40 How often the scorching heat ravaged me by day, and the frost by night, while sleep fled from my eyes! 41 Of the twenty years that I have now spent in your house-hold, I slaved fourteen years for your two daughters and six years for your flock, while you changed my wages time after time. 42* If my ancestral God, the God of Abraham and the Awesome One of Isaac, had not been on my side, you would now have sent me away empty-handed. But God saw my plight and the fruits of my toil, and last night he gave judgment."

43† Laban replied to Jacob: "The women are mine, their children are mine, and the flocks are mine; everything you see belongs to me. But since these women are my daughters, I will now do something for them and for the children they have borne. 44 Come, then, we will make a pact, you and I; the LORD shall be a witness between us."

45* Then Jacob took a stone and set it up as a me-morial stone. 46 Jacob said to his kinsmen, "Gather some stones." So they got some stones and made a mound; and they had a meal there at the mound. 47† Laban called it Jegar-sahadutha, but Jacob named it Galeed. 48 "This mound," said Laban, "shall be a witness from now on between you and

---

31, 20: *Hoodwinked:* literally "stolen the heart of," i.e., lulled the mind of. *Aramean:* The earliest extra-biblical references to the Arameans date from several centuries after the time of Jacob; to call Laban an *Aramean* and to have him speak Aramaic (v 47) would seem to be an anachronism.

31, 23: *For seven days:* literally "a way of seven days," a general term to designate a long distance; it would have taken a camel car-avan many more days to travel from Haran to Gilead, the region east of the northern half of the Jordan.

31, 26: *War captives:* literally "women captured by the sword"; the women of a conquered people were treated as part of the victor's booty; cf 1 Sm 30, 2; 2 Kgs 5, 2.

31, 39: Laban's actions were contrary to the customs of the an-cient Near East, as recorded in the Code of Hammurabi: "If in a sheepfold an act of god has occurred, or a lion has made a kill, the shepherd shall clear himself before the deity, and the owner of the fold must accept the loss" (par. 266); cf Ex 22, 12.

31, 43–54: In this account of the treaty between Laban and Jacob, the Yahwist and Elohist sources are closely interwoven. The *mound* or cairn of stones comes from the Yahwist source, the *me-morial stone* or stele comes from the Elohist one.

31, 47: *Jegar-sahadutha:* an Aramaic term meaning "mound of witness." *Galeed:* in Hebrew, *galed,* with the same meaning; also of-fers an explanation of the regional name Gilead.

31, 24: Wis 10, 12.   31, 42: Gn 19, 24.29.
31, 34: Gn 31, 19.   31, 45: Gn 28, 18; 35, 14.
31, 39: Ex 22, 12.

me." That is why it was named Galeed— 49† and also Mizpah, for he said: "May the LORD keep watch between you and me when we are out of each other's sight. 50 If you mistreat my daughters, or take other wives besides my daughters, remember that even though no one else is about, God will be witness between you and me."

51 Laban said further to Jacob: "Here is this mound, and here is the memorial stone that I have set up between you and me. 52 This mound shall be witness, and this memorial stone shall be witness, that, with hostile intent, neither may I pass beyond this mound into your territory nor may you pass beyond it into mine. 53 May the God of Abraham and the god of Nahor [their ancestral deities] maintain justice between us!" Jacob took the oath by the Awesome One of Isaac. 54 He then offered a sacrifice on the mountain and invited his kinsmen to share in the meal. When they had eaten, they passed the night on the mountain.

32 1 Early the next morning, Laban kissed his grandchildren and his daughters goodbye; then he set out on his journey back home, 2 while Jacob continued on his own way. Then God's messengers encountered Jacob. 3† When he saw them he said, "This is God's encampment." So he named that place Mahanaim.

Embassy to Esau

4* Jacob sent messengers ahead to his brother Esau in the land of Seir, the country of Edom, 5 with this message: "Thus shall you say to my lord Esau: 'Your servant Jacob speaks as follows: I have been staying with Laban and have been detained there until now. 6 I own cattle, asses and sheep, as well as male and female servants. I am sending my lord this information in the hope of gaining your favor.'"
7 When the messengers returned to Jacob, they said, "We reached your brother Esau. He is now coming to meet you, accompanied by four hundred men."

8 Jacob was very much frightened. In his anxiety, he divided the people who were with him, as well as his flocks, herds, and camels, into two camps. 9 "If Esau should attack and overwhelm one camp," he reasoned, "the remaining camp may still survive." 10* Then he prayed, "O God of my father Abraham and God of my father Isaac! You told me, O LORD, 'Go back to the land of your birth, and I will be good to you.' 11 I am unworthy of all the acts of kindness that you have loyally performed for your servant: although I crossed the Jordan here with nothing but

Wrestling with God

Even after twenty years, Jacob is anxious about meeting Esau again. This time, Jacob uses his craftiness not to deceive Esau but to gain Esau's good graces. Then while on the way home, he has an amazing religious experience. Many Scripture scholars believe that the strange wrestling encounter is a symbol that Jacob has become a changed person. He finally realizes that in all his troubles, God was his true opponent.

Perhaps at times you have wrestled with yourself or with God. It is not so much that God is your opponent or that you are in a contest. It is the wrestling itself that matters. When you face the challenges, especially the big ones, you wrestle between the person you are now and the person God is calling you to be.

In your prayer, reflect or journal on the following questions:

- When does it seem like God is trying to wrestle with you? What does it feel like?
- Is God challenging you about something in your life right now?
- What blessings might you gain in accepting God's challenge and changing your life?

▸ Gn 32, 23–33

my staff, I have now grown into two companies. 12* Save me, I pray, from the hand of my brother Esau! Otherwise I fear that when he comes he will strike me down and slay the mothers and children. 13 You yourself said, 'I will be very good to you, and I will make your descendants like the sands of the sea, which are too numerous to count.'"

14 After passing the night there, Jacob selected from what he had with him the following presents for his brother Esau: 15 two hundred she-goats and twenty he-goats; two hundred ewes and twenty rams; 16 thirty milch camels and their young; forty cows and ten bulls; twenty she-asses and ten he-asses. 17 He put these animals in charge of his

---

† **31, 49:** *Mizpah:* a town in Gilead; cf Jgs 10, 17; 11, 11.34; Hos 5, 1. The Hebrew name *mispa* ("lookout") is allied to *yisep yhwh* ("may the LORD keep watch"), and also echoes the word *masseba* ("memorial pillar").
  32, 3: *Mahanaim:* a town in Gilead (Jos 13, 26.30; 21, 38; 2 Sm

2, 8; etc.). The Hebrew name means "two camps." There are other allusions to the name in vv 8.11.

32, 4: Gn 36, 6.   **32, 12:** Gn 28, 14; 48, 16; Ex
32, 10: Gn 31, 3.   32, 13; Heb 11, 12.

servants, in separate droves, and he told the servants, "Go on ahead of me, but keep a space between one drove and the next." 18 To the servant in the lead he gave this instruction: "When my brother Esau meets you, he may ask you, 'Whose man are you? Where are you going? To whom do these animals ahead of you belong?' 19 Then you shall answer, 'They belong to your brother Jacob, but they have been sent as a gift to my lord Esau; and Jacob himself is right behind us.' " 20 He gave similar instructions to the second servant and the third and to all the others who followed behind the droves, namely: "Thus and thus shall you say to Esau, when you reach him; 21 and be sure to add, 'Your servant Jacob is right behind us.' " For Jacob reasoned, "If I first appease him with gifts that precede me, then later, when I face him, perhaps he will forgive me." 22 So the gifts went on ahead of him, while he stayed that night in the camp.

Struggle with the Angel

23 In the course of that night, however, Jacob arose, took his two wives, with the two maidservants and his eleven children, and crossed the ford of the Jabbok. 24 After he had taken them across the stream and had brought over all his possessions, 25† Jacob was left there alone. Then some man wrestled with him until the break of dawn. 26* When the man saw that he could not prevail

over him, he struck Jacob's hip at its socket, so that the hip socket was wrenched as they wrestled. 27 The man then said, "Let me go, for it is daybreak." But Jacob said, "I will not let you go until you bless me." 28* "What is your name?" the man asked. He answered, "Jacob." 29† Then the man said, "You shall no longer be spoken of as Jacob, but as Israel, because you have contended with divine and human beings and have prevailed." 30 Jacob then asked him, "Do tell me your name, please." He answered, "Why should you want to know my name?" With that, he bade him farewell. 31*† Jacob named the place Peniel, "Because I have seen God face to face," he said, "yet my life has been spared."

32 At sunrise, as he left Penuel, Jacob limped along because of his hip. 33 That is why, to this day, the Israelites do not eat the sciatic muscle that is on the hip socket, inasmuch as Jacob's hip socket was struck at the sciatic muscle.

Jacob and Esau Meet

33 1 Jacob looked up and saw Esau coming, accompanied by four hundred men. So he divided his children among Leah, Rachel and the two maidservants, 2 putting the maids and their children first, Leah and her children next, and Rachel and Joseph last. 3 He himself went on ahead of them, bowing to the ground seven times, until he reached his brother. 4 Esau ran to meet him,

---

Letting Go of the Past

 LIVE IT!

Jacob is understandably apprehensive as he approaches his long-estranged twin brother. How will Esau react? But Esau, who was wronged by Jacob, runs to meet him and gives him a hug. All is forgiven, and the two are reconciled at last. This story is like the parable of the prodigal son in Lk 15, 11–32.

All of us have wronged others, especially the people we care about most. All of us have also experienced forgiveness. Nothing is quite like the freedom that comes with genuine forgiveness and reconciliation. A burden is lifted. A heavy heart is made lighter. A vengeful attitude is transformed into a feeling of inner peace and harmony. This is the work of God's grace. Forgiveness and reconciliation are powerful signs of the presence of God. We can almost feel the enormous sense of relief experienced by Jacob as he realizes that his brother holds no grudge.

Does a relationship in your life need forgiveness and reconciliation? If so, what can you do to bring about healing in this relationship?

▶ Gn 33, 1–17

32, 25: *Some man:* a messenger of the Lord in human form, as is clear from vv 29ff.
32, 29: *Israel:* the first part of the Hebrew name *Yisrael* is given a popular explanation in the word *sarita,* "you contended"; the second part is the first syllable of *elohim,* "divine beings." The present incident, with a similar allusion to the name Israel, is referred to in Hos 12, 5, where the mysterious wrestler is explicitly called an angel.

32, 31: *Peniel:* a variant of the word Penuel (v 32), the name of a town on the north bank of the Jabbok in Gilead (Jgs 8, 8f.17; 1 Kgs 12, 25). The name is explained as meaning "the face of God," *peniel. Yet my life has been spared:* see note on Gn 16, 13.

32, 26: Hos 12, 4.
32, 28: Gn 35, 10; 1 Kgs

18, 31; 2 Kgs 17, 34.
32, 31: Jgs 13, 22.

embraced him, and flinging himself on his neck, kissed him as he wept.

⁵ When Esau looked about, he saw the women and children. "Who are these with you?" he asked. Jacob answered, "They are the children whom God has graciously bestowed on your servant." ⁶ Then the maidservants and their children came forward and bowed low; ⁷ next, Leah and her children came forward and bowed low; lastly, Rachel and her children came forward and bowed low. ⁸ Then Esau asked, "What did you intend with all those droves that I encountered?" Jacob answered, "It was to gain my lord's favor." ⁹ "I have plenty," replied Esau;

herds, which now have sucklings; if overdriven for a single day, the whole flock will die. ¹⁴ Let my lord, then, go on ahead of me, while I proceed more slowly at the pace of the livestock before me and at the pace of my children, until I join my lord in Seir." ¹⁵ Esau replied, "Let me at least put at your disposal some of the men who are with me." But Jacob said, "For what reason? Please indulge me in this, my lord." ¹⁶ So on the same day that Esau began his journey back to Seir, ¹⁷† Jacob journeyed to Succoth. There he built a home for himself and made booths for his livestock. That is why the place was called Succoth.

No Way, Shechem!

A news article reported on the rape of a girl by a group of high school boys. The girl was dating one of the boys and went to a party where she became intoxicated. The boys decided to take advantage of her and one-by-one raped her. The next day, she told her parents what had happened, the police were contacted, and the boys were arrested. Many people were left wondering how this could have happened in their little town.

Rape is more about power than it is about sex. The story in Genesis, chapter 34, tells us of Shechem, a local prince, who rapes Dinah. Because of his power, he figured he could do what he wanted to her. But in the end, his life is taken.

The boys in the story above felt that they had the power to do what they wanted, but in the end, they were arrested and sentenced to serve time in a juvenile facility. We are to respect one another. Position or power does not give us the right to commit sexual violence. Rape and any other sexual abuse are an outrage to God.

▸ **Gn 34, 1–31**

"you should keep what is yours, brother." ¹⁰ "No, I beg you!" said Jacob. "If you will do me the favor, please accept this gift from me, since to come into your presence is for me like coming into the presence of God, now that you have received me so kindly. ¹¹ Do accept the present I have brought you; God has been generous toward me, and I have an abundance." Since he so urged him, Esau accepted.

¹² Then Esau said, "Let us break camp and be on our way; I will travel alongside you." ¹³ But Jacob replied: "As my lord can see, the children are frail. Besides, I am encumbered with the flocks and

¹⁸* Having thus come from Paddan-aram, Jacob arrived safely at the city of Shechem, which is in the land of Canaan, and he encamped in sight of the city. ¹⁹*† The plot of ground on which he had pitched his tent he bought for a hundred pieces of bullion from the descendants of Hamor, the founder of Shechem. ²⁰* He set up a memorial stone there and invoked "El, the God of Israel."

The Rape of Dinah

34 ¹† Dinah, the daughter whom Leah had borne to Jacob, went out to visit some of

33, 17: *Succoth:* an important town near the confluence of the Jabbok and the Jordan (Jos 13, 27; Jgs 8, 5–16; 1 Kgs 7, 46). *Booths:* in Hebrew, *sukkot*, of the same sound as the name of the town.

33, 19: *Pieces of bullion:* in Hebrew, *kesita*, a monetary unit of which the value is now unknown. *Descendants of Hamor:* Hamorites, "the men of Hamor"; cf Jgs 9, 28. Hamor was regarded as the eponymous ancestor of the pre-Israelite inhabitants of Shechem.

34, 1–31: Behind the story of the rape of Dinah and the revenge of Jacob's sons on the men of the city of Shechem there probably lies a dimly recollected historical event connected with an armed conflict between the earliest Israelite tribes invading central Canaan and the Hurrian inhabitants of the Shechem region.

33, 18: Gn 12, 6; Jn 4, 6.   Acts 7, 16.
33, 19: Jos 24, 32; Jn 4, 5;   **33, 20:** Jgs 6, 24.

the women of the land. 2† When Shechem, son of Hamor the Hivite, who was chief of the region, saw her, he seized her and lay with her by force. 3 Since he was strongly attracted to Dinah, daughter of Jacob, indeed was really in love with the girl, he endeavored to win her affection. 4 Shechem also asked his father Hamor, "Get me this girl for a wife."

5 Meanwhile, Jacob heard that Shechem had defiled his daughter Dinah; but since his sons were out in the fields with his livestock, he held his peace until they came home. 6 Now Hamor, the father of Shechem, went out to discuss the matter with Jacob, 7* just as Jacob's sons were coming in from the fields. When they heard the news, the men were shocked and seethed with indignation. What Shechem had done was an outrage in Israel; such a thing could not be tolerated.

8 Hamor appealed to them, saying, "My son Shechem has his heart set on your daughter. Please give her to him in marriage. 9 Intermarry with us; give your daughters to us, and take our daughters for yourselves. 10 Thus you can live among us. The land is open before you; you can settle and move about freely in it, and acquire landed property here." 11 Then Shechem, too, appealed to Dinah's father and brothers: "Do me this favor, and I will pay whatever you demand of me. 12 No matter how high you set the bridal price, I will pay you whatever you ask; only give me the maiden in marriage."

Revenge of Jacob's Sons

13 Jacob's sons replied to Shechem and his father Hamor with guile, speaking as they did because their sister Dinah had been defiled. 14 "We could not do such a thing," they said, "as to give our sister to an uncircumcised man; that would be a disgrace for us. 15 We will agree with you only on this condition, that you become like us by having every male among you circumcised. 16 Then we will give you our daughters and take yours in marriage; we will settle among you and become one kindred people with you. 17 But if you do not comply with our terms regarding circumcision, we will take our daughter and go away."

18 Their proposal seemed fair to Hamor and his son Shechem. 19 The young man lost no time in acting in the matter, since he was deeply in love with Jacob's daughter. Moreover, he was more highly

respected than anyone else in his clan. 20 So Hamor and his son Shechem went to their town council and thus presented the matter to their fellow townsmen: 21 "These men are friendly toward us. Let them settle in the land and move about in it freely; there is ample room in the country for them. We can marry their daughters and give our daughters to them in marriage. 22 But the men will agree to live with us and form one kindred people with us only on this condition, that every male among us be circumcised as they themselves are. 23 Would not the livestock they have acquired—all their animals—then be ours? Let us, therefore, give in to them, so that they may settle among us."

24† All the able-bodied men of the town agreed with Hamor and his son Shechem, and all the males, including every able-bodied man in the community, were circumcised. 25* On the third day, while they were still in pain, Dinah's full brothers Simeon and Levi, two of Jacob's sons, took their swords, advanced against the city without any trouble, and massacred all the males. 26* After they had put Hamor and his son Shechem to the sword, they took Dinah from Shechem's house and left. 27 Then the other sons of Jacob followed up the slaughter and sacked the city in reprisal for their sister Dinah's defilement. 28 They seized their flocks, herds and asses, whatever was in the city and in the country around. 29* They carried off all their wealth, their women, and their children, and took for loot whatever was in the houses.

30 Jacob said to Simeon and Levi: "You have brought trouble upon me by making me loathsome to the inhabitants of the land, the Canaanites and the Perizzites. I have so few men that, if these people unite against me and attack me, I and my family will be wiped out." 31 But they retorted, "Should our sister have been treated like a harlot?"

Bethel Revisited

35 1* God said to Jacob: "Go up now to Bethel. Settle there and build an altar there to the God who appeared to you while you were fleeing from your brother Esau." 2† So Jacob told his family and all the others who were with him: "Get rid of the foreign gods that you have among you; then purify yourselves and put on fresh clothes. 3 We are now to go up to Bethel, and I will build an altar there to the God who answered me in

---

34, 2: *Hivite:* The Greek text has "Horite"; the terms were apparently used indiscriminately to designate the Hurrian or other non-Semitic elements in Palestine.

34, 24: *Every able-bodied man in the community:* literally "all those who go out at the gate of the city," apparently meaning the men who go out to war. By temporarily crippling them through circumcision, Jacob's sons deprived the city of its defenders.

35, 2: *Foreign gods:* pagan images, including household idols

(see note on Gn 31, 19), that Jacob's people brought with them from Paddan-aram.

34, 7: 2 Sm 13, 12.   34, 29: Jdt 9, 3f.
34, 25: Gn 49, 6.   35, 1: Gn 28, 12f.
34, 26: Jdt 9, 2.

my hour of distress and who has been with me wherever I have gone." 4† They therefore handed over to Jacob all the foreign gods in their possession and also the rings they had in their ears. 5 Then, as they set out, a terror from God fell upon the towns round about, so that no one pursued the sons of Jacob.

6* Thus Jacob and all the people who were with him arrived in Luz [that is, Bethel] in the land of Canaan. 7* There he built an altar and named the place Bethel, for it was there that God had revealed himself to him when he was fleeing from his brother.

8† Death came to Rebekah's nurse Deborah; she was buried under the oak below Bethel, and so it was called Allon-bacuth.

9 On Jacob's arrival from Paddan-aram, God appeared to him again and blessed him. 10* God said to him:

"You whose name is Jacob
　　shall no longer be called Jacob,
　　but Israel shall be your name."

Thus he was named Israel. 11 God also said to him:

"I am God Almighty;
　　be fruitful and multiply.
A nation, indeed an assembly of nations,
　　shall stem from you,
　　and kings shall issue from your loins.
12* The land I once gave
　　to Abraham and Isaac
　　I now give to you;
And to your descendants after you
　　will I give this land."

13 Then God departed from him. 14* On the site where God had spoken with him, Jacob set up a memorial stone, and upon it he made a libation and poured out oil. 15 Jacob named the site Bethel, because God had spoken with him there.

Jacob's Family

16 Then they departed from Bethel: but while they still had some distance to go on the way to Ephrath, Rachel began to be in labor and to suffer great distress. 17 When her pangs were most severe, her midwife said to her, "Have no fear! This time, too, you have a son." 18† With her last breath—for she was at the point of death—she called him Ben-oni; his father, however, named him Benjamin. 19*† Thus Rachel died; and she was buried on the road to Ephrath [that is, Bethlehem]. 20 Jacob set up a memorial stone on her grave, and the same monument marks Rachel's grave to this day.

21 Israel moved on and pitched his tent beyond Migdal-eder. 22* While Israel was encamped in that region, Reuben went and lay with Bilhah, his father's concubine. When Israel heard of it, he was greatly offended.

The sons of Jacob were now twelve. 23 The sons of Leah: Reuben, Jacob's first-born, Simeon, Levi, Judah, Issachar, and Zebulun; 24† the sons of Rachel: Joseph and Benjamin; 25 the sons of Rachel's maid Bilhah: Dan and Naphtali; 26 the sons of Leah's maid Zilpah: Gad and Asher. These are the sons of Jacob who were born to him in Paddan-aram.

27 Jacob went home to his father Isaac at Mamre, in Kiriath-arba [that is, Hebron], where Abraham and Isaac had stayed. 28 The lifetime of Isaac was one hundred and eighty years; 29 then he breathed his last. After a full life, he died as an old man and was taken to his kinsmen. His sons Esau and Jacob buried him.

Edomite Lists

36 1 These are the descendants of Esau [that is, Edom]. 2*† Esau took his wives from among the Canaanite women: Adah, daughter of Elon the Hittite; Oholibamah, granddaughter through Anah of Zibeon the Hivite; 3 and Basemath, daughter of Ishmael and sister of Nebaioth. 4* Adah bore Eliphaz to Esau; Basemath bore Reuel; 5* and Oholibamah bore Jeush, Jalam and Korah. These are the sons of Esau who were born to him in the land of Canaan.

6* Esau took his wives, his sons, his daughters,

35, 4: *Rings:* Earrings were often worn as amulets connected with pagan magic.

35, 8: This verse may have stood originally in some other context. Rebekah's nurse is spoken of without a name, in Gn 24, 59. *Allon-bacuth:* the Hebrew name means "oak of weeping."

35, 18: *Ben-oni:* means either "son of my vigor" or, more likely in the context, "son of affliction." *Benjamin:* "son of the right hand." This may be interpreted to signify a son who is his father's help and support, but more likely its original meaning was "southerner." In the Hebrew idiom, the south lies to one's right hand, and Benjamin was the southernmost of the Rachel tribes.

35, 19: *Bethlehem:* the gloss comes from a later tradition that identified the site with Bethlehem, also called Ephrath or Ephratha (Jos 15, 59; Ru 4, 11; Mi 5, 1). But Rachel's grave was actually near Ramah (Jer 31, 15), a few miles north of Jerusalem, in the territory of Benjamin (1 Sm 20, 2).

35, 24ff: Benjamin is here said to have been born in *Paddan-aram,* either because all twelve sons of Jacob are considered as a unit, or because the Priestly source, from which vv 23–29 are taken, follows a tradition different from that of the Elohistic source found in vv 16–20.

36, 2–14: The names of Esau's wives and of their fathers given here differ considerably from their names cited from other old sources in Gn 26, 34 and 28, 9. *Zibeon the Hivite:* In v 20 he is called a *Horite;* see note on Gn 34, 2.

35, 6: Gn 28, 19; Jos 18, 13; Jgs 1, 22f.	**35, 19:** Gn 48, 7; 1 Sm 10, 2; Mi 5, 2.
35, 7: Gn 28, 12f.	**35, 22:** Gn 49, 4; 1 Chr 5, 1.
35, 10: 1 Kgs 18, 31; 2 Kgs 17, 34.	**36, 2:** Gn 26, 34.
35, 12: Ex 32, 13; Heb 11, 9.	**36, 4:** 1 Chr 1, 35.
35, 14: Gn 28, 18; 31, 45.	**36, 5:** 1 Chr 1, 35.
	36, 6: Gn 32, 4.

and all the members of his household, as well as his livestock comprising various animals and all the property he had acquired in the land of Canaan, and went to the land of Seir, out of the way of his brother Jacob. 7 Their possessions had become too great for them to dwell together, and the land in which they were staying could not support them because of their livestock. 8* So Esau settled in the highlands of Seir. [Esau is Edom.] 9 These are the descendants of Esau, ancestor of the Edomites, in the highlands of Seir.

10 These are the names of Esau's sons: Eliphaz, son of Esau's wife Adah; and Reuel, son of Esau's wife Basemath. 11* The sons of Eliphaz were Teman, Omar, Zepho, Gatam and Kenaz. 12 (Esau's son Eliphaz had a concubine Timna, and she bore Amalek to Eliphaz.) These are the descendants of Esau's wife Adah. 13* The sons of Reuel were Nahath, Zerah, Shammah and Mizzah. These are the descendants of Esau's wife Basemath. 14* The descendants of Esau's wife Oholibamah—granddaughter through Anah of Zibeon—whom she bore to Esau were Jeush, Jalam and Korah.

15 The following are the clans of Esau's descendants. The descendants of Eliphaz, Esau's first-born: the clans of Teman, Omar, Zepho, Kenaz, 16 Korah, Gatam and Amalek. These are the clans of Eliphaz in the land of Edom; they are descended from Adah. 17 The descendants of Esau's son Reuel: the clans of Nahath, Zerah, Shammah and Mizzah. These are the clans of Reuel in the land of Edom; they are descended from Esau's wife Basemath. 18 The descendants of Esau's wife Oholibamah: the clans of Jeush, Jalam and Korah. These are the clans of Esau's wife Oholibamah, daughter of Anah. 19 Such are the descendants of Esau [that is, Edom] according to their clans.

20*† The following are the descendants of Seir the Horite, the original settlers in the land: Lotan, Shobal, Zibeon, Anah, 21 Dishon, Ezer and Dishan; they are the Horite clans descended from Seir, in the land of Edom. 22* Lotan's descendants were Hori and Hemam, and Lotan's sister was Timna. 23 Shobal's descendants were Alvan, Mahanath, Ebal, Shepho and Onam. 24 Zibeon's descendants were Aiah and Anah. (He is the Anah who found water in the desert while he was pasturing the asses of his father Zibeon.) 25 The descendants of Anah were Dishon and Oholibamah, daughter of Anah. 26 The descendants of Dishon were Hemdan, Eshban, Ithran and Cheran. 27 The descendants of Ezer

were Bilhan, Zaavan and Akan. 28 The descendants of Dishan were Uz and Aran. 29 These are the Horite clans: the clans of Lotan, Shobal, Zibeon, Anah, 30 Dishon, Ezer and Dishan; they were the clans of the Horites, clan by clan, in the land of Seir.

31*† The following are the kings who reigned in the land of Edom before any king reigned over the Israelites. 32 Bela, son of Beor, became king in Edom; the name of his city was Dinhabah. 33 When Bela died, Jobab, son of Zerah, from Bozrah, succeeded him as king. 34 When Jobab died, Husham, from the land of the Temanites, succeeded him as king. He defeated the Midianites in the country of Moab; the name of his city was Avith. 35 When Husham died, Hadad, son of Bedad, succeeded him as king. 36 When Hadad died, Samlah, from Masrekah, succeeded him as king. 37 When Samlah died, Shaul, from Rehoboth-on-the-River, succeeded him as king. 38 When Shaul died, Baal-hanan, son of Achbor, succeeded him as king. 39 When Baal-hanan died, Hadar succeeded him as king; the name of his city was Pau. (His wife's name was Mehetabel; she was the daughter of Matred, son of Mezahab.)

40 The following are the names of the clans of Esau individually according to their subdivisions and localities: the clans of Timna, Alvah, Jetheth, 41 Oholibamah, Elah, Pinon, 42 Kenaz, Teman, Mibzar, 43 Magdiel and Iram. These are the clans of the Edomites, according to their settlements in their territorial holdings. [Esau was the father of the Edomites.]

IV: Joseph and His Brothers

Joseph Sold into Egypt

37 1 Jacob settled in the land where his father had stayed, the land of Canaan. 2 This is his family history. When Joseph was seventeen years old, he was tending the flocks with his brothers; he was an assistant to the sons of his father's wives Bilhah and Zilpah, and he brought his father bad reports about them.

3 Israel loved Joseph best of all his sons, for he was the child of his old age; and he had made him a long tunic. 4 When his brothers saw that their father loved him best of all his sons, they hated him so much that they would not even greet him.

5* Once Joseph had a dream, which he told to his brothers: 6 "Listen to this dream I had. 7 There we were, binding sheaves in the field, when

---

36, 20: *Seir the Horite:* According to Dt 2, 12, the highlands of Seir were inhabited by Horites before they were occupied by the Edomites.
36, 31: *Before any king reigned over the Israelites:* obviously this statement was written after the time of Saul, Israel's first king.

36, 8: Dt 2, 4f; Jos 24, 4.   36, 20f: 1 Chr 1, 38.
36, 11f: 1 Chr 1, 36.   36, 22–28: 1 Chr 1, 39–42.
36, 13: 1 Chr 1, 37.   36, 31–43: 1 Chr 1, 45–54.
36, 14: 1 Chr 1, 35.   37, 5: Gn 42, 9.

GN

suddenly my sheaf rose to an upright position, and your sheaves formed a ring around my sheaf and bowed down to it." 8* "Are you really going to make yourself king over us?" his brothers asked him. "Or impose your rule on us?" So they hated him all the more because of his talk about his dreams.

him off from the valley of Hebron. When Joseph reached Shechem, 15 a man met him as he was wandering about in the fields. "What are you looking for?" the man asked him. 16 "I am looking for my brothers," he answered. "Could you please tell me where they are tending the flocks?" 17 The man told him, "They have moved on from here; in fact,

Introducing ▶ JOSEPH

The timeless power of Joseph's story is reaffirmed by the long and successful run of the Broadway play *Joseph and the Amazing Technicolor Dreamcoat.* (In other Bible versions, the "long tunic" in Gn 37, 3 is translated as a "coat of many colors.") The play is based on chapters 37–50 of Genesis, which contains one of the world's greatest stories of family, jealousy, betrayal, and forgiveness.

A son of Jacob and Rachel, Joseph carries to Egypt the divine promises of land and descendants, and eventually becomes the link with the story of Moses and the Exodus. As Jacob's favorite son, Joseph experiences the jealousy of his brothers, who sell him to Egyptian merchants. In Egypt, Joseph rises to power, becoming second in command to the Pharaoh. Later, when Joseph's brothers come to Egypt looking for food, he forgives them and becomes reconciled with them.

Joseph's story encourages us to forgive others, even when we have been unjustly treated by them. Whenever we have been greatly wronged, remembering Joseph will offer us hope and courage.

▶ Gn 37, 1—50, 26

9 Then he had another dream, and this one, too, he told to his brothers. "I had another dream," he said; "this time, the sun and the moon and eleven stars were bowing down to me." 10 When he also told it to his father, his father reproved him. "What is the meaning of this dream of yours?" he asked. "Can it be that I and your mother and your brothers are to come and bow to the ground before you?" 11 So his brothers were wrought up against him but his father pondered the matter.

12 One day, when his brothers had gone to pasture their father's flocks at Shechem, 13 Israel said to Joseph, "Your brothers, you know, are tending our flocks at Shechem. Get ready; I will send you to them." "I am ready," Joseph answered. 14 "Go then," he replied; "see if all is well with your brothers and the flocks, and bring back word." So he sent

I heard them say, 'Let us go on to Dothan.' " So Joseph went after his brothers and caught up with them in Dothan. 18 They noticed him from a distance, and before he came up to them, they plotted to kill him. 19 They said to one another: "Here comes that master dreamer! 20* Come on, let us kill him and throw him into one of the cisterns here; we could say that a wild beast devoured him. We shall then see what comes of his dreams."

21† When Reuben heard this, he tried to save him from their hands, saying, "We must not take his life. 22* Instead of shedding blood," he continued, "just throw him into that cistern there in the desert; but don't kill him outright." His purpose was to rescue him from their hands and restore him to his father. 23 So when Joseph came up to them, they stripped him of the long tunic he had on; 24 then they took

---

† **37, 21–36:** The chapter thus far is from the Yahwist source, as are also vv 25–28a. But vv 21–24 and 28b–36 are from the Elohist source. In the latter, Reuben tries to rescue Joseph, who is taken in Reuben's absence by certain Midianites; in the Yahwist source, it is Judah who saves Joseph's life by having him sold to certain Ishmaelites. Although the two variant forms in which the story was

handed down in early oral tradition differ in these minor points, they agree on the essential fact that Joseph was brought as a slave into Egypt because of the jealousy of his brothers.

*
37, 8: Gn 50, 17.   **37, 22:** Gn 42, 22.
37, 20: Gn 44, 28.

him and threw him into the cistern, which was empty and dry.

25* They then sat down to their meal. Looking up, they saw a caravan of Ishmaelites coming from Gilead, their camels laden with gum, balm and resin to be taken down to Egypt. 26* Judah said to his brothers: "What is to be gained by killing our brother and concealing his blood? 27 Rather, let us sell him to these Ishmaelites, instead of doing away with him ourselves. After all, he is our brother, our own flesh." His brothers agreed. 28*† They sold Joseph to the Ishmaelites for twenty pieces of silver.

Some Midianite traders passed by, and they pulled Joseph up out of the cistern and took him to Egypt. 29 When Reuben went back to the cistern and saw that Joseph was not in it, he tore his clothes, 30 and returning to his brothers, he exclaimed: "The boy is gone! And I—where can I turn?" 31 They took Joseph's tunic, and after slaughtering a goat, dipped the tunic in its blood. 32 They then sent someone to bring the long tunic to their father, with the message: "We found this. See whether it is your son's tunic or not." 33* He recognized it and exclaimed: "My son's tunic! A wild beast has devoured him! Joseph has been torn to pieces!" 34 Then Jacob rent his clothes, put sackcloth on his loins, and mourned his son many days. 35* Though his sons and daughters tried to console him, he refused all consolation, saying, "No, I will go down mourning to my son in the nether world." Thus did his father lament him.

36* The Midianites, meanwhile, sold Joseph in Egypt to Potiphar, a courtier of Pharaoh and his chief steward.

Judah and Tamar

38 1† About that time Judah parted from his brothers and pitched his tent near a certain Adullamite named Hirah. 2* There he met the daughter of a Canaanite named Shua, married her, and had relations with her. 3 She conceived and bore a son, whom she named Er. 4 Again she conceived and bore a son, whom she named Onan. 5*† Then she bore still another son, whom she named Shelah. They were in Chezib when he was born.

?did you KNOW?

Levirate Marriage

Why does Onan have to marry his dead brother's wife and have a son by her? One of the laws specified in Dt 25, 5–10 regulates what is called levirate marriage. *Levirate* means "brother-in-law." When a man's married brother dies without a son, that man is obligated to marry the wife who was left, and the first son whom she bears shall "continue the line of the deceased" (verse 6). This marriage practice seems to have developed in Israel for several reasons:

- A male child was needed to be heir to the dead man's property because women generally did not own property.
- The dead man's widow needed support and protection.
- A male heir ensured that the family property was kept within the immediate family.

▶ Gn 38, 8

---

6 Judah got a wife named Tamar for his first-born, Er. 7* But Er, Judah's first-born, greatly offended the LORD; so the LORD took his life. 8*† Then Judah said to Onan, "Unite with your brother's widow, in fulfillment of your duty as brother-in-law, and thus preserve your brother's line." 9 Onan, however, knew that the descendants would not be counted as his; so whenever he had relations with his brother's widow, he wasted his seed on the ground, to avoid contributing offspring for his brother. 10 What he did greatly offended the LORD, and the LORD took his life too. 11 Thereupon Judah said to his daughter-in-law Tamar, "Stay as a widow in your father's house until my son Shelah grows up"—for he feared that Shelah also might die like his brothers. So Tamar went to live in her father's house.

---

† 37, 28: *They sold Joseph . . . silver:* in the Hebrew text, these words occur between *out of the cistern* and *(they) took him to Egypt* at the end of the verse.
  38, 1–30: This chapter, from the Yahwist source, has nothing to do with the Joseph story in which Judah is still living with his father and brothers. The sacred author inserted this independent account from the life of Judah at this place to mark the long lapse of time during which Joseph's family knew nothing of his life in Egypt. This is apparently a personalized history of the early days of the tribe of Judah, which interbred with several Canaanite clans, though some of these soon became extinct.
  38, 5: *Chezib:* a variant form of Achzib (Jos 15, 44; Mi 1, 14), a town in the Judean Shephelah.

38, 8: *Preserve your brother's line:* literally, "raise up seed for your brother." The ancient Israelites regarded as very important their law of levirate, or "brother-in-law" marriage; see notes on Dt 25, 5; Ru 2, 20. In the present story, it is primarily Onan's violation of this law, rather than the means he used to circumvent it, that brought on him God's displeasure (vv 9f).

37, 25: Gn 43, 11.
37, 26: Jb 16, 18.
37, 28: Ps 105, 17; Wis 10, 13; Acts 7, 9.
37, 33: Gn 44, 28.
37, 35: Gn 42, 38.

37, 36: Ps 105, 17.
38, 2: 1 Chr 2, 3.
38, 5: 1 Chr 4, 21.
38, 7: 1 Chr 2, 3.
38, 8: Dt 25, 5; Mt 22, 24; Mk 12, 19; Lk 20, 28.

¹² Years passed, and Judah's wife, the daughter of Shua, died. After Judah completed the period of mourning, he went up to Timnah for the shearing of his sheep, in company with his friend Hirah the Adullamite. ¹³ When Tamar was told that her father-in-law was on his way up to Timnah to shear his sheep, ¹⁴* she took off her widow's garb, veiled her face by covering herself with a shawl, and sat down at the entrance to Enaim, which is on the way to Timnah; for she was aware that, although Shelah was now grown up, she had not been given to him in marriage. ¹⁵ When Judah saw her, he mistook her for a harlot, since she had covered her face. ¹⁶ So he went over to her at the roadside, and not realizing that she was his daughter-in-law, he said, "Come, let me have intercourse with you." She replied, "What will you pay me for letting you have intercourse with me?" ¹⁷ He answered, "I will send you a kid from the flock." "Very well," she said, "provided you leave a pledge until you send it." ¹⁸† Judah asked, "What pledge am I to give you?" She answered, "Your seal and cord, and the staff you carry." So he gave them to her and had intercourse with her, and she conceived by him. ¹⁹ When she went away, she took off her shawl and put on her widow's garb again.

²⁰ Judah sent the kid by his friend the Adullamite to recover the pledge from the woman; but he could not find her. ²¹† So he asked the men of the place, "Where is the temple prostitute, the one by the roadside in Enaim?" But they answered, "There has never been a temple prostitute here." ²² He went back to Judah and told him, "I could not find her; and besides, the men of the place said there was no temple prostitute there." ²³ "Let her keep the things," Judah replied; "otherwise we shall become a laughingstock. After all, I did send her the kid, even though you were unable to find her."

²⁴ About three months later, Judah was told that his daughter-in-law Tamar had played the harlot and was then with child from her harlotry. "Bring her out," cried Judah; "she shall be burned." ²⁵ But as they were bringing her out, she sent word to her father-in-law, "It is by the man to whom these things belong that I am with child. Please verify,"

she added, "whose seal and cord and whose staff these are." ²⁶ Judah recognized them and said, "She is more in the right than I am, since I did not give her to my son Shelah." But he had no further relations with her.

²⁷* When the time of her delivery came, she was found to have twins in her womb. ²⁸ While she was giving birth, one infant put out his hand; and the midwife, taking a crimson thread, tied it on his hand, to note that this one came out first. ²⁹*† But as he withdrew his hand, his brother came out; and she said, "What a breach you have made for yourself!" So he was called Perez. ³⁰*† Afterward his brother came out; he was called Zerah.

Joseph's Temptation

39 ¹† When Joseph was taken down to Egypt, a certain Egyptian (Potiphar, a courtier of Pharaoh and his chief steward) bought him from the Ishmaelites who had brought him there. ²* But since the LORD was with him, Joseph got on very well and was assigned to the household of his Egyptian master. ³ When his master saw that the LORD was with him and brought him success in whatever he did, ⁴* he took a liking to Joseph and made him his personal attendant; he put him in charge of his household and entrusted to him all his possessions. ⁵ From the moment that he put him in charge of his household and all his possessions, the LORD blessed the Egyptian's house for Joseph's sake; in fact, the LORD's blessing was on everything he owned, both inside the house and out. ⁶ Having left everything he owned in Joseph's charge, he gave no thought, with Joseph there, to anything but the food he ate.

Now Joseph was strikingly handsome in countenance and body. ⁷ After a time, his master's wife began to look fondly at him and said, "Lie with me." ⁸ But he refused. "As long as I am here," he told her, "my master does not concern himself with anything in the house, but has entrusted to me all he owns. ⁹ He wields no more authority in this house than I do, and he has withheld from me nothing but yourself, since you are his wife. How, then, could I commit so great a wrong and thus stand condemned

---

† **38, 18:** *Seal and cord:* the cylinder seal, through which a hole was bored lengthwise so that it could be worn from the neck by a cord, was a distinctive means of identification. Apparently a man's staff was also marked with his name (Nm 17, 16f) or other sign of identification.

38, 21: *Temple prostitute:* the Hebrew term *qedesha,* literally "consecrated woman," designates a woman who had ritual intercourse with men in pagan fertility rites; cf Dt 23, 18; Hos 4, 14, where the same Hebrew word is used. Hirah the Adullamite uses a word that refers to a higher social class than that designated by the term *zona,* common "harlot," used in vv 15.24.

38, 29: *He was called Perez:* the Hebrew word means "breach."

38, 30: *He was called Zerah:* a name connected here by popular etymology with a Hebrew verb for the red light of dawn, alluding apparently to the crimson thread.

---

† **39, 1:** *(Potiphar . . . chief steward):* These words in the text serve to harmonize ch 39 from the Yahwist source, with Gn 37, 36, and 40, 1–23, from the Elohist. In the former, the Ishmaelites who bought Joseph from his brothers (Gn 37, 28) sold him to the unnamed "Egyptian master" of ch 39. In the latter, the Midianites who kidnaped Joseph (Gn 37, 28; 40, 15) sold him to Potiphar, Pharaoh's chief steward (Gn 37, 36), whose house was used as a royal prison (Gn 40, 2f).

38, 14: Prv 7, 10.
38, 27: 1 Chr 2, 4.
38, 29: Rv 4, 12; Mt 1, 3; Lk 3, 33.
38, 30: Nm 26, 20; 1 Chr 2, 4;

Mt 1, 3.
39, 2: 1 Sm 3, 19; 10, 7; 18, 14; 2 Sm 5, 10; 2 Kgs 18, 7; Acts 7, 9.
39, 4: Dn 1, 9.

before God?" 10* Although she tried to entice him day after day, he would not agree to lie beside her, or even stay near her.

11 One such day, when Joseph came into the house to do his work, and none of the household servants were then in the house, 12 she laid hold of him by his cloak, saying, "Lie with me!" But leaving the cloak in her hand, he got away from her and ran outside. 13 When she saw that he had left his cloak in her hand as he fled outside, 14 she screamed for her household servants and told them, "Look! My husband has brought in a Hebrew slave to make sport of us! He came in here to lie with me, but I cried out as loud as I could. 15 When he heard me scream for help, he left his cloak beside me and ran away outside."

16 She kept the cloak with her until his master came home. 17 Then she told him the same story: "The Hebrew slave whom you brought here broke in on me, to make sport of me. 18 But when I screamed for help, he left his cloak beside me and fled outside." 19 As soon as the master heard his wife's story about how his slave had treated her, he became enraged. 20* He seized Joseph and threw him into the jail where the royal prisoners were confined.

But even while he was in prison, 21* the LORD remained with Joseph; he showed him kindness by making the chief jailer well-disposed toward him. 22 The chief jailer put Joseph in charge of all the prisoners in the jail, and everything that had to be done there was done under his management. 23 The chief jailer did not concern himself with anything at all that was in Joseph's charge, since the LORD was with him and brought success to all he did.

The Dreams Interpreted

40 1 Some time afterward, the royal cupbearer and baker gave offense to their lord, the king of Egypt. 2 Pharaoh was angry with his two courtiers, the chief cupbearer and the chief baker, 3 and he put them in custody in the house of the chief steward (the same jail where Joseph was confined). 4 The chief steward assigned Joseph to them, and he became their attendant.

After they had been in custody for some time, 5 the cupbearer and the baker of the king of Egypt who were confined in the jail both had dreams on the same night, each dream with its own meaning. 6 When Joseph came to them in the morning, he noticed that they looked disturbed. 7 So he asked Pharaoh's courtiers who were with him in custody in his master's house, "Why do you look so sad

today?" 8* They answered him, "We have had dreams, but there is no one to interpret them for us." Joseph said to them, "Surely, interpretations come from God. Please tell the dreams to me."

9 Then the chief cupbearer told Joseph his dream. "In my dream," he said, "I saw a vine in front of me, 10 and on the vine were three branches. It had barely budded when its blossoms came out, and its clusters ripened into grapes. 11 Pharaoh's cup was in my hand; so I took the grapes, pressed them out into his cup, and put it in Pharaoh's hand." 12 Joseph said to him: "This is what it means. The three branches are three days; 13† within three days Pharaoh will lift up your head and restore you to your post. You will be handing Pharaoh his cup as you formerly used to do when you were his cupbearer. 14 So if you will still remember, when all is well with you, that I was here with you, please do me the favor of mentioning me to Pharaoh, to get me out of this place. 15 The truth is that I was kidnaped from the land of the Hebrews, and here I have not done anything for which I should have been put into a dungeon."

16 When the chief baker saw that Joseph had given this favorable interpretation, he said to him: "I too had a dream. In it I had three wicker baskets on my head; 17 in the top one were all kinds of bakery products for Pharaoh, but the birds were pecking at them out of the basket on my head." 18 Joseph said to him in reply: "This is what it means. The three baskets are three days; 19 within three days Pharaoh will lift up your head and have you impaled on a stake, and the birds will be pecking the flesh from your body."

20 And in fact, on the third day, which was Pharaoh's birthday, when he gave a banquet to all his staff, with his courtiers around him, he lifted up the heads of the chief cupbearer and chief baker. 21 He restored the chief cupbearer to his office, so that he again handed the cup to Pharaoh; 22 but the chief baker he impaled—just as Joseph had told them in his interpretation. 23 Yet the chief cupbearer gave no thought to Joseph; he had forgotten him.

Pharaoh's Dream

41 1 After a lapse of two years, Pharaoh had a dream. He saw himself standing by the Nile, 2 when up out of the Nile came seven cows, handsome and fat; they grazed in the reed grass. 3 Behind them seven other cows, ugly and gaunt, came up out of the Nile; and standing on the bank of the Nile beside the others, 4 the ugly, gaunt cows ate up the seven handsome, fat cows. Then Pharaoh woke up.

40, 13: *Lift up your head:* signifying "pardon you." In v 19 "to lift up the head" means "to behead"; and finally, in v 20, the same expression means "to review the case (of someone)." Joseph couches his interpretation of the dreams in equivocal terms.

39, 10: 1 Mc 2, 53.
39, 20: Ps 105, 18.
39, 21: Acts 7, 9f.
40, 8: Gn 41, 16.

G
N

5 He fell asleep again and had another dream. He saw seven ears of grain, fat and healthy, growing on a single stalk. 6 Behind them sprouted seven ears of grain, thin and blasted by the east wind; 7 and the seven thin ears swallowed up the seven fat, healthy ears. Then Pharaoh woke up, to find it was only a dream.

8 Next morning his spirit was agitated. So he summoned all the magicians and sages of Egypt and recounted his dreams to them; but no one could interpret his dreams for him. 9 Then the chief cupbearer spoke up and said to Pharaoh: "On this occasion I am reminded of my negligence. 10 Once, when Pharaoh was angry, he put me and the chief baker in custody in the house of the chief steward. 11 Later, we both had dreams on the same night, and each of our dreams had its own meaning. 12* There with us was a Hebrew youth, a slave of the chief steward; and when we told him our dreams, he interpreted them for us and explained for each of us the meaning of his dream. 13 And it turned out just as he had told us: I was restored to my post, but the other man was impaled."

14* Pharaoh therefore had Joseph summoned, and they hurriedly brought him from the dungeon. After he shaved and changed his clothes, he came into Pharaoh's presence. 15 Pharaoh then said to him: "I had certain dreams that no one can interpret. But I hear it said of you that the moment you are told a dream you can interpret it." 16* "It is not I," Joseph replied to Pharaoh, "but God who will give Pharaoh the right answer."

17 Then Pharaoh said to Joseph: "In my dream, I was standing on the bank of the Nile, 18 when up from the Nile came seven cows, fat and well-formed; they grazed in the reed grass. 19 Behind them came seven other cows, scrawny, most ill-formed and gaunt. Never have I seen such ugly specimens as these in all the land of Egypt! 20 The gaunt, ugly cows ate up the first seven fat cows. 21 But when they had consumed them, no one could tell that they had done so, because they looked as ugly as before. Then I woke up. 22 In another dream, I saw seven ears of grain, fat and healthy, growing on a single stalk. 23 Behind them sprouted seven ears of grain, shriveled and thin and blasted by the east wind; 24 and the seven thin ears swallowed up the seven healthy ears. I have spoken to the magicians, but none of them can give me an explanation."

25 Joseph said to Pharaoh: "Both of Pharaoh's dreams have the same meaning. God has thus foretold to Pharaoh what he is about to do. 26 The seven healthy cows are seven years, and the seven healthy ears are seven years—the same in each dream. 27 So

did you KNOW?

Dreams

In the ancient world, belief in the reality and significance of dreams was widespread. The ancients believed that dreams and visions revealed messages, prophecies, and healing from their gods. Israel shared this view of the importance of dreams. Joseph is described as an interpreter of dreams, and this skill earns him Pharaoh's respect (Gn 41, 37–45), as well as his brothers' jealousy (37, 5–11).

In the Old Testament, the prophets are often referred to as seers because the word of God so often comes to them through dreams and visions. The focus, however, is always on the word of God and its meaning, not on the dream itself. In fact, God usually gives a character in the story the interpretation of the dream, which aims to lead the people to more faithful observance of the covenant. If the dream does not do this, it is to be considered a false dream. (See other references to dreams in Gn 28, 10–22; Dt 13, 2–6; Sir 34, 1–4; Jer 27, 9–10; 29, 8–9; Jl 3, 1; Zec 1, 8; Mt 1, 20; 2, 13.)

▸ Gn 37, 1–11; 40, 1—41, 36

also, the seven thin, ugly cows that came up after them are seven years, as are the seven thin, windblasted ears; they are seven years of famine. 28 It is just as I told Pharaoh: God has revealed to Pharaoh what he is about to do. 29 Seven years of great abundance are now coming throughout the land of Egypt; 30 but these will be followed by seven years of famine, when all the abundance in the land of Egypt will be forgotten. When the famine has ravaged the land, 31 no trace of the abundance will be found in the land because of the famine that follows it—so utterly severe will that famine be. 32 That Pharaoh had the same dream twice means that the matter has been reaffirmed by God and that God will soon bring it about.

33 "Therefore, let Pharaoh seek out a wise and discerning man and put him in charge of the land of Egypt. 34 Pharaoh should also take action to appoint overseers, so as to regiment the land during the seven years of abundance. 35 They should

---

41, 12: Dn 1, 17.   41, 16: Gn 40, 8.
41, 14: Ps 105, 20.

husband all the food of the coming good years, collecting the grain under Pharaoh's authority, to be stored in the towns for food. 36 This food will serve as a reserve for the country against the seven years of famine that are to follow in the land of Egypt, so that the land may not perish in the famine."

37* This advice pleased Pharaoh and all his officials. 38 "Could we find another like him," Pharaoh asked his officials, "a man so endowed with the spirit of God?" 39 So Pharaoh said to Joseph: "Since God has made all this known to you, no one can be as wise and discerning as you are. 40* You shall be in charge of my palace, and all my people shall dart at your command. Only in respect to the throne shall I outrank you. 41 Herewith," Pharaoh told Joseph, "I place you in charge of the whole land of Egypt." 42† With that, Pharaoh took off his signet ring and put it on Joseph's finger. He had him dressed in robes of fine linen and put a gold chain about his neck. 43† He then had him ride in the chariot of his vizier, and they shouted "Abrek!" before him.

Thus was Joseph installed over the whole land of Egypt. 44 "I, Pharaoh, proclaim," he told Joseph, "that without your approval no one shall move hand or foot in all the land of Egypt." 45† Pharaoh also bestowed the name of Zaphenath-paneah on Joseph, and he gave him in marriage Asenath, the daughter of Potiphera, priest of Heliopolis. 46 Joseph was thirty years old when he entered the service of Pharaoh, king of Egypt.

After Joseph left Pharaoh's presence, he traveled throughout the land of Egypt. 47 During the seven years of plenty, when the land produced abundant crops, 48 he husbanded all the food of these years of plenty that the land of Egypt was enjoying and stored it in the towns, placing in each town the crops of the fields around it. 49 Joseph garnered grain in quantities like the sands of the sea, so vast that at last he stopped measuring it, for it was beyond measure.

50* Before the famine years set in, Joseph became the father of two sons, born to him by Asenath, daughter of Potiphera, priest of Heliopolis. 51† He named his first-born Manasseh, meaning, "God has

made me forget entirely the sufferings I endured at the hands of my family"; 52† and the second he named Ephraim, meaning, "God has made me fruitful in the land of my affliction."

53 When the seven years of abundance enjoyed by the land of Egypt came to an end, 54* the seven years of famine set in, just as Joseph had predicted. Although there was famine in all the other countries, food was available throughout the land of Egypt. 55 When hunger came to be felt throughout the land of Egypt and the people cried to Pharaoh for bread, Pharaoh directed all the Egyptians to go to Joseph and do whatever he told them. 56 When the famine had spread throughout the land, Joseph opened all the cities that had grain and rationed it to the Egyptians, since the famine had gripped the land of Egypt. 57 In fact, all the world came to Joseph to obtain rations of grain, for famine had gripped the whole world.

The Brothers' First Journey to Egypt

42 1 When Jacob learned that grain rations were available in Egypt, he said to his sons: "Why do you keep gaping at one another? 2* I hear," he went on, "that rations of grain are available in Egypt. Go down there and buy some for us, that we may stay alive rather than die of hunger." 3 So ten of Joseph's brothers went down to buy an emergency supply of grain from Egypt. 4 It was only Joseph's full brother Benjamin that Jacob did not send with the rest, for he thought some disaster might befall him. 5* Thus, since there was famine in the land of Canaan also, the sons of Israel were among those who came to procure rations.

6* It was Joseph, as governor of the country, who dispensed the rations to all the people. When Joseph's brothers came and knelt down before him with their faces to the ground, 7 he recognized them as soon as he saw them. But he concealed his own identity from them and spoke sternly to them. "Where do you come from?" he asked them. They answered, "From the land of Canaan, to procure food."

8 When Joseph recognized his brothers, although

41, 42: *Signet ring:* a finger ring in which was set a stamp seal, different from the cylinder seal such as Judah wore; see note on Gn 38, 18. This is an authentic detail. By receiving Pharaoh's signet ring, Joseph was made vizier of Egypt (v 43); the vizier was known as "seal-bearer of the king of Lower Egypt." Another authentic detail is the *gold chain,* a symbol of high office in ancient Egypt.
41, 43: *Abrek:* apparently a cry of homage, though the word's derivation and actual meaning are uncertain.
41, 45: *Zaphenath-paneah:* a Hebrew transcription of an Egyptian name meaning "the god speaks and he (the new-born child) lives." *Asenath:* means "belonging to (the Egyptian goddess) Neith." *Potiphera:* means "he whom Ra (the Egyptian god) gave"; a shorter form of the same name was borne by Joseph's master (Gn 37, 36). *Heliopolis:* in Hebrew, *On,* a city seven miles northeast of modern

Cairo, site of the chief temple of the sun god; it is mentioned also in v 50; Gn 46, 20; Ez 30, 17.
41, 51: *Manasseh:* allusion to this name is in the Hebrew expression, *nishshani,* "he made me forget."
41, 52: *Ephraim:* related to the Hebrew expression *hiphrani,* "(God) has made me fruitful."

41, 37: Acts 7, 10.
41, 40: Ps 105, 21; Wis 10, 14; 1 Mc 2, 53; Acts 7, 10.
41, 50: Gn 46, 20; 48, 5.
41, 54: Ps 105, 16; Acts 7, 11.
42, 2: Acts 7, 12.
42, 5: Jdt 5, 10; Acts 7, 11.
42, 6: Ps 105, 21.

they did not recognize him, 9*† he was reminded of the dreams he had about them. He said to them: "You are spies. You have come to see the nakedness of the land." 10 "No, my lord," they replied. "On the contrary, your servants have come to procure food. 11 All of us are sons of the same man. We are honest men; your servants have never been spies." 12 But he answered them: "Not so! You have come to see the nakedness of the land." 13* "We your servants," they said, "were twelve brothers, sons of a certain man in Canaan; but the youngest one is at present with our father, and the other one is gone." 14 "It is just as I said," Joseph persisted; "you are spies. 15 This is how you shall be tested: unless your youngest brother comes here, I swear by the life of Pharaoh that you shall not leave here. 16 So send one of your number to get your brother, while the rest of you stay here under arrest. Thus shall your words be tested for their truth; if they are untrue, as Pharaoh lives, you are spies!" 17 With that, he locked them up in the guardhouse for three days.

18 On the third day Joseph said to them: "Do this, and you shall live; for I am a God-fearing man. 19 If you have been honest, only one of your brothers need be confined in this prison, while the rest of you may go and take home provisions for your starving families. 20* But you must come back to me with your youngest brother. Your words will thus be verified, and you will not die." To this they agreed. 21* To one another, however, they said: "Alas, we are being punished because of our brother. We saw the anguish of his heart when he pleaded with us, yet we paid no heed; that is why this anguish has now come upon us." 22* "Didn't I tell you," broke in Reuben, "not to do wrong to the boy? But you wouldn't listen! Now comes the reckoning for his blood." 23 They did not know, of course, that Joseph understood what they said, since he spoke with them through an interpreter. 24 But turning away from them, he wept. When he was able to speak to them again, he had Simeon taken from them and bound before their eyes. 25 Then Joseph gave orders to have their containers filled with grain, their money replaced in each one's sack, and provisions given them for their journey. After this had been done for them, 26 they loaded their donkeys with the rations and departed.

27† At the night encampment, when one of them opened his bag to give his donkey some fodder, he was surprised to see his money in the mouth of his bag. 28 "My money has been returned!" he cried out to his brothers. "Here it is in my bag!" At that their hearts sank. Trembling, they asked one another, "What is this that God has done to us?"

29 When they got back to their father Jacob in the land of Canaan, they told him all that had happened to them. 30 "The man who is lord of the country," they said, "spoke to us sternly and put us in custody as if we were spying on the land. 31 But we said to him: 'We are honest men; we have never been spies. 32 There were twelve of us brothers, sons of the same father; but one is gone, and the youngest one is at present with our father in the land of Canaan.' 33 Then the man who is lord of the country said to us: 'This is how I shall know if you are honest men: leave one of your brothers with me, while the rest of you go home with rations for your starving families. 34 When you come back to me with your youngest brother, and I know that you are honest men and not spies, I will restore your brother to you, and you may move about freely in the land.'"

35 When they were emptying their sacks, there in each one's sack was his moneybag! At the sight of their moneybags, they and their father were dismayed. 36 Their father Jacob said to them: "Must you make me childless? Joseph is gone, and Simeon is gone, and now you would take away Benjamin! Why must such things always happen to me!" 37 Then Reuben told his father: "Put him in my care, and I will bring him back to you. You may kill my own two sons if I do not return him to you." 38* But Jacob replied: "My son shall not go down with you. Now that his full brother is dead, he is the only one left. If some disaster should befall him on the journey you must make, you would send my white head down to the nether world in grief."

The Second Journey to Egypt

43

1† Now the famine in the land grew more severe. 2 So when they had used up all the rations they had brought from Egypt, their father said to them, "Go back and procure us a little more food." 3* But Judah replied: "The man strictly warned us, 'You shall not appear in my presence unless your brother is with you.' 4 If you are willing to let our brother go with us, we will go down to procure food for you. 5* But if you are not willing, we will not go down, because the man told us, 'You shall not appear in my presence unless your

---

† 42, 9.12: *The nakedness of the land:* the military weakness of the land, like human nakedness, should not be seen by strangers.

42, 27–28: These two verses are from the Yahwist source, whereas the rest of the chapter is from the Elohist source, in which the men find the money in their sacks (not "bags"—a different Hebrew word) only when they arrive home (v 35); cf Gn 43, 21.

43, 1–34: This chapter and the following one are from the Yahwist source, in which Judah, not Reuben as in the Elohist source, volunteers to go surety for Benjamin.

---

*
42, 9: Gn 37, 5.	42, 22: Gn 37, 22.
42, 13: Gn 44, 20.	42, 38: Gn 37, 35.
42, 20: Gn 43, 5.	43, 3: Gn 44, 23.
42, 21: Gn 37, 18–27.	43, 5: Gn 42, 20.

brother is with you.' " 6 Israel demanded, "Why did you bring this trouble on me by telling the man that you had another brother?" 7 They answered: "The man kept asking about ourselves and our family: 'Is your father still living? Do you have another brother?' We had to answer his questions. How could we know that he would say, 'Bring your brother down here'?"

8* Then Judah urged his father Israel: "Let the boy go with me, that we may be off and on our way if you and we and our children are to keep from starving to death. 9* I myself will stand surety for him. You can hold me responsible for him. If I fail to bring him back, to set him in your presence, you can hold it against me forever. 10 Had we not dilly-dallied, we could have been there and back twice by now!"

11* Their father Israel then told them: "If it must be so, then do this: Put some of the land's best products in your baggage and take them down to the man as gifts: some balm and honey, gum and resin, and pistachios and almonds. 12 Also take extra money along, for you must return the amount that was put back in the mouths of your bags; it may have been a mistake. 13 Take your brother, too, and be off on your way back to the man. 14 May God Almighty dispose the man to be merciful toward you, so that he may let your other brother go, as well as Benjamin. As for me, if I am to suffer bereavement, I shall suffer it."

15 So the men got the gifts, took double the amount of money with them, and, accompanied by Benjamin, were off on their way down to Egypt to present themselves to Joseph. 16 When Joseph saw Benjamin with them, he told his head steward, "Take these men into the house, and have an animal slaughtered and prepared, for they are to dine with me at noon." 17 Doing as Joseph had ordered, the steward conducted the men to Joseph's house. 18 But on being led to his house, they became apprehensive. "It must be," they thought, "on account of the money put back in our bags the first time, that we are taken inside; they want to use it as a pretext to attack us and take our donkeys and seize us as slaves." 19 So they went up to Joseph's head steward and talked to him at the entrance of the house. 20* "If you please, sir," they said, "we came down here once before to procure food. 21* But when we arrived at a night's encampment and opened our bags, there was each man's money

in the mouth of his bag—our money in the full amount! We have now brought it back. 22 We have brought other money to procure food with. We do not know who put the first money in our bags." 23 "Be at ease," he replied; "you have no need to fear. Your God and the God of your father must have put treasures in your bags for you. As for your money, I received it." With that, he led Simeon out to them.

24 The steward then brought the men inside Joseph's house. He gave them water to bathe their feet, and got fodder for their donkeys. 25 Then they set out their gifts to await Joseph's arrival at noon, for they had heard that they were to dine there. 26 When Joseph came home, they presented him with the gifts they had brought inside, while they bowed down before him to the ground. 27* After inquiring how they were, he asked them, "And how is your aged father, of whom you spoke? Is he still in good health?" 28 "Your servant our father is thriving and still in good health," they said, as they bowed respectfully. 29* When Joseph's eye fell on his full brother Benjamin, he asked, "Is this your youngest brother, of whom you told me?" Then he said to him, "May God be gracious to you, my boy!" 30 With that, Joseph had to hurry out, for he was so overcome with affection for his brother that he was on the verge of tears. He went into a private room and wept there.

31 After washing his face, he reappeared and, now in control of himself, gave the order, "Serve the meal." 32† It was served separately to him, to the brothers, and to the Egyptians who partook of his board. (Egyptians may not eat with Hebrews; that is abhorrent to them.) 33 When they were seated by his directions according to their age, from the oldest to the youngest, they looked at one another in amazement; 34† and as portions were brought to them from Joseph's table, Benjamin's portion was five times as large as anyone else's. So they drank freely and made merry with him.

Final Test

44 1† Then Joseph gave his head steward these instructions: "Fill the men's bags with as much food as they can carry, and put each man's money in the mouth of his bag. 2 In the mouth of the youngest one's bag put also my silver goblet, together with the money for his rations." The steward carried out Joseph's instructions. 3 At

---

43, 32: *Separately to him:* that Joseph did not eat with the other Egyptians was apparently a matter of rank.
43, 34: *Five times as large as:* probably an idiomatic expression for "much larger than."
44, 1f: Replacement of the money in the men's bags is probably a redactional addition here, taken from the Yahwist account of the

first visit. It is only the goblet in Benjamin's bag, not any replaced money, that plays a part in the rest of the chapter.

43, 8: Gn 42, 37.	**43, 21:** Gn 42, 27f.
43, 9: Gn 44, 32.	**43, 27:** Tb 7, 4.
43, 11: Gn 45, 23.	**43, 29:** Gn 42, 13.
43, 20: Gn 42, 3.	

GN

daybreak the men and their donkeys were sent off. [4] They had not gone far out of the city when Joseph said to his head steward: "Go at once after the men! When you overtake them, say to them, 'Why did you repay good with evil? Why did you steal the silver goblet from me? [5]† It is the very one from which my master drinks and which he uses for divination. What you have done is wrong.' "

[6] When the steward overtook them and repeated these words to them, [7] they remonstrated with him: "How can my lord say such things? Far be it from your servants to do such a thing! [8] We even brought back to you from the land of Canaan the money that we found in the mouths of our bags. Why, then, would we steal silver or gold from your master's house? [9] If any of your servants is found to have the goblet, he shall die, and as for the rest of us, we shall become my lord's slaves." [10] But he replied, "Even though it ought to be as you propose, only the one who is found to have it shall become my slave, and the rest of you shall be exonerated." [11] Then each of them eagerly lowered his bag to the ground and opened it; [12] and when a search was made, starting with the oldest and ending with the youngest, the goblet turned up in Benjamin's bag. [13] At this, they tore their clothes. Then, when each man had reloaded his donkey, they returned to the city.

[14] As Judah and his brothers reentered Joseph's house, he was still there; so they flung themselves on the ground before him. [15] "How could you do such a thing?" Joseph asked them. "You should have known that such a man as I could discover by divination what happened." [16]† Judah replied: "What can we say to my lord? How can we plead or how try to prove our innocence? God has uncovered your servants' guilt. Here we are, then, the slaves of my lord—the rest of us no less than the one in whose possession the goblet was found." [17] "Far be it from me to act thus!" said Joseph. "Only the one in whose possession the goblet was found shall become my slave; the rest of you may go back safe and sound to your father."

[18] Judah then stepped up to him and said: "I beg you, my lord, let your servant speak earnestly to my lord, and do not become angry with your servant, for you are the equal of Pharaoh. [19]† My lord asked your servants, 'Have you a father, or another brother?' [20]* So we said to my lord, 'We have an aged father, and a young brother, the child of his old age.

This one's full brother is dead, and since he is the only one by that mother who is left, his father dotes on him.' [21] Then you told your servants, 'Bring him down to me that my eyes may look on him.' [22] We replied to my lord, 'The boy cannot leave his father; his father would die if he were to leave him.' [23]* But you told your servants, 'Unless your youngest brother comes back with you, you shall not come into my presence again.' [24] When we returned to your servant our father, we reported to him the words of my lord.

[25] "Later, our father told us to come back and buy some food for the family. [26] So we reminded him, 'We cannot go down there; only if our youngest brother is with us can we go, for we may not see the man if our youngest brother is not with us.' [27] Then your servant our father said to us, 'As you know, my wife bore me two sons. [28]* One of them, however, disappeared, and I had to conclude that he must have been torn to pieces by wild beasts; I have not seen him since. [29] If you now take this one away from me, too, and some disaster befalls him, you will send my white head down to the nether world in grief.'

[30] "If then the boy is not with us when I go back to your servant my father, whose very life is bound up with his, he will die as soon as he sees that the boy is missing; [31] and your servants will thus send the white head of our father down to the nether world in grief. [32]* Besides, I, your servant, got the boy from his father by going surety for him, saying, 'If I fail to bring him back to you, father, you can hold it against me forever.' [33] Let me, your servant, therefore, remain in place of the boy as the slave of my lord, and let the boy go back with his brothers. [34] How could I go back to my father if the boy were not with me? I could not bear to see the anguish that would overcome my father."

The Truth Revealed

45 [1] Joseph could no longer control himself in the presence of all his attendants, so he cried out, "Have everyone withdraw from me!" Thus no one else was about when he made himself known to his brothers. [2] But his sobs were so loud that the Egyptians heard him, and so the news reached Pharaoh's palace. [3]* "I am Joseph," he said to his brothers. "Is my father still in good health?" But his brothers could give him no answer, so dumbfounded were they at him.

44, 5: *Divination:* seeking omens through liquids poured into a cup or bowl was a common practice in the ancient Near East; cf v 15. Even though divination was frowned on in later Israel (Lv 19, 31), it is in this place an authentic touch which the sacred author does not hesitate to ascribe to Joseph, the wisest man in Egypt.
44, 16: *Guilt:* in trying to do away with Joseph when he was young.

44, 19: *My lord . . . your servants:* such frequently repeated expressions in Judah's speech show the formal court style used by a subject in speaking to a high official.

44, 20: Gn 42, 13.   44, 32: Gn 43, 9.
44, 23: Gn 43, 3.   45, 3f: Acts 7, 13.
44, 28: Gn 37, 20.33.

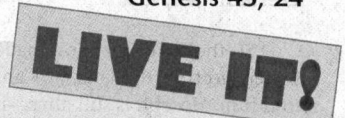

God's Master Plan

After Joseph's tearful reconciliation with his brothers, he tells them that their past treatment of him enabled him to save them from the famine. Because he ended up in Egypt and rose to power, he can now invite them to stay as guests of the Pharaoh.

Joseph realizes that good has come out of an evil act. He sees the events of his family's life as part of God's plan to preserve life and to make sure that the Covenant continues. Joseph's insight does not justify what his brothers did, but it does help us realize that good can come out of a tragic event. It is often hard for us to understand why something bad is happening, but as time passes, we often gain perspective and insight. These are the rewards of trust and faith. Joseph remained faithful, despite many difficulties. Let us strive to do the same, assured that not even human sinfulness can thwart God's saving plans.

When have you experienced good things coming out of a bad situation? Has it ever seemed like God has upset part of your life, only to result in something better than you expected?

▸ Gn 45, 5–8

---

⁴ "Come closer to me," he told his brothers. When they had done so, he said: "I am your brother Joseph, whom you once sold into Egypt. ⁵* But now do not be distressed, and do not reproach yourselves for having sold me here. It was really for the sake of saving lives that God sent me here ahead of you. ⁶ For two years now the famine has been in the land, and for five more years tillage will yield no harvest. ⁷ God, therefore, sent me on ahead of you to ensure for you a remnant on earth and to save your lives in an extraordinary deliverance. ⁸† So it was not really you but God who had me come here; and he has made of me a father to Pharaoh, lord of all his household, and ruler over the whole land of Egypt.

⁹*† "Hurry back, then, to my father and tell him: 'Thus says your son Joseph: God has made me lord of all Egypt; come to me without delay. ¹⁰† You will settle in the region of Goshen, where you will be near me—you and your children and grandchildren, your flocks and herds, and everything that you own. ¹¹ Since five years of famine still lie ahead, I will provide for you there, so that you and your family and all that are yours may not suffer want.' ¹² Surely, you can see for yourselves, and Benjamin can see for himself, that it is I, Joseph, who am speaking to you. ¹³ Tell my father all about my high position in Egypt and what you have seen. But hurry and bring my father down here." ¹⁴ Thereupon he flung himself on the neck of his brother Benjamin and wept, and Benjamin wept in his arms. ¹⁵ Joseph then kissed all his brothers, crying over each of them; and only then were his brothers able to talk with him.

¹⁶ When the news reached Pharaoh's palace that Joseph's brothers had come, Pharaoh and his courtiers were pleased. ¹⁷ So Pharaoh told Joseph: "Say to your brothers: 'This is what you shall do: Load up your animals and go without delay to the land of Canaan. ¹⁸* There get your father and your families, and then come back here to me; I will assign you the best land in Egypt, where you will live off the fat of the land.' ¹⁹ Instruct them further: 'Do this. Take wagons from the land of Egypt for your children and your wives and to transport your father on your way back here. ²⁰ Do not be concerned about your belongings, for the best in the whole land of Egypt shall be yours.' "

²¹ The sons of Israel acted accordingly. Joseph gave them the wagons, as Pharaoh had ordered, and he supplied them with provisions for the journey. ²² He also gave to each of them fresh clothing, but to Benjamin he gave three hundred shekels of silver and five sets of garments. ²³ Moreover, what he sent to his father was ten jackasses loaded with the finest products of Egypt and ten jennies loaded with grain and bread and other provisions for his journey. ²⁴ As he sent his brothers on their way, he told them, "Let there be no recriminations on the way."

---

† **45, 8:** *Father to Pharaoh:* a term applied to a vizier in ancient Egypt.

45, 9–15: In these verses, as in Gn 46, 31—47, 5a, all from the Yahwist source, Joseph in his own name invites his father and brothers to come to Egypt. Only after their arrival is Pharaoh informed of the fact. On the other hand, in 45, 16–20, from the Elohist source, it is Pharaoh himself who invites Joseph's kinsmen to migrate to his domain.

45, 10: *The region of Goshen:* modern Wadi Tumilât in the eastern part of the Nile Delta.

45, 5: Gn 50, 20; Sir 49, 15.   **45, 18:** Acts 7, 14.
45, 9: Acts 7, 14.

GN

25 So they left Egypt and made their way to their father Jacob in the land of Canaan. 26 When they told him, "Joseph is still alive—in fact, it is he who is ruler of all the land of Egypt," he was dumbfounded; he could not believe them. 27 But when they recounted to him all that Joseph had told them, and when he saw the wagons that Joseph had sent for his transport, the spirit of their father Jacob revived. 28 "It is enough," said Israel. "My son Joseph is still alive! I must go and see him before I die."

Migration to Egypt

46 1 Israel set out with all that was his. When he arrived at Beer-sheba, he offered sacrifices to the God of his father Isaac. 2 There God, speaking to Israel in a vision by night, called, "Jacob! Jacob!" "Here I am," he answered. 3† Then he said: "I am God, the God of your father. Do not be afraid to go down to Egypt, for there I will make you a great nation. 4 Not only will I go down to Egypt with you; I will also bring you back here, after Joseph has closed your eyes."

5 So Jacob departed from Beer-sheba, and the sons of Israel put their father and their wives and children on the wagons that Pharaoh had sent for his transport. 6* They took with them their livestock and the possessions they had acquired in the land of Canaan. Thus Jacob and all his descendants migrated to Egypt. 7 His sons and his grandsons, his daughters and his granddaughters—all his descendants—he took with him to Egypt.

8* These are the names of the Israelites, Jacob and his descendants, who migrated to Egypt.

Reuben, Jacob's first-born, 9*† and the sons of Reuben: Hanoch, Pallu, Hezron and Carmi. 10* The sons of Simeon: Nemuel, Jamin, Ohad, Jachin, Zohar, and Shaul, son of a Canaanite woman. 11* The sons of Levi: Gershon, Kohath and Merari. 12* The sons of Judah: Er, Onan, Shelah, Perez and Zerah—but Er and Onan had died in the land of Canaan; and the sons of Perez were Hezron and Hamul. 13* The sons of Issachar: Tola, Puah, Jashub and Shimron. 14* The sons of Zebulun: Sered, Elon and Jahleel. 15 These were the sons whom Leah bore to Jacob in Paddan-aram, along with his daughter Dinah—thirty-three persons in all, male and female.

16* The sons of Gad: Zephon, Haggi, Shuni, Ezbon, Eri, Arod and Areli. 17* The sons of Asher: Imnah, Ishvah, Ishvi and Beriah, with their sister Serah; and the sons of Beriah: Heber and Malchiel. 18 These were the descendants of Zilpah, whom Laban had given to his daughter Leah; these she bore to Jacob—sixteen persons in all.

19 The sons of Jacob's wife Rachel: Joseph and Benjamin. 20* In the land of Egypt Joseph became the father of Manasseh and Ephraim, whom Asenath, daughter of Potiphera, priest of Heliopolis, bore to him. 21* The sons of Benjamin: Bela, Becher, Ashbel, Gera, Naaman, Ahiram, Shupham, Hupham and Ard. 22 These were the sons whom Rachel bore to Jacob—fourteen persons in all.

23* The sons of Dan: Hushim. 24* The sons of Naphtali: Jahzeel, Guni, Jezer and Shillem. 25 These were the sons of Bilhah, whom Laban had given to his daughter Rachel; these she bore to Jacob—seven persons in all.

26* Jacob's people who migrated to Egypt—his direct descendants, not counting the wives of Jacob's sons—numbered sixty-six persons in all. 27*† Together with Joseph's sons who were born to him in Egypt—two persons—all the people comprising Jacob's family who had come to Egypt amounted to seventy persons in all.

28 Israel had sent Judah ahead to Joseph, so that he might meet him in Goshen. On his arrival in the region of Goshen, 29 Joseph hitched the horses to his chariot and rode to meet his father Israel in Goshen. As soon as he saw him, he flung himself on his neck and wept a long time in his arms. 30 And Israel said to Joseph, "At last I can die, now that I have seen for myself that Joseph is still alive."

31 Joseph then said to his brothers and his father's household: "I will go and inform Pharaoh, telling him: 'My brothers and my father's household, whose home is in the land of Canaan, have come to me. 32 The men are shepherds, having long been keepers of livestock; and they have brought with them their flocks and herds, as well as everything else they own.' 33 So when Pharaoh summons you and asks what your occupation is, 34 you must answer, 'We your servants, like our ancestors, have been keepers of livestock from the beginning until now,' in order that you may stay in the region of

---

46, 3: *I am God:* more precisely according to the Hebrew text, "I am El." "El" is here a divine name, not the common noun "god."

46, 9–27: This genealogical list here has been inserted by a redactor who bases it on the clan lists (Nm 26, 5–50) at the time of Moses. Therefore it includes some of Jacob's grandchildren, who would hardly have been born when Joseph was still a relatively young man. The number *fourteen* (v 22) is based on a garbled version of the genealogical list.

46, 27: *Seventy persons:* either to be understood as a round number, or arrived at by including Jacob and Joseph with the preceding persons, who add up to sixty-eight.

46, 6: Ex 1, 1; Jos 24, 4; Jdt 5, 10; Acts 7, 15.
46, 8: Ex 1, 2.
46, 9: Ex 6, 14; Nm 26, 5; 1 Chr 5, 3.
46, 10: Ex 6, 15; Nm 26, 12; 1 Chr 4, 24.
46, 11: Ex 6, 16; Nm 3, 17; 26, 57; 1 Chr 6, 1.
46, 12: Gn 38, 3–10.29f; Nm 26, 19; Rv 4, 18–22; 1 Chr 2, 5.
46, 13: Nm 26, 23f; 1 Chr 7, 1.
46, 14: Nm 26, 26.
46, 16: Nm 26, 15f.
46, 17: Nm 26, 44; 1 Chr 7, 30f.
46, 20: Gn 41, 50; Nm 26, 28. 35.
46, 21: Nm 26, 38; 1 Chr 7, 6; 8, 1–4.
46, 23: Nm 26, 42.
46, 24: Nm 26, 48f; 1 Chr 7, 13.
46, 26: Ex 1, 5.
46, 27: Ex 1, 5; Dt 10, 22; Acts 7, 14.

Goshen, since all shepherds are abhorrent to the Egyptians."

Settlement in Goshen

47 [1] Joseph went and told Pharaoh, "My father and my brothers have come from the land of Canaan, with their flocks and herds and everything else they own; and they are now in the region of Goshen." [2] He then presented to Pharaoh five of his brothers whom he had selected from their full number. [3] When Pharaoh asked them what their occupation was, they answered, "We, your servants, like our ancestors, are shepherds. [4]* We have come," they continued, "in order to stay in this country, for there is no pasture for your servants' flocks in the land of Canaan, so severe has the famine been there. Please, therefore, let your servants settle in the region of Goshen." [5] Pharaoh said to Joseph, "They may settle in the region of Goshen; and if you know any of them to be qualified, you may put them in charge of my own livestock."

Thus, when Jacob and his sons came to Joseph in Egypt, and Pharaoh, king of Egypt, heard about it, Pharaoh said to Joseph, "Now that your father and brothers have come to you, [6] the land of Egypt is at your disposal; settle your father and brothers in the pick of the land." [7] Then Joseph brought his father Jacob and presented him to Pharaoh. After Jacob had paid his respects to Pharaoh, [8] Pharaoh asked him, "How many years have you lived?" [9]† Jacob replied: "The years I have lived as a wayfarer amount to a hundred and thirty. Few and hard have been these years of my life, and they do not compare with the years that my ancestors lived as wayfarers." [10] Then Jacob bade Pharaoh farewell and withdrew from his presence.

[11]† As Pharaoh had ordered, Joseph settled his father and brothers and gave them holdings in Egypt on the pick of the land, in the region of Rameses. [12] And Joseph sustained his father and brothers and his father's whole household, down to the youngest, with food.

Joseph's Land Policy

[13] Since there was no food in any country because of the extreme severity of the famine, and the lands of Egypt and Canaan were languishing from hunger, [14] Joseph gathered in, as payment for the rations that were being dispensed, all the money that was to be found in Egypt and Canaan, and he put it in Pharaoh's palace. [15] When all the money in Egypt and Canaan was spent, all the Egyptians came to Joseph, pleading, "Give us food or we shall perish under your eyes; for our money is gone." [16] "Since your money is gone," replied Joseph, "give me your livestock, and I will sell you bread in return for your livestock." [17] So they brought their livestock to Joseph, and he sold them food in return for their horses, their flocks of sheep and herds of cattle, and their donkeys. Thus he got them through that year with bread in exchange for all their livestock. [18] When that year ended, they came to him in the following one and said: "We cannot hide from my lord that, with our money spent and our livestock made over to my lord, there is nothing left to put at my lord's disposal except our bodies and our farm land. [19] Why should we and our land perish before your very eyes? Take us and our land in exchange for food, and we will become Pharaoh's slaves and our land his property; only give us seed, that we may survive and not perish, and that our land may not turn into a waste."

[20] Thus Joseph acquired all the farm land of Egypt for Pharaoh, since with the famine too much for them to bear, every Egyptian sold his field; so the land passed over to Pharaoh, [21] and the people were reduced to slavery, from one end of Egypt's territory to the other. [22] Only the priests' lands Joseph did not take over. Since the priests had a fixed allowance from Pharaoh and lived off the allowance Pharaoh had granted them, they did not have to sell their land.

[23] Joseph told the people: "Now that I have acquired you and your land for Pharaoh, here is your seed for sowing the land. [24] But when the harvest is in, you must give a fifth of it to Pharaoh, while you keep four-fifths as seed for your fields, and as food for yourselves and your families [and as food for your children]." [25] "You have saved our lives!" they answered. "We are grateful to my lord that we can be Pharaoh's slaves." [26] Thus Joseph made it a law for the land in Egypt, which is still in force, that a fifth of its produce should go to Pharaoh. Only the land of the priests did not pass over to Pharaoh.

Jacob Blesses Ephraim and Manasseh

[27]* Thus Israel settled in the land of Egypt, in the

---

† **47, 9:** *Wayfarer . . . wayfarers:* man is merely a sojourner on earth; cf Ps 39, 13.

47, 11: *The region of Rameses:* same as the region of Goshen; see note on Gn 45, 10. The name Rameses, however, is an anachronism, since this royal name did not come into use before the end of the fourteenth century B.C., long after the time of Joseph.

47, 4: Ex 23, 9; Dt 23, 8.   **47, 27:** Ex 1, 7.

GN

region of Goshen. There they acquired property, were fertile, and increased greatly. 28 Jacob lived in the land of Egypt for seventeen years; the span of his life came to a hundred and forty-seven years. 29 When the time approached for Israel to die, he called his son Joseph and said to him: "If you really wish to please me, put your hand under my thigh as a sign of your constant loyalty to me; do not let me be buried in Egypt. 30* When I lie down with my ancestors, have me taken out of Egypt and buried in their burial place." 31†."I will do as you say," he replied. But his father demanded, "Swear it to me!" So Joseph swore to him. Then Israel bowed at the head of the bed.

48 1 Some time afterward, Joseph was informed, "Your father is failing." So he took along with him his two sons, Manasseh and Ephraim. 2 When Jacob was told, "Your son Joseph has come to you," he rallied his strength and sat up in bed.

3*† Jacob then said to Joseph: "God Almighty appeared to me at Luz in the land of Canaan, and blessing me, 4 he said, 'I will make you fertile and numerous and raise you into an assembly of tribes, and I will give this land to your descendants after you as a permanent possession.' 5 Your two sons, therefore, who were born to you in the land of Egypt before I joined you here, shall be mine; Ephraim and Manasseh shall be mine as much as Reuben and Simeon are mine. 6 Progeny born to you after them shall remain yours; but their heritage shall be recorded in the names of their two brothers. 7*† I do this because, when I was returning from Paddan, your mother Rachel died, to my sorrow, during the journey in Canaan, while we were still a short distance from Ephrath; and I buried her there on the way to Ephrath [that is, Bethlehem]."

8 When Israel saw Joseph's sons, he asked, "Who are these?" 9 "They are my sons," Joseph answered his father, "whom God has given me here." "Bring them to me," said his father, "that I may bless them." 10 (Now Israel's eyes were dim from age, and he could not see well.) When Joseph brought his sons close to him, he kissed and embraced them. 11 Then Israel said to Joseph, "I never expected to see your face again, and now God has allowed me to see your descendants as well!"

12 Joseph removed them from his father's knees and bowed down before him with his face to the ground. 13 Then Joseph took the two, Ephraim with his right hand, to Israel's left, and Manasseh with his left hand, to Israel's right, and led them to him. 14 But Israel, crossing his hands, put out his right hand and laid it on the head of Ephraim, although he was the younger, and his left hand on the head of Manasseh, although he was the first-born. 15* Then he blessed them with these words:

"May the God in whose ways
　　my fathers Abraham and Isaac walked,
The God who has been my shepherd
　　from my birth to this day,
16　The Angel who has delivered me from
　　　all harm,
　　bless these boys
That in them my name be recalled,
　　and the names of my fathers, Abraham
　　　and Isaac,
And they may become teeming multitudes
　　upon the earth!"

17 When Joseph saw that his father had laid his right hand on Ephraim's head, this seemed wrong to him; so he took hold of his father's hand, to remove it from Ephraim's head to Manasseh's, 18 saying, "That is not right, father; the other one is the first-born; lay your right hand on his head!" 19 But his father resisted. "I know it, son," he said, "I know. That one too shall become a tribe, and he too shall be great. Nevertheless, his younger brother shall surpass him, and his descendants shall become a multitude of nations." 20* So when he blessed them that day and said, "By you shall the people of Israel pronounce blessings; may they say, 'God make you like Ephraim and Manasseh,' " he placed Ephraim before Manasseh.

21 Then Israel said to Joseph: "I am about to die. But God will be with you and will restore you to the land of your fathers. 22*† As for me, I give to you, as to the one above his brothers, Shechem, which I captured from the Amorites with my sword and bow."

47, 31: *Israel bowed at the head of the bed:* meaning perhaps that he gave a nod of assent and appreciation as he lay on his bed. By reading with different vowels the Hebrew word for "bed," the Greek version translated it as "staff," and understood the phrase to mean that he bowed in worship, leaning on the top of his staff; it is thus quoted in Heb 11, 21.

48, 3: *Luz:* an older name of Bethel (Gn 28, 19).

48, 7: Since her early death prevented Rachel from bearing more than two sons, Jacob feels justified in treating her two grandsons as if they were his own offspring.

48, 22: Both the meaning of the Hebrew and the historical reference in this verse are obscure. By taking the Hebrew word for Shechem as a common noun meaning shoulder or mountain slope, some translators render the verse, "I give you one portion more than your brothers, which I captured . . ." The reference may be to the capture of Shechem by the sons of Jacob (Gn 34, 24–29). Shechem lay near the border separating the tribal territory of Manasseh from that of Ephraim (Jos 16, 4–9; 17, 1f.7).

47, 30: Gn 50, 5.　　　　　　　48, 15: Heb 11, 21.
48, 3f: Gn 28, 12–15; 35, 6.　　48, 20: Heb 11, 21.
48, 7: Gn 35, 19.　　　　　　　48, 22: Jos 17, 14.17f; Jn 4, 5.

Cultural Connections

ASSEMBLE AND HEAR!

Genesis 49, 1–2 is the first reading at Mass on the ninth day before Christmas. This is an important day for Filipino Catholics because it marks the beginning of Simbang Gabi, or Dawn Worship.

On the nine days before Christmas, people gather to celebrate Mass in the dark of the predawn—usually between four and five o'clock in the morning. Mass ends with chocolate and buns and socializing. In fact, this is such a popular custom that even people who don't come to Mass all year will make it for the nine Masses of Simbang Gabi! It is a special celebration of thankfulness for the gift of their Catholic faith.

This Philippine tradition is an example of a Catholic custom called a novena. A novena is a public or private prayer repeated nine times. It can be a prayer said every day for nine days, one day a week for nine weeks, one day a month for nine months, or in any other pattern of nine. Why not make up your own personal novena? Just think of a prayer in a form you find meaningful (journaling, singing, reading the Scriptures, or even praying silently), and repeat it once a day for nine days or once a week for nine weeks. Happy praying!

▶ Gn 49, 1–2

Jacob's Testament

49 ¹ Jacob called his sons and said: "Gather around, that I may tell you what is to happen to you in days to come.

² "Assemble and listen, sons of Jacob,
    listen to Israel, your father.

³ "You, Reuben, my first-born,
    my strength and the first fruit of
      my manhood,
    excelling in rank and excelling in power!
⁴* Unruly as water, you shall no longer excel,
    for you climbed into your father's bed
    and defiled my couch to my sorrow.

⁵† "Simeon and Levi, brothers indeed,
    weapons of violence are their knives.
⁶* Let not my soul enter their council,
    or my spirit be joined with their company;

For in their fury they slew men,
    in their willfulness they maimed oxen.
⁷ Cursed be their fury so fierce,
    and their rage so cruel!
I will scatter them in Jacob,
    disperse them throughout Israel.
⁸ "You, Judah, shall your brothers praise
    —your hand on the neck of your
      enemies;
    the sons of your father shall bow down
      to you.
⁹* Judah, like a lion's whelp,
    you have grown up on prey, my son.
He crouches like a lion recumbent,
    the king of beasts—who would dare
      rouse him?
¹⁰† The scepter shall never depart from Judah,
    or the mace from between his legs,
While tribute is brought to him,
    and he receives the people's homage.

49, 5: *Knives:* if this is the meaning of the obscure Hebrew word here, the reference may be to the knives used in circumcising the men of Shechem (Gn 34, 24; cf Jos 5, 2).

49, 10: *While tribute is brought to him:* this translation is based on a slight change in the Hebrew text, which, as it stands, would seem to mean, "until he comes to Shiloh." A somewhat different reading of the Hebrew text would be, "until he comes to whom it be-

longs." This last has been traditionally understood in a Messianic sense. In any case, the passage foretells the supremacy of the tribe of Judah, which found its fulfillment in the Davidic dynasty and ultimately in the Messianic Son of David, Jesus Christ.

49, 4: Gn 35, 22; 1 Chr 5, 1f.   49, 9: 1 Chr 5, 2.
49, 6: Gn 34, 25.

GN

11† He tethers his donkey to the vine,
    his purebred ass to the choicest stem.
In wine he washes his garments,
    his robe in the blood of grapes.
12 His eyes are darker than wine,
    and his teeth are whiter than milk.

13 "Zebulun shall dwell by the seashore
    [This means a shore for ships],
    and his flank shall be based on Sidon.

14 "Issachar is a rawboned ass,
    crouching between the saddlebags.
15 When he saw how good a settled life was,
    and how pleasant the country,
He bent his shoulder to the burden
    and became a toiling serf.

16† "Dan shall achieve justice for his kindred
    like any other tribe of Israel.
17 Let Dan be a serpent by the roadside,
    a horned viper by the path,
That bites the horse's heel,
    so that the rider tumbles backward.

18 "[I long for your deliverance, O LORD!]

19† "Gad shall be raided by raiders,
    but he shall raid at their heels.

20 "Asher's produce is rich,
    and he shall furnish dainties for kings.

21 "Naphtali is a hind let loose,
    which brings forth lovely fawns.

22 "Joseph is a wild colt,
    a wild colt by a spring,
    a wild ass on a hillside.
23 Harrying and attacking,
    the archers opposed him;
24 But each one's bow remained stiff,
    as their arms were unsteady,
By the power of the Mighty One of Jacob,
    because of the Shepherd, the Rock of Israel,
25† The God of your father, who helps you,
    God Almighty, who blesses you,
With the blessings of the heavens above,
    the blessings of the abyss that
        crouches below,

The blessings of breasts and womb,
26   the blessings of fresh grain and blossoms,
The blessings of the everlasting mountains,
    the delights of the eternal hills.
May they rest on the head of Joseph,
    on the brow of the prince among
        his brothers.

27 "Benjamin is a ravenous wolf;
    mornings he devours the prey,
    and evenings he distributes the spoils."

Farewell and Death

28 All these are the twelve tribes of Israel, and this is what their father said about them, as he bade them farewell and gave to each of them an appropriate message. 29 Then he gave them this charge: "Since I am about to be taken to my kindred, bury me with my fathers in the cave that lies in the field of Ephron the Hittite, 30* the cave in the field of Machpelah, facing on Mamre, in the land of Canaan, the field that Abraham bought from Ephron the Hittite for a burial ground. 31 There Abraham and his wife Sarah are buried, and so are Isaac and his wife Rebekah, and there, too, I buried Leah— 32 the field and the cave in it that had been purchased from the Hittites."

33 When Jacob had finished giving these instructions to his sons, he drew his feet into the bed, breathed his last, and was taken to his kindred.

Jacob's Funeral

50 1 Joseph threw himself on his father's face and wept over him as he kissed him. 2 Then he ordered the physicians in his service to embalm his father. When they embalmed Israel, 3 they spent forty days at it, for that is the full period of embalming; and the Egyptians mourned him for seventy days. 4 When that period of mourning was over, Joseph spoke to Pharaoh's courtiers. "Please do me this favor," he said, "and convey to Pharaoh this request of mine. 5* Since my father, at the point of death, made me promise on oath to bury him in the tomb that he had prepared for himself in the land of Canaan, may I go up there to bury my father and then come back?" 6 Pharaoh replied, "Go and bury your father, as he made you promise on oath."

7 So Joseph left to bury his father; and with him went all of Pharaoh's officials who were senior

---

49, 11: *In wine . . . the blood of grapes:* Judah's clothes are poetically pictured as soaked with grape juice from trampling in the wine press, the rich vintage of his land; cf Is 63, 2.
49, 16: In Hebrew the verb for *achieve justice* is from the same root as the name Dan.
49, 19: In Hebrew there is a certain assonance between the name

Gad and the words for "raided," "raiders" and "raid."
49, 25f: A very similar description of the agricultural riches of the tribal land of Joseph is given in Dt 33, 13–16.

49, 30: Gn 23, 17.   50, 5: Gn 47, 30.

members of his court and all the other dignitaries of Egypt, [8] as well as Joseph's whole household, his brothers, and his father's household; only their children and their flocks and herds were left in the region of Goshen. [9] Chariots, too, and charioteers went up with him; it was a very large retinue.

[10]† When they arrived at Goren-ha-atad, which is beyond the Jordan, they held there a very great and solemn memorial service; and Joseph observed seven days of mourning for his father. [11] When the Canaanites who inhabited the land saw the mourning at Goren-ha-atad, they said, "This is a solemn funeral the Egyptians are having." That is why the place was named Abel-mizraim. It is beyond the Jordan.

[12] Thus Jacob's sons did for him as he had instructed them. [13]* They carried him to the land of Canaan and buried him in the cave in the field of Machpelah, facing on Mamre, the field that Abraham had bought for a burial ground from Ephron the Hittite.

[14] After Joseph had buried his father he returned to Egypt, together with his brothers and all who had gone up with him for the burial of his father.

Plea for Forgiveness

[15] Now that their father was dead, Joseph's brothers became fearful and thought, "Suppose Joseph has been nursing a grudge against us and now plans to pay us back in full for all the wrong we did him!" [16] So they approached Joseph and said: "Before your father died, he gave us these instructions: [17] 'You shall say to Joseph, Jacob begs you to forgive the criminal wrongdoing of your brothers, who treated you so cruelly.' Please, therefore, forgive the crime that we, the servants of your father's God, committed." When they spoke these words to him, Joseph broke into tears. [18] Then his brothers proceeded to fling themselves down before him and said, "Let us be your slaves!" [19] But Joseph replied to them: "Have no fear. Can I take the place of God? [20]* Even though you meant harm to me, God meant it for good, to achieve his present end, the survival of many people. [21]* Therefore have no fear. I will provide for you and for your children." By thus speaking kindly to them, he reassured them.

---

†
   50, 10f: *Goren-ha-atad:* "Threshing Floor of the Brambles." *Abel-mizraim:* although the name really means "watercourse of the Egyptians," it is understood here, by a play on the first part of the term, to mean "mourning of the Egyptians." The site has not been identified through either reading of the name. But it is difficult to see why the mourning rites should have been held in the land *beyond the Jordan* when the burial was at Hebron. Perhaps an earlier form of the story placed the mourning rites beyond the Wadi of Egypt, the traditional boundary between Canaan and Egypt (Nm 34, 5; Jos 15, 4.47).

50, 13: Gn 23, 16; Acts 7, 16.   **50, 21:** Gn 47, 12.
50, 20: Gn 45, 5; Sir 49, 15.

did you KNOW?

Israel's Ancestry

Although the Israelites descended from many different kin, the Book of Genesis traces their origins back to a series of common ancestors, which served to unite them as a people. Genesis tells the stories of those great ancestors, men and women called patriarchs and matriarchs, who were the founders of what later became the people of Israel. The twelve tribes of Israel are understood to be descendants from Jacob's twelve sons (see Jacob's last words in Genesis, chapter 49, for a description of those tribes). Twelve becomes an important number that comes up again and again in the Bible. For example, the twelve Apostles are Jesus' closest followers in the New Testament.

It can be confusing to remember who is related to whom, so here's a chart to keep everyone straight:

Hagar (Sarah's slave)
├── Ishmael
Abraham
├── Isaac
Sarah
├── Esau (Edom)
└── Jacob (Israel)
Rebekah

Leah
├── Reuben
├── Simeon
├── Levi
├── Judah
├── Issachar
├── Zebulun
└── Dinah (only daughter)

Bilhah (Rachel's maid)
├── Dan
└── Naphtali

Zilpah (Leah's maid)
├── Gad
└── Asher

Rachel
├── Joseph
└── Benjamin
├── Ephraim
└── Manasseh

■ Levi's tribe was set aside as priests and was not assigned land after the conquest of Canaan.
■ Because Jacob adopted Joseph's sons Ephraim and Manasseh, Joseph is the father of two tribes.

22 Joseph remained in Egypt, together with his father's family. He lived a hundred and ten years. 23* He saw Ephraim's children to the third generation, and the children of Manasseh's son Machir were also born on Joseph's knees.

Death of Joseph

24* Joseph said to his brothers: "I am about to

die. God will surely take care of you and lead you out of this land to the land that he promised on oath to Abraham, Isaac and Jacob." 25* Then, putting the sons of Israel under oath, he continued, "When God thus takes care of you, you must bring my bones up with you from this place." 26* Joseph died at the age of a hundred and ten. He was embalmed and laid to rest in a coffin in Egypt.

50, 23: Nm 32, 39; Jos 17, 1.   **50, 25:** Ex 13, 19; Heb 11, 22.
50, 24: Ex 3, 8; Jos 24, 32;   **50, 26:** Sir 49, 15.
Heb 11, 22.

Click! Chains snap shut around your ankles. Crack! The tip of a whip whistles past your head. Bang! A door shuts, leaving you in darkness. These are the sounds of slavery, and they come as a surprise at the beginning of the Book of Exodus. What happened after the happy ending in Genesis? Like an action-packed drama, Exodus tells a story of deceit and broken promises, and of how God's miraculous interventions delivered the Israelites from their slavery in Egypt.

At a Glance

I. The Israelites in Egypt (1, 1—12, 36).

II. The Exodus from Egypt and the Journey to Sinai (12, 37—18, 27).

III. The Covenant at Mount Sinai (19, 1—24, 18).

IV. The Dwelling and Its Furnishings (25, 1—40, 38).

In-depth

The Book of Exodus is the story of Israel's liberation. Exodus literally means "departure," and this book's central story is of how God liberates the people from slavery in Egypt (an event called the Exodus). Its central character is Moses, who is chosen by God to become God's voice and the instrument of God's power. Exodus was written hundreds of years after these events, using oral traditions that described the origin of many of the Israelites' beliefs and religious rituals.

Exodus is divided into four main sections. The first two sections, chapters 1–18, begin with the Israelites enslaved in Egypt and prohibited from worshiping their God. Israel cries out to God, and God answers by sending Moses. When Pharaoh refuses to let the Israelites go, God sends ten devastating plagues, and Pharaoh finally gives in. Later, Pharaoh changes his mind and chases the Israelites, only to have his army destroyed after the Israelites' escape through the Red Sea. This section ends with the people wandering through the wilderness, sustained by food and water miraculously provided by God.

Sections three and four of Exodus, chapters 19–40, occur at Mount Sinai. There, God enters into a covenant with all the people. God's part of the Sinai Covenant is to guarantee continued protection. Israel's part is to be faithful to God alone, a faithfulness marked by special laws (chapters 20–23) and special worship (chapters 24–31) that unite them as a people. Exodus ends with Israel still encamped at Mount Sinai, struggling to become a people of the Covenant.

The stories and laws in Exodus are at the heart of both Jewish and Christian belief in a God who saves, a God of freedom. You cannot fully appreciate the meaning of Jesus' life, death, and Resurrection without knowing these stories.

Quick Facts

Period Covered
sometime from 1500 to 1250 B.C.

Author
unknown author gathering oral traditions and stories from various tribal peoples

Themes
God liberates people from slavery and oppression. God sustains the Israelites in the wilderness. God forms a covenant marked by laws and rituals.

Exodus

The Book of

Exodus

14, 21

I: The Israelites In Egypt

Jacob's Descendants in Egypt

1 [1]† These are the names of the sons of Israel who, accompanied by their households, migrated with Jacob into Egypt: [2]† Reuben, Simeon, Levi and Judah; [3] Issachar, Zebulun and Benjamin; [4] Dan and Naphtali; Gad and Asher. [5]*† The total number of the direct descendants of Jacob was seventy. Joseph was already in Egypt.

[6]* Now Joseph and all his brothers and that whole generation died. [7] But the Israelites were fruitful and prolific. They became so numerous and strong that the land was filled with them.

The Oppression

[8]*† Then a new king, who knew nothing of Joseph, came to power in Egypt. [9] He said to his subjects, "Look how numerous and powerful the Israelite people are growing, more so than we ourselves! [10] Come, let us deal shrewdly with them to stop their increase; otherwise, in time of war they too may join our enemies to fight against us, and so leave our country."

[11]*† Accordingly, taskmasters were set over the Israelites to oppress them with forced labor. Thus they had to build for Pharaoh the supply cities of Pithom and Raamses. [12] Yet the more they were oppressed, the more they multiplied and spread. The Egyptians, then, dreaded the Israelites [13] and reduced them to cruel slavery, [14]† making life bitter for them with hard work in mortar and brick and all kinds of field work—the whole cruel fate of slaves.

Command to the Midwives

[15] The king of Egypt told the Hebrew midwives, one of whom was called Shiphrah and the other Puah, [16]† "When you act as midwives for the Hebrew women and see them giving birth, if it is a boy, kill him; but if it is a girl, she may live." [17] The midwives, however, feared God; they did not do as the king of Egypt had ordered them, but let the boys live. [18] So the king summoned the midwives and asked them, "Why have you acted thus, allowing the boys to live?" [19] The midwives answered Pharaoh, "The Hebrew women are not like the Egyptian women. They are robust and give birth before the

---

1, 1: *Sons of Israel:* here literally the first-generation sons of Jacob. Cf v 5. However, beginning with Ex 1, 7 the same Hebrew phrase refers to the more remote descendants of Jacob; hence, from there on, it is ordinarily rendered as "the Israelites." *Households:* the family in its fullest sense, including wives, children and servants.
1, 2: The sons of Jacob are listed here according to the respective mothers. Cf Gn 29, 31; 30, 20; 35, 16–26.
1, 5: *Direct descendants:* literally, persons coming from the loins of Jacob; hence, wives and servants are here excluded. Cf Gn 46, 26.
1, 8: *Who knew nothing of Joseph:* this king ignored the services that Joseph had rendered to Egypt.

1, 11: *Pharaoh:* not a personal name, but a title common to all the kings of Egypt.
1, 14: *Mortar:* either the wet clay with which the bricks were made, as in Na 3, 14, or the cement used between the bricks in building, as in Gn 11, 3.
1, 16: *And see them giving birth:* the Hebrew text is uncertain.

1, 5: Gn 46, 27; Dt 10, 22;
    Acts 7, 14.
1, 6: Gn 50, 26.
1, 8ff: Acts 7, 18.
1, 11: Dt 26, 6.

Saving Lives

In the story of the birth of Moses, Pharaoh ordered the Egyptian midwives to kill all the male Israelite babies at birth. The midwives recognized such killing as an atrocity and refused to obey Pharaoh. Their actions might be considered civil disobedience against unjust laws.

Some people claim that the right to have an abortion is a just law. Aren't they right? Consider this incident: At a youth group gathering, abortion was discussed, and a video was shown on how abortions are performed. One young man shared that although he did not believe in abortion, he used to believe exceptions could be made, such as in the case of rape or incest. After watching the video, he said that he no longer believed that such exceptions could be morally justified. A young woman said that the video had convinced her that abortion is in the same moral category as serial murder. These young people, like the midwives in Exodus, recognized that all human life is sacred.

▸ Ex 1, 15–22

midwife arrives." ²⁰ Therefore God dealt well with the midwives. The people, too, increased and grew strong. ²¹ And because the midwives feared God, he built up families for them. ²²*† Pharaoh then commanded all his subjects, "Throw into the river every boy that is born to the Hebrews, but you may let all the girls live."

Birth and Adoption of Moses

2 ¹* Now a certain man of the house of Levi married a Levite woman, ²* who conceived and bore a son. Seeing that he was a goodly child, she hid him for three months. ³† When she could hide him no longer, she took a papyrus basket, daubed it with bitumen and pitch, and putting the child in it, placed it among the reeds on the river bank. ⁴ His sister stationed herself at a distance to find out what would happen to him.

⁵ Pharaoh's daughter came down to the river to bathe, while her maids walked along the river bank. Noticing the basket among the reeds, she sent her handmaid to fetch it. ⁶ On opening it, she looked, and lo, there was a baby boy, crying! She was moved with pity for him and said, "It is one of the Hebrews' children." ⁷ Then his sister asked Pharaoh's daughter, "Shall I go and call one of the Hebrew women to nurse the child for you?" ⁸ "Yes, do so," she answered. So the maiden went and called the child's own mother. ⁹ Pharaoh's daughter said

to her, "Take this child and nurse it for me, and I will repay you." The woman therefore took the child and nursed it. ¹⁰*† When the child grew, she brought him to Pharaoh's daughter, who adopted him as her son and called him Moses; for she said, "I drew him out of the water."

Moses' Flight to Midian

¹¹*† On one occasion, after Moses had grown up, when he visited his kinsmen and witnessed their forced labor, he saw an Egyptian striking a Hebrew, one of his own kinsmen. ¹² Looking about and seeing no one, he slew the Egyptian and hid him in the sand. ¹³ The next day he went out again, and now two Hebrews were fighting! So he asked the culprit, "Why are you striking your fellow Hebrew?" ¹⁴ But he replied, "Who has appointed you ruler and judge over us? Are you thinking of killing me as you killed the Egyptian?" Then Moses became afraid and thought, "The affair must certainly be known."

¹⁵* Pharaoh, too, heard of the affair and sought to put him to death. But Moses fled from him and stayed in the land of Midian. As he was seated there by a well, ¹⁶ seven daughters of a priest of Midian came to draw water and fill the troughs to water their father's flock. ¹⁷ But some shepherds came and drove them away. Then Moses got up and defended them and watered their flock. ¹⁸† When

---

1, 22: *The river:* the Nile, which was "the" river for the Egyptians.
2, 3: *Basket:* literally, "chest" or "ark"; the same Hebrew word is used in Gn 6, 14 for Noah's ark. Here, however, the chest was made of papyrus stalks.
2, 10: *When the child grew:* probably when he was weaned or a little later. *Moses:* in Hebrew, *Mosheh;* the Hebrew word for "draw out" is *mashah.* This explanation of the name is not intended as a scientific etymology but as a play on words. The name is probably derived from an Egyptian word for "has been born," referring the birth to a god thought to be its sponsor.

2, 11: *After Moses had grown up:* Acts 7, 23 indicates that this was after an interval of nearly forty years. Cf Ex 7, 7. *Striking:* probably in the sense of "flogging"; according to some, "slaying."
2, 18: *Reuel:* he was also called Jethro. Cf Ex 3, 1; 4, 18; 18, 1.

1, 22: Acts 7, 19.   2, 10: Acts 7, 21; Heb 11, 24.
2, 1: Ex 6, 20; Nm 26, 59.   2, 11–14: Acts 7, 23–28.
2, 2: Acts 7, 20; Heb 11, 23.   2, 15: Acts 7, 29; Heb 11, 27.

EX

they returned to their father Reuel, he said to them, "How is it you have returned so soon today?" [19]† They answered, "An Egyptian saved us from the interference of the shepherds. He even drew water for us and watered the flock!" [20] "Where is the man?" he asked his daughters. "Why did you leave him there? Invite him to have something to eat." [21] Moses agreed to live with him, and the man gave him his daughter Zipporah in marriage. [22]*† She bore him a son, whom he named Gershom; for he said, "I am a stranger in a foreign land."

The Burning Bush

[23]* A long time passed, during which the king of Egypt died. Still the Israelites groaned and cried out because of their slavery. As their cry for release went up to God, [24]* he heard their groaning and was mindful of his covenant with Abraham, Isaac and Jacob. [25] He saw the Israelites and knew. . . .

3 [1]† Meanwhile Moses was tending the flock of his father-in-law Jethro, the priest of Midian. Leading the flock across the desert, he came to Horeb, the mountain of God. [2]*† There an angel of the LORD appeared to him in fire flaming out of a bush. As he looked on, he was surprised to see that the bush, though on fire, was not consumed. [3] So Moses decided, "I must go over to look at this remarkable sight, and see why the bush is not burned."

The Call of Moses

[4] When the LORD saw him coming over to look at it more closely, God called out to him from the bush, "Moses! Moses!" He answered, "Here I am." [5]* God said, "Come no nearer! Remove the sandals from your feet, for the place where you stand is holy ground. [6]*† I am the God of your father," he continued, "the God of Abraham, the God of Isaac, the God of Jacob." Moses hid his face, for he was afraid to look at God. [7] But the LORD said, "I have witnessed the affliction of my people in Egypt and have heard their cry of complaint against their slave drivers, so I know well what they are suffering.

Introducing ▶ MOSES

Moses is, without doubt, the most important character in the Pentateuch, if not the entire Old Testament. Struggling to find language to describe his greatness, Dt 34, 10 says, "Since then no prophet has arisen in Israel like Moses, whom the LORD knew face to face." Born to a couple from the tribe of Levi and raised as an Egyptian by the Pharaoh's daughter, Moses was perfectly suited to negotiate Israel's freedom from slavery in Egypt. In event after event, the author of Exodus shows us Moses' wonder-working power, his prophetic skill, and his intimacy with God.

Despite all of Moses' great accomplishments, he never loses his humanness. He lacks confidence in his ability to speak (Ex 4, 10); he is angry and frustrated with his people (17, 4), and he bargains with God out of love for his people (32, 11–14). Moses, noble but also knowing sadness, is elegantly portrayed in the passage where he dies within sight of the Promised Land (Deuteronomy, chapter 34). These qualities paint a picture of someone whose perseverance and trust allowed God to work through him.

A prophet is literally God's voice, and Moses was indeed God's voice, which shaped Israel to be a people of the Covenant. All other leaders and figures in the Old Testament are compared with Moses. In the New Testament, even Jesus is compared with Moses.

---

† **2, 19:** *An Egyptian:* Moses was probably wearing Egyptian dress, or spoke Egyptian to Reuel's daughters.
2, 22: *Gershom:* the name is explained as if it came from the Hebrew word *ger,* "stranger," joined to the Hebrew word *sham,* "there." Some Greek and Latin manuscripts add here a passage taken from Ex 18, 4.
3, 1: *The mountain of God:* probably given this designation because of the divine apparitions which took place there, such as on this occasion and when the Israelites were there after the departure from Egypt.
3, 2: *An angel of the LORD:* the visual form under which God appeared and spoke to men is referred to indifferently in some Old Testament texts either as God's angel or as God himself. Cf Gn 16, 7.13; Ex 14, 19.24f; Nm 22, 22–35; Jgs 6, 11–18.
3, 6: The appearance of God caused fear of death, since it was believed that no one could see God and live; cf Gn 32, 30. *The God of Abraham . . . Jacob:* cited by Christ in proof of the resurrection since the patriarchs, long dead, live on in God who is the God of the living. Cf Mt 22, 32; Mk 12, 26; Lk 20, 37.

2, 22: Ex 18, 3.
2, 23: Ex 3, 7.9; Dt 26, 7.
2, 24: Ex 6, 5; Pss 105, 8f; 106, 44f.
3, 2–10: Acts 7, 30–35.
3, 5: Jos 5, 15.
3, 6: Ex 4, 5; Mt 22, 32; Mk 12, 36; Lk 20, 37.

HOLY GROUND

In many Asian cultures, before people enter a home, they remove their shoes. People do this before entering a mosque too. Perhaps you remove your shoes before entering your home as well. Removing one's shoes is a common sign of respect. Moses is commanded to remove his sandals in Ex 3, 5. Why? Because he is standing on holy ground. Why is the ground holy? Because God is present.

Moses is awestruck and humbled by his experience of God's presence. In today's multimedia culture, we are rarely awed by anything. Even the burning bush would be just another special effect. How can we regain our sense of awe at God's majesty? Some people experience it in nature, looking at a star-filled sky or the waves rolling in on the ocean. Others experience it in getting to know other people deeply. Still others find it in the amazing patterns that science reveals. The one common element to experiencing awe seems to be the ability to slow down, look closely, and appreciate what we discover.

So slow down, find your own holy ground, take your shoes off, and let God fill you with awe!

▶ Ex 3, 1–6

8*† Therefore I have come down to rescue them from the hands of the Egyptians and lead them out of that land into a good and spacious land, a land flowing with milk and honey, the country of the Canaanites, Hittites, Amorites, Perizzites, Hivites and Jebusites. 9 So indeed the cry of the Israelites has reached me, and I have truly noted that the Egyptians are oppressing them. 10 Come, now! I will send you to Pharaoh to lead my people, the Israelites, out of Egypt."

11† But Moses said to God, "Who am I that I should go to Pharaoh and lead the Israelites out of Egypt?" 12 He answered, "I will be with you; and this shall be your proof that it is I who have sent you: when you bring my people out of Egypt, you will worship God on this very mountain." 13 "But," said Moses to God, "when I go to the Israelites and say to them, 'The God of your fathers has sent me

to you,' if they ask me, 'What is his name?' what am I to tell them?" 14† God replied, "I am who am." Then he added, "This is what you shall tell the Israelites: I AM sent me to you."

15* God spoke further to Moses, "Thus shall you say to the Israelites: The LORD, the God of your fathers, the God of Abraham, the God of Isaac, the God of Jacob, has sent me to you.

"This is my name forever;
    this is my title for all generations.

16† "Go and assemble the elders of the Israelites, and tell them: The LORD, the God of your fathers, the God of Abraham, Isaac and Jacob, has appeared to me and said: I am concerned about you and about the way you are being treated in Egypt; 17 so I have decided to lead you up out of the misery of

---

3, 8: *I have come down:* a figure of speech signifying an extraordinary divine intervention in human affairs. Cf Gn 11, 5.7. *Flowing with milk and honey:* an expression denoting agricultural prosperity, which seems to have been proverbial in its application to Palestine. Cf Ex 13, 5; Nm 13, 27; Jos 5, 6; Jer 11, 5; 32, 22; Ez 20, 6.15.

3, 11: *Who am I:* besides naturally shrinking from such a tremendous undertaking, Moses realized that, as a fugitive from Pharaoh, he could hardly hope to carry out a mission to him. Perhaps he also recalled that on one occasion even his own kinsmen questioned his authority. Cf Ex 2, 14.

3, 14: *I am who am:* apparently this utterance is the source of the word *Yahweh,* the proper personal name of the God of Israel. It is

commonly explained in reference to God as the absolute and necessary Being. It may be understood of God as the Source of all created beings. Out of reverence for this name, the term *Adonai,* "my Lord," was later used as a substitute. The word LORD in the present version represents this traditional usage. The word "Jehovah" arose from a false reading of this name as it is written in the current Hebrew text.

3, 16: *Elders:* the Israelite leaders, who were usually older men. They were representatives of the people.

3, 8f: Gn 15, 19ff.   3, 15: Ps 135, 13.

EX

Egypt into the land of the Canaanites, Hittites, Amorites, Perizzites, Hivites and Jebusites, a land flowing with milk and honey.

18* "Thus they will heed your message. Then you and the elders of Israel shall go to the king of Egypt and say to him: The LORD, the God of the Hebrews, has sent us word. Permit us, then, to go a three-days' journey in the desert, that we may offer sacrifice to the LORD, our God.

19 "Yet I know that the king of Egypt will not allow you to go unless he is forced. 20 I will stretch out my hand, therefore, and smite Egypt by doing all kinds of wondrous deeds there. After that he will send you away. 21 I will even make the Egyptians so well-disposed toward this people that, when you leave, you will not go empty-handed. 22*† Every woman shall ask her neighbor and her house guest for silver and gold articles and for clothing to put on your sons and daughters. Thus you will despoil the Egyptians."

Confirmation of Moses' Mission

4 1"But," objected Moses, "suppose they will not believe me, nor listen to my plea? For they may say, 'The LORD did not appear to you.' " 2 The LORD therefore asked him, "What is that in your

did you KNOW?

God's Mysterious Name

"I am who am"—one possible translation of Yahweh from Ex 3, 14—seems more like a definition than a name. Some scholars have suggested Yahweh might be better translated "he causes to be what exists." In any case, the four Hebrew letters YHWH (or Yahweh in English) are difficult to translate. Over the centuries, the Jewish people stopped pronouncing the four letters out of reverence for God and replaced them with the word Adonai, meaning "my Lord." Most English translations of the Bible respect this long-standing tradition, translating the original YHWH as LORD. This mysterious name of God reminds us that no name or symbol can fully express who God is.

▶ Ex 3, 13–15

THE NAME OF GOD

Many Native American peoples, such as the Lakota and the Sioux, have several names for God. Wakan-Tanka and Tun-ka-shi-la are still commonly used today. These words for God are often translated as Great Spirit.

This is a good translation because Wakan is a word that brings together the concepts of mystery, sacredness, holiness, awe, and inspiration. Tanka describes something that is great.

Tun-ka-shi-la is often used the same way as Wakan-Tanka, but its meaning is slightly different. Tun-ka-shi-la is often translated as Grandfather or Great Grandfather, but it means the "one who is the oldest, so old that nothing or no one is older." Tun-ka-shi-la is a name that reflects the Great Spirit as the source of all things, the one who has existed from the beginning.

▶ Ex 3, 13–15

---

† **3, 22:** *Articles:* probably jewelry. *Despoil:* this was permissible, that the Israelites might compensate themselves for their many years of servitude; besides, the Egyptians would give these things willingly. Cf Ex 12, 33–36.

* **3, 18:** Ex 5, 3.   **3, 22:** 21f; Ex 11, 2f; 12, 35f.

Cultural Connections

GOD SENDS PROPHETS TO LIBERATE HIS PEOPLE!

God responded to the cry of his people, choosing Moses as a prophet and commissioning him to lead the Israelites to freedom. Despite Moses' first doubts, with God's assistance, Moses became an effective and powerful leader. God would not let Moses' excuses stand in the way of God's mission of liberation.

Christians share in Jesus Christ's prophetic work as well. We too need to speak out against injustice and help the victims of oppression. Like the prophets before us, we can only succeed with God's help.

In our time, great spiritual leaders have risen up to lead people to freedom: Mohandas Gandhi, Martin Luther King Jr., Dorothy Day, Archbishop Oscar Romero, and Cesar Chavez are just a few. As in the case of Moses, God inspired these leaders to see their people experiencing injustice and to seek to liberate them from oppressive powers. You can be sure that these people also had their doubts and relied on God for their strength and hope.

■ Are you aware of any group that is being oppressed today? How might God be calling you to help?

■ Ask God for wisdom, strength, and help in your mission.

▸ Ex 4, 1–17

---

hand?" "A staff," he answered. ³* The LORD then said, "Throw it on the ground." When he threw it on the ground it was changed into a serpent, and Moses shied away from it. ⁴ "Now, put out your hand," the LORD said to him, "and take hold of its tail." So he put out his hand and laid hold of it, and it became a staff in his hand. ⁵ "This will take place so that they may believe," he continued, "that the LORD, the God of their fathers, the God of Abraham, the God of Isaac, the God of Jacob, did appear to you."

⁶ Again the LORD said to him, "Put your hand in your bosom." He put it in his bosom, and when he withdrew it, to his surprise his hand was leprous, like snow. ⁷ The LORD then said, "Now, put your hand back in your bosom." Moses put his hand back in his bosom, and when he withdrew it, to his surprise it was again like the rest of his body. ⁸ "If they will not believe you, nor heed the message of the first sign, they should believe the message of the second. ⁹* And if they will not believe even these two signs, nor heed your plea, take some water from the river and pour it on the dry land. The wa-

ter you take from the river will become blood on the dry land."

Aaron's Office as Assistant

¹⁰* Moses, however, said to the LORD, "If you please, Lord, I have never been eloquent, neither in the past, nor recently, nor now that you have spoken to your servant; but I am slow of speech and tongue." ¹¹ The LORD said to him, "Who gives one man speech and makes another deaf and dumb? Or who gives sight to one and makes another blind? Is it not I, the LORD? ¹² Go, then! It is I who will assist you in speaking and will teach you what you are to say." ¹³† Yet he insisted, "If you please, Lord, send someone else!" ¹⁴ Then the LORD became angry with Moses and said, "Have you not your brother, Aaron the Levite? I know that he is an eloquent speaker. Besides, he is now on his way to meet you. ¹⁵ When he sees you, his heart will be glad. You are to speak to him, then, and put the words in his mouth. I will assist both you and him in speaking and will teach the two of you what you are to do.

---

† 4, 13: *Send someone else:* literally, "Send by means of him whom you will send," that is, "Send whom you will."

4, 3: Ex 7, 10.　　　　4, 10: Ex 6, 12.
4, 9: Ex 7, 17.19f.

16*† He shall speak to the people for you: he shall be your spokesman, and you shall be as God to him. 17† Take this staff in your hand; with it you are to perform the signs."

Moses' Return to Egypt

18† After this Moses returned to his father-in-law Jethro and said to him, "Let me go back, please, to my kinsmen in Egypt, to see whether they are still living." Jethro replied, "Go in peace." 19* In Midian the LORD said to Moses, "Go back to Egypt, for all the men who sought your life are dead." 20 So Moses took his wife and his sons, and started back to the land of Egypt, with them riding the ass. The staff of God he carried with him. 21† The LORD said to him, "On your return to Egypt, see that you perform before Pharaoh all the wonders I have put in your power. I will make him obstinate, however, so that he will not let the people go. 22* So you shall say to Pharaoh: Thus says the LORD: Israel is my son, my first-born. 23* Hence I tell you: Let my son go, that he may serve me. If you refuse to let him go, I warn you, I will kill your son, your first-born."

24† On the journey, at a place where they spent the night, the Lord came upon Moses and would have killed him. 25* But Zipporah took a piece of flint and cut off her son's foreskin and, touching his person, she said, "You are a spouse of blood to me." 26 Then God let Moses go. At that time she said, "A spouse of blood," in regard to the circumcision.

27 The LORD said to Aaron, "Go into the desert to meet Moses." So he went, and when they met at the mountain of God, Aaron kissed him. 28 Moses informed him of all the LORD had said in sending him, and of the various signs he had enjoined upon him. 29 Then Moses and Aaron went and assembled all the elders of the Israelites. 30 Aaron told them everything the LORD had said to Moses, and he performed the signs before the people. 31 The people believed, and when they heard that the LORD was concerned about them and had seen their affliction, they bowed down in worship.

Pharaoh's Obduracy

5 1 After that, Moses and Aaron went to Pharaoh and said, "Thus says the LORD, the God of Israel: Let my people go, that they may celebrate a feast to me in the desert." 2 Pharaoh answered, "Who is the LORD, that I should heed his plea to let Israel go? I do not know the LORD; even if I did, I would not let Israel go." 3* They replied, "The God of the Hebrews has sent us word. Let us go a three days' journey in the desert, that we may offer sacrifice to the LORD, our God; otherwise he will punish us with pestilence or the sword."

4 The king of Egypt answered them, "What do you mean, Moses and Aaron, by taking the people away from their work? Off to your labor! 5 Look how numerous the people of the land are already," continued Pharaoh, "and yet you would give them rest from their labor!"

6† That very day Pharaoh gave the taskmasters and foremen of the people this order: 7† "You shall no longer supply the people with straw for their brickmaking as you have previously done. Let them go and gather straw themselves! 8 Yet you shall levy upon them the same quota of bricks as they have previously made. Do not reduce it. They are lazy; that is why they are crying, 'Let us go to offer sacrifice to our God.' 9 Increase the work for the men, so that they keep their mind on it and pay no attention to lying words."

10 So the taskmasters and foremen of the people went out and told them, "Thus says Pharaoh: I will not provide you with straw. 11 Go and gather the straw yourselves, wherever you can find it. Yet there must not be the slightest reduction in your work." 12 The people, then, scattered throughout the land of Egypt to gather stubble for straw, 13 while the taskmasters kept driving them on, saying, "Finish your work, the same daily amount as when your straw was supplied."

Complaint of the Foremen

14 The foremen of the Israelites, whom the taskmasters of Pharaoh had placed over them, were beaten, and were asked, "Why have you not completed your prescribed amount of bricks yesterday and today, as before?"

15 Then the Israelite foremen came and made this appeal to Pharaoh: "Why do you treat your servants in this manner? 16 No straw is supplied to

---

4, 16: *Spokesman:* literally, "mouth"; Aaron was to serve as a mouthpiece for Moses, as a prophet does for God; hence the relation between Moses and Aaron is compared to that between God and his prophet. Cf Ex 7, 1.

4, 17: *This staff:* probably the same as that of vv 2ff; but some understand it here of a new staff now given by God to Moses.

4, 18: Moses did not tell his father-in-law his main reason for returning to Egypt, but this secondary motive which he offered was also true.

4, 21: *Make him obstinate:* literally, "harden his heart." God permitted Pharaoh to be stubborn in his opposition to the departure of the Israelites. Cf Rom 9, 17f.

4, 24ff: Apparently God was angry with Moses for having failed to keep the divine command given to Abraham in Gn 17, 10ff. Moses' life is spared when his wife circumcises their son.

5, 6: *The taskmasters and foremen:* the former were higher officials and probably Egyptians; the latter were lower officials, chosen from the Israelites themselves. Cf v 14.

5, 7: Straw was mixed with the clay to give the sun-dried bricks greater consistency.

4, 16: 15f: Ex 7, 1.　　　　　4, 23: Ex 11, 5; 12, 29.
4, 19: Ex 2, 15.23.　　　　　4, 25: Is 6, 2; 7, 20.
4, 22: Sir 36, 11.　　　　　　5, 3: Ex 3, 18.

Why Me?

Read Ex 5, 22–23. Can you imagine how Moses must have felt? He did what God told him to do, and things only got worse for the Israelites. But Moses was still able to talk to God, even if only to say, "Why did you send me?"

Thomas Merton, a famous Trappist monk and spiritual writer, knew that Christians sometimes feel like Moses did:

> The Christian
> must have the courage
> to follow Christ.
> The Christian
> who is risen in Christ
> must dare
> to be like Christ:
> he must dare
> to follow conscience
> even in unpopular causes.
> He must, if necessary,
> be able to disagree with the majority
> and make decisions
> that he knows
> to be according to the Gospel
> and teaching of Christ,
> even when others
> do not understand
> why he is acting this way.
>   (He Is Risen, p. 22)

The next time you are feeling a little like Moses and wondering, Why me? try this prayer:

Faithful God, help me to trust in you during times of disappointment and disillusion. I want to believe you are working in ways I cannot see. Please help my disbelief, for I know that you will honor my best efforts and make things come out right in the end. Amen.

▶ Ex 5, 22–23

your servants, and still we are told to make bricks. Look how your servants are beaten! It is you who are at fault." [17] Pharaoh answered, "It is just because you are lazy that you keep saying, 'Let us go and offer sacrifice to the LORD.' [18] Off to work, then! Straw shall not be provided for you, but you must still deliver your quota of bricks."

[19] The Israelite foremen knew they were in a sorry plight, having been told not to reduce the daily amount of bricks. [20] When, therefore, they left Pharaoh and came upon Moses and Aaron, who were waiting to meet them, [21] they said to them, "The LORD look upon you and judge! You have brought us into bad odor with Pharaoh and his servants and have put a sword in their hands to slay us."

Renewal of God's Promise

[22] Moses again had recourse to the LORD and said, "Lord, why do you treat this people so badly? And why did you send me on such a mission? [23] Ever since I went to Pharaoh to speak in your name, he has maltreated this people of yours, and you have done nothing to rescue them."

6 [1] Then the LORD answered Moses, "Now you shall see what I will do to Pharaoh. Forced by my mighty hand, he will send them away; compelled by my outstretched arm, he will drive them from his land."

[2] God also said to Moses, "I am the LORD. [3]* As God the Almighty I appeared to Abraham, Isaac and Jacob, but my name, LORD, I did not make known to them. [4]* I also established my covenant with them, to give them the land of Canaan, the land in which they were living as aliens. [5]* And now that I have heard the groaning of the Israelites, whom the Egyptians are treating as slaves, I am mindful of my covenant. [6] Therefore, say to the Israelites: I am the LORD. I will free you from the forced labor of the Egyptians and will deliver you from their slavery. I will rescue you by my outstretched arm and with mighty acts of judgment. [7]* I will take you as my own people, and you shall have me as your God. You will know that I, the LORD, am your God when I free you from the labor of the Egyptians [8] and bring you into the land which I swore to give to Abraham, Isaac and Jacob. I will give it to you as your own possession—I, the LORD!" [9] But when Moses told this to the Israelites, they would not listen to him because of their dejection and hard slavery.

[10] Then the LORD said to Moses, [11] "Go and tell Pharaoh, king of Egypt, to let the Israelites leave his

---

6, 3: Gn 17, 1; 35, 11.   6, 5: Ex 2, 24.
6, 4: Gn 15, 18; 17, 4–8.   6, 7: Lv 26, 12.

You Promised, God

The Israelite people had been slaves for so long, they were discouraged and did not believe Moses' liberating message in Ex 6, 1–9. Moses probably sounded crazy to them. The writer of Exodus reminds us of God's faithfulness to God's promises and that God's plans cannot be stopped by human weakness. We too may find it hard to believe in God's power in our life when we feel burdened and oppressed, especially over a long time.

In your prayer, reflect or journal on the following questions and suggestion:

- When do you find it hard to believe in God's promises?
- What people do you know who find it hard to accept God's power in their life?
- What barriers are keeping them from accepting God?
- Make up your own prayer expressing your desire to count on God's promises.

▸ Ex 6, 1–9

land." 12* But Moses protested to the LORD, "If the Israelites would not listen to me, how can it be that Pharaoh will listen to me, poor speaker that I am!" 13 Still, the LORD, to bring the Israelites out of Egypt, spoke to Moses and Aaron and gave them his orders regarding both the Israelites and Pharaoh, king of Egypt.

Genealogy of Moses and Aaron

14*† These are the heads of the ancestral houses. The sons of Reuben, the first-born of Israel, were Hanoch, Pallu, Hezron and Carmi; these are the clans of Reuben. 15* The sons of Simeon were Jemuel, Jamin, Ohad, Jachin, Zohar and Shaul, who was the son of a Canaanite woman; these are the clans of Simeon. 16* The names of the sons of Levi, in their genealogical order, are Gershon, Kohath and Merari. Levi lived one hundred and thirty-seven years.

17* The sons of Gershon, as heads of clans, were Libni and Shimei. 18* The sons of Kohath were Amram, Izhar, Hebron and Uzziel. Kohath lived one hundred and thirty-three years. 19* The sons of Merari were Mahli and Mushi. These are the clans of Levi in their genealogical order.

20*† Amram married his aunt Jochebed, who bore him Aaron, Moses and Miriam. Amram lived one hundred and thirty-seven years. 21 The sons of Izhar were Korah, Nepheg and Zichri. 22 The sons of Uzziel were Mishael, Elzaphan and Sithri. 23* Aaron married Amminadab's daughter, Elisheba, the sister of Nahshon; she bore him Nadab, Abihu, Eleazar and Ithamar. 24 The sons of Korah were Assir, Elkanah and Abiasaph. These are the clans of the Korahites. 25 Aaron's son, Eleazar, married one of Putiel's daughters, who bore him Phinehas. These are the heads of the ancestral clans of the Levites. 26 This is the Aaron and this the Moses to whom the LORD said, "Lead the Israelites from the land of Egypt, company by company." 27 These are the ones who spoke to Pharaoh, king of Egypt, to bring the Israelites out of Egypt—the same Moses and Aaron.

Moses and Aaron before Pharaoh

28 On the day the LORD spoke to Moses in Egypt 29 he said, "I am the LORD. Repeat to Pharaoh, king of Egypt, all that I tell you." 30* But Moses protested to the LORD, "Since I am a poor speaker, how can it be that Pharaoh will listen to me?"

7 1*† The LORD answered him, "See! I have made you as God to Pharaoh, and Aaron your brother shall act as your prophet. 2 You shall tell him all that I command you. In turn, your brother Aaron shall tell Pharaoh to let the Israelites leave his land. 3 Yet I will make Pharaoh so obstinate that, despite the many signs and wonders that I will work in the land of Egypt, 4 he will not listen to you. Therefore I will lay my hand on Egypt and by great acts of judgment I will bring the hosts of my people, the Israelites, out of the land of Egypt, 5 so that the

---

6, 14: The purpose of the genealogy here is to give the line from which Moses and Aaron sprang. Reuben and Simeon are first mentioned because, as older brothers of Levi, their names occur before his in the genealogy.

6, 20: *His aunt:* more exactly, "his father's sister." Later on such a marriage was forbidden. Cf Lv 18, 12. Hence, the Greek and Latin versions render here, "his cousin."

7, 1: Just as God had his prophets to speak to men in his name, so Moses had Aaron as his "prophet" to speak to Pharaoh. Cf Ex 4, 16.

6, 12: Ex 6, 30.
6, 14: Nm 26, 5f; 1 Chr 5, 3.
6, 15: Nm 26, 12; 1 Chr 4, 24.
6, 16: Nm 3, 17; 1 Chr 6, 1.
6, 17: Nm 3, 21; 1 Chr 6, 17; 23, 7.
6, 18: Nm 3, 27; 1 Chr 6, 2. 18.
6, 19: Nm 3, 20; 1 Chr 6, 19; 23, 21.
6, 20: Nm 26, 59.
6, 23: Ru 4, 19f; 1 Chr 2, 10.
6, 30: Ex 6, 12.
7, 1: Ex 4, 15f.

Egyptians may learn that I am the LORD, as I stretch out my hand against Egypt and lead the Israelites out of their midst."

⁶ Moses and Aaron did as the LORD had commanded them. ⁷ Moses was eighty years old and Aaron eighty-three when they spoke to Pharaoh.

The Staff Turned into a Snake

⁸ The LORD told Moses and Aaron, ⁹* "If Pharaoh demands that you work a sign or wonder, you shall say to Aaron: Take your staff and throw it down before Pharaoh, and it will be changed into a snake." ¹⁰ Then Moses and Aaron went to Pharaoh and did as the LORD had commanded. Aaron threw his staff down before Pharaoh and his servants, and it was changed into a snake. ¹¹* Pharaoh, in turn, summoned wise men and sorcerers, and they also, the magicians of Egypt, did likewise by their magic arts. ¹² Each one threw down his staff, and it was changed into a snake. But Aaron's staff swallowed their staffs. ¹³ Pharaoh, however, was obstinate and would not listen to them, just as the LORD had foretold.

First Plague: Water Turned into Blood

¹⁴† Then the LORD said to Moses, "Pharaoh is obdurate in refusing to let the people go. ¹⁵ Tomorrow morning, when he sets out for the water, go and present yourself by the river bank, holding in your hand the staff that turned into a serpent. ¹⁶ Say to him: The LORD, the God of the Hebrews, sent me to you with the message: Let my people go to worship me in the desert. But as yet you have not listened. ¹⁷* The LORD now says: This is how you shall know that I am the LORD. I will strike the water of the river with the staff I hold, and it shall be changed into blood. ¹⁸ The fish in the river shall die, and the river itself shall become so polluted that the Egyptians will be unable to drink its water."

¹⁹ The LORD then said to Moses, "Say to Aaron: Take your staff and stretch out your hand over the waters of Egypt—their streams and canals and pools, all their supplies of water—that they may become blood. Throughout the land of Egypt there shall be blood, even in the wooden pails and stone jars."

²⁰ Moses and Aaron did as the LORD had commanded. Aaron raised his staff and struck the waters of the river in full view of Pharaoh and his servants, and all the water of the river was changed into blood. ²¹ The fish in the river died, and the river itself became so polluted that the Egyptians could not drink its water. There was blood throughout the land of Egypt. ²² But the Egyptian magicians did the same by their magic arts. So Pharaoh remained obstinate and would not listen to Moses and Aaron, just as the LORD had foretold. ²³ He turned away and went into his house, with no concern even for this. ²⁴ All the Egyptians had to dig in the neighborhood of the river for drinking water, since they could not drink the river water.

Second Plague: the Frogs

²⁵ Seven days passed after the LORD had struck the river. ²⁶*† Then the LORD said to Moses, "Go to Pharaoh and tell him: Thus says the LORD: Let my people go to worship me. ²⁷ If you refuse to let them go, I warn you, I will send a plague of frogs over all your territory. ²⁸ The river will teem with frogs. They will come up into your palace and into your bedroom and onto your bed, into the houses of your servants, too, and your subjects, even into your ovens and your kneading bowls. ²⁹ The frogs will swarm all over you and your subjects and your servants."

8 ¹ The LORD then told Moses, "Say to Aaron: Stretch out your hand and your staff over the streams and canals and pools, to make frogs overrun the land of Egypt." ² Aaron stretched out his hand over the waters of Egypt, and the frogs came up and covered the land of Egypt. ³ But the magicians did the same by their magic arts. They, too, made frogs overrun the land of Egypt.

⁴ Then Pharaoh summoned Moses and Aaron and said, "Pray the LORD to remove the frogs from me and my subjects, and I will let the people go to offer sacrifice to the LORD." ⁵ Moses answered Pharaoh, "Do me the favor of appointing the time when I am to pray for you and your servants and your subjects, that the frogs may be taken away from you and your houses and be left only in the river." ⁶ "Tomorrow," said Pharaoh. Then Moses replied, "It shall be as you have said, so that you may learn that there is none like the LORD, our God. ⁷ The frogs shall leave you and your houses, your servants and your subjects; only in the river shall they be left."

⁸ After Moses and Aaron left Pharaoh's presence, Moses implored the LORD to fulfill the promise he had made to Pharaoh about the frogs; ⁹† and the LORD did as Moses had asked. The frogs in the

---

† **7, 14:** Most of the ten plagues of Egypt seem to be similar to certain natural phenomena of that country; but they are represented as supernatural at least in their greater intensity and in their occurring exactly according to Moses' commands.
7, 26—8, 28: This is Ex 8, 1–32 in the verse enumeration of the Vulgate.

8, 9: *Courtyards:* some render "farmhouses."

7, 9: Ex 4, 3.   105, 29; Wis 11, 5–7.
7, 11: 2 Tm 3, 8.   7, 26–29: Pss 78, 45; 105, 30.
7, 17–21: Ex 4, 9; Pss 78, 45;

?did you KNOW?

Plagues and the Crossing of the Red Sea

The writer of Exodus combines several versions of what happened in describing the ten plagues and the crossing of the Red Sea. Like in a fine tapestry, the different strands are carefully woven together to produce a suspenseful story. When Pharaoh refuses to let the Israelites go, God sends ten plagues to convince Pharaoh to cooperate. The first nine plagues are exaggerations of naturally occurring events. For example, Exodus says that the first plague is the water of the Nile turning to blood. At times, silt and microbes pollute and redden the Nile, making the water undrinkable. The Israelite people see God at work in the miraculous timing of these natural events.

Finally, God must resort to drastic measures. For the tenth plague, God sends the angel of death to kill the firstborn children of the Egyptians. Moses has the Israelites mark their doorposts with the blood of a lamb so that the angel of death "passes over" their homes. Pharaoh is now eager to get rid of the Israelites and releases them from service. They gladly begin their journey to God's Promised Land.

After the Israelites leave, Pharaoh regrets his decision and sends his army after them. As the Egyptians close in, the Israelites seem to be trapped at the marshlands by the Red Sea (see map 2, "The Exodus from Egypt"). Although the prose version of this situation in Exodus, chapter 14, and the poetic version in chapter 15 differ in many details, both stress that the Israelites are able to pass through a section of wetlands that was made nearly dry by a strong east wind. The chariot wheels of the Egyptians get stuck in the mud, and as the water returns, they drown. Again, it is the timing of God's help that enables the miraculous escape. God hears God's people and sets them free!

▶ Ex 7, 1—14, 31

houses and courtyards and fields died off. 10 Heaps and heaps of them were gathered up, and there was a stench in the land. 11 But when Pharaoh saw that there was a respite, he became obdurate and would not listen to them, just as the LORD had foretold.

Third Plague: the Gnats

12*† Thereupon the LORD said to Moses, "Tell Aaron to stretch out his staff and strike the dust of the earth, that it may be turned into gnats throughout the land of Egypt." 13 They did so. Aaron stretched out his hand, and with his staff he struck the dust of the earth, and gnats came upon man and beast. The dust of the earth was turned into gnats throughout the land of Egypt. 14* Though the magicians tried to bring forth gnats by their magic arts, they could not do so. As the gnats infested man and beast, 15† the magicians said to Pharaoh, "This is the finger of God." Yet Pharaoh remained obstinate and would not listen to them, just as the LORD had foretold.

Fourth Plague: the Flies

16 Again the LORD told Moses, "Early tomorrow morning present yourself to Pharaoh when he goes forth to the water, and say to him: Thus says the LORD: Let my people go to worship me. 17 If you will not let my people go, I warn you, I will loose swarms of flies upon you and your servants and your subjects and your houses. The houses of the Egyptians and the very ground on which they stand shall be filled with swarms of flies. 18 But on that day I will make an exception of the land of Goshen: there shall be no flies where my people dwell, that you may know that I am the LORD in the midst of the earth. 19 I will make this distinction between my people and your people. This sign shall take place tomorrow." 20* This the LORD did. Thick swarms of flies entered the house of Pharaoh and houses of his servants; throughout Egypt the land was infested with flies.

21 Then Pharaoh summoned Moses and Aaron and said to them, "Go and offer sacrifice to your God in this land." 22† But Moses replied, "It is not right to do so, for the sacrifices we offer to the LORD, our God, are an abomination to the Egyptians. If before their very eyes we offer sacrifices which are an abomination to them, will not the Egyptians

---

8, 12.17: *Gnats, flies*: it is uncertain what species of troublesome insects are here meant.

8, 15: *The finger of God*: understood by the magicians as the *staff* mentioned in Ex 8, 13. Cf Lk 11, 20.

8, 22: The Egyptians would fiercely resent the sacrifice of any animal they considered sacred. Certain animals were worshiped in Egypt, at least as the symbols of various deities.

8, 12f: Ps 105, 31.   8, 20: Pss 78, 45; 105, 31;
8, 14: Wis 17, 7.   Wis 16, 9.

stone us? 23 We must go a three days' journey in the desert to offer sacrifice to the LORD, our God, as he commands us." 24 "Well, then," said Pharaoh, "I will let you go to offer sacrifice to the LORD, your God, in the desert, provided that you do not go too far away and that you pray for me." 25 Moses answered, "As soon as I leave your presence I will pray to the LORD that the flies may depart tomorrow from Pharaoh and his servants and his subjects. Pharaoh, however, must not play false again by refusing to let the people go to offer sacrifice to the LORD." 26 When Moses left Pharaoh's presence, he prayed to the LORD; 27 and the LORD did as Moses had asked. He removed the flies from Pharaoh and his servants and subjects. Not one remained. 28 But once more Pharaoh became obdurate and would not let the people go.

Fifth Plague: the Pestilence

9 ¹ Then the LORD said to Moses, "Go to Pharaoh and tell him: Thus says the LORD, the God of the Hebrews: Let my people go to worship me. ² If you refuse to let them go and persist in holding them, ³ I warn you, the LORD will afflict all your livestock in the field—your horses, asses, camels, herds and flocks—with a very severe pestilence. ⁴ But the LORD will distinguish between the livestock of Israel and that of Egypt, so that none belonging to the Israelites will die." ⁵ And setting a definite time, the LORD added, "Tomorrow the LORD shall do this in the land." 6* And on the next day the LORD did so. All the livestock of the Egyptians died, but not one beast belonging to the Israelites. ⁷ But though Pharaoh's messengers informed him that not even one beast belonging to the Israelites had died, he still remained obdurate and would not let the people go.

Sixth Plague: the Boils

⁸ Then the LORD said to Moses and Aaron, "Take a double handful of soot from a furnace, and in the presence of Pharaoh let Moses scatter it toward the sky. ⁹ It will then turn into fine dust over the whole land of Egypt and cause festering boils on man and beast throughout the land."

¹⁰ So they took soot from a furnace and stood in the presence of Pharaoh. Moses scattered it toward the sky, and it caused festering boils on man and beast. ¹¹ The magicians could not stand in Moses' presence, for there were boils on the magicians no less than on the rest of the Egyptians. ¹² But the LORD made Pharaoh obstinate, and he would not listen to them, just as the LORD had foretold to Moses.

Seventh Plague: the Hail

¹³ Then the LORD told Moses, "Early tomorrow morning present yourself to Pharaoh and say to him: Thus says the LORD, the God of the Hebrews: Let my people go to worship me, ¹⁴ or this time I will hurl all my blows upon you and your servants and your subjects, that you may know that there is none like me anywhere on earth. ¹⁵ For by now I would have stretched out my hand and struck you and your subjects with such pestilence as would wipe you from the earth. 16*† But this is why I have spared you: to show you my power and to make my name resound throughout the earth! ¹⁷ Will you still block the way for my people by refusing to let them go? ¹⁸ I warn you, then, tomorrow at this hour I will rain down such fierce hail as there has never been in Egypt from the day the nation was founded up to the present. ¹⁹ Therefore, order all your livestock and whatever else you have in the open fields to be brought to a place of safety. Whatever man or beast remains in the fields and is not brought to shelter shall die when the hail comes upon them." ²⁰ Some of Pharaoh's servants feared the warning of the LORD and hurried their servants and livestock off to shelter. ²¹ Others, however, did not take the warning of the LORD to heart and left their servants and livestock in the fields.

²² The LORD then said to Moses, "Stretch out your hand toward the sky, that hail may fall upon the entire land of Egypt, on man and beast and every growing thing in the land of Egypt." 23* When Moses stretched out his staff toward the sky, the LORD sent forth hail and peals of thunder. Lightning flashed toward the earth, and the LORD rained down hail upon the land of Egypt; ²⁴ and lightning constantly flashed through the hail, such fierce hail as had never been seen in the land since Egypt became a nation. ²⁵ It struck down every man and beast that was in the open throughout the land of Egypt; it beat down every growing thing and splintered every tree in the fields. ²⁶ Only in the land of Goshen, where the Israelites dwelt, was there no hail.

²⁷ Then Pharaoh summoned Moses and Aaron and said to them, "I have sinned again! The LORD is just; it is I and my subjects who are at fault. ²⁸ Pray to the LORD, for we have had enough of God's thunder and hail. Then I will let you go; you need stay no longer." ²⁹ Moses replied, "As soon as I leave the city I will extend my hands to the LORD; the thunder will cease, and there will be no more hail. Thus you shall learn that the earth is the LORD'S. ³⁰ But you and your servants, I know, do not yet fear the LORD God."

---

† **9, 16:** *To show you:* some ancient versions read, "to show through you." Cf Rom 9, 17.

9, 6: Ps 78, 48.   **9, 23f:** Pss 78, 47; 105, 32f.
9, 16: Rom 9, 17.

31 Now the flax and the barley were ruined, because the barley was in ear and the flax in bud. 32 But the wheat and the spelt were not ruined, for they grow later.

33 When Moses had left Pharaoh's presence and had gone out of the city, he extended his hands to the LORD. Then the thunder and the hail ceased, and the rain no longer poured down upon the earth. 34 But Pharaoh, seeing that the rain and hail and thunder had ceased, sinned again: he with his servants became obdurate, 35 and in his obstinacy he would not let the Israelites go, as the LORD had foretold through Moses.

Eighth Plague: the Locusts

10 1 Then the LORD said to Moses, "Go to Pharaoh, for I have made him and his servants obdurate in order that I may perform these signs of mine among them 2* and that you may recount to your son and grandson how ruthlessly I dealt with the Egyptians and what signs I wrought among them, so that you may know that I am the LORD."

3 So Moses and Aaron went to Pharaoh and told him, "Thus says the LORD, the God of the Hebrews: How long will you refuse to submit to me? Let my people go to worship me. 4 If you refuse to let my people go, I warn you, tomorrow I will bring locusts into your country. 5 They shall cover the ground, so that the ground itself will not be visible. They shall eat up the remnant you saved unhurt from the hail, as well as all the foliage that has since sprouted in your fields. 6 They shall fill your houses and the houses of your servants and of all the Egyptians; such a sight your fathers or grandfathers have not seen from the day they first settled on this soil up to the present day." With that he turned and left Pharaoh.

7 But Pharaoh's servants said to him, "How long must he be a menace to us? Let the men go to worship the LORD, their God. Do you not yet realize that Egypt is being destroyed?" 8 So Moses and Aaron were brought back to Pharaoh, who said to them, "You may go and worship the LORD, your God. But how many of you will go?" 9 "Young and old must go with us," Moses answered, "our sons and daughters as well as our

flocks and herds must accompany us. That is what a feast of the LORD means to us." 10† "The LORD help you," Pharaoh replied, "if I ever let your little ones go with you! Clearly, you have some evil in mind. 11† No, no! Just you men can go and worship the LORD. After all, that is what you want." With that they were driven from Pharaoh's presence.

12* The LORD then said to Moses, "Stretch out your hand over the land of Egypt, that locusts may swarm over it and eat up all the vegetation and whatever the hail has left." 13† So Moses stretched out his staff over the land of Egypt, and the LORD sent an east wind blowing over the land all that day and all that night. At dawn the east wind brought the locusts. 14 They swarmed over the whole land of Egypt and settled down on every part of it. Never before had there been such a fierce swarm of locusts, nor will there ever be. 15 They covered the surface of the whole land, till it was black with them. They ate up all the vegetation in the land and the fruit of whatever trees the hail had spared. Nothing green was left on any tree or plant throughout the land of Egypt.

16 Hastily Pharaoh summoned Moses and Aaron and said, "I have sinned against the LORD, your God, and against you. 17 But now, do forgive me my sin once more, and pray the LORD, your God, to take at least this deadly pest from me." 18 When Moses left the presence of Pharaoh, he prayed to the LORD, 19† and the LORD changed the wind to a very strong west wind, which took up the locusts and hurled them into the Red Sea. But though not a single locust remained within the confines of Egypt, 20 the LORD made Pharaoh obstinate, and he would not let the Israelites go.

Ninth Plague: the Darkness

21† Then the LORD said to Moses, "Stretch out your hand toward the sky, that over the land of Egypt there may be such intense darkness that one can feel it." 22* So Moses stretched out his hand toward the sky, and there was dense darkness throughout the land of Egypt for three days. 23 Men could not see one another, nor could they move from where they were, for three days. But all the Israelites had light where they dwelt.

10, 10: *The LORD help you* . . . : literally, "May the LORD be with you in the same way as I let you . . ."; a sarcastic blessing intended as a curse.

10, 11: Pharaoh realized that if the men alone went they would have to return to their families. He suspected that the Hebrews had no intention of returning.

10, 13: *East wind:* coming across the desert from Arabia, the strong east wind brings Egypt the burning sirocco and, at times, locusts. Cf Ex 14, 21.

10, 19: *The Red Sea:* according to the traditional translation, but the Hebrew is literally, "the Reed Sea"; hence the Red Sea of Exodus

was probably a body of shallow water somewhat to the north of the present deep Red Sea.

10, 21: *Darkness:* at times a storm from the south, called the *khamsin,* blackens the sky of Egypt with sand from the Sahara; the dust in the air is then so thick that the darkness can, in a sense, "be felt."

10, 2: Dt 6, 20ff.   **10, 22:** Ps 105, 28.
10, 12ff: Pss 78, 46; 105, 34f.

²⁴ Pharaoh then summoned Moses and Aaron and said, "Go and worship the LORD. Your little ones, too, may go with you. But your flocks and herds must remain." ²⁵ Moses replied, "You must also grant us sacrifices and holocausts to offer up to the LORD, our God. ²⁶ Hence, our livestock also must go with us. Not an animal must be left behind. Some of them we must sacrifice to the LORD, our God, but we ourselves shall not know which ones we must sacrifice to him until we arrive at the place itself." ²⁷ But the LORD made Pharaoh obstinate, and he would not let them go. ²⁸ "Leave my presence," Pharaoh said to him, "and see to it that you do not appear before me again! The day you appear before me you shall die!" ²⁹ Moses replied, "Well said! I will never appear before you again."

Tenth Plague: the Death of the First-born

11 ¹ Then the LORD told Moses, "One more plague will I bring upon Pharaoh and upon Egypt. After that he will let you depart. In fact, he will not merely let you go; he will drive you away. ²* Instruct your people that every man is to ask his neighbor, and every woman her neighbor, for silver and gold articles and for clothing." ³ The LORD indeed made the Egyptians well-disposed toward the people; Moses himself was very highly regarded by Pharaoh's servants and the people in the land of Egypt.

⁴* Moses then said, "Thus says the LORD: At midnight I will go forth through Egypt. ⁵* Every first-born in this land shall die, from the first-born of Pharaoh on the throne to the first-born of the slave-girl at the handmill, as well as all the first-born of the animals. ⁶ Then there shall be loud wailing throughout the land of Egypt, such as has never been, nor will ever be again. ⁷ But among the Israelites and their animals not even a dog shall growl, so that you may know how the LORD distinguishes between the Egyptians and the Israelites. ⁸* All these servants of yours shall then come down to me, and prostrate before me, they shall beg me, 'Leave us, you and all your followers!' Only then will I depart." With that he left Pharaoh's presence in hot anger.

⁹ The LORD said to Moses, "Pharaoh refuses to listen to you that my wonders may be multiplied in the land of Egypt." ¹⁰ Thus, although Moses and Aaron performed these various wonders in Pharaoh's presence, the LORD made Pharaoh obstinate, and he would not let the Israelites leave his land.

The Passover Ritual Prescribed

12 ¹ The LORD said to Moses and Aaron in the land of Egypt, ²*† "This month shall stand at the head of your calendar; you shall reckon it the first month of the year. ³ Tell the whole community of Israel: On the tenth of this month every one of your families must procure for itself a lamb, one apiece for each household. ⁴† If a family is too small for a whole lamb, it shall join the nearest household in procuring one and shall share in the lamb in proportion to the number of persons who partake of it. ⁵ The lamb must be a year-old male and without blemish. You may take it from either the sheep or the goats. ⁶ You shall keep it until the fourteenth day of this month, and then, with the whole assembly of Israel present, it shall be slaughtered during the evening twilight. ⁷ They shall take some of its blood and apply it to the two doorposts and the lintel of every house in which they partake of the lamb. ⁸ That same night they shall eat its roasted flesh with unleavened bread and bitter herbs. ⁹ It shall not be eaten raw or boiled, but roasted whole, with its head and shanks and inner organs. ¹⁰ None of it must be kept beyond the next morning; whatever is left over in the morning shall be burned up.

¹¹† "This is how you are to eat it: with your loins girt, sandals on your feet and your staff in hand, you shall eat like those who are in flight. It is the Passover of the LORD. ¹² For on this same night I will go through Egypt, striking down every first-born of the land, both man and beast, and executing judgment on all the gods of Egypt—I, the LORD! ¹³* But the blood will mark the houses where you are. Seeing the blood, I will pass over you; thus, when I strike the land of Egypt, no destructive blow will come upon you.

¹⁴ "This day shall be a memorial feast for you, which all your generations shall celebrate with pilgrimage to the LORD, as a perpetual institution. ¹⁵ For seven days you must eat unleavened bread. From the very first day you shall have your houses clear of all leaven. Whoever eats leavened bread from the first day to the seventh shall be cut off from Israel. ¹⁶ On the first day you shall hold a sacred assembly, and likewise on the seventh. On

12, 2: *This month:* Abib, the month of "ripe grain." Cf Ex 13, 4; 23, 15; 34, 18; Dt 16, 1. It occurred near the vernal equinox, March-April. Later it was known by the Babylonian name of Nisan. Cf Neh 2, 1; Est 3, 7.

12, 4: *Share in the lamb:* probably, in the expenses of its purchase. Some explain, "reckon for the lamb the number of persons required to eat it." Cf Ex 12, 10.

12, 11: *Passover:* in Hebrew, *pesach,* in Aramaic, *pascha.* In the following verses the same root is used in the verb "to pass over." The

word may be originally Egyptian, *pesach,* "the blow," i.e., the final plague which destroyed the Egyptian first-born.

11, 2f: Ex 3, 21f; 12, 35f.	**12, 2–20:** Lv 23, 5–8; Nm 9,
11, 4: Ex 12, 12.	2–5; 28, 16ff; Dt 16,
11, 5f: Ex 12, 29f.	1–8.
11, 8: Ex 12, 31ff.	**12, 13:** Heb 11, 28.

? did you KNOW?

The Passover

"Why is this night so different from all other nights?" This question, asked by the youngest member of the family, is part of the Jewish celebration of the Passover. Jewish people continue to celebrate the Passover today in fulfillment of Moses' command, "You shall observe this as a perpetual ordinance for yourselves and your descendants" (Ex 12, 24).

The Passover is celebrated around a meal including lamb and unleavened bread. The lamb recalls the Passover lamb whose blood was placed on the doorpost to protect the firstborn from the angel of death. The unleavened bread recalls the haste in which the people prepared to depart. Retelling the ancient story, generations of Jews have remembered that "night of nights" when the angel of death passed over the Israelites' houses and struck down the firstborn of the Egyptians. On that night, the people of God were finally released from slavery. Thus, Passover is a celebration of God's gift of freedom—a religious Independence Day, so to speak.

It was during the Passover celebration that Jesus had his farewell dinner (see Jn 13, 1), placing himself as the paschal sacrifice. Christians see Jesus as the new Passover; through his death and Resurrection, we are finally liberated from all bondage, including sin and death.

▶ Ex 12, 14–28

these days you shall not do any sort of work, except to prepare the food that everyone needs.

17* "Keep, then, this custom of the unleavened bread. Since it was on this very day that I brought your ranks out of the land of Egypt, you must celebrate this day throughout your generations as a perpetual institution. 18 From the evening of the fourteenth day of the first month until the evening of the twenty-first day of this month you shall eat unleavened bread. 19 For seven days no leaven may be found in your houses. Anyone, be he a resident alien or a native, who eats leavened food shall be cut off from the community of Israel. 20 Nothing leavened may you eat; wherever you dwell you may eat only unleavened bread."

Promulgation of the Passover

21 Moses called all the elders of Israel and said to them, "Go and procure lambs for your families, and slaughter them as Passover victims. 22*† Then take a bunch of hyssop, and dipping it in the blood that is in the basin, sprinkle the lintel and the two doorposts with this blood. But none of you shall go outdoors until morning. 23 For the LORD will go by, striking down the Egyptians. Seeing the blood on the lintel and the two doorposts, the LORD will pass over that door and not let the destroyer come into your houses to strike you down.

24 "You shall observe this as a perpetual ordinance for yourselves and your descendants. 25 Thus, you must also observe this rite when you have entered the land which the LORD will give you as he promised. 26* When your children ask you, 'What does this rite of yours mean?' 27 you shall reply, 'This is the Passover sacrifice of the LORD, who passed over the houses of the Israelites in Egypt; when he struck down the Egyptians, he spared our houses.' "

Then the people bowed down in worship, 28 and the Israelites went and did as the LORD had commanded Moses and Aaron.

Death of the First-born

29* At midnight the LORD slew every first-born in the land of Egypt, from the first-born of Pharaoh on the throne to the first-born of the prisoner in the dungeon, as well as all the first-born of the animals. 30 Pharaoh arose in the night, he and all his servants and all the Egyptians; and there was loud wailing throughout Egypt, for there was not a house without its dead.

Permission To Depart

31 During the night Pharaoh summoned Moses and Aaron and said, "Leave my people at once, you and the Israelites with you! Go and worship the LORD as you said. 32 Take your flocks, too, and your herds, as you demanded, and begone; and you will be doing me a favor."

33 The Egyptians likewise urged the people on, to hasten their departure from the land; they thought that otherwise they would all die. 34 The people,

---

† **12, 22:** Hyssop: a plant with many woody branchlets that made a convenient sprinkler.

12, 17: Ex 13, 3.
12, 22f: Ex 12, 7.13.
12, 26f: Ex 13, 8.14; Dt 6, 20f.
12, 29f: Ex 11, 4ff; Pss 78, 51; 105, 36; 136, 10; Wis 18, 10–16.

therefore, took their dough before it was leavened, in their kneading bowls wrapped in their cloaks on their shoulders. 35* The Israelites did as Moses had commanded: they asked the Egyptians for articles of silver and gold and for clothing. 36 The LORD indeed had made the Egyptians so well-disposed toward the people that they let them have whatever they asked for. Thus did they despoil the Egyptians.

II: The Exodus From Egypt and the Journey to Sinai

Departure from Egypt

37* The Israelites set out from Rameses for Succoth, about six hundred thousand men on foot, not counting the children. 38† A crowd of mixed ancestry also went up with them, besides their livestock, very numerous flocks and herds. 39 Since the dough they had brought out of Egypt was not leavened, they baked it into unleavened loaves. They had been rushed out of Egypt and had no opportunity even to prepare food for the journey.

40*† The time the Israelites had stayed in Egypt was four hundred and thirty years. 41 At the end of four hundred and thirty years, all the hosts of the LORD left the land of Egypt on this very date. 42 This was a night of vigil for the LORD, as he led them out of the land of Egypt; so on this same night all the Israelites must keep a vigil for the LORD throughout their generations.

Passover Regulations

43 The LORD said to Moses and Aaron, "These are the regulations for the Passover. No foreigner may partake of it. 44 However, any slave who has been bought for money may partake of it, provided you have first circumcised him. 45 But no transient alien or hired servant may partake of it. 46*† It must be eaten in one and the same house; you may not take any of its flesh outside the house. You shall not break any of its bones. 47 The whole community of Israel must keep this feast. 48* If any aliens living among you wish to celebrate the Passover of the LORD, all the males among them must first be circumcised, and then they may join in its observance just like the natives. But no man who is uncircumcised may partake of it. 49 The law shall be the same for the resident alien as for the native."

50 All the Israelites did just as the LORD had commanded Moses and Aaron. 51 On that same day the LORD brought the Israelites out of Egypt company by company.

Consecration of First-born

13 1 The LORD spoke to Moses and said, 2* "Consecrate to me every first-born that opens the womb among the Israelites, both of man and beast, for it belongs to me."

3* Moses said to the people, "Remember this day on which you came out of Egypt, that place of slavery. It was with a strong hand that the LORD brought you away. Nothing made with leaven must be eaten. 4 This day of your departure is in the month of Abib. 5 Therefore, it is in this month that you must celebrate this rite, after the LORD, your God, has brought you into the land of the Canaanites, Hittites, Amorites, Hivites and Jebusites, which he swore to your fathers he would give you, a land flowing with milk and honey. 6 For seven days you shall eat unleavened bread, and the seventh day shall also be a festival to the LORD. 7 Only unleavened bread may be eaten during the seven days; no leaven and nothing leavened may be found in all your territory. 8 On this day you shall explain to your son, 'This is because of what the LORD did for me when I came out of Egypt.' 9* It shall be as a sign on your hand and as a reminder on your forehead; thus the law of the LORD will ever be on your lips, because with a strong hand the LORD brought you out of Egypt. 10 Therefore, you shall keep this prescribed rite at its appointed time from year to year.

11 "When the LORD, your God, has brought you into the land of the Canaanites, which he swore to you and your fathers he would give you, 12* you shall dedicate to the LORD every son that opens the womb; and all the male firstlings of your animals shall belong to the LORD. 13 Every first-born of an ass you shall redeem with a sheep. If you do not redeem it, you shall break its neck. Every first-born son you must redeem. 14 If your son should ask you later on, 'What does this mean?' you shall tell him, 'With a strong hand the LORD brought us out of Egypt, that place of slavery. 15 When Pharaoh stubbornly refused to let us go, the LORD killed every first-born in the land of Egypt, every first-born of man and of beast. That is why I sacrifice to the LORD everything of the male sex that opens the womb, and why I redeem every first-born of my sons.'

---

† **12, 38:** *Mixed ancestry:* half-Hebrew and half-Egyptian. Cf Nm 11, 4; Lv 24, 10f.

12, 40: *In Egypt:* according to some ancient sources, "in Canaan and Egypt," thus reckoning from the time of Abraham. Cf Gal 3, 17.

12, 46: *You shall not break any of its bones:* the application of these words to our Lord on the cross shows that the Paschal lamb was a prophetic type of Christ, immolated to free men from the bondage of sin. Cf also 1 Cor 5, 7; 1 Pt 1, 19.

* 12, 35f: Ex 3, 21f; 11, 2f; Ps   13, 2: Ex 13, 12–15.
   105, 37f.   13, 3–10: Ex 12, 2–20.
12, 37: Nm 33, 3ff.   13, 9: Ex 13, 16; Dt 6, 8; 11,
12, 40: Gn 15, 13; Acts 7, 6;   18.
   Gal 3, 17.   13, 12–15: Ex 13, 2; 22, 29f; 34,
12, 46: Nm 9, 12; Jn 19, 36.   19f; Nm 3, 12f; 8, 16;
12, 48: 47f: Nm 9, 14.   18, 15; Dt 15, 19.

EX

God Liberates Us from Oppression!

Many centuries before Christ, the Israelites migrated to Egypt from Canaan, seeking food because of an extreme drought in their land. The Egyptians, taking advantage of the Israelites' need for food and shelter, set taskmasters to rule over them and made their lives bitter with hard service.

■ Have you, your family, or your people ever experienced oppression through forced labor?

■ Are you aware of situations in which people are being oppressed or exploited because of their immigrant status, their educational level, or their need for food and shelter?

■ Pray for God's liberating power, and ask God to give you the strength to fight unjust situations and oppression.

The Israelite people groaned under their slavery and asked God for help. God responded to their plight and sent Moses to lead them into freedom. But they needed to overcome their fear of the unknown future and to step out in trust. Their liberation was accomplished when they responded to God's initiative to free themselves from a life of bondage. To be free, we must first be willing to admit that we are enslaved to something.

■ What types of oppression or pressures have taken away your freedom to live according to God's will?

■ How can your community help young people to recognize when they are enslaved by social and peer pressures?

■ Pray with Psalm 54 to ask for God's help in your struggle. Or pray with Psalm 146 to praise and thank God for liberation that you have experienced.

▶ Ex 14, 1–31

16* Let this, then, be as a sign on your hand and as a pendant on your forehead: with a strong hand the LORD brought us out of Egypt."

Toward the Red Sea

17† Now, when Pharaoh let the people go, God did not lead them by way of the Philistines' land, though this was the nearest; for he thought, should the people see that they would have to fight, they might change their minds and return to Egypt. 18 Instead, he rerouted them toward the Red Sea by way of the desert road. In battle array the Israelites marched out of Egypt. 19* Moses also took Joseph's bones along, for Joseph had made the Israelites swear solemnly that, when God should come to them, they would carry his bones away with them. 20* Setting out from Succoth, they camped at Etham near the edge of the desert. 21*† The LORD preceded them, in the daytime by means of a column of cloud to show them the way, and at night by means of a column of fire to give them light. Thus they could travel both day and night. 22 Neither the column of cloud by day nor the column of fire by night ever left its place in front of the people.

14 1 Then the LORD said to Moses, 2*† "Tell the Israelites to turn about and camp before Pi-hahiroth, between Migdol and the sea. You shall camp in front of Baal-zephon, just opposite, by

---

† 13, 17: By way of the Philistines' land: the most direct route from Egypt to Palestine, along the shore of the Mediterranean.

13, 21: A column of cloud . . . a column of fire: probably one and the same preternatural phenomenon, a central nucleus of fire surrounded by smoke; only at night was its luminous nature visible. Cf Ex 40, 38.

14, 2: These places have not been definitively identified. Even the relative position of Pi-hahiroth and Baal-zephon is not clear; perhaps the former was on the west shore of the sea, where the Israelites were, and the latter on the opposite shore.

* 13, 16: Ex 13, 9.
13, 19: Gn 50, 25; Jos 24, 32.
13, 20: Nm 33, 6.
13, 21f: Ex 40, 38; Nm 9,

15–22; Dt 1, 33; Neh 9, 19; Pss 78, 14; 105, 39; Wis 10, 17.
14, 2: Nm 33, 7f.

the sea. ³ Pharaoh will then say, 'The Israelites are wandering about aimlessly in the land. The desert has closed in on them.' ⁴ Thus will I make Pharaoh so obstinate that he will pursue them. Then I will receive glory through Pharaoh and all his army, and the Egyptians will know that I am the LORD."

This the Israelites did. ⁵ When it was reported to the king of Egypt that the people had fled, Pharaoh and his servants changed their minds about them. "What have we done!" they exclaimed. "Why, we have released Israel from our service!" ⁶ So Pharaoh made his chariots ready and mustered his soldiers— ⁷ six hundred first-class chariots and all the other chariots of Egypt, with warriors on them all. ⁸* So obstinate had the LORD made Pharaoh that he pursued the Israelites even while they were marching away in trumph. ⁹ The Egyptians, then, pursued them;

Pharaoh's whole army, his horses, chariots and charioteers, caught up with them as they lay encamped by the sea, at Pi-hahiroth, in front of Baal-zephon.

Crossing of the Red Sea

¹⁰ Pharaoh was already near when the Israelites looked up and saw that the Egyptians were on the march in pursuit of them. In great fright they cried out to the LORD. ¹¹ And they complained to Moses, "Were there no burial places in Egypt that you had to bring us out here to die in the desert? Why did you do this to us? Why did you bring us out of Egypt? ¹² Did we not tell you this in Egypt, when we said, 'Leave us alone. Let us serve the Egyptians'? Far better for us to be the slaves of the Egyptians than to die in the desert." ¹³ But Moses answered the people, "Fear not! Stand your ground, and you will

LOOK TO THE HILLS

An African American theology professor tells a story about two Israelites who, while crossing the Red Sea, kept looking down at their feet. One said: "Look at my feet. They're covered with mud. This is some fine mess that Moses led us into." They crossed the sea without ever looking up. They never saw the sea parted on either side. As they wiped the mud from their feet and garments, they completely missed the sea's closing and the Egyptians' being swallowed up at God's command!

Although it seems like it would have been impossible to miss something so fantastic as the parting of the Red Sea, it is sometimes easy to focus so much on the negative that the positive is missed. Some people—especially those facing oppression, rejection, injustice, and hardship—keep looking down and miss seeing God's power and their own talents and gifts. Looking down can almost become second nature, poisoning a person's whole attitude. People can waste a lot of time looking down at life's struggles and never looking up.

Brothers and sisters, the resurrected Christ has won victory for all, for people of every race and culture—so look up! Keep your eyes on the prize of the high calling of God in Christ Jesus. Remember the hopeful words in Psalm 121, 1–2:

I raise my eyes toward the mountains.
   From where will my help come?
My help comes from the LORD,
   the maker of heaven and earth.

What do you do when self-doubt and negativity tempt you to keep looking down? How can you encourage others when it seems that the injustices and struggles of life have beaten them down?

▶ Ex 14, 1–31

14, 8: 5–8: Wis 19, 3; 1 Mc 4, 9.

EX

see the victory the LORD will win for you today. These Egyptians whom you see today you will never see again. ¹⁴ The LORD himself will fight for you; you have only to keep still."

¹⁵ Then the LORD said to Moses, "Why are you crying out to me? Tell the Israelites to go forward. ¹⁶ And you, lift up your staff and, with hand outstretched over the sea, split the sea in two, that the Israelites may pass through it on dry land. ¹⁷ But I will make the Egyptians so obstinate that they will go in after them. Then I will receive glory through Pharaoh and all his army, his chariots and charioteers. ¹⁸ The Egyptians shall know that I am the LORD, when I receive glory through Pharaoh and his chariots and charioteers."

¹⁹ The angel of God, who had been leading Israel's camp, now moved and went around behind them. The column of cloud also, leaving the front, took up its place behind them, ²⁰† so that it came between the camp of the Egyptians and that of Israel. But the cloud now became dark, and thus the night passed without the rival camps coming any closer together all night long. ²¹* Then Moses stretched out his hand over the sea, and the LORD swept the sea with a strong east wind throughout the night and so turned it into dry land. When the water was thus divided, ²² the Israelites marched into the midst of the sea on dry land, with the water like a wall to their right and to their left.

Destruction of the Egyptians

²³ The Egyptians followed in pursuit; all Pharaoh's horses and chariots and charioteers went after them right into the midst of the sea. ²⁴ In the night watch just before dawn the LORD cast through the column of the fiery cloud upon the Egyptian force a glance that threw it into a panic; ²⁵ and he so clogged their chariot wheels that they could hardly drive. With that the Egyptians sounded the retreat before Israel, because the LORD was fighting for them against the Egyptians.

²⁶ Then the LORD told Moses, "Stretch out your hand over the sea, that the water may flow back upon the Egyptians, upon their chariots and their charioteers." ²⁷ So Moses stretched out his hand over the sea, and at dawn the sea flowed back to its normal depth. The Egyptians were fleeing head on toward the sea, when the LORD hurled them into its midst. ²⁸* As the water flowed back, it covered the chariots and the charioteers of Pharaoh's whole army which had followed the Israelites into the sea.

Not a single one of them escaped. ²⁹ But the Israelites had marched on dry land through the midst of the sea, with the water like a wall to their right and to their left. ³⁰ Thus the LORD saved Israel on that day from the power of the Egyptians. When Israel saw the Egyptians lying dead on the seashore ³¹* and beheld the great power that the LORD had shown against the Egyptians, they feared the LORD and believed in him and in his servant Moses.

PRAYING

Miriam Leads the People in Praise

The Song at the Sea in Ex 15, 1–21 is probably the oldest writing in the Bible. It is an example of how the Israelite people put stories of God's mighty deeds into song so that they could be remembered and passed on from generation to generation.

Verses 20–21 tell us that the prophetess Miriam led the prayer—singing and dancing. Miriam was Moses and Aaron's sister. The three of them formed a leadership team. Many biblical scholars believe that she may be the author of the song. This is one of the few biblical stories that clearly show a woman serving as a prayer leader.

▸ Ex 15, 1–21

15 ¹*† Then Moses and the Israelites sang this song to the LORD:

> I will sing to the LORD, for he is
> gloriously triumphant;
> horse and chariot he has cast into
> the sea.
> ²* My strength and my courage is the LORD,
> and he has been my savior.
> He is my God, I praise him;
> the God of my father, I extol him.
> ³ The LORD is a warrior,
> LORD is his name!

and leading them to the victorious conquest of the Promised Land.

14, 20: *The cloud now became dark:* the light which it ordinarily cast at night would now have been a help to the Egyptians; its present obscurity serves as a shield for the Israelites. However, the reading of the original text here is not quite certain.

15, 1–21: This canticle (used in Christian liturgy) celebrates God's saving power, miraculously delivering his people from their enemies,

14, 21f: Ex 15, 19; Pss 66, 6; 78, 13; 136, 13f; Wis 10, 18; 19, 7f; Is 63, 12f; Heb 11, 29.
14, 28f: Dt 11, 4; Ps 106, 11.
14, 31f: Ps 106, 12; Wis 10, 20.
15, 1: Ex 15, 21.
15, 2: Ps 118, 14; Is 12, 2.

4   Pharaoh's chariots and army he hurled into
        the sea;
    the elite of his officers were submerged in
        the Red Sea.

5* The flood waters covered them,
        they sank into the depths like a stone.

6   Your right hand, O LORD, magnificent in power,
        your right hand, O LORD, has shattered
        the enemy.

7   In your great majesty you overthrew
        your adversaries;
    you loosed your wrath to consume them
        like stubble.

8   At a breath of your anger the waters piled up,
        the flowing waters stood like a mound,
    the flood waters congealed in the midst of
        the sea.

9   The enemy boasted, "I will pursue and
        overtake them;
    I will divide the spoils and have my fill
        of them;
    I will draw my sword; my hand shall
        despoil them!"

10   When your wind blew, the sea covered them;
        like lead they sank in the mighty waters.

11   Who is like to you among the gods, O LORD?
        Who is like to you, magnificent in holiness?
    O terrible in renown, worker of wonders,

12   when you stretched out your right hand,
        the earth swallowed them!

13   In your mercy you led the people you
        redeemed;
        in your strength you guided them to your
        holy dwelling.

14   The nations heard and quaked:
        anguish gripped the dwellers in Philistia.

15   Then were the princes of Edom dismayed;
        trembling seized the chieftains of Moab;
    All the dwellers in Canaan melted away;

16*   terror and dread fell upon them.
    By the might of your arm they were frozen
        like stone,
    while your people, O LORD, passed over,
    while the people you had made your own
        passed over.

17   And you brought them in and planted them
        on the mountain of your inheritance—
    the place where you made your seat, O LORD,
    the sanctuary, O LORD, which your
        hands established.

18   The LORD shall reign forever and ever.

19* They sang thus because Pharaoh's horses and
chariots and charioteers had gone into the sea, and
the LORD made the waters of the sea flow back upon
them, though the Israelites had marched on dry
land through the midst of the sea. 20 The prophetess Miriam, Aaron's sister, took a tambourine in her
hand, while all the women went out after her with
tambourines, dancing; 21*† and she led them in
the refrain:

Sing to the LORD, for he is gloriously
    triumphant;
    horse and chariot he has cast into the sea.

At Marah and Elim

22* Then Moses led Israel forward from the Red
Sea, and they marched out to the desert of Shur. After traveling for three days through the desert without finding water, 23 they arrived at Marah, where
they could not drink the water, because it was too
bitter. Hence this place was called Marah. 24 As the
people grumbled against Moses, saying, "What are
we to drink?" 25* he appealed to the LORD, who
pointed out to him a certain piece of wood. When
he threw this into the water, the water became fresh.

It was here that the LORD, in making rules and
regulations for them, put them to the test. 26* "If
you really listen to the voice of the LORD, your
God," he told them, "and do what is right in his
eyes: if you heed his commandments and keep all
his precepts, I will not afflict you with any of the
diseases with which I afflicted the Egyptians; for I,
the LORD, am your healer."

27* Then they came to Elim, where there were
twelve springs of water and seventy palm trees, and
they camped there near the water.

The Desert of Sin

16 1† Having set out from Elim, the whole
Israelite community came into the desert
of Sin, which is between Elim and Sinai, on the

15, 21: *She led them:* Miriam's refrain re-echoes the first verse of
this song and was probably sung as an antiphon after each verse.
16, 1: *On the fifteenth day of the second month:* just one full
month after their departure from Egypt. Cf Ex 12, 2.51; Nm 33, 3f.
They encamped in the desert of Sin on a Friday; the murmuring
(vv 2f) occurred on the sabbath, the arrival of the quail (v 13) the
evening before Sunday, followed by six mornings (vv 14–27) of collecting manna before the next sabbath.

15, 5: Neh 9, 11.
15, 16f: Ps 78, 53ff.
15, 19: Ex 14, 21-29.
15, 21: Ex 15, 1.
15, 22f: Nm 33, 8.
15, 25: Sir 38, 5.
15, 26: Dt 7, 15.
15, 27: Nm 33, 9.

fifteenth day of the second month after their departure from the land of Egypt. 2 Here in the desert the whole Israelite community grumbled against Moses and Aaron. 3 The Israelites said to them, "Would that we had died at the LORD'S hand in the land of Egypt, as we sat by our fleshpots and ate our fill of bread! But you had to lead us into this desert to make the whole community die of famine!"

munity, they turned toward the desert, and lo, the glory of the LORD appeared in the cloud! 11 The LORD spoke to Moses and said, 12 "I have heard the grumbling of the Israelites. Tell them: In the evening twilight you shall eat flesh, and in the morning you shall have your fill of bread, so that you may know that I, the LORD, am your God."

13* In the evening quail came up and covered the

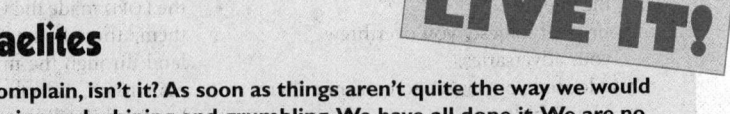

Those Whiny Israelites

LIVE IT!

It's so easy to complain, isn't it? As soon as things aren't quite the way we would like, we start fussing and whining and grumbling. We have all done it. We are no different from the Israelites who, despite having just been miraculously delivered from slavery, start complaining after a few days in the wilderness. "Why," they ask, "would God lead us through the Red Sea only to let us die of hunger?"

Perspective. Faith. That's what it takes. Once we have been through a crisis or spent time in a place where people are truly poor and hungry, we gain a perspective on our own culture, on our own tendency to want everything just the way we like it and as soon as possible. The next time we hear ourselves complaining about something, let's pause and try to see a bigger picture, perhaps the one that God sees. Then we can ask ourselves, Is this really worth complaining about?

▸ Ex 16, 1–3

The Quail and Manna

4*† Then the LORD said to Moses, "I will now rain down bread from heaven for you. Each day the people are to go out and gather their daily portion; thus will I test them, to see whether they follow my instructions or not. 5 On the sixth day, however, when they prepare what they bring in, let it be twice as much as they gather on the other days." 6 So Moses and Aaron told all the Israelites, "At evening you will know that it was the LORD who brought you out of the land of Egypt; 7* and in the morning you will see the glory of the LORD, as he heeds your grumbling against him. But what are we that you should grumble against us? 8 When the LORD gives you flesh to eat in the evening," continued Moses, "and in the morning your fill of bread, as he heeds the grumbling you utter against him, what then are we? Your grumbling is not against us, but against the LORD."

9 Then Moses said to Aaron, "Tell the whole Israelite community: Present yourselves before the LORD, for he has heard your grumbling." 10 When Aaron announced this to the whole Israelite com-

camp. In the morning a dew lay all about the camp, 14 and when the dew evaporated, there on the surface of the desert were fine flakes like hoarfrost on the ground. 15*† On seeing it, the Israelites asked one another, "What is this?" for they did not know what it was. But Moses told them, "This is the bread which the LORD has given you to eat.

Regulations Regarding the Manna

16 "Now, this is what the LORD has commanded. So gather it that everyone has enough to eat, an omer for each person, as many of you as there are, each man providing for those of his own tent." 17 The Israelites did so. Some gathered a large and some a small amount. 18*† But when they measured it out by the omer, he who had gathered a large amount did not have too much, and he who had gathered a small amount did not have too little. They so gathered that everyone had enough to eat. 19 Moses also told them, "Let no one keep any of it over until tomorrow morning." 20 But they would not listen to him. When some kept a part of

---

16, 4: *Bread from heaven:* as a gift from God, the manna is said to come down from the sky. Cf Ps 78, 25; Wis 16, 20. Perhaps it was similar to a natural substance that is still found in small quantities on the Sinai peninsula, but here it is, at least in part, clearly miraculous. Our Lord referred to the manna as a type of the Blessed Eucharist. Cf Jn 6, 32.49–52.

16, 15: *What is this:* the original *man hu* is thus rendered by the ancient versions, which understood the phrase as a popular etymology of the Hebrew word *man,* "manna"; some render, "This is manna."

16, 18: St. Paul cites this passage as an example of equitable sharing. Cf 2 Cor 8, 15.

16, 4: Pss 78, 24f; 105, 40;	16, 13: Nm 11, 31; Ps 78, 27f.
Jn 6, 31f; 1 Cor 10, 3.	16, 15: Dt 8, 3.
16, 7: 6f; Ex 16, 12.	16, 18: 2 Cor 8, 15.

it over until the following morning, it became wormy and rotten. Therefore Moses was displeased with them.

21 Morning after morning they gathered it, till each had enough to eat; but when the sun grew hot, the manna melted away. 22 On the sixth day they gathered twice as much food, two omers for each person. When all the leaders of the community came and reported this to Moses, 23 he told them, "That is what the LORD prescribed. Tomorrow is a day of complete rest, the sabbath, sacred to the LORD. You may either bake or boil the manna, as you please; but whatever is left put away and keep for the morrow." 24 When they put it away for the morrow, as Moses commanded, it did not become rotten or wormy. 25 Moses then said, "Eat it today, for today is the sabbath of the LORD. On this day you will not find any of it on the ground. 26 On the other six days you can gather it, but on the seventh

day, the sabbath, none of it will be there." 27 Still, on the seventh day some of the people went out to gather it, although they did not find any. 28 Then the LORD said to Moses, "How long will you refuse to keep my commandments and laws? 29 Take note! The LORD has given you the sabbath. That is why on the sixth day he gives you food for two days. On the seventh day everyone is to stay home and no one is to go out." 30 After that the people rested on the seventh day.

31*† The Israelites called this food manna. It was like coriander seed, but white, and it tasted like wafers made with honey.

32 Moses said, "This is what the LORD has commanded. Keep an omerful of manna for your descendants, that they may see what food I gave you to eat in the desert when I brought you out of the land of Egypt." 33*† Moses then told Aaron, "Take an urn and put an omer of manna in it. Then place it before

MANNA AND RICE

Rice is the symbol of our life
We eat rice daily
There are different kinds of rice
But we are one
as the rice-eating community
Rice is the symbol of celebration
We express our joy of harvest with it
There are many sufferings in Asia
but we anticipate the time of cosmic celebration.

(From Maren C. Tirabassi and
Kathy Wonson Eddy, editors,
Gifts of Many Cultures, p. 186)

This poem from Japan by Masao and Fumiko Takenaka expresses their appreciation for rice, the most basic food of the Japanese. It unites them as a people and reminds them to be joyful. In a similar way, Exodus tells how the gift of manna united the Israelites and gave them a reason for celebration despite their many trials. What foods unite you and your friends? family? culture? What connections do you see between manna, rice, and the Eucharist?

▸ Ex 16, 1–36

16, 31: *Coriander seed:* small, round, aromatic seeds of bright brown color; the comparison, therefore, refers merely to the size and shape, not to the taste or color of the manna.
16, 33: *Urn:* according to the Greek translation, which is fol-

lowed in Heb 9, 4, this was a golden vessel.

16, 31: Nm 11, 7.   16, 33: Heb 9, 4.

the LORD in safekeeping for your descendants." 34† So Aaron placed it in front of the commandments for safekeeping, as the LORD had commanded Moses.

35* The Israelites ate this manna for forty years, until they came to settled land; they ate manna until they reached the borders of Canaan. 36 [An omer is one tenth of an ephah.]

Water from the Rock

17 1* From the desert of Sin the whole Israelite community journeyed by stages, as the LORD directed, and encamped at Rephidim. Here there was no water for the people to drink. 2* They quarreled, therefore, with Moses and said, "Give us water to drink." Moses replied, "Why do you quarrel with me? Why do you put the LORD to a test?" 3 Here, then, in their thirst for water, the people grumbled against Moses, saying, "Why did you ever make us leave Egypt? Was it just to have us die here of thirst with our children and our livestock?" 4 So Moses cried out to the LORD, "What shall I do with this people? A little more and they will stone me!" 5 The LORD answered Moses, "Go over there in front of the people, along with some of the elders of Israel, holding in your hand, as you go, the staff with which you struck the river. 6* I will be standing there in front of you on the rock in Horeb. Strike the rock, and the water will flow from it for the people to drink." This Moses did, in the presence of the elders of Israel. 7*† The place was called Massah and Meribah, because the Israelites quarreled there and tested the LORD, saying, "Is the LORD in our midst or not?"

Battle with Amalek

8*† At Rephidim, Amalek came and waged war against Israel. 9 Moses, therefore, said to Joshua, "Pick out certain men, and tomorrow go out and engage Amalek in battle. I will be standing on top of the hill with the staff of God in my hand." 10 So Joshua did as Moses told him: he engaged Amalek in battle after Moses had climbed to the top of the hill with Aaron and Hur. 11 As long as Moses kept his hands raised up, Israel had the better of the fight, but when he let his hands rest, Amalek had the better of the fight. 12 Moses' hands, however, grew tired; so they put a rock in place for him to sit on. Meanwhile Aaron and Hur supported his hands, one on one side and one on the other, so that his hands remained steady till sunset. 13 And Joshua mowed down Amalek and his people with the edge of the sword.

14* Then the LORD said to Moses, "Write this down in a document as something to be remembered, and recite it in the ears of Joshua. I will completely blot out the memory of Amalek from under the heavens." 15† Moses also built an altar there, which he called Yahweh-nissi; 16 for he said, "The LORD takes in hand his banner; the LORD will war against Amalek through the centuries."

Meeting with Jethro

18 1 Now Moses' father-in-law Jethro, the priest of Midian, heard of all that God had done for Moses and for his people Israel: how the LORD had brought Israel out of Egypt. 2 So his father-in-law Jethro took along Zipporah, Moses' wife, whom Moses had sent back to him, 3* and her two

Prayer in Support of Others

During the battle against Amalek, Moses' outstretched arms could be understood as a prayer of support for the Israelites. It was an effective prayer, too, because as long as he was able to maintain it, the Israelites were winning. When he could not maintain the prayer by himself, Aaron and Hur helped.

Prayer makes a difference. Research has shown that prayer helps people's emotional and physical health and healing, though it cannot explain why. Spiritual energy is a proven, powerful force.

Prayer doesn't even need words. To hold someone in prayer, just think of her or him and quietly take the pain or joy into your heart.

▶ Ex 17, 8–16

---

†
16, 34: *The commandments:* the two tablets of the ten commandments, which were kept in the ark. Cf Ex 25, 16.21f.

17, 7: *Massah . . . Meribah:* Hebrew words meaning respectively, "the (place of the) test," and, "the (place of the) quarreling."

17, 8: *Amalek:* the Amalekites were an aboriginal people of southern Palestine and the Sinai peninsula. Cf Nm 24, 20.

17, 15: *Yahweh-nissi:* meaning, "the LORD is my banner."

*
16, 35: Jos 5, 12.
17, 1: Nm 33, 12ff.
17, 2–7: Nm 20, 2–13.
17, 6: 5f: Dt 8, 15; Pss 78, 15f;
  105, 41; Wis 11, 4; Is
  43, 20; 48, 21.

17, 7: Ps 95, 8f.
17, 8: Dt 25, 17; 1 Sm 15, 2.
17, 14: Nm 24, 20; 1 Sm 15,
  3.20.
18, 3: Ex 2, 22.

sons. One of these was called Gershom; for he said, "I am a stranger in a foreign land." 4 The other was called Eliezer; for he said, "My father's God is my helper; he has rescued me from Pharaoh's sword." 5 Together with Moses' wife and sons, then, his father-in-law Jethro came to him in the desert where he was encamped near the mountain of God, 6 and he sent word to Moses, "I, Jethro, your father-in-law, am coming to you, along with your wife and her two sons."

7 Moses went out to meet his father-in-law, bowed down before him, and kissed him. Having greeted each other, they went into the tent. 8 Moses then told his father-in-law of all that the LORD had done to Pharaoh and the Egyptians for the sake of Israel, and of all the hardships they had had to endure on their journey, and how the LORD had come to their rescue. 9 Jethro rejoiced over all the goodness that the LORD had shown Israel in rescuing them from the hands of the Egyptians. 10 "Blessed be the LORD," he said,

evening. 14 When his father-in-law saw all that he was doing for the people, he inquired, "What sort of thing is this that you are doing for the people? Why do you sit alone while all the people have to stand about you from morning till evening?" 15 Moses answered his father-in-law, "The people come to me to consult God. 16 Whenever they have a disagreement, they come to me to have me settle the matter between them and make known to them God's decisions and regulations."

17 "You are not acting wisely," his father-in-law replied. 18* "You will surely wear yourself out, and not only yourself but also these people with you. The task is too heavy for you; you cannot do it alone. 19 Now, listen to me, and I will give you some advice, that God may be with you. Act as the people's representative before God, bringing to him whatever they have to say. 20 Enlighten them in regard to the decisions and regulations, showing

Sharing Responsibility **LIVE IT!**

Was Moses a workaholic (see Ex 18, 18)? Maybe he just found himself suddenly overwhelmed by too many responsibilities. Fortunately for Moses, he had a wise father-in-law who could see an alternative that Moses could not see—or maybe did not want to see.

Who in this story do you feel most like?
- Moses, surrounded by people clamoring for your attention
- Jethro, concerned about Moses but able to offer some advice
- one of the people, hoping that Moses has a few minutes to listen to your problem
- one of the trustworthy judges, chosen by Moses to make sure that the Israelites experience justice in all their day-to-day business

When leaders share responsibility, they are saying to other people, "I trust you, we're in this together, and you are needed." When you are in a leadership position, remember Jethro's advice to Moses, and don't be a lone ranger; ask others to help!

▶ Ex 18, 13–26

"who has rescued his people from the hands of Pharaoh and the Egyptians. 11 Now I know that the LORD is a deity great beyond any other; for he took occasion of their being dealt with insolently to deliver the people from the power of the Egyptians." 12 Then Jethro, the father-in-law of Moses, brought a holocaust and other sacrifices to God, and Aaron came with all the elders of Israel to participate with Moses' father-in-law in the meal before God.

Appointment of Minor Judges

13 The next day Moses sat in judgment for the people, who waited about him from morning until

them how they are to live and what they are to do. 21* But you should also look among all the people for able and God-fearing men, trustworthy men who hate dishonest gain, and set them as officers over groups of thousands, of hundreds, of fifties, and of tens. 22 Let these men render decisions for the people in all ordinary cases. More important cases they should refer to you, but all the lesser cases they can settle themselves. Thus, your burden will be lightened, since they will bear it with you. 23 If you do this, when God gives you orders you will be able to stand the strain, and all these people will go home satisfied."

18, 18: Nm 11, 14.   18, 21.25: Dt 1, 15; 16, 18.

?did you KNOW?

The Ten Commandments

The Covenant God made with the Israelites is often called the Sinai Covenant. The Ten Commandments are a handy summary of the Sinai Covenant—literally handy because they can be counted off on one's fingers. Because the Commandments are short (so short that they are sometimes called the Ten Words) and most of them begin with a similar phrase ("You shall not"), they are easily committed to memory. The ancient Israelites believed that everyone had to know and observe these basic rules if God's people were to live together in peace and security. Today, three major world religions—Jewish, Christian, and Islamic—continue to revere the Ten Commandments as basic building blocks of human community.

For the ancient Israelites, the Ten Commandments covered specific behaviors that made them different from the neighboring cultures. Over the centuries, Christians have applied the moral principles of the Ten Commandments to many other moral questions. In fact, the *Catechism of the Catholic Church* presents the Ten Commandments as the structure for teaching about many moral issues. For Jesus' teaching on the Commandments, see Mt 5, 1—7, 29; 22, 34–40; Mk 12, 28–34.

▶ Ex 20, 1–17

---

24 Moses followed the advice of his father-in-law and did all that he had suggested. 25 He picked out able men from all Israel and put them in charge of the people as officers over groups of thousands, of hundreds, of fifties, and of tens. 26 They rendered decisions for the people in all ordinary cases. The more difficult cases they referred to Moses, but all the lesser cases they settled themselves. 27 Then

Moses bade farewell to his father-in-law, who went off to his own country.

III: The Covenant at Mount Sinai

Arrival at Sinai

19 1* In the third month after their departure from the land of Egypt, on its first day, the Israelites came to the desert of Sinai. 2 After the journey from Rephidim to the desert of Sinai, they pitched camp.

While Israel was encamped here in front of the mountain, 3 Moses went up the mountain to God. Then the LORD called to him and said, "Thus shall you say to the house of Jacob; 4* tell the Israelites: You have seen for yourselves how I treated the Egyptians and how I bore you up on eagle wings and brought you here to myself. 5* Therefore, if you hearken to my voice and keep my covenant, you shall be my special possession, dearer to me than all other people, though all the earth is mine. 6*† You shall be to me a kingdom of priests, a holy nation. That is what you must tell the Israelites." 7 So Moses went and summoned the elders of the people. When he set before them all that the LORD had ordered him to tell them, 8 the people all answered together, "Everything the LORD has said, we will do." Then Moses brought back to the LORD the response of the people.

9* The LORD also told him, "I am coming to you in a dense cloud, so that when the people hear me speaking with you, they may always have faith in you also." When Moses, then, had reported to the LORD the response of the people, 10 the LORD added, "Go to the people and have them sanctify themselves today and tomorrow. Make them wash their garments 11 and be ready for the third day; for on the third day the LORD will come down on Mount Sinai before the eyes of all the people. 12* Set limits for the people all around the mountain, and tell them: Take care not to go up the mountain, or even to touch its base. If anyone touches the mountain he must be put to death. 13 No hand shall touch him; he must be stoned to death or killed with arrows. Such a one, man or beast, must not be allowed to live. Only when the ram's horn resounds may they go up to the mountain." 14 Then Moses came down from the mountain to the people and had them sanctify themselves and wash their garments. 15 He warned

---

19, 6: *Kingdom of priests:* inasmuch as the whole Israelite nation was consecrated to God in a special way, it formed a race of royal priests who participated in the liturgical sacrifices, even though the actual offering of the sacrifices was the exclusive prerogative of the Aaronic priesthood. The same condition exists in the New Dispensation as regards the whole Christian people and the Christian priest-

hood in the strict sense. Cf Is 61, 6; 1 Pt 2, 5.9.

19, 1f: Nm 33, 15.   19, 6: 1 Pt 2, 9.
19, 4: Dt 32, 11.   19, 9: Ex 20, 21; 24, 15–18.
19, 5: Dt 7, 6; 14, 2; 26, 18f; 19, 12f: Ex 34, 3; Heb 12, 18f.
   32, 8f.

them, "Be ready for the third day. Have no intercourse with any woman."

The Great Theophany

¹⁶ On the morning of the third day there were peals of thunder and lightning, and a heavy cloud over the mountain, and a very loud trumpet blast, so that all the people in the camp trembled. ¹⁷* But Moses led the people out of the camp to meet God, and they stationed themselves at the foot of the mountain. ¹⁸ Mount Sinai was all wrapped in smoke, for the LORD came down upon it in fire. The smoke rose from it as though from a furnace, and the whole mountain trembled violently. ¹⁹ The trumpet blast grew louder and louder, while Moses was speaking and God answering him with thunder.

²⁰ When the LORD came down to the top of Mount Sinai, he summoned Moses to the top of the mountain, and Moses went up to him. ²¹ Then the LORD told Moses, "Go down and warn the people not to break through toward the LORD in order to see him; otherwise many of them will be struck down. ²² The priests, too, who approach the LORD must sanctify themselves; else he will vent his anger upon them." ²³ Moses said to the LORD, "The people cannot go up to Mount Sinai, for you yourself warned us to set limits around the mountain to make it sacred." ²⁴ The LORD repeated, "Go down now! Then come up again along with Aaron. But the priests and the people must not break through to come up to the LORD; else he will vent his anger upon them." ²⁵ So Moses went down to the people and told them this.

The Ten Commandments

20 ¹† Then God delivered all these commandments:

²* "I, the LORD, am your God, who brought you out of the land of Egypt, *that place of slavery. ³ You shall not have other gods besides me. ⁴* You shall not carve idols for yourselves in the shape of anything in the sky above or on the earth below or in the waters beneath the earth; ⁵*† you shall not bow down before them or worship them. For I, the LORD, your God, am a jealous God, inflicting punishment for their fathers' wickedness on the children of those who hate me, down to the third and fourth generation; ⁶ but bestowing mercy down to the thousandth generation, on the children of those who love me and keep my commandments.

⁷* "You shall not take the name of the LORD, your God, in vain. For the LORD will not leave unpunished him who takes his name in vain.

⁸ "Remember to keep holy the sabbath day. ⁹ Six days you may labor and do all your work, ¹⁰* but the seventh day is the sabbath of the LORD, your God. No work may be done then either by you, or your son or daughter, or your male or female slave, or your beast, or by the alien who lives with you. ¹¹* In six days the LORD made the heavens and the earth, the sea and all that is in them; but on the seventh day he rested. That is why the LORD has blessed the sabbath day and made it holy.

¹²* "Honor your father and your mother, that you may have a long life in the land which the LORD, your God, is giving you.*

Living the Ten Commandments

God gave the Israelites the Ten Commandments, which united them and required from them certain attitudes and behaviors toward God and their fellow Israelites. Obedience to the Commandments became the sign of faithfulness to the Covenant with God. Later, the prophets again and again held the Israelites accountable for this Covenant, calling them to repent and reconcile with God when they disobeyed God's Law.

The Ten Commandments continue to be the moral foundation for Jews and Christians today. How do you use them in making your moral decisions? How familiar are you with church teaching that applies the Ten Commandments today? Ask God for the understanding and the strength to keep God's Commandments, especially those that are the most difficult for you.

▶ Ex 20, 1–17

---

† **20, 1–17:** The precise division of these precepts into "ten commandments" is somewhat uncertain. Traditionally among Catholics vv 1–6 are considered as only one commandment, and v 17 as two. Cf Dt 5, 6–21.

20, 5: *Jealous:* demanding exclusive allegiance, such as a wife must have for her husband.

* 19:17: 16ff: Dt 4, 10ff.
20, 2–17: Dt 5, 6–21.
  20, 2: Lv 26, 13; Ps 81, 10; Hos 13, 4.
  20, 4: Ex 34, 17; Lv 26, 1; Dt 4, 15–19; 27, 15.
  20, 5: Ex 34, 7.14; Nm 14, 18; Dt 4, 24; 6, 15.

  20, 7: Lv 19, 12; 24, 16.
20, 10: 8ff: Ex 23, 12; 31, 13–16; 34, 21; 35, 2; Lv 23, 3.
  20, 11: Ex 31, 17; Gn 2, 2f.
20, 12–16: Mt 19, 18f; Mk 10, 19; Lk 18, 20; Rom 13, 9.
  20, 12: Mt 15, 4; Mk 7, 10; Eph 6, 2f.

The TEN Commandments

1 I, the LORD, am your God . . . You shall not have other gods besides me. **2** You shall not take the name of the LORD, your God, in vain. **3** Remember to keep holy the Sabbath day. **4** Honor your father and your mother. **5** You shall not kill. **6** You shall not commit adultery. **7** You shall not steal. **8** You shall not bear false witness against your neighbor. **9 & 10** You shall not covet your neighbor's house. You shall not covet your neighbor's wife . . . nor anything else that belongs to him.

20, 2-17

13* "You shall not kill.

14* "You shall not commit adultery.

15* "You shall not steal.

16* "You shall not bear false witness against your neighbor.

17* "You shall not covet your neighbor's house. You shall not covet your neighbor's wife, nor his male or female slave, nor his ox or ass, nor anything else that belongs to him."

The Fear of God

18* When the people witnessed the thunder and lightning, the trumpet blast and the mountain smoking, they all feared and trembled. So they took up a position much farther away 19 and said to Moses, "You speak to us, and we will listen; but let not God speak to us, or we shall die." 20 Moses answered the people, "Do not be afraid, for God has come to you only to test you and put his fear upon you, lest you should sin." 21 Still the people remained at a distance, while Moses approached the cloud where God was.

22 The LORD told Moses, "Thus shall you speak to the Israelites: You have seen for yourselves that I have spoken to you from heaven. 23* Do not make anything to rank with me; neither gods of silver nor gods of gold shall you make for yourselves.

20, 13: Mt 5, 21.
20, 14: Lv 18, 20; 20, 10; Dt 22, 22; Mt 5, 27.
20, 15: Lv 19, 11.
20, 16: Ex 23, 1; Dt 19, 16ff; Prv 19, 5.9; 24, 28.
20, 17: Rom 7, 7.
20, 18–21: Dt 4, 11; 5, 22–27; 18,
16; Heb 12, 18f.
20, 23: Ex 20, 3f.

²⁴*† "An altar of earth you shall make for me, and upon it you shall sacrifice your holocausts and peace offerings, your sheep and your oxen. In whatever place I choose for the remembrance of my name I will come to you and bless you. ²⁵* If you make an altar of stone for me, do not build it of cut stone, for by putting a tool to it you desecrate it. ²⁶ You shall not go up by steps to my altar, on which you must not be indecently uncovered.

Laws Regarding Slaves

21 ¹† "These are the rules you shall lay before them. ²* When you purchase a Hebrew slave, he is to serve you for six years, but in the seventh year he shall be given his freedom without cost. ³ If he comes into service alone, he shall leave alone; if he comes with a wife, his wife shall leave with him. ⁴ But if his master gives him a wife and she bears him sons or daughters, the woman and her children shall remain the master's property and the man shall leave alone. ⁵ If, however, the slave declares, 'I am devoted to my master and my wife and children; I will not go free,' ⁶† his master shall bring him to God and there, at the door or doorpost, he shall pierce his ear with an awl, thus keeping him as his slave forever.

⁷ "When a man sells his daughter as a slave, she shall not go free as male slaves do. ⁸† But if her master, who had destined her for himself, dislikes her, he shall let her be redeemed. He has no right to sell her to a foreigner, since he has broken faith with her. ⁹ If he destines her for his son, he shall treat her like a daughter. ¹⁰ If he takes another wife, he shall not withhold her food, her clothing, or her conjugal rights. ¹¹ If he does not grant her these three things, she shall be given her freedom absolutely, without cost to her.

Personal Injury

¹²* "Whoever strikes a man a mortal blow must be put to death. ¹³ He, however, who did not hunt a man down, but caused his death by an act of God, may flee to a place which I will set apart for this purpose. ¹⁴ But when a man kills another after maliciously scheming to do so, you must take him even from my altar and put him to death. ¹⁵ Whoever strikes his father or mother shall be put to death.

¹⁶* "A kidnaper, whether he sells his victim or still has him when caught, shall be put to death.

¹⁷* "Whoever curses his father or mother shall be put to death.

¹⁸ "When men quarrel and one strikes the other with a stone or with his fist, not mortally, but enough to put him in bed, ¹⁹ the one who struck the blow shall be acquitted, provided the other can get up and walk around with the help of his staff. Still, he must compensate him for his enforced idleness and provide for his complete cure.

²⁰ "When a man strikes his male or female slave with a rod so hard that the slave dies under his hand, he shall be punished. ²¹ If, however, the slave survives for a day or two, he is not to be punished, since the slave is his own property.

²²* "When men have a fight and hurt a pregnant woman, so that she suffers a miscarriage, but no further injury, the guilty one shall be fined as much as the woman's husband demands of him, and he shall pay in the presence of the judges. ²³† But if injury ensues, you shall give life for life, ²⁴ eye for eye, tooth for tooth, hand for hand, foot for foot, ²⁵ burn for burn, wound for wound, stripe for stripe.

²⁶ "When a man strikes his male or female slave in the eye and destroys the use of the eye, he shall let the slave go free in compensation for the eye. ²⁷ If he knocks out a tooth of his male or female slave, he shall let the slave go free in compensation for the tooth.

²⁸ "When an ox gores a man or a woman to death, the ox must be stoned; its flesh may not be eaten. The owner of the ox, however, shall go unpunished. ²⁹ But if an ox was previously in the habit of goring people and its owner, though warned, would not keep it in; should it then kill a man or a woman, not only must the ox be stoned, but its owner also must be put to death. ³⁰ If, however, a fine is imposed on him, he must pay in ransom for his life whatever amount is imposed on him. ³¹ This law applies if it is a boy or a girl that the ox gores. ³² But if it is a male or a female slave that it gores, he must pay the owner of the slave thirty shekels of silver, and the ox must be stoned.

20, 24: *I choose for the remembrance of my name:* literally, "where I make my name to be remembered": at the sacred site where God wishes to be worshiped and his name revered.

21, 1: *Rules:* judicial precedents to be used in settling questions of law and custom. This introductory phrase serves as the title of the following collection of civil and religious laws (chapters 21–23) which is called in Ex 24, 7, *the book of the covenant.*

21, 6: *To God:* to the sanctuary; or perhaps the phrase is to be rendered, "to the gods," in the sense of "to the judges." Cf Ps 82, 1. Since the expression "to have an open ear" meant "to obey," a pierced ear lobe was an ancient symbol of obedience. Cf Ps 40, 7.

21, 8: *Destined her:* intended her as a wife of second rank.

21, 23ff: This section is known as the *lex talionis,* the law of tit for

tat. The purpose of this law was not merely the enforcement of rigorous justice, but also the prevention of greater penalties than would be just. Christ refers to this passage when he exhorts Christians to cede their lawful rights for the sake of charity. Cf Mt 5, 38ff.

20, 24: Dt 12, 5.11; 14, 23; 16, 6.
20, 25: Dt 27, 5; Jos 8, 31.
21, 2–6: Lv 25, 39ff; Dt 15, 12–18; Jer 34, 14.
21, 12ff: Lv 24, 17; Nm 35, 15–29; Dt 4, 41f; 19, 2–5.
21, 16: Dt 24, 7.
21, 17: Lv 20, 9; Prv 20, 20; Mt 15, 4; Mk 7, 10.
21, 22–25: Lv 24, 18–21; Dt 19, 21; Mt 5, 38.

EX

Property Damage

33 "When a man uncovers or digs a cistern and does not cover it over again, should an ox or an ass fall into it, 34 the owner of the cistern must make good by restoring the value of the animal to its owner; the dead animal, however, he may keep.

35 "When one man's ox hurts another's ox so badly that it dies, they shall sell the live ox and divide this money as well as the dead animal equally between them. 36 But if it was known that the ox was previously in the habit of goring and its owner would not keep it in, he must make full restitution, an ox for an ox; but the dead animal he may keep.

37*† "When a man steals an ox or a sheep and slaughters or sells it, he shall restore five oxen for the one ox, and four sheep for the one sheep.

22 1† "[If a thief is caught in the act of housebreaking and beaten to death, there is no bloodguilt involved. 2 But if after sunrise he is thus beaten, there is bloodguilt.] He must make full restitution. If he has nothing, he shall be sold to pay for his theft. 3 If what he stole is found alive in his possession, be it an ox, an ass or a sheep, he shall restore two animals for each one stolen.

4† "When a man is burning over a field or a vineyard, if he lets the fires spread so that it burns in another's field, he must make restitution with the best produce of his own field or vineyard. 5 If the fire spreads further, and catches on to thorn bushes, so that shocked grain or standing grain or the field itself is burned up, the one who started the fire must make full restitution.

Trusts and Loans

6 "When a man gives money or any article to another for safekeeping and it is stolen from the latter's house, the thief, if caught, must make twofold restitution. 7† If the thief is not caught, the owner of the house shall be brought to God, to swear that he himself did not lay hands on his neighbor's property. 8 In every question of dishonest appropriation, whether it be about an ox, or an ass, or a sheep, or a garment, or anything else that has disappeared, where another claims that the thing is his, both parties shall present their case before God;

the one whom God convicts must make two-fold restitution to the other.

9 "When a man gives an ass, or an ox, or a sheep, or any other animal to another for safekeeping, if it dies, or is maimed or snatched away, without anyone witnessing the fact, 10 the custodian shall swear by the LORD that he did not lay hands on his neighbor's property; the owner must accept the oath, and no restitution is to be made. 11 But if the custodian is really guilty of theft, he must make restitution to the owner. 12* If it has been killed by a wild beast, let him bring it as evidence, and he need not make restitution for the mangled animal.

13 "When a man borrows an animal from his neighbor, if it is maimed or dies while the owner is not present, the man must make restitution. 14 But if the owner is present, he need not make restitution. If it was hired, this was covered by the price of its hire.

Social Laws

15* "When a man seduces a virgin who is not betrothed, and lies with her, he shall pay her marriage price and marry her. 16† If her father refuses to give her to him, he must still pay him the customary marriage price for virgins.

17* "You shall not let a sorceress live.

18* "Anyone who lies with an animal shall be put to death.

19* "Whoever sacrifices to any god, except to the LORD alone, shall be doomed.

20* "You shall not molest or oppress an alien, for you were once aliens yourselves in the land of Egypt. 21 You shall not wrong any widow or orphan. 22 If ever you wrong them and they cry out to me, I will surely hear their cry. 23 My wrath will flare up, and I will kill you with the sword; then your own wives will be widows, and your children orphans.

24* "If you lend money to one of your poor neighbors among my people, you shall not act like an extortioner toward him by demanding interest from him. 25 If you take your neighbor's cloak as a pledge, you shall return it to him before sunset; 26 for this cloak of his is the only covering he has for his body. What else has he to sleep in? If he cries out to me, I will hear him; for I am compassionate.

21, 37—22, 30: In the Vulgate, 22, 1–31.
22, 1f: *If a thief is caught:* this seems to be a fragment of what was once a longer law on housebreaking, which has been inserted here into the middle of a law on stealing animals. At night the householder would be justified in killing a burglar outright, but not so in the daytime, when the burglar could more easily be caught alive. *He must make full restitution:* this stood originally immediately after 21, 37.
22, 4: The Greek and Latin versions understood this verse as a prohibition against allowing one's cattle to graze in the field of another.

22, 7: *Brought to God:* see note on Ex 21, 6. Cf also Ex 22, 10.
22, 16: *The customary marriage price for virgins:* fifty shekels according to Dt 22, 29.

21, 37: 2 Sm 12, 6.   **22, 20–23:** Ex 23, 9; Lv 19, 33f;
22, 12: Gn 31, 39.   Dt 10, 18f; 24, 17f; 27,
22, 15f: Dt 22, 28f.   19; Zec 7, 10.
22, 17: Lv 19, 26.31; 20, 6.27; **22, 24–26:** Lv 25, 35–38; Dt 23,
        Dt 18, 10f.   19f; 24, 10–13; Ez 18,
22, 18: Lv 18, 23; Dt 27, 21.   7f.17f.
22, 19: Dt 13; 17, 2–7.

Would You Do It?

"You shall not molest or oppress an alien. . . . You shall not wrong any widow or orphan" (Ex 22, 20–21). This section of the Sinai laws reminds the Israelites to take care of the poor and vulnerable in their midst. It reminds the Israelites not to become abusive like the Egyptians.

How can we care for poor people? Consider this story: Mike and Dave were spending some time in New York City. During a walk, they went by the train station, a place where many runaways and homeless people found refuge. They came across a young man hunched over with his back to the wall. His clothes were wet, and he was shivering. He was holding a cup, panhandling. Dave took out some change and threw it into the cup. Mike just stood and stared. Dave motioned to Mike to keep on moving, but Mike didn't move. Then Mike did something that amazed Dave. He sat down and took off his shoes, an almost brand-new pair of insulated leather hiking boots he had received for Christmas. He motioned to the young homeless man to do the same. He took his boots and socks and put them on the young man. Mike put on the young man's old canvas sneakers, stood up, and walked away. Dave followed in silence.

▶ Ex 22, 20–26

27*† "You shall not revile God, nor curse a prince of your people.

28 "You shall not delay the offering of your harvest and your press. You shall give me the first-born of your sons. 29* You must do the same with your oxen and your sheep; for seven days the firstling may stay with its mother, but on the eighth day you must give it to me.

30* "You shall be men sacred to me. Flesh torn to pieces in the field you shall not eat; throw it to the dogs.

23

1* "You shall not repeat a false report. Do not join the wicked in putting your hand, as an unjust witness, upon anyone. 2 Neither shall you allege the example of the many as an excuse for doing wrong, nor shall you, when testifying in a lawsuit, side with the many in perverting justice. 3* You shall not favor a poor man in his lawsuit.

4* "When you come upon your enemy's ox or ass going astray, see to it that it is returned to him. 5 When you notice the ass of one who hates you lying prostrate under its burden, by no means desert him; help him, rather, to raise it up.

6 "You shall not deny one of your needy fellow men his rights in his lawsuit. 7 You shall keep away from anything dishonest. The innocent and the just you shall not put to death, nor shall you acquit the guilty. 8* Never take a bribe, for a bribe blinds even the most clear-sighted and twists the words even of the just. 9* You shall not oppress an alien; you well know how it feels to be an alien, since you were once aliens yourselves in the land of Egypt.

Religious Laws

10* "For six years you may sow your land and gather in its produce. 11 But the seventh year you shall let the land lie untilled and unharvested, that the poor among you may eat of it and the beasts of the field may eat what the poor leave. So also shall you do in regard to your vineyard and your olive grove.

12* "For six days you may do your work, but on the seventh day you must rest, that your ox and your ass may also have rest, and that the son of your maidservant and the alien may be refreshed. 13 Give heed to all that I have told you.

"Never mention the name of any other god; it shall not be heard from your lips.

14*† "Three times a year you shall celebrate a pilgrim feast to me. 15† You shall keep the feast of Unleavened Bread. As I have commanded you, you must eat unleavened bread for seven days at the prescribed time in the month of Abib, for it was then that you came out of Egypt. No one shall appear before me empty-handed. 16 You shall also keep the

† 22, 27: God: or perhaps "the gods," in the sense of "the judges," as the parallel with a prince of your people suggests.
23, 14: These three feasts are elsewhere called the Passover, Pentecost and Booths. Cf Ex 34, 18–26; Lv 23; Dt 16.
23, 15: Appear before me: the original expression was "see my face"; so also in several other places, as Ex 23, 17; 34, 23f; Dt 16, 16; 31, 11.

* 22, 27: Acts 23, 5.
22, 29: Ex 13, 2; 34, 19; Lv 22, 27; Dt 15, 19.
22, 30: Lv 7, 24; 17, 15; 22, 8.
23, 1f: Dt 19, 16ff.
23, 3: Lv 19, 15.
23, 4: Dt 22, 1ff.
23, 8: Dt 16, 19; 27, 25; Sir 20, 28.
23, 9: Ex 22, 21.
23, 10f: Lv 25, 3–7.
23, 12: Ex 20, 8.
23, 14–17: Ex 34, 18.22ff; Lv 23; Dt 16, 1–17.

feast of the grain harvest with the first of the crop that you have sown in the field; and finally, the feast at the fruit harvest at the end of the year, when you gather in the produce from the fields. [17] Thrice a year shall all your men appear before the LORD God.

[18]* "You shall not offer the blood of my sacrifice with leavened bread; nor shall the fat of my feast be kept overnight till the next day. [19]† The choicest first fruits of your soil you shall bring to the house of the LORD, your God.

"You shall not boil a kid in its mother's milk.

Reward of Fidelity

[20]* "See, I am sending an angel before you, to guard you on the way and bring you to the place I have prepared. [21]† Be attentive to him and heed his voice. Do not rebel against him, for he will not forgive your sin. My authority resides in him. [22] If you heed his voice and carry out all I tell you, I will be an enemy to your enemies and a foe to your foes.

[23] "My angel will go before you and bring you to the Amorites, Hittites, Perizzites, Canaanites, Hivites and Jebusites; and I will wipe them out. [24]*† Therefore, you shall not bow down in worship before their gods, nor shall you make anything like them; rather, you must demolish them and smash their sacred pillars. [25] The LORD, your God, you shall worship; then I will bless your food and drink, and I will remove all sickness from your midst; [26] no woman in your land will be barren or miscarry; and I will give you a full span of life.

[27]* "I will have the fear of me precede you, so that I will throw into panic every nation you reach. I will make all your enemies turn from you in flight, [28]† and ahead of you I will send hornets to drive the Hivites, Canaanites and Hittites out of your way. [29] But not in one year will I drive them all out before you; else the land will become so desolate that the wild beasts will multiply against you. [30] Instead, I will drive them out little by little before you, until you have grown numerous enough to take possession of the land. [31]*† I will set your boundaries from the Red Sea to the sea of the Philistines, and from the desert to the River; all who dwell in this land I will hand over to you to be driven out of your way. [32] You shall not make a covenant with them or their gods. [33]* They must not abide in your land, lest they make you sin against me by ensnaring you into worshiping their gods."

? did you KNOW?
Sacrifice and the Eucharist

Sacrifice is defined as an offering made to God that becomes holy by being set apart, blessed, and burned or consumed. Just as food and gifts were brought to a king as a form of tribute and worship, so too in Israel animals were brought to God and sacrificed, their blood splattered on the altar, and their meat cooked and eaten as a form of worship that brought communion with God. The blood symbolized God's gift of life, and when the blessed sacrifice was eaten, communion occurred between God and people. In Exodus, chapter 24, when Israel is about to ratify the Covenant with God, Moses smears the blood of the animal on the altar to assert the Israelites' union with God through the observance of the Covenant.

In the New Testament, the language Jesus uses at his Last Supper seems to reflect this sacrificial understanding. Jesus shares bread and wine as his body and blood and speaks about a New Covenant that will be ratified by the giving of his body and the shedding of his blood. Even today, Catholics celebrating the Eucharist in Jesus' memory encounter the real presence of Jesus in the sacred food of bread and wine, recalling the New Covenant of love he established through giving his body and shedding his blood.

▶ Ex 24, 1–8

Ratification of the Covenant

24 [1] Moses himself was told, "Come up to the LORD, you and Aaron, with Nadab, Abihu, and seventy of the elders of Israel. You shall all worship at some distance, [2] but Moses alone is to come close to the LORD; the others shall not come too near, and the people shall not come up at all with Moses."

23, 19: *Boil a kid in its mother's milk:* this was part of a Canaanite ritual; hence it is forbidden here as a pagan ceremony.

23, 21: *My authority resides in him:* literally, "My name is within him."

23, 24: *Make anything like them:* some render, "act according to their conduct." *Sacred pillars:* objects of religious veneration at Canaanite sanctuaries.

23, 28: *Hornets:* some understand this figuratively of various troublesome afflictions; others translate the Hebrew word as "leprosy." Cf Dt 7, 20; Jos 24, 12; Wis 12, 8.

23, 31: *The sea of the Philistines:* the Mediterranean. *The River:* the Euphrates. Only in the time of David and Solomon did the territory of Israel come near to reaching such distant borders.

23, 18f: Ex 34, 25f.
23, 20: Ex 14, 19; 32, 34; 33, 2.
23, 24: 23f: Ex 34, 10–16; Nm 33, 51f; Dt 7, 24ff.
23, 27f: Dt 2, 25; 7, 20ff.
23, 31: Gn 15, 18; Dt 11, 24; Jos 1, 4.
23, 33:32f: Ex 34, 12–16; Dt 7, 2ff.

3* When Moses came to the people and related all the words and ordinances of the LORD, they all answered with one voice, "We will do everything that the LORD has told us." 4† Moses then wrote down all the words of the LORD and, rising early the next day, he erected at the foot of the mountain an altar and twelve pillars for the twelve tribes of Israel. 5 Then, having sent certain young men of the Israelites to offer holocausts and sacrifice young bulls as peace offerings to the LORD, 6 Moses took half of the blood and put it in large bowls; the other half he splashed on the altar. 7 Taking the book of the covenant, he read it aloud to the people, who answered, "All that the LORD has said, we will heed and do." 8* Then he took the blood and sprinkled it on the people, saying, "This is the blood of the covenant which the LORD has made with you in accordance with all these words of his."

9 Moses then went up with Aaron, Nadab, Abihu, and seventy elders of Israel, 10 and they beheld the God of Israel. Under his feet there appeared to be sapphire tilework, as clear as the sky itself. 11† Yet he did not smite these chosen Israelites. After gazing on God, they could still eat and drink.

Moses on the Mountain

12* The LORD said to Moses, "Come up to me on the mountain and, while you are there, I will give you the stone tablets on which I have written the commandments intended for their instruction." 13 So Moses set out with Joshua, his aide, and went up to the mountain of God. 14 The elders, however, had been told by him, "Wait here for us until we return to you. Aaron and Hur are staying with you. If anyone has a complaint, let him refer the matter to them." 15 After Moses had gone up, a cloud covered the mountain. 16* The glory of the LORD settled upon Mount Sinai. The cloud covered it for six days, and on the seventh day he called to Moses from the midst of the cloud. 17* To the Israelites the glory of the LORD was seen as a consuming fire on the mountaintop. 18* But Moses passed into the midst of the cloud as he went up on the mountain; and there he stayed for forty days and forty nights.

IV: The Dwelling and Its Furnishings

Collection of Materials

25 1* This is what the LORD then said to Moses: 2 "Tell the Israelites to take up a collection for me. From every man you shall accept the contribution that his heart prompts him to give me. 3* These are the contributions you shall accept from them: gold, silver and bronze; 4 violet, purple and scarlet yarn; fine linen and goat hair; 5† rams' skins dyed red, and tahash skins; acacia wood; 6 oil for the light; spices for the anointing oil and for the fragrant incense; 7 onyx stones and other gems for mounting on the ephod and the breastpiece.

8* "They shall make a sanctuary for me, that I may dwell in their midst. 9* This Dwelling and all its furnishings you shall make exactly according to the pattern that I will now show you.

Plan of the Ark

10* "You shall make an ark of acacia wood, two and a half cubits long, one and a half cubits wide, and one and a half cubits high. 11 Plate it inside and outside with pure gold, and put a molding of gold around the top of it. 12 Cast four gold rings and fasten them on the four supports of the ark, two rings on one side and two on the opposite side. 13 Then make poles of acacia wood and plate them with gold. 14 These poles you are to put through the rings on the sides of the ark, for carrying it; 15 they must remain in the rings of the ark and never be withdrawn. 16 In the ark you are to put the commandments which I will give you.

17† "You shall then make a propitiatory of pure gold, two cubits and a half long, and one and a half cubits wide. 18† Make two cherubim of beaten gold for the two ends of the propitiatory, 19 fastening them so that one cherub springs direct from each end. 20 The cherubim shall have their wings spread out above, covering the propitiatory with them; they shall be turned toward each other, but with their faces looking toward the propitiatory. 21 This propitiatory you shall then place on top of the ark. In the ark itself you are to put the commandments

---

24, 4: *Pillars:* stone shafts or slabs, erected as symbols of the fact that each of the twelve tribes had entered into this covenant with God; not idolatrous as in Ex 23, 24, although the same Hebrew word is used in both passages. See note on Gn 28, 18.

24, 11: *After gazing on God:* the ancients thought that the sight of God would bring merely instantaneous death. Cf Ex 33, 20; Gn 16, 13; 32, 31; Jgs 6, 22f; 13, 22. *Eat and drink:* partake of the sacrificial meal.

25, 5: *Tahash:* perhaps the name of a marine animal, such as the dugong or the porpoise. The Greek and Latin versions took it for the color hyacinth.

25, 17: *Propitiatory:* this traditional rendering of the Hebrew term, which may mean merely "cover," is derived from its connection with the ceremony of the Day of Atonement whereby God was rendered "propitious." Cf Lv 16, 14ff.

25, 18ff: *Cherubim:* probably in the form of human-headed winged lions. The cherubim over the ark formed the throne for the invisible Lord. Cf Ps 80, 2. For a more detailed description of the somewhat different cherubim in the temple of Solomon, see 1 Kgs 6, 23–28; 2 Chr 3, 10–13.

24, 3: Ex 19, 8.
24, 8: 5ff: Heb 9, 18ff.
24, 12: Ex 31, 18; 32, 15f; Dt 5, 22.
24, 16: Sir 45, 4.
24, 17: Ex 19, 18; Heb 12, 18.
24, 18: Ex 34, 28; Dt 9, 9.

25, 1–7: Ex 35, 4–9.20–29.
25, 3: Ex 35, 4–9.
25, 8f: Ex 26, 1–30; 36, 8–38.
25, 9: Acts 7, 44.
25, 10–22: Ex 37, 1–9; Heb 9, 1–5.

25, 10–22

which I will give you. 22 There I will meet you and there, from above the propitiatory, between the two cherubim on the ark of the commandments, I will tell you all the commands that I wish you to give the Israelites.

The Table

23* "You shall also make a table of acacia wood, two cubits long, a cubit wide, and a cubit and a half high. 24 Plate it with pure gold and make a molding of gold around it. 25† Surround it with a frame, a handbreadth high, with a molding of gold around the frame. 26 You shall also make four rings of gold for it and fasten them at the four corners, one at each leg, 27 on two opposite sides of the frame as holders for the poles to carry the table. 28 These poles for carrying the table you shall make of acacia wood and plate with gold. 29† Of pure gold you shall make its plates and cups, as well as its pitchers and bowls for pouring libations. 30* On the table you shall always keep showbread set before me.

The Lampstand

31* "You shall make a lampstand of pure beaten gold—its shaft and branches—with its cups and knobs and petals springing directly from it. 32 Six branches are to extend from the sides of the lampstand, three branches on one side, and three on the other. 33† On one branch there are to be three cups, shaped like almond blossoms, each with its knob and petals; on the opposite branch there are to be three cups, shaped like almond blossoms, each with its knob and petals; and so for the six branches that extend from the lampstand. 34† On the shaft there are to be four cups, shaped like almond blossoms, with their knobs and petals, 35 including a knob below each of the three pairs of branches that extend from the lampstand. 36 Their knobs and branches shall so spring from it that the whole will form but a single piece of pure beaten gold. 37*† You shall then make seven lamps for it and so set up the lamps that they shed their light on the space in front of the lampstand. 38† These, as well as the trimming shears and trays, must be of pure gold. 39 Use a talent of pure gold for the lampstand and all its appurtenances. 40* See that you make them according to the pattern shown you on the mountain.

The Tent Cloth

26 1*† "The Dwelling itself you shall make out of sheets woven of fine linen twined and of violet, purple and scarlet yarn, with cherubim embroidered on them. 2 The length of each shall be twenty-eight cubits, and the width four cubits; all the sheets shall be of the same size. 3 Five of the sheets are to be sewed together, edge to edge; and the same for the other five. 4 Make loops of violet yarn along the edge of the end sheet in one set, and the same along the edge of the end sheet in the other set. 5 There are to be fifty loops along the edge of the end sheet in the first set, and fifty loops along the edge of the corresponding sheet in the second set, and so placed that the loops are directly opposite each other. 6 Then make fifty clasps of gold, with which to join the two sets of sheets, so that the Dwelling forms one whole.

25, 25: *A frame:* probably placed near the bottom of the legs to keep them steady. The golden table of Herod's temple is pictured thus on the Arch of Titus.

25, 29f: The *plates* held the showbread, that is, the holy bread which was placed upon the table every sabbath as an offering to God, and was later eaten by the priests. The *cups* held the incense which was strewn upon the bread. Cf Lv 24, 5–9. The libation wine was poured from the *pitchers* into the *bowls*. All these vessels were kept on the golden table.

25, 33: In keeping with the arrangement of the ornaments on the shaft, the three sets of ornaments on each branch were probably so placed that one was at the top and the other two equally spaced along the length of the branch. *Knob:* the cup-shaped seed capsule at the base of a flower.

25, 34f: Of the four ornaments on the shaft, one was at the top and one was below each of the three sets of side branches.

25, 37: The lamps were probably shaped like small boats, with the wick at one end; the end with the wick was turned toward the front of the lampstand.

25, 38: *Trays:* small receptacles for the burnt-out wicks.

26, 1: *Sheets:* strips of tapestry, woven of white linen, the colored threads being used for the cherubim which were embroidered on them. These sheets were stretched across the top of the Dwelling to form a roof, their free ends hanging down inside the boards which formed walls.

25, 23–30: Ex 37, 10–16.　　　　25, 37: Lv 24, 2ff; Nm 8, 2.
25, 30: Lv 24, 5ff.　　　　　　　25, 40: Heb 8, 5.
25, 31–40: Ex 37, 17–24.　　　　26, 1–14: Ex 36, 8–19.

EX

⁷† "Also make sheets woven of goat hair, to be used as a tent covering over the Dwelling. ⁸ Eleven such sheets are to be made; the length of each shall be thirty cubits, and the width four cubits: all eleven sheets shall be of the same size. ⁹† Sew five of the sheets, edge to edge, into one set, and the other six sheets into another set. Use the sixth sheet double at the front of the tent. ¹⁰ Make fifty loops along the edge of the end sheet in one set, and fifty loops along the edge of the end sheet in the second set. ¹¹ Also make fifty bronze clasps and put them into the loops, to join the tent into one whole. ¹² There will be an extra half sheet of tent covering, which shall be allowed to hang down over the rear of the Dwelling. ¹³ Likewise, the sheets of the tent will have an extra cubit's length to be left hanging down on either side of the Dwelling to protect it. ¹⁴ Over the tent itself you shall make a covering of rams' skins dyed red, and above that, a covering of tahash skins.

The Wooden Walls

¹⁵* "You shall make boards of acacia wood as walls for the Dwelling. ¹⁶ The length of each board is to be ten cubits, and its width one and a half cubits. ¹⁷† Each board shall have two arms that shall serve to fasten the boards in line. In this way all the boards of the Dwelling are to be made. ¹⁸ Set up the boards of the Dwelling as follows: twenty boards on the south side, ¹⁹ with forty silver pedestals under the twenty boards, so that there are two pedestals under each board, at its two arms; ²⁰ twenty boards on the other side of the Dwelling, the north side, ²¹ with their forty silver pedestals, two under each board; ²² six boards for the rear of the Dwelling, to the west; ²³ and two boards for the corners at the rear of the Dwelling. ²⁴ These two shall be double at the bottom, and likewise double at the top, to the first ring. That is how both boards in the corners are to be made. ²⁵ Thus, there shall be in the rear eight boards, with their sixteen silver pedestals, two pedestals under each board. ²⁶ Also make bars of acacia wood: five for the boards on one side of the Dwelling, ²⁷ five for those on the other side, and five for those at the rear, toward the west. ²⁸ The center bar, at the middle of the boards, shall reach across from end to end. ²⁹ Plate the boards with gold, and make gold rings on them as holders for the bars, which are also to be plated with gold. ³⁰ You shall erect the Dwelling according to the pattern shown you on the mountain.

The Veils

³¹* "You shall have a veil woven of violet, purple and scarlet yarn, and of fine linen twined, with cherubim embroidered on it.* ³²† It is to be hung on four gold-plated columns of acacia wood, which shall have hooks of gold and shall rest on four silver pedestals. ³³ Hang the veil from clasps. The ark of the commandments you shall bring inside, behind this veil which divides the holy place from the holy of holies. ³⁴ Set the propitiatory on the ark of the commandments in the holy of holies.

³⁵ "Outside the veil you shall place the table and the lampstand, the latter on the south side of the Dwelling, opposite the table, which is to be put on the north side. ³⁶† For the entrance of the tent make a variegated curtain of violet, purple and scarlet yarn and of fine linen twined. ³⁷ Make five columns of acacia wood for this curtain; have them plated with gold, with their hooks of gold; and cast five bronze pedestals for them.

The Altar of Holocausts

27 ¹* "You shall make an altar of acacia wood, on a square, five cubits long and five cubits wide; it shall be three cubits high. ² At the four corners there are to be horns, so made that they spring directly from the altar. You shall then plate it with bronze. ³ Make pots for removing the ashes, as well as shovels, basins, forks and fire pans, all of which shall be of bronze. ⁴† Make a grating of bronze network for it; this to have four bronze rings, one at each of its four corners. ⁵ Put it down around the altar, on the ground. This network is to be half as high as the altar. ⁶ You shall also make poles of acacia wood for the altar, and plate them with bronze. ⁷ These poles are to be put through the rings, so that they are on either side of the altar when it is carried. ⁸† Make the altar itself in the form of a hollow box, just as it was shown you on the mountain.

26, 7: *Tent covering:* the cloth made of sheets of goat hair to cover the Dwelling.

26, 9: Half the width of the end strip was folded back at the front of the Dwelling, thus leaving another half-strip to hang down at the rear. Cf v 12.

26, 17: *Arms:* literally, "hands." According to some, they served as "tongue and groove" to mortise the boards together; according to others, they were pegs at the bottom of the boards and fitted into sockets in the pedestals.

26, 32: *Hooks:* probably placed near the tops of the columns, to hold the rope from which the veils and curtains hung.

26, 36: *Variegated:* without definite designs such as the cherubim on the inner veil.

27, 4: *Grating:* it is not clear whether this was flush with the altar or at some small distance from it; in the latter case the space between the altar and the grating would be filled with stones and serve as a platform around the altar, which would otherwise be too high for the priest to reach conveniently.

27, 8: *Hollow:* probably filled with earth or stones when in use. Cf Ex 20, 24f.

26, 15–30: Ex 36, 20–34.   26, 31–37: Ex 36, 35–38.
26, 31: 2 Chr 3, 14.   27, 1–8: Ex 38, 1–7.

Court of the Dwelling

9* "You shall also make a court for the Dwelling. On the south side the court shall have hangings a hundred cubits long, woven of fine linen twined, 10 with twenty columns and twenty pedestals of bronze; the hooks and bands on the columns shall be of silver. 11 On the north side there shall be similar hangings, a hundred cubits long, with twenty columns and twenty pedestals of bronze; the hooks and bands on the columns shall be of silver. 12 On the west side, across the width of the court, there shall be hangings, fifty cubits long, with ten columns and ten pedestals. 13 The width of the court on the east side shall be fifty cubits. 14 On one side there shall be hangings to the extent of fifteen cubits, with three columns and three pedestals; 15 on the other side there shall be hangings to the extent of fifteen cubits, with three columns and three pedestals.

16 "At the entrance of the court there shall be a variegated curtain, twenty cubits long, woven of violet, purple and scarlet yarn and of fine linen twined. It shall have four columns and four pedestals.

17 "All the columns around the court shall have bands and hooks of silver, and pedestals of bronze. 18 The enclosure of the court is to be one hundred cubits long, fifty cubits wide, and five cubits high. Fine linen twined must be used, and the pedestals must be of bronze. 19 All the fittings of the Dwelling, whatever be their use, as well as all its tent pegs and all the tent pegs of the court, must be of bronze.

Oil for the Lamps

20* "You shall order the Israelites to bring you clear oil of crushed olives, to be used for the light, so that you may keep lamps burning regularly. 21 From evening to morning Aaron and his sons shall maintain them before the LORD in the meeting tent, outside the veil which hangs in front of the commandments. This shall be a perpetual ordinance for the Israelites throughout their generations.

The Priestly Vestments

28 1* "From among the Israelites have your brother Aaron, together with his sons Nadab, Abihu, Eleazar and Ithamar, brought to you, that they may be my priests. 2 For the glorious adornment of your brother Aaron you shall have sacred vestments made. 3 Therefore, to the various expert workmen whom I have endowed with skill, you shall give instructions to make such vestments for Aaron as will set him apart for his sacred service as my priest. 4 These are the vestments they shall make: a breastpiece, an ephod, a robe, a brocaded tunic, a miter and a sash. In making these sacred vestments which your brother Aaron and his sons are to wear in serving as my priests, 5 they shall use gold, violet, purple and scarlet yarn and fine linen.

The Ephod and Breastpiece

6*† "The ephod they shall make of gold thread and of violet, purple and scarlet yarn, embroidered on cloth of fine linen twined. 7 It shall have a pair of shoulder straps joined to its two upper ends. 8 The embroidered belt on the ephod shall extend out from it and, like it, be made of gold thread, of violet, purple and scarlet yarn, and of fine linen twined.

9 "Get two onyx stones and engrave on them the names of the sons of Israel: 10 six of their names on one stone, and the other six on the other stone, in the order of their birth. 11 As a gem-cutter engraves a seal, so shall you have the two stones engraved with the names of the sons of Israel and then mounted in gold filigree work. 12 Set these two stones on the shoulder straps of the ephod as memorial stones of the sons of Israel. Thus Aaron shall bear their names on his shoulders as a reminder before the LORD. 13* Make filigree rosettes of gold, 14 as well as two chains of pure gold, twisted like cords, and fasten the cordlike chains to the filigree rosettes.

15*† "The breastpiece of decision you shall also have made, embroidered like the ephod with gold thread and violet, purple and scarlet yarn on cloth of fine linen twined. 16 It is to be square when folded double, a span high and a span wide. 17† On it you shall mount four rows of precious stones: in the first row, a carnelian, a topaz and an emerald; 18 in the second row, a garnet, a sapphire and a beryl; 19 in the third row, a jacinth, an agate and an amethyst; 20 in the fourth row, a chrysolite, an onyx and a jasper. These stones are to be mounted in gold filigree work, 21 twelve of them to match the names of the sons of Israel, each stone engraved like a seal with the name of one of the twelve tribes.

---

† **28, 6:** *Ephod:* this Hebrew word is retained in the translation because it is the technical term for a peculiar piece of the priestly vestments, the exact nature of which is uncertain. It seems to have been a sort of apron that hung from the shoulders of the priest by *shoulder straps* (v 7) and was tied around his waist by the loose ends of the attached belt (v 8).

28, 15–30: *Breastpiece:* in shape like a modern altar burse, it was a pocketlike receptacle for holding the *Urim* and *Thummim* (v 30), and formed an integral part of the ephod, to which it was attached

by an elaborate system of rings and chains. Both the ephod and its breastpiece were made of brocaded linen.

28, 17–20: The translation of the Hebrew names of some of these gems is quite conjectural.

27, 9–19: Ex 38, 9–20.   Sir 45, 8–14.
27, 20f: Lv 24, 1–4.
28, 1–5: Ex 39, 1; Sir 45, 7.   28, 13f: Ex 28, 22.25;
                                         39, 15.18.
28, 6–12: Ex 39, 2–7;   28, 15–21: Ex 39, 15–21.

22 "When the chains of pure gold, twisted like cords, have been made for the breastpiece, 23 you shall then make two rings of gold for it and fasten them to the two upper ends of the breastpiece. 24 The gold cords are then to be fastened to the two rings at the upper ends of the breastpiece, 25 the other two ends of the cords being fastened in front to the two filigree rosettes which are attached to the shoulder straps of the ephod. 26 Make two other rings of gold and put them on the two lower ends of the breastpiece, on its edge that faces the ephod. 27 Then make two more rings of gold and fasten them to the bottom of the shoulder straps next to where they join the ephod in front, just above its embroidered belt. 28 Violet ribbons shall bind the rings of the breastpiece to the rings of the ephod, so that the breastpiece will stay right above the embroidered belt of the ephod and not swing loose from it.

29 "Whenever Aaron enters the sanctuary, he will thus bear the names of the sons of Israel on the breastpiece of decision over his heart as a constant reminder before the LORD. 30*† In this breastpiece of decision you shall put the Urim and Thummim, that they may be over Aaron's heart whenever he enters the presence of the LORD. Thus he shall always bear the decisions for the Israelites over his heart in the LORD's presence.

Other Vestments

31* "The robe of the ephod you shall make entirely of violet material. 32 It shall have an opening for the head in the center, and around this opening there shall be a selvage, woven as at the opening of a shirt, to keep it from being torn. 33 All around the hem at the bottom you shall make pomegranates, woven of violet, purple and scarlet yarn and fine linen twined, with gold bells between them; 34 first a gold bell, then a pomegranate, and thus alternating all around the hem of the robe. 35 Aaron shall wear it when ministering, that its tinkling may be heard as he enters and leaves the LORD's presence in the sanctuary; else he will die.

36 "You shall also make a plate of pure gold and engrave on it, as on a seal engraving, "Sacred to the LORD." 37* This plate is to be tied over the miter with a violet ribbon in such a way that it rests on the front of the miter, 38 over Aaron's forehead. Since Aaron bears whatever guilt the Israelites may incur in consecrating any of their sacred gifts, this plate must always be over his forehead, so that they may find favor with the LORD.

39* "The tunic of fine linen shall be brocaded. The miter shall be made of fine linen. The sash shall be of variegated work.

40 "Likewise, for the glorious adornment of Aaron's sons you shall have tunics and sashes and turbans made. 41† With these you shall clothe your brother Aaron and his sons. Anoint and ordain them, consecrating them as my priests. 42* You must also make linen drawers for them, to cover their naked flesh from their loins to their thighs. 43 Aaron and his sons shall wear them whenever they go into the meeting tent or approach the altar to minister in the sanctuary, lest they incur guilt and die. This shall be a perpetual ordinance for him and for his descendants.

Consecration of the Priests

29 1* "This is the rite you shall perform in consecrating them as my priests. Procure a young bull and two unblemished rams. 2 With fine wheat flour make unleavened cakes mixed with oil, and unleavened wafers spread with oil, 3 and put them in a basket. Take the basket of them along with the bullock and the two rams. 4 Aaron and his sons you shall also bring to the entrance of the meeting tent, and there wash them with water. 5 Take the vestments and clothe Aaron with the tunic, the robe of the ephod, the ephod itself, and the breastpiece, fastening the embroidered belt of the ephod around him. 6 Put the miter on his head, the sacred diadem on the miter. 7 Then take the anointing oil and anoint him with it, pouring it on his head. 8 Bring forward his sons also and clothe them with the tunics, 9* gird them with the sashes, and tie the turbans on them. Thus shall the priesthood be theirs by perpetual law, and thus shall you ordain Aaron and his sons.

Ordination Sacrifices

10* "Now bring forward the bullock in front of the meeting tent. There Aaron and his sons shall lay their hands on its head. 11 Then slaughter the bullock before the LORD, at the entrance of the meeting tent. 12 Take some of its blood and with your finger put it on the horns of the altar. All the rest of the blood you shall pour out at the base of the altar.

28, 30: *Urim and Thummim:* both the meaning of these Hebrew words and the exact nature of the objects so designated are uncertain. They were apparently lots of some kind which were drawn or cast by the priest to ascertain God's decision in doubtful matters. Hence, the burse in which they were kept was called "the breastpiece of decision."

28, 41: *Ordain them:* literally, "fill their hands," a technical expression used solely for the installation of priests. The phrase probably originated in the custom of placing in the priests' hands the instruments or other symbols of the sacerdotal office.

28, 30: Lv 8, 8; Sir 45, 11.	**28, 42:** Ez 44, 18.
28, 31–35: Ex 39, 20ff; Lv 8, 9; Sir 45, 10.	**29, 1–8:** Lv 8, 1–9.
	29, 9: Lv 8, 13.
28, 37: Ex 39, 31; Lv 8, 9.	**29, 10–26:** Lv 8, 14–30.
28, 39–43: Ex 39, 27ff.	

13 All the fat that covers its inner organs, as well as the lobe of its liver and its two kidneys, together with the fat that is on them, you shall take and burn on the altar. 14* But the flesh and hide and offal of the bullock you must burn up outside the camp, since this is a sin offering.

15 "Then take one of the rams, and after Aaron and his sons have laid their hands on its head, 16 slaughter it. The blood you shall take and splash on all the sides of the altar. 17 Cut the ram into pieces; its inner organs and shanks you shall first wash, and then put them with the pieces and with the head. 18 The entire ram shall then be burned on the altar, since it is a holocaust, a sweet-smelling oblation to the LORD.

19 "After this take the other ram, and when Aaron and his sons have laid their hands on its head, 20 slaughter it. Some of its blood you shall take and put on the tip of Aaron's right ear and on the tips of his sons' right ears and on the thumbs of their right hands and the great toes of their right feet. Splash the rest of the blood on all the sides of the altar. 21 Then take some of the blood that is on the altar, together with some of the anointing oil, and sprinkle this on Aaron and his vestments, as well as on his sons and their vestments, that his sons and their vestments may be sacred.

22† "Now, from this ram you shall take its fat: its fatty tail, the fat that covers its inner organs, the lobe of its liver, its two kidneys with the fat that is on them, and its right thigh, since this is the ordination ram; 23 then, out of the basket of unleavened food that you have set before the LORD, you shall take one of the loaves of bread, one of the cakes made with oil, and one of the wafers. 24† All these things you shall put into the hands of Aaron and his sons, so that they may wave them as a wave offering before the LORD. 25 After you have received them back from their hands, you shall burn them on top of the holocaust on the altar as a sweet-smelling oblation to the LORD. 26 Finally, take the breast of Aaron's ordination ram and wave it as a wave offering before the LORD; this is to be your own portion.

27*† "Thus shall you set aside the breast of whatever wave offering is waved, as well as the thigh of whatever raised offering is raised up, whether this be the ordination ram or anything else belonging to Aaron or to his sons. 28 Such things are due to Aaron and his sons from the Israelites by a perpetual ordinance as a contribution. From their peace offerings, too, the Israelites shall make a contribution, their contribution to the LORD.

29* "The sacred vestments of Aaron shall be passed down to his descendants, that in them they may be anointed and ordained. 30 The descendant who succeeds him as priest and who is to enter the meeting tent to minister in the sanctuary shall be clothed with them for seven days.

31* "You shall take the flesh of the ordination ram and boil it in a holy place. 32 At the entrance of the meeting tent Aaron and his sons shall eat the flesh of the ram and the bread that is in the basket. 33 They themselves are to eat of these things by which atonement was made at their ordination and consecration; but no layman may eat of them, since they are sacred. 34 If some of the flesh of the ordination sacrifice or some of the bread remains over on the next day, this remnant must be burned up; it is not to be eaten, since it is sacred. 35* Carry out all these orders in regard to Aaron and his sons just as I have given them to you.

"Seven days you shall spend in ordaining them, 36*† sacrificing a bullock each day as a sin offering, to make atonement. Thus also shall you purge the altar in making atonement for it; you shall anoint it in order to consecrate it. 37 Seven days you shall spend in making atonement for the altar and in consecrating it. Then the altar will be most sacred, and whatever touches it will become sacred.

38*† "Now, this is what you shall offer on the altar: two yearling lambs as the sacrifice established for each day; 39 one lamb in the morning and the other lamb at the evening twilight. 40 With the first lamb there shall be a tenth of an ephah of fine flour mixed with a fourth of a hin of oil of crushed olives and, as its libation, a fourth of a hin of wine. 41 The other lamb you shall offer at the evening twilight, with the same cereal offering and libation as in the morning. You shall offer this as a sweet-smelling oblation to the LORD. 42 Throughout your generations this established holocaust shall be offered before the LORD at the entrance of the meeting tent, where I will meet you and speak to you.

43* "There, at the altar, I will meet the Israelites; hence, it will be made sacred by my glory. 44 Thus I will consecrate the meeting tent and the altar, just

---

† 29, 22: *Fatty tail:* the thick layer of fat surrounding the tails of sheep and rams bred in Palestine even today. It is regarded as a choice food. Cf Lv 3, 9.

29, 24–26: *Wave offering:* the portions of a peace offering, breast and right thigh, which the officiating priest moved to and fro (waved) in the presence of the Lord. They were reserved for Aaron and his sons.

29, 27–30: These verses are a parenthetical interruption of the ordination ritual; v 31 belongs logically immediately after v 26.

29, 36f: *Purge the altar:* the construction of an altar by profane

hands rendered it impure. The anointing and consecration of the altar purified it and made it sacred.

29, 38–42: A parenthesis inserted into the rubrics for consecrating the altar; v 43 belongs directly after v 37.

29, 14: Heb 13, 11.
29, 27f: Lv 7, 31–34; 10, 14f; Nm 18, 18f; Dt 18, 3.
29, 29: Nm 20, 26.28.
29, 31–34: Lv 8, 31f.
29, 35: Lv 8, 36.
29, 36f: Lv 8, 33ff.
29, 38–42: Nm 28, 3–8.
29, 43: Ex 25, 22.

as I also consecrate Aaron and his sons to be my priests. [45] I will dwell in the midst of the Israelites and will be their God. [46] They shall know that I, the LORD, am their God who brought them out of the land of Egypt, so that I, the LORD, their God, might dwell among them.

Altar of Incense

30 [1]* "For burning incense you shall make an altar of acacia wood, [2] with a square surface, a cubit long, a cubit wide, and two cubits high, with horns that spring directly from it. [3] Its grate on top, its walls on all four sides, and its horns you shall plate with pure gold. Put a gold molding around it. [4] Underneath the molding you shall put gold rings, two on one side and two on the opposite side, as holders for the poles used in carrying it. [5] Make the poles, too, of acacia wood and plate them with gold. [6]* This altar you are to place in front of the veil that hangs before the ark of the commandments where I will meet you.

[7] "On it Aaron shall burn fragrant incense. Morning after morning, when he prepares the lamps, [8] and again in the evening twilight, when he lights the lamps, he shall burn incense. Throughout your generations this shall be the established incense offering before the LORD. [9] On this altar you shall not offer up any profane incense, or any holocaust or cereal offering; nor shall you pour out a libation upon it. [10]* Once a year Aaron shall perform the atonement rite on its horns. Throughout your generations this atonement is to be made once a year with the blood of the atoning sin offering. This altar is most sacred to the LORD."

Census Tax

[11] The LORD also said to Moses, [12]* "When you take a census of the Israelites who are to be registered, each one, as he is enrolled, shall give the LORD a forfeit for his life, so that no plague may come upon them for being registered. [13]* Everyone who enters the registered group must pay a half-shekel, according to the standard of the sanctuary shekel, twenty gerahs to the shekel. This payment of a half-shekel is a contribution to the LORD. [14] Everyone of twenty years or more who enters the registered group must give this contribution to the LORD. [15] The rich need not give more, nor shall the poor give less, than a half-shekel in this contribution to the LORD to pay the forfeit for their lives. [16]* When you receive this forfeit money from the Israelites, you shall donate it to the service of the meeting tent,

that there it may be the Israelites' reminder, before the LORD, of the forfeit paid for their lives."

The Laver

[17] The LORD said to Moses, [18]* "For ablutions you shall make a bronze laver with a bronze base. Place it between the meeting tent and the altar, and put water in it. [19]* Aaron and his sons shall use it in washing their hands and feet. [20] When they are about to enter the meeting tent, they must wash with water, lest they die. Likewise when they approach the altar in their ministry, to offer an oblation to the LORD, [21] they must wash their hands and feet, lest they die. This shall be a perpetual ordinance for him and his descendants throughout their generations."

The Anointing Oil

[22] The LORD said to Moses, [23] "Take the finest spices: five hundred shekels of free-flowing myrrh; half that amount, that is, two hundred and fifty shekels, of fragrant cinnamon; two hundred and fifty shekels of fragrant cane; [24] five hundred shekels of cassia—all according to the standard of the sanctuary shekel; together with a hin of olive oil; [25]* and blend them into sacred anointing oil, perfumed ointment expertly prepared. [26]* With this sacred anointing oil you shall anoint the meeting tent and the ark of the commandments, [27] the table and all its appurtenances, the lampstand and its appurtenances, the altar of incense [28] and the altar of holocausts with all its appurtenances, and the laver with its base. [29] When you have consecrated them, they shall be most sacred; whatever touches them shall be sacred. [30]* Aaron and his sons you shall also anoint and consecrate as my priests. [31] To the Israelites you shall say: As sacred anointing oil this shall belong to me throughout your generations. [32] It may not be used in any ordinary anointing of the body, nor may you make any other oil of a like mixture. It is sacred, and shall be treated as sacred by you. [33] Whoever prepares a perfume like this, or whoever puts any of this on a layman, shall be cut off from his kinsmen."

The Incense

[34]* The LORD told Moses, "Take these aromatic substances: storax and onycha and galbanum, these and pure frankincense in equal parts; [35] and blend them into incense. This fragrant powder, expertly prepared, is to be salted and so kept pure and sacred. [36] Grind some of it into fine dust and put this before the commandments in the meeting tent where I will meet you. This incense shall be treated

---

30, 1–5: Ex 37, 25–28.
30, 6: Ex 40, 26.
30, 10: Lv 16, 18.
30, 12: Nm 1, 2f; 26, 2.

30, 13: Mt 17, 24–27.
30, 16: Ex 38, 25.
30, 18: Ex 38, 8; 40, 7.30.
30, 19ff: Ex 40, 31f.

30, 25: Ex 37, 29.
30, 26–29: Ex 40, 9ff; Lv 8, 10;
Nm 7, 1.

30, 30: Ex 29, 7; Lv 8, 12.
30, 34ff: Ex 25, 6; 37, 29.

as most sacred by you. 37 You may not make incense of a like mixture for yourselves; you must treat it as sacred to the LORD. 38 Whoever makes an incense like this for his own enjoyment of its fragrance, shall be cut off from his kinsmen."

Choice of Artisans

31 1* The LORD said to Moses, 2 "See, I have chosen Bezalel, son of Uri, son of Hur, of the tribe of Judah, 3 and I have filled him with a divine spirit of skill and understanding and knowledge in every craft: 4 in the production of embroidery, in making things of gold, silver or bronze, 5 in cutting and mounting precious stones, in carving wood, and in every other craft. 6 As his assistant I have appointed Oholiab, son of Ahisamach, of the tribe of Dan. I have also endowed all the experts with the necessary skill to make all the things I have ordered you to make: 7* the meeting tent, the ark of the commandments with the propitiatory on top of it, all the furnishings of the tent, 8 the table with its appurtenances, the pure gold lampstand with all its appurtenances, the altar of incense, 9 the altar of holocausts with all its appurtenances, the laver with its base, 10† the service cloths, the sacred vestments for Aaron the priest, the vestments for his sons in

their ministry, 11 the anointing oil, and the fragrant incense for the sanctuary. All these things they shall make just as I have commanded you."

Sabbath Laws

12* The LORD said to Moses, 13 "You must also tell the Israelites: Take care to keep my sabbaths, for that is to be the token between you and me throughout the generations, to show that it is I, the LORD, who make you holy. 14 Therefore, you must keep the sabbath as something sacred. Whoever desecrates it shall be put to death. If anyone does work on that day, he must be rooted out of his people. 15 Six days there are for doing work, but the seventh day is the sabbath of complete rest, sacred to the LORD. Anyone who does work on the sabbath day shall be put to death. 16 So shall the Israelites observe the sabbath, keeping it throughout their generations as a perpetual covenant. 17 Between me and the Israelites it is to be an everlasting token; for in six days the LORD made the heavens and the earth, but on the seventh day he rested at his ease."

18* When the LORD had finished speaking to Moses on Mount Sinai, he gave him the two tablets of the commandments, the stone tablets inscribed by God's own finger.

Caught Up in the Moment

Now that I think about it, it was a stupid thing to do. But it is so hard to be objective when you are caught up in the excitement of the moment. We had been waiting a long time for Moses—too long, it seems. We got bored and restless. You know how it is. Someone came up with the idea of the golden calf. It sounded like fun, something to pass the time and remind us of the old gods. And I have to admit, that calf did look pretty good!

I do feel sorry for Aaron. Moses saw what we had done and hurled the stone tablets to the ground in a fit of rage. Aaron tried to explain how it was, but Moses would hear none of it. He was upset. He had a right to be. There is no valid excuse for what we did. Aaron tried to pretend that the calf sort of formed itself, but it was a feeble excuse. We all knew it. And when we learned what was on the stone tablets, we knew we had done wrong. Moses had those tablets from the hands of God. This was to have been a solemn moment, followed by a great celebration. But instead, we had to face the wrath of Moses and pick up the shattered pieces of stone.

It is so easy to lose sight of what we are all about. It is so easy to do something stupid when we are bored and tired of waiting. And then we wonder how we could have let ourselves get so far off track. It is too easy, isn't it? We are all too human at times.

No, I don't blame Moses for losing his temper. He had every right. We let him down. We let ourselves down. But most of all, we let God down.

▶ Ex 32, 1–35

31, 10: *The service cloths:* so the Greek. They were perhaps the colored cloths mentioned in Nm 4, 4–15.

31, 1–6: Ex 35, 30–35.
31, 7–11: Ex 35, 10–19.
31, 12–17: Ex 20, 8–11; 35, 1–3.

31, 18: Ex 24, 12; 32, 15f; Dt 5, 22.

EX

The Golden Calf

32 [1]* When the people became aware of Moses' delay in coming down from the mountain, they gathered around Aaron and said to him, "Come, make us a god who will be our leader; as for the man Moses who brought us out of the land of Egypt, we do not know what has happened to him." [2] Aaron replied, "Have your wives and sons and daughters take off the golden earrings they are wearing, and bring them to me." [3] So all the people took off their earrings and brought them to Aaron, [4]* who accepted their offering, and fashioning this gold with a graving tool, made a molten calf. Then they cried out, "This is your God, O Israel, who brought you out of the land of Egypt." [5]† On seeing this, Aaron built an altar before the calf and proclaimed, "Tomorrow is a feast of the LORD." [6]* Early the next day the people offered holocausts and brought peace offerings. Then they sat down to eat and drink, and rose up to revel.

[7] With that, the LORD said to Moses, "Go down at once to your people, whom you brought out of the land of Egypt, for they have become depraved. [8]* They have soon turned aside from the way I pointed out to them, making for themselves a molten calf and worshiping it, sacrificing to it and crying out, 'This is your God, O Israel, who brought you out of the land of Egypt!' [9]* I see how stiff-necked this people is," continued the LORD to Moses. [10] "Let me alone, then, that my wrath may blaze up against them to consume them. Then I will make of you a great nation."

[11]* But Moses implored the LORD, his God, saying, "Why, O LORD, should your wrath blaze up against your own people, whom you brought out of the land of Egypt with such great power and with so strong a hand? [12] Why should the Egyptians say, 'With evil intent he brought them out, that he might kill them in the mountains and exterminate them from the face of the earth'? Let your blazing wrath die down; relent in punishing your people. [13]* Remember your servants Abraham, Isaac and Israel, and how you swore to them by your own self, saying, 'I will make your descendants as numerous as the stars in the sky; and all this land that I promised, I will give your descendants as their perpetual heritage.' " [14] So the LORD relented in the punishment he had threatened to inflict on his people.

[15]* Moses then turned and came down the mountain with the two tablets of the commandments in his hands, tablets that were written on both sides, front and back; [16]* tablets that were made by God, having inscriptions on them that were engraved by God himself. [17] Now, when Joshua heard the noise of the people shouting, he said to Moses, "That sounds like a battle in the camp." [18] But Moses answered, "It does not sound like cries of victory, nor does it sound like cries of defeat; the sounds that I hear are cries of revelry." [19]* As he drew near the camp, he saw the calf and the dancing. With that, Moses' wrath flared up, so that he threw the tablets down and broke them on the base of the mountain. [20]*† Taking the calf they had made, he fused it in the fire and then ground it down to powder, which he scattered on the water and made the Israelites drink.

[21] Moses asked Aaron, "What did this people ever do to you that you should lead them into so grave a sin?" Aaron replied, "Let not my lord be angry. [22] You know well enough how prone the people are to evil. [23] They said to me, 'Make us a god to be our leader; as for the man Moses who brought us out of the land of Egypt, we do not know what has happened to him.' [24] So I told them, 'Let anyone who has gold jewelry take it off.' They gave it to me, and I threw it into the fire, and this calf came out."

[25] When Moses realized that, to the scornful joy of their foes, Aaron had let the people run wild, [26]* he stood at the gate of the camp and cried, "Whoever is for the LORD, let him come to me!" All the Levites then rallied to him, [27]† and he told them, "Thus says the LORD, the God of Israel: Put your sword on your hip, every one of you! Now go up and down the camp, from gate to gate, and slay your own kinsmen, your friends and neighbors!" [28] The Levites carried out the command of Moses, and that day there fell about three thousand of the people. [29]† Then Moses said, "Today you have been dedicated to the LORD, for you were against your own sons and kinsmen, to bring a blessing upon yourselves this day."

The Atonement

[30]* On the next day Moses said to the people, "You have committed a grave sin. I will go up to the LORD, then; perhaps I may be able to make atone-

---

† **32, 5:** *The calf . . . a feast of the LORD:* from this it is clear that the golden calf was intended as an image, not of a false god, but of the LORD himself, his strength being symbolized by the strength of a young bull. The Israelites, however, had been forbidden to represent the Lord under any visible form. Cf Ex 20, 4.

32, 20: *The water:* the stream that flowed down Mount Sinai. Cf Dt 9, 21.

32, 27: *Slay your own kinsmen . . . :* those who were especially guilty of the idolatry.

32, 29: *Dedicated to the LORD:* because of their zeal for the true worship of the Lord, the Levites were chosen to be special ministers of the ritual service. However, the meaning of the Hebrew here is somewhat disputed.

---

*
32, 1: Ex 32, 23; Acts 7, 40.	**32, 15:** Dt 9, 15.
32, 4: Ex 32, 8; 1 Kgs 12, 28.	**32, 16:** Ex 31, 18.
32, 6: 1 Cor 10, 7.	**32, 19:** Dt 9, 16f.
32, 8: 7f: Dt 9, 12.16.	**32, 20:** Dt 9, 21.
32, 9f: Dt 9, 13; Ps 106, 23.	**32, 26–29:** Dt 33, 8f.
32, 11f: Nm 14, 13ff; Dt 9, 28.	**32, 30–34:** Dt 9, 18ff.
32, 13: Gn 22, 16f.	

EX

ment for your sin." 31 So Moses went back to the LORD and said, "Ah, this people has indeed committed a grave sin in making a god of gold for themselves! 32† If you would only forgive their sin! If you will not, then strike me out of the book that you have written." 33 The LORD answered, "Him only who has sinned against me will I strike out of my book. 34 Now, go and lead the people whither I have told you. My angel will go before you. When it is time for me to punish, I will punish them for their sin."

35 Thus the LORD smote the people for having had Aaron make the calf for them.

33

1* The LORD told Moses, "You and the people whom you have brought up from the land of Egypt, are to go up from here to the land which I swore to Abraham, Isaac and Jacob I would give to their descendants. 2* Driving out the Canaanites, Amorites, Hittites, Perizzites, Hivites and Jebusites, I will send an angel before you 3 to the land flowing with milk and honey. But I myself will not go up in your company, because you are a stiff-necked people; otherwise I might exterminate you on the way." 4 When the people heard this bad news, they went into mourning, and no one wore his ornaments.

5 The LORD said to Moses, "Tell the Israelites: You are a stiff-necked people. Were I to go up in your company even for a moment, I would exterminate you. Take off your ornaments, therefore; I will then see what I am to do with you." 6 So, from Mount Horeb onward, the Israelites laid aside their ornaments.

Moses' Intimacy with God

7*† The tent, which was called the meeting tent, Moses used to pitch at some distance away, outside the camp. Anyone who wished to consult the LORD would go to this meeting tent outside the camp. 8 Whenever Moses went out to the tent, the people would all rise and stand at the entrance of their own tents, watching Moses until he entered the tent. 9 As Moses entered the tent, the column of cloud would come down and stand at its entrance while the LORD spoke with Moses. 10 On seeing the column of cloud stand at the entrance of the tent, all the people would rise and worship at the entrance of their own tents. 11* The LORD used to speak to Moses face to face, as one man speaks to another.

Moses would then return to the camp, but his young assistant, Joshua, son of Nun, would not move out of the tent.

12* Moses said to the LORD, "You, indeed, are telling me to lead this people on; but you have not let me know whom you will send with me. Yet you have said, 'You are my intimate friend,' and also, 'You have found favor with me.' 13 Now, if I have found favor with you, do let me know your ways so that, in knowing you, I may continue to find favor with you. Then, too, this nation is, after all, your own people." 14† "I myself," the LORD answered, "will go along, to give you rest." 15 Moses replied, "If you are not going yourself, do not make us go up

God Passing By

How close can we get to God without actually seeing God's face? If anyone would know, it is Moses. His rather amazing encounter with God is recorded in Ex 33, 18–23.

We too can experience, as many saints and mystics have, a deep intimacy with God. It is significant that God and Moses most often met in nature. If you are lucky, you have a favorite outdoor spot. Perhaps it is a place where you can simply sit and ponder as you gaze at the scenery before you. Perhaps during a sunset on a lovely summer evening or while gazing at the sea or a flowing stream, you somehow connect with God. You may not actually see or feel the hand of God, but somehow you know that God is with you and you are catching a glimpse of God's glory. You feel yourself held in the palm of God's gracious hand. And sometimes, like Moses (see 34, 29), you are transformed by the power of God's presence.

Where do you most fully experience the presence of God?

▶ Ex 33, 18–23

---

† **32, 32:** *The book that you have written:* the list of God's intimate friends. In a similar sense St. Paul wished to be anathema from Christ for the sake of his brethren. Cf Rom 9, 3.

33, 7–11: *The meeting tent* is mentioned here by anticipation; its actual construction is described in the following chapters.

33, 14: *I myself:* literally, "my face," that is, "my presence." *To give you rest:* in the Promised Land; some understand, "to put your

mind at rest"; others, by a slight emendation in the text, render, "to lead you."

33, 1: Gn 12, 7.
33, 2: Ex 23, 23.
33, 7: Ex 29, 42f.
33, 11: Nm 12, 8; Dt 34, 10; Sir 45, 4–6.
33, 12: Ex 32, 34.

from here. [16] For how can it be known that we, your people and I, have found favor with you, except by your going with us? Then we, your people and I, will be singled out from every other people on the earth." [17] The LORD said to Moses, "This request, too, which you have just made, I will carry out, because you have found favor with me and you are my intimate friend."

[18] Then Moses said, "Do let me see your glory!" [19]* He answered, "I will make all my beauty pass before you, and in your presence I will pronounce my name, 'LORD'; I who show favors to whom I will, I who grant mercy to whom I will. [20]* But my face you cannot see, for no man sees me and still lives. [21] Here," continued the LORD, "is a place near me where you shall station yourself on the rock. [22] When my glory passes I will set you in the hollow of the rock and will cover you with my hand until I have passed by. [23]† Then I will remove my hand, so that you may see my back; but my face is not to be seen."

Renewal of the Tablets

34 [1]* The LORD said to Moses, "Cut two stone tablets like the former, that I may write on them the commandments which were on the former tablets that you broke. [2] Get ready for tomorrow morning, when you are to go up Mount Sinai and there present yourself to me on the top of the mountain. [3]* No one shall come up with you, and no one is even to be seen on any part of the mountain; even the flocks and the herds are not to go grazing toward this mountain." [4] Moses then cut two stone tablets like the former, and early the next morning he went up Mount Sinai as the LORD had commanded him, taking along the two stone tablets.

[5] Having come down in a cloud, the LORD stood with him there and proclaimed his name, "LORD." [6] Thus the LORD passed before him and cried out, "The LORD, the LORD, a merciful and gracious God, slow to anger and rich in kindness and fidelity, [7]* continuing his kindness for a thousand generations, and forgiving wickedness and crime and sin; yet not declaring the guilty guiltless, but punishing children and grandchildren to the third and fourth generation for their fathers' wickedness!" [8] Moses at once bowed down to the ground in worship. [9] Then he said, "If I find favor with you, O LORD, do come

along in our company. This is indeed a stiff-necked people; yet pardon our wickedness and sins, and receive us as your own."

Religious Laws

[10] "Here, then," said the LORD, "is the covenant I will make. Before the eyes of all your people I will work such marvels as have never been wrought in any nation anywhere on earth, so that this people among whom you live may see how awe-inspiring are the deeds which I, the LORD, will do at your side. [11]* But you, on your part, must keep the commandments I am giving you today.

"I will drive out before you the Amorites, Canaanites, Hittites, Perizzites, Hivites, and Jebusites. [12]* Take care, therefore, not to make a covenant with these inhabitants of the land that you are to enter; else they will become a snare among you. [13]† Tear down their altars; smash their sacred pillars, and cut down their sacred poles. [14]† You shall not worship any other god, for the LORD is 'the Jealous One'; a jealous God is he. [15] Do not make a covenant with the inhabitants of that land; else, when they render their wanton worship to their gods and sacrifice to them, one of them may invite you and you may partake of his sacrifice. [16] Neither shall you take their daughters as wives for your sons; otherwise, when their daughters render their wanton worship to their gods, they will make your sons do the same.

[17]* "You shall not make for yourselves molten gods.

[18]* "You shall keep the feast of Unleavened Bread. For seven days at the prescribed time in the month of Abib you are to eat unleavened bread, as I commanded you; for in the month of Abib you came out of Egypt.

[19]* "To me belongs every first-born male that opens the womb among all your livestock, whether in the herd or in the flock. [20] The firstling of an ass you shall redeem with one of the flock; if you do not redeem it, you must break its neck. The first-born among your sons you shall redeem.

"No one shall appear before me empty-handed.

[21]* "For six days you may work, but on the seventh day you shall rest; on that day you must rest even during the seasons of plowing and harvesting.

[22]*† "You shall keep the feast of Weeks with the

33, 23: *You may see my back:* man can see God's glory as reflected in creation, but his "face," that is, God as he is in himself, mortal man cannot behold. Cf 1 Cor 13, 12.

34, 13: *Sacred poles:* "Ashera" was the name of a Canaanite goddess. In her honor wooden poles (*asherot*) were erected, just as stone pillars (*massebot*) were erected in honor of the god Baal. Both were placed near the altar in a Canaanite shrine.

34, 14: *The LORD is 'the Jealous One':* see note on Ex 20, 5. Some, by a slight emendation, render, "The LORD is jealous for his name." Cf Ez 39, 25.

34, 22: *Feast of Weeks:* the festival of thanksgiving for the harvest,

celebrated seven weeks or fifty days after the beginning of the harvest. It was also called Pentecost (fiftieth) and coincided with the giving of the law on Mount Sinai, fifty days after the offering of the first fruits (Lv 23 10f; Dt 16, 9).

33, 19: Rom 9, 15.	12, 2f.
33, 20: Jn 1, 18; 1 Tm 6, 16.	**34, 17:** Lv 19, 4; 5, 8f.
34, 1: Dt 10, 1f.	**34, 18:** Ex 12, 15ff; 13, 3f.
34, 3: Ex 19, 12f.21.	**34, 19f:** Ex 13, 2.12f;
34, 7: 6f: Ex 20, 5f; Nm 14, 18;	23, 15.
Dt 5, 9f; Jer 32, 18.	**34, 21:** Ex 20, 9f.
34, 11: Ex 13, 5; 33, 2.	**34, 22f:** Ex 23, 16f; Dt 16,
34, 12–16: Ex 23, 32f; Dt 7, 1–5;	10.13.16.

first of the wheat harvest; likewise, the feast at the fruit harvest at the close of the year. 23 Three times a year all your men shall appear before the Lord, the LORD God of Israel. 24 Since I will drive out the nations before you to give you a large territory, there will be no one to covet your land when you go up three times a year to appear before the LORD, your God.

25 "You shall not offer me the blood of sacrifice with leavened bread, nor shall the sacrifice of the Passover feast be kept overnight for the next day.

26* "The choicest first fruits of your soil you shall bring to the house of the LORD, your God.

"You shall not boil a kid in its mother's milk."

Radiance of Moses' Face

27 Then the LORD said to Moses, "Write down these words, for in accordance with them I have made a covenant with you and with Israel." 28* So Moses stayed there with the LORD for forty days and forty nights, without eating any food or drinking any water, and he wrote on the tablets the words of the covenant, the ten commandments.

29 As Moses came down from Mount Sinai with the two tablets of the commandments in his hands, he did not know that the skin of his face had become radiant while he conversed with the LORD. 30 When Aaron, then, and the other Israelites saw Moses and noticed how radiant the skin of his face had become, they were afraid to come near him. 31 Only after Moses called to them did Aaron and all the rulers of the community come back to him. Moses then spoke to them. 32 Later on, all the Israelites came up to him, and he enjoined on them all that the LORD had told him on Mount Sinai. 33† When he finished speaking with them, he put a veil over his face. 34* Whenever Moses entered the presence of the LORD to converse with him, he removed the veil until he came out again. On coming out, he would tell the Israelites all that had been commanded. 35 Then the Israelites would see that the skin of Moses' face was radiant; so he would again put the veil over his face until he went in to converse with the LORD.

Sabbath Regulations

35 1* Moses assembled the whole Israelite community and said to them, "This is what the LORD has commanded to be done. 2 On

---

did you KNOW?
Major Jewish Feasts

The joyful anticipation that we feel before a major holiday seems to be shared by people of all cultures and religious traditions. Certainly, the Israelites had that feeling before the three festivals described in Ex 34, 18–26 (and in 23, 14–17). They looked forward to them the way we might look forward to Christmas or Easter.

The *feast of Unleavened Bread*, which began on the day after Passover and lasted a week, marked the beginning of the barley harvest. This feast probably originated in a pre-Passover agricultural holiday. Originally, unleavened bread—bread made without yeast—was eaten during this week to symbolize a fresh start. Later, the feast was connected to the Passover celebration, and the custom of eating unleavened bread came to be seen as a reminder of the haste with which the people had left Egypt—before having time to leaven their bread.

The *feast of Weeks*, or Pentecost, began seven weeks after the barley harvest, to celebrate the start of the wheat harvest. Later, the feast of Weeks took on added significance. Because the Israelites had arrived at Mount Sinai in the third month after their departure from Egypt (19, 1), this weeklong feast came to be seen as a celebration of God's Covenant with Israel.

The third weeklong festival, the *feast of Booths*, also called the festival of Tabernacles, was celebrated as the produce of the land was gathered. Much like our own Thanksgiving Day, it was a time set aside to thank God for the bounty of the earth. It is the most popular of these feasts. Because booths are tents, this feast reminded the Israelites of the time they spent wandering in the desert. In Exodus, it is called the feast at the fruit harvest, and in other places, simply the festival (1 Kgs 8, 2).

▶ Ex 34, 18–26

---

† **34, 33:** *He put a veil over his face:* St. Paul sees in this a symbol of the failure of the Jews to recognize Jesus as the promised Messiah; the true spiritual meaning of the writings of Moses and the prophets is still veiled from the unbelieving Jews. Cf 2 Cor 3, 7–18.

34, 26: 25f: Ex 23, 18f.   34, 34: 33f: 2 Cor 3, 13.16.
34, 28: Ex 24, 18; Dt 9, 9.18;   35, 1–3: Ex 31, 13–17.
   10, 2.4.

six days work may be done, but the seventh day shall be sacred to you as the sabbath of complete rest to the LORD. Anyone who does work on that day shall be put to death. 3 You shall not even light a fire in any of your dwellings on the sabbath day."

Collection of Materials

4 Moses told the whole Israelite community, "This is what the LORD has commanded: 5* Take up among you a collection for the LORD. Everyone, as his heart prompts him, shall bring, as a contribution to the LORD, gold, silver and bronze; 6 violet, purple and scarlet yarn; fine linen and goat hair; 7 rams' skins dyed red, and tahash skins; acacia wood; 8 oil for the light; spices for the anointing oil and for the fragrant incense; 9 onyx stones and other gems for mounting on the ephod and on the breastpiece.

Call for Artisans

10* "Let every expert among you come and make all that the LORD has commanded: 11 the Dwelling, with its tent, its covering, its clasps, its boards, its bars, its columns and its pedestals; 12 the ark, with its poles, the propitiatory, and the curtain veil; 13 the table, with its poles and all its appurtenances, and the showbread; 14 the lampstand, with its appurtenances, the lamps, and the oil for the light; 15 the altar of incense, with its poles; the anointing oil, and the fragrant incense; the entrance curtain for the entrance of the Dwelling; 16 the altar of holocausts, with its bronze grating, its poles, and all its appurtenances; the laver, with its base; 17 the hangings of the court, with their columns and pedestals; the curtain for the entrance of the court; 18 the tent pegs for the Dwelling and for the court, with their ropes; 19 the service cloths for use in the sanctuary; the sacred vestments for Aaron, the priest, and the vestments worn by his sons in their ministry."

The Contribution

20 When the whole Israelite community left Moses' presence, 21 everyone, as his heart suggested and his spirit prompted, brought a contribution to the LORD for the construction of the meeting tent, for all its services, and for the sacred vestments. 22* Both the men and the women, all as their hearts prompted them, brought brooches, earrings, rings, necklaces and various other gold articles. Everyone who could presented an offering of gold to the LORD. 23 Everyone who happened to have violet, purple or scarlet yarn, fine linen or goat hair, rams' skins dyed red or tahash skins, brought them. 24 Whoever could make a contribution of silver or

bronze offered it to the LORD; and everyone who happened to have acacia wood for any part of the work, brought it. 25 All the women who were expert spinners brought hand-spun violet, purple and scarlet yarn and fine linen thread. 26 All the women who possessed the skill, spun goat hair. 27 The princes brought onyx stones and other gems for mounting on the ephod and on the breastpiece; 28 as well as spices, and oil for the light, anointing oil, and fragrant incense. 29 Every Israelite man and woman brought to the LORD such voluntary offerings as they thought best, for the various kinds of work which the LORD had commanded Moses to have done.

The Artisans

30* Moses said to the Israelites, "See, the LORD has chosen Bezalel, son of Uri, son of Hur, of the tribe of Judah, 31 and has filled him with a divine spirit of skill and understanding and knowledge in every craft: 32 in the production of embroidery, in making things of gold, silver or bronze, 33 in cutting and mounting precious stones, in carving wood, and in every other craft. 34 He has also given both him and Oholiab, son of Ahisamach, of the tribe of Dan, the ability to teach others. 35 He has endowed them with skill to execute all types of work: engraving, embroidering, the making of variegated cloth of violet, purple and scarlet yarn and fine linen thread, weaving, and all other arts and crafts.

36 1* "Bezalel, therefore, will set to work with Oholiab and with all the experts whom the LORD has endowed with skill and understanding in knowing how to execute all the work for the service of the sanctuary, just as the LORD has commanded."

2 Moses then called Bezalel and Oholiab and all the other experts whom the LORD had endowed with skill, men whose hearts moved them to come and take part in the work. 3 They received from Moses all the contributions which the Israelites had brought for establishing the service of the sanctuary. Still, morning after morning the people continued to bring their voluntary offerings to Moses. 4 Thereupon the experts who were executing the various kinds of work for the sanctuary, all left the work they were doing, 5 and told Moses, "The people are bringing much more than is needed to carry out the work which the LORD has commanded us to do." 6 Moses, therefore, ordered a proclamation to be made throughout the camp: "Let neither man nor woman make any more contributions for the sanctuary." So the people stopped bringing their offerings; 7 there

35, 5–9: Ex 25, 2–7.
35, 10–19: Ex 31, 6–11.
35, 22–28: Ex 25, 3–7.
35, 30–35: Ex 31, 1–6.
36, 1f: Ex 31, 1.6.

was already enough at hand, in fact, more than enough, to complete the work to be done.

The Tent Cloth and Coverings

8* The various experts who were executing the work, made the Dwelling with its ten sheets woven of fine linen twined, having cherubim embroidered on them with violet, purple and scarlet yarn. 9 The length of each sheet was twenty-eight cubits, and the width four cubits; all the sheets were of the same size. 10 Five of the sheets were sewed together, edge to edge; and the same for the other five. 11 Loops of violet yarn were made along the edge of the end sheet in the first set, and the same along the edge of the end sheet in the second set. 12 Fifty loops were thus put on one inner sheet, and fifty loops on the inner sheet in the other set, with the loops directly opposite each other. 13 Then fifty clasps of gold were made, with which the sheets were joined so that the Dwelling formed one whole.

14 Sheets of goat hair were also woven as a tent over the Dwelling. Eleven such sheets were made. 15 The length of each sheet was thirty cubits and the width four cubits; all eleven sheets were of the same size. 16 Five of these sheets were sewed edge to edge into one set; and the other six sheets into another set. 17 Fifty loops were made along the edge of the end sheet in one set, and fifty loops along the edge of the corresponding sheet in the other set. 18 Fifty bronze clasps were made with which the tent was joined so that it formed one whole. 19 A covering for the tent was made of rams' skins dyed red, and above that, a covering of tahash skins.

The Boards

20* Boards of acacia wood were made as walls for the Dwelling. 21 The length of each board was ten cubits, and the width one and a half cubits. 22 Each board had two arms, fastening them in line. In this way all the boards of the Dwelling were made. 23 They were set up as follows: twenty boards on the south side, 24 with forty silver pedestals under the twenty boards, so that there were two pedestals under each board, at its two arms; 25 twenty boards on the other side of the Dwelling, the north side, 26 with their forty silver pedestals, two under each board; 27 six boards at the rear of the Dwelling, to the west; 28 and two boards at the corners in the rear of the Dwelling. 29 These were double at the bottom, and likewise double at the top, to the first ring. That is how both boards in the corners were made. 30 Thus, there were in the rear eight boards, with their sixteen silver pedestals, two pedestals under

each board. 31 Bars of acacia wood were also made, five for the boards on one side of the Dwelling, 32 five for those on the other side, and five for those at the rear, to the west. 33 The center bar, at the middle of the boards, was made to reach across from end to end. 34 The boards were plated with gold, and gold rings were made on them as holders for the bars, which were also plated with gold.

The Veil

35* The veil was woven of violet, purple and scarlet yarn, and of fine linen twined, with cherubim embroidered on it. 36 Four gold-plated columns of

did you KNOW?

The Ark of the Covenant

The ark of the Covenant, which Bezalel made in fulfillment of God's command, was a portable box in which the Israelites kept the tablets of the Law (see Dt 10, 1–5; 1 Kgs 8, 9) and possibly other sacred items. The large box was made of gold-plated wood, with four rings attached to its lower corners; through these rings, gold-plated poles were inserted for carrying the ark in procession. On top of the ark sat two golden angels facing each other, their wings touching over their heads.

The ark of the Covenant was a symbol of God's saving presence among the Israelites. It accompanied them during their forty years in the desert (Nm 10, 33–36) and was solemnly carried through the Jordan River when they entered the Promised Land (Jos 3, 1–17). Later, the Israelite soldiers took the ark into battle, invoking God's strength against their enemies (1 Sm 4, 1–11). After the ark was lost in battle to the Philistines, David retrieved it and brought it to Jerusalem (2 Sm 6, 1–23), where his son Solomon eventually enthroned it in the Temple, in the holy of holies (1 Kgs 8, 1–11). The ark remained there until the destruction of Jerusalem in 587 B.C., when it was lost to history.

▸ Ex 37, 1–9

acacia wood, with gold hooks, were made for it, and four silver pedestals were cast for them. ^37 The curtain for the entrance of the tent was made of violet, purple and scarlet yarn, and of fine linen twined, woven in a variegated manner. ^38 Its five columns, with their hooks as well as their capitals and bands, were plated with gold; their five pedestals were of bronze.

The Ark

37 ^1 Bezalel made the ark of acacia wood, two and a half cubits long, one and a half cubits wide, and one and a half cubits high. ^2 The inside and outside were plated with gold, and a molding of gold was put around it. ^3 Four gold rings were cast and put on its four supports, two rings for one side and two for the opposite side. ^4 Poles of acacia wood were made and plated with gold; ^5 these were put through the rings on the sides of the ark, for carrying it.

^6 The propitiatory was made of pure gold, two and a half cubits long and one and a half cubits wide. ^7 Two cherubim of beaten gold were made for the two ends of the propitiatory, ^8 one cherub fastened at one end, the other at the other end, springing directly from the propitiatory at its two ends. ^9* The cherubim had their wings spread out above, covering the propitiatory with them. They were turned toward each other, but with their faces looking toward the propitiatory.

The Table

^10* The table was made of acacia wood, two cubits long, one cubit wide, and one and a half cubits high. ^11 It was plated with pure gold, and a molding of gold was put around it. ^12 A frame a handbreadth high was also put around it, with a molding of gold around the frame. ^13 Four rings of gold were cast for it and fastened, one at each of the four corners. ^14 The rings were alongside the frame as holders for the poles to carry the table. ^15 These poles were made of acacia wood and plated with gold. ^16 The vessels that were set on the table, its plates and cups, as well as its pitchers and bowls for pouring libations, were of pure gold.

The Lampstand

^17* The lampstand was made of pure beaten gold—its shaft and branches as well as its cups and knobs and petals springing directly from it. ^18 Six branches extended from its sides, three branches on one side and three on the other.

^19 On one branch there were three cups, shaped like almond blossoms, each with its knob and petals; on the opposite branch there were three cups, shaped like almond blossoms, each with its knob and petals; and so for the six branches that extended from the lampstand. ^20 On the shaft there were four cups, shaped like almond blossoms, with their knobs and petals, ^21 including a knob below each of the three pairs of branches that extended from the lampstand. ^22 The knobs and branches sprang so directly from it that the whole formed but a single piece of pure beaten gold. ^23 Its seven lamps, as well as its trimming shears and trays, were made of pure gold. ^24 A talent of pure gold was used for the lampstand and its various appurtenances.

The Altar of Incense

^25* The altar of incense was made of acacia wood, on a square, a cubit long, a cubit wide, and two cubits high, having horns that sprang directly from it. ^26 Its grate on top, its walls on all four sides, and its horns were plated with pure gold; and a molding of gold was put around it. ^27 Underneath the molding gold rings were placed, two on one side and two on the opposite side, as holders for the poles to carry it. ^28 The poles, too, were made of acacia wood and plated with gold.

^29* The sacred anointing oil and the fragrant incense were prepared in their pure form by a perfumer.

The Altar of Holocausts

38 ^1* The altar of holocausts was made of acacia wood, on a square, five cubits long and five cubits wide; its height was three cubits. ^2 At the four corners horns were made that sprang directly from the altar. The whole was plated with bronze. ^3 All the utensils of the altar, the pots, shovels, basins, forks and fire pans, were likewise made of bronze. ^4 A grating of bronze network was made for the altar and placed round it, on the ground, half as high as the altar itself. ^5 Four rings were cast for the four corners of the bronze grating, as holders for the poles, ^6 which were made of acacia wood and plated with bronze. ^7 The poles were put through the rings on the sides of the altar for carrying it. The altar was made in the form of a hollow box.

^8*† The bronze laver, with its bronze base, was made from the mirrors of the women who served at the entrance of the meeting tent.

---

† **38, 8:** The reflecting surface of ancient mirrors was usually of polished bronze. *The women who served:* cf 1 Sm 2, 22.

* 37, 9: 1–9: Ex 25, 10–22.
37, 10–16: Ex 25, 23–30.
37, 17–24: Ex 25, 31–39.
37, 25–28: Ex 30, 1–5.

37, 29: Ex 30, 23ff.34ff.
38, 1–7: Ex 27, 1–8; 2 Chr 1, 5.
38, 8: Ex 30, 18–21.

The Court

9* The court was made as follows. On the south side of the court there were hangings, woven of fine linen twined, a hundred cubits long, 10 with twenty columns and twenty pedestals of bronze, the hooks and bands of the columns being of silver. 11 On the north side there were similar hangings, one hundred cubits long, with twenty columns and twenty pedestals of bronze, the hooks and bands of the columns being of silver. 12 On the west side there were hangings, fifty cubits long, with ten columns and ten pedestals, the hooks and bands of the columns being of silver. 13 On the east side the court was fifty cubits long. 14 Toward one side there were hangings to the extent of fifteen cubits, with three columns and three pedestals; 15 toward the other side, beyond the entrance of the court, there were likewise hangings to the extent of fifteen cubits, with three columns and three pedestals. 16 The hangings on all sides of the court were woven of fine linen twined. 17 The pedestals of the columns were of bronze, while the hooks and bands of the columns were of silver; the capitals were silver-plated, and all the columns of the court were banded with silver.

18 At the entrance of the court there was a variegated curtain, woven of violet, purple and scarlet yarn and of fine linen twined, twenty cubits long and five cubits wide, in keeping with the hangings of the court. 19 There were four columns and four pedestals of bronze for it, while their hooks were of silver. 20 All the tent pegs for the Dwelling and for the court around it were of bronze.

Amount of Metal Used

21 The following is an account of the various amounts used on the Dwelling, the Dwelling of the commandments, drawn up at the command of Moses by the Levites under the direction of Ithamar, son of Aaron the priest. 22* However, it was Bezalel, son of Uri, son of Hur, of the tribe of Judah, who made all that the Lord commanded Moses, 23 and he was assisted by Oholiab, son of Ahisamach, of the tribe of Dan, who was an engraver, an embroiderer, and a weaver of variegated cloth of violet, purple and scarlet yarn and of fine linen.

24 All the gold used in the entire construction of the sanctuary, having previously been given as an offering, amounted to twenty-nine talents and seven hundred and thirty shekels, according to the standard of the sanctuary shekel. 25 The amount of the silver received from the community was one hundred talents and one thousand seven hundred and seventy-five shekels, according to the standard of the sanctuary shekel; 26* one bekah apiece, that is, a half-shekel apiece, according to the standard of the sanctuary shekel, was received from every man of twenty years or more who entered the registered group; the number of these was six hundred and three thousand five hundred and fifty men. 27 One hundred talents of silver were used for casting the pedestals of the sanctuary and the pedestals of the veil, one talent for each pedestal, or one hundred talents for the one hundred pedestals. 28 The remaining one thousand seven hundred and seventy-five shekels were used for making the hooks on the columns, for plating the capitals, and for banding them with silver. 29 The bronze, given as an offering, amounted to seventy talents and two thousand four hundred shekels. 30 With this were made the pedestals at the entrance of the meeting tent, the bronze altar with its bronze gratings and all the appurtenances of the altar, 31 the pedestals around the court, the pedestals at the entrance of the court, and all the tent pegs for the Dwelling and for the court around it.

The Vestments

39 1* With violet, purple and scarlet yarn were woven the service cloths for use in the sanctuary, as well as the sacred vestments for Aaron, as the LORD had commanded Moses.

2* The ephod was woven of gold thread and of violet, purple and scarlet yarn and of fine linen twined. 3 Gold was first hammered into gold leaf and then cut up into threads, which were woven with the violet, purple and scarlet yarn into an embroidered pattern on the fine linen. 4 Shoulder straps were made for it and joined to its two upper ends. 5 The embroidered belt on the ephod extended out from it, and like it, was made of gold thread, of violet, purple and scarlet yarn, and of fine linen twined, as the LORD had commanded Moses. 6 The onyx stones were prepared and mounted in gold filigree work; they were engraved like seal engravings with the names of the sons of Israel. 7 These stones were set on the shoulder straps of the ephod as memorial stones of the sons of Israel, just as the LORD had commanded Moses.

8* The breastpiece was embroidered like the ephod, with gold thread and violet, purple and scarlet yarn on cloth of fine linen twined. 9 It was square and folded double, a span high and a span wide in its folded form. 10 Four rows of precious stones were mounted on it: in the first row a carnelian, a topaz and an emerald; 11 in the second row, a garnet, a sapphire and a beryl; 12 in the third row a jacinth, an agate and an amethyst; 13 in the

UMBRELLAS, ARKS, AND TENTS

Umbrellas offer protection from the sun or rain. In Asian cultures, servants would hold umbrellas over emperors and kings. Catholics in Indonesia have adapted this custom for their worship. Often, an umbrella is set up over the tabernacle. Umbrellas are held over a priest when he carries the Blessed Sacrament or over the statue of Jesus' Sacred Heart when it is carried in a procession. The umbrella has become a sign of reverence for something that symbolizes God's presence.

The ark of the Covenant was built to act like an umbrella, to protect and reverence the tablets of the Law (the Commandments). When the ark was not being carried, it rested in the tabernacle in the holy of holies, which was a special tent at the center of the Israelites' camp. The ark and the tent served the same practical purpose as an umbrella and had the same deeper meaning of reverencing God's presence.

The next time you use an umbrella, remember how umbrellas are used to show respect for that which is holy: the body of Christ, the Ten Commandments, and one of God's greatest creations, you!

▸ Ex 40, 1–15

---

fourth row a chrysolite, an onyx and a jasper. They were mounted in gold filigree work. 14 These stones were twelve, to match the names of the sons of Israel, and each stone was engraved like a seal with the name of one of the twelve tribes.

15* Chains of pure gold, twisted like cords, were made for the breastpiece, 16 together with two gold filigree rosettes and two gold rings. The two rings were fastened to the two upper ends of the breastpiece. 17 The two gold chains were then fastened to the two rings at the ends of the breastpiece. 18 The other two ends of the two chains were fastened in front to the two filigree rosettes, which were attached to the shoulder straps of the ephod. 19 Two other gold rings were made and put on the two lower ends of the breastpiece, on the edge facing the ephod. 20 Two more gold rings were made and fastened to the bottom of the two shoulder straps next to where they joined the ephod in front, just above its embroidered belt. 21 Violet ribbons bound the rings of the breastpiece to the rings of the ephod, so that the breastpiece stayed right above the embroidered belt of the ephod and did not swing loose from it. All this was just as the LORD had commanded Moses.

The Other Vestments

22 The robe of the ephod was woven entirely of violet yarn, 23 with an opening in its center like the opening of a shirt, with selvage around the opening to keep it from being torn. 24 At the hem of the robe pomegranates were made of violet, purple and scarlet yarn and of fine linen twined; 25 bells of pure gold were also made and put between the pomegranates all around the hem of the robe: 26 first a bell, then a pomegranate, and thus alternating all around the hem of the robe which was to be worn in performing the ministry—all this, just as the LORD had commanded Moses.

27* For Aaron and his sons there were also woven tunics of fine linen; 28 the miter of fine linen; the ornate turbans of fine linen; drawers of linen [of fine linen twined]; 29 and sashes of variegated work made of fine linen twined and of violet, purple and scarlet yarn, as the LORD had commanded Moses. 30* The plate of the sacred diadem was made of pure gold and inscribed, as on a seal engraving: "Sacred to the LORD." 31 It was tied over the miter with a violet ribbon, as the LORD had commanded Moses.

39, 15–21: Ex 28, 31–35.   39, 30f: Ex 28, 36f.
39, 27ff: Ex 28, 39–42.

Presentation of the Work to Moses

³² Thus the entire work of the Dwelling of the meeting tent was completed. The Israelites did the work just as the LORD had commanded Moses. ³³ They then brought to Moses the Dwelling, the tent with all its appurtenances, the clasps, the boards, the bars, the columns, the pedestals, ³⁴ the covering of rams' skins dyed red, the covering of tahash skins, the curtain veil; ³⁵ the ark of the commandments with its poles, the propitiatory, ³⁶ the table with all its appurtenances and the showbread, ³⁷ the pure gold lampstand with its lamps set up on it and with all its appurtenances, the oil for the light, ³⁸ the golden altar, the anointing oil, the fragrant incense; the curtain for the entrance of the tent, ³⁹ the altar of bronze with its bronze grating, its poles and all its appurtenances, the laver with its base, ⁴⁰ the hangings of the court with their columns and pedestals, the curtain for the entrance of the court with its ropes and tent pegs, all the equipment for the service of the Dwelling of the meeting tent; ⁴¹ the service cloths for use in the sanctuary, the sacred vestments for Aaron the priest, and the vestments to be worn by his sons in their ministry. ⁴² The Israelites had carried out all the work just as the LORD had commanded Moses. ⁴³ So when Moses saw that all the work was done just as the LORD had commanded, he blessed them.

Erection of the Dwelling

40 ¹ Then the LORD said to Moses, ²*† "On the first day of the first month you shall erect the Dwelling of the meeting tent.* ³* Put the ark of the commandments in it, and screen off the ark with the veil. ⁴ Bring in the table and set it. Then bring in the lampstand and set up the lamps on it. ⁵ Put the golden altar of incense in front of the ark of the commandments, and hang the curtain at the entrance of the Dwelling. ⁶ Put the altar of holocausts in front of the entrance of the Dwelling of the meeting tent. ⁷ Place the laver between the meeting tent and the altar, and put water in it. ⁸ Set up the court round about, and put the curtain at the entrance of the court.

⁹* "Take the anointing oil and anoint the Dwelling and everything in it, consecrating it and all its furnishings, so that it will be sacred. ¹⁰ Anoint the altar of holocausts and all its appurtenances, consecrating it, so that it will be most sacred. ¹¹ Likewise, anoint the laver with its base, and thus consecrate it.

¹²* "Then bring Aaron and his sons to the entrance of the meeting tent, and there wash them with water. ¹³ Clothe Aaron with the sacred vestments and anoint him, thus consecrating him as my priest. ¹⁴ Bring forward his sons also, and clothe them with the tunics. ¹⁵ As you have anointed their father, anoint them also as my priests. Thus, by being anointed, they shall receive a perpetual priesthood throughout all future generations."

¹⁶ Moses did exactly as the LORD had commanded him. ¹⁷ On the first day of the first month of the second year the Dwelling was erected. ¹⁸ It was Moses who erected the Dwelling. He placed its pedestals, set up its boards, put in its bars, and set up its columns. ¹⁹ He spread the tent over the Dwelling and put the covering on top of the tent, as the LORD had commanded him. ²⁰* He took the commandments and put them in the ark; he placed poles alongside the ark and set the propitiatory upon it. ²¹ He brought the ark into the Dwelling and hung the curtain veil, thus screening off the ark of the commandments, as the LORD had commanded him. ²² He put the table in the meeting tent, on the north side of the Dwelling, outside the veil, ²³* and arranged the bread on it before the LORD, as the LORD had commanded him. ²⁴ He placed the lampstand in the meeting tent, opposite the table, on the south side of the Dwelling, ²⁵ and he set up the lamps before the LORD, as the LORD had commanded him. ²⁶ He placed the golden altar in the meeting tent, in front of the veil, ²⁷ and on it he burned fragrant incense, as the LORD had commanded him. ²⁸ He hung the curtain at the entrance of the Dwelling. ²⁹ He put the altar of holocausts in front of the entrance of the Dwelling of the meeting tent, and offered holocausts and cereal offerings on it, as the LORD had commanded him. ³⁰* He placed the laver between the meeting tent and the altar, and put water in it for washing. ³¹ Moses and Aaron and his sons used to wash their hands and feet there, ³² for they washed themselves whenever they went into the meeting tent or approached the altar, as the LORD commanded Moses. ³³ Finally, he set up the court around the Dwelling and the altar and hung the curtain at the entrance of the court. Thus Moses finished all the work.

God's Presence in the Dwelling

³⁴* Then the cloud covered the meeting tent, and the glory of the LORD filled the Dwelling. ³⁵ Moses could not enter the meeting tent, because the cloud settled down upon it and the glory of the LORD

40, 2: *On the first day of the first month:* almost a year after the departure of the Israelites from Egypt. Cf v 17.

* 40, 2–8: Ex 40, 16–33.
  40, 2: Ex 26, 30.
  40, 3ff: Ex 26, 33ff.
  40, 9ff: Ex 30, 26–29.
  40, 12–15: Ex 28, 41; 29, 4–9; Lv

8, 1–13.
40, 20ff: Ex 25, 16.21; 26, 33ff.
  40, 23: Ex 25, 30.
  40, 30ff: Ex 30, 18ff.
  40, 34–38: Nm 9, 15–22.

filled the Dwelling. ³⁶ Whenever the cloud rose from the Dwelling, the Israelites would set out on their journey. ³⁷ But if the cloud did not lift, they would not go forward; only when it lifted did they go forward. ³⁸ In the daytime the cloud of the LORD was seen over the Dwelling; whereas at night, fire was seen in the cloud by the whole house of Israel in all the stages of their journey.

Leviticus

When approaching a stop sign, come to a complete stop before proceeding." "You are not allowed to pass when a yellow line is on your side of the road." Sometime soon you will be given a book to learn these rules of driving—unless you have already had the pleasure! These laws may be a pain to memorize, but without them driving would be chaos. The Book of Leviticus has a similar function. It is primarily a list of laws, rules, and instructions to ensure holiness and order in worship and the people's way of life.

At a Glance

I. Ritual of Sacrifices (chapters 1—7).

II. Ceremony of Ordination (chapters 8—10).

III. Laws regarding Legal Purity (chapters 11—16).

IV. Code of Legal Holiness (chapters 17—26).

V. Redemption of Offerings (chapter 27).

In-depth

Leviticus, the third book of the Pentateuch, or Torah, is named after the tribe of Levi, whose male members were designated priests in Israel. It was their responsibility to conduct appropriate worship of God. For that reason, the book has often been referred to as the Torah (Law) of the Priests.

Most Scripture scholars believe that the laws and regulations in Leviticus developed over hundreds of years after the people entered the Promised Land. The book was composed at a time when the priests were struggling to unify Israel as it lay in ruins from its Babylonian conquerers. They wished to gather the various traditions and regulations that governed Israel's way of life. The author of Leviticus, referred to as the Priestly writer, writes as if these gathered traditions and regulations were given by God to Moses at Mount Sinai as part of the original Law. The author wishes to show that these laws are an extension of the Sinai Covenant.

If the goal of Israel's existence is to "be holy, because I [the Lord] am holy" (Lv 11, 45), then the Book of Leviticus records how holiness becomes part of every aspect of Israel's existence. Chapters 17–26 are described as the Code of Legal Holiness. The words on love of neighbor in 19, 18 are quoted several times in the New Testament. The purpose of Leviticus is to call Israel to follow the Law and thus become a holy people and make its land a suitable place for God to dwell.

The customs and rites in Jesus' time are observances of the laws in Leviticus. Many of those customs and rites were left behind as Christianity emerged as a distinct religion.

Quick Facts

Period Covered
after the Exodus, during the Israelites' encampment at Mount Sinai

Author
the Priestly writer writing after the Babylonian Exile

Theme
to teach the way of holiness through observance of the Law and religious ritual

Leviticus

I: Ritual of Sacrifices

Holocausts

1 ¹ The LORD called Moses, and from the meeting tent gave him this message: ²*† "Speak to the Israelites and tell them: When any one of you wishes to bring an animal offering to the LORD, such an offering must be from the herd or from the flock.

³*† "If his holocaust offering is from the herd, it must be a male without blemish. To find favor with the LORD, he shall bring it to the entrance of the meeting tent ⁴* and there lay his hand on the head of the holocaust, so that it may be acceptable to make atonement for him. ⁵* He shall then slaughter the bull before the LORD, but Aaron's sons, the priests, shall offer up its blood by splashing it on the sides of the altar which is at the entrance of the meeting tent. ⁶ Then he shall skin the holocaust and cut it up into pieces. ⁷ After Aaron's sons, the priests, have put some burning embers on the altar and laid some wood on them, ⁸ they shall lay the pieces of meat, together with the head and the suet, on top of the wood and embers on the altar. ⁹* The inner organs and the shanks, however, the offerer

shall first wash with water. The priest shall then burn the whole offering on the altar as a holocaust, a sweet-smelling oblation to the LORD.

¹⁰ "If his holocaust offering is from the flock, that is, a sheep or a goat, he must bring a male without blemish. ¹¹ This he shall slaughter before the LORD at the north side of the altar. Then Aaron's sons, the priests, shall splash its blood on the sides of the altar. ¹² When the offerer has cut it up into pieces, the priest shall lay these, together with the head and suet, on top of the wood and the fire on the altar. ¹³ The inner organs and the shanks, however, the offerer shall first wash with water. The priest shall offer them up and then burn the whole offering on the altar as a holocaust, a sweet-smelling oblation to the LORD.

¹⁴* "If he offers a bird as a holocaust to the LORD, he shall choose a turtledove or a pigeon as his offering. ¹⁵* Having brought it to the altar where it is to be burned, the priest shall snap its head loose and squeeze out its blood against the side of the altar. ¹⁶ Its crop and feathers shall be removed and thrown on the ash heap at the east side of the altar. ¹⁷ Then, having split the bird down the middle

---

1, 2: *From the herd or from the flock:* the only animals which could be used as sacrificial victims were either of the bovine class (bulls, cows and calves) or the ovine class (sheep and lambs, goats and kids). Excluded, therefore, were not only all wild animals, but also such "unclean" domestic animals as the camel and the ass. See note on Lv 11, 1ff.

1, 3: *Holocaust:* from the Greek word meaning "wholly burned," this is the technical term for the special type of sacrifice in which an

entire animal except its hide was consumed in the fire on the altar. The primary purpose of this complete gift was to render glory and praise to God.

1, 2: Lv 22, 18.19.
1, 3: Ex 12, 5.
1, 4: Lv 3, 2.8.13; 4, 15; 8, 14.22; 16, 21; Ex 29, 10.15.
1, 5: Lv 3, 8.
1, 9: Lv 3, 5.16; Ex 29, 18.
1, 14: Lv 5, 7; 12, 8; Lk 2, 24.
1, 15: Lv 5, 8.

without separating the halves, the priest shall burn it on the altar, over the wood on the fire, as a holocaust, a sweet-smelling oblation to the LORD.

Cereal Offerings

2 1* "When anyone wishes to bring a cereal offering to the LORD, his offering must consist of fine flour. He shall pour oil on it and put frankincense over it. 2*† When he has brought it to Aaron's sons, the priests, one of them shall take a handful of this fine flour and oil, together with all the frankincense, and this he shall burn on the altar as a token offering, a sweet-smelling oblation to the LORD. 3* The rest of the cereal offering belongs to Aaron and his sons. It is a most sacred oblation to the LORD.

4 "When the cereal offering you present is baked in an oven, it must be in the form of unleavened cakes made of fine flour mixed with oil, or of unleavened wafers spread with oil. 5* If you present a cereal offering that is fried on a griddle, it must be of fine flour mixed with oil and unleavened. 6 Such a cereal offering must be broken into pieces, and oil must be poured over it. 7 If you present a cereal offering that is prepared in a pot, it must be of fine flour, deep-fried in oil. 8 A cereal offering that is made in any of these ways you shall bring to the LORD, offering it to the priest, who shall take it to the altar. 9 Its token offering the priest shall then lift from the cereal offering and burn on the altar as a sweet-smelling oblation to the LORD. 10 The rest of the cereal offering belongs to Aaron and his sons. It is a most sacred oblation to the LORD.

11* "Every cereal offering that you present to the LORD shall be unleavened, for you shall not burn any leaven or honey as an oblation to the LORD. 12 Such you may indeed present to the LORD in the offering of first fruits, but they are not to be placed on the altar for a pleasing odor. 13*† However, every cereal offering that you present to the LORD shall be seasoned with salt. Do not let the salt of the covenant of your God be lacking from your cereal offering. On every offering you shall offer salt.

14 "If you present a cereal offering of first fruits to the LORD, you shall offer it in the form of fresh grits of new ears of grain, roasted by fire. 15 On this cereal offering you shall put oil and frankincense. 16 For its token offering the priest shall then burn

---

did you KNOW?

The Covenant Laws

Even though Christians are not bound by the Jewish religion—see the Letters to the Hebrews and to the Romans—the laws in Leviticus help us understand the meaning of life for the Israelites. These laws developed out of their experience of striving to be faithful to God and were interpreted and taught by the priests of the tribe of Levi.

The purity laws may seem the strangest to us today. They defined who or what was pure—that is, free from contamination—and therefore acceptable to God for the purpose of liturgical worship. They included laws on sickness, especially leprosy, because physical disease was understood as a symptom of sin or spiritual contamination. Purity laws also covered food, animals, bodily discharges, and corpses.

Other laws described proper relationships between people. These laws reflected more the intentions of the heart. Later, the prophets and Jesus would emphasize that impurity comes from the heart, not from something outside the person (Mk 7, 1–23). Other laws regulated priestly ministry, and still others regulated social institutions. Nothing was left to chance. The laws of the Covenant made it clear that God was present in every aspect of the people's lives.

---

some of the grits and oil, together with all the frankincense, as an oblation to the LORD.

Peace Offerings

3 1*† "If someone in presenting a peace offering makes his offering from the herd, he may offer before the LORD either a male or a female animal, but it must be without blemish. 2* He shall lay his hand on the head of his offering, and then

---

† **2, 2:** *Token offering:* literally, "reminder." Instead of burning the whole cereal offering, they burned only this part of it on the altar; it thus corresponded to the fat of the peace offering. See note on Lv 3, 1.

2, 13: *The salt of the covenant of your God:* the partaking in common of salt by those seated together at table was an ancient symbol of friendship and alliance. Cf Mk 9, 49 and Col 4, 6; and see note on Nm 18, 19.

3, 1: *Peace offering:* thus the ancient versions have rendered the Hebrew word, which perhaps means more exactly, "fulfillment sac-

rifice," offered up in fulfillment of a vow. Cf Prv 7, 14. Its characteristic feature was the sacred banquet at which the offerer and his guests partook of the meat of the sacrificed animal. Cf Lv 7, 11–21.

2, 1: Nm 15, 4.
2, 2: Lv 6, 15.
2, 3: Lv 7, 9f; Sir 7, 31;
  1 Cor 9, 13.
2, 5: 1 Chr 23, 29.
2, 11: Lv 6, 16f; Mt 16, 12;

Mk 8, 15; Lk 12, 1;
  1 Cor 5, 7; Gal 5, 9.
2, 13: Ez 43, 24.
3, 1: Lv 22, 21.
3, 2: Lv 1, 4.

slaughter it at the entrance of the meeting tent; but Aaron's sons, the priests, shall splash its blood on the sides of the altar. ³* From the peace offering he shall offer as an oblation to the LORD the fatty membrane over the inner organs, and all the fat that adheres to them, ⁴† as well as the two kidneys, with the fat on them near the loins, and the lobe of the liver, which he shall sever above the kidneys. ⁵* All this Aaron's sons shall then burn on the altar with the holocaust, on the wood over the fire, as a sweet-smelling oblation to the LORD.

⁶ "If the peace offering he presents to the LORD is from the flock, he may offer either a male or a female animal, but it must be without blemish. ⁷ If he presents a lamb as his offering, he shall bring it before the LORD, ⁸ and after laying his hand on the head of his offering, he shall slaughter it before the meeting tent; but Aaron's sons shall splash its blood on the sides of the altar. ⁹*† As an oblation to the LORD he shall present the fat of the peace offering: the whole fatty tail, which he must sever close to the spine, the fatty membrane over the inner organs, and all the fat that adheres to them, ¹⁰ as well as the two kidneys, with the fat on them near the loins, and the lobe of the liver, which he must sever above the kidneys. ¹¹ All this the priest shall burn on the altar as the food of the LORD's oblation.

¹² "If he presents a goat, he shall bring it before the LORD, ¹³ and after laying his hand on its head, he shall slaughter it before the meeting tent; but Aaron's sons shall splash its blood on the sides of the altar. ¹⁴ From it he shall offer as an oblation to the LORD the fatty membrane over the inner organs, and all the fat that adheres to them, ¹⁵ as well as the two kidneys, with the fat on them near the loins, and the lobe of the liver, which he must sever above the kidneys. ¹⁶ All this the priest shall burn on the altar as the food of the sweet-smelling oblation. All the fat belongs to the LORD. ¹⁷*† This shall be a perpetual ordinance for your descendants wherever they may dwell. You shall not partake of any fat or any blood."

Sin Offerings: For Priests

4 ¹ The LORD said to Moses, ²*† "Tell the Israelites: When a person inadvertently commits a sin against some command of the LORD by doing one of the forbidden things, ³*† if it is the anointed priest who thus sins and thereby makes the people also become guilty, he shall present to the LORD a young, unblemished bull as a sin offering for the sin he committed. ⁴* Bringing the bullock to the entrance of the meeting tent, before the LORD, he shall lay his hand on its head and slaughter it before the LORD. ⁵ The anointed priest shall then take some of the bullock's blood and bring it into the meeting tent, ⁶* where, dipping his finger in the blood, he shall sprinkle it seven times before the LORD, toward the veil of the sanctuary. ⁷* The priest shall also put some of the blood on the horns of the altar of fragrant incense which is before the

Sin Offering

The sin-offering laws probably seem strange to you. Because of Jesus' sacrifice, Christians have never had to make sin offerings. But they do serve an important role in understanding what Jesus' death and Resurrection mean for our own sin and salvation.

The Israelites understood that sin affects not only the sinner but also those whose lives the sinner touches. They understood sin as incurring a debt that must be repaid. The sinner made a guilt offering to atone for the sin.

Isaiah said that God made the life of the suffering servant a guilt offering for those who were too far into debt to repay (Is 53, 10). At the Last Supper, Jesus told the Apostles, "This is my blood . . . which will be shed on behalf of many for the forgiveness of sins" (Mt 26, 28). Jesus became our sin offering to take on the debt of our sin. In prayerful thanks for this great gift, read Eph 1, 3–14.

▸ Lv 4, 1—5, 26

LV

† 3, 4: *The lobe of the liver:* some render, "the fatty covering of the liver."

3, 9: *The whole fatty tail:* see note on Ex 29, 22.

3, 17: *Any fat:* only the fat mentioned in vv 9f.14f is meant; other fat could be eaten by the Israelites.

4, 2: *A sin:* not necessarily a moral fault; included are all the cases of ritual uncleanness which people necessarily incurred in certain unavoidable circumstances.

4, 3: *The anointed priest:* his violation of the ceremonial law

brought a sort of collective guilt on all the people whom he represented before God. *Sin offering:* more exactly, "sacrifice for remitting sin"; sin is here understood as explained above.

3, 3: Ex 29, 13.22.
3, 5: Lv 6, 12.
3, 9: Lv 9, 19.
3, 17: Lv 17, 10–14; Gn 9, 4; Dt 12, 16.23; 15, 23.
4, 2: Lv 5, 15.17; Nm 15, 22–29.
4, 3: Heb 7, 27.
4, 4: Lv 1, 3f.
4, 6: Lv 8, 11.
4, 7: Lv 8, 15; 9, 9; 16, 18; Ex 29, 12.

LORD in the meeting tent. The rest of the bullock's blood he shall pour out at the base of the altar of holocausts which is at the entrance of the meeting tent. 8 From the sin-offering bullock he shall remove all the fat: the fatty membrane over the inner organs, and all the fat that adheres to them, 9 as well as the two kidneys, with the fat on them near the loins, and the lobe of the liver, which he must sever above the kidneys. 10 This is the same as is removed from the ox of the peace offering; and the priest shall burn it on the altar of holocausts. 11* The hide of the bullock and all its flesh, with its head, legs, inner organs and offal, 12 in short, the whole bullock, shall be brought outside the camp to a clean place where the ashes are deposited and there be burned up in a wood fire. At the place of the ash heap, there it must be burned.

For the Community

13* "If the whole community of Israel inadvertently and without even being aware of it does something that the LORD has forbidden and thus makes itself guilty, 14 should it later on become known that the sin was committed, the community shall present a young bull as a sin offering. They shall bring it before the meeting tent, 15* and here, before the LORD, the elders of the community shall lay their hands on the bullock's head. When the bullock has been slaughtered before the LORD, 16 the anointed priest shall bring some of its blood into the meeting tent, 17 and dipping his finger in the blood, he shall sprinkle it seven times before the LORD, toward the veil. 18 He shall also put some of the blood on the horns of the altar of fragrant incense which is before the LORD in the meeting tent. The rest of the blood he shall pour out at the base of the altar of holocausts which is at the entrance of the meeting tent. 19 All of its fat he shall take from it and burn on the altar, 20 doing with this bullock just as he did with the other sin-offering bullock. Thus the priest shall make atonement for them, and they will be forgiven. 21 This bullock must also be brought outside the camp and burned, just as has been prescribed for the other one. This is the sin offering for the community.

For the Princes

22 "Should a prince commit a sin inadvertently by doing one of the things which are forbidden by some commandment of the LORD, his God, and thus become guilty, 23 if later on he learns of the sin he committed, he shall bring as his offering an unblemished male goat. 24 Having laid his hands on its head, he shall slaughter the goat as a sin offering before the LORD, in the place where the holocausts are slaughtered. 25 The priest shall then take some of the blood of the sin offering on his finger and put it on the horns of the altar of holocausts. The rest of the blood he shall pour out at the base of this altar. 26* All of the fat he shall burn on the altar like the fat of the peace offering. Thus the priest shall make atonement for the prince's sin, and it will be forgiven.

For Private Persons

27* "If a private person commits a sin inadvertently by doing one of the things which are forbidden by the commandments of the LORD, and thus becomes guilty, 28 should he later on learn of the sin he committed, he shall bring an unblemished she-goat as the offering for his sin. 29* Having laid his hand on the head of the sin offering, he shall slaughter it at the place of the holocausts. 30 The priest shall then take some of its blood on his finger and put it on the horns of the altar of holocausts. The rest of the blood he shall pour out at the base of the altar. 31* All the fat shall be removed, just as the fat is removed from the peace offering, and the priest shall burn it on the altar for an odor pleasing to the LORD. Thus the priest shall make atonement for him, and he will be forgiven.

32 "If, however, for his sin offering he presents a lamb, he shall bring an unblemished female. 33 Having laid his hand on its head, he shall slaughter this sin offering in the place where the holocausts are slaughtered. 34 The priest shall then take some of the blood of the sin offering on his finger and put it on the horns of the altar of holocausts. The rest of the blood he shall pour out at the base of the altar. 35* All the fat shall be removed, just as the fat is removed from the peace-offering lamb, and the priest shall burn it on the altar with the other oblations of the LORD. Thus the priest shall make atonement for the man's sin, and it will be forgiven.

For Special Cases

5 1* "If any person refuses to give the information which, as a witness of something he has seen or learned, he has been adjured to give, and thus commits a sin and has guilt to bear; 2* or if someone, without being aware of it, touches any unclean thing, as the carcass of an unclean wild animal, or that of an unclean domestic animal, or that of an unclean swarming creature, and thus becomes unclean and guilty; 3 or if someone, without being

4, 11: Lv 8, 17; 9, 11; Ex 29, 14; Nm 19, 5.
4, 13: Lv 5, 2–4; Nm 15, 24–26.
4, 15: Lv 1, 4.
4, 26: Lv 3, 3–5.
4, 27: Nm 15, 27.
4, 29: Lv 1, 4.
4, 31: Lv 1, 9; 3, 3–5.
4, 35: Lv 3, 3.9.
5, 1: Prv 29, 24.
5, 2: Lv 11, 24.31.39; 12; 13; 15.

aware of it, touches some human uncleanness, whatever kind of uncleanness this may be, and then recognizes his guilt; 4* or if someone, without being aware of it, rashly utters an oath to do good or evil, such as men are accustomed to utter rashly, and then recognizes that he is guilty of such an oath; 5* then whoever is guilty in any of these cases shall confess the sin he has incurred, 6 and as his sin offering for the sin he has committed he shall bring to the LORD a female animal from the flock, a ewe lamb or a she-goat. The priest shall then make atonement for his sin.

7* "If, however, he cannot afford an animal of the flock, he shall bring to the LORD as the sin offering for his sin two turtledoves or two pigeons, one for a sin offering and the other for a holocaust. 8* He shall bring them to the priest, who shall offer the one for the sin offering first. Snapping its head loose at the neck, yet without breaking it off completely, 9* he shall sprinkle some of the blood of the sin offering against the side of the altar. The rest of the blood shall be squeezed out against the base of the altar. Such is the offering for sin. 10 The other bird shall be offered as a holocaust in the usual way. Thus the priest shall make atonement for the sin the man committed, and it will be forgiven.

11 "If he is unable to afford even two turtledoves or two pigeons, he shall present as a sin offering for his sin one tenth of an ephah of fine flour. He shall not put oil or frankincense on it, because it is a sin offering. 12 When he has brought it to the priest, the latter shall take a handful of this flour as a token offering, and this he shall burn as a sin offering on the altar with the other oblations of the LORD. 13* Thus the priest shall make atonement for the sin that the man committed in any of the above cases, and it will be forgiven. The rest of the flour, like the cereal offerings, shall belong to the priest."

Guilt Offerings

14 The LORD said to Moses, 15† "If someone commits a sin by inadvertently cheating in the LORD's sacred dues, he shall bring to the LORD as his guilt offering an unblemished ram from the flock, valued at two silver shekels according to the standard of the sanctuary shekel. 16* He shall also restore what he has sinfully withheld from the sanctuary, adding to it a fifth of its value. This is to be given to the priest, who shall then make atonement for

him with the guilt-offering ram, and he will be forgiven.

17*† "If someone, without being aware of it, commits such a sin by doing one of the things which are forbidden by some commandment of the LORD, that he incurs guilt for which he must answer, 18 he shall bring as a guilt offering to the priest an unblemished ram of the flock of the established value. The priest shall then make atonement for the fault which was unwittingly committed, and it will be forgiven. 19 Such is the offering for guilt; the penalty of the guilt must be paid to the LORD."

20 The LORD said to Moses, 21 "If someone commits a sin of dishonesty against the LORD by denying his neighbor a deposit or a pledge for a stolen article, or by otherwise retaining his neighbor's goods unjustly, 22 or if, having found a lost article, he denies the fact and swears falsely about it with any of the sinful oaths that men make in such cases, 23 he shall therefore, since he has incurred guilt by his sin, restore the thing that was stolen or unjustly retained by him or the deposit left with him or the lost article he found 24 or whatever else he swore falsely about; on the day of his guilt offering he shall make full restitution of the thing itself, and in addition, give the owner one fifth of its value. 25 As his guilt offering he shall bring to the LORD an unblemished ram of the flock of the established value. When he has presented this as his guilt offering to the priest, 26 the latter shall make atonement for him before the LORD, and he will be forgiven whatever guilt he may have incurred."

The Daily Holocaust

6 1 The LORD said to Moses, 2† "Give Aaron and his sons the following command: This is the ritual for holocausts. The holocaust is to remain on the hearth of the altar all night until the next morning, and the fire is to be kept burning on the altar. 3 The priest, clothed in his linen robe and wearing linen drawers on his body, shall take away the ashes to which the fire has reduced the holocaust on the altar, and lay them at the side of the altar. 4 Then, having taken off these garments and put on other garments, he shall carry the ashes to a clean place outside the camp. 5 The fire on the altar is to be kept burning; it must not go out. Every morning the priest shall put firewood on it. On this he shall lay out the holocaust and burn the fat of the peace

---

5, 15: *Cheating:* not offering the full amount in tithes, first fruits, etc. *Guilt offering:* its characteristic was a certain additional penalty imposed as reparation for the injustice involved in the fault which was atoned for by this sacrifice. However, in certain passages, e.g., Lv 14, 12f; Nm 6, 12; Ezr 10, 19, the term "guilt offering" is used for more important cases of "sin offerings" where no apparent injustice is involved.

5, 17: *Without being aware of it:* the case naturally presupposes that later on the offender learns of his mistake. Cf Lv 4, 13f.

6, 2: *Ritual:* literally, "law, instruction." Here, and in the following paragraphs, are given additional prescriptions for various kinds of sacrifices which were, in part, treated of in the preceding chapters.

5, 4: Jgs 11, 30f; 1 Sm 14, 24; Mk 6, 23; Acts 23, 12.
5, 5: Lv 26, 40; Nm 5, 7.
5, 7: Lv 12, 8; Lk 2, 24.
5, 8: Lv 1, 15.17.
5, 9: Lv 1, 15.
5, 13: Lv 4, 26.35.
5, 16: Lv 22, 14.
5, 17: Lv 4, 2.

offerings. 6 The fire is to be kept burning continuously on the altar; it must not go out.

Daily Cereal Offering

7 "This is the ritual of the cereal offering. One of Aaron's sons shall first present it before the LORD, in front of the altar. 8 Then he shall take from it a handful of its fine flour and oil, together with all the frankincense that is on it, and this he shall burn on the altar as its token offering, a sweet-smelling oblation to the LORD. 9 The rest of it Aaron and his sons may eat; but it must be eaten in the form of unleavened cakes and in a sacred place: in the court of the meeting tent they shall eat it. 10 It shall not be baked with leaven. I have given it to them as their portion from the oblations of the LORD; it is most sacred, like the sin offering and the guilt offering. 11 All the male descendants of Aaron may partake of it as their rightful share in the oblations of the LORD perpetually throughout your generations. Whatever touches the oblations becomes sacred."

12† The LORD said to Moses, 13 "This is the offering that Aaron and his sons shall present to the LORD [on the day he is anointed]: one tenth of an ephah of fine flour for the established cereal offering, half in the morning and half in the evening. 14 It shall be well kneaded and fried in oil on a griddle when you bring it in. Having broken the offering into pieces, you shall present it as a sweet-smelling oblation to the LORD. 15 Aaron's descendant who succeeds him as the anointed priest shall do likewise. This is a perpetual ordinance: for the Lord the whole offering shall be burned. 16 Every cereal offering of a priest shall be a whole burnt offering; it may not be eaten."

Sin Offerings

17 The LORD said to Moses, 18* "Tell Aaron and his sons: This is the ritual for sin offerings. At the place where holocausts are slaughtered, there also, before the LORD, shall the sin offering be slaughtered. It is most sacred. 19* The priest who presents the sin offering may partake of it; but it must be eaten in a sacred place, in the court of the meeting tent. 20 Whatever touches its flesh shall become sacred. If any of its blood is spilled on a garment, the stained part must be washed in a sacred place. 21* A clay vessel in which it has been cooked shall thereafter be broken; if it is cooked in a bronze ves-

sel, this shall be scoured afterward and rinsed with water. 22* All the males of the priestly line may partake of the sin offering, since it is most sacred. 23* But no one may partake of any sin offering of which some blood has been brought into the meeting tent to make atonement in the sanctuary; such an offering must be burned up in the fire.

Guilt Offerings

7 1 "This is the ritual for guilt offerings, which are most sacred. 2* At the place where holocausts are slaughtered, there also shall the guilt offering be slaughtered. Its blood shall be splashed on the sides of the altar. 3* All of its fat shall be taken from it and offered up: the fatty tail, the fatty membrane over the inner organs, 4 as well as the two kidneys with the fat on them near the loins, and the lobe of the liver, which must be severed above the kidneys. 5 All this the priest shall burn on the altar as an oblation to the LORD. This is the guilt offering. 6* All the males of the priestly line may partake of it; but it must be eaten in a sacred place, since it is most sacred.

7 "Because the sin offering and the guilt offering are alike, both having the same ritual, the guilt offering likewise belongs to the priest who makes atonement with it. 8 Similarly, the priest who offers a holocaust for someone may keep for himself the hide of the holocaust that he has offered. 9* Also, every cereal offering that is baked in an oven or deep-fried in a pot or fried on a griddle shall belong to the priest who offers it, 10* whereas all cereal offerings that are offered up dry or mixed with oil shall belong to all of Aaron's sons without distinction.

Peace Offerings

11 "This is the ritual for the peace offerings that are presented to the LORD. 12 When anyone makes a peace offering in thanksgiving, together with his thanksgiving sacrifice he shall offer unleavened cakes mixed with oil, unleavened wafers spread with oil, and cakes made of fine flour mixed with oil and well kneaded. 13† His offering shall also include loaves of leavened bread along with the victim of his peace offering for thanksgiving. 14 From each of his offerings he shall present one portion as a contribution to the LORD; this shall belong to the priest who splashes the blood of the peace offering.

6, 12–16: This is another law about the daily or "established" cereal offering. It differs in some respects from the preceding law (vv 7–11) and also from the law in Ex 29, 38–42. Hence, the words *on the day he is anointed* were probably added by some later scribe in order to avoid the difficulty of harmonizing this law with the other two laws on the same matter.

7, 13: *Leavened bread:* these loaves were not burned on the altar (cf Lv 2, 11), but were eaten at the "communion" meal which followed the sacrifice. See note on Lv 3, 1.

6, 18: Lv 7, 2.
6, 19: Lv 10, 17.
6, 21: Lv 11, 33; 15, 12.
6, 22: Lv 7, 6; Nm 18, 10.
6, 23: Lv 4, 5; Heb 13, 11.
7, 2: Lv 6, 18.

7, 3–5: Lv 3, 4.9f.14–16; 4, 8f.
7, 6: Lv 6, 22.
7, 9: Lv 2, 3–10; Nm 18, 9; Ez 44, 29.
7, 10: Lv 2, 14f.

15* "The flesh of the thanksgiving sacrifice shall be eaten on the day it is offered; none of it may be kept till the next day. 16 However, if the sacrifice is a votive or a free-will offering, it should indeed be eaten on the day the sacrifice is offered, but what is left over may be eaten on the next day. 17 Should any flesh from the sacrifice be left over on the third day, it must be burned up in the fire. 18 If, therefore, any of the flesh of the peace offering is eaten on the third day, it shall not win favor for him nor shall it be reckoned to his credit; rather, it shall be considered as refuse, and anyone who eats of it shall have his guilt to bear. 19 Should the flesh touch anything unclean, it may not be eaten, but shall be burned up in the fire.

"All who are clean may partake of this flesh. 20 If, however, someone while in a state of uncleanness eats any of the flesh of a peace offering belonging to the LORD, that person shall be cut off from his people. 21 Likewise, if someone touches anything unclean, whether the uncleanness be of human or of animal origin or from some loathsome crawling creature, and then eats of a peace offering belonging to the LORD, that person, too, shall be cut off from his people."

Prohibition against Blood and Fat

22 The LORD said to Moses, 23*† "Tell the Israelites: You shall not eat the fat of any ox or sheep or goat. 24* Although the fat of an animal that has died a natural death or has been killed by wild beasts may be put to any other use, you may not eat it. 25 If anyone eats the fat of an animal from which an oblation is made to the LORD, such a one shall be cut off from his people. 26 Wherever you dwell, you shall not partake of any blood, be it of bird or of animal. 27* Every person who partakes of any blood shall be cut off from his people."

The Portions for Priests

28 The LORD said to Moses, 29 "Tell the Israelites: He who presents a peace offering to the LORD shall bring a part of it as his special offering to him, 30† carrying in with his own hands the oblations to the LORD. The fat is to be brought in, together with the breast, which is to be waved as a wave offering before the LORD. 31* The priest shall burn the fat on the altar, but the breast belongs to Aaron and his sons. 32 Moreover, from your peace offering you shall give to the priest the right leg as a raised offering. 33 The descendant of Aaron who offers up the blood and fat of the peace offering shall have the right leg as his portion, 34* for from the peace offerings of the Israelites I have taken the breast that is waved and the leg that is raised up, and I have given them to Aaron, the priest, and to his sons by a perpetual ordinance as a contribution from the Israelites."

35† This is the priestly share from the oblations of the LORD, allotted to Aaron and his sons on the day he called them to be the priests of the LORD; 36 on the day he anointed them the LORD ordered the Israelites to give them this share by a perpetual ordinance throughout their generations.

37 This is the ritual for holocausts, cereal offerings, sin offerings, guilt offerings, [ordination offerings] and peace offerings, 38 which the LORD enjoined on Moses at Mount Sinai at the time when he commanded the Israelites in the wilderness of Sinai to bring their offerings to the LORD.

II: Ceremony of Ordination

Ordination of Aaron and His Sons

8 1*† The LORD said to Moses, 2† "Take Aaron and his sons, together with the vestments, the anointing oil, the bullock for a sin offering, the two rams, and the basket of unleavened food. 3 Then assemble the whole community at the entrance of the meeting tent." 4 And Moses did as the LORD had commanded. When the community had assembled at the entrance of the meeting tent, 5 Moses told them what the LORD had ordered to be done. 6* Bringing forward Aaron and his sons, he first washed them with water. 7* Then he put the tunic on Aaron, girded him with the sash, clothed him with the robe, placed the ephod on him, and girded him with the embroidered belt of the ephod, fastening it around him. 8*† He then set the breastpiece on him, with the Urim and Thummim in it, 9* and put the miter on his head, attaching the gold plate, the sacred diadem, over the front of the miter, at his forehead, as the LORD had commanded him to do.

10* Taking the anointing oil, Moses anointed and consecrated the Dwelling, with all that was in it.

7, 23: *The fat:* only the particular portions specified in Lv 3, 9f. 14f are meant. *Ox or sheep or goat:* such animals as could be sacrificed; the fat of other clean animals could be eaten.

7, 30–34: *A wave offering . . . a raised offering:* these ceremonies are described in Ex 29, 24–28. The Hebrew word for "raised offering" is also rendered, in certain contexts, as "contribution."

7, 35: *The priestly share:* literally, "the anointed part."

8, 1–9.21: Though presented in the form of a narrative, this description of Aaron's ordination was intended to serve as a guide for all future ordinations.

8, 2: *The vestments,* etc.: already described in Ex 28–29.
8, 8: *The Urim and Thummim:* see note on Ex 28, 30.

7, 15–18: Lv 19, 6f.
7, 23: Lv 3, 17.
7, 24: Lv 22, 8.
7, 27: Lv 17, 10.
7, 31: Lv 3, 11.16.
7, 34: Ex 29, 27f.

8, 1–36: cf Ex 29.
8, 6f: Ex 40, 12f.
8, 7ff: Sir 45, 8–13.
8, 8: Ex 28, 30.
8, 9: Ex 28, 36.
8, 10: Ex 30, 26.

11 Then he sprinkled some of this oil seven times on the altar, and anointed the altar, with all its appurtenances, and the laver, with its base, thus consecrating them. 12* He also poured some of the anointing oil on Aaron's head, thus consecrating him. 13 Moses likewise brought forward Aaron's sons, clothed them with tunics, girded them with sashes, and put turbans on them, as the LORD had commanded him to do.

Ordination Sacrifices

14 When he had brought forward the bullock for a sin offering, Aaron and his sons laid their hands on its head. 15* Then Moses slaughtered it, and taking some of its blood, with his finger he put it on the horns around the altar, thus purifying the altar. He also made atonement for the altar by pouring out the blood at its base when he consecrated it. 16* Taking all the fat that was over the inner organs, as well as the lobe of the liver and the two kidneys with their fat, Moses burned them on the altar. 17 The bullock, however, with its hide and flesh and offal he burned in the fire outside the camp, as the LORD had commanded him to do.

18 He next brought forward the holocaust ram, and Aaron and his sons laid their hands on its head. 19 When he had slaughtered it, Moses splashed its blood on all sides of the altar. 20 After cutting up the ram into pieces, he burned the head, the cut-up pieces and the suet; 21 then, having washed the inner organs and the shanks with water, he also burned these remaining parts of the ram on the altar as a holocaust, a sweet-smelling oblation to the LORD, as the LORD had commanded him to do.

22 Then he brought forward the second ram, the ordination ram, and Aaron and his sons laid their hands on its head. 23* When he had slaughtered it, Moses took some of its blood and put it on the tip of Aaron's right ear, on the thumb of his right hand, and on the big toe of his right foot. 24 Moses had the sons of Aaron also come forward, and he put some of the blood on the tips of their right ears, on the thumbs of their right hands, and on the big toes of their right feet. The rest of the blood he splashed on the sides of the altar. 25 He then took the fat: the fatty tail and all the fat over the inner organs, the lobe of the liver and the two kidneys with their fat, and likewise the right leg; 26 from the basket of unleavened food that was set before the LORD he took one unleavened cake, one loaf of bread made with oil, and one wafer; these he placed on top of the portions of fat and the right leg. 27 He then put all these things into the hands of Aaron and his sons, whom he had wave them as a wave offering before the LORD. 28 When he had received them back, Moses burned them with the holocaust on the altar as the ordination offering, a sweet-smelling oblation to the LORD. 29 He then took the breast and waved it as a wave offering before the LORD; this was Moses' own portion of the ordination ram. All this was in keeping with the LORD's command to Moses. 30 Taking some of the anointing oil and some of the blood that was on the altar, Moses sprinkled with it Aaron and his vestments, as well as his sons and their vestments, thus consecrating both Aaron and his vestments and his sons and their vestments.

31 Finally, Moses said to Aaron and his sons, "Boil the flesh at the entrance of the meeting tent, and there eat it with the bread that is in the basket of the ordination offering, in keeping with the command I have received: 'Aaron and his sons shall eat of it.' 32 What is left over of the flesh and the bread you shall burn up in the fire. 33 Moreover, you are not to depart from the entrance of the meeting tent for seven days, until the days of your ordination are completed; for your ordination is to last for seven days. 34† The LORD has commanded that what has been done today be done to make atonement for you. 35 Hence you must remain at the entrance of the meeting tent day and night for seven days, carrying out the prescriptions of the LORD; otherwise you shall die; for this is the command I have received." 36 So Aaron and his sons did all that the LORD had commanded through Moses.

Octave of the Ordination

9 1 On the eighth day Moses summoned Aaron and his sons, together with the elders of Israel, 2 and said to Aaron, "Take a calf for a sin offering and a ram for a holocaust, both without blemish, and offer them before the LORD. 3 Tell the elders of Israel, too: Take a he-goat for a sin offering, a calf and a lamb, both unblemished yearlings, for a holocaust, 4 and an ox and a ram for a peace offering, to sacrifice them before the LORD, along with a cereal offering mixed with oil; for today the LORD will reveal himself to you." 5 So they brought what Moses had ordered. When the whole community had come forward and stood before the LORD, 6 Moses said, "This is what the LORD orders you to do, that the glory of the LORD may be revealed to

---

† **8, 34:** The sense is not quite clear. Either the verse gives merely the reason why God ordered this ceremony, or it contains God's command that the same ceremony be used in all future ordinations, or it decrees a repetition of the entire ceremony on each of the seven days. At least a sin offering for atonement was made on each of these days. Cf Ex 29, 29–36.

8, 12: Sir 45, 15.
8, 15: Lv 4, 7; Heb 9, 22.
8, 16f: Lv 3, 4; 4, 8–11.
8, 23: Lv 14, 14.

you. ⁷ Come up to the altar," Moses then told Aaron, "and offer your sin offering and your holocaust in atonement for yourself and for your family; then present the offering of the people in atonement for them, as the LORD has commanded."

⁸ Going up to the altar, Aaron first slaughtered the calf that was his own sin offering. ⁹ When his sons presented the blood to him, he dipped his finger in the blood and put it on the horns of the altar. The rest of the blood he poured out at the base of the altar. ¹⁰ He then burned on the altar the fat, the kidneys and the lobe of the liver that were taken from the sin offering, as the LORD had commanded Moses; ¹¹ but the flesh and the hide he burned up in the fire outside the camp. ¹² Then Aaron slaughtered his holocaust. When his sons brought him the blood, he splashed it on all sides of the altar. ¹³ They then brought him the pieces and the head of the holocaust, and he burned them on the altar. ¹⁴ Having washed the inner organs and the shanks, he burned these also with the holocaust on the altar.

¹⁵ Thereupon he had the people's offering brought up. Taking the goat that was for the people's sin offering, he slaughtered it and offered it up for sin as before. ¹⁶ Then he brought forward the holocaust, other than the morning holocaust, and offered it in the usual manner. ¹⁷ He then presented the cereal offering; taking a handful of it, he burned it on the altar. ¹⁸ Finally he slaughtered the ox and the ram, the peace offering of the people. When his sons brought him the blood, Aaron splashed it on all sides of the altar. ¹⁹* The portions of fat from the ox and from the ram, the fatty tail, the fatty membrane over the inner organs, the two kidneys, with the fat that is on them, and the lobe of the liver, ²⁰ he placed on top of the breasts and burned them on the altar, ²¹* having first waved the breasts and the right legs as a wave offering before the LORD, in keeping with the LORD's command to Moses.

Revelation of the Lord's Glory

²² Aaron then raised his hands over the people and blessed them. When he came down from offering the sin offering and holocaust and peace offering, ²³* Moses and Aaron went into the meeting tent. On coming out they again blessed the people. Then the glory of the LORD was revealed to all the people. ²⁴* Fire came forth from the LORD'S presence and consumed the holocaust and the remnants of the fat on the altar. Seeing this, all the people cried out and fell prostrate.

Nadab and Abihu

10 ¹*† During this time Aaron's sons Nadab and Abihu took their censers and, strewing incense on the fire they had put in them, they offered up before the LORD profane fire, such as he had not authorized. ²*† Fire therefore came forth from the LORD'S presence and consumed them, so that they died in his presence. ³*† Moses then said to Aaron, "This is as the LORD said:

Through those who approach me I will
    manifest my sacredness;
    In the sight of all the people I will reveal
    my glory."

But Aaron said nothing. ⁴ Then Moses summoned Mishael and Elzaphan, the sons of Aaron's uncle Uzziel, with the order, "Come, remove your kinsmen from the sanctuary and carry them to a place outside the camp." ⁵† So they went in and took them, in their tunics, outside the camp, as Moses had commanded.

Conduct of the Priests

⁶*† Moses said to Aaron and his sons Eleazar and Ithamar, "Do not bare your heads or tear your garments, lest you bring not only death on yourselves but God's wrath also on the whole community. Your kinsmen, the rest of the house of Israel, shall mourn for those whom the LORD'S fire has smitten; ⁷ but do not you go beyond the entry of the meeting tent, else you shall die; for the anointing oil of the LORD is upon you." So they did as Moses told them.

⁸ The LORD said to Aaron, ⁹* "When you are to go to the meeting tent, you and your sons are forbidden under pain of death, by a perpetual ordinance throughout your generations, to drink any wine or strong drink. ¹⁰* You must be able to distinguish between what is sacred and what is profane, between what is clean and what is unclean; ¹¹* you must teach the Israelites all the laws that the LORD has given them through Moses."

---

† **10, 1:** *Nadab and Abihu:* the older sons of Aaron. Cf Ex 6, 23f.
10, 2: *Fire:* perhaps after the manner of lightning.
10, 3: *I will manifest my sacredness:* the presence of God is so sacred that it strikes dead those who approach him without the proper holiness. Cf Nm 20, 13; Ez 28, 22.
10, 5: *In their tunics:* they were buried just as they were, with no shroud or funeral solemnities.
10, 6: *Bare your heads:* go without the customary head covering, as a sign of mourning. Some interpreters, however, understand it as the cutting off of one's hair, which ordinarily all the Israelites, men as

well as women, let grow long. Cf Is 15, 2; Jer 7, 29. Still others understand the verb to mean "to let one's hair hang loose and wild." Cf Lv 13, 45; 21, 10, where the same phrase is used.

9, 19f: Lv 3, 3ff.
9, 21: Lv 7, 31f.
9, 23: Nm 6, 23–26.
9, 24: 1 Kgs 18, 38; 2 Chr 7, 1.
10, 1: Lv 16, 1; Nm 3, 4; 26, 61; 1 Chr 24, 2.
10, 2: Nm 16, 35.
10, 3: Lv 21, 17.21.
10, 6: Lv 21, 10.
10, 9: Ez 44, 21.
10, 10: Lv 11, 47; 20, 25; Ez 22, 26; 44, 23.
10, 11: Sir 45, 16.

L
V

The Eating of the Priestly Portions

12* Moses said to Aaron and his surviving sons, Eleazar and Ithamar, "Take the cereal offering left over from the oblations of the LORD, and eat it beside the altar in the form of unleavened cakes. Since it is most sacred, 13 you must eat it in a sacred place. This is your due from the oblations of the LORD, and that of your sons; such is the command I have received. 14* With your sons and daughters you shall also eat the breast of the wave offering and the leg of the raised offering, in a clean place; for these have been assigned to you and your children as your due from the peace offerings of the Israelites. 15 The leg of the raised offering and the breast of the wave offering shall first be brought in with the oblations, the fatty portions, that are to be waved as a wave offering before the LORD. Then they shall belong to you and your children by a perpetual ordinance, as the LORD has commanded."

16† When Moses inquired about the goat of the sin offering, he discovered that it had all been burned. So he was angry with the surviving sons of Aaron, Eleazar and Ithamar, and said, 17* "Why did you not eat the sin offering in the sacred place, since it is most sacred? It has been given to you that you might bear the guilt of the community and make atonement for them before the LORD. 18 If its blood was not brought into the inmost part of the sanctuary, you should certainly have eaten the offering in the sanctuary, in keeping with the command I had received." 19 Aaron answered Moses, "Even though they presented their sin offering and holocaust before the LORD today, yet this misfortune has befallen me. Had I then eaten of the sin offering today, would it have been pleasing to the LORD?" 20 On hearing this, Moses was satisfied.

III: Laws Regarding Legal Purity

Clean and Unclean Food

11 1† The LORD said to Moses and Aaron, 2 "Speak to the Israelites and tell them: Of all land animals these are the ones you may eat: 3 any animal that has hoofs you may eat, provided it is cloven-footed and chews the cud. 4 But you shall not eat any of the following that only chew the cud or only have hoofs: the camel, which indeed chews the cud, but does not have hoofs and is

did you KNOW?

The Israelite Diet

The diet of the ancient Israelites consisted mainly of breads, cereals, fruits, vegetables, and dairy products. Meat was served only on special occasions because it was expensive. A typical family meal was made up of barley or wheat bread, grapes, figs, olive oil, beans, cucumbers, onions, and cheese. On festive occasions, beef or lamb might grace the table.

The laws in Leviticus, chapter 11, contain many restrictions regarding the eating of animals. The reasons for these restrictions are not clear, although many scholars believe that one purpose was to keep the Israelites from consuming animals used in pagan worship (for example, the pig offered in Babylonian services). Hygiene was likely another consideration.

The basic "meat laws" were as follows:

- Of the larger animals, those that chewed their cud and had split hooves could be eaten. Therefore, lamb was acceptable, but pork was not.
- Sea creatures only with both fins and scales could be eaten. Thus, catfish and eels were to be avoided.
- Eagles, vultures, buzzards, and many other birds were excluded from the table.
- Rodents, reptiles, and insects (except locusts and grasshoppers) were spurned altogether.

The blood from all animals had to be drained completely before cooking because blood was seen as the life force and therefore as belonging to God alone. In addition, it was unlawful to touch or eat any animal found dead; contact with any dead body made one impure.

▶ Lv 11, 1–47

10, 16–19: *Eleazar and Ithamar* burned the entire goat of the sin offering (Lv 9, 15) instead of eating it in a sacred place (Lv 6, 19) to bear the guilt of the community. Aaron defends this action of his sons against Moses' displeasure by implying that they did not have sufficient sanctity to eat the flesh of the victim and thus perform the expiation of the people. They themselves still labored under the blow of the divine anger which struck their brothers Nadab and Abihu.

11, 1ff: These distinctions between edible and inedible meats were probably based on traditional ideas of hygiene, but they are here given a moral, religious basis: the inedible varieties are classified as "unclean" to remind the Israelites that they are to be a pure and holy people, dedicated to the Lord.

10, 12: Lv 6, 16.   **10, 17:** Lv 6, 18f.
10, 14f: Lv 7, 34.

therefore unclean for you; [5]† the rock badger, which indeed chews the cud, but does not have hoofs and is therefore unclean for you; [6] the hare, which indeed chews the cud, but does not have hoofs and is therefore unclean for you; and the pig, [7] which does indeed have hoofs and is cloven-footed, but does not chew the cud and is therefore unclean for you. [8] Their flesh you shall not eat, and their dead bodies you shall not touch; they are unclean for you.

[9] "Of the various creatures that live in the water, you may eat the following: whatever in the seas or in river waters has both fins and scales you may eat. [10] But of the various creatures that crawl or swim in the water, whether in the sea or in the rivers, all those that lack either fins or scales are loathsome for you, [11] and you shall treat them as loathsome. Their flesh you shall not eat, and their dead bodies you shall loathe. [12] Every water creature that lacks fins or scales is loathsome for you.

[13]† "Of the birds, these you shall loathe and, as loathsome, they shall not be eaten: the eagle, the vulture, the osprey, [14] the kite, the various species of falcons, [15] the various species of crows, [16] the ostrich, the nightjar, the gull, the various species of hawks, [17] the owl, the cormorant, the screech owl, [18] the barn owl, the desert owl, the buzzard, [19]† the stork, the various species of herons, the hoopoe, and the bat.

[20] "The various winged insects that walk on all fours are loathsome for you. [21] But of the various winged insects that walk on all fours you may eat those that have jointed legs for leaping on the ground; [22]† hence of these you may eat the following: the various kinds of locusts, the various kinds of grasshoppers, the various kinds of katydids, and the various kinds of crickets. [23] All other winged insects that have four legs are loathsome for you.

[24]† "Such is the uncleanness that you contract, that everyone who touches their dead bodies shall be unclean until evening, [25] and everyone who picks up any part of their dead bodies shall wash his garments and be unclean until evening. [26]† All hoofed animals that are not cloven-footed or do not chew the cud are unclean for you; everyone who touches them becomes unclean. [27]† Of the various quadrupeds, all those that walk on paws are unclean for you; everyone who touches their dead bodies shall be unclean until evening, [28] and everyone who picks up their dead bodies shall wash his garments and be unclean until evening. Such is their uncleanness for you.

[29] "Of the creatures that swarm on the ground, the following are unclean for you: the rat, the mouse, the various kinds of lizards, [30] the gecko, the chameleon, the agama, the skink, and the mole. [31] Among the various swarming creatures, these are unclean for you. Everyone who touches them when they are dead shall be unclean until evening. [32] Everything on which one of them falls when dead becomes unclean. Any such article that men use, whether it be an article of wood, cloth, leather or goat hair, must be put in water and remain unclean until evening, when it again becomes clean. [33] Should any of these creatures fall into a clay vessel, everything in it becomes unclean, and the vessel itself you must break. [34] Any solid food that was in contact with water, and any liquid that men drink, in any such vessel become unclean. [35] Any object on which one of their dead bodies falls, becomes unclean; if it is an oven or a jar-stand, this must be broken to pieces; they are unclean and shall be treated as unclean by you. [36]† However, a spring or a cistern for collecting water remains clean; but whoever touches the dead body becomes unclean. [37] Any sort of cultivated grain remains clean even though one of their dead bodies falls on it; [38] but if the grain has become moistened, it becomes unclean when one of these falls on it.

[39] "When one of the animals that you could otherwise eat, dies of itself, anyone who touches its dead body shall be unclean until evening; [40]* and anyone who eats of its dead body shall wash his garments and be unclean until evening; so also, anyone who removes its dead body shall wash his garments and be unclean until evening.

[41] "All the creatures that swarm on the ground are loathsome and shall not be eaten. [42] Whether it crawls on its belly, goes on all fours, or has many legs, you shall eat no swarming creature: they are loathsome. [43]* Do not make yourselves loathsome or unclean with any swarming creature through

L V

11, 5f: According to modern zoology, *the rock badger* (hyrax Syriacus) is classified as an ungulate, and *the hare* as a rodent; neither is a ruminant. They appear to chew their food as the true ruminants do, and it is upon this appearance that the classification in the text is based.
11, 13–19.30: The identification of the various Hebrew names for these birds and reptiles is in many cases uncertain.
11, 19: *The bat:* actually a mammal, but listed here with the birds because of its wings.
11, 22: The Hebrew distinguishes four classes of edible locust-like insects, but the difference between them is quite uncertain. Cf Mt 3, 4.

11, 24–28: This paragraph sharpens the prohibition against unclean animals: not only is their meat unfit for food, but contact with their dead bodies makes a person ritually unclean.
11, 26: *All hoofed animals that are not cloven-footed:* such as the horse and the ass.
11, 27: *All those that walk on paws:* such as dogs and cats.
11, 36: *Whoever touches the dead body:* to remove the dead insect from the water supply.

11, 40: Lv 17, 15; 22, 8.   **11, 43f:** Lv 20, 25f.

LV

being contaminated by them. 44* For I, the LORD, am your God; and you shall make and keep yourselves holy, because I am holy. You shall not make yourselves unclean, then, by any swarming creature that crawls on the ground. 45 Since I, the LORD, brought you up from the land of Egypt that I might be your God, you shall be holy, because I am holy.

46 "This is the law for animals and birds and for all the creatures that move about in the water or swarm on the ground, 47* that you may distinguish between the clean and the unclean, between creatures that may be eaten and those that may not be eaten."

Uncleanness of Childbirth

12 1 The LORD said to Moses, 2*† "Tell the Israelites: When a woman has conceived and gives birth to a boy, she shall be unclean for seven days, with the same uncleanness as at her menstrual period. 3* On the eighth day, the flesh of the boy's foreskin shall be circumcised, 4 and then she shall spend thirty-three days more in becoming purified of her blood; she shall not touch anything sacred nor enter the sanctuary till the days of her purification are fulfilled. 5 If she gives birth to a girl, for fourteen days she shall be as unclean as at her

A MOTHER'S PRAYER AT CHILDBIRTH

Sun, moon, stars,
you that move in the heavens,
hear this mother!
A new life has come among you.
Make its path smooth that it may reach
the brow of the first hill.

Winds, clouds, rain, mist,
all that move in the air,
hear this mother!
A new life has come among you.
Make its path smooth that it may reach
the brow of the second hill.

Hills, valleys, rivers, lakes, trees, grasses,
all of the earth,
hear this mother!
A new life has come among you.
Make its path smooth that it may reach
the brow of the third hill.

Birds that fly in the air,
animals that dwell in the forest,
insects that creep in the grasses and burrow
*   in the ground,*
hear this mother!
A new life has come among you.
Make its path smooth that it may reach
the brow of the fourth hill.

All the heavens, air and earth,
hear this mother!
A new life has come among you.
Make its path smooth—then shall it travel
*   beyond the four hills!*

(From Suzanne Slesin and
Emily Gwathmey, compilers, Amen, n.p.)

Like the Israelites, with their purification ritual described in Leviticus, chapter 12, most cultures have rituals and prayers associated with childbirth. In this mother's prayer of the Omaha tribe, the four hills refer to the four parts of human life—childhood, youth, adulthood, and old age. What a wonderful reminder that life is a journey and that all creation is invited to celebrate new life!

▶ Lv 12, 1–8

---

† **12, 2f:** The uncleanness of the woman was more serious during the first period, the seven days after the birth of a boy or the fourteen days after the birth of a girl; only during this period would the rules given in Lv 15, 19–24 apply.

11, 44: Lv 19, 2; 20, 7.26;
    Mt 5, 48; 1 Pt 1, 16.
11, 47: Lv 10, 10.

12, 2: Lv 15, 19.
12, 3: Gn 17, 12; Jn 7, 22.

menstruation, after which she shall spend sixty-six days in becoming purified of her blood.

6* "When the days of her purification for a son or for a daughter are fulfilled, she shall bring to the priest at the entrance of the meeting tent a yearling lamb for a holocaust and a pigeon or a turtledove for a sin offering. 7 The priest shall offer them up before the LORD to make atonement for her, and thus she will be clean again after her flow of blood. Such is the law for the woman who gives birth to a boy or a girl child. 8*† If, however, she cannot afford a lamb, she may take two turtledoves or two pigeons, the one for a holocaust and the other for a sin offering. The priest shall make atonement for her, and thus she will again be clean."

Leprosy

13 1 The LORD said to Moses and Aaron, 2*† "If someone has on his skin a scab or pustule or blotch which appears to be the sore of leprosy, he shall be brought to Aaron, the priest, or to one of the priests among his descendants, 3 who shall examine the sore on his skin. If the hair on the sore has turned white and the sore itself shows that it has penetrated below the skin, it is indeed the sore of leprosy; the priest, on seeing this, shall declare the man unclean. 4 If, however, the blotch on the skin is white, but does not seem to have penetrated below the skin, nor has the hair turned white, the priest shall quarantine the stricken man for seven days. 5 On the seventh day the priest shall again examine him. If he judges that the sore has remained unchanged and has not spread on the skin, the priest shall quarantine him for another seven days, 6 and once more examine him on the seventh day. If the sore is now dying out and has not spread on the skin, the priest shall declare the man clean; it was merely eczema. The man shall wash his garments and so become clean. 7 But if, after he has shown himself to the priest to be declared clean, the eczema spreads at all on his skin, he shall once more show himself to the priest. 8 Should the priest, on examining it, find that the eczema has indeed spread on the skin, he shall declare the man unclean; it is leprosy.

9 "When someone is stricken with leprosy, he shall be brought to the priest. 10 Should the priest, on examining him, find that there is a white scab on the skin which has turned the hair white and that there is raw flesh in it, 11 it is skin leprosy that

has long developed. The priest shall declare the man unclean without first quarantining him, since he is certainly unclean. 12† If leprosy breaks out on the skin and, as far as the priest can see, covers all the skin of the stricken man from head to foot, 13 should the priest then, on examining him, find that the leprosy does cover his whole body, he shall declare the stricken man clean; since it has all turned white, the man is clean. 14 But as soon as raw flesh appears on him, he is unclean; 15 on observing the raw flesh, the priest shall declare him unclean, because raw flesh is unclean; it is leprosy. 16 If, however, the raw flesh again turns white, he shall return to the priest; 17 should the latter, on examining him, find that the sore has indeed turned white, he shall declare the stricken man clean, and thus he will be clean.

18 "If a man who had a boil on his skin which later healed, 19 should now in the place of the boil have a white scab or a pink blotch, he shall show himself to the priest. 20 If the latter, on examination, sees that it is deeper than the skin and that the hair has turned white, he shall declare the man unclean: it is the sore of leprosy that has broken out in the boil. 21 But if the priest, on examining him, finds that there is no white hair in it and that it is not deeper than the skin and is already dying out, the priest shall quarantine him for seven days. 22 If it has then spread on the skin, the priest shall declare him unclean; the man is stricken. 23 But if the blotch remains in its place without spreading, it is merely the scar of the boil; the priest shall therefore declare him clean.

24 "If a man had a burn on his skin, and the proud flesh of the burn now becomes a pink or a white blotch, 25 the priest shall examine it. If the hair has turned white on the blotch and this seems to have penetrated below the skin, it is leprosy that has broken out in the burn; the priest shall therefore declare him unclean and stricken with leprosy. 26 But if the priest, on examining it, finds that there is no white hair on the blotch and that this is not deeper than the skin and is already dying out, the priest shall quarantine him for seven days. 27 Should the priest, when examining it on the seventh day, find that it has spread at all on the skin, he shall declare the man unclean and stricken with leprosy. 28 But if the blotch remains in its place without spreading on the skin and is already dying out, it is merely the scab of the burn; the priest shall

---

12, 8: Forty days after the birth of Jesus, his Virgin Mother made this offering of the poor (Lk 2, 22.24); since the holocaust was offered in thanksgiving for the birth of the child, this was most fittingly offered by Mary. However, because of her miraculous delivery, she was not really obliged to make the sin offering of purification.

13, 2ff: Various kinds of skin blemishes are treated here which were not contagious but simply disqualified their subjects from association with others, especially in public worship, until they were

declared ritually clean. The Hebrew term used does not refer to Hansen's disease, currently called leprosy.

13, 12ff: *If leprosy breaks out on the skin:* the symptoms described here point to a form of skin disease which is merely on the surface and therefore easily cured.

12, 6: Lk 2, 22.   13, 2: Dt 24, 8.
12, 8: Lv 1, 14; Lk 2, 24.

therefore declare the man clean, since it is only the scar of the burn.

29 "When a man or a woman has a sore on the head or cheek, 30† should the priest, on examining it, find that the sore has penetrated below the skin and that there is fine yellow hair on it, the priest shall declare the person unclean, for this is scall, a leprous disease of the head or cheek. 31 But if the priest, on examining the scall sore, finds that it has not penetrated below the skin, though the hair on it may not be black, the priest shall quarantine the person with scall sore for seven days, 32 and on the seventh day again examine the sore. If the scall has not spread and has no yellow hair on it and does not seem to have penetrated below the skin, 33 the man shall shave himself, but not on the diseased spot. Then the priest shall quarantine him for another seven days. 34 If the priest, when examining the scall on the seventh day, finds that it has not spread on the skin and that it has not penetrated below the skin, he shall declare the man clean; the latter shall wash his garments, and thus he will be clean. 35 But if the scall spreads at all on his skin after he has been declared clean, 36 the priest shall again examine it. If the scall has indeed spread on the skin, he need not look for yellow hair; the man is surely unclean. 37 If, however, he judges that the scall has remained in its place and that black hair has grown on it, the disease has been healed; the man is clean, and the priest shall declare him clean.

38 "When the skin of a man or a woman is spotted with white blotches, 39† the priest shall make an examination. If the blotches on the skin are white and already dying out, it is only tetter that has broken out on the skin, and the person therefore is clean.

40 "When a man loses the hair of his head, he is not unclean merely because of his bald crown. 41 So too, if he loses the hair on the front of his head, he is not unclean merely because of his bald forehead. 42 But when there is a pink sore on his bald crown or bald forehead, it is leprosy that is breaking out there. 43 The priest shall examine him; and if the scab on the sore of the bald spot has the same pink appearance as that of skin leprosy of the fleshy part of the body, 44 the man is leprous and unclean, and the priest shall declare him unclean by reason of the sore on his head.

45 "The one who bears the sore of leprosy shall keep his garments rent and his head bare, and shall muffle his beard; he shall cry out, 'Unclean, unclean!' 46* As long as the sore is on him he shall declare himself unclean, since he is in fact unclean.

He shall dwell apart, making his abode outside the camp.

Leprosy of Clothes

47† "When a leprous infection is on a garment of wool or of linen, 48 or on woven or knitted material of linen or wool, or on a hide or anything made of leather, 49 if the infection on the garment or hide, or on the woven or knitted material, or on any leather article is greenish or reddish, the thing is indeed infected with leprosy and must be shown to the priest. 50 Having examined the infection, the priest shall quarantine the infected article for seven days.

51 "On the seventh day the priest shall again examine the infection. If it has spread on the garment, or on the woven or knitted material, or on the leather, whatever be its use, the infection is malignant leprosy, and the article is unclean. 52 He shall therefore burn up the garment, or the woven or knitted material of wool or of linen, or the leather article, whatever it may be, which is infected; since it has malignant leprosy, it must be destroyed by fire. 53 But if the priest, on examining the infection, finds that it has not spread on the garment, or on the woven or knitted material, or on the leather article, 54 he shall give orders to have the infected article washed and then quarantined for another seven days.

55 "Then the priest shall again examine the infected article after it has been washed. If the infection has not changed its appearance, even though it may not have spread, the article is unclean and shall be destroyed by fire. 56 But if the priest, on examining the infection, finds that it is dying out after the washing, he shall tear the infected part out of the garment, or the leather, or the woven or knitted material. 57 If, however, the infection again appears on the garment, or on the woven or knitted material, or on the leather article, it is still virulent and the thing infected shall be destroyed by fire. 58 But if, after the washing, the infection has left the garment, or the woven or knitted material, or the leather article, the thing shall be washed a second time, and thus it will be clean. 59* This is the law for leprous infection on a garment of wool or linen, or on woven or knitted material, or on any leather article, to determine whether it is clean or unclean."

Purification after Leprosy

14 1 The LORD said to Moses, 2* "This is the law for the victim of leprosy at the time of his purification. He shall be brought to the

---

13, 30: *Scall:* a scabby or scaly eruption of the scalp. According to some, "ringworm."

13, 39: *Tetter:* vitiligo, a harmless form of skin disease.

13, 47: *A leprous infection:* some mold or fungus growth resembling human leprosy.

13, 46: Nm 5, 2; 12, 14f;
 2 Kgs 15, 5; Lk 17, 12.
13, 59: Lv 14, 54.
14, 2: Mt 8, 4; Mk 1, 44;
 Lk 5, 14.

priest, [3] who is to go outside the camp to examine him. If the priest finds that the sore of leprosy has healed in the leper, [4]† he shall order the man who is to be purified, to get two live, clean birds, as well as some cedar wood, scarlet yarn, and hyssop. [5]† The priest shall then order him to slay one of the birds over an earthen vessel with spring water in it. [6] Taking the living bird with the cedar wood, the scarlet yarn and the hyssop, the priest shall dip them all in the blood of the bird that was slain over the spring water, [7] and then sprinkle seven times the man to be purified from his leprosy. When he has thus purified him, he shall let the living bird fly away over the countryside. [8] The man being purified shall then wash his garments and shave off all his hair and bathe in water; only when he is thus made clean may he come inside the camp; but he shall still remain outside his tent for seven days. [9] On the seventh day he shall again shave off all the hair of his head, his beard, his eyebrows, and any other hair he may have, and also wash his garments and bathe his body in water; and so he will be clean.

Purification Sacrifices

[10] "On the eighth day he shall take two unblemished male lambs, one unblemished yearling ewe lamb, three tenths of an ephah of fine flour mixed with oil for a cereal offering, and one log of oil. [11] The priest who performs the purification ceremony shall place the man who is being purified, as well as all these offerings, before the LORD at the entrance of the meeting tent. [12] Taking one of the male lambs, the priest shall present it as a guilt offering, along with the log of oil, waving them as a wave offering before the LORD. [13] (This lamb he shall slaughter in the sacred place where the sin offering and the holocaust are slaughtered; because, like the sin offering, the guilt offering belongs to the priest and is most sacred.) [14]* Then the priest shall take some of the blood of the guilt offering and put it on the tip of the man's right ear, the thumb of his right hand, and the big toe of his right foot. [15] The priest shall also take the log of oil and pour some of it into the palm of his own left hand; [16] then, dipping his right forefinger in it, he shall sprinkle it seven times before the LORD. [17] Of the oil left in his hand the priest shall put some on the tip of the man's right ear, the thumb of his right hand, and the big toe of his right foot, over the blood of the guilt offering. [18] The rest of the oil in his hand the priest shall put on the head of the man being

purified. Thus shall the priest make atonement for him before the LORD. [19] Only after he has offered the sin offering in atonement for the man's uncleanness shall the priest slaughter the holocaust [20] and offer it, together with the cereal offering, on the altar before the LORD. When the priest has thus made atonement for him, the man will be clean.

Poor Leper's Sacrifice

[21] "If a man is poor and cannot afford so much, he shall take one male lamb for a guilt offering, to be used as a wave offering in atonement for himself, one tenth of an ephah of fine flour mixed with oil for a cereal offering, a log of oil, [22]† and two turtledoves or pigeons, which he can more easily afford, the one as a sin offering and the other as a holocaust. [23] On the eighth day of his purification he shall bring them to the priest, at the entrance of the meeting tent before the LORD. [24] Taking the guilt-offering lamb, along with the log of oil, the priest shall wave them as a wave offering before the LORD. [25] When he has slaughtered the guilt-offering lamb, he shall take some of its blood, and put it on the tip of the right ear of the man being purified, on the thumb of his right hand, and on the big toe of his right foot. [26] The priest shall then pour some of the oil into the palm of his own left hand [27] and with his right forefinger sprinkle it seven times before the LORD. [28] Some of the oil in his hand the priest shall also put on the tip of the man's right ear, the thumb of his right hand, and the big toe of his right foot, over the blood of the guilt offering. [29] The rest of the oil in his hand the priest shall put on the man's head. Thus shall he make atonement for him before the LORD. [30] Then, of the turtledoves or pigeons, such as the man can afford, [31] the priest shall offer up one as a sin offering and the other as a holocaust, along with the cereal offering. Thus shall the priest make atonement before the LORD for the man who is to be purified. [32] This is the law for one afflicted with leprosy who has insufficient means for his purification."

Leprosy of Houses

[33] The LORD said to Moses and Aaron, [34] "When you come into the land of Canaan, which I am giving you to possess, if I put a leprous infection on any house of the land you occupy, [35] the owner of the house shall come and report to the priest, 'It looks to me as if my house were infected.' [36] The priest shall then order the house to be cleared out before he goes in to examine the infection, lest everything in the

---

14, 4: *Scarlet yarn:* probably used for tying the hyssop sprig to the cedar branchlet.
14, 5: *Spring water:* literally, "living water," taken from some source of running water, not from a cistern.

14, 22: *Two turtledoves:* substitutes for the two additional lambs, similar to the offering of a poor woman after childbirth. Cf Lv 12, 8.

14, 14: Lv 8, 23f.

house become unclean. Only after this is he to go in to examine the house. 37 If the priest, on examining it, finds that the infection on the walls of the house consists of greenish or reddish depressions which seem to go deeper than the surface of the wall, 38 he shall close the door of the house behind him and quarantine the house for seven days. 39 On the seventh day the priest shall return to examine the house again. If he finds that the infection has spread on the walls, 40 he shall order the infected stones to be pulled out and cast in an unclean place outside the city. 41 The whole inside of the house shall then be scraped, and the mortar that has been scraped off shall be dumped in an unclean place outside the city. 42 Then new stones shall be brought and put in the place of the old stones, and new mortar shall be made and plastered on the house.

43 "If the infection breaks out once more after the stones have been pulled out and the house has been scraped and replastered, 44 the priest shall come again; and if he finds that the infection has spread in the house, it is corrosive leprosy, and the house is unclean. 45 It shall be pulled down, and all its stones, beams and mortar shall be hauled away to an unclean place outside the city. 46 Whoever enters a house while it is quarantined shall be unclean until evening. 47 Whoever sleeps or eats in such a house shall also wash his garments. 48 If the priest finds, when he comes to examine the house, that the infection has in fact not spread after the plastering, he shall declare the house clean, since the infection has been healed. 49 To purify the house, he shall take two birds, as well as cedar wood, scarlet yarn, and hyssop. 50 One of the birds he shall slay over an earthen vessel with spring water in it. 51 Then, taking the cedar wood, the hyssop and the scarlet yarn, together with the living bird, he shall dip them all in the blood of the slain bird and the spring water, and sprinkle the house seven times. 52 Thus shall he purify the house with the bird's blood and the spring water, along with the living bird, the cedar wood, the hyssop, and the scarlet yarn. 53 He shall then let the living bird fly away over the countryside outside the city. When he has thus made atonement for it, the house will be clean.

54 "This is the law for every kind of human leprosy and scall, 55* for leprosy of garments and houses, 56 as well as for scabs, pustules and blotches, 57 so that it may be manifest when there is a state of uncleanness and when a state of cleanness. This is the law for leprosy."

Personal Uncleanness

15 1 The LORD said to Moses and Aaron, 2* "Speak to the Israelites and tell them:

Every man who is afflicted with a chronic flow from his private parts is thereby unclean. 3 Such is his uncleanness from this flow that it makes no difference whether the flow drains off or is blocked up; his uncleanness remains. 4 Any bed on which the man afflicted with the flow lies, is unclean, and any piece of furniture on which he sits, is unclean. 5 Anyone who touches his bed shall wash his garments, bathe in water, and be unclean until evening. 6 Whoever sits on a piece of furniture on which the afflicted man was sitting, shall wash his garments, bathe in water, and be unclean until evening. 7 Whoever touches the body of the afflicted man shall wash his garments, bathe in water, and be unclean until evening. 8 If the afflicted man spits on a clean man, the latter shall wash his garments, bathe in water, and be unclean until evening. 9 Any saddle on which the afflicted man rides, is unclean. 10 Whoever touches anything that was under him shall be unclean until evening; whoever lifts up any such thing shall wash his garments, bathe in water, and be unclean until evening. 11 Anyone whom the afflicted man touches with unrinsed hands shall wash his garments, bathe in water, and be unclean until evening. 12 Earthenware touched by the afflicted man shall be broken; and every wooden article shall be rinsed with water.

13 "When a man who has been afflicted with a flow becomes free of his affliction, he shall wait seven days for his purification. Then he shall wash his garments and bathe his body in fresh water, and so he will be clean. 14 On the eighth day he shall take two turtledoves or two pigeons, and going before the LORD, to the entrance of the meeting tent, he shall give them to the priest, 15 who shall offer them up, the one as a sin offering and the other as a holocaust. Thus shall the priest make atonement before the LORD for the man's flow.

16 "When a man has an emission of seed, he shall bathe his whole body in water and be unclean until evening. 17 Any piece of cloth or leather with seed on it shall be washed with water and be unclean until evening.

18 "If a man lies carnally with a woman, they shall both bathe in water and be unclean until evening.

19* "When a woman has her menstrual flow, she shall be in a state of impurity for seven days. Anyone who touches her shall be unclean until evening. 20 Anything on which she lies or sits during her impurity shall be unclean. 21 Anyone who touches her bed shall wash his garments, bathe in water, and be unclean until evening. 22 Whoever touches any article of furniture on which she was

---

did you KNOW?

Monthly Periods

Not every woman suffers pain and swelling as part of her menstrual cycle, but many do. Imagine the life of women in Old Testament days. No sanitary supplies, just strips of cloth. Not much privacy. Not much sympathy from men. No understanding of human biology. Just the monthly flow of blood and the trouble and discomfort of dealing with it.

And on top of the discomfort, women were seen as unclean during their menstrual period. How unfair! How uncaring! How did this unclean concept in Lv 15, 19–33 develop, anyway? It probably had to do with blood's being a powerful sign of life. To the ancient Israelites, the loss of blood may have symbolized illness and death.

Thankfully, we do not apply all the Mosaic laws to our life today. We have grown in our understanding of human biology and of human dignity. Let's never stop growing.

▸ Lv 15, 19–33

sitting, shall wash his garments, bathe in water, and be unclean until evening. [23]† But if she is on the bed or on the seat when he touches it, he shall be unclean until evening. [24]* If a man dares to lie with her, he contracts her impurity and shall be unclean for seven days; every bed on which he then lies also becomes unclean.

[25]* "When a woman is afflicted with a flow of blood for several days outside her menstrual period, or when her flow continues beyond the ordinary period, as long as she suffers this unclean flow she shall be unclean, just as during her menstrual period. [26] Any bed on which she lies during such a flow becomes unclean, as it would during her menstruation, and any article of furniture on which she

sits becomes unclean just as during her menstruation. [27] Anyone who touches them becomes unclean; he shall wash his garments, bathe in water, and be unclean until evening.

[28] "If she becomes freed from her affliction, she shall wait seven days, and only then is she to be purified. [29] On the eighth day she shall take two turtledoves or two pigeons and bring them to the priest at the entrance of the meeting tent. [30] The priest shall offer up one of them as a sin offering and the other as a holocaust. Thus shall the priest make atonement before the LORD for her unclean flow.

[31] "You shall warn the Israelites of their uncleanness, lest by defiling my Dwelling, which is in their midst, their uncleanness be the cause of their death.

[32] "This is the law for the man who is afflicted with a chronic flow, or who has an emission of seed, and thereby becomes unclean; [33] as well as for the woman who has her menstrual period, or who is afflicted with a chronic flow; the law for male and female; and also for the man who lies with an unclean woman."

The Day of Atonement

16 [1] After the death of Aaron's two sons, who died when they approached the LORD'S presence, the LORD spoke to Moses [2]*† and said to him, "Tell your brother Aaron that he is not to come whenever he pleases into the sanctuary, inside the veil, in front of the propitiatory on the ark; otherwise, when I reveal myself in a cloud above the propitiatory, he will die. [3] Only in this way may Aaron enter the sanctuary. He shall bring a young bullock for a sin offering and a ram for a holocaust. [4] He shall wear the sacred linen tunic, with the linen drawers next his flesh, gird himself with the linen sash and put on the linen miter. But since these vestments are sacred, he shall not put them on until he has first bathed his body in water. [5]* From the Israelite community he shall receive two male goats for a sin offering and one ram for a holocaust.

[6] "Aaron shall bring in the bullock, his sin offering to atone for himself and for his household. [7] Taking the two male goats, and setting them before the LORD at the entrance of the meeting tent, [8]† he shall cast lots to determine which one is for the LORD and which for Azazel. [9] The goat that is determined by lot for the LORD, Aaron shall bring

---

† **15, 23:** What is added to the legislation by this verse is uncertain in both the Hebrew and the Greek.
16, 2: *The sanctuary, inside the veil:* the innermost part of the sanctuary, known also as "the holy of holies." Cf Ex 26, 33f. Here the high priest was allowed to enter only once a year, on Yom Kippur, the Day of Atonement. In Heb 9, 3–12 this ceremony is applied to Christ's single act of Redemption, whereby he won for us an everlasting atonement. *Propitiatory:* see note on Ex 25, 17.

16, 8: *Azazel:* perhaps a name for Satan, used only in this chapter. The ancient versions translated this word as "the escaping goat," whence the English word "scapegoat."

15, 24: Lv 18, 19.   **16, 2:** Heb 9, 6–12.
15, 25: Mt 9, 20; Mk 5, 25;   **16, 5:** Nm 29, 11.
     Lk 8, 43.

in and offer up as a sin offering. [10] But the goat determined by lot for Azazel he shall set alive before the LORD, so that with it he may make atonement by sending it off to Azazel in the desert.

[11] "Thus shall Aaron offer up the bullock, his sin offering, to atone for himself and for his family. When he has slaughtered it, [12] he shall take a censer full of glowing embers from the altar before the LORD, as well as a double handful of finely ground fragrant incense, and bringing them inside the veil, [13]† there before the LORD he shall put incense on the fire, so that a cloud of incense may cover the propitiatory over the commandments; else he will die. [14]* Taking some of the bullock's blood, he shall sprinkle it with his finger on the fore part of the propitiatory and likewise sprinkle some of the blood with his finger seven times in front of the propitiatory.

[15]* "Then he shall slaughter the people's sin-offering goat, and bringing its blood inside the veil, he shall do with it as he did with the bullock's blood, sprinkling it on the propitiatory and before it. [16] Thus he shall make atonement for the sanctuary because of all the sinful defilements and faults of the Israelites. He shall do the same for the meeting tent, which is set up among them in the midst

of their uncleanness. [17] No one else may be in the meeting tent from the time he enters the sanctuary to make atonement until he departs. When he has made atonement for himself and his household, as well as for the whole Israelite community, [18]* he shall come out to the altar before the LORD and make atonement for it also. Taking some of the bullock's and the goat's blood, he shall put it on the horns around the altar, [19] and with his finger sprinkle some of the blood on it seven times. Thus he shall render it clean and holy, purged of the defilements of the Israelites.

The Scapegoat

[20] "When he has completed the atonement rite for the sanctuary, the meeting tent and the altar, Aaron shall bring forward the live goat. [21]* Laying both hands on its head, he shall confess over it all the sinful faults and transgressions of the Israelites, and so put them on the goat's head. He shall then have it led into the desert by an attendant. [22]* Since the goat is to carry off their iniquities to an isolated region, it must be sent away into the desert.

[23]† "After Aaron has again gone into the meeting tent, he shall strip off and leave in the sanctuary the linen vestments he had put on when he entered

The Scapegoat

What an interesting tradition! In the Israelite ritual described in Lv 16, 20–21, the leader symbolically transfers all the people's sins onto a goat and drives it away. It is a liberating act that allows a fresh start.

But today, the idea of a scapegoat conveys oppression rather than freedom. A person becomes the scapegoat when other people blame him or her for their problems. Here is an example:

Suppose you are on a soccer team that expects this week's game to be easy, so no one works hard at practice. On game day, the score is tied near the end of the game. Your team is already thinking about going home when the other team scores a goal and wins the game. Everyone gets mad at the goalie for not preventing the goal. The goalie is the scapegoat, but everyone should share in the fault for the loss because they did not practice well or play their best.

■ Have you ever been the scapegoat for someone else's problems? If so, how did that feel? What did you do?

■ Have you ever scapegoated someone else when you were partly to blame for some situation? What happened? How will you prevent scapegoating in the future?

▶ Lv 16, 20–21

16, 13: *Else he will die;* the smoke is to conceal the resplendent majesty of God, the sight of which would strike any man dead.
16, 23: This verse is best read after v 25. According to later Jewish practice the high priest again went into the holy of holies to remove the censer.

16, 14: Heb 9, 13.25.
16, 15: Heb 5, 1; 6, 19.
16, 18: Ex 30, 12.
16, 21: Is 53, 6; 2 Cor 5, 21.
16, 22: Is 53, 11.12; Jn 1, 29; 1 Pt 2, 24.

there. 24 After bathing his body with water in a sacred place, he shall put on his vestments, and then come out and offer his own and the people's holocaust, in atonement for himself and for the people, 25 and also burn the fat of the sin offering on the altar.

26 "The man who has led away the goat for Azazel shall wash his garments and bathe his body in water; only then may he enter the camp. 27* The sin-offering bullock and goat whose blood was brought into the sanctuary to make atonement, shall be taken outside the camp, where their hides and flesh and offal shall be burned up in the fire. 28 The one who burns them shall wash his garments and bathe his body in water; only then may he enter the camp.

The Fast

29*† "This shall be an everlasting ordinance for you: on the tenth day of the seventh month every one of you, whether a native or a resident alien, shall mortify himself and shall do no work. 30 Since on this day atonement is made for you to make you clean, so that you may be cleansed of all your sins before the LORD, 31 by everlasting ordinance it shall be a most solemn sabbath for you, on which you must mortify yourselves.

32 "This atonement is to be made by the priest who has been anointed and ordained to the priesthood in succession to his father. He shall wear the linen garments, the sacred vestments, 33 and make atonement for the sacred sanctuary, the meeting tent and the altar, as well as for the priests and all the people of the community. 34* This, then, shall be an everlasting ordinance for you: once a year atonement shall be made for all the sins of the Israelites."

Thus was it done, as the LORD had commanded Moses.

IV: Code of Legal Holiness

Sacredness of Blood

17 1 The LORD said to Moses, 2 "Speak to Aaron and his sons, as well as to all the Israelites, and tell them: This is what the LORD has commanded. 3† Any Israelite who slaughters an ox

or a sheep or a goat, whether in the camp or outside of it, 4 without first bringing it to the entrance of the meeting tent to present it as an offering to the LORD in front of his Dwelling, shall be judged guilty of bloodshed; and for this, such a man shall be cut off from among his people. 5 Therefore, such sacrifices as they used to offer up in the open field the Israelites shall henceforth offer to the LORD, bringing them to the priest at the entrance of the meeting tent and sacrificing them there as peace offerings to the LORD. 6 The priest shall splash the blood on the altar of the LORD at the entrance of the meeting tent and there burn the fat for an odor pleasing to the LORD. 7* No longer shall they offer their sacrifices to the satyrs to whom they used to render their wanton worship. This shall be an everlasting ordinance for them and their descendants.

8 "Tell them, therefore: Anyone, whether of the house of Israel or of the aliens residing among them, who offers a holocaust or sacrifice 9 without bringing it to the entrance of the meeting tent to offer it to the LORD, shall be cut off from his kinsmen. 10* And if anyone, whether of the house of Israel or of the aliens residing among them, partakes of any blood, I will set myself against that one who partakes of blood and will cut him off from among his people. 11*† Since the life of a living body is in its blood, I have made you put it on the altar, so that atonement may thereby be made for your own lives, because it is the blood, as the seat of life, that makes atonement. 12 That is why I have told the Israelites: No one among you, not even a resident alien, may partake of blood.

13 "Anyone hunting, whether of the Israelites or of the aliens residing among them, who catches an animal or a bird that may be eaten, shall pour out its blood and cover it with earth. 14* Since the life of every living body is its blood, I have told the Israelites: You shall not partake of the blood of any meat. Since the life of every living body is its blood, anyone who partakes of it shall be cut off.

15* Everyone, whether a native or an alien, who eats of an animal that died of itself or was killed by a wild beast, shall wash his garments, bathe in water, and be unclean until evening, and then he will be clean. 16 If he does not wash or does not bathe his body, he shall have the guilt to bear."

---

† **16, 29:** *Mortify himself:* literally, "afflict his soul"; traditionally understood by the Jews as signifying abstinence from all food. This is the only fast day prescribed in the Mosaic law.

17, 3ff: The ancients considered blood the seat and sign of life, and therefore something sacred, even in animals. Cf Gn 9, 4f. Hence, even the ordinary butchering of an animal for meat was looked upon as having a sacrificial character, so that it should be performed at the sanctuary. This law, however, could not be carried out without great difficulty when the Israelites were scattered throughout Palestine, and so was modified in Dt 12, 20ff.

17, 11: *That atonement may thereby be made for your own lives:* hence, the sacrifice of an animal was a symbolic act which substi-

tuted the victim's life for the life of the offerer, who thus acknowledged that he deserved God's punishments for his sins. This idea of sacrifice is applied in Heb 9–10 to the death of Christ, inasmuch as "without the shedding of blood there is no forgiveness" (Heb 9, 22).

16, 27: Heb 13, 11.   **17, 10:** Lv 3, 17.
16, 29: Lv 23, 27.32; Nm   **17, 11:** Gn 9, 4.
   29, 7.   **17, 14:** Lv 7, 26f.
16, 34: Heb 9, 7.25.   **17, 15:** Lv 11, 39f; 22, 8.
17, 7: Ex 34, 15; Dt 32, 17;
   2 Chr 11, 15; 1 Cor
   10, 20.

The Sanctity of Sex

18 [1] The LORD said to Moses, [2] "Speak to the Israelites and tell them: I, the LORD, am your God. [3] You shall not do as they do in the land of Egypt, where you once lived, nor shall you do as they do in the land of Canaan, where I am bringing you; do not conform to their customs. [4] My decrees

daughter's daughter, for that would be a disgrace to your own family. [11] You shall not have intercourse with the daughter whom your father's wife bore to him, since she, too, is your sister. [12]* You shall not have intercourse with your father's sister, since she is your father's relative. [13] You shall not have intercourse with your mother's sister, since she is your

LIVE IT!

A Very Special Gift

The laws about sexual relations in Leviticus, chapter 18, are another example of how holiness extended to all aspects of life for the Israelites. The people had experienced the sexual promiscuity of other cultures (see Genesis, chapter 19). To become a great nation, the children of God, they had to abandon unhealthy and unholy sexual practices and follow God's way.

Young people today also receive many confusing cultural messages about when it is okay to have sex. In movies, television, and music, sex happens all the time between unmarried people, with no consequences. But the church, parents, and teachers are saying to wait until marriage. What is a person to believe?

Think about this: Suppose you are receiving a special gift for Christmas. The gift has been wrapped up and then hidden until Christmas Day. How would it feel if you discovered the present and opened it before Christmas? You probably would initially feel some excitement and pleasure in opening the gift. But the special meaning of opening it on the right day would be lost—for both you and the one presenting it to you.

Sex is a wonderful gift from God, meant for that day when you say, "I do," to someone you are committed to in marriage. Only in marriage can sex unite a couple as God intended. Marriage provides the place where children can be properly raised. That is why the Bible tells us to wait until we are married to have sex—so this gift will be as special as it is meant to be.

▶ Lv 18, 1–30

you shall carry out, and my statutes you shall take care to follow. I, the LORD, am your God. [5]* Keep, then, my statutes and decrees, for the man who carries them out will find life through them. I am the LORD.

[6]† "None of you shall approach a close relative to have sexual intercourse with her. I am the LORD. [7]* You shall not disgrace your father by having intercourse with your mother. Besides, since she is your own mother, you shall not have intercourse with her. [8]* You shall not have intercourse with your father's wife, for that would be a disgrace to your father. [9] You shall not have intercourse with your sister, your father's daughter or your mother's daughter, whether she was born in your own household or born elsewhere. [10] You shall not have intercourse with your son's daughter or with your

mother's relative. [14]* You shall not disgrace your father's brother by being intimate with his wife, since she, too, is your aunt. [15] You shall not have intercourse with your daughter-in-law; she is your son's wife, and therefore you shall not disgrace her. [16]*† You shall not have intercourse with your brother's wife, for that would be a disgrace to your brother. [17] You shall not have intercourse with a woman and also with her daughter, nor shall you marry and have intercourse with her son's daughter or her daughter's daughter; this would be shameful, because they are related to her. [18] While your wife is still living you shall not marry her sister as her rival; for thus you would disgrace your first wife.

[19] "You shall not approach a woman to have intercourse with her while she is unclean from menstruation. [20] You shall not have carnal relations

---

† **18, 6–18:** These laws are formulated as directed to the male Israelites only, but naturally the same norms of consanguinity and affinity would apply to the women as well. Marriage, as well as casual intercourse, is here forbidden between men and women of the specified degrees of relationship.
18, 16: *With your brother's wife:* it was the violation of this law

which aroused the wrath of John the Baptist against Herod Antipas. Cf Mk 6, 18. An exception to this law is made in Dt 25, 5.

18, 5: Gal 3, 12.
18, 7–16: Lv 20, 11–21.
18, 8: Dt 23, 1; 27, 20; 1 Cor 5, 1.
18, 12f: Lv 20, 19.
18, 14: Lv 20, 20.
18, 16: Lv 20, 21; Mt 14, 3f; Mk 6, 18.

LV

with your neighbor's wife, defiling yourself with her. [21]*† You shall not offer any of your offspring to be immolated to Molech, thus profaning the name of your God. I am the LORD. [22]* You shall not lie with a male as with a woman; such a thing is an abomination. [23]* You shall not have carnal relations with an animal, defiling yourself with it; nor shall a woman set herself in front of an animal to mate with it; such things are abhorrent.

[24] "Do not defile yourselves by any of these things by which the nations whom I am driving out of your way have defiled themselves. [25] Because their land has become defiled, I am punishing it for its wickedness, by making it vomit out its inhabitants. [26] You, however, whether natives or resident aliens, must keep my statutes and decrees forbidding all such abominations [27] by which the previous inhabitants defiled the land; [28] otherwise the land will vomit you out also for having defiled it, just as it vomited out the nations before you. [29] Everyone who does any of these abominations shall be cut off from among his people. [30]* Heed my charge, then, not to defile yourselves by observing the abominable customs that have been observed before you. I, the LORD, am your God."

Various Rules of Conduct

19 [1] The LORD said to Moses, [2]* "Speak to the whole Israelite community and tell them: Be holy, for I, the LORD, your God, am holy. [3]* Revere your mother and father, and keep my sabbaths. I, the LORD, am your God.

[4]* "Do not turn aside to idols, nor make molten gods for yourselves. I, the LORD, am your God.

[5] "When you sacrifice your peace offering to the LORD, if you wish it to be acceptable, [6] it must be eaten on the very day of your sacrifice or on the following day. Whatever is left over until the third day shall be burned up in the fire. [7]* If any of it is eaten on the third day, the sacrifice will be unacceptable as refuse; [8] whoever eats of it then shall pay the penalty for having profaned what is sacred to the LORD. Such a one shall be cut off from his people.

[9]* "When you reap the harvest of your land, you shall not be so thorough that you reap the field to its very edge, nor shall you glean the stray ears of grain. [10] Likewise, you shall not pick your vineyard bare, nor gather up the grapes that have fallen. These things you shall leave for the poor and the alien. I, the LORD, am your God.

[11]* "You shall not steal. You shall not lie or speak falsely to one another. [12]* You shall not swear falsely by my name, thus profaning the name of your God. I am the LORD.

[13]* "You shall not defraud or rob your neighbor. You shall not withhold overnight the wages of your day laborer. [14] You shall not curse the deaf, or put a stumbling block in front of the blind, but you shall fear your God. I am the LORD.

[15]* "You shall not act dishonestly in rendering judgment. Show neither partiality to the weak nor deference to the mighty, but judge your fellow men justly. [16] You shall not go about spreading slander among your kinsmen; nor shall you stand by idly when your neighbor's life is at stake. I am the LORD.

[17]* "You shall not bear hatred for your brother in your heart. Though you may have to reprove your fellow man, do not incur sin because of him. [18]*† Take no revenge and cherish no grudge against your fellow countrymen. You shall love your neighbor as yourself. I am the LORD.

[19] "Keep my statutes: do not breed any of your domestic animals with others of a different species; do not sow a field of yours with two different kinds of seed; and do not put on a garment woven with two different kinds of thread.

[20]† "If a man has carnal relations with a female slave who has already been living with another man but has not yet been redeemed or given her freedom, they shall be punished but not put to death, because she is not free. [21] The man, moreover, shall bring to the entrance of the meeting tent a ram as his guilt offering to the LORD. [22] With this ram the priest shall make atonement before the LORD for the sin he has committed, and it will be forgiven him.

[23]† "When you come into the land and plant any fruit tree there, first look upon its fruit as if it were uncircumcised. For three years, while its fruit remains uncircumcised, it may not be eaten. [24] In the

---

†
18, 21: *Immolated to Molech:* the reference is to the Canaanite custom of sacrificing children to the god Molech. The little victims were first slain and then cremated. Cf Ez 16, 20ff; 20, 26.31; 23, 37.

19, 18: *You shall love your neighbor as yourself:* cited by our Lord as the second of the two most important commandments of God. Cf Mt 22, 39; Mk 12, 31. Although in the present context the word "neighbor" is restricted to "fellow countrymen," in Lk 10, 29–37 Christ extends its meaning to embrace all men, even enemies. Cf also Mt 5, 43ff.

19, 20ff: This law seems out of its proper context here; perhaps it stood originally after Lv 20, 12. *Female slave . . . given her freedom:* reference is to the case treated of in Ex 21, 7–11.

19, 23ff: *Uncircumcised:* by analogy with a newborn boy, the newly planted tree was considered impure until "circumcised" by offering to the Lord all the fruit it bore in the fourth year.

*
18, 21: Lv 20, 2–5; Dt 18, 10;
2 Kgs 16, 3; 21, 6.
18, 22: Lv 20, 13; Rom 1, 27;
1 Cor 6, 9f.
18, 23: Lv 20, 15f; Ex 22, 18.
18, 30: Lv 20, 13; Dt 18, 9.
19, 2: Lv 11, 44; Mt 5, 48;
1 Pt 1, 16.
19, 3: Ex 20, 12.
19, 4: Lv 26, 1; Ex 20, 3–5;
34, 17; Dt 27, 15.
19, 7: Lv 7, 18.
19, 9: Lv 23, 22; Dt 24, 19ff.

19, 11: Ex 20, 15f.
19, 12: Ex 20, 7; Mt 5, 33.
19, 13: Dt 24, 14f.
19, 15: Ex 23, 2f; Dt 1, 17; 16,
19; Ps 82, 2; Prv 24,
23.
19, 17: Mt 18, 15; Lk 17, 3;
Gal 6, 1; 1 Jn 3, 14.
19, 18: Mt 5, 43; 19, 19; 22,
39; Mk 12, 31; Rom
13, 9; Gal 5, 14; Jas
2, 8.

You Shall Be Holy

As the Israelites' image of God developed, so did their sense of how they needed to live as God's people. As God's chosen people, they felt called to behave according to God's plan for them by keeping themselves pure as individuals and as a community. The laws in the Book of Leviticus are examples of how they lived out the call to be holy. For them, holiness was not just for the Sabbath or the Temple but for every day and everything.

Think about the choices you make in the following areas. How do your choices help you to be holy as God is holy?

- what you eat
- what you watch
- what you wear
- what you buy
- what you listen to
- how you relate to other people

▶ Leviticus, chapters 19–20

fourth year, however, all of its fruit shall be sacred to the LORD as a thanksgiving feast to him. 25 Not until the fifth year may you eat its fruit. Thus it will continue its yield for you. I, the LORD, am your God.

26* "Do not eat meat with the blood still in it. Do not practice divination or soothsaying. 27*† Do not clip your hair at the temples, nor trim the edges of your beard. 28 Do not lacerate your bodies for the dead, and do not tattoo yourselves. I am the LORD.

29 "You shall not degrade your daughter by making a prostitute of her; else the land will become corrupt and full of lewdness. 30* Keep my sabbaths, and reverence my sanctuary. I am the LORD.

31* "Do not go to mediums or consult fortune-tellers, for you will be defiled by them. I, the LORD, am your God.

32 "Stand up in the presence of the aged, and show respect for the old; thus shall you fear your God. I am the LORD.

33* "When an alien resides with you in your land, do not molest him. 34* You shall treat the alien who resides with you no differently than the natives born among you; have the same love for him as for yourself; for you too were once aliens in the land of Egypt. I, the LORD, am your God.

35 "Do not act dishonestly in using measures of length or weight or capacity. 36* You shall have a true scale and true weights, an honest ephah and an honest hin. I, the LORD, am your God, who brought you out of the land of Egypt. 37 Be careful, then, to observe all my statutes and decrees. I am the LORD."

Penalties for Various Sins

20 1 The LORD said to Moses, 2* "Tell the Israelites: Anyone, whether an Israelite or an alien residing in Israel, who gives any of his offspring to Molech shall be put to death. Let his fellow citizens stone him. 3* I myself will turn against such a man and cut him off from the body of his people; for in giving his offspring to Molech, he has defiled my sanctuary and profaned my holy name. 4 Even if his fellow citizens connive at such a man's crime of giving his offspring to Molech, and fail to put him to death, 5 I myself will set my face against that man and his family and will cut off from their people both him and all who join him in his wanton worship of Molech. 6* Should anyone turn to mediums and fortune-tellers and follow their wanton ways, I will turn against such a one and cut him off from his people. 7* Sanctify yourselves, then, and be holy; for I, the LORD, your God, am holy. 8 Be careful, therefore, to observe what I, the LORD, who make you holy, have prescribed.

9* "Anyone who curses his father or mother shall be put to death; since he has cursed his father or mother, he has forfeited his life. 10* If a man commits adultery with his neighbor's wife, both the adulterer and the adulteress shall be put to death. 11* If a man disgraces his father by lying with his father's wife, both the man and his stepmother shall be put to death; they have forfeited their lives. 12* If a man lies with his daughter-in-law, both of them shall be put to death; since they have committed an abhorrent deed, they have forfeited their lives. 13* If a man lies with a male as with a woman, both of them shall be put to death for their abominable deed; they have forfeited their lives. 14* If a man marries a woman and her mother also, the man and the two women as well shall be burned to death for their shameful conduct, so that such shamefulness may not be found among you. 15* If a man has carnal relations with an animal, the man

†
19, 27: See note on Lv 21, 5.

*
19, 26: Lv 3, 17; Dt 18, 10; 2 Kgs 17, 17; 21, 6; 2 Chr 33, 6.
19, 27: Lv 21, 5.
19, 30: Lv 26, 2; Ex 20, 8.
19, 31: Lv 20, 6.27; Dt 18, 11; Is 8, 19.
19, 33: Ex 22, 20; 23, 9; Jer 22, 3; Mal 3, 5.
19, 34: Dt 10, 19.

19, 36: Dt 25, 13.15; Prv 11, 1; 16, 11; 20, 10; Ez 45, 10.
20, 2: Lv 18, 21.
20, 3: Ez 23, 39.
20, 6: Lv 19, 31.
20, 7: Lv 11, 44; 19, 2; 1 Pt 1, 16.
20, 9: Ex 21, 17; Prv 20, 20;
Mt 15, 4; Mk 7, 10.
20, 10: Lv 18, 20; Dt 22, 22; Jn 8, 5.
20, 11: Lv 18, 7f.
20, 12: Lv 18, 15.
20, 13: Lv 18, 22.
20, 14: Lv 18, 17; Dt 27, 23.
20, 15: Ex 22, 18; Dt 27, 21.

shall be put to death, and the animal shall be slain. 16* If a woman goes up to any animal to mate with it, the woman and the animal shall be slain; let them both be put to death; their lives are forfeit. 17* If a man consummates marriage with his sister or his half-sister, they shall be publicly cut off from their people for this shameful deed; the man shall pay the penalty of having had intercourse with his own sister. 18* If a man lies in sexual intercourse with a woman during her menstrual period, both of them shall be cut off from their people, because they have laid bare the flowing fountain of her blood. 19* You shall not have intercourse with your mother's sister or your father's sister; whoever does so shall pay the penalty of incest. 20 If a man disgraces his uncle by having intercourse with his uncle's wife, the man and his aunt shall pay the penalty by dying childless. 21 If a man marries his brother's wife and thus disgraces his brother, they shall be childless because of this incest.

22 "Be careful to observe all my statutes and all my decrees; otherwise the land where I am bringing you to dwell will vomit you out. 23* Do not conform, therefore, to the customs of the nations whom I am driving out of your way, because all these things that they have done have filled me with disgust for them. 24* But to you I have said: Their land shall be your possession, a land flowing with milk and honey. I am giving it to you as your own, I, the LORD, your God, who have set you apart from the other nations. 25* You, too, must set apart, then, the clean animals from the unclean, and the clean birds from the unclean, so that you may not be contaminated with the uncleanness of any beast or bird or of any swarming creature in the land that I have set apart for you. 26* To me, therefore, you shall be sacred; for I, the LORD, am sacred, I, who have set you apart from the other nations to be my own.

27*† "A man or a woman who acts as a medium or fortune-teller shall be put to death by stoning; they have no one but themselves to blame for their death."

Sanctity of the Priesthood

21 1*† The LORD said to Moses, "Speak to Aaron's sons, the priests, and tell them: None of you shall make himself unclean for any dead person among his people, 2 except for his nearest relatives, his mother or father, his son or daughter, his brother 3 or his maiden sister, who is of his own family while she remains unmarried; for these he may make himself unclean. 4 But for a sister who has married out of his family he shall not make himself unclean; this would be a profanation.

5*† "The priests shall not make bare the crown of the head, nor shave the edges of the beard, nor lacerate the body. 6† To their God they shall be sacred, and not profane his name; since they offer up the oblations of the LORD, the food of their God, they must be holy.

7* "A priest shall not marry a woman who has been a prostitute or has lost her honor, nor a woman who has been divorced by her husband; for the priest is sacred to his God. 8 Honor him as sacred who offers up the food of your God; treat him as sacred, because I, the LORD, who have consecrated him, am sacred.

9 "A priest's daughter who loses her honor by committing fornication and thereby dishonors her father also, shall be burned to death.

10† "The most exalted of the priests, upon whose head the anointing oil has been poured and who has been ordained to wear the special vestments, shall not bare his head or rend his garments, 11 nor shall he go near any dead person. Not even for his father or mother may he thus become unclean 12* or leave the sanctuary; otherwise he will profane the sanctuary of his God, for with the anointing oil upon him, he is dedicated to his God, to me, the LORD.

13 "The priest shall marry a virgin. 14* Not a widow or a woman who has been divorced or a woman who has lost her honor as a prostitute, but a virgin, taken from his own people, shall he marry; 15 otherwise he will have base offspring among his people. I, the LORD, have made him sacred."

Irregularities

16 The LORD said to Moses, 17 "Speak to Aaron and tell him: None of your descendants, of whatever generation, who has any defect shall come forward to offer up the food of his God. 18 Therefore, he who has any of the following defects may not come forward: he who is blind, or lame, or who has any disfigurement or malformation, 19 or a crippled foot or hand, 20 or who is humpbacked or weakly

20, 16: Lv 18, 23.
20, 17: Lv 18, 9; Dt 27, 22.
20, 18: Lv 18, 19.
20, 19: Lv 18, 12f.
20, 23: Lv 18, 30.
20, 24: Ex 3, 8.17; 6, 8.
20, 25: Lv 11, 2–47; Dt 14, 4–20.
20, 26: Lv 11, 44; Ex 19, 6;

1 Pt 1, 16.
20, 27: Lv 19, 31; Ex 22, 17; Dt 18, 11.
21, 1: Ez 44, 25.
21, 5: Ez 44, 20.
21, 7: Ez 44, 22.
21, 12: Lv 10, 7.
21, 14: Ez 44, 22.

or walleyed, or who is afflicted with eczema, ring-worm or hernia. 21 No descendant of Aaron the priest who has any such defect may draw near to of-fer up the oblations of the LORD; on account of his defect he may not draw near to offer up the food of his God. 22 He may, however, partake of the food of his God: of what is most sacred as well as of what is sacred. 23 Only, he may not approach the veil nor go up to the altar on account of his defect; he shall not profane these things that are sacred to me, for it is I, the LORD, who make them sacred."

24 Moses, therefore, told this to Aaron and his sons and to all the Israelites.

Sacrificial Banquets

22 ¹ The LORD said to Moses, ² "Tell Aaron and his sons to respect the sacred offer-ings which the Israelites consecrate to me; else they will profane my holy name. I am the LORD.

³ "Tell them: If any one of you, or of your de-scendants in any future generation, dares, while he is in a state of uncleanness, to draw near the sacred offerings which the Israelites consecrate to the LORD, such a one shall be cut off from my presence. I am the LORD.

⁴* "No descendant of Aaron who is stricken with leprosy, or who suffers from a flow, may eat of these sacred offerings, unless he again becomes clean. Moreover, if anyone touches a person who has become unclean by contact with a corpse, or if any-one has had an emission of seed, ⁵* or if anyone touches any swarming creature or any man whose uncleanness, of whatever kind it may be, is conta-gious, ⁶* the one who touches such as these shall be unclean until evening and may not eat of the sacred portions until he has first bathed his body in water; ⁷ then, when the sun sets, he again becomes clean. Only then may he eat of the sacred offerings, which are his food. ⁸* He shall not make himself unclean by eating of any animal that has died of itself or has been killed by wild beasts. I am the LORD.

⁹ "They shall keep my charge and not do wrong in this matter; else they will die for their profana-tion. I am the LORD who have consecrated them.

¹⁰* "Neither a lay person nor a priest's tenant or hired servant may eat of any sacred offering. ¹¹ But a slave whom a priest acquires by purchase or who is born in his house may eat of his food. ¹² A priest's daughter who is married to a layman may not eat of the sacred contributions. ¹³ But if a priest's daughter is widowed or divorced and, hav-ing no children, returns to her father's house, she may then eat of her father's food as in her youth.

No layman, however, may eat of it. ¹⁴* If such a one eats of a sacred offering through inadvertence, he shall make restitution to the priest for the sacred offering, with an increment of one fifth of the amount. ¹⁵* The sacred offerings which the Israelites contribute to the LORD the priests shall not allow to be profaned ¹⁶ nor in the eating of the sacred offer-ing shall they bring down guilt that must be pun-ished; it is I, the LORD, who make them sacred."

Unacceptable Victims

¹⁷ The LORD said to Moses, ¹⁸ "Speak to Aaron and his sons and to all the Israelites, and tell them: When anyone of the house of Israel, or any alien re-siding in Israel, who wishes to offer a sacrifice, brings a holocaust as a votive offering or as a free-will offering to the LORD, ¹⁹* if it is to be accept-able, the ox or sheep or goat that he offers must be an unblemished male. ²⁰* You shall not offer one that has any defect, for such a one would not be ac-ceptable for you. ²¹* When anyone presents a peace offering to the LORD from the herd or the flock in fulfillment of a vow, or as a free-will offering, if it is to find acceptance, it must be unblemished; it shall not have any defect. ²² One that is blind or crippled or maimed, or one that has a running sore or mange or ringworm, you shall not offer to the LORD; do not put such an animal on the altar as an oblation to the LORD. ²³ An ox or a sheep that is in any way ill-proportioned or stunted you may in-deed present as a free-will offering, but it will not be acceptable as a votive offering. ²⁴ One that has its testicles bruised or crushed or torn out or cut off you shall not offer to the LORD. You shall neither do this in your own land ²⁵* nor receive from a for-eigner any such animals to offer up as the food of your God; since they are deformed or defective, they will not be acceptable for you."

²⁶ The LORD said to Moses, ²⁷* "When an ox or a lamb or a goat is born, it shall remain with its mother for seven days; only from the eighth day on-ward will it be acceptable, to be offered as an obla-tion to the LORD. ²⁸ You shall not slaughter an ox or a sheep on one and the same day with its young. ²⁹ Whenever you offer a thanksgiving sacrifice to the LORD, so offer it that it may be acceptable for you; ³⁰* it must, therefore, be eaten on the same day; none of it shall be left over until the next day. I am the LORD.

³¹ "Be careful to observe the commandments which I, the LORD, give you, ³² and do not profane my holy name; in the midst of the Israelites I, the LORD, must be held as sacred. It is I who made you

22, 4: Lv 7, 20; 15, 16.
22, 5: Lv 11, 24.43.
22, 6: Heb 10, 22.
22, 8: Lv 17, 15; Dt 14, 21;

Ez 44, 31.
22, 10: 1 Sm 21, 6; Mt 12, 4.
22, 14: Lv 5, 16; 27, 13.15.
19.

22, 15: Lv 19, 8; Nm 18, 32.
22, 19: Lv 1, 3.10.
22, 20: Dt 15, 21; 17, 1; Mal
1, 8.14.

22, 21: Lv 3, 1.6.
22, 25: Mal 1, 14.
22, 27: Ex 22, 29.
22, 30: Lv 7, 15.

sacred [33] and led you out of the land of Egypt, that I, the LORD, might be your God."

Holy Days

23 [1] The LORD said to Moses, [2] "Speak to the Israelites and tell them: The following are the festivals of the LORD, my feast days, which you shall celebrate with a sacred assembly.

[3]* "For six days work may be done; but the seventh day is the sabbath rest, a day for sacred assembly, on which you shall do no work. The sabbath shall belong to the LORD wherever you dwell.

Passover

[4]* "These, then, are the festivals of the LORD which you shall celebrate at their proper time with a sacred assembly. [5]* The Passover of the LORD falls on the fourteenth day of the first month, at the evening twilight. [6]* The fifteenth day of this month is the LORD'S feast of Unleavened Bread. For seven days you shall eat unleavened bread. [7]* On the first of these days you shall hold a sacred assembly and do no sort of work. [8] On each of the seven days you shall offer an oblation to the LORD. Then on the seventh day you shall again hold a sacred assembly and do no sort of work."

[9] The LORD said to Moses, [10] "Speak to the Israelites and tell them: When you come into the land which I am giving you, and reap your harvest, you shall bring a sheaf of the first fruits of your harvest to the priest, [11]† who shall wave the sheaf before the LORD that it may be acceptable for you. On the day after the sabbath the priest shall do this. [12] On this day, when your sheaf is waved, you shall offer to the LORD for a holocaust an unblemished yearling lamb. [13] Its cereal offering shall be two tenths of an ephah of fine flour mixed with oil, as a sweet-smelling oblation to the LORD; and its libation shall be a fourth of a hin of wine. [14]† Until this day, when you bring your God this offering, you shall not eat any bread or roasted grain or fresh kernels. This shall be a perpetual statute for you and your descendants wherever you dwell.

Pentecost

[15]* "Beginning with the day after the sabbath, the day on which you bring the wave-offering sheaf, you shall count seven full weeks, [16]*† and then on the day after the seventh week, the fiftieth day, you shall present the new cereal offering to the LORD. [17] For the wave offering of your first fruits to the LORD, you shall bring with you from wherever you live two loaves of bread made of two tenths of an ephah of fine flour and baked with leaven. [18] Besides the bread, you shall offer to the LORD a holocaust of seven unblemished yearling lambs, one young bull, and two rams, along with their cereal offering and libations, as a sweet-smelling oblation to the LORD. [19]* One male goat shall be sacrificed as a sin offering, and two yearling lambs as a peace offering. [20] The priest shall wave the bread of the first fruits and the two lambs as a wave offering before the LORD; these shall be sacred to the LORD and belong to the priest. [21] On this same day you shall by proclamation have a sacred assembly, and no sort of work may be done. This shall be a perpetual statute for you and your descendants wherever you dwell.

[22] "When you reap the harvest of your land, you shall not be so thorough that you reap the field to its very edge, nor shall you glean the stray ears of your grain. These things you shall leave for the poor and the alien. I, the LORD, am your God."

New Year's Day

[23] The LORD said to Moses, [24] "Tell the Israelites: On the first day of the seventh month you shall keep a sabbath rest, with a sacred assembly and with the trumpet blasts as a reminder; [25] you shall then do no sort of work, and you shall offer an oblation to the LORD."

The Day of Atonement

[26]* The LORD said to Moses, [27]* "The tenth of this seventh month is the Day of Atonement, when you shall hold a sacred assembly and mortify yourselves and offer an oblation to the LORD. [28] On this day you shall not do any work, because it is the Day of Atonement, when atonement is made for you before the LORD, your God. [29] Anyone who does not mortify himself on this day shall be cut off from his people; [30] and if anyone does any work on this day, I will remove him from the midst of his people. [31] This is a perpetual statute for you and your descendants wherever you dwell: you shall do no work, [32] but shall keep a sabbath of complete rest and mortify yourselves. Beginning on the evening

23, 11: *The sabbath:* according to the Jewish tradition this was the feast day itself, the fifteenth of Nisan, which was a special day of rest. Cf v 7. However, some understand here the Saturday of the Passover week, or even the Saturday following it; cf Jn 19, 31.
23, 14: *Any bread:* made from the new grain. The harvest had first to be sanctified for man's use by this offering to God.
23, 16: *The fiftieth:* from the Greek word for this we have the name "Pentecost." Cf 2 Mc 12, 31; Acts 2, 1. It was also called "the feast of the Seven Weeks," or simply "the feast of Weeks" (Nm 28, 26; Dt 16, 10; Tb 2, 1). *The new cereal offering:* of flour made

from the new grain. Pentecost was the thanksgiving feast at the end of the grain harvest, which began after Passover. Later tradition made it a commemoration of the giving of the law at Sinai.

23, 3: Ex 20, 8–11; 23, 12; 31, 14f; 34, 21; Dt 5, 12–15; Lk 13, 14.	23, 7: Ex 12, 15; Nm 28, 18.25.
23, 4: Ex 23, 14–19.	23, 15: Ex 34, 22; Nm 28, 26; Dt 16, 9.
23, 5: Nm 9, 2f; 28, 16.	23, 16: Acts 2, 1.
23, 6: Ex 12, 18; 13, 3.10; 23, 15; 34, 18.	23, 19: Nm 28, 30.
	23, 26: Lv 25, 9.
	23, 27: Lv 16, 29f; Nm 29, 7.

L
V

KOREAN FESTIVAL CUSTOMS

In preparation for the Lunar New Year (in January or February) and for the Moon Festival (a feast of thanksgiving in August), Korean families follow some traditional customs. These customs are similar to those of the Israelite festivals described in Leviticus, chapter 23.

In Korea, the day before each feast is used for purification. People take ceremonial baths symbolizing the total cleansing of their body, their spirit, and their attitudes. The baths wash away meanness, carelessness, and other faults. The people also wear new clothes and often get a haircut.

Before sunrise on the day of the feast, the people bow before a table holding name cards of their ancestors. They use incense, pour out wine, and pray to their ancestors, asking for their intercession and help. Family members pray silently for all their individual and family needs. During the day, families visit the homes of their extended family. During these visits, the prayer ritual is often repeated.

After a day of visiting, families return home for a feast of the best food and drink possible. The sharing of food is the most significant part of the meal. Neighbors exchange portions of food with one another and bring food to poor families. Families set food on a small table near the door as an offering of thanks to the Creator and sprinkle rice on the ground around their house in gratitude for the crops.

▶ Lv 23, 4–44

of the ninth of the month, you shall keep this sabbath of yours from evening to evening."

The Feast of Booths

33 The LORD said to Moses, 34*† "Tell the Israelites: The fifteenth day of this seventh month is the LORD's feast of Booths, which shall continue for seven days. 35 On the first day there shall be a sacred assembly, and you shall do no sort of work. 36 For seven days you shall offer an oblation to the LORD, and on the eighth day you shall again hold a sacred assembly and offer an oblation to the LORD. On that solemn closing you shall do no sort of work.

37 "These, therefore, are the festivals of the LORD on which you shall proclaim a sacred assembly, and offer as an oblation to the LORD holocausts and cereal offerings, sacrifices and libations, as prescribed for each day, 38 in addition to those of the LORD's sabbaths, your donations, your various votive offerings and the free-will offerings that you present to the LORD.

39* "On the fifteenth day, then, of the seventh month, when you have gathered in the produce of the land, you shall celebrate a pilgrim feast of the LORD for a whole week. The first and the eighth day shall be days of complete rest. 40† On the first day you shall gather foliage from majestic trees, branches of palms and boughs of myrtles and of valley poplars, and then for a week you shall make merry before the LORD, your God. 41* By perpetual statute for you and your descendants you shall keep this pilgrim feast of the

---

23, 34: *Feast of Booths:* the joyful observance of the vintage and fruit harvest. Cf Dt 16, 13. During the seven days of the feast the Israelites camped in booths of branches erected on the roofs of their houses or in the streets in commemoration of their wanderings in the desert, where they dwelt in booths.

23, 40: *Foliage:* literally, "fruit," but here probably used in the general sense of "produce, growth." These branches were used for constructing the "booths" or huts in which the people lived during

the feast. Cf Neh 8, 15. However, from about the time of Christ on, the Jews have understood this of "fruit" in the strict sense; hence, branches of lemons and oranges were carried with the other branches in joyous procession.

23, 34: Nm 29, 12; Dt 16, 13;   23, 39: Ex 23, 16; Dt 16, 13.
2 Mc 1, 9.18; Jn 7, 2.   23, 41: Nm 29, 12–38.

LORD for one whole week in the seventh month of the year. 42 During this week every native Israelite among you shall dwell in booths, 43* that your descendants may realize that, when I led the Israelites out of the land of Egypt, I made them dwell in booths. I, the LORD, am your God."

44 Thus did Moses announce to the Israelites the festivals of the LORD.

The Sanctuary Light

24 1 The LORD said to Moses, 2* "Order the Israelites to bring you clear oil of crushed olives for the light, so that you may keep lamps burning regularly. 3 In the meeting tent, outside the veil that hangs in front of the commandments, Aaron shall set up the lamps to burn before the LORD regularly, from evening till morning. Thus, by a perpetual statute for you and your descendants, 4* the lamps shall be set up on the pure gold lampstand, to burn regularly before the LORD.

The Showbread

5* "You shall take fine flour and bake it into twelve cakes, using two tenths of an ephah of flour for each cake. 6 These you shall place in two piles, six in each pile, on the pure gold table before the LORD. 7 On each pile put some pure frankincense, which shall serve as an oblation to the LORD, a token offering for the bread. 8* Regularly on each sabbath day this bread shall be set out afresh before the LORD, offered on the part of the Israelites by an everlasting agreement. 9 It shall belong to Aaron and his sons, who must eat it in a sacred place, since, as something most sacred among the various oblations to the LORD, it is his by perpetual right."

Punishment of Blasphemy

10 Among the Israelites there was a man born of an Israelite mother (Shelomith, daughter of Dibri, of the tribe of Dan) and an Egyptian father. 11 This man quarreled publicly with another Israelite and cursed and blasphemed the LORD'S name. So the people brought him to Moses, 12 who kept him in custody till a decision from the LORD should settle the case for them. 13 The LORD then said to Moses, 14 "Take the blasphemer outside the camp, and when all who heard him have laid their hands on his head, let the whole community stone him.

15 Tell the Israelites: Anyone who curses his God shall bear the penalty of his sin; 16* whoever blasphemes the name of the LORD shall be put to death. The whole community shall stone him; alien and native alike must be put to death for blaspheming the LORD'S name.

17* "Whoever takes the life of any human being shall be put to death; 18* whoever takes the life of an animal shall make restitution of another animal. A life for a life! 19 Anyone who inflicts an injury on his neighbor shall receive the same in return. 20* Limb for limb, eye for eye, tooth for tooth! The same injury that a man gives another shall be inflicted on him in return. 21 Whoever slays an animal shall make restitution, but whoever slays a man shall be put to death. 22* You shall have but one rule, for alien and native alike. I, the LORD, am your God."

23* When Moses told this to the Israelites, they took the blasphemer outside the camp and stoned him; they carried out the command that the LORD had given Moses.

The Sabbatical Year

25 1 The LORD said to Moses on Mount Sinai, 2 "Speak to the Israelites and tell them: When you enter the land that I am giving you, let the land, too, keep a sabbath for the LORD. 3* For six years you may sow your field, and for six years prune your vineyard, gathering in their produce. 4* But during the seventh year the land shall have a complete rest, a sabbath for the LORD, when you may neither sow your field nor prune your vineyard. 5† The aftergrowth of your harvest you shall not reap, nor shall you pick the grapes of your untrimmed vines in this year of sabbath rest for the land. 6 While the land has its sabbath, all its produce will be food equally for you yourself and for your male and female slaves, for your hired help and the tenants who live with you, 7 and likewise for your livestock and for the wild animals on your land.

The Jubilee Year

8 "Seven weeks of years shall you count—seven times seven years—so that the seven cycles amount to forty-nine years. 9 Then, on the tenth day of the seventh month let the trumpet resound; on this, the Day of Atonement, the trumpet blast shall re-echo throughout your land. 10*† This fiftieth year you

---

25, 5ff: As long as the produce of the sabbatical year remains on the field, it remains available to everyone; cf v 12. In Ex 23, 10f the poor and the wild beasts that have no other source of nourishment are alone mentioned.

25, 10: *Fiftieth year:* to arrive at this number, the preceding year of jubilee is included in the count, and therefore this is more exactly the forty-ninth year, the seventh sabbatical year. *Liberty:* Israelite slaves were set free (v 50) and landed property was returned to its original owner (v 13): two important laws for preserving the social and economic equilibrium. *Jubilee:* derived from the Hebrew word *yobel,* "ram's horn," which was blown on this occasion.

23, 43: Dt 31, 10-13.
24, 2: Ex 27, 20f.
24, 4: Ex 25, 31.
24, 5: Ex 25, 30; 1 Kgs 7, 48; 2 Chr 4, 19; 13, 11; Heb 9, 2.
24, 8: 1 Chr 9, 32.
24, 16: 1 Kgs 21, 10.13; Mt 26, 65f; Jn 10, 33.
24, 17: Gn 9, 5f; Ex 21, 12;

Nm 35, 31; Dt 19, 11f.
24, 18: Ex 21, 33f.
24, 20: Dt 19, 21; Mt 5, 38.
24, 22: Lv 19, 34; Ex 12, 49; Nm 15, 16.
24, 23: Acts 7, 57f.
25, 3: Ex 23, 10f.
25, 4: 1 Mc 6, 49.53.
25, 10: Nm 36, 4; Is 61, 2; Ez 46, 17; Lk 4, 19.

did you KNOW?

7 x 7 + 1 = Jubilee!

In the Bible, seven is a special number. Just as the seventh day of the week was set aside as a day of rest in ancient Israel, so the seventh year was set aside as a year of rest for the land. Fields were to remain uncultivated during the seventh year; whatever fruits or grains grew on their own were to be left for the poor. The "sabbatical year" was a reminder to the people that the land actually belonged to God, not to them.

Seven may be a special number, but seven times seven plus one is very special. The fiftieth year—the year after seven times seven years—was declared the Jubilee year, and God's Law demanded some very special things to happen. The people were to take a year of vacation from their normal routine. This meant no planting for a farmer, no lending for a banker, and no big sales for a merchant. Why this break? Because God wanted the Jubilee year to be a time when everyone started over with a clean slate. During the Jubilee, all land was to be returned to its original owners, and all Israelite slaves were to be set free. Debts were to be forgiven and justly settled. The year of Jubilee was like the reset button on a computer, stopping everything and returning it to its original setting. It was a check against the unjust distribution of property and wealth.

The Catholic church has continued the custom of celebrating the fiftieth year, especially when it marks the end of a century. Faithful to its Jewish roots, the church sees the Jubilee year as a special time for renewal. In preparation for a Jubilee year, it asks individuals and communities to commit themselves to following Jesus more faithfully.

▸ Leviticus, chapter 25

when every one of you shall return to his own property, every one to his own family estate. ¹¹ In this fiftieth year, your year of jubilee, you shall not sow, nor shall you reap the aftergrowth or pick the grapes from the untrimmed vines. ¹² Since this is the jubilee, which shall be sacred for you, you may not eat of its produce, except as taken directly from the field.

¹³ "In this year of jubilee, then, every one of you shall return to his own property. ¹⁴ Therefore, when you sell any land to your neighbor or buy any from him, do not deal unfairly. ¹⁵* On the basis of the number of years since the last jubilee shall you purchase the land from him; and so also, on the basis of the number of years for crops, shall he sell it to you. ¹⁶ When the years are many, the price shall be so much the more; when the years are few, the price shall be so much the less. For it is really the number of crops that he sells you. ¹⁷ Do not deal unfairly, then; but stand in fear of your God. I, the LORD, am your God.

¹⁸ "Observe my precepts and be careful to keep my regulations, for then you will dwell securely in the land. ¹⁹* The land will yield its fruit and you will have food in abundance, so that you may live there without worry. ²⁰* Therefore, do not say, 'What shall we eat in the seventh year, if we do not then sow or reap our crop?' ²¹ I will bestow such blessings on you in the sixth year that there will then be crop enough for three years. ²²* When you sow in the eighth year, you will continue to eat from the old crop; and even into the ninth year, when the crop comes in, you will still have the old to eat from.

Redemption of Property

²³* "The land shall not be sold in perpetuity; for the land is mine, and you are but aliens who have become my tenants. ²⁴ Therefore, in every part of the country that you occupy, you must permit the land to be redeemed. ²⁵* When one of your countrymen is reduced to poverty and has to sell some of his property, his closest relative, who has the right to redeem it, may go and buy back what his kinsman has sold. ²⁶ If, however, the man has no relative to redeem his land, but later on acquires sufficient means to buy it back in his own name, ²⁷ he shall make a deduction from the price in proportion to the number of years since the sale, and then pay back the balance to the one to whom he sold it, so that he may thus regain his own property. ²⁸* But if he does not acquire sufficient means to buy back his land, what he has sold shall remain in the possession of the purchaser until the jubilee, when it must be released and returned to its original owner.

shall make sacred by proclaiming liberty in the land for all its inhabitants. It shall be a jubilee for you,

---

25, 15: Lv 27, 18.23.
25, 19: Lv 26, 5.

25, 20: Mt 6, 25.31; Lk 12, 22.29.

25, 22: Lv 26, 10.
25, 23: 1 Pt 2, 11.

25, 25: Ru 2, 20; 4, 4.6; Jer 32, 7f.
25, 28: Lv 27, 24.

29 "When someone sells a dwelling in a walled town, he has the right to buy it back during the time of one full year from its sale. 30 But if such a house in a walled town has not been redeemed at the end of a full year, it shall belong in perpetuity to the purchaser and his descendants; nor shall it be released in the jubilee. 31 However, houses in villages that are not encircled by walls shall be considered as belonging to the surrounding farm land; they may be redeemed at any time, and in the jubilee they must be released.

32 "In levitical cities the Levites shall always have the right to redeem the town houses that are their property. 33 Any town house of the Levites in their cities that had been sold and not redeemed, shall be released in the jubilee; for the town houses of the Levites are their hereditary property in the midst of the Israelites. 34* Moreover, the pasture land belonging to their cities shall not be sold at all; it must always remain their hereditary property.

35* "When one of your fellow countrymen is reduced to poverty and is unable to hold out beside you, extend to him the privileges of an alien or a tenant, so that he may continue to live with you. 36 Do not exact interest from your countryman either in money or in kind, but out of fear of God let him live with you. 37* You are to lend him neither money at interest nor food at a profit. 38 I, the LORD, am your God, who brought you out of the land of Egypt to give you the land of Canaan and to be your God.

39* "When, then, your countryman becomes so impoverished beside you that he sells you his services, do not make him work as a slave. 40 Rather, let him be like a hired servant or like your tenant, working with you until the jubilee year, 41 when he, together with his children, shall be released from your service and return to his kindred and to the property of his ancestors. 42 Since those whom I brought out of the land of Egypt are servants of mine, they shall not be sold as slaves to any man. 43 Do not lord it over them harshly, but stand in fear of your God.

44 "Slaves, male and female, you may indeed possess, provided you buy them from among the neighboring nations. 45 You may also buy them from among the aliens who reside with you and from their children who are born and reared in your land. Such slaves you may own as chattels, 46* and leave to your sons as their hereditary property, making them perpetual slaves. But you shall not lord it harshly over any of the Israelites, your kinsmen.

47 "When one of your countrymen is reduced to such poverty that he sells himself to a wealthy alien who has a permanent or a temporary residence among you, or to one of the descendants of an immigrant family, 48 even after he has thus sold his services he still has the right of redemption; he may be redeemed by one of his own brothers, 49 or by his uncle or cousin, or by some other relative or fellow clansman; or, if he acquires the means, he may redeem himself. 50 With his purchaser he shall compute the years from the sale to the jubilee, distributing the sale price over these years as though he had been hired as a day laborer. 51 The more such years there are, the more of the sale price he shall pay back as ransom; 52 the fewer years there are left before the jubilee year, the more he has to his credit; in proportion to his years of service shall he pay his ransom. 53 The alien shall treat him as a servant hired on an annual basis, and he shall not lord it over him harshly under your very eyes. 54* If he is not thus redeemed, he shall nevertheless be released, together with his children, in the jubilee year. 55 For to me the Israelites belong as servants; they are servants of mine, because I brought them out of the land of Egypt, I, the LORD, your God.

The Reward of Obedience

26 1* "Do not make false gods for yourselves. You shall not erect an idol or a sacred pillar for yourselves, nor shall you set up a stone figure for worship in your land; for I, the LORD, am your God. 2* Keep my sabbaths, and reverence my sanctuary. I am the LORD.

3† "If you live in accordance with my precepts and are careful to observe my commandments, 4* I will give you rain in due season, so that the land will bear its crops, and the trees their fruit; 5 your threshing will last till vintage time, and your vintage till the time for sowing, and you will have food to eat in abundance, so that you may dwell securely in your land. 6 I will establish peace in the land, that you may lie down to rest without anxiety. I will rid the country of ravenous beasts, and keep the sword of war from sweeping across your land. 7 You will rout your enemies and lay them low with your sword. 8 Five of you will put a hundred of your foes to flight, and a hundred of you will chase ten thousand of them, till they are cut down by your sword. 9 I will look with favor upon you, and make you

---

† **26, 3–45:** Since God's covenant was with the Israelite nation as a whole, these promises and threats are made primarily to the entire community. The rewards and punishments are of a temporal nature because the community as such exists only here on earth, not in the hereafter.

25, 34: Nm 35, 3.
25, 35: Dt 15, 7.8.
25, 37: Dt 23, 19.
25, 39: 1 Kgs 9, 22.
25, 46: Is 14, 1f.
25, 54: Ex 21, 2f.
26, 1: Lv 19, 4; Ex 20, 4;
    Nm 33, 52; Dt 5, 8.
26, 2: Ex 20, 8.
26, 4: Ps 85, 13.

fruitful and numerous, as I carry out my covenant with you. 10* So much of the old crops will you have stored up for food that you will have to discard them to make room for the new. 11* I will set my Dwelling among you, and will not disdain you. 12 Ever present in your midst, I will be your God, and you will be my people; 13 for it is I, the LORD, your God, who brought you out of the land of the Egyptians and freed you from their slavery, breaking the yoke they had laid upon you and letting you walk erect.

Punishment of Disobedience

14 "But if you do not heed me and do not keep all these commandments, 15 if you reject my precepts and spurn my decrees, refusing to obey all my commandments and breaking my covenant, 16 then I, in turn, will give you your deserts. I will punish you with terrible woes—with wasting and fever to dim the eyes and sap the life. You will sow your seed in vain, for your enemies will consume the crop. 17* I will turn against you, till you are beaten down before your enemies and lorded over by your foes. You will take to flight though no one pursues you.

18 "If even after this you do not obey me, I will increase the chastisement for your sins sevenfold, 19 to break your haughty confidence. I will make the sky above you as hard as iron, and your soil as hard as bronze, 20 so that your strength will be spent in vain; your land will bear no crops, and its trees no fruit.

21 "If then you become defiant in your unwillingness to obey me, I will multiply my blows another sevenfold, as your sins deserve. 22 I will unleash the wild beasts against you, to rob you of your children and wipe out your livestock, till your population dwindles away and your roads become deserted.

23 "If, with all this, you still refuse to be chastened by me and continue to defy me, 24* I, too, will defy you and will smite you for your sins seven times harder than before. 25 I will make the sword, the avenger of my covenant, sweep over you. Though you then huddle together in your walled cities, I will send in pestilence among you, till you are forced to surrender to the enemy. 26* And as I cut off your supply of bread, ten women will need but one oven for baking all the bread they dole out to you in rations—not enough food to still your hunger.

27 "If, despite all this, you still persist in disobeying and defying me, 28 I, also, will meet you with fiery defiance and will chastise you with sevenfold fiercer punishment for your sins, 29*† till you begin to eat the flesh of your own sons and daughters. 30* I will demolish your high places, overthrow your incense stands, and cast your corpses on those of your idols. In my abhorrence of you, 31 I will lay waste your cities and devastate your sanctuaries, refusing to accept your sweet-smelling offerings. 32* So devastated will I leave the land that your very enemies who come to live there will stand aghast at the sight of it. 33* You yourselves I will scatter among the nations at the point of my drawn sword, leaving your countryside desolate and your cities deserted. 34* Then shall the land retrieve its lost sabbaths during all the time it lies waste, while you are in the land of your enemies; then shall the land have rest and make up for its sabbaths 35 during all the time that it lies desolate, enjoying the rest that you would not let it have on the sabbaths when you lived there.

36 "Those of you who survive in the lands of their enemies I will make so fainthearted that, if leaves rustle behind them, they will flee headlong, as if from the sword, though no one pursues them; 37 stumbling over one another as if to escape a weapon, while no one is after them—so helpless will you be to take a stand against your foes! 38 You will be lost among the Gentiles, swallowed up in your enemies' country. 39* Those of you who survive in the lands of their enemies will waste away for their own and their fathers' guilt.

40 "Thus they will have to confess that they and their fathers were guilty of having rebelled against me and of having defied me, 41 so that I, too, had to defy them and bring them into their enemies' land. Then, when their uncircumcised hearts are humbled and they make amends for their guilt, 42* I will remember my covenant with Jacob, my covenant with Isaac, and my covenant with Abraham; and of the land, too, I will be mindful. 43 But the land must first be rid of them, that in its desolation it may make up its lost sabbaths, and that they, too, may make good the debt of their guilt for having spurned my precepts and abhorred my statutes. 44 Yet even so, even while they are in their enemies' land, I will not reject or spurn them, lest, by wiping them out, I make void my covenant with them; for I, the LORD, am their God. 45* I will remember them because of the covenant I made with

---

† **26, 29:** *Eat the flesh of your own sons and daughters:* extreme famine in cities under siege often forced their inhabitants to such dire means of subsistence. Cf Dt 28, 53; Jer 19, 9; Ez 5, 10; 2 Kgs 6, 28f.

26, 10: Lv 25, 22.
26, 11f: Ex 29, 45; Ez 39, 26ff;

2 Cor 6, 16.
26, 17: Dt 28, 25.

26, 24f: Jer 2, 30;
 Ez 5, 17; 14, 17.
26, 26: Is 9, 19; Ez 4, 16; 5,
 16; 14, 13; Mi 6, 14.
26, 29: Is 9, 18.
26, 30: 2 Chr 14, 5; 34, 3.4.7;
 Ez 6, 3–6.
26, 32: 1 Kgs 9, 8; Jer 9, 11;
 18, 16; 19, 8; 25, 18;

 Ez 5, 15.
26, 33: Jer 9, 16; Zec 7, 14.
26, 34: Lv 25, 2; 2 Chr 36, 21.
26, 39: Ez 4, 17; 24, 23; 33,
 10.
26, 42: Ex 6, 5; 2 Kgs 13, 23;
 Ps 106, 45; Ez 16, 60.
26, 45: Ex 12, 51.

their forefathers, whom I brought out of the land of Egypt under the very eyes of the Gentiles, that I, the LORD, might be their God."

⁴⁶† These are the precepts, decrees and laws which the LORD had Moses promulgate on Mount Sinai in the pact between himself and the Israelites.

V: Redemption of Offerings

Redemption of Votive Offerings

27 ¹ The LORD said to Moses, ² "Speak to the Israelites and tell them: When anyone fulfills a vow of offering one or more persons to the LORD, who are to be ransomed at a fixed sum of money, ³ for persons between the ages of twenty and sixty, the fixed sum, in sanctuary shekels, shall be fifty silver shekels for a man, ⁴ and thirty shekels for a woman; ⁵ for persons between the ages of five and twenty, the fixed sum shall be twenty shekels for a youth, and ten for a maiden; ⁶ for persons between the ages of one month and five years, the fixed sum shall be five silver shekels for a boy, and three for a girl; ⁷ for persons of sixty or more, the fixed sum shall be fifteen shekels for a man, and ten for a woman. ⁸ However, if the one who took the vow is too poor to meet the fixed sum, the person must be set before the priest, who shall determine the sum for his ransom in keeping with the means of the one who made the vow.

⁹ "If the offering vowed to the LORD is an animal that may be sacrificed, every such animal, when vowed to the LORD, becomes sacred. ¹⁰ The offerer shall not present a substitute for it by exchanging either a better for a worse one or a worse for a better one. If he attempts to offer one animal in place of another, both the original and its substitute shall be treated as sacred. ¹¹ If the animal vowed to the LORD is unclean and therefore unfit for sacrifice, it must be set before the priest, ¹²† who shall determine its value in keeping with its good or bad qualities, and the value set by the priest shall stand. ¹³* If the offerer wishes to redeem the animal, he shall pay one fifth more than this valuation.

¹⁴ "When someone dedicates his house as sacred to the LORD, the priest shall determine its value in keeping with its good or bad points, and the value set by the priest shall stand. ¹⁵ If the one who dedicated his house wishes to redeem it, he shall pay one fifth more than the price thus established, and then it will again be his.

¹⁶ "If the object which someone dedicates to the LORD is a piece of his hereditary land, its valuation shall be made according to the amount of seed required to sow it, the acreage sown with a homer of barley seed being valued at fifty silver shekels. ¹⁷ If the dedication of a field is made at the beginning of a jubilee period, the full valuation shall hold; ¹⁸* but if it is some time after this, the priest shall estimate its money value according to the number of years left until the next jubilee year, with a corresponding rebate on the valuation. ¹⁹ If the one who dedicated his field wishes to redeem it, he shall pay one fifth more than the price thus established, and so reclaim it. ²⁰ If, instead of redeeming such a field, he sells it to someone else, it may no longer be redeemed; ²¹ but at the jubilee it shall be released as sacred to the LORD; like a field that is doomed, it shall become priestly property.

²² "If the field that some man dedicates to the LORD is one he had purchased and not a part of his hereditary property, ²³ the priest shall compute its value in proportion to the number of years until the next jubilee, and on the same day the price thus established shall be given as sacred to the LORD; ²⁴* at the jubilee, however, the field shall revert to the hereditary owner of this land from whom it had been purchased.

²⁵ "Every valuation shall be made according to the standard of the sanctuary shekel. There are twenty gerahs to the shekel.

Offerings Not To Be Redeemed

²⁶* "Note that a first-born animal, which as such already belongs to the LORD, may not be dedicated by vow to him. If it is an ox or a sheep, it shall be ceded to the LORD; ²⁷† but if it is an unclean animal, it may be redeemed by paying one fifth more than its fixed value. If it is not redeemed, it shall be sold at its fixed value.

²⁸* "Note, also, that any one of his possessions which a man vows as doomed to the LORD, whether it is a human being or an animal or a hereditary field, shall be neither sold nor ransomed; everything that is thus doomed becomes most sacred to the LORD. ²⁹† All human beings that are doomed

---

† **26, 46:** The Book of Leviticus seems originally to have ended here; the following chapter is an appendix.

27, 12: *Determine its value:* fix the price at which the animal may be sold to someone else. Only the original owner must pay the twenty percent tax, as a penalty for buying back what he had vowed to God. So also for houses and fields that are vowed to the Lord, as treated of in the following verses. The money from the sale or from the redemption of such vowed property naturally goes to the sanctuary.

27, 27: *An unclean animal:* such as the first-born of an ass, which was unfit for sacrifice. According to Ex 13; 34, 20, a first-born ass was to be redeemed by offering a sheep in its stead, or was to have

its neck broken. The present law is probably a later modification of the earlier one.

27, 29: *All human beings that are doomed:* according to some interpreters, this signifies the idolatrous Canaanites, who were doomed to destruction by divine authority; according to others, this drastic law was enacted for the purpose of discouraging private persons from rashly vowing their slaves or other dependents as offerings to God. Cf Ex 22, 19; Dt 13, 13–19.

* 27, 13: Lv 22, 14.   27, 26: Ex 13, 2.
27, 18: Lv 25, 15f.   27, 28: 1 Sm 15, 21.
27, 24: Lv 25, 10.28.41.

lose the right to be redeemed; they must be put to death.

30* "All tithes of the land, whether in grain from the fields or in fruit from the trees, belong to the LORD, as sacred to him. 31 If someone wishes to buy back any of his tithes, he shall pay one fifth more than their value. 32 The tithes of the herd and the flock shall be determined by ceding to the LORD as

27, 30: Nm 18, 21.24;
      2 Chr 31, 5f.12; Mal 3,
      8.10.

sacred every tenth animal as they are counted by the herdsman's rod. 33 It shall not matter whether good ones or bad ones are thus chosen, and no exchange may be made. If any exchange is attempted, both the original animal and its substitute shall be treated as sacred, without the right of being bought back."

34 These are the commandments which the LORD gave Moses on Mount Sinai for the Israelites.

Sound the trumpet, beat the drum, we are going to war! The call to arms brings out the best and the worst in people—courage and cowardice, love and hate, hope and fear. The Book of Numbers records the varied experiences of the Israelites as they prepare for the armed conquest of the Promised Land. But most important, it tells of God's insistence that they maintain their purity and holiness to be worthy recipients of God's promises.

At a Glance

I. Preparation for the Departure from Sinai (1, 1—10, 10).

II. From Sinai to the Plains of Moab (10, 11—22, 1).

III. On the Plains of Moab (22, 2—36, 13).

In-depth

Although the Book of Numbers is named for the two censuses mentioned in it (chapters 1 and 26), the book's original Hebrew name, meaning "in the desert," describes it better. Numbers picks up the story of the Israelites where Exodus leaves off. The first section begins with a census at Mount Sinai to determine who is eligible for military service. As the people prepare to enter the Promised Land, their leaders review the laws and regulations with them.

In the second section, the Israelites begin their journey to the Promised Land. Unfortunately, they have not learned to put their faith in God, and their journey is marked by grumbling, rebellion, and even idolatry. When the first army refuses to enter the Promised Land because of reports that it is inhabited by a race of giants (Nm 13, 33), God decrees that none of the older generation who left Egypt shall enter the Promised Land. So, the Israelites begin their desert wandering, which lasts thirty-eight years (see map 2, "The Exodus from Egypt").

The third section of Numbers paints a more hopeful picture. The people of the new generation are faithful and obedient as they prepare to enter the Land. They experience victory against the Midianites (chapter 31) and conquer the land east of the Jordan (chapter 32). The God who liberated their ancestors from Egypt, sustained and led them through the wilderness with Moses, is the same God who now makes ready to fulfill the promise of the Land to Israel.

Numbers was written by priestly scribes hundreds of years after these events, after the people had lost the Promised Land to the Babylonians. They fully appreciated the gift of the Land only after they had lost it. For the Israelites in the Babylonian Exile, Numbers portrayed the hopeful, grateful, and faithful hearts required of those whom God blesses.

Quick Facts

Period Covered
the thirty-eight years of wandering in the desert after the Exodus

Authors
priestly scribes writing during the Babylonian Exile (587–538 B.C.)

Theme
Faithfulness and grateful-ness to God are neces-sary for Israel to obtain the Promised Land.

The Book of *Numbers*

Numbers

Chap. 31

I: Preparation for the Departure from Sinai

The Census

1 ¹ In the year following that of the Israelites' departure from the land of Egypt, on the first day of the second month, the LORD said to Moses in the meeting tent in the desert of Sinai: ²*† "Take a census of the whole community of the Israelites, by clans and ancestral houses, registering each male individually. ³ You and Aaron shall enroll in companies all the men in Israel of twenty years or more who are fit for military service.

Moses' Assistants

⁴ "To assist you there shall be a man from each tribe, the head of his ancestral house. ⁵* These are the names of those who are to assist you:

from Reuben: Elizur, son of Shedeur;
⁶ from Simeon: Shelumiel, son of Zurishaddai;
⁷ from Judah: Nahshon, son of Amminadab;
⁸ from Issachar: Nethanel, son of Zuar;
⁹ from Zebulun: Eliab, son of Helon;
¹⁰ from Ephraim: Elishama, son of Ammihud,
and from Manasseh: Gamaliel, son of Pedahzur,
for the descendants of Joseph;

¹¹ from Benjamin: Abidan, son of Gideoni;
¹² from Dan: Ahiezer, son of Ammishaddai;
¹³ from Asher: Pagiel, son of Ochran;
¹⁴ from Gad: Eliasaph, son of Reuel;
¹⁵ from Naphtali: Ahira, son of Enan."

¹⁶*† These were councilors of the community, princes of their ancestral tribes, chiefs of the troops of Israel. ¹⁷ So Moses and Aaron took these men who had been designated, ¹⁸ and assembled the whole community on the first day of the second month. Every man of twenty years or more then declared his name and lineage according to clan and ancestral house, ¹⁹ as the LORD had commanded Moses.

Count of the Twelve Tribes

This is their census as taken in the desert of Sinai. ²⁰ Of the descendants of Reuben, the first-born of Israel, registered by lineage in clans and ancestral houses: when all the males of twenty years or more who were fit for military service were polled, ²¹ forty-six thousand five hundred were enrolled in the tribe of Reuben.

²² Of the descendants of Simeon, registered by lineage in clans and ancestral houses: when all the males of twenty years or more who were fit for mil-

---

1, 2: All Israel was divided into tribes, each tribe into clans, and each clan into ancestral houses.

1, 16: *Troops:* literally "thousands"; this division of the Israelites, with its subdivisions of "hundreds, fifties and tens," was primarily for military and judicial purposes. Cf Ex 18, 21: 2 Sm 18, 1.

1, 2f: Nm 14, 29; 26, 2–51. **1, 16:** Ex 18, 21.25.
1, 5–15: Nm 10, 14–27.

itary service were polled, 23 fifty-nine thousand three hundred were enrolled in the tribe of Simeon.

24 Of the descendants of Gad, registered by lineage in clans and ancestral houses: when all the males of twenty years or more who were fit for military service were polled, 25 forty-five thousand six hundred and fifty were enrolled in the tribe of Gad.

26 Of the descendants of Judah, registered by lineage in clans and ancestral houses: when all the males of twenty years or more who were fit for military service were polled, 27 seventy-four thousand six hundred were enrolled in the tribe of Judah.

28 Of the descendants of Issachar, registered by lineage in clans and ancestral houses: when all the males of twenty years or more who were fit for military service were polled, 29 fifty-four thousand four hundred were enrolled in the tribe of Issachar.

30 Of the descendants of Zebulun, registered by lineage in clans and ancestral houses: when all the males of twenty years or more who were fit for military service were polled, 31 fifty-seven thousand four hundred were enrolled in the tribe of Zebulun.

32 Of the descendants of Joseph—

Of the descendants of Ephraim, registered by lineage in clans and ancestral houses: when all the males of twenty years or more who were fit for military service were polled, 33 forty thousand five hundred were enrolled in the tribe of Ephraim.

34 Of the descendants of Manasseh, registered by lineage in clans and ancestral houses: when all the males of twenty years or more who were fit for military service were polled, 35 thirty-two thousand two hundred were enrolled in the tribe of Manasseh.

36 Of the descendants of Benjamin, registered by lineage in clans and ancestral houses: when all the males of twenty years or more who were fit for military service were polled, 37 thirty-five thousand four hundred were enrolled in the tribe of Benjamin.

38 Of the descendants of Dan, registered by lineage in clans and ancestral houses: when all the males of twenty years or more who were fit for military service were polled, 39 sixty-two thousand seven hundred were enrolled in the tribe of Dan.

40 Of the descendants of Asher, registered by lineage in clans and ancestral houses: when all the males of twenty years or more who were fit for military service were polled, 41 forty-one thousand five hundred were enrolled in the tribe of Asher.

42 Of the descendants of Naphtali, registered by lineage in clans and ancestral houses: when all the males of twenty years or more who were fit for

military service were polled, 43 fifty-three thousand four hundred were enrolled in the tribe of Naphtali.

44 It was these who were registered, each according to his ancestral house, in the census taken by Moses and Aaron and the twelve princes of Israel. 45 The total number of the Israelites of twenty years or more who were fit for military service, registered by ancestral houses, 46 was six hundred and three thousand five hundred and fifty.

Levites Omitted in the Census

47*† The Levites, however, were not registered by ancestral tribe with the others. 48 For the LORD had told Moses, 49 "The tribe of Levi alone you shall not enroll nor include in the census along with the other Israelites. 50* You are to give the Levites charge of the Dwelling of the commandments with all its equipment and all that belongs to it. It is they who shall carry the Dwelling with all its equipment and who shall be its ministers. They shall therefore camp around the Dwelling. 51* When the Dwelling is to move on, the Levites shall take it down; when the Dwelling is to be pitched, it is the Levites who shall set it up. Any layman who comes near it shall be put to death. 52* While the other Israelites shall camp by companies, each in his own division of the camp, 53* the Levites shall camp around the Dwelling of the commandments. Otherwise God's wrath will strike the Israelite community. The Levites, then, shall have charge of the Dwelling of the commandments." 54 All this the Israelites fulfilled as the LORD had commanded Moses.

Arrangement of the Tribes

2 1 The LORD said to Moses and Aaron: 2* "The Israelites shall camp, each in his own division, under the ensigns of their ancestral houses. They shall camp around the meeting tent, but at some distance from it.

3† "Encamped on the east side, toward the sunrise, shall be the divisional camp of Judah, arranged in companies. [The prince of the Judahites was Nahshon, son of Amminadab, 4 and his soldiers amounted in the census to seventy-four thousand six hundred.] 5 With Judah shall camp the tribe of Issachar [their prince was Nethanel, son of Zuar, 6 and his soldiers amounted in the census to fifty-four thousand four hundred] 7 and the tribe of Zebulun. [Their prince was Eliab, son of Helon, 8 and his soldiers amounted in the census to fifty-seven thousand four hundred. 9 The total number of those registered by companies in the camp of

---

1, 47: The Levites were not enrolled in this census, which was principally for military purposes, but a separate census was made of them. Cf Nm 3, 15f.39.

2, 3–31: A similar arrangement of the tribes around the central sanctuary in the ideal Israelite state is given in Ez 48.

1, 47: Nm 2, 33; 3, 14–39;
   26, 57–62.
1, 50: Nm 3, 7f; 4, 2–49;
   1 Chr 6, 48.
1, 51: Nm 3, 10.38; 18, 7;

2 Sm 6, 6f; 1 Chr 13, 10.
1, 52: Nm 2, 34.
1, 53: Nm 3, 7f.38; 8, 19;
   18, 4f.
2, 2: Nm 1, 52.

did you KNOW?

Holy War

The Book of Numbers begins with a census of "all the men in Israel of twenty years or more who are fit for military service" (1, 3). The people of Israel are preparing to take over the land God had promised to them, the Chosen People. This is no ordinary war but a holy war, a war that they believe is divinely inspired, even a war God commands. In 31, 2, God says to Moses, "Avenge the Israelites on the Midianites." The Israelites go on to kill every Midianite except for the young girls who are virgins.

How are we to understand this? Does God really order the killing of innocent people? To answer this, let's first remember that the writers of the Bible were influenced by their own cultural background and understanding of God. Three main things were probably on the mind of the writer of Numbers. First, the early Israelites viewed God as a warrior god fighting for them. Second, they believed the Canaanites were a wicked and idolatrous people who deserved punishment. And finally, they believed the Midianites deserved special punishment because they had led the Israelites into idolatry and sin at Shittim (see 25, 1–5).

Holy wars are dangerous. Throughout history, people have committed atrocities in the name of God. Christians must interpret the Old Testament in the light of Jesus' teachings in the New Testament. Jesus clearly taught about a God of mercy and love, not a God of war and vengeance. This is one area where the New Testament teaching replaces an earlier Old Testament understanding. Holy wars have no place in the lives of Christians.

Judah was one hundred and eighty-six thousand four hundred.] These shall be first on the march.

10 "On the south side shall be the divisional camp of Reuben, arranged in companies. [Their prince was Elizur, son of Shedeur, 11 and his soldiers amounted in the census to forty-six thousand five hundred.] 12 Beside them shall camp the tribe of Simeon [their prince was Shelumiel, son of Zurishaddai, 13 and his soldiers amounted in the census to fifty-nine thousand three hundred] 14 and next the tribe of Gad. [Their prince was Eliasaph, son of Reuel, 15 and his soldiers amounted in the census to forty-five thousand six hundred and fifty. 16 The total number of those registered by companies in the camp of Reuben was one hundred and fifty-one thousand four hundred and fifty.] These shall be second on the march.

17 "Then the meeting tent and the camp of the Levites shall set out in the middle of the line. As in camp, so also on the march, every man shall be in his proper place, with his own division.

18 "On the west side shall be the divisional camp of Ephraim, arranged in companies. [Their prince was Elishama, son of Ammihud, 19 and his soldiers amounted in the census to forty thousand five hundred.] 20 Beside them shall camp the tribe of Manasseh [their prince was Gamaliel, son of Pedahzur, 21 and his soldiers amounted in the census to thirty-two thousand two hundred] 22 and the tribe of Benjamin. [Their prince was Abidan, son of Gideoni, 23 and his soldiers amounted in the census to thirty-five thousand four hundred. 24 The total number of those registered by companies in the camp of Ephraim was one hundred and eight thousand one hundred.] These shall be third on the march.

25 "On the north side shall be the divisional camp of Dan, arranged in companies. [Their prince was Ahiezer, son of Ammishaddai, 26 and his soldiers amounted in the census to sixty-two thousand seven hundred.] 27 Beside them shall camp the tribe of Asher [their prince was Pagiel, son of Ochran, 28 and his soldiers amounted in the census to forty-one thousand five hundred] 29 and next the tribe of Naphtali. [Their prince was Ahira, son of Enan, 30 and his soldiers amounted in the census to fifty-three thousand four hundred. 31 The total number of those registered by companies in the camp of Dan was one hundred and fifty-seven thousand six hundred.] These shall be the last of the divisions on the march."

32* This was the census of the Israelites taken by ancestral houses. The total number of those registered by companies in the camps was six hundred and three thousand five hundred and fifty. 33 The Levites, however, were not registered with the other Israelites, for so the LORD had commanded Moses. 34 The Israelites did just as the LORD had commanded Moses; both in camp and on the march they were in their own divisions, every man according to his clan and his ancestral house.

The Sons of Aaron

3 [1] The following were the descendants of Aaron and Moses at the time that the LORD spoke to Moses on Mount Sinai. [2]* The sons of Aaron were Nadab his first-born, Abihu, Eleazar, and Ithamar. [3] These are the names of the sons of Aaron, the anointed priests who were ordained to exercise the priesthood. [4]* But when Nadab and Abihu offered profane fire before the LORD in the desert of Sinai, they met death in the presence of the LORD, and left no sons. Thereafter only Eleazar and Ithamar performed the priestly functions under the direction of their father Aaron.

Levites in Place of the First-born

[5] Now the LORD said to Moses: [6]* "Summon the tribe of Levi and present them to Aaron the priest, as his assistants. [7]* They shall discharge his obligations and those of the whole community before the meeting tent by serving at the Dwelling. [8] They shall have custody of all the furnishings of the meeting tent and discharge the duties of the Israelites in the service of the Dwelling. [9]* You shall give the Levites to Aaron and his sons; they have been set aside from among the Israelites as dedicated to me. [10]* But only Aaron and his descendants shall you appoint to have charge of the priestly functions. Any layman who comes near shall be put to death."

[11] The LORD said to Moses, [12]* "It is I who have chosen the Levites from the Israelites in place of every first-born that opens the womb among the Israelites. The Levites, therefore, are mine, [13] because every first-born is mine. When I slew all the first-born in the land of Egypt, I made all the first-born in Israel sacred to me, both of man and of beast. They belong to me; I am the LORD."

Census of the Levites

[14] The LORD said to Moses in the desert of Sinai, [15]* "Take a census of the Levites by ancestral houses and clans, registering every male of a month or more." [16] Moses, therefore, took their census in accordance with the command the LORD had given him.

[17]* The sons of Levi were named Gershon, Kohath and Merari. [18] The descendants of Gershon, by clans, were named Libni and Shimei. [19] The descendants of Kohath, by clans, were Amram, Izhar, Hebron and Uzziel. [20] The descendants of Merari, by clans, were Mahli and Mushi. These were the clans of the Levites by ancestral houses.

Duties of the Levitical Clans

[21] To Gershon belonged the clan of the Libnites and the clan of the Shimeites; these were the clans of the Gershonites. [22] When all their males of a month or more were registered, they numbered seven thousand five hundred. [23] The clans of the Gershonites camped behind the Dwelling, to the west. [24] The prince of their ancestral house was Eliasaph, son of Lael. [25]*† At the meeting tent they had charge of whatever pertained to the Dwelling, the tent and its covering, the curtain at the entrance of the meeting tent, [26] the hangings of the court, the curtain at the entrance of the court enclosing both the Dwelling and the altar, and the ropes.

[27] To Kohath belonged the clans of the Amramites, the Izharites, the Hebronites, and the Uzzielites; these were the clans of the Kohathites. [28] When all their males of a month or more were registered, they numbered eight thousand three hundred. They had charge of the sanctuary. [29] The clans of the Kohathites camped at the south side of the Dwelling. [30] The prince of their ancestral house was Elizaphan, son of Uzziel. [31]† They had charge of whatever pertained to the ark, the table, the lampstand, the altars, the utensils with which the ministry of the sanctuary was exercised, and the veil. [32] The chief prince of the Levites, however, was Eleazar, son of Aaron the priest; he was supervisor over those who had charge of the sanctuary.

[33] To Merari belonged the clans of the Mahlites and the Mushites; these were the clans of Merari. [34] When all their males of a month or more were registered, they numbered six thousand two hundred. [35] The prince of the ancestral house of the clans of Merari was Zuriel, son of Abihail. They camped at the north side of the Dwelling. [36]† The Merarites were charged with the care of whatever pertained to the boards of the Dwelling, its bars, columns, pedestals, and all its fittings, [37] as well as the columns of the surrounding court with their pedestals, pegs and ropes.

[38] East of the Dwelling, that is, in front of the

3, 25f: The Gershonites had two wagons for transporting these things; cf Nm 7, 7. For a description of the Dwelling, see Ex 26, 1–6; the tent, Ex 26, 7–13; its covering, Ex 26, 14; the curtain at the entrance, Ex 26, 36; the hangings of the court, Ex 27, 9–15; the curtain at the entrance of the court, Ex 27, 16; the ropes of the Dwelling, Ex 35, 18.

3, 31: The Kohathites had to carry these sacred objects on their shoulders; cf Nm 7, 9. For a description of the ark, see Ex 25, 10–22; the table, Ex 25, 23–30; the lampstand, Ex 25, 31–40; the altars, Ex 27, 1–8; 30, 1–10.

3, 36f: The Merarites had four wagons for transporting this heavy material; cf Nm 7, 8. For a description of the boards, bars, etc., of the Dwelling, see Ex 26, 15–30; the columns, pedestals, etc., of the court, Ex 27, 9–19.

3, 2: Ex 6, 23.
3, 4: Nm 26, 61; Lv 10, 1f; 1 Chr 24, 2.
3, 6: Nm 18, 2.
3, 7: Nm 8, 24.
3, 9: Nm 8, 19.
3, 10: Nm 1, 51; 18, 7.

3, 12f: Nm 3, 41; 8, 16f; Ex 13, 2.12.15.
3, 15: Nm 3, 39; 26, 62.
3, 17–20: Nm 26, 57; Gn 46, 11; Ex 6, 16–19; 1 Chr 6, 1f.16–19.
3, 25–26: Ex 26, 7.14.36; 36, 14.

N
M

meeting tent, toward the sunrise, were camped Moses and Aaron and the latter's sons. They discharged the obligations of the sanctuary for the Israelites. Any layman who came near was to be put to death.

39 The total number of male Levites a month old or more whom Moses had registered by clans in keeping with the LORD's command, was twenty-two thousand.

Census and Ransom of First-born

40 The LORD then said to Moses, "Take a census of all the first-born males of the Israelites a month old or more, and compute their total number. 41 Then assign the Levites to me, the LORD, in place of all the first-born of the Israelites, as well as their cattle in place of all the first-born among the cattle of the Israelites." 42 So Moses took a census of all the first-born of the Israelites, as the LORD had commanded him. 43 When all the first-born males of a month or more were registered, they numbered twenty-two thousand two hundred and seventy-three.

44 The LORD said to Moses: 45 "Take the Levites in place of all the first-born of the Israelites, and the Levites' cattle in place of their cattle, that the Levites may belong to me. I am the LORD. 46 As ransom for the two hundred and seventy-three first-born of the Israelites who outnumber the Levites, 47* you shall take five shekels for each individual, according to the standard of the sanctuary shekel, twenty gerahs to the shekel. 48 Give this silver to Aaron and his sons as ransom for the extra number." 49 So Moses took the silver as ransom from those who were left when the rest had been redeemed by the Levites. 50 From the first-born of the Israelites he received in silver one thousand three hundred and sixty-five shekels according to the sanctuary standard. 51 He then gave this ransom silver to Aaron and his sons, as the LORD had commanded him.

Duties Further Defined

4 1 The LORD said to Moses and Aaron: 2 "Among the Levites take a total of the Kohathites, by clans and ancestral houses, all the men of the Kohathites 3*† between thirty and fifty years of age; these are to undertake obligatory tasks in the meeting tent.

4 "The service of the Kohathites in the meeting tent concerns the most sacred objects. 5† In breaking camp, Aaron and his sons shall go in and take down the screening curtain and cover the ark of the commandments with it. 6 Over these they shall put a cover of tahash skin, and on top of this spread an all-violet cloth. They shall then put the poles in place. 7 On the table of the Presence they shall spread a violet cloth and put on it the plates and cups, as well as the bowls and pitchers for libations; the established bread offering shall remain on the table. 8 Over these they shall spread a scarlet cloth and cover all this with tahash skin. They shall then put the poles in place. 9 They shall use a violet cloth to cover the lampstand with its lamps, trimming shears, and trays, as well as the various containers of oil from which it is supplied. 10 The lampstand with all its utensils they shall then enclose in a covering of tahash skin, and place on a litter. 11† Over the golden altar they shall spread a violet cloth, and cover this also with a covering of tahash skin. They shall then put the poles in place. 12 Taking the utensils of the sanctuary service, they shall wrap them all in violet cloth and cover them with tahash skin. They shall then place them on a litter. 13† After cleansing the altar of its ashes, they shall spread a purple cloth over it. 14† On this they shall put all the utensils with which it is served: the fire pans, forks, shovels, basins, and all the utensils of the altar. They shall then spread a covering of tahash skin over this, and put the poles in place.

15* "Only after Aaron and his sons have finished covering the sacred objects and all their utensils on breaking camp, shall the Kohathites enter to carry them. But they shall not touch the sacred objects; if they do they will die. These, then, are the objects in the meeting tent that the Kohathites shall carry.

16 "Eleazar, son of Aaron the priest, shall be in charge of the oil for the light, the fragrant incense, the established cereal offering, and the anointing oil. He shall be in charge of the whole Dwelling with all the sacred objects and utensils that are in it."

17 The LORD said to Moses and Aaron: 18 "Do not let the group of Kohathite clans perish from the body of the Levites. 19 That they may live and not die when they approach the most sacred objects, this is what you shall do for them: Aaron and his sons shall go in and assign to each of them his task and what he must carry; 20* but the Kohathites shall not go in to look upon the sacred objects, even for an instant; if they do, they will die."

21 The LORD said to Moses, 22 "Take a total

4, 3: *Thirty:* at a later period the Levites began to serve when they were twenty-five (Nm 8, 24) or even only twenty years old (1 Chr 23, 24.27; 2 Chr 31, 17; Ezr 3, 8; but cf 1 Chr 23, 3).
4, 5: *The screening curtain:* the veil between the inner and the outer rooms of the sanctuary. Cf Ex 26, 31–33.
4, 11: *The golden altar:* the altar of incense. Cf Ex 30, 1–6.
4, 13: *The altar:* the bronze altar of holocausts. Cf Ex 27, 1–8.

4, 14: *Forks:* used in turning over the sacrificed animal on the fire of the altar. *Basins:* to receive the sacrificial blood; cf Zec 9, 15.

3, 47: Nm 18, 16; Ex 30, 13;   4, 15: 2 Sm 6, 6f; 1 Chr
  Lv 27, 25; Ez 45, 12.   13, 9f.
4, 3: Nm 8, 24; 1 Chr 23,   4, 20: 1 Sm 6, 19.
  24–27.

among the Gershonites also, by ancestral houses and clans, 23 of all the men between thirty and fifty years of age; these are to undertake obligatory tasks in the meeting tent. 24 This is the task of the clans of the Gershonites, what they must do and what they must carry: 25 they shall carry the sheets of the Dwelling, the meeting tent with its covering and the outer wrapping of tahash skin, the curtain at the entrance of the meeting tent, 26 the hangings of the court, the curtain at the entrance of the court that encloses both the Dwelling and the altar, together with their ropes and all other objects necessary in their use. Whatever is to be done with these things shall be their task. 27 The service of the Gershonites shall be entirely under the direction of Aaron and his sons, with regard to what they must do and what they must carry; you shall make each man of them responsible for what he is to carry. 28 This, then, is the task of the Gershonites in the meeting tent; and they shall be under the supervision of Ithamar, son of Aaron the priest.

29 "Among the Merarites, too, you shall enroll by clans and ancestral houses 30 all their men between thirty and fifty years of age; these are to undertake obligatory tasks in the meeting tent. 31* This is what they shall be responsible for carrying, all the years of their service in the meeting tent: the boards of the Dwelling with its bars, columns and pedestals, 32 and the columns of the surrounding court with their pedestals, pegs and ropes. You shall designate for each man of them all the objects connected with his service, which he shall be responsible for carrying. 33 This, then, is the task of the clans of the Merarites during all their service in the meeting tent under the supervision of Ithamar, son of Aaron the priest."

Number of Adult Levites

34 So Moses and Aaron and the princes of the community made a registration among the Kohathites, by clans and ancestral houses, 35 of all the men between thirty and fifty years of age. These were to undertake obligatory tasks in the meeting tent; 36 as registered by clans, they numbered two thousand seven hundred and fifty. 37 Such was the census of all the men of the Kohathite clans who were to serve in the meeting tent, which Moses took, together with Aaron, as the LORD bade him. 38 The registration was then made among the

Gershonites, by clans and ancestral houses, 39 of all the men between thirty and fifty years of age. These were to undertake obligatory tasks in the meeting tent; 40 as registered by clans and ancestral houses, they numbered two thousand six hundred and thirty. 41 Such was the census of all the men of the Gershonite clans who were to serve in the meeting tent, which Moses took, together with Aaron, at the LORD's bidding.

42 Then the registration was made among the Merarites, by clans and ancestral houses, 43 of all the men from thirty up to fifty years of age. These were to undertake obligatory tasks in the meeting tent; 44 as registered by clans, they numbered three thousand two hundred. 45 Such was the census of the men of the Merarite clans which Moses took, together with Aaron, as the LORD bade him.

46 Therefore, when Moses and Aaron and the Israelite princes had completed the registration among the Levites, by clans and ancestral houses, 47 of all the men between thirty and fifty years of age who were to undertake tasks of service or transport of the meeting tent, 48 the total number registered was eight thousand five hundred and eighty. 49 According to the LORD's bidding to Moses, they gave them their individual assignments for service and for transport; so the LORD had commanded Moses.

The Unclean Expelled

5 1 The LORD said to Moses: 2*† "Order the Israelites to expel from camp every leper, and everyone suffering from a discharge, and everyone who has become unclean by contact with a corpse. 3* Male and female alike, you shall compel them to go out of the camp; they are not to defile the camp in which I dwell." 4 The Israelites obeyed the command that the LORD had given Moses; they expelled them from the camp.

Unjust Possession

5† The LORD said to Moses, 6* "Tell the Israelites: If a man (or woman) commits a fault against his fellow man and wrongs him, thus breaking faith with the LORD, 7 he shall confess the wrong he has done, restore his ill-gotten goods in full, and in addition give one fifth of their value to the one he has wronged. 8† However, if the latter has no next of kin to whom restoration of the ill-gotten goods can

---

5, 2: For the laws regarding victims of leprosy, see Lv 13–14; those suffering from a discharge, Lv 15; the unclean by contact with a corpse, Nm 19, 11–22; Lv 21, 1–4.

5, 5–10: The basic law on unjust possession is given in Lv 5, 14–26. The new item here concerns the case where the injured party has died and left no heirs, in which case the restitution must be made to the priest.

5, 8: Next of kin: literally, "redeemer," a technical term denoting

the nearest relative, upon whom devolved the obligation of "redeeming" the family property, in order to keep it within the family. Cf Lv 25, 25; Ru 4, 1–6.

4, 31: Nm 3, 36f.
5, 2: Nm 19, 11.13; Lv 13, 46; 21, 1; 22, 4.
5, 3: Nm 35, 34.
5, 6ff: Lv 5, 21–25.

be made, the goods to be restored shall be the LORD'S and shall fall to the priest; this is apart from the atonement ram with which the priest makes amends for the guilty man. 9* Likewise, every sacred contribution that the Israelites are bound to make shall fall to the priest. 10* Each Israelite man may dispose of his own sacred contributions; they become the property of the priest to whom he gives them."

Ordeal for a Suspected Adulteress

11 The LORD said to Moses, 12 "Speak to the Israelites and tell them: If a man's wife goes astray and becomes unfaithful to him 13* by having intercourse with another man, though her husband has not sufficient evidence of the fact, so that her impurity remains unproved for lack of a witness who might have caught her in the act; 14 or if a man is overcome by a feeling of jealousy that makes him suspect his wife, whether she was actually impure or not: 15 he shall bring his wife to the priest and shall take along as an offering for her a tenth of an ephah of barley meal. However, he shall not pour oil on it nor put frankincense over it, since it is a cereal offering of jealousy, a cereal offering for an appeal in a question of guilt.

16 "The priest shall first have the woman come forward and stand before the LORD. 17*† In an earthen vessel he shall meanwhile put some holy water, as well as some dust that he has taken from the floor of the Dwelling. 18† Then, as the woman stands before the LORD, the priest shall uncover her head and place in her hands the cereal offering of her appeal, that is, the cereal offering of jealousy, while he himself shall hold the bitter water that brings a curse. 19 Then he shall adjure the woman, saying to her, 'If no other man has had intercourse with you, and you have not gone astray by impurity while under the authority of your husband, be immune to the curse brought by this bitter water. 20 But if you have gone astray while under the authority of your husband and have acted impurely by letting a man other than your husband have intercourse with you'— 21† so shall the priest adjure the woman with this oath of imprecation—'may the

LORD make you an example of malediction and imprecation among your people by causing your thighs to waste away and your belly to swell! 22*† May this water, then, that brings a curse, enter your body to make your belly swell and your thighs waste away!' And the woman shall say, 'Amen, amen!' 23 The priest shall put these imprecations in writing and shall then wash them off into the bitter water, 24 which he is to have the woman drink, so that it may go into her with all its bitter curse. 25 But first he shall take the cereal offering of jealousy from the woman's hand, and having waved this offering before the LORD, shall put it near the altar, 26* where he shall take a handful of the cereal offering as its token offering and burn it on the altar. Only then shall he have the woman drink the water. 27 Once she has done so, if she has been impure and unfaithful to her husband, this bitter water that brings a curse will go into her, and her belly will swell and her thighs will waste away, so that she will become an example of imprecation among her people. 28 If, however, the woman has not defiled herself, but is still pure, she will be immune and will still be able to bear children.

29 "This, then, is the law for jealousy: When a woman goes astray while under the authority of her husband and acts impurely, 30 or when such a feeling of jealousy comes over a man that he becomes suspicious of his wife, he shall have her stand before the LORD, and the priest shall apply this law in full to her. 31† The man shall be free from guilt, but the woman shall bear such guilt as she may have."

Laws Concerning Nazirites

6 1 The LORD said to Moses: 2† "Speak to the Israelites and tell them: When a man (or a woman) solemnly takes the nazirite vow to dedicate himself to the LORD, 3* he shall abstain from wine and strong drink; he may neither drink wine vinegar, other vinegar, or any kind of grape juice, nor eat either fresh or dried grapes. 4 As long as he is a nazirite he shall not eat anything of the produce of the vine; not even unripe grapes or grapeskins. 5* While he is under the nazirite vow, no razor shall touch his hair. Until the period of his dedication to

---

5, 17: *Holy water:* water from the laver that stood in the court of the Dwelling.
5, 18: *Appeal:* by which she invokes the Lord and refers her case to his decision.
5, 21: *An example of malediction and imprecation:* the woman's name would be used in curses and oaths to invoke a similar misfortune on another person or on oneself. Cf Is 65, 15; Jer 29, 22.
5, 22: *Amen:* a Hebrew word meaning, "certainly, truly," used to give assent to a statement, a curse, a blessing, a prayer, or the like; in this sense of "so be it," the Christian liturgy also uses it after prayers and blessings.
5, 31: *Free from guilt:* by fulfilling his obligation of obtaining a decision in the matter.
6, 1ff: *Nazirite:* from the Hebrew word *nazir*, meaning "set apart

as sacred, dedicated, vowed." The nazirite vow could be either for a limited period or for life. Those bound by this vow had to abstain from all the products of the grapevine, from cutting or shaving their hair, and from contact with a corpse. They were regarded as men of God like the prophets; cf Am 2, 11f. Examples of lifelong nazirites were Samson (Jgs 13, 4f.7; 16, 17), Samuel (1 Sm 1, 11), and John the Baptizer (Lk 1, 15). At the time of Christ the practice of taking the nazirite vow for a limited period seems to have been quite common, even among the early Christians; cf Acts 18, 18; 21, 23f.26.

5, 9: Dt 18, 3f; Ex 44, 29f. 5, 26: Lv 5, 12.
5, 10: Lv 10, 12–15. 6, 3f: Jgs 13, 7.14.
5, 13: Lv 18, 20; Jn 8, 4. 6, 5: Jgs 13, 5; 16, 17; 1 Sm
5, 17: Nm 19, 17. 1, 11.
5, 22: Ps 109, 18.

the LORD is over, he shall be sacred, and shall let the hair of his head grow freely. 6* As long as he is dedicated to the LORD, he shall not enter where a dead person is. 7 Not even for his father or mother, his sister or brother, should they die, may he become unclean, since his head bears his dedication to God. 8 As long as he is a nazirite he is sacred to the LORD.

9 "If someone dies very suddenly in his presence, so that his dedicated head becomes unclean, he shall shave his head on the day of his purification, that is, on the seventh day. 10 On the eighth day he shall bring two turtledoves or two pigeons to the priest at the entrance of the meeting tent. 11 The priest shall offer up the one as a sin offering and the other as a holocaust, thus making atonement for him for the sin he has committed by reason of the dead person. On the same day he shall reconsecrate his head 12 and begin anew the period of his dedication to the LORD as a nazirite, bringing a yearling lamb as a guilt offering. The previous period is not valid, because his dedicated head became unclean.

13* "This is the ritual for the nazirite: On the day he completes the period of his dedication he shall go to the entrance of the meeting tent, 14 bringing as his offering to the LORD one unblemished yearling lamb for a holocaust, one unblemished yearling ewe lamb for a sin offering, one unblemished ram as a peace offering, along with their cereal offerings and libations, 15 and a basket of unleavened cakes of fine flour mixed with oil and of unleavened wafers spread with oil. 16 The priest shall present them before the LORD, and shall offer up the sin offering and the holocaust for him. 17 He shall then offer up the ram as a peace offering to the LORD, with its cereal offering and libation, and the basket of unleavened cakes. 18* Then at the entrance of the meeting tent the nazirite shall shave his dedicated head, collect the hair, and put it in the fire that is under the peace offering. 19 After the nazirite has shaved off his dedicated hair, the priest shall take a boiled shoulder of the ram, as well as one unleavened cake and one unleavened wafer from the basket, and shall place them in the hands of the nazirite. 20 The priest shall then wave them as a wave offering before the LORD. They become sacred and shall belong to the priest, along with the breast of the wave offering and the leg of the raised offering. Only after this may the nazirite drink wine.

21 "This, then, is the law for the nazirite; this is the offering to the LORD which is included in his vow of dedication apart from anything else which his means may allow. Thus shall he carry out the law of his dedication in keeping with the vow he has taken."

The Priestly Blessing

22 The LORD said to Moses: 23 "Speak to Aaron and his sons and tell them: This is how you shall bless the Israelites. Say to them:

24   The LORD bless you and keep you!
25†   The LORD let his face shine upon you, and be
          gracious to you!
26†   The LORD look upon you kindly and give
          you peace!

27 So shall they invoke my name upon the Israelites, and I will bless them."

God Bless You

A very old blessing in Nm 6, 22–27 (some of which is repeated in Ps 4, 7 and 67, 1) was not originally a Christian blessing, but its three parts remind us of Christian blessings calling on the Trinity.

This blessing is a good one for special occasions. You could write it on a card for a birthday, Mother's Day or Father's Day, a wedding anniversary, or any other special event. Or you could use it to make a poster or an engraving for a first Communion, a wedding, or a Confirmation.

If this blessing sounds familiar, maybe it's because on New Year's Day (the feast of Mary, mother of God), we hear it as the first reading. It's the perfect way to start the new year.

▶ Nm 6, 22–27

Offerings of Princes

7 1* Now, when Moses had completed the erection of the Dwelling and had anointed and consecrated it with all its equipment (as well as the altar with all its equipment), 2 an offering was made by the princes of Israel, who were heads of ancestral houses; the same princes of the tribes who supervised the census. 3 The offering they brought

---

6, 25: *Let his face shine:* a Hebrew idiom for "smile."
6, 26: *Peace:* the Hebrew word includes the idea of "prosperity, happiness."

6, 6: Nm 19, 11.16; Lv 21, 11.
6, 13: Acts 21, 24.26.

6, 18: Acts 18, 18; 21, 24.
7, 1: Ex 40, 17.

before the LORD consisted of six baggage wagons and twelve oxen, that is, a wagon for every two princes, and an ox for every prince. These they presented as their offering before the Dwelling.

4 The LORD then said to Moses, 5 "Accept their offering, that these things may be put to use in the service of the meeting tent. Assign them to the Levites, to each group in proportion to its duties." 6 So Moses accepted the wagons and oxen, and assigned them to the Levites. 7* He gave two wagons and four oxen to the Gershonites in proportion to their duties, 8 and four wagons and eight oxen to the Merarites in proportion to their duties, under the supervision of Ithamar, son of Aaron the priest. 9* He gave none to the Kohathites, because they had to carry on their shoulders the sacred objects which were their charge.

10* For the dedication of the altar also, the princes brought offerings before the altar on the day it was anointed. 11 But the LORD said to Moses, "Let one prince a day present his offering for the dedication of the altar."

12† The one who presented his offering on the first day was Nahshon, son of Amminadab, prince of the tribe of Judah. 13 His offering consisted of one silver plate weighing a hundred and thirty shekels according to the sanctuary standard and one silver basin weighing seventy shekels, both filled with fine flour mixed with oil for a cereal offering; 14 one gold cup of ten shekels' weight filled with incense; 15 one young bull, one ram, and one yearling lamb for a holocaust; 16 one goat for a sin offering; 17 and two oxen, five rams, five goats, and five yearling lambs for a peace offering. This was the offering of Nahshon, son of Amminadab.

18 On the second day Nethanel, son of Zuar, prince of Issachar, made his offering. 19 He presented as his offering one silver plate weighing a hundred and thirty shekels according to the sanctuary standard and one silver basin weighing seventy shekels, both filled with fine flour mixed with oil for a cereal offering; 20 one gold cup of ten shekels' weight filled with incense; 21 one young bull, one ram, and one yearling lamb for a holocaust; 22 one goat for a sin offering; 23 and two oxen, five rams, five goats, and five yearling lambs for a peace offering. This was the offering of Nethanel, son of Zuar.

24 On the third day it was the turn of Eliab, son of Helon, prince of the Zebulunites. 25 His offering consisted of one silver plate weighing a hundred and thirty shekels according to the sanctuary standard and one silver basin weighing seventy shekels, both filled with fine flour mixed with oil for a ce-

real offering; 26 one gold cup of ten shekels' weight filled with incense; 27 one young bull, one ram, and one yearling lamb for a holocaust; 28 one goat for a sin offering; 29 and two oxen, five rams, five goats, and five yearling lambs for a peace offering. This was the offering of Eliab, son of Helon.

30 On the fourth day it was the turn of Elizur, son of Shedeur, prince of the Reubenites. 31 His offering consisted of one silver plate weighing a hundred and thirty shekels according to the sanctuary standard and one silver basin weighing seventy shekels, both filled with fine flour mixed with oil for a cereal offering; 32 one gold cup of ten shekels' weight filled with incense; 33 one young bull, one ram, and one yearling lamb for a holocaust; 34 one goat for a sin offering; 35 and two oxen, five rams, five goats, and five yearling lambs for a peace offering. This was the offering of Elizur, son of Shedeur.

36 On the fifth day it was the turn of Shelumiel, son of Zurishaddai, prince of the Simeonites. 37 His offering consisted of one silver plate weighing a hundred and thirty shekels according to the sanctuary standard and one silver basin weighing seventy shekels, both filled with fine flour mixed with oil for a cereal offering; 38 one gold cup of ten shekels' weight filled with incense; 39 one young bull, one ram, and one yearling lamb for a holocaust; 40 one goat for a sin offering; 41 and two oxen, five rams, five goats, and five yearling lambs for a peace offering. This was the offering of Shelumiel, son of Zurishaddai.

42 On the sixth day it was the turn of Eliasaph, son of Reuel, prince of the Gadites. 43 His offering consisted of one silver plate weighing a hundred and thirty shekels according to the sanctuary standard and one silver basin weighing seventy shekels, both filled with fine flour mixed with oil for a cereal offering; 44 one gold cup of ten shekels' weight filled with incense; 45 one young bull, one ram, and one yearling lamb for a holocaust; 46 one goat for a sin offering; 47 and two oxen, five rams, five goats, and five yearling lambs for a peace offering. This was the offering of Eliasaph, son of Reuel.

48 On the seventh day it was the turn of Elishama, son of Ammihud, prince of the Ephraimites. 49 His offering consisted of one silver plate weighing a hundred and thirty shekels according to the sanctuary standard and one silver basin weighing seventy shekels, both filled with fine flour mixed with oil for a cereal offering; 50 one gold cup of ten shekels' weight filled with incense; 51 one young bull, one ram, and one yearling lamb for a holocaust; 52 one goat for a sin offering; 53 and two oxen, five rams, five goats, and five yearling lambs

---

7, 12–88: The repetitive account of the same offerings brought by each of the twelve tribal princes and the summary of them are characteristic of an official registration.

7, 7f: Nm 4, 24–33.   7, 10: Nm 7, 84.
7, 9: Nm 3, 31; 4, 4–15.

for a peace offering. This was the offering of Elishama, son of Ammihud.

54 On the eighth day it was the turn of Gamaliel, son of Pedahzur, prince of the Manassehites. 55 His offering consisted of one silver plate weighing a hundred and thirty shekels according to the sanctuary standard and one silver basin weighing seventy shekels, both filled with fine flour mixed with oil for a cereal offering; 56 one gold cup of ten shekels' weight filled with incense; 57 one young bull, one ram, and one yearling lamb for a holocaust; 58 one goat for a sin offering; 59 and two oxen, five rams, five goats, and five yearling lambs for a peace offering. This was the offering of Gamaliel, son of Pedahzur.

60 On the ninth day it was the turn of Abidan, son of Gideoni, prince of the Benjaminites. 61 His offering consisted of one silver plate weighing a hundred and thirty shekels according to the sanctuary standard and one silver basin weighing seventy shekels, both filled with fine flour mixed with oil for a cereal offering; 62 one gold cup of ten shekels' weight filled with incense; 63 one young bull, one ram, and one yearling lamb for a holocaust; 64 one goat for a sin offering; 65 and two oxen, five rams, five goats, and five yearling lambs for a peace offering. This was the offering of Abidan, son of Gideoni.

66 On the tenth day it was the turn of Ahiezer, son of Ammishaddai, prince of the Danites. 67 His offering consisted of one silver plate weighing a hundred and thirty shekels according to the sanctuary standard and one silver basin weighing seventy shekels, both filled with fine flour mixed with oil for a cereal offering; 68 one gold cup of ten shekels' weight filled with incense; 69 one young bull, one ram, and one yearling lamb for a holocaust; 70 one goat for a sin offering; 71 and two oxen, five rams, five goats, and five yearling lambs for a peace offering. This was the offering of Ahiezer, son of Ammishaddai.

72 On the eleventh day it was the turn of Pagiel, son of Ochran, prince of the Asherites. 73 His offering consisted of one silver plate weighing a hundred and thirty shekels according to the sanctuary standard and one silver basin weighing seventy shekels, both filled with fine flour mixed with oil for a cereal offering; 74 one gold cup of ten shekels' weight filled with incense; 75 one young bull, one ram, and one yearling lamb for a holocaust; 76 one goat for a sin offering; 77 and two oxen, five rams, five goats, and five yearling lambs for a peace offering. This was the offering of Pagiel, son of Ochran.

78 On the twelfth day it was the turn of Ahira, son of Enan, prince of the Naphtalites. 79 His offering consisted of one silver plate weighing a hundred and thirty shekels according to the sanctuary standard and one silver basin weighing seventy shekels, both filled with fine flour mixed with oil for a cereal offering; 80 one gold cup of ten shekels' weight filled with incense; 81 one young bull, one ram, and one yearling lamb for a holocaust; 82 one goat for a sin offering; 83 and two oxen, five rams, five goats, and five yearling lambs for a peace offering. This was the offering of Ahira, son of Enan.

84 These were the offerings for the dedication of the altar, given by the princes of Israel on the occasion of its anointing: twelve silver plates, twelve silver basins, and twelve gold cups. 85 Each silver plate weighed a hundred and thirty shekels, and each silver basin seventy, so that all the silver of these vessels amounted to two thousand four hundred shekels, according to the sanctuary standard. 86 The twelve gold cups that were filled with incense weighed ten shekels apiece, according to the sanctuary standard, so that all the gold of the cups amounted to one hundred and twenty shekels. 87 The animals for the holocausts were, in all, twelve young bulls, twelve rams, and twelve yearling lambs, with their cereal offerings; those for the sin offerings were twelve goats. 88 The animals for the peace offerings were, in all, twenty-four oxen, sixty rams, sixty goats, and sixty yearling lambs. These, then, were the offerings for the dedication of the altar after it was anointed.

The Voice

89* When Moses entered the meeting tent to speak with him, he heard the voice addressing him from above the propitiatory on the ark of the commandments, from between the two cherubim; and it spoke to him. . . .

The Lamps Set Up

8 1 The LORD spoke to Moses, and said, 2* "Give Aaron this command: When you set up the seven lamps, have them throw their light toward the front of the lampstand." 3 Aaron did so, setting up the lamps to face toward the front of the lampstand, just as the LORD had commanded Moses. 4* The lampstand was made of beaten gold in both its shaft and its branches, according to the pattern which the LORD had shown Moses.

Purification of the Levites

5 The LORD said to Moses: 6† "Take the Levites from among the Israelites and purify them. 7† This is what

---

8, 6: *Purify them:* in the language of the Pentateuch only the priests were "consecrated," that is, made sacred or set aside for the Lord, in an elaborate ceremony described in Ex 29; Lv 8. The Levites were merely "purified," that is, made ritually clean for their special work.

8, 7: *Water of remission:* literally, "water of sin," that is, for the remission of sin.

7, 89: Ex 25, 22.   8, 4: Ex 25, 31.40.
8, 2: Ex 25, 37.

you shall do to them to purify them. Sprinkle them with the water of remission; then have them shave their whole bodies and wash their clothes, and so purify themselves. 8 They shall take a young bull, along with its cereal offering of fine flour mixed with oil; you shall take another young bull for a sin offering. 9 Then have the Levites come forward in front of the meeting tent, where you shall assemble also the whole community of the Israelites. 10 While the Levites are present before the LORD, the Israelites shall lay their hands upon them. 11 Let Aaron then offer the Levites before the LORD as a wave offering from the Israelites, thus devoting them to the service of the LORD. 12 The Levites in turn shall lay their hands on the heads of the bullocks, which shall then be immolated, the one as a sin offering and the other as a holocaust to the LORD, in atonement for the Levites. 13 Thus, then, shall you have the Levites stand before Aaron and his sons, to be offered as a wave offering to the LORD; 14* and thus shall you set aside the Levites from the rest of the Israelites, that they may be mine.

15 "Only then shall the Levites enter upon their service in the meeting tent. You shall purify them and offer them as a wave offering; 16* because they, among the Israelites, are strictly dedicated to me; I have taken them for myself in place of every first-born that opens the womb among the Israelites. 17* Indeed, all the first-born among the Israelites, both of man and of beast, belong to me; I consecrated them to myself on the day I slew all the first-born in the land of Egypt. 18 But in place of all the first-born Israelites I have taken the Levites; 19* and I have given these dedicated Israelites to Aaron and his sons to discharge the duties of the Israelites in the meeting tent and to make atonement for them, so that no plague may strike among the Israelites should they come near the sanctuary."

20 Thus, then, did Moses and Aaron and the whole community of the Israelites deal with the Levites, carrying out exactly the command which the LORD had given Moses concerning them. 21† When the Levites had cleansed themselves of sin and washed their clothes, Aaron offered them as a wave offering before the LORD, and made atonement for them to purify them. 22 Only then did they enter upon their service in the meeting tent under the supervision of Aaron and his sons. The command which the LORD had given Moses concerning the Levites was carried out.

Age Limits for Levitical Service

23 The LORD said to Moses: 24* "This is the rule for the Levites. Each from his twenty-fifth year onward shall perform the required service in the meeting tent. 25 When he is fifty years old, he shall retire from the required service and work no longer. 26 His service with his fellow Levites shall consist in sharing their responsibilities in the meeting tent, but he shall not do the work. This, then, is how you are to regulate the duties of the Levites."

Second Passover

9 1 In the first month of the year following their departure from the land of Egypt, the LORD said to Moses in the desert of Sinai, 2 "Tell the Israelites to celebrate the Passover at the prescribed time. 3* The evening twilight of the fourteenth day of this month is the prescribed time when you shall celebrate it, observing all its rules and regulations." 4 Moses, therefore, told the Israelites to celebrate the Passover. 5 And they did so, celebrating the Passover in the desert of Sinai during the evening twilight of the fourteenth day of the first month, just as the LORD had commanded Moses.

6 There were some, however, who were unclean because of a human corpse and so could not keep the Passover that day. These men came up to Moses and Aaron that same day 7 and said, "Although we are unclean because of a corpse, why should we be deprived of presenting the LORD'S offering at its proper time along with the other Israelites?" 8 Moses answered them, "Wait until I learn what the LORD will command in your regard."

9 The LORD then said to Moses: 10 "Speak to the Israelites and say: If any one of you or of your descendants is unclean because of a corpse, or if he is absent on a journey, he may still keep the LORD'S Passover. 11* But he shall keep it in the second month, during the evening twilight of the fourteenth day of that month, eating it with unleavened bread and bitter herbs, 12* and not leaving any of it over till morning, nor breaking any of its bones, but observing all the rules of the Passover. 13 However, anyone who is clean and not away on a journey, who yet fails to keep the Passover, shall be cut off from his people, because he did not present the LORD'S offering at the prescribed time. That man shall bear the consequences of his sin.

14*† "If an alien who lives among you wishes to keep the LORD'S Passover, he too shall observe the

---

8, 21: *Cleansed themselves of sin:* by having the "water of remission" sprinkled on them as prescribed in v 7.
9, 14: *An alien:* this passage presupposes that he is already circumcised as prescribed in Ex 12, 48.

8, 14: Nm 3, 45.
8, 16: Nm 3, 12.45.
8, 17: Nm 3, 13; 13, 2; Lk 2, 23.
8, 19: Nm 3, 9f.
8, 24: Nm 4, 3.23.
9, 3: Ex 12, 6; Lv 23, 5.
9, 11: 2 Chr 30, 2–15.
9, 12: Ex 12, 46; Jn 19, 36.
9, 14: Ex 12, 48f.

rules and regulations for the Passover. You shall have the same law for the resident alien as for the native of the land."

The Fiery Cloud

15*† On the day when the Dwelling was erected, the cloud covered the Dwelling, the tent of the commandments; but from evening until morning it took on the appearance of fire over the Dwelling. 16 It was always so: during the day the Dwelling was covered by the cloud, which at night had the appearance of fire. 17* Whenever the cloud rose from the tent, the Israelites would break camp; wherever the cloud came to rest, they would pitch camp. 18* At the bidding of the LORD the Israelites moved on, and at his bidding they encamped. As long as the cloud stayed over the Dwelling, they remained in camp.

19 Even when the cloud tarried many days over the Dwelling, the Israelites obeyed the LORD and would not move on; 20 yet sometimes the cloud was over the Dwelling only for a few days. It was at the bidding of the LORD that they stayed in camp, and it was at his bidding that they departed. 21 Sometimes the cloud remained there only from evening until morning; and when it rose in the morning, they would depart. Or if the cloud lifted during the day, or even at night, they would then set out. 22 Whether the cloud tarried over the Dwelling for two days or for a month or longer, the Israelites remained in camp and did not depart; but when it lifted, they moved on. 23 Thus, it was always at the bidding of the LORD that they encamped, and at his bidding that they set out; ever heeding the charge of the LORD, as he had bidden them through Moses.

The Silver Trumpets

10 1 The LORD said to Moses: 2 "Make two trumpets of beaten silver, which you shall use in assembling the community and in breaking camp. 3 When both are blown, the whole community shall gather round you at the entrance of the meeting tent; 4 but when one of them is blown, only the princes, the chiefs of the troops of Israel, shall gather round you. 5 When you sound the first alarm, those encamped on the east side shall set out; 6 when you sound the second alarm, those encamped on the south side shall set out; when you sound the third alarm, those encamped on the west side shall set out; when you sound the fourth alarm, those encamped on the north side shall set out. Thus shall the alarm be sounded for

them to depart. 7 But in calling forth an assembly you are to blow an ordinary blast, without sounding the alarm.

8 "It is the sons of Aaron, the priests, who shall blow the trumpets; and the use of them is prescribed by perpetual statute for you and your descendants. 9* When in your own land you go to war against an enemy that is attacking you, you shall sound the alarm on the trumpets, and the LORD, your God, will remember you and save you from your foes. 10*† On your days of celebration, your festivals, and your new-moon feasts, you shall blow the trumpets over your holocausts and your peace offerings; this will serve as a reminder of you before your God. I, the LORD, am your God."

II: From Sinai to the Plains of Moab

Departure from Sinai

11 In the second year, on the twentieth day of the second month, the cloud rose from the Dwelling of the commandments. 12 The Israelites moved on from the desert of Sinai by stages, until the cloud came to rest in the desert of Paran.

13 The first time that they broke camp at the bidding of the LORD through Moses, 14* the camp of the Judahites, under its own standard and arranged in companies, was the first to set out. Nahshon, son of Amminadab, was over their host, 15 and Nethanel, son of Zuar, over the host of the tribe of Issachar, 16 and Eliab, son of Helon, over the host of the tribe of Zebulun. 17 Then, after the Dwelling was dismantled, the clans of Gershon and Merari set out, carrying the Dwelling. 18 The camp of the Reubenites, under its own standard and arranged in companies, was the next to set out, with Elizur, son of Shedeur, over their host, 19 and Shelumiel, son of Zurishaddai, over the host of the tribe of Simeon, 20 and Eliasaph, son of Reuel, over the host of the tribe of Gad. 21 The clan of Kohath then set out, carrying the sacred objects for the Dwelling, which was to be erected before their arrival. 22 The camp of the Ephraimites next set out, under its own standard and arranged in companies, with Elishama, son of Ammihud, over their host, 23 and Gamaliel, son of Pedahzur, over the host of the tribe of Manasseh, 24 and Abidan, son of Gideoni, over the host of the tribe of Benjamin. 25 Finally, as rear guard for all the camps, the camp of the Danites set out, under its own standard and arranged in companies, with Ahiezer, son of Amishaddai, over their host, 26 and

---

9, 15: *The cloud:* already mentioned at the departure from Egypt; cf Ex 13, 21f.

10, 10: *Days of celebration:* special holidays, such as the occasion of a victory. *Festivals:* the great annual feasts of the Passover, Pentecost and Booths described in Lv 23; Nm 28–29.

9, 15: Ex 13, 21.
9, 17: Wis 18, 3.
9, 18: 1 Cor 10, 1.
10, 9: 2 Chr 13, 14.

10, 10: Nm 29, 1; 2 Chr 29, 26ff.
10, 14ff: Nm 2, 3.5.7.

Pagiel, son of Ochran, over the host of the tribe of Asher, 27 and Ahira, son of Enan, over the host of the tribe of Naphtali. 28 This was the order of departure for the Israelites, company by company.

Hobab as Guide

As they were setting out, 29 Moses said to his brother-in-law Hobab, son of Reuel the Midianite, "We are setting out for the place which the LORD has promised to give us. Come with us, and we will be generous toward you, for the LORD has promised prosperity to Israel." 30† But he answered, "No, I will not come. I am going instead to my own country and to my own kindred." 31 Moses said, "Please, do not leave us; you know where we can camp in the desert, and you will serve as eyes for us. 32 If you come with us, we will share with you the prosperity the LORD will bestow on us."

Into the Desert

33*† They moved on from the mountain of the LORD, a three days' journey, and the ark of the covenant of the LORD which was to seek out their resting place went the three days' journey with them. 34 And when they set out from camp, the cloud of the LORD was over them by day.

35 Whenever the ark set out, Moses would say,

"Arise, O LORD, that your enemies may
     be scattered,
and those who hate you may flee
     before you."

36 And when it came to rest, he would say,

"Return, O LORD, you who ride upon
     the clouds,
to the troops of Israel."

Discontent of the People

11 1* Now the people complained in the hearing of the LORD; and when he heard it his wrath flared up so that the fire of the LORD burned among them and consumed the outskirts of the camp. 2 But when the people cried out to Moses, he prayed to the LORD and the fire died out. 3† Hence that place was called Taberah, because there the fire of the LORD burned among them.

4* The foreign elements among them were so greedy for meat that even the Israelites lamented

again, "Would that we had meat for food! 5 We remember the fish we used to eat without cost in Egypt, and the cucumbers, the melons, the leeks, the onions, and the garlic. 6* But now we are famished; we see nothing before us but this manna."

7*† Manna was like coriander seed and had the appearance of bdellium. 8 When they had gone about and gathered it up, the people would grind it between millstones or pound it in a mortar, then cook it in a pot and make it into loaves, which tasted like cakes made with oil. 9* At night, when the dew fell upon the camp, the manna also fell.

10 When Moses heard the people, family after family, crying at the entrance of their tents, so that the LORD became very angry, he was grieved. 11 "Why do you treat your servant so badly?" Moses asked the LORD. "Why are you so displeased with me that you burden me with all this people? 12 Was it I who conceived all this people? or was it I who gave them birth, that you tell me to carry them at my bosom, like a foster father carrying an infant, to the land you have promised under oath to their fathers? 13 Where can I get meat to give to all this people? For they are crying to me, 'Give us meat for our food.' 14 I cannot carry all this people by myself, for they are too heavy for me. 15 If this is the way you will deal with me, then please do me the favor of killing me at once, so that I need no longer face this distress."

The Seventy Elders

16 Then the LORD said to Moses, "Assemble for me seventy of the elders of Israel, men you know for true elders and authorities among the people, and bring them to the meeting tent. When they are in place beside you, 17 I will come down and speak with you there. I will also take some of the spirit that is on you and will bestow it on them, that they may share the burden of the people with you. You will then not have to bear it by yourself.

18 "To the people, however, you shall say: Sanctify yourselves for tomorrow, when you shall have meat to eat. For in the hearing of the LORD you have cried, 'Would that we had meat for food! Oh, how well off we were in Egypt!' Therefore the LORD will give you meat for food, 19 and you will eat it, not for one day, or two days, or five, or ten, or twenty days, 20 but for a whole month—until it comes out of your very nostrils and becomes loathsome to you. For you have spurned the LORD who is in your

---

10, 30ff: Hobab wished to be coaxed before granting the favor. From Jgs 1, 16 it seems probable that he did accede to Moses' request.
10, 33: *The mountain of the LORD:* Sinai (Horeb), elsewhere always called "the mountain of God."
11, 3: *Taberah:* means "the burning."
11, 7: *Coriander seed:* see note on Ex 16, 31. *Bdellium:* a trans-

parent, amber-colored gum resin, which is also mentioned in Gn 2, 12.

10, 33: Dt 1, 33.	11, 7f: Ex 16, 14f.31; Ps 78,
11, 1: Dt 9, 22.	24; Wis 16, 20; Jn
11, 4: Ps 78, 18.	6, 31.
11, 6: 5f: Nm 21, 5; Ex 16, 3;	11, 9: Ex 16, 14f.
Acts 7, 39.	

midst, and in his presence you have wailed, 'Why did we ever leave Egypt?' "

²¹ But Moses said, "The people around me include six hundred thousand soldiers; yet you say, 'I will give them meat to eat for a whole month.' ²² Can enough sheep and cattle be slaughtered for them? If all the fish of the sea were caught for them, would they have enough?" ²³ The LORD answered Moses, "Is this beyond the LORD's reach? You shall see now whether or not what I have promised you takes place."

The Spirit on the Elders

²⁴ So Moses went out and told the people what the LORD had said. Gathering seventy elders of the people, he had them stand around the tent. ²⁵† The LORD then came down in the cloud and spoke to him. Taking some of the spirit that was on Moses, he bestowed it on the seventy elders; and as the spirit came to rest on them, they prophesied.

²⁶ Now two men, one named Eldad and the other Medad, were not in the gathering but had been left in the camp. They too had been on the list, but had not gone out to the tent; yet the spirit came to rest on them also, and they prophesied in the camp. ²⁷ So, when a young man quickly told Moses, "Eldad and Medad are prophesying in the camp," ²⁸ Joshua, son of Nun, who from his youth had been Moses' aide, said, "Moses, my lord, stop them." ²⁹ But Moses answered him, "Are you jealous for my sake? Would that all the people of the LORD were prophets! Would that the LORD might bestow his spirit on them all!" ³⁰ Then Moses retired to the camp, along with the elders of Israel.

The Quail

³¹*† There arose a wind sent by the LORD, that drove in quail from the sea and brought them down over the camp site at a height of two cubits from the ground for the distance of a day's journey all around the camp. ³²*† All that day, all night, and all the next day the people gathered in the quail. Even the one who got the least gathered ten homers of them. Then they spread them out all around the

camp. ³³ But while the meat was still between their teeth, before it could be consumed, the LORD's wrath flared up against the people, and he struck them with a very great plague. ³⁴† So that place was named Kibroth-hattaavah, because it was there that the greedy people were buried.

³⁵ From Kibroth-hattaavah the people set out for Hazeroth.

Jealousy of Aaron and Miriam

12 While they were in Hazeroth, ¹† Miriam and Aaron spoke against Moses on the pretext of the marriage he had contracted with a Cushite woman. ²† They complained, "Is it through Moses alone that the LORD speaks? Does he not speak through us also?" And the LORD heard this. ³* Now, Moses himself was by far the meekest man on the face of the earth. ⁴ So at once the LORD said to Moses and Aaron and Miriam, "Come out, you three, to the meeting tent." And the three of them went. ⁵ Then the LORD came down in the column of cloud, and standing at the entrance of the tent, called Aaron and Miriam. When both came forward, ⁶ he said, "Now listen to the words of the LORD:

> Should there be a prophet among you,
>   in visions will I reveal myself to him,
>   in dreams will I speak to him;
> ⁷* Not so with my servant Moses!
>   Throughout my house he bears my trust:
> ⁸*   face to face I speak to him,
>   plainly and not in riddles.
> The presence of the LORD he beholds.

Why, then, did you not fear to speak against my servant Moses?"

Miriam's Leprosy

⁹ So angry was the LORD against them that when he departed, ¹⁰*† and the cloud withdrew from the tent, there was Miriam, a snow-white leper! When Aaron turned and saw her a leper, ¹¹ "Ah, my lord!" he said to Moses, "please do not charge us with the

---

---

† **11, 25:** *They prophesied:* in the sense, not of foretelling the future, but of speaking in enraptured enthusiasm. Such manifestations of mystic exaltation occurred in the early days of Hebrew prophecy (1 Sm 10, 10ff; 19, 20ff) and in the first years of the Church (Acts 2, 6–11.17; 19, 6; 1 Cor 12–14).

11, 31: *At a height of two cubits from the ground:* exhausted by the storm, the quail could take but short, low flights, so that they were easily captured. To give food to the hungry people, God may have used the natural phenomenon of the annual migration of quail across the Sinai Peninsula. In the spring large flocks of these birds cross the Gulf of Aqabah flying toward the west; in the fall they fly back eastward from the Mediterranean. The sea mentioned here probably refers to the former body of water.

11, 32: *They spread them out:* to cure by drying.

11, 34: *Kibroth-hattaavah:* means "graves of greed."

12, 1: *Cushite woman:* apparently Zipporah, the Midianitess, is meant; cf Ex 2, 21. Perhaps the term is used here merely in the sense of "despised foreigner."

12, 2: The real reason for Miriam's quarrel with her brother Moses was her jealousy of his superior position; his Cushite wife served only as an occasion for the dispute. Aaron merely followed his sister in her rebellion; hence she alone was punished.

12, 10: *A snow-white leper:* afflicted with "white leprosy," a skin disease that generally is not serious or of long duration. Cf Lv 13, 3–6.

11, 31: Ps 78, 26ff.
11, 32f: Nm 78, 26–31; 1 Cor 10, 6–7.
12, 3: Sir 45, 1f.
12, 7: Sir 45, 3; Heb 3, 2.5.
12, 8: Ex 33, 11; Dt 34, 10.
12, 10: Dt 24, 9.

The Jealousy of Miriam and Aaron

Miriam. I don't know, Aaron. Sometimes Moses really gets to me. He seems to forget that we're all in this together.

Aaron. Yes, we are God's chosen people. All of us, not just Moses. And, of course, he married outside the fold. A Cushite, of all people.

Miriam. It really is a scandal. He is the self-appointed leader of our people, and yet he is not even married to an Israelite woman. That just doesn't sit well with our people.

Aaron. And he can be so aloof. I know he has a special connection with God, and I know it isn't easy being a leader. But he always seems to set himself apart, acting like he's better than the rest of us.

Miriam. What bothers me most is that Moses assumes that God speaks only through him.

Aaron. Yes, it's as if the rest of us have no role to play. What if I receive a revelation from God? Will Moses respond the same way we are expected to whenever he speaks? I doubt it!

Miriam. So do I. He pretends to be humble and to speak for God. I'm tired of it. We need to have a voice also.

Jealousy is like a dangerous cancer, growing until it affects your whole outlook on life (see what happens to Miriam in Nm 12, 9–10). What happens inside of you when you feel jealous? How does jealousy affect your attitudes toward other people?

▸ Numbers, chapter 12

sin that we have foolishly committed! 12 Let her not thus be like the stillborn babe that comes forth from its mother's womb with its flesh half consumed." 13 Then Moses cried to the LORD, "Please, not this! Pray, heal her!" 14 But the LORD answered Moses, "Suppose her father had spit in her face, would she not hide in shame for seven days? Let her be confined outside the camp for seven days; only then may she be brought back." 15 So Miriam was confined outside the camp for seven days, and the people did not start out again until she was brought back.

16 After that the people set out from Hazeroth and encamped in the desert of Paran.

The Twelve Scouts

13 1 The LORD said to Moses, 2 "Send men to reconnoiter the land of Canaan, which I am giving the Israelites. You shall send one man from each ancestral tribe, all of them princes." 3* So Moses dispatched them from the desert of Paran, as the LORD had ordered. All of them were leaders among the Israelites; 4 by name they were:

Shammua, son of Zaccur, of the tribe of Reuben;

5 Shaphat, son of Hori, of the tribe of Simeon;
6 Caleb, son of Jephunneh, of the tribe of Judah;
7 Igal [son of Joseph] of the tribe of Issachar;
10 Gaddiel, son of Sodi, of the tribe of Zebulun;
11 Gaddi, son of Susi, of the tribe of Manasseh, for the Josephites, with
8 Hoshea, son of Nun, of the tribe of Ephraim;
9 Palti, son of Raphu, of the tribe of Benjamin;
12 Ammiel, son of Gemalli, of the tribe of Dan;
13 Sethur, son of Michael, of the tribe of Asher;
14 Nahbi, son of Vophsi, of the tribe of Naphtali;
15 Geuel, son of Machi, of the tribe of Gad.

16† These are the names of the men whom Moses sent out to reconnoiter the land. But Hoshea, son of Nun, Moses called Joshua.

17 In sending them to reconnoiter the land of Canaan, Moses said to them, "Go up here in the Negeb, up into the highlands, 18 and see what kind of land it is. Are the people living there strong or weak, few or many? 19 Is the country in which they live good or bad? Are the towns in which they dwell open or fortified? 20 Is the soil fertile or barren, wooded or clear? And do your best to get some of the fruit of the land." It was then the season for early grapes.

13, 16: *Joshua:* in Hebrew, "Jehoshua," which was later modified to "Jeshua," the Hebrew pronunciation of the name "Jesus." Hoshea and Joshua are variants of one original name meaning "the LORD saves." Cf Mt 1, 21.

13, 3–33: Dt 1, 22–28.

²¹† So they went up and reconnoitered the land from the desert of Zin as far as where Rehob adjoins Labo of Hamath. ²²*† Going up by way of the Negeb, they reached Hebron, where Ahiman, Sheshai and Talmai, descendants of the Anakim, were living. [Hebron had been built seven years before Zoan in Egypt.] ²³† They also reached the Wadi Eshcol, where they cut down a branch with a single cluster of grapes on it, which two of them carried on a pole, as well as some pomegranates and figs. ²⁴* It was because of the cluster the Israelites cut there that they called the place Wadi Eshcol.

Their Return

²⁵ After reconnoitering the land for forty days they returned, ²⁶* met Moses and Aaron and the whole community of the Israelites in the desert of Paran at Kadesh, made a report to them all, and showed them the fruit of the country. ²⁷ They told Moses: "We went into the land to which you sent us. It does indeed flow with milk and honey, and here is its fruit. ²⁸* However, the people who are living in the land are fierce, and the towns are fortified and very strong. Besides, we saw descendants of the Anakim there. ²⁹ Amalekites live in the region of the Negeb; Hittites, Jebusites and Amorites dwell in the highlands, and Canaanites along the seacoast and the banks of the Jordan."

³⁰ Caleb, however, to quiet the people toward Moses, said, "We ought to go up and seize the land, for we can certainly do so." ³¹ But the men who had gone up with him said, "We cannot attack these people; they are too strong for us." ³²* So they spread discouraging reports among the Israelites about the land they had scouted, saying, "The land that we explored is a country that consumes its inhabitants. And all the people we saw there are huge men, ³³*† veritable giants [the Anakim were a race of giants]; we felt like mere grasshoppers, and so we must have seemed to them."

Threats of Revolt

14 ¹ At this, the whole community broke out with loud cries, and even in the night the people wailed. ²* All the Israelites grumbled against Moses and Aaron, the whole community saying to them, "Would that we had died in the land of Egypt, or that here in the desert we were dead! ³ Why is the LORD bringing us into this land only to have us fall by the sword? Our wives and little ones will be taken as booty. Would it not be better for us to return to Egypt?" ⁴ So they said to one another, "Let us appoint a leader and go back to Egypt."

⁵ But Moses and Aaron fell prostrate before the whole assembled community of the Israelites; ⁶ while Joshua, son of Nun, and Caleb, son of Jephunneh, who had been in the party that scouted the land, tore their garments ⁷* and said to the whole community of the Israelites, "The country which we went through and explored is a fine, rich land. ⁸ If the LORD is pleased with us, he will bring us in and give us that land, a land flowing with milk and honey. ⁹*† But do not rebel against the LORD! You need not be afraid of the people of that land; they are but food for us! Their defense has left them, but the LORD is with us. Therefore, do not be afraid of them." ¹⁰ In answer, the whole community threatened to stone them.

The Lord's Sentence

But then the glory of the LORD appeared at the meeting tent to all the Israelites. ¹¹* And the LORD said to Moses, "How long will this people spurn me? How long will they refuse to believe in me, despite all the signs I have performed among them? ¹²* I will strike them with pestilence and wipe them out. Then I will make of you a nation greater and mightier than they."

¹³* But Moses said to the LORD: "Are the Egyptians to hear of this? For by your power you brought out this people from among them. ¹⁴* And are they to tell of it to the inhabitants of this land? It has been heard that you, O LORD, are in the midst of this people; you, LORD, who plainly reveal yourself! Your cloud stands over them, and you go before them by day in a column of cloud and by night in a column of fire. ¹⁵ If now you slay this whole people, the nations who have heard such reports of you will say, ¹⁶* 'The LORD was not able to bring this people into the land he swore to give them;

13, 21: *The desert of Zin:* north of Paran and southwest of the Dead Sea. It is quite distinct from "the desert of Sin" near the border of Egypt (Ex 16, 1; 17, 1; Nm 33, 11). *Labo of Hamath:* a town near Riblah (Jer 39, 5f) at the southern border of Hamath, an independent kingdom in southern Syria. David's conquests extended as far as Hamath (2 Sm 8, 9ff), and Labo thus formed the northern border of the ideal extent of Israel's possessions (Nm 34, 7ff; Ez 47, 15; 48, 1). Some commentators think that this verse is a later addition to the text; cf Dt 1, 24.
13, 22.28: *Anakim:* an aboriginal race in southern Palestine, largely absorbed by the Canaanites before the Israelite invasion. Either because of their tall stature or because of the massive stone structures left by them the Israelites regarded them as giants.
13, 23: *Eshcol:* means "cluster."

13, 33: *Giants:* in Hebrew, "nephilim." Cf Gn 6, 4.
14, 9: *They are but food for us:* that is, "we can easily consume and destroy them." This is the answer to the pessimistic report that this land "consumes its inhabitants" (Nm 13, 32).

13, 22: Jos 11, 21f.
13, 24: Nm 32, 9; Dt 1, 24f.
13, 26f: Ex 3, 8.17.
13, 28f: Dt 9, 1f.
13, 32: Nm 32, 9; Jos 14, 8.
13, 33: Dt 2, 10.
14, 2: Ex 16, 3; Ps 106, 25.
14, 7f: Dt 1, 25.
14, 9: Dt 7, 18.
14, 11: Ps 78, 22.32.
14, 12: Ex 32, 10.
14, 13–16: Ex 32, 12; Dt 9, 26ff; Ps 106, 23.
14, 14: Ex 13, 21; Jos 2, 9f.
14, 16: Ex 32, 12; Dt 9, 28.

that is why he slaughtered them in the desert.'
17 Now then, let the power of my Lord be displayed
in its greatness, even as you have said, 18* 'The LORD
is slow to anger and rich in kindness, forgiving
wickedness and crime; yet not declaring the guilty
guiltless, but punishing children to the third and
fourth generation for their fathers' wickedness.'
19* Pardon, then, the wickedness of this people in
keeping with your great kindness, even as you have
forgiven them from Egypt until now."

20 The LORD answered: "I pardon them as you
have asked. 21 Yet, by my life and the LORD's glory
that fills the whole earth, 22* of all the men who
have seen my glory and the signs I worked in Egypt
and in the desert, and who nevertheless have put
me to the test ten times already and have failed to
heed my voice, 23 not one shall see the land which
I promised on oath to their fathers. None of these
who have spurned me shall see it. 24* But because
my servant Caleb has a different spirit and follows
me unreservedly, I will bring him into the land
where he has just been, and his descendants shall
possess it. 25† But now, since the Amalekites and
Canaanites are living in the valleys, turn away tomorrow and set out in the desert on the Red
Sea road."

26 The LORD also said to Moses and Aaron:
27* "How long will this wicked community grumble against me? I have heard the grumblings of the
Israelites against me. 28† Tell them: By my life, says
the LORD, I will do to you just what I have heard
you say. 29* Here in the desert shall your dead bodies fall. Of all your men of twenty years or more,
registered in the census, who grumbled against me,
30 not one shall enter the land where I solemnly
swore to settle you, except Caleb, son of Jephunneh,
and Joshua, son of Nun. 31* Your little ones, however, who you said would be taken as booty, I will
bring in, and they shall appreciate the land you
spurned. 32 But as for you, your bodies shall fall
here in the desert, 33* here where your children
must wander for forty years, suffering for your faithlessness, till the last of you lies dead in the desert.
34 Forty days you spent in scouting the land; forty
years shall you suffer for your crimes: one year for
each day. Thus you will realize what it means to oppose me. 35 I, the LORD, have sworn to do this to all
this wicked community that conspired against me:
here in the desert they shall die to the last man."

36* And so it happened to the men whom Moses
had sent to reconnoiter the land and who on returning had set the whole community grumbling
against him by spreading discouraging reports
about the land; 37 these men who had given out the
bad report about the land were struck down by the
LORD and died. 38* Of all the men who had gone to
reconnoiter the land, only Joshua, son of Nun, and
Caleb, son of Jephunneh, survived.

Unsuccessful Invasion

39 When Moses repeated these words to all the
Israelites, the people felt great remorse. 40* Early
the next morning they started up into the foothills,
saying, "Here we are, ready to go up to the place
that the LORD spoke of: for we were indeed doing
wrong." 41 But Moses said, "Why are you again disobeying the LORD's orders? This cannot succeed.
42* Do not go up, because the LORD is not in your
midst; if you go, you will be beaten down before
your enemies. 43 For there the Amalekites and
Canaanites face you, and you will fall by the sword.
You have turned back from following the LORD;
therefore the LORD will not be with you."

44* Yet they dared to go up into the foothills,
even though neither the ark of the covenant of the
LORD nor Moses left the camp. 45† And the
Amalekites and Canaanites who dwelt in that hill
country came down and defeated them, beating
them back as far as Hormah.

Secondary Offerings

15 1 The LORD said to Moses, 2† "Give the
Israelites these instructions: When you
have entered the land that I will give you for your
homesteads, 3 if you make to the LORD a sweet-
smelling oblation from the herd or from the flock,
in holocaust, in fulfillment of a vow, or as a
freewill offering, or for one of your festivals,
4 whoever does so shall also present to the LORD a
cereal offering consisting of a tenth of an ephah of
fine flour mixed with a fourth of a hin of oil, 5 as
well as a libation of a fourth of a hin of wine, with
each lamb sacrificed in holocaust or otherwise.
6 With each sacrifice of a ram you shall present a

14, 25: *The valleys:* the low-lying plains in the Negeb and along
the seacoast and in the Jordan depression as well as the higher valleys in the mountains farther north; cf Nm 14, 45.

14, 28f: God punished the malcontents by giving them their
wish; cf v 2. Their lack of faith and of confidence in God is cited in
1 Cor 10, 10, and Heb 3, 12–18, as a warning for Christians.

14, 45: *Hormah:* one of the Canaanite royal cities in southern
Judea (Jos 12, 14), known at this time as "Zephath"; the origin of the
later name is told in Nm 21, 3; Jgs 1, 17.

15, 2–16: These laws on sacrifice are complementary to those of
Lv 1–3. Since the food of the Israelites consisted not only of meat but

---

also of bread, oil and wine, so, besides the animal oblations, they offered flour, wine and oil in sacrifice to the Lord.

14, 18: Ex 20, 5; 34, 6f; Pss 103, 8; 145, 8.
14, 19: Ps 78, 38.
14, 22f: Dt 1, 35.
14, 24: Jos 14, 8f.
14, 27: Ex 16, 7.12.
14, 29: Dt 1, 35; Heb 3, 17.
14, 31: Dt 1, 39.
14, 33f: Nm 13, 26; 32, 13; Ps 95, 10; Ez 4, 6.
14, 36f: Nm 13, 17.32f; 1 Cor 10, 10.
14, 38: Nm 26, 65.
14, 40: Nm 13, 18; Dt 1, 42.
14, 42: Dt 1, 42.
14, 44: Dt 1, 43.

cereal offering of two tenths of an ephah of fine flour mixed with a third of a hin of oil, [7] and a libation of a third of a hin of wine, thus making a sweet-smelling offering to the LORD. [8] When you sacrifice an ox as a holocaust, or in fulfillment of a vow, or as a peace offering to the LORD, [9] with it you shall present a cereal offering of three tenths of an ephah of fine flour mixed with half a hin of oil, [10] and a libation of half a hin of wine, as a sweet-smelling oblation to the LORD. [11] The same is to be done for each ox, ram, lamb or goat. [12] Whatever the number you offer, do the same for each of them.

[13] "All the native-born shall make these offerings in the same way, whenever they present a sweet-smelling oblation to the LORD. [14] Likewise, in any future generation, any alien residing with you permanently or for a time, who presents a sweet-smelling oblation to the LORD, shall do as you do. [15] There is but one rule for you and for the resident alien, a perpetual rule for all your descendants. Before the LORD you and the alien are alike, [16] with the same law and the same application of it for the alien residing among you as for yourselves."

[17] The LORD said to Moses, [18] "Speak to the Israelites and tell them: When you enter the land into which I will bring you [19] and begin to eat of the food of that land, you shall offer the LORD a contribution [20]*† consisting of a cake of your first batch of dough. You shall offer it just as you offer a contribution from the threshing floor. [21] Throughout your generations you shall give a contribution to the LORD from your first batch of dough.

Sin Offerings

[22]*† "When through inadvertence you fail to carry out any of these commandments which the LORD gives to Moses, [23] and through Moses to you, from the time the LORD first issues the commandment down through your generations: [24] if the community itself unwittingly becomes guilty of the fault of inadvertence, the whole community shall offer the holocaust of one young bull as a sweet-smelling oblation pleasing to the LORD, along with its prescribed cereal offering and libation, as well as one he-goat as a sin offering. [25]* Then the priest shall make atonement for the whole Israelite community; thus they will be for-

given the inadvertence for which they have brought their holocaust as an oblation to the LORD. [26] Not only the whole Israelite community, but also the aliens residing among you, shall be forgiven, since the fault of inadvertence affects all the people.

[27]* "However, if it is an individual who sins inadvertently, he shall bring a yearling she-goat as a sin offering, [28] and the priest shall make atonement before the LORD for him who sinned inadvertently; when atonement has been made for him, he will be forgiven. [29] You shall have but one law for him who sins inadvertently, whether he be a native Israelite or an alien residing with you.

[30]* "But anyone who sins defiantly, whether he be a native or an alien, insults the LORD, and shall be cut off from among his people. [31]* Since he has despised the word of the LORD and has broken his commandment, he must be cut off. He has only himself to blame."

The Sabbath-breaker

[32] While the Israelites were in the desert, a man was discovered gathering wood on the sabbath day. [33] Those who caught him at it brought him to Moses and Aaron and the whole assembly. [34]*† But they kept him in custody, for there was no clear decision as to what should be done with him. [35] Then the LORD said to Moses, "This man shall be put to death; let the whole community stone him outside the camp." [36] So the whole community led him outside the camp and stoned him to death, as the LORD had commanded Moses.

Tassels on the Cloak

[37] The LORD said to Moses, [38]*† "Speak to the Israelites and tell them that they and their descendants must put tassels on the corners of their garments, fastening each corner tassel with a violet cord. [39] When you use these tassels, let the sight of them remind you to keep all the commandments of the LORD, without going wantonly astray after the desires of your hearts and eyes. [40] Thus you will remember to keep all my commandments and be holy to your God. [41]* I, the LORD, am your God who, as God, brought you out of Egypt that I, the LORD, may be your God."

15, 20: *Dough:* some render, "barley grits." This word is used elsewhere only in Ez 44, 30 and Neh 10, 33; a related Hebrew word is used in Lv 2, 14.

15, 22ff: Although no moral guilt is incurred by an inadvertent violation of God's commandments, the sanctity of the law can require some reparation even for such violations.

15, 34: *No clear decision:* they already knew that a willful violation of the sabbath was a capital offense, but they did not yet know how the death penalty was to be inflicted.

15, 38: *Tassels:* at the time of Christ these tassels were worn by all pious Jews, including our Lord (Mt 9, 20f; Mk 6, 56); the Pharisees wore very large ones in ostentation of their zeal for the law (Mt 23, 5).

15, 20: 19–20: Ez 44, 30.   15, 31: Prv 13, 13.
15, 22f: Lv 4, 13f.   15, 34: Lv 24, 12.
15, 25: Lv 4, 20.   15, 38: Dt 22, 12.
15, 27f: Lv 4, 27f.   15, 41: Lv 22, 32f.
15, 30: Dt 17, 12.

Rebellion of Korah

16 [1] † Korah, son of Izhar, son of Kohath, son of Levi, [and Dathan and Abiram, sons of Eliab, son of Pallu, son of Reuben] took [2] two hundred and fifty Israelites who were leaders in the community, members of the council and men of note. They stood before Moses, [3]* and held an assembly against Moses and Aaron, to whom they said, "Enough from you! The whole community, all of them, are holy; the LORD is in their midst. Why then should you set yourselves over the LORD's congregation?"

[4] When Moses heard this, he fell prostrate. [5] Then he said to Korah and to all his band, "May the LORD make known tomorrow morning who belongs to him and who is the holy one and whom he will have draw near to him! Whom he chooses, he will have draw near him. [6] Do this: take your censers [Korah and all his band] [7] and put fire in them and place incense in them before the LORD tomorrow. He whom the LORD then chooses is the holy one. Enough from you Levites!"

[8] Moses also said to Korah, "Listen to me, you Levites! [9]* Is it too little for you that the God of Israel has singled you out from the community of Israel, to have you draw near him for the service of the LORD's Dwelling and to stand before the community to minister for them? [10] He has allowed you and your kinsmen, the descendants of Levi, to approach him, and yet you now seek the priesthood too. [11] It is therefore against the LORD that you and all your band are conspiring. For what has Aaron done that you should grumble against him?"

Rebellion of Dathan and Abiram

[12]† Moses summoned Dathan and Abiram, sons of Eliab, but they answered, "We will not go. [13] Are you not satisfied with having led us here away from a land flowing with milk and honey, to make us perish in the desert, that you must now lord it over us? [14]† Far from bringing us to a land flowing with milk and honey, or giving us fields and vineyards for our inheritance, will you also gouge out our eyes? No, we will not go."

[15]* Then Moses became very angry and said to the LORD, "Pay no heed to their offering. I have never taken a single ass from them, nor have I wronged any one of them."

Korah

[16] Moses said to Korah, "You and all your band shall appear before the LORD tomorrow—you and they and Aaron too. [17] Then each of your two hundred and fifty followers shall take his own censer, put incense in it, and offer it to the LORD; and you and Aaron, each with his own censer, shall do the same." [18] So they all took their censers, and laying incense on the fire they had put in them, they took their stand by the entrance of the meeting tent along with Moses and Aaron. [19] Then, when Korah had assembled all his band against them at the entrance of the meeting tent, the glory of the LORD appeared to the entire community, [20] and the LORD said to Moses and Aaron, [21] "Stand apart from this band, that I may consume them at once." [22] But they fell prostrate and cried out, "O God, God of the spirits of all mankind, will one man's sin make you angry with the whole community?" [23] The LORD answered Moses, [24] "Speak to the community and tell them: Withdraw from the space around the Dwelling" [of Korah, Dathan and Abiram].

Punishment of Dathan and Abiram

[25]† Moses, followed by the elders of Israel, arose and went to Dathan and Abiram. [26] Then he warned the community, "Keep away from the tents of these wicked men and do not touch anything that is theirs: otherwise you too will be swept away because of all their sins." [27] When Dathan and Abiram had come out and were standing at the entrances of their tents with their wives and sons and little ones, [28] Moses said, "This is how you shall know that it was the LORD who sent me to do all I have done, and that it was not I who planned it: [29] if these men die an ordinary death, merely suffering the fate common to all mankind, then it was not the LORD who sent me. [30] But if the LORD does something entirely new, and the ground opens its mouth and swallows them alive down into the nether world, with all belonging to them, then you will know that these men have defied the LORD." [31]* No sooner had he finished saying all this than

---

† **16, 1ff:** The evidence seems to show that there were two distinct rebellions: one of Korah and his band (Nm 27, 3) and the other of Dathan and Abiram (Dt 11, 6); cf Ps 106. The present account combines both events into one narrative; but even here it is rather easy to separate the two, once certain proper names (vv 1.6.24.32.35) have been identified as glosses. The rebellion of the Reubenites, Dathan and Abiram, was of a political nature, against Moses alone as the civil leader; these rebels were punished by being swallowed alive in an earthquake. The rebellion of Korah was of a religious nature, against the religious leadership of both Moses and Aaron; about two hundred and fifty malcontents joined Korah's band; they were punished by fire. The parts of the present section which refer to the rebellion of Dathan and Abiram are vv 12–15 and vv 25–34 of chapter 16; the rest of chapter 16 and all of chapter 17 concern the rebellion of Korah.

16, 12: *We will not go:* to appear before Moses' tribunal.

16, 14: *Gouge out our eyes:* blind us to the real state of affairs.

16, 25: Since Dathan and Abiram had refused to go to Moses (vv 12ff), he, with the elders as witnesses, was obliged to go to their tent.

16, 3: Ps 106, 16ff; Sir 45,
   19; 1 Cor 10, 10.
16, 9: Dt 10, 8.

16, 15: 1 Sm 12, 3.
16, 31ff: Nm 26, 10; Lv 10, 2;
   Dt 11, 6; Ps 106, 7f.

the ground beneath them split open, 32 and the earth opened its mouth and swallowed them and their families [and all of Korah's men] and all their possessions. 33 They went down alive to the nether world with all belonging to them; the earth closed over them, and they perished from the community. 34 But all the Israelites near them fled at their shrieks, saying, "The earth might swallow us too!"

Punishment of Korah

35† So they withdrew from the space around the Dwelling [of Korah, Dathan and Abiram]. And fire from the LORD came forth which consumed the two hundred and fifty men who were offering the incense.

17 1 The LORD said to Moses, 2 "Tell Eleazar, son of Aaron the priest, to remove the censers from the embers; and scatter the fire some distance away, 3† for these sinners have consecrated the censers at the cost of their lives. Have them hammered into plates to cover the altar, because in being presented before the LORD they have become sacred. In this way they shall serve as a sign to the Israelites." 4 So Eleazar the priest had the bronze censers of those burned during the offering hammered into a covering for the altar, 5 in keeping with the orders which the LORD had given him through Moses. This cover was to be a reminder to the Israelites that no layman, no one who was not a descendant of Aaron, should approach the altar to offer incense before the LORD, lest he meet the fate of Korah and his band.

6 The next day the whole Israelite community grumbled against Moses and Aaron, saying, "It is you who have slain the LORD'S people." 7 But while the community was deliberating against them, Moses and Aaron turned toward the meeting tent, and the cloud now covered it and the glory of the LORD appeared. 8 Then Moses and Aaron came to the front of the meeting tent, 9 and the LORD said to Moses and Aaron, 10 "Depart from this community, that I may consume them at once." But they fell prostrate.

11* Then Moses said to Aaron, "Take your censer, put fire from the altar in it, lay incense on it, and bring it quickly to the community to make atonement for them; for wrath has come forth from the LORD and the blow is falling." 12 Obeying the orders of Moses, Aaron took his censer and ran in among the community, where the blow was already falling on the people. Then, as he offered the incense and made atonement for the people, 13 standing there between the living and the dead, the scourge was checked. 14 Yet fourteen thousand seven hundred died from the scourge, in addition to those who died because of Korah. 15 When the scourge had been checked, Aaron returned to Moses at the entrance of the meeting tent.

Aaron's Staff

16 The LORD now said to Moses, 17† "Speak to the Israelites and get one staff from them for each ancestral house, twelve staffs in all, one from each of their tribal princes. Mark each man's name on his staff; 18† and mark Aaron's name on Levi's staff, for the head of Levi's ancestral house shall also have a staff. 19 Then lay them down in the meeting tent, in front of the commandments, where I meet you. 20 There the staff of the man of my choice shall sprout. Thus will I suppress from my presence the Israelites' grumbling against you."

21 So Moses spoke to the Israelites, and their princes gave him staffs, twelve in all, one from each tribal prince; and Aaron's staff was with them. 22 Then Moses laid the staffs down before the LORD in the tent of the commandments. 23 The next day, when Moses entered the tent, Aaron's staff, representing the house of Levi, had sprouted and put forth not only shoots, but blossoms as well, and even bore ripe almonds! 24 Moses thereupon brought out all the staffs from the LORD'S presence to the Israelites. After each prince identified his own staff and took it, 25 the LORD said to Moses, "Put back Aaron's staff in front of the commandments, to be kept there as a warning to the rebellious, so that their grumbling may cease before me; if it does not, they will die." 26 And Moses did as the LORD had commanded him.

Charge of the Sacred Things

27† Then the Israelites cried out to Moses, "We are perishing; we are lost, we are all lost! 28 Every time anyone approaches the Dwelling of the LORD, he dies! Are we to perish to the last man?"

---

† **16, 35:** This verse continues v 24; the first sentence is transposed from v 27.

17, 3: Whatever was brought into intimate contact with something sacred shared in its sacredness. See note on Nm 19, 20.

17, 17: The staff was not merely an article of practical use, but also a symbol of authority; cf Gn 49, 10; Nm 24, 17; Jer 48, 17. Hence, the staff of a leader of a tribe was considered the emblem of his tribe; in fact, certain Hebrew words for "staff" also mean "tribe." Perhaps for this reason, to avoid confusion, the author here uses the term "ancestral house" instead of the ordinary word for "tribe."

17, 18: *Levi's staff:* it is not clear whether this is considered as one

of the twelve mentioned in the preceding verse, or as a thirteenth staff. Sometimes Levi is reckoned as one of the twelve tribes (e.g., Dt 27, 12f), but more often the number twelve is arrived at by counting the two sub-tribes of Joseph, i.e., Ephraim and Manasseh, as distinct tribes. In this passage also it seems probable that the tribe of Levi is considered apart from the other twelve.

17, 27f: Logically these two verses belong immediately after Nm 16, 35.

---

* **17, 11:** Wis 18, 20f.

18 [1] † The LORD said to Aaron, "You and your sons as well as the other members of your ancestral house shall be responsible for the sanctuary; but the responsibility of the priesthood shall rest on you and your sons alone. [2]† Bring with you also your other kinsmen of the tribe of Levi, your ancestral tribe, as your associates and assistants, while you and your sons are in front of the tent of the commandments. [3] They shall look after your persons and the whole tent; however, they shall not come near the sacred vessels or the altar, lest both they and you die. [4]† As your associates they shall have charge of all the work connected with the meeting tent. But no layman shall come near you. [5] You shall have charge of the sanctuary and of the altar, that wrath may not fall again upon the Israelites.

[6]* "Remember, it is I who have taken your kinsmen, the Levites, from the body of the Israelites; they are a gift to you, dedicated to the LORD for the service of the meeting tent. [7]*† But only you and your sons are to have charge of performing the priestly functions in whatever concerns the altar and the room within the veil. I give you the priesthood as a gift. Any layman who draws near shall be put to death."

The Priests' Share of the Sacrifices

[8]*† The LORD said to Aaron, "I myself have given you charge of the contributions made to me in the various sacred offerings of the Israelites; by perpetual ordinance I have assigned them to you and to your sons as your priestly share. [9] You shall have the right to share in the oblations that are most sacred, in whatever they offer me as cereal offerings or sin offerings or guilt offerings; these shares shall accrue to you and to your sons. [10] In eating them you shall treat them as most sacred; every male among you may partake of them. As sacred, they belong to you.

[11]*† "You shall also have what is removed from the gift in every wave offering of the Israelites; by perpetual ordinance I have assigned it to you and to your sons and daughters. All in your family who are clean may partake of it. [12]* I have also as-signed to you all the best of the new oil and of the new wine and grain that they give to the LORD as their first fruits; [13] and likewise, of whatever grows on their land, the first products that they bring in to the LORD shall be yours; all of your family who are clean may partake of them. [14]† Whatever is doomed in Israel shall be yours. [15]* Every living thing that opens the womb, whether of man or of beast, such as are to be offered to the LORD, shall be yours; but you must let the first-born of man, as well as of unclean animals, be redeemed. [16] The ransom for a boy is to be paid when he is a month old; it is fixed at five silver shekels according to the sanctuary standard, twenty gerahs to the shekel. [17] But the first-born of cattle, sheep or goats shall not be redeemed; they are sacred. Their blood you must splash on the altar and their fat you must burn as a sweet-smelling oblation to the LORD. [18]* Their meat, however, shall be yours, just as the breast and the right leg of the wave offering belong to you. [19]† By perpetual ordinance I have assigned to you and to your sons and daughters all the contributions from the sacred gifts which the Israelites make to the LORD; this is an inviolable covenant to last forever before the LORD, for you and for your descendants." [20]*† Then the LORD said to Aaron, "You shall not have any heritage in the land of the Israelites nor hold any portion among them; I will be your portion and your heritage among them.

Tithes Due the Levites

[21]* "To the Levites, however, I hereby assign all tithes in Israel as their heritage in recompense for the service they perform in the meeting tent. [22] The Israelites may no longer approach the meeting tent; else they will incur guilt deserving death. [23] Only the Levites are to perform the service of the meeting tent, and they alone shall be held responsible; this is a perpetual ordinance for all your generations. The Levites, therefore, shall not have any heritage among the Israelites, [24] for I have assigned to them as their heritage the tithes which the Israelites give as a contribution to the LORD. That is why I have or-

---

18, 1ff: This law, which kept unqualified persons from contact with sacred things, is the answer to the Israelites' cry in Nm 17, 28. It is followed by other laws concerning priests and Levites.

18, 2: *Associates:* in Hebrew this word alludes to the popular etymology of the name "Levi." Cf Gn 29, 34.

18, 4: *Layman:* here, "one who is not a Levite"; in v 7, "one who is not a priest."

18, 7: *Veil:* the outer veil, or "curtain," is probably meant.

18, 8ff: Two classes of offerings are here distinguished: the most sacred offering, which only the male members of the priestly families could eat (vv 8ff), and the other offerings, which even the women of the priestly families could eat (vv 11–19).

18, 11: *Wave offering:* this included the breast and right leg (v 18), the shoulder of the peace offering (Lv 7, 30–34), and portions of the nazirite sacrifice (Nm 6, 19f).

18, 14: *Doomed:* in Hebrew, *herem,* which means here "set aside from profane use and made sacred to the Lord." Cf Lv 27, 21.28.

18, 19: *An inviolable covenant:* literally, "a covenant of salt." Cf 2 Chr 13, 5. The reference may perhaps be to the preservative power of salt (cf Mt 5, 13); but more likely the phrase refers to the custom of partaking of the same salt in common to render a contract unbreakable. See note on Lv 2, 13.

18, 20: The priests and Levites were forbidden to own hereditary land such as the other Israelites possessed; therefore in the allotment of the land they were not to receive any portion of it. Certain cities, however, were assigned to them for their residence; cf Nm 35, 1–8.

18, 6: Nm 3, 9; 8, 19.
18, 7: Nm 3, 10.
18, 8: Nm 5, 9.
18, 11: Ex 29, 27f; Lv 7, 34; 10, 14.
18, 12f: Dt 18, 4; 26, 2.
18, 15: Ex 13, 2.
18, 18: Lv 7, 31–34.
18, 20: Dt 10, 9; 18, 1f; Jos 13, 33; Ez 44, 28.
18, 21: Heb 7, 5.

dered that they are not to have any heritage among the Israelites."

Tithes Paid by the Levites

25 The LORD said to Moses, 26 "Give the Levites these instructions: When you receive from the Israelites the tithes I have assigned you from them as your heritage, you are to make a contribution from them to the LORD, a tithe of the tithes; 27 and your contribution will be credited to you as if it were grain from the threshing floor or new wine from the press. 28 Thus you too shall make a contribution from all the tithes you receive from the Israelites, handing over to Aaron the priest the part to be contributed to the LORD. 29 From all the gifts that you receive, and from the best parts, you are to consecrate to the LORD your own full contribution.

30 "Tell them also: Once you have made your contribution from the best part, the rest of the tithes will be credited to you Levites as if it were produce of the threshing floor or of the wine press. 31 Your families, as well as you, may eat them anywhere, since they are your recompense for service at the meeting tent. 32 You will incur no guilt so long as you make a contribution of the best part. Do not profane the sacred gifts of the Israelites and so bring death on yourselves."

Ashes of the Red Heifer

19 1 The LORD said to Moses and Aaron: 2 "This is the regulation which the law of the LORD prescribes. Tell the Israelites to procure for you a red heifer that is free from every blemish and defect and on which no yoke has ever been laid. 3† This is to be given to Eleazar the priest, to be led outside the camp and slaughtered in his presence. 4† Eleazar the priest shall take some of its blood on his finger and sprinkle it seven times toward the front of the meeting tent. 5 Then the heifer shall be burned in his sight, with its hide and flesh, its blood and offal; 6 and the priest shall take some cedar wood, hyssop and scarlet yarn and throw them into the fire in which the heifer is being burned. 7 The priest shall then wash his garments and bathe his body in water. He remains unclean until the evening, and only afterward may he return to the camp. 8 Likewise, he who burned the heifer shall wash his garments, bathe his body in water, and be unclean until evening. 9 Finally, a man who

is clean shall gather up the ashes of the heifer and deposit them in a clean place outside the camp. There they are to be kept for preparing lustral water for the Israelite community. The heifer is a sin offering. 10 He who has gathered up the ashes of the heifer shall also wash his garments and be unclean until evening. This is a perpetual ordinance, both for the Israelites and for the aliens residing among them.

Use of the Ashes

11 "Whoever touches the dead body of any human being shall be unclean for seven days; 12 he shall purify himself with the water on the third and on the seventh day, and then he will be clean again. But if he fails to purify himself on the third and on the seventh day, he will not become clean. 13* Everyone who fails to purify himself after touching the body of any deceased person, defiles the Dwelling of the LORD and shall be cut off from Israel. Since the lustral water has not been splashed over him, he remains unclean: his uncleanness still clings to him.

14 "This is the law: When a man dies in a tent, everyone who enters the tent, as well as everyone already in it, shall be unclean for seven days; 15 likewise, every vessel that is open, or with its lid unfastened, shall be unclean. 16 Moreover, everyone who in the open country touches a dead person, whether he was slain by the sword or died naturally, or who touches a human bone or a grave, shall be unclean for seven days. 17† For anyone who is thus unclean, ashes from the sin offering shall be put in a vessel, and spring water shall be poured on them. 18 Then a man who is clean shall take some hyssop, dip it in this water, and sprinkle it on the tent and on all the vessels and persons that were in it, or on him who touched a bone, a slain person or other dead body, or a grave. 19 The clean man shall sprinkle the unclean on the third and on the seventh day; thus purified on the seventh day, he shall wash his garments and bathe his body in water, and in the evening he will be clean again. 20† Any unclean man who fails to have himself purified shall be cut off from the community, because he defiles the sanctuary of the LORD. As long as the lustral water has not been splashed over him, he remains unclean. 21 This shall be a perpetual ordinance for you.

19, 3: *Outside the camp:* several Fathers of the Church saw in this a prefiguring of the sacrificial death of Christ outside the walls of Jerusalem; cf Jn 19, 20; Heb 13, 12; in the purifying water, into which the ashes of the red heifer were put, they saw a type of the water of Baptism.
19, 4: *Toward the front of the meeting tent:* since the tabernacle faced the east (Ex 26, 15–30), the killing of the heifer took place east of the camp; in later times it was done on the Mount of Olives, east of the Temple.

19, 17ff: "If . . . the sprinkled ashes of a heifer sanctify the unclean unto the cleansing of the flesh, how much more will the blood of Christ . . . cleanse your conscience from dead works?" (Heb 9, 13f).
19, 20: Ritual uncleanness is, as it were, contagious; so also sacredness; see note on Nm 17, 3.

---

* 19, 13: Lv 15, 31.

"One who sprinkles the lustral water shall wash his garments, and anyone who comes in contact with this water shall be unclean until evening. 22 Moreover, whatever the unclean person touches becomes unclean itself, and anyone who touches it becomes unclean until evening."

Death of Miriam

20 1 † The whole Israelite community arrived in the desert of Zin in the first month, and the people settled at Kadesh. It was here that Miriam died, and here that she was buried.

Water Famine at Kadesh

2 As the community had no water, they held a council against Moses and Aaron. 3 The people contended with Moses, exclaiming, "Would that we too had perished with our kinsmen in the LORD's presence! 4 Why have you brought the LORD's community into this desert where we and our livestock are dying? 5 Why did you lead us out of Egypt, only to bring us to this wretched place which has neither grain nor figs nor vines nor pomegranates? Here there is not even water to drink!" 6 But Moses and Aaron went away from the assembly to the entrance of the meeting tent, where they fell prostrate.

Sin of Moses and Aaron

Then the glory of the LORD appeared to them, 7 and the LORD said to Moses, 8 "Take the staff and assemble the community, you and your brother Aaron, and in their presence order the rock to yield its waters. From the rock you shall bring forth water for the community and their livestock to drink." 9 So Moses took the staff from its place before the LORD, as he was ordered. 10* He and Aaron assembled the community in front of the rock, where he said to them, "Listen to me, you rebels! Are we to bring water for you out of this rock?" 11*† Then, raising his hand, Moses struck the rock twice with his staff, and water gushed out in abundance for the community and their livestock to drink. 12† But the LORD said to Moses and Aaron, "Because you were not faithful to me in

showing forth my sanctity before the Israelites, you shall not lead this community into the land I will give them."

13* These are the waters of Meribah, where the Israelites contended against the LORD, and where he revealed his sanctity among them.

Edom's Refusal

14† From Kadesh Moses sent men to the king of Edom with the message: "Your brother Israel has this to say: You know of all the hardships that have befallen us, 15 how our fathers went down to Egypt, where we stayed a long time, how the Egyptians maltreated us and our fathers, 16* and how, when we cried to the LORD, he heard our cry and sent an angel who led us out of Egypt. Now here we are at the town of Kadesh at the edge of your territory. 17† Kindly let us pass through your country. We will not cross any fields or vineyards, nor drink any well water, but we will go straight along the royal road without turning to the right or to the left, until we have passed through your territory."

18 But Edom answered him, "You shall not pass through here; if you do, I will advance against you with the sword." 19 The Israelites insisted, "We want only to go up along the highway. If we or our livestock drink any of your water, we will pay for it. Surely there is no harm in merely letting us march through." 20* But Edom still said, "No, you shall not pass through," and advanced against them with a large and heavily armed force. 21 Therefore, since Edom refused to let them pass through their territory, Israel detoured around them.

Death of Aaron

22*† Setting out from Kadesh, the whole Israelite community came to Mount Hor. 23 There at Mount Hor, on the border of the land of Edom, the LORD said to Moses and Aaron, 24 "Aaron is about to be taken to his people; he shall not enter the land I am giving to the Israelites, because you both rebelled against my commandment at the waters of Meribah. 25* Take Aaron and his son Eleazar and bring them up on Mount Hor. 26 Then strip Aaron

---

20, 1: *The first month:* we would expect the mention also of the day and of the year (after the exodus) when this took place; cf similar dates in Nm 1, 1; 10, 11; 33, 38; Dt 1, 3. Here the full date seems to have been lost. Probably the Israelites arrived in Kadesh in the third year after the exodus. Cf Dt 1, 46. *The desert of Zin:* a barren region with a few good oases, southwest of the Dead Sea. See note on Nm 13, 21.

20, 11: *Twice:* perhaps because he had not sufficient faith to work the miracle with the first blow. Cf v 12.

20, 12f: The sin of Moses and Aaron consisted in doubting God's mercy toward the ever-rebellious people. *In showing forth my sanctity:* God's sacred power and glory: an allusion to the name of the place, Kadesh, which means "sanctified, sacred." Meribah means "contention." Cf Ex 17, 7.

20, 14: *Your brother Israel:* the Edomites were descended from

Esau, the brother of Jacob. Their country, to the southeast of the Dead Sea, was also known as Seir; cf Gn 25, 24ff; 36, 1.8f.

20, 17: *The royal road:* an important highway, running north and south along the plateau east of the Dead Sea. In ancient times it was much used by caravans and armies; later it was improved by the Romans, and large stretches of it are still clearly recognizable.

20, 22: *Mount Hor:* not definitively identified, but probably to be sought in the vicinity of Kadesh. According to Dt 10, 6, Aaron died at Moserah (cf "Moseroth" in Nm 33, 30f), which is apparently the name of the region in which Mount Hor is situated.

20, 10: Ex 17, 5f.   20, 16: Ex 2, 23.
20, 11: Ps 78, 15f; Wis 11, 4;   20, 20: Jgs 11, 17.
    1 Cor 10, 4.   20, 22: 21f; Nm 33, 37.
20, 13: Nm 27, 14; Ex 17, 7.   20, 25f: Dt 32, 50.

of his garments and put them on his son Eleazar; for there Aaron shall be taken in death."

27 Moses did as the LORD commanded. When they had climbed Mount Hor in view of the whole community, 28* Moses stripped Aaron of his garments and put them on his son Eleazar. Then Aaron died there on top of the mountain. When Moses and Eleazar came down from the mountain, 29 all the community understood that Aaron had passed away; and for thirty days the whole house of Israel mourned him.

Victory over Arad

21 1 *† When the Canaanite king of Arad, who lived in the Negeb, heard that the Israelites were coming along the way of Atharim, he engaged them in battle and took some of them captive. 2* Israel then made this vow to the LORD: "If you deliver this people into my hand, I will doom their cities." 3*† Later, when the LORD heeded Israel's prayer and delivered up the Canaanites, they doomed them and their cities. Hence that place was named Hormah.

The Bronze Serpent

4 From Mount Hor they set out on the Red Sea road, to bypass the land of Edom. But with their patience worn out by the journey, 5*† the people complained against God and Moses, "Why have you brought us up from Egypt to die in this desert, where there is no food or water? We are disgusted with this wretched food!"

6*† In punishment the LORD sent among the people saraph serpents, which bit the people so that many of them died. 7 Then the people came to Moses and said, "We have sinned in complaining against the LORD and you. Pray the LORD to take the serpents from us." So Moses prayed for the people, 8† and the LORD said to Moses, "Make a saraph and mount it on a pole, and if anyone who has been bitten looks at it, he will recover." 9*† Moses accordingly made a bronze serpent and mounted it on a pole, and whenever anyone who had been bitten by a serpent looked at the bronze serpent, he recovered.

Chap. 21

Journey around Moab

10* The Israelites moved on and encamped in Oboth. 11† Setting out from Oboth, they encamped in Iye-abarim in the desert fronting Moab on the east. 12 Setting out from there, they encamped in the Wadi Zered. 13 Setting out from there, they encamped on the other side of the Arnon, in the desert that extends from the territory of the Amorites; for the Arnon forms Moab's boundary with the Amorites. 14† Hence it is said in the "Book of the Wars of the LORD":

> "Waheb in Suphah and the wadies,
> 15　　Arnon and the wadi gorges
> That reach back toward the site of Ar
> 　　and slant to the border of Moab."

16† From there they went to Beer, where there was the well of which the LORD said to Moses, "Bring the people together, and I will give them water." 17 Then it was that Israel sang this song:

> "Spring up, O well!—so sing to it—
> 18　　The well that the princes sank,

21, 1–3: The account of this episode seems to be a later insertion here, for Nm 21, 4, belongs logically immediately after Nm 20, 29. Perhaps this is the same event as that mentioned in Jgs 1, 16f.

21, 3: *Hormah:* related to the Hebrew word *herem,* meaning "doomed." See notes on Nm 14, 45; 18, 14.

21, 5: *This wretched food:* apparently the manna is meant.

21, 6: *Saraph:* the Hebrew name for a certain species of venomous snakes; the word probably signifies "the fiery one," these snakes being so called from the burning effect of their poisonous bite.

21, 8: *If anyone who has been bitten looks at it, he will recover:* "and as Moses lifted up the serpent in the desert, even so must the Son of Man be lifted up, that those who believe in him may not perish, but may have life everlasting" (Jn 3, 14f).

21, 9: King Hezekiah, in his efforts to abolish idolatry, "smashed the bronze serpent which Moses had made" (2 Kgs 18, 4).

21, 11: *Iye-abarim:* probably means "the ruins in the Abarim (Mountains)." See note on Nm 27, 12.

21, 14: *The "Book of the Wars of the LORD":* an ancient collection of Israelite songs, now lost. *Waheb in Suphah:* since neither place is mentioned elsewhere, it is quite uncertain whether these dubious Hebrew words are even to be considered as place names; some Hebrew words apparently lost must have preceded this phrase.

21, 16: *Beer:* means "a well."

20, 28: Nm 33, 38.　　　　21, 6: Dt 8, 15; Wis 16, 5;
21, 1: Nm 33, 40.　　　　　　1 Cor 10, 9.
21, 2: Jos 6, 17; Jgs 1, 17.　21, 9: Wis 16, 6f.10; Jn 3,
21, 3: Nm 14, 45.　　　　　　14f.
21, 5: Nm 11, 6; Ex 16, 3.　21, 10: Nm 33, 43f.

that the nobles of the people dug,
with their scepters and their staffs."

From Beer they went to Mattanah, 19 from Mattanah to Nahaliel, from Nahaliel to Bamoth, 20† from Bamoth to the cleft in the plateau of Moab at the headland of Pisgah that overlooks Jeshimon.

Victory over Sihon

21 Now Israel sent men to Sihon, king of the Amorites, with the message, 22 "Let us pass through your country. We will not turn aside into any field or vineyard, nor will we drink any well water, but we will go straight along the royal road until we have passed through your territory." 23* Sihon, however, would not let Israel pass through his territory, but mustered all his forces and advanced into the desert against Israel. When he reached Jahaz, he engaged Israel in battle. 24 But Israel defeated him at the point of the sword, and took possession of his land from the Arnon to the Jabbok and as far as the country of the Ammonites, whose boundary was at Jazer. 25* Israel seized all the towns here and settled in these towns of the Amorites, in Heshbon and all its dependencies. 26 Now Heshbon was the capital of Sihon, king of the Amorites, who had fought against the former king of Moab and had seized all his land from Jazer to the Arnon. 27 That is why the poets say:

"Come to Heshbon, let it be rebuilt,
    let Sihon's capital be firmly constructed.
28   For fire went forth from Heshbon
    and a blaze from the city of Sihon;
  It consumed the cities of Moab
    and swallowed up the high places of
      the Arnon.
29† Woe to you, O Moab!
    You are ruined, O people of Chemosh!
  He let his sons become fugitives
    and his daughters be taken captive
    by the Amorite king Sihon.
30   Their plowland is ruined from Heshbon
    to Dibon;
  Ar is laid waste; fires blaze as far as Medeba."

31 When Israel had settled in the land of the Amorites, 32 Moses sent spies to Jazer; Israel then captured it with its dependencies and dispossessed the Amorites who were there.

Victory over Og

33* Then they turned and went up along the road to Bashan. But Og, king of Bashan, advanced against them with all his people to give battle at Edrei. 34* The LORD, however, said to Moses, "Do not be afraid of him; for into your hand I will deliver him with all his people and his land. Do to him as you did to Sihon, king of the Amorites, who lived in Heshbon." 35 So they struck him down with his sons and all his people, until not a survivor was left to him, and they took possession of his land.

22

1† Then the Israelites moved on and encamped in the plains of Moab on the other side of the Jericho stretch of the Jordan.

III: On the Plains of Moab

Balaam Summoned

2 Now Balak, son of Zippor, saw all that Israel did to the Amorites. 3 Indeed, Moab feared the Israelites greatly because of their numbers, and detested them. 4 So Moab said to the elders of Midian, "Soon this horde will devour all the country around us as an ox devours the grass of the field." And Balak, Zippor's son, who was king of Moab at that time, 5 sent messengers to Balaam, son of Beor, at Pethor on the Euphrates, in the land of the Amawites, summoning him with these words, "A people has come here from Egypt who now cover the face of the earth and are settling down opposite us! 6† Please come and curse this people for us; they are stronger than we are. We may then be able to defeat them and drive them out of the country. For I know that whoever you bless is blessed and whoever you curse is cursed." 7 Then the elders of Moab and of Midian left with the divination fee in hand and went to Balaam. When they had given him Balak's message, 8 he said to them in reply, "Stay here overnight, and I will give you whatever answer the LORD gives me." So the princes of Moab lodged with Balaam.

9 Then God came to Balaam and said, "Who are these men visiting you?" 10 Balaam answered God, "Balak, son of Zippor, king of Moab, sent me the

---

21, 20: *Jeshimon:* "the wasteland"; in 1 Sm 23, 19.24, and 26, 1.3, this is the desert of Judah, on the western side of the Dead Sea, but here and in Nm 23, 28, it seems to refer to the southern end of the Jordan valley where Beth-jeshimoth was situated.
21, 29: *Chemosh:* the chief god of the Moabites, and mentioned as such in the famous inscription of Mesha, king of Moab, who was the contemporary of the dynasty of Omri in Israel. Cf 1 Kgs 11, 7.33; 2 Kgs 23, 13; Jer 48, 7.13.
22, 1: *The plains of Moab:* the lowlands to the northeast of the Dead Sea, between the Jordan and the foothills below Mount Nebo.

Here the Israelites remained until they crossed the Jordan, as told in Jos 1–4. Jericho lay to the west of the Jordan.
22, 6: *Curse this people for us:* Balak believed that if Balaam forecast an evil omen for Israel, this evil would come to pass, as if by magic. Balaam was a soothsayer or foreteller; cf Jos 13, 22.

21, 23: Dt 2, 32; Jgs 11, 20.   21, 33: Dt 3, 1ff.
21, 25f: Jos 21, 39; Jgs 11, 26.   21, 34: Ps 136, 17ff.

message: [11] 'This people that came here from Egypt now cover the face of the earth. Please come and lay a curse on them for us; we may then be able to give them battle and drive them out.' " [12] But God said to Balaam, "Do not go with them and do not curse this people, for they are blessed." [13] The next morning Balaam arose and told the princes of Balak, "Go back to your own country, for the LORD has refused to let me go with you." [14] So the princes of Moab went back to Balak with the report, "Balaam refused to come with us."

Second Appeal to Balaam

[15] Balak again sent princes, who were more numerous and more distinguished than the others. [16] On coming to Balaam they told him, "This is what Balak, son of Zippor, has to say: Please do not refuse to come to me. [17] I will reward you very handsomely and will do anything you ask of me. Please come and lay a curse on this people for me." [18]* But Balaam replied to Balak's officials, "Even if Balak gave me his house full of silver and gold, I could not do anything, small or great, contrary to the command of the LORD, my God. [19] But, you too shall stay here overnight, till I learn what else the LORD may tell me."

[20] That night God came to Balaam and said to him, "If these men have come to summon you, you may go with them; yet only on the condition that you do exactly as I tell you." [21] So the next morning when Balaam arose, he saddled his ass, and went off with the princes of Moab.

The Talking Ass

[22]† But now the anger of God flared up at him for going, and the angel of the LORD stationed himself on the road to hinder him as he was riding along on his ass, accompanied by two of his servants. [23] When the ass saw the angel of the LORD standing on the road with sword drawn, she turned off the road and went into the field, and Balaam had to beat her to bring her back on the road. [24] Then the angel of the LORD took his stand in a narrow lane between vineyards with a stone wall on each side. [25] When the ass saw the angel of the LORD there, she shrank against the wall; and since she squeezed Balaam's leg against it, he beat her again. [26] The angel of the LORD then went ahead, and stopped next in a passage so narrow that there was no room to move either to the right or to the left. [27] When the ass saw the angel of the LORD

The Talking Donkey

Balaam is an interesting biblical character. He is not an Israelite and seems to be a sort of prophet for hire. Balak, the king of Moab, hires him to prophesy against Israel. But Balaam, hearing a message from God through his "ass," or donkey, instead of cursing the Israelites, blesses them four times. Even though the Israelites were unfaithful, God continues to be with them, to bless them.

Balaam is a sign of the universal character of God's call, and the donkey is a symbol of the poor and oppressed. The complaining and whining donkey represents those who usually are not heard but are given a voice through the prophets.

This story gives us two insights into prayer. First, if God can use a donkey to talk to Balaam, God can use anything to talk to us. God speaks to us in many ways—through our experiences, the Scriptures, poetry and music, our relationship with nature, and more. Are we paying attention? Second, God wants us to hear the often unheard voice of the poor and oppressed. Do you hear God's voice expressed through them?

▶ Nm 22, 22–35

there, she cowered under Balaam. So, in anger, he again beat the ass with his stick.

[28]* But now the LORD opened the mouth of the ass, and she asked Balaam, "What have I done to you that you should beat me these three times?" [29] "You have acted so willfully against me," said Balaam to the ass, "that if I but had a sword at hand, I would kill you here and now." [30] But the ass said to Balaam, "Am I not your own beast, and have you not always ridden upon me until now? Have I been in the habit of treating you this way before?" "No," replied Balaam.

[31] Then the LORD removed the veil from Balaam's eyes, so that he too saw the angel of the

---

† **22, 22:** *The anger of God flared up:* not merely because Balaam was going to Balak, for he had God's permission for the journey (v 20), but perhaps because he was tempted by avarice to curse Israel against God's command. "They have followed the way of Balaam, son of Bosor, who loved the wages of wrongdoing" (2 Pt 1, 15);

"abandoned themselves to Balaam's error for the sake of gain" (Jude 11). Cf v 32 and compare Ex 4, 18–26.

22, 18: Nm 24, 13.   22, 28: 2 Pt 2, 16.

LORD standing on the road with sword drawn; and he fell on his knees and bowed to the ground. 32 But the angel of the LORD said to him, "Why have you beaten your ass these three times? It is I who have come armed to hinder you because this rash journey of yours is directly opposed to me. 33 When the ass saw me, she turned away from me these three times. If she had not turned away from me, I would have killed you; her I would have spared." 34 Then Balaam said to the angel of the LORD, "I have sinned. Yet I did not know that you stood against me to oppose my journey. Since it has displeased you, I will go back home." 35 But the angel of the LORD said to Balaam, "Go with the men; but you may say only what I tell you." So Balaam went on with the princes of Balak.

36 When Balak heard that Balaam was coming, he went out to meet him at the boundary city Ir-Moab on the Arnon at the end of the Moabite territory. 37 And he said to Balaam, "I sent an urgent summons to you! Why did you not come to me? Did you think I could not reward you?" 38 Balaam answered him, "Well, I have come to you after all. But what power have I to say anything? I can speak only what God puts in my mouth." 39 Then Balaam went with Balak, and they came to Kiriath-huzoth. 40 Here Balak slaughtered oxen and sheep, and sent portions to Balaam and to the princes who were with him.

The First Oracle

41 The next morning Balak took Balaam up on Bamoth-baal, and from there he saw some of the clans.

23 1 Then Balaam said to Balak, "Build me seven altars, and prepare seven bullocks and seven rams for me here." 2 So he did as Balaam had ordered, offering a bullock and a ram on each altar. And Balak said to him, "I have erected the seven altars, and have offered a bullock and a ram on each." 3 Balaam then said to him, "Stand here by your holocaust while I go over there. Perhaps the LORD will meet me, and then I will tell you whatever he lets me see." He went out on the barren height, 4 and God met him. 5 When he had put an utterance in Balaam's mouth, the LORD said to him, "Go back to Balak, and speak accordingly." 6 So he went back to Balak, who was still standing by his holocaust together with all the princes of Moab.

7*† Then Balaam gave voice to his oracle:

From Aram has Balak brought me here,
    Moab's king, from the Eastern Mountains:
"Come and lay a curse for me on Jacob,
    come and denounce Israel."
8   How can I curse whom God has not cursed?
    How denounce whom the LORD has
      not denounced?
9† For from the top of the crags I see him,
    from the heights I behold him.
Here is a people that lives apart
    and does not reckon itself among
      the nations.
10† Who has ever counted the dust of Jacob,
    or numbered Israel's wind-borne particles?
May I die the death of the just,
    may my descendants be as many as theirs!

11 "What have you done to me?" cried Balak to Balaam. "It was to curse my foes that I brought you here; instead, you have even blessed them." 12 Balaam replied, "Is it not what the LORD puts in my mouth that I must repeat with care?"

The Second Oracle

13† Then Balak said to him, "Please come with me to another place from which you can see only some and not all of them, and from there curse them for me." 14 So he brought him to the lookout field on the top of Pisgah, where he built seven altars and offered a bullock and a ram on each of them. 15 Balaam then said to Balak, "Stand here by your holocaust, while I seek a meeting over there." 16 Then the LORD met Balaam, and having put an utterance in his mouth, he said to him, "Go back to Balak, and speak accordingly." 17 So he went back to Balak, who was still standing by his holocaust together with the princes of Moab. When Balak asked him, "What did the LORD say?" 18 Balaam gave voice to his oracle:

Be aroused, O Balak, and hearken;
    give ear to my testimony, O son of Zippor!
19   God is not man that he should speak falsely,
    nor human, that he should change
      his mind.
Is he one to speak and not act,
    to decree and not fulfill?

23, 7: *Aram:* the ancient name of the region later known as Syria. *The Eastern Mountains:* the low ranges in the Syrian desert near the Euphrates and Balaam's town of Pethor; cf Nm 22, 5.

23, 9: *A people that lives apart:* Israel, as the chosen people of God, occupied a unique place among the nations, from which they kept themselves aloof.

23, 10: *The dust of Jacob . . . Israel's wind-borne particles:* the Israelites will be as numerous as dust in a desert sandstorm. *May I . . .*

as many as theirs: a formula by which Balaam swears he is speaking the truth; he sees the reward of virtue in having numerous descendants.

23, 13: *To another place:* Balak thought that if Balaam would view Israel from a different site, he could forecast a different kind of omen.

23, 7: Nm 22, 6.

20   It is a blessing I have been given
            to pronounce;
        a blessing which I cannot restrain.
21† Misfortune is not observed in Jacob,
        nor misery seen in Israel.
     The LORD, his God, is with him;
        with him is the triumph of his King.
22*†It is God who brought him out of Egypt,
        a wild bull of towering might.
23   No, there is no sorcery against Jacob,
        nor omen against Israel.
     It shall yet be said of Jacob,
        and of Israel, "Behold what God
            has wrought!"
24* Here is a people that springs up
            like a lioness,
        and stalks forth like a lion;
     It rests not till it has devoured its prey
        and has drunk the blood of the slain.

25 "Even though you cannot curse them," said
Balak to Balaam, "at least do not bless them." 26 But
Balaam answered Balak, "Did I not warn you that I
must do all that the LORD tells me?"

The Third Oracle

27 Then Balak said to Balaam, "Come, let me
bring you to another place; perhaps God will approve of your cursing them for me from there."
28 So he took Balaam to the top of Peor, that overlooks Jeshimon. 29 Balaam then said to him, "Here
build me seven altars; and here prepare for me sev-
en bullocks and seven rams." 30 And Balak did as
Balaam had ordered, offering a bullock and a ram
on each altar.

24 1 Balaam, however, perceiving that the
LORD was pleased to bless Israel, did not
go aside as before to seek omens, but turned his
gaze toward the desert. 2 When he raised his eyes
and saw Israel encamped, tribe by tribe, the spirit of
God came upon him, 3 and he gave voice to his oracle:

     The utterance of Balaam, son of Beor,
        the utterance of the man whose eye is true,
4   The utterance of one who hears what
            God says,
        and knows what the Most High knows,

Of one who sees what the Almighty sees,
        enraptured, and with eyes unveiled:
5   How goodly are your tents, O Jacob;
        your encampments, O Israel!
6   They are like gardens beside a stream,
        like the cedars planted by the LORD.
7   His wells shall yield free-flowing waters,
        he shall have the sea within reach;
     His king shall rise higher than. . . .
        and his royalty shall be exalted.
8*   It is God who brought him out of Egypt,
        a wild bull of towering might.
     He shall devour the nations like grass,
        their bones he shall strip bare.
9*   He lies crouching like a lion,
        or like a lioness; who shall arouse him?
     Blessed is he who blesses you,
        and cursed is he who curses you!

10*† Balak beat his palms together in a blaze of
anger at Balaam and said to him, "It was to curse
my foes that I summoned you here; yet three times
now you have even blessed them instead! 11 Be off
at once, then, to your home. I promised to reward
you richly, but the LORD has withheld the reward
from you!" 12 Balaam replied to Balak, "Did I not
warn the very messengers whom you sent to me,
13* 'Even if Balak gave me his house full of silver
and gold, I could not of my own accord do anything, good or evil, contrary to the command of the
LORD'? Whatever the LORD says I must repeat.

The Fourth Oracle

14 "But now that I am about to go to my own
people, let me first warn you what this people will
do to your people in the days to come." 15 Then Balaam gave voice to his oracle:

     The utterance of Balaam, son of Beor,
        the utterance of the man whose eye is true,
16   The utterance of one who hears what
            God says,
        and knows what the Most High knows,
     Of one who sees what the Almighty sees,
        enraptured and with eyes unveiled.
17*† I see him, though not now;
        I behold him, though not near:
     A star shall advance from Jacob,
        and a staff shall rise from Israel,

N
M

---

† **23, 21:** *Misfortune . . . misery:* Balaam admits that he is unable to
predict any evils for Israel.
    23, 22: *A wild bull of towering might:* the reference is to Israel,
rather than to God.
    24, 10: *Balak beat his palms:* a sign of disclaiming any responsi-
bility for paying the promised reward.
    24, 17: *A star . . . a staff:* many of the Fathers have understood
this as a Messianic prophecy, although it is not referred to anywhere
in the New Testament; in this sense the star is Christ himself, just as

he is the staff from Israel; cf Is 11, 1. But it is doubtful whether this
passage is to be connected with the "star of the Magi" in Mt 2, 1–12.
The Shuthites: mentioned in other documents of this period as nomads on the border of Palestine.

*
23, 22: Nm 24, 8.   27, 29; 49, 9.
23, 24: Nm 24, 9; Gn 49, 9.   **24, 10:** Nm 23, 11.
24, 8: Nm 23, 22.   **24, 13:** Nm 22, 18.
24, 9: Nm 23, 24; Gn 12, 3;   **24, 17:** 2 Sm 8, 2.

That shall smite the brows of Moab,
and the skulls of all the Shuthites,

18 Till Edom is dispossessed,
and no fugitive is left in Seir.
Israel shall do valiantly,

19 and Jacob shall overcome his foes.

20 *†Upon seeing Amalek, Balaam gave voice to his oracle:

First of the peoples was Amalek,
but his end is to perish forever.

21† Upon seeing the Kenites, he gave voice to his oracle:

Your abode is enduring, O smith,
and your nest is set on a cliff;

22 Yet destined for burning—
even as I watch—are your inhabitants.

23† Upon seeing . . . he gave voice to his oracle:

Alas, who shall survive of Ishmael,

24 to deliver his people from the hands of the Kittim?
When they have conquered Asshur and conquered Eber,
He too shall perish forever.

25 Then Balaam set out on his journey home; and Balak also went his way.

Worship of Baal of Peor

25 1 *†While Israel was living at Shittim, the people degraded themselves by having illicit relations with the Moabite women. 2* These then invited the people to the sacrifices of their god, and the people ate of the sacrifices and worshiped their god. 3* When Israel thus submitted to the rites of Baal of Peor, the LORD's anger flared up against Israel, 4*† and he said to Moses, "Gather all the leaders of the people, and hold a public execution of the guilty ones before the LORD, that his blazing wrath may be turned away from Israel." 5 So Moses told the Israelite judges, "Each of you shall kill those of his men who have submitted to the rites of Baal of Peor."

Zeal of Phinehas

6† Yet a certain Israelite came and brought in a Midianite woman to his clansmen in the view of Moses and of the whole Israelite community, while they were weeping at the entrance of the meeting tent. 7* When Phinehas, son of Eleazar, son of Aaron the priest, saw this, he left the assembly, and taking a lance in hand, 8 followed the Israelite into his retreat where he pierced the pair of them, the Israelite and the woman. Thus the slaughter of Israelites was checked; 9 but only after twenty-four thousand had died.

10 Then the LORD said to Moses, 11† "Phinehas, son of Eleazar, son of Aaron the priest, has turned my anger from the Israelites by his zeal for my honor among them; that is why I did not put an end to the Israelites for the offense to my honor. 12* Announce, therefore, that I hereby give him my pledge of friendship, 13 which shall be for him and for his descendants after him the pledge of an everlasting priesthood, because he was zealous on behalf of his God and thus made amends for the Israelites."

14† The Israelite slain with the Midianite woman was Zimri, son of Salu, prince of an ancestral house of the Simeonites. 15 The slain Midianite woman was Cozbi, daughter of Zur, who was head of a clan, an ancestral house, in Midian.

Vengeance on the Midianites

16† The LORD then said to Moses, 17* "Treat the Midianites as enemies and crush them, 18 for they have been your enemies by their wily dealings with you as regards Peor and as regards their kinswoman Cozbi, the daughter of the Midianite prince, who was killed at the time of the slaughter because of Peor."

---

† **24, 20:** *First:* literally "the beginning." Amalek was an aboriginal people in Palestine and therefore considered as of great antiquity. There is a deliberate contrast here between the words first and end.

24, 21: The Kenites lived in high strongholds in the mountains of southern Palestine and the Sinai Peninsula, and were skilled in working the various metals found in their territory. Their name is connected, at least by popular etymology, with the Hebrew word for "smith"; of similar sound is the Hebrew word for "nest"—hence the play on words in the present passage.

24, 23f: The translation of this short oracle is based on a reconstructed text and is rather uncertain. *Ishmael:* the survival of Ishmael is indicated in Gn 17, 20; 21, 13.18.

25, 1: *Shittim:* the full name was Abel-shittim, a locality at the foot of the mountains in the northeastern corner of the plains of Moab (Nm 33, 49). *Illicit relations:* perhaps as part of the licentious worship of Baal of Peor.

25, 4: *Hold a public execution:* the same phrase occurs in 2 Sm 21, 6–14, where the context shows that at least a part of the penalty consisted in being denied honorable burial. In both passages, dis-

memberment as a punishment for the breaking of covenant pledges is a current understanding of the phrase.

25, 6: *Midianite woman:* at this time the Midianites were leagued with the Moabites in opposing Israel; cf Nm 22, 4.7. Balaam had induced both the Midianites (Nm 31, 16) and the Moabites (Rv 2, 14) to lure the Israelites to the obscene rites of Baal of Peor. *They were weeping:* on account of the plague that had struck them; cf v 8.

25, 11: *For my honor:* by taking vengeance on those who had made Baal of Peor a rival of the Lord.

25, 14f: The nobility of the slain couple is mentioned in order to stress the courage of Phinehas in punishing them. The zeal of Phinehas became proverbial; cf Ps 106, 30; Sir 45, 23; 1 Mc 2, 26.54.

25, 16ff: The account of the execution of this command is given in Nm 31, 1–18.

24, 20: Ex 17, 14; 1 Sm 15, 3.
25, 1: Nm 31, 16.
25, 2: Ex 34, 15f.
25, 3: Ps 106, 28; Hos 9, 10.
25, 4: Dt 4, 3.

25, 7: Ps 106, 30.
25, 12f: Sir 45, 23f; Ps 106, 31;
1 Mc 2, 26.54.
25, 17f: Nm 31, 2–12.

The Second Census

26 [19]† After the slaughter [1] the LORD said to Moses and Eleazar, son of Aaron the priest, [2]* "Take a census, by ancestral houses, throughout the community of the Israelites of all those of twenty years or more who are fit for military service in Israel." [3] So on the plains of Moab along the Jericho stretch of the Jordan, Moses and the priest Eleazar registered [4] those of twenty years or more, as the LORD had commanded Moses.

The Israelites who came out of the land of Egypt were as follows:

[5]* Of Reuben, the first-born of Israel, the Reubenites by clans were: through Hanoch the clan of the Hanochites, through Pallu the clan of the Palluites, [6] through Hezron the clan of the Hezronites, through Carmi the clan of the Carmites. [7] These were the clans of the Reubenites, of whom forty-three thousand seven hundred and thirty men were registered.

[8] From Pallu descended Eliab, [9]* and the descendants of Eliab were Dathan and Abiram—the same Dathan and Abiram, councilors of the community, who revolted against Moses and Aaron [like Korah's band when it rebelled against the LORD]. [10] The earth opened its mouth and swallowed them as a warning [Korah too and the band that died when the fire consumed two hundred and fifty men. [11] The descendants of Korah, however, did not die out].

[12]† The Simeonites by clans were: through Nemuel the clan of the Nemuelites, through Jamin the clan of the Jaminites, through Jachin the clan of the Jachinites, [13] through Sohar the clan of the Soharites, through Shaul the clan of the Shaulites. [14] These were the clans of the Simeonites, of whom twenty-two thousand two hundred men were registered.

[15] The Gadites by clans were: through Zephon the clan of the Zephonites, through Haggi the clan of the Haggites, through Shuni the clan of the Shunites, [16] through Ozni the clan of the Oznites, through Eri the clan of the Erites, [17] through Arod the clan of the Arodites, through Areli the clan of the Arelites. [18] These were the clans of the Gadites, of whom forty thousand five hundred men were registered.

[19]* The sons of Judah who died in the land of Canaan were Er and Onan. [20] The Judahites by clans were: through Shelah the clan of the Shelahites, through Perez the clan of the Perezites, through Zerah the clan of the Zerahites. [21] The Perezites were: through Hezron the clan of the Hezronites, through Hamul the clan of the Hamulites. [22] These were the clans of Judah, of whom seventy-six thousand five hundred men were registered.

[23] The Issacharites by clans were: through Tola the clan of the Tolaites, through Puvah the clan of the Puvahites, [24] through Jashub the clan of the Jashubites, through Shimron the clan of the Shimronites. [25] These were the clans of Issachar, of whom sixty-four thousand three hundred men were registered.

[26] The Zebulunites by clans were: through Sered the clan of the Seredites, through Elon the clan of the Elonites, through Jahleel the clan of the Jahleelites. [27] These were the clans of the Zebulunites, of whom sixty thousand five hundred men were registered.

[28] The sons of Joseph were Manasseh, and Ephraim. [29] The Manassehites by clans were: through Machir the clan of the Machirites, through Gilead, a descendant of Machir, the clan of the Gileadites. [30] The Gileadites were: through Abiezer the clan of the Abiezrites, through Helek the clan of the Helekites, [31] through Asriel the clan of the Asrielites, through Shechem the clan of the Shechemites, [32] through Shemida the clan of the Shemidaites, through Hepher the clan of the Hepherites. [33]* Zelophehad, son of Hepher, had no sons, but only daughters, whose names were Mahlah, Noah, Hoglah, Milcah and Tirzah. [34] These were the clans of Manasseh, of whom fifty-two thousand seven hundred men were registered.

[35] The Ephraimites by clans were: through Shuthelah the clan of the Shuthelahites, through Becher the clan of the Bechrites, through Tahan the clan of the Tahanites. [36] The Shuthelahites were: through Eran the clan of the Eranites. [37] These were the clans of the Ephraimites, of whom thirty-two thousand five hundred men were registered.

These were the descendants of Joseph by clans.

[38] The Benjaminites by clans were: through Bela the clan of the Belaites, through Ashbel the clan of the Ashbelites, through Ahiram the clan of the Ahiramites, [39] through Shupham the clan of the Shuphamites, through Hupham the clan of the Huphamites. [40] The descendants of Bela were Arad and Naaman: through Arad the clan of the Aradites, through Naaman the clan of the Naamanites. [41] These were the Benjaminites by clans, of whom forty-five thousand six hundred men were registered.

---

† **26, 19:** This is the last verse of Ch 25.
26, 12: *Nemuel:* so also in Gn 46, 10; 1 Chr 4, 24. In Ex 6, 15, the same man is called "Jemuel"; it is uncertain which form is correct.

* **26, 2:** Nm 1, 2f.   1 Chr 2, 3.
26, 5f: 1 Chr 5, 3.   **26, 33:** Nm 27, 1; 36, 11;
26, 9f: Nm 16, 1.32.   Jos 17, 3.
26, 19: Gn 38, 7.10; 46, 12;

42 The Danites by clans were: through Shuham the clan of the Shuhamites. These were the clans of Dan, 43 of whom sixty-four thousand four hundred men were registered.

44 The Asherites by clans were: through Imnah the clan of the Imnites, through Ishvi the clan of the Ishvites, through Beriah the clan of the Beriites, 45 through Heber the clan of the Heberites, through Malchiel the clan of the Malchielites. 46 The name of Asher's daughter was Serah. 47 These were the clans of Asher, of whom fifty-three thousand four hundred men were registered.

48 The Naphtalites by clans were: through Jahzeel the clan of the Jahzeelites, through Guni the clan of the Gunites, 49 through Jezer the clan of the Jezerites, through Shillem the clan of the Shillemites. 50 These were the clans of Naphtali, of whom forty-five thousand four hundred men were registered.

51 These six hundred and one thousand seven hundred and thirty were the Israelites who were registered.

Allotment of the Land

52† The LORD said to Moses, 53* "Among these groups the land shall be divided as their heritage in keeping with the number of individuals in each group. 54* To a large group you shall assign a large heritage, to a small group a small heritage, each group receiving its heritage in proportion to the number of men registered in it. 55 But the land shall be divided by lot, as the heritage of the various ancestral tribes. 56 As the lot falls shall each group, large or small, be assigned its heritage."

Census of the Levites

57 The Levites registered by clans were: through Gershon the clan of the Gershonites, through Kohath the clan of the Kohathites, through Merari the clan of the Merarites. 58 These also were clans of Levi: the clan of the Libnites, the clan of the Hebronites, the clan of the Mahlites, the clan of the Mushites, the clan of the Korahites.

Among the descendants of Kohath was Amram, 59 whose wife was named Jochebed. She also was of the tribe of Levi, born to the tribe in Egypt. To Amram she bore Aaron and Moses and their sister Miriam. 60 To Aaron were born Nadab and Abihu,

Eleazar and Ithamar. 61 But Nadab and Abihu died when they offered profane fire before the LORD.

62* The total number of male Levites one month or more of age, who were registered, was twenty-three thousand. They were not registered with the other Israelites, however, for no heritage was given them among the Israelites.

63 These, then, were the men registered by Moses and the priest Eleazar in the census of the Israelites taken on the plains of Moab along the Jericho stretch of the Jordan. 64 Among them there was not a man of those who had been registered by Moses and the priest Aaron in the census of the Israelites taken in the desert of Sinai. 65* For the LORD had told them that they would surely die in the desert, and not one of them was left except Caleb, son of Jephunneh, and Joshua, son of Nun.

Zelophehad's Daughters

27 1* Zelophehad, son of Hepher, son of Gilead, son of Machir, son of Manasseh, son of Joseph, had daughters named Mahlah, Noah, Hoglah, Milcah and Tirzah. They came forward, 2 and standing in the presence of Moses, the priest Eleazar, the princes, and the whole community at the entrance of the meeting tent, said: 3† "Our father died in the desert. Although he did not join those who banded together against the LORD [in Korah's band], he died for his own sin without leaving any sons. 4 But why should our father's name be withdrawn from his clan merely because he had no son? Let us, therefore, have property among our father's kinsmen."

Laws Concerning Heiresses

5† When Moses laid their case before the LORD, 6 the LORD said to him, 7 "The plea of Zelophehad's daughters is just; you shall give them hereditary property among their father's kinsmen, letting their father's heritage pass on to them. 8 Therefore, tell the Israelites: If a man dies without leaving a son, you shall let his heritage pass on to his daughter; 9 if he has no daughter, you shall give his heritage to his brothers; 10 if he has no brothers, you shall give his heritage to his father's brothers; 11* if his father had no brothers, you shall give his heritage to his nearest relative in his

---

26, 52–56: The division of Canaan among the various tribes and clans and families was determined partly by the size of each group and partly by lot. Perhaps the lots determined the respective locality of each tribal land and the section reserved for each clan, while the relative size of the allotted locality and section depended on the numerical strength of each group. The Hebrews considered the outcome of the drawing of lots as an expression of God's will; cf Acts 1, 23–26.

27, 3: *He did not join . . . against the LORD:* had he done so, he and his heirs could have rightly been deprived of the privilege of receiving a portion in the Promised Land.

27, 5–11: The purpose of this law, as also that of the related laws in Nm 36, 2–10 (heiresses to marry within the same tribe), Dt 25, 5–10 (levirate marriage), and Lv 25, 10 (return of property in the jubilee year), was to keep the landed property within the proper domain of each tribe.

26, 53: Jos 11, 23.   26, 65: Nm 14, 22ff.29.
26, 54: Nm 33, 54; 35, 8.   27, 1: Nm 26, 33; Jos 17, 3.
26, 62: Nm 3, 39.   27, 11: Jer 32, 6–9.

clan, who shall then take possession of it." This is the legal norm for the Israelites, as the LORD commanded Moses.

Joshua To Succeed Moses

¹²*† The LORD said to Moses, "Go up here into the Abarim Mountains and view the land that I am giving to the Israelites. ¹³* When you have viewed it, you too shall be taken to your people, as was your brother Aaron, ¹⁴* because in the rebellion of the community in the desert of Zin you both rebelled against my order to manifest my sanctity to them by means of the water." [This is the water of Meribah of Kadesh in the desert of Zin.]

¹⁵ Then Moses said to the LORD, ¹⁶† "May the LORD, the God of the spirits of all mankind, set over the community a man ¹⁷ who shall act as their leader in all things, to guide them in all their actions; that the LORD'S community may not be like sheep without a shepherd." ¹⁸*† And the LORD replied to Moses, "Take Joshua, son of Nun, a man of spirit, and lay your hand upon him. ¹⁹ Have him stand in the presence of the priest Eleazar and of the whole community, and commission him before their eyes. ²⁰ Invest him with some of your own dignity, that the whole Israelite community may obey him. ²¹† He shall present himself to the priest Eleazar, to have him seek out for him the decisions of the Urim in the LORD'S presence; and as he directs, Joshua, all the Israelites with him, and the community as a whole shall perform all their actions."

²² Moses did as the LORD had commanded him. Taking Joshua and having him stand in the presence of the priest Eleazar and of the whole community, ²³ he laid his hands on him and gave him his commission, as the LORD had directed through Moses.

General Sacrifices

28 ¹ The LORD said to Moses, ² "Give the Israelites this commandment: At the times I have appointed, you shall be careful to present to me the food offerings that are offered to me as sweet-smelling oblations.

Each Morning and Evening

³*† "You shall tell them therefore: This is the oblation which you shall offer to the LORD: two unblemished yearling lambs each day as the established holocaust, ⁴ offering one lamb in the morning and the other during the evening twilight, ⁵† each with a cereal offering of one tenth of an ephah of fine flour mixed with a fourth of a hin of oil of crushed olives. ⁶ This is the established holocaust that was offered at Mount Sinai as a sweet-smelling oblation to the LORD. ⁷† And as the libation for the first lamb, you shall pour out to the LORD in the sanctuary a fourth of a hin of wine. ⁸ The other lamb, to be offered during the evening twilight, you shall offer with the same cereal offering and the same libation as in the morning, as a sweet-smelling oblation to the LORD.

On the Sabbath

⁹ "On the sabbath day you shall offer two unblemished yearling lambs, with their cereal offering, two tenths of an ephah of fine flour mixed with oil, and with their libations. ¹⁰ Each sabbath there shall be the sabbath holocaust in addition to the established holocaust and its libation.

At the New Moon Feast

¹¹† "On the first of each month you shall offer as a holocaust to the LORD two bullocks, one ram, and seven unblemished yearling lambs, ¹² with three tenths of an ephah of fine flour mixed with oil as the cereal offering for each bullock, two tenths of an ephah of fine flour mixed with oil as the cereal offering for the ram, ¹³ and one tenth of an ephah of fine flour mixed with oil as the cereal offering for each lamb, that the holocaust may be a sweet-smelling oblation to the LORD. ¹⁴ Their libations shall be half a hin of wine for each bullock, a third of a hin for the ram, and a fourth of a hin for each lamb. This is the new moon holocaust for every new moon of the year. ¹⁵ Moreover, one goat shall be sacrificed as a sin offering to the LORD. These are to be offered in addition to the established holocaust and its libation.

---

† **27, 12:** *The Abarim Mountains:* the range on the eastern side of the Dead Sea.

27, 16: *The God of the spirits of all mankind:* the sense is either that God knows the character and abilities of all men and therefore knows best whom to appoint (cf Acts 1, 24), or, more probably, that God is Master of life and death and therefore can call Moses from this world whenever he wishes; cf the same phrase in Nm 16, 22, where "spirit" evidently means "the life principle."

27, 18: *A man of spirit:* literally, "a man in whom there is spirit": one who has the qualities of a good leader—courage, prudence, and strength of will. Cf Gn 41, 38; Dt 34, 9.

27, 21: *The Urim:* certain sacred objects which the Hebrew priests employed to ascertain the divine will, probably by obtaining a positive or negative answer to a given question. The full expression was "the Urim and Thummim"; cf Ex 28, 30; Lv 8, 8; Dt 33, 8; Ezr

2, 63; Neh 7, 65. Joshua was ordinarily not to receive direct revelations from God as Moses had received them.

28, 3: *The established holocaust:* "the tamid holocaust," the technical term for the daily sacrifice.

28, 5: *Oil of crushed olives:* this oil, made in a mortar, was purer and more expensive than oil extracted in the olive press.

28, 7: *In the sanctuary:* according to Sir 50, 15, it was at the base of the altar.

28, 11: *On the first of each month:* literally, "at the new moons"; beginning on the evening when the crescent of the new moon first appeared.

27, 12: Dt 3, 27; 32, 49; 34, 1.   27, 18: Dt 34, 9.
27, 13f: Nm 20, 12.24.   28, 3–8: Ex 29, 38–42.
27, 14: Dt 32, 51.

At the Passover

16*† "On the fourteenth day of the first month falls the Passover of the LORD, 17 and the fifteenth day of this month is the pilgrimage feast. For seven days unleavened bread is to be eaten. 18* On the first of these days you shall hold a sacred assembly, and do no sort of work. 19 As an oblation you shall offer a holocaust to the LORD, which shall consist of two bullocks, one ram, and seven yearling lambs that you are sure are unblemished, 20 with their cereal offerings of fine flour mixed with oil, offering three tenths of an ephah for each bullock, two tenths for the ram, 21 and one tenth for each of the seven lambs; 22 and offer one goat as a sin offering in atonement for yourselves. 23 These offerings you shall make in addition to the established morning holocaust: 24 you shall make exactly the same offerings each day for seven days as food offerings, in addition to the established holocaust with its libation, for a sweet-smelling oblation to the LORD. 25* On the seventh day you shall hold a sacred assembly, and do no sort of work.

At Pentecost

26*† "On the day of first fruits, on your feast of Weeks, when you present to the LORD the new cereal offering, you shall hold a sacred assembly, and do no sort of work. 27 You shall offer as a sweet-smelling holocaust to the LORD two bullocks, one ram, and seven yearling lambs that you are sure are unblemished, 28 with their cereal offerings of fine flour mixed with oil; offering three tenths of an ephah for each bullock, two tenths for the ram, 29 and one tenth for each of the seven lambs. 30 Moreover, one goat shall be offered as a sin offering in atonement for yourselves. 31 You shall make these offerings, together with their libations, in addition to the established holocaust with its cereal offering.

On New Year's Day

29 1*† "On the first day of the seventh month you shall hold a sacred assembly, and do no sort of work; it shall be a day on which you sound the trumpet. 2 You shall offer as a sweet-smelling holocaust to the LORD one bullock, one ram, and seven unblemished yearling lambs, 3 with

did you KNOW?

Other Jewish Feasts

In chapter 29 of Numbers, we find the instructions for two more Jewish festivals. (For other Jewish festivals, see Ex 34, 18–26.) The *feast of Trumpets* is a fall celebration prescribed for "the first day of the seventh month" (Nm 29, 1). This day of rest, marked by trumpet blasts and sacrifices, came to be called Rosh Hashanah (head of the year), the beginning of the Jewish New Year.

On the tenth day of the seventh month, the Israelites celebrated the Day of Atonement (Yom Kippur). On this solemn day of penance and fasting, the high priest laid the sins of the people on a so-called scapegoat (see Lv 16, 20–21), then ran the beast into the wilderness, thus symbolically purifying the nation.

▶ Nm 29, 1–11

their cereal offerings of fine flour mixed with oil; offering three tenths of an ephah for the bullock, two tenths for the ram, 4 and one tenth for each of the seven lambs. 5 Moreover, one goat shall be offered as a sin offering in atonement for yourselves. 6 These are to be offered in addition to the ordinary new moon holocaust with its cereal offering, and in addition to the established holocaust with its cereal offering, together with the libations prescribed for them, as a sweet-smelling oblation to the LORD.

On the Day of Atonement

7*† "On the tenth day of this seventh month you shall hold a sacred assembly, and mortify yourselves, and do no sort of work. 8 You shall offer as a sweet-smelling holocaust to the LORD one bullock, one ram, and seven yearling lambs that you are sure are unblemished, 9 with their cereal offerings of

---

† **28, 16:** *On the fourteenth day:* toward evening at the end of this day; cf Ex 12, 6.18.

28, 26: *The day of first fruits:* a unique term for this feast, which is usually called "the feast of Weeks"; it was celebrated as a thanksgiving for the wheat harvest seven weeks after the barley harvest (Passover). In the time of Christ it was commonly known by the Greek word "Pentecost," that is, "fiftieth" (day after the Passover); see note on Lv 23, 16.

29, 1: *The first day of the seventh month:* (about September-October) is now the Jewish New Year's Day. In the older calendar the year began with the first of Nisan (March-April); cf Ex 12, 2.

29, 7: *The tenth day of this seventh month:* the Day of Atonement. *Mortify yourselves:* literally, "afflict your souls," that is, with fasting.

28, 16: Ex 12, 18; Lv 23, 5; Dt 16, 1.	Lv 23, 8.
28, 18: Ex 12, 16; Lv 23, 7.	**28, 26:** Ex 34, 22.
28, 25: Ex 12, 16; 13, 6;	**29, 1:** Nm 10; Lv 23, 24.
	29, 7: Lv 16, 29; 23, 27f.32.

fine flour mixed with oil; offering three tenths of an ephah for the bullock, two tenths for the ram, [10] and one tenth for each of the seven lambs. [11]† Moreover, one goat shall be sacrificed as a sin offering. These are to be offered in addition to the atonement sin offering, the established holocaust with its cereal offering, and their libations.

On the Feast of Booths

[12]*† "On the fifteenth day of the seventh month you shall hold a sacred assembly, and do no sort of work; then, for seven days following, you shall celebrate a pilgrimage feast to the LORD. [13]† You shall offer as a sweet-smelling holocaust to the LORD thirteen bullocks, two rams, and fourteen yearling lambs that are unblemished, [14] with their cereal offerings of fine flour mixed with oil; offering three tenths of an ephah for each of the thirteen bullocks, two tenths for each of the two rams, [15] and one tenth for each of the fourteen lambs. [16] Moreover, one goat shall be sacrificed as a sin offering. These are to be offered in addition to the established holocaust with its cereal offering and libation.

[17] "On the second day you shall offer twelve bullocks, two rams, and fourteen unblemished yearling lambs, [18] with their cereal offerings and libations as prescribed for the bullocks, rams and lambs in proportion to their number, [19] as well as one goat for a sin offering, besides the established holocaust with its cereal offering and libation.

[20] "On the third day you shall offer eleven bullocks, two rams, and fourteen unblemished yearling lambs, [21] with their cereal offerings and libations as prescribed for the bullocks, rams and lambs in proportion to their number, [22] as well as one goat for a sin offering, besides the established holocaust with its cereal offering and libation.

[23] "On the fourth day you shall offer ten bullocks, two rams, and fourteen unblemished yearling lambs, [24] with their cereal offerings and libations as prescribed for the bullocks, rams and lambs in proportion to their number, [25] as well as one goat for a sin offering, besides the established holocaust with its cereal offering and libation.

[26] "On the fifth day you shall offer nine bullocks, two rams, and fourteen unblemished yearling lambs, [27]* with their cereal offerings and libations as prescribed for the bullocks, rams and lambs in

proportion to their number, [28] as well as one goat for a sin offering, besides the established holocaust with its cereal offering and libation.

[29] "On the sixth day you shall offer eight bullocks, two rams, and fourteen unblemished yearling lambs, [30] with their cereal offerings and libations as prescribed for the bullocks, rams and lambs in proportion to their number, [31] as well as one goat for a sin offering, besides the established holocaust with its cereal offering and libation.

[32] "On the seventh day you shall offer seven bullocks, two rams, and fourteen unblemished yearling lambs, [33] with their cereal offerings and libations as prescribed for the bullocks, rams and lambs in proportion to their number, [34] as well as one goat for a sin offering, besides the established holocaust with its cereal offering and libation.

[35]*† "On the eighth day you shall hold a solemn meeting, and do no sort of work. [36] You shall offer up in holocaust as a sweet-smelling oblation to the LORD one bullock, one ram, and seven unblemished yearling lambs, [37] with their cereal offerings and libations as prescribed for the bullocks, rams and lambs in proportion to their number, [38] as well as one goat for a sin offering, besides the established holocaust with its cereal offering and libation.

[39] "These are the offerings you shall make to the LORD on your festivals, besides whatever holocausts, cereal offerings, libations, and peace offerings you present as your votive or free-will offerings."

30 [1] Moses then gave the Israelites these instructions, just as the LORD had ordered him.

Validity and Annulment of Vows

[2] Moses said to the heads of the Israelite tribes, "This is what the LORD has commanded: [3]*† When a man makes a vow to the LORD or binds himself under oath to a pledge of abstinence, he shall not violate his word, but must fulfill exactly the promise he has uttered.

[4] "When a woman, while still a maiden in her father's house, makes a vow to the LORD, or binds herself to a pledge, [5] if her father learns of her vow or the pledge to which she bound herself and says nothing to her about it, then any vow or any pledge

---

† **29, 11:** *The atonement sin offering:* the bullock prescribed in Lv 16, 11f.

29, 12: This feast of Booths celebrating the vintage harvest was the most popular of all and therefore had the most elaborate ritual. See note on Lv 23, 34.

29, 13: *Thirteen bullocks:* the number of bullocks sacrificed before the octave day was seventy, arranged on a descending scale so that the number on the seventh day was the sacred number seven.

29, 35: *A solemn meeting:* the Hebrew word is the technical term for the closing celebration of the three major feasts of the Passover,

Pentecost and Booths, or of other special feasts that lasted for a week. Cf Lv 23, 36; Dt 16, 8; 2 Chr 7, 9; Neh 8, 18.

30, 3: *A vow . . . a pledge:* here the former signifies the doing of some positive good deed, in particular the offering of some sacrifice; the latter signifies the abstaining from some otherwise licit action or pleasure; cf v 14.

29, 12: Lv 23, 34f.   **29, 35:** Lv 23, 36; Jn 7, 37.
29, 27: Nm 29, 30.37.   **30, 3:** Dt 23, 22; Eccl 5, 3f.

did you KNOW?

Making a Vow

Vow.

Such a simple word, really. Three letters. One syllable. But its simplicity masks its meaning. If a word's length were directly related to its significance, vow would have to become a long word indeed. It is a heavy word, one that we use sparingly. We tend to associate it with marriage or the life commitment of priests and religious sisters and brothers. Vows can be public or private, solemn or simple.

From a faith perspective, a person making a vow is making a deep, binding promise before God. A vow cannot really be captured on paper. A vow must be lived out. It must be internalized. It is the foundation for a life choice. We know, deep in our heart, that God is part of our vows.

The Israelites also took vows seriously. Numbers, chapter 30, is devoted to laws about vows. The laws were sexist by our standards. For example, a father or a husband could veto a woman's vows. Such laws were deemed acceptable in the Israelites' patriarchal society, but they are not in ours.

▸ Nm 30, 2–6

she has made remains valid. 6 But if on the day he learns of it her father expresses to her his disapproval, then any vow or any pledge she has made becomes null and void; and the LORD releases her from it, since her father has expressed to her his disapproval.

7 "If she marries while under a vow or under a rash pledge to which she bound herself, 8 and her husband learns of it, yet says nothing to her that day about it, then the vow or pledge she had made remains valid. 9 But if on the day he learns of it her husband expresses to her his disapproval, he thereby annuls the vow she had made or the rash pledge

to which she had bound herself, and the LORD releases her from it. 10 The vow of a widow or of a divorced woman, or any pledge to which such a woman binds herself, is valid.

11† "If it is in her husband's house that she makes a vow or binds herself under oath to a pledge, 12 and her husband learns of it yet says nothing to express to her his disapproval, then any vow or any pledge she has made remains valid. 13 But if on the day he learns of them her husband annuls them, then whatever she has expressly promised in her vow or in her pledge becomes null and void; since her husband has annulled them, the LORD releases her from them.

14 "Any vow or any pledge that she makes under oath to mortify herself, her husband can either allow to remain valid or render null and void. 15 But if her husband, day after day, says nothing at all to her about them, he thereby allows as valid any vow or any pledge she has made; he has allowed them to remain valid, because on the day he learned of them he said nothing to her about them. 16† If, however, he countermands them some time after he first learned of them, he is responsible for her guilt."

17 These are the statutes which the LORD prescribed through Moses concerning the relationship between a husband and his wife, as well as between a father and his daughter while she is still a maiden in her father's house.

Extermination of the Midianites

31 1† The LORD said to Moses, 2 "Avenge the Israelites on the Midianites, and then you shall be taken to your people." 3 So Moses told the people, "Select men from your midst and arm them for war, to attack the Midianites and execute the LORD'S vengeance on them. 4 From each of the tribes of Israel you shall send a band of one thousand men to war." 5 From the clans of Israel, therefore, a thousand men of each tribe were levied, so that there were twelve thousand men armed for war. 6 Moses sent them out on the campaign, a thousand from each tribe, with Phinehas, son of Eleazar, the priest for the campaign, who had with him the sacred vessels and the trumpets for sounding the alarm. 7 They waged war against the Midianites, as the LORD had commanded Moses, and killed every male among them. 8† Besides those slain in battle, they killed the five Midianite kings: Evi, Rekem, Zur, Hur and Reba; and they also executed Balaam, son of Beor, with the sword. 9 But the Israelites kept

---

† **30, 11:** *In her husband's house:* after her marriage. This contrasts with the case given in vv 7ff.
30, 16: *He countermands them:* he prevents their fulfillment. Since he has first allowed the vows to remain valid, he can no longer annul them.

31, 1ff: The narrative of Israel's relations with Midian, which was interrupted after Nm 25, 18, is now resumed.
31, 8: *The five Midianite kings:* they are called "Midianite princes, Sihon's vassals" in Jos 13, 21.

the women of the Midianites with their little ones as captives, and all their herds and flocks and wealth as spoil, ¹⁰ while they set on fire all the towns where they had settled and all their encampments. ¹¹ Then they took all the booty, with the people and beasts they had captured, and brought the captives, together with the spoils and booty, ¹² to Moses and the priest Eleazar and to the Israelite community at their camp on the plains of Moab, along the Jericho stretch of the Jordan.

Treatment of the Captives

¹³ When Moses and the priest Eleazar, with all the princes of the community, went outside the camp to meet them, ¹⁴ Moses became angry with the officers of the army, the clan and company commanders, who were returning from combat. ¹⁵ "So you have spared all the women!" he exclaimed. ¹⁶* "Why, they are the very ones who on Balaam's advice prompted the unfaithfulness of the Israelites toward the LORD in the Peor affair, which began the slaughter of the LORD's community. ¹⁷† Slay, therefore, every male child and every woman who has had intercourse with a man. ¹⁸ But you may spare and keep for yourselves all girls who had no intercourse with a man.

Purification after Combat

¹⁹ "Moreover, you shall stay outside the camp for seven days, and those of you who have slain anyone or touched anyone slain in battle shall purify yourselves on the third and on the seventh day. This applies both to you and to your captives. ²⁰ You shall also purify every article of cloth, leather, goats' hair, or wood."

²¹ Eleazar the priest told the soldiers who had returned from combat: "This is what the law, as prescribed by the LORD to Moses, ordains: ²² Whatever can stand fire, such as gold, silver, bronze, iron, tin and lead, ²³† you shall put into the fire, that it may become clean; however, it must also be purified with lustral water. But whatever cannot stand fire you shall put into the water. ²⁴ On the seventh day you shall wash your clothes, and then you will again be clean. After that you may enter the camp."

Division of the Booty

²⁵ The LORD said to Moses: ²⁶ "With the help of the priest Eleazar and of the heads of the ancestral houses, count up all the human captives and the beasts that have been taken; ²⁷† then divide them evenly, giving half to those who took active part in the war by going out to combat, and half to the rest of the community. ²⁸ You shall levy a tax for the LORD on the warriors who went out to combat: one out of every five hundred persons, oxen, asses and sheep ²⁹ in their half of the spoil you shall turn over to the priest Eleazar as a contribution to the LORD. ³⁰ From the Israelites' half you shall take one out of every fifty persons, and the same from the different beasts, oxen, asses and sheep, and give them to the Levites, who have charge of the LORD's Dwelling." ³¹ So Moses and the priest Eleazar did this, as the LORD had commanded Moses.

Amount of Booty

³² This booty, what was left of the loot which the soldiers had taken, amounted to six hundred and seventy-five thousand sheep, ³³ seventy-two thousand oxen, ³⁴ sixty-one thousand asses, ³⁵ and thirty-two thousand girls who were still virgins.

³⁶ The half that fell to those who had gone out to combat was: three hundred and thirty-seven thousand five hundred sheep, ³⁷ of which six hundred and seventy-five fell as tax to the LORD; ³⁸ thirty-six thousand oxen, of which seventy-two fell as tax to the LORD; ³⁹ thirty thousand five hundred asses, of which sixty-one fell as tax to the LORD; ⁴⁰ and sixteen thousand persons, of whom thirty-two fell as tax to the LORD. ⁴¹ The taxes contributed to the LORD, Moses gave to the priest Eleazar, as the LORD had commanded him.

⁴² The half for the other Israelites, which fell to the community when Moses had taken it from the soldiers, was: ⁴³ three hundred and thirty-seven thousand five hundred sheep, ⁴⁴ thirty-six thousand oxen, ⁴⁵ thirty thousand five hundred asses, ⁴⁶ and sixteen thousand persons. ⁴⁷ From this, the Israelites' share, Moses, as the LORD had ordered, took one out of every fifty, both of persons and of beasts, and gave them to the Levites, who had charge of the LORD's Dwelling.

Gifts of the Officers

⁴⁸ Then the officers who had been clan and company commanders of the army came up to Moses ⁴⁹ and said to him, "Your servants have counted up the soldiers under our command, and not one is

---

31, 17: There are later references to Midian in Jgs 6–8; 1 Kgs 11, 18; Is 60, 6. The present raid was only against those Midianites who were dwelling at this time near the encampment of the Israelites.

31, 23: *Lustral water:* water mixed with the ashes of the red heifer as prescribed in Nm 19, 9.

31, 27: *Divide them evenly:* for a similar division of the booty into two equal parts, between those who engaged in the fray and

those who stayed with the baggage, cf 1 Sm 30, 24. But note that here the tax on the booty of the non-combatants is ten times as much as that on the soldier's booty.

31, 16: 2 Pt 2, 15; Rv 2, 14.

missing. [50]† So, to make atonement for ourselves before the LORD, each of us will bring as an offering to the LORD some gold article he has picked up, such as an anklet, a bracelet, a ring, an earring, or a necklace." [51] Moses and the priest Eleazar accepted this gold from them, all of it in well-wrought articles. [52] The gold that they gave as a contribution to the LORD amounted in all to sixteen thousand seven hundred and fifty shekels. This was from the clan and company commanders; [53] what the common soldiers had looted each one kept for himself. [54] Moses, then, and the priest Eleazar accepted the gold from the clan and company commanders, and put it in the meeting tent as a memorial for the Israelites before the LORD.

Request of Gad and Reuben

32 [1] † Now the Reubenites and Gadites had a very large number of livestock. Noticing that the land of Jazer and of Gilead was grazing country, [2] they came to Moses and the priest Eleazar and to the princes of the community and said, [3]† "The region of Ataroth, Dibon, Jazer, Nimrah, Heshbon, Elealeh, Sebam, Nebo and Baal-meon, [4] which the LORD has laid low before the community of Israel, is grazing country. Now, since your servants have livestock," [5] they continued, "if we find favor with you, let this land be given to your servants as their property. Do not make us cross the Jordan."

Moses' Rebuke

[6] But Moses answered the Gadites and Reubenites: "Are your kinsmen, then, to engage in war, while you remain here? [7] Why do you wish to discourage the Israelites from crossing to the land the LORD has given them? [8]* That is just what your fathers did when I sent them from Kadesh-barnea to reconnoiter the land. [9] They went up to the Wadi Eshcol and reconnoitered the land, then so discouraged the Israelites that they would not enter the land the LORD had given them. [10]* At that time the wrath of the LORD flared up, and he swore, [11] 'Because they have not followed me unreservedly, none of these men of twenty years or more who have come up from Egypt shall ever see this country I promised under oath to Abraham and Isaac

and Jacob, [12]*† except the Kenizzite Caleb, son of Jephunneh, and Joshua, son of Nun, who have followed the LORD unreservedly.' [13] So in his anger with the Israelites the LORD made them wander in the desert forty years, until the whole generation that had done evil in the sight of the LORD had died out. [14] And now here you are, a brood of sinners, rising up in your fathers' place to add still more to the LORD'S blazing wrath against the Israelites. [15] If you turn away from following him, he will make them stay still longer in the desert, and so you will bring about the ruin of this whole nation."

Counter Proposal

[16] But they were insistent with him: "We wish only to build sheepfolds here for our flocks, and towns for our families; [17]* but we ourselves will march as troops in the van of the Israelites, until we have led them to their destination. Meanwhile our families can remain here in the fortified towns, safe from attack by the natives. [18] We will not return to our homes until every one of the Israelites has taken possession of his heritage, [19]* and will not claim any heritage with them once we cross the Jordan, so long as we receive a heritage for ourselves on this eastern side of the Jordan."

Agreement Reached

[20]† Moses said to them in reply: "If you keep your word to march as troops in the LORD'S vanguard [21] and to cross the Jordan in full force before the LORD until he has driven his enemies out of his way [22]* and the land is subdued before him, then you may return here, quit of every obligation to the LORD and to Israel, and this region shall be your possession before the LORD. [23] But if you do not do this, you will sin against the LORD, and you can be sure that you will not escape the consequences of your sin. [24] Build the towns, then, for your families, and the folds for your flocks, but also fulfill your express promise."

[25] The Gadites and Reubenites answered Moses, "Your servants will do as you command, my lord. [26]* While our wives and children, our herds and other livestock remain in the towns of Gilead, [27] all your servants will go across as armed troops to battle before the LORD, just as your lordship says."

---

† **31, 50:** The precise nature and use of some of these articles of gold is not certain.

32, 1: *Gilead:* the name of the western part of the plateau east of the Jordan, sometimes signifying the whole region from the Yarmuk to the Jordan, sometimes only the northern part of this region, and sometimes, as here, only its southern part. Jazer lay to the east of southern Gilead.

32, 3: The places named in this verse, as well as the additional ones given in vv 34–38, were all in the former kingdom of Sihon, that is, in the region between the Jabbok and the Arnon. Cf Nm 21, 23f; Jos 13, 19–21.24–27.

32, 12: *Kenizzite:* a member of the clan of Kenaz, which, according to Gn 36, 11.15.42, was Edomitic; hence, although Caleb belonged to the tribe of Judah (Nm 13, 6; 34, 19), he must have had Edomite blood in his veins; cf also Jos 14, 6.14.

32, 20ff: Since the ark of the Lord was borne into battle with the Israelite army, the vanguard was said to march before the Lord.

32, 8f: Nm 13, 31ff; Dt 1, 22.
32, 10f: Dt 1, 34f.
32, 12: Nm 14, 24; Dt 1, 36.
32, 17: Jos 4, 12f.
32, 19: Jos 13, 8.
32, 22: Jos 1, 15.
32, 26: Jos 1, 14.

28 Moses, therefore, gave this order in their regard to the priest Eleazar, to Joshua, son of Nun, and to the heads of the ancestral tribes of the Israelites: 29 "If all the Gadites and Reubenites cross the Jordan with you as combat troops before the LORD, you shall give them Gilead as their property when the land has been subdued before you. 30 But if they will not go across with you as combat troops before the LORD, you shall bring their wives and children and livestock across before you into Canaan, and they shall have their property with you in the land of Canaan."

31 To this the Gadites and Reubenites replied, "We will do what the LORD has commanded us, your servants. 32 We ourselves will go across into the land of Canaan as troops before the LORD, but we will retain our hereditary property on this side of the Jordan." 33*† So Moses gave them [the Gadites and Reubenites, as well as half the tribe of Manasseh, son of Joseph, the kingdom of Sihon, king of the Amorites, and the kingdom of Og, king of Bashan,] the land with its towns and the districts that surrounded them.

34 The Gadites rebuilt the fortified towns of Dibon, Ataroth, Aroer, 35 Atroth-shophan, Jazer, Jogbehah, 36 Beth-nimrah and Beth-haran, and they built sheepfolds. 37 The Reubenites rebuilt Heshbon, Elealeh, Kiriathaim, 38† Nebo, Baal-meon [names to be changed!], and Sibmah. These towns, which they rebuilt, they called by their old names.

Other Conquests

39 The descendants of Machir, son of Manasseh, invaded Gilead and captured it, driving out the Amorites who were there. 40* [Moses gave Gilead to Machir, son of Manasseh, and he settled there.] 41* Jair, a Manassehite clan, campaigned against the tent villages, captured them and called them Havvoth-jair. 42 Nobah also campaigned against Kenath, captured it with its dependencies and called it Nobah after his own name.

Stages on the Journey

33 1 † The following are the stages by which the Israelites journeyed up by companies

from the land of Egypt under the guidance of Moses and Aaron. 2 By the LORD'S command Moses recorded the starting places of the various stages. The starting places of the successive stages were:

3† They set out from Rameses in the first month,
on the fifteenth day of the first month.
On the Passover morrow the Israelites
went forth
in triumph, in view of all Egypt,
4* While the Egyptians buried their first-born
all of whom the LORD had struck down;
on their gods, too, the LORD
executed judgments.

From Egypt to Sinai

5 Setting out from Rameses, the Israelites camped at Succoth. 6 Setting out from Succoth, they camped at Etham near the edge of the desert. 7* Setting out from Etham, they turned back to Pi-hahiroth, which is opposite Baal-zephon, and they camped opposite Migdol. 8* Setting out from Pi-hahiroth, they crossed over through the sea into the desert, and after a three days' journey in the desert of Etham, they camped at Marah. 9* Setting out from Marah, they came to Elim, where there were twelve springs of water and seventy palm trees, and they camped there. 10 Setting out from Elim, they camped beside the Red Sea. 11 Setting out from the Red Sea, they camped in the desert of Sin. 12 Setting out from the desert of Sin, they camped at Dophkah. 13 Setting out from Dophkah, they camped at Alush. 14* Setting out from Alush, they camped at Rephidim, where there was no water for the people to drink. 15* Setting out from Rephidim, they camped in the desert of Sinai.

From Sinai to Kadesh

16 Setting out from the desert of Sinai, they camped at Kibroth-hattaavah. 17* Setting out from Kibroth-hattaavah, they camped at Hazeroth. 18 Setting out from Hazeroth, they camped at Rithmah. 19 Setting out from Rithmah, they camped at Rimmon-perez. 20 Setting out from Rimmon-perez, they camped at Libnah. 21 Setting out

---

32, 33: The preceding is concerned solely with the two tribes of Gad and Reuben and with the land of the former kingdom of Sihon; hence it seems probable that the sudden reference here to the half-tribe of Manasseh and to their territory in Bashan, the former kingdom of Og, is a later addition to the text.

32, 38: The phrase in brackets is a gloss, warning the reader either to change the order of the preceding names, or, more probably, to read some other word, such as bosheth, "shame," for Baal. *They called by their old names:* literally, "they called by their names" (see Textual Notes); however, some understand the current Hebrew text to mean, "they called by new names."

33, 1ff: This list of camping sites was drawn up by Moses, as v 2 expressly states. However, in its present form it probably includes some glosses. Moreover, a comparison with the more detailed accounts of the journey as given elsewhere shows that this is not com-

plete. It records just forty camping sites, not counting the starting place, Rameses, and the terminus, the plains of Moab. This number, which corresponds exactly to the forty years of wandering in the desert, is probably a schematic device. Besides, it seems that in its present form the order of some of these names has been disturbed. Several names listed here are not recorded elsewhere.

33, 3f: These two verses were probably borrowed from some ancient song celebrating the exodus from Egypt.

32, 33: Dt 3, 12; 29, 7; Jos 12, 6; 13, 8.
32, 40: Dt 3, 15.
32, 41: Dt 3, 14.
33, 4f: Ex 12. 12.29.37.
33, 7: Ex 14, 2.
33, 8: Ex 15, 22.
33, 9: Ex 15, 27.
33, 14: Ex 17, 1.
33, 15: Ex 19, 2.
33, 17f: Nm 11, 34f.

from Libnah, they camped at Rissah. 22 Setting out from Rissah, they camped at Kehelathah. 23 Setting out from Kehelathah, they camped at Mount Shepher. 24 Setting out from Mount Shepher, they camped at Haradah. 25 Setting out from Haradah, they camped at Makheloth. 26 Setting out from Makheloth, they camped at Tahath. 27 Setting out from Tahath, they camped at Terah. 28 Setting out from Terah, they camped at Mithkah. 29 Setting out from Mithkah, they camped at Hashmonah. 30† Setting out from Hashmonah,—

From Mount Hor to Ezion-geber

They camped at Moseroth. 31 Setting out from Moseroth, they camped at Bene-jaakan. 32 Setting out from Bene-jaakan, they camped at Mount Gidgad. 33 Setting out from Mount Gidgad, they camped at Jotbathah. 34 Setting out from Jotbathah, they camped at Abronah. 35 Setting out from Abronah, they camped at Ezion-geber. 36* Setting out from Ezion-geber,—

From Kadesh to Mount Hor

They camped in the desert of Zin, at Kadesh. 37 Setting out from Kadesh, they camped at Mount Hor on the border of the land of Edom. 38* [Aaron the priest ascended Mount Hor at the LORD's command, and there he died in the fortieth year from the departure of the Israelites from the land of Egypt, on the first day of the fifth month. 39 Aaron was a hundred and twenty-three years old when he died on Mount Hor. 40† Now, when the Canaanite king of Arad, who lived in the Negeb in the land of Canaan, heard that the Israelites were coming. . . .] 41 Setting out from Mount Hor,—

From Ezion-geber to the Plains of Moab

† They camped at Zalmonah. 42 Setting out from Zalmonah, they camped at Punon. 43 Setting out from Punon, they camped at Oboth. 44 Setting out from Oboth, they camped at Iye-abarim on the border of Moab. 45 Setting out from Iye-abarim, they camped at Dibon-gad. 46 Setting out from Dibon-gad, they camped at Almon-diblathaim. 47 Setting out from Almon-diblathaim, they camped in the Abarim Mountains opposite Nebo. 48 Setting out from the Abarim Mountains, they camped on the plains of Moab along the Jericho stretch of the Jordan. 49 Their camp along the Jordan on the plains

of Moab extended from Beth-jeshimoth to Abel-shittim.

Conquest and Division of Canaan

50 The LORD spoke to Moses on the plains of Moab beside the Jericho stretch of the Jordan and said to him: 51 "Tell the Israelites: When you go across the Jordan into the land of Canaan, 52* drive out all the inhabitants of the land before you; destroy all their stone figures and molten images, and demolish all their high places.

53 "You shall take possession of the land and settle in it, for I have given you the land as your property. 54* You shall apportion the land among yourselves by lot, clan by clan, assigning a large heritage to a large group and a small heritage to a small group. Wherever anyone's lot falls, there shall his property be within the heritage of his ancestral tribe.

55* "But if you do not drive out the inhabitants of the land before you, those whom you allow to remain will become as barbs in your eyes and thorns in your sides, and they will harass you in the country where you live, 56 and I will treat you as I had intended to treat them."

The Boundaries

34 1 The LORD said to Moses, 2 "Give the Israelites this order: When you enter the land of Canaan, this is the territory that shall fall to you as your heritage—the land of Canaan with its boundaries:

3* "Your southern boundary shall be at the desert of Zin along the border of Edom; on the east it shall begin at the end of the Salt Sea, 4* and turning south of the Akrabbim Pass, it shall cross Zin, and extend south of Kadesh-barnea to Hazar-addar; thence it shall cross to Azmon, 5* and turning from Azmon to the Wadi of Egypt, shall terminate at the Sea.

6† "For your western boundary you shall have the Great Sea with its coast; this shall be your western boundary.

7† "The following shall be your boundary on the north: from the Great Sea you shall draw a line to Mount Hor, 8 and shall continue it from Mount Hor to Labo in the land of Hamath, with the boundary extending through Zedad. 9 Thence the boundary shall reach to Ziphron and termi-

---

33, 30–36: Moseroth is mentioned in Dt 10, 6 (in the form of "Moserah"), as the place where Aaron died. It must therefore have been close to Mount Hor; cf Nm 20, 22ff. It seems very probable that the section vv 36b–41a stood originally immediately after v 30a.

33, 40: The verse begins the same account of the victory over Arad as is given in Nm 21, 1ff, where it also follows the account of Aaron's death.

33, 41b–49: It seems that this section stood originally immediately after v 36a.

34, 6: The Great Sea: the Mediterranean.
34, 7f: Mount Hor: different from the one where Aaron died; cf Nm 20, 22; 33, 37f.

33, 36f: Nm 20, 1.22.   33, 55: Jos 23, 13; Jgs 2, 3.
33, 38: Nm 20, 25; Dt 32, 50.   34, 3: Jos 15, 1f.
33, 52: Ex 23, 31; 34, 13; Dt   34, 4: Jos 15, 3.
  7, 5; 12, 3.   34, 5: Jos 15, 4.
33, 54: Nm 26, 53ff.

nate at Hazar-enan. This shall be your northern boundary.

¹⁰ "For your eastern boundary you shall draw a line from Hazar-enan to Shepham. ¹¹ From Shepham the boundary shall go down to Ar-Baal, east of Ain, and descending further, shall strike the ridge on the east side of the Sea of Chinnereth; ¹² thence the boundary shall continue along the Jordan and terminate with the Salt Sea.

"This is the land that shall be yours, with the boundaries that surround it."

¹³ Moses also gave this order to the Israelites: "This is the land, to be apportioned among you by lot, which the LORD has commanded to be given to the nine and one half tribes. ¹⁴ For all the ancestral houses of the tribe of Reuben, and the ancestral houses of the tribe of Gad, as well as half of the tribe of Manasseh, have already received their heritage; ¹⁵ these two and one half tribes have received their heritage on the eastern side of the Jericho stretch of the Jordan, toward the sunrise."

Supervisors of the Allotment

¹⁶ The LORD said to Moses, ¹⁷ "These are the names of the men who shall apportion the land among you: Eleazar the priest, and Joshua, son of Nun, ¹⁸* and one prince from each of the tribes whom you shall designate for this task. ¹⁹ These shall be as follows:

from the tribe of Judah: Caleb, son
    of Jephunneh;
²⁰ from the tribe of Simeon: Samuel, son
    of Ammihud;
²¹ from the tribe of Benjamin: Elidad, son
    of Chislon;
²² from the tribe of Dan: Bukki, son of Jogli;
²³ from the tribe of Manasseh: Hanniel, son of
    Ephod; and
²⁴ from the tribe of Ephraim: Kemuel, son of
    Shiphtan, for the descendants of Joseph;
²⁵ from the tribe of Zebulun: Elizaphan, son
    of Parnach;
²⁶ from the tribe of Issachar: Paltiel, son of Azzan;
²⁷ from the tribe of Asher: Ahihud, son of Shelomi;
²⁸ from the tribe of Naphtali: Pedahel, son
    of Ammihud."

²⁹ These are they whom the LORD commanded to assign the Israelites their heritage in the land of Canaan.

Cities for the Levites

35 ¹ The LORD gave these instructions to Moses on the plains of Moab beside the Jericho stretch of the Jordan: ²* "Tell the Israelites that out of their hereditary property they shall give the Levites cities for homes, as well as pasture lands around the cities. ³ The cities shall serve them to dwell in, and the pasture lands shall serve their herds and flocks and other animals. ⁴ The pasture lands of the cities to be assigned the Levites shall extend a thousand cubits from the city walls in each direction. ⁵ Thus you shall measure out two thousand cubits outside the city along each side—east, south, west and north—with the city lying in the center. This shall serve them as the pasture lands of their cities.

⁶* "Now these are the cities you shall give to the Levites: the six cities of asylum which you must establish as places where a homicide can take refuge, and in addition forty-two other cities— ⁷ a total of forty-eight cities with their pasture lands to be assigned the Levites. ⁸† In assigning the cities from the property of the Israelites, take more from a larger group and fewer from a smaller one, so that each group will cede cities to the Levites in proportion to its own heritage."

Cities of Asylum

⁹ The LORD said to Moses, ¹⁰ "Tell the Israelites: When you go across the Jordan into the land of Canaan, ¹¹* select for yourselves cities to serve as cities of asylum, where a homicide who has killed someone unintentionally may take refuge. ¹²† These cities shall serve you as places of asylum from the avenger of blood, so that a homicide shall not be put to death unless he is first tried before the community. ¹³ Six cities of asylum shall you assign: ¹⁴ three beyond the Jordan, and three in the land of Canaan. ¹⁵ These six cities of asylum shall serve not only the Israelites but all the resident or transient aliens among them, so that anyone who has killed another unintentionally may take refuge there.

Murder and Manslaughter

¹⁶*† "If a man strikes another with an iron instrument and causes his death, he is a murderer and shall be put to death. ¹⁷ If a man strikes another with a death-dealing stone in his hand and causes his death, he is a murderer and shall be put to death. ¹⁸ If a man strikes another with a death-dealing club in his hand and causes his death, he is a murderer

---

35, 8: This provision was hardly observed in the actual assignment of the levitical cities as narrated in Jos 21.

35, 12: *The avenger of blood:* one of the close relatives of the slain (2 Sm 14, 7) who, as executor of public justice, had the right and duty to take the life of the murderer; cf Dt 19, 6. 12; Jos 20, 3. 5.9.

35, 16–25: Here, as also in Dt 19, 1–13, there is a casuistic development of the original law as stated in Ex 21, 12ff.

34, 18: Nm 1, 4.   35, 11: 10ff: Dt 19, 2; Jos 20, 2ff.
35, 2: Jos 14, 3f; 21, 2.   35, 16: Ex 21, 12; Lv 24, 17.
35, 6: Dt 4, 41f; Jos 20, 2.

and shall be put to death. 19 The avenger of blood may execute the murderer, putting him to death on sight.

20* "If a man pushes another out of hatred, or after lying in wait for him throws something at him, and causes his death, 21 or if he strikes another out of enmity and causes his death, he shall be put to death as a murderer. The avenger of blood may execute the murderer on sight.

22* "However, if a man pushes another accidentally and not out of enmity, or if without lying in wait for him he throws some object at him, 23 or without seeing him throws a death-dealing stone which strikes him and causes his death, although he was not his enemy nor seeking to harm him: 24 then the community, deciding the case between the slayer and the avenger of blood in accordance with these norms, 25* shall free the homicide from the avenger of blood and shall remand him to the city of asylum where he took refuge; and he shall stay there until the death of the high priest who has been anointed with sacred oil. 26 If the homicide of his own accord leaves the bounds of the city of asylum where he has taken refuge, 27 and the avenger of blood finds him beyond these bounds and kills him, the avenger incurs no blood-guilt; 28 the homicide was bound to stay in his city of asylum until the death of the high priest. Only after the death of the high priest may the homicide return to his own district.

29 "These shall be norms for you and all your descendants, wherever you live, for rendering judgment.

Witnesses

30* "Whenever someone kills another, the evidence of witnesses is required for the execution of the murderer. The evidence of a single witness is not sufficient for putting a person to death.

No Indemnity

31 "You shall not accept indemnity in place of the life of a murderer who deserves the death penalty; he must be put to death. 32 Nor shall you accept indemnity to allow a refugee to leave his city of asylum and again dwell elsewhere in the land before the death of the high priest. 33 You shall not desecrate the land where you live. Since bloodshed desecrates the land, the land can have no atonement for the blood shed on it except through the blood of him who shed it. 34* Do not defile the land in which you live and in the midst of which I dwell; for I am the LORD who dwells in the midst of the Israelites."

Property of Heiresses

36 1 The heads of the ancestral houses in the clan of descendants of Gilead, son of Machir, son of Manasseh—one of the Josephite clans—came up and laid this plea before Moses and the priest Eleazar and before the princes who were the heads of the ancestral houses of the other Israelites. 2* They said: "The LORD commanded you, my lord, to apportion the land by lot among the Israelites; and you, my lord, were also commanded by the LORD to give the heritage of our kinsman Zelophehad to his daughters. 3 But if they marry into one of the other Israelite tribes, their heritage will be withdrawn from our ancestral heritage and will be added to that of the tribe into which they marry; thus the heritage that fell to us by lot will be diminished. 4† When the Israelites celebrate the jubilee year, the heritage of these women will be permanently added to that of the tribe into which they marry and will be withdrawn from that of our ancestral tribe."

5† So Moses gave this regulation to the Israelites according to the instructions of the LORD: "The tribe of the Josephites are right in what they say. 6 This is what the LORD commands with regard to the daughters of Zelophehad: They may marry anyone they please, provided they marry into a clan of their ancestral tribe, 7 so that no heritage of the Israelites will pass from one tribe to another, but all the Israelites will retain their own ancestral heritage. 8 Therefore, every daughter who inherits property in any of the Israelite tribes shall marry someone belonging to a clan of her own ancestral tribe, in order that all the Israelites may remain in possession of their own ancestral heritage. 9 Thus, no heritage can pass from one tribe to another, but all the Israelite tribes will retain their own ancestral heritage."

10 The daughters of Zelophehad obeyed the command which the LORD had given to Moses. 11 Mahlah, Tirzah, Hoglah, Milcah and Noah, Zelophehad's daughters, married relatives on their father's side 12 within the clans of the descendants of Manasseh, son of Joseph; hence their heritage remained in the tribe of their father's clan.

Conclusion

13 These are the commandments and decisions which the LORD prescribed for the Israelites through Moses, on the plains of Moab beside the Jericho stretch of the Jordan.

---

† **36, 4:** Before the jubilee year various circumstances, such as divorce, could make such property revert to its original tribal owners; but in the jubilee year it became irrevocably attached to its new owners.

36, 5–9: This is a supplement to the law given in Nm 27, 5–11.

* **35, 20:** Ex 21, 14; Dt 19, 11.   1 Tm 5, 19.
35, 22: Jos 20, 3.   **35, 34:** Ex 29, 45.
35, 25: Jos 20, 6.   **36, 2:** Nm 26, 55; 27, 6; Jos
35, 30: Dt 17, 6; 19, 15; Jn 8,   17, 3f.
17; 2 Cor 13, 1;

Imagine this touching scene: You are standing at the bedside of your aging grandparent with all your cousins and family members. Your grandfather or grandmother begins to speak, sharing stories about the lessons he or she has learned from life. You listen to the familiar stories as if for the first time, and you are awed by the wisdom and love they contain. This is the scene Deuteronomy sets up—Moses is like the wise, aging grandparent, sharing his instructions and encouragement before dying.

At a Glance

I. Historical Review and Exhortation (1, 1—4, 43).

II. God and His Covenant (4, 44—11, 32).

III. Exposition of the Law (12, 1—26, 19).

IV. Final Words of Moses (27, 1—34, 12).

In-depth

The word Deuteronomy means "second law" in Greek. The first Law given on Mount Sinai was proposed by God to guide Israel in its wilderness journey. Written at a time when Israel was settled in the Promised Land and in need of religious reformation, Deuteronomy is a "second Law," adapted to the new situation of a people that needs to be reminded of its Covenant with God.

Deuteronomy has four divisions:

- In the first section (1, 1—4, 43), Moses addresses Israel by reviewing its history since Mount Horeb (Deuteronomy's term for Mount Sinai). Moses calls Israel to faithfulness and loyalty.
- In the second section (4, 44—11, 32), Moses reviews the Ten Commandments and the essence of the Law. He reminds the Israelites of the rewards for obeying and the consequences of disobeying the Law.
- In the third section (chapters 12–26), the most important section of Deuteronomy, Moses spells out a law to shape and govern the Israelites' new life as they settle in the Land.
- Finally, in the fourth section (chapters 27–34), Moses gives his last will and testament, offers a final blessing, and dies. His death is portrayed as the "sealing" of the second Law.

More than anything else, Deuteronomy stresses Israel as one people, with one God, one sanctuary, and now one land. These elements not only make Israel a unique people but bind it together in unity and solidarity. The Land of Promise now becomes a symbol of God's blessing and favor, the fulfillment of God's promises in the Covenant.

Quick Facts

Period Covered
just before the Israelites enter the Promised Land

Authors
scribes from the eighth century B.C. adapting the earlier Covenant Law to Israel's changing situation

Theme
the importance of the Covenant, the total commitment required by God's law

Deuteronomy

1, 1

I: Historical Review and Exhortation

Introduction

1 [1]† These are the words which Moses spoke to all Israel beyond the Jordan [in the desert, in the Arabah, opposite Suph, between Paran and Tophel, Laban, Hazeroth and Dizahab; [2] it is a journey of eleven days from Horeb to Kadesh-barnea by way of the highlands of Seir].

[3] In the fortieth year, on the first day of the eleventh month, Moses spoke to the Israelites all the commands that the LORD had given him in their regard. [4]* After he had defeated Sihon, king of the Amorites, who lived in Heshbon, and Og, king of Bashan, who lived in Ashtaroth and in Edrei, [5] Moses began to explain the law in the land of Moab beyond the Jordan, as follows:

Departure from Horeb

[6] "The LORD, our God, said to us at Horeb, 'You have stayed long enough at this mountain. [7]*† Leave here and go to the hill country of the Amorites and to all the surrounding regions, the land of the Canaanites in the Arabah, the mountains, the foothills, the Negeb and the seacoast; to

Lebanon, and as far as the Great River [the Euphrates]. [8]* I have given that land over to you. Go now and occupy the land I swore to your fathers, Abraham, Isaac and Jacob, I would give to them and to their descendants.'

Appointment of Elders

[9]† "At that time I said to you, 'Alone, I am unable to carry you. [10]* The LORD, your God, has so multiplied you that you are now as numerous as the stars in the sky. [11] May the LORD, the God of your fathers, increase you a thousand times over, and bless you as he promised! [12] But how can I alone bear the crushing burden that you are, along with your bickering? [13]* Choose wise, intelligent and experienced men from each of your tribes, that I may appoint them as your leaders.' [14] You answered me, 'We agree to do as you have proposed.' [15] So I took outstanding men of your tribes, wise and experienced, and made them your leaders as officials over thousands, over hundreds, over fifties and over tens, and other tribal officers. [16]* I charged your judges at that time, 'Listen to complaints among your kinsmen, and administer true justice to both parties even if one of them is an alien. [17] In rendering judg-

†
1, 1: The local setting of all these discourses is in the land of Moab beyond the Jordan (cf v 5), also known as the plains of Moab (Nm 36, 13).
1, 7: The Amorites and the Canaanites formed the principal part of the pre-Israelite population of Palestine. *The foothills:* the hills on the western slope of the Judean mountain range. *The Arabah:* the valley of the Jordan and the depression south of the Dead Sea. *The Negeb:* the arid land in southern Palestine.

1, 9: *Carry you:* cf v 31.

1, 4: Dt 3, 2; Nm 21, 21–35.
1, 7: Nm 13, 29.
1, 8: Gn 12, 7; 15, 18; 17, 7f; 28, 13f.
1, 10: Dt 10, 22; Gn 15, 5.
1, 13ff: Ex 18, 21–25.
1, 16f: Ex 18, 26; 2 Chr 19, 6f; Prv 24, 23; Jn 7, 24; Jas 2, 9.

ment, do not consider who a person is; give ear to the lowly and to the great alike, fearing no man, for judgment is God's. Refer to me any case that is too hard for you and I will hear it.' 18 Thereupon I gave you all the commands you were to fulfill.

The Twelve Scouts

19* "Then, in obedience to the command of the LORD, our God, we set out from Horeb and journeyed through the whole desert, vast and fearful as you have seen, in the direction of the hill country of the Amorites. We had reached Kadesh-barnea 20 when I said to you, 'You have come to the hill country of the Amorites, which the LORD, our God, is giving us. 21 The LORD, your God, has given this land over to you. Go up and occupy it, as the LORD, the God of your fathers, commands you. Do not fear or lose heart.' 22* Then all of you came up to me and said, 'Let us send men ahead to reconnoiter the land for us and report to us on the road we must follow and the cities we must take.' 23 Agreeing with the proposal, I chose twelve men from your number, one from each tribe. 24 They set out into the hill country as far as the Wadi Eshcol, and explored it. 25 Then, taking along some of the fruit of the land, they brought it down to us and reported, 'The land which the LORD, our God, gives us is good.'

Threats of Revolt

26* "But you refused to go up, and after defying the command of the LORD, your God, 27*† you set to murmuring in your tents, 'Out of hatred for us the LORD has brought us up out of the land of Egypt, to deliver us into the hands of the Amorites and destroy us. 28* What shall we meet with up there? Our kinsmen have made us fainthearted by reporting that the people are stronger and taller than we, and their cities are large and fortified to the sky; besides, they saw the Anakim there.' 29 "But I said to you, 'Have no dread or fear of them. 30 The LORD, your God, who goes before you, will himself fight for you, just as he took your part before your very eyes in Egypt, 31 as well as in the desert, where you saw how the LORD, your God, carried you, as a man carries his child, all along your journey until you arrived at this place.' 32 Despite this, you would not trust the LORD, your God, 33* who journeys before you to find you a resting place—by day in the cloud, and by night in the fire, to show the way you must go. 34 When the LORD

heard your words, he was angry; 35* and he swore, 'Not one man of this evil generation shall look upon the good land I swore to give to your fathers, 36† except Caleb, son of Jephunneh; he shall see it. For to him and to his sons I will give the land he trod upon, because he has followed the LORD unreservedly.'

37* "The LORD was angered against me also on your account, and said, 'Not even you shall enter there, 38* but your aide Joshua, son of Nun, shall enter. Encourage him, for he is to give Israel its heritage. 39* Your little ones, who you said would become booty, and your children, who as yet do not know good from bad—they shall enter; to them I will give it, and they shall occupy it. 40 But as for yourselves: turn about and proceed into the desert on the Red Sea road.'

Unsuccessful Invasion

41* "In reply you said to me, 'We have sinned against the LORD. We will go up ourselves and fight, just as the LORD, our God, commanded us.' And each of you girded on his weapons, making light of going up into the hill country. 42 But the LORD said to me, 'Warn them: Do not go up and fight, lest you be beaten down before your enemies, for I will not be in your midst.' 43 I gave you this warning but you would not listen. In defiance of the LORD's command you arrogantly marched off into the hill country. 44 Then the Amorites living there came out against you and, like bees, chased you, cutting you down in Seir as far as Hormah. 45 On your return you wept before the LORD, but he did not listen to your cry or give ear to you. 46 That is why you had to stay as long as you did at Kadesh.

Northward along Edom

2 1* "When we did turn and proceed into the desert on the Red Sea road, as the LORD had commanded me, we circled around the highlands of Seir for a long time. 2 Finally the LORD said to me, 3 'You have wandered round these highlands long enough; turn and go north. 4 Give this order to the people: You are now about to pass through the territory of your kinsmen, the descendants of Esau, who live in Seir. Though they are afraid of you, be very careful 5 not to come in conflict with them, for I will not give you so much as a foot of their land, since I have already given Esau possession of the highlands of Seir. 6 You shall purchase from them

DT

---

†
1, 27: *In your tents:* among yourselves.
1, 36: *Except Caleb:* Joshua also was allowed to enter, but he is not referred to here because special mention is made of him in v 38 as the successor of Moses.

*
1, 19: Dt 8, 15; 32, 10.
1, 22–28: Nm 13, 2–34.
1, 26: Dt 9, 23.
1, 27: Dt 9, 28; Nm 14, 1–4;

Ps 106, 25.
1, 28: Dt 9, 1f.
1, 33: Ex 13, 21; Nm 10, 33f;
14, 14.
1, 35: 34ff; Nm 14, 22f.28–38; Jos
14, 9.
1, 37: Dt 4, 21; 34, 4;

Nm 20, 12.
1, 38: Dt 31, 3.7; Nm 27,
18ff; 34, 17.
1, 39: Nm 14, 31.
1, 41–45: Nm 14, 40.42–45.
2, 1: Dt 1, 40; Nm 14, 25;
21, 4.

with silver the food you eat and the well water you drink. 7* The LORD, your God, has blessed you in all your undertakings; he has been concerned about your journey through this vast desert. It is now forty years that he has been with you, and you have never been in want.'

Along Moab

8* "Then we left behind us the Arabah route, Elath, Ezion-geber, and Seir, where our kinsmen, the descendants of Esau, live; and we went on toward the desert of Moab. 9* And the LORD said to me, 'Do not show hostility to the Moabites or engage them in battle, for I will not give you possession of any of their land, since I have given Ar to the descendants of Lot as their own. 10* [Formerly the Emim lived there, a people strong and numerous and tall like the Anakim; 11 like them they were considered Rephaim. It was the Moabites who called them Emim. 12* In Seir, however, the former inhabitants were the Horites; the descendants of Esau dispossessed them, clearing them out of the way and taking their place, just as the Israelites have done in the land of their heritage which the LORD has given them.] 13* Get ready, then, to cross the Wadi Zered.' So we crossed it. 14* Thirty-eight years had elapsed between our departure from Kadesh-barnea and that crossing; in the meantime the whole generation of soldiers had perished from the camp, as the LORD had sworn they should. 15 For it was the LORD's hand that was against them, till he wiped them out of the camp completely.

Along Ammon

16 "When at length death had put an end to all the soldiers among the people, 17 the LORD said to me, 18 'You are now about to leave Ar and the territory of Moab behind. 19* As you come opposite the Ammonites, do not show hostility or come in conflict with them, for I will not give you possession of any land of the Ammonites, since I have given it to the descendants of Lot as their own. 20 [This also was considered a country of the Rephaim from its former inhabitants, whom the Ammonites called Zamzummim, 21 a people strong and numerous and tall like the Anakim. But these, too, the LORD cleared out of the way for the Ammonites, who ousted them and took their place. 22 He had done the same for the descendants of Esau, who dwell in

Seir, by clearing the Horites out of their way, so that the descendants of Esau have taken their place down to the present. 23† So also the Caphtorim, migrating from Caphtor, cleared away the Avvim, who once dwelt in villages as far as Gaza, and took their place.]

Defeat of Sihon

24* " 'Advance now across the Wadi Arnon. I now deliver into your hands Sihon, the Amorite king of Heshbon, and his land. Begin the occupation; engage him in battle. 25 This day I will begin to put a fear and dread of you into every nation under the heavens, so that at the mention of your name they will quake and tremble before you.'

26 "So I sent messengers from the desert of Kedemoth to Sihon, king of Heshbon, with this offer of peace: 27 'Let me pass through your country by the highway; I will go along it without turning aside to the right or to the left. 28 For the food I eat which you will supply, and for the water you give me to drink, you shall be paid in silver. Only let me march through, 29* as the descendants of Esau who dwell in Seir and the Moabites who dwell in Ar have done, until I cross the Jordan into the land which the LORD, our God, is about to give us.' 30 But Sihon, king of Heshbon, refused to let us pass through his land, because the LORD, your God, made him stubborn in mind and obstinate in heart that he might deliver him up to you, as indeed he has now done.

31 "Then the LORD said to me, 'Now that I have already begun to hand over to you Sihon and his land, begin the actual occupation.' 32 So Sihon and all his people advanced against us to join battle at Jahaz; 33* but since the LORD, our God, had delivered him to us, we defeated him and his sons and all his people. 34*† At that time we seized all his cities and doomed them all, with their men, women and children; we left no survivor. 35 Our only booty was the livestock and the loot of the captured cities. 36* From Aroer on the edge of the Wadi Arnon and from the city in the wadi itself, as far as Gilead, no city was too well fortified for us to whom the LORD had delivered them up. 37* However, in obedience to the command of the LORD, our God, you did not encroach upon any of the Ammonite land, neither the region bordering on the Wadi Jabbok, nor the cities of the highlands.

2, 23: *The Caphtorim:* members of one of the groups of sea peoples who invaded the coast of Egypt and the southern part of Palestine about 1200 B.C. *Caphtor:* the ancient name of the island of Crete. Cf Am 9, 7.

2, 34: *Doomed:* see notes on Nm 18, 14; 21, 3.

2, 7: Dt 8, 2ff.
2, 8: Jgs 11, 18.
2, 9: Gn 19, 36f.
2, 10: Dt 1, 28.
2, 12: Gn 36, 20f.
2, 13: Nm 21, 12.
2, 14: Nm 14, 29.33.35.
2, 19: Gn 19, 38.
2, 24: Nm 21, 13; Jgs 11, 19–22.
2, 29: Dt 2, 5.8f; Jgs 11, 17.
2, 33: Dt 29, 7; Nm 21, 23–32.
2, 34: Dt 3, 6; 29, 7f.
2, 36: Dt 3, 12; Jos 13, 9.16; Jgs 11, 26.
2, 37: Nm 21, 24; Jos 12, 2.

Defeat of Og

3 1* "Then we turned and proceeded toward Bashan. But Og, king of Bashan, advanced against us with all his people to give battle at Edrei. 2* The LORD, however, said to me, 'Do not be afraid of him, for I have delivered him into your hand with all his people and his land. Do to him as you did to Sihon, king of the Amorites, who lived in Heshbon.' 3 And thus the LORD, our God, delivered into our hands Og, king of Bashan, with all his people. We defeated him so completely that we left him no survivor. 4 At that time we captured all his cities, none of them eluding our grasp, the whole region of Argob, the kingdom of Og in Bashan: sixty cities in all, 5 to say nothing of the great number of unwalled towns. All the cities were fortified with high walls and gates and bars. 6* As we had done to Sihon, king of Heshbon, so also here we doomed all the cities, with their men, women and children; 7 but all the livestock and the loot of each city we took as booty for ourselves.

8 "And so at that time we took from the two kings of the Amorites beyond the Jordan the territory from the Wadi Arnon to Mount Hermon 9 [which is called Sirion by the Sidonians and Senir by the Amorites], 10 comprising all the cities of the plateau and all Gilead and all the cities of the kingdom of Og in Bashan including Salecah and Edrei. 11† [Og, king of Bashan, was the last remaining survivor of the Rephaim. He had a bed of iron, nine regular cubits long and four wide, which is still preserved in Rabbah of the Ammonites.]

Allotment of the Conquered Lands

12* "When we occupied the land at that time, I gave Reuben and Gad the territory from Aroer, on the edge of the Wadi Arnon, halfway up into the highlands of Gilead, with the cities therein. 13 The rest of Gilead and all of Bashan, the kingdom of Og, the whole Argob region, I gave to the half-tribe of Manasseh. [All this region of Bashan was once called a land of the Rephaim. 14* Jair, a Manassehite clan, took all the region of Argob as far as the border of the Geshurites and Maacathites, and called it after his own name Bashan Havvoth-jair, the name it bears today.] 15 To Machir I gave Gilead, 16 and to Reuben and Gad the territory from Gilead to the Wadi Arnon—including the wadi bed and its banks—and to the Wadi Jabbok, which is the border of the Ammonites, 17* as well as the Arabah with the Jordan and its eastern banks from Chin-

nereth to the Salt Sea of the Arabah, under the slopes of Pisgah.

18*† "At that time I charged them as follows: 'The LORD, your God, has given you this land as your own. But all you troops equipped for battle must cross over in the vanguard of your brother Israelites. 19* Only your wives and children, as well as your livestock, of which I know you have a large number, shall remain behind in the towns I have given you, 20* until the LORD has settled your kinsmen as well, and they too possess the land which the LORD, your God, will give them on the other side of the Jordan. Then you may all return to the possessions I have given you.'

21 "It was then that I instructed Joshua, 'Your eyes have seen all that the LORD, your God, has done to both these kings; so, too, will the LORD do to all the kingdoms which you will encounter over there. 22 Fear them not, for the LORD, your God, will fight for you.'

Refusal to Moses

23 "And it was then that I besought the LORD, 24 'O Lord GOD, you have begun to show to your servant your greatness and might. For what god in heaven or on earth can perform deeds as mighty as yours? 25 Ah, let me cross over and see this good land beyond the Jordan, this fine hill country, and the Lebanon!' 26* But the LORD was angry with me on your account and would not hear me. 'Enough!' the LORD said to me. 'Speak to me no more of this. 27* Go up to the top of Pisgah and look out to the west, and to the north, and to the south, and to the east. Look well, for you shall not cross this Jordan. 28* Commission Joshua, and encourage and strengthen him, for he shall cross at the head of this people and shall put them in possession of the land you are to see.' 29 This was while we were in the ravine opposite Beth-peor.

Advantages of Fidelity

4 1 "Now, Israel, hear the statutes and decrees which I am teaching you to observe, that you may live, and may enter in and take possession of the land which the LORD, the God of your fathers, is giving you 2* In your observance of the commandments of the LORD, your God, which I enjoin upon you, you shall not add to what I command you nor subtract from it 3* You have seen with your own eyes what the LORD did at Baal-peor: the LORD, your God, destroyed from your midst everyone that

---

3, 11: *Bed of iron:* some translate, "a sarcophagus of basalt."
3, 18: *I charged them:* the words which follow were spoken to the men of Reuben and Gad (cf Nm 32).

3, 1: Dt 29, 6; Nm 21, 33.
3, 2f: Nm 21, 34f.
3, 6: Ps 135, 10ff.
3, 12f: Nm 32, 29.32f;

Jos 13, 8.29.
3, 14: Nm 32, 41; Jos 13, 11. 13.
3, 17: Dt 4, 49; Jos 12, 3.
3, 18: Jos 1, 14; 4, 12.
3, 19: Nm 32, 1.4; Jos 1, 14.
3, 20: Jos 22, 4.
3, 26: Dt 4, 21.
3, 27: Dt 34, 4; Nm 27, 12f.
3, 28: Dt 1, 38; 31, 7; Nm 27, 22f.
4, 2: Dt 13, 1.
4, 3: Nm 25, 3–9.

followed the Baal of Peor; 4 but you, who clung to the LORD, your God, are all alive today 5 Therefore, I teach you the statutes and decrees as the LORD, my God, has commanded me, that you may observe them in the land you are entering to occupy 6 Observe them carefully, for thus will you give evidence of your wisdom and intelligence to the nations, who will hear of all these statutes and say, 'This great nation is truly a wise and intelligent people' 7* For what great nation is there that has gods so close to it as the Lord, our God, is to us whenever we call upon him? 8 Or what great nation has statutes and decrees that are as just as this whole law which I am setting before you today?

Revelation at Horeb

9* "However, take care and be earnestly on your guard not to forget the things which your own eyes have seen, nor let them slip from your memory as long as you live, but teach them to your children and to your children's children: 10*† There was the day on which you stood before the LORD, your God, at Horeb, and he said to me, 'Assemble the people for me; I will have them hear my words, that they may learn to fear me as long as they live in the land and may so teach their children.' 11* You came near and stood at the foot of the mountain, which blazed to the very sky with fire and was enveloped in a dense black cloud. 12* Then the LORD spoke to you from the midst of the fire. You heard the sound of the words, but saw no form; there was only a voice. 13 He proclaimed to you his covenant, which he commanded you to keep: the ten commandments, which he wrote on two tablets of stone. 14 The LORD charged me at that time to teach you the statutes and decrees which you are to observe over in the land you will occupy.

Danger of Idolatry

15* "You saw no form at all on the day the LORD spoke to you at Horeb from the midst of the fire. Be strictly on your guard, therefore, 16* not to degrade yourselves by fashioning an idol to represent any figure, whether it be the form of a man or of a woman, 17 of any animal on the earth or of any bird that flies in the sky, 18 of anything that crawls on the ground or of any fish in the waters under the earth. 19* And when you look up to the heavens and behold the

sun or the moon or any star among the heavenly hosts, do not be led astray into adoring them and serving them. These the LORD, your God, has let fall to the lot of all other nations under the heavens; 20*† but you he has taken and led out of that iron foundry, Egypt, that you might be his very own people, as you are today. 21* Since the LORD was angered against me on your account and swore that I should not cross the Jordan nor enter the good land which he is giving you as a heritage, 22* I myself shall die in this country without crossing the Jordan; but you will cross over and take possession of that good land. 23* Take heed, therefore, lest, forgetting the covenant which the LORD, your God, has made with you, you fashion for yourselves against his command an idol in any form whatsoever. 24 For the LORD, your God, is a consuming fire, a jealous God.

God's Fidelity

25† "When you have children and grandchildren, and have grown old in the land, should you then degrade yourselves by fashioning an idol in any form and by this evil done in his sight provoke the LORD, your God, 26 I call heaven and earth this day to witness against you, that you shall all quickly perish from the land which you will occupy when you cross the Jordan. You shall not live in it for any length of time but shall be promptly wiped out. 27* The LORD will scatter you among the nations, and there shall remain but a handful of you among the nations to which the LORD will lead you. 28* There you shall serve gods fashioned by the hands of man out of wood and stone, gods which can neither see nor hear, neither eat nor smell. 29* Yet there too you shall seek the LORD, your God; and you shall indeed find him when you search after him with your whole heart and your whole soul. 30 In your distress, when all these things shall have come upon you, you shall finally return to the LORD, your God, and heed his voice. 31* Since the LORD, your God, is a merciful God, he will not abandon and destroy you, nor forget the covenant which under oath he made with your fathers.

Proofs of God's Love

32 "Ask now of the days of old, before your time, ever since God created man upon the earth; ask from one end of the sky to the other: Did anything

---

4, 10: Beginning here and continuing on for several verses (at least to the end of v 14) is the "reminiscence," the account of the things that the Israelites should recall and teach their children.
4, 20: Egypt is called an *iron foundry,* or furnace for smelting iron, because God allowed the Israelites to be afflicted there for the sake of their spiritual purification; the same expression for Egypt occurs also in 1 Kgs 8, 51; Jer 11, 4; compare the expression, "the furnace of affliction," in Is 48, 10.
4, 25: *Grown old:* Israel will lose the freshness of its youthful fervor.

4, 7: 2 Sm 7, 23.
4, 9: Dt 11, 19; Ps 78, 3–6.
4, 10: Heb 12, 18f.
4, 11: Ex 19, 17f.
4, 12: Dt 4, 33.36; 5, 4.
4, 15: Ex 24, 12; 31, 18; 34, 28.
4, 16: Dt 5, 8; Ex 20, 4.
4, 19: Dt 17, 3; Jb 31, 26ff.
4, 20: 1 Kgs 8, 51; Jer 11, 4.
4, 21: Dt 1, 37; 3, 26.
4, 22: Dt 3, 27.
4, 23: Dt 4, 16.
4, 27f: Dt 28, 36.62.64.
4, 28: Ps 135, 15ff; Is 44, 9.
4, 29: Jer 29, 13.
4, 31: Dt 31, 8.

so great ever happen before? Was it ever heard of? [33]* Did a people ever hear the voice of God speaking from the midst of fire, as you did, and live? [34]*† Or did any god venture to go and take a nation for himself from the midst of another nation, by testings, by signs and wonders, by war, with his strong hand and outstretched arm, and by great terrors, all of which the LORD, your God, did for you in Egypt before your very eyes? [35] All this you were allowed to see that you might know the LORD is God and there is no other. [36] Out of the heavens he let you hear his voice to discipline you; on earth he let you see his great fire, and you heard him speaking out of the fire. [37] For love of your fathers he chose their descendants and personally led you out of Egypt by his great power, [38] driving out of your way nations greater and mightier than you, so as to bring you in and to make their land your heritage, as it is today. [39]* This is why you must now know, and fix in your heart, that the LORD is God in the heavens above and on earth below, and that there is no other. [40]* You must keep his statutes and commandments which I enjoin on you today, that you and your children after you may prosper, and that you may have long life on the land which the LORD, your God, is giving you forever."

Cities of Refuge

[41]* Then Moses set apart three cities in the region east of the Jordan, [42] that a homicide might take refuge there if he unwittingly killed his neighbor to whom he had previously borne no malice, and that he might save his life by fleeing to one of these cities: [43] Bezer in the desert, in the region of the plateau, for the Reubenites; Ramoth in Gilead for the Gadites; and Golan in Bashan for the Manassehites.

II: God and His Covenant

Introduction

[44] This is the law which Moses set before the Israelites. [45] These are the ordinances, statutes and decrees which he proclaimed to them when they had come out of Egypt [46] and were beyond the Jordan in the ravine opposite Beth-peor, in the land of Sihon, king of the Amorites, who dwelt in Heshbon and whom Moses and the Israelites defeated after

coming out of Egypt. [47] They occupied his land and the land of Og, king of Bashan, as well—the land of these two kings of the Amorites in the region east of the Jordan: [48]† from Aroer on the edge of the Wadi Arnon to Mount Sion (that is, Hermon) [49]* and all the Arabah east of the Jordan, as far as the Arabah Sea under the slopes of Pisgah.

The Covenant at Horeb

5 [1] Moses summoned all Israel and said to them, "Hear, O Israel, the statutes and decrees which I proclaim in your hearing this day, that you may learn them and take care to observe them. [2]* The LORD, our God, made a covenant with us at Horeb; [3] not with our fathers did he make this covenant, but with us, all of us who are alive here this day. [4] The LORD spoke with you face to face on the mountain from the midst of the fire. [5]* Since you were afraid of the fire and would not go up the mountain, I stood between the LORD and you at that time, to announce to you these words of the LORD:

The Decalogue

[6]* 'I, the LORD, am your God, who brought you out of the land of Egypt,* that place of slavery. [7]* You shall not have other gods besides me. [8]* You shall not carve idols for yourselves in the shape of anything in the sky above or on the earth below or in the waters beneath the earth; [9]*† you shall not bow down before them or worship them. For I, the LORD, your God, am a jealous God, inflicting punishments for their fathers' wickedness on the children of those who hate me, down to the third and fourth generation [10]* but bestowing mercy, down to the thousandth generation, on the children of those who love me and keep my commandments.

[11]* 'You shall not take the name of the LORD, your God, in vain. For the LORD will not leave unpunished him who takes his name in vain.

[12] 'Take care to keep holy the sabbath day as the LORD, your God, commanded you. [13] Six days you may labor and do all your work; [14]* but the seventh day is the sabbath of the LORD, your God. No work may be done then, whether by you, or your son or daughter, or your male or female slave, or your ox or ass or any of your beasts, or the alien who lives with you. Your male and female slave should rest as

---

4, 34: *Testings:* the demonstrations of God's power as in the ten great plagues of Egypt; cf Dt 7, 19; 29, 2.

4, 48: *Sion:* another name for Mount Hermon, besides those mentioned in Dt 3, 9.

5, 9f: God does not punish us for another's sins, but because of the solidarity of human society, the good or evil deeds of one generation may make their effects felt even in later generations. Yet note how God's mercy allows the good effects of virtue to last much longer than the bad effects of vice: a thousand generations compared to three or four.

4, 33: Dt 4, 36; 5, 24.26; Ex 20, 19.
4, 34: Dt 7, 19; 26, 8; 29, 2; Ex 7, 3; 15, 3–10; Jer 32, 21.
4, 39: Dt 4, 35.
4, 40: Dt 6, 2f; 12, 28.
4, 41ff: Dt 19, 2–13; Nm 35, 6–29; Jos 20, 8; 21, 27.36f; 1 Chr 6, 71. 80.
4, 49: Dt 3, 17.

5, 2: Dt 28, 69.
5, 5: Ex 24, 2.
5, 6–21: Ex 20, 2–17.
5, 6: Ps 81, 11.
5, 7: Ps 81, 10.
5, 8: Dt 27, 15; Lv 26, 1; Ps 97, 7.
5, 9: Ex 34, 14.
5, 10: Dt 7, 9; Ex 20, 6.
5, 11: Mt 5, 33.
5, 14: Gn 2, 2; Ex 20, 8; 23, 12; Heb 4, 4.

D
T

THE LAKOTA CODE

See how similar these guidelines from a Native American tribal code are to the Ten Commandments (Dt 5, 1–21), not to mention our own civil laws, school policies, and even family rules. What can we learn from them?

- Love one another.
- Pity orphan children. Be kind to them because they are poor; feed them and clothe them.
- Do not kill one another.
- Do not steal anything from anyone, especially from your own people.
- Do not tell lies to anyone, or lie about anyone.
- Respect your brothers and sisters. Do not marry in your own family.
- The ability to make good speech is a great gift from their maker, owner of all things, to the people. This is why you should not talk badly about anyone. Bad talk can hurt one's family or everyday life.
- Never quarrel among one another. Be good to others and always be friendly to whomever you meet, wherever you meet them.
- Do not brag about yourself, or try to hurt another's feelings. The generous person is the one who is respected.

(Ron Zeilinger, *Sacred Ground*, pp. 74–75)

▶ **Dt 5, 1–21**

you do. ¹⁵* For remember that you too were once slaves in Egypt, and the LORD, your God, brought you from there with his strong hand and outstretched arm. That is why the LORD, your God, has commanded you to observe the sabbath day.

¹⁶* 'Honor your father and your mother, as the LORD, your God, has commanded you, that you may have a long life and prosperity in the land which the LORD, your God, is giving you.

¹⁷* 'You shall not kill.

¹⁸ 'You shall not commit adultery.

¹⁹ 'You shall not steal.

²⁰ 'You shall not bear dishonest witness against your neighbor.

²¹ 'You shall not covet your neighbor's wife.

'You shall not desire your neighbor's house or field, nor his male or female slave, nor his ox or ass, nor anything that belongs to him.'

Moses as Mediator

²² "These words, and nothing more, the LORD spoke with a loud voice to your entire assembly on the mountain from the midst of the fire and the dense cloud. He wrote them upon two tablets of stone and gave them to me. ²³ But when you heard the voice from the midst of the darkness, while the mountain was ablaze with fire, you came to me in the person of all your tribal heads and elders, ²⁴* and said, 'The LORD, our God, has indeed let us see his glory and his majesty! We have heard his voice from the midst of the fire and have found out today that a man can still live after God has spoken with him. ²⁵* But why should we die now? Surely this great fire will consume us. If we hear the voice of the LORD, our God, any more, we shall die. ²⁶ For what mortal has heard, as we have, the voice of the living God speaking from the midst of

5, 15: Dt 15, 15; 16, 12; 24,
18.22.
5, 16: Sir 3, 2–16; Mt 15, 4;

Mk 7, 10; Lk 18, 20;
Eph 6, 2.
5, 17–20: Mt 5, 21.27;

Lk 18, 20; Jas 2, 11.   5, 25: Dt 18, 16.
5, 24: Dt 4, 33.

fire, and survived? ²⁷* Go closer, you, and hear all that the LORD, our God, will say, and then tell us what the LORD, our God, tells you; we will listen and obey.'

²⁸* "The LORD heard your words as you were speaking to me and said to me, 'I have heard the words these people have spoken to you, which are all well said. ²⁹ Would that they might always be of such a mind, to fear me and to keep all my commandments! Then they and their descendants would prosper forever. ³⁰ Go, tell them to return to their tents. ³¹ Then you wait here near me and I will give you all the commandments, the statutes and decrees you must teach them, that they may observe them in the land which I am giving them to possess.'

³² "Be careful, therefore, to do as the LORD, your God, has commanded you, not turning aside to the right or to the left, ³³* but following exactly the way prescribed for you by the LORD, your God, that you may live and prosper, and may have long life in the land which you are to occupy.

6 ¹* "These then are the commandments, the statutes and decrees which the LORD, your God, has ordered that you be taught to observe in the land into which you are crossing for conquest, ²* so that you and your son and your grandson may fear the LORD, your God, and keep, throughout the days of your lives, all his statutes and commandments which I enjoin on you, and thus have long life. ³ Hear then, Israel, and be careful to observe them, that you may grow and prosper the more, in keeping with the promise of the LORD, the God of your fathers, to give you a land flowing with milk and honey.

The Great Commandment

⁴*† "Hear, O Israel! The LORD is our God, the LORD alone! ⁵* Therefore, you shall love the LORD, your God, with all your heart, and with all your soul, and with all your strength. ⁶ Take to heart these words which I enjoin on you today. ⁷* Drill them into your children. Speak of them at home and abroad, whether you are busy or at rest. ⁸*† Bind them at your wrist as a sign and let them be as a pendant on your forehead. ⁹* Write them on the doorposts of your houses and on your gates.

Fidelity in Prosperity

¹⁰* "When the LORD, your God, brings you into the land which he swore to your fathers, Abraham, Isaac and Jacob, that he would give you, a land with fine, large cities that you did not build, ¹¹ with houses full of goods of all sorts that you did not garner, with cisterns that you did not dig, with vineyards and olive groves that you did not plant; and when, therefore, you eat your fill, ¹²* take care not to forget the

The Shema: Putting God First

Deuteronomy 6, 4 is the most famous declaration of faith in the Old Testament: "Hear, O Israel! The LORD is our God, the LORD alone!" This short verse, part of a prayer called the Shema, is uttered daily by faithful Jews. It has been so important that the commands of verses 8–9 often have been interpreted literally. The Pharisees of Jesus' day, for example, wore miniature copies of the prayer on their bodies and attached other copies to their doorposts. Orthodox Jews today continue this tradition. Keeping the law of God is a privilege—something to be "worn" with pride!

The Shema reminds Jewish people to put God first and to love God with all their heart, soul, and might. Think about people who seem to carry God in their heart all the time. Are they lost and frustrated? Do they seem angry and hate filled? Chances are they seem more relaxed and sure of themselves than most people do. Having God in your sights at all times will help in more ways than you could ever imagine!

▶ Dt 6, 4–9

---

† **6, 4f:** This passage contains the basic principle of the whole Mosaic law, the keynote of the Book of Deuteronomy: since the Lord alone is God, we must love him with an undivided heart. Christ cited these words as "the greatest and the first commandment," embracing in itself the whole law of God (Mt 22, 37f and parallels).

6, 8: *Bind them . . . as a sign:* these injunctions were probably meant merely in a figurative sense; cf Ex 13, 9.16. However, the later Jews understood them literally, and tied on their wrists and foreheads "phylacteries," boxes containing strips of parchment on which the words were inscribed; cf Mt 23, 5.

5, 27: Ex 20, 19.
5, 28: Dt 18, 17.
5, 33: Dt 4, 40.
6, 1: Dt 4, 1; 5, 31; 12, 1.
6, 2: Dt 4, 40; 5, 29; 10, 12f.
6, 4: Mk 12, 29.
6, 5: Dt 10, 12; 11, 13; Mt 22, 37; Mk 12, 30; Lk 10, 27.
6, 7: 6f: Dt 4, 9; 11, 18; 32, 46.
6, 8: Dt 11, 18; Ex 13, 9. 16; Mt 23, 5.
6, 9: Dt 11, 20.
6, 10f: Jos 24, 13.
6, 12: Dt 5, 6.

LORD, who brought you out of the land of Egypt, that place of slavery. 13*† The LORD, your God, shall you fear; him shall you serve, and by his name shall you swear. 14 You shall not follow other gods, such as those of the surrounding nations, 15* lest the wrath of the LORD, your God, flare up against you and he destroy you from the face of the land; for the LORD, your God, who is in your midst, is a jealous God.

16* "You shall not put the LORD, your God, to the test, as you did at Massah. 17 But keep the commandments of the LORD, your God, and the ordinances and statutes he has enjoined on you. 18 Do what is right and good in the sight of the LORD, that you may, according to his word, prosper, and may enter in and possess the good land which the LORD promised on oath to your fathers, 19* thrusting all your enemies out of your way.

Instruction to Children

20* "Later on, when your son asks you what these ordinances, statutes and decrees mean which the LORD, our God, has enjoined on you, 21* you shall say to your son, 'We were once slaves of Pharaoh in Egypt, but the LORD brought us out of Egypt with his strong hand 22 and wrought before our eyes signs and wonders, great and dire, against Egypt and against Pharaoh and his whole house. 23 He brought us from there to lead us into the land he promised on oath to our fathers, and to give it to us. 24 Therefore, the LORD commanded us to observe all these statutes in fear of the LORD, our God, that we may always have as prosperous and happy a life as we have today; 25 and our justice before the LORD, our God, is to consist in carefully observing all these commandments he has enjoined on us.'

Destruction of Pagans

7 1* "When the LORD, your God, brings you into the land which you are to enter and occupy, and dislodges great nations before you—the

DON'T LOSE YOUR LANGUAGE!

"Qui perd sa langue, perd sa foi." This French Canadian proverb means, "Lose your language, lose your faith."

As Canada was being settled, the French were afraid that the English culture would dominate the land and culture. Most of the French were Catholic, and most of the English were Protestant. The French believed their faith was so tied to their language that the loss of their language would mean a loss to their faith and how they expressed it culturally.

This same fear is present in the Bible. Peter was afraid to eat with the Gentiles—those who were not Jews (see Gal 2, 12). The Samaritan woman at the well knew that Jesus, a Jew, should have nothing to do with her because Samaritans were considered "half-Jews" due to intermarriage (see Jn 4, 9).

Chapter 7 of Deuteronomy portrays this fear in a frightening way. Israelites were told not just to avoid pagans but to destroy them. Intermarriage would mean losing Jewish language, culture, and faith—and sooner or later would lead to worshiping false gods. (See also Ex 23, 23-26.)

Yet Jesus treated the Samaritan woman with dignity. Paul challenged Peter to eat with the uncircumcised and to let them become Christians without first becoming Jews. We need not be afraid of those who are different from us. We can treat others with dignity and even build friendships without the fear of losing our language or our faith.

▶ Dt 7, 1–5

---

† 6, 13: *Him shall you serve:* here, to "serve" God means especially to "worship" him; in this sense it is quoted by our Lord (Mt 4, 10) as an argument against worshiping the devil.

6, 13: Dt 10, 20; Mt 4, 10;
    Lk 4, 8.
6, 15: 14f: Dt 8, 19; 11, 16.28.
6, 16: Nm 20, 1–13.

6, 19: Ex 23, 27; 34, 11.
6, 20: Ex 12, 26; 13, 14.
6, 21: Ex 20, 2.
7, 1: Ex 23, 23; 33, 2.

Hittites, Girgashites, Amorites, Canaanites, Per-izzites, Hivites and Jebusites: seven nations more numerous and powerful than you— 2* and when the LORD, your God, delivers them up to you and you defeat them, you shall doom them. Make no covenant with them and show them no mercy. 3* You shall not intermarry with them, neither giving your daughters to their sons nor taking their daughters for your sons. 4 For they would turn your sons from following me to serving other gods, and then the wrath of the LORD would flare up against you and quickly destroy you.

5*† "But this is how you must deal with them: Tear down their altars, smash their sacred pillars, chop down their sacred poles, and destroy their idols by fire. 6* For you are a people sacred to the LORD, your God; he has chosen you from all the nations on the face of the earth to be a people pe-culiarly his own. 7 It was not because you are the largest of all nations that the LORD set his heart on you and chose you, for you are really the smallest of all nations. 8 It was because the LORD loved you and because of his fidelity to the oath he had sworn to your fathers, that he brought you out with his strong hand from the place of slavery, and ran-somed you from the hand of Pharaoh, king of Egypt. 9* Understand, then, that the LORD, your God, is God indeed, the faithful God who keeps his merciful covenant down to the thousandth genera-tion toward those who love him and keep his com-mandments, 10 but who repays with destruction the person who hates him; he does not dally with such a one, but makes him personally pay for it. 11 You shall therefore carefully observe the command-ments, the statutes and the decrees which I enjoin on you today.

Blessings of Obedience

12* "As your reward for heeding these decrees and observing them carefully, the LORD, your God, will keep with you the merciful covenant which he promised on oath to your fathers. 13* He will love and bless and multiply you; he will bless the fruit of your womb and the produce of your soil, your grain and wine and oil, the issue of your herds and the young of your flocks, in the land which he swore to your fathers he would give you. 14 You will be blessed above all peoples; no man or woman among you shall be childless nor shall your live-stock be barren. 15 The LORD will remove all sick-ness from you; he will not afflict you with any of the malignant diseases that you know from Egypt, but will leave them with all your enemies.

16 "You shall consume all the nations which the LORD, your God, will deliver up to you. You are not to look on them with pity, lest you be ensnared into serving their gods. 17* Perhaps you will say to your-selves, 'These nations are greater than we. How can we dispossess them?' 18 But do not be afraid of them. Rather, call to mind what the LORD, your God, did to Pharaoh and to all Egypt: 19* the great test-ings which your own eyes have seen, the signs and wonders, his strong hand and outstretched arm with which the LORD, your God, brought you out. The same also will he do to all the nations of whom you are now afraid. 20* Moreover, the LORD, your God, will send hornets among them, until the survivors who have hidden from you are destroyed. 21 There-fore, do not be terrified by them, for the LORD, your God, who is in your midst, is a great and awesome God. 22* He will dislodge these nations before you little by little. You cannot exterminate them all at once, lest the wild beasts become too numerous for you. 23* The LORD, your God, will deliver them up to you and will rout them utterly until they are an-nihilated. 24* He will deliver their kings into your hand, that you may make their names perish from under the heavens. No man will be able to stand up against you, till you have put an end to them. 25 The images of their gods you shall destroy by fire. Do not covet the silver or gold on them, nor take it for your-selves, lest you be ensnared by it; for it is an abomi-nation to the LORD, your God. 26 You shall not bring any abominable thing into your house, lest you be doomed with it; loathe and abhor it utterly as a thing that is doomed.

God's Care

8 1* "Be careful to observe all the command-ments I enjoin on you today, that you may live and increase, and may enter in and possess the land which the LORD promised on oath to your fa-thers. 2* Remember how for forty years now the LORD, your God, has directed all your journeying in the desert, so as to test you by affliction and find out whether or not it was your intention to keep his commandments. 3*† He therefore let you be afflict-ed with hunger, and then fed you with manna, a food unknown to you and your fathers, in order to show you that not by bread alone does man live,

---

7, 5: *Sacred pillars . . . poles:* see note on Ex 34, 13.
8, 3: *Not by bread alone, etc.:* quoted by our Lord in Mt 4, 4. The sense is: God takes care of those who love him even when natural means seem to fail them.

7, 2: Ex 34, 12.
7, 3f: Ex 34, 16; 1 Kgs 11, 1f.
7, 5: Dt 12, 3; Ex 34, 13.
7, 6: Dt 14, 2; 26, 18; Ex 19, 6.
7, 9f: Dt 5, 9f.
7, 12–16: Dt 28, 1–14; Ex 23, 22–26; Lv 26, 3–13.
7, 13: Dt 30, 9.
7, 17f: Dt 1, 28ff.
7, 19: Dt 4, 34.
7, 20: Ex 23, 28ff.
7, 22: Ex 23, 29f.
7, 23: Dt 7, 2.
7, 24: Dt 11, 25.
8, 1: Dt 4, 1; 6, 1.
8, 2: Dt 2, 7; 29, 4; Am 2, 10.
8, 3: Ex 16, 12–15.35; Nm 11, 6–9; Mt 4, 4; Lk 4, 4.

THE PRINCIPLE OF *UJIMA*

Decades before the Civil War, the Underground Railroad helped thousands of African slaves find their way to freedom. The Underground Railroad was not a real railroad but a loose network of antislavery northerners—mostly African Americans—who helped escaped slaves reach safety in the free states or Canada. People called conductors guided groups of fugitive slaves through isolated areas at night so that they wouldn't be spotted. Others opened their homes and farms to give them safe places to stay during the day. It was dangerous work because professional slave catchers and local officials were always looking for escaped slaves to return for financial rewards.

The Underground Railroad is just one example of what can be accomplished through the Kwanzaa principle of *ujima* (see "Kwanzaa as a Way of Life," Dt 10, 12–22), which is collective work and responsibility. Our African American ancestors in this country worked together bravely for the common good. Many members of the Underground Railroad were former slaves themselves and took responsibility for freeing others as they had been freed. Today, we need young people with the same sense of responsibility and the willingness to work together to free others from poverty, violence, and addiction.

Martin Luther King Jr. did this. In his last speech, he said to you and me: "I've been to the Mountain top, and I've seen the Promised Land. I may not get there with you, but I want you to know that we as a people will get to the Promised Land." He knew that he would not live to see his people freed from prejudice and discrimination. But he spent his whole life working with others toward that goal.

The author of Deuteronomy wrote long after Moses' time. Many of the Chosen People had indeed become wealthy, so he used Moses' authority to remind them of how they had gotten to where they were. Their ancestors—escaped, impoverished slaves—trusted in God and worked together over a long time to bring prosperity to the nation. This is the mentality we too must cultivate in order to bring success to ourselves and our people.

▶ Dt 8, 11–18

---

but by every word that comes forth from the mouth of the LORD. [4]* The clothing did not fall from you in tatters, nor did your feet swell these forty years. [5] So you must realize that the LORD, your God, disciplines you even as a man disciplines his son.

Danger of Prosperity

[6] "Therefore, keep the commandments of the LORD, your God, by walking in his ways and fearing him. [7]* For the LORD, your God, is bringing you into a good country, a land with streams of water, with springs and fountains welling up in the hills and valleys, [8] a land of wheat and barley, of vines and fig trees and pomegranates, of olive trees and of honey, [9] a land where you can eat bread without stint and

where you will lack nothing, a land whose stones contain iron and in whose hills you can mine copper. [10] But when you have eaten your fill, you must bless the LORD, your God, for the good country he has given you. [11] Be careful not to forget the LORD, your God, by neglecting his commandments and decrees and statutes which I enjoin on you today: [12] lest, when you have eaten your fill, and have built fine houses and lived in them, [13] and have increased your herds and flocks, your silver and gold, and all your property, [14] you then become haughty of heart and unmindful of the LORD, your God, who brought you out of the land of Egypt, that place of slavery; [15]* who guided you through the vast and terrible desert with its saraph serpents and scorpions, its

---

8, 4: Dt 29, 4; Neh 9, 21.   8, 15: Wis 11, 4.
8, 7: Dt 11, 10ff.

D
T

parched and waterless ground; who brought forth water for you from the flinty rock [16] and fed you in the desert with manna, a food unknown to your fathers, that he might afflict you and test you, but also make you prosperous in the end. [17]* Otherwise, you might say to yourselves, 'It is my own power and the strength of my own hand that has obtained for me this wealth.' [18] Remember then, it is the LORD, your God, who gives you the power to acquire wealth, by fulfilling, as he has now done, the covenant which he swore to your fathers. [19]* But if you forget the LORD, your God, and follow other gods, serving and worshiping them, I forewarn you this day that you will perish utterly. [20] Like the nations which the LORD destroys before you, so shall you too perish for not heeding the voice of the LORD, your God.

Unmerited Success

9 [1]* "Hear, O Israel! You are now about to cross the Jordan to enter in and dispossess nations greater and stronger than yourselves, having large cities fortified to the sky, [2]* the Anakim, a people great and tall. You know of them and have heard it said of them, 'Who can stand up against the Anakim?' [3]* Understand, then, today that it is the LORD, your God, who will cross over before you as a consuming fire; he it is who will reduce them to nothing and subdue them before you, so that you can drive them out and destroy them quickly, as the LORD promised you. [4]* After the LORD, your God, has thrust them out of your way, do not say to yourselves, 'It is because of my merits that the LORD has brought me in to possess this land'; for it is really because of the wickedness of these nations that the LORD is driving them out before you. [5] No, it is not because of your merits or the integrity of your heart that you are going in to take possession of their land; but the LORD, your God, is driving these nations out before you on account of their wickedness and in order to keep the promise which he made on oath to your fathers, Abraham, Isaac and Jacob. [6] Understand this, therefore: it is not because of your merits that the LORD, your God, is giving you this good land to possess, for you are a stiff-necked people.

The Golden Calf

[7]* "Bear in mind and do not forget how you angered the LORD, your God, in the desert. From the day you left the land of Egypt until you arrived in this place, you have been rebellious toward the LORD. [8]* At Horeb you so provoked the LORD that

he was angry enough to destroy you, [9]* when I had gone up the mountain to receive the stone tablets of the covenant which the LORD made with you. Meanwhile I stayed on the mountain forty days and forty nights without eating or drinking, [10]* till the LORD gave me the two tablets of stone inscribed, by God's own finger, with a copy of all the words that the LORD spoke to you on the mountain from the midst of the fire on the day of the assembly. [11] Then, at the end of the forty days and forty nights, when the LORD had given me the two stone tablets of the covenant, [12]* he said to me, 'Go down from here now, quickly, for your people whom you have brought out of Egypt have become depraved; they have already turned aside from the way I pointed out to them and have made for themselves a molten idol. [13] I have seen now how stiff-necked this people is,' the LORD said to me. [14] 'Let me be, that I may destroy them and blot out their name from under the heavens. I will then make of you a nation mightier and greater than they.'

[15]* "When I had come down again from the blazing, fiery mountain, with the two tablets of the covenant in both my hands, [16] I saw how you had sinned against the LORD, your God: you had already turned aside from the way which the LORD had pointed out to you by making for yourselves a molten calf! [17]* Raising the two tablets with both hands I threw them from me and broke them before your eyes. [18]* Then, as before, I lay prostrate before the LORD for forty days and forty nights without eating or drinking, because of all the sin you had committed in the sight of the LORD and the evil you had done to provoke him. [19]* For I dreaded the fierce anger of the LORD against you: his wrath would destroy you. Yet once again the LORD listened to me. [20] With Aaron, too, the LORD was deeply angry, and would have killed him had I not prayed for him also at that time. [21]* Then, taking the calf, the sinful object you had made, and fusing it with fire, I ground it down to powder as fine as dust, which I threw into the wadi that went down the mountainside.

[22]* "At Taberah, at Massah, and at Kibroth-hattaavah likewise, you provoked the LORD to anger. [23]* And when he sent you up from Kadesh-barnea to take possession of the land he was giving you, you rebelled against this command of the LORD, your God, and would not trust or obey him. [24] Ever since I have known you, you have been rebels against the LORD.

8, **17:** Dt 9, 4.
8, **19:** Dt 4, 25f; 30, 18.
9, **1:** Dt 1, 28; 4, 38.
9, **2:** Nm 13, 33.
9, **3:** Dt 31, 3; Ex 23, 27.
9, **4:** Dt 8, 17.
9, **7:** Dt 31, 27; Ex 14, 11; Nm 14, 11.
9, **8:** Ex 32, 4; Ps 106, 19.
9, **9:** Ex 24, 12.18; 34, 28.
9, **10:** Ex 31, 18.
9, **12ff:** Ex 32, 7–10.
9, **15:** Ex 32, 15.
9, **17: 16f:** Ex 32, 19.
9, **18:** Ex 32, 31; 34, 28.
9, **19:** Dt 10, 10; Ex 32, 10.
9, **21:** Ex 32, 20.
9, **22:** Ex 17, 7; Nm 11, 1ff.34.
9, **23:** Nm 14, 1–4; Ps 106, 24f.

KWANZAA AS A WAY OF LIFE

The heart of the Law is love, our love for God and God's love for us. We express that love through the values we live out. Conflicts occur when the way we rank our values comes into conflict with the way others rank their values.

For example: You may place a value on completing all your schoolwork, studying, and excelling in school. Another person sitting near you in class may not place the same high value on school. The two of you may come into conflict because this person disrupts the class and makes it difficult for you to understand what the teacher is explaining.

This is why a universal value system is important. It is why the Book of Deuteronomy has laws on everything from worship to sanitation. These laws gave the Israelites a common value system.

Kwanzaa is the name of a value system accepted by many African peoples. It was developed by Maulana Karenga after studying many different cultures throughout Africa. In 1965, he codified the unifying aspects of each of these cultures into the seven principles of Kwanzaa (also known as the Nguzo Saba). The seven principles are written in Swahili (an African trade and business language) and speak to the holistic development of the individual, family, community, nation, and race. Kwanzaa is celebrated from 26 December to 1 January. It is good that more and more African Americans are celebrating it each year, but these principles must be fully put into practice year-round as a way of life.

Kwanzaa is not a religion or a religious holiday, but it can strengthen the faith that you already practice. Look up the Bible passages listed with the following Kwanzaa principles to learn more about each one:

1. *umoja* (unity): Psalm 133; I Cor 12, 12–26
2. *kujichagulia* (self-determination): Jdt 8, 9–36
3. *ujima* (collective work and responsibility): Dt 8, 11–18
4. *ujamaa* (cooperative economics): Mt 16, 25
5. *nia* (purpose): Rom 8, 28
6. *kuumba* (creativity): Mt 25, 14–30
7. *imani* (faith): Gal 6, 9

▸ Dt 10, 12–22

25 "Those forty days, then, and forty nights, I lay prostrate before the LORD, because he had threatened to destroy you. 26 This was my prayer to him: O Lord GOD, destroy not your people, the heritage which your majesty has ransomed and brought out of Egypt with your strong hand. 27 Remember your servants, Abraham, Isaac and Jacob. Look not upon the stubbornness of this people nor upon their wickedness and sin, 28* lest the people from whose land you have brought us say, 'The LORD was not able to bring them into the land he promised them'; or 'Out of hatred for them he brought them out to slay them in the desert.' 29* They are, after all, your people and your heritage, whom you have brought out by your great power and with your outstretched arm.

10 1* "At that time the LORD said to me, 'Cut two tablets of stone like the former; then

---

9, 28: Nm 14, 14ff.   10, 1: Ex 34, 1.
9, 29: Dt 4, 20; Ex 6, 6f.

come up the mountain to me. Also make an ark of wood. ² I will write upon the tablets the commandments that were on the former tablets that you broke, and you shall place them in the ark.' ³* So I made an ark of acacia wood, and cut two tablets of stone like the former, and went up the mountain carrying the two tablets. ⁴* The LORD then wrote on them, as he had written before, the ten commandments which he spoke to you on the mountain from the midst of the fire on the day of the assembly. After the LORD had given them to me, ⁵* I turned and came down the mountain, and placed the tablets in the ark I had made. There they have remained, in keeping with the command the LORD gave me.

⁶* [The Israelites set out from Beeroth Benejaakan for Moserah, where Aaron died and was buried, his son Eleazar succeeding him in the priestly office. ⁷* From there they set out for Gudgodah, and from Gudgodah for Jotbathah, a region where there is water in the wadies.]

⁸* "At that time the LORD set apart the tribe of Levi to carry the ark of the covenant of the LORD, to be in attendance before the LORD and minister to him, and to give blessings in his name, as they have done to this day. ⁹* For this reason, Levi has no share in the heritage with his brothers; the LORD himself is his heritage, as the LORD, your God, has told him.

¹⁰ "After I had spent these other forty days and forty nights on the mountain, and the LORD had once again heard me and decided not to destroy you, ¹¹* he said to me, 'Go now and set out at the head of your people, that they may enter in and occupy the land which I swore to their fathers I would give them.'

The Lord's Majesty

¹²* "And now, Israel, what does the LORD, your God, ask of you but to fear the LORD, your God, and follow his ways exactly, to love and serve the LORD, your God, with all your heart and all your soul, ¹³ to keep the commandments and statutes of the LORD which I enjoin on you today for your own good? ¹⁴*† Think! The heavens, even the highest heavens, belong to the LORD, your God, as well as the earth and everything on it. ¹⁵* Yet in his love for your fathers the LORD was so attached to them as to

choose you, their descendants, in preference to all other peoples, as indeed he has now done. ¹⁶† Circumcise your hearts, therefore, and be no longer stiff-necked. ¹⁷* For the LORD, your God, is the God of gods, the LORD of lords, the great God, mighty and awesome, who has no favorites, accepts no bribes; ¹⁸ who executes justice for the orphan and the widow, and befriends the alien, feeding and clothing him. ¹⁹* So you too must befriend the alien, for you were once aliens yourselves in the land of Egypt. ²⁰* The LORD, your God, shall you fear, and him shall you serve; hold fast to him and swear by his name. ²¹ He is your glory, he, your God, who has done for you those great and terrible things which your own eyes have seen. ²²* Your ancestors went down to Egypt seventy strong, and now the LORD, your God, has made you as numerous as the stars of the sky.

The Wonders of the Lord

11 ¹ "Love the LORD, your God, therefore, and always heed his charge: his statutes, decrees and commandments. ² It is not your children, who have not known it from experience, but you yourselves who must now understand the discipline of the LORD, your God; his majesty, his strong hand and outstretched arm; ³* the signs and deeds he wrought among the Egyptians, on Pharaoh, king of Egypt, and on all his land; ⁴* what he did to the Egyptian army and to their horses and chariots, engulfing them in the water of the Red Sea as they pursued you, and bringing ruin upon them even to this day; ⁵ what he did for you in the desert until you arrived in this place; ⁶* and what he did to the Reubenites Dathan and Abiram, sons of Eliab, when the ground opened its mouth and swallowed them up out of the midst of Israel, with their families and tents and every living thing that belonged to them. ⁷ With your own eyes you have seen all these great deeds that the LORD has done. ⁸ Keep all the commandments, then, which I enjoin on you today, that you may be strong enough to enter in and take possession of the land into which you are crossing, ⁹ and that you may have long life on the land which the LORD swore to your fathers he would give to them and their descendants, a land flowing with milk and honey.

---

† **10, 14:** *Even the highest heavens:* literally, "and the heavens of the heavens"; compare the phrase, "the third heaven," in 2 Cor 12, 2.
10, 16: *Circumcise your hearts:* cf Dt 30, 6; Jer 4, 4; Rom 2, 29. The "uncircumcised heart" (Lv 26, 41; Jer 9, 25; Ez 44, 7.9) is closed and unreceptive to divine grace and guidance, just as "uncircumcised ears" (Jer 6, 10) are closed to sound, and "uncircumcised lips" (Ex 6, 12.30) do not open well in speech.

---

*
10, 3: Ex 34, 4.
10, 4: Ex 20, 1–17; 34, 28.
10, 5: Ex 40, 20; 1 Kgs 8, 9.
10, 6: Nm 33, 31.

10, 7: Nm 33, 32f.
10, 8: Nm 3, 6; 6, 23–27; 16, 9.
10, 9: Nm 18, 20.
10, 11: Ex 32, 34; 33, 1.
10, 12: Dt 6, 2.5.
10, 14: Neh 9, 6.
10, 15: Dt 7, 6ff.
10, 17: 2 Chr 19, 7; Jb 34, 19; Wis 6, 7; Acts 10, 34; Rom 2, 11; Gal 2, 6.

10, 19: Ex 22, 21; 23, 9; Lv 19, 33f.
10, 20: Dt 6, 13; Mt 4, 10; Lk 4, 8.
10, 22: Gn 46, 27; Ex 1, 5; Acts 7, 14.
11, 3: Dt 6, 22; Ps 78, 42–51.
11, 4: Ex 14, 26ff; 15, 9; Pss 78, 53; 106, 11.
11, 6: Nm 16, 31ff.

The Gift of Rain

10 "For the land which you are to enter and occupy is not like the land of Egypt from which you have come, where you would sow your seed and then water it by hand, as in a vegetable garden. 11* No, the land into which you are crossing for conquest is a land of hills and valleys that drinks in rain from the heavens, 12 a land which the LORD, your God, looks after; his eyes are upon it continually from the beginning of the year to the end. 13*† If, then, you truly heed my commandments which I enjoin on you today, loving and serving the LORD, your God, with all your heart and all your soul, 14† I will give the seasonal rain to your land, the early rain and the late rain, that you may have your grain, wine and oil to gather in; 15* and I will bring forth grass in your fields for your animals. Thus you may eat your fill. 16* But be careful lest your heart be so lured away that you serve other gods and worship them. 17 For then the wrath of the LORD will flare up against you and he will close up the heavens, so that no rain will fall, and the soil will not yield its crops, and you will soon perish from the good land he is giving you.

Reward of Fidelity

18* "Therefore, take these words of mine into your heart and soul. Bind them at your wrist as a sign, and let them be a pendant on your forehead. 19 Teach them to your children, speaking of them at home and abroad, whether you are busy or at rest. 20 And write them on the doorposts of your houses and on your gates, 21 so that, as long as the heavens are above the earth, you and your children may live on in the land which the LORD swore to your fathers he would give them.

22 "For if you are careful to observe all these commandments I enjoin on you, loving the LORD, your God, and following his ways exactly, and holding fast to him, 23* the LORD will drive all these nations out of your way, and you will dispossess nations greater and mightier than yourselves. 24*† Every place where you set foot shall be yours: from the desert and from Lebanon, from the Euphrates River to the Western Sea, shall be your territory. 25* None shall stand up against you; the LORD, your God, will spread the fear and dread of you through any land where you set foot, as he promised you.

A Blessing and a Curse

26* "I set before you here, this day, a blessing and a curse: 27 a blessing for obeying the commandments of the LORD, your God, which I enjoin on you today; 28 a curse if you do not obey the commandments of the LORD, your God, but turn aside from the way I ordain for you today, to follow other gods, whom you have not known. 29*† When the LORD, your God, brings you into the land which you are to enter and occupy, then you shall pronounce the blessing on Mount Gerizim, the curse on Mount Ebal. 30 [Are they not beyond the Jordan, on the other side of the western road in the country of the Canaanites who live in the Arabah, opposite the Gilgal beside the terebinth of Moreh?] 31 For you are about to cross the Jordan to enter and occupy the land which the LORD, your God, is giving you. When therefore, you take possession of it and settle there, 32 be careful to observe all the statutes and decrees that I set before you today.

III: Exposition of the Law

One Sanctuary

12 1 "These are the statutes and decrees which you must be careful to observe in the land which the LORD, the God of your fathers, has given you to occupy, as long as you live on its soil. 2* Destroy without fail every place on the high mountains, on the hills, and under every leafy tree where the nations you are to dispossess worship their gods. 3 Tear down their altars, smash their sacred pillars, destroy by fire their sacred poles, and shatter the idols of their gods, that you may stamp out the remembrance of them in any such place.

4 "That is not how you are to worship the LORD, your God. 5* Instead, you shall resort to the place which the LORD, your God, chooses out of all your tribes and designates as his dwelling 6 and there you shall bring your holocausts and sacrifices, your tithes and personal contributions, your votive and freewill offerings, and the firstlings of your herds and flocks. 7 There, too, before the LORD, your God, you and your families shall eat and make merry over all your undertakings, because the LORD, your God, has blessed you. 8 You shall not do as we are now doing; here, everyone does what seems right to himself, 9 since you have not yet reached your

---

† **11, 13ff:** As often in the Prophets, the discourse passes into the words of God himself. Cf Dt 7, 4; 17, 3; 28, 20; 29, 4f.

11, 14: *The early rain:* the rains which begin in October or November and continue intermittently throughout the winter. *The late rain:* the heavy showers of March and April. In Palestine the crops are sown in the autumn and reaped in the spring.

11, 24: *The Western Sea:* the Mediterranean.

11, 29: *You shall pronounce the blessing . . . the curse:* for the full ceremony, see chapters 27 and 28. *Gerizim . . . Ebal:* adjacent mountains in Samaria with a deep ravine between them. Their sum-

mits command an excellent view of the entire country.

11, 11f: Dt 8, 7.　　　　　**11, 26ff:** Dt 28, 2–45; 30, 1.
11, 13f: Dt 10, 12; Lv 26, 4.　　　15.19.
11, 15: Ps 104, 14.　　　　　**11, 29:** Dt 27, 12f.
11, 16f: Dt 4, 25f; 6, 14.　　　**12, 2f:** Dt 7, 5; Ex 23, 24;
11, 18–21: Dt 6, 9.　　　　　34, 13.
11, 23: Dt 7, 1; 9, 1.　　**12, 5–7.11f:** Dt 14, 22–26; 15,
11, 24: Ex 23, 31.　　　　　19f; 16, 2.10f.14f;
11, 25: Dt 2, 25; 7, 24; Ex 23,　　26, 2.
　　27.

resting place, the heritage which the LORD, your God, will give you. 10 But after you have crossed the Jordan and dwell in the land which the LORD, your God, is giving you as a heritage, when he has given you rest from all your enemies round about and you live there in security, 11 then to the place which the LORD, your God, chooses as the dwelling place for his name you shall bring all the offerings I command you: your holocausts and sacrifices, your tithes and personal contributions, and every special offering you have vowed to the LORD. 12 You shall make merry before the LORD, your God, with your sons and daughters, your male and female slaves, as well as with the Levite who belongs to your community but has no share of his own in your heritage. 13 Take care not to offer up your holocausts in any place you fancy, 14 but offer them up in the place which the LORD chooses from among your tribes; there you shall make whatever offerings I enjoin upon you.

Profane and Sacred Meals

15 "However, in any of your communities you may slaughter and eat to your heart's desire as much meat as the LORD, your God, has blessed you with; and the unclean as well as the clean may eat it, as they do the gazelle or the deer. 16* Only, you shall not partake of the blood, but must pour it out on the ground like water. 17 Moreover, you shall not, in your own communities, partake of your tithe of grain or wine or oil, of the first-born of your herd or flock, of any offering you have vowed, of your freewill offerings, or of your personal contributions. 18 These you must eat before the LORD, your God, in the place he chooses, along with your son and daughter, your male and female slave, and the Levite who belongs to your community; and there, before the LORD, you shall make merry over all your undertakings. 19* Take care, also, that you do not neglect the Levite as long as you live in the land.

20*† "After the LORD, your God, has enlarged your territory, as he promised you, when you wish meat for food, you may eat it at will, to your heart's desire; 21 and if the place which the LORD, your God, chooses for the abode of his name is too far, you may slaughter in the manner I have told you any of your herd or flock that the LORD has given you, and eat it to your heart's desire in your own community. 22 You may eat it as you would the gazelle or the deer: the unclean and the clean eating

it alike. 23 But make sure that you do not partake of the blood; for blood is life, and you shall not consume this seat of life with the flesh. 24 Do not partake of the blood, therefore, but pour it out on the ground like water. 25 Abstain from it, that you and your children after you may prosper for doing what is right in the sight of the LORD. 26 However, any sacred gifts or votive offerings that you may have, you shall bring with you to the place which the LORD chooses, 27* and there you must offer both the flesh and the blood of your holocausts on the altar of the LORD, your God; of your other sacrifices the blood indeed must be poured out against the altar of the LORD, your God, but their flesh may be eaten. 28 Be careful to heed all these commandments I enjoin on you, that you and your descendants may always prosper for doing what is good and right in the sight of the LORD, your God.

Pagan Rites

29 "When the LORD, your God, removes the nations from your way as you advance to dispossess them, be on your guard! Otherwise, once they have been wiped out before you and you have replaced them and are settled in their land, 30 you will be lured into following them. Do not inquire regarding their gods, 'How did these nations worship their gods? I, too, would do the same.' 31* You shall not thus worship the LORD, your God, because they offered to their gods every abomination that the LORD detests, even burning their sons and daughters to their gods.

Penalties for Idolatry

13 1 "Every command that I enjoin on you, you shall be careful to observe, neither adding to it nor subtracting from it.

2† "If there arises among you a prophet or a dreamer who promises you a sign or wonder, 3 urging you to follow other gods, whom you have not known, and to serve them: even though the sign or wonder he has foretold you comes to pass, 4 pay no attention to the words of that prophet or that dreamer; for the LORD, your God, is testing you to learn whether you really love him with all your heart and with all your soul. 5 The LORD, your God, shall you follow, and him shall you fear; his commandment shall you observe, and his voice shall you heed, serving him and holding fast to him alone. 6* But that prophet or that dreamer shall be put to death, because, in order to lead you astray from the way which the LORD, your God, has directed you to

---

12, 20: *Meat for food:* as on special feasts. Meat was not eaten every day in Israel, even by the wealthy.
13, 2.4.6: *Dreamer:* a false prophet who pretended to have received revelations from God in his dreams; cf Jer 23, 25–32; Zec 10, 2. But dreams could also be a channel of true prophecy (Nm 12, 6; Jl 3, 1) and of genuine revelations (Gn 20, 3.6;

31, 10.24; 37, 5.9; Mt 1, 20; 2, 12f.19; etc.).

12, 16: Dt 15, 23; Gn 9, 4; Lv	Ex 34, 24.
3, 17.	12, 27: Lv 17, 11.
12, 19: Dt 14, 27.	12, 31: Lv 18, 21; Jer 7, 31.
12, 20: Dt 19, 8; Gn 28, 14;	13, 6–10.14: Dt 6, 14; 17, 2–7.

take, he has preached apostasy from the LORD, your God, who brought you out of the land of Egypt and ransomed you from that place of slavery. Thus shall you purge the evil from your midst.

7 "If your own full brother, or your son or daughter, or your beloved wife, or your intimate friend, entices you secretly to serve other gods, whom you and your fathers have not known, 8 gods of any other nation, near at hand or far away, from one end of the earth to the other: 9 do not yield to him or listen to him, nor look with pity upon him, to spare or shield him, 10 but kill him. Your hand shall be the first raised to slay him; the rest of the people shall join in with you. 11 You shall stone him to death, because he sought to lead you astray from the LORD, your God, who brought you out of the land of Egypt, that place of slavery. 12 And all Israel, hearing of it, shall fear and never again do such evil as this in your midst.

13 "If, in any of the cities which the LORD, your God, gives you to dwell in, you hear it said 14 that certain scoundrels have sprung up among you and have led astray the inhabitants of their city to serve other gods whom you have not known, 15 you must inquire carefully into the matter and investigate it thoroughly. If you find that it is true and an established fact that this abomination has been committed in your midst, 16* you shall put the inhabitants of that city to the sword, dooming the city and all life that is in it, even its cattle, to the sword. 17 Having heaped up all its spoils in the middle of its square, you shall burn the city with all its spoils as a whole burnt offering to the LORD, your God. Let it be a heap of ruins forever, never to be rebuilt. 18 You shall not retain anything that is doomed, that the blazing wrath of the LORD may die down and he may show you mercy and in his mercy for you may multiply you as he promised your fathers on oath; 19 because you have heeded the voice of the LORD, your God, keeping all his commandments which I enjoin on you today, doing what is right in his sight.

Pagan Mourning Rites

14 1* "You are children of the LORD, your God. You shall not gash yourselves nor shave the hair above your foreheads for the dead. 2* For you are a people sacred to the LORD, your God, who has chosen you from all the nations on the face of the earth to be a people peculiarly his own.

Clean and Unclean Animals

3* "You shall not eat any abominable thing.

4* These are the animals you may eat: the ox, the sheep, the goat, 5† the red deer, the gazelle, the roe deer, the ibex, the addax, the oryx, and the mountain sheep. 6 Any animal that has hoofs you may eat, provided it is cloven-footed and chews the cud. 7 But you shall not eat any of the following that only chew the cud or only have cloven hoofs: the camel, the hare and the rock badger, which indeed chew the cud, but do not have hoofs and are therefore unclean for you; 8* and the pig, which indeed has hoofs and is cloven-footed, but does not chew the cud and is therefore unclean for you. Their flesh you shall not eat, and their dead bodies you shall not touch.

14, 3–21

9 "Of the various creatures that live in the water, whatever has both fins and scales you may eat, 10 but all those that lack either fins or scales you shall not eat; they are unclean for you.

11 "You may eat all clean birds. 12 But you shall not eat any of the following: the eagle, the vulture, the osprey, 13 the various kites and falcons, 14 all the various species of crows, 15 the ostrich, the nightjar, the gull, the various species of hawks, 16 the owl, the screech owl, the ibis, 17 the desert owl, the buzzard, the cormorant, 18 the stork, the various species of herons, the hoopoe, and the bat. 19† All winged insects, too, are unclean for you and shall not be eaten. 20 But you may eat any clean winged creatures.

---

† **14, 5:** *The gazelle, the addax, the oryx:* species of antelopes. *The ibex:* a species of wild goat.
14, 19f: The apparent contradiction is to be resolved in the light of Lv 11, 20–23; the unclean winged insects are those that walk on the ground; the clean winged creatures are those that leap on the ground, such as certain species of locusts.

* **13, 16f:** Jos 6, 18.24; 7, 26; 8, 28.
14, 1: Lv 19, 28.
14, 2: Dt 7, 6.
14, 3: Ez 4, 14; Acts 10, 14.
14, 4–20: Lv 11, 2–23.
14, 8: Lv 11, 26.

21*† "You must not eat any animal that has died of itself, for you are a people sacred to the LORD, your God. But you may give it to an alien who belongs to your community, and he may eat it, or you may sell it to a foreigner.

"You shall not boil a kid in its mother's milk.

Tithes

22* "Each year you shall tithe all the produce that grows in the field you have sown; 23* then in the place which the LORD, your God, chooses as the dwelling place of his name you shall eat in his presence your tithe of the grain, wine and oil, as well as the firstlings of your herd and flock, that you may learn always to fear the LORD, your God. 24† If, however, the journey is too much for you and you are not able to bring your tithe, because the place which the LORD, your God, chooses for the abode of his name is too far for you, considering how the LORD has blessed you, 25 you may exchange the tithe for money and, with the purse of money in hand, go to the place which the LORD, your God, chooses. 26 You may then exchange the money for whatever you desire, oxen or sheep, wine or strong drink, or anything else you would enjoy, and there before the LORD, your God, you shall partake of it and make merry with your family. 27* But do not neglect the Levite who belongs to your community, for he has no share in the heritage with you.

28 "At the end of every third year you shall bring out all the tithes of your produce for that year and deposit them in community stores, 29* that the Levite who has no share in the heritage with you, and also the alien, the orphan and the widow who belong to your community, may come and eat their fill; so that the LORD, your God, may bless you in all that you undertake.

Debts and the Poor

15 1*† "At the end of every seven-year period you shall have a relaxation of debts, 2 which shall be observed as follows. Every creditor shall relax his claim on what he has loaned his neighbor; he must not press his neighbor, his kinsman, because a relaxation in honor of the LORD has been proclaimed. 3* You may press a foreigner, but you shall relax the claim on your kinsman for what

is yours. 4 Nay, more! since the LORD, your God, will bless you abundantly in the land he will give you to occupy as your heritage, there should be no one of you in need. 5 If you but heed the voice of the LORD, your God, and carefully observe all these commandments which I enjoin on you today, 6* you will lend to many nations, and borrow from none; you will rule over many nations, and none will rule over you, since the LORD, your God, will bless you as he promised. 7 If one of your kinsmen in any community is in need in the land which the LORD, your God, is giving you, you shall not harden your heart nor close your hand to him in his need. 8* Instead, you shall open your hand to him and freely lend him enough to meet his need. 9 Be on your guard lest, entertaining the mean thought that the seventh year, the year of relaxation, is near, you grudge help to your needy kinsman and give him nothing; else he will cry to the LORD against you and you will be held guilty. 10 When you give to him, give freely and not with ill will; for the LORD, your God, will bless you for this in all your works and undertakings. 11*† The needy will never be lacking in the land; that is why I command you to open your hand to your poor and needy kinsman in your country.

Hebrew Slaves

12* "If your kinsman, a Hebrew man or woman, sells himself to you, he is to serve you for six years, but in the seventh year you shall dismiss him from your service, a free man. 13 When you do so, you shall not send him away empty-handed, 14 but shall weight him down with gifts from your flock and threshing floor and wine press, in proportion to the blessing the LORD, your God, has bestowed on you. 15* For remember that you too were once slaves in the land of Egypt, and the LORD, your God, ransomed you. That is why I am giving you this command today. 16 If, however, he tells you that he does not wish to leave you, because he is devoted to you and your household, since he fares well with you, 17*† you shall take an awl and thrust it through his ear into the door, and he shall then be your slave forever. Your female slave, also, you shall treat in the same way. 18 You must not be reluctant to let your slave go free, since the service he has given you

---

14, 21: *Boil a kid in its mother's milk:* see note on Ex 23, 19.

14, 24: *Considering how the LORD has blessed you:* should the Israelite farmer be blessed with an abundant harvest, a tenth of this would be too much to transport for a great distance.

15, 1: *At the end of every seven-year period:* in every seventh, or sabbatical, year. Cf Dt 15, 9; 31, 10; and compare Jer 34, 14 with Dt 15, 12. *A relaxation of debts:* it is uncertain whether a full cancellation of debts is meant, or merely a suspension of payment on them or on their interest among the Israelites. Cf Ex 23, 11 where the same Hebrew root is used of a field that is "let lie fallow" in the sabbatical year.

15, 11: *The needy will never be lacking:* compare the words of Christ, "The poor you have always with you" (Mt 26, 11).

15, 17: *His ear:* cf Ex 21, 6 and the note there.

14, 21: Ex 22, 30; 23, 19; 34, 26.
14, 22: Lv 27, 30.
14, 23f: Dt 12, 5ff.
14, 27: Dt 12, 12.19.
14, 29: 28f: Dt 26, 12.
15, 1: Neh 10, 31.
15, 3: Dt 23, 20.

15, 6: Dt 28, 12f.
15, 8: Lv 25, 35; Sir 29, 1f; Mt 5, 42.
15, 11: Dt 15, 8; Sir 29, 12.
15, 12: Ex 21, 2; Jer 34, 14.
15, 15: Dt 5, 15.
15, 17: 16f: Ex 21, 5f.

for six years was worth twice a hired man's salary; then also the LORD, your God, will bless you in everything you do.

Firstlings

19* "You shall consecrate to the LORD, your God, all the male firstlings of your herd and of your flock. You shall not work the firstlings of your cattle, nor shear the firstlings of your flock. 20* Year after year you and your family shall eat them before the LORD, your God, in the place he chooses. 21 If, however, a firstling is lame or blind or has any other serious defect, you shall not sacrifice it to the LORD, your God, 22 but in your own communities you may eat it, the unclean and the clean eating it alike, as you would a gazelle or a deer. 23* Only, you shall not partake of its blood, which must be poured out on the ground like water.

Feast of the Passover

16 1*† "Observe the month of Abib by keeping the Passover of the LORD, your God, since it was in the month of Abib that he brought you by night out of Egypt. 2 You shall offer the Passover sacrifice from your flock or your herd to the LORD, your God, in the place which he chooses as the dwelling place of his name. 3* You shall not eat leavened bread with it. For seven days you shall eat with it only unleavened bread, the bread of affliction, that you may remember as long as you live the day of your departure from the land of Egypt; for in frightened haste you left the land of Egypt. 4 Nothing leavened may be found in all your territory for seven days, and none of the meat which you sacrificed on the evening of the first day shall be kept overnight for the next day.

5 "You may not sacrifice the Passover in any of the communities which the LORD, your God, gives you; 6 only at the place which he chooses as the dwelling place of his name, and in the evening at sunset, on the anniversary of your departure from Egypt, shall you sacrifice the Passover. 7 You shall cook and eat it at the place the LORD, your God, chooses; then in the morning you may return to your tents. 8 For six days you shall eat unleavened bread, and on the seventh there shall be a solemn meeting in honor of the LORD, your God; on that day you shall not do any sort of work.

Feast of Weeks

9* "You shall count off seven weeks, computing them from the day when the sickle is first put to the standing grain. 10† You shall then keep the feast of Weeks in honor of the LORD, your God, and the measure of your own freewill offering shall be in proportion to the blessing the LORD, your God, has bestowed on you. 11* In the place which the LORD, your God, chooses as the dwelling place of his name, you shall make merry in his presence together with your son and daughter, your male and female slave, and the Levite who belongs to your community, as well as the alien, the orphan and the widow among you. 12 Remember that you too were once slaves in Egypt, and carry out these statutes carefully.

Feast of Booths

13*† "You shall celebrate the feast of Booths for seven days, when you have gathered in the produce from your threshing floor and wine press. 14* You shall make merry at your feast, together with your son and daughter, your male and female slave, and also the Levite, the alien, the orphan and the widow who belong to your community. 15 For seven days you shall celebrate this pilgrim feast in honor of the LORD, your God, in the place which he chooses; since the LORD, your God, has blessed you in all your crops and in all your undertakings, you shall do naught but make merry.

16* "Three times a year, then, every male among you shall appear before the LORD, your God, in the place which he chooses: at the feast of Unleavened Bread, at the feast of Weeks, and at the feast of Booths. No one shall appear before the LORD empty-handed, 17 but each of you with as much as he can give, in proportion to the blessings which the LORD, your God, has bestowed on you.

Judges

18 "You shall appoint judges and officials throughout your tribes to administer true justice for the people in all the communities which the LORD, your God, is giving you. 19* You shall not distort justice; you must be impartial. You shall not take a bribe; for a bribe blinds the eyes even of the wise and twists the words even of the just. 20 Justice and justice alone shall be your aim, that you may have life and may possess the land which the LORD, your God, is giving you.

16, 1: *Abib:* "ear of grain, ripe grain," the name of the month in which the barley harvest fell, corresponding to our March and April; at a later period this month received the Babylonian name of "Nisan."

16, 10: *Feast of Weeks:* later known more commonly as "Pentecost."

16, 13: See note on Lv 23, 34.

15, 19: Ex 13, 11.
15, 20: Dt 14, 23.
15, 23: 21ff: Dt 12, 15f; Lv 22, 20.
16, 1–8: Ex 12, 2–20; 23, 15; Nm 28, 16ff.24f.
16, 3f: Ex 13, 6f; 34, 18.
16, 9–12: Lv 23, 15–21.

16, 11: Dt 12, 5.7.12.18.
16, 13–15: Ex 23, 16; Lv 23, 34–43; Nm 29, 12–38.
16, 14: Dt 16, 11.
16, 16: Ex 23, 14f.17; 34, 23; 2 Chr 8, 13.
16, 19: Dt 1, 17; Ex 23, 8.

Pagan Worship

21*† "You shall not plant a sacred pole of any kind of wood beside the altar of the LORD, your God, which you will build; 22† nor shall you erect a sacred pillar, such as the LORD, your God, detests.

17

1* "You shall not sacrifice to the LORD, your God, from the herd or from the flock an animal with any serious defect; that would be an abomination to the LORD, your God.

2* "If there is found among you, in any one of the communities which the LORD, your God, gives you, a man or a woman who does evil in the sight of the LORD, your God, and transgresses his covenant, 3* by serving other gods, or by worshiping the sun or the moon or any of the host of the sky, against my command; 4 and if, on being informed of it, you find by careful investigation that it is true and an established fact that this abomination has been committed in Israel: 5† you shall bring the man (or woman) who has done the evil deed out to your city gates and stone him to death. 6* The testimony of two or three witnesses is required for putting a person to death; no one shall be put to death on the testimony of only one witness. 7* At the execution, the witnesses are to be the first to raise their hands against him; afterward all the people are to join in. Thus shall you purge the evil from your midst.

Judges

8 "If in your own community there is a case at issue which proves too complicated for you to decide, in a matter of bloodshed or of civil rights or of personal injury, you shall then go up to the place which the LORD, your God, chooses, 9* to the levitical priests or to the judge who is in office at that time. They shall study the case and then hand down to you their decision. 10 According to this decision that they give you in the place which the LORD chooses, you shall act, being careful to do exactly as they direct. 11 You shall carry out the directions they give you and the verdict they pronounce for you, without turning aside to the right or to the left from the decision they hand down to you. 12† Any man who has the insolence to refuse to listen to the priest who officiates there in the ministry of the

---

?did you KNOW?

The Torah

The Hebrew word Torah means "instruction" or "teaching," and only over time has come to mean "the Law." Torah refers most fundamentally to the Law that was recorded as given by God to Moses on Mount Sinai. As the people of Israel lived the Torah, it became equated with their very life and existence. It was the key for their organization as a people and gave consistency to their struggle to live their Covenant with God.

Jewish people refer to the first five books of the Bible (the Pentateuch) as the Torah because those books contain the Law and instructions on how to live it. The other books of the Old Testament are also strongly connected to the Torah. The historical books record how the people and their kings kept the Torah or disobeyed it. When they obeyed, they were blessed with happiness, health, and prosperity. When they disobeyed, they were punished with barrenness, destruction, and death. The prophets in the prophetic books call the people to faithfulness to the Law. They condemn idolatry and injustice and call the people to live the spirit of the Torah.

What law are Christians called to live by? For a hint, see the Letter of Paul to the Galatians and the Letter of James.

▸ **Dt 17, 8–11**

LORD, your God, or to the judge, shall die. Thus shall you purge the evil from your midst. 13 And all the people, on hearing of it, shall fear, and never again be so insolent.

---

† **16, 21—17, 7:** This section seems to be out of its proper place, since it interrupts the natural sequence of the laws for the judges (Dt 16, 18—20 and 17, 8—13). It probably belongs to the similar section, Dt 12, 29—14, 2.

16, 22: 21f: *Sacred pole . . . sacred pillar:* see note on Ex 34, 13.

17, 5: *Out to your city gates:* outside the gates in an unclean place; cf Lv 24, 14; Nm 15, 36; Acts 7, 58; Heb 13, 12.

17, 12: *The priest:* the high priest; *the judge:* a layman. The for-

mer presided over the court in cases which directly concerned religion, the latter in cases of a more secular nature; cf 2 Chr 19, 8–11.

16, 21: 1 Kgs 14, 15; 2 Chr 33, 3.
17, 1: Lv 22, 20.
17, 2–7: Dt 13, 6–15.
17, 3: Dt 4, 19.

17, 6: Dt 19, 15; Nm 35, 30; Mt 18, 16; Jn 8, 17; 2 Cor 13, 1.
17, 7: Dt 13, 10.
17, 9: Dt 21, 5; 2 Chr 19, 8.

The King

14* "When you have come into the land which the LORD, your God, is giving you, and have occupied it and settled in it, should you then decide to have a king over you like all the surrounding nations, 15* you shall set that man over you as your king whom the LORD, your God, chooses. He whom you set over you as king must be your kinsman; a foreigner, who is no kin of yours, you may not set over you. 16*† But he shall not have a great number of horses; nor shall he make his people go back again to Egypt to acquire them, against the LORD's warning that you must never go back that way again. 17* Neither shall he have a great number of wives, lest his heart be estranged, nor shall he accumulate a vast amount of silver and gold. 18* When he is enthroned in his kingdom, he shall have a copy of this law made from the scroll that is in the custody of the levitical priests. 19 He shall keep it with him and read it all the days of his life that he may learn to fear the LORD, his God, and to heed and fulfill all the words of this law and these statutes. 20 Let him not become estranged from his countrymen through pride, nor turn aside to the right or to the left from these commandments. Then he and his descendants will enjoy a long reign in Israel.

Priests

18 1* "The whole priestly tribe of Levi shall have no share in the heritage with Israel; they shall live on the oblations of the LORD and the portions due to him. 2 Levi shall have no heritage among his brothers; the LORD himself is his heritage, as he has told him. 3 The priests shall have a right to the following things from the people: from those who are offering a sacrifice, whether the victim is from the herd or from the flock, the priest shall receive the shoulder, the jowls and the stomach. 4* You shall also give him the first fruits of your grain and wine and oil, as well as the first fruits of the shearing of your flock; 5 for the LORD, your God, has chosen him and his sons out of all your tribes to be always in attendance to minister in the name of the LORD.

6 "When a Levite goes from one of your communities anywhere in Israel in which he ordinarily resides, to visit, as his heart may desire, the place which the LORD chooses, 7 he may minister there in the name of the LORD, his God, like all his fellow Levites who are in attendance there before the LORD. 8 He shall then receive the same portions to eat as the rest, along with his monetary offerings and heirlooms.

Prophets

9* "When you come into the land which the LORD, your God, is giving you, you shall not learn to imitate the abominations of the peoples there. 10*† Let there not be found among you anyone who immolates his son or daughter in the fire, nor a fortune-teller, soothsayer, charmer, diviner, 11 or caster of spells, nor one who consults ghosts and spirits or seeks oracles from the dead. 12* Anyone who does such things is an abomination to the LORD, and because of such abominations the LORD, your God, is driving these nations out of your way. 13 You, however, must be altogether sincere toward the LORD, your God. 14 Though these nations whom you are to dispossess listen to their soothsayers and fortune-tellers, the LORD, your God, will not permit you to do so.

15*† "A prophet like me will the LORD, your God, raise up for you from among your own kinsmen; to him you shall listen. 16* This is exactly what you requested of the LORD, your God, at Horeb on the day of the assembly, when you said, 'Let us not again hear the voice of the LORD, our God, nor see this great fire any more, lest we die.' 17 And the LORD said to me, 'This was well said. 18 I will raise up for them a prophet like you from among their kinsmen, and will put my words into his mouth; he shall tell them all that I command him. 19* If any man will not listen to my words which he speaks in my name, I myself will make him answer for it. 20* But if a prophet presumes to speak in my name an ora-

---

17, 16: *Horses:* chariotry for war. *The LORD's warning:* the same warning is also referred to in Dt 28, 68, although it is not mentioned explicitly elsewhere in the Pentateuch. We know from other sources that Egypt used to export war horses to Palestine. The danger envisioned here is that some king might make Israel a vassal of Egypt for the sake of such military aid.

18, 10f: *Immolates his son or daughter in the fire:* to Molech. See note on Lv 18, 21. Such human sacrifices are classed here with other pagan superstitions because they were believed to possess magical powers for averting a calamity; cf 2 Kgs 3, 27. Three other forms of superstition are listed here: augury (by a fortune-teller, a soothsayer or a diviner); black magic (by a charmer . . . or caster of spells); and necromancy (by one who consults ghosts and spirits or seeks oracles from the dead).

18, 15: *A prophet like me:* from the context (opposition to the pagan soothsayers) it seems that Moses is referring in general to all

the true prophets who were to succeed him. But since Christ is the Great Prophet in whom the prophetic office finds its fulfillment and completion, this passage was understood in a special Messianic sense both by the Jews (Jn 6, 14; 7, 40) and by the Apostles (Acts 3, 22; 7, 37).

17, 14: 1 Sm 8, 5.19f.
17, 15: 1 Sm 9, 16; 10, 24; 16, 12.
17, 16: Dt 28, 68; 1 Kgs 4, 26; 10, 26.
17, 17: 1 Kgs 11; 3f; Neh 13, 26.
17, 18: Dt 31, 9.26.
18, 1: Nm 18, 8f.20–24; 1 Cor 9, 13.
18, 4: Nm 18, 12; 2 Chr 31, 5.

18, 9: Dt 12, 29ff; Lv 18, 26–30.
18, 10f: Lv 18, 21; 19, 31; 20, 27; 1 Sm 28, 7; 2 Kgs 17, 17; 21, 6.
18, 12: Dt 9, 4.
18, 15: Jn 1, 45; 6, 14; Acts 3, 22; 7, 37.
18, 16: Ex 20, 19.
18, 19: Acts 3, 23.
18, 20.22: Dt 13, 2ff.

cle that I have not commanded him to speak, or speaks in the name of other gods, he shall die.'

²¹ "If you say to yourselves, 'How can we recognize an oracle which the LORD has spoken?', ²² know that, even though a prophet speaks in the name of the LORD, if his oracle is not fulfilled or verified, it is an oracle which the LORD did not speak. The prophet has spoken it presumptuously, and you shall have no fear of him.

Cities of Refuge

19 ¹ "When the LORD, your God, removes the nations whose land he is giving you, and you have taken their place and are settled in their cities and houses, ²*† you shall set apart three cities in the land which the LORD, your God, is giving you to occupy. ³ You shall thereby divide into three regions the land which the LORD, your God, will give you as a heritage, and so arrange the routes that every homicide will be able to find a refuge.

⁴* "It is in the following case that a homicide may take refuge in such a place to save his life: when someone unwittingly kills his neighbor to whom he had previously borne no malice. ⁵ For example, if he goes with his neighbor to a forest to cut wood, and as he swings his ax to fell a tree, its head flies off the handle and hits his neighbor a mortal blow, he may take refuge in one of these cities to save his life. ⁶† Should the distance be too great, the avenger of blood may in the heat of his anger pursue the homicide and overtake him and strike him dead, even though he does not merit death since he had previously borne the slain man no malice. ⁷ That is why I order you to set apart three cities.

⁸* "But if the LORD, your God, enlarges your territory, as he swore to your fathers, and gives you all the land he promised your fathers he would give ⁹ in the event that you carefully observe all these commandments which I enjoin on you today, loving the LORD, your God, and ever walking in his ways: then add three cities to these three. ¹⁰ Thus, in the land which the LORD, your God, is giving you as a heritage, innocent blood will not be shed and you will not become guilty of bloodshed.

¹¹* "However, if someone lies in wait for his neighbor out of hatred for him, and rising up against him, strikes him mortally, and then takes refuge in one of these cities, ¹² the elders of his own city shall send for him and have him taken from there, and shall hand him over to be slain by the avenger of blood. ¹³ Do not look on him with pity, but purge from Israel the stain of shedding innocent blood, that you may prosper.

Removal of Landmarks

¹⁴* "You shall not move your neighbor's landmarks erected by your forefathers in the heritage you receive in the land which the LORD, your God, is giving you to occupy.

False Witnesses

¹⁵* "One witness alone shall not take the stand against a man in regard to any crime or any offense of which he may be guilty; a judicial fact shall be established only on the testimony of two or three witnesses.

¹⁶ "If an unjust witness takes the stand against a man to accuse him of a defection from the law, ¹⁷* the two parties in the dispute shall appear before the LORD in the presence of the priests or judges in office at that time; ¹⁸ and if after a thorough investigation the judges find that the witness is a false witness and has accused his kinsman falsely, ¹⁹* you shall do to him as he planned to do to his kinsman. Thus shall you purge the evil from your midst. ²⁰ The rest, on hearing of it, shall fear, and never again do a thing so evil among you. ²¹* Do not look on such a man with pity. Life for life, eye for eye, tooth for tooth, hand for hand, and foot for foot!

Courage in War

20 ¹ "When you go out to war against your enemies and you see horses and chariots and an army greater than your own, do not be afraid of them, for the LORD, your God, who brought you up from the land of Egypt, will be with you.

² "When you are about to go into battle, the priest shall come forward and say to the soldiers: ³ 'Hear, O Israel! Today you are going into battle against your enemies. Be not weakhearted or afraid; be neither alarmed nor frightened by them. ⁴* For it is the LORD, your God, who goes with you to fight for you against your enemies and give you victory.'

⁵* "Then the officials shall say to the soldiers, 'Is

19, 2: *Set apart three cities:* the Israelites were to have at least six cities of refuge, three in the land east of the Jordan and three in the land of Canaan west of the Jordan (Nm 35, 9–34); but since the three cities east of the Jordan had now been appointed (Dt 4, 41–43), reference is made here only to the three west of the Jordan. The execution of this command is narrated in Jos 20.
19, 6: *The avenger of blood:* see note on Nm 35, 12.

19, 2: Dt 4, 41ff; Ex 21, 13; Nm 35, 10–15; Jos 20, 2.8.
19, 4: Dt 4, 42; Nm 35, 15; Jos 20, 3.5.
19, 8: Gn 15, 18–21; 28, 14; Ex 23, 31; 34, 24.
19, 11ff: Ex 21, 12.14; Nm 35, 20f.
19, 14: Dt 27, 17; Prv 23, 10; Hos 5, 10.
19, 15: Dt 17, 6; Nm 35, 30; Mt 18, 16; Jn 8, 17; 2 Cor 13, 1.
19, 17: Dt 17, 8f.
19, 19: 18f; Dn 13, 61f.
19, 21: Ex 21, 23f; Lv 24, 20; Mt 5, 38.
20, 4: Dt 1, 30; 3, 22; Jos 23, 10.
20, 5ff: 1 Mc 3, 56.

Facing Life's Battles

What are the wars in your life? Where do you experience conflict and lack of peace? We all hope that we will not face war in armed conflict. But in a sense, war is around us in the conflicts of everyday life.

We have fights with family and friends. We battle the pressures of society and our peers. We are at odds with the future. Deuteronomy 20, 1 tells us that we are not to fear times of war because our God is with us and will be our strength.

When we face conflict, our faith will be tested, but we must hold strong and true to what God tells us. If we let our heart be filled with God, the wars that we face will become opportunities for God's love to triumph.

What conflicts do you encounter these days? Do you sense that God is with you in these conflicts? If so, how? Pray for peace-filled ways to resolve conflict.

▶ **Dt 20, 1**

there anyone who has built a new house and not yet had the housewarming? Let him return home, lest he die in battle and another dedicate it. 6 Is there anyone who has planted a vineyard and never yet enjoyed its fruits? Let him return home, lest he die in battle and another enjoy its fruits in his stead. 7* Is there anyone who has betrothed a woman and not yet taken her as his wife? Let him return home, lest he die in battle and another take her to wife.' 8* In fine, the officials shall say to the soldiers, 'Is there anyone who is afraid and weakhearted? Let him return home, lest he make his fellows as fainthearted as himself.'

9 "When the officials have finished speaking to the soldiers, military officers shall be appointed over the army.

Cities of the Enemy

10 "When you march up to attack a city, first offer it terms of peace. 11 If it agrees to your terms of peace and opens its gates to you, all the people to be found in it shall serve you in forced labor. 12 But if it refuses to make peace with you and instead offers you battle, lay siege to it, 13 and when the LORD, your God, delivers it into your hand, put every male in it to the sword; 14* but the women and children and livestock and all else in it that is worth plundering you may take as your booty, and you may use this plunder of your enemies which the LORD, your God, has given you.

15 "That is how you shall deal with any city at a considerable distance from you, which does not belong to the peoples of this land. 16 But in the cities of those nations which the LORD, your God, is giving you as your heritage, you shall not leave a single soul alive. 17* You must doom them all— the Hittites, Amorites, Canaanites, Perizzites, Hivites and Jebusites—as the LORD, your God, has commanded you, 18 lest they teach you to make any such abominable offerings as they make to their gods, and you thus sin against the LORD, your God.

Trees of a Besieged City

19 "When you are at war with a city and have to lay siege to it for a long time before you capture it, you shall not destroy its trees by putting an ax to them. You may eat their fruit, but you must not cut down the trees. After all, are the trees of the field men, that they should be included in your siege? 20 However, those trees which you know are not fruit trees you may destroy, cutting them down to build siegeworks with which to reduce the city that is resisting you.

Expiation of Untraced Murder

21 1† "If the corpse of a slain man is found lying in the open on the land which the LORD, your God, is giving you to occupy, and it is not known who killed him, 2 your elders and judges shall go out and measure the distances to the cities that are in the neighborhood of the corpse. 3 When it

---

† **21, 1–9:** This paragraph is best read immediately after Dt 19, 21. The slain man may not necessarily have been murdered; he may have been killed by a wild beast. But the blood of the slain cries out to God from the soil where it was shed; cf Gn 4, 10. Therefore a religious ceremony of propitiation is here prescribed in order to avert God's anger on the community.

* 20, 7: Dt 24, 5.   20, 17: 16f: Dt 7, 1f; Jos 10, 40;
  20, 8: Jgs 7, 3.   11, 14.
20, 14: 13f: Nm 31, 7.9.11;
        Jos 22, 8.

is established which city is nearest the corpse, the elders of that city shall take a heifer that has never been put to work as a draft animal under a yoke, [4]† and bringing it down to a wadi with an ever-flowing stream at a place that has not been plowed or sown, they shall cut the heifer's throat there in the wadi. [5]* The priests, the descendants of Levi, shall also be present, for the LORD, your God, has chosen them to minister to him and to give blessings in his name, and every case of dispute or violence must be settled by their decision. [6]† Then all the elders of that city nearest the corpse shall wash their hands over the heifer whose throat was cut in the wadi, [7]† and shall declare, 'Our hands did not shed this blood, and our eyes did not see the deed. [8] Absolve, O LORD, your people Israel, whom you have ransomed, and let not the guilt of shedding innocent blood remain in the midst of your people Israel.' Thus they shall be absolved from the guilt of bloodshed, [9] and you shall purge from your midst the guilt of innocent blood, that you may prosper for doing what is right in the sight of the LORD.

Marriage with a Female Captive

[10] "When you go out to war against your enemies and the LORD, your God, delivers them into your hand, so that you take captives, [11] if you see a comely woman among the captives and become so enamored of her that you wish to have her as wife, [12]† you may take her home to your house. But before she may live there, she must shave her head and pare her nails [13] and lay aside her captive's garb. After she has mourned her father and mother for a full month, you may have relations with her, and you shall be her husband and she shall be your wife. [14] However, if later on you lose your liking for her, you shall give her her freedom, if she wishes it; but you shall not sell her or enslave her, since she was married to you under compulsion.

Rights of the First-born

[15] "If a man with two wives loves one and dislikes the other; and if both bear him sons, but the first-born is of her whom he dislikes: [16] when he comes to bequeath his property to his sons he may not consider as his first-born the son of the wife he loves, in preference to his true first-born, the son of the wife whom he dislikes. [17] On the contrary, he shall recognize as his first-born the son of her whom he dislikes, giving him a double share of whatever he happens to own, since he is the first fruits of his manhood, and to him belong the rights of the first-born.

The Incorrigible Son

[18] "If a man has a stubborn and unruly son who will not listen to his father or mother, and will not obey them even though they chastise him, [19]† his father and mother shall have him apprehended and brought out to the elders at the gate of his home city, [20] where they shall say to those city elders, 'This son of ours is a stubborn and unruly fellow who will not listen to us; he is a glutton and a drunkard.' [21] Then all his fellow citizens shall stone him to death. Thus shall you purge the evil from your midst, and all Israel, on hearing of it, shall fear.

Corpse of a Criminal

[22]† "If a man guilty of a capital offense is put to death and his corpse hung on a tree, [23]*† it shall not remain on the tree overnight. You shall bury it the same day; otherwise, since God's curse rests on him who hangs on a tree, you will defile the land which the LORD, your God, is giving you as an inheritance.

Care for Lost Animals

22

[1]* "You shall not see your kinsman's ox or sheep driven astray without showing concern about it; see to it that it is returned to your kinsman. [2] If this kinsman does not live near you, or you do not know who he may be, take it to your own place and keep it with you until he claims it; then give it back to him. [3] You shall do the same with his ass, or his garment, or anything else which your kinsman loses and you happen to find; you may not be unconcerned about them. [4] You shall not see your kinsman's ass or ox foundering on the road without showing concern about it; see to it that you help him lift it up.

DT

21, 4: *They shall cut the heifer's throat in the wadi:* its blood is to be carried away by the stream, signifying thereby the removal of the human blood from the soil. This is not a sacrifice but a symbolic action; the priests are present merely as official witnesses.

21, 6: *Wash their hands:* a symbolic gesture in protestation of one's own innocence when human blood is unjustly shed; cf Mt 27, 24.

21, 7: *This blood:* the blood of the slain man as symbolized by the heifer's blood.

21, 12f: *Shave her head . . . :* these symbolic actions are meant to signify the purification of the woman from her pagan defilement or perhaps the end of her period of mourning for her previous husband.

21, 19: *The gate:* in the city walls. This open space served as the forum for the administration of justice. Cf Dt 22, 15; 25, 7; Ru 4, 1f.11; Is 29, 21; Am 5, 10.12.15.

21, 22: *Hung on a tree:* some understand, "impaled on a stake." In any case the hanging or impaling was not the means used to execute the criminal; he was first put to death by the ordinary means, stoning, and his corpse was then exposed on high as a salutary warning for others. Cf Jos 8, 29; 10, 26; 1 Sm 31, 10; 2 Sm 21, 9.

21, 23: *God's curse rests on him who hangs on a tree:* St. Paul quotes these words in Gal 3, 13, where he applies them to the crucified Savior, who "redeemed us from the curse of the law, becoming a curse for us."

21, 5: Dt 19, 17.   22, 1–4: Ex 23, 4f.
21, 23: Gal 3, 13.

Various Precepts

5 "A woman shall not wear an article proper to a man, nor shall a man put on a woman's dress; for anyone who does such things is an abomination to the LORD, your God.

6 "If, while walking along, you chance upon a bird's nest with young birds or eggs in it, in any tree or on the ground, and the mother bird is sitting on them, you shall not take away the mother bird along with her brood; 7 you shall let her go, although you may take her brood away. It is thus that you shall have prosperity and a long life.

8 "When you build a new house, put a parapet around the roof; otherwise, if someone falls off, you will bring blood-guilt upon your house.

9*† "You shall not sow your vineyard with two different kinds of seed; if you do, its produce shall become forfeit, both the crop you have sown and the yield of the vineyard. 10 You shall not plow with an ox and an ass harnessed together. 11 You shall not wear cloth of two different kinds of thread, wool and linen, woven together.

12*† "You shall put twisted cords on the four corners of the cloak that you wrap around you.

Crimes against Marriage

13 "If a man, after marrying a woman and having relations with her, comes to dislike her, 14 and makes monstrous charges against her and defames her by saying, 'I married this woman, but when I first had relations with her I did not find her a virgin,' 15† the father and mother of the girl shall take the evidence of her virginity and bring it to the elders at the city gate. 16 There the father of the girl shall say to the elders, 'I gave my daughter to this man in marriage, but he has come to dislike her, 17 and now brings monstrous charges against her, saying: I did not find your daughter a virgin. But here is the evidence of my daughter's virginity!' And they shall spread out the cloth before the elders of the city. 18† Then these city elders shall take the man and chastise him, 19 besides fining him one hundred silver shekels, which they shall give to the girl's father, because the man defamed a virgin in Israel. Moreover, she shall remain his wife, and he may not divorce her as long as he lives.

20 "But if this charge is true, and evidence of the girl's virginity is not found, 21 they shall bring the girl to the entrance of her father's house and there her townsmen shall stone her to death, because she committed a crime against Israel by her unchasteness in her father's house. Thus shall you purge the evil from your midst.

22* "If a man is discovered having relations with a woman who is married to another, both the man and the woman with whom he has had relations shall die. Thus shall you purge the evil from your midst.

23† "If within the city a man comes upon a maiden who is betrothed, and has relations with her, 24 you shall bring them both out to the gate of the city and there stone them to death: the girl because she did not cry out for help though she was in the city, and the man because he violated his neighbor's wife. Thus shall you purge the evil from your midst.

25 "If, however, it is in the open fields that a man comes upon such a betrothed maiden, seizes her and has relations with her, the man alone shall die. 26 You shall do nothing to the maiden, since she is not guilty of a capital offense. This case is like that of a man who rises up against his neighbor and murders him: 27 it was in the open fields that he came upon her, and though the betrothed maiden may have cried out for help, there was no one to come to her aid.

28* "If a man comes upon a maiden that is not betrothed, takes her and has relations with her, and their deed is discovered, 29 the man who had relations with her shall pay the girl's father fifty silver shekels and take her as his wife, because he has deflowered her. Moreover, he may not divorce her as long as he lives.

23

1† "A man shall not marry his father's wife, nor shall he dishonor his father's bed.

Membership in the Community

2 "No one whose testicles have been crushed or whose penis has been cut off, may be admitted into the community of the LORD. 3 No child of an incestuous union may be admitted into the community of the LORD, nor any descendant of his even to the tenth generation. 4* No Ammonite or Moabite may ever be admitted into the community of the LORD, nor any descendants of theirs even to the tenth generation, 5* because they would not succor you with food and water on your journey after you left Egypt, and because Moab hired Balaam, son of Beor, from

---

† 　**22, 9:** *Become forfeit:* to the sanctuary; cf Lv 19, 19; Jos 6, 19.
　22, 12: *Twisted cords:* referred to as "tassels" on "violet cords" in Nm 15, 38. See note there.
　22, 15: *The evidence of her virginity:* the bridal garment or sheet stained with a little blood from the first nuptial relations.
　22, 18: *Chastise him:* flog him, as prescribed in Dt 25, 1–3.
　22, 23: *A maiden who is betrothed:* a girl who is married but not

yet brought to her husband's home and whose marriage is therefore still unconsummated.
　23, 1: *Father's wife:* stepmother. *Dishonor:* cf Dt 27, 20.

22, 9: Dt 9.11, Lv 19, 19.	**22, 28f:** Ex 22, 16.
22, 12: Nm 15, 38; Mt 23, 5.	**23, 4:** Neh 13, 1f.
22, 22: Lv 20, 10; Jn 8, 4f.	**23, 5:** Nm 24, 10.

DT

Pethor in Aram Naharaim, to curse you; ⁶ though the LORD, your God, would not listen to Balaam and turned his curse into a blessing for you, because he loves you. ⁷ Never promote their peace and prosperity as long as you live. ⁸* But do not abhor the Edomite, since he is your brother, nor the Egyptian, since you were an alien in his country. ⁹ Children born to them may in the third generation be admitted into the community of the LORD.

Cleanliness in Camp

¹⁰ "When you are in camp during an expedition against your enemies, you shall keep yourselves from everything offensive. ¹¹ If one of you becomes unclean because of a nocturnal emission, he shall go outside the camp, and not return until, ¹² toward evening, he has bathed in water; then, when the sun has set, he may come back into the camp. ¹³ Outside the camp you shall have a place set aside to be used as a latrine. ¹⁴ You shall also keep a trowel in your equipment and with it, when you go outside to ease nature, you shall first dig a hole and afterward cover up your excrement. ¹⁵ Since the LORD, your God, journeys along within your camp to defend you and to put your enemies at your mercy, your camp must be holy; otherwise, if he sees anything indecent in your midst, he will leave your company.

Various Precepts

¹⁶ "You shall not hand over to his master a slave who has taken refuge from him with you. ¹⁷† Let him live with you wherever he chooses, in any one of your communities that pleases him. Do not molest him.

¹⁸*† "There shall be no temple harlot among the Israelite women, nor a temple prostitute among the Israelite men. ¹⁹ You shall not offer a harlot's fee or a dog's price as any kind of votive offering in the house of the LORD, your God; both these things are an abomination to the LORD, your God.

²⁰* "You shall not demand interest from your countrymen on a loan of money or of food or of anything else on which interest is usually demanded. ²¹ You may demand interest from a foreigner,

but not from your countryman, so that the LORD, your God, may bless you in all your undertakings on the land you are to enter and occupy.

²² "When you make a vow to the LORD, your God, you shall not delay in fulfilling it; otherwise you will be held guilty, for the LORD, your God, is strict in requiring it of you. ²³ Should you refrain from making a vow, you will not be held guilty. ²⁴ But you must keep your solemn word and fulfill the votive offering you have freely promised to the LORD.

²⁵ "When you go through your neighbor's vineyard, you may eat as many of his grapes as you wish, but do not put them in your basket. ²⁶ When you go through your neighbor's grainfield, you may pluck some of the ears with your hand, but do not put a sickle to your neighbor's grain.

Marriage Laws

24 ¹† "When a man, after marrying a woman and having relations with her, is later displeased with her because he finds in her something indecent, and therefore he writes out a bill of divorce and hands it to her, thus dismissing her from his house: ² if on leaving his house she goes and becomes the wife of another man, ³ and the second husband, too, comes to dislike her and dismisses her from his house by handing her a written bill of divorce; ⁴ or if this second man who has married her, dies; then her former husband, who dismissed her, may not again take her as his wife after she has become defiled. That would be an abomination before the LORD, and you shall not bring such guilt upon the land which the LORD, your God, is giving you as a heritage.

⁵* "When a man is newly wed, he need not go out on a military expedition, nor shall any public duty be imposed on him. He shall be exempt for one year for the sake of his family, to bring joy to the wife he has married.

Justice, Equity and Charity

⁶† "No one shall take a hand mill or even its upper stone as a pledge for debt, for he would be taking the debtor's sustenance as a pledge.

D
T

23, 17: *In any one of your communities:* from this it would seem that the slave in question is a fugitive from a foreign country.

23, 18f: The pagans believed that they could enter into special relationship with their gods and goddesses by having sexual relations with the pagan priests and priestesses who prostituted themselves for this purpose. The money paid for this was considered a sort of votive offering made to the pagan sanctuary. Such abominations were naturally forbidden in Israel. *A dog's price:* the money paid the pagan priest for his indecent service.

24, 1–4: This law is directly concerned only with forbidding divorced couples to remarry each other, and indirectly with checking hasty divorces, by demanding sufficient cause and certain legal formalities. Divorce itself is taken for granted and tolerated as an existing custom whose evils this law seeks to lessen. Cf Dt 22, 19.29; Mal

2, 14ff. Christ gave the authentic interpretation of this law: "Moses, by reason of the hardness of your heart, permitted you to put away your wives; but it was not so from the beginning" (Mt 19, 8f).

24, 1: *Something indecent:* a rather indefinite phrase, meaning perhaps "immodest conduct." At the time of Christ the rabbis differed in opinion concerning the sufficient grounds for divorce; cf Mt 19, 3.

24, 6: Since the Israelites ground their grain into flour only in sufficient quantity for their current need, to deprive a debtor of his hand mill was virtually equivalent to condemning him to starve to death.

23, 8: Gn 25, 24ff.   23, 20: Ex 22, 25; Lv 25, 37;
23, 18: 1 Kgs 14, 24; 22, 46;   Lk 6, 34f.
    2 Kgs 23, 7.   24, 5: Dt 20, 7.

7* "If any man is caught kidnaping a fellow Is-raelite in order to enslave him and sell him, the kid-naper shall be put to death. Thus shall you purge the evil from your midst.

8* "In an attack of leprosy you shall be careful to observe exactly and to carry out all the directions of the levitical priests. Take care to act in accordance with the instructions I have given them. 9* Remem-ber what the LORD, your God, did to Miriam on the journey after you left Egypt.

10† "When you make a loan of any kind to your neighbor, you shall not enter his house to receive a pledge from him, 11 but shall wait outside until the man to whom you are making the loan brings his pledge outside to you. 12 If he is a poor man, you shall not sleep in the mantle he gives as a pledge, 13* but shall return it to him at sunset that he him-self may sleep in it. Then he will bless you, and it will be a good deed of yours before the LORD, your God.

14 "You shall not defraud a poor and needy hired servant, whether he be one of your own country-men or one of the aliens who live in your commu-nities. 15* You shall pay him each day's wages before sundown on the day itself, since he is poor and looks forward to them. Otherwise he will cry to the LORD against you, and you will be held guilty.

16* "Fathers shall not be put to death for their children, nor children for their fathers; only for his own guilt shall a man be put to death.

17* "You shall not violate the rights of the alien or of the orphan, nor take the clothing of a widow as a pledge. 18 For, remember, you were once slaves in Egypt, and the LORD, your God, ransomed you from there; that is why I command you to observe this rule.

19* "When you reap the harvest in your field and overlook a sheaf, you shall not go back to get it; let it be for the alien, the orphan or the widow, that the LORD, your God, may bless you in all your undertakings. 20 When you knock down the fruit of your olive trees, you shall not go over the branches a second time; let what remains be for the alien, the orphan and the widow. 21 When you pick your grapes, you shall not go over the vineyard a second time; let what remains be for the alien, the orphan, and the widow. 22 For remember that you were once slaves in Egypt; that is why I command you to ob-serve this rule.

? did you KNOW?

The Poor, the Strangers, the Widows, and the Orphans

One remarkable aspect of Israel's Cov-enant was the command to care for the poor, the "aliens" or strangers, the widows, and the orphans. These four groups were the outsiders in ancient Israel because they fell outside Israel's socioeconomic system. The poor often had no means to sustain themselves. Strangers, or aliens, were not part of Israel's tribal organiza-tion. Widows depended on the charity of others. Orphans were destitute because they had no family to help them survive.

God provides a reason why Israel must care for the poor and oppressed. Just as the Israelites were enslaved in Egypt—when they were poor, oppressed, orphans in a foreign land—and God responded to their cry for help, so they must care for the poor, oppressed, forgotten, and mar-ginalized in their midst. Can this be any less true for us today?

▶ Dt 24, 10–21

25 1 "When men have a dispute and bring it to court, and a decision is handed down to them acquitting the innocent party and condemning the guilty party, 2 if the latter de-serves stripes, the judge shall have him lie down and in his presence receive the number of stripes his guilt deserves. 3*† Forty stripes may be given him, but no more; lest, if he were beaten with more stripes than these, your kinsman should be looked upon as disgraced because of the severity of the beating.

24, 10f: The debtor had the right to select the pledge that the creditor demanded as a guarantee for his loan.

25, 3: *Forty stripes:* a relatively mild punishment in ancient times. Later Jewish practice limited the number to thirty-nine; cf 2 Cor 11, 24.

24, 7: Ex 21, 16.
24, 8: Lv 13, 1–14.
24, 9: Nm 12, 10–15.
24, 13: Ex 22, 26.
24, 15: 14f: Lv 19, 13; Tb 4, 15; Sir 34, 25f; Jer 22, 13.
24, 16: 2 Kgs 14, 6; 2 Chr 25, 4; Ez 18, 20.
24, 17: Ex 22, 22; 23, 9.
24, 19ff: Lv 19, 9f; 23, 22.
25, 3: 2 Cor 11, 24.

[4]*† "You shall not muzzle an ox when it is treading out grain.

Levirate Marriage

[5]*† "When brothers live together and one of them dies without a son, the widow of the deceased shall not marry anyone outside the family; but her husband's brother shall go to her and perform the duty of a brother-in-law by marrying her. [6]* The first-born son she bears shall continue the line of the deceased brother, that his name may not be blotted out from Israel. [7] If, however, a man does not care to marry his brother's wife, she shall go up to the elders at the gate and declare, 'My brother-in-law does not intend to perform his duty toward me and refuses to perpetuate his brother's name in Israel.' [8] Thereupon the elders of his city shall summon him and admonish him. If he persists in saying, 'I am not willing to marry her,' [9]† his sister-in-law, in the presence of the elders, shall go up to him and strip his sandal from his foot and spit in his face, saying publicly, 'This is how one should be treated who will not build up his brother's family!' [10] And his lineage shall be spoken of in Israel as 'the family of the man stripped of his sandal.'

Various Precepts

[11] "When two men are fighting and the wife of one intervenes to save her husband from the blows of his opponent, if she stretches out her hand and seizes the latter by his private parts, [12] you shall chop off her hand without pity.

[13]* "You shall not keep two differing weights in your bag, one large and the other small; [14] nor shall you keep two different measures in your house, one large and the other small. [15] But use a true and just weight, and a true and just measure, that you may have a long life on the land which the LORD, your God, is giving you. [16] Everyone who is dishonest in any of these matters is an abomination to the LORD, your God.

[17]*† "Bear in mind what Amalek did to you on the journey after you left Egypt, [18] how without fear of any god he harassed you along the way, weak and weary as you were, and cut off at the rear all those who lagged behind. [19]* Therefore, when the LORD, your God, gives you rest from all your enemies round about in the land which he is giving you to occupy as your heritage, you shall blot out the memory of Amalek from under the heavens. Do not forget!

Thanksgiving for the Harvest

26 [1] "When you have come into the land which the LORD, your God, is giving you as a heritage, and have occupied it and settled in it, [2]* you shall take some first fruits of the various products of the soil which you harvest from the land which the LORD, your God, gives you, and putting them in a basket, you shall go to the place which the LORD, your God, chooses for the dwelling place of his name. [3] There you shall go to the priest in office at that time and say to him, 'Today I acknowledge to the LORD, my God, that I have indeed come into the land which he swore to our fathers he would give us.' [4] The priest shall then receive the basket from you and shall set it in front of the altar of the LORD, your God. [5]*† Then you shall declare before the LORD, your God, 'My father was a wandering Aramean who went down to Egypt with a small household and lived there as an alien. But there he became a nation great, strong and numerous. [6]* When the Egyptians maltreated and oppressed us, imposing hard labor upon us, [7] we cried to the LORD, the God of our fathers, and he heard our cry and saw our affliction, our toil and our oppression. [8]* He brought us out of Egypt with his strong hand and outstretched arm, with terrifying power, with signs and wonders; [9]* and bringing us into this country, he gave us this land flowing with milk and honey. [10] Therefore, I have now brought you the first fruits of the products of the soil which you, O LORD, have given me.' And having set them before the LORD, your God, you shall bow down in his presence. [11]* Then you and your family,

---

25, 4: St Paul argues from this verse that a laborer has the right to live on the fruits of his labor; cf 1 Cor 9, 9; 1 Tm 5, 18.

25, 5: *When brothers live together:* when relatives of the same clan, though married, hold their property in common. It was only in this case that the present law was to be observed, since one of its purposes was to keep the property of the deceased within the same clan. Such a marriage of a widow with her brother-in-law is known as a "levirate" marriage from the Latin word *levir*, meaning "a husband's brother."

25, 9f: The penalty decreed for a man who refuses to comply with this law of family loyalty is public disgrace (the widow is to spit in his face) and the curse of poverty; sandals were proverbially a man's cheapest possession (cf Am 2, 6; 8, 6), and therefore "a man without sandals" was the poorest of the poor. Some commentators, however, connect this symbolic act with the ceremony mentioned in Ru 4, 7f.

25, 17–19: This attack on Israel by Amalek is not mentioned elsewhere in the Old Testament, although it probably was connected with the battle mentioned in Ex 17, 8. A campaign against Amalek was carried out by Saul; cf 1 Sm 15.

26, 5: *Aramean:* either in reference to the origin of the patriarchs from Aram Naharaim (cf Gn 24, 10; 25, 20; 28, 5; 31, 20.24), or merely in the sense of "nomad," in the same way as "Arab" was later used; cf Jer 3, 2.

25, 4: 1 Cor 9, 9; 1 Tm 5, 18.
25, 5: Mt 22, 24; Mk 12, 19; Lk 20, 28.
25, 6–9: Ru 4, 5–10.
25, 13ff: Lv 19, 35f; Prv 16, 11; Ez 45, 10; Ml 6, 11.
25, 17: Ex 17, 8.
25, 19: Ex 17, 14; 1 Sm 15, 2f.

26, 2: Ex 23, 19; 34, 26.
26, 5: Gn 46, 6f; Acts 7, 14f.
26, 6f: Ex 1, 8–22; 2, 23ff; 3, 9; Nm 20, 15f.
26, 8: Ex 12, 51.
26, 9: Ex 3, 8.
26, 11: Dt 12, 7.12.

together with the Levite and the aliens who live among you, shall make merry over all these good things which the LORD, your God, has given you.

Prayer with the Tithes

12*† "When you have finished setting aside all the tithes of your produce in the third year, the year of the tithes, and you have given them to the Levite, the alien, the orphan and the widow, that they may eat their fill in your own community, 13 you shall declare before the LORD, your God, 'I have purged my house of the sacred portion and I have given it to the Levite, the alien, the orphan and the widow, just as you have commanded me. In this I have not broken or forgotten any of your commandments: 14† I have not eaten any of the tithe as a mourner; I have not brought any of it out as one unclean; I have not offered any of it to the dead. I have thus hearkened to the voice of the LORD, my God, doing just as you have commanded me. 15 Look down, then, from heaven, your holy abode, and bless your people Israel and the soil you have given us in the land flowing with milk and honey which you promised on oath to our fathers.'

The Covenant

16 "This day the LORD, your God, commands you to observe these statutes and decrees. Be careful, then, to observe them with all your heart and with all your soul. 17* Today you are making this agreement with the LORD: he is to be your God and you are to walk in his ways and observe his statutes, commandments and decrees, and to hearken to his voice. 18* And today the LORD is making this agreement with you: you are to be a people peculiarly his own, as he promised you; and provided you keep all his commandments, 19 he will then raise you high in praise and renown and glory above all other nations he has made, and you will be a people sacred to the LORD, your God, as he promised."

IV: Final Words of Moses

Ceremonies

27 1 Then Moses, with the elders of Israel, gave the people this order: "Keep all these commandments which I enjoin on you today. 2 On the day you cross the Jordan into the land which the LORD, your God, is giving you, set up some large stones and coat them with plaster.

3* Also write on them, at the time you cross, all the words of this law, that you may thus enter into the land flowing with milk and honey, which the LORD, your God, and the God of your fathers, is giving you as he promised you. 4 When, moreover, you have crossed the Jordan, besides setting up on Mount Ebal these stones concerning which I command you today, and coating them with plaster, 5* you shall also build to the LORD, your God, an altar made of stones that no iron tool has touched. 6 You shall make this altar of the LORD, your God, with undressed stones, and shall offer on it holocausts to the LORD, your God. 7 You shall also sacrifice peace offerings and eat them there, making merry before the LORD, your God. 8† On the stones you shall inscribe all the words of this law very clearly."

9* Moses, with the levitical priests, then said to all Israel: "Be silent, O Israel, and listen! This day you have become the people of the LORD, your God. 10 You shall therefore hearken to the voice of the LORD, your God, and keep his commandments and statutes which I enjoin on you today."

11 That same day Moses gave the people this order: 12* "When you cross the Jordan, Simeon, Levi, Judah, Issachar, Joseph and Benjamin shall stand on Mount Gerizim to pronounce blessings over the people, 13 while Reuben, Gad, Asher, Zebulun, Dan and Naphtali shall stand on Mount Ebal to pronounce curses.

The Twelve Curses

14 "The Levites shall proclaim aloud to all the men of Israel: 15*† 'Cursed be the man who makes a carved or molten idol—an abomination to the LORD, the product of a craftsman's hands—and sets it up in secret!' And all the people shall answer, 'Amen!'

16* 'Cursed be he who dishonors his father or his mother!' And all the people shall answer, 'Amen!'

17* 'Cursed be he who moves his neighbor's landmarks!' And all the people shall answer, 'Amen!'

18* 'Cursed be he who misleads a blind man on his way!' And all the people shall answer, 'Amen!'

19* 'Cursed be he who violates the rights of the alien, the orphan or the widow!' And all the people shall answer, 'Amen!'

20* 'Cursed be he who has relations with his father's wife, for he dishonors his father's bed!' And all the people shall answer, 'Amen!'

---

† **26, 12:** *And you have given them to the Levite . . . :* as prescribed in Dt 14, 28f.
26, 14: These are allusions to pagan religious practices.
27, 8: *On the stones:* cf vv 3f; not the stones of the altar.
27, 15–26: *Amen:* see note on Nm 5, 22.

26, 12: Dt 14, 28f.
26, 17: Ex 24, 7.
26, 18f: Dt 7, 6; 14, 2; 28, 1; Ex 19, 5.
27, 3: Jos 8, 32.
27, 5: Ex 20, 25; Jos 8, 31.
27, 9: Dt 26, 17ff.
27, 12f: Dt 11, 29; Jos 8, 33f.

27, 15: Ex 20, 4.23; Lv 19, 4; Wis 14, 8.
27, 16: Dt 21, 18–21; Ex 21, 17; Lv 20, 9.
27, 17: Dt 19, 14.
27, 18: Lv 19, 14.
27, 19: Dt 24, 17; Ex 22, 21f.
27, 20: Dt 22; 23, 1; Lv 18, 8; 20, 11.

21* 'Cursed be he who has relations with any animal!' And all the people shall answer, 'Amen!'

22* 'Cursed be he who has relations with his sister or his half-sister!' And all the people shall answer, 'Amen!'

23* 'Cursed be he who has relations with his mother-in-law!' And all the people shall answer, 'Amen!'

24* 'Cursed be he who slays his neighbor in secret!' And all the people shall answer, 'Amen!'

25 'Cursed be he who accepts payment for slaying an innocent man!' And all the people shall answer, 'Amen!'

26* 'Cursed be he who fails to fulfill any of the provisions of this law!' And all the people shall answer, 'Amen!'

Blessings for Obedience

28 †1* "Thus, then, shall it be:* if you continue to heed the voice of the LORD, your God, and are careful to observe all his commandments which I enjoin on you today, the LORD, your God, will raise you high above all the nations of the earth.* 2 When you hearken to the voice of the LORD, your God, all these blessings will come upon you and overwhelm you:

3   "May you be blessed in the city,
    and blessed in the country!
4* "Blessed be the fruit of your womb,
    the produce of your soil and the offspring
      of your livestock,
    the issue of your herds and the young of
      your flocks!
5   "Blessed be your grain bin and your
    kneading bowl!
6† "May you be blessed in your coming in,
    and blessed in your going out!

Victory and Prosperity

7† "The LORD will beat down before you the enemies that rise up against you; though they come out against you from but one direction, they will flee before you in seven. 8 The LORD will affirm his blessing upon you, on your barns and on all your undertakings, blessing you in the land that the LORD, your God, gives you. 9* Provided that you

keep the commandments of the LORD, your God, and walk in his ways, he will establish you as a people sacred to himself, as he swore to you; 10*† so that, when all the nations of the earth see you bearing the name of the LORD, they will stand in awe of you. 11 The LORD will increase in more than goodly measure the fruit of your womb, the offspring of your livestock, and the produce of your soil, in the land which he swore to your fathers he would give you. 12* The LORD will open up for you his rich treasure house of the heavens, to give your land rain in due season, blessing all your undertakings, so that you will lend to many nations and borrow from none. 13† The LORD will make you the head,

Catholic Connections

HAIL MARY

Deuteronomy 28, 4 might sound familiar to you. These words, also found in Lk 1, 42, are part of a prayer called the Hail Mary. In this passage, Moses reminds the Israelites that they shall be blessed because of their obedience, and Mary is the ultimate example of the blessings that come from obedience to God's will.

▶ Dt 28, 1–6

not the tail, and you will always mount higher and not decline, as long as you obey the commandments of the LORD, your God, which I order you today to observe carefully; 14 not turning aside to

---

† **28, 1–69:** This chapter would read better immediately after chapter 26.

28, 6: *In your coming in . . . in your going out:* at the beginning and end of every action, or in all actions in general.

28, 7.25: *From but one direction . . . in seven:* in one compact mass, contrasted with many scattered groups.

28, 10: *You bearing the name of the LORD:* literally, "The LORD's name is called over you," an expression signifying ownership and protection. Cf 2 Sm 12, 28; 1 Kgs 8, 43; Is 4, 1; 63, 19; Jer 7, 10f; 14, 9; 15, 16; 25, 29; Am 9, 12.

28, 13: *The head, not the tail:* in the honorable position as leader. Cf Is 9, 14; 19, 15.

27, 21: Ex 22, 18; Lv 18, 23; 20, 15.	28, 1–68: Lv 26, 1–45.
27, 22: Lv 18, 9; 20, 17.	28, 1–14: Dt 7, 12–16.
27, 23: Lv 18, 17; 20, 14.	28, 1: Dt 26, 19.
27, 24: Ex 20, 13; 21, 12; Nm 35, 20f.	28, 4: Dt 7, 13; 30.9.
	28, 9: Dt 26, 18; Ex 19, 5f.
27, 26: Gal 3, 10.	28, 10: Dt 2, 25; 11, 25.
	28, 12: Dt 15, 6.

the right or to the left from any of the command-ments which I now give you, in order to follow other gods and serve them.

Curses for Disobedience

15* "But if you do not hearken to the voice of the LORD, your God, and are not careful to observe all his commandments which I enjoin on you today, all these curses shall come upon you and over-whelm you:

16   "May you be cursed in the city,
         and cursed in the country!

17   "Cursed be your grain bin and your
         kneading bowl!

18   "Cursed be the fruit of your womb,
         the produce of your soil and the offspring
            of your livestock,
         the issue of your herds and the young of
            your flocks!

19   "May you be cursed in your coming in,
         and cursed in your going out!

Sickness and Defeat

20 "The LORD will put a curse on you, defeat and frustration in every enterprise you undertake, until you are speedily destroyed and perish for the evil you have done in forsaking me. 21 The LORD will bring a pestilence upon you that will persist until he has exterminated you from the land you are en-tering to occupy. 22 The LORD will strike you with wasting and fever, with scorching, fiery drought, with blight and searing wind, that will plague you until you perish. 23* The sky over your heads will be like bronze and the earth under your feet like iron. 24 For rain the LORD will give your land powdery dust, which will come down upon you from the sky until you are destroyed. 25* The LORD will let you be beaten down before your enemies; though you advance against them from one direction, you will flee before them in seven, so that you will become a terrifying example to all the kingdoms of the earth. 26 Your carcasses will become food for all the birds of the air and for the beasts of the field, with no one to frighten them off. 27* The LORD will strike you with Egyptian boils and with tumors, eczema and the itch, until you cannot be cured.

28 And the LORD will strike you with madness, blindness and panic, 29 so that even at midday you will grope like a blind man in the dark, unable to find your way.

Despoilment

"You will be oppressed and robbed continually, with no one to come to your aid. 30 Though you be-troth a wife, another man will have her. Though you build a house, you will not live in it. Though you plant a vineyard, you will not enjoy its fruits. 31 Your ox will be slaughtered before your eyes, and you will not eat of its flesh. Your ass will be stolen in your presence, but you will not recover it. Your flocks will be given to your enemies, with no one to come to your aid. 32 Your sons and daughters will be given to a foreign nation while you look on and grieve for them in constant helplessness. 33 A peo-ple whom you do not know will consume the fruit of your soil and of all your labor, and you will be oppressed and crushed at all times without surcease, 34 until you are driven mad by what your eyes must look upon. 35† The LORD will strike you with malignant boils of which you cannot be cured, on your knees and legs, and from the soles of your feet to the crown of your head.

Exile

36* "The LORD will bring you, and your king whom you have set over you, to a nation which you and your fathers have not known, and there you will serve strange gods of wood and stone, 37 and will call forth amazement, reproach and barbed scorn from all the nations to which the LORD will lead you.

Fruitless Labors

38* "Though you spend much seed on your field, you will harvest but little, for the locusts will devour the crop. 39* Though you plant and cultivate vine-yards, you will not drink or store up the wine, for the grubs will eat the vines clean. 40* Though you have olive trees throughout your country, you will have no oil for ointment, for your olives will drop off unripe. 41* Though you beget sons and daugh-ters, they will not remain with you, but will go into captivity. 42 Buzzing insects will infest all your trees and the crops of your soil. 43 The alien residing among you will rise higher and higher above you,

---

28, 35: This verse is best read with v 27.

28, 15: Bar 1, 20; Dn 9, 11;
    Mal 2, 2.
28, 23: 22f: Lv 26, 19.
28, 25: Lv 26, 17.37.

28, 27: Ex 9, 9ff.
28, 36: 1 Kgs 9, 7ff; 2 Chr 7,
    20ff; 33, 11; 36, 6.20.
28, 38: Mi 6, 15; Hg 1, 6.
28, 39: Zep 1, 13.
28, 40: Mi 6, 15.
28, 41: Lam 1, 5.

DT

while you sink lower and lower. 44 He will lend to you, not you to him. He will become the head, you the tail.

45 "All these curses will come upon you, pursuing you and overwhelming you, until you are destroyed, because you would not hearken to the voice of the LORD, your God, nor keep the commandments and statutes he gave you. 46† They will light on you and your descendants as a sign and a wonder for all time. 47 Since you would not serve the LORD, your God, with joy and gratitude for abundance of every kind, 48 therefore in hunger and thirst, in nakedness and utter poverty, you will serve the enemies whom the LORD will send against you. He will put an iron yoke on your neck, until he destroys you.

Invasion and Siege

49* "The LORD will raise up against you a nation from afar, from the end of the earth, that swoops down like an eagle, a nation whose tongue you do not understand, 50 a nation of stern visage, that shows neither respect for the aged nor pity for the young. 51 They will consume the offspring of your livestock and the produce of your soil, until you are destroyed; they will leave you no grain or wine or oil, no issue of your herds or young of your flocks, until they have brought about your ruin. 52 They will besiege you in each of your communities, until the great, unscalable walls you trust in come tumbling down all over your land. They will so besiege you in every community throughout the land which the LORD, your God, has given you, 53* that in the distress of the siege to which your enemy subjects you, you will eat the fruit of your womb, the flesh of your own sons and daughters whom the LORD, your God, has given you. 54 The most refined and fastidious man among you will begrudge his brother and his beloved wife and his surviving children 55 any share in the flesh of his children that he himself is using for food when nothing else is left him in the straits of the siege to which your enemy will subject you in all your communities. 56 The most refined and delicate woman among you, so delicate and refined that she would not venture to set the sole of her foot on the ground, will begrudge her beloved husband

and her son and daughter 57 the afterbirth that issues from her womb and the infant she brings forth when she secretly uses them for food for want of anything else, in the straits of the siege to which your enemy will subject you in your communities.

Plagues

58 "If you are not careful to observe every word of the law which is written in this book, and to revere the glorious and awesome name of the LORD, your God, 59 he will smite you and your descendants with severe and constant blows, malignant and lasting maladies. 60*† He will again afflict you with all the diseases of Egypt which you dread, and they will persist among you. 61 Should there be any kind of sickness or calamity not mentioned in this book of the law, that too the LORD will bring upon you until you are destroyed. 62* Of you who were numerous as the stars in the sky, only a few will be left, because you would not hearken to the voice of the LORD, your God.

Exile

63* "Just as the LORD once took delight in making you grow and prosper, so will he now take delight in ruining and destroying you, and you will be plucked out of the land you are now entering to occupy. 64* The LORD will scatter you among all the nations from one end of the earth to the other, and there you will serve strange gods of wood and stone, such as you and your fathers have not known. 65† Among these nations you will find no repose, not a foot of ground to stand upon, for there the LORD will give you an anguished heart and wasted eyes and a dismayed spirit. 66 You will live in constant suspense and stand in dread both day and night, never sure of your existence. 67 In the morning you will say, 'Would that it were evening!' and in the evening you will say, 'Would that it were morning!' for the dread that your heart must feel and the sight that your eyes must see. 68*† The LORD will send you back in galleys to Egypt, to the region I told you that you were never to see again; and there you will offer yourselves for sale to your enemies as male and female slaves, but there will be no buyer."

D
T

† **28, 46:** *A sign and a wonder:* an ominous example, attracting attention; cf Dt 29, 21–28.

28, 60: *He will again afflict you with all the diseases of Egypt:* such as the Lord had promised to remove from his people; cf Dt 7, 15.

28, 65: *Wasted eyes:* worn out and disappointed in their longing gaze.

28, 68: *In galleys:* in the ships of the Phoenician slave traders (Ez 27, 13; Jl 4, 6; Am 1, 9), who also dealt with Egypt (Is 23, 3).

*
28, 49–52: Jer 5, 15ff; Bar 4, 15f.　　28, 62: Dt 1, 10; Jer 42, 2.
　28, 53: Lv 26, 29; 2 Kgs 6,　　28, 63: Dt 30, 9.
　　　28f; Jer 19, 9; Lam 4,　　28, 64: Lv 26, 33.
　　　10; Bar 2, 3.　　　　28, 68: Hos 8, 13; 9, 3.
　28, 60: Dt 28, 27.

69 These are the words of the covenant which the LORD ordered Moses to make with the Israelites in the land of Moab, in addition to the covenant which he made with them at Horeb.

Past Favors Recalled

29 1 Moses summoned all Israel and said to them, "You have seen all that the LORD did in the land of Egypt before your very eyes to Pharaoh and all his servants and to all his land; 2* the great testings your own eyes have seen, and those great signs and wonders. 3† But not even at the present day has the LORD yet given you a mind to understand, or eyes to see, or ears to hear. 4* 'I led you for forty years in the desert. Your clothes did not fall from you in tatters nor your sandals from your feet; 5 bread was not your food, nor wine or beer your drink. Thus you should know that I, the LORD, am your God.' 6* When we came to this place, Sihon, king of Heshbon, and Og, king of Bashan, came out to engage us in battle, but we defeated them 7* and took over their land, which we then gave as a heritage to the Reubenites, Gadites, and half the tribe of Manasseh. 8 Keep the terms of this covenant, therefore, and fulfill them, that you may succeed in whatever you do.

All Israel Bound to the Covenant

9 "You are all now standing before the LORD, your God—your chiefs and judges, your elders and officials, and all of the men of Israel, 10 together with your wives and children and the aliens who live in your camp, down to those who hew wood and draw water for you— 11† that you may enter into the covenant of the LORD, your God, which he concluded with you today under this sanction of a curse; 12 so that he may now establish you as his people and he may be your God, as he promised you and as he swore to your fathers Abraham, Isaac and Jacob. 13 But it is not with you alone that I am making this covenant, under this sanction of a curse; 14† it is just as much with those who are not here among us today as it is with those of us who are now here present before the LORD, our God.

Warning against Idolatry

15 "You know in what surroundings we lived in the land of Egypt and what we passed by in the nations we traversed, 16 and you saw the loathsome idols of wood and stone, of gold and silver, that they possess. 17 Let there be, then, no man or woman, no clan or tribe among you, who would now turn away their hearts from the LORD, our God, to go and serve these pagan gods! Let there be no root that would bear such poison and wormwood among you! 18† If any such person, upon hearing the words of this curse, should beguile himself into thinking that he can safely persist in his stubbornness of heart, as though to sweep away both the watered soil and the parched ground, 19 the LORD will never consent to pardon him. Instead, the LORD's wrath and jealousy will flare up against that man, and every curse mentioned in this book will alight on him. The LORD will blot out his name from under the heavens 20 and will single him out from all the tribes of Israel for doom, in keeping with all the curses of the covenant inscribed in this book of the law.

Punishment for Infidelity

21 "Future generations, your own descendants who will rise up after you, as well as the foreigners who will come here from far-off lands, when they see the calamities of this land and the ills with which the LORD has smitten it— 22* all its soil being nothing but sulphur and salt, a burnt-out waste, unsown and unfruitful, without a blade of grass, destroyed like Sodom and Gomorrah, Admah and Zeboiim, which the LORD overthrew in his furious wrath— 23* they and all the nations will ask, 'Why has the LORD dealt thus with this land? Why this fierce outburst of wrath?' 24 And the answer will be, 'Because they forsook the covenant which the LORD, the God of their fathers, had made with them when he brought them out of the land of Egypt, 25 and they went and served other gods and adored them, gods whom they did not know and whom he had not let fall to their lot; 26 that is why the LORD was angry with this land and brought on it all the imprecations listed in this book; 27* in his furious

---

29, 3: *Eyes to see . . . ears to hear:* with inner, spiritual discernment. Cf Mt 13, 43.

29, 11: *Sanction of a curse:* the present pact binds under penalty of the curses mentioned in this book. Cf v 20.

29, 14: *Not here among us:* this includes their descendants.

29, 18: *To sweep away both the watered soil and the parched ground:* apparently a proverb signifying that such an unfaithful Israelite will cause God to punish the good with the wicked, to root

out the good plants growing in irrigated soil, together with the worthless plants growing in the dry ground.

29, 2: Dt 4, 34; Ex 19, 4.
29, 4: Dt 8, 2.4.
29, 6: Dt 2, 24.32; 3, 1; Nm 21, 33ff.
29, 7: Dt 3, 16; Nm 32, 33.
29, 22: Gn 14, 10f; 19, 24f.
29, 23f: 1 Kgs 9, 8f; Jer 22, 8f.
29, 27: Dn 9, 11-14.

wrath and tremendous anger the LORD uprooted them from their soil and cast them out into a strange land, where they are today.' 28† [Both what is still hidden and what has already been revealed concern us and our descendants forever, that we may carry out all the words of this law.]

Mercy for the Repentant

30 1* "When all these things which I have set before you, the blessings and the curses, are fulfilled in you, and from among whatever nations the LORD, your God, may have dispersed you, you ponder them in your heart: 2* then, provided that you and your children return to the LORD, your God, and heed his voice with all your heart and all your soul, just as I now command you, 3 the LORD, your God, will change your lot; and taking pity on you, he will again gather you from all the nations wherein he has scattered you. 4 Though you may have been driven to the farthest corner of the world, even from there will the LORD, your God, gather you; even from there will he bring you back. 5 The LORD, your God, will then bring you into the land which your fathers once occupied, that you too may occupy it, and he will make you more prosperous and numerous than your fathers. 6*† The LORD, your God, will circumcise your hearts and the hearts of your descendants, that you may love the LORD, your God, with all your heart and all your soul, and so may live. 7 But all those curses the LORD, your God, will assign to your enemies and the foes who persecuted you. 8 You, however, must again heed the LORD'S voice and carry out all his commandments which I now enjoin on you. 9* Then the LORD, your God, will increase in more than goodly measure the returns from all your labors, the fruit of your womb, the offspring of your livestock, and the produce of your soil; for the LORD, your God, will again take delight in your prosperity, even as he took delight in your fathers', 10 if only you heed the voice of the LORD, your God, and keep his commandments and statutes that are written in this book of the law, when you return to the LORD, your God, with all your heart and all your soul.

God's Command Clear

11† "For this command which I enjoin on you today is not too mysterious and remote for you.

12 It is not up in the sky, that you should say, 'Who will go up in the sky to get it for us and tell us of it, that we may carry it out?' 13 Nor is it across the sea, that you should say, 'Who will cross the sea to get it for us and tell us of it, that we may carry it out?' 14† No, it is something very near to you, already in your mouths and in your hearts; you have only to carry it out.

The Choice before Israel

15 "Here, then, I have today set before you life and prosperity, death and doom. 16 If you obey the commandments of the LORD, your God, which I enjoin on you today, loving him, and walking in his ways, and keeping his commandments, statutes and decrees, you will live and grow numerous, and the LORD, your God, will bless you in the land you are entering to occupy. 17 If, however, you turn away your hearts and will not listen, but are led astray and adore and serve other gods, 18 I tell you now that you will certainly perish; you

will not have a long life on the land which you are crossing the Jordan to enter and occupy. 19* I call heaven and earth today to witness against you: I have set before you life and death, the blessing and the curse.* Choose life, then, that you and

---

"Choose Life"

This statement is a powerful summons to all of us who are believers. We live in a culture that is constantly filled and refilled with images of violence and death, especially in the media and entertainment. Many people seem to choose options that lead to death rather than life. Temptations to do so are everywhere.

God calls us to choose life—every time. What options before us lead to life rather than death? What choices give life to others?

Life is what we are called to—a full life, lived out in God's presence, a life lived in service to others. Think about the choices you make each day. Your decision to greet someone or smile at someone can make a big difference. That difference can be life giving. Choose life. It is always the right choice!

▶ Dt 30, 19

---

your descendants may live, 20 by loving the LORD, your God, heeding his voice, and holding fast to him. For that will mean life for you, a long life for you to live on the land which the LORD swore he would give to your fathers Abraham, Isaac and Jacob."

The Lord's Leadership

31 1 When Moses had finished speaking these words to all Israel, 2* he said to them, "I am now one hundred and twenty years old and am no longer able to move about freely; besides, the LORD has told me that I shall not cross this Jordan. 3* It is the LORD your God, who will cross before you; he will destroy these nations before you, that you may supplant them. [It is Joshua who will cross before you, as the LORD promised.] 4* The LORD will deal with them just as he dealt with Sihon and Og, the kings of the Amorites whom he destroyed, and with their country. 5* When, therefore, the LORD delivers them up to you, you must deal with them exactly as I have ordered you. 6* Be brave and steadfast; have no fear or dread of them, for it is the LORD, your God, who marches with you; he will never fail you or forsake you."

Call of Joshua

7* Then Moses summoned Joshua and in the presence of all Israel said to him, "Be brave and steadfast, for you must bring this people into the land which the LORD swore to their fathers he

would give them; you must put them in possession of their heritage. 8 It is the LORD who marches before you; he will be with you and will never fail you or forsake you. So do not fear or be dismayed."

The Reading of the Law

9 When Moses had written down this law, he entrusted it to the levitical priests who carry the ark of the covenant of the LORD, and to all the elders of Israel, 10*† giving them this order: "On the feast of Booths, at the prescribed time in the year of relaxation which comes at the end of every seven-year period, 11† when all Israel goes to appear before the LORD, your God, in the place which he chooses, you shall read this law aloud in the presence of all Israel. 12 Assemble the people—men, women and children, as well as the aliens who live in your communities—that they may hear it and learn it, and so fear the LORD, your God, and carefully observe all the words of this law. 13 Their children also, who do not know it yet, must hear it and learn it, that they too may fear the LORD, your God, as long as you live on the land which you will cross the Jordan to occupy."

Commission of Joshua

14† The LORD said to Moses, "The time is now approaching for you to die. Summon Joshua, and present yourselves at the meeting tent that I may give him his commission." So Moses and Joshua went

---

31, 10: *The year of relaxation:* cf Dt 15, 1ff and the note there.
31, 11ff: Reading the law not only instructed the people but also consoled them by the assurance of the divine goodness.
31, 14f.23: V 23 is best read immediately after v 15; perhaps the original order was vv 7–8.14–15.23.

31, 2: Dt 34, 7; Nm 20, 12.   **31, 6:** Dt 20, 3f.
31, 3: Dt 9, 3.   **31, 7f:** Jos 1, 6f.9.
31, 4: Nm 21, 21–35.   **31, 10f:** Dt 16, 13ff.
31, 5: Dt 7, 2.

Cultural Connections

HISPANICS LIVE THE HISTORY OF SALVATION!

As Moses did, Hispanics express their faith in the Lord of history:

Lord, you who are the Lord of all,
we, the Hispanic people of the United States,
conscious of being a people with its own identity,
born of common roots,
cultural traditions, language, and faith,
and in diversity united,
direct this prayer to you.

Lord and master of history,
we, a people, as we experience the same hungers and hurts,
make a preferential option for the poor,
and we stand in solidarity with this suffering humanity.

From your creative womb, we have been born;
we are your family, your believing people.
In this moment of grace, we feel ourselves called
to a "prophetic mission";
working together and participating in community,
we speak in your name to church and society.

Raised up as a people, intent on being authors
of our own history,
we walk with hope and in a progressive process.
Together we contribute to the coming of
the Kingdom of God here and now,
struggling to establish the new society, with an economy, relationships, and values
based on the love and the justice of your Son, Jesus Christ.

We ask this in company with Mary,
the mother of all believers.
Amen.

(Secretariat for Hispanic Affairs, *Prophetic Voices*, p. 23)

---

and presented themselves at the meeting tent. [15] And the LORD appeared at the tent in a column of cloud, which stood still at the entrance of the tent.

A Command to Moses

[16]* The LORD said to Moses, "Soon you will be at rest with your fathers, and then this people will take to rendering wanton worship to the strange gods among whom they will live in the land they are about to enter. They will forsake me and break the covenant which I have made with them. [17] At that time my anger will flare up against them; I will forsake them and hide my face from them, so that they will become a prey to be devoured, and many evils and troubles will befall them. At that time they will indeed say, 'Is it not because our God is not among us that these evils have befallen us?' [18] Yet I will be hiding my face from them at that time only because

D
T

31, 16: Jgs 2, 12.17.

of all the evil they have done in turning to other gods. [19]* Write out this song, then, for yourselves. Teach it to the Israelites and have them recite it, so that this song may be a witness for me against the Israelites. [20] For when I have brought them into the land flowing with milk and honey which I promised on oath to their fathers, and they have eaten their fill and grown fat, if they turn to other gods and serve them, despising me and breaking my covenant; [21] then, when many evils and troubles befall them, this song, which their descendants will not have forgotten to recite, will bear witness against them. For I know what they are inclined to do even at the present time, before I have brought them into the land which I promised on oath to their fathers." [22] So Moses wrote this song that same day, and he taught it to the Israelites.

Commission of Joshua

[23]* Then the LORD commissioned Joshua, son of Nun, and said to him, "Be brave and steadfast, for it is you who must bring the Israelites into the land which I promised them on oath. I myself will be with you."

The Law Placed in the Ark

[24] When Moses had finished writing out on a scroll the words of the law in their entirety, [25]* he gave the Levites who carry the ark of the covenant of the LORD this order: [26] "Take this scroll of the law and put it beside the ark of the covenant of the LORD, your God, that there it may be a witness against you. [27] For I already know how rebellious and stiff-necked you will be. Why, even now, while I am alive among you, you have been rebels against the LORD! How much more, then, after I am dead! [28]* Therefore, assemble all your tribal elders and your officials before me, that I may speak these words for them to hear, and so may call heaven and earth to witness against them. [29]* For I know that after my death you are sure to become corrupt and to turn aside from the way along which I directed you, so that evil will befall you in some future age because you have done evil in the LORD's sight, and provoked him by your deeds."

The Song of Moses

[30] Then Moses recited the words of this song from beginning to end, for the whole assembly of Israel to hear:

A

32 [1]† Give ear, O heavens, while I speak;
    let the earth hearken to the words of
    my mouth!
[2]   May my instruction soak in like the rain,
    and my discourse permeate like the
    dew,
Like a downpour upon the grass,
    like a shower upon the crops:
[3]   For I will sing the LORD's renown.
    Oh, proclaim the greatness of our God!
[4]* The Rock—how faultless are his deeds,
    how right all his ways!
A faithful God, without deceit,
    how just and upright he is!

[5]* Yet basely has he been treated by his
    degenerate children,
    a perverse and crooked race!
[6]* Is the LORD to be thus repaid by you,
    O stupid and foolish people?
Is he not your father who created you?
    Has he not made you and established
    you?

[7]* Think back on the days of old,
    reflect on the years of age upon age.
Ask your father and he will inform you,
    ask your elders and they will tell you:
[8]*† When the Most High assigned the nations
    their heritage,
    when he parceled out the descendants
    of Adam,
He set up the boundaries of the peoples
    after the number of the sons of God;
[9]* While the LORD's own portion was Jacob,
    his hereditary share was Israel.

[10]* He found them in a wilderness,
    a wasteland of howling desert.

32, 1–43: In the style of the great prophets, the speaker is often God himself. The whole song is a poetic sermon, having for its theme God's benefits to Israel (vv 1–14) and Israel's ingratitude and idolatry in turning to the gods of the pagans, which sins will be punished by the pagans themselves (vv 15–29); in turn, the foolish pride of the pagans will be punished, and the Lord's honor will be vindicated (vv 30–43).

32, 8: *The sons of God:* the angels; cf Jb 1, 6; 2, 1; 38, 7; Ps 89, 7f. Here the various nations are portrayed as having their respective guardian angels. Cf Dn 10, 20f; 12, 1.

31, 19: Dt 31, 21; 32, 1–43.
31, 23: Dt 31, 7f; Jos 1, 5ff.
31, 25: 24f: Dt 31, 9.
31, 28: Dt 32, 1–43.
31, 29: Jgs 2, 19.
32, 4: Ps 92, 15; Rv 15, 3.
32, 5: Dt 31, 29; Ps 78, 8; Lk 9, 41.
32, 6: Ex 4, 22; Is 63, 16; 64, 8; Jer 31, 9.
32, 7: Dt 4, 32; Ps 44, 2.
32, 8: Gn 10, 1–32; Acts 17, 26.
32, 9: Ex 19, 5; Ps 33, 12.
32, 10: Dt 8, 15; Jer 2, 6; Zec 2, 8.

He shielded them and cared for them,
   guarding them as the apple of his eye.

11* As an eagle incites its nestlings forth
   by hovering over its brood,
So he spread his wings to receive them
   and bore them up on his pinions.
12 The LORD alone was their leader,
   no strange god was with him.
13† He had them ride triumphant over the
     summits of the land
   and live off the products of its fields,
Giving them honey to suck from its rocks
   and olive oil from its hard, stony ground;

14† Butter from its cows and milk from its
     sheep,
   with the fat of its lambs and rams;
Its Bashan bulls and its goats,
   with the cream of its finest wheat;
   and the foaming blood of its grapes
     you drank.

B

15*† [So Jacob ate his fill,]
   the darling grew fat and frisky;
   you became fat and gross and gorged.
They spurned the God who made them
   and scorned their saving Rock.
16* They provoked him with strange gods
   and angered him with abominable idols.

17 They offered sacrifice to demons, to
     "no-gods,"
   to gods whom they had not known before,
To newcomers just arrived,
   of whom their fathers had never stood
     in awe.
18* You were unmindful of the Rock that
     begot you,
   You forgot the God who gave you birth.
19 When the LORD saw this, he was filled
     with loathing
   and anger toward his sons and daughters.
20* "I will hide my face from them," he said,
   "and see what will then become
     of them.
What a fickle race they are,
   sons with no loyalty in them!

21* "Since they have provoked me with their
     'no god'
   and angered me with their vain idols,
I will provoke them with a 'no-people';
   with a foolish nation I will anger them.

22* "For by my wrath a fire is enkindled
   that shall rage to the depths of
     the netherworld,
Consuming the earth with its yield,
   and licking with flames the roots of
     the mountains.
23 I will spend on them woe upon woe
   and exhaust all my arrows against them:

24 "Emaciating hunger and consuming fever
   and bitter pestilence,
And the teeth of wild beasts I will send
     among them,
   with the venom of reptiles gliding in
     the dust.

25* "Snatched away by the sword in the street
   and by sheer terror at home
Shall be the youth and the maiden alike,
   the nursing babe as well as the hoary old
     man.

26 "I would have said, 'I will make an end
     of them
   and blot out their name from
     men's memories,'
27 Had I not feared the insolence of
     their enemies,
   feared that these foes would
     mistakenly boast,
'Our own hand won the victory;
   the LORD had nothing to do with it.' "

28† For they are a people devoid of reason,
   having no understanding.
29 If they had insight they would realize
     what happened,
   they would understand their future and say,

C

30 "How could one man rout a thousand,
   or two men put ten thousand to flight,

32, 13: *The land:* Canaan.
32, 14: *Bashan:* a fertile grazing land east of the Jordan, famous for its strong cattle. Cf Ps 22, 13; Ez 39, 18; Am 4, 1.
32, 15: *The darling:* a probable meaning of the Hebrew word *yeshurun,* a term of endearment for "Israel." Cf Dt 33, 5.26; Is 44, 2.
32, 28–35: The reference is to the pagan nations, not to Israel.

32, 11: Ex 19, 4.   **32, 20:** Dt 31, 17.
32, 15: Dt 31, 20.   **32, 21:** Rom 10, 19.
32, 16: Nm 25, 2f; Ps 78, 58.   **32, 22:** Lam 4, 11.
32, 18: Jer 2, 32.   **32, 25:** Lv 26, 25.

Unless it was because their Rock sold them
and the LORD delivered them up?"

31 Indeed, their "rock" is not like our Rock,
and our foes are under condemnation.

32 They are a branch of Sodom's vine-stock,
from the vineyards of Gomorrah.
Poisonous are their grapes
and bitter their clusters.

33 Their wine is the venom of dragons
and the cruel poison of cobras.

34 "Is not this preserved in my treasury,
sealed up in my storehouse,

35 Against the day of vengeance and requital,
against the time they lose their footing?"
Close at hand is the day of their disaster,
and their doom is rushing upon them!

36*†Surely, the LORD shall do justice for his people;
on his servants he shall have pity.
When he sees their strength failing,
and their protected and unprotected alike
disappearing,

37* He will say, "Where are their gods
whom they relied on as their 'rock'?

38 Let those who ate the fat of your sacrifices
and drank the wine of your libations
Rise up now and help you!
Let them be your protection!

39* "Learn then that I, I alone, am God,
and there is no god besides me.
It is I who bring both death and life,
I who inflict wounds and heal them,
and from my hand there is no rescue.

40 "To the heavens I raise my hand and swear:
As surely as I live forever,

41 I will sharpen my flashing sword,
and my hand shall lay hold of my quiver.

"With vengeance I will repay my foes
and requite those who hate me.

42 I will make my arrows drunk with blood,
and my sword shall gorge itself with flesh—
With the blood of the slain and the captured,
Flesh from the heads of the
enemy leaders."

43 Exult with him, you heavens,
glorify him, all you angels of God;
For he avenges the blood of his servants
and purges his people's land.

44 So Moses, together with Joshua, son of Nun, went and recited all the words of this song for the people to hear.

Final Appeal

45 When Moses had finished speaking all these words to all Israel, 46* he said, "Take to heart all the warning which I have now given you and which you must impress on your children, that you may carry out carefully every word of this law. 47 For this is no trivial matter for you; rather, it means your very life, since it is by this means that you are to enjoy a long life on the land which you will cross the Jordan to occupy."

Moses to View Canaan

48 On that very day the LORD said to Moses, 49* "Go up on Mount Nebo, here in the Abarim Mountains [it is in the land of Moab facing Jericho], and view the land of Canaan, which I am giving to the Israelites as their possession. 50* Then you shall die on the mountain you have climbed, and shall be taken to your people, just as your brother Aaron died on Mount Hor and there was taken to his people; 51* because both of you broke faith with me among the Israelites at the waters of Meribath-kadesh in the desert of Zin by failing to manifest my sanctity among the Israelites. 52* You may indeed view the land at a distance, but you shall not enter that land which I am giving to the Israelites."

Blessing upon the Tribes

33 1 This is the blessing which Moses, the man of God, pronounced upon the Israelites before he died. 2*† He said:

32, 36: *Their protected and unprotected:* the meaning of the Hebrew is uncertain; according to some, the idea is "slaves and freemen."

33, 2–5.26–29: These verses seem to form an independent hymn describing, in the form of a theophany, the conquest of Canaan. The first section of this hymn (vv 2–5) serves here as an introduction to the various "blessings"; the second section (vv 26–29), as their conclusion.

32, 36: 2 Mc 7, 6.
32, 37f: Jgs 10, 14; Jer 2, 28.
32, 39: Dt 4, 35; Tb 13, 2; Wis 16, 13.
32, 46: Dt 4, 9.
32, 49: Nm 27, 12; 33, 47f.
32, 50: Nm 20, 24ff.28; 27, 13; 33, 38.
32, 51: Nm 20, 12; 27, 14.
32, 52: Dt 3, 27; 34, 4.
33, 2: Ex 19, 18.20; Jgs 5, 4f.

"The LORD came from Sinai
     and dawned on his people from Seir;
He shone forth from Mount Paran
     and advanced from Meribath-kadesh,
While at his right hand a fire blazed forth
     and his wrath devastated the nations.
3† But all his holy ones were in his hand;
     they followed at his feet
     and he bore them up on his pinions.
4* A law he gave to us;
     he made the community of Jacob his domain,
5†   and he became king of his darling,
When the chiefs of the people assembled
     and the tribes of Israel came together.
6*† "May Reuben live and not die out,
     but let his men be few."

7*† The following is for Judah. He said:
"The LORD hears the cry of Judah;
     you will bring him to his people.
His own hands defend his cause
     and you will be his help against his foes."

8*† Of Levi he said:
"To Levi belong your Thummim,
     to the man of your favor your Urim;
For you put him to the test at Massah
     and you contended with him at the waters
         of Meribah.
9† He said of his father, 'I regard him not';
     his brothers he would not acknowledge,
     and his own children he refused
         to recognize.
Thus the Levites keep your words,
     and your covenant they uphold.
10* They promulgate your decisions to Jacob
     and your law to Israel.
They bring the smoke of sacrifice to
         your nostrils,
     and burnt offerings to your altar.
11 Bless, O LORD, his possessions
     and accept the ministry of his hands.
Break the backs of his adversaries
     and of his foes, that they may not rise."

12* Of Benjamin he said:
"Benjamin is the beloved of the LORD,
     who shelters him all the day,
     while he abides securely at his breast."

13* Of Joseph he said:
"Blessed by the LORD is his land
     with the best of the skies above
     and of the abyss crouching beneath;
14 With the best of the produce of the year,
     and the choicest sheaves of the months;
15 With the finest gifts of the age-old
         mountains
     and the best from the timeless hills;
16† With the best of the earth and its fullness,
     and the favor of him who dwells in
         the bush.
These shall come upon the head of Joseph
     and upon the brow of the prince among
         his brothers,
17 The majestic bull, his father's first-born,
     whose horns are those of the wild ox
With which to gore the nations,
     even those at the ends of the earth."
[These are the myriads of Ephraim,
     and these the thousands of Manasseh.]

18* Of Zebulun he said:
"Rejoice, O Zebulun, in your pursuits,
     and you, Issachar, in your tents!
19† You who invite the tribes to the mountains
     where feasts are duly held,
Because you suck up the abundance of
         the seas
     and the hidden treasures of the sand."

20* Of Gad he said:
"Blessed be he who has made Gad so vast!
     He lies there like a lion
     that has seized the arm and head of
         the prey.

33, 3: *His holy ones were in his hand:* the Israelites were protected by the Lord.

33, 5.26: *The darling:* see note on Dt 32, 15.

33, 6: In keeping with the other blessings, probably this verse was once introduced by the phrase, "Of Reuben he said." It is to be noted that there is no blessing here for Simeon.

33, 7: *Bring him to his people:* this probably refers to the isolated position of the tribe of Judah during the conquest of the Promised Land (cf Jgs 1, 17–19); according to some commentators the reference is to the divided kingdom.

33, 8: *Thummim . . . Urim:* see note on Ex 28, 30.

33, 9: The reference is probably to the Levites' slaughter of their brethren after the affair of the golden calf in the desert; cf Ex 32, 27–29.

33, 16: *Him who dwells in the bush:* a title given to the Lord because of his appearance to Moses in the burning bush; cf Ex 3.

33, 19: *The abundance of the seas:* perhaps the wealth that comes from sea-borne trade or from fishing. *The hidden treasures of the sand:* possibly an allusion to the valuable purple dye extracted from certain marine shells found on the coast of northern Palestine.

33, 4: Jn 1, 17; 7, 19.   **33, 10:** Ex 30, 7f.
33, 6: Gn 49, 3f.   **33, 12:** Gn 49, 27.
33, 7: Gn 49, 8–12.   **33, 13–17:** Gn 49, 22–26.
33, 8: Gn 49, 5; Ex 17; 7; 28,   **33, 18f:** Gn 49, 13ff.
30; Nm 20, 13.   **33, 20f:** Gn 49, 19.

21 *†He saw that the best should be his
    when the princely portion was assigned,
    while the heads of the people were gathered.
He carried out the justice of the LORD
    and his decrees respecting Israel."

22 *†Of Dan he said:
"Dan is a lion's whelp,
    that springs forth from Bashan!"

23 *†Of Naphtali he said:
"Naphtali is enriched with favors
    and filled with the blessings of the LORD;
The lake and south of it are his
    possession!"

24 *†Of Asher he said:
"More blessed than the other sons
    be Asher!
May he be the favorite among his brothers,
    as the oil of his olive trees runs over
    his feet!

25 May your bolts be of iron and bronze;
    may your strength endure through all
    your days!"

26 "There is no god like the God of the
    darling,
who rides the heavens in his power,
    and rides the skies in his majesty;

27 He spread out the primeval tent;
    he extended the ancient canopy.
He drove the enemy out of your way
    and the Amorite he destroyed.

28 * Israel has dwelt securely,
    and the fountain of Jacob has
    been undisturbed.
In a land of grain and wine,
    where the heavens drip with dew.

29 * How fortunate you are, O Israel!
    Where else is a nation victorious in
    the LORD?
The LORD is your saving shield,
    and his sword is your glory.
Your enemies fawn upon you,
    as you stride upon their heights."

Death and Burial of Moses

34 1 * Then Moses went up from the plains of Moab to Mount Nebo, the headland of Pisgah which faces Jericho, and the LORD showed him all the land—Gilead, and as far as Dan, 2 all Naphtali, the land of Ephraim and Manasseh, all the land of Judah as far as the Western Sea, 3 the Negeb, the circuit of the Jordan with

MOSES' DEATH

Why did Moses die on the brink of entering the Promised Land? This question has disturbed many generations of believers. The one who received God's call to lead the Israelites out of slavery, who amazed Pharaoh with wonders and called down plagues on Egypt, who opened the Red Sea and received the tablets of the Law on Mount Sinai—this great leader did not get to enjoy the success of his work (Nm 20, 12)! Deuteronomy 34, 1–6 simply tells us that Moses died on Mount Nebo and that his burial place was forgotten.

But consider this: By the time Deuteronomy was written, Moses had become a legendary figure. Many of the details of his life had been forgotten. Perhaps it is fitting that Moses' story ends as it began: shrouded in mystery, tragedy, and hope. What hope? The hope for another prophet like Moses (18, 15) that remained alive and strong in the Israelites' hearts.

▸ Deuteronomy, chapter 34

the lowlands at Jericho, city of palms, and as far as Zoar. 4 * The LORD then said to him, "This is the land which I swore to Abraham, Isaac and Jacob that I would give to their descendants. I have let you feast your eyes upon it, but you shall not

---

† **33, 21:** The princely portion: Moses gave the tribe of Gad their land on the east of the Jordan only on condition that they would help the other tribes conquer the land west of the river; cf Nm 32; Jos 22.
33, 22: The sense is, "May he leap up like a lion of Bashan"; the heavily wooded hills of Bashan were notorious for their lions, but the tribe of Dan was not settled in this region.
33, 23: The lake: the Lake of Gennesaret on which the land of this tribe bordered.

33, 24: The land of the tribe of Asher was covered with olive groves.

* 33, 21: Nm 32, 1.5.16–19.   33, 24f: Gn 49, 20.
  31f; Jos 1, 12–15;   33, 28: Gn 27, 28.
  1 Chr 5, 18–22.   33, 29: Dt 4, 7f.
33, 22: Gn 49, 16f.   34, 1: Dt 3, 27.
33, 23: Gn 49, 21; Jos 19,   34, 4: Dt 3, 27; 32, 52; Gn
  32–39.   12, 7; 15, 18.

DT

cross over." 5* So there, in the land of Moab, Moses, the servant of the LORD, died as the LORD had said; 6 and he was buried in the ravine opposite Beth-peor in the land of Moab, but to this day no one knows the place of his burial. 7* Moses was one hundred and twenty years old when he died, yet his eyes were undimmed and his vigor unabated. 8 For thirty days the Israelites wept for Moses in the plains of Moab, till they had completed the period of grief and mourning for Moses.

9* Now Joshua, son of Nun, was filled with the spirit of wisdom, since Moses had laid his hands upon him; and so the Israelites gave him their obedience, thus carrying out the LORD'S command to Moses.

10* Since then no prophet has arisen in Israel like Moses, whom the LORD knew face to face. 11* He had no equal in all the signs and wonders the LORD sent him to perform in the land of Egypt against Pharaoh and all his servants and against all his land, 12 and for the might and the terrifying power that Moses exhibited in the sight of all Israel.

34, 5: Dt 32, 50.
34, 7: Dt 31, 2.
34, 9: Nm 27, 18.23; Jos 1, 17.
34, 10: Ex 33, 11.
34, 11: Dt 4, 34.

Introduction to the

Historical
Books

Have you ever noticed that many older people enjoy telling stories about the past? Sometimes, it seems that their past experiences are more real to them than present-day events. Those of us who are younger may get tired of hearing about the "good old days." Still, a lot is to be gained from listening carefully to the memories of our elders. The sixteen historical books of the Old Testament, like the voices of respected elders, tell the stories of God at work in ancient Israel. In reading these stories, we can see more clearly how God works in today's world.

In-depth

THE HISTORICAL BOOKS RECOUNT THE PERIOD of Israelite history from 1250 to 100 B.C. In those books, we read about the following events:

- the Israelites' settlement in the Promised Land and their struggle to protect themselves from their enemies (the Books of Joshua and Judges)
- the rise of a united kingdom under David (1 and 2 Samuel, 1 Kings)
- the division of the kingdom into northern and southern kingdoms, and the various kings and prophets of each, until the fall of Jerusalem in 587 B.C. (1 and 2 Kings, 1 and 2 Chronicles)
- the return from Exile and the rebuilding of the nation (Ezra and Nehemiah)
- the Jewish resistance to Greek domination in the second century before Christ (1 and 2 Maccabees)

In addition, the books contain three "novels" about the human challenge to trust God in difficult times (Tobit, Judith, and Esther).

The historical books of the Old Testament are not like the history books that we read in school. Those who write history books today generally try to report the facts with little interpretation. "Let the events speak for themselves," they say. However, those who wrote the historical books of the Old Testament had a different purpose: "Let us tell you what the events *mean in the light of our faith in God."* Thus, the history contained in these books is often called sacred history because it reveals God's message and God's purpose in history.

Scripture scholars find evidence of two general groups shaping the final form of the historical books. The first group is called the Deuteronomic school of writers because it was responsible for the highly influential Book of Deuteronomy. This group also wrote Joshua, Judges, 1 and 2 Samuel, and 1 and 2 Kings. The Deuteronomists were convinced that God rewarded the good and punished the wicked in this world. Thus, you will find in these books a repeated pattern of (1) God's offer of love, (2) the people's faithlessness and sin, (3) God's just punishment, (4) the people's repentance and cry for help, (5) God's forgiveness and mercy, and (6) the people's repeated sin.

The second group (or person), sometimes called the Chronicler, is responsible for 1 and 2 Chronicles, and probably Ezra and Nehemiah. The Chronicler still emphasized that God rewards the faithful and punishes the unfaithful, but the measurement for what is faithful had changed. Instead of emphasizing faithfulness to the Sinai Covenant, the Chronicler emphasized faithfulness to proper worship, particularly worship at the Temple in Jerusalem. The Chronicler wrote after the destruction of the northern and southern kingdoms, to nurture the faith of a small community trying to rebuild itself.

Some of the religious truths you will learn from reading these books are as follows:

- God is not removed from the affairs of this world but cares deeply about what is happening in human history.
- People are happier when they follow the law of God than when they turn away from the Law.
- All human beings, from the beginning of history, are joined in a common struggle to find sense and meaning in the ups and downs of life.

As you read these books, remember that the authors' understanding of God is not the same as Jesus' understanding. Although not denying the truths about God taught by these books, Christians have a larger context for understanding God's unconditional love and unlimited mercy: Jesus' teaching in the New Testament.

Other Background

- **The Book of Ruth was not originally one of the historical books. It was written later than the books it is now sandwiched between.**

- **The Books of 1 and 2 Chronicles review the same historical period as 1 and 2 Samuel and 1 and 2 Kings.**

- **Tobit, Judith, and Esther are fictional works that use history only as a backdrop. Their purpose is to encourage fidelity to God's law in hard times.**

- **Tobit, Judith, 1 and 2 Maccabees, and parts of Esther are not found in every translation of the Old Testament and are not contained in many Protestant Bibles. See "The Case of the Missing Books," near Tb 1, 16.**

When you were young, did you ask to hear your favorite book over and over again? Do you remember feeling secure because you knew how the story would turn out? Often, familiar stories appeal to us because of their simple justice: evil is punished, and good is rewarded. The author of the Book of Joshua applies this simple justice to the conquest of the Promised Land: those who follow God are rewarded, and those who do not are destroyed.

At a Glance

In-depth

The Book of Joshua is named after the Israelite hero who succeeds Moses and leads the people in their takeover of the Promised Land. At the beginning of the book, Joshua promises the Israelites that they will conquer the land of Canaan and make it their own if they are faithful to the Covenant of Moses. They respond with enthusiasm, "We will obey you as completely as we obeyed Moses" (1, 16). The author describes how by remaining true to the Commandments of God, the various Israelite tribes, under Joshua's leadership, take over the land and settle in it with their families and livestock (see map 2, "The Exodus from Egypt").

Today, biblical scholars doubt that the conquest of the Promised Land by the twelve tribes of Israel was as complete and easy as it is written in Joshua. Archaeologists have found evidence that Canaanites continued to live in the area after the "conquest." The historical memories preserved in the book were reshaped by the author to emphasize an important lesson of faith: God would preserve the Israelites on their land as long as they obeyed the Commandments.

The belief in the triumph of good and the punishment of evil is at the heart of the Book of Joshua. Like Judges, 1 and 2 Samuel, and 1 and 2 Kings, the Book of Joshua is inspired by the Book of Deuteronomy, which insists that God rewards the just and punishes the wicked in this world (see Dt 30, 15–20). The Book of Joshua challenges us to remember that God is our surest hope in all the ups and downs of history.

Quick Facts

Period Covered
after the desert wandering, from about 1250 to 1200 B.C.

Author
unknown, from the Deuteronomic tradition, writing in the seventh or sixth century B.C.

Themes
Israel's conquest of the Promised Land, the triumph of good and the punishment of evil

Of Note
The name Jesus is the Greek form of Joshua, which means "God saves."

The Book of Joshua

Joshua

I: Conquest of Canaan

Divine Promise of Assistance

1 ¹ After Moses, the servant of the LORD, had died, the LORD said to Moses' aid Joshua, son of Nun: ² "My servant Moses is dead. So prepare to cross the Jordan here, with all the people, into the land I will give the Israelites. ³ As I promised Moses, I will deliver to you every place where you set foot. ⁴*† Your domain is to be all the land of the Hittites, from the desert and from Lebanon east to the great river Euphrates and west to the Great Sea. ⁵* No one can withstand you while you live. I will be with you as I was with Moses: I will not leave you nor forsake you. ⁶ Be firm and steadfast, so that you may give this people possession of the land which I swore to their fathers I would give them. ⁷ Above all, be firm and steadfast, taking care to observe the entire law which my servant Moses enjoined on you. Do not swerve from it either to the right or to the left, that you may succeed wherever you go. ⁸ Keep this book of the law on your lips. Recite it by day and by night, that you may observe carefully all that is written in it; then you will successfully attain your goal. ⁹* I command you: be firm and steadfast! Do not fear nor be dismayed, for the LORD, your God, is with you wherever you go."

¹⁰ So Joshua commanded the officers of the people: ¹¹* "Go through the camp and instruct the people, 'Prepare your provisions, for three days from now you shall cross the Jordan here, to march in and take possession of the land which the LORD, your God, is giving you.' "

The Transjordan Tribes

¹² Joshua reminded the Reubenites, the Gadites, and the half-tribe of Manasseh: ¹³ "Remember what Moses, the servant of the LORD, commanded you when he said, 'The LORD, your God, will permit you to settle in this land.' ¹⁴* Your wives, your children, and your livestock shall remain in the land Moses gave you here beyond the Jordan. But all the warriors among you must cross over armed ahead of your kinsmen and you must help them ¹⁵* until the LORD has settled your kinsmen, and they like you possess the land which the LORD, your God, is giving them. Afterward you may return and occupy your own land, which Moses, the servant of the LORD, has given you east of the Jordan." ¹⁶ "We will do all you have commanded us," they answered Joshua, "and we will go wherever you send us. We will obey you as completely as we obeyed Moses. ¹⁷ But may the LORD, your God, be with you as he was with Moses. ¹⁸ If anyone rebels against your orders and does not obey every command you give him, he shall be put to death. But be firm and steadfast."

---

† **1, 4:** The ideal frontiers are given: in the south the desert of Sinai, in the north the Lebanon range, in the east the Euphrates, and in the west the Great Sea, the Mediterranean.

* **1, 4:** 3f: Jos 14, 9; Gn 15, 18; Dt 11, 24.
1, 5: Dt 31, 8; Heb 13, 5.
1, 9: 7f: Dt 31, 7f.
1, 11: Dt 11, 31.
1, 14: Nm 32, 26.
1, 15: Jos 22, 4; Dt 3, 20.

Be Not Afraid

"Be firm and steadfast! Do not fear nor be dismayed, for the LORD, your God, is with you wherever you go" (Jos 1, 9).

Living proof:

Saint Joan of Arc was a humble, uneducated peasant maiden from fifteenth-century France. Inspired by saintly voices, she overcame numerous obstacles to lead the French troops into battle against British invaders.

Saint Thomas More, a distinguished scholar and lawyer, refused to approve King Henry VIII's divorce and remarriage and establishment of the Church of England.

Dorothy Day, twentieth-century American cofounder of the Catholic Worker Movement, challenged all Christians to serve poor and homeless people and dedicated her life to nonviolence.

Archbishop Oscar Romero of El Salvador was shot while saying Mass in 1980 because he dared to speak against the military groups that were terrorizing and killing the poor people of his diocese.

These four people, along with many others, have taken to heart God's words to Joshua. If you are not familiar with their stories, take time to learn more about these Catholic heroes.

▶ Jos 1, 5–9

Spies Saved by Rahab

2 ¹*† Then Joshua, son of Nun, secretly sent out two spies from Shittim, saying, "Go, reconnoiter the land and Jericho." When the two reached Jericho, they went into the house of a harlot named Rahab, where they lodged. 2 But a report was brought to the king of Jericho that some Israelites had come there that night to spy out the land. 3 So the king of Jericho sent Rahab the order, "Put out the visitors who have entered your house, for they have come to spy out the entire land." 4* The woman had taken the two men and hidden them, so she said, "True, the men you speak of came to me, but I did not know where they came from. 5 At dark, when it was time for the gate to be shut, they left, and I do not know where they went. You will have to pursue them immediately to overtake them." 6† Now, she had led them to the roof, and hidden them among her stalks of flax spread out there. 7 But the pursuers set out along the way to the fords of the Jordan, and once they had left, the gate was shut.

8† Before the spies fell asleep, Rahab came to them on the roof 9* and said: "I know that the LORD has given you the land, that a dread of you has come upon us, and that all the inhabitants of the land are overcome with fear of you. 10* For we have heard how the LORD dried up the waters of the Red Sea before you when you came out of Egypt, and how you dealt with Sihon and Og, the two kings of the Amorites beyond the Jordan, whom you doomed to destruction. 11* At these reports, we are disheartened; everyone is discouraged because of you, since the LORD, your God, is God in heaven above and on earth below. 12* Now then, swear to me by the LORD that, since I am showing kindness to you, you in turn will show kindness to my family; and give me an unmistakable token 13 that you are to spare my father and mother, brothers and sisters, and all their kin, and save us from death." 14 "We pledge our lives for yours," the men answered her. "If you do not betray this errand of ours, we will be faithful in showing kindness to you when the LORD gives us the land."

15† Then she let them down through the window with a rope; for she lived in a house built into the city wall. 16 "Go up into the hill country," she sug-

---

2, 1: *Harlot:* this is the regular equivalent of the Hebrew word, but perhaps it is used here of Rahab in the broader sense of a woman who kept a public house. Joshua's spies hoped to remain undetected at such an inn.

2, 6: *Stalks of flax spread out:* to dry in the sun, after they had been soaked in water, according to the ancient process of preparing flax for linen-making. In the Near East the flax harvest occurs near the time of the feast of the Passover (Jos 4, 19; 5, 10); cf Ex 9, 31.

2, 8–11: Rahab's faith and good works are praised in the New Testament; cf Heb 11, 31; Jas 2, 25.

2, 15: *A house built into the city wall:* such houses, which used the city wall for their own inner walls, have been found at ancient sites. The upper story of Rahab's house was evidently higher than the city wall. It was through the window of such a house that St. Paul escaped from Damascus; cf Acts 9, 25; 2 Cor 11, 33.

2, 1: Mt 1, 5; Jas 2, 25.   Nm 21, 23–26.33ff.
2, 4: Jos 6, 17.   2, 11: Dt 4, 39.
2, 9: Ex 15, 15f; 23, 27.   2, 12: Jos 2, 18; 6, 23.25.
2, 10: Jos 4, 23; Ex 14, 21;

A Prayer Against Prejudice

Creator of diverse people, the Israelites united themselves with Rahab, someone outside their group, and trusted her. Lead me to be open to befriending those who are different from me so that I may learn to trust them as well.

Forgive my friends and me for every time we have looked at someone different and considered that person to be of lesser quality. Forgive us for each time we have talked about certain people as if we were superior. Forgive our cliques that look down on others and won't associate with them. And help us forgive those who have looked down on us. Amen.

▶ Joshua, chapter 2

gested to them, "that your pursuers may not find you. Hide there for three days, until they return; then you may proceed on your way." 17 The men answered her, "This is how we will fulfill the oath you made us take: 18 When we come into the land, tie this scarlet cord in the window through which you are letting us down; and gather your father and mother, your brothers and all your family into your house. 19 Should any of them pass outside the doors of your house, he will be responsible for his own death, and we shall be guiltless. But we shall be responsible if anyone in the house with you is harmed. 20 If, however, you betray this errand of ours, we shall be quit of the oath you have made us take." 21 "Let it be as you say," she replied, and bade them farewell. When they were gone, she tied the scarlet cord in the window.

22 They went up into the hills, where they stayed three days until their pursuers, who had sought them all along the road without finding them, returned. 23 Then the two came back down from the hills, crossed the Jordan to Joshua, son of Nun, and reported all that had befallen them. 24 They assured

Joshua, "The LORD has delivered all this land into our power; indeed, all the inhabitants of the land are overcome with fear of us."

Preparations for Crossing the Jordan

3 1* Early the next morning, Joshua moved with all the Israelites from Shittim to the Jordan, where they lodged before crossing over. 2 Three days later the officers went through the camp 3 and issued these instructions to the people: "When you see the ark of the covenant of the LORD, your God, which the levitical priests will carry, you must also break camp and follow it, 4 that you may know the way to take, for you have not gone over this road before. But let there be a space of two thousand cubits between you and the ark. Do not come nearer to it." 5 Joshua also said to the people, "Sanctify yourselves, for tomorrow the LORD will perform wonders among you." 6 And he directed the priests to take up the ark of the covenant and go on ahead of the people; and they did so.

7* Then the LORD said to Joshua, "Today I will begin to exalt you in the sight of all Israel, that they may know I am with you, as I was with Moses. 8 Now command the priests carrying the ark of the covenant to come to a halt in the Jordan when they reach the edge of the waters."

9 So Joshua said to the Israelites, "Come here and listen to the words of the LORD, your God." 10* He continued: "This is how you will know that there is a living God in your midst, who at your approach will dispossess the Canaanites, Hittites, Hivites, Perizzites, Girgashites, Amorites and Jebusites. 11 The ark of the covenant of the LORD of the whole earth will precede you into the Jordan. 12* [Now choose twelve men, one from each of the tribes of Israel.] 13 When the soles of the feet of the priests carrying the ark of the LORD, the Lord of the whole earth, touch the water of the Jordan, it will cease to flow; for the water flowing down from upstream will halt in a solid bank."

The Crossing Begun

14 The people struck their tents to cross the Jordan, with the priests carrying the ark of the covenant ahead of them. 15† No sooner had these priestly bearers of the ark waded into the waters at the edge of the Jordan, which overflows all its banks during the entire season of the harvest, 16*† than

---

3, 15: *Season of the harvest:* toward the end of March and the beginning of April, when the grain and other crops that grew during the rainy season of winter were reaped. The crossing took place "on the tenth day of the first month" of the Hebrew year, which began with the first new moon after the spring equinox; cf Jos 4, 19. At this time of the year the Jordan would be swollen as a result of the winter rains and the melting snow of Mount Hermon.

3, 16: The sudden damming of the river could have been caused by a landslide, as has happened on other occasions. The miraculous

character of this event would not thereby be removed because God, who foretold it (Jos 3, 13), also caused it to take place at precisely the right moment (Jos 3, 15), whether or not he used natural forces to accomplish his will.

3, 1: Jos 2, 1.
3, 7: Jos 1, 5; 4, 14.
3, 10: Ex 33, 2; Dt 7, 1.
3, 12: Jos 4, 2.4.
3, 16: Ps 114, 3.

J
O
S

the waters flowing from upstream halted, backing up in a solid mass for a very great distance indeed, from Adam, a city in the direction of Zarethan; while those flowing downstream toward the Salt Sea of the Arabah disappeared entirely. Thus the people crossed over opposite Jericho. 17* While all Israel crossed over on dry ground, the priests carrying the ark of the covenant of the LORD remained motionless on dry ground in the bed of the Jordan until the whole nation had completed the passage.

Memorial Stones

4 1 After the entire nation had crossed the Jordan, the LORD said to Joshua, 2* "Choose twelve men from the people, one from each tribe, 3* and instruct them to take up twelve stones from this spot in the bed of the Jordan where the priests have been standing motionless. Carry them over with you, and place them where you are to stay tonight."

4 Summoning the twelve men whom he had selected from among the Israelites, one from each tribe, 5 Joshua said to them: "Go to the bed of the Jordan in front of the ark of the LORD, your God; lift to your shoulders one stone apiece, so that they will equal in number the tribes of the Israelites. 6 In the future, these are to be a sign among you. When your children ask you what these stones mean to you, 7* you shall answer them, 'The waters of the Jordan ceased to flow before the ark of the covenant of the LORD when it crossed the Jordan.' Thus these stones are to serve as a perpetual memorial to the Israelites." 8 The twelve Israelites did as Joshua had commanded: they took up as many stones from the bed of the Jordan as there were tribes of the Israelites, and carried them along to the camp site, where they placed them, according to the LORD's direction. 9 Joshua also had twelve stones set up in the bed of the Jordan on the spot where the priests stood who were carrying the ark of the covenant. They are there to this day.

10† The priests carrying the ark remained in the bed of the Jordan until everything had been done that the LORD had commanded Joshua to tell the people. The people crossed over quickly, 11 and when all had reached the other side, the ark of the LORD, borne by the priests, also crossed to its place in front of them. 12* The Reubenites, Gadites, and half-tribe of Manasseh, armed, marched in the vanguard of the Israelites, as Moses had ordered. 13 About forty thousand troops equipped for battle passed over before the LORD to the plains of Jericho.

14* That day the LORD exalted Joshua in the sight of all Israel, and thenceforth during his whole life they respected him as they had respected Moses.

15 Then the LORD said to Joshua, 16* "Command the priests carrying the ark of the commandments to come up from the Jordan." 17 Joshua did so, 18 and when the priests carrying the ark of the covenant of the LORD had come up from the bed of the Jordan, as the soles of their feet regained the dry ground, the waters of the Jordan resumed their course and as before overflowed all its banks.

19 The people came up from the Jordan on the tenth day of the first month, and camped in Gilgal on the eastern limits of Jericho. 20 At Gilgal Joshua set up the twelve stones which had been taken from the Jordan, 21 saying to the Israelites, "In the future, when the children among you ask their fathers what these stones mean, 22 you shall inform them, 'Israel crossed the Jordan here on dry ground.' 23* For the LORD, your God, dried up the waters of the Jordan in front of you until you crossed over, just as the LORD, your God, had done at the Red Sea, which he dried up in front of us until we crossed over; 24 in order that all the peoples of the earth may learn that the hand of the LORD is mighty, and that you may fear the LORD, your God, forever."

Rites at Gilgal

5 1 When all the kings of Amorites to the west of the Jordan and all the kings of the Canaanites by the sea heard that the LORD had dried up the waters of the Jordan before the Israelites until they crossed over, they were disheartened and lost courage at their approach.

2 On this occasion the LORD said to Joshua, "Make flint knives and circumcise the Israelite nation for the second time." 3† So Joshua made flint knives and circumcised the Israelites at Gibeath-haaraloth, 4* under these circumstances: Of all the people who came out of Egypt, every man of military age had died in the desert during the journey after they left Egypt. 5 Though all the men who came out were circumcised, none of those born in the desert during the journey after the departure from Egypt were circumcised. 6* Now the Israelites had wandered forty years in the desert, until all the warriors among the people that came forth from Egypt died off because they had not obeyed the command of the LORD. For the LORD swore* that he would not let them see the land flowing

---

4, 10–18: After the digression about the two sets of memorial stones, the author resumes the narrative by briefly repeating the story of the crossing, which he had already told in Jos 3, 14–17.

5, 3: *Gibeath-haaraloth:* "Hill of the Foreskins."

3, 17: Jos 4, 7.22.
4, 2: Jos 3, 12.
4, 3: Jos 3, 13; 4, 8f; Dt 27, 2.
4, 7: Jos 3, 13.16.
4, 12: Dt 3, 18.
4, 14: Jos 3, 7.
4, 16: Jos 3, 6.
4, 23: Ex 14, 21.
5, 4: Nm 14, 29; 26, 64f; Dt 2, 16; Ps 106, 26; 1 Cor 10, 5.
5, 6: Nm 14, 29.
5, 6: Heb 3, 11.17.

with milk and honey which he had promised their fathers he would give us. 7*† It was the children whom he raised up in their stead whom Joshua circumcised, for these were yet with foreskins, not having been circumcised on the journey. 8 When the rite had been performed, the whole nation remained in camp where they were, until they recovered. 9*† Then the LORD said to Joshua, "Today I have removed the reproach of Egypt from you." Therefore the place is called Gilgal to the present day.

10*† While the Israelites were encamped at Gilgal on the plains of Jericho, they celebrated the Passover on the evening of the fourteenth of the month. 11 On the day after the Passover they ate of the produce of the land in the form of unleavened cakes and parched grain. On that same day 12* after the Passover on which they ate of the produce of the land, the manna ceased. No longer was there manna for the Israelites, who that year ate of the yield of the land of Canaan.

Siege at Jericho

13*† While Joshua was near Jericho, he raised his eyes and saw one who stood facing him, drawn sword in hand. Joshua went up to him and asked, "Are you one of us or of our enemies?" 14 He replied, "Neither. I am the captain of the host of the LORD and I have just arrived." Then Joshua fell prostrate to the ground in worship, and said to him, "What has my lord to say to his servant?" 15* The captain of the host of the LORD replied to Joshua, "Remove your sandals from your feet, for the place on which you are standing is holy." And Joshua obeyed.

6 1 Now Jericho was in a state of siege because of the presence of the Israelites, so that no one left or entered. 2 And to Joshua the LORD said, "I have delivered Jericho and its king into your power. 3 Have all the soldiers circle the city, marching once around it. Do this for six days, 4* with seven priests carrying ram's horns ahead of the ark. On the seventh day march around the city seven times, and have the priests blow the horns. 5 When they give a long blast on the ram's horns and you hear that signal, all the people shall shout aloud. The wall of the city will collapse, and they will be able to make a frontal attack."

6 Summoning the priests, Joshua, son of Nun, then ordered them to take up the ark of the covenant with seven of the priests carrying ram's horns in front of the ark of the LORD. 7 And he ordered the people to proceed in a circle around the city, with the picked troops marching ahead of the ark of the LORD. 8 At this order they proceeded, with the seven priests who carried the ram's horns before the LORD blowing their horns, and the ark of the covenant of the LORD following them. 9 In front of the priests with the horns marched the picked troops; the rear guard followed the ark, and the blowing of horns was kept up continually as they marched. 10 But the people had been commanded by Joshua not to shout or make any noise or outcry until he gave the word: only then were they to shout. 11 So he had the ark of the LORD circle the city, going once around it, after which they returned to camp for the night.

12 Early the next morning, Joshua had the priests take up the ark of the LORD. 13 The seven priests bearing the ram's horns marched in front of the ark of the LORD, blowing their horns. Ahead of these marched the picked troops, while the rear guard followed the ark of the LORD, and the blowing of horns was kept up continually. 14 On this second day they again marched around the city once before returning to camp; and for six days in all they did the same.

15 On the seventh day, beginning at daybreak, they marched around the city seven times in the same manner; on that day only did they march around the city seven times. 16 The seventh time around, the priests blew the horns and Joshua said to the people, "Now shout, for the LORD has given you the city 17* and everything in it. It is under the LORD's ban. Only the harlot Rahab and all who are in the house with her are to be spared, because she hid the messengers we sent. 18*† But be careful not to take, in your greed, anything that is under the ban; else you will bring upon the camp of Israel this ban and the misery of it. 19 All silver and gold, and the articles of bronze or iron, are sacred to the LORD. They shall be put in the treasury of the LORD."

5, 9: *The place is called Gilgal:* by popular etymology, because of the similarity of sound with the Hebrew word *gallothi,* "I have removed." Gilgal probably means "(the place of) the circle of standing stones." Cf Jos 4, 4–8.

5, 10: *The month:* the first month of the year, later called Nisan; see note on Jos 3, 15. The crossing of the Jordan occurred, therefore, about the same time of the year as did the equally miraculous crossing of the Red Sea; cf Ex 12–14.

5, 13—6, 26: The account of the siege of Jericho embraces: (1) the command of the Lord, through his angel, to Joshua (Jos 5, 13—6, 5); (2) Joshua's instructions to the Israelites, with a brief summary of how these orders were carried out (Jos 6, 6–11); (3) a description of the action on each of the first six days (Jos 6, 12–14); (4) the events on the seventh day (Jos 6, 15–26).

6, 18: *That is under the ban:* that is doomed to destruction; see notes on Lv 27, 29; Nm 18, 14; 21, 3.

5, 7: Dt 1, 39.
5, 9: Jos 4, 19.
5, 10: Ex 12, 6; Lv 23, 5; Nm 9, 3–5.
5, 12: Ex 16, 35.
5, 13: Ex 23, 20.
5, 15: Ex 3, 5; Acts 7, 33.
6, 4: Nm 10, 8f.
6, 17: Jos 2, 4; Dt 20, 17; Heb 11, 31.
6, 18: Jos 7, 12.25; Dt 13, 18.

JOS

The Fall of Jericho

20*† As the horns blew, the people began to shout. When they heard the signal horn, they raised a tremendous shout. The wall collapsed, and the people stormed the city in a frontal attack and took it. 21* They observed the ban by putting to the sword all living creatures in the city: men and women, young and old, as well as oxen, sheep and asses. 22* Joshua directed the two men who had spied out the land, "Go into the harlot's house and bring out the woman with all her kin, as you swore to her you would do." 23* The spies entered and brought out Rahab, with her father, mother, brothers, and all her kin. Her entire family they led forth and placed them outside the camp of Israel. 24* The city itself they burned with all that was in it, except the silver, gold, and articles of bronze and iron, which were placed in the treasury of the house of the LORD. 25† Because Rahab the harlot had hidden the messengers whom Joshua had sent to reconnoiter Jericho, Joshua spared her with her family and all her kin, who continue in the midst of Israel to this day.

26*† On that occasion Joshua imposed the oath: Cursed before the LORD be the man who attempts to rebuild this city, Jericho. He shall lose his first-born when he lays its foundation, and he shall lose his youngest son when he sets up its gates.

27* Thus the LORD was with Joshua so that his fame spread throughout the land.

Defeat at Ai

7 1* But the Israelites violated the ban; Achan, son of Carmi, son of Zerah, son of Zara of the tribe of Judah, took goods that were under the ban, and the anger of the LORD flared up against the Israelites.

2 Joshua next sent men from Jericho to Ai, which is near Bethel on its eastern side, with instructions to go up and reconnoiter the land. When they had explored Ai, 3 they returned to Joshua and advised, "Do not send all the people up; if only about two or three thousand go up, they can overcome Ai. The enemy there are few; you need not call for an effort from all the people." 4 About three thousand of the people made the attack, but they were defeated by those at Ai, 5 who killed some thirty-six of them. They pressed them back across the clearing in front of the city gate till they broke ranks, and defeated them finally on the descent, so that the confidence of the people melted away like water.

6 Joshua, together with the elders of Israel, rent his garments and lay prostrate before the ark of the LORD until evening; and they threw dust on their heads. 7 "Alas, O Lord GOD," Joshua prayed, "why did you ever allow this people to pass over the Jordan, delivering us into the power of the Amorites, that they might destroy us? Would that we had been content to dwell on the other side of the Jordan. 8 Pray, Lord, what can I say, now that Israel has turned its back to its enemies? 9 When the Canaanites and the other inhabitants of the land hear of it, they will close in around us and efface our name from the earth. What will you do for your great name?"

10 The LORD replied to Joshua: "Stand up. Why are you lying prostrate? 11* Israel has sinned: they have violated the covenant which I enjoined on them. They have stealthily taken goods subject to the ban, and have deceitfully put them in their baggage. 12* If the Israelites cannot stand up to their enemies, but must turn their back to them, it is because they are under the ban. I will not remain with you unless you remove from among you whoever has incurred the ban. 13* Rise, sanctify the people. Tell them to sanctify themselves before tomorrow, for the LORD, the God of Israel, says: You are under the ban, O Israel. You cannot stand up to your enemies until you remove from among you whoever has incurred the ban. 14 In the morning you must present yourselves by tribes. The tribe which the LORD designates shall come forward by clans; the clan which the LORD designates shall come forward by families; the family which the LORD designates shall come forward one by one. 15 He who is designated as having incurred the ban shall be destroyed by fire, with all that is his, because he has violated the covenant of the LORD and has committed a shameful crime in Israel."

Achan's Guilt and Punishment

16† Early the next morning Joshua had Israel come forward by tribes, and the tribe of Judah was

---

† **6, 20:** *The wall collapsed:* by the miraculous intervention of God. The blowing of the horns and the shouting of the people were a customary feature of ancient warfare, here intended by God as a test of the people's obedience and of their faith in his promise; cf Heb 11, 30.

6, 25: From Mt 1, 5, we learn that Rahab married Salmon of the tribe of Judah and thus became the great-great-grandmother of David, Christ's ancestor; cf Ru 4, 18–22.

6, 26: *He shall lose his first-born . . . its gates:* this curse was fulfilled when Hiel rebuilt Jericho as a fortified city during the reign of Ahab, king of Israel, cf 1 Kgs 16, 34. Till then Jericho was merely an unwalled village; cf Jos 18, 12.21; Jgs 3, 13; 2 Sm 10, 5.

7, 16ff: *Was designated:* probably by means of the Urim and Thummim; cf 1 Sm 14, 38–42. See note on Ex 28, 30.

6, 20: 2 Mc 12, 15; Heb 11, 30.
6, 21: Dt 7, 2.
6, 22: Jos 2, 14.
6, 23: Jos 2, 13; Heb 11, 31.
6, 24: Jos 8, 2.
6, 26: 1 Kgs 16, 34.
6, 27: Jos 1, 5.
7, 1: Jos 6, 18; 22, 20; 1 Chr 2, 7.
7, 11: Jos 6, 17–19.
7, 12: Jos 6, 18.
7, 13: Jos 3, 5; Lv 20, 7; 1 Sm 16, 5.

designated. [17]* Then he had the clans of Judah come forward, and the clan of Zerah was designated. He had the clan of Zerah come forward by families, and Zabdi was designated. [18] Finally he had that family come forward one by one, and Achan, son of Carmi, son of Zabdi, son of Zerah of the tribe of Judah, was designated. [19] Joshua said to Achan, "My son, give to the LORD, the God of Israel, glory and honor by telling me what you have done; do not hide it from me." [20] Achan answered Joshua, "I have indeed sinned against the LORD, the God of Israel. This is what I have done: [21] Among the spoils, I saw a beautiful Babylonian mantle, two hundred shekels of silver, and a bar of gold fifty shekels in weight; in my greed I took them. They are now hidden in the ground inside my tent, with the silver underneath." [22] The messengers whom Joshua sent hastened to the tent and found them hidden there, with the silver underneath. [23] They took them from the tent, brought them to Joshua and all the Israelites, and spread them out before the LORD.

[24] Then Joshua and all Israel took Achan, son of Zerah, with the silver, the mantle, and the bar of gold, and with his sons and daughters, his ox, his ass and his sheep, his tent, and all his possessions, and led them off to the Valley of Achor. [25]* Joshua said, "The LORD bring upon you today the misery with which you have afflicted us!" And all Israel stoned him to death [26]*† and piled a great heap of stones over him, which remains to the present day. Then the anger of the LORD relented. That is why the place is called the Valley of Achor to this day.

Capture of Ai

8 [1]* The LORD then said to Joshua, "Do not be afraid or dismayed. Take all the army with you and prepare to attack Ai. I have delivered the king of Ai into your power, with his people, city, and land. [2]* Do to Ai and its king what you did to Jericho and its king; except that you may take its spoil and livestock as booty. Set an ambush behind the city." [3]† So Joshua and all the soldiers prepared to attack Ai. Picking out thirty thousand warriors, Joshua sent them off by night [4] with these orders: "See that you ambush the city from the rear, at no great distance; then all of you be on the watch. [5] The rest of the people and I will come up to the city, and when they make a sortie against us as they did the last time, we will flee from them. [6] They will keep coming out after us until we have drawn them

away from the city, for they will think we are fleeing from them as we did the last time. When this occurs, [7] rise from ambush and take possession of the city, which the LORD, your God, will deliver into your power. [8] When you have taken the city, set it afire in obedience to the LORD'S command. These are my orders to you." [9] Then Joshua sent them away. They went to the place of ambush, taking up their position to the west of Ai, toward Bethel. Joshua, however, spent that night in the plain.

[10] Early the next morning Joshua mustered the army and went up to Ai at its head, with the elders of Israel. [11] When all the troops he led were drawn up in position before the city, they pitched camp north of Ai, on the other side of the ravine. [12] [He took about five thousand men and set them in ambush between Bethel and Ai, west of the city.] [13] Thus the people took up their stations, with the main body north of the city and the ambush west of it, and Joshua waited overnight among his troops. [14] The king of Ai saw this, and he and all his army came out very early in the morning to engage Israel in battle at the descent toward the Arabah, not knowing that there was an ambush behind the city. [15] Joshua and the main body of the Israelites fled in seeming defeat toward the desert, [16] till the last of the soldiers in the city had been called out to pursue them. [17] Since they were drawn away from the city, with every man engaged in this pursuit of Joshua and the Israelites, not a soldier remained in Ai [or Bethel], and the city was open and unprotected.

[18] Then the LORD directed Joshua, "Stretch out the javelin in your hand toward Ai, for I will deliver it into your power." Joshua stretched out the javelin in his hand toward the city, [19] and as soon as he did so, the men in ambush rose from their post, rushed in, captured the city, and immediately set it on fire. [20] By the time the men of Ai looked back, the smoke from the city was already sky-high. Escape in any direction was impossible, because the Israelites retreating toward the desert now turned on their pursuers; [21] for when Joshua and the main body of Israelites saw that the city had been taken from ambush and was going up in smoke, they struck back at the men of Ai. [22]* Since those in the city came out to intercept them, the men of Ai were hemmed in by Israelites on either side, who cut them down without any fugitives or survivors [23] except the king, whom they took alive and brought to Joshua.

† —

7, 26: *Achor:* "misery, affliction." The reference is to the saying of Joshua in v 25, with an allusion also to the similar-sounding name of Achan.

8, 3: *Thirty thousand warriors:* this figure of the Hebrew text, which seems extremely high, may be due to a copyist's error; some manuscripts of the Septuagint have "three thousand," which is the

number of the whole army in the first, unsuccessful attack (Jos 7, 4); the variant reading in v 12 mentions "five thousand."

* —

7, 17: Nm 26, 20.   8, 1: Jos 2, 24.
7, 25: Jos 6, 18; 22, 20;   8, 2: Jos 6, 21.24; Dt 20,
    1 Chr 2, 7.   14.
7, 26: Jos 8, 29.   8, 22: Dt 7, 2.

JOS

24 All the inhabitants of Ai who had pursued the Israelites into the desert were slain by the sword there in the open, down to the last man. Then all Israel returned and put to the sword those inside the city. 25 There fell that day a total of twelve thousand men and women, the entire population of Ai. 26* Joshua kept the javelin in his hand stretched out until he had fulfilled the doom on all the inhabitants of Ai. 27 However, the Israelites took for themselves as booty the livestock and the spoil of that city, according to the command of the LORD issued to Joshua. 28* Then Joshua destroyed the place by fire, reducing it to an everlasting mound of ruins, as it remains today. 29* He had the king of Ai hanged on a tree until evening; then at sunset Joshua ordered the body removed from the tree and cast at the entrance of the city gate, where a great heap of stones was piled up over it, which remains to the present day.

Altar on Mount Ebal

30† Later Joshua built an altar to the LORD, the God of Israel, on Mount Ebal, 31* of unhewn stones on which no iron tool had been used, in keeping with the command to the Israelites of Moses, the servant of the LORD, as recorded in the book of the law. On this altar they offered holocausts and peace offerings to the LORD. 32* There, in the presence of the Israelites, Joshua inscribed upon the stones a copy of the law written by Moses. 33* And all Israel, stranger and native alike, with their elders, officers and judges, stood on either side of the ark facing the levitical priests who were carrying the ark of the covenant of the LORD. Half of them were facing Mount Gerizim and half Mount Ebal, thus carrying out the instructions of Moses, the servant of the LORD, for the blessing of the people of Israel on this first occasion. 34* Then were read aloud all the words of the law, the blessings and the curses, exactly as written in the book of the law. 35* Every single word that Moses had commanded, Joshua read aloud to the entire community, including the women and children, and the strangers who had accompanied Israel.

Confederacy against Israel

9 1* When the news reached the kings west of the Jordan, in the mountain regions and in the foothills, and all along the coast of the Great Sea as far as Lebanon: Hittites, Amorites, Canaanites, Perizzites, Hivites and Jebusites, 2 they all

Catholic Connections

THE IMPORTANCE OF ALTARS

As soon as the Israelites were able, they built an altar in the Promised Land and renewed their Covenant with God. The altar was a visible sign of the constant need for rededication and renewal.

The altar is an important symbol for Catholics. Catholics gather around the altar to remember and celebrate Jesus' sacrificial death, his Resurrection, and our new Covenant with God. We gather around the altar to share a meal. We remember the story of our faith, and we are joined together as a community of faith.

The next time you are in church, look at the altar and think about all the other altars in Catholic churches around the world. Think about all the other people who are celebrating the Mass even as you sit there. Think about all the people, beginning with Jesus and the Apostles, who have celebrated their Christian faith around an altar. You are united with them just as surely as the Israelite people were united with one another at Mount Ebal.

▶ Jos 8, 30–35

formed an alliance to launch a common attack against Joshua and Israel.

The Gibeonite Deception

3* On learning what Joshua had done to Jericho and Ai, the inhabitants of Gibeon 4 put into effect a device of their own. They chose provisions for a journey, making use of old sacks for their asses, and old wineskins, torn and mended. 5 They wore old,

---

† **8, 30–35:** These ceremonies were prescribed in Dt 11, 29, and Dt 27, 2–26. See notes on those passages.

* **8, 26:** Ex 17, 11ff. **8, 29:** Jos 10, 26f; Dt 21, 22f; Jn 19, 31. **8, 28:** Dt 13, 16.

8, 31: Ex 20, 24f; Dt 27, 5f. **8, 32:** Dt 27, 2.8. **8, 33:** Jos 3, 3; Dt 11, 27; 27, 12; 31, 9.12. **8, 34:** Dt 28, 2–68; 30, 19; 31, 11; Neh 8, 2f. **8, 35:** Dt 31, 12. **9, 1:** Jos 3, 10; Ex 3, 8.17; 23, 23; Dt 1, 7. **9, 3:** Jos 6, 21.24; 11, 19.

patched sandals and shabby garments; and all the bread they took was dry and crumbly. 6* Thus they journeyed to Joshua in the camp at Gilgal, where they said to him and to the men of Israel, "We have come from a distant land to propose that you make an alliance with us." 7† But the men of Israel replied to the Hivites, "You may be living in land that is ours. How, then, can we make an alliance with you?" 8 But they answered Joshua, "We are your servants." Then Joshua asked them, "Who are you? Where do you come from?" 9* They answered him, "Your servants have come from a far-off land, because of the fame of the LORD, your God. For we have heard reports of all that he did in Egypt 10* and all that he did to the two kings of the Amorites beyond the Jordan, Sihon, king of Heshbon, and Og, king of Bashan, who lived in Ashtaroth. 11 So our elders and all the inhabitants of our country said to us, 'Take along provisions for the journey and go to meet them. Say to them: We are your servants; we propose that you make an alliance with us.' 12 This bread of ours was still warm when we brought it from home as provisions the day we left to come to you, but now it is dry and crumbled. 13 Here are our wineskins, which were new when we filled them, but now they are torn. Look at our garments and sandals, which are worn out from the very long journey." 14* Then the Israelite princes partook of their provisions, without seeking the advice of the LORD. 15* So Joshua made an alliance with them and entered into an agreement to spare them, which the princes of the community sealed with an oath.

Gibeonites Made Vassals

16 Three days after the agreement was entered into, the Israelites learned that these people were from nearby, and would be living in Israel. 17 The third day on the road, the Israelites came to their cities of Gibeon, Chephirah, Beeroth and Kiriath-jearim, 18 but did not attack them, because the princes of the community had sworn to them by the LORD, the God of Israel. When the entire community grumbled against the princes, 19 these all remonstrated with the people, "We have sworn to them by the LORD, the God of Israel, and so we cannot harm them. 20 Let us therefore spare their lives and so deal with them that we shall not be pun-

ished for the oath we have sworn to them." 21† Thus the princes recommended that they be let live, as hewers of wood and drawers of water for the entire community; and the community did as the princes advised them.

22 Joshua summoned the Gibeonites and said to them, "Why did you lie to us and say that you lived at a great distance from us, when you will be living in our very midst? 23 For this are you accursed: every one of you shall always be a slave [hewers of wood and drawers of water] for the house of my God." 24* They answered Joshua, "Your servants were fully informed of how the LORD, your God, commanded his servant Moses that you be given the entire land and that all its inhabitants be destroyed before you. Since, therefore, at your advance, we were in great fear for our lives, we acted as we did. 25 And now that we are in your power, do with us what you think fit and right." 26† Joshua did what he had decided: while he saved them from being killed by the Israelites, 27* at the same time he made them, as they still are, hewers of wood and drawers of water for the community and for the altar of the LORD, in the place of the LORD's choice.

The Siege of Gibeon

10 1* Now Adonizedek, king of Jerusalem, heard that, in the capture and destruction of Ai, Joshua had done to that city and its king as he had done to Jericho and its king. He heard also that the inhabitants of Gibeon had made their peace with Israel, remaining among them, 2 and that there was great fear abroad, because Gibeon was large enough for a royal city, larger even than the city of Ai, and all its men were brave. 3 So Adonizedek, king of Jerusalem, sent for Hoham, king of Hebron, Piram, king of Jarmuth, Japhia, king of Lachish, and Debir, king of Eglon, 4* to come to his aid for an attack on Gibeon, since it had concluded peace with Joshua and the Israelites. 5† The five Amorite kings, of Jerusalem, Hebron, Jarmuth, Lachish and Eglon, united all their forces and marched against Gibeon, where they took up siege positions. 6* Thereupon, the men of Gibeon sent an appeal to Joshua in his camp at Gilgal: "Do not abandon your servants. Come up here quickly and save us. Help us, because all the Amorite kings of the mountain country have joined forces against us."

9, 7: *The Hivites:* apparently the Gibeonites belonged to this larger ethnic group (cf also Jos 11, 19), although in 2 Sm 21, 2 they are classed as Amorites; both groups are listed among the seven nations in Canaan whom the Israelites were to exterminate; cf Dt 7, 1f.

9, 21: *Hewers of wood and drawers of water:* proverbial terms for the lowest social class in the Israelite community; cf Dt 29, 10f.

9, 26f: Later on, Saul violated the immunity of the Gibeonites, but David vindicated it; cf 2 Sm 21, 1–9.

10, 5: *Hebron . . . Eglon:* these four cities were to the south and southwest of Jerusalem.

9, 6: Ex 23, 32; Dt 7, 2.	**9, 27:** Dt 12, 5.
9, 9: Jos 2, 10.	**10, 1:** Jos 9, 15; 6, 21.24; 8,
9, 10: Nm 21, 25.33.	26–29.
9, 14: Nm 27, 21.	**10, 4:** Jos 9, 15.
9, 15: Jos 11, 19; 2 Sm 21, 2.	**10, 6:** Jos 9, 6.
9, 24: Ex 23, 27f; Dt 7, 1f.	

J
O
S

Joshua's Victory

7 So Joshua marched up from Gilgal with his picked troops and the rest of his soldiers. 8 Meanwhile the LORD said to Joshua, "Do not fear them, for I have delivered them into your power. Not one of them will be able to withstand you." 9 And when Joshua made his surprise attack upon them after an all-night march from Gilgal, 10 the LORD threw them into disorder before him. The Israelites inflicted a great slaughter on them at Gibeon and pursued them down the Beth-horon slope, harassing them as far as Azekah and Makkedah.

11*† While they fled before Israel along the descent from Beth-horon, the LORD hurled great stones from the sky above them all the way to Azekah, killing many. More died from these hailstones than the Israelites slew with the sword. 12 On this day, when the LORD delivered up the Amorites to the Israelites,

> Joshua prayed to the LORD,
>   and said in the presence of Israel:
> Stand still, O sun, at Gibeon,
>   O moon, in the valley of Aijalon!

13*† And the sun stood still,
    and the moon stayed,
    while the nation took vengeance on
        its foes.

Is this not recorded in the Book of Jashar? The sun halted in the middle of the sky; not for a whole day did it resume its swift course. 14 Never before or since was there a day like this, when the LORD obeyed the voice of a man; for the LORD fought for Israel. 15 [Then Joshua and all Israel returned to the camp at Gilgal.]

Execution of Amorite Kings

16 Meanwhile the five kings who had fled, hid in a cave at Makkedah. 17 When Joshua was told that the five kings had been discovered hiding in a cave at Makkedah, 18 he said, "Roll large stones to the mouth of the cave and post men over it to guard them. 19 But do not remain there yourselves. Pursue your enemies, and harry them in the rear. Do not allow them to escape to their cities, for the LORD, your God, has delivered them into your power."

20 Once Joshua and the Israelites had finally inflicted the last blows in this very great slaughter,

and the survivors had escaped from them into the fortified cities, 21 all the army returned safely to Joshua and the camp at Makkedah, no man uttering a sound against the Israelites. 22 Then Joshua said, "Open the mouth of the cave and bring out those five kings to me." 23 Obediently, they brought out to him from the cave the five kings, of Jerusalem, Hebron, Jarmuth, Lachish and Eglon. 24 When they had done so, Joshua summoned all the men of Israel and said to the commanders of the soldiers who had marched with him, "Come forward and put your feet on the necks of these kings." They came forward and put their feet upon their necks. 25 Then Joshua said to them, "Do not be afraid or dismayed, be firm and steadfast. This is what the LORD will do to all the enemies against whom you fight." 26* Thereupon Joshua struck and killed them, and hanged them on five trees, where they remained hanging until evening. 27 At sunset they were removed from the trees at the command of Joshua and cast into the cave where they had hidden; over the mouth of the cave large stones were placed, which remain until this very day.

Conquest of Southern Canaan

28* Makkedah, too, Joshua captured and put to the sword at that time. He fulfilled the doom on the city, on its king, and on every person in it, leaving no survivors. Thus he did to the king of Makkedah what he had done to the king of Jericho. 29 Joshua then passed on with all Israel from Makkedah to Libnah, which he attacked. 30 Libnah also, with its king, the LORD delivered into the power of Israel. He put it to the sword with every person there, leaving no survivors. Thus he did to its king what he had done to the king of Jericho. 31 Joshua next passed on with all Israel from Libnah to Lachish, where they set up a camp during the attack. 32 The LORD delivered Lachish into the power of Israel, so that on the second day Joshua captured it and put it to the sword with every person in it, just as he had done to Libnah. 33 At that time Horam, king of Gezer, came up to help Lachish, but Joshua defeated him and his people, leaving him no survivors. 34 From Lachish, Joshua passed on with all Israel to Eglon; encamping near it, they attacked it 35 and captured it the same day, putting it to the sword. He fulfilled the doom that day on every person in it, just as he had done at Lachish. 36 From Eglon,

---

† **10, 11:** *Great stones from the sky:* the hailstones mentioned in the next sentence.

10, 13: *Is this not recorded:* the reference is to the preceding, poetic passage. Evidently the Book of Jashar, like the Book of the Wars of the LORD (Nm 21, 14), recounted in epic style the exploits of Israel's early heroes. *The sun halted:* though it is widely supposed that this passage describes in popular language and according to external appearances a miraculous lengthening of the day, it is equally probable that Joshua's prayer was rather for an abrupt obscuration of

the sun, which would impede his enemies in their flight homeward and also prevent them from rallying their forces; this request would have been answered by the hailstorm (cf Sir 46, 5) and by a darkness relieved only twenty-four hours later, well into the next day.

10, 11: Jb 38, 22.   **10, 26f:** Jos 8, 29; Dt 21, 22f.
10, 13: Sir 46, 4; Is 28, 21;   **10, 28:** Jos 6, 21.
    Heb 3, 11.

Joshua went up with all Israel to Hebron, which they attacked ³⁷ and captured. They put it to the sword with its king, all its towns, and every person there, leaving no survivors, just as Joshua had done to Eglon. He fulfilled the doom on it and on every person there. ³⁸ Then Joshua and all Israel turned back to Debir and attacked it, ³⁹ capturing it with its king and all its towns. They put them to the sword and fulfilled the doom on every person there, leaving no survivors. Thus was done to Debir and its king what had been done to Hebron, as well as to Libnah and its king.

⁴⁰* Joshua conquered the entire country; the mountain regions, the Negeb, the foothills, and the mountain slopes, with all their kings. He left no survivors, but fulfilled the doom on all who lived there, just as the LORD, the God of Israel, had commanded. ⁴¹† Joshua conquered from Kadesh-barnea to Gaza, and all the land of Goshen to Gibeon. ⁴² All these kings and their lands Joshua captured in a single campaign, for the LORD, the God of Israel, fought for Israel. ⁴³ Thereupon Joshua with all Israel returned to the camp at Gilgal.

Northern Confederacy

11 ¹† When Jabin, king of Hazor, learned of this, he sent a message to Jobab, king of Madon, to the king of Shimron, to the king of Achshaph, ²* and to the northern kings in the mountain regions and in the Arabah near Chinneroth, in the foothills, and in Naphath-dor to the west. ³ These were Canaanites to the east and west, Amorites, Hittites, Perizzites and Jebusites in the mountain regions, and Hivites at the foot of Hermon in the land of Mizpah. ⁴ They came out with all their troops, an army numerous as the sands on the seashore, and with a multitude of horses and chariots. ⁵† All these kings joined forces and marched to the waters of Merom, where they encamped together to fight against Israel.

⁶ The LORD said to Joshua, "Do not fear them, for by this time tomorrow I will stretch them slain before Israel. You must hamstring their horses and burn their chariots." ⁷ Joshua with his whole army came upon them at the waters of Merom in a surprise attack. ⁸* The LORD delivered them into the power of the Israelites, who defeated them and pursued them to Greater Sidon, to Misrephoth-maim, and eastward to the valley of Mizpeh. They struck them all down, leaving no survivors. ⁹ Joshua did to them as the LORD had commanded: he hamstrung their horses and burned their chariots.

Conquest of Northern Canaan

¹⁰ At that time Joshua, turning back, captured Hazor and slew its king with the sword; for Hazor formerly was the chief of all those kingdoms. ¹¹ He also fulfilled the doom by putting every person there to the sword, till none was left alive. Hazor itself he burned. ¹²* Joshua thus captured all those kings with their cities and put them to the sword, fulfilling the doom on them, as Moses, the servant of the LORD, had commanded. ¹³ However, Israel did not destroy by fire any of the cities built on raised sites, except Hazor, which Joshua burned. ¹⁴ The Israelites took all the spoil and livestock of these cities as their booty; but the people they put to the sword, until they had exterminated the last of them, leaving none alive. ¹⁵* As the LORD had commanded his servant Moses, so Moses commanded Joshua, and Joshua acted accordingly. He left nothing undone that the LORD had commanded Moses should be done.

Survey of the Conquest

¹⁶* So Joshua captured all this land: the mountain regions, the entire Negeb, all the land of Goshen, the foothills, the Arabah, as well as the mountain regions and foothills of Israel, ¹⁷* from Mount Halak that rises toward Seir as far as Baal-gad in the Lebanon valley at the foot of Mount Hermon. All their kings he captured and put to death. ¹⁸ Joshua waged war against all these kings for a long time. ¹⁹* With the exception of the Hivites who lived in Gibeon, no city made peace with the Israelites; all were taken in battle. ²⁰* For it was the design of the LORD to encourage them to wage war against Israel, that they might be doomed to destruction and thus receive no mercy, but be exterminated, as the LORD had commanded Moses.

²¹*† At that time Joshua penetrated the mountain regions and exterminated the Anakim in Hebron, Debir, Anab, the entire mountain region of

---

† **10, 41:** Goshen: a town and its surrounding district at the southern end of the Judean mountains (cf Jos 11, 16; 15, 51); not to be confused with the land of Goshen in northeastern Egypt (Gen 45, 10), although in the current Hebrew Bible both names are spelled the same.

11, 1ff: Hazor, Madon, Shimron, and Chinneroth: cities and their surrounding districts in eastern Galilee. Achshaph and Naphath-dor: southwest of Galilee. The mountain regions: in central and northern Galilee.

11, 5: The waters of Merom: a stream in central Galilee that flows southeast to water the fertile Arabah, or plain of Chinneroth on the western shore of the lake of Gennesaret.

11, 21ff: Most of the land assigned to the tribe of Judah was not conquered by it till the early period of the Judges. See note on Jgs 1, 1–36.

*
10, 40: Dt 20, 16f.   11, 17: Jos 12, 7; Dt 7, 24.
11, 2: Jos 12, 3; Jgs 1, 27. 11, 19: Jos 9, 3.7.15.
11, 8: Jos 13, 6.   11, 20: Dt 2, 30; 20, 16f.
11, 12: Dt 7, 2; 20, 16f.   11, 21: Jos 15, 13f; Nm 13,
11, 15: Jos 7, 2.   22; Dt 1, 28.
11, 16: Jos 10, 41; 12, 8.

JOS

Judah, and the entire mountain region of Israel. Joshua fulfilled the doom on them and on their cities, 22 so that no Anakim were left in the land of the Israelites. However, some survived in Gaza, in Gath, and in Ashdod. 23*† Thus Joshua captured the whole country, just as the LORD had foretold to Moses. Joshua gave it to Israel as their heritage, apportioning it among the tribes. And the land enjoyed peace.

Lists of Conquered Kings

12 †1 The kings of the land east of the Jordan, from the River Arnon to Mount Hermon, including all the eastern section of the Arabah, whom the Israelites conquered and whose lands they occupied, were: 2* First, Sihon, king of the Amorites, who lived in Heshbon. His domain extended from Aroer, which is on the bank of the Wadi Arnon, to include the wadi itself, and the land northward through half of Gilead to the Wadi Jabbok, 3* as well as the Arabah from the eastern side of the Sea of Chinnereth, as far south as the eastern side of the Salt Sea of the Arabah in the direction of Beth-jeshimoth, to a point under the slopes of Pisgah. 4* Secondly, Og, king of Bashan, a survivor of the Rephaim, who lived at Ashtaroth and Edrei. 5 He ruled over Mount Hermon, Salecah, and all Bashan as far as the boundary of the Geshurites and Maacathites, and over half of Gilead as far as the territory of Sihon, king of Heshbon. 6* After Moses, the servant of the LORD, and the Israelites conquered them, he assigned their land to the Reubenites, the Gadites, and the half-tribe of Manasseh, as their property.

7 This is a list of the kings whom Joshua and the Israelites conquered west of the Jordan and whose land, from Baal-gad in the Lebanon valley to Mount Halak which rises toward Seir, Joshua apportioned to the tribes of Israel. 8 It included the mountain regions and foothills, the Arabah, the slopes, the desert, and the Negeb, belonging to the Hittites, Amorites, Canaanites, Perizzites, Hivites and Jebusites. 9* They were the kings of Jericho, Ai (which is near Bethel), 10 Jerusalem, Hebron, 11* Jarmuth, Lachish, 12* Eglon, Gezer, 13* Debir, Geder, 14 Hormah, Arad, 15* Libnah, Adullam, 16* Makkedah, Bethel, 17* Tappuah, Hepher, 18* Aphek, Lasharon, 19* Madon, Hazor, 20* Shimron, Achshaph, 21* Taanach, Megiddo, 22 Kedesh, Jokneam (at Carmel),

?did you KNOW?

The Conquest of Canaan

A strong parallel connects the beginning of the story of Joshua—the crossing of the Jordan River, God's direction and protection of the Israelites (symbolized by the ark), and the renewal of the Covenant at Mount Ebal—and the events of the Exodus from Egypt. The parallel reinforces how the conquest of Canaan was part of God's continued liberation of the Chosen People and a key moment in the history of Israel.

As the Israelites moved in on the Promised Land, the Canaanites were one of several groups of people that the Israelites had to deal with. Joshua 12, 8 also mentions Hittites, Amorites, Perizzites, Hivites, and Jebusites. But the Canaanites seemed to be the dominant inhabitants. They were primarily an agricultural society and believed that their gods, called baals, controlled the rains, the seasons, and the fertility of the soil. For the Israelites, God was revealed as the only God over all creation and history.

The conquest of the Canaanites through violence might make you wonder what the Israelites believed about God. Basically, they believed that the Canaanite baals were an offense against God. Because the Canaanites would not change, the Israelites felt justified in killing them and taking their land. (See "Holy War," near Nm 2, 1.) Later, Christians would not be able to justify such actions because of Jesus' teaching that everyone is loved by God and that we must love even our enemies. But at the time Joshua was written, God and God's plan for humanity had not yet been fully revealed.

▶ Joshua, chapter 12

---

†11, 23: *The land enjoyed peace:* of a limited and temporary nature. Many of the individual tribes had still to fight against the remaining Canaanites; cf Jos 15, 13–17; 17, 12f. This verse forms the conclusion to the first part of the book. Cf note on Jos 12, 1–24.

12, 1–24: This chapter, inserted between the two principal parts of the book (chapters 1–11 and 13–21), resembles the lists of conquered cities which are inscribed on monuments of the Egyptian and Assyrian monarchs. Perhaps it was copied here from some such public Israelite record.

11, 23: Jos 14, 1–19, 51; Nm 34, 2–12.
12, 2–5: Nm 21, 21–26.33ff.
12, 3: Jos 13, 20.
12, 4: Jos 13, 11f.
12, 6: Nm 32, 33; Dt 3, 12f.
12, 9: Jos 6, 2; 8, 23.
12, 11: 10f; Jos 10, 23.
12, 12: Jos 10, 23.33.

12, 13: Jos 10, 38f; 15, 36.
12, 15: Jos 10, 29f; 15, 35.
12, 16: Jos 8, 17; 10, 28.
12, 17: Jos 15, 34.
12, 18: Jos 15, 53.
12, 19: Jos 11, 1.10.
12, 20: Jos 11, 1.
12, 21: Jos 17, 11.
12, 22: Jos 19, 37.

23* and Dor (in Naphath-dor), the foreign king at Gilgal, 24 and the king of Tirzah, thirty-one kings in all.

II: Division of the Land

Division of Land Commanded

13 1* When Joshua was old and advanced in years, the LORD said to him: "Though now you are old and advanced in years, a very large part of the land still remains to be conquered. 2† This additional land includes all Geshur and all the districts of the Philistines 3* (from the stream adjoining Egypt to the boundary of Ekron in the north is reckoned Canaanite territory, though held by the five lords of the Philistines in Gaza, Ashdod, Ashkelon, Gath and Ekron); also where the Avvim are in the south; 4 all the land of the Canaanites from Mearah of the Sidonians to Aphek, and the boundaries of the Amorites; 5 and the Gebalite territory; and all the Lebanon on the east, from Baal-gad at the foot of Mount Hermon to Labo in the land of Hamath. 6* At the advance of the Israelites I will drive out all the Sidonian inhabitants of the mountain regions between Lebanon and Misrephoth-maim; at least include these areas in the division of the Israelite heritage, just as I have commanded you. 7 Now, therefore, apportion among the nine tribes and the half-tribe of Manasseh the land which is to be their heritage."

The Eastern Tribes

8* Now the other half of the tribe of Manasseh, as well as the Reubenites and Gadites, had received their heritage which Moses, the servant of the LORD, had given them east of the Jordan: 9 from Aroer on the bank of the Wadi Arnon and the city in the wadi itself, through the tableland of Medeba and Dibon, 10 with the rest of the cities of Sihon, king of the Amorites, who reigned in Heshbon, to the boundary of the Ammonites; 11 also Gilead and the territory of the Geshurites and Maacathites, all Mount Hermon, and all Bashan as far as Salecah, 12 the entire kingdom in Bashan of Og, a survivor of the Rephaim, who reigned at Ashtaroth and Edrei. Though Moses conquered and occupied these territories, 13 the Israelites did not dislodge the Geshurites and Maacathites, so that Geshur and Maacath survive in the midst of Israel to this day. 14* However, to the tribe of Levi Moses assigned no heritage

since, as the LORD had promised them, the LORD, the God of Israel, is their heritage.

Reuben

15* What Moses gave to the Reubenite clans:* 16 Their territory reached from Aroer, on the bank of the Wadi Arnon, and the city in the wadi itself, through the tableland about Medeba, 17 to include Heshbon and all its towns which are on the tableland, Dibon, Bamoth-baal, Beth-baal-meon, 18 Jahaz, Kedemoth, Mephaath, 19 Kiriathaim, Sibmah, Zereth-shahar on the knoll within the valley, 20 Beth-peor, the slopes of Pisgah, Beth-jeshimoth, 21* and the other cities of the tableland and, generally, of the kingdom of Sihon. This Amorite king, who reigned in Heshbon, Moses had killed, with his vassals, the princes of Midian, who were settled in the land: Evi, Rekem, Zur, Hur and Reba; 22* and among their slain followers the Israelites put to the sword also the soothsayer Balaam, son of Beor. 23 The boundary of the Reubenites was the bank of the Jordan. These cities and their villages were the heritage of the clans of the Reubenites.

Gad

24* What Moses gave to the Gadite clans: 25 Their territory included Jazer, all the cities of Gilead, and half the land of the Ammonites as far as Aroer, toward Rabbah 26 (that is, from Heshbon to Ramath-mizpeh and Betonim, and from Mahanaim to the boundary of Lodebar); 27 and in the Jordan valley: Beth-haram, Beth-nimrah, Succoth, Zaphon, the other part of the kingdom of Sihon, king of Heshbon, with the bank of the Jordan to the southeastern tip of the Sea of Chinnereth. 28 These cities and their villages were the heritage of the clans of the Gadites.

Manasseh

29* What Moses gave to the clans of the half-tribe of Manasseh: 30* Their territory included Mahanaim, all of Bashan, the entire kingdom of Og, king of Bashan, and all the villages of Jair, which are sixty cities in Bashan. 31 Half of Gilead, with Ashtaroth and Edrei, once the royal cities of Og in Bashan, fell to the descendants of Machir, son of Manasseh, for half the clans descended from Machir.

32 These are the portions which Moses gave when he was in the plains of Moab, beyond the Jordan

---

† **13, 2:** *Geshur:* not to be confused with the large Aramaean district of the same name in Bashan (vv 11–13; Dt 3, 14); here it is a region to the south of the Philistine country, since vv 2–5 list the unconquered lands along the coast from south to north; cf also 1 Sm 27, 8.

12, 23: Jos 11, 2.
13, 1: Jos 23, 1.
13, 3: Jgs 3, 3.
13, 6: Jos 11, 8.
13, 8: Jos 12, 6; Nm 32, 33.
13, 14: Jos 14, 3f; Nm 18, 20–24.
13, 15–31: Dt 3, 12–17.
13, 15–23: Nm 21, 25–31; 32, 37f.
13, 21: Nm 21, 24; 31, 8; Dt 3, 10.
13, 22: Nm 31, 8.
13, 24–28: Nm 32, 34ff.
13, 29–31: Nm 32, 39ff.
13, 30: Nm 32, 41.

east of Jericho. ³³* However, Moses gave no heritage to the tribe of Levi, since the LORD himself, the God of Israel, is their heritage, as he promised.

The Western Tribes

14 ¹* Here follow the portions which the Israelites received in the land of Canaan. Eleazar the priest, Joshua, son of Nun, and the heads of families in the tribes of the Israelites determined ²* their heritage by lot, in accordance with the instructions the LORD had given through Moses concerning the remaining nine and a half tribes. ³* For to two and a half tribes Moses had already given a heritage beyond the Jordan; and though the Levites were given no heritage among the tribes, ⁴* the descendants of Joseph formed two tribes, Manasseh and Ephraim. The Levites themselves received no share of the land except cities to live in, with their pasture lands for the cattle and flocks.

⁵ Thus, in apportioning the land, did the Israelites carry out the instructions of the LORD to Moses.

Caleb's Portion

⁶* When the Judahites came up to Joshua in Gilgal, the Kenizzite Caleb, son of Jephunneh, said to him: "You know what the LORD said to the man of God, Moses, about you and me in Kadesh-barnea. ⁷* I was forty years old when the servant of the LORD, Moses, sent me from Kadesh-barnea to reconnoiter the land; and I brought back to him a conscientious report. ⁸* My fellow scouts who went up with me discouraged the people, but I was completely loyal to the LORD, my God. ⁹ On that occasion Moses swore this oath, "The land where you have set foot shall become your heritage and that of your descendants forever, because you have been completely loyal to the LORD, my God." ¹⁰* Now, as he promised, the LORD has preserved me while Israel was journeying through the desert, for the forty-five years since the LORD spoke thus to Moses; and although I am now eighty-five years old, ¹¹* I am still as strong today as I was the day Moses sent me forth, with no less vigor whether for war or for ordinary tasks. ¹²* Give me, therefore, this mountain region which the LORD promised me that day, as you yourself heard. True, the Anakim are there, with large fortified cities, but if the LORD is with me

I shall be able to drive them out, as the LORD promised." ¹³* Joshua blessed Caleb, son of Jephunneh, and gave him Hebron as his heritage. ¹⁴ Therefore Hebron remains the heritage of the Kenizzite Caleb, son of Jephunneh, to the present day, because he was completely loyal to the LORD, the God of Israel. ¹⁵* Hebron was formerly called Kiriath-arba, for Arba, the greatest among the Anakim. And the land enjoyed peace.

Boundaries of Judah

15 ¹* The lot for the clans of the Judahite tribe fell in the extreme south toward the boundary of Edom, the desert of Zin in the Negeb. ²* The boundary there ran from the bay that forms the southern end of the Salt Sea, ³ southward below the pass of Akrabbim, across through Zin, up to a point south of Kadesh-barnea, across to Hezron, and up to Addar; from there, looping around Karka, ⁴ it crossed to Azmon and then joined the Wadi of Egypt before coming out at the sea. [This is your southern boundary.] ⁵ The eastern boundary was the Salt Sea as far as the mouth of the Jordan.

⁶* The northern boundary climbed from the bay where the Jordan meets the sea, up to Beth-hoglah, and ran north of Beth-arabah, up to Eben-Bohan-ben-Reuben. ⁷* Thence it climbed up to Debir, north of the vale of Achor, in the direction of the Gilgal that faces the pass of Adummim, on the south side of the wadi; from there it crossed to the waters of En-shemesh and emerged at En-rogel. ⁸*† Climbing again to the Valley of Ben-Hinnom on the southern flank of the Jebusites [that is, Jerusalem], the boundary rose to the top of the mountain at the northern end of the Valley of Rephaim, which bounds the Valley of Hinnom on the west. ⁹* From the top of the mountain it ran to the fountain of waters of Nephtoah, extended to the cities of Mount Ephron, and continued to Baalah, or Kiriath-jearim. ¹⁰ From Baalah the boundary curved westward to Mount Seir and passed north of the ridge of Mount Jearim (that is, Chesalon); thence it descended to Beth-shemesh, and ran across to Timnah. ¹¹ It then extended along the northern flank of Ekron, continued through Shikkeron, and across to Mount Baalah, thence to include Jabneel, before it came out at the sea. ¹² The western boundary was the Great Sea and its coast. This was the complete boundary of the clans of the Judahites.

---

† **15, 8:** *The Valley of Ben-hinnom:* the southern limit of Jerusalem. Ben-hinnom means "son of Hinnom." The place was also called Valley of Hinnom, in Hebrew *ge-hinnom,* whence the word "Gehenna" is derived.

13, 33: Jos 18, 7; Nm 18, 20.
14, 1: Jos 17, 4; 21, 1; Nm 34, 17f.
14, 2: Nm 26, 55; 33, 54; 34, 13.
14, 3: Jos 13, 8.14.33.
14, 4: Jos 21, 3–40; Gn 48, 5.
14, 6: Nm 14, 24.30; 32, 12; Dt 1, 36.38.
14, 7: Nm 14, 6–9.
14, 8: Nm 13, 31ff; 14, 24; 32, 12; Dt 1, 36.
14, 10: Nm 14, 30.
14, 11: Sir 46, 1ff.
14, 12: Jos 11, 21.
14, 13: Jos 10, 36f; 15, 13–19; 21, 11f.
14, 15: Jgs 1, 10.
15, 1: Nm 34, 3.
15, 2–4: Nm 34, 3ff.
15, 6: Jos 18, 18f.22.
15, 7: Jos 7, 26; 18, 16ff; 2 Sm 17, 17.
15, 8: Jos 18, 16.
15, 9: Jos 18, 15.

Conquest by Caleb

13* As the LORD had commanded, Joshua gave Caleb, son of Jephunneh,* a portion among the Judahites, namely, Kiriath-arba (Arba was the father of Anak), that is, Hebron. 14* And Caleb drove out from there the three Anakim, the descendants of Anak: Sheshai, Ahiman and Talmai. 15* From there he marched up against the inhabitants of Debir, which was formerly called Kiriath-sepher. 16 Caleb said, "I will give my daughter Achsah in marriage to the one who attacks Kiriath-sepher and captures it." 17† Othniel, son of Caleb's brother Kenaz, captured it, and so Caleb gave him his daughter Achsah in marriage. 18 On the day of her marriage to Othniel, she induced him to ask her father for some land. Then, as she alighted from the ass, Caleb asked her, "What is troubling you?" 19 She answered, "Give me an additional gift! Since you have assigned to me land in the Negeb, give me also pools of water." So he gave her the upper and the lower pools.

Cities of Judah

20† This is the heritage of the clans of the tribe of Judahites: 21 The cities of the tribe of the Judahites in the extreme southern district toward Edom were: Kabzeel, Eder, Jagur, 22 Kinah, Dimonah, Adadah, 23 Kedesh, Hazor and Ithnan; 24 Ziph, Telem, Bealoth, 25 Hazor-hadattah, and Kerioth-hezron (that is, Hazor); 26 Amam, Shema, Moladah, 27 Hazar-gaddah, Heshmon, Beth-pelet, 28 Hazar-shual, Beer-sheba, and Biziothiah, 29 Baalah, Iim, Ezem, 30 Eltolad, Chesil, Hormah, 31* Ziklag, Madmannah, Sansannah, 32 Lebaoth, Shilhim and En-rimmon; a total of twenty-nine cities with their villages. 33† In the foothills: Eshtaol, Zorah, Ashnah, 34 Zanoah, Engannim, Tappuah, Enam, 35 Jarmuth, Adullam, Socoh, Azekah, 36 Shaaraim, Adithaim, Gederah, and Gederothaim; fourteen cities and their villages. 37 Zenan, Hadashah, Migdal-gad, 38 Dilean, Mizpeh, Joktheel, 39 Lachish, Bozkath, Eglon, 40 Cabbon, Lahmam, Chitlish, 41 Gederoth, Beth-dagon, Naamah and Makkedah; sixteen cities and their villages. 42 Libnah, Ether, Ashan, 43 Iphtah, Ashnah, Nezib, 44 Keilah, Achzib and Mareshah; nine cities and their villages. 45 Ekron and its towns and villages; 46 from Ekron to the sea, all the towns that lie alongside Ashdod and their villages; 47 Ashdod and its towns and villages; Gaza and its towns and villages, as far as the Wadi of Egypt and the coast of the Great Sea.

48 In the mountain regions: Shamir, Jattir, Socoh, 49 Dannah, Kiriath-sannah (that is, Debir), 50 Anab, Eshtemoh, Anim, 51 Goshen, Holon and Giloh; eleven cities and their villages. 52 Arab, Dumah, Eshan, 53 Janim, Beth-tappuah, Aphekah, 54 Humtah, Kiriath-arba (that is, Hebron), and Zior; nine cities and their villages. 55 Maon, Carmel, Ziph, Juttah, 56 Jezreel, Jokdeam, Zanoah, 57 Kain, Gibbeah and Timnah; ten cities and their villages. 58 Halhul, Beth-zur, Gedor, 59 Maarath, Beth-anoth and El-tekon; six cities and their villages. Tekoa, Ephrathah (that is, Bethlehem), Peor, Etam, Kulom, Tatam, Zores, Karim, Gallim, Bether and Manoko; eleven cities and their villages. 60* Kiriath-baal (that is, Kiriath-jearim) and Rabbah: two cities and their villages.

61† In the desert: Beth-arabah, Middin, Secacah, 62 Nibshan, Ir-hamelah and En-gedi; six cities and their villages. 63* [But the Jebusites who lived in Jerusalem the Judahites could not drive out; so the Jebusites dwell in Jerusalem beside the Judahites to the present day.]

The Joseph Tribes

16 1† The lot that fell to the Josephites extended from the Jordan at Jericho to the waters of Jericho east of the desert; then the boundary went up from Jericho to the heights at Bethel. 2 Leaving Bethel for Luz, it crossed the ridge to the border of the Archites at Ataroth, 3* and descended westward to the border of the Japhletites, to that of Lower Beth-horon, and to Gezer, ending thence at the sea.

Ephraim

4 Within the heritage of Manasseh and Ephraim, sons of Joseph, 5*† the dividing line for the heritage of the clans of the Ephraimites ran from east of Ataroth-addar to Upper Beth-horon 6* and thence to the sea. From Michmethath on the north,

---

15, 17–19: The story of Othniel is told again in Jgs 1, 13–15; cf also Jgs 3, 9–11.

15, 20–62: This elaborate list of the cities of Judah was probably taken from a document made originally for administrative purposes; the cities are divided into four provincial districts, some of which have further subdivisions. For similar lists of the cities of Judah, cf Jos 19, 2–7; 1 Chr 4, 28–32; Neh 11, 25–30. This list has suffered in transmission, so that the totals given in vv 32 and 36 are not exact, and some of the names are probably misspelled; many of the cities cannot be identified.

15, 33: In the foothills: see note on Dt 1, 7.

15, 61: In the desert: in the Jordan rift near the Dead Sea.

16, 1–17.18: The boundaries and cities of Judah, the most important tribe, having been given, the land of the next most important group, the two Josephite tribes of Ephraim and Manasseh, is now described, though it was separated from Judah by the territories of Benjamin (Jos 18, 11–20) and Dan (Jos 19, 40–48).

16, 1–3: This line formed the southern boundary of Ephraim and the northern boundaries of Benjamin and of Dan.

16, 5: The dividing line: separating Ephraim from Manasseh. Ephraim's northern border (v 5) is given in an east-to-west direction; its eastern border (v 6f) in a north-to-south direction.

15, 13–19: Jgs 1, 10–15.
15, 13: Jgs 1, 13ff.
15, 14: Nm 13, 22; Jgs 1, 20.
15, 15: Jos 10, 38.
15, 31: 1 Sm 27, 6.
15, 60: Jos 18, 14.
15, 63: Jgs 1, 21; 2 Sm 5, 6.
16, 3: Jos 10, 10.33.
16, 5: Jos 18, 13.
16, 6: Jos 17, 7.

their boundary curved eastward around Taanath-shiloh, and continued east of it to Janoah; [7] from there it descended to Ataroth and Naarah, and skirting Jericho, it ended at the Jordan. [8]* From Tappuah the boundary ran westward to the Wadi Kanah and ended at the sea. This was the heritage of the clans of the Ephraimites, [9]* including the villages that belonged to each city set aside for the Ephraimites within the territory of the Manassehites. [10]* But they did not drive out the Canaanites living in Gezer, who live on within Ephraim to the present day, though they have been impressed as laborers.

Manasseh

17 [1]* Now as for the lot that fell to the tribe of Manasseh as the first-born of Joseph: since his eldest son, Machir, the father of Gilead, was a warrior, who had already obtained Gilead and Bashan, [2]* the allotment was now made to the other descendants of Manasseh, the clans of Abiezer, Helek, Asriel, Shechem, Hepher and Shemida, the other male children of Manasseh, son of Joseph.

[3]* Furthermore, Zelophehad, son of Hepher, son of Gilead, son of Machir, son of Manasseh, had had no sons, but only daughters, whose names were Mahlah, Noah, Hoglah, Milcah, and Tirzah. [4]* These presented themselves to Eleazar the priest, to Joshua, son of Nun, and to the princes, saying, "The LORD commanded Moses to give us a heritage among our kinsmen." So in obedience to the command of the LORD a heritage was given to each of them among their father's kinsmen. [5]* Thus ten shares fell to Manasseh apart from the land of Gilead and Bashan beyond the Jordan, [6] since these female descendants of Manasseh received each a portion among his sons. The land of Gilead fell to the rest of the Manassehites.

[7]† Manasseh bordered on Asher. From Michmethath, near Shechem, another boundary ran southward to include the natives of En-Tappuah, [8] because the district of Tappuah belonged to Manasseh, although Tappuah itself was an Ephraimite city on the border of Manasseh. [9]* This same boundary continued down to the Wadi Kanah. The cities that belonged to Ephraim from among the cities of Manasseh were those to the south of the wadi; thus the territory of Manasseh ran north of the wadi and ended at the sea. [10] The land on the south belonged to Ephraim and that on the north to Manasseh; with the sea as their common boundary, they reached Asher on the north and Issachar on the east.

[11]* Moreover, in Issachar and in Asher Manasseh was awarded Beth-shean* and its towns, Ibleam and its towns, Dor and its towns and the natives there, Endor and its towns and natives, Taanach and its towns and natives, and Megiddo and its towns and natives [the third is Naphath-dor]. [12] Since the Manassehites could not conquer these cities, the Canaanites persisted in this region. [13] When the Israelites grew stronger they impressed the Canaanites as laborers, but they did not drive them out.

Protest of Joseph Tribes

[14]* The descendants of Joseph said to Joshua, "Why have you given us only one lot and one share as our heritage? Our people are too many, because of the extent to which the LORD has blessed us." [15] Joshua answered them, "If you are too many, go up to the forest and clear out a place for yourselves there in the land of the Perizzites and Rephaim, since the mountain regions of Ephraim are so narrow." [16]* For the Josephites said, "Our mountain regions are not enough for us; on the other hand, the Canaanites living in the valley region all have iron chariots, in particular those in Beth-shean and its towns, and those in the valley of Jezreel." [17] Joshua therefore said to Ephraim and Manasseh, the house of Joseph, "You are a numerous people and very strong. You shall have not merely one share, [18] for the mountain region which is now forest shall be yours when you clear it. Its adjacent land shall also be yours if, despite their strength and iron chariots, you drive out the Canaanites."

18 [1]* After they had subdued the land, the whole community of the Israelites assembled at Shiloh, where they set up the meeting tent.

The Seven Remaining Portions

[2] Seven tribes among the Israelites had not yet received their heritage. [3] Joshua therefore said to the Israelites, "How much longer will you put off taking steps to possess the land which the LORD, the God of your fathers, has given you? [4] Choose three men from each of your tribes; I will commission them to begin a survey of the land, which they shall describe

---

17, 7: *Manasseh bordered on Asher:* only at the extreme northwestern section of Manasseh's territory. The boundary given in the following sentences (vv 7–10) is a more detailed description of the one already mentioned in Jos 16, 5ff, as separating Manasseh from Ephraim.

16, 8: Jos 17, 7.
16, 9: Jos 17, 9.
16, 10: Jgs 1, 29.
17, 1: Gn 41, 51; 46, 20; 48, 18; 50, 23; Nm 26, 29; Dt 3, 13.15.
17, 2: Nm 26, 29–32.
17, 3: Nm 26, 33; 27, 1; 36, 2.
17, 4: Nm 27, 6f; 36, 2.
17, 5: Jos 13, 30f.
17, 9: Jos 16, 8f.
17, 11: 1 Chr 7, 29.
17, 11ff: Jgs 1, 27f.
17, 14: Jos 16, 4; Gn 48, 19f.22.
17, 16: Jgs 6, 33.
18, 1: Jos 19, 51.

for purposes of inheritance. When they return to me, [5]* you shall divide it into seven parts. Judah is to retain its territory in the south, and the house of Joseph its territory in the north. [6] You shall bring here to me the description of the land in seven sections. I will then cast lots for you here before the LORD, our God. [7]* For the Levites have no share among you, because the priesthood of the LORD is their heritage; while Gad, Reuben, and the half-tribe of Manasseh have already received the heritage east of the Jordan which Moses, the servant of the LORD, gave them."

[8] When those who were to map out the land were ready for the journey, Joshua instructed them to survey the land, prepare a description of it, and return to him; then he would cast lots for them there before the LORD in Shiloh. [9] So they went through the land, listed its cities in writing in seven sections, and returned to Joshua in the camp at Shiloh. [10] Joshua then divided up the land for the Israelites into their separate shares, casting lots for them before the LORD in Shiloh.

Benjamin

[11] One lot fell to the clans of the tribe of Benjaminites. The territory allotted them lay between the descendants of Judah and those of Joseph. [12]*† Their northern boundary began at the Jordan and went over the northern flank of Jericho, up westward into the mountains, till it reached the desert of Beth-aven. [13]* From there it crossed over to the southern flank of Luz (that is, Bethel). Then it ran down to Ataroth-addar, on the mountaintop south of Lower Beth-horon. [14] For the western border, the boundary line swung south from the mountaintop opposite Beth-horon till it reached Kiriath-baal (that is, Kiriath-jearim), which city belonged to the Judahites. This was the western boundary. [15] The southern boundary began at the limits of Kiriath-jearim and projected to the spring at Nephtoah. [16]* It went down to the edge of the mountain on the north of the Valley of Rephaim, where it faces the Valley of Ben-hinnom; and continuing down the Valley of Hinnom along the southern flank of the Jebusites, reached En-rogel. [17] Inclining to the north, it extended to En-shemesh, and thence to Geliloth, opposite the pass of Adummim. Then it dropped to Eben-Bohan-ben-Reuben, [18]* across the northern flank of the Arabah

overlook, down into the Arabah. [19] From there the boundary continued across the northern flank of Beth-hoglah and extended to the northern tip of the Salt Sea, at the southern end of the Jordan. This was the southern boundary. [20] The Jordan bounded it on the east. This was how the heritage of the clans of the Benjaminites was bounded on all sides.

[21] Now the cities belonging to the clans of the tribe of the Benjaminites were: Jericho, Beth-hoglah, Emek-keziz, [22] Beth-arabah, Zemaraim, Bethel, [23] Avvim, Parah, Ophra, [24] Chephar-ammoni, Ophni and Geba; twelve cities and their villages. [25] Also Gibeon, Ramah, Beeroth, [26] Mizpeh, Chephirah, Mozah, [27] Rekem, Irpeel, Taralah, [28] Zela, Haeleph, the Jebusite city (that is, Jerusalem), Gibeah and Kiriath; fourteen cities and their villages. This was the heritage of the clans of Benjaminites.

Simeon

19

[1] The second lot fell to Simeon. The heritage of the clans of the tribe of Simeonites lay within that of the Judahites. [2]* For their heritage they received Beer-sheba, Shema, Moladah, [3] Hazar-shual, Balah, Ezem, [4] Eltolad, Bethul, Hormah, [5] Ziklag, Bethmar-caboth, Hazar-susah, [6] Beth-lebaoth and Sharuhen; thirteen cities and their villages. [7] Also En-rimmon, Ether and Ashan; four cities and their villages, [8] besides all the villages around these cities as far as Baalath-beer (that is, Ramoth-negeb). This was the heritage of the clans of the tribe of the Simeonites. [9] This heritage of the Simeonites was within the confines of the Judahites; for since the portion of the latter was too large for them, the Simeonites obtained their heritage within it.

Zebulun

[10]† The third lot fell to the clans of the Zebulunites. The limit of their heritage was at Sarid. [11] Their boundary went up west . . . and through Mareal, reaching Dabbesheth and the wadi that is near Jokneam. [12] From Sarid eastward it ran to the district of Chisloth-tabor, on to Daberath, and up to Japhia. [13] From there it continued eastward to Gath-hepher and to Eth-kazin, extended to Rimmon, and turned to Neah. [14] Skirting north of Hannathon, the boundary ended at the valley of Iphtahel. [15] Thus, with Kattath, Nahalal, Shimron,

---

18, 12–20: Benjamin's northern boundary (vv 12f) corresponded to part of the southern boundary of Ephraim (Jos 16, 1f). Their western border (v 14) was the eastern border of Dan (cf Jos 19, 40–47). Their southern boundary (vv 15–19) corresponded to part of the northern boundary of Judah (Jos 15, 6–9).
   19, 10–16: Zebulun's territory was in the central section of the Plain of Esdraelon and of southern Galilee; it was bounded on the south by Manasseh, on the southeast by Issachar, on the northeast and north by Naphtali, and on the west by Asher. The site of the later

city of Nazareth was within its borders. Bethlehem of Zebulun was, of course, distinct from the city of the same name in Judah. *Twelve cities:* apparently seven of the names are missing from v 15, unless some of the places mentioned in vv 12–14 are to be included in the number.

18, 5: Jos 15, 1—17, 18.   28, 19.
18, 7: Jos 13, 8.33.   **18, 16:** Jos 15, 7f.
18, 12: Jos 16, 1.   **18, 18:** Jos 15, 6.
18, 13: Jos 16, 2f.5; Gn   **19, 2–8:** 1 Chr 4, 28–33.

Idalah and Bethlehem, there were twelve cities and their villages 16 to comprise the heritage of the clans of the Zebulunites.

Issachar

17† The fourth lot fell to Issachar. The territory of the clans of the Issacharites 18 included Jezreel, Chesulloth, Shunem, 19 Hapharaim, Shion, Anaharath, 20 Rabbith, Kishion, Ebez, 21 Remeth, En-gannim, En-haddah and Beth-pazzez. 22 The boundary reached Tabor, Shahazumah and Beth-shemesh, ending at the Jordan. These sixteen cities and their villages 23 were the heritage of the clans of the Issacharites.

Asher

24† The fifth lot fell to the clans of the tribe of the Asherites. 25 Their territory included Helkath, Hali, Beten, Achshaph, 26 Allammelech, Amad and Mishal, and reached Carmel on the west, and Shihor-libnath. 27 In the other direction, it ran eastward of Beth-dagon, reached Zebulun and the valley of Iphtahel; then north of Beth-emek and Neiel, it extended to Cabul, 28* Mishal, Abdon, Rehob, Hammon and Kanah, near Greater Sidon. 29 Then the boundary turned back to Ramah and to the fortress city of Tyre; thence it cut back to Hosah and ended at the sea. Thus, with Mahalab, Achzib, 30 Ummah, Acco, Aphek and Rehob, there were twenty-two cities and their villages 31 to comprise the heritage of the clans of the tribe of the Asherites.

Naphtali

32† The sixth lot fell to the Naphtalites. The boundary of the clans of the Naphtalites 33 extended from Heleph, from the oak at Zaanannim to Lakkum, including Adami-nekeb and Jabneel, and ended at the Jordan. 34 In the opposite direction, westerly, it ran through Aznoth-tabor and from there extended to Hukkok; it touched Zebulun on the south, Asher on the west, and the Jordan on the east. 35 The fortified cities were Ziddim, Zer, Hammath, Rakkath, Chinnereth, 36 Adamah, Ramah, Hazor, 37 Kedesh, Edrei, En-hazor, 38* Yiron, Migdal-el, Horem, Beth-anath and Beth-shemesh; nineteen cities and their villages, 39 to comprise the heritage of the clans of the tribe of the Naphtalites.

Dan

40† The seventh lot fell to the clans of the tribe of Danites. 41 Their heritage was the territory of Zorah, Eshtaol, Ir-shemesh, 42* Shaalabbin, Aijalon, Ithlah, 43 Elon, Timnah, Ekron, 44 Eltekoh, Gibbethon, Baalath, 45 Jehud, Bene-berak, Gath-rimmon, 46 Me-jarkon and Rakkon, with the coast at Joppa. 47*† But the territory of the Danites was too small for them; so the Danites marched up and attacked Leshem, which they captured and put to the sword. Once they had taken possession of Leshem, they renamed the settlement after their ancestor Dan. 48 These cities and their villages were the heritage of the clans of the tribe of the Danites.

Joshua's City

49 When the last of them had received the portions of the land they were to inherit, the Israelites assigned a heritage in their midst to Joshua, son of Nun. 50* In obedience to the command of the LORD, they gave him the city which he requested, Timnah-serah in the mountain region of Ephraim. He rebuilt the city and made it his home.

51 These are the final portions into which Eleazar the priest, Joshua, son of Nun, and the heads of families in the tribes of the Israelites divided the land by lot in the presence of the LORD, at the door of the meeting tent in Shiloh.

Cities of Asylum

20 1† The LORD said to Joshua: 2* "Tell the Israelites to designate the cities of which I spoke to them through Moses, 3 to which one guilty of accidental and unintended homicide may flee for asylum from the avenger of blood. 4 To one of these cities the killer shall flee, and standing at the entrance of the city gate, he shall plead his case before the elders, who must receive him and assign him a place in which to live among them. 5 Though the avenger of blood pursues him, they are not to deliver up the homicide who slew his fellow man unintentionally and not out of previous hatred. 6* Once he has stood judgment before the community, he shall live on in that city till the death of the high priest who is in office at the time. Then the killer may go back home to his own city from which he fled."

19, 17–23: Issachar's land was on the eastern watershed of the Plain of Esdraelon, but also included the southeastern end of the Galilean mountains. It was surrounded by Manasseh on the south and east, by Naphtali on the north, and by Zebulun on the west. Jezreel (v 18) dominated the plain to which it gave its name, the later form of which was Esdraelon.

19, 24–31: Asher inherited the western slope of the Galilean hills as far as the sea, with Manasseh to the south, Zebulun and Naphtali to the east, and Phoenicia to the north.

19, 32–39: Naphtali received eastern Galilee; Asher was to the west and Zebulun and Issachar were to the south, while the upper Jordan and Mount Hermon formed the eastern border. Part of the

tribe of Dan later on occupied the northern extremity of Naphtali's lands, at the sources of the Jordan (v 47).

19, 40–46: The original territory of Dan was a small enclave between Judah, Benjamin, Ephraim and the Philistines.

19, 47: Leshem: called Laish in Jgs 18, where the story of the migration of the Danites is told at greater length.

20, 1–9: The laws concerning the cities of refuge are given in Nm 35, 9–28; Dt 19, 1–13; see notes on Nm 35, 16–25; Dt 19, 2.

19, 28f: Jgs 1, 31.
19, 38: Jgs 1, 33.
19, 42: Jgs 1, 35.
19, 47: Jgs 18, 27–29.

19, 50: Jos 24, 30; Jgs 2, 9.
20, 2: Ex 21, 13; Nm 35, 10–14; Dt 4, 41–43; 19, 2–9.
20, 6: Nm 35, 12.24f.

List of Cities

7* So they set apart Kedesh in Galilee in the mountain region of Naphtali, Shechem in the mountain region of Ephraim, and Kiriath-arba (that is, Hebron) in the mountain region of Judah. 8* And beyond the Jordan east of Jericho they designated Bezer on the open tableland in the tribe of Reuben, Ramoth in Gilead in the tribe of Gad, and Golan in Bashan in the tribe of Manasseh. 9* These were the designated cities to which any Israelite or stranger living among them who had killed a person accidentally might flee to escape death at the hand of the avenger of blood, until he could appear before the community.

Levitical Cities

21

1*† The heads of the Levite families came up to Eleazar the priest, to Joshua, son of Nun, and to the heads of families of the other tribes of the Israelites 2* at Shiloh in the land of Canaan, and said to them, "The LORD commanded, through Moses, that cities be given us to dwell in, with pasture lands for our livestock." 3 Out of their own heritage, in obedience to this command of the LORD, the Israelites gave the Levites the following cities with their pasture lands.

4 When the first lot among the Levites fell to the clans of the Kohathites, the descendants of Aaron the priest obtained thirteen cities by lot from the tribes of Judah, Simeon and Benjamin. 5 The rest of the Kohathites obtained ten cities by lot from the clans of the tribe of Ephraim, from the tribe of Dan, and from the half-tribe of Manasseh. 6 The Gershonites obtained thirteen cities by lot from the clans of the tribe of Issachar, from the tribe of Asher, from the tribe of Naphtali, and from the half-tribe of Manasseh. 7 The clans of the Merarites obtained twelve cities from the tribes of Reuben, Gad and Zebulun. 8* These cities with their pasture lands the Israelites allotted to the Levites in obedience to the LORD's command through Moses.

Cities of the Priests

9* From the tribes of the Judahites and Simeonites they designated the following cities, 10 and assigned them to the descendants of Aaron in the Kohathite clan of the Levites, since the first lot fell to them: 11 first, Kiriath-arba (Arba was the father of Anak), that is, Hebron, in the mountain region of Judah, with the adjacent pasture lands, 12* al-

though the open country and villages belonging to the city had been given to Caleb, son of Jephunneh, as his property. 13 Thus to the descendants of Aaron the priest were given the city of asylum for homicides at Hebron, with its pasture lands; also, Libnah with its pasture lands, 14 Jattir with its pasture lands, Eshtemoa with its pasture lands, 15 Holon with its pasture lands, Debir with its pasture lands, 16 Ashan with its pasture lands, Juttah with its pasture lands, and Beth-shemesh with its pasture lands: nine cities from the two tribes mentioned. 17 From the tribe of Benjamin they obtained the four cities of Gibeon with its pasture lands, Geba with its pasture lands, 18* Anathoth with its pasture lands, and Almon with its pasture lands. 19 These cities which with their pasture lands belonged to the priestly descendants of Aaron, were thirteen in all.

Cities of the Other Kohathites

20* The rest of the Kohathite clans among the Levites obtained by lot, from the tribe of Ephraim, four cities. 21 They were assigned, with its pasture lands, the city of asylum for homicides at Shechem in the mountain region of Ephraim; also Gezer with its pasture lands, 22 Kibzaim with its pasture lands, and Beth-horon with its pasture lands. 23 From the tribe of Dan they obtained the four cities of Elteke with its pasture lands, Gibbethon with its pasture lands, 24 Aijalon with its pasture lands, and Gath-rimmon with its pasture lands; 25 and from the half-tribe of Manasseh the two cities of Taanach with its pasture lands and Ibleam with its pasture lands. 26 These cities which with their pasture lands belonged to the rest of the Kohathite clans were ten in all.

Cities of the Gershonites

27* The Gershonite clan of the Levites received from the half-tribe of Manasseh two cities: the city of asylum for homicides at Golan with its pasture lands; and also Beth-Astharoth with its pasture lands. 28 From the tribe of Issachar they obtained the four cities of Kishion with its pasture lands, Daberath with its pasture lands, 29 Jarmuth with its pasture lands, and En-gannim with its pasture lands; 30 from the tribe of Asher, the four cities of Mishal with its pasture lands, Abdon with its pasture lands, 31 Helkath with its pasture lands, and Rehob with its pasture lands; 32 and from the tribe

---

21, 1: The order to establish special cities for the Levites is given in Nm 35, 1–8. The forty-eight cities listed here were hardly the exclusive possession of the Levites; at least the more important of them, such as Hebron, Shechem and Ramoth in Gilead, were certainly peopled for the most part by the tribe in whose territory they were situated. But in all these cities the Levites had special property rights which they did not possess in other cities; cf Lv 25, 32ff.

20, 7: Jos 15, 13; 19, 37; 21, 21.
20, 8: Jos 21, 27.36f.
20, 9: Nm 35, 15.
21, 1: Ex 6, 16–19; Nm 3, 17–20.
21, 2: Nm 35, 2.
21, 8: Nm 35, 2.
21, 9–19: 1 Chr 6, 54–60.
21, 12: Jos 14, 14; 15, 13.
21, 18: Jer 1, 1.
21, 20–26: 1 Chr 6, 66–70.
21, 27–33: 1 Chr 6, 71–76.

of Naphtali, three cities: the city of asylum for homicides at Kedesh in Galilee, with its pasture lands; also Hammath with its pasture lands, and Rakkath with its pasture lands. 33 These cities which with their pasture lands belonged to the Gershonite clans were thirteen in all.

Cities of the Merarites

34* The Merarite clans, the last of the Levites, received from the tribe of Zebulun the four cities of Jokneam with its pasture lands, Kartah with its pasture lands, 35 Rimmon with its pasture lands, and Nahalal with its pasture lands; 36 also, across the Jordan, from the tribe of Reuben, four cities: the city of asylum for homicides at Bezer with its pasture lands, Jahaz with its pasture lands, 37 Kedemoth with its pasture lands, and Mephaath with its pasture lands; 38 and from the tribe of Gad a total of four cities: the city of asylum for homicides at Ramoth in Gilead with its pasture lands, also Mahanaim with its pasture lands, 39 Heshbon with its pasture lands, and Jazer with its pasture lands. 40 The cities which were allotted to the Merarite clans, the last of the Levites, were therefore twelve in all.

41* Thus the total number of cities within the territory of the Israelites which, with their pasture lands, belonged to the Levites, was forty-eight. 42 With each and every one of these cities went the pasture lands round about it.

43* And so the LORD gave Israel all the land he had sworn to their fathers he would give them. Once they had conquered and occupied it, 44 the LORD gave them peace on every side, just as he had promised their fathers. Not one of their enemies could withstand them; the LORD brought all their enemies under their power. 45* Not a single promise that the LORD made to the house of Israel was broken; every one was fulfilled.

III: Return of the Transjordan Tribes and Joshua's Farewell

The Eastern Tribes Dismissed

22 1 At that time Joshua summoned the Reubenites, the Gadites, and the half-tribe of Manasseh 2* and said to them: "You have done all that Moses, the servant of the LORD, commanded you, and have obeyed every command I gave you. 3 For many years now you have not once abandoned your kinsmen, but have faithfully carried out the commands of the LORD, your God. 4* Since, therefore, the LORD, your God, has settled your kinsmen as he promised them, you may now return to your tents beyond the Jordan; to your own land, which Moses, the servant of the LORD, gave you. 5* But be very careful to observe the precept and law which Moses, the servant of the LORD, enjoined upon you: love the LORD, your God; follow him faithfully; keep his commandments; remain loyal to him; and serve him with your whole heart and soul." 6 Joshua then blessed them and sent them away to their own tents.

7* (For, to half the tribe of Manasseh Moses had assigned land in Bashan; and to the other half Joshua had given a portion along with their kinsmen west of the Jordan.) What Joshua said to them when he sent them off to their tents with his blessing was, 8* "Now that you are returning to your own tents with great wealth, with very numerous livestock, with silver, gold, bronze and iron, and with a very large supply of clothing, divide these spoils of your enemies with your kinsmen there." 9* So the Reubenites, the Gadites, and the half-tribe of Manasseh left the other Israelites at Shiloh in the land of Canaan and returned to the land of Gilead, their own property, which they had received according to the LORD's command through Moses.

The Altar beside the Jordan

10 When the Reubenites, the Gadites, and the half-tribe of Manasseh came to the region of the Jordan in the land of Canaan, they built there at the Jordan a conspicuously large altar. 11*† The other Israelites heard the report that the Reubenites, the Gadites, and the half-tribe of Manasseh had built an altar in the region of the Jordan facing the land of Canaan, across from them, 12† and therefore they assembled their whole community at Shiloh to declare war on them.

Accusation of the Western Tribes

13* First, however, they sent to the Reubenites, the Gadites, and the half-tribe of Manasseh in the

---

† **22, 11:** In the region of the Jordan facing the land of Canaan: on the eastern side of the Jordan valley. The river itself formed the boundary between these eastern tribes and the rest of the tribes who lived in what was formerly Canaan—though the term Canaan could also be used of both sides of the Jordan valley (cf v 10). The Transjordan tribes naturally built their altar in their own territory.

22, 12: To declare war on them: the western Israelites considered this altar, which seemed to violate the customary unity of the sanctuary (cf Lv 17, 1–9; Dt 12, 4–14), as a sign of secession and dangerous to national unity. The motives for the war were political as well as religious.

* 21, 34–38: 1 Chr 6, 77–81.
    21, 41: Nm 35, 7.
    21, 43: Gn 12, 7; 13, 15; 15, 18; 26, 3; 28, 4.13.
    21, 45: Jos 23, 14f.
    22, 2: Jos 1, 16f; Nm 32, 20ff; Dt 3, 18ff.
    22, 4: Jos 1, 13; 13, 8; Nm 32, 33.
    22, 5: Dt 6, 5f.17; 10, 12; 11, 1.13.22.
    22, 7: Jos 17, 5.
    22, 8: Nm 31, 27.
    22, 9: Jos 18, 1; Nm 32, 1.26.29.
    22, 11: Dt 13, 13ff.
    22, 13: Ex 6, 25; Sir 45, 28.

A Prayer for Understanding

When the Israelite tribes located east of the Jordan build a large altar to worship God, the Israelite tribes who settled west of the Jordan become concerned. They think that by building more altars, the tribes to the east are compromising their belief in one God. Some are ready to go to war over this issue. But maintaining unity among the tribes is also important. So, the western tribes wisely send Phinehas and others to insist on the importance of one place of worship. Listening to the eastern tribes, Phinehas understands their good intentions, and war is avoided.

Think about times when you have jumped to conclusions about other people's actions. Then say the following prayer:

God of love and wisdom, a misunderstanding almost led to war among the Israelites. Help me to avoid jumping to conclusions about the actions of others. Help me to listen and understand their intentions, as Phinehas did. And let me be gracious in recognizing when I am wrong. Amen.

▶ Jos 22, 13–20

land of Gilead an embassy consisting of Phinehas, son of Eleazar the priest, 14 and ten princes, one from every tribe of Israel, each one being both prince and military leader of his ancestral house. 15 When these came to the Reubenites, the Gadites, and the half-tribe of Manasseh in the land of Gilead, they said to them: 16* "The whole community of the LORD sends this message: What act of treachery is this you have committed against the God of Israel? You have seceded from the LORD this day, and rebelled against him by building an altar of your own! 17* For the sin of Peor, a plague came upon the community of the LORD. 18 We are still not free of that; must you now add to it? You are rebelling against the LORD today and by tomorrow he will be angry with the whole community of Israel! 19*† If you consider the land you now possess unclean, cross over to the land the LORD possesses, where the Dwelling of the LORD stands, and share that with us. But do not rebel against the LORD, nor involve us in rebellion, by building an altar of your own in addition to the altar of the LORD, our God. 20*† When Achan, son of Zerah, violated the ban, did not wrath fall upon the entire community of Israel? Though he was but a single man, he did not perish alone for his guilt!"

Reply of the Eastern Tribes

21 The Reubenites, the Gadites, and the half-tribe of Manasseh replied to the military leaders of the Israelites: "The LORD is the God of gods. 22† The LORD, the God of gods, knows and Israel shall know. If now we have acted out of rebellion or treachery against the LORD, our God, 23 and if we have built an altar of our own to secede from the LORD, or to offer holocausts, grain offerings or peace offerings upon it, the LORD himself will exact the penalty. 24 We did it rather out of our anxious concern lest in the future your children should say to our children: 'What have you to do with the LORD, the God of Israel? 25 For the LORD has placed the Jordan as a boundary between you and us. You descendants of Reuben and Gad have no share in the LORD.' Thus your children would prevent ours from revering the LORD. 26 So we decided to guard our interests by building this altar of our own: not for holocausts or for sacrifices, 27* but as evidence for you on behalf of ourselves and our descendants, that we have the right to worship the LORD in his presence with our holocausts, sacrifices, and peace offerings. Now in the future your children cannot say to our children, 'You have no share in the LORD.' 28† Our thought was, that if in the future they should speak thus to us or to our descendants, we could answer: 'Look at the model of the altar of the LORD which our fathers made, not for holocausts or for sacrifices, but to witness between you and us.' 29 Far be it from us to rebel against the LORD or to

---

22, 19: *Unclean:* not sanctified by the Dwelling of the Lord.

22, 20: *Achan . . . did not perish alone:* his guilt caused the failure of the first attack on Ai (Jos 7, 4–23); this fact is adduced as an argument for the solidarity and mutual responsibility of all the Israelites.

22, 22: *The LORD, the God of gods:* the Hebrew, which cannot be adequately rendered in English here, adds to the divine name Yahweh ("the LORD") two synonymous words for "God," *el* and *elohim.* The repetition of these three sacred words adds force to the protestations of fidelity and innocence.

22, 28: *To witness:* far from being destined to form a rival sanctuary, the model of the altar was intended by the eastern tribes solely as a means of teaching their children to be faithful to the one true sanctuary beyond the Jordan.

22, 16: Lv 17, 8f. 22, 20: Jos 7, 1.5.
22, 17: Nm 25, 3f; Dt 4, 3. 22, 27: Dt 12, 5f.17f.
22, 19: Jos 18, 1.

secede now from the LORD by building an altar for holocaust, grain offering, or sacrifice in addition to the altar of the LORD, our God, which stands before his Dwelling."

30 When Phinehas the priest and the princes of the community, the military leaders of the Israelites, heard what the Reubenites, the Gadites and the Manassehites had to say, they were satisfied. 31 Phinehas, son of Eleazar the priest, said to the Reubenites, the Gadites and the Manassehites, "Now we know that the LORD is with us. Since you have not committed this act of treachery against the LORD, you have kept the Israelites free from punishment by the LORD."

32 Phinehas, son of Eleazar the priest, and the princes returned from the Reubenites and the Gadites in the land of Gilead to the Israelites in the land of Canaan, and reported the matter to them. 33 The report satisfied the Israelites, who blessed God and decided against declaring war on the Reubenites and Gadites or ravaging the land they occupied.

34† The Reubenites and the Gadites gave the altar its name as a witness among them that the LORD is God.

Joshua's Final Plea

23 1* Many years later, after the LORD had given the Israelites rest from all their enemies round about them, and when Joshua was old and advanced in years, 2 he summoned all Israel (including their elders, leaders, judges and officers) and said to them: "I am old and advanced in years. 3 You have seen all that the LORD, your God, has done for you against all these nations; for it has been the LORD, your God, himself who fought for you. 4* Bear in mind that I have apportioned among your tribes as their heritage the nations that survive [as well as those I destroyed] between the Jordan and the Great Sea in the west. 5 The LORD, your God, will drive them out and dislodge them at your approach, so that you will take possession of their land as the LORD, your God, promised you. 6* Therefore strive hard to observe and carry out all that is written in the book of the law of Moses, not straying from it in any way, 7* or mingling with these nations while they survive among you. You must not invoke their gods, or swear by them, or serve them, or worship them, 8 but you must remain loyal to the LORD, your God, as you have been

to this day. 9 At your approach the LORD has driven out large and strong nations, and to this day no one has withstood you. 10* One of you puts to flight a thousand, because it is the LORD, your God, himself who fights for you, as he promised you. 11 Take great care, however, to love the LORD, your God. 12* For if you ever abandon him and ally yourselves with the remnant of these nations while they survive among you, by intermarrying and intermingling with them, 13 know for certain that the LORD, your God, will no longer drive these nations out of your way. Instead they will be a snare and a trap for you, a scourge for your sides and thorns for your eyes, until you perish from this good land which the LORD, your God, has given you.

14† "Today, as you see, I am going the way of all men. So now acknowledge with your whole heart and soul that not one of all the promises the LORD, your God, made to you has remained unfulfilled. Every promise has been fulfilled for you, with not one single exception. 15*† But just as every promise the LORD, your God, made to you has been fulfilled for you, so will he fulfill every threat, even so far as to exterminate you from this good land which the LORD, your God, has given you. 16 If you transgress the covenant of the LORD, your God, which he enjoined on you, serve other gods and worship them, the anger of the LORD will flare up against you and you will quickly perish from the good land which he has given you."

Reminder of the Divine Goodness

24 1 Joshua gathered together all the tribes of Israel at Shechem, summoning their elders, their leaders, their judges and their officers. When they stood in ranks before God, 2*† Joshua addressed all the people: "Thus says the LORD, the God of Israel: In times past your fathers, down to Terah, father of Abraham and Nahor, dwelt beyond the River and served other gods. 3* But I brought your father Abraham from the region beyond the River and led him through the entire land of Canaan. I made his descendants numerous, and gave him Isaac. 4* To Isaac I gave Jacob and Esau. To Esau I assigned the mountain region of Seir in which to settle, while Jacob and his children went down to Egypt.

5* "Then I sent Moses and Aaron, and smote Egypt with the prodigies which I wrought in her midst. 6* Afterward I led you out of Egypt, and

---

† **22, 34:** The name of this altar was the Hebrew word for "witness," c ed.

23, 14: *Going the way of all men:* drawing near to death, the inevitable goal of all; cf 1 Kgs 2, 1f.

23, 15: *Every threat:* mentioned especially in Dt 28, 15–68.

24, 2: *Beyond the River:* east of the Euphrates; cf Gn 11, 28–31.

23, 1: Jos 13, 1.
23, 4: Jos 13, 2–7; 14, 2; 18, 10; Ps 78, 55.
23, 6: Jos 1, 7.
23, 7: Dt 7, 2ff.
23, 10: Ex 14, 14; Lv 26, 8; Dt 3, 22.
23†, 12: Ex 34, 16; Dt 7, 3.
23, 15: Lv 26, 14–39; Dt 28, 15–68.
24, 2: Gn 11, 26.31; 31, 53.
24, 3: Gn 12, 1; Acts 7, 2–4.
24, 4: Gn 25, 24ff; 36, 8; 46, 1.6; Acts 7, 15.
24, 5: Ex 3, 10; 7, 14—12, 30.
24, 6: Ex 12, 37.51; 14, 9.

LIVE IT!

Living the Covenant Today!

Some people think that the Israelites were completely homogenous and without differences, but nothing could be further from the truth. Joshua 24, 1 tells how Joshua summoned the leaders of the twelve tribes to present themselves before God. In this gathering, they embraced their common faith in God and renewed the Covenant of Sinai, setting aside their differences and political struggles.

But the twelve tribes were not unlike schools and neighborhoods in many parts of this country, where young people gather in clubs, cliques, and even gangs, oftentimes dividing themselves by ethnic group or social class. Such division frequently leads to conflict, turf war, and violence.

People don't have to be identical, or even similar, to be united. They just have to be tolerant of one another's differences and see a reason to celebrate the richness of their diversity.

Imagine if all Christian churches could come together, as the tribes did in Joshua's time, and embrace a common identity before God. Imagine if all the clubs, cliques, and gangs in our schools and neighborhoods could come together that way. What strength we would have to help one another face life's challenges!

■ What can you do to foster this type of unity in your local schools, churches, and neighborhoods?

■ Who are some adults and young people you know who might help you work toward this goal?

▶ Jos 24, 1–28

---

when you reached the sea, the Egyptians pursued your fathers to the Red Sea with chariots and horsemen. 7* Because they cried out to the LORD, he put darkness between your people and the Egyptians, upon whom he brought the sea so that it engulfed them. After you witnessed what I did to Egypt, and dwelt a long time in the desert, 8* I brought you into the land of the Amorites who lived east of the Jordan. They fought against you, but I delivered them into your power. You took possession of their land, and I destroyed them [the two kings of the Amorites] before you. 9* Then Balak, son of Zippor, king of Moab, prepared to war against Israel. He summoned Balaam, son of Beor, to curse you; 10* but I would not listen to Balaam. On the contrary, he had to bless you, and I saved you from him. 11* Once you crossed the Jordan and came to Jericho, the men of Jericho fought against you, but I delivered them also into your power. 12*† And I sent the hornets ahead of you which drove them [the Amorites, Perizzites, Canaanites, Hittites, Girgashites, Hivites and Jebusites] out of your way; it was not your sword or your bow.

13* "I gave you a land which you had not tilled and cities which you had not built, to dwell in; you have eaten of vineyards and olive groves which you did not plant.

14* "Now, therefore, fear the LORD and serve him completely and sincerely. Cast out the gods your fathers served beyond the River and in Egypt, and serve the LORD. 15*† If it does not please you to serve the LORD, decide today whom you will serve, the gods your fathers served beyond the River or the gods of the Amorites in whose country you are dwelling. As for me and my household, we will serve the LORD."

Renewal of the Covenant

16 But the people answered, "Far be it from us to forsake the LORD for the service of other gods. 17 For it was the LORD, our God, who brought us and our fathers up out of the land of Egypt, out of a state of slavery. He performed those great miracles before our very eyes and protected us along our entire journey and among all the peoples through whom we passed. 18 At our approach the LORD drove out [all the peoples, including] the Amorites who dwelt

---

† 24, 12: *The hornets:* see note on Ex 23, 28.
24, 15: *The gods your fathers served:* Abraham's ancestors were polytheists.

* 24, 7: Ex 14, 10.20.27f.
24, 8: Nm 21, 21–35.
24, 9: Nm 22, 2–5.
24, 10: Nm 23, 1—24, 25.
24, 11: Jos 3, 14; 6, 1.

24, 12: Jos 11, 20; Ex 23, 28; Dt 7, 20.
24, 13: Dt 6, 10f.
24, 14: Dt 10, 12; 1 Sm 7, 3; 12, 24; Tb 14, 9.
24, 15: Dt 30, 15–19.

JOS

Fear the LORD

and serve him

completely

and

sincerely

24, 14

in the land. Therefore we also will serve the LORD, for he is our God."

19*† Joshua in turn said to the people, "You may not be able to serve the LORD, for he is a holy God; he is a jealous God who will not forgive your transgressions or your sins. 20 If, after the good he has done for you, you forsake the LORD and serve strange gods, he will do evil to you and destroy you."

21 But the people answered Joshua, "We will still serve the LORD." 22 Joshua therefore said to the people, "You are your own witnesses that you have chosen to serve the LORD." They replied, "We are, indeed!" 23 "Now, therefore, put away the strange

gods that are among you and turn your hearts to the LORD, the God of Israel." 24 Then the people promised Joshua, "We will serve the LORD, our God, and obey his voice."

25 So Joshua made a covenant with the people that day and made statutes and ordinances for them at Shechem, 26* which he recorded in the book of the law of God. Then he took a large stone and set it up there under the oak that was in the sanctuary of the LORD. 27* And Joshua said to all the people, "This stone shall be our witness, for it has heard all the words which the LORD spoke to us. It shall be a witness against you, should you wish to deny your God." 28* Then Joshua dismissed the people, each to his own heritage.

Death of Joshua

29* After these events, Joshua, son of Nun, servant of the LORD, died at the age of a hundred and ten. 30* He was buried within the limits of his heritage at Timnath-serah in the mountain region of Ephraim north of Mount Gaash. 31 Israel served the LORD during the entire lifetime of Joshua and that of the elders who outlived Joshua and knew all that the LORD had done for Israel. 32*† The bones of Joseph, which the Israelites had brought up from Egypt, were buried in Shechem in the plot of ground Jacob had bought from the sons of Hamor, father of Shechem, for a hundred pieces of money. This was a heritage of the descendants of Joseph. 33* When Eleazar, son of Aaron, also died, he was buried on the hill which had been given to his son Phinehas in the mountain region of Ephraim.

24, 19: *You may not be able:* fidelity to God's service is not easy, and therefore those who take such solemn obligations on themselves must be ever vigilant against human weakness.

24, 32: *The bones of Joseph:* the mummified body of Joseph (Gn 50, 25f), which the Israelites took with them as they left Egypt (Ex 13, 19), was fittingly buried at the ancient city of Shechem, near the border between the two Josephite tribes of Ephraim and Manasseh.

24, 19: Ex 20, 5; 23, 21; 34, 14; Lv 19, 2.
24, 26: Gn 28, 18; 31, 45; Jgs 9, 6.
24, 27: Gn 31, 48.52; Dt 31, 19.21.26.
24, 28: Jgs 2, 6.
24, 29ff: Jgs 2, 7ff.
24, 30: Jos 19, 50; Jgs 2, 9.
24, 32: Gn 33, 19; 50, 24; Ex 13, 19.
24, 33: Jos 22, 13.

Mom and Dad treat me like such a child." "I can't get a job without experience, but how can I get experience if I can't get a job?" The teenage years often feel like an in-between time, when young people pass from being children to becoming adults who must take responsibility for their own life. This time of transition holds many challenges. In some ways, the Book of Judges is about Israel's "teenage years." It tells about the difficulties faced by God's people in an in-between time: the two hundred years between the conquest of Canaan under Joshua and the establishment of the kingdom of Israel under Saul.

At a Glance

I. Palestine after the Death of Joshua (1, 1—3, 6).

II. Stories of the Judges (3, 7—16, 31).

III. The Tribes of Dan and Benjamin in the Days of the Judges (17, 1—21, 25).

In-depth

In the Book of Judges, the twelve tribes of Israel face two especially difficult challenges: how to live peacefully with one another and how to withstand the attacks of foreign armies. God answers the Israelites' prayers for help by raising up extraordinary men and women to lead the tribes. These famous leaders—Gideon, Deborah, Samson, and nine others—are called judges, but they aren't judges in courtrooms wearing black robes. They are local elders and military heroes who are chosen by God's spirit to lead the Israelites in times of crisis.

The pattern that we observed in the Book of Joshua also appears in the Book of Judges: when the people obey God's laws, they thrive; when they are disobedient, they suffer and need to be rescued by a leader raised up by God's spirit. The stories in Judges probably began as regional tales about local heroes. As they were collected and edited by the author of Judges, they became national stories influenced by the message of Deuteronomy: faithfulness to God is the only road to personal and tribal security.

Judges reminds us that the challenges of life, especially in the in-between times, are best handled through prayer and reliance on God. God can be trusted to lead us through all difficulties, both great and small.

Quick Facts

Period Covered
from 1220 to 1000 B.C.

Author
The book was put into final form by an unknown person from the Deuteronomic school, sometime during the Israelite monarchy.

Themes
God raises up mighty heroes to protect the people. God works even through flawed heroes.

The Book of *Judges*

Judges

Chap. 5

I: Palestine after the Death of Joshua

Pagan Survivors in Palestine

1 [1]*† After the death of Joshua the Israelites consulted the LORD, asking, "Who shall be first among us to attack the Canaanites and to do battle with them?" [2] The LORD answered, "Judah shall attack: I have delivered the land into his power." [3] Judah then said to his brother Simeon, "Come up with me into the territory allotted to me, and let us engage the Canaanites in battle. I will likewise accompany you into the territory allotted to you." So Simeon went with him.

[4] When the forces of Judah attacked, the LORD delivered the Canaanites and Perizzites into their power, and they slew ten thousand of them in Bezek. [5] It was in Bezek that they came upon Adonibezek and fought against him. When they defeated the Canaanites and Perizzites, [6] Adonibezek fled. They set out in pursuit, and when they caught him, cut off his thumbs and his big toes. [7] At this Adonibezek said, "Seventy kings, with their thumbs and big toes cut off, used to pick up scraps under my table. As I have done, so has God repaid me."

He was brought to Jerusalem, and there he died. [8] [The Judahites fought against Jerusalem and captured it, putting it to the sword; then they destroyed the city by fire.]

[9]* Afterward the Judahites went down to fight against the Canaanites who lived in the mountain region, in the Negeb, and in the foothills, [10]* Judah also marched against the Canaanites who dwelt in Hebron, which was formerly called Kiriath-arba, and defeated Sheshai, Ahiman and Talmai.* [11] From there they marched against the inhabitants of Debir, which was formerly called Kiriath-sepher. [12] And Caleb said, "I will give my daughter Achsah in marriage to the one who attacks Kiriath-sepher and captures it." [13]* Othniel, son of Caleb's younger brother Kenaz, captured it; so Caleb gave him his daughter Achsah in marriage. [14] On the day of her marriage to Othniel she induced him to ask her father for some land. Then, as she alighted from the ass, Caleb asked her, "What is troubling you?" [15] "Give me an additional gift," she answered. "Since you have assigned land in the Negeb to me, give me also pools of water." So Caleb gave her the upper and the lower pool. [16]*† The descendants of

---

† **1, 1–36:** This chapter summarizes events most of which occurred shortly after the death of Joshua. Perhaps because they were planned and inaugurated by him, they are also attributed to him in the last half of the preceding book (Jos 14–22).
1, 16: *Moses' father-in-law:* Reuel; cf Nm 10, 29–32 and note. *City of palms:* Jericho (cf Dt 34, 3), or a town in the Negeb.

* **1, 1:** Jgs 20, 18; Nm 27, 21.
1, 9: Jos 10, 40; 11, 16; 12, 8.
1, 10: Jos 15, 13–19.
1, 10: Nm 13, 22; Jos 14, 15.
1, 13: Jgs 3, 9.
1, 16: Jgs 4, 11; Nm 10, 29–32.

Water in the Desert

Caleb's daughter, Achsah, asks for pools of water (Jgs 1, 15) as her wedding present. Presumably, she is asking for a place with springs of fresh water. Achsah's new home will be in the desert, and she knows that her family will need water. She's not afraid to ask for what she needs.

In your prayer, reflect or journal on the following questions:

- What parts of your life are like a barren desert, that is, dry and lifeless?
- What could act as a spring for these parts of your life, bringing new life to them? Be bold in asking God to bring that new life.

▸ Jgs 1, 14–15

the Kenite, Moses' father-in-law, came up with the Judahites from the city of palms to the desert at Arad [which is in the Negeb]. But they later left and settled among the Amalekites.

17* Judah then went with his brother Simeon, and they defeated the Canaanites who dwelt in Zephath. After having doomed the city to destruction, they renamed it Hormah. 18* Judah, however, did not occupy Gaza with its territory, Ashkelon with its territory, or Ekron with its territory. 19* Since the LORD was with Judah, he gained possession of the mountain region. Yet he could not dislodge those who lived on the plain, because they had iron chariots. 20* As Moses had commanded, Hebron was given to Caleb, who then drove from it the three sons of Anak.

21*† The Benjaminites did not dislodge the Jebusites who dwelt in Jerusalem, with the result that the Jebusites live in Jerusalem beside the Benjaminites to the present day.

22 The house of Joseph, too, marched up against Bethel, and the LORD was with them. 23* The house of Joseph had a reconnaissance made of Bethel,

which formerly was called Luz. 24 The scouts saw a man coming out of the city and said to him, "Show us a way into the city, and we will spare you." 25 He showed them a way into the city, which they then put to the sword; but they let the man and his whole clan go free. 26 He then went to the land of the Hittites, where he built a city and called it Luz, as it is still called.

27* Manasseh did not take possession of Beth-shean with its towns or of Taanach with its towns. Neither did he dislodge the inhabitants of Dor and its towns, those of Ibleam and its towns, or those of Megiddo and its towns. The Canaanites kept their hold in this district. 28 When the Israelites grew stronger, they impressed the Canaanites as laborers, but did not drive them out. 29* Similarly, the Ephraimites did not drive out the Canaanites living in Gezer, and so the Canaanites live in Gezer in their midst.

30 Zebulun did not dislodge the inhabitants of Kitron or those of Nahalol; the Canaanites live among them, but have become forced laborers.

31* Nor did Asher drive out the inhabitants of Acco or those of Sidon, or take possession of Mahaleb, Achzib, Helbah, Aphik or Rehob. 32 The Asherites live among the Canaanite natives of the land, whom they have not dislodged.

33* Naphtali did not drive out the inhabitants of Beth-shemesh or those of Beth-anath, and so they live among the Canaanite natives of the land. However, the inhabitants of Beth-shemesh and Beth-anath have become forced laborers for them.

34* The Amorites hemmed in the Danites in the mountain region, not permitting them to go down into the plain. 35 The Amorites had a firm hold in Harheres, Aijalon and Shaalbim, but as the house of Joseph gained the upper hand, they were impressed as laborers.

36 The territory of the Amorites extended from the Akrabbim pass to Sela and beyond.

Infidelities of the Israelites

2 1* An angel of the LORD went up from Gilgal to Bochim and said, "It was I who brought you up from Egypt and led you into the land which I promised on oath to your fathers. I said that I would never break my covenant with you, 2* but that you were not to make a pact with the inhabitants of this land, and you were to pull down their altars. Yet you have not obeyed me. What did you

---

1, 21: According to Jos 18, 16, Jerusalem was assigned to the tribe of Benjamin. But it was not actually taken from the Jebusites until David captured it (2 Sm 5, 6–9) and made it his capital, outside the tribal organization.

1, 17: Nm 21, 3.
1, 18: Jos 11, 22.
1, 19: Jos 17, 16ff.
1, 20: Jos 14, 9.13; 15, 14.
1, 21: Jos 15, 63.
1, 23: Gn 28, 19; 35, 6; 48, 3; Jos 18, 13.
1, 27f: Jos 17, 11ff.
1, 29: Jos 16, 10.
1, 31f: Jos 19, 24–31.
1, 33: Jos 19, 32–39.
1, 34: Jos 19, 47f.
2, 1ff: Jgs 6, 8ff.
2, 2: Ex 34, 12f.15; Dt 7, 2.5; 21, 2f.

mean by this? 3* For now I tell you, I will not clear them out of your way; they shall oppose you and their gods shall become a snare for you."

4 When the angel of the LORD had made these threats to all the Israelites, the people wept aloud; 5† and so that place came to be called Bochim. They offered sacrifice there to the LORD.

6* When Joshua dismissed the people, each Israelite went to take possession of his own hereditary land. 7 The people served the LORD during the entire lifetime of Joshua, and of those elders who outlived Joshua and who had seen all the great work which the LORD had done for Israel. 8 Joshua, son of Nun, the servant of the LORD, was a hundred and ten years old when he died; 9* and they buried him within the borders of his heritage at Timnathheres in the mountain region of Ephraim north of Mount Gaash.

10 But once the rest of that generation were gathered to their fathers, and a later generation arose that did not know the LORD, or what he had done for Israel, 11*† the Israelites offended the LORD by serving the Baals. 12 Abandoning the LORD, the God of their fathers, who had led them out of the land of Egypt, they followed the other gods of the various nations around them, and by their worship of these gods provoked the LORD.

13† Because they had thus abandoned him and served Baal and the Ashtaroth, 14 the anger of the LORD flared up against Israel, and he delivered them over to plunderers who despoiled them. He allowed them to fall into the power of their enemies round about whom they were no longer able to withstand. 15* Whatever they undertook, the LORD turned into disaster for them, as in his warning he had sworn he would do, till they were in great distress. 16 Even when the LORD raised up judges to deliver them from the power of their despoilers, 17 they did not listen to their judges, but abandoned themselves to the worship of other gods. They were quick to stray from the way their fathers had taken, and did not follow their example of obedience to the commandments of the LORD. 18 Whenever the LORD raised up judges for them, he would be with the judge and save them from the power of their enemies as long as the judge lived; it was thus the LORD took pity on their distressful cries of affliction under their oppressors. 19* But when the judge died, they would relapse and do worse than their fathers, following other gods in service and worship, relinquishing none of their evil practices or stubborn conduct.

20* In his anger toward Israel the LORD said, "Inasmuch as this nation has violated my covenant which I enjoined on their fathers, and has disobeyed me, 21 I for my part will not clear away for them any more of the nations which Joshua left when he died." 22 Through these nations the Israelites were to be made to prove whether or not

Obeying Authority   LIVE IT!

Have you ever decided to disobey your parents, your teachers, or maybe a boss at work? What were the consequences? Disobedience to legitimate authority tends to bring about bad consequences. Just read Jgs 2, 10–15. The people turned from God, and their separation from God led to defeat at the hands of their enemies.

God places parents, teachers, and other authority figures in our life to protect and support us. Their love and caring are an extension of God's love and caring. From their vantage point, they often see a bigger picture than we do. When we disobey their reasonable requests, we build walls between them and us, preventing God's love from reaching us. On the other hand, obedience leads to more trust, responsibility, and freedom. Of course, as Jesus himself showed us, no one is obligated to obey requests or directions that are abusive, demeaning, or immoral.

So, the next time you are having a problem with a person in authority, ask yourself, "Might obedience in this situation somehow bring me closer to God?"

▶ Jgs 2, 10–15

---

† 2, 5: Bochim: the Hebrew word for "weepers."
2, 11: Baals: the chief god of the Canaanites and the Phoenicians was called "Baal," a word meaning "lord." He was honored by various titles, hence the plural form here, equivalent to "the pagan gods."
2, 13: Ashtaroth: the Canaanite Phoenician goddess of love and

fertility was Astarte. The plural form used here refers to her various titles and images and is equivalent to "goddesses."

2, 3: Nm 33, 55; Jos 23, 13.
2, 6–9: Jos 24, 28–31.
2, 9: Jos 19, 50.
2, 11.14: Jgs 3, 7f; 4, 1f; 6, 1;
10, 6f; 13, 1.
2, 15: Dt 28, 15–68.
2, 19: Jgs 3, 12; 4, 1; 6, 1; 8, 33.
2, 20f: Jos 23, 16.

they would keep to the way of the LORD and continue in it as their fathers had done; 23 therefore the LORD allowed them to remain instead of expelling them immediately, or delivering them into the power of Israel.

3 1 The following are the nations which the LORD allowed to remain, so that through them he might try all those Israelites who had no experience of the battles with Canaan 2 [just to instruct, by training them in battle, those generations only of the Israelites who would not have had that previous experience]: 3*† the five lords of the Philistines; and all the Canaanites, the Sidonians, and the Hivites who dwell in the mountain region of Lebanon between Baal-hermon and the entrance to Hamath. 4 These served to put Israel to the test, to determine whether they would obey the commandments the LORD had enjoined on their fathers through Moses. 5 Besides, the Israelites were living among the Canaanites, Hittites, Amorites, Perizzites, Hivites and Jebusites. 6 In fact, they took their daughters in marriage, and gave their own daughters to their sons in marriage, and served their gods.

II: Stories of the Judges

Othniel

7*† Because the Israelites had offended the LORD by forgetting the LORD, their God, and serving the Baals and the Asherahs, 8 the anger of the LORD flared up against them, and he allowed them to fall into the power of Cushan-rishathaim, king of Aram Naharaim, whom they served for eight years. 9 But when the Israelites cried out to the LORD, he raised up for them a savior, Othniel, son of Caleb's younger brother Kenaz, who rescued them. 10* The spirit of the LORD came upon him, and he judged Israel. When he went out to war, the LORD delivered Cushan-rishathaim, king of Aram, into his power, so that he made him subject. 11* The land then was at rest for forty years, until Othniel, son of Kenaz, died.

Ehud

12 Again the Israelites offended the LORD, who because of this offense strengthened Eglon, king of Moab, against Israel. 13 In alliance with the Ammonites and Amalekites, he attacked and defeated Israel, taking possession of the city of palms. 14 The Israelites then served Eglon, king of Moab, for eighteen years.

15 But when the Israelites cried out to the LORD, he raised up for them a savior, the Benjaminite Ehud, son of Gera, who was left-handed. It was by him that the Israelites sent their tribute to Eglon, king of Moab. 16 Ehud made himself a two-edged dagger a foot long, and wore it under his clothes over his right thigh. 17 He presented the tribute to Eglon, king of Moab, who was very fat, 18 and after the presentation went off with the tribute bearers. 19 He returned, however, from where the idols are, near Gilgal, and said, "I have a private message for you, O king." And the king said, "Silence!" Then when all his attendants had left his presence, 20 and Ehud went in to him where he sat alone in his cool upper room, Ehud said, "I have a message from God for you." So the king rose from his chair, 21 and then Ehud with his left hand drew the dagger from his right thigh, and thrust it into Eglon's belly. 22 The hilt also went in after the blade, and the fat closed over the blade because he did not withdraw the dagger from his body.

23 Then Ehud went out into the hall, shutting the doors of the upper room on him and locking them. 24 When Ehud had left and the servants came, they saw that the doors of the upper room were locked, and thought, "He must be easing himself in the cool chamber." 25 They waited until they finally grew suspicious. Since he did not open the doors of the upper room, they took the key and opened them. There on the floor, dead, lay their lord!

26 During their delay Ehud made good his escape and, passing the idols, took refuge in Seirah. 27 On his arrival he sounded the horn in the mountain region of Ephraim, and the Israelites went down from the mountains with him as their leader. 28* "Follow me," he said to them, "for the LORD has delivered your enemies the Moabites into your power." So they followed him down and seized the fords of the Jordan leading to Moab, permitting no one to cross. 29 On that occasion they slew about ten thousand Moabites, all of them strong and valiant men. Not a man escaped. 30 Thus was Moab brought under the power of Israel at that time; and the land had rest for eighty years.

Shamgar

31 After him there was Shamgar, son of Anath, who slew six hundred Philistines with an oxgoad. He, too, rescued Israel.

† 3, 3: *The Philistines:* non-Semitic invaders, who gave their name to all Palestine, although they occupied only its southwestern plains. Their confederation embraced the five leading cities of Gaza, Ashkelon, Ashdod, Gath and Ekron.
3, 7: *Asherahs:* elsewhere rendered "sacred poles." See note on Ex 34, 13 and on Dt 7, 5. Here the word seems to mean "goddesses."

3, 3: Jos 13, 2–6.   25; 14, 6.19; 15, 14.
3, 7: Jgs 2, 11ff.   3, 11: Jgs 5, 31; 8, 28.
3, 10: Jgs 6, 34; 11, 29; 13,   3, 28: Jgs 4, 7.14; 7, 9.15.

Deborah and Barak

4 [1] After Ehud's death, however, the Israelites again offended the LORD. [2]* So the LORD allowed them to fall into the power of the Canaanite king, Jabin, who reigned in Hazor. The general of his army was Sisera, who dwelt in Harosheth-ha-goiim. [3] But the Israelites cried out to the LORD; for with his nine hundred iron chariots he sorely oppressed the Israelites for twenty years.

[4] At this time the prophetess Deborah, wife of Lappidoth, was judging Israel. [5] She used to sit under Deborah's palm tree, situated between Ramah

Wartime Women

In Judges, chapter 4, Deborah, a judge and prophet, rallies Barak and the Israelites to war, and Jael, another woman (who is not an Israelite), delivers the final blow to the enemy's commander, Sisera. In chapter 5, Deborah leads the victory celebration with an elaborate prayer-song that is probably one of the oldest texts in the Bible (see also Exodus, chapter 15).

In the Bible, women are often innocent victims of war. Usually, they do not do the fighting but are raped, killed, or widowed. Is Jael's violence the answer to this abuse? Is Jael a hero? Or is she still a victim of war, forced to make a violent choice in order to survive in a violent world? The writer of the Book of Judges gives no judgment on her actions.

When we are no longer victims but have become people who abuse others, has the situation really improved? Or are we just doing to others what we would never want done to ourselves? In light of Jesus' teachings, these are important questions to ask. Let us pray:

God of love, please deliver us from being both victims of violence and agents of violence. Amen.

▶ Judges, chapter 4

and Bethel in the mountain region of Ephraim, and there the Israelites came up to her for judgment. [6]* She sent and summoned Barak, son of Abinoam, from Kedesh of Naphtali. "This is what the LORD, the God of Israel, commands," she said to him; "go, march on Mount Tabor, and take with you ten thousand Naphtalites and Zebulunites. [7]* I will lead Sisera, the general of Jabin's army, out to you at the Wadi Kishon, together with his chariots and troops, and will deliver them into your power." [8] But Barak answered her, "If you come with me, I will go; if you do not come with me, I will not go." [9] "I will certainly go with you," she replied, "but you shall not gain the glory in the expedition on which you are setting out, for the LORD will have Sisera fall into the power of a woman." So Deborah joined Barak and journeyed with him to Kedesh. [10]* Barak summoned Zebulun and Naphtali to Kedesh, and ten thousand men followed him. Deborah also went up with him. [11]*† Now the Kenite Heber had detached himself from his own people, the descendants of Hobab, Moses' brother-in-law, and had pitched his tent by the terebinth of Zaanannim, which was near Kedesh.

[12] It was reported to Sisera that Barak, son of Abinoam, had gone up to Mount Tabor. [13] So Sisera assembled from Harosheth-ha-goiim at the Wadi Kishon all nine hundred of his iron chariots and all his forces. [14] Deborah then said to Barak, "Be off, for this is the day on which the LORD has delivered Sisera into your power. The LORD marches before you." So Barak went down Mount Tabor, followed by his ten thousand men. [15]* And the LORD put Sisera and all his chariots and all his forces to rout before Barak. Sisera himself dismounted from his chariot and fled on foot. [16] Barak, however, pursued the chariots and the army as far as Harosheth-ha-goiim. The entire army of Sisera fell beneath the sword, not even one man surviving.

[17]† Sisera, in the meantime, had fled on foot to the tent of Jael, wife of the Kenite Heber, since Jabin, king of Hazor, and the family of the Kenite Heber were at peace with one another. [18] Jael went out to meet Sisera and said to him, "Come in, my lord, come in with me; do not be afraid." So he went into her tent, and she covered him with a rug. [19]* He said to her, "Please give me a little water to drink. I am thirsty." But she opened a jug of milk for him to drink, and then covered him over. [20] "Stand at the entrance of the tent," he said to her. "If anyone comes and asks, 'Is there someone here?' say, 'No!' "

4, 11: Most of the Kenites occupied a district in the southern part of Judah (Jgs 1, 16). A group of them, however, had detached themselves and settled in lower Galilee.
4, 17–22: It is to be noted that the sacred author merely records the fact of the murder of Sisera. We must not construe this as approval of Jael's action.

4, 2: Jos 11, 1.10; Ps 83, 10;
    1 Sm 12, 9.
4, 6: Heb 11, 32.
4, 7: Jgs 5, 21; Ps 83, 10.
4, 10: Jgs 5, 18.
4, 11: Nm 10, 29.
4, 15: Ps 83, 10.
4, 19: Jgs 5, 25.

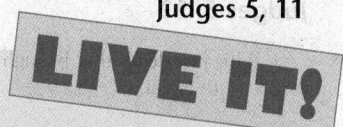

The Battle Within

Although the story of Deborah is inspiring, partly because so few women leaders are portrayed in the Bible, it is also a story of war and violence. The Book of Judges records one battle after another. It is wearying to read of so much fighting and of rejoicing over someone's having a tent peg pounded into his head.

We need to keep our perspective here and understand that the way the Israelites viewed life at that time was simple: If they were victorious, God was with them. If they were defeated, God had been offended and had turned away from them.

What can we learn from this story? It teaches that God never turns away from us. The real victories to celebrate are the personal battles that we win each day as we strive to become more faithful to God. Jesus calls us to make peace rather than war. Our greatest enemy is often within, as we strive to be the person God wants us to be, whether our name is Deborah or Joshua, Jennifer or Carlos.

What battle is going on inside you today? What choice in this battle leads to greater faithfulness to God?

▶ Judges, chapter 4

21* Instead Jael, wife of Heber, got a tent peg and took a mallet in her hand. While Sisera was sound asleep, she stealthily approached him and drove the peg through his temple down into the ground, so that he perished in death. 22 Then when Barak came in pursuit of Sisera, Jael went out to meet him and said to him, "Come, I will show you the man you seek." So he went in with her, and there lay Sisera dead, with the tent peg through his temple.

23 Thus on that day God humbled the Canaanite king, Jabin, before the Israelites; 24 their power weighed ever heavier upon him, till at length they destroyed the Canaanite king, Jabin.

Canticle of Deborah

5 1 On that day Deborah [and Barak, son of Abinoam] sang this song:

2† Of chiefs who took the lead in Israel,
     of noble deeds by the people who bless
        the LORD,
3 Hear, O kings! Give ear, O princes!
    I to the LORD will sing my song,
     my hymn to the LORD, the God of Israel.

4 O LORD, when you went out from Seir,
     when you marched from the land of Edom,
The earth quaked and the heavens were shaken,
     while the clouds sent down showers.

5* Mountains trembled
     in the presence of the LORD, the One
     of Sinai,
     in the presence of the LORD, the God of
     Israel.*

6* In the days of Shamgar, son of Anath,
     in the days of slavery caravans ceased;
Those who traveled the roads
     went by roundabout paths.

7 Gone was freedom beyond the walls
     gone indeed from Israel.

When I, Deborah, rose,
     when I rose, a mother in Israel,
8† New gods were their choice;
     then the war was at their gates.
Not a shield could be seen, nor a lance,
     among forty thousand in Israel!

9 My heart is with the leaders of Israel,
     nobles of the people who bless the LORD;
10 They who ride on white asses,
     seated on saddlecloths as they
       go their way;
11 Sing of them to the strains of the harpers at
     the wells,
     where men recount the just deeds of
       the LORD,

5, 2–31: This canticle is an excellent example of early Hebrew poetry, even though some of its verses are now obscure.

5, 8: *New gods:* pagan deities; cf Dt 32, 16–18. God punished the idolatry of the Israelites by leaving them relatively unarmed before the attacks of their enemies, who had better weapons, made of iron; cf 1 Sm 13, 19–22.

4, 21: Jgs 5, 26.
5, 5: Dt 33, 2; 2 Sm 22, 8;
    Pss 18, 8; 68, 9.
5, 5: Ex 19, 16; Dt 4, 11; Ps
    97, 5.
5, 6: Jgs 3, 31.

his just deeds that brought freedom
    to Israel.

12 Awake, awake, Deborah!
    awake, awake, strike up a song.
    Strength! arise, Barak,
    make despoilers your spoil, son
        of Abinoam.

13 Then down came the fugitives with
        the mighty,
    the people of the LORD came down for me
        as warriors.

14† From Ephraim, princes were in the valley;
    behind you was Benjamin, among
        your troops.
    From Machir came down commanders,
    from Zebulun wielders of the
        marshal's staff.

15* With Deborah were the princes of Issachar;
    Barak, too, was in the valley, his
        course unchecked.

    Among the clans of Reuben
        great were the searchings of heart.

16 Why do you stay beside your hearths
    listening to the lowing of the herds?
    Among the clans of Reuben
        great were the searchings of heart!

17 Gilead, beyond the Jordan, rests;
    why does Dan spend his time in ships?
    Asher, who dwells along the shore,
        is resting in his coves.

18* Zebulun is the people defying death;
    Naphtali, too, on the open heights!

19* The kings came and fought;
    then they fought, those kings of Canaan,
    At Taanach by the waters of Megiddo;
    no silver booty did they take.

20*† From the heavens the stars, too, fought;
    from their courses they fought against Sisera.

21* The Wadi Kishon swept them away;
    a wadi . . . , the Kishon.

22 Then the hoofs of the horses pounded,
    with the dashing, dashing of his steeds.

23† "Curse Meroz," says the LORD,
    "hurl a curse at its inhabitants!
    For they came not to my help,
    as warriors to the help of the LORD."

24* Blessed among women be Jael,
    blessed among tent-dwelling women.
25* He asked for water, she gave him milk;
    in a princely bowl she offered curds.
26 With her left hand she reached for the peg,
    with her right, for the workman's mallet.

    She hammered Sisera, crushed his head;
    she smashed, stove in his temple.
27 At her feet he sank down, fell, lay still;
    down at her feet he sank and fell;
    where he sank down, there he fell, slain.

28 From the window peered down and wailed
    the mother of Sisera, from the lattice:
    "Why is his chariot so long in coming?
    why are the hoofbeats of his
        chariots delayed?"
29 The wisest of her princesses answers her,
    and she, too, keeps answering herself:
30 "They must be dividing the spoil they took:
    there must be a damsel or two for
        each man,
    Spoils of dyed cloth as Sisera's spoil,
    an ornate shawl or two for me in
        the spoil."
31* May all your enemies perish thus, O LORD!
    but your friends be as the sun rising in
        its might!

And the land was at rest for forty years.

The Call of Gideon

6 ¹ The Israelites offended the LORD, who therefore delivered them into the power of Midian
for seven years, ² so that Midian held Israel subject.
For fear of Midian the Israelites established the fire
signals on the mountains, the caves for refuge, and
the strongholds. ³* And it used to be that when the
Israelites had completed their sowing, Midian,
Amalek and the Kedemites would come up, ⁴ encamp opposite them, and destroy the produce of
the land as far as the outskirts of Gaza, leaving no
sustenance in Israel, nor sheep, oxen or asses. ⁵ For

5, 14–22: Praise for the tribes which formed the Israelite league against Sisera: Ephraim, Benjamin, Manasseh (represented by Machir), Zebulun, Issachar, and Naphtali (led by Barak). The tribes of Reuben, Gad (Gilead), Dan, and Asher are chided for their lack of co-operation. The more distant tribes of Judah and Simeon are not mentioned.

5, 20f: It would seem that nature aided the Hebrews in some way. Perhaps the torrential rains swelled the waters of Kishon, which then overwhelmed the Canaanites.

5, 23: *Meroz:* an unknown locality in which Hebrews probably resided, since its inhabitants are cursed for their failure to proffer aid.

5, 15: Jgs 4, 14.
5, 18: Jgs 4, 10.
5, 19: Jgs 1, 27; Jos 17, 11.
5, 20: Jgs 4, 15; Jos 10, 14.
5, 21: Jgs 4, 7.13.
5, 24: Jgs 4, 17; Jdt 13, 17; Lk 1, 28.42.
5, 25f: Jgs 4, 19.21.
5, 31: Ps 83, 10–19.
6, 3f: Jgs 7, 12; Dt 28, 30ff.

they would come up with their livestock, and their tents would become as numerous as locusts; and neither they nor their camels could be numbered, when they came into the land to lay it waste. 6 Thus was Israel reduced to misery by Midian, and so the Israelites cried out to the LORD.

7 When Israel cried out to the LORD because of Midian, 8* he sent a prophet to the Israelites who said to them, "The LORD, the God of Israel, says: I led you up from Egypt; I brought you out of the place of slavery. 9 I rescued you from the power of Egypt and of all your other oppressors. I drove them out before you and gave you their land. 10 And I said to you: I, the LORD, am your God; you shall not venerate the gods of the Amorites in whose land you are dwelling. But you did not obey me."

11 Then the angel of the LORD came and sat under the terebinth in Ophrah that belonged to Joash the Abiezrite. While his son Gideon was beating out wheat in the wine press to save it from the Midianites, 12 the angel of the LORD appeared to him and said, "The LORD is with you, O champion!" 13 "My LORD," Gideon said to him, "if the LORD is with us, why has all this happened to us? Where are his wondrous deeds of which our fathers told us when they said, 'Did not the LORD bring us up from Egypt?' For now the LORD has abandoned us and has delivered us into the power of Midian." 14 The LORD turned to him and said, "Go with the strength you have and save Israel from the power of Midian. It is I who send you." 15 But he answered him, "Please, my lord, how can I save Israel? My family is the meanest in Manasseh, and I am the most insignificant in my father's house." 16 "I shall be with you," the LORD said to him, "and you will cut down Midian to the last man." 17 He answered him, "If I find favor with you, give me a sign that you are speaking with me. 18 Do not depart from here, I pray you, until I come back to you and bring out my offering and set it before you." He answered, "I will await your return."

19 So Gideon went off and prepared a kid and an ephah of flour in the form of unleavened cakes. Putting the meat in a basket and the broth in a pot, he brought them out to him under the terebinth and presented them. 20* The angel of God said to him, "Take the meat and unleavened cakes and lay them on this rock; then pour out the broth." When he had done so, 21 the angel of the LORD stretched out the tip of the staff he held, and touched the meat and unleavened cakes. Thereupon a fire came up from the rock which consumed the meat and

unleavened cakes, and the angel of the LORD disappeared from sight. 22* Gideon, now aware that it had been the angel of the LORD, said, "Alas, Lord GOD, that I have seen the angel of the LORD face to face!" 23 The LORD answered him, "Be calm, do not fear. You shall not die." 24† So Gideon built there an altar to the LORD and called it Yahweh-shalom. To this day it is still in Ophrah of the Abiezrites.

25† That same night the LORD said to him, "Take the seven-year-old spare bullock and destroy your father's altar to Baal and cut down the sacred pole that is by it. 26 You shall build, instead, the proper kind of altar to the LORD, your God, on top of this stronghold. Then take the spare bullock and offer it as a holocaust on the wood from the sacred pole you have cut down." 27 So Gideon took ten of his servants and did as the LORD had commanded him. But through fear of his family and of the townspeople, he would not do it by day, but did it at night. 28 Early the next morning the townspeople found that the altar of Baal had been destroyed, the sacred pole near it cut down, and the spare bullock offered on the altar that was built. 29 They asked one another, "Who did this?" Their inquiry led them to the conclusion that Gideon, son of Joash, had done it. 30 So the townspeople said to Joash, "Bring out your son that he may die, for he has destroyed the altar of Baal and has cut down the sacred pole that was near it." 31 But Joash replied to all who were standing around him, "Do you intend to act in Baal's stead, or be his champion? If anyone acts for him, he shall be put to death by morning. If he whose altar has been destroyed is a god, let him act for himself!" 32*† So on that day Gideon was called Jerubbaal, because of the words, "Let Baal take action against him, since he destroyed his altar."

33 Then all Midian and Amalek and the Kedemites mustered and crossed over into the valley of Jezreel, where they encamped. 34 The spirit of the LORD enveloped Gideon; he blew the horn that summoned Abiezer to follow him. 35 He sent messengers, too, throughout Manasseh, which also obeyed his summons; through Asher, Zebulun and Naphtali, likewise, he sent messengers and these tribes advanced to meet the others. 36 Gideon said to God, "If indeed you are going to save Israel through me, as you promised, 37 I am putting this woolen fleece on the threshing floor. If dew comes on the fleece alone, while all the ground is dry, I shall know that you will save Israel through me, as you promised." 38 That is what took place. Early the next morning he wrung the dew from the fleece,

† ——————————————————————
6, 24: *Yahweh-shalom:* Hebrew for "the LORD is peace," a reference to the LORD's words, "Be calm," literally, "Peace be to you!"
6, 25: *The sacred pole:* see note on Ex 34, 13.
6, 32: *Jerubbaal:* similar in sound to the Hebrew words meaning, "Let Baal take action."

* ——————————————————————
6, 8ff: Jgs 2, 1f; 10, 11–14.   Dt 5, 24ff.
6, 20: Jgs 13, 19.
6, 22f: Gn 32, 31;   6, 32: 1 Sm 12, 11.

Trusting God

The true test of love is loving without testing.

Gideon keeps testing God; he cannot bring himself to believe God's promises. Judges, chapters 6–8, gives a full picture of this hero who never quite understands what loving God is all about. Even after his victory and his words of devotion to God, he makes a gold idol (Jgs 8, 22–28).

Most people are tempted to test God in some way: "God, I'll know you are there for me if I get this job." Fortunately, God is big enough to accept our testing. Just do not expect God to answer every request—at least not exactly the way you would like God to answer it.

How do you test God? Is your prayer more trusting than Gideon's prayer? The next time you feel anxious or afraid, use one of these Scripture passages for your prayer: Psalm 25; Psalm 27; John, chapter 14; 1 Jn 4, 7–21. Challenge yourself to trust God without testing.

▶ Jgs 6, 36–40

squeezing out of it a bowlful of water. 39 Gideon then said to God, "Do not be angry with me if I speak once more. Let me make just one more test with the fleece. Let the fleece alone be dry, but let there be dew on all the ground." 40 That night God did so; the fleece alone was dry, but there was dew on all the ground.

Defeat of Midian

7 1* Early the next morning Jerubbaal (that is, Gideon) encamped by En-harod with all his soldiers. The camp of Midian was in the valley north of Gibeath-hammoreh. 2 The LORD said to Gideon, "You have too many soldiers with you for me to deliver Midian into their power, lest Israel vaunt itself against me and say, 'My own power brought me the victory.' 3* Now proclaim to all the soldiers, 'If anyone is afraid or fearful, let him

leave.' " When Gideon put them to this test on the mountain, twenty-two thousand of the soldiers left, but ten thousand remained. 4 The LORD said to Gideon, "There are still too many soldiers. Lead them down to the water and I will test them for you there. If I tell you that a certain man is to go with you, he must go with you. But no one is to go if I tell you he must not." 5† When Gideon led the soldiers down to the water, the LORD said to him, "You shall set to one side everyone who laps up the water as a dog does with its tongue; to the other, everyone who kneels down to drink." 6 Those who lapped up the water raised to their mouths by hand numbered three hundred, but all the rest of the soldiers knelt down to drink the water. 7 The LORD said to Gideon, "By means of the three hundred who lapped up the water I will save you and will deliver Midian into your power. So let all the other soldiers go home." 8 Their horns, and such supplies as the soldiers had with them, were taken up, and Gideon ordered the rest of the Israelites to their tents, but kept the three hundred men. Now the camp of Midian was beneath him in the valley.

9 That night the LORD said to Gideon, "Go, descend on the camp, for I have delivered it up to you. 10 If you are afraid to attack, go down to the camp with your aide Purah. 11 When you hear what they are saying, you will have the courage to descend on the camp." So he went down with his aide Purah to the outposts of the camp. 12 The Midianites, Amalekites, and all the Kedemites lay in the valley, as numerous as locusts. Nor could their camels be counted, for these were as many as the sands on the seashore. 13† When Gideon arrived, one man was telling another about a dream. "I had a dream," he said, "that a round loaf of barley bread was rolling into the camp of Midian. It came to our tent and struck it, and as it fell it turned the tent upside down." 14 "This can only be the sword of the Israelite Gideon, son of Joash," the other replied. "God has delivered Midian and all the camp into his power." 15 When Gideon heard the description and explanation of the dream, he prostrated himself. Then returning to the camp of Israel, he said, "Arise, for the LORD has delivered the camp of Midian into your power."

16 He divided the three hundred men into three companies, and provided them all with horns and with empty jars and torches inside the jars. 17 "Watch me and follow my lead," he told them. "I shall go to the edge of the camp, and as I do, you

---

7, 5: The Lord desired not numerous but reliable soldiers. Those who drank from their hands were alert, standing ready to resist attack, whereas the others were careless and undependable. The cowardly soldiers had already been dismissed (v 3); cf Dt 20, 8.
7, 13: The barley loaf represents the agricultural Hebrews while

the tent refers to the nomadic Midianites. The overthrow of the tent indicates the victory of the Hebrews over their Midianite oppressors.

7, 1: Jgs 6, 32.   7, 3: Dt 20, 8.

must do also. 18 When I and those with me blow horns, you too must blow horns all around the camp and cry out, 'For the LORD and for Gideon!' " 19† So Gideon and the hundred men who were with him came to the edge of the camp at the beginning of the middle watch, just after the posting of the guards. They blew the horns and broke the jars they were holding. 20 All three companies blew horns and broke their jars. They held the torches in their left hands, and in their right the horns they were blowing, and cried out, "A sword for the LORD and Gideon!" 21 They all remained standing in place around the camp, while the whole camp fell to running and shouting and fleeing. 22* But the three hundred men kept blowing the horns, and throughout the camp the LORD set the sword of one against another. The army fled as far as Beth-shittah in the direction of Zarethan, near the border of Abel-meholah at Tabbath.

23 The Israelites were called to arms from Naphtali, from Asher, and from all Manasseh, and they pursued Midian. 24 Gideon also sent messengers throughout the mountain region of Ephraim to say, "Go down to confront Midian, and seize the water courses against them as far as Beth-barah, as well as the Jordan." So all the Ephraimites were called to arms, and they seized the water courses as far as Beth-barah, and the Jordan as well. 25* They captured the two princes of Midian, Oreb and Zeeb, killing Oreb at the rock of Oreb and Zeeb at the wine press of Zeeb. Then they pursued Midian and carried the heads of Oreb and Zeeb to Gideon beyond the Jordan.

8 1 But the Ephraimites said to him, "What have you done to us, not calling us when you went to fight against Midian?" And they quarreled bitterly with him. 2* "What have I accomplished now in comparison with you?" he answered them. "Is not the gleaning of Ephraim better than the vintage of Abiezer? 3 Into your power God delivered the princes of Midian, Oreb and Zeeb. What have I been able to do in comparison with you?" When he said this, their anger against him subsided.

4 When Gideon reached the Jordan and crossed it with his three hundred men, they were exhausted and famished. 5 So he said to the men of Succoth, "Will you give my followers some loaves of bread? They are exhausted, and I am pursuing Zebah and Zalmunna, kings of Midian." 6† But the princes of Succoth replied, "Are the hands of Zebah and Zal-

munna already in your possession, that we should give food to your army?" 7 Gideon said, "Very well; when the LORD has delivered Zebah and Zalmunna into my power, I will grind your flesh in with the thorns and briers of the desert." 8 He went up from there to Penuel and made the same request of them, but the men of Penuel answered him as had the men of Succoth. 9 So to the men of Penuel, too, he said, "When I return in triumph, I will demolish this tower."

10 Now Zebah and Zalmunna were in Karkor with their force of about fifteen thousand men; these were all who were left of the whole Kedemite army, a hundred and twenty thousand swordsmen having fallen. 11 Gideon went up by the route of the nomads east of Nobah and Jogbehah, and attacked the camp when it felt secure. 12 Zebah and Zalmunna fled. He pursued them and took the two kings of Midian, Zebah and Zalmunna, captive, throwing the entire army into panic.

13 Then Gideon, son of Joash, returned from battle by the pass of Heres. 14 He captured a young man of Succoth, who upon being questioned listed for him the seventy-seven princes and elders of Succoth. 15 So he went to the men of Succoth and said, "Here are Zebah and Zalmunna, with whom you taunted me, 'Are the hands of Zebah and Zalmunna already in your possession, that we should give food to your weary followers?' " 16 He took the elders of the city, and thorns and briers of the desert, and ground these men of Succoth into them. 17 He also demolished the tower of Penuel and slew the men of the city.

18 Then he said to Zebah and Zalmunna, "Where now are the men you killed at Tabor?" "They all resembled you," they replied. "They appeared to be princes." 19 "They were my brothers, my mother's sons," he said. "As the LORD lives, if you had spared their lives, I should not kill you." 20 Then he said to his first-born, Jether, "Go, kill them." Since Jether was still a boy, he was afraid and did not draw his sword. 21 Zebah and Zalmunna said, "Come, kill us yourself, for a man's strength is like the man." So Gideon stepped forward and killed Zebah and Zalmunna. He also took the crescents that were on the necks of their camels.

22 The Israelites then said to Gideon, "Rule over us—you, your son, and your son's son—for you rescued us from the power of Midian." 23 But Gideon answered them, "I will not rule over you, nor shall my son rule over you. The LORD must rule over you."

J
G
S

---

† **7, 19:** *At the beginning of the middle watch:* about two hours before midnight. The ancient Hebrews divided the night into three watches of about four hours each. At the beginning of a watch the sentinels were changed.

8, 6: *Are the hands . . . in your possession . . . ?:* i.e., can you already boast of victory? The hands as well as the heads of slain

enemies were cut off and counted as trophies; cf 2 Sm 4, 8; 2 Kgs 10, 7f; and the Ugaritic Anath Epic, V AB, II 10ff.

7, 22f: Ps 83, 10; Is 9, 4.
7, 25: Jgs 8, 3; Ps 83, 12;   Is 10, 26.
                                             8, 2: Jgs 6, 34.

24† Gideon went on to say, "I should like to make a request of you. Will each of you give me a ring from his booty?" (For being Ishmaelites, the enemy had gold rings.) 25 "We will gladly give them," they replied, and spread out a cloak into which everyone threw a ring from his booty. 26 The gold rings that he requested weighed seventeen hundred gold shekels, in addition to the crescents and pendants, the purple garments worn by the kings of Midian, and the trappings that were on the necks of their camels. 27 Gideon made an ephod out of the gold and placed it in his city Ophrah. However, all Israel paid idolatrous homage to it there, and caused the ruin of Gideon and his family.

28 Thus was Midian brought into subjection by the Israelites; no longer did they hold their heads high. And the land had rest for forty years, during the lifetime of Gideon.

Gideon's Son Abimelech

29 Then Jerubbaal, son of Joash, went back home to stay. 30* Now Gideon had seventy sons, his direct descendants, for he had many wives. 31† His concubine who lived in Shechem also bore him a son, whom he named Abimelech. 32 At a good old age Gideon, son of Joash, died and was buried in the tomb of his father Joash in Ophrah of the Abiezrites. 33† But after Gideon was dead, the Israelites again abandoned themselves to the Baals, making Baal of Berith their god 34 and forgetting the LORD, their God, who had delivered them from the power of their enemies all around them. 35 Nor were they grateful to the family of Jerubbaal [Gideon] for all the good he had done for Israel.

9 1* Abimelech, son of Jerubbaal, went to his mother's kinsmen in Shechem, and said to them and to the whole clan to which his mother's family belonged, 2 "Put this question to all the citizens of Shechem: 'Which is better for you: that seventy men, or all Jerubbaal's sons, rule over you, or that one man rule over you?' You must remember that I am your own flesh and bone." 3 When his mother's kin repeated these words to them on his behalf, all the citizens of Shechem sympathized with Abimelech, thinking, "He is our kinsman." 4 They also gave him seventy silver shekels from the temple of Baal of Berith, with which Abimelech hired shiftless men and ruffians as his followers. 5 He then went to his ancestral house in Ophrah, and slew his brothers, the seventy sons of Jerubbaal, on one stone. Only the youngest son of Jerubbaal, Jotham, escaped, for he was hidden. 6 Then all the citizens of Shechem and all Beth-millo came together and proceeded to make Abimelech king by the terebinth at the memorial pillar in Shechem.

7 When this was reported to him, Jotham went to the top of Mount Gerizim, and standing there, cried out to them in a loud voice: "Hear me, citizens of Shechem, that God may then hear you! 8* Once the trees went to anoint a king over themselves. So they said to the olive tree, 'Reign over us.' 9† But the olive tree answered them, 'Must I give up my rich oil, whereby men and gods are honored, and go to wave over the trees?' 10 Then the trees said to the fig tree, 'Come; you reign over us!' 11 But the fig tree answered them, 'Must I give up my sweetness and my good fruit, and go to wave over the trees?' 12 Then the trees said to the vine, 'Come you, and reign over us.' 13† But the vine answered them, 'Must I give up my wine that cheers gods and men, and go to wave over the trees?' 14 Then all the trees said to the buckthorn, 'Come; you reign over us!' 15 But the buckthorn replied to the trees, 'If you wish to anoint me king over you in good faith, come and take refuge in my shadow. Otherwise, let fire come from the buckthorn and devour the cedars of Lebanon.'

16† "Now then, if you have acted in good faith and honorably in appointing Abimelech your king, if you have dealt well with Jerubbaal and with his family, and if you have treated him as he deserved— 17 for my father fought for you at the risk of his life when he saved you from the power of Midian; 18* but you have risen against his family this day and have killed his seventy sons upon one stone, and have made Abimelech, the son of his handmaid, king over the citizens of Shechem, because he is your kinsman— 19 if, then, you have acted in good faith and with honor toward Jerubbaal and his family this day, rejoice in Abimelech and may he in turn rejoice in you. 20 But if not, let fire come forth from Abimelech to devour the citizens of Shechem and Beth-millo, and let fire come forth from the citizens and from Beth-millo to devour

---

8, 24: *Ishmaelites:* here as in Gn 37, 25–28, the designation is not ethnic; it refers rather to their status as nomads.

8, 31: *Concubine:* a wife of secondary rank.

8, 33: *Baal of Berith:* one of the titles of Baal as worshiped by the Canaanites of Shechem, meaning "the lord of the covenant."

9, 9: *Whereby men and gods are honored:* oil was used in the worship both of the true God and of false gods; it was prescribed in the worship of Yahweh (Lv 2, 1.6.15; 24, 2). It was also used to consecrate prophets, priests and kings (Ex 30, 25.30; 1 Sm 10, 1; 16, 13).

9, 13: *Cheers gods:* wine was used in the libations both of the Temple of Jerusalem and of pagan temples.

9, 16: Just as the noble trees refused the honor of royalty and were made subject to a mean plant, so did Abimelech of less noble birth than the seventy sons of Gideon now tyrannize over the people.

8, 30: Jgs 9, 2.5.	9, 8: Jgs 8, 22f.
9, 1: Jgs 8, 31.	9, 18: Jgs 8, 31.

Abimelech." 21 Then Jotham went in flight to Beer, where he remained for fear of his brother Abimelech.

22 When Abimelech had ruled Israel for three years, 23 God put bad feelings between Abimelech and the citizens of Shechem, who rebelled against Abimelech. 24 This was to repay the violence done to the seventy sons of Jerubbaal and to avenge their blood upon their brother Abimelech, who killed them, and upon the citizens of Shechem, who encouraged him to kill his brothers. 25 The citizens of Shechem then set men in ambush for him on the mountaintops, and these robbed all who passed them on the road. But it was reported to Abimelech.

26 Now Gaal, son of Ebed, came over to Shechem with his kinsmen. The citizens of Shechem put their trust in him, 27 and went out into the fields, harvested their grapes and trod them out. Then they held a festival and went to the temple of their god, where they ate and drank and cursed Abimelech. 28* Gaal, son of Ebed, said, "Who is Abimelech? And why should we of Shechem serve him? Were not the son of Jerubbaal and his lieutenant Zebul once subject to the men of Hamor, father of Shechem? Why should we serve him? 29 Would that this people were entrusted to my command! I would depose Abimelech. I would say to Abimelech, 'Get a larger army and come out!' "

30 At the news of what Gaal, son of Ebed, had said, Zebul, the ruler of the city, was angry 31 and sent messengers to Abimelech in Arumah with the information: "Gaal, son of Ebed, and his kinsmen have come to Shechem and are stirring up the city against you. 32 Now rouse yourself; set an ambush tonight in the fields, you and the men who are with you. 33 Promptly at sunrise tomorrow morning, make a raid on the city. When he and his followers come out against you, deal with him as best you can."

34 During the night Abimelech advanced with all his soldiers and set up an ambush for Shechem in four companies. 35 Gaal, son of Ebed, went out and stood at the entrance of the city gate. When Abimelech and his soldiers rose from their place of ambush, 36 Gaal saw them and said to Zebul, "There are men coming down from the hilltops!" But Zebul answered him, "You see the shadow of the hills as men." 37 But Gaal went on to say, "Men are coming down from the region of Tabbur-Haares, and one company is coming by way of Elon-Meonenim." 38 Zebul said to him, "Where now is the boast you uttered, 'Who is Abimelech that we should serve him?' Are these not the men for whom you expressed contempt? Go out now

and fight with them." 39 So Gaal went out at the head of the citizens of Shechem and fought against Abimelech. 40 But Abimelech routed him, and he fled before him; and many fell slain right up to the entrance of the gate. 41 Abimelech returned to Arumah, but Zebul drove Gaal and his kinsmen from Shechem, which they had occupied.

42 The next day, when the people were taking the field, it was reported to Abimelech, 43 who divided the men he had into three companies, and set up an ambush in the fields. He watched till he saw the people leave the city, and then rose against them for the attack. 44 Abimelech and the company with him dashed in and stood by the entrance of the city gate, while the other two companies rushed upon all who were in the field and attacked them. 45† That entire day Abimelech fought against the city, and captured it. He then killed its inhabitants and demolished the city, sowing the site with salt.

46 When they heard of this, all the citizens of Migdal-shechem went into the crypt of the temple of El-berith. 47 It was reported to Abimelech that all the citizens of Migdal-shechem were gathered together. 48 So he went up Mount Zalmon with all his soldiers, took his ax in his hand, and cut down some brushwood. This he lifted to his shoulder, then said to the men with him, "Hurry! Do just as you have seen me do." 49 So all the men likewise cut down brushwood, and following Abimelech, placed it against the crypt. Then they set the crypt on fire over their heads, so that every one of the citizens of Migdal-shechem, about a thousand men and women, perished.

50 Abimelech proceeded to Thebez, which he invested and captured. 51 Now there was a strong tower in the middle of the city, and all the men and women, in a word all the citizens of the city, fled there, shutting themselves in and going up to the roof of the tower. 52 Abimelech came up to the tower and fought against it, advancing to the very entrance of the tower to set it on fire. 53* But a certain woman cast the upper part of a millstone down on Abimelech's head, and it fractured his skull. 54* He immediately called his armor-bearer and said to him, "Draw your sword and dispatch me, lest they say of me that a woman killed me." So his attendant ran him through and he died. 55 When the Israelites saw that Abimelech was dead, they all left for their homes.

56 Thus did God requite the evil Abimelech had done to his father in killing his seventy brothers. 57 God also brought all their wickedness home to the Shechemites, for the curse of Jotham, son of Jerubbaal, overtook them.

---

† 9, 45: *Sowing the site with salt:* a severe measure, which was a symbol of desolation, and even more, since it actually rendered the ground barren and useless.

* 9, 28: Gn 34, 2.6.
9, 53: 2 Sm 11, 21.

9, 54: 1 Sm 31, 4; 1 Chr 10, 4.

J
G
S

Tola

10 [1] After Abimelech there rose to save Israel the Issacharite Tola, son of Puah, son of Dodo, a resident of Shamir in the mountain region of Ephraim. [2] When he had judged Israel twenty-three years, he died and was buried in Shamir.

Jair

[3] Jair the Gileadite came after him and judged Israel twenty-two years. [4]*† He had thirty sons who rode on thirty saddle-asses and possessed thirty cities in the land of Gilead; these are called Havvoth-jair to the present day. [5] Jair died and was buried in Kamon.

Oppression by the Ammonites

[6] The Israelites again offended the LORD, serving the Baals and Ashtaroths, the gods of Aram, the gods of Sidon, the gods of Moab, the gods of the Ammonites, and the gods of the Philistines. Since they had abandoned the LORD and would not serve him, [7] the LORD became angry with Israel and allowed them to fall into the power of [the Philistines and] the Ammonites. [8] For eighteen years they afflicted and oppressed the Israelites in Bashan, and all the Israelites in the Amorite land beyond the Jordan in Gilead. [9] The Ammonites also crossed the Jordan to fight against Judah, Benjamin, and the house of Ephraim, so that Israel was in great distress.

[10] Then the Israelites cried out to the LORD, "We have sinned against you; we have forsaken our God and have served the Baals." [11]* The LORD answered the Israelites: "Did not the Egyptians, the Amorites,* the Ammonites, the Philistines, [12]* the Sidonians, the Amalekites, and the Midianites oppress you? Yet when you cried out to me, and I saved you from their grasp, [13] you still forsook me and worshiped other gods. Therefore I will save you no more. [14] Go and cry out to the gods you have chosen; let them save you now that you are in distress." [15] But the Israelites said to the LORD, "We have sinned. Do to us whatever you please. Only save us this day." [16] And they cast out the foreign gods from their midst and served the LORD, so that he grieved over the misery of Israel.

[17]* The Ammonites had gathered for war and encamped in Gilead, while the Israelites assembled and encamped in Mizpah. [18]* And among the people the princes of Gilead said to one another, "The one who begins the war against the Ammonites shall be leader of all the inhabitants of Gilead."

Jephthah

11 [1] There was a chieftain, the Gileadite Jephthah, born to Gilead of a harlot. [2] Gilead's wife had also borne him sons, and on growing up the sons of the wife had driven Jephthah away, saying to him, "You shall inherit nothing in our family, for you are the son of another woman." [3] So Jephthah had fled from his brothers and had taken up residence in the land of Tob. A rabble had joined company with him, and went out with him on raids.

[4] Some time later, the Ammonites warred on Israel. [5] When this occurred the elders of Gilead went to bring Jephthah from the land of Tob. [6] "Come," they said to Jephthah, "be our commander that we

PRAY IT

The Effects of Sin

Once again, the Israelites lapse into sin and worship other gods (Jgs 10, 6). Once again, they cry out to God to save them (verse 10). Did they think their sins would have no effect on their lives?

Listen to these words from **Pope John Paul II:**

> There is no sin, not even the most intimate and secret one, the most strictly individual one, that exclusively concerns the person committing it. With greater or lesser violence, with greater or lesser harm, every sin has repercussions on the . . . whole human family.

Have you done anything today that brought harm to you or others? Have you used your gifts and talents as God intended them to be used? Have you neglected an opportunity to share God's love with another person?

LORD, you know all things. Look on me with love, and hear my prayer. Forgive my sins, and give me strength to turn away from the lure of sin. Help me to be more generous in serving you and my neighbor. Help me to be a true follower of your Son, Jesus. Amen.

▸ Jgs 10, 10–16

---

†
  10, 4: *Saddle-asses:* a sign of rank and wealth; cf Jgs 5, 10; 12, 14.

*
  10, 4: Dt 3, 14.
  10, 11–14: Jgs 2, 1ff; 6, 8ff.
  10, 11: Nm 21, 21–32.
  10, 12: Jgs 6, 3.
  10, 17: Jgs 11, 29.
  10, 18: Jgs 11, 5–11.

may be able to fight the Ammonites." 7 "Are you not the ones who hated me and drove me from my father's house?" Jephthah replied to the elders of Gilead. "Why do you come to me now, when you are in distress?" 8 The elders of Gilead said to Jephthah, "In any case, we have now come back to you; if you go with us to fight against the Ammonites, you shall be the leader of all of us who dwell in Gilead." 9 Jephthah answered the elders of Gilead, "If you bring me back to fight against the Ammonites and the LORD delivers them up to me, I shall be your leader." 10 The elders of Gilead said to Jephthah, "The LORD is witness between us that we will do as you say."

11* So Jephthah went with the elders of Gilead, and the people made him their leader and commander. In Mizpah, Jephthah settled all his affairs before the LORD. 12 Then he sent messengers to the king of the Ammonites to say, "What have you against me that you come to fight with me in my land?" 13* He answered the messengers of Jephthah, "Israel took away my land from the Arnon to the Jabbok and the Jordan when they came up from Egypt. Now restore the same peaceably."

14 Again Jephthah sent messengers to the king of the Ammonites, 15* saying to him, "This is what Jephthah says: Israel did not take the land of Moab or the land of the Ammonites. 16 For when they came up from Egypt, Israel went through the desert to the Red Sea and came to Kadesh. 17* Israel then sent messengers to the king of Edom saying, 'Let me pass through your land.' But the king of Edom did not give consent. They also sent to the king of Moab, but he too was unwilling. So Israel remained in Kadesh. 18* Then they went through the desert, and by-passing the land of Edom and the land of Moab, went east of the land of Moab and encamped across the Arnon. Thus they did not go through the territory of Moab, for the Arnon is the boundary of Moab. 19* Then Israel sent messengers to Sihon, king of the Amorites, king of Heshbon. Israel said to him, 'Let me pass through your land to my own place.' 20 But Sihon refused to let Israel pass through his territory. On the contrary, he gathered all his soldiers, who encamped at Jahaz and fought Israel. 21 But the LORD, the God of Israel, delivered Sihon and all his men into the power of Israel, who defeated them and occupied all the land of the

Amorites dwelling in that region, 22 the whole territory from the Arnon to the Jabbok, from the desert to the Jordan. 23 If now the LORD, the God of Israel, has cleared the Amorites out of the way of his people, are you to dislodge Israel? 24*† Should you not possess that which your god Chemosh gave you to possess, and should we not possess all that the LORD, our God, has cleared out for us? 25* Again, are you any better than Balak, son of Zippor, king of Moab? Did he ever quarrel with Israel, or did he war against them 26* when Israel occupied Heshbon and its villages, Aroer and its villages, and all the cities on the banks of the Arnon? Three hundred years have passed; why did you not recover them during that time? 27 I have not sinned against you, but you wrong me by warring against me. Let the LORD, who is judge, decide this day between the Israelites and the Ammonites!" 28 But the king of the Ammonites paid no heed to the message Jephthah sent him.

Jephthah's Vow

29 The spirit of the LORD came upon Jephthah. He passed through Gilead and Manasseh, and through Mizpah-Gilead as well, and from there he went on to the Ammonites. 30† Jephthah made a vow to the LORD. "If you deliver the Ammonites into my power," he said, 31 "whoever comes out of the doors of my house to meet me when I return in triumph from the Ammonites shall belong to the LORD. I shall offer him up as a holocaust."

32 Jephthah then went on to the Ammonites to fight against them, and the LORD delivered them into his power, 33 so that he inflicted a severe defeat on them, from Aroer to the approach of Minnith (twenty cities in all) and as far as Abel-keramim. Thus were the Ammonites brought into subjection by the Israelites. 34 When Jephthah returned to his house in Mizpah, it was his daughter who came forth, playing the tambourines and dancing. She was an only child: he had neither son nor daughter besides her. 35* When he saw her, he rent his garments and said, "Alas, daughter, you have struck me down and brought calamity upon me. For I have made a vow to the LORD and I cannot retract." 36 "Father," she replied, "you have made a vow to the LORD. Do with me as you have vowed, because the LORD has wrought vengeance for you on your

---

11, 24: *Chemosh:* the chief god of the Moabites—not of the Ammonites, whose leading deity was called Molech or Milcom; cf Nm 21, 29; 1 Kgs 11, 7; 2 Kgs 23, 13. The error is probably due to an ancient copyist. Jephthah argues from the viewpoint of his adversaries, the Ammonites, that they were entitled to all the land they had conquered with the aid of their god. It does not necessarily follow that Jephthah himself believed in the actual existence of this pagan god.

11, 30–40: The text clearly implies that Jephthah vowed a human sacrifice, according to the custom of his pagan neighbors; cf 2 Kgs

3, 27. The inspired author merely records the fact; he does not approve of the action.

11, 11: Jgs 10, 18.
11, 13: Nm 21, 13.24ff.
11, 15: Dt 2, 9.19.
11, 17: Nm 20, 1.14.18–21;
    Dt 1, 46.
11, 18: Nm 21, 4.11.13; 22,
    36; Dt 2, 8.

11, 19–22: Nm 21, 21–26; Dt 2,
    26–36.
11, 24: Nm 21, 29; 1 Kgs 11, 7.
11, 25: Nm 22, 2; Jos 24, 9;
    Mi 6, 5.
11, 26: Nm 21, 25; Dt 2, 36.
11, 35: Nm 30, 3.

enemies the Ammonites." [37]† Then she said to her father, "Let me have this favor. Spare me for two months, that I may go off down the mountains to mourn my virginity with my companions." [38] "Go," he replied, and sent her away for two months. So she departed with her companions and mourned her virginity on the mountains. [39] At the end of the two months she returned to her father, who did to her as he had vowed. She had not been intimate with man. It then became a custom in Israel [40] for Israelite women to go yearly to mourn the daughter of Jephthah the Gileadite for four days of the year.

The Shibboleth Incident

12 [1]* The men of Ephraim gathered together and crossed over to Zaphon. They said to Jephthah, "Why do you go on to fight with the Ammonites without calling us to go with you? We will burn your house over you." [2] Jephthah answered them, "My soldiers and I were engaged in a critical contest with the Ammonites. I summoned you, but you did not rescue me from their power. [3] When I saw that you would not effect a rescue, I took my life in my own hand and went on to the Ammonites, and the LORD delivered them into my power. Why, then, do you come up against me this day to fight with me?"

[4] Then Jephthah called together all the men of Gilead and fought against Ephraim, whom they defeated; for the Ephraimites had said, "You of Gilead are Ephraimite fugitives in territory belonging to Ephraim and Manasseh." [5] The Gileadites took the fords of the Jordan toward Ephraim. When any of the fleeing Ephraimites said, "Let me pass," the men of Gilead would say to him, "Are you an Ephraimite?" If he answered, "No!" [6]† they would ask him to say "Shibboleth." If he said "Sibboleth," not being able to give the proper pronunciation, they would seize him and kill him at the fords of the Jordan. Thus forty-two thousand Ephraimites fell at that time.

[7] After having judged Israel for six years, Jephthah the Gileadite died and was buried in his city in Gilead.

Ibzan

[8] After him Ibzan of Bethlehem judged Israel. [9] He had thirty sons. He also had thirty daughters married outside the family, and he brought in as wives for his sons thirty young women from outside the family. After having judged Israel for seven years, [10] Ibzan died and was buried in Bethlehem.

Elon

[11] After him the Zebulunite Elon judged Israel. When he had judged Israel for ten years, [12] the Zebulunite Elon died and was buried in Elon in the land of Zebulun.

Abdon

[13] After him the Pirathonite Abdon, son of Hillel, judged Israel. [14] He had forty sons and thirty grandsons who rode on seventy saddle-asses. After having judged Israel for eight years, [15] the Pirathonite Abdon, son of Hillel, died and was buried in Pirathon in the land of Ephraim on the mountain of the Amalekites.

The Birth of Samson

13 [1]* The Israelites again offended the LORD, who therefore delivered them into the power of the Philistines for forty years.

[2] There was a certain man from Zorah, of the clan of the Danites, whose name was Manoah. His wife was barren and had borne no children. [3]* An angel of the LORD appeared to the woman and said to her, "Though you are barren and have had no children, yet you will conceive and bear a son. [4] Now, then, be careful to take no wine or strong drink and to eat nothing unclean. [5]*† As for the son you will conceive and bear, no razor shall touch his head, for this boy is to be consecrated to God from the womb. It is he who will begin the deliverance of Israel from the power of the Philistines."

[6] The woman went and told her husband, "A man of God came to me; he had the appearance of an angel of God, terrible indeed. I did not ask him where he came from, nor did he tell me his name. [7] But he said to me, 'You will be with child and will bear a son. So take neither wine nor strong drink, and eat nothing unclean. For the boy shall be consecrated to God from the womb, until the day of his death.' " [8] Manoah then prayed to the LORD. "O LORD, I beseech you," he said, "may the man of God whom you sent, return to us to teach us what to do for the boy who will be born."

[9] God heard the prayer of Manoah, and the angel

11, 37: *Mourn my virginity:* to bear children was woman's greatest pride; to be childless was regarded as a great misfortune. Hence Jephthah's daughter asks permission to mourn the fact that she will be put to death before she can bear children.

12, 6: *Shibboleth:* "an ear of grain." But this Hebrew word can also mean "flood water" as in Ps 69, 3.16. Apparently the Gileadites engaged the Ephraimites in conversation about the "flood water" of the Jordan. Differences in enunciating the initial sibilant of the Hebrew word betrayed different tribal affinities.

13, 5: *Consecrated:* In Hebrew, *nazir.* Samson therefore was for life to be under the nazirite vow, which obliged him to abstain from drinking wine or having his hair cut; cf Nm 6, 2–8.

12, 1: Jgs 8, 1.
13, 1: Jgs 10, 6.
13, 3f: 1 Sm 1, 20; Lk 1, 31.
13, 5: Nm 6, 5.

of God came again to the woman as she was sitting in the field. Since her husband Manoah was not with her, 10 the woman ran in haste and told her husband. "The man who came to me the other day has appeared to me," she said to him; 11 so Manoah got up and followed his wife. When he reached the man, he said to him, "Are you the one who spoke to my wife?" "Yes," he answered. 12 Then Manoah asked, "Now, when that which you say comes true, what are we expected to do for the boy?" 13 The angel of the LORD answered Manoah, "Your wife is to abstain from all the things of which I spoke to her. 14 She must not eat anything that comes from the vine, nor take wine or strong drink, nor eat anything unclean. Let her observe all that I have commanded her." 15 Then Manoah said to the angel of

the sky from the altar, the angel of the LORD ascended in the flame of the altar. When Manoah and his wife saw this, they fell prostrate to the ground; 21 but the angel of the LORD was seen no more by Manoah and his wife. Then Manoah, realizing that it was the angel of the LORD, 22* said to his wife, "We will certainly die, for we have seen God." 23 But his wife pointed out to him, "If the LORD had meant to kill us, he would not have accepted a holocaust and cereal offering from our hands! Nor would he have let us see all this just now, or hear what we have heard."

24* The woman bore a son and named him Samson. The boy grew up and the LORD blessed him; 25 the spirit of the LORD first stirred him in Mahanehdan, which is between Zorah and Eshtaol.

Introducing ▶ SAMSON

The story of Samson in Judges, chapters 13–16, is one of the most well-known in the Bible. Most of us know Samson for his great feats of strength, such as killing a lion bare-handed and slaying a thousand men with the jawbone of a donkey. But did you also know that Samson's birth was announced by an angel and that the Book of Judges says "the spirit of the LORD stirred him" more often for Samson than for any other judge? Samson was a Nazirite as well as a judge. Nazirites took vows to abstain from alcohol, avoid contact with dead bodies, and refrain from cutting their hair.

Like many of the other judges, Samson was a flawed hero. He broke all his Nazirite vows, was controlled by lust, and used his great strength for personal revenge. Despite these flaws, God chose to use Samson. Samson paid for his sins, but ultimately, his tragic death brought victory over the Philistines. Once again, God's purposes were accomplished, even through a flawed and sinful human being.

the LORD, "Can we persuade you to stay, while we prepare a kid for you?" 16 But the angel of the LORD answered Manoah, "Although you press me, I will not partake of your food. But if you will, you may offer a holocaust to the LORD." Not knowing that it was the angel of the LORD, 17 Manoah said to him, "What is your name, that we may honor you when your words come true?" 18*† The angel of the LORD answered him, "Why do you ask my name, which is mysterious?" 19* Then Manoah took the kid with a cereal offering and offered it on the rock to the LORD, whose works are mysteries. While Manoah and his wife were looking on, 20 as the flame rose to

Marriage of Samson

14 1† Samson went down to Timnah and saw there one of the Philistine women. 2 On his return he told his father and mother, "There is a Philistine woman I saw in Timnah whom I wish you to get as a wife for me." 3 His father and mother said to him, "Can you find no wife among your kinsfolk or among all our people, that you must go and take a wife from the uncircumcised Philistines?" But Samson answered his father, "Get her for me, for she pleases me." 4* Now his father and mother did not know that this had been brought about by the LORD, who was providing an

---

13, 18: *Mysterious:* incomprehensible, above human understanding. Hence, the angel speaks in the name of the Lord himself, to whom Manoah at once offers a sacrifice.

14, 1–3: Marriages were arranged by the parents of the bridegroom as well as of the bride; cf Gn 24, 2–8; 34, 3–6. The Mosaic law specified only seven pagan nations, not including the Philistines,

in the prohibition against mixed marriages; cf Dt 7, 1–4. But national and religious sentiment was against any marriage with a non-Israelite; cf Gn 28, 1f; 1 Kgs 11, 1–10.

*
13, 18: Gn 32, 29.	**13, 22:** 21f; Jgs 6, 22f.
13, 19f: Jgs 6, 19ff.	**13, 24:** Heb 11, 32.
	14, 4: Jgs 15, 11.

opportunity against the Philistines; for at that time they had dominion over Israel.

5† So Samson went down to Timnah with his father and mother. When they had come to the vineyards of Timnah, a young lion came roaring to meet him. 6 But the spirit of the LORD came upon Samson, and although he had no weapons, he tore the lion in pieces as one tears a kid. 7 However, on the journey to speak for the woman, he did not mention to his father or mother what he had done. 8 Later, when he returned to marry the woman who pleased him, he stepped aside to look at the remains of the lion and found a swarm of bees and honey in the lion's carcass. 9 So he scooped the honey out into his palms and ate it as he went along. When he came to his father and mother, he gave them some to eat, without telling them that he had scooped the honey from the lion's carcass.

10 His father also went down to the woman, and Samson gave a banquet there, since it was customary for the young men to do this. 11† When they met him, they brought thirty men to be his companions. 12 Samson said to them, "Let me propose a riddle to you. If within the seven days of the feast you solve it for me successfully, I will give you thirty linen tunics and thirty sets of garments. 13 But if you cannot answer it for me, you must give me thirty tunics and thirty sets of garments." "Propose your riddle," they responded; "we will listen to it." 14 So he said to them,

"Out of the eater came forth food,
and out of the strong came forth sweetness."

After three days' failure to answer the riddle, 15 they said on the fourth day to Samson's wife, "Coax your husband to answer the riddle for us, or we will burn you and your family. Did you invite us here to reduce us to poverty?" 16 At Samson's side, his wife wept and said, "You must hate me; you do not love me, for you have proposed a riddle to my countrymen, but have not told me the answer." He said to her, "If I have not told it even to my father or my mother, must I tell it to you?" 17 But she wept beside him during the seven days the feast lasted. On the seventh day, since she importuned him, he told her the answer, and she explained the riddle to her countrymen.

18 On the seventh day, before the sun set, the men of the city said to him,

"What is sweeter than honey,
and what is stronger than a lion?"

He replied to them,

"If you had not plowed with my heifer,
you would not have solved my riddle."

19 The spirit of the LORD came upon him, and he went down to Ashkelon, where he killed thirty of their men and despoiled them; he gave their garments to those who had answered the riddle. Then he went off to his own family in anger, 20* and Samson's wife was married to the one who had been best man at his wedding.

Samson Defeats the Philistines

15 1 After some time, in the season of the wheat harvest, Samson visited his wife, bringing a kid. But when he said, "Let me be with my wife in private," her father would not let him enter, 2 saying, "I thought it certain you wished to repudiate her; so I gave her to your best man. Her younger sister is more beautiful than she; you may have her instead." 3 Samson said to them, "This time the Philistines cannot blame me if I harm them." 4 So Samson left and caught three hundred foxes. Turning them tail to tail, he tied between each pair of tails one of the torches he had at hand. 5 He then kindled the torches and set the foxes loose in the standing grain of the Philistines, thus burning both the shocks and the standing grain, and the vineyards and olive orchards as well.

6* When the Philistines asked who had done this, they were told, "Samson, the son-in-law of the Timnite, because his wife was taken and given to his best man." So the Philistines went up and destroyed her and her family by fire. 7 Samson said to them, "If this is how you act, I will not stop until I have taken revenge on you." 8 And with repeated blows, he inflicted a great slaughter on them. Then he went down and remained in a cavern of the cliff of Etam.

9 The Philistines went up and, from a camp in Judah, deployed against Lehi. 10 When the men of Judah asked, "Why have you come up against us?" they answered, "To take Samson prisoner; to do to him as he has done to us." 11 Three thousand men of Judah went down to the cavern in the cliff of Etam and said to Samson, "Do you not know that

---

14, 5ff: Although Samson was accompanied by his parents on the journey to Timnah, v 7 implies that he was not near them when he tore the lion in pieces.
14, 11: *Companions:* known at a later period as "the friends of the bridegroom" (1 Mc 9, 39; Mk 2, 19), the best man and his fel-

lows. Here they are Philistines (v 16), appointed by the family of the bride, who would also have several bridesmaids; cf Mt 25, 1–13.

14, 20: Jgs 15, 2.6.   15, 6: Jgs 14, 20.

the Philistines are our rulers? Why, then, have you done this to us?" He answered them, "As they have done to me, so have I done to them." 12 They said to him, "We have come to take you prisoner, to deliver you over to the Philistines." Samson said to them, "Swear to me that you will not kill me yourselves." 13* "No," they replied, "we will certainly not kill you but will only bind you and deliver you over to them." So they bound him with two new ropes and brought him up from the cliff. 14 When he reached Lehi, and the Philistines came shouting to meet him, the spirit of the LORD came upon him: the ropes around his arms became as flax that is consumed by fire and his bonds melted away from his hands. 15 Near him was the fresh jawbone of an ass; he reached out, grasped it, and with it killed a thousand men. 16 Then Samson said,

"With the jawbone of an ass
　　I have piled them in a heap;
With the jawbone of an ass
　　I have slain a thousand men."

17† As he finished speaking he threw the jawbone from him; and so that place was named Ramath-lehi. 18 Being very thirsty, he cried to the LORD and said, "You have granted this great victory by the hand of your servant. Must I now die of thirst or fall into the hands of the uncircumcised?" 19† Then God split the cavity in Lehi, and water issued from it, which Samson drank till his spirit returned and he revived. Hence that spring in Lehi is called En-hakkore to this day.

20* Samson judged Israel for twenty years in the days of the Philistines.

16 1 Once Samson went to Gaza, where he saw a harlot and visited her. 2 Informed that Samson had come there, the men of Gaza surrounded him with an ambush at the city gate all night long. And all the night they waited, saying, "Tomorrow morning we will kill him." 3 Samson rested there until midnight. Then he rose, seized the doors of the city gate and the two gateposts, and tore them loose, bar and all. He hoisted them on his shoulders and carried them to the top of the ridge opposite Hebron.

Samson and Delilah

4 After that he fell in love with a woman in the Wadi Sorek whose name was Delilah. 5 The lords of the Philistines came to her and said, "Beguile him and find out the secret of his great strength, and

how we may overcome and bind him so as to keep him helpless. We will each give you eleven hundred shekels of silver."

6 So Delilah said to Samson, "Tell me the secret of your great strength and how you may be bound so as to be kept helpless." 7 "If they bind me with seven fresh bowstrings which have not dried," Samson answered her, "I shall be as weak as any other man." 8 So the lords of the Philistines brought her seven fresh bowstrings which had not dried, and she bound him with them. 9* She had men lying in wait in the chamber and so she said to him, "The Philistines are upon you, Samson!" But he snapped the strings as a thread of tow is severed by a whiff of flame; and the secret of his strength remained unknown.

10 Delilah said to Samson, "You have mocked me and told me lies. Now tell me how you may be bound." 11* "If they bind me tight with new ropes, with which no work has been done," he answered her, "I shall be as weak as any other man." 12 So Delilah took new ropes and bound him with them. Then she said to him, "The Philistines are upon you, Samson!" For there were men lying in wait in the chamber. But he snapped them off his arms like thread.

13 Delilah said to Samson again, "Up to now you have mocked me and told me lies. Tell me how you may be bound." He said to her, "If you weave my seven locks of hair into the web and fasten them with the pin, I shall be as weak as any other man." 14 So while he slept, Delilah wove his seven locks of hair into the web, and fastened them in with the pin. Then she said, "The Philistines are upon you, Samson!" Awakening from his sleep, he pulled out both the weaver's pin and the web.

15 Then she said to him, "How can you say that you love me when you do not confide in me? Three times already you have mocked me, and not told me the secret of your great strength!" 16 She importuned him continually and vexed him with her complaints till he was deathly weary of them. 17* So he took her completely into his confidence and told her, "No razor has touched my head, for I have been consecrated to God from my mother's womb. If I am shaved, my strength will leave me, and I shall be as weak as any other man!" 18 When Delilah saw that he had taken her completely into his confidence, she summoned the lords of the Philistines, saying, "Come up this time, for he has opened his heart to me." So the lords of the Philistines came and brought up the money with them. 19 She had him sleep on her lap, and called for a

J
G
S

---

† **15, 17:** *Ramath-lehi:* "heights of the jawbone."
　15, 19: *En-hakkore:* "the spring of him who cries out," an allusion to Samson's cry in v 18.

* 15, 13: Jgs 16, 11f.　　　　16, 11: Jgs 15, 13.
　15, 20: Jgs 16, 31.　　　　16, 17: Jgs 13, 5.
　16, 9: Jgs 15, 14.

Manipulation

JGS

You'd think that Samson would catch on, wouldn't you? Delilah tries to coax from Samson the secret of his strength. By the third attempt, it seems rather obvious that she wants to betray him to the Philistines. Nonetheless, Samson finally is pestered into revealing his secret, and Delilah uses the information to betray him.

Have you ever had a confidence betrayed? Have you ever trusted someone with a secret only to discover later that your secret is out? It makes it that much harder to trust again, to be open and to share yourself with another. When the person who betrays your confidence is someone you love, the betrayal is even more painful.

We need to do some soul-searching here. Ask yourself: Am I the kind of person who can be trusted with someone's secret? Have I ever betrayed a confidence?

It is easier than we like to think to be like Delilah—abusing the trust built up in a relationship and manipulating another person, even someone we care deeply about. We need to resolve to be people of integrity, who would never betray a confidence for personal gain.

▸ Jgs 16, 4–22

man who shaved off his seven locks of hair. Then she began to mistreat him, for his strength had left him. 20 When she said, "The Philistines are upon you, Samson!", and he woke from his sleep, he thought he could make good his escape as he had done time and again, for he did not realize that the LORD had left him. 21 But the Philistines seized him and gouged out his eyes. Then they brought him down to Gaza and bound him with bronze fetters, and he was put to grinding in the prison. 22 But the hair of his head began to grow as soon as it was shaved off.

The Death of Samson

23*† The lords of the Philistines assembled to offer a great sacrifice to their god Dagon and to make merry. They said,

> "Our god has delivered into our power
> Samson our enemy."

25 When their spirits were high, they said, "Call Samson that he may amuse us." So they called Samson from the prison, and he played the buffoon before them. 24 When the people saw him, they praised their god. For they said,

> "Our god has delivered into our power
> our enemy, the ravager of our land,
> the one who has multiplied our slain."

Then they stationed him between the columns. 26 Samson said to the attendant who was holding

his hand, "Put me where I may touch the columns that support the temple and may rest against them." 27 The temple was full of men and women: all the lords of the Philistines were there, and from the roof about three thousand men and women looked on as Samson provided amusement. 28 Samson cried out to the LORD and said, "O Lord GOD, remember me! Strengthen me, O God, this last time that for my two eyes I may avenge myself once and for all on the Philistines." 29 Samson grasped the two middle columns on which the temple rested and braced himself against them, one at his right hand, the other at his left. 30 And Samson said, "Let me die with the Philistines!" He pushed hard, and the temple fell upon the lords and all the people who were in it. Those he killed at his death were more than those he had killed during his lifetime.

31* All his family and kinsmen went down and bore him up for burial in the grave of his father Manoah between Zorah and Eshtaol. He had judged Israel for twenty years.

III: The Tribes of Dan and Benjamin in the Days of the Judges

Micah and the Levite

17 1 There was a man in the mountain region of Ephraim whose name was Micah. 2 He said to his mother, "The eleven hundred shekels of silver over which you pronounced a curse in my hearing when they were taken from you, are in my possession. It was I who took them; so now I

16, 23: Dagon was originally a Mesopotamian deity, whom the Philistines came to worship as their own god of grain.

16, 23: 1 Sm 5, 2–5.   16, 31: Jgs 15, 20.

will restore them to you." [3*†] When he restored the eleven hundred shekels of silver to his mother, she took two hundred of them and gave them to the silversmith, who made of them a carved idol overlaid with silver. [4] Then his mother said, "May the LORD bless my son! I have consecrated the silver to the LORD as my gift in favor of my son, by making a carved idol overlaid with silver." It remained in the house of Micah. [5*] Thus the layman Micah had a sanctuary. He also made an ephod and household idols, and consecrated one of his sons, who became his priest. [6*] In those days there was no king in Israel; everyone did what he thought best.

16, 28—31

[7] There was a young Levite who had resided within the tribe of Judah at Bethlehem of Judah. [8] From that city he set out to find another place of residence. On his journey he came to the house of Micah in the mountain region of Ephraim. [9] Micah said to him, "Where do you come from?" He answered him, "I am a Levite from Bethlehem in Judah, and am on my way to find some other place of residence." [10*] "Stay with me," Micah said to him. "Be father and priest to me, and I will give you ten silver shekels a year, a set of garments, and your food." [11] So the young Levite decided to stay with the man, to whom he became as one of his own sons. [12†] Micah consecrated the young Levite, who became his priest, remaining in his house. [13] Therefore Micah said, "Now I know that the LORD will prosper me, since the Levite has become my priest."

Migration of the Danites

18 [1*†] At that time there was no king in Israel. Moreover the tribe of Danites were in search of a district to dwell in, for up to that time they had received no heritage among the tribes of Israel.

[2] So the Danites sent from their clan a detail of five valiant men of Zorah and Eshtaol, to reconnoiter the land and scout it. With their instructions to go and scout the land, they traveled as far as the house of Micah in the mountain region of Ephraim, where they passed the night. [3*†] Near the house of Micah, they recognized the voice of the young Levite and turned in that direction. "Who brought you here and what are you doing here?" they asked him. "What is your interest here?" [4*] "This is how Micah treats me," he replied to them. "He pays me a salary and I am his priest." [5] They said to him, "Consult God, that we may know whether the undertaking we are engaged in will succeed." [6] The priest said to them, "Go and prosper: the LORD is favorable to the undertaking you are engaged in."

[7] So the five men went on and came to Laish. They saw that the people dwelling there lived securely after the manner of the Sidonians, quiet and trusting, with no lack of any natural resources. They were distant from the Sidonians and had no contact with other people. [8] When the five returned to their kinsmen in Zorah and Eshtaol and were asked for a report, [9] they replied, "Come, let us attack them, for we have seen the land and it is very good. Are you going to hesitate? Do not be slothful about beginning your expedition to possess the land. [10] Those against whom you go are a trusting people, and the land is ample. God has indeed given it into your power: a place where no natural resource is lacking."

[11] So six hundred men of the clan of the Danites, fully armed with weapons of war, set out from where they were in Zorah and Eshtaol, [12*] and camped in Judah, up near Kiriath-jearim; hence to this day the place, which lies west of Kiriath-jearim, is called Mahaneh-dan.

[13] From there they went on to the mountain region of Ephraim and came to the house of Micah. [14*] The five men who had gone to reconnoiter the land of Laish said to their kinsmen, "Do you know that in these houses there are an ephod, household idols, and a carved idol overlaid with silver? Now decide what you must do!" [15] So turning in that direction, they went to the house of the young Levite

---

17, 3: *Idol:* an image, not of a pagan god, but of the Lord. The Mosaic law forbade the making of an image even of the true God.

17, 12f: According to Nm 18, 1–7 only those Levites who were descended from Aaron could be consecrated as priests.

18, 1: The tribe of Dan had been assigned a territory with definite limits in central Palestine. However they were unable to gain possession of the better portion of their land (Jgs 1, 34). So they now seek territory elsewhere in Palestine.

18, 3: *Recognized the voice:* perhaps they noticed the peculiar pronunciation of his south Hebrew dialect.

17, 3: Ex 20, 4; Lv 19, 4.	18, 3: Jgs 17, 7.
17, 5: Jgs 18, 14.17.	18, 4: Jgs 17, 10.
17, 6: Jgs 18, 1; 21, 25.	18, 12: Jgs 13, 25.
17, 10: Jgs 18, 19.	18, 14: Jgs 17, 4f.
18, 1: Jos 19, 40–48.	

at the home of Micah and greeted him. 16 The six hundred men girt with weapons of war, who were Danites, stood by the entrance of the gate, and the priest stood there also. 17 Meanwhile the five men who had gone to reconnoiter the land went up and entered the house of Micah. 18 When they had gone in and taken the ephod, the household idols, and the carved idol overlaid with silver, the priest said to them, "What are you doing?" 19* They said to him, "Be still: put your hand over your mouth. Come with us and be our father and priest. Is it better for you to be priest for the family of one man or to be priest for a tribe and a clan in Israel?" 20 The priest, agreeing, took the ephod, household idols, and carved idol and went off in the midst of the band. 21 As they turned to depart, they placed their little ones, their livestock, and their goods at the head of the column.

22 The Danites had already gone some distance, when those in the houses near that of Micah took up arms and overtook them. 23 They called to the Danites, who turned about and said to Micah, "What do you want, that you have taken up arms?" 24 "You have taken my god, which I made, and have gone off with my priest as well," he answered. "What is left for me? How, then, can you ask me what I want?" 25 The Danites said to him, "Let us hear no further sound from you, lest fierce men fall upon you and you and your family lose your lives." 26 The Danites then went on their way, and Micah, seeing that they were stronger than he, returned home.

27 Having taken what Micah had made, and the priest he had had, they attacked Laish, a quiet and trusting people; they put them to the sword and destroyed their city by fire. 28 No one came to their aid, since the city was far from Sidon and they had no contact with other people. The Danites then rebuilt the city, which was in the valley that belongs to Beth-rehob, and lived there. 29 They named it Dan after their ancestor Dan, son of Israel. However, the name of the city was formerly Laish. 30† The Danites set up the carved idol for themselves, and Jonathan, son of Gershom, son of Moses, and his descendants were priests for the tribe of the Danites until the time of the captivity of the land. 31 They maintained the carved idol Micah had made as long as the house of God was in Shiloh.

The Levite from Ephraim

19 1* At that time, when there was no king in Israel, there was a Levite residing in re-mote parts of the mountain region of Ephraim who had taken for himself a concubine from Bethlehem of Judah. 2 His concubine was unfaithful to him and left him for her father's house in Bethlehem of Judah, where she stayed for some four months. 3 Her husband then set out with his servant and a pair of asses, and went after her to forgive her and take her back. She brought him into her father's house, and on seeing him, the girl's father joyfully made him welcome. 4 He was detained by the girl's father, and so he spent three days with this father-in-law of his, eating and drinking and passing the night there. 5† On the fourth day they rose early in the morning and he prepared to go. But the girl's father said to his son-in-law, "Fortify yourself with a little food; you can go later on." 6 So they stayed and the two men ate and drank together. Then the girl's father said to the husband, "Why not decide to spend the night here and enjoy yourself?" 7 The man still made a move to go, but when his father-in-law pressed him he went back and spent the night there.

8 On the fifth morning he rose early to depart, but the girl's father said, "Fortify yourself and tarry until the afternoon." When he and his father-in-law had eaten, 9 and the husband was ready to go with his concubine and servant, the girl's father said to him, "It is already growing dusk. Stay for the night. See, the day is coming to an end. Spend the night here and enjoy yourself. Early tomorrow you can start your journey home." 10 The man, however, refused to stay another night; he and his concubine set out with a pair of saddled asses, and traveled till they came opposite Jebus, which is Jerusalem. 11 Since they were near Jebus with the day far gone, the servant said to his master, "Come, let us turn off to this city of the Jebusites and spend the night in it." 12* But his master said to him, "We will not turn off to a city of foreigners, who are not Israelites, but will go on to Gibeah. 13* Come," he said to his servant, "let us make for some other place, either Gibeah or Ramah, to spend the night." 14 So they continued on their way till the sun set on them when they were abreast of Gibeah of Benjamin.

15*† There they turned off to enter Gibeah for the night. The man waited in the public square of the city he had entered, but no one offered them the shelter of his home for the night. 16 In the evening, however, an old man came from his work in the field; he was from the mountain region of Ephraim, though he lived among the Benjaminite townspeople of Gibeah. 17 When he noticed the

---

†
18, 30: *Until . . . land:* about the year 734 B.C., when the Assyr-ian emperor Tiglath-pileser III subjected northern Palestine.

19, 5–9: Such importuning of guests to prolong their stay at the home of their host is characteristic of Oriental hospitality.

19, 15: Private hospitality was the customary means of providing comfort to travelers where public facilities were so rare.

*
18, 19: Jgs 17, 10.   19, 13: Jos 18, 25.
19, 1: Jgs 17, 6.   19, 15: Jgs 20, 4.
19, 12: Jgs 1, 21.

traveler in the public square of the city, the old man asked where he was going, and whence he had come. ¹⁸ He said to him, "We are traveling from Bethlehem of Judah far up into the mountain region of Ephraim, where I belong. I have been to Bethlehem of Judah and am now going back home; but no one has offered us the shelter of his house. ¹⁹ We have straw and fodder for our asses, and bread and wine for the woman and myself and for our servant; there is nothing else we need." ²⁰ "You are welcome," the old man said to him, "but let me provide for all your needs, and do not spend the night in the public square." ²¹* So he led them to his house and provided fodder for the asses. Then they washed their feet, and ate and drank.

The Outrage at Gibeah

²²*† While they were enjoying themselves, the men of the city, who were corrupt, surrounded the house and beat on the door. They said to the old man whose house it was, "Bring out your guest, that we may abuse him." ²³ The owner of the house went out to them and said, "No, my brothers; do not be so wicked. Since this man is my guest, do not commit this crime. ²⁴ Rather let me bring out my maiden daughter or his concubine. Ravish them, or do whatever you want with them; but against the man you must not commit this wanton crime." ²⁵ When the men would not listen to his host, the husband seized his concubine and thrust her outside to them. They had relations with her and abused her all night until the following dawn, when they let her go. ²⁶ Then at daybreak the woman came and collapsed at the entrance of the house in which her husband was a guest, where she lay until the morning. ²⁷ When her husband rose that day and opened the door of the house to start out again on his journey, there lay the woman, his concubine, at the entrance of the house with her hands on the threshold. ²⁸ He said to her, "Come, let us go"; but there was no answer. So the man placed her on an ass and started out again for home.

²⁹† On reaching home, he took a knife to the body of his concubine, cut her into twelve pieces, and sent them throughout the territory of Israel. ³⁰* Everyone who saw this said, "Nothing like this has been done or seen from the day the Israelites came up from the land of Egypt to this day. Take note of it, and state what you propose to do."

Assembly of Israelites

20 ¹† So all the Israelites came out as one man: from Dan to Beer-sheba, and from the land of Gilead, the community was gathered to the LORD at Mizpah. ² The leaders of all the people and all the tribesmen of Israel, four hundred thousand foot soldiers who were swordsmen, presented themselves in the assembly of the people of God. ³ Meanwhile, the Benjaminites heard that the Israelites had gone up to Mizpah. The Israelites asked to be told how the crime had taken place, ⁴* and the Levite, the husband of the murdered woman, testified: "My concubine and I went into Gibeah of Benjamin for the night. ⁵* But the citizens of Gibeah rose up against me by night and surrounded the house in which I was. Me they attempted to kill, and my concubine they abused so that she died. ⁶* So I took my concubine and cut her up and sent her through every part of the territory of Israel, because of the monstrous crime they had committed in Israel. ⁷*† Now that you are all here, O Israelites, state what you propose to do." ⁸ All the people rose as one man to say, "None of us is to leave for his tent or return to his home. ⁹ Now as for Gibeah, this is what we will do: We will proceed against it by lot, ¹⁰ taking from all the tribes of Israel ten men for every hundred, a hundred for every thousand, a thousand for every ten thousand, and procuring supplies for the soldiers who will go to deal fully and suitably with Gibeah of Benjamin for the crime it committed in Israel."

¹¹ When, therefore, all the men of Israel without exception were leagued together against the city, ¹²† the tribes of Israel sent men throughout the tribe of Benjamin to say, "What is this evil which has occurred among you? ¹³ Now give up these corrupt men of Gibeah, that we may put them to death and thus purge the evil from Israel." But the Benjaminites refused to accede to the demand of their brothers, the Israelites. ¹⁴ Instead, the Benjaminites assembled from their other cities to Gibeah, to do battle with the Israelites. ¹⁵ The number of the Benjaminite swordsmen from the other cities on that occasion was twenty-six thousand, in addition to the inhabitants of Gibeah. ¹⁶ Included in this total were seven hundred picked men who were left-handed, every one of them able to sling a stone at a hair without missing. ¹⁷ Meanwhile the other

---

19, 22: *Who were corrupt:* literally "sons of Belial," indicating extreme perversion; cf Gn 19, 4–8. This crime and its punishment made the name Gibeah proverbial as a place of shameful wickedness; cf Hos 9, 9; 10, 9.

19, 29: A drastic means for arousing the tribes to avenge the unheard of crime of the Benjaminites.

20, 1: *From Dan to Beer-sheba:* from north to south. *The land of Gilead:* all the territory east of the Jordan.

20, 7: The Israelites were asked to decide at once what action to take concerning this crime; cf 2 Sm 16, 20. The Levite undoubtedly addressed the tribal heads who would speak in behalf of the multitude.

20, 12: Before the crime at Gibeah was punished, the Benjaminites were invited to join their brethren, the Israelites, in punishing the crime. Since they failed to respond, special messengers were sent asking them to deliver up the guilty ones. They replied by gathering their forces for combat.

19, 21: Gn 18, 4; 24, 32;   20, 4: Jgs 19, 14f.
    43, 24.   20, 5: Jgs 19, 22–27.
19, 22–25: Gn 19, 4–9.   20, 6: Jgs 19, 29.
19, 30: Hos 9, 9; 10, 9.   20, 7: Jgs 19, 30.

Israelites who, without Benjamin, mustered four hundred thousand swordsmen ready for battle, 18*† moved on to Bethel and consulted God. When the Israelites asked who should go first in the attack on the Benjaminites, the LORD said, "Judah shall go first." 19 The next day the Israelites advanced on Gibeah with their forces.

War with Benjamin

20 On the day the Israelites drew up in battle array at Gibeah for the combat with Benjamin, 21 the Benjaminites came out of the city and felled twenty-two thousand men of Israel. 23 Then the Israelites went up and wept before the LORD until evening. "Shall I again engage my brother Benjamin in battle?" they asked the LORD; and the LORD answered that they should. 22 But though the Israelite soldiers took courage and again drew up for combat in the same place as on the previous day, 24 when they met the Benjaminites for the second time, 25 once again the Benjaminites who came out of Gibeah against them felled eighteen thousand Israelites, all of them swordsmen. 26 So the entire Israelite army went up to Bethel, where they wept and remained fasting before the LORD until evening of that day, besides offering holocausts and peace offerings before the LORD. 27* When the Israelites consulted the LORD (for the ark of the covenant of God was there in those days, 28 and Phinehas, son of Eleazar, son of Aaron, was ministering to him in those days), and asked, "Shall I go out again to battle with Benjamin, my brother, or shall I desist?" the LORD said, "Attack! for tomorrow I will deliver him into your power." 29*† So Israel set men in ambush around Gibeah.

30 The Israelites went up against the Benjaminites for the third time and formed their line of battle at Gibeah as on other occasions. 31 The Benjaminites went out to meet them, and in the beginning they killed off about thirty of the Israelite soldiers in the open field, just as on the other occasions. 32 Therefore the Benjaminites thought, "We are defeating them as before"; not realizing that disaster was about to overtake them. The Israelites, however, had planned the flight so as to draw them away from the city onto the highways. They were drawn away from the city onto the highways, of which the one led to Bethel, the other to Gibeon. 33 And then all the men of Israel rose from their places. They reformed their ranks at Baal-tamar, and the Israelites in ambush rushed from their place west of Gibeah,

34 ten thousand picked men from all Israel, and advanced against the city itself. In a fierce battle, 35 the LORD defeated Benjamin before Israel; and on that day the Israelites killed twenty-five thousand one hundred men of Benjamin, all of them swordsmen.

36 To the Benjaminites it had looked as though the enemy were defeated, for the men of Israel gave ground to Benjamin, trusting in the ambush they had set at Gibeah. 37 But then the men in ambush made a sudden dash into Gibeah, overran it, and put the whole city to the sword. 38 Now, the other Israelites had agreed with the men in ambush on a smoke signal they were to send up from the city. 39 And though the men of Benjamin had begun by killing off some thirty of the men of Israel, under the impression that they were defeating them as surely as in the earlier fighting, the Israelites wheeled about to resist 40 as the smoke of the signal column began to rise up from the city. It was when Benjamin looked back and saw the whole city in flames against the sky 41 that the men of Israel wheeled about. Therefore the men of Benjamin were thrown into confusion, for they realized the disaster that had overtaken them. 42 They retreated before the men of Israel in the direction of the desert, with the fight being pressed against them. In their very midst, meanwhile, those who had been in the city were spreading destruction. 43 The men of Benjamin had been surrounded, and were now pursued to a point east of Gibeah, 44 while eighteen thousand of them fell, warriors to a man. 45* The rest turned and fled through the desert to the rock Rimmon. But on the highways the Israelites picked off five thousand men among them, and chasing them up to Gidom, killed another two thousand of them there. 46 Those of Benjamin who fell on that day were in all twenty-five thousand swordsmen, warriors to a man. 47 But six hundred others who turned and fled through the desert reached the rock Rimmon, where they remained for four months.

48 The men of Israel withdrew through the territory of the Benjaminites, putting to the sword the inhabitants of the cities, the livestock, and all they chanced upon. Moreover they destroyed by fire all the cities they came upon.

Wives for the Survivors

21 1† Now the men of Israel had sworn at Mizpah that none of them would give his

---

20, 18: *Judah shall go first:* the same response as in Jgs 1, 1f, but without the assurance of immediate success. Only after the Israelites were punished at the hands of the Benjaminites for their own grossness, and had performed penance, did they succeed in punishing the latter for their part in the crime of rape and murder, by gaining the victory over them.
20, 29–46: This stratagem proved more useful to the Israelites than force, as in the siege of Ai (Jos 8, 3–21). In the parallel accounts

the first (vv 29–35) is a summary of the second (vv 36–46).
21, 1–3: The anger of the Israelites led them to destroy their brethren, the Benjaminites. Having realized their goal, however, they were soon filled with dismay, and sought to restore the tribe they had all but exterminated.

20, 18: Jgs 1, 1f.   20, 29–46: Jos 8, 4–24.
20, 27: 1 Sm 4, 3f.   20, 45: Jgs 21, 13.

daughter in marriage to anyone from Benjamin. 2* So the people went to Bethel and remained there before God until evening, raising their voices in bitter lament. 3 They said, "LORD, God of Israel, why has it come to pass in Israel that today one tribe of Israel should be lacking?" 4 Early the next day the people built an altar there and offered holocausts and peace offerings. 5* Then the Israelites asked, "Are there any among all the tribes of Israel who did not come up to the LORD for the assembly?" For they had taken a solemn oath that anyone who did not go up to the LORD at Mizpah should be put to death without fail.

6† The Israelites were disconsolate over their brother Benjamin and said, "Today one of the tribes of Israel has been cut off. 7 What can we do about wives for the survivors, since we have sworn by the LORD not to give them any of our daughters in marriage?" 8 And when they asked whether anyone among the tribes of Israel had not come up to the LORD in Mizpah, they found that none of the men of Jabesh-gilead had come to the encampment for the assembly. 9 A roll call of the army established that none of the inhabitants of that city were present. 10 The community, therefore, sent twelve thousand warriors with orders to go to Jabesh-gilead and put those who lived there to the sword, including the women and children. 11*† They were told to include under the ban all males and every woman who was not still a virgin. 12 Finding among the inhabitants of Jabesh-gilead four hundred young virgins, who had had no relations with men, they brought them to the camp at Shiloh in the land of Canaan. 13* Then the whole community sent a message to the Benjaminites at the rock Rimmon,

offering them peace. 14 When Benjamin returned at that time, they gave them as wives the women of Jabesh-gilead whom they had spared; but these proved to be not enough for them.

15† The people were still disconsolate over Benjamin because the LORD had made a breach among the tribes of Israel. 16 And the elders of the community said, "What shall we do for wives for the survivors? For every woman in Benjamin has been put to death." 17 They said, "Those of Benjamin who survive must have heirs, else one of the Israelite tribes will be wiped out. 18† Yet we cannot give them any of our daughters in marriage, because the Israelites have sworn, 'Cursed be he who gives a woman to Benjamin!' " 19 Then they thought of the yearly feast of the LORD at Shiloh, north of Bethel, east of the highway that goes up from Bethel to Shechem, and south of Lebonah. 20 And they instructed the Benjaminites, "Go and lie in wait in the vineyards. 21 When you see the girls of Shiloh come out to do their dancing, leave the vineyards and each of you seize one of the girls of Shiloh for a wife, and go to the land of Benjamin. 22 When their fathers or their brothers come to complain to us, we shall say to them, 'Release them to us as a kindness, since we did not take a woman apiece in the war. Had you yourselves given them these wives, you would now be guilty.' "

23 The Benjaminites did this; they carried off a wife for each of them from their raid on the dancers, and went back to their own territory, where they rebuilt and occupied the cities. 24 Also at that time the Israelites dispersed; each of them left for his own heritage in his own clan and tribe.

25*† In those days there was no king in Israel; everyone did what he thought best.

---

† **21, 6–9:** This account is summarized in the parallel passage in vv 2–5.

21, 11: *Under the ban:* see note on Nm 21, 3.

21, 15: *Had made a breach:* what is here attributed to God was in reality the free and deliberate act of the Israelites and happened only by the permissive will of God. The ancients attributed to the first primary cause what is more directly due to secondary causes.

21, 18: Regardless of the serious consequences of their vow, the

Israelites considered themselves obliged to fulfill it; cf Jgs 11, 31. 35f.39.

21, 25: Cf Jgs 17, 6; 18, 1; 19, 1. The verse gives the reason why the lawlessness of the period of judges, and the events described herein, were possible.

---

*
21, 2: Jgs 20, 26.
21, 5: Jgs 20, 8ff.
21, 11: Nm 31, 17.

21, 13: Jgs 20, 47.
21, 25: Jgs 17, 6; 18, 1; 19, 1.

Tracing one's family tree has become a popular pastime. People comb through courthouse files, study old tombstones in search of names and dates, and write to churches in foreign countries looking for baptismal and marriage records. In learning about our ancestors, we gain a better sense of our place in history and who we should be in light of that history. Ruth is a beautiful story of love and loyalty about one of Israel's ancestors. The story helps God's people understand who they are and how they should live.

At a Glance

I. Naomi in Moab (chapter 1).

II. The Meeting (chapters 2–3).

III. Boaz Marries Ruth (chapter 4).

In-depth

The Book of Ruth offers a surprising revelation about the family tree of King David: Ruth, King David's great-grandmother, was a foreigner, born and reared in the land of Moab. The Book of Ruth was written long after the death of her famous great-grandson, but it seems to preserve an accurate memory: King David was of mixed ancestry. Many Israelites were probably shocked that God worked through a member of an enemy tribe to advance the divine plan.

The Book of Ruth is sandwiched between Judges and 1 Samuel because its events take place during the time of the judges. It teaches some extremely important lessons:

- Ruth was faithful to Naomi, her mother-in-law, even though she was of a different race and different faith. Ruth challenged the ancient Israelites, who tended to view foreigners with suspicion and to see nothing good in their enemies.

- If God's plan included a Moabite woman among David's ancestors, then God's love and favor must extend beyond the boundaries of Israel. After the Exile, when Jewish marriages to foreigners were outlawed, the little Book of Ruth presented a huge challenge!

- God works through the faithfulness of ordinary people living ordinary lives. No kings, wars, or dramatic miracles appear in the Book of Ruth.

The Book of Ruth is action packed and full of dialog; it is a dramatic story like the Books of Judith and Tobit. Some of the traditions of ancient Israel may seem strange to us today, but we can still gain a deeper understanding of ourselves and our faith by reading the story of King David's great-grandmother.

Quick Facts

Period Covered
sometime from 1200 to 1000 B.C.

Author
unknown, probably writing sometime during the monarchy (1000–800 B.C.)

Themes
God's plan includes non-Israelites. God works through ordinary people.

Ruth

Naomi in Moab

1 [1]† Once in the time of the judges there was a famine in the land; so a man from Bethlehem of Judah departed with his wife and two sons to reside on the plateau of Moab. [2] The man was named Elimelech, his wife Naomi, and his sons Mahlon and Chilion; they were Ephrathites from Bethlehem of Judah. Some time after their arrival on the Moabite plateau, [3] Elimelech, the husband of Naomi, died, and she was left with her two sons, [4] who married Moabite women, one named Orpah, the other Ruth. When they had lived there about ten years, [5] both Mahlon and Chilion died also, and the woman was left with neither her two sons nor her husband. [6] She then made ready to go back from the plateau of Moab because word reached her there that the LORD had visited his people and given them food.

[7] She and her two daughters-in-law left the place where they had been living. Then as they were on the road back to the land of Judah, [8]† Naomi said to her two daughters-in-law, "Go back, each of you, to your mother's house! May the LORD be kind to you as you were to the departed and to me! [9] May the LORD grant each of you a husband and a home in which you will find rest." She kissed them good-by, but they wept with loud sobs, [10] and told her they would return with her to her people. [11]† "Go back, my daughters!" said Naomi. "Why should you come with me? Have I other sons in my womb who may become your husbands? [12] Go back, my daughters! Go, for I am too old to marry again. And even if I could offer any hopes, or if tonight I had a husband or had borne sons, [13] would you then wait and deprive yourselves of husbands until those sons grew up? No, my daughters! my lot is too bitter for you, because the LORD has extended his hand against me." [14] Again they sobbed aloud and wept; and Orpah kissed her mother-in-law good-by, but Ruth stayed with her.

[15] "See now!" she said, "your sister-in-law has gone back to her people and her god. Go back after your sister-in-law!" [16]† But Ruth said, "Do not ask me to abandon or forsake you! for wherever you go I will go, wherever you lodge I will lodge, your people shall be my people, and your God my God.

---

† **1, 1f:** *In the time of the judges:* three generations before the end of the period of Judges; cf Ru 4, 21f. *Bethlehem of Judah:* to distinguish it from the town of the same name in the tribe of Zebulun (Jos 19, 15). *Ephrathites from Bethlehem:* belonging to a Judean clan which settled in Bethlehem; cf 1 Sm 17, 12; 1 Chr 2, 50f; 4, 4.

1, 8: *Mother's house:* the women's part of the dwelling; cf Jgs 4, 17; Song 3, 4.

1, 11: *Have I other sons . . . husbands?:* Naomi insisted that her daughters-in-law remain in their own country only for the sake of posterity. If she had had other sons, the levirate law would have obliged them to marry the widows of her deceased sons to perpetuate the names of the deceased; cf Gn 38, 8; Dt 25, 5f.

1, 16: An example of heroic fidelity and piety. Ruth's decision, confirmed with an oath, to adhere to her mother-in-law impelled her to abandon her country and its pagan worship.

Stand by Me

Loyalty is one of those old-fashioned words, isn't it? How often do we hear it mentioned these days? And what exactly does it mean to be loyal? The story of Naomi and Ruth gives us an inspiring example of loyalty. After Ruth's husband dies and her mother-in-law decides to return home to Bethlehem, Naomi tells her two widowed daughters-in-law that they should return to their homes and marry again. But Ruth decides to stay with Naomi, which means leaving her own land of Moab and settling in Judea, a foreign land. Ruth's words to Naomi are a powerful statement of what it means to be loyal: "Wherever you go I will go, wherever you lodge I will lodge, your people shall be my people, and your God my God" (Ru 1, 16). In other words, "No matter what, I will stand by you."

We are also called to be loyal—especially to our families and friends. In other words, we are to stand by the people we are close to, especially when they are experiencing hard times. Even when it's tough to do so, we are to remain faithful. Loyalty creates trust and deepens relationships.

None of us wants to be disloyal. Think about Peter's reaction at Jesus' Passion when he realized he had denied knowing Jesus three times!

Reflect on the times in your life when you have experienced loyalty. How have your friends or family members proven their loyalty to you? How and when have you proven your loyalty to another? God is always loyal to us; are we loyal to God?

▶ Ru 1, 1–18

R
U

17 Wherever you die I will die, and there be buried. May the Lord do so and so to me, and more besides, if aught but death separates me from you!" 18 Naomi then ceased to urge her, for she saw she was determined to go with her.

The Return to Bethlehem

19 So they went on together till they reached Bethlehem. On their arrival there, the whole city was astir over them, and the women asked, "Can this be Naomi?" 20*† But she said to them, "Do not call me Naomi. Call me Mara, for the Almighty has made it very bitter for me. 21 I went away with an abundance, but the Lord has brought me back destitute. Why should you call me Naomi, since the Lord has pronounced against me and the Almighty has brought evil upon me?" 22† Thus it was that Naomi returned with the Moabite daughter-in-law, Ruth, who accompanied her back from the plateau of Moab. They arrived in Bethlehem at the beginning of the barley harvest.

The Meeting

2 1* Naomi had a prominent kinsman named Boaz, of the clan of her husband Elimelech. 2*† Ruth the Moabite said to Naomi, "Let me go and glean ears of grain in the field of anyone who will allow me that favor." Naomi said to her, "Go, my daughter," 3 and she went. The field she entered to glean after the harvesters happened to be the section belonging to Boaz of the clan of Elimelech. 4† Boaz himself came from Bethlehem and said to the harvesters, "The Lord be with you!" and they replied, "The Lord bless you!" 5 Boaz asked the overseer of his harvesters, "Whose girl is this?" 6* The overseer of the harvesters answered, "She is the Moabite girl who returned from the plateau of Moab with Naomi. 7 She asked leave to gather the gleanings into sheaves after the harvesters; and ever since she came this morning she has remained here until now, with scarcely a moment's rest."

8 Boaz said to Ruth, "Listen, my daughter! Do not go to glean in anyone else's field; you are not to

---

1, 20f: *Naomi:* means "amiable" or "pleasant," suggesting God's favor toward her. *The Almighty has brought evil upon me:* the ancients regarded adversity as a punishment from God for personal sin, as if good and evil were always repaid in a temporal and material manner.

1, 22: *Barley harvest:* early April. This circumstance favored the events of the narrative that follow.

2, 2: *Let me go and glean . . . grain:* even the poor, the widow, the

stranger, and the orphan had a right to glean at harvest time; cf Lv 19, 9f, 23; 22; Dt 24, 19–22.

2, 4: *The Lord be with you:* courtesy and religious feeling characterize the salutations of the Hebrews. This greeting is used in the Christian liturgy.

1, 20: Ex 15, 23.
2, 1: Ru 3, 2.12; 4, 21; Mt 1, 5.
2, 2: Dt 24, 19.
2, 6: Ru 1, 22.

leave here. Stay here with my women servants. [9] Watch to see which field is to be harvested, and follow them; I have commanded the young men to do you no harm. When you are thirsty, you may go and drink from the vessels the young men have filled." [10] Casting herself prostrate upon the ground, she said to him, "Why should I, a foreigner, be favored with your notice?" [11]* Boaz answered her: "I have had a complete account of what you have done for your mother-in-law after your husband's death; you have left your father and your mother and the land of your birth, and have come to a people whom you did not know previously. [12] May the LORD reward what you have done! May you receive a full reward from the LORD, the God of Israel, under whose wings you have come for refuge." [13] She said, "May I prove worthy of your kindness, my lord: you have comforted me, your servant, with your consoling words; would indeed that I were a servant of yours!" [14] At mealtime Boaz said to her, "Come here and have some food; dip your bread in the sauce." Then as she sat near the reapers, he handed her some roasted grain and she ate her fill and had some left over. [15] She rose to

glean, and Boaz instructed his servants to let her glean among the sheaves themselves without scolding her, [16] and even to let drop some handfuls and leave them for her to glean without being rebuked.

[17] She gleaned in the field until evening, and when she beat out what she had gleaned it came to about an ephah of barley, [18] which she took into the city and showed to her mother-in-law. Next she brought out and gave her what she had left over from lunch. [19] So her mother-in-law said to her, "Where did you glean today? Where did you go to work? May he who took notice of you be blessed!" Then she told her mother-in-law with whom she had worked. "The man at whose place I worked today is named Boaz," she said. [20]*† "May he be blessed by the LORD, who is ever merciful to the living and to the dead," Naomi exclaimed to her daughter-in-law; and she continued, "He is a relative of ours, one of our next of kin." [21] "He even told me," added Ruth the Moabite, "that I should stay with his servants until they complete his entire harvest." [22] "You would do well, my dear," Naomi rejoined, "to go out with his servants; for in someone else's field you might be insulted." [23] So she

Service to the Poor and the Community!

The story of Ruth was a challenge to the Israelites' tendency to distrust foreigners. It is also an example of how service to the poor was an integral part of Israel's society. For in the story, Boaz, a wealthy and respected person, both provides for the poor and looks beyond the differences of race and faith to marry Ruth. Boaz's goal is to do God's will. His marriage to Ruth ensures that Naomi's land is redeemed and that she will have descendants to claim the land. Ruth's faithfulness and Boaz's integrity serve to gradually restore Naomi's hope in God's care.

In the New Testament, it becomes even clearer that God makes no distinctions between people of different races and cultures. And Jesus teaches that caring for the poor is one of the requirements for being God's people.

■ How do you treat people of different races, and how much is service to poor people a part of your life?

■ Pray that you can follow Ruth and Boaz's example and be an instrument of faith, hope, and justice for people in need.

2, 20: *One of our next of kin:* literally "our redeemer," a near relative of the same clan who had the right and duty to restore the land which an impoverished kinsman had alienated (Lv 25, 25–28), and to marry the widow of a relative who had died without male offspring so as to raise up posterity to his name (Dt 25, 5–10).

2, **11:** Ru 1, 14–17.   2, **20:** Ru 3, 9.

stayed gleaning with the servants of Boaz until the end of the barley and wheat harvests.

Ruth Again Presents Herself

3 When she was back with her mother-in-law, [1] Naomi said to her, "My daughter, I must seek a home for you that will please you. [2]* Now is not Boaz, with whose servants you were, a relative of ours? This evening he will be winnowing barley at the threshing floor. [3] So bathe and anoint yourself; then put on your best attire and go down to the threshing floor. Do not make yourself known to the man before he has finished eating and drinking. [4]† But when he lies down, take note of the place where he does so. Then go, uncover a place at his feet, and lie down. He will tell you what to do." [5] "I will do whatever you advise," Ruth replied. [6] So she went down to the threshing floor and did just as her mother-in-law had instructed her.

[7] Boaz ate and drank to his heart's content. Then when he went and lay down at the edge of the sheaves, she stole up, uncovered a place at his feet, and lay down. [8] In the middle of the night, however, the man gave a start and turned around to find a woman lying at his feet. [9]† He asked, "Who are you?" And she replied, "I am your servant Ruth. Spread the corner of your cloak over me, for you are my next of kin." [10]* He said, "May the LORD bless you, my daughter! You have been even more loyal now than before in not going after the young men, whether poor or rich. [11] So be assured, daughter, I will do for you whatever you say; all my towns-people know you for a worthy woman. [12]*† Now, though indeed I am closely related to you, you have another relative still closer. [13]* Stay as you are for tonight, and tomorrow, if he wishes to claim you, good! let him do so. But if he does not wish to claim you, as the LORD lives, I will claim you myself. Lie there until morning." [14] So she lay at his feet until morning, but rose before men could recognize one another. Boaz said, "Let it not be known that this woman came to the threshing floor." [15]* Then he said to her, "Take off your cloak and hold it out." When she did so, he poured out six measures of barley, helped her lift the bundle, and left for the city.

[16] Ruth went home to her mother-in-law, who asked, "How have you fared, my daughter?" So she told her all the man had done for her, [17] and concluded, "He gave me these six measures of barley because he did not wish me to come back to my mother-in-law empty-handed!" [18] Naomi then said, "Wait here, my daughter, until you learn what happens, for the man will not rest, but will settle the matter today."

Boaz Marries Ruth

4 [1]*† Boaz went and took a seat at the gate; and when he saw the closer relative of whom he had spoken come along, he called to him by name, "Come and sit beside me!" And he did so. [2]† Then Boaz picked out ten of the elders of the city and asked them to sit nearby. When they had done this, [3] he said to the near relative: "Naomi, who has come back from the Moabite plateau, is putting up for sale the piece of land that belonged to our kinsman Elimelech. [4]*† So I thought I would inform you, bidding you before those here present,

Wherever You Go

Ruth is under no obligation to leave her homeland and go to Israel with her mother-in-law, very likely facing a life of poverty. But her loyalty is rewarded, and she finds new life among God's people.

After reading Ruth's story, reflect on these questions:
- What do you find inspiring in Ruth's story?
- To whom are you faithful?
- What would have to be present in a relationship for you to have the kind of loyalty Ruth showed to Naomi?
- Can you make Ruth's words to Naomi your prayer to God?

Where you lead, I will follow; where you direct me, I will live; your people shall be my family, and you shall always be my God. (Adapted from Ru 1, 16)

---

† 3, 4: *Uncover a place at his feet* . . . : confident of the virtue of Ruth and Boaz, Naomi advises this unusual expedient to her daughter-in-law for the purpose of introducing her claim.

3, 9: *Spread the corner of your cloak over me:* be my protector by marrying me according to the duty of a near kinsman; cf Dt 25, 5; Ez 16, 8.

3, 12: *Relative still closer:* who had a prior right and duty to marry Ruth.

4, 1: *Took a seat at the gate:* i.e., of the city, where business affairs were settled.

4, 2: *Ten of the elders:* to serve as judges in legal matters as well as witnesses of the settlement of business affairs; cf Dt 25, 7–9.

4, 4: Poverty had obliged Naomi to sell the land of her deceased husband. The law permitted the nearest kinsman to redeem the land and thus preserve the family patrimony; cf Lv 25, 25.

3, 2: Ru 1.   3, 15: Ru 2, 17.
3, 10: Dt 25, 5.   4, 1: Ru 3, 12.
3, 12: Ru 4, 1.   4, 4: Lv 25, 25.
3, 13: Ru 4, 5; Dt 25, 5.

including the elders of my people, to put in your claim for it if you wish to acquire it as next of kin. But if you do not wish to claim it, tell me so, that I may be guided accordingly, for no one has a prior claim to yours, and mine is next." He answered, "I will put in my claim."

5*† Boaz continued, "Once you acquire the field from Naomi, you must take also Ruth the Moabite, the widow of the late heir, and raise up a family for the departed on his estate." 6 The near relative replied, "I cannot exercise my claim lest I depreciate my own estate. Put in a claim yourself in my stead, for I cannot exercise my claim." 7† Now it used to be the custom in Israel that, to make binding a contract of redemption or exchange, one party would take off his sandal and give it to the other. This was the form of attestation in Israel. 8 So the near relative, in saying to Boaz, "Acquire it for yourself," drew off his sandal. 9 Boaz then said to the elders and to all the people, "You are witnesses today that I have acquired from Naomi all the holdings of Elimelech, Chilion and Mahlon. 10 I also take Ruth the Moabite, the widow of Mahlon, as my wife, in order to raise up a family for her late husband on his estate, so that the name of the departed may not perish among his kinsmen and fellow citizens. Do you witness this today?" 11* All those at the gate, including the elders, said, "We do so. May the LORD make this wife come into your house like Rachel and Leah, who between them built up the house of Israel. May you do well in Ephrathah and win fame in Bethlehem. 12*† With the offspring the LORD will give you from this girl, may your house become like the house of Perez, whom Tamar bore to Judah."

13 Boaz took Ruth. When they came together as man and wife, the LORD enabled her to conceive and she bore a son. 14 Then the women said to Naomi, "Blessed is the LORD who has not failed to provide you today with an heir! May he become famous in Israel! 15 He will be your comfort and the support of your old age, for his mother is the daughter-in-law who loves you. She is worth more to you than seven sons!" 16† Naomi took the child, placed him on her lap, and became his nurse. 17*† And the neighbor women gave him his name, at the news that a grandson had been born to Naomi. They called him Obed. He was the father of Jesse, the father of David.

18* These are the descendants of Perez: Perez was the father of Hezron,* 19 Hezron was the father of Ram, Ram was the father of Amminadab, 20* Amminadab was the father of Nahshon, Nahshon was the father of Salmon, 21 Salmon was the father of Boaz, Boaz was the father of Obed, 22* Obed was the father of Jesse, and Jesse became the father of David.

4, 5f: The heir of Elimelech's field had died without children (Ru 1, 5). The nearest of kin could now redeem the land but he must also take Ruth, the widow of the late heir, to wife to perpetuate the family of the deceased; cf Dt 25, 5f. The first male child of such a marriage would be the legal son of Mahlon and grandson of Elimelech.

4, 7: Take off his sandal . . . : by this act the near relative renounced his legal right, both to the field of Elimelech and to the marriage with Ruth. The custom mentioned in Dt 25, 6 is somewhat different.

4, 12: Perez, whom Tamar bore to Judah: the right which Judah unwittingly satisfied for his daughter-in-law Tamar (Gn 38), Boaz willingly rendered to Ruth.

4, 16: Placed him on her lap: took him as her own; cf Gn 30, 3; 48, 12; Nm 11, 12.

4, 17: The father of Jesse, the father of David: indicating the place of Obed, Jesse and David in the line of Judah and the ancestry of Christ, the Messiah; cf Mt 1, 5f.

4, 5: Ru 3, 13; Dt 25, 5.	**4, 18–22:** 1 Chr 2, 4–15;
4, 11: Gn 29, 31—30, 24;	Mt 1, 3–6.
35, 19.	**4, 18:** Gn 46, 12; 1 Chr 4, 1.
4, 12: Gn 38, 29.	**4, 20:** Ex 6, 23; Nm 1, 7.
4, 17: Lk 1, 58.	**4, 22:** 1 Sm 16, 10–13.

The First Book of Samuel

An ongoing national debate these days involves, on the one side, those who want more laws to protect workers, poor people, and the environment, and on the other side, those who want fewer laws and less government. The First Book of Samuel reflects a similar tension in Israel as the days of the judges come to an end and the first kings make their appearance. This period of Israelite history is filled with mighty struggles and colorful personalities, including a king who gradually loses his sanity and the shining hero who replaces him.

At a Glance

I. History of the Last Judges, Eli and Samuel (1, 1—7, 17).

II. Establishment of the Monarchy in Israel (8, 1—12, 25).

III. Saul and David (13, 1—31, 13).

In-depth

This book is named after Samuel, the last of the judges and a reluctant king-maker. Samuel, a prophet anointed to speak God's word to the nation, represents one way of governing. God works through the prophet's words to remind the people of Israel to be faithful to the terms of the Covenant. A second way of governing is represented by Saul, the first king anointed by Samuel to rule over the whole nation. God works through the king's laws and regulations to ensure that the people of Israel are faithful to the terms of the Covenant. In 1 Samuel, the former way of governing the Israelite nation gradually gives way to the latter, with an obvious gain and an obvious loss for the people.

When kings begin to rule Israel in place of judges and prophets, the people gain a more structured way of life and develop a greater national identity. These changes also make them stronger in facing threats from other nations. But at the same time, the people lose a great deal of personal freedom and independence. They are taxed and even forced into labor to support the king's government and building plans. Echoes of this debate on governing styles can be found throughout 1 Samuel (see "Doublets," near 9, 1).

Israel's kings were understood as being chosen by God and as being responsible for God's interests. First Samuel clearly emphasizes that the success of kings depends on their obedience to God's law. First Samuel reminds us that final authority in human affairs rests in no human being, but in God alone. Human systems are never perfect, but must constantly be reviewed and renewed.

Quick Facts

Period Covered
approximately 1080 to 1040 B.C.

Author
unknown, from the Deuteronomic tradition, probably using ancient court records and hero stories

Theme
tension between the need for a king and the people's reliance on God

Of Note
First and Second Samuel, originally one book, were made into two books when they were translated from Hebrew into Greek.

1 Samuel

I: History of the Last Judges, Eli and Samuel

Elkanah and His Family at Shiloh

1 ¹* There was a certain man from Ramathaim, Elkanah by name, a Zuphite from the hill country of Ephraim. He was the son of Jeroham, son of Elihu, son of Tohu, son of Zuph, an Ephraimite. ² He had two wives, one named Hannah, the other Peninnah; Peninnah had children, but Hannah was childless. ³* This man regularly went on pilgrimage from his city to worship the LORD of hosts and to sacrifice to him at Shiloh, where the two sons of Eli, Hophni and Phinehas, were ministering as priests of the LORD. ⁴ When the day came for Elkanah to offer sacrifice, he used to give a portion each to his wife Peninnah and to all her sons and daughters, ⁵* but a double portion to Hannah because he loved her, though the LORD had made her barren. ⁶* Her rival, to upset her, turned it into a constant reproach to her that the LORD had left her barren. ⁷ This went on year after year; each time they made their pilgrimage to the sanctuary of the LORD, Peninnah would approach her, and Hannah would weep and refuse to eat. ⁸* Her husband Elkanah used to ask her: "Hannah, why do you weep, and why do you refuse to eat? Why do you grieve? Am I not more to you than ten sons?"

Hannah's Prayer

⁹ Hannah rose after one such meal at Shiloh, and presented herself before the LORD; at the time, Eli the priest was sitting on a chair near the doorpost of the LORD's temple. ¹⁰ In her bitterness she prayed to the LORD, weeping copiously, ¹¹*† and she made a vow, promising: "O LORD of hosts, if you look with pity on the misery of your handmaid, if you remember me and do not forget me, if you give your handmaid a male child, I will give him to the LORD for as long as he lives; neither wine nor liquor shall he drink, and no razor shall ever touch his head." ¹² As she remained long at prayer before the LORD, Eli watched her mouth, ¹³ for Hannah was praying silently; though her lips were moving, her voice could not be heard. Eli, thinking her drunk, ¹⁴ said to her, "How long will you make a drunken show of yourself? Sober up from your wine!" ¹⁵ "It isn't that, my lord," Hannah answered. "I am an unhappy woman. I have had neither wine nor liquor; I was only pouring out my troubles to the LORD. ¹⁶ Do not think your handmaid a ne'er-do-well; my prayer has been prompted by my deep sorrow and misery." ¹⁷ Eli said, "Go in peace, and may the God of Israel grant you what you have asked of him." ¹⁸ She replied, "Think kindly of your maidservant," and left. She went to her quarters, ate and drank with her husband, and no longer appeared down-

---

† **1, 11:** *Give him to the LORD:* some ancient texts call Samuel a *nazir* in this context; see note on Nm 6, 1ff.

1, 1: 1 Chr 6, 19f.
1, 3: Ex 23, 14–17; 34, 23; Dt 16, 16; Jgs 21, 19.
1, 5: Dt 21, 15ff.
1, 6: Gn 16, 4f.
1, 8: Ru 4, 15.
1, 11: Nm 6, 1–5; Jgs 13, 2–5; 16, 17; Lk 1, 15.

cast. [19] Early the next morning they worshiped before the LORD, and then returned to their home in Ramah.

Hannah Bears a Son

When Elkanah had relations with his wife Hannah, the LORD remembered her. [20]† She conceived, and at the end of her term bore a son whom she called Samuel, since she had asked the LORD for him. [21] The next time her husband Elkanah was going up with the rest of his household to offer the customary sacrifice to the LORD and to fulfill his vows, [22] Hannah did not go, explaining to her husband, "Once the child is weaned, I will take him to appear before the LORD and to remain there forever; I will offer him as a perpetual nazirite." [23] Her husband Elkanah answered her: "Do what you think best; wait until you have weaned him. Only, may the LORD bring your resolve to fulfillment!" And so she remained at home and nursed her son until she had weaned him.

Samuel Is Offered to God

[24]† Once he was weaned, she brought him up with her, along with a three-year-old bull, an ephah of flour, and a skin of wine, and presented him at the temple of the LORD in Shiloh. [25] After the boy's father had sacrificed the young bull, Hannah, his mother, approached Eli [26] and said: "Pardon, my lord! As you live, my lord, I am the woman who stood near you here, praying to the LORD. [27] I prayed for this child, and the LORD granted my request. [28] Now I, in turn, give him to the LORD; as long as he lives, he shall be dedicated to the LORD." She left him there; [1]† and as she worshiped the LORD, she said:

2 * "My heart exults in the LORD,†
my horn† is exalted in my God.
I have swallowed up my enemies;
I rejoice in my victory.
[2]* There is no Holy One like the LORD;
there is no Rock like our God.

[3]*† "Speak boastfully no longer,
nor let arrogance issue from your mouths.

For an all-knowing God is the LORD,
a God who judges deeds.
[4]* The bows of the mighty are broken,
while the tottering gird on strength.
[5] The well-fed hire themselves out for bread,
while the hungry batten on spoil.
The barren wife bears seven sons,
while the mother of many languishes.
[6]* "The LORD puts to death and gives life;
he casts down to the nether world;
he raises up again.
[7] The LORD makes poor and makes rich,
he humbles, he also exalts.
[8]* He raises the needy from the dust;
from the ash heap he lifts up the poor,
To seat them with nobles
and make a glorious throne their heritage.
He gives to the vower his vow,
and blesses the sleep of the just.

"For the pillars of the earth are the LORD's,
and he has set the world upon them.

Prayers of Strong and Holy Women

Compare Hannah's prayer in 1 Sm 2, 1–10 to Mary's prayer in Lk 1, 46–55. Notice the joy, the confident faith in God's way, and the understanding that God will raise up those who are hungry, poor, and in need. Notice also how God will deal with the proud, the powerful, and the rich, especially in Mary's prayer. These holy women identify in their lives and in their prayers the bigger picture of what God is all about.

What strong and holy women in your life keep you in their prayers?

▶ 1 Sm 2, 1–10

---

† **1, 20:** *Since she had asked:* this explanation would be more directly appropriate for the name Saul, which means "asked"; Samuel means "name of God."
1, 24: *An ephah:* a little more than a bushel.
1, 1: *And . . . said:* this belongs to ch 2.
2, 1–10: A hymn attributed to Hannah, the mother of Samuel, as her thanksgiving to God because she has borne a son despite her previous sterility. She praises God as the helper of the weak (1ff), who casts down the mighty and raises up the lowly (3ff), and who alone is the source of true strength (8ff); the hymn ends with a prayer for the king (v 10). This canticle has several points of resemblance with our Lady's Magnificat.

2, 1: *Horn:* the symbol of strength; cf Pss 18, 3; 75, 5; 89, 18; 112, 9.
2, 3: *Speak . . . mouths:* addressed to the enemies mentioned in v 1.

2, 1: Dt 33, 17; 2 Sm 22, 3; Ps 18, 2; Is 61, 10; Lk 1, 47.69.
2, 2: 2 Sm 22, 3; Ps 18, 2.
2, 3: Ps 75, 4.
2, 4: Is 40, 29.
2, 6: Dt 32, 39; Tb 4, 19; Jb 5, 11; Ps 30, 4; Wis 16, 13; Lk 1, 52.
2, 8: Jb 9, 6; 38, 6; Ps 104, 5; 121, 3.

9 He will guard the footsteps of his
    faithful ones,
but the wicked shall perish in the darkness.
For not by strength does man prevail;
10*   the LORD's foes shall be shattered.
The Most High in heaven thunders;
    the LORD judges the ends of the earth.
Now may he give strength to his king
    and exalt the horn of his anointed!"

11 When Elkanah returned home to Ramah, the child remained in the service of the LORD under the priest Eli.

Wickedness of Eli's Sons

12 Now the sons of Eli were wicked; they had respect neither for the LORD 13* nor for the priests' duties toward the people. When someone offered a sacrifice, the priest's servant would come with a three-pronged fork, while the meat was still boiling, 14 and would thrust it into the basin, kettle, caldron, or pot. Whatever the fork brought up, the priest would keep. That is how all the Israelites were treated who came to the sanctuary at Shiloh. 15 In fact, even before the fat was burned, the priest's servant would come and say to the man offering the sacrifice, "Give me some meat to roast for the priest. He will not accept boiled meat from you, only raw meat." 16* And if the man protested to him, "Let the fat be burned first as is the custom, then take whatever you wish," he would reply, "No, give it to me now, or else I will take it by force." 17 Thus the young men sinned grievously in the presence of the LORD; they treated the offerings to the LORD with disdain.

The LORD Rewards Hannah

18† Meanwhile the boy Samuel, girt with a linen apron, was serving in the presence of the LORD. 19 His mother used to make a little garment for him, which she would bring him each time she went up with her husband to offer the customary sacrifice. 20 And Eli would bless Elkanah and his wife, as they were leaving for home. He would say, "May the LORD repay you with children from this woman for the gift she has made to the LORD!" 21* The LORD favored Hannah so that she conceived

and gave birth to three more sons and two daughters, while young Samuel grew up in the service of the LORD.

Eli's Futile Rebuke

22† When Eli was very old, he heard repeatedly how his sons were treating all Israel [and that they were having relations with the women serving at the entry of the meeting tent.] 23 So he said to them: "Why are you doing such things? 24 No, my sons, you must not do these things! It is not a good report that I hear the people of the LORD spreading about you. 25 If a man sins against another man, one can intercede for him with the LORD; but if a man sins against the LORD, who can intercede for him?" But they disregarded their father's warning, since the LORD had decided on their death. 26* Meanwhile, young Samuel was growing in stature and in worth in the estimation of the LORD and of men.

Doom of Eli's House

27† A man of God came to Eli and said to him: "This is what the LORD says: 'I went so far as to reveal myself to your father's family when they were in Egypt as slaves to the house of Pharaoh. 28*† I chose them out of all the tribes of Israel to be my priests, to go up to my altar, to burn incense, and to wear the ephod before me; and I assigned all the oblations of the Israelites to your father's family. 29 Why do you keep a greedy eye on my sacrifices and on the offerings which I have prescribed? And why do you honor your sons in preference to me, fattening yourselves with the choicest part of every offering of my people Israel?' 30* This, therefore, is the oracle of the LORD, the God of Israel: 'I said in the past that your family and your father's family should minister in my presence forever. But now,' the LORD declares, 'away with this! for I will honor those who honor me, but those who spurn me shall be accursed. 31 Yes, the time is coming when I will break your strength and the strength of your father's family, so that no man in your family shall reach old age. 32 You shall witness as a disappointed rival all the benefits enjoyed by Israel, but there shall never be an old man in your family. 33 I will permit some of your family to remain at my altar, to wear

2, 18: *Linen apron:* called in Hebrew "ephod," but not the same as the high priest's ephod (Ex 28, 6–14) or the ephod used in divination (v 28). Samuel wore a simple apron such as was worn by the priests (1 Sm 22, 18), and on one occasion also by David (2 Sm 6, 14).

2, 22: The bracketed words, which recall Ex 38, 8, are a gloss in the received text; they are lacking in the oldest Greek translation, and in a Hebrew manuscript from Qumran.

2, 27–36: These verses propose the punishment of Eli from a point of view contemporary with the reform of Josiah (2 Kgs 23, 9; cf v 36); they hint at the events recorded in 1 Sm 22, 18–23 and 1 Kgs 2, 27. The older story of this divine warning is that in 1 Sm 3, 11–14.

2, 28: *Ephod:* a portable container, presumably of cloth, for the lots used in ritual consultation of God during the days of the Judges (Jgs 17, 5; 18, 14–15) and down into the time of David (1 Sm 14, 3ff; 23, 6ff; 30, 7f). The ephod of the high priest described in Ex 28, 6ff becomes a garment upon which a breastpiece of decision symbolizes, but no longer serves for, such consultation. The Exodus text codifies a later form of the tradition.

2, 10: Ps 98, 9.   2, 26: Lk 2, 52.
2, 13–15: Ex 29, 27f; Lv 7,   2, 28: 1 Sm 23, 9; 30, 7f; Jgs
  29–36; Dt 18, 3.   17, 5.
2, 16: Lv 3, 3ff.   2, 30f: 2 Sm 22, 26; 1 Kgs 2,
2, 21: 1 Sm 3, 19.   27; Ps 18, 25.

out their eyes in consuming greed; but the rest of the men of your family shall die by the sword. 34* You shall have a sign in what will happen to your two sons, Hophni and Phinehas: both shall die on the same day. 35 I will choose a faithful priest who shall do what I have in heart and mind. I will establish a lasting house for him which shall function in the presence of my anointed forever. 36* Then whoever is left of your family will come to grovel before him for a piece of silver or a loaf of bread, and will say: Appoint me, I beg you, to a priestly function, that I may have a morsel of bread to eat.' "

Revelation to Samuel

3 1† During the time young Samuel was minister to the LORD under Eli, a revelation of the LORD was uncommon and vision infrequent. 2 One day Eli was asleep in his usual place. His eyes had lately grown so weak that he could not see. 3* The lamp of God was not yet extinguished, and Samuel was sleeping in the temple of the LORD where the ark of God was. 4 The LORD called to Samuel, who answered, "Here I am." 5 He ran to Eli and said, "Here I am. You called me." "I did not call you," Eli said. "Go back to sleep." So he went back to sleep. 6 Again the LORD called Samuel, who rose and went to Eli. "Here I am," he said. "You called me." But he answered, "I did not call you, my son. Go back to sleep."

7 At that time Samuel was not familiar with the LORD, because the LORD had not revealed anything to him as yet. 8 The LORD called Samuel again, for the third time. Getting up and going to Eli, he said, "Here I am. You called me." Then Eli understood that the LORD was calling the youth. 9 So he said to Samuel, "Go to sleep, and if you are called, reply, 'Speak, LORD, for your servant is listening.' " When Samuel went to sleep in his place, 10 the LORD came and revealed his presence, calling out as before, "Samuel, Samuel!" Samuel answered, "Speak, for your servant is listening." 11 The LORD said to Samuel: "I am about to do something in Israel that will cause the ears of everyone who hears it to ring. 12 On that day I will carry out in full against Eli everything I threatened against his family. 13* I announce to him that I am condemning his family once and for all, because of this crime: though he knew his sons were blaspheming God, he did not reprove them. 14 Therefore, I swear to the family of Eli that no sacrifice or offering will ever expiate its crime." 15 Samuel then slept until morning, when he got up early and opened the doors of the temple

of the LORD. He feared to tell Eli the vision, 16 but Eli called to him, "Samuel, my son!" He replied, "Here I am." 17† Then Eli asked, "What did he say to you? Hide nothing from me! May God do thus and so to you if you hide a single thing he told you." 18 So Samuel told him everything, and held nothing back. Eli answered, "He is the LORD. He will do what he judges best."

Samuel Acknowledged as Prophet

19* Samuel grew up, and the LORD was with him, not permitting any word of his to be without effect. 20* Thus all Israel from Dan to Beer-sheba came to know that Samuel was an accredited prophet of the LORD. 21 The LORD continued to appear at Shiloh; he manifested himself to Samuel at Shiloh through his word, 1† and Samuel spoke to all Israel.

Eli Teaches Samuel How to Pray

Eli taught Samuel to listen to God's voice with a simple sentence: "Speak, LORD, for your servant is listening" (1 Sm 3, 9). Let's look at that sentence as a prayer:

"Speak, LORD . . ." This is an invitation. It shows openness and readiness. It shows your recognition of God: "You are the Almighty, and I am ready to hear what you have to say."

". . . for your servant . . ." This shows humility. It is a recognition of yourself: "I am your servant. It is my desire to do what you want. My life's purpose is to serve you."

". . . is listening." This demonstrates your response: "I am not going to ignore you. I am not going to daydream or just pretend to pay attention. I will take in your message, and it will become part of me."

▶ 1 Sm 3, 1–19

---

†
3, 1: *Uncommon:* prophetic communications from God were almost unknown.
3, 17: *May God do thus and so to you:* the Biblical writers avoid repeating for us the specific terms of a curse as the speaker would have uttered it.

3, 1: *And . . . Israel:* this belongs to ch 4.

2, 34: 1 Sm 4, 11.
2, 36: 2 Kgs 23, 9.
3, 3: Ex 25, 22; 27, 20f; Lv 24, 2.4; 2 Chr 13, 11.
3, 13: 1 Sm 2, 27–36.
3, 19: 1 Sm 2, 21.
3, 20: Jgs 20, 1.

Defeat of the Israelites

4 At that time, the Philistines gathered for an attack on Israel. Israel went out to engage them in battle and camped at Ebenezer, while the Philistines camped at Aphek. 2 The Philistines then drew up in battle formation against Israel. After a fierce struggle Israel was defeated by the Philistines, who slew about four thousand men on the battlefield. 3 When the troops retired to the camp, the elders of Israel said, "Why has the LORD permitted us to be defeated today by the Philistines? Let us fetch the ark of the LORD from Shiloh that it may go into battle among us and save us from the grasp of our enemies."

Loss of the Ark

4*† So the people sent to Shiloh and brought from there the ark of the LORD of hosts, who is enthroned upon the cherubim. The two sons of Eli, Hophni and Phinehas, were with the ark of God. 5 When the ark of the LORD arrived in the camp, all Israel shouted so loudly that the earth resounded. 6 The Philistines, hearing the noise of shouting, asked, "What can this loud shouting in the camp of the Hebrews mean?" On learning that the ark of the LORD had come into the camp, 7 the Philistines were frightened. They said, "Gods have come to their camp." They said also, "Woe to us! This has never happened before. 8† Woe to us! Who can deliver us from the power of these mighty gods? These are the gods that struck the Egyptians with various plagues and with pestilence. 9 Take courage and be manly, Philistines; otherwise you will become slaves to the Hebrews, as they were your slaves. So fight manfully!" 10* The Philistines fought and Israel was defeated; every man fled to his own tent. It was a disastrous defeat, in which Israel lost thirty thousand foot soldiers. 11* The ark of God was captured, and Eli's two sons, Hophni and Phinehas, were among the dead.

Death of Eli

12* A Benjaminite fled from the battlefield and reached Shiloh that same day, with his clothes torn and his head covered with dirt. 13 When he arrived, Eli was sitting in his chair beside the gate, watching the road, for he was troubled at heart about the ark of God. The man, however, went into the city to divulge his news, which put the whole city in an uproar. 14 Hearing the outcry of the men standing near him, Eli inquired, "What does this commotion mean?" 15 (Eli was ninety-eight years old, and his eyes would not focus, so that he could not see.) 16 The man quickly came up to Eli and said, "It is I who have come from the battlefield; I fled from there today." He asked, "What happened, my son?" 17 And the messenger answered: "Israel fled from the Philistines; in fact, the troops suffered heavy losses. Your two sons, Hophni and Phinehas, are among the dead, and the ark of God has been captured." 18 At this mention of the ark of God, Eli fell backward from his chair into the gateway; since he was an old man and heavy, he died of a broken neck. He had judged Israel for forty years.

19 His daughter-in-law, the wife of Phinehas, was with child and at the point of giving birth. When she heard the news concerning the capture of the ark and the deaths of her father-in-law and her husband, she was seized with the pangs of labor, and gave birth. 20* She was about to die when the women standing around her said to her, "Never fear! You have given birth to a son." Yet she neither answered nor paid any attention. 21 [She named the child Ichabod, saying, "Gone is the glory from Israel," with reference to the capture of the ark of God and to her father-in-law and her husband.] 22* She said, "Gone is the glory from Israel," because the ark of God had been captured.

The Ark in the Temple of Dagon

5 1* The Philistines, having captured the ark of God, transferred it from Ebenezer to Ashdod. 2 They then took the ark of God and brought it into the temple of Dagon, placing it beside Dagon. 3 When the people of Ashdod rose early the next morning, Dagon was lying prone on the ground before the ark of the LORD. So they picked Dagon up and replaced him. 4 But the next morning early, when they arose, Dagon lay prone on the ground before the ark of the LORD, his head and hands broken off and lying on the threshold, his trunk alone intact. 5 For this reason, neither the priests of Dagon nor any others who enter the temple of Dagon tread on the threshold of Dagon in Ashdod to this very day; they always step over it.

The Ark Is Carried About

6*† Now the LORD dealt severely with the people of Ashdod. He ravaged and afflicted the city and its

---

4, 4: *Enthroned upon the cherubim:* this title of the Lord seems to have originated in the sanctuary at Shiloh; it represents the divine Majesty as seated upon a throne on which he can be borne through the heavens by winged creatures somewhat as in the visions of Ez 1 and 10.

4, 8: *These mighty gods:* the Philistines, who were polytheists, are represented as supposing the Israelites honored several gods.

5, 6: *Hemorrhoids . . . mice:* a double calamity fell upon them—

a plague of mice or rats, and a severe epidemic of pestilential tumors, probably the bubonic plague.

4, 4: Ex 25, 22.	35, 16ff.
4, 10: Ps 78, 61.	**4, 22:** Ps 78, 61.
4, 11: 1 Sm 2, 34.	**5, 1–5:** Jgs 16, 23–30; Is 45,
4, 12: Jos 7, 6; 2 Sm 1, 2; Jer	5f.20f.
7, 12.	**5, 6:** Ps 78, 66.
4, 20: 1 Sm 14, 3; Gn	

vicinity with hemorrhoids; he brought upon the city a great and deadly plague of mice that swarmed in their ships and overran their fields. 7 On seeing how matters stood, the men of Ashdod decided, "The ark of the God of Israel must not remain with us, for he is handling us and our god Dagon severely." 8 So they summoned all the Philistine lords and inquired of them, "What shall we do with the ark of the God of Israel?" The men of Gath replied, "Let them move the ark of the God of Israel on to us." 9 So they moved the ark of the God of Israel to Gath! But after it had been brought there, the LORD threw the city into utter turmoil: he afflicted its inhabitants, young and old, and hemorrhoids broke out on them. 10 The ark of God was next sent to Ekron; but as it entered that city, the people there cried out, "Why have they brought the ark of the God of Israel here to kill us and our kindred?" 11 Then they, too, sent a summons to all the Philistine lords and pleaded: "Send away the ark of the God of Israel. Let it return to its own place, that it may not kill us and our kindred." A deadly panic had seized the whole city, since the hand of God had been very heavy upon it. 12 Those who escaped death were afflicted with hemorrhoids, and the outcry from the city went up to the heavens.

The Ark To Be Returned

6 1 The ark of the LORD had been in the land of the Philistines seven months 2 when they summoned priests and fortune-tellers to ask, "What shall we do with the ark of the LORD? Tell us what we should send back with it." 3† They replied: "If you intend to send away the ark of the God of Israel, you must not send it alone, but must, by all means, make amends to him through a guilt offering. Then you will be healed, and will learn why he continues to afflict you." 4 When asked further, "What guilt offering should be our amends to him?", they replied:

"Five golden hemorrhoids and five golden mice to correspond to the number of Philistine lords, since the same plague has struck all of you and your lords. 5 Therefore, make images of the hemorrhoids and of the mice that are infesting your land and give them as a tribute to the God of Israel. Perhaps then he will cease to afflict you, your gods, and your land. 6* Why should you become stubborn, as the Egyptians and Pharaoh were stubborn? Was it not after he had dealt ruthlessly with them that the Israelites were released and departed? 7* So now set to work and make a new cart. Then take two milch cows that have not borne the yoke; hitch them to

the cart, but drive their calves indoors away from them. 8 You shall next take the ark of the LORD and place it on the cart, putting in a box beside it the golden articles that you are offering, as amends for your guilt. Start it on its way, and let it go. 9 Then watch! If it goes up to Beth-shemesh along the route to his own territory, he has brought this great calamity upon us; if not, we will know it was not he who struck us, but that an accident happened to us."

The Ark in Beth-shemesh

10 They acted upon this advice. Taking two milch cows, they hitched them to the cart but shut up their calves indoors. 11 Then they placed the ark of the LORD on the cart, along with the box containing the golden mice and the images of the hemorrhoids. 12 The cows went straight for the route to Beth-shemesh and continued along this road, mooing as they went, without turning right or left. The Philistine lords followed them as far as the border of Beth-shemesh. 13 The people of Beth-shemesh were harvesting the wheat in the valley. When they looked up and spied the ark, they greeted it with rejoicing. 14* The cart came to the field of Joshua the Beth-shemite and stopped there. At a large stone in the field, the wood of the cart was split up and the cows were offered as a holocaust to the LORD. 15 The Levites, meanwhile, had taken down the ark of God and the box beside it, in which the golden articles were, and had placed them on the great stone. The men of Beth-shemesh also offered other holocausts and sacrifices to the LORD that day. 16 After witnessing this, the five Philistine lords returned to Ekron the same day.

Guilt Offering

17 The golden hemorrhoids the Philistines sent back as a guilt offering to the LORD were as follows: one for Ashdod, one for Gaza, one for Ashkelon, one for Gath, and one for Ekron. 18 The golden mice, however, corresponded to the number of all the cities of the Philistines belonging to the five lords, including fortified cities and open villages. The large stone on which the ark of the LORD was placed is still in the field of Joshua the Beth-shemite at the present time.

Penalty for Irreverence

19 The descendants of Jeconiah did not join in the celebration with the inhabitants of Beth-shemesh when they greeted the ark of the LORD, and seventy of them were struck down. The people

---

6, 3: A guilt offering: a propitiatory offering customary after unwitting transgression of the ordinances of God regarding holy things or property rights; cf Lv 6, 1ff.

6, 6: Ex 7, 14; 8, 15; 9, 34.
6, 7: Nm 19, 2; Dt 21, 3;
2 Sm 6, 3.
6, 14: 2 Sm 24, 21ff.

went into mourning at this great calamity with which the LORD had afflicted them. 20 The men of Beth-shemesh asked, "Who can stand in the presence of this Holy One? To whom shall he go from us?" 21 They then sent messengers to the inhabitants of Kiriath-jearim, saying, "The Philistines have returned the ark of the LORD; come down and get it."

7 1 So the inhabitants of Kiriath-jearim came for the ark of the LORD and brought it into the house of Abinadab on the hill, appointing his son Eleazar as guardian of the ark of the LORD.

Religious Reform

2 From the day the ark came to rest in Kiriath-jearim a long time, twenty years, elapsed, and the whole Israelite population turned to the LORD. 3* Samuel said to them: "If you wish with your whole heart to return to the LORD, put away your foreign gods and your Ashtaroth, devote yourselves to the LORD, and worship him alone. Then he will deliver you from the power of the Philistines." 4 So the Israelites put away their Baals and Ashtaroth, and worshiped the LORD alone. 5* Samuel then gave orders, "Gather all Israel to Mizpah, that I may pray to the LORD for you." 6*† When they were gathered at Mizpah, they drew water and poured it out on the ground before the LORD, and they fasted that day, confessing, "We have sinned against the LORD." It was at Mizpah that Samuel began to judge the Israelites.

Rout of the Philistines

7 When the Philistines heard that the Israelites had gathered at Mizpah, their lords went up against Israel. Hearing this, the Israelites became afraid of the Philistines 8* and said to Samuel, "Implore the LORD our God unceasingly for us, to save us from the clutches of the Philistines." 9* Samuel therefore took an unweaned lamb and offered it entire as a holocaust to the LORD. He implored the LORD for Israel, and the LORD heard him. 10 While Samuel was offering the holocaust, the Philistines advanced to join battle with Israel. That day, however, the LORD thundered loudly against the Philistines, and threw them into such confusion that they were defeated by Israel. 11 Thereupon the Israelites sallied

forth from Mizpah and pursued the Philistines, harrying them down beyond Beth-car. 12† Samuel then took a stone and placed it between Mizpah and Jeshanah; he named it Ebenezer, explaining, "To this point has the LORD helped us." 13* Thus were the Philistines subdued, never again to enter the territory of Israel, for the LORD was severe with them as long as Samuel lived. 14 The cities from Ekron to Gath which the Philistines had taken from Israel were restored to them. Israel also freed the territory of these cities from the dominion of the Philistines. Moreover there was peace between Israel and the Amorites.

15 Samuel judged Israel as long as he lived. 16 He made a yearly journey, passing through Bethel, Gilgal and Mizpah and judging Israel at each of these sanctuaries. 17* Then he used to return to Ramah, for that was his home. There, too, he judged Israel and built an altar to the LORD.

II: Establishment of the Monarchy in Israel

Request for a King

8 †1 In his old age Samuel appointed his sons judges over Israel. 2 His first-born was named Joel, his second son, Abijah; they judged at Beersheba. 3* His sons did not follow his example but sought illicit gain and accepted bribes, perverting justice. 4 Therefore all the elders of Israel came in a body to Samuel at Ramah 5* and said to him, "Now that you are old, and your sons do not follow your example, appoint a king over us, as other nations have, to judge us."

God Grants the Request

6 Samuel was displeased when they asked for a king to judge them. He prayed to the LORD, however, 7* who said in answer: "Grant the people's every request. It is not you they reject, they are rejecting me as their king. 8 As they have treated me constantly from the day I brought them up from Egypt to this day, deserting me and worshiping strange gods, so do they treat you too. 9 Now grant their request; but at the same time, warn them solemnly and inform them of the rights of the king who will rule them."

---

† **7, 6:** *Poured it out on the ground:* for the symbolism, cf 2 Sm 14, 14.

7, 12: *Ebenezer:* or *eben ha-ezer,* means "stone of help."

8, 1: From this chapter on, the First Book of Samuel gives us two and sometimes three viewpoints on most of the events with which it is concerned, such as the appointment of Saul as king, the reasons for his downfall, his relationship with David, even the circumstances of Saul's death (1 Sm 31; 2 Sm 1). The choice of Saul as king is seen, in ch 8, followed by 10, 17–27 and ch 12, as motivated by the people's defection from the proper service of God; this later editorial approach incorporates not only narratives with which it is consistent,

but also early traditions (9, 1–10.16; ch 11) which portray the events and their motivation quite differently.

7, 3: 1 Sm 12, 10.20.24; Jos 24, 23; Jgs 6, 6–10; 10, 10–16.
7, 5: 1 Sm 10, 17; Jgs 20, 1.
7, 6: Jgs 20, 26; Ps 22, 14; Lam 2, 19.
7, 8: Ex 17, 9–13.
7, 9f: 2 Sm 22, 14f; Sir 46, 16ff.
7, 13: Jgs 3, 30; 8, 28; 11, 33.
7, 17: 1 Sm 9, 12; 14, 35.
8, 3: Ex 23, 8; Dt 16, 19; Prv 17, 23.
8, 5f: Dt 17, 14f; Hos 13, 10; Acts 13, 21.
8, 7f: 1 Sm 12, 1.12f; Jgs 8, 22f; 10, 13; 1 Kgs 9, 9.

The Rights of a King

10 Samuel delivered the message of the LORD in full to those who were asking him for a king. 11* He told them: "The rights of the king who will rule you will be as follows: He will take your sons and assign them to his chariots and horses, and they will run before his chariot. 12* He will also appoint from among them his commanders of groups of a thousand and of a hundred soldiers. He will set them to do his plowing and his harvesting, and to make his implements of war and the equipment of his chariots. 13 He will use your daughters as ointment-makers, as cooks, and as bakers. 14* He will take the best of your fields, vineyards, and olive groves, and give them to his officials. 15 He will tithe your crops and your vineyards, and give the revenue to his eunuchs and his slaves. 16 He will take your male and female servants, as well as your best oxen and your asses, and use them to do his work. 17* He will tithe your flocks and you yourselves will become his slaves. 18 When this takes place, you will complain against the king whom you have chosen, but on that day the LORD will not answer you."

Persistent Demand

19* The people, however, refused to listen to Samuel's warning and said, "Not so! There must be a king over us. 20 We too must be like other nations, with a king to rule us and to lead us in warfare and fight our battles." 21 When Samuel had listened to all the people had to say, he repeated it to the LORD, 22 who then said to him, "Grant their request and appoint a king to rule them." Samuel thereupon said to the men of Israel, "Each of you go to his own city."

9 1* There was a stalwart man from Benjamin named Kish, who was the son of Abiel, son of Zeror, son of Becorath, son of Aphiah, a Benjaminite. 2* He had a son named Saul, who was a handsome young man. There was no other Israelite handsomer than Saul; he stood head and shoulders above the people.

The Lost Asses

3 Now the asses of Saul's father, Kish, had wandered off. Kish said to his son Saul, "Take one of the servants with you and go out and hunt for the asses." 4 Accordingly they went through the hill country of Ephraim, and through the land of Shalishah. Not finding them there, they continued through the land of Shaalim without success. They also went through the land of Benjamin, but they failed to find the animals. 5 When they came to the land of Zuph, Saul said to the servant who was with him, "Come, let us turn back, lest my father forget about the asses and become anxious about us." 6 The servant replied, "Listen! There is a man of God in this city, a man held in high esteem; all that he says is sure to come true. Let us go there now! Perhaps he can tell us how to accomplish our errand." 7* But Saul said to his servant, "If we go, what can we offer the man? There is no bread in our bags, and we have no present to give the man of God. What have we?" 8† Again the servant answered Saul, "I have a quarter of a silver shekel. If I give that to the man of God, he will tell us our way." 10 Saul then said to his servant, "Well said! Come on, let us go!" And they went to the city where the man of God lived.

Quest for Samuel's Aid

11* As they were going up the ascent to the city, they met some girls coming out to draw water and inquired of them, "Is the seer in town?" 9*† (In former times in Israel, anyone who sent to consult God used to say, "Come, let us go to the seer." For he who is now called prophet was formerly called

did you KNOW?

Doublets

Often, more than one version of a story is recorded in the Bible. Genesis has two stories of the Creation (1, 1—2, 4; 2, 4–25). The First Book of Samuel has two different attitudes toward the request to have a king in Israel. Compare the anti-king passages of 8, 10–22 and 10, 17–19 with the pro-king passages of 9, 15–16 and chapter 11. Most likely, the difference of opinion comes from different parts of Israel. The Bible often combines two versions of a story, called doublets, to allow consideration of both sides of an issue.

9, 8: *A quarter of a silver shekel:* about a tenth of an ounce of silver.
9, 9: This verse is a later explanation of the term *seer,* first used in the text in 1 Sm 9, 11.

8, 11: 1 Sm 10, 25; Dt 17, 14–20; 1 Kgs 12.
8, 12: 2 Sm 15, 1; 1 Kgs 1, 5.
8, 14: 1 Sm 22, 7; 1 Kgs 21, 1–24; Ez 46, 18.
8, 17: 1 Kgs 12, 4.
8, 19: 1 Sm 10, 19.
9, 1: 1 Sm 14, 51; 1 Chr 8, 33.
9, 2: 1 Sm 10, 23.
9, 7f: Nm 22, 7; 1 Kgs 14, 3; 2 Kgs 4, 42; 5, 15; 8, 8f.
9, 11: Gn 24, 11ff; Ex 2, 16.
9, 9: Sir 46, 15.

seer.) [12]*† The girls answered, "Yes, there—straight ahead. Hurry now; just today he came to the city, because the people have a sacrifice today on the high place. [13] When you enter the city, you may reach him before he goes up to the high place to eat. The people will not eat until he arrives; only after he blesses the sacrifice will the invited guests eat. Go up immediately, for you should find him right now."

Samuel's Revelation about Saul

[14] So they went up to the city. As they entered it, Samuel was coming toward them on his way to the high place. [15]* The day before Saul's arrival, the LORD had given Samuel the revelation: [16]* "At this time tomorrow I will send you a man from the land of Benjamin whom you are to anoint as commander of my people Israel. He shall save my people from the clutches of the Philistines, for I have witnessed their misery and accepted their cry for help." [17] When Samuel caught sight of Saul, the LORD assured him, "This is the man of whom I told you; he is to govern my people." [18] Saul met Samuel in the gateway and said, "Please tell me where the seer lives." [19] Samuel answered Saul: "I am the seer. Go up ahead of me to the high place and eat with me today. In the morning, before dismissing you, I will tell you whatever you wish. [20] As for the asses you lost three days ago, do not worry about them, for they have been found. Whom does Israel desire ardently if not you and your father's family?" [21]* Saul replied: "Am I not a Benjaminite, of one of the smallest tribes of Israel, and is not my clan the least among the clans of the tribe of Benjamin? Why say such things to me?"

[22] Samuel then took Saul and his servant and brought them to the room, where he placed them at the head of the guests, of whom there were about thirty. [23] He said to the cook, "Bring the portion I gave you and told you to put aside." [24]† So the cook took up the leg and what went with it, and placed it before Saul. Samuel said: "This is a reserved portion that has been set before you. Eat, for it was kept for you until your arrival; I explained that I was inviting

some guests." Thus Saul dined with Samuel that day. [25] When they came down from the high place into the city, a mattress was spread for Saul on the roof, [26] and he slept there.

Saul's Anointing

At daybreak Samuel called to Saul on the roof, "Get up, and I will start you on your journey." Saul rose, and he and Samuel went outside the city together. [27] As they were approaching the edge of the town, Samuel said to Saul, "Tell the servant to go on ahead of us, but stay here yourself for the moment, that I may give you a message from God."

10 [1]* Then, from a flask he had with him, Samuel poured oil on Saul's head; he also kissed him, saying: "The LORD anoints you commander over his heritage. You are to govern the LORD's people Israel, and to save them from the grasp of their enemies roundabout.

"This will be the sign for you that the LORD has anointed you commander over his heritage: [2]*† When you leave me today, you will meet two men near Rachel's tomb at Zelzah in the territory of Benjamin, who will say to you, 'The asses you went to look for have been found. Your father is no longer worried about the asses, but is anxious about you and says, What shall I do about my son?' [3] Farther on, when you arrive at the terebinth of Tabor, you will be met by three men going up to God at Bethel; one will be bringing three kids, another three loaves of bread, and the third a skin of wine. [4] They will greet you and offer you two wave offerings of bread, which you will take from them. [5]*† After that you will come to Gibeath-elohim, where there is a garrison of the Philistines. As you enter that city, you will meet a band of prophets, in a prophetic state, coming down from the high place preceded by lyres, tambourines, flutes and harps. [6]* The spirit of the LORD will rush upon you, and you will join them in their prophetic state and will be changed into another man. [7] When you see these signs fulfilled, do whatever you judge feasible, because God is with you. [8]*† Now go down ahead of

---

9, 12: *On the high place:* the local sanctuary on the top of a hill, where the sacrifice was offered and the sacrificial meal eaten.

9, 24: *And what went with it:* a slight change would give "and the fatty tail" as perhaps the original reading. Sheep in the Near East are exceptionally fat-tailed, and such a portion would be thought a special delicacy by the Hebrews. However, the ritual legislation as we know it (Lv 3, 9) would require that the fat tail be burned on the altar. If this general rule was later than the time of Samuel, the present text may have been retouched so as not to seem to contravene it. A Qumran text has "the festive (leg)" here.

10, 2: Here, as in Jer 31, 15, Rachel's tomb is placed north of Jerusalem. Later tradition understood Gn 35, 19f in the sense given by Mt 2, 16ff, and placed the tomb at Bethlehem, farther south.

10, 5: *A garrison of the Philistines:* the Hebrew word for "garrison" has been explained alternatively to mean a pillar erected to mark the Philistine occupation, or an inspector or officer for the col-

lection of taxes. *In a prophetic state:* in an ecstatic condition due to strong feelings of religious enthusiasm induced by a communal observance, possibly accompanied by music and dancing.

10, 8: By inserting this verse, with its seven days, an editor has prepared for one narrative of the rejection of Saul (1 Sm 13, 8–15) in the very context of Saul's anointing.

9, 12: 1 Sm 7, 17; 16, 2.5;
20, 6.29; Dt 12, 13;
1 Kgs 3, 2.4.
9, 15: Acts 13, 21.
9, 16: 1 Sm 10, 1.
9, 21: 1 Sm 15, 17.
10, 1: 1 Sm 9, 16f; 24, 7;
Jgs 9, 9; 1 Kgs 1, 39;

Acts 13, 21.
10, 2: Jer 31, 15; Mk 14, 13.
10, 5f: 1 Sm 13, 3; 16, 13; 19,
20f.
10, 6: 1 Sm 11, 6; 16, 13; Jgs
14, 6.19; 15, 14; 2 Kgs
3, 15.
10, 8: 1 Sm 13, 8; Lv 3, 1.

me to Gilgal, for I shall come down to you, to offer holocausts and to sacrifice peace offerings. Wait seven days until I come to you; I shall then tell you what you must do."

Fulfillment of the Signs

9 As Saul turned to leave Samuel, God gave him another heart. That very day all these signs came to pass. . . . 10*† When they were going from there to Gibeah, a band of prophets met him, and the spirit of God rushed upon him, so that he joined them in their prophetic state. 11* When all who had known him previously saw him in a prophetic state among the prophets, they said to one another, "What has happened to the son of Kish? Is Saul also among the prophets?" 12 And someone from that district added, "And who is their father?" Thus the proverb arose, "Is Saul also among the prophets?" 13 When he came out of the prophetic state, he went home.

Silence about the Kingship

14 Saul's uncle inquired of him and his servant, "Where have you been?" Saul replied, "To look for the asses. When we could not find them, we went to Samuel." 15 Then Saul's uncle said, "Tell me, then, what Samuel said to you." 16 Saul said to his uncle, "He assured us that the asses had been found." But he mentioned nothing to him of what Samuel had said about the kingship.

Saul Chosen King by Lot

17* Samuel called the people together to the LORD at Mizpah 18* and addressed the Israelites: "Thus says the LORD, the God of Israel, 'It was I who brought Israel up from Egypt and delivered you from the power of the Egyptians and from the power of all the kingdoms that oppressed you.' 19* But today you have rejected your God, who delivers you from all your evils and calamities, by saying to him, 'Not so, but you must appoint a king over us.' Now, therefore, take your stand before the LORD according to tribes and families." 20 So Samuel had all the tribes of Israel come forward, and the tribe of Benjamin was chosen. 21 Next he had the tribe of Benjamin come forward in clans, and the clan of Matri was chosen, and finally Saul, son of Kish, was chosen. But they looked for him in vain. 22* Again they consulted the LORD, "Has he come here?" The LORD

answered, "He is hiding among the baggage." 23* They ran to bring him from there; and when he stood among the people, he was head and shoulders above all the crowd. 24* Samuel said to all the people, "Do you see the man whom the LORD has chosen? There is none like him among all the people!" Then all the people shouted, "Long live the king!"

25*† Samuel next explained to the people the law of royalty and wrote it in a book, which he placed in the presence of the LORD. This done, Samuel dismissed the people, each to his own place. 26 Saul also went home to Gibeah, accompanied by warriors whose hearts the LORD had touched. 27* But certain worthless men said, "How can this fellow save us?" They despised him and brought him no present.

Defeat of the Ammonites

11 1*† About a month later, Nahash the Ammonite went up and laid siege to Jabesh-gilead. All the men of Jabesh begged Nahash, "Make a treaty with us, and we will be your subjects." 2 But Nahash the Ammonite replied, "This is my condition for a treaty with you: I must gouge out every man's right eye, that I may thus bring ignominy on all Israel." 3 The elders of Jabesh said to him: "Give us seven days to send messengers throughout the territory of Israel. If no one rescues us, we will surrender to you." 4 When the messengers arrived at Gibeah of Saul, they related the news to the people, all of whom wept aloud. 5 Just then Saul came in from the field, behind his oxen. "Why are the people weeping?" he asked. The message of the inhabitants of Jabesh was repeated to him. 6* As he listened to this report, the spirit of God rushed upon him and he became very angry. 7* Taking a yoke of oxen, he cut them into pieces, which he sent throughout the territory of Israel by couriers with the message, "If anyone does not come out to follow Saul [and Samuel], the same as this will be done to his oxen!" In dread of the LORD, the people turned out to a man. 8 When he reviewed them in Bezek, there were three hundred thousand Israelites and seventy thousand Judahites.

9 To the messengers who had come he said, "Tell the inhabitants of Jabesh-gilead that tomorrow, while the sun is hot, they will be rescued." The messengers came and reported this to the inhabitants of

---

† **10, 10:** The story has here been abridged by omitting the fulfillment of the first two signs given by Samuel (1 Sm 10, 2ff).

10, 25: *The law of royalty:* the charter defining the rights of the king.

11, 1: *About a month later:* there is ancient evidence for a longer introduction to this campaign. The time indication here may refer to its earlier stages rather than to the events of ch 10.

* **10, 10:** 1 Sm 19, 20–24; Nm 11, 25.
10, 11: 1 Sm 19, 24.
10, 17: 1 Sm 7, 5.
10, 18: Ex 20, 2; Lv 11, 45; 25, 38; Nm 15, 41; Dt 5, 6; Jgs 6, 8f.
10, 19: 1 Sm 8, 19.
10, 22: 1 Sm 30, 24.

10, 23: 1 Sm 9, 2; 16, 7.
10, 24: 2 Sm 16, 16; 1 Kgs 1, 25; 2 Kgs 11, 12.
10, 25: 1 Sm 8, 11; Dt 17, 14–20.
10, 27: 1 Sm 11, 12.
11, 1: 1 Sm 12, 12; 31, 11.
11, 6: 1 Sm 16, 13; Jgs 14, 6.19.
11, 7: 1 Kgs 11, 30; 2 Kgs 13, 18.

Jabesh, who were jubilant, [10] and said to Nahash, "Tomorrow we will surrender to you, and you may do whatever you please with us." [11] On the appointed day, Saul arranged his troops in three companies and invaded the camp during the dawn watch. They slaughtered Ammonites until the heat of the day; by then the survivors were so scattered that no two were left together.

Saul Accepted as King

[12]*† The people then said to Samuel: "Who questioned whether Saul should rule over us? Hand over the men and we will put them to death." [13]* But Saul broke in to say, "No man is to be put to death this day, for today the LORD has saved Israel." [14] Samuel said to the people, "Come, let us go to Gilgal to inaugurate the kingdom there." [15] So all the people went to Gilgal, where, in the presence of the LORD, they made Saul king. They also sacrificed peace offerings there before the LORD, and Saul and all the Israelites celebrated the occasion with great joy.

Samuel's Integrity

12 [1]* Samuel addressed all Israel: "I have granted your request in every respect," he said. "I have set a king over you [2] and now the king is your leader. As for me, I am old and gray, and have sons among you. I have lived with you from my youth to the present day. [3]* Here I stand! Answer me in the presence of the LORD and of his anointed. Whose ox have I taken? Whose ass have I taken? Whom have I cheated? Whom have I oppressed? From whom have I accepted a bribe and overlooked his guilt? I will make restitution to you." [4] They replied, "You have neither cheated us, nor oppressed us, nor accepted anything from anyone." [5] So he said to them, "The LORD is witness against you this day, and his anointed as well, that you have found nothing in my possession." "He is witness," they agreed.

Samuel Upbraids the People

[6]* Continuing, Samuel said to the people: "The LORD is witness, who appointed Moses and Aaron, and who brought your fathers up from the land of Egypt. [7] Now, therefore, take your stand, and I shall arraign you before the LORD, and shall recount for you all the acts of mercy the LORD has done for you and your fathers. [8]* When Jacob and his sons went to Egypt and the Egyptians oppressed them, your fathers appealed to the LORD, who sent Moses and Aaron to bring them out of Egypt, and he gave them this place to live in. [9]* But they forgot the LORD their God; and he allowed them to fall into the clutches of Sisera, the captain of the army of Jabin, king of Hazor, into the grasp of the Philistines, and into the grip of the king of Moab, who made war against them. [10]* Each time they appealed to the LORD and said, 'We have sinned in forsaking the LORD and worshiping Baals and Ashtaroth; but deliver us now from the power of our enemies, and we will worship you.' [11]* Accordingly, the LORD sent Jerubbaal, Barak, Jephthah, and Samuel; he delivered you from the power of your enemies on every side, so that you were able to live in security. [12]* Yet, when you saw Nahash, king of the Ammonites, advancing against you, you said to me, 'Not so, but a king must rule us,' even though the LORD your God is your king.

Warnings for People and King

[13]* "Now you have the king you want, a king the LORD has given you. [14] If you fear the LORD and worship him, if you are obedient to him and do not rebel against the LORD's command, if both you and the king who rules you follow the LORD your God—well and good. [15] But if you do not obey the LORD and if you rebel against his command, the LORD will deal severely with you and your king, and destroy you. [16] Now then, stand ready to witness the great marvel the LORD is about to accomplish before your eyes. [17]* Are we not in the harvest time for wheat? Yet I shall call to the LORD, and he will send thunder and rain. Thus you will see and understand how greatly the LORD is displeased that you have asked for a king." [18] Samuel then called to the LORD, and the LORD sent thunder and rain that day.

Assistance Promised

As a result, all the people dreaded the LORD and Samuel. [19] They said to Samuel, "Pray to the LORD your God for us, your servants, that we may not die for having added to all our other sins the evil of asking for a king." [20] "Do not fear," Samuel answered them. "It is true you have committed all this evil; still, you must not turn from the LORD, but must worship him with your whole heart. [21]* Do not turn to meaningless idols which can

† **11, 12–14:** With these verses, an editor has harmonized the account of the acknowledgment of Saul as king at Mizpah (1 Sm 10, 17–24) with the public acclamation at Gilgal (1 Sm 11, 15) after the defeat of the Ammonites (1 Sm 11, 1–11). The Greek text of 1 Sm 11, 15 reads "and Samuel anointed Saul as king," instead of they made Saul king.

11, 12: 1 Sm 10, 27.
11, 13: 2 Sm 19, 23.
12, 1: 1 Sm 8, 7.9.22.
12, 3: Ex 20, 17; 23, 8; Nm 16, 15; Dt 16, 19; Sir 46, 19.
12, 6: Mi 6, 4.
12, 8: Gn 46, 5; Ex 1, 11; 2, 23ff.
12, 9: Jgs 3, 12ff; 4, 2f; 10, 7;
      13, 1.
12, 10: 1 Sm 7, 3f.
12, 11: Jgs 6, 14.32; 11, 1.
12, 12: 1 Sm 8, 6f.19; 11, 1f;
      Jgs 8, 23.
12, 13: 1 Sm 8, 7.
12, 17: Ex 9, 23.28ff; 1 Kgs 18, 1.
12, 21: Dt 32, 37ff.

neither profit nor save; they are nothing. 22*For the sake of his own great name the LORD will not abandon his people, since the LORD himself chose to make you his people. 23*As for me, far be it from me to sin against the LORD by ceasing to pray for you and to teach you the good and right way. 24 But you must fear the LORD and worship him faithfully with your whole heart; keep in mind the great things he has done among you. 25 If instead you continue to do evil, both you and your king shall perish."

III: Saul and David

13 1†[Saul was . . . years old when he became king and he reigned . . . (two) years over Israel.]

Saul Offers Sacrifice

2 Saul chose three thousand men of Israel, of whom two thousand remained with him in Michmash and in the hill country of Bethel, and one thousand were with Jonathan in Gibeah of Benjamin. He sent the rest of the people back to their tents. 3*† Now Jonathan overcame the Philistine garrison which was in Gibeah, and the Philistines got word of it. Then Saul sounded the horn throughout the land, with a proclamation, "Let the Hebrews hear!" 4 Thus all Israel learned that Saul had overcome the garrison of the Philistines and that Israel had brought disgrace upon the Philistines; and the soldiers were called up to Saul in Gilgal. 5 The Philistines also assembled for battle, with three thousand chariots, six thousand horsemen, and foot soldiers as numerous as the sands of the seashore. Moving up against Israel, they encamped in Michmash, east of Beth-aven. 6*Some Israelites, aware of the danger and of the difficult situation, hid themselves in caves, in thickets, among rocks, in caverns, and in cisterns, 7† and other Hebrews passed over the Jordan into the land of Gad and Gilead. Saul, however, held out at Gilgal, although all his followers were seized with fear. 8*He waited seven days—the time Samuel had determined. When Samuel did not arrive at Gilgal, the men began to slip away from Saul. 9 He then said, "Bring me the holocaust and peace offerings," and he offered up the holocaust.

King Saul Reproved

10 He had just finished this offering when Samuel arrived. Saul went out to greet him, 11 and Samuel asked him, "What have you done?" Saul replied: "When I saw that the men were slipping away from me, since you had not come by the specified time, and with the Philistines assembled at Michmash, 12 I said to myself, 'Now the Philistines will come down against me at Gilgal, and I have not yet sought the LORD's blessing.' So in my anxiety I offered up the holocaust." 13 Samuel's response was: "You have been foolish! Had you kept the command the LORD your God gave you, the LORD would now establish your kingship in Israel as lasting; 14* but as things are, your kingdom shall not endure. The LORD has sought out a man after his own heart and has appointed him commander of his people, because you broke the LORD's command."

Philistine Invasion

15* Then Samuel set out from Gilgal and went his own way; but the rest of the people went up after Saul to meet the soldiers, going from Gilgal to Gibeah of Benjamin. Saul then numbered the soldiers he had with him, who were about six hundred. 16 Saul, his son Jonathan, and the soldiers they had with them were now occupying Geba of Benjamin, and the Philistines were encamped at Michmash. 17* Meanwhile, raiders left the camp of the Philistines in three bands. One band took the Ophrah road toward the district of Shual; 18 another turned in the direction of Beth-horon; and the third took the road for Geba that overlooks the Valley of the Hyenas toward the desert.

Disarmament of Israel

19* Not a single smith was to be found in the whole land of Israel, for the Philistines had said, "Otherwise the Hebrews will make swords or spears." 20 All Israel, therefore, had to go down to the Philistines to sharpen their plowshares, mattocks, axes, and sickles. 21 The price for the plowshares and mattocks was two-thirds of a shekel, and a third of a shekel for sharpening the axes and for setting the ox-goads. 22 And so on the day of battle neither sword nor spear could be found in the possession

13, 1: A formula like that of 2 Sm 5, 4 was introduced here at some time; but the age of Saul when he became king remains a blank, and the two years assigned for his reign in the received text cannot be correct. Tradition (Acts 13, 21) offers the round number, "forty years."

13, 3–4: *The Philistine garrison:* see note on 1 Sm 10, 5. *Let the Hebrews hear:* a different reading of these verses, based on the Greek, would yield: "And the Philistines heard that the Hebrews (or: the slaves) had revolted. Saul in the meantime sounded the trumpet throughout all the land (v 4), and all Israel heard that Saul. . . ."

13, 7–15: These verses, like 1 Sm 10, 8, anticipate the rejection

of Saul; a different occasion and motivation for this are given in ch 15, resumed in 1 Sm 28, 17f.

12, 22: Jer 14, 21; Ex 20, 9; Dn 3, 34.
12, 23: Ex 32, 11.
13, 3: 1 Sm 14, 1–15; Jgs 3, 27; 6, 34; 2 Sm 20, 1f.
13, 6: 1 Sm 14, 22.
13, 8: 1 Sm 10, 8.
13, 14: 1 Sm 25, 30; 2 Sm 7, 15f; Ps 78, 70; Acts 13, 22.
13, 15: 1 Sm 14, 2.
13, 17: 1 Sm 14, 15.
13, 19: Jgs 5, 8.

of any of the soldiers with Saul or Jonathan. Only Saul and his son Jonathan had them.

Jonathan's Exploit

23* An outpost of the Philistines had pushed forward to the pass of Michmash.

14 1* One day Jonathan, son of Saul, said to his armor-bearer, "Come, let us go over to the Philistine outpost on the other side." But he did not inform his father. 2 (Saul's command post was under the pomegranate tree near the threshing floor on the outskirts of Geba; those with him numbered about six hundred men. 3* Ahijah, son of Ahitub, brother of Ichabod, who was the son of Phinehas, son of Eli, the priest of the LORD at Shiloh, was wearing the ephod.) Nor did the soldiers know that Jonathan had gone. 4 Flanking the ravine through which Jonathan intended to get over to the Philistine outpost there was a rocky crag on each side, one called Bozez, the other Seneh. 5 One crag was to the north, toward Michmash, the other to the south, toward Geba. 6* Jonathan said to his armor-bearer: "Come, let us go over to that outpost of the uncircumcised. Perhaps the LORD will help us, because it is no more difficult for the LORD to grant victory through a few than through many." 7 His armor-bearer replied, "Do whatever you are inclined to do; I will match your resolve." 8 Jonathan continued: "We shall go over to those men and show ourselves to them. 9 If they say to us, 'Stay there until we can come to you,' we shall stop where we are; we shall not go up to them. 10 But if they say, 'Come up to us,' we shall go up, because the LORD has delivered them into our grasp. That will be our sign." 11 Accordingly, the two of them appeared before the outpost of the Philistines, who said, "Look, some Hebrews are coming out of the holes where they have been hiding." 12 The men of the outpost called to Jonathan and his armor-bearer. "Come up here," they said, "and we will teach you a lesson." So Jonathan said to his armor-bearer, "Climb up after me, for the LORD has delivered them into the grasp of Israel." 13 Jonathan clambered up with his armor-bearer behind him; as the Philistines turned to flee him, he cut them down, and his armor-bearer followed him and finished them off. 14 In this first exploit Jonathan and his armor-bearer slew about twenty men within half a furlong. 15 Then panic spread to the army and

to the countryside, and all the soldiers, including the outpost and the raiding parties, were terror-stricken. The earth also shook, so that the panic was beyond human endurance.

Rout of the Philistines

16 The lookouts of Saul in Geba of Benjamin saw that the enemy camp had scattered and were running about in all directions. 17 Saul said to those around him, "Count the troops and find out if any of us are missing." When they had investigated, they found Jonathan and his armor-bearer missing. 18† Saul then said to Ahijah, "Bring the ephod here." (Ahijah was wearing the ephod in front of the Israelites at that time.) 19 While Saul was speaking to the priest, the tumult in the Philistine camp kept increasing. So he said to the priest, "Withdraw your hand." 20* And Saul and all his men shouted and rushed into the fight, where the Philistines, wholly confused, were thrusting swords at one another. 21* In addition, the Hebrews who had previously sided with the Philistines and had gone up with them to the camp, turned to join the Israelites under Saul and Jonathan. 22* Likewise, all the Israelites who were hiding in the hill country of Ephraim, on hearing that the Philistines were fleeing, pursued them in the rout. 23 Thus the LORD saved Israel that day.

Saul's Oath

† The battle continued past Beth-horon; 24 the whole people, about ten thousand combatants, were with Saul, and there was scattered fighting in every town in the hill country of Ephraim And Saul swore a very rash oath that day, putting the people under this ban: "Cursed be the man who takes food before evening, before I am able to avenge myself on my enemies" So none of the people tasted food 25 Indeed, there was a honeycomb lying on the ground, 26 and when the soldiers came to the comb the swarm had left it; yet no one would raise a hand to his mouth from it, because the people feared the oath.

Violation of the Oath

27 Jonathan, who had not heard that his father had put the people under oath, thrust out the end of the staff he was holding and dipped it into the honey. Then he raised it to his mouth and his eyes lit up. 28 At this one of the soldiers spoke up: "Your

---

† **14, 18:** *Ephod:* to be used in consulting God; see note on v 41, and that on 1 Sm 2, 28, above.

14, 23: *Past Beth-horon:* this is a textual correction influenced by 1 Sm 13, 18; the received Hebrew text refers to Bethel (Beth-aven), but the effect of the victory would seem to have been that the main ridge of mountains in the territories of Benjamin and Ephraim was cleared of Philistines.

* **13, 23:** 1 Sm 14, 15.
14, 1: 1 Sm 13, 3.
14, 3: 1 Sm 2, 28; 4, 21; 14, 18; 23, 9; 30, 7.
14, 6: 1 Sm 17, 26.36.47; Sir 39, 18; 1 Mc 3, 19.
14, 20: Jgs 7, 22.
14, 21: 1 Sm 29, 4.
14, 22: 1 Sm 13, 6.

father put the people under a strict oath, saying, 'Cursed be the man who takes food this day!' As a result the people are weak." 29 Jonathan replied: "My father brings trouble to the land. Look how bright my eyes are from this small taste of honey I have had. 30 What is more, if the people had eaten freely today of their enemy's booty when they came across it, would not the slaughter of the Philistines by now have been the greater for it?"

Use of Flesh with Blood Forbidden

31 After the Philistines were routed that day from Michmash to Aijalon, the people were completely exhausted. 32* So they pounced upon the spoil and took sheep, oxen and calves, slaughtering them on the ground and eating the flesh with blood. 33 Informed that the people were sinning against the LORD by eating the flesh with blood, Saul said: "You have broken faith. Roll a large stone here for me." 34 He continued: "Mingle with the people and tell each of them to bring his ox or his sheep to me. Slaughter it here and then eat, but you must not sin against the LORD by eating the flesh with blood." So everyone brought to the LORD whatever ox he had seized, and they slaughtered them there; 35* and Saul built an altar to the LORD—this was the first time he built an altar to the LORD.

Jonathan in Danger of Death

36 Then Saul said, "Let us go down in pursuit of the Philistines by night, to plunder among them until daybreak and to kill them all off." They replied, "Do what you think best." But the priest said, "Let us consult God." 37* So Saul inquired of God: "Shall I go down in pursuit of the Philistines? Will you deliver them into the power of Israel?" But he received no answer on this occasion. 38 Saul then said, "Come here, all officers of the army. We must investigate and find out how this sin was committed today. 39 As the LORD lives who has given victory to Israel, even if my son Jonathan has committed it, he shall surely die!" But none of the people answered him. 40* So he said to all Israel, "Stand on one side, and I and my son Jonathan will stand on the other." The people responded, "Do what you think best." 41*† And Saul said to the LORD, the God of Israel: "Why did you not answer your servant this time? If the blame for this resides in me or my son Jonathan, LORD, God of Israel, respond

with Urim; but if this guilt is in your people Israel, respond with Thummim." Jonathan and Saul were designated, and the people went free. 42 Saul then said, "Cast lots between me and my son Jonathan." And Jonathan was designated. 43 Saul said to Jonathan, "Tell me what you have done." Jonathan replied, "I only tasted a little honey from the end of the staff I was holding. Am I to die for this?" 44* Saul said, "May God do thus and so to me if you do not indeed die, Jonathan!"

Rescue of Jonathan

45*† But the army said to Saul: "Is Jonathan to die, though it was he who brought Israel this great victory? This must not be! As the LORD lives, not a single hair of his head shall fall to the ground, for God was with him in what he did today!" Thus the soldiers were able to rescue Jonathan from death. 46 After that Saul gave up the pursuit of the Philistines, who returned to their own territory.

Wars and Victories

47* After taking over the kingship of Israel, Saul waged war on all their surrounding enemies— Moab, the Ammonites, Aram, Beth-rehob, the king of Zobah, and the Philistines. Wherever he turned, he was successful 48 and fought bravely. He defeated Amalek and delivered Israel from the hands of those who were plundering them.

Saul's Family

49*† The sons of Saul were Jonathan, Ishvi, and Malchishua; his two daughters were named, the elder, Merob, and the younger, Michal. 50 Saul's wife, who was named Ahinoam, was the daughter of Ahimaaz. The name of his general was Abner, son of Saul's uncle, Ner; 51* Kish, Saul's father, and Ner, Abner's father, were sons of Abiel.

52 An unremitting war was waged against the Philistines during Saul's lifetime. When Saul saw any strong or brave man, he took him into his service.

15 1 Samuel said to Saul: "It was I the LORD sent to anoint you king over his people Israel. Now, therefore, listen to the message of the LORD. 2* This is what the LORD of hosts has to say: 'I will punish what Amalek did to Israel when he barred his way as he was coming up from Egypt.

14, 41: The *Urim* and *Thummim*, or sacred lots, were a device for ascertaining the will of God; they ceased to be used after the time of David. The material and the shape of these objects, and the manner in which they were used, are unknown. They gave a "yes" or "no" answer to specific questions.
14, 45: *Rescue:* the Hebrew word used is that for the "redemption" of the first-born (Ex 13, 13ff).
14, 49: *Ishvi:* known also as Ishbaal, in 2 Sm 2, 8 and elsewhere. The name may once have read "Ishyo" here.

14, 32: 1 Sm 15, 19.21; Lv 3, 17; 7, 26f; 17, 10–14; Acts 15, 20.29.
14, 35: 1 Sm 7, 17; Jgs 6, 24.
14, 37: 1 Sm 28, 6.15.
14, 40: Jos 7, 13ff.
14, 41: 1 Sm 28, 6; Ex 28, 30; Dt 33, 8.
14, 44: 1 Sm 3, 17; Ru 1, 17.
14, 45: 2 Sm 14, 11; 1 Kgs 1, 52.
14, 47: 2 Sm 1, 22; 8, 2–5.
14, 49: 1 Sm 18, 20.25; 31, 2; 1 Chr 8, 33; 9, 39; 10, 2.
14, 51: 1 Sm 9, 1.
15, 2: Ex 17, 8–10.16; Dt 25, 17ff.

³*† Go, now, attack Amalek, and deal with him and all that he has under the ban. Do not spare him, but kill men and women, children and infants, oxen and sheep, camels and asses.' "

Disobedience of Saul

⁴† Saul alerted the soldiers, and at Telaim reviewed two hundred thousand foot soldiers and ten thousand men of Judah. ⁵ Saul went to the city of Amalek, and after setting an ambush in the wadi, ⁶* warned the Kenites: "Come! Leave Amalek and withdraw, that I may not have to destroy you with them, for you were kind to the Israelites when they came up from Egypt." After the Kenites left, ⁷* Saul routed Amalek from Havilah to the approaches of Shur, on the frontier of Egypt. ⁸ He took Agag, king of Amalek, alive, but on the rest of the people he put into effect the ban of destruction by the sword. ⁹ He and his troops spared Agag and the best of the fat sheep and oxen, and the lambs. They refused to carry out the doom on anything that was worthwhile, dooming only what was worthless and of no account.

Saul Is Reproved

¹⁰ Then the LORD spoke to Samuel: ¹¹† "I regret having made Saul king, for he has turned from me and has not kept my command." At this Samuel grew angry and cried out to the LORD all night. ¹² Early in the morning he went to meet Saul, but was informed that Saul had gone to Carmel, where he erected a trophy in his own honor, and that on his return he had passed on and gone down to Gilgal. ¹³ When Samuel came to him, Saul greeted him: "The LORD bless you! I have kept the command of the LORD." ¹⁴ But Samuel asked, "What, then, is the meaning of this bleating of sheep that comes to my ears, and the lowing of oxen that I hear?" ¹⁵ Saul replied: "They were brought from Amalek. The men spared the best sheep and oxen to sacrifice to the LORD, your God; but we have carried out the ban on the rest." ¹⁶ Samuel said to Saul: "Stop! Let me tell you what the LORD said to me last night." "Speak!" he replied. ¹⁷* Samuel then said: "Though little in your own esteem, are you not leader of the tribes of Israel? The LORD anointed you king of Israel ¹⁸* and sent you on a mission, saying, 'Go and put the sinful Amalekites under a ban of destruction. Fight against them until you have exterminated them.' ¹⁹* Why then have you disobeyed the LORD? You have pounced on the spoil, thus displeasing the LORD." ²⁰ Saul answered Samuel: "I did indeed obey the LORD and fulfill the mission on which the LORD sent me. I have brought back Agag, and I have destroyed Amalek under the ban. ²¹* But from the spoil the men took sheep and oxen, the best of what had been banned, to sacrifice to the LORD their God in Gilgal." ²²*† But Samuel said:

> "Does the LORD so delight in holocausts
>   and sacrifices

Power and Corruption

Power corrupts. We have often heard that phrase. And in 1 Sm 15, 22–23, we have a vivid example. King Saul once again has decided to take matters in his own hands and goes against the word of the LORD. He seems to assume that his role as king exempts him from obedience to God. But Samuel reminds Saul that he has assumed way too much. No king, no president, no prime minster is above the law. Especially when that Law comes from God.

Have you ever been in a position of leadership and been tempted to abuse your privileges?

▶ **1 Sm 15, 22–23**

15, 3: *Under the ban:* in such wars of extermination, all things (men, cities, beasts, etc.) were to be blotted out; nothing could be reserved for private use. The interpretation of God's will here attributed to Samuel is in keeping with the abhorrent practices of blood revenge prevalent among pastoral, seminomadic peoples such as the Hebrews had recently been. The slaughter of the innocent has never been in conformity with the will of God.

15, 4: The numbers here are not realistic; compare 1 Sm 14, 24 above.

15, 11: *I regret:* God manifests "regret" when, offended by men, he takes away his benefits, graces and favors. It is not God, but men, who change, to their own detriment.

15, 22: Samuel is disapproving, not of sacrifices in general, but of merely external sacrifices offered in defiance of God's commandment and without heartfelt obedience.

15, 3: 1 Sm 27, 8; 30, 17; Ex 17, 16; Nm 24, 20.
15, 6: Nm 24, 21.
15, 7: 1 Sm 27, 8.
15, 17: 1 Sm 9, 21.
15, 18: 1 Sm 28, 18.
15, 19: 14, 32.
15, 21: Lv 27, 28.
15, 22: Prv 21, 3; Hos 6, 6; Am 5, 21–25; Zec 10, 2; Mt 9, 13; 12, 7; Heb 10, 9.

as in obedience to the command of
   the LORD?
Obedience is better than sacrifice,
   and submission than the fat of rams.
23 For a sin like divination is rebellion,
   and presumption is the crime of idolatry.
Because you have rejected the command of
   the LORD,
   he, too, has rejected you as ruler."

Saul Asks Forgiveness

24* Saul replied to Samuel: "I have sinned, for I have disobeyed the command of the LORD and your instructions. In my fear of the people, I did what they said. 25 Now forgive my sin, and return with me, that I may worship the LORD." 26* But Samuel said to Saul, "I will not return with you, because you rejected the command of the LORD and the LORD rejects you as king of Israel." 27* As Samuel turned to go, Saul seized a loose end of his mantle, and it tore off. 28* So Samuel said to him: "The LORD has torn the kingdom of Israel from you this day, and has given it to a neighbor of yours, who is better than you. 29* The Glory of Israel neither retracts nor repents, for he is not man that he should repent." 30 But he answered: "I have sinned, yet honor me now before the elders of my people and before Israel. Return with me that I may worship

the LORD your God." 31 And so Samuel returned with him, and Saul worshiped the LORD.

Agag Is Cut Down

32 Afterward Samuel commanded, "Bring Agag, king of Amalek, to me." Agag came to him struggling and saying, "So it is bitter death!" 33* And Samuel said,

"As your sword has made women childless,
   so shall your mother be childless
     among women."

Then he cut Agag down before the LORD in Gilgal.

34 Samuel departed for Ramah, while Saul went up to his home in Gibeah of Saul. 35* Never again, as long as he lived, did Samuel see Saul. Yet he grieved over Saul, because the LORD regretted having made him king of Israel.

Samuel Sent to Bethlehem

16 1*† The LORD said to Samuel: "How long will you grieve for Saul, whom I have rejected as king of Israel? Fill your horn with oil, and be on your way. I am sending you to Jesse of Bethlehem, for I have chosen my king from among his sons." 2 But Samuel replied: "How can I go? Saul will hear of it and kill me." To this the LORD answered: "Take a heifer along and say, 'I have come to sacrifice to the LORD.' 3 Invite Jesse to the sacrifice, and I myself will tell you what to do; you are to anoint for me the one I point out to you."

4 Samuel did as the LORD had commanded him. When he entered Bethlehem, the elders of the city came trembling to meet him and inquired, "Is your visit peaceful, O seer?" 5* He replied: "Yes! I have come to sacrifice to the LORD. So cleanse yourselves and join me today for the banquet." He also had Jesse and his sons cleanse themselves and invited them to the sacrifice. 6 As they came, he looked at Eliab and thought, "Surely the LORD's anointed is here before him." 7* But the LORD said to Samuel: "Do not judge from his appearance or from his lofty stature, because I have rejected him. Not as man sees does God see, because man sees the appearance but the LORD looks into the heart." 8* Then Jesse called Abinadab and presented him before Samuel, who said, "The LORD has not chosen him." 9 Next Jesse presented Shammah, but Samuel said, "The LORD has not chosen this one either."

But the LORD said to Samuel: "Do not judge from his appearance or from his lofty stature, because I have rejected him. Not as man sees does God see, because man sees the appearance,

but the LORD looks into the heart

16, 7

---

† **16, 1:** The anointing here prepared for is unknown to David's brother Eliab in the next chapter (1 Sm 17, 28), and David is twice anointed after Saul's death (2 Sm 2, 4; 5, 3).

15, 24: 1 Sm 26, 21.
15, 26: 1 Kgs 11, 11.30f.
15, 27: 1 Sm 24, 6.
15, 28: 1 Sm 28, 17; 2 Sm 7, 15f.
15, 29: Nm 23, 19.
15, 33: Ex 21, 23.
15, 35: Gn 6, 6.
16, 1: 1 Kgs 1, 39; Ru 4, 17–22; 1 Chr 11, 3; Is 11, 1; Lk 2, 4.
16, 5: 1 Sm 9, 12f; 20, 26; Ex 19, 10; Jb 1, 5.
16, 7: 1 Sm 10, 23f; 1 Chr 28, 9; Prv 15, 11; Jer 17, 10; 20, 12; Lk 16, 15; Acts 1, 24.
16, 8ff: 1 Sm 17, 12f; 1 Chr 2, 13ff.

¹⁰ In the same way Jesse presented seven sons before Samuel, but Samuel said to Jesse, "The LORD has not chosen any one of these." ¹¹* Then Samuel asked Jesse, "Are these all the sons you have?" Jesse replied, "There is still the youngest, who is tending the sheep." Samuel said to Jesse, "Send for him; we will not begin the sacrificial banquet until he arrives here." ¹²* Jesse sent and had the young man brought to them. He was ruddy, a youth handsome to behold and making a splendid appearance. The LORD said, "There—anoint him, for this is he!" ¹³* Then Samuel, with the horn of oil in hand, anointed him in the midst of his brothers; and from that day on, the spirit of the LORD rushed upon David. When Samuel took his leave, he went to Ramah.

Saul's Spirit of Melancholy

¹⁴*† The spirit of the LORD had departed from Saul, and he was tormented by an evil spirit sent by the LORD. ¹⁵ So the servants of Saul said to him: "Please! An evil spirit from God is tormenting you. ¹⁶ If your lordship will order it, we, your servants here in attendance on you, will look for a man skilled in playing the harp. When the evil spirit from God comes over you, he will play and you will feel better." ¹⁷ Saul then told his servants, "Find me a skillful harpist and bring him to me." ¹⁸*† A servant spoke up to say: "I have observed that one of the sons of Jesse of Bethlehem is a skillful harpist. He is also a stalwart soldier, besides being an able speaker, and handsome. Moreover, the LORD is with him."

David Made Armor-Bearer

¹⁹ Accordingly, Saul dispatched messengers to ask Jesse to send him his son David, who was with the flock. ²⁰* Then Jesse took five loaves of bread, a skin of wine, and a kid, and sent them to Saul by his son David. ²¹* Thus David came to Saul and entered his service. Saul became very fond of him, made him his armor-bearer, ²² and sent Jesse the message, "Allow David to remain in my service, for he meets with my approval." ²³ Whenever the spirit from God seized Saul, David would take the harp and play, and Saul would be relieved and feel better, for the evil spirit would leave him.

The Challenge of Goliath

17 ¹ The Philistines rallied their forces for battle at Socoh in Judah and camped between Socoh and Azekah at Ephes-dammim. ² Saul and the Israelites also gathered and camped in the Vale of the Terebinth, drawing up their battle line to meet the Philistines. ³ The Philistines were stationed on one hill and the Israelites on an opposite hill, with a valley between them.

⁴ A champion named Goliath of Gath came out from the Philistine camp; he was six and a half feet tall. ⁵ He had a bronze helmet on his head and wore a bronze corselet of scale armor weighing five thousand shekels, ⁶† and bronze greaves, and had a bronze scimitar slung from a baldric. ⁷*† The shaft of his javelin was like a weaver's heddle-bar, and its iron head weighed six hundred shekels. His shield-bearer went before him. ⁸ He stood and shouted to the ranks of Israel: "Why come out in battle formation? I am a Philistine, and you are Saul's servants. Choose one of your men, and have him come down to me. ⁹ If he beats me in combat and kills me, we will be your vassals; but if I beat him and kill him, you shall be our vassals and serve us." ¹⁰ The Philistine continued: "I defy the ranks of Israel today.

16, 14: *An evil spirit sent by the* LORD: the Lord permitted Saul to be tormented with violent fits of rage.

16, 18: Of the two traditions which describe the coming of David into Saul's service, the oldest Greek translation retains only the one comprised in 1 Sm 16, 14–23; 17, 1–11.32–54. This effort at consistency is not in accord with the character of the rest of the book; see note on 1 Sm 8, 1. Though square brackets are used in this edition to indicate the passages lacking in the oldest translation, this is meant only to help the reader follow one account at a time. Both are equally a part of the inspired text, as are also the various amplifications and retouchings of the narrative given within brackets in chs 18 and 19.

17, 6: *Scimitar:* the Hebrew word for this is rather rare, and the nature of the weapon was in doubt until recent years. It is not the same as the sword of v 45.

17, 7: *Six hundred shekels:* over 15 pounds.

16, 11: 1 Sm 17, 15.28.34; 2 Sm 7, 8.
16, 12: 1 Sm 9, 2.
16, 13: 1 Sm 10, 6; 11, 6; Jgs 3, 10; 9, 9; Sir 46, 13.
16, 14: 1 Sm 18, 10f.
16, 18: 2 Sm 17, 8.
16, 20: 1 Sm 9, 7f; 10, 4.27; 16, 1; 17, 27ff.
16, 21: 1 Sm 18, 2.
17, 7: 2 Sm 21, 19; 1 Chr 11, 23; 20, 5.

Give me a man and let us fight together." [11] Saul and all the men of Israel, when they heard this challenge of the Philistine, were dismayed and terror-stricken.

David Comes to the Camp

[12]*† [David was the son of an Ephrathite named Jesse, who was from Bethlehem in Judah. He had eight sons, and in the days of Saul was old and well on in years. [13] The three oldest sons of Jesse had followed Saul to war; these three sons who had gone off to war were named, the first-born Eliab, the second son Abinadab, and the third Shammah. [14] David was the youngest. While the three oldest had joined Saul, [15]* David would go and come from Saul to tend his father's sheep at Bethlehem.

some token from them. [19] Saul, and they, and all Israel are fighting against the Philistines in the Vale of the Terebinth." [20]* Early the next morning, having left the flock with a shepherd, David set out on his errand, as Jesse had commanded him. He reached the barricade of the camp just as the army, on their way to the battleground, were shouting their battle cry. [21] The Israelites and the Philistines drew up opposite each other in battle array. [22]* David entrusted what he had brought to the keeper of the baggage and hastened to the battle line where he greeted his brothers. [23] While he was talking with them, the Philistine champion, by name Goliath of Gath, came up from the ranks of the Philistines and spoke as before, and David listened. [24] When the Israelites saw the man, they all retreated before him,

Introducing ► DAVID

Who cannot love David? This shepherd-turned-king is one of the great tragic heroes of the Old Testament. David, whose name means "beloved," was the successor to Saul and the second king (1000–961 B.C.) of the new nation formed out of the twelve tribes of Israel. The youngest son of Jesse of the tribe of Judah, David was a member of Saul's court as a young man. Later, when Saul disappointed God, Samuel the prophet anointed David as Saul's successor. After Saul was killed, David established the neutral city of Jerusalem as his capital (see map 3, "The Kingdom Years"). He moved the ark of the LORD there, making this city the new religious center of Israel. Jerusalem is also known as the City of David.

David was a successful warrior, a capable king, and a gifted poet, having himself written some of the Psalms. He was also capable of great sin. His affair with Bathsheba seemed to lead to a string of violence and betrayal affecting his whole family. One of his sons, Absalom, even inspired a revolt against David. But through it all, David was passionately in love with God. God recognized this and promised David that someone from his house would sit upon the throne in Israel.

When Israel was destroyed and its kings taken prisoners, the people developed a hope that another anointed one, a messiah from the house of David, would rise up and lead Israel in God's ways once again. It is this hope for the Davidic messiah that is fulfilled by Jesus in the New Testament.

[16] [Meanwhile the Philistine came forward and took his stand morning and evening for forty days. [17] [Now Jesse said to his son David: "Take this ephah of roasted grain and these ten loaves for your brothers, and bring them quickly to your brothers in the camp. [18] Also take these ten cheeses for the field officer. Greet your brothers and bring home

very much afraid. [25]* The Israelites had been saying: "Do you see this man coming up? He comes up to insult Israel. If anyone should kill him, the king would give him great wealth, and his daughter as well, and would grant exemption to his father's family in Israel." [26]* David now said to the men standing by: "What will be done for the man who

---

† **17, 12–31:** An alternative account of how David came to undertake the combat with the Philistine is here inserted; it is continued in 1 Sm 17, 55—18, 6. See note on 1 Sm 16, 18.

17, 12: 1 Sm 16, 1.10; Ru 1, 2.
17, 15: 1 Sm 18, 2; 2 Sm 7, 8.
17, 20: 1 Sm 26, 5.
17, 22: 1 Sm 25, 13.

17, 25: 1 Sm 18, 17; Jos 15, 16.
17, 26: 1 Sm 18, 25; Jgs 15, 18; 2 Kgs 19, 4; Is 37, 4.

kills this Philistine and frees Israel of the disgrace? Who is this uncircumcised Philistine in any case, that he should insult the armies of the living God?" 27 They repeated the same words to him and said, "That is how the man who kills him will be rewarded." 28 When Eliab, his oldest brother, heard him speaking with the men, he grew angry with David and said: "Why did you come down? With whom have you left those sheep in the desert meanwhile? I know your arrogance and your evil intent. You came down to enjoy the battle!" 29 David replied, "What have I done now?—I was only talking." 30 Yet he turned from him to another and asked the same question; and everyone gave him

37* David continued: "The LORD, who delivered me from the claws of the lion and the bear, will also keep me safe from the clutches of this Philistine." Saul answered David, "Go! the LORD will be with you."

Preparation for the Encounter

38 Then Saul clothed David in his own tunic, putting a bronze helmet on his head and arming him with a coat of mail. 39 David also girded himself with Saul's sword over the tunic. He walked with difficulty, however, since he had never tried armor before. He said to Saul, "I cannot go in these, because I have never tried them before." So

Taking On Goliath

David makes it look so easy. A slingshot, a stone, a skillful aim, and it is all over. Goliath is dead, and the Israelites win the day. It is a story that gives hope to anyone who has ever been bullied or harassed.

A David lives in each of us, and plenty of Goliaths are out there ready to defeat us. The Goliaths we encounter can include peer pressure, an addiction, an abusive situation, or simply self-doubt. We may feel overpowered by these Goliaths, sure that they are too big for us to handle. But they are not! Those of us who believe in God, as David did, know that we are not alone. As followers of Jesus, we rely not on violence but on love and the support of the Christian community to defeat the Goliaths in our life. We can make David's story our own.

Identify a Goliath in your life right now, and journal about it. What stepping-stone can you take in defeating it?

▶ **I Samuel, chapter 17**

the same answer as before. 31 The words that David had spoken were overheard and reported to Saul, who sent for him.]

David Fights Goliath

32 Then David spoke to Saul: "Let your majesty not lose courage. I am at your service to go and fight this Philistine." 33 But Saul answered David, "You cannot go up against this Philistine and fight with him, for you are only a youth, while he has been a warrior from his youth." 34* Then David told Saul: "Your servant used to tend his father's sheep, and whenever a lion or bear came to carry off a sheep from the flock, 35 I would go after it and attack it and rescue the prey from its mouth. If it attacked me, I would seize it by the jaw, strike it, and kill it. 36 Your servant has killed both a lion and a bear, and this uncircumcised Philistine will be as one of them, because he has insulted the armies of the living God."

he took them off. 40 Then, staff in hand, David selected five smooth stones from the wadi and put them in the pocket of his shepherd's bag. With his sling also ready to hand, he approached the Philistine.

David's Victory

41 With his shield-bearer marching before him, the Philistine also advanced closer and closer to David. 42 When he had sized David up, and seen that he was youthful, and ruddy, and handsome in appearance, he held him in contempt. 43 The Philistine said to David, "Am I a dog that you come against me with a staff?" Then the Philistine cursed David by his gods 44* and said to him, "Come here to me, and I will leave your flesh for the birds of the air and the beasts of the field." 45 David answered him: "You come against me with sword and spear and scimitar, but I come against you in the name of

---

17, 34f: Jgs 14, 6; Sir 47, 3.
17, 37: Prv 28, 1.

17, 44: Dt 28, 26; Is 18, 6;
Jer 15, 3.

the LORD of hosts, the God of the armies of Israel that you have insulted. ⁴⁶ Today the LORD shall deliver you into my hand; I will strike you down and cut off your head. This very day I will leave your corpse and the corpses of the Philistine army for the birds of the air and the beasts of the field; thus the whole land shall learn that Israel has a God. ⁴⁷* All this multitude, too, shall learn that it is not by sword or spear that the LORD saves. For the battle is the LORD'S, and he shall deliver you into our hands."

⁴⁸ The Philistine then moved to meet David at close quarters, while David ran quickly toward the battle line in the direction of the Philistine. ⁴⁹ David put his hand into the bag and took out a stone, hurled it with the sling, and struck the Philistine on the forehead. The stone embedded itself in his brow, and he fell prostrate on the ground. ⁵⁰* [Thus David overcame the Philistine with sling and stone; he struck the Philistine mortally, and did it without a sword.] ⁵¹* Then David ran and stood over him; with the Philistine's own sword [which he drew from its sheath] he dispatched him and cut off his head.

Flight of the Philistines

When they saw that their hero was dead, the Philistines took to flight. ⁵² Then the men of Israel and Judah, with loud shouts, went in pursuit of the Philistines to the approaches of Gath and to the gates of Ekron, and Philistines fell wounded along the road from Shaaraim as far as Gath and Ekron. ⁵³ On their return from the pursuit of the Philistines, the Israelites looted their camp. ⁵⁴*† David took the head of the Philistine and brought it to Jerusalem; but he kept Goliath's armor in his own tent.

David Presented to Saul

⁵⁵ [When Saul saw David go out to meet the Philistine, he asked his general Abner, "Abner, whose son is that youth?" Abner replied, "As truly as your majesty is alive, I have no idea." ⁵⁶ And the king said, "Find out whose son the lad is." ⁵⁷ So when David returned from slaying the Philistine, Abner took him and presented him to Saul. David was still holding the Philistine's head. ⁵⁸ Saul then asked him, "Whose son are you, young man?" David replied, "I am the son of your servant Jesse of Bethlehem."

David and Jonathan

18 ¹* [By the time David finished speaking with Saul, Jonathan had become as fond of David as if his life depended on him; he loved him as he loved himself. ²* Saul laid claim to David that day and did not allow him to return to his father's house. ³ And Jonathan entered into a bond with David, because he loved him as himself. ⁴* Jonathan divested himself of the mantle he was wearing and gave it to David, along with his military dress, and his sword, his bow and his belt. ⁵ David then carried out successfully every mission on which Saul sent him. So Saul put him in charge of his soldiers, and this was agreeable to the whole army, even to Saul's own officers.]

Saul's Jealousy

⁶* At the approach of Saul and David (on David's return after slaying the Philistine), women came out from each of the cities of Israel to meet King Saul, singing and dancing, with tambourines, joyful songs, and sistrums. ⁷* The women played and sang:

"Saul has slain his thousands,
    and David his ten thousands."

⁸ Saul was very angry and resentful of the song, for he thought: "They give David ten thousands, but only thousands to me. All that remains for him is the kingship." ⁹ [And from that day on, Saul was jealous of David.

¹⁰* [The next day an evil spirit from God came over Saul, and he raged in his house. David was in attendance, playing the harp as at other times, while Saul was holding his spear. ¹¹ Saul poised the spear, thinking to nail David to the wall, but twice David escaped him.] ¹² Saul then began to fear David, [because the LORD was with him, but had departed from Saul himself.] ¹³ Accordingly, Saul removed him from his presence by appointing him a field officer. So David led the people on their military expeditions, ¹⁴ and prospered in all his enterprises, for the LORD was with him. ¹⁵ Seeing how successful he was, Saul conceived a fear of David; ¹⁶* on the other hand, all Israel and Judah loved him, since he led them on their expeditions.

¹⁷* [Saul said to David, "There is my older daughter, Merob, whom I will give you in marriage if you become my champion and fight the battles of

---

† **17, 54:** At the time supposed by this narrative, Jerusalem was still Jebusite, and David had no military tent of his own; the verse is a later gloss.

17, 47: 1 Sm 14, 6; Ps 33, 16. **17, 51:** 1 Sm 21, 10.
17, 50: Sir 47, 4; 1 Mc 4, 30. **17, 54:** 1 Sm 31, 9.

18, 1: 1 Sm 19, 1–7; 20, 17;   **18, 7:** 1 Sm 21, 12; 29, 5; Sir
  23, 16; 2 Sm 1, 26; 9, 1.   47, 6f.
18, 2: 1 Sm 16, 21; 17, 15. **18, 10f:** 1 Sm 16, 14; 19, 9f;
18, 4: 2 Sm 1, 22.   20, 33; 22, 6; 26, 8.
18, 6: Ex 15, 20f; Jgs 11, 34; **18, 16:** 2 Sm 5, 2.
  Jdt 15, 12.   **18, 17:** 1 Sm 14, 49; 17, 25.

the LORD." Saul had in mind, "I shall not touch him; let the Philistines strike him." 18 But David answered Saul: "Who am I? And who are my kin or my father's clan in Israel that I should become the king's son-in-law?" 19* However, when it was time for Saul's daughter Merob to be given to David, she was given in marriage to Adriel the Meholathite instead.]

20* Now Saul's daughter Michal loved David, and it was reported to Saul, who was pleased at this, 21 for he thought, "I will offer her to him to become a snare for him, so that the Philistines may strike him." [Thus for the second time Saul said to David, "You shall become my son-in-law today."] 22 Saul then ordered his servants to speak to David privately and to say: "The king is fond of you, and all his officers love you. You should become the king's son-in-law." 23 But when Saul's servants mentioned this to David, he said: "Do you think it easy to become the king's son-in-law? I am poor and insignificant." 24 When his servants reported to him the nature of David's answer, 25* Saul commanded them to say this to David: "The king desires no other price for the bride than the foreskins of one hundred Philistines, that he may thus take vengeance on his enemies." Saul intended in this way to bring about David's death through the Philistines. 26 When the servants reported this offer to David, he was pleased with the prospect of becoming the king's son-in-law. [Before the year was up,] 27 David made preparations and sallied forth with his men and slew two hundred Philistines. He brought back their foreskins and counted them out before the king, that he might thus become the king's son-in-law. So Saul gave him his daughter Michal in marriage. 28 Saul thus came to recognize that the LORD was with David; besides, his own daughter Michal loved David. 29 Therefore Saul feared David all the more [and was his enemy ever after].

30 [The Philistine chiefs continued to make forays, but each time they took the field, David was more successful against them than any other of Saul's officers, and as a result acquired great fame.]

Persecution of David

19 1* Saul discussed his intention of killing David with his son Jonathan and with all his servants. But Saul's son Jonathan, who was very fond of David, 2 told him: "My father Saul is trying to kill you. Therefore, please be on your guard tomorrow morning; get out of sight and remain in

hiding. 3 I, however, will go out and stand beside my father in the countryside where you are, and will speak to him about you. If I learn anything, I will let you know."

4 Jonathan then spoke well of David to his father Saul, saying to him: "Let not your majesty sin against his servant David, for he has committed no offense against you, but has helped you very much by his deeds. 5* When he took his life in his hands and slew the Philistine, and the LORD brought about a great victory for all Israel through him, you were glad to see it. Why, then, should you become guilty of shedding innocent blood by killing David without cause?" 6 Saul heeded Jonathan's plea and swore, "As the LORD lives, he shall not be killed." 7 So Jonathan summoned David and repeated the whole conversation to him. Jonathan then brought David to Saul, and David served him as before.

8 When war broke out again, David went out to fight against the Philistines and inflicted a great defeat upon them, putting them to flight. 9* Then an evil spirit from the LORD came upon Saul as he was sitting in his house with spear in hand and David was playing the harp nearby. 10 Saul tried to nail David to the wall with the spear, but David eluded Saul, so that the spear struck only the wall, and David got away safe.

11† The same night, Saul sent messengers to David's house to guard it, that he might kill him in the morning. David's wife Michal informed him, "Unless you save yourself tonight, tomorrow you will be killed." 12* Then Michal let David down through a window, and he made his escape in safety. 13* Michal took the household idol and laid it in the bed, putting a net of goat's hair at its head and covering it with a spread. 14 When Saul sent messengers to arrest David, she said, "He is sick." 15 Saul, however, sent the messengers back to see David and commanded them, "Bring him up to me in the bed, that I may kill him." 16 But when the messengers entered, they found the household idol in the bed, with the net of goat's hair at its head. 17 Saul therefore asked Michal: "Why did you play this trick on me? You have helped my enemy to get away!" Michal answered Saul: "He threatened me, 'Let me go or I will kill you.' "

David and Samuel in Ramah

18 Thus David got safely away; he went to Samuel in Ramah, informing him of all that Saul had done to him. Then he and Samuel went to stay in the

† **19, 11:** This story in all probability originally followed 1 Sm 18, 29, placing the episode of David's escape on the night of his marriage with Michal.

* **18, 19:** 1 Sm 21, 8; 24, 16.
18, 20: 1 Sm 14, 49; 25, 44; 26, 23; 2 Sm 3, 13.
18, 25: 1 Sm 17, 26; Gn 34, 12.
19, 1: 1 Sm 18, 1; 20, 1ff.
19, 5: Dt 19, 10; Ps 119, 109.
19, 9f: 1 Sm 16, 14; 18, 10f.
19, 12: Jos 2, 15; Acts 9, 25; 2 Cor 11, 33.
19, 13: Gn 31, 19; Jos 17, 5; 18, 14.18.20.

sheds. ¹⁹ When Saul was told that David was in the sheds near Ramah, ²⁰* he sent messengers to arrest David. But when they saw the band of prophets, presided over by Samuel, in a prophetic frenzy, they too fell into the prophetic state. ²¹ Informed of this, Saul sent other messengers, who also fell into the prophetic state. For the third time Saul sent messengers, but they too fell into the prophetic state.

Saul among the Prophets

²² Saul then went to Ramah himself. Arriving at the cistern of the threshing floor on the bare hilltop, he inquired, "Where are Samuel and David?", and was told, "At the sheds near Ramah." ²³ As he set out from the hilltop toward the sheds, the spirit of God came upon him also, and he continued on in a prophetic condition until he reached the spot. At the sheds near Ramah ²⁴* he, too, stripped himself of his garments and he, too, remained in the prophetic state in the presence of Samuel; all that day and night he lay naked. That is why they say, "Is Saul also among the prophets?"

David Consults with Jonathan

20 ¹* David fled from the sheds near Ramah, and went to Jonathan. "What have I done?" he asked him. "What crime or what offense does your father hold against me that he seeks my life?" ² Jonathan answered him: "Heaven forbid that you should die! My father does nothing, great or small, without disclosing it to me. Why, then, should my father conceal this from me? This cannot be so!" ³ But David replied: "Your father is well aware that I am favored with your friendship, so he has decided, 'Jonathan must not know of this lest he be grieved.' Nevertheless, as the LORD lives and as you live, there is but a step between me and death." ⁴ Jonathan then said to David, "I will do whatever you wish." ⁵* David answered: "Tomorrow is the new moon, when I should in fact dine with the king. Let me go and hide in the open country until evening. ⁶ If it turns out that your father misses me, say, 'David urged me to let him go on short notice to his city Bethlehem, because his whole clan is holding its seasonal sacrifice there.' ⁷ If he says, 'Very well,' your servant is safe. But if he becomes quite angry, you can be sure he has planned some harm. ⁸* Do this kindness for your servant because of the LORD's bond between us, into which you brought me: if I am guilty, kill me yourself! Why should you give me up to your father?" ⁹ But Jonathan

answered: "Not I! If ever I find out that my father is determined to inflict injury upon you, I will certainly let you know." ¹⁰ David then asked Jonathan, "Who will tell me if your father gives you a harsh answer?"

Mutual Agreement

¹¹ [Jonathan replied to David, "Come, let us go out into the field." When they were out in the open country together, ¹² Jonathan said to David: "As the LORD, the God of Israel, lives, I will sound out my father about this time tomorrow. Whether he is well disposed toward David or not, I will send you the information. ¹³* Should it please my father to bring any injury upon you, may the LORD do thus and so to Jonathan if I do not apprise you of it and send you on your way in peace. May the LORD be with you even as he was with my father. ¹⁴ Only this: if I am still alive, may you show me the kindness of the LORD. But if I die, ¹⁵ never withdraw your kindness from my house. And when the LORD exterminates all the enemies of David from the surface of the earth, ¹⁶ the name of Jonathan must never be allowed by the family of David to die out from among you, or the LORD will make you answer for it." ¹⁷ And in his love for David, Jonathan renewed his oath to him, because he loved him as his very self.]

¹⁸ Jonathan then said to him: "Tomorrow is the new moon; and you will be missed, since your place will be vacant. ¹⁹* On the following day you will be missed all the more. Go to the spot where you hid on the other occasion and wait near the mound there. ²⁰ On the third day of the month I will shoot arrows, as though aiming at a target. ²¹ I will then send my attendant to go and recover the arrows. If in fact I say to him, 'Look, the arrow is this side of you; pick it up,' come, for you are safe. As the LORD lives, there will be nothing to fear. ²² But if I say to the boy, 'Look, the arrow is beyond you,' go, for the LORD sends you away. ²³ However, in the matter which you and I have discussed, the LORD shall be between you and me forever." ²⁴ So David hid in the open country.

On the day of the new moon, when the king sat at table to dine, ²⁵ taking his usual place against the wall, Jonathan sat facing him, while Abner sat at the king's side, and David's place was vacant. ²⁶*† Saul, however, said nothing that day, for he thought, "He must have become unclean by accident, and not yet have been cleansed." ²⁷ On the next day, the second

---

19, 20: 1 Sm 10, 5f.10; Nm 11, 25.
19, 24: 1 Sm 10, 10ff.
20, 1: 1 Sm 19, 1–7.11–17.
20, 5: Nm 10, 10; 28, 11–15.
20, 8f: 1 Sm 23, 17f.
20, 13–16: 1 Sm 24, 22f; 2 Sm 9, 1–13; 21, 7.
20, 19: 1 Sm 19, 1–7.
20, 26: 1 Sm 16, 5; Lv 7, 20f; 15, 1ff.

Friends Forever

David and Jonathan have one of the most touching stories of friendship in the Bible. In 1 Sm 18, 1–4, Jonathan makes a special covenant with David. In chapter 20, their deep love leads them to risk their lives for each other. Saul, the king and Jonathan's father, is acting like a madman. He is insanely jealous of David and wants him dead.

Yet, Jonathan and David bring God into their relationship. This gives them the wisdom to see what is right and do it. When they have to part (see 20, 41–42), they weep and kiss and remind each other of their vows.

Not many teenagers deal with situations as drastic as this, but tension with parents over your choice of friends can be common. Parents may not understand why you like a person whom they dislike. It can leave you with a sense of being stuck in the middle.

Your response should be like David and Jonathan's, keeping God part of all your relationships. Each friendship then becomes a living prayer, and God will guide you through conflicts and help you make good decisions.

▶ 1 Samuel, chapter 20

day of the month, David's place was vacant. Saul inquired of his son Jonathan, "Why has the son of Jesse not come to table yesterday or today?" 28 Jonathan answered Saul: "David urgently asked me to let him go to his city, Bethlehem. 29 'Please let me go,' he begged, 'for we are to have a clan sacrifice in our city, and my brothers insist on my presence. Now, therefore, if you think well of me, give me leave to visit my brothers.' That is why he has not come to the king's table." 30 But Saul was extremely angry with Jonathan and said to him: "Son of a rebellious woman, do I not know that, to your own shame and to the disclosure of your mother's shame, you are the companion of Jesse's son? 31* Why, as long as the son of Jesse lives upon the earth, you cannot make good your claim to the kingship! So send for him, and bring him to me, for

he is doomed." 32 But Jonathan asked his father Saul: "Why should he die? What has he done?" 33* At this Saul brandished his spear to strike him, and thus Jonathan learned that his father was resolved to kill David. 34 Jonathan sprang up from the table in great anger and took no food that second day of the month, for he was grieved on David's account, since his father had railed against him.

Jonathan's Farewell

35 The next morning Jonathan went out into the field with a little boy for his appointment with David. 36 There he said to the boy, "Run and fetch the arrow." And as the boy ran, he shot an arrow beyond him in the direction of the city. 37 When the boy made for the spot where Jonathan had shot the arrow, Jonathan called after him, "The arrow is farther on!" 38 Again he called to his lad, "Hurry, be quick, don't delay!" Jonathan's boy picked up the arrow and brought it to his master. 39 The boy knew nothing; only Jonathan and David knew what was meant. 40 Then Jonathan gave his weapons to this boy of his and said to him, "Go, take them to the city." 41 When the boy had left, David rose from beside the mound and prostrated himself on the ground three times before Jonathan in homage. They kissed each other and wept aloud together. 42* At length Jonathan said to David, "Go in peace, in keeping with what we two have sworn by the name of the LORD: 'The LORD shall be between you and me, and between your posterity and mine forever.' "

21

1 Then David departed on his way, while Jonathan went back into the city.

The Holy Bread

2* David went to Ahimelech, the priest of Nob, who came trembling to meet him and asked, "Why are you alone? Is there no one with you?" 3 David answered the priest: "The king gave me a commission and told me to let no one know anything about the business on which he sent me or the commission he gave me. For that reason I have arranged a meeting place with my men. 4* Now what have you on hand? Give me five loaves, or whatever you can find." 5† But the priest replied to David, "I have no ordinary bread on hand, only holy bread; if the men have abstained from women, you may eat some of that." 6 David answered the

---

† **21, 5f:** *From women:* the high priest, willing to distribute the holy bread to David and his men, requires that they be free from ritual uncleanness, associated in Old Testament times (Lv 15, 18) with the marriage act. David's answer supposes the discipline of a military campaign under the conditions of "holy war" (Dt 23, 10).

20, 31: 2 Sm 12, 5.   21, 2: Is 10, 32; Mk 2, 26.
20, 33: 1 Sm 18, 11.   21, 4: Lv 24, 5.9.
20, 42: 2 Sm 9, 1; 21, 7.

1 S M

priest: "We have indeed been segregated from women as on previous occasions. Whenever I go on a journey, all the young men are consecrated—even for a secular journey. All the more so today, when they are consecrated at arms!" 7* So the priest gave him holy bread, for no other bread was on hand except the showbread which had been removed from the LORD's presence and replaced by fresh bread when it was taken away. 8 One of Saul's servants was there that day, detained before the LORD; his name was Doeg the Edomite, and he was Saul's chief henchman.

The Sword of Goliath

9 David then asked Ahimelech: "Do you have a spear or a sword on hand? I brought along neither my sword nor my weapons, because the king's business was urgent." 10* The priest replied: "The sword of Goliath the Philistine, whom you killed in the Vale of the Terebinth, is here [wrapped in a mantle] behind an ephod. If you wish to take that, take it; there is no sword here except that one." David said: "There is none to match it. Give it to me!"

David a Fugitive

11* That same day David took to flight from Saul, going to Achish, king of Gath. 12* But the servants of Achish said, "Is this not David, the king of the land? During their dances do they not sing,

'Saul has slain his thousands,
  but David his ten thousands'?"

13 David took note of these remarks and became very much afraid of Achish, king of Gath. 14 So, as they watched, he feigned insanity and acted like a madman in their hands, drumming on the doors of the gate and drooling onto his beard. 15 Finally Achish said to his servants: "You see the man is mad. Why did you bring him to me? 16 Do I not have enough madmen, that you bring in this one to carry on in my presence? Should this fellow come into my house?"

22 1* David left Gath and escaped to the cave of Adullam. When his brothers and the rest of his family heard about it, they came down to him there. 2 He was joined by all those who were in difficulties or in debt, or who were embittered, and he became their leader. About four hundred men were with him.

3 From there David went to Mizpeh of Moab and said to the king of Moab, "Let my father and mother stay with you, until I learn what God will do for me." 4† He left them with the king of Moab, and they stayed with him as long as David remained in the refuge.

5 But the prophet Gad said to David: "Do not remain in the refuge. Leave, and go to the land of Judah." And so David left and went to the forest of Hereth.

Doeg Betrays Ahimelech

6* Now Saul heard that David and his men had been located. At the time he was sitting in Gibeah under a tamarisk tree on the high place, holding his spear, while all his servants were standing by. 7* So he said to them: "Listen, men of Benjamin! Will the son of Jesse give all of you fields and vineyards? Will he make each of you an officer over a thousand or a hundred men, 8 that you have all conspired against me and no one tells me that my son has made an agreement with the son of Jesse? None of you shows sympathy for me or discloses to me that my son has stirred up my servant to be an enemy against me, as is the case today." 9* Then Doeg the Edomite, who was standing with the officers of Saul, spoke up: "I saw the son of Jesse come to Ahimelech, son of Ahitub, in Nob. 10 He consulted the LORD for him and gave him supplies, and the sword of Goliath the Philistine as well."

Slaughter of the Priests

11 At this the king sent a summons to Ahimelech the priest, son of Ahitub, and to all his family who were priests in Nob; and they all came to the king. 12 Then Saul said, "Listen, son of Ahitub!" He replied, "Yes, my lord." 13 Saul asked him, "Why did you conspire against me with the son of Jesse by giving him food and a sword and by consulting God for him, that he might rebel against me and become my enemy, as is the case today?" 14 Ahimelech answered the king: "And who among all your servants is as loyal as David, the king's son-in-law, captain of your bodyguard, and honored in your own house? 15 Is this the first time I have consulted God for him? No indeed! Let not the king accuse his servant or anyone in my family of such a thing. Your servant knows nothing at all, great or small, about the whole matter." 16 But the king said, "You shall die, Ahimelech, with all your family." 17* The king then commanded his henchmen standing by:

† **22, 4–5:** *Refuge:* seemingly connected with the cave complex spoken of in v 1.

21, 7: 1 Sm 22, 9; Lv 24,   5–9; Mt 12, 3f; Mk 2,

26; Lk 6, 3ff.   Mi 1, 15.
21, 10: 1 Sm 17, 51.54.   22, 6: Ps 52.
21, 11: 1 Sm 27, 2; 29, 5.   22, 7: 1 Sm 8, 14.
21, 12: 1 Sm 18, 7; 29, 5.   22, 9f: 1 Sm 21, 2–10.
22, 1: 2 Sm 23, 13; Ps 63;   22, 17: 1 Sm 2, 31.33; 21, 7.

"Make the rounds and kill the priests of the LORD, for they assisted David. They knew he was a fugitive and yet failed to inform me." But the king's servants refused to lift a hand to strike the priests of the LORD. 18 The king therefore commanded Doeg, "You make the rounds and kill the priests!" So Doeg the Edomite went from one to the next and killed the priests himself, slaying on that day eighty-five who wore the linen ephod. 19 Saul also put the priestly city of Nob to the sword, including men and women, children and infants, and oxen, asses and sheep.

Abiathar Escapes

20* One son of Ahimelech, son of Ahitub, named Abiathar, escaped and fled to David. 21 When Abiathar told David that Saul had slain the priests of the LORD, 22 David said to him: "I knew that day, when Doeg the Edomite was there, that he would surely tell Saul. I am responsible for the death of all your family. 23 Stay with me. Fear nothing; he that seeks your life must seek my life also. You are under my protection."

Keilah Liberated

23 1* David received information that the Philistines were attacking Keilah and plundering the threshing floors. 2* So he consulted the LORD, inquiring, "Shall I go and defeat these Philistines?" The LORD answered, "Go, for you will defeat the Philistines and rescue Keilah." 3 But David's men said to him: "We are afraid here in Judah. How much more so if we go to Keilah against the forces of the Philistines!" 4 Again David consulted the LORD, who answered, "Go down to Keilah, for I will deliver the Philistines into your power." 5 David then went with his men to Keilah and fought with the Philistines. He drove off their cattle and inflicted a severe defeat on them, and thus rescued the inhabitants of Keilah.

6* Abiathar, son of Ahimelech, who had fled to David, went down with David to Keilah, taking the ephod with him.

Flight from Keilah

7 When Saul was told that David had entered Keilah, he said: "God has put him in my grip. Now he has shut himself in, for he has entered a city with gates and bars." 8 Saul then called all the people to war, in order to go down to Keilah and besiege David and his men. 9* When David found out that Saul was planning to harm him, he said to the priest Abiathar, "Bring forward the ephod."

10 David then said: "O LORD God of Israel, your servant has heard a report that Saul plans to come to Keilah, to destroy the city on my account. 11 Will they hand me over? And now: will Saul come down as your servant has heard? O LORD God of Israel, tell your servant." The LORD answered, "He will come down." 12 David then asked, "Will the citizens of Keilah deliver me and my men into the grasp of Saul?" And the LORD answered, "Yes." 13 So David and his men, about six hundred in number, left Keilah and wandered from place to place. When Saul was informed that David had escaped from Keilah, he abandoned the expedition.

David and Jonathan in Horesh

14 David now lived in the refuges in the desert, or in the barren hill country near Ziph. Though Saul sought him continually, the LORD did not deliver David into his grasp. 15 David was apprehensive because Saul had come out to seek his life; but while he was at Horesh in the barrens near Ziph, 16* Saul's son, Jonathan, came down there to David and strengthened his resolve in the LORD. 17 He said to him: "Have no fear, my father Saul shall not lay a hand to you. You shall be king of Israel and I shall be second to you. Even my father Saul knows this." 18* They made a joint agreement before the LORD in Horesh, where David remained, while Jonathan returned to his home.

Treachery of the Ziphites

19* Some of the Ziphites went up to Saul in Gibeah and said, "David is hiding among us, now in the refuges, and again at Horesh, or on the hill of Hachilah, south of the wasteland. 20 Therefore, whenever the king wishes to come down, let him do so. It will be our task to deliver him into the king's grasp." 21* Saul replied: "The LORD bless you for your sympathy toward me. 22 Go now and make sure once more! Take note of the place where he sets foot" (for he thought, perhaps they are playing some trick on me). 23 "Look around and learn in which of all the various hiding places he is holding out. Then come back to me with sure information, and I will go with you. If he is in the region, I will search him out among all the families of Judah." 24* So they went off to Ziph ahead of Saul. At this time David and his men were in the desert below Maon, in the Arabah south of the wasteland.

Escape from Saul

25 When Saul and his men came looking for him, David got word of it and went down to the

22, 20: 1 Sm 23, 6; 30, 7;
    1 Kgs 2, 28f.
23, 1: Jos 15, 44.

23, 2: 1 Sm 28, 6.
23, 6: 1 Sm 22, 20; 30, 7.
23, 9: 1 Sm 2, 28.

23, 16: 1 Sm 18, 1.
23, 18: 1 Sm 18, 3; 20, 8.
23, 19: 1 Sm 26, 1–3; Ps 54.

23, 21: 2 Sm 2, 5.
23, 24: 1 Sm 25, 2.

gorge in the desert below Maon. Saul heard of this and pursued David into the desert below Maon. 26 As Saul moved along one rim of the gorge, David and his men took to the other. David was in anxious flight to escape Saul, and Saul and his men were attempting to outflank David and his men in order to capture them, 27 when a messenger came to Saul, saying, "Come quickly, because the Philistines have invaded the land." 28 Saul interrupted his pursuit of David and went to meet the Philistines. This is how that place came to be called the Gorge of Divisions.

David Spares Saul

24 1 David then went up from there and stayed in the refuges behind Engedi. 2 And when Saul returned from the pursuit of the Philistines, he was told that David was in the desert near Engedi. 3 So Saul took three thousand picked men from all Israel and went in search of David and his men in the direction of the wild goat crags. 4* When he came to the sheepfolds along the way, he found a cave, which he entered to ease nature. David and his men were occupying the inmost recesses of the cave.

5 David's servants said to him, "This is the day of which the LORD said to you, 'I will deliver your enemy into your grasp; do with him as you see fit.' " So David moved up and stealthily cut off an end of Saul's mantle. 6* Afterward, however, David regretted that he had cut off an end of Saul's mantle. 7* He said to his men, "The LORD forbid that I should do such a thing to my master, the LORD'S anointed, as to lay a hand on him, for he is the LORD'S anointed." 8 With these words David restrained his men and would not permit them to attack Saul. Saul then left the cave and went on his way. 9 David also stepped out of the cave, calling to Saul, "My lord the king!" When Saul looked back, David bowed to the ground in homage 10 and asked Saul: "Why do you listen to those who say, 'David is trying to harm you'? 11 You see for yourself today that the LORD just now delivered you into my grasp in the cave. I had some thought of killing you, but I took pity on you instead. I decided, 'I will not raise a hand against my lord, for he is the LORD'S anointed and a father to me.' 12* Look here at this end of your mantle which I hold. Since I cut off an end of your mantle and did not kill you, see and be convinced that I plan no harm and no rebellion. I have done you no wrong, though you are hunting me down to take my life. 13 The LORD will judge between me and you, and the LORD will exact justice from you in my case. I shall not touch you. 14 The old

proverb says, 'From the wicked comes forth wickedness.' So I will take no action against you. 15 Against whom are you on campaign, O king of Israel? Whom are you pursuing? A dead dog, or a single flea! 16* The LORD will be the judge; he will decide between me and you. May he see this, and take my part, and grant me justice beyond your reach!"

did you KNOW?

The LORD's Anointed

Throughout human history, oil has been used as medicine, perfume, and a symbol of blessing. The Israelite kings and prophets were anointed with oil to symbolize the powerful spirit of God present to them as they fulfilled their important role. Often it was olive oil mixed with a small amount of perfume. Oil plays a symbolic role throughout the Bible and has historically played an important role in the life of the church. In many Old Testament texts, oil was reserved for priests, kings, and people of high importance. Today we use oil in most of the sacraments of the church because we are the "priestly people."

The Hebrew word *mashiah*, translated in 1 Sm 24, 7 as "anointed [one]," is the root of the English word *messiah*. Often applied to kings in the Old Testament, this title was attached in the second century B.C. to the one "like David" who was expected to come (see Dn 9, 25). *Mashiah* translated into Greek is *christos*, which became the title given to Jesus by his followers: Jesus, the Christ; Jesus, the anointed one; Jesus, the Messiah.

Saul's Remorse

17 When David finished saying these things to Saul, Saul answered, "Is that your voice, my son David?" And he wept aloud. 18 Saul then said to David: "You are in the right rather than I; you have treated me generously, while I have done you harm.

24, 4: Ps 57.
24, 6: 1 Sm 15, 27.

24, 7: 1 Sm 10, 1; 31, 4;
    2 Sm 1, 14.

24, 12: Rom 12, 19.

24, 16: 1 Sm 18, 19.31; 26, 19;
    Pss 35, 1ff; 43, 1.

¹⁹ Great is the generosity you showed me today, when the LORD delivered me into your grasp and you did not kill me. ²⁰ For if a man meets his enemy, does he send him away unharmed? May the LORD reward you generously for what you have done this day. ²¹* And now, since I know that you shall surely be king and that sovereignty over Israel shall come into your possession, ²²* swear to me by the LORD that you will not destroy my descendants and that you will not blot out my name and family." ²³ David gave Saul his oath and Saul returned home, while David and his men went up to the refuge.

Death of Samuel

25

¹* Samuel died, and all Israel gathered to mourn him; they buried him at his home in Ramah.

Nabal and Abigail

²* Then David went down to the desert of Maon. There was a man of Maon who had property in Carmel; he was very wealthy, owning three thousand sheep and a thousand goats. At this time he was present for the shearing of his flock in Carmel. ³* The man was named Nabal, his wife, Abigail. The woman was intelligent and attractive, but Nabal himself, a Calebite, was harsh and ungenerous in his behavior. ⁴ When David heard in the desert that Nabal was shearing his flock, ⁵ he sent ten young men, instructing them: "Go up to Carmel. Pay Nabal a visit and greet him in my name. ⁶ Say to him, 'Peace be with you, my brother, and with your family, and with all who belong to you. ⁷ I have just heard that shearers are with you. Now, when your shepherds were with us, we did them no injury, neither did they miss anything all the while they were in Carmel. ⁸ Ask your servants and they will tell you so. Look kindly on these young men, since we come at a festival time. Please give your servants and your son David whatever you can manage.' "

⁹ When David's young men arrived, they delivered this message fully to Nabal in David's name, and then waited. ¹⁰ But Nabal answered the servants of David: "Who is David? Who is the son of Jesse? Nowadays there are many servants who run away from their masters. ¹¹ Must I take my bread, my wine, my meat that I have slaughtered for my own shearers, and give them to men who come from I know not where?" ¹² So David's young men retraced their steps and on their return reported to him all that had been said. ¹³ Thereupon David said

to his men, "Let everyone gird on his sword." And so everyone, David included, girded on his sword. About four hundred men went up after David, while two hundred remained with the baggage.

¹⁴ But Nabal's wife Abigail was informed of this by one of the servants, who said: "David sent messengers from the desert to greet our master, but he flew at them screaming. ¹⁵ Yet these men were very good to us. We were done no injury, neither did we miss anything all the while we were living among them during our stay in the open country. ¹⁶ For us they were like a rampart night and day the whole time we were pasturing the sheep near them. ¹⁷ Now, see what you can do, for you must realize that otherwise evil is in store for our master and for his whole family. He is so mean that no one can talk to him." ¹⁸ Abigail quickly got together two hundred loaves, two skins of wine, five dressed sheep, five seahs of roasted grain, a hundred cakes of pressed raisins, and two hundred cakes of pressed figs, and loaded them on asses. ¹⁹ She then said to her servants, "Go on ahead; I will follow you." But she did not tell her husband Nabal.

²⁰ As she came down through a mountain defile riding on an ass, David and his men were also coming down from the opposite direction. When she met them, ²¹ David had just been saying: "Indeed, it was in vain that I guarded all this man's possessions in the desert, so that he missed nothing. He has repaid good with evil. ²²* May God do thus and so to David, if by morning I leave a single male alive among all those who belong to him." ²³ As soon as Abigail saw David, she dismounted quickly from the ass and, falling prostrate on the ground before David, did him homage. ²⁴ As she fell at his feet she said:

"My lord, let the blame be mine. Please let your handmaid speak to you, and listen to the words of your handmaid. ²⁵† Let not my lord pay attention to that worthless man Nabal, for he is just like his name. Fool is his name, and he acts the fool. I, your handmaid, did not see the young men whom my lord sent. ²⁶† Now, therefore, my lord, as the LORD lives, and as you live, it is the LORD who has kept you from shedding blood and from avenging yourself personally. May your enemies and those who seek to harm my lord become as Nabal! ²⁷ Accept this present, then, which your maidservant has brought for my lord, and let it be given to the young men who follow my lord. ²⁸ Please forgive the transgression of your handmaid, for the LORD shall certainly establish a lasting dynasty for my lord, because your

---

25, 25: *Fool is his name:* Nabal in Hebrew means "a fool."
25, 26: Abigail anticipates that some misfortune will shortly overtake Nabal, as in fact it does (vv 37–38).

24, 21: 1 Sm 26, 25.
24, 22: 2 Sm 9, 1ff.
25, 1: 1 Sm 28, 3; Sir 46, 13–20.
25, 2: 1 Sm 23, 24; Jos 15, 55.
25, 3: 1 Sm 27, 3; Jos 14, 6; 1 Chr 2, 42.45.
25, 22: 1 Kgs 16, 11; 21, 21; 2 Kgs 9, 8.

lordship is fighting the battles of the LORD, and there is no evil to be found in you your whole life long. 29*† If anyone rises to pursue you and to seek your life, may the life of my lord be bound in the bundle of the living in the care of the LORD your God; but may he hurl out the lives of your enemies as from the hollow of a sling. 30* And when the LORD carries out for my lord the promise of success he has made concerning you, and appoints you as commander over Israel, 31 you shall not have this as a qualm or burden on your conscience, my lord, for having shed innocent blood or for having avenged yourself personally. When the LORD confers this benefit on your lordship, remember your handmaid." 32 David said to Abigail: "Blessed be the LORD, the God of Israel, who sent you to meet me today. 33 Blessed be your good judgment and blessed be you yourself, who this day have prevented me from shedding blood and from avenging myself personally. 34 Otherwise, as the LORD, the God of Israel, lives, who has restrained me from harming you, if you had not come so promptly to meet me, by dawn Nabal would not have had a single man or boy left alive." 35 David then took from her what she had brought him and said to her: "Go up to your home in peace! See, I have granted your request as a personal favor."

Nabal's Death

36 When Abigail came to Nabal, there was a drinking party in his house like that of a king, and Nabal was merry because he was very drunk. So she told him nothing at all before daybreak the next morning. 37 But then, when Nabal had become sober, his wife told him what had happened. At this his courage died within him, and he became like a stone. 38 About ten days later the LORD struck him and he died. 39 On hearing that Nabal was dead, David said: "Blessed be the LORD, who has requited the insult I received at the hand of Nabal, and who restrained his servant from doing evil, but has punished Nabal for his own evil deeds."

David Marries Abigail and Ahinoam

David then sent a proposal of marriage to Abigail. 40 When David's servants came to Abigail in Carmel, they said to her, "David has sent us to you that he may take you as his wife." 41 Rising and bowing to the ground, she answered, "Your handmaid would become a slave to wash the feet of my lord's servants." 42 She got up immediately, mounted an ass,

and followed David's messengers, with her five maids following in attendance upon her. She became his wife, 43* and David also married Ahinoam of Jezreel. Thus both of them were his wives; but Saul gave David's wife Michal, Saul's own daughter, to Palti, son of Laish, who was from Gallim.*

Saul's Life Again Spared

26 1* Men from Ziph came to Saul in Gibeah, reporting that David was hiding on the hill of Hachilah at the edge of the wasteland. 2 So Saul went off down to the desert of Ziph with three thousand picked men of Israel, to search for David in the desert of Ziph. 3 Saul camped beside the road on the hill of Hachilah, at the edge of the wasteland. David, who was living in the desert, saw that Saul had come into the desert after him 4 and sent out scouts, who confirmed Saul's arrival. 5* David himself then went to the place where Saul was encamped and examined the spot where Saul and Abner, son of Ner, the general, had their sleeping quarters. Saul's were within the barricade, and all his soldiers were camped around him. 6* David asked Ahimelech the Hittite, and Abishai, son of Zeruiah and brother of Joab, "Who will go down into the camp with me to Saul?" Abishai replied, "I will." 7 So David and Abishai went among Saul's soldiers by night and found Saul lying asleep within the barricade, with his spear thrust into the ground at his head and Abner and his men sleeping around him.

8* Abishai whispered to David: "God has delivered your enemy into your grasp this day. Let me nail him to the ground with one thrust of the spear; I will not need a second thrust!" 9 But David said to Abishai, "Do not harm him, for who can lay hands on the LORD'S anointed and remain unpunished? 10 As the LORD lives," David continued, "it must be the LORD himself who will strike him, whether the time comes for him to die, or he goes out and perishes in battle. 11 But the LORD forbid that I touch his anointed! Now take the spear which is at his head and the water jug, and let us be on our way." 12 So David took the spear and the water jug from their place at Saul's head, and they got away without anyone's seeing or knowing or awakening. All remained asleep, because the LORD had put them into a deep slumber.

David Taunts Abner

13 Going across to an opposite slope, David stood on a remote hilltop at a great distance from

---

25, 29: The bundle of the living: the figure is perhaps taken from the practice of tying up valuables in a kerchief or bag for safekeeping. Abigail desires that David enjoy permanent peace and security, but that his enemies be subject to constant agitation and humiliation like a stone whirled about, cast out of the sling, and thereafter disregarded.

25, 29: Ps 69, 28.
25, 30: 1 Sm 13, 14; 2 Sm 3, 10.
25, 43: 1 Sm 27, 3.
25, 43: 1 Sm 18, 20; 27, 3; 30, 5; 2 Sm 3, 2.13ff;

1 Chr 3, 1.
26, 1f: 1 Sm 23, 19f; Ps 54.
26, 5: 1 Sm 17, 20.
26, 6: 1 Chr 2, 16.
26, 8: 1 Sm 18, 11; 19, 10.

Abner, son of Ner, and the troops. ¹⁴ He then shouted, "Will you not answer, Abner?" And Abner answered, "Who is it that calls me?" ¹⁵ David said to
Abner: "Are you not a man whose like does not exist in Israel? Why, then, have you not guarded your
lord the king when one of his subjects went to kill
the king, your lord? ¹⁶ This is no creditable service
you have performed. As the LORD lives, you people
deserve death because you have not guarded your
lord, the LORD's anointed. Go, look: where are the
king's spear and the water jug that was at his head?"

Saul Admits His Guilt

¹⁷ Saul recognized David's voice and asked, "Is
that your voice, my son David?" David answered,
"Yes, my lord the king." ¹⁸ He continued: "Why
does my lord pursue his servant? What have I done?
What evil do I plan? ¹⁹*† Please, now, let my lord
the king listen to the words of his servant. If the
LORD has incited you against me, let an offering appease him; but if men, may they be cursed before
the LORD, because they have exiled me so that this
day I have no share in the LORD's inheritance, but
am told: 'Go, serve other gods!' ²⁰ Do not let my
blood flow to the ground far from the presence of
the LORD. For the king of Israel has come out to
seek a single flea as if he were hunting partridge in
the mountains." ²¹ Then Saul said: "I have done
wrong. Come back, my son David, I will not harm
you again, because you have held my life precious
today. Indeed, I have been a fool and have made a
serious mistake." ²² But David answered: "Here is
the king's spear. Let an attendant come over to get
it. ²³* The LORD will reward each man for his justice
and faithfulness. Today, though the LORD delivered
you into my grasp, I would not harm the LORD's
anointed. ²⁴ As I valued your life highly today, so
may the LORD value my life highly and deliver me
from all difficulties." ²⁵* Then Saul said to David:
"Blessed are you, my son David! You shall certainly
succeed in whatever you undertake." David went
his way, and Saul returned to his home.

Refuge among Philistines

27 ¹ But David said to himself: "I shall perish some day at the hand of Saul. I have
no choice but to escape to the land of the Philistines; then Saul will give up his continuous search
for me throughout the land of Israel, and I shall be
out of his reach." ²* Accordingly, David departed

with his six hundred men and went over to Achish,
son of Maoch, king of Gath. ³* David and his men
lived in Gath with Achish; each one had his family,
and David had his two wives, Ahinoam from Jezreel
and Abigail, the widow of Nabal from Carmel.
⁴ When Saul was told that David had fled to Gath,
he no longer searched for him.

In Ziklag

⁵ David said to Achish: "If I meet with your approval, let me have a place to live in one of the
country towns. Why should your servant live with
you in the royal city?" ⁶*† That same day Achish
gave him Ziklag, which has, therefore, belonged to
the kings of Judah up to the present time. ⁷* In all,
David lived a year and four months in the country
of the Philistines.

Raids on Israel's Foes

⁸* David and his men went up and made raids on
the Geshurites, Girzites, and Amalekites—peoples living in the land between Telam, on the approach to
Shur, and the land of Egypt. ⁹ In attacking the land
David would not leave a man or woman alive, but
would carry off sheep, oxen, asses, camels, and
clothes. On his return he brought these to Achish,
¹⁰* who asked, "Whom did you raid this time?" And
David answered, "The Negeb of Judah," or "The
Negeb of Jarahmeel," or "The Negeb of the Kenites."
¹¹ But David would not leave a man or woman alive
to be brought to Gath, fearing that they would betray him by saying, "This is what David did." This
was his custom as long as he lived in the country of
the Philistines. ¹² And Achish trusted David, thinking, "He must certainly be detested by his people Israel. I shall have him as my vassal forever."

28 ¹ In those days the Philistines mustered
their military forces to fight against Israel.
So Achish said to David, "You realize, of course, that
you and your men must go out on campaign with
me to Jezreel." ² David answered Achish, "Good!
Now you shall learn what your servant can do."
Then Achish said to David, "I shall appoint you my
permanent bodyguard."

³* Now Samuel had died and, after being
mourned by all Israel, was buried in his city,
Ramah. Meanwhile Saul had driven mediums and
fortune-tellers out of the land.

---

† **26, 19:** *The LORD's inheritance:* the land of Israel (Dt 32, 8f),
under the Lord's special protection, where he could be freely worshiped.
27, 6: *Has . . . belonged to the kings of Judah:* as a personal
holding, outside the system of tribal lands; Jerusalem, when taken by
David, had a similar status (2 Sm 5, 7–9).

26, 19: 1 Sm 24, 16.   27, 6: 1 Sm 30, 1.
26, 23: 1 Sm 18, 20.   27, 7: 1 Sm 29, 3.
26, 25: 1 Sm 24, 21.   27, 8: 1 Sm 15, 3.7.
27, 2: 1 Sm 21, 11–16.   27, 10: 1 Sm 30, 14.29; 1 Chr
27, 3: 1 Sm 25, 3.44; 30, 3ff;   2, 9.25.42.
   2 Sm 2, 3.   28, 3: 1 Sm 25, 1; Sir 46, 20.

Saul in Dismay

⁴ The Philistine levies advanced to Shunem and encamped. Saul, too, mustered all Israel; they camped on Gilboa. ⁵ When Saul saw the camp of the Philistines, he was dismayed and lost heart completely. ⁶* He therefore consulted the LORD; but the LORD gave no answer, whether in dreams or by the Urim or through prophets. ⁷* Then Saul said to his servants, "Find me a woman who is a medium, to whom I can go to seek counsel through her." His servants answered him, "There is a woman in Endor who is a medium."

The Witch of Endor

⁸* So he disguised himself, putting on other clothes, and set out with two companions. They came to the woman by night, and Saul said to her, "Tell my fortune through a ghost; conjure up for me the one I ask you to." ⁹ But the woman answered him, "You are surely aware of what Saul has done, in driving the mediums and fortune-tellers out of the land. Why, then, are you laying snares for my life, to have me killed?" ¹⁰ But Saul swore to her by the LORD, "As the LORD lives, you shall incur no blame for this." ¹¹ Then the woman asked him, "Whom do you want me to conjure up?" and he answered, "Samuel."

Samuel Appears

¹²† When the woman saw Samuel, she shrieked at the top of her voice and said to Saul, "Why have you deceived me? You are Saul!" ¹³ But the king said to her, "Have no fear. What do you see?" The woman answered Saul, "I see a preternatural being rising from the earth." ¹⁴ "What does he look like?" asked Saul. And she replied, "It is an old man who is rising, clothed in a mantle." Saul knew that it was Samuel, and so he bowed face to the ground in homage.

Saul's Doom

¹⁵* Samuel then said to Saul, "Why do you disturb me by conjuring me up?" Saul replied: "I am in great straits, for the Philistines are waging war against me and God has abandoned me. Since he no longer answers me through prophets or in dreams, I have called you to tell me what I should do." ¹⁶* To this Samuel said: "But why do you ask

me, if the LORD has abandoned you and is with your neighbor? ¹⁷ The LORD has done to you what he foretold through me: he has torn the kingdom from your grasp and has given it to your neighbor David. ¹⁸* "Because you disobeyed the LORD's directive and would not carry out his fierce anger against Amalek, the LORD has done this to you today. ¹⁹* Moreover, the LORD will deliver Israel, and you as well, into the clutches of the Philistines. By tomorrow you and your sons will be with me, and the LORD will have delivered the army of Israel into the hands of the Philistines."

Saul's Despair

²⁰ Immediately Saul fell full length on the ground, for he was badly shaken by Samuel's message. Moreover, he had no bodily strength left, since he had eaten nothing all that day and night. ²¹ Then the woman came to Saul, and seeing that he was quite terror-stricken, said to him: "Remember, your maidservant obeyed you: I took my life in my hands and fulfilled the request you made of me. ²² Now you, in turn, please listen to your maidservant. Let me set something before you to eat, so that you may have strength when you go on your way." ²³ But he refused, saying, "I will not eat." However, when his servants joined the woman in urging him, he listened to their entreaties, got up from the ground, and sat on a couch. ²⁴ The woman had a stall-fed calf in the house, which she now quickly slaughtered. Then taking flour, she kneaded it and baked unleavened bread. ²⁵ She set the meal before Saul and his servants, and they ate. Then they stood up and left the same night.

David's Aid Rejected

29 ¹* Now the Philistines had mustered all their forces in Aphek, and the Israelites were encamped at the spring of Harod near Jezreel. ² As the Philistine lords were marching their groups of a hundred and a thousand, David and his men were marching in the rear guard with Achish. ³* The Philistine chiefs asked, "What are those Hebrews doing here?" And Achish answered them: "Why, that is David, the officer of Saul, king of Israel. He has been with me now for a year or two, and I have no fault to find with him from the day he came over to me until the present." ⁴* But the Philistine chiefs

---

† **28, 12:** Human beings cannot communicate at will with the souls of the dead. God may, however, permit a departed soul to appear to the living and even to disclose things unknown to them. Saul's own prohibition of necromancy and divination (v 3) was in keeping with the consistent teaching of the Old Testament. If we are to credit the reality of the apparition to Saul, it was due, not to the summons of the witch, but to God's will; the woman merely furnished the occasion.

28, 6: 1 Sm 14, 37.41; Ex 28, 30; Lv 8, 8.
28, 7: Lv 19, 31; 20, 27; Dt 18, 10ff; 1 Chr 10, 13f; Acts 16, 16.
28, 8: 1 Kgs 14, 2.
28, 15: Sir 46, 20.
28, 16: 1 Sm 15, 27f.
28, 18: 1 Sm 15, 18f.26.
28, 19: 1 Sm 31, 2-6; Sir 46, 20.
29, 1: 1 Sm 4, 1.
29, 3: 1 Sm 27, 7.
29, 4: 1 Chr 12, 19f.

were angered at this and said to him: "Send that man back! Let him return to the place you picked out for him. He must not go down into battle with us, lest during the battle he become our enemy. For how else can he win back his master's favor, if not with the heads of these men of ours? [5]* Is this not the David of whom they sing during their dances,

'Saul has slain his thousands,
    but David his ten thousands'?"

[6] So Achish summoned David and said to him: "As the LORD lives, you are honest, and I should be pleased to have you active with me in the camp, for I have found nothing wrong with you from the day of your arrival to this day. But you are not welcome to the lords. [7] Withdraw peaceably, now, and do nothing that might displease the Philistine lords." [8] But David said to Achish: "What have I done? Or what have you against your servant from the first day I have been with you to this day, that I cannot go to fight against the enemies of my lord the king?" [9] "You know," Achish answered David, "that you are acceptable to me. But the Philistine chiefs have determined you are not to go up with us to battle. [10] So the first thing tomorrow, you and your lord's servants who came with you, go to the place I picked out for you. Do not decide to take umbrage at this; you are as acceptable to me as an angel of God. But make an early morning start, as soon as it grows light, and be on your way." [11] So David and his men left early in the morning to return to the land of the Philistines. The Philistines, however, went on up to Jezreel.

Ziklag in Ruins

30 [1]* Before David and his men reached Ziklag on the third day, the Amalekites had raided the Negeb and Ziklag, had stormed the city, and had set it on fire. [2] They had taken captive the women and all who were in the city, young and old, killing no one; they had carried them off when they left. [3] David and his men arrived at the city to find it burned to the ground and their wives, sons and daughters taken captive. [4] Then David and those who were with him wept aloud until they could weep no more. [5]* David's two wives, Ahinoam of Jezreel and Abigail, the widow of Nabal from Carmel, had also been carried off with the rest. [6] Now David found himself in great difficulty, for the men spoke of stoning him, so bitter were they over the fate of their sons and daughters. But with renewed trust in the LORD his God, [7]* David

said to Abiathar, the priest, son of Ahimelech, "Bring me the ephod!" When Abiathar brought him the ephod, [8] David inquired of the LORD, "Shall I pursue these raiders? Can I overtake them?" The LORD answered him, "Go in pursuit, for you shall surely overtake them and effect a rescue."

Raid of the Amalekites

[9] So David went off with his six hundred men and came as far as the Wadi Besor, where those who were to remain behind halted. [10] David continued the pursuit with four hundred men, but two hundred were too exhausted to cross the Wadi Besor and remained behind. [11] An Egyptian was found in the open country and brought to David. He was provided with food, which he ate, and given water to drink; [12] a cake of pressed figs and two cakes of pressed raisins were also offered to him. When he had eaten, he revived; he had not taken food nor drunk water for three days and three nights. [13] Then David asked him, "To whom do you belong, and where do you come from?" He replied: "I am an Egyptian, the slave of an Amalekite. My master abandoned me because I fell sick three days ago today. [14]* We raided the Negeb of the Cherethites, the territory of Judah, and the Negeb of Caleb; and we set Ziklag on fire." [15] David then asked him, "Will you lead me down to this raiding party?" He answered, "Swear to me by God that you will not kill me or deliver me to my master, and I will lead you to the raiding party." [16] He did lead them, and there were the Amalekites scattered all over the ground, eating, drinking, and in a festive mood because of all the rich booty they had taken from the land of the Philistines and from the land of Judah.

The Booty Recovered

[17]* From dawn to sundown David attacked them, putting them under the ban so that none escaped except four hundred young men, who mounted their camels and fled. [18] David recovered everything the Amalekites had taken, and rescued his two wives. [19] Nothing was missing, small or great, booty or sons or daughters, of all that the Amalekites had taken. David brought back everything. [20] Moreover, David took all the sheep and oxen, and as they drove them before him, they shouted, "This is David's spoil."

Division of the Spoils

[21] When David came to the two hundred men who had been too exhausted to follow him, and whom he had left behind at the Wadi Besor, they

29, 5: 1 Sm 18, 6f; 21, 11.
30, 1: 1 Sm 27, 6.10; 1 Chr 12, 21.

30, 5: 1 Sm 25, 42; 27, 3; 30, 5.
30, 7f: 1 Sm 2, 28; 23, 6; Ex 28, 30.

30, 14: 1 Sm 27, 10; Ez 25, 16.

30, 17: 1 Sm 15, 3; Jos 6, 17; Jgs 7, 12.

Suicide Is Not an Answer

In 1 Sm 31, 4, Saul commits suicide out of fear of what his enemies would do to him. His death leaves a gap for the Israelites, and David, Saul's enemy, deeply mourns his death in 2 Samuel, chapter 1.

A popular newspaper advice columnist printed a letter from someone who was writing to share a thought on suicide. He had decided that his life was not worth living anymore and planned to kill himself. The moment before he was about to do it, he thought about who would find him, and then he stopped. He realized that he couldn't put someone through the pain and suffering of finding him dead from suicide. Because he thought of another, he no longer looked at his life as hopeless.

No life is worthless! No pain is invincible! No matter how overwhelming your struggles and challenges seem, there are people who can help you and people who could not bear to lose you. Seek God for help, seek others for help—suicide is never a solution!

For more on suicide, see "Judas's Suicide," Mt 27, 3–10.

▶ I Sm 31, 1–6

came out to meet David and the men with him. On nearing them David greeted them. 22 But all the stingy and worthless men among those who had accompanied David spoke up to say, "Since they did not accompany us, we will not give them anything from the booty, except to each man his wife and children. Let them take those along and be on their way." 23 But David said: "You must not do this, my brothers, after what the LORD has given us. He has protected us and delivered into our grip the band that came against us. 24* Who could agree with this proposal of yours? Rather, the share of the one who goes down to battle and that of the one who remains with the baggage shall be the same; they shall share alike." 25* And from that day forward he made it a law and a custom in Israel, as it still is today.

David's Gifts to Judah

26 When David came to Ziklag, he sent part of the spoil to the elders of Judah, city by city, saying, "This is a gift to you from the spoil of the enemies of the LORD": 27 to those in Bethel, to those in Ramoth-negeb, to those in Jattir, 28 to those in Aroer, to those in Siphmoth, to those in Eshtemoa, 29* to those in Racal, to those in the Jerahmeelite cities, to those in the Kenite cities, 30 to those in Hormah, to those in Borashan, to those in Athach, 31 to those in Hebron, and to all the places frequented by David and his men.

Death of Saul and His Sons

31 1* As they pressed their attack on Israel, with the Israelites fleeing before them and falling mortally wounded on Mount Gilboa, 2* the Philistines pursued Saul and his sons closely, and slew Jonathan, Abinadab, and Malchishua, sons of Saul. 3 The battle raged around Saul, and the archers hit him; he was pierced through the abdomen. 4* Then Saul said to his armor-bearer, "Draw your sword and run me through, lest these uncircumcised come and make sport of me." But his armor-bearer, badly frightened, refused to do it. So Saul took his own sword and fell upon it. 5*† When the armor-bearer saw that Saul was dead, he too fell upon his sword and died with him. 6 Thus Saul, his three sons, and his armor-bearer died together on that same day.

7 When the Israelites on the slope of the valley and those along the Jordan saw that the men of Israel had fled and that Saul and his sons were dead, they too abandoned their cities and fled. Then the Philistines came and lived in those cities.

8 The day after the battle the Philistines came to strip the slain, and found Saul and his three sons lying on Mount Gilboa. 9* They cut off Saul's head and stripped him of his armor, and then sent the good news throughout the land of the Philistines to their idols and to the people. 10 They put his

---

31, 5: This report of the suicidal act of Saul is presented as a part of his downfall, to be judged accordingly.

30, 24: 1 Sm 17, 22; 25, 13.   30, 25: Nm 31, 27.

30, 29: 1 Sm 27, 10.
31, 1–13: 1 Chr 10, 1–12; 2 Sm
  1, 1–16; 4, 4.
31, 2: 1 Sm 14, 49; 28, 19;
  1 Chr 10, 2f.
31, 4: 1 Sm 24, 7; Jgs 9, 54;

1 Chr 10, 4.
31, 5: 1 Sm 10, 1; 26, 9;
  2 Mc 14, 42.
31, 9: 1 Sm 17, 54; 2 Sm 1,
  20; 2 Mc 15, 35.

armor in the temple of Astarte, but impaled his body on the wall of Beth-shan.

Burial of Saul

[11]* When the inhabitants of Jabesh-gilead heard what the Philistines had done to Saul, [12]† all their warriors set out, and after marching throughout the night, removed the bodies of Saul and his sons from the wall of Beth-shan, and brought them to Jabesh, where they cremated them. [13] Then they took their bones and buried them under the tamarisk tree in Jabesh, and fasted for seven days.

---

† **31, 12:** *Cremated them:* cremation was not normally practiced in Israel, though it was known in the country from pre-Israelite times.

31, 11ff: 1 Sm 11, 1–11; 2 Sm 2, 4–7.

Politician Guilty of Taking Foreign Bribes!" "Minister Accused of Sexual Misconduct!" "Athlete Arrested on Drug Charges!" Sometimes it seems as if the news is filled with one scandal after another. "What's happening in the world today?" we may ask in despair. "Are there no honest, decent people left?" After reading 2 Samuel, you will realize that scandals among the rich and powerful are nothing new. But somehow, God's will is accomplished despite human sin.

At a Glance

David Mourns Saul's Death (1, 1—2, 7).

IV. The Reign of David (2, 8—20, 25).

V. Appendixes (21, 1—24, 25).

In-depth

The main character in 2 Samuel is King David, whom we already met in 1 Samuel. The youngest of Jesse's sons, David is secretly anointed to succeed King Saul; he kills Goliath, plays music in Saul's court, and is befriended by the king's son Jonathan. At the beginning of 2 Samuel, when David takes the throne and quickly extends Israel's boundaries in every direction, everything looks hopeful for the nation.

As 2 Samuel continues, however, we discover that this hero is far from perfect: he sleeps with Bathsheba, the wife of one of his soldiers, and then tries to deceive the man when Bathsheba reports that she is pregnant. Later, he has the soldier killed and takes Bathsheba as his own. Soon, several tragedies befall his family, and further bad decisions hurt his reign, leaving us with a mixed picture of the second king of Israel. Was David a great saint or a great sinner?

It was through David that God established a new Covenant with the people of Israel (7, 1–17). This fact is underlined in a memorable way when David, after completing his own magnificent palace, declares that he will build a house for God. But God does not want a temple; God wishes to maintain a covenantal relationship with the people of Israel through all history: "Your throne shall stand firm forever" (verse 16).

Although a talented military leader and a powerful ruler, King David shared our broken human nature. The author of 2 Samuel reminds us that even the great and the mighty stand in need of God's help and mercy; even they must keep God's Covenant. Because of David's reliance on God, he became a symbol of the ideal king and of the future messiah. David's greatness—and our own—comes from a willing reliance on God.

Quick Facts

Period Covered
from 1000 to 961 B.C.

Author
same as for 1 Samuel

Theme
David's rise to power and his fall into sin

Of Note
Samuel does not appear in this book, although it carries his name.

The Second Book of *Samuel*

2 Samuel

Report of Saul's Death

1 [1]* After the death of Saul, David returned from his defeat of the Amalekites and spent two days in Ziklag. [2] On the third day a man came from Saul's camp, with his clothes torn and dirt on his head. Going to David, he fell to the ground in homage. [3] David asked him, "Where do you come from?" He replied, "I have escaped from the Israelite camp." [4] "Tell me what happened," David bade him. He answered that the soldiers had fled the battle and that many of them had fallen and were dead, among them Saul and his son Jonathan. [5] Then David said to the youth who was reporting to him, "How do you know that Saul and his son Jonathan are dead?" [6]* The youthful informant replied: "It was by chance that I found myself on Mount Gilboa and saw Saul leaning on his spear, with chariots and horsemen closing in on him. [7] He turned around and, seeing me, called me to him. When I said, 'Here I am,' [8] he asked me, 'Who are you?' and I replied, 'An Amalekite.' [9] Then he said to me, 'Stand up to me, please, and finish me off, for I am in great suffering, yet fully alive.' [10] So I stood up to him and dispatched him, for I knew that he could not survive his wound. I removed the crown from his head and the armlet from his arm and brought them here to my lord."

[11]* David seized his garments and rent them, and all the men who were with him did likewise. [12]* They mourned and wept and fasted until evening for Saul and his son Jonathan, and for the soldiers of the LORD of the clans of Israel, because they had fallen by the sword. [13] Then David said to the young man who had brought him the information, "Where are you from?" He replied, "I am the son of an Amalekite immigrant." [14]* David said to him, "How is it that you were not afraid to put forth your hand to desecrate the LORD's anointed?" [15] David then called one of the attendants and said to him, "Come, strike him down"; and the youth struck him a mortal blow. [16] Meanwhile David said to him, "You are responsible for your own death, for you testified against yourself when you said, 'I dispatched the LORD's anointed.' "

Elegy for Saul and Jonathan

[17] Then David chanted this elegy for Saul and his son Jonathan, [18]* which is recorded in the Book of Jashar to be taught to the Judahites. He sang:

[19]   "Alas! the glory of Israel, Saul,
    slain upon your heights;
  how can the warriors have fallen!

[20]*   "Tell it not in Gath,
    herald it not in the streets of Ashkelon,

1, 1: 1 Sm 30, 17–20; 31, 1-13.
1, 6–10: 2 Sm 4, 10; 1 Sm 31,

1–4; 1 Chr 10, 1-4.

1, 11: 2 Sm 13, 31.

1, 12: 1 Sm 31, 13.
1, 14: 1 Sm 10, 1; 24, 7; Ps 105, 15.

1, 18: Jos 10, 13.
1, 20: Jgs 16, 23; 1 Sm 31, 9; Mi 1, 10.

David the Musician

Most of us know that music can be a powerful force. Most of us listen to music every day. It helps us get through hard times. It is also an essential part of most celebrations. What would a wedding be like without music? What would a party be like without music? No doubt each of us has a favorite song or musician we turn to often, especially when we need a lift. And no doubt God works through music to touch our hearts.

David also knew the power of music. His song of mourning for Saul and Jonathan is an emotional tribute to both men, but especially to his close friend, Jonathan. If you are a musician, you know that God also works through you to touch the hearts of others and speak to them. Let David be your inspiration. He played the lyre (harp), sang, and wrote beautiful songs, which we call psalms. He prayed through music. There is a saying that goes, "Those who sing pray twice." David seemed to live that out in his life.

What are the songs and music that help you to pray and to recall God's presence? If you are a musician, when have you felt God's presence while making music?

▶ 2 Sm 1, 17–27

Lest the Philistine maidens rejoice,
   lest the daughters of the strangers exult!
21*†Mountains of Gilboa,
    may there be neither dew nor rain upon you,
    nor upsurgings of the deeps!
Upon you lie begrimed the warriors' shields,
    the shield of Saul, no longer anointed
      with oil.

22* "From the blood of the slain,
    from the bodies of the valiant,
The bow of Jonathan did not turn back,
    or the sword of Saul return unstained.
23 Saul and Jonathan, beloved and cherished,
    separated neither in life nor in death,
    swifter than eagles, stronger than lions!
24 Women of Israel, weep over Saul,
    who clothed you in scarlet and in finery,
    who decked your attire with ornaments
      of gold.

25 "How can the warriors have fallen—
    in the thick of the battle,
    slain upon your heights!
26* "I grieve for you, Jonathan my brother!
    most dear have you been to me;
More precious have I held love for you
    than love for women.

27 "How can the warriors have fallen,
    the weapons of war have perished!"

David Anointed King

2 ¹ After this David inquired of the LORD, "Shall I go up into one of the cities of Judah?" The LORD replied to him, "Yes." Then David asked, "Where shall I go?" He replied, "To Hebron." ²* So David went up there accompanied by his two wives, Ahinoam of Jezreel and Abigail, the widow of Nabal of Carmel. ³ David also brought up his men with their families, and they dwelt in the cities near Hebron. ⁴* Then the men of Judah came there and anointed David king of the Judahites.

A report reached David that the men of Jabesh-gilead had buried Saul. ⁵ So David sent messengers to the men of Jabesh-gilead and said to them: "May you be blessed by the LORD for having done this kindness to your lord Saul in burying him. ⁶ And now may the LORD be kind and faithful to you. I, too, will be generous to you for having done this. ⁷ Take courage, therefore, and prove yourselves valiant men, for though your lord Saul is dead, the Judahites have anointed me their king."

IV: The Reign of David

Ishbaal King of Israel

⁸* Abner, son of Ner, Saul's general, took Ishbaal, son of Saul, and brought him over to Mahanaim, ⁹ where he made him king over Gilead, the Ashurites, Jezreel, Ephraim, Benjamin, and the rest of Israel. ¹⁰ Ishbaal, son of Saul, was forty years old

---

1, 21: *Upsurgings of the deeps:* this reading attempts to recover from an unintelligible Hebrew phrase the poetic parallel to dew and rain. The sense would be a wish that the mountain should have neither moisture from above nor water from springs or wells.

1, 21: Gn 27, 28.
1, 22: 1 Sm 14, 47.
1, 26: 1 Sm 18, 1; 1 Mc 9, 21.
2, 2: 1 Sm 25, 42f.
2, 4: 1 Sm 31, 11ff.
2, 8: 1 Sm 14, 50.

when he became king over Israel, and he reigned for two years. The Judahites alone followed David. ¹¹* In all, David spent seven years and six months in Hebron as king of the Judahites.

Combat near Gibeon

¹² Now Abner, son of Ner, and the servants of Ishbaal, Saul's son, left Mahanaim for Gibeon. ¹³ Joab, son of Zeruiah, and David's servants also set out and met them at the pool of Gibeon. And they sat down, one group on one side of the pool and the other on the opposite side. ¹⁴ Then Abner said to Joab, "Let the young men rise and perform for us." Joab replied, "All right!" ¹⁵ So they rose and were counted off: twelve of the Benjaminites of Ishbaal, son of Saul, and twelve of David's servants. ¹⁶† Then each one grasped his opponent's head and thrust his sword into his opponent's side, and all fell down together. And so that place, which is in Gideon, was named the Field of the Sides.

Death of Asahel

¹⁷ After a very fierce battle that day, Abner and the men of Israel were defeated by David's servants. ¹⁸* The three sons of Zeruiah were there—Joab, Abishai, and Asahel. Asahel, who was as fleet of foot as a gazelle in the open field, ¹⁹* set out after Abner, turning neither right nor left in his pursuit. ²⁰ Abner turned around and said, "Is that you, Asahel?" He replied, "Yes." ²¹ Abner said to him, "Turn right or left; seize one of the young men and take what you can strip from him." But Asahel would not desist from his pursuit. ²²* Once more Abner said to Asahel: "Stop pursuing me! Why must I strike you to the ground? How could I face your brother Joab?" ²³ Still he refused to stop. So Abner struck him in the abdomen with the heel of his javelin, and the weapon protruded from his back. He fell there and died on the spot. And all who came to the place where Asahel had fallen and died, came to a halt. ²⁴ Joab and Abishai, however, continued the pursuit of Abner. The sun had gone down when they came to the hill of Ammah which lies east of the valley toward the desert near Geba.

Truce between Joab and Abner

²⁵ Here the Benjaminites rallied around Abner, forming a single group, and made a stand on the hilltop. ²⁶ Then Abner called to Joab and said: "Must the sword destroy to the utmost? Do you not know that afterward there will be bitterness? How much longer will you refrain from ordering the

people to stop the pursuit of their brothers?" ²⁷ Joab replied, "As God lives, if you had not spoken, the soldiers would not have been withdrawn from the pursuit of their brothers until morning." ²⁸ Joab then sounded the horn, and all the soldiers came to a halt, pursuing Israel no farther and fighting no more. ²⁹ Abner and his men marched all night long through the Arabah, crossed the Jordan, marched all through the morning, and came to Mahanaim. ³⁰ Joab, after interrupting the pursuit of Abner, assembled all the men. Besides Asahel, nineteen other servants of David were missing. ³¹ But David's servants had fatally wounded three hundred and sixty men of Benjamin, followers of Abner. ³² They took up Asahel and buried him in his father's tomb in Bethlehem. Joab and his men made an all-night march, and dawn found them in Hebron.

3 ¹ There followed a long war between the house of Saul and that of David, in which David grew stronger, but the house of Saul weaker.

Sons Born in Hebron

²* Sons were born to David in Hebron: his firstborn, Amnon, of Ahinoam from Jezreel; ³* the second, Chileab, of Abigail the widow of Nabal of Carmel; the third, Absalom, son of Maacah the daughter of Talmai, king of Geshur; ⁴* the fourth, Adonijah, son of Haggith; the fifth, Shephatiah, son of Abital; ⁵ and the sixth, Ithream, of David's wife Eglah. These were born to David in Hebron.

Ishbaal and Abner Quarrel

⁶ During the war between the house of Saul and of David, Abner was gaining power in the house of Saul. ⁷* Now Saul had had a concubine, Rizpah, the daughter of Aiah. And Ishbaal, son of Saul, said to Abner, "Why have you been intimate with my father's concubine?" ⁸ Enraged at the words of Ishbaal, Abner said, "Am I a dog's head in Judah? At present I am doing a kindness to the house of your father Saul, to his brothers and his friends, by keeping you out of David's clutches; yet this day you charge me with a crime involving a woman! ⁹* May God do thus and so to Abner if I do not carry out for David what the Lord swore to him— ¹⁰* that is, take away the kingdom from the house of Saul and establish the throne of David over Israel and over Judah from Dan to Beer-sheba." ¹¹ In his fear of Abner, Ishbaal was no longer able to say a word to him.

2, 16: The nature of this gruesome game is not clear, and the place name is variously given in the older texts.

2, 11: 2 Sm 5, 5; 1 Kgs 2, 11.   **2, 18:** 2 Sm 23, 24, 1 Chr 2, 16.

2, 19: 1 Chr 27, 7.
2, 22: 2 Sm 3, 27f.30.
3, 2–5: 1 Chr 3, 14.
3, 3: 2 Sm 13, 37; 15, 8.

3, 4: 1 Kgs 1, 5.
3, 7: 2 Sm 21, 8ff.
3, 9: Ru 1, 17.
3, 10: 2 Sm 5, 2; 1 Sm 25, 30.

Abner and David Reconciled

12 Then Abner sent messengers to David in Telam, where he was at the moment, to say, "Make an agreement with me, and I will aid you by bringing all Israel over to you." 13* He replied, "Very well, I will make an agreement with you. But one thing I require of you. You must not appear before me unless you bring back Michal, Saul's daughter, when you come to present yourself to me." 14 At the same time David sent messengers to Ishbaal, son of Saul, to say, "Give me my wife Michal, whom I espoused by paying a hundred Philistine foreskins." 15* Ishbaal sent for her and took her away from her husband Paltiel, son of Laish, 16 who followed her weeping as far as Bahurim. But Abner said to him, "Go back!" And he turned back.

17 Abner then said in discussion with the elders of Israel: "For a long time you have been seeking David as your king. 18 Now take action, for the LORD has said of David, 'By my servant David I will save my people Israel from the grasp of the Philistines and from the grasp of all their enemies.' " 19 Abner also spoke personally to Benjamin, and then went to make his own report to David in Hebron concerning all that would be agreeable to Israel and to the whole house of Benjamin. 20 When Abner, accompanied by twenty men, came to David in Hebron, David prepared a feast for Abner and for the men who were with him. 21 Then Abner said to David, "I will now go to assemble all Israel for my lord the king, that they may make an agreement with you; you will then be king over all whom you wish to rule." So David bade Abner farewell, and he went away in peace.

Death of Abner

22 Just then David's servants and Joab were coming in from an expedition, bringing much plunder with them. Abner, having been dismissed by David, was no longer with him in Hebron but had gone his way in peace. 23 When Joab and the whole force he had with him arrived, he was informed, "Abner, son of Ner, came to David; he has been sent on his way in peace." 24 So Joab went to the king and said: "What have you done? Abner came to you. Why did you let him go peacefully on his way? 25 Are you not aware that Abner came to deceive you and to learn the ins and outs of all that you are doing?" 26 Joab then left David, and without David's knowledge sent messengers after Abner, who brought him back from the cistern of Sirah. 27* When Abner returned to Hebron, Joab took him aside within the city gate as

though to speak with him privately. There he stabbed him in the abdomen, and he died in revenge for the killing of Joab's brother Asahel. 28* Later David heard of it and said: "Before the LORD, I and my kingdom are forever innocent. 29 May the full responsibility for the death of Abner, son of Ner, be laid to Joab and to all his family. May the men of Joab's family never be without one suffering from a discharge, or a leper, or one unmanly, one falling by the sword, or one in need of bread!" 30 [Joab and his brother Abishai had lain in wait for Abner because he killed their brother Asahel in battle at Gibeon.]

David Mourns Abner

31* Then David said to Joab and to all the people who were with him, "Rend your garments, gird yourselves with sackcloth, and mourn over Abner." King David himself followed the bier. 32 When they had buried Abner in Hebron, the king wept aloud at the grave of Abner, and the people also wept. 33 And the king sang this elegy over Abner:

"Would Abner have died like a fool?
34 Your hands were not bound with chains,
       nor your feet placed in fetters;
    As men fall before the wicked, you fell."

And all the people continued to weep for him. 35* Then they went to console David with food while it was still day. But David swore, "May God do thus and so to me if I eat bread or anything else before sunset." 36 All the people noted this with approval, just as they were pleased with everything that the king did. 37 So on that day all the people and all Israel came to know that the king had no part in the killing of Abner, son of Ner. 38 The king then said to his servants: "You must recognize that a great general has fallen today in Israel. 39* Although I am the anointed king, I am weak this day, and these men, the sons of Zeruiah, are too ruthless for me. May the LORD requite the evildoer in accordance with his evil deed."

Death of Ishbaal

4 1 When Ishbaal, son of Saul, heard that Abner had died in Hebron, he ceased to resist and all Israel was alarmed. 2* Ishbaal, son of Saul, had two company leaders named Baanah and Rechab, sons of Rimmon the Beerothite, of the tribe of Benjamin. [Beeroth, too, was ascribed to Benjamin: 3* the Beerothites fled to Gittaim, where they have been resident aliens to this day. 4*† Jonathan, son

---

† **4, 4:** Saul's grandson *Meribbaal* is the subject of ch 9 below. The text of this verse may owe its present place to the fact that pre-Christian copies of the Books of Samuel tended to confuse his name with that of his uncle Ishbaal, Saul's son and successor, a principal figure in chapters 2–4.

3, 13: 1 Sm 18, 20–27.
3, 15: 1 Sm 25, 44.
3, 27: 1 Kgs 2, 5.32.
3, 28.30: 2 Sm 2, 22f.
3, 31: 2 Sm 21, 10.
3, 35: Ru 1, 17.
3, 39: Ps 28, 4; Is 3, 11.
4, 2: 2 Sm 9, 3; Jos 9, 17f.
4, 3: Jos 18, 25.
4, 4: 2 Sm 9, 3; 19, 25.

of Saul, had a son named Meribbaal with crippled feet. He was five years old when the news about Saul and Jonathan came from Jezreel, and his nurse took him up and fled. But in their hasty flight, he fell and became lame.] ⁵ The sons of Rimmon the Beerothite, Rechab and Baanah, came into the house of Ishbaal during the heat of the day, while he was taking his siesta. ⁶ The portress of the house had dozed off while sifting wheat, and was asleep. So Rechab and his brother Baanah slipped past ⁷ and entered the house while Ishbaal was lying asleep in his bedroom. They struck and killed him, and cut off his head. Then, taking the head, they traveled on the Arabah road all night long.

The Murder Avenged

⁸ They brought the head of Ishbaal to David in Hebron and said to the king: "This is the head of Ishbaal, son of your enemy Saul, who sought your life. Thus has the LORD this day avenged my lord the king on Saul and his posterity." ⁹ But David replied to Rechab and his brother Baanah, sons of Rimmon the Beerothite: "As the LORD lives, who rescued me from all difficulty, ¹⁰* in Ziklag I seized and put to death the man who informed me of Saul's death, thinking himself the bearer of good news for which I ought to give him a reward. ¹¹ How much more now, when wicked men have slain an innocent man in bed at home, must I hold you responsible for his death and destroy you from the earth!" ¹²* So at a command from David, the young men killed them and cut off their hands and feet, hanging them up near the pool in Hebron. But he took the head of Ishbaal and buried it in Abner's grave in Hebron.

David King of Israel

5 ¹* All the tribes of Israel came to David in Hebron and said: "Here we are, your bone and your flesh. ²* In days past, when Saul was our king, it was you who led the Israelites out and brought them back. And the LORD said to you, 'You shall shepherd my people Israel and shall be commander of Israel.'" ³ When all the elders of Israel came to David in Hebron, King David made an agreement with them there before the LORD, and they anointed him king of Israel. ⁴ David was thirty years old when he became king, and he reigned for forty

years: ⁵* seven years and six months in Hebron over Judah, and thirty-three years in Jerusalem over all Israel and Judah.

Capture of Zion

⁶*† Then the king and his men set out for Jerusalem against the Jebusites who inhabited the region. David was told, "You cannot enter here: the blind and the lame will drive you away!" which was their way of saying, "David cannot enter here."* ⁷ But David did take the stronghold of Zion, which is the City of David. ⁸* On that day David said: "All who wish to attack the Jebusites must strike at them through the water shaft. The lame and the blind shall be the personal enemies of David." That is why it is said, "The blind and the lame shall not enter the palace." ⁹* David then dwelt in the stronghold, which is called the City of David; he built up the area from Millo to the palace. ¹⁰* David grew steadily more powerful, for the LORD of hosts was with him. ¹¹* Hiram, king of Tyre, sent ambassadors to David; he furnished cedar wood, as well as carpenters and masons, who built a palace for David.* ¹² And David knew that the LORD had established him as king of Israel and had exalted his rule for the sake of his people Israel.

David's Family in Jerusalem

¹³* David took more concubines and wives in Jerusalem after he had come from Hebron, and more sons and daughters were born to him in Jerusalem. ¹⁴ These are the names of those who were born to him in Jerusalem: Shammua, Shobab, Nathan, Solomon, ¹⁵ Ibhar, Elishua, Nepheg, Japhia, ¹⁶ Elishama, Baaliada, and Eliphelet.

Rout of the Philistines

¹⁷† When the Philistines heard that David had been anointed king of Israel, they all took the field in search of him. On hearing this, David went down to the refuge. ¹⁸† The Philistines came and overran the valley of Rephaim. ¹⁹ David inquired of the LORD, "Shall I attack the Philistines—will you deliver them into my grip?" The LORD replied to David, "Attack, for I will surely deliver the Philistines into your grip." ²⁰† David then went to Baal-perazim, where he defeated them. He said, "The

---

5, 6–12: David's most important military exploit, the taking of Jerusalem, is here presented before his battles with the Philistines, vv 17–25, which were earlier in time. The sense of vv 6 and 8 is in doubt.

5, 17: *Refuge:* probably near Adullam (1 Sm 22, 1–5).

5, 18–25: The successive defeats of the Philistines in the valley of Rephaim southwest of Jerusalem had the effect of blocking their access to the mountain ridge near Gibeon, and confining them to their holdings on the coast and in the foothills beyond Gezer to the west and south.

5, 20: *Baal-perazim:* means approximately "the lord of scatterings."

4, 10: 2 Sm 1, 6–10.14.16.
4, 12: Dt 21, 22f; 1 Sm 31, 10.
5, 1ff: 1 Chr 11, 1ff.
5, 2: 2 Sm 3, 10; Dt 17, 15; 1 Sm 18, 16.
5, 5: 2 Sm 2, 11; 1 Kgs 2, 11; 1 Chr 3, 4.
5, 6–10: 1 Chr 11, 4–9.
5, 6: Jos 15, 63; Jgs 1,
19.21; Is 29, 3.
5, 8: Lv 21, 18; Mt 21, 14f.
5, 9: 1 Kgs 3, 1; 11, 27.
5, 10: Pss 78, 70ff.89; 132, 13.
5, 11–25: 1 Chr 14, 1–16.
5, 11f: 1 Kgs 5, 15; 1 Chr 14, 1f.
5, 13–16: 1 Chr 3, 5–8; 14, 3–7.

LORD has scattered my enemies before me like waters that have broken free." That is why the place is called Baal-perazim. 21 They abandoned their gods there, and David and his men carried them away. 22 But the Philistines came up again and overran the valley of Rephaim. 23 So David inquired of the LORD, who replied: "You must not attack frontally, but circle their rear and meet them before the mastic trees. 24† When you hear a sound of marching in the tops of the mastic trees, act decisively, for the LORD will have gone forth before you to attack the camp of the Philistines." 25 David obeyed the LORD'S command and routed the Philistines from Gibeon as far as Gezer.

The Ark Brought to Jerusalem

6 1* David again assembled all the picked men of Israel, thirty thousand in number. 2* Then David and all the people who were with him set out for Baala of Judah to bring up from there the ark of God, which bears the name of the LORD of hosts enthroned above the cherubim. 3* The ark of God was placed on a new cart and taken away from the house of Abinadab on the hill. Uzzah and Ahio, sons of Abinadab, guided the cart, 4 with Ahio walking before it, 5* while David and all the Israelites made merry before the LORD with all their strength, with singing and with citharas, harps, tambourines, sistrums and cymbals. 6 When they came to the threshing floor of Nodan, Uzzah reached out his hand to the ark of God and steadied it, for the oxen were making it tip. 7 But the LORD was angry with Uzzah; God struck him on that spot, and he died there before God. 8* David was disturbed because the LORD had vented his anger on Uzzah. (The place has been called Perez-uzzah down to the present day.) 9 David feared the LORD that day and said, "How can the ark of the LORD come to me?" 10 So David would not have the ark of the LORD brought to him in the City of David, but diverted it to the house of Obed-edom the Gittite.

11* The ark of the LORD remained in the house of Obed-edom the Gittite for three months, and the LORD blessed Obed-edom and his whole house. 12* When it was reported to King David that the LORD had blessed the family of Obed-edom and all that belonged to him, David went to bring up the ark of God from the house of Obed-edom into the City of David amid festivities. 13 As soon as the bearers of the ark of the LORD had advanced six steps, he sacrificed an ox and a fatling. 14* Then David, girt with a linen apron, came dancing before the LORD with abandon, 15 as he and all the Israelites were bringing up the ark of the LORD with shouts of joy and to the sound of the horn. 16 As the ark of the LORD was entering the City of David, Saul's daughter Michal looked down through the window and saw King David leaping and dancing before the LORD, and she despised him in her heart. 17* The ark of the LORD was brought in and set in its place within the tent David had pitched for it. Then David offered holocausts and peace of-

The Dance of Life

LIVE IT!

It's a party! How else could we describe the festivities surrounding the triumphant bringing of the ark of the LORD into Jerusalem? And King David is leading the way, dancing before the LORD "with abandon" (2 Sm 6, 14). What a scene that must have been! What a wonderfully uninhibited way for David to express his great joy at escorting the ark into the city he has made his own.

So often we attend religious rituals as mere observers, much like Michal, David's wife, being critical and uninvolved. David shows us the true way to celebrate—with singing and dancing and eating. We need to celebrate together the presence of the LORD in our life! Here, David is our role model. Let us sing the song in our heart and dance to the music God has planted within us.

How can we do a better job of celebrating the LORD in our life? Are we observers or participants in the dance of life?

▶ 2 Sm 6, 11–19

---

† **5, 24:** *Sound of marching:* the wind in the treetops suggestive of the Lord's footsteps.

6, 1–11: 1 Chr 13, 1–14.   6, 2: Ex 25, 10; Jos 15, 9; Ps 132, 8ff; 1 Chr 1, 4.

6, 3: 1 Sm 4, 3f; 6, 7f; 7, 1; Dn 3, 55.
6, 5: Pss 68, 25f; 150, 3.5.
6, 8: 1 Kgs 8, 1.
6, 11: 1 Chr 26, 4.

6, 12–23: 1 Chr 15, 1–29; Ps 24, 7–10.
6, 14: 1 Sm 2, 18.
6, 17ff: Lv 1, 1–17; 3, 1–17; 1 Chr 16, 1ff.

ferings before the LORD. [18] When he finished making these offerings, he blessed the people in the name of the LORD of hosts. [19] He then distributed among all the people, to each man and each woman in the entire multitude of Israel, a loaf of bread, a cut of roast meat, and a raisin cake. With this, all the people left for their homes.

[20]* When David returned to bless his own family, Saul's daughter Michal came out to meet him and said, "How the king of Israel has honored himself today, exposing himself to the view of the slave girls of his followers, as a commoner might do!" [21]* But David replied to Michal: "I was dancing before the LORD. As the LORD lives, who preferred me to your father and his whole family when he appointed me commander of the LORD's people, Israel, not only will I make merry before the LORD, [22] but I will demean myself even more. I will be lowly in your esteem, but in the esteem of the slave girls you spoke of I will be honored." [23] And so Saul's daughter Michal was childless to the day of her death.

David's Concern for the Ark

7 [1]* When King David was settled in his palace, and the LORD had given him rest from his enemies on every side,* [2]* he said to Nathan the prophet, "Here I am living in a house of cedar, while the ark of God dwells in a tent!" [3]* Nathan answered the king, "Go, do whatever you have in mind, for the LORD is with you." [4] But that night the LORD spoke to Nathan and said: [5]* "Go, tell my servant David, 'Thus says the LORD: Should you build me a house to dwell in? [6] I have not dwelt in a house from the day on which I led the Israelites out of Egypt to the present, but I have been going about in a tent under cloth. [7] In all my wanderings everywhere among the Israelites, did I ever utter a word to any one of the judges whom I charged to tend my people Israel, to ask: Why have you not built me a house of cedar?'

The LORD's Promises

[8]*† "Now then, speak thus to my servant David, 'The LORD of hosts has this to say: It was I who took

you from the pasture and from the care of the flock to be commander of my people Israel. [9]* I have been with you wherever you went, and I have destroyed all your enemies before you. And I will make you famous like the great ones of the earth. [10] I will fix a place for my people Israel; I will plant them so that they may dwell in their place without further disturbance. Neither shall the wicked continue to afflict them as they did of old, [11]* since the time I first appointed judges over my people Israel. I will give you rest from all your enemies. The LORD also reveals to you that he will establish a house for you. [12]* And when your time comes and you rest with your ancestors, I will raise up your heir after you, sprung from your loins, and I will make his kingdom firm. [13] It is he who shall build a house for my name. And I will make his royal throne firm forever. [14] I will be a father to him, and he shall be a son to me. And if he does wrong, I will correct him with the rod of men and with human chastisements; [15]* but I will not withdraw my favor from him as I withdrew it from your predecessor Saul, whom I removed from my presence. [16]* Your house and your kingdom shall endure forever before me; your throne shall stand firm forever.' " [17] Nathan reported all these words and this entire vision to David.

King David's Prayer

[18]* Then King David went in and sat before the LORD and said, "Who am I, Lord GOD, and who are the members of my house, that you have brought me to this point? [19]† Yet even this you see as too little, Lord GOD; you have also spoken of the house of your servant for a long time to come: this too you have shown to man, Lord GOD! [20] What more can David say to you? You know your servant, Lord GOD! [21] For your servant's sake and as you have had at heart, you have brought about this entire magnificent disclosure to your servant. [22]* And so—

"Great are you, Lord GOD! There is none like you and there is no God but you, just as we have heard it told. [23]* What other nation on earth is there like your people Israel, which God has led, redeeming it as his people; so that you have made yourself

† **7, 8–16:** The prophecy to David contained in these verses is cited again, in poetic form, in Ps 89, 20–38, and alluded to in Ps 132. The promise regarding the people of Israel, vv 10–11, is a part of the promise to David at least as old as the composition of this chapter of Samuel, where it is anticipated in vv 6–7, and alluded to in David's thanksgiving, vv 23–24; it applies to the people an expression used of David in Ps 89, 23. The prophecy to David is the basis for Jewish expectation of a messiah, son of David, which Jesus Christ fulfilled in a transcendent way; cf Acts 2, 30; Heb 1, 5.

7, 19: *This too you have shown to man:* the text as transmitted has, rather, "and this is instruction for (or: the law of) mankind." The author of Chronicles (1 Chr 17, 17) saw approximately the same phrase, which he endeavored to fit into the context in a quite different sense. The above is conjectural; cf Dt 5, 24.

6, 20: 1 Chr 16, 43.
6, 21: 1 Sm 13, 14; 15, 28.
7, 1–29: 1 Chr 17, 1–27.
7, 1: 1 Kgs 5, 4.
7, 2: Dt 12, 10; 25, 19.
7, 3: Ps 132, 1–5.
7, 5: 1 Kgs 5, 17; 8, 16.27; 1 Chr 22, 8; 28, 3; Is 66, 1; Acts 7, 48.
7, 8: 1 Sm 16, 13; 17, 15–20; Ps 78, 70f; Am 7, 14.
7, 9: Ps 89, 27.
7, 11: 2 Sm 23, 5; 1 Kgs 2, 4–24.

7, 12ff: 1 Kgs 5, 19; 8, 19; 1 Chr 22, 10; 2 Chr 7, 18; Ps 89, 5.27f.30. 37f; Lk 1, 32; Heb 1, 5.
7, 15: 2 Sm 23, 5; 1 Sm 13, 14; 15, 26.28; 2 Kgs 19, 34; 1 Chr 17, 11–14; Ps 89, 34.
7, 16: 2 Sm 23, 5; Dn 2, 45; 1 Mc 2, 57; Mk 11, 10; Lk 1, 32f; Heb 1, 8.
7, 18: 1 Chr 17, 16.
7, 22: Ex 15, 11; Is 45, 5.
7, 23: Dt 4, 7.34.

2
S
M

David Praises God

Then King David went in and sat before the LORD and said, "Who am I, Lord GOD, and who are the members of my house, that you have brought me to this point?" (2 Sm 7, 18). When was the last time you brought yourself before God, like King David, simply to offer praise for all God has done for you?

It is easy for us to feel too busy to take time for God. Then we complain and get frustrated because God does not seem to be around, giving our life direction. Taking quiet moments to place ourselves in humility before our God and to praise God for the good we experience is important.

Find a quiet place, take just fifteen minutes. No radio, no television, no book. Think of all the positive and happy things in your life, and in your own words, say, "Thank you, God, for caring for me and the people I love!"

▸ 2 Sm 7, 18–29

renowned by doing this magnificent deed, and by doing awe-inspiring things as you have cleared nations and their gods out of the way of your people, which you redeemed for yourself from Egypt? 24* You have established for yourself your people Israel as yours forever, and you, LORD, have become their God. 25 And now, LORD God, confirm for all time the prophecy you have made concerning your servant and his house, and do as you have promised. 26 Your name will be forever great, when men say, 'The LORD of hosts is God of Israel,' and the house of your servant David stands firm before you. 27 It is you, LORD of hosts, God of Israel, who said in a revelation to your servant, 'I will build a house for you.' Therefore your servant now finds the courage to make this prayer to you. 28* And now, Lord GOD, you are God and your words are truth;

you have made this generous promise to your servant. 29 Do, then, bless the house of your servant that it may be before you forever; for you, Lord GOD, have promised, and by your blessing the house of your servant shall be blessed forever."

Summary of David's Wars

8 1*† After this David attacked the Philistines and conquered them, wresting . . . from the Philistines. 2† He also defeated Moab and then measured them with a line, making them lie down on the ground. He told off two lengths of line for execution, and a full length to be spared. Thus the Moabites became tributary to David. 3* Next David defeated Hadadezer, son of Rehob, king of Zobah, when he went to reestablish his dominion at the Euphrates River.* 4* David captured from him one thousand seven hundred horsemen and twenty thousand foot soldiers. And he hamstrung all the chariot horses, preserving only enough for a hundred chariots. 5 When the Arameans of Damascus came to the aid of Hadadezer, king of Zobah, David slew twenty-two thousand of them. 6 David then placed garrisons in Aram of Damascus, and the Arameans became subjects, tributary to David. The LORD brought David victory in all his undertakings. 7 David also took away the golden shields used by Hadadezer's servants and brought them to Jerusalem. [These Shishak, king of Egypt, took away when he came to Jerusalem in the days of Rehoboam, son of Solomon.] 8 From Tebah and Berothai, towns of Hadadezer, King David removed a very large quantity of bronze. 9 When Toi, king of Hamath, heard that David had defeated all the forces of Hadadezer, 10 he sent his son Hadoram to King David to greet him and to congratulate him for his victory over Hadadezer in battle, because Toi had been in many battles with Hadadezer. Hadoram also brought with him articles of silver, gold, and bronze. 11 These, too, King David consecrated to the LORD, together with the silver and gold he had taken from every nation he had conquered: 12 from Edom and Moab, from the Ammonites, from the Philistines, from the Amalekites, and from the plunder of Hadadezer, son of Rehob, king of Zobah.

13*† On his return, David became famous for having slain eighteen thousand Edomites in the Salt Valley; 14 after which he placed garrisons in Edom.

8, 1: *Wresting . . .* : the Hebrew text here gives "the bridle of the cubit"; 1 Chr 18, 1 understood "Gath and its dependent villages"; others implausibly read "dominion of the capital city."

8, 2: *Two lengths . . . a full length:* usually taken to mean that two-thirds of them were executed; but it could mean that two-thirds were spared, if the line was used full length in their case but doubled on itself to make "two lines" for those to be put to death.

8, 13: *On his return:* possibly to Jerusalem, after the revolt of

Absalom, a circumstance which this catalogue of victories would avoid mentioning. 1 Chr 18, 13 attributes the defeat of the Edomites to Abishai.

7, 24f: Ex 6, 7; Dt 7, 6; 26, 17; 29, 12.
7, 28: Nm 23, 19; Jn 17, 17.
8, 1–18: 1 Chr 18, 1–17.
8, 3–8: 2 Sm 10, 15–19.

8, 3: 2 Sm 10, 6; 1 Kgs 11, 23.
8, 4: Jos 11, 6.9.
8, 13: 2 Kgs 14, 7.

Thus all the Edomites became David's subjects, and the LORD brought David victory in all his undertakings.

David's Officials

15* David reigned over all Israel, judging and administering justice to all his people. 16 Joab, son of Zeruiah, was in command of the army. Jehoshaphat, son of Ahilud, was chancellor. 17 Zadok, son of Ahitub, and Ahimelech, son of Abiathar, were priests. Shawsha was scribe. 18* Benaiah, son of Jehoiada, was in command of the Cherethites and Pelethites. And David's sons were priests.

David and Meribbaal

9 1* David asked, "Is there any survivor of Saul's house to whom I may show kindness for the sake of Jonathan?" 2* Now there was a servant of the family of Saul named Ziba. He was summoned to David, and the king asked him, "Are you Ziba?" He replied, "Your servant." 3* Then the king inquired, "Is there any survivor of Saul's house to whom I may show God's kindness?" Ziba answered the king, "There is still Jonathan's son, whose feet are crippled." 4* The king said to him, "Where is he?" and Ziba answered, "He is in the house of Machir, son of Ammiel, in Lodebar." 5 So King David sent for him and had him brought from the house of Machir, son of Ammiel, in Lodebar. 6 When Meribbaal, son of Jonathan, son of Saul, came to David, he fell prostrate in homage. David said, "Meribbaal," and he answered, "Your servant." 7 "Fear not," David said to him, "I will surely be kind to you for the sake of your father Jonathan. I will restore to you all the lands of your grandfather Saul, and you shall always eat at my table." 8* Bowing low, he answered, "What is your servant that you should pay attention to a dead dog like me?" 9 The king then called Ziba, Saul's attendant, and said to him: "I am giving your lord's son all that belonged to Saul and to all his family. 10 You and your sons and servants must till the land for him. You shall bring in the produce, which shall be food for your lord's family to eat. But Meribbaal, your lord's son, shall always eat at my table." Ziba, who had fifteen sons and twenty servants, 11* said to the king, "Your servant shall do just as my lord the king has commanded him." And so Meribbaal ate at David's table like one of the king's sons. 12* Meribbaal had

a young son whose name was Mica; and all the tenants of Ziba's family worked for Meribbaal. 13* But Meribbaal lived in Jerusalem, because he always ate at the king's table. He was lame in both feet.

Insult of the Ammonites

10 1*† Some time later the king of the Ammonites died, and his son Hanun succeeded him as king. 2 David thought, "I will be kind to Hanun, son of Nahash, as his father was kind to me." So David sent his servants with condolences to Hanun for the loss of his father. But when David's servants entered the country of the Ammonites, 3 the Ammonite princes said to their lord Hanun: "Do you think that David is honoring your father by sending men with condolences? Is it not rather to explore the city, to spy on it, and to overthrow it, that David has sent his messengers to you?" 4* Hanun, therefore, seized David's servants and, after shaving off half their beards and cutting away the lower halves of their garments at the buttocks, sent them away. 5 When he was told of it, King David sent out word to them, since the men were quite ashamed. "Stay in Jericho until your beards grow," he said, "and then come back."

Ammonites Defeated

6*† In view of the offense they had given to David, the Ammonites sent for and hired twenty thousand Aramean foot soldiers from Beth-rehob and Zobah, as well as the king of Maacah with one thousand men, and twelve thousand men from Tob. 7* On learning this, David sent out Joab with the entire levy of trained soldiers. 8 The Ammonites came out and drew up in battle formation at the entrance of their city gate, while the Arameans of Zobah and Rehob and the men of Tob and Maacah remained apart in the open country. 9 When Joab saw the battle lines drawn up against him, both front and rear, he made a selection from all the picked troops of Israel and arrayed them against the Arameans. 10 He placed the rest of the soldiers under the command of his brother Abishai, who arrayed them against the Ammonites. 11 Joab said, "If the Arameans are stronger than I, you shall help me. But if the Ammonites are stronger than you, I will come to help you. 12 Be brave; let us prove our valor for the sake of our people and the cities of our God; the LORD will do what he judges best."

10, 1: *Some time later:* early in the reign of David, since Hanun's father had been ruling in Ammon at the beginning of Saul's reign (1 Sm 11) and Solomon was as yet unborn (2 Sm 11, 1; 12, 24).

10, 6–9: A Hebrew text from Qumran (4Q Sam^a) comes closer in these verses to what is given in 1 Chr 19, 6–9. The scene of the conflict is more likely Rabbath-Ammon, with Josephus (Ant., vii, 123), than Madeba, as in 1 Chronicles; compare ch 11.

8, 15–18: 2 Sm 20, 23–26; 1 Kgs 4, 1–6; 1 Chr 18, 14–17.
8, 18: 2 Sm 15, 18; 20, 7.23; 23, 20.
9, 1: 2 Sm 21, 7; 1 Sm 18, 1–4; 20, 8ff.15f.42.
9, 2: 2 Sm 16, 1–4; 19, 27.
9, 3: 2 Sm 4, 4.
9, 4: 2 Sm 17, 27.
9, 8: 1 Sm 24, 15.
9, 11: 2 Sm 19, 29.
9, 12: 1 Chr 8, 34.
9, 13: 2 Sm 21, 7.
10, 1–19: 1 Chr 19, 1–19.
10, 4: Is 20, 4.
10, 6: 2 Sm 8, 3; 1 Sm 14, 47.
10, 7: 2 Sm 11, 1.

13 When Joab and the soldiers who were with him approached the Arameans for battle, they fled before him. 14 The Ammonites, seeing that the Arameans had fled, also fled from Abishai and withdrew into the city. Joab then ceased his attack on the Ammonites and returned to Jerusalem.

Arameans Defeated

15* Then the Arameans responded to their defeat by Israel with a full mustering of troops; 16 Hadadezer sent for and enlisted Arameans from beyond the Euphrates. They came to Helam, with Shobach, general of Hadadezer's army, at their head. 17 On receiving this news, David assembled all Israel, crossed the Jordan, and went to Helam. The Arameans drew up in formation against David and fought with him. 18 But the Arameans gave way

they ravaged the Ammonites and besieged Rabbah. David, however, remained in Jerusalem. 2 One evening David rose from his siesta and strolled about on the roof of the palace. From the roof he saw a woman bathing, who was very beautiful. 3* David had inquiries made about the woman and was told, "She is Bathsheba, daughter of Eliam, and wife of [Joab's armor-bearer] Uriah the Hittite." 4* Then David sent messengers and took her. When she came to him, he had relations with her, at a time when she was just purified after her monthly period. She then returned to her house. 5 But the woman had conceived, and sent the information to David, "I am with child."

6 David therefore sent a message to Joab, "Send me Uriah the Hittite." So Joab sent Uriah to David. 7 When he came, David questioned him about

Lust and Its Consequences

LIVE IT!

> **What the king wants, the king gets.**
> That seems to be the message of 2 Sm 11, 1–5. We are spared many of the details about the encounter between David and Bathsheba, but we do know this: Bathsheba is married to Uriah, so David has coveted another man's wife and committed adultery. When Bathsheba becomes pregnant, David attempts to deceive Uriah into thinking the baby is Uriah's, by bringing him home to have sex with Bathsheba. But Uriah refuses to do so because he and his comrades are in the midst of a war. Finally, David arranges for Uriah to be murdered in battle.
>
> In one brief episode, David has broken four commandments. He has given in to lust, and it has led him into a situation that will affect his family, his kingship, and the whole nation of Israel.
>
> It is so easy to give in to temptation, especially lust, because it can be so alluring, and because we generally fail to think beyond the moment. A dangerous thing.
>
> However, God can still use us, despite our sinfulness, as God used David.
>
> ▶ 2 Sm 11, 1–5

before Israel, and David's men killed seven hundred charioteers and forty thousand of the Aramean foot soldiers. Shobach, general of the army, was struck down and died on the field. 19 All of Hadadezer's vassal kings, in view of their defeat by Israel, then made peace with the Israelites and became their subjects. And the Arameans were afraid to give further aid to the Ammonites.

David's Sin

11 1*† At the turn of the year, when kings go out on campaign, David sent out Joab along with his officers and the army of Israel, and

Joab, the soldiers, and how the war was going, and Uriah answered that all was well. 8 David then said to Uriah, "Go down to your house and bathe your feet." Uriah left the palace, and a portion was sent out after him from the king's table. 9 But Uriah slept at the entrance of the royal palace with the other officers of his lord, and did not go down to his own house. 10 David was told that Uriah had not gone home. So he said to Uriah, "Have you not come from a journey? Why, then, did you not go down to your house?" 11* Uriah answered David, "The ark and Israel and Judah are lodged in tents, and my lord Joab and your majesty's servants are encamped

---

11, 1: *At the turn of the year: in the spring.*

10, 15–19: 2 Sm 8, 3–8; 1 Chr 9, 16–19.
11, 1: 2 Sm 10, 7; 1 Chr 20, 1.

11, 3: 2 Sm 23, 39.
11, 4: Lv 15, 19.
11, 11: 1 Sm 4, 3f.

in the open field. Can I go home to eat and to drink and to sleep with my wife? As the LORD lives and as you live, I will do no such thing." 12 Then David said to Uriah, "Stay here today also, I shall dismiss you tomorrow." So Uriah remained in Jerusalem that day. On the day following, 13 David summoned him, and he ate and drank with David, who made him drunk. But in the evening he went out to sleep on his bed among his lord's servants, and did not go down to his home. 14 The next morning David wrote a letter to Joab which he sent by Uriah. 15 In it he directed: "Place Uriah up front, where the fighting is fierce. Then pull back and leave him to be struck down dead." 16 So while Joab was besieging the city, he assigned Uriah to a place where he knew the defenders were strong. 17 When the men of the city made a sortie against Joab, some officers of David's army fell, and among them Uriah the Hittite died.

18 Then Joab sent David a report of all the details of the battle, 19 instructing the messenger, "When you have finished giving the king all the details of the battle, 20 the king may become angry and say to you: 'Why did you go near the city to fight? Did you not know that they would shoot from the wall above? 21* Who killed Abimelech, son of Jerubbaal? Was it not a woman who threw a millstone down on him from the wall above, so that he died in Thebez? Why did you go near the wall?' Then you in turn shall say, 'Your servant Uriah the Hittite is

also dead.' " 22† The messenger set out, and on his arrival he relayed to David all the details as Joab had instructed him. 23 He told David: "The men had us at a disadvantage and came out into the open against us, but we pushed them back to the entrance of the city gate. 24 Then the archers shot at your servants from the wall above, and some of the king's servants died, among them your servant Uriah." 25 David said to the messenger: "This is what you shall convey to Joab: 'Do not be chagrined at this, for the sword devours now here and now there. Strengthen your attack on the city and destroy it.' Encourage him."

26 When the wife of Uriah heard that her husband had died, she mourned her lord. 27 But once the mourning was over, David sent for her and brought her into his house. She became his wife and bore him a son. But the LORD was displeased with what David had done.

Nathan's Parable

12 1*† The LORD sent Nathan to David, and when he came to him, he said: "Judge this case for me! In a certain town there were two men, one rich, the other poor. 2 The rich man had flocks and herds in great numbers. 3 But the poor man had nothing at all except one little ewe lamb that he had bought. He nourished her, and she grew up with him and his children. She shared the little food he had and drank from his cup and slept in his

The Power of a Good Story

A story can be a powerful thing. Jesus knew the power of stories, so he often responded to questions by telling a story.

The prophet Nathan also knew the power of stories. His challenge was to force David to come to grips with what he had done with Bathsheba and Uriah. In 2 Samuel, Nathan cleverly creates a story in which David is to assume his familiar role as judge. David hears the case and is furious at the actions of the rich man in it, declaring that he should die for what he has done. Then, with four words, Nathan turns David's world upside down:

"You are the man!" (12, 7).

What can David say? He just condemned himself, and he knows it. Nathan has cleverly forced him into a moment of truth. You may want to read Psalm 51, which poetically records David's confession.

Yes, a story can be a powerful thing. Just ask Nathan. Or David. Or Jesus.

▶ 2 Sm 12, 1–12

†
  11, 22: After this verse, the Greek text, which is here the older form, has David, angry with Joab, repeat exactly the questions Joab had foreseen in vv 20ff. In v 24 of our oldest Greek text, the messenger specifies that about eighteen men were killed.

12, 1–4: This utterance of Nathan is in regular lines in Hebrew, resembling English blank verse.

*

11, 21: Jgs 9, 50–54.   **12, 1:** Sir 47, 1.

bosom. She was like a daughter to him. 4 Now, the rich man received a visitor, but he would not take from his own flocks and herds to prepare a meal for the wayfarer who had come to him. Instead he took the poor man's ewe lamb and made a meal of it for his visitor." 5 David grew very angry with that man and said to Nathan: "As the LORD lives, the man who has done this merits death! 6* He shall restore the ewe lamb fourfold because he has done this and has had no pity."

David's Punishment

7* Then Nathan said to David: "You are the man! Thus says the LORD God of Israel: 'I anointed you king of Israel. I rescued you from the hand of Saul. 8 I gave you your lord's house and your lord's wives for your own. I gave you the house of Israel and of Judah. And if this were not enough, I could count up for you still more. 9 Why have you spurned the LORD and done evil in his sight? You have cut down Uriah the Hittite with the sword; you took his wife as your own, and him you killed with the sword of the Ammonites. 10* Now, therefore, the sword shall never depart from your house, because you have despised me and have taken the wife of Uriah to be your wife.' 11* Thus says the LORD: 'I will bring evil upon you out of your own house. I will take your wives while you live to see it, and will give them to your neighbor. He shall lie with your wives in broad daylight. 12 You have done this deed in secret, but I will bring it about in the presence of all Israel, and with the sun looking down.' "

David's Repentance

13* Then David said to Nathan, "I have sinned against the LORD." Nathan answered David: "The LORD on his part has forgiven your sin: you shall not die. 14 But since you have utterly spurned the LORD by this deed, the child born to you must surely die." 15 Then Nathan returned to his house.

The LORD struck the child that the wife of Uriah had borne to David, and it became desperately ill. 16 David besought God for the child. He kept a fast, retiring for the night to lie on the ground clothed in sackcloth. 17 The elders of his house stood beside him urging him to rise from the ground; but he would not, nor would he take food with them. 18 On the seventh day, the child died. David's servants, however, were afraid to tell him that the child was dead, for they said: "When the child was alive, we spoke to him, but he would not listen to what we said. How can we tell him the child is dead? He may

do some harm!" 19 But David noticed his servants whispering among themselves and realized that the child was dead. He asked his servants, "Is the child dead?" They replied, "Yes, he is." 20 Rising from the ground, David washed and anointed himself, and changed his clothes. Then he went to the house of the LORD and worshiped. He returned to his own house, where at his request food was set before him, and he ate. 21 His servants said to him: "What is this you are doing? While the child was living, you fasted and wept and kept vigil; now that the child is dead you rise and take food." 22 He replied: "While the child was living, I fasted and wept, thinking, 'Perhaps the LORD will grant me the child's life.' 23* But now he is dead. Why should I fast? Can I bring him back again? I shall go to him, but he will not return to me." 24 Then David comforted his wife Bathsheba. He went and slept with her; and she conceived and bore him a son, who was named Solomon. The LORD loved him 25 and sent the prophet Nathan to name him Jedidiah, on behalf of the LORD.

Ammonite War Ends

26* Joab fought against Rabbah of the Ammonites and captured this royal city. 27 He sent messengers to David with the word: "I have fought against Rabbah and have taken the water-city. 28 Therefore, assemble the rest of the soldiers, join the siege against the city and capture it, lest it be I that capture the city and it be credited to me." 29 So David assembled the rest of the soldiers and went to Rabbah. When he had fought against it and captured it, 30† he took the crown from Milcom's head. It weighed a talent, of gold and precious stones; it was placed on David's head. He brought out immense booty from the city, 31 and also led away the inhabitants, whom he assigned to work with saws, iron picks, and iron axes, or put to work at the brickmold. This is what he did to all the Ammonite cities. David and all the soldiers then returned to Jerusalem.

The Crime of Amnon

13 1* Some time later the following incident occurred. David's son Absalom had a beautiful sister named Tamar, and David's son Amnon loved her. 2 He was in such straits over his sister Tamar that he became sick; since she was a virgin, Amnon thought it impossible to carry out his designs toward her. 3* Now Amnon had a friend named Jonadab, son of David's brother Shimeah, who was very clever. 4 He asked him, "Prince, why are you so dejected morning after morning? Why

†————————————————
12, 30: *Weighed a talent:* since this would be more than 75 pounds, some commentators picture the idol's crown as displaying a single precious stone of large size, which David took to wear; but the text does not say this.

*————————————————
12, 6: Ex 21, 37; Lk 19, 8.   5; 50, 6; Sir 47, 11.
12, 7: 1 Sm 16, 13.   12, 23: Jb 7, 9.
12, 10: 2 Sm 13, 28f; 18, 14.   12, 26–31: 1 Chr 20, 1–3.
12, 11: 2 Sm 16, 11.22.   13, 1: 2 Sm 3, 2f; 1 Chr 3, 9.
12, 13: 1 Kgs 21, 29; Pss 32,   13, 3: 1 Sm 21, 21.

2
S
M

Family Violence

How should we react to the story of the rape of Tamar by her half-brother, Amnon, and the subsequent murder of Amnon by Absalom to avenge his sister's disgrace? This brutal story of lust, cruelty, and revenge has all the makings of a TV movie or a best-selling paperback. So, what is it doing in the Bible?

We have to remind ourselves that these are all David's children. We also have to remind ourselves that after Nathan confronts David about his affair with Bathsheba and his arrangement of Uriah's death, he tells David that "the sword shall never depart from your house" (2 Sm 12, 10).

This prophecy finds fulfillment with the deaths of David's sons Amnon (2 Sm 13, 28-29) and Absalom (2 Sm 18, 14). Just as David allowed his lust for Bathsheba to get the best of him, Amnon follows in his father's footsteps, but by deceiving and forcing himself upon his sister, he has magnified the offense. And then in disgust, he wants nothing to do with Tamar. Tamar's brother Absalom bides his time, and when the opportunity presents itself, he has Amnon killed in front of the rest of his brothers to avenge his sister. Absalom himself dies shortly thereafter when he gets tangled up in a tree and an enemy takes advantage of his misfortune.

This is a tragic story and, unfortunately, all too human. The men and women of the Scriptures had to deal with the same horrors and family violence that we do, three thousand years later. The words of Ecclesiastes seem sadly true in this case: "What has been, that will be; what has been done, that will be done. Nothing is new under the sun" (Eccl 1, 9). At least in this story, the old axiom "Those who live by the sword die by the sword" has come true.

▸ 2 Sm 13

---

not tell me?" So Amnon said to him, "I am in love with Tamar, my brother Absalom's sister." ⁵ Then Jonadab replied, "Lie down on your bed and pretend to be sick. When your father comes to visit you, say to him, 'Please let my sister Tamar come and encourage me to take food. If she prepares something appetizing in my presence, for me to see, I will eat it from her hand.' " ⁶ So Amnon lay down and pretended to be sick. When the king came to visit him, Amnon said to the king, "Please let my sister Tamar come and prepare some fried cakes before my eyes, that I may take nourishment from her hand."

⁷ David then sent home a message to Tamar, "Please go to the house of your brother Amnon and prepare some nourishment for him." ⁸ Tamar went to the house of her brother Amnon, who was in bed. Taking dough and kneading it, she twisted it into cakes before his eyes and fried the cakes. ⁹ Then she took the pan and set out the cakes before him. But Amnon would not eat; he said, "Have everyone leave me." When they had all left him, ¹⁰ Amnon said to Tamar, "Bring the nourishment into the bedroom, that I may have it from your hand." So Tamar picked up the cakes she had

prepared and brought them to her brother Amnon in the bedroom. ¹¹ But when she brought them to him to eat, he seized her and said to her, "Come! Lie with me, my sister!" ¹²* But she answered him, "No, my brother! Do not shame me! That is an intolerable crime in Israel. Do not commit this insensate deed. ¹³* Where would I take my shame? And you would be a discredited man in Israel. So please, speak to the king; he will not keep me from you."

¹⁴ Not heeding her plea, he overpowered her; he shamed her and had relations with her. ¹⁵ Then Amnon conceived an intense hatred for her, which far surpassed the love he had had for her. "Get up and leave," he said to her. ¹⁶ She replied, "No, brother, because to drive me out would be far worse than the first injury you have done me." He would not listen to her, ¹⁷ but called the youth who was his attendant and said, "Put her outside, away from me, and bar the door after her." ¹⁸ Now she had on a long tunic, for that is how maiden princesses dressed in olden days. When his attendant put her out and barred the door after her, ¹⁹ Tamar put ashes on her head and tore the long tunic in which she was clothed. Then, putting her hands to her

---

13, 12: Lv 18, 9; 20, 17; Dt 27, 22.   13, 13: Gn 34, 7.

head, she went away crying loudly. 20 Her brother Absalom said to her: "Has your brother Amnon been with you? Be still now, my sister; he is your brother. Do not take this affair to heart." But Tamar remained grief-stricken and forlorn in the house of her brother Absalom. 21 King David, who got word of the whole affair, became very angry. He did not, however, spark the resentment of his son Amnon, whom he favored because he was his first-born. 22 Absalom, moreover, said nothing at all to Amnon, although he hated him for having shamed his sister Tamar.

Absalom's Plot

23 After a period of two years Absalom had shearers in Baal-hazor near Ephraim, and he invited all the princes. 24 Absalom went to the king and said: "Your servant is having shearers. Please, your majesty, come with all your retainers to your servant." 25 But the king said to Absalom, "No, my son, all of us should not go lest we be a burden to you." And though Absalom urged him, he refused to go and began to bid him goodbye. 26 Absalom then said, "If you will not come yourself, please let my brother Amnon come to us." The king asked him, "Why should he go to you?" 27 At Absalom's urging, however, he sent Amnon and all the other princes with him. Absalom prepared a banquet fit for royalty. 28* But he had instructed his servants: "Now watch! When Amnon is merry with wine and I say to you, 'Kill Amnon,' put him to death. Do not be afraid, for it is I who order you to do it. Be resolute and act manfully."

Death of Amnon

29 When the servants did to Amnon as Absalom had commanded, all the other princes rose, mounted their mules, and fled. 30 While they were still on the road, a report reached David that Absalom had killed all the princes and that not one of them had survived. 31* The king stood up, rent his garments, and then lay on the ground. All his servants standing by him also rent their garments. 32 But Jonadab, son of David's brother Shimeah, spoke up: "Let not my lord think that all the young princes have been killed! Amnon alone is dead, for Absalom was determined on this ever since Amnon shamed his sister Tamar. 33 So let not my lord the king put faith in the report that all the princes are dead. Amnon alone is dead." 34 Meanwhile, Absalom had taken flight. Then the servant on watch looked about and saw a large group coming down the slope from the direction of Bahurim. He came in and reported this,

telling the king that he had seen some men coming down the mountainside from the direction of Bahurim. 35 So Jonadab said to the king: "There! The princes have come. It is as your servant said." 36 No sooner had he finished speaking than the princes came in, weeping aloud. The king, too, and all his servants wept very bitterly. 37* But Absalom, who had taken flight, went to Talmai, son of Ammihud, king of Geshur, 38 and stayed in Geshur for three years.

Efforts for Absalom's Return

39 The king continued during all that time to mourn over his son; but his longing reached out for Absalom as he became reconciled to the death of Amnon.

14 1 When Joab, son of Zeruiah, observed how the king felt toward Absalom, 2 he sent to Tekoa and brought from there a gifted woman, to whom he said: "Pretend to be in mourning. Put on mourning apparel and do not anoint yourself with oil, that you may appear to be a woman who has been long in mourning for a departed one. 3 Then go to the king and speak to him in this manner." And Joab instructed her what to say.

4 So the woman of Tekoa went to the king and fell prostrate to the ground in homage, saying, "Help, your majesty!" 5* The king said to her, "What do you want?" She replied: "Alas, I am a widow; my husband is dead. 6 Your servant had two sons, who quarreled in the field. There being no one to part them, one of them struck his brother and killed him. 7*† Then the whole clan confronted your servant and demanded: 'Give up the one who killed his brother. We must put him to death for the life of his brother whom he has slain; we must extinguish the heir also.' Thus they will quench my remaining hope and leave my husband neither name nor posterity upon the earth." 8 The king then said to the woman: "Go home. I will issue a command on your behalf." 9 The woman of Tekoa answered him, "Let me and my family be to blame, my lord king; you and your throne are innocent." 10 Then the king said, "If anyone says a word to you, have him brought to me, and he shall not touch you again." 11 But she went on to say, "Please, your majesty, keep in mind the LORD your God, that the avenger of blood may not go too far in destruction and that my son may not be done away with." He replied, "As the LORD lives, not a hair of your son shall fall to the ground."

14, 7: *Hope:* literally, "glowing coal." The image is similar to that of the lighted lamp, e.g., Ps 89, 17, to keep alive the ancestral name.

13, 28f: 2 Sm 12, 10.
13, 31: 2 Sm 1, 11.
13, 37: 2 Sm 3, 3; 15, 8.

14, 5f: 2 Kgs 6, 26f.
14, 7: Nm 35, 19.

¹² The woman continued, "Please let your servant say still another word to my lord the king." He replied, "Speak." ¹³ So the woman said: "Why, then, do you think of this same kind of thing against the people of God? In pronouncing as he has, the king shows himself guilty, for not bringing back his own banished son. ¹⁴*† We must indeed die; we are then like water that is poured out on the ground and cannot be gathered up. Yet, though God does not bring back life, he does take thought how not to banish anyone from him. ¹⁵ And now, if I have presumed to speak of this matter to your majesty, it is because the people have given me cause to fear. And so your servant thought: 'Let me speak to the king. Perhaps he will grant the petition of his maidservant. ¹⁶ For the king must surely consent to free his servant from the grasp of one who would seek to destroy me and my son as well from God's inheritance.' " ¹⁷*† And the woman concluded: "Let the word of my lord the king provide a resting place; indeed, my lord the king is like an angel of God, evaluating good and bad. The LORD your God be with you."

¹⁸ The king answered the woman, "Now do not conceal from me anything I may ask you!" The woman said, "Let my lord the king speak." ¹⁹ So the king asked, "Is Joab involved with you in all this?" And the woman answered: "As you live, my lord the king, it is just as your majesty has said, and not otherwise. It was your servant Joab who instructed me and told your servant all these things she was to say. ²⁰ Your servant Joab did this to come at the issue in a roundabout way. But my lord is as wise as an angel of God, so that he knows all things on earth."

Absalom's Return

²¹ Then the king said to Joab: "I hereby grant this request. Go, therefore, and bring back young Absalom." ²² Falling prostrate to the ground in homage and blessing the king, Joab said, "This day I know that I am in good favor with you, my lord the king, since the king has granted the request of his servant." ²³ Joab then went off to Geshur and brought Absalom to Jerusalem. ²⁴ But the king said, "Let him go to his own house; he shall not appear before me." So Absalom went off to his house and did not appear before the king.

²⁵ In all Israel there was not a man who could so be praised for his beauty as Absalom, who was without blemish from the sole of his foot to the crown of his head. ²⁶ When he shaved his head—which he used to do at the end of every year, because his hair became too heavy for him—the hair

weighed two hundred shekels according to the royal standard. ²⁷* Absalom had three sons born to him, besides a daughter named Tamar, who was a beautiful woman.

Absalom Is Pardoned

²⁸ Absalom lived in Jerusalem for two years without appearing before the king. ²⁹ Then he summoned Joab to send him to the king, but Joab would not come to him. Although he summoned him a second time, Joab refused to come. ³⁰* He therefore instructed his servants: "You see Joab's field that borders mine, on which he has barley. Go, set it on fire." And so Absalom's servants set the field on fire. Joab's farmhands came to him with torn garments and reported to him what had been done. ³¹ At this, Joab went to Absalom in his house and asked him, "Why have your servants set my field on fire?" ³² Absalom answered Joab: "I was summoning you to come here, that I may send you to the king to say: 'Why did I come back from Geshur? I would be better off if I were still there!' Now, let me appear before the king. If I am guilty, let him put me to death." ³³ Joab went to the king and reported this. The king then called Absalom, who came to him and in homage fell on his face to the ground before the king. Then the king kissed him.

Absalom's Plot

15 ¹* After this Absalom provided himself with chariots, horses, and fifty henchmen. ² Moreover, Absalom used to rise early and stand alongside the road leading to the gate. If someone had a lawsuit to be decided by the king, Absalom would call to him and say, "From what city are you?" And when he replied, "Your servant is of such and such a tribe of Israel," ³ Absalom would say to him, "Your suit is good and just, but there is no one to hear you in the king's name." ⁴ And he would continue: "If only I could be appointed judge in the land! Then everyone who has a lawsuit to be decided might come to me and I would render him justice." ⁵ Whenever a man approached him to show homage, he would extend his hand, hold him, and kiss him. ⁶ By behaving in this way toward all the Israelites who came to the king for judgment, Absalom was stealing away the loyalties of the men of Israel.

Conspiracy in Hebron

⁷ After a period of four years, Absalom said to the king: "Allow me to go to Hebron and fulfill a vow I made to the LORD. ⁸* For while living in Geshur in Aram, your servant made this vow: 'If the LORD ever

---

† **14, 14:** *How not to banish:* a possible allusion to the religious institution of cities of refuge for involuntary murderers; see Nm 35, 9–15.
14, 17: *A resting place:* cf Ps 95, 11; Heb 3, 7—4, 11. The reference here is to a return home for Absalom to Israel.

14, 14: Jb 7, 9; 14, 7–12; Ps 88, 5.11ff.
14, 17.20: 1 Sm 29, 9.
14, 27: 2 Sm 18, 18.

14, 30: Jgs 15, 4f.
15, 1: 1 Sm 8, 11; 1 Kgs 1, 5.
15, 8: 2 Sm 3, 3; 13, 37.

brings me back to Jerusalem, I will worship him in Hebron.' " [9] The king wished him a safe journey, and he went off to Hebron. [10] Then Absalom sent spies throughout the tribes of Israel to say, "When you hear the sound of the horn, declare Absalom king in Hebron." [11] Two hundred men had accompanied Absalom from Jerusalem. They had been invited and went in good faith, knowing nothing of the plan. [12]* Absalom also sent to Ahithophel the Gilonite, David's counselor, an invitation to come from his town, Giloh, for the sacrifices he was about to offer. So the conspiracy gained strength, and the people with Absalom increased in numbers.

David Flees Jerusalem

[13]* An informant came to David with the report, "The Israelites have transferred their loyalty to Absalom." [14] At this, David said to all his servants who were with him in Jerusalem: "Up! Let us take flight, or none of us will escape from Absalom. Leave quickly, lest he hurry and overtake us, then visit disaster upon us and put the city to the sword." [15] The king's officers answered him, "Your servants are ready, whatever our lord the king chooses to do." [16]* Then the king set out, accompanied by his entire household, except for ten concubines whom he left behind to take care of the palace. [17] As the king left the city, with all his officers accompanying him, they halted opposite the ascent of the Mount of Olives, at a distance, [18]* while the whole army marched past him.

David and Ittai

As all the Cherethites and Pelethites, and the six hundred men of Gath who had accompanied him from that city, were passing in review before the king, [19] he said to Ittai the Gittite: "Why should you also go with us? Go back and stay with the king, for you are a foreigner and you, too, are an exile from your own country. [20] You came only yesterday, and shall I have you wander about with us today, wherever I have to go? Return and take your brothers with you, and may the LORD be kind and faithful to you." [21]* But Ittai answered the king, "As the LORD lives, and as my lord the king lives, your servant shall be wherever my lord the king may be, whether for death or for life." [22] So the king said to Ittai, "Go, then, march on." And Ittai the Gittite, with all his men and all the dependents that were with him, marched on. [23] Everyone in the countryside wept aloud as the last of the soldiers went by, and the king crossed the Kidron Valley with all the soldiers

moving on ahead of him by way of the Mount of Olives, toward the desert.

David and the Priests

[24] Zadok, too [with all the Levite bearers of the ark of the covenant of God], and Abiathar brought the ark of God to a halt until the soldiers had marched out of the city. [25] Then the king said to Zadok: "Take the ark of God back to the city. If I find favor with the LORD, he will bring me back and permit me to see it and its lodging. [26]* But if he should say, 'I am not pleased with you,' I am ready; let him do to me as he sees fit." [27] The king also said to the priest Zadok: "See to it that you and Abiathar return to the city in peace, and both your sons with you, your own son Ahimaaz, and Abiathar's son Jonathan. [28] Remember, I shall be waiting at the fords near the desert until I receive information from you." [29] So Zadok and Abiathar took the ark of God back to Jerusalem and remained there.

[30]* As David went up the Mount of Olives, he wept without ceasing. His head was covered, and he was walking barefoot. All those who were with him also had their heads covered and were weeping as they went. [31]* When David was informed that Ahithophel was among the conspirators with Absalom, he said, "O LORD, turn the counsel of Ahithophel to folly!"

David and Hushai

[32]* When David reached the top, where men used to worship God, Hushai the Archite was there to meet him, with rent garments and dirt upon his head. [33] David said to him: "If you come with me, you will be a burden to me. [34]* But if you return to the city and say to Absalom, 'Let me be your servant, O king; I was formerly your father's servant, but now I will be yours,' you will undo for me the counsel of Ahithophel. [35] You will have the priests Zadok and Abiathar there with you. If you hear anything from the royal palace, you shall report it to the priests Zadok and Abiathar, [36] who have there with them both Zadok's son Ahimaaz and Abiathar's son Jonathan. Through them you shall send on to me whatever you hear." [37] So David's friend Hushai went into the city of Jerusalem as Absalom was about to enter it.

David and Ziba

16 [1]* David had gone a little beyond the top when Ziba, the servant of Meribbaal, met him with saddled asses laden with two hundred loaves of bread, an ephah of cakes of pressed

15, 12: 2 Sm 16, 23.
15, 13: Ps 3.
15, 16: 2 Sm 16, 21f; 20, 3.
15, 18: 2 Sm 8, 18.
15, 21: Ru 1, 16.
15, 26: 2 Sm 16, 10.
15, 30: 2 Sm 19, 5; Mi 1, 8.
15, 31: 2 Sm 16, 23; 17, 14. 23.
15, 32: 2 Sm 16, 16.
15, 34: 2 Sm 16, 19.
16, 1: 2 Sm 4, 4; 9, 1–13; 19, 18.25.

raisins, an ephah of summer fruits, and a skin of wine. ² The king said to Ziba, "What do you plan to do with these?" Ziba replied: "The asses are for the king's household to ride on. The bread and summer fruits are for your servants to eat, and the wine for those to drink who are weary in the desert." ³* Then the king said, "And where is your lord's son?" Ziba answered the king, "He is staying in Jerusalem, for he said, 'Now the Israelites will restore to me my father's kingdom.' " ⁴* The king therefore said to Ziba, "So! Everything Meribbaal had is yours." Then Ziba said: "I pay you homage, my lord the king. May I find favor with you!"

David and Shimei

⁵* As David was approaching Bahurim, a man named Shimei, the son of Gera of the same clan as Saul's family, was coming out of the place, cursing as he came. ⁶ He threw stones at David and at all the king's officers, even though all the soldiers, including the royal guard, were on David's right and on his left. ⁷ Shimei was saying as he cursed: "Away, away, you murderous and wicked man! ⁸† The LORD has requited you for all the bloodshed in the family of Saul, in whose stead you became king, and the LORD has given over the kingdom to your son Absalom. And now you suffer ruin because you are a murderer." ⁹* Abishai, son of Zeruiah, said to the king: "Why should this dead dog curse my lord the king? Let me go over, please, and lop off his head." ¹⁰* But the king replied: "What business is it of mine or of yours, sons of Zeruiah, that he curses? Suppose the LORD has told him to curse David; who then will dare to say, 'Why are you doing this?' " ¹¹* Then the king said to Abishai and to all his servants: "If my own son, who came forth from my loins, is seeking my life, how much more might this Benjaminite do so? Let him alone and let him curse, for the LORD has told him to. ¹² Perhaps the LORD will look upon my affliction and make it up to me with benefits for the curses he is uttering this day." ¹³* David and his men continued on the road, while Shimei kept abreast of them on the hillside, all the while cursing and throwing stones and dirt as he went. ¹⁴ The king and all the soldiers with him arrived at the Jordan tired out, and stopped there for a rest.

Absalom's Counselors

¹⁵ In the meantime Absalom, accompanied by Ahithophel, entered Jerusalem with all the Israelites. ¹⁶* When David's friend Hushai the Archite

came to Absalom, he said to him: "Long live the king! Long live the king!" ¹⁷ But Absalom asked Hushai: "Is this your devotion to your friend? Why did you not go with your friend?" ¹⁸ Hushai replied to Absalom: "On the contrary, I am his whom the LORD and all this people and all Israel have chosen, and with him I will stay. ¹⁹* Furthermore, as I was in attendance upon your father, so will I be before you. Whom should I serve, if not his son?" ²⁰ Then Absalom said to Ahithophel, "Offer your counsel on what we should do." ²¹* Ahithophel replied to Absalom: "Have relations with your father's concubines, whom he left behind to take care of the palace. When all Israel hears how odious you have made yourself to your father, all your partisans will take courage." ²²* So a tent was pitched on the roof for Absalom, and he visited his father's concubines in view of all Israel.

Counsel of Ahithophel

²³* Now the counsel given by Ahithophel at that time was as though one had sought divine revelation. Such was all his counsel both to David and to Absalom.

17 ¹ Ahithophel went on to say to Absalom: "Please let me choose twelve thousand men, and be off in pursuit of David tonight. ² If I come upon him when he is weary and discouraged, I shall cause him to panic. When all the people with him flee, I shall strike down the king alone. ³ Then I can bring back the rest of the people to you, as a bride returns to her husband. It is the death of only one man you are seeking; then all the people will be at peace." ⁴ This plan was agreeable to Absalom and to all the elders of Israel.

Counsel of Hushai

⁵ Then Absalom said, "Now call Hushai the Archite also; let us hear what he too has to say." ⁶ When Hushai came to Absalom, Absalom said to him: "This is what Ahithophel proposed. Shall we follow his proposal? If not, speak up." ⁷ Hushai replied to Absalom, "This time Ahithophel has not given good counsel." ⁸* And he went on to say: "You know that your father and his men are warriors, and that they are as fierce as a bear in the wild robbed of her cubs. Moreover, since your father is skilled in warfare, he will not spend the night with the people. ⁹ Even now he lies hidden in one of the caves or in some other place. And if some of our soldiers should fall at the first attack, whoever hears

---

† **16, 8:** *Bloodshed . . . Saul:* refers to the episode recounted in 2 Sm 21, 1–14.

16, 3: 2 Sm 19, 26f.
16, 4: 2 Sm 19, 30.

16, 5: 2 Sm 3, 16; 19, 17.
  22f; 1 Kgs 2, 8.

16, 9: 2 Sm 19, 23.29; 1 Sm
  24, 15; 26, 6.
16, 10: 2 Sm 15, 25f; 19, 23.
16, 11: 2 Sm 12, 11.
16, 13: 2 Sm 19, 19–24.
16, 16: 2 Sm 15, 32–37.

16, 19: 2 Sm 15, 34.
16, 21: 2 Sm 15, 16; 20, 3.
16, 22: 2 Sm 12, 11f.
16, 23: 2 Sm 15, 12.31; 17,
  23.
17, 8: Hos 13, 8.

of it will say, 'Absalom's followers have been slaughtered.' [10] Then even the brave man with the heart of a lion will lose courage. For all Israel knows that your father is a warrior and that those who are with him are brave.

[11] "This is what I counsel: Let all Israel from Dan to Beer-sheba, who are as numerous as the sands by the sea, be called up for combat; and go with them yourself. [12] We can then attack him wherever we find him, settling down upon him as dew alights on the ground. None shall survive—neither he nor any of his followers. [13] And if he retires into a city, all Israel shall bring ropes to that city and we can drag it into the gorge, so that not even a pebble of it can be found." [14]* Then Absalom and all the Israelites pronounced the counsel of Hushai the Archite better than that of Ahithophel. For the LORD had decided to undo Ahithophel's good counsel, in order thus to bring Absalom to ruin.

David Told of the Plan

[15] Then Hushai said to the priests Zadok and Abiathar: "This is the counsel Ahithophel gave Absalom and the elders of Israel, and this is what I counseled. [16] So send a warning to David immediately, not to spend the night at the fords near the desert, but to cross over without fail. Otherwise the king and all the people with him will be destroyed." [17] Now Jonathan and Ahimaaz were staying at En-rogel, since they could not risk being seen entering the city. A maidservant was to come with information for them, and they in turn were to go and report to King David. [18] But an attendant saw them and informed Absalom. They sped on their way and reached the house of a man in Bahurim who had a cistern in his courtyard. They let themselves down into this, [19] and the housewife took the cover and spread it over the cistern, strewing ground grain on the cover so that nothing could be noticed. [20] When Absalom's servants came to the woman at the house, they asked, "Where are Ahimaaz and Jonathan?" The woman replied, "They went by a short while ago toward the water." They searched, but found no one, and so returned to Jerusalem. [21] As soon as they left, Ahimaaz and Jonathan came up out of the cistern and went on to inform King David. They said to him: "Leave! Cross the water at once, for Ahithophel has given the following counsel in regard to you." [22] So David and all his people moved on and crossed the Jordan. By daybreak, there was no one left who had not crossed.

[23]* When Ahithophel saw that his counsel was not acted upon, he saddled his ass and departed, going to his home in his own city. Then, having left orders concerning his family, he hanged himself. And so he died and was buried in his father's tomb.

[24] Now David had gone to Mahanaim when Absalom crossed the Jordan accompanied by all the Israelites. [25]* Absalom had put Amasa in command of the army in Joab's place. Amasa was the son of an Ishmaelite named Ithra, who had married Abigail, daughter of Jesse and sister of Joab's mother Zeruiah. [26] Israel and Absalom encamped in the territory of Gilead.

[27]* When David came to Mahanaim, Shobi, son of Nahash from Rabbah of the Ammonites, Machir, son of Ammiel from Lodebar, and Barzillai, the Gileadite from Rogelim, [28]* brought couches, coverlets, basins and earthenware, as well as wheat, barley, flour, roasted grain, beans, lentils, [29] honey, butter and cheese from the flocks and herds, for David and those who were with him to eat; for they said, "The people have been hungry and tired and thirsty in the desert."

Preparation for Battle

18 [1] After mustering the troops he had with him, David placed officers in command of groups of a thousand and groups of a hundred. [2] David then put a third part of the soldiers under Joab's command, a third under command of Abishai, son of Zeruiah and brother of Joab, and a third under command of Ittai the Gittite. The king then said to the soldiers, "I intend to go out with you myself." [3] But they replied: "You must not come out with us. For if we should flee, we shall not count; even if half of us should die, we shall not count. You are equal to ten thousand of us. Therefore it is better that we have you to help us from the city." [4] So the king said to them, "I will do what you think best"; and he stood by the gate as all the soldiers marched out in units of a hundred and of a thousand. [5] But the king gave this command to Joab, Abishai and Ittai: "Be gentle with young Absalom for my sake." All the soldiers heard the king instruct the various leaders with regard to Absalom.

Defeat of Absalom

[6] David's army then took the field against Israel, and a battle was fought in the forest near Mahanaim. [7] The forces of Israel were defeated by David's servants, and the casualties there that day were heavy—twenty thousand men. [8] The battle spread out over that entire region, and the thickets consumed more combatants that day than did the sword.

17, 14: 2 Sm 15, 31.   17, 23: 2 Sm 15, 31; 16, 23.

17, 25: 2 Sm 19, 14; 20, 4-13.   1 Kgs 2, 7.
17, 27: 2 Sm 9, 4; 19, 32;
17, 28: 2 Sm 19, 32; Ezr 2, 61.

Death of Absalom

⁹ Absalom unexpectedly came up against David's servants. He was mounted on a mule, and, as the mule passed under the branches of a large terebinth, his hair caught fast in the tree. He hung between heaven and earth while the mule he had been riding ran off. ¹⁰ Someone saw this and reported to Joab that he had seen Absalom hanging from a terebinth. ¹¹ Joab said to his informant: "If you saw him, why did you not strike him to the ground on the spot? Then it would have been my duty to give you fifty pieces of silver and a belt." ¹² But the man replied to Joab: "Even if I already held a thousand pieces of silver in my two hands, I would not harm the king's son, for the king charged you and Abishai and Ittai in our hearing to protect the youth Absalom for his sake. ¹³ Had I been disloyal and killed him, the whole matter would have come to the attention of the king, and you would stand aloof." ¹⁴* Joab replied, "I will not waste time with you in this way." And taking three pikes in hand, he thrust for the heart of Absalom, still hanging from the tree alive. ¹⁵ Next, ten of Joab's young armor-bearers closed in on Absalom, and killed him with further blows. ¹⁶* Joab then sounded the horn, and the soldiers turned back from the pursuit of the Israelites, because Joab called on them to halt. ¹⁷* Absalom was taken up and cast into a deep pit in the forest, and a very large mound of stones was erected over him. And all the Israelites fled to their own tents.

¹⁸* During his lifetime Absalom had taken a pillar and erected it for himself in the King's Valley, for he said, "I have no son to perpetuate my name." The pillar which he named for himself is called Yadabshalom to the present day.

David Told of Absalom's Death

¹⁹ Then Ahimaaz, son of Zadok, said, "Let me run to take the good news to the king that the LORD has set him free from the grasp of his enemies." ²⁰ But Joab said to him: "You are not the man to bring the news today. On some other day you may take the good news, but today you would not be bringing good news, for in fact the king's son is dead." ²¹ Then Joab said to a Cushite, "Go, tell the king what you have seen." The Cushite bowed to Joab and sped away. ²² But Ahimaaz, son of Zadok, said to Joab again, "Come what may, permit me also to run after the Cushite." Joab replied: "Why do you want to run, my son? You will receive no reward." ²³ But he insisted, "Come what may, I want to run." Joab said to him, "Very well." Ahimaaz sped off by way of the Jordan plain and outran the Cushite.

²⁴ Now David was sitting between the two gates, and a lookout mounted to the roof of the gate above the city wall, where he looked about and saw a man running all alone. ²⁵ The lookout shouted to inform the king, who said, "If he is alone, he has good news to report." As he kept coming nearer, ²⁶ the lookout spied another runner. From his place atop the gate he cried out, "There is another man running by himself." And the king responded, "He, too, is bringing good news." ²⁷* Then the lookout said, "I notice that the first one runs like Ahimaaz, son of Zadok." The king replied, "He is a good man; he comes with good news." ²⁸ Then Ahimaaz called out and greeted the king. With face to the ground he paid homage to the king and said, "Blessed be the LORD your God, who has delivered up the men who rebelled against my lord the king." ²⁹ But the king asked, "Is the youth Absalom safe?" And Ahimaaz replied, "I saw a great disturbance when the king's servant Joab sent your servant on, but I do not know what it was." ³⁰ The king said, "Step aside and remain in attendance here." So he stepped aside and remained there. ³¹ When the Cushite came in, he said, "Let my lord the king receive the good news that this day the LORD has taken your part, freeing you from the grasp of all who rebelled against you." ³² But the king asked the Cushite, "Is young Absalom safe?" The Cushite replied, "May the enemies of my lord the king and all who rebel against you with evil intent be as that young man!"

19 ¹ The king was shaken, and went up to the room over the city gate to weep. He said as he wept, "My son Absalom! My son, my son Absalom! If only I had died instead of you, Absalom, my son, my son!"

18, 14: 2 Sm 12, 10; 13, 28f.   **18, 17:** Jos 7, 26; 8, 29; 10, 27.   **18, 27:** 2 Kgs 9, 20.
18, 16: 2 Sm 20, 23–26.   **18, 18:** 2 Sm 14, 27.

Surviving Grief

It is a cold winter day when the state trooper comes to the door with the news that James Washington has just lost his son in an automobile accident. James falls to the ground in utter pain. Michael was just sixteen years old. James weeps as the trooper helps him up; the young officer begins to cry as he thinks of his own son, just three years of age.

There is no greater loss for parents than the death of a child. In 2 Sm 19, 1, King David is devastated by the death of his son Absalom, despite Absalom's betrayal. There is no easy answer or explanation when someone we love dies. How could God allow this? It is too hard to understand. What helps is to allow ourselves to mourn like David and to place ourselves into God's healing hands.

Life continues. Joab challenges David not to forget the people who have served him faithfully and count on his leadership (verses 6–8). In our grief, we must not forget the family and friends who grieve with us. We need them, and they need us to heal the pain of loss.

▶ 2 Sm 19, 1–9

Joab Reproves David

2 Joab was told that the king was weeping and mourning for Absalom; 3 and that day's victory was turned into mourning for the whole army when they heard that the king was grieving for his son. 4 The soldiers stole into the city that day like men shamed by flight in battle. 5* Meanwhile the king covered his face and cried out in a loud voice, "My son Absalom! Absalom! My son, my son!" 6 Then Joab went to his residence and said: "Though they saved your life and your sons' and daughters' lives, also the lives of your wives and those of your concubines, you have put all your servants to shame today 7 by loving those who hate you and hating those who love you. For you have shown today that officers and servants mean nothing to you. Indeed I am now certain that if Absalom were alive today and all of us dead, you would think that more suitable. 8 Now then, get up! Go out and speak kindly to your servants. I swear by the LORD that if you do not go out, not a single man will remain with you overnight, and this will be a far greater disaster for you than any that has afflicted you from your youth until now." 9 So the king stepped out and sat at the gate. When all the people were informed that the king was sitting at the gate, they came into his presence.

The Reconciliation

Now the Israelites had fled to their separate tents, 10 but throughout the tribes of Israel all the people were arguing among themselves, saying to one another: "The king delivered us from the clutches of our enemies, and it was he who rescued us from the grip of the Philistines. But now he has fled from the country before Absalom, 11 and Absalom, whom we anointed over us, died in battle. Why, then, should you remain silent about restoring the king to his palace?" When the talk of all Israel reached the king, 12 David sent word to the priests Zadok and Abiathar: "Say to the elders of Judah: 'Why should you be last to restore the king to his palace? 13 You are my brothers, you are my bone and flesh. Why should you be last to restore the king?' 14* Also say to Amasa: 'Are you not my bone and flesh? May God do thus and so to me, if you do not become my general permanently in place of Joab.' " 15 He won over all the Judahites as one man, and so they summoned the king to return, with all his servants.

David and Shimei

16 When the king, on his return, reached the Jordan, Judah had come to Gilgal to meet him and to escort him across the Jordan. 17* Shimei, son of Gera, the Benjaminite from Bahurim, hurried down with the Judahites to meet King David, 18* accompanied by a thousand men from Benjamin. Ziba, too, the servant of the house of Saul, accompanied by his fifteen sons and twenty servants, hastened to the Jordan before the king. 19* They crossed over the ford to bring the king's household over and to do whatever he wished. When Shimei, son of Gera, crossed the Jordan, he fell down before the king 20 and said to him: "May my lord not hold me guilty, and may he not remember and take to heart

19, 5: 2 Sm 15, 30.   19, 17: 2 Sm 16, 5–13.   19, 18: 2 Sm 16, 1–4; 19,   19, 19ff: 2 Sm 16, 13; Ex 22,
19, 14: 2 Sm 17, 25; 20, 4.   25–31.   27; 1 Kgs 2, 8.

the wrong that your servant did the day my lord the king left Jerusalem. 21 For your servant knows that he has done wrong. Yet realize that I have been the first of the whole house of Joseph to come down today to meet my lord the king." 22 But Abishai, son of Zeruiah, countered: "Shimei must be put to death for this. He cursed the LORD'S anointed." 23* David replied: "What has come between you and me, sons of Zeruiah, that you would create enmity for me this day? Should anyone die today in Israel? Am I not aware that today I am king of Israel?" 24 Then the king said to Shimei, "You shall not die." And the king gave him his oath.

David and Meribbaal

25 Meribbaal, son of Saul, also went down to meet the king. He had not washed his feet nor trimmed his mustache nor washed his clothes from the day the king left until he returned safely. 26* When he came from Jerusalem to meet the king, the king asked him, "Why did you not go with me, Meribbaal?" 27* He replied: "My lord the king, my servant betrayed me. For your servant, who is lame, said to him, 'Saddle the ass for me, that I may ride on it and go with the king.' 28 But he slandered your servant before my lord the king. But my lord the king is like an angel of God. Do what you judge best. 29* For though my father's entire house deserved only death from my lord the king, yet you placed your servant among the guests at your table. What right do I still have to make further appeal to the king?" 30* But the king said to him: "Why do you go on talking? I say, 'You and Ziba shall divide the property.'" 31 Meribbaal answered the king, "Indeed let him have it all, now that my lord the king has returned safely to his palace."

David and Barzillai

32* Barzillai the Gileadite also came down from Rogelim and escorted the king to the Jordan for his crossing, taking leave of him there. 33 It was Barzillai, a very old man of eighty and very wealthy besides, who had provisioned the king during his stay in Mahanaim. 34 The king said to Barzillai, "Cross over with me, and I will provide for your old age as my guest in Jerusalem." 35 But Barzillai answered the king: "How much longer have I to live, that I should go up to Jerusalem with the king? 36 I am now eighty years old. Can I distinguish between good and bad? Can your servant taste what he eats and drinks, or still appreciate the voices of singers and songstresses? Why should your servant be any further burden to my

lord the king? 37 In escorting the king across the Jordan, your servant is doing little enough! Why should the king give me this reward? 38 Please let your servant go back to die in his own city by the tomb of his father and mother. Here is your servant Chimham. Let him cross over with my lord the king. Do for him whatever you will." 39 Then the king said to him, "Chimham shall come over with me, and I will do for him as you would wish. And anything else you would like me to do for you, I will do." 40 Then all the people crossed over the Jordan, but the king remained; he kissed Barzillai and bade him Godspeed as he returned to his own district. 41 Finally the king crossed over to Gilgal, accompanied by Chimham.

Israel and Judah Quarrel

All the people of Judah and half of the people of Israel had escorted the king across. 42 But all these Israelites began coming to the king and saying, "Why did our brothers the Judahites steal you away and escort the king and his household across the Jordan, along with all David's men?" 43 All the Judahites replied to the men of Israel: "Because the king is our relative. Why are you angry over this affair? Have we had anything to eat at the king's expense? Or have portions from his table been given to us?" 44* The Israelites answered the Judahites: "We have ten shares in the king. Also, we are the first-born rather than you. Why do you slight us? Were we not first to speak of restoring the king?" Then the Judahites in turn spoke even more fiercely than the Israelites.

Sheba's Rebellion

20 1* Now a rebellious individual from Benjamin named Sheba, the son of Bichri, happened to be there. He sounded the horn and cried out,

"We have no portion in David,
    nor any share in the son of Jesse.
    Every man to his tent, O Israel!"

2 So all the Israelites left David for Sheba, son of Bichri. But from the Jordan to Jerusalem the Judahites remained loyal to their king. 3* When King David came to his palace in Jerusalem, he took the ten concubines whom he had left behind to take care of the palace and placed them in confinement. He provided for them, but had no further relations with them. And so they remained in confinement to the day of their death, lifelong widows.

19, 23: 2 Sm 16, 9f; 1 Sm 11, 13; 1 Kgs 2, 8.38.46.
19, 26: 2 Sm 16, 3.
19, 27: 2 Sm 9, 2–13; Dt 21, 12f.
19, 29: 2 Sm 9, 9ff.

19, 30: 2 Sm 16, 4.
19, 32: 2 Sm 17, 27ff; 1 Kgs 2, 7; Ezr 2, 61.
19, 44: 1 Kgs 11, 31.
20, 1: 1 Kgs 12, 16.
20, 3: 2 Sm 15, 16; 16, 20ff.

Amasa's Death

4* Then the king said to Amasa: "Summon the Judahites for me within three days. Then present yourself here." 5 Accordingly Amasa set out to summon Judah, but delayed beyond the time set for him by David. 6 Then David said to Abishai: "Sheba, son of Bichri, may now do us more harm than Absalom did. Take your lord's servants and pursue him, lest he find fortified cities and take shelter while we look on." 7* So Joab and the Cherethites and Pelethites and all the warriors marched out behind Abishai from Jerusalem to campaign in pursuit of Sheba, son of Bichri. 8*† They were at the great stone in Gibeon when Amasa met them. Now Joab had a belt over his tunic, from which was slung, in its sheath near his thigh, a sword that could be drawn with a downward movement. 9 And Joab asked Amasa, "How are you, my brother?" With his right hand Joab held Amasa's beard as if to kiss him. 10* And since Amasa was not on his guard against the sword in Joab's other hand, Joab stabbed him in the abdomen with it, so that his entrails burst forth to the ground, and he died without receiving a second thrust. Then Joab and his brother Abishai pursued Sheba, son of Bichri. 11 One of Joab's attendants stood by Amasa and said, "Let him who favors Joab and is for David follow Joab." 12 Amasa lay covered with blood in the middle of the highroad, and the man noticed that all the soldiers were stopping. So he removed Amasa from the road to the field and placed a garment over him, because all who came up to him were stopping. 13 When he had been removed from the road, everyone went on after Joab in pursuit of Sheba, son of Bichri.

Joab Pursues Sheba

14 Sheba passed through all the tribes of Israel to Abel Beth-maacah. Then all the Bichrites assembled and they too entered the city after him. 15 So David's servants came and besieged him in Abel Beth-maacah. They threw up a mound against the city, and all the soldiers who were with Joab began battering the wall to throw it down. 16 Then a wise woman from the city stood on the outworks and called out, "Listen, listen! Tell Joab to come here, that I may speak with him." 17 When Joab had come near her, the woman said, "Are you Joab?" And he replied, "Yes." She said to him, "Listen to what your maidservant has to say." He replied, "I am listening." 18*† Then she went on to say: "There is an ancient saying, 'Let them ask if they will in

Abel 19 or in Dan whether loyalty is finished or ended in Israel.' You are seeking to beat down a city that is a mother in Israel. Why do you wish to destroy the inheritance of the LORD?" 20 Joab answered, "Not at all, not at all! I do not wish to destroy or to ruin anything. 21 That is not the case at all. A man named Sheba, son of Bichri, from the hill country of Ephraim has rebelled against King David. Surrender him alone, and I will withdraw from the city." Then the woman said to Joab, "His head shall be thrown to you across the wall." 22 She went to all the people with her advice, and they cut off the head of Sheba, son of Bichri, and threw it out to Joab. He then sounded the horn, and they scattered from the city to their own tents, while Joab returned to Jerusalem to the king.

David's Officials

23* Joab was in command of the whole army of Israel. Banaiah, son of Jehoiada, was in command of the Cherethites and Pelethites. 24 Adoram was in charge of the forced labor. Jehoshaphat, son of Ahilud, was the chancellor. 25* Shawsha was the scribe. Zadok and Abiathar were priests. 26 Ira the Jairite was also David's priest.

V: Appendixes

Gibeonite Vengeance

21 1* During David's reign there was a famine for three successive years. David had recourse to the LORD, who said, "There is bloodguilt on Saul and his family because he put the Gibeonites to death." 2* So the king called the Gibeonites and spoke to them. (Now the Gibeonites were not Israelites, but survivors of the Amorites; and although the Israelites had given them their oath, Saul had attempted to kill them off in his zeal for the men of Israel and Judah.) 3 David said to the Gibeonites, "What must I do for you and how must I make atonement, that you may bless the inheritance of the LORD?" 4 The Gibeonites answered him, "We have no claim against Saul and his house for silver or gold, nor is it our place to put any man to death in Israel." Then he said, "I will do for you whatever you propose." 5 They said to the king, "As for the man who was exterminating us and who intended to destroy us that we might have no place in all the territory of Israel, 6 let seven men from among his descendants be given to us, that we may dismember them before the LORD in Gibeon, on the

---

† **20, 8:** The text of this verse is quite uncertain.
20, 18f: The proverbial expression here has been poorly transmitted, and its sense is doubtful.

20, 4: 2 Sm 17, 25; 19, 14.
20, 7: 2 Sm 8, 18.
20, 8: 2 Sm 2, 13.
20, 10: 1 Kgs 2, 5.
20, 18: Gn 49, 16.
20, 23: 2 Sm 8, 16ff; 23, 20.
20, 25: 2 Sm 8, 17f.
21, 1: 2 Sm 24, 13.
21, 2: Jos 9, 3–27.

LORD'S mountain." The king replied, "I will give them up." [7]* The king, however, spared Meribbaal, son of Jonathan, son of Saul, because of the LORD'S oath that formed a bond between David and Saul's son Jonathan. [8]* But the king took Armoni and Meribbaal, the two sons that Aiah's daughter Rizpah had borne to Saul, and the five sons of Saul's daughter Merob that she had borne to Adriel, son of Barzillai the Meholathite, [9] and surrendered them to the Gibeonites. They then dismembered them on the mountain before the LORD. The seven fell at the one time; they were put to death during the first days of the harvest—that is, at the beginning of the barley harvest.

[10]* Then Rizpah, Aiah's daughter, took sackcloth and spread it out for herself on the rock from the beginning of the harvest until rain came down on them from the sky, fending off the birds of the sky from settling on them by day, and the wild animals by night. [11] When David was informed of what Rizpah, Aiah's daughter, the concubine of Saul, had done, [12]* he went and obtained the bones of Saul and of his son Jonathan from the citizens of Jabesh-gilead, who had carried them off secretly from the public square of Beth-shan, where the Philistines had hanged them at the time they killed Saul on Gilboa. [13] When he had brought up from there the bones of Saul and of his son Jonathan, the bones of those who had been dismembered were also gathered up. [14]* Then the bones of Saul and of his son Jonathan were buried

in the tomb of his father Kish at Zela in the territory of Benjamin. After all that the king commanded had been carried out, God granted relief to the land.

Exploits in Philistine Wars

[15] There was another battle between the Philistines and Israel. David went down with his servants and fought the Philistines, but David grew tired. [16] Dadu, one of the Rephaim, whose bronze spear weighed three hundred shekels, was about to take him captive. Dadu was girt with a new sword and planned to kill David, [17]* but Abishai, son of Zeruiah, came to his assistance and struck and killed the Philistine. Then David's men swore to him, "You must not go out to battle with us again, lest you quench the lamp of Israel."

[18]* After this there was another battle with the Philistines in Gob. On that occasion Sibbecai, from Husha, killed Saph, one of the Rephaim.* [19]* There was another battle with the Philistines in Gob, in which Elhanan, son of Jair from Bethlehem, killed Goliath of Gath, who had a spear with a shaft like a weaver's heddle-bar. [20] There was another battle at Gath in which there was a man of large stature with six fingers on each hand and six toes on each foot—twenty-four in all. He too was one of the Rephaim. [21]* And when he insulted Israel, Jonathan, son of David's brother Shimei, killed him. [22] These four were Rephaim in Gath, and they fell at the hands of David and his servants.

LIVE IT!

The Lord Is My Rock

Build on the rock! What exactly does that mean? Have you ever watched a house being built? One of the first things that a contractor does is level the ground and put in a foundation. Upon the foundation, the structure begins to grow. A solid foundation will enable that house to stand for many years.

The same goes for our life, both personally and communally. What is your foundation—the rock—that your life is built on? In 2 Sm 22, 2, King David says to the LORD, "[You are] my rock, my fortress, my deliverer." David built his life on the rock and foundation of the LORD. As a result, he found refuge in times of fear. It was this rock that saved David and the people of Israel from the hands of their enemies. Because of David's reliance on God, his kingdom is seen by later generations of Jews as the ideal kingdom for Israel.

You too can find this same refuge, this same saving grace. Starting today, build your life with the Lord as your foundation (see Mt 7, 24–27). The next time you face a battle, be it drugs or envy or anger or lust, *stand on the rock!*

▶ 2 Sm 22, 1–4

21, 7: 2 Sm 9, 13; 1 Sm 18, 3; 20, 8ff.15f.42.
21, 8: 2 Sm 3, 7.
21, 10: 2 Sm 3, 31; 12, 16.
21, 12: 1 Sm 31, 10–13.
21, 14: 2 Sm 24, 25.
21, 17: 1 Kgs 11, 36; 15, 4; 2 Kgs 8, 19.
21, 18–22: 1 Chr 20, 4–8.
21, 18: 2 Sm 23, 27.
21, 19f: 1 Sm 17, 4.7.
21, 21: 2 Sm 13, 3.

Song of Thanksgiving

22 1*† David sang the words of this song to the LORD when the LORD had rescued him from the grasp of all his enemies and from the hand of Saul. 2* This is what he sang:

A

I

"O LORD, my rock, my fortress, my deliverer,
3*† my God, my rock of refuge!
My shield, the horn of my salvation,
my stronghold, my refuge,
my savior, from violence you keep me safe.
4 'Praised be the LORD,' I exclaim,
and I am safe from my enemies.

II

5† "The breakers of death surged round
about me,
the floods of perdition overwhelmed me;
6 The cords of the nether world enmeshed me,
the snares of death overtook me.
7† In my distress I called upon the LORD
and cried out to my God;
From his temple he heard my voice,
and my cry reached his ears.

III

8† "The earth swayed and quaked;
the foundations of the heavens trembled
and shook when his wrath flared up.
9 Smoke rose from his nostrils,
and a devouring fire from his mouth;
he kindled coals into flame.
10* He inclined the heavens and came down,
with dark clouds under his feet.

11*† He mounted a cherub and flew,
borne on the wings of the wind.
12 He made darkness the shelter about him,
with spattering rain and thickening clouds.

13 From the brightness of his presence
coals were kindled to flame.

14 "The LORD thundered from heaven;
the Most High gave forth his voice.
15* He sent forth arrows to put them to flight;
he flashed lightning and routed them.
16 Then the wellsprings of the sea appeared,
the foundations of the earth were
laid bare,
At the rebuke of the LORD,
at the blast of the wind of his wrath.

17* "He reached out from on high and
grasped me;
he drew me out of the deep waters.
18 He rescued me from my mighty enemy,
from my foes, who were too powerful
for me.
19 They attacked me on my day of calamity,
but the LORD came to my support.
20 He set me free in the open,
and rescued me, because he loves me.

IV

21 "The LORD rewarded me according to
my justice;
according to the cleanness of my hands he
requited me.
22 For I kept the ways of the LORD
and was not disloyal to my God.
23 For his ordinances were all present to me,
and his statutes I put not from me;
24 But I was wholehearted toward him,
and I was on my guard against guilt.
25 And the LORD requited me according to
my justice,
according to my innocence in his sight.

26*† "Toward the faithful you are faithful;
toward the wholehearted you
are wholehearted;

22, 1–51: This song of thanksgiving is also given, with a few small variants, in Ps 18. In both places it is attributed to David. Two main sections can be distinguished. In the first part, after an introductory stanza of praise to God (2–4), David describes the peril he was in (5–7), and then poetically depicts, under the form of a theophany, God's intervention in his behalf (8–20), concluding with an acknowledgment of God's justice (21–31). In the second part, God is praised for having prepared the psalmist for war (32–35), given him victory over his enemies (36–39), whom he put to flight (40–43), and bestowed on him dominion over many peoples (44–46). The entire song ends with paean of grateful praise (47–51).

22, 3: *The horn of my salvation:* my strong savior. The horn, the dreadful weapon of an enraged bull, was a symbol of strength; cf Lk 1, 69.

22, 5f: These verses are to be understood figuratively.

22, 7: *His temple:* his heavenly abode.

22, 8ff: God's intervention is graphically portrayed under the figures of an earthquake (vv 8.16) and a thunderstorm (vv 9–15); cf Jgs 5, 4f; Pss 29; 97, 2–6; Hb 3.

22, 11: *He mounted a cherub:* since God makes the winds his messengers, or "angels" (Ps 104, 4), he is spoken of poetically as riding on the clouds, or on the angelic creatures called "cherubim." His earthly throne above the ark of the covenant was likewise associated with two winged cherubim; cf Ex 37, 7ff. In both senses the Lord is enthroned upon the cherubim; cf Pss 79, 2; 99, 1.

22, 26f: Men are treated by God in the same way they treat him and their fellow men.

22, 1: Ps 18, 1.   22, 11: Ex 25, 18.
22, 2–51: Ps 18, 3–51.   22, 15: Ps 144, 6.
22, 3: 1 Sm 2, 1f.   22, 17: Ps 144, 7.
22, 10: Ps 144, 5.   22, 26f: 1 Sm 2, 30.

2
S
M

27 Toward the sincere you are sincere;
        but toward the crooked you are astute.
28 You save lowly people,
        though on the lofty your eyes look down.
29† You are my lamp, O LORD!
        O my God, you brighten the darkness
        about me.
30 For with your aid I run against an
        armed band,
        and by the help of my God I leap over
        a wall.
31* God's way is unerring;
        the promise of the LORD is fire-tried;
        he is a shield to all who take refuge
        in him."

B

I

32 "For who is God except the LORD?
        Who is a rock save our God?
33 The God who girded me with strength
        and kept my way unerring;
34† Who made my feet swift as those of hinds
        and set me on the heights;
35 Who trained my hands for war
        till my arms could bend a bow of brass.

II

36 "You have given me your saving shield,
        and your help has made me great.
37 You made room for my steps;
        unwavering was my stride.
38 I pursued my enemies and destroyed them,
        nor did I turn again till I made an end
        of them.
39 I smote them and they did not rise;
        they fell beneath my feet.

III

40 "You girded me with strength for war;
        you subdued my adversaries beneath me.
41 My enemies you put to flight before me
        and those who hated me I destroyed.
42 They cried for help—but no one saved them;
        to the LORD—but he answered them not.
43 I ground them fine as the dust of the earth;
        like the mud in the streets I trampled
        them down.

IV

44 "You rescued me from the strife of my people;
        you made me head over nations.
        A people I had not known became my slaves;
45 as soon as they heard me, they obeyed.
46 The foreigners fawned and cringed before me;
        they staggered forth from their fortresses."

C

47 "The LORD live! And blessed be my Rock!
        Extolled be my God, Rock of my salvation.
48 O God, who granted me vengeance,
        who made peoples subject to me
49 and helped me escape from my enemies,
        Above my adversaries you exalt me
        and from the violent man you rescue me.
50* Therefore will I proclaim you, O LORD, among
        the nations,
        and I will sing praise to your name,
51 You who gave great victories to your king
        and showed kindness to your anointed,
        to David and his posterity forever."

The Last Words of David

23 ¹*† These are the last words of David:
        "The utterance of David, son of Jesse;
        the utterance of the man God raised up,
        Anointed of the God of Jacob,
        favorite of the Mighty One of Israel.
2* The spirit of the LORD spoke through me;
        his word was on my tongue.
3* The God of Israel spoke;
        of me the Rock of Israel said,
        'He that rules over men in justice,
        that rules in the fear of God,
4* Is like the morning light at sunrise
        on a cloudless morning,
        making the greensward sparkle after rain.'
5* Is not my house firm before God?
        He has made an eternal covenant with me,
        set forth in detail and secured.
        Will he not bring to fruition
        all my salvation and my every desire?
6* But the wicked are all like thorns to be
        cast away;
        they cannot be taken up by hand.
7   He who wishes to touch them
        must arm himself with iron and the shaft
        of a spear,
        and they must be consumed by fire."

---

†
22, 29: *My lamp:* a figure of life and happiness; cf 1 Kgs 11, 36.
  22, 34: *The heights:* a natural stronghold safe from attack; cf Ps 62, 3; Hb 3, 19.
  23, 1–7: The text of this short composition in the spirit of the wisdom writers (Prv 30, 1–6) is difficult in places; it views David's career in retrospect.

*
22, 31: Prv 30, 5.
22, 50: Ps 22, 23; Rom 15, 9.
23, 1: 1 Kgs 2, 3–9; Sir 47, 8.
23, 2: Is 59, 21; Jer 1, 9.
23, 3: Ps 72, 1–4.

23, 4: Jgs 5, 31; Ps 72, 6.
23, 5: 2 Sm 7, 11.15f; Ps 89, 30; Is 55, 3.
23, 6: Dt 13, 14.

David's Warriors

8*† These are the names of David's warriors. Ishbaal, son of Hachamoni, was the first of the Three. It was he who brandished his battle-ax over eight hundred slain in a single encounter. 9* Next to him, among the Three warriors, was Eleazar, son of Dodo the Ahohite. He was with David at Ephesdammim when the Philistines assembled there for battle. The Israelites had retreated, 10 but he stood his ground and fought the Philistines until his hand grew tired and became cramped, holding fast to the sword. The LORD brought about a great victory on that day; the soldiers turned back after Eleazar, but only to strip the slain. 11* Next to him was Shammah, son of Agee the Hararite. The Philistines had assembled at Lehi, where there was a plot of land full of lentils. When the soldiers fled from the Philistines, 12 he took his stand in the middle of the plot and defended it. He slew the Philistines, and the LORD brought about a great victory. Such were the deeds of the Three warriors.

13* During the harvest three of the Thirty went down to David in the cave of Adullam, while a Philistine clan was encamped in the Vale of Rephaim. 14 At that time David was in the refuge, and there was a garrison of Philistines in Bethlehem. 15 Now David had a strong craving and said, "Oh, that someone would give me a drink of water from the cistern that is by the gate of Bethlehem!" 16 So the Three warriors broke through the Philistine camp and drew water from the cistern that is by the gate of Bethlehem. But when they brought it to David he refused to drink it, and instead poured it out to the LORD, 17 saying: "The LORD forbid that I do this! Can I drink the blood of these men who went at the risk of their lives?" So he refused to drink it.

18 Abishai, brother of Joab, son of Zeruiah, was at the head of the Thirty. It was he who brandished his spear over three hundred slain. He was listed among the Thirty 19 and commanded greater respect than the Thirty, becoming their leader. However, he did not attain to the Three.

20* Benaiah, son of Jehoiada, a stalwart from Kabzeel, was a man of great achievements. It was he who slew the two lions in Moab. He also went down and killed the lion in the cistern at the time of the snow. 21 It was he, too, who slew an Egyptian of large stature. Although the Egyptian was armed with a spear, he went against him with a club and wrested the spear from the Egyptian's hand, then killed him with his own spear. 22 Such were the deeds performed by Benaiah, son of Jehoiada. He was listed among the Thirty warriors 23* and commanded greater respect than the Thirty. However, he did not attain to the Three. David put him in command of his bodyguard. 24*† Asahel, brother of Joab. . . .

Among the Thirty were: Elhanan, son of Dodo, from Bethlehem; 25 Shammah from En-harod; Elika from En-harod; 26 Helez from Beth-pelet; Ira, son of Ikkesh, from Tekoa; 27* Abiezer from Anathoth; Sibbekai from Hushah; 28 Zalmon from Ahoh; Maharai from Netophah; 29 Heled, son of Baanah, from Netophah; Ittai, son of Ribai, from Gibeah of the Benjaminites; 30 Benaiah from Pirathon; Hiddai from Nahale-gaash; 31 Abibaal from Beth-arabah; Azmaveth from Bahurim; 32 Eliahba from Shaalbon; Jashen the Gunite; Jonathan, 33 son of Shammah the Hararite; Ahiam, son of Sharar the Hararite; 34 Eliphelet, son of Ahasbai, from Bethmaacah; Eliam, son of Ahithophel, from Gilo; 35 Hezrai from Carmel; Paarai the Arbite; 36 Igal, son of Nathan, from Zobah; Bani the Gadite; 37 Zelek the Ammonite; Naharai from Beeroth, armor-bearer of Joab, son of Zeruiah; 38 Ira from Jattir; Gareb from Jattir; 39* Uriah the Hittite—thirty-seven in all.

Census of the People

24 1*† The LORD's anger against Israel flared again, and he incited David against the Israelites by prompting him to number Israel and Judah. 2 Accordingly the king said to Joab and the leaders of the army who were with him, "Tour all the tribes in Israel from Dan to Beer-sheba and register the people, that I may know their number." 3 But Joab said to the king: "May the LORD your God increase the number of people a hundredfold for your royal majesty to see it with his own eyes. But why does it please my lord the king to order a thing of this kind?" 4 The king, however, overruled Joab and the leaders of the army, so they left the king's presence in order to register the people of Israel. 5 Crossing the Jordan, they began near Aroer, south of the city in the wadi, and went in the direc-

---

23, 8ff: There are thirty-seven warriors in all mentioned in this list. First there are the Three warriors most noted for singlehanded exploits (vv 8–12). Then comes the story of a daring adventure by three unnamed members of the larger group (vv 13–17). Next come the commanders of the king's bodyguard, Abishai (vv 18–19) and Benaiah (vv 20–23), with whom must be counted Asahel (v 24) and Joab (vv 18.24.37), and finally the group of the Thirty (vv 24–39).

23, 24: A more complete notice about Asahel, who died early in his career (2 Sm 2, 16–23), is to be presumed lost at this point. Elhanan is the first of the Thirty.

24, 1ff: This story was probably joined at one time to 2 Sm 21, 1–14.

23, 8–39: 1 Chr 11, 41; 27, 1–15.
23, 9: 1 Sm 17, 1.
23, 11: Jgs 15, 9.
23, 13: 1 Sm 22, 1; Mi 1, 15.
23, 20: 2 Sm 8, 18; 20, 23; Jgs 14, 6; 1 Kgs 2, 29f.
23, 23: 1 Sm 22, 14.
23, 24: 2 Sm 2, 18–23.
23, 27: 2 Sm 21, 18.
23, 39: 2 Sm 11, 3f.
24, 1–25: 1 Chr 21, 1–27.

tion of Gad, toward Jazer. 6 They continued on to Gilead and to the district below Mount Hermon. Then they proceeded to Dan; from there they turned toward Sidon, 7 going to the fortress of Tyre and to all the cities of the Hivites and Canaanites, and ending up at Beer-sheba in the Negeb of Judah. 8 Thus they toured the whole country, reaching Jerusalem again after nine months and twenty days. 9 Joab then reported to the king the number of people registered: in Israel, eight hundred thousand men fit for military service; in Judah, five hundred thousand.

The Pestilence

10*† Afterward, however, David regretted having numbered the people, and said to the LORD: "I have sinned grievously in what I have done. But now, LORD, forgive the guilt of your servant, for I have been very foolish." 11 When David rose in the morning, the LORD had spoken to the prophet Gad, David's seer, saying: 12 "Go and say to David, 'This is what the LORD says: I offer you three alternatives; choose one of them, and I will inflict it on you.' " 13* Gad then went to David to inform him. He asked: "Do you want a three years' famine to come upon your land, or to flee from your enemy three months while he pursues you, or to have a three days' pestilence in your land? Now consider and decide what I must reply to him who sent me." 14 David answered Gad: "I am in very serious difficulty. Let us fall by the hand of God, for he is most merciful; but let me not fall by the hand of man." 15 Thus David chose the pestilence. Now it was the time of the wheat harvest when the plague broke out among the people. [The LORD then sent a pestilence over Israel from morning until the time appointed, and seventy thousand of the people from Dan to Beer-sheba died.] 16* But when the angel stretched forth his hand toward Jerusalem to destroy it, the LORD regretted the calamity and said to the angel causing the destruction among the people, "Enough now! Stay your hand." The angel of the LORD was then standing at the threshing floor of Araunah the Jebusite. 17† When David saw the angel who was striking the people, he said to the LORD: "It is I who have sinned; it is I, the shepherd, who have done wrong. But these are sheep; what have they done? Punish me and my kindred."

Sacrifice of Atonement

18 On the same day Gad went to David and said to him, "Go up and build an altar to the LORD on the threshing floor of Araunah the Jebusite." 19 Following Gad's bidding, David went up as the LORD had commanded. 20 Now Araunah looked down and noticed the king and his servants coming toward him while he was threshing wheat. So he went out and paid homage to the king, with face to the ground. 21 Then Araunah asked, "Why does my lord the king come to his servant?" David replied, "To buy the threshing floor from you, to build an altar to the LORD, that the plague may be checked among the people." 22* But Araunah said to David: "Let my lord the king take and offer up whatever he may wish. Here are oxen for holocausts, and threshing sledges and the yokes of the oxen for wood. 23 All this does Araunah give to the king." Araunah then said to the king, "May the LORD your God accept your offering." 24 The king, however, replied to Araunah, "No, I must pay you for it, for I cannot offer to the LORD my God holocausts that cost nothing." So David bought the threshing floor and the oxen for fifty silver shekels. 25 Then David built an altar there to the LORD, and offered holocausts and peace offerings. The LORD granted relief to the country, and the plague was checked in Israel.

---

† **24, 10:** The narrative supposes that since the people belonged to the Lord rather than to the king, only the Lord should know their exact number.
24, 17: Before this verse a Qumran manuscript (4Q Sam^a) gives the fuller text of 1 Chr 21, 16, an alternative to the words "When David saw the angel who was striking the people."

* **24, 10:** 1 Sm 24, 6; 1 Chr 21, 7.
24, 13: 2 Sm 21, 1.
24, 16: Ex 12, 23; 2 Kgs 19, 35.
24, 22f: 1 Sm 6, 14; 1 Kgs 19, 21.

The ancient Egyptians had an advanced civilization, yet today the remains of their handiwork lie buried under centuries of sand. The great Roman Empire spanned the Western world at the time of Jesus, yet today only scattered ruins testify to its existence. The same is true of the glorious but short-lived Israelite kingdom. The Books of 1 and 2 Kings trace its tragic collapse from the glories of Solomon's Temple to the Babylonian Exile.

In-depth

If the kingships of Saul and David could be described as the spring and summer of the Israelite kingdom, the Books of 1 and 2 Kings describe its fall and winter. The beginning of 1 Kings covers the glorious late summer under King Solomon. Solomon accumulated great riches, constructed a beautiful Temple, and built Jerusalem into a city rivaling any other center of power. But the summer was quickly over at Solomon's death, when the kingdom was split in two (see map 3, "The Kingdom Years"). The northern kingdom, called Israel, and the southern kingdom, called Judah, were ruled by a succession of kings, most of whom proved to be weak and sinful leaders. Their incompetence had disastrous consequences: the two kingdoms fell to foreign powers. Israel fell to the Assyrians in 722 B.C., and Judah to the Babylonians in 587 B.C.

The sorrow that we hear in 1 and 2 Kings is accompanied by a clear explanation: the people have fallen because of their wickedness and the wickedness of their leaders. Not surprisingly, the author of 1 and 2 Kings fashioned the history of God's people into a kind of morality tale, emphasizing the importance of faithfulness to the Covenant and the Law.

Of special interest in these books is the appearance of the classical prophet. Unlike the prophets of other lands, who were mere tools in the ruler's hand, the great prophets of Israel and Judah, like Elijah and Elisha, often directly opposed royal decisions and actions. Their job was not to pamper the ruler's pride but to speak God's word clearly and boldly.

As we read about the terrible crises that the kingdoms of Judah and Israel faced, we can reflect on one of the basic truths of human history: Apart from God there is no hope. Only one thing remains as history passes: God's promise.

At a Glance

I. The Reign of Solomon (1 Kgs 1, 1—11, 43).

II. Judah and Israel to the Time of Ahab (1 Kgs 12, 1—16, 34).

III. Stories of the Prophets (1 Kgs 17, 1—22, 54).

I. The Kingdoms of Israel and Judah (2 Kgs 1, 1—17, 41).

II. The Kingdom of Judah after 721 B.C. (2 Kgs 18, 1—25, 30).

Quick Facts

Period Covered
from 961 to 587 B.C.

Author
unknown, from the Deuteronomic tradition, writing after the fall of Jerusalem

Theme
the history of Israel's and Judah's kings from Solomon until the fall of Jerusalem

Of Note
The two books of Kings were originally one book.

1 Kings

I: The Reign of Solomon

1 ¹ When King David was old and advanced in years, though they spread covers over him he could not keep warm. ² His servants therefore said to him, "Let a young virgin be sought to attend you, lord king, and to nurse you. If she sleeps with your royal majesty, you will be kept warm." ³ So they sought for a beautiful girl throughout the territory of Israel, and found Abishag the Shunamite, whom they brought to the king. ⁴ The maiden, who was very beautiful, nursed the king and cared for him, but the king did not have relations with her.

Ambition of Adonijah

⁵ Adonijah, son of Haggith, began to display his ambition to be king. He acquired chariots, drivers, and fifty henchmen. ⁶ Yet his father never rebuked him or asked why he was doing this. Adonijah was also very handsome, and next in age to Absalom by the same mother. ⁷ He conferred with Joab, son of Zeruiah, and with Abiathar the priest, and they supported him. ⁸ However, Zadok the priest, Benaiah, son of Jehoiada, Nathan the prophet, and Shimei and his companions, the pick of David's army, did not side with Adonijah. ⁹† When he slaughtered sheep, oxen, and fatlings at the stone Zoheleth, near En-rogel, Adonijah invited all his brothers, the king's sons, and all the royal officials of Judah. ¹⁰ But he did not invite the prophet Nathan, or Benaiah, or the pick of the army, or his brother Solomon.

Solomon Proclaimed King

¹¹ Then Nathan said to Bathsheba, Solomon's mother: "Have you not heard that Adonijah, son of Haggith, has become king without the knowledge of our lord David? ¹² Come now, let me advise you so that you may save your life and that of your son Solomon. ¹³ Go, visit King David, and say to him, 'Did you not, lord king, swear to your handmaid: Your son Solomon shall be king after me and shall sit upon my throne? Why, then, has Adonijah become king?' ¹⁴ And while you are still there speaking to the king, I will come in after you and confirm what you have said."

¹⁵ So Bathsheba visited the king in his room, while Abishag the Shunamite was attending him because of his advanced age. ¹⁶ Bathsheba bowed in homage to the king, who said to her, "What do you wish?" ¹⁷ She answered him: "My lord, you swore to me your handmaid by the LORD, your God, that my son Solomon should reign after you and sit upon your throne. ¹⁸ But now Adonijah has become

---

† **1, 9:** *En-rogel:* the modern Job's Well southeast of Jerusalem. It marked the ancient boundary between the tribes of Benjamin and Judah (Jos 15, 7; 18, 16). Here David's men sought information about Absalom's revolt (2 Sm 17, 17).

king, and you, my lord king, do not know it. [19] He has slaughtered oxen, fatlings, and sheep in great numbers; he has invited all the king's sons, Abiathar the priest, and Joab, the general of the army, but not your servant Solomon. [20]† Now, my lord king, all Israel is waiting for you to make known to them who is to sit on the throne after your royal majesty. [21] If this is not done, when my lord the king sleeps with his fathers, I and my son Solomon will be considered criminals."

[22] While she was still speaking to the king, the prophet Nathan came in. [23] When he had been announced, the prophet entered the king's presence and, bowing to the floor, did him homage. [24] Then Nathan said: "Have you decided, my lord king, that Adonijah is to reign after you and sit on your throne? [25] He went down today and slaughtered oxen, fatlings, and sheep in great numbers; he invited all the king's sons, the commanders of the army, and Abiathar the priest, and they are eating and drinking in his company and saying, 'Long live King Adonijah!' [26] But me, your servant, he did not invite; nor Zadok the priest, nor Benaiah, son of Jehoiada, nor your servant Solomon. [27] Was this done by my royal master's order without my being told who was to succeed to your majesty's kingly throne?"

[28] King David answered, "Call Bathsheba here." When she re-entered the king's presence and stood before him, [29] the king swore, "As the LORD lives, who has delivered me from all distress, [30] this very day I will fulfill the oath I swore to you by the LORD, the God of Israel, that your son Solomon should reign after me and should sit upon my throne in my place." [31] Bowing to the floor in homage to the king, Bathsheba said, "May my lord, King David, live forever!" [32] Then King David summoned Zadok the priest, Nathan the prophet, and Benaiah, son of Jehoiada. When they had entered the king's presence, [33] he said to them: "Take with you the royal attendants. Mount my son Solomon upon my own mule and escort him down to Gihon. [34] There Zadok the priest and Nathan the prophet are to anoint him king of Israel, and you shall blow the horn and cry, 'Long live King Solomon!' [35] When you come back in his train, he is to go in and sit upon my throne and reign in my place. I designate him ruler of Israel and of Judah." [36] In answer to the king, Benaiah, son of Jehoiada, said: "So be it! May the LORD, the God of my lord the king, so decree! [37] As the LORD has been with your royal majesty, so may he be with Solomon, and exalt his throne even more than that of my lord, King David!"

[38]† So Zadok the priest, Nathan the prophet, Benaiah, son of Jehoiada, and the Cherethites and Pelethites went down, and mounting Solomon on King David's mule, escorted him to Gihon. [39] Then Zadok the priest took the horn of oil from the tent

Introducing ►SOLOMON

Solomon was one of the sons of David and Bathsheba. He ruled for forty years after King David died, and he was the third and last king to rule over the united kingdom of Israel.

There is an old saying that often our personal strengths are our greatest weaknesses. This is true of Solomon. He was a tremendous organizer, an able ruler, a clever politician, and a great builder—it was during his reign that the first Temple was built in Jerusalem. To fulfill these great accomplishments, however, Solomon taxed his people heavily, married foreign women to seal political alliances with other nations, and used forced labor to complete his building projects. These things offended God and made Solomon unpopular with the people of Israel.

When Solomon died, ten of the original twelve tribes from the northern part of Israel left the kingdom owing to these harsh practices and set up their own kingdom. Israel never again existed as a united kingdom ruled by an Israelite king. The author of Kings attributes this more to Solomon's acceptance of other gods near the end of his life than to his political mistakes.

---

† **1, 20:** At this time, neither law nor the right of primogeniture, but the will of the ruling monarch, determined succession to the throne.
1, 38: *Cherethites and Pelethites:* mercenaries in David's body-guard. They became part of his retinue after he defeated the Philistines and established himself in Jerusalem; cf 2 Sm 8, 18; 15, 18; 20, 23.

and anointed Solomon. They blew the horn and all the people shouted, "Long live King Solomon!" ⁴⁰ Then all the people went up after him, playing flutes and rejoicing so much as to split open the earth with their shouting.

⁴¹ Adonijah and all the guests who were with him heard it, just as they ended their banquet. When Joab heard the sound of the horn, he asked, "What does this uproar in the city mean?" ⁴² As he was speaking, Jonathan, son of Abiathar the priest, arrived. "Come," said Adonijah, "you are a man of worth and must bring good news." ⁴³ "On the contrary!" Jonathan answered him. "Our lord, King David, has made Solomon king. ⁴⁴ The king sent with him Zadok the priest, Nathan the prophet, Benaiah, son of Jehoiada, and the Cherethites and Pelethites, and they mounted him upon the king's own mule. ⁴⁵ Zadok the priest and Nathan the prophet anointed him king at Gihon, and they went up from there rejoicing, so that the city is in an uproar. That is the noise you heard. ⁴⁶ Besides, Solomon took his seat on the royal throne, ⁴⁷ and the king's servants went in and paid their respects to our lord, King David, saying, 'May God make Solomon more famous than you and exalt his throne more than your own!' And the king in his bed worshiped God, ⁴⁸ and this is what he said: 'Blessed be the LORD, the God of Israel, who has this day seated one of my sons upon my throne, so that I see it with my own eyes.' "

⁴⁹ All the guests of Adonijah left in terror, each going his own way. ⁵⁰† Adonijah, in fear of Solomon, also left; he went and seized the horns of the altar. ⁵¹ It was reported to Solomon that Adonijah, in his fear of King Solomon, had seized the horns of the altar and said, "Let King Solomon first swear that he will not kill me, his servant, with the sword." ⁵² Solomon answered, "If he proves himself worthy, not a hair shall fall from his head. But if he is found guilty of crime, he shall die." ⁵³ King Solomon sent to have him brought down from the altar, and he came and paid homage to the king. Solomon then said to him, "Go to your home."

David's Last Instructions and Death

2 ¹† When the time of David's death drew near, he gave these instructions to his son Solomon: ² "I am going the way of all mankind. Take courage and be a man. ³* Keep the mandate of the LORD, your God, following his ways and observing his statutes, commands, ordinances, and decrees as they are written in the law of Moses, that you may succeed in whatever you do, wherever you turn, ⁴* and the LORD may fulfill the promise he made on my behalf when he said, 'If your sons so conduct themselves that they remain faithful to me with their whole heart and with their whole soul, you shall always have someone of your line on the throne of Israel.' ⁵* You yourself know what Joab, son of Zeruiah, did to me when he slew the two generals of Israel's armies, Abner, son of Ner, and Amasa, son of Jether. He took revenge for the blood of war in a time of peace, and put blood shed without provocation on the belt about my waist and on the sandal on my foot. ⁶ Act with the wisdom you possess; you must not allow him to go down to the grave in peaceful old age.

⁷* "But be kind to the sons of Barzillai the Gileadite, and have them eat at your table. For they received me kindly when I was fleeing your brother Absalom.

⁸* "You also have with you Shimei, son of Gera, the Benjaminite of Bahurim, who cursed me balefully when I was going to Mahanaim. Because he came down to meet me at the Jordan, I swore to him by the LORD that I would not put him to the sword. ⁹ But you must not let him go unpunished. You are a prudent man and will know how to deal with him to send down his hoary head in blood to the grave."

¹⁰* David rested with his ancestors and was buried in the City of David. ¹¹* The length of David's reign over Israel was forty years: he reigned seven years in Hebron and thirty-three years in Jerusalem.

The Kingdom Made Secure

¹² When Solomon was seated on the throne of his father David, with his sovereignty firmly established, ¹³ Adonijah, son of Haggith, went to Bathsheba, the mother of Solomon. "Do you come as a friend?" she asked. "Yes," he answered, ¹⁴ and added, "I have something to say to you." She replied, "Say it." ¹⁵ So he said: "You know that the kingdom was mine, and all Israel expected me to be king. But the kingdom escaped me and became my brother's, for the LORD gave it to him. ¹⁶ But now there is one favor I would ask of you. Do not refuse

---

1, 50: *Horns of the altar:* the protuberances on each of the four corners of the altar were surrounded with a special degree of holiness (Ex 27, 2; 29, 12), and constituted a place of asylum for transgressors of the law (Ex 21, 13f; 1 Kgs 2, 28).

2, 1–6.8–9: Solomon is expected to remove from his father's family the imputation of blood guilt brought upon it by Joab in the unwarranted killings of Abner (2 Sm 3, 27–29) and Amasa (2 Sm 19, 9–10); and likewise to punish Shimei for his curse, the effects of which David had pledged himself not to avenge in person (2 Sm 19, 21–23). The standards of morality presumed in these verses are far from the Christian ones.

2, 3: Dt 17, 19.
2, 4: 2 Sm 7, 11–16; Ps 132, 11f.
2, 5: 2 Sm 3, 27; 20, 10.
2, 7: 2 Sm 19, 33ff.
2, 8: 2 Sm 16, 5; 19, 19.
2, 10: Acts 2, 29.
2, 11: 1 Chr 29, 27.

me." And she said, "Speak on." 17† He said, "Please ask King Solomon, who will not refuse you, to give me Abishag the Shunamite for my wife." 18 "Very well," replied Bathsheba, "I will speak to the king for you."

19 Then Bathsheba went to King Solomon to speak to him for Adonijah, and the king stood up to meet her and paid her homage. Then he sat down upon his throne, and a throne was provided for the king's mother, who sat at his right. 20 "There is one small favor I would ask of you," she said. "Do not refuse me." "Ask it, my mother," the king said to her, "for I will not refuse you." 21 So she said, "Let Abishag the Shunamite be given to your brother Adonijah for his wife." 22 "And why do you ask Abishag the Shunamite for Adonijah?" King Solomon answered his mother. "Ask the kingdom for him as well, for he is my elder brother and has with him Abiathar the priest and Joab, son of Zeruiah." 23 And King Solomon swore by the LORD: "May God do thus and so to me, and more besides, if Adonijah has not proposed this at the cost of his life. 24 And now, as the LORD lives, who has seated me firmly on the throne of my father David and made of me a dynasty as he promised, this day

shall Adonijah be put to death." 25 Then King Solomon sent Benaiah, son of Jehoiada, who struck him dead.

26 The king said to Abiathar the priest: "Go to your land in Anathoth. Though you deserve to die, I will not put you to death this time, because you carried the ark of the Lord GOD before my father David and shared in all the hardships my father endured." 27* So Solomon deposed Abiathar from his office of priest of the LORD, thus fulfilling the prophecy which the LORD had made in Shiloh about the house of Eli.

28 When the news came to Joab, who had sided with Adonijah, though not with Absalom, he fled to the tent of the LORD and seized the horns of the altar. 29 King Solomon was told that Joab had fled to the tent of the LORD and was at the altar. He sent Benaiah, son of Jehoiada, with the order, "Go, strike him down." 30 Benaiah went to the tent of the LORD and said to him, "The king says, 'Come out.' " But he answered, "No! I will die here." Benaiah reported to the king, "This is what Joab said to me in reply." 31 The king answered him: "Do as he has said. Strike him down and bury him, and you will remove from me and from my family the blood

God, Give Me Wisdom!

LIVE IT!

At the beginning of his reign, Solomon asked God for wisdom to govern his people. Under the advice of the prophet Nathan, Solomon became a great king. His failure came later because he betrayed God by accepting other gods and exploiting his people with work and taxes to build his magnificent royal city of Jerusalem.

Whenever you are in a leadership position, remember that you must use the power or authority you have in service to God and God's people; never use it to exploit others or for your own selfishness.

■ Ask God for the wisdom necessary to discern how to respond to the needs of people you lead.

■ Examine your leadership style frequently to see if you remain faithful to God's call to be a servant of those in need.

▶ 1 Kgs 3, 4–15

2, 17.22–25: Abishag had been the concubine of King David (1 Kgs 1, 4). His successor, Solomon, inherited his father's harem. When Adonijah requested Abishag as his wife, he was subtly undermining the security of Solomon's throne and exposing himself to the suspicion of insurrection that would cost him his life; cf 2 Sm 3, 6–11; 16, 22.

2, 27: 1 Sm 2, 31.

which Joab shed without provocation. 32* The LORD will hold him responsible for his own blood, because he struck down two men better and more just than himself, and slew them with the sword without my father David's knowledge: Abner, son of Ner, general of Israel's army, and Amasa, son of Jether, general of Judah's army. 33 Joab and his descendants shall be responsible forever for their blood. But there shall be the peace of the LORD forever for David, and his descendants, and his house, and his throne." 34 Benaiah, son of Jehoiada, went back, struck him down and killed him; he was buried in his house in the desert. 35 The king appointed Benaiah, son of Jehoiada, over the army in his place, and put Zadok the priest in place of Abiathar.

36 Then the king summoned Shimei and said to him: "Build yourself a house in Jerusalem and live there. Do not go anywhere else. 37 For if you leave, and cross the Kidron Valley, be certain you shall die without fail. You shall be responsible for your own blood." 38 Shimei answered the king: "I accept. Your servant will do just as the king's majesty has said." So Shimei stayed in Jerusalem for a long time. 39 But three years later, two of Shimei's servants ran away to Achish, son of Maacah, king of Gath, and Shimei was informed that his servants were in Gath. 40 So Shimei rose, saddled his ass, and went to Achish in Gath in search of his servants, whom he brought back. 41 When Solomon was informed that Shimei had gone from Jerusalem to Gath, and had returned, 42 the king summoned Shimei and said to him: "Did I not have you swear by the LORD to your clear understanding of my warning that, if you left and went anywhere else, you should die without fail? And you answered, 'I accept and obey'. 43 Why, then, have you not kept the oath of the LORD and the command that I gave you?" 44 And the king said to Shimei: "You know in your heart the evil that you did to my father David. Now the LORD requites you for your own wickedness. 45 But King Solomon shall be blessed, and David's throne shall endure before the LORD forever." 46 The king then gave the order to Benaiah, son of Jehoiada, who struck him dead as he left.

Wisdom of Solomon

3 1* With the royal power firmly in his grasp, Solomon allied himself by marriage with Pharaoh, king of Egypt. The daughter of Pharaoh, whom he married, he brought to the City of David, until he should finish building his palace, and the temple of the LORD, and the wall around Jerusalem. 2 However, the people were sacrificing on the high places, for up to that time no temple had been

A Wise Heart

A famous prayer, often called the Peace Prayer, by Saint Francis of Assisi (A.D. 1181–1226), contains the line "LORD, grant that I may not so much seek to be . . . understood, as to understand."

It is almost as if Saint Francis is echoing the prayer of King Solomon, who lived two thousand years before him. The request is the same. Both men ask God to give them the gift of a wise heart—the ability to see things as God sees them.

What a difference wisdom can make in our life. What a wonderful thing to pray for. What a blessing to increase the amount of wisdom in our world. What inspiring examples we have in the prayers of Solomon a millennium before Jesus, and of Francis a millennium after.

Let us ask God daily for a wise heart.

▶ 1 Kgs 3, 9

built to the name of the LORD. 3 Solomon loved the LORD, and obeyed the statutes of his father David; yet he offered sacrifice and burned incense on the high places.

4 The king went to Gibeon to sacrifice there, because that was the most renowned high place. Upon its altar Solomon offered a thousand holocausts. 5 In Gibeon the LORD appeared to Solomon in a dream at night. God said, "Ask something of me and I will give it to you." 6 Solomon answered: "You have shown great favor to your servant, my father David, because he behaved faithfully toward you, with justice and an upright heart; and you have continued this great favor toward him, even today, seating a son of his on his throne. 7 O LORD, my God, you have made me, your servant, king to succeed my father David; but I am a mere youth, not knowing at all how to act. 8 I serve you in the midst of the people whom you have chosen, a people so vast that it cannot be numbered or counted. 9* Give your servant, therefore, an understanding heart to judge your people and to distinguish right from wrong. For who is able to govern this vast people of yours?"

10 The LORD was pleased that Solomon made this request. 11 So God said to him: "Because you have asked for this—not for a long life for yourself, nor for riches, nor for the life of your enemies, but for understanding so that you may know what is right— 12 I do as you requested. I give you a heart so wise and understanding that there has never been anyone like you up to now, and after you there will come no one to equal you. 13* In addition, I give you what you have not asked for, such riches and glory that among kings there is not your like. 14 And if you follow me by keeping my statutes and commandments, as your father David did, I will give you a long life."

15 When Solomon awoke from his dream, he went to Jerusalem, stood before the ark of the covenant of the LORD, offered holocausts and peace offerings, and gave a banquet for all his servants.

Solomon's Judgment

16 Later, two harlots came to the king and stood before him. 17 One woman said: "By your leave, my lord, this woman and I live in the same house, and I gave birth in the house while she was present. 18 On the third day after I gave birth, this woman also gave birth. We were alone in the house; there was no one there but us two. 19 This woman's son died during the night; she smothered him by lying on him. 20 Later that night she got up and took my son from my side, as I, your handmaid, was sleeping. Then she laid him in her bosom, after she had laid her dead child in my bosom. 21 I rose in the morning to nurse my child, and I found him dead. But when I examined him in the morning light, I saw it was not the son whom I had borne."

22 The other woman answered, "It is not so! The living one is my son, the dead one is yours." But the first kept saying, "No, the dead one is your child, the living one is mine!" Thus they argued before the king. 23 Then the king said: "One woman claims, 'This, the living one, is my child, and the dead one is yours.' The other answers, 'No! The dead one is your child; the living one is mine.' " 24 The king continued, "Get me a sword." When they brought the sword before him, 25 he said, "Cut the living child in two, and give half to one woman and half to the other." 26 The woman whose son it was, in the anguish she felt for it, said to the king, "Please, my lord, give her the living child—please do not kill it!" The other, however, said, "It shall be neither mine nor yours. Divide it!" 27 The king then answered, "Give the first one the living child! By no means kill it, for she is the mother."

28 When all Israel heard the judgment the king had given, they were in awe of him, because they saw that the king had in him the wisdom of God for giving judgment.

Chief Officers of the Kingdom

4 1 Solomon was king over all Israel, 2 and these were the officials he had in his service:

Azariah, son of Zadok, priest;
3 Elihoreph and Ahijah, sons of Shisha, scribes;
Jehoshaphat, son of Ahilud, chancellor;
4 [Benaiah, son of Jehoiada, commander of the army;
Zadok and Abiathar, priests;]
5 Azariah, son of Nathan, chief of the commissaries;
Zabud, son of Nathan, companion to the king;
6 Ahishar, major-domo of the palace; and
Adoniram, son of Abda, superintendent of the forced labor.

Solomon's Royal State

7† Solomon had twelve commissaries for all Israel who supplied food for the king and his household, each having to provide for one month in the year. 8 Their names were:

the son of Hur in the hill country of Ephraim;
9 the son of Deker in Makaz, Shaalbim, Beth-shemesh, Elon and Beth-hanan;
10 the son of Hesed in Arubboth, as well as in Socoh and the whole region of Hepher;
11 the son of Abinadab, who was married to Solomon's daughter Taphath, in all the Naphath-dor;
12 Baana, son of Ahilud, in Taanach and Megiddo, and beyond Jokmeam, and in all Beth-shean, and in the country around Zarethan below Jezreel from Beth-shean to Abel-meholah;
13 the son of Geber in Ramoth-Gilead, having charge of the villages of Jair, son of Manasseh, in Gilead; and of the district of Argob in Bashan—sixty large walled cities with gates barred with bronze;
14 Ahinadab, son of Iddo, in Mahanaim;
15 Ahimaaz, who was married to Basemath, another daughter of Solomon, in Naphtali;
16 Baana, son of Hushai, in Asher and along the rocky coast;
17 Jehoshaphat, son of Paruah, in Issachar;
18 Shimei, son of Ela, in Benjamin;

---

† **4, 7–19:** The administration of the kingdom thus initiated by Solomon continued in its main features for the duration of the monarchy in Israel and Judah.

* **3, 13:** Wis 7, 11; Mt 6, 29.

HOW EXCELLENT

The First Book of Kings says, "Solomon surpassed all the Cedemites and all the Egyptians in wisdom" (5, 10).

This should be a source of pride for young African Americans. The people of Egypt and of the East are dark-skinned people. Ancient southern Egypt included the country of modern Ethiopia. The people in these countries must have been well known for their wisdom in order for the biblical author to use them in a comparison with Solomon. African Americans can praise God for their African ancestors: the wise, black people from Egypt and the East.

▸ **I Kgs 5, 10**

---

¹⁹† Geber, son of Uri, in the land of Gilead, the land of Sihon, king of the Amorites, and of Og, king of Bashan.

There was one prefect besides, in the king's own land.

5 ⁷ These commissaries, one for each month, provided food for King Solomon and for all the guests at the royal table. They left nothing unprovided. ⁸ For the chariot horses and draft animals also, each brought his quota of barley and straw to the required place.

²⁰† Judah and Israel were as numerous as the sands by the sea; they ate and drank and made merry. ¹* Solomon ruled over all the kingdoms from the River to the land of the Philistines, down to the border of Egypt; they paid Solomon tribute and were his vassals as long as he lived.

² Solomon's supplies for each day were thirty kors of fine flour, sixty kors of meal, ³ ten fatted oxen, twenty pasture-fed oxen, and a hundred sheep, not counting harts, gazelles, roebucks, and fatted fowl.

⁴ He ruled over all the land west of the Euphrates, from Tiphsah to Gaza, and over all its kings, and he had peace on all his borders round about. ⁵ Thus Judah and Israel lived in security, every man under his vine or under his fig tree from Dan to Beersheba, as long as Solomon lived.

⁶* Solomon had four thousand stalls for his twelve thousand chariot horses.

⁹* Moreover, God gave Solomon wisdom and exceptional understanding and knowledge, as vast as the sand on the seashore. ¹⁰ Solomon surpassed all the Cedemites and all the Egyptians in wisdom. ¹¹ He was wiser than all other men—than Ethan the Ezrahite, or Heman, Chalcol, and Darda, the musicians—and his fame spread throughout the neighboring nations. ¹²* Solomon also uttered three thousand proverbs, and his songs numbered a thousand and five. ¹³ He discussed plants, from the cedar on Lebanon to the hyssop growing out of the wall, and he spoke about beasts, birds, reptiles, and fishes. ¹⁴ Men came to hear Solomon's wisdom from all nations, sent by all the kings of the earth who had heard of his wisdom.

Preparations for the Temple

¹⁵ When Hiram, king of Tyre, heard that Solomon had been anointed king in place of his father, he sent an embassy to him; for Hiram had always been David's friend. ¹⁶ Solomon sent back this message to Hiram: ¹⁷ "You know that my father David, because of the enemies surrounding him on all sides, could not build a temple in honor of the LORD, his God, until such a time as the LORD should put these enemies under the soles of his feet. ¹⁸ But now the LORD, my God, has given me peace on all sides. There is no enemy or threat of

---

4, 19: *One prefect . . . in the king's own land:* the royal territory of Judah had its own peculiar administration different from that of the twelve districts which had to supply the king and his household with a month's provisions of food each year (v 7).

5, 20: This verse belongs to ch 4.

5, 1: Sir 47, 15f; 2 Chr 9, 26.
5, 6: 2 Chr 9, 25f.
5, 9–14: Sir 47, 16f.
5, 12: 1 Kgs 3, 12.

1
K
G
S

danger. [19]* So I propose to build a temple in honor of the LORD, my God, as the LORD predicted to my father David when he said: 'It is your son whom I will put upon your throne in your place who shall build the temple in my honor.' [20] Give orders, then, to have cedars from the Lebanon cut down for me. My servants shall accompany yours, since you know that there is no one among us who is skilled in cutting timber like the Sidonians, and I will pay you whatever you say for your servants' salary."

[21] When he had heard the words of Solomon, Hiram was pleased and said, "Blessed be the LORD this day, who has given David a wise son to rule this numerous people." [22] Hiram then sent word to Solomon, "I agree to the proposal you sent me, and I will provide all the cedars and fir trees you wish. [23] My servants shall bring them down from the Lebanon to the sea, and I will arrange them into rafts in the sea and bring them wherever you say. There I will break up the rafts, and you shall take the lumber. You, for your part, shall furnish the provisions I desire for my household."

[24] So Hiram continued to provide Solomon with all the cedars and fir trees he wished; [25] while Solomon every year gave Hiram twenty thousand kors of wheat to provide for his household, and twenty thousand measures of pure oil. [26] The LORD, moreover, gave Solomon wisdom as he promised him, and there was peace between Hiram and Solomon, since they were parties to a treaty.

[27] King Solomon conscripted thirty thousand workmen from all Israel. [28] He sent them to the Lebanon each month in relays of ten thousand, so that they spent one month in the Lebanon and two months at home. Adoniram was in charge of the draft. [29] Solomon had seventy thousand carriers and eighty thousand stonecutters in the mountain, [30] in addition to three thousand three hundred overseers, answerable to Solomon's prefects for the work, directing the people engaged in the work. [31] By order of the king, fine, large blocks were quarried to give the temple a foundation of hewn stone. [32] Solomon's and Hiram's builders, along with the Gebalites, hewed them out, and prepared the wood and stones for building the temple.

Building of the Temple

6 [1]*† In the four hundred and eightieth year from the departure of the Israelites from the land of Egypt, in the fourth year of Solomon's reign over Israel, in the month of Ziv, which is the second month, the construction of the temple of the LORD was begun.

[2] The temple which King Solomon built for the LORD was sixty cubits long, twenty wide, and twenty-five high. [3] The porch in front of the temple was twenty cubits from side to side, along the width of the nave, and ten cubits deep in front of the temple. [4] Splayed windows with trellises were made for the temple, [5] and adjoining the wall of the temple, which enclosed the nave and the sanctuary, an annex of several stories was built. [6] Its lowest story was five cubits wide, the middle one six cubits wide, the third seven cubits wide, because there were offsets along the outside of the temple so that the beams would not be fastened into the walls of the temple. [7] (The temple was built of stone dressed at the quarry, so that no hammer, axe, or iron tool was to be heard in the temple during its construction.) [8] The entrance to the lowest floor of the annex was at the right side of the temple, and stairs with intermediate landings led up to the middle story and from the middle story to the third. [9] When the temple was built to its full height, it was roofed in with rafters and boards of cedar. [10] The annex, with its lowest story five cubits high, was built all along the outside of the temple, to which it was joined by cedar beams.

[11]† This word of the LORD came to Solomon: [12]* "As to this temple you are building—if you observe my statutes, carry out my ordinances, keep and obey all my commands, I will fulfill toward you the promise I made to your father David. [13]* I will dwell in the midst of the Israelites and will not forsake my people Israel."

[14] When Solomon finished building the temple, [15] its walls were lined from floor to ceiling beams with cedar paneling, and its floor was laid with fir planking. [16] At the rear of the temple a space of twenty cubits was set off by cedar partitions from the floor to the rafters, enclosing the sanctuary, the holy of holies. [17] The nave, or part of the temple in front of the sanctuary, was forty cubits long. [18] The cedar in the interior of the temple was carved in the form of gourds and open flowers; all was of cedar, and no stone was to be seen.

[19]† In the innermost part of the temple was located the sanctuary to house the ark of the LORD's

---

6, 1: *Construction of the temple of the LORD* is here paralleled in importance with the founding of the nation after the departure from Egypt. In both, God is the central figure who chose Israel as his people, and now chooses the place where his temple should be built (Dt 12, 4–18.26). The year is given in a round number, 480, which corresponds to twelve generations. *The fourth year of Solomon's reign:* c. 968 B.C.

6, 11ff: *This word of the LORD . . . my people Israel:* the oracle, which came as a climax at the completion of the work, was an expression of God's acceptance and approval. Nevertheless the fulfill-

ment of God's promises to David and his royal descendants will depend on their observance of his ordinances and commands.

6, 19: *The innermost part of the temple:* the sanctuary or holy of holies reserved exclusively for the Lord. Here through his presence he dwelt as on a throne between the cherubim above the ark of the covenant (2 Kgs 6, 23–28; 2 Chr 3, 10–13). See note on Ex 25, 18ff.

5, 19: 2 Sm 7, 13; 1 Chr 22, 10.
6, 1: 2 Chr 3, 1.
6, 12: 2 Sm 7, 13.
6, 13: 1 Chr 22, 9f.

The Temple of Solomon

1 Kings, chap. 6

Holy of Holies

Storeroom

Storeroom

Holy Place
(Nave)

Porch

Pillar

Pillar

Steps

Sea of Bronze

Altar

in size and shape, 26 and each was exactly ten cubits high. 27 The cherubim were placed in the inmost part of the temple, with their wings spread wide, so that one wing of each cherub touched a side wall while the other wing, pointing toward the middle of the room, touched the corresponding wing of the second cherub. 28 The cherubim, too, were overlaid with gold.

29 The walls on all sides of both the inner and the outer rooms had carved figures of cherubim, palm trees, and open flowers. 30 The floor of both the inner and the outer rooms was overlaid with gold. 31 At the entrance of the sanctuary, doors of olive wood were made; the doorframes had beveled posts. 32 The two doors were of olive wood, with carved figures of cherubim, palm trees, and open flowers. The doors were overlaid with gold, which was also molded to the cherubim and the palm trees. 33 The same was done at the entrance to the nave, where the doorposts of olive wood were rectangular. 34 The two doors were of fir wood; each door was banded by a metal strap, front and back, 35 and had carved cherubim, palm trees, and open flowers, over which gold was evenly applied.

36 The inner court was walled off by means of three courses of hewn stones and one course of cedar beams.

37 The foundations of the LORD's temple were laid in the month of Ziv 38 in the fourth year, and it was completed in all particulars, exactly according to plan, in the month of Bul, the eighth month, in the eleventh year. Thus it took Solomon seven years to build it.

Building of the Palace

7 1* His own palace Solomon completed after thirteen years of construction. 2 He built the hall called the Forest of Lebanon one hundred cubits long, fifty wide, and thirty high; it was supported by four rows of cedar columns, with cedar capitals upon the columns. 3 Moreover, it had a ceiling of cedar above the beams resting on the columns; these beams numbered forty-five, fifteen to a row. 4 There were three window frames at either end, with windows in strict alignment. 5 The posts of all the doorways were rectangular, and the doorways faced each other, three at either end. 6 The porch of the columned hall he made fifty cubits long and thirty wide. The porch extended the width of the columned hall, and there was a canopy in front. 7 He also built the vestibule of the throne where he gave judgment—that is, the tribunal; it

covenant, 20† twenty cubits long, twenty wide, and twenty high. 21 Solomon overlaid the interior of the temple with pure gold. He made in front of the sanctuary a cedar altar, overlaid it with gold, and looped it with golden chains. 22 The entire temple was overlaid with gold so that it was completely covered with it; the whole altar before the sanctuary was also overlaid with gold. 23 In the sanctuary were two cherubim, each ten cubits high, made of olive wood. 24 Each wing of a cherub measured five cubits so that the space from wing tip to wing tip of each was ten cubits. 25 The cherubim were identical

---

† **6, 20:** *Twenty (cubits) high:* it is usually supposed that the holy of holies was of this height because it had a raised floor, five cubits above the floor level of the nave, rather than a dropped ceiling. The building was *twenty-five cubits high* (v 2) according to the reading here followed.

---

* 7, 1: 1 Kgs 9, 10.

was paneled with cedar from floor to ceiling beams.
8* His living quarters were in another court, set in
deeper than the tribunal and of the same construction. A palace like this tribunal was built for
Pharaoh's daughter, whom Solomon had married.

9 All these buildings were of fine stones, hewn to
size and trimmed front and back with a saw, from
the foundation to the bonding course. 10 (The foundation was made of fine, large blocks, some ten
cubits and some eight cubits. 11 Above were fine
stones hewn to size, and cedar wood.) 12 The great
court was enclosed by three courses of hewn stones
and a bonding course of cedar beams. So also were
the inner court of the temple of the LORD and the
temple porch.

Furnishing of the Temple

13 King Solomon had Hiram brought from Tyre.
14 He was a bronze worker, the son of a widow from
the tribe of Naphtali; his father had been from Tyre.
He was endowed with skill, understanding, and
knowledge of how to produce any work in bronze. He
came to King Solomon and did all his metal work.

15*† Two hollow bronze columns were cast, each
eighteen cubits high and twelve cubits in circumference; their metal was of four fingers' thickness.
16 There were also two capitals cast in bronze, to
place on top of the columns, each of them five cubits
high. 17 Two pieces of network with a chainlike mesh
were made to cover the (nodes of the) capitals on top
of the columns, one for each capital. 18 Four hundred
pomegranates were also cast; two hundred of them
in a double row encircled the piece of network on
each of the two capitals. 19 The capitals on top of the
columns were finished wholly in a lotus pattern
20 above the level of the nodes and their enveloping
network. 21 The columns were then erected adjacent
to the porch of the temple, one to the right, called
Jachin, and the other to the left, called Boaz. 22 Thus
the work on the columns was completed.

23*† The sea was then cast; it was made with a
circular rim, and measured ten cubits across, five in
height, and thirty in circumference. 24 Under the
brim, gourds encircled it, ten to the cubit all the
way around; the gourds were in two rows and were
cast in one mold with the sea. 25 This rested on
twelve oxen, three facing north, three facing west,
three facing south, and three facing east, with their
haunches all toward the center, where the sea was
set upon them. 26 It was a handbreadth thick, and
its brim resembled that of a cup, being lily-shaped.
Its capacity was two thousand measures.

27 Ten stands were also made of bronze, each
four cubits long, four wide, and three high. 28 When
these stands were constructed, panels were set within the framework. 29 On the panels between the
frames there were lions, oxen, and cherubim; and
on the frames likewise, above and below the lions
and oxen, there were wreaths in relief.

30 Each stand had four bronze wheels and
bronze axles. 32 The four wheels were below the
paneling, and the axletrees of the wheels and the
stand were of one piece. Each wheel was a cubit and
a half high. 33 The wheels were constructed like
chariot wheels; their axles, fellies, spokes, and hubs
were all cast.

The four legs of each stand had cast braces, which
were under the basin; they had wreaths on each
side. 34 These four braces, extending to the corners
of each stand, were of one piece with the stand.

35 On top of the stand there was a raised collar
half a cubit high, with supports and panels which
were of one piece with the top of the stand. 31 This
was surmounted by a crown one cubit high within
which was a rounded opening to provide a receptacle a cubit and a half in depth. There was carved
work at the opening, on panels that were angular,
not curved. 36 On the surfaces of the supports and
on the panels, wherever there was a clear space,
cherubim, lions, and palm trees were carved, as well
as wreaths all around. 37 This was how the ten
stands were made, all of the same casting, the same
size, the same shape. 38 Ten bronze basins were
then made, each four cubits in diameter with a
capacity of forty measures, one basin for the top of
each of the ten stands. 39 The stands were placed,
five on the south side of the temple and five on the
north. The sea was placed off to the southeast from
the south side of the temple.

40 When Hiram made the pots, shovels, and
bowls, he therewith completed all his work for
King Solomon in the temple of the LORD: 41 two
columns, two nodes for the capitals on top of the
columns, two pieces of network covering the nodes
for the capitals on top of the columns, 42 four
hundred pomegranates in double rows on both
pieces of network that covered the two nodes of the
capitals where they met the columns, 43 ten stands,
ten basins on the stands, 44 one sea, twelve oxen
supporting the sea, 45 pots, shovels, and bowls. All
these articles which Hiram made for King Solomon
in the temple of the LORD were of burnished bronze.
46 The king had them cast in the neighborhood of
the Jordan, in the clayey ground between Succoth

---

† 7, 15–21: The *two hollow bronze columns*, Jachin and Boaz
(2 Chr 3, 17), stood free to the right and left of the temple porch. The
names are related to God's power (Boaz) founding (Jachin) the temple and his people.

7, 23–26: *The sea . . . rested on twelve oxen*: this was a large circular tank containing about twelve thousand gallons of water.

7, 8: 1 Kgs 3, 1.
7, 15: Jer 52, 21.

7, 23: 2 Chr 4, 2.

and Zarethan. [47] Solomon did not weigh all the articles because they were so numerous; the weight of the bronze, therefore, was not determined.

[48] Solomon had all the articles made for the interior of the temple of the LORD: the golden altar; the golden table on which the showbread lay; [49] the lampstands of pure gold, five to the right and five to the left before the sanctuary, with their flowers, lamps, and tongs of gold; [50] basins, snuffers, bowls, cups, and fire pans of pure gold; and hinges of gold for the doors of the inner room, or holy of holies, and for the doors of the outer room, the nave.

[51]* When all the work undertaken by King Solomon in the temple of the LORD was completed, he brought in the dedicated offerings of his father David, putting the silver, gold, and other articles in the treasuries of the temple of the LORD.

Dedication of the Temple

8 [1]* At the order of Solomon, the elders of Israel and all the leaders of the tribes, the princes in the ancestral houses of the Israelites, came to King Solomon in Jerusalem, to bring up the ark of the LORD's covenant from the City of David [which is Zion]. [2] All the men of Israel assembled before King Solomon during the festival in the month of Ethanim (the seventh month). [3] When all the elders of Israel had arrived, the priests took up the ark; [4] they carried the ark of the LORD and the meeting tent with all the sacred vessels that were in the tent. (The priests and Levites carried them.)

[5] King Solomon and the entire community of Israel present for the occasion sacrificed before the ark sheep and oxen too many to number or count. [6]† The priests brought the ark of the covenant of the LORD to its place beneath the wings of the cherubim in the sanctuary, the holy of holies of the temple. [7] The cherubim had their wings spread out over the place of the ark, sheltering the ark and its poles from above. [8] The poles were so long that their ends could be seen from that part of the holy place adjoining the sanctuary; however, they could not be seen beyond. (They have remained there to this day.) [9]* There was nothing in the ark but the two stone tablets which Moses had put there at Horeb, when the LORD made a covenant with the Israelites at their departure from the land of Egypt.

[10] When the priests left the holy place, the cloud filled the temple of the LORD [11] so that the priests could no longer minister because of the cloud, since the LORD's glory had filled the temple of the

LORD. [12]* Then Solomon said, "The LORD intends to dwell in the dark cloud; [13] I have truly built you a princely house, a dwelling where you may abide forever."

[14] The king turned and greeted the whole community of Israel as they stood. [15] He said to them: "Blessed be the LORD, the God of Israel, who with his own mouth made a promise to my father David and by his hand has brought it to fulfillment. It was he who said, [16] 'Since the day I brought my people Israel out of Egypt, I have not chosen a city out of any tribe of Israel for the building of a temple to my honor; but I choose David to rule my people Israel.' [17]* When my father David wished to build a temple to the honor of the LORD, the God of Israel, [18] the Lord said to him, 'In wishing to build a temple to my honor, you do well. [19] It will not be you, however, who will build the temple; but the son who will spring from you, he shall build the temple to my honor.' [20] And now the LORD has fulfilled the promise that he made: I have succeeded my father

PRAY IT!

Holy Places

Solomon knows that the Temple will not hold God. Holy places are not cages to keep God contained. People need holy places more than God does. We gather together in public holy places to experience God's presence as a community. But we can also meet God one-on-one in private holy places, special to us alone.

Try creating a holy space in your bedroom. Clear out a corner, and put in it a small table and a chair or rug to sit on. On the table, put your Bible and an object or two to help you focus on God. You might use a candle, a special picture or statue, or something from a retreat or a special place. Try to spend a little time each day in your holy space with God.

▶ 1 Kgs 8, 27–30

---

† **8, 6–9:** The transfer of the ark of the covenant into the newly constructed temple building, and the oracle of God's acceptance (1 Kgs 9, 3–9), and his act of possession (1 Kgs 8, 10–13), constituted the temple's solemn dedication, and made of it the abiding dwelling of God among his people for which David had hoped (2 Sm 6, 12–15; 7, 1–3). The concurrence of the feast of Booths marks an appropriate transition of God's dwelling among nomadic tribes to his permanent abode among a settled people.

7, 51: 2 Chr 5, 1.　　　　　　8, 12: 2 Chr 6, 1.
8, 1: 2 Chr 5, 2.　　　　　　8, 17: 2 Sm 7, 5.
8, 9: Ex 34, 27; Heb 9, 4.

David and sit on the throne of Israel, as the LORD foretold, and I have built this temple to honor the LORD, the God of Israel. 21 I have provided in it a place for the ark in which is the covenant of the LORD, which he made with our fathers when he brought them out of the land of Egypt."

Solomon's Prayer

22 Solomon stood before the altar of the LORD in the presence of the whole community of Israel, and stretching forth his hands toward heaven, 23 he said, "LORD, God of Israel, there is no God like you in heaven above or on earth below; you keep your covenant of kindness with your servants who are faithful to you with their whole heart. 24 You have kept the promise you made to my father David, your servant. You who spoke that promise, have this day, by your own power, brought it to fulfillment. 25* Now, therefore, LORD, God of Israel, keep the further promise you made to my father David, your servant, saying, 'You shall always have someone from your line to sit before me on the throne of Israel, provided only that your descendants look to their conduct so that they live in my presence, as you have lived in my presence.' 26 Now, LORD, God of Israel, may this promise which you made to my father David, your servant, be confirmed.

27 "Can it indeed be that God dwells among men on earth? If the heavens and the highest heavens cannot contain you, how much less this temple which I have built! 28 Look kindly on the prayer and petition of your servant, O LORD, my God, and listen to the cry of supplication which I, your servant, utter before you this day. 29 May your eyes watch night and day over this temple, the place where you have decreed you shall be honored; may you heed the prayer which I, your servant, offer in this place. 30 Listen to the petitions of your servant and of your people Israel which they offer in this place. Listen from your heavenly dwelling and grant pardon.

31 "If a man sins against his neighbor and is required to take an oath sanctioned by a curse, when he comes and takes the oath before your altar in this temple, 32 listen in heaven; take action and pass judgment on your servants. Condemn the wicked and punish him for his conduct, but acquit the just and establish his innocence.

33† "If your people Israel sin against you and are defeated by an enemy, and if then they return to you, praise your name, pray to you, and entreat you in this temple, 34 listen in heaven and forgive the sin of your people Israel, and bring them back to the land you gave their fathers.

35 "If the sky is closed, so that there is no rain, because they have sinned against you and you afflict them, and if then they repent of their sin, and pray, and praise your name in this place, 36 listen in heaven and forgive the sin of your servant and of your people Israel, teaching them the right way to live and sending rain upon this land of yours which you have given to your people as their heritage.

37 "If there is famine in the land or pestilence; or if blight comes, or mildew, or a locust swarm, or devouring insects; if an enemy of your people besieges them in one of their cities; whatever plague or sickness there may be, 38 if then any one [of your entire people Israel] has remorse of conscience and offers some prayer or petition, stretching out his hands toward this temple, 39 listen from your heavenly dwelling place and forgive. You who alone know the hearts of all men, render to each one of them according to his conduct; knowing their hearts, so treat them 40 that they may fear you as long as they live on the land you gave our fathers.

41 "To the foreigner, likewise, who is not of your people Israel, but comes from a distant land to honor you 42 (since men will learn of your great name and your mighty hand and your outstretched arm), when he comes and prays toward this temple, 43 listen from your heavenly dwelling. Do all that the foreigner asks of you, that all the peoples of the earth may know your name, may fear you as do your people Israel, and may acknowledge that this temple which I have built is dedicated to your honor.

44 "Whatever the direction in which you may send your people forth to war against their enemies, if they pray to you, O LORD, toward the city you have chosen and the temple I have built in your honor, 45 listen in heaven to their prayer and petition, and defend their cause.

46* "When they sin against you (for there is no man who does not sin), and in your anger against them you deliver them to the enemy, so that their captors deport them to a hostile land, far or near, 47 may they repent in the land of their captivity and be converted. If then they entreat you in the land of their captors and say, 'We have sinned and done wrong; we have been wicked'; 48 if with their whole heart and soul they turn back to you in the land of the enemies who took them captive, pray to you toward the land you gave their fathers, the city you have chosen, and the temple I have built in your honor, 49 listen from your heavenly dwelling. 50 Forgive your people their sins and all the offenses they have committed against you, and grant

---

† **8, 33–34.46–53:** These references to deportation of Israelites to a hostile land are an expansion of Solomon's prayer dating from the Babylonian exile four centuries later.

8, 25: 2 Sm 7, 12.

8, 46: 2 Chr 6, 36; Eccl 7, 20; 1 Jn 1, 8.

them mercy before their captors, so that these will be merciful to them. [51] For they are your people and your inheritance, whom you brought out of Egypt, from the midst of an iron furnace.

[52] "Thus may your eyes be open to the petition of your servant and to the petition of your people Israel. Hear them whenever they call upon you, [53] because you have set them apart among all the peoples of the earth for your inheritance, as you declared through your servant Moses when you brought our fathers out of Egypt, O Lord GOD."

[54] When Solomon finished offering this entire prayer of petition to the LORD, he rose from before the altar of the LORD, where he had been kneeling with his hands outstretched toward heaven. [55] He stood and blessed the whole community of Israel, saying in a loud voice: [56] "Blessed be the LORD who has given rest to his people Israel, just as he promised. Not a single word has gone unfulfilled of the entire generous promise he made through his servant Moses. [57] May the LORD, our God, be with us as he was with our fathers and may he not forsake us nor cast us off. [58] May he draw our hearts to himself, that we may follow him in everything and keep the commands, statutes, and ordinances which he enjoined on our fathers. [59] May this prayer I have offered to the LORD, our God, be present to him day and night, that he may uphold the cause of his servant and of his people Israel as each day requires, [60] that all the peoples of the earth may know the LORD is God and there is no other. [61] You must be wholly devoted to the LORD, our God, observing his statutes and keeping his commandments, as on this day."

[62] The king and all Israel with him offered sacrifices before the LORD. [63] Solomon offered as peace offerings to the LORD twenty-two thousand oxen and one hundred twenty thousand sheep. Thus the king and all the Israelites dedicated the temple of the LORD. [64] On that day the king consecrated the middle of the court facing the temple of the LORD; he offered there the holocausts, the cereal offerings, and the fat of the peace offerings, because the bronze altar before the LORD was too small to hold these offerings.

[65] On this occasion Solomon and all the Israelites, who had assembled in large numbers from Labo of Hamath to the wadi of Egypt, celebrated the festival before the LORD, our God, for seven days. [66] On the eighth day he dismissed the people, who bade the king farewell and went to their homes, rejoicing and happy over all the blessings the LORD had given to his servant David and to his people Israel.

Catholic Connections

BLESSING THE COMMUNITY

The community is a phrase used to describe people gathered to pray together. Think of how the community is blessed at the end of Mass. With raised hands, the priest speaks with words similar to Solomon's in 1 Kgs 8, 56–61. The people are sent forth to know God's love and to do what God wants.

Let us praise God, who loves us, and let us go in peace to love and serve God and one another.

▶ 1 Kgs 8, 56–61

Promise and Warning to Solomon

9 [1] After Solomon finished building the temple of the LORD, the royal palace, and everything else that he had planned, [2]* the LORD appeared to him a second time, as he had appeared to him in Gibeon. [3] The LORD said to him: "I have heard the prayer of petition which you offered in my presence. I have consecrated this temple which you have built; I confer my name upon it forever, and my eyes and my heart shall be there always. [4] As for you, if you live in my presence as your father David lived, sincerely and uprightly, doing just as I have commanded you, keeping my statutes and decrees, [5]* I will establish your throne of sovereignty over Israel forever, as I promised your father David when I said, 'You shall always have someone from your line on the throne of Israel.' [6] But if you and your descendants ever withdraw from me, fail to keep the commandments and statutes which I set before you, and proceed to venerate and worship strange gods, [7] I will cut off Israel from the land I gave them and repudiate the temple I have consecrated to my honor. Israel shall become a proverb and a byword among all nations, [8]* and this temple shall become a heap of ruins. Every passerby shall catch his

---

9, 2: 1 Kgs 3, 5; 11, 9;   9, 5: 2 Sm 7, 12–16.
      2 Chr 7, 12.   9, 8: Dt 29, 23; Jer 22, 8.

breath in amazement, and ask, 'Why has the LORD done this to the land and to this temple?' 9 Men will answer: 'They forsook the LORD, their God, who brought their fathers out of the land of Egypt; they adopted strange gods which they worshiped and served. That is why the LORD has brought down upon them all this evil.' "

Other Acts of the King

10 After the twenty years during which Solomon built the two houses, the temple of the LORD and the palace of the king— 11 Hiram, king of Tyre, supplying Solomon with all the cedar wood, fir wood, and gold he wished—King Solomon gave Hiram twenty cities in the land of Galilee. 12 Hiram left Tyre to see the cities Solomon had given him, but was not satisfied with them. 13 So he said, "What are these cities you have given me, my brother?" And he called them the land of Cabul, as they are called to this day. 14† Hiram, however, had sent King Solomon one hundred and twenty talents of gold.

15† This is an account of the forced labor which King Solomon levied in order to build the temple of the LORD, his palace, Millo, the wall of Jerusalem, Hazor, Megiddo, Gezer 16 (Pharaoh king of Egypt, had come up and taken Gezer and, after destroying it by fire and slaying all the Canaanites living in the city, had given it as dowry to his daughter, Solomon's wife; 17 Solomon then rebuilt Gezer), Lower Beth-horon, 18 Baalath, Tamar in the desert of Judah, 19 all his cities for supplies, cities for chariots and for horses, and whatever else Solomon decided should be built in Jerusalem, in Lebanon, and in the entire land under his dominion. 20 All the non-Israelite people who remained in the land, descendants of the Amorites, Hittites, Perizzites, Hivites, and Jebusites 21 whose doom the Israelites had been unable to accomplish, Solomon conscripted as forced laborers, as they are to this day. 22 But Solomon enslaved none of the Israelites, for they were his fighting force, his ministers, commanders, adjutants, chariot officers, and charioteers. 23 The supervisors of Solomon's works who policed the people engaged in the work numbered five hundred and fifty.

24 As soon as Pharaoh's daughter went up from the City of David to her palace, which he had built for her, Solomon built Millo.

25 Three times a year Solomon used to offer holocausts and peace offerings on the altar which he had built to the LORD, and to burn incense before the LORD; and he kept the temple in repair.

26† King Solomon also built a fleet at Ezion-geber, which is near Elath on the shore of the Red Sea in the land of Edom. 27 In this fleet Hiram placed his own expert seamen with the servants of Solomon. 28 They went to Ophir, and brought back four hundred and twenty talents of gold to King Solomon.

Visit of the Queen of Sheba

10 1*† The queen of Sheba, having heard of Solomon's fame, came to test him with subtle questions. 2 She arrived in Jerusalem with a very numerous retinue, and with camels bearing spices, a large amount of gold, and precious stones. She came to Solomon and questioned him on every subject in which she was interested. 3 King Solomon explained everything she asked about, and there remained nothing hidden from him that he could not explain to her.

4 When the queen of Sheba witnessed Solomon's great wisdom, the palace he had built, 5 the food at his table, the seating of his ministers, the attendance and garb of his waiters, his banquet service, and the holocausts he offered in the temple of the LORD, she was breathless. 6 "The report I heard in my country about your deeds and your wisdom is true," she told the king. 7 "Though I did not believe the report until I came and saw with my own eyes, I have discovered that they were not telling me the half. Your wisdom and prosperity surpass the report I heard. 8 Happy are your men, happy these servants of yours, who stand before you always and listen to your wisdom. 9 Blessed be the LORD, your God, whom it has pleased to place you on the throne of Israel. In his enduring love for Israel, the LORD has made you king to carry out judgment and justice." 10 Then she gave the king one hundred and twenty gold talents, a very large quantity of spices, and precious stones. Never again did anyone bring such an abundance of spices as the queen of Sheba gave to King Solomon.

11† Hiram's fleet, which used to bring gold from Ophir, also brought from there a large quantity of cabinet wood and precious stones. 12 With the wood the king made supports for the temple of the

---

† **9, 14:** *One hundred and twenty talents of gold:* approximately three million six hundred thousand dollars.

9, 15: *Millo:* probably means a filling, and may refer to an artificial earthwork or platform of stamped ground south of the temple area. It was begun by David (2 Sm 5, 9); cf 1 Kgs 9, 24; 11, 27.

9, 26: *Ezion-geber . . . Edom:* the first mention of maritime commerce in the Israelite kingdom (to which the land of Edom was subject after its conquest by King David; cf 2 Sm 8, 14).

10, 1: *Queen of Sheba:* women rulers among the Arabs are recorded in eighth-century-B.C. Assyrian inscriptions. Sheba was for centuries the leading principality in what is now the Yemen.

10, 11f: *Cabinet:* an unknown wood, probably fragrant.

10, 1: 2 Chr 9, 1; Mt 12, 42; Lk 11, 31.

LORD and for the palace of the king, and harps and lyres for the chanters. No more such wood was brought or seen to the present day.

13 King Solomon gave the queen of Sheba everything she desired and asked for, besides such presents as were given her from Solomon's royal bounty. Then she returned with her servants to her own country.

Solomon's Wealth

14 The gold that Solomon received every year weighed six hundred and sixty-six gold talents, 15 in addition to what came from the Tarshish fleet, from the traffic of merchants, and from all the kings of Arabia and the governors of the country. 16* Moreover, King Solomon made two hundred shields of beaten gold (six hundred gold shekels went into each shield) 17 and three hundred bucklers of beaten gold (three minas of gold went into each buckler); and he put them in the hall of the Forest of Lebanon. 18 The king also had a large ivory throne made, and overlaid it with refined gold. 19 The throne had six steps, a back with a round top, and an arm on each side of the seat. Next to each arm stood a lion; 20 and twelve other lions stood on the steps, two to a step, one on either side of each step. Nothing like this was produced in any other kingdom. 21 In addition, all King Solomon's drinking vessels were of gold, and all the utensils in the hall of the Forest of Lebanon were of pure gold. There was no silver, for in Solomon's time it was considered worthless. 22† The king had a fleet of Tarshish ships at sea with Hiram's fleet. Once every three years the fleet of Tarshish ships would come with a cargo of gold, silver, ivory, apes, and monkeys. 23 Thus King Solomon surpassed in riches and wisdom all the kings of the earth. 24 And the whole world sought audience with Solomon, to hear from him the wisdom which God had put in his heart. 25 Each one brought his yearly tribute: silver or gold articles, garments, weapons, spices, horses and mules.

26* Solomon collected chariots and drivers; he had one thousand four hundred chariots and twelve thousand drivers; these he allocated among the chariot cities and to the king's service in Jerusalem. 27 The king made silver as common in Jerusalem as stones, and cedars as numerous as the sycamores of the foothills. 28 Solomon's horses were imported from Cilicia, where the king's agents purchased them. 29 A chariot imported from Egypt cost six hundred shekels, a horse one hundred and fifty shekels; they were exported at these rates to all the Hittite and Aramean kings.

Solomon's Sin

Sometimes, when we think we are strongest, we are actually weakest. Solomon replaces his poverty of spirit with pride (see 1 Kgs 3, 4–14). He seems to believe that he is strong enough to go against God's command not to take foreign wives and that he can withstand the influence of their foreign gods. But Solomon falls into the sin of idolatry (worshiping other gods), breaking the Covenant.

Have you ever considered doing something that you knew was wrong? Did you tell yourself, "It won't hurt to do it just this once"? Maybe that is what Solomon said when he took his first foreign wife.

In your prayer time, reflect or journal on the following questions:
- What takes your attention away from God?
- Have you ever used the excuse, "I'm strong enough to handle this," to lead you into doing something wrong?
- Pray Ps 86, 11 to end your prayer.

▸ 1 Kgs 11, 1–8

The Sins of Solomon

11 1*† King Solomon loved many foreign women besides the daughter of Pharaoh (Moabites, Ammonites, Edomites, Sidonians, and Hittites), 2* from nations with which the LORD had forbidden the Israelites to intermarry, "because," he said, "they will turn your hearts to their gods." 3 But Solomon fell in love with them. He had seven

---

10, 22: *Tarshish ships:* large, strong vessels for long voyages. Tarshish was the ancient Tartessus, a Phoenician colony in southern Spain, the name of which denotes a center for smelting metallic ore.

11, 1–3.7: The glorious rise of Solomon, his piety and wisdom, administrative skill and wealth, the extension of his kingdom, his prestige among neighboring rulers, his reign of peace, above all his friendship with God—these are now eclipsed by his sins of intermarriage with great numbers of pagan wives and the consequent forbidden worship of their gods (Ex 34, 11–16; Dt 7, 1–5). His construction of temples in their honor merited the punishment of loss of

a united kingdom to his posterity, and the opposition of adversaries to himself (vv 14.23–27). Hadad the Edomite rebelled against Solomon at the beginning of his reign (v 25). Rezon of Syria established a new kingdom in Dàmascus; Jeroboam of Israel constituted the greatest threat because of his revolt from within. This threefold threat culminated in the breakup of Solomon's kingdom.

10, 16: 1 Kgs 14, 26.   11, 1: Dt 17, 17; Sir 47, 19f.
10, 26: 2 Chr 1, 14.   11, 2: Ex 34, 16.

hundred wives of princely rank and three hundred concubines, and his wives turned his heart.

4 When Solomon was old his wives had turned his heart to strange gods, and his heart was not entirely with the LORD, his God, as the heart of his father David had been. 5 By adoring Astarte, the goddess of the Sidonians, and Milcom, the idol of the Ammonites, 6 Solomon did evil in the sight of the LORD; he did not follow him unreservedly as his father David had done. 7 Solomon then built a high place to Chemosh, the idol of Moab, and to Molech, the idol of the Ammonites, on the hill opposite Jerusalem. 8 He did the same for all his foreign wives who burned incense and sacrificed to their gods. 9* The LORD, therefore, became angry with Solomon, because his heart was turned away from the LORD, the God of Israel, who had appeared to him twice 10 (for though the LORD had forbidden him this very act of following strange gods, Solomon had not obeyed him).

11 So the LORD said to Solomon: "Since this is what you want, and you have not kept my covenant and my statutes which I enjoined on you, I will deprive you of the kingdom and give it to your servant. 12* I will not do this during your lifetime, however, for the sake of your father David; it is your son whom I will deprive. 13 Nor will I take away the whole kingdom. I will leave your son one tribe for the sake of my servant David and of Jerusalem, which I have chosen."

14 The LORD then raised up an adversary to Solomon: Hadad the Edomite, who was of the royal line in Edom. 15* Earlier, when David had conquered Edom, Joab, the general of the army, while going to bury the slain, put to death every male in Edom. 16 Joab and all Israel remained there six months until they had killed off every male in Edom. 17 Meanwhile, Hadad, who was only a boy, fled toward Egypt with some Edomite servants of his father. 18 They left Midian and passing through Paran, where they picked up additional men, they went into Egypt to Pharaoh, king of Egypt, who gave Hadad a house, appointed him rations, and assigned him land.

19 Hadad won great favor with Pharaoh, so that he gave him in marriage the sister of Queen Tahpenes, his own wife. 20 Tahpenes' sister bore Hadad a son, Genubath. After his weaning, the queen kept him in Pharaoh's palace, where he then lived with Pharaoh's own sons. 21 When Hadad in Egypt heard that David rested with his ancestors and that Joab, the general of the army, was dead, he said to Pharaoh, "Give me leave to return to my own country." 22 Pharaoh said to him, "What do you lack with me, that you are seeking to return to your own country?" "Nothing," he said, "but please let me go!"

23 God raised up against Solomon another adversary, in Rezon, the son of Eliada, who had fled from his lord, Hadadezer, king of Zobah, 24 when David defeated them with slaughter. Rezon gathered men about him and became leader of a band, went to Damascus, settled there, and became king in Damascus. 25 He was an enemy of Israel as long as Solomon lived; this added to the harm done by Hadad, who made a rift in Israel by becoming king over Edom.

26* Solomon's servant Jeroboam, son of Nebat, an Ephraimite from Zeredah with a widowed mother, Zeruah, also rebelled against the king. 27 This is why he rebelled. King Solomon was building Millo, closing up the breach of his father's City of David. 28 Jeroboam was a man of means, and when Solomon saw that he was also an industrious young man, he put him in charge of the entire labor force of the house of Joseph. 29* At that time Jeroboam left Jerusalem, and the prophet Ahijah the Shilonite met him on the road. The two were alone in the area, and the prophet was wearing a new cloak. 30 Ahijah took off his new cloak, tore it into twelve pieces, 31* and said to Jeroboam:

"Take ten pieces for yourself; the LORD, the God of Israel, says: 'I will tear away the kingdom from Solomon's grasp and will give you ten of the tribes. 32 One tribe shall remain to him for the sake of David my servant, and of Jerusalem, the city I have chosen out of all the tribes of Israel. 33 The ten I will give you because he has forsaken me and has worshiped Astarte, goddess of the Sidonians, Chemosh, god of Moab, and Milcom, god of the Ammonites; he has not followed my ways or done what is pleasing to me according to my statutes and my decrees, as his father David did. 34 Yet I will not take any of the kingdom from Solomon himself, but will keep him a prince as long as he lives for the sake of my servant David, whom I chose, who kept my commandments and statutes. 35 But I will take the kingdom from his son and will give it to you—that is, the ten tribes. 36 I will give his son one tribe, that my servant David may always have a lamp before me in Jerusalem, the city in which I choose to be honored. 37 I will take you; you shall reign over all that you desire and shall become king of Israel. 38 If, then, you heed all that I command you, follow my ways, and please me by keeping my statutes and my commandments like my servant David, I will be with you. I will establish for you, as I did for David, a lasting dynasty; I will give Israel to you. 39 I will punish David's line for this, but not forever.' "

40 When Solomon tried to have Jeroboam killed for his rebellion, he escaped to King Shishak, in Egypt, where he remained until Solomon's death.

11, 9: 1 Kgs 9, 2.   11, 15: 2 Sm 8, 14.   11, 29: 1 Kgs 14, 2;   11, 31: 1 Kgs 12, 15.
11, 12: 1 Kgs 12, 15.   11, 26: 2 Chr 13, 6.   2 Chr 10, 15.

?did you KNOW?

The Kingdom of Israel Splits

When the people of Israel first came to settle in Canaan, they organized into twelve tribes, ruled by chieftains, that supported and protected one another. As Israel grew in size, it was necessary to have one central ruler who would unite the tribes into one nation. Saul was the first king of this united Israel. David followed Saul and expanded the kingdom's territory. David's son Solomon continued ruling over the expanded kingdom and engaged in expensive building projects.

At Solomon's death, many Israelites wanted a less demanding king. They had suffered under the burden of heavy taxes and forced labor. When Solomon's son Rehoboam refused to make any changes (1 Kgs 12, 11), ten of the northern tribes pulled away and placed their own king, Jeroboam, on the throne. The northern kingdom was called Israel. The southern kingdom, composed of two tribes, was called Judah (see map 3, "The Kingdom Years"). The kingdom was now split in two, and it was never again reunited.

Saul (1020 B.C.)
|
David (1000 B.C.)
|
Solomon (961 B.C.)
|
Kingdom splits (931 B.C.)

JUDAH (south)	ISRAEL (north)
Capital: Jerusalem	Capital: Samaria
Twenty kings	Twenty kings
Falls to Babylonians (587 B.C.)	Falls to Assyrians (721 B.C.)
Exile to Babylon	Exile to Assyria

▶ 1 Kgs 12, 1–19

---

41 The rest of the acts of Solomon, with all his deeds and his wisdom, are recorded in the book of the chronicles of Solomon. 42 The time that Solomon reigned in Jerusalem over all Israel was forty years. 43 Solomon rested with his ancestors; he was buried in his father's City of David, and his son Rehoboam succeeded him as king.

II: Judah and Israel to the Time of Ahab

Secession of Israel

12 1*† Rehoboam went to Shechem, where all Israel had come to proclaim him king. 3 They said to Rehoboam: 4 "Your father put on us a heavy yoke. If you now lighten the harsh service and the heavy yoke your father imposed on us, we will serve you." 5 "Come back to me in three days," he answered them. When the people had departed, 6 King Rehoboam consulted the elders who had been in his father's service while he was alive, and asked, "What answer do you advise me to give this people?" 7 They replied, "If today you will be the servant of this people and submit to them, giving them a favorable answer, they will be your servants forever." 8 But he ignored the advice the elders had given him, and consulted the young men who had grown up with him and were in his service. 9 He said to them, "What answer do you advise me to give this people, who have asked me to lighten the yoke my father imposed on them?" 10 The young men who had grown up with him replied, "This is what you must say to this people who have asked you to lighten the yoke your father put on them: 'My little finger is thicker than my father's body. 11 Whereas my father put a heavy yoke on you, I will make it heavier. My father beat you with whips, but I will beat you with scorpions.' "

12 On the third day all Israel came back to King Rehoboam, as he had instructed them to do. 13 Ignoring the advice the elders had given him, the king gave the people a harsh answer. 14 He said to them, as the young men had advised: "My father put on you a heavy yoke, but I will make it heavier. My father beat you with whips, but I will beat you with scorpions." 15* The king did not listen to the people, for the LORD brought this about to fulfill the prophecy he had uttered to Jeroboam, son of Nebat, through Ahijah the Shilonite.

16† When all Israel saw that the king did not listen to them, the people answered the king:

12, 1: *Shechem:* chief city of the northern tribes, where a covenant of fidelity had previously been made between the Lord and his people and a stone of witness had been erected in memory of the event (Jos 24, 25ff).

12, 16: *What share have we in David:* even in David's time the northern tribes seemed ready to withdraw from Judah (2 Sm 20, 1). The unreasonable attitude of Rehoboam toward them intensified the discontent caused by the oppression of Solomon (v 4) and thus precipitated the establishment of a rival monarchy (v 20).

12, 1: 2 Chr 10, 1.   **12, 15:** 1 Kgs 11, 12.31.

"What share have we in David?
We have no heritage in the son of Jesse.
To your tents, O Israel!
Now look to your own house, David."

So Israel went off to their tents, 17 but Rehoboam reigned over the Israelites who lived in the cities of Judah. 18 King Rehoboam then sent out Adoram, superintendent of the forced labor, but all Israel stoned him to death. Rehoboam managed to mount his chariot to flee to Jerusalem, 19 and Israel went into rebellion against David's house to this day. 2 Jeroboam, son of Nebat, who was still in Egypt, where he had fled from King Solomon, returned from Egypt as soon as he learned this. 20 When all Israel heard that Jeroboam had returned, they summoned him to an assembly and made him king over all Israel. None remained loyal to David's house except the tribe of Judah alone.

21 On his arrival in Jerusalem, Rehoboam gathered together all the house of Judah and the tribe of Benjamin—one hundred eighty thousand seasoned warriors—to fight against the house of Israel, to restore the kingdom to Rehoboam, son of Solomon. 22* However, the LORD spoke to Shemaiah, a man of God: 23 "Say to Rehoboam, son of Solomon, king of Judah, and to the house of Judah and to Benjamin, and to the rest of the people: 24 'Thus says the LORD: You must not march out to fight against your brother Israelites. Let every man return home, for I have brought this about.' " They accepted this message of the LORD and gave up the expedition accordingly.

25 Jeroboam built up Shechem in the hill country of Ephraim and lived there. Then he left it and built up Penuel.

Religious Rebellion

26† Jeroboam thought to himself: "The kingdom will return to David's house. 27 If now this people go up to offer sacrifices in the temple of the LORD in Jerusalem, the hearts of this people will return to their master, Rehoboam, king of Judah, and they will kill me." 28* After taking counsel, the king made two calves of gold and said to the people: "You have been going up to Jerusalem long enough. Here is your God, O Israel, who brought you up from the

land of Egypt." 29† And he put one in Bethel, the other in Dan. 30 This led to sin, because the people frequented these calves in Bethel and in Dan. 31* He also built temples on the high places and made priests from among the people who were not Levites. 32 Jeroboam established a feast in the eighth month on the fifteenth day of the month to duplicate in Bethel the pilgrimage feast of Judah, with sacrifices to the calves he had made; and he stationed in Bethel priests of the high places he had built.

Message of the Prophet from Judah

33 Jeroboam ascended the altar he built in Bethel on the fifteenth day of the eighth month, the month in which he arbitrarily chose to establish a feast for the Israelites; he was going to offer sacrifice.

13 1 A man of God came from Judah to Bethel by the word of the LORD, while Jeroboam was standing at the altar to offer sacrifice. 2* He cried out against the altar the word of the LORD: "O altar, altar, the LORD says, 'A child shall be born to the house of David, Josiah by name, who shall slaughter upon you the priests of the high places who offer sacrifice upon you, and he shall burn human bones upon you.' " 3 He gave a sign that same day and said: "This is the sign that the LORD has spoken: The altar shall break up and the ashes on it shall be strewn about."

4 When King Jeroboam heard what the man of God was crying out against the altar, he stretched forth his hand from the altar and said, "Seize him!" But the hand he stretched forth against him withered, so that he could not draw it back. 5 Moreover, the altar broke up and the ashes from it were strewn about—the sign the man of God had given as the word of the LORD. 6 Then the king appealed to the man of God. "Entreat the LORD, your God," he said, "and intercede for me that I may be able to withdraw my hand." So the man of God entreated the LORD, and the king recovered the normal use of his hand. 7 "Come home with me for some refreshment," the king invited the man of God, "and I will give you a present." 8 "If you gave me half your kingdom," the man of God said to the king, "I would not go with you, nor eat bread or drink water in this place. 9 For I was instructed by the word of the LORD not to eat bread or drink water and not to return by

---

† **12, 26–32:** Jeroboam feared reunification of the divided kingdom through worship in the single temple in Jerusalem. To prevent this he encouraged shrines on the high places, and appointed false priests to supplement those of levitical descent. The golden bullocks he installed in two of his sanctuaries, though probably intended as bearers of the invisible Divine Majesty, quickly became occasions for idolatry. Thus Jeroboam caused Israel to sin, and sealed his doom and that of his royal house (1 Kgs 13, 34; 14, 7–14).

12, 29: *Bethel* and *Dan:* at the southern and northern boundaries of the separate kingdom of Israel, where sanctuaries had existed in the past (Gn 12, 8; 13, 3; 18, 10–22; 25, 1–16; Jgs 18, 1–31).

12, 22–24: 2 Chr 11, 2ff.   **12, 31:** 2 Chr 11, 15.
12, 28: Tb 1, 5; Ex 32, 8.   **13, 2:** 2 Kgs 23, 16.

the way I came." ¹⁰ So he departed by another road and did not go back the way he had come to Bethel.

¹¹ There was an old prophet living in the city, whose sons came and told him all that the man of God had done that day in Bethel. When they repeated to their father the words he had spoken to the king, ¹² the father asked them, "Which way did he go?" And his sons pointed out to him the road taken by the man of God who had come from Judah. ¹³ Then he said to his sons, "Saddle the ass for me." When they had saddled it, he mounted ¹⁴ and followed the man of God, whom he found seated under a terebinth. When he asked him, "Are you the man of God who came from Judah?" he answered, "Yes." ¹⁵ Then he said, "Come home with me and have some bread." ¹⁶ "I cannot go back with you, and I cannot eat bread or drink water with you in this place," he answered, ¹⁷ "for I was told by the word of the LORD neither to eat bread nor drink water here, and not to go back the way I came." ¹⁸ But he said to him, "I, too, am a prophet like you, and an angel told me in the word of the LORD to bring you back with me to my house and to have you eat bread and drink water." He was lying to him, however.

¹⁹ So he went back with him, and ate bread and drank water in his house. ²⁰ But while they were sitting at table, the LORD spoke to the prophet who had brought him back, ²¹ and he cried out to the man of God who had come from Judah: "The LORD says, 'Because you rebelled against the command of the LORD and did not keep the command which the LORD, your God, gave you, ²² but returned and ate bread and drank water in the place where he told you to do neither, your corpse shall not be brought to the grave of your ancestors.' "

²³ After he had eaten bread and drunk water, the ass was saddled for him, and he again ²⁴ set out. But a lion met him on the road, and killed him. His corpse lay sprawled on the road, and the ass remained standing by it, and so did the lion. ²⁵ Some passers-by saw the body lying in the road, with the lion standing beside it, and carried the news to the city where the old prophet lived. ²⁶ On hearing it, the prophet who had brought him back from his journey said: "It is the man of God who rebelled against the command of the LORD. He has delivered him to a lion, which mangled and killed him, as the LORD predicted to him." ²⁷ Then he said to his sons, "Saddle the ass for me." When they had saddled it, ²⁸ he went off and found the body lying in the road with the ass and the lion standing beside it. The lion had not eaten the body nor had it harmed the ass. ²⁹ The prophet lifted up the body of the man of God and put it on the ass, and brought it back to

the city to mourn over it and to bury it. ³⁰ He laid the man's body in his own grave, and they mourned over it: "Alas, my brother!" ³¹ After he had buried him, he said to his sons, "When I die, bury me in the grave where the man of God is buried. Lay my remains beside his. ³² For the word of the LORD which he proclaimed against the altar in Bethel and against all the shrines on the high places in the cities of Samaria shall certainly come to pass."

³³ Jeroboam did not give up his evil ways after this event, but again made priests for the high places from among the common people. Whoever desired it was consecrated and became a priest of the high places. ³⁴ This was a sin on the part of the house of Jeroboam for which it was to be cut off and destroyed from the earth.

Death of Abijah

14 ¹ At that time Abijah, son of Jeroboam, took sick. ²* So Jeroboam said to his wife, "Get ready and disguise yourself so that none will recognize you as Jeroboam's wife. Then go to Shiloh, where you will find the prophet Ahijah. It is he who predicted my reign over this people. ³ Take along ten loaves, some cakes, and a jar of preserves, and go to him. He will tell you what will happen to the child." ⁴ The wife of Jeroboam obeyed. She made the journey to Shiloh and entered the house of Ahijah who could not see because age had dimmed his sight.

⁵ The LORD had said to Ahijah: "Jeroboam's wife is coming to consult you about her son, for he is sick. This is what you must tell her. When she comes, she will be in disguise." ⁶ So Ahijah, hearing the sound of her footsteps as she entered the door, said, "Come in, wife of Jeroboam. Why are you in disguise? I have been commissioned to give you bitter news. ⁷ Go, tell Jeroboam, 'This is what the LORD, the God of Israel, says: I exalted you from among the people and made you ruler of my people Israel. ⁸ I deprived the house of David of the kingdom and gave it to you. Yet you have not been like my servant David, who kept my commandments and followed me with his whole heart, doing only what pleased me. ⁹ You have done worse than all who preceded you: you have gone and made for yourself strange gods and molten images to provoke me; but me you have cast behind your back. ¹⁰* Therefore, I am bringing evil upon the house of Jeroboam: I will cut off every male in Jeroboam's line, whether slave or freeman in Israel, and will burn up the house of Jeroboam completely, as though dung were being burned. ¹¹* When one of Jeroboam's line dies in the city, dogs will devour

1
K
G
S

14, 2: 1 Kgs 11, 29.   14, 11: 1 Kgs 16, 4.
14, 10: 1 Kgs 15, 29.

him; when one of them dies in the field, he will be devoured by the birds of the sky. For the LORD has spoken!' [12] So leave; go home! As you step inside the city, the child will die, [13] and all Israel will mourn him and bury him, for he alone of Jeroboam's line will be laid in the grave, since in him alone of Jeroboam's house has something pleasing to the LORD, the God of Israel, been found. [14] Today, at this very moment, the LORD will raise up for himself a king of Israel who will destroy the house of Jeroboam. [15] The LORD will strike Israel like a reed tossed about in the water and will pluck out Israel from this good land which he gave their fathers, scattering them beyond the River, because they made sacred poles for themselves and thus provoked the LORD. [16] He will give up Israel because of the sins Jeroboam has committed and caused Israel to commit."

[17] So Jeroboam's wife started back; when she reached Tirzah and crossed the threshold of her house, the child died. [18] He was buried with all Israel mourning him, as the LORD had prophesied through his servant the prophet Ahijah.

[19] The rest of the acts of Jeroboam, with his warfare and his reign, are recorded in the book of the chronicles of the kings of Israel. [20] The length of Jeroboam's reign was twenty-two years. He rested with his ancestors, and his son Nadab succeeded him as king.

Reign of Rehoboam

[21]* Rehoboam, son of Solomon, reigned in Judah. He was forty-one years old when he became king, and he reigned seventeen years in Jerusalem, the city in which, out of all the tribes of Israel, the LORD chose to be honored. His mother was the Ammonite named Naamah.

[22] Judah did evil in the sight of the LORD, and by their sins angered him even more than their fathers had done. [23] They, too, built for themselves high places, pillars, and sacred poles, upon every high hill and under every green tree. [24] There were also cult prostitutes in the land. Judah imitated all the abominable practices of the nations whom the LORD had cleared out of the Israelites' way.

[25]† In the fifth year of King Rehoboam, Shishak, king of Egypt, attacked Jerusalem. [26]* He took everything, including the treasures of the temple of the LORD and those of the royal palace, as well as all the gold shields made under Solomon. [27] To

replace them, King Rehoboam had bronze shields made, which he entrusted to the officers of the guard on duty at the entrance of the royal palace. [28] Whenever the king visited the temple of the LORD, those on duty would carry the shields, and then return them to the guardroom.

[29] The rest of the acts of Rehoboam, with all that he did, are recorded in the book of the chronicles of the kings of Judah. [30] There was constant warfare between Rehoboam and Jeroboam. [31] Rehoboam rested with his ancestors; he was buried with them in the City of David. His mother was the Ammonite named Naamah. His son Abijam succeeded him as king.

Reign of Abijam

15 [1]* In the eighteenth year of King Jeroboam, son of Nebat, Abijam became king of Judah; [2] he reigned three years in Jerusalem. His mother's name was Maacah, daughter of Abishalom. [3] He imitated all the sins his father had committed before him, and his heart was not entirely with the LORD, his God, like the heart of his grandfather David. [4] Yet for David's sake the LORD, his God, gave him a lamp in Jerusalem, raising up his son after him and permitting Jerusalem to endure; [5]* because David had pleased the LORD and did not disobey any of his commands as long as he lived, except in the case of Uriah the Hittite.

[7]* The rest of Abijam's acts, with all that he did, are written in the book of the chronicles of the kings of Judah. [6] There was war between Abijam and Jeroboam. [8] Abijam rested with his ancestors; he was buried in the City of David, and his son Asa succeeded him as king.

Reign of Asa

[9] In the twentieth year of Jeroboam, king of Israel, Asa, king of Judah, began to reign; [10] he reigned forty-one years in Jerusalem. His grandmother's name was Maacah, daughter of Abishalom. [11] Asa pleased the LORD like his forefather David, [12] banishing the temple prostitutes from the land and removing all the idols his father had made. [13] He also deposed his grandmother Maacah from her position as queen mother, because she had made an outrageous object for Asherah. Asa cut down this object and burned it in the Kidron Valley. [14] The high places did not disappear; yet Asa's heart was entirely with the LORD as long as he lived. [15] He

---

† **14, 25:** *In the fifth year . . . Shishak, king of Egypt, attacked Jerusalem:* c. 926 B.C. According to 2 Chr 12, 1–12, the repentance of King Rehoboam and of the princes of Israel after the warning of the prophet Shemaiah diverted the actual attack on Jerusalem. Shishak, however, carried off the treasures of the temple of the Lord and of the king's palace (2 Chr 12, 9). A bas-relief of this Pharaoh in the temple of Aman at Karnak commemorates his conquest of some hundred and fifty Palestinian and Trans-Jordanian cities and towns.

*

14, 21: 2 Chr 12, 13.	**15, 5:** 2 Sm 11, 4.
14, 26: 1 Kgs 10, 16.	**15, 7:** 2 Chr 13, 2.
15, 1: 2 Chr 13, 1f.	

brought into the temple of the LORD his father's and his own votive offerings of silver, gold, and various utensils.

16 There was war between Asa and Baasha, king of Israel, as long as they both reigned. 17* Baasha, king of Israel, attacked Judah and fortified Ramah to prevent communication with Asa, king of Judah. 18† Asa then took all the silver and gold remaining in the treasuries of the temple of the LORD and of the royal palace. Entrusting them to his ministers, King Asa sent them to Ben-hadad, son of Tabrimmon, son of Hezion, king of Aram, resident in Damascus. He said: 19 "There is a treaty between you and me, as there was between your father and my father. I am sending you a present of silver and gold. Go, break your treaty with Baasha, king of Israel, that he may withdraw from me." 20 Ben-hadad agreed with King Asa and sent the leaders of his troops against the cities of Israel. They attacked Ijon, Dan, Abel-beth-maacah, and all Chinnereth, besides all the land of Naphtali. 21 When Baasha heard of it, he left off fortifying Ramah, and stayed in Tirzah. 22 Then King Asa summoned all Judah without exception, and they carried away the stones and beams with which Baasha was fortifying Ramah. With them King Asa built Geba of Benjamin and Mizpeh.

23 The rest of the acts of Asa, with all his valor and accomplishments, and the cities he built, are written in the book of the chronicles of the kings of Judah. In his old age, Asa had an infirmity in his feet. 24* He rested with his ancestors; he was buried in his forefather's City of David, and his son Jehoshaphat succeeded him as king.

Reign of Nadab

25 In the second year of Asa, king of Judah, Nadab, son of Jeroboam, became king of Israel; he reigned over Israel two years. 26 He did evil in the LORD's sight, imitating his father's conduct and the sin which he had caused Israel to commit. 27 Baasha, son of Ahijah, of the house of Issachar, plotted against him and struck him down at Gibbethon of the Philistines, which Nadab and all Israel were besieging. 28 Baasha killed him in the third year of Asa, king of Judah, and reigned in his stead. 29* Once he was king, he killed off the entire house of Jeroboam, not leaving a single soul to Jeroboam but destroying him utterly, according to the warning which the LORD had pronounced through his servant, Ahijah the Shilonite, 30 because of the sins Jeroboam committed and caused Israel to

commit, by which he provoked the LORD, the God of Israel, to anger.

31 The rest of the acts of Nadab, with all that he did, are written in the book of the chronicles of the kings of Israel. 32 [There was war between Asa and Baasha, king of Israel, as long as they lived.]

Reign of Baasha

33 In the third year of Asa, king of Judah, Baasha, son of Ahijah, began his twenty-four-year reign over Israel in Tirzah. 34 He did evil in the LORD's sight, imitating the conduct of Jeroboam and the sin he had caused Israel to commit.

16 1 The LORD spoke against Baasha to Jehu, son of Hanani, and said: 2 "Inasmuch as I lifted you up from the dust and made you ruler of my people Israel, but you have imitated the conduct of Jeroboam and have caused my people Israel to sin, provoking me to anger by their sins, 3* I will destroy you, Baasha, and your house; 4* I will make your house like that of Jeroboam, son of Nebat. If anyone of Baasha's line dies in the city, dogs shall devour him; if he dies in the field, he shall be devoured by the birds of the sky."

5* The rest of the acts of Baasha, with all his valor and accomplishments, are written in the book of the chronicles of the kings of Israel. 6 Baasha rested with his ancestors; he was buried in Tirzah, and his son Elah succeeded him as king. 7 [Through the prophet Jehu, son of Hanani, the LORD had threatened Baasha and his house, because of all the evil Baasha did in the sight of the LORD, provoking him to anger by his evil deeds, so that he became like the house of Jeroboam; and because he killed Nadab.]

Reign of Elah

8 In the twenty-sixth year of Asa, king of Judah, Elah, son of Baasha, began his two-year reign over Israel in Tirzah. 9 His servant Zimri, commander of half his chariots, plotted against him. As he was in Tirzah, drinking to excess in the house of Arza, superintendent of his palace in Tirzah, 10* Zimri entered; he struck and killed him in the twenty-seventh year of Asa, king of Judah, and reigned in his place. 11 Once he was seated on the royal throne, he killed off the whole house of Baasha, not sparing a single male relative or friend of his. 12 Zimri destroyed the entire house of Baasha, as the LORD had prophesied to Baasha through the prophet Jehu, 13 because of all the sins which Baasha and his son Elah committed and caused

---

† **15, 18:** *Ben-hadad . . . king of Aram:* Ben-hadad I, third successor of Rezon, who had thrown off the yoke of the Israelites during the reign of Solomon and become king of Aram (11, 23f).

15, 17: 2 Chr 16, 1.
15, 24: 2 Chr 17, 1.
15, 29: 1 Kgs 14, 10; 21, 22.
16, 3: 1 Kgs 21, 22.
16, 4: 1 Kgs 14, 11.
16, 5: 2 Chr 16, 1.
16, 10: 2 Kgs 9, 31.

Israel to commit, provoking the LORD, the God of Israel, to anger by their idols.

[14] The rest of the acts of Elah, with all that he did, are written in the book of the chronicles of the kings of Israel.

Reign of Zimri

[15] In the twenty-seventh year of Asa, king of Judah, Zimri reigned seven days in Tirzah. The army was besieging Gibbethon of the Philistines [16] when they heard that Zimri had formed a conspiracy and had killed the king. So that day in the camp all Israel proclaimed Omri, general of the army, king of Israel. [17] Omri marched up from Gibbethon, accompanied by all Israel, and laid siege to Tirzah. [18] When Zimri saw the city was captured, he entered the citadel of the royal palace and burned down the palace over him. He died [19] because of the sins he had committed, doing evil in the sight of the LORD by imitating the sinful conduct of Jeroboam, thus causing Israel to sin.

[20] The rest of the acts of Zimri, with the conspiracy he carried out, are written in the book of the chronicles of the kings of Israel.

[21] At that time the people of Israel were divided, half following Tibni, son of Ginath, to make him king, and half for Omri. [22] The partisans of Omri prevailed over those of Tibni, son of Ginath. Tibni died and Omri became king.

Reign of Omri

[23] In the thirty-first year of Asa, king of Judah, Omri became king; he reigned over Israel twelve years, the first six of them in Tirzah. [24] He then bought the hill of Samaria from Shemer for two silver talents and built upon the hill, naming the city he built Samaria after Shemer, the former owner. [25] But Omri did evil in the LORD'S sight beyond any of his predecessors. [26] He closely imitated the sinful conduct of Jeroboam, son of Nebat, causing Israel to sin and to provoke the LORD, the God of Israel, to anger by their idols.

[27] The rest of the acts of Omri, with all his valor and accomplishments, are written in the book of the chronicles of the kings of Israel. [28] Omri rested with his ancestors; he was buried in Samaria, and his son Ahab succeeded him as king.

Reign of Ahab

[29] In the thirty-eighth year of Asa, king of Judah, Ahab, son of Omri, became king of Israel; he reigned over Israel in Samaria for twenty-two years. [30] Ahab, son of Omri, did evil in the sight of the LORD more than any of his predecessors. [31] It was not enough for him to imitate the sins of Jeroboam, son of Nebat. He even married Jezebel, daughter of Ethbaal, king of the Sidonians, and went over to the veneration and worship of Baal. [32] Ahab erected an altar to Baal in the temple of Baal which he built in Samaria, [33] and also made a sacred pole. He did more to anger the LORD, the God of Israel, than any of the kings of Israel before him.

[34]* During his reign, Hiel from Bethel rebuilt Jericho. He lost his first-born son, Abiram, when he laid the foundation, and his youngest son, Segub, when he set up the gates, as the LORD had foretold through Joshua, son of Nun.

III: Stories of the Prophets

Drought Predicted by Elijah

17 [1]*† Elijah the Tishbite, from Tishbe in Gilead, said to Ahab: "As the LORD, the God of Israel, lives, whom I serve, during these years there shall be no dew or rain except at my word." [2] The LORD then said to Elijah: [3] "Leave here, go east and hide in the Wadi Cherith, east of the Jordan. [4] You shall drink of the stream, and I have commanded ravens to feed you there." [5] So he left and did as the LORD had commanded. He went and remained by the Wadi Cherith, east of the Jordan. [6] Ravens brought him bread and meat in the morning, and bread and meat in the evening, and he drank from the stream.

Elijah and the Widow

[7] After some time, however, the brook ran dry, because no rain had fallen in the land. [8] So the LORD said to him: [9] "Move on to Zarephath of Sidon and stay there. I have designated a widow there to provide for you." [10]* He left and went to Zarephath. As he arrived at the entrance of the city, a widow was gathering sticks there; he called out to her, "Please bring me a small cupful of water to drink." [11] She left to get it, and he called out after her, "Please bring along a bit of bread." [12] "As the LORD, your God, lives," she answered, "I have nothing baked; there is only a handful of flour in my jar and a little oil in my jug. Just now I was collecting a couple of sticks, to go in and prepare something for myself and my son; when we have eaten it, we shall

---

†
17, 1: *Elijah the Tishbite:* one of the most important figures in Old Testament history. As his name indicates ("Yahweh is my God"), Elijah was the successful leader in the struggle to preserve the knowledge and worship of Yahweh against the encroaching worship of Baal introduced into Israel by Jezebel, the Tyrian wife of Ahab. The Elijah cycle of narratives includes, besides the above struggle, miracle stories, denunciations of kings, and a preparation for the

prophet's role as eschatological forerunner of the "great day of the Lord"; cf Mal 3, 23–24; Mt 17, 10–13; Lk 1, 17.

16, 34: Jos 6, 26.　　　　　　**17, 10:** Lk 4, 26.
17, 1: Sir 48, 3; Jas 5, 17.

die." 13 "Do not be afraid," Elijah said to her. "Go and do as you propose. But first make me a little cake and bring it to me. Then you can prepare something for yourself and your son. 14 For the LORD, the God of Israel, says, 'The jar of flour shall not go empty, nor the jug of oil run dry, until the day when the LORD sends rain upon the earth.' " 15 She left and did as Elijah had said. She was able to eat for a year, and he and her son as well; 16 the jar of flour did not go empty, nor the jug of oil run dry, as the LORD had foretold through Elijah.

17 Some time later the son of the mistress of the house fell sick, and his sickness grew more severe until he stopped breathing. 18 So she said to Elijah, "Why have you done this to me, O man of God? Have you come to me to call attention to my guilt and to kill my son?" 19 "Give me your son," Elijah said to her. Taking him from her lap, he carried him to the upper room where he was staying, and laid him on his own bed. 20 He called out to the LORD: "O LORD, my God, will you afflict even the widow with whom I am staying by killing her son?" 21 Then he stretched himself out upon the child three times and called out to the LORD: "O LORD, my God, let the life breath return to the body of this child." 22 The LORD heard the prayer of Elijah; the life breath returned to the child's body and he revived. 23 Taking the child, Elijah brought him down into the house from the upper room and gave him to his mother. "See!" Elijah said to her, "your son is alive." 24 "Now indeed I know that you are a man of God," the woman replied to Elijah. "The word of the LORD comes truly from your mouth."

Elijah and the Prophets of Baal

18 1 Long afterward, in the third year, the LORD spoke to Elijah. "Go, present yourself to Ahab," he said, "that I may send rain upon the earth." 2 So Elijah went to present himself to Ahab.

3 Now the famine in Samaria was bitter, 4 and Ahab had summoned Obadiah, his vizier, who was a zealous follower of the LORD. When Jezebel was murdering the prophets of the LORD, Obadiah took a hundred prophets, hid them away fifty each in two caves, and supplied them with food and drink. 5 Ahab said to Obadiah, "Come, let us go through the land to all sources of water and to all the streams. We may find grass and save the horses and mules, so that we shall not have to slaughter any of the beasts." 6 Dividing the land to explore between them, Ahab went one way by himself, Obadiah another way by himself.

7 As Obadiah was on his way, Elijah met him.

Introducing....

►ELIJAH AND ELISHA

You didn't want to mess with Elijah and Elisha. They were take-no-prisoners kinds of prophets. According to 1 Kings, Elijah has 450 prophets of Baal killed after publicly humiliating them (18, 40). And when a bunch of boys call Elisha "baldhead," they are attacked by bears (2 Kgs 2, 23–24).

Elijah, whose name means "Yahweh is my God," shows up in the second half of 1 Kings reminding the Israelites that God is their God alone and that keeping God's Covenant means not worshiping the Canaanite baals (gods). In a dramatic story, he shows the idol-worshiping King Ahab and Queen Jezebel that God is superior to their false gods (1 Kgs 18, 21–40).

Elijah was recorded as being carried to heaven in a fiery chariot (2 Kgs 2, 11) as a sign of his greatness, and he was expected to reappear before the "day of the LORD" arrived (Mal 3, 23). By New Testament times, Elijah had come to represent the prophets as Moses had come to represent the Law. Referring to Moses and Elijah was a way of summarizing everything that God had revealed before Christ.

Elisha was Elijah's disciple and successor. He plays an important role in the first half of 2 Kings. Elisha's name means "God is salvation." He was a man of wisdom and a miracle worker.

These "tough guys" also had tender hearts. Both miraculously multiplied food for widows (1 Kgs 17, 16; 2 Kgs 4, 5), and both brought a dead child back to life (1 Kgs 17, 22; 2 Kgs 4, 34). Elijah and Elisha are revered both for their uncompromising faith and for their compassion for the "little ones."

Recognizing him, Obadiah fell prostrate and asked, "Is it you, my lord Elijah?" 8 "Yes," he answered. "Go tell your master, 'Elijah is here!'" 9 But Obadiah said, "What sin have I committed, that you are handing me over to Ahab to have me killed? 10 As the LORD, your God, lives, there is no nation or kingdom where my master has not sent in search of you. When they replied, 'He is not here,' he made each kingdom and nation swear they could not find you. 11 And now you say, 'Go tell your master: Elijah is here!' 12 After I leave you, the spirit of the LORD will carry you to some place I do not know, and when I go to inform Ahab and he does not find you, he will kill me. Your servant has revered the LORD from his youth. 13 Have you not been told, my lord, what I did when Jezebel was murdering the prophets of the LORD—that I hid a hundred of the prophets of the LORD, fifty each in two caves, and supplied them with food and drink? 14 And now you say, 'Go tell your master: Elijah is here!' He will kill me!" 15 Elijah answered, "As the LORD of hosts lives, whom I serve, I will present myself to him today."

16 So Obadiah went to meet Ahab and informed him. Ahab came to meet Elijah, 17 and when he saw Elijah, said to him, "Is it you, you disturber of Israel?" 18 "It is not I who disturb Israel," he answered, "but you and your family, by forsaking the commands of the LORD and following the Baals. 19 Now summon all Israel to me on Mount Carmel, as well as the four hundred and fifty prophets of Baal and the four hundred prophets of Asherah who eat at Jezebel's table." 20 So Ahab sent to all the Israelites and had the prophets assemble on Mount Carmel.

21 Elijah appealed to all the people and said, "How long will you straddle the issue? If the LORD is God, follow him; if Baal, follow him." The people, however, did not answer him. 22 So Elijah said to the people, "I am the only surviving prophet of the LORD, and there are four hundred and fifty prophets of Baal. 23 Give us two young bulls. Let them choose one, cut it into pieces, and place it on the wood, but start no fire. I shall prepare the other and place it on the wood, but shall start no fire. 24 You shall call on the name of your gods, and I will call on the name of the LORD. The God who answers with fire is God." All the people answered, "Agreed!"

25 Elijah then said to the prophets of Baal, "Choose one young bull and prepare it first, for there are more of you. Call upon your gods, but do not start the fire." 26 Taking the young bull that was turned over to them, they prepared it and called on Baal from morning to noon, saying, "Answer us, Baal!" But there was no sound, and no one answering. And they hopped around the altar they had prepared. 27 When it was noon, Elijah taunted them: "Call louder, for he is a god and may be

meditating, or may have retired, or may be on a journey. Perhaps he is asleep and must be awakened." 28 They called out louder and slashed themselves with swords and spears, as was their custom, until blood gushed over them. 29 Noon passed and they remained in a prophetic state until the time for offering sacrifice. But there was not a sound; no one answered, and no one was listening.

30 Then Elijah said to all the people, "Come here to me." When they had done so, he repaired the altar of the LORD which had been destroyed. 31 He took twelve stones, for the number of tribes of the sons of Jacob, to whom the LORD had said, "Your name shall be Israel." 32 He built an altar in honor of the LORD with the stones, and made a trench around the altar large enough for two seahs of grain. 33 When he had arranged the wood, he cut up the young bull and laid it on the wood. 34 "Fill four jars with water," he said, "and pour it over the holocaust and over the wood." "Do it again," he said, and they did it again. "Do it a third time," he said, and they did it a third time. 35 The water flowed around the altar, and the trench was filled with the water.

36 At the time for offering sacrifice, the prophet Elijah came forward and said, "LORD, God of Abraham, Isaac, and Israel, let it be known this day that you are God in Israel and that I am your servant and have done all these things by your command. 37 Answer me, LORD! Answer me, that this people may know that you, LORD, are God and that you have brought them back to their senses." 38 The LORD'S fire came down and consumed the holocaust, wood, stones, and dust, and it lapped up the water in the trench. 39 Seeing this, all the people fell prostrate and said, "The LORD is God! The LORD is God!" 40 Then Elijah said to them, "Seize the prophets of Baal. Let none of them escape!" They were seized, and Elijah had them brought down to the brook Kishon and there he slit their throats.

41 Elijah then said to Ahab, "Go up, eat and drink, for there is the sound of a heavy rain." 42 So Ahab went up to eat and drink, while Elijah climbed to the top of Carmel, crouched down to the earth, and put his head between his knees. 43 "Climb up and look out to sea," he directed his servant, who went up and looked, but reported, "There is nothing." Seven times he said, "Go, look again!" 44 And the seventh time the youth reported, "There is a cloud as small as a man's hand rising from the sea." Elijah said, "Go and say to Ahab, 'Harness up and leave the mountain before the rain stops you.'" 45 In a trice, the sky grew dark with clouds and wind, and a heavy rain fell. Ahab mounted his chariot and made for Jezreel. 46 But the hand of the LORD was on Elijah, who girded up his clothing and ran before Ahab as far as the approaches to Jezreel.

Flight to Horeb

19 [1] Ahab told Jezebel all that Elijah had done—that he had put all the prophets to the sword. [2] Jezebel then sent a messenger to Elijah and said, "May the gods do thus and so to me if by this time tomorrow I have not done with your life what was done to each of them." [3] Elijah was afraid and fled for his life, going to Beer-sheba of Judah. He left his servant there [4] and went a day's journey into the desert, until he came to a broom tree and sat beneath it. He prayed for death: "This is enough, O LORD! Take my life, for I am no better than my fathers." [5] He lay down and fell asleep under the broom tree, but then an angel touched him and ordered him to get up and eat. [6] He looked and there at his head was a hearth cake and a jug of water. After he ate and drank, he lay down again, [7] but the angel of the LORD came back a second time, touched him, and ordered, "Get up and eat, else the journey will be too long for you!" [8] He got up, ate and drank; then strengthened by that food, he walked forty days and forty nights to the mountain of God, Horeb.

[9] There he came to a cave, where he took shelter. But the word of the LORD came to him, "Why are you here, Elijah?" [10] He answered: "I have been most zealous for the LORD, the God of hosts, but the Israelites have forsaken your covenant, torn down your altars, and put your prophets to the sword. I alone am left, and they seek to take my life." [11]† Then the LORD said, "Go outside and stand on the mountain before the LORD; the LORD will be passing by." A strong and heavy wind was rending the mountains and crushing rocks before the LORD—but the LORD was not in the wind. After the wind there was an earthquake—but the LORD was not in the earthquake. [12] After the earthquake there was fire—but the LORD was not in the fire. After the fire there was a tiny whispering sound. [13] When he heard this, Elijah hid his face in his cloak and went and stood at the entrance of the cave. A voice said to him, "Elijah, why are you here?" [14]* He replied, "I have been most zealous for the LORD, the God of hosts. But the Israelites have forsaken your covenant, torn down your altars, and put your prophets to the sword. I alone am left, and they seek to take my life." [15]† "Go, take the road back to the desert near Damascus," the LORD said to him. "When you arrive,

---

Looking for God

E lijah was told to meet God on the mountain. God's presence could have been in fire, an earthquake, a great wind, but God was in none of these. God was in the tiny whispering sound.

All of us have a need for God. We might not know it, but it is there: a God-shaped hole in our soul that no one and nothing else can fill. Without God we will always feel empty.

Sometimes we look for loud and spectacular things to fill that empty space. We buy expensive clothing or toys. Or we smoke cigarettes, drink alcohol, use other illegal drugs, or have sex without commitment. And we still feel empty.

The irony is that through all this, God is there, in the quiet depths of our heart. We need to be like Elijah—tuning out things that are not God and tuning in to God's presence. Taking quiet time to think and pray is a great start.

▶ 1 Kgs 19, 9–13

---

you shall anoint Hazael as king of Aram. [16]* Then you shall anoint Jehu, son of Nimshi, as king of Israel, and Elisha, son of Shaphat of Abel-meholah, as prophet to succeed you. [17] If anyone escapes the sword of Hazael, Jehu will kill him. If he escapes the sword of Jehu, Elisha will kill him. [18]* Yet I will leave seven thousand men in Israel—all those who have not knelt to Baal or kissed him."

Call of Elisha

[19]† Elijah set out, and came upon Elisha, son of Shaphat, as he was plowing with twelve yoke of oxen; he was following the twelfth. Elijah went over to him and threw his cloak over him. [20] Elisha left the oxen, ran after Elijah, and said, "Please, let me

---

19, 11ff: Compare these divine manifestations to Elijah with those to Moses (Ex 19, 1–23; 33, 21ff; 34, 5) on the same Mount Horeb (Sinai) (Dt 4, 10–15). Though various phenomena, such as wind, storms, earthquakes, fire (Ex 19, 18f), herald the divine presence, they do not constitute the presence itself which, like the tiny whispering sound, is imperceptible and bespeaks the spirituality of God. It was fitting that Elijah, whose mission it was to reestablish the covenant and restore the pure faith, should have returned to Horeb where the covenant was revealed to Moses and through him to the Israelite people (Ex 3, 1–4.17; 33, 18—34, 9). Moses and Elijah appeared with Christ at the time of his transfiguration (Mt 17, 1–9; Mk 9, 1–7; Lk 9, 28–36).

19, 15–17: Elijah himself carried out only the third of the commissions entrusted to him (vv 19–21); Elisha was deputed to perform the first in person (2 Kgs 8, 7–19), and the second through one of his followers (2 Kgs 9, 1–10).

19, 19–21: Elijah's act of throwing his mantle over the shoulders of Elisha expressed the divine call to share the prophetic mission. Elisha's prompt response through destruction of his plow and oxen is an example of total obedience and detachment from his former manner of living in order to promote the glory of God.

19, 14: Rom 11, 3.   19, 18: Rom 11, 4.
19, 16: 2 Kgs 9, 2.

kiss my father and mother goodbye, and I will follow you." "Go back!" Elijah answered. "Have I
done anything to you?" ²¹ Elisha left him and, taking the yoke of oxen, slaughtered them; he used the
plowing equipment for fuel to boil their flesh, and
gave it to his people to eat. Then he left and followed Elijah as his attendant.

Ahab's Victories over Ben-hadad

20 ¹ Ben-hadad, king of Aram, gathered all
his forces, and accompanied by thirty-
two kings with horses and chariotry, proceeded to
invest and attack Samaria. ² He sent couriers to
Ahab, king of Israel, within the city, ³ and said to
him, "This is Ben-hadad's message: 'Your silver and
gold are mine, and your wives and your promising
sons are mine.' " ⁴ The king of Israel answered, "As
you say, my lord king, I and all I have are yours."
⁵ But the couriers came again and said, "This is Ben-
hadad's message: 'I sent you word to give me your
silver and gold, your wives and your sons. ⁶ Now,
however, at this time tomorrow I will send my servants to you, and they shall ransack your house and
the houses of your servants. They shall seize and
take away whatever they consider valuable.' "

⁷ The king of Israel then summoned all the elders
of the land and said: "Understand clearly that this
man wants to ruin us. When he sent to me for my
wives and sons, my silver and my gold, I did not refuse him." ⁸ All the elders and all the people said to
him, "Do not listen. Do not give in." ⁹ Accordingly he
directed the couriers of Ben-hadad, "Say to my lord
the king, 'I will do all that you demanded of your servant the first time. But this I cannot do.' " The couriers
left and reported this. ¹⁰ Ben-hadad then sent him the
message, "May the gods do thus and so to me if there
is enough dust in Samaria to make handfuls for all
my followers." ¹¹ The king of Israel replied, "Tell him,
'It is not for the man who is buckling his armor to
boast as though he were taking it off.' " ¹² Ben-hadad
was drinking in the pavilions with the kings when he
heard this reply. "Prepare the assault," he commanded his servants; and they made ready to storm the city.

¹³ Then a prophet came up to Ahab, king of Israel,
and said: "The LORD says, 'Do you see all this huge
army? When I deliver it up to you today, you will
know that I am the LORD.' " ¹⁴ But Ahab asked,
"Through whom will it be delivered up?" He answered, "The LORD says, 'Through the retainers of the
governors of the provinces.' " Then Ahab asked,
"Who is to attack?" He replied, "You are." ¹⁵ So Ahab
called up the retainers of the governors of the
provinces, two hundred thirty-two of them. Behind
them he mustered all the Israelite soldiery, who

numbered seven thousand. ¹⁶ They marched out at
noon, while Ben-hadad was drinking heavily in the
pavilions with the thirty-two kings who were his allies. ¹⁷ When the retainers of the governors of the
provinces marched out first, Ben-hadad received
word that some men had marched out of Samaria.
¹⁸ He answered, "Whether they have come out for
peace or for war, in any case take them alive." ¹⁹ But
when these had come out of the city—the soldiers of
the governors of the provinces with the army following them— ²⁰ each of them struck down his man.
The Arameans fled with Israel pursuing them, while
Ben-hadad, king of Aram, escaped on a chariot steed.
²¹ The king of Israel went out, took the horses and
chariots, and inflicted a severe defeat on Aram.

²²† Then the prophet went up to the king of Israel
and said to him: "Go, regroup your forces. Mark well
what you do, for at the beginning of the year the king
of Aram will attack you." ²³ On the other hand, the
servants of the king of Aram said to him: "Their gods
are gods of mountains. That is why they defeated us.
But if we fight them on level ground, we shall be sure
to defeat them. ²⁴ This is what you must do: Take the
kings from their posts and put prefects in their
places. ²⁵ Mobilize an army as large as the army that
has deserted you, horse for horse, chariot for chariot.
Let us fight them on level ground, and we shall surely defeat them." He took their advice and did this.

²⁶ At the beginning of the year, Ben-hadad mobi-
lized Aram and went up to Aphek to fight against
Israel. ²⁷ The Israelites, too, were called to arms and
supplied with provisions; then they went out to engage the foe. The Israelites, encamped opposite
them, seemed like a couple of small flocks of goats,
while Aram covered the countryside. ²⁸ A man of
God came up and said to the king of Israel: "The
LORD says, 'Because Aram has said the LORD is a god
of mountains, not a god of plains, I will deliver up
to you all this large army, that you may know I am
the LORD.' " ²⁹ They were encamped opposite each
other for seven days. On the seventh day battle was
joined, and the Israelites struck down one hundred
thousand foot soldiers of Aram in one day. ³⁰ The
survivors, twenty-seven thousand of them, fled into
the city of Aphek, and there the wall collapsed. Ben-
hadad, too, fled, and took refuge within the city, in
an inside room.

³¹ His servants said to him: "We have heard that
the kings of the land of Israel are merciful kings. Allow us, therefore, to garb ourselves in sackcloth, with
cords around our heads, and go out to the king of
Israel. Perhaps he will spare your life." ³² So they
dressed in sackcloth girded at the waist, and wearing
cords around their heads, they went to the king of

20, 22: *At the beginning of the year:* in the spring.

Israel. "Your servant Ben-hadad pleads for his life,"
they said. "Is he still alive?" the king asked. "He is my
brother." 33 Hearing this as a good omen, the men
quickly took him at his word and said, "Ben-hadad is
your brother." He answered, "Go and get him."
When Ben-hadad came out to him, the king had him
mount his chariot. 34 Ben-hadad said to him, "I will
restore the cities which my father took from your
father, and you may make yourself bazaars in Damascus, as my father did in Samaria." "On these
terms," Ahab replied, "I will set you free." So he
made an agreement with him and then set him free.
35 One of the guild prophets was prompted by the
LORD to say to his companion, "Strike me." But he
refused to strike him. 36 Then he said to him, "Since
you did not obey the voice of the LORD, a lion will
kill you when you leave me." When they parted
company, a lion came upon him and killed him.
37 The prophet met another man and said, "Strike
me." The man struck him a blow and wounded him.
38 The prophet went on and waited for the king on
the road, having disguised himself with a bandage
over his eyes. 39 As the king was passing, he called
out to the king and said, "Your servant went into the
thick of the battle, and suddenly someone turned
and brought me a man and said, 'Guard this man. If
he is missing, you shall have to pay for his life with
your life or pay out a talent of silver.' 40 But while
your servant was looking here and there, the man
disappeared." The king of Israel said to him, "That is
your sentence. You have decided it yourself." 41 He
immediately removed the bandage from his eyes,
and the king of Israel recognized him as one of the
prophets. 42* He said to him: "The LORD says, 'Because you have set free the man I doomed to destruction, your life shall pay for his life, your people
for his people.' " Disturbed and angry, the king of Israel went off homeward and entered Samaria.

Seizure of Naboth's Vineyard

21 1 Some time after this, as Naboth the
Jezreelite had a vineyard in Jezreel next to
the palace of Ahab, king of Samaria, 2 Ahab said to
Naboth, "Give me your vineyard to be my vegetable
garden, since it is close by, next to my house. I will
give you a better vineyard in exchange, or, if you
prefer, I will give you its value in money." 3 "The
LORD forbid," Naboth answered him, "that I should
give you my ancestral heritage." 4 Ahab went home

disturbed and angry at the answer Naboth the
Jezreelite had made to him: "I will not give you my
ancestral heritage." Lying down on his bed, he
turned away from food and would not eat.
5 His wife Jezebel came to him and said to him,
"Why are you so angry that you will not eat?" 6 He
answered her, "Because I spoke to Naboth the
Jezreelite and said to him, 'Sell me your vineyard, or,
if you prefer, I will give you a vineyard in exchange.'
But he refused to let me have his vineyard." 7 "A fine
ruler over Israel you are indeed!" his wife Jezebel
said to him. "Get up. Eat and be cheerful. I will obtain the vineyard of Naboth the Jezreelite for you."
8 So she wrote letters in Ahab's name and, having
sealed them with his seal, sent them to the elders and
to the nobles who lived in the same city with
Naboth. 9 This is what she wrote in the letters: "Proclaim a fast and set Naboth at the head of the people.
10 Next, get two scoundrels to face him and accuse
him of having cursed God and king. Then take him
out and stone him to death." 11 His fellow citizens—
the elders and the nobles who dwelt in his city—did
as Jezebel had ordered them in writing, through the
letters she had sent them. 12 They proclaimed a fast
and placed Naboth at the head of the people. 13 Two
scoundrels came in and confronted him with the accusation, "Naboth has cursed God and king." And
they led him out of the city and stoned him to death.
14 Then they sent the information to Jezebel that
Naboth had been stoned to death.
15 When Jezebel learned that Naboth had been
stoned to death, she said to Ahab, "Go on, take possession of the vineyard of Naboth the Jezreelite
which he refused to sell you, because Naboth is not
alive, but dead." 16 On hearing that Naboth was
dead, Ahab started off on his way down to the vineyard of Naboth the Jezreelite, to take possession of it.
17 But the LORD said to Elijah the Tishbite:
18 "Start down to meet Ahab, king of Israel, who
rules in Samaria. He will be in the vineyard of
Naboth, of which he has come to take possession.
19*† This is what you shall tell him, 'The LORD says:
After murdering, do you also take possession? For
this, the LORD says: In the place where the dogs
licked up the blood of Naboth, the dogs shall lick
up your blood, too.' " 20† "Have you found me out,
my enemy?" Ahab said to Elijah. "Yes," he answered. "Because you have given yourself up to doing evil in the LORD'S sight, 21* I am bringing evil

---

21, 19: The response of Ahab to this divine judgment is described
in v 27, and the consequences are given in vv 28–29, and in 2 Kgs
9, 21–26.
21, 20–26: In these verses the Judean editor of the Books of Kings
substitutes, for the message of Elijah prepared for in v 19, a sweeping and definitive judgment against the whole family of Ahab in the
same terms as were used against the families of Jeroboam I (1 Kgs
14, 9–11) and Baasha (1 Kgs 16, 2–4). This judgment is the fruit of

later theological reflection; it is not occasioned directly by the crime
against Naboth, but by the idolatry of Ahab and Jezebel. The judgment on Jezebel herself (v 23) may have been uttered by Elijah during the Naboth episode; it finds its fulfillment in 2 Kgs 9, 36–37. Still
another theological explanation for the death of Ahab is given by the
north Israelite writer of 1 Kgs 20, 35–42 above.

20, 42: 1 Kgs 22, 35.   21, 21: 2 Kgs 9, 8.
21, 19: 1 Kgs 22, 38.

upon you: I will destroy you and will cut off every male in Ahab's line, whether slave or freeman, in Israel. [22]* I will make your house like that of Jeroboam, son of Nebat, and like that of Baasha, son of Ahijah, because of how you have provoked me by leading Israel into sin." [23]* (Against Jezebel, too, the LORD declared, "The dogs shall devour Jezebel in the district of Jezreel.") [24] "When one of Ahab's line dies in the city, dogs will devour him; when one of them dies in the field, the birds of the sky will devour him." [25] Indeed, no one gave himself up to the doing of evil in the sight of the LORD as did Ahab, urged on by his wife Jezebel. [26] He became completely abominable by following idols, just as the Amorites had done, whom the LORD drove out before the Israelites.

[27] When Ahab heard these words, he tore his garments and put on sackcloth over his bare flesh. He fasted, slept in the sackcloth, and went about subdued. [28] Then the LORD said to Elijah the Tishbite, [29]* "Have you seen that Ahab has humbled himself before me? Since he has humbled himself before me, I will not bring the evil in his time. I will bring the evil upon his house during the reign of his son."

Campaign against Ramoth-gilead

22 [1]* Three years passed without war between Aram and Israel. [2] In the third year, however, King Jehoshaphat of Judah came down to the king of Israel, [3] who said to his servants, "Do you not know that Ramoth-gilead is ours and we are doing nothing to take it from the king of Aram?" [4] He asked Jehoshaphat, "Will you come with me to fight against Ramoth-gilead?" Jehoshaphat answered the king of Israel, "You and I are as one, and your people and my people, your horses and my horses as well." [5] Jehoshaphat also said to the king of Israel, "Seek the word of the LORD at once."

[6] The king of Israel gathered together the prophets, about four hundred of them, and asked, "Shall I go to attack Ramoth-gilead or shall I refrain?" "Go up," they answered. "The LORD will deliver it over to the king." [7] But Jehoshaphat said, "Is there no other prophet of the LORD here whom we may consult?" [8] The king of Israel answered, "There is one other through whom we might consult the LORD, Micaiah, son of Imlah; but I hate him because he prophesies not good but evil about me." Jehoshaphat said, "Let not your majesty speak of evil against you."

[9] So the king of Israel called an official and said to him, "Get Micaiah, son of Imlah, at once." [10] The king of Israel and King Jehoshaphat of Judah were seated, each on his throne, clothed in their robes of state on a threshing floor at the entrance of the gate of Samaria, and all the prophets were prophesying before them. [11] Zedekiah, son of Chenaanah, made himself horns of iron and said, "The LORD says, 'With these you shall gore Aram until you have destroyed them.'" [12] The other prophets prophesied in a similar vein, saying: "Go up to Ramoth-gilead; you shall succeed. The LORD will deliver it over to the king."

[13] The messenger who had gone to call Micaiah said to him, "Look now, the prophets are unanimously predicting good for the king. Let your word be the same as any of theirs; predict good." [14] "As the LORD lives," Micaiah answered, "I shall say whatever the LORD tells me."

[15] When he came to the king, the king said to him, "Micaiah, shall we go to fight against Ramoth-gilead, or shall we refrain?" "Go up," he answered, "you shall succeed! The LORD will deliver it over to the king." [16] But the king answered him, "How many times must I adjure you to tell me nothing but the truth in the name of the LORD?" [17] So Micaiah said:

"I see all Israel
 scattered on the mountains,
 like sheep without a shepherd,
 and the LORD saying, 'These have no master!
 Let each of them go back home in peace.' "

[18] The king of Israel said to Jehoshaphat, "Did I not tell you he prophesies not good but evil about me?" [19]† Micaiah continued: "Therefore hear the word of the LORD: I saw the LORD seated on his throne, with the whole host of heaven standing by to his right and to his left. [20] The LORD asked, 'Who will deceive Ahab, so that he will go up and fall at Ramoth-gilead?' And one said this, another that, [21] until one of the spirits came forth and presented himself to the LORD, saying, 'I will deceive him.' The LORD asked, 'How?' [22] He answered, 'I will go forth and become a lying spirit in the mouths of all his prophets.' The LORD replied, 'You shall succeed in deceiving him. Go forth and do this.' [23] So now, the LORD has put a lying spirit in the mouths of all these prophets of yours, but the LORD himself has decreed evil against you."

22, 19–23: The prophet Micaiah uses as a last resort to deter Ahab from his foolhardy design of fighting against Ramoth-gilead the literary device of describing false prophets as messengers of a lying spirit which God, after holding counsel with his angels, permits to deceive them.

21, 22: 1 Kgs 15, 29; 16, 3.   21, 29: 2 Kgs 9, 26.
21, 23: 2 Kgs 9, 36.   22, 1: 2 Chr 18, 1.

24 Thereupon Zedekiah, son of Chenaanah, came up and slapped Micaiah on the cheek, saying, "Has the spirit of the LORD, then, left me to speak with you?" 25 "You shall find out," Micaiah replied, "on that day when you retreat into an inside room to hide." 26 The king of Israel then said, "Seize Micaiah and take him back to Amon, prefect of the city, and to Joash, the king's son, 27 and say, 'This is the king's order: Put this man in prison and feed him scanty rations of bread and water until I return in safety.' " 28† But Micaiah said, "If ever you return in safety, the LORD has not spoken through me."

29 The king of Israel and King Jehoshaphat of Judah went up to Ramoth-gilead, 30 and the king of Israel said to Jehoshaphat, "I will disguise myself and go into battle, but you put on your own clothes." So the king of Israel disguised himself and entered the fray. 31 In the meantime the king of Aram had given his thirty-two chariot commanders the order, "Do not fight with anyone at all except the king of Israel." 32 When the chariot commanders saw Jehoshaphat, they cried out, "That must be the king of Israel!" and shifted to fight him. But Jehoshaphat shouted his battle cry, 33 and the chariot commanders, aware that he was not the king of Israel, gave up pursuit of him. 34 Someone, however, drew his bow at random, and hit the king of Israel between the joints of his breastplate. He ordered his charioteer, "Rein about and take me out of the ranks, for I am disabled." 35* The battle grew fierce during the day, and the king, who was propped up in his chariot facing the Arameans, died in the evening. The blood from his wound flowed to the bottom of the chariot. 36 At sunset a cry went through the army, "Every man to his city, every man to his land, 37 for the king is dead!" So they went to Samaria, where they buried the king. 38* When the chariot was washed at the pool of Samaria, the dogs licked up his blood and harlots bathed there, as the LORD had prophesied.

39 The rest of the acts of Ahab, with all that he did, including the ivory palace and all the cities he built, are recorded in the book of the chronicles of the kings of Israel. 40 Ahab rested with his ancestors, and his son Ahaziah succeeded him as king.

Reign of Jehoshaphat

41 Jehoshaphat, son of Asa, began to reign over Judah in the fourth year of Ahab, king of Israel. 42 Jehoshaphat was thirty-five years old when he began to reign, and he reigned twenty-five years in Jerusalem. His mother's name was Azubah, daughter of Shilhi. 43 He followed all the ways of his father Asa unswervingly, doing what was right in the LORD's sight. 44 Nevertheless, the high places did not disappear, and the people continued to sacrifice and to burn incense on the high places. 45 Jehoshaphat also made peace with the king of Israel. 46 The rest of the acts of Jehoshaphat, with his prowess, what he did and how he fought, are recorded in the book of the chronicles of the kings of Judah.

47 He removed from the land the rest of the cult prostitutes who had remained in the reign of his father Asa. 48 There was no king in Edom, but an appointed regent. 49 Jehoshaphat made Tarshish ships to go to Ophir for gold; but in fact the ships did not go, because they were wrecked at Ezion-geber. 50 Then Ahaziah, son of Ahab, said to Jehoshaphat, "Let my servants accompany your servants in the ships." But Jehoshaphat would not agree. 51 Jehoshaphat rested with his ancestors; he was buried in his forefathers' City of David. His son Jehoram succeeded him as king.

Reign of Ahaziah

52† Ahaziah, son of Ahab, began to reign over Israel in Samaria in the seventeenth year of Jehoshaphat, king of Judah; he reigned two years over Israel. 53 He did evil in the sight of the LORD, behaving like his father, his mother, and Jeroboam, son of Nebat, who caused Israel to sin. 54 He served and worshiped Baal, thus provoking the LORD, the God of Israel, just as his father had done.

22, 28: A note in the Hebrew text after this verse attributes to Micaiah ben Imlah the first words of the book of a different Micaiah, the minor prophet of Moresheth.

22, 52: *Seventeenth year:* so the present Hebrew text. More consistent with 2 Kgs 1, 17 would be a date in the twenty-fourth year of Jehoshaphat for Ahab's death; see note on 2 Kgs 1, 1.

22, 35: 1 Kgs 20, 42.   **22, 38:** 1 Kgs 21, 19.

2 Kings

For background on this book, see the introduction to 1 and 2 Kings.

Chap. 25

I: The Kingdoms of Israel and Judah

Ahaziah Consults Baalzebub

1 ¹* After Ahab's death, Moab rebelled against Israel. ²† Ahaziah had fallen through the lattice of his roof terrace at Samaria and had been injured. So he sent out messengers with the instructions: "Go and inquire of Baalzebub, the god of Ekron, whether I shall recover from this injury."

³ Meanwhile, the angel of the LORD said to Elijah the Tishbite: "Go, intercept the messengers of Samaria's king, and ask them, 'Is it because there is no God in Israel that you are going to inquire of Baalzebub, the god of Ekron?' ⁴ For this, the LORD says: 'You shall not leave the bed upon which you lie; instead, you shall die.' " And with that, Elijah departed. ⁵ The messengers then returned to Ahaziah, who asked them, "Why have you returned?" ⁶ "A man came up to us," they answered, "who said to us, 'Go back to the king who sent you and tell him: The LORD says, Is it because there is no God in Israel that you are sending to inquire of Baalzebub,

the god of Ekron? For this you shall not leave the bed upon which you lie; instead, you shall die.' " ⁷ The king asked them, "What was the man like who came up to you and said these things to you?" ⁸*† "Wearing a hairy garment," they replied, "with a leather girdle about his loins." "It is Elijah the Tishbite!" he exclaimed.

Death of Two Captains

⁹ Then the king sent a captain with his company of fifty men after Elijah. The prophet was seated on a hilltop when he found him. "Man of God," he ordered, "the king commands you to come down." ¹⁰* "If I am a man of God," Elijah answered the captain, "may fire come down from heaven and consume you and your fifty men." And fire came down from heaven and consumed him and his fifty men. ¹¹ Ahaziah sent another captain with his company of fifty men after Elijah. "Man of God," he called out to Elijah, "the king commands you to come down immediately." ¹²† "If I am a man of God," Elijah answered him, "May fire come down

---

1, 2: *Baalzebub:* in this form, "Baal of flies." The name in the Hebrew text is a derisive alteration of Baalzebul, "Prince Baal." The best New Testament evidence supports the latter form in Mt 10, 25; Lk 11, 15. Later associations with Aramaic *beeldebaba,* "enemy," gave the ancient name its connotation of "devil."

1, 8: *Hairy garment:* a sign of ascetical and prophetic calling, imitated by John the Baptizer; see Mt 3, 4; Mk 1, 6.

1, 12: *Divine fire:* literally, "fire of God," which in Hebrew sounds quite like man of God. The play on words is the basis for

Elijah's alleged retort. This story was told among the people to enhance the dignity of the prophet and to reflect the power of God whom he served. The mercy which God extends even to the wicked is described in Wis 11, 17—12, 22, and the prophet Elijah was well aware of it (1 Kgs 21, 28f).

*
1, 1: 2 Kgs 3, 4–27.
1, 8: Zec 13, 4.

1, 10: Lv 10, 2; Sir 48, 3f; Lk 9, 54f.

from heaven and consume you and your fifty men."
And divine fire came down from heaven, consuming him and his fifty men.

Death of the King

13 Again, for the third time, Ahaziah sent a captain with his company of fifty men. When the third captain arrived, he fell to his knees before Elijah, pleading with him. "Man of God," he implored him, "let my life and the lives of these fifty men, your servants, count for something in your sight! 14 Already fire has come down from heaven, consuming two captains with their companies of fifty men. But now, let my life mean something to you!" 15 Then the angel of the LORD said to Elijah, "Go down with him; you need not be afraid of him."

16* So Elijah left and went down with him and stated to the king: "Thus says the LORD: 'Because you sent messengers to inquire of Baalzebub, the god of Ekron, you shall not leave the bed upon which you lie; instead you shall die.'"

17† Ahaziah died in fulfillment of the prophecy of the LORD spoken by Elijah. Since he had no son, his brother Joram succeeded him as king, in the second year of Jehoram, son of Jehoshaphat, king of Judah. 18 The rest of the acts of Ahaziah are recorded in the book of chronicles of the kings of Israel.

Elijah and Elisha

2 1† When the LORD was about to take Elijah up to heaven in a whirlwind, he and Elisha were on their way from Gilgal. 2 "Stay here, please," Elijah said to Elisha. "The LORD has sent me on to Bethel." "As the LORD lives, and as you yourself live," Elisha replied, "I will not leave you." So they went down to Bethel, 3 where the guild prophets went out to Elisha and asked him, "Do you know that the LORD will take your master from over you today?" "Yes, I know it," he replied. "Keep still."

4 Then Elijah said to him, "Stay here, please, Elisha, for the LORD has sent me on to Jericho." "As the LORD lives, and as you yourself live," Elisha

Elijah, Prophet of God in Solidarity with the People!

Elijah was a passionate prophet who read the history of the monarchy (Israel's kings) from the perspective of God. He saw division in the people of Israel. On the one hand were the kings, the noblemen, and the leaders of the army; on the other hand were the peasants, the widows, and the persecuted prophets. The Covenant had been broken. Elijah denounced the unfaithfulness of Queen Jezebel and Kings Ahab and Ahaziah. They had introduced idolatry in the form of the false god Baal, who favored the powerful and allowed injustices.

Elijah's faithfulness to the Covenant and his solidarity with the poor led him to speak against kings and queens, to fight false prophets, and to intervene in national affairs. The powerful rulers wanted to kill him and silence his voice. After his dramatic departure (2 Kgs 2, 11), the people never forgot him; they always expected his return.

■ If you saw today's world through the prism that Elijah used to view the world of his time, what would you see? Whom would you support with your words and actions? Whom would you challenge?

■ Through your Baptism, you are called to be a prophet. As a prophet, how can you promote justice in society?

---

† **1, 17:** *Joram:* in the Second Book of Kings the name Joram *(yoram),* alternately Jehoram *(yehoram),* appears in numerous passages to designate both the king of Judah, son and successor of Jehoshaphat (848–841 B.C.), and the contemporary king of Israel, son of Ahab (852–841 B.C.). For the convenience of the reader in distinguishing these two kings, the longer form, Jehoram, is used to designate the king of Judah and the shorter form, Joram, to designate the king of Israel. See note on 2 Kgs 3, 1.

2, 1: *Gilgal:* commonly identified with Jiljulieh, about seven miles north of Bethel, and different from the Gilgal in Dt 11, 30 near Shechem, and that in Jos 4 and 5, *passim,* near Jericho.

* **1, 16:** Sir 48, 6.

replied, "I will not leave you." [5] They went on to Jericho, where the guild prophets approached Elisha and asked him, "Do you know that the LORD will take your master from over you today?" "Yes, I know it," he replied. "Keep still."

[6] Elijah said to Elisha, "Please stay here; the LORD has sent me on to the Jordan." "As the LORD lives, and as you yourself live," Elisha replied, "I will not leave you." And so the two went on together. [7] Fifty of the guild prophets followed, and when the two stopped at the Jordan, stood facing them at a distance. [8]* Elijah took his mantle, rolled it up and struck the water, which divided, and both crossed over on dry ground.

Elisha Succeeds Elijah

[9]† When they had crossed over, Elijah said to Elisha, "Ask for whatever I may do for you, before I am taken from you." Elisha answered, "May I receive a double portion of your spirit." [10]* "You have asked something that is not easy," he replied. "Still, if you see me taken up from you, your wish will be granted; otherwise not." [11]* As they walked on conversing, a flaming chariot and flaming horses came between them, and Elijah went up to heaven in a whirlwind. [12]*† When Elisha saw it happen he cried out, "My father! my father! Israel's chariots and drivers!" But when he could no longer see him, Elisha gripped his own garment and tore it in two.

[13]* Then he picked up Elijah's mantle which had fallen from him, and went back and stood at the bank of the Jordan. [14] Wielding the mantle which had fallen from Elijah, he struck the water in his turn and said, "Where is the LORD, the God of Elijah?" When Elisha struck the water it divided and he crossed over.

[15] The guild prophets in Jericho, who were on the other side, saw him and said, "The spirit of Elijah rests on Elisha." They went to meet him, bowing to the ground before him. [16]* "Among your servants are fifty brave men," they said. "Let them go in search of your master. Perhaps the spirit of the LORD has carried him away to some mountain or some valley." "Do not send them," he answered. [17] However, they kept urging him, until he was embarrassed and said, "Send them." So they sent the fifty men, who searched for three days without finding him. [18] When they returned to Elisha in Jericho, where he was staying, he said to them, "Did I not tell you not to go?"

Healing of the Water

[19] Once the inhabitants of the city complained to Elisha, "The site of the city is fine indeed, as my lord can see, but the water is bad and the land unfruitful." [20] "Bring me a new bowl," Elisha said, "and put salt into it." When they had brought it to him, [21] he went out to the spring and threw salt into it, saying, "Thus says the LORD, 'I have purified this water. Never again shall death or miscarriage spring from it.' " [22] And the water has stayed pure even to this day, just as Elisha prophesied.

The Prophet's Curse

[23]† From there Elisha went up to Bethel. While he was on the way, some small boys came out of the city and jeered at him. "Go up, baldhead," they shouted, "go up, baldhead!" [24] The prophet turned and saw them, and he cursed them in the name of the LORD. Then two she-bears came out of the woods and tore forty-two of the children to pieces.

[25] From there he went to Mount Carmel, and thence he returned to Samaria.

Campaign of Joram against Moab

3 [1]† Joram, son of Ahab, became king of Israel in Samaria [in the eighteenth year of Jehoshaphat, king of Judah, and he reigned for twelve

2, 9: *Double portion of your spirit:* as the first-born son inherited a double portion of his father's property (Dt 21, 17), so Elisha asks to inherit from Elijah his spirit of prophecy in the degree befitting his principal disciple. In Nm 11, 17.25, God bestows some of the spirit of Moses on others.

2, 12: *My father:* a religious title accorded prophetic leaders; cf 2 Kgs 6, 21; 8, 9. *Israel's chariots and drivers:* Elijah was worth more than a whole army in defending Israel and the true religion. King Joash of Israel uses the same phrase of Elisha himself (2 Kgs 13, 14).

2, 23f: This story, like the one about Elijah and the captains (ch 1), is preserved for us in Scripture to convey a popular understanding of the dignity of the prophet. Told in popular vein, it becomes a caricature, in which neither Elisha nor the bears behave in character. See note on 2 Kgs 1, 12 and the contrasting narrative in ch 4.

3, 1: The sequence of the reigns between Ahab and Jehu of Israel may be reconstructed as follows: Jehoshaphat of Judah outlived Ahab by a short time, so that Ahaziah of Israel was his contemporary. Jehoram of Judah succeeded his father Jehoshaphat while Ahaziah of Israel was still alive. Jehoram (Joram) of Israel became king, following his brother Ahaziah, in the second year of Jehoram of Judah (2 Kgs 1, 17); this is one datum on which the earliest Greek evidence and the standard Hebrew text are in agreement.

The two Jehorams were contemporary for much of their reigns; Jehoram of Judah was succeeded by Ahaziah something more than a year before Jehu did away with the rulers of both kingdoms (2 Kgs 9, 1–29).

The Moabite campaign of 2 Kgs 3, 4–27 is thus best placed under the two Kings Jehoram, before the Edomite rebellion mentioned in 2 Kgs 8, 20. In the received Hebrew text, Jehoshaphat has been made the Judahite protagonist in the campaign against Moab as a tribute to his piety; this assimilates the story of 2 Kgs 3 to that of 1 Kgs 22, but creates difficulties in the chronology which the extant data leave partly unresolved. An older practice for stories of the Israelite kings was to leave them and their fellow kings without identification by name; cf 2 Kgs 6, 8–7, 20. The name of Jehoshaphat has been omitted from a number of places in 2 Kgs 3–8, in this translation; cf 1 Kgs 22, 51.

2, 8: Ex 14, 16.22.
2, 10: Nm 11, 17.25.
2, 11: Gn 5, 24; 1 Mc 2, 58; Acts 1, 9.
2, 12: 2 Kgs 13, 14; Sir 48, 9.12.
2, 13: 1 Kgs 19, 19.
2, 16: 1 Kgs 18, 12.

years]. 2 He did evil in the LORD's sight, though not as much as his father and mother. He did away with the pillar of Baal, which his father had made, 3 but he still clung to the sin to which Jeroboam, son of Nebat, had lured Israel; this he did not give up.

4 Now Mesha, king of Moab, who raised sheep, used to pay the king of Israel as tribute a hundred thousand lambs and the wool of a hundred thousand rams. 5 But when Ahab died, the king of Moab had rebelled against the king of Israel. 6 Joram as king mustered all Israel, and when he set out on a campaign from Samaria, 7* he sent the king of Judah the message: "The king of Moab is in rebellion against me. Will you join me in battle against Moab?" "I will," he replied. "You and I shall be as one, your people and mine, and your horses and mine as well." 8 They discussed the route for their attack, and settled upon the route through the desert of Edom.

9 So the king of Israel set out, accompanied by the king of Judah and the king of Edom. After their roundabout journey of seven days the water gave out for the army and for the animals with them. 10 "Alas!" exclaimed the king of Israel. "The LORD has called together these three kings to put them in the grasp of Moab." 11* But the king of Judah asked, "Is there no prophet of the LORD here through whom we may inquire of the LORD?" One of the officers of the king of Israel replied, "Elisha, son of Shaphat, who poured water on the hands of Elijah, is here." 12 "He has the word of the LORD," the king of Judah agreed. So the kings of Israel, Judah, and Edom went down to Elisha. 13 "What do you want with me?" Elisha asked the king of Israel. "Go to the prophets of your father and to the prophets of your mother." "No," the king of Israel replied. "The LORD has called these three kings together to put them in the grasp of Moab." 14* Then Elisha said, "As the LORD of hosts lives, whom I serve, were it not that I respect the king of Judah, I should neither look at you nor notice you at all. 15 Now get me a minstrel."

When the minstrel played, the power of the LORD came upon Elisha 16 and he announced: "Thus says the LORD, 'Provide many catch basins in this wadi.' 17 For the LORD says, 'Though you will see neither wind nor rain, yet this wadi will be filled with water for you, your livestock, and your pack animals to drink.' 18 And since the LORD does not consider this enough, he will also deliver Moab into your grasp.

19* You shall destroy every fortified city, fell every fruit tree, stop up all the springs, and ruin every fertile field with stones."

20* In the morning, at the time of the sacrifice, water came from the direction of Edom and filled the land. 21 Meanwhile, all Moab heard that the kings had come to give them battle; every man capable of bearing arms was called up and stationed at the border. 22† Early that morning, when the sun shone on the water, the Moabites saw the water at a distance as red as blood. 23 "This is blood!" they exclaimed. "The kings have fought among themselves and killed one another. Quick! To the spoils, Moabites!" 24 But when they reached the camp of Israel, the Israelites rose up and attacked the Moabites, who fled from them. They ranged through the countryside striking down the Moabites, and 25*† destroying the cities; each of them cast stones onto every fertile field till they had loaded it down; all the springs they stopped up and every useful tree they felled. Finally only Kir-hareseth was left behind its stone walls, and the slingers had surrounded it and were attacking it. 26 When he saw that he was losing the battle, the king of Moab took seven hundred swordsmen to break through to the king of Aram, but he failed. 27*† So he took his firstborn, his heir apparent, and offered him as a holocaust upon the wall. The wrath against Israel was so great that they gave up the siege and returned to their own land.

The Widow's Oil

4 1*† A certain woman, the widow of one of the guild prophets, complained to Elisha: "My husband, your servant, is dead. You know that he was a God-fearing man, yet now his creditor has come to take my two children as his slaves." 2 "How can I help you?" Elisha answered her. "Tell me what you have in the house." "This servant of yours has nothing in the house but a jug of oil," she replied. 3 "Go out," he said, "borrow vessels from all your neighbors—as many empty vessels as you can. 4 Then come back and close the door on yourself and your children; pour the oil into all the vessels, and as each is filled, set it aside." 5 She went and did so, closing the door on herself and her children. As they handed her the vessels, she would pour in oil. 6 When all the vessels were filled, she said to her son, "Bring me another vessel." "There is none left," he answered her. And

---

3, 22: *Red as blood:* possibly caused by the red sandstone of the Wadi Zered (Dt 2, 13), south of Moab.
3, 25: *Kir-hareseth:* modern Kerak, east of the Dead Sea; cf Is 16, 7.11; Jer 48, 31.36.
3, 27: *The wrath against Israel:* probably the wrath of Chemosh, the Moabite god to whom the child was offered. He was feared by the Israelites who lost heart on foreign soil.

4, 1: *His creditor . . . slaves:* Hebrew law permitted the selling of wife and children as chattels for debt; cf. Ex 21, 7; Am 2, 6; 8, 6; Is 50.

3, 7: 1 Kgs 22, 4.
3, 11: 1 Kgs 22, 7.
3, 14: 1 Kgs 18, 15.
3, 19: Dt 20, 19.
3, 20: 1 Kgs 18, 29.
3, 25: Jb 5, 23.
3, 27: Jgs 11, 30f.
4, 1: 1 Kgs 17, 8–16.

4, 1—7

then the oil stopped. 7 She went and told the man of God, who said, "Go and sell the oil to pay off your creditor; with what remains, you and your children can live."

Elisha and the Shunammite

8 One day Elisha came to Shunem, where there was a woman of influence, who urged him to dine with her. Afterward, whenever he passed by, he used to stop there to dine. 9 So she said to her husband, "I know that he is a holy man of God. Since he visits us often, 10 let us arrange a little room on the roof and furnish it for him with a bed, table, chair, and lamp, so that when he comes to us he can stay there." 11 Some time later Elisha arrived and stayed in the room overnight. 12 Then he said to his servant Gehazi, "Call this Shunammite woman." He did so, and when she stood before Elisha, 13 he told Gehazi, "Say to her, 'You have lavished all this care on us; what can we do for you? Can we say a good word for you to the king or to the commander of the army?'" She replied, "I am living among my own people." 14 Later Elisha asked, "Can something be done for her?" "Yes!" Gehazi answered. "She has no son, and her husband is getting on in years." 15 "Call her," said Elisha. When she had been called, and stood at the door, 16* Elisha promised, "This time next year you will be fondling a baby son." "Please, my lord," she protested, "you are a man of God; do not deceive your servant." 17 Yet the woman conceived, and by the same time the

following year she had given birth to a son, as Elisha promised.

18* The day came when the child was old enough to go out to his father among the reapers. 19 "My head hurts!" he complained to his father. "Carry him to his mother," the father said to a servant. 20 The servant picked him up and carried him to his mother; he stayed with her until noon, when he died in her lap. 21 The mother took him upstairs and laid him on the bed of the man of God. Closing the door on him, she went out 22 and called to her husband, "Let me have a servant and a donkey. I must go quickly to the man of God, and I will be back." 23 "Why are you going to him today?" he asked. "It is neither the new moon nor the sabbath." But she bade him good-bye, 24 and when the donkey was saddled, said to her servant: "Lead on! Do not stop my donkey unless I tell you to." 25 She kept going till she reached the man of God on Mount Carmel. When he spied her at a distance, the man of God said to his servant Gehazi: "There is the Shunammite! 26† Hurry to meet her, and ask if all is well with her, with her husband, and with the boy." "Greetings," she replied. 27 But when she reached the man of God on the mountain, she clasped his feet. Gehazi came near to push her away, but the man of God said: "Let her alone, she is in bitter anguish; the LORD hid it from me and did not let me know." 28 "Did I ask my lord for a son?" she cried out. "Did I not beg you not to deceive me?" 29† "Gird your loins," Elisha said to Gehazi, "take my staff with you and be off; if you meet anyone, do not greet him, and if anyone greets you, do not answer. Lay my staff upon the boy." 30 But the boy's mother cried out: "As the LORD lives and as you yourself live, I will not release you." So he started to go back with her.

31* Meanwhile, Gehazi had gone on ahead and had laid the staff upon the boy, but there was no sound or sign of life. He returned to meet Elisha and informed him that the boy had not awakened. 32 When Elisha reached the house, he found the boy lying dead. 33* He went in, closed the door on them both, and prayed to the LORD. 34 Then he lay upon the child on the bed, placing his mouth upon the child's mouth, his eyes upon the eyes, and his hands upon the hands. As Elisha stretched himself over the child, the body became warm. 35* He arose, paced up and down the room, and then once more lay down upon the boy, who now sneezed seven times and opened his eyes. 36 Elisha summoned Gehazi

---

†
4, 26: *Greetings:* the conventional answer to Gehazi's question, which tells him nothing.

4, 29: *Do not greet him:* the profuse exchange of compliments among Orientals meeting and greeting one another consumed time. Urgency necessitated their omission, as our Lord counseled his disciples (Lk 10, 4).

*
4, 16: Gn 18, 10.
4, 18: 1 Kgs 17, 17–24.
4, 31–36: Acts 20, 10ff.
4, 33: 1 Kgs 17, 21–23.
4, 35: Heb 11, 35.

and said, "Call the Shunammite." She came at his call, and Elisha said to her, "Take your son." [37] She came in and fell at his feet in gratitude; then she took her son and left the room.

The Poisoned Stew

[38] When Elisha returned to Gilgal, there was a famine in the land. Once, when the guild prophets were seated before him, he said to his servant, "Put the large pot on, and make some vegetable stew for the guild prophets." [39] Someone went out into the field to gather herbs and found a wild vine, from which he picked a clothful of wild gourds. On his return he cut them up into the pot of vegetable stew without anybody's knowing it. [40] The stew was poured out for the men to eat, but when they began to eat it, they exclaimed, "Man of God, there is poison in the pot!" And they could not eat it. [41] "Bring some meal," Elisha said. He threw it into the pot and said, "Serve it to the people to eat." And there was no longer anything harmful in the pot.

Multiplication of Loaves

[42] A man came from Baal-shalishah bringing the man of God twenty barley loaves made from the first-fruits, and fresh grain in the ear. "Give it to the people to eat," Elisha said. [43] But his servant objected, "How can I set this before a hundred men?" "Give it to the people to eat," Elisha insisted. "For thus says the LORD, 'They shall eat and there shall be some left over.' " [44] And when they had eaten, there was some left over, as the LORD had said.

Cure of Naaman

5 [1] Naaman, the army commander of the king of Aram, was highly esteemed and respected by his master, for through him the LORD had brought victory to Aram. But valiant as he was, the man was a leper. [2] Now the Arameans had cap-

tured from the land of Israel in a raid a little girl, who became the servant of Naaman's wife. [3] "If only my master would present himself to the prophet in Samaria," she said to her mistress, "he would cure him of his leprosy." [4] Naaman went and told his lord just what the slave girl from the land of Israel had said. [5] "Go," said the king of Aram. "I will send along a letter to the king of Israel." So Naaman set out, taking along ten silver talents, six thousand gold pieces, and ten festal garments. [6] To the king of Israel he brought the letter, which read: "With this letter I am sending my servant Naaman to you, that you may cure him of his leprosy."

7* When he read the letter, the king of Israel tore his garments and exclaimed: "Am I a god with power over life and death, that this man should send someone to me to be cured of leprosy? Take note! You can see he is only looking for a quarrel with me!" 8 When Elisha, the man of God, heard that the king of Israel had torn his garments, he sent word to the king: "Why have you torn your garments? Let him come to me and find out that there is a prophet in Israel."

9 Naaman came with his horses and chariots and stopped at the door of Elisha's house. 10* The prophet sent him the message: "Go and wash seven times in the Jordan, and your flesh will heal, and you will be clean." 11 But Naaman went away angry, saying, "I thought that he would surely come out and stand there to invoke the LORD his God, and would move his hand over the spot, and thus cure the leprosy. 12† Are not the rivers of Damascus, the Abana and the Pharpar, better than all the waters of Israel? Could I not wash in them and be cleansed?" With this, he turned about in anger and left.

13 But his servants came up and reasoned with him. "My father," they said, "if the prophet had told you to do something extraordinary, would you not have done it? All the more now, since he said to you, 'Wash and be clean,' should you do as he said." 14* So Naaman went down and plunged into the Jordan seven times at the word of the man of God. His flesh became again like the flesh of a little child, and he was clean.

15 He returned with his whole retinue to the man of God. On his arrival he stood before him and said, "Now I know that there is no God in all the earth, except in Israel. Please accept a gift from your servant."

16 "As the LORD lives whom I serve, I will not take it," Elisha replied; and despite Naaman's urging, he still refused. 17† Naaman said: "If you will not accept, please let me, your servant, have two muleloads of earth, for I will no longer offer holocaust or sacrifice to any other god except to the LORD. 18 But I trust the LORD will forgive your servant this: when my master enters the temple of Rimmon to worship there, then I, too, as his adjutant, must bow down in the temple of Rimmon. May the LORD forgive your servant this." 19† "Go in peace," Elisha said to him.

20 Naaman had gone some distance when Gehazi, the servant of Elisha, the man of God, thought to himself: "My master was too easy with this Aramean Naaman, not accepting what he brought. As the LORD lives, I will run after him and get something out of him." 21 So Gehazi hurried after Naaman. Aware that someone was running after him, Naaman alighted from his chariot to wait for him. "Is everything all right?" he asked. 22 "Yes," Gehazi replied, "but my master sent me to say, 'Two young men have just come to me, guild prophets from the hill country of Ephraim. Please give them a talent of silver and two festal garments.' " 23 "Please take two talents," Naaman said, and pressed them upon him. He tied up these silver talents in bags and gave them, with the two festal garments, to two of his servants, who carried them before Gehazi. 24 When they reached the hill, Gehazi took what they had, carried it into the house, and sent the men on their way.

25 He went in and stood before Elisha his master, who asked him, "Where have you been, Gehazi?" He answered, "Your servant has not gone anywhere." 26 But Elisha said to him: "Was I not present in spirit when the man alighted from his chariot to wait for you? Is this a time to take money or to take garments, olive orchards or vineyards, sheep or cattle, male or female servants? 27* The leprosy of Naaman shall cling to you and your descendants forever." And Gehazi left Elisha, a leper white as snow.

Recovery of the Lost Ax

6 1 The guild prophets once said to Elisha: "There is not enough room for us to continue to live here with you. 2 Let us go to the Jordan, where by getting one beam apiece we can build ourselves a place to live." "Go," Elisha said. 3 "Please agree to accompany your servants," one of them requested. "Yes, I will come," he replied.

4 So he went with them, and when they arrived at the Jordan they began to fell trees. 5 While one of them was felling a tree trunk, the iron axhead slipped into the water. "O master," he cried out, "it was borrowed!" 6 "Where did it fall?" asked the man of God. When he pointed out the spot, Elisha cut off a stick, threw it into the water, and brought the iron to the surface. 7 "Pick it up," he said. And the man reached down and grasped it.

5, 12: *Wash in them and be cleansed:* typical of the ambiguity in ritual healing or cleanliness. The muddy waters of the Jordan are no match hygienically for the mountain spring waters of Damascus; ritually, it is the other way around.

5, 17: *Two mule-loads of earth:* Israelite earth on which to erect in Aram an altar to the God of Israel.

5, 19: *Go in peace:* Elisha understands and approves the situation of Naaman who, though a proselyte as regards belief in and worship of the God of Israel, is required by his office to assist his master, the king, worshiping in the pagan temple of Rimmon.

*
5, 7: Gn 30, 2; 1 Sm 2, 6; Jn   5, 14: Lk 4, 27.
      5, 21.   5, 27: Ex 4, 6; Nm 12, 10.
5, 10: Jn 9, 7.

Aramean Ambush

[8] When the king of Aram was waging war on Israel, he would make plans with his servants to attack a particular place. [9] But the man of God would send word to the king of Israel, "Be careful! Do not pass by this place, for Aram will attack there." [10] So the king of Israel would send word to the place which the man of God had indicated, and alert it; then they would be on guard. This happened several times.

[11] Greatly disturbed over this, the king of Aram called together his officers. "Will you not tell me," he asked them, "who among us is for the king of Israel?" [12] "No one, my lord king," answered one of the officers. "The Israelite prophet Elisha can tell the king of Israel the very words you speak in your bedroom." [13] "Go, find out where he is," he said, "so that I may take him captive."

Blinded Aramean Soldiers

Informed that Elisha was in Dothan, [14] he sent there a strong force with horses and chariots. They arrived by night and surrounded the city. [15] Early the next morning, when the attendant of the man of God arose and went out, he saw the force with its horses and chariots surrounding the city. "Alas!" he said to Elisha. "What shall we do, my lord?" [16] "Do not be afraid," Elisha answered. "Our side outnumbers theirs." [17]* Then he prayed, "O LORD, open his eyes, that he may see." And the LORD opened the eyes of the servant, so that he saw the mountainside filled with horses and fiery chariots around Elisha.

[18] When the Arameans came down to get him, Elisha prayed to the LORD, "Strike this people blind, I pray you." And in answer to the prophet's prayer the LORD struck them blind. [19] Then Elisha said to them: "This is the wrong road, and this is the wrong city. Follow me! I will take you to the man you want." And he led them to Samaria. [20] When they entered Samaria, Elisha prayed, "O LORD, open their eyes that they may see." The LORD opened their eyes, and they saw that they were inside Samaria. [21] When the king of Israel saw them, he asked, "Shall I kill them, my father?" [22]† "You must not kill them," replied Elisha. "Do you slay those whom you have taken captive with your sword or bow? Serve them bread and water. Let them eat and drink, and then go back to their master." [23] The king spread a great feast for them. When they had

eaten and drunk he sent them away, and they went back to their master. No more Aramean raiders came into the land of Israel.

Siege of Samaria

[24] After this, Ben-hadad, king of Aram, mustered his whole army and laid siege to Samaria. [25] Because of the siege the famine in Samaria was so severe that an ass's head sold for eighty pieces of silver, and a fourth of a kab of wild onion for five pieces of silver.

[26] One day, as the king of Israel was walking on the city wall, a woman cried out to him, "Help, my lord king!" [27] "No," he replied, "the LORD help you! Where could I find help for you: from the threshing floor or the winepress?" [28]* Then the king asked her, "What is your trouble?" She replied: "This woman said to me, 'Give up your son that we may eat him today; then tomorrow we will eat my son.' [29] So we boiled my son and ate him. The next day I said to her, 'Now give up your son that we may eat him.' But she hid her son." [30]* When the king heard the woman's words, he tore his garments. And as he was walking on the wall, the people saw that he was wearing sackcloth underneath, next to his skin.

[31] "May God do thus and so to me," the king exclaimed, "if the head of Elisha, son of Shaphat, stays on him today!" [32] Meanwhile, Elisha was sitting in his house in conference with the elders. The king had sent a man ahead before he himself should come to him. Elisha had said to the elders: "Do you know that this son of a murderer is sending someone to cut off my head? When the messenger comes, see that you close the door and hold it fast against him. His master's footsteps are echoing behind him." [33] While Elisha was still speaking, the king came down to him and said, "This evil is from the LORD. Why should I trust in the LORD any longer?"

7 [1]† Elisha said: "Hear the word of the LORD! Thus says the LORD, 'At this time tomorrow a seah of fine flour will sell for a shekel, and two seahs of barley for a shekel, in the market of Samaria.'" [2]* But the adjutant on whose arm the king leaned, answered the man of God, "Even if the LORD were to make windows in heaven, how could this happen?" "You shall see it with your own eyes," Elisha said, "but you shall not eat of it."

6, 22: *With your sword or bow:* since the king would not slay prisoners who had surrendered to his power, much less should he slay prisoners captured by God's power. By Oriental custom they became guests within Samaria's walls.

7, 1: *Market:* literally "gate," the principal place of trading in ancient walled cities in time of peace.

6, 17: 2 Kgs 7, 6; Ps 67, 18.
6, 28: Dt 28, 53–57.
6, 30: 1 Kgs 20, 31; 21, 27.

7, 2: 2 Kgs 7, 17; Ps 78, 23; Is 24, 18.

The Lepers at the Gate

3 * At the city gate were four lepers who were deliberating, "Why should we sit here until we die? 4 If we decide to go into the city, we shall die there, for there is famine in the city. If we remain here, we shall die too. Come, let us desert to the camp of the Arameans. If they spare us, we live; if they kill us, we die." 5 At twilight they left for the Arameans; but when they reached the edge of the camp, no one was there. 6 * † The LORD had caused the army of the Arameans to hear the sound of chariots and horses, the din of a large army, and they had reasoned among themselves, "The king of Israel has hired the kings of the Hittites and the kings of the borderlands to fight us." 7 Then in the twilight they fled, abandoning their tents, their horses, and their asses, the whole camp just as it was, and fleeing for their lives.

8 After the lepers reached the edge of the camp, they went first into one tent, ate and drank, and took silver, gold, and clothing from it, and went out and hid them. Back they came into another tent, took things from it, and again went out and hid them. 9 Then they said to one another: "We are not doing right. This is a day of good news, and we are keeping silent. If we wait until morning breaks, we shall be blamed. Come, let us go and inform the palace."

10 They came and summoned the city gatekeepers. "We went to the camp of the Arameans," they said, "but no one was there—not a human voice, only the horses and asses tethered, and the tents just as they were left." 11 The gatekeepers announced this and it was reported within the palace. 12 Though it was night, the king got up; he said to his servants: "Let me tell you what the Arameans have done to us. Knowing that we are in famine, they have left their camp to hide in the field, hoping to take us alive and enter our city when we leave it." 13 One of his servants, however, suggested: "Since those who are left in the city are no better off than all the throng that has perished, let some of us take five of the abandoned horses and send scouts to investigate."

End of the Siege

14 They took two chariots, and horses, and the king sent them to reconnoiter the Aramean army. "Go and find out," he ordered. 15 They followed the Arameans as far as the Jordan, and the whole route was strewn with garments and other objects that the Arameans had thrown away in their haste. The messengers returned and told the king.

16 The people went out and plundered the camp of the Arameans; and then a seah of fine flour sold for a shekel and two seahs of barley for a shekel, as the LORD had said.

17 The king put in charge of the gate the officer who was his adjutant; but the people trampled him to death at the gate, just as the man of God had predicted when the king visited him. 18 Thus was fulfilled the prophecy of the man of God to the king, "Two seahs of barley will sell for a shekel, and one seah of fine flour for a shekel at this time tomorrow at the gate of Samaria." 19 The adjutant had answered the man of God, "Even if the LORD were to make windows in heaven, how could this happen?" And Elisha had replied, "You shall see it with your own eyes, but you shall not eat of it." 20 And that is what happened to him, for the people trampled him to death at the gate.

Prediction of Famine

8 1 * Elisha once said to the woman whose son he had restored to life: "Get ready! Leave with your family and settle wherever you can, because the LORD has decreed a seven-year famine which is coming upon the land." 2 The woman got ready and did as the man of God said, setting out with her family and settling in the land of the Philistines for seven years. 3 At the end of the seven years, the woman returned from the land of the Philistines and went out to the king to claim her house and her field. 4 The king was talking with Gehazi, the servant of the man of God. "Tell me," he said, "all the great things that Elisha has done." 5 Just as he was relating to the king how his master had restored a dead person to life, the very woman whose son Elisha had restored to life came to the king to claim her house and field. "My lord king," Gehazi said, "this is the woman, and this is that son of hers whom Elisha restored to life." 6 † The king questioned the woman, and she told him her story. With that the king placed an official at her disposal, saying, "Restore all her property to her, with all that the field produced from the day she left the land until now."

Death of Ben-hadad Foretold

7 Elisha came to Damascus at a time when Ben-hadad, king of Aram, lay sick. When he was told that the man of God had come there, 8 the king said to Hazael, "Take a gift with you and go call on the man of God. Have him consult the LORD as to whether I shall recover from this sickness." 9 Hazael went to visit him, carrying a present, and with

---

7, 6: *Kings of the borderlands:* from Musur in Anatolia rather than Egypt.
8, 6: *An official:* Literally "eunuch," and perhaps actually so in this instance.

7, 3: Lv 13, 46.
7, 6f: 2 Kgs 6, 17; 19, 35f;
8, 1: 2 Kgs 4, 36.
2 Sm 5, 24.

forty camel loads of the best goods of Damascus. On his arrival, he stood before the prophet and said, "Your son Ben-hadad, king of Aram, has sent me to ask you whether he will recover from his sickness." 10 "Go and tell him," Elisha answered, "that he will surely recover. However, the LORD has showed me that he will in fact die." 11 Then he stared him down until Hazael became ill at ease. The man of God wept, 12* and Hazael asked, "Why are you weeping, my lord?" Elisha replied, "Because I know the evil that you will inflict upon the Israelites. You will burn their fortresses, you will slay their youth with the sword, you will dash their little children to pieces, you will rip open their pregnant women."

13*† Hazael exclaimed, "How can a dog like me, your servant, do anything so important?" "The LORD has showed you to me as king over Aram," replied Elisha.

14 Hazael left Elisha and returned to his master. "What did Elisha tell you?" asked Ben-hadad. "He told me that you would surely recover," replied Hazael. 15 The next day, however, Hazael took a cloth, dipped it in water, and spread it over the king's face, so that he died. And Hazael reigned in his stead.

Reign of Jehoram of Judah

16† In the fifth year of Joram, son of Ahab, king of Israel, Jehoram, son of Jehoshaphat, king of Judah, became king. 17* He was thirty-two years old when he began to reign, and he reigned eight years in Jerusalem. 18 He conducted himself like the kings of Israel of the line of Ahab, since the sister of Ahab was his wife; and he did evil in the LORD's sight. 19* Even so, the LORD was unwilling to destroy Judah, because of his servant David. For he had promised David that he would leave him a lamp in the LORD's presence for all time. 20 During Jehoram's reign, Edom revolted against the sovereignty of Judah and chose a king of its own. 21 Thereupon Jehoram with all his chariots crossed over to Zair. He arose by night and broke through the Edomites when they had surrounded him and the commanders of his chariots. Then his army fled homeward. 22* To this day Edom has been in revolt against the rule of Judah. Libnah also revolted at that time. 23 The rest of the acts of Jehoram, with all that he did, are recorded in the book of the chronicles of the kings of Judah. 24 Jehoram rested with

Grading Kings

As you read the remaining chapters of Second Kings, notice that the author gives a kind of report card for each of the rulers of Israel and Judah. Jehoram, for example, receives an F: "He did evil in the LORD's sight" (8, 18). Josiah receives an A: "He pleased the LORD and conducted himself unswervingly" (22, 2). The author, who wrote after the fall of both kingdoms, provides a theological reason for Israel's and Judah's failure. Because most of the rulers continually violated God's law, they were largely responsible for the fall of the kingdoms.

his ancestors and was buried with them in the City of David. His son Ahaziah succeeded him as king.

Accession of Ahaziah

25† Ahaziah, son of Jehoram, king of Judah, became king in the twelfth year of Joram, son of Ahab, king of Israel. 26 He was twenty-two years old when he began his reign, and he reigned one year in Jerusalem. His mother's name was Athaliah; she was the daughter of Omri, king of Israel. 27 He conducted himself like the house of Ahab, doing evil in the LORD's sight as they did, since he was related to them by marriage. 28* He joined Joram, son of Ahab, in battle against Hazael, king of Aram, at Ramoth-gilead, where the Arameans wounded Joram. 29 King Joram returned to Jezreel to be healed of the wounds which the Arameans had inflicted on him at Ramah in his battle against Hazael, king of Aram. Then Ahaziah, son of Jehoram, king of Judah, went down to Jezreel to visit him there in his illness.

Anointing of Jehu

9 1* The prophet Elisha called one of the guild prophets and said to him: "Gird your loins, take this flask of oil with you, and go to Ramoth-gilead. 2* When you get there, look for Jehu, son of

---

8, 13: *A dog . . . your servant:* Hazael feigns humility (1 Sm 24, 14; 2 Sm 9, 8), without attending to the crimes he would commit after usurping the royal power as the prophet predicts. *Anything so important:* literally "a great deed" for a patriotic Syrian.

8, 16: Jehoram of Judah succeeded his father Jehoshaphat during the reign of Ahaziah of Israel. See note on 2 Kgs 3, 1.

8, 25: *Twelfth year of Joram:* i.e., of Israel, who probably reigned only eight years.

8, 12: 2 Kgs 13, 7.
8, 13: 2 Kgs 15, 16; 1 Kgs 19, 15.
8, 17ff: 2 Chr 21, 5ff.
8, 19: 2 Sm 7, 11–16; 21, 17; 1 Kgs 11, 36; 15, 4;
2 Chr 21, 7.
8, 22: Gn 27, 40; 2 Chr 21, 8ff.
8, 28: 2 Kgs 9, 14f.
9, 1: 1 Kgs 21, 29; Hos 1, 4.
9, 2: 1 Kgs 19, 16.

Jehoshaphat, son of Nimshi. Enter and take him away from his companions into an inner chamber. 3* From the flask you have, pour oil on his head, and say, 'Thus says the LORD: I anoint you king over Israel.' Then open the door and flee without delay." 4 The young man (the guild prophet) went to Ramoth-gilead. 5 When he arrived, the commanders of the army were in session. "I have a message for you, commander," he said. "For which one of us?" asked Jehu. "For you, commander," he answered. 6 Jehu got up and went into the house. Then the young man poured the oil on his head and said, "Thus says the LORD, the God of Israel: 'I anoint you king over the people of the LORD, over Israel. 7† You shall destroy the house of Ahab your master; thus will I avenge the blood of my servants the prophets, and the blood of all the other servants of the LORD shed by Jezebel, 8* and by all the rest of the family of Ahab. I will cut off every male in Ahab's line, whether slave or freeman in Israel. 9 I will deal with the house of Ahab as I dealt with the house of Jeroboam, son of Nebat, and with the house of Baasha, son of Ahijah. 10 Dogs shall devour Jezebel at the confines of Jezreel, so that no one can bury her.'" Then he opened the door and fled.

11 When Jehu rejoined his master's servants, they asked him, "Is all well? Why did that madman come to you?" "You know that kind of man and his talk," he replied. 12 But they said, "Not at all! Come, tell us." So he told them what the young man had said to him, and finally, "Thus says the LORD: 'I anoint you king over Israel.'" 13* At once each took his garment, spread it under Jehu on the bare steps, blew the trumpet, and cried out, "Jehu is king!"

14* Thus Jehu, son of Jehoshaphat, son of Nimshi, formed a conspiracy against Joram. Joram, with all Israel, had been besieging Ramoth-gilead against Hazael, king of Aram, 15 but had returned to Jezreel to be healed of the wounds the Arameans had inflicted on him in the battle against Hazael, king of Aram.

Murder of Joram

"If you are truly with me," Jehu said, "see that no one escapes from the city to report in Jezreel." 16 Then Jehu mounted his chariot and drove to Jezreel, where Joram lay ill and Ahaziah, king of Judah, had come to visit him.

17 The watchman standing on the tower in Jezreel saw the troop of Jehu coming and reported, "I see chariots." "Get a driver," Joram said, "and send him

to meet them and to ask whether all is well." 18 So a driver went out to meet him and said, "The king asks whether all is well." "What does it matter to you how things are?" Jehu said. "Get behind me." The watchman reported to the king, "The messenger has reached them, but is not returning."

19 Joram sent a second driver, who went to them and said, "The king asks whether all is well." "What does it matter to you how things are?" Jehu replied. "Get behind me."

20 The watchman reported, "The messenger has reached them, but is not returning. The driving is like that of Jehu, son of Nimshi, in its fury." 21 "Prepare my chariot," said Joram. When they had done so, Joram, king of Israel, and Ahaziah, king of Judah, set out, each in his own chariot, to meet Jehu. They reached him near the field of Naboth the Jezreelite. 22† When Joram recognized Jehu, he asked, "Is all well, Jehu?" "How can all be well," Jehu replied, "as long as the many fornications and witchcrafts of your mother Jezebel continue?" 23 Joram reined about and fled, crying to Ahaziah, "Treason, Ahaziah!" 24 But Jehu drew his bow and shot Joram between the shoulders, so that the arrow went through his heart and he collapsed in his chariot. 25* Then Jehu said to his adjutant Bidkar, "Take him and throw him into the field of Naboth the Jezreelite. For I remember that when we were driving teams behind his father Ahab, the LORD delivered this oracle against him: 26 'As surely as I saw yesterday the blood of Naboth and the blood of his sons,' says the LORD, 'I will repay you for it in that very plot of ground, says the LORD.' So now take him into this plot of ground, in keeping with the word of the LORD."

Death of Ahaziah

27* Seeing what was happening, Ahaziah, king of Judah, fled toward Beth-haggan. Jehu pursued him, shouting, "Kill him too!" And they pierced him as he rode through the pass of Gur near Ibleam. He continued his flight as far as Megiddo and died there. 28 His servants brought him in a chariot to Jerusalem and buried him in the tomb of his ancestors in the City of David. 29 Ahaziah had become king of Judah in the eleventh year of Joram, son of Ahab.

Death of Jezebel

30 When Jezebel learned that Jehu had arrived in Jezreel, she shadowed her eyes, adorned her hair,

---

† **9, 7–10:** The editors of the Books of Kings have here added to the prophet's message the same type of indictment and sanctions against the family of Ahab as were invoked against the dynasties of Jeroboam (1 Kgs 14, 10f), Baasha (1 Kgs 16, 3f), and Ahab on a previous occasion (1 Kgs 21, 21–24).

9, 22: *Fornications and witchcrafts:* the worship of foreign gods.

9, 3: 1 Kgs 19, 16.
9, 8ff: 1 Kgs 14, 10f; 16, 3f;
21, 21–24.
9, 13: Mt 21, 8.
9, 14f: 2 Kgs 8, 28f; 1 Kgs 22, 3f.
9, 25f: 1 Kgs 21, 9–16.
9, 27ff: 2 Chr 22, 7ff.

and looked down from her window. 31* As Jehu came through the gate, she cried out, "Is all well, Zimri, murderer of your master?" 32 Jehu looked up to the window and shouted, "Who is on my side? Anyone?" At this, two or three eunuchs looked down toward him. 33 "Throw her down," he ordered. They threw her down, and some of her blood spurted against the wall and against the horses. Jehu rode in over her body 34 and, after eating and drinking, he said: "Attend to that accursed woman and bury her; after all, she was a king's daughter." 35 But when they went to bury her, they found nothing of her but the skull, the feet, and the hands. 36* They returned to Jehu, and when they told him, he said, "This is the sentence which the LORD pronounced through his servant Elijah the Tishbite: 'In the confines of Jezreel dogs shall eat the flesh of Jezebel. 37 The corpse of Jezebel shall be like dung in the field in the confines of Jezreel, so that no one can say: This was Jezebel.'"

Killing of Ahab's Descendants

10 1* Ahab had seventy descendants in Samaria. Jehu prepared letters and sent them to the city rulers, to the elders, and to the guardians of Ahab's descendants in Samaria. 2 "Since your master's sons are with you," he wrote, "and you have the chariots, the horses, a fortified city, and the weapons, when this letter reaches you 3 decide which is the best and the fittest of your master's offspring, place him on his father's throne, and fight for your master's house." 4 They were overcome with fright and said, "If two kings could not withstand him, how can we?" 5 So the vizier and the ruler of the city, along with the elders and the guardians, sent this message to Jehu: "We are your servants, and we will do everything you tell us. We will proclaim no one king; do whatever you think best." 6 So Jehu wrote them a second letter: "If you are on my side and will obey me, count the heads of your master's sons and come to me in Jezreel at this time tomorrow." [The seventy princes were in the care of prominent men of the city, who were rearing them.]

7 When the letter arrived, they took the princes and slew all seventy of them, put their heads in baskets, and sent them to Jehu in Jezreel. 8 "They have brought the heads of the princes," a messenger came in and told him. "Pile them in two heaps at the entrance of the city until morning," he ordered. 9 Going out in the morning, he stopped and said to all the people: "You are not responsible, and although I conspired against my lord and slew him,

yet who killed all these? 10* Know that not a single word which the LORD has spoken against the house of Ahab shall go unfulfilled. The LORD has accomplished all that he foretold through his servant Elijah." 11* Thereupon Jehu slew all who were left of the family of Ahab in Jezreel, as well as all his powerful supporters, intimates, and priests, leaving him no survivor.

Ahaziah's Kinsmen

12* Then he set out for Samaria, and at Beth-eked-haroim on the way, 13 he came across kinsmen of Ahaziah, king of Judah. "Who are you?" he asked. "We are kinsmen of Ahaziah," they replied. "We are going down to visit the princes and the family of the queen mother." 14 "Take them alive," Jehu ordered. They were taken alive, forty-two in number, then slain at the pit of Beth-eked. Not one of them was spared.

Jehu in Samaria

15* When he had left there, Jehu met Jehonadab, son of Rechab, on the road. He greeted him and asked, "Are you sincerely disposed toward me, as I am toward you?" "Yes," replied Jehonadab. "If you are," continued Jehu, "give me your hand." Jehonadab gave him his hand, and Jehu drew him up into his chariot. 16 "Come with me," he said, "and see my zeal for the LORD." And he took him along in his own chariot.

17 When he arrived in Samaria, Jehu slew all who remained there of Ahab's line, doing away with them completely and thus fulfilling the prophecy which the LORD had spoken to Elijah.

Baal's Temple Destroyed

18* Jehu gathered all the people together and said to them: "Ahab served Baal to some extent, but Jehu will serve him yet more. 19 Now summon for me all Baal's prophets, all his worshipers, and all his priests. See that no one is absent, for I have a great sacrifice for Baal. Whoever is absent shall not live." This Jehu did as a ruse, so that he might destroy the worshipers of Baal. 20 Jehu said further, "Proclaim a solemn assembly in honor of Baal." They did so, 21 and Jehu sent word of it throughout the land of Israel. All the worshipers of Baal without exception came into the temple of Baal, which was filled to capacity. 22* Then Jehu said to the custodian of the wardrobe, "Bring out the garments for all the worshipers of Baal." When he had brought out the garments for them, 23 Jehu, with Jehonadab, son of Rechab, entered the temple of Baal and

---

9, 31: 1 Kgs 16, 9ff.
9, 36: 1 Kgs 21, 23.
10, 1: Jgs 9, 5; 1 Kgs 15, 29;

16, 11.
10, 10: 1 Kgs 21, 17–24.29.
10, 11: Hos 1, 4.

10, 12ff: 2 Chr 22, 8f.
10, 15: 1 Chr 2, 55; Jer 35, 1–11.

10, 18: 1 Kgs 16, 30ff.
10, 22: 1 Kgs 16, 32.

said to the worshipers of Baal, "Search and be sure that there is no worshiper of the LORD here with you, but only worshipers of Baal." 24 Then they proceeded to offer sacrifices and holocausts. Now Jehu had stationed eighty men outside with this warning, "If one of you lets anyone escape of those whom I shall deliver into your hands, he shall pay life for life." 25 As soon as he finished offering the holocaust, Jehu said to the guards and officers, "Go in and slay them. Let no one escape." So the guards and officers put them to the sword and cast them out. Afterward they went into the inner shrine of the temple of Baal, 26 took out the stele of Baal, and burned the shrine. 27 Then they smashed the stele of Baal, tore down the building, and turned it into a latrine, as it remains today.

28 Thus Jehu rooted out the worship of Baal from Israel. 29* However, he did not desist from the sins which Jeroboam, son of Nebat, had caused Israel to commit, as regards the golden calves at Bethel and at Dan. 30* The LORD said to Jehu, "Because you have done well what I deem right, and have treated the house of Ahab as I desire, your sons to the fourth generation shall sit upon the throne of Israel." 31 But Jehu was not careful to observe wholeheartedly the law of the LORD, the God of Israel, since he did not desist from the sins which Jeroboam caused Israel to commit.

32* At that time the LORD began to dismember Israel. Hazael defeated the Israelites throughout their territory 33 east of the Jordan (all the land of Gilead, of the Gadites, Reubenites and Manassehites), from Aroer on the river Arnon up through Gilead and Bashan.

34 The rest of the acts of Jehu, his valor and all his accomplishments, are written in the book of the chronicles of the kings of Israel. 35 Jehu rested with his ancestors and was buried in Samaria. His son Jehoahaz succeeded him as king. 36 The length of Jehu's reign over Israel in Samaria was twenty-eight years.

Rule of Athaliah

11 1* When Athaliah, the mother of Ahaziah, saw that her son was dead, she began to kill off the whole royal family. 2† But Jehosheba, daughter of King Jehoram and sister of Ahaziah, took Joash, his son, and spirited him away, along with his nurse, from the bedroom where the princes were about to be slain. She concealed him from Athaliah, and so he did not die. 3 For six years he

remained hidden in the temple of the LORD, while Athaliah ruled the land.

4* But in the seventh year, Jehoiada summoned the captains of the Carians and of the guards. He had them come to him in the temple of the LORD, exacted from them a sworn commitment, and then showed them the king's son. 5 He gave them these orders: "This is what you must do: the third of you who come on duty on the sabbath shall guard the king's palace; 6 another third shall be at the gate Sur; and the last third shall be at the gate behind the guards. 7 The two of your divisions who are going off duty that week shall keep guard over the temple of the LORD for the king. 8 You shall surround the king, each with drawn weapons, and if anyone tries to approach the cordon, kill him; stay with the king, whatever he may do."

9* The captains did just as Jehoiada the priest commanded. Each one with his men, both those going on duty for the sabbath and those going off duty that week, came to Jehoiada the priest. 10* He gave the captains King David's spears and shields, which were in the temple of the LORD. 11 And the guards, with drawn weapons, lined up from the southern to the northern limit of the enclosure, surrounding the altar and the temple on the king's behalf. 12* Then Jehoiada led out the king's son and put the crown and the insignia upon him. They proclaimed him king and anointed him, clapping their hands and shouting, "Long live the king!"

13* Athaliah heard the noise made by the people, and appeared before them in the temple of the LORD. 14† When she saw the king standing by the pillar, as was the custom, and the captains and trumpeters near him, with all the people of the land rejoicing and blowing trumpets, she tore her garments and cried out, "Treason, treason!" 15 Then Jehoiada the priest instructed the captains in command of the force: "Bring her outside through the ranks. If anyone follows her," he added, "let him die by the sword." He had given orders that she should not be slain in the temple of the LORD. 16 She was led out forcibly to the horse gate of the royal palace, where she was put to death.

17* Then Jehoiada made a covenant between the LORD as one party and the king and the people as the other, by which they would be the LORD's people; and another covenant, between the king and the people. 18 Thereupon all the people of the land went to the temple of Baal and demolished it. They shattered its altars and images completely, and slew

---

11, 2: *Jehosheba* was the wife of Jehoida, the high priest; cf 2 Chr 22, 11.

11, 14: *By the pillar:* see note on 2 Chr 23, 13.

10, 29: 1 Kgs 12, 28f.
10, 30: 2 Kgs 15, 12ff.
10, 32: Am 1, 3.
11, 1: Jgs 9, 5.
11, 4–8: 2 Chr 23, 1–7.
11, 9–12: 2 Chr 23, 8–11.
11, 10ff: 2 Sm 8, 7; 1 Kgs 1, 33f.
11, 12: 2 Sm 1, 10.
11, 13–16: 2 Chr 23, 12–15.
11, 17–20: 2 Chr 23, 16–21.

Mattan, the priest of Baal, before the altars. After appointing a detachment for the temple of the LORD, Jehoiada ¹⁹ with the captains, the Carians, the guards, and all the people of the land, led the king down from the temple of the LORD through the guards' gate to the palace, where Joash took his seat on the royal throne. ²⁰ All the people of the land rejoiced and the city was quiet, now that Athaliah had been slain with the sword at the royal palace.

Reign of Joash

12 ¹* Joash was seven years old when he became king. ² Joash began to reign in the seventh year of Jehu, and he reigned forty years in Jerusalem. His mother, who was named Zibiah, was from Beer-sheba. ³ Joash did what was pleasing to the LORD as long as he lived, because the priest Jehoiada guided him. ⁴ Still, the high places did not disappear; the people continued to sacrifice and to burn incense there.

⁵* For the priests Joash made this rule: "All the funds for sacred purposes that are brought to the temple of the LORD—the census tax, personal redemption money, and whatever funds are freely brought to the temple of the LORD— ⁶ the priests may take for themselves, each from his own clients. However, they must make whatever repairs on the temple may prove necessary." ⁷ Nevertheless, as late as the twenty-third year of the reign of King Joash, the priests had not made needed repairs on the temple. ⁸ Accordingly, King Joash summoned the priest Jehoiada and the other priests. "Why do you not repair the temple?" he asked them. "You must no longer take funds from your clients, but you shall turn them over for the repairs." ⁹* So the priests agreed that they would neither take funds from the people nor make the repairs on the temple.

¹⁰ The priest Jehoiada then took a chest, bored a hole in its lid, and set it beside the stele, on the right as one entered the temple of the LORD. The priests who guarded the entry would put into it all the funds that were brought to the temple of the LORD. ¹¹ When they noticed that there was a large amount of silver in the chest, the royal scribe [and the priest] would come up, and they would melt down all the funds that were in the temple of the LORD, and weigh them. ¹² The amount thus realized they turned over to the master workmen in the temple of the LORD. They in turn would give it to the carpenters and builders working in the temple of the LORD, ¹³ and to the lumbermen and stone cutters,

and for the purchase of the wood and hewn stone used in repairing the breaches, and for any other expenses that were necessary to repair the temple. ¹⁴ None of the funds brought to the temple of the LORD were used there to make silver cups, snuffers, basins, trumpets, or any gold or silver article. ¹⁵ Instead, they were given to the workmen, and with them they repaired the temple of the LORD. ¹⁶ Moreover, no reckoning was asked of the men who were provided with the funds to give to the workmen, because they held positions of trust. ¹⁷ The funds from guilt-offerings and from sin-offerings, however, were not brought to the temple of the LORD; they belonged to the priests.

¹⁸* Then King Hazael of Aram mounted a siege against Gath. When he had taken it, Hazael decided to go on to attack Jerusalem.* ¹⁹ But King Jehoash of Judah took all the dedicated offerings presented by his forebears, Jehoshaphat, Jehoram, and Ahaziah, kings of Judah, as well as his own, and all the gold there was in the treasuries of the temple and the palace, and sent them to King Hazael of Aram, who then led his forces away from Jerusalem. ²⁰ The rest of the acts of Joash, with all that he did, are recorded in the book of the chronicles of the kings of Judah. ²¹ Certain of his officials entered into a plot against him and killed him at Beth-millo. ²² Jozacar, son of Shimeath, and Jehozabad, son of Shomer, were the officials who killed him. He was buried in his forefathers' City of David, and his son Amaziah succeeded him as king.

Reign of Jehoahaz of Israel

13 ¹ In the twenty-third year of Joash, son of Ahaziah, king of Judah, Jehoahaz, son of Jehu, began his seventeen-year reign over Israel in Samaria. ² He did evil in the LORD's sight, conducting himself like Jeroboam, son of Nebat, and not renouncing the sin he had caused Israel to commit. ³ The LORD was angry with Israel and for a long time left them in the power of Hazael, king of Aram, and of Ben-hadad, son of Hazael. ⁴* Then Jehoahaz entreated the LORD, who heard him, since he saw the oppression to which the king of Aram had subjected Israel. ⁵† So the LORD gave Israel a savior, and the Israelites, freed from the power of Aram, dwelt in their own homes as formerly. ⁶*† Nevertheless, they did not desist from the sins which the house of Jeroboam had caused Israel to commit, but persisted in them. The sacred pole also remained standing in Samaria. ⁷ No soldiers were left

---

† **13, 5:** *A savior:* by this language, typical of the Book of Judges (Jgs 3, 9.15), Jeroboam II of Israel is meant; cf 2 Kgs 14, 27.
    13, 6: *Sacred pole:* see note on Ex 34, 13.

12, 1f: 2 Chr 24, 1f.   **12, 18–22:** 2 Chr 24, 23–27.
12, 5–8: 2 Chr 24, 5–10.   **13, 4:** 2 Kgs 14, 26f.
12, 9–16: 2 Chr 24, 11–14.   **13, 6:** Ex 34, 13.
12, 18: 2 Kgs 8, 12.

to Jehoahaz, except fifty horsemen with ten chariots and ten thousand foot soldiers, since the king of Aram had destroyed them and trampled them like dust. 8 The rest of the acts of Jehoahaz, with all his valor and accomplishments, are recorded in the book of the chronicles of the kings of Israel. 9 Jehoahaz rested with his ancestors and was buried in Samaria. His son Joash succeeded him as king.

Reign of Joash of Israel

10 In the thirty-seventh year of Joash, king of Judah, Jehoash, son of Jehoahaz, began his sixteen-year reign over Israel in Samaria. 11 He did evil in the sight of the LORD; he did not desist from any of the sins which Jeroboam, son of Nebat, had caused Israel to commit, but persisted in them. 12*† [The rest of the acts of Joash, the valor with which he fought against Amaziah, king of Judah, and all his accomplishments, are recorded in the book of the chronicles of the kings of Israel. 13 Joash rested with his ancestors, and Jeroboam occupied the throne. Joash was buried with the kings of Israel in Samaria.]

14*† When Elisha was suffering from the sickness of which he was to die, King Joash of Israel went down to visit him. "My father, my father!" he exclaimed, weeping over him. "Israel's chariots and horsemen!" 15 "Take a bow and some arrows," Elisha said to him. When he had done so, 16† Elisha said to the king of Israel, "Put your hand on the bow." As the king held the bow, Elisha placed his hands over the king's hands 17 and said, "Open the window toward the east." He opened it, Elisha said, "Shoot," and he shot. The prophet exclaimed, "The LORD'S arrow of victory! The arrow of victory over Aram! You will completely conquer Aram at Aphec." 18 Then he said to the king of Israel, "Take the arrows," which he did. Elisha said to him, "Strike the ground!" He struck the ground three times and stopped. 19 Angry with him, the man of God said: "You should have struck five or six times; you would have defeated Aram completely. Now, you will defeat Aram only three times."

20 Elisha died and was buried. At the time, bands of Moabites used to raid the land each year. 21* Once some people were burying a man, when suddenly they spied such a raiding band. So they cast the dead man into the grave of Elisha, and everyone went off. But when the man came in contact with the bones of Elisha, he came back to life and rose to his feet.

22 King Hazael of Aram oppressed Israel during the entire reign of Jehoahaz. 23* But the LORD was merciful with Israel and looked on them with compassion because of his covenant with Abraham, Isaac, and Jacob. He was unwilling to destroy them or to cast them out from his presence. 24 So when King Hazael of Aram died and his son Ben-hadad succeeded him as king, 25 Joash, son of Jehoahaz, took back from Ben-hadad, son of Hazael, the cities which Hazael had taken in battle from his father Jehoahaz. Joash defeated Ben-hadad three times, and thus recovered the cities of Israel.

Amaziah of Judah

14 1† In the second year of Joash, son of Jehoahaz, king of Israel, Amaziah, son of Joash, king of Judah, began to reign. 2* He was twenty-five years old when he became king, and he reigned twenty-nine years in Jerusalem. His mother, whose name was Jehoaddin, was from Jerusalem. 3 He pleased the LORD, yet not like his forefather David, since he did just as his father Joash had done. 4 Thus the high places did not disappear, but the people continued to sacrifice and to burn incense on them. 5* When Amaziah had the kingdom firmly in hand, he slew the officials who had murdered the king, his father. 6* But the children of the murderers he did not put to death, obeying the LORD'S command written in the book of the law of Moses, "Fathers shall not be put to death for their children, nor shall children be put to death for their fathers; each one shall die for his own sin."

7* Amaziah slew ten thousand Edomites in the Salt Valley, and took Sela in battle. He renamed it Joktheel, the name it has to this day.

8* Then Amaziah sent messengers to Jehoash, son of Jehoahaz, son of Jehu, king of Israel, with this challenge, "Come, let us meet face to face." 9 King Jehoash of Israel sent this reply to the king of Judah: "The thistle of Lebanon sent word to the cedar of Lebanon, 'Give your daughter to my son in marriage,' but an animal of Lebanon passed by and trampled the thistle underfoot. 10 You have indeed

---

13, 12f: The conclusion to the reign of Joash is given again in 2 Kgs 14, 15f, where it is more appropriate.

13, 14: *My father, my father:* the king expresses here the same sentiments as those with which Elisha addressed Elijah.

13, 16–19: Symbolic acts similar to these are seen in Ex 17, 8ff; Jos 8, 18ff; Ez 4, 1ff.

14, 1f: *In the second year . . . twenty-nine years in Jerusalem:* the reigns of the kings of Judah between Athaliah and Ahaz are assigned too many years in all to correspond to the reigns in Israel from Jehu to the fall of Samaria. It seems probable that Amaziah was murdered as soon as his son Azaiah was old enough to rule, and that Amazi-

ah's reign was nearer nineteen than twenty-nine years. The correlation, in 2 Kgs 15, 1, of the beginning of Azariah's reign with the 27th year of Jeroboam II can hardly be correct; and the sixteen-year reign of Jotham of Judah (2 Kgs 15, 33) consisted for the most part of a regency during the illness of his father (2 Kgs 15, 5).

13, 12: 2 Kgs 14, 8–16.
13, 14: 2 Kgs 2, 12.
13, 21: Sir 48, 14.
13, 23: Dt 9, 27.
14, 2f: 2 Chr 25, 1f.
14, 5f: 2 Chr 25, 3f.

14, 6: Dt 24, 16; Ez 18, 20.
14, 7: 2 Sm 8, 13f; 2 Chr 25, 11.
14, 8: 2 Kgs 13, 12; Jgs 9, 8–15.

conquered Edom, and you have become ambitious. Enjoy your glory, but stay at home! Why involve yourself and Judah with you in misfortune and failure?"

[11] But Amaziah would not listen. King Jehoash of Israel then advanced, and he and King Amaziah of Judah met in battle at Beth-shemesh of Judah. [12] Judah was defeated by Israel, and all the Judean soldiery fled homeward. [13] King Jehoash of Israel captured Amaziah, son of Jehoash, son of Ahaziah, king of Judah, at Beth-shemesh. He went on to Jerusalem where he tore down four hundred cubits of the city wall, from the Gate of Ephraim to the Corner Gate. [14] He took all the gold and silver and all the utensils there were in the temple of the LORD and in the treasuries of the palace, and hostages as well. Then he returned to Samaria. [15]* The rest of the acts of Jehoash, his valor, and how he fought Amaziah, king of Judah, are recorded in the book of the chronicles of the kings of Israel. [16] Jehoash rested with his ancestors; he was buried in Samaria with the kings of Israel. His son Jeroboam succeeded him as king.

[17]† Amaziah, son of Joash, king of Judah, survived Jehoash, son of Jehoahaz, king of Israel, by fifteen years. [18] The rest of the acts of Amaziah are written in the book of the chronicles of the kings of Judah. [19] When a conspiracy was formed against him in Jerusalem, he fled to Lachish. But he was pursued to Lachish and killed there. [20] He was brought back on horses and buried with his ancestors in the City of David in Jerusalem. [21]*† Thereupon all the people of Judah took the sixteen-year-old Azariah and proclaimed him king to succeed his father Amaziah. [22] It was Azariah who rebuilt Elath and restored it to Judah, after King Amaziah rested with his ancestors.

Jeroboam II of Israel

[23] In the fifteenth year of Amaziah, son of Joash, king of Judah, Jeroboam, son of Joash, king of Israel, began his forty-one-year reign in Samaria. [24] He did evil in the sight of the LORD; he did not desist from any of the sins which Jeroboam, son of Nebat, had caused Israel to commit. [25]† He restored the boundaries of Israel from Labo-of-Hamath to the sea of the Arabah, just as the LORD, the God of Israel, had prophesied through his servant, the prophet Jonah, son of Amittai, from Gath-hepher. [26]* For the LORD saw the very bitter affliction of Israel, where there was neither slave nor freeman, no

one at all to help Israel. [27] Since the LORD had not determined to blot out the name of Israel from under the heavens, he saved them through Jeroboam, son of Joash. [28] The rest of the acts of Jeroboam, his valor and all his accomplishments, how he fought with Damascus and turned back Hamath from Israel, are recorded in the book of the chronicles of the kings of Israel. [29] Jeroboam rested with his ancestors, the kings of Israel, and his son Zechariah succeeded him as king.

Azariah of Judah

15 [1]*† Azariah, son of Amaziah, king of Judah, became king in the twenty-seventh year of Jeroboam, king of Israel. [2] He was sixteen years old when he began to reign, and he reigned fifty-two years in Jerusalem. His mother, whose name was Jecholiah, was from Jerusalem. [3] He pleased the LORD just as his father Amaziah had done. [4] Yet the high places did not disappear; the people continued to sacrifice and to burn incense on them. [5]* The LORD afflicted the king, and he was a leper to the day of his death. He lived in a house apart, while Jotham, the king's son, was vizier and regent for the people of the land. [6] The rest of the acts of Azariah, and all his accomplishments, are recorded in the book of the chronicles of the kings of Judah. [7] Azariah rested with his ancestors, and was buried with them in the City of David. His son Jotham succeeded him as king.

Zechariah of Israel

[8] In the thirty-eighth year of Azariah, king of Judah, Zechariah, son of Jeroboam, was king of Israel in Samaria for six months. [9] He did evil in the sight of the LORD as his fathers had done, and did not desist from the sins which Jeroboam, son of Nebat, had caused Israel to commit. [10] Shallum, son of Jabesh, conspired against Zechariah, attacked and killed him at Ibleam, and reigned in his place. [11] The rest of the acts of Zechariah are recorded in the book of the chronicles of the kings of Israel. [12]* Thus the LORD's promise to Jehu, "Your descendants to the fourth generation shall sit upon the throne of Israel," was fulfilled.

Shallum of Israel

[13] Shallum, son of Jabesh, became king in the thirty-ninth year of Uzziah, king of Judah; he reigned one month in Samaria. [14] Menahem, son of Gadi, came up from Tirzah to Samaria, where he attacked

14, 17: See note on 2 Kgs 14, 1f.
14, 21: *Azariah:* also called Uzziah in many texts.
14, 25: *Sea of the Arabah:* the Dead Sea. *Jonah:* see note on Jon 1, 1.
15, 1: *Twenty-seventh year:* see note on 2 Kgs 14, 1f.

14, 15: 2 Kgs 13, 12f.
14, 21: 2 Chr 26, 1f.
14, 26: 2 Kgs 13, 4f; 1 Kgs 14, 10.
15, 1ff: 2 Chr 26, 3f.
15, 5ff: 2 Chr 26, 21ff.
15, 12: 2 Kgs 10, 30.

and killed Shallum, son of Jabesh, and reigned in his place. 15 The rest of the acts of Shallum, and the fact of his conspiracy, are recorded in the book of the chronicles of the kings of Israel. 16 At that time, Menahem punished Tappuah, all the inhabitants of the town and of its whole district, because on his way from Tirzah they did not let him in. He punished them even to ripping open all the pregnant women.

Menahem of Israel

17 In the thirty-ninth year of Azariah, king of Judah, Menahem, son of Gadi, began his ten-year reign over Samaria. 18 He did evil in the sight of the LORD, not desisting from the sins which Jeroboam, son of Nebat, had caused Israel to commit. During his reign, 19† Pul, king of Assyria, invaded the land, and Menahem gave him a thousand talents of silver to have his assistance in strengthening his hold on the kingdom. 20 Menahem secured the money to give to the king of Assyria by exacting it from all the men of substance in the country, fifty silver shekels from each. The king of Assyria did not remain in the country but withdrew. 21 The rest of the acts of Menahem, and all his accomplishments, are recorded in the book of the chronicles of the kings of Israel. 22 Menahem rested with his ancestors, and his son Pekahiah succeeded him as king.

Pekahiah of Israel

23 In the fiftieth year of Azariah, king of Judah, Pekahiah, son of Menahem, began his two-year reign over Israel in Samaria. 24 He did evil in the sight of the LORD, not desisting from the sins which Jeroboam, son of Nebat, had caused Israel to commit. 25 His adjutant Pekah, son of Remaliah, who had with him fifty men from Gilead, conspired against him, killed him within the palace stronghold in Samaria, and reigned in his place. 26 The rest of the acts of Pekahiah, and all his accomplishments, are recorded in the book of the chronicles of the kings of Israel.

Pekah of Israel

27† In the fifty-second year of Azariah, king of Judah, Pekah, son of Remaliah, began his twenty-year reign over Israel in Samaria. 28 He did evil in the sight of the LORD, not desisting from the sins which Jeroboam, son of Nebat, had caused Israel to commit. 29 During the reign of Pekah, king of Israel, Tiglath-pileser, king of Assyria, came and took Ijon,

Abel-beth-maacah, Janoah, Kedesh, Hazor, all the territory of Naphtali, Gilead, and Galilee, deporting the inhabitants to Assyria. 30 Hoshea, son of Elah, conspired against Pekah, son of Remaliah; he attacked and killed him, and reigned in his place [in the twentieth year of Jotham, son of Uzziah]. 31 The rest of the acts of Pekah, and all his accomplishments, are recorded in the book of the chronicles of the kings of Israel.

Jotham of Judah

32* In the second year of Pekah, son of Remaliah, king of Israel, Jotham, son of Uzziah, king of Judah, began to reign. 33 He was twenty-five years old when he became king, and he reigned sixteen years in Jerusalem. His mother's name was Jerusha, daughter of Zadok. 34 He pleased the LORD, just as his father Uzziah had done. 35† Nevertheless the high places did not disappear and the people continued to sacrifice and to burn incense on them. It was he who built the Upper Gate of the temple of the LORD. 36 The rest of the acts of Jotham, and all his accomplishments, are recorded in the book of the chronicles of the kings of Judah. 37 It was at that time that the LORD first loosed Rezin, king of Aram, and Pekah, son of Remaliah, against Judah. 38 Jotham rested with his ancestors and was buried with them in his forefather's City of David. His son Ahaz succeeded him as king.

Ahaz of Judah

16 1* In the seventeenth year of Pekah, son of Remaliah, Ahaz, son of Jotham, king of Judah, began to reign. 2 Ahaz was twenty years old when he became king, and he reigned sixteen years in Jerusalem. He did not please the LORD, his God, like his forefather David, 3* but conducted himself like the kings of Israel, and even immolated his son by fire, in accordance with the abominable practice of the nations whom the LORD had cleared out of the way of the Israelites. 4* Further, he sacrificed and burned incense on the high places, on hills, and under every leafy tree.

5* Then Rezin, king of Aram, and Pekah, son of Remaliah, king of Israel, came up to Jerusalem to attack it. Although they besieged Ahaz, they were unable to conquer him. 6* At the same time the king of Edom recovered Elath for Edom, driving the Judeans out of it. The Edomites then entered Elath, which they have occupied until the present.

---

† **15, 19:** *Pul:* the Babylonian throne name of the Assyrian Tiglath-pileser III; cf 2 Kgs 15, 29.

15, 27: The *twenty* years here ascribed to Pekah are an impossibility; the calculation which made his reign, of five years at most, appear so long may have been based on the attempt to give Jotham of Judah a full sixteen-year reign independently of his regency. See 2 Kgs 16, 1 and the note on 2 Kgs 14, 1f.

15, 35: *The Upper Gate:* also the Gate of Benjamin; cf Jer 20, 2; Ez 9, 2.

15, 32–38: 2 Chr 27, 1–4.7–9.   16, 4: Dt 12, 2.
   16, 1–4: 2 Chr 28, 1–4.   16, 5: 2 Chr 28, 5f.
   16, 3: Lv 18, 21.   16, 6: 2 Chr 28, 17.

⁷* Meanwhile, Ahaz sent messengers to Tiglath-pileser, king of Assyria, with the plea: "I am your servant and your son. Come up and rescue me from the clutches of the king of Aram and the king of Israel, who are attacking me." ⁸* Ahaz took the silver and gold that were in the temple of the LORD and in the palace treasuries and sent them as a present to the king of Assyria, ⁹† who listened to him and moved against Damascus, which he captured. He deported its inhabitants to Kir and put Rezin to death.

¹⁰ King Ahaz went to Damascus to meet Tiglath-pileser, king of Assyria. When he saw the altar in Damascus, King Ahaz sent to Uriah the priest a model of the altar and a detailed design of its construction. ¹¹ Uriah the priest built an altar according to the plans which King Ahaz sent him from Damascus, and had it completed by the time the king returned home. ¹² On his arrival from Damascus, the king inspected this altar, then went up to it and offered sacrifice on it, ¹³* burning his holocaust and cereal-offering, pouring out his libation, and sprinkling the blood of his peace-offerings on the altar. ¹⁴ The bronze altar that stood before the LORD he brought from the front of the temple—that is, from the space between the new altar and the temple of the LORD—and set it on the north side of his altar. ¹⁵*† "Upon the large altar," King Ahaz commanded Uriah the priest, "burn the morning holocaust and the evening cereal-offering, the royal holocaust and cereal-offering, as well as the holocausts, cereal-offerings, and libations of the people. You must also sprinkle on it all the blood of holocausts and sacrifices. But the old bronze altar shall be mine for consultation." ¹⁶ Uriah the priest did just as King Ahaz had commanded. ¹⁷* King Ahaz detached the frames from the bases and removed the lavers from them; he also took down the bronze sea from the bronze oxen that supported it, and set it on a stone pavement. ¹⁸† In deference to the king of Assyria he removed from the temple of the LORD the emplacement which had been built in the temple for a throne, and the outer entrance for the king. ¹⁹* The rest of the acts of Ahaz are recorded in the book of the chronicles of the kings of Judah.

²⁰ Ahaz rested with his ancestors and was buried with them in the City of David. His son Hezekiah succeeded him as king.

Hoshea of Israel

17 ¹ In the twelfth year of Ahaz, king of Judah, Hoshea, son of Elah, began his nine-year reign over Israel in Samaria. ² He did evil in the sight of the LORD, yet not to the extent of the kings of Israel before him. ³*† Shalmaneser, king of Assyria, advanced against him, and Hoshea became his vassal and paid him tribute. ⁴ But the king of Assyria found Hoshea guilty of conspiracy for sending envoys to the king of Egypt at Sais, and for failure to pay the annual tribute to his Assyrian overlord. ⁵ For this, the king of Assyria arrested and imprisoned Hoshea; he then occupied the whole land and attacked Samaria, which he besieged for three years. ⁶*† In the ninth year of Hoshea, the king of Assyria took Samaria, and deported the Israelites to Assyria, settling them in Halah, at the Habor, a river of Gozan, and in the cities of the Medes.

⁷ This came about because the Israelites sinned against the LORD, their God, who had brought them up from the land of Egypt, from under the domination of Pharaoh, king of Egypt, and because they venerated other gods. ⁸ They followed the rites of the nations whom the LORD had cleared out of the way of the Israelites [and the kings of Israel whom they set up]. ⁹ They adopted unlawful practices toward the LORD, their God. They built high places in all their settlements, the watchtowers as well as the walled cities. ¹⁰* They set up pillars and sacred poles for themselves on every high hill and under every leafy tree. ¹¹ There, on all the high places, they burned incense like the nations whom the LORD had sent into exile at their coming. They did evil things that provoked the LORD, ¹² and served idols, although the LORD had told them, "You must not do this."

¹³ And though the LORD warned Israel and Judah by every prophet and seer, "Give up your evil ways and keep my commandments and statutes, in accordance with the entire law which I enjoined on your fathers and which I sent you by my servants

---

16, 9: Firmly dated events bearing on chapters 16 through 20 are: the fall of Damascus (16, 9) in 732 B.C., the fall of Samaria (18, 9–11) in 721 B.C., and Sennacherib's invasion of Judah (18, 13) in 701 B.C., which is equated both in Kings and in Is 36, 1 with the 14th year of Hezekiah. These data make it necessary to credit Ahaz with at least a twenty-year reign, between 735 and c. 715 B.C., and to exclude the correlations between Hoshea of Israel and Hezekiah in chapter 18.

If the 14th-year correspondence for 701 B.C. is given up, other arrangements are possible. The alleged ages of Jotham (15, 33), Ahaz (16, 2), and Hezekiah (18, 2) at their successive accessions to the throne do not argue for an early date for Hezekiah; but one or more of these may be artificial. Azariah (15, 1–7; Is 6, 1) was still on the throne of Judah in 743 B.C.

16, 15: For consultation: perhaps the introduction into Judah of the Babylonian practice of omen sacrifices; cf Ez 21, 16.

16, 18: Emplacement . . . for a throne, and the outer entrance for the king: signs of sovereignty for the Hebrew kings.

17, 3: Shalmaneser: son and successor of Tiglath-pileser.

17, 6: The king of Assyria: Shalmaneser's successor and usurper, Sargon II.

16, 7: 2 Chr 28, 16.
16, 8: 2 Chr 28, 21.
16, 13: 2 Chr 28, 23.
16, 15: Ex 29, 38f; Nm 28, 3f.
16, 17: 2 Chr 28, 24.
16, 19: 2 Chr 28, 26f.
17, 3: 2 Kgs 18, 9; Tb 1, 2.
17, 6: 2 Kgs 18, 10f.
17, 10: Ex 23, 24; 34, 13; Dt 12, 2.

? did you KNOW?

The First Captivity

The Second Book of Kings describes two captivities and exiles. The first one is the Assyrian conquest of the northern kingdom, Israel, which occurred in 721 B.C. (see map 4, "The Assyrian Empire"). According to the author of 2 Kings, Israel fell first because its kings and people were even less faithful to God than the kings and people of Judah, the southern kingdom. Notice that the Assyrian conquest is described in the briefest detail (17, 5–6), but the reasons for it are described in great detail (verses 7–18).

▶ **2 Kgs 17, 5–18**

the prophets," 14* they did not listen, but were as stiff-necked as their fathers, who had not believed in the LORD, their God. 15* They rejected his statutes, the covenant which he had made with their fathers, and the warnings which he had given them. The vanity they pursued, they themselves became: they followed the surrounding nations whom the LORD had commanded them not to imitate. 16* They disregarded all the commandments of the LORD, their God, and made for themselves two molten calves; they also made a sacred pole and worshiped all the host of heaven, and served Baal. 17* They immolated their sons and daughters by fire, practiced fortune-telling and divination, and sold themselves into evildoing in the LORD's sight, provoking him 18 till, in his great anger against Israel, the LORD put them away out of his sight. Only the tribe of Judah was left.

19 Even the people of Judah, however, did not keep the commandments of the LORD, their God, but followed the rites practiced by Israel. 20 So the LORD rejected the whole race of Israel. He afflicted them and delivered them over to plunderers, finally casting them out from before him. 21* When he tore Israel away from the house of David, they made Jeroboam, son of Nebat, king: he drove the Israelites away from the LORD, causing them to commit a great sin. 22 The Israelites imitated Jeroboam in all the sins he committed, nor would they desist from them. 23* Finally, the LORD put Israel away out of his sight as he had foretold through all his servants, the prophets; and Israel went into exile from their native soil to Assyria, an exile lasting to the present.

24 The king of Assyria brought people from Babylon, Cuthah, Avva, Hamath, and Sepharvaim, and settled them in the cities of Samaria in place of the Israelites. They took possession of Samaria and dwelt in its cities. 25 When they first settled there, they did not venerate the LORD, so he sent lions among them that killed some of their number. 26 A report reached the king of Assyria: "The nations whom you deported and settled in the cities of Samaria do not know how to worship the God of the land, and he has sent lions among them that are killing them, since they do not know how to worship the God of the land." 27 The king of Assyria gave the order, "Send back one of the priests whom I deported, to go there and settle, to teach them how to worship the God of the land." 28 So one of the priests who had been deported from Samaria returned and settled in Bethel, and taught them how to venerate the LORD.

29* But these peoples began to make their own gods in the various cities in which they were living; in the shrines on the high places which the Samaritans had made, each people set up gods. 30 Thus the Babylonians made Marduk and his consort; the men of Cuth made Nergal; the men of Hamath made Ashima; 31 the men of Avva made Nibhaz and Tartak; and the men of Sepharvaim immolated their children by fire to their city gods, King Hadad and his consort Anath. 32* They also venerated the LORD, choosing from their number priests for the high places, who officiated for them in the shrines on the high places. 33 But, while venerating the LORD, they served their own gods, following the worship of the nations from among whom they had been deported.

34*† To this day they worship according to their ancient rites. [They did not venerate the LORD nor observe the statutes and regulations, the law and commandments, which the LORD enjoined on the descendants of Jacob, whom he had named Israel. 35* When he made a covenant with them, he commanded them: "You must not venerate other gods, nor worship them, nor serve them, nor offer sacrifice to them. 36 The LORD, who brought you up

---

† **17, 34–40:** *They did not . . . earlier manner:* this passage is an adaptation of language denouncing the Israelites to make it applicable to the later Samaritan sect of postexilic times. The original bearing of the discourse (vv 13–15) can be seen by reading it between vv 22 and 23. Cf also 2 Kgs 18, 12.

17, 14: Jer 25, 5; Dt 9, 13.
17, 15: Jer 2, 5.
17, 16: 1 Kgs 12, 28; Ex 34, 13; Dt 4, 19; 17, 2f.
17, 17: Lv 18, 21; Dt 18, 10.
17, 21: 1 Kgs 12, 19f; 12,

26–33.
17, 23: Jer 25, 9.
17, 29: Jn 4, 9.
17, 32: 1 Kgs 12, 31.
17, 34: Gn 32, 29.
17, 35: Ex 20, 3ff.

from the land of Egypt with great power and outstretched arm: him shall you venerate, him shall you worship, and to him shall you sacrifice. 37 You must be careful to observe forever the statutes and regulations, the law and commandment, which he wrote for you, and you must not venerate other gods. 38 The covenant which I made with you, you must not forget; you must not venerate other gods. 39 But the LORD, your God, you must venerate; it is he who will deliver you from the power of all your enemies." 40 They did not listen, however, but continued in their earlier manner.] 41 Thus these nations venerated the LORD, but also served their idols. And their sons and grandsons, to this day, are doing as their fathers did.

II: The Kingdom of Judah after 721 B.C.

Hezekiah

18 1* In the third year of Hoshea, son of Elah, king of Israel, Hezekiah, son of Ahaz, king of Judah, began to reign. 2 He was twenty-five years old when he became king, and he reigned twenty-nine years in Jerusalem. His mother's name was Abi, daughter of Zechariah. 3 He pleased the LORD, just as his forefather David had done. 4* It was he who removed the high places, shattered the pillars, and cut down the sacred poles. He smashed the bronze serpent called Nehushtan which Moses had made, because up to that time the Israelites were burning incense to it. 5 He put his trust in the LORD, the God of Israel; and neither before him nor after him was there anyone like him among all the kings of Judah. 6 Loyal to the LORD, Hezekiah never turned away from him, but observed the commandments which the LORD had given Moses. 7 The LORD was with him, and he prospered in all that he set out to do. He rebelled against the king of Assyria and did not serve him. 8 He also subjugated the watchtowers and walled cities of the Philistines, all the way to Gaza and its territory.

9† In the fourth year of King Hezekiah, which was the seventh year of Hoshea, son of Elah, king of Israel, Shalmaneser, king of Assyria, attacked Samaria, laid siege to it, 10* and after three years captured it. In the sixth year of Hezekiah, the ninth year of Hoshea, king of Israel, Samaria was taken.

11 The king of Assyria then deported the Israelites to Assyria and settled them in Halah, at the Habor, a river of Gozan, and in the cities of the Medes. 12* This came about because they had not heeded the warning of the LORD, their God, but violated his covenant, not heeding and not fulfilling the commandments of Moses, the servant of the LORD.

Invasion of Sennacherib

13*† In the fourteenth year of King Hezekiah, Sennacherib,† king of Assyria, went on an expedition against all the fortified cities of Judah and captured them. 14 Hezekiah, king of Judah, sent this message to the king of Assyria at Lachish: "I have done wrong. Leave me, and I will pay whatever tribute you impose on me." The king of Assyria exacted three hundred talents of silver and thirty talents of gold from Hezekiah, king of Judah. 15 Hezekiah paid him all the funds there were in the temple of the LORD and in the palace treasuries. 16* He broke up the door panels and the uprights of the temple of the LORD which he himself had ordered to be overlaid with gold, and gave the gold to the king of Assyria.

17*† The king of Assyria sent the general, the lord chamberlain, and the commander from Lachish with a great army to King Hezekiah at Jerusalem. They went up, and on their arrival in Jerusalem, stopped at the conduit of the upper pool on the highway of the fuller's field. 18* They called for the king, who sent out to them Eliakim, son of Hilkiah, the master of the palace; Shebnah the scribe; and the herald Joah, son of Asaph. 19 The commander said to them, "Tell Hezekiah, 'Thus says the great king, the king of Assyria: On what do you base this confidence of yours? 20 Do you think mere words substitute for strategy and might in war? On whom, then, do you rely, that you rebel against me? 21* This Egypt, the staff on which you rely, is in fact a broken reed which pierces the hand of anyone who leans on it. That is what Pharaoh, king of Egypt, is to all who rely on him. 22 But if you say to me, We rely on the LORD, our God, is not he the one whose high places and altars Hezekiah has removed, commanding Judah and Jerusalem to worship before this altar in Jerusalem?'

23 "Now, make a wager with my lord, the king of Assyria: I will give you two thousand horses if you can put riders on them. 24 How then can you

18, 9: See note on 2 Kgs 16, 9.

18, 13—20, 11: Duplication of Is 36, 1—38, 8.21.22.

18, 13: *Sennacherib* succeeded Sargon II as king of Assyria. His Judean campaign was waged in 701 B.C. See note on 2 Kgs 16, 9.

18, 17: *General, the lord chamberlain . . . commander:* the text lists three major functionaries by their Assyrian titles, of which only the first, more nearly "lord lieutenant," is military in origin; the commander was technically the king's chief butler.

18, 1ff: 2 Chr 28, 27; 29, 1f.
18, 4: Ex 23, 24; 34, 13; Nm 21, 9; Dt 12, 2; 2 Chr 31, 1; Wis 16, 6; Jn 3, 14.
18, 10f: 2 Kgs 17, 6; Tb 1, 2.
18, 12: 2 Kgs 17, 7–18.

18, 13: 2 Chr 32, 1ff; Sir 48, 18; Is 36, 1.
18, 16: 1 Kgs 6, 20–22.
18, 17: 2 Chr 32, 9; Is 36, 1ff.
18, 18: Is 22, 13–25.
18, 21: Is 30, 1–7; 31, 1–3; Ez 29, 6–7.

repulse even one of the least servants of my lord, relying as you do on Egypt for chariots and horsemen? 25 Was it without the LORD'S will that I have come up to destroy this place? The LORD said to me, 'Go up and destroy that land!' "

26 Then Eliakim, son of Hilkiah, and Shebnah and Joah said to the commander: "Please speak to your servants in Aramaic; we understand it. Do not speak to us in Judean within earshot of the people who are on the wall."

27 But the commander replied: "Was it to your master and to you that my lord sent me to speak these words? Was it not rather to the men sitting on the wall, who, with you, will have to eat their own excrement and drink their urine?" 28 Then the commander stepped forward and cried out in a loud voice in Judean, "Listen to the words of the great king, the king of Assyria. 29 Thus says the king: 'Do not let Hezekiah deceive you, since he cannot deliver you out of my hand. 30 Let not Hezekiah induce you to rely on the LORD, saying, The LORD will surely save us; this city will not be handed over to the king of Assyria. 31 Do not listen to Hezekiah, for the king of Assyria says: Make peace with me and surrender! Then each of you will eat of his own vine and of his own fig-tree, and drink the water of his own cistern, 32 until I come to take you to a land like your own, a land of grain and wine, of bread and orchards, of olives, oil and fruit syrup. Choose life, not death. Do not listen to Hezekiah when he would seduce you by saying, The LORD will rescue us. 33 Has any of the gods of the nations ever rescued his land from the hand of the king of Assyria? 34* Where are the gods of Hamath and Arpad? Where are the gods of Sepharvaim, Hena, and Avva? Where are the gods of the land of Samaria? 35 Which of the gods for all these lands ever rescued his land from my hand? Will the LORD then rescue Jerusalem from my hand?' " 36 But the people remained silent and did not answer him one word, for the king had ordered them not to answer him.

37 Then the master of the palace, Eliakim, son of Hilkiah, Shebnah the scribe, and the herald Joah, son of Asaph, came to Hezekiah with their garments torn, and reported to him what the commander had said.

Hezekiah and Isaiah

19 1* When King Hezekiah heard this, he tore his garments, wrapped himself in sackcloth, and went into the temple of the LORD. 2 He sent Eliakim, the master of the palace, Shebnah

the scribe, and the elders of the priests, wrapped in sackcloth, to tell the prophet Isaiah, son of Amoz, 3† "Thus says Hezekiah: 'This is a day of distress, of rebuke, and of disgrace. Children are at the point of birth, but there is no strength to bring them forth. 4 Perhaps the LORD, your God, will hear all the words of the commander, whom his master, the king of Assyria, sent to taunt the living God, and will rebuke him for the words which the LORD, your God, has heard. So send up a prayer for the remnant that is here.' " 5 When the servants of King Hezekiah had come to Isaiah, 6* he said to them, "Tell this to your master: 'Thus says the LORD: Do not be frightened by the words you have heard, with which the servants of the king of Assyria have blasphemed me. 7 I am about to put in him such a spirit that, when he hears a certain report, he will return to his own land, and there I will cause him to fall by the sword.' "

8 When the commander, on his return, heard that the king of Assyria had withdrawn from Lachish, he found him besieging Libnah. 9 The king of Assyria heard a report that Tirhakah, king of Ethiopia, had come out to fight against him. Again he sent envoys to Hezekiah with this message: 10 "Thus shall you say to Hezekiah, king of Judah: 'Do not let your God on whom you rely deceive you by saying that Jerusalem will not be handed over to the king of Assyria. 11 You have heard what the kings of Assyria have done to all other countries: they doomed them! Will you, then, be saved? 12* Did the gods of the nations whom my fathers destroyed save them? Gozan, Haran, Rezeph, or the Edenites in Telassar? 13* Where are the king of Hamath, the king of Arpad, or the kings of the cities Sepharvaim, Hena and Avva?' "

14* Hezekiah took the letter from the hand of the messengers and read it; then he went up to the temple of the LORD, and spreading it out before him, 15* he prayed in the LORD'S presence: "O LORD, God of Israel, enthroned upon the cherubim! You alone are God over all the kingdoms of the earth. You have made the heavens and the earth. 16 Incline your ear, O LORD, and listen! Open your eyes, O LORD, and see! Hear the words of Sennacherib which he sent to taunt the living God. 17 Truly, O LORD, the kings of Assyria have laid waste the nations and their lands, 18* and cast their gods into the fire; they destroyed them because they were not gods, but the work of human hands, wood and stone. 19* Therefore, O LORD, our God, save us from the power of this man, that all the kingdoms of the earth may know that you alone, O LORD, are God."

† **19, 3:** See note on Is 37, 3.

* **18, 34:** 2 Kgs 17, 24.
19, 1-7: Is 37, 1-7.

19, 6: Is 10, 5–19.
19, 12: 2 Kgs 17, 6.

19, 13: 2 Kgs 18, 34.
19, 14–19: 2 Chr 32, 20; Is 37,
14–20.

19, 15: Ex 25, 18.
19, 18: Jer 10, 3.
19, 19: 1 Kgs 18, 24.

Punishment of Sennacherib

20 Then Isaiah, son of Amoz, sent this message to Hezekiah: "Thus says the LORD, the God of Israel, in answer to your prayer for help against Sennacherib, king of Assyria: I have listened! [21]† This is the word the LORD has spoken concerning him:

" 'She despises you, laughs you to scorn,
    the virgin daughter Zion!
Behind you she wags her head,
    daughter Jerusalem.
[22] Whom have you insulted and blasphemed,
    against whom have you raised your voice
And lifted up your eyes on high?
    Against the Holy One of Israel!
[23] Through your servants you have insulted the
    LORD.
    You said: With my many chariots
I climbed the mountain heights,
    the recesses of Lebanon;
I cut down its lofty cedars,
    its choice cypresses;
I reached the remotest heights,
    its forest park.
[24] I dug wells and drank water in foreign lands;
I dried up with the soles of my feet
    all the rivers of Egypt.

[25] " 'Have you not heard?
    Long ago I prepared it,
From days of old I planned it.
    Now I have brought it to pass:
That you should reduce fortified cities
    into heaps of ruins,
[26] While their inhabitants, shorn of power,
    are dismayed and ashamed,
Becoming like the plants of the field, like the
    green growth,
    like the scorched grass on the housetops.
[27]* I am aware whether you stand or sit;
    I know whether you come or go,
[28]   and also your rage against me.
Because of your rage against me
    and your fury which has reached my ears,
I will put my hook in your nose
    and my bit in your mouth,
    and make you return the way you came.

[29] " 'This shall be a sign for you:
    this year you shall eat the aftergrowth,
    next year, what grows of itself;
But in the third year, sow and reap,
    plant vineyards and eat their fruit!

[30] The remaining survivors of the house of Judah
    shall again strike root below
    and bear fruit above.
[31] For out of Jerusalem shall come a remnant,
    and from Mount Zion, survivors.
    The zeal of the LORD of hosts shall do this.'

[32] "Therefore, thus says the LORD concerning the king of Assyria: 'He shall not reach this city, nor shoot an arrow at it, nor come before it with a shield, nor cast up siege-works against it. [33] He shall return by the same way he came, without entering the city, says the LORD. [34]* I will shield and save this city for my own sake, and for the sake of my servant David.' "

[35]* That night the angel of the LORD went forth and struck down one hundred and eighty-five thousand men in the Assyrian camp. Early the next morning, there they were, all the corpses of the dead. [36] So Sennacherib, the king of Assyria, broke camp, and went back home to Nineveh.

[37] When he was worshiping in the temple of his god Nisroch, his sons Adrammelech and Sharezer slew him with the sword and fled into the land of Ararat. His son Esar-haddon reigned in his stead.

Hezekiah's Illness

20 [1]* In those days, when Hezekiah was mortally ill, the prophet Isaiah, son of Amoz, came and said to him: "Thus says the LORD: 'Put your house in order, for you are about to die; you shall not recover.' " [2] He turned his face to the wall and prayed to the LORD: [3] "O LORD, remember how faithfully and wholeheartedly I conducted myself in your presence, doing what was pleasing to you!" And Hezekiah wept bitterly.

[4] Before Isaiah had left the central courtyard, the word of the LORD came to him: [5] "Go back and tell Hezekiah, the leader of my people: 'Thus says the LORD, the God of your forefather David: I have heard your prayer and seen your tears. I will heal you. In three days you shall go up to the LORD's temple; [6] I will add fifteen years to your life. I will rescue you and this city from the hand of the king of Assyria; I will be a shield to this city for my own sake, and for the sake of my servant David.' "

[7] Isaiah then ordered a poultice of figs to be brought and applied to the boil, that he might recover. [8] Then Hezekiah asked Isaiah, "What is the sign that the LORD will heal me and that I shall go up to the temple of the LORD on the third day?" [9] Isaiah replied, "This will be the sign for you from the LORD that he will do what he has promised: Shall the shadow go forward or back ten steps?"

---

† **19, 21–31:** vv 21–28 are addressed to Sennacherib, vv 29–31 to Judah.

* **19, 27:** Ps 139, 2f.
19, 34: 2 Sm 7, 12; Hos 1, 7.
19, 35: Sir 48, 21; 2 Chr 32, 21f; Is 37, 36–38;
1 Mc 7, 41; 2 Mc 8, 19.
20, 1–9: 2 Chr 32, 24; Is 38, 1–8.

10 "It is easy for the shadow to advance ten steps," Hezekiah answered. "Rather, let it go back ten steps." 11 So the prophet Isaiah invoked the LORD, who made the shadow retreat the ten steps it had descended on the staircase to the terrace of Ahaz.

12*† At that time, when Merodach-baladan, son of Baladan, king of Babylon, heard that Hezekiah had been ill, he sent letters and gifts to him. 13 Hezekiah was pleased at this, and therefore showed the messengers his whole treasury, his silver, gold, spices and fine oil, his armory, and all that was in his storerooms; there was nothing in his house or in all his realm that Hezekiah did not show them.

14 Then Isaiah the prophet came to King Hezekiah and asked him: "What did these men say to you? Where did they come from?" "They came from a distant land, from Babylon," replied Hezekiah. 15 "What did they see in your house?" the prophet asked. "They saw everything in my house," answered Hezekiah. "There is nothing in my storerooms that I did not show them."

16 Then Isaiah said to Hezekiah: "Hear the word of the LORD: 17 The time is coming when all that is in your house, and everything that your fathers have stored up until this day, shall be carried off to Babylon; nothing shall be left, says the LORD. 18 Some of your own bodily descendants shall be taken and made servants in the palace of the king of Babylon."

19 Hezekiah replied to Isaiah, "The word of the LORD which you have spoken is favorable." For he thought, "There will be peace and security in my lifetime."

20*† The rest of the acts of Hezekiah, all his valor, and his construction of the pool and conduit by which water was brought into the city, are written in the book of the chronicles of the kings of Judah. 21 Hezekiah rested with his ancestors and his son Manasseh succeeded him as king.

Reign of Manasseh

21 1* Manasseh was twelve years old when he began to reign, and he reigned fifty-five years in Jerusalem. His mother's name was Hephzibah. 2 He did evil in the sight of the LORD, following the abominable practices of the nations whom the LORD had cleared out of the way of the Israelites. 3* He rebuilt the high places which his father Hezekiah had destroyed. He erected altars to Baal, and also set up a sacred pole, as Ahab, king of Israel, had done. He worshiped and served the whole host of heaven. 4 He built altars in the temple of the LORD, about which the LORD had said, "I will establish my name in Jerusalem"— 5* altars for the whole host of heaven, in the two courts of the temple.

6 He immolated his son by fire. He practiced soothsaying and divination, and reintroduced the consulting of ghosts and spirits. He did much evil in the LORD's sight and provoked him to anger.

7* The Asherah idol he had made, he set up in the temple, of which the LORD had said to David and to his son Solomon: "In this temple and in Jerusalem, which I have chosen out of all the tribes of Israel, I shall place my name forever. 8 I will not in future allow Israel to be driven off the land I gave their fathers, provided that they are careful to observe all I have commanded them, the entire law which my servant Moses enjoined upon them." 9 But they did not listen, and Manasseh misled them into doing even greater evil than the nations whom the LORD had destroyed at the coming of the Israelites.

10 Then the LORD spoke through his servants the prophets: 11* "Because Manasseh, king of Judah, has practiced these abominations and has done greater evil than all that was done by the Amorites before him, and has led Judah into sin by his idols, 12 therefore thus says the LORD, the God of Israel: 'I will bring such evil on Jerusalem and Judah that, whenever anyone hears of it, his ears shall ring. 13* I will measure Jerusalem with the same cord as I did Samaria, and with the plummet I used for the house of Ahab. I will wipe Jerusalem clean as one wipes a dish, wiping it inside and out. 14 I will cast off the survivors of my inheritance and deliver them into enemy hands, to become a prey and a booty for all their enemies, 15 because they have done evil in my sight and provoked me from the day their fathers came forth from Egypt until today.'"

16 In addition to the sin which he caused Judah to commit, Manasseh did evil in the sight of the LORD, shedding so much innocent blood as to fill the length and breadth of Jerusalem. 17* The rest of the acts of Manasseh, the sin he committed and all that he did, are written in the book of the chronicles of the kings of Judah. 18 Manasseh rested with his ancestors and was buried in his palace garden, the garden of Uzza. His son Amon succeeded him as king.

---

† **20, 12–19:** Duplication of Is 39, 1–8.
20, 20: *Pool and conduit:* Hezekiah's tunnel; cf 2 Chr 32, 30.

* **20, 12f:** Is 39, 1f; 2 Chr 32, 27ff.   **20, 20:** 2 Chr 32, 30; Sir 48, 17.

21, 1–10: 2 Chr 33, 1–10.
21, 3: 2 Kgs 17, 16; 1 Kgs 18, 4; 16, 32f.
21, 5: Lv 18, 21.
21, 7: 2 Sm 7, 13; 1 Kgs 8,

16; 9, 3.
21, 11: 1 Kgs 21, 26; Jer 15, 4.
21, 13: Is 34, 11; Am 7, 7–9; Lam 2, 8.
21, 17: 2 Chr 33, 18ff.

Reign of Amon

19* Amon was twenty-two years old when he began to reign, and he reigned two years in Jerusalem. His mother's name was Meshullemeth, daughter of Haruz of Jotbah. 20 He did evil in the sight of the LORD, as his father Manasseh had done. 21 He followed exactly the path his father had trod, serving and worshiping the idols his father had served. 22 He abandoned the LORD, the God of his fathers, and did not follow the path of the LORD. 23 Subjects of Amon conspired against him and slew the king in his palace, 24 but the people of the land then slew all who had conspired against King Amon, and proclaimed his son Josiah king in his stead. 25 The rest of the acts that Amon did are written in the book of the chronicles of the kings of Judah. 26 He was buried in his own grave in the garden of Uzza, and his son Josiah succeeded him as king.

Reign of Josiah

22 1* Josiah was eight years old when he began to reign, and he reigned thirty-one years in Jerusalem. His mother's name was Jedidah, daughter of Adaiah of Bozkath. 2 He pleased the LORD and conducted himself unswervingly just as his ancestor David had done.

3*† In his eighteenth year, King Josiah sent the scribe Shaphan, son of Azaliah, son of Meshullam, to the temple of the LORD with orders to 4* go to the high priest Hilkiah and have him smelt down the precious metals that had been donated to the temple of the Lord, which the doorkeepers had collected from the people. 5 They were to be consigned to the master workmen in the temple of the LORD, who should then pay them out to the carpenters, builders, and lumbermen making repairs on the temple, 6 and for the purchase of wood and hewn stone for the temple repairs. 7 No reckoning was asked of them regarding the funds consigned to them, because they held positions of trust.

The Book of the Law

8 The high priest Hilkiah informed the scribe Shaphan, "I have found the book of the law in the temple of the LORD." Hilkiah gave the book to Shaphan, who read it. 9 Then the scribe Shaphan went to the king and reported, "Your servants have smelted down the metals available in the temple and have consigned them to the master workmen in the temple of the LORD." 10 The scribe Shaphan also informed the king that the priest Hilkiah had

Josiah Brings Back the Ways of God

What happened to the Covenant? What happened to the Israelites' true traditions and prayer rituals? After worshiping false gods for so long, it seems as if people just forgot about the Covenant! Then in 2 Kgs 22, 8, Hilkiah discovers an old book, King Josiah reads it, and a religious reform is started. Josiah's reform is an effort to know and obey God's law and to restore worship to the one, true God. The holy days and holy ways of God are back—at least for a while (see also 2 Chronicles, chapters 34–35).

Reading can be powerful. Christians have a tremendous tradition of spiritual writings that inspire and renew faith. Spiritual autobiographies like *The Confessions of Saint Augustine; The Story of a Soul*, by Saint Thérèse of Lisieux; and *The Seven Storey Mountain*, by Thomas Merton, are classics. You might try starting with entertaining fictional books with a strong spiritual message, like the seven volumes of *The Chronicles of Narnia*, by C. S. Lewis, or the *Joshua* books, by Joseph F. Girzone. For other suggestions of spiritual writings you might enjoy, ask a parent, youth minister, teacher, or pastor.

▸ **2 Kings, chapters 22–23**

given him a book, and then read it aloud to the king. 11* When the king had heard the contents of the book of the law, he tore his garments 12 and issued this command to Hilkiah the priest, Ahikam, son of Shaphan, Achbor, son of Micaiah, the scribe Shaphan, and the king's servant Asaiah: 13 "Go, consult the LORD for me, for the people, for all Judah, about the stipulations of this book that has been found, for the anger of the LORD has been set furiously ablaze against us, because our fathers did not obey the stipulations of this book, nor fulfill our written obligations."

---

† **22, 3:** *Shaphan:* head of a prominent family in the reign of Josiah, secretary to the king, bearer and reader of the newfound book of the law (vv 3–13; 2 Chr 34, 8f.15–20). He and his sons favored the reform of King Josiah and supported the prophet Jeremiah; cf Jer 26, 24.

* 21, 19–26: 2 Chr 33, 21–25.   22, 4–7: 2 Kgs 12, 11–16.
   22, 1f: 2 Chr 34, 1f.   22, 11–20: 2 Chr 34, 19–28.
22, 3–13: 2 Chr 34, 8–21.

14 So Hilkiah the priest, Ahikam, Achbor, Shaphan, and Asaiah betook themselves to the Second Quarter in Jerusalem, where the prophetess Huldah resided. She was the wife of Shallum, son of Tikvah, son of Harhas, keeper of the wardrobe. When they had spoken to her, 15 she said to them, "Thus says the LORD, the God of Israel: 'Say to the man who sent you to me, 16 Thus says the LORD: I will bring upon this place and upon its inhabitants all the evil that is threatened in the book which the king of Judah has read. 17 Because they have forsaken me and have burned incense to other gods, provoking me by everything to which they turn their hands, my anger is ablaze against this place and it cannot be extinguished.'

18 "But to the king of Judah who sent you to consult the LORD, give this response: 'Thus says the LORD, the God of Israel: As for the threats you have heard, 19 because you were heartsick and have humbled yourself before the LORD when you heard my threats that this place and its inhabitants would become a desolation and a curse; because you tore your garments and wept before me; I in turn have listened, says the LORD. 20 I will therefore gather you to your ancestors; you shall go to your grave in peace, and your eyes shall not see all the evil I will bring upon this place.'" This they reported to the king.

23 1* The king then had all the elders of Judah and of Jerusalem summoned together before him. 2 The king went up to the temple of the LORD with all the men of Judah and all the inhabitants of Jerusalem: priests, prophets, and all the people, small and great. He had the entire contents of the book of the covenant that had been found in the temple of the LORD, read out to them. 3 Standing by the column, the king made a covenant before the LORD that they would follow him and observe his ordinances, statutes and decrees with their whole hearts and souls, thus reviving the terms of the covenant which were written in this book. And all the people stood as participants in the covenant.

4* Then the king commanded the high priest Hilkiah, his vicar, and the doorkeepers to remove from the temple of the LORD all the objects that had been made for Baal, Asherah, and the whole host of heaven. He had these burned outside Jerusalem on the slopes of the Kidron and their ashes carried to Bethel. 5* He also put an end to the pseudo-priests whom the kings of Judah had appointed to burn incense on the high places in the cities of Judah and in the vicinity of Jerusalem, as well as those who burned incense to Baal, to the sun, moon, and signs of the Zodiac, and to the whole host of heaven. 6* From the temple of the LORD he also removed the sacred pole, to the Kidron Valley, outside Jerusalem; there he had it burned and beaten to dust, which was then scattered over the common graveyard. 7*† He tore down the apartments of the cult prostitutes which were in the temple of the LORD, and in which the women wove garments for the Asherah.

8* He brought in all the priests from the cities of Judah, and then defiled, from Geba to Beer-sheba, the high places where they had offered incense. He also tore down the high place of the satyrs, which was at the entrance of the Gate of Joshua, governor of the city, to the left as one enters the city gate. 9 The priests of the high places could not function at the altar of the LORD in Jerusalem; but they, along with their relatives, ate the unleavened bread.

10*† The king also defiled Topheth in the Valley of Ben-hinnom, so that there would no longer be any immolation of sons or daughters by fire in honor of Molech. 11† He did away with the horses which the kings of Judah had dedicated to the sun; these were at the entrance of the temple of the LORD, near the chamber of Nathan-melech the eunuch, which was in the large building. The chariots of the sun he destroyed by fire. 12* He also demolished the altars made by the kings of Judah on the roof (the roof terrace of Ahaz), and the altars made by Manasseh in the two courts of the temple of the LORD. He pulverized them and threw the dust into the Kidron Valley. 13*† The king defiled the high places east of Jerusalem, south of the Mount of Misconduct, which Solomon, king of Israel, had built in honor of Astarte, the Sidonian horror, of Chemosh, the Moabite horror, and of Milcom, the idol of the Ammonites. 14* He broke to pieces the pillars, cut down the sacred poles, and filled the places where they had been with human bones. 15* Likewise the altar which was at Bethel, the high place

†
23, 7: *Cult prostitutes:* of both sexes; cf 1 Kgs 14, 24.
23, 10: *Topheth . . . by fire:* condemned by Deuteronomic law and denounced by Jeremiah (Dt 12, 31; Jer 7, 29ff; Jer 19).
23, 11: *Large building:* to the west of the temple area (1 Chr 26, 18), named in the Hebrew by an Egyptian name for a similar construction.
23, 13: *Mount of Misconduct:* a paranomasia on "Mount of Olives" (in Hebrew *Maschit/mishcheh*) as suggested by the Targum. Cf Vulgate, "Mount of Offense." *Horror . . . idol:* in all three phrases here the Hebrew uses a pejorative designation meaning "abomination."

*
23, 1–5: 2 Chr 34, 29–33.
23, 4: 2 Chr 34, 3–5; Sir 49, 3.
23, 5: Dt 17, 3ff.
23, 6: Dt 16, 21; 1 Kgs 14, 23.
23, 7: 1 Kgs 14, 24; Dt 23, 18f.
23, 8: Dt 12, 2f.
23, 10: Lv 18, 21.
23, 12: 2 Kgs 21, 5.
23, 13: 1 Kgs 11, 7.
23, 14: Dt 16, 21f; 1 Kgs 14, 23.
23, 15: 1 Kgs 12, 31f; 13, 32.

built by Jeroboam, son of Nebat, who caused Israel to sin—this same altar and high place he tore down, breaking up the stones and grinding them to powder, and burning the Asherah.

¹⁶ When Josiah turned and saw the graves there on the mountainside, he ordered the bones taken from the graves and burned on the altar, and thus defiled it in fulfillment of the word of the LORD which the man of God had proclaimed as Jeroboam was standing by the altar on the feast day. When the king looked up and saw the grave of the man of God who had proclaimed these words, ¹⁷ he asked, "What is that tombstone I see?" The men of the city replied, "It is the grave of the man of God who came from Judah and predicted the very things you have done to the altar of Bethel." ¹⁸*† "Let him be," he said, "let no one move his bones." So they left his bones undisturbed together with the bones of the prophet who had come from Samaria.

¹⁹* Josiah also removed all the shrines on the high places near the cities of Samaria which the kings of Israel had erected, thereby provoking the LORD; he did the very same to them as he had done in Bethel. ²⁰ He slaughtered upon the altars all the priests of the high places that were at the shrines, and burned human bones upon them. Then he returned to Jerusalem.

²¹* The king issued a command to all the people to observe the Passover of the LORD, their God, as it was prescribed in that book of the covenant. ²² No Passover such as this had been observed during the period when the Judges ruled Israel, or during the entire period of the kings of Israel and the kings of Judah, ²³ until the eighteenth year of King Josiah, when this Passover of the LORD was kept in Jerusalem.

²⁴*† Further, Josiah did away with the consultation of ghosts and spirits, with the household gods, idols, and all the other horrors to be seen in the land of Judah and in Jerusalem, so that he might carry out the stipulations of the law written in the book that the priest Hilkiah had found in the temple of the LORD.

²⁵* Before him there had been no king who turned to the LORD as he did, with his whole heart, his whole soul, and his whole strength, in accord with the entire law of Moses; nor could any after him compare with him.

²⁶ Yet, because of all the provocations that Manasseh had given, the LORD did not desist from his fiercely burning anger against Judah. ²⁷* The LORD said: "Even Judah will I put out of my sight as I did Israel. I will reject this city, Jerusalem, which I chose, and the temple of which I said, 'There shall my name be.'"

²⁸* The rest of the acts of Josiah, with all that he did, are written in the book of the chronicles of the kings of Judah. ²⁹* In his time Pharaoh Neco, king of Egypt, went up toward the river Euphrates to the king of Assyria. King Josiah set out to confront him, but was slain at Megiddo at the first encounter. ³⁰† His servants brought his body on a chariot from Megiddo to Jerusalem, where they buried him in his own grave. Then the people of the land took Jehoahaz, son of Josiah, anointed him, and proclaimed him king to succeed his father.

Reign of Jehoahaz

³¹* Jehoahaz was twenty-three years old when he began to reign, and he reigned three months in Jerusalem. His mother, whose name was Hamutal, daughter of Jeremiah, was from Libnah. ³² He did evil in the sight of the LORD, just as his forebears had done. ³³† Pharaoh Neco took him prisoner at Riblah in the land of Hamath, thus ending his reign in Jerusalem. He imposed a fine upon the land of a hundred talents of silver and a talent of gold. ³⁴ Pharaoh Neco then appointed Eliakim, son of Josiah, king in place of his father Josiah; he changed his name to Jehoiakim. Jehoahaz he took away with him to Egypt, where he died. ³⁵ Jehoiakim gave the silver and gold to Pharaoh, but taxed the land to raise the amount Pharaoh demanded. He exacted the silver and gold from the people of the land, from each proportionately, to pay Pharaoh Neco.

Reign of Jehoiakim

³⁶* Jehoiakim was twenty-five years old when he began to reign, and he reigned eleven years in Jerusalem. His mother's name was Zebidah, daughter of Pedaiah, from Rumah. ³⁷ He did evil in the sight of the LORD, just as his forebears had done.

24 ¹* During his reign Nebuchadnezzar, king of Babylon, moved against him, and Jehoiakim became his vassal for three years. Then

---

†   **23, 18:** *From Samaria:* more narrowly, from Bethel; cf 1 Kgs 13, 31f.

     23, 24: *Household gods . . . idols:* teraphim. See note on Gn 31, 19.

     23, 30.35: *People of the land:* in this period, the phrase referred to "landed gentry"; in later times it meant "the poor." Cf 2 Kgs 24, 14.

     23, 33: *A talent of gold:* some manuscripts of the Greek and Syriac texts have "ten talents."

*   **23, 18:** 1 Kgs 13, 31.
     23, 19: 2 Chr 34, 6f.
     23, 21: Dt 16, 1–8; 2 Chr 35, 1ff.18f.
     23, 24: 2 Kgs 21, 6; Gn 31, 19; Dt 18, 11; Jgs 18, 14.
     23, 25: Dt 6, 5.
     23, 27: 2 Kgs 24, 2.
     23, 28: 2 Chr 35, 26f.
     23, 29: 2 Chr 35, 20–24.
     23, 31: 2 Chr 36, 2f.
     23, 36f: 2 Chr 36, 4f.
     24, 1–5: 2 Chr 36, 6ff.

Jehoiakim turned and rebelled against him. ² * The LORD loosed against him bands of Chaldeans, Arameans, Moabites, and Ammonites; he loosed them against Judah to destroy it, as the LORD had threatened through his servants the prophets. ³ This befell Judah because the LORD had stated that he would inexorably put them out of his sight for the sins Manasseh had committed in all that he did; ⁴ * and especially because of the innocent blood he shed, with which he filled Jerusalem, the LORD would not forgive.

⁵ * The rest of the acts of Jehoiakim, with all that he did, are written in the book of the chronicles of the kings of Judah. ⁶ Jehoiakim rested with his ancestors, and his son Jehoiachin succeeded him as king. ⁷ The king of Egypt did not again leave his own land, for the king of Babylon had taken all that belonged to the king of Egypt from the wadi of Egypt to the Euphrates River.

Reign of Jehoiachin

⁸† Jehoiachin was eighteen years old when he began to reign, and he reigned three months in Jerusalem. His mother's name was Nehushta, daughter of Elnathan of Jerusalem. ⁹ He did evil in the sight of the LORD, just as his forebears had done.

¹⁰ * At that time the officials of Nebuchadnezzar, king of Babylon, attacked Jerusalem, and the city came under siege. ¹¹ Nebuchadnezzar, king of Babylon, himself arrived at the city while his servants were besieging it. ¹² Then Jehoiachin, king of Judah, together with his mother, his ministers, officers, and functionaries, surrendered to the king of Babylon, who, in the eighth year of his reign, took him captive. ¹³ * He carried off all the treasures of the temple of the LORD and those of the palace, and broke up all the gold utensils that Solomon, king of Israel, had provided in the temple of the LORD, as the LORD had foretold. ¹⁴ He deported all Jerusalem: all the officers and men of the army, ten thousand in number, and all the craftsmen and smiths. None were left among the people of the land except the poor. ¹⁵ * He deported Jehoiachin to Babylon, and also led captive from Jerusalem to Babylon the king's mother and wives, his functionaries, and the chief men of the land. ¹⁶ The king of Babylon also led captive to Babylon all seven thousand men of the army, and a thousand craftsmen and smiths, all of them trained soldiers. ¹⁷ In place of Jehoiachin, the king of Babylon appointed his uncle Mattaniah king, and changed his name to Zedekiah.

Reign of Zedekiah

¹⁸ * Zedekiah was twenty-one years old when he became king, and he reigned eleven years in Jerusalem. His mother's name was Hamutal, daughter of Jeremiah of Libnah. ¹⁹ He also did evil in the sight of the LORD, just as Jehoiakim had done. ²⁰ * The LORD'S anger befell Jerusalem and Judah till he cast them out from his presence. Thus Zedekiah rebelled against the king of Babylon.

25 ¹ *† In the tenth month of the ninth year of Zedekiah's reign, on the tenth day of the month, Nebuchadnezzar, king of Babylon, and his whole army advanced against Jerusalem, encamped around it, and built siege walls on every side. ² The siege of the city continued until the eleventh year of Zedekiah. ³ On the ninth day of the fourth month, when famine had gripped the city, and the people had no more bread, ⁴ the city walls were breached. Then the king and all the soldiers left the city by night through the gate between the two walls which was near the king's garden. Since

did you KNOW?
The Fall of Jerusalem

The second conquest and exile described in 2 Kings (see "The First Captivity," 17, 5–18, for the first) involves the southern kingdom, Judah. Judah was conquered by the Babylonians in 587 B.C., which is why that event is often referred to as the Babylonian Exile (see map 5, "The Babylonian Empire"). The author of Kings implies that the kingdom of Judah lasted longer than the kingdom of Israel because it had faithful reformer kings like Hezekiah and Josiah. The fall of Judah was particularly devastating because both Jerusalem, David's city, and the Temple, the central place of worship, were destroyed. The whole Book of Lamentations is an expression of the sorrow and grief the people experienced as a result.

▶ **2 Kgs 25, 1–21**

---

† **24, 8:** *He reigned three months:* in the year 597 B.C.
25, 1–30: This chapter parallels Jer 39 and 52; see notes to those parts of Jeremiah.

* 24, 2: 2 Kgs 23, 27.
24, 4: 2 Kgs 21, 16.
24, 5: 2 Chr 36, 8.
24, 10: 2 Chr 36, 10; Dn 1, 1f.
24, 13: 2 Kgs 20, 17; Is 39, 6.
24, 15: Est A, 3; 2, 6.
24, 18: 2 Chr 36, 9; Jer 37, 1f; 52, 1ff.
24, 20: 2 Kgs 22, 17; 23, 27.
25, 1–21: Jer 39, 1–10; 52, 4–28.

the Chaldeans had the city surrounded, they went in the direction of the Arabah. [5] But the Chaldean army pursued the king and overtook him in the desert near Jericho, abandoned by his whole army.

[6] The king was therefore arrested and brought to Riblah to the king of Babylon, who pronounced sentence on him. [7] He had Zedekiah's sons slain before his eyes. Then he blinded Zedekiah, bound him with fetters, and had him brought to Babylon.

[8] On the seventh day of the fifth month (this was in the nineteenth year of Nebuchadnezzar, king of Babylon), Nebuzaradan, captain of the bodyguard, came to Jerusalem as the representative of the king of Babylon. [9]* He burned the house of the LORD, the palace of the king, and all the houses of Jerusalem; every large building was destroyed by fire. [10] Then the Chaldean troops who were with the captain of the guard tore down the walls that surrounded Jerusalem.

[11]† Then Nebuzaradan, captain of the guard, led into exile the last of the people remaining in the city, and those who had deserted to the king of Babylon, and the last of the artisans. [12] But some of the country's poor, Nebuzaradan, captain of the guard, left behind as vinedressers and farmers.

[13]* The bronze pillars that belonged to the house of the LORD, and the wheeled carts and the bronze sea in the house of the LORD, the Chaldeans broke into pieces; they carried away the bronze to Babylon. [14]* They took also the pots, the shovels, the snuffers, the bowls, the pans and all the bronze vessels used for service. [15] The fire-holders and the bowls which were of gold or silver the captain of the guard also carried off. [16] The weight in bronze of the two pillars, the bronze sea, and the wheeled carts, all of them furnishings which Solomon had made for the house of the LORD, was never calculated. [17]* Each of the pillars was eighteen cubits high; a bronze capital five cubits high surmounted each pillar, and a network with pomegranates encircled the capital, all of bronze; and so for the other pillar, as regards the network.

[18] The captain of the guard also took Seraiah the high priest, Zephaniah the second priest, and the three keepers of the entry. [19] And from the city he took one courtier, a commander of soldiers, five men in the personal service of the king who were still in the city, the scribe of the army commander, who mustered the people of the land, and sixty of the common people still remaining in the city. [20] The captain of the guard, Nebuzaradan, arrested these and brought them to the king of Babylon at Riblah; [21] the king had them struck down and put to death in Riblah, in the land of Hamath. Thus was Judah exiled from her land.

Governorship of Gedaliah

[22]* As for the people whom he had allowed to remain in the land of Judah, Nebuchadnezzar, king of Babylon, appointed as their governor Gedaliah, son of Ahikam, son of Shaphan. [23] Hearing that the king of Babylon had appointed Gedaliah governor, all the army commanders with their men came to him at Mizpah: Ishmael, son of Nethaniah, Johanan, son of Kareah, Seraiah, son of Tanhumeth the Netophathite, and Jaazaniah, from Bethmaacah. [24] Gedaliah gave the commanders and their men his oath. "Do not be afraid of the Chaldean officials," he said to them. "Remain in the country and serve the king of Babylon, and all will be well with you."

[25] But in the seventh month Ishmael, son of Nethaniah, son of Elishama, of royal descent, came with ten men, attacked Gedaliah and killed him, along with the Jews and Chaldeans who were in Mizpah with him. [26] Then all the people, great and small, left with the army commanders and went to Egypt for fear of the Chaldeans.

Release of Jehoiachin

[27]* In the thirty-seventh year of the exile of Jehoiachin, king of Judah, on the twenty-seventh day of the twelfth month, Evil-merodach, king of Babylon, in the inaugural year of his own reign, raised up Jehoiachin, king of Judah, from prison. [28] He spoke kindly to him and gave him a throne higher than that of the other kings who were with him in Babylon. [29] Jehoiachin took off his prison garb and ate at the king's table as long as he lived. [30] The allowance granted him by the king was a perpetual allowance, in fixed daily amounts, for as long as he lived.

25, 11: *Those who had deserted:* perhaps on the advice of Jeremiah; cf Jer 38, 2f.

25, 9: 2 Chr 36, 19; Ps 74, 7.
25, 13: 2 Kgs 16, 17; 1 Kgs 7,
  15–39; 2 Chr 3, 15;
  36, 18; Jer 27, 19.
25, 14: 1 Kgs 7, 48ff.
25, 17: 1 Kgs 7, 15; Jer 52,
  21ff.
25, 22–26: Jer 40, 5.7—41, 1–3.
25, 27–30: Jer 52, 31–34.

Have you ever had a friendly disagreement with someone over the interpretation of a movie? Did you each emphasize different aspects of the movie to support your interpretation? The First and Second Books of Chronicles are another interpretation of the history of the people of Israel. These books downplay the Covenant and emphasize the importance of institutional ritual and worship of God.

At a Glance

I. Genealogical Tables (1 Chr 1, 1—9, 34).

II. The History of David (1 Chr 9, 35—29, 30).

I. The Reign of Solomon (2 Chr 1, 1—9, 31).

II. The Monarchy before Hezekiah (2 Chr 10, 1—27, 9).

III. Reforms of Hezekiah and Josiah (2 Chr 28, 1—36, 1).

IV. End of the Kingdom (2 Chr 36, 2–23).

In-depth

The Chronicler is the name given to the unknown author (or authors) of 1 and 2 Chronicles. The Chronicler, writing after the Israelites returned from the Exile in Babylon, has a unique perspective, so unique that he almost never mentions the Sinai Covenant or Moses (central themes throughout other parts of the Old Testament). Because the Israelites cannot have their own king, the Chronicler emphasizes a new type of reign, one governed by priests instead of kings.

The Chronicler uses two types of material—genealogies and lively sermons—to summarize Israel's history from the Creation to around 525 B.C. But he primarily focuses on Kings David and Solomon. They are praised extensively because of their role in centralizing worship in Jerusalem and building the Temple. Many of the negative stories about David from 2 Samuel—such as his affair with Bathsheba—are not even mentioned. The Chronicler wants nothing to tarnish the people's memory of an ideal kingdom that might one day be restored.

Second Chronicles also focuses on the southern kingdom of Judah and ignores the northern kingdom of Israel after Solomon's death. This may well be due to a bias of the priestly class in Jerusalem against the religious practice of the northern tribes. This bias lasted into Jesus' time.

The goal of 1 and 2 Chronicles was to give the Israelites hope for the future after returning from the Exile. The Chronicler reminded them that if they maintained their religious practices and worship of God, they would continue to be God's people.

Quick Facts

Period Covered
Creation to the end of the Babylonian captivity

Author
a Levite cantor and scribe writing after the return to Jerusalem around 400 B.C.

Theme
Israel can secure its future by continuing its worship in the pattern established by David.

1 Chronicles

Chap. 15

I: Genealogical Tables

From Adam to Abraham

1 1*† Adam, Seth, Enosh, 2* Kenan, Mahalalel, Jared, 3* Enoch, Methuselah, Lamech, 4* Noah, Shem, Ham, and Japheth. 5* The descendants of Japheth were Gomer, Magog, Madai, Javan, Tubal, Meshech, and Tiras. 6 The descendants of Gomer were Ashkenaz, Riphath, and Togarmah. 7 The descendants of Javan were Elishah, Tarshis, the Kittim, and the Rodanim.

8* The descendants of Ham were Cush, Mesraim, Put, and Canaan. 9 The descendants of Cush were Seba, Havilah, Sabta, Raama, and Sabteca. The descendants of Raama were Sheba and Dedan. 10 Cush became the father of Nimrod, who was the first to be a conqueror on the earth. 11* Mesraim became the father of the Ludim, Anamim, Lehabim, Naphtuhim, 12 Pathrusim, Casluhim, and Caphtorim, from whom the Philistines sprang. 13 Canaan became the father of Sidon, his first-born, and Heth, 14 and the Jebusite, the Amorite, the Girgashite, 15 the Hivite, the Arkite, the Sinite, 16 the Arvadite, the Zemarite, and the Hamathite.

17* The descendants of Shem were Elam, Asshur, Arpachshad, Lud, and Aram. The descendants of Aram were Uz, Hul, Gether, and Mash. 18 Arpachshad became the father of Shelah, and Shelah became the father of Eber. 19 Two sons were born to Eber; the first was named Peleg (for in his time the world was divided), and his brother was Joktan. 20 Joktan became the father of Almodad, Sheleph, Hazarmaveth, Jerah, 21 Hadoram, Uzal, Diklah, 22 Ebal, Abimael, Sheba, 23 Ophir, Havilah, and Jobab; all these were the sons of Joktan.

24* Shem, Arpachshad, Shelah, 25 Eber, Peleg, Reu, 26 Serug, Nahor, Terah, 27* Abram, who was Abraham.

From Abraham to Jacob

28* The sons of Abraham were Isaac and Ishmael. 29* These were their descendants:

Nebaioth, the first-born of Ishmael, then Kedar, Adbeel, Mibsam, 30 Mishma, Dumah, Massa, Hadad, Tema, 31 Jetur, Naphish, and Kedemah. These were the descendants of Ishmael.

† **1, 1—9, 34:** The Chronicler set as his task the retelling, from his particular viewpoint, of the story of God's people from the beginning to his own day. Since his primary interest was the history of David and the Davidic dynasty of Judah, he presents through mere genealogical lists a summary of what preceded the reign of Saul, David's predecessor in the kingdom. The sources for these genealogies are mostly the canonical Hebrew Scriptures that were already in their present form in his time. The cross references in this book indicate in each case the scriptural sources used.

1, 1: 1 Chr 4, 25f; Gn 5, 3.6.9.
1, 2ff: Gn 5, 9–32; 10, 2ff.
1, 3: Gn 4, 25.
1, 4: Gn 5, 32; 6, 10; 9, 18.
1, 5ff: Gn 10, 2ff.
1, 8: Gn 10, 8.
1, 11–16: Gn 10, 13–18.
1, 17–23: Gn 10, 22–29; 11, 10–18.
1, 24–27: Gn 11, 10–26; Lk 3, 34ff.
1, 27: Gn 17, 5; Neh 9, 7.
1, 28: Gn 16, 11.15; 21, 2f; Gal 4, 22f; Heb 11, 11.
1, 29ff: Gn 25, 13–16.

³²* The descendants of Keturah, Abraham's concubine: she bore Zimran, Jokshan, Medan, Midian, Ishbak, and Shuah. The sons of Jokshan were Sheba and Dedan. ³³ The descendants of Midian were Ephah, Epher, Hanoch, Abida, and Eldaah. All these were the descendants of Keturah.

³⁴* Abraham became the father of Isaac. The sons of Isaac were Esau and Israel.

³⁵* The sons of Esau were Eliphaz, Reuel, Jeush, Jalam, and Korah. ³⁶ The sons of Eliphaz were Teman, Omar, Zephi, Gatam, Kenaz, [Timna,] and Amalek. ³⁷ The sons of Reuel were Nahath, Zerah, Shammah, and Mizzah.

³⁸*† The descendants of Seir were Lotan, Shobal, Zibeon, Anah, Dishon, Ezer, and Dishan. ³⁹ The sons of Lotan were Hori and Homam; Timna was the sister of Lotan. ⁴⁰ The sons of Shobal were Alian, Manahath, Ebal, Shephi, and Onam. The sons of Zibeon were Aiah and Anah. ⁴¹ The sons of Anah: Dishon. The sons of Dishon were Hemdan, Eshban, Ithran, and Cheran. ⁴² The sons of Ezer were Bilhan, Zaavan, and Jaakan. The sons of Dishan were Uz and Aran.

⁴³* The kings who reigned in the land of Edom before they had Israelite kings were the following: Bela, son of Beor, the name of whose city was Ninhabah. ⁴⁴* When Bela died, Jobab, son of Zerah, from Bozrah, succeeded him. ⁴⁵* When Jobab died, Husham, from the land of the Temanites, succeeded him. ⁴⁶ Husham died and Hadad, son of Bedad, succeeded him. He overthrew the Midianites on the Moabite plateau, and the name of his city was Avith. ⁴⁷ Hadad died and Samlah of Masrekah succeeded him. ⁴⁸ Samlah died and Shaul from Rehoboth-han-nahar succeeded him. ⁴⁹ When Shaul died, Baalhanan, son of Achbor, succeeded him. ⁵⁰ Baalhanan died and Hadad succeeded him. The name of his city was Pai, and his wife's name was Mehetabel. She was the daughter of Matred, who was the daughter of Mezahab. ⁵¹* After Hadad died. . . .

These were the chiefs of Edom: the chiefs of Timna, Aliah, Jetheth, ⁵² Oholibamah, Elah, Pinon, ⁵³ Kenaz, Teman, Mibzar, ⁵⁴ Magdiel, and Iram were the chiefs of Edom.

2 ¹* These were the sons of Israel: Reuben, Simeon, Levi, Judah, Issachar, Zebulun, ²* Dan, Joseph, Benjamin, Naphtali, Gad, and Asher.

Judah

³*† The sons of Judah were: Er, Onan, and Shelah; these three were born to him of Bathshua, a Canaanite woman. But Judah's first-born, Er, was wicked in the sight of the LORD, so he killed him. ⁴* Judah's daughter-in-law Tamar bore him Perez and Zerah, so that he had five sons in all.

⁵* The sons of Perez were Hezron and Hamul. ⁶* The sons of Zerah were Zimri, Ethan, Heman, Calcol, and Darda—five in all. ⁷* The sons of Zimri: Carmi. The sons of Carmi: Achar, who brought trouble upon Israel by violating the ban. ⁸ The sons of Ethan: Azariah. ⁹*† The sons born to Hezron were Jerahmeel, Ram, and Chelubai.

¹⁰*† Ram became the father of Amminadab, and Amminadab became the father of Nahshon, a prince of the Judahites. ¹¹* Nahshon became the father of Salma. Salma became the father of Boaz. ¹² Boaz became the father of Obed. Obed became the father of Jesse. ¹³* Jesse became the father of Eliab, his first-born, of Abinadab, the second son, Shimea, the third,* ¹⁴ Nethanel, the fourth, Raddai, the fifth, ¹⁵ Ozem, the sixth, and David, the seventh. ¹⁶* Their sisters were Zeruiah and Abigail. Zeruiah had three sons: Abishai, Joab, and Asahel. ¹⁷* Abigail bore Amasa, whose father was Jether the Ishmaelite.

¹⁸*† By his wife Azubah, Caleb, son of Hezron, became the father of a daughter, Jerioth. Her sons were Jesher, Shobab, and Ardon. ¹⁹* When Azubah died, Caleb married Ephrath, who bore him Hur. ²⁰* Hur became the father of Uri, and Uri became the father of Bezalel. ²¹* Then Hezron had relations with the daughter of Machir, the father of Gilead, having married her when he was sixty years old. She bore him Segub. ²²* Segub became the father of

---

1, 38: *Seir:* another name for Esau (v 35) or Edom (v 43).

2, 3—4, 23: For two reasons, the Chronicler places the genealogy of the tribe of Judah before that of the other tribes, giving it also at greater length than the others: because of his interest in David and because in the Chronicler's time the people of God were almost exclusively Jews. Both David and the Jews were of the tribe of Judah.

2, 9: *Chelubai:* a variant form of the name Caleb (vv 18.42), distinct from Chelub of 1 Chr 4, 11.

2, 10–17: Immediate ancestors of David. A similar list is given in Ru 4, 19–22; each list, independent of the other, derives from a common source.

2, 18–24: Descendants of Caleb. In 1 Chr 4, 15, as is often the case in the Pentateuch (Nm 13, 6; 14, 6.30; 26, 65; etc.), Caleb is called son of Jephunneh. Here he is called son of Hezron, perhaps because the Calebites were reckoned as part of the clan of the Hezronites.

1, 32f: Gn 25, 1–4.   32, 28f; Mt 1, 2; Lk 3,
1, 34: Gn 21, 2f; 25, 19.25f.   34.

1, 35ff: Gn 36, 4f.10–13.15ff.   22, 20.
1, 38–42: Gn 36, 20–28.   2, 9: Rv 4, 19; Mt 1, 3.
1, 43–54: Gn 36, 31–43.   2, 10: Rv 4, 19; Mt 1, 4.
  1, 44: Is 34, 6; 63, 1; Jer 49,   2, 11f: Nm 1, 7; Rv 4, 20f; Mt
    13.22.   1, 4f.
  1, 45: Gn 36, 11; Jb 2, 11; Jer   2, 13ff: 1 Sm 16, 6–13; 17,
    49, 7.20.   13f.
1, 51–54: Gn 36, 40–43.   2, 13: 2 Chr 11, 18.
  2, 1: Gn 29, 32–35; 30,   2, 16: 2 Sm 2, 18.
    18.20; 35, 23.   2, 17: 2 Sm 17, 25; 19, 14;
  2, 2: Gn 30, 6.8.11.13.24;   20, 4–13.
    35, 18.24ff.   2, 18: 1 Chr 2, 24.
  2, 3: 1 Chr 4, 21; Gn 38,   2, 19: 1 Chr 2, 24.
    1–5; 46, 12.   2, 20: Ex 24, 14; 31, 2; 35,
  2, 4: Gn 38, 7.13–30; 46,   30; 2 Chr 1, 5.
    12; Rv 4, 12.18; Mt   2, 21: Nm 26, 29; 27, 1; 32,
    1, 3.   32; Jos 13, 31; Jgs 5,
  2, 5: Gn 46, 12.   14.
  2, 6: 1 Kgs 5, 11.   2, 22: Nm 32, 41; 1 Kgs 4,
  2, 7: Jos 7, 1.18ff.24f.   13.

Jair, who possessed twenty-three cities in the land of Gilead. 23* Geshur and Aram took from them the villages of Jair, that is, Kenath and its towns, sixty cities in all, which had belonged to the sons of Machir, the father of Gilead. 24* After the death of Hezron, Caleb had relations with Ephrathah, the widow of his father Hezron, and she bore him Ashhur, the father of Tekoa.

25*† The sons of Jerahmeel, the first-born of Hezron, were Ram, the first-born, then Bunah, Oren, and Ozem, his brothers. 26 Jerahmeel also had another wife, Atarah by name, who was the mother of Onam. 27 The sons of Ram, the first-born of Jerahmeel, were Maaz, Jamin, and Eker. 28 The sons of Onam were Shammai and Jada. The sons of Shammai were Nadab and Abishur. 29 Abishur's wife, who was named Abihail, bore him Ahban and Molid. 30 The sons of Nadab were Seled and Appaim. Seled died without sons. 31* The sons of Appaim: Ishi. The sons of Ishi: Sheshan. The sons of Sheshan: Ahlai. 32 The sons of Jada, the brother of Shammai, were Jether and Jonathan. Jether died without sons. 33 The sons of Jonathan were Peleth and Zaza. These were the descendants of Jerahmeel. 34 Sheshan, who had no sons, only daughters, had an Egyptian slave named Jarha. 35 Sheshan gave his daughter in marriage to his slave Jarha, and she bore him Attai. 36 Attai became the father of Nathan. Nathan became the father of Zabad. 37 Zabad became the father of Ephlal. Ephlal became the father of Obed. 38 Obed became the father of Jehu. Jehu became the father of Azariah. 39 Azariah became the father of Helez. Helez became the father of Eleasah. 40 Eleasah became the father of Sismai. Sismai became the father of Shallum. 41 Shallum became the father of Jekamiah. Jekamiah became the father of Elishama.

42† The descendants of Caleb, the brother of Jerahmeel: [Mesha] his first-born, who was the father of Ziph. Then the sons of Mareshah, who was the father of Hebron. 43 The sons of Hebron were Korah, Tappuah, Rekem, and Shema. 44 Shema became the father of Raham, who was the father of Jorkeam. Rekem became the father of Shammai. 45 The sons of Shammai: Maon, who was the father of Beth-zur. 46 Ephah, Caleb's concubine, bore Ha-

ran, Moza, and Gazez. Haran became the father of Gazez. 47 The sons of Jahdai were Regem, Jotham, Geshan, Pelet, Ephah, and Shaaph. 48 Maacah, Caleb's concubine, bore Sheber and Tirhanah. 49* She also bore Shaaph, the father of Madmannah, Sheva, the father of Machbenah, and the father of Gibea. Achsah was Caleb's daughter.

50† These were descendants of Caleb, sons of Hur, the first-born of Ephrathah: Shobal, the father of Kiriath-jearim, 51 Salma, the father of Bethlehem, and Hareph, the father of Bethgader. 52 The sons of Shobal, the father of Kiriath-jearim, were Reaiah, half the Manahathites, 53* and the clans of Kiriath-jearim: the Ithrites, the Puthites, the Shumathites, and the Mishraites. From these the people of Zorah and the Eshtaolites derived. 54 The descendants of Salma were Bethlehem, the Netophathites, Atrothbeth-Joab, half the Manahathites, and the Zorites. 55* The clans of the Sopherim dwelling in Jabez were the Tirathites, the Shimeathites, and the Sucathites. They were the Kenites, who came from Hammath of the ancestor of the Rechabites.

3 1*† The following were the sons of David who were born to him in Hebron: the first-born, Amnon, by Ahinoam of Jezreel; the second, Daniel,† by Abigail of Carmel; 2 the third, Absalom, son of Maacah, who was the daughter of Talmai, king of Geshur; the fourth, Adonijah, son of Haggith; 3 the fifth, Shephatiah, by Abital; the sixth, Ithream, by his wife Eglah. 4* Six in all were born to him in Hebron, where he reigned seven years and six months. Then he reigned thirty-three years in Jerusalem, 5*† where the following were born to him: Shimea, Shobab, Nathan, Solomon—four by Bathsheba, the daughter of Ammiel,* 6 Ibhar, Elishua, Eliphelet, 7 Nogah, Nepheg, Japhia, 8 Elishama, Eliada, and Eliphelet—nine. 9* All these were sons of David, in addition to other sons by concubines; and Tamar was their sister.

10*† The son of Solomon was Rehoboam, whose son was Abijah, whose son was Asa, whose son was Jehoshaphat,* 11* whose son was Joram, whose son was Ahaziah, whose son was Joash, 12* whose son was Amaziah, whose son was Azariah, whose son was Jotham, 13* whose son was Ahaz, whose son

---

2, 25–41: The Jerahmeelites were a clan in the Negeb of Judah.
2, 42–49: Another list, dating from preexilic times, of the Calebites, a clan that inhabited the south of Judah.
2, 50–55: The Hurites, a clan dwelling to the south and west of Jerusalem and related to the Calebites.
3, 1–9: David's sons.
3, 1: *Daniel:* called Chileab in 2 Sm 3, 3.
3, 5: *Shimea:* called Shammua in 2 Sm 5, 14. *Ammiel:* called Eliam in 2 Sm 11, 3.
3, 10–16: The kings of Judah from Solomon to the destruction of Jerusalem by the Babylonians.

2, 23: Dt 3, 14; Jos 13, 30; Jgs 10, 4.
2, 24: 1 Chr 2, 19; 2 Sm 14, 2; 2 Chr 11, 6.
2, 25: 1 Sm 27, 10; 30, 29; Jb 32, 2.
2, 31: 1 Chr 4, 20.
2, 49: Jos 15, 16; Jgs 1, 12.
2, 53: Jgs 18, 2.
2, 55: Nm 24, 21; Jgs 1, 16; 4, 11; 1 Sm 15, 6.
3, 1–4: 2 Sm 3, 2–5.
3, 4: 2 Sm 2, 11; 5, 5.
3, 5–8: 2 Sm 5, 14ff.
3, 5: 2 Sm 5, 5.

3, 9: 2 Sm 13, 1f.
3, 10–17: Mt 1, 7–12.
3, 10: 1 Kgs 11, 43; 14, 31; 15, 1.8.24; 2 Chr 9, 31; 12, 16; 13, 23; 17, 1.
3, 11: 1 Kgs 22, 51; 2 Chr 21, 1; 22, 1; 24, 1.27.
3, 12: 2 Kgs 12, 21; 14, 21; 15, 7; 2 Chr 25, 1; 26, 1.23; 27, 1.
3, 13: 2 Kgs 15, 38; 16, 20; 20, 21; 2 Chr 28, 1.27; 32, 33.

did you KNOW?

Genealogies

Look at all these names! Our present-day interest in family trees obviously has ancient roots. The first nine chapters of 1 Chronicles consist entirely of family trees—or genealogies—tracing the history of Israel from Adam to Saul. In a culture where not only money and identity but also the offices of priest and king passed from one generation to another, it was essential to be able to trace one's bloodline.

The many genealogies of the Old Testament answer important questions: How were the various tribes related to one another? Who were a particular tribe's ancestors? What right did a certain group or person have to the office of priest or king? The Chronicler lists the genealogies of David and Levi in considerable detail. The kingship and the priesthood were clearly of special interest to him.

▶ 1 Chronicles, chapters 1–9

was Hezekiah, whose son was Manasseh, ¹⁴* whose son was Amon, whose son was Josiah. ¹⁵*† The sons of Josiah were: the first-born, Johanan; the second, Jehoiakim; the third, Zedekiah; the fourth, Shallum. ¹⁶* The sons of Jehoiakim were: Jeconiah, his son; Zedekiah, his son.

¹⁷*† The sons of Jeconiah the captive were: Shealtiel, ¹⁸† Malchiram, Pedaiah, Shenazzar, Jekamiah, Shama, and Nedabiah. ¹⁹† The sons of Pedaiah were Zerubbabel and Shimei. The sons of Zerubbabel were Meshullam and Hananiah; Shelomith was their sister. ²⁰ The sons of Meshullam were Hashubah, Ohel, Berechiah, Hasadiah, Jushab-hesed—five. ²¹ The sons of Hananiah were Pelatiah, Jeshaiah, Rephaiah, Arnan, Obadiah, and Shecaniah. ²²* The sons of Shecaniah were Shemaiah, Hattush, Igal, Bariah, Neariah, Shaphat—six. ²³ The sons of Neariah were Elioenai, Hizkiah, and Azrikam—three. ²⁴ The sons of Elioenai were Hodaviah, Eliashib, Pelaiah, Akkub, Johanan, Delaiah, and Anani—seven.

4 ¹*† The descendants of Judah were: Perez, Hezron, Carmi, Hur, and Shobal. ² Reaiah, the son of Shobal, became the father of Jahath, and Jahath became the father of Ahumai and Lahad. These were the clans of the Zorathites.

³ These were the descendants of Hareph, the father of Etam: Jezreel, Ishma, and Idbash; their sister was named Hazzelelponi. ⁴ Penuel was the father of Gedor, and Ezer the father of Hushah. These were the descendants of Hur, the first-born of Ephrathah, the father of Bethlehem.

⁵* Ashhur, the father of Tekoa, had two wives, Helah and Naarah. ⁶ Naarah bore him Ahuzzam, Hepher, the Temenites and the Ahashtarites. These were the descendants of Naarah. ⁷ The sons of Helah were Zereth, Izhar, Ethnan, and Koz. ⁸ Koz became the father of Anub and Zobebah, as well as of the clans of Aharhel, son of Harum. ⁹ Jabez was the most distinguished of the brothers. His mother had named him Jabez, saying, "I bore him with pain." ¹⁰ Jabez prayed to the God of Israel: "Oh, that you may truly bless me and extend my boundaries! Help me and make me free of misfortune, without pain!" And God granted his prayer.

¹¹ Chelub, the brother of Shuhah, became the father of Mehir, who was the father of Eshton. ¹² Eshton became the father of Beth-rapha, Paseah, and Tehinnah, the father of the city of Nahash. These were the men of Recah.

¹³* The sons of Kenaz were Othniel and Seraiah. The sons of Othniel were Hathath and Meonothai; ¹⁴ Meonothai became the father of Ophrah. Seraiah became the father of Joab, the father of Geharashim, so called because they were craftsmen. ¹⁵* The sons of Caleb, son of Jephunneh, were Ir,

---

3, 15: *Shallum:* the same as Jehoahaz, Josiah's successor; cf Jer 22, 11.

3, 17–24: The descendants of King Jechoniah up to the time of the Chronicler. If twenty-five years are allowed to each generation, the ten generations between Jechoniah and Anani (the last name on the list) would bring the birth of the latter to about 405 B.C.—an important item in establishing the approximate date of the Chronicler.

3, 18: *Shenazzar:* presumably the same as Sheshbazzar of Ezr 1, 8.11; 5, 14ff, the prince of Judah who was the first Jewish governor of Judah after the exile. Both forms of the name probably go back to the Babylonian name *Sin-ab-ussar* signifying, "O [god] Sin, protect [our] father!"

3, 19: *Zerubbabel:* here called the son of Pedaiah, though elsewhere (Hg 1, 12.14; 2, 2.23; Ezr 3, 2.8; 5, 2; Neh 12, 1) called son of Shealtiel. The latter term may merely mean that Zerubbabel succeeded Shealtiel as head of the house of David.

4, 1–43: The southern tribes.

3, 14: 2 Kgs 21, 18.26; 2 Chr 33, 20.25.	**3, 22:** Neh 3, 29.
3, 15: 2 Kgs 23, 34; 24, 17; 2 Chr 36, 4.10.	**4, 1:** 1 Chr 2, 4f.7.9.50; Gn 38, 29; 46, 12; Mt 1, 3.
3, 16: 2 Kgs 24, 6.17; 2 Chr 36, 8.10.	**4, 5:** 1 Chr 2, 24.
3, 17.19: Ezr 2, 2; 3, 2.8; 5, 2; Sir 49, 11; Hg 1, 1.12.14; Mt 1, 12f; Lk 3, 27.	**4, 13:** Jos 15, 17; Jgs 1, 13; 3, 9.11.
	4, 15: Nm 13, 6; 14, 6; 32, 12; Jos 14, 6.14.

Elah, and Naam. The sons of Elah were . . . and Kenaz. [16] The sons of Jehallelel were Ziph, Ziphah, Tiria, and Asarel. [17]* The sons of Ezrah were Jether, Mered, Epher, and Jalon. Jether became the father of Miriam, Shammai, and Ishbah, the father of Eshtemoa. [. . . . . .] [18] His (Mered's) Egyptian wife bore Jared, the father of Gedor, Heber, the father of Soco, and Jekuthiel, the father of Zanoah. These were the sons of Bithiah, the daughter of Pharaoh, whom Mered married. [19] The sons of his Jewish wife, the sister of Naham, the father of Keilah, were Shimon the Garmite and Ishi the Maacathite. [20] The sons of Shimon were Amnon, Rinnah, Benhanan, and Tilon. The son of Ishi was Zoheth and the son of Zoheth. . . .

[21]* The descendants of Shelah, son of Judah, were: Er, the father of Lecah; Laadah, the father of Mareshah; the clans of the linen weavers' guild in Beth-ashbea; [22] Jokim; the men of Cozeba; and Joash and Saraph, who held property in Moab, but returned to Bethlehem. [These are events of old.] [23] They were potters and inhabitants of Netaim and Gederah, where they lived in the king's service.

Simeon

[24]* The sons of Simeon were Nemuel, Jamin, Jachin, Zerah, and Shaul, [25] whose son was Shallum, whose son was Mibsam, whose son was Mishma. [26] The descendants of Mishma were his son Hammuel, whose son was Zaccur, whose son was Shimei. [27] Shimei had sixteen sons and six daughters. His brothers, however, did not have many sons, and as a result all their clans did not equal the number of the Judahites.

[28]* They dwelt in Beer-sheba, Moladah, Hazarshual, [29] Bilhah, Ezem, Tolad, [30] Bethuel, Hormah, Ziklag, [31] Beth-marcaboth, Hazar-susim, Bethbiri, and Shaaraim. Until David came to reign, these were their cities [32] and their villages. Etam, also, and Ain, Rimmon, Tochen, and Ashan—five cities, [33] together with all their outlying villages as far as Baal. Here is where they dwelt, and so it was inscribed of them in their family records.

[34] Meshobab, Jamlech, Joshah, son of Amaziah, [35] Joel, Jehu, son of Joshibiah, son of Seraiah, son of Asiel, [36] Elioenai, Jaakobath, Jeshohaiah, Asaiah, Adiel, Jesimiel, Benaiah, [37] Ziza, son of Shiphi, son of Allon, son of Jedaiah, son of Shimri, son of Shemaiah— [38]* these just named were princes in their clans, and their ancestral houses spread out to such an extent [39]† that they went to the approaches of Gedor, east of the valley, seeking pasture for their flocks. [40] They found abundant and good pastures, and the land was spacious, quiet, and peaceful. [41]* They who have just been listed by name set out during the reign of Hezekiah, king of Judah, and attacked the tents of Ham (for Hamites dwelt there formerly) and also the Meunites who were there. They pronounced against them the ban that is still in force and dwelt in their place because they found pasture there for their flocks.

[42] Five hundred of them (the Simeonites) went to Mount Seir under the leadership of Pelatiah, Neariah, Rephaiah, and Uzziel, sons of Ishi. [43]* They attacked the surviving Amalekites who had escaped, and have resided there to the present day.

Reuben

5 [1]*† The sons of Reuben, the first-born of Israel. (He was indeed the first-born, but because he disgraced the couch of his father his birthright was given to the sons of Joseph, son of Israel, so that he is not listed in the family records according to birthright. [2]* Judah, in fact, became powerful among his brothers, so that the ruler came from him, though the birthright had been Joseph's.) [3]* The sons of Reuben, the first-born of Israel, were Hanoch, Pallu, Hezron, and Carmi. [4] His son was Joel, whose son was Shemaiah, whose son was Gog, whose son was Shimei, [5] whose son was Micah, whose son was Reaiah, whose son was Baal, [6]* whose son was Beerah, whom Tiglathpileser, the king of Assyria, took into exile; he was a prince of the Reubenites. [7] His brothers who belonged to his clans, when they were listed in the family records according to their descendants, were: Jeiel, the chief, and Zechariah, [8]* and Bela, son of Azaz, son of Shema, son of Joel. The Reubenites lived in Aroer and as far as Nebo and Baal-meon; [9]* toward the east they dwelt as far as the desert which extends from the Euphrates River, for they had much livestock in the land of Gilead. [10]* During the reign of Saul they waged war with the Hagrites, and when they had defeated them they occupied their tents throughout the region east of Gilead.

Gad

[11]* The Gadites lived alongside them in the land of Bashan as far as Salecah. [12]* Joel was chief,

---

†
4, 39: *Gedor:* in the Greek, Gerar, no doubt correct.
5, 1–26: The Transjordan tribes.

4, 17: 1 Sm 30, 28.
4, 21: 1 Chr 2, 3; Gn 38, 5; 46, 12; Nm 26, 20.
4, 24: Gn 46, 10; Ex 6, 15; Nm 26, 12f.
4, 28–32: Jos 19, 2–8.
4, 38: Nm 1, 2.
4, 41: 2 Kgs 18, 1f; 2 Chr 29, 1.
4, 43: Ex 17, 8.14; Dt 25,

17ff; 1 Sm 14, 48; 15, 3.7f; 2 Sm 8, 12.
5, 1: Gn 35, 22; 48, 5.15–22; 49, 3f; Dt 33, 6.
5, 2: 1 Chr 28, 4; Gn 49, 8ff.
5, 3: Gn 46, 9; Ex 6, 14; Nm 26, 5f.
5, 6: 2 Kgs 15, 29.
5, 8: Jos 13, 9.16f; Nm 32, 3.38.
5, 9: Jos 22, 9.
5, 10: Ps 83, 6.
5, 11: Jos 13, 11.24–28.
5, 12: Gn 46, 16.

Shapham was second in command, and Janai was judge in Bashan. 13 Their brothers, corresponding to their ancestral houses, were: Michael, Meshullam, Sheba, Jorai, Jacan, Zia, and Eber—seven. 14 These were the sons of Abihail, son of Huri, son of Jaroah, son of Gilead, son of Michael, son of Jeshishai, son of Jahdo, son of Buz. 15 Ahi, son of Abdiel, son of Guni, was the head of their ancestral houses. 16 They dwelt in Gilead, in Bashan and its towns, and in all the pasture lands of Sirion to the borders. 17 All were listed in the family records in the time of Jotham, king of Judah, and of Jeroboam, king of Israel.

18 The Reubenites, Gadites, and half-tribe of Manasseh were warriors, men who bore shield and sword and who drew the bow, trained in warfare—forty-four thousand seven hundred and sixty men fit for military service. 19* When they waged war against the Hagrites and against Jetur, Naphish, and Nodab, 20* they received help so that they mastered the Hagrites and all who were with them. For during the battle they called on God, and he heard them because they had put their trust in him. 21 Along with one hundred thousand men they also captured their livestock: fifty thousand camels, two hundred fifty thousand sheep, and two thousand asses. 22* Many had fallen in battle, for victory is from God; and they took over their dwelling place until the time of the exile.

East Manasseh

23 The numerous members of the half-tribe of Manasseh lived in the land of Bashan as far as Baal-hermon, Senir, and Mount Hermon. 24 The following were the heads of their ancestral houses: Epher, Ishi, Eliel, Azriel, Jeremiah, Hodaviah, and Jahdiel—men who were warriors, famous men, and heads over their ancestral houses.

25* However, they offended the God of their fathers by lusting after the gods of the natives of the land, whom God had cleared out of their way. 26*† Therefore the God of Israel incited against them the anger of Pul, king of Assyria, and of Tiglath-pileser, king of Assyria, who deported the Reubenites, the Gadites, and the half-tribe of Manasseh and brought them to Halah, Habor, and Hara, and to the river Gozan, where they have remained to this day.

Levi

27*† The sons of Levi were Gershon, Kohath, and Merari. 28* The sons of Kohath were Amram, Izhar, Hebron, and Uzziel. 29* The children of Amram were Aaron, Moses, and Miriam. The sons of Aaron were Nadab, Abihu, Eleazar, and Ithamar. 30† Eleazar, became the father of Phinehas. Phinehas became the father of Abishua. 31 Abishua became the father of Bukki. Bukki became the father of Uzzi. 32 Uzzi became the father of Zerahiah. Zerahiah became the father of Meraioth. 33 Meraioth became the father of Amariah. Amariah became the father of Ahitub. 34 Ahitub became the father of Zadok. Zadok became the father of Ahimaaz. 35 Ahimaaz became the father of Azariah. Azariah became the father of Johanan. 36 Johanan became the father of Azariah, who served as priest in the temple Solomon built in Jerusalem. 37 Azariah became the father of Amariah. Amariah became the father of Ahitub. 38 Ahitub became the father of Zadok. Zadok became the father of Shallum. 39 Shallum became the father of Hilkiah. Hilkiah became the father of Azariah. 40 Azariah became the father of Seraiah. Seraiah became the father of Jehozadak. 41 Jehozadak was one of those who went into the exile which the LORD inflicted on Judah and Jerusalem through Nebuchadnezzar.

6 1* The sons of Levi were Gershon, Kohath, and Merari. 2* The sons of Gershon were named Libni and Shimei. 3* The sons of Kohath were Amram, Izhar, Hebron, and Uzziel. 4* The sons of Merari were Mahli and Mushi.

The following were the clans of Levi, distributed according to their ancestors: 5 of Gershon: his son Libni, whose son was Jahath, whose son was Zimmah, 6 whose son was Joah, whose son was Iddo, whose son was Zerah, whose son was Jetherai.

7 The descendants of Kohath were: his son Amminadab, whose son was Korah, whose son was Assir, 8 whose son was Elkanah, whose son was Ebiasaph, whose son was Assir, 9 whose son was Tahath, whose son was Uriel, whose son was Uzziah, whose son was Shaul. 10 The sons of Elkanah were Amasai and Ahimoth, 11 whose son was Elkanah, whose son was Zophai, whose son was Nahath, 12 whose son was Eliab, whose son was Jeroham, whose son was Elkanah, whose son was

---

5, 26: *Pul:* the name which the Assyrian king Tiglath-pileser III (745–727 B.C.) took as king of Babylon.

5, 27—6, 66: The tribe of Levi. The list gives special prominence to Levi's son Kohath, from whom were descended both the Aaronite priests (1 Chr 5, 28–41) and the leading group of temple singers (1 Chr 6, 18–23).

5, 30–41: The line of preexilic priests. The list seems to be confused in vv 36ff, which repeat the names, mostly in inverse order, that occur in vv 34f. A similar but shorter list is given, with variations, in Ezr 7, 1–5.

5, 19: 1 Chr 1, 31; 5, 10; Gn 25, 15; Ps 83, 6.
5, 20: Dt 33, 20f.
5, 22: Nm 32, 39; Dt 3, 8ff; Jgs 3, 3.
5, 25: Ex 34, 14ff; 2 Kgs 17, 7.
5, 26: 2 Kgs 15, 9.29; 17, 6.
5, 27: 1 Chr 6, 1; 23, 6; Gn 46, 11; Ex 6, 16; Nm 26, 57.
5, 28: 1 Chr 6, 3; Ex 6, 18.
5, 29: Ex 6, 20; Nm 26, 59f.
6, 1: 1 Chr 5, 27; 23, 6; Gn 46, 11; Ex 6, 16; Nm 26, 57.
6, 2: Ex 6, 17.
6, 3: 1 Chr 6, 18; Nm 3, 19; 26, 59.
6, 4: 1 Chr 6, 14; Ex 6, 19; Nm 3, 20; 26, 58.

Samuel. ¹³ The sons of Samuel were Joel, the first-born, and Abijah, the second.

¹⁴* The descendants of Merari were Mahli, whose son was Libni, whose son was Shimei, whose son was Uzzah, ¹⁵ whose son was Shimea, whose son was Haggiah, whose son was Asaiah.

¹⁶† The following were entrusted by David with the choir services in the LORD's house from the time when the ark had obtained a permanent resting place. ¹⁷ They served as singers before the Dwelling of the meeting tent until Solomon built the temple of the LORD in Jerusalem, and they performed their services in an order prescribed for them. ¹⁸ Those who so performed are the following, together with their descendants.

Among the Kohathites: Heman, the chanter, son of Joel, son of Samuel, ¹⁹ son of Elkanah, son of Jeroham, son of Eliel, son of Toah, ²⁰ son of Zuth, son of Elkanah, son of Mahath, son of Amasi, ²¹ son of Elkanah, son of Joel, son of Azariah, son of Zephaniah, ²²* son of Tahath, son of Assir, son of Ebiasaph, son of Korah, ²³ son of Izhar, son of Kohath, son of Levi, son of Israel.

²⁴ His brother Asaph stood at his right hand. Asaph was the son of Berechiah, son of Shimea, ²⁵ son of Michael, son of Baaseiah, son of Malchijah, ²⁶ son of Ethni, son of Zerah, son of Adaiah, ²⁷* son of Ethan, son of Zimmah, son of Shimei, ²⁸ son of Jahath, son of Gershon, son of Levi.

²⁹ Their brothers, the Merarites, stood at the left: Ethan, son of Kishi, son of Abdi, son of Malluch, ³⁰ son of Hashabiah, son of Amaziah, son of Hilkiah, ³¹ son of Amzi, son of Bani, son of Shemer, ³²* son of Mahli, son of Mushi, son of Merari, son of Levi.

³³* Their brother Levites were appointed to all other services of the Dwelling of the house of God. ³⁴* However, it was Aaron and his descendants who burnt the offerings on the altar of holocausts and on the altar of incense; they alone had charge of the holy of holies and of making atonement for Israel, as Moses, the servant of God, had ordained.

³⁵ These were the descendants of Aaron: his son Eleazer, whose son was Phinehas, whose son was Abishua, ³⁶ whose son was Bukki, whose son was Uzzi, whose son was Zerahiah, ³⁷ whose son was Meraioth, whose son was Amariah, whose son was Ahitub, ³⁸ whose son was Zadok, whose son was Ahimaaz.

³⁹† The following were their dwelling places to which their encampment was limited. To the de-

scendants of Aaron who belonged to the clan of the Kohathites, since the first lot fell to them, ⁴⁰ was assigned Hebron with its adjacent pasture lands in the land of Judah, ⁴¹ although the open country and the villages belonging to the city had been given to Caleb, the son of Jephunneh. ⁴² There were assigned to the descendants of Aaron: Hebron, a city of asylum, Libnah with its pasture lands, Jattir with its pasture lands, Eshtemoa with its pasture lands, ⁴³ Holon with its pasture lands, Debir with its pasture lands, ⁴⁴ Ashan with its pasture lands, Jetta with its pasture lands, and Beth-shemesh with its pasture lands. ⁴⁵ Also from the tribe of Benjamin: Gibeon with its pasture lands, Geba with its pasture lands, Almon with its pasture lands, Anathoth with its pasture lands. In all, they had thirteen cities with their pasture lands. ⁴⁹ The Israelites assigned these cities with their pasture lands to the Levites, ⁵⁰ designating them by name and assigning them by lot from the tribes of the Judahites, Simeonites, and Benjaminites.

⁴⁶ The other Kohathites obtained ten cities by lot for their clans from the tribe of Ephraim, from the tribe of Dan, and from the half-tribe of Manasseh. ⁴⁷ The clans of the Gershonites obtained thirteen cities from the tribes of Issachar, Asher, and Naphtali, and from the half-tribe of Manasseh in Bashan. ⁴⁸ The clans of the Merarites obtained twelve cities by lot from the tribes of Reuben, Gad, and Zebulun.

⁵¹ The clans of the Kohathites obtained cities by lot from the tribe of Ephraim. ⁵² They were assigned: Shechem in the mountain region of Ephraim, a city of asylum, with its pasture lands, Gezer with its pasture lands, ⁵³ Kibzaim with its pasture lands, and Beth-horon with its pasture lands. ⁵⁴ From the tribe of Dan: Elteke with its pasture lands, Gibbethon with its pasture lands, Aijalon with its pasture lands, and Gath-rimmon with its pasture lands. ⁵⁵ From the half-tribe of Manasseh: Taanach with its pasture lands and Ibleam with its pasture lands. These belonged to the rest of the Kohathite clan.

⁵⁶ The clans of the Gershonites received from the half-tribe of Manasseh: Golan in Bashan with its pasture lands and Ashtaroth with its pasture lands. ⁵⁷ From the tribe of Issachar: Kedesh with its pasture lands, Daberath with its pasture lands, ⁵⁸ Ramoth with its pasture lands, and Engannim with its pasture lands. ⁵⁹ From the tribe of Asher: Mashal with its pasture lands, Abdon with its pasture lands, ⁶⁰ Hilkath with its pasture lands, and

---

† **6, 16–32:** The origin of the choir services performed by the levitical families in the postexilic temple at the time of the Chronicler is here attributed to David, somewhat as all the laws in the Pentateuch are attributed to Moses.

6, 39–66: Regarding the nature of the rights of Levites in the cities assigned to them, see note on Jos 21, 1.

* **6, 14:** 1 Chr 6, 4; Ex 6, 19; Nm 3, 20; 26, 58.
6, 22: Ex 6, 24.
6, 27: 1 Chr 6, 2.5.
6, 32: Ex 6, 19; Nm 26, 58.
6, 33: 1 Chr 15, 17.19; 16, 41f; 2 Chr 5, 12.
6, 34: 1 Chr 16, 39f.

Rehob with its pasture lands. [61] From the tribe of Naphtali: Kedesh in Galilee with its pasture lands, Hammon with its pasture lands, and Kiriathaim with its pasture lands.

[62] The rest of the Merarites received from the tribe of Zebulun: Jokneam with its pasture lands, Kartah with its pasture lands, Rimmon with its pasture lands, and Tabor with its pasture lands. [63] Across the Jordan at Jericho [that is, east of the Jordan] they received from the tribe of Reuben: Bezer in the desert with its pasture lands, Jahzah with its pasture lands, [64] Kedemoth with its pasture lands, and Mephaath with its pasture lands. [65] From the tribe of Gad: Ramoth in Gilead with its pasture lands, Mahanaim with its pasture lands, [66] Heshbon with its pasture lands, and Jazer with its pasture lands.

Issachar

7 [1]† The sons of Issachar were Tola, Puah, Jashub, and Shimron: four. [2]* The sons of Tola were Uzzi, Rephaiah, Jeriel, Jahmai, Ibsam, and Shemuel, warrior heads of the ancestral houses of Tola. Their kindred numbered twenty-two thousand six hundred in the time of David. [3] The sons of Uzzi: Izrahiah. The sons of Izrahiah were Michael, Obadiah, Joel, and Isshiah. All five of these were chiefs. [4] Their kindred, by ancestral houses, numbered thirty-six thousand men in organized military troops, since they had more wives and sons [5] than their fellow tribesmen. In all the clans of Issachar there was a total of eighty-seven thousand warriors in their family records.

Benjamin

[6]* The sons of Benjamin were Bela, Becher, and Jediael—three. [7] The sons of Bela were Ezbon, Uzzi, Uzziel, Jerimoth, and Iri—five. They were heads of their ancestral houses and warriors. Their family records listed twenty-two thousand and thirty-four. [8]* The sons of Becher were Zemirah, Joash, Eliezer, Elioenai, Omri, Jeremoth, Abijah, Anathoth, and Alemeth—all these were sons of Becher. [9] Their family records listed twenty thousand two hundred of their kindred who were heads of their ancestral houses and warriors. [10] The sons of Jediael: Bilhan. The sons of Bilhan were Jeush, Benjamin, Ehud, Chenaanah, Zethan, Tarshish, and Ahishahar. [11]* All these were descendants of Jediael, heads of ancestral houses and warriors. They numbered seventeen thousand two hundred men fit for military service . . . Shupham and Hupham.

Dan, Naphtali and Manasseh

[12]* The sons of Dan: Hushim. [13] The sons of Naphtali were Jahziel, Guni, Jezer, and Shallum. These were descendants of Bilhah. [14]* The sons of Manasseh, whom his Aramean concubine bore: she bore Machir, the father of Gilead.* [15]* Machir took a wife whose name was Maacah; his sister's name was Molecheth. Manasseh's second son was named Zelophehad, but to Zelophehad only daughters were born. [16] Maacah, Machir's wife, bore a son whom she named Peresh. He had a brother named Sheresh, whose sons were Ulam and Rakem. [17] The sons of Ulam: Bedan. These were the descendants of Gilead, the son of Machir, the son of Manasseh. [18] His sister Molecheth bore Ishhod, Abiezer, and Mahlah. [19] The sons of Shemida were Ahian, Shechem, Likhi, and Aniam.

Ephraim

[20]* The sons of Ephraim: Shuthelah, whose son was Bered, whose son was Tahath, whose son was Eleadah, whose son was Tahath, [21] whose son was Zabad. Ephraim's son Shuthelah, and Ezer and Elead, who were born in the land, were slain by the inhabitants of Gath because they had gone down to take away their livestock. [22] Their father Ephraim mourned a long time, but after his kinsmen had come and comforted him, [23]* he visited his wife, who conceived and bore a son whom he named Beriah, since evil had befallen his house. [24] He had a daughter, Sheerah, who built lower and upper Beth-horon and Uzzen-sheerah. [25] Zabad's son was Rephah, whose son was Resheph, whose son was Telah, whose son was Tahan, [26]* whose son was Ladan, whose son was Ammihud, whose son was Elishama, [27] whose son was Nun, whose son was Joshua.

[28]* Their property and their dwellings were in Bethel and its towns, Naaran to the east, Gezer and its towns to the west, and also Shechem and its towns as far as Ayyah and its towns. [29]* Manasseh, however, had possession of Beth-shean and its towns, Taanach and its towns, Megiddo and its towns, and Dor and its towns. In these dwelt the descendants of Joseph, the son of Israel.

Asher

[30]* The sons of Asher were Imnah, Iishvah, Ishvi, and Beriah; their sister was Serah. [31] Beriah's sons were Heber and Malchiel, who was the father of Birzaith. [32] Heber became the father of Japhlet, Shomer, Hotham, and their sister Shua. [33] The sons

---

7, 1–40: The northern tribes.

7, 1: Gn 46, 13.
7, 2: Nm 26, 23f; Jgs 10, 1.
7, 6: 1 Chr 7, 6; Gn 46, 21;
  Nm 26, 38.

7, 8: 1 Chr 7, 8.
7, 11: Nm 26, 39.
7, 12f: Gn 46, 24; Nm 26,
  48f.

7, 14–19: Nm 26, 29–32.
7, 14: Nm 26, 29; Jos 17, 1.
7, 15: Nm 26, 33; Jos 17, 3.
7, 20: Nm 26, 35.
7, 23: 1 Chr 8, 13.
7, 26: Nm 1, 10; 2, 18; 7, 48;

10, 22.
7, 28: Gn 12, 8; 1 Kgs 9, 16.
7, 29: Jos 17, 11.
7, 30: Gn 46, 17; Nm 26,
  44ff.

of Japhlet were Pasach, Bimhal, and Ashvath; these were the sons of Japhlet. 34 The sons of Shomer were Ahi, Rohgah, Jehubbah, and Aram. 35 The sons of his brother Hotham were Zophah, Imna, Shelesh, and Amal. 36 The sons of Zophah were Suah, Harnepher, Shual, Beri, Imrah, 37 Bezer, Hod, Shamma, Shilshah, Ithran, and Beera. 38 The sons of Jether were Jephunneh, Pispa, and Ara. 39 The sons of Ulla were Arah, Hanniel, and Rizia. 40 All these were descendants of Asher, heads of ancestral houses, distinguished men, warriors, and chiefs among the princes. Their family records numbered twenty-six thousand men fit for military service.

Benjamin

8 1*† Benjamin became the father of Bela, his first-born, Ashbel, the second son, Aharah, the third, 2 Nohah, the fourth, and Rapha, the fifth. 3 The sons of Bela were Addar and Gera, the father of Ehud. 4* The sons of Ehud were Abishua, Naaman, Ahoah, 5 Gera, Shephuphan, and Huram. 6 These were the sons of Ehud, family heads over those who dwelt in Geba and were deported to Manahath. 7 Also Naaman, Ahijah, and Gera. The last, who led them into exile, became the father of Uzza and Ahihud. 8 Shaharaim became a father on the Moabite plateau after he had put away his wives Hushim and Baara. 9 By his wife Hodesh he became the father of Jobab, Zibia, Mesha, Malcam, 10 Jeuz, Sachia, and Mirmah. These were his sons, family heads. 11 By Hushim he became the father of Abitub and Elpaal. 12* The sons of Elpaal were Eber, Misham, Shemed, who built Ono and Lod with its nearby towns, 13 Beriah, and Shema. They were family heads of those who dwelt in Aijalon, and they put the inhabitants of Gath to flight. 14 Their brethren were Elpaal, Shashak, and Jeremoth. 15 Zebadiah, Arad, Eder, 16 Michael, Ishpah, and Joha were the sons of Beriah. 17 Zebadiah, Meshullam, Hizki, Heber, 18 Ishmerai, Izliah, and Jobab were the sons of Elpaal. 19 Jakim, Zichri, Zabdi, 20 Elienai, Zillethai, Eliel, 21 Adaiah, Beraiah, and Shimrath were the sons of Shimei. 22 Ishpan, Eber, Eliel, 23 Abdon, Zichri, Hanan, 24 Hananiah, Elam, Anthothijah, 25 Iphdeiah, and Penuel were the sons of Shashak. 26 Shamsherai, Shehariah, Athaliah, 27 Jaareshiah, Elijah, and Zichri were the sons of Jeroham. 28 These were family heads over their kindred, chiefs who dwelt in Jerusalem.
29* In Gibeon dwelt Jeiel, the founder of Gibeon,

whose wife's name was Maacah; 30 also his first-born son, Abdon, and Zur, Kish, Baal, Ner, Nadab, 31 Gedor, Ahio, Zecher, and Mikloth. 32 Mikloth became the father of Shimeah. These, too, dwelt with their relatives in Jerusalem, opposite their fellow tribesmen. 33* Ner became the father of Kish, and Kish became the father of Saul. Saul became the father of Jonathan, Malchishua, Abinadab, and Eshbaal.* 34* The son of Jonathan was Meribbaal, and Meribbaal became the father of Micah. 35 The sons of Micah were Pithon, Melech, Tarea, and Ahaz. 36* Ahaz became the father of Jehoaddah, and Jehoaddah became the father of Alemeth, Azmaveth, and Zimri. Zimri became the father of Moza. 37* Moza became the father of Binea, whose son was Raphah, whose son was Eleasah, whose son was Azel. 38 Azel had six sons, whose names were Azrikam, his first-born, Ishmael, Sheariah, Azariah, Obadiah, and Hanan; all these were the sons of Azel. 39 The sons of Eshek, his brother, were Ulam, his first-born, Jeush, the second son, and Eliphelet, the third. 40 The sons of Ulam were combat archers, and many were their sons and grandsons: one hundred and fifty. All these were the descendants of Benjamin.

9 1* Thus all Israel was inscribed in its family records which are recorded in the book of the kings of Israel.
Now Judah had been carried in captivity to Babylon because of its rebellion. 2*† The first to settle again in their cities and dwell there were certain lay Israelites, the priests, the Levites, and the temple slaves.*

Jerusalemites

3 In Jerusalem lived Judahites and Benjaminites; also Ephraimites and Manassehites. 4 Among the Judahites was Uthai, son of Ammihud, son of Omri, son of Imri, son of Bani, one of the descendants of Perez, son of Judah. 5 Among the Shelanites were Asaiah, the first-born, and his sons. 6 Among the Zerahites were Jeuel and six hundred and ninety of their brethren. 7 Among the Benjaminites were Sallu, son of Meshullam, son of Hodaviah, son of Hassenuah; 8 Ibneiah, son of Jeroham; Elah, son of Uzzi, son of Michri; Meshullam, son of Shephatiah, son of Reuel, son of Ibnijah. 9 Their kindred of various families were nine hundred and fifty-six. All those named were heads of their ancestral houses.

---

†

8, 1–40: A second, variant list of the Benjaminites, with special prominence given to Saul's family (vv 33–40).
9, 2–34: The inhabitants of Jerusalem after the exile. A similar list, with many variants in the names, is given in Neh 11, 3–24.

*

8, 1: 1 Chr 7, 6; Gn 46, 21; Nm 26, 38ff.
8, 4: Jgs 3, 15.
8, 12: Neh 11, 35.

8, 29–32: 1 Chr 9, 35–38.
8, 33–38: 1 Chr 9, 39–44.
 8, 33: 1 Chr 10, 2; 1 Sm 9, 1; 14, 49.51; 31, 2.
8, 34: 2 Sm 4, 4; 9, 6.10.12.
8, 36: 1 Chr 9, 42.
8, 37: 1 Chr 9, 43.

9, 1: 2 Chr 16, 11; 20, 34; 25, 26; 27, 7; 33, 18; 36, 8.
9, 2–22: Neh 11, 3–19.
 9, 2: Ezr 2, 70; 7, 7; Neh 11, 3.

10 Among the priests were Jedaiah; Jehoiarib; Jachin; 11 Azariah, son of Hilkiah, son of Meshullam, son of Zadok, son of Meraioth, son of Ahitub, the ruler of the house of God; 12 Adaiah, son of Jeroham, son of Pashhur, son of Malchijah; Maasai, son of Adiel, son of Jahzerah, son of Meshullam, son of Meshillemith, son of Immer. 13 Their brethren, heads of their ancestral houses, were one thousand seven hundred and sixty, valiant for the work of the service of the house of God.

14 Among the Levites were Shemaiah, son of Hasshub, son of Azrikam, son of Hashabiah, one of the descendants of Merari; 15 Bakbakkar; Heresh; Galal; Mattaniah, son of Mica, son of Zichri, a descendant of Asaph; 16 Obadiah, son of Shemaiah, son of Galal, a descendant of Jeduthun; and Berechiah, son of Asa, son of Elkanah, whose family lived in the villages of the Netophathites.

17 The gatekeepers were Shallum, Akkub, Talmon, Ahiman, and their brethren; Shallum was the chief. 18 Previously they had stood guard at the king's gate on the east side; now they became gatekeepers for the encampments of the Levites. 19 Shallum, son of Kore, son of Ebiasaph, a descendant of Korah, and his brethren of the same ancestral house of the Korahites had as their assigned task the guarding of the threshold of the tent, just as their fathers had guarded the entrance to the encampment of the LORD. 20* Phinehas, son of Eleazar, had been their chief in times past—the LORD be with him! 21* Zechariah, son of Meshelemiah, guarded the gate of the meeting tent. 22 In all, those who were chosen for gatekeepers at the threshold were two hundred and twelve. They were inscribed in the family records of their villages. David and Samuel the seer had established them in their position of trust. 23 Thus they and their sons kept guard over the gates of the house of the LORD, the house which was then a tent. 24* The gatekeepers were stationed at the four sides, to the east, the west, the north, and the south. 25* Their kinsmen who lived in their own villages took turns in assisting them for seven-day periods, 26 while the four chief gatekeepers were on constant duty. These were the Levites who also had charge of the chambers and treasures of the house of God. 27 At night they lodged about the house of God, for it was in their charge and they had the duty of opening it each morning.

28 Some of them had charge of the liturgical equipment, tallying it as it was brought in and taken out. 29 Others were appointed to take care of the utensils and all the sacred vessels, as well as the fine flour, the wine, the oil, the frankincense, and the spices. 30* It was the sons of priests, however, who mixed the spiced ointments. 31* Mattithiah, one of the Levites, the first-born of Shallum the Koreite, was entrusted with preparing the cakes. 32* Benaiah the Kohathite, one of their brethren, was in charge of setting out the showbread each sabbath.

33 These were the chanters and the gatekeepers, family heads over the Levites. They stayed in the chambers when free of duty, for day and night they had to be ready for service. 34 These were the levitical family heads over their kindred, chiefs who dwelt in Jerusalem.

II: The History of David

Genealogy of Saul

35* In Gibeon dwelt Jeiel, the founder of Gibeon, whose wife's name was Maacah. 36 His first-born son was Abdon; then came Zur, Kish, Baal, Ner, Nadab, 37 Gedor, Ahio, Zechariah, and Mikloth. 38 Mikloth became the father of Shimeam. These, too, with their brethren, dwelt opposite their brethren in Jerusalem. 39 Ner became the father of Kish, and Kish became the father of Saul. Saul became the father of Jonathan, Malchishua, Abinadab, and Eshbaal. 40 The son of Jonathan was Meribbaal, and Meribbaal became the father of Micah. 41 The sons of Micah were Pithon, Melech, Tahrea, and Ahaz. 42 Ahaz became the father of Jehoaddah, and Jehoaddah became the father of Alemeth, Azmaveth, and Zimri. Zimri became the father of Moza. 43 Moza became the father of Binea, whose son was Rephaiah, whose son was Eleasah, whose son was Azel. 44 Azel had six sons, whose names were Azrikam, his first-born, Ishmael, Sheariah, Azariah, Obadiah, and Hanan; these were the sons of Azel.

His Death and Burial

10 1* Now the Philistines were at war with Israel; the Israelites fled before the Philistines, and a number of them fell, slain on Mount Gilboa. 2 The Philistines pressed hard after Saul and his sons. When the Philistines had killed Jonathan, Abinadab, and Malchishua, sons of Saul, 3 the whole fury of the battle descended upon Saul. Then the archers found him, and wounded him with their arrows.

4 Saul said to his armor-bearer, "Draw your sword and thrust me through with it, that these uncircumcised may not come and maltreat me." But the armor-bearer, in great fear, refused. So Saul took his own sword and fell on it; 5 and seeing him dead,

---

9, 20: Ex 6, 25; Nm 25, 7.11;   9, 24: 1 Chr 26, 13.
Jgs 20, 28.   9, 25: 2 Chr 23, 4f.
9, 21: 1 Chr 26, 2.14.   9, 30: Ex 30, 22–33.

9, 31f: 1 Chr 23, 29; Lv 2, 1ff;   9, 35–44: 1 Chr 8, 29–38.
6, 13ff; 7, 11.   10, 1–12: 1 Sm 31, 1–13.
9, 32: Ex 25, 30; Lv 24, 5–8.

the armor-bearer also fell on his sword and died. 6 Thus, with Saul and his three sons, his whole house died at one time. 7 When all the Israelites who were in the valley saw that Saul and his sons had died in the rout, they left their cities and fled; thereupon the Philistines came and occupied them.

8 On the following day, when the Philistines came to strip the slain, they found Saul and his sons where they had fallen on Mount Gilboa. 9 They stripped him, cut off his head, and took his armor; these they sent throughout the land of the Philistines to convey the good news to their idols and their people. 10 His armor they put in the house of their gods, but his skull they impaled on the temple of Dagon.

11 When all the inhabitants of Jabesh-gilead had heard what the Philistines had done to Saul, 12* its warriors rose to a man, recovered the bodies of Saul and his sons, and brought them to Jabesh. They buried their bones under the oak of Jabesh, and fasted seven days.

13*† Thus Saul died because of his rebellion against the LORD in disobeying his command, and also because he had sought counsel of a necromancer, 14* and had not rather inquired of the LORD. Therefore the LORD slew him, and transferred his kingdom to David, the son of Jesse.

David Is Made King

11 1* Then all Israel gathered about David in Hebron, and they said: "Surely, we are of the same bone and flesh as you. 2* Even formerly, when Saul was still the king, it was you who led Israel in all its battles. And now the LORD, your God, has said to you, 'You shall shepherd my people Israel and be ruler over them.' " 3* Then all the elders of Israel came to the king at Hebron, and there David made a covenant with them in the presence of the LORD; and they anointed him king over Israel, in accordance with the word of the LORD as revealed through Samuel.

Jerusalem Captured

4* Then David and all Israel went to Jerusalem, that is, Jebus, where the natives of the land were called Jebusites. 5 The inhabitants of Jebus said to David, "You shall not enter here." David nevertheless captured the fortress of Zion, which is the City of David. 6* David said, "Whoever strikes the Jebusites first shall be made the chief commander." Joab, the son of Zeruiah, was the first to go up; and so he became chief. 7 David took up his residence in the fortress, which thenceforth was called the City of David. 8* He rebuilt the city on all sides, from the Millo all the way around, while Joab restored the rest of the city. 9 David became more and more powerful, for the LORD of hosts was with him.

David's Warriors

10* These were David's chief warriors who, together with all Israel, supported him in his reign in order to make him true king, even as the LORD had commanded concerning Israel. 11† Here is the list of David's warriors:

Ishbaal, the son of Hachamoni, chief of the Three. He brandished his spear against three hundred, whom he slew in a single encounter. 12* Next to him Eleazar, the son of Dodo the Ahohite, one of the Three warriors. 13* He was with David at Pasdammim, where the Philistines had massed for battle. The plowland was fully planted with barley, but its defenders were retreating before the Philistines. 14 He made a stand on the sown ground, kept it safe, and cut down the Philistines. Thus the LORD brought about a great victory.

15* Three of the Thirty chiefs went down to the rock, to David, who was in the cave of Adullam while the Philistines were encamped in the valley of Rephaim. 16 David was then in the stronghold, and a Philistine garrison was at Bethlehem. 17 David expressed a desire: "Oh, that someone would give me a drink from the cistern that is by the gate at Bethlehem!" 18 Thereupon the Three broke through the encampment of the Philistines, drew water from the cistern by the gate at Bethlehem, and carried it back to David. But David refused to drink it. Instead, he poured it out as a libation to the LORD, 19 saying, "God forbid that I should do such a thing! Could I drink the blood of these men who risked their lives?" For at the risk of their lives they brought it; and so he refused to drink it. Such deeds as these the Three warriors performed.

20*† Abishai, the brother of Joab. He was the chief of the Thirty; he brandished his spear against three hundred, and slew them. Thus he had a reputation like that of the Three.* 21 He was twice as

10, 13f: The Chronicler's comment on why Saul met his tragic end: he had disobeyed the Lord's command given through the prophet Samuel (1 Sm 15, 3–9), and had sought counsel of a necromancer (1 Sm 28, 6–19), contrary to the Mosaic law against necromancy (Dt 18, 10f).

11, 11f: *The Three:* the Chronicler names only two of them: Ishbaal and Eleazar. According to 2 Sm 23, 8–12, the Three were Ishbaal, Eleazar, and Shammah.

11, 20: listed by name in vv 26–47. The list given in 2 Sm 23, 8–39 often differs in names and spellings; for the numbers, see the note there.

10, 12: 2 Sm 2, 5.
10, 13: Dt 18, 10ff; 1 Sm 13, 13f; 15, 3.11.26.
10, 14: 1 Sm 15, 28; 2 Sm 3, 9f.
11, 1–9: 2 Sm 5, 1–10.
11, 2: 1 Sm 16, 5.13–16.30; 19, 8.
11, 3: 1 Sm 16, 1.13; 2 Sm 2, 4.
11, 4: Jos 15, 8; Jgs 1, 21; 19, 10f.

11, 6: 2 Sm 2, 13ff; 8, 16.
11, 8: 1 Kgs 9, 15.24; 11, 27; 2 Chr 32, 5.
11, 12: 1 Chr 27, 4.
11, 10–41: 2 Sm 23, 8–39.
11, 13: 1 Sm 17, 1.
11, 15: 1 Chr 14, 9; 2 Sm 5, 18.22.
11, 20f: 2 Sm 23, 18f.
11, 20: 1 Chr 18, 12; 1 Sm 26, 6ff; 2 Sm 16, 9; 18, 2; 21, 17.

famous as any of the Thirty and became their commander, but he did not attain to the Three.

22 Benaiah, the son of Jehoiada, a valiant man of mighty deeds, from Kabzeel. He killed the two sons of Ariel of Moab, and also, on a snowy day, he went down and killed the lion in the cistern. 23 He likewise slew the Egyptian, a huge man five cubits tall. The Egyptian carried a spear that was like a weaver's heddle-bar, but he came against him with a staff, wrested the spear from the Egyptian's hand, and killed him with his own spear. 24 Such deeds as these of Benaiah, the son of Jehoiada, gave him a reputation like that of the Three. 25* He was more famous than any of the Thirty, but he did not attain to the Three. David put him in charge of his bodyguard.

26* Also these warriors: Asahel, the brother of Joab; Elhanan, son of Dodo, from Bethlehem; 27 Shammoth, from En-harod; Helez, from Palti; 28 Ira, son of Ikkesh, from Tekoa; Abiezer, from Anathoth; 29* Sibbecai, from Husha; Ilai, from Ahoh; 30* Maharai, from Netophah; Heled, son of Baanah, from Netophah; 31* Ithai, son of Ribai, from Gibeah of Benjamin; Benaiah, from Pirathon; 32 Hurai, from the valley of Gaash; Abiel, from Betharabah; 33 Azmaveth, from Bahurim; Eliahba, from Shaalbon; 34 Jashen the Gunite; Jonathan, son of Shagee, from En-harod; 35 Ahiam, son of Sachar, from En-harod; Elipheleth, son of 36 Ahasabi, from Beth-maacah; Ahijah, from Gilo; 37 Hezro, from Carmel; Naarai, the son of Ezbai; 38 Joel, brother of Nathan, from Rehob, the Gadite; 39 Zelek the Ammonite; Naharai, from Beeroth, the armor-bearer of Joab, son of Zeruiah; 40 Ira, from Jattir; Gareb, from Jattir; 41 Uriah the Hittite; Zabad, son of Ahlai, 42 and, in addition to the Thirty, Adina, son of Shiza, the Reubenite, chief of the tribe of Reuben; 43 Hanan, from Beth-maacah; Joshaphat the Mithnite; 44 Uzzia, from Ashterath; Shama and Jeiel, sons of Hotham, from Aroer; 45 Jediael, son of Shimri, and Joha, his brother, the Tizite; 46 Eliel the Mahavite; Jeribai and Joshaviah, sons of Elnaam; Ithmah, from Moab; 47 Eliel, Obed, and Jaasiel the Mezobian.

David's Early Followers

12 1* The following men came to David in Ziklag while he was still under banishment from Saul, son of Kish; they, too, were among the warriors who helped him in his battles. 2 They were archers who could use either the right or the left hand, both in slinging stones and in shooting arrows with the bow. They were some of Saul's kinsmen, from Benjamin. 3* Ahiezer was their chief, along with Joash, both sons of Shemaah of Gibeah; also Jeziel and Pelet, sons of Azmaveth; Beracah; Jehu, from Anathoth; 4 Ishmaiah the Gibeonite, a warrior on the level of the Thirty, and in addition to their number: 5 Jeremiah; Jahaziel; Johanan; Jozabad, from Gederah; 6 Eluzai; Jerimoth; Bealiah; Shemariah; Shephatiah the Haruphite; 7 Elkanah, Isshiah, Azarel, Joezer, and Ishbaal, who were Korahites; 8 Joelah, finally, and Zebadiah, sons of Jeroham, from Gedor.

9* Some of the Gadites also went over to David when he was at the stronghold in the wilderness. They were valiant warriors, experienced soldiers equipped with shield and spear, who bore themselves like lions, and were as swift as the gazelles on the mountains. 10 Ezer was their chief, Obadiah was second, Eliab third, 11 Mishmannah fourth, Jeremiah fifth, 12 Attai sixth, Eliel seventh, 13 Johanan eighth, Elzabad ninth, 14 Jeremiah tenth, and Machbannai eleventh. 15 These Gadites were army commanders, the lesser placed over hundreds and the greater over thousands. 16 It was they who crossed over the Jordan when it was overflowing both its banks in the first month, and dispersed all who were in the valleys to the east and to the west.

17 Some Benjaminites and Judahites also came to David at the stronghold. 18 David went out to meet them and addressed them in these words: "If you come peacefully, to help me, I am of a mind to have you join me. But if you have come to betray me to my enemies though my hands have done no wrong, may the God of our fathers see and punish you."

19 Then spirit enveloped Amasai, the chief of the Thirty, who spoke:

> "We are yours, O David,
>   we are with you, O son of Jesse.
> Peace, peace to you,
>   and peace to him who helps you;
>   your God it is who helps you."

So David received them and placed them among the leaders of his troops.

20 Men from Manasseh also deserted to David when he came with the Philistines to battle against Saul. However, he did not help the Philistines, for their lords took counsel and sent him home, saying, "At the cost of our heads he will desert to his master Saul." 21 As he was returning to Ziklag, therefore, these deserted to him from Manasseh: Adnah, Jozabad, Jediael, Michael, Jozabad, Elihu, and Zillethai, chiefs of thousands of Manasseh. 22 They

11, 25: 2 Sm 8, 18; 20, 23.   11, 29: 1 Chr 27, 11.
11, 26: 1 Chr 2, 16; 27, 7.   11, 30: 1 Chr 27, 13.

11, 31: 1 Chr 27, 14.   12, 3: 1 Chr 27, 12.
12, 1: 1 Sm 27, 1–7.   12, 9: Dt 33, 20.

helped David by taking charge of his troops, for they were all warriors and became commanders of his army. 23 And from day to day men kept coming to David's help until there was a vast encampment, like an encampment of angels.

The Assembly at Hebron

24 This is the muster of the detachments of armed troops that came to David at Hebron to transfer to him Saul's kingdom, as the LORD had ordained. 25† Judahites bearing shields and spears: six thousand eight hundred armed troops. 26 Of the Simeonites, warriors fit for battle: seven thousand one hundred. 27 Of the Levites: four thousand six hundred, 28 along with Jehoiada, leader of the line of Aaron, with another three thousand seven hundred, 29 and Zadok, a young warrior, with twenty-two princes of his father's house. 30 Of the Benjaminites, the brethren of Saul: three thousand—until this time, most of them had held their allegiance to the house of Saul. 31 Of the Ephraimites: twenty thousand eight hundred warriors, men renowned in their ancestral houses. 32 Of the half-tribe of Manasseh: eighteen thousand, designated by name to come and make David king. 33 Of the Issacharites, their chiefs who were endowed with an understanding of the times and who knew what Israel had to do: two hundred chiefs, together with all their brethren under their command. 34 From Zebulun, men fit for military service, set in battle array with every kind of weapon for war: fifty thousand men rallying with a single purpose. 35 From Naphtali: one thousand captains, and with them, armed with shield and lance, thirty-seven thousand men. 36 Of the Danites, set in battle array: twenty-eight thousand six hundred. 37 From Asher, fit for military service and set in battle array: forty thousand. 38 From the other side of the Jordan, of the Reubenites, Gadites, and the half-tribe of Manasseh, men equipped with every kind of weapon of war: one hundred and twenty thousand.

39 All these soldiers, drawn up in battle order, came to Hebron with the resolute intention of making David king over all Israel. The rest of Israel was likewise of one mind to make David king. 40 They remained with David for three days, feasting and drinking, for their brethren had prepared for them. 41 Moreover, their neighbors from as far as Issachar, Zebulun, and Naphtali came bringing food on

asses, camels, mules, and oxen—provisions in great quantity of meal, pressed figs, raisins, wine, oil, oxen, and sheep. For there was rejoicing in Israel.

Transfer of the Ark

13 1* After David had taken counsel with his commanders of thousands and of hundreds, that is to say, with every one of his leaders, 2* he said to the whole assembly of Israel: "If it seems good to you, and is so decreed by the LORD our God, let us summon the rest of our brethren from all the districts of Israel, and also the priests and the Levites from their cities with pasture lands, that they may join us; 3 and let us bring the ark of our God here among us, for in the days of Saul we did not visit it." 4 And the whole assembly agreed to do this, for the idea was pleasing to all the people.

5*† Then David assembled all Israel, from Shihor of Egypt to Labo of Hamath, to bring the ark of God from Kiriath-jearim. 6* David and all Israel went up to Baalah, that is, to Kiriath-jearim, of Judah, to bring back the ark of God, which was known by the name "LORD enthroned upon the cherubim." 7 They transported the ark of God on a new cart from the house of Abinadab; Uzzah and Ahio were guiding the cart, 8 while David and all Israel danced before God with great enthusiasm, amid songs and music on lyres, harps, tambourines, cymbals, and trumpets.

9† As they reached the threshing floor of Chidon, Uzzah stretched out his hand to steady the ark, for the oxen were upsetting it. 10 Then the LORD became angry with Uzzah and struck him; he died there in God's presence, because he had laid his hand on the ark. 11† David was disturbed because the LORD's anger had broken out against Uzzah. Therefore that place has been called Perez-uzza even to this day.

12 David was now afraid of God, and he said, "How can I bring the ark of God with me?" 13 Therefore he did not take the ark back with him to the City of David, but he took it instead to the house of Obed-edom the Gittite. 14* The ark of God remained in the house of Obed-edom with his family for three months, and the LORD blessed Obed-edom's household and all that he possessed.

David in Jerusalem

14 1* Hiram, king of Tyre, sent envoys to David along with masons and carpenters,

---

†
12, 25–38: The Chronicler fills out the pageantry of joyous occasions in keeping with his much later appreciation of the significance of the event in the history of God's people: the numbers in attendance at David's crowning in Hebron (cf 2 Sm 5, 1ff) are recounted in the same spirit of enthusiasm which in v 23 compares David's band of desert freebooters to a numerous encampment of angels.
13, 5: *Shihor of Egypt:* the eastern branch of the Nile delta. *Labo of Hamath:* in southern Syria.
13, 9: *Chidon:* in 2 Sm 6, 6, Nodan.

13, 11: *Perez-uzza:* A Hebrew term meaning "the breaking out against Uzza."

13, 1–14: 2 Sm 6, 1–11.
13, 2: Nm 35, 1ff; Jos 14, 4; 21, 2ff.
13, 5: 1 Chr 15, 3; Jos 13, 3.5; 1 Sm 6, 21; 7, 1f;
2 Sm 6, 1–11.
13, 6: Jos 15, 9; 18, 14; 1 Sm 4, 4; 7, 1.
13, 14: 1 Chr 26, 4f.
14, 1–16: 2 Sm 5, 11–25.

and cedar wood to build him a house.* ² David now understood that the LORD had truly confirmed him as king over Israel, for his kingdom was greatly exalted for the sake of his people Israel. ³* David took other wives in Jerusalem and became the father of more sons and daughters. ⁴ These are the names of those who were born to him in Jerusalem: Shammua, Shobab, Nathan, Solomon, ⁵ Ibhar, Elishua, Elpelet, ⁶ Nogah, Nepheg, Japhia, ⁷ Elishama, Beeliada, and Eliphelet.

The Philistine Wars

⁸ When the Philistines had heard that David was anointed king over all Israel, they went up in unison to seek him out. But when David heard of this, he marched out against them. ⁹* Meanwhile the Philistines had come and raided the valley of Rephaim. ¹⁰ David inquired of God, "Shall I advance against the Philistines, and will you deliver them into my power?" The LORD answered him, "Advance, for I will deliver them into your power." ¹¹ They advanced, therefore, to Baal-perazim, and David defeated them there. Then David said, "God has used me to break through my enemies just as water breaks through a dam." Therefore that place was called Baal-perazim. ¹²* The Philistines had left their gods there, and David ordered them to be burnt.

¹³ Once again the Philistines raided the valley, ¹⁴ and again David inquired of God. But God answered him: "Do not try to pursue them, but go around them and come upon them from the direction of the mastic trees. ¹⁵ When you hear the sound of marching in the tops of the mastic trees, then go forth to battle, for God has already gone before you to strike the army of the Philistines." ¹⁶ David did as God commanded him, and they routed the Philistine army from Gibeon to Gezer.

¹⁷ Thus David's fame was spread abroad through every land, and the LORD made all the nations fear him.

The Ark Brought to Jerusalem

15 ¹ David built houses for himself in the City of David and prepared a place for the ark of God, pitching a tent for it there. ²* At that time he said, "No one may carry the ark of God except the Levites, for the LORD chose them to carry the ark of the LORD and to minister to him forever." ³* Then David assembled all Israel in Jerusalem to bring the ark of the LORD to the place which he had prepared for it. ⁴ David also called together the sons of Aaron and the Levites: ⁵ of the sons of Kohath, Uriel, their chief, and one hundred and twenty of his brethren; ⁶ of the sons of Merari, Asaiah, their chief, and two hundred and twenty of his brethren; ⁷ of the sons of Gershon, Joel, their chief, and one hundred and thirty of his brethren; ⁸ of the sons of Elizaphan, Shemaiah, their chief, and two hundred of his brethren; ⁹ of the sons of Hebron, Eliel, their chief, and eighty of his brethren; ¹⁰ of the sons of Uzziel, Amminadab, their chief, and one hundred and twelve of his brethren.

¹¹* David summoned the priests Zadok and Abiathar, and the Levites Uriel, Asaiah, Joel, Shemaiah, Eliel, and Amminadab, ¹²* and said to them: "You, the heads of the levitical families, must sanctify yourselves along with your brethren and bring the ark of the LORD, the God of Israel, to the place which I have prepared for it. ¹³* Because you were not with us the first time, the wrath of the LORD our God burst upon us, for we did not seek him aright." ¹⁴ Accordingly, the priests and the Levites sanctified themselves to bring up the ark of the LORD, the God of Israel. ¹⁵* The Levites bore the ark of God on their shoulders with poles, as Moses had ordained according to the word of the LORD.

¹⁶* David commanded the chiefs of the Levites to appoint their brethren as chanters, to play on musical instruments, harps, lyres, and cymbals, to make a loud sound of rejoicing. ¹⁷* Therefore the Levites appointed Heman, son of Joel, and, among his brethren, Asaph, son of Berechiah; and among the sons of Merari, their brethren, Ethan, son of Kushaiah; ¹⁸ and, together with these, their brethren of the second rank: the gatekeepers Zechariah, Uzziel, Shemiramoth, Jehiel, Unni, Eliab, Benaiah, Maaseiah, Mattithiah, Eliphelehu, Mikneiah, Obed-edom, and Jeiel. ¹⁹ The chanters, Heman, Asaph, and Ethan, sounded brass cymbals. ²⁰† Zechariah, Uzziel, Shemiramoth, Jehiel, Unni, Eliab, Maaseiah, and Benaiah played on harps set to "Alamoth." ²¹ But Mattithiah, Eliphelehu, Mikneiah, Obed-edom, and Jeiel led the chant on lyres set to "the eighth." ²²* Chenaniah was the chief of the Levites in the chanting; he directed the chanting, for he was skillful. ²³ Berechiah and Elkanah were gatekeepers before the ark. ²⁴* The priests, Shebaniah, Joshaphat, Nethanel, Amasai, Zechariah, Benaiah, and Eliezer, sounded the trumpets before the ark of

---

† **15, 20:** *Alamoth:* a musical term (literally, "young women") of uncertain meaning, occurring also in Ps 46, 1, where it is rendered as virgins. Perhaps it may mean something like "soprano," whereas the term "eighth" (Hebrew *sheminith*, v 21) may then mean "bass"; cf Pss 6, 1; 12, 1.

14, 1: 1 Kgs 5, 1; 2 Chr 2, 3.
14, 3-7: 1 Chr 3, 5-8; 2 Sm 5, 13-16.
14, 9: 1 Chr 11, 15.

14, 12: Dt 7, 5.25.
15, 2: Nm 1, 50; 7, 9; Dt 10, 8; 31, 25; 1 Sm 6, 15; Jos 3, 8.
15, 3: 1 Chr 13, 5; 2 Sm 6, 15.17.
15, 11: 1 Chr 16, 39; 2 Sm 8, 17; 15, 29.35.
15, 12: 2 Chr 29, 5.15.34; 30, 3.15.24.

15, 13: 1 Chr 13, 3.
15, 15: Ex 25, 13ff; Nm 1, 50; 7, 9; 2 Chr 35, 3.
15, 16: 1 Chr 13, 8; 16, 5; 2 Chr 5, 12; 29, 25; Neh 12, 27.
15, 17: 1 Chr 6, 31-47; 25, 1-8.
15, 22: 1 Chr 26, 29.
15, 24: Nm 10, 8; Jos 6, 4ff.

God. Obed-edom and Jeiel were also gatekeepers before the ark.

25* Thus David, the elders of Israel, and the commanders of thousands went to bring up the ark of the covenant of the LORD with joy from the house of Obed-edom. 26* While the Levites, with God's help, were bearing the ark of the covenant of the LORD, seven bulls and seven rams were sacrificed. 27* David was clothed in a robe of fine linen, as were all the Levites who carried the ark, the singers, and Chenaniah, the leader of the chant; David was also wearing a linen ephod. 28 Thus all Israel brought back the ark of the covenant of the LORD with joyful shouting, and to the sound of horns, trumpets, and cymbals, and the music of harps and lyres. 29* But as the ark of the covenant of the LORD was entering the City of David, Michal, daughter of Saul, looked down from her window, and when she saw King David leaping and dancing, she despised him in her heart.

16 1* They brought in the ark of God and set it within the tent which David had pitched for it. Then they offered up holocausts and peace offerings to God.* 2 When David had finished offering up the holocausts and peace offerings, he blessed the people in the name of the LORD, 3 and distributed to every Israelite, to every man and to every woman, a loaf of bread, a piece of meat, and a raisin cake.

The Ministering Levites

4* He now appointed certain Levites to minister before the ark of the LORD, to celebrate, thank, and praise the LORD, the God of Israel. 5 Asaph was their chief, and second to him were Zechariah, Uzziel, Shemiramoth, Jehiel, Mattithiah, Eliab, Benaiah, Obed-edom, and Jeiel. These were to play on harps and lyres, while Asaph was to sound the cymbals, 6 and the priests Benaiah and Jahaziel were to be the regular trumpeters before the ark of the covenant of God.

7 Then, on that same day, David appointed Asaph and his brethren to sing for the first time these praises of the LORD:

8*† Give thanks to the LORD, invoke his name;
    make known among the nations his
      deeds.
9 Sing to him, sing his praise,
    proclaim all his wondrous deeds.

10 Glory in his holy name;
    rejoice, O hearts that seek the LORD!
11 Look to the LORD in his strength;
    seek to serve him constantly.
12 Recall the wondrous deeds that he has wrought,
    his portents, and the judgments he
      has uttered,
13 You descendants of Israel, his servants,
    sons of Jacob, his chosen ones!

14 He, the LORD, is our God;
    throughout the earth his judgments prevail.
15 He remembers forever his covenant
    which he made binding for a
      thousand generations—
16 Which he entered into with Abraham
    and by his oath to Isaac;
17 Which he established for Jacob by statute,
    for Israel as an everlasting covenant,
18 Saying, "To you will I give the land of Canaan
    as your allotted inheritance."

19 When they were few in number,
    a handful, and strangers there,
20 Wandering from nation to nation,
    from one kingdom to another people,
21 He let no one oppress them,
    and for their sake he rebuked kings:
22 "Touch not my anointed,
    and to my prophets do no harm."

23* Sing to the LORD, all the earth,
    announce his salvation, day after day.
24 Tell his glory among the nations;
    among all peoples, his wondrous deeds.

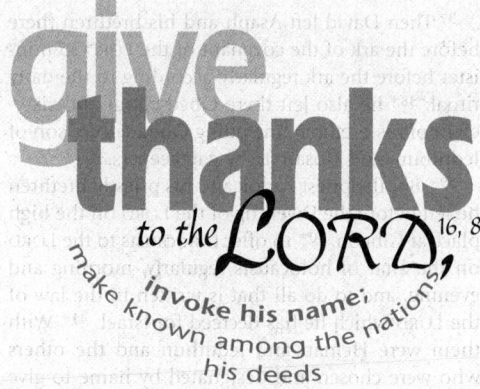

give thanks to the LORD, invoke his name; make known among the nations his deeds 16, 8

---

† **16, 8–36:** A hymn composed of parts, with textual variants, from several Psalms; vv 8–22 = Ps 105, 1–15; vv 23–33 = Ps 96, 1–13; vv 34–36 = Ps 106, 1,47f.

* 15, 25–29: 2 Sm 6, 12–16.
  15, 26: 2 Sm 6, 17; 2 Chr 29, 21.
  15, 27: 1 Sm 2, 18; 2 Sm 6, 14.
  15, 29: 2 Sm 6, 20ff.

16, 1–3: 2 Sm 6, 17ff.
16, 1: 1 Chr 15, 1.
16, 4: Sir 47, 9.
16, 8–22: Ps 105, 1–15.
16, 23–33: Ps 96, 1–13.

25 For great is the LORD and highly to be praised;
  and awesome is he, beyond all gods.
26 For all the gods of the nations are things
      of nought,
  but the LORD made the heavens.
27 Splendor and majesty go before him;
  praise and joy are in his holy place.

28 Give to the LORD, you families of nations,
  give to the LORD glory and praise;
29 Give to the LORD the glory due his name!
  Bring gifts, and enter his presence;
  worship the LORD in holy attire.
30 Tremble before him, all the earth;
  he has made the world firm, not to
      be moved.

31 Let the heavens be glad and the earth rejoice;
  let them say among the nations: The LORD
      is king.
32 Let the sea and what fills it resound;
  let the plains rejoice and all that is in them!
33 Then shall all the trees of the forest exult
  before the LORD, for he comes:
  he comes to rule the earth.

34* Give thanks to the LORD, for he is good,
  for his kindness endures forever;
35 And say, "Save us, O God, our savior,
  gather us and deliver us from the nations,
  That we may give thanks to your holy name
  and glory in praising you."
36 Blessed be the LORD, the God of Israel,
  through all eternity!
  Let all the people say, Amen!
      Alleluia.

37 Then David left Asaph and his brethren there
before the ark of the covenant of the LORD to minister before the ark regularly according to the daily
ritual; 38* he also left there Obed-edom and sixty-
eight of his brethren, including Obed-edom, son of
Jeduthun, and Hosah, to be gatekeepers.
39* But the priest Zadok and his priestly brethren
he left before the Dwelling of the LORD on the high
place at Gibeon, 40* to offer holocausts to the LORD
on the altar of holocausts regularly, morning and
evening, and to do all that is written in the law of
the LORD which he has decreed for Israel. 41* With
them were Heman and Jeduthun and the others
who were chosen and designated by name to give
thanks to the LORD, "because his kindness endures

RITUAL PRAYER

King David established times of regular,
ritual prayer at the ark. Regular, ritual
prayer is a practice of many of the world's
great religions and, in the eyes of the
Chronicler, is a key ingredient of true religious practice. Catholics also have ancient
traditions of regular, ritual prayer. (Regular,
in this instance, does not mean "ordinary,"
but rather "at certain, established times.")
We start the day with prayer, we end the
day with prayer, we have special blessings
for special occasions, and we gather to celebrate the Eucharist each week. Regular,
ritual prayer helps to remind us of God's
presence and of our identity as God's people.
  How do you pray? Do you pray regularly? Do you have any personal rituals as part
of your prayer life?

▶ 1 Chr 16, 37–43

forever," 42* with trumpets and cymbals for accompaniment, and instruments for the sacred chant.
The sons of Jeduthun kept the gate.
43* Then all the people departed, each to his own
home, and David returned to bless his household.

The Oracle of Nathan

17 1* After David had taken up residence in
his house, he said to Nathan the prophet,
"See, I am living in a house of cedar, but the ark of
the covenant of the LORD dwells under tentcloth."*
2 Nathan replied to David, "Do, therefore, whatever
you desire, for God is with you."
3 But that same night the word of God came to
Nathan: 4* "Go and tell my servant David, Thus
says the LORD: It is not you who are to build a house
for me to dwell in. 5 For I have never dwelt in a

16, 34ff: Ps 106, 1.47f.   Nm 28, 3.6; 2 Chr 13,   16, 42: 2 Chr 29, 27.   2 Sm 5, 11.
16, 38: 1 Chr 15, 24.   11.   16, 43: 2 Sm 6, 19f.   17, 4: 1 Chr 28, 3; 1 Kgs 8,
16, 39: 1 Kgs 3, 4.   16, 41: 2 Chr 5, 12; 7, 3.6; 20,   17, 1–27: 2 Sm 7, 1–29.   19.
16, 40: Ex 29, 38–42; Lv 6, 9;   21; Ezr 3, 11.   17, 1: 1 Chr 15, 1;

house, from the time when I led Israel onward, even to this day, but I have been lodging in tent or pavilion ⁶ as long as I have wandered about with all of Israel. Did I ever say a word to any of the judges of Israel whom I commanded to guide my people, such as, 'Why have you not built me a house of cedar?' ⁷* Therefore, tell my servant David, Thus says the LORD of hosts: I took you from the pasture, from following the sheep, that you might become ruler over my people Israel. ⁸ I was with you wherever you went, and I cut down all your enemies before you. I will make your name great like that of the greatest on the earth. ⁹ I will assign a place for my people Israel and I will plant them in it to dwell there henceforth undisturbed; nor shall wicked men ever again oppress them, as they did at first, ¹⁰ and during all the time when I appointed judges over my people Israel. And I will subdue all your enemies. Moreover, I declare to you that I, the LORD, will build you a house; ¹¹* so that when your days have been completed and you must join your fathers, I will raise up your offspring after you who will be one of your own sons, and I will establish his kingdom. ¹²* He it is who shall build me a house, and I will establish his throne forever. ¹³* I will be a father to him, and he shall be a son to me, and I will not withdraw my favor from him as I withdrew it from him who preceded you; ¹⁴ but I will maintain him in my house and in my kingdom forever, and his throne shall be firmly established forever."

¹⁵ All these words and this whole vision Nathan related exactly to David.

David's Thanksgiving

¹⁶ Then David came in and sat in the LORD'S presence, saying: "Who am I, O LORD God, and what is my family, that you should have brought me as far as I have come? ¹⁷* And yet, even this you now consider too little, O God! For you have made a promise regarding your servant's family reaching into the distant future, and you have looked on me as henceforth the most notable of men, O LORD God. ¹⁸ What more can David say to you? You know your servant. ¹⁹ O LORD, for your servant's sake and in keeping with your purpose, you have done this great thing. ²⁰* O LORD, there is no one like you and there is no God but you, just as we have always understood.

²¹* "Is there, like your people Israel, whom you redeemed from Egypt, another nation on earth whom a god went to redeem as his people? You won for yourself a name for great and awesome deeds by driving out the nations before your people. ²² You made your people Israel your own forever, and you, O LORD, became their God. ²³ Therefore, O LORD, may the promise that you have uttered concerning your servant and his house remain firm forever. Bring about what you have promised, ²⁴ that your renown as LORD of hosts, God of Israel, may be great and abide forever, while the house of David, your servant, is established in your presence.

²⁵* "Because you, O my God, have revealed to your servant that you will build him a house, your servant has made bold to pray before you. ²⁶ Since

Where Do We Place God?

How the world loves boxes and containers and compartments! Remember the old saying, A place for everything and everything in its place? There is something comforting in knowing that everything is where it should be.

Don't we often try to put God away in a special place? Isn't it more convenient to think of God as residing "up there" in the tabernacle or sanctuary? Perhaps that is why in 1 Chr 17, 4–6, God seems less than enthusiastic about David's desire to build a temple. The danger is clear: identify God with a building, however grand and beautiful, and in people's minds, God *stays* there.

When we enter a chapel or a church, we become reverent, sensing that we are in the presence of God. And, indeed, we are. But we need to remember that we do not leave God behind when we step out of that structure. Simply put, God cannot and will not be confined, despite our best efforts.

Our God walks with us. God's place is everywhere.

How can you practice living in the constant presence of God?

▶ 1 Chr 17, 1–15

17, 7: 1 Sm 16, 11.   17, 12: 1 Chr 22, 10; 28, 6.10.   17, 17: 2 Sm 7, 19.   17, 21: Dt 4, 7; 2 Sm 7, 23.
17, 11: 2 Sm 7, 12f.   17, 13: 2 Sm 7, 14.   17, 20: Sir 36, 4.   17, 25: 2 Sm 7, 27.

you, O LORD, are truly God and have promised this good thing to your servant, ²⁷* and since you have deigned to bless the house of your servant, so that it will remain forever—since it is you, O LORD, who blessed it, it is blessed forever."

David's Victories

18 ¹* After this, David defeated the Philistines and subdued them; and he took Gath and its towns away from the control of the Philistines. ² He also defeated Moab, and the Moabites became his subjects, paying tribute.

³ David then defeated Hadadezer, king of Zobah toward Hamath, when the latter was on his way to set up his victory stele at the river Euphrates. ⁴* David took from him twenty thousand foot soldiers, one thousand chariots, and seven thousand horsemen. Of the chariot horses, David hamstrung all but one hundred. ⁵ The Arameans of Damascus came to the aid of Hadadezer, king of Zobah, but David also slew twenty-two thousand of their men. ⁶ Then David set up garrisons in the Damascus region of Aram, and the Arameans became his subjects, paying tribute. Thus the LORD made David victorious in all his campaigns.

⁷ David took the golden shields that were carried by Hadadezer's attendants and brought them to Jerusalem. ⁸* He likewise took away from Tibhath and Cun, cities of Hadadezer, large quantities of bronze, which Solomon later used to make the bronze sea and the pillars and the vessels of bronze.

⁹ When Tou, king of Hamath, heard that David had defeated the entire army of Hadadezer, king of Zobah, ¹⁰* he sent his son Hadoram to wish King David well and to congratulate him on having waged a victorious war against Hadadezer; for Hadadezer had been at war with Tou. He also sent David gold, silver and bronze utensils of every sort. ¹¹ These also King David consecrated to the LORD along with all the silver and gold that he had taken from the nations: from Edom, Moab, the Ammonites, the Philistines, and Amalek.

¹²* Abishai, the son of Zeruiah, also slew eighteen thousand Edomites in the Valley of Salt. ¹³ He set up garrisons in Edom, and all the Edomites became David's subjects. Thus the LORD made David victorious in all his campaigns.

David's Officials

¹⁴* David reigned over all Israel and dispensed justice and right to all his people. ¹⁵* Joab, son of Zeruiah, was in command of the army; Jehoshaphat, son of Ahilud, was herald; ¹⁶*† Zadok, son of Ahitub, and Ahimelech, son of Abiathar, were priests; Shavsha was scribe; ¹⁷*† Benaiah, son of Jehoiada, was in command of the Cherethites and the Pelethites; and David's sons were the chief assistants to the king.

Campaigns against Ammon

19 ¹* Afterward Nahash, king of the Ammonites, died and his son succeeded him as king. ² David said, "I will show kindness to Hanun, the son of Nahash, for his father treated me with kindness." Therefore he sent envoys to him to comfort him over the death of his father. But when David's servants had entered the land of the Ammonites to comfort Hanun, ³ the Ammonite princes said to Hanun, "Do you think David is doing this—sending you these consolers—to honor your father? Have not his servants rather come to you to explore the land, spying it out for its overthrow?" ⁴ Thereupon Hanun seized David's servants and had them shaved and their garments cut off half-way at the hips. Then he sent them away. ⁵ When David was informed of what had happened to his men, he sent messengers to meet them, for the men had been greatly disgraced. "Remain at Jericho," the king told them, "until your beards have grown again; and then you may come back here."

⁶ When the Ammonites realized that they had put themselves in bad odor with David, Hanun and the Ammonites sent a thousand talents of silver to hire chariots and horsemen from Aram Naharaim, from Aram-maacah, and from Zobah. ⁷ They hired thirty-two thousand chariots along with the king of Maacah and his army, who came and encamped before Medeba. The Ammonites also assembled from their cities and came out for war.

⁸ When David heard of this, he sent Joab and his

18, 16: *Zadok . . . and Ahimelech, son of Abiathar, were priests:* as in the Chronicler's source, 2 Sm 8, 17. But according to 2 Sm 15, 24.29.35; 17, 15; 19, 11; 20, 25, and even 1 Chr 15, 11, it was Abiathar who shared the priestly office with Zadok, and he remained in this office even during the early years of Solomon's reign (1 Kgs 2, 26; 4, 4). Moreover, according to 1 Sm 22, 20; 23, 6; 30, 7, Ahimelech was the father, not the son, of Abiathar. If the text Ahimelech, son of Abiathar, is not due to a scribal change, one must assume that Abiathar had a son who was named after his grandfather and who shared the priestly office with his father during the last years of David's reign.

18, 17: *David's sons were the chief assistants to the king:* in the parallel passage, 2 Sm 8, 18, which was the Chronicler's source,

David's sons were priests. The change is characteristic of the Chronicler, for whom only Aaron's descendants could be priests.

17, 27: Nm 22, 6.
18, 1–13: 2 Sm 8, 1–14.
18, 4: 2 Sm 8, 14; Jos 11, 6.9.
18, 8: 2 Sm 8, 8; 1 Kgs 7, 15.23.27.
18, 10: 2 Sm 8, 10.
18, 12: 2 Sm 8, 13; 2 Kgs 14, 7.
18, 14–17: 2 Sm 8, 15–18.
18, 15: 1 Chr 11, 6; 2 Sm 8, 16; 1 Kgs 4, 3.
18, 16: 1 Chr 24, 3.6.31; 2 Sm 8, 17.
18, 17: 1 Chr 11, 22; 2 Sm 8, 18; 1 Kgs 1, 38.44.
19, 1–19: 2 Sm 10, 1–19.

whole army of warriors against them. 9 The Ammonites marched out and lined up for battle at the gate of the city, while the kings who had come to their help remained apart in the open field. 10* When Joab saw that there was a battle line both in front of and behind him, he chose some of the best fighters among the Israelites and set them in array against the Arameans; 11* the rest of the army, which he placed under the command of his brother Abishai, then lined up to oppose the Ammonites. 12 And he said: "If the Arameans prove too strong for me, you must come to my help; and if the Ammonites prove too strong for you, I will save you. 13 Hold steadfast and let us show ourselves courageous for the sake of our people and the cities of our God; then may the LORD do what seems best to him." 14 Joab therefore advanced with his men to engage the Arameans in battle; but they fled before him. 15 And when the Ammonites saw that the Arameans had fled, they also took to flight before his brother Abishai, and reentered the city. Joab then returned to Jerusalem.

16 Seeing themselves vanquished by Israel, the Arameans sent messengers to bring out the Arameans from the other side of the River, with Shophach, the general of Hadadezer's army, at their head. 17 When this was reported to David, he gathered all Israel together, crossed the Jordan, and met them. With the army of David drawn up to fight the Arameans, they gave battle. 18 But the Arameans fled before Israel, and David slew seven thousand of their chariot fighters and forty thousand of their foot soldiers; he also killed Shophach, the general of the army. 19 When the vassals of Hadadezer saw themselves vanquished by Israel, they made peace with David and became his subjects. After this, the Arameans refused to come to the aid of the Ammonites.

20 1 At the beginning of the following year, the time when kings go to war, Joab led the army out in force, laid waste the land of the Ammonites, and went on to besiege Rabbah, while David himself remained in Jerusalem. When Joab had attacked Rabbah and destroyed it, 2* David took the crown of Milcom from the idol's head. It was found to weigh a talent of gold; and it contained precious stones, which David wore on his own head.

He also brought out a great amount of booty from the city. 3 He deported the people of the city and set them to work with saws, iron picks, and axes. Thus David dealt with all the cities of the Ammonites. Then he and his whole army returned to Jerusalem.

Victories over the Philistines

4* Afterward there was another battle with the Philistines, at Gezer. At that time, Sibbecai the Hushathite slew Sippai, one of the descendants of the Raphaim, and the Philistines were subdued.* 5*† Once again there was war with the Philistines, and Elhanan, the son of Jair, slew Lahmi, the brother of Goliath of Gath, whose spear shaft was like a weaver's heddle-bar.

6 In still another battle, at Gath, they encountered a giant, also a descendant of the Raphaim, who had six fingers to each hand and six toes to each foot; twenty-four in all. 7 He defied Israel, and Jonathan, the son of Shimea, David's brother, slew him. 8 These were the descendants of the Raphaim of Gath who died at the hands of David and his servants.

David's Census; the Plague

21 1*† A satan rose up against Israel, and he enticed David into taking a census of Israel.* 2 David therefore said to Joab and to the other generals of the army, "Go, find out the number of the Israelites from Beer-sheba to Dan, and report back to me that I may know their number." 3 But Joab replied: "May the LORD increase his people a hundredfold! My lord king, are not all of them my lord's subjects? Why does my lord seek to do this thing? Why will he bring guilt upon Israel?" 4 However, the king's command prevailed over Joab, who departed and traversed all of Israel, and then returned to Jerusalem. 5 Joab reported the result of the census to David: of men capable of wielding a sword, there were in all Israel one million one hundred thousand, and in Judah four hundred and seventy thousand. 6* Levi and Benjamin, however, he did not include in the census, for the king's command was repugnant to Joab. 7 This command displeased God, who began to punish Israel. 8 Then David said to God, "I have sinned greatly in doing this thing. Take away your servant's guilt, for I have acted very foolishly."

20, 5: *Elhanan . . . slew Lahmi, the brother of Goliath:* the Chronicler thus solves the difficulty of the apparent contradiction between 1 Sm 17, 49ff (David killed Goliath) and 2 Sm 21, 19 (Elhanan killed Goliath).

21, 1: *A satan:* in the parallel passage of 2 Sm 24, 1, the Lord's anger. The change in the term reflects the changed theological outlook of postexilic Israel, when evil could no longer be attributed directly to God. At an earlier period the Hebrew word *satan* ("adversary," or, especially in a court of law, "accuser"), when not used of men, designated an angel who accused men before God (Jb

1, 6–12; 2, 1–7; Zec 3, 1f). Here, as in later Judaism (Wis 2, 24) and in the New Testament, satan, or the "devil" (from the Greek translation of the word), designates an evil spirit who tempts men to wrongdoing.

19, 10: 1 Chr 20, 23; 1 Kgs 2, 28.34.
19, 11: 1 Chr 23, 18f.
20, 2f: 2 Sm 12, 30f.
20, 4–8: 2 Sm 21, 18–22.
20, 4: 1 Chr 11, 29; 27, 11.

20, 5: 1 Chr 11, 26; 1 Sm 17, 4.23.
21, 1–7: 2 Sm 24, 1–25.
21, 1: Zec 3, 1f.
21, 6: 1 Chr 27, 24; Nm 1, 49.

9* Then the LORD spoke to Gad, David's seer, in these words: 10 "Go, tell David: Thus says the LORD: I offer you three alternatives; choose one of them, and I will inflict it on you." 11 Accordingly, Gad went to David and said to him: "Thus says the LORD: Decide now— 12 will it be three years of famine; or three months of fleeing your enemies, with the sword of your foes ever at your back; or three days of the LORD's own sword, a pestilence in the land, with the LORD's destroying angel in every part of Israel? Therefore choose: What answer am I to give him who sent me?" 13 Then David said to Gad: "I am in dire straits. But I prefer to fall into the hand of the LORD, whose mercy is very great, than into the hands of men."

14 Therefore the LORD sent pestilence upon Israel, and seventy thousand men of Israel died. 15* God also sent an angel to destroy Jerusalem; but as he was on the point of destroying it, the LORD saw and decided against the calamity, and said to the destroying angel, "Enough now! Stay your hand!"

Ornan's Threshing Floor

The angel of the LORD was then standing by the threshing floor of Ornan the Jebusite. 16 When David raised his eyes, he saw the angel of the LORD standing between earth and heaven, with a naked sword in his hand stretched out against Jerusalem. David and the elders, clothed in sackcloth, prostrated themselves face to the ground, 17 and David prayed to God: "Was it not I who ordered the census of the people? I am the one who sinned, I did this wicked thing. But these sheep, what have they done? O LORD, my God, strike me and my father's family, but do not afflict your people with this plague!"

18* Then the angel of the LORD commanded Gad to tell David to go up and erect an altar to the LORD on the threshing floor of Ornan the Jebusite. 19 David went up at Gad's command, given in the name of the LORD. 20 While Ornan was threshing wheat, he turned around and saw the king, and his four sons who were with him, without recognizing them. 21 But as David came on toward him, he looked up and saw that it was David. Then he left the threshing floor and bowed down before David, his face to the ground. 22 David said to Ornan: "Sell me the ground of this threshing floor, that I may build on it an altar to the LORD. Sell it to me at its full price, that the plague may be stayed from the people." 23 But Ornan said to David: "Take it as your own, and let my lord the king do what seems best to him. See, I also give you the oxen for the holocausts, the threshing sledges for the wood, and the wheat for the cereal offering. I give it all to you." 24 But King David replied to Ornan: "No! I will buy it from you properly, at its full price. I will not take what is yours for the LORD, nor offer up holocausts that cost me nothing." 25† So David paid Ornan six hundred shekels of gold for the place.

Altar of Holocausts

26* David then built an altar there to the LORD, and offered up holocausts and peace offerings. When he called upon the LORD, he answered him by sending down fire from heaven upon the altar of holocausts. 27 Then the LORD gave orders to the angel to return his sword to its sheath.

28 Once David saw that the LORD had heard him on the threshing floor of Ornan the Jebusite, he continued to offer sacrifices there. 29* The Dwelling

PRAY IT!

True Repentance

Think of a time when you said, "I'm sorry," just because you felt you had to. Now think of a time when you were truly sorry for causing harm to another by doing something God had commanded you not to do. There is a big difference between going through the motions of repentance and being truly repentant before another and before God. For example, David sinned by ordering a census to count his people (1 Chr 21, 2). He accepted a consequence that he hoped would be the easiest (verse 13). But when he saw the harm he had caused, he became truly repentant and asked God's mercy upon the Israelites (verse 17).

Repentance requires true sorrow and asking God to change our heart. It leads to an active response to make amends with God and with the church. Such repentance is called reconciliation, and Catholics celebrate it in the sacrament of Reconciliation.

▶ 1 Chr 21, 1–17

21, 25: *Six hundred shekels of gold:* about 10,000 dollars. According to 2 Sm 24, 24, David paid 50 shekels of silver, about 20 dollars, for Ornan's threshing floor; but for the Chronicler the site of the temple was much more precious than that.

21, 9: 1 Chr 29, 29; 1 Sm 9, 9; 2 Chr 29, 25.
21, 15: Gn 6, 6; Ex 32, 14; 2 Sm 24, 16; Jon 3, 10.
21, 18: 2 Chr 3, 1.
21, 26: Lv 9, 24; Jgs 6, 21; 1 Kgs 18, 38; 2 Chr 7, 1; 2 Mc 2, 10ff.
21, 29: 1 Chr 16, 39; 1 Kgs 8, 4; 2 Chr 1, 8.

of the LORD, which Moses had built in the desert, and the altar of holocausts were at that time on the high place at Gibeon. 30 But David could not go there to worship God, for he was fearful of the sword of the angel of the LORD. 1*† Therefore David said, "This is the house of the LORD God, and this is the altar of holocausts for Israel."

Material for the Temple

22 2*† David then ordered that all the aliens who lived in the land of Israel be brought together, and he appointed them stonecutters to hew out stone blocks for building the house of God. 3* He also laid up large stores of iron to make nails for the doors of the gates, and clamps, together with so much bronze that it could not be weighed, 4* and cedar trees without number. The Sidonians and Tyrians brought great stores of cedar logs to David, 5* who said: "My son Solomon is young and immature; but the house that is to be built for the LORD must be made so magnificent that it will be renowned and glorious in all countries. Therefore I will make preparations for it." Thus before his death David laid up materials in abundance.

Charge to Solomon

6 Then he called for his son Solomon and commanded him to build a house for the LORD, the God of Israel. 7* David said to Solomon: "My son, it was my purpose to build a house myself for the honor of the LORD, my God. 8 But this word of the LORD came to me: 'You have shed much blood, and you have waged great wars. You may not build a house in my honor, because you have shed too much blood upon the earth in my sight. 9*† However, a son is to be born to you. He will be a peaceful man, and I will give him rest from all his enemies on every side. For Solomon shall be his name, and in his time I will bestow peace and tranquility on Israel. 10* It is he who shall build a house in my honor; he shall be a son to me, and I will be a father to him, and I will establish the throne of his kingship over Israel forever.' 11 Now, my son, the

LORD be with you, and may you succeed in building the house of the LORD your God, as he has said you shall. 12 May the LORD give you prudence and discernment when he brings you to rule over Israel, so that you keep the law of the LORD, your God. 13* Only then shall you succeed, if you are careful to observe the precepts and decrees which the LORD gave Moses for Israel. Be brave and steadfast; do not fear or lose heart. 14*† See, with great effort I have laid up for the house of the LORD a hundred thousand talents of gold, a million talents of silver, and bronze and iron in such great quantities that they cannot be weighed. I have also stored up wood and stones, to which you must add. 15 Moreover, you have available an unlimited supply of workmen, stonecutters, masons, carpenters, and every kind of craftsman 16 skilled in gold, silver, bronze, and iron. Set to work, therefore, and the LORD be with you!"

Charge to the Leaders

17 David also commanded all of Israel's leaders to help his son Solomon: 18* "Is not the LORD your God with you? Has he not given you rest on every side? Indeed, he has delivered the occupants of the land into my power, and the land is subdued before the LORD and his people. 19* Therefore, devote your hearts and souls to seeking the LORD your God. Proceed to build the sanctuary of the LORD God, that the ark of the covenant of the LORD and God's sacred vessels may be brought into the house built in honor of the LORD."

The Levitical Classes

23 1* When David had grown old and was near the end of his days, he made his son Solomon king over Israel. 2 He then gathered together all the leaders of Israel, together with the priests and the Levites.

3* The Levites thirty years old and above were counted, and their total number was found to be thirty-eight thousand men. 4 Of these, twenty-four thousand were to direct the service of the house of the LORD, six thousand were to be officials and judges, 5* four thousand were to be gatekeepers,

21, 1: This belongs to ch 22.

22, 2ff: According to 1 Kgs 5, 15–32, it was Solomon who made the material preparations for building the temple, even though David had wished to do so (1 Kgs 5, 17ff). The Chronicler, however, sought to have David, who was Israel's ideal king, more closely connected with Israel's most sacred sanctuary, the temple of Jerusalem.

22, 9: The Hebrew word for peace, *shalom*, is reflected here in the name Solomon, in Hebrew, *Shelomo*. A contrast is drawn here between Solomon, the peaceful man, and David, who waged great wars (v 8). David was prevented from building the temple, not only because all his time was taken up in waging war (1 Kgs 5, 17), but also because he shed much blood (v 8), and in the eyes of the Chronicler this made him ritually unfit for the task.

22, 14: *A hundred thousand talents of gold:* about 3,775 tons of gold. *A million talents of silver:* about 37,750 tons of silver. The fantastically exaggerated figures are intended merely to stress the

inestimable value of the temple as the center of Israelite worship. More modest figures are given in 1 Kgs 9, 14.28; 10, 10.14.

21, 1: 1 Chr 21, 18.26.28; 2 Chr 3, 1.
22, 2: 1 Kgs 5, 31f; 9, 20f; 2 Chr 2, 16f.
22, 3: 1 Chr 18, 8; 1 Kgs 7, 47.
22, 4: 1 Chr 10, 27; Ezr 3, 7.
22, 5: 1 Chr 29, 1.
22, 7–10: 1 Chr 17, 1–14; 28, 2–7; 2 Sm 7, 1–16; 1 Kgs 5, 3ff; 8, 17–21.
22, 9: 2 Sm 12, 24.
22, 10: Heb 1, 5.
22, 13: 1 Chr 28, 7.20; Dt 31,
6.23; Jos 1, 6f.9; 1 Kgs 2, 2f.
22, 14: 1 Chr 29, 2ff.
22, 18: 1 Chr 23, 25; Jos 21, 44; 23, 1; 2 Sm 7, 1.
22, 19: 1 Kgs 8, 6.21; 2 Chr 5, 7; 6, 11.
23, 1: 1 Chr 28, 5; 1 Kgs 1, 30.
23, 3: Nm 4, 3.23.30.35.39. 43.47; 8, 23–26; 2 Chr 31, 17.
23, 5: 1 Chr 9, 22.

and four thousand were to praise the LORD with the instruments which David had devised for praise. 6* David divided them into classes according to the sons of Levi: Gershon, Kohath, and Merari.

7 To the Gershonites belonged Ladan and Shimei. 8* The sons of Ladan: Jehiel the chief, then Zetham and Joel; three in all. 9 The sons of Shimei were Shelomoth, Haziel, and Haran; three. These were the heads of the families of Ladan. 10 The sons of Shimei were Jahath, Zizah, Jeush, and Beriah; these were the sons of Shimei, four in all. 11 Jahath was the chief and Zizah was second to him; but Jeush and Beriah had not many sons, and therefore they were classed as a single family, fulfilling a single office.

12* The sons of Kohath: Amram, Izhar, Hebron, and Uzziel; four in all. 13* The sons of Amran were Aaron and Moses. Aaron was set apart to be consecrated as most holy, he and his sons forever, to offer sacrifice before the LORD, to minister to him, and to bless his name forever. 14 As for Moses, however, the man of God, his sons were counted as part of the tribe of Levi. 15* The sons of Moses were Gershon and Eliezer. 16* The sons of Gershon: Shubael the chief. 17 The sons of Eliezer were Rehabiah the chief—Eliezer had no other sons, but the sons of Rehabiah were very numerous. 18 The sons of Izhar: Shelomith the chief. 19* The sons of Hebron: Jeriah, the chief, Amariah, the second, Jahaziel, the third, and Jekameam, the fourth. 20* The sons of Uzziel: Micah, the chief, and Isshiah, the second.

21* The sons of Merari: Mahli and Mushi. The sons of Mahli: Eleazar and Kish. 22* Eleazar died leaving no sons, only daughters; the sons of Kish, their kinsmen, married them. 23* The sons of Mushi: Mahli, Eder, and Jeremoth; three in all.

24* These were the sons of Levi according to their ancestral houses, the family heads as they were enrolled one by one according to their names. They performed the work of the service of the house of the LORD from twenty years of age upward, 27 for David's final orders were to enlist the Levites from the time they were twenty years old.

25* David said: "The LORD, the God of Israel, has given rest to his people, and has taken up his dwelling in Jerusalem. 26* Henceforth the Levites need not carry the Dwelling or any of its furnishings or equipment. 28 Rather, their duty shall be to assist the sons of Aaron in the service of the house of the

LORD, having charge of the courts, the chambers, and the preservation of everything holy: they shall take part in the service of the house of God. 29* They shall also have charge of the showbread, of the fine flour for the cereal offering, of the wafers of unleavened bread, and of the baking and mixing, and of all measures of quantity and size. 30* They must be present every morning to offer thanks and to praise the LORD, and likewise in the evening; 31* and at every offering of holocausts to the LORD on sabbaths, new moons, and feast days, in such numbers as are prescribed, they must always be present before the LORD. 32* They shall observe what is prescribed for them concerning the meeting tent, the sanctuary, and the sons of Aaron, their brethren, in the service of the house of the LORD."

The Priestly Classes

24 1* The descendants of Aaron also were divided into classes. The sons of Aaron were Nadab, Abihu, Eleazar, and Ithamar. 2* Nadab and Abihu died before their father, leaving no sons; therefore only Eleazar and Ithamar served as priests. 3* David, with Zadok, a descendant of Eleazar, and Ahimelech, a descendant of Ithamar, assigned the functions for the priestly service. 4 But since the descendants of Eleazar were found to be more numerous than those of Ithamar, the former were divided into sixteen groups, and the latter into eight groups, each under its family head. 5 Their functions were assigned impartially by lot, for there were officers of the holy place, and officers of the divine presence, descended both from Eleazar and from Ithamar. 6*† The scribe Shemaiah, son of Nethanel, a Levite, made a record of it in the presence of the king, and of the leaders, of Zadok the priest, and of Ahimelech, son of Abiathar, and of the heads of the ancestral houses of the priests and of the Levites, listing two successive family groups from Eleazar before each one from Ithamar.

7* The first lot fell to Jehoiarib, the second to Jedaiah, 8 the third to Harim, the fourth to Seorim, 9 the fifth to Malchijah, the sixth to Mijamin, 10* the seventh to Hakkoz, the eighth to Abijah, 11 the ninth to Jeshua, the tenth to Shecaniah, 12 the eleventh to Eliashib, the twelfth to Jakim, 13 the thirteenth to Huppah, the fourteenth to Ishbaal, 14 the fifteenth to Bilgah, the sixteenth to Immer, 15 the seventeenth to Hezir, the eighteenth to Hap-

† **24, 6:** *Ahimelech, son of Abiathar:* see note on 1 Chr 18, 16.

23, 6: 1 Chr 6, 1.16–30; 26, 1–19; Ex 6, 16; Nm 3, 17; 26, 57.
23, 8: 1 Chr 6, 21f; 29, 8.
23, 12: 1 Chr 26, 23; Ex 6, 18; Nm 3, 19; 26, 23ff.
23, 13: 1 Chr 6, 49; Ex 6, 20; 28, 1; Nm 6, 23.
23, 15: Ex 2, 22; 18, 3f.
23, 16: 1 Chr 26, 24.
23, 19: 1 Chr 24, 23.
23, 20: 1 Chr 24, 24f.
23, 21: 1 Chr 6, 29; 24, 26.28f; Ex 6, 19; Nm 3, 20.33.
23, 22: 1 Chr 24, 28f.
23, 23: 1 Chr 6, 47; 24, 30.

23, 24: 2 Chr 31, 17; Ezr 3, 8.
23, 25: 1 Chr 22, 18; Ps 132, 13.
23, 26: 1 Chr 15, 15; 2 Chr 35, 3.
23, 29: 1 Chr 9, 29.31f; Lv 2, 1.4f; 24, 5–8.
23, 30: Nm 28, 3–8.
23, 31: Nm 28, 2–29.39.
23, 32: Nm 3, 6–9; 18, 2–5.
24, 1: Ex 6, 23; Nm 3, 2ff;

26, 60.
24, 2: Lv 10, 1–7.12; Nm 3, 2.4.
24, 3: 1 Chr 18, 16; 2 Sm 8, 17; 2 Chr 8, 14.
24, 6: 1 Chr 18, 16; 2 Sm 8, 17.
24, 7–10: 1 Chr 9, 10ff; Ezr 2, 36ff; Neh 7, 39ff; 11, 10ff.
24, 10: Lk 1, 5.

pizzez, [16] the nineteenth to Pethahiah, the twentieth to Jehezkel, [17] the twenty-first to Jachin, the twenty-second to Gamul, [18] the twenty-third to Delaiah, the twenty-fourth to Maaziah. [19]* This was the appointed order of their service when they functioned in the house of the LORD in keeping with the precepts given them by Aaron, their father, as the LORD, the God of Israel, had commanded him.

Other Levites

[20]* Of the remaining Levites, there were Shubael, of the descendants of Amram, and Jehdeiah, of the descendants of Shubael; [21] Isshiah, the chief, of the descendants of Rehabiah; [22] Shelomith of the Izharites, and Jahath of the descendants of Shelomith. [23] The descendants of Hebron were Jeriah, the chief, Amariah, the second, Jahaziel, the third, Jekameam, the fourth. [24] The descendants of Uzziel were Micah; Shamir, of the descendants of Micah; [25] Isshiah, the brother of Micah; and Zechariah, a descendant of Isshiah. [26] The descendants of Merari were Mahli, Mushi, and the descendants of his son Uzziah. [27] The descendants of Merari through his son Uzziah: Shoham, Zaccur, and Ibri. [28] Descendants of Mahli were Eleazar, who had no sons, [29] and Jerahmeel, of the descendants of Kish. [30] The descendants of Mushi were Mahli, Eder, and Jerimoth.

These were the descendants of the Levites according to their ancestral houses. [31]* They too, in the same manner as their relatives, the descendants of Aaron, cast lots in the presence of King David, Zadok, Ahimelech, and the heads of the priestly and levitical families; the more important family did so in the same way as the less important one.

The Singers

25 [1]* David and the leaders of the liturgical cult set apart for service the descendants of Asaph, Heman, and Jeduthun, as singers of inspired song to the accompaniment of lyres and harps and cymbals.

This is the list of those who performed this service: [2]† Of the sons of Asaph: Zaccur, Joseph, Nethaniah, and Asharelah, sons of Asaph, under the direction of Asaph, who sang inspired songs under the guidance of the king. [3] Of Jeduthun, these sons of Jeduthun: Gedaliah, Zeri, Jeshaiah, Shimei, Hashabiah, and Mattithiah; six, under the direction

of their father Jeduthun, who sang inspired songs to the accompaniment of a lyre, to give thanks and praise to the LORD. [4] Of Heman, these sons of Heman: Bukkiah, Mattaniah, Uzziel, Shubael, and Jerimoth; Hananiah, Hanani, Eliathah, Giddalti, Romamti-ezer, Joshbekashah, Mallothi, Hothir, and Mahazioth. [5]* All these were the sons of Heman, the king's seer in divine matters; to enhance his prestige, God gave Heman fourteen sons and three daughters. [6]* All these, whether of Asaph, Jeduthun, or Heman, were under their fathers' direction in the singing in the house of the LORD to accompaniment of cymbals, harps and lyres, serving in the house of God, under the guidance of the king. [7] Their number, together with that of their brethren who were trained in singing to the LORD, all of them skilled men, was two hundred and eighty-eight. [8]* They cast lots for their functions equally, young and old, master and pupil alike.

[9] The first lot fell to Asaph, the family of Joseph; he and his sons and his brethren were twelve. Gedaliah was the second; he and his brethren and his sons were twelve. [10] The third was Zaccur, his sons, and his brethren: twelve. [11] The fourth fell to Izri, his sons, and his brethren: twelve. [12] The fifth was Nethaniah, his sons, and his brethren: twelve. [13] The sixth was Bukkiah, his sons, and his brethren: twelve. [14] The seventh was Jesarelah, his sons, and his brethren: twelve. [15] The eighth was Jeshaiah, his sons, and his brethren: twelve. [16] The ninth was Mattaniah, his sons, and his brethren: twelve. [17] The tenth was Shimei, his sons, and his brethren: twelve. [18] The eleventh was Uzziel, his sons, and his brethren: twelve. [19] The twelfth fell to Hashabiah, his sons, and his brethren: twelve. [20] The thirteenth was Shubael, his sons, and his brethren: twelve. [21] The fourteenth was Mattithiah, his sons, and his brethren: twelve. [22] The fifteenth fell to Jeremoth, his sons, and his brethren: twelve. [23] The sixteenth fell to Hananiah, his sons, and his brethren: twelve. [24] The seventeenth fell to Joshbekashah, his sons, and his brethren: twelve. [25] The eighteenth fell to Hanani, his sons, and his brethren: twelve. [26] The nineteenth fell to Mallothi, his sons, and his brethren: twelve. [27] The twentieth fell to Eliathah, his sons, and his brethren: twelve. [28] The twenty-first fell to Hothir, his sons, and his brethren: twelve. [29] The twenty-second fell to Giddalti, his sons, and his brethren: twelve. [30] The

---

† **25, 2–31:** This list of twenty-four classes of temple singers balances the list of the twenty-four classes of priests (1 Chr 24, 4–19). The last nine names in 1 Chr 25, 4, which seem to form a special group, appear to have been originally fragments or incipits of hymns. With some slight changes in the vocalization, the names would mean: "Have mercy on me, O LORD," "Have mercy on me," "You are my God," "I magnify," "I extol the help of . . . ," "Sitting in adversity," "I have fulfilled," "He made abundant," and "Visions."

* 24, 19: 2 Chr 23, 8.
24, 20–31: 1 Chr 23, 7–23.
  24, 31: 1 Chr 25, 8; 26, 13.
    25, 1: 1 Chr 6, 31ff; 15,
      16f.19; 16, 37; 2 Chr

5, 12; 35, 15; Neh 12,
  27.45.
25, 5: 2 Chr 35, 15.
25, 6: 1 Chr 15, 16.
25, 8: 1 Chr 24, 31.

twenty-third fell to Mahazioth, his sons, and his brethren: twelve. 31 The twenty-fourth fell to Romamti-ezer, his sons, and his brethren: twelve.

Classes of Gatekeepers

26 1* As for the classes of gatekeepers. Of the Korahites was Meshelemiah, the son of Kore, one of the sons of Abiasaph. 2 Meshelemiah's sons: Zechariah, the first-born, Jediael, the second son, Zebadiah, the third, Jathniel, the fourth, 3 Elam, the fifth, Jehohanan, the sixth, Eliehoenai, the seventh. 4 Obed-edom's sons: Shemaiah, the first-born, Jehozabad, a second son, Joah, the third, Sachar, the fourth, Nethanel, the fifth, 5 Ammiel, the sixth, Issachar, the seventh, Peullethai, the eighth, for God blessed him. 6 To his son Shemaiah were born sons who ruled over their family, for they were warriors. 7 The sons of Shemaiah were Othni, Rephael, Obed, and Elzabad; also his brethren who were men of might, Elihu and Semachiah. 8 All these were of the sons of Obed-edom, who, together with their sons and their brethren, were mighty men, fit for the service. Of Obed-edom, sixty-two. 9 Of Meshelemiah, eighteen sons and brethren, mighty men.

10* Hosah, a descendant of Merari, had these sons: Shimri, the chief (for though he was not the first-born, his father made him chief), 11 Hilkiah, the second son, Tebaliah, the third, Zechariah, the fourth. All the sons and brethren of Hosah were thirteen.

12 To these classes of gatekeepers, under their chief men, were assigned watches in the service of the house of the LORD, for each group in the same way. 13 They cast lots for each gate, the small and the large families alike. 14* When the lot was cast for the east side, it fell to Meshelemiah. Then they cast lots for his son Zechariah, a prudent counselor, and the north side fell to his lot. 15 To Obed-edom fell the south side, and to his sons the storehouse. 16 To Hosah fell the west side with the Shallecheth gate at the ascending highway. For each family, watches were established. 17 On the east, six watched each day, on the north, four each day, on the south, four each day, and at the storehouse they were two and two; 18† as for the large building on the west, there were four at the highway and two at the large building. 19 These were the classes of the gatekeepers, descendants of Kore and Merari.

Treasurers

20* Their brother Levites superintended the stores for the house of God and the stores of votive offerings. 21* Among the descendants of Ladan the Gershonite, the family heads were descendants of Jehiel: the descendants of Jehiel, 22* Zetham and his brother Joel, who superintended the treasures of the house of the LORD. 23 From the Amramites, Izharites, Hebronites, and Uzzielites, 24 Shubael, son of Gershon, son of Moses, was chief superintendent over the treasures. 25* His associate pertained to Eliezer, whose son was Rehabiah, whose son was Jeshaiah, whose son was Joram, whose son was Zichri, whose son was Shelomith. 26* This Shelomith and his brethren superintended all the stores of the votive offerings dedicated by King David, the heads of the families, the commanders of thousands and of hundreds, and the commanders of the army, 27 from the booty they had taken in the wars, for the enhancement of the house of the LORD. 28 Also, whatever Samuel the seer, Saul, son of Kish, Abner, son of Ner, Joab, son of Zeruiah, and all others had consecrated, was under the charge of Shelomith and his brethren.

Magistrates

29* Among the Izharites, Chananiah and his sons were in charge of Israel's civil affairs as officials and judges. 30* Among the Hebronites, Hashabiah and his brethren, one thousand seven hundred police officers, had the administration of Israel on the western side of the Jordan in all the work of the LORD and in the service of the king. 31* Among the Hebronites, Jerijah was their chief according to their family records. In the fortieth year of David's reign search was made, and there were found among them outstanding officers at Jazer of Gilead. 32 His brethren were also police officers, two thousand seven hundred heads of families. King David appointed them to the administration of the Reubenites, the Gadites, and the half-tribe of Manasseh in everything pertaining to God and to the king.

Army Commanders

27 1† This is the list of the Israelite family heads, commanders of thousands and of hundreds, and other officers who served the king in all that pertained to the divisions, of twenty-four

---

26, 18: *The large building* (in the Hebrew text *Parbar*): see note on 2 Kgs 23, 11.

27, 1–15: This list of army commanders is similar to, but distinct from, the list of David's warriors as given in 1 Chr 11, 10–47. The schematic enumeration of the soldiers as presented here is, no doubt, artificial and grossly exaggerated (12 x 24,000 = 288,000 men!), unless the Hebrew word *(eleph)* for thousand is understood as designating a military unit of much smaller size; see note on 1 Chr 12, 25–38.

26, 1: 1 Chr 9, 19; 2 Chr 8, 14; 23, 19; 35, 15; Neh 12, 45.
26, 10: 1 Chr 16, 38.
26, 14: 1 Chr 9, 24.
26, 20: 1 Chr 28, 12; 1 Kgs 7, 51.
26, 21: 1 Chr 23, 7f; 29, 8.

26, 22ff: 1 Chr 23, 8.12.16.
26, 25: 1 Chr 23, 17f; 24, 21.
26, 26: 2 Sm 8, 11.
26, 29: 1 Chr 23, 4.
26, 30: 1 Chr 27, 17; Neh 11, 15f.
26, 31: 1 Chr 23, 19; 29, 27; Jos 13, 25.

thousand men each, that came and went month by month throughout the year.

2 Over the first division for the first month was Ishbaal, son of Zabdiel, and in his division were twenty-four thousand men; 3 a descendant of Perez, he was chief over all the commanders of the army for the first month. 4* Over the division of the second month was Eleazar, son of Dodo, from Ahoh, and in his division were twenty-four thousand men. 5* The third army commander, chief for the third month, was Benaiah, son of Jehoiada the priest, and in his division were twenty-four thousand men. 6 This Benaiah was a warrior among the Thirty and over the Thirty. His son Ammizabad was over his division. 7* Fourth, for the fourth month, was Asahel, brother of Joab, and after him his son Zebadiah, and in his division were twenty-four thousand men. 8 Fifth, for the fifth month, was the commander Shamhuth, a descendant of Zerah, and in his division were twenty-four thousand men. 9 Sixth, for the sixth month, was Ira, son of Ikkesh, from Tekoa, and in his division were twenty-four thousand men. 10 Seventh, for the seventh month, was Helles, from Beth-pheleth, of the sons of Ephraim, and in his division were twenty-four thousand men. 11*Eighth, for the eighth month, was Sibbecai the Hushathite, a descendant of Zerah, and in his division were twenty-four thousand men. 12 Ninth, for the ninth month, was Abiezer from Anathoth, of Benjamin, and in his division were twenty-four thousand men. 13 Tenth, for the tenth month, was Maharai from Netophah, a descendant of Zerah, and in his division were twenty-four thousand men. 14 Eleventh, for the eleventh month, was Benaiah the Pirathonite, of Ephraim, and in his division were twenty-four thousand men. 15 Twelfth, for the twelfth month, was Heldai the Netophathite, of the family of Othniel, and in his division were twenty-four thousand men.

Tribal Heads

16 Over the tribes of Israel, for the Reubenites the leader was Eliezer, son of Zichri; for the Simeonites, Shephatiah, son of Maacah; 17 for Levi, Hashabiah, son of Kemuel; for Aaron, Zadok; 18* for Judah, Eliab, one of David's brothers; for Issachar, Omri, son of Michael; 19 for Zebulun, Ishmaiah, son of Obadiah; for Naphtali, Jeremoth, son of Azriel; 20 for the sons of Ephraim, Hoshea, son of Azaziah;

for the half-tribe of Manasseh, Joel, son of Pedaiah; 21 for the half-tribe of Manasseh in Gilead, Iddo, son of Zechariah; for Benjamin, Jaasiel, son of Abner; 22 for Dan, Azarel, son of Jeroham. These were the commanders of the tribes of Israel.

23* David did not count those who were twenty years of age or younger, for the LORD had promised to multiply Israel like the stars of the heavens. 24* Joab, son of Zeruiah, began to take the census, but he did not complete it, for because of it wrath fell upon Israel. Therefore the number did not enter into the book of chronicles of King David.

Overseers

25* Over the treasures of the king was Azmaveth, the son of Adiel. Over the stores in the country, the cities, the villages, and the towers was Jonathan, son of Uzziah. 26 Over the farm workers who tilled the soil was Ezri, son of Chelub. 27 Over the vineyards was Shimei from Ramah, and over their produce for the wine cellars was Zabdi the Shiphmite. 28 Over the olive trees and sycamores of the foothills was Baal-hanan the Gederite, and over the stores of oil was Joash. 29 Over the cattle that grazed in Sharon was Shitrai the Sharonite, and over the cattle in the valleys was Shaphat, the son of Adlai; 30 over the camels was Obil the Ishmaelite; over the she-asses was Jehdeiah the Meronothite; 31 and over the flocks was Jaziz the Hagrite. All these were the overseers of King David's possessions.

David's Court

32 Jonathan, David's uncle and a man of intelligence, was counselor and scribe; he and Jehiel, the son of Hachmoni, were tutors of the king's sons. 33* Ahithophel was also the king's counselor, and Hushai the Archite was the king's confidant. 34† After Ahithophel came Jehoiada, the son of Benaiah, and Abiathar. The commander of the king's army was Joab.

The Assembly at Jerusalem

28 1* David assembled at Jerusalem all the leaders of Israel, the heads of the tribes, the commanders of the divisions who were in the service of the king, the commanders of thousands and of hundreds, the overseers of all the king's estates and possessions, and his sons, together with the courtiers, the warriors, and every important

---

† **27, 34:** *After Ahithophel:* after his suicide (2 Sm 17, 23). Jehoiada then succeeded him as the king's counselor. *Abiathar:* the priest. The Chronicler does not mention his office because he regards only the Zadokites as legitimate high priests.

* 27, 4: 1 Chr 9, 37; 11, 12;
  2 Sm 23, 9.
27, 5f: 1 Chr 11, 22ff; 18, 17;
  2 Sm 23, 20ff.
27, 7: 2 Sm 2, 18; 23, 24.
27, 11: 1 Chr 11, 29; 20, 4;
  2 Sm 21, 18.
27, 18: 1 Chr 2, 13.

27, 23: 1 Chr 22, 17.
27, 24: 2 Sm 24, 10.
27, 25: 2 Sm 23, 31.
27, 33: 2 Sm 15, 12.32–37;
  16, 16–19.23; 17,
  5–16.23.
28, 1: 1 Chr 27, 2–22.25–31;
  11, 10ff.

man. ²*† King David rose to his feet and said: "Hear me, my brethren and my people. It was my purpose to build a house of repose myself for the ark of the covenant of the LORD, the footstool for the feet of our God; and I was preparing to build it. ³ But God said to me, 'You may not build a house in my honor, for you are a man who fought wars and shed blood.' ⁴* However, the LORD, the God of Israel, chose me from all my father's family to be king over Israel forever. For he chose Judah as leader, then one family of Judah, that of my father; and finally, among all the sons of my father, it pleased him to make me king over all Israel. ⁵* And of all my sons—for the LORD has given me many sons—he has chosen my son Solomon to sit on the LORD's royal throne over Israel. ⁶* For he said to me: 'It is your son Solomon who shall build my house and my courts, for I have chosen him for my son, and I will be a father to him. ⁷ I will establish his kingdom forever, if he perseveres in keeping my commandments and decrees as he keeps them now.' ⁸* Therefore in the presence of all Israel, the assembly of the LORD, and in the hearing of our God, I exhort you to keep and to carry out all the commandments of the LORD, your God, that you may continue to possess this good land and afterward leave it as an inheritance to your children forever.

⁹* "As for you, Solomon, my son, know the God of your father and serve him with a perfect heart and a willing soul, for the LORD searches all hearts and understands all the mind's thoughts. If you seek him, he will let himself be found by you; but if you abandon him, he will cast you off forever. ¹⁰ See, then! The LORD has chosen you to build a house as his sanctuary. Take courage and set to work."

Temple Plans Given to Solomon

¹¹* Then David gave to his son Solomon the pattern of the portico and of the building itself, with its storerooms, its upper rooms and inner chambers, and the room with the propitiatory. ¹² He provided also the pattern for all else that he had in mind by way of courts for the house of the LORD, with the surrounding compartments for the stores for the house of God and the stores of the votive offerings, ¹³ as well as for the divisions of the priests and Levites, for all the work of the service of the house

of the LORD, and for all the liturgical vessels of the house of the LORD. ¹⁴ He specified the weight of gold to be used in the golden vessels for the various services and the weight of silver to be used in the silver vessels for the various services; ¹⁵* likewise for the golden lampstands and their lamps he specified the weight of gold for each lampstand and its lamps, and for the silver lampstands he specified the weight of silver for each lampstand and its lamps, depending on the use to which each lampstand was to be put. ¹⁶ He specified the weight of gold for each table to hold the showbread, and the silver for the silver tables; ¹⁷ the pure gold to be used for the forks and pitchers; the amount of gold for each golden bowl and the silver for each silver bowl; ¹⁸*† the refined gold, and its weight, to be used for the altar of incense; and, finally, gold for what would suggest a chariot throne: the cherubim that spread their wings and covered the ark of the covenant of the LORD. ¹⁹ He had successfully committed to writing the exact specifications of the pattern, because the hand of the LORD was upon him.

²⁰* Then David said to his son Solomon: "Be firm and steadfast; go to work without fear or discouragement, for the LORD God, my God, is with you. He will not fail you or abandon you before you have completed all the work for the service of the house of the LORD. ²¹* The classes of the priests and Levites are ready for all the service of the house of God; they will help you in all your work with all those who are eager to show their skill in every kind of craftsmanship. Also the leaders and all the people will do everything that you command."

Offerings for the Temple

29 ¹* King David then said to the whole assembly: "My son Solomon, whom alone God has chosen, is still young and immature; the work, however, is great, for this castle is not intended for man, but for the LORD God. ²* For this reason I have stored up for the house of my God, as far as I was able, gold for what will be made of gold, silver for what will be made of silver, bronze for what will be made of bronze, iron for what will be made of iron, wood for what will be made of wood, onyx stones and settings for them, carnelian and mosaic stones, every other

---

28, 2: *The ark . . . the footstool . . . of our God:* the Lord, who was invisibly enthroned upon the cherubim that were associated with the ark of the covenant at Shiloh and later in the Jerusalem temple, had the ark as his footstool; cf Pss 99, 5; 132, 7. The propitiatory (1 Chr 28, 11) and the chariot throne (1 Chr 28, 18) reflect the different circumstances of the postexilic community, for whom only the place of the ark was a focal point of worship, though the ark itself was no longer present.

28, 18: *Chariot throne:* probably suggested by Ez 1, 4–24; 10, 1–22.

28, 2f: 1 Chr 17, 4; 22, 7ff;
  2 Sm 7, 5; 1 Kgs 5, 3;
  Ps 132, 3–7.
28, 4: 1 Chr 17, 23; Gn 49,
  8ff; 1 Sm 16, 6–13.
28, 5: 1 Chr 3, 1–9; 14, 3–7;
  22, 9; 23, 1; Wis 9, 7.
28, 6: 1 Chr 17, 11ff; 22, 9f;
  2 Sm 7, 12f.
28, 8: Dt 4, 5.
28, 9: 1 Chr 29, 17; 2 Chr

15, 2; 1 Kgs 8, 61.
28, 11: Ex 25, 9.40; 26, 30.
28, 15: Ex 25, 31–37.
28, 18: Ex 25, 18–22; 30,
  1–10; 1 Kgs 6, 23–28.
28, 20: 1 Chr 22, 13.16; Jos
  1, 5.
28, 21: Ex 36, 1–5.
29, 1: 1 Chr 22, 5; 28, 5.
29, 2: 1 Chr 22, 14.

GOD'S NAME

As David neared the end of his life and reign, he blessed God's name in the midst of the people. The Israelites, who believed in one God, were surrounded by other cultures who believed in many different gods, both good and evil. The name of the Israelites' one God was sacred and precious to them, and they often associated God's name with power, glory, majesty, and victory over all creation.

In Hmong, the name of God is Huab Tais Ntuj, which can be translated as Highest One or Emperor Spirit or Overriding Spirit. The Hmong culture developed as a subculture within the Central Highlands of China. The Hmong believed in different spirits, both good and evil, angelic and demonic. So, in naming God Highest Emperor, overriding all other spirits, they clearly also developed a belief in one God with power over all creation.

▸ 1 Chr 29, 10–22

kind of precious stone, and great quantities of marble. ³ But now, because of the delight I take in the house of my God, in addition to all that I stored up for the holy house, I give to the house of my God my personal fortune in gold and silver: ⁴* three thousand talents of Ophir gold, and seven thousand talents of refined silver, for overlaying the walls of the rooms, ⁵* for the various utensils to be made of gold and silver, and for every work that is to be done by artisans. Now, who else is willing to contribute generously this day to the LORD?"

⁶* Then the heads of the families, the leaders of the tribes of Israel, the commanders of thousands and of hundreds, and the overseers of the king's affairs came forward willingly ⁷* and contributed for the service of the house of God five thousand talents and ten thousand darics of gold, ten thousand talents of silver, eighteen thousand talents of bronze, and one hundred thousand talents of iron. ⁸* Those who had precious stones gave them into the keeping of Jehiel the Gershonite for the treasury of the house of the LORD. ⁹* The people rejoiced over these free-will offerings, which had been contributed to the LORD wholeheartedly. King David also rejoiced greatly.

David's Prayer

¹⁰ Then David blessed the LORD in the presence of the whole assembly, praying in these words:

> "Blessed may you be, O LORD,
>   God of Israel our father,
>   from eternity to eternity.

¹¹   "Yours, O LORD, are grandeur and power,
>   majesty, splendor, and glory.
> For all in heaven and on earth is yours;
>   yours, O LORD, is the sovereignty;
>   you are exalted as head over all.

¹²*   "Riches and honor are from you,
>   and you have dominion over all.
> In your hand are power and might;
>   it is yours to give grandeur and strength
>   to all.

¹³   Therefore, our God, we give you thanks
>   and we praise the majesty of your name."

¹⁴ "But who am I, and who are my people, that we should have the means to contribute so freely? For everything is from you, and we only give you what we have received from you. ¹⁵* For we stand

---

29, 4: 2 Chr 9, 10; 1 Kgs 9, 28; 10, 11.
29, 5: Ex 25, 2; 35, 5f.
29, 6: 1 Chr 27, 1.25–31; 28, 1.
29, 7: Ezr 2, 69; 8, 27; Neh 7, 70ff.
29, 8: 1 Chr 23, 8; 26, 21.
29, 9: 2 Kgs 12, 4.
29, 12: 2 Chr 20, 6; Wis 6, 3.
29, 15: Lv 25, 23; Wis 2, 5; 5, 9.

1

C
H
R

before you as aliens: we are only your guests, like all our fathers. Our life on earth is like a shadow that does not abide. 16 O LORD our God, all this wealth that we have brought together to build you a house in honor of your holy name comes from you and is entirely yours. 17 I know, O my God, that you put hearts to the test and that you take pleasure in uprightness. With a sincere heart I have willingly given all these things, and now with joy I have seen your people here present also giving to you generously. 18* O LORD, God of our fathers Abraham, Isaac, and Israel, keep such thoughts in the hearts and minds of your people forever, and direct their hearts toward you. 19 Give to my son Solomon a wholehearted desire to keep your commandments, precepts, and statutes, that he may carry out all these plans and build the castle for which I have made preparation."

20 Then David besought the whole assembly, "Now bless the LORD your God!" And the whole assembly blessed the LORD, the God of their fathers, bowing down and prostrating themselves before the LORD and before the king. 21 On the following day they offered sacrifices and holocausts to the LORD, a thousand bulls, a thousand rams, and a thousand lambs, together with their libations and many other sacrifices for all Israel; 22 and on that day they ate and drank in the LORD's presence with great rejoicing.

Solomon Anointed

† Then for a second time they proclaimed David's son Solomon king, and they anointed him as the LORD's prince, and Zadok as priest. 23* Thereafter Solomon sat on the throne of the LORD as king in place of his father David; he prospered, and all Israel obeyed him. 24 All the leaders and warriors, and also all the other sons of King David, swore allegiance to King Solomon. 25* And the LORD exalted Solomon greatly in the eyes of all Israel, giving him a glorious reign such as had not been enjoyed by any king over Israel before him.

Death of David

26 Thus David, the son of Jesse, had reigned over all Israel. 27* The time that he reigned over Israel was forty years: in Hebron he reigned seven years, and in Jerusalem thirty-three. 28* He died at a ripe old age, rich in years and wealth and glory, and his son Solomon succeeded him as king.

29* Now the deeds of King David, first and last, can be found written in the history of Samuel the seer, the history of Nathan the prophet, and the history of Gad the seer, 30 together with the particulars of his reign and valor, and of the events that affected him and all Israel and all the kingdoms of the surrounding lands.

29, 22: *For a second time:* the first time is referred to in 1 Chr 23, 1. Here there is a solemn public ratification of David's earlier appointment of Solomon as his successor.

29, 18: Ex 3, 6.15f; 4, 5; 1 Kgs 18, 36.
29, 23: 1 Chr 28, 5; 2 Chr 9, 8; 1 Kgs 2, 10ff.
29, 25: 2 Chr 1, 12; 1 Kgs 3, 13.
29, 27: 2 Sm 5, 5; 1 Kgs 2, 11.
29, 28: 1 Chr 23, 1.
29, 29: 1 Chr 21, 9; 1 Sm 22, 5.

2 Chronicles

For background on this book, see the introduction to 1 and 2 Chronicles.

Chap. 3

I: The Reign of Solomon

Solomon at Gibeon

1 [1] Solomon, son of David, strengthened his hold on the kingdom, for the LORD, his God, was with him, constantly making him more renowned. [2] He sent a summons to all Israel, to the commanders of thousands and of hundreds, the judges, the princes of all Israel, and the family heads; [3]* and, accompanied by the whole assembly, he went to the high place at Gibeon, because the meeting tent of God, made in the desert by Moses, the LORD'S servant, was there. [4] (The ark of God, however, David had brought up from Kiriath-jearim to Jerusalem, where he had provided a place and pitched a tent for it.) [5]*† The bronze altar made by Bezalel, son of Uri, son of Hur, he put in front of the LORD'S Dwelling on the high place. There Solomon and the assembly consulted the LORD, [6] and Solomon offered sacrifice in the LORD'S presence on the bronze altar at the meeting tent; he offered a thousand holocausts upon it.

[7] That night God appeared to Solomon and said to him, "Make a request of me, and I will grant it to

you." [8] Solomon answered God: "You have shown great favor to my father David, and you have allowed me to succeed him as king. [9] Now, LORD God, may your promise to my father David be fulfilled, for you have made me king over a people as numerous as the dust of the earth. [10] Give me, therefore, wisdom and knowledge to lead this people, for otherwise who could rule this great people of yours?" [11] God then replied to Solomon: "Since this has been your wish and you have not asked for riches, treasures and glory, nor for the life of those who hate you, nor even for a long life for yourself, but have asked for wisdom and knowledge in order to rule my people over whom I have made you king, [12] wisdom and knowledge are given you; but I will also give you riches, treasures and glory, such as kings before you never had, nor will those have them who come after you."

Solomon's Wealth

[13] Solomon returned to Jerusalem from the high place at Gibeon, from the meeting tent, and became king over Israel. [14]* He gathered together chariots and drivers, so that he had one thousand four hundred chariots and twelve thousand drivers he

---

† **1, 5:** *The bronze altar . . . the LORD's Dwelling:* the Chronicler justifies Solomon's worship at the high place of Gibeon. He pictures *the LORD's Dwelling,* i.e., the Mosaic meeting tent, and *the bronze altar* made at Moses' command (Ex 31, 1–9) as still at Gibeon after David had removed the ark of the covenant from there to a new tent in Jerusalem (1 Chr 15, 1.25; 16, 1). The altar made by Bezalel is described as being of acacia wood plated with bronze (Ex 27, 1f).

Solomon later made an all-bronze altar for the temple in Jerusalem (2 Chr 4, 1).

*

1, 3–12: 1 Kgs 3, 4–15; 1 Chr 21, 29.
1, 5: Ex 27, 1f; 31, 2; 1 Chr

2, 20.
1, 14: 2 Chr 9, 25; 10, 26–29.

did you KNOW?

Wisdom and the Torah

What a deal for Solomon! God tells him to ask for anything and Solomon will have it (2 Chr 1, 7). Solomon prays to be wise (verse 10), which pleases God because it indicates Solomon's desire to rule God's people according to God's will. But what is wisdom? For the Chronicler, wisdom is ultimately living one's life in conformity with God's instruction, or the Torah (see Dt 17, 8–11). Wisdom is evident in the person who worships God correctly and lives a moral life in keeping with the Law, and in the king who governs justly. To learn more about the Israelites' view of wisdom, take a look at the wisdom books in the next section of the Old Testament. For a New Testament perspective, see Lk 2, 41–52; 1 Cor 1, 18–31.

▶ 2 Chr 1, 7–12

could station in the chariot cities and with the king in Jerusalem. ¹⁵* The king made silver and gold as common in Jerusalem as stones, while cedars became as numerous as the sycamores of the foothills. ¹⁶*† Solomon also imported horses from Egypt and Cilicia. The king's agents would acquire them by purchase from Cilicia, ¹⁷* and would then bring up chariots from Egypt and export them at six hundred silver shekels, with the horses going for a hundred and fifty shekels. At these rates they served as middlemen for all the Hittite and Aramean kings.

Preparations for the Temple

¹⁸ Solomon gave orders for the building of a house to honor the LORD and also of a house for his own royal estate.

2 ¹* He conscripted seventy thousand men to carry stone and eighty thousand to cut the stone in the mountains, and over these he placed

three thousand six hundred overseers. ²* Moreover, Solomon sent this message to Huram, king of Tyre: "As you dealt with my father David, sending him cedars to build a house for his dwelling, so deal with me. ³* I intend to build a house for the honor of the LORD, my God, and to consecrate it to him, for the burning of fragrant incense in his presence, for the perpetual display of the showbread, for holocausts morning and evening, and for the sabbaths, new moons, and festivals of the LORD, our God: such is Israel's perpetual obligation. ⁴ And the house I intend to build must be large, for our God is greater than all other gods. ⁵* Yet who is really able to build him a house, since the heavens and even the highest heavens cannot contain him? And who am I that I should build him a house, unless it be to offer incense in his presence? ⁶ Now, send me men skilled at work in gold, silver, bronze and iron, in purple, crimson, and violet fabrics, and who know how to do engraved work, to join the craftsmen who are with me in Judah and Jerusalem, whom my father David appointed. ⁷ Also send me boards of cedar, cypress and cabinet wood from Lebanon, for I realize that your servants know how to cut the wood of the Lebanon. My servants will labor with yours ⁸ in order to prepare for me a great quantity of wood, since the house I intend to build must be lofty and wonderful. ⁹* I will furnish as food for your servants, the hewers who cut the wood, twenty thousand kors of wheat, twenty thousand kors of barley, twenty thousand measures of wine, and twenty thousand measures of oil."

¹⁰ Huram, king of Tyre, wrote an answer which he sent to Solomon: "Because the LORD loves his people, he has placed you over them as king." ¹¹* He added: "Blessed be the LORD, the God of Israel, who made heaven and earth, for having given King David a wise son of intelligence and understanding, who will build a house for the LORD and also a house for his royal estate. ¹²* I am now sending you a craftsman of great skill, Huram-abi, ¹³† son of a Danite woman and of a father from Tyre; he knows how to work with gold, silver, bronze and iron, with stone and wood, with purple, violet, fine linen and crimson, and also how to do all kinds of engraved work and to devise every type of artistic work that may be given him and your craftsmen and the craftsmen of my lord David your father. ¹⁴* And now, let my lord send to his servants the wheat, barley, oil and wine

---

1, 16f: *Egypt . . . Cilicia:* it seems likely that the horses came from Cilicia and the chariots from Egypt. Some read the source of these data in 1 Kgs 10, 28f as containing the name (Musur) of a mountain district north of Cilicia, rather than of Egypt; but the author of Chronicles surely understood Egypt; cf 2 Chr 9, 28.
2, 13: *A Danite woman:* a widow of the tribe of Naphtali (1 Kgs 7, 14). The Danites had settled in the northern section of Naphtali's territory (Jgs 18, 27ff). Bezalel's fellow craftsman was of the tribe of Dan (Ex 31, 6).

1, 15: 1 Kgs 10, 27.	Nm 28–29.
1, 16: 1 Kgs 10, 28.	2, 5: 2 Chr 6, 18.
1, 17: 1 Kgs 10, 29.	2, 9: 1 Kgs 5, 25; Ezr 3, 7.
2, 1: 2 Chr 2, 17; 5, 29f.	2, 11: 1 Kgs 5, 21.
2, 2–9: 1 Kgs 5, 15–20; 1 Chr 14, 1.	2, 12f: 1 Kgs 7, 13f; Ex 31, 1–5.
2, 3: Lv 24, 5–8;	2, 14f: 1 Kgs 5, 22–26.

which he has promised. ¹⁵* For our part, we will cut trees on Lebanon, as many as you need, and float them down to you at the port of Joppa, whence you may take them up to Jerusalem."

¹⁶* Thereupon Solomon took a census of all the alien men who were in the land of Israel (following the census David his father had taken of them), who were found to number one hundred fifty-three thousand six hundred. ¹⁷* Of these he made seventy thousand carriers and eighty thousand cutters in the mountains, and three thousand six hundred overseers to keep the people working.

Building of the Temple

3 ¹*† Then Solomon began to build the house of the LORD in Jerusalem on Mount Moriah, which had been pointed out to his father David, on the spot which David had selected, the threshing-floor of Ornan the Jebusite. ² He began to build in the second month of the fourth year of his reign. ³* These were the specifications laid down by Solomon for building the house of God: the length was sixty cubits according to the old measure, and the width was twenty cubits; ⁴*† the porch which lay before the nave along the width of the house was also twenty cubits, and it was twenty cubits high. He overlaid its interior with pure gold. ⁵* The nave he overlaid with cypress wood which he covered with fine gold, embossing on it palms and chains. ⁶ He also decorated the building with precious stones. ⁷ The house; its beams and thresholds, as well as its walls and its doors, he overlaid with gold, and he engraved cherubim upon the walls. (The gold was from Parvaim.) ⁸* He also made the room of the holy of holies. Its length corresponded to the width of the house, twenty cubits, and its width was also twenty cubits. He overlaid it with fine gold to the amount of six hundred talents. ⁹ The weight of the nails was fifty gold shekels. The upper chambers he likewise covered with gold.

¹⁰* For the room of the holy of holies he made two cherubim of carved workmanship, which were then overlaid with gold. ¹¹ The wings of the cherubim spanned twenty cubits: ¹² one wing of each

cherub, five cubits in length, extended to a wall of the building, while the other wing, also five cubits in length, touched the corresponding wing of the second cherub. ¹³ The combined wingspread of the two cherubim was thus twenty cubits. They stood upon their own feet, facing toward the nave. ¹⁴*† He made the veil of violet, purple, crimson and fine linen, and had cherubim embroidered upon it.

¹⁵* In front of the building he set two columns thirty-five cubits high; the capital topping each was of five cubits. ¹⁶ He worked out chains in the form of a collar with which he encircled the capitals of the columns, and he made a hundred pomegranates which he set on the chains. ¹⁷ He set up the columns to correspond with the nave, one for the right side and the other for the left, and he called the one to the right Jachin and the one to the left Boaz.

4 ¹* Then he made a bronze altar twenty cubits long, twenty cubits wide and ten cubits high. ²* He also made the molten sea. It was perfectly round, ten cubits in diameter, five in depth, and thirty in circumference; ³† below the rim a ring of figures of oxen encircled the sea, ten to the cubit, all the way around; there were two rows of these cast in the same mold with the sea. ⁴ It rested on twelve oxen, three facing north, three west, three south, and three east, with their haunches all toward the center; the sea rested on their backs. ⁵† It was a handbreadth thick, and its brim was made like that of a cup, being lily-shaped. It had a capacity of three thousand measures.

⁶* Then he made ten basins for washing, placing five of them to the right and five to the left. Here were cleansed the victims for the holocausts; but the sea was for the priests to wash in.

⁷* He made the lampstands of gold, ten of them as was prescribed, and placed them in the nave, five to the right and five to the left. ⁸* He made ten tables and had them set in the nave, five to the right and five to the left; and he made a hundred golden bowls. ⁹* He made the court of the priests and the

---

† 3, 1: *Mount Moriah:* the height in the land of Moriah (Gn 22, 2). This is the only place in the Bible where the temple mount is identified with the site where Abraham was to sacrifice Isaac.

3, 4: *The porch . . . twenty cubits high:* this measurement, not given in the Books of Kings, is here based on a variant Greek text that may be a later revision. The received Hebrew text says, "one hundred and twenty cubits high." The height of the two freestanding columns adjacent to the porch (1 Kgs 7, 15–16) is nearly doubled by the Chronicler (2 Chr 3, 15).

3, 14: *The veil:* at the entrance of the holy of holies, as also in the Mosaic meeting tent (Ex 26, 31f). Solomon's temple had doors at this place (1 Kgs 6, 31). Apparently there was a veil here in the temple of the Chronicler's time as there was also in Herod's temple (Mt 27, 51; Mk 15, 38; Lk 23, 45).

4, 3: *Oxen:* in 1 Kgs 7, 24 this double row of ornaments is described as being gourds. The text of Kings available to the Chronicler

may have been faulty on this point as the words are similar in sound. In 2 Chr 4, 16 the forks correspond in a similar way to bowls in the text of 1 Kings (7, 40).

4, 5: *Three thousand measures:* according to 1 Kgs 7, 26, "two thousand measures."

2, 15: Ezr 3, 7.
2, 16f: 1 Chr 22, 2.
2, 17: 2 Chr 2, 1.
3, 1f: Gn 22, 2; 1 Kgs 6, 1; 1 Chr 21, 22–26.
3, 3: 1 Kgs 6, 2; Ez 40, 5.
3, 4: 1 Kgs 6, 3; Ez 40, 48.
3, 5: 1 Kgs 6, 15; Ez 41, 16.
3, 8: 1 Kgs 6, 16f.20; Ez 41, 3.
3, 10–31: 1 Kgs 6, 23–27.
3, 14: Mt 27, 51.
3, 15ff: 1 Kgs 7, 15–22; Ez 40, 49.
4, 1: Ez 43, 13–17.
4, 2–5: 1 Kgs 7, 23–26; Ez 43, 13.
4, 6: 1 Kgs 7, 38f; Ez 40, 38.
4, 7: 1 Kgs 7, 49.
4, 8: 1 Kgs 7, 50; 1 Chr 28, 16.
4, 9: 1 Kgs 7, 12.

great courtyard and the gates of the courtyard; the gates he overlaid with bronze. 10* The sea was placed off to the southeast from the right side of the temple.

11* Huram also made the pots, the shovels and the bowls. Huram thus completed the work he had to do for King Solomon in the house of God: 12 two columns, two nodes for the capitals topping these two columns, and two networks covering the nodes of the capitals topping the columns; 13 also four hundred pomegranates for the two networks, with two rows of pomegranates to each network, to cover the two nodes of the capitals topping the columns. 14 He made the stands, and the basins on the stands; 15 one sea, and the twelve oxen under it; 16 likewise the pots, the shovels and the forks. Huram-abi made all these articles for King Solomon from polished bronze for the house of the LORD. 17 The king had them cast in the Jordan region, in the clayey ground between Succoth and Zeredah. 18 Solomon made all these vessels, so many in number that the weight of the bronze was not ascertained.

19 Solomon had all these articles made for the house of God: the golden altar, the tables on which the showbread lay, 20 the lampstands and their lamps of pure gold which were to burn according to prescription before the sanctuary, 21 flowers, lamps and gold tongs [this was the purest gold], 22 snuffers, bowls, cups and firepans of pure gold. As for the entry to the house, its inner doors to the holy of holies, as well as the doors to the nave, were of gold.

Dedication of the Temple

5 1* When all the work undertaken by Solomon for the temple of the LORD had been completed, he brought in the dedicated offerings of his father David, putting the silver, the gold and all the other articles in the treasuries of the house of God. 2 At Solomon's order the elders of Israel and all the leaders of the tribes, the princes of the Israelite ancestral houses, came to Jerusalem to bring up the ark of the LORD's covenant from the City of David (which is Zion). 3 All the men of Israel assembled before the king during the festival of the seventh month. 4*† When all the elders of Israel had arrived, the Levites took up the ark, 5 and they carried the ark and the meeting tent with all the sacred vessels that were in the tent; it was the levitical priests who carried them.

6 King Solomon and the entire community of Israel gathered about him before the ark were sacrificing sheep and oxen so numerous that they could not be counted or numbered. 7 The priests brought the ark of the covenant of the LORD to its place beneath the wings of the cherubim in the sanctuary, the holy of holies of the temple. 8 The cherubim had their wings spread out over the place of the ark, sheltering the ark and its poles from above. 9† The poles were long enough so that their ends could be seen from that part of the holy place nearest the sanctuary; however, they could not be seen beyond. The ark has remained there to this day. 10 There was nothing in it but the two tablets which Moses put there on Horeb, the tablets of the covenant which the LORD made with the Israelites at their departure from Egypt.

11 When the priests came out of the holy place (all the priests who were present had purified themselves without reference to the rotation of their various classes), 12 the Levites who were singers, all who belonged to Asaph, Heman, Jeduthun, and their sons and brothers, clothed in fine linen, with cymbals, harps and lyres, stood east of the altar, and with them a hundred and twenty priests blowing trumpets.

13 When the trumpeters and singers were heard as a single voice praising and giving thanks to the LORD, and when they raised the sound of the trumpets, cymbals and other musical instruments to "give thanks to the LORD, for he is good, for his mercy endures forever," the building of the LORD's temple was filled with a cloud. 14* The priests could not continue to minister because of the cloud, since the LORD's glory filled the house of God.

6 1* Then Solomon said: "The LORD intends to dwell in the dark cloud. 2 I have truly built you a princely house and dwelling, where you may abide forever." 3* Turning about, the king greeted the whole community of Israel as they stood. 4 He said: "Blessed be the LORD, the God of Israel, who with his own mouth made a promise to my father David and by his own hands brought it to fulfillment. He said: 5 'Since the day I brought my people out of the land of Egypt, I have not chosen any city from among all the tribes of Israel for the building of a temple to my honor, nor have I chosen any man to be commander of my people Israel; 6 but now I choose Jerusalem, where I shall be honored,

† ——————
5, 4: *The Levites:* The parallel passage in 1 Kgs 8, 3 has the priests; but see 2 Chr 5, 5, where the Deuteronomic term levitical priests is used, as also in 2 Chr 23, 18; 30, 27.
5, 9: *The ark has remained there to this day:* the Chronicler must have copied this from his source (1 Kgs 8, 8) without reflecting that the ark was lost in the Babylonian destruction of Jerusalem; cf 2 Mc 2, 4–8.

* ——————
4, 10: 1 Kgs 7, 39.
4, 11–22: 1 Kgs 7, 40–51.
5, 1–14: 1 Kgs 7, 51—8, 13.
5, 4f: 2 Chr 35, 3.

5, 14: 2 Chr 7, 2; 1 Kgs 8,
      10f.
6, 1f: 1 Kgs 8, 12f.
6, 3–11: 1 Kgs 8, 14–21.

and I choose David to rule my people Israel.' [7] My father David wished to build a temple to the honor of the LORD, the God of Israel, [8] but the LORD said to him: 'In wishing to build a temple to my honor, you do well. [9] However, you shall not build the temple; rather, your son whom you will beget shall build the temple to my honor.'

[10] "Now the LORD has fulfilled the promise that he made. I have succeeded my father David and have taken my seat on the throne of Israel, as the LORD foretold, and I have built the temple to the honor of the LORD, the God of Israel. [11] And I have placed there the ark, in which abides the covenant of the LORD which he made with the Israelites."

Solomon's Prayer

[12]* Solomon then took his place before the altar of the LORD in the presence of the whole community of Israel and stretched forth his hands. [13]† He had made a bronze platform five cubits long, five cubits wide, and three cubits high, which he had placed in the middle of the courtyard. Having ascended it, Solomon knelt in the presence of the whole of Israel and stretched forth his hands toward heaven. [14] Thus he prayed: "LORD, God of Israel, there is no god like you in heaven or on earth; you keep your covenant and show kindness to your servants who are wholeheartedly faithful to you. [15] You have kept the promise you made to my father David, your servant. With your own mouth you spoke it, and by your own hand you have brought it to fulfillment this day. [16] Now, therefore, LORD, God of Israel, keep the further promise you made to my father David, your servant, when you said, 'You shall always have someone from your line to sit before me on the throne of Israel, provided only that your descendants look to their conduct so as always to live according to my law, even as you have lived in my presence.' [17] Now, LORD, God of Israel, may this promise which you made to your servant David be confirmed.

[18] "Can it indeed be that God dwells with mankind on earth? If the heavens and the highest heavens cannot contain you, how much less this temple which I have built! [19] Look kindly on the prayer and petition of your servant, O LORD, my God, and listen to the cry of supplication your servant makes before you. [20] May your eyes watch day and night over this temple, the place where you have decreed you shall be honored; may you heed the prayer which I your servant offer toward this place. [21] Listen to the petitions of your servant and of your people Israel which they direct toward this place. Listen from your heavenly dwelling, and when you have heard, pardon.

[22] "When any man sins against his neighbor and is required to take an oath of execration against himself, and when he comes for the oath before your altar in this temple, [23] listen from heaven: take action and pass judgment on your servants, requiting the wicked man and holding him responsible for his conduct, but absolving the innocent and rewarding him according to his virtue. [24] When your people Israel have sinned against you and are defeated by the enemy, but afterward they return and praise your name, and they pray to you and entreat you in this temple, [25] listen from heaven and forgive the sin of your people Israel, and bring them back to the land which you gave them and their fathers. [26] When the sky is closed so that there is no rain, because they have sinned against you, but then they pray toward this place and praise your name, and they withdraw from sin because you afflict them, [27] listen in heaven and forgive the sin of your servants and of your people Israel. But teach them the right way to live, and send rain upon your land which you gave your people as their heritage. [28] When there is famine in the land, when there is pestilence, or blight, or mildew, or locusts, or caterpillars; when their enemies besiege them at any of their gates; whenever there is a plague or sickness of any kind; [29] when any Israelite of all your people offers a prayer or petition of any kind, and in awareness of his affliction and pain, stretches out his hands toward this temple, [30] listen from your heavenly dwelling place, and forgive. Knowing his heart, render to everyone according to his conduct, for you alone know the hearts of men. [31] So may they fear you and walk in your ways as long as they live on the land you gave our fathers.

[32] "For the foreigner, too, who is not of your people Israel, when he comes from a distant land to honor your great name, your mighty power, and your outstretched arm, when they come in prayer to this temple, [33] listen from your heavenly dwelling place, and do whatever the foreigner entreats you, that all the peoples of the earth may know your name, fearing you as do your people Israel, and knowing that this house which I have built is dedicated to your honor.

[34] "When your people go forth to war against their enemies, wherever you send them, and pray to you in the direction of this city and of the

---

6, 13: This verse is not found in the Chronicler's source; cf 1 Kgs 8, 22f. He has Solomon praying on a bronze platform . . . in the middle of the courtyard because at the time of the Chronicler only the priests prayed before the altar.

6, 12–41: 1 Kgs 8, 22–53.

house I have built to your honor, ³⁵ listen from heaven to their prayer and petition, and defend their cause. ³⁶ When they sin against you (for there is no man who does not sin), and in your anger against them you deliver them to the enemy, so that their captors deport them to another land, far or near, ³⁷ when they repent in the land where they are captive and are converted, when they entreat you in the land of their captivity and say, 'We have sinned and done wrong; we have been wicked,' ³⁸ and with their whole heart and with their whole soul they turn back to you in the land of those who hold them captive, when they pray in the direction of their land which you gave their fathers, and of the city you have chosen, and of the house which I have built to your honor, ³⁹ listen from your heavenly dwelling place, hear their prayer and petitions, and uphold their cause. Forgive your people who have sinned against you. ⁴⁰ My God, may your eyes be open and your ears attentive to the prayer of this place. ⁴¹ And now,

"Advance, LORD God, to your resting place,
    you and the ark of your majesty.
May your priests, LORD God, be clothed with salvation,
    may your faithful ones rejoice in good things.
⁴² LORD God, reject not the plea of your anointed,
    remember the devotion of David, your servant."

7 ¹* When Solomon had ended his prayer, fire came down from heaven and consumed the holocaust and the sacrifices, and the glory of the LORD filled the house. ²* But the priests could not enter the house of the LORD, for the glory of the LORD had filled the house of the LORD. ³ All the Israelites looked on while the fire came down and the glory of the LORD was upon the house, and they fell down upon the pavement with their faces to the earth and adored, praising the LORD, "for he is good, for his mercy endures forever." ⁴* The king and all the people were offering sacrifices before the LORD. ⁵* King Solomon offered as sacrifice twenty-

two thousand oxen, and one hundred twenty thousand sheep.

End of the Dedication

⁶* Thus the king and all the people dedicated the house of God. The priests were standing at their stations, as were the Levites, with the musical instruments of the LORD which King David had made for "praising the LORD, for his mercy endures forever," when David used them to accompany the hymns. Across from them the priests blew the trumpets and all Israel stood.

⁷* Then Solomon consecrated the middle part of the court which lay before the house of the LORD; there he offered the holocausts and the fat of the peace offerings, since the bronze altar which Solomon had made could not hold the holocausts, the cereal offerings and the fat.

⁸* On this occasion Solomon and with him all Israel, who had assembled in very large numbers from Labo of Hamath to the Wadi of Egypt, celebrated the festival for seven days. ⁹*† On the eighth day they held a special meeting, for they had celebrated the dedication of the altar for seven days and the feast for seven days. ¹⁰ On the twenty-third day of the seventh month he sent the people back to their tents, rejoicing and glad at heart at the good things the LORD had done for David, for Solomon, and for his people Israel. ¹¹* Solomon completed the house of the LORD and the royal palace; he successfully accomplished everything he had planned to do in regard to the house of the LORD and his own house.

God's Promise to Solomon

¹² The LORD appeared to Solomon during the night and said to him: "I have heard your prayer, and I have chosen this place for my house of sacrifice. ¹³ If I close heaven so that there is no rain, if I command the locust to devour the land, if I send pestilence among my people, ¹⁴ and if my people, upon whom my name has been pronounced, humble themselves and pray, and seek my presence and turn from their evil ways, I will hear them from heaven and pardon their sins and revive their land. ¹⁵ Now my eyes shall be open and my ears attentive to the prayer of this place. ¹⁶ And now I have chosen and consecrated this house that my name may be there forever; my eyes and my heart also shall be there always.

7, 9f: *The feast:* of Booths, celebrated on the fifteenth day of the seventh month and followed by a solemn octave lasting through the twenty-second day (Lv 23, 33–36; Nm 29, 12–35); the people are therefore sent home on the twenty-third day (v 10). The festival (v 8) for the dedication of the altar and of the temple lasted for seven days before the feast of Booths, from the seventh to the fourteenth day. According to 1 Kgs 8, 65f, the people are dismissed at the end of these seven days.

7, 1–10: 1 Kgs 8, 54–66; Jgs 6,
    21; 1 Chr 21, 26;
    2 Mc 2, 10.
7, 2: 2 Chr 5, 14; Ex 24, 16;
    1 Kgs 8, 10f.
7, 4: 2 Chr 5, 13; 1 Kgs 8,
    62; Ps 136, 1.

7, 5: 1 Kgs 8, 62f.
7, 6: Nm 10, 8.10;
    Ps 136, 1.
7, 7: 1 Kgs 8, 64.
7, 8: 1 Kgs 8, 65.
7, 9f: 1 Kgs 8, 66.
7, 11–22: 1 Kgs 9, 1–9.

[17] "As for you, if you live in my presence as your father David did, doing all that I have commanded you and keeping my statutes and ordinances, [18] I will establish your royal throne as I covenanted with your father David when I said, 'There shall never be lacking someone of yours as ruler in Israel.' [19] But if you turn away and forsake my statutes and commands which I placed before you, if you proceed to venerate and worship strange gods, [20] then I will uproot the people from the land I gave them; I will cast from my sight this house which I have consecrated to my honor, and I will make it a proverb and a byword among all peoples. [21] This temple which is so exalted—everyone passing by it will be amazed and ask: 'Why has the LORD done this to this land and to this house?' [22] And men will answer: 'They forsook the LORD, the God of their fathers, who brought them out of the land of Egypt, and they adopted strange gods and worshiped them and served them. That is why he has brought down upon them all this evil.' "

Public Works

8 [1]* After the twenty years during which Solomon built the house of the LORD and his own house, [2]† he built up the cities which Huram had given him, and settled Israelites there. [3] Then Solomon went to Hamath of Zoba and conquered it. [4]† He built Tadmor in the desert region and all the supply cities, which he built in Hamath. [5]* He built Upper Beth-horon and Lower Beth-horon, fortified cities with walls, gates and bars; [6] also Baalath, all the supply cities belonging to Solomon, and all the cities for the chariots, the cities for the horsemen, and whatever else Solomon decided should be built in Jerusalem, in the Lebanon, and in the entire land under his dominion. [7] All the people that remained of the Hittites, Amorites, Perizzites, Hivites, and Jebusites, who were not of Israel— [8] that is, their descendants remaining in the land, whom the Israelites had not destroyed—Solomon subjected to forced labor, as they continue to this day. [9] But Solomon did not enslave the Israelites for his works. They became soldiers, commanders of his warriors, and commanders of his chariots and his horsemen. [10] They were also King Solomon's two hundred and fifty overseers who had charge of the people.

Solomon's Piety

[11] Solomon brought the daughter of Pharaoh up from the City of David to the palace which he had built for her, for he said, "No wife of mine shall dwell in the house of David, king of Israel, for the places where the ark of the LORD has come are holy."

[12] In those times Solomon offered holocausts to the LORD upon the altar of the LORD which he had built in front of the porch, [13]* as was required day by day according to the command of Moses, and in particular on the sabbaths, at the new moons, and on the fixed festivals three times a year: on the feast of the Unleavened Bread, the feast of Weeks and the feast of Booths.

[14]* And according to the ordinance of his father David he appointed the various classes of the priests for their service, and the Levites according to their functions of praise and ministry alongside the priests, as the daily duty required. The gatekeepers of the various classes stood guard at each gate, since such was the command of David, the man of God. [15] There was no deviation from the king's command in any respect relating to the priests and Levites or the treasuries. [16] All of Solomon's work was carried out successfully from the day the foundation of the house of the LORD was laid until the house of the LORD had been completed in every detail.

Glories of the Court

[17]* In those times Solomon went to Ezion-geber and to Elath on the seashore of the land of Edom. [18]* Huram, through his servants, sent him ships and crewmen acquainted with the sea, who accompanied Solomon's servants to Ophir and brought back from there four hundred and fifty talents of gold to King Solomon.

9 [1]* When the queen of Sheba heard of Solomon's fame, she came to Jerusalem to test him with subtle questions, accompanied by a very numerous retinue and by camels bearing spices, much gold, and precious stones. She came to Solomon and questioned him on every subject in which she was interested. [2] Solomon explained to her everything she asked about, and there remained nothing hidden from Solomon that he could not explain to her.

8, 2: *The cities which Huram had given him:* according to 1 Kgs 9, 10–14, Solomon had ceded the cities as payment for the timber and gold received from Tyre. But since Huram was dissatisfied, he may have returned the cities to Solomon.

8, 4: *Tadmor:* later known as Palmyra, an important caravan city in the Syrian desert. The parallel passage in 1 Kgs 9, 18 has Tamar, in southern Judah; cf Ez 47, 19; 48, 28. But Solomon may well have fortified Tadmor against the Arameans.

8, 1f: 1 Kgs 9, 10f.
8, 5–12: 1 Kgs 9, 18–25.
8, 13: 1 Kgs 9, 25; Ex 23, 14; Nm 28—29.
8, 14: 1 Chr 23—26; Neh 12, 46.
8, 17: 1 Kgs 9, 26; Mt 12, 42; Lk 11, 31.
8, 18: 1 Kgs 9, 27f.
9, 1: 1 Kgs 10, 1f; Mt 12, 42; Lk 11, 31.

2
CHR

Chap. 9

you always and listen to your wisdom. ⁸ Blessed be the LORD, your God, who has been so pleased with you as to place you on his throne as king for the LORD, your God. Because your God has so loved Israel as to will to make it last forever, he has appointed you over them as king to administer right and justice." ⁹ Then she gave the king one hundred and twenty gold talents and a very large quantity of spices, as well as precious stones. There was no other spice like that which the queen of Sheba gave to King Solomon.

¹⁰ The servants of Huram and of Solomon who brought gold from Ophir also brought cabinet wood and precious stones. ¹¹ With the cabinet wood the king made stairs for the temple of the LORD and the palace of the king; also lyres and harps for the chanters. The like of these had not been seen before in the land of Judah.

¹² King Solomon gave the queen of Sheba everything she desired and asked him for, more than she had brought to the king. Then she returned to her own country with her servants.

¹³* The gold that Solomon received each year weighed six hundred and sixty-six gold talents, ¹⁴ in addition to what was collected from travelers and what the merchants brought. All the kings of Arabia also, and the governors of the country, brought gold and silver to Solomon.

¹⁵ Moreover, King Solomon made two hundred large shields of beaten gold, six hundred shekels of beaten gold going into each shield, ¹⁶ and three hundred bucklers of beaten gold, three hundred shekels of gold going into each buckler; these the king put in the hall of the Forest of Lebanon.

³ When the queen of Sheba witnessed Solomon's wisdom, the palace he had built, ⁴ the food at his table, the seating of his ministers, the attendance of his servants and their dress, his cupbearers and their dress, and the holocausts he offered in the house of the LORD, it took her breath away. ⁵ "The account I heard in my country about your deeds and your wisdom is true," she told the king. ⁶ "Yet I did not believe the report until I came and saw with my own eyes. I have discovered that they did not tell me the half of your great wisdom; you have surpassed the stories I heard. ⁷ Happy are your men, happy these servants of yours, who stand before

Money Talks

LIVE IT!

You can't take it with you.

How often have we heard this statement? We know it's true. Yet we are so easily impressed with wealth and riches. King Solomon, whose wealth is described in 2 Chr 9, 13–28, would be right at home in our world, which seems so taken with the rich and the famous.

The Chronicler seems to suggest that Solomon's wealth is a sign of his being blessed by God (see 1, 12). And some Jews and Christians still see wealth as a sign of God's blessing. But we need to remember Jesus' words, "For where your treasure is, there also will your heart be" (Mt 6, 21), and "Blessed are you who are poor, / for the kingdom of God is yours" (Lk 6, 20). Jesus saw that the accumulation of wealth in his time was frequently the result of injustice (see "The Greed Trap," Lk 12, 13–21). Simply put, Jesus probably would not have approved of Solomon's wealth. How do you view wealth? What is your attitude toward poor people?

▶ 2 Chr 9, 13–28

9, 13–28: 1 Kgs 10, 14–28.

¹⁷ King Solomon also made a large ivory throne which he overlaid with fine gold. ¹⁸ The throne had six steps; a footstool of gold was fastened to it, and there was an arm on each side of the seat, with two lions standing beside the arms. ¹⁹ Twelve other lions also stood there, one on either side of each step. Nothing like this had ever been produced in any other kingdom. ²⁰ Furthermore, all of King Solomon's drinking vessels were of gold, and all the utensils in the hall of the Forest of Lebanon were of pure gold; silver was not considered of value in Solomon's time. ²¹ For the king had ships that went to Tarshish with the servants of Huram. Once every three years the fleet of Tarshish would return with a cargo of gold and silver, ivory, apes and monkeys. ²² Thus King Solomon surpassed all the other kings of the earth in riches as well as in wisdom.

²³ All the kings of the earth sought audience with Solomon, to hear from him the wisdom which God had put in his heart. ²⁴ Year in and year out, each one would bring his tribute—silver and gold articles, garments, weapons, spices, horses and mules. ²⁵ Solomon also had four thousand stalls of horses, chariots, and twelve thousand horsemen, which he assigned to the chariot cities and to the king in Jerusalem. ²⁶ He was ruler over all the kings from the River to the land of the Philistines and down to the border of Egypt. ²⁷ The king made silver as common in Jerusalem as stones, while cedars became as numerous as the sycamores of the foothills. ²⁸† Horses were imported for Solomon from Egypt and from all the lands.

The Death of Solomon

²⁹* The rest of the acts of Solomon, first and last, are written, as is well known, in the acts of Nathan the prophet, in the prophecy of Ahijah the Shilonite, and in the visions of Iddo the seer which concern Jeroboam, son of Nebat. ³⁰ Solomon reigned in Jerusalem over all Israel for forty years. ³¹ He rested with his ancestors; he was buried in his father's City of David, and his son Rehoboam succeeded him as king.

II: The Monarchy before Hezekiah

Division of the Kingdom

10 ¹*† Rehoboam went to Shechem, for all Israel had come to Shechem to proclaim him king. ² When Jeroboam, son of Nebat, heard of this in Egypt where he had fled from King Solomon, he returned from Egypt. ³ Jeroboam was summoned to the assembly, and he and all Israel said to Rehoboam: ⁴ "Your father laid a heavy yoke upon us. If you now lighten the harsh service and the heavy yoke that your father imposed on us, we will serve you." ⁵ "In three days," he answered them, "come back to me."

When the people had departed, ⁶ King Rehoboam consulted the elders who had been in the service of his father during Solomon's lifetime, asking, "What answer do you advise me to give this people?" ⁷ They replied, "If you will deal kindly with this people and give in to them, acceding to their request, they will be your servants forever." ⁸ But he ignored the advice the elders had given him and consulted the young men who had grown up with him and were in his service. ⁹ He said to them, "What answer do you advise me to give this people, who have asked me to lighten the yoke my father imposed on them?" ¹⁰ The young men who had grown up with him replied: "This is the answer you should give to this people who have said to you, 'Your father laid a heavy yoke upon us, but do you lighten our yoke'; this you should say to them: 'My little finger is thicker than my father's body. ¹¹ Whereas my father put a heavy yoke on you, I will make it heavier! My father beat you with whips, but I will beat you with scorpions!'"

¹² On the third day, Jeroboam and all the people came back to King Rehoboam as he had instructed them to do. ¹³ Ignoring the advice the elders had given him, the king gave them a harsh answer, ¹⁴ speaking to them according to the advice of the young men: "My father laid a heavy yoke on you, but I will make it heavier. My father beat you with whips, but I will beat you with scorpions." ¹⁵* The king would not listen to the people, for this turn of events was divinely ordained to fulfill the prophecy the LORD had uttered to Jeroboam, the son of Nebat, through Ahijah the Shilonite.

¹⁶* When all Israel saw that the king would not listen to them, the people answered the king,

"What share have we in David?
We have no heritage in the son of Jesse.
Everyone to your tents, O Israel!
Now look to your own house, David!"

So all Israel went off to their tents. ¹⁷ Rehoboam, therefore, reigned over only those Israelites who lived in the cities of Judah. ¹⁸ King Rehoboam then

---

† **9, 28:** See note on 2 Chr 1, 16f.
10, 1: *All Israel:* as in the original source (1 Kgs 12, 1), the northern tribes, distinct from Judah and Benjamin. Contrast the Chronicler's own terms, those Israelites who lived in the cities of Judah (v 17), and all the Israelites [literally, all Israel] in Judah and Benjamin (2 Chr 11, 3).

* **9, 29ff:** 1 Kgs 11, 41ff.   12, 15.
10, 1–14: 1 Kgs 12, 1–14.   **10, 16–19:** 1 Kgs 12, 16–19.
    10, 15: 1 Kgs 11, 29–39;

sent out Hadoram, who was superintendent of the forced labor, but the Israelites stoned him to death. Rehoboam himself managed to mount his chariot and flee to Jerusalem. 19 Thus Israel has been in rebellion against David's house to this day.

11 1* On his arrival in Jerusalem Rehoboam gathered together the house of Judah and Benjamin, a hundred and eighty thousand seasoned warriors, to have them fight against Israel and restore the kingdom to him. 2 However, the word of the LORD came to Shemiah, a man of God: 3 "Say to Rehoboam, son of Solomon, king of Judah, and to all the Israelites in Judah and Benjamin: 4 Thus says the LORD: You must not march out to fight against your brothers. Let every man return home, for what has occurred I have brought about.' " They obeyed this message of the LORD and gave up the expedition against Jeroboam.

Rehoboam's Works

5† Rehoboam took up residence in Jerusalem and built fortified cities in Judah. 6 He built up Bethlehem, Etam, Tekoa, 7 Beth-zur, Soco, Adullam, 8 Gath, Mareshah, Ziph, 9 Adoraim, Lachish, Azekah, 10 Zorah, Aijalon, and Hebron; these were fortified cities in Judah and Benjamin. 11 Then he strengthened the fortifications and put commanders in them, with supplies of food, oil and wine. 12 In every city were shields and spears, and he made them very strong. Thus Judah and Benjamin remained his.

Refugees from the North

13 Now the priests and Levites throughout Israel presented themselves to him from all parts of their land, 14* for the Levites left their assigned pasture lands and their holdings and came to Judah and Jerusalem, because Jeroboam and his sons repudiated them as priests of the LORD. 15* In their place, he himself appointed priests for the high places and satyrs and calves he had made. 16 After them, all those of the Israelite tribes who firmly desired to seek the LORD, the God of Israel, came to Jerusalem to sacrifice to the LORD, the God of their fathers. 17 Thus they strengthened the kingdom of Judah and made Rehoboam, son of Solomon, prevail for three years; for they walked in the way of David and Solomon three years.

Rehoboam's Family

18 Rehoboam took to himself as wife Mahalath, daughter of Jerimoth, son of David and of Abihail,

daughter of Eliab, son of Jesse. 19 She bore him sons: Jehush, Shemariah and Zaham. 20* After her, he married Maacah, daughter of Absalom, who bore him Abijah, Attai, Ziza and Shelomith. 21 Rehoboam loved Maacah, daughter of Absalom, more than all his other wives and concubines; he had taken eighteen wives and sixty concubines, and he fathered twenty-eight sons and sixty daughters. 22 Rehoboam constituted Abijah, son of Maacah, commander among his brothers, for he intended to make him king. 23 He acted prudently, distributing various of his sons throughout all the districts of Judah and Benjamin, in all the fortified cities; and he furnished them with copious provisions and sought an abundance of wives for them.

His Apostasy

12 1* After Rehoboam had consolidated his rule and had become powerful, he abandoned the law of the LORD, he and all Israel with him. 2* Thus it happened that in the fifth year of King Rehoboam, Shishak, king of Egypt, attacked Jerusalem, for they had been unfaithful to the LORD. 3† He came up with twelve hundred chariots and sixty thousand horsemen, and there was no counting the army that came with him from Egypt—Libyans, Sukkites and Ethiopians. 4 They captured the fortified cities of Judah and came as far as Jerusalem. 5* Then Shemaiah the prophet came to Rehoboam and the commanders of Judah who had gathered at Jerusalem because of Shishak, and said to them: "Thus says the LORD: 'You have abandoned me, and therefore I have abandoned you to the power of Shishak.' "

6 However, the commanders of Israel and the king humbled themselves, saying, "The LORD is just." 7 When the LORD saw that they had humbled themselves, the word of the LORD came to Shemaiah: "Because they have humbled themselves, I will not destroy them; I will give them some deliverance, and my wrath shall not be poured out upon Jerusalem through Shishak. 8 But they shall be his servants, that they may know what it is to serve me and what it is to serve earthly kingdoms." 9* Therefore Shishak, king of Egypt, attacked Jerusalem and carried off the treasures of the temple of the LORD and of the king's palace. He took everything, including the gold bucklers that Solomon had made. 10 (To replace them, King Rehoboam made bronze bucklers, which he entrusted to the officers of the guard on duty at the entrance of the royal palace. 11 Whenever the king visited the temple of the LORD, the troops would come bearing them, and

---

† **11, 5–12:** These verses, though not found in 1 Kings, are apparently based on a reliable, ancient source.
12, 3: *Sukkites:* foreign mercenaries in the Egyptian army.

11, 1–4: 1 Kgs 12, 21–24.
11, 14: 1 Kgs 12, 32.
11, 15: 1 Kgs 12, 32; Lv 17, 7.
11, 20: 1 Kgs 15, 2.
12, 1: 1 Kgs 11, 4; 14, 22.
12, 2: 1 Kgs 14, 25.
12, 5: 2 Chr 11, 2.
12, 9ff: 1 Kgs 14, 25–28.

Selling Out

King Rehoboam, son of Solomon, sold out and abandoned the law of the LORD after he thought his rule was secure (2 Chr 12, 1). The Chronicler tells us that the LORD abandoned Rehoboam to the Egyptians because of this. Fortunately, Rehoboam and his officers repented, and the LORD showed mercy on them.

It is tempting to compromise our values in order to succeed and become popular, even though doing this ends up hurting the people around us. Maybe you have experienced some success like Rehoboam and figure you can have even more if you just bend the rules a bit. Maybe you feel life has given you a rotten deal and the only way to get ahead is to forget your principles. But before you sell out, think again. Ultimately, abandoning your good and holy principles won't get you ahead; it will only lead to your downfall.

▶ **2 Chr 12, 1–12**

then they would return them to the guardroom.) ¹² Because he had humbled himself, the anger of the LORD turned from him so that it did not destroy him completely; and in Judah, moreover, good deeds were found.

¹³* King Rehoboam consolidated his power in Jerusalem and continued to rule; he was forty-one years old when he became king, and he reigned seventeen years in Jerusalem, the city in which, out of all the tribes of Israel, the LORD chose to be honored. Rehoboam's mother was named Naamah, an Ammonite. ¹⁴ He did evil, for he had not truly resolved to seek the LORD. ¹⁵* The acts of Rehoboam, first and last, are written, as is well known, in the history of Shemaiah the prophet and of Iddo the seer [his family record]. There was war continually between Rehoboam and Jeroboam. ¹⁶ Rehoboam rested with his ancestors; he was buried in the City of David. His son Abijah succeeded him as king.

War between Abijah and Jeroboam

13 ¹* In the eighteenth year of King Jeroboam, Abijah became king of Judah; ² he reigned three years in Jerusalem. His mother was named Michaiah, daughter of Uriel of Gibeah. There was war between Abijah and Jeroboam.

³ Abijah joined battle with a force of four hundred thousand picked warriors, while Jeroboam lined up against him in battle with eight hundred thousand picked and valiant warriors. ⁴† Abijah stood on Mount Zemaraim, which is in the highlands of Ephraim, and said: "Listen to me, Jeroboam and all Israel! ⁵ Do you not know that the LORD, the God of Israel, has given the kingdom of Israel to David forever, to him and to his sons, by a covenant made in salt? ⁶* Yet Jeroboam, son of

Nebat, the servant of Solomon, son of David, has stood up and rebelled against his lord! ⁷ Worthless men, scoundrels, joined him and overcame Rehoboam, son of Solomon, when Rehoboam was young and unthinking, and no match for them. ⁸ But now, do you think you are a match for the kingdom of the LORD commanded by the sons of David, simply because you are a huge multitude and have with you the golden calves which Jeroboam made you for gods?

⁹ "Have you not expelled the priests of the LORD, the sons of Aaron, and the Levites, and made for yourselves priests like the peoples of foreign lands? Everyone who comes to consecrate himself with a young bull and seven rams becomes a priest of no-gods. ¹⁰ But as for us, the LORD is our God, and we have not forsaken him. The priests ministering to the LORD are sons of Aaron, and the Levites also have their offices. ¹¹ They burn holocausts to the LORD and fragrant incense morning after morning and evening after evening; they display the showbread on the pure table, and the lamps of the golden lampstand burn evening after evening; for we observe our duties to the LORD, our God, but you have abandoned him. ¹² See, God is with us, at our head, and his priests are here with trumpets to sound the attack against you. Do not battle against the LORD, the God of your fathers, O Israelites, for you will not succeed!"

¹³ But Jeroboam had an ambush go around them to come at them from the rear; so that while his army faced Judah, his ambush lay behind them. ¹⁴ When Judah turned and saw that they had to battle on both fronts, they cried out to the LORD and the priests sounded the trumpets. ¹⁵ Then the men of Judah shouted; and when they did so, God defeated

---

13, 4–12: This is a free composition of the Chronicler to show that this was a religious, rather than a political, war.

12, 13: 1 Kgs 14, 21.
12, 15f: 1 Kgs 14, 29ff.

13, 1f: 1 Kgs 15, 1f.
13, 6: 1 Kgs 11, 26.

Jeroboam and all Israel before Abijah and Judah. 16 The Israelites fled before Judah, and God delivered them into their hands. 17 Abijah and his people inflicted a severe defeat upon them; five hundred thousand picked men of Israel fell slain. 18 The Israelites were subdued on that occasion and the Judahites were victorious because they relied on the LORD, the God of their fathers. 19 Abijah pursued Jeroboam and took cities from him: Bethel and its dependencies, Jeshanah and its dependencies, and Ephron and its dependencies. 20 Jeroboam did not regain power during the time of Abijah; the LORD struck him down and he died, 21 while Abijah continued to grow stronger. He took to himself fourteen wives and fathered twenty-two sons and sixteen daughters.

Death of Abijah

22* The rest of Abijah's acts, his deeds and his words, are written in the midrash of the prophet Iddo. 23 Abijah rested with his ancestors; they buried him in the City of David. His son Asa succeeded him as king. During his time, ten years of peace began in the land.

Asa the Reformer

14 1* Asa did what was good and pleasing to the LORD, his God, 2 removing the heathen altars and the high places, breaking to pieces the sacred pillars, and cutting down the sacred poles. 3 He commanded Judah to seek the LORD, the God of their fathers, and to observe the law and its commands. 4 He removed the high places and incense stands from all the cities of Judah, and under him the kingdom had peace. 5 He built fortified cities in Judah, for the land had peace and no war was waged against him during these years, because the LORD had given him peace. 6 He said to Judah: "Let us build these cities and surround them with walls, towers, gates and bars. The land is still ours, for we have sought the LORD, our God; we sought him, and he has given us rest on every side." So they built and prospered.

The Ethiopian Invasion

7† Asa had an army of three hundred thousand shield- and lance-bearers from Judah, and two hundred and eighty thousand from Benjamin who carried bucklers and were archers, all of them valiant warriors. 8* Zerah the Ethiopian moved against them with a force of one million men and

three hundred chariots, and he came as far as Mareshah. 9 Asa went out to meet him and set himself in battle array in the valley of Zephathah, near Mareshah. 10* Asa called upon the LORD, his God, praying: "O LORD, there is none like you to help the powerless against the strong. Help us, O LORD, our God, for we rely on you, and in your name we have come against this multitude. You are the LORD, our God; let no man prevail against you." 11* And so the LORD defeated the Ethiopians before Asa and Judah, and they fled. 12 Asa and those with him pursued them as far as Gerar, and the Ethiopians fell until there were no survivors, for they were crushed before the LORD and his army, which carried away enormous spoils. 13 Then the Judahites conquered all the cities around Gerar, for the fear of the LORD was upon them; they despoiled all the cities, for there was much booty in them. 14 They attacked also the tents of the cattle-herders and carried off a great number of sheep and camels. Then they returned to Jerusalem.

Cult Reform

15 1 Upon Azariah, son of Oded, came the spirit of God. 2* He went forth to meet Asa and said to him: "Hear me, Asa and all Judah and Benjamin! The LORD is with you when you are with him, and if you seek him he will be present to you; but if you abandon him, he will abandon you. 3 For a long time Israel had no true God, no priest-teacher and no law, 4* but when in their distress they turned to the LORD, the God of Israel, and sought him, he was present to them. 5 In that former time there was no place for anyone to go or come, but there were many terrors upon the inhabitants of the lands. 6* Nation crushed nation and city crushed city, for God destroyed them by every kind of adversity. 7* But as for you, be strong and do not relax, for your work shall be rewarded."

8 When Asa heard these words and the prophecy [Oded the prophet], he was encouraged to remove the detestable idols from the whole land of Judah and Benjamin and from the cities he had taken in the highlands of Ephraim, and to restore the altar of the LORD which was before the vestibule of the LORD. 9 Then he convened all Judah and Benjamin, together with those of Ephraim, Manasseh and Simeon who sojourned with them; for many had fled to him from Israel when they saw that the LORD, his God, was with him. 10† They gathered at

---

† **14, 7–14:** An Ethiopian invasion of Judah is mentioned only in 1 Chronicles. This account may be a legend contrived to show how the pious King Asa was rewarded through divine assistance. There may, however, have been an incursion of nomads from the Negeb at this time; cf vv 13f.

15, 10ff: With this description of a covenant ceremony in the third month of a year beginning in the spring, the Chronicler lays a

13, 22f: 2 Chr 12, 15; 1 Kgs 7ff.
14, 1f: 2 Chr 13, 15; Ex 23, 24; 34, 13; 1 Kgs 15, 11f.
14, 8: 2 Chr 16, 8.

14, 10: 2 Chr 32, 8.
14, 11: Pss 20, 7f; 60, 11f.
15, 2: Jer 29, 13f; Hos 3, 4f.
15, 4: Dt 4, 29f.
15, 6: Is 19, 2.
15, 7: Is 7, 4; Jer 31, 16.

Keep On Turning

Conversion.

A very important word for Christians. Its Latin root means "to turn around." We turn from sin and toward God, as individuals and as a people. In 2 Chr 15, 8–15, we read about King Asa and his people hearing the words of the prophet Azariah and then turning away from idols and turning back to God.

Conversion is not a one-time event. It is a process all of us go through again and again as our faith and understanding grow. We are reminded of that especially during the season of Lent. On Ash Wednesday, as individuals and as a community, we hear the words, "Turn away from sin and be faithful to the gospel" (*Sacramentary*, p. 77). The Israelites went through the same thing. Again and again, they were called to turn back to God.

If we are committed to following Jesus, conversion is a lifelong process of deepening our faith. Where are you most in need of conversion? Where is our nation most in need of conversion?

▶ **2 Chr 15, 8–15**

Jerusalem in the third month of the fifteenth year of Asa's reign, 11 and sacrificed to the LORD at that time seven hundred oxen and seven thousand sheep of the booty they had brought. 12 They entered into a covenant to seek the LORD, the God of their fathers, with all their heart and soul; 13* and everyone who would not seek the LORD, the God of Israel, was to be put to death, whether small or great, whether man or woman. 14 They swore to the LORD with a loud voice, with shouting and with trumpets and horns. 15* All Judah rejoiced over the oath, for they had sworn with their whole heart and sought him with complete desire, so that he was present to them. And the LORD gave them rest on every side.

16* Maacah, the mother of King Asa, he deposed as queen mother because she had made an outrageous object for Asherah; Asa cut this down, smashed it, and burnt it in the Kidron Valley. 17 Although the high places did not disappear from Israel, yet Asa's heart was undivided as long as he lived. 18 He brought into the house of God his father's votive offerings and his own: silver, gold, and various utensils. 19 There was no war until the thirty-fifth year of Asa's reign.

Asa's Infidelity

16 1* In the thirty-sixth year of Asa's reign, Baasha, king of Israel, attacked Judah and fortified Ramah to prevent any communication with Asa, king of Judah. 2 Asa then brought out silver and gold from the treasuries of the temple of the LORD and of the royal palace and sent them to Ben-hadad, king of Aram, who lived in Damascus, with this message: 3 "There is a treaty between you and me, as there was between your father and my father. See, I am sending you silver and gold. Go, break your treaty with Baasha, king of Israel, that he may withdraw from me." 4 Ben-hadad agreed to King Asa's request and sent the leaders of his troops against the cities of Israel. They attacked Ijon, Dan, Abel-maim, and all the store cities of Naphtali. 5 When Baasha heard of it, he left off fortifying Ramah; he stopped his work. 6 Then King Asa commandeered all of Judah to carry away the stone and wood with which Baasha had been fortifying Ramah, and with them he fortified Geba and Mizpah.

7† At that time Hanani the seer came to Asa, king of Judah, and said to him: "Because you relied on the king of Aram and did not rely on the LORD, your God, the army of the king of Aram has escaped your hand. 8* Were not the Ethiopians and Libyans a vast army, with great numbers of chariots and drivers? And yet, because you relied on the LORD, he delivered them into your power. 9* The eyes of the LORD roam over the whole earth, to encourage those who are devoted to him wholeheartedly. You have acted foolishly in this matter, for from now on you will have wars." 10 But Asa became angry with the seer and imprisoned him in the stocks, so greatly was he enraged at him over this. Asa also oppressed some of his people at this time.

---

foundation for celebrating the ancient feast of Pentecost (Weeks) as the time for a solemn renewal of the people's covenant with God on Mount Sinai; see Ex 19, 1ff; Lv 23, 16 and the note there. This is also the background for Pentecost as the "birthday of the Church."
16, 7: *The king of Aram . . . escaped:* according to the Lucianic

recension, "the king of Israel escaped": this may well be the original reading; Asa was friendly with Aram.

15, 13: Neh 10, 30.   16, 1–6: 1 Kgs 15, 16–21.
15, 15: Dt 4, 29.   16, 8: 2 Chr 14, 8–14.
15, 16ff: 1 Kgs 15, 13ff.   16, 9: Ps 33, 13ff.

11* Now the acts of Asa, first and last, can be found recorded in the book of the kings of Judah and Israel. 12 In the thirty-ninth year of his reign, Asa contracted a serious disease in his feet. But even in his sickness he did not seek the LORD, but only the physicians. 13 Asa rested with his ancestors; he died in the forty-first year of his reign. 14 They buried him in the tomb he had hewn for himself in the City of David, having laid him upon a couch which was filled with spices and various kinds of aromatics compounded into an ointment. They also burned a very great funeral pyre for him.

Zeal of Jehoshaphat for the Law

17 1* His son Jehoshaphat succeeded him as king and strengthened his hold against Israel. 2 He placed armed forces in all the fortified cities of Judah, and put garrisons in the land of Judah and in the cities of Ephraim which his father Asa had taken. 3† The LORD was with Jehoshaphat, for he walked in the ways his father had pursued in the beginning, and he did not consult the Baals. 4 Rather, he sought the God of his father and observed his commands, and not the practices of Israel. 5 As a result, the LORD made his kingdom secure, and all Judah gave Jehoshaphat gifts, so that he enjoyed great wealth and glory. 6* Thus he was encouraged to follow the LORD'S ways, and again he removed the high places and the sacred poles from Judah.

7 In the third year of his reign he sent his leading men, Ben-hail, Obadiah, Zechariah, Nethanel and Micaiah, to teach in the cities of Judah. 8* With them he sent the Levites Shemaiah, Nethaniah, Zebadiah, Asahel, Shemiramoth, Jehonathan, Adonijah and Tobijah, together with the priests Elishama and Jehoram. 9* They taught in Judah, having with them the book containing the law of the LORD; they traveled through all the cities of Judah and taught among the people.

His Power

10 Now the fear of the LORD was upon all the kingdoms of the countries surrounding Judah, so that they did not war against Jehoshaphat. 11 Some of the Philistines brought Jehoshaphat gifts and a tribute of silver; and the Arabs also brought him a flock of seven thousand seven hundred rams and seven thousand seven hundred he-goats. 12 Jehoshaphat grew steadily greater. He built strongholds and store cities in Judah. 13 He carried out many works in the cities of Judah, and he had soldiers, valiant warriors, in Jerusalem. 14 This was

their mustering according to their ancestral houses. Of Judah, the commanders of thousands: Adnah the commander, and with him three hundred thousand valiant warriors. 15 Next to him, Jehohanan the commander, and with him two hundred eighty thousand. 16 Next to him, Amasiah, son of Zichri, who offered himself to the LORD, and with him two hundred thousand valiant warriors. 17 From Benjamin: Eliada, a valiant warrior, and with him two hundred thousand armed with bow and buckler. 18 Next to him, Jozabad, and with him one hundred and eighty thousand equipped for war. 19 These were at the service of the king; in addition were those whom the king had placed in the fortified cities throughout all Judah.

Alliance with Israel

18 1* Jehoshaphat therefore had wealth and glory in abundance; but he became related to Ahab by marriage. 2 After some years he went down to Ahab at Samaria; Ahab offered numerous sheep and oxen for him and the people with him, and persuaded him to go up against Ramoth-gilead. 3 Ahab, king of Israel, asked Jehoshaphat, king of Judah, "Will you come with me to Ramoth-gilead?" "You and I are as one," was his answer; "your people and my people as well. We will be with you in the battle." 4 But Jehoshaphat also said to the king of Israel, "Seek the word of the LORD at once."

The Prophets

5 The king of Israel gathered his prophets, four hundred in number, and asked them, "Shall we go to attack Ramoth-gilead, or shall I refrain?" "Go up," they answered. "God will deliver it over to the king." 6 But Jehoshaphat said, "Is there no other prophet of the LORD here whom we may consult?" 7 The king of Israel answered Jehoshaphat, "There is still another through whom we may consult the LORD, but I hate him, for he prophesies not good but always evil about me. That is Micaiah, son of Imlah." Jehoshaphat said, "Let not your Majesty speak of evil against you." 8 So the king of Israel called an official, to whom he said, "Get Micaiah, son of Imlah, at once." 9 The king of Israel and King Jehoshaphat of Judah were seated each on his throne, clothed in their robes of state on a threshing floor at the entrance of the gate of Samaria, and all the prophets were prophesying before them.

10 Zedekiah, son of Chenaanah, made iron horns for himself and said: "The LORD says, 'With these you shall gore Aram until you have destroyed them.' " 11 The other prophets prophesied in the

---

17, 3: *The LORD was with Jehoshaphat:* along with Hezekiah and Josiah, Jehoshaphat was one of the Chronicler's favorite kings.

16, 11–14: 1 Kgs 15, 23f.   17, 8: 2 Chr 19, 8.
17, 1: 1 Kgs 15, 24.   17, 9: Ezr 7, 25.
17, 6: 2 Chr 20, 33; Ex 34, 13.   18, 1–34: 1 Kgs 22, 1–35.

same vein, saying: "Go up to Ramoth-gilead. You shall succeed; the LORD will deliver it over to the king." 12† The messenger who had gone to call Micaiah said to him: "Look now, the prophets unanimously predict good for the king. Let your word, like each of theirs, predict good." 13 "As the LORD lives," Micaiah answered, "I will say what my God tells me."

14 When he came to the king, the king said to him, "Micaiah, shall we go to fight against Ramoth-gilead, or shall I refrain?" "Go up," he answered, "and succeed; they will be delivered into your power." 15 But the king said to him, "How many times must I adjure you to tell me nothing but the truth in the name of the LORD?" 16 Then Micaiah answered:

> "I see all Israel
>   scattered on the mountains,
> like sheep without a shepherd,
>   and the LORD saying, 'These have
>   no master!
> Let each of them go back home in peace.' "

17 The king of Israel said to Jehoshaphat, "Did I not tell you that he prophesies no good about me, but only evil?" 18 But Micaiah continued: "Therefore hear the word of the LORD: I saw the LORD seated on his throne, with the whole host of heaven standing by to his right and to his left. 19 The LORD asked, 'Who will deceive Ahab, king of Israel, so that he will go up and fall at Ramoth-gilead?' And one said this, another that, 20 until a spirit came forward and presented himself to the LORD, saying, 'I will deceive him.' The LORD asked, 'How?' 21 He answered, 'I will go forth and become a lying spirit in the mouths of all his prophets.' The LORD agreed: 'You shall succeed in deceiving him. Go forth and do this.' 22 So now the LORD has put a lying spirit in the mouths of these your prophets, but the LORD himself has decreed evil against you."

23 Thereupon Zedekiah, son of Chenaanah, came up and slapped Micaiah on the cheek, saying, "Which way did the spirit of the LORD go when he left me to speak to you?" 24 "You shall find out," Micaiah replied, "on that day when you enter an innermost chamber to hide." 25 The king of Israel then said: "Seize Micaiah and take him back to Amon, prefect of the city, and to Joash the king's son, 26 and say, 'This is the king's order: Put this man in prison and feed him scanty rations of bread

and water until I return in safety!' " 27† But Micaiah said, "If ever you return in safety, the LORD has not spoken through me." And he said, "Hear, O peoples, all of you!"

Ahab's Death

28 The king of Israel and King Jehoshaphat of Judah went up to Ramoth-gilead 29 and the king of Israel said to Jehoshaphat, "I will go into battle disguised, but you put on your own clothes." So the king of Israel disguised himself and they entered the fray. 30 Meanwhile, the king of Aram had given his chariot commanders the order, "Fight with no one, small or great, except the king of Israel." 31 When the commanders saw Jehoshaphat, they exclaimed, "That must be the king of Israel!" and shifted to fight him. But Jehoshaphat cried out and the LORD helped him; God induced them to leave him. 32 The chariot commanders became aware that he was not the king of Israel and gave up their pursuit of him. 33* Someone, however, drew his bow at random and hit the king of Israel between the joints of his breastplate. He ordered his charioteer, "Rein about and take me out of the ranks, for I am disabled." 34 The battle grew fierce during the day, and the king of Israel braced himself up on his chariot facing the Arameans until evening. He died as the sun was setting.

Jehoshaphat Rebuked

19 1 King Jehoshaphat of Judah returned in safety to his house in Jerusalem. 2† Jehu the seer, son of Hanani, met King Jehoshaphat and said to him: "Should you help the wicked and love those who hate the LORD? For this reason, wrath is upon you from the LORD. 3 Yet some good things are to be found in you, since you have removed the sacred poles from the land and have been determined to seek God."

Judges Appointed

4 Jehoshaphat dwelt in Jerusalem; but he went out again among the people from Beer-sheba to the highlands of Ephraim and brought them back to the LORD, the God of their fathers. 5 He appointed judges in the land, in all the fortified cities of Judah, city by city, 6* and he said to them: "Take care what you do, for you are judging, not on behalf of man, but on behalf of the LORD; he judges with you. 7* And now, let the fear of the LORD be upon you. Act carefully, for with the LORD, our God, there is

---

18, 12–22: See note on 1 Kgs 22, 19–23.
18, 27: *"Hear, O peoples, all of you!":* this quotation, which appears in some texts of 1 Kgs 22, 28, ascribes to the prophet Micaiah ben Imlah the opening words of the prophetic utterance of Micah of Moresheth (Mi 1, 2), a century later.

19, 2: *Jehu the seer, son of Hanani:* hardly the same seer as Jehu, son of Hanani, who prophesied against Baasha almost 50 years earlier (1 Kgs 16, 1).

18, 33: 2 Chr 35, 23; 1 Kgs	19, 6: Dt 1, 16ff; 16, 19f.
22, 34.	19, 7: Dt 10, 17.

no injustice, no partiality, no bribe-taking." 8* In Jerusalem also, Jehoshaphat appointed some Levites and priests and some of the family heads of Israel to judge in the name of the LORD and to settle quarrels among the inhabitants of Jerusalem. 9 He gave them this command: "You shall act faithfully and wholeheartedly in the fear of the LORD. 10* And in every dispute that your brethren living in their cities bring to you, whether it concerns bloodguilt or questions of law, command, statutes, or judgments, warn them lest they become guilty before the LORD and his wrath come upon you and your brethren. Do that and you shall be guiltless. 11 See now, Amariah is high priest over you in everything that pertains to the LORD, and Zebadiah, son of Ishmael, is leader of the house of Judah in all that pertains to the king; and the Levites will be your officials. Act firmly, and the LORD will be with the good."

Invasion from Edom

20 1† After this the Moabites, the Ammonites, and with them some Meunites came to fight against Jehoshaphat. 2 The message was brought to Jehoshaphat: "A great multitude is coming against you from across the sea, from Edom; they are already in Hazazon-tamar" (which is Engedi). 3 Jehoshaphat was frightened, and he hastened to consult the LORD. He proclaimed a fast for all Judah. 4* Then Judah gathered to seek help from the LORD; from every one of the cities of Judah they came to seek the LORD.

Prayer of Jehoshaphat

5 Jehoshaphat stood up in the assembly of Judah and Jerusalem in the house of the LORD before the new court, 6* and he said: "LORD, God of our fathers, are you not the God in heaven, and do you not rule over all the kingdoms of the nations? In your hand is power and might, and no one can withstand you. 7* Was it not you, our God, who drove out the inhabitants of this land before your people Israel and gave it forever to the descendants of Abraham, your friend? 8 They have dwelt in it and they built in it a sanctuary to your honor, saying, 9 'When evil comes upon us, the sword of judgment, or pestilence, or famine, we will stand before this house and before you, for your name is in this

house, and we will cry out to you in our affliction, and you will hear and save!' 10* And now, see the Ammonites, Moabites, and those of Mount Seir whom you did not allow Israel to invade when they came from the land of Egypt, but instead they passed them by and did not destroy them. 11 See how they are now repaying us by coming to drive us out of the possession you have given us. 12 O our God, will you not pass judgment on them? We are powerless before this vast multitude that comes against us. We are at a loss what to do, hence our eyes are turned toward you."

Victory Prophesied

13 All Judah was standing before the LORD, with their little ones, their wives, and their young sons. 14 And the spirit of the LORD came upon Jahaziel, son of Zechariah, son of Benaiah, son of Jeiel, son of Mattaniah, a Levite of the clan of Asaph, in the midst of the assembly, 15 and he said: "Listen, all of Judah, inhabitants of Jerusalem, and King Jehoshaphat! The LORD says to you: 'Do not fear or lose heart at the sight of this vast multitude, for the battle is not yours but God's. 16 Go down against them tomorrow. You will see them coming up by the ascent of Ziz, and you will come upon them at the end of the wadi which opens on the wilderness of Jeruel. 17* You will not have to fight in this encounter. Take your places, stand firm, and see how the LORD will be with you to deliver you, Judah and Jerusalem. Do not fear or lose heart. Tomorrow go out to meet them, and the LORD will be with you.' " 18 Then Jehoshaphat knelt down with his face to the ground, and all Judah and the inhabitants of Jerusalem fell down before the LORD in worship. 19 Levites from among the Kohathites and Korahites rose to sing the praises of the LORD, the God of Israel, in a resounding chorus.

The Invaders Destroyed

20* In the early morning they hastened out to the wilderness of Tekoa. As they were going out, Jehoshaphat halted and said: "Listen to me, Judah and inhabitants of Jerusalem! Trust in the LORD, your God, and you will be found firm. Trust in his prophets and you will succeed." 21*† After consulting with the people, he appointed some to sing to the LORD and some to praise the holy Appearance

---

20, 1–30: Although the account here seems to be a free composition of the Chronicler, there is probably a basis in fact for it; there could well have been a raid of nomads against Judah in the reign of Jehoshaphat, similar to Zerah's attack on Asa (2 Chr 14, 8–14). The story may also, in some way, be connected with the campaign of Israel and Judah against Moab through the territory of Edom (2 Kgs 3, 4–27).

20, 21: *Holy Appearance:* the Lord, who is with the Israelite army

(v 17), manifests himself (the same language is in Ps 29, 2) in bringing Israel the victory (Ex 14, 14.24).

19, 8: 2 Chr 17, 8f; Dt 17,
    8–13; Ps 122, 3ff.
19, 10: Nm 35, 19.
20, 4: Jer 36, 6; Jb 1, 14.
20, 6: 2 Chr 32, 7; Dt 4, 39.

20, 7: Dn 3, 35.
20, 10: Dt 2, 4f.9f.18f.
20, 17: Is 8, 10.
20, 20: Is 7, 9.
20, 21: Ps 136, 1.

as it went forth at the head of the army. They sang: "Give thanks to the LORD, for his mercy endures forever." 22 At the moment they began their jubilant hymn, the LORD laid an ambush against the Ammonites, Moabites, and those of Mount Seir who were coming against Judah, so that they were vanquished. 23* For the Ammonites and Moabites set upon the inhabitants of Mount Seir and completely exterminated them. And when they had finished with the inhabitants of Seir, they began to destroy each other.

24 When Judah came to the watchtower of the desert and looked toward the throng, they saw only corpses fallen on the ground, with no survivors. 25 Jehoshaphat and his people came to take plunder, and they found an abundance of cattle and personal property, garments and precious vessels. They took so much that they were unable to carry it all; they were three days taking the spoil, so great was it. 26† On the fourth day they held an assembly in the Valley of Beracah—for there they blessed the LORD; therefore that place has ever since been called the Valley of Beracah. 27 Then all the men of Judah and Jerusalem, with Jehoshaphat at their head, turned back toward Jerusalem celebrating the joyful victory the LORD had given them over their enemies. 28 They came to Jerusalem, to the house of the LORD, with harps, lyres and trumpets. 29 And the fear of God came upon all the kingdoms of the surrounding lands when they heard how the LORD had fought against the enemies of Israel. 30 Thereafter Jehoshaphat's kingdom enjoyed peace, for his God gave him rest on every side.

Jehoshaphat's Other Deeds

31* Thus Jehoshaphat reigned over Judah. He was thirty-five years old when he became king, and he reigned twenty-five years in Jerusalem. His mother was named Azubah, daughter of Shilhi. 32 He followed the path of his father Asa unswervingly, doing what was right in the LORD's sight. 33 But the high places were not removed, nor as yet had the people fixed their hearts on the God of their fathers.

34 The rest of the acts of Jehoshaphat, first and last, can be found written in the chronicle of Jehu, son of Hanani, which is inserted in the book of the kings of Israel. 35 After this, King Jehoshaphat of Judah allied himself with King Ahaziah of Israel, who did evil. 36* He joined with him in building

ships to sail to Tarshish; the fleet was built at Ezion-geber. 37 But Eliezer, son of Dodavahu from Mareshah, prophesied against Jehoshaphat, saying, "Because you have joined with Ahaziah, the LORD will shatter your work." And the ships were wrecked and were unable to sail to Tarshish.

21 1* Jehoshaphat rested with his ancestors; he was buried with them in the City of David. Jehoram, his son, succeeded him as king. 2 His brothers, sons of Jehoshaphat, were Azariah, Jehiel, Zechariah, Azariah, Michael and Shephatiah; all these were sons of King Jehoshaphat of Judah. 3 Their father gave them numerous gifts of silver, gold and precious objects, together with fortified cities in Judah, but the kingship he gave to Jehoram because he was the first-born.

Evil Deeds of Jehoram

4 When Jehoram had come into his father's kingdom and had consolidated his power, he put to the sword all his brothers and also some of the princes of Israel. 5* Jehoram was thirty-two years old when he became king, and he reigned eight years in Jerusalem. 6† He conducted himself like the kings of Israel of the line of Ahab, because one of Ahab's daughters was his wife. He did evil in the sight of the LORD, 7* but the LORD would not destroy the house of David because of the covenant he had made with David and because of his promise to give him and his sons a lamp for all time.

8* During his time Edom revolted against the sovereignty of Judah; they chose a king of their own. 9 Thereupon Jehoram crossed over with his officers and all the chariots he had. He arose by night and broke through the Edomites when they had surrounded him and the commanders of his chariots. 10 However, Edom has continued in revolt against the sovereignty of Judah down to the present time. Libnah also revolted at that time against Jehoram's sovereignty because he had forsaken the LORD, the God of his fathers. 11 He also set up high places in the mountains of Judah; he led the inhabitants of Jerusalem into idolatry and seduced Judah.

Retribution

12† He received a letter from the prophet Elijah with this message: Thus says the LORD, the God of your ancestor David: 'Because you have not followed the path of your father Jehoshaphat, nor of

---

20, 26: *Beracah:* the Hebrew word for "blessing."

21, 6: *One of Ahab's daughters:* Athaliah. In 2 Chr 22, 2 (and its source, 2 Kgs 8, 26) she is called Omri's daughter; but this should probably be understood in the sense of granddaughter.

21, 12: *Elijah:* the only mention by the Chronicler of this prophet of the northern kingdom of Israel. It is doubtful that Elijah was still living in the reign of Jehoram of Judah; in any case, the attribution

of the letter to him is most likely an imaginative filling out of the narration.

20, 23: Jos 6, 17; Ez 38, 21.
20, 31–34: 1 Kgs 22, 41–45.
20, 36f: 1 Kgs 22, 48f.
21, 1: 1 Kgs 22, 51.
21, 5ff: 2 Kgs 8, 17ff.

21, 7: 1 Kgs 11, 36; 2 Kgs 8, 19.
21, 8ff: Gn 27, 40; 2 Kgs 8, 20ff.

?did you KNOW?

The Role of the Prophet

The letter from Elijah to King Jehoram discussed in 2 Chr 21, 12–15 underscores the principal role of the Hebrew prophet: to be God's voice, the one who speaks for God. Although many early figures are called prophets, including Moses and Deborah, the classical prophet—*nabi'* in Hebrew—appeared later in Israelite history. The primary function of the prophet was not to foretell the future but to announce God's judgment, to confront those who violated God's law, and to console those who suffered. In short, the prophets were the conscience of the Israelite nation.

▸ 2 Chr 21, 12–15

Asa, king of Judah, 13 but instead have walked in the way of the kings of Israel and have led Judah and the inhabitants of Jerusalem into idolatry, as did the house of Ahab, and also because you have murdered your brothers of your father's house who were better than you, 14 the LORD will strike your people, your children, your wives, and all that is yours with a great plague; 15 and you shall have severe pains from a disease in your bowels, while your bowels issue forth because of the disease, day after day.' "

16 Then the LORD stirred up against Jehoram the animosity of the Philistines and of the Arabs who bordered on the Ethiopians. 17 They came up against Judah, invaded it, and carried away all the wealth found in the king's palace, along with his sons and his wives; there was left to him only one son, Jehoahaz, his youngest. 18 After these events, the LORD afflicted him with an incurable disease of the bowels. 19 As time went on until a period of two years had elapsed, his bowels issued forth because of the disease and he died in great pain. His people did not make a pyre for him like that of his fathers. 20* He was thirty-two years old when he became king, and he reigned eight years in Jerusalem. He departed unloved and was buried in the City of David, but not in the tombs of the kings.

Ahaziah

22 1* Then the inhabitants of Jerusalem made Ahaziah, his youngest son, king in his stead, since all the older sons had been slain by the band that had come into the fort with the Arabs. Thus Ahaziah, son of Jehoram, reigned as king of Judah. 2 He was twenty-two years old when he became king, and he reigned one year in Jerusalem. His mother was named Athaliah, daughter of Omri. 3 He, too, followed the ways of the house of Ahab, because his mother counseled him to act sinfully. 4 To his own destruction, he did evil in the sight of the LORD, as did the house of Ahab, since they were his counselors after the death of his father.

5 He was also following their counsel when he accompanied Jehoram, son of Ahab, king of Israel, to battle against Hazael, king of Aram, at Ramoth-gilead. There Jehoram was wounded by the Arameans. 6 He returned to Jezreel to be healed of the wounds he had received at Rama in his battle against Hazael, king of Aram. Because of this illness, Ahaziah, son of Jehoram, king of Judah, went down to visit Jehoram, son of Ahab, in Jezreel. 7* Now it was willed by God for Ahaziah's downfall that he should join Jehoram, for after his arrival he rode out with Jehoram to Jehu, son of Nimshi, whom the LORD had anointed to cut down the house of Ahab. 8* While Jehu was executing judgment on the house of Ahab, he also encountered the princes of Judah and the nephews of Ahaziah who were his attendants, and he slew them. 9*† Then he looked for Ahaziah himself. They caught him where he was hiding in Samaria and brought him to Jehu, who put him to death. They buried him, for they said, "He was the grandson of Jehoshaphat, who sought the LORD with his whole heart." There remained in Ahaziah's house no one powerful enough to wield the kingship.

Usurpation of Athaliah

10* When Athaliah, mother of Ahaziah, learned that her son was dead, she proceeded to kill off all the royal offspring of the house of Judah. 11 But Jehosheba, a royal princess, secretly took Ahaziah's son Joash from among the king's sons who were about to be slain, and put him and his nurse in a bedroom. In this way Jehosheba, who was the daughter of King Jehoram, a sister of Ahaziah, and wife of Jehoiada the priest, hid the child from Athaliah's sight, so that she did not put him to death. 12 For six years he remained hidden with them in the house of God, while Athaliah ruled over the land.

---

† **22, 9:** This account of the death of Ahaziah of Judah is not derived from 2 Kgs 9, 27f, with which it is at variance.

21, 20: 2 Kgs 8, 24.   22, 8: 2 Kgs 10, 12ff.
22, 1–6: 2 Kgs 8, 24–29.   22, 9: 2 Kgs 9, 27f.
22, 7: 2 Kgs 9, 21; 10, 12ff.   22, 10ff: 2 Kgs 11, 1ff.

Athaliah Overthrown

23 ¹* In the seventh year, Jehoiada took courage and entered a conspiracy with certain captains: Azariah, son of Jehoram; Ishmael, son of Jehohanan; Azariah, son of Obed; Masseiah, son of Adaiah; and Elishaphat, son of Zichri. ² They journeyed about Judah, gathering the Levites from all the cities of Judah and also the heads of the Israelite families. When they had come to Jerusalem, ³ the whole assembly made a covenant with the king in the house of God. Jehoiada said to them: "Here is the king's son who must reign, as the LORD promised concerning the sons of David. ⁴ This is what you must do: a third of your number, both priests and Levites, who come in on the sabbath must guard the thresholds, ⁵ another third must be at the king's palace, and the final third at the Foundation Gate, when all the people will be in the courts of the LORD's temple. ⁶ Let no one enter the LORD's house except the priests and those Levites who are ministering. They may enter because they are holy; but all the other people must observe the prescriptions of the LORD. ⁷ The Levites shall surround the king on all sides, each with his weapon drawn. Whoever tries to enter the house must be slain. Stay with the king wherever he goes."

⁸* The Levites and all Judah did just as Jehoiada the priest commanded. Each brought his men, those who were to come in on the sabbath as well as those who were to depart on the sabbath, since Jehoiada the priest had not dismissed any of the divisions. ⁹ Jehoiada the priest gave the captains the spears, shields and bucklers of King David which were in the house of God. ¹⁰ He stationed all the people, each with his spear in hand, from the southern to the northern extremity of the enclosure, around the altar and the temple on the king's behalf. ¹¹ Then they brought out the king's son, set the crown and the insignia upon him, and made him king. Jehoiada and his sons anointed him, and they cried, "Long live the king!"

¹² When Athaliah heard the din of the people running and acclaiming the king, she went to the people in the temple of the LORD. ¹³† She looked, and there was the king standing beside his pillar at the entrance, the officers and the trumpeters around him, and all the people of the land rejoicing and blowing trumpets, while the singers with their musical instruments were leading the acclaim. Athaliah

tore her garments and cried out, "Treason! treason!" ¹⁴ Then Jehoiada the priest sent out the captains who were in command of the army; he said to them: "Take her outside through the ranks, and if anyone tries to follow her, let him die by the sword. For," the priest continued, "you must not put her to death in the LORD's temple." ¹⁵ So they seized her, and when she arrived at the entrance to the Horse Gate of the palace, they put her to death there.

¹⁶ Then Jehoiada made a covenant between himself and all the people and the king, that they should be the LORD's people. ¹⁷ And all the people went to the temple of Baal and tore it down. They smashed its altars and images, and they slew Mattan, the priest of Baal, before the altars. ¹⁸* Then Jehoiada gave the charge of the LORD's temple into the hands of the levitical priests, to whom David had assigned turns in the temple for offering the holocausts of the LORD, as is written in the law of Moses, with rejoicing and song, as David had provided. ¹⁹ Moreover, he stationed guards at the gates of the LORD's temple, so that no one unclean in any respect might enter. ²⁰ Then he took the captains, the nobles, the rulers among the people, and all the people of the land, and led the king out of the LORD's house. When they had come within the upper gate of the king's house, they seated the king upon the royal throne. ²¹ All the people of the land rejoiced and the city was quiet, now that Athaliah had been put to death by the sword.

The Temple Restored

24 ¹* Joash was seven years old when he became king, and he reigned forty years in Jerusalem. His mother, named Zibiah, was from Beer-sheba. ² Joash did what was pleasing to the LORD as long as Jehoiada the priest lived. ³ Jehoiada provided him with two wives, and he became the father of sons and daughters.

⁴ After some time, Joash decided to restore the LORD's temple. ⁵† He called together the priests and Levites and said to them: "Go out to all the cities of Judah and collect money from all Israel that you may repair the house of your God over the years. You must hasten this affair." But the Levites did not hasten. ⁶* Then the king summoned Jehoiada, who was in charge, and said to him: "Why have you not required the Levites to bring in from Judah and Jerusalem the tax levied by Moses, the servant of the

---

23, 13: *Beside his pillar:* the king had a special place in the eastern gateway of the temple court that contained the altar of holocausts. He occupied this place on feasts and sabbaths at the time of the statutory offerings, or when he made freewill offerings of his own; cf 2 Kgs 11, 4 and also Ez 46, 1–8 for a later reflection of this.

24, 5: *Collect money:* according to 2 Kgs 12, 5, the people themselves brought the money to the temple; it consisted, at least in part, of voluntary contributions. At the time of the Chronicler (see Neh

10, 32) there was a fixed head tax for the upkeep of the temple (2 Chr 34, 9), based on Ex 30, 12–16. This was still in force in New Testament times (Mt 17, 24f).

23, 1–17.19ff: 2 Kgs 11, 4–20.   24, 1–14: 2 Kgs 12, 1–13.
  23, 8: 2 Kgs 11, 9; 1 Chr 24,   24, 6: Ex 25, 1–9; Neh 10,
  19.   33.
  23, 18: 1 Chr 23, 13.

LORD, and by the assembly of Israel, for the tent of the testimony?" [7] For the wicked Athaliah and her sons had damaged the house of God and had even turned over to the Baals the dedicated resources of the LORD's temple.

[8]* At the king's command, therefore, they made a chest, which they put outside the gate of the LORD's temple. [9]* They had it proclaimed throughout Judah and Jerusalem that the tax which Moses, the servant of God, had imposed on Israel in the desert should be brought to the LORD. [10] All the princes and the people rejoiced; they brought what was asked and cast it into the chest until it was filled. [11] Whenever the chest was brought to the royal officials by the Levites and they saw that it contained much money, the royal scribe and an overseer for the high priest came, emptied the chest, then took it back and returned it to its place. This they did day after day until they had collected a large sum of money. [12] Then the king and Jehoiada gave it to the workmen in charge of the labor on the LORD's temple, who hired masons and carpenters to restore the temple, and also iron- and bronze-smiths to repair it. [13] The workmen labored, and the task of restoration progressed under their hands. They restored the house of God according to its original form, and reinforced it. [14] After they had finished, they brought the rest of the money to the king and to Jehoiada, who had it made into utensils for the LORD's temple, utensils for the service and the holocausts, and basins and other gold and silver utensils. They offered holocausts in the LORD's temple continually throughout the lifetime of Jehoiada. [15] Jehoiada lived to a ripe old age; he was a hundred and thirty years old when he died. [16] He was buried in the City of David with the kings, because he had done good in Israel, in particular with respect to God and his temple.

Apostasy of King Joash

[17] After the death of Jehoiada, the princes of Judah came and paid homage to the king, and the king then listened to them. [18]* They forsook the temple of the LORD, the God of their fathers, and began to serve the sacred poles and the idols; and because of this crime of theirs, wrath came upon Judah and Jerusalem. [19] Although prophets were sent to them to convert them to the LORD, the people would not listen to their warnings. [20] Then the spirit of God possessed Zechariah, son of Jehoiada the priest. He took his stand above the people and said to them: "God says, 'Why are you transgressing the LORD's commands, so that you cannot prosper?

Because you have abandoned the LORD, he has abandoned you.' " [21] But they conspired against him, and at the king's order they stoned him to death in the court of the LORD's temple. [22] Thus King Joash was unmindful of the devotion shown him by Jehoiada, Zechariah's father, and slew his son. And as he was dying, he said, "May the LORD see and avenge."

Retribution

[23]* At the turn of the year a force of Arameans came up against Joash. They invaded Judah and Jerusalem, did away with all the princes of the people, and sent all their spoil to the king of Damascus. [24]* Though the Aramean force came with few men, the LORD surrendered a very large force into their power, because Judah had abandoned the LORD, the God of their fathers. So punishment was meted out to Joash. [25]* After the Arameans had departed from him, leaving him in grievous suffering, his servants conspired against him because of the murder of the son of Jehoiada the priest. They killed him on his sickbed. He was buried in the City of David, but not in the tombs of the kings.

[26] These conspired against him: Zabad, son of Shimeath from Ammon, and Jehozabad, son of Shimrith from Moab. [27]* Of his sons, and the great tribute imposed on him, and of his rebuilding of the house of God, there is a written account in the midrash of the book of the kings. His son Amaziah succeeded him as king.

Campaign in Edom

25 [1]* Amaziah was twenty-five years old when he became king, and he reigned twenty-nine years in Jerusalem. His mother, named Jehoaddan, was from Jerusalem. [2] He did what was pleasing in the sight of the LORD, though not wholeheartedly. [3] After he had strengthened his hold on the kingdom, he slew those of his servants who had killed the king, his father; [4]* but he did not put their children to death, for he acted according to what is written in the law, in the Book of Moses, as the LORD commanded: "Fathers shall not be put to death for their children, nor children for their fathers; but only for his own guilt shall a man be put to death."

[5] Amaziah mustered Judah and placed them, out of all Judah and Benjamin according to their ancestral houses, under leaders of thousands and of hundreds. When he had counted those of twenty years and over, he found them to be three hundred thousand picked men fit for war, capable of handling

24, 8: 2 Chr 34, 9.
24, 9: Ex 30, 13.
24, 18: Ex 34, 13.

24, 23: 2 Kgs 12, 17f.
24, 24: Dt 32, 30.
24, 25f: 2 Kgs 12, 21f.

24, 27: 2 Kgs 12, 19.22.
25, 1-4: 2 Kgs 14, 1-6.

25, 4: Dt 24, 16; 2 Kgs 14,
5f; Ez 18, 20.

lance and shield. 6 He also hired a hundred thousand valiant warriors from Israel for a hundred talents of silver. 7 But a man of God came to him and said: "O king, let not the army of Israel go with you, for the LORD is not with Israel, with any Ephraimite. 8 Instead, go on your own, strongly prepared for the conflict; otherwise the LORD will defeat you in the face of the enemy. It is God who has the power to reinforce or to defeat." 9 Amaziah answered the man of God, "But what is to be done about the hundred talents that I paid for the troops of Israel?" The man of God replied, "The LORD can give you much more than that." 10 Amaziah then disbanded the troops that had come to him from Ephraim, and sent them home. They, however, became furiously angry with Judah, and returned home blazing with resentment.

11* Amaziah now assumed command of his army. They proceeded to the Valley of Salt, and there they killed ten thousand men of Seir. 12 The Judahites also brought back another ten thousand alive, whom they led to the summit of the Rock and then cast down, so that they were all crushed. 13 Meanwhile, the mercenaries whom Amaziah had dismissed from battle service with him raided the cities of Judah from Samaria to Beth-horon. They killed three thousand of the inhabitants and took away much booty.

Infidelity of Amaziah

14 When Amaziah returned from his conquest of the Edomites he brought back with him the gods of the people of Seir, which he set up as his own gods; he bowed down before them and offered sacrifice to them. 15 Then the anger of the LORD blazed out against Amaziah, and he sent a prophet to him who said: "Why have you had recourse to this people's gods that could not save their own people from your hand?" 16 While he was still speaking, however, the king said to him: "Have you been made the king's counselor? Be silent! Why should it be necessary to kill you?" Therefore the prophet desisted. "I know, however," he said, "that God has let you take counsel to your own destruction, because you have done this thing and have refused to hear my counsel."

Retribution

17* Having taken counsel, King Amaziah of Judah sent messengers to Joash, son of Jehoahaz, son of Jehu, the king of Israel, saying, "Come, let us meet each other face to face." 18* King Joash of Israel sent this reply to King Amaziah of Judah: "The thistle of the Lebanon sent a message to the cedar of the Lebanon, saying, 'Give your daughter to my son for his wife.' But the wild beasts of the Lebanon passed by and trampled the thistle down. 19 You are thinking, 'See, I have beaten Edom!', and thus ambition makes you proud. Remain at home. Why involve yourself, and Judah with you, in misfortune and failure?" 20 But Amaziah would not listen, for God had determined to hand them over because they had had recourse to the gods of Edom.

21 Therefore King Joash of Israel advanced and he and King Amaziah met in battle at Bethshemesh of Judah. 22 There Judah was defeated by Israel, and all the Judean soldiers fled homeward. 23 King Joash of Israel captured Amaziah, king of Judah, son of Joash, son of Jehoahaz, at Bethshemesh and brought him to Jerusalem. Then he tore down the wall of Jerusalem from the Ephraim Gate to the Corner Gate, a distance of four hundred cubits. 24† He took away all the gold and silver and all the vessels he found in the house of God with Obed-edom, together with the treasures of the palace, and hostages as well. Then he returned to Samaria.

25* Amaziah, son of Joash, king of Judah, survived Joash, son of Jehoahaz, king of Israel, by fifteen years. 26 The rest of the acts of Amaziah, first and last, can be found written, as is well known, in the book of the kings of Judah and Israel. 27 Now from the time that Amaziah ceased to follow the LORD, a conspiracy was formed against him in Jerusalem; hence he fled to Lachish. But they pursued him to Lachish and put him to death there. 28† They brought him back on horses and buried him with his ancestors in the City of Judah.

The Works of Uzziah

26 1* All the people of Judah chose Uzziah, though he was but sixteen years of age, and proclaimed him king to succeed his father Amaziah. 2 He rebuilt Elath and restored it to Judah; this was after King Amaziah had gone to rest with his ancestors. 3 Uzziah was sixteen years old when he became king, and he reigned fifty-two years in Jerusalem. His mother, named Jecoliah, was from Jerusalem. 4 He pleased the LORD, just as his father Amaziah had done.

25, 24: *With Obed-edom:* possibly a reference to the priest of an Edomite false worship (cf v 14), if not to a levitical family of gatekeepers; cf 1 Chr 15, 18; 26, 12–15.
25, 28: *The City of Judah:* in the parallel passage of 2 Kgs 14, 20, the City of David. The Chronicler is referring, by this term, to the capital of Judah, Jerusalem.

25, 11: 2 Kgs 14, 7.
25, 17–24: 2 Kgs 14, 8–14.   2 Kgs 14, 9.
25, 18: Jgs 9, 7–15;   25, 25–28: 2 Kgs 14, 17–20.
                              26, 1–4: 2 Kgs 14, 21f; 15, 1ff.

⁵*† He was prepared to seek God as long as Zechariah lived, who taught him to fear God; and as long as he sought the LORD, God made him prosper. ⁶* He went out and fought the Philistines and razed the walls of Gath, Jabneh and Ashdod [and built cities in the district of Ashdod and in Philistia]. ⁷ God helped him against the Philistines, against the Arabs who dwelt in Gurbaal, and against the Meunites. ⁸ The Ammonites paid tribute to Uzziah and his fame spread as far as Egypt, for he grew stronger and stronger. ⁹ Moreover, Uzziah built towers in Jerusalem at the Corner Gate, at the Valley Gate, and at the Angle, and he fortified them. ¹⁰ He built towers in the desert and dug numerous cisterns, for he had many cattle. He had plowmen in the foothills and the plains, and vinedressers in the highlands and the garden land. He was a lover of the soil.

¹¹ Uzziah also had a standing army of fit soldiers divided into bands according to the number in which they were mustered by Jeiel the scribe and Maaseiah the recorder, under the command of Hananiah, one of the king's officials. ¹² The entire number of family heads over these valiant warriors was two thousand six hundred, ¹³ and at their disposal was a mighty army of three hundred seven thousand five hundred fighting men of great valor to help the king against his enemies. ¹⁴ Uzziah provided for them—for the entire army—bucklers, lances, helmets, breastplates, bows and slingstones. ¹⁵ He also built machines in Jerusalem, devices contrived to stand on the towers and at the angles of the walls to shoot arrows and cast large stones. His fame spread far and wide, and his power was ascribed to the marvelous help he had received.

Pride and Fall

¹⁶ But after he had become strong, he became proud to his own destruction and broke faith with the LORD, his God. He entered the temple of the LORD to make an offering on the altar of incense. ¹⁷ But Azariah the priest, and with him eighty other priests of the LORD, courageous men, followed him. ¹⁸* They opposed King Uzziah, saying to him: "It is not for you, Uzziah, to burn incense to the LORD, but for the priests, the sons of Aaron, who have been consecrated for this purpose. Leave the sanctuary, for you have broken faith and no longer have a part in the glory that comes from the LORD God." ¹⁹* Uzziah, who was holding a censer for burning the incense, became angry, but at the moment he showed his anger to the priests, while they were looking at him in the house of the LORD beside the altar of incense, leprosy broke out on his forehead. ²⁰ Azariah the chief priest and all the other priests examined him, and when they saw that his forehead was leprous, they expelled him from the temple. He himself fled willingly, for the LORD had afflicted him. ²¹* King Uzziah remained a leper to the day of his death. As a leper he dwelt in a segregated house, for he was excluded from the house of the LORD. Therefore his son Jotham was regent of the palace and ruled the people of the land.

²² The prophet Isaiah, son of Amos, wrote the rest of the acts of Uzziah, first and last. ²³ Uzziah rested with his ancestors; he was buried with them in the field adjoining the royal cemetery, for they said, "He was a leper." His son Jotham succeeded him as king.

Jotham

27 ¹* Jotham was twenty-five years old when he became king, and he reigned sixteen years in Jerusalem. His mother was named Jerusa, daughter of Zadok. ² He pleased the LORD just as his father Uzziah had done, though he did not enter the temple of the LORD; the people, however, continued to act sinfully.

³ He built the upper gate of the LORD's house and had much construction done on the wall of Ophel. ⁴ Moreover, he built cities in the hill country of Judah, and in the forest land he set up fortresses and towers. ⁵ He fought with the king of the Ammonites and conquered them. That year the Ammonites paid him one hundred talents of silver, together with ten thousand kors of wheat and ten thousand of barley. They brought the same to him also in the second and in the third year. ⁶ Thus Jotham continued to grow strong because he lived resolutely in the presence of the LORD, his God. ⁷* The rest of the acts of Jotham, his wars and his activities, can be found written in the book of the kings of Israel and Judah. ⁸ He was twenty-five years old when he became king, and he reigned sixteen years in Jerusalem. ⁹ Jotham rested with his ancestors and was buried in the City of David, and his son Ahaz succeeded him as king.

III: Reforms of Hezekiah and Josiah

Impiety of Ahaz

28 ¹* Ahaz was twenty years old when he became king, and he reigned sixteen years in Jerusalem. He did not please the LORD as his forefather David had done, ² but conducted himself

†
26, 5: *Zechariah:* this person, not otherwise identified, is referred to in language suggesting a pious layman rather than a priest or prophet; cf 2 Chr 29, 1.

26, 5: 2 Chr 24, 2.
26, 6: Am 1, 8.
26, 18: Ex 30, 7.
26, 19: Nm 12, 10.
26, 21ff: 2 Kgs 15, 5ff;

Lv 13, 46; Nm 19, 20.
27, 1–3: 2 Kgs 15, 32–35.
27, 7–9: 2 Kgs 15, 36ff.
28, 1–4: 2 Kgs 16, 1–4.

like the kings of Israel and even made molten idols of the Baals. 3* Moreover, he offered sacrifice in the Valley of Ben-hinnom, and immolated his sons by fire according to the abominable practice of the nations which the LORD had cleared out before the Israelites. 4 He offered sacrifice and incense on the high places, on hills, and under every leafy tree.

Retribution

5* Therefore the LORD, his God, delivered him into the power of the king of Aram. The Arameans defeated him and carried away captive a large number of his people, whom they brought to Damascus. He was also delivered into the power of the king of Israel, who defeated him with great slaughter. 6 For Pekah, son of Remaliah, slew one hundred and twenty thousand of Judah in a single day, all of them valiant men, because they had abandoned the LORD, the God of their fathers. 7 Zichri, an Ephraimite warrior, killed Maaseiah, the king's son, and Azrikam, the master of the palace, and also Elkanah, who was second to the king. 8 The Israelites took away as captives two hundred thousand of their brethren's wives, sons and daughters; they also took from them much plunder, which they brought to Samaria.

The Prophecy of Oded

9 In Samaria there was a prophet of the LORD by the name of Oded. He went out to meet the army returning to Samaria and said to them: "It was because the LORD, the God of your fathers, was angry with Judah that he delivered them into your hands. You, however, have slaughtered them with a fury that has reached up to heaven. 10 And now you are planning to make the children of Judah and Jerusalem your slaves and bondwomen. Are not you yourselves, therefore, guilty of a crime against the LORD, your God? 11 Now listen to me: send back the captives you have carried off from among your brethren, for the burning anger of the LORD is upon you."

12 At this, some of the Ephraimite leaders, Azariah, son of Johanan, Berechiah, son of Meshillemoth, Jehizkiah, son of Shallum, and Amasa, son of Hadlai, themselves stood up in opposition to those who had returned from the war. 13 They said to them: "Do not bring the captives here, for what you propose will make us guilty before the LORD and increase our sins and our guilt. Our guilt is already great, and there is a burning anger upon

Israel." 14 Therefore the soldiers left their captives and the plunder before the princes and the whole assembly. 15* Then the men just named proceeded to help the captives. All of them who were naked they clothed from the booty; they clothed them, put sandals on their feet, gave them food and drink, anointed them, and all who were weak they set on asses. They brought them to Jericho, the city of palms, to their brethren. Then they returned to Samaria.

Further Sins of Ahaz

16* At that time King Ahaz sent an appeal for help to the kings of Assyria. 17* The Edomites had returned, attacked Judah, and carried off captives. 18 The Philistines too had raided the cities of the foothills and the Negeb of Judah; they captured Beth-shemesh, Aijalon, Gederoth, Soco and its dependencies, Timnah and its dependencies, and Gimzo and its dependencies, and occupied them. 19† For the LORD had brought Judah low because of Ahaz, king of Israel, who let Judah go its own way and proved utterly faithless to the LORD. 20* Tilgath-pilneser, king of Assyria, did indeed come to him, but to oppress him rather than to help him. 21* Though Ahaz plundered the LORD's house and the houses of the king and the princes to make payment to the king of Assyria, it availed him nothing.

22 While he was already in distress, the same King Ahaz became even more unfaithful to the LORD. 23* He sacrificed to the gods of Damascus who had defeated him, saying, "Since it was the gods of the kings of Aram who helped them, I will sacrifice to them that they may help me also." However, they only caused further disaster to him and to all Israel. 24* Ahaz gathered up the utensils of God's house and broke them in pieces. He closed the doors of the LORD's house and had altars made for himself in every corner of Jerusalem. 25 In every city throughout Judah he set up high places to offer sacrifice to other gods. Thus he angered the LORD, the God of his fathers.

26* The rest of his deeds and his activities, first and last, can be found written in the book of the kings of Judah and Israel. 27 Ahaz rested with his ancestors and was buried in Jerusalem—in the city, for they did not bring him to the tombs of the kings of Israel. His son Hezekiah succeeded him as king.

28, 19: *Ahaz, king of Israel:* in the period of the divided kingdom the term king of Israel would elsewhere mean "king of the northern Kingdom of Israel."

28, 3: 2 Kgs 16, 3; Lv 18, 21.
28, 5: 2 Kgs 16, 5; Is 7, 1–9.

28, 15: Lk 10, 25–37.
28, 16: 2 Kgs 16, 7.

28, 17: 2 Kgs 16, 6.
28, 20: 2 Kgs 16, 10; Is 7, 17–20; 8, 5–8.
28, 21: 2 Kgs 16, 8.
28, 23: 2 Kgs 16, 12f;

Is 10, 20.
28, 24: 2 Chr 29, 3; 30, 14; 2 Kgs 16, 17.
28, 26f: 2 Kgs 16, 19f.

Reforms of Hezekiah

29

[1]* Hezekiah was twenty-five years old when he became king, and he reigned twenty-nine years in Jerusalem. His mother was named Abia, daughter of Zechariah. [2] He pleased the LORD just as his forefather David had done. [3]* It was he who, in the first month of the first year of his reign, opened the doors of the LORD's house and repaired them. [4] He summoned the priests and Levites, gathered them in the open space to the east, [5] and said to them: "Listen to me, you Levites! Sanctify yourselves now and sanctify the house of the LORD, the God of your fathers, and clean out the filth from the sanctuary. [6] Our fathers acted faithlessly and did evil in the eyes of the LORD, our God. They abandoned him, turned away their faces from the LORD's dwelling, and turned their backs on him. [7]* They also closed the doors of the vestibule, extinguished the lamps, and refused to burn incense and offer holocausts in the sanctuary to the honor of the God of Israel. [8]* Therefore the anger of the LORD has come upon Judah and Jerusalem; he has made them an object of terror, astonishment and mockery, as you see with your own eyes. [9] For our fathers, as you know, fell by the sword, and our sons, our daughters and our wives have been taken captive because of this. [10] Now, I intend to make a covenant with the LORD, the God of Israel, that his burning anger may withdraw from us. [11] My sons, be not negligent any longer, for it is you whom the LORD has chosen to stand before him, to minister to him, to be his ministers and to offer incense."

[12] Then the Levites arose: Mahath, son of Amasai, and Joel, son of Azariah, descendants of the Kohathites; of the sons of Merari: Kish, son of Abdi, and Azariah, son of Jehallel; of the Gershonites: Joah, son of Zimmah, and Eden, son of Joah; [13] of the sons of Elizaphan: Shimri and Jeuel; of the sons of Asaph: Zechariah and Mattaniah; [14] of the sons of Heman: Jehuel and Shimei; of the sons of Jeduthun: Shemaiah and Uzziel. [15] They gathered their brethren together and sanctified themselves; then they came as the king had ordered, to cleanse the LORD's house in keeping with his words.

[16] The priests entered the interior of the LORD's house to cleanse it; and whatever they found in the LORD's temple that was unclean they brought out to the court of the LORD's house, where the Levites took it from them and carried it out to the Kidron Valley. [17] They began the work of consecration on the first day of the first month, and on the eighth day of the month they arrived at the vestibule of the LORD; they consecrated the LORD's house during eight days, and on the sixteenth day of the first month, they had finished.

[18] Then they went inside to King Hezekiah and said: "We have cleansed the entire house of the LORD, the altar of holocausts with all its utensils, and the table for the showbread with all its utensils. [19] All the articles which King Ahaz during his reign had thrown away because of his apostasy, we have restored and consecrated, and they are now before the LORD's altar."

The Rite of Expiation

[20] Then King Hezekiah hastened to convoke the princes of the city and went up to the LORD's house. [21] Seven bulls, seven rams, seven lambs and seven he-goats were brought for a sin offering for the kingdom, for the sanctuary, and for Judah, and he ordered the sons of Aaron, the priests, to offer them on the altar of the LORD. [22] They slaughtered the bulls, and the priests collected the blood and cast it

Renewing Your Prayer Life

Hezekiah was one of Judah's reformer kings. Before he became king, the people had neglected the Temple in Jerusalem for a long time. At the beginning of Hezekiah's reign, the Temple needed some intense effort to get it back in order.

Sometimes our prayer life suffers from neglect too. We get busy and do not take enough time to pray, or we forget to pray altogether. When we decide to commit ourselves to regular prayer, it may take some intense effort to get rid of our bad habits.

Imagine your prayer life as being like the Temple. How does it look? Is it in need of a little dusting? full of cobwebs? ready for major renovation? What steps can you take to make sure you do not neglect your prayer life?

▸ 2 Chr 29, 1–11

29, 1ff: 2 Kgs 18, 1ff.   **29, 8f:** Lv 26, 32f; Dt 28, 25;
29, 3: 2 Chr 28, 24.   Jer 25, 18.
29, 7: 2 Kgs 16, 15.

on the altar. Then they slaughtered the rams and cast the blood on the altar; then they slaughtered the lambs and cast the blood on the altar. 23 Then the he-goats for the sin offering were led before the king and the assembly, who laid their hands upon them. 24 The priests then slaughtered them and offered their blood on the altar to atone for the sin of all Israel; for "The holocaust and the sin offering," the king had said, "is for all Israel."

25 He stationed the Levites in the LORD'S house with cymbals, harps and lyres according to the prescriptions of David, of Gad the king's seer, and of Nathan the prophet; for the prescriptions were from the LORD through his prophets. 26 The Levites were stationed with the instruments of David, and the priests with the trumpets. 27 Then Hezekiah ordered the holocaust to be sacrificed on the altar, and in the same instant that the holocaust began, they also began the song of the LORD, to the accompaniment of the trumpets and the instruments of David, king of Israel. 28 The entire assembly prostrated itself, and they continued to sing the song and to sound the trumpets until the holocaust had been completed. 29 As the holocaust was completed, the king and all who were with him knelt and prostrated themselves. 30 King Hezekiah and the princes then commanded the Levites to sing the praises of the LORD in the words of David and of Asaph the seer. They sang praises till their joy was full, then fell down and prostrated themselves.

31 Hezekiah now spoke out this command: "You have undertaken a work for the LORD. Approach, and bring forward the sacrifices and thank offerings for the house of the LORD." Then the assembly brought forward the sacrifices and thank offerings and all the holocausts which were free-will offerings. 32 The number of holocausts that the assembly brought forward was seventy oxen, one hundred rams, and two hundred lambs: all of these as a holocaust to the LORD. 33 As consecrated gifts there were six hundred oxen and three thousand sheep. 34* Since the priests were too few in number to be able to skin all the victims for the holocausts, their brethren the Levites assisted them until the task was completed and the priests had sanctified themselves; the Levites, in fact, were more willing than the priests to sanctify themselves. 35 Also, the holocausts were many, along with the fat of the peace offerings and the libations for the holocausts. Thus the service of the house of the LORD was reestablished. 36 Hezekiah and all the people rejoiced over what God had reestablished for the people, and at how suddenly this had been done.

Invitation to the Passover

30 1* Hezekiah sent a message to all Israel and Judah, and even wrote letters to Ephraim and Manasseh saying that they should come to the house of the LORD in Jerusalem to celebrate the Passover in honor of the LORD, the God of Israel. 2* The king, his princes, and the entire assembly in Jerusalem had agreed to celebrate the Passover during the second month, 3 for they could not celebrate it at the time of the restoration: the priests had not sanctified themselves in sufficient numbers, and the people were not gathered at Jerusalem. 4 When this proposal had been approved by the king and the entire assembly, 5 they issued a decree to be proclaimed throughout all Israel from Beer-sheba to Dan, that everyone should come to Jerusalem to celebrate the Passover in honor of the LORD, the God of Israel; for not many had kept it in the manner prescribed. 6 Accordingly the couriers, with the letters written by the king and his princes, traversed all Israel and Judah, and at the king's command they said: "Israelites, return to the LORD, the God of Abraham, Isaac and Israel, that he may return to you, the remnant left from the hands of the Assyrian kings. 7* Be not like your fathers and your brethren who proved faithless to the LORD, the God of their fathers, so that he delivered them over to desolation, as you yourselves now see. 8 Be not obstinate, as your fathers were; extend your hands to the LORD and come to his sanctuary that he has consecrated forever, and serve the LORD, your God, that he may turn away his burning anger from you. 9* For when you return to the LORD, your brethren and your children will find mercy with their captors and return to this land; for merciful and compassionate is the LORD, your God, and he will not turn away his face from you if you return to him."

10 So the couriers passed from city to city in the land of Ephraim and Manasseh and as far as Zebulun, but they were derided and scoffed at. 11 Nevertheless, some from Asher, Manasseh and Zebulun humbled themselves and came to Jerusalem. 12 In Judah, however, the power of God brought it about that the people were of one mind to carry out the command of the king and the princes in accordance with the word of the LORD. 13 Thus many people gathered in Jerusalem to celebrate the feast of Unleavened Bread in the second month; it was a very great assembly.

The Passover Celebrated

14* They proceeded to take down the altars that were in Jerusalem; also they removed all the altars

---

29, 34: 1 Chr 15, 12.   30, 2ff: Nm 9, 6–13.   30, 9: 1 Kgs 8, 50.   30, 14: 2 Chr 28, 42f.
30, 1: Ex 12, 1–28.   30, 7: Acts 7, 51.

of incense and cast them into the Kidron Valley. [15] They slaughtered the Passover on the fourteenth day of the second month. The priests and Levites, touched with shame, sanctified themselves and brought holocausts into the house of the LORD. [16] They stood in the places prescribed for them according to the law of Moses, the man of God. The priests sprinkled the blood given them by the Levites; [17]* for many in the assembly had not sanctified themselves, and the Levites were in charge of slaughtering the Passover victims for all who were unclean and therefore could not consecrate them to the LORD. [18] The greater part of the people, in fact, chiefly from Ephraim, Manasseh, Issachar and Zebulun, had not cleansed themselves. Nevertheless they ate the Passover, contrary to the prescription; for Hezekiah prayed for them, saying, "May the LORD, who is good, grant pardon to [19] everyone who has resolved to seek God, the LORD, the God of his fathers, though he be not clean as holiness requires." [20] The LORD heard Hezekiah and spared the people.

[21] Thus the Israelites who were in Jerusalem celebrated the feast of Unleavened Bread with great rejoicing for seven days, and the Levites and the priests sang the praises of the LORD day after day with all their strength. [22] Hezekiah spoke encouragingly to all the Levites who had shown themselves well skilled in the service of the LORD. And when they had completed the seven days of festival, slaying peace offerings and singing praises to the LORD, the God of their fathers, [23] the whole assembly agreed to celebrate another seven days. With joy, therefore, they continued the festivity seven days longer. [24] King Hezekiah of Judah had contributed a thousand bulls and seven thousand sheep to the assembly, and the princes had contributed to the assembly a thousand bulls and ten thousand sheep. The priests sanctified themselves in great numbers, [25] and the whole assembly of Judah rejoiced, together with the priests and Levites and the rest of the assembly that had come from Israel, as well as the sojourners from the land of Israel and those that lived in Judah. [26] There was great rejoicing in Jerusalem, for since the days of Solomon, son of David, king of Israel, there had not been the like in the city. [27] Then the levitical priests rose and blessed the people; their voice was heard and their prayer reached heaven, God's holy dwelling.

Liturgical Reform

31 [1]* After all this was over, those Israelites who had been present went forth to the cities of Judah and smashed the sacred pillars, cut down the sacred poles, and tore down the high places and altars throughout Judah, Benjamin, Ephraim and Manasseh, until all were destroyed. Then the Israelites returned to their various cities, each to his own possession.

[2] Hezekiah reestablished the classes of the priests and the Levites according to their former classification, assigning to each priest and Levite his proper service, whether in regard to holocausts or peace offerings, thanksgiving or praise, or ministering in the gates of the encampment of the LORD. [3]* From his own wealth the king allotted a portion for holocausts, those of morning and evening and those on sabbaths, new moons and festivals, as prescribed in the law of the LORD. [4] He also commanded the people living in Jerusalem to provide the support of the priests and Levites, that they might devote themselves entirely to the law of the LORD.

[5]* As soon as the order was promulgated, the Israelites brought, in great quantities, the best of their grain, wine, oil and honey, and all the produce of the fields; they gave a generous tithe of everything. [6]* Israelites and Judahites living in other cities of Judah also brought in tithes of oxen, sheep, and things that had been consecrated to the LORD, their God; these they brought in and set out in heaps. [7]† It was in the third month that they began to establish these heaps, and they completed them in the seventh month. [8] When Hezekiah and the princes had come and seen the heaps, they blessed the LORD and his people Israel. [9] Then Hezekiah questioned the priests and the Levites concerning the heaps, [10]* and the priest Azariah, head of the house of Zadoc, answered him, "Since they began to bring the offerings to the house of the LORD, we have eaten to the full and have had much left over, for the LORD has blessed his people. This great supply is what was left over."

[11] Hezekiah then gave orders that chambers should be constructed in the house of the LORD. When this had been done, [12] the offerings, tithes and consecrated things were deposited there in safekeeping. The overseer of these things was Conaniah the Levite, and his brother Shimei was second in charge. [13] Jehiel, Azaziah, Nathan, Asahel, Jerimoth, Jozabad, Eliel, Ismachiah, Mahath and

---

31, 7: *Third month . . . seventh month:* between the feast of Pentecost and that of Booths, an interval without rain in Palestine, at the end of which the problem of storage (v 11) would become more urgent.

30, 17: 2 Chr 35, 6.
31, 1: 2 Chr 34, 3f; 2 Kgs
       18, 4.
31, 3: 1 Chr 29, 3; Ez 45, 17;
       Nm 28—29.

31, 5: Nm 18, 8–24;
       Dt 14, 22f.
31, 6: Nm 12, 44–47; 13,
       10–13.
31, 10: Lv 25, 19–22.

Giving the Best of the Best

In 2 Chr 31, 5, we read about how the people "brought, in great quantities, the best of their grain, wine, oil and honey, and all the produce of the fields." They gave the best of the best, in gratitude for the gifts from God. That is what being generous is all about. True generosity springs from the heart and motivates us to give the best of what we have, not just what we do not want or need anymore.

The word *tithe* appears in this verse. For the Israelites, to tithe meant to give 10 percent of one's earnings as a tax for the upkeep of the Temple. Some Christians continue the spirit of tithing by giving 10 percent of all they earn to the church and other charities. They are offering God their best, the firstfruits of their labor (see Lk 21, 1–4 and Acts 4, 32–37).

We all need to search our heart and continue this tradition of offering our best back to God—not because it makes us look good and gives us "extra points" with God, but because it comes from our gratitude for the gifts we have received.

▶ 2 Chr 31, 2–10

Benaiah were supervisors subject to Conaniah and his brother Shimei by appointment of King Hezekiah and of Azariah, the prefect of the house of God. 14 Kore, the son of Imnah, a Levite and the keeper of the eastern gate, was in charge of the free-will gifts made to God; he distributed the offerings made to the LORD and the most holy of the consecrated things. 15 Under him in the priestly cities were Eden, Miniamin, Jeshua, Shemaiah, Amariah and Shecaniah, who faithfully made the distribution to their brethren, great and small alike, according to their classes.

16* There was also a register by ancestral houses of males thirty years of age and over, for all priests who were eligible to enter the house of the LORD according to the daily rule to fulfill their service in the order of their classes. 17* The priests were inscribed in their family records according to their ancestral houses, and the Levites of twenty years and over according to their various offices and classes. 18 A distribution was also made to all who were inscribed in the family records, for their little ones, wives, sons and daughters—thus for the entire assembly, since they were to sanctify themselves by sharing faithfully in the consecrated things. 19 The sons of Aaron, the priests who lived on the lands attached to their cities, had in every city men designated by name to distribute portions to every male among the priests and to every Levite listed in the family records.

20 This Hezekiah did in all Judah. He did what was good, upright and faithful before the LORD, his God. 21* Everything that he undertook, for the service of the house of God or for the law and the commandments, was to do the will of his God. He did this wholeheartedly, and he prospered.

Invasion of Sennacherib

32 1* But after he had proved his fidelity by such deeds, Sennacherib, king of Assyria, came. He invaded Judah, besieged the fortified cities, and proposed to take them by storm. 2 When Hezekiah saw that Sennacherib was coming with the intention of attacking Jerusalem, 3 he decided in counsel with his princes and warriors to stop the waters of the springs outside the city. When they had pledged him their support, 4* a large crowd was gathered which stopped all the springs and also the running stream in the valley nearby. For they said, "Why should the kings of Assyria come and find an abundance of water?" 5* He then looked to his defenses: he rebuilt the wall where it was broken down, raised towers upon it, and built another wall outside. He strengthened the Millo of the City of David and had a great number of spears and shields prepared. 6 Then he appointed army commanders over the people. He gathered them together in his presence in the open space at the gate of the city and encouraged them with these words: 7* "Be brave and steadfast; do not be afraid or dismayed because of the king of Assyria and all the throng that is coming with him, for there is more with us than with him. 8* For he has only an arm of flesh, but we have the LORD, our God, to help us and to fight our battles." And the people took confidence from the words of King Hezekiah of Judah.

31, 16: 1 Chr 23, 3f.
31, 17: 1 Chr 23, 6–24.
31, 21: Ps 119, 2f.
32, 1: 2 Kgs 18, 13.

32, 4: Is 22, 9.11.
32, 5: Neh 2, 17f.
32, 7: 2 Chr 14, 10;
20, 6–12.
32, 8: Is 31, 3.

Threat of Sennacherib

⁹* After this, while Sennacherib, king of Assyria, himself remained at Lachish with all his forces, he sent his officials to Jerusalem with this message for King Hezekiah of Judah, and all the Judahites who were in Jerusalem: ¹⁰ "King Sennacherib of Assyria has this to say: On what are you relying, while you remain under siege in Jerusalem? ¹¹ Has not Hezekiah deceived you, delivering you over to a death of famine and thirst, by his claim that 'the LORD, our God, will save us from the grasp of the king of Assyria'? ¹² Has not this same Hezekiah removed his high places and altars and commanded Judah and Jerusalem, 'You shall prostrate yourselves before one altar only, and on it alone you shall offer incense'? ¹³ Do you not know what my fathers and I have done to all the peoples of other lands? Were the gods of the nations in those lands able to save their lands from my hand? ¹⁴ Who among all the gods of those nations which my fathers put under the ban was able to save his people from my hand? Will your god, then, be able to save you from my hand? ¹⁵ Let not Hezekiah mislead you further and deceive you in any such way. Do not believe him! Since no other god of any other nation or kingdom has been able to save his people from my hand or the hands of my fathers, how much the less shall your god save you from my hand!"

¹⁶ His officials said still more against the LORD God and against his servant Hezekiah, ¹⁷* for he had written letters to deride the LORD, the God of Israel, speaking of him in these terms: "As the gods of the nations in other lands have not saved their people from my hand, neither shall Hezekiah's god save his people from my hand." ¹⁸ In a loud voice they shouted in the Judean language to the people of Jerusalem who were on the wall, to frighten and terrify them so that they might capture their city. ¹⁹ They spoke of the God of Israel as though he were one of the gods of the other peoples of the earth, a work of human hands. ²⁰* But because of this, King Hezekiah and the prophet Isaiah, son of Amos, prayed and called out to heaven.

Defeat of Sennacherib

²¹* Then the LORD sent an angel, who destroyed every valiant warrior, leader and commander in the camp of the Assyrian king, so that he had to return shamefaced to his own country. And when he entered the temple of his god, some of his own offspring struck him down there with the sword.

²² Thus the LORD saved Hezekiah and the inhabitants of Jerusalem from the hand of Sennacherib, king of Assyria, as from every other power; he gave them rest on every side. ²³* Many brought gifts for the LORD to Jerusalem and costly objects for King Hezekiah of Judah, who thereafter was exalted in the eyes of all the nations.

Hezekiah's Other Deeds

²⁴* In those days Hezekiah became mortally ill. He prayed to the LORD, who answered him by giving him a sign. ²⁵ Hezekiah, however, did not then discharge his debt of gratitude, for he had become proud. Therefore anger descended upon him and upon Judah and Jerusalem. ²⁶* But then Hezekiah humbled himself for his pride—both he and the inhabitants of Jerusalem; and therefore the LORD did not vent his anger on them during the time of Hezekiah.

²⁷* Hezekiah possessed very great wealth and glory. He had treasuries made for his silver, gold, precious stones, spices, jewels, and other precious things of all kinds; ²⁸ also storehouses for the harvest of grain, for wine and oil, and barns for the various kinds of cattle and for the flocks. ²⁹ He built cities for himself, and he acquired sheep and oxen in great numbers, for God gave him very great riches. ³⁰* This same Hezekiah stopped the upper outflow of water from Gihon and led it underground westward to the City of David. Hezekiah prospered in all his undertakings. ³¹ Nevertheless, in respect to the ambassadors [princes] sent to him from Babylon to investigate the sign that had occurred in the land, God forsook him to test him, that he might know all that was in his heart.

³² The rest of Hezekiah's acts, including his pious works, can be found written in the Vision of the Prophet Isaiah, son of Amos, and in the book of the kings of Judah and Israel. ³³† Hezekiah rested with his ancestors; he was buried at the approach to the tombs of the descendants of David. All Judah and the inhabitants of Jerusalem paid him honor at his death. His son Manasseh succeeded him as king.

Impiety of Manasseh

33 ¹* Manasseh was twelve years old when he became king, and he reigned fifty-five years in Jerusalem. ² He did evil in the sight of the LORD, following the abominable practices of the nations whom the LORD had cleared out of the way of the Israelites. ³ He rebuilt the high places which his

---

† **32, 33:** The approach to the tombs: literally, "the ascent of the tombs," which may mean "the upper section of the tombs," their most prominent and honored place.

32, 9–20: 2 Kgs 18, 17–37; Is 36, 1–22.
32, 17: 2 Kgs 19, 9–13; Is 37, 9–13.
32, 20: 2 Kgs 19, 14–19; Is 37, 14–20.
32, 21: 2 Kgs 19, 35ff; Is 37, 36ff.
32, 23: 2 Chr 14, 6.
32, 24: 2 Kgs 20, 1–11;
Is 38, 1–8.
32, 26.31: 2 Kgs 20, 12–19; Is 39, 1–8.
32, 27f: 2 Kgs 20, 13; Is 39, 2.
32, 30: 2 Kgs 20, 20f.
33, 1: 2 Kgs 21, 1–9.

Perseverance in Leadership

King Hezekiah persevered and prospered. He had many riches and provided for the people in his kingdom. One great accomplishment was a tunnel he had dug under the City of David (2 Chr 32, 30). The tunnel allowed the springs of Gihon to flow into the city so that the people had easier access to the water. That tunnel, more than seventeen hundred feet long, was carved through the stone. Today, it would not take much to complete such a task, but in Hezekiah's time, it was done little by little with simple tools.

A great leader needs perseverance. People can get discouraged and lose heart when faced with difficult tasks. A good leader provides the encouragement and vision to get the job done. Who is an encouraging leader in your life? How do you encourage other people you work or go to school or live with?

▸ **2 Chr 32, 27–33**

---

father Hezekiah had torn down, erected altars for the Baals, made sacred poles, and prostrated himself before the whole host of heaven and worshiped them. 4 He even built altars in the temple of the LORD, of which the LORD had said, "In Jerusalem shall my name be forever": 5 he built altars to the whole host of heaven in the two courts of the LORD'S house. 6 It was he, too, who immolated his sons by fire in the Valley of Ben-hinnom. He practiced augury, divination and magic, and appointed necromancers and diviners of spirits, so that he provoked the LORD with the great evil that he did in his sight. 7 He placed an idol that he had carved in the house of God, of which God had said to David and his son Solomon: "In this house and in Jerusalem which I have chosen from all the tribes of Israel I shall place my name forever. 8 I will not again allow Israel's feet to leave the land which I assigned to your fathers, provided they are careful to observe all that I commanded them, keeping the whole law and the statutes and the ordinances given by Moses." 9 Manasseh misled Judah and the inhabitants of Jerusalem into doing even greater evil than the nations which the LORD had destroyed at the coming of the Israelites. 10 The LORD spoke to Manasseh and his people, but they paid no attention.

His Conversion

11*† Therefore the LORD brought against them the army commanders of the Assyrian king; they took Manasseh with hooks, shackled him with chains, and transported him to Babylon. 12 In this

distress, he began to appease the LORD, his God. He humbled himself abjectly before the God of his fathers 13† and prayed to him. The LORD let himself be won over: he heard his prayer and restored him to his kingdom in Jerusalem. Then Manasseh understood that the LORD is indeed God.

14 Afterward he built an outer wall for the City of David to the west of Gihon in the valley, extending to the Fish Gate and encircling Ophel; he built it very high. He stationed army officers in all the fortified cities of Judah. 15* He removed the foreign gods and the idol from the LORD's house and all the altars he had built on the mount of the LORD's house and in Jerusalem, and he cast them outside the city. 16 He restored the altar of the LORD, and sacrificed on it peace offerings and thank offerings, and commanded Judah to serve the LORD, the God of Israel. 17 Though the people continued to sacrifice on the high places, they now did so to the LORD, their God.

18* The rest of the acts of Manasseh, his prayer to his God, and the words of the seers who spoke to him in the name of the LORD, the God of Israel, can be found written in the chronicles of the kings of Israel. 19 His prayer and how his supplication was heard, all his sins and his infidelity, the sites where he built high places and erected sacred poles and carved images before he humbled himself, all can be found written down in the history of his seers. 20 Manasseh rested with his ancestors and was buried in his own palace. His son Amon succeeded him as king.

33, 11: There is no evidence elsewhere for an imprisonment of King Manasseh in Babylon. However, according to the Assyrian inscriptions, he paid tribute to the Assyrian kings Esarhaddon (680–669 B.C.) and Asshurbanipal (668–627 B.C.). He may well have been obliged to go to Nineveh to take the oath of allegiance as vassal to the king of Assyria.

33, 13: *And prayed to him:* these words led an unknown writer to compose the apocryphal "Prayer of Manasseh," which is added as an appendix to many editions of the Vulgate Bible and is used in the public prayers of the church.

33, 11: Jb 36, 7f; Ez 19, 9.   **33, 18.20:** 2 Kgs 21, 17f.
33, 15: 2 Chr 14, 2.

Amon

21* Amon was twenty-two years old when he became king, and he reigned two years in Jerusalem. 22 He did evil in the sight of the LORD, just as his father Manasseh had done. Amon offered sacrifice to all the idols which his father Manasseh had made, and worshiped them. 23 Moreover, he did not humble himself before the LORD as his father Manasseh had done; on the contrary, Amon only increased his guilt. 24 His servants conspired against him and put him to death in his own house. 25 But the people of the land slew all those who had conspired against King Amon, and then they, the people of the land, made his son Josiah king in his stead.

Reforms of Josiah

34 1* Josiah was eight years old when he became king, and he reigned thirty-one years in Jerusalem. 2 He pleased the LORD, following the path of his ancestor David. 3*† In the eighth year of his reign, while he was still a youth, he began to seek after the God of his forefather David, and in his twelfth year he began to purge Judah and Jerusalem of the high places, the sacred poles and the carved and molten images. 4 In his presence, the altars of the Baals were destroyed; the incense stands erected above them were torn down; the sacred poles and the carved and molten images were shattered and beaten into dust, which was strewn over the tombs of those who had sacrificed to them; 5 and the bones of the priests he burned upon their altars. Thus he purged Judah and Jerusalem. 6 He did likewise in the cities of Manasseh, Ephraim, Simeon, and in the ruined villages of the surrounding country as far as Naphtali; 7 he destroyed the altars, broke up the sacred poles and carved images and beat them into dust, and tore down the incense stands throughout the land of Israel. Then he returned to Jerusalem.

The Temple Restored

8* In the eighteenth year of his reign, in order to cleanse the temple as well as the land, he sent Shaphan, son of Azaliah, Maaseiah, the ruler of the city, and Joah, son of Joahaz, the chamberlain, to restore the house of the LORD, his God. 9* They came to Hilkiah the high priest and turned over the money brought to the house of God which the Levites, the guardians of the threshold, had collected from Manasseh, Ephraim, and all the remnant

of Israel, as well as from all of Judah, Benjamin, and the inhabitants of Jerusalem. 10 They turned it over to the master workmen in the house of the LORD, and these in turn used it to pay the workmen in the LORD's house who were restoring and repairing the temple. 11 They also gave it to the carpenters and the masons to buy hewn stone and timber for the tie beams and rafters of the buildings which the kings of Judah had allowed to fall into ruin. 12 The men worked faithfully at their tasks; their overseers were Jahath and Obadiah, Levites of the line of Merari, and Zechariah and Meshullam, of the Kohathites, who directed them. All those Levites who were skillful with musical instruments 13 were in charge of the men who carried the burdens, and they directed all the workers in every kind of labor. Some of the other Levites were scribes, officials and gatekeepers.

The Finding of the Law

14* When they brought out the money that had been deposited in the house of the LORD, Hilkiah the priest found the book of the law of the LORD given through Moses. 15 He reported this to Shaphan the scribe, saying, "I have found the book of the law in the house of the LORD." Hilkiah gave the book to Shaphan, 16 who brought it to the king at the same time that he was making his report to him. He said, "Your servants are doing everything that has been entrusted to them; 17 they have turned into bullion the metals deposited in the LORD's house and have handed it over to the overseers and the workmen." 18 Then Shaphan the scribe announced to the king, "Hilkiah the priest has given me a book." And Shaphan read from it before the king.

19 When the king heard the words of the law, he tore his garments 20 and issued this command to Hilkiah, to Ahikam, son of Shaphan, to Abdon, son of Michah, to Shaphan the scribe, and to Asaiah, the king's servant: 21 "On behalf of myself and those who are left in Israel and Judah, go, consult the LORD concerning the words of the book that has been found. For the anger of the LORD has been set furiously ablaze against us, since our fathers have not kept the word of the LORD and have not done all that is written in this book." 22 Then Hilkiah and the other men from the king went to the prophetess Huldah, the wife of Shallum, son of Tokhath, son of Hasrah, the guardian of the wardrobe; she dwelt

---

† **34, 3:** *In his twelfth year:* c. 628 B.C., the year after Asshurbanipal's death, when Judah could free itself from Assyrian domination. From 2 Kgs 22, 1—23, 25 alone, one might think that Josiah's reform began only after the discovery of the book of the law in the temple, in the eighteenth year of his reign. But the Chronicler is no doubt right in placing the beginning of the reform at an earlier period. The

very repair of the temple, which led to the finding of the book of the law, must have been occasioned by a cultic reform.

33, 21–25: 2 Kgs 21, 19–26.   34, 8–13: 2 Kgs 22, 3–7.
  34, 1f: 2 Kgs 22, 1f.   34, 9: 2 Chr 24, 8f.
34, 3–7: 2 Chr 14, 1–4; 31, 1;   34, 14–28: 2 Kgs 22, 8–20.
  2 Kgs 23, 4–20.

in Jerusalem, in the new quarter. They spoke to her as they had been instructed, 23 and she said to them: "Thus says the LORD, the God of Israel: 'Tell the one who sent you to me, 24 The LORD says: I am prepared to bring evil upon this place and upon its inhabitants, all the curses written in the book that has been read before the king of Judah. 25 Because they have abandoned me and have offered incense to other gods, provoking me by every deed that they have performed, my anger is ablaze against this place and cannot be extinguished.'

26 "But to the king of Judah who sent you to consult the LORD, give this response: 'Thus says the LORD, the God of Israel, concerning the threats you have heard: 27 Because you were heartsick and have humbled yourself before God on hearing his words spoken against this place and its inhabitants; because you have humbled yourself before me, have torn your garments, and have wept before me, I in turn have listened—so declares the LORD. 28 I will gather you to your ancestors and you shall be taken to your grave in peace. Your eyes shall not see all the evil I will bring upon this place and upon its inhabitants.' "

They brought back this message to the king.

Renewal of the Covenant

29* The king now convened all the elders of Judah and Jerusalem. 30 He went up to the house of the LORD with all the men of Judah and the inhabitants of Jerusalem, the priests, the Levites, and all the people, great and small; and he had read aloud to them the entire text of the book of the covenant that had been found in the house of the LORD. 31† Standing at his post, the king made a covenant before the LORD to follow the LORD and to keep his commandments, decrees, and statutes with his whole heart and soul, thus observing the terms of the covenant written in this book. 32 He thereby committed all who were of Jerusalem and Benjamin, and the inhabitants of Jerusalem conformed themselves to the covenant of God, the God of their fathers. 33* Josiah removed every abominable thing from all the territory belonging to the Israelites, and he obliged all who were in Israel to serve the LORD, their God. During his lifetime they did not desert the LORD, the God of their fathers.

The Passover

35 1* Josiah celebrated in Jerusalem a Passover to honor the LORD; the Passover sacrifice was slaughtered on the fourteenth day of the first month.* 2 He reappointed the priests to their duties and encouraged them in the service of the LORD's house. 3* He said to the Levites who were to instruct all Israel, and who were consecrated to the LORD: "Put the holy ark in the house built by Solomon, son of David, king of Israel. It shall no longer be a burden on your shoulders. Serve now the LORD, your God, and his people Israel. 4 Prepare yourselves in your ancestral houses and your classes according to the prescriptions of King David of Israel and his son Solomon. 5* Stand in the sanctuary according to the divisions of the ancestral houses of your brethren, the common people, so that the distribution of the Levites and the families may be the same. 6* Slay the Passover sacrifice, sanctify yourselves, and be at the disposition of your brethren, that all may be carried out according to the word of the LORD given through Moses."

7* Josiah contributed to the common people a flock of lambs and kids, thirty thousand in number, each to serve as a Passover victim for any who were present, and also three thousand oxen; these were from the king's property. 8* His princes also gave a free-will gift to the people, the priests and the Levites. Hilkiah, Zechariah and Jehiel, prefects of the house of God, gave to the priests two thousand six hundred Passover victims together with three hundred oxen. 9 Conaniah and his brothers Shemaiah, Nethanel, Hashabiah, Jehiel and Jozabad, the rulers of the Levites, contributed to the Levites five thousand Passover victims, together with five hundred oxen.

10 When the service had been arranged, the priests took their places, as did the Levites in their classes according to the king's command. 11 The Passover sacrifice was slaughtered, whereupon the priests sprinkled some of the blood and the Levites proceeded to the skinning. 12 They separated what was destined for the holocaust and gave it to various groups of the ancestral houses of the common people to offer to the LORD, as is prescribed in the book of Moses. They did the same with the oxen. 13* They cooked the Passover on the fire as prescribed, and also cooked the sacred meals in pots, cauldrons and pans, then brought them quickly to all the common people. 14 Afterward they prepared the Passover for themselves and for the priests. Indeed the priests, the sons of Aaron, were busy offering holocausts and the fatty portions until night; therefore the Levites prepared for themselves and for the priests, the sons of Aaron. 15 The singers, the sons of Asaph, were at their posts as prescribed by David: Asaph, Heman and

---

34, 31: *Standing at his post:* see note on 2 Chr 23, 13.

34, 29–32: 2 Kgs 23, 1ff.   35, 1–19: 2 Kgs 23, 21ff.
34, 33: 2 Kgs 23, 4–20.   35, 1: Ex 12, 1–28;

2 Kgs 23, 21.   35, 6: 2 Chr 30, 17.
35, 3: 2 Chr 5, 4; 1 Chr 15,   35, 7: Ex 12, 5.
   12.15.   35, 8: Nm 7, 1–83.
35, 5: 1 Chr 24—26.   35, 13: Nm 12, 8f.

Jeduthun, the king's seer. The gatekeepers were at every gate; there was no need for them to leave their stations, for their brethren, the Levites, prepared for them. 16 Thus the entire service of the LORD was arranged that day so that the Passover could be celebrated and the holocausts offered on the altar of the LORD, as King Josiah had commanded. 17 The Israelites who were present on that occasion kept the Passover and the feast of the Unleavened Bread for seven days. 18* No such Passover had been observed in Israel since the time of the prophet Samuel, nor had any king of Israel kept a Passover like that of Josiah, the priests and Levites, all of Judah and Israel that were present, and the inhabitants of Jerusalem. 19 It was in the eighteenth year of Josiah's reign that this Passover was observed.

Josiah's Reign Ends

20 After Josiah had done all this to restore the temple, Neco, king of Egypt, came up to fight at Carchemish on the Euphrates, and Josiah went out to intercept him. 21 Neco sent messengers to him, saying: "What quarrel is between us, king of Judah? I have not come against you this day, for my war is with another kingdom, and God has told me to hasten. Do not interfere with God who is with me, as otherwise he will destroy you." 22 But Josiah would not withdraw from him, for he had sought a pretext for fighting with him. Therefore he would not listen to the words of Neco that came from the mouth of God, but went out to fight in the plain of Megiddo. 23* Then the archers shot King Josiah, who said to his servants, "Take me away, for I am seriously wounded." 24 His servants removed him from his own chariot, placed him in another he had in reserve, and brought him to Jerusalem, where he died. He was buried in the tombs of his ancestors, and all Judah and Jerusalem mourned him. 25† Jeremiah also composed a lamentation over Josiah, which is recited to this day by all the male and female singers in their lamentations over Josiah. These have been made obligatory for Israel, and can be found written in the Lamentations.

26* The rest of the chronicle of Josiah, his pious deeds in regard to what is written in the law of the LORD, and his acts, first and last, can be found written in the book of the kings of Israel and Judah.

36

1* The people of the land took Jehoahaz, son of Josiah, and made him king in Jerusalem in his father's stead.

IV: End of the Kingdom

Jehoahaz

2 Jehoahaz was twenty-three years old when he became king, and he reigned three months in Jerusalem. 3 The king of Egypt deposed him in Jerusalem and fined the land one hundred talents of silver and a talent of gold. 4 Then the king of Egypt made his brother Eliakim king over Judah and Jerusalem, and changed his name to Jehoiakim. Neco took his brother Jehoahaz away and brought him to Egypt.

Jehoiakim

5* Jehoiakim was twenty-five years old when he became king, and he reigned eleven years in Jerusalem. He did evil in the sight of the LORD, his God. 6*† Nebuchadnezzar, king of Babylon, came up against him and bound him with chains to take him to Babylon. 7 Nebuchadnezzar also carried away to Babylon some of the vessels of the house of the LORD and put them in his palace in Babylon. 8* The rest of the acts of Jehoiakim, the abominable things that he did, and what therefore happened to him, can be found written in the book of the kings of Israel and Judah. His son Jehoiachin succeeded him as king.

Jehoiachin

9* Jehoiachin was eighteen years old when he became king, and he reigned three months [and ten days] in Jerusalem. He did evil in the sight of the LORD. 10*† At the turn of the year, King Nebuchadnezzar sent for him and had him brought to Babylon, along with precious vessels from the temple of the LORD. He made his brother Zedekiah king over Judah and Jerusalem.

Zedekiah

11* Zedekiah was twenty-one years old when he became king, and he reigned eleven years in Jerusalem. 12* He did evil in the sight of the LORD, his God, and he did not humble himself before the

---

35, 25: The reference to a lamentation over Josiah composed by Jeremiah is not found either in 2 Kgs or Jer; but see note on Zec 12, 11. *Their lamentations:* probably a reference to the canonical Book of Lamentations.

36, 6: *Nebuchadnezzar . . . bound him with chains to take him to Babylon:* the Chronicler does not say that Jehoiakim was actually taken to Babylon. According to 2 Kgs 24, 1–6, Jehoiakim revolted after being Nebuchadnezzar's vassal for three years; he died in Jerusalem before the Babylonian king could reach the city. However, Dn 1, 1f, apparently based on 2 Chr 36, 6f, speaks of Jehoiakim's deportation to Babylon.

36, 10: *His brother Zedekiah:* Zedekiah was actually the brother of Jehoiakim and the uncle of Jehoiachin (2 Kgs 24, 17; Jer 37, 1), though scarcely older than his nephew (2 Kgs 24, 8.18; 2 Chr 36, 9.11).

35, 18f: 2 Kgs 23, 22f.
35, 23: 2 Chr 18, 33f.
35, 28: 2 Kgs 23, 28.
36, 1–4: 2 Kgs 23, 30–34; 1 Chr 3, 15f.
36, 5: 2 Kgs 23, 36f; Jer 22, 18f.
36, 6: 2 Kgs 24, 1f.
36, 8: 2 Kgs 24, 5.
36, 9: 2 Kgs 24, 8f.
36, 10: 2 Kgs 24, 10–16.
36, 11: 2 Kgs 24, 18ff; Jer 52, 1ff.
36, 12: Jer 37, 1ff.

prophet Jeremiah, who spoke the word of the LORD. ¹³* He also rebelled against King Nebuchadnezzar, who had made him swear by God. He became stiff-necked and hardened his heart rather than return to the LORD, the God of Israel. ¹⁴ Likewise all the princes of Judah, the priests and the people added infidelity to infidelity, practicing all the abominations of the nations and polluting the LORD's temple which he had consecrated in Jerusalem.

Dissolution of Judah

¹⁵* Early and often did the LORD, the God of their fathers, send his messengers to them, for he had compassion on his people and his dwelling place. ¹⁶* But they mocked the messengers of God, despised his warnings, and scoffed at his prophets, until the anger of the LORD against his people was so inflamed that there was no remedy. ¹⁷* Then he brought up against them the king of the Chaldeans, who slew their young men in their own sanctuary building, sparing neither young man nor maiden, neither the aged nor the decrepit; he delivered all of them over into his grip. ¹⁸* All the utensils of the house of God, the large and the small, and the

treasures of the LORD's house and of the king and his princes, all these he brought to Babylon. ¹⁹* They burnt the house of God, tore down the walls of Jerusalem, set all its palaces afire, and destroyed all its precious objects. ²⁰ Those who escaped the sword he carried captive to Babylon, where they became his and his sons' servants until the kingdom of the Persians came to power. ²¹ All this was to fulfill the word of the LORD spoken by Jeremiah: "Until the land has retrieved its lost sabbaths, during all the time it lies waste it shall have rest while seventy years are fulfilled."

Decree of Cyrus

²²*† In the first year of Cyrus, king of Persia, in order to fulfill the word of the LORD spoken by Jeremiah, the LORD inspired King Cyrus of Persia to issue this proclamation throughout his kingdom, both by word of mouth and in writing: ²³ "Thus says Cyrus, king of Persia: 'All the kingdoms of the earth the LORD, the God of heaven, has given to me, and he has also charged me to build him a house in Jerusalem, which is in Judah. Whoever, therefore, among you belongs to any part of his people, let him go up, and may his God be with him!' "

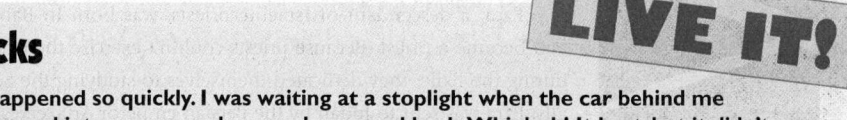

Stiff Necks

It happened so quickly. I was waiting at a stoplight when the car behind me slammed into my car and my neck snapped back. Whiplash! It hurt, but it didn't seem very serious. I was much more upset at the damage that had been done to my car. But by the next morning, I was in agony. I could barely move my head, and my neck was stiff and sore. By the end of the day, my neck was in a brace, and I was taking pain medication.

Now I understand a little better why the Bible so often uses the metaphor of stiff-necked people (2 Chr 36, 13). To be unable or unwilling to turn their heads deprives people of the ability to look toward God. They just keep looking straight ahead as if it were not possible to look in any other direction. You miss out on a lot if you don't or can't look from side to side, believe me!

How often have you refused to turn toward God or to gain a new perspective on life?

▶ 2 Chr 36, 11–14

36, 22f: The words of these verses are identical with those of Ezr 1, 1–3a. Originally Ezra-Nehemiah formed the last part of the single work of the Chronicler, of which 1 and 2 Chronicles formed the first part. But when Ezra-Nehemiah was regarded as a natural sequence to the Books of Samuel and of Kings, it was separated from 1 and 2 Chronicles and placed before them. Thus, 1 and 2 Chronicles became the last part of the Hebrew Bible. To prevent this work from ending on a note of doom, Ezr 1, 1–3a was repeated as 2 Chr 36, 22f.

36, 13: 2 Kgs 25, 1; Jer 52, 4; Ex 17, 13–16.
36, 15: Jer 7, 25; Heb 1, 1.
36, 16: Mt 23, 34ff.
36, 17: Lam 1, 15; 5, 11–14.
36, 18: 2 Kgs 25, 14f.
36, 19: 2 Kgs 25, 9f; Lam 2, 8.
36, 22: Ezr 1, 1ff.

The Books of Ezra and Nehemiah

Imagine the worst vacation ever. The car breaks down twice, you are sick almost the whole time, and the weather is awful. You can't wait to get home—but when you walk in the front door, the house is trashed. Now, imagine how the Israelites felt. They didn't just have a bad vacation; they spent fifty years as captives in a foreign land. When they finally returned home, they faced the overwhelming task of rebuilding Jerusalem and starting their new life. Fortunately, they had Ezra and Nehemiah to help lead and encourage them.

At a Glance

I. The Return from Exile (Ezr 1, 1—6, 22).

II. The Deeds of Ezra (Ezr 7, 1—10, 44).

I. The Deeds of Nehemiah (Neh 1, 1—7, 72).

II. Promulgation of the Law (Neh 8, 1—13, 31).

In-depth

In 587 B.C., the land of Judah and the city of Jerusalem were conquered by the Babylonians, and many Israelites were exiled to Babylon. The Books of Ezra and Nehemiah pick up the story with the return of some Israelites from Babylon to Judah in 538 B.C. The two books were originally a single work, perhaps written in their final form by the same person (or persons) who wrote 1 and 2 Chronicles.

Ezra, a descendant of Israelite priests, was born in Babylonian captivity and became a priest. Because priests couldn't exercise their religious functions during the Exile, they dedicated themselves to studying the Scriptures. Eventually, Ezra was sent to Judah by the Persian emperor Artaxerxes to restore Israel's faithfulness to God. Ezra appointed scribes and judges to establish civil and moral order in the new community returned from Exile.

Nehemiah was a Jewish cupbearer for Emperor Artaxerxes (a cupbearer tastes the contents of whatever the emperor drinks to assure it is not poisoned). When Nehemiah heard reports of Jerusalem's poverty and ruin, he persuaded the emperor to appoint him governor of Judah to help rebuild the city. Nehemiah turned out to be a gifted governor. Under Nehemiah's direction, Jerusalem's walls were rebuilt, and economic and social reforms helped restore order and hope to the community.

Ezra and Nehemiah's leadership was extremely important to Israel as the people returned and began the difficult task of rebuilding Jerusalem. The need to save the faith and customs of the Israelites led to a strict observance of the Law and the beginnings of modern Judaism.

Quick Facts

Period Covered
from the Exiles' return to Jerusalem through Nehemiah's tenure as governor of Judah, from 538 to about 400 B.C.

Author
a scribe (the Chronicler) drawing on Ezra's and Nehemiah's memoirs and other sources

Themes
the return of the Israelites from captivity, the rebuilding of Jerusalem and the Temple

478

Ezra

6, 3

I: The Return from Exile

The Decree of Cyrus

1 ¹*† In the first year of Cyrus, king of Persia, in order to fulfill the word of the LORD spoken by Jeremiah, the LORD inspired King Cyrus of Persia to issue this proclamation throughout his kingdom, both by word of mouth and in writing: ² "Thus says Cyrus, king of Persia: 'All the kingdoms of the earth the LORD, the God of heaven, has given to me, and he has also charged me to build him a house in Jerusalem, which is in Judah. ³ Whoever, therefore, among you belongs to any part of his people, let him go up, and may his God be with him! ⁴ Let everyone who has survived, in whatever place he may have dwelt, be assisted by the people of that place with silver, gold, goods, and cattle, together with free will offerings for the house of God in Jerusalem.' "

⁵ Then the family heads of Judah and Benjamin and the priests and Levites—everyone, that is, whom God had inspired to do so—prepared to go up to build the house of the LORD in Jerusalem. ⁶* All their neighbors gave them help in every way, with silver, gold, goods, and cattle, and with many precious gifts besides all their free-will offerings. ⁷ King Cyrus, too, had the utensils of the house of the LORD brought forth which Nebuchadnezzar had taken away from Jerusalem and placed in the house of his god. ⁸† Cyrus, king of Persia, had them brought forth by the treasurer Mithredath, and counted out to Sheshbazzar, the prince of Judah. ⁹ This was the inventory: sacks of goldware, thirty; sacks of silverware, one thousand and twenty-nine; ¹⁰ golden bowls, thirty; silver bowls, four hundred and ten; other ware, one thousand pieces. ¹¹† Total of the gold- and silverware: five thousand four hundred pieces. All these Sheshbazzar took with him when the exiles were brought back from Babylon to Jerusalem.

Census of the Province

2 ¹*† These are the inhabitants of the province who returned from the captivity of the exiles, whom Nebuchadnezzar, king of Babylon, had carried away to Babylon, and who came back to Jerusalem and Judah, each man in his own city ² (those who returned with Zerubbabel, Jeshua, Nehemiah, Seraiah, Reelaiah, Mordecai, Bilshan, Mispereth, Bigvai, Rehum, and Baanah):

1, 1: *In the first year of Cyrus:* as sovereign over the world empire which began with his conquest of Babylon; that is, 538 B.C.

1, 8: *Sheshbazzar:* very probably the fourth son of Jehoiachin, king of Judah, taken captive to Babylon in 598 B.C., listed in 1 Chr 3, 18 as Senneser; if so, he was the uncle of Zerubbabel (Ezr 3, 2ff); see note on 1 Chr 3, 18.

1, 11: *Total . . . five thousand four hundred pieces:* either this figure or the figures given for one or more of the items listed (vv 9f) have been corrupted in the transmission of the text.

2, 1–67: As it now stands, this list is an expanded form of the lists of returned captives from the sixth century B.C.; see Neh 7, 6–72, where it reappears.

1, 1ff: 2 Chr 36, 22f; Jer 25, 11f; 29, 10; Zec 1, 12.
1, 6: Ex 3, 22; 11, 2; 12, 35.
2, 1: Neh 7, 6–67.

The Spirit of Giving

LIVE IT!

Nine eleven.

Whenever we hear those two words, we are reminded of a horrible day in the history of the United States. The image of the twin towers of the World Trade Center burning and collapsing will stay with us forever. That event affected all of us, but it especially affected the citizens of New York City. Many stories of heroism surround that awful time. The people of New York City and the entire nation came together to grieve and especially to rebuild. Countless people volunteered untold hours to help with rescue efforts and clean-up. Countless more donated money to the families of those directly affected by the tragedy. Despite the horror of the attack, the aftermath of September 11, 2001, brought millions of people together to help rebuild a broken city. It was perhaps one of our finest hours as a nation.

For the Jews returning to Jerusalem, the task of rebuilding their ruined city must have seemed just as overwhelming if not more. (Their whole city was destroyed.) King Cyrus understood this and asked that family, friends, and neighbors help by giving whatever they could to the rebuilding effort.

Who has been there to help you when you have felt completely overwhelmed? How do you offer help to others in their times of tragedy and crisis?

▶ Ezr 1, 6–11

The census of the men of Israel: 3 sons of Parosh, two thousand one hundred and seventy-two; 4 sons of Shephatiah, three hundred and seventy-two; 5 sons of Arah, seven hundred and seventy-five; 6 sons of Pahath-moab, who were sons of Jeshua and Joab, two thousand eight hundred and twelve; 7 sons of Elam, one thousand two hundred and fifty-four; 8 sons of Zattu, nine hundred and forty-five; 9 sons of Zaccai, seven hundred and sixty; 10 sons of Bani, six hundred and forty-two; 11 sons of Bebai, six hundred and twenty-three; 12 sons of Azgad, one thousand two hundred and twenty-two; 13 sons of Adonikam, six hundred and sixty-six; 14 sons of Bigvai, two thousand and fifty-six; 15 sons of Adin, four hundred and fifty-four; 16 sons of Ater, who were sons of Hezekiah, ninety-eight; 17 sons of Bezai, three hundred and twenty-three; 18 sons of Jorah, one hundred and twelve; 19 sons of Hashum, two hundred and twenty-three; 20 sons of Gibeon, ninety-five; 21 sons of Bethlehem, one hundred and twenty-three; 22 men of Netophah, fifty-six; 23 men of Anathoth, one hundred and twenty-eight; 24 men of Beth-azmaveth, forty-two; 25 men of Kiriath-jearim, Chephirah, and Beeroth, seven hundred and forty-three; 26 men of Ramah and Geba, six hundred and twenty-one; 27 men of Michmas, one hundred and twenty-two; 28 men of Bethel and Ai, two hundred and twenty-three; 29 sons of Nebo, fifty-two; 30 sons of Magbish, one hundred and fifty-six; 31 sons of the other Elam, one thousand two hundred and fifty-four; 32 sons of Harim, three hundred and twenty; 33 sons of Lod, Hadid, and Ono, seven hundred and twenty-five; 34 sons of Jericho, three hundred and forty-five; 35 sons of Senaah, three thousand six hundred and thirty.

36 The priests: sons of Jedaiah, who were of the house of Jeshua, nine hundred and seventy-three; 37 sons of Immer, one thousand and fifty-two; 38 sons of Pashhur, one thousand two hundred and forty-seven; 39 sons of Harim, one thousand and seventeen.

40* The Levites: sons of Jeshua, Kadmiel, Binnui, and Hodaviah, seventy-four.

41 The singers: sons of Asaph, one hundred and twenty-eight.

42 The gatekeepers: sons of Shallum, sons of Ater, sons of Talmon, sons of Akkub, sons of Hatita, sons of Shobai, one hundred and thirty-nine in all.

43 The temple slaves: sons of Ziha, sons of Hasupha, sons of Tabbaoth, 44 sons of Keros, sons of Siaha, sons of Padon, 45 sons of Lebanah, sons of Hagabah, sons of Akkub, 46 sons of Hagab, sons of Shamlai, sons of Hanan, 47 sons of Giddel, sons of Gahar, sons of Reaiah, 48 sons of Rezin, sons of Nekoda, sons of Gazzam, 49 sons of Uzza, sons of Paseah, sons of Besai, 50 sons of Asnah, sons of the Meunites, sons of the Nephusites, 51 sons of Bakbuk, sons of

Hakupha, sons of Harhur, 52 sons of Bazluth, sons of Mehida, sons of Harsha, 53 sons of Barkos, sons of Sisera, sons of Temah, 54 sons of Neziah, sons of Hatipha.

55 Descendants of the slaves of Solomon: sons of Sotai, sons of Hassophereth, sons of Peruda, 56 sons of Jaalah, sons of Darkon, sons of Giddel, 57 sons of Shephatiah, sons of Hattil, sons of Pochereth-hazzebaim, sons of Ami. 58 The total of the temple slaves and the descendants of the slaves of Solomon was three hundred and ninety-two.

59 The following who returned from Tel-melah, Tel-harsha, Cherub, Addan, and Immer were unable to prove that their ancestral houses and their descent were Israelite: 60 sons of Delaiah, sons of Tobiah, sons of Nekoda, six hundred and fifty-two. 61* Also, of the priests: sons of Habaiah, sons of Hakkoz, sons of Barzillai (he had married one of the daughters of Barzillai the Gileadite and became known by his name). 62 These men searched their family records, but their names could not be found written there; hence they were degraded from the priesthood, 63† and His Excellency ordered them not to partake of the most holy foods until there should be a priest bearing the Urim and Thummim.

64 The entire assembly taken together came to forty-two thousand three hundred and sixty, 65 not counting their male and female slaves, who were seven thousand three hundred and thirty-seven. They also had two hundred male and female singers. 66 Their horses were seven hundred and thirty-six, their mules two hundred and forty-five, 67 their camels four hundred and thirty-five, their asses six thousand seven hundred and twenty.

68 When they arrived at the house of the LORD in Jerusalem, some of the family heads made free-will offerings for the house of God, to rebuild it in its place. 69 According to their means they contributed to the treasury for the temple service: sixty-one thousand drachmas of gold, five thousand minas of silver, and one hundred garments for the priests. 70 The priests, the Levites, and some of the common people took up residence in Jerusalem; but the singers, the gatekeepers, and the temple slaves dwelt in their cities. Thus all the Israelites dwelt in their cities.

Restoration of the Altar

3 1*† Now when the seventh month came, after the Israelites had settled in their cities, the people gathered at Jerusalem as one man. 2 Then Jeshua, son of Jozadak, together with his brethren the priests, and Zerrubbabel, son of Shealtiel, together with his brethren, set about rebuilding the altar of the God of Israel in order to offer on it the holocausts prescribed in the law of Moses, the man of God. 3* Despite their fear of the peoples of the land, they replaced the altar on its foundations and offered holocausts to the LORD on it, both morning and evening. 4* They also kept the feast of Booths in the manner prescribed, and they offered the daily holocausts in the proper number required for each day. 5 Thereafter they offered the established holocaust, the sacrifices prescribed for the new moons and all the festivals sacred to the LORD, and those which anyone might offer as a free-will gift to the LORD. 6 From the first day of the seventh month they began to offer holocausts to the LORD, though the foundation of the temple of the LORD had not yet been laid.

Founding of the Temple

7* Then they hired stonecutters and carpenters, and sent food and drink and oil to the Sidonians and Tyrians that they might ship cedar trees from the Lebanon to the port of Joppa, as Cyrus, king of Persia, had authorized. 8 In the year after their coming to the house of God in Jerusalem, in the second month, Zerubbabel, son of Shealtiel, and Jeshua, son of Jozadak, together with the rest of their brethren, the priests and Levites and all who had come from the captivity to Jerusalem, began by appointing the Levites twenty years of age and over to supervise the work on the house of the LORD. 9 Jeshua and his sons and brethren, with Kadmiel and Binnui, son of Henadad, and their sons and their brethren, the Levites, stood as one man to supervise those who were engaged in the work on the house of God. 10* When the builders had laid the foundation of the LORD'S temple, the vested priests with the trumpets and the Levites, sons of Asaph, were stationed there with the cymbals to praise the LORD in the manner laid down by David, king of Israel. 11* They alternated in songs of praise and

---

2, 63: *His Excellency:* the deputy of the Persian government; from the context, he was one of the Jewish exile leaders. Nehemiah as governor receives the same title (Neh 8, 9; 10, 2). *Urim and Thummim:* see note on Ex 28, 30.

3, 1f: *The seventh month:* Tishri (September–October), apparently of 538 B.C.; cf Ezr 1, 1; 4, 5. In this case, it was Sheshbazzar who erected the first altar, since he began the work on the foundations of the temple in Jerusalem; cf Ezr 5, 16. It was in the second year of Darius I, i.e., in 520 B.C., that Jeshua and Zerubbabel resumed the work on the temple that had been temporarily interrupted (Ezr 4, 24—5, 1; Hg 1, 1; 2, 1). The Chronicler or a later editor of the text here attributes to them the beginning of the work which, in reality,

they merely completed. *Shealtiel:* the oldest son of King Jehoiachin of Judah and the brother of Sheshbazzar (1 Chr 3, 18f); Zerubbabel was therefore the grandson of Jehoiachin; see note on Ezr 1, 8.

2, 61: 2 Sm 17, 27; 19, 32f; 1 Kgs 2, 7.
3, 1: Neh 7, 73—8, 1.
3, 3: 1 Kgs 8, 64; Dn 9, 25.
3, 4: Ex 23, 16; Nm 28, 3–8.
3, 7: 1 Chr 22, 4; 2 Chr 2, 9.
3, 10: Ezr 2, 41.
3, 11: Pss 100, 5; 136; Jer 33, 11.

Holy Tears

Ezra 3, 12 tells us that many of the older Israelites who remembered the first Temple wept at the grand celebration that marked its rebirth. Were they shedding tears of joy that the Temple was being built again? Or were they shedding tears of sorrow over what they had lost and never regained? Most likely, they were doing both.

Weeping can be a holy and healing part of life. Unfortunately, some people believe that strong men and women never cry. But tears are appropriate on many occasions: the loss of a dear friend or family member, a reconciliation with someone after a long separation, and the moment we recognize we have sinned and hurt someone deeply, to name a few. We should bring our tears to God in prayer. They will turn into holy tears as God's healing love enters our life.

▸ Ezr 3, 10–13

thanksgiving to the LORD, "for he is good, for his kindness to Israel endures forever"; and all the people raised a great shout of joy, praising the LORD because the foundation of the LORD'S house had been laid. 12* Many of the priests, Levites, and family heads, the old men who had seen the former house, cried out in sorrow as they watched the foundation of the present house being laid. Many others, however, lifted up their voices in shouts of joy, 13* and no one could distinguish the sound of the joyful shouting from the sound of those who were weeping; for the people raised a mighty clamor which was heard afar off.

Samaritan Interference

4 1 When the enemies of Judah and Benjamin heard that the exiles were building a temple for the LORD, the God of Israel, 2 they approached Zerubbabel and the family heads and said to them, "Let us build with you, for we seek your God just as you do, and we have sacrificed to him since the days of Esarhaddon, king of Assyria, who had us brought here." 3 But Zerubbabel, Jeshua, and the rest of the family heads of Israel answered them, "It is not your responsibility to build with us a house for our God, but we alone must build it for the LORD, the God of Israel, as King Cyrus of Persia has commanded us." 4 Thereupon the people of the land set out to intimidate and dishearten the people of Judah so as to keep them from building. 5† They also suborned counselors to work against them and thwart their plans during the remaining years of Cyrus, king of Persia, and until the reign of Darius, king of Persia.

Later Hostility

6 Also at the beginning of the reign of Ahashuerus they prepared a written accusation against the inhabitants of Judah and Jerusalem.

7† Again, in the time of Artaxerxes, Mithredath wrote in concert with Tabeel and the rest of his fellow officials to Artaxerxes, king of Persia. The document was written in Aramaic and was accompanied by a translation. [Aramaic:]

8† Then Rehum, the governor, and Shimshai, the scribe, wrote the following letter against Jerusalem to King Artaxerxes: 9 "Rehum, the governor, Shimshai, the scribe, and their fellow judges, officials, and agents from among the Persian, Urukian, Babylonian, Susian (that is, Elamite), 10 and the other peoples whom the great and illustrious Assurbanipal transported and settled in the city of Samaria and elsewhere in the province West-of-Euphrates, as follows. . . . ." 11 This is a copy of the letter that they sent to him:

"To King Artaxerxes, your servants, the men of West-of-Euphrates, as follows: 12 Let it be known to the king that the Jews who came up from you to us have arrived at Jerusalem and are now rebuilding this rebellious and evil city. They are raising up its walls, and the foundations have already been laid. 13 Now let it be known to the king that if this city is rebuilt and its walls are raised up again, they will no longer pay taxes, tributes, or tolls; thus it can only result in harm to the throne. 14 Now, since we partake of the salt of the palace, we ought not simply to look on while the king is being

---

4, 5: *Darius:* Darius I (521–485 B.C.). The temple-building narrative continues in Ezr 4, 24. In between (Ezr 4, 6–23) is a series of notes about the opposition to the returned exiles voiced at the Persian court in the early fifth century B.C., after the temple had been reestablished.

4, 7: *Aramaic:* this word in the original text seems to be a note indicating a change of language from Hebrew to Aramaic, which in fact takes place here. The Aramaic section ends with Ezr 6, 18, but

again in Ezr 7, 12–26 a royal letter is cited in Aramaic.

4, 8–23: The central question here is the rebuilding of the fortification walls of Jerusalem, not the building of the temple. The interruption of work on the city wall some time before 445 B.C. was the occasion for the coming of Nehemiah to Palestine (Neh 1, 1–4; 2, 1–5). *Artaxerxes:* Artaxerxes I (464–423 B.C.).

3, 12: Hg 2, 3.   3, 13: Tb 14, 5.

dishonored. Therefore we have sent this message to inform you, O king, [15] so that inquiry may be made in the historical records of your fathers. In the historical records you can discover and verify that this city is a rebellious city which has proved fatal to kings and provinces, and that sedition has been fostered there since ancient times. For that reason this city was destroyed. [16] We inform you, O king, that if this city is rebuilt and its walls are raised up again, by that very fact you will no longer own any part of West-of-Euphrates."

[17] The king sent this answer: "To Rehum, the governor, Shimshai, the scribe, and their fellow officials living in Samaria and elsewhere in the province West-of-Euphrates, greetings and the following: [18] The communication which you sent us has been read plainly in my presence. [19] When at my command inquiry was made, it was verified that from ancient times this city has risen up against kings and that rebellion and sedition have been fostered there. [20] Powerful kings were once in Jerusalem who ruled over all West-of-Euphrates, and taxes, tributes, and tolls were paid to them. [21] Give orders, therefore, that will stop the work of these men. This city may not be rebuilt until a further decree has been issued by me. [22] Take care that you do not neglect this matter, lest the evil grow to the detriment of the throne."

[23]* As soon as a copy of King Artaxerxes' letter had been read before Rehum, the governor, Shimshai, the scribe, and their fellow officials, they went in all haste to the Jews in Jerusalem and stopped their work by force of arms.

Rebuilding of the Temple

[24]† Thus it was that the work on the house of God in Jerusalem was halted. This inaction lasted until the second year of the reign of Darius, king of Persia.

5 [1]*† Then the prophets Haggai and Zechariah, son of Iddo, began to prophesy to the Jews in Judah and Jerusalem in the name of the God of Israel. [2] Thereupon Zerubbabel, son of Shealtiel, and Jeshua, son of Jozadak, began again to build the house of God in Jerusalem, with the prophets of God giving them support. [3] At that time there came to them Tattenai, governor of West-of-Euphrates, and Shethar-bozenai, and their fellow officials, who asked of them: "Who issued the decree for you to build this house and

raise this edifice? [4] What are the names of the men who are building this structure?" [5] But their God watched over the elders of the Jews so that they were not hindered, until a report could go to Darius and then a written order be sent back concerning this matter.

[6] A copy of the letter sent to King Darius by Tattenai, governor of West-of-Euphrates, and Shethar-bozenai, and their fellow officials from West-of-Euphrates; [7] they sent him a report in which was written the following:

"To King Darius, all good wishes! [8] Let it be known to the king that we have visited the province of Judah and the house of the great God: it is being rebuilt of cut stone and the walls are being reinforced with timber; the work is being carried on diligently and is making good progress under their hands. [9] We then questioned the elders, addressing to them the following words: 'Who issued the decree for you to build this house and raise this edifice?' [10] We also asked them their names, to report them to you in a list of the men who are their leaders. [11] This was their answer to us: 'We are the servants of the God of heaven and earth, and we are rebuilding the house built here long years ago, which a great king of Israel built and finished. [12] But because our fathers provoked the wrath of the God of heaven, he delivered them into the power of the Chaldean, Nebuchadnezzar, king of Babylon, who destroyed this house and led the people captive to Babylon. [13] However, in the first year of Cyrus, king of Babylon, King Cyrus issued a decree for the rebuilding of this house of God. [14] Moreover, the gold and silver utensils of the house of God which Nebuchadnezzar had taken from the temple in Jerusalem and carried off to the temple in Babylon, King Cyrus ordered to be removed from the temple in Babylon and consigned to a certain Sheshbazzar, whom he named governor. [15] And he commanded him: Take these utensils and deposit them in the temple of Jerusalem, and let the house of God be rebuilt on its former site. [16] Then this same Sheshbazzar came and laid the foundations of the house of God in Jerusalem. Since that time the building has been going on, and it is not yet completed.' [17] Now, if it please the king, let a search be made in the royal archives of Babylon to discover whether a decree really was issued by King Cyrus for the rebuilding of this house of God in Jerusalem. And may the king's pleasure in this matter be communicated to us."

4, 24: *The second year . . . of Darius:* 520 B.C.; it marks the beginning of the successful restoration of the temple, which was accomplished within the five years following (Ezr 5, 1—6, 18).

5, 1: *The prophets Haggai and Zechariah:* two of the Minor Prophets, whose books record their role in the encouragement of this work.

4, 23: Neh 1, 3.

5, 1: Hg 1, 14—2, 9; Zec 4, 9.

EZR

Cultural Connections

THE REBIRTH OF A NATION

Among the first things oppressive governments often do, historically speaking, is destroy or shut down religious establishments and make religious gatherings illegal. This is what happened to the Israelites taken into exile. But when oppressive governments can no longer hold the people down, when oppressive methods lose their grip, among the first things the people do is bring back religious establishments and religious gatherings. This is what the Israelites did upon return to their land.

The reopening of the Catholic Cathedral in Moscow, Russia, in December 1999, marked the symbolic end of Roman Catholic religious persecution in Russia. For over eighty years, radical socialist, Marxist, and communist political leaders persecuted almost all religious communities in Russia, especially Roman Catholics. Faith and religion were seen as not just unimportant but as unnecessary and unwanted, to say the least.

Russia now struggles to rise above those years of oppression, and not just the religious oppression but the social and economic oppression as well. Many see the reopening of the Catholic Cathedral as an important step toward rebuilding the wounded country and leading it out of its past woes.

Have you ever felt uncomfortable speaking about your beliefs in a group of people? What kinds of statements did people make that caused you to feel uncomfortable sharing your beliefs? How can you help eliminate intolerance of this kind?

▸ **Ezra, chapter 5**

The Decree of Darius

6 ¹ Thereupon King Darius issued an order to search the archives in which the Babylonian records were stored away; ²* and in Ecbatana, the stronghold in the province of Media, a scroll was found containing the following text: "Memorandum. ³ In the first year of King Cyrus, King Cyrus issued a decree: The house of God in Jerusalem. The house is to be rebuilt as a place for offering sacrifices and bringing burnt offerings. Its height is to be sixty cubits and its width sixty cubits. ⁴ It shall have three courses of cut stone for each one of timber. The costs are to be borne by the royal palace. ⁵ Also, the gold and silver utensils of the house of God which Nebuchadnezzar took from the temple of Jerusalem and brought to Babylon are to be sent back: to be returned to their place in the temple of Jerusalem and deposited in the house of God.

⁶ "Now, therefore, Tattenai, governor of West-of-Euphrates, and Shethar-bozenai, and you, their fellow officials in West-of-Euphrates, do not interfere

in that place. ⁷ Let the governor and the elders of the Jews continue the work on that house of God; they are to rebuild it on its former site. ⁸ I also issue this decree concerning your dealing with these elders of the Jews in the rebuilding of that house of God: From the royal revenue, the taxes of West-of-Euphrates, let these men be repaid for their expenses, in full and without delay. ⁹ Whatever else is required—young bulls, rams, and lambs for holocausts to the God of heaven, wheat, salt, wine, and oil, according to the requirements of the priests who are in Jerusalem—is to be delivered to them day by day without fail, ¹⁰ that they may continue to offer sacrifices of pleasing odor to the God of heaven and pray for the life of the king and his sons. ¹¹ I also issue this decree: If any man violates this edict, a beam is to be taken from his house, and he is to be lifted up and impaled on it; and his house is to be reduced to rubble for this offense. ¹² And may the God who causes his name to dwell there overthrow every king or people who may undertake to alter this or to destroy this house of God in Jerusalem. I, Darius, have issued this decree; let it be carefully executed."

13 Then Tattenai, the governor of West-of-Euphrates, and Shethar-bozenai, and their fellow officials carried out fully the instructions King Darius had sent them. 14 The elders of the Jews continued to make progress in the building, supported by the message of the prophets, Haggai and Zechariah, son of Iddo. They finished the building according to the command of the God of Israel and the decrees of Cyrus and Darius [and of Artaxerxes, king of Persia]. 15 They completed this house on the third day of the month Adar, in the sixth year of the reign of King Darius. 16 The Israelites—priests, Levites, and the other returned exiles—celebrated the dedication of this house of God with joy. 17 For the dedication of this house of God, they offered one hundred bulls, two hundred rams, and four hundred lambs, together with twelve he-goats as a sin-offering for all Israel, in keeping with the number of the tribes of Israel. 18 Finally, they set up the priests in their classes and the Levites in their divisions for the service of God in Jerusalem, as is prescribed in the book of Moses.

did you KNOW?
The Second Temple

The first Temple, built during Solomon's reign, was destroyed in 587 B.C. when the southern kingdom of Judah was conquered by the Babylonians. The Persian king, Cyrus II, conquered Babylon in 539 B.C. and a year later liberated the Jewish exiles in Babylon. He also decreed that the Temple in Jerusalem be rebuilt (Ezr 6, 3). Between the years 520 and 515, the second Temple was rebuilt in Jerusalem. The second Temple was an essential aspect of the Israelites' rebuilding of their life, culture, and religion after the Babylonian Exile. This Temple, rather than a king, became the central focus of Jewish identity.

The Passover

19* The exiles kept the Passover on the fourteenth day of the first month. 20 The Levites, every one of whom had purified himself for the occasion, sacrificed the Passover for the rest of the exiles, for their brethren the priests, and for themselves. 21* The Israelites who had returned from the exile partook of it together with all those who had separated themselves from the uncleanness of the peoples of the land to join them in seeking the LORD, the God of Israel. 22† They joyfully kept the feast of Unleavened Bread for seven days, for the LORD had filled them with joy by making the king of Assyria favorable to them, so that he gave them help in their work on the house of God, the God of Israel.

II: The Deeds of Ezra

Ezra the Scribe

7 1† After these events, during the reign of Artaxerxes, king of Persia, Ezra, son of Seraiah, son of Azariah, son of Hilkiah, 2 son of Shallum, son of Zadok, son of Ahitub, 3 son of Amariah, son of Azariah, son of Meraioth, 4 son of Zerahiah, son of Uzzi, son of Bukki, 5 son of Abishua, son of Phinehas, son of Eleazar, son of the high priest Aaron— 6* this Ezra came up from Babylon. He was a scribe, well-versed in the law of Moses which was given by the LORD, the God of Israel. Because the hand of the LORD, his God, was upon him, the king granted him all that he requested.

7 Some of the Israelites and some priests, Levites, singers, gatekeepers, and temple slaves also came up to Jerusalem in the seventh year of King Artaxerxes. 8 Ezra came to Jerusalem in the fifth month of that seventh year of the king. 9 On the first day of the first month he resolved on the journey up from Babylon, and on the first day of the fifth month he arrived at Jerusalem, for the favoring hand of his God was upon him. 10* Ezra had set his heart on the study and practice of the law of the LORD and on teaching statutes and ordinances in Israel.

The Decree of Artaxerxes

11 This is a copy of the rescript which King Artaxerxes gave to Ezra the priest-scribe, the scribe of the text of the LORD's commandments and statutes for Israel:

6, 22: *Assyria:* used here in a broad sense for the Persian Empire.
7, 1–8: The date of Ezra's journey to Palestine is not known with certainty. The seventh year of King Artaxerxes I would be 458 B.C., and the present order of the text suggests that date. The narratives of Ezra and Nehemiah make it seem to many, however, that the arrival of Nehemiah in 445 B.C. should precede that of Ezra. If so, Ezra may be thought to have come in 398 B.C., the seventh year of King

Artaxerxes II. Others argue for the thirty-seventh year of Artaxerxes I, that is, 428 B.C.; this would suppose that the date given in the text has suffered in transmission.

6, 19–22: Ex 12, 1–20.   7, 6: Ezr 7, 28; 8, 18; Neh
6, 21: Ps 47, 9.   2, 8.18.
                               7, 10: Ps 119, 45.

12* "Artaxerxes, king of kings, to Ezra the priest, scribe of the law of the God of heaven (then, after greetings): 13 I have issued this decree, that anyone in my kingdom belonging to the people of Israel, its priests or Levites, who is minded to go up to Jerusalem with you, may do so. 14 You are the envoy from the king and his seven counselors to supervise Judah and Jerusalem in respect of the law of your God which is in your possession, 15 and to bring with you the silver and gold which the king and his counselors have freely contributed to the God of Israel, whose dwelling is in Jerusalem, 16 as well as all the silver and gold which you may receive throughout the province of Babylon, together with the freewill offerings which the people and priests freely contribute for the house of their God in Jerusalem. 17 You must take care, therefore, to use this money to buy bulls, rams, lambs, and the cereal offerings and libations proper to these, and offer them on the altar of the house of your God in Jerusalem. 18 You and your brethren may do whatever seems best to you with the remainder of the silver and gold, conformably to the will of your God. 19 The utensils consigned to you for the service of the house of your God you are to deposit before the God of Jerusalem. 20 Whatever else you may be required to supply for the needs of the house of your God, you may draw from the royal treasury. 21 I, Artaxerxes the king, issue this decree to all the treasurers of West-of-Euphrates: Whatever Ezra the priest, scribe of the law of the God of heaven, requests of you, dispense to him accurately, 22 within these limits: silver, one hundred talents; wheat, one hundred kors; wine, one hundred baths; oil, one hundred baths; salt, without limit. 23 Let everything that is ordered by the God of heaven be carried out exactly for the house of the God of heaven, that wrath may not come upon the realm of the king and his sons. 24 We also inform you that it is not permitted to impose taxes, tributes, or tolls on any priest, Levite, singer, gatekeeper, temple slave, or any other servant of that house of God.

25*† "As for you, Ezra, in accordance with the wisdom of your God which is in your possession, appoint magistrates and judges to administer justice to all the people in West-of-Euphrates, to all, that is, who know the laws of your God. Instruct those who do not know these laws. 26 Whoever does not obey the law of your God and the law of the king, let strict judgment be executed upon him, whether death, or corporal punishment, or a fine on his goods, or imprisonment."

Ezra and His Companions

27 Blessed be the LORD, the God of our fathers, who thus disposed the mind of the king to glorify the house of the LORD in Jerusalem, 28* and who let me find favor with the king, with his counselors, and with all the most influential royal officials. I therefore took courage and, with the hand of the LORD, my God, upon me, I gathered together Israelite family heads to make the return journey with me.

8 1 This is the list of the family heads who returned with me from Babylon during the reign of King Artaxerxes:

2 Of the sons of Phinehas, Gershon; of the sons of Ithamar, Daniel; of the sons of David, Hattush, 3 son of Shecaniah; of the sons of Parosh, Zechariah, and with him one hundred and fifty males were enrolled; 4 of the sons of Pahath-moab, Eliehoenai, son of Zerahiah, and with him two hundred males; 5 of the sons of Zattu, Shecaniah, son of Jahaziel, and with him three hundred males; 6 of the sons of Adin, Ebed, son of Jonathan, and with him fifty males; 7 of the sons of Elam, Jeshaiah, son of Athaliah, and with him seventy males; 8 of the sons of Shephatiah, Zebadiah, son of Michael, and with him eighty males; 9 of the sons of Joab, Obadiah, son of Jehiel, and with him two hundred and eighteen males; 10 of the sons of Bani, Shelomith, son of Josiphiah, and with him one hundred and sixty males; 11 of the sons of Bebai, Zechariah, son of Bebai, and with him twenty-eight males; 12 of the sons of Azgad, Johanan, son of Hakkatan, and with him one hundred and ten males; 13 of the sons of Adonikam, younger sons, whose names were Eliphelet, Jeiel, and Shemaiah, and with them sixty males; 14 of the sons of Bigvai, Uthai, son of Zakkur, and with him seventy males.

The Journey to Jerusalem

15† I had them assemble by the river that flows toward Ahava, where we made camp for three days. There I perceived that both laymen and priests were present, but I could not discover a single Levite. 16 Therefore I sent Eliezer, Ariel, Shemaiah, Jarib, Elnathan, Nathan, Zechariah, and Meshullam, wise leaders, 17 with a command for Iddo, the leader in the place Casiphia, instructing them what to say to Iddo and his brethren, and to the temple slaves in Casiphia, in order to procure for us ministers for the house of our God. 18* They sent to us—for the favoring hand of our God was upon

---

7, 25: *The wisdom of your God:* the Mosaic law; cf vv 6, 14.

8, 15: *Ahava:* a town at an unidentified site in Babylonia. The river that flowed toward it was probably a branch or canal of the Euphrates.

7, 12–17: Ezr 1, 2ff.   7, 28: Ezr 7, 6.
7, 25: 2 Chr 17, 9.   8, 18: Ezr 7, 6.

us—a well-instructed man, one of the sons of Mahli, son of Levi, son of Israel, namely Sherebiah, with his sons and brethren, eighteen men. 19 They also sent us Hashabiah, and with him Jeshaiah, sons of Merari, and their brethren and their sons, twenty men. 20* Of the temple slaves (those whom David and the princes appointed to serve the Levites) there were two hundred and twenty. All these men were enrolled by name.

21 Then I proclaimed a fast, there by the river of Ahava, that we might humble ourselves before our God to petition from him a safe journey for ourselves, our children, and all our possessions. 22* For I would have been ashamed to ask the king for troops and horsemen to protect us against enemies along the way, since we had said to the king, "The favoring hand of our God is upon all who seek him, but his mighty wrath is against all who forsake him." 23 So we fasted, and prayed to our God for this, and our petition was granted. 24 Next I selected twelve of the priestly leaders along with Sherebiah, Hashabiah, and ten of their brethren, 25 and I weighed out before them the silver and the gold and the utensils offered for the house of our God by the king, his counselors, his officials, and all the Israelites of that region. I consigned it to them in these amounts: 26 silver, six hundred and fifty talents; silver utensils, one hundred; gold, one hundred talents; 27 twenty golden bowls valued at a thousand darics; two vases of excellent polished bronze, as precious as gold. 28 I addressed them in these words: "You are consecrated

to the LORD, and the utensils are also consecrated; the silver and the gold are a free-will offering to the LORD, the God of your fathers. 29 Keep good watch over them till you weigh them out in Jerusalem in the presence of the chief priests and Levites and the family leaders of Israel, in the chambers of the house of the LORD." 30 The priests and the Levites then took over the silver, the gold, and the utensils that had been weighed out, to bring them to Jerusalem, to the house of our God.

31 We set out for Jerusalem from the river of Ahava on the twelfth day of the first month. The hand of our God remained upon us, and he protected us from enemies and bandits along the way. 32 Thus we arrived at Jerusalem, where we first rested for three days. 33 On the fourth day, the silver, the gold, and the utensils were weighed out in the house of our God and consigned to the priest Meremoth, son of Uriah, who was assisted by Eleazar, son of Phinehas; they were assisted by the Levites Jozabad, son of Jeshua, and Noadiah, son of Binnui. 34 Everything was in order as to number and weight, and the total weight was registered. At that same time, 35 those who had returned from the captivity, the exiles, offered as holocausts to the God of Israel twelve bulls for all Israel, ninety-six rams, seventy-seven lambs, and twelve goats as sin-offerings: all these as a holocaust to the LORD. 36† Finally, the orders of the king were presented to the king's satraps and to the governors in West-of-Euphrates, who gave their support to the people and to the house of God.

EZR

Who Belongs, and Who Does Not?

In Ezra, chapters 9–10, Ezra tells the people to reject their foreign wives and children. Nehemiah does the same in Neh 13, 23–27. This probably strikes us as harsh, but we can try to understand the Israelites' situation. Only a remnant of the Israelites was left to re-establish Israel's identity. History had taught the Israelites that intermarriage led to a watering down of their faith and of the people's loyalty to their religious practices. The only way to survive as a people was to separate themselves from outsiders.

This separation led to an even greater animosity between the Jews from Judah and their cousins in faith, the Samaritans. We see some of this prejudice in the Gospels (see Jn 4, 1–42 and "Discrimination in Jesus' Time," Lk 10, 25–37). Christians have had similar separations throughout our history. Today, the church teaches us to be faithful to our beliefs but also to be open to others who believe differently and discover together what we have in common.

▸ Ezra, chapters 9–10

8, 36: The story of Ezra's mission is seemingly continued from this point by Neh 7, 72b—8, 18, which may be read before Ezr 9, 1.

8, 20: Ezr 2, 43.   **8, 22:** Neh 2, 9.

Denunciation of Mixed Marriages

9 1* When these matters had been concluded, the leaders approached me with this report: "Neither the Israelite laymen nor the priests nor the Levites have kept themselves aloof from the peoples of the land and their abominations [Canaanites, Hittites, Perizzites, Jebusites, Ammonites, Moabites, Egyptians, and Amorites]; 2 for they have taken some of their daughters as wives for themselves and their sons, and thus they have desecrated the holy race with the peoples of the land. Furthermore, the leaders and rulers have taken a leading part in this apostasy!"

Ezra's Exhortation

3* When I had heard this thing, I tore my cloak and my mantle, plucked hair from my head and beard, and sat there stupefied. 4* Around me gathered all who were in dread of the sentence of the God of Israel on this apostasy of the exiles, while I remained motionless until the evening sacrifice. 5 Then, at the time of the evening sacrifice, I rose in my wretchedness, and with cloak and mantle torn I fell on my knees, stretching out my hands to the LORD, my God.

6* I said: "My God, I am too ashamed and confounded to raise my face to you, O my God, for our wicked deeds are heaped up above our heads and our guilt reaches up to heaven. 7† From the time of our fathers even to this day great has been our guilt, and for our wicked deeds we have been delivered over, we and our kings and our priests, to the will of the kings of foreign lands, to the sword, to captivity, to pillage, and to disgrace, as is the case today.

8* "And now, but a short time ago, mercy came to us from the LORD, our God, who left us a remnant and gave us a stake in his holy place; thus our God has brightened our eyes and given us relief in our servitude. 9* For slaves we are, but in our servitude our God has not abandoned us; rather, he has turned the good will of the kings of Persia toward us. Thus he has given us new life to raise again the house of our God and restore its ruins, and has granted us a fence in Judah and Jerusalem. 10 But now, O our God, what can we say after all this? For we have abandoned your commandments, 11* which you gave through your servants the prophets: the land which you are entering to take as your possession is a land unclean with the filth of the peoples of the land, with the abominations with which they have filled it from one end to the other in their uncleanness. 12* Do not, then, give your daughters to their sons in marriage, and do not take their daughters for your sons. Never promote their peace and prosperity; thus you will grow strong, enjoy the produce of the land, and leave it as an inheritance to your children forever.

13 "After all that has come upon us for our evil deeds and our great guilt—though you, our God, have made less of our sinfulness than it deserved and have allowed us to survive as we do— 14 shall we again violate your commandments by intermarrying with these abominable peoples? Would you not become so angered with us as to destroy us without remnant or survivor? 15 O LORD, God of Israel, you are just; yet we have been spared, the remnant we are today. Here we are before you in our sins. Because of all this, we can no longer stand in your presence."

The People's Response

10 1 While Ezra prayed and acknowledged their guilt, weeping and prostrate before the house of God, a very large assembly of Israelites gathered about him, men, women, and children; and the people wept profusely. 2 Then Shecaniah, the son of Jehiel, one of the sons of Elam, made this appeal to Ezra: "We have indeed betrayed our God by taking as wives foreign women of the peoples of the land. Yet even now there remains a hope for Israel. 3 Let us therefore enter into a covenant before our God to dismiss all our foreign wives and the children born of them, in keeping with what you, my lord, advise, and those who fear the commandments of our God. Let the law be observed! 4 Rise, then, for this is your duty! We will stand by you, so have courage and take action!"

5 Ezra rose to his feet and demanded an oath from the chiefs of the priests, from the Levites and from all Israel that they would do as had been proposed; and they swore it. 6† Then Ezra retired from his place before the house of God and entered the chamber of Johanan, son of Eliashib, where he spent the night neither eating food nor drinking water, for he was in mourning over the betrayal by the exiles. 7 A proclamation was made throughout Judah and Jerusalem that all the exiles should gather together in Jerusalem, 8 and that

---

9, 7: After this verse, the next part of the prayer attributed to Ezra is perhaps to be found in Neh 9, 6–37, which may be read as leading up to Ezr 9, 8–15.

10, 6: *Johanan, son of Eliashib:* actually, the grandson of Eliashib; the father of Johanan was Eliashib's son Joiada (Neh 12, 10f.22). Since Eliashib was high priest at the time of Nehemiah (Neh 3, 1. 20f; 13, 4.7) and Johanan, if not yet high priest, was at least old enough to have his own separate quarters (chamber) in the temple at

the time of Ezra, it is practically certain that Nehemiah's activity in Jerusalem must have preceded that of Ezra.

9, 1f: Dt 7, 1; Neh 9, 2.	9, 8: Is 4, 3.
9, 3: Ps 119, 136.	9, 9: Ps 106, 46.
9, 4: Is 66, 2.	9, 11: Lv 18, 24f; Ez 36, 17.
9, 6: Ps 38, 4.	9, 12: Dt 7, 3.

whoever failed to appear within three days would, according to the judgment of the leaders and elders, suffer the confiscation of all his possessions, and himself be excluded from the assembly of the exiles.

⁹† All the men of Judah and Benjamin gathered together in Jerusalem within the three-day period: it was in the ninth month, on the twentieth day of the month. All the people, standing in the open place before the house of God, were trembling both over the matter at hand and because it was raining. ¹⁰ Then Ezra, the priest, stood up and said to them: "Your unfaithfulness in taking foreign women as wives has added to Israel's guilt. ¹¹* But now, give praise to the LORD, the God of your fathers, and do his will: separate yourselves from the peoples of the land and from these foreign women." ¹² In answer, the whole assembly cried out with a loud voice: "Yes, it is our duty to do as you say! ¹³ But the people are numerous and it is the rainy season, so that we cannot remain out-of-doors; besides, this is not a task that can be performed in a single day or even two, for those of us who have sinned in this regard are many. ¹⁴ Let our leaders represent the whole assembly; then let all those in our cities who have taken foreign women for wives appear at appointed times, accompanied by the elders and magistrates of each city in question, till we have turned away from us our God's burning anger over this affair." ¹⁵ Only Jonathan, son of Asahel, and Jahzeiah, son of Tikvah, were against this proposal, with Meshullam and Shabbethai the Levite supporting them.

The Guilty

¹⁶† The exiles did as agreed. Ezra appointed as his assistants men who were family heads, one for each family, all of them designated by name. They held sessions to examine the matter, beginning with the first day of the tenth month. ¹⁷ By the first day of the first month they had passed judgment on all the men who had taken foreign women for wives.

¹⁸ Among the priests, the following were found to have taken foreign women for wives: Of the sons of Jeshua, son of Jozadak, and his brethren: Maaseiah, Eliezer, Jarib, and Gedaliah. ¹⁹ They pledged themselves to dismiss their wives, and as a guilt-offering for their guilt they gave a ram from the flock. ²⁰ Of the sons of Immer: Hanani and Zebadiah; ²¹ of the sons of Harim: Maaseiah, Elijah, Shemaiah, Jehiel, and Uzziah; ²² of the sons of Pashhur: Elioenai, Maaseiah, Ishmael, Nethanel, Jozabad, and Elasah.

²³* Of the Levites: Jozabad, Shemei, Kelaiah (also called Kelita), Pethahiah, Judah, and Eliezer.

²⁴ Of the singers: Eliashib and Zakkur; of the gatekeepers: Shallum, Telem, and Uri.

²⁵ Among the other Israelites: Of the sons of Parosh: Ramiah, Izziah, Malchijah, Mijamin, Eleazar, Malchijah, and Benaiah; ²⁶ of the sons of Elam: Mattaniah, Zechariah, Jehiel, Abdi, Jeremoth, and Elijah; ²⁷ of the sons of Zattu: Elioenai, Eliashib, Mattaniah, Jeremoth, Zabad, and Aziza; ²⁸ of the sons of Bebai: Jehohanan, Hananiah, Zabbai, and Athlai; ²⁹ of the sons of Bani: Meshullam, Malluch, Adaiah, Jashub, Sheal, and Jeremoth; ³⁰ of the sons of Pahath-moab: Adna, Chelal, Benaiah, Maaseiah, Mattaniah, Bezalel, Binnui, and Manasseh; ³¹ of the sons of Harim: Eliezer, Isshijah, Malchijah, Shemaiah, Shimeon, ³² Benjamin, Malluch, Shemariah; ³³ of the sons of Hashum: Mattenai, Mattattah, Zabad, Eliphelet, Jeremai, Manasseh, Shimei; ³⁴ of the sons of Begui: Maadai, Amram, Uel, ³⁵ Benaiah, Bedeiah, Cheluhi, ³⁶ Vaniah, Meremoth, Eliashib, ³⁷ Mattaniah, Mattenai, and Jaasu; ³⁸ of the sons of Binnui: Shimei, ³⁹ Shelemiah, Nathan, and Adaiah; ⁴⁰ of the sons of Zachai: Shashai, Sharai, ⁴¹ Azarel, Shelemiah, Shemariah, ⁴² Shallum, Amariah, Joseph; ⁴³ of the sons of Nebo: Jeiel, Mattithiah, Zabad, Zebina, Jaddai, Joel, Benaiah.

⁴⁴† All these had taken foreign wives; but they sent them away, both the women and their children.

---

† **10, 9:** *Ninth month:* Chislev (November–December), during the "early rains" in Palestine. Since the assembly took place *in the open . . . all the people . . . were trembling . . . because it was raining.*

10, 16f: The work of the committee lasted three months, from the first day of the tenth month, Tebet (December–January), to the first day of the first month, Nisan (March–April), of the following Jewish year.

10, 44: The account of the problem of mixed marriages at the time of Ezra is continued in Neh 9, 1–5; this may be read immediately after Ezr 10, 44, though the date given in Neh 9, 1 fits more precisely after Ezr 10, 15; cf Hg 2, 10–14.

10, 11: Neh 9, 2.   **10, 23:** Neh 8, 7; 10, 11.

Nehemiah

For background on this book, see the introduction to Ezra and Nehemiah.

I: The Deeds of Nehemiah

Nehemiah's Vocation

1 ¹† The words of Nehemiah, the son of Hacaliah.

In the month Chislev of the twentieth year, I was in the citadel of Susa ² when Hanani, one of my brothers, came with other men from Judah. I asked them about the Jews, the remnant preserved after the captivity, and about Jerusalem, ³ and they answered me: "The survivors of the captivity there in the province are in great distress and under reproach. Also, the wall of Jerusalem lies breached, and its gates have been gutted with fire." ⁴ When I heard this report, I began to weep and continued mourning for several days; I fasted and prayed before the God of heaven.

⁵* I prayed: "O LORD, God of heaven, great and awesome God, you who preserve your covenant of mercy toward those who love you and keep your commandments, ⁶* may your ear be attentive, and your eyes open, to heed the prayer which I, your servant, now offer in your presence day and night for your servants the Israelites, confessing the sins which we of Israel have committed against you, I and my father's house included. ⁷* Grievously have we offended you, not keeping the commandments, the statutes, and the ordinances which you committed to your servant Moses. ⁸* But remember, I pray, the promise which you gave through Moses, your servant, when you said: 'Should you prove faithless, I will scatter you among the nations; ⁹ but should you return to me and carefully keep my commandments, even though your outcasts have been driven to the farthest corner of the world, I will gather them from there, and bring them back to the place which I have chosen as the dwelling place for my name.' ¹⁰* They are your servants, your people, whom you freed by your great might and your strong hand. ¹¹*† O LORD, may your ear be attentive to my prayer and that of all your willing servants who revere your name. Grant success to your servant this day, and let him find favor with this man"—for I was cupbearer to the king.

Appointment by the King

2 ¹ In the month Nisan of the twentieth year of King Artaxerxes, when the wine was in my charge, I took some and offered it to the king. As I had never before been sad in his presence, ² the

---

† **1, 1:** The first mission of Nehemiah, from the twentieth year of Artaxerxes I, lasted from the spring (Neh 2, 1) of 445 B.C. until 433 B.C. (Neh 5, 14). It is recounted in Neh 1, 1—6, 15; 12, 27–43; 6, 16—7, 5; 11, 1–21, which may be read in that order.

1, 11: *Cupbearer to the king:* an important official in the royal household. Because Nehemiah could appear in the queen's presence (Neh 2, 6), it is commonly presumed that he was a eunuch; but this is not necessarily so.

* **1, 5:** Dt 7, 9.12; Dn 9, 4.   **1, 8f:** Dt 30, 1–5.
1, 6: 2 Chr 6, 40.   **1, 10:** Dt 9, 29.
1, 7: Dn 3, 29f.   **1, 11:** Ps 118, 25.

Nehemiah Prepares for Action

Do you ever watch the news and think, Why bother trying to make the world a better place? Christians are called to social action—action for justice, action to make the world a better place. But social sin can scare Christians away from social action. Social sin—such as poverty, racism, violence, materialism, and indifference—seems too big for any individual to do much about. In the overwhelming face of social sin, it is easy to say, "I give up."

But then we have Nehemiah's example. When Nehemiah heard of the results of Israel's collective sin, he could have said, "I give up." Instead, he turned to God in fasting and prayer. Fasting and prayer help us focus on what is important. Fasting and prayer help us remember that God calls us only to be faithful in taking action. Let God worry about the results.

In your prayer, reflect or journal on the following questions:
- What social issue are you concerned about?
- What can you fast from to help yourself gain a new perspective on that issue? (You can fast from many things: food, television, a particular activity, a particular place.)
- What group can you get involved with to address this concern?
- What do you need to bring to God in prayer?

▶ Nehemiah, chapter 1

king asked me, "Why do you look sad? If you are not sick, you must be sad at heart." Though I was seized with great fear, ³ I answered the king: "May the king live forever! How could I not look sad when the city where my ancestors are buried lies in ruins, and its gates have been eaten out by fire?" ⁴ The king asked me, "What is it, then, that you wish?" I prayed to the God of heaven ⁵ and then answered the king: "If it please the king, and if your servant is deserving of your favor, send me to Judah, to the city of my ancestors' graves, to rebuild it." ⁶ Then the king, and the queen seated beside him, asked me how long my journey would take and when I would return. I set a date that was acceptable to him, and the king agreed that I might go.

⁷ I asked the king further: "If it please the king, let letters be given to me for the governors of West-of-Euphrates, that they may afford me safe-conduct till I arrive in Judah; ⁸* also a letter for Asaph, the keeper of the royal park, that he may give me wood for timbering the gates of the temple-citadel and for the city wall and the house that I shall occupy." The king granted my requests, for the favoring hand of my God was upon me. ⁹* Thus I proceeded to the governors of West-of-Euphrates and presented the king's letters to them. The king also sent with me army officers and cavalry.

¹⁰† When Sanballat the Horonite and Tobiah the Ammonite slave had heard of this, they were very much displeased that someone had come to seek the welfare of the Israelites.

Circuit of the City

¹¹ When I had arrived in Jerusalem, I first rested there for three days. ¹² Then I set out by night with only a few other men (for I had not told anyone what my God had inspired me to do for Jerusalem) and with no other animals but my own mount. ¹³† I rode out at night by the Valley Gate, passed by the Dragon Spring, and came to the Dung Gate, observing how the walls of Jerusalem lay in ruins and its gates had been eaten out by fire. ¹⁴ Then I passed over to the Spring Gate and to the King's Pool. Since there was no room here for my mount

---

2, 10: *Sanballat the Horonite:* the governor of the province of Samaria (Neh 3, 33f), apparently a native of one of the Beth-horons. A letter from the Jews living at Elephantine in southern Egypt, dated 408–407 B.C., mentions "Delayah and Shelemyah, the sons of Sanballat, the governor of Samaria." Although his own name was Babylonian—Sin-uballit, i.e., "Sin (the moon god) has given life"—two sons had names referring to Yahweh. *Tobiah the Ammonite slave:* the governor of the province of Ammon in Transjordan. His honorary title, "servant" (in Hebrew, *ebed*), i.e., of the king, could also be understood as slave, and Nehemiah no doubt meant it in this derogatory sense. The Tobiads remained a powerful family even in Maccabean times (2 Mc 3, 11). Sanballat and Tobiah together with Geshem the Arab (Neh 2, 19; 6, 1f), who was probably in charge of Edom and the regions to the south and southeast of Judah, opposed

the rebuilding of Jerusalem's walls on political grounds; the city was the capital of a rival province.

2, 13ff: Nehemiah left Jerusalem by the Valley Gate near the northwestern end of the old City of David and went south down the Tyropoean Valley toward the Dragon Spring (or the En-rogel of Jos 15, 7; 18, 16; 2 Sm 17, 17; 1 Kgs 1, 9, now known as Job's Well) at the juncture of the Valley of Hinnom and the Kidron Valley; he then turned north at the Dung Gate (or the Potsherd Gate of Jer 19, 2) at the southern end of the city and proceeded up the wadi, that is, the Kidron Valley, passing the Spring Gate (at the Spring of Gihon) and the King's Pool (unidentified); finally he turned west and then south to his starting point.

2, 8: Ezr 7, 6.   2, 9: Ezr 8, 22.

to pass with me astride, [15] I continued on foot up the wadi by night, inspecting the wall all the while till I once more reached the Valley Gate, by which I went back in. [16] The magistrates knew nothing of where I had gone or what I was doing, for as yet I had disclosed nothing to the Jews, neither to the priests, nor to the nobles, nor to the magistrates, nor to the others who would be concerned about the matter.

Rebuilding Jerusalem's Walls

[17] Afterward I said to them: "You see the evil plight in which we stand: how Jerusalem lies in ruins and its gates have been gutted by fire. Come, let us rebuild the wall of Jerusalem, so that we may no longer be an object of derision!" [18]* Then I explained to them how the favoring hand of my God had rested upon me, and what the king had said to me. They replied, "Let us be up and building!" And they undertook the good work with vigor.

[19] On hearing of this, Sanballat the Horonite, Tobiah the Ammonite slave, and Geshem the Arab mocked us and ridiculed us. "What is this that you are about?" they asked. "Are you rebelling against the king?" [20]† My answer to them was this: "It is the God of heaven who will grant us success. We, his servants, shall set about the rebuilding; but for you there is to be neither share nor claim nor memorial in Jerusalem."

List of Workers

3 [1]*† Eliashib the high priest and his priestly brethren took up the task of rebuilding the Sheep Gate. They timbered it and set up its doors, its bolts, and its bars, then continued the rebuilding to the Tower of Hananel. [2] At their side the men of Jericho were rebuilding, and next to them was Zaccur, son of Imri. [3]* The Fish Gate was rebuilt by the sons of Hassenaah; they timbered it and set up its doors, its bolts, and its bars. [4] At their side Meremoth, son of Uriah, son of Hakkoz, carried out the work of repair; next to him was Meshullam, son of Berechiah, son of Meshezabel; and next to him was Zadok, son of Baana. [5] Next to him the Tekoites carried out the work of repair; however, some of their outstanding men would not submit to the labor asked by their lords. [6] The New City Gate was repaired by Joiada, son of Paseah; and Meshullam, son of Besodeiah; they timbered it and set up its doors, its bolts, and its bars. [7] At their side were Melatiah the Gibeonite,

? did you KNOW?
Rebuilding Hiroshima and Nagasaki

Nehemiah faced the difficult task of rebuilding a city completely destroyed by war. Unfortunately, this type of destruction has happened too many times in human history. We all remember how the twin towers of the destroyed World Trade Center were virtual cities that were utterly destroyed in a terrorist attack. But the most dramatic destruction of entire cities in modern times was the atomic bombing of Hiroshima and Nagasaki, Japan, on 6 August 1945 and 9 August 1945. The bombings flattened those cities and melted and destroyed objects and people within 1.5 miles of its epicenter. The Catholic Church condemns all such indiscriminate destruction—whether by atomic, biological, or chemical weapons.

Although the effects of these bombings were catastrophic, they did not wipe out the human spirit. Since that day, citizens of Hiroshima and Nagasaki have been recovering and rebuilding, first by burying the dead, then by rebuilding homes, stores, churches, and temples. Today, Hiroshima and Nagasaki are thriving cities. The destruction and rebuilding of these cities are probably best summarized in this haiku, written by Yasuhiko Shigemoto, who was a teenager when the bomb hit Hiroshima:

How freely
butterflies are flying about
in the A-bomb Dome!

("My Haiku of Hiroshima")

▶ Neh 2, 17–18

Jadon the Meronothite, and the men of Gibeon and of Mizpah, who were under the jurisdiction of the Sheep Gate (to the north of the temple). The exact sites of many of the topographical points mentioned are uncertain.

---

† **2, 20:** *Neither share nor claim nor memorial:* although Sanballat and Tobiah were Yahwist, Nehemiah would not let them participate in any of the rights of the religious community in Jerusalem.
3, 1–32: The construction work on the gates and walls of the city is described in counterclockwise direction, beginning and ending at

2, 18: Ezr 7, 6. **3, 3:** Ezr 2, 35; Zep 1, 10.
3, 1: Jer 31, 38.

the governor of West-of-Euphrates. 8† Next to them the work of repair was carried out by Uzziel, son of Harhaiah, a member of the goldsmiths' guild, and at his side was Hananiah, one of the perfumers' guild. They restored Jerusalem as far as the wall of the public square. 9 Next to them the work of repair was carried out by Rephaiah, son of Hur, leader of half the district of Jerusalem, 10 and at his side was Jedaiah, son of Harumaph, who repaired opposite his own house. Next to him Hattush, son of Hashabneiah, carried out the work of repair. 11 The adjoining sector, as far as the Oven Tower, was repaired by Malchijah, son of Harim, and Hasshub, of Pahath-moab. 12 At their side the work of repair was carried out by Shallum, son of Hallohesh, leader of half the district of Jerusalem, by himself and his daughters. 13 The Valley Gate was repaired by Hanun and the inhabitants of Zanoah; they rebuilt it and set up its doors, its bolts, and its bars. They also repaired a thousand cubits of the wall up to the Dung Gate. 14 The Dung Gate was repaired by Malchijah, son of Rechab, leader of the district of Beth-haccherem; he rebuilt it and set up its doors, its bolts, and its bars. 15 The Spring Gate was repaired by Shallum, son of Colhozeh, leader of the district of Mizpah; he rebuilt it, roofed it over, and set up its doors, its bolts, and its bars. He also repaired the wall of the Aqueduct Pool near the king's garden as far as the steps that lead down from the City of David. 16 After him, the work of repair was carried out by Nehemiah, son of Azbuk, leader of half the district of Beth-zur, to a place opposite the tombs of David, as far as the artificial pool and the barracks.

17 After him, the Levites carried out the work of repair: Rehum, son of Bani. Next to him, for his own district, was Hashabiah, leader of half the district of Keilah. 18 After him, their brethren carried out the work of repair: Binnui, son of Henadad, leader of half the district of Keilah; 19 next to him Ezer, son of Jeshua, leader of Mizpah, who repaired the adjoining sector, the Corner, opposite the ascent to the arsenal. 20 After him, Baruch, son of Zabbai, repaired the adjoining sector from the Corner to the entrance of the house of Eliashib, the high priest. 21 After him, Meremoth, son of Uriah, son of Hakkoz, repaired the adjoining sector from the entrance of Eliashib's house to the end of the house.

22 After him, the work of repair was carried out by the priests, men of the surrounding country. 23 After them, Benjamin and Hasshub carried out the repair in front of their houses; after them, Aza-riah, son of Maaseiah, son of Ananiah, made the repairs alongside his house. 24 After him, Binnui, son of Henadad, repaired the adjoining sector from the house of Azariah to the Corner [that is, to the Angle]. 25 After him, Palal, son of Uzai, carried out the work of repair opposite the Corner and the tower projecting from the Upper Palace at the quarters of the guard. After him, Pedaiah, son of Parosh, carried out the work of repair 26 to a point opposite the Water Gate on the east, and the projecting tower. 27 After him, the Tekoites repaired the adjoining sector opposite the great projecting tower, to the wall of Ophel [the temple slaves were dwelling on Ophel].

28 Above the Horse Gate the priests carried out the work of repair, each before his own house. 29* After them Zadok, son of Immer, carried out the repair before his house, and after him the repair was carried out by Shemaiah, son of Shecaniah, keeper of the East Gate. 30 After him, Hananiah, son of Shelemiah, and Hanun, the sixth son of Zalaph, repaired the adjoining sector; after them, Meshullam, son of Berechiah, repaired the place opposite his own lodging. 31 After him, Malchijah, a member of the goldsmiths' guild, carried out the work of repair as far as the quarters of the temple slaves and the merchants, before the Gate of Inspection and as far as the upper chamber of the Angle. 32 Between the upper chamber of the Angle and the Sheep Gate, the goldsmiths and the merchants carried out the work of repair.

Opposition from Judah's Foes

33 When Sanballat heard that we were rebuilding the wall, it roused his anger and he became very much incensed. He ridiculed the Jews, 34 saying in the presence of his brethren and the troops of Samaria: "What are these miserable Jews trying to do? Will they complete their restoration in a single day? Will they recover these stones, burnt as they are, from the heaps of dust?" 35 Tobiah the Ammonite was beside him, and he said: "It is a rubble heap they are building. Any fox that attacked it would breach their wall of stones!" 36 Take note, O our God, how we were mocked! Turn back their derision upon their own heads and let them be carried away to a land of captivity! 37* Hide not their crime and let not their sin be blotted out in your sight, for they insulted the builders to their face! 38 We, however, continued to build the wall, which was soon filled in and completed up to half its height. The people worked with a will.

---

† **3, 8:** *Wall of the public square:* that is, the section of wall bounding the place of assembly outside the Gate of Ephraim, or New City Gate; cf Neh 3, 6; 8, 16.

* 3, 29: Ez 40, 6.

3, 37: Jer 18, 23.

4 [1] When Sanballat, Tobiah, the Arabs, the Ammonites, and the Ashdodites heard that the restoration of the walls of Jerusalem was progressing—for the gaps were beginning to be closed up—they became extremely angry. [2] Thereupon they all plotted together to come and fight against Jerusalem and thus to throw us into confusion. [3] We prayed to our God and posted a watch against them day and night for fear of what they might do. [4] Meanwhile the Judahites were saying:

"Slackened is the bearers' strength,
    there is no end to the rubbish;
Never shall we be able
    the wall to rebuild."

[5] Our enemies thought, "Before they are aware of it or see us, we shall come into their midst, kill them, and put an end to the work." [6] When the Jews who lived near them had come to us from one place after another, and had told us ten times over that they were about to attack us, [7] I stationed guards down below, behind the wall, near the exposed points, assigning them by family groups with their swords, their spears, and their bows. [8] I made an inspection, then addressed these words to the nobles, the magistrates, and the rest of the people: "Have no fear of them! Keep in mind the LORD, who is great and to be feared, and fight for your brethren, your sons and daughters, your wives and your homes." [9] When our enemies became aware that we had been warned and that God had upset their plan, we all went back, each to his own task at the wall.

[10]* From that time on, however, only half my able men took a hand in the work, while the other half, armed with spears, bucklers, bows, and breastplates, stood guard behind the whole house of Judah [11] as they rebuilt the wall. The load carriers, too, were armed; each did his work with one hand and held a weapon with the other. [12] Every builder, while he worked, had his sword girt at his side. Also, a trumpeter stood beside me, [13] for I had said to the nobles, the magistrates, and the rest of the people: "Our work is scattered and extensive, and we are widely separated from one another along the wall; [14] wherever you hear the trumpet sound, join us there; our God will fight with us." [15] Thus we went on with the work, half of the men with spears at the ready, from daybreak till the stars came out.

[16] At the same time I told the people to spend the nights inside Jerusalem, each man with his own attendant, so that they might serve as a guard by night and a working force by day. [17] Neither I, nor my kinsmen, nor any of my attendants, nor any of the bodyguard that accompanied me took off his clothes; everyone kept his weapon at his right hand.

Antisocial Conduct

5 [1]* Then there rose a great outcry of the common people and their wives against certain of their fellow Jews. [2] Some said: "We are forced to pawn our sons and daughters in order to get grain to eat that we may live." [3] Others said: "We are

Nehemiah's Strength

LIVE IT!

Many young people have traumatic experiences, such as the divorce of their parents, domestic and community violence, the death of a parent or sibling, prejudice, and poverty. Some young people come through these experiences as victims, unable to take any control of their life. Others take the attitude If you can't beat them, join them, and become cynical, violent, or antisocial. But some rise above their hurt to live a happy and healthy life. What can account for the difference in people's reactions?

Perhaps Nehemiah provides a clue. He was confronted by cynical people (Neh 3, 33–35) and violent people (4, 1–3). But he trusted in something bigger than himself. "It is the God of heaven who will grant us success" (2, 20), he proclaimed to those with negative attitudes.

Prayer and faith in God gave Nehemiah strength to take action in difficult times. They can work for us too. Don't let life's traumas make you powerless. Don't let them make you cynical and part of the problem. Pray and have faith, and you too will have the strength to meet your problems with action.

▸ Neh 3, 33—4, 17

4, 10: Ps 149, 6.   5, 1f: Jer 34, 8–22.

Hunger Pains

LIVE IT!

"I'm hungry."

"Yeah, I'm starved. Let's go get something to eat."

How many times have we uttered those words or heard them said? It's so easy. If we're hungry, we eat. If we're thirsty, we grab something to drink. If we're not feeling well, we get something to make us feel better. We forget sometimes that our way of doing things is the exception in the world, not the rule. Right now, people in this country and in the rest of the world are starving and have no idea where their next meal is coming from.

When Nehemiah's people were hungry, he saw the problem right away. The problem was not a lack of food. It was that some people were using their wealth and influence to control who got the food (Neh 5, 7–8). Nehemiah took the radical step of demanding that the powerful and wealthy stop taking advantage of those less well off. He demanded that the wealthy restore the money and property that they had taken from others through unjust charging of interest (verses 10–11).

Experts tell us that much the same is true today. People are starving not because food is scarce but because political and economic conditions prevent them from getting the food. If only we could be like Nehemiah and demand that the powerful and wealthy reform. Well, you know what? We can! We can educate ourselves and speak out through letters and phone calls to elected officials. And while we are calling for society to change, let's volunteer at a neighborhood pantry or soup kitchen to help feed the poor people in our own backyard.

▶ Nehemiah, chapter 5

---

forced to pawn our fields, our vineyards, and our houses, that we may have grain during the famine." ⁴ Still others said: "To pay the king's tax we have borrowed money on our fields and our vineyards. ⁵* And though these are our own kinsmen and our children are as good as theirs, we have had to reduce our sons and daughters to slavery, and violence has been done to some of our daughters! Yet we can do nothing about it, for our fields and our vineyards belong to others."

Nehemiah's Action

⁶ I was extremely angry when I heard the reasons they had for complaint. ⁷† After some deliberation, I called the nobles and magistrates to account, saying to them, "You are exacting interest from your own kinsmen!" I then rebuked them severely, ⁸* saying to them: "As far as we were able, we bought back our fellow Jews who had been sold to Gentiles; you, however, are selling your own brothers, to have them bought back by us." They remained silent, for they could find no answer. ⁹ I continued: "What you are doing is not good. Should you not walk in the fear of our God, and put an end to the derision of our Gentile enemies? ¹⁰ I

myself, my kinsmen, and my attendants have lent the people money and grain without charge. Let us put an end to this usury! ¹¹ I ask that you return to them this very day their fields, their vineyards, their olive groves, and their houses, together with the interest on the money, the grain, the wine, and the oil that you have lent them." ¹² They answered: "We will return everything and exact nothing further from them. We will do just what you ask." Then I called for the priests and had them administer an oath to these men that they would do as they had promised. ¹³ I also shook out the folds of my garment, saying, "Thus may God shake from his home and his fortune every man who fails to keep this promise, and may he thus be shaken out and emptied!" And the whole assembly answered, "Amen," and praised the LORD. Then the people did as they had promised.

Nehemiah's Lack of Self-Interest

¹⁴ Moreover, from the time that King Artaxerxes appointed me governor in the land of Judah, from his twentieth to his thirty-second year—during these twelve years neither I nor my brethren lived from the governor's allowance. ¹⁵ The earlier

---

† 5, 7: *You are exacting interest from your own kinsmen!*: contrary to the Mosaic law (Dt 23, 20).

5, 5: Ez 21, 7; Lv 25, 39.   5, 8: Lv 25, 48.

governors, my predecessors, had laid a heavy burden on the people, taking from them each day forty
silver shekels for their food; then too, their men oppressed the people. But I, because I feared God, did
not act thus. 16 Moreover, though I had acquired no
land of my own, I did my part in this work on the
wall, and all my men were gathered there for the
work. 17 Though I set my table for a hundred and
fifty persons, Jews and magistrates, as well as those
who came to us from the nations round about,
18 and though the daily preparations were made at
my expense—one beef, six choice muttons, poul-
try—besides all kinds of wine in abundance every
ten days, despite this I did not claim the governor's
allowance, for the labor lay heavy upon this people.
19 Keep in mind, O my God, in my favor all that I
did for this people.

Plots against Nehemiah

6 1 When it had been reported to Sanballat, Tobiah, Geshem the Arab, and our other enemies that I had rebuilt the wall and that there was
no breach left in it (though up to that time I had
not yet set up the doors in the gates), 2 Sanballat
and Geshem sent me this message: "Come, let us
hold council together at Caphirim in the plain of
Ono." They were planning to do me harm. 3 However, I sent messengers to them with this reply: "I
am engaged in a great enterprise and am unable to
come down; why should the work stop, while I
leave it to come down to you?" 4 Four times they
sent me this same proposal, and each time I gave
the same reply. 5 Then, the fifth time, Sanballat sent
me the same message by one of his servants, who
bore an unsealed letter 6 containing this text:
"Among the nations it has been reported—Geshem
is witness to this—that you and the Jews are planning a rebellion; that for this reason you are rebuilding the wall; and that you are to be their
king"—and so on. 7 "Also, that you have set up
prophets in Jerusalem to proclaim you king of Judah. Now, since matters like these must reach the
ear of the king, come, let us hold council together."
8 I sent him this answer: "Nothing of what you report has taken place; rather, it is the invention of
your own mind." 9 They were all trying to frighten
us, thinking, "Their hands will slacken in the work,
and it will never be completed." But instead, I now
redoubled my efforts.

10 I went to the house of Shemaiah, son of Delaiah, son of Mehetabel, who was unable to go about,
and he said:

"Let us meet in the house of God,
   inside the temple building;
   let us lock the doors of the temple.
For men are coming to kill you;
   by night they are coming coming to
   kill you."

11 My answer was: "A man like me take flight? Can
a man like me enter the temple to save his life? I
will not go!" 12 For on consideration it was plain to
me that God had not sent him; rather, because Tobiah and Sanballat had bribed him, he voiced this
prophecy concerning me 13 that I might act on it
out of fear and commit this sin. Then they would
have had a shameful story with which to discredit
me. 14* Keep in mind Tobiah and Sanballat, O my
God, because of these things they did; keep in
mind as well Noadiah the prophetess and the other prophets who were trying to frighten me.

Conclusion of the Work

15† The wall was finished on the twenty-fifth day
of Elul; it had taken fifty-two days. 16* When all our
enemies had heard of this, and all the nations round
about had taken note of it, our enemies lost much
face in the eyes of the nations, for they knew that it
was with our God's help that this work had been
completed. 17† At that same time, however, many letters were going to Tobiah from the nobles of Judah,
and Tobiah's letters were reaching them, 18 for many
in Judah were in league with him, since he was the
son-in-law of Shecaniah, son of Arah, and his son Jehohanan had married the daughter of Meshullam,
son of Berechiah. 19 Thus they would praise his good
deeds in my presence and relate to him whatever I
said; and Tobiah sent letters trying to frighten me.

7 1 When the wall had been rebuilt, I had the
doors set up, and the gatekeepers [and the
singers and the Levites] were put in charge of them.
2 Over Jerusalem I placed Hanani, my brother, and
Hananiah, the commander of the citadel, who was a
more trustworthy and God-fearing man than most.
3 I said to them: "The gates of Jerusalem are not to be
opened until the sun is hot, and while the sun is still
shining they shall shut and bar the doors. Appoint as
watchmen the inhabitants of Jerusalem, some at their
watch posts, and others before their own houses."

Census of the Province

4 Now the city was quite wide and spacious, but
its population was small, and none of the houses

---

† **6, 15:** *Elul:* the sixth month (August–September). *Fifty-two days:*
according to Josephus (*Antiquities* XI, v 8), the rebuilding of the walls
of Jerusalem by Nehemiah took two years and four months, which
seems more probable.

6, 17ff: These verses should be read immediately after v 14.

6, 14: Jer 23, 9–40;   **6, 16:** Pss 118, 22f; 127, 1.
        Zec 13, 3.

had been rebuilt. [5] When my God had put it into my mind to gather together the nobles, the magistrates, and the common people, and to examine their family records, I came upon the family list of those who had returned in the earliest period. There I found the following written:

[6]*† These are the inhabitants of the province who returned from the captivity of the exiles whom Nebuchadnezzar, king of Babylon, had carried away, and who came back to Jerusalem and Judah, each man to his own city [7] (those who returned with Zerubbabel, Jeshua, Nehemiah, Azariah, Raamiah, Nahamani, Mordecai, Bilshan, Mispereth, Bigvai, Nehum, and Baanah).

The census of the men of Israel: [8] sons of Parosh, two thousand one hundred and seventy-two; [9] sons of Shephatiah, three hundred and seventy-two; [10] sons of Arah, six hundred and fifty-two; [11] sons of Pahath-moab who were sons of Jeshua and Joab, two thousand eight hundred and eighteen; [12] sons of Elam, one thousand two hundred and fifty-four; [13] sons of Zattu, eight hundred and forty-five; [14] sons of Zaccai, seven hundred and sixty; [15] sons of Binnui, six hundred and forty-eight; [16] sons of Bebai, six hundred and twenty-eight; [17] sons of Azgad, two thousand three hundred and twenty-two; [18] sons of Adonikam, six hundred and sixty-seven; [19] sons of Bigvai, two thousand and sixty-seven; [20] sons of Adin, six hundred and fifty-five; [21] sons of Ater who were sons of Hezekiah, ninety-eight; [22] sons of Hashum, three hundred and twenty-eight; [23] sons of Bezai, three hundred and twenty-four; [24] sons of Hariph, one hundred and twelve; [25] sons of Gibeon, ninety-five; [26] men of Bethlehem and Netophah, one hundred and eighty-eight; [27] men of Anathoth, one hundred and twenty-eight; [28] men of Beth-azmaveth, forty-two; [29] men of Kiriath-jearim, Chephirah, and Beeroth, seven hundred and forty-three; [30] men of Ramah and Geba, six hundred and twenty-one; [31] men of Michmas, one hundred and twenty-two; [32] men of Bethel and Ai, one hundred and twenty-three; [33] men of Nebo, fifty-two; [34] sons of another Elam, one thousand two hundred and fifty-four; [35] sons of Harim, three hundred and twenty; [36] sons of Jericho, three hundred and forty-five; [37] sons of Lod, Hadid, and Ono, seven hundred and twenty-one; [38] sons of Senaah, three thousand nine hundred and thirty.

[39] The priests: sons of Jedaiah who were of the house of Jeshua, nine hundred and seventy-three; [40] sons of Immer, one thousand and fifty-two; [41] sons of Pashhur, one thousand two hundred and forty-seven; [42] sons of Harim, one thousand and seventeen.

[43] The Levites: sons of Jeshua, Kadmiel, Binnui, Hodeviah, seventy-four.

[44] The singers: sons of Asaph, one hundred and forty-eight.

[45] The gatekeepers: sons of Shallum, sons of Ater, sons of Talmon, sons of Akkub, sons of Hatita, sons of Shobai, one hundred and thirty-eight.

[46] The temple slaves: sons of Ziha, sons of Hasupha, sons of Tabbaoth, [47] sons of Keros, sons of Sia, sons of Padon, [48] sons of Lebana, sons of Hagaba, sons of Shalmai, [49] sons of Hanan, sons of Giddel, sons of Gahar, [50] sons of Reaiah, sons of Rezin, sons of Nekoda, [51] sons of Gazzam, sons of Uzza, sons of Paseah, [52] sons of Besai, sons of the Meunites, sons of the Nephusites, [53] sons of Bakbuk, sons of Hakupha, sons of Harhur, [54] sons of Bazlith, sons of Mehida, sons of Harsha, [55] sons of Barkos, sons of Sisera, sons of Temah, [56] sons of Neziah, sons of Hatipha.

[57] Descendants of the slaves of Solomon: sons of Sotai, sons of Sophereth, sons of Perida, [58] sons of Jaala, sons of Darkon, sons of Giddel, [59] sons of Shephatiah, sons of Hattil, sons of Pochereth-hazzebaim, sons of Amon. [60] The total of the temple slaves and the descendants of the slaves of Solomon was three hundred and ninety-two.

[61] The following who returned from Telmelah, Tel-harsha, Cherub, Addon, and Immer were unable to prove that their ancestral houses and their descent were Israelite: [62] sons of Delaiah, sons of Tobiah, sons of Nekoda, six hundred and forty-two. [63] Also, of the priests: sons of Hobaiah, sons of Hakkoz, sons of Barzillai (he had married one of the daughters of Barzillai the Gileadite and became known by his name). [64] These men searched their family records, but their names could not be found written there; hence they were degraded from the priesthood, [65]† and His Excellency ordered them not to partake of the most holy foods until there should be a priest bearing the Urim and Thummim.

[66] The entire assembly taken together came to forty-two thousand three hundred and sixty, [67] not counting their male and female slaves, who were seven thousand three hundred and thirty-seven. They also had two hundred male and female singers. Their horses were seven hundred and thirty-six, their mules two hundred and forty-five, [68] their camels four hundred and thirty-five, their asses six thousand seven hundred and twenty.

[69] Certain of the family heads contributed to the service. His Excellency put into the treasury one

---

7, 6–72a: See note on Ezr 2, 1–67.
7, 65.69: *His Excellency:* see note on Ezr 2, 63.

7, 6–72: Ezr 2, 1–70.

NEH

thousand drachmas of gold, fifty basins, thirty gar-ments for priests, and five hundred minas of silver. 70 Some of the family heads contributed to the treasury for the temple service: twenty thousand drachmas of gold and two thousand two hundred minas of silver. 71 The contributions of the rest of the people amounted to twenty thousand drachmas of gold, two thousand minas of silver, and sixty-seven garments for priests.

72† The priests, the Levites, the gatekeepers, the singers, the temple slaves, and all Israel took up res-idence in their cities.

II: Promulgation of the Law

Ezra Reads the Law

8 Now when the seventh month came, 1* the whole people gathered as one man in the open space before the Water Gate, and they called upon Ezra the scribe to bring forth the book of the law of Moses which the LORD prescribed for Israel. 2 On the first day of the seventh month, therefore, Ezra the priest brought the law before the assembly, which consisted of men, women, and those chil-dren old enough to understand. 3 Standing at one end of the open place that was before the Water Gate, he read out of the book from daybreak till midday, in the presence of the men, the women, and those children old enough to understand; and all the people listened attentively to the book of the law. 4 Ezra the scribe stood on a wooden platform that had been made for the occasion; at his right side stood Mattithiah, Shema, Anaiah, Uriah, Hilki-ah, and Maaseiah, and on his left Pedaiah, Mishael, Malchijah, Hashum, Hashbaddanah, Zechariah, Meshullam. 5 Ezra opened the scroll so that all the people might see it (for he was standing higher up than any of the people); and, as he opened it, all the people rose. 6 Ezra blessed the LORD, the great God, and all the people, their hands raised high, answered, "Amen, amen!" Then they bowed down and prostrated themselves before the LORD, their faces to the ground. 7* [The Levites Jeshua, Bani, Sherebiah, Jamin, Akkub, Shabbethai, Hodiah, Maaseiah, Kelita, Azariah, Jozabad, Hanan, and Pelaiah explained the law to the people, who re-mained in their places.] 8* Ezra read plainly from the book of the law of God, interpreting it so that all could understand what was read. 9 Then

[Nehemiah, that is, His Excellency, and] Ezra the priest-scribe [and the Levites who were instructing the people] said to all the people: "Today is holy to the LORD your God. Do not be sad, and do not weep"—for all the people were weeping as they heard the words of the law. 10* He said further: "Go, eat rich foods and drink sweet drinks, and allot por-tions to those who had nothing prepared; for today is holy to our LORD. Do not be saddened this day, for rejoicing in the LORD must be your strength!" 11 [And the Levites quieted all the people, saying, "Hush, for today is holy, and you must not be sad-dened."] 12 Then all the people went to eat and drink, to distribute portions, and to celebrate with great joy, for they understood the words that had been expounded to them.

The Feast of Booths

13 On the second day, the family heads of the whole people and also the priests and the Levites gathered around Ezra the scribe and examined the words of the law more closely. 14* They found it written in the law prescribed by the LORD through Moses that the Israelites must dwell in booths dur-ing the feast of the seventh month; 15* and that they should have this proclamation made through-out their cities and in Jerusalem: "Go out into the hill country and bring in branches of olive trees, oleasters, myrtle, palm, and other leafy trees, to make booths, as the law prescribes." 16 The people went out and brought in branches with which they made booths for themselves, on the roofs of their houses, in their courtyards, in the courts of the house of God, and in the open spaces of the Water Gate and the Gate of Ephraim. 17 Thus the entire as-sembly of the returned exiles made booths and dwelt in them. Now the Israelites had done nothing of this sort from the days of Jeshua, son of Nun, un-til this occasion; therefore there was very great joy. 18 Ezra read from the book of the law of God day af-ter day, from the first day to the last. They kept the feast for seven days, and the solemn assembly on the eighth day, as was required.

Confession of the People

9 1*† On the twenty-fourth day of this month, the Israelites gathered together fasting and in sackcloth, their heads covered with dust. 2* Those of Israelite descent separated themselves from all

---

7, 72b—8, 18: To be read after Ezr 8, 36. The gloss mentioning Nehemiah in v 9 was inserted in this Ezra section after the disloca-tion of several parts of Ezra-Nehemiah had occurred. There is no clear evidence of a simultaneous presence of Nehemiah and Ezra in Jerusalem; Neh 12, 26 and 12, 36 are also scribal glosses.

9, 1–5: This is a continuation of the account concerning the prob-lem of mixed marriages at the time of Ezra; it should be read imme-diately after Ezr 10, 44.

8, 1: Ezr 3, 1.	33–36.
8, 7: Neh 10, 11.	8, 15: Ps 118, 27.
8, 8: Ezr 7, 6.	9, 1: Dn 9, 3.
8, 10: Est 9, 19.	9, 2: Ezr 9, 1f; 10, 11.
8, 14: Ex 23, 14; Lv 23,	

who were of foreign extraction, then stood forward and confessed their sins and the guilty deeds of their fathers. ³ When they had taken their places, they read from the book of the law of the LORD their God, for a fourth part of the day, and during another fourth part they made their confession and prostrated themselves before the LORD their God. ⁴ Standing on the platform of the Levites were Jeshua, Binnui, Kadmiel, Shebaniah, Bunni, Sherebiah, Bani, and Chenani, who cried out to the LORD their God with a loud voice. ⁵* The Levites Jeshua, Kadmiel, Bani, Hashabneiah, Sherebiah, Hodiah, Shebaniah, and Pethahiah said,

> "Arise, bless the LORD, your God,
> from eternity to eternity!"

The Israelites answered with the blessing,

> "Blessed is your glorious name,
> and exalted above all blessing and praise."

⁶† Then Ezra said: "It is you, O LORD, you are the only one; you made the heavens, the highest heavens and all their host, the earth and all that is upon it, the seas and all that is in them. To all of them you give life, and the heavenly hosts bow down before you.

⁷* "You, O LORD, are the God who chose Abram, who brought him out from Ur of the Chaldees, and named him Abraham. ⁸* When you had found his heart faithful in your sight, you made the covenant with him to give to him and his posterity the land of the Canaanites, Hittites, Amorites, Perizzites, Jebusites, and Girgashites. These promises of yours you fulfilled, for you are just.

⁹* "You saw the affliction of our fathers in Egypt,
> you heard their cry by the Red Sea;

from eternity to eternity!

9, 5

¹⁰* You worked signs and wonders
> against Pharoah,
> against all his servants and the people of
>   his land,
> Because you knew of their insolence
>   toward them;
> thus you made for yourself a name even to
>   this day.
¹¹* The sea you divided before them,
> on dry ground they passed through the
>   midst of the sea;
> Their pursuers you hurled into the depths,
> like a stone into the mighty waters.
¹²* With a column of cloud you led them by day,
> and by night with a column of fire,
> To light the way of their journey,
> the way in which they must travel.
¹³* On Mount Sinai you came down,
> you spoke with them from heaven;
> You gave them just ordinances, firm laws,
> good statutes, and commandments;
¹⁴* Your holy sabbath you made known to them,
> commandments, statutes, and law you
>   prescribed for them,
> by the hand of Moses your servant.
¹⁵* Food from heaven you gave them in
>   their hunger,
> water from a rock you sent them in
>   their thirst.
> You bade them enter and occupy the land
> which you had sworn with upraised hand
>   to give them.

¹⁶ "But they, our fathers, proved to be insolent; they held their necks stiff and would not obey your commandments. ¹⁷* They refused to obey and no longer remembered the miracles you had worked for them. They stiffened their necks and turned their heads to return to their slavery in Egypt. But you are a God of pardons, gracious and compassionate, slow to anger and rich in mercy; you did not forsake them. ¹⁸* Though they made for themselves a molten calf, and proclaimed, 'Here is your God who brought you up out of Egypt,' and were guilty of great effronteries, ¹⁹ yet in your great mercy you did not forsake them in the desert. The column of cloud did not cease to lead them by day on their journey, nor did the column of fire by night cease to light for them the way by which they were to travel.

²⁰* "Your good spirit you bestowed on them, to

---

† **9, 6–37:** The prayer of Ezra which began in Ezr 9, 6f is here continued; see note on Ezr 9, 7.

9, 5: Dn 2, 20; 3, 52.   9, 7: Gn 12, 1; 17, 5.

9, 8: Gn 15, 18f.   9, 14: Ex 20, 8.
9, 9: Ex 2, 23f.   9, 15: Ex 16, 4; 17, 1f.
9, 10: Ex 7–11; 14.   9, 17: Nm 14, 1–4; Ex 34, 6;
9, 11: Ex 15, 5.10.   Dn 9, 9.
9, 12: Ex 13, 21f.   9, 18: Ex 32, 4.
9, 13: Ex 19–20.   9, 20: Dt 2, 7.

give them understanding; your manna you did not withhold from their mouths, and you gave them water in their thirst. 21* Forty years in the desert you sustained them: they did not want; their garments did not become worn, and their feet did not become swollen. 22* You gave them kingdoms and peoples, which you divided up among them as border lands. They possessed the land of Sihon, king of Heshbon, and the land of Og, king of Bashan.

23* "You made their children as numerous as the stars of the heavens, and you brought them into the land which you had commanded their fathers to enter and possess. 24 The sons went in to take possession of the land, and you humbled before them the Canaanite inhabitants of the land and delivered them over into their power, their kings as well as the peoples of the land, to do with them as they would. 25* They captured fortified cities and fertile land; they took possession of houses filled with all good things, cisterns already dug, vineyards, olive groves, and fruit trees in abundance. They could eat and have their fill, fatten and feast themselves on your immense good gifts.

26* "But they were contemptuous and rebellious: they cast your law behind their backs, they slew your prophets who bore witness against them in order to bring them back to you, and they were guilty of great effronteries. 27* Therefore you delivered them into the power of their enemies, who oppressed them. But in the time of their oppression they would cry out to you, and you would hear them from heaven, and according to your great mercy give them saviors to deliver them from the power of their enemies.

28 "As soon as they had relief, they would go back to doing evil in your sight. Then again you abandoned them to the power of their enemies, who crushed them. Then they cried out to you, and you heard them from heaven and delivered them according to your mercy, many times over. 29* You bore witness against them, in order to bring them back to your law. But they were insolent and would not obey your commandments; they sinned against your ordinances, from which men draw life when they practice them. They turned stubborn backs, stiffened their necks, and would not obey. 30 You were patient with them for many years, bearing witness against them through your spirit, by means of your prophets; still they would not listen. Thus you delivered them over

into the power of the peoples of the lands. 31 Yet in your great mercy you did not completely destroy them and you did not forsake them, for you are a kind and merciful God.

32* "Now, therefore, O our God, great, mighty, and awesome God, you who in your mercy preserve the covenant, take into account all the disasters that have befallen us, our kings, our princes, our priests, our prophets, our fathers, and your entire people, from the time of the kings of Assyria until this day! 33* In all that has come upon us you have been just, for you kept faith while we have done evil. 34 Yes, our kings, our princes, our priests, and our fathers have not kept your law; they paid no attention to your commandments and the obligations of which you reminded them. 35 While they were yet in their kingdom, in the midst of the many good things that you had given them and in the wide and fertile land that you had spread out before them, they did not serve you nor did they turn away from their evil deeds. 36 But, see, we today are slaves; and as for the land which you gave our fathers that they might eat its fruits and good things—see, we have become slaves upon it! 37 Its rich produce goes to the kings whom you set over us because of our sins, who rule over our bodies and our cattle as they please. We are in great distress!"

Agreement of the People

10 1*† In view of all this, we are entering into a firm pact, which we are putting into writing. On the sealed document appear the names of our princes, our Levites, and our priests.

2 On the sealed document: His Excellency Nehemiah, son of Hacaliah, and Zedekiah.

3 Seraiah, Azariah, Jeremiah, 4 Pashhur, Amariah, Malchijah, 5 Hattush, Shebaniah, Malluch, 6 Harim, Meremoth, Obadiah, 7 Daniel, Ginnethon, Baruch, 8 Meshullam, Abijah, Mijamin, 9 Maaziah, Bilgai, Shemaiah: these are the priests.

10 The Levites: Jeshua, son of Azaniah; Binnui, of the sons of Henadad; Kadmiel; 11* and their brethren Shebaniah, Hodiah, Kelita, Pelaiah, Hanan, 12 Mica, Rehob, Hashabiah, 13 Zaccur, Sherebiah, Shebaniah, 14 Hodiah, Bani, Beninu.

15 The leaders of the people: Parosh, Pahath-moab, Elam, Zattu, Bani, 16 Bunni, Azgad, Bebai, 17 Adonijah, Bigvai, Adin, 18 Ater, Hezekiah, Azzur, 19 Hodiah, Hashum, Bezai, 20 Hariph, Anathoth, Nebai, 21 Magpiash, Meshullam, Hazir, 22 Meshezabel, Zadok, Jaddua, 23 Pelatiah, Hanan, Anaiah,

---

10, 1–40: This section belongs to the Nehemiah narrative rather than to that of Ezra. It is best read after Neh 13, 31. *In view of all this:* considering the situation described in Neh 13, 4–31.

9, 21: Dt 8, 4.
9, 22: Nm 21, 21–35; Dt 1, 4; 2, 26—3, 11.
9, 23: Dt 1, 10.
9, 25: Dt 3, 5; 6, 10f; 11, 11; 32, 15.
9, 26: Wis 2, 10–20.
9, 27: Dn 9, 19.
9, 29: Lv 18, 5; Dt 30, 16; 32, 47.
9, 32: Lam 5.
9, 33: Dn 3, 27; 9, 14.
10, 1: Neh 12, 12–26.
10, 11: Ezr 10, 23.

24 Hoshea, Hananiah, Hasshub, 25 Hallohesh, Pilha, Shobek, 26 Rehum, Hashabnah, Maaseiah, 27 Ahiah, Hanan, Anan, 28 Malluch, Harim, Baanah.

Provisions of the Pact

29 The rest of the people, priests, Levites, gatekeepers, singers, temple slaves, and all others who have separated themselves from the peoples of the lands in favor of the law of God, with their wives, their sons, their daughters, all who are of the age of discretion, 30* join with their brethren who are their princes, and with the sanction of a curse take this oath to follow the law of God which was given through Moses, the servant of God, and to observe carefully all the commandments of the LORD, our Lord, his ordinances and his statutes.

31* Agreed, that we will not marry our daughters to the peoples of the land, and that we will not take their daughters for our sons.

32* When the peoples of the land bring in merchandise or any kind of grain for sale on the sabbath day, we will not buy from them on the sabbath or on any other holy day. We will forgo the seventh year, as well as every kind of debt.

33* We impose these commandments on ourselves: to give a third of a shekel each year for the service of the house of our God, 34 for the showbread, for the daily cereal offering, for the daily holocaust, for the sabbaths, new moons, and festivals, for the holy offerings, for sin offerings to make atonement for Israel, and for every service of the house of our God. 35* We, priests, Levites, and people, have determined by lot concerning the procurement of wood: it is to be brought to the house of our God by each of our family houses at stated times each year, to be burnt on the altar of the LORD, our God, as the law prescribes. 36* We have agreed to bring each year to the house of the LORD the first fruits of our fields and of our fruit trees, of whatever kind; 37 also, as is prescribed in the law, to bring to the house of our God, to the priests who serve in the house of our God, the first-born of our children and our animals, including the first-born of our flocks and herds. 38* The first batch of our dough, and our offerings of the fruit of every tree, of wine and of oil, we will bring to the priests, to the chambers of the house of our God. The tithe of our fields we will bring to the Levites; they, the Levites, shall take the tithe in all the cities of our service. 39 An Aaronite priest shall be with the Levites when they take the tithe, and the Levites shall bring the tithe of the tithes to the house of our God, to the chambers of the treasury. 40 For to these chambers the Israelites and Levites bring the offerings of grain, wine, and oil; there also are housed the utensils of the sanctuary, and the ministering priests, the gatekeepers, and the singers. We will not neglect the house of our God.

Repeopling of Jerusalem

11 1* † The leaders of the people took up residence in Jerusalem, and the rest of the people cast lots to bring one man in ten to reside in Jerusalem, the holy city, while the other nine would remain in the other cities. 2 The people applauded all those men who willingly agreed to take up residence in Jerusalem.

The Residents of Jerusalem

3* These are the heads of the province who took up residence in Jerusalem. (In the cities of Judah dwelt lay Israelites, priests, Levites, temple slaves, and the descendants of the slaves of Solomon, each man on the property he owned in his own city.)

4 In Jerusalem dwelt both Judahites and Benjaminites. Of the Judahites: Athaiah, son of Uzziah, son of Zechariah, son of Amariah, son of Shephatiah, son of Mehallalel, of the sons of Perez; 5 Maaseiah, son of Baruch, son of Colhozeh, son of Hazaiah, son of Adaiah, son of Joiarib, son of Zechariah, a son of the Shelanites. 6 The total of the sons of Perez who dwelt in Jerusalem was four hundred and sixty-eight valiant men.

7 These were the Benjaminites: Sallu, son of Meshullam, son of Joed, son of Pedaiah, son of Kolaiah, son of Maaseiah, son of Ithiel, son of Jeshaiah, 8 and his brethren, warriors, nine hundred and twenty-eight in number. 9 Joel, son of Zichri, was their commander, and Judah, son of Hassenuah, was second in charge of the city.

10 Among the priests were: Jedaiah; Joiarib; Jachin; 11 Seraiah, son of Hilkiah, son of Meshullam, son of Zadok, son of Meraioth, son of Ahitub, the ruler of the house of God, 12 and their brethren who carried out the temple service, eight hundred and twenty-two; Adaiah, son of Jeroham, son of Pelaliah, son of Amzi, son of Zechariah, son of Pashhur, son of Malchijah, 13 and his brethren, family heads, two hundred and forty-two; and

11, 1–19: This list of the family heads who lived in Jerusalem at the time of Nehemiah is best read after Neh 7, 72a. It is basically the same as that given in 1 Chr 9, 2–17, but there are many differences between the two lists.

10, 30: Neh 13, 23–27.
10, 31: Neh 13, 15–22.
10, 32: Neh 5, 1–13; Ex 20, 8; Lv 25, 2–7.
10, 33: 2 Chr 24, 6.9f; Lv 24, 5–9.
10, 35: Neh 13, 31.
10, 36f: Ex 13, 1.11ff; Dt 26, 1.
10, 38: Neh 13, 10–14; Nm 18, 21.24ff.
11, 1: Neh 7, 4.
11, 3–19: 1 Chr 9, 2–34.

Amasai, son of Azarel, son of Ahzai, son of Meshillemoth, son of Immer, 14 and his brethren, warriors, one hundred and twenty-eight. Their commander was Zabdiel, son of Haggadol.

15 Among the Levites were Shemaiah, son of Hasshub, son of Azrikam, son of Hashabiah, son of Bunni; 16 Shabbethai and Jozabad, levitical chiefs who were placed over the external affairs of the house of God; 17 Mattaniah, son of Micah, son of Zabdi, son of Asaph, director of the psalms, who led the thanksgiving at prayer; Bakbukiah, second in rank among his brethren; and Abda, son of Shammua, son of Galal, son of Jeduthun. 18 The total of the Levites in the holy city was two hundred and eighty-four.

19 The gatekeepers were Akkub, Talmon, and their brethren, who kept watch over the gates; one hundred and seventy-two in number.

20 The rest of Israel, including priests and Levites, were in all the other cities of Judah, each man in his inheritance.

21 The temple slaves lived on Ophel. Ziha and Gishpa were in charge of the temple slaves.

22* The prefect of the Levites in Jerusalem was Uzzi, son of Bani, son of Hashabiah, son of Mattaniah, son of Mica; he was one of the sons of Asaph, the singers appointed to the service of the house of God— 23 for they had been appointed by royal decree, and there was a fixed schedule for the singers assigning them their daily duties.

24 Pethahiah, son of Meshezabel, a descendant of Zerah, son of Judah, was royal deputy in all affairs that concerned the people.

The Other Cities

25 As concerns their villages in the country: Judahites lived in Kiriath-arba and its dependencies, in Dibon and its dependencies, in Jekabzeel and its villages, 26 in Jeshua, Moladah, Beth-pelet, 27 in Hazar-shual, in Beer-sheba and its dependencies, 28 in Ziklag, in Meconah and its dependencies, 29 in En-rimmon, Zorah, Jarmuth, 30 Zanoah, Adullam, and their villages, Lachish and its countryside, Azekah and its dependencies. They were settled from Beer-sheba to Ge-hinnom.

31 Benjaminites were in Geba, Michmash, Aija, Bethel and its dependencies, 32 Anathoth, Nob, Ananiah, 33 Hazor, Ramah, Gittaim, 34 Hadid,

Zeboim, Neballat, 35 Lod, Ono, and the Valley of the Artisans.

36 Some sections of the Levites from Judah settled in Benjamin.

Priests and Levites under Zerubbabel

12 1* The following are the priests and Levites who returned with Zerubbabel, son of Shealtiel, and Jeshua: Seraiah, Jeremiah, Ezra, 2 Amariah, Malluch, Hattush, 3 Shecaniah, Rehum, Meremoth, 4 Iddo, Ginnethon, Abijah, 5 Mijamin, Maadiah, Bilgah, 6 Shemaiah, and Joiarib, Jedaiah, 7 Sallu, Amok, Hilkiah, Jedaiah. These were the priestly heads and their brethren in the days of Jeshua.

8 The Levites were Jeshua, Binnui, Kadmiel, Sherebiah, Judah, Mattaniah; the last-mentioned, together with his brethren, was in charge of the hymns, 9 while Bakbukiah and Unno and their brethren ministered opposite them by turns.

High Priests

10† Jeshua became the father of Joiakim, Joiakim became the father of Eliashib, and Eliashib became the father of Joiada. 11 Joiada became the father of Johanan, and Johanan became the father of Jaddua.

Priests and Levites under Joiakim

12* In the days of Joiakim these were the priestly family heads: for Seraiah, Meraiah; for Jeremiah, Hananiah; 13 for Ezra, Meshullam; for Amariah, Jehohanan; 14 for Malluch, Jonathan; for Shebaniah, Joseph; 15 for Harim, Adna; for Meremoth, Helkai; 16 for Iddo, Zechariah; for Ginnethon, Meshullam; 17 for Abijah, Zichri; for Miamin, . . . ; for Maadiah, Piltai; 18 for Bilgah, Shammua; for Shemaiah, Jehonathan; 19 and for Joiarib, Mattenai; for Jedaiah, Uzzi; 20 for Sallu, Kallai; for Amok, Eber; 21 for Hilkiah, Hashabiah; for Jedaiah, Nethanel.

22 In the time of Eliashib, Joiada, Johanan, and Jaddua, the family heads of the priests were written down in the Book of Chronicles, up until the reign of Darius the Persian. 23 The sons of Levi: the family heads were written down in the Book of Chronicles, up until the time of Johanan, the son of Eliashib.

24* The heads of the Levites were Hashabiah, Sherebiah, Jeshua, Binnui, Kadmiel. Their brethren

---

† **12, 10f:** *Jeshua:* the high priest when Zerubbabel was governor, i.e., the last decades of the sixth century B.C. (Hg 1, 1.12.14; 2, 2.4). He was the grandfather of Eliashib, the high priest at least in the early period of Nehemiah's governorship, i.e., 445–433 B.C. (Ezr 10, 6; Neh 3, 1.20f; 13, 4.7). Eliashib, in turn, was the grandfather of Johanan, a grown man, if not yet a high priest, at the time of Ezra, i.e., c. 400 B.C. (Ezr 10, 6, and note). According to Josephus (*Antiquities* XI, v), whose testimony here is doubtful, Jaddua, son of Johanan, died as an old man about the same time that Alexander the Great

died, i.e., 323 B.C. If this list of the postexilic high priests, at least as far as Johanan, comes, as seems probable (cf v 23), from the Chronicler himself and not from a later scribe, it is of prime importance for dating the Chronicler's work in the first decades of the fourth century B.C.

11, 22: 2 Chr 20, 14.   **12, 12–22:** Neh 10, 3–9; 12, 1–6.
12, 1–6: Neh 12, 12–22.   **12, 24:** Ezr 2, 40.

who stood opposite them to sing praises and thanksgiving in fulfillment of the command of David, the man of God, one section opposite the other, 25* were Mattaniah, Bakbukiah, Obadiah.

Meshullam, Talmon, and Akkub were gatekeepers. They kept watch over the storerooms at the gates.

26 All these lived in the time of Joiakim, son of Jeshua, son of Jozadak [and in the time of Nehemiah the governor and of Ezra the priest-scribe].

Dedication of the City Wall

27† At the dedication of the wall of Jerusalem, the Levites were sought out wherever they lived and were brought to Jerusalem to celebrate a joyful dedication with thanksgiving hymns and the music of cymbals, harps, and lyres. 28 The levitical singers gathered together from the region about Jerusalem, from the villages of the Netophathites, 29 from Beth-gilgal, and from the plains of Geba and Azmaveth (for the singers had built themselves settlements about Jerusalem). 30 The priests and Levites first purified themselves, then they purified the people, the gates, and the wall.

31 I had the princes of Judah mount the wall, and I arranged two great choirs. The first of these proceeded to the right, along the top of the wall, in the direction of the Dung Gate, 32 followed by Hoshaiah and half the princes of Judah, 33 along with Azariah, Ezra, Meshullam, 34 Judah, Benjamin, Shemaiah, and Jeremiah, 35 priests with the trumpets, and also Zechariah, son of Jonathan, son of Shemaiah, son of Mattaniah, son of Micaiah, son of Zaccur, son of Asaph, 36 and his brethren Shemaiah, Azarel, Milalai, Gilalai, Maai, Nethanel, Judah, and Hanani, with the musical instruments of David, the man of God. [Ezra the scribe was at their head.] 37 At the Spring Gate they went straight up by the steps of the City of David and continued along the top of the wall above the house of David until they came to the Water Gate on the east.

38 The second choir proceeded to the left, followed by myself and the other half of the princes of the people, along the top of the wall past the Oven Tower as far as the Broad Wall, 39 then past the Ephraim Gate [the New City Gate], the Fish Gate, the Tower of Hananel, and the Hundred Tower, as far as the Sheep Gate [and they came to a halt at the Prison Gate].

40 The two choirs took up a position in the house of God; I, too, who had with me half the magistrates, 41 the priests Eliakim, Maaseiah, Minjamin, Micaiah, Elioenai, Zechariah, Hananiah, with the trumpets, 42 and Maaseiah, Shemaiah, Eleazar, Uzzi, Jehohanan, Malchijah, Elam, and Ezer. The singers were heard under the leadership of Jezrahiah. 43 Great sacrifices were offered on that day, and there was rejoicing over the great feast of the LORD in which they shared. The women and the children joined in, and the rejoicing at Jerusalem could be heard from afar off.

Offerings for Priests and Levites

44*† At that time men were appointed over the chambers set aside for stores, offerings, first fruits, and tithes; in them they were to collect from the fields of the various cities the portions legally assigned to the priests and Levites. For Judah rejoiced in its appointed priests and Levites 45 who carried out the ministry of their God and the ministry of purification (as did the singers and the gatekeepers) in accordance with the prescriptions of David and of Solomon, his son. 46* For the heads of the families of the singers and the hymns of praise and thanksgiving to God came down from the days of David and Asaph in times of old. 47* Thus all Israel, in the days of Zerubbabel [and in the days of Nehemiah], gave the singers and the gatekeepers their portions, according to their daily needs. They made their consecrated offering to the Levites, and the Levites made theirs to the sons of Aaron.

Separation from Aliens

13 1*† At that time, when there was reading from the book of Moses in the hearing of the people, it was found written there that "no Ammonite or Moabite may ever be admitted into the assembly of God; 2* for they would not succor the Israelites with food and water, but they hired Balaam to curse them, though our God turned the curse into a blessing." 3* When they had heard the law, they separated from Israel every foreign element.

---

† **12, 27–43:** The dedication of the wall of Jerusalem took place, no doubt, soon after the restoration of the wall and its gates had been completed. Therefore, this section is best read after Neh 6, 15.

12, 44–47: This account of the provisions made for the temple services is apparently a composition of the Chronicler. *At that time:* a mere connective; no particular time is meant, but the account fits best after that of the restoration of the temple (Ezr 6, 13–18) in the days of Zerubbabel (v 47). The gloss mentioning Nehemiah is not in the ancient Greek version.

13, 1ff: These verses were composed by the Chronicler to serve as an introduction to the reforms that Nehemiah instituted during his second mission in Jerusalem (vv 4–31). The part of the book of Moses read to the people is freely quoted here from Dt 23, 3–6.

* 12, 25: Neh 11, 17.
12, 44f: 1 Chr 23–26; 2 Chr 8, 14.
12, 46: 2 Chr 29, 30; 35, 15.
12, 47: Neh 13, 10f; 10, 39; Nm 18, 26.
13, 1ff: Dt 23, 3–6.
13, 2: Nm 22–24.
13, 3: Neh 13, 23–28.

Reform in the Temple

4† Before this, the priest Eliashib, who had been placed in charge of the chambers of the house of our God and who was an associate of Tobiah, 5* had set aside for the latter's use a large chamber in which had previously been stored the cereal offerings, incense and utensils, the tithes in grain, wine, and oil allotted to the Levites, singers, and gatekeepers, and the offerings due the priests. 6† During all this time I had not been in Jerusalem, for in the thirty-second year of Artaxerxes, king of Babylon, I had gone back to the king. After due time, however, I asked leave of the king 7 and returned to Jerusalem, where I discovered the evil thing that Eliashib had done for Tobiah, in setting aside for him a chamber in the courts of the house of God. 8 This displeased me very much, and I had all of Tobiah's household goods thrown outside the chamber. 9 Then I gave orders to purify the chambers, and I had them replace there the utensils of the house of God, the cereal offerings, and the incense.

10 I learned, too, that the portions due the Levites were no longer being given, so that the Levites and the singers who should have been carrying out the services had deserted, each man to his own field. 11 I took the magistrates to task, demanding, "Why is the house of God abandoned?" Then I brought the Levites together and had them resume their stations. 12* All Judah once more brought in the tithes of grain, wine, and oil to the storerooms; 13 and in charge of the storerooms I appointed the priest Shelemiah, Zadok the scribe, and Pedaiah, one of the Levites, together with Hanan, son of Zaccur, son of Mattaniah, as their assistant; for these men were held to be trustworthy. It was their duty to make the distribution to their brethren. 14 Remember this to my credit, O my God! Let not the devotion which I showed for the house of my God and its services be forgotten!

Sabbath Observance

15* In those days I perceived that men in Judah were treading the winepresses on the sabbath; that they were bringing in sheaves of grain, loading them on their asses, together with wine, grapes, figs, and every other kind of burden, and bringing them to Jerusalem on the sabbath day. I warned them to sell none of these victuals. 16 In Jerusalem itself the Tyrians who were resident there were importing fish and every other kind of merchandise and selling it to the Judahites on the sabbath. 17 I took the nobles of Judah to task, demanding of them: "What is this evil thing that you are doing, profaning the sabbath day? 18 Did not your fathers act in this same way, with the result that our God has brought all this evil upon us and upon this city? Would you add to the wrath against Israel by once more profaning the sabbath?"

19 When the shadows were falling on the gates of Jerusalem before the sabbath, I ordered the doors to be closed and forbade them to be reopened till after the sabbath. I posted some of my own men at the gates so that no burden might enter on the sabbath day. 20 The merchants and sellers of various kinds of merchandise spent the night once or twice outside Jerusalem, 21 but then I warned them, saying to them: "Why do you spend the night alongside the wall? If you keep this up, I will lay hands on you!" From that time on, they did not return on the sabbath. 22 Then I ordered the Levites to purify themselves and to go and watch the gates, so that the sabbath day might be kept holy. This, too, remember in my favor, O my God, and have mercy on me in accordance with your great mercy!

Mixed Marriages

23* Also in those days I saw Jews who had married Ashdodite, Ammonite, or Moabite wives. 24† Of their children, half spoke Ashdodite, and none of them knew how to speak Jewish; and so it was in regard to the languages of the various other peoples. 25 I took them to task and cursed them; I had some of them beaten and their hair pulled out; and I adjured them by God: "You shall not marry your daughters to their sons nor take any of their daughters for your sons or for yourselves! 26* Did not Solomon, the king of Israel, sin because of them? Though among the many nations there was no king like him, and though he was beloved of his God and God had made him king over all Israel, yet even he was made to sin by foreign women. 27 Must it also be heard of you that you have done this same very great evil, betraying our God by marrying foreign women?"

---

† **13, 4–31:** This is part of the "Memoirs of Nehemiah"; it is continued in Neh 10, 1–40.

13, 6: *After due time:* It is not known when Nehemiah returned to Jerusalem or how long his second period of activity there lasted, but it probably ended before Ezra came to Palestine; see note on Ezr 7, 1–8.

13, 24: *Ashdodite:* the language spoken at Ashdod, more likely an Aramaic rather than a Philistine dialect. *Jewish:* Hebrew as spoken in postexilic Judah.

13, 5: Neh 12, 44.
13, 12: Neh 10, 38f; 12, 44f.47; 2 Chr 31, 6.
13, 15: Neh 10, 32; Ex 20, 8.
13, 23: Neh 10, 31; 13, 1ff; Dt 23, 3.
13, 26: 1 Kgs 11, 1–13.

28* One of the sons of Joiada, son of Eliashib the high priest, was the son-in-law of Sanballat the Horonite! I drove him from my presence. 29 Remember against them, O my God, how they defiled the priesthood and the covenant of the priesthood and the Levites!

30 Thus I cleansed them of all foreign contamination. I established the various functions for the priests and Levites, so that each had his appointed task. 31* I also provided for the procurement of wood at stated times and for the first fruits. Remember this in my favor, O my God!

13, 28: Neh 2, 10; 13, 4f.7ff.   13, 31: Neh 10, 35f.

The Book of Tobit

G**ood people suffering, love that must overcome a frightening obstacle, an undercover angel—the Book of Tobit has it all. Part fairy tale, part love story, this book will bring a smile to your face and perhaps a tear to your eye. Enjoy!**

In-depth

For the author of the Book of Tobit, understanding God's will was not difficult. The conviction that God rewards good people, especially those who have experienced great suffering, is evident on every page. In the story, the faithful Tobit, who is blinded after doing a good deed, and the virtuous Sarah, who is ridiculed because she has had seven husbands die on their wedding night, pray for death because of their suffering and humiliation. In answer to their prayers, God sends the angel Raphael to lead Tobit's son Tobias on a journey to Sarah's town. The story ends happily—but you will have to read it yourself to find out exactly how.

The Book of Tobit is a novel, that is, a fiction book. The author was writing at a time when the Jews were governed by oppressive Greek rulers, and the people needed the reassurance of this happy tale. They had not forgotten the fall of Jerusalem or the Exile in Babylon, and Israel's suffering weighed heavily on them. What was the advantage of following God's law if all they had to look forward to was more suffering? (Belief in an afterlife had not yet developed among the Jewish people.) The book assured the faithful that God would eventually reward them: it was just a matter of time.

Although the book's miraculous answers may seem too simple to modern-day readers, its insistence on God's presence in human life and God's concern for those who suffer remains as important as ever. All people—even Christians who believe in life after death—need encouragement to face the challenges of this world with faith and hope.

At a Glance

I. Tobit's Ordeals (1, 3—3, 6).

II. Sarah's Plight (3, 7–17).

III. Tobiah's Journey and Marriage to Sarah (4, 1—9, 6).

IV. Tobiah's Return; Cure of Tobit's Blindness (10, 1—11, 18).

V. Raphael Reveals His Identity (12, 1–22).

VI. Tobit's Song of Praise (13, 1–18).

VII. Epilogue (14, 1–15).

Quick Facts

Setting
although fictional, the book reflects the historical situation of Israelites deported from Israel to Nineveh in 721 B.C.

Author
unknown, writing sometime in the second century B.C.

Theme
In time, God will aid the faithful who suffer.

Of Note
Raphael is one of only three angels named in the Bible; the others are Michael and Gabriel.

506

Tobit

Tobit

1 ¹† This book tells the story of Tobit, son of Tobiel, son of Hananiel, son of Aduel, son of Gabael of the family of Asiel, of the tribe of Naphtali, ²*† who during the reign of Shalmaneser, king of Assyria, was taken captive from Thisbe, which is south of Kedesh Naphtali in upper Galilee, above and to the west of Asser, north of Phogor.

I: Tobit's Ordeals

His Virtue

³ I, Tobit, have walked all the days of my life on the paths of truth and righteousness. I performed many charitable works for my kinsmen and my people who had been deported with me to Nineveh, in Assyria. ⁴ When I lived as a young man in my own country, Israel, the entire tribe of my forefather Naphtali had broken away from the house of David and from Jerusalem. This city had been singled out of all Israel's tribes, so that they all might offer sacrifice in the place where the temple, God's dwelling, had been built and consecrated for all generations to come. ⁵*† All my kinsmen, like the rest of the tribe of my forefather Naphtali, used to offer sacrifice on all the mountains of Galilee as well as to the young bull which Jeroboam, king of Israel, had made in Dan.

⁶*† I, for my part, would often make the pilgrimage alone to Jerusalem for the festivals, as is prescribed for all Israel by perpetual decree. Bringing with me the first fruits of the field and the firstlings of the flock, together with a tenth of my income and the first shearings of the sheep,* I would hasten to Jerusalem ⁷* and present them to the priests, Aaron's sons, at the altar. To the Levites who were doing service in Jerusalem I would give the tithe of grain, wine, olive oil, pomegranates, figs, and other fruits. And except for sabbatical years, I used to give a second tithe in money, which each year I would go and disburse in Jerusalem. ⁸ The third tithe I gave to orphans and widows, and to converts who were living with the Israelites. Every third year I would bring them this offering, and we

---

† **1, 1:** *Tobit:* in the fragments of the book found at Qumran, is given as *Tobi,* an abbreviated form of *Tobiyah* (v 9; Ezr 2, 60) or of *Tobiyahu* (2 Chr 17, 8), a name which means "Yahweh is good." *Tobiel,* "God is good"; *Hananiel,* "God is merciful." The book abounds in theophoric names.

1, 2: Shalmaneser V (727–722 B.C.): began the siege of Samaria; the inhabitants of the northern kingdom were taken into captivity by his successor, Sargon II (722–705). *Thisbe* and *Phogor:* towns of Galilee that have not been identified; *Thisbe* in Gilead was perhaps the birthplace of Elijah. *Kedesh:* cf Jos 20, 7. *Asser:* Hazor (Jos 11, 1).

1, 5: Jeroboam established sanctuaries in *Dan* and Bethel so that the people would no longer go to Jerusalem for the festivals. The gold statues of bulls which he placed in the sanctuaries were considered the throne of Yahweh; but the people soon came to worship the images themselves. Jeroboam also encouraged the high places or hilltop shrines (1 Kgs 12, 26–33).

1, 6ff: *Perpetual decree:* Dt 12, 11.13–14. Refusing to worship at Jeroboam's shrines, the faithful Tobit continued to bring his offerings to Jerusalem; see 2 Chr 11, 16. For the various tithes, cf Nm 18, 20–32; 2 Chr 31, 4–6; Dt 14, 22–29; 26, 12f.

1, 2: 2 Kgs 17, 3; 18, 9ff.
1, 5: 1 Kgs 12, 26–32.
1, 6: Ex 23, 14f.17; 34, 23.
1, 6: Dt 16, 16.
1, 7f: Nm 18, 12f.24; Dt 14, 22–29; 18, 4f.

ate it in keeping with the decree of the Mosaic law
and the commands of Deborah, the mother of my
father Tobiel; for when my father died, he left me
an orphan.

9 When I reached manhood, I married Anna, a
woman of our own lineage. By her I had a son
whom I named Tobiah. 10* Now after I had been
deported to Nineveh, all my brothers and relatives
ate the food of heathens, 11 but I refrained from eating that kind of food. 12 Because of this wholehearted service of God, 13* the Most High granted
me favor and status with Shalmaneser, so that I became purchasing agent for all his needs. 14† Every
now and then until his death I would go to Media
to buy goods for him. I also deposited several
pouches containing a great sum of money with my
kinsman Gabael, son of Gabri, who lived at Rages,
in Media. 15† But when Shalmaneser died and his
son Sennacherib succeeded him as king, the roads
to Media became unsafe, so I could no longer go
there.

Courage in Burying the Dead

16 During Shalmaneser's reign I performed many
charitable works for my kinsmen and my people.
17*† I would give my bread to the hungry and my
clothing to the naked. If I saw one of my people who
had died and been thrown outside the walls of Nineveh, I would bury him. 18 I also buried anyone
whom Sennacherib slew when he returned as a fugitive from Judea during the days of judgment decreed
against him by the heavenly King because of the blasphemies he had uttered. In his rage he killed many Israelites, but I used to take their bodies by stealth and
bury them; so when Sennacherib looked for them, he
could not find them. 19 But a certain citizen of Nineveh informed the king that it was I who buried the
dead. When I found out that the king knew all about
me and wanted to put me to death, I went into hiding; then in my fear I took to flight. 20 Afterward, all
my property was confiscated; I was left with nothing.
All that I had was taken to the king's palace, except for
my wife Anna and my son Tobiah.

21*† But less than forty days later the king was assassinated by two of his sons, who then escaped

---

1, 14: *A great sum of money:* literally, "ten silver talents," about
ten thousand dollars. *Rages:* modern Rai, about five miles southeast
of Teheran. *Media:* the northwestern part of modern Iran.

1, 15: *Sennacherib* (705–681 B.C.): the son of Sargon (722–
705 B.C.); neither was descended from Shalmaneser. Inconsistencies
such as this point to the fact that the Book of Tobit is a religious novel
(see Introduction; also notes on 5, 6 and 14, 15).

1, 17–18: Tobit risked his own life to bury the dead. Deprivation
of burial was viewed with horror by the Jews. Cf Tb 4, 3–4; 6, 15;
14, 12–13.

1, 21: *Esarhaddon:* 681–669 B.C. *Ahiqar:* a hero of ancient folklore, known for his outstanding wisdom. The Story (or Wisdom) of
Ahiqar was very popular in antiquity and is extant in many different
forms: Aramaic, Syriac, Armenian, Arabic (Arabian Nights), Greek
(Aesop's Fables), Slavonic, Ethiopic, and Romanian. The sacred

did you KNOW?

The Case of the Missing Books

The Book of Tobit is treated differently in
some versions of the Bible. Some put it in
a section of books separated from the rest
of the Old Testament. Some do not include it at all. We can find an explanation
to this puzzle if we look back in time.

Sometime in the second or third
century B.C., Jewish scholars translated
the Scriptures from Hebrew and Aramaic
into Greek. Many Jews living throughout
the Mediterranean world spoke Greek,
which had become a common language
in that area at the time. For Greek-speaking Jews, this translation, called the Septuagint, was the Bible that they used.
Because most of the early Christians
spoke Greek, including Jews such as Paul,
the Septuagint was adopted by the
church as its Bible (Old Testament).

After the destruction of the Jerusalem
Temple by the Romans in A.D. 70, leading
rabbis strove to reorganize Jewish worship,
which could no longer center on the Temple in Jerusalem. They reviewed the existing editions of the Bible and developed an
official list of thirty-nine holy books. They
rejected certain books contained in the
Greek Sepuagint for which there was no
existing original Hebrew or Aramaic text,
such as Tobit, Judith, 1 and 2 Maccabees,
Wisdom, Sirach, Baruch, and additions to
the Books of Esther and Daniel.

Many centuries later, the Christian
reformer Martin Luther used the Jewish
canon of the Old Testament in his translation of the Bible. He placed the additional
books in a separate section, entitling them
the Apocrypha (from the Greek for "hidden"). The Catholic church and the Orthodox churches continue to use the fuller
Greek canon, preferring the term *deuterocanonical* (from the Greek for "second
canon") for the disputed books.

author makes Tobit the uncle of the famous Ahiqar in order to enhance Tobit's own prestige. See note on Tb 14, 10.

1, 10: Lv 11; Dt 14, 3–21;
Acts 15, 29; 1 Cor 8,
7ff.
1, 13: Dn 2, 48f.
1, 17: Jb 31, 16–20.
1, 21: 2 Kgs 19, 37; 2 Chr
32, 21; Sir 48, 21; Is
37, 38; 2 Mc 8, 19.

into the mountains of Ararat. His son Esarhaddon, who succeeded him as king, placed Ahiqar, my brother Anael's son, in charge of all the accounts of his kingdom, so that he took control over the entire administration. 22 Then Ahiqar interceded on my behalf, and I was able to return to Nineveh. For under Sennacherib, king of Assyria, Ahiqar had been chief cupbearer, keeper of the seal, administrator, and treasurer; and Esarhaddon reappointed him. He was a close relative—in fact, my nephew.

2 1*† Thus under King Esarhaddon I returned to my home, and my wife Anna and my son Tobiah were restored to me. Then on our festival of Pentecost, the feast of Weeks, a fine dinner was prepared for me, and I reclined to eat. 2† The table was set for me, and when many different dishes were placed before me, I said to my son Tobiah: "My son, go out and try to find a poor man from among our kinsmen exiled here in Nineveh. If he is a sincere worshiper of God, bring him back with you, so that he can share this meal with me. Indeed, son, I shall wait for you to come back."

3 Tobiah went out to look for some poor kinsman of ours. When he returned he exclaimed, "Father!" I said to him, "What is it, son?" He answered, "Father, one of our people has been murdered! His body lies in the market place where he was just strangled!" 4 I sprang to my feet, leaving the dinner untouched; and I carried the dead man from the street and put him in one of the rooms, so that I might bury him after sunset. 5*† Returning to my own quarters, I washed myself and ate my food in sorrow. 6* I was reminded of the oracle pronounced by the prophet Amos against Bethel:

"Your festivals shall be turned
      into mourning,
And all your songs into lamentation."

7 And I wept. Then at sunset I went out, dug a grave, and buried him.

8 The neighbors mocked me, saying to one another: "Will this man never learn! Once before he was hunted down for execution because of this very thing; yet now that he has escaped, here he is again burying the dead!"

Tobit's Blindness

9 That same night I bathed, and went to sleep next to the wall of my courtyard. Because of the heat I left my face uncovered. 10† I did not know there were birds perched on the wall above me, till their warm droppings settled in my eyes, causing cataracts. I went to see some doctors for a cure, but the more they anointed my eyes with various salves, the worse the cataracts became, until I could see no more. For four years I was deprived of eyesight, and all my kinsmen were grieved at my condition. Ahiqar, however, took care of me for two years, until he left for Elymais.

11 At that time my wife Anna worked for hire at weaving cloth, the kind of work women do. 12† When she sent back the goods to their owners, they would pay her. Late in winter she finished the cloth and sent it back to the owners. They paid her the full salary, and also gave her a young goat for the table. 13 On entering my house the goat began to bleat. I called to my wife and said: "Where did this goat come from? Perhaps it was stolen! Give it back to its owners; we have no right to eat stolen food!" 14*† But she said to me, "It was given to me as a bonus over and above my wages." Yet I would not believe her; and told her to give it back to its owners. I became very angry with her over this. So she retorted: "Where are your charitable deeds now? Where are your virtuous acts? See! Your true character is finally showing itself!"

3 1 Grief-stricken in spirit, I groaned and wept aloud. Then with sobs I began to pray:

Tobit's Prayer for Death

2* "You are righteous, O Lord,
      and all your deeds are just;
All your ways are mercy and truth;
      you are the judge of the world.
3* And now, O Lord, may you be mindful
      of me,
      and look with favor upon me.
Punish me not for my sins,
      nor for my inadvertent offenses,
      nor for those of my fathers.

† 2, 1: *The feast of Weeks:* also called by its Greek name Pentecost, was celebrated fifty days after the Passover. Cf Lv 23, 15–21; Dt 16, 9–12.

2, 2: Almsgiving and charity to the poor are important virtues taught by the book (Tb 4, 7–11.16f; 12, 8f; 14, 10f).

2, 5: *I washed myself:* because of ritual defilement from touching a corpse (Nm 19, 11–13).

2, 10: *Cataracts:* literally, "white scales, or films." *Elymais:* the Greek name of ancient Elam, a district northeast of the head of the Persian Gulf.

2, 12: *Late in winter:* literally, "seventh of Dystros," the

Macedonian month which corresponds to the Jewish month of Shebat (January–February). *For the table:* literally, "for the hearth"; the gift had probably been made in view of some springtime festival like the Jewish Purim.

2, 14: Anna's sharp rebuke calls to mind the words of Job's wife (Jb 2, 9).

*
2, 1: Lv 23, 15–21; Nm 28,	2, 14: Jb 2, 9.
26–31; Dt 16, 9–12.	3, 2: Pss 25, 10; 119, 137;
2, 5: Nm 19, 11–22.	Dn 3, 27.
2, 6: Am 8, 10; 1 Mc 1, 39.	3, 3: Ex 34, 7.

"They sinned against you,

4 * and disobeyed your commandments.
So you handed us over to plundering, exile,
and death,
till we were an object lesson, a byword,
a reproach
in all the nations among whom you
scattered us.

5 "Yes, your judgments are many and true
in dealing with me as my sins
and those of my fathers deserve.
For we have not kept your commandments,
nor have we trodden the paths of truth
before you.

6 * † "So now, deal with me as you please,
and command my life breath to be taken
from me,
that I may go from the face of the earth
into dust.
It is better for me to die than to live,
because I have heard insulting calumnies,
and I am overwhelmed with grief.

"Lord, command me to be delivered from
such anguish;
let me go to the everlasting abode;
Lord, refuse me not.
For it is better for me to die
than to endure so much misery in life,
and to hear these insults!"

II: Sarah's Plight

Sarah Falsely Accused

7 † On the same day, at Ecbatana in Media, it so
happened that Raguel's daughter Sarah also had to
listen to abuse, from one of her father's maids.
8 † For she had been married to seven husbands, but
the wicked demon Asmodeus killed them off before
they could have intercourse with her, as it is prescribed for wives. So the maid said to her: "You are
the one who strangles your husbands! Look at you!
You have already been married seven times, but you
have had no joy with any one of your husbands.
9 Why do you beat us? Because your husbands are

dead? Then why not join them! May we never see a
son or daughter of yours!"

10 * That day she was deeply grieved in spirit. She
went in tears to an upstairs room in her father's
house with the intention of hanging herself. But she
reconsidered, saying to herself: "No! People would
level this insult against my father: 'You had only
one beloved daughter, but she hanged herself because of ill fortune!' And thus would I cause my father in his old age to go down to the nether world
laden with sorrow. It is far better for me not to hang
myself, but to beg the Lord to have me die, so that
I need no longer live to hear such insults."

Praying for Death?

Tobit and Sarah are at the end of their
rope. They have experienced such suffering and disgrace that life no longer has
any meaning for them. They know suicide
is wrong, so they each pray that God will
send death to end their suffering and humiliation (Tb 3, 6–10).

It is not uncommon for people who
are very sick or in great pain or very old
to pray for death, like Tobit. Unfortunately, young people who have experienced
great loss or trauma often wish for death
too, like Sarah. No one can completely
explain the mystery of why we—both
young and old—suffer. But through our
loving actions and prayers, we can support one another in our suffering.

What people do you know who are
suffering to the point of despair? Take a
few moments every day to remember
those people in prayer, and call or write
to let them know you are thinking of
them.

▶ Tobit, chapter 3

3, 6: *It is better for me to die than to live:* in his distress Tobit uses
the words of the petulant Jonah (Jon 4, 3.8), who wished to die because God did not destroy the hated Ninevites. In similar circumstances, Moses (Nm 11, 15), Elijah (1 Kgs 19, 4), and Job (Jb 7, 15)
also prayed for death. *Everlasting abode:* a reference to Sheol, the
dismal abode of the dead from which no one returns (Jb 7, 9–10;
14, 12; Is 26, 14). The revelation of a blessed immortality had not yet
been made. See note on Tb 4, 6.
3, 7: From here on, the story is told in the third person. V 7
relates one of the several marvelous coincidences which the story-
teller uses to heighten interest; see also vv 16.17; 4, 1; 5, 4. Ec-

batana: Hamadan in modern Iran; this was the capital of ancient
Media. *Raguel:* "friend of God."
3, 8: *Asmodeus:* in Persian *aeshma daeva,* "demon of wrath,"
adopted into Aramaic with the sense of "the Destroyer." He will be
subdued (Tb 8, 3) by Raphael (v 17), "God heals."

3, 4: Dt 28, 15; Bar 1,   4; Jb 7, 15; Jon 4, 3.8.
    16–22; 2, 4f; 3, 8; Dn   **3, 10:** Tb 6, 15; Gn 37, 35;
    9, 5f.   42, 38; 44, 29.31.
3, 6: Nm 11, 15; 1 Kgs 19,

¹¹*† At that time, then, she spread out her hands, and facing the window, poured out this prayer:

Sarah's Prayer for Death

"Blessed are you, O Lord, merciful God!
    Forever blessed and honored is your
        holy name;
    may all your works forever bless you.
¹² And now, O Lord, to you I turn my face
        and raise my eyes.
¹³ Bid me to depart from the earth,
        never again to hear such insults.

¹⁴ "You know, O Master, that I am innocent
        of any impure act with a man,
¹⁵ And that I have never defiled my own name
        or my father's name in the land of
            my exile.

"I am my father's only daughter,
    and he has no other child to make his heir,
Nor does he have a close kinsman or
        other relative
    whom I might bide my time to marry.
I have already lost seven husbands;
    why then should I live any longer?
But if it please you, Lord, not to slay me,
    look favorably upon me and have pity on me;
    never again let me hear these insults!"

An Answer to Prayer

¹⁶ At that very time, the prayer of these two suppliants was heard in the glorious presence of Almighty God. ¹⁷*† So Raphael was sent to heal them both: to remove the cataracts from Tobit's eyes, so that he might again see God's sunlight; and to marry Raguel's daughter Sarah to Tobit's son Tobiah, and then drive the wicked demon Asmodeus from her. For Tobiah had the right to claim her before any other who might wish to marry her.

In the very moment that Tobit returned from the courtyard to his house, Raguel's daughter Sarah came downstairs from her room.

III: Tobiah's Journey and Marriage to Sarah

A Father's Instruction

4 ¹ That same day Tobit remembered the money he had deposited with Gabael at Rages in Media, and he thought, ² "Now that I have asked for death, why should I not call my son Tobiah and let him know about this money before I die?" ³*† So he called his son Tobiah; and when he came, he said to him: "My son, when I die, give me a decent burial. Honor your mother, and do not abandon her as long as she lives. Do whatever pleases her, and do not grieve her spirit in any way. ⁴ Remember, my son, that she went through many trials for your sake while you were in her womb. And when she dies, bury her in the same grave with me.

⁵ "Through all your days, my son, keep the Lord in mind, and suppress every desire to sin or to break his commandments. Perform good works all the days of your life, and do not tread the paths of wrongdoing. ⁶*† For if you are steadfast in your service, your good works will bring success, not only to you, but also to all those who live uprightly.

⁷* "Give alms from your possessions. Do not turn your face away from any of the poor, and God's face will not be turned away from you. ⁸ Son, give alms in proportion to what you own. If you have great wealth, give alms out of your abundance; if you have but little, distribute even some of that. But do not hesitate to give alms; ⁹* you will be storing up a goodly treasure for yourself against the day of adversity. ¹⁰ Almsgiving frees one from death, and keeps one from going into the dark abode. ¹¹* Alms are a worthy offering in the sight of the Most High for all who give them.

¹²* "Be on your guard, son, against every form of immorality, and above all, marry a woman of the lineage of your forefathers. Do not marry a stranger who is not of your father's tribe, because we are sons of the prophets. My boy, keep in mind Noah, Abraham, Isaac, and Jacob, our

---

3, 11: *Facing the window:* that is, looking toward Jerusalem; cf Dn 6, 11. *Blessed are you* and "Blessed be God" are traditional openings of Jewish prayers (Tb 8, 5.15; 11, 14; 13, 1).
3, 17: *Tobiah had the right:* according to the patriarchal custom of marriage within the family group. Tobiah was Sarah's closest eligible relative (Tb 6, 12). Cf Tb 4, 12–13; Gn 24.
4, 3–19: A collection of maxims which parallel those in the wisdom literature, especially Proverbs and Sirach (see Introduction): duties toward parents (3–4); cf also Tb 14, 13; perseverance in virtue and avoidance of evil (5–6.14b); necessity and value of almsgiving and charity (7–11.16–17); marriage to a kinsman (12–13a); industry (13b); prompt payment of wages (14a); the golden rule (15a); temperance (15b); docility (18); prayer (19).
4, 6: Before the revelation of retribution for all men in the after-

life—a doctrine taught in the Book of Wisdom—Old Testament man believed that virtue guaranteed earthly prosperity, and sin earthly disaster (cf Dt 28).

3, 11: 1 Kgs 8, 44.48; Pss 28, 2; 134, 2; Dn 6, 11.
3, 17: Tb 4, 12f; 6, 12f; Gn 24, 3f.
4, 3: Ex 20, 12; Prv 23, 22; Sir 7, 27.
4, 6: Tb 12, 8ff; Jn 3, 21; Eph 4, 15.
4, 7f: Tb 12, 8ff; Dt 15,

7f.11; Prv 19, 17; Sir 4, 1–6; 14, 13; Lk 14, 13; 1 Jn 3, 17.
4, 9: Mt 6, 20f.
4, 11: Sir 3, 30; 29, 12.
4, 12: Tb 3, 15.17; 6, 12; Gn 11, 29.31; 25, 20; 28, 1–4; 29, 15–30; Ex 34, 16; Dt 7, 3; Jgs 14, 3.

fathers from of old: all of them took wives from among their own kinsmen and were blessed in their children. Remember that their posterity shall inherit the land. 13 Therefore, my son, love your kinsmen. Do not be so proudhearted toward your kinsmen, the sons and daughters of your people, as to refuse to take a wife for yourself from among them. For in such arrogance there is ruin and great disorder. Likewise, in worthlessness there is decay and dire poverty, for worthlessness is the mother of famine.

14* "Do not keep with you overnight the wages of any man who works for you, but pay him immediately. If you thus behave as God's servant, you will receive your reward. Keep a close watch on yourself, my son, in everything you do, and discipline yourself in all your conduct. 15* Do to no one what you yourself dislike. Do not drink wine till you become drunk, nor let drunkenness accompany you on your way.

16* "Give to the hungry some of your bread, and to the naked some of your clothing. Whatever you have left over, give away as alms; and do not begrudge the alms you give. 17*† Be lavish with your bread and wine at the burial of the virtuous, but do not share them with sinners.

18 "Seek counsel from every wise man, and do not think lightly of any advice that can be useful. 19*† At all times bless the Lord God, and ask him to make all your paths straight and to grant success to all your endeavors and plans. For no pagan nation possesses good counsel, but the Lord himself gives all good things. If the Lord chooses, he raises a man up; but if he should decide otherwise, he casts him down to the deepest recesses of the nether world. So now, my son, keep in mind my commandments, and never let them be erased from your heart.

20 "And now, son, I wish to inform you that I have deposited a great sum of money with Gabri's son Gabael at Rages in Media. 21* Do not be discouraged, my child, because of our poverty. You will be a rich man if you fear God, avoid all sin, and do what is right before the Lord your God."

The Angel Raphael

5 1 Then Tobiah replied to his father Tobit: "Everything that you have commanded me, father, I will do. 2 But how shall I be able to obtain the money from him, since he does not know me nor do I know him? What can I show him to make him recognize me and trust me, so that he will give

GIVE FOOD TO THE HUNGRY

In China, whenever you see a friend, it is customary to ask whether he or she has eaten a meal yet. If your friend responds, "No, I haven't eaten yet," it may mean that his or her last meal was yesterday or even the day before that. Then, you invite your friend to your home and share whatever food you have. This custom goes back to the great famine of China (1958–59), when people were dying of starvation and even eating tree bark.

Tobit gives his son good advice when he instructs him to share his food with the hungry and his clothing with the poor (Tb 4, 16). Read Mt 25, 31–46 to hear how seriously Jesus wants us to follow this advice.

▶ Tb 4, 16

4, 17: Tobit counsels his son either to give alms in honor of the dead, or, more probably, to give the "bread of consolation" to the family of the deceased. Cf Jer 16, 7; Ez 24, 17.

4, 19: Prayer is the foundation of a moral life.

4, 14: Lv 19, 13; Dt 24, 15.
4, 15: Mt 7, 12; Lk 6, 31.
4, 16: Dt 15, 10; Is 58, 7; Mt 25, 35f; 2 Cor 9, 7.
4, 17: Jer 16, 7; Lk 14, 13.
4, 19: Dt 4, 6; Ps 119, 10.
4, 21: 1 Tm 6, 6ff.

me the money? I do not even know which roads to take for the journey into Media!" ³† Tobit answered his son Tobiah: "We exchanged signatures on a document written in duplicate; I divided it into two parts, and each of us kept one; his copy I put with the money. Think of it, twenty years have already passed since I deposited that money! So now, my son, find yourself a trustworthy man who will make the journey with you. We will, of course, give him a salary when you return; but get back that money from Gabael."

⁴*† Tobiah went to look for someone acquainted with the roads who would travel with him to Media. As soon as he went out, he found the angel Raphael standing before him, though he did not know that this was an angel of God. ⁵ Tobiah said to him, "Who are you, young man?" He replied, "I am an Israelite, one of your kinsmen. I have come here to work." Tobiah said, "Do you know the way to Media?" ⁶† The other replied: "Yes, I have been there many times. I know the place well and I know all the routes. I have often traveled to Media; I used to stay with our kinsman Gabael, who lives at Rages in Media. It is a good two days' travel from Ecbatana to Rages, for Rages is situated at the mountains, Ecbatana out on the plateau." ⁷* Tobiah said to him, "Wait for me, young man, till I go back and tell my father; for I need you to make the journey with me. I will, of course, pay you." ⁸ Raphael replied, "Very well, I will wait for you; but do not be long."

⁹ Tobiah went back to tell his father Tobit what had happened. He said to him, "I have just found a man who is one of our own Israelite kinsmen!" Tobit said, "Call the man, so that I may find out what family and tribe he comes from, and whether he is trustworthy enough to travel with you, son." Tobiah went out to summon the man saying, "Young man, my father would like to see you."

¹⁰† When Raphael entered the house, Tobit greeted him first. Raphael said, "Hearty greetings to you!" Tobit replied: "What joy is left for me any more? Here I am, a blind man who cannot see God's sunlight, but must remain in darkness, like the dead who no longer see the light! Though alive, I am among the dead. I can hear a man's voice, but I cannot see him." Raphael said, "Take courage! God has healing in store for you; so take courage!" Tobit then said: "My son Tobiah wants to go to Media. Can you go with him to show him the way? I will of course pay you, brother." Raphael answered: "Yes, I can go with him, for I know all the routes. I have often traveled to Media and crossed all its plains and mountains; so I know every road well." ¹¹ Tobit asked, "Brother, tell me, please, what family and tribe are you from?" ¹²* Raphael said: "Why? Do you need a tribe and a family? Or are you looking for a hired man to travel with your son?" Tobit replied, "I wish to know truthfully whose son you are, brother, and what your name is."

¹³† Raphael answered, "I am Azariah, son of Hananiah the elder, one of your own kinsmen." ¹⁴ Tobit exclaimed: "Welcome! God save you, brother! Do not be provoked with me, brother, for wanting to learn the truth about your family. So it turns out that you are a kinsman, and from a noble and good line! I knew Hananiah and Nathaniah, the two sons of Shemaiah the elder; with me they used to make the pilgrimage to Jerusalem, where we would worship together. No, they did not stray from the right path; your kinsmen are good men. You are certainly of good lineage, and welcome!"

¹⁵† Then he added: "For each day you are away I will give you the normal wages, plus expenses for you and for my son. If you go with my son, ¹⁶ I will even add a bonus to your wages!" Raphael replied: "I will go with him; have no fear. In good health we shall leave you, and in good health we shall return to you, for the way is safe." ¹⁷ Tobit said, "God bless you, brother." Then he called his son and said to him: "My son, prepare whatever you need for the journey, and set out with your kinsman. May God in heaven protect you on the way and bring you back to me safe and sound; and may his angel accompany you for safety, my son."

Before setting out on his journey, Tobiah kissed his father and mother. Tobit said to him, "Have a safe journey." ¹⁸ But his mother began to weep. She said to Tobit: "Why have you decided to send my child away? Is he not the staff to which we cling,

5, 3: *Document:* in Greek *cheirographon.* In the Middle Ages, notably in England, a deed and its duplicate were written on one piece of parchment, with the Latin word *chirographum* inscribed across the top of the sheet or between the two copies of the text. The document was then cut in two in either a straight or a wavy line, the parts being given to the persons concerned. Perhaps this procedure derived from the present verse of Tobit. Duplicate documents, usually one open and the other sealed, are well known from the ancient Near East.
5, 4: *He did not know:* the theme of an angel in disguise occurs frequently in folklore as well as in the Old Testament (Gn 18; cf Heb 13, 2).
5, 6: *It is a good two days' travel from Echatana to Rages:* Alexan-

der's army need eleven days in forced marches to cover this distance, about 180 miles. The author is merely using popular impressions about faraway places; he is not teaching geography. (See notes on Tb 1, 15; 3, 7 and Introduction.)
5, 10: *Hearty greetings* and *what joy* form a wordplay on the Greek verb *chairein,* "to greet" and "to be joyful."
5, 13–14: *Azariah,* "Yahweh helps"; *Hananiah,* "Yahweh is merciful"; *Nathaniah,* "Yahweh gives"; *Shemaiah,* "Yahweh hears."
5, 15: *The normal wages:* literally, "a drachma," about seventeen cents, a day's wage for a workingman.

5, 4: Heb 13, 2.   **5, 12:** Jgs 13, 17f.
5, 7: Tb 12, 2.

ever there with us in all that we do? ¹⁹ I hope more money is not your chief concern! Rather let it be a ransom for our son! ²⁰ What the Lord has given us to live on is certainly enough for us." ²¹ Tobit reassured her: "Have no such thought. Our son will leave in good health and come back to us in good health. Your own eyes will see the day when he returns to you safe and sound. ²²† So, no such thought; do not worry about them, my love. For a good angel will go with him, his journey will be successful, and he will return unharmed." ¹† Then she stopped weeping.

Journey to Rages

6 ² When the boy left home, accompanied by the angel, the dog followed Tobiah out of the house and went with him. The travelers walked till nightfall, and made camp beside the Tigris River. ³ Now when the boy went down to wash his feet in the river, a large fish suddenly leaped out of the water and tried to swallow his foot. He shouted in alarm. ⁴ But the angel said to him, "Take hold of the fish and don't let it get away!" The boy seized the fish and hauled it up on the shore. ⁵† The angel then told him: "Cut the fish open and take out its gall, heart, and liver, and keep them with you; but throw away the entrails. Its gall, heart, and liver make useful medicines." ⁶ After the lad had cut the fish open, he put aside the gall, heart, and liver. Then he broiled and ate part of the fish; the rest he salted and kept for the journey.

Raphael's Instructions

⁷ Afterward they traveled on together till they were near Media. The boy asked the angel this question: "Brother Azariah, what medicinal value is there in the fish's heart, liver, and gall?" ⁸ He answered: "As regards the fish's heart and liver, if you burn them so that the smoke surrounds a man or a woman who is afflicted by a demon or evil spirit, the affliction will leave him completely, and no demons will ever return to him again. ⁹ And as for the gall, if you rub it on the eyes of a man who has cataracts, blowing into his eyes right on the cataracts, his sight will be restored."

¹⁰ When they had entered Media and were getting close to Ecbatana, ¹¹ Raphael said to the boy, "Brother Tobiah!" He answered, "Yes, what is it?" Raphael continued: "Tonight we must stay with Raguel, who is a relative of yours. He has a daughter

named Sarah, ¹²* but no other child. Since you are Sarah's closest relative, you before all other men have the right to marry her. Also, her father's estate is rightfully yours to inherit. Now the girl is sensible, courageous, and very beautiful; and her father loves her dearly." ¹³† He continued: "Since you have the right to marry her, listen to me, brother. Tonight I will ask the girl's father to let us have her as your bride. When we return from Rages, we will hold the wedding feast for her. I know that Raguel cannot keep her from you or let her become engaged to another man; that would be a capital crime according to the decree in the Book of Moses, and he knows that it is your right, before all other men, to marry his daughter. So heed my words, brother; tonight we must speak for the girl, so that we may have her engaged to you. And when we return from Rages, we will take her and bring her back with us to your house."

¹⁴ Tobiah objected, however: "Brother Azariah, I have heard that this woman has already been married seven times, and that her husbands died in their bridal chambers. On the very night they approached her, they dropped dead. And I have heard it said that it was a demon who killed them. ¹⁵* So now I too am afraid of this demon. Because he loves her, he does not harm her; but he does slay any man who wishes to come close to her. I am my father's only child. If I should die, I would bring my father and mother down to their grave in sorrow over me. And they have no other son to bury them!"

¹⁶ Raphael said to him: "Do you not remember your father's orders? He commanded you to marry a woman from your own family. So now listen to me, brother; do not give another thought to this demon, but marry Sarah. I know that tonight you shall have her for your wife! ¹⁷ When you go into the bridal chamber, take the fish's liver and heart, and place them on the embers for the incense. ¹⁸† As soon as the demon smells the odor they give off, he will flee and never again show himself near her. Then when you are about to have intercourse with her, both of you first rise up to pray. Beg the Lord of heaven to show you mercy and grant you deliverance. But do not be afraid, for she was set apart for you before the world existed. You will save her, and she will go with you. And I suppose that you will have children by her, who will take the place of brothers for you. So do not worry."

5, 22: *My love:* literally, "sister," a term of endearment applied to one's wife; cf Tb 7, 11.15; 8, 4.21; 10, 6.13; Song 4, 9.10.12; 5, 1f. *A good angel:* a reference to the guardian angel, though Tobit does not know, of course, that Raphael himself, disguised as Azariah, is the good angel in this case.
5, 1: *Then . . . weeping:* this verse belongs to ch 6.
6, 5: *Its gall . . . medicines:* belief in the healing power of these

organs was common among even the physicians of antiquity.
6, 13: *Raguel . . . Book of Moses:* Nm 36, 6–8 prescribed marriage within the ancestral tribe, but no death penalty is mentioned.
6, 18: *Rise up to pray:* prayer is needed to drive out the demon.

6, 12: Tb 4, 12f; Nm 36, 8.   6, 15: Tb 3, 10.

When Tobiah heard Raphael say that she was his kinswoman, of his own family's lineage, he fell deeply in love with her, and his heart became set on her.

At the House of Raguel

7 [1] When they entered Ecbatana, Tobiah said, "Brother Azariah, lead me straight to our kinsman Raguel." So he brought him to the house of Raguel, whom they found seated by his courtyard gate. They greeted him first. He said to them, "Greetings to you too, brothers! Good health to you, and welcome!" When he brought them into his home, [2] he said to his wife Edna, "This young man looks just like my kinsman Tobit!" [3] So Edna asked them, "Who are you, brothers?" They answered, "We are of the exiles from Naphtali at Nineveh." [4] She said, "Do you know our kinsman Tobit?" They answered, "Indeed we do!" She asked, "Is he well?" [5] They answered, "Yes, he is alive and well." Then Tobiah exclaimed, "He is my father!" [6] Raguel sprang up and kissed him, shedding tears of joy. [7] But when he heard that Tobit had lost his eyesight, he was grieved and wept aloud. He said to Tobiah: "My child, God bless you! You are the son of a noble and good father. But what a terrible misfortune that such a righteous and charitable man should be afflicted with blindness!" He continued to weep in the arms of his kinsman Tobiah. [8] His wife Edna also wept for Tobit; and even their daughter Sarah began to weep.

Marriage of Tobiah and Sarah

[9] Afterward, Raguel slaughtered a ram from the flock and gave them a cordial reception. When they had bathed and reclined to eat, Tobiah said to Raphael, "Brother Azariah, ask Raguel to let me marry my kinswoman Sarah." [10] Raguel overheard the words; so he said to the boy: "Eat and drink and be merry tonight, for no man is more entitled to marry my daughter Sarah than you, brother. Besides, not even I have the right to give her to anyone but you, because you are my closest relative. But I will explain the situation to you very frankly. [11] I have given her in marriage to seven men, all of whom were kinsmen of ours, and all died on the very night they approached her. But now, son, eat and drink. I am sure the Lord will look after you both." Tobiah answered, "I will eat or drink nothing until you set aside what belongs to me."

Raguel said to him: "I will do it. She is yours according to the decree of the Book of Moses. Your marriage to her has been decided in heaven! Take your kinswoman; from now on you are her love, and she is your beloved. She is yours today and ever after. And tonight, son, may the Lord of heaven prosper you both. May he grant you mercy and peace." [12]* Then Raguel called his daughter Sarah, and she came to him. He took her by the hand and gave her to Tobiah with the words: "Take her according to the law. According to the decree written in the Book of Moses she is your wife. Take her and bring her back safely to your father. And may the God of heaven grant both of you peace and prosperity." [13]* He then called her mother and told her to bring a scroll, so that he might draw up a marriage contract stating that he gave Sarah to Tobiah as his wife according to the decree of the Mosaic law. Her mother brought the scroll, and he drew up the contract, to which they affixed their seals.

[14] Afterward they began to eat and drink. [15] Later Raguel called his wife Edna and said, "My love, prepare the other bedroom and bring the girl there." [16] She went and made the bed in the room, as she was told, and brought the girl there. After she had cried over her, she wiped away the tears and said: [17] "Be brave, my daughter. May the Lord of heaven grant you joy in place of your grief. Courage, my daughter." Then she left.

Expulsion of the Demon

8 [1] When they had finished eating and drinking, the girl's parents wanted to retire. They brought the young man out of the dining room and led him into the bedroom. [2]† At this point Tobiah, mindful of Raphael's instructions, took the fish's liver and heart from the bag which he had with him, and placed them on the embers for the incense. [3]† The demon, repelled by the odor of the fish, fled into Upper Egypt; Raphael pursued him there and bound him hand and foot. Then Raphael returned immediately.

[4] When the girl's parents left the bedroom and closed the door behind them, Tobiah arose from bed and said to his wife, "My love, get up. Let us pray and beg our Lord to have mercy on us and to grant us deliverance." [5]* She got up, and they started to pray and beg that deliverance might be theirs. He began with these words:

"Blessed are you, O God of our fathers;
     praised be your name forever and ever.

T
B

---

† **8, 2f:** The manner of coping with demonic influences among the ancients seems quaint to us. However, the fish here is part of the story, and not a recipe for exorcism. It is clear that the author places primary emphasis on the value of prayer to God (Tb 6, 18; 8, 4–8), on the role of the angel as God's agent, and on the pious dispositions of Tobiah.

8, 3: *Into Upper Egypt:* to the desert there. The desert was considered the dwelling place of demons. Cf Is 13, 21; 34, 14; Mt 4, 1; 12, 43.

7, 12: Gn 24, 50f.   **8, 5:** Dn 3, 26.
7, 13: Tb 6, 12.

Angels Among Us

Many older Catholics were taught as children that they were to leave a bit of space on their chair for their guardian angel. We smile at that story, partly because it was a creative way to make angels real in the lives of children, and partly because it points to a truth about God's presence in our life.

In the fictional story of Tobit, we meet the angel Raphael. In other parts of the Bible, angels serve primarily as God's messengers. But Raphael is much more than a messenger. He disguises himself as a kindly but unknown relative who guides Tobias to the secrets he needs to know to relieve both Tobit's and Sarah's suffering.

The truth is that many angels are around us. Most of us have heard stories about kind strangers who appear seemingly out of nowhere to help and then disappear. Our seat may not have a lot of room for an angel, but our world certainly does. They remind us that God is with us, protecting us and guiding us.

Have you or someone you know been touched by an angel? In return, why don't you look for opportunities to be someone else's "angel"?

Let the heavens and all your creation
    praise you forever.
6* You made Adam and you gave him his
      wife Eve
    to be his help and support;
    and from these two the human
      race descended.
You said, 'It is not good for the man to
      be alone;
    let us make him a partner like himself.'
7 Now, Lord, you know that I take this wife
    of mine
    not because of lust,
    but for a noble purpose.
Call down your mercy on me and on her,
    and allow us to live together to a happy
      old age."

8 They said together, "Amen, amen," 9 and went to bed for the night.

But Raguel got up and summoned his servants. With him they went out to dig a grave, 10 for he said, "I must do this, because if Tobiah should die, we would be subjected to ridicule and insult." 11 When they had finished digging the grave, Raguel went back into the house and called his wife, 12 saying, "Send one of the maids in to see whether Tobiah is alive or dead, so that if necessary we may bury him without anyone's knowing about it." 13 She sent the maid, who lit a lamp, opened the bedroom door, went in, and found them sound asleep

together. 14 The maid went out and told the girl's parents that Tobiah was alive, and that there was nothing wrong. 15 Then Raguel praised the God of heaven in these words:

"Blessed are you, O God, with every holy and
    pure blessing!
Let all your chosen ones praise you;
let them bless you forever!
16 Blessed are you, who have made
    me glad;
what I feared did not happen.
Rather you have dealt with us
    according to your great mercy.
17 Blessed are you, for you were merciful
    toward two only children.
Grant them, Master, mercy and
    deliverance,
and bring their lives to fulfillment
    with happiness and mercy."

18 Then he told his servants to fill in the grave before dawn.

Wedding Feast

19 He asked his wife to bake many loaves of bread; he himself went out to the herd and picked out two steers and four rams which he ordered to be slaughtered. So the servants began to prepare the feast. 20† He summoned Tobiah and made an oath in his presence, saying: "For fourteen days you shall not stir

---

8, 20: *For fourteen days:* because of the happy, and unexpected, turn of events, Raguel doubles the time of the wedding feast. When Tobiah returns home, the usual seven-day feast is held (Tb 11, 18). Cf Jgs 14, 12.

8, 6: Gn 2, 18–23.

from here, but shall remain here eating and drinking with me; and you shall bring joy to my daughter's sorrowing spirit. ²¹ Take, to begin with, half of whatever I own when you go back in good health to your father; the other half will be yours when I and my wife die. Be of good cheer, my son! I am your father, and Edna is your mother; and we belong to you and to your beloved now and forever. So be happy, son!"

The Money Recovered

9 ¹ Then Tobiah called Raphael and said to him: ² "Brother Azariah, take along with you four servants and two camels and travel to Rages. Go to Gabael's house and give him this bond. Get the money and then bring him along with you to the wedding celebration. ⁴ For you know that my father is counting the days. If I should delay my return by a single day, I would cause him intense grief. ³ You witnessed the oath that Raguel has sworn; I cannot violate his oath." ⁵ So Raphael, together with the four servants and two camels, traveled to Rages in Media, where they stayed at Gabael's house. Raphael gave Gabael his bond and told him about Tobit's son Tobiah, and that he had married and was inviting him to the wedding celebration. Gabael promptly checked over the sealed money-bags, and they placed them on the camels.

⁶ The following morning they got an early start and traveled to the wedding celebration. When they entered Raguel's house, they found Tobiah reclining at table. He sprang up and greeted Gabael, who wept and blessed him, exclaiming: "O noble and good child, son of a noble and good, upright and charitable man, may the Lord grant heavenly blessing to you and to your wife, and to your wife's father and mother. Blessed be God, because I have seen the very image of my cousin Tobit!"

IV: Tobiah's Return; Cure of Tobit's Blindness

Anxiety of the Parents

10 ¹ Meanwhile, day by day, Tobit was keeping track of the time Tobiah would need to go and to return. When the number of days was reached and his son did not appear, ² he said, "I wonder what has happened. Perhaps he has been detained there; or perhaps Gabael is dead, and there is no one to give him the money." ³ And he began to worry. ⁴ His wife Anna said, "My son has perished and is no longer among the living!" And she began to weep aloud and to wail over her son: ⁵ "Alas, my child, light of my eyes, that I let you make this journey!" ⁶ But Tobit kept telling her: "Hush, do not think about it, my love; he

is safe! Probably they have to take care of some unexpected business there. The man who is traveling with him is trustworthy, and is one of our own kinsmen. So do not worry over him, my love. He will be here soon." ⁷* But she retorted, "Stop it, and do not lie to me! My child has perished!" She would go out and keep watch all day at the road her son had taken, and she ate nothing. At sunset she would go back home to wail and cry the whole night through, getting no sleep at all.

Departure from Ecbatana

Now at the end of the fourteen-day wedding celebration which Raguel had sworn to hold for his daughter, Tobiah went to him and said: "Please let me go, for I know that my father and mother do not believe they will ever see me again. So I beg you, father, let me go back to my father. I have already told you how I left him." ⁸ Raguel said to Tobiah: "Stay, my child, stay with me. I am sending messengers to your father Tobit, and they will give him news of you." ⁹ But Tobiah insisted, "No, I beg you to let me go back to my father."

¹⁰ Raguel then promptly handed over to Tobiah Sarah his wife, together with half of all his property: male and female slaves, oxen and sheep, asses and camels, clothing, money, and household goods. ¹¹ Bidding them farewell, he let them go. He embraced Tobiah and said to him: "Good-bye, my son. Have a safe journey. May the Lord of heaven grant prosperity to you and to your wife Sarah. And may I see children of yours before I die!" ¹² Then he kissed his daughter Sarah and said to her: "My daughter, honor your father-in-law and your mother-in-law, because from now on they are as much your parents as the ones who brought you into the world. Go in peace, my daughter; let me hear good reports about you as long as I live." Finally he said good-bye to them and sent them away.

¹³ Then Edna said to Tobiah: "My child and beloved kinsman, may the Lord bring you back safely, and may I live long enough to see children of you and of my daughter Sarah before I die. Before the Lord, I entrust my daughter to your care. Never cause her grief at any time in your life. Go in peace, my child. From now on I am your mother, and Sarah is your beloved. May all of us be prosperous all the days of our lives." She kissed them both and sent them away in peace.

¹⁴ When Tobiah left Raguel, he was full of happiness and joy, and he blessed the Lord of heaven and earth, the King of all, for making his journey so successful. Finally he said good-bye to Raguel and his wife Edna, and added, "May I honor you all the days of my life!"

10, 7: Gn 45, 26.

Homeward Journey

11 [1] Then they left and began their return journey. When they were near Kaserin, just before Nineveh, [2] Raphael said: "You know how we left your father. [3] Let us hurry on ahead of your wife to prepare the house while the rest of the party are still on the way." [4] So they both went on ahead and Raphael said to Tobiah, "Have the gall in your hand!" And the dog ran along behind them.

[5] Meanwhile, Anna sat watching the road by which her son was to come. [6] When she saw him coming, she exclaimed to his father, "Tobit, your son is coming, and the man who traveled with him!"

[7] Raphael said to Tobiah before he reached his father: "I am certain that his eyes will be opened. [8] Smear the fish gall on them. This medicine will make the cataracts shrink and peel off from his eyes; then your father will again be able to see the light of day."

Sight Restored

[9]* Then Anna ran up to her son, threw her arms around him, and said to him, "Now that I have seen you again, son, I am ready to die!" And she sobbed aloud. [10] Tobit got up and stumbled out through the courtyard gate. Tobiah went up to him [11] with the fish gall in his hand, and holding him firmly, blew into his eyes. "Courage, father," he said. [12] Next he smeared the medicine on his eyes, [13] and it made them smart. Then, beginning at the corners of Tobit's eyes, Tobiah used both hands to peel off the cataracts. When Tobit saw his son, he threw his arms around him [14] and wept. He exclaimed, "I can see you, son, the light of my eyes!" Then he said:

"Blessed be God,
   and praised be his great name,
   and blessed be all his holy angels.
May his holy name be praised
   throughout all the ages,
[15]* Because it was he who scourged me,
   and it is he who has had mercy on me.
Behold, I now see my son Tobiah!"

Then Tobit went back in, rejoicing and praising God with full voice. Tobiah told his father that his journey had been a success; that he had brought back the money; and that he had married Raguel's daughter Sarah, who would arrive shortly, for she was approaching the gate of Nineveh.

[16] Rejoicing and praising God, Tobit went out to the gate of Nineveh to meet his daughter-in-law. When the people of Nineveh saw him walking along briskly, with no one leading him by the hand, they were amazed. [17] Before them all Tobit proclaimed how God had mercifully restored sight to his eyes. When Tobit reached Sarah, the wife of his son Tobiah, he greeted her: "Welcome, my daughter! Blessed be your God for bringing you to us, daughter! Blessed are your father and your mother. Blessed is my son Tobiah, and blessed are you, daughter! Welcome to your home with blessing and joy. Come in, daughter!" That day there was joy for all the Jews who lived in Nineveh. [18] Ahiqar and his nephew Nadab also came to rejoice with Tobit. They celebrated Tobiah's wedding feast for seven happy days, and he received many gifts.

V: Raphael Reveals His Identity

Raphael's Wages

12 [1]† When the wedding celebration came to an end, Tobit called his son Tobiah and said to him, "Son, see to it that you give what is due to the man who made the journey with you; give him a bonus too." [2]* Tobiah said: "Father, how much shall I pay him? It would not hurt me at all to give him half of all the wealth he brought back with me. [3] He led me back safe and sound; he cured my wife; he brought the money back with me; and he cured you. How much of a bonus should I give him?" [4] Tobit answered, "It is only fair, son, that he should receive half of all that he brought back." [5] So Tobiah called Raphael and said, "Take as your wages half of all that you have brought back, and go in peace."

Exhortation

[6]† Raphael called the two men aside privately and said to them: "Thank God! Give him the praise and the glory. Before all the living, acknowledge the many good things he has done for you, by blessing and extolling his name in song. Before all men, honor and proclaim God's deeds, and do not be slack in praising him. [7] A king's secret it is prudent to keep, but the works of God are to be declared and made known. Praise them with due honor. Do good, and evil will not find its way to

---

12, 1–5: *Tobit* and *his son* generously agree to give Azariah far more than the wages agreed upon in Tb 5, 15–16.

12, 6–10: In the fashion of a wisdom teacher, *Raphael* gives the two men a short exhortation similar to the one Tobit gave his son in Tb 4, 3–19.

12, 6f: The Jews considered the duty of praising God their most esteemed privilege. Without praise of God, life was meaningless. Cf Is 38, 16–20.

11, 9: Gn 33, 4; 45, 14; 46, 29f; Lk 15, 20.

11, 15: Tb 13, 2; Dt 32, 39; 1 Sm 2, 6.

12, 2: Tb 5, 3.7.15f.

you. 8*† Prayer and fasting are good, but better than either is almsgiving accompanied by righteousness. A little with righteousness is better than abundance with wickedness. It is better to give alms than to store up gold; 9* for almsgiving saves one from death and expiates every sin. Those who regularly give alms shall enjoy a full life; 10 but those habitually guilty of sin are their own worst enemies.

Raphael's Identity

11 "I will now tell you the whole truth; I will conceal nothing at all from you. I have already said to you, 'A king's secret it is prudent to keep, but the works of God are to be made known with due honor.' 12*† I can now tell you that when you, Tobit, and Sarah prayed, it was I who presented and read the record of your prayer before the Glory of the Lord; and I did the same thing when you used to bury the dead. 13 When you did

not hesitate to get up and leave your dinner in order to go and bury the dead, 14† I was sent to put you to the test. At the same time, however, God commissioned me to heal you and your daughter-in-law Sarah. 15* I am Raphael, one of the seven angels who enter and serve before the Glory of the Lord."

16 Stricken with fear, the two men fell to the ground. 17 But Raphael said to them: "No need to fear; you are safe. Thank God now and forever. 18 As for me, when I came to you it was not out of any favor on my part, but because it was God's will. So continue to thank him every day; praise him with song. 19 Even though you watched me eat and drink, I did not really do so; what you were seeing was a vision. 20* So now get up from the ground and praise God. Behold, I am about to ascend to him who sent me; write down all these things that have happened to you." 21 When Raphael ascended, they rose to their feet and could no longer see him.

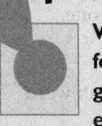

Hope for the Faithful!   **LIVE IT!**

When the Jews lived under the influence of Greek culture, there was a great need for hope. The story of Tobit and Tobias, whose names mean "goodness" and "God is good," was written to give hope to those who continue to be faithful to God, even in difficult times.

Tobit is the model of the good Israelite at all times and places. God's saving actions for him and his family symbolize God's actions toward Israel. In this spirit, before his death, Tobit sings a beautiful hymn in thanksgiving for God's goodness and with hope in the triumph of Jerusalem over its oppressors.

- Recognize the goodness of God in your life and the way in which you fail God.
- Take a moment to pray in Tobit's style. Praise God for the blessings in your life; ask forgiveness for the times you have failed God; give thanks for the times God has answered your prayers in a wiser way than what you had asked for. Pray not only for yourself but for all people, with hope for the triumph of God's love and peace over the egoism, hatred, and violence so common today.

▶ Tobit, chapter 13

†

12, 8: *Prayer . . . fasting . . . almsgiving . . . righteousness:* these, together with the proper attitude toward wealth, are treated in great detail by Christ our Lord in the Sermon on the Mount (Mt 6).

12, 12.15: *Raphael* is one of the seven specially designated intercessors who present man's prayers to God. Angelology was developing in this period. The names of two other angels are given in the Bible: Gabriel (Dn 8, 16; 9, 21; Lk 1, 19.26) and Michael (Dn 10, 13.21; 12, 1; Jude 9; Rv 12, 7).

12, 14: *I was sent . . . test:* God often sends trials to purify his faithful servants further. Cf Jb 1–2.

12, 8: Tb 4, 7–11; Sir 29,   12, 12: Jb 33, 23f; Acts 10, 4;
   8–13.   Rv 8, 3f.
12, 9: Dn 4, 24.   12, 15: Lk 1, 19; Rv 8, 2.
                            12, 20: Jgs 13, 20.

22 They kept thanking God and singing his praises; and they continued to acknowledge these marvelous deeds which he had done when the angel of God appeared to them.

VI: Tobit's Song of Praise

13 1*† Then Tobit composed this joyful prayer:

Blessed be God who lives forever,
> because his kingdom lasts for all ages.
2* For he scourges and then has mercy;
> he casts down to the depths of
> > the netherworld,
> and he brings up from the great abyss.
No one can escape his hand.

3 Praise him, you Israelites, before the Gentiles,
> for though he has scattered you among them,
4 he has shown you his greatness even there.
Exalt him before every living being,
> because he is the Lord our God,
> our Father and God forever.
5* He scourged you for your iniquities,
> but will again have mercy on you all.
He will gather you from all the Gentiles
> among whom you have been scattered.

6* When you turn back to him with all
> > your heart,
> to do what is right before him,
Then he will turn back to you,
> and no longer hide his face from you.

So now consider what he has done for you,
> and praise him with full voice.
Bless the Lord of righteousness,
> and exalt the King of the ages.

In the land of my exile I praise him,
> and show his power and majesty to a
> > sinful nation.
"Turn back, you sinners! do the right
> > before him:
perhaps he may look with favor upon you
and show you mercy.

7 "As for me, I exalt my God,
> and my spirit rejoices in the King
> > of heaven.

8 Let all men speak of his majesty,
> and sing his praises in Jerusalem."

9*† O Jerusalem, holy city,
> he scourged you for the works of
> > your hands,
> but will again pity the children of
> > the righteous.
10* Praise the Lord for his goodness,
> and bless the King of the ages,
> so that his tent may be rebuilt in you
> > with joy.
May he gladden within you all who
> were captives;
all who were ravaged may he cherish
> within you
for all generations to come.

11* A bright light will shine to all parts of
> the earth;
> many nations shall come to you from afar,
And the inhabitants of all the limits of
> the earth,
> drawn to you by the name of the Lord God,
Bearing in their hands their gifts for the King
> of heaven.
Every generation shall give joyful praise
> in you,
> and shall call you the chosen one,
through all ages forever.

12* Accursed are all who speak a harsh word
> against you;
> accursed are all who destroy you
> and pull down your walls,
And all who overthrow your towers
> and set fire to your homes;
> but forever blessed are all those who build
> you up.

13 Go, then, rejoice over the children of
> the righteous,
> who shall all be gathered together
> and shall bless the Lord of the ages.
14* Happy are those who love you,
> and happy those who rejoice in
> > your prosperity.

Happy are all the men who shall grieve
> over you,
> over all your chastisements,

13, 1–18: Tobit's hymn of praise (cf Ex 15, 1–18; Jdt 16, 1–17) is divided into two parts. The first part (vv 1–8) is a song of praise that echoes themes from the hymns and psalms of the kingdom; the second (vv 9–18) is addressed to Jerusalem in the style of the prophets who spoke of a new and ideal Jerusalem (Is 60); cf Rv 21.
13, 9: *Works of your hands:* idols.

13, 1: Tb 3, 11; 8, 5.15; 1 Chr 29, 10; Dn 3, 26.
13, 2: Tb 11, 15; 13, 9; Dt 32, 39; 1 Sm 2, 6; Wis 16, 13.
13, 5: Dt 30, 3; Neh 1, 9.
13, 6: Dt 30, 2.
13, 9: Tb 11, 15; Mi 7, 19; Rv 21.
13, 10: Is 44, 26.28; Am 9, 11; Zec 1, 16.
13, 11: Is 2, 3f; 9, 1; 49, 6; 60, 1; Mi 4, 2; Zec 8, 22.
13, 12: Bar 4, 31f.
13, 14: Ps 122, 6; Is 66, 10.

For they shall rejoice in you
    as they behold all your joy forever.

15 My spirit blesses the Lord, the great King;
16*   Jerusalem shall be rebuilt as his home
    forever.
  Happy for me if a remnant of my
    offspring survive
    to see your glory and to praise the King
    of heaven!

The gates of Jerusalem shall be built with
    sapphire and emerald,
  and all your walls with precious stones.
The towers of Jerusalem shall be built
    with gold,
  and their battlements with pure gold.
17 The streets of Jerusalem shall be paved
    with rubies and stones of Ophir;
18 The gates of Jerusalem shall sing hymns
    of gladness,
  and all her houses shall cry out, "Alleluia!"

"Blessed be God who has raised you up!
  may he be blessed for all ages!"
For in you they shall praise his holy
    name forever.

The end of Tobit's hymn of praise.

VII: Epilogue

Parting Advice

14 1 Tobit died peacefully at the age of a hundred and twelve, and received an honorable burial in Nineveh. 2 He was sixty-two years old when he lost his eyesight, and after he recovered it he lived in prosperity, giving alms and continually blessing God and praising the divine Majesty. 3* Just before he died, he called his son Tobiah and Tobiah's seven sons, and gave him this command: "Son, take your children 4*† and flee into Media, for I believe God's word which was spoken by Nahum against Nineveh. It shall all happen, and shall overtake Assyria and Nineveh; indeed,

whatever was said by Israel's prophets, whom God commissioned, shall occur. Not one of all the oracles shall remain unfulfilled, but everything shall take place in the time appointed for it. So it will be safer in Media than in Assyria or Babylon. For I know and believe that whatever God has spoken will be accomplished. It shall happen, and not a single word of the prophecies shall prove false.

"As for our kinsmen who dwell in Israel, they shall all be scattered and led away into exile from the Good Land. The entire country of Israel shall become desolate; even Samaria and Jerusalem shall become desolate! God's temple there shall be burnt to the ground and shall be desolate for a while. 5*† But God will again have mercy on them and bring them back to the land of Israel. They shall rebuild the temple, but it will not be like the first one, until the era when the appointed times shall be completed. Afterward all of them shall return from their exile, and they shall rebuild Jerusalem with splendor. In her the temple of God shall also be rebuilt; yes, it will be rebuilt for all generations to come, just as the prophets of Israel said of her. 6*† All the nations of the world shall be converted and shall offer God true worship; all shall abandon their idols which have deceitfully led them into error, 7* and shall bless the God of the ages in righteousness. Because all the Israelites who are to be saved in those days will truly be mindful of God, they shall be gathered together and go to Jerusalem; in security shall they dwell forever in the land of Abraham, which will be given over to them. Those who sincerely love God shall rejoice, but those who become guilty of sin shall completely disappear from the land.

9 "Now, children, I give you this command: serve God faithfully and do what is right before him; you must tell your children to do what is upright and to give alms, to be mindful of God and at all times to bless his name sincerely and with all their strength.

8 "Now, as for you, my son, depart from Nineveh; do not remain here. 10*† The day you bury your mother next to me, do not even stay overnight within the confines of the city. For I see that people here shamelessly commit all sorts of wickedness and treachery. Think, my son, of all that Nadab did to

---

† **14, 4f:** *Nahum:* one of the minor prophets, whose book contains oracles of doom against *Nineveh*. Here, in keeping with the period to which he assigns his story, the sacred author makes Tobit speak as if the punishment of *Nineveh*, the destruction of Jerusalem (587 B.C.), the exile from Judah and the return, would all take place in the future. The technique of using the facts of past history as seemingly future predictions, is a frequent device of apocalyptic writers. *The Good Land:* a favorite name for the promised land. Cf Dt 1, 35; 3, 25; 4, 21.22.
14, 5: *Until the era . . . completed:* a reference to the advent of messianic times, in which a new, more perfect temple was to be expected. Cf Heb 9, 1–14.
14, 6: Conversion of the Gentiles is also to come in the messianic era.
14, 10: *Nadab:* In the story of *Ahiqar,* the hero *Ahiqar,* chancel-

lor under the Assyrian kings Sennacherib and Esarhaddon, adopts his nephew *Nadab* and prepares him to become his successor. But *Nadab* treacherously plots to have his uncle put to death. *Ahiqar* hides in a friend's house, and is finally vindicated (came out again into the light) when *Nadab's* scheme is discovered. Thereupon *Nadab* is thrown into a dungeon where he dies (went into everlasting darkness). It was *Ahiqar's* almsgiving that delivered him from death; see note on Tb 2, 2.

13, 16: Tb 14, 5; Is 54, 11–13;
    62, 2; Rv 21, 10–21.
14, 3: Gn 47, 29f.
14, 4: Na 2, 2—3, 19.
14, 5: Neh 12, 27; Jer 31, 38.
14, 6: Tb 45, 14; Is 60, 1–4.
14, 7: Is 60, 21; Jer 32, 37;
    Ex 34, 28; 37, 25;
    39, 26.
14, 10: Tb 1, 21f.

Ahiqar, the very one who brought him up: Ahiqar went down alive into the earth! Yet God made Nadab's disgraceful crime rebound against him. Ahiqar came out again into the light, but Nadab went into the everlasting darkness, for he had tried to kill Ahiqar. Because Ahiqar had given alms to me, he escaped from the deadly trap Nadab had set for him. But Nadab himself fell into the deadly trap, and it destroyed him. [11] So, my children, note well what almsgiving does, and also what wickedness does—it kills! But now my spirit is about to leave me."

Death of Tobit and Tobiah

[12]* They placed him on his bed and he died; and he received an honorable burial. When Tobiah's mother died, he buried her next to his father. He then departed with his wife and children for Media, where he settled in Ecbatana with his father-in-law Raguel. [13] He took respectful care of his aging father-in-law and mother-in-law; and he buried them at Ecbatana in Media. Then he inherited Raguel's estate as well as that of his father Tobit. [14] He died at the venerable age of a hundred and seventeen. [15]† But before he died, he heard of the destruction of Nineveh and saw its effects. He witnessed the exile of the city's inhabitants when Cyaxares, king of Media, led them captive into Media. Tobiah praised God for all that he had done against the citizens of Nineveh and Assyria. Before dying he rejoiced over Nineveh's destruction, and he blessed the Lord God forever and ever. Amen.

14, 15: *Cyaxares:* Nabopolassar, king of Babylon, and *Cyaxares* conquered and destroyed *Nineveh* in 612 B.C.; see note on Tb 1, 15.

14, 12: Tb 4, 4.

Do you like to cheer for the underdog? If so, you are like most people. Whether in a law court, on a football field, or in politics, we get a thrill from seeing the high and mighty toppled by a courageous and determined underdog. This theme is evident in some of the most popular stories of the Old Testament: a group of Hebrew slaves escapes from Pharaoh's army; the teenage David topples the giant Goliath; the prophet Daniel escapes injury in the lions' den. Judith's story is another in which the little people —against all odds—somehow come out on top.

In-depth

As the Book of Judith opens, the mighty Assyrian army is on the march against Jerusalem. To block the advance, the citizens of the small town of Bethulia are asked by the high priest to resist the army's movement. With little hope of success but a great deal of courage, the Bethulians accept the challenge. When they are at the point of surrender, a childless widow named Judith steps forward. Putting all her trust in "the God of the lowly, the helper of the oppressed, the supporter of the weak, the protector of the forsaken, the savior of those without hope" (Jdt 9, 11), she bravely delivers her nation from certain defeat.

The story of Judith must have presented a challenge to the male-dominated world of the Israelites. As a childless widow, Judith would have had little social standing. Yet she succeeds where the king, the priests, and the leaders of the city fail. It is interesting that the name Judith is probably not even a proper name. It simply means "Jewish woman." In a sense, Judith stands for all the Jewish women of the past who have served God through their faith, courage, and decisive action.

Because of its many historical errors, the Book of Judith is clearly a fictional work. With remarkable storytelling flair, the author underlines one of the major elements of Hebrew faith: "O LORD, great are you and glorious, / wonderful in power and unsurpassable" (16, 13). This was the kind of faith that the underdog people of God needed as they faced the growing might of the Roman Empire.

At a Glance

I. Peril of the Jews (1, 1—7, 32).

II. Deliverance of the Jews (8, 1—14, 10).

III. Victory (14, 11—16, 25).

Quick Facts

Setting
a fictional book without a clear historical setting

Author
unknown, writing at the end of the second or the beginning of the first century B.C.

Themes
a woman of faith and courage, God's saving power

The Book of Judith

Judith

Chap. 10

I: Peril of the Jews

War against the Medes

1 ¹ It was the twelfth year of the reign of Nebuchadnezzar, king of the Assyrians in the great city of Nineveh. At that time Arphaxad ruled over the Medes in Ecbatana. ² Around this city he built a wall of blocks of stone, each three cubits in height and six in length. He made the wall seventy cubits high and fifty thick. ³ At the gates he raised towers of a hundred cubits, with a thickness of sixty cubits at the base. ⁴ The gateway he built to a height of seventy cubits, with an opening forty cubits wide for the passage of his chariot forces and the marshaling of his infantry. ⁵ Then King Nebuchadnezzar waged war against King Arphaxad in the vast plain, in the district of Ragae. ⁶† To him there rallied all the inhabitants of the mountain region, all who dwelt along the Euphrates, the Tigris, and the Hydaspes, and King Arioch of the Elamites, in the plain. Thus many nations came together to resist the people of Cheleoud.

Ultimatum to the West

⁷ Now Nebuchadnezzar, king of the Assyrians, sent messengers to all the inhabitants of Persia, and to all those who dwelt in the West: to the inhabitants of Cilicia and Damascus, Lebanon and Anti-Lebanon, to all who dwelt along the seacoast, ⁸ to the peoples of Carmel, Gilead, Upper Galilee, and the vast plain of Esdraelon, ⁹ to all those in Samaria and its cities, and west of the Jordan as far as Jerusalem, Bethany, Chelous, Kadesh, and the River of Egypt; to Tahpanhes, Raamses, all the land of Goshen, ¹⁰ Tanis, Memphis and beyond, and to all the inhabitants of Egypt as far as the borders of Ethiopia.

¹¹ But the inhabitants of all that land disregarded the summons of Nebuchadnezzar, king of the Assyrians, and would not go with him to the war. They were not afraid of him but regarded him as a lone individual opposed to them, and turned away his envoys empty-handed, in disgrace. ¹²† Then Nebuchadnezzar fell into a violent rage against all that land, and swore by his throne and his kingdom that he would avenge himself on all the territories of Cilicia and Damascus and Syria, and also destroy with his sword all the inhabitants of Moab, Ammon, the whole of Judea, and those living anywhere in Egypt as far as the borders of the two seas.

Defeat of Arphaxad

¹³ In the seventeenth year he proceeded with his army against King Arphaxad, and was victorious in his campaign. He routed the whole force of Arphax-

---

1, 6: *Cheleoud:* probably the Chaldeans are meant.
1, 12: *The two seas:* the ancient rulers in Mesopotamia often des-ignated the limits of their realm as extending from the Upper Sea (the Mediterranean) to the Lower Sea (the Persian Gulf).

ad, his entire cavalry and all his chariots, 14 and took possession of his cities. He pressed on to Ecbatana and took its towers, sacked its marketplaces, and turned its glory into shame. 15 Arphaxad himself he overtook in the mountains of Ragae, ran him through with spears, and utterly destroyed him. 16* Then he returned home with all his numerous, motley horde of warriors; and there he and his army relaxed and feasted for a hundred and twenty days.

Council of War against the West

2 1 In the eighteenth year, on the twenty-second day of the first month, there was a discussion in the palace of Nebuchadnezzar, king of the Assyrians, about taking revenge on the whole world, as he had threatened. 2 He summoned all his ministers and nobles, laid before them his secret plan, and urged the total destruction of those countries. 3 They decided to do away with all those who had refused to comply with the order he had issued.

4 When he had completed his plan, Nebuchadnezzar, king of the Assyrians, summoned Holofernes, general in chief of his forces, second to himself in command, and said to him: 5* "Thus says the great king, the lord of all the earth: Go forth from my presence, take with you men of proven valor, a hundred and twenty thousand infantry and twelve thousand cavalry, 6 and proceed against all the land of the West, because they did not comply with the order I issued. 7† Tell them to have earth and water ready, for I will come against them in my wrath; I will cover all the land with the feet of my soldiers, to whom I will deliver them as spoils. 8 Their slain shall fill their ravines and wadies, the swelling torrent shall be choked with their dead; 9 and I will deport them as exiles to the very ends of the earth.

10 "You go before me and take possession of all their territories for me. If they surrender to you, guard them for me till the day of their punishment. 11 As for those who resist, show them no quarter, but deliver them up to slaughter and plunder in each country you occupy. 12† For as I live, and by the strength of my kingdom, what I have spoken I will accomplish by my power. 13 Do not disobey a single one of the orders of your lord; fulfill them exactly as I have commanded you, and do it without delay."

Campaign of Holofernes

14 So Holofernes left the presence of his lord, and summoned all the princes, and the generals and officers of the Assyrian army. 15 He mustered a hundred and twenty thousand picked troops, as his lord had commanded, and twelve thousand mounted archers, 16 and grouped them into a complete combat force. 17 He took along a very large number of camels, asses, and mules for their baggage; innumerable sheep, cattle, and goats for their food supply; 18 abundant provisions for each man, and much gold and silver from the royal palace.

19 Then he and his whole army proceeded on their expedition in advance of King Nebuchadnezzar, to cover all the western region with their chariots and cavalry and regular infantry. 20* A huge, irregular force, too many to count, like locusts or the dust of the earth, went along with them.

21 After a three-day march from Nineveh, they reached the plain of Bectileth, and from Bectileth they next encamped near the mountains to the north of Upper Cilicia. 22 From there Holofernes took his whole force, the infantry, calvary, and chariots, and marched into the mountain region. 23† He devastated Put and Lud, and plundered all the Rassisites and the Ishmaelites on the border of the desert toward the south of Chaldea.

24 Then, following the Euphrates, he went through Mesopotamia, and battered down every fortified city along the Wadi Abron, until he reached the sea. 25 He seized the territory of Cilicia, and cut down everyone who resisted him. Then he proceeded to the southern borders of Japheth, toward Arabia. 26 He surrounded all the Midianites, burned their tents, and plundered their sheepfolds. 27 Descending to the plain of Damascus at the time of the wheat harvest, he set fire to all their fields, destroyed their flocks and herds, despoiled their cities, devastated their plains, and put all their youths to the sword.

28 The fear and dread of him fell upon all the inhabitants of the coastland, upon those in Sidon and Tyre, and those who dwelt in Sur and Ocina, and the inhabitants of Jamnia. Those in Azotus and Ascalon also feared him greatly.

Submission of the West

3 1 They therefore sent messengers to him to sue for peace in these words: 2 "We, the servants of

---

†
2, 7: *Earth and water:* in the Persian period, the offering of these to a conqueror was a symbolic gesture of unconditional surrender.

2, 12: *As I live:* in the Old Testament, an oath proper to divinity; cf Dt 32, 40. Nebuchadnezzar is making himself equal to God; see Jdt 6, 2. *By my power:* literally "by my hand." The hand of Nebuchadnezzar raised in opposition to God and to his people is the occasion for Judith's intervention by a woman's hand; cf Jdt 9, 9f; Is 10, 5–14.

2, 23: *Put and Lud:* the same as the "Put and Lud" mentioned in Ez 30, 5 as allies of Egypt, and in Ez 27, 10 as supplying mercenary soldiers to Tyre. Here they seem inserted to embellish the narrative with assonance and prophetic associations rather than to indicate definite localities.

*
1, 16: Est 1, 3f.   **2, 20:** Jgs 7, 12.
2, 5f: Est 3, 8f.

Nebuchadnezzar the great king, lie prostrate before you; do with us as you will. ³ Our dwellings and all our wheat fields, our flocks and herds, and all our encampments are at your disposal; make use of them as you please. ⁴ Our cities and their inhabitants are also at your service; come and deal with them as you see fit."

⁵ After the spokesmen had reached Holofernes and given him this message, ⁶ he went down with his army to the seacoast, and stationed garrisons in the fortified cities; from them he impressed picked troops as auxiliaries. ⁷ The people of these cities and all the inhabitants of the countryside received him with garlands and dancing to the sound of timbrels. ⁸* Nevertheless, he devastated their whole territory and cut down their sacred groves, for he had been commissioned to destroy all the gods of the earth, so that every nation might worship Nebuchadnezzar alone, and every people and tribe invoke him as a god. ⁹ At length Holofernes reached Esdraelon in the neighborhood of Dothan, the approach to the main ridge of the Judean mountains; ¹⁰† he set up his camp between Geba and Scythopolis, and stayed there a whole month to refurbish all the equipment of his army.

Israelite Defense

4 ¹ When the Israelites who dwelt in Judea heard of all that Holofernes, commander in chief of Nebuchadnezzar, king of the Assyrians, had done to the nations, and how he had despoiled all their temples and destroyed them, ² they were in extreme dread of him, and greatly alarmed for Jerusalem and the temple of the LORD, their God. ³† Now, they had lately returned from exile, and only recently had all the people of Judea been gathered together, and the vessels, the altar, and the temple been purified from profanation. ⁴ So they sent word to the whole region of Samaria, to Kona, Beth-horon, Belmain, and Jericho, to Choba and Aesora, and to the valley of Salem. ⁵ The people there posted guards on all the summits of the high mountains, fortified their villages, and since their fields had recently been harvested, stored up provisions in preparation for war.

⁶† Joakim, who was high priest in Jerusalem in those days, wrote to the inhabitants of Bethulia

[and Betomesthaim], which is on the way to Esdraelon, facing the plain near Dothan, ⁷ and instructed them to keep firm hold of the mountain passes, since these offered access to Judea. It would be easy to ward off the attacking forces, as the defile was only wide enough for two abreast. ⁸† The Israelites carried out the orders given them by Joakim, the high priest, and the senate of the whole people of Israel, which met in Jerusalem.

Prayer and Penance

⁹ All the men of Israel cried to God with great fervor and did penance— ¹⁰*† they, along with their wives, and children, and domestic animals. All their resident aliens, hired laborers, and slaves also girded themselves with sackcloth. ¹¹† And all the Israelite men, women, and children who lived in Jerusalem prostrated themselves in front of the temple building, with ashes strewn on their heads, displaying their sackcloth covering before the LORD. ¹²* The altar, too, they draped in sackcloth; and with one accord they cried out fervently to the God of Israel not to allow their children to be seized, their wives to be taken captive, the cities of their inheritance to be ruined, or the sanctuary to be profaned and mocked for the nations to gloat over.

¹³* The LORD heard their cry and had regard for their distress. For the people observed a fast of many days' duration throughout Judea, and before the sanctuary of the LORD Almighty in Jerusalem. ¹⁴ The high priest Joakim, and all the priests in attendance on the LORD who served his altar, were also girded with sackcloth as they offered the daily holocaust, the votive offerings, and the free-will offerings of the people. ¹⁵ With ashes upon their turbans, they cried to the LORD with all their strength to look with favor on the whole house of Israel.

Council against the Israelites

5 ¹ It was reported to Holofernes, commander in chief of the Assyrian army, that the Israelites were ready for battle, and had blocked the mountain passes, fortified the summits of all the higher peaks, and placed roadblocks in the plains. ² In great anger he summoned all the rulers of the Moabites, the generals of the Ammonites, and all the satraps of the seacoast ³ and said to them: "Now

---

3, 10: *Geba:* perhaps originally "Gelboe," the mountain range near the eastern end of which lay Scythopolis, the Greek name for ancient Beth-shean (Jos 17, 11).

4, 3: *Returned from exile . . . profanation:* these allusions are variously attributed—to the Persian period (538–323 B.C.), or even to a condition in the days of Antiochus Epiphanes (175–164 B.C.).

4, 6: *Joakim, who was high priest:* see Bar 1, 7 and the footnote on Bar 1, 8f; this name for a high priest cannot be used in dating the events in Judith.

4, 8: The organization of the Jewish nation as subject to a high priest and a senate, or council of elders, was proper to the Greek

period (after 323 B.C.), and is reflected in the coinage of John Hyrcanus (135–104 B.C.).

4, 10: *Domestic animals:* see note on Jon 3, 8.

4, 11: *Prostrated themselves in front of the temple building:* for a parallel to this ceremony of entreaty, see Jl 1, 13f; 2, 15ff, and the note on Jl 2, 17.

3, 8: Ex 34, 13. 4, 12: Est 4, 1f.
4, 10f: Jon 3, 7f. 4, 13: Est 4, 16.

tell me, you Canaanites, what sort of people is this that dwells in the mountains? Which cities do they inhabit? How large is their army? In what does their power and strength consist? Who has set himself up as their king and the leader of their army? 4 Why have they refused to come out to meet me along with all the other inhabitants of the West?"

Achior's Speech

5* Then Achior, the leader of all the Ammonites, said to him: "My lord, hear this account from your servant; I will tell you the truth about this people that lives near you [that inhabits this mountain region]; no lie shall escape your servant's lips.

6† "These people are descendants of the Chaldeans. 7* They formerly dwelt in Mesopotamia, for they did not wish to follow the gods of their forefathers who were born in the land of the Chaldeans. 8 Since they abandoned the way of their ancestors, and acknowledged with divine worship the God of heaven, their forefathers expelled them from the presence of their gods. So they fled to Mesopotamia and dwelt there a long time. 9* Their God bade them leave their abode and proceed to the land of Canaan. Here they settled, and grew very rich in gold, silver, and a great abundance of livestock. 10* Later, when famine had gripped the whole land of Canaan, they went down into Egypt. They stayed there as long as they found sustenance, and grew into such a great multitude that the number of their race could not be counted. 11* The king of Egypt, however, rose up against them, shrewdly forced them to labor at brickmaking, oppressed and enslaved them. 12 But they cried to their God, and he struck the land of Egypt with plagues for which there was no remedy. When the Egyptians expelled them, 13* God dried up the Red Sea before them, 14 and led them along the route to Sinai and Kadesh-barnea. First they drove out all the inhabitants of the desert; 15* then they settled in the land of the Amorites, destroyed all the Heshbonites by main force, crossed the Jordan, and took possession of the whole mountain region. 16* They expelled the Canaanites, the Perizzites, the Jebusites, the Shechemites, and all the Gergesites; and they lived in these mountains a long time.

17* "As long as the Israelites did not sin in the sight of their God, they prospered, for their God, who hates wickedness, was with them. 18* But when they deviated from the way he prescribed for them, they were ground down steadily, more and more, by frequent wars, and finally taken as captives into foreign lands. The temple of their God was razed to the ground, and their cities were occupied by their enemies. 19 But now that they have returned to their God, they have come back from the Dispersion wherein they were scattered, and have repossessed Jerusalem, where their sanctuary is, and have settled again in the mountain region which was unoccupied.

20* "So now, my lord and master, if these people are at fault, and are sinning against their God, and if we verify this offense of theirs, then we shall be able to go up and conquer them. 21 But if they are not a guilty nation, then your lordship should keep his distance; otherwise their LORD and God will shield them, and we shall become the laughingstock of the whole world."

22 Now when Achior had concluded his recommendation, all the people standing round about the tent murmured; and the officers of Holofernes and all the inhabitants of the seacoast and of Moab alike said he should be cut to pieces. 23 "We are not afraid of the Israelites," they said, "for they are a powerless people, incapable of a strong defense. 24* Let us therefore attack them; your great army, Lord Holofernes, will swallow them up."

Holofernes' Answer

6 1 When the noise of the crowd surrounding the council had subsided, Holofernes, commander in chief of the Assyrian army, said to Achior, in the presence of the whole throng of coastland peoples, of the Moabites, and of the Ammonite mercenaries: 2* "Who are you, Achior, to prophesy among us as you have done today, and to tell us not to fight against the Israelites because their God protects them? What god is there beside Nebuchadnezzar? He will send his force and destroy them from the face of the earth. Their God will not save them; 3* but we, the servants of Nebuchadnezzar, will strike them down as one man, for they will be unable to withstand the force of our cavalry. 4* We will overwhelm them with it, and the mountains shall be drunk with their blood, and their plains filled with their corpses. Not a trace of them shall survive our attack: they shall utterly perish, says King Nebuchadnezzar, lord of all the earth;

---

† **5, 6–9:** Achior outlines the early history of the Hebrews, whose forefather, Abraham, first lived in Ur of the Chaldeans (Gn 11, 28) and then migrated to Haran (Gn 11, 31) in Aram Naharaim (Gn 24, 10), which was called Mesopotamia by the Greeks. The gods of their forefathers were the pagan deities worshiped by Abraham's relatives (Jos 24, 2).

5, 5: Jdt 11, 9–19.
5, 7: Gn 11, 31.
5, 9: Gn 11, 31—12, 5.
5, 10: Gn 42, 1–5; 46, 1–7; Ex 1, 7.
5, 11f: Ex 5, 4–21; 7, 1–9.
5, 13f: Ex 14, 21f.29.
5, 15: Nm 21, 21–32; Jos 2, 10.
5, 16: Dt 7, 1.
5, 17f: Dt 28—30; Ps 106, 40–46; Is 59, 7.
5, 18: 2 Kgs 25.
5, 20f: Jdt 8, 18ff; 11, 10.
5, 24: Jdt 6, 2; 9, 7; 16, 2.
6, 2: Jdt 3, 8; 9, 7.
6, 3: Is 36, 18ff.
6, 4: Jdt 6, 17.

for he has spoken, and his words shall not remain unfulfilled. 5 As for you, Achior, you Ammonite mercenary, for saying these things in a moment of perversity you shall not see my face after today, until I have taken revenge on this race of people from Egypt. 6* Then at my return, the sword of my army or the spear of my servants will pierce your sides, and you shall fall among their slain. 7 My servants will now conduct you to the mountain region, and leave you at one of the towns along the ascent. 8 You shall not die till you are destroyed together with them. 9 If you still cherish the hope that they will not be taken, then there is no need for you to be downcast. I have spoken, and my words shall not prove false in any respect."

Achior in Bethulia

10 Then Holofernes ordered the servants who were standing by in his tent to seize Achior, conduct him to Bethulia, and hand him over to the Israelites. 11 So the servants took him in custody and brought him out of the camp into the plain. From there they led him into the mountain region till they reached the springs below Bethulia. 12 When the men of the city saw them, they seized their weapons and ran out of the city to the crest of the ridge; and all the slingers blocked the ascent of Holofernes' servants by hurling stones upon them. 13 So they took cover below the mountain, where they bound Achior and left him lying at the foot of the mountain; then they returned to their lord.

14 The Israelites came down to him from their city, loosed him, and brought him into Bethulia. They haled him before the rulers of the city, 15 who in those days were Uzziah, son of Micah of the tribe of Simeon, Chabris, son of Gothoniel, and Charmis, son of Melchiel. 16 They then convened all the elders of the city; and all their young men, as well as the women, gathered in haste at the place of assembly. They placed Achior in the center of the throng, and Uzziah questioned him about what had happened. 17 He replied by giving them an account of what was said in the council of Holofernes, and of all his own words among the Assyrian officers, and of all the boasting threats of Holofernes against the house of Israel. 18 At this the people fell prostrate and worshiped God; and they cried out: 19† "LORD, God of heaven, behold their arrogance! Have pity on the lowliness of our people, and look with favor this day on those

who are consecrated to you." 20 Then they reassured Achior and praised him highly. 21 Uzziah brought him from the assembly to his home, where he gave a banquet for the elders. That whole night they called upon the God of Israel for help.

Siege of Bethulia

7 1 The following day Holofernes ordered his whole army, and all the allied troops that had come to his support, to move against Bethulia, seize the mountain passes, and engage the Israelites in battle. 2 That same day all their fighting men went into action. Their forces numbered a hundred and seventy thousand infantry and twelve thousand horsemen, not counting the baggage train or the men who accompanied it on foot—a very great army. 3 They encamped at the spring in the valley near Bethulia, and spread out in breadth toward Dothan as far as Balbaim, and in length from Bethulia to Cyamon, which faces Esdraelon.

4 When the Israelites saw how many there were, they said to one another in great dismay: "Soon they will devour the whole country. Neither the high mountains nor the valleys and hills can support the mass of them." 5† Yet they all seized their weapons, lighted fires on their bastions, and kept watch throughout the night.

6 On the second day Holofernes led out all his cavalry in the sight of the Israelites who were in Bethulia. 7 He reconnoitered the approaches to their city and located their sources of water; these he seized, stationing armed detachments around them, while he himself returned to his troops.

8 All the commanders of the Edomites and all the leaders of the Ammonites, together with the generals of the seacoast, came to Holofernes and said: 9 "Sir, listen to what we have to say, that there may be no losses among your troops. 10* These Israelites do not rely on their spears, but on the height of the mountains where they dwell; it is not easy to reach the summit of their mountains. 11 Therefore, sir, do not attack them in regular formation; thus not a single one of your troops will fall. 12 Stay in your camp, and spare all your soldiers. Have some of your servants keep control of the source of water that flows out at the base of the mountain, 13* for that is where the inhabitants of Bethulia get their water. Then thirst will begin to carry them off, and they will surrender their city. Meanwhile, we and our men will go up to the summits of the nearby

---

6, 19: The Latin Vulgate (6, 15) has a longer form of this prayer: "Lord, God of heaven and earth, behold their arrogance; regard our lowliness and look with favor on your holy ones; show that you do not abandon those who trust in you, but that you humble those who trust in themselves and glory in their own strength."

7, 5: *Lighted fires on their bastions:* to serve as signals for alerting the neighboring towns. Reference to fire signals in time of siege is

made in the Lachish ostraca at the beginning of the sixth century B.C. *Kept watch throughout the night:* to prevent a surprise attack.

6, 6: Jdt 5, 22.   **7, 13:** Ex 5, 21.
7, 10: 1 Kgs 20, 23.28.

mountains, and encamp there to guard against anyone's leaving the city. 14 They and their wives and children will languish with hunger, and even before the sword strikes them they will be laid low in the streets of their city. 15 Thus you will render them dire punishment for their rebellion and their refusal to meet you peacefully."

16 Their words pleased Holofernes and all his ministers, and he ordered their proposal to be carried out. 17 Thereupon the Moabites moved camp, together with five thousand Assyrians. They encamped in the valley, and held the water supply and the springs of the Israelites. 18 The Edomites and the Ammonites went up and encamped in the mountain region opposite Dothan; and they sent some of their men to the south and to the east opposite Egrebel, near Chusi, which is on Wadi Mochmur. The rest of the Assyrian army was encamped in the plain, covering the whole countryside. Their enormous store of tents and equipment was spread out in profusion everywhere.

19* The Israelites cried to the LORD, their God, for they were disheartened, since all their enemies had them surrounded, and there was no way of slipping through their lines. 20 The whole Assyrian camp, infantry, chariots, and cavalry, kept them thus surrounded for thirty-four days. All the reservoirs of water failed the inhabitants of Bethulia, 21 and the cisterns ran dry, so that on no day did they have enough to drink, but their drinking water was rationed. 22 Their children fainted away, and the women and youths were consumed with thirst and were collapsing in the streets and gateways of the city, with no strength left in them.

23 All the people, therefore, including youths, women, and children, went in a crowd to Uzziah and the rulers of the city. They set up a great clamor and said before the elders: 24 "God judge between you and us! You have done us grave injustice in not making peace with the Assyrians. 25 There is no help for us now! Instead, God has sold us into their power by laying us prostrate before them in thirst and utter exhaustion. 26 Therefore, summon them and deliver the whole city as booty to the troops of Holofernes and to all his forces; 27 we would be better off to become their prey. We should indeed be made slaves, but at least we should live, and not have to behold our little ones dying before our eyes and our wives and children breathing out their souls. 28 We adjure you by heaven and earth, and by our God, the LORD of our forefathers, who is punishing us for our sins and those of our forefathers, to do as we have proposed, this very day."

29 All in the assembly with one accord broke into shrill wailing and loud cries to the LORD their God. 30 But Uzziah said to them, "Courage, my brothers! Let us wait five days more for the LORD our God, to show his mercy toward us; he will not utterly forsake us. 31 But if those days pass without help coming to us, I will do as you say." 32 Then he dispersed the men to their posts, and they returned to the walls and towers of the city; the women and children he sent to their homes. Throughout the city they were in great misery.

II: Deliverance of the Jews

Judith

8 ¹ † Now in those days Judith, daughter of Merari, son of Joseph, son of Oziel, son of Elkiah, son of Ananias, son of Gideon, son of Raphain, son of Ahitob, son of Elijah, son of Hilkiah, son of Eliab, son of Nathanael, son of Salamiel, son of Sarasadai, son of Simeon, son of Israel, heard of this. 2 Her husband, Manasseh, of her own tribe and clan, had died at the time of the barley harvest. 3 While he was in the field supervising those who bound the sheaves, he suffered sunstroke; and he died of this illness in Bethulia, his native city. He was buried with his forefathers in the field between Dothan and Balamon. 4 The widowed Judith remained three years and four months at home, 5† where she set up a tent for herself on the roof of her house. She put sackcloth about her loins and wore widow's weeds. 6* She fasted all the days of her widowhood, except sabbath eves and sabbaths, new moon eves and new moons, feastdays and holidays of the house of Israel. 7 She was beautifully formed and lovely to behold. Her husband, Manasseh, had left her gold and silver, servants and maids, livestock and fields, which she was maintaining. 8 No one had a bad word to say about her, for she was a very God-fearing woman.

Her Words to the Elders

9 When Judith, therefore, heard of the harsh words which the people, discouraged by their lack of water, had spoken against their ruler, and of all that Uzziah had said to them in reply, swearing that he would hand over the city to the Assyrians at the end of five days, 10 she sent the maid who was in charge of all her things to ask Uzziah, Chabris, and Charmis, the elders of the city, to visit her. 11 When

---

8, 1: *Salamiel, son of Sarasadai:* head of the tribe of Simeon during the wanderings of the Israelites in the desert (Nm 1, 6).

8, 5: *A tent:* erected by Judith on the roof of her house (v 5); it was here that the elders came to confer with her (v 11).

7, 19: Ps 106, 6.   8, 6: Lk 2, 37.

THE PRINCIPLE OF *KUJICHAGULIA*

"That man over there says that women need to be helped into carriages, and lifted over ditches, and to have the best place everywhere. Nobody ever helps me into carriages, or over mud puddles, or gives me any best place! And ain't I a woman?" (Sojourner Truth, 1851)

When people who are abused cower quietly in corners, injustice lives on. Bent heads, muffled voices, and terrified spirits invite wrongs to continue.

Judith was a biblical heroine who refused to let her role be determined by others. As a woman and a widow, she had little social standing in ancient Israel. Yet, she did not let this keep her from speaking out and challenging the community leaders to action.

Sojourner Truth was a modern hero who refused to keep quiet despite being mistreated and devalued. Her womanhood was slighted, and her personhood was trampled, yet she traveled America to tell all who would listen about the evils of slavery.

The Kwanzaa principle of *kujichagulia* (see "Kwanzaa as a Way of Life," Dt 10, 12–22), or self-determination, sometimes requires us to stand up and speak out. Silence can be compliance. Thank God for the gift of boldness of speech! It gives us the power to speak the truth even in the most oppressive situations.

Dear God, give me the boldness of Judith and Sojourner Truth to address the wrongs of this world. Amen.

▶ Jdt 8, 9–36

they came, she said to them: "Listen to me, you rulers of the people of Bethulia. What you said to the people today is not proper. When you promised to hand over the city to our enemies at the end of five days unless within that time the LORD comes to our aid, you interposed between God and yourselves this oath which you took. 12* Who are you, then, that you should have put God to the test this day, setting yourselves in the place of God in human affairs? 13 It is the LORD Almighty for whom you are laying down conditions; will you never understand anything? 14* You cannot plumb the depths of the human heart or grasp the workings of the human mind; how then can you fathom God, who has made all these things, discern his mind, and understand his plan?

"No, my brothers, do not anger the LORD our God. 15 For if he does not wish to come to our aid within the five days, he has it equally within his power to protect us at such time as he pleases, or to destroy us in the face of our enemies. 16 It is not for you to make the LORD our God give surety for his plans.

"God is not man that he should be moved
    by threats,
    nor human, that he may be given an ultimatum.

17 "So while we wait for the salvation that comes from him, let us call upon him to help us, and he will hear our cry if it is his good pleasure. 18* For there has not risen among us in recent generations, nor does there exist today, any tribe, or clan, or town, or city of ours that worships gods made by hands, as happened in former days. 19* It was for such conduct that our forefathers were handed over to the sword and to pillage, and fell with great destruction before our enemies. 20 But since we acknowledge no other god but the LORD, we hope that he will not disdain us or any of our people. 21 If

8, 12: Jb 38, 2; 40, 2.7f;
42, 3.
8, 14: Jb 41, 3; Prv 14, 10;

Wis 9, 13; Is 40, 13;
Rom 11, 33f; 1 Cor 2,
11

8, 18: Jdt 5, 20f; 11, 10.

8, 19: Pss 78, 56f; 106, 13f;
Jer 7, 16–20; 14, 7.

we are taken, all Judea will fall, our sanctuary will be plundered, and God will make us pay for its profanation with our life's blood. 22 For the slaughter of our kinsmen, for the taking of exiles from the land, and for the devastation of our inheritance, he will lay the guilt on our heads. Wherever we shall be enslaved among the nations, we shall be a mockery and a reproach in the eyes of our masters. 23 Our enslavement will not be turned to our benefit, but the LORD our God will maintain it to our disgrace.

24 "Therefore, my brothers, let us set an example for our kinsmen. Their lives depend on us, and the defense of the sanctuary, the temple, and the altar rests with us. 25* Besides all this, we should be grateful to the LORD our God, for putting us to the test, as he did our forefathers. 26 Recall how he dealt with Abraham, and how he tried Isaac, and all that happened to Jacob in Syrian Mesopotamia while he was tending the flocks of Laban, his mother's brother. 27* Not for vengeance did the LORD put them in the crucible to try their hearts, nor has he done so with us. It is by way of admonition that he chastises those who are close to him."

Uzziah's Response

28 Then Uzziah said to her: "All that you have said was spoken with good sense, and no one can gainsay your words. 29 Not today only is your wisdom made evident, but from your earliest years all the people have recognized your prudence, which corresponds to the worthy dispositions of your heart. 30 The people, however, were so tortured with thirst that they forced us to speak to them as we did, and to bind ourselves by an oath that we cannot break. 31 But now, God-fearing woman that you are, pray for us that the LORD may send rain to fill up our cisterns, lest we be weakened still further."

32 Then Judith said to them: "Listen to me! I will do something that will go down from generation to generation among the descendants of our race. 33 Stand at the gate tonight to let me pass through with my maid; and within the days you have specified before you will surrender the city to our enemies, the LORD will rescue Israel by my hand. 34 You must not inquire into what I am doing, for I will not tell you until my plan has been accomplished." 35 Uzziah and the rulers said to her, "Go in peace, and may the LORD God go before you to take vengeance upon our enemies!" 36 Then they withdrew from the tent and returned to their posts.

THE BODY PRAYER

To pray, Judith prostrated herself, which means she lay face down on the ground. This position demonstrates humility and surrender. Judith also wore ashes and sackcloth, additional symbols of repentance and sorrow.

You will see this prayer posture on Good Friday, when the priests lie down on the floor at the beginning of the service. It is a sign of reverence and humility as we remember in a special way Jesus' sacrifice on the cross. You will see priest and deacon candidates prostrate themselves during the ordination ceremony as a sign of humility and their dependence on God's strength to carry out their ministry—a sign not just for themselves but for the whole Christian community.

▶ Jdt 9, 1

The Prayer of Judith

9 1* Judith threw herself down prostrate, with ashes strewn upon her head, and wearing nothing over her sackcloth. While the incense was being offered in the temple of God in Jerusalem that evening, Judith prayed to the LORD with a loud voice: 2*† "LORD, God of my forefather Simeon! You put a sword into his hand to take revenge upon the foreigners who had immodestly loosened the maiden's girdle, shamefully exposed her thighs, and disgracefully violated her body. This they did, though you forbade it. 3† Therefore you had their rulers slaughtered; and you covered with their blood the bed in which they lay deceived, the same bed that had felt the shame of their own deceiving. You smote the slaves together with their princes,

---

9, 2: *The maiden:* Dinah, Jacob's daughter, who was violated by Shechem, the Hivite (Gn 34, 2).
9, 3: Because Shechem had deceived and violated Dinah, her brothers, Simeon and Levi, tricked Shechem and the men of his city into being circumcised, and then slew them while they were confined to bed from the circumcision; cf Gn 34, 13–29.

8, 25f: Gn 22, 1–12; 29,
22–30.
8, 27: Dt 4, 7.

9, 1: Ex 30, 7f; Ps 141, 2.
9, 2: Gn 34.

JDT

and the princes together with their servants. ⁴ Their wives you handed over to plunder, and their daughters to captivity; and all the spoils you divided among your favored sons, who burned with zeal for you, and in their abhorrence of the defilement of their kinswoman, called on you for help.

⁵* "O God, my God, hear me also, a widow. It is you who were the author of those events and of what preceded and followed them. The present, also, and the future you have planned. Whatever you devise comes into being; ⁶* the things you decide on come forward and say, 'Here we are!' All your ways are in readiness, and your judgment is made with foreknowledge.

⁷* "Here are the Assyrians, a vast force, priding themselves on horse and rider, boasting of the power of their infantry, trusting in shield and spear, bow and sling. They do not know that

8   " 'You, the LORD, crush warfare;
        Lord is your name.'

"Shatter their strength in your might, and crush their force in your wrath; for they have resolved to profane your sanctuary, to defile the tent where your glorious name resides, and to overthrow with iron the horns of your altar. ⁹* See their pride, and send forth your wrath upon their heads. Give me, a widow, the strong hand to execute my plan. ¹⁰ With the guile of my lips, smite the slave together with the ruler, the ruler together with his servant; crush their pride by the hand of a woman.

¹¹ "Your strength is not in numbers, nor does your power depend upon stalwart men; but you are the God of the lowly, the helper of the oppressed, the supporter of the weak, the protector of the forsaken, the savior of those without hope.

¹² "Please, please, God of my forefather, God of the heritage of Israel, LORD of heaven and earth, Creator of the waters, King of all you have created, hear my prayer! ¹³* Let my guileful speech bring wound and wale on those who have planned dire things against your covenant, your holy temple, Mount Zion, and the homes your children have inherited. ¹⁴ Let your whole nation and all the tribes know clearly that you are the God of all power and might, and that there is no other who protects the people of Israel but you alone."

Judith's Departure

10 ¹ As soon as Judith had thus concluded, and ceased her invocation to the God of Israel, ² she rose from the ground. She called her maid and they went down into the house, which she used only on sabbaths and feast days. ³* She took off the sackcloth she had on, laid aside the garments of her widowhood, washed her body with water, and anointed it with rich ointment. She arranged her hair and bound it with a fillet, and put on the festive attire she had worn while her husband, Manasseh, was living. ⁴* She chose sandals for her feet, and put on her anklets, bracelets, rings, earrings, and all her other jewelry. Thus she made herself very beautiful, to captivate the eyes of all the men who should see her.

⁵* She gave her maid a leather flask of wine and a cruse of oil. She filled a bag with roasted grain, fig cakes, bread and cheese; all these provisions she wrapped up and gave to the maid to carry.

⁶ Then they went out to the gate of the city of Bethulia and found Uzziah and the elders of the city, Chabris and Charmis, standing there. ⁷ When these men saw Judith transformed in looks and differently dressed, they were very much astounded at her beauty and said to her, ⁸ "May the God of our fathers bring you to favor, and make your undertaking a success, for the glory of the Israelites and the exaltation of Jerusalem."

Judith bowed down to God. Then she said to them, ⁹ "Order the gate of the city opened for me, that I may go to carry out the business we discussed." So they ordered the youths to open the gate for her as she requested. ¹⁰ When they did so, Judith and her maid went out. The men of the city kept her in view as she went down the mountain and crossed the valley; then they lost sight of her.

Judith Captured

¹¹ As Judith and her maid walked directly across the valley, they encountered the Assyrian outpost. ¹²† The men took her in custody and asked her, "To what people do you belong? Where do you come from, and where are you going?" She replied: "I am a daughter of the Hebrews, and I am fleeing from them, because they are about to be delivered up to you as prey. ¹³* I have come to see Holofernes, the general in chief of your forces, to give him a trustworthy report; I will show him the route by which he can ascend and take possession of the whole mountain district without a single one of his men suffering injury or loss of life."

¹⁴ When the men heard her words and gazed upon her face, which appeared wondrously beautiful to them, they said to her, ¹⁵ "By coming down

10, 12f: The deceitful means used by Judith against Holofernes, here and in Jdt 11, 5–19, are to be judged in the light of the moral concepts of Old Testament times; cf Gn 27, 1–25; 34, 13–29; 37, 32ff; Jos 2, 1–7; Jgs 4, 17–22.

9, 5: Is 44, 7.
9, 6: Jb 38, 35; Is 46, 9–13; Bar 3, 35.
9, 7f: Jdt 5, 23; 6, 2; 16, 2.
9, 9: Ps 33, 16.
9, 13: Jdt 10, 4; 11, 20.23; 16, 6.9.
10, 3: Jdt 8, 6ff.
10, 4: Jdt 9, 13.
10, 5: Jdt 12, 2.
10, 13: Jdt 11, 5f.

thus promptly to see our master, you have saved your life. Now go to his tent; some of our men will accompany you to present you to him. [16] When you stand before him, have no fear in your heart; give him the report you speak of, and he will treat you well." [17] So they detailed a hundred of their men as an escort for her and her maid, and these conducted them to the tent of Holofernes.

[18] When the news of her arrival spread among the tents, a crowd gathered in the camp. They came and stood around her as she waited outside the tent of Holofernes, while he was being informed about her. [19] They marveled at her beauty, regarding the Israelites with wonder because of her, and they said to one another, "Who can despise this people that has such women among them? It is not wise to leave one man of them alive, for if any were to be spared they could beguile the whole world."

Judith Meets Holofernes

[20] The guard of Holofernes and all his servants came out and ushered her into the tent. [21] Now Holofernes was reclining on his bed under a canopy with a netting of crimson and gold, emeralds and other precious stones. [22] When they announced her to him, he came out to the antechamber, preceded by silver lamps; [23] and when Holofernes and his servants beheld Judith, they all marveled at the beauty of her face. She threw herself down prostrate before him, but his servants raised her up.

11 [1] Then Holofernes said to her: "Take courage, lady; have no fear in your heart! Never have I harmed anyone who chose to serve Nebuchadnezzar, king of all the earth. [2] Nor would I have raised my spear against your people who dwell in the mountain region, had they not despised me and brought this upon themselves. [3] But now tell me why you fled from them and came to us. In any case, you have come to safety. Take courage! Your life is spared tonight and for the future. [4] No one at all will harm you. Rather, you will be well treated, as are all the servants of my lord, King Nebuchadnezzar."

[5]* Judith answered him: "Listen to the words of your servant, and let your handmaid speak in your presence! I will tell no lie to my lord this night, [6] and if you follow out the words of your handmaid, God will give you complete success, and my lord will not fail in any of his undertakings. [7]* By the life of Nebuchadnezzar, king of all the earth, and by the power of him who has sent you to set all creatures aright! not only do men serve him

through you; but even the wild beasts and the cattle and the birds of the air, because of your strength, will live for Nebuchadnezzar and his whole house. [8] Indeed, we have heard of your wisdom and sagacity, and all the world is aware that throughout the kingdom you alone are competent, rich in experience, and distinguished in military strategy.

[9]* "As for Achior's speech in your council, we have heard of it. When the men of Bethulia spared him, he told them all he had said to you. [10]* So then, my lord and master, do not disregard his word, but bear it in mind, for it is true. For our people are not punished, nor does the sword prevail against them, except when they sin against their God. [11] But now their guilt has caught up with them by which they bring the wrath of their God upon them whenever they do wrong; so that my lord will not be repulsed and fail, but death will overtake them. [12] Since their food gave out and all their water ran low, they decided to kill their animals, and determined to consume all the things which God in his laws forbade them to eat. [13] They decreed that they would use up the first fruits of grain and the tithes of wine and oil which they had sanctified and reserved for the priests who minister in the presence of our God in Jerusalem: things which no layman should even touch with his hands. [14] They have sent messengers to Jerusalem to bring back to them authorization from the council of the elders; for the inhabitants there have also done these things. [15] On the very day when the response reaches them and they act upon it, they will be handed over to you for destruction.

[16] "As soon as I, your handmaid, learned all this, I fled from them. God has sent me to perform with you such deeds that people throughout the world will be astonished on hearing of them. [17] Your handmaid is, indeed, a God-fearing woman, serving the God of heaven night and day. Now I will remain with you, my lord; but each night your handmaid will go out to the ravine and pray to God. He will tell me when the Israelites have committed their crimes. [18] Then I will come and let you know, so that you may go out with your whole force, and not one of them will be able to withstand you. [19] I will lead you through Judea, till you come to Jerusalem, and there I will set up your judgment seat. You will drive them like sheep that have no shepherd, and not even a dog will growl at you. This was told me, and announced to me in advance, and I in turn have been sent to tell you."

[20]* Her words pleased Holofernes and all his servants; they marveled at her wisdom and exclaimed, [21] "No other woman from one end of the world to

11, 5f: Jdt 10, 13.   **11, 7:** Jer 27, 6; Bar 3, 16f; Dn 2, 38.

11, 9f: Jdt 5, 5.   **11, 20:** Jdt 9, 13.
11, 10: Jdt 5, 21; 8, 18.

the other looks so beautiful and speaks so wisely!" 22 Then Holofernes said to her: "God has done well in sending you ahead of your people, to bring victory to our arms, and destruction to those who have despised my lord. 23* You are fair to behold, and your words are well spoken. If you do as you have said, your God will be my God; you shall dwell in the palace of King Nebuchadnezzar, and shall be renowned throughout the earth."

Judith's Conduct

12 1 Then he ordered them to lead her into the room where his silverware was kept, and bade them set a table for her with his own delicacies to eat and his own wine to drink. 2* But Judith said, "I will not partake of them, lest it be an occasion of sin; but I shall be amply supplied from the things I brought with me." 3 Holofernes asked her: "But if your provisions give out, where shall we get more of the same to provide for you? None of your people are with us." 4 Judith answered him, "As surely as you, my lord, live, your handmaid will not use up her supplies till the LORD accomplishes by my hand what he has determined."

5 Then the servants of Holofernes led her into the tent, where she slept till midnight. In the night watch just before dawn, she rose 6 and sent this message to Holofernes, "Give orders, my lord, to let your handmaid go out for prayer." 7 So Holofernes ordered his bodyguard not to hinder her. Thus she stayed in the camp three days. Each night she went out to the ravine of Bethulia, where she washed herself at the spring of the camp. 8 After bathing, she besought the LORD, the God of Israel, to direct her way for the triumph of his people. 9 Then she returned purified to the tent, and remained there until her food was brought to her toward evening.

Holofernes' Banquet

10† On the fourth day Holofernes gave a banquet for his servants alone, to which he did not invite any of the officers. 11 And he said to Bagoas, the eunuch in charge of his household: "Go and persuade this Hebrew woman in your care to come and to eat and drink with us. 12 It would be a disgrace for us to have such a woman with us without enjoying her company. If we do not entice her, she will laugh us to scorn."

13 So Bagoas left the presence of Holofernes, and came to Judith and said, "So fair a maiden should not be reluctant to come to my lord to be honored by him, to enjoy drinking wine with us, and to be like one of the Assyrian women who live in the palace of Nebuchadnezzar." 14 She replied, "Who am I to refuse my lord? Whatever is pleasing to him I will promptly do. This will be a joy for me till the day of my death."

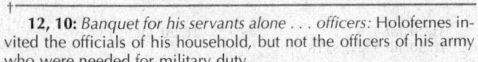

Dead Drunk!

Have you ever wondered why people get drunk? Why would anyone want to drink enough alcohol to pass out? Getting drunk has lots of negative consequences, and getting very drunk can even be fatal.

In the Book of Judith, chapter 13, Judith takes advantage of Holofernes' drunkenness to kill him. She gives the term *dead drunk* a whole new meaning. If you do not believe that getting drunk can destroy your life, then think again. It doesn't take a widow with a sword to help drunkenness destroy your life.

▶ Jdt 12, 15—13, 10

---

† **12, 10:** *Banquet for his servants alone . . . officers:* Holofernes invited the officials of his household, but not the officers of his army who were needed for military duty.

* **11, 23:** Jdt 9, 13.   **12, 2:** Jdt 10, 5; Dn 1, 8.

15 Thereupon she proceeded to put on her festive garments and all her feminine adornments. Meanwhile her maid went ahead and spread out on the ground for her in front of Holofernes the fleece Bagoas had furnished for her daily use in reclining at her dinner. 16 Then Judith came in and reclined on it. The heart of Holofernes was in rapture over her, and his spirit was shaken. He was burning with the desire to possess her, for he had been biding his time to seduce her from the day he saw her. 17 Holofernes said to her, "Drink and be merry with us!" 18 Judith replied, "I will gladly drink, my lord, for at no time since I was born have I ever enjoyed life as much as I do today." 19 She then took the things her maid had prepared, and ate and drank in his presence. 20 Holofernes, charmed by her, drank a great quantity of wine, more than he had ever drunk on one single day in his life.

13 1 When it grew late, his servants quickly withdrew. Bagoas closed the tent from the outside and excluded the attendants from their master's presence. They went off to their beds, for they were all tired from the prolonged banquet. 2 Judith was left alone in the tent with Holofernes, who lay prostrate on his bed, for he was sodden with wine. 3 She had ordered her maid to stand outside the bedroom and wait, as on the other days, for her to come out; she said she would be going out for her prayer. To Bagoas she had said this also.

Beheading of Holofernes

4 When all had departed, and no one, small or great, was left in the bedroom, Judith stood by Holofernes' bed and said within herself: "O LORD, God of all might, in this hour look graciously on my undertaking for the exaltation of Jerusalem; 5 now is the time for aiding your heritage and for carrying out my design to shatter the enemies who have risen against us." 6 She went to the bedpost near the head of Holofernes, and taking his sword from it, 7 drew close to the bed, grasped the hair of his head, and said, "Strengthen me this day, O God of Israel!" 8* Then with all her might she struck him twice in the neck and cut off his head. 9 She rolled his body off the bed and took the canopy from its supports. Soon afterward, she came out and handed over the head of Holofernes to her maid, 10 who put it into her food pouch; and the two went off together as they were accustomed to do for prayer.

The Return to Bethulia

They passed through the camp, and skirting the ravine, reached Bethulia on the mountain. As they

did you KNOW?

Is God a Fan of Violence?

Is it hard to believe that God strengthened Judith to cut off Holofernes' head (Jdt 13, 7–8)? Or that God was angry at Saul for not destroying Agag and his possessions (1 Sm 15, 18–19)? Or that Jephthah had to sacrifice his daughter because of a vow he had made (Jdg 11, 29–40)? The violence portrayed in the Old Testament is often horrifying, especially when the Old Testament authors view it as part of God's will.

In the ancient world, tribes and nations viewed their gods as the leaders of their armies. The Hebrews were no exception. One of God's oldest titles is "LORD, God of hosts" (Ps 89, 9; Is 6, 3); the image is of an almighty warrior who fought on Israel's side (see Ex 15, 3; 1 Sm 14, 23). The enemies of Israel were seen as God's enemies, and their destruction as God's will. The military victories of Joshua, Saul, and David were understood as proof of heaven's blessing on the nation.

Later in history, as the Israelites experienced one agonizing defeat after another and the prophets challenged them to consider God's love for all nations, a new understanding of God's will began to develop in certain Jewish circles. Later prophets spoke of beating "swords into plowshares" (Is 2, 4), of making "a covenant of peace" (Ez 37, 26), of seeking "to do the right and to love goodness, / and to walk humbly with your God" (Mi 6, 8). From their own painful history, the Chosen People started to see that war and violence always meant unspeakable suffering for many, and they began to question whether holy war was part of God's will.

▶ Jdt 13, 1–10

approached its gates, 11 Judith shouted to the guards from a distance: "Open! Open the gate! God, our

J
D
T

God, is with us. Once more he has made manifest his strength in Israel and his power against our enemies; he has done it this very day." [12] When the citizens heard her voice, they quickly descended to their city gate and summoned the city elders. [13] All the people, from the least to the greatest, hurriedly assembled, for her return seemed unbelievable. They opened the gate and welcomed the two women. They made a fire for light; and when they gathered around the two, [14] Judith urged them with a loud voice: "Praise God, praise him! Praise God, who has not withdrawn his mercy from the house of Israel, but has shattered our enemies by my hand this very night." [15]* Then she took the head out of the pouch, showed it to them, and said: "Here is the head of Holofernes, general in charge of the Assyrian army, and here is the canopy under which he lay in his drunkenness. The LORD struck him down by the hand of a woman. [16] As the LORD lives, who has protected me in the path I have followed, I swear that it was my face that seduced Holofernes to his ruin, and that he did not sin with me to my defilement or disgrace."

[17] All the people were greatly astonished. They bowed down and worshiped God, saying with one accord, "Blessed are you, our God, who today have brought to nought the enemies of your people." [18]* Then Uzziah said to her: "Blessed are you, daughter, by the Most High God, above all the women on earth; and blessed be the LORD God, the creator of heaven and earth, who guided your blow at the head of the chief of our enemies. [19] Your deed of hope will never be forgotten by those who tell of the might of God. [20] May God make this redound to your everlasting honor, rewarding you with blessings, because you risked your life when your people were being oppressed, and you averted our disaster, walking uprightly before our God." And all the people answered, "Amen! Amen!"

Judith's Counsel

14 [1] Then Judith said to them: "Listen to me, my brothers. Take this head and hang it on the parapet of your wall. [2] At daybreak, when the sun rises on the earth, let each of you seize his weapons, and let all the able-bodied men rush out of the city under command of a captain, as if about to go down into the plain against the advance guard of the Assyrians, but without going down. [3] They will seize their armor and hurry to their camp to awaken the generals of the Assyrian army. When they run to the tent of Holofernes and do not find him, panic will seize them, and they will flee before

you. [4] Then you and all the other inhabitants of the whole territory of Israel will pursue them and strike them down in their tracks. [5] But before doing this, summon for me Achior the Ammonite, that he may see and recognize the one who despised the house of Israel and sent him here to meet his death."

Achior Summoned

[6]† So they called Achior from the house of Uzziah. When he came and saw the head of Holofernes in the hand of one of the men in the assembly of the people, he fell forward in a faint. [7] Then, after they lifted him up, he threw himself at the feet of Judith in homage, saying: "Blessed are you in every tent of Judah; and in every foreign nation, all who hear of you will be struck with terror. [8] But now, tell me all that you did during these days." So Judith told him, in the presence of the people, all that she had been doing from the day she left till the time she began speaking to them. [9] When she finished her account, the people cheered loudly, and their city resounded with shouts of joy. [10] Now Achior, seeing all that the God of Israel had done, believed firmly in him. He had the flesh of his foreskin circumcised, and he has been united with the house of Israel to the present day.

III: Victory

Consternation in the Camp

[11] At daybreak they hung the head of Holofernes on the wall. Then all the Israelite men took up their arms and went to the slopes of the mountain. [12] When the Assyrians saw them, they notified their captains; these, in turn, went to the generals and division leaders and all their other commanders. [13] They came to the tent of Holofernes and said to the one in charge of all his things, "Waken our master, for the slaves have dared come down to give us battle, to their utter destruction." [14] Bagoas went in, and knocked at the entry of the tent, presuming that he was sleeping with Judith. [15] As no one answered, he parted the curtains, entered the bedroom, and found him lying on the floor, a headless corpse. [16] He broke into a loud clamor of weeping, groaning, and howling, and rent his garments. [17] Then he entered the tent where Judith had her quarters; and, not finding her, he rushed out to the troops and cried: [18]* "The slaves have duped us! A single Hebrew woman has brought disgrace on the house of King Nebuchadnezzar. Here is Holofernes headless on the ground!"

† **14, 6–10:** In recognizing the head of Holofernes, whom he had known personally, Achior was so overcome with the evidence of the Lord's power exerted through a woman that he believed in the God of Israel.

13, 15: Jdt 14, 18.
13, 18: Jgs 5, 24; Lk 1, 28.42.
14, 18: Jdt 13, 15; 16, 5–9; Jgs 9, 54.

[19] When the commanders of the Assyrian army heard these words, they rent their tunics and were seized with consternation. Loud screaming and howling arose in the camp.

15 [1] On hearing what had happened, those still in their tents were amazed, [2] and overcome with fear and trembling. No one kept ranks any longer; they scattered in all directions, and fled along every road, both through the valley and in the mountains. [3] Those also who were stationed in the mountain district around Bethulia took to flight. Then all the Israelite warriors overwhelmed them.

Pursuit

[4] Uzziah sent messengers to Betomasthaim, to Choba and Kona, and to the whole country of Israel to report what had happened, that all might fall upon the enemy and destroy them. [5] On hearing this, all the Israelites, with one accord, attacked them and cut them down as far as Choba. Even those from Jerusalem and the rest of the mountain region took part in this, for they too had been notified of the happenings in the camp of their enemies. The Gileadites and the Galileans struck the enemy's flanks with great slaughter, even beyond Damascus and its territory. [6] The remaining inhabitants of Bethulia swept down on the camp of the Assyrians, plundered it, and acquired great riches. [7]* The Israelites who returned from the slaughter took possession of what was left, till the towns and villages in the mountains and on the plain were crammed with the enormous quantity of booty they had seized.

[8]* The high priest Joakim and the elders of the Israelites, who dwelt in Jerusalem, came to see for themselves the good things that the LORD had done for Israel, and to meet and congratulate Judith. [9]† When they had visited her, all with one accord blessed her, saying:

"You are the glory of Jerusalem,
    the surpassing joy of Israel;
    you are the splendid boast of our people.
[10]   With your own hand you have done all this;
    you have done good to Israel,
    and God is pleased with what you
        have wrought.
May you be blessed by the LORD Almighty
    forever and ever!"

And all the people answered, "Amen!"

[11] For thirty days the whole populace plundered the camp, giving Judith the tent of Holofernes, with all his silver, his couches, his dishes, and all his furniture, which she accepted. She harnessed her mules, hitched her wagons to them, and loaded these things on them.

[12]* All the women of Israel gathered to see her; and they blessed her and performed a dance in her honor. She took branches in her hands and distributed them to the women around her, [13] and she and the other women crowned themselves with garlands of olive leaves. At the head of all the people, she led the women in the dance, while the men of Israel followed in their armor, wearing garlands and singing hymns.

Hymn of Praise

[14] Judith led all Israel in this song of thanksgiving, and the people swelled this hymn of praise:

16 [1]* "Strike up the instruments,
        a song to my God with timbrels,
    chant to the LORD with cymbals;
    Sing to him a new song,
        exalt and acclaim his name.
[2]*   For the LORD is God; he crushes warfare,
        and sets his encampment among
            his people;
    he snatched me from the hands of my
        persecutors.

Judith Leads the Prayer-Song

In the Book of Judith, chapter 16, Judith sings praises to God and leads the people in a holy celebration after victory over the enemy.

Notice the similarity to Miriam's song (Exodus, chapter 15), Deborah's song (Judges, chapter 5), and even Tobit's song (Tobit, chapter 13).

Singing, dancing, and retelling special stories go hand in hand with praising God.

▸ Jdt 16, 1–20

J
D
T

15, 9: *You are the glory of Jerusalem, the surpassing joy of Israel; you are the splendid boast of our people:* these words are used in the liturgy of the Church in regard to the Blessed Virgin Mary.

15, 7: Est 9, 5.16.
15, 8: Est 9, 10.
15, 12: Ex 15, 20f; Jgs 11, 34;
    1 Sm 18, 6; Jer 31, 4.13.
16, 1: Pss 81, 2f; 135, 1ff;
    149, 1ff.
16, 2: Jdt 5, 23; 6, 2; 9, 7f;
    Ex 15, 3; Ps 46, 10.

3 "The Assyrian came from the mountains of
the north,
with the myriads of his forces he came;
Their numbers blocked the torrents, their
horses covered the hills.

4 He threatened to burn my land,
put my youths to the sword,
Dash my babes to the ground,
make my children a prey,
and seize my virgins as spoil.

5* "But the LORD Almighty thwarted them,
by a woman's hand he confounded them.

6* Not by youths was their mighty one
struck down,
nor did titans bring him low,
nor huge giants attack him;
But Judith, the daughter of Merari,
by the beauty of her countenance
disabled him.

7 She took off her widow's garb
to raise up the afflicted in Israel.
She anointed her face with fragrant oil;

8 with a fillet she fastened her tresses
and put on a linen robe to beguile him.

9* Her sandals caught his eyes,
and her beauty captivated his mind.
The sword cut through his neck.

10 "The Persians were dismayed at her daring,
the Medes appalled at her boldness.

11 When my lowly ones shouted, they
were terrified;
when my weaklings cried out,
they trembled;
at the sound of their war cry, they took
to flight.

12 The sons of slave girls pierced them through;
the supposed sons of rebel mothers cut
them down;
they perished before the ranks of
my LORD.

13* "A new hymn I will sing to my God.
O LORD, great are you and glorious,
wonderful in power and unsurpassable.

14* Let your every creature serve you;
for you spoke, and they were made,
You sent forth your spirit, and they
were created;
no one can resist your word.

15* The mountains to their bases, and the seas,
are shaken;
the rocks, like wax, melt before your
glance.

"But to those who fear you,
you are very merciful.

16* Though the sweet odor of every sacrifice is
a trifle,
and the fat of all holocausts but little in
your sight,
one who fears the LORD is forever great.

17*† "Woe to the nations that rise against
my people!
The LORD Almighty will requite them;
in the day of judgment he will
punish them:
He will send fire and worms into their flesh,
and they shall burn and suffer forever."

Thanksgiving

18 The people then went to Jerusalem to worship
God; when they were purified, they offered their
holocausts, free-will offerings, and gifts. 19* Judith
dedicated, as a votive offering to God, all the things
of Holofernes that the people had given her, as well
as the canopy that she herself had taken from his
bedroom. 20 For three months the people continued their celebration in Jerusalem before the sanctuary, and Judith remained with them.

Judith's Renown

21 When those days were over, each one returned
to his inheritance. Judith went back to Bethulia and
remained on her estate. For the rest of her life she
was renowned throughout the land. 22 Many
wished to marry her, but she gave herself to no man
all the days of her life from the time of the death
and burial of her husband, Manasseh. 23* She lived
to be very old in the house of her husband, reaching the advanced age of a hundred and five. She
died in Bethulia, where they buried her in the tomb
of her husband, Manasseh; 24 and the house of Israel mourned her for seven days. Before she died,
she distributed her goods to the relatives of her husband, Manasseh, and to her own relatives; and to
the maid she gave her freedom.

25*† During the life of Judith and for a long time
after her death, no one again disturbed the Israelites.

---

†
16, 17: *Fire and worms into their flesh:* see footnote on Is 66, 24.
16, 25: The Vulgate adds: "The feast day of this victory was adopted by the Hebrews into the calendar of their holy days, and has been
celebrated by the Jews from that time to the present." However, there
is no other evidence of such a festivity; and it is the ancient feast of
Passover to which the narrative is especially suited.

*
16, 5: Jdt 14, 8.
16, 6: Jdt 9, 13.
16, 9: Jdt 9, 13.
16, 13: Ps 144, 9.
16, 14: Pss 33, 9; 104, 30;
148, 5.
16, 15: Jgs 5, 5; Ps 97, 5.
16, 16: Ps 86, 11; Sir 34,
13–17.
16, 17: Is 66, 24.
16, 19: Nm 31, 48–54; Dt 13,
13–18; Jos 6, 18f.
16, 23: Gn 23, 19; 49, 29–32.
16, 25: Jgs 3, 11.30; 5, 31; 8, 28.

Most of us cannot understand what would possess a group of people to plot the complete destruction of another group of people. Yet, in our own time, ethnic groups have been targeted for extinction through wars, concentration camps, and death squads. The Book of Esther is the story of a genocidal plot against a Jewish population and how that plot was prevented by Mordecai and his courageous cousin Esther.

In-depth

In the five centuries before Jesus, many of the Jewish people who were uprooted from their homeland had to be on the lookout for their safety. Several of the late Old Testament books—Sirach, Tobit, and Daniel—reflect the challenges that these emigrant Jews had to face.

The fictional story of Queen Esther belongs to this group. Like Joseph in Egypt, Esther rose to a position of power in a foreign government. When a plot was hatched to destroy the Jews, she used her influence with the king of Persia to save her people. Each year, Esther's victory is celebrated in the Jewish feast of Purim (Est 9, 18–32)—the feast of little people who have triumphed over larger forces.

Like Daniel, the Book of Esther has come down to us in two versions: the Hebrew and the Greek. The difference in style between these two versions is obvious:

- The shorter Hebrew text is clearly fictional and does not even mention God's name. The Greek text, a later reworking of the Hebrew, adds sections to bring out the religious dimension of the story and to make the book appear more historical.
- The Hebrew version emphasizes the human actors; the Greek version, the divine Actor. The two versions stress different aspects of the same truth: God is the savior of the Chosen People (Greek) but works through human beings to achieve that goal (Hebrew).

In the present translation, the portions preceded by the letters A through F indicate the underlying Greek additions referred to above. The regular chapter numbers apply to the Hebrew text. Despite the confusing numbering, the book reads as a unified story; it's full of action and has a happy ending. What is more, it challenges us to recognize in our hatred of others the seeds of unthinkable destruction.

At a Glance

I. **Prologue (A, 1–17).**

II. **Elevation of Esther (1, 1—2, 23).**

III. **Haman's Plot Against the Jews (3, 1–13; B, 1–7; 3, 14—4, 8; B, 8; 4, 9–16; C, 1—D, 16; 5, 1–14).**

IV. **Vindication of the Jews (6, 1—8, 12; E, 1–24; 8, 13—10, 3).**

V. **Epilogue (F, 1–10).**

Quick Facts

Setting
Persia after the Babylonian Exile

Authors
Hebrew version. unknown, probably writing in the late fourth century B.C.
Greek version. unknown, writing about two centuries later

Themes
God's love for the little ones, the origin of the feast of Purim

Of Note
Catholic Bibles include the Greek version of Esther, inserted as additions A to F.

The Book of Esther

Esther

Chap. D

I: Prologue

Dream of Mordecai

A ¹*† In the second year of the reign of the great King Ahasuerus, on the first day of Nisan, Mordecai, son of Jair, son of Shimei, son of Kish, of the tribe of Benjamin, had a dream. ² He was a Jew residing in the city of Susa, a prominent man who served at the king's court, ³* and one of the captives whom Nebuchadnezzar, king of Babylon, had taken from Jerusalem with Jeconiah, king of Judah.

⁴*† This was his dream. There was noise and tumult, thunder and earthquake—confusion upon the earth. ⁵ Two great dragons came on, both poised for combat. They uttered a mighty cry, ⁶ and at their cry every nation prepared for war, to fight against the race of the just. ⁷ It was a dark and gloomy day. Tribulation and distress, evil and great confusion, lay upon the earth. ⁸ The whole race of the just were dismayed with fear of the evils to come upon them, and were at the point of destruction. ⁹* Then they cried out to God, and as they cried, there appeared to come forth a great river, a flood of water from a little spring. ¹⁰ The light of the sun broke forth; the lowly were exalted and they devoured the nobles.

¹¹ Having seen this dream and what God intended to do, Mordecai awoke. He kept it in mind, and tried in every way, until night, to understand its meaning.

The Plot Discovered

¹²* Mordecai lodged at the court with Bagathan and Thares, two eunuchs of the king who were court guards. ¹³ He overheard them plotting, investigated their plans, and discovered that they were preparing to lay hands on King Ahasuerus. So he informed the king about them, ¹⁴ and the king had the two eunuchs questioned and, upon their confession, put to death. ¹⁵ Then the king had these things recorded; Mordecai, too, put them into writing. ¹⁶*† The king also appointed Mordecai to serve at the court, and rewarded him for his actions.

A, 1: *King Ahasuerus:* Xerxes I (485–464 B.C.). *Mordecai:* a Babylonian name, after the God Marduk. The genealogy of Mordecai is designed to reflect opposition to Israel's enemy, as narrated in 1 Sm 15, 7ff, where Saul (whose father's name was Kish, of the Tribe of Benjamin) conquered Agag the Amalekite; in A, 17 Haman is said to be the son of an Agagite. Further emphasis on the Benjaminite-Agagite opposition can be seen in Shimei, the Benjaminite who reviled David (2 Sm 16, 5ff). Jair appears to be the minor Judge, a Transjordan Manassehite (Jgs 10, 3). The chronology of the book would make Mordecai well over one hundred years old, since he was deported with Jehoiachin about 598 B.C.; cf Est 2, 5f.

A, 4: The interpretation of this dream is given in Est F, 1–6.
A, 16: *Rewarded him:* this reward comes only later; see the sequence of events from the Hebrew text of Esther at 2, 22f, and 6, 3, below.

---

*
A, 1: Est 2, 5.	**A, 4ff:** Est F, 2.4ff.
A, 3: Est 2, 6; 2 Kgs 24, 15; 2 Chr 36, 9f; Jer 22, 24ff; 24, 1; 29, 1f.	**A, 9f:** Est F, 3.
	A, 12–15: Est 2, 21ff; 6, 1ff.
	A, 16: Est 6, 3.

17*† Haman, however, son of Hammedatha the Agagite, who was in high honor with the king, sought to harm Mordecai and his people because of the two eunuchs of the king.

II: Elevation of Esther

The Banquet of Ahasuerus

1 1† During the reign of Ahasuerus—this was the Ahasuerus who ruled over a hundred and twenty-seven provinces from India to Ethiopia— 2† while he was occupying the royal throne in the stronghold of Susa, 3* in the third year of his reign, he presided over a feast for all his officers and ministers: the Persian and Median aristocracy, the nobles, and the governors of the provinces. 4 For as many as a hundred and eighty days, he displayed the glorious riches of his kingdom and the resplendent wealth of his royal estate.

5 At the end of this time the king gave a feast of seven days in the garden court of the royal palace for all the people, great and small, who were in the stronghold of Susa. 6 There were white cotton draperies and violet hangings, held by cords of crimson byssus from silver rings on marble pillars. Gold and silver couches were on the pavement, which was of porphyry, marble, mother-of-pearl, and colored stones. 7 Liquor was served in a variety of golden cups, and the royal wine flowed freely, as befitted the king's munificence. 8 By ordinance of the king the drinking was unstinted, for he had instructed all the stewards of his household to comply with the good pleasure of everyone.

9† Queen Vashti also gave a feast for the women inside the royal palace of King Ahasuerus.

Deposal of Vashti

10* On the seventh day, when the king was merry with wine, he instructed Mehuman, Biztha, Harbona, Bigtha, Abagtha, Zethar, and Carkas, the seven eunuchs who attended King Ahasuerus, 11 to bring Queen Vashti into his presence wearing the royal crown, that he might display her beauty to the populace and the officials, for she was lovely to behold. 12 But Queen Vashti refused to come at the royal order issued through the eunuchs. At this the king's wrath flared up, and he burned with fury.

13 He conferred with the wise men versed in the law, because the king's business was conducted in general consultation with lawyers and jurists. 14* He summoned Carshena, Shethar, Admatha, Tarshish, Meres, Marsena and Memucan, the seven Persian and Median officials who were in the king's personal service and held first rank in the realm, 15 and asked them, "What is to be done by law with Queen Vashti for disobeying the order of King Ahasuerus issued through the eunuchs?"

16 In the presence of the king and of the officials, Memucan answered: "Queen Vashti has not wronged the king alone, but all the officials and the populace throughout the provinces of King Ahasuerus. 17 For the queen's conduct will become known to all the women, and they will look with disdain upon their husbands when it is reported, 'King Ahasuerus commanded that Queen Vashti be ushered into his presence, but she would not come.' 18 This very day the Persian and Median ladies who hear of the queen's conduct will rebel against all the royal officials, with corresponding disdain and rancor. 19*† If it please the king, let an irrevocable royal decree be issued by him and inscribed among the laws of the Persians and Medes, forbidding Vashti to come into the presence of King Ahasuerus and authorizing the king to give her royal dignity to one more worthy than she. 20 Thus, when the decree which the king will issue is published throughout his realm, vast as it is, all wives will honor their husbands, from the greatest to the least."

21 This proposal found acceptance with the king and the officials, and the king acted on the advice of Memucan. 22† He sent letters to all the royal provinces, to each province in its own script and to each people in its own language, to the effect that every man should be lord in his own home.

Esther Made Queen

2 1 After this, when King Ahasuerus' wrath had cooled, he thought over what Vashti had done and what had been decreed against her. 2 Then the king's personal attendants suggested: "Let beautiful young virgins be sought for the king. 3 Let the king appoint commissaries in all the provinces of his realm to bring together all beautiful young virgins to the harem in the stronghold of Susa. Under the

---

† **A, 17:** *Haman . . . the Agagite:* opposed Mordecai the Benjaminite, by whom, however, he was overcome (Est 7, 9f), just as King Agag the Amalekite, was conquered by King Saul ancestor of Mordecai (1 Sm 15, 7ff).

1, 1: *From India to Ethiopia:* from western India to Upper Egypt, the greatest extent of the Persian Empire achieved under Darius the Great, father of Ahasuerus.

1, 2: *Susa:* ancient capital of Elam (Gn 14, 1); under the Achamenid kings, one of the two capitals of the Persian Empire. The other was Persepolis, the summer palace of the kings.

1, 9: *Queen Vashti:* Herodotus (Histories 7, 61) relates that the wife of Ahasuerus was Amestris.

1, 19: *Irrevocable royal decree:* the historian Siculus indicates that such a concept of irrevocable laws existed in the time of Darius III (335–331 B.C.), the last of the Persian kings, cf Est 8, 8.

1, 22: *To each province . . . script and to each people . . . language:* many languages were spoken in the Persian Empire, the principal ones being Persian, Elamite, Babylonian, Aramaic, Phoenician, Egyptian, and Greek. Each of them had its own script.

---

*
A, 17: Est 3, 1–15; B, 1–7; E,	**1, 10:** Dn 5, 1.
13.	**1, 14:** Ezr 7, 14.
1, 3: Jdt 1, 16.	**1, 19:** Est 8, 5.8; Dn 6, 8f.

did you KNOW?

Diaspora Jews

The fictional story of Esther implies that Mordecai and Esther were members of the Diaspora. The Greek word *diaspora* means "scattered abroad." It refers to the Jews who lived outside of Palestine. When the Babylonians destroyed Jerusalem (587 B.C.), many of the Jews who were forced to leave the land of Israel decided to settle in various Greco-Roman cities and not return home. They maintained their Jewish identity by adapting the language and customs of their new home into their Jewish traditions. The Diaspora Jews were responsible for the translation of the Hebrew Bible into Greek, a translation called the Septuagint.

care of the royal eunuch Hegai, custodian of the women, let cosmetics be given them. 4 Then the girl who pleases the king shall reign in place of Vashti." This suggestion pleased the king, and he acted accordingly.

5 There was in the stronghold of Susa a certain Jew named Mordecai, son of Jair, son of Shimei, son of Kish, a Benjaminite, 6* who had been exiled from Jerusalem with the captives taken with Jeconiah, king of Judah, whom Nebuchadnezzar, king of Babylon, had deported. 7*† He was foster father to Hadassah, that is, Esther, his cousin; for she had lost both father and mother. The girl was beautifully formed and lovely to behold. On the death of her father and mother, Mordecai had taken her as his own daughter.

8 When the king's order and decree had been obeyed and many maidens brought together to the stronghold of Susa under the care of Hegai, Esther also was brought in to the royal palace under the care of Hegai, custodian of the women. 9 The girl pleased him and won his favor. So he promptly furnished her with cosmetics and provisions. Then picking out seven maids for her from the royal

palace, he transferred both her and her maids to the best place in the harem. 10 Esther did not reveal her nationality or family, for Mordecai had commanded her not to do so.

11 Day by day Mordecai would walk about in front of the court of the harem, to learn how Esther was faring and what was to become of her.

12 Each girl went in turn to visit King Ahasuerus after the twelve months' preparation decreed for the women. Of this period of beautifying treatment, six months were spent with oil of myrrh, and the other six months with perfumes and cosmetics. 13 Then, when the girl was to visit the king, she was allowed to take with her from the harem to the royal palace whatever she chose. 14* She would go in the evening and return in the morning to a second harem under the care of the royal eunuch Shaashgaz, custodian of the concubines. She could not return to the king unless he was pleased with her and had her summoned by name.

15 As for Esther, daughter of Abihail and adopted daughter of his nephew Mordecai, when her turn came to visit the king, she did not ask for anything but what the royal eunuch Hegai, custodian of the women, suggested. Yet she won the admiration of all who saw her. 16 Esther was led to King Ahasuerus in his palace in the tenth month, Tebeth, in the seventh year of his reign. 17 The king loved Esther more than all other women, and of all the virgins she won his favor and benevolence. So he placed the royal diadem on her head and made her queen in place of Vashti. 18† Then the king gave a great feast in honor of Esther to all his officials and ministers, granting a holiday to the provinces and bestowing gifts with royal bounty.

The Plot Discovered

19*† [To resume: From the time the virgins had been brought together, and while Mordecai was passing his time at the king's gate, 20 Esther had not revealed her family or nationality, because Mordecai had told her not to; and Esther continued to follow Mordecai's instructions, just as she had when she was being brought up by him. 21*† And during the time that Mordecai spent at the king's gate, Bagathan and Thares, two of the royal eunuchs who guarded the entrance, had plotted in anger to lay hands on King Ahasuerus. 22 When the plot became known to Mordecai, he told Queen Esther, who in

---

2, 7: *Hadassah* (the feminine form of hadas, myrtle), was the name by which this woman would be known among her Jewish compatriots. Esther is a variant of the name of the Babylonian goddess Ishtar.

2, 18: *A holiday:* or perhaps, "a remission of taxes."

2, 19–23: This is a resumption, in a slightly different form, of the story already told in Est A, 12–15.

2, 21: *Mordecai . . . at the king's gate:* to exercise watchful care for Esther. Some understand this to mean that Mordecai was stationed at the gate to render royal service; cf Est A, 2.

2, 6: Est A, 3; 2 Kgs 24, 15; 2 Chr 36, 9f; Jer 22, 24ff; 24, 1; 29, 1f.
2, 7: Est 2, 15.
2, 14: Est 2, 19f; 4, 11.16.
2, 19f: Est 2, 14.
2, 21ff: Est A, 12–15; 6, 1ff.

turn informed the king for Mordecai. 23†‡ The matter was investigated and verified, and both of them were hanged on a gibbet. This was written in the annals for the king's use.]

III: Haman's Plot Against the Jews

Mordecai Refuses To Honor Haman

3 1* After these events King Ahasuerus raised Haman, son of Hammedatha the Agagite, to high rank, seating him above all his fellow officials. 2*† All the king's servants who were at the royal gate would kneel and bow down to Haman, for that is what the king had ordered in his regard. Mordecai, however, would not kneel and bow down. 3* The king's servants who were at the royal gate said to Mordecai, "Why do you disobey the king's order?" 4 When they had reminded him day after day and he would not listen to them, they informed Haman, to see whether Mordecai's explanation was acceptable, since he had told them that he was a Jew.

Haman's Reprisal

5 When Haman observed that Mordecai would not kneel and bow down to him, he was filled with anger. 6 Moreover, he thought it was not enough to lay hands on Mordecai alone. Since they had told Haman of Mordecai's nationality, he sought to destroy all the Jews, Mordecai's people, throughout the realm of King Ahasuerus. 7*† In the first month, Nisan, in the twelfth year of King Ahasuerus, the *pur*, or lot, was cast in Haman's presence, to determine the day and the month for the destruction of Mordecai's people on a single day, and the lot fell on the thirteenth day of the twelfth month, Adar.

Decree against the Jews

8* Then Haman said to King Ahasuerus: "Dispersed among the nations throughout the provinces of your kingdom, there is a certain people living apart, with laws differing from those of every other people. They do not obey the laws of the king, and so it is not proper for the king to tolerate them. 9* If it please the king, let a decree be issued to destroy them; and I will deliver to the procurators ten thousand silver talents for deposit in the royal treasury." 10*† The king took the signet ring from his hand and gave it to Haman, son of Hammedatha the Agagite, the enemy of the Jews. 11 "The silver you may keep," the king said to Haman, "but

Body Count

LIVE IT!

Genocide. Such a frightening word. The complete destruction of a people. This is what King Ahasuerus plots in the Book of Esther: to destroy all the Jews in his kingdom. Fortunately, he does not succeed.

In our time, we know only too well that the past two centuries have been marked by many attempts to exterminate whole groups of people. The most systematic and ambitious of these attempts was that of Adolf Hitler and the Third Reich. Six million Jews were put to death in Nazi concentration camps, along with four million other "undesirables." Yet, we in the Americas need to look no farther than our own shores. Many Native American peoples were slaughtered simply because they were defending their homes and way of life. Others were wiped out by diseases brought by European settlers in the name of progress, civilization, and Christianity.

Such atrocities begin with a them-and-us attitude. The first step is to set apart a group of people and blame them for whatever is going wrong. The second is to give them a label, like "savages" or "communists," to make them seem less human and easier to destroy. The ghosts of too many victims of genocide remind us that the only accurate pronoun to describe our human family is *we*.

▸ Est 3, 1–7

E
S
T

2, 23: *Hanged on a gibbet:* impaled, perhaps, after the Babylonian manner.
3, 2: *Mordecai . . . would not kneel and bow down:* in order not to render to man, the homage which he regarded as belonging to God alone; cf Est C, 5ff.
3, 7: *Pur:* a Babylonian word which the Hebrew translates as goral, "lot." This word is preserved in the text because its plural, purim, became the name of the feast of Purim commemorating the deliverance of the Jews; cf Est 9, 24.26.

3, 10: *Signet ring:* a ring containing a seal which was impressed on documents to authenticate them. By giving this ring to Haman, the king bestowed on him the power to authenticate royal decrees.

3, 1: Est B, 3; 5, 11; E, 11.
3, 2: Est C, 5; 5, 9.13; 6, 10.12.
3, 3: Est 4, 16.
3, 7: Est 9, 24ff; F, 10.

3, 8: Est 3, 13; B, 4; E, 24; Dn 3, 8–12; Wis 2, 14f.
3, 9: Est 7, 4.
3, 10: Gn 41, 42.

as for this people, do with them whatever you please."

12 So the royal scribes were summoned; and on the thirteenth day of the first month they wrote, at the dictation of Haman, an order to the royal satraps, the governors of every province, and the officials of every people, to each province in its own script and to each people in its own language. It was written in the name of King Ahasuerus and sealed with the royal signet ring. 13* Letters were sent by couriers to all the royal provinces, that all the Jews, young and old, including women and children, should be killed, destroyed, wiped out in one day, the thirteenth day of the twelfth month, Adar, and that their goods should be seized as spoil.

B 1 This is a copy of the letter:

"The great King Ahasuerus writes to the satraps of the hundred and twenty-seven provinces from India to Ethiopia, and the governors subordinate to them, as follows: 2* When I came to rule many peoples and to hold sway over the whole world, I determined not to be carried away with the sense of power, but always to deal fairly and with clemency; to provide for my subjects a life of complete tranquillity; and by making my government humane and effective as far as the borders, to restore the peace desired by all men. 3* When I consulted my counselors as to how this might be accomplished, Haman, who excels among us in wisdom, who is outstanding for constant devotion and steadfast loyalty, and who has gained the second rank in the kingdom, 4* brought it to our attention that, mixed in with all the races throughout the world, there is one people of bad will, which by its laws is opposed to every other people and continually disregards the decrees of kings, so that the unity of empire blamelessly designed by us cannot be established.

5 "Having noted, therefore, that this most singular people is continually at variance with all men, lives by divergent and alien laws, is inimical to our interests, and commits the worst crimes, so that stability of government cannot be obtained, 6*† we hereby decree that all those who are indicated to you in the letters of Haman, who is in charge of the administration and is a second father to us, shall, together with their wives and children, be utterly destroyed by the swords of their enemies, without any pity or mercy, on the fourteenth day of the twelfth month, Adar, of the current year; 7 so that when these

people, whose present ill will is of long standing, have gone down into the nether world by a violent death on one same day, they may at last leave our affairs stable and undisturbed for the future."

(3) 14 A copy of the decree to be promulgated as law in every province was published to all the peoples, that they might be prepared for that day. 15 The couriers set out in haste at the king's command; meanwhile, the decree was promulgated in the stronghold of Susa. The king and Haman then sat down to feast, but the city of Susa was thrown into confusion.

Esther's Aid Sought by Mordecai

4 1* When Mordecai learned all that was happening, he tore his garments, put on sackcloth and ashes, and walked through the city, crying out loudly and bitterly, 2 till he came before the royal gate, which no one clothed in sackcloth might enter. 3 (Likewise in each of the provinces, wherever the king's legal enactment reached, the Jews went into deep mourning, with fasting, weeping, and lament; they all slept on sackcloth and ashes.)

4 Queen Esther's maids and eunuchs came and told her. Overwhelmed with anguish, she sent garments for Mordecai to put on, so that he might take off his sackcloth; but he refused. 5 Esther then summoned Hathach, one of the king's eunuchs whom he had placed at her service, and commanded him to find out what this action of Mordecai meant and the reason for it. 6 So Hathach went out to Mordecai in the public square in front of the royal gate, 7 and Mordecai told him all that had happened, as well as the exact amount of silver Haman had promised to pay to the royal treasury for the slaughter of the Jews. 8 He also gave him a copy of the written decree for their destruction which had been promulgated in Susa, to show and explain to Esther. He was to instruct her to go to the king; she was to plead and intercede with him in behalf of her people. 8† "Remember the days of your lowly estate," Mordecai had him say, "when you were brought up in my charge; for Haman, who is second to the king, has asked for our death. 9 Invoke the LORD and speak to the king for us; save us from death."

Hathach returned to Esther and told her what Mordecai had said. 10 Then Esther replied to Hathach and gave him this message for Mordecai: 11* "All the servants of the king and the people of his provinces know that any man or woman who

---

B, 6: *Fourteenth day:* the Hebrew text, as in Est 2, 13 above, and the Greek text here translated do not agree on the day of the month specified by the king; in fact, a two-day celebration is decreed in chapter 9, and the 13th, 14th and 15th of Adar are all mentioned; see Est 9, 15.18.

4, 8: This verse belongs to chapter B.

3, 13: Est B, 6; 7, 4.
B, 2: Est E, 8f.
B, 3: Est 3, 1; 5, 11; E, 11.
B, 4: Est 3, 8; E, 24.

B, 6: Est 3, 13; 7, 4; E, 11ff.
4, 1: Jdt 4, 12.
4, 11: Est 2, 14; 4, 12; D, 12.

did you KNOW?

The Silent Women of the Bible

"Mordecai went away and did exactly as Esther had commanded" (Est C, 1). What a surprise: to hear of a man in the ancient world taking orders from a woman! Esther, like Judith, has an exceptional role in the Old Testament. Many other important women are not even named: Jephthah's daughter, Samson's mother, and Job's wife, for instance. Even the Hebrew women whose names have become famous—Sarah, Rebekah, Rachel, Miriam, Bathsheba—played second fiddle to their more famous husbands. They depended on indirect influence or trickery to get what they wanted.

In the biblical world, a woman was defined by her relationships with men. Before marriage, she belonged to her father's household and had no status outside of it. Once married, a woman left her father's family and joined the family of her husband. If her husband died, she remained in the new family, rearing children for her deceased spouse or, if childless, marrying a brother-in-law. Although many women undoubtedly lived happily under this system, many others just as surely suffered abuse or felt oppressed. The stories of Lot's daughters (Gn 19, 8) and the woman of Gibeah (Jgs 19, 22–30) testify to this horrifying truth.

A system of scriptural interpretation that was developed during recent decades attempts to give voice to the many silent, forgotten, abused women of the Bible. More and more biblical scholars reread the familiar stories, searching for quiet messages that have long been overlooked. All of us—males and females alike—can benefit from this effort to listen to the voices of these women who have been silenced for so many centuries.

▶ Est 4, 15—C, 1

goes to the king in the inner court without being summoned, suffers the automatic penalty of death, unless the king extends to him the golden scepter, thus sparing his life. Now as for me, I have not been summoned to the king for thirty days."

12 When Esther's words were reported to Mordecai, 13 he had this reply brought to her: "Do not imagine that because you are in the king's palace, you alone of all the Jews will escape. 14† Even if you now remain silent, relief and deliverance will come to the Jews from another source; but you and your father's house will perish. Who knows but that it was for a time like this that you obtained the royal dignity?"

15 Esther sent back to Mordecai the response: 16* "Go and assemble all the Jews who are in Susa; fast on my behalf, all of you, not eating or drinking, night or day, for three days. I and my maids will also fast in the same way. Thus prepared, I will go to the king, contrary to the law. If I perish, I perish!"

Prayer of Mordecai

Mordecai went away and did exactly as Esther had commanded. 1 Recalling all that the LORD had done, he prayed to him 2 and said: "O Lord God, almighty King, all things are in your power, and there is no one to oppose you in your will to save Israel. 3 You made heaven and earth and every wonderful thing under the heavens. 4 You are LORD of all, and there is no one who can resist you, LORD. 5* You know all things. You know, O LORD, that it was not out of insolence or pride or desire for fame that I acted thus in not bowing down to the proud Haman. 6 Gladly would I have kissed the soles of his feet for the salvation of Israel. 7 But I acted as I did so as not to place the honor of man above that of God. I will not bow down to anyone but you, my LORD. It is not out of pride that I am acting thus. 8 And now, LORD God, King, God of Abraham, spare your people, for our enemies plan our ruin and are bent upon destroying the inheritance that was yours from the beginning. 9 Do not spurn your portion, which you redeemed for yourself out of Egypt. 10 Hear my prayer; have pity on your inheritance and turn our sorrow into joy: thus we shall live to sing praise to your name, O LORD. Do not silence those who praise you."

11 All Israel, too, cried out with all their strength, for death was staring them in the face.

Prayer of Esther

12* Queen Esther, seized with mortal anguish, likewise had recourse to the LORD. 13 Taking off her

---

4, 14: *From another source:* very probably Mordecai refers to divine aid; the Greek additions (C) are explicit about this.

4, 16: Est C, 12f.   **C, 12f:** Est 4, 16.
C, 5ff: Est 3, 2; 5, 9.

splendid garments, she put on garments of distress and mourning. In place of her precious ointments she covered her head with dirt and ashes. She afflicted her body severely; all her festive adornments were put aside, and her hair was wholly disheveled.

14 Then she prayed to the LORD, the God of Israel, saying: "My LORD, our King, you alone are God. Help me, who am alone and have no help but you, 15* for I am taking my life in my hand. 16* As a child I was wont to hear from the people of the land of my forefathers that you, O LORD, chose Israel from among all peoples, and our fathers from among all their ancestors, as a lasting heritage, and that you fulfilled all your promises to them. 17 But now we have sinned in your sight, and you have delivered us into the hands of our enemies, 18 because we worshiped their gods. You are just, O LORD. 19 But now they are not satisfied with our bitter servitude, but have undertaken 20 to do away with the decree you have pronounced, and to destroy your heritage; to close the mouths of those who praise you, and to extinguish the glory of your temple and your altar; 21 to open the mouths of the heathen to acclaim their false gods, and to extol an earthly king forever.

22 "O LORD, do not relinquish your scepter to those that are nought. Let them not gloat over our ruin, but turn their own counsel against them and make an example of our chief enemy. 23 Be mindful of us, O LORD. Manifest yourself in the time of our distress and give me courage, King of gods and Ruler of every power. 24 Put in my mouth persuasive words in the presence of the lion and turn his heart to hatred for our enemy, so that he and those who are in league with him may perish. 25 Save us by your power, and help me, who am alone and have no one but you, O LORD.

"You know all things. 26 You know that I hate the glory of the pagans, and abhor the bed of the uncircumcised or of any foreigner. 27 You know that I am under constraint, that I abhor the sign of grandeur which rests on my head when I appear in public; abhor it like a polluted rag, and do not wear it in private. 28† I, your handmaid, have never eaten at the table of Haman, nor have I graced the banquet of the king or drunk the wine of libations. 29 From the day I was brought here till now, your handmaid has had no joy except in you, O LORD, God of Abraham. 30 O God, more powerful than all, hear the voice of those in despair. Save us from the power of the wicked, and deliver me from my fear."

Esther Is Received by the King

D 1 On the third day, putting an end to her prayers, she took off her penitential garments and arrayed herself in her royal attire. 2 In making her state appearance, after invoking the all-seeing God and savior, she took with her two maids; 3 on the one she leaned gently for support, 4 while the other followed her, bearing her train. 5 She glowed with the perfection of her beauty and her countenance was as joyous as it was lovely, though her heart was shrunk with fear. 6 She passed through all the portals till she stood face to face with the king, who was seated on his royal throne, clothed in full robes of state, and covered with gold and precious stones, so that he inspired great awe. 7 As he looked up, his features ablaze with the height of majestic anger, the queen staggered, changed color, and leaned weakly against the head of the maid in front of her. 8 But God changed the king's anger to gentleness. In great anxiety he sprang from his throne, held her in his arms until she recovered, and comforted her with reassuring words. 9 "What is it, Esther?" he said to her. "I am your brother. Take courage! 10 You shall not die because of this general decree of ours. 11 Come near!" 12* Raising the golden scepter, he touched her neck with it, embraced her, and said, "Speak to me."

13 She replied: "I saw you, my lord, as an angel of God, and my heart was troubled with fear of your majesty. 14 For you are awesome, my lord, though your glance is full of kindness." 15 As she said this, she fainted. 16 The king became troubled and all his attendants tried to revive her.

5 1† [Now on the third day, Esther put on her royal garments and stood in the inner courtyard, looking toward the royal palace, while the king was seated on his royal throne in the audience chamber, facing the palace doorway. 2 He saw Queen Esther standing in the courtyard, and made her welcome by extending toward her the golden staff which he held. She came up to him, and touched the top of the staff.]

3* Then the king said to her, "What is it, Queen Esther? What is your request? Even if it is half of my kingdom, it shall be granted you." 4 "If it please your majesty," Esther replied, "come today with Haman to a banquet I have prepared." 5 And the king ordered, "Have Haman make haste to fulfill the wish of Esther."

First Banquet of Esther

So the king went with Haman to the banquet Esther had prepared. 6* During the drinking of the

---

C, 28: *Wine of libations:* offered in sacrifice to the gods.
5, 1f: The Hebrew text here translated is a short form of the account already given in Greek.

C, 15: Est 4, 16.
C, 16: Dt 4, 20; 7, 6; 9, 29; 14, 2; 26, 18; 32, 9.

D, 12: Est 4, 11.
5, 3: Est 5, 6; 7, 2; 9, 12.
5, 6: Est 5, 3.

wine, the king said to Esther, "Whatever you ask for shall be granted, and whatever request you make shall be honored, even if it is for half my kingdom." [7] Esther replied: "This is my petition and request: [8] if I have found favor with the king and if it pleases your majesty to grant my petition and honor my request, come with Haman tomorrow to a banquet which I shall prepare for you; and then I will do as you ask."

Haman's Plot against Mordecai

[9]* That day Haman left happy and in good spirits. But when he saw that Mordecai at the royal gate did not rise, and showed no fear of him, he was filled with anger toward him. [10] Haman restrained himself, however, and went home, where he summoned his friends and his wife Zeresh. [11]* He recounted the greatness of his riches, the large number of his sons, and just how the king had promoted him and placed him above the officials and royal servants. [12] "Moreover," Haman added, "Queen Esther invited no one but me to the banquet with the king; again tomorrow I am to be her guest, with the king. [13]* Yet none of this satisfies me as long as I continue to see the Jew Mordecai sitting at the royal gate." [14]* His wife Zeresh and all his friends said to him, "Have a gibbet set up, fifty cubits in height, and in the morning ask the king to have Mordecai hanged on it. Then go to the banquet with the king in good cheer." This suggestion pleased Haman, and he had the gibbet erected.

IV: Vindication of the Jews

Mordecai's Reward from the King

6 [1] That night the king, unable to sleep, asked that the chronicle of notable events be brought in. While this was being read to him, [2]* the passage occurred in which Mordecai reported Bagathan and Teresh, two of the royal eunuchs who guarded the entrance, for seeking to lay hands on King Ahasuerus. [3]* The king asked, "What was done to reward and honor Mordecai for this?" The king's attendants replied, "Nothing was done for him." [4]* "Who is in the court?" the king asked. Now Haman had entered the outer court of the king's palace to suggest to the king that Mordecai should be hanged on the gibbet he had raised for him. [5] The king's servants answered him, "Haman is waiting in the court." "Let him come in," the king said. [6] When Haman entered, the king said to him, "What should be done for the man whom the king wishes to reward?" Now Haman thought to himself, "Whom would the king more probably wish to reward than me?" [7] So he replied to the king: "For the man whom the king wishes to reward [8] there should be brought the royal robe which the king wore and the horse on which the king rode when the royal crown was placed on his head. [9]* The robe and the horse should be consigned to one of the noblest of the king's officials, who must clothe the man the king wishes to reward, have him ride on the horse in the public square of the city, and cry out before him, 'This is what is done for the man whom the king wishes to reward.'" [10]* Then the king said to Haman: "Hurry! Take the robe and horse as you have proposed, and do this for the Jew Mordecai, who is sitting at the royal gate. Do not omit anything you proposed." [11] So Haman took the robe and horse, clothed Mordecai, had him ride in the public square of the city, and cried out before him, "This is what is done for the man whom the king wishes to reward."

[12]* Mordecai then returned to the royal gate, while Haman hurried home, his head covered in grief. [13] When he told his wife Zeresh and all his friends everything that had happened to him, his advisers and his wife Zeresh said to him, "If Mordecai, before whom you are beginning to decline, is of the Jewish race, you will not prevail against him, but will surely be defeated by him."

Esther's Second Banquet

[14] While they were speaking with him, the king's eunuchs arrived and hurried Haman off to the banquet Esther had prepared.

7 [1] So the king and Haman went to the banquet with Queen Esther. [2]* Again, on this second day, during the drinking of the wine, the king said to Esther, "Whatever you ask, Queen Esther, shall be granted you. Whatever request you make shall be honored, even for half the kingdom." [3] Queen Esther replied: "If I have found favor with you, O king, and if it pleases your majesty, I ask that my life be spared, and I beg that you spare the lives of my people. [4]* For my people and I have been delivered to destruction, slaughter, and extinction. If we were to be sold into slavery I would remain silent, but as it is, the enemy will be unable to compensate for the harm done to the king." [5]* "Who and where," said King Ahasuerus to Queen Esther, "is the man who has dared to do this?" [6] Esther replied, "The enemy oppressing us is this wicked Haman." At this, Haman was seized with dread of the king and queen.

5, 9: Est 3, 2f; C, 5ff; 6, 10.12.
5, 11: Est 3, 1; B, 3; E, 11; 9, 6–10.
5, 13: Est 3, 2f; 6, 10.12.
5, 14: Est 6, 4; 7, 9f.
6, 2: Est A, 12ff; 2, 21ff.
6, 3: Est A, 16.
6, 4: Est 5, 14; 7, 9f.
6, 9: Gn 41, 42f; 1 Kgs 1, 33; Dn 5, 29.
6, 10: Est 2, 21; 3, 2f; 5, 9.13.
6, 12: Est 2, 21; 3, 2f; 5, 9.13.
7, 2: Est 5, 3.
7, 4: Est 3, 13; B, 6.
7, 5: Est 3, 8f.

7 The king left the banquet in anger and went into the garden of the palace, but Haman stayed to beg Queen Esther for his life, since he saw that the king had decided on his doom. 8 When the king returned from the garden of the palace to the banquet hall, Haman had thrown himself on the couch on which Esther was reclining; and the king exclaimed, "Will he also violate the queen while she is with me in my own house!" Scarcely had the king spoken, when the face of Haman was covered over.

Punishment of Haman

9* Harbona, one of the eunuchs who attended the king, said, "At the house of Haman stands a gibbet fifty cubits high. Haman prepared it for Mordecai, who gave the report that benefited the king." The king answered, "Hang him on it." 10 So they hanged Haman on the gibbet which he had made ready for Mordecai, and the anger of the king abated.

8 1* That day King Ahasuerus gave the house of Haman, enemy of the Jews, to Queen Esther; and Mordecai was admitted to the king's presence, for Esther had revealed his relationship to her. 2* The king removed his signet ring from Haman, and transferred it into the keeping of Mordecai; and Esther put Mordecai in charge of the house of Haman.

The Second Royal Decree

3 In another audience with the king, Esther fell at his feet and tearfully implored him to revoke the harm done by Haman the Agagite, and the plan he had devised against the Jews. 4 The king stretched forth the golden scepter to Esther. So she rose and, standing in his presence, 5* said: "If it pleases your majesty and seems proper to you, and if I have found favor with you and you love me, let a document be issued to revoke the letters which that schemer Haman, son of Hammedatha the Agagite, wrote for the destruction of the Jews in all the royal provinces. 6 For how can I witness the evil that is to befall my people, and how can I behold the destruction of my race?"

7 King Ahasuerus then said to Queen Esther and to the Jew Mordecai: "Now that I have given Esther the house of Haman, and they have hanged him on the gibbet because he attacked the Jews, 8*† you in turn may write in the king's name what you see fit concerning the Jews and seal the letter with the royal signet ring." For whatever is written in the name of the king and sealed with the royal signet ring cannot be revoked.

9 At that time, on the twenty-third day of the third month, Sivan, the royal scribes were summoned. Exactly as Mordecai dictated, they wrote to the Jews and to the satraps, governors, and officials of the hundred and twenty-seven provinces from India to Ethiopia: to each province in its own script and to each people in its own language, and to the Jews in their own script and language. 10 These letters, which he wrote in the name of King Ahasuerus and sealed with the royal signet ring, he sent by mounted couriers riding thoroughbred royal steeds. 11* In these letters the king authorized the Jews in each and every city to group together and defend their lives, and to kill, destroy, wipe out, along with their wives and children, every armed group of any nation or province which should attack them, and to seize their goods as spoil 12 throughout the provinces of King Ahasuerus, on a single day, the thirteenth of the twelfth month, Adar.

E 1 The following is a copy of the letter:

"King Ahasuerus the Great to the governors of the provinces in the hundred and twenty-seven satrapies from India to Ethiopia, and to those responsible for our interests: Greetings!

2 "Many have become the more ambitious the more they were showered with honors through the bountiful generosity of their patrons. 3 Not only do they seek to do harm to our subjects; incapable of bearing such greatness, they even begin plotting against their own benefactors. 4 Not only do they drive out gratitude from among men; with the arrogant boastfulness of those to whom goodness has no meaning, they suppose they will escape the vindictive judgment of the all-seeing God.

5 "Often, too, the fair speech of friends entrusted with the administration of affairs has induced many placed in authority to become accomplices in the shedding of innocent blood, and has involved them in irreparable calamities 6 by deceiving with malicious slander the sincere good will of rulers. 7 This can be verified in the ancient stories that have been handed down to us, but more fully when one considers the wicked deeds perpetrated in your midst by the pestilential influence of those undeserving of authority. 8* We must provide for the future, so as to render the kingdom undisturbed and peaceful for all men, 9 taking advantage of changing

---

† **8, 8:** *Whatever is written . . . cannot be revoked:* the king cannot directly grant Esther's request (v 5) to revoke the previous decree against the Jews because of the irrevocable character of the laws of the Medes and Persians (Est 1, 19; Dn 6, 9); but he empowers Esther to issue a new decree in his name which renders the earlier decree without effect; cf Est 3, 12f.

7, 9f: Est 5, 14; 6, 4.
8, 1: Est 9, 1; Prv 11, 8; 26, 27; Mt 7, 2.
8, 2: Prv 13, 22; Dn 2, 48f.
8, 5: Est 1, 19.
8, 8: Est 1, 19.
8, 11f: Est 9, 1–4.
E, 8f: Est B, 2.

conditions and deciding always with equitable treatment matters coming to our attention.

10† "For instance, Haman, son of Hammedatha, a Macedonian, certainly not of Persian blood, and very different from us in generosity, was hospitably received by us. 11* He so far enjoyed the good will which we have toward all peoples that he was proclaimed 'father of the king,' before whom everyone was to bow down; he attained the rank second to the royal throne. 12 But, unequal to this dignity, he strove to deprive us of kingdom and of life; 13* and by weaving intricate webs of deceit, he demanded the destruction of Mordecai, our savior and constant benefactor, and of Esther, our blameless royal consort, together with their whole race. 14 For by such measures he hoped to catch us defenseless and to transfer the rule of the Persians to the Macedonians. 15 But we find that the Jews, who were doomed to extinction by this arch-criminal, are not evildoers, but rather are governed by very just laws 16 and are the children of the Most High, the living God of majesty, who has maintained the kingdom in a flourishing condition for us and for our forebears.

17 "You will do well, then, to ignore the letter sent by Haman, son of Hammedatha, 18* for he who composed it has been hanged, together with his entire household, before the gates of Susa. Thus swiftly has God, who governs all, brought just punishment upon him.

19 "You shall exhibit a copy of this letter publicly in every place, to certify that the Jews may follow their own laws, 20 and that you may help them on the day set for their ruin, the thirteenth day of the twelfth month, Adar, to defend themselves against those who attack them. 21 For God, the ruler of all, has turned that day for them from one of destruction of the chosen race into one of joy. 22 Therefore, you too must celebrate this memorable day among your designated feasts with all rejoicing, 23 so that both now and in the future it may be, for us and for loyal Persians, a celebration of victory, and for those who plot against us a reminder of destruction.

24* "Every city and province, without exception, that does not observe this decree shall be ruthlessly destroyed with fire and sword, so that it will be left not merely untrodden by men, but even shunned by wild beasts and birds forever."

(8) 13† A copy of the letter to be promulgated as law in each and every province was published among all the peoples, so that the Jews might be prepared on that day to avenge themselves on their enemies. 14 Couriers mounted on royal steeds sped forth in haste at the king's order, and the decree was promulgated in the stronghold of Susa.

15* Mordecai left the king's presence clothed in a royal robe of violet and of white cotton, with a large crown of gold and a cloak of crimson byssus. The city of Susa shouted with joy, 16 and there was splendor and merriment for the Jews, exultation and triumph. 17* In each and every province and in each and every city, wherever the king's order arrived, there was merriment and exultation, banqueting and feasting for the Jews. And many of the peoples of the land embraced Judaism, for they were seized with a fear of the Jews.

Victory of the Jews

9 1* When the day arrived on which the order decreed by the king was to be carried out, the thirteenth day of the twelfth month, Adar, on which the enemies of the Jews had expected to become masters of them, the situation was reversed: the Jews became masters of their enemies. 2 The Jews mustered in their cities throughout the provinces of King Ahasuerus to attack those who sought to do them harm, and no one could withstand them, but all peoples were seized with a fear of them. 3 Moreover, all the officials of the provinces, the satraps, governors, and royal procurators supported the Jews from fear of Mordecai; 4 for Mordecai was powerful in the royal palace, and the report was spreading through all the provinces that he was continually growing in power.

5* The Jews struck down all their enemies with the sword, killing and destroying them; they did to their enemies as they pleased. 6* In the stronghold of Susa, the Jews killed and destroyed five hundred men. 7 They also killed Parshandatha, Dalphon, Aspatha, 8 Porathai, Adalia, Aridatha, 9 Parmashta, Arisai, Aridai, and Vaizatha, 10*† the ten sons of Haman, son of Hammedatha, the foe of the Jews. However, they did not engage in plundering.

11 On the same day, when the number of those killed in the stronghold of Susa was reported to the king, 12 he said to Queen Esther: "In the stronghold

---

E, 10: *Macedonian:* a redactor of the book in the Hellenistic period used the designation Macedonian, here and in v 14, to express, after Macedonia's conquest of Persia, the most odious kind of man that a Persian ruler could be supposed to think of; the Hebrew text, for a similar reason, called Haman an Agagite. See note on Est A, 17.

8, 13: *Avenge themselves on their enemies:* partly in self-defense (Est E, 20), and partly to express the fact that the extreme cruelty designed against the Jews by their enemies now recoiled upon the latter as a punishment. Cf 9, 1f.

9, 10: *They did not engage in plundering:* in contrast to the Israelites who fought Agag (1 Sm 15, 9); cf also vv 15f.

E, 11: Est B, 3.6.	8, 17: Est 9, 27.
E, 13: Est A, 17.	9, 1f: Est 8, 11f.
E, 18: Est 7, 10; 9, 14.	9, 5: Jdt 15, 6.
E, 24: Est 3, 8f; B, 4.	9, 6–10: Est 5, 11; B, 3; E, 11.
8, 15: Dn 5, 7.	9, 10: Est 9, 15; Jdt 15, 7.11.

of Susa the Jews have killed and destroyed five hundred men, as well as the ten sons of Haman. What must they have done in the other royal provinces! You shall again be granted whatever you ask, and whatever you request shall be honored." [13] So Esther said, "If it pleases your majesty, let the Jews in Susa be permitted again tomorrow to act according to today's decree, and let the ten sons of Haman be hanged on gibbets." [14]* The king then gave an order to this effect, and the decree was published in Susa. So the ten sons of Haman were hanged, [15]*† and the Jews in Susa mustered again on the fourteenth of the month of Adar and killed three hundred men in Susa. However, they did not engage in plundering.

[16]*† The other Jews, who dwelt in the royal provinces, also mustered and defended themselves, and obtained rest from their enemies. They killed seventy-five thousand of their foes, without engaging in plunder, [17] on the thirteenth day of the month of Adar. On the fourteenth of the month they rested, and made it a day of feasting and rejoicing.

[18] (The Jews in Susa, however, mustered on the thirteenth and fourteenth of the month. But on the fifteenth they rested, and made it a day of feasting and rejoicing.) [19] That is why the rural Jews, who dwell in villages, celebrate the fourteenth of the month of Adar as a day of rejoicing and feasting, a holiday on which they send gifts of food to one another.

The Feast of Purim

[20] Mordecai recorded these events and sent letters to all the Jews, both near and far, in all the provinces of King Ahasuerus. [21] He ordered them to celebrate every year both the fourteenth and the fifteenth of the month of Adar [22] as the days on which the Jews obtained rest from their enemies and as the month which was turned for them from sorrow into joy, from mourning into festivity. They were to observe these days with feasting and gladness, sending food to one another and gifts to the poor. [23]* The Jews took upon themselves for the future this observance which they instituted at the written direction of Mordecai.

[24]* Haman, son of Hammedatha the Agagite, the foe of all the Jews, had planned to destroy them and had cast the *pur*, or lot, for the time of their defeat

and destruction. [25]* Yet, when Esther entered the royal presence, the king ordered in writing that the wicked plan Haman had devised against the Jews should instead be turned against Haman and that he and his sons should be hanged on gibbets. [26] And so these days have been named Purim after the word *pur*.

Thus, because of all that was contained in this letter, and because of what they had witnessed and experienced in this affair, [27]* the Jews established and took upon themselves, their descendants, and all who should join them, the inviolable obligation of celebrating these two days every year in the manner prescribed by this letter, and at the time appointed. [28] These days were to be commemorated and kept in every generation, by every clan, in every province, and in every city. These days of Purim were never to fall into disuse among the Jews, nor into oblivion among their descendants.

did you KNOW?

Purim

The feast of Purim ("lots" in Hebrew) commemorates the legendary victory of Queen Esther and Mordecai. A minor festival in the Jewish calendar, Purim is celebrated in late winter and is marked by the exchange of gifts and the sharing of meals.

▸ Est 9, 20–32

[29]† Queen Esther, daughter of Abihail and of Mordecai the Jew, wrote to confirm with full authority this second letter about Purim, [30]* when Mordecai sent documents concerning peace and security to all the Jews in the hundred and twenty-seven provinces of Ahasuerus' kingdom. [31]† Thus were established, for their appointed time, these days of Purim which Mordecai the Jew and Queen

E
S
T

---

† **9, 15:** This second slaughter explains the two dates (13th and 14th) of the Purim celebration by Jews in Susa (v 18).

9, 16: *Seventy-five thousand:* according to the Greek text this number was fifteen thousand.

9, 29: *Queen Esther, daughter of Abihail and of Mordecai:* the natural offspring of Abihail and adopted daughter of Mordecai; cf Est 2, 15. *This second letter:* for the burden of this letter see Est 9, 20ff. It was endorsed by Queen Esther. The first letter, written in the king's name, is referred to in Est 8, 9.

9, 31: *Fasting and supplication:* as the Jews had previously un-

dertaken the duty of fasting and supplication to prevent the impending disaster, they now observe days of festival to commemorate their deliverance—in both cases (cf Est 4, 3.15f) at the request of Mordecai and Esther.

9, 14: Est 7, 10; E, 18.
9, 15: Est 9, 10.
9, 16: Jdt 15, 6.
9, 23: Est 9, 29.
9, 24ff: Est 3, 7; E, 10.
9, 25: Est 6, 5–13.
9, 27: Est 8, 12.17.
9, 30: Est 9, 23–26.

Esther had designated for the Jews, just as they had previously enjoined upon themselves and upon their race the duty of fasting and supplication. [32] The command of Esther confirmed these prescriptions for Purim and was recorded in the book.

10 [1] King Ahasuerus laid tribute on the land and on the islands of the sea. [2] All the acts of his power and valor, as well as a detailed account of the greatness of Mordecai, whom the king promoted, are recorded in the chronicles of the kings of Media and Persia. [3]* The Jew Mordecai was next in rank to King Ahasuerus, in high standing among the Jews, and was regarded with favor by his many brethren, as the promoter of his people's welfare and the herald of peace for his whole race.

V: Epilogue

Mordecai's Dream Fulfilled

F [1]* Then Mordecai said: "This is the work of God. [2] I recall the dream I had about these very things, and not a single detail has been left unfulfilled— [3] the tiny spring that grew into a river, the light of the sun, the many waters. The river is Esther, whom the king married and made queen. [4] The two dragons are myself and Haman. [5] The nations are those who assembled to destroy the name of the Jews, [6] but my people is Israel, who cried to God and was saved.

"The LORD saved his people and delivered us from all these evils. God worked signs and great wonders, such as have not occurred among the nations. [7]† For this purpose he arranged two lots: one for the people of God, the second for all the other nations. [8] These two lots were fulfilled in the hour, the time, and the day of judgment before God and among all the nations. [9]* God remembered his people and rendered justice to his inheritance.

[10]† "Gathering together with joy and happiness before God, they shall celebrate these days on the fourteenth and fifteenth of the month Adar throughout all future generations of his people Israel."

---

† **F, 7:** *Two lots:* in this passage of the Greek text, which gives a more religious interpretation of the feast, the two lots are drawn by God to determine, respectively, the destiny of Israel and that of the nations. In Est 3, 7 above, translated from the Hebrew text, the feast is called Purim because of the lots which Aman cast to determine the day for the extinction of the Jews.

F, 10: The Greek text of Esther contains a postscript as follows: In the fourth year of the reign of Ptolemy and Cleopatra, Dositheus, who said he was a priest and Levite, and his son Ptolemy brought the present letter of Purim, saying that it was genuine and that Lysimachus, son of Ptolemy, of the community of Jerusalem, had translated it. The date referred to in this postscript is most probably 78–77 B.C., in the reign of Ptolemy XII and Cleopatra V.

10, 3: 2 Mc 15, 14.
F, 1–6: Est A, 4–10.

F, 9: Est 3, 7; 9, 17f.21.24–28.

Have you ever listened as two fighting siblings tell their parents about a conflict? Usually, each child blames the other one and protests his or her complete innocence. Sometimes you have to wonder if they are even talking about the same fight. In a similar way, the author of 1 Maccabees, reporting on the Jewish resistance to the persecution of the Seleucid (Greek) rulers, tells one version of the story. The book defends the violent resistance of the family of Mattathias. Second Maccabees, on the other hand, has a broader perspective in telling of other forms of Jewish resistance.

At a Glance

In-depth

The writer of 1 Maccabees has a clear purpose in mind: to defend the family of Mattathias, whose sons—the Maccabees—held positions of authority in the Jewish community. The most famous of them, Judas Maccabeus, led the Jews in a successful revolt (167–164 B.C.) against the Greek persecution—an incredible feat given the military might of the Greeks. After Judas's death, his brothers and nephews held positions of power, and Israel remained free from foreign domination for the next hundred years.

For traditional Jews, the power of the Maccabees posed a problem: because Mattathias's bloodline could be traced to neither King David nor Aaron the priest, by what right had his descendants assumed kingly and priestly authority? Against such criticism, the author of 1 Maccabees tries to prove that God's plan was accomplished through Mattathias's family.

The interpretation of Jewish history contained in 1 Maccabees invites us to believe in God's choice of Mattathias's sons as saviors of the nation. Even more important, it invites us to believe in the utter reliability of God: "And so, consider this from generation to generation, that none who hope in him shall fail in strength" (2, 61).

Quick Facts

Period Covered
from 175 to 134 B.C.

Author
unknown, writing around 100 B.C.

Theme
God brings Israel to freedom through the family of Mattathias.

Of Note
First Maccabees is not found in some Protestant Bibles (see "The Case of the Missing Books," near Tb 1, 16).

Maccabees

1 Maccabees

I: Introduction: Hellenism In Asia Minor

Conquests and Death of Alexander

1 ¹*† After Alexander the Macedonian, Philip's son, who came from the land of Kittim, had defeated Darius, king of the Persians and Medes, he became king in his place, having first ruled in Greece. ² He fought many campaigns, captured fortresses, and put kings to death. ³ He advanced to the ends of the earth, gathering plunder from many nations; the earth fell silent before him, and his heart became proud and arrogant. ⁴ He collected a very strong army and conquered provinces, nations, and rulers, and they became his tributaries. ⁵ But after all this he took to his bed, realizing that he was going to die. ⁶ He therefore summoned his officers, the nobles, who had been brought up with him from his youth, to divide his kingdom among them while he was still alive. ⁷† Alexander had reigned twelve years when he died.

⁸ So his officers took over his kingdom, each in his own territory, ⁹ and after his death they all put on royal crowns, and so did their sons after them for many years, causing much distress over the earth.

II: The Maccabean Revolt

Pact between Jews and Gentiles

¹⁰*† There sprang from these a sinful offshoot, Antiochus Epiphanes, son of King Antiochus, once a hostage at Rome. He became king in the year one hundred and thirty-seven of the kingdom of the Greeks.

¹¹* In those days there appeared in Israel men who were breakers of the law, and they seduced many people, saying: "Let us go and make an alliance with the Gentiles all around us; since we separated from them, many evils have come upon us." ¹² The proposal was agreeable; ¹³* some from among the people promptly went to the king, and he authorized them to introduce the way of living of the Gentiles. ¹⁴† Thereupon they built a gymnasium

---

1, 1: *Land of Kittim:* Greece. The name referred originally to inhabitants of Kiti, capital of the isle of Cyprus, then to any Cypriots (Is 23, 1; Jer 2, 10), later to Greeks in general, and finally even to Romans. See note on Dn 11, 30. *Darius:* Darius III, Codoman (336–331 B.C.).

1, 7: *Twelve years:* 336–323 B.C.

1, 10: *The year one hundred and thirty-seven:* Antiochus IV seized the throne in September, 175 B.C. Dates are given in this book according to the Seleucid era, which however was reckoned in two different ways. Antiochians considered this date to be October, 312 B.C. (Syrian calendar), while Babylonians and Jewish priests accepted April, 311 B.C. as the commencement of the era (temple calendar). The author of 1 Maccabees dates political events by the

Syrian calendar but religious events by the temple calendar. Accordingly, the civil New Year occurred variously in September or October, the religious New Year in March or April.

1, 14: *Gymnasium:* symbol and center of athletic and intellectual life, it was the chief instrument of Hellenistic propaganda. Jewish youth were attracted by sports and encouraged to join youth clubs. They received training in military skills and in the duties of citizens. Through participation in the intellectual life, many were gradually won over to paganism.

1, 1–10: Dn 8, 20ff; 11, 3f.21.   **1, 11:** 2 Mc 4, 9–17.
1, 10: 2 Mc 4, 7.   **1, 13ff:** 2 Mc 4, 7–17.

---

in Jerusalem according to the Gentile custom. [15]* They covered over the mark of their circumcision and abandoned the holy covenant; they allied themselves with the Gentiles and sold themselves to wrongdoing.

Egyptian Campaign of Antiochus

[16] When his kingdom seemed secure, Antiochus proposed to become king of Egypt, so as to rule over both kingdoms. [17]*† He invaded Egypt with a strong force, with chariots and elephants, and with a large fleet, [18] to make war on Ptolemy, king of Egypt. Ptolemy was frightened at his presence and fled, leaving many casualties. [19] The fortified cities in the land of Egypt were captured, and Antiochus plundered the land of Egypt.

Persecution of the Jews

[20]*† After Antiochus had defeated Egypt in the year one hundred and forty-three, he returned and went up to Israel and to Jerusalem with a strong force. [21] He insolently invaded the sanctuary and took away the golden altar, the lampstand for the light with all its fixtures, [22] the offering table, the cups and the bowls, the golden censers, the curtain, the crowns, and the golden ornament on the façade of the temple. He stripped off everything, [23] and took away the gold and silver and the precious vessels; he also took all the hidden treasures he could find. [24] Taking all this, he went back to his own country, after he had spoken with great arrogance and shed much blood.

[25] And there was great mourning for Israel, in
    every place where they dwelt,
[26] and the rulers and the elders groaned.
    Virgins and young men languished,
    and the beauty of the women was disfigured.
[27] Every bridegroom took up lamentation,
    she who sat in the bridal
      chamber mourned,
[28] And the land was shaken on account of
    its inhabitants,
    and all the house of Jacob was covered
    with shame.

[29]* Two years later, the king sent the Mysian commander to the cities of Judah, and he came to

Jerusalem with a strong force. [30] He spoke to them deceitfully in peaceful terms, and won their trust. Then he attacked the city suddenly, in a great onslaught, and destroyed many of the people in Israel. [31] He plundered the city and set fire to it, demolished its houses and its surrounding walls, [32] took captive the women and children, and seized the cattle. [33]*† Then they built up the City of David with a high, massive wall and strong towers, and it became their citadel. [34] There they installed a sinful race, perverse men, who fortified themselves inside it, [35] storing up weapons and provisions, and depositing there the plunder they had collected from Jerusalem. And they became a great threat.

[36] The citadel became an ambush against
    the sanctuary,
    and a wicked adversary to Israel at all times.
[37] And they shed innocent blood around
    the sanctuary;
    they defiled the sanctuary.
[38] Because of them the inhabitants of Jerusalem
    fled away,
    and she became the abode of strangers.
    She became a stranger to her own offspring,
    and her children forsook her.
[39]* Her sanctuary was as desolate as a wilderness;
    her feasts were turned into mourning,
    Her sabbaths to shame,
    her honor to contempt.
[40] Her dishonor was as great as her glory
    had been,
    and her exaltation was turned
    into mourning.

Prohibitions against Religion

[41] Then the king wrote to his whole kingdom that all should be one people, [42] each abandoning his particular customs. All the Gentiles conformed to the command of the king, [43] and many Israelites were in favor of his religion; they sacrificed to idols and profaned the sabbath.

[44]* The king sent messengers with letters to Jerusalem and to the cities of Judah, ordering them to follow customs foreign to their land: [45] to prohibit holocausts, sacrifices, and libations in the sanctuary, to profane the sabbaths and feast days, [46]* to desecrate the sanctuary and the sacred

---

† **1, 17:** *Elephants:* an important part of Seleucid armament. About 300 B.C. Seleucus I, founder of the dynasty, procured five hundred of them from India; cf 1 Mc 6, 34–37.

1, 20: *Defeated Egypt in the year one hundred and forty-three:* 169 B.C. No mention is made in 1 Maccabees of the second expedition to Egypt a year later, described in 2 Mc 5, 1.11. Dn 11, 25.29 records both.

1, 33: *City of David:* not Mount Zion on the eastern hill of Jerusalem, which David captured from the Jebusites (2 Sm 5, 7), but a new fortress built on the western hill and overlooking the temple

and its courts on Mount Zion. It was occupied for twenty-six years by the Syro-Macedonian garrison, together with apostate Jews, and was a continual threat to the temple and the Jewish people (v 36); cf 1 Mc 13, 49ff.

1, 15: 1 Cor 7, 18.	**1, 33:** 1 Mc 6, 18.
1, 17: 2 Mc 5, 1; Dn 11,	**1, 39f:** Tb 2, 6; Am 8, 10.
25–28.	**1, 44–63:** 2 Mc 6, 1–11.
1, 20–24: 2 Mc 5, 11–21.	**1, 46:** 2 Mc 6, 2; Dn 9, 27.
1, 29–32: 2 Mc 5, 24ff.	

ministers, to build pagan altars and temples and shrines, [47] to sacrifice swine and unclean animals, [48] to leave their sons uncircumcised, and to let themselves be defiled with every kind of impurity and abomination, [49] so that they might forget the law and change all their observances. [50]* Whoever refused to act according to the command of the king should be put to death.

[51] Such were the orders he published throughout his kingdom. He appointed inspectors over all the people, and he ordered the cities of Judah to offer sacrifices, each city in turn. [52] Many of the people, those who abandoned the law, joined them and committed evil in the land. [53] Israel was driven into hiding, wherever places of refuge could be found.

[54]*† On the fifteenth day of the month Chislev, in the year one hundred and forty-five, the king erected the horrible abomination upon the altar of holocausts, and in the surrounding cities of Judah they built pagan altars. [55] They also burnt incense at the doors of houses and in the streets. [56]† Any scrolls of the law which they found they tore up and burnt. [57]* Whoever was found with a scroll of the covenant, and whoever observed the law, was condemned to death by royal decree. [58] So they used their power against Israel, against those who were caught, each month, in the cities. [59] On the twenty-fifth day of each month they sacrificed on the altar erected over the altar of holocausts. [60]* Women who had had their children circumcised were put to death, in keeping with the decree, [61] with the babies hung from their necks; their families also and those who had circumcised them were killed. [62] But many in Israel were determined and resolved in their hearts not to eat anything unclean; [63]* they preferred to die rather than to be defiled with unclean food or to profane the holy covenant; and they did die. Terrible affliction was upon Israel.

Mattathias and His Sons

2 [1]† In those days Mattathias, son of John, son of Simeon, a priest of the family of Joarib, left Jerusalem and settled in Modein. [2]* He had five sons: John, who was called Gaddi; [3] Simon, who was called Thassi; [4] Judas, who was called Maccabeus; [5] Eleazar, who was called Avaran; and Jonathan, who was called Apphus. [6] When he saw the sacrileges that were being committed in Judah and in Jerusalem, [7] he said: "Woe is me! Why was I born to see the ruin of my people and the ruin of the holy city, and to sit idle while it is given into the hands of enemies, and the sanctuary into the hands of strangers?

[8]   "Her temple has become like a man disgraced,
[9]*   her glorious ornaments have been carried
            off as spoils,
        Her infants have been murdered in her streets,
            her young men by the sword of the enemy.
[10]   What nation has not taken its share of
            her realm,
        and laid its hand on her possessions?
[11]   All her adornment has been taken away.
        From being free, she has become a slave.
[12]   We see our sanctuary and our beauty
            and our glory laid waste,
        And the Gentiles have defiled them!
[13]   Why are we still alive?"

[14] Then Mattathias and his sons tore their garments, put on sackcloth, and mourned bitterly.

Pagan Worship Refused

[15] The officers of the king in charge of enforcing the apostasy came to the city of Modein to organize the sacrifices. [16] Many of Israel joined them, but Mattathias and his sons gathered in a group apart. [17] Then the officers of the king addressed Mattathias: "You are a leader, an honorable and great man in this city, supported by sons and kinsmen. [18]† Come now, be the first to obey the king's command, as all the Gentiles and the men of Judah and those who are left in Jerusalem have done. Then you and your sons shall be numbered among the King's Friends, and shall be enriched with silver and gold and many gifts." [19] But Mattathias answered in a loud voice: "Although all the Gentiles in the king's realm obey him, so that each forsakes the religion of his fathers and consents to the king's orders, [20] yet I and my sons and my kinsmen will keep to the covenant of our fathers. [21] God forbid that we should forsake the law and the commandments. [22] We will not obey the words of the king nor depart from our religion in the slightest degree."

[23] As he finished saying these words, a certain Jew came forward in the sight of all to offer sacrifice on the altar in Modein according to the king's order. [24] When Mattathias saw him, he was filled with

---

† **1, 54:** *Fifteenth day of the month Chislev, in the year one hundred and forty-five:* early December, 167 B.C. *Horrible abomination:* in the original Hebrew, a contemptuous pun on the title "Lord of heaven" given to the god Zeus Olympios, to whom an image or perhaps an altar was erected upon the altar of holocausts in the temple of Jerusalem; cf Dn 9, 27; 11, 31.
1, 56f: *Scrolls of the law:* one or more of the first five books of the Old Testament.
2, 1: *Modein:* a village twenty miles northwest of Jerusalem.

2, 18: *The King's Friends:* a regular order of nobility at Hellenistic courts. The various grades are frequently mentioned in this book: Friends, Chief Friends, Kinsmen.

*
1, 50: 2 Mc 6, 18—7, 41.   1, 60f: 2 Mc 6, 10.
1, 54: 1 Mc 6, 7; Dn 9, 27;   1, 63: 2 Mc 6, 10.
    11, 31.   2, 2: 1 Chr 24, 7.
1, 57: 2 Mc 2, 14.   2, 9: Lam 2, 11.21.

Religious Persecution

The Jews were facing a societal attack on their faith. But Mattathias and his sons chose to fight the official and cultural pressure to turn away from their faith.
Are there times when you feel persecuted because of your belief in God? In what subtle ways does contemporary society ridicule people with religious beliefs? If you were to be persecuted because of your religion, how would you respond?

▸ 1 Mc 2, 19–22

zeal; his heart was moved and his just fury was aroused; he sprang forward and killed him upon the altar. 25 At the same time, he also killed the messenger of the king who was forcing them to sacrifice, and he tore down the altar. 26* Thus he showed his zeal for the law, just as Phinehas did with Zimri, son of Salu.

27 Then Mattathias went through the city shouting, "Let everyone who is zealous for the law and who stands by the covenant follow after me!" 28* Thereupon he fled to the mountains with his sons, leaving behind in the city all their possessions. 29† Many who sought to live according to righteousness and religious custom went out into the desert to settle there, 30 they and their sons, their wives and their cattle, because misfortunes pressed so hard on them.

31 It was reported to the officers and soldiers of the king who were in the City of David, in Jerusalem, that certain men who had flouted the king's order had gone out to the hiding places in the desert. 32* Many hurried out after them, and having caught up with them, camped opposite and prepared to attack them on the sabbath. 33 "Enough of this!" the pursuers said to them. "Come out and obey the king's command, and your lives will be spared." 34 But they replied, "We will not come out, nor will we obey the king's command to profane the sabbath." 35 Then the enemy attacked them at once; 36 but they did not retaliate; they neither threw stones, nor blocked up their own hiding places. 37 They said, "Let us all die without reproach; heaven and earth are our witnesses that you destroy us unjustly." 38 So the officers and soldiers attacked them on the sabbath, and they died with their wives, their children and their cattle, to the number of a thousand persons.

39 When Mattathias and his friends heard of it,

they mourned deeply for them. 40 "If we all do as our kinsmen have done," they said to one another, "and do not fight against the Gentiles for our lives and our traditions, they will soon destroy us from the earth." 41 On that day they came to this decision: "Let us fight against anyone who attacks us on the sabbath, so that we may not all die as our kinsmen died in the hiding places."

42† Then they were joined by a group of Hasideans, valiant Israelites, all of them devout followers of the law. 43 And all those who were fleeing from the disaster joined them and supported them. 44* They gathered an army and struck down sinners in their anger and lawbreakers in their wrath, and the survivors fled to the Gentiles for safety. 45 Mattathias and his friends went about and tore down the pagan altars; 46 they also forcibly circumcised any uncircumcised boys whom they found in the territory of Israel. 47 They put to flight the arrogant, and the work prospered in their hands. 48 They saved the law from the hands of the Gentiles and of the kings and did not let the sinner triumph.

Death of Mattathias

49 When the time came for Mattathias to die, he said to his sons: "Arrogance and scorn have now grown strong; it is a time of disaster and violent anger. 50 Therefore, my sons, be zealous for the law and give your lives for the covenant of our fathers.

51 "Remember the deeds that our fathers did in
          their times,
        and you shall win great glory and an
          everlasting name.
52* Was not Abraham found faithful in trial,
        and it was reputed to him as uprightness?
53* Joseph, when in distress, kept
        the commandment,

2, 29: *The desert:* the sparsely inhabited mountain country southward from Jerusalem and west of the Dead Sea. It was an arid region with some perennial springs and a fair amount of rain in winter.
2, 42: *Hasideans:* in Hebrew *hasidim,* "pious ones," a religious group devoted to the strict observance of the law. They were the forerunners of both the Pharisees and the Essenes. They first supported

the Maccabean movement, but subsequently opposed it, regarding it as too political.

2, 26: 1 Mc 2, 54; Nm 25,
    6–14.
2, 28: 2 Mc 5, 27.
2, 32–38: 2 Mc 6, 11.
2, 44: Is 63, 3.
2, 52: Gn 15, 6; 22, 1ff.
2, 53: Gn 39, 7–10; 41,
    39–43.

and he became master of Egypt.
54* Phinehas our father, for his burning
    zeal,
    received the covenant of an
    everlasting priesthood.
55* Joshua, for executing his commission,
    became a judge in Israel.
56* Caleb, for bearing witness before
    the assembly,
    received an inheritance in the land.
57* David, for his piety,
    received as a heritage a throne of
    everlasting royalty.
58* Elijah, for his burning zeal for the law,
    was taken up to heaven.
59* Hananiah, Azariah and Mishael, for
    their faith,
    were saved from the fire.
60* Daniel, for his innocence,
    was delivered from the jaws of lions.
61 And so, consider this from generation
    to generation,
    that none who hope in him shall fail
    in strength.
62 Do not fear the words of a sinful man,
    for his glory ends in corruption
    and worms.
63 Today he is exalted, and tomorrow he is not
    to be found,
    because he has returned to his dust,
    and his schemes have perished.
64 Children! be courageous and strong in
    keeping the law,
    for by it you shall be glorified.

65 "Here is your brother Simeon who I know is a wise man; listen to him always, and he will be a father to you. 66 And Judas Maccabeus, a warrior from his youth, shall be the leader of your army and direct the war against the nations. 67 You shall also gather about you all who observe the law, and you shall avenge the wrongs of your people. 68 Pay back the Gentiles what they deserve, and observe the precepts of the law."

69 Then he blessed them, and he was united with his fathers. 70† He died in the year one hundred and forty-six, and was buried in the tombs of his fathers in Modein, and all Israel mourned him greatly.

III: Leadership of Judas Maccabeus

Defeat of Apollonius and Seron

3 1 Then his son Judas, who was called Maccabeus, took his place. 2 All his brothers and all who had joined his father supported him, and they carried on Israel's war joyfully.

3* He spread abroad the glory of his people,
    and put on his breastplate like a giant.
He armed himself with weapons of war;
    he planned battles and protected the camp
    with his sword.
4 In his actions he was like a lion,
    like a young lion roaring for prey.
5 He pursued the wicked, hunting them out,
    and those who troubled his people he
    destroyed by fire.
6 The lawbreakers were cowed by fear of him,
    and all evildoers were dismayed.
By his hand redemption was
    happily achieved,
7 and he afflicted many kings;
He made Jacob glad by his deeds,
    and his memory is blessed forever.
8 He went about the cities of Judah
    destroying the impious there.
He turned away wrath from Israel
9 and was renowned to the ends of the earth;
    he gathered together those who
    were perishing.

10† Then Apollonius gathered the Gentiles, together with a large army from Samaria, to fight against Israel. 11 When Judas learned of it, he went out to meet him and defeated and killed him. Many fell wounded, and the rest fled. 12 Their possessions were seized and the sword of Apollonius was taken by Judas, who fought with it the rest of his life.

13 But Seron, commander of the Syrian army, heard that Judas had gathered many about him, an assembly of faithful men ready for war. 14 So he said, "I will make a name for myself and win glory in the kingdom by defeating Judas and his followers, who have despised the king's command." 15 And again a large company of renegades advanced with him to help him take revenge on the Israelites. 16† When he reached the ascent of Beth-horon, Judas went out to meet him with a few

1
M
C

2, 70: *In the year one hundred and forty-six:* 166 B.C.
3, 10: *Apollonius:* the Mysian commander mentioned in 1 Mc 1, 29 and in 2 Mc 5, 24.
3, 16: *Beth-horon:* the famous pass leading up from the coastal plain to the Judean hill country. Here Joshua won an important battle (Jos 10, 10f), and in 66 A.D. a Roman force under Cestius was trapped and massacred.

2, 54: Nm 25, 10–13; Sir 45,   2, 58: 1 Kgs 19, 10.14; 2 Kgs
    28ff.   2, 11.
2, 55: Jos 1, 2.5.   2, 59: Dn 3, 50.
2, 56: Nm 13, 30; 14, 6–9.   2, 60: Dn 6, 23; 14, 31–42.
    24; Jos 14, 14.   3, 3: 2 Mc 8, 5.
2, 57: 2 Sm 2, 4; 7, 16.

men. [17] But when they saw the army coming against them, they said to Judas: "How can we, few as we are, fight such a mighty host as this? Besides, we are weak today from fasting." [18] But Judas said: "It is easy for many to be overcome by a few; in the sight of Heaven there is no difference between deliverance by many or by few; [19]* for victory in war does not depend upon the size of the army, but on strength that comes from Heaven. [20] With great presumption and lawlessness they come against us to destroy us and our wives and children and to despoil us; [21] but we are fighting for our lives and our laws. [22]† He himself will crush them before us; so do not be afraid of them." [23] When he finished speaking, he rushed suddenly upon Seron and his army, who were crushed before him. [24]*† He pursued Seron down the descent of Beth-horon into the plain. About eight hundred of their men fell, and the rest fled to the country of the Philistines. [25] Then Judas and his brothers began to be feared, and dread fell upon the Gentiles about them. [26] His fame reached the king, and all the Gentiles talked about the battles of Judas.

Regency of Lysias

[27] When Antiochus heard about these events, he was angry; so he ordered a muster of all the forces of his kingdom, a very strong army. [28] He opened his treasure chests, gave his soldiers a year's pay, and commanded them to be prepared for anything. [29] He then found that this exhausted the money in his treasury; moreover the income from the province was small, because of the dissension and distress he had brought upon the land by abolishing the laws which had been in effect from of old. [30] He feared that, as had happened more than once, he would not have enough for his expenses and for the gifts that he had previously given with a more liberal hand than the preceding kings. [31] Greatly perplexed, he decided to go to Persia and levy tribute on those provinces, and so raise a large sum of money. [32] He left Lysias, a nobleman of royal blood, in charge of the king's affairs from the Euphrates River to the frontier of Egypt, [33] and commissioned him to take care of his son Antiochus until his own return. [34] He entrusted to him half of the army, and the elephants, and gave him instructions concerning

everything he wanted done. As for the inhabitants of Judea and Jerusalem, [35] Lysias was to send an army against them to crush and destroy the power of Israel and the remnant of Jerusalem and efface their memory from the land. [36] He was to settle foreigners in all their territory and distribute their land by lot.

[37]† The king took the remaining half of the army and set out from Antioch, his capital, in the year one hundred and forty-seven; he crossed the Euphrates River and advanced inland.

The Victories of Judas

[38]*† Lysias chose Ptolemy, son of Dorymenes, and Nicanor and Gorgias, capable men among the King's Friends,* [39] and with them he sent forty thousand men and seven thousand cavalry to invade the land of Judah and ravage it according to the king's orders. [40]† Setting out with all their forces, they came and pitched their camp near Emmaus in the plain. [41] When the merchants of the country heard of their fame, they came to the camp, bringing fetters and a large sum of silver and gold, to buy the Israelites as slaves. A force from Idumea and from Philistia joined with them.

[42] Judas and his brothers saw that the situation had become critical now that armies were encamped within their territory; they knew of the orders which the king had given to destroy and utterly wipe out the people. [43] So they said to one another, "Let us restore our people from their ruined estate, and fight for our people and our sanctuary!"

[44] The assembly gathered together to prepare for battle and to pray and implore mercy and compassion.

[45]   Jerusalem was uninhabited, like a desert;
   not one of her children entered or
      came out.
The sanctuary was trampled on,
   and foreigners were in the citadel;
   it was a habitation of Gentiles.
Joy had disappeared from Jacob,
   and the flute and the harp were silent.

[46]*† Thus they assembled and went to Mizpah near Jerusalem, because there was formerly at

---

3, 22: *He himself:* out of reverence for God, the author of 1 Maccabees prefers to use this and other expressions, such as "Heaven," instead of the divine name. Cf 1 Mc 3, 50.

3, 24: *About eight hundred:* the figures given in this book for strength of armies and number of casualties are not to be taken literally. In accordance with biblical usage, they indicate rather the importance of the battle described or the greatness of the victory.

3, 37: This expedition, in the spring of 165 B.C., resulted in failure; cf ch 6.

3, 38: *Nicanor:* the leader of another attack against the Jews four years later. He was finally killed by Judas; cf 1 Mc 7, 26–46.

3, 40: *Emmaus:* probably not the village mentioned in Lk 24, 13, but a settlement about twenty miles west of Jerusalem at the edge of the hill country.

3, 46: . . . *Mizpah a place of prayer for Israel:* a holy place established of old eight miles north and slightly west of Jerusalem. It was here that Samuel began to judge the Israelites (1 Sm 7, 5–11; 10, 17).

3, 19: 1 Sm 14, 16.
3, 24: Jos 10, 10.
3, 38–44: 2 Mc 8, 8–15.
3, 38f: 1 Mc 7, 26; 2 Mc 4,
45; 8, 8f; 10, 14.
3, 46ff: 1 Sm 7, 5f; 2 Mc 8,
16–23.

Mizpah a place of prayer for Israel. [47] That day they fasted and wore sackcloth; they sprinkled ashes on their heads and tore their clothes. [48]† They unrolled the scroll of the law, to learn about the things for which the Gentiles consulted the images of their idols. [49]*† They brought with them the priestly vestments, the first fruits, and the tithes; and they brought forward the nazirites who had completed the time of their vows. [50] And they cried aloud to Heaven: "What shall we do with these men, and where shall we take them? [51] For your sanctuary has been trampled on and profaned, and your priests are in mourning and humiliation. [52] Now the Gentiles are gathered together against us to destroy us. You know what they plot against us. [53] How shall we be able to resist them unless you help us?" [54] Then they blew the trumpets and cried out loudly.

[55] After this Judas appointed officers among the people, over thousands, over hundreds, over fifties, and over tens. [56]* He proclaimed that those who were building houses, or were just married, or were planting vineyards, and those who were afraid, could each return to his home, according to the law. [57] Then the army moved off, and they camped to the south of Emmaus. [58] Judas said: "Arm yourselves and be brave; in the morning be ready to fight these Gentiles who have assembled against us to destroy us and our sanctuary. [59]* It is better for us to die in battle than to witness the ruin of our nation and our sanctuary. Whatever Heaven wills, he will do."

4 [1] Now Gorgias took five thousand infantry and a thousand picked cavalry, and this detachment set out at night [2] in order to attack the camp of the Jews and take them by surprise. Some men from the citadel were their guides. [3] Judas heard of it, and himself set out with his soldiers to attack the king's army at Emmaus, [4] while the latter's forces were still scattered away from the camp. [5] During the night Gorgias came into the camp of Judas, and found no one there; so he began to hunt for them in the mountains, saying, "They are fleeing from us."

[6] But at daybreak Judas appeared in the plain with three thousand men, who lacked such armor and swords as they would have wished. [7] They saw the army of the Gentiles, strong and breastplated,

flanked with cavalry, and made up of expert soldiers. [8] Judas said to the men with him: "Do not be afraid of their numbers or dread their attack. [9]* Remember how our fathers were saved in the Red Sea, when Pharaoh pursued them with an army. [10]* So now let us cry to Heaven in the hope that he will favor us, remember his covenant with our fathers, and destroy this army before us today. [11] All the Gentiles shall know that there is One who redeems and delivers Israel."

[12] When the foreigners looked up and saw them marching toward them, [13] they came out of their camp for battle, and the men with Judas blew the trumpet. [14] The battle was joined and the Gentiles were defeated and fled toward the plain. [15]† Their whole rearguard fell by the sword, and they were pursued as far as Gazara and the plains of Judea, to Azotus and Jamnia. About three thousand of their men fell.

[16] When Judas and the army returned from the pursuit, [17] he said to the people: "Do not be greedy for the plunder, for there is a fight ahead of us, [18] and Gorgias and his army are near us on the mountain. But now stand firm against our enemies and overthrow them. Afterward you can freely take the plunder."

[19] As Judas was finishing this speech, a detachment appeared, looking down from the mountain. [20] They saw that their army had been put to flight and their camp was being burned. The smoke that could be seen indicated what had happened. [21] When they realized this, they were terrified; and when they also saw the army of Judas in the plain ready to attack, [22]† they all fled to Philistine territory.

[23] Then Judas went back to plunder the camp, and his men collected much gold and silver, violet and crimson cloth, and great treasure. [24]* As they returned, they were singing hymns and glorifying Heaven, "for he is good, for his mercy endures forever." [25] Thus Israel had a great deliverance that day.

Victory over Lysias

[26]* But those of the foreigners who had escaped went and told Lysias all that had occurred. [27] When he heard it he was disturbed and discouraged, because things in Israel had not turned out as he intended and as the king had ordered.

[28] So the following year he gathered together

---

†
3, 48: *To learn . . . idols:* favorable omens for the coming battle. A contrast is intended between the idol worship of the pagans and the consultation of the word of God by the Jews; cf 2 Mc 8, 23.

3, 49: *Nazirites:* see note on Nm 6, 1ff.

4, 15: *Gazara:* Gezer of the Hebrew Bible, five miles northwest of Emmaus: *Azotus,* Hebrew Ashdod, lay to the southwest; and *Jamnia,* Hebrew Jabneel (Jos 15, 11) or Jabneh (2 Chr 26, 6), to the west of Gazara.

4, 22: *Philistine territory:* the coastal cities of southern Palestine,

traditionally hostile to Jerusalem. Jamnia in particular was an important base for the Seleucid power.

*
3, 49: Nm 6, 2–5.	**4, 10:** 1 Mc 2, 21.
3, 56: Dt 20, 5–8; Jgs 7, 3.	**4, 24:** Ps 118, 1ff.29.
3, 59: 1 Mc 2, 21f.	**4, 26–35:** 2 Mc 11, 1–12.
4, 9: Ex 14, 21ff.	

sixty thousand picked men and five thousand cavalry, to subdue them. 29† They came into Idumea and camped at Beth-zur, and Judas met them with ten thousand men. 30* Seeing that the army was strong, he prayed thus:

"Blessed are you, O Savior of Israel, who broke the rush of the mighty one by the hand of your servant David and delivered the camp of the Philistines into the hand of Jonathan, the son of Saul, and his armor-bearer. 31 Give this army into the hands of your people Israel; make them ashamed of their troops and their cavalry. 32 Strike them with fear, weaken the boldness of their strength, and let them tremble at their own destruction. 33 Strike them down by the sword of those who love you, that all who know your name may hymn your praise."

34 Then they engaged in battle, and about five thousand of Lysias' men fell in hand-to-hand fighting. 35† When Lysias saw his ranks beginning to give way, and the increased boldness of Judas, whose men were ready either to live or to die bravely, he withdrew to Antioch and began to recruit mercenaries so as to return to Judea with greater numbers.

Purification of the Temple

36*† Then Judas and his brothers said, "Now that our enemies have been crushed, let us go up to purify the sanctuary and rededicate it." 37 So the whole army assembled, and went up to Mount Zion. 38* They found the sanctuary desolate, the altar desecrated, the gates burnt, weeds growing in the courts as in a forest or on some mountain, and the priests' chambers demolished. 39 Then they tore their clothes and made great lamentation; they sprinkled their heads with ashes 40 and fell with their faces to the ground. And when the signal was given with trumpets, they cried out to Heaven.

41 Judas appointed men to attack those in the citadel, while he purified the sanctuary. 42 He chose blameless priests, devoted to the law; 43 these purified the sanctuary and carried away the stones of the Abomination to an unclean place. 44* They deliberated what ought to be done with the altar of holocausts that had been desecrated. 45* The happy thought came to them to tear it down, lest it be a lasting shame to them that the Gentiles had defiled it; so they tore down the altar. 46 They stored the stones in a suitable place on the temple hill, until a prophet should come and decide what to do with them. 47* Then they took uncut stones, according to the law, and built a new altar like the former one. 48 They also repaired the sanctuary and the interior of the temple and purified the courts. 49* They made new sacred vessels and brought the lampstand, the altar of incense, and the table into the temple. 50* Then they burned incense on the altar and lighted the lamps on the lampstand, and these illuminated the temple. 51 They also put loaves on the table and hung up the curtains. Thus they finished all the work they had undertaken.

52† Early in the morning on the twenty-fifth day of the ninth month, that is, the month of Chislev, in the year one hundred and forty-eight, 53* they arose and offered sacrifice according to the law on the new altar of holocausts that they had made. 54 On the anniversary of the day on which the Gentiles had defiled it, on that very day it was reconsecrated with songs, harps, flutes, and cymbals. 55 All the people prostrated themselves and adored and praised Heaven, who had given them success.

56 For eight days they celebrated the dedication of the altar and joyfully offered holocausts and

did you KNOW?

Hanukkah

Hanukkah, or the feast of Dedication, is a joyful eight-day celebration in the month of Chislev (December). On each night of the festival, a candle is lit in joyful remembrance of the Maccabees' rededication of the Temple in Jerusalem after it was robbed and desecrated by Antiochus IV Epiphanes (1 Mc 4, 56). Even more deeply, the candlelight symbolizes the gratitude of the Jewish people for the survival, often against great odds, of their age-old faith.

▶ 1 Mc 4, 52–59

---

† 4, 29: *Beth-zur:* an important frontier city in the mountain area, fifteen miles southwest of Jerusalem. Its inhabitants were sympathetic to the Maccabees and refused to receive Lysias.

4, 35: According to 2 Mc 11, 13–15, peace negotiations followed between Lysias and Judas.

4, 36: *The sanctuary:* the whole temple area with its walls, courts and outbuildings, to be distinguished from the temple proper, the oblong edifice with porch, main room and inner shrine.

4, 52: *Twenty-fifth day of the ninth month . . . in the year one hundred and forty-eight:* December 14, 164 B.C.

4, 30: 1 Sm 17, 48ff.
4, 36–59: 2 Mc 10, 1–8.
4, 38: Ps 74, 2–7.
4, 44: 1 Kgs 8, 64.
4, 45: 1 Mc 6, 7.
4, 47: Ex 20, 25.
4, 49: Ex 25, 23–39; 30, 1–6.
4, 50: Ex 30, 7ff.
4, 53.56: Ex 30, 10; Ez 43, 18–27.

sacrifices of deliverance and praise. [57] They ornamented the façade of the temple with gold crowns and shields; they repaired the gates and the priests' chambers and furnished them with doors. [58] There was great joy among the people now that the disgrace of the Gentiles was removed. [59]*† Then Judas and his brothers and the entire congregation of Israel decreed that the days of the dedication of the altar should be observed with joy and gladness on the anniversary every year for eight days, from the twenty-fifth day of the month Chislev.

[60] At that time they built high walls and strong towers around Mount Zion, to prevent the Gentiles from coming and trampling over it as they had done before. [61] Judas also placed a garrison there to protect it, and likewise fortified Beth-zur, that the people might have a stronghold facing Idumea.

Punishment of Hostile Acts

5 [1]*† When the Gentiles round about heard that the altar had been rebuilt and the sanctuary consecrated as before, they were very angry. [2] So they decided to destroy the descendants of Jacob who were among them, and they began to massacre and persecute the people. [3]*† Then Judas attacked the sons of Esau at Akrabattene in Idumea, because they were blockading Israel; he defeated them heavily, overcame and despoiled them. [4]† He also remembered the malice of the sons of Baean, who had become a snare and a stumblingblock to the people by ambushing them along the roads. [5] He forced them to take refuge in towers, which he besieged; he vowed their annihilation and burned down the towers along with all the persons in them. [6]† Then he crossed over to the Ammonites, where he found a strong army and a large body of people with Timothy as their leader. [7] He fought many battles with them, routed them, and struck them down. [8] After seizing Jazer and its villages, he returned to Judea.

Liberation of Galilean Jews

[9] The Gentiles in Gilead assembled to attack and destroy the Israelites who were in their territory; these then fled to the stronghold of Dathema. [10] They sent a letter to Judas and his brothers

saying: "The Gentiles around us have combined against us to destroy us, [11] and they are preparing to come and seize this stronghold to which we have fled. Timothy is the leader of their army. [12] Come at once and rescue us from them, for many of us have fallen. [13]* All our kinsmen who were among the Tobiads have been killed; the Gentiles have carried away their wives and children and their goods, and they have slain there about a thousand men."

[14] While they were reading this letter, suddenly other messengers, in torn clothes, arrived from Galilee to deliver a similar message: [15]† that the inhabitants of Ptolemais, Tyre, and Sidon, and the whole of Gentile Galilee had joined forces to destroy them. [16] When Judas and the people heard this, a great assembly convened to consider what they should do for their unfortunate kinsmen who were being attacked by enemies.

[17] Judas said to his brother Simon: "Choose men for yourself, and go, rescue your kinsmen in Galilee; I and my brother Jonathan will go to Gilead."

[18] In Judea he left Joseph, son of Zechariah, and Azariah, leader of the people, with the rest of the army to guard it. [19] "Take charge of these people," he commanded them, "but do not fight against the Gentiles until we return." [20] Three thousand men were allotted to Simon, to go into Galilee, and eight thousand men to Judas, for Gilead.

[21] Simon went into Galilee and fought many battles with the Gentiles. They were crushed before him, [22] and he pursued them to the very gate of Ptolemais. About three thousand men of the Gentiles fell, and he gathered their spoils. [23] He took with him the Jews who were in Galilee and in Arbatta, with their wives and children and all that they had, and brought them to Judea with great rejoicing.

Rescue in Gilead

[24]* Judas Maccabeus and his brother Jonathan crossed the Jordan and marched for three days through the desert. [25]† There they met some Nabateans, who received them peacefully and told them all that had happened to the Jews in Gilead: [26] "Many of them have been imprisoned in Bozrah,

---

4, 59: *Days of the dedication . . . Chislev:* institution of the feast of Hanukkah, also called the feast of Dedication (Jn 10, 22). Josephus Flavius calls it the feast of Lights.
5, 1: The events of this chapter occurred within the year 163 B.C.
5, 3: *Akrabattene:* a district southwest of the Dead Sea.
5, 4: *Sons of Baean:* 2 Mc 10, 15–23 calls them simply Idumeans.
5, 6ff: This summary anticipates the order of events and would fit better between vv 36 and 37. It corresponds to 2 Mc 12, 17–23. The action was probably a reprisal for the massacre referred to in v 13. Timothy was the Seleucid governor of Transjordan. *Jazer:* a town on the road from the Jordan to Amman.
5, 15: *Ptolemais:* Hebrew Acco (Jgs 1, 31), modern Acre, on the coast north of Haifa.

5, 25: *Nabateans:* an Arab people who acquired wealth and power as caravan merchants in the final two centuries B.C. They settled down, established Petra as their capital, and for a time controlled all of Transjordan, even as far as Damascus. It was from a Nabatean governor that St. Paul escaped about 38 A.D. (2 Cor 11, 32f).

4, 59: Jn 10, 22.   5, 13: 2 Mc 12, 17.
5, 1f: 1 Mc 13, 6.   5, 24–36: 2 Mc 12, 10ff.
5, 3ff: 2 Mc 10, 15–23.

in Bosor near Alema, in Chaspho, Maked, and Carnaim"—all of these are large, fortified cities— 27 "and some have been imprisoned in the other cities of Gilead. Tomorrow their enemies plan to attack the strongholds and to seize and destroy all these people in one day."

28 Thereupon Judas suddenly changed direction with his army, marched across the desert to Bozrah, and captured the city. He slaughtered all the male population, took all their possessions, and set fire to the city. 29 He led his army from that place by night, and they marched toward the stronghold of Dathema. 30 When morning came, they looked ahead and saw a countless multitude of people, with ladders and devices for capturing the stronghold, and beginning to attack the people within. 31 When Judas perceived that the struggle had begun and that the noise of the battle was resounding to heaven with trumpet blasts and loud shouting, 32 he said to the men of his army, "Fight for our kinsmen today."

33 He came up behind them with three columns blowing their trumpets and shouting in prayer. 34 When the army of Timothy realized that it was Maccabeus, they fell back before him, and he inflicted on them a crushing defeat. About eight thousand of their men fell that day. 35 Then he turned toward Alema and attacked and captured it; he killed all the male population, plundered the place, and burned it down. 36 From there he moved on and took Chaspho, Maked, Bosor, and the other cities of Gilead.

37* After these events Timothy assembled another army and camped opposite Raphon, on the other side of the stream. 38 Judas sent men to spy on the camp, and they reported to him: "All the Gentiles around us have rallied to him, making a very large force; 39 they have also hired Arabs to help them, and have camped beyond the stream, ready to attack you." So Judas went forward to attack them.

40* As Judas and his army were approaching the running stream, Timothy said to the officers of his army: "If he crosses over to us first, we shall not be able to resist him; he will certainly defeat us. 41 But if he is afraid and camps on the other side of the river, we will cross over to him and defeat him."

42 But when Judas reached the running stream, he stationed the officers of the people beside the stream and gave them this order: "Do not allow any man to pitch a tent; all must go into battle." 43 He was the first to cross to the attack, with all the people behind him, and the Gentiles were crushed before them; they threw away their arms and fled to the temple enclosure at Carnaim. 44* The Jews captured that city and burnt the enclosure with all who were in it. So Carnaim was subdued, and Judas met with no more resistance.

45 Then he assembled all the Israelites, great and small, who were in Gilead, with their wives and children and their goods, a great crowd of people, to go into the land of Judah. 46*† When they reached Ephron, a large and strongly fortified city along the way, they found it impossible to encircle it on either the right or the left; they would have to march right through it. 47* But the men in the city shut them out and blocked up the gates with stones. 48 Then Judas sent them this peaceful message: "We wish to cross your territory in order to reach our own; no one will harm you; we will only march through." But they would not open to him.

49 So Judas ordered a proclamation to be made in the camp that everyone make an attack from the place where he was. 50 When the men of the army took up their positions, he assaulted the city all that day and night, and it was delivered to him. 51 He slaughtered every male, razed and plundered the city, and passed through it over the slain.

52 Then they crossed the Jordan to the great plain in front of Beth-shan; 53 and Judas kept rounding up the stragglers and encouraging the people the whole way, until he reached the land of Judah. 54 They ascended Mount Zion in joy and gladness and offered holocausts, because not one of them had fallen; they returned in safety.

Joseph and Azariah Defeated

55 During the time that Judas and Jonathan were in the land of Gilead, and Simon his brother was in Galilee opposite Ptolemais, 56 Joseph, son of Zechariah, and Azariah, the leaders of the army, heard about the brave deeds and the fighting that they were doing. 57 They said, "Let us also make a name for ourselves by going out and fighting against the Gentiles around us."

58 They gave orders to the men of their army who were with them, and marched toward Jamnia. 59 But Gorgias and his men came out of the city to meet them in battle. 60 Joseph and Azariah were beaten, and were pursued to the frontiers of Judea, and about two thousand Israelites fell that day. 61 It was a bad defeat for the people, because they had not obeyed Judas and his brothers, thinking that they would do brave deeds. 62 But they did not belong to the family of those men to whom it was granted to achieve Israel's salvation. 63 The valiant

---

† **5, 46:** *Ephron:* a city in Transjordan opposite Beth-shan, about five miles east of the Jordan River. Situated on a height, it dominated the valleys of the two tributaries of the Jordan.

5, 37–44: 2 Mc 12, 20–26.   5, 46–54: 2 Mc 12, 27–31.
5, 40: 1 Sm 14, 9f.   5, 47: Nm 20, 17–21; 21,
5, 44: 2 Mc 12, 21.   21–25.

Judas and his brothers were greatly renowned in all Israel and among all the Gentiles, wherever their name was heard; 64 and men gathered about them and praised them.

65† Then Judas and his brothers went out and attacked the sons of Esau in the country toward the south; he took Hebron and its villages, and he destroyed its strongholds and burned the towers around it. 66 He then set out for the land of the Philistines and passed through Marisa. 67 At that time some priests fell in battle who had gone out rashly to fight in their desire to distinguish themselves. 68 Judas then turned toward Azotus in the land of the Philistines. He destroyed their altars and burned the statues of their gods; and after plundering their cities he returned to the land of Judah.

Defeat and Death of Antiochus IV

6 1*† As King Antiochus was traversing the inland provinces, he heard that in Persia there was a city called Elymais, famous for its wealth in silver and gold, 2 and that its temple was very rich, containing gold helmets, breastplates, and weapons left there by Alexander, son of Philip, king of Macedon, the first king of the Greeks. 3 He went therefore and tried to capture and pillage the city. But he could not do so, because his plan became known to the people of the city 4 who rose up in battle against him. So he retreated and in great dismay withdrew from there to return to Babylon.

5 While he was in Persia, a messenger brought him news that the armies sent into the land of Judah had been put to flight; 6 that Lysias had gone at first with a strong army and been driven back by the Israelites; that they had grown strong by reason of the arms, men, and abundant possessions taken from the armies they had destroyed; 7* that they had pulled down the Abomination which he had built upon the altar in Jerusalem; and that they had surrounded with high walls both the sanctuary, as it had been before, and his city of Beth-zur.

8 When the king heard this news, he was struck with fear and very much shaken. Sick with grief because his designs had failed, he took to his bed. 9 There he remained many days, overwhelmed with sorrow, for he knew he was going to die.

10 So he called in all his Friends and said to them: "Sleep has departed from my eyes, for my heart is sinking with anxiety. 11 I said to myself: 'Into what tribulation have I come, and in what floods of sorrow am I now! 12 Yet I was kindly and beloved in my rule.' But I now recall the evils I did in Jerusalem, when I carried away all the vessels of gold and silver that were in it, and for no cause gave orders that the inhabitants of Judah be destroyed. 13 I know that this is why these evils have overtaken me; and now I am dying, in bitter grief, in a foreign land."

14 Then he summoned Philip, one of his Friends, and put him in charge of his whole kingdom. 15 He gave him his crown, his robe, and his signet ring, so that he might guide the king's son Antiochus and bring him up to be king. 16† King Antiochus died in Persia in the year one hundred and forty-nine.

The Citadel Besieged

17*† When Lysias learned that the king was dead, he set up the king's son Antiochus, whom he had reared as a child, to be king in his place; and he gave him the title Eupator.

18* The men in the citadel were hemming in Israel around the sanctuary, continually trying to harm them and to strengthen the Gentiles. 19 But Judas planned to destroy them, and called all the people together to besiege them. 20† So in the year one hundred and fifty they assembled and stormed the citadel, for which purpose he constructed catapults and other devices. 21 Some of the besieged escaped, joined by impious Israelites; 22 they went to the king and said:

"How long will you fail to do justice and avenge our kinsmen? 23 We agreed to serve your father and to follow his orders and obey his edicts. 24 And for this the sons of our people have become our enemies; they have put to death as many of us as they could find and have plundered our estates. 25 They have acted aggressively not only against us, but throughout their whole territory. 26 Look! They have now besieged the citadel in Jerusalem in order to capture it, and they have fortified the sanctuary and Beth-zur. 27 Unless you quickly forestall them, they will do even worse things than these, and you will not be able to stop them."

Campaign against Judas

28* When the king heard this he was angry, and he called together all his Friends, the officers of his

---

5, 65: *Sons of Esau:* Idumeans.

6, 1: *Elymais:* the mountainous region of Elam, north of the Persian Gulf. This section continues the story from 1 Mc 3, 37 and pertains to events preceding those in 1 Mc 4, 37ff.

6, 16: *The year one hundred and forty-nine:* September 22, 164, to October 9, 163 B.C. A Babylonian list of the Seleucid kings indicates that Antiochus died in November or early December of 164.

6, 17: *The king's son Antiochus:* Antiochus V Eupator, then about nine years old. He was in Antioch, still in the charge of Lysias, who proceeded to govern and wage wars in his name. Both were put to

death two years later, when Demetrius, brother of Antiochus IV, arrived to claim the kingship; cf 1 Mc 7, 1ff.

6, 20: *The year one hundred and fifty:* October, 163, to September, 162 B.C.

6, 1–13: 2 Mc 1, 12–17; 9, 1–29.　　**6, 17:** 2 Mc 10, 10f.
　　　　　　　　　　　　　　　6, 18: 1 Mc 1, 33ff.
6, 7: 1 Mc 1, 54; 4, 41ff.60f.　**6, 28–54:** 2 Mc 13, 1–23.

1
M
C

army, and the commanders of the cavalry.* ²⁹ Mercenary forces also came to him from other kingdoms and from the islands of the seas. ³⁰ His army numbered a hundred thousand foot-soldiers, twenty thousand cavalry, and thirty-two elephants trained for war. ³¹ They passed through Idumea and camped before Beth-zur. For many days they attacked it; they constructed siege-devices, but the besieged made a sortie and burned these, and they fought bravely.

³² Then Judas marched away from the citadel and moved his camp to Beth-zechariah, on the way to the king's camp. ³³ The king, rising before dawn, moved his force hastily along the road to Beth-zechariah; and the armies prepared for battle, while the trumpets sounded. ³⁴ They made the elephants drunk on grape and mulberry wine to provoke them to fight. ³⁵ The beasts were distributed along the phalanxes, each elephant having assigned to it a thousand men in coats of mail, with bronze helmets, and five hundred picked cavalry. ³⁶ These anticipated the beast wherever it was; and wherever it moved, they moved too and never left it. ³⁷ A strong wooden tower covering each elephant, and fastened to it by a harness, held, besides the Indian mahout, three soldiers who fought from it. ³⁸ The remaining cavalry were stationed on one or the other of the two flanks of the army, to harass the enemy and to be protected from the phalanxes. ³⁹ When the sun shone on the gold and bronze shields, the mountains gleamed with their brightness and blazed like flaming torches. ⁴⁰ Part of the king's army extended over the heights, while some were on low ground, but they marched forward steadily and in good order. ⁴¹ All who heard the noise of their numbers, the tramp of their marching, and the clashing of the arms, trembled; for the army was very great and strong.

⁴² Judas with his army advanced to fight, and six hundred men of the king's army fell. ⁴³* Eleazar, called Avaran, saw one of the beasts bigger than any of the others and covered with royal armor, and he thought the king must be on it. ⁴⁴ So he gave up his life to save his people and win an everlasting name for himself. ⁴⁵ He dashed up to it in the middle of the phalanx, killing men right and left, so that they fell back from him on both sides. ⁴⁶ He ran right under the elephant and stabbed it in the belly, killing it. The beast fell to the ground on top of him, and he died there.

⁴⁷ When the Jews saw the strength of the royal army and the ardor of its forces, they retreated from them. ⁴⁸* A part of the king's army went up to

did you KNOW?

A Just War

Have you ever believed in something so strongly that you could justify a war to protect it? The Maccabees did, and they led a violent resistance against terrible religious persecution.

The Catholic church teaches that "all citizens and all governments are obliged to work for the avoidance of war" (*Catechism*, no. 2308). But it also teaches that there can be occasions for legitimate defense by military force (no. 2309), or what is sometimes called a just war. The criteria for a just war are as follows:

- All other means to avoid war must be exhausted.
- The damage done by the aggressor must be grave and certain.
- There must be serious prospects of success.
- The use of arms must not produce evils that are greater than the evil to be eliminated.

No one should be required to participate in any war that does not meet all these criteria.

War is not the answer; peace is. But at times in history, some Christians have felt that the only response to a grave injustice was violent resistance. However, no Christian is obligated to fight in a war if doing so goes against his or her conscience—although he or she may be required to serve the community in some other way—and nonviolent resistance is always an option (see "Nonviolent Resistance," 2 Mc 7, 42).

Jerusalem to attack them, and the king established camps in Judea and at Mount Zion. ⁴⁹*† He made peace with the men of Beth-zur, and they evacuated the city, because they had no food there to enable them to stand a siege, for that was a sabbath year in the land. ⁵⁰ The king took Beth-zur and stationed a garrison there to hold it. ⁵¹ For many days he besieged the sanctuary, setting up artillery and

---

† **6, 49:** *A sabbath year in the land:* when sowing and reaping were prohibited (Ex 23, 10f; Lv 25, 2–7). The year without a harvest (autumn of 164 to autumn of 163) was followed by a food shortage.

6, 28ff: 2 Mc 13, 1f.
6, 43: 2 Mc 13, 15.

6, 48f: 2 Mc 13, 22–23.
6, 49: Lv 25, 2.

machines, fire-throwers, catapults and mechanical bows for shooting arrows and slingstones. 52 The Jews countered by setting up machines of their own, and kept up the fight a long time. 53 But there were no provisions in the storerooms, because it was the seventh year, and the tide-over provisions had been eaten up by those who had been rescued from the Gentiles and brought to Judea. 54 Few men remained in the sanctuary; the rest scattered, each to his own home, for the famine was too much for them.

Peace Treaty

55* Lysias heard that Philip, whom King Antiochus, before his death, had appointed to train his son Antiochus to be king, 56 had returned from Persia and Media with the army that accompanied the king, and that he was seeking to take over the government. 57* So he hastily resolved to withdraw. He said to the king, the leaders of the army, and the soldiers: "We are growing weaker every day, our provisions are scanty, the place we are besieging is strong, and it is our duty to take care of the affairs of the kingdom. 58 Therefore let us now come to terms with these men, and make peace with them and all their nation. 59 Let us grant them freedom to live according to their own laws as formerly; it was on account of their laws, which we abolished, that they became angry and did all these things."

60 The proposal found favor with the king and the leaders; he sent peace terms to the Jews, and they accepted. 61 So the king and the leaders swore an oath to them, and on these terms they evacuated the fortification. 62 But when the king entered Mount Zion and saw how the place was fortified, he broke the oath he had sworn and gave orders for the encircling wall to be destroyed. 63 Then he departed in haste and returned to Antioch, where he found Philip in possession of the city. He fought against him and took the city by force.

Expedition of Bacchides and Alcimus

7 1*† In the year one hundred and fifty-one, Demetrius, son of Seleucus, set out from Rome, arrived with a few men in a city on the seacoast, and began to rule there. 2 As he was preparing to enter the royal palace of his ancestors, the soldiers seized Antiochus and Lysias to bring them to him. 3 When he was informed of this, he said, "Do not show me

their faces." 4 So the soldiers killed them, and Demetrius sat on the royal throne.

5† Then all the lawless and impious men of Israel came to him. They were led by Alcimus, who desired to be high priest. 6 They made this accusation to the king against the people: "Judas and his brothers have destroyed all your friends and have driven us out of our country. 7 So now, send a man whom you trust to go and see all the havoc Judas has done to us and to the king's land, and let him punish them and all their supporters."

8 Then the king chose Bacchides, one of the King's Friends, governor of West-of-Euphrates, a great man in the kingdom, and faithful to the king. 9* He sent him and the impious Alcimus, to whom he granted the high priesthood, with orders to take revenge on the Israelites. 10 They set out and, on arriving in the land of Judah with a great army, sent messengers who spoke deceitfully to Judas and his brothers in peaceful terms. 11 But these paid no attention to their words, seeing that they had come with a great army. 12 A group of scribes, however, gathered about Alcimus and Bacchides to ask for a just agreement. 13* The Hasideans were the first among the Israelites to seek peace with them, 14 for they said, "A priest of the line of Aaron has come with the army, and he will not do us any wrong." 15 He spoke with them peacefully and swore to them, "We will not try to injure you or your friends." 16 So they trusted him. But he arrested sixty of them and killed them in one day, according to the text of Scripture:

17* "The flesh of your saints they have strewn,
    and their blood they have shed round
      about Jerusalem,
    and there was no one to bury them."

18 Then fear and dread of them came upon all the people, who said: "There is no truth or justice among them; they violated the agreement and the oath that they swore."

19† Bacchides withdrew from Jerusalem and pitched his camp in Beth-zaith. He had many of the men arrested who deserted to him, throwing them into the great pit. 20 He handed the province over to Alcimus, leaving troops to help him, while he himself returned to the king.

7, 1ff: *The year one hundred and fifty-one:* the spring of 161 B.C. Demetrius, son of Seleucus, was the lawful heir to the kingdom; but when only nine years old, he was taken as a hostage at Rome in place of his uncle, who ruled as Antiochus IV Epiphanes. At the age of twenty-five Demetrius fled secretly from Rome and, with the support of the Syrians, overcame his rival Antiochus V and put him to death. *The royal palace:* at Antioch.

7, 5f: *Alcimus:* a renegade Jew hostile to the Maccabees, who became high priest after the death of Menelaus (2 Mc 14, 3). He received confirmation in his office from the new King Demetrius (v 9),

and brought malicious charges against Judas and his brothers and the people (v 6). He wrought more evils on the Israelites than the Gentiles had done (v 23).

7, 19: *Beth-zaith:* about three miles north of Beth-zur and twelve miles south of Jerusalem.

6, 55–63: 2 Mc 13, 23–26.   7, 9ff: 2 Mc 14, 46.
  6, 57: 2 Mc 11, 13ff.   7, 13f: 1 Mc 2, 42.
  7, 1–7: 2 Mc 14, 1–11.   7, 17: Ps 79, 1ff.

21 Alcimus spared no pains to maintain his high priesthood, 22 and all those who were disturbing their people gathered about him. They took possession of the land of Judah and caused great distress in Israel. 23 When Judas saw all the evils that Alcimus and his men were bringing upon the Israelites, more than even the Gentiles had done, 24 he went about all the borders of Judea and took revenge on the men who had deserted, preventing them from going out into the country. 25 But when Alcimus saw that Judas and his followers were gaining strength and realized that he could not oppose them, he returned to the king and accused them of grave crimes.

Defeat of Nicanor

26* Then the king sent Nicanor, one of his famous officers, who was a bitter enemy of Israel, with orders to destroy the people. 27† Nicanor came to Jerusalem with a large force and deceitfully sent to Judas and his brothers this peaceable message: 28 "Let there be no fight between me and you. I will come with a few men to meet you peaceably."

29 So he came to Judas, and they greeted one another peaceably. But Judas' enemies were prepared to seize him. 30* When he became aware that Nicanor had come to him with treachery in mind, Judas was afraid and would not meet him again. 31† When Nicanor saw that his plan had been discovered, he went out to fight Judas near Capharsalama. 32 About five hundred men of Nicanor's army fell; the rest fled to the City of David.

33* After this, Nicanor went up to Mount Zion. Some of the priests from the sanctuary and some of the elders of the people came out to greet him peaceably and to show him the holocaust that was being offered for the king. 34† But he mocked and ridiculed them, defiled them, and spoke disdainfully. 35 In a rage he swore: "If Judas and his army are not delivered to me at once, when I return victorious I will burn this temple down." He went away in great anger. 36* The priests, however, went in and stood before the altar and the sanctuary. They wept and said: 37 "You have chosen this house to bear your name, to be a house of prayer and petition for your people. 38 Take revenge on this man and his army, and let them fall by the sword. Remember their blasphemies, and do not let them continue."

39 Nicanor left Jerusalem and pitched his camp at Beth-horon, where the Syrian army joined him. 40† But Judas camped in Adasa with three thousand men. Here Judas uttered this prayer: 41* "When they who were sent by the king blasphemed, your angel went out and killed a hundred and eighty-five thousand of them. 42* In the same way, crush this army before us today, and let the rest know that Nicanor spoke wickedly against your sanctuary; judge him according to his wickedness."

43* The armies met in battle on the thirteenth day of the month Adar. Nicanor's army was crushed, and he himself was the first to fall in the battle. 44 When his army saw that Nicanor was dead, they threw down their arms and fled. 45 The Jews pursued them a day's journey, from Adasa to near Gazara, blowing the trumpets behind them as signals. 46 From all the surrounding villages of Judea people came out and closed in on them. They hemmed them in, and all the enemies fell by the sword; not a single one escaped.

47 Then the Jews collected the spoils and the booty; they cut off Nicanor's head and his right arm, which he had lifted up so arrogantly. These they brought to Jerusalem and displayed there. 48 The people rejoiced greatly, and observed that day as a great festival. 49† They decreed that it should be observed every year on the thirteenth of Adar. 50† And for a short time the land of Judah was quiet.

Treaty with the Romans

8 1† Judas had heard of the reputation of the Romans. They were valiant fighters and acted

---

7, 27: *Nicanor . . . deceitfully sent to Judas:* a more favorable picture of Nicanor, as an honest man who became a personal friend of Judas, is given in 2 Mc 14, 17–25. Their friendship was broken by the intrigues of Alcimus (2 Mc 14, 26–30).

7, 31: *Caphar-salama:* a village seven miles north-northwest of Jerusalem, on the road leading to Beth-horon.

7, 34: *Defiled them:* spitting on the priests caused them to become legally defiled.

7, 40: *Adasa:* a village southeast of Caphar-salama.

7, 49: *The thirteenth of Adar:* March 27, 160 B.C. This day in the Jewish calendar was called the "Day of Nicanor" (2 Mc 15, 36), but it was not long celebrated by the Jews.

7, 50: *A short time:* about one month following the death of Nicanor. After that began the attack of Bacchides resulting in the death of Judas (1 Mc 9, 1–18).

8, 1: This chapter contains the account of the embassy which Judas sent to Rome, probably before the death of Nicanor, to conclude a treaty of alliance between Rome and the Jewish nation. Without precise chronology, the pertinent data are gathered into a unified theme.

The image of the Roman Republic greatly impressed the smaller Eastern peoples seeking support against their overlords (1–16), because of Roman success in war (2–11) and effective aid to their allies (12–13). Numerous interventions by Rome in the politics of the Near East bear witness to its power and prestige in the second century B.C. Cf 1 Mc 1, 10; 7, 2; 12, 3; 15, 15–24; 2 Mc 11, 34. With the Roman control of Palestine in 63 B.C., the Republic and later the Empire became heartily detested. The eulogy of Rome in this chapter is one of the reasons why 1 Maccabees was not preserved by the Palestinian Jews of the century that followed.

7, 26f: 1 Mc 3, 38; 2 Mc 8, 9;   7, 36: Jl 2, 17.
    14, 12f.   7, 41f: 2 Mc 8, 19; 15, 22ff.
7, 30: 2 Mc 14, 30.   7, 42: Is 37, 36ff.
7, 33–38: 2 Mc 14, 31–36.   7, 43: 2 Mc 15, 25–35.

amiably to all who took their side. They established a friendly alliance with all who applied to them. [2]† He was also told of their battles and the brave deeds that they had performed against the Gauls, conquering them and forcing them to pay tribute. [3] They had gotten possession of the silver and gold mines in Spain, [4] and by planning and persistence had conquered the whole country, although it was very remote from their own. They had crushed the kings who had come against them from the far corners of the earth and had inflicted on them severe defeat, and the rest paid tribute to them every year. [5]† Philip and Perseus, king of the Macedonians, and the others who opposed them in battle had been overwhelmed and subjugated. [6]† Antiochus the Great, king of Asia, who had fought against them with a hundred and twenty elephants and with cavalry and chariots and a very great army, had been defeated by them. [7] They had taken him alive and obliged him and the kings who succeeded him to pay a heavy tribute, to give hostages and a section of [8]† Lycia, Mysia, and Lydia from among their best provinces. The Romans took these from him and gave them to King Eumenes. [9]† When the men of Greece had planned to come and destroy them, [10] the Romans discovered it, and sent against the Greeks a single general who made war on them. Many were wounded and fell, and the Romans took their wives and children captive. They plundered them, took possession of their land, tore down their strongholds and reduced them to slavery even to this day. [11] All the other kingdoms and islands that had ever opposed them they destroyed and enslaved; [12] with their friends, however, and those who relied on them, they maintained friendship. They had conquered kings both far and near, and all who heard of their fame were afraid of them. [13] In truth, those whom they desired to help to a kingdom became kings, and those whom they wished to depose they deposed; and they were greatly exalted. [14] Yet with all this, none of them put on a crown or wore purple as a display of grandeur. [15] They had made for themselves a senate

house, and every day three hundred and twenty men took counsel, deliberating on all that concerned the people and their well-being. [16]† They entrusted their government to one man every year, to rule over their entire country, and they all obeyed that one, and there was no envy or jealousy among them.

[17]* So Judas chose Eupolemus, son of John, son of Accos, and Jason, son of Eleazar, and sent them to Rome to establish an alliance of friendship with them. [18] He did this to get rid of the yoke, for it was obvious that the kingdom of the Greeks was subjecting Israel to slavery. [19] After making a very long journey to Rome, the envoys entered the senate and spoke as follows: [20] "Judas, called Maccabeus, and his brothers, with the Jewish people, have sent us to you to make a peaceful alliance with you, and to enroll ourselves among your allies and friends." [21] The proposal pleased the Romans, [22]*† and this is a copy of the reply they inscribed on bronze tablets and sent to Jerusalem, to remain there with the Jews as a record of peace and alliance:

[23] "May it be well with the Romans and the Jewish nation at sea and on land forever; may sword and enemy be far from them. [24] But if war is first made on Rome, or any of its allies in any of their dominions, [25] the Jewish nation will help them wholeheartedly, as the occasion shall demand; [26] and to those who wage war they shall not give nor provide grain, arms, money, or ships; this is Rome's decision. They shall fulfill their obligations without receiving any recompense. [27] In the same way, if war is made first on the Jewish nation, the Romans will help them willingly, as the occasion shall demand, [28] and to those who are attacking them there shall not be given grain, arms, money, or ships; this is Rome's decision. They shall fulfill their obligations without deception. [29] On these terms the Romans have made an agreement with the Jewish people. [30] But if both parties hereafter decide to add or take away anything, they shall do as they choose, and whatever they shall add or take away shall be valid.

---

† **8, 2:** *Gauls:* probably the Celts of northern Italy and southern France, subdued by the Romans in 222 B.C., and again in 200–191 B.C.; but perhaps also those in Asia Minor (the Galatians), whom the Romans defeated in 189 B.C.

8, 5: *Philip:* Philip V of Macedonia, defeated by a Graeco-Roman alliance at Cynoscephalae in 197 B.C. Perseus, his son, was defeated at Pydna in 168 B.C., and died a prisoner. With this, the kingdom of Macedonia came to an end.

8, 6: *Antiochus:* Antiochus III, greatest of the Seleucid kings. He was defeated at Magnesia in 190 B.C. By the Treaty of Apamea in 189, he was obliged to pay Rome a crushing indemnity of 15,000 talents. It was the weakening of Antiochene power and the growing military and economic influence of Rome that led Antiochus IV to adopt the policy of political, religious and cultural unification of Syria and Palestine.

8, 8: *Lycia, Mysia:* regions in western Asia Minor. These names are restored here by conjectural emendation; the Greek text has "India, Media," most likely through scribal error. *Eumenes:* Eumenes II

(197–158), king of Pergamum, an ally of Rome who benefited greatly from Antiochus' losses.

8, 9f: The revolt of the Achaean League, inserted here, occurred in 146 B.C., after Judas' time. It was crushed by the Roman consul Lucius Mummius and marked the end of Greek independence. The author regards all Greeks as the enemies of God.

8, 16: *They entrusted their government to one man:* actually the Roman Republic always had two consuls as joint heads of the government. Presumably, a single one dealt with embassies and answered letters, hence the impression the Jews received; cf 1 Mc 15, 16.

8, 22: *The reply . . . on bronze tablets and sent to Jerusalem:* the decree of the Senate would be inscribed on bronze and kept in the Roman Capitol, with only a later form sent to Jerusalem. The translation of the decree into Hebrew and then into Greek, as found here in 1 Maccabees, may have occasioned this error.

---

*

8, 17: 1 Mc 12, 1f; 15, 15–22.   8, 22: 1 Mc 14, 18.

31 "Moreover, concerning the wrongs that King Demetrius has done to them, we have written to him thus: 'Why have you made your yoke heavy upon our friends and allies the Jews? 32 If they complain about you again, we will do them justice and make war on you by land and sea.' "

Invasion of Judah

9 1 When Demetrius heard that Nicanor and his army had fallen in battle, he again sent Bacchides and Alcimus into the land of Judah, along with the right wing of his army. 2† They took the road to Galilee, and camping opposite the ascent at Arbela, they captured it and killed many people. 3† In the first month of the year one hundred and fifty-two, they encamped against Jerusalem. 4 Then they set out for Berea with twenty thousand men and two thousand cavalry. 5 Judas, with three thousand picked men, had camped at Elasa. 6 When his men saw the great number of the troops, they were very much afraid, and many slipped away from the camp, until only eight hundred men remained.

7 As Judas saw that his army was melting away just when the battle was imminent, he was panic-stricken, because he had no time to gather them together. 8 But in spite of his discouragement, he said to those who remained: "Let us go forward to meet our enemies; perhaps we can put up a good fight against them." 9 They tried to dissuade him, saying: "We certainly cannot. Let us save our lives now, and come back with our kinsmen, and then fight against them. Now we are too few." 10 But Judas said: "Far be it from me to do such a thing as to flee from them! If our time has come, let us die bravely for our kinsmen and not leave a stain upon our glory!"

Death of Judas

11 Then the army of Bacchides moved out of camp and took its position for combat. The cavalry were divided into two squadrons, and the slingers and the archers came on ahead of the army, and all the valiant men were in the front line. 12 Bacchides was on the right wing. Flanked by the two squadrons, the phalanx attacked as they blew their trumpets. Those who were on Judas' side also blew their trumpets. 13 The earth shook with the noise of the armies, and the battle raged from morning until evening. 14 Seeing that Bacchides was on the right, with the main force of his army, Judas, with all the most stouthearted rallying to him, 15† drove back the right wing and pursued them as far as the mountain slopes. 16 But when the men on the left wing saw that the right wing was driven back, they turned and followed Judas and his men, taking them in the rear. 17 The battle was fought desperately, and many on both sides fell wounded. 18 Then Judas fell, and the rest fled.

19 Jonathan and Simon took their brother Judas and buried him in the tomb of their fathers at Modein. 20 All Israel bewailed him in great grief. They mourned for him many days, and they said, 21* "How the mighty one has fallen, the savior of Israel!" 22 The other acts of Judas, his battles, the brave deeds he performed, and his greatness have not been recorded; but they were very many.

IV: Leadership of Jonathan

Bacchides and Jonathan

23 After the death of Judas, the transgressors of the law raised their heads in every part of Israel, and all kinds of evildoers appeared. 24 In those days there was a very great famine, and the country deserted to them. 25 Bacchides chose impious men and made them masters of the country. 26 These sought out and hunted down the friends of Judas and brought them to Bacchides, who punished and derided them. 27 There had not been such great distress in Israel since the time prophets ceased to appear among the people.

28 Then all the friends of Judas came together and said to Jonathan: 29 "Since your brother Judas died, there has been no one like him to oppose our enemies, Bacchides and those who are hostile to our nation. 30 Now therefore we have chosen you today to be our ruler and leader in his place, and to fight our battle." 31 From that moment Jonathan accepted the leadership, and took the place of Judas his brother.

32 When Bacchides learned of it, he sought to kill him. 33† But Jonathan and his brother Simon and all the men with him discovered this, and they fled to the desert of Tekoa and camped by the waters of the pool of Asphar.

9, 2: *They took the road . . . Arbela, they captured it:* this passage is restored, in part, by conjectural emendation. The present Greek text could be translated, "They took the road to Gilgal, and camping opposite Mesaloth at Arbela, they captured it." But Arbela (modern Khirbet Irbid) was in Galilee—on a high hill overlooking the western shore of the Sea of Galilee. Gilgal, on the contrary, was in the Jordan valley near Jericho. "Mesaloth" is probably a corrupt form of a Hebrew word meaning "steps, ascent."

9, 3: *The first month of the year one hundred and fifty-two:* April/May 160 B.C., by the temple calendar.

9, 15: *As far as the mountain slopes:* conjectural emendation. The Greek text has "as far as Mount Azotus"; this is most unlikely. Apparently the Greek translator mistook the Hebrew word *ashdot,* "slopes," for *asdod,* "Azotus."

9, 33: *Tekoa:* Home of the prophet Amos in the wild country above the Dead Sea, southeast of Jerusalem.

9, 34: Omitted, it is a dittography of verse 43.

9, 21: 2 Sam 1, 27.

What Makes a Hero?

History is full of heroes, those bigger-than-life men and women like Judas Maccabeus who have made a difference because of their courageous acts and their willingness to take risks that frighten other people. What makes someone a hero? Is each of us capable of heroism?

Someone we have grown up with, who now seems ordinary, could one day be a hero. None of us knows when we could be called on to do something heroic. We need an openness to God's call and a willingness to take a risk—to let go of our fears and to reach deep within ourselves for courage and strength. You may amaze yourself at what you can accomplish in extraordinary situations. The stuff of heroes, of great and brave persons such as Judas Maccabeus, is already within us. We need only to believe in ourselves and believe that God is with us.

You may not end up in a history book or be memorialized in a statue, but you can make a difference in the life of one or perhaps many people. What really counts is to be a hero in the eyes of God.

▶ 1 Mc 9, 19–22

---

³⁵*† Jonathan sent his brother as leader of the convoy to ask permission of his friends, the Nabateans, to deposit with them their great quantity of baggage. ³⁶† But the sons of Jambri from Medaba made a raid and seized and carried off John and everything he had. ³⁷ After this, word was brought to Jonathan and his brother Simon: "The sons of Jambri are celebrating a great wedding, and with a large escort they are bringing the bride, the daughter of one of the great princes of Canaan, from Nadabath." ³⁸ Remembering the blood of John their brother, they went up and hid themselves under cover of the mountain. ³⁹ They watched, and suddenly saw a noisy crowd with baggage; the bridegroom and his friends and kinsmen had come out to meet the bride's party with tambourines and musicians and much equipment. ⁴⁰ The Jews rose up against them from their ambush and killed them. Many fell wounded, and after the survivors fled toward the mountain, all their spoils were taken. ⁴¹ Thus the wedding was turned into mourning, and the sound of music into lamentation. ⁴² Having taken their revenge for the blood of their brother, the Jews returned to the marshes of the Jordan.

⁴³ When Bacchides heard of it, he came on the sabbath to the banks of the Jordan with a large force. ⁴⁴ Then Jonathan said to his companions, "Let us get up now and fight for our lives, for today is not like yesterday and the day before. ⁴⁵† The battle is before us, and behind us are the waters of the

Jordan on one side, marsh and thickets on the other, and there is no way of escape. ⁴⁶ Cry out now to Heaven for deliverance from our enemies." ⁴⁷ When they joined battle, Jonathan raised his arm to strike Bacchides, but Bacchides backed away from him. ⁴⁸ Jonathan and his men jumped into the Jordan and swam across to the other side, but the enemy did not pursue them across the Jordan. ⁴⁹ A thousand men on Bacchides' side fell that day.

⁵⁰† On returning to Jerusalem, Bacchides built strongholds in Judea: the Jericho fortress, as well as Emmaus, Beth-horon, Bethel, Timnath, Pharathon, and Tephon, with high walls and gates and bars. ⁵¹ In each he put a garrison to oppose Israel. ⁵² He fortified the city of Beth-zur, Gazara and the citadel, and put soldiers in them and stores of provisions. ⁵³* He took as hostages the sons of the leaders of the country and put them in custody in the citadel at Jerusalem.

⁵⁴† In the year one hundred and fifty-three, in the second month, Alcimus ordered the wall of the inner court of the sanctuary to be torn down, thus destroying the work of the prophets. But he only began to tear it down. ⁵⁵ Just at that time he had a stroke, and his work was interrupted; his mouth was closed and he was paralyzed, so that he could no longer utter a word to give orders concerning his house. ⁵⁶ Finally he died in great agony. ⁵⁷ Seeing that Alcimus was dead, Bacchides returned to the king, and the land of Judah was quiet for two years.

---

† **9, 35:** *Jonathan sent his brother:* this was John who was called Gaddi (1 Mc 2, 2; cf 9, 36.38).
9, 36: *Medaba:* northeast of the Dead Sea.
9, 45: Jonathan's force was apparently trapped in one of the many oxbows of the lower Jordan. Bacchides had crossed and caught them still on the east bank.

9, 50: These sites constitute a ring on the edges of the province of Judea.
9, 54: *In the year . . . second month:* May 159 B.C.
* ———
9, 35: 1 Mc 5, 25.   **9, 53:** 1 Mc 10, 9.

1
M
C

58 Then all the transgressors of the law held a council and said: "Jonathan and his companions are living in peace and security. Now then, let us have Bacchides return, and he will capture all of them in a single night." 59 So they went and took counsel with him. 60 When Bacchides was setting out with a large force, he sent letters secretly to all his allies in Judea, telling them to seize Jonathan and his companions. They were not able to do this, however, because their plot became known. 61 In fact, Jonathan's men seized about fifty of the men of the country who were ringleaders in the mischief and put them to death. 62† Then Jonathan and Simon and their companions withdrew to Bethbasi in the desert; they rebuilt and strengthened its fortifications that had been demolished. 63 When Bacchides learned of this, he gathered together his whole force and sent word to those who were in Judea. 64 He came and pitched his camp before Bethbasi, and constructing siege-machines, he fought against it for many days.

65 Leaving his brother Simon in the city, Jonathan, accompanied by a small group of men, went out into the field. 66 He struck down Odomera and his kinsmen and the sons of Phasiron in their encampment; these men had set out to go up to the siege with their forces. 67 Simon and his men then sallied forth from the city and set fire to the machines. 68 They fought against Bacchides, and he was beaten. This caused him great distress. Because the enterprise he had planned came to naught, 69 he was angry with the lawless men who had advised him to invade the province. He killed many of them and resolved to return to his own country.

70 Jonathan learned of this and sent ambassadors to make peace with him and to obtain the release of the prisoners. 71 He agreed to do as Jonathan had asked. He swore an oath to him that he would never try to injure him for the rest of his life; 72 and he released the prisoners he had previously taken from the land of Judah. He returned to his own country and never came into their territory again.

73† Then the sword ceased in Israel. Jonathan settled in Michmash; he began to judge the people, and he destroyed the impious in Israel.

Revolt of Alexander

10 1† In the year one hundred and sixty, Alexander, who was called Epiphanes, son of Antiochus, came up and took Ptolemais. He was accepted and began to reign there. 2 When King Demetrius heard of it, he mustered a very large army and marched out to engage him in combat. 3 Demetrius sent a letter to Jonathan written in peaceful terms, to pay him honor; 4 for he said: "Let us be the first to make peace with him, before he makes peace with Alexander against us, 5 since he will remember all the wrongs we have done to him, his brothers, and his nation."

6 So Demetrius authorized Jonathan, as his ally, to gather an army and procure arms; and he ordered that the hostages in the citadel be released to him. 7 Accordingly Jonathan went up to Jerusalem and read the letter to all the people. The men in the citadel 8 were struck with fear when they heard that the king had given him authority to gather an army. 9* They released the hostages to Jonathan, and he gave them back to their parents. 10 Thereafter Jonathan dwelt in Jerusalem, and began to build and restore the city. 11 He ordered the workmen to build the walls and encircle Mount Zion with square stones for its fortification, which they did. 12 The foreigners in the strongholds that Bacchides had built, took flight; 13 each one of them left his place and returned to his own country. 14 Only in Beth-zur did some remain of those who had abandoned the law and the commandments, for they used it as a place of refuge.

Jonathan Supports Alexander

15 King Alexander heard of the promises that Demetrius had made to Jonathan; he was also told of the battles and valiant deeds of Jonathan and his brothers and the troubles that they had endured. 16 He said, "Shall we ever find another man like him? Let us now make him our friend and ally." 17 So he sent Jonathan a letter written in these terms: 18 "King Alexander sends greetings to his brother Jonathan. 19 We have heard of you, that you are a mighty warrior and worthy to be our friend. 20* We have therefore appointed you today to be high priest of your nation; you are to be called the King's Friend, and you are to look after our interests and preserve amity with us." He also sent him a purple robe and a crown of gold.

21† Jonathan put on the sacred vestments in the seventh month of the year one hundred and sixty at the feast of Booths, and he gathered an army and

---

9, 62: *Bethbasi:* two miles east of Bethlehem, and six miles north of Tekoa.

9, 73: *Began to judge:* exercise the governing authority as in the book of Judges. With Jerusalem and the garrison towns (v 50) firmly in Seleucid hands, Jonathan's freedom of action was greatly restricted. Michmash, southeast of Bethel, famous for the exploit of the former Jonathan, son of Saul; cf 1 Sm 14.

10, 1: *The year one hundred and sixty:* 152 B.C. *Alexander . . . Antiochus:* Alexander Balas claimed to be a son of Antiochus IV. He

had the backing of the Romans, who had never forgiven Demetrius for becoming king without their permission. The latter meanwhile had become unpopular with his own people as well as with the Jews.

10, 21: *Jonathan . . . feast of Booths:* Jonathan began to discharge the office of high priest October 23–30, 152 B.C. For seven years after the death of Alcimus there had been no high priest in Jerusalem.

procured many arms. 22 When Demetrius heard of these things, he was distressed and said: 23 "Why have we allowed Alexander to get ahead of us by gaining the friendship of the Jews and thus strengthening himself? 24 I too will write them conciliatory words and offer dignities and gifts, so that they may be an aid to me."

25 So he sent them this message: "King Demetrius sends greetings to the Jewish nation. 26 We have heard how you have kept the treaty with us and continued in our friendship and not gone over to our enemies, and we are glad. 27 Continue, therefore, to keep faith with us, and we will reward you with favors in return for what you do in our behalf. 28 We will grant you many exemptions and will bestow gifts on you.

29* "I now free you, as I also exempt all the Jews, from the tribute, the salt tax, and the crown levies. 30*† Instead of collecting the third of the grain and the half of the fruit of the trees that should be my share, I renounce the right from this day forward. Neither now nor in the future will I collect them from the land of Judah or from the three districts annexed from Samaria. 31 Let Jerusalem and her territory, her tithes and her tolls, be sacred and free from tax. 32 I also yield my authority over the citadel in Jerusalem, and I transfer it to the high priest, that he may put in it such men as he shall choose to guard it. 33 Every one of the Jews who has been carried into captivity from the land of Judah into any part of my kingdom I set at liberty without ransom; and let all their taxes, even those on their cattle, be canceled. 34 Let all feast days, sabbaths, new moon festivals, appointed days, and the three days that precede each feast day, and the three days that follow, be days of immunity and exemption for every Jew in my kingdom. 35 Let no man have authority to exact payment from them or to molest any of them in any matter.

36 "Let thirty thousand Jews be enrolled in the king's army and allowances be given them, as is due to all the king's soldiers. 37 Let some of them be stationed in the king's principal strongholds, and of these let some be given positions of trust in the affairs of the kingdom. Let their superiors and their rulers be taken from among them, and let them follow their own laws, as the king has commanded in the land of Judah.

38 "Let the three districts that have been added to Judea from the province of Samaria be incorporated with Judea so that they may be under one man

and obey no other authority than the high priest. 39 Ptolemais and its confines I give as a present to the sanctuary in Jerusalem for the necessary expenses of the sanctuary. 40 I make a yearly personal grant of fifteen thousand silver shekels out of the royal revenues, from appropriate places. 41 All the additional funds that the officials did not hand over as they had done in the first years, shall henceforth be handed over for the services of the temple. 42 Moreover, the dues of five thousand silver shekels that used to be taken from the revenue of the sanctuary every year shall be canceled, since these funds belong to the priests who perform the services. 43 Whoever takes refuge in the temple of Jerusalem or in any of its precincts, because of money he owes the king, or because of any other debt, shall be released, together with all the goods he possesses in my kingdom. 44 The cost of rebuilding and restoring the structures of the sanctuary shall be covered out of the royal revenue. 45 Likewise the cost of building the walls of Jerusalem and fortifying it all around, and of building walls in Judea, shall be donated from the royal revenue."

46 When Jonathan and the people heard these words, they neither believed nor accepted them, for they remembered the great evil that Demetrius had done in Israel, and how sorely he had afflicted them. 47 They therefore decided in favor of Alexander, for he had been the first to address them peaceably, and they remained his allies for the rest of his life.

48 King Alexander gathered together a large army and encamped opposite Demetrius. 49 The two kings joined battle, and when the army of Demetrius fled, Alexander pursued him, and overpowered his soldiers. 50 He pressed the battle hard until sunset, and Demetrius fell that day.

Treaty of Ptolemy and Alexander

51 Alexander sent ambassadors to Ptolemy, king of Egypt, with this message: 52 "Now that I have returned to my realm, taken my seat on the throne of my fathers, and established my rule by crushing Demetrius and gaining control of my country— 53 for I engaged him in battle, defeated him and his army, and recovered the royal throne— 54 let us now establish friendship with each other. Give me your daughter for my wife; and as your son-in-law, I will give to you and to her gifts worthy of you."

55 King Ptolemy answered in these words: "Happy the day on which you returned to the land of

†
It was taken for granted that the king, though a Gentile, had the power to appoint one. The Maccabees, though a priestly family, were not of the line of Zadok, and some in Israel regarded Jonathan's tenure as a usurpation.

10, 30: *The three districts annexed from Samaria:* mentioned by

name in 1 Mc 11, 34. The present Greek text, by a scribal error, has added "and Galilee" after "Samaria."

*

10, 29: 1 Mc 11, 28f.35.   **10, 30:** 1 Mc 11, 28.34.

your fathers and took your seat on their royal throne! 56 I will do for you what you have written; but meet me in Ptolemais, so that we may see each other, and I will become your father-in-law as you have proposed."

57† So Ptolemy with his daughter Cleopatra set out from Egypt and came to Ptolemais in the year one hundred and sixty-two. 58 There King Alexander met him, and Ptolemy gave him his daughter Cleopatra in marriage. Their wedding was celebrated at Ptolemais with great splendor according to the custom of kings.

59 King Alexander also wrote to Jonathan to come and meet him. 60* So he went with pomp to Ptolemais, where he met the two kings and gave them and their friends silver and gold and many gifts and thus won their favor. 61 Some pestilent Israelites, transgressors of the law, united against him to accuse him, but the king paid no heed to them. 62 He ordered Jonathan to be divested of his ordinary garments and to be clothed in royal purple; and so it was done. 63 The king also had him seated at his side. He said to his magistrates: "Go with him to the center of the city and make a proclamation that no one is to bring charges against him on any grounds or be troublesome to him in any way."

64* When his accusers saw the honor paid to him in the proclamation, and the purple with which he was clothed, they all fled. 65 The king also honored him by numbering him among his Chief Friends and made him military commander and governor of the province. 66 So Jonathan returned in peace and happiness to Jerusalem.

Victory over Apollonius

67† In the year one hundred and sixty-five, Demetrius, son of Demetrius, came from Crete to the land of his fathers. 68 When King Alexander heard of it he was greatly troubled, and returned to Antioch. 69 Demetrius appointed Apollonius governor of Coelesyria. Having gathered a large army, Apollonius pitched his camp at Jamnia. From there he sent this message to Jonathan the high priest:

70 "You are the only one who resists us. I am laughed at and put to shame on your account. Why are you displaying power against us in the mountains? 71 If you have confidence in your forces, come down now to us in the plain, and let us test each other's strength there; the city forces are on my side. 72 Inquire and learn who I am and who the others are who are helping me. Men say that you

cannot make a stand against us because your fathers were twice put to flight in their own land. 73 Now you too will be unable to withstand our cavalry and such a force as this in the plain, where there is not a stone or a pebble or a place to flee."

74 When Jonathan heard the message of Apollonius, he was roused. Choosing ten thousand men, he set out from Jerusalem, and Simon his brother joined him to help him. 75 He pitched camp near Joppa, but the men in the city shut him out because Apollonius had a garrison there. When the Jews besieged it, 76† the men of the city became afraid and opened the gates, and so Jonathan took possession of Joppa.

77 When Apollonius heard of it, he drew up three thousand horsemen and an innumerable infantry. He marched on Azotus as though he were going on through the country, but at the same time he advanced into the plain, because he had such a large number of horsemen to rely on. 78 Jonathan followed him to Azotus, and they engaged in battle. 79 Apollonius, however, had left a thousand cavalry in hiding behind them. 80 When Jonathan discovered that there was an ambush behind him, his army was surrounded. From morning until evening they showered his men with arrows. 81 But his men held their ground, as Jonathan had commanded, whereas the enemy's horses became tired out. 82 When the horsemen were exhausted, Simon attacked the phalanx, overwhelmed it and put it to flight. 83 The horsemen too were scattered over the plain. The enemy fled to Azotus and entered Bethdagon, the temple of their idol, to save themselves. 84* But Jonathan burned and plundered Azotus with its neighboring towns, and destroyed by fire both the temple of Dagon and the men who had taken refuge in it. 85 Those who fell by the sword, together with those who were burned alive, came to about eight thousand men. 86 Then Jonathan left there and pitched his camp at Ashkalon, and the people of that city came out to meet him with great pomp. 87 He and his men then returned to Jerusalem, laden with much booty. 88 When King Alexander heard of these events, he accorded new honors to Jonathan. 89† He sent him a gold buckle, such as is usually given to King's Kinsmen; he also gave him Ekron and all its territory as a possession.

Alliance of Demetrius and Ptolemy

11 1 The king of Egypt gathered his forces, as numerous as the sands of the seashore,

†

10, 57: *Cleopatra:* Cleopatra Thea, then about fifteen years old. She later married Demetrius II, and later still, his brother Antiochus VII. *The year one hundred and sixty-two:* 151/150 B.C.

10, 67: *The year one hundred and sixty-five:* 147 B.C. *Demetrius:* Demetrius II Nicator.

10, 76: *Joppa:* about forty miles northwest of Jerusalem. For the

first time the Maccabees took possession of a seaport; nominally it was on behalf of King Alexander.

10, 89: *Kinsmen:* a class higher than Chief Friends.

10, 60: 1 Mc 2, 18.   10, 84: 1 Mc 11, 4; 1 Sm 5,
10, 64f: 1 Mc 2, 18; 11, 27.   2–5.

and many ships; and he sought by deceit to take Alexander's kingdom and add it to his own. 2 He entered Syria with peaceful words, and the people in the cities opened their gates to welcome him, as King Alexander had ordered them to do, since Ptolemy was his father-in-law. 3 But when Ptolemy entered the cities, he stationed garrison troops in each one. 4* When he reached Azotus, he was shown the temple of Dagon destroyed by fire, Azotus and its suburbs demolished, corpses lying about, and the charred bodies of those burned by Jonathan in the war and stacked up along his route. 5 To prejudice the king against Jonathan, he was told what the latter had done; but the king said nothing. 6 Jonathan met the king with pomp at Joppa, and they greeted each other and spent the night there. 7† Jonathan accompanied the king as far as the river called Eleutherus and then returned to Jerusalem.

8† Plotting evil against Alexander, King Ptolemy took possession of the cities along the seacoast as far as Seleucia-by-the-Sea. 9 He sent ambassadors to King Demetrius, saying: "Come, let us make a pact with each other; I will give you my daughter whom Alexander has married, and you shall reign over your father's kingdom. 10† I regret that I gave him my daughter, for he has sought to kill me." 11 His real reason for accusing Alexander, however, was that he coveted Alexander's kingdom. 12 After taking his daughter away and giving her to Demetrius, Ptolemy broke with Alexander; their enmity became open. 13 Then Ptolemy entered Antioch and assumed the crown of Asia; he thus wore two crowns on his head, that of Egypt and that of Asia.

Deaths of Alexander and Ptolemy

14 King Alexander was in Cilicia at that time, because the people of that region had revolted. 15 When Alexander heard the news, he came to challenge Ptolemy in battle. Ptolemy marched out and met him with a strong force and put him to flight. 16 Alexander fled to Arabia to seek protection. King Ptolemy's triumph was complete 17 when the Arab Zabdiel cut off Alexander's head and sent it to Ptolemy. 18 But three days later King Ptolemy

himself died, and his men in the fortified cities were killed by the inhabitants of the strongholds. 19† Thus Demetrius became king in the year one hundred and sixty-seven.

Pact with Demetrius

20 At that time Jonathan gathered together the men of Judea to attack the citadel in Jerusalem, and they set up many machines against it. 21 Some transgressors of the law, enemies of their own nation, went to the king and informed him that Jonathan was besieging the citadel. 22 When Demetrius heard this, he was furious, and set out immediately for Ptolemais. He wrote to Jonathan to discontinue the siege and to meet him for a conference at Ptolemais as soon as possible.

23 On hearing this, Jonathan ordered the siege to continue. He selected some elders and priests of Israel and exposed himself to danger 24 by going to the king at Ptolemais. He brought with him silver, gold apparel, and many other presents, and found favor with the king. 25 Although some impious men of his own nation brought charges against him, 26 the king treated him just as his predecessors had done and showed him great honor in the presence of all his Friends. 27 He confirmed him in the high priesthood and in all the honors he had previously held, and had him enrolled among his Chief Friends.

28* Jonathan asked the king to exempt Judea and the three districts of Samaria from tribute, promising him in return three hundred talents. 29 The king agreed and wrote the following letter to Jonathan about all these matters:

30*† "King Demetrius sends greetings to his brother Jonathan and to the Jewish nation. 31† We are sending you, for your information, a copy of the letter that we wrote to Lasthenes our kinsman concerning you. 32 'King Demetrius sends greetings to his father Lasthenes. 33 Because of the good will they show us, we have decided to bestow benefits on the Jewish nation, who are our friends and who observe their obligations to us. 34*† Therefore we confirm their possession, not only of the territory of Judea, but also of the three districts of Aphairema, Lydda,

---

11, 7: *Eleutherus:* modern Nahr el-Kebir, the northern border of modern Lebanon; in the second century B.C. the northern limit of Coelesyria.

11, 8: *Seleucia-by-the-Sea:* at the mouth of the Orontes, the port city of Antioch.

11, 10: *I regret . . . to kill me:* according to Josephus, Ammonius, a friend of Alexander, had tried to assassinate Ptolemy, and the latter claimed that Alexander was the instigator, thus calumniating him to gain his kingdom (v 11).

11, 19: *The year one hundred and sixty-seven:* 146/145 B.C. The two deaths (vv 17–18) occurred in the summer of 145 B.C.

11, 30: *Brother:* this title and *father* in v 32 are honorific titles used of the Kinsmen.

11, 31: *Lasthenes:* leader of the mercenary troops who had come

with Demetrius from Crete. He was now the young king's chief minister and was apparently responsible for the disastrous policy (v 38) of disbanding the national army.

11, 34: *Aphairema:* the Ophrah of Jos 18, 23; 1 Sm 23, 6; the Ephron of 2 Chr 13, 19; and the Ephraim of Jn 11, 54—modern et-Taiyibeh, five miles northeast of Bethel. *Lydda:* the Lod of the postexilic Jews (Ez 2, 33; Neh 11, 35) and the hometown of Aeneas, who was cured by Peter (Acts 9, 32ff). It is ten miles southeast of Joppa. *Ramathaim:* the Ramathaim-zophim of 1 Sm 1, 1, and the Arimathea of Mt 27, 57—modern Rentis, nine miles northeast of Lydda.

11, 4: 1 Mc 10, 84.   **11, 30–37:** 1 Mc 10, 26–45.
11, 28: 1 Mc 10, 29; 11, 34.   **11, 34f:** 1 Mc 10, 29; 11, 28.

and Ramathaim. These districts, together with all their dependencies, were transferred from Samaria to Judea in favor of all those who offer sacrifices for us in Jerusalem instead of paying the royal taxes that formerly the king received from them each year from the produce of the soil and the fruit of the trees. 35 From this day on we grant them release from payment of all other things that would henceforth be due to us, that is, of tithes and tribute and of the tax on the salt pans and the crown tax. 36 Henceforth none of these provisions shall ever be revoked. 37 Be sure, therefore, to have a copy of these instructions made and given to Jonathan, that it may be displayed in a conspicuous place on the holy hill.' "

The Intrigue of Trypho

38 When King Demetrius saw that the land was peaceful under his rule and that he had no opposition, he dismissed his entire army, every man to his home, except the foreign troops which he had hired from the islands of the nations. So all the soldiers who had served under his predecessors hated him. 39* When a certain Trypho, who had previously belonged to Alexander's party, saw that all the troops were grumbling at Demetrius, he went to Imalkue the Arab, who was bringing up Alexander's young son Antiochus. 40 Trypho kept urging Imalkue to hand over the boy to him, that he might make him king in his father's place. During his stay there of many days, he told him of all that Demetrius had done and of the hatred that his soldiers had for him.

Jonathan Aids Demetrius

41 Meanwhile Jonathan sent the request to King Demetrius to withdraw his troops from the citadel of Jerusalem and from the other strongholds, for they were constantly hostile to Israel. 42 Demetrius, in turn, sent this word to Jonathan: "I will not only do this for you and your nation, but I will greatly honor you and your nation when I find the opportunity. 43 Do me the favor, therefore, of sending men to fight for me, because all my troops have revolted."

44 So Jonathan sent three thousand good fighting men to him at Antioch. When they came to the king, he was delighted over their arrival, 45 for the populace, one hundred and twenty thousand strong, had massed in the center of the city in an attempt to kill him. 46 But he took refuge in the

palace, while the populace gained control of the main streets and began to fight. 47 So the king called the Jews to his aid. They all rallied around him and spread out through the city. On that day they killed about a hundred thousand men in the city, 48 which, at the same time, they set on fire and plundered on a large scale. Thus they saved the king's life. 49 When the populace saw that the Jews held the city at their mercy, they lost courage and cried out to the king in supplication, 50 "Give us your terms and let the Jews stop attacking us and our city." So they threw down their arms and made peace. 51 The Jews thus gained glory in the eyes of the king and all his subjects, and they became renowned throughout his kingdom. Finally they returned to Jerusalem with much spoil.

52 But when King Demetrius was sure of his royal throne, and the land was peaceful under his rule, 53 he broke all his promises and became estranged from Jonathan. Instead of rewarding Jonathan for all the favors he had received from him, he caused him much trouble.

Alliance with Trypho

54* After this, Trypho returned and brought with him the young boy Antiochus, who became king and wore the royal crown. 55 All the soldiers whom Demetrius had discharged rallied around Antiochus and fought against Demetrius, who was routed and fled. 56 Trypho captured the elephants and occupied Antioch. 57 Then young Antiochus wrote to Jonathan: "I confirm you in the high priesthood and appoint you ruler over the four districts and wish you to be one of the King's Friends." 58* He also sent him gold dishes and a dinner service, gave him the right to drink from gold cups, to dress in royal purple, and to wear a gold buckle. 59† Likewise, he made Jonathan's brother Simon governor of the region from the Ladder of Tyre to the frontier of Egypt.

60† Jonathan set out and traveled through West-of-Euphrates and its cities, and all the forces of Syria espoused his cause as allies. When he arrived at Ashkalon, the citizens welcomed him with pomp. 61 But when he set out for Gaza, the people of Gaza locked their gates against him. So he besieged it and burned and plundered its suburbs. 62 Then the people of Gaza appealed to him for mercy, and he granted them peace. He took the sons of their chief men as hostages and sent them to Jerusalem. He then traveled on through the province as far as Damascus.

---

† **11, 59:** *Ladder of Tyre:* modern Ras en-Naquurah, on the border between Lebanon and Israel, where the mountains reach the sea, so that the coastal road must ascend in a series of steps.

11, 60: *West-of-Euphrates:* refers here to the territory of Palestine and Coelesyria, but not Upper Syria; cf 1 Mc 3, 32; 7, 8.

* **11, 39:** 1 Mc 12, 39.   **11, 58:** 1 Mc 2, 18.
11, 54: 1 Mc 11, 39; 12, 39.

War with Demetrius

63 Jonathan heard that the generals of Demetrius had come with a strong force to Kadesh in Galilee, intending to remove him from office. 64 So he went to meet them, leaving his brother Simon in the province. 65 Simon besieged Beth-zur, attacked it for many days, and blockaded the inhabitants. 66 When they sued for peace, he granted it to them. He expelled them from the city, took possession of it, and put a garrison there.

67† Meanwhile, Jonathan and his army pitched their camp near the waters of Gennesaret, and at daybreak they went to the plain of Hazor. 68 There, in front of him on the plain, was the army of the foreigners. This army attacked him in the open, having first detached an ambush against him in the mountains. 69 Then the men in ambush rose out of their places and joined in the battle. 70 All of Jonathan's men fled; no one stayed except the army commanders Mattathias, son of Absalom, and Judas, son of Chalphi. 71 Jonathan tore his clothes, threw earth on his head, and prayed. 72 Then he went back to the combat and so overwhelmed the enemy that they took to flight. 73 Those of his men who were running away saw it and returned to him; and with him they pursued the enemy as far as their camp in Kadesh, where they pitched their own camp. 74 Three thousand of the foreign troops fell on that day. Then Jonathan returned to Jerusalem.

Alliances with Rome and Sparta

12 1* When Jonathan saw that the times favored him, he sent selected men to Rome to confirm and renew his friendship with the Romans. 2 He also sent letters to Sparta and other places for the same purpose.

3 After reaching Rome, the men entered the senate chamber and said, "The high priest Jonathan and the Jewish people have sent us to renew the earlier friendship and alliance between you and them." 4 The Romans gave them letters addressed to the authorities in the various places, requesting them to provide the envoys with safe conduct to the land of Judah.

5 This is a copy of the letter that Jonathan wrote to the Spartans: 6 "Jonathan the high priest, the senate of the nation, the priests, and the rest of the Jewish people send greetings to their brothers the Spartans. 7*† Long ago a letter was sent to the high priest Onias from Arius, who then reigned over you, stating that you are our brothers, as the attached copy shows. 8 Onias welcomed the envoy with honor and received the letter, which clearly referred to alliance and friendship. 9*† Though we have no need of these things, since we have for our encouragement the sacred books that are in our possession, 10 we have ventured to send word to you for the renewal of brotherhood and friendship, so as not to become strangers to you altogether; a long time has passed since your mission to us. 11 We, on our part, have never ceased to remember you in the sacrifices and prayers that we offer on our feasts and other appropriate days, as it is right and proper to remember brothers. 12 We likewise rejoice in your renown. 13 But many hardships and wars have beset us, and the kings around us have attacked us. 14 We did not wish to be troublesome to you and to the rest of our allies and friends in these wars; 15 with the help of Heaven for our support, we have been saved from our enemies, and they have been humbled. 16* So we have chosen Numenius, son of Antiochus, and Antipater, son of Jason, and we have sent them to the Romans to renew our former friendship and alliance with them. 17 We have also ordered them to come to you and greet you, and to deliver to you our letter about the renewal of our brotherhood. 18 Therefore kindly send us an answer on this matter."

19 This is a copy of the letter that was sent to Onias: 20* "Arius, king of the Spartans, sends greetings to Onias the high priest. 21 A document has been found stating that the Spartans and the Jews are brothers; both nations descended from Abraham. 22 Now that we have learned this, kindly write to us about your welfare. 23 We, on our part, are informing you that your cattle and your possessions are ours, and ours are yours. We have, therefore, given orders that you should be told of this."

Demetrius Repelled

24 Jonathan heard that the generals of Demetrius had returned to attack him with a stronger army than before. 25† He set out from Jerusalem and went into the country of Hamath to meet them, giving them no time to enter his province. 26 The spies he had sent into their camp came back and reported that the enemy had made ready to attack the Jews that very night. 27 Therefore, when the sun set,

† **11, 67:** *Plain of Hazor:* the site of the ancient Canaanite city (Jos 11, 10), ten miles north of the Lake of Gennesaret.

12, 7: *Onias:* Onias I, high priest from 323–300 or 290 B.C. *Arius:* Arius I, king from 309 to 265 B.C. The letter was sent long ago, i.e., a century and a half before.

12, 9: *The sacred books . . . in our possession:* a reference to "the law, the prophets and other books," as mentioned in the Prologue to Sirach (v 1), after 132 B.C.

12, 25: *Country of Hamath:* the Seleucid territory of Upper Syria northeast of Coelesyria and separated from it by the Eleutherus River. The latter territory was under the command of Jonathan (1 Mc 11, 59f).

12, 1: 1 Mc 8, 17.	**12, 16:** 1 Mc 14, 22; 15, 15.
12, 7: 1 Mc 12, 20–23.	**12, 20–23:** 1 Mc 12, 6f.
12, 9: Rom 15, 4.	

Jonathan ordered his men to be on guard and to remain armed, ready for combat, throughout the night. He also set outposts all around the camp. ²⁸ When the enemy heard that Jonathan and his men were ready for battle, their hearts sank with fear and dread. They lighted fires and then withdrew. ²⁹ But because Jonathan and his men were watching the lights burning, they did not know what had happened until morning. ³⁰ Then Jonathan pursued them, but he could not overtake them, for they had crossed the river Eleutherus. ³¹ So Jonathan turned aside against the Arabs who are called Zabadeans, overwhelming and plundering them. ³² Then he marched on to Damascus and traversed that whole region.

³³ Simon also set out and went as far as Ashkalon and its neighboring strongholds. He then turned to Joppa and occupied it, ³⁴ for he heard that its men had intended to hand over this stronghold to the supporters of Demetrius. He left a garrison there to guard it.

³⁵ When Jonathan returned, he assembled the elders of the people, and with them he made plans for building strongholds in Judea, ³⁶ for making the walls of Jerusalem still higher, and for erecting a high barrier between the citadel and the city, that would isolate the citadel and so prevent its garrison from commerce with the city. ³⁷ The people therefore worked together on building up the city, for part of the east wall above the ravine had collapsed. The quarter called Chaphenatha was also repaired. ³⁸ Simon likewise built up Adida in the Shephelah, and strengthened its fortifications by providing them with gates and bars.

Capture of Jonathan

³⁹* Trypho was determined to become king of Asia, assume the crown, and do away with King Antiochus. ⁴⁰ But he was afraid that Jonathan would not permit him, but would fight against him. Looking for a way to seize and kill him, he set out and reached Beth-shan. ⁴¹ Jonathan marched out against him with forty thousand picked fighting men and came to Beth-shan. ⁴² But when Trypho saw that Jonathan had arrived with a large army, he was afraid to offer him violence. ⁴³ Instead, he received him with honor, introduced him to all his friends, and gave him presents. He also ordered his friends and soldiers to obey him as they would himself. ⁴⁴ Then he said to Jonathan: "Why have you put all your soldiers to so much trouble when we are not at war? ⁴⁵ Pick out a few men to stay with you, send the rest back home, and then come with me to Ptolemais. I will hand it over to you together

with other strongholds and their garrisons, as well as the officials, then I will leave and go home. That is why I came here."

⁴⁶ Jonathan believed him and did as he said. He dismissed his troops, and they returned to the land of Judah. ⁴⁷ But he kept with him three thousand men, of whom he sent two thousand to Galilee while one thousand accompanied him. ⁴⁸ Then as soon as Jonathan had entered Ptolemais, the men of the city closed the gates and seized him; all who had entered with him, they killed with the sword.

⁴⁹† Trypho sent soldiers and cavalry to Galilee and the Great Plain to destroy all Jonathan's men. ⁵⁰ These, upon learning that Jonathan had been captured and his companions killed, encouraged one another and went out in compact body ready to fight. ⁵¹ As their pursuers saw that they were ready to fight for their lives, they turned back. ⁵² Thus all these men of Jonathan came safely into the land of Judah. They mourned over Jonathan and his men, and were in great fear, and all Israel fell into deep mourning.

⁵³* All the nations round about sought to destroy them. They said, "Now that they have no leader to help them, let us make war on them and wipe out their memory from among men."

V: Simon, High Priest and Ethnarch

Simon, Leader of the Jews

13 ¹ When Simon heard that Trypho was gathering a large army to invade and ravage the land of Judah, ² and saw that the people

---

12, 49: *The Great Plain:* of Beth-shan (v 41), where Jonathan's disbanded troops remained.

12, 39: 1 Mc 11, 39f.54f.   **12, 53:** 1 Mc 5, 2; 13, 6.

1
M
C

were in dread and terror, he went up to Jerusalem. There he assembled the people 3 and exhorted them in these words: "You know what I, my brothers, and my father's house have done for the laws and the sanctuary; what battles and disasters we have been through. 4 It was for the sake of these, for the sake of Israel, that all my brothers have perished, and I alone am left. 5 Far be it from me, then, to save my own life in any time of distress, for I am not better than my brothers. 6* Rather will I avenge my nation and the sanctuary, as well as your wives and children, for all the nations out of hatred have united to destroy us."

7 As the people heard these words, their spirit was rekindled. 8 They shouted in reply: "You are our leader in place of your brothers Judas and Jonathan. 9 Fight our battles, and we will do everything that you tell us." 10 So Simon mustered all the men able to fight, and quickly completing the walls of Jerusalem, fortified it on every side. 11 He sent Jonathan, son of Absalom, to Joppa with a large force; Jonathan drove out the occupants and remained there.

Deceit and Treachery of Trypho

12 Then Trypho moved from Ptolemais with a large army to invade the land of Judah, bringing Jonathan with him as prisoner. 13 But Simon pitched his camp at Adida, facing the plain. 14 When Trypho learned that Simon had succeeded his brother Jonathan, and that he intended to fight him, he sent envoys to him with this message: 15 "We have detained your brother Jonathan on account of the money that he owed the royal treasury in connection with the offices that he held. 16 Therefore, if you send us a hundred talents of silver, and two of his sons as hostages to guarantee that when he is set free he will not revolt against us, we will release him."

17 Although Simon knew that they were speaking deceitfully to him, he gave orders to get the money and the boys, for fear of provoking much hostility among the people, who might say 18 that Jonathan perished because Simon would not send Trypho the money and the boys. 19 So he sent the boys and the hundred talents; but Trypho broke his promise and would not let Jonathan go. 20† Next he began to invade and ravage the country. His troops went around by the road that leads to Adora, but Simon and his army moved along opposite him everywhere he went. 21 The men in the citadel sent messengers to Trypho, urging him to come to them by way of the desert, and to send them provisions. 22 Although Trypho got all his cavalry ready to go, there was a heavy fall of snow that night, and he could not go. So he left for Gilead. 23† When he was approaching Baskama, he had Jonathan killed and buried there. 24 Then Trypho returned to his own country.

Jonathan's Tomb

25 Simon sent for the remains of his brother Jonathan, and buried him in Modein, the city of his fathers. 26 All Israel bewailed him with solemn lamentation, mourning over him for many days. 27 Then Simon erected over the tomb of his father and his brothers a monument of stones, polished front and back, and raised high enough to be seen at a distance. 28 He set up seven pyramids facing one another for his father and his mother and his four brothers. 29 For the pyramids he devised a setting of big columns, on which he carved suits of armor as a perpetual memorial, and next to the armor he placed carved ships, which could be seen by all who sailed the sea. 30 This tomb which he built at Modein is there to the present day.

Pact between Simon and Demetrius

31 Trypho dealt treacherously with the young King Antiochus. He killed him 32 and assumed the kingship in his place, putting on the crown of Asia. Thus he brought much evil on the land. 33 Simon, on his part, built up the strongholds of Judea, strengthening their fortifications with high towers, thick walls, and gates with bars, and he stored up provisions in the fortresses. 34 Simon also sent chosen men to King Demetrius with the request that he grant the land a release from taxation, for all that Trypho did was to plunder the land. 35 In reply, King Demetrius sent him the following letter:

36 "King Demetrius sends greetings to Simon the high priest, the friend of kings, and to the elders and the Jewish people. 37 We have received the gold crown and the palm branch that you sent. We are willing to be on most peaceful terms with you and to write to our official to grant you release from tribute. 38 Whatever we have guaranteed to you remains in force, and the strongholds that you have built shall remain yours. 39 We remit any oversights and defaults incurred up to now, as well as the crown tax that you owe. Any other tax that may have been collected in Jerusalem shall no longer be collected there. 40 If any of you are qualified for enrollment in our service, let them be enrolled. Let there be peace between us."

† **13, 20f:** The invaders made a wide flanking movement to invade Judea from the south. *Adora* was a few miles southwest of Beth-zur. They would avoid Beth-zur itself and other strongholds of the Maccabees by following the way of the desert.

13, 23: *Baskama:* northeast of the Sea of Galilee.

* **13, 6:** 1 Mc 5, 2; 12, 53.

41† Thus in the year one hundred and seventy, the yoke of the Gentiles was removed from Israel, **42** and the people began to write in their records and contracts, "In the first year of Simon, high priest, governor, and leader of the Jews."

Capture of Gazara and the Citadel

43*† In those days Simon besieged Gazara and surrounded it with troops. He made a siege machine, pushed it up against the city, and attacked and captured one of the towers. **44** The men who had been on the siege machine jumped down into the city and caused a great tumult there. **45** The men of the city, joined by their wives and children, went up on the wall, with their garments rent, and cried out in loud voices, begging Simon to grant them peace. **46** "Do not treat us according to our evil deeds," they said, "but according to your mercy."

47 So Simon came to terms with them and did not destroy them. He made them leave the city, however, and he purified the houses in which there were idols. Then he entered the city with hymns and songs of praise. **48** After removing from it everything that was impure, he settled there men who observed the law. He improved its fortifications and built himself a residence.

49 The men in the citadel in Jerusalem were prevented from going out into the country and back for the purchase of food; they suffered greatly from hunger, and many of them died of starvation. **50** They finally cried out to Simon for peace, and he gave them peace. He expelled them from the citadel and cleansed it of impurities. **51*†** On the twenty-third day of the second month, in the year one hundred and seventy-one, the Jews entered the citadel with shouts of jubilation, waving of palm branches, the music of harps and cymbals and lyres, and the singing of hymns and canticles, because a great enemy of Israel had been destroyed. **52** Simon decreed that this day should be celebrated every year with rejoicing. He also strengthened the fortifications of the temple hill alongside the citadel, and he and his companions dwelt there. **53†** Seeing that his son John was now a grown man, Simon made him commander of all his soldiers, with his residence in Gazara.

Capture of Demetrius

14 **1†** In the year one hundred and seventy-two, King Demetrius assembled his army and marched into Media to obtain help so that he could fight Trypho. **2†** When Arsaces, king of Persia and Media, heard that Demetrius had invaded his territory, he sent one of his generals to take him alive. **3** The general went forth and defeated the army of Demetrius; he captured him and brought him to Arsaces, who put him in prison.

Glory of Simon

4* The land was at rest all the days of Simon,
 who sought the good of his nation.
 His people were delighted with his power
 and his magnificence throughout his reign.
5 As his crowning glory he captured the port
 of Joppa
 and made it a gateway to the isles of
 the sea.
6* He enlarged the borders of his nation
 and gained control of the country.
7 He took many enemies prisoners of war
 and made himself master of Gazara,
 Beth-zur, and the citadel.
 He cleansed the citadel of its impurities;
 there was no one to withstand him.
8* The people cultivated their land in peace;
 the land yielded its produce
 and the trees of the field their fruit.
9* Old men sat in the squares,
 all talking about the good times,
 while the young men wore the glorious
 apparel of war.
10 He supplied the cities with food
 and equipped them with means of defense,
 till his glorious name reached the ends of
 the earth.
11* He brought peace to the land,
 and Israel was filled with happiness.
12* Every man sat under his vine and his fig tree,
 with no one to disturb him.
13 No one was left to attack them in their land;
 the kings in those days were crushed.
14 He strengthened all the lowly among
 his people

13, 41: *The year one hundred and seventy:* March, 142, to April, 141 B.C., by the temple calendar.
13, 43: *Gazara:* a key position in the Shephelah, fortified by Bacchides in 160 B.C.; cf 1 Mc 9, 52.
13, 51: *The twenty-third day of the second month:* June 3, 141 B.C.
13, 53: *John:* John Hyrcanus, who was to succeed his father as ruler and high priest; cf 1 Mc 16, 23f.
14, 1: *The year one hundred and seventy-two:* 141–140 B.C. The expedition began most probably in the spring of 140.
14, 2: *Arsaces:* Arsaces VI, also called Mithridates I, the Parthian

king (171–138 B.C.). Parthians had overrun Persia and now held Babylonia, both of which had hitherto belonged to the Seleucid empire. The Greeks and Macedonians in these countries had appealed to Demetrius for help.

13, 43: 2 Mc 10, 32–38.   14, 8: Zec 8, 12.
13, 51: 1 Mc 1, 36.   14, 9: Zec 8, 4f.
14, 4: 1 Mc 3, 3–9.   14, 11: Lv 26, 6.
14, 6: Ex 34, 24.   14, 12: Mi 4, 4; Zec 3, 10.

and was zealous for the law;

　he suppressed all the lawless and

　　the wicked.

15 　He made the temple splendid

　　and enriched its equipment.

Alliance with Rome and Sparta

16† When people heard in Rome and even in Sparta that Jonathan had died, they were deeply grieved. 17 But when the Romans heard that his brother Simon had been made high priest in his place and was master of the country and the cities, 18* they sent him inscribed tablets of bronze to renew with him the friendship and alliance that they had established with his brothers Judas and Jonathan. 19 These were read before the assembly in Jerusalem.

20 This is a copy of the letter that the Spartans sent: "The rulers and the citizens of Sparta send greetings to Simon the high priest, the elders, the priests, and the rest of the Jewish people, our brothers. 21 The envoys you sent to our people have informed us of your glory and fame, and we were happy that they came. 22* In accordance with what they said we have recorded the following in the public decrees: Since Numenius, son of Antiochus, and Antipater, son of Jason, envoys of the Jews, have come to us to renew their friendship with us, 23 the people have voted to receive the men with honor, and to deposit a copy of their words in the public archives, so that the people of Sparta may have a record of them. A copy of this decree has been made for Simon the high priest."

24* After this, Simon sent Numenius to Rome with a great gold shield weighing a thousand minas, to confirm the alliance with the Romans.

Decree of Honor

25 When the people heard of these things, they said, "How can we thank Simon and his sons? 26 He and his brothers and his father's house have stood firm and repulsed Israel's enemies. They have thus preserved its liberty." So they made an inscription on bronze tablets, which they affixed to pillars on Mount Zion. 27† The following is a copy of the inscription:

"On the eighteenth day of Elul, in the year one hundred and seventy-two, that is, the third year under Simon the high priest in Asaramel, 28 in a great assembly of priests, people, rulers of the nation, and elders of the country, the following proclamation was made:

29 " 'Since there have often been wars in our country, Simon, son of the priest Mattathias, descendant of Joarib, and his brothers have put themselves in danger and resisted the enemies of their nation, so that their sanctuary and law might be maintained, and they have thus brought great glory to their nation. 30 After Jonathan had rallied his nation and become their high priest, he was gathered to his kinsmen. 31 When the enemies of the Jews sought to invade and devastate their country and to lay hands on their temple, 32 Simon rose up and fought for his nation, spending large sums of his own money to equip the men of his nation's armed forces and giving them their pay. 33 He fortified the cities of Judea, especially the frontier city of Bethzur, where he stationed a garrison of Jewish soldiers, and where previously the enemy's arms had been stored. 34 He also fortified Joppa by the sea and Gazara on the border of Azotus, a place previously occupied by the enemy; these cities he resettled with Jews, and furnished them with all that was necessary for their restoration. 35 When the Jewish people saw Simon's loyalty and the glory he planned to bring to his nation, they made him their leader and high priest because of all he had accomplished and the loyalty and justice he had shown his nation. In every way he sought to exalt his people.

36 " 'In his time and under his guidance they succeeded in driving the Gentiles out of their country, especially those in the City of David in Jerusalem, who had built for themselves a citadel from which they used to sally forth to defile the environs of the temple and inflict grave injury on its purity. 37 In this citadel he stationed Jewish soldiers, and he strengthened its fortifications for the defense of the land and the city, while he also raised the wall of Jerusalem to a greater height. 38 Consequently, King Demetrius confirmed him in the high priesthood, 39* made him one of his Friends, and conferred the highest honors on him. 40 He had indeed heard that the Romans had addressed the Jews as friends, allies, and brothers and that they had received Simon's envoys with honor.

41 " 'The Jewish people and their priest have, therefore, made the following decisions. Simon shall be their permanent leader and high priest until a true prophet arises. 42 He shall act as governor general over them, and shall have charge of the temple, to make regulations concerning its functions and concerning the country, its weapons and

---

14, 16: The embassy to *Rome* and *Sparta* was sent soon after Simon's accession to power, and the replies were received before Demetrius' expedition (vv 1–3) — probably in 142 B.C.

14, 27: *Eighteenth day of Elul:* September 13, 140 B.C. *Asaramel:* a Hebrew name meaning "court of the people of God."

14, 18: 1 Mc 8, 22.　　　　　　　14, 24: 1 Mc 12, 16; 15, 15.

14, 22: 1 Mc 12, 16; 15, 15.　　　14, 39f: 1 Mc 2, 18.

strongholds; [43] he shall be obeyed by all. All contracts made in the country shall be dated by his name. He shall have the right to wear royal purple and gold ornaments. [44] It shall not be lawful for any of the people or priests to nullify any of these decisions, or to contradict the orders given by him, or to convene an assembly in the country without his consent, to be clothed in royal purple or wear an official gold brooch. [45] Whoever acts otherwise or violates any of these prescriptions shall be liable to punishment.

[46] " 'All the people approved of granting Simon the right to act in accord with these decisions, [47]† and Simon accepted and agreed to act as high priest, governor general, and ethnarch of the Jewish people and priests and to exercise supreme authority over all.' "

[48] It was decreed that this inscription should be engraved on bronze tablets, to be set up in a conspicuous place in the precincts of the temple, [49] and that copies of it should be deposited in the treasury, where they would be available to Simon and his sons.

Letter of Antiochus

15 [1]† Antiochus, son of King Demetrius, sent a letter from the islands of the sea to Simon, the priest and ethnarch of the Jews, and to all the nation, [2] which read as follows:

"King Antiochus sends greetings to Simon, the priest and ethnarch, and to the Jewish nation. [3] Whereas certain villains have gained control of the kingdom of my ancestors, I intend to reclaim it, that I may restore it to its former state. I have recruited a large number of mercenary troops and equipped warships [4] to make a landing in my country and take revenge on those who have ruined it and laid waste many cities in my realm.

[5] "Now, therefore, I confirm to you all the tax exemptions that the kings before me granted you and whatever other privileges they conferred on you. [6] I authorize you to coin your own money, as legal tender in your country. [7] Jerusalem and its temple shall be free. All the weapons you have prepared and all the strongholds you have built and now occupy shall remain in your possession. [8] All debts, present or future, due to the royal treasury shall be canceled for you, now and for all time. [9] When we recover our kingdom, we will greatly honor you and your

nation and the temple, so that your glory will be manifest in all the earth."

[10]† In the year one hundred and seventy-four, Antiochus invaded the land of his ancestors, and all the troops rallied to him, so that few were left with Trypho. [11]† Pursued by Antiochus, Trypho fled to Dor, by the sea, [12] realizing what a mass of troubles had come upon him now that his soldiers had deserted him. [13] Antiochus encamped before Dor with a hundred and twenty thousand infantry and eight thousand horsemen. [14] While he invested the city, his ships closed in along the coast, so that he blockaded it by land and sea and let no one go in or out.

Roman Alliance Renewed

[15]* Meanwhile, Numenius and his companions left Rome with letters such as this addressed to various kings and countries:

[16]† "Lucius, Consul of the Romans, sends greetings to King Ptolemy. [17] Certain envoys of the Jews, our friends and allies, have come to us to renew their earlier alliance of friendship. They had been sent by Simon the high priest and the Jewish people, [18]* and they brought with them a gold shield worth a thousand minas. [19] Therefore we have decided to write to various kings and countries, that they are not to harm them, or wage war against them or their cities or their country, and are not to assist those who fight against them. [20] We have also decided to accept the shield from them. [21] If, then, any troublemakers from their country take refuge with you, hand them over to Simon the high priest, so that he may punish them according to their law."

[22]† The consul sent similar letters to Kings Demetrius, Attalus, Ariarthes and Arsaces; [23] to all the countries—Sampsames, Sparta, Delos, Myndos, Sicyon, Caria, Samos, Pamphylia, Lycia, Halicarnassus, Rhodes, Phaselis, Cos, Side, Aradus, Gortyna, Cnidus, Cyprus, and Cyrene. [24] A copy of the letter was also sent to Simon the high priest.

Hostility of Antiochus

[25] When King Antiochus was encamped before Dor, he assaulted it continuously both with troops and with the siege machines he had made. He blockaded Trypho by preventing anyone from going in or out. [26] Simon sent to Antiochus' support two thousand elite troops, together with gold and

---

14, 47: *Ethnarch:* a subaltern ruler over a racial group whose office needed confirmation by a higher authority within the empire.

15, 1: *Antiochus:* Antiochus VII Sidetes, son of Demetrius I, and younger brother of Demetrius II, now a prisoner of the Parthians. At the age of twenty he set out from the island of Rhodes to take his brother's place and drive out the usurper Trypho.

15, 10: *The year one hundred and seventy-four:* 138 B.C.

15, 11: *Dor, by the sea:* a fortress on the Palestinian coast, fifteen miles south of Carmel.

15, 16: *Lucius:* perhaps Lucius Caecilius Metellus, consul in 142 B.C., or Lucius Calpurnicus Piso, consul in 140–139 B.C. This document pertains to Simon's first year as leader.

15, 22: *Attalus:* Attalus II of Pergamum, reigned 159–138 B.C. *Ariarthes:* Ariarthes V of Cappadocia, reigned 162–130 B.C. *Arsaces:* see note on 1 Mc 14, 2.

15, 15: 1 Mc 8, 17; 12, 16; 14, 22.24.   **15, 18:** 1 Mc 14, 24.

silver and much equipment. 27 But he refused to accept the aid; in fact, he broke all the agreements he had previously made with Simon and became hostile toward him.

28 He sent Athenobius, one of his Friends, to confer with Simon and say: "You are occupying Joppa and Gazara and the citadel of Jerusalem; these are cities of my kingdom. 29 You have laid waste their territories, done great harm to the land, and taken possession of many districts in my realm. 30 Therefore, give up the cities you have seized and the tribute money of the districts outside the territory of Judea of which you have taken possession; 31 or instead, pay me five hundred talents of silver for the devastation you have caused and five hundred talents more for the tribute money of the cities. If you do not do this, we will come and make war on you."

32 So Athenobius, the king's Friend, came to Jerusalem, and on seeing the splendor of Simon's court, the gold and silver plate on the sideboard, and the rest of his rich display, he was amazed. When he gave him the king's message, 33 Simon said to him in reply:

"We have not seized any foreign land; what we took is not the property of others, but our ancestral heritage which for a time had been unjustly held by our enemies. 34 Now that we have the opportunity, we are holding on to the heritage of our ancestors. 35 As for Joppa and Gazara, which you demand, the men of these cities were doing great harm to our people and laying waste our country; however, we are willing to pay you a hundred talents for these cities."

36 Athenobius made no reply, but returned to the king in anger. When he told him of Simon's words, of his splendor, and of all he had seen, the king fell into a violent rage.

Victory over Cendebeus

37† Trypho had gotten aboard a ship and escaped to Orthosia. 38 Then the king appointed Cendebeus commander in chief of the seacoast, and gave him infantry and cavalry forces. 39† He ordered him to move his troops against Judea and to fortify Kedron and strengthen its gates, so that he could launch attacks against the Jewish people. Meanwhile the king went in pursuit of Trypho. 40 When Cendebeus came to Jamnia, he began to harass the people and to make incursions into Judea, where he took people captive or massacred them. 41 As the king ordered, he fortified Kedron and stationed horsemen

and infantry there, so that they could go out and patrol the roads of Judea.

16 1 John then went up from Gazara and told his father Simon what Cendebeus was doing. 2 Simon called his two oldest sons, Judas and John, and said to them: "I and my brothers and my father's house have fought the battles of Israel from our youth until today, and many times we succeeded in saving Israel. 3 I have now grown old, but you, by the mercy of Heaven, have come to man's estate. Take my place and my brother's, and go out and fight for our nation; and may the help of Heaven be with you!"

4 John then mustered in the land twenty thousand warriors and horsemen. Setting out against Cendebeus, they spent the night at Modein, 5 rose early, and marched into the plain. There, facing them, was an immense army of foot soldiers and horsemen, and between the two armies was a stream. 6 John and his men took their position against the enemy. Seeing that his men were afraid to cross the stream, John crossed first. When his men saw this, they crossed over after him. 7 Then he divided his infantry into two corps and put his cavalry between them, for the enemy's horsemen were very numerous. 8 They blew the trumpets, and Cendebeus and his army were put to flight; many of them fell wounded, and the rest fled toward the stronghold. 9 It was then that John's brother Judas fell wounded; but John pursued them until Cendebeus reached Kidron, which he had fortified. 10 Some took refuge in the towers on the plain of Azotus, but John set fire to these, and about two thousand of the enemy perished. He then returned to Judea in peace.

Murder of Simon and His Sons

11 Ptolemy, son of Abubus, had been appointed governor of the plain of Jericho, and he had much silver and gold, 12 being the son-in-law of the high priest. 13 But he became ambitious and sought to get control of the country. So he made treacherous plans to do away with Simon and his sons. 14† As Simon was inspecting the cities of the country and providing for their needs, he and his sons Mattathias and Judas went down to Jericho in the year one hundred and seventy-seven, in the eleventh month (that is, the month Shebat). 15† The son of Abubus gave them a deceitful welcome in the little stronghold called Dok which he had built. While serving them a sumptuous banquet, he had his men

---

15, 37: *Orthosia:* a port between Tripoli and the Eleutherus River.

15, 39: *Kedron:* a few miles southeast of Jamnia and facing the fortress of Gazara held by John Hyrcanus.

16, 14: *In the year one hundred and seventy-seven, in the eleventh month:* January–February, 134 B.C., by the temple calendar.

16, 15: *Dok:* a fortress built on a cliff three miles northwest of Jericho, near modern Ain Duq.

hidden there. [16] Then, when Simon and his sons had drunk freely, Ptolemy and his men sprang up, weapons in hand, rushed upon Simon in the banquet hall, and killed him, his two sons, and some of his servants. [17] By this vicious act of treason he repaid good with evil.

[18] Then Ptolemy wrote an account of this and sent it to the king, asking that troops be sent to help him and that the country be turned over to him. [19] He sent other men to Gazara to do away with John. To the army officers he sent letters inviting them to come to him so that he might present them with silver, gold, and gifts. [20] He also sent others to seize Jerusalem and the mount of the temple. [21] But someone ran ahead and brought word to John at Gazara that his father and his brothers had perished, and that Ptolemy had sent men to kill him also. [22] On hearing this, John was utterly astounded. When the men came to kill him, he had them arrested and put to death, for he knew what they meant to do. [23]† Now the rest of the history of John, his wars and the brave deeds he performed, his rebuilding of the walls, and his other achievements— [24] these things are recorded in the chronicle of his pontificate, from the time that he succeeded his father as high priest.

---

† **16, 23f:** John Hyrcanus was ruler and high priest from 134 B.C. till his death in 104 B.C. These Verses suggest that the book was written, or at least completed, only after he died.

When you are suffering, what is your first response? to escape? to look for relief? to cry out in pain? These are normal and healthy responses: no well-adjusted person chooses to suffer willingly. Sometimes, though, people inflict unspeakable suffering on one another, especially through violence such as rape and torture. What meaning could there be in such suffering? In response, 2 Maccabees insists that God will vindicate all those who suffer innocently at the hands of the unjust.

At a Glance

I. Letters to the Jews in Egypt (1, 1—2, 18).

II. Author's Preface (2, 19–32).

III. Heliodorus' Attempt To Profane the Temple (3, 1–40).

IV. Profanation and Persecution (4, 1—7, 42).

V. Victories of Judas and Purification of the Temple (8, 1—10, 8).

VI. Renewed Persecution (10, 9—15, 36).

VII. Epilogue (15, 37–39).

In-depth

In 167 B.C., the Jewish people faced a new persecution under the Seleucid (Greek) king Antiochus IV Epiphanes. In an effort to unify the many different peoples under his rule, Antiochus imposed his own language, customs, and religion on all of them, including the Jews. Second Maccabees covers some of the same history as First Maccabees but with different purposes: to show the variety of ways the Jews resisted persecution and to give hope to persecuted Jews in the author's time.

The Book of Job had already struggled with the mystery of human suffering and concluded that only God could understand it. Not content with this answer, the author of 2 Maccabees presses forward with new insights:

- In the famous story of the martyrdom of a Jewish mother and her seven sons (7, 1–42), 2 Maccabees talks about the resurrection of the dead.

- In chapter 12, the value of praying for the dead is commended.

- In chapter 15, the book speaks confidently of the prayers of the saints in heaven for those on earth.

Second Maccabees is less concerned with the facts of history than with the meaning of history. It insists that whenever God's faithful people suffer, they can be assured of receiving justice—if not in this life, then in the resurrection. The book shows how the Jewish faith continued to develop as it faced the sometimes painful events of history.

Quick Facts

Period Covered
from 180 to 161 B.C.

Author
someone around 100 B.C., summarizing a lost work by Jason of Cyrene

Themes
differing responses to persecution, the just and suffering

Of Note
Second Maccabees is not found in every translation of the Old Testament (see "The Case of the Missing Books," near Tb 1, 16).

Maccabees

2 Maccabees

I: Letters to the Jews In Egypt

First Letter 124 B.C.

1 [1] The Jews in Jerusalem and in the land of Judea send greetings to their brethren, the Jews in Egypt, and wish them true peace! [2] May God bless you and remember his covenant with his faithful servants, Abraham, Isaac and Jacob. [3] May he give to all of you a heart to worship him and to do his will readily and generously. [4] May he open your heart to his law and his commandments and grant you peace. [5] May he hear your prayers, and be reconciled to you, and never forsake you in time of adversity. [6] Even now we are praying for you here.

[7]*† In the reign of Demetrius, the year one hundred and sixty-nine, we Jews wrote to you during the trouble and violence that overtook us in those years after Jason and his followers had revolted against the holy land and the kingdom, [8]*† setting fire to the gatehouse and shedding innocent blood.

But we prayed to the LORD, and our prayer was heard; we offered sacrifices and fine flour; we lighted the lamps and set out the loaves of bread. [9]† We are now reminding you to celebrate the feast of Booths in the month of Chislev. [10]† Dated in the year one hundred and eighty-eight.

Festival Letter 164 B.C.

The people of Jerusalem and Judea, the senate, and Judas send greetings and good wishes to Aristobulus, counselor of King Ptolemy and member of the family of the anointed priests, and to the Jews in Egypt. [11]† Since we have been saved by God from grave dangers, we give him great thanks for having fought on our side against the king; [12]* it was he who drove out those who fought against the holy city. [13]† When their leader arrived in Persia with his seemingly irresistible army, they were cut to pieces in the temple of the goddess Nanea through a deceitful stratagem employed by Nanea's priests.

1, 7: *Demetrius:* Demetrius II, king of Syria (145–139, 129–125 B.C.). *The year one hundred and sixty-nine* of the Seleucid era, 143 B.C. Regarding the dates in 1 and 2 Maccabees, see note on 1 Mc 1, 10. On the troubles caused by Jason and his revolt against the kingdom, i.e., the rule of the legitimate high priest, see 2 Mc 4, 7–22.

1, 8: *Our prayer was heard:* in the ultimate victory of the Maccabees.

1, 9: *Feast of Booths in the month of Chislev:* really the feast of the Dedication of the temple (2 Mc 10, 1–8), celebrated on the twenty-fifth of Chislev (Nov.-Dec.). Its solemnity resembles that of the true feast of Booths (Lv 23, 33–43), celebrated on the fifteenth of Tishri (Sept.-Oct.); cf 2 Mc 1, 18.

1, 10: 124 B.C. The date pertains to the preceding, not the following letter. *King Ptolemy:* Ptolemy VI Philometor, ruler of Egypt from 180 to 145 B.C.; he is mentioned also in 1 Mc 1, 18; 10, 51–59.

1, 11f: *The king:* Antiochus IV of Syria, the bitter persecutor of the Jews, who, as leader of the Syrian army that invaded Persia, perished there in 164 B.C.

1, 13: *Nanea:* an oriental goddess comparable to Artemis of the Greeks.

*

1, 7: 2 Mc 4, 7–20.
1, 8: 1 Mc 4, 38.

1, 12–17: 2 Mc 9, 1–29; 1 Mc 6, 1–13.

¹⁴† On the pretext of marrying the goddess, Antiochus with his Friends had come to the place to get its great treasures by way of dowry. ¹⁵ When the priests of the Nanaeon had displayed the treasures, Antiochus with a few attendants came to the temple precincts. As soon as he entered the temple, the priests locked the doors. ¹⁶ Then they opened a hidden trapdoor in the ceiling, hurled stones at the leader and his companions and struck them down. They dismembered the bodies, cut off their heads and tossed them to the people outside. ¹⁷ Forever blessed be our God, who has thus punished the wicked!

¹⁸† We shall be celebrating the purification of the temple on the twenty-fifth day of the month Chislev, so we thought it right to inform you that you too may celebrate the feast of Booths and of the fire that appeared when Nehemiah, the rebuilder of the temple† and the altar, offered sacrifices. ¹⁹† When our fathers were being exiled to Persia, devout priests of the time took some of the fire from the altar and hid it secretly in the hollow of a dry cistern, making sure that the place would be unknown to anyone. ²⁰ Many years later, when it so pleased God, Nehemiah, commissioned by the king of Persia, sent the descendants of the priests who had hidden the fire to look for it. ²¹ When they informed us that they could not find any fire, but only muddy water, he ordered them to scoop some out and bring it. After the material for the sacrifices had been prepared, Nehemiah ordered the priests to sprinkle with the water the wood and what lay on it. ²² When this was done and in time the sun, which had been clouded over, began to shine, a great fire blazed up, so that everyone marveled. ²³ While the sacrifice was being burned, the priests recited a prayer, and all present joined in with them, Jonathan leading and the rest responding with Nehemiah.

²⁴ The prayer was as follows: "LORD, LORD God, creator of all things, awesome and strong, just and merciful, the only king and benefactor, ²⁵ who alone are gracious, just, almighty, and eternal, Israel's savior from all evil, who chose our forefathers and sanctified them: ²⁶ accept this sacrifice on behalf of all your people Israel and guard and sanctify your heritage. ²⁷ Gather together our scattered people, free those who are the slaves of the Gentiles, look kindly on those who are despised and detested, and let the Gentiles know that you are our God. ²⁸ Punish those who tyrannize over us and arrogantly mistreat us. ²⁹* Plant your people in your holy place, as Moses promised."

³⁰ Then the priests began to sing hymns. ³¹ After the sacrifice was burned, Nehemiah ordered the rest of the liquid to be poured upon large stones. ³² As soon as this was done, a flame blazed up, but its light was lost in the brilliance cast from a light on the altar. ³³ When the event became known and the king of the Persians was told that, in the very place where the exiled priests had hidden the fire, a liquid was found with which Nehemiah and his people had burned the sacrifices, ³⁴ the king, after verifying the fact, fenced the place off and declared it sacred. ³⁵ To those on whom the king wished to bestow favors he distributed the large revenues he received there. ³⁶† Nehemiah and his companions called the liquid nephthar, meaning purification, but most people named it naphtha.

2 ¹† You will find in the records, not only that Jeremiah the prophet ordered the deportees to take some of the aforementioned fire with them, ²* but also that the prophet, in giving them the law, admonished them not to forget the commandments of the LORD or be led astray in their thoughts, when seeing the gold and silver idols and their ornaments. ³ With other similar words he urged them not to let the law depart from their hearts. ⁴*† The same document also tells how the prophet, following a divine revelation, ordered that the tent and the ark should accompany him and how he went off to the mountain which Moses climbed to see God's inheritance. ⁵ When Jeremiah arrived there, he found a room in a cave in which he put the tent, the ark, and the altar of incense; then he blocked up the entrance. ⁶ Some of those who followed him came up intending to mark the path, but they could not find it. ⁷ When Jeremiah heard of this, he reproved them: "The place is to remain unknown

1, 14–17: A different account of the death of Antiochus IV is given in 2 Mc 9, 1–29, and another variant account in 1 Mc 6, 1–16. The writer of this letter had probably heard a distorted rumor of the king's death. This fact and other indications show that the letter was written very soon after Antiochus IV died, hence in 164 B.C.

1, 18–36: This purely legendary account of Nehemiah's miraculous fire is incorporated in the letter because of its connection with the temple and its rededication.

1, 18: *Nehemiah, the rebuilder of the temple:* he rebuilt the walls of Jerusalem, but the temple had been rebuilt by Zerubbabel almost a century before.

1, 19: *Persia:* actually Babylonia, which later became part of the Persian Empire.

1, 36: By a play on words, the Greek term *naphtha* (petroleum) is assimilated to some Semitic word, perhaps *nephthar,* meaning "loosened."

2, 1–8: This legendary account of how Jeremiah hid the sacred tent (which was not mentioned after the time of Solomon!), the ark and the altar is given for the purpose of explaining why the postexilic temple was the legitimate place of worship even without these sacred objects.

2, 4: *The mountain:* Nebo; cf Dt 34, 1.

1, 29: 2 Mc 2, 18; Dt 30, 3ff.	**2, 4f:** Dt 32, 49; 34, 1; Rv 11, 19.
2, 2: Bar 6, 3–72.	

until God gathers his people together again and shows them mercy. [8]*† Then the LORD will disclose these things, and the glory of the LORD will be seen in the cloud, just as it appeared in the time of Moses and when Solomon prayed that the Place might be gloriously sanctified."

[9] It is also related how Solomon in his wisdom offered a sacrifice at the dedication and the completion of the temple. [10]* Just as Moses prayed to the LORD and fire descended from the sky and consumed the sacrifices, so Solomon also prayed and fire came down and burned up the holocausts. [11]*† Moses had said, "Because it had not been eaten, the sin offering was burned up." [12] Solomon also celebrated the feast in the same way for eight days.

[13]† Besides these things, it is also told in the records and in Nehemiah's Memoirs how he collected the books about the kings, the writings of the prophets and of David, and the royal letters about sacred offerings. [14]* In like manner Judas also collected for us the books that had been scattered because of the war, and we now have them in our possession. [15] If you need them, send messengers to get them for you.

[16] As we are about to celebrate the feast of the purification of the temple, we are writing to you requesting you also to please celebrate the feast. [17] It is God who has saved all his people and has restored to all of them their heritage, the kingdom, the priesthood, and the sacred rites, [18]* as he promised through the law. We trust in God, that he will soon have mercy on us and gather us together from everywhere under the heavens to his holy Place, for he has rescued us from great perils and has purified his Place.

II: Author's Preface

[19] This is the story of Judas Maccabeus and his brothers, of the purification of the great temple, the dedication of the altar, [20]† the campaigns against Antiochus Epiphanes and his son Eupator, [21] and of the heavenly manifestations accorded to the heroes who fought bravely for Judaism, so that, few as they were, they seized the whole land, put to flight the barbarian hordes, [22] regained possession of the world-famous temple, liberated the city, and re-

established the laws that were in danger of being abolished, while the LORD favored them with all his generous assistance. [23] All this, which Jason of Cyrene set forth in detail in five volumes, we will try to condense into a single book.

Purpose and Method

[24] In view of the flood of statistics, and the difficulties encountered by those who wish to plunge into historical narratives where the material is abundant, [25] we have aimed to please those who prefer simple reading, as well as to make it easy for the studious who wish to commit things to memory, and to be helpful to all. [26] For us who have taken upon ourselves the labor of making this digest, the task, far from being easy, is one of sweat and of sleepless nights, [27] just as the preparation of a festive banquet is no light matter for one who thus seeks to give enjoyment to others. Similarly, to win the gratitude of many we will gladly endure these inconveniences, [28] while we leave the responsibility for exact details to the original author, and confine our efforts to giving only a summary outline. [29] As the architect of a new house must give his attention to the whole structure, while the man who undertakes the decoration and the frescoes has only to concern himself with what is needed for ornamentation, so I think it is with us. [30] To enter into questions and examine them thoroughly from all sides is the task of the professional historian; [31] but the man who is making an adaptation should be allowed to aim at brevity of expression and to omit detailed treatment of the matter. [32] Here, then, we shall begin our account without further ado; it would be nonsense to write a long preface to a story and then abbreviate the story itself.

III: Heliodorus' Attempt to Profane the Temple†

Treachery of Simon

3 [1]* While the holy city lived in perfect peace and the laws were strictly observed because of the piety of the high priest Onias† and his hatred of evil, [2] the kings themselves honored the Place and glorified the temple with the most magnificent

---

2, 8: *The Place:* the temple of Jerusalem.

2, 11: The statement attributed here to Moses seems to be based on Lv 10, 16–20.

2, 13: *Nehemiah's Memoirs:* a lost apocryphal work.

2, 20: For the account of the campaigns against Antiochus IV Epiphanes, see 2 Mc 4, 7—10, 9; and for the account of those against his son Antiochus V Eupator, see 2 Mc 10, 10—13, 26.

3, 1–40: This legendary episode about Heliodorus is recounted here for the purpose of stressing the inviolability of the temple of

Jerusalem; its later profanation was allowed by God because of the people's sins; cf 2 Mc 5, 17f.

3, 1: *The high priest Onias:* Onias III, who was priest from 196 to 175 B.C., and died in 171 B.C. He was the son of Simon, whose praises are sung in Sir 50, 1–21.

2, 8: 1 Kgs 8, 11.	**2, 14:** 1 Mc 1, 57.
2, 10: Lv 9, 23f; 2 Chr 7, 1.	**2, 18:** Dt 30, 3ff.
2, 11: Lv 10, 16–20.	**3, 1ff:** 2 Mc 5, 19f; 15, 12.

gifts. [3†] Thus Seleucus, king of Asia, defrayed from his own revenues all the expenses necessary for the sacrificial services. [4*†] But a certain Simon, of the priestly course of Bilgah, who had been appointed superintendent of the temple, had a quarrel with the high priest about the supervision of the city market. [5] Since he could not prevail against Onias, he went to Apollonius of Tarsus, who at that time was governor of Coelesyria and Phoenicia, [6] and reported to him that the treasury in Jerusalem was so full of untold riches that the total sum of money was incalculable and out of all proportion to the cost of the sacrifices, and that it would be possible to bring it all under the control of the king.

Mission of Heliodorus

[7] When Apollonius had an audience with the king, he informed him about the riches that had been reported to him. The king chose his minister Heliodorus and sent him with instructions to expropriate the aforesaid wealth. [8] So Heliodorus immediately set out on his journey, ostensibly to visit the cities of Coelesyria and Phoenicia, but in reality to carry out the king's purpose. [9] When he arrived in Jerusalem and had been graciously received by the high priest of the city, he told him about the information that had been given, and explained the reason for his presence, and he asked if these things were really true. [10*] The high priest explained that part of the money was a care fund for widows and orphans, [11†] and a part was the property of Hyrcanus, son of Tobias, a man who occupied a very high position. Contrary to the calumnies of the impious Simon, the total amounted to four hundred talents of silver and two hundred of gold. [12] He added that it was utterly unthinkable to defraud those who had placed their trust in the sanctity of the Place and in the sacred inviolability of a temple venerated all over the world. [13] But because of the orders he had from the king, Heliodorus said that in any case the money must be confiscated for the royal treasury. [14] So on the day he had set he went in to take an inventory of the funds.

Anguish of the Faithful

There was great distress throughout the city. [15] Priests prostrated themselves in their priestly robes before the altar, and loudly begged him in heaven who had given the law about deposits to keep the deposits safe for those who had made

them. [16] Whoever saw the appearance of the high priest was pierced to the heart, for the changed color of his face manifested the anguish of his soul. [17] The terror and bodily trembling that had come over the man clearly showed those who saw him the pain that lodged in his heart. [18] People rushed out of their houses in crowds to make public supplication, because the Place was in danger of being profaned. [19] Women, girded with sackcloth below their breasts, filled the streets; maidens secluded indoors ran together, some to the gates, some to the walls, others peered through the windows, [20] all of them with hands raised toward heaven, making supplication. [21] It was pitiful to see the populace variously prostrated in prayer and the high priest full of dread and anguish.

Divine Intervention

[22] While they were imploring the almighty LORD to keep the deposits safe and secure for those who had placed them in trust, [23] Heliodorus went on with his plan. [24] But just as he was approaching the treasury with his bodyguards, the LORD of spirits who holds all power manifested himself in so striking a way that those who had been bold enough to follow Heliodorus were panic-stricken at God's power and fainted away in terror. [25] There appeared to them a richly caparisoned horse, mounted by a dreadful rider. Charging furiously, the horse attacked Heliodorus with its front hoofs. The rider was seen to be wearing golden armor. [26] Then two other young men, remarkably strong, strikingly beautiful, and splendidly attired, appeared before him. Standing on each side of him, they flogged him unceasingly until they had given him innumerable blows. [27] Suddenly he fell to the ground, enveloped in great darkness. Men picked him up and laid him on a stretcher. [28] The man who a moment before had entered that treasury with a great retinue and his whole bodyguard was carried away helpless, having clearly experienced the sovereign power of God. [29] While he lay speechless and deprived of all hope of aid, due to an act of God's power, [30] the Jews praised the LORD who had marvelously glorified his holy Place; and the temple, charged so shortly before with fear and commotion, was filled with joy and gladness, now that the almighty LORD had manifested himself.

[31] Soon some of the companions of Heliodorus begged Onias to invoke the Most High, praying that

3, 3: *Seleucus*: Seleucus IV Philopator, who reigned from 187 to 175 B.C.
3, 4: *Bilgah*: a priestly family mentioned in Neh 12, 5.18.
3, 11: *Son of Tobias*: a member of the Tobiad family of Transjor-

dan (Neh 2, 10; 6, 17ff; 13, 4–8). Hyrcanus' father was Joseph, whose mother was the sister of the high priest Onias II.

3, 4: 2 Mc 4, 23.   3, 10: Dt 14, 29.

the life of the man who was about to expire might be spared. 32 Fearing that the king might think that Heliodorus had suffered some foul play at the hands of the Jews, the high priest offered a sacrifice for the man's recovery. 33 While the high priest was offering the sacrifice of atonement, the same young men in the same clothing again appeared and stood before Heliodorus. "Be very grateful to the high priest Onias," they told him. "It is for his sake that the LORD has spared your life. 34 Since you have been scourged by Heaven, proclaim to all men the majesty of God's power." When they had said this, they disappeared.

Testimony of Heliodorus

35 After Heliodorus had offered a sacrifice to the LORD and made most solemn vows to him who had spared his life, he bade Onias farewell, and returned with his soldiers to the king. 36 Before all men he gave witness to the deeds of the most high God that he had seen with his own eyes. 37 When the king asked Heliodorus who would be a suitable man to be sent to Jerusalem next, he answered: 38 "If you have an enemy or a plotter against the government, send him there, and you will receive him back well-flogged, if indeed he survives at all; for there is certainly some special divine power about the Place. 39 He who has his dwelling in heaven watches over that Place and protects it, and he strikes down and destroys those who come to harm it." 40 This was how the matter concerning Heliodorus and the preservation of the treasury turned out.

IV: Profanation and Persecution

Onias Appeals to the King

4 1 The Simon mentioned above as the informer about the funds against his own country, made false accusations that it was Onias who threatened Heliodorus and instigated the whole miserable affair. 2 He dared to brand as a plotter against the government the man who was a benefactor of the city, a protector of his compatriots, and a zealous defender of the laws. 3 When Simon's hostility reached such a point that murders were being committed by one of his henchmen, 4 Onias saw that the opposition was serious and that Apollonius, son of Menestheus, the governor of Coelesyria and Phoenicia, was abetting Simon's wickedness. 5 So he had recourse to the king, not as an accuser of his countrymen, but as a

Arrogance

Arrogance seems to run in the family of Simon. First, Simon seeks to embarrass the high priest, Onias, because of a minor disagreement (2 Mc 3, 1–14). When that fails, he falsely accuses Onias of a crime (4, 1–6). Several years later, Simon's brother bribes his way into power (verses 23–29).

We have all encountered arrogant people who think that they can do no wrong, and when they do err, cover it up by attacking others. Many of us are intimidated by such people and resent that we felt talked down to or easily dismissed as unimportant. So, how should we respond to arrogant people? The most obvious solution is to ignore them. If that is not possible, then we need to react to them calmly and confidently. Finally, we should keep them in our prayers. Their arrogance can be masking an insecurity or a hurt that needs God's healing touch.

In your prayer, reflect or journal on the following questions:
- Who intimidates you by her or his arrogant behavior?
- How could you respond in a loving and just way?
- What do you need to bring to God in prayer?

▶ 2 Mc 3, 1—4, 29

man looking to the general and particular good of all the people. 6 He saw that, unless the king intervened, it would be impossible to have a peaceful government, and that Simon would not desist from his folly.

Jews Led by Jason To Apostatize

7*† But Seleucus died, and when Antiochus surnamed Epiphanes succeeded him on the throne, Onias' brother Jason obtained the high priesthood by corrupt means: 8 in an interview, he promised the king three hundred and sixty talents of silver, as

---

† **4, 7:** *Seleucus died:* he was murdered by Heliodorus. Antiochus Epiphanes was his younger brother. Onias' brother showed his love

for the Greek way of life (v 10) by changing his Hebrew name Joshua, or Jesus, to the Greek name Jason.

well as eighty talents from another source of income. [9]† Besides this he agreed to pay a hundred and fifty more, if he were given authority to establish a gymnasium and a youth club for it and to enroll men in Jerusalem as Antiochians.

[10] When Jason received the king's approval and came into office, he immediately initiated his countrymen into the Greek way of life. [11]*† He set aside the royal concessions granted to the Jews through the mediation of John, father of Eupolemus (that Eupolemus who would later go on an embassy to the Romans to establish a treaty of friendship with them); he abrogated the lawful institutions and introduced customs contrary to the law. [12]*† He quickly established a gymnasium at the very foot of the acropolis, where he induced the noblest young men to wear the Greek hat. [13] The craze for Hellenism and foreign customs reached such a pitch, through the outrageous wickedness of the ungodly pseudo-high-priest Jason, [14] that the priests no longer cared about the service of the altar. Disdaining the temple and neglecting the sacrifices, they hastened, at the signal for the discus-throwing, to take part in the unlawful exercises on the athletic field. [15] They despised what their ancestors had regarded as honors, while they highly prized what the Greeks esteemed as glory. [16] Precisely because of this, they found themselves in serious trouble: the very people whose manner of life they emulated, and whom they desired to imitate in everything, became their enemies and oppressors. [17] It is no light matter to flout the laws of God, as the following period will show.

[18] When the quinquennial games were held at Tyre in the presence of the king, [19] the vile Jason sent envoys as representatives of the Antiochians of Jerusalem, to bring there three hundred silver drachmas for the sacrifice to Hercules. But the bearers themselves decided that the money should not be spent on a sacrifice, as that was not right, but should be used for some other purpose. [20]† So the contribution destined by the sender for the sacrifice to Hercules was in fact applied, by those who brought it, to the construction of triremes.

[21]† When Apollonius, son of Menestheus, was sent to Egypt for the coronation of King Philometor,

Antiochus learned that the king was opposed to his policies; so he took measures for his own security. [22] After going to Joppa, he proceeded to Jerusalem. There he was received with great pomp by Jason and the people of the city, who escorted him with torchlights and acclamations; following this, he led his army into Phoenicia.

Menelaus Supplants Jason

[23]† Three years later Jason sent Menelaus, brother of the aforementioned Simon, to deliver the money to the king, and to obtain decisions on some important matters. [24] When he had been introduced to the king, he flattered him with such an air of authority that he secured the high priesthood for himself, outbidding Jason by three hundred talents of silver. [25] He returned with the royal commission, but with nothing that made him worthy of the high priesthood; he had the temper of a cruel tyrant and the rage of a wild beast. [26] Then Jason, who had cheated his own brother and now saw himself cheated by another man, was driven out as a fugitive to the country of the Ammonites.

[27] Although Menelaus had obtained the office, he did not make any payments of the money he had promised to the king, [28] in spite of the demand of Sostratus, the commandant of the citadel, whose duty it was to collect the taxes. For this reason, both were summoned before the king. [29] Menelaus left his brother Lysimachus as his substitute in the high priesthood, while Sostratus left Crates, commander of the Cypriots, as his substitute.

Murder of Onias

[30]† While these things were taking place, the people of Tarsus and Mallus rose in revolt, because their cities had been given as a gift to Antiochis, the king's mistress. [31] The king, therefore, went off in haste to settle the affair, leaving Andronicus, one of his nobles, as his deputy. [32] Then Menelaus, thinking this a good opportunity, stole some gold vessels from the temple and presented them to Andronicus; he had already sold some other vessels in Tyre and in the neighboring cities. [33] When Onias had clear evidence of the facts, he made a public protest, after withdrawing to the inviolable sanctuary at

---

† **4, 9:** *Youth club:* an educational institution in which young men were trained both in Greek intellectual culture and in physical fitness. *Antiochians:* honorary citizens of Antioch, a Hellenistic city of the Seleucid Kingdom that had a corporation of such Antiochians, who enjoyed certain political and commercial privileges.
4, 11: *Eupolemus:* one of the two envoys sent to Rome by Judas Maccabeus (1 Mc 8, 17).
4, 12: Since the *gymnasium,* where the youth exercised naked (Greek *gymnos*), lay in the Tyropoeon Valley to the east of the citadel, it was directly next to the temple on its eastern side. *The Greek hat:* a wide-brimmed hat, traditional headgear of Hermes,

the patron god of athletic contests; it formed part of the distinctive costume of the members of the "youth club."
4, 20: *Triremes:* war vessels with three banks of oars.
4, 21: *Philometor:* Ptolemy VI, king of Egypt, c. 172 to c. 145 B.C.
4, 23: *Menelaus:* Jewish high priest from c. 172 to his execution in 162 B.C. (2 Mc 13, 3–8).
4, 30: *Mallus:* a city of Cilicia (v 36) in southeastern Asia Minor, about thirty miles east of Tarsus.

4, 11: 1 Mc 8, 17.   **4, 12:** 1 Mc 1, 14.

Daphne, near Antioch. 34 Thereupon Menelaus approached Andronicus privately and asked him to lay hands on Onias. So Andronicus went to Onias, and by treacherously reassuring him through sworn pledges with right hands joined, persuaded him, in spite of his suspicions, to leave the sanctuary. Then, without any regard for justice, he immediately put him to death.

35 As a result, not only the Jews, but many people of other nations as well, were indignant and angry over the unjust murder of the man. 36† When the king returned from the region of Cilicia, the Jews of the city, together with the Greeks who detested the crime, went to see him about the murder of Onias. 37 Antiochus was deeply grieved and full of pity; he wept as he recalled the prudence and noble conduct of the deceased. 38 Inflamed with anger, he immediately stripped Andronicus of his purple robe, tore off his other garments, and had him led through the whole city to the very place where he had committed the outrage against Onias; and there he put the murderer to death. Thus the LORD rendered him the punishment he deserved.

Riot against Lysimachus

39† Many sacrilegious thefts had been committed by Lysimachus in the city with the connivance of Menelaus. When word was spread that a large number of gold vessels had been stolen, the people assembled in protest against Lysimachus. 40 As the crowds, now thoroughly enraged, began to riot, Lysimachus launched an unjustified attack against them with about three thousand armed men under the leadership of Auranus, a man as advanced in folly as he was in years. 41 Reacting against Lysimachus' attack, the people picked up stones or pieces of wood or handfuls of the ashes lying there and threw them in wild confusion at Lysimachus and his men. 42 As a result, they wounded many of them and even killed a few, while they put all the rest to flight. The sacrilegious thief himself they slew near the treasury.

43 Charges about this affair were brought against Menelaus. 44† When the king came to Tyre, three men sent by the senate presented to him the justice of their cause. 45* But Menelaus, seeing himself on the losing side, promised Ptolemy, son of

Dorymenes, a substantial sum of money if he would win the king over. 46 So Ptolemy retired with the king under a colonnade, as if to get some fresh air, and persuaded him to change his mind. 47 Menelaus, who was the cause of all the trouble, the king acquitted of the charges, while he condemned to death those poor men who would have been declared innocent even if they had pleaded their case before Scythians. 48 Thus, those who had prosecuted the case for the city, for the people, and for the sacred vessels, quickly suffered unjust punishment. 49 For this reason, even some Tyrians were indignant over the crime and provided sumptuously for their burial. 50 But Menelaus, thanks to the covetousness of the men in power, remained in office, where he grew in wickedness and became the chief plotter against his fellow citizens.

Sedition and Death of Jason

5 1† About this time Antiochus sent his second expedition into Egypt. 2* It then happened that all over the city, for nearly forty days, there appeared horsemen charging in midair, clad in garments interwoven with gold—companies fully armed with lances 3 and drawn swords; squadrons of cavalry in battle array, charges and countercharges on this side and that, with brandished shields and bristling spears, flights of arrows and flashes of gold ornaments, together with armor of every sort. 4 Therefore all prayed that this vision might be a good omen.

5† But when a false rumor circulated that Antiochus was dead, Jason gathered fully a thousand men and suddenly attacked the city. As the defenders on the walls were forced back and the city was finally being taken, Menelaus took refuge in the citadel. 6 Jason then slaughtered his fellow citizens without mercy, not realizing that triumph over one's own kindred was the greatest failure, but imagining that he was winning a victory over his enemies, not his fellow countrymen. 7 Even so, he did not gain control of the government, but in the end received only disgrace for his treachery, and once again took refuge in the country of the Ammonites. 8† At length he met a miserable end. Called to account before Aretas, king of the Arabs, he fled from city to city, hunted by all men, hated

---

† **4, 36:** *The city:* Antioch. But some understand the Greek to mean "each city."
4, 39: *The city:* Jerusalem. Menelaus was still in Syria.
4, 44: *The senate:* the council of Jewish elders at Jerusalem; cf 1 Mc 12, 6.
5, 1: *Second expedition:* the first invasion of Egypt by Antiochus in 169 B.C. (1 Mc 1, 16–20) is not mentioned in 2 Maccabees, unless the coming of the Syrian army to Palestine (2 Mc 4, 21f) is regarded as the first invasion. The author of 2 Maccabees apparently combines the first pillage of Jerusalem in 169 B.C. after Antiochus' first invasion

of Egypt (1 Mc 1, 20–28; cf 2 Mc 5, 5ff) with the second pillage of the city two years later (167 B.C.), following the king's second invasion of Egypt in 168 B.C. (1 Mc 1, 29–35; cf 2 Mc 5, 24ff).
5, 5: *Jason:* brother of Onias III, was claimant of the high priesthood (2 Mc 4, 7–10). Later he was supplanted by Menelaus who drove him into Transjordan (2 Mc 4, 26).
5, 8: *Aretas:* King Aretas I of the Nabateans; cf 1 Mc 5, 25.

*
4, 45: 2 Mc 8, 8; 1 Mc 3, 38.   5, 2f: 2 Mc 3, 24ff; 10, 29f;
5, 1: 1 Mc 1, 17.   11, 8.

as a transgressor of the laws, abhorred as the butcher of his country and his countrymen. After being driven into Egypt, [9] he crossed the sea to the Spartans, among whom he hoped to find protection because of his relations with them. There he who had exiled so many from their country perished in exile; [10] and he who had cast out so many to lie unburied went unmourned himself with no funeral of any kind or any place in the tomb of his ancestors.

The City Ravaged

[11]* When these happenings were reported to the king, he thought that Judea was in revolt. Raging like a wild animal, he set out from Egypt and took Jerusalem by storm. [12] He ordered his soldiers to cut down without mercy those whom they met and to slay those who took refuge in their houses. [13] There was a massacre of young and old, a killing of women and children, a slaughter of virgins and infants. [14] In the space of three days, eighty thousand were lost, forty thousand meeting a violent death, and the same number being sold into slavery. [15] Not satisfied with this, the king dared to enter the holiest temple in the world; Menelaus, that traitor both to the laws and to his country, served as guide. [16] He laid his impure hands on the sacred vessels and gathered up with profane hands the votive offerings made by other kings for the advancement, the glory, and the honor of the Place. [17]* Puffed up in spirit, Antiochus did not realize that it was because of the sins of the city's inhabitants that the LORD was angry for a little while and hence disregarded the holy Place. [18] If they had not become entangled in so many sins, this man, like Heliodorus, who was sent by King Seleucus to inspect the treasury, would have been flogged and turned back from his presumptuous action as soon as he approached. [19]*† The LORD, however, had not chosen the people for the sake of the Place, but the Place for the sake of the people. [20] Therefore, the Place itself, having shared in the people's misfortunes, afterward participated in their good fortune; and what the Almighty had forsaken in his anger was restored in all its glory, once the great Sovereign became reconciled.

[21]* Antiochus carried off eighteen hundred talents from the temple, and hurried back to Antioch. In his arrogance he planned to make the land navigable and the sea passable on foot, so carried away was he with pride. [22]† But he left governors to harass the nation: at Jerusalem, Philip, a Phrygian by birth, and in character more cruel than the man who appointed him; [23]† at Mount Gerizim, Andronicus; and besides these, Menelaus, who lorded it over his fellow citizens worse than the others did. Out of hatred for the Jewish citizens, [24]*† the king sent Apollonius, commander of the Mysians, at the head of an army of twenty-two thousand men, with orders to kill all the grown men and sell the women and young men into slavery. [25] When this man arrived in Jerusalem, he pretended to be peacefully disposed and waited until the holy day of the sabbath; then, finding the Jews refraining from work, he ordered his men to parade fully armed. [26] All those who came out to watch, he massacred, and running through the city with armed men, he cut down a large number of people.

[27]* But Judas Maccabeus with about nine others withdrew to the wilderness where he and his companions lived like wild animals in the hills, continuing to eat what grew wild to avoid sharing the defilement.

The Temple Desecrated

6 [1]* Not long after this the king sent an Athenian senator to force the Jews to abandon the customs of their ancestors and live no longer by the laws of God; [2]*† also to profane the temple in Jerusalem and dedicate it to Olympian Zeus, and that on Mount Gerizim to Zeus the Hospitable, as the inhabitants of the place requested. [3] This intensified the evil in an intolerable and utterly disgusting way. [4]† The Gentiles filled the temple with debauchery and revelry; they amused themselves with prostitutes and had intercourse with women even in the sacred court. They also brought into the temple things that were forbidden, [5] so that the altar was covered with abominable offerings prohibited by the laws.

---

†
5, 19: Man is more important than even the most sacred institutions; cf Mk 2, 27.

5, 22: *Philip, a Phrygian by birth:* the Philip of 2 Mc 6, 11 and 8, 8, but probably not the same as Philip the regent of 2 Mc 9, 29 and 1 Mc 6, 14.

5, 23: *Mount Gerizim:* the sacred mountain of the Samaritans at Shechem; cf 2 Mc 6, 2.

5, 24: *Apollonius:* the Mysian commander of 1 Mc 1, 29; mentioned also in 2 Mc 3, 5; 4, 4.

6, 2: *Olympian Zeus:* equated with the Syrian Baal *shomem* ("the lord of the heavens"), a term which the Jews rendered as "Shiqqus

shomem," horrible abomination (Dn 9, 27; 11, 31; 12, 11; 1 Mc 1, 54).

6, 4: *Amused themselves with prostitutes:* as in the fertility cults of the ancient Near East; see notes on Bar 6, 10.42f.

---

*
5, 11–21: 1 Mc 1, 20–24.   **5, 21:** 1 Mc 1, 23f.
  5, 17: 2 Mc 6, 12–16; 7,   **5, 24ff:** 1 Mc 1, 29f.
    16–19.32–38.   **5, 27:** 1 Mc 2, 28.
  5, 19ff: 2 Mc 3, 1ff; 1 Chr 17,   **6, 1–11:** 1 Mc 1, 44–63.
    9; Mk 2, 27.   **6, 2:** 1 Mc 1, 46; Dn 9, 27.

Abolition of the Law

⁶ A man could not keep the sabbath or celebrate the traditional feasts, nor even admit that he was a Jew. ⁷† Moreover, at the monthly celebration of the king's birthday the Jews had, from bitter necessity, to partake of the sacrifices, and when the festival of Dionysus was celebrated, they were compelled to march in his procession, wearing wreaths of ivy.

⁸ At the suggestion of the citizens of Ptolemais, a decree was issued ordering the neighboring Greek cities to act in the same way against the Jews: oblige them to partake of the sacrifices, ⁹ and put to death those who would not consent to adopt the customs of the Greeks. It was obvious, therefore, that disaster impended. ¹⁰* Thus, two women who were arrested for having circumcised their children were publicly paraded about the city with their babies hanging at their breasts and then thrown down from the top of the city wall. ¹¹* Others, who had assembled in nearby caves to observe the sabbath in secret, were betrayed to Philip and all burned to death. In their respect for the holiness of that day, they had scruples about defending themselves.

Purpose of Divine Judgment

¹²* Now I beg those who read this book not to be disheartened by these misfortunes, but to consider that these chastisements were meant not for the ruin but for the correction of our nation. ¹³ It is, in fact, a sign of great kindness to punish sinners promptly instead of letting them go for long. ¹⁴* Thus, in dealing with other nations, the LORD patiently waits until they reach the full measure of their sins before he punishes them; but with us he has decided to deal differently, ¹⁵ in order that he may not have to punish us more severely later, when our sins have reached their fullness. ¹⁶ He never withdraws his mercy from us. Although he disciplines us with misfortunes, he does not abandon his own people. ¹⁷ Let these words suffice for recalling this truth. Without further ado we must go on with our story.

Martyrdom of Eleazar

¹⁸*† Eleazar, one of the foremost scribes, a man of advanced age and noble appearance, was being forced to open his mouth to eat pork. ¹⁹ But preferring a glorious death to a life of defilement, he spat out the meat, and went forward of his own accord to the instrument of torture, ²⁰ as men ought to do who have the courage to reject the food which it is unlawful to taste even for love of life. ²¹ Those in charge of that unlawful ritual meal took the man aside privately, because of their long acquaintance with him, and urged him to bring meat of his own providing, such as he could legitimately eat, and to

Teaching by Example

LIVE IT!

Second Maccabees tells the story of Eleazar, a dignified, elderly scribe who has followed God his whole life. Rather than compromise his principles, Eleazar courageously accepts death by torture. He knows that his example will influence younger people (6, 28). His example gives others courage (verse 31).

Young people watch and learn. An old television commercial showed a father and son driving along in a car. The son had a toy steering wheel in front of him and imitated his father's driving. When the father turned the wheel, so did the son. When the father switched the turn signal, so did the son.

Then the father pulled a cigarette from a pack. He lit it and began smoking. The next scene showed the son going for the pack of cigarettes.

The next time you find yourself struggling to make the right choice, think about the example you might be giving to someone younger than you.

▶ 2 Mc 6, 18–31

6, 7: *Dionysus:* called also Bacchus the god of the grape harvest and of wine; ivy was one of his symbols.

6, 18—7, 42: The stories of Eleazar and of the mother and her seven sons, among the earliest models of "martyrology," were understandably popular among the Christians of the early centuries. Written originally to encourage God's people in times of persecution, they add gruesome details to the record of tortures, and place long speeches in the mouths of the martyrs.

6, 10: 1 Mc 1, 60f.	16–19.32–38.
6, 11: 1 Mc 2, 32–38.	**6, 14:** Wis 11, 9f; 12, 2.22.
6, 12–16: 2 Mc 5, 17; 7,	**6, 18:** Lv 11, 7f; Heb 11, 35.

pretend to be eating some of the meat of the sacrifice prescribed by the king; [22] in this way he would escape the death penalty, and be treated kindly because of their old friendship with him. [23] But he made up his mind in a noble manner, worthy of his years, the dignity of his advanced age, the merited distinction of his gray hair, and of the admirable life he had lived from childhood; and so he declared that above all he would be loyal to the holy laws given by God.

He told them to send him at once to the abode of the dead, explaining: [24] "At our age it would be unbecoming to make such a pretense; many young men would think the ninety-year-old Eleazar had gone over to an alien religion. [25] Should I thus dissimulate for the sake of a brief moment of life, they would be led astray by me, while I would bring shame and dishonor on my old age. [26] Even if, for the time being, I avoid the punishment of men, I shall never, whether alive or dead, escape the hands of the Almighty. [27] Therefore, by manfully giving up my life now, I will prove myself worthy of my old age, [28] and I will leave to the young a noble example of how to die willingly and generously for the revered and holy laws."

He spoke thus, and went immediately to the instrument of torture. [29] Those who shortly before had been kindly disposed, now became hostile toward him because what he had said seemed to them utter madness. [30] When he was about to die under the blows, he groaned and said: "The LORD in his holy knowledge knows full well that, although I could have escaped death, I am not only enduring terrible pain in my body from this scourging, but also suffering it with joy in my soul because of my devotion to him." [31] This is how he died, leaving in his death a model of courage and an unforgettable example of virtue not only for the young but for the whole nation.

Martyrdom of a Mother and Her Sons

7 [1*] It also happened that seven brothers with their mother were arrested and tortured with

I WILL SACRIFICE MYSELF

If I were a bird
and able to fly afar,
I would like to be a white dove
to guide the people to freedom.
If I were the cloud in the sky,
I would shelter and bring rains
to the rice field.
If I were a grain of sand,

I would throw myself down
to make a path for the people.
I will sacrifice my life
for the suffering people.
I would sacrifice myself
no matter how many times
I would have to die.

(From "For the People,"
by Nid Thialand, in
Your Will Be Done)

This song was written by a twenty-two-year-old Thai student. He was later shot and killed by police officers at a demonstration against the return of a corrupt leader. His love for Thailand echoes the love of the mother and her seven sons for God and their Jewish faith in chapter 7 of 2 Maccabees.

▶ **2 Maccabees, chapter 7**

7, 1: Jer 15, 9.

whips and scourges by the king, to force them to eat pork in violation of God's law. 2 One of the brothers, speaking for the others, said: "What do you expect to achieve by questioning us? We are ready to die rather than transgress the laws of our ancestors." 3 At that the king, in a fury, gave orders to have pans and caldrons heated. 4 While they were being quickly heated, he commanded his executioners to cut out the tongue of the one who had spoken for the others, to scalp him and cut off his hands and feet, while the rest of his brothers and his mother looked on. 5 When he was completely maimed but still breathing, the king ordered them to carry him to the fire and fry him. As a cloud of smoke spread from the pan, the brothers and their mother encouraged one another to die bravely, saying such words as these: 6* "The LORD God is looking on, and he truly has compassion on us, as Moses declared in his canticle, when he protested openly with the words, 'And he will have pity on his servants.' "

7 When the first brother had died in this manner, they brought the second to be made sport of. After tearing off the skin and hair of his head, they asked him, "Will you eat the pork rather than have your body tortured limb by limb?" 8 Answering in the language of his forefathers, he said, "Never!" So he too in turn suffered the same tortures as the first. 9*† At the point of death he said: "You accursed fiend, you are depriving us of this present life, but the King of the world will raise us up to live again forever. It is for his laws that we are dying."

10 After him the third suffered their cruel sport. He put out his tongue at once when told to do so, and bravely held out his hands, 11* as he spoke these noble words: "It was from Heaven that I received these; for the sake of his laws I disdain them; from him I hope to receive them again." 12 Even the king and his attendants marveled at the young man's courage, because he regarded his sufferings as nothing.

13 After he had died, they tortured and maltreated the fourth brother in the same way. 14 When he was near death, he said, "It is my choice to die at the hands of men with the God-given hope of being restored to life by him; but for you, there will be no resurrection to life."

15 They next brought forward the fifth brother and maltreated him. 16* Looking at the king, he said: "Since you have power among men, mortal though you are, do what you please. But do not think that our nation is forsaken by God. 17 Only wait, and you will see how his great power will torment you and your descendants."

18 After him they brought the sixth brother. When he was about to die, he said: "Have no vain illusions. We suffer these things on our own account, because we have sinned against our God; that is why such astonishing things have happened to us. 19* Do not think, then, that you will go unpunished for having dared to fight against God."

20 Most admirable and worthy of everlasting remembrance was the mother, who saw her seven sons perish in a single day, yet bore it courageously because of her hope in the LORD. 21 Filled with a noble spirit that stirred her womanly heart with manly courage, she exhorted each of them in the language of their forefathers with these words: 22 "I do not know how you came into existence in my womb; it was not I who gave you the breath of life, nor was it I who set in order the elements of which each of you is composed. 23 Therefore, since it is the Creator of the universe who shapes each man's beginning, as he brings about the origin of everything, he, in his mercy, will give you back both breath and life, because you now disregard yourselves for the sake of his law."

24 Antiochus, suspecting insult in her words, thought he was being ridiculed. As the youngest brother was still alive, the king appealed to him, not with mere words, but with promises on oath, to make him rich and happy if he would abandon his ancestral customs: he would make him his Friend and entrust him with high office. 25 When the youth paid no attention to him at all, the king appealed to the mother, urging her to advise her boy to save his life. 26 After he had urged her for a long time, she went through the motions of persuading her son. 27 In derision of the cruel tyrant, she leaned over close to her son and said in their native language: "Son, have pity on me, who carried you in my womb for nine months, nursed you for three years, brought you up, educated and supported you to your present age. 28† I beg you, child, to look at the heavens and the earth and see all that is in them; then you will know that God did not make them out of existing things; and in the same way the human race came into existence.

7, 9: *The King of the world will raise us up:* here, and in vv 11.14.23.29.36, belief in the future resurrection of the body, at least for the just, is clearly stated; cf also 2 Mc 12, 44; 14, 46; Dn 12, 2.

7, 28: *God did not make them out of existing things:* that is, God made all things solely by his omnipotent will and his creative word; cf Heb 11, 3.

7, 6: Dt 32, 36.
7, 9: 2 Mc 12, 44; 14, 46.
7, 11: 2 Mc 12, 43ff.

7, 16–19: 2 Mc 5, 17; 6, 12–16.
7, 19: Acts 5, 39.

29 Do not be afraid of this executioner, but be worthy of your brothers and accept death, so that in the time of mercy I may receive you again with them."

30 She had scarcely finished speaking when the youth said: "What are you waiting for? I will not obey the king's command. I obey the command of the law given to our forefathers through Moses. 31 But you, who have contrived every kind of affliction for the Hebrews, will not escape the hands of God. 32* We, indeed, are suffering because of our sins. 33 Though our living LORD treats us harshly for a little while to correct us with chastisements, he will again be reconciled with his servants. 34 But you, wretch, vilest of all men! do not, in your insolence, concern yourself with unfounded hopes, as you raise your hand against the children of Heaven. 35 You have not yet escaped the judgment of the almighty and all-seeing God. 36 My brothers, after enduring brief pain, have drunk of never-failing life, under God's covenant, but you, by the judgment of God, shall receive just punishments for your arrogance. 37 Like my brothers, I offer up my body and my life for our ancestral laws, imploring God to show mercy soon to our nation, and by afflictions and blows to make you confess that he alone is God. 38 Through me and my brothers, may there be an end to the wrath of the Almighty that has justly fallen on our whole nation." 39 At that, the king became enraged and treated him even worse than the others, since he bitterly resented the boy's contempt. 40* Thus he too died undefiled, putting all his trust in the LORD. 41 The mother was last to die, after her sons.

42 Enough has been said about the sacrificial meals and the excessive cruelties.

V: Victories of Judas and Purification of the Temple

Judas Maccabeus

8 1* Judas Maccabeus and his companions entered the villages secretly, summoned their kinsmen, and by also enlisting others who remained faithful to Judaism, assembled about six thousand men. 2 They implored the LORD to look kindly upon his people, who were being oppressed on all sides; to have pity on the temple, which was profaned by godless men; 3 to have mercy on the city, which was being destroyed and about to be leveled to the ground; to hearken to the blood that

did you KNOW?
Nonviolent Resistance

The article "A Just War," 1 Mc 6, 32, discusses just war as a response to the Seleucid persecution of the Jews. Second Maccabees, chapters 6–7, hints at another response—nonviolent resistance. Despite being ordered to forsake their faith and to adopt Greek customs, Jews resisted. We read of women continuing to have their baby boys circumcised (6, 10), of secret gatherings to celebrate the Sabbath (6, 11), and of martyrs refusing to eat unlawful meat (6, 19; 7, 1). Although the stories focus on the violent responses and tortures inflicted by the Greeks, they indicate that at least part of the population neither gave up their religious practices nor took up arms in violent conflict.

Christians have continued to develop the concept of nonviolent resistance—sometimes called pacifism. Nonviolent resistance is rooted in Jesus' teachings to turn the other cheek (Mt 5, 39) and "love your enemies" (5, 44). Nonviolent resistance is not passive. It confronts evil and refuses to cooperate with it without resorting to violence. Those who practice nonviolent resistance accept the suffering that results because they know God can bring good out of the suffering of the just. The Catholic church teaches that nonviolent resistance gives witness to God's redeeming love and that no person who objects to committing violence should be forced into military service.

Christian nonviolence is a challenge for everyone. How do you practice it in your relationships with others? In what situations, if any, do you think it is necessary to respond with violence? In what situations would you refuse to participate in military service?

cried out to him; 4 to remember the criminal slaughter of innocent children and the blasphemies uttered against his name; and to manifest his hatred

---

7, 32.38: 2 Mc 5, 17; 6, 12–16; 17, 16–19.
7, 40f: Heb 11, 35.

8, 1–7: 2 Mc 5, 27; 1 Mc 3, 10–26.

of evil. 5* Once Maccabeus got his men organized, the Gentiles could not withstand him, for the LORD's wrath had now changed to mercy. 6 Coming unexpectedly upon towns and villages, he would set them on fire. He captured strategic positions, and put to flight a large number of the enemy. 7 He preferred the nights as being especially helpful for such attacks. Soon the fame of his valor spread everywhere.

First Victory over Nicanor

8*† When Philip saw that Judas was gaining ground little by little and that his successful advances were becoming more frequent, he wrote to Ptolemy, governor of Coelesyria and Phoenicia, to come to the aid of the king's government. 9* Ptolemy promptly selected Nicanor, son of Patroclus, one of the Chief Friends, and sent him at the head of at least twenty thousand armed men of various nations to wipe out the entire Jewish race. With him he associated Gorgias, a professional military commander, well-versed in the art of war. 10 Nicanor planned to raise the two thousand talents of tribute owed by the king to the Romans by selling captured Jews into slavery. 11 So he immediately sent word to the coastal cities, inviting them to buy Jewish slaves and promising to deliver ninety slaves for a talent— little did he dream of the punishment that was to fall upon him from the Almighty.

12 When Judas learned of Nicanor's advance and informed his companions about the approach of the army, 13 the cowardly and those who lacked faith in God's justice deserted and got away. 14 But the others sold everything they had left, and at the same time besought the LORD to deliver those whom the ungodly Nicanor had sold before even meeting them. 15 They begged the LORD to do this, if not for their sake, at least for the sake of the covenants made with their forefathers, and because they themselves bore his holy, glorious name. 16 Maccabeus assembled his men, six thousand strong, and exhorted them not to be panic stricken before the enemy, nor to fear the large number of the Gentiles attacking them unjustly, but to fight courageously, 17 keeping before their eyes the lawless outrage perpetrated by the Gentiles against the holy Place and the affliction of the humiliated city, as well as the subversion of their ancestral way of life. 18 "They trust in weapons and acts of daring,"

he said, "but we trust in almighty God, who can by a mere nod destroy not only those who attack us, but the whole world." 19* He went on to tell them of the times when help had been given their ancestors: both the time of Sennacherib, when a hundred and eighty-five thousand of his men were destroyed, 20 and the time of the battle in Babylonia against the Galatians, when only eight thousand Jews fought along with four thousand Macedonians; yet when the Macedonians were hard pressed, the eight thousand routed one hundred and twenty thousand and took a great quantity of booty, because of the help they received from Heaven. 21 With such words he encouraged them and made them ready to die for their laws and their country.

Then Judas divided his army into four, 22† placing his brothers, Simon, Joseph, and Jonathan, each over a division, assigning to each fifteen hundred men. 23* (There was also Eleazar.) After reading to them from the holy book and giving them the watchword, "The Help of God," he himself took charge of the first division and joined in battle with Nicanor. 24 With the Almighty as their ally, they killed more than nine thousand of the enemy, wounded and disabled the greater part of Nicanor's army, and put all of them to flight. 25 They also seized the money of those who had come to buy them as slaves. When they had pursued the enemy for some time, 26 they were obliged to return by reason of the late hour. It was the day before the sabbath, and for that reason they could not continue the pursuit. 27 They collected the enemy's arms and stripped them of their spoils, and then observed the sabbath with fervent praise and thanks to the LORD who kept them safe for that day on which he let descend on them the first dew of his mercy. 28 After the sabbath, they gave a share of the booty to the persecuted and to widows and orphans; the rest they divided among themselves and their children. 29 When this was done, they made supplication in common, imploring the merciful LORD to be completely reconciled with his servants.

Timothy and Bacchides Defeated

30 They also challenged the forces of Timothy and Bacchides, killed more than twenty thousand of them, and captured some very high fortresses.

8, 8–29.34ff: This account of the campaign of *Nicanor* and *Gorgias* against Judas is paralleled, with certain differences, in 1 Mc 3, 38—4, 24.

8, 22: *Joseph:* called John in 1 Mc 2, 2; 9, 36.38. This paragraph interrupts the story of Nicanor's defeat, which is resumed in v 34. The purpose of the author apparently is to group together the defeats suffered by the Syrians on various occasions. Battles against Timothy are

recounted in 1 Mc 5, 37–44 and 2 Mc 12, 10–25; against Bacchides in 1 Mc 7, 8–20.

8, 5ff: 1 Mc 3, 3–9.	8, 19: 2 Mc 15, 22; 2 Kgs 19,
8, 8: 2 Mc 4, 45; 1 Mc 3, 38.	35; Is 37, 36.
8, 9: 1 Mc 7, 26.	8, 23: 1 Mc 3, 48.

They divided the enormous plunder, allotting half to themselves and the rest to the persecuted, to orphans, widows, and the aged. 31 They collected the enemies' weapons and carefully stored them in suitable places; the rest of the spoils they carried to Jerusalem. 32 They also killed the commander of Timothy's forces, a most wicked man, who had done great harm to the Jews. 33 While celebrating the victory in their ancestral city, they burned both those who had set fire to the sacred gates and Callisthenes, who had taken refuge in a little house; so he received the reward his wicked deeds deserved.

Humiliation of Nicanor

34* The accursed Nicanor, who had brought the thousand slave dealers to buy the Jews, 35 after being humbled through the LORD's help by those whom he had thought of no account, laid aside his fine clothes and fled alone across country like a runaway slave, until he reached Antioch. He was eminently successful in destroying his own army. 36 So he who had promised to provide tribute for the Romans by the capture of the people of Jerusalem testified that the Jews had a champion, and that they were invulnerable for the very reason that they followed the laws laid down by him.

Punishment and Death of Antiochus

9 1*† About that time Antiochus retreated in disgrace from the region of Persia. 2 He had entered the city called Persepolis and attempted to rob the temple and gain control of the city. Thereupon the people had swift recourse to arms, and Antiochus' men were routed, so that in the end Antiochus was put to flight by the natives and forced to beat a shameful retreat. 3 On his arrival in Ecbatana, he learned what had happened to Nicanor and to Timothy's forces. 4 Overcome with anger, he planned to make the Jews suffer for the injury done by those who had put him to flight. Therefore he ordered his charioteer to drive without stopping until he finished the journey.

Yet the condemnation of Heaven rode with him, since he said in his arrogance, "I will make Jerusalem the common graveyard of the Jews as soon as I arrive there." 5* So the all-seeing LORD, the God of Israel, struck him down with an unseen but incurable blow; for scarcely had he uttered those words when he was seized with excruciating

pains in his bowels and sharp internal torment, 6 a fit punishment for him who had tortured the bowels of others with many barbarous torments. 7 Far from giving up his insolence, he was all the more filled with arrogance. Breathing fire in his rage against the Jews, he gave orders to drive even faster. As a result he hurtled from the dashing chariot, and every part of his body was racked by the violent fall. 8* Thus he who previously, in his superhuman presumption, thought he could command the waves of the sea, and imagined he could weigh the mountaintops in his scales, was now thrown to the ground and had to be carried on a litter, clearly manifesting to all the power of God. 9* The body of this impious man swarmed with worms, and while he was still alive in hideous torments, his flesh rotted off, so that the entire army was sickened by the stench of his corruption. 10 Shortly before, he had thought that he could reach the stars of heaven, and now, no one could endure to transport the man because of this intolerable stench.

11 At last, broken in spirit, he began to give up his excessive arrogance, and to gain some understanding, under the scourge of God, for he was racked with pain unceasingly. 12 When he could no longer bear his own stench, he said, "It is right to be subject to God, and not to think one's mortal self divine." 13 Then this vile man vowed to the LORD, who would no longer have mercy on him, 14 that he would set free the holy city, toward which he had been hurrying with the intention of leveling it to the ground and making it a common graveyard; 15 he would put on perfect equality with the Athenians all the Jews, whom he had judged not even worthy of burial, but fit only to be thrown out with their children to be eaten by vultures and wild animals; 16 he would adorn with the finest offerings the holy temple which he had previously despoiled; he would restore all the sacred vessels many times over; and would provide from his own revenues the expenses required for the sacrifices. 17 Besides all this, he would become a Jew himself and visit every inhabited place to proclaim there the power of God. 18 But since God's punishment had justly come upon him, his sufferings were not lessened, so he lost hope for himself and wrote the following letter to the Jews in the form of a supplication. It read thus:

---

† **9, 1–28:** In order to keep together the various accounts of God's punishment of the persecutors of his people, the author places here the stories of Antiochus' illness and death (in actuality the king died only after the purification of the temple; cf 1 Mc 4, 36–59; 6, 1–16; 2 Mc 10, 1–8); of Judas' campaigns in Idumea and Transjordan (cf 2 Mc 5, 1–51; 2 Mc 10, 14–38); and of the first expedition of Lysias (1 Mc 4, 26–35; 2 Mc 11, 1–15).

* 8, 34f: 2 Mc 8, 23f; 1 Mc 7, 26.
9, 1–29: 2 Mc 1, 12–17; 1 Mc
　6, 1–13.
9, 5: Acts 12, 20–23.

9, 8: Jb 38, 8–11; Ps 65, 6f;
　Is 40, 12.
9, 9: Acts 12, 23.

[19]† "To my esteemed Jewish citizens, Antiochus, their king and general, sends hearty greetings and best wishes for their health and happiness. [20] If you and your children are well and your affairs are going as you wish, I thank God very much, for my hopes are in heaven. [21] Now that I am ill, I recall with affection the esteem and good will you bear me. On returning from the regions of Persia, I fell victim to a troublesome illness; so I thought it necessary to form plans for the general welfare of all. [22] Actually, I do not despair about my health, since I have great hopes of recovering from my illness. [23] Nevertheless, I know that my father, whenever he went on campaigns in the hinterland, would name his successor, [24] so that, if anything unexpected happened or any unwelcome news came, the people throughout the realm would know to whom the government had been entrusted, and so not be disturbed. [25]† I am also bearing in mind that the neighboring rulers, especially those on the borders of our kingdom, are on the watch for opportunities and waiting to see what will happen. I have therefore appointed as king my son Antiochus, whom I have often before entrusted and commended to most of you, when I made hurried visits to the outlying provinces. I have written to him the letter copied below. [26] Therefore I beg and entreat each of you to remember the general and individual benefits you have received, and to continue to show good will toward me and my son. [27] I am confident that, following my policy, he will treat you with mildness and kindness in his relations with you."

[28] So this murderer and blasphemer, after extreme sufferings, such as he had inflicted on others, died a miserable death in the mountains of a foreign land. [29] His foster brother Philip brought the body home; but fearing Antiochus' son, he later withdrew into Egypt, to Ptolemy Philometor.

Purification of Temple and City

10 [1]* When Maccabeus and his companions, under the LORD's leadership, had recovered the temple and the city, [2] they destroyed the altars erected by the Gentiles in the marketplace and the sacred enclosures. [3]† After purifying the temple, they made a new altar. Then, with fire struck from flint, they offered sacrifice for the first time in two

years, burned incense, and lighted lamps. They also set out the showbread. [4] When they had done this, they prostrated themselves and begged the LORD that they might never again fall into such misfortunes, and that if they should sin at any time, he might chastise them with moderation and not hand them over to blasphemous and barbarous Gentiles. [5] On the anniversary of the day on which the temple had been profaned by the Gentiles, that is, the twenty-fifth of the same month Chislev, the purification of the temple took place. [6] The Jews celebrated joyfully for eight days as on the feast of Booths, remembering how, a little while before, they had spent the feast of Booths living like wild animals in caves on the mountains. [7] Carrying rods entwined with leaves, green branches and palms, they sang hymns of grateful praise to him who had brought about the purification of his own Place. [8] By public edict and decree they prescribed that the whole Jewish nation should celebrate these days every year.

10, 6

VI: Renewed Persecution

Death of Ptolemy

[9]* Such was the end of Antiochus surnamed Epiphanes. [10] Now we shall relate what happened under Antiochus Eupator, the son of that godless man, and shall give a summary of the chief evils caused by the wars. [11] When Eupator succeeded to

---

9, 19–27: Despite the statement in v 18, this letter is not really a supplication. It is rather a notification to all the king's subjects of the appointment of his son as his successor and a request that they be loyal to the new king. Apparently the same letter, which has every appearance of being authentic, was sent to the various peoples throughout the kingdom, with only a few words of address changed for each group.

9, 25: *The letter copied below:* not included in the text of 2 Maccabees.
   10, 3: *Two years:* three years according to 1 Mc 1, 54 and 4, 52.

10, 1–8: 1 Mc 4, 36–59.   10, 9: 2 Mc 2, 21; 1 Mc 6, 17.

the kingdom, he put a certain Lysias in charge of the government as commander in chief of Coelesyria and Phoenicia. [12]† Ptolemy, surnamed Macron, had taken the lead in treating the Jews fairly because of the previous injustice that had been done them, and he endeavored to have peaceful relations with them. [13] As a result, he was accused before Eupator by the King's Friends. In fact, on all sides he heard himself called a traitor for having abandoned Cyprus, which Philometor had entrusted to him, and for having gone over to Antiochus Epiphanes. Since he could not command the respect due to his high office, he ended his life by taking poison.

Victory over the Idumeans

[14]† When Gorgias became governor of the region, he employed foreign troops and used every opportunity to attack the Jews. [15]* At the same time the Idumeans, who held some important strongholds, were harassing the Jews; they welcomed fugitives from Jerusalem and endeavored to continue the war. [16] Maccabeus and his companions, after public prayers asking God to be their ally, moved quickly against the strongholds of the Idumeans. [17] Attacking vigorously, they gained control of the places, drove back all who manned the walls, and cut down those who opposed them, killing as many as twenty thousand men. [18] When at least nine thousand took refuge in two very strong towers, containing everything necessary to sustain a siege, [19] Maccabeus left Simon and Joseph, along with Zacchaeus and his men, in sufficient numbers to besiege them, while he himself went off to places where he was more urgently needed. [20] But some of the men in Simon's force who were money lovers let themselves be bribed by some of the men in the towers; on receiving seventy thousand drachmas, they allowed a number of them to escape. [21] When Maccabeus was told what had happened, he assembled the rulers of the people and accused those men of having sold their kinsmen for money by setting their enemies free to fight against them. [22] So he put them to death as traitors, and without delay captured the two towers. [23] As he was successful at arms in all his undertakings, he destroyed more than twenty thousand men in the two strongholds.

Victory over Timothy

[24]† Timothy, who had previously been defeated by the Jews, gathered a tremendous force of foreign troops and collected a large number of cavalry from Asia; then he appeared in Judea, ready to conquer it by force. [25] At his approach, Maccabeus and his men made supplication to God, sprinkling earth upon their heads and girding their loins in sackcloth. [26]* Lying prostrate at the foot of the altar, they begged him to be gracious to them, and to be an enemy to their enemies, and a foe to their foes, as the law declares.

[27] After the prayer, they took up their arms and advanced a considerable distance from the city, halting when they were close to the enemy. [28]† As soon as dawn broke, the armies joined battle, the one having as pledge of success and victory not only their valor but also their reliance on the LORD, and the other taking fury as their leader in the fight.

[29]* In the midst of the fierce battle, there appeared to the enemy from the heavens five majestic men riding on golden-bridled horses, who led the Jews on. [30] They surrounded Maccabeus, and shielding him with their own armor, kept him from being wounded. They shot arrows and hurled thunderbolts at the enemy, who were bewildered and blinded, thrown into confusion and routed. [31] Twenty-five hundred of their foot soldiers and six hundred of their horsemen were slain. [32]* Timothy, however, fled to a well-fortified stronghold called Gazara, where Chaereas was in command. [33] For four days Maccabeus and his men eagerly besieged the fortress. [34] Those inside, relying on the strength of the place, kept repeating outrageous blasphemies and uttering abominable words. [35] When the fifth day dawned, twenty young men in the army of Maccabeus, angered over such blasphemies, bravely stormed the wall and with savage fury cut down everyone they encountered. [36] Others who climbed up the same way swung around on the defenders, taking the besieged in the rear; they put the towers to the torch, spread the fire and burned the blasphemers alive. Still others broke down the gates and let in the rest of the troops, who took possession of the city. [37]† Timothy had hidden in a cistern, but they killed him, along with his brother Chaereas, and Apollophanes. [38] On completing these exploits, they blessed, with hymns of grateful

†
10, 12: *Ptolemy. . . Macron:* son of Dorymenes (2 Mc 4, 45), was formerly hostile to the Jews (2 Mc 6, 8).
10, 14–23: Probably the same campaign of Judas against the Idumeans that is mentioned in 1 Mc 5, 1–3.
10, 24: *Timothy . . . previously . . . defeated by the Jews:* as recounted in 2 Mc 8, 30ff.
10, 28: *As soon as dawn broke:* the same battle at dawn as in 1 Mc 5, 30–34.

10, 37: *Timothy . . . they killed:* apparently, the same Timothy is still alive in 2 Mc 12, 2.18–25. The present passage is not in chronological order, Gazara, v 32 (Gezer) was not captured by the Jews until much later (cf 1 Mc 9, 50ff; 13, 53).

*
10, 15–23: 1 Mc 5, 3ff.
   10, 26: Ex 23, 22.
                        10, 29f: 2 Mc 3, 24ff; 5, 2f; 10, 29f; 11, 8.
                        10, 32: 1 Mc 13, 43–48.

praise, the LORD who shows great kindness to Israel and grants them victory.

Defeat of Lysias

11 [1]†Very soon afterward, Lysias, guardian and kinsman of the king and head of the government, being greatly displeased at what had happened, [2] mustered about eighty thousand infantry and all his cavalry and marched against the Jews. His plan was to make Jerusalem a Greek settlement; [3] to levy tribute on the temple, as he did on the sanctuaries of the other nations; and to put the high priesthood up for sale every year. [4] He did not take God's power into account at all, but felt exultant confidence in his myriads of foot soldiers, his thousands of horsemen, and his eighty elephants. [5] So he invaded Judea, and when he reached Beth-zur, a fortified place about twenty miles from Jerusalem, launched a strong attack against it. [6]* When Maccabeus and his men learned that Lysias was besieging the strongholds, they and all the people begged the LORD with lamentations and tears to send a good angel to save Israel. [7] Maccabeus himself was the first to take up arms, and he exhorted the others to join him in risking their lives to help their kinsmen. Then they resolutely set out together. [8]* Suddenly, while they were still near Jerusalem, a horseman appeared at their head, clothed in white garments and brandishing gold weapons. [9] Then all of them together thanked God for his mercy, and their hearts were filled with such courage that they were ready to assault not only men, but the most savage beasts, yes, even walls of iron. [10] Now that the LORD had shown his mercy toward them, they advanced in battle order with the aid of their heavenly ally. [11] Hurling themselves upon the enemy like lions, they laid low eleven thousand foot soldiers and sixteen hundred horsemen, and put all the rest to flight. [12] Most of those who got away were wounded and stripped of their arms, while Lysias himself escaped only by shameful flight.

Peace with the Syrians

[13]* But Lysias was not a stupid man. He reflected on the defeat he had suffered, and came to realize that the Hebrews were invincible because the mighty God was their ally. He therefore sent a message [14] persuading them to settle everything on just terms, and promising to persuade the king also, and to induce him to become their friend. [15] Maccabeus, solicitous for the common good, agreed to all that Lysias proposed; and the king, on his part, granted in behalf of the Jews all the written requests of Maccabeus to Lysias.

Official Letters

[16] These are the terms of the letter which Lysias wrote to the Jews: "Lysias sends greetings to the Jewish people. [17] John and Absalom, your envoys, have presented your signed communication and asked about the matters contained in it. [18] Whatever had to be referred to the king I called to his attention, and the things that were acceptable he has granted. [19] If you maintain your loyalty to the government, I will endeavor to further your interests in the future. [20] On the details of these matters I have authorized my representatives, as well as your envoys, to confer with you. [21]† Farewell." The year one hundred and forty-eight, the twenty-fourth of Dioscorinthius.

[22] The king's letter read thus: "King Antiochus sends greetings to his brother Lysias. [23] Now that our father has taken his place among the gods, we wish the subjects of our kingdom to be undisturbed in conducting their own affairs. [24] We understand that the Jews do not agree with our father's policy concerning Greek customs but prefer their own way of life. They are petitioning us to let them retain their own customs. [25] Since we desire that this people too should be undisturbed, our decision is that their temple be restored to them and that they live in keeping with the customs of their ancestors. [26] Accordingly, please send them messengers to give them our assurances of friendship, so that, when they learn of our decision, they may have nothing to worry about but may contentedly go about their own business."

[27] The king's letter to the people was as follows: "King Antiochus sends greetings to the Jewish senate and to the rest of the Jews. [28] If you are well, it is what we desire. We too are in good health. [29] Menelaus has told us of your wish to return home and attend to your own affairs. [30] Therefore, those who return by the thirtieth of Xanthicus will have our assurance of full permission [31] to observe their dietary laws and other laws, just as before, and none of the Jews shall be molested in any way for faults committed through ignorance. [32] I have also sent Menelaus to reassure you. [33]† Farewell." In the year

2
M
C

† **11, 1–12:** The defeat of Lysias at Beth-zur probably occurred before the purification of the temple; cf 1 Mc 4, 26–35.
11, 21: *The year one hundred and forty-eight:* 164 B.C. The reading of the name of the month and its position in the calendar are uncertain.
11, 33: The date, which is the same as the date of the Romans' letter (v 38) cannot be correct. The king's letter must be connected with the peace treaty of the year 149 of the Seleucid era, i.e., 163

B.C. Perhaps the mention of the month of Xanthicus in the body of the letter (v 30) caused the date of the Romans' letter to be transferred to this one.

* **11, 1–12:** 1 Mc 4, 26–35.   **11, 8:** 2 Mc 3, 24ff; 5, 2f; 10,
11, 6: Ex 23, 20.   29f.
                           11, 13–33: 1 Mc 6, 57–61.

one hundred and forty-eight, the fifteenth of Xanthicus.

34 The Romans also sent them a letter as follows: "Quintus Memmius and Titus Manius, legates of the Romans, send greetings to the Jewish people. 35 Whatever Lysias, kinsman of the king, has granted you, we also approve. 36 But the matters on which he passed judgment should be submitted to the king. As soon as you have considered them, send someone to us with your decisions so that we may present them to your advantage, for we are on our way to Antioch. 37 Make haste, then, to send us those who can inform us of your intentions. 38† Farewell." In the year one hundred and forty-eight, the fifteenth of Xanthicus.

Persecution Renewed

12 1 After these agreements were made, Lysias returned to the king, and the Jews went about their farming. 2† But some of the local governors, Timothy and Apollonius, son of Gennaeus, as also Hieronymus and Demophon, to say nothing of Nicanor, the commander of the Cyprians, would not allow them to live in peace.

3 Some people of Joppa also committed this outrage: they invited the Jews who lived among them, together with their wives and children, to embark on boats which they had provided. There was no hint of enmity toward them: 4 this was done by public vote of the city. When the Jews, not suspecting treachery and wishing to live on friendly terms, accepted the invitation, the people of Joppa took them out to sea and drowned at least two hundred of them.

Activity of Judas

5 As soon as Judas heard of the barbarous deed perpetrated against his countrymen, he summoned his men; 6 and after calling upon God, the just judge, he marched against the murderers of his kinsmen. In a night attack he set the harbor on fire, burnt the boats, and put to the sword those who had taken refuge there. 7 When the gates of the town were shut, he withdrew, intending to come back later and wipe out the entire population of Joppa.

8 On hearing that the men of Jamnia planned to give like treatment to the Jews who lived among them, 9 he attacked the Jamnian populace by night, setting fire to the harbor and the fleet, so that the glow of the flames was visible as far as Jerusalem, thirty miles away.

10*† When the Jews had gone about a mile from there in the campaign against Timothy, they were attacked by Arabs numbering at least five thousand foot soldiers, and five hundred horsemen. 11 After a hard fight, Judas and his companions, with God's help, were victorious. The defeated nomads begged Judas to make friends with them and promised to supply the Jews with cattle and to help them in every other way. 12 Realizing that they could indeed be useful in many respects, Judas agreed to make peace with them. After the pledge of friendship had been exchanged, the Arabs withdrew to their tents.

13 He also attacked a certain city called Caspin, fortified with earthworks and ramparts and inhabited by a mixed population of Gentiles. 14 Relying on the strength of their walls and their supply of provisions, the besieged treated Judas and his men with contempt, insulting them and even uttering blasphemies and profanity. 15* But Judas and his men invoked the aid of the great Sovereign of the world, who, in the day of Joshua, overthrew Jericho without battering-ram or siege machine; then they furiously stormed the ramparts. 16 Capturing the city by the will of God, they inflicted such indescribable slaughter on it that the adjacent pool, which was about a quarter of a mile wide, seemed to be filled with the blood that flowed into it.

17*† When they had gone on some ninety miles, they reached Charax,* where there were certain Jews known as Toubiani. 18 But they did not find Timothy in that region, for he had already departed from there without having done anything except to leave behind in one place a very strong garrison. 19 But Dositheus and Sosipater, two of Maccabeus' captains, marched out and destroyed the force of more than ten thousand men that Timothy had left in the stronghold. 20 Meanwhile, Maccabeus divided his army into cohorts, with a commander over each cohort, and went in pursuit of Timothy, who had a force of a hundred and twenty thousand foot soldiers and twenty-five hundred horsemen. 21 When Timothy learned of the approach of Judas, he sent on ahead of him the women and children, as well as the baggage, to a place called Karnion, which was hard to besiege and even hard to reach because of the difficult terrain of that region. 22 But

---

11, 38: The date is April 12, 164 B.C.

12, 2: *Apollonius, son of Gennaeus:* not the Apollonius who was the son of Menestheus (2 Mc 4, 21). *Nicanor:* probably distinct from the Nicanor of 2 Mc 14, 2.

12, 10: *From there:* not from the aforesaid Jamnia (vv 8f) or Joppa (vv 3–7), but from a place in Transjordan; vv 10–26 parallel the account given in 1 Mc 5, 9–13.24–54 of Judas' campaign in northern Transjordan.

12, 17: *Certain Jews known as Toubiani:* because they lived "in the land of Tob" (1 Mc 5, 13).

12, 10–16: 1 Mc 5, 24–36.   12, 17–26: 1 Mc 5, 37–44.
  12, 15: Jos 6, 1–21.   12, 17: 1 Mc 5, 13.

when Judas' first cohort appeared, the enemy was overwhelmed with fear and terror at the manifestation of the All-seeing. Scattering in every direction, they rushed away in such headlong flight that in many cases they wounded one another, pierced by the swords of their own men. 23 Judas pressed the pursuit vigorously, putting the sinners to the sword and destroying as many as thirty thousand men.

24 Timothy himself fell into the hands of the men under Dositheus and Sosipater; but with great cunning, he asked them to spare his life and let him go, because he had in his power the parents and relatives of many of them, and could make these suffer. 25 When he had fully confirmed his solemn pledge to restore them unharmed, they let him go for the sake of saving their brethren.

Further Successes

26† Judas then marched to Karnion and the shrine of Atargatis, where he killed twenty-five thousand people. 27* After the defeat and destruction of these, he moved his army to Ephron, a fortified city inhabited by people of many nationalities. Robust young men took up their posts in defense of the walls, from which they fought valiantly; inside were large supplies of machines and missiles. 28 But the Jews, invoking the Sovereign who forcibly shatters the might of his enemies, got possession of the city and slaughtered twenty-five thousand of the people in it. 29† Then they set out from there and hastened on to Scythopolis, seventy-five miles from Jerusalem. 30 But when the Jews who lived there testified to the good will shown by the Scythopolitans and to their kind treatment even in times of adversity, 31 Judas and his men thanked them and exhorted them to be well disposed to their race in the future also. Finally they arrived in Jerusalem, shortly before the feast of Weeks.

32 After this feast called Pentecost, they lost no time in marching against Gorgias, governor of Idumea, 33 who opposed them with three thousand foot soldiers and four hundred horsemen. 34 In the ensuing battle, a few of the Jews were slain. 35† A man called Dositheus, a powerful horseman and one of Bacenor's men, caught hold of Gorgias, grasped his military cloak and dragged him along by main strength, intending to capture the vile wretch alive, when a Thracian horseman attacked Dositheus and cut off his arm at the shoulder. Then

Catholic Connections

PRAYERS FOR THE DEAD

The story of Judas Maccabeus and his men praying for their fallen comrades provides an early witness to the practice of praying for the dead. Some Christian churches maintain that prayers for the dead have absolutely no effect. The Roman Catholic church, on the contrary, has always taught that prayers for the dead do have an effect and should be an important part of Christian practice.

This belief is related to the Catholic doctrine of Purgatory. The church teaches that when a person dies, there is a moment of judgment—particular judgment. While some people immediately enter heaven and others may be condemned to hell, some souls need a further cleansing of the effects of sin. They need to grow in holiness. This process is called Purgatory.

The members of the church, those already in heaven and those still on earth, pray and intercede for those who are in this transitional state. The prayers of the faithful call on God's mercy and grace to bring home to glory those who long for total union with God.

Did you know that the church prays for the dead at every celebration of the Eucharist? Usually toward the end of the Eucharistic prayer, the priest offers a remembrance for the dead. One of the prayers reads, "Remember those who have died in the peace of Christ and all the dead whose faith is known to you alone" (*Sacramentary*, p. 560). Praying for the dead is also one of the spiritual works of mercy. Try to include prayers for the dead as part of your daily spiritual practice.

▶ 2 Mc 12, 38–46

---

† **12, 26:** *Atargatis:* a Syrian goddess, represented by the body of a fish.
12, 29: *Scythopolis:* the Greek name of the city of Beth-shan; cf 1 Mc 5, 52.
12, 35: *One of Bacenor's men:* certain ancient witnesses to the text have "one of the Toubiani"; cf v 17.

12, 27–31: 2 Mc 5, 45–54.

Gorgias fled to Marisa. ³⁶ After Esdris and his men had been fighting for a long time and were weary, Judas called upon the LORD to show himself their ally and leader in the battle. ³⁷ Then, raising a battle cry in his ancestral language, and with songs, he charged Gorgias' men when they were not expecting it and put them to flight.

Expiation for the Dead

³⁸ Judas rallied his army and went to the city of Adullam. As the week was ending, they purified themselves according to custom and kept the sabbath there. ³⁹ On the following day, since the task had now become urgent, Judas and his men went to gather up the bodies of the slain and bury them with their kinsmen in their ancestral tombs. ⁴⁰* But under the tunic of each of the dead they found amulets sacred to the idols of Jamnia, which the law forbids the Jews to wear. So it was clear to all that this was why these men had been slain. ⁴¹ They all therefore praised the ways of the LORD, the just judge who brings to light the things that are hidden. ⁴²† Turning to supplication, they prayed that the sinful deed might be fully blotted out. The noble Judas warned the soldiers to keep themselves free from sin, for they had seen with their own eyes what had happened because of the sin of those who had fallen. ⁴³ He then took up a collection among all his soldiers, amounting to two thousand silver drachmas, which he sent to Jerusalem to provide for an expiatory sacrifice. In doing this he acted in a very excellent and noble way, inasmuch as he had the resurrection of the dead in view; ⁴⁴ for if he were not expecting the fallen to rise again, it would have been useless and foolish to pray for them in death. ⁴⁵ But if he did this with a view to the splendid reward that awaits those who had gone to rest in godliness, it was a holy and pious thought. ⁴⁶ Thus he made atonement for the dead that they might be freed from this sin.

The Syrians Invade Judea

13 ¹† In the year one hundred and forty-nine, Judas and his men learned that Antiochus Eupator was invading Judea with a large force, ²*† and that with him was Lysias, his guardian, who was in charge of the government.

They led a Greek army of one hundred and ten thousand foot soldiers, fifty-three hundred horsemen, twenty-two elephants, and three hundred chariots armed with scythes.

Death of Menelaus

³ Menelaus also joined them, and with great duplicity kept urging Antiochus on, not for the welfare of his country, but in the hope of being established in office. ⁴*† But the King of kings aroused the anger of Antiochus against the scoundrel. When the king was shown by Lysias that Menelaus was to blame for all the trouble, he ordered him to be taken to Beroea and executed there in the customary local method. ⁵† There is at that place a tower seventy-five feet high, full of ashes, with a circular rim sloping down steeply on all sides toward the ashes. ⁶ A man guilty of sacrilege or notorious for certain other crimes is brought up there and then hurled down to destruction. ⁷ In such a manner was Menelaus, the transgressor of the law, fated to die; he was deprived even of decent burial. ⁸ It was altogether just that he who had committed so many sins against the altar with its pure fire and ashes should meet his death in ashes.

Skirmish near Modein

⁹ The king was advancing, his mind full of savage plans for inflicting on the Jews worse things than those they suffered in his father's time. ¹⁰ When Judas learned of this, he urged the people to call upon the LORD night and day, to help them now, if ever, ¹¹ when they were about to be deprived of their law, their country, and their holy temple; and not to allow this nation, which had just begun to revive, to be subjected again to blasphemous Gentiles. ¹² When they had all joined in doing this, and had implored the merciful LORD continuously with weeping and fasting and prostrations for three days, Judas encouraged them and told them to stand ready. ¹³ After a private meeting with the elders, he decided that, before the king's army could invade Judea and take possession of the city, the Jews should march out and settle the matter with God's help. ¹⁴ Leaving the outcome to the Creator of the world, and exhorting his followers to fight nobly to death for the laws, the temple, the city, the country, and the government, he pitched his camp near

---

† **12, 42–46:** This is the earliest statement of the doctrine that prayers (v 42) and sacrifices (v 43) for the dead are beneficial. The statement is made here, however, only for the purpose of proving that Judas believed in the resurrection of the just (2 Mc 7, 9.14.23.36). That is, he believed that expiation could be made for certain sins of otherwise good men—soldiers who had given their lives for God's cause. Thus, they could share in the resurrection. His belief was similar to, but not quite the same as, the Catholic doctrine of purgatory.

13, 1: *In the year one hundred and forty-nine:* 163–162 B.C.

13, 2: *They led:* the Greek means literally "Each (of them) led," but it is unlikely that the author meant the already immense numbers to be doubled; the numbers are similar to those in 1 Mc 6, 30.

13, 4: *Beroea:* the Greek name of Aleppo.

13, 5: *Ashes:* probably smoldering ashes; the tower resembles the ancient Persian fire towers.

---

* 12, 40: Dt 7, 25.
13, 2: 1 Mc 6, 30.

13, 4: 1 Tm 6, 15; Rv 17, 14;
19, 16.

Modein. [15]*† Giving his men the battle cry "God's Victory," he made a night attack on the king's pavilion with a picked force of the bravest young men and killed about two thousand in the camp. They also slew the lead elephant and its rider. [16]† Finally they withdrew in triumph, having filled the camp with terror and confusion. [17] Day was just breaking when this was accomplished with the help and protection of the LORD.

Treaty with Antiochus V

[18]* The king, having had a taste of the Jews' daring, tried to take their positions by a stratagem. [19] So he marched against Beth-zur, a strong fortress of the Jews; but he was driven back, checked, and defeated. [20] Judas then sent supplies to the men inside, [21]† but Rhodocus, of the Jewish army, betrayed military secrets to the enemy. He was found out, arrested, and imprisoned. [22] The king made a second attempt by negotiating with the men of Beth-zur. After giving them his pledge and receiving theirs, he withdrew [23] and attacked Judas and his men. But he was defeated. Next he heard that Philip, who was left in charge of the government in Antioch, had rebelled. Dismayed, he parleyed with the Jews, submitted to their terms, and swore to observe their rights. Having come to this agreement, he offered a sacrifice, and honored the temple with a generous donation. [24]† He approved of Maccabeus and left him as military and civil governor of the territory from Ptolemais to the region of the Gerrenes. [25] When he came to Ptolemais, the people of that city were angered by the peace treaty; in fact they were so indignant that they wanted to annul its provisions. [26] But Lysias took the platform, defended the treaty as well as he could, and won them over by persuasion. After calming them and gaining their good will, he returned to Antioch.

That is how the king's attack and withdrawal went.

Antagonism of Alcimus

14 [1]*† Three years later, Judas and his men learned that Demetrius, son of Seleucus, had sailed into the port of Tripolis with a powerful army and a fleet, [2] and that he had occupied the country, after doing away with Antiochus and his guardian Lysias.

[3] A certain Alcimus, a former high priest, who had willfully incurred defilement at the time of the revolt, realized that there was no way for him to salvage his position and regain access to the holy altar. [4]* So he went to King Demetrius in the year one hundred and fifty-one and presented him with a gold crown and a palm branch, as well as some of the customary olive branches from the temple. On that occasion he kept quiet. [5] But he found an opportunity to further his mad scheme when he was invited to the council by Demetrius and questioned about the dispositions and intentions of the Jews. He replied: [6] "Those Jews called Hasideans, led by Judas Maccabeus, are warmongers, who stir up sedition and keep the kingdom from enjoying peace and quiet. [7] For this reason, now that I am deprived of my ancestral dignity, that is to say, the high priesthood, I have come here— [8] first, out of my genuine concern for the king's interests, and secondly, out of consideration for my own countrymen, since our entire nation is suffering great affliction from the unreasonable conduct of the people just mentioned. [9] When you have informed yourself in detail on these matters, O king, act in the interest of our country and its hard-pressed people with the same gracious consideration that you show toward all. [10] As long as Judas is around, it is impossible for the state to enjoy peace." [11] When he had said this, the other Friends who were hostile to Judas quickly added fuel to Demetrius' indignation.

Dealings with Nicanor

[12]* The king immediately chose Nicanor, who had been in command of the elephants, and appointed him governor of Judea. He sent him off [13] with orders to put Judas to death, to disperse his followers, and to set up Alcimus as high priest of the great temple. [14]† The Gentiles from Judea, who would have banished Judas, came flocking to Nicanor, thinking that the misfortunes and calamities of the Jews would mean prosperity for themselves. [15]* When the Jews heard of Nicanor's coming, and that the Gentiles were rallying to him, they sprinkled themselves with earth and prayed to him who established his people forever, and who always comes to the aid of his heritage. [16] At their leader's command, they set

---

†
13, 15: *Slew:* literally "stabbed"; the deed was done by Eleazar (1 Mc 6, 43–46).

13, 16: *They withdrew in triumph:* according to 1 Mc 6, 47 they fled.

13, 21: *Military secrets:* probably about the lack of provisions in the besieged city; cf 1 Mc 6, 49.

13, 24: The Greek text is uncertain and may be rendered: "He approved of Maccabeus, then left Hegemonides as governor of the territory . . ." *Gerrenes:* probably the inhabitants of Gerar, southeast of Gaza.

14, 1: *Three years later:* actually, Demetrius (I Soter), son of Seleucus (IV), landed at Tripolis in the year 151 of the Seleucid era (v 4), i.e., 162–161 B.C.; cf 1 Mc 7, 1–7.

14, 14: *Who would have banished Judas:* the meaning of the Greek is uncertain; some render it: "who had fled before Judas."

*
13, 15: 1 Mc 6, 43–46.	**14, 4:** 1 Mc 7, 25.
13, 18–23: 1 Mc 6, 48–53.	**14, 12f:** 2 Mc 8, 9; 1 Mc 3, 38f.
14, 1–11: 1 Mc 7, 1–7.	**14, 15–19:** 1 Mc 7, 26–32.

out at once and came upon the enemy at the village of Adasa. ¹⁷ Judas' brother Simon had engaged Nicanor, but because of the sudden appearance of the enemy suffered a slight repulse. ¹⁸ However, when Nicanor heard of the valor of Judas and his men, and the great courage with which they fought for their country, he shrank from deciding the issue by bloodshed. ¹⁹ So he sent Posidonius, Theodotus and Mattathias to arrange an agreement. ²⁰ After a long discussion of the terms, each leader communicated them to his troops; and when general agreement was expressed, they assented to the treaty. ²¹ A day was set on which the leaders would meet by themselves. From each side a chariot came forward and thrones were set in place. ²² Judas had posted armed men in readiness at suitable points for fear that the enemy might suddenly carry out some treacherous plan. But the conference was held in the proper way. ²³ Nicanor stayed on in Jerusalem, where he did nothing out of place. He got rid of the throngs of ordinary people who gathered around him; ²⁴ but he always kept Judas in his company, for he had a cordial affection for the man. ²⁵ He urged him to marry and have children; so Judas married, settled down, and shared the common life.

Threats against Judas

²⁶ When Alcimus saw their friendship for each other, he took the treaty that had been made, went to Demetrius, and said that Nicanor was plotting against the state, and that he had appointed Judas, the conspirator against the kingdom, to be his successor. ²⁷ Stirred up by the villain's calumnies, the king became enraged. He wrote to Nicanor, stating that he was displeased with the treaty, and ordering him to send Maccabeus as a prisoner to Antioch without delay. ²⁸ When this message reached Nicanor he was dismayed, for he hated to break his agreement with a man who had done no wrong. ²⁹ However, there was no way of opposing the king, so he watched for an opportunity to carry out this order by a stratagem. ³⁰ But Maccabeus noticed that Nicanor was becoming cool in his dealings with him, and acting with unaccustomed rudeness when they met; he concluded that this coldness betokened no good. So he gathered together a large number of his men, and went into hiding from Nicanor.

³¹* When Nicanor realized that he had been disgracefully outwitted by the man, he went to the great and holy temple, at a time when the priests were offering the customary sacrifices, and ordered them to surrender Judas. ³² As they declared under oath that they did not know where the wanted man was, ³³ he raised his right hand toward the temple and swore this oath: "If you do not hand Judas over to me as prisoner, I will level this shrine of God to the ground; I will tear down the altar, and erect here a splendid temple to Dionysus." ³⁴ With these words he went away. The priests stretched out their hands toward heaven, calling upon the unfailing defender of our nation in these words: ³⁵* "LORD of all, though you are in need of nothing, you have approved of a temple for your dwelling place among us. ³⁶ Therefore, O holy One, LORD of all holiness, preserve forever undefiled this house, which has been so recently purified."

The Story of Razis

³⁷† A certain Razis, one of the elders of Jerusalem, was denounced to Nicanor as a patriot. A man highly regarded, he was called a father of the Jews because of his love for them. ³⁸ In the early days of the revolt, he had been convicted of Judaism, and had risked body and life in his ardent zeal for it. ³⁹ Nicanor, to show his detestation of the Jews, sent more than five hundred soldiers to arrest him. ⁴⁰ He thought that by arresting such a man he would deal the Jews a hard blow. ⁴¹ But when these troops, on the point of capturing the tower, were forcing the outer gate and calling for fire to set the door ablaze, Razis, now caught on all sides, turned his sword against himself, ⁴² preferring to die nobly rather than fall into the hands of vile men and suffer outrages unworthy of his noble birth. ⁴³ In the excitement of the struggle he failed to strike exactly. So while the troops rushed in through the doors, he gallantly ran up to the top of the wall and with manly courage threw himself down into the crowd. ⁴⁴ But as they quickly drew back and left an opening, he fell into the middle of the empty space. ⁴⁵ Still breathing, and inflamed with anger, he got up and ran through the crowd, with blood gushing from his frightful wounds. ⁴⁶* Then, standing on a steep rock, as he lost the last of his blood, he tore out his entrails and flung them with both hands into the crowd, calling upon the LORD of life and of spirit to give these back to him again. Such was the manner of his death.

Nicanor's Blasphemy

15 ¹ When Nicanor learned that Judas and his companions were in the territory of Samaria, he decided to attack them in all safety on the day of rest. ² The Jews who were forced to follow

---

† **14, 37–46:** The story of Razis belongs to the "martyrology" class of literature; it is similar to the stories in 2 Mc 6, 18—7, 42.

* **14, 31–36:** 1 Mc 7, 33–38. **14, 35:** Acts 17, 25. **14, 46:** 2 Mc 7, 9ff.

him pleaded, "Do not massacre them in that way, like a savage barbarian, but show respect for the day which the All-seeing has exalted with holiness above all other days." ³* At this the thrice-sinful wretch asked if there was a ruler in heaven who prescribed the keeping of the sabbath day. ⁴ When they replied that there was indeed such a ruler in heaven, the living LORD himself, who commanded the observance of the sabbath day, ⁵ he said, "I, on my part, am ruler on earth, and my orders are that you take up arms and carry out the king's business." Nevertheless he did not succeed in carrying out his cruel plan.

Fresh Hope

⁶† In his utter boastfulness and arrogance Nicanor had determined to erect a public monument of victory over Judas and his men. ⁷ But Maccabeus remained confident, fully convinced that he would receive help from the LORD. ⁸ He urged his men not to fear the enemy, but mindful of the help they had received from Heaven in the past, to expect that now, too, victory would be given them by the Almighty. ⁹† By encouraging them with words from the law and the prophets, and by reminding them of the battles they had already won, he filled them with fresh enthusiasm. ¹⁰ Having stirred up their courage, he gave his orders and pointed out at the same time the perfidy of the Gentiles and their violation of oaths. ¹¹ When he had armed each of them, not so much with the safety of shield and spear as with the encouragement of noble words, he cheered them all by relating a dream, a kind of vision, worthy of belief.

Introducing

▶ JEWISH SECTS

In the last two centuries before Christ, a diversity of ways of being Jewish emerged. Different groups arose emphasizing different ways of remaining faithful to their Jewish heritage. These groups, or factions, within a religion are sometimes called sects. Primarily three sects emerged within Judaism.

Pharisees. The Pharisees were descendants of the Hasidim, Jews devoted to a strict observance of the Law who opposed King Antiochus IV Epiphanes' attempts to destroy the Jewish religion. Pharisee means "separated" and probably reflects the Pharisees' rigorous observance of the Law. They were often greatly respected. In the New Testament, Jesus argues with some Pharisees but is also a guest of others. Saint Paul was a Pharisee. Not surprisingly, some of the Pharisees' teachings were similar to those of the early Christians.

Sadducees. The Sadducees were a conservative Jewish sect that emerged in the first century B.C. and lasted only to around A.D 70. The Sadducees were wealthy and politically influential landowners, and some of them had important roles in the Temple. They emphasized the necessity of worshiping at the Temple in Jerusalem. Unlike the Pharisees, they did not believe in the resurrection of the body.

Essenes. The Essenes, like the Pharisees, seem to have descended from the Hasidim. They existed in the first century B.C. and disappeared after A.D. 70. The name Essene can mean "healer" or "pious." The Essenes did not believe in the necessity of Temple sacrifice and often lived together in isolated communities where they practiced a simple lifestyle. Some of them were connected with the desert monastery at Qumran and were responsible for writing the Dead Sea Scrolls. John the Baptist's preaching and some of Jesus' teaching in the Gospels closely reflected the writings and teachings of the Essenes.

---

† **15, 6:** *Public monument of victory:* a heap of stones covered with the arms and armor of the fallen enemy.
15, 9: *The law and the prophets:* the first of the three parts of the Hebrew Scriptures, called the sacred books (1 Mc 12, 9).

* **15, 3:** 1 Mc 7, 34.

12*† What he saw was this: Onias, the former high priest, a good and virtuous man, modest in appearance, gentle in manners, distinguished in speech, and trained from childhood in every virtuous practice, was praying with outstretched arms for the whole Jewish community. 13 Then in the same way another man appeared, distinguished by his white hair and dignity, and with an air about him of extraordinary, majestic authority. 14† Onias then said of him, "This is God's prophet Jeremiah, who loves his brethren and fervently prays for his people and their holy city." 15 Stretching out his right hand, Jeremiah presented a gold sword to Judas. As he gave it to him he said, 16 "Accept this holy sword as a gift from God; with it you shall crush your adversaries."

Defeat and Death of Nicanor

17 Encouraged by Judas' noble words, which had power to instill valor and stir young hearts to courage, the Jews determined not to delay, but to charge gallantly and decide the issue by hand-to-hand combat with the utmost courage, since their city and its temple with the sacred vessels were in danger. 18* They were not so much concerned about their wives and children or their brothers and kinsmen; their first and foremost fear was for the consecrated sanctuary. 19 Those who remained in the city suffered a like agony, anxious as they were about the battle in the open country.

20 Everyone now awaited the decisive moment. The enemy were already drawing near with their troops drawn up in battle line, their elephants placed in strategic positions, and their cavalry stationed on the flanks. 21 Maccabeus, contemplating the hosts before him, their elaborate equipment, and the fierceness of their elephants, stretched out his hands toward heaven and called upon the LORD who works miracles; for he knew that it is not through arms but through the LORD's decision that victory is won by those who deserve it. 22* He prayed to him thus: "You, O LORD, sent your angel in the days of King Hezekiah of Judea, and he slew a hundred and eighty-five thousand men of Sennacherib's army. 23 Sovereign of the heavens, send a good angel now to spread fear and dread before us. 24 By the might of your arm may those be struck down who have blasphemously come against your holy people!" With this he ended his prayer.

25* Nicanor and his men advanced to the sound of trumpets and battle songs. 26 But Judas and his men met the army with supplication and prayers. 27 Fighting with their hands and praying to God with their hearts, they laid low at least thirty-five thousand, and rejoiced greatly over this manifestation of God's power. 28 When the battle was over and they were joyfully departing, they discovered Nicanor lying there in all his armor; 29 so they raised tumultuous shouts in their native tongue in praise of the divine Sovereign.

30 Then Judas, who was ever in body and soul the chief defender of his fellow citizens, and had maintained from youth his affection for his countrymen, ordered Nicanor's head and whole right arm to be cut off and taken to Jerusalem. 31† When he arrived there, he assembled his countrymen, stationed the priests before the altar, and sent for those in the citadel. 32 He showed them the vile Nicanor's head and the wretched blasphemer's arm that had been boastfully stretched out against the holy dwelling of the Almighty. 33 He cut out the tongue of the godless Nicanor, saying he would feed it piecemeal to the birds and would hang up the other wages of his folly opposite the temple. 34 At this, everyone looked toward heaven and praised the LORD who manifests his divine power, saying, "Blessed be he who has kept his own Place undefiled!"

35* Judas hung up Nicanor's head on the wall of the citadel, a clear and evident proof to all of the Lord's help. 36*† By public vote it was unanimously decreed never to let this day pass unobserved, but to celebrate it on the thirteenth day of the twelfth month, called Adar in Aramaic, the eve of Mordecai's Day.

VII: Epilogue

Author's Apology

37 Since Nicanor's doings ended in this way, with the city remaining in possession of the Hebrews from that time on, I will bring my own story to an end here too. 38 If it is well written and to the point, that is what I wanted; if it is poorly done and mediocre, that is the best I could do. 39 Just as it is harmful to drink wine alone or water alone, whereas mixing wine with water makes a more pleasant drink that increases delight, so a skillfully composed story delights the ears of those who read the work. Let this, then, be the end.

15, 12: *Onias, the former high priest:* Onias III (2 Mc 3, 1–40). Evidently the author believed that the departed just were in some way alive even before the resurrection.
15, 14: *Jeremiah:* regarded by the postexilic Jews as one of the greatest figures in their history; cf 2 Mc 2, 1; Mt 16, 14. *Who . . . prays for his people:* a clear belief in the intercession of the saints.
15, 31: *Those in the citadel:* presumably Jewish soldiers; actually, the citadel was still in the possession of the Syrians.

15, 36: *Mordecai's Day:* the feast of Purim, celebrated on the fourteenth and fifteenth days of Adar (Est 9, 17–22).

15, 12: 2 Mc 3, 1ff.
15, 18: 1 Mc 4, 36.
15, 22f: 2 Mc 8, 19; 2 Kgs 19, 35; Is 37, 36; 1 Mc 7, 40f.
15, 25–36: 2 Mc 8, 39–50.
15, 35: 1 Sm 31, 9f.
15, 36: 1 Mc 7, 49.

Introduction to the

Wisdom

and Poetry Books

The LORD is my shepherd; there is nothing I lack.

(Ps 23, 1)

A mild answer calms wrath,
   but a harsh word stirs up anger.

(Prov 15, 1)

There is an appointed time for everything,
   and a time for every affair under the heavens.

(Eccl 3, 1)

The books these words are taken from, the wisdom and poetry books of the Old Testament, are among the most quoted books of the Bible. The distilled wisdom they contain and the beauty of the language they use have universal appeal. Across cultures and across time, these books touch thoughtful minds and inquiring hearts.

In-depth

THIS SECTION OF THE BIBLE CONTAINS A VARIETY of books. The Book of Psalms consists of religious hymns, many written for use in Jewish worship. The Song of Songs is a love poem. The Book of Job is a debate on why innocent people suffer. The Book of Wisdom, Proverbs, and Sirach give advice on moral and virtuous living. And Ecclesiastes is a sort of journal on the purpose of human life. The most obvious common element among these books is the use of poetic language to convey their message. Not that these are the only books of the Old Testament that use poetry. But they make such extensive application of it that a little background on the nature of Hebrew poetry is helpful for reading them.

The most important feature of Hebrew poetry is parallelism. Parallelism involves the repetition of words or ideas in successive lines of a verse. Sometimes, the second line contrasts with the first:

The LORD watches over the way of the just,
   but the way of the wicked leads to ruin.

(Ps 1, 6)

Other times, the second line completes the thought of the first:

> The LORD looks down from heaven upon the
> human race,
> To see if even one is wise, if even one seeks
> God.
>
> (14, 2)

Still other times, the second line seems to restate the first line more forcefully:

> For I know my offense;
> my sin is always before me.
>
> (51, 5)

In its many forms, parallelism—not a rhythmic pattern or rhyming words—is the organizing principle of Hebrew poetry.

Hebrew poetry also uses symbolic language that is characteristic of poetry in any language. This includes metaphors ("LORD, my rock, my fortress, my deliverer" [18, 3]) and similes ("As a deer longs for streams of water, / so my soul longs for you, O God" [Pss 42–43, 2]). To appreciate the beauty of Old Testament poetry and feel its impact, one must be willing to wrestle with symbolic ways of interpreting words and phrases.

Whereas the other books of the Old Testament emphasize ancient Israel's distinctive religious values, the wisdom and poetry books focus on its unique view of wisdom. Wisdom literature is something the ancient Israelites shared with neighboring cultures. The Egyptians, Sumerians, and Babylonians all had literature that offered practical, time-tested advice for people seeking trustworthy guidance. For the Israelites, however, true wisdom was more than mere common sense: it was a gift from God given to those who sought it. Some passages of the wisdom literature even describe wisdom as a divine person, a beautiful, eternal, holy, and feminine depiction of God (see Wis 7, 22—8, 8 and Sirach, chapter 1).

In general, the wisdom writings have these characteristics:

- few references to the Law or the Covenant
- a minimal interest in Israel's history
- a search for harmony and the meaning of life
- a willingness to explore the difficult mysteries of life, such as suffering and death
- a commitment to discovering the moral lessons of everyday experiences
- a fundamental belief that good and wise living is rewarded whereas evil and foolish ways lead to ruin

The poetry and wisdom books of the Old Testament had an enormous influence on the writers of the New Testament and continue to be popular. Their poetic structure, which often makes them difficult to comprehend, also gives them a richness and depth that centuries of reading and rereading have not exhausted. Each time you read from these books, you will discover new treasures to enrich your life.

Other Background

- **The Book of Psalms is quoted more often in the New Testament than is any other Old Testament book. Also, it is used extensively in the church's liturgy.**

- **Job and Ecclesiastes posed serious challenges to the traditional understanding of Israelite faith. For help in understanding why, see the introductions to these books.**

- **Solomon's reputation for wisdom was so great that he was indicated as the author of four books actually written by others: Proverbs, Ecclesiastes, Song of Songs, and Wisdom.**

- **The Book of Wisdom and Sirach are not found in all translations of the Old Testament (see "The Case of the Missing Books," near Tb 1, 16).**

You've seen the picture—a mother holding her poor, dead child, against the background of a country ravaged by drought. Or perhaps you have watched someone you love suffer from a devastating illness. And you found yourself wondering, Why, God? This is the basic question struggled with in the Book of Job. How can God allow innocent people to suffer?

In-depth

At the time Job was written, most Israelites believed that if they obeyed God's commandments, God would bless them and protect them. The Israelites also believed that if people were suffering or poor, God was punishing them for some sin they or their parents had committed, even if they did not know what that sin was. The Israelites' thinking was extremely logical—because God is all-powerful and completely just, God will not allow people or communities to suffer unless they have sinned in some way.

The Book of Job challenges that way of thinking. Job is a good man who has received great wealth and a wonderful family from God. In fact, Job's final defense in chapter 31 is one of the finest summaries of the Old Testament vision of a righteous person. The Book of Job begins with God allowing Job's wealth and children and health to be taken from him. Three friends come to mourn with Job. In a series of lengthy debates, they point out that his misfortunes must be the result of some sin or wrong he has committed. Job maintains his innocence, sometimes forcefully, and demands another explanation from God. Finally, God appears to Job and overwhelms him with questions about the nature of the universe. Job realizes that God is beyond human knowledge and that some mysteries—including suffering—can never be completely understood; they can only be accepted.

The Book of Job does not give the final answer about why bad things happen to good people. But it does make it clear that good people do suffer and their suffering is not a punishment sent by God. And Job is a reminder to the Israelites and to us that God's purposes are too far beyond human understanding for anyone to claim to know everything there is to know about God.

Quick Facts

Author
unknown, writing between the 7th and 5th centuries B.C.

Theme
Why do good people suffer?

Of Note
Job is a story within a story: chapters 1–2 and 42, 7–17 constitute a folktale; set within that tale, in 3, 1—42, 6, is a poetic debate about the cause of suffering.

The Book of Job

Job

1, 20

I: Prologue

Job's Wealth and Piety

1 ¹*† In the land of Uz there was a blameless and upright man named Job, who feared God and avoided evil. ²† Seven sons and three daughters were born to him; ³† and he had seven thousand sheep, three thousand camels, five hundred yoke of oxen, five hundred she-asses, and a great number of work animals, so that he was greater than any of the men of the East. ⁴ His sons used to take turns giving feasts, sending invitations to their three sisters to eat and drink with them. ⁵ And when each feast had run its course, Job would send for them and sanctify them, rising early and offering holocausts for every one of them. For Job said, "It may be that my sons have sinned and blasphemed God in their hearts." This Job did habitually.

⁶*† One day, when the sons of God came to present themselves before the LORD, Satan also came among them.* ⁷* And the LORD said to Satan, "Whence do you come?" Then Satan answered the LORD and said, "From roaming the earth and patrolling it." ⁸ And the LORD said to Satan, "Have you noticed my servant Job, and that there is no one on earth like him, blameless and upright, fearing God and avoiding evil?" ⁹ But Satan answered the LORD and said, "Is it for nothing that Job is God-fearing?

¹⁰ Have you not surrounded him and his family and all that he has with your protection? You have blessed the work of his hands, and his livestock are spread over the land. ¹¹* But now put forth your hand and touch anything that he has, and surely he will blaspheme you to your face." ¹² And the LORD said to Satan, "Behold, all that he has is in your power; only do not lay a hand upon his person." So Satan went forth from the presence of the LORD.

The First Trial

¹³ And so one day, while his sons and his daughters were eating and drinking wine in the house of their eldest brother, ¹⁴ a messenger came to Job and said, "The oxen were plowing and the asses grazing beside them, ¹⁵† and the Sabeans carried them off in a raid. They put the herdsmen to the sword, and I alone have escaped to tell you." ¹⁶† While he was yet speaking, another came and said, "Lightning has fallen from heaven and struck the sheep and their shepherds and consumed them; and I alone have escaped to tell you." ¹⁷ While he was yet speaking, another came and said, "The Chaldeans formed three columns, seized the camels, carried them off, and put those tending them to the sword, and I alone have escaped to tell you." ¹⁸ While he was yet speaking, another came and said, "Your sons and daughters were eating and drinking wine

In Good Times and Bad

Have you ever felt so angry at the loss of something that you cursed and swore at God? Have you ever felt like just giving up on God because of your loss? In Jb 1, 13–19, a man named Job experiences an unimaginable loss. His children, his home, and his property are all destroyed at the same time. Job responds with great anger and great pain, but instead of cursing or blaming God, he blesses (praises) God (verse 21).

Job never loses his faith in God, even when he loses so much else. Through most of the rest of this book, he struggles to understand why this has happened to him. Job is an important model. When faced with great suffering, he does not lose his belief in the goodness of God, nor does he let his friends talk him into false confessions of sinfulness. Like Job, we must not fall into the trap of thinking that when bad things happen, God is punishing us.

▶ Jb 1, 13–21

---

in the house of their eldest brother, [19] when suddenly a great wind came across the desert and smote the four corners of the house. It fell upon the young people and they are dead; and I alone have escaped to tell you." [20] Then Job began to tear his cloak and cut off his hair. He cast himself prostrate upon the ground, [21]*† and said,

> "Naked I came forth from my mother's womb,
> and naked shall I go back again.

> The LORD gave and the LORD has taken away;
> blessed be the name of the LORD!"

[22]* In all this Job did not sin, nor did he say anything disrespectful of God.

The Second Trial

2 [1]* Once again the sons of God came to present themselves before the LORD, and Satan also came with them. [2] And the LORD said to Satan,

---

Introducing ▶ SATAN

Does the word Satan conjure for you an image of a demon with horns and a tail, torturing people in the fires of hell? or perhaps an evil presence wandering the world looking for souls to corrupt? Does it surprise you that Jb 1, 6 and Zec 3, 1 present Satan as actually working for God? In fact, the word Satan is more of a job description than a name; it means "adversary." In the Old Testament, Satan is depicted as a member of God's court whose responsibility it was to accuse or test humans before God. (Although, contrary to popular belief, the snake in the Garden of Eden is never identified as Satan in the Bible!)

It is only much later that Satan is seen as the enemy of God and the controller of the forces of evil. The notion of Satan as an evildoer seems to have been borrowed from a similar figure in Persian religion and developed in Israel as time passed. By the New Testament period, Satan is identified as a powerful agent of evil fighting against God (1 Thes 2, 18), is instrumental in Jesus' death (Lk 22, 3), tempts people to sin (1 Cor 7, 5), and is called the devil (Rv 12, 9). The good news is that in the death and Resurrection of Jesus, God overcomes the evil associated with Satan, both now and forever.

▶ Jb 1, 6—2, 10

1, 21: *Go back again:* to the earth; cf Gn 2, 7; Sir 40, 1.

1, 21: Eccl 5, 14; 1 Tm 6, 7.   2, 1: Jb 1, 6.
1, 22: Jb 2, 10; Jas 5, 11.

"Whence do you come?" And Satan answered the LORD and said, "From roaming the earth and patrolling it." ³* And the LORD said to Satan, "Have you noticed my servant Job, and that there is no one on earth like him, faultless and upright, fearing God and avoiding evil? He still holds fast to his innocence although you incited me against him to ruin him without cause." ⁴† And Satan answered the LORD and said, "Skin for skin! All that a man has will he give for his life. ⁵* But now put forth your hand and touch his bone and his flesh, and surely he will blaspheme you to your face." ⁶ And the LORD said to Satan, "He is in your power; only spare his life." ⁷ So Satan went forth from the presence of the LORD and smote Job with severe boils from the soles of his feet to the crown of his head. ⁸ And he took a potsherd to scrape himself, as he sat among the ashes. ⁹*† Then his wife said to him, "Are you still holding to your innocence? Curse God and die." ¹⁰* But he said to her, "Are even you going to speak as senseless women do? We accept good things from God; and should we not accept evil?" Through all this, Job said nothing sinful.

Job's Three Friends

¹¹† Now when three of Job's friends heard of all the misfortune that had come upon him, they set out each one from his own place: Eliphaz from Teman, Bildad from Shuh, and Zophar from Naamath. They met and journeyed together to give him sympathy and comfort. ¹² But when, at a distance, they lifted up their eyes and did not recognize him, they began to weep aloud; they tore their cloaks and threw dust upon their heads. ¹³ Then they sat down upon the ground with him seven days and seven nights, but none of them spoke a word to him; for they saw how great was his suffering.

II: First Cycle of Speeches

Job's Plaint

3 ¹ After this, Job opened his mouth and cursed his day. ² Job spoke out and said:

³* Perish the day on which I was born,
    the night when they said, "The child is
    a boy!"
⁴ May that day be darkness:
    let not God above call for it,
    nor light shine upon it!
⁵ May darkness and gloom claim it,
    clouds settle upon it,
    the blackness of night affright it!
⁶ May obscurity seize that day;
    let it not occur among the days of the year,
    nor enter into the count of the months!

LIVE IT!

Being There

What is the best way to respond to the suffering of another? Many of us shy away from funerals and hospitals because we just don't know what to say or how to act.

In Jb 2, 11–13, Job was visited by three friends. They did not recognize him at first because of his great suffering; then they cried. And then something remarkable happened: "They sat down upon the ground with him seven days and seven nights, but none of them spoke a word to him; for they saw how great was his suffering."

We must give Job's friends credit for being there, for spending time with him, and for letting him know they cared, especially when they first arrived. That is all we have to do for a friend who is hurting—offer a hug and a simple "I'm sorry," and then just stay around. Though this sounds easy, it can be very hard; we can feel so helpless. We need to keep in mind that what matters most is that we are there. That is what will be remembered.

If you know people are suffering or grieving, don't avoid them. Go up to them, let them know how you feel, and just be there for them. That is all. And that is a lot.

▶ Jb 2, 11–13

---

† **2, 4:** *Skin for skin:* an expression which, as applied to Job, means that he has borne his suffering patiently thus far only because he seeks to avoid greater suffering and to receive greater favors from God.
2, 9: *Curse God and die:* you have nothing to hope for from God and therefore nothing to live for.
2, 11: The names of Job's friends suggest Edomite origin. The Edomites (Ob 8f) and more specifically the Temanites (Jer 49, 7) enjoyed a reputation for wisdom.

2, 3: Jb 1, 1.
2, 5: Jb 1, 11.
2, 9: Jb 19, 17.
2, 10: Jb 1, 22; Sir 2, 4; Jas 5, 11.
3, 3: Jer 20, 14.

7 May that night be barren;
  let no joyful outcry greet it!

8† Let them curse it who curse the sea,
  the appointed disturbers of Leviathan!

9 May the stars of its twilight be darkened;
  may it look for daylight, but have none,
  nor gaze on the eyes of the dawn,

10 Because it kept not shut the doors of
  the womb
  to shield my eyes from trouble!

11* Why did I not perish at birth,
  come forth from the womb and expire?

16† Or why was I not buried away like an
  untimely birth,
  like babes that have never seen the light?

12 Wherefore did the knees receive me?
  or why did I suck at the breasts?

13 For then I should have lain down and
  been tranquil;
  had I slept, I should then have been at rest

14 With kings and counselors of the earth
  who built where now there are ruins

15 Or with princes who had gold
  and filled their houses with silver.

17† There the wicked cease from troubling,
  there the weary are at rest.

18 There the captives are at ease together,
  and hear not the voice of the slave driver.

19 Small and great are there the same,
  and the servant is free from his master.

20 Why is light given to the toilers,
  and life to the bitter in spirit?

21 They wait for death and it comes not;
  they search for it rather than for
  hidden treasures,

22 Rejoice in it exultingly,
  and are glad when they reach the grave:

23 Men whose path is hidden from them,
  and whom God has hemmed in!

24 For sighing comes more readily to me
  than food,
  and my groans well forth like water.

25 For what I fear overtakes me,
  and what I shrink from comes upon me.

26 I have no peace nor ease;
  I have no rest, for trouble comes!

Eliphaz's First Speech

4 ¹ Then spoke Eliphaz the Temanite, who said:

2 If someone attempts a word with you, will
  you mind?
  For how can anyone refrain from speaking?

3 Behold, you have instructed many,
  and have made firm their feeble hands.

4 Your words have upheld the stumbler;
  you have strengthened his faltering knees.

5 But now that it comes to you, you
  are impatient;
  when it touches yourself, you are dismayed.

6 Is not your piety a source of confidence,
  and your integrity of life your hope?

7* Reflect now, what innocent person perishes?
  Since when are the upright destroyed?

8 As I see it, those who plow for mischief
  and sow trouble, reap the same.

9* By the breath of God they perish,
  and by the blast of his wrath they
  are consumed.

10† Though the lion roars, though the king of
  beasts cries out,
  yet the teeth of the young lions are broken;

11 The old lion perishes for lack of prey,
  and the cubs of the lioness are scattered.

12† For a word was stealthily brought to me,
  and my ear caught a whisper of it.

13* In my thoughts during visions of the night,
  when deep sleep falls on men,

14 Fear came upon me, and shuddering,
  that terrified me to the bones.

15 Then a spirit passed before me,
  and the hair of my flesh stood up.

16 It paused, but its likeness I could not discern;
  a figure was before my eyes,
  and I heard a still voice:

17* "Can a man be righteous as against God?
  Can a mortal be blameless against his Maker?

18* Lo, he puts no trust in his servants,
  and with his angels he can find fault.

19 How much more with those that dwell in
  houses of clay,
  whose foundation is in the dust,

3, 8: *Leviathan:* in Jb 40, 25, the crocodile; here the reference is probably to a mythological sea monster symbolizing primeval chaos. Cf Jb 9, 13; 26, 13; Pss 74, 13f; 104, 26; Is 27, 1.

3, 16: This verse has been placed between vv 11 and 12 where it probably stood originally. There is reason to believe that here, as well as in several other places in Job, the original order of the poetic lines was accidentally disturbed in the early transmission of the text; so in chapters 12–15; 19–21; 24–31; 34; 36; 38–42. The verse numbers given in such cases are always those of the current Hebrew text, though the arrangement may differ. The footnotes will advise the reader of the difficulties and provide him with further indications for following the progress of thought in the book.

3, 17: *There:* in death.
4, 10: *The lion:* used figuratively here for the violent, rapacious sinner who cannot prevail against God.
4, 12–21: A dramatic presentation of the idea of man's nothingness in contrast to God's greatness.

3, 11: Jb 10, 18f.
4, 7: Ps 37, 25.
4, 9: Ps 18, 16; Is 11, 4; 2 Thes 2, 8.
4, 13: Jb 33, 15.
4, 17: Jb 9, 2; 15, 14ff; 25, 4; Pss 130, 3; 143, 2.
4, 18: Jb 15, 15; 2 Pt 2, 4; Jude 6.

who are crushed more easily than
the moth!

20 Morning or evening they may be shattered;
with no heed paid to it, they perish forever.

21 The pegs of their tent are plucked up;
they die without knowing wisdom."

5 1 Call now! Will anyone respond to you?
To which of the holy ones will you
appeal?

2 Nay, impatience kills the fool
and indignation slays the simpleton.

3* I have seen a fool spreading his roots,
but his household suddenly decayed.

4† His children shall be far from safety;
they shall be crushed at the gate without
a rescuer.

5 What they have reaped the hungry shall
eat up;
[or God shall take it away by blight;]
and the thirsty shall swallow
their substance.

6 For mischief comes not out of the earth,
nor does trouble spring out of the ground;

7† But man himself begets mischief,
as sparks fly upward.

8 In your place, I would appeal to God,
and to God I would state my plea.†

10 He gives rain upon the earth
and sends water upon the fields;

11* He sets up on high the lowly,
and those who mourn he exalts to safety.

12 He frustrates the plans of the cunning,
so that their hands achieve no success;

13* He catches the wise in their own ruses,
and the designs of the crafty are routed.

14 They meet with darkness in the daytime,
and at noonday they grope as though it
were night.

15 But the poor from the edge of the sword
and from the hand of the mighty, he saves.

16 Thus the unfortunate have hope,
and iniquity closes her mouth.

17 Happy is the man whom God reproves!
The Almighty's chastening do not reject.

18* For he wounds, but he binds up;
he smites, but his hands give healing.

19† Out of six troubles he will deliver you,
and at the seventh no evil shall touch you.

20 In famine he will deliver you from death,
and in war from the threat of the sword;

21 From the scourge of the tongue you shall
be hidden,
and shall not fear approaching ruin.

22 At destruction and want you shall laugh;
the beasts of the earth you need not dread.

23 You shall be in league with the stones of
the field,
and the wild beasts shall be at peace
with you.

24 And you shall know that your tent is secure;
taking stock of your household, you shall
miss nothing.

25 You shall know that your descendants
are many,
and your offspring as the grass of
the earth.

26 You shall approach the grave in full vigor,
as a shock of grain comes in at its season.

27 Lo, this we have searched out; so it is!
This we have heard, and you should know.

Job's First Reply

6 1 Then Job answered and said:

2 Ah, could my anguish but be measured
and my calamity laid with it in the scales,

3 They would now outweigh the sands of
the sea!
Because of this I speak without restraint.

4* For the arrows of the Almighty pierce me,
and my spirit drinks in their poison;
the terrors of God are arrayed against me.

5† Does the wild ass bray when he has grass?
Does the ox low over his fodder?

6 Can a thing insipid be eaten without salt?
Is there flavor in the white of an egg?

7 I refuse to touch them;
they are loathsome food to me.

8 Oh, that I might have my request,
and that God would grant what I long for:

9 Even that God would decide to crush me,
that he would put forth his hand and cut
me off!

10 Then I should still have consolation
and could exult through unremitting pain,
because I have not transgressed the
commands of the Holy One.

5, 4: *At the gate:* of the city, where justice was administered.
5, 7: *Sparks:* in Hebrew, "sons of resheph," which the ancient versions took as the name of a bird.
5, 9: Omitted here; it is a duplicate of Jb 9, 10.
5, 19: *Six . . . the seventh:* proverbial expression for any large number; cf Prv 24, 16; Lk 17, 4.
6, 5f: Job would not complain if his life were as pleasant to him as fodder to a hungry animal; but his life is as disagreeable as insipid

food. *White of an egg:* thus the obscure Hebrew has been understood in Jewish tradition; some render it "mallow juice."

5, 3: Ps 37, 35f.   **5, 13:** 1 Cor 3, 19.
5, 11: 1 Sm 2, 7f; Ps 113, 7;   **5, 18:** Hos 6, 1f.
Lk 1, 52.   **6, 4:** Ps 88, 17.

J
B

11 What strength have I that I should endure,
       and what is my limit that I should
          be patient?
12 Have I the strength of stones,
       or is my flesh of bronze?
13* Have I no helper,
       and has advice deserted me?
14 A friend owes kindness to one in despair,
       though he have forsaken the fear of
          the Almighty.
15 My brethren are undependable as a brook,
       as watercourses that run dry in the wadies;
16 Though they may be black with ice,
       and with snow heaped upon them,
17 Yet once they flow, they cease to be;
       in the heat, they disappear from their place.
18 Caravans turn aside from their routes;
       they go into the desert and perish.
19† The caravans of Tema search,
       the companies of Sheba have hopes;
20 They are disappointed, though they
          were confident;
       they come there and are frustrated.
21 It is thus that you have now become for me;
       you see a terrifying thing and are afraid.
22 Have I asked you to give me anything,
       to offer a gift for me from your possessions,
23 Or to deliver me from the enemy,
       or to redeem me from oppressors?
24 Teach me, and I will be silent;
       prove to me wherein I have erred.
25 How agreeable are honest words;
       yet how unconvincing is your argument!
26 Do you consider your words as proof,
       but the sayings of a desperate man as
          wind?
27 You would even cast lots for the orphan,
       and would barter away your friend!
28 Come, now, give me your attention;
       surely I will not lie to your face.
29 Think it over; let there be no injustice.
       Think it over; I still am right.
30 Is there insincerity on my tongue,
       or cannot my taste discern falsehood?

7 1*† Is not man's life on earth a drudgery?
       Are not his days those of a hireling?
2 He is a slave who longs for the shade,
       a hireling who waits for his wages.
3 So I have been assigned months of misery,
       and troubled nights have been told off
          for me.

PRAY IT!

Suffering

Job's words in Job, chapter 7, are almost a prayer describing his suffering and asking, Why me? Job isn't worried about being polite; he says it like it is. What can you learn from Job about prayer during suffering?

First, you need to be honest with God and yourself. If you are hurt or in pain, don't play games with God. Tell God what you are feeling in your own words. Write it down in a journal if you want to. And be honest. Because if you aren't honest with God, you probably aren't being honest with yourself.

Second, let all your feelings out, just like Job did—including your anger. God is big enough to handle it. When you suppress your negative feelings, they may come out in unhealthy ways. So, let God help you deal with them.

Finally, let your prayer lead you to take some action. Job debated with his friends. That's probably how people did counseling back then! Your prayer to God for help might lead you to a counselor, a minister, or a support group. God works in many ways.

▶ Jb 7, 1–21

4 If in bed I say, "When shall I arise?"
       Then the night drags on;
       I am filled with restlessness until the dawn.
5* My flesh is clothed with worms and scabs;
       my skin cracks and festers;
6 My days are swifter than a weaver's shuttle;
       they come to an end without hope.
7* Remember that my life is like the wind;
       I shall not see happiness again.
8 The eye that now sees me shall no more
          behold me;
       as you look at me, I shall be gone.
9* As a cloud dissolves and vanishes,
       so he who goes down to the nether world
          shall come up no more.

6, 19: *Tema:* in northwest Arabia. *Sheba:* see note on Jb 1, 15.
7, 1: *Drudgery:* taken by some to refer to military service; cf also Jb 14, 14.

6, 13: Jb 19, 14f.
7, 1: Jb 14, 14.
7, 5: Jb 2, 7f.
7, 7: Pss 8, 5; 144, 3.

7, 9f: Jb 10, 21; 14, 10ff;
2 Sm 12, 23; 14, 14;
Wis 2, 1.

10   He shall not again return to his house;
    his place shall know him no more.
11   My own utterance I will not restrain;
    I will speak in the anguish of my spirit;
    I will complain in the bitterness of
       my soul.
12† Am I the sea, or a monster of the deep,
    that you place a watch over me?†
    Why have you set me up as an object
       of attack
    or why should I be a target for you?
13   When I say, "My bed shall comfort me,
    my couch shall ease my complaint,"
14   Then you affright me with dreams
    and with visions terrify me,
15   So that I should prefer choking
    and death rather than my pains.
16* I waste away: I cannot live forever;
    let me alone, for my days are but a breath.
17   What is man, that you make much of him,
    or pay him any heed?
18* You observe him with each new day
    and try him at every moment!
19   How long will it be before you look away
       from me,
    and let me alone long enough to swallow
       my spittle?
20   Though I have sinned, what can I do to you,
    O watcher of men?
21   Why do you not pardon my offense,
    or take away my guilt?
    For soon I shall lie down in the dust;
    and should you seek me I shall then
       be gone.

Bildad's First Speech

8 1 Bildad the Shuhite spoke out and said:

2   How long will you utter such things?
    The words from your mouth are like a
       mighty wind!
3* Does God pervert judgment,
    and does the Almighty distort justice?
4   If your children have sinned against him
    and he has left them in the grip of
       their guilt,
5   Still, if you yourself have recourse to God
    and make supplication to the Almighty,
6   Should you be blameless and upright,
    surely now he will awake for you
    and restore your rightful domain;

7   Your former state will be of little moment,
    for in time to come you will
       flourish indeed.
8* If you inquire of the former generations,
    and give heed to the experience of
       the fathers
9* (As we are but of yesterday and have
       no knowledge,
    because our days on earth are but
       a shadow),
10   Will they not teach you and tell you
    and utter their words of understanding?
11† Can the papyrus grow up without mire?
    Can the reed grass flourish without water?
12   While it is yet green and uncut,
    it withers quicker than any grass.
13   So is the end of everyone who forgets God,
    and so shall the hope of the godless
       man perish.
14   His confidence is but a gossamer thread
    and his trust is a spider's web.
15   He shall rely upon his family, but it shall
       not last;
    he shall cling to it, but it shall not endure.
16   He is full of sap before sunrise,
    and beyond his garden his shoots go forth;
17   About a heap of stones are his roots entwined;
    among the rocks he takes hold.
18   Yet if one tears him from his place,
    it will disown him: "I have never seen you!"
19   There he lies rotting beside the road,
    and out of the soil another sprouts.
20   Behold, God will not cast away the upright;
    neither will he take the hand of the wicked.
21   Once more will he fill your mouth
       with laughter,
    and your lips with rejoicing.
22   They that hate you shall be clothed
       with shame,
    and the tent of the wicked shall be
       no more.

Job's Second Reply

9 1 Then Job answered and said:

2   I know well that it is so;
    but how can a man be justified
       before God?
3   Should one wish to contend with him,
    he could not answer him once in a
       thousand times.

7, 12: An allusion in poetic imagery to primeval chaos as a monstrous ocean vanquished by God at the world's creation.
   7, 12–21: Job now speaks, not to his friends, but to God.
   8, 11ff: As marsh plants need water, so man needs God. These verses are taken by some as a quotation from the teaching of the forefathers; cf v 10.

7, 16: Jb 14, 1ff.5.
7, 18: Ps 17, 3.
8, 3: Jb 34, 10ff.
8, 8: Dt 4, 32; 32, 7.
8, 9: Jb 14, 2; Pss 102, 12;
     109, 23; 144, 4;
     Wis 2, 5.

4 God is wise in heart and mighty in strength;
who has withstood him and
remained unscathed?

5 He removes the mountains before they
know it;
he overturns them in his anger.

6* He shakes the earth out of its place,
and the pillars beneath it tremble.

7 He commands the sun, and it rises not;
he seals up the stars.

8* He alone stretches out the heavens
and treads upon the crests of the sea.

9 He made the Bear and Orion,
the Pleiades and the constellations of
the south;

10 He does great things past finding out,
marvelous things beyond reckoning.

11 Should he come near me, I see him not;
should he pass by, I am not aware of him;

12 Should he seize me forcibly, who can say
him nay?
Who can say to him, "What are you
doing?"

13† He is God and he does not relent;
the helpers of Rahab bow beneath him.

14 How much less shall I give him any answer,
or choose out arguments against him!

15* Even though I were right, I could not
answer him,
but should rather beg for what was due me.

16 If I appealed to him and he answered my call,
I could not believe that he would hearken
to my words;

17 With a tempest he might overwhelm me,
and multiply my wounds without cause;

18 He need not suffer me to draw breath,
but might fill me with bitter griefs.

19 If it be a question of strength, he is mighty;
and if of judgment, who will call him
to account?

20* Though I were right, my own mouth might
condemn me;
were I innocent, he might put me in
the wrong.

21 Though I am innocent, I myself cannot
know it;
I despise my life.

22* It is all one! therefore I say:
Both the innocent and the wicked
he destroys.

23 When the scourge slays suddenly,
he laughs at the despair of the innocent.

24 The earth is given into the hands of
the wicked;
he covers the faces of its judges.
If it is not he, who then is it?

25* My days are swifter than a runner,
they flee away; they see no happiness;

26 They shoot by like skiffs of reed,
like an eagle swooping upon its prey.

27 If I say: I will forget my complaining,
I will lay aside my sadness and be of
good cheer,

28† Then I am in dread of all my pains;
I know that you will not hold me innocent.

29 If I must be accounted guilty,
why then should I strive in vain?

30 If I should wash myself with snow
and cleanse my hands with lye,

31 Yet you would plunge me in the ditch,
so that my garments would abhor me.

32 For he is not a man like myself, that I should
answer him,
that we should come together in judgment.

33 Would that there were an arbiter between us,
who could lay his hand upon us both

34 and withdraw his rod from me.
Would that his terrors did not frighten me;

35 that I might speak without being afraid
of him.
Since this is not the case with me,

1*† I loathe my life.

10 I will give myself up to complaint;
I will speak from the bitterness of
my soul.

2 I will say to God: Do not put me in
the wrong!
Let me know why you oppose me.

3 Is it a pleasure for you to oppress,
to spurn the work of your hands,
and smile on the plan of the wicked?

4 Have you eyes of flesh?
Do you see as man sees?

5* Are your days as the days of a mortal,
and are your years as a man's lifetime,

6 That you seek for guilt in me
and search after my sins,

7* Even though you know that I am not wicked,
and that none can deliver me out of
your hand?

8 Your hands have formed me and
fashioned me;
will you then turn and destroy me?

9, 13: *Rahab:* cf Jb 26, 12. See note on Ps 89, 11.
9, 28–31: *You:* refers to God.
10, 1: *I loathe my life:* this is the first verse of ch 10.

9, 6: Jb 26, 11.
9, 8: Ps 104, 2; Is 40, 22.
9, 15: Jb 10, 15.
9, 20: Jb 15, 6.
9, 22: Eccl 9, 2.

9, 25: Jb 7, 6.
10, 1: Jb 9, 21.
10, 5: Jb 36, 26.
10, 7: Jb 2, 3.9; Dt 32, 39;
Wis 16, 15.

9* Oh, remember that you fashioned me
    from clay!
    Will you then bring me down to
    dust again?

10 Did you not pour me out as milk,
    and thicken me like cheese?

11 With skin and flesh you clothed me,
    with bones and sinews knit me together.

12 Grace and favor you granted me,
    and your providence has preserved
    my spirit.

13 Yet these things you have hidden in your heart;
    I know that they are your purpose:

14 If I should sin, you would keep a watch
    against me,
    and from my guilt you would not
    absolve me.

15 If I should be wicked, alas for me!
    if righteous, I dare not hold up my head,
    filled with ignominy and sodden
    with affliction!

16 Should it lift up, you hunt me like a lion:
    repeatedly you show your wondrous power
    against me,

17 You renew your attack upon me
    and multiply your harassment of me;
    in waves your troops come against me.

18* Why then did you bring me forth from
    the womb?
    I should have died and no eye have seen me.

19 I should be as though I had never lived;
    I should have been taken from the womb
    to the grave.

20 Are not the days of my life few?
    Let me alone, that I may recover a little

21* Before I go whence I shall not return,
    to the land of darkness and of gloom,

22 The black, disordered land
    where darkness is the only light.

Zophar's First Speech

11
1 And Zophar the Naamathite spoke out
and said:

2 Should not the man of many words
    be answered,
    or must the garrulous man necessarily
    be right?

3 Shall your babblings keep men silent,
    and shall you deride and no one
    give rebuke?

4 Shall you say: "My teaching is pure,
    and I am clean in your sight"?

5 But oh, that God would speak,
    and open his lips against you,

6 And tell you that the secrets of wisdom
    are twice as effective:
    So you might learn that God
    will make you answer for your guilt.

7* Can you penetrate the designs of God?
    Dare you vie with the perfection of
    the Almighty?

8 It is higher than the heavens; what can
    you do?
    It is deeper than the nether world; what can
    you know?

9 It is longer than the earth in measure,
    and broader than the sea.

10 If he seize and imprison
    or call to judgment, who then can say
    him nay?

11 For he knows the worthlessness of men
    and sees iniquity; will he then ignore it?

12* Will empty man then gain understanding,
    and the wild jackass be made docile?

13 If you set your heart aright
    and stretch out your hands toward him,

14 If you remove all iniquity from your conduct,
    and let not injustice dwell in your tent,

15 Surely then you may lift up your face
    in innocence;
    you may stand firm and unafraid.

16 For then you shall forget your misery,
    or recall it like waters that have ebbed away.

17 Then your life shall be brighter than
    the noonday;
    its gloom shall become as the morning,

18* And you shall be secure, because there
    is hope;
    you shall look round you and lie down
    in safety,

19 and you shall take your rest with none
    to disturb.
    Many shall entreat your favor,

20 but the wicked, looking on, shall be
    consumed with envy.
    Escape shall be cut off from them,
    they shall wait to expire.

Job's Third Reply

12
1 Then Job replied and said:

2 No doubt you are the intelligent folk,
    and with you wisdom shall die!

3* But I have intelligence as well as you;
    for who does not know such things
    as these?

10, 9: Jb 4, 19; 33, 6; Gn 2,   10, 18: Jb 3, 3.11.
7; 3, 19; Ps 146, 4.   10, 21: Jb 7, 9f; 16, 22.

11, 7: Rom 11, 33.   11, 18: Lv 26, 6; Ps 4, 9.
11, 12: Jb 39, 5-8.   12, 3: Jb 13, 2; 15, 9.

4 *†I have become the sport of my neighbors:
"The one whom God answers when he calls
upon him,
the just, the perfect man," is a
laughingstock;

5 The undisturbed esteem my downfall
a disgrace
such as awaits unsteady feet;

6 Yet the tents of robbers are prosperous,
and those who provoke God are secure.

7 But now ask the beasts to teach you,
and the birds of the air to tell you;

8 Or the reptiles on earth to instruct you,
and the fish of the sea to inform you.

9 Which of all these does not know
that the hand of God has done this?

10 * In his hand is the soul of every living thing,
and the life breath of all mankind.

11 * Does not the ear judge words
as the mouth tastes food?

12 * So with old age is wisdom,
and with length of days understanding.

13 With him are wisdom and might;
his are counsel and understanding.

14 * If he breaks a thing down, there is
no rebuilding;
if he imprisons a man, there is no release.

15 * He holds back the waters and there
is drought;
he sends them forth and they overwhelm
the land.

18 † He loosens the bonds imposed by kings
and leaves but a waistcloth to bind the
king's own loins.

21 He breaks down the barriers of the streams

19 and lets their never-failing waters
flow away.

16 With him are strength and prudence;
the misled and the misleaders are his.

17 He sends counselors away barefoot,
and of judges he makes fools.

20 He silences the trusted adviser,
and takes discretion from the aged.

22 The recesses of the darkness he discloses,
and brings the gloom forth to the light.

23 He makes nations great and he destroys
them;
he spreads peoples abroad and he
abandons them.

24 He takes understanding from the leaders of
the land,

25 till they grope in the darkness
without light;
he makes them stagger like drunken men.

13 1 Lo, all this my eye has seen;
my ear has heard and perceived it.

2 * What you know, I also know;
I fall not short of you.

3 * But I would speak with the Almighty;
I wish to reason with God.

4 You are glossing over falsehoods
and offering vain remedies, every one
of you!

5 Oh, that you would be altogether silent!
This for you would be wisdom.

6 Hear now the rebuke I shall utter
and listen to the reproof from my lips.

7 Is it for God that you speak falsehood?
Is it for him that you utter deceit?

8 Is it for him that you show partiality?
Do you play advocate on behalf of God?

9 Will it be well when he shall search
you out?
Would you impose on him as one does
on men?

10 He will openly rebuke you
if even in secret you show partiality.

11 Surely will his majesty affright you
and the dread of him fall upon you.

12 Your reminders are ashy maxims,
your fabrications are mounds of clay.

13 Be silent, let me alone! that I may speak
and give vent to my feelings.

14 † I will carry my flesh between my teeth,
and take my life in my hand.

15 * Slay me though he might, I will wait
for him;
I will defend my conduct before him.

16 And this shall be my salvation,
that no impious man can come into
his presence.

17 Pay careful heed to my speech,
and give my statement a hearing.

18 * Behold, I have prepared my case,
I know that I am in the right.

19 If anyone can make a case against me,
then I shall be silent and die.

---

† **12, 4f:** The Hebrew is somewhat obscure, but the general sense
is that the wicked mock at the pious when the latter appear to be
abandoned by God; cf Ps 22, 7ff; Mt 27, 39–43.

12, 18: *Waistcloth . . . loins:* he reduces kings to the condition of
slaves, who wear only a cloth wrapped about the waist.

13, 14: The second half of the verse is a common biblical expression for risking one's life; cf Jgs 12, 3; 1 Sm 19, 5; 28, 21; Ps
119, 109; the first half of the verse must have a similar meaning. Job

is so confident of his innocence that he is willing to risk his life by
going to judgment with God.

12, 4: Jb 21, 3; 30, 1.	12, 15: Gn 7, 11–24.
12, 10: Acts 17, 28.	13, 2: Jb 12, 3; 15, 9.
12, 11: Jb 34, 3.	13, 3: Jb 23, 4.
12, 12: Jb 32, 7.	13, 15: Jb 27, 5.
12, 14: Rv 3, 7.	13, 18: Jb 33, 9.

20† These things only do not use against me,
   then from your presence I need not hide:

21 Withdraw your hand far from me,
   and let not the terror of you frighten me.

22 Then call me, and I will respond;
   or let me speak first, and answer me.

23 What are my faults and my sins?
   My misdeeds and my sins make known
      to me!

24* Why do you hide your face
   and consider me your enemy?

25 Will you harass a wind-driven leaf,
   or pursue a withered straw?

26 For you draw up bitter indictments
      against me,
   and punish in me the faults of my youth.

27 You put my feet in the stocks;
   you watch all my paths
   and trace out all my footsteps.

14 ¹* Man born of woman
      is short-lived and full of trouble,

2* Like a flower that springs up and fades,
   swift as a shadow that does not abide.

3 Upon such a one will you cast your eyes
   so as to bring him into judgment
      before you,

28† Though he wears out like a leather bottle,
   like a garment that the moth
      has consumed?

4* Can a man be found who is clean
      of defilement?
   There is none, 5 however short his days.
   You know the number of his months;
   you have fixed the limit which he
      cannot pass.

6 Look away from him and let him be,
   while, like a hireling, he completes
      his day.

7 For a tree there is hope,
   if it be cut down, that it will sprout again
   and that its tender shoots will not cease.

8 Even though its root grow old in the earth,
   and its stump die in the dust,

9 Yet at the first whiff of water it may
      flourish again
   and put forth branches like a young plant.

10* But when a man dies, all vigor leaves him;
   when man expires, where then is he?

11 As when the waters of a lake fail,
   or a stream grows dry and parches,

12* So men lie down and rise not again.
   Till the heavens are no more, they shall
      not awake,
   nor be roused out of their sleep.

13 Oh, that you would hide me in the
      nether world
   and keep me sheltered till your wrath
      is past;
   would fix a time for me, and then
      remember me!

14* When a man has died, were he to live again,
   all the days of my drudgery I would wait,
   until my relief should come.

15 You would call, and I would answer you;
   you would esteem the work of your hands.

16* Surely then you would count my steps,
   and not keep watch for sin in me.

17† My misdeeds would be sealed up in a pouch,
   and you would cover over my guilt.

18 But as a mountain falls at last
   and its rock is moved from its place,

19 As waters wear away the stones
   and floods wash away the soil of the land,
   so you destroy the hope of man.

20 You prevail once for all against him and he
      passes on;
   with changed appearance you send
      him away.

21 If his sons are honored, he is not aware of it;
   if they are in disgrace, he does not know
      about them.

22 Only his own flesh pains him,
   and his soul grieves for him.

III: Second Cycle of Speeches

Second Speech of Eliphaz

15 ¹ Then Eliphaz the Temanite spoke and
      said:

2 Should a wise man answer with airy opinions,
   or puff himself up with wind?

3 Should he argue in speech which does not avail,
   and in words which are to no profit?

4 You in fact do away with piety,
   and you lessen devotion toward God,

5 Because your wickedness instructs
      your mouth,
   and you choose to speak like the crafty.

6* Your own mouth condemns you, not I;
   your own lips refute you.

---

† **13, 20:** From here to the end of chapter 14, Job pleads his case,
addressing God rather than his three friends.
14, 28: This verse has been transposed from ch 13.
14, 17: *Sealed up in a pouch:* hidden away and forgotten.

13, 24: Jb 19, 11; 33, 10.
14, 1: Jb 10, 20; 15, 14; Pss
39, 5f; 89, 46; Wis
2, 1.
14, 2: Jb 8, 9; Pss 90, 6; 102,
12; 103, 15; 109, 23;
144, 4; Is 40, 6f; Jas

1, 10.
14, 4: Ps 51, 4.7.
14, 10: Jb 20, 7.
14, 12: Jb 7, 10.
14, 14: Jb 7, 1.
14, 16: Jb 31, 4; 34, 21.
15, 6: Jb 9, 20.

7 Are you indeed the first-born of mankind,
  or were you brought forth before the hills?

8* Are you privy to the counsels of God,
  and do you restrict wisdom to yourself?

9* What do you know that we do not know?
  What intelligence have you which we
  have not?

10 There are gray-haired old men among us
  more advanced in years than your father.

11 Are the consolations of God not enough
  for you,
  and speech that deals gently with you?

12 Why do your notions carry you away,
  and why do your eyes blink,

13 So that you turn your anger against God
  and let such words escape your mouth!

14* What is a man that he should be blameless,
  one born of woman that he should
  be righteous?*

15* If in his holy ones God places no confidence,
  and if the heavens are not clean in
  his sight,

16 How much less so is the abominable,
  the corrupt:
  man, who drinks in iniquity like water!

17 I will show you, if you listen to me;
  what I have seen I will tell—

18 What wise men relate
  and have not contradicted since the days of
  their fathers,

19 To whom alone the land was given,
  when no foreigner moved among them.

20 The wicked man is in torment all his days,
  and limited years are in store for the tyrant;

21 The sound of terrors is in his ears;
  when all is prosperous, the spoiler comes
  upon him.

22 He despairs of escaping the darkness,
  and looks ever for the sword;

23 A wanderer, food for the vultures,
  he knows that his destruction is imminent.

24 By day the darkness fills him with dread;
  distress and anguish overpower him.

25 Because he has stretched out his hand
  against God
  and bade defiance to the Almighty,

26 One shall rush sternly upon him
  with the stout bosses of his shield,
  like a king prepared for the charge.

27 Because he has blinded himself with
  his crassness,
  padding his loins with fat,

28 He shall dwell in ruinous cities,
  in houses that are deserted,
  That are crumbling into clay

29 with no shadow to lengthen over the ground.
  He shall not be rich, and his possessions shall
  not endure;

31 for vain shall be his bartering.

30 A flame shall wither him up in his
  early growth,
  and with the wind his blossoms
  shall disappear.

32 His stalk shall wither before its time,
  and his branches shall be green no more.

33 He shall be like a vine that sheds its
  grapes unripened,
  and like an olive tree casting off its bloom.

34* For the breed of the impious shall be sterile,
  and fire shall consume the tents
  of extortioners.

35*†They conceive malice and bring
  forth emptiness;
  they give birth to failure.

Job's Fourth Reply

16 ¹ Then Job answered and said:

2* I have heard this sort of thing many times.
  Wearisome comforters are you all!

3 Is there no end to windy words?
  Or what sickness have you that you
  speak on?

4 I also could talk as you do,
  were you in my place.
  I could declaim over you,
  or wag my head at you;

5 I could strengthen you with talk,
  or shake my head with silent lips.

6 If I speak, this pain I have will not be checked;
  if I leave off, it will not depart from me.

7 But now that I am exhausted and stunned,
  all my company has closed in on me.

8 As a witness there rises up
  my traducer, speaking openly against me;

9 I am the prey his wrath assails,
  he gnashes his teeth against me.
  My enemies lord it over me;

10 their mouths are agape to bite me.
  They smite me on the cheek insultingly;
  they are all enlisted against me.

11 God has given me over to the impious;
  into the clutches of the wicked he has
  cast me.

15, 35: *They give birth to failure:* their wicked plans yield nothing but futile results. Cf Ps 7, 15; Is 59, 4.

15, 8: Jb 11, 7; Wis 9, 13; Jer
    23, 18; Rom 11, 34;
    1 Cor 2, 11.16.
15, 9: Jb 12, 3; 13, 2.
15, 14ff: Jb 25, 4ff.
15, 14: Jb 14, 4.
15, 15: Jb 4, 18f.
15, 34: Wis 3, 11.18.
15, 35: Ps 7, 15; Is 59, 4.
16, 2: Jb 12, 3.

12 I was in peace, but he dislodged me;
   he seized me by the neck and dashed me
     to pieces.
He has set me up for a target;
13   his arrows strike me from all directions,
He pierces my sides without mercy,
   he pours out my gall upon the ground.
14 He pierces me with thrust upon thrust;
   he attacks me like a warrior.
15 I have fastened sackcloth over my skin,
   and have laid my brow in the dust.
16 My face is inflamed with weeping
   and there is darkness over my eyes,
17 Although my hands are free from violence,
   and my prayer is sincere.
18† O earth, cover not my blood,
   nor let my outcry come to rest!
19† Even now, behold, my witness is in heaven,
   and my spokesman is on high.
20 My friends it is who wrong me;
   before God my eyes drop tears,
21 That he may do justice for a mortal in
    his presence
   and decide between a man and
    his neighbor.
22 For my years are numbered now,
   and I am on a journey from which I shall
    not return.

17

1 My spirit is broken, my lamp of life
    extinguished;
my burial is at hand.
2 I am indeed mocked,
   and, as their provocation mounts, my eyes
    grow dim.
3† Grant me one to offer you a pledge on
    my behalf:
who is there that will give surety for me?
4 You darken their minds to knowledge;
   therefore they do not understand.
5 My lot is described as evil,
6*   and I am made a byword of the people;
   their object lesson I have become.
7 My eye has grown blind with anguish,
   and all my frame is shrunken to a
    shadow.
8 Upright men are astonished at this,
   and the innocent aroused against
    the wicked.

9 Yet the righteous shall hold to his way,
   and he who has clean hands increase
    in strength.
10 But turn now, and come on again;
   for I shall not find a wise man among you!
11 My days are passed away, my plans are at
    an end,
   the cherished purposes of my heart.
12 Such men change the night into day;
   where there is darkness they talk of
    approaching light.
13 If I look for the nether world as my dwelling,
   if I spread my couch in the darkness,
14 If I must call corruption "my father,"
   and the maggot "my mother" and
    "my sister,"
15 Where then is my hope,
   and my prosperity, who shall see?
16 Will they descend with me into the
    nether world?
   Shall we go down together into the dust?

Bildad's Second Speech

18

1 Then Bildad the Shuhite replied and
   said:

2 When will you put an end to words?
   Reflect, and then we can have discussion.
3 Why are we accounted like the beasts,
   their equals in your sight?
4† You who tear yourself in your anger,
   shall the earth be neglected on
    your account
   [or the rock be moved out of its place]?
5 Truly, the light of the wicked is
    extinguished;
   no flame brightens his hearth.
6* The light is darkened in his tent;
   in spite of him, his lamp goes out.
7 His vigorous steps are hemmed in,
   and his own counsel casts him down.
8 For he rushes headlong into a net,
   and he wanders into a pitfall.
9 A trap seizes him by the heel,
   and a snare lays hold of him.
10 A noose for him is hid on the ground,
   and the toils for him on the way.
11* On every side terrors affright him;
   they harry him at each step.
12 Disaster is ready at his side,

16, 18: As the blood of those who were unjustly slain cries to heaven for vengeance (Gn 4, 10; Ez 24, 6–9), so Job's sufferings demand redress.

16, 19: *Witness:* refers either to God or, more probably, to Job's prayer.

17, 3: Addressed to God; v 10 to Job's friends.

18, 4: Job himself is portrayed as having the heedless rage of wild beasts, despite which God does not forsake the usual course of Divine Providence.

17, 6: Jb 30, 9.   24, 20.
18, 6: Jb 21, 17; Prv 13, 9;   18, 11: Jb 15, 20–24; 27, 20.

13†   the first-born of death consumes his limbs.

14† Fiery destruction lodges in his tent,
    and marches him off to the king of terrors.
    He is plucked from the security of his tent;

15   over his abode brimstone is scattered.

16 Below, his roots dry up,
    and above, his branches wither.

17* His memory perishes from the land,
    and he has no name on the earth.

18 He is driven from light into darkness,
    and banished out of the world.

19 He has neither son nor grandson among
    his people,
    nor any survivor where once he dwelt.

20 They who come after shall be appalled at
    his fate;
    they who went before are struck
    with horror.

21 So is it then with the dwelling of the
    impious man,
    and such is the place of him who knows
    not God!

Job's Fifth Reply

19 ¹ Then Job answered and said:

2   How long will you vex my soul,
    grind me down with words?

3   These ten times you have reviled me,
    have assailed me without shame!

4   Be it indeed that I am at fault
    and that my fault remains with me.

5   Even so, if you would vaunt yourselves
    against me
    and cast up to me my reproach,

6   Know then that God has dealt unfairly
    with me,
    and compassed me round with his net.

7* If I cry out "Injustice!" I am not heard.
    I cry for help, but there is no redress.

8   He has barred my way and I cannot pass;
    he has veiled my path in darkness;

9   He has stripped me of my glory,
    and taken the diadem from my brow.

10 He breaks me down on every side, and I
    am gone;

    my hope he has uprooted like a tree.

11* His wrath he has kindled against me;
    he counts me among his enemies.

12 His troops advance as one man;
    they build up their road to attack me,
    and they encamp around my tent.

13* My brethren have withdrawn from me,
    and my friends are wholly estranged.

14 My kinsfolk and companions neglect me,
    and my guests have forgotten me.

15 Even my handmaids treat me as a stranger;
    I am an alien in their sight.

16 I call my servant, but he gives no answer,
    though in my speech I plead with him.

17* My breath is abhorred by my wife;
    I am loathsome to the men of my family.

18 The young children, too, despise me;
    when I appear, they speak against me.

19* All my intimate friends hold me in horror;
    those whom I loved have turned
    against me!

20† My bones cleave to my skin,
    and I have escaped with my flesh between
    my teeth.

21 Pity me, pity me, O you my friends,
    for the hand of God has struck me!

22† Why do you hound me as though you
    were divine,
    and insatiably prey upon me?

23*† Oh, would that my words were written down!
    Would that they were inscribed in a record:

24 That with an iron chisel and with lead
    they were cut in the rock forever!

25*† But as for me, I know that my Vindicator lives,
    and that he will at last stand forth upon
    the dust;

27 Whom I myself shall see:
    my own eyes, not another's, shall
    behold him.

26 And from my flesh I shall see God;
    my inmost being is consumed
    with longing.

28 But you who say, "How shall we
    persecute him,
    seeing that the root of the matter is found
    in him?"

---

†   **18, 13:** *First-born of death:* that is, disease, plague.
   18, 14: *The king of terrors:* of the nether world, death; however, the Hebrew is obscure.
   19, 20: *With my flesh between my teeth:* meaning perhaps that Job has been reduced to such an extremity that he scarcely has thin lips over his teeth. But the current Hebrew text of this line is probably corrupt.
   19, 22: *Divine:* possessing God's attributes of judgment and authority to punish.
   19, 23f: Job regards what he is about to say as so important that he wishes it recorded in a permanent manner.
   19, 25.27: The meaning of this passage is obscure because the original text has been poorly preserved and the ancient versions do

not agree among themselves. It is certain that Job expresses his belief in a future vindication by God (called here in the Hebrew "Goel"), but the time and manner of this vindication are undefined. In the Vulgate Job is made to indicate a belief in physical resurrection after death, but the Hebrew and the other ancient versions are less specific.

---

*

18, 17: Ps 34, 17; Prv 2, 22;	**19, 17:** Jb 2, 9.
10, 7.	**19, 19:** Sir 6, 8.
19, 7: Jb 30, 20.	**19, 23:** Jb 31, 35.
19, 11: Jb 13, 24; 33, 10.	**19, 25ff:** Phil 3, 20; Ti 2, 13.
19, 13: Jb 6, 13.	

29 Be afraid of the sword for yourselves,
        for these crimes deserve the sword;
        that you may know that there is
            a judgment.

Zophar's Second Speech

20 ¹ Then Zophar the Naamathite spoke
         and said:

3   A rebuke which puts me to shame I hear,
2   and because of this I am disturbed.
    So now my thoughts provide me with
            an answer,
        and from my understanding a spirit gives
            me a reply.
4   Do you not know this from olden time,
        since man was placed upon the earth,
5* That the triumph of the wicked is short
        and the joy of the impious but for
            a moment?
6   Though his pride mount up to the heavens
        and his head reach to the clouds,
7* Yet he perishes forever like the fuel of his fire,
        and the onlookers say, "Where is he?"
8   Like a dream he takes flight and is not
            found again;
        he fades away like a vision of the night.
9   The eye which saw him does so no more;
        nor shall his dwelling again behold him.
11 Though his frame is full of youthful vigor,
        this shall lie with him in the dust.
12 Though wickedness is sweet in his mouth,
        and he hides it under his tongue,
13 Though he retains it and will not let it go
        but keeps it still within his mouth,
14 Yet in his stomach the food shall turn;
        it shall be venom of asps inside him.
15 The riches he swallowed he shall disgorge;
        God shall compel his belly to disown them.
16 The poison of asps he shall drink in;
        the viper's fangs shall slay him.
17† He shall see no streams of oil,
        no torrents of honey or milk.
18 Restoring his gains, he shall not enjoy them;
        though his wealth increases, he shall
            not rejoice.
19 Because he has oppressed the poor,
        and stolen a patrimony he had not
            built up,
21 Therefore his prosperity shall not endure,
10*   and his hands shall yield up his riches.

20* Though he has known no quiet in his greed,
        his treasures shall not save him.
22* When he abounds to overflowing, he shall be
            brought into straits,
        and nought shall be left of his goods.
23 God shall send against him the fury of
            his wrath
        and rain down his missiles of war upon him.
24 Should he escape the iron weapon,
        the bow of bronze shall pierce
            him through;
25 The dart shall come out of his back;
        terrors shall fall upon him.
26* Complete darkness is in store for him;
        the fire which shall consume him needs not
            to be fanned.
27 The heavens shall reveal his guilt,
        and the earth shall rise up against him.
28 The flood shall sweep away his house
        with the waters that run off in the day of
            God's anger.
29* This is the portion of a wicked man,
        and the heritage appointed him by God.

Job's Sixth Reply

21 ¹ Then Job said in reply:

2* At least listen to my words,
        and let that be the consolation you offer.
3   Bear with me while I speak;
        and after I have spoken, you can mock!
4   Is my complaint toward man?
        And why should I not be impatient?
5   Look at me and be astonished,
        put your hands over your mouths.
6   When I think of it, I am dismayed,
        and horror takes hold on my flesh.

7* Why do the wicked survive,
        grow old, become mighty in power?
8   Their progeny is secure in their sight;
        they see before them their kinsfolk and
            their offspring.
9   Their homes are safe and without fear,
        nor is the scourge of God upon them.
10 Their bulls gender without fail;
        their cows calve and do not miscarry.
11 These folk have infants numerous as lambs,
        and their children dance.
12 They sing to the timbrel and harp,
        and make merry to the sound of the flute.

---

† **20, 17:** *Oil:* olive oil, one of the main agricultural products of
Palestine, a land proverbially rich in honey and milk.

20, 5: Jb 21, 13; Ps 37, 35f.
20, 7: Jb 14, 10; Ps 37,
    10.36.
20, 10: Jb 27, 14.
20, 20: Eccl 5, 9; Lk 12, 20.
20, 22: Jb 15, 20–35.

20, 26: Dt 32, 22.
20, 29: Jb 27, 13.
21, 2: Jb 13, 17.
21, 7: Jb 12, 6; Pss 37, 35;
    73, 3; Eccl 8, 14; Jer
    12, 1f; Mal 3, 14f.

13* They live out their days in prosperity,
and tranquilly go down to the
nether world.
14* Yet they say to God, "Depart from us,
for we have no wish to learn your ways!
15* What is the Almighty that we should
serve him?
And what gain shall we have if we pray
to him?"
16* If their happiness is not in their own hands
and if the counsel of the wicked is repulsive
to God,
17 How often is the lamp of the wicked put out?
How often does destruction come
upon them,
the portion he allots in his anger?

18 Let them be like straw before the wind,
and like chaff which the storm
snatches away!
19 May God not store up the man's misery for
his children;
let him requite the man himself so that he
feels it,
20 Let his own eyes see the calamity,
and the wrath of the Almighty let
him drink!
21 For what interest has he in his family
after him,
when the number of his months
is finished?

23 One dies in his full vigor,
wholly at ease and content;
24 His figure is full and nourished,
and his bones are rich in marrow.
25 Another dies in bitterness of soul,
having never tasted happiness.
26 Alike they lie down in the dust,
and worms cover them both.

27 Behold, I know your thoughts,
and the arguments you rehearse against me.
28 For you say, "Where is the house of
the magnate,
and where the dwelling place of the wicked?"
29 Have you not asked the wayfarers
and do you not recognize
their monuments?
30 Nay, the evil man is spared calamity when
it comes;
32 and on the day he is carried to the grave

31 Who will charge him with his conduct to
his face,
and for what he has done who will
repay him?
33 Sweet to him are the clods of the valley,
and over him the funeral mound
keeps watch,
While all the line of mankind follows him,
and the countless others who have
gone before.
34 How then can you offer me vain comfort,
while in your answers perfidy remains?

IV: Third Cycle of Speeches

Eliphaz's Third Speech

22 ¹ Then Eliphaz the Temanite answered
and said:

2* Can a man be profitable to God?
Though to himself a wise man be profitable!
22† Can anyone teach God knowledge,
seeing that he judges those on high?
3* Is it of advantage to the Almighty if you
are just?
Or is it a gain to him if you make your
ways perfect?
4 Is it because of your piety that he
reproves you—
that he enters with you into judgment?
5 Is not your wickedness manifold?
Are not your iniquities endless?

6*†You have unjustly kept your kinsmen's goods
in pawn,
left them stripped naked of their clothing.
7 To the thirsty you have given no water to drink,
and from the hungry you have
withheld bread;
8 As if the land belonged to the man of might,
and only the privileged were to dwell in it.
9* You have sent widows away empty-handed,
and the resources of orphans you
have destroyed.
10* Therefore snares are round about you,
and a sudden terror causes you dismay,
11 Or darkness, in which you cannot see;
a deluge of waters covers you.

12* Does not God, in the heights of the heavens,
behold the stars, high though they are?

22, 22: *Those on high:* the angels. This verse has been transposed
from ch 21.
22, 6ff: This criticism of Job by Eliphaz is altogether untrue, but it
is made to dramatize the latter's argument that God always acts justly when he causes someone to suffer. Verse 8 is misplaced.

21, 13: Jb 34, 20.
21, 14: Jb 22, 17.
21, 15: Mal 3, 14.
21, 16: Jb 22, 18.
22, 2: Jb 9, 2.
22, 3: Jb 35, 7.

22, 6: Jb 24, 3; Dt 24, 6.17;
Ez 18, 12.16.
22, 9: Dt 24, 17; 27, 19.
22, 10: Jb 18, 8ff.
22, 12: Jb 11, 8.

13* Yet you say, "What does God know?
    Can he judge through the thick darkness?
14 Clouds hide him so that he cannot see;
    he walks upon the vault of the heavens!"

15 Do you indeed keep to the ancient way
    trodden by worthless men,
16 Who were snatched away before their time;
    whose foundations a flood swept away?
17 These men said to God, "Depart from us!"
    and, "What can the Almighty do to us?"
18*† [Yet he had filled their houses with
    good things!
    But far be from me the mind of
    the impious!]
19* The just look on and are gladdened,
    and the innocent deride them:
20 "Truly these have been destroyed where
    they stood,
    and such as were left, fire has consumed!"

21 Come to terms with him to be at peace.
    In this shall good come to you:
22 Receive instruction from his mouth,
    and lay up his words in your heart.
23 If you return to the Almighty, you will
    be restored;
    if you put iniquity far from your tent,
24† And treat raw gold like dust,
    and the fine gold of Ophir as pebbles from
    the brook,
25 Then the Almighty himself shall be your gold
    and your sparkling silver.

26 For then you shall delight in the Almighty
    and you shall lift up your face toward God.
27* You shall entreat him and he will hear you,
    and your vows you shall fulfill.
28 When you make a decision, it shall succeed
    for you,
    and upon your ways the light shall shine.
29* For he brings down the pride of the haughty,
    but the man of humble mien he saves.
30* God delivers him who is innocent;
    you shall be delivered through cleanness
    of hands.

Job's Seventh Reply

23 ¹ Again Job answered and said:

2 Though I know my complaint is bitter,

his hand is heavy upon me in my groanings.
3 Oh, that today I might find him,
    that I might come to his judgment seat!
4 I would set out my cause before him,
    and fill my mouth with arguments;
5 I would learn the words with which he
    would answer,
    and understand what he would reply to me.
6 Even should he contend against me with his
    great power,
    yet, would that he himself might heed!
7 There the upright man might reason
    with him,
    and I should once and for all preserve
    my rights.

8 But if I go to the east, he is not there;
    or to the west, I cannot perceive him;
9 Where the north enfolds him, I behold him not;
    by the south he is veiled, and I see him not.
10* Yet he knows my way;
    if he proved me, I should come forth
    as gold.
11 My foot has always walked in his steps;
    his way I have kept and have not
    turned aside.
12 From the commands of his lips I have
    not departed;
    the words of his mouth I have treasured in
    my heart.
13* But he has decided, and who can say
    him nay?
    What he desires, that he does.
14 For he will carry out what is appointed
    for me;
    and many such things may yet be in
    his mind.
15 Therefore am I dismayed before him;
    when I take thought, I fear him.
16 Indeed God has made my courage fail;
    the Almighty has put me in dismay.
17 Yes, would that I had vanished in darkness,
    and that thick gloom were before me to
    conceal me.

24 ¹† Why are not times set by the Almighty,
    and why do his friends not see
    his days?
2 The wicked remove landmarks;
    they steal away herds and pasture them.

22, 18: A gloss, taken partly from Jb 21, 16.
22, 24: *Ophir:* cf note to Ps 45, 10.
24, 1: Why does not God favor his friends by the speedy punishment of his enemies? (The text and order of verses in this chapter are not certain; note the omission of v 9 which duplicates words of vv 2–4.)

22, 13f: Pss 10, 11; 73, 11; 94,
    7; Is 29, 15; Ez 8, 12;
    9, 9.
22, 18: Jb 21, 16.
22, 19: Ps 107, 42.
22, 27: Jb 33, 26.
22, 29: Ps 138, 6; Prv 29, 23;

Mt 23, 12; Lk 1, 52;
    Jas 4, 10; 1 Pt 5, 5.
22, 30: Jb 17, 9; Ps 18, 21.25.
23, 10: Ps 66, 10; Prv 17, 3;
    Mal 3, 3; 1 Pt 1, 7.
23, 13: Jb 42, 2; Ps 115, 3;
    135, 6.

did you KNOW?

A Long Debate

Why are Job's friends so insistent that sin and suffering are connected? Why do they go on, chapter after chapter, telling Job that his suffering is a punishment for his sins? The author of the Book of Job uses the debate of Job and his friends to contrast two positions. The position of Job's friends is that God rewards people who are good and punishes those who are wicked: if Job is suffering terribly, then Job must have sinned terribly. Job's repeated denial of sin reveals the second position, which is that sometimes innocent people suffer. This second position is harder to argue because it leaves a huge question: Why?

Because Job has too much integrity to repent for sins he never committed (Jb 27, 1–6), he keeps searching for another answer. Finally, Job makes an oath of innocence. Such an oath has God as its witness, and if it is false, it requires God to strike down the person who made it. But God appears to Job in an awesome show of power (chapters 38–41) and reminds Job that human intelligence is too limited to comprehend the deeper mysteries of creation. God alone knows why innocent people suffer; Job must trust God's plan.

Read chapters 20–24 to get a sense of the long debate in Job about human suffering. This debate reflects the long history of the Israelites wrestling with this complex question.

3   The asses of orphans they drive away;
     they take the widow's ox for a pledge.
4   They force the needy off the road;
     all the poor of the land are driven
       into hiding.
5   Like wild asses in the desert, these go forth
     to their task of seeking food;

     The steppe provides food for the young
       among them;
6   they harvest at night in the untilled land.
7   They pass the night naked, without clothing,
     for they have no covering against the cold;
8   They are drenched with the rain of
       the mountains,
     and for want of shelter they cling to
       the rock.
11   Between the rows they press out the oil;
     they glean in the vineyard of the wicked.
     They tread the wine presses, yet suffer thirst,
10   and famished are those who carry
       the sheaves.

12   From the dust the dying groan,
     and the souls of the wounded cry out
     [yet God does not treat it as unseemly].
13* There are those who are rebels against
       the light;
     they know not its ways;
     they abide not in its paths.
14   When there is no light the murderer rises,
     to kill the poor and needy.
15* The eye of the adulterer watches for the twilight;
     he says, "No eye will see me."
     In the night the thief roams about,
     and he puts a mask over his face;
16   in the dark he breaks into houses.
     By day they shut themselves in;
     none of them know the light,
17† for daylight they regard as darkness.

          * * *

18   Their portion in the land is accursed,
20   and wickedness is splintered like wood.
19.21. . . . .
22   To him who rises without assurance of his life
23   he gives safety and support.
     He sustains the mighty by his strength,
     and his eyes are on their ways.
24   They are exalted for a while, and then they
       are gone;
     they are laid low and, like all others, are
       gathered up;
     like ears of grain they shrivel.

          * * *

25   If this be not so, who will confute me,
     and reduce my argument to nought?

---

† **24, 17:** The asterisks which follow this verse mark off a passage (vv 18–24) which cannot be ascribed to Job with certainty. Vv 17–24 are in general poorly preserved; and much of vv 18–21 has not been translated because these verses are obscure. St. Jerome renders them as follows: (18) "He is light upon the face of the water, cursed be his portion on the earth; let him not walk by the way of vineyards. (19) Let him pass from the snow waters to excessive heat, and his sin even to hell. (20) Let mercy forget him; may worms be his sweetness; let him be remembered no more, but be broken in pieces as an unfruitful tree. (21) For he has fed the barren that bears not, and to the widow he has done no good."

24, 13: Jn 3, 19f.   24, 15: Prv 7, 9f.

Bildad's Third Speech

25

¹ Then Bildad the Shuhite answered and
said:

2　Dominion and awesomeness are his
　　who brings about harmony in his heavens.
³†　Is there any numbering of his troops?
　　Yet to which of them does not his
　　　light extend?
⁴*　How can a man be just in God's sight,
　　or how can any woman's child
　　　be innocent?
5　Behold, even the moon is not bright
　　and the stars are not clear in his sight.
⁶*　How much less man, who is but a maggot,
　　the son of man, who is only a worm?

Job's Reply

26

¹† Then Job spoke again and said:

2　What help you give to the powerless,
　　what strength to the feeble arm!
3　How you counsel, as though he had
　　　no wisdom;
　　how profuse is the advice you offer!
⁴*　With whose help have you uttered
　　　those words,
　　and whose is the breath that comes forth
　　　from you?
⁵*†The shades beneath writhe in terror,
　　the waters, and their inhabitants.
⁶*†Naked before him is the nether world,
　　and Abaddon has no covering.
⁷†　He stretches out the North over empty space,
　　and suspends the earth over nothing at all;
8　He binds up the waters in his clouds,
　　yet the cloud is not rent by their weight;
9　He holds back the appearance of the
　　　full moon
　　by spreading his clouds before it.

¹⁰*†He has marked out a circle on the surface of
　　the deep
　　as the boundary of light and darkness.

¹¹*　The pillars of the heavens tremble
　　and are stunned at his thunderous rebuke;
¹²†　By his power he stirs up the sea,
　　and by his might he crushes Rahab;
¹³*†With his angry breath he scatters the water,
　　and he hurls the lightning against
　　　it relentlessly;
　　His hand pierces the fugitive dragon
　　　as from his hand it strives to flee.
14　Lo, these are but the outlines of his ways,
　　and how faint is the word we hear!

Job's Reply

27

¹¹ I will teach you the manner of God's
　　　dealings,
　　and the way of the Almighty I will
　　　not conceal.
²*†As God lives, who withholds my deserts,
　　the Almighty, who has made bitter
　　　my soul,
3　So long as I still have life in me
　　and the breath of God is in my nostrils,
4　My lips shall not speak falsehood,
　　nor my tongue utter deceit!
⁵*　Far be it from me to account you right;
　　till I die I will not renounce my innocence.
6　My justice I maintain and I will not
　　　relinquish it;
　　my heart does not reproach me for any of
　　　my days.
7　Let my enemy be as the wicked
　　and my adversary as the unjust!
8　For what can the impious man expect when
　　　he is cut off,
　　when God requires his life?
9　Will God then attend to his cry
　　when calamity comes upon him?
10　Will he then delight in the Almighty
　　and call upon him constantly?
12　Behold, you yourselves have all seen it;
　　why then do you spend yourselves in
　　　idle words!

* * *

25, 3: *His troops:* the heavenly hosts, the stars or the angels. *His light:* compare the wording in Jb 24, 13: those who are rebels against the light.

26, 1–14: Probably to be read as Job's reply to Bildad's short speech. Some, however, would make it the reply to Zophar (Jb 27, 13–21); it would thus lead up to the poem of ch 28.

26, 5: *Shades:* the dead in Sheol, the nether world; cf Pss 6, 6; 88, 11.

26, 6: *Nether world:* cf note to Ps 6, 6. *Abaddon:* Hebrew for "(place of) destruction," a synonym for *nether world:* cf Jb 28, 22; Rv 9, 11.

26, 7: *The North:* used here as a synonym for the firmament, the heavens; cf Is 14, 13.

26, 10: *Circle:* the horizon of the ocean which serves as the boundary for the activity of light and darkness.

26, 12: *Rahab:* cf Jb 9, 13; see note on Ps 89, 11.

26, 13: *The fugitive dragon:* the same term occurs in Is 27, 1 in apposition to Leviathan; see note on Jb 3, 8. This is actually Jb 27, 22.

27, 2–12: This is probably to be read as Job's reply to Zophar's speech of Jb 27, 13–21. In the current Hebrew text the heading for this chapter (Jb 27, 1, here omitted) is identical with Jb 29, 1; we should expect rather such a heading as is Jb 21, 1; 23, 1; 26, 1.

25, 4: Jb 4, 17ff; 9, 2.	26, 11: Jb 9, 6.
25, 6: Jb 4, 19; 15, 16.	26, 13: Is 27, 1.
26, 4: Gn 2, 7.	27, 2: Jb 34, 5.
26, 5: Prv 9, 18.	27, 5: Jb 2, 3.9; 13, 15;
26, 6: Ps 139, 7–12.	33, 9.
26, 10: Jb 38, 8–11; Prv 8, 29.	

13*†This is the portion of a wicked man
　　　from God,
　　　the inheritance an oppressor receives from
　　　the Almighty:

14　Though his children be many, the sword is
　　　their destiny.
　　　His offspring shall not be filled
　　　with bread.

15　His survivors, when they die, shall have
　　　no burial,
　　　and their widows shall not be mourned.

16　Though he heap up silver like dust
　　　and store away mounds of clothing,

17　What he has stored the just man shall wear,
　　　and the innocent shall divide the silver.

18　He builds his house as of cobwebs,
　　　or like a booth put up by the vinekeeper.

19*　He lies down a rich man, one last time;
　　　he opens his eyes and nothing remains
　　　to him.

20　Terrors rush upon him by day;
　　　at night the tempest carries him off.

21†　The storm wind seizes him and
　　　he disappears;
　　　it sweeps him out of his place.

* * *

The Inaccessibility of Wisdom

28 1† There is indeed a mine for silver,
　　　and a place for gold which men refine.

2　Iron is taken from the earth,
　　　and copper is melted out of stone.

4　. . . . .

5　The earth, though out of it comes forth
　　　bread,
　　　is in fiery upheaval underneath.

6　Its stones are the source of sapphires,
　　　and there is gold in its dust.

12*　But whence can wisdom be obtained,
　　　and where is the place of understanding?

13　Man knows nothing to equal it,
　　　nor is it to be had in the land of the living.

15*　Solid gold cannot purchase it,

　　　nor can its price be paid with silver.

16†　It cannot be bought with gold of Ophir,
　　　with the precious onyx or the sapphire.

17　Gold or crystal cannot equal it,
　　　nor can golden vessels reach its worth.

18　Neither coral nor jasper should be thought of;
　　　it surpasses pearls and 19 Arabian topaz.

20　Whence, then, comes wisdom,
　　　and where is the place of
　　　understanding?

21　It is hid from the eyes of any beast;
　　　from the birds of the air it is concealed.

7　The path to it no bird of prey knows,
　　　nor has the hawk's eye seen that path.

8　The proud beasts have not trodden it,
　　　nor has the lion gone that way.

14　The abyss declares, "It is not in me";
　　　and the sea says, "I have it not."

22†　Abaddon and Death say,
　　　"Only by rumor have we heard of it."

23*　God knows the way to it;
　　　it is he who is familiar with its place.*

24　For he beholds the ends of the earth
　　　and sees all that is under the heavens.

3　He has set a boundary for the darkness;
　　　to the farthest confines he penetrates.

9　He sets his hand to the flinty rock,
　　　and overturns the mountains at
　　　their foundations.

10　He splits channels in the rocks;
　　　his eyes behold all that is precious.

11　He probes the wellsprings of the streams,
　　　and brings hidden things to light.

25　He has weighed out the wind,
　　　and fixed the scope of the waters;

26*　When he made rules for the rain
　　　and a path for the thunderbolts,

27　Then he saw wisdom and appraised it,
　　　gave it its setting, knew it through
　　　and through.

28*　And to man he said:
　　　Behold, the fear of the LORD is wisdom;
　　　and avoiding evil is understanding.

---

† 　**27, 13–21:** This is probably to be read as Zophar's third speech. The asterisks are present to indicate it is not likely that the sacred writer intended these words to be ascribed to Job.
　　27, 21: The Hebrew has two more verses: v 22 (read above with Jb 26, 13); and v 23, which is a variant form of v 21.
　　28, 1–28: Note the changed order of verses; v 4 is uncertain.
　　This chapter contains a beautifully vivid description of that Wisdom which is beyond the attainment of creatures; known only to God, it is reflected in the order and majesty of his creation. Man, however, can, in a way, participate in this Wisdom by fearing the LORD and avoiding evil. Scholars are not agreed regarding the authorship of this poem, though it is altogether worthy of the author of the Book of Job. Used here as a counterpoise to ch 3 at the begin-

ning of the dialogue, it may have been first conceived as an independent poem.
　　28, 16: *Ophir:* cf note to Ps 45, 10.
　　28, 22: *Abaddon:* cf note to Jb 26, 6.

27, 13: Jb 20, 4–29.
27, 19: Pss 49, 18; 76, 6.
28, 12: Eccl 7, 24f; Bar 3,
　　14f.29–33.
28, 15: Prv 3, 14; 8, 10f.19;
　　16, 16; Wis 7, 7–11.
28, 23–27: Prv 8, 22–31.
28, 23: Prv 2, 6; Sir 1, 1;
　　Jas 1, 5.
28, 26: Jb 38, 25; Prv 3, 20.
28, 28: Ps 111, 10; Prv 1, 7; 9,
　　10; Sir 1, 16.

V: Job's Final Summary of His Cause

29 ¹ Job took up his theme anew and said:

2* Oh, that I were as in the months past!
    as in the days when God watched over me,

3 While he kept his lamp shining above
    my head,
    and by his light I walked through darkness;

4 As I was in my flourishing days,
    when God sheltered my tent;

5 When the Almighty was yet with me,
    and my children were round about me;

6† When my footsteps were bathed in milk,
    and the rock flowed with streams of oil;

7 When I went forth to the gate of the city
    and set up my seat in the square—

8 Then the young men saw me and withdrew,
    while the elders rose up and stood;

9* The chief men refrained from speaking
    and covered their mouths with their hands;

10 The voice of the princes was silenced,
    and their tongues stuck to the roofs of
    their mouths.

21 For me they listened and waited;
    they were silent for my counsel.

22 Once I spoke, they said no more,
    but received my pronouncement drop
    by drop.

23 They waited for me as for the rain;
    they drank in my words like the
    spring rains.

24 When I smiled on them they were reassured;
25   mourners took comfort from my
    cheerful glance.
I chose out their way and presided;
    I took a king's place in the armed forces.

11 Whoever heard of me blessed me;
    those who saw me commended me.

12 For I rescued the poor who cried out for
    help,
    the orphans, and the unassisted;

13 The blessing of those in extremity came
    upon me,
    and the heart of the widow I made joyful.

14 I wore my honesty like a garment;

justice was my robe and my turban.

15 I was eyes to the blind,
    and feet to the lame was I;

16 I was a father to the needy;
    the rights of the stranger I studied,

17 And I broke the jaws of the wicked man;
    from his teeth I forced the prey.

18† Then I said: "In my own nest I shall grow old;
    I shall multiply years like the phoenix.

19 My root is spread out to the waters;
    the dew rests by night on my branches.

20 My glory is fresh within me,
    and my bow is renewed in my hand!"

30 ¹* But now they hold me in derision
    who are younger in years than I;
Whose fathers I should have disdained
    to rank with the dogs of my flock.

2 Such strength as they had, to me
    meant nought;
    they were utterly destitute.

3* In want and hunger was their lot,
    they who fled to the parched wastelands:

4† They plucked saltwort and shrubs;
    the roots of the broom plant were
    their food.

5 They were banished from among men,
    with an outcry like that against a thief—

6 To dwell on the slopes of the wadies,
    in caves of sand and stone;

7 Among the bushes they raised their
    raucous cry;
    under the nettles they huddled together.

8 Irresponsible, nameless men,
    they were driven out of the land.

9* Yet now they sing of me in mockery;
    I am become a byword among them.

10 They abhor me, they stand aloof from me,
    they do not hesitate to spit in my face!

11 Indeed, they have loosed their bonds; they
    lord it over me,
    and have thrown off restraint in my presence.

12 To subvert my paths they rise up;
    they build their approaches for my ruin.

13 To destroy me, they attack with none to
    stay them;

---

† **29, 6:** Hyperbole to express abundance; see note on Jb 20, 17.
29, 18: *Phoenix:* a legendary bird which, after several centuries of life, consumed itself in fire, then rose from its ashes in youthful freshness. This meaning, originally intended in the Greek, later came to mean "palm tree." Some render the Hebrew as "sand."
30, 4: *Saltwort:* found in salt marshes and very sour to the taste; eaten by the extremely poor as a cooked vegetable. *Broom plant:* the

juniper or brushwood; cf Ps 120, 4; a figure of bitterness and poverty, because of its bitter-tasting roots which are practically inedible.

29, 2: Jb 1, 10.   30, 3–8: Jb 24, 5f.
29, 9: Wis 8, 10ff.   30, 9: Jb 17, 6.
30, 1: Jb 12, 4; 19, 18.

Hey, God! Did You Hear Me?

How do we know that God hears and answers our prayers? The Books of Job and the Psalms describe many instances of both cries for help and God's responses to those cries. In our day-to-day reality, however, we can't always tell when God is answering our prayers. It isn't like we walk by trees that burn and speak to us, hear whispers in the wind that call our name, or see and hear angels who give us God's answer. But God does hear and answer our prayers. One way to determine how God is answering our prayers is through discernment.

In the discernment process, an adult mentor or spiritual director can help you figure out what God is trying to say to you. If you don't already have someone who can help you in this way (like a priest, religion teacher, campus or youth minister, or parent), you can ask at your parish or school for help in finding an adult mentor. This spiritual director will be able to tell you more about the discernment process and whether it is the right process for you at this time in your life.

With a spiritual director, you will learn how to hear God's answers to your prayers.

▶ Jb 30, 20

---

14   as through a wide breach they advance.
Amid the uproar they come on in waves;
15   over me rolls the terror.
My dignity is borne off on the wind,
and my welfare vanishes like a cloud.
18† One with great power lays hold of
my clothing;
by the collar of my tunic he seizes me:
19   He has cast me into the mire;
I am leveled with the dust and ashes.

20* I cry to you, but you do not answer me;
you stand off and look at me,
21   Then you turn upon me without mercy
and with your strong hand you buffet me.
22   You raise me up and drive me before
the wind;
I am tossed about by the tempest.
23* Indeed I know you will turn me back in death
to the destined place of everyone alive.
24   Yet should not a hand be held out
to help a wretched man in his calamity?
25* Or have I not wept for the hardships
of others;
was not my soul grieved for the destitute?
26   Yet when I looked for good, then evil came;
when I expected light, then came darkness.

16   My soul ebbs away from me;

27   days of affliction have overtaken me.
17   My frame takes no rest by night;
my inward parts seethe and will not
be stilled.
28   I go about in gloom, without the sun;
I rise up in public to voice my grief.

29   I have become the brother of jackals,
companion to the ostrich.
30   My blackened skin falls away from me;
the heat scorches my very frame.
31   My harp is turned to mourning,
and my reed pipe to sounds of weeping.

31   2 But what is man's lot from God above,
his inheritance from the Almighty
on high?
3   Is it not calamity for the unrighteous,
and woe for evildoers?
4* Does he not see my ways,
and number all my steps?
6* Let God weigh me in the scales of justice;
thus will he know my innocence!

5† If I have walked in falsehood
and my foot has hastened to deceit;
7   If my steps have turned out of the way,
and my heart has followed my eyes,
or any stain clings to my hands,

---

† 30, 18–23: Job here refers to God's stern treatment of him.
31, 5–34: Job's final protestation of his innocence.

* 30, 20: Jb 19, 7.
30, 23: Heb 9, 27.
30, 25: Jb 29, 12–16.

31, 4: Jb 14, 16; 34, 21; Ps
139, 3; Prv 5, 21.
31, 6: Jb 23, 10.

8   Then may I sow, but another eat of it,
    or may my planting be rooted up!

38 If my land has cried out against me
    till its very furrows complained;
39 If I have eaten its produce without payment
    and grieved the hearts of its tenants;
40 Then let the thistles grow instead of wheat
    and noxious weeds instead of barley!

1† If I have made an agreement with my eyes
    and entertained any thoughts against
        a maiden;
9   If my heart has been enticed toward a woman,
    and I have lain in wait at my
        neighbor's door;
10 Then may my wife grind for another,
    and may others cohabit with her!

11* For that would be heinous,
    a crime to be condemned;
12* A fire that should burn down to the abyss
    till it consumed all my possessions to
        the roots.
13 Had I refused justice to my manservant
    or to my maid, when they had a claim
        against me,
14 What then should I do when God rose up;
    what could I answer when he demanded
        an account?
15 Did not he who made me in the womb
        make him?
    Did not the same One fashion us before
        our birth?

16* If I have denied anything to the poor,
    or allowed the eyes of the widow
        to languish
17 While I ate my portion alone,
    with no share in it for the fatherless,
18 Though like a father God has reared me from
        my youth,
    guiding me even from my
        mother's womb—
19 If I have seen a wanderer without clothing,
    or a poor man without covering,
20 Whose limbs have not blessed me

when warmed with the fleece of my sheep;
21† If I have raised my hand against the innocent
    because I saw that I had supporters at
        the gate—
22 Then may my arm fall from the shoulder,
    my forearm be broken at the elbow!
23 For the dread of God will be upon me,
    and his majesty will overpower me.
24 Had I put my trust in gold
    or called fine gold my security;
25 Or had I rejoiced that my wealth was great,
    or that my hand had acquired abundance—
26*†Had I looked upon the sun as it shone,
    or the moon in the splendor of its progress,
27 And had my heart been secretly enticed
    to waft them a kiss with my hand;
28* This too would be a crime for condemnation,
    for I should have denied God above.

29* Had I rejoiced at the destruction of my enemy
    or exulted when evil fell upon him,
30 Even though I had not suffered my mouth
        to sin
    by uttering a curse against his life—

31† Had not the men of my tent exclaimed,
    "Who has not been fed with his meat!"
32 Because no stranger lodged in the street,
    but I opened my door to wayfarers—

33† Had I, out of human weakness, hidden
        my sins
    and buried my guilt in my bosom
34 Because I feared the noisy multitude
    and the scorn of the tribes terrified me—
    then I should have remained silent, and not
        come out of doors!

35* Oh, that I had one to hear my case,
    and that my accuser would write out
        his indictment!
36† Surely, I should wear it on my shoulder
    or put it on me like a diadem;
37† Of all my steps I should give him an account;
    like a prince I should present myself
        before him.

This is my final plea; let the Almighty answer me!
The words of Job are ended.

† ———————
  31, 1.9: Note the gradation: avoidance of sinful glances and
thoughts against a maiden; desire for another's wife.
  31, 21: *Gate:* cf notes on Jb 5, 4; Ru 4, 1.
  31, 26ff: Job never sinned by worshiping the sun or the moon;
waft them a kiss: an act of idolatrous worship.
  31, 31: The members of his household will testify to his hospitality.
  31, 33f: Job's present protest is made, not in spite of hidden sins
which he had been unwilling to disclose, but out of genuine innocence.
  31, 36: *On my shoulder:* i.e., boldly, proudly.

  31, 37: *Like a prince:* not as a frightened criminal. *Final plea:* literally, "tau," the last letter of the Hebrew alphabet; in the current
Hebrew text this line is in v 35, while the following one ends v 40.

* ———————
  31, 11: Ex 20, 14; Lv 20, 10;   **31, 26f:** Dt 4, 19.
        Dt 22, 22.   **31, 28:** Dt 17, 2–7.
  31, 12: Sir 9, 8f.   **31, 29:** Prv 24, 17.
  31, 16–23: Jb 29, 12–16.   **31, 35:** Jb 19, 23; 23, 3–7.

VI: Elihu's Speeches

32 ¹* Then the three men ceased to answer Job, because he was righteous in his own eyes. ²*† But the anger of Elihu, son of Barachel the Buzite, of the family of Ram, was kindled. He was angry with Job for considering himself rather than God to be in the right. ³* He was angry also with the three friends because they had not found a good answer and had not condemned Job. ⁴ But since these men were older than he, Elihu bided his time before addressing Job. ⁵ When, however, Elihu saw that there was no reply in the mouths of the three men, his wrath was inflamed. ⁶ So Elihu, son of Barachel the Buzite, spoke out and said:

> I am young and you are very old;
>> therefore I held back and was afraid
>> to declare to you my knowledge.
> ⁷* Days should speak, I thought,
>> and many years teach wisdom!
> ⁸* But it is a spirit in man,
>> the breath of the Almighty, that gives
>> him understanding.
> ⁹ It is not those of many days who are wise,
>> nor the aged who understand the right.
> ¹⁰ Therefore I say, hearken to me;
>> let me too set forth my knowledge!

> ¹¹ Behold, I have waited for your
>> discourses,
>> and have given ear to your arguments.
> ¹² Yes, I followed you attentively
>> as you searched out what to say;
>> And behold, there is none who has
>> convicted Job,
>> not one of you who could refute
>> his statements.
> ¹³† Yet do not say, "We have met wisdom.
>> God may vanquish him but not man!"
> ¹⁴ For had he addressed his words to me,
>> I should not then have answered him as
>> you have done.

> ¹⁵ They are dismayed, they make no more reply;
>> words fail them.
> ¹⁶ Must I wait? Now that they speak no more,
>> and have ceased to make reply,
> ¹⁷ I too will speak my part;
>> I also will show my knowledge!

> ¹⁸ For I am full of matters to utter;
>> the spirit within me compels me.
> ¹⁹ Like a new wineskin with wine
>> under pressure,
>> my bosom is ready to burst.
> ²⁰ Let me speak and obtain relief;
>> let me open my lips, and make reply.
> ²¹ I would not be partial to anyone,
>> nor give flattering titles to any.
> ²² For I know nought of flattery;
>> if I did, my Maker would soon take
>> me away.

But it is a spirit in man, the breath of the Almighty, that gives him understanding. 32, 8

33 ¹ Therefore, O Job, hear my discourse,
>> and hearken to all my words.
> ² Behold, now I open my mouth;
>> my tongue and my voice form words.
> ³ I will state directly what is in my mind,
>> my lips shall utter knowledge sincerely;
> ⁴* For the spirit of God has made me,
>> the breath of the Almighty keeps me alive.

> ⁵ If you are able, refute me;
>> draw up your arguments and stand forth.
> ⁶* Behold I, like yourself, have been taken
>> from the same clay by God.
> ⁷ Therefore no fear of me should dismay you,
>> nor should my presence weigh heavily
>> upon you.

> ⁸ But you have said in my hearing,
>> as I listened to the sound of your words:

---

† **32, 2:** Elihu means "My God is he." This speaker was from Buz, which, according to Jer 25, 23, was near Tema and Dedan. A young man, he impetuously and impatiently upbraids Job for his boldness toward God, and the three friends for not successfully answering Job. He undertakes to defend God's absolute justice and to explain more clearly why there is suffering. While fundamentally his position is the same as that of the three friends, he does locate more definitely, though not perfectly, the place of suffering in the divine plan.
32, 13: *Met wisdom:* in Job's arguments.

32, 1: Jb 33, 9.
32, 2: Jb 13, 18; 27, 6; 34, 5; 35, 2.
32, 3: Jb 22, 5.
32, 7: Jb 12, 12.
32, 8: Jb 33, 4.
33, 4: Jb 32, 8.
33, 6: Jb 31, 15.

9* "I am clean and without transgression;
　　I am innocent; there is no guilt in me.
10* Yet he invents pretexts against me
　　and reckons me as his enemy.
11* He puts my feet in the stocks;
　　he watches all my ways!"

12 In this you are not just, let me tell you;
　　for God is greater than man.
13* Why, then, do you make complaint
　　　against him
　　that he gives no account of his doings?
14 For God does speak, perhaps once,
　　or even twice, though one perceive it not.

15 In a dream, in a vision of the night,
　　[when deep sleep falls upon men]
　　as they slumber in their beds,
16 It is then he opens the ears of men
　　and as a warning to them, terrifies them;
17 By turning man from evil
　　and keeping pride away from him,
18 He withholds his soul from the pit
　　and his life from passing to the grave.

19 Or a man is chastened on his bed by pain
　　and unceasing suffering within his frame,
20* So that to his appetite food
　　　becomes repulsive,
　　and his senses reject the choicest
　　　nourishment.
21 His flesh is wasted so that it cannot be seen,
　　and his bones, once invisible, appear;
22 His soul draws near to the pit,
　　his life to the place of the dead.

23† If then there be for him an angel,
　　one out of a thousand, a mediator,
　　To show him what is right for him
　　and bring the man back to justice,
24 He will take pity on him and say,
　　"Deliver him from going down to
　　　the pit;
　　I have found him a ransom."

25 Then his flesh shall become soft as a boy's;
　　he shall be again as in the days of
　　　his youth.
26* He shall pray and God will favor him;

he shall see God's face with rejoicing.
27 He shall sing before men and say,
　　"I sinned and did wrong,
　　yet he has not punished me accordingly.
28 He delivered my soul from passing to the pit,
　　and I behold the light of life."

29 Lo, all these things God does,
　　twice, or thrice, for a man,
30 Bringing back his soul from the pit
　　to the light, in the land of the living.
31 Be attentive, O Job; listen to me!
　　Be silent and I will speak.
32 If you have aught to say, then answer me.
　　Speak out! I should like to see you
　　　justified.
33 If not, then do you listen to me;
　　be silent while I teach you wisdom.

34

1 Then Elihu continued and said:

2 Hear, O wise men, my discourse,
　　and you that have knowledge, hear me!
3* For the ear tests words,
　　as the taste does food.
4 Let us discern for ourselves what is right;
　　let us learn between us what is good.
5* For Job has said, "I am innocent,
　　but God has taken what is my due.
6* Notwithstanding my right I am set at nought;
　　in my wound the arrow rankles, sinless
　　　though I am."

7 What man is like Job?
　　He drinks in blasphemies like water,
8 Keeps company with evildoers
　　and goes along with wicked men,
9* When he says, "It profits a man nought
　　that he is pleasing to God."

10* Therefore, men of understanding, hearken
　　　to me:
　　far be it from God to do wickedness;
　　far from the Almighty to do wrong!
11* Rather, he requites men for their conduct,
　　and brings home to a man his way of life.
12* Surely, God cannot act wickedly,
　　the Almighty cannot violate justice.
13* Who gave him government over the earth,
　　or who else set all the land in its place?

---

†
33, 23: *Angel:* one of the thousands who stand between God and man as intermediaries, reminding man of his duties and giving God an account of their fulfillment.

33, 9: Jb 10, 7; 13, 18; 27,
　5f; 29, 14; 32, 1; 34, 5.
33, 10: Jb 13, 24; 19, 11.
33, 11: Jb 13, 27; 31, 4.

33, 13: Jb 31, 35.
33, 20: Jb 6, 7.
33, 26: Jb 22, 26–29.
34, 3: Jb 12, 11.
34, 5: Jb 33, 9f.
34, 6: Jb 9, 20.
34, 9: Jb 9, 22f.30f; 21, 15;

35, 3.
34, 10: Jb 36, 23.
34, 11: Ps 62, 13; Prv 24, 12;
　Mt 16, 27; Rom 2, 6;
　2 Cor 5, 10; Rv 22, 12.
34, 12: Jb 8, 3.
34, 13: Jb 38, 4–7.

14 If he were to take back his spirit to himself,
     withdraw to himself his breath,

15* All flesh would perish together,
     and man would return to the dust.

16 Now, do you, O Job, hear this!
     Hearken to the words I speak!

17 Can an enemy of justice indeed be in control,
     or will you condemn the supreme
         Just One,

18 Who says to a king, "You are worthless!"
     and to nobles, "You are wicked!"

19* Who neither favors the person of princes,
     nor respects the rich more than the
         poor?
     For they are all the work of his hands;

20*   in a moment they die, even at midnight.
     He brings on nobles, and takes them away,
         removing the powerful without lifting
         a hand;

21 For his eyes are upon the ways of man,
     and he beholds all his steps.

22 There is no darkness so dense
     that evildoers can hide in it.

25 Therefore he discerns their works;
     he turns at night and crushes them.

23 For he forewarns no man of his time
     to come before God in judgment.

24* Without a trial he breaks the mighty,
     and sets others in their stead,

27 Because they turned away from him
     and heeded none of his ways,

28 But caused the cries of the poor to reach him,
     so that he heard the plea of the afflicted.

29† If he remains tranquil, who then can
         condemn?
     If he hides his face, who then can
         behold him?

30 . . . .

31 When anyone says to God,
     "I was misguided; I will offend no more.

32 Teach me wherein I have sinned;
     if I have done wrong, I will do so
         no more,"

33 Would you then say that God must punish,
     since you reject what he is doing?

It is you who must choose, not I;
     speak, therefore, what you know.

34 Men of understanding will say to me,
     every wise man who hears my views:

35* "Job speaks without intelligence,
     and his words are without sense."

36 Let Job be tried to the limit,
     since his answers are those of the impious;

37 For he is adding rebellion to his sin
     by brushing off our arguments
     and addressing many words to God.

35

1 Then Elihu proceeded and said:

2* Do you think it right to say,
     "I am just rather than God"?

3* To say, "What does it profit me;
     what advantage have I more than if I
         had sinned?"

4† I have words for a reply to you
     and your three companions as well.

5 Look up to the skies and behold;
     regard the heavens high above you.

6 If you sin, what injury do you do to God?
     Even if your offenses are many, how do you
         hurt him?

7* If you are righteous, what do you give him,
     or what does he receive from your hand?

8 Your wickedness can affect only a man
         like yourself;
     and your justice only a fellow
         human being.

9 In great oppression men cry out;
     they call for help because of the power of
         the mighty,

10 Saying, "Where is God, my Maker,
     who has given visions in the night,

11 Taught us rather than the beasts of the earth,
     and made us wise rather than the birds of
         the heavens?"

12 Though thus they cry out, he answers not
     against the pride of the wicked.

13 But it is idle to say God does not hear
     or that the Almighty does not take notice.

14† Even though you say that you see him not,
     the case is before him; with trembling
         should you wait upon him.

34, 26.29f: The extant Hebrew text of these verses contains several added phrases which either represent duplication or are very obscure.

35, 4: *A reply to you:* Elihu refers to Job's statement that the innocent suffer as much as the wicked, and especially to Eliphaz's words in Jb 22, 2f.

35, 14f: The text here is uncertain. It seems to indicate that Job should have realized God's indifference is only apparent, and that, because he has not done so, God will punish him.

34, 15: Jb 10, 9.
34, 19: Dt 10, 17; 2 Chr 19, 7;
     Wis 6, 7; Acts 10, 34;
     Rom 2, 11; Eph 6, 9;
     Col 3, 25; 1 Pt 1, 17.
34, 20: Jb 21, 3.

34, 24: Ps 2, 9.
34, 35: Jb 35, 16; 38, 2; 42, 3.
35, 2: Jb 32, 2.
35, 3: Jb 34, 9.
35, 7: Jb 22, 3; 41, 2; Lk 17,
     10; Rom 11, 35.

15 But now that you have done otherwise, God's
    anger punishes,
    nor does he show concern that a man
      will die.

16* Yet Job to no purpose opens his mouth,
    and without knowledge multiplies
      words.

36

1 Elihu proceeded further and said:

2 Wait yet a little and I will instruct you,
    for there are still words to be said on
      God's behalf.

3 I will bring my knowledge from afar,
    and to my Maker I will accord the right.

4 For indeed, my theme cannot fail me:
    the one perfect in knowledge I set
      before you.

5† Behold, God rejects the obstinate
    in heart;
    he preserves not the life of the wicked,

6* He withholds not the just man's rights,
    but grants vindication to the oppressed

7* And with kings upon thrones
    he sets them, exalted forever.

8 Or if they are bound with fetters
    and held fast by bonds of affliction,

9 Then he makes known to them what they
    have done
    and their sins of boastful pride.

10 He opens their ears to correction
    and exhorts them to turn back from evil.

11 If they obey and serve him,
    they spend their days in prosperity,
    their years in happiness.

12† But if they obey not, they perish;
    they die for lack of knowledge.

13 The impious in heart lay up anger
    for themselves;
    they cry not for help when he
      enchains them;

14† Therefore they expire in youth,
    and perish among the reprobate.

15 But he saves the unfortunate through
    their affliction,
    and instructs them through distress.

16-20† . . . .

21 Take heed, turn not to evil;
    for you have preferred carousal to affliction.

22 Behold, God is sublime in his power.
    What teacher is there like him?

23* Who prescribes for him his conduct,
    or who can say, "You have done wrong"?

24 Remember, you should extol his work,
    which men have praised in song.

25 All men contemplate it;
    man beholds it from afar.

26 Lo, God is great beyond our knowledge;
    the number of his years is past
      searching out.

27 He holds in check the waterdrops
    that filter in rain through his mists,

28 Till the skies run with them
    and the showers rain down on mankind.

31† For by these he nourishes the nations,
    and gives them food in abundance.

29.30† Lo! he spreads the clouds in layers
    as the carpeting of his tent.

32 In his hands he holds the lightning,
    and he commands it to strike the mark.

33 His thunder speaks for him
    and incites the fury of the storm.

37

1 At this my heart trembles
    and leaps out of its place,

2† To hear his angry voice
    as it rumbles forth from his mouth!

3 Everywhere under the heavens he sends it,
    with his lightning, to the ends of the earth.

4 Again his voice roars—
    the majestic sound of his thunder.

5 He does great things beyond our knowing;
    wonders past our searching out.

6 For he says to the snow, "Fall to the earth";
    likewise to his heavy, drenching rain.

7 He shuts up all mankind indoors;
8   the wild beasts take to cover
    and remain quietly in their dens.

36, 5–21: Perhaps this section should be read between vv 6 and 7 of chapter 34.

36, 12: *Knowledge:* practical wisdom in serving God, which they lack because they refused it when warned (cf v 10).

36, 14: *Reprobate:* cf Dt 23, 18f.

36, 16–20: The Hebrew text here is in disorder. The Vulgate has: "(16) Therefore he will give you most ample salvation from the narrow mouth which has no foundations beneath it; but the repose of your table will be filled with fatness. (17) Your case has been judged as that of the wicked; case and judgment you will receive. (18) Let no wrath, then, overcome you, that you oppress anyone; nor let nu- merous gifts mislead you. (19) Lay down your greatness without tribulation, and all who are mighty in strength. (20) Do not draw out the night, that people may go in place of them."

36, 31: *These:* refers to the showers of v 28, if the verse order in- dicated above is correct.

36, 29f: Because of the uncertainty of the text, no translation of these verses has received unanimous approval from exegetes.

37, 2: *Voice:* the thunder.

35, 16: Jb 34, 35; 38, 2; 42, 3.   36, 7: Ps 113, 7f.
36, 6: Ps 72, 4.12f.   36, 23: Jb 34, 10; Is 40, 13.

J
B

9† Out of its chamber comes forth the tempest;
      from the north winds, the cold.
10* With his breath God brings the frost,
      and the broad waters become congealed.
11 With hail, also, the clouds are laden,
      as they scatter their flashes of light.
12† He it is who changes their rounds, according
      to his plans,
      in their task upon the surface of the earth,
13   whether for punishment or mercy, as
      he commands.

14 Hearken to this, O Job!
      Stand and consider the wondrous works
      of God!
15 Do you know how God lays his commands
      upon them,
      and makes the light shine forth from
      his clouds?
16 Do you know how the clouds are banked,
      the wondrous work of him who is perfect
      in knowledge?
17 You, whom the streams of water fail
      when a calm from the south comes over
      the land,
18† Do you spread out with him the firmament of
      the skies,
      hard as a brazen mirror?

19 Teach us then what we shall say to him;
      we cannot, for the darkness, make our plea.
20† Will he be told about it when I speak,
      or when a man says he is being destroyed?
21† Nay, rather, it is as the light which men
      see not
      while it is obscured among the clouds,
      till the wind comes by and sweeps the
      clouds away.
22† From the North the splendor comes,
      surrounding God's awesome majesty!
23 The Almighty! we cannot discover him,
      pre-eminent in power and judgment;
      his great justice owes no one an accounting.
24 Therefore men revere him,
      though none can see him, however wise
      their hearts.

?did you KNOW?

Heaven and Earth

The questions God asks Job about the formation of the cosmos (Jb 38, 4–38) give us a clue about how the ancient Israelites thought the universe was put together. They believed that God had created it in three levels: the heavens, which were contained in a giant vault above the earth; the earth itself, which was a disk that rested on the waters of the abyss; and the abyss, which was the underworld. Over time, the heavens and the earth developed symbolic meanings. The heavens became known as the place where God dwells and the earth as the place that humans inhabit. Even later, the abyss became known as the place of the dead.

▶ Jb 38, 4–38

VII: The LORD's Speech

38 1† Then the LORD addressed Job out of the storm and said:

2   Who is this that obscures divine plans
      with words of ignorance?
3*†Gird up your loins now, like a man;
      I will question you, and you tell me
      the answers!
4   Where were you when I founded the earth?
      Tell me, if you have understanding.
5   Who determined its size; do you know?
      Who stretched out the measuring line for it?
6   Into what were its pedestals sunk,
      and who laid the cornerstone,

---

† **37, 9:** *Chamber:* where it was popularly believed storms were kept enclosed.
37, 12: *Their rounds:* of rain (Jb 36, 27), of clouds (Jb 36, 29f), of lightning and thunder (Jb 36, 32f), of snow (Jb 37, 6), of winds (Jb 37, 9).
37, 18: *The firmament . . . mirror:* the ancients thought of the sky as a ceiling above which were the "upper waters" (cf Gn 1, 6f; 7, 11); when this ceiling became as hard as metal, the usual rain failed to fall on the earth (cf Lv 26, 19; Dt 28, 23).
37, 20: Will an angel bring this to God's attention?
37, 21: Even though God seems not to know our circumstances, he does know them, just as surely as the sun shines, unseen by man, behind the clouds.

37, 22: Now the storms of doubt and ignorance disappear, and from the North, used here as a symbol for God's mysterious abode, comes the splendor of the manifestation of God's majestic ways.
38, 1: Now the LORD enters the debate and addresses two discourses (38–39 and 40–41) to Job, in which he speaks of his wisdom and power, which are altogether beyond the capacity of Job, who therefore should never dare to demand a reason for the divine actions. *Out of the storm:* frequently the background of the appearances of the LORD in the Old Testament; cf Pss 18; 50; Na 1, 3; Hb 3.
38, 3: *Gird up your loins:* prepare for combat—figuratively, be ready to defend yourself in debate.

37, 10: Ps 148, 17.   **38, 3:** Jb 40, 1.

J
B

7† While the morning stars sang in chorus
  and all the sons of God shouted for joy?

8* And who shut within doors the sea,
  when it burst forth from the womb;
9 When I made the clouds its garment
  and thick darkness its swaddling bands?
10 When I set limits for it
  and fastened the bar of its door,
11 And said: Thus far shall you come but
   no farther,
  and here shall your proud waves be stilled!

12 Have you ever in your lifetime commanded
   the morning
  and shown the dawn its place
13 For taking hold of the ends of the earth,
  till the wicked are shaken from its surface?
14 The earth is changed as is clay by the seal,
  and dyed as though it were a garment;
15 But from the wicked the light is withheld,
  and the arm of pride is shattered.

16 Have you entered into the sources of the sea,
  or walked about in the depths of the abyss?
17 Have the gates of death been shown to you,
  or have you seen the gates of darkness?
18 Have you comprehended the breadth of
   the earth?
  Tell me, if you know all:
19 Which is the way to the dwelling place
   of light,
  and where is the abode of darkness,
20 That you may take them to their boundaries
  and set them on their homeward paths?
21† You know, because you were born
   before them,
  and the number of your years is great!
22† Have you entered the storehouse of the snow,
  and seen the treasury of the hail
23 Which I have reserved for times of stress,
  for the days of war and of battle?
24 Which way to the parting of the winds,
  whence the east wind spreads over
   the earth?
25 Who has laid out a channel for the downpour
  and for the thunderstorm a path
26 To bring rain to no man's land,
  the unpeopled wilderness;
27 To enrich the waste and desolate ground

  till the desert blooms with verdure?
28 Has the rain a father;
  or who has begotten the drops of dew?
29 Out of whose womb comes the ice,
  and who gives the hoarfrost its birth in
   the skies,
30 When the waters lie covered as though
   with stone
  that holds captive the surface of the deep?
31† Have you fitted a curb to the Pleiades,
  or loosened the bonds of Orion?
32 Can you bring forth the Mazzaroth in
   their season,
  or guide the Bear with its train?
33 Do you know the ordinances of the heavens;
  can you put into effect their plan on the earth?

34† Can you raise your voice among the clouds,
  or veil yourself in the waters of the storm?
35† Can you send forth the lightnings on
   their way,
  or will they say to you, "Here we are"?
37 Who counts the clouds in his wisdom?
  Or who tilts the water jars of heaven
38 So that the dust of earth is fused into a mass
  and its clods made solid?
39 Do you hunt the prey for the lioness
  or appease the hunger of her cubs,
40 While they crouch in their dens,
  or lie in wait in the thicket?
36† Who puts wisdom in the heart,
  and gives the cock its understanding?
41* Who provides nourishment for the ravens
  when their young ones cry out to God,
  and they rove abroad without food?

39 ¹ Do you know about the birth of the
   mountain goats,
  watch for the birth pangs of the hinds,
2 Number the months that they must fulfill,
  and fix the time of their bringing forth?
3 They crouch down and bear their young;
  they deliver their progeny in the desert.
4 When their offspring thrive and grow,
  they leave and do not return.

5 Who has given the wild ass his freedom,
  and who has loosed him from bonds?
6 I have made the wilderness his home

---

†
38, 7: *Sons of God:* angels; cf Jb 1, 6.
38, 21: Divine irony.
38, 22f: *Hail . . . of war:* thus God used a hailstorm to rout
Joshua's foes in the battle of Gibeon; cf Jos 10, 11; Sir 46, 5.
38, 31f: *Pleiades . . . Orion . . . Bear:* cf Jb 9, 9. *Mazzaroth:* it is
uncertain what astronomical group is meant by this Hebrew word;
perhaps a southern constellation (cf Jb 9, 9).

38, 34: *Veil yourself . . . storm:* wrap yourself in a cloud, as God
comes in a theophany; cf Ps 18, 12.
38, 35: *Here we are:* at your service.
38, 36: *Understanding:* the reflection of divine Wisdom discernible in the created animal instincts of the cock.

*
38, 8: Gn 1, 9.   **38, 41:** Ps 147, 9.

J
B

and the salt flats his dwelling.
7 He scoffs at the uproar of the city,
   and hears no shouts of a driver.
8 He ranges the mountains for pasture,
   and seeks out every patch of green.

9 Will the wild ox consent to serve you,
   and to pass the nights by your manger?
10 Will a rope bind him in the furrow,
    and will he harrow the valleys after you?
11 Will you trust him for his great strength
    and leave to him the fruits of your toil?
12 Can you rely on him to thresh out your grain
    and gather in the yield of your
    threshing floor?
13† The wings of the ostrich beat idly;
    her plumage is lacking in pinions.
14† When she leaves her eggs on the ground
    and deposits them in the sand,
15 Unmindful that a foot may crush them,
    that the wild beasts may trample them,
16 She cruelly disowns her young
    and ruthlessly makes nought of her brood;
17 For God has withheld wisdom from her
    and has given her no share
    in understanding.
18 Yet in her swiftness of foot
    she makes sport of the horse and his rider.

19† Do you give the horse his strength,
    and endow his neck with splendor?
20 Do you make the steed to quiver
    while his thunderous snorting
    spreads terror?
21 He jubilantly paws the plain
    and rushes in his might against
    the weapons.
22 He laughs at fear and cannot be deterred;
    he turns not back from the sword.
23 Around him rattles the quiver,
    flashes the spear and the javelin.
24 Frenzied and trembling he devours
    the ground;
    he holds not back at the sound of
    the trumpet,
25 but at each blast he cries, "Aha!"
    Even from afar he scents the battle,
    the roar of the chiefs and the shouting.

26 Is it by your discernment that the hawk soars,
    that he spreads his wings toward the south?

27 Does the eagle fly up at your command
    to build his nest aloft?
28 On the cliff he dwells and spends the night,
    on a spur of the cliff or the fortress.
29 From thence he watches for his prey;
    his eyes behold it afar off.
30* His young ones greedily drink blood;
    where the slain are, there is he.

40 ¹ The LORD then said to Job:

2* Will we have arguing with the Almighty by
    the critic?
    Let him who would correct God give answer!

³ Then Job answered the LORD and said:

4 Behold, I am of little account; what can I
    answer you?
    I put my hand over my mouth.
5 Though I have spoken once, I will not do
    so again;
    though twice, I will do so no more.

⁶ Then the LORD addressed Job out of the storm
and said:

7 Gird up your loins now, like a man.
    I will question you, and you tell me
    the answers!
8 Would you refuse to acknowledge my right?
    Would you condemn me that you may
    be justified?
9 Have you an arm like that of God,
    or can you thunder with a voice like his?
10 Adorn yourself with grandeur and majesty,
    and array yourself with glory and splendor.
11 Let loose the fury of your wrath;
12 tear down the wicked and shatter them.
    Bring down the haughty with a glance;
13 bury them in the dust together;
    in the hidden world imprison them.
14 Then will I too acknowledge
    that your own right hand can save you.

15† See, besides you I made Behemoth,
    that feeds on grass like an ox.
16 Behold the strength in his loins,
    and his vigor in the sinews of his belly.
17 He carries his tail like a cedar;
    the sinews of his thighs are like cables.

39, 13: The wings of the ostrich cannot raise her from the ground,
but they help her to run swiftly.
39, 14ff: It was popularly believed that, because the ostrich laid
her eggs on the sand, she was thereby cruelly abandoning them;
cf Lam 4, 3.

39, 19–25: The famous description of a war horse.
40, 15: Behemoth: the hippopotamus.

39, 30: Mt 24, 28; Lk 17, 37.   **40, 2:** Jb 38, 3.

Too Big to Understand

All the questions God asks Job about creation and good and evil in Job, chapters 38–41, are intended to make one simple point: "You can never understand me. I am too big. You are too small."

The author of Job seems to be saying to readers, "If you think you've got God all figured out—like Job's friends thought they had or like even Job wanted to have—you're wrong." The author is reminding readers that God is a mystery —powerful and awesome beyond our imagination and control.

In your prayer, reflect or journal on the following questions:

- Do you expect God to provide you with happiness? peace? friends?
- What happens if God doesn't meet your expectations in the way you want them to be met? Can you let go of your expectations and trust in God's love? Why or why not?

▶ Job, chapters 38–41

---

18   His bones are like tubes of bronze;
         his frame is like iron rods.

19   He came at the beginning of God's ways,
         and was made the taskmaster of
              his fellows;
20   For the produce of the mountains is brought
              to him,
         and of all wild animals he makes sport.
21   Under the lotus trees he lies,
         in coverts of the reedy swamp.
22   The lotus trees cover him with their shade;
         all about him are the poplars on the bank.
23   If the river grows violent, he is not disturbed;
         he is tranquil though the torrent surges
              about his mouth.
24† Who can capture him by his eyes,
         or pierce his nose with a trap?

25† Can you lead about Leviathan with a hook,

or curb his tongue with a bit?
26   Can you put a rope into his nose,
         or pierce through his cheek with a gaff?
27   Will he then plead with you, time after time,
         or address you with tender words?
28   Will he make an agreement with you
         that you may have him as a slave forever?
29   Can you play with him, as with a bird?
         Can you put him in leash for
              your maidens?
30† Will the traders bargain for him?
         Will the merchants divide him up?

31   Can you fill his hide with barbs,
         or his head with fish spears?
32   Once you but lay a hand upon him,
         no need to recall any other conflict!

41
2†   Is he not relentless when aroused;
         who then dares stand before him?
1   Whoever might vainly hope to do so
         need only see him to be overthrown.
3   Who has assailed him and come off safe—
         who under all the heavens?

4   I need hardly mention his limbs,
         his strength, and the fitness of his armor.
5   Who can strip off his outer garment,
         or penetrate his double corselet?
6   Who can force open the doors of
              his mouth,
         close to his terrible teeth?
7   Rows of scales are on his back,
         tightly sealed together;
8   They are fitted each so close to the next
         that no space intervenes;
9   So joined one to another
         that they hold fast and cannot be parted.

10   When he sneezes, light flashes forth;
         his eyes are like those of the dawn.
11   Out of his mouth go forth firebrands;
         sparks of fire leap forth.
12   From his nostrils issues steam,
         as from a seething pot or bowl.
13   His breath sets coals afire;
         a flame pours from his mouth.
14   Strength abides in his neck,
         and terror leaps before him.

15.16 His heart is hard as stone:
         his flesh, as the lower millstone.

40, 24: Eyes . . . nose: the only exposed parts of the submerged beast.
40, 25: Leviathan here is the crocodile. But cf Jb 3, 8.
40, 30: Merchants: literally, "Canaanites," whose reputation for

trading was so widespread that their name came to be used for merchants; cf Prv 31, 24. The meaning of this verse is that the crocodile is too powerful a creature to be sold like common fish.
41, 2: Before him: some read, "before me," i.e., God; also in v 3.

Why?

So, that's it? God just shows up, overwhelms Job with a bunch of questions he can't answer, and then gives Job back double everything he lost? God doesn't even answer Job's question about why he had to suffer!

And what about *our* questions? Why do innocent children die? Why is someone we love taken from us? Why do people die from hunger in a world that has so much? Why did that plane crash? Why did our friend die?

Why was Job satisfied with God's response? Perhaps Job's mind and his heart struggled with God's answer, and his heart won. Maybe his heart told him to trust in God's love even when his mind couldn't understand the mystery of his suffering.

With Job, the Israelite people began to see the suffering of innocent people as mystery and not as punishment. In the New Testament, this suffering would continue to be seen as mystery but also as something more. The death of Jesus—the ultimate innocent suffering person—and his Resurrection led to the understanding that God ultimately brings good out of the suffering of faithful people (see Jn 12, 24–25 and the introduction to 1 Peter).

▶ Jb 38, 1—42, 6

17† When he rises up, the mighty are afraid;
   the waves of the sea fall back.
18 Should the sword reach him, it will
      not avail;
   nor will the spear, nor the dart, nor
      the javelin.
19 He regards iron as straw,
   and bronze as rotten wood.
20 The arrow will not put him to flight;
   slingstones used against him are
      but straws.
21 Clubs he esteems as splinters;
   he laughs at the crash of the spear.

22 His belly is sharp as pottery fragments;
   he spreads like a threshing sledge upon
      the mire.
23 He makes the depths boil like a pot;
   the sea he churns like perfume in
      a kettle.
24 Behind him he leaves a shining path;
   you would think the deep had the hoary
      head of age.
25 Upon the earth there is not his like,
   intrepid he was made.
26 All, however lofty, fear him;
   he is king over all proud beasts.

42 ¹ Then Job answered the LORD and said:
2† I know that you can do all things,
   and that no purpose of yours can
      be hindered.
3* I have dealt with great things that I do
      not understand;
   things too wonderful for me, which I
      cannot know.
5 I had heard of you by word of mouth,
   but now my eye has seen you.
6 Therefore I disown what I have said,
   and repent in dust and ashes.

VIII: Epilogue

Job's Restoration

7† And it came to pass after the LORD had spoken these words to Job, that the LORD said to Eliphaz the Temanite, "I am angry with you and with your two friends; for you have not spoken rightly concerning me, as has my servant Job. 8† Now, therefore, take seven bullocks and seven rams, and go to my servant Job, and offer up a holocaust for yourselves; and let my servant Job pray for you; for his prayer I will accept, not to punish you

---

† **41, 17:** The text here is uncertain.
42, 2–6: In the current Hebrew text, this final utterance of Job is interrupted by words ascribed to God (vv 3f) which are in large part a duplication of Jb 38, 2f.
42, 7: The three friends of Job (Elihu is ignored in the Epilogue) are criticized by the LORD because they had (even though in good faith) leveled false charges against him.

42, 8: Job becomes the intercessor for his friends, as were other great Old Testament characters, e.g., Abraham and Moses, and as our Lord would be, whom he prefigured. *Seven:* a symbolic number.

42, 3: Jb 34, 35; 35, 16;
   38, 2.

severely. For you have not spoken rightly concerning me, as has my servant Job." 9 Then Eliphaz the Temanite, and Bildad the Shuhite, and Zophar the Naamathite, went and did as the LORD had commanded them. And the LORD accepted the intercession of Job.

10 Also, the LORD restored the prosperity of Job, after he had prayed for his friends; the LORD even gave to Job twice as much as he had before. 11† Then all his brethren and his sisters came to him, and all his former acquaintances, and they dined with him in his house. They condoled with him and comforted him for all the evil which the LORD had brought upon him; and each one gave him a piece of money and a gold ring.

12* Thus the LORD blessed the latter days of Job more than his earlier ones. For he had fourteen thousand sheep, six thousand camels, a thousand yoke of oxen, and a thousand she-asses. 13 And he had seven sons and three daughters, 14† of whom he called the first Jemimah, the second Keziah, and the third Keren-happuch. 15† In all the land no other women were as beautiful as the daughters of Job; and their father gave them an inheritance among their brethren. 16*† After this, Job lived a hundred and forty years; and he saw his children, his grandchildren, and even his great-grandchildren. 17 Then Job died, old and full of years.

---

† **42, 11:** *A piece of money:* the term is the same as that used in Gn 33, 19; Jos 24, 32. *Gold ring:* for the nose or ear.

42, 14: Job's daughters had names symbolic of their charms: Jemimah, dove; Keziah, precious perfume (cf Ps 45, 9); Kerenhappuch, cosmetic jar—more precisely, a container for a black powder that was used like modern mascara.

42, 15: Ordinarily daughters did not inherit property unless there were no sons; cf Nm 27, 1–11.

42, 16: As his other rewards were twice as much as he had before (v 10), so Job's hundred and forty years were double the expected span of human life; cf Ps 90, 10.

42, 12: Jb 1, 3.   **42, 16:** Jb 5, 25f.

Rock! Pop! Salsa! Rhythm and blues! Hip-hop! Rap! Jazz! Country! Alternative! We each have our own favorite music that somehow resonates with our being, and maybe even expresses our attitude and philosophy toward life. So much so that we often refer to it as *our* music, even though it was written by someone else. In the same way, we can say that the Psalms are Israel's music. They are the hymns or songs that Israel used in its Temple worship. They give voice to the souls of the Israelites and tell about the ups and downs of the Israelites' relationship with God.

At a Glance

Psalms is divided into five books without any particular organizing theme:

I. First Book
(Psalms 1—41).

II. Second Book
(Psalms 42—72).

III. Third Book
(Psalms 73—89).

IV. Fourth Book
(Psalms 90—106).

V. Fifth Book
(Psalms 107—150).

In-depth

The Hebrew version of Psalms is titled Tehillim, or Praises, because its hymns praise God. The Greek translation calls them Psalmoi, or Psalms, which means "religious songs performed to music." The 150 Psalms can be grouped into one or more of five general categories:

- The *hymns of praise and thanksgiving* sing of God's majesty, power, and wisdom (for example, Psalms 8, 24, 47, 93, 95–99, 113–118, 136, and 150).
- The *hymns of lament or petition* include both individual and communal cries to God for help in some need (for example, Psalms 38, 51, 55, 58, 59, 74, 78, 105, and 106).
- The *hymns of wisdom* sing of Israel's insights into how to live according to God's law and what brings true happiness (for example, Psalms 1, 34, 37, 49, 73, 112, and 128).
- The *liturgical or worship psalms* are used for entrance hymns at liturgies or during worship services at the Temple (for example, Psalms 15, 24, and 134).
- The *historical psalms* sing of the great wonders God has worked throughout the history of Israel (for example, Psalms 78, 105, 106, 135, and 136).

Quick Facts

Authors
many, sometimes called psalmists

Themes
a variety

Of Note
The psalms are used by Catholic Christians regularly at Mass and in the church's official prayer, the liturgy of the hours.

Because of King David's reputation for writing and performing music, he is named as the author of many of the Psalms. Actually, though, many of them were written long after his death. It is more accurate to understand the Psalms as a collection of songs that reflect different times and experiences throughout Israel's existence. Just as your favorite music might tell others what you value as a person, the Psalms tell us about Israel and its wondrous relationship with God.

The Book of *Psalms*

Psalms

FIRST BOOK — PSALMS 1–41

PSALM 1 †

True Happiness in God's Law

I

1† Happy those who do not follow
   the counsel of the wicked,
Nor go the way of sinners,
   nor sit in company with scoffers.*
2† Rather, the law of the LORD is their joy;
   God's law they study day and night.*
3 They are like a tree*
   planted near streams of water,
   that yields its fruit in season;
Its leaves never wither;
   whatever they do prospers.

II

4† But not the wicked!

They are like chaff driven by the wind.*
5 Therefore the wicked will not survive
      judgment,
   nor will sinners in the assembly of the just.
6 The LORD watches over the way of the just,*
   but the way of the wicked leads to ruin.

PSALM 2 †

A Psalm for a Royal Coronation

1 Why do the nations protest
   and the peoples grumble in vain?*
2† Kings on earth rise up
   and princes plot together
   against the LORD and his anointed:*
3 "Let us break their shackles
   and cast off their chains!"*
4 The one enthroned in heaven laughs;
   the LORD derides them,*

† **Ps 1:** A preface to the whole Book of Psalms, contrasting with striking similes the destiny of the good and the wicked. The psalm views life as activity, as choosing either the good or the bad. Each "way" brings its inevitable consequences. The wise through their good actions will experience rootedness and life, and the wicked, rootlessness and death.
1, 1: *Those:* literally, "the man." That word is used here and in many of the Psalms as typical, and therefore is translated "they." *The way:* a common biblical term for manner of living or moral conduct (Pss 32, 8; 101, 2.6; Prv 2, 20; 1 Kgs 8, 36).
1, 2: *The law of the LORD:* either the Torah, the first five books of the Bible, or, more probably, divine teaching or instruction.
1, 4: *The wicked:* those who by their actions distance themselves from God's life-giving presence.
Ps 2: A royal psalm. To rebellious kings (1–3) God responds vig-

orously (4–6). A speaker proclaims the divine decree (in the legal adoption language of the day), making the Israelite king the earthly representative of God (7–9) and warning kings to obey (10–11). The psalm has a messianic meaning for the Church; the New Testament understands it of Christ (Acts 4, 25–27; 13, 33; Heb 1, 5).
2, 2: *Anointed:* in Hebrew *mashiah*, "anointed"; in Greek *christos*, whence English Messiah and Christ. In Israel kings (Jgs 9, 8; 1 Sm 9, 16; 16, 12–13) and high priests (Lv 8, 12; Nm 3, 3) received the power of their office through anointing.

*
1, 1: Pss 26, 4–5; 40, 5. | **1, 6:** Ps 37, 18.
1, 2: Jos 1, 8; Ps 119; Sir 39, 1. | **2, 1:** Rv 11, 18.
1, 3: Pss 52, 10; 92, 13–15; | **2, 2:** Ps 83, 6.
Jer 17, 8. | **2, 3:** Ps 149, 8.
1, 4: Pss 35, 5; 83, 14–16; | **2, 4:** Pss 37, 13; 59, 9; Wis
Jb 21, 18. | 4, 18.

5 Then speaks to them in anger,
    terrifies them in wrath:
6 "I myself have installed my king
    on Zion, my holy mountain."
7 I will proclaim the decree of the LORD,
    who said to me, "You are my son;
    today I am your father.*
8 Only ask it of me,
    and I will make your inheritance the
      nations,
    your possession the ends of the earth.
9 With an iron rod you shall shepherd them,
    like a clay pot you will shatter them."*
10 And now, kings, give heed;
    take warning, rulers on earth.
11 Serve the LORD with fear;
    with trembling bow down in homage,
Lest God be angry and you perish from the
     way
    in a sudden blaze of anger.
Happy are all who take refuge in God!*

PSALM 3†

Threatened but Trusting

1† A psalm of David, when he fled
    from his son Absalom.*

I

2 How many are my foes, LORD!
    How many rise against me!
3† How many say of me,
    "God will not save that one."*   *Selah*
4 But you, LORD, are a shield around me;
    my glory, you keep my head high.*

II

5† Whenever I cried out to the LORD,
    I was answered from the holy mountain.
                 Selah
6 Whenever I lay down and slept,
    the LORD preserved me to rise again.*
7 I do not fear, then, thousands of people
    arrayed against me on every side.

III

8 Arise, LORD! Save me, my God!
    You will shatter the jaws of all my foes;
    you will break the teeth of the wicked.*

? did you KNOW?

Understanding the Psalms

"Praise God!" "Why am I suffering?"
"Save us from oppression and injustice."
"God, give me rest." These phrases illustrate types of prayer: praise, lament, and
petition. The Book of Psalms includes
these and many other kinds of prayer,
made by individuals, small groups, or the
whole Jewish nation. Yet, throughout the
Psalms, there is one constant: human
experience is viewed through the eyes of
faith. For example, Psalm 3 reflects the
human experience of being attacked by
others (verses 2–3). The writer of this
psalm, rather than losing all hope, calls
God to the rescue (verse 8). In a similar
way, all the Psalms teach us that every
human experience can also be a faith
experience.

9† Safety comes from the LORD!
    Your blessing for your people!*   *Selah*

PSALM 4†

Trust in God

1† For the leader; with stringed instruments.
    A psalm of David.

I

2 Answer when I call, my saving God.
    In my troubles, you cleared a way;
    show me favor; hear my prayer.*

II

3 How long will you people mock my honor,
    love what is worthless, chase after lies?*
                 Selah
4 Know that the LORD works wonders for the
    faithful;
    the LORD hears when I call out.

Ps 3: An individual lament complaining of enemies who deny that God will come to the rescue (2–3). Despite such taunts the psalmist hopes for God's protection even in sleep (4–7). The psalm prays for an end to the enemies' power to speak maliciously (8) and closes peacefully with an expression of trust (9).

3, 1: The superscription, added later, relates the psalm to an incident in the life of David.

3, 3.5.9: *Selah:* the term is generally considered a direction to the cantor or musicians but its exact meaning is not known. It occurs 71 times in 39 psalms.

Ps 4: An individual lament emphasizing trust in God. The petition is based upon the psalmist's vivid experience of God as savior (2). That experience of God is the basis for the warning to the wicked:

revere God who intervenes on the side of the faithful (3–6). The faithful psalmist exemplifies the blessings given to the just (7–9).

4, 1: *For the leader:* many psalm headings contain this rubric. Its exact meaning is unknown but may signify that such psalms once stood together in a collection of "the choirmaster." Cf 1 Chr 15, 21.

2, 7: Pss 89, 27; 110, 2–3;
  Is 49, 1.
2, 9: Rv 2, 27; 12, 5; 19, 15.
2, 11: Pss 34, 9; 146, 5; Prv
  16, 20.
3, 1: 2 Sm 15, 13ff.
3, 3: Ps 71, 11.
3, 4: Pss 7, 11; 18, 3; 62,

7–8; Dt 33, 29; Is 60,
  19.
3, 6: Ps 4, 9; Prv 3, 24.
3, 8: Ps 58, 7.
3, 9: Ps 28, 9; Jon 2, 10.
4, 2: Ps 118, 5.
4, 3: Ps 62, 4.

5† Tremble and do not sin;
    upon your beds ponder in silence.*
6 Offer fitting sacrifice
    and trust in the LORD.*

III

7 Many say, "May we see better times!
    LORD, show us the light of your face!"*

                          Selah

8 But you have given my heart more joy
    than they have when grain and wine
      abound.
9 In peace I shall both lie down and sleep,*
    for you alone, LORD, make me secure.

PSALM 5†

Prayer for Divine Help

1 For the leader; with wind instruments.
    A psalm of David.

I

2 Hear my words, O LORD;
    listen to my sighing.*
3 Hear my cry for help,
    my king, my God!
  To you I pray, O LORD;
4   at dawn you will hear my cry;
    at dawn I will plead before you and
      wait.*

II

5 You are not a god who delights in evil;
    no wicked person finds refuge with you;
6   the arrogant cannot stand before you.
  You hate all who do evil;
7   you destroy all who speak falsely.*
  Murderers and deceivers
    the LORD abhors.

III

8 But I can enter your house
    because of your great love.
  I can worship in your holy temple
    because of my reverence for you, LORD.*

9 Guide me in your justice because of my foes;
    make straight your way before me.*

IV

10† For there is no sincerity in their mouths;
    their hearts are corrupt.
  Their throats are open graves;*
    on their tongues are subtle lies.
11 Declare them guilty, God;
    make them fall by their own devices.*
  Drive them out for their many sins;
    they have rebelled against you.

V

12 Then all who take refuge in you will be glad
    and forever shout for joy.*
  Protect them that you may be the joy
    of those who love your name.
13 For you, LORD, bless the just;
    you surround them with favor like a
      shield.

PSALM 6†

Prayer in Distress

1† For the leader; with stringed instruments,
    "upon the eighth." A psalm of David.

I

2 Do not reprove me in your anger, LORD,
    nor punish me in your wrath.*
3 Have pity on me, LORD, for I am weak;
    heal me, LORD, for my bones are
      trembling.*
4† In utter terror is my soul—
    and you, LORD, how long . . . ?*
5† Turn, LORD, save my life;
    in your mercy rescue me.
6† For who among the dead remembers you?
    Who praises you in Sheol?*

II

7 I am wearied with sighing;
    all night long tears drench my bed;
    my couch is soaked with weeping.

4, 5: *Tremble:* be moved deeply with religious awe. The Greek translation understood the emotion to be anger, and it is so cited in Eph 4, 26.

Ps 5: A lament contrasting the security of the house of God (8–9.12–13) with the danger of the company of evildoers (5–7.10–11). The psalmist therefore prays that God will hear (2–4) and grant the protection and joy of the temple.

5, 10: *Their throats:* their speech brings harm to their hearers (cf Jer 5, 16). The verse mentions four parts of the body, each a source of evil to the innocent.

Ps 6: The first of the seven Penitential Psalms (Pss 6, 32, 38, 51, 102, 130, 143), a designation dating from the seventh century A.D. for psalms suitable to express repentance. The psalmist does not, as in many laments, claim to be innocent but appeals to God's mercy (5). Sin here, as often in the Bible, is both the sinful act and its injurious consequences; here it is physical sickness (3–4.7–8) and the attacks of enemies (8.9.11). The psalmist prays that the effects of personal and social sin be taken away.

6, 1: *"Upon the eighth":* apparently a musical notation, now lost.
6, 4: *How long?:* elliptical for "How long will it be before you answer my prayer?" Cf Ps 13, 2–3.

6, 5: *Mercy:* Hebrew *hesed,* translated as "mercy" or "love," describes God's affectionate fidelity to human beings, which is rooted in divine and not human integrity.

6, 6: A motive for God to preserve the psalmist from death: in the shadowy world of the dead no one offers you praise. Sheol is the biblical term for the underworld where the insubstantial souls of dead human beings dwelt. It was similar to the Hades of Greek and Latin literature. In the second century B.C., biblical books begin to speak positively of life with God after death (Dn 12, 1–3; Wis 3).

4, 5: Eph 4, 26.	5, 9: Ps 23, 3; Prv 4, 11; Is
4, 6: Ps 51, 19.	26, 7.
4, 7: Pss 31, 17; 44, 4; 67,	5, 10: Rom 3, 13.
1; 80, 4; Jb 13, 24;	5, 11: Ps 141, 10.
Nm 6, 25; Dn 9, 17.	5, 12: Ps 64, 11.
4, 9: Ps 3, 6.	6, 2: Ps 38, 2.
5, 2: Pss 86, 6; 130, 1–2.	6, 3: Jer 17, 14–15.
5, 4: Wis 16, 28.	6, 4: Pss 13, 2–3; 74, 10;
5, 7: Pss 101, 7; Wis 14, 9;	89, 47.
Hb 1, 13.	6, 6: Pss 30, 10; 88, 11;
5, 8: Ps 138, 2; Jon 2, 5.	115, 17; Is 38, 18.

Our Cross to Bear

In Psalm 6, the psalmist is praying for deliverance from physical and mental suffering. Christians often refer to the suffering or sacrifice that comes as part of life as their cross to bear, because they see it as connected to Jesus' own suffering on the cross. Indeed, we all have crosses to bear. Some crosses are heavier than others, and like the psalmist, we ask God to deliver us from them. But unlike the psalmist, Christians also pray that God will transform their suffering and use it in some way for the good of others.

What are some of the crosses that you have had to bear? How were you saved from your suffering? How has someone else's suffering or sacrifice helped or inspired you?

▶ Psalm 6

8 My eyes are dimmed with sorrow,
    worn out because of all my foes.*
                    III
9 Away from me, all who do evil!*
    The LORD has heard my weeping.
10 The LORD has heard my prayer;
    the LORD takes up my plea.
11 My foes will be terrified and disgraced;
    all will fall back in sudden shame.*

PSALM 7 †

God the Vindicator

1 A plaintive song of David, which he sang to the LORD
    concerning Cush, the Benjaminite.
                    I
2 LORD my God, in you I take refuge;
    rescue me; save me from all who pursue
    me,*
3 Lest they maul me like lions,
    tear me to pieces with none to save.
                    II
4† LORD my God, if I am at fault in this,
    if there is guilt on my hands,
5 If I have repaid my friend with evil—
    I spared even those who hated me without
    cause—
6 Then let my enemy pursue and overtake me,
    trample my life to the ground,
    and leave me dishonored in the dust.* Selah
                    III
7 Rise up, LORD, in your anger;
    rise against the fury of my foes.*

Wake to judge as you have decreed.
8 Have the assembly of the peoples gather
    about you;
    sit on your throne high above them,
9 O LORD, judge of the nations.
    Grant me justice, LORD, for I am blameless,
    free of any guilt.
10 Bring the malice of the wicked to an end;
    uphold the innocent,
    O God of justice,
    who tries hearts and minds.*
                    IV
11 A shield before me is God
    who saves the honest heart.*
12 God is a just judge,
    who rebukes in anger every day.
13 If sinners do not repent,
    God sharpens his sword,
    strings and readies the bow,*
14 Prepares his deadly shafts,
    makes arrows blazing thunderbolts.*
                    V
15 Sinners conceive iniquity;
    pregnant with mischief,
    they give birth to failure.*
16 They open a hole and dig it deep,
    but fall into the pit they have dug.*
17 Their mischief comes back upon themselves;
    their violence falls on their own heads.
                    VI
18 I praise the justice of the LORD;
    I celebrate the name of the LORD Most High.*

Ps 7: An individual lament. The psalmist flees to God's presence in the sanctuary for justice and protection (2–3) and takes an oath that only the innocent can swear (4–6). The innocent psalmist can thus hope for the just God's protection (7–14) and be confident that the actions of the wicked will come back upon their own heads (15–17). The justice of God leads the psalmist to praise (18).

7, 4: *At fault in this:* in the accusation the enemies have made against the psalmist.

6, 8: Pss 31, 10; 38, 11; 40, 13.
6, 9: Ps 119, 115; Mt 7, 23; Lk 13, 27.
6, 11: Pss 35, 4.26; 40, 15; 71, 13.
7, 2: Pss 6, 5; 22, 21.
7, 6: Ps 143, 3.
7, 7: Pss 9, 4; 19, 20.
7, 10: Pss 17, 3; 26, 2; 35, 24; 43, 1; 139, 23; Jer
17, 10; 20, 12.
7, 11: Ps 3, 4.
7, 13: Ps 11, 2.
7, 14: Is 50, 11.
7, 15: Jb 15, 35; Is 59, 4.
7, 16: Pss 9, 16; 35, 8; 57, 7; Prv 26, 27; Eccl 10, 8; Sir 27, 26.
7, 18: Pss 18, 50; 30, 5; 135, 3; 146, 2.

PSALM 8†

Divine Majesty and Human Dignity

¹† For the leader; "upon the *gittith*."
A psalm of David.

2 O LORD, our Lord,
how awesome is your name through all the
earth!
You have set your majesty above the heavens!

³† Out of the mouths of babes* and infants
you have drawn a defense against your foes,
to silence enemy and avenger.

4 When I see your heavens, the work of your
fingers,
the moon and stars that you set in place—

⁵† What are humans that you are mindful of them,*
mere mortals that you care for them?*

⁶† Yet you have made them little less than a god,
crowned them with glory and honor.

7 You have given them rule over the works of
your hands,*
put all things at their feet:

8 All sheep and oxen,
even the beasts of the field,

9 The birds of the air, the fish of the sea,
and whatever swims the paths of the seas.

10 O LORD, our Lord,
how awesome is your name through all the
earth!

PSALMS 9–10†

Thanksgiving for Victory and Prayer for Justice

¹† For the leader; according to *Muth Labben*.
A psalm of David.

A
I

2 I will praise you, LORD, with all my heart;
I will declare all your wondrous deeds.

3 I will delight and rejoice in you;
I will sing hymns to your name, Most High.

4 For my enemies turn back;
they stumble and perish before you.

II

5 You upheld my right and my cause,
seated on your throne, judging justly.

6 You rebuked the nations, you destroyed the
wicked;
their name you blotted out for all time.*

7 The enemies have been ruined forever;
you destroyed their cities;
their memory has perished.

III

8 The LORD rules forever,
has set up a throne for judgment.

9 It is God who governs the world with justice,*
who judges the peoples with fairness.

10 The LORD is a stronghold for the oppressed,
a stronghold in times of trouble.*

11 Those who honor your name trust in you;
you never forsake those who seek you,
LORD.

IV

12 Sing hymns to the LORD enthroned on Zion;
proclaim God's deeds among the nations!

13 For the avenger of bloodshed remembers,
does not forget the cry of the afflicted.*

V

14 Have mercy on me, LORD;
see how my foes afflict me!
You alone can raise me from the gates of
death.*

15† Then I will declare all your praises,
sing joyously of your salvation
in the gates of daughter Zion.

VI

16 The nations fall into the pit they dig;
in the snare they hide, their own foot is
caught.

---

† **Ps 8:** While marvelling at the limitless grandeur of God (2–3), the psalmist is struck first by the smallness of human beings in creation (4–5), and then by the royal dignity and power that God has graciously bestowed upon them (6–10).

8, 1: *"Upon the gittith"*: probably the title of the melody to which the psalm was to be sung or a musical instrument.

8, 3: *Babes and infants:* the text is obscure. Some join this line to the last line of 2 (itself obscure) to read: "(you) whose majesty is exalted above the heavens / by the mouths of babes and infants." *Drawn a defense:* some prefer the Septuagint's "fashioned praise," which is quoted in Mt 21, 16. *Enemy and avenger:* probably cosmic enemies. The primeval powers of watery chaos are often personified in poetic texts (Pss 74, 13–14; 89, 11; Jb 9, 13; 26, 12–13; Is 51, 9).

8, 5: *Humans . . . mere mortals:* literally, "(mortal) person" . . . "son of man (in sense of a human being, Hebrew *'adam*)." The emphasis is on the fragility and mortality of human beings to whom God has given great dignity.

8, 6: *Little less than a god:* Hebrew *'elohim*, the ordinary word for "God" or "the gods" or members of the heavenly court. The Greek version translated *'elohim* by "angel, messenger"; several ancient and modern versions so translate. The meaning seems to be that God created human beings almost at the level of the beings in the heav-

enly world. Heb 2, 9 finds the eminent fulfillment of this verse in Jesus Christ, who was humbled before being glorified. Cf also 1 Cor 15, 27, where St. Paul applies to Christ the closing words of v 7.

Pss 9–10: Pss 9 and 10 in the Hebrew text have been transmitted as separate poems but they actually form a single acrostic poem and are so transmitted in the Greek and Latin tradition. Each verse of the two psalms begins with a successive letter of the Hebrew alphabet (though several letters have no corresponding stanza). The psalm states loosely connected themes: the rescue of the helpless poor from their enemies, God's worldwide judgment and rule over the nations, the psalmist's own concern for rescue (14–15).

9, 1: *Muth Labben:* probably the melodic accompaniment of the psalm, now lost.

9, 15: *Daughter Zion:* an ancient Near Eastern city could sometimes be personified as a woman or a queen, the spouse of the god of the city.

8, 3: Mt 21, 16; Wis 10, 21.
8, 5: Ps 144, 3; Jb 7, 17.
8, 5: Heb 2, 6ff.
8, 7ff: Gn 1, 26.28; Wis 9, 2;
1 Cor 15, 27.

9, 6: Jb 18, 17.
9, 9: Pss 96, 10; 98, 9.
9, 10: Ps 37, 39; Is 25, 4.
9, 13: Jb 16, 18.
9, 14: Wis 16, 13.

Write Your Own Psalm

As you may know, there are many types of psalms (see the introduction to the Book of Psalms). You may also know that more than one person wrote the Psalms. Even today there are psalmists, people who write songs or poems similar in tone and style to the Psalms in the Bible. Would you like to write your own psalm? Try it in your journal:

- Choose the type of psalm you want to write.
- Use poetic language and symbolism.
- Illustrate your psalm.
- Set it to music (like the original ones).
- Or, choose an existing Psalm and rewrite it to reflect a current issue.

17† The LORD is revealed in this divine rule:
  by the deeds they do the wicked are
    trapped.*   *Higgaion. Selah*

VII

18 To Sheol the wicked will depart,
  all the nations that forget God.
19 The needy will never be forgotten,
  nor will the hope of the afflicted ever fade.*
20 Arise, LORD, let no mortal prevail;
  let the nations be judged in your presence.
21 Strike them with terror, LORD;
  show the nations they are mere mortals.
                                        Selah

B

I

1 Why, LORD, do you stand at a distance
  and pay no heed to these troubled times?
2 Arrogant scoundrels pursue the poor;
  they trap them by their cunning schemes.*

II

3 The wicked even boast of their greed;
  these robbers curse and scorn the LORD.*
4 In their insolence the wicked boast:
  "God doesn't care, doesn't even exist."*
5 Yet their affairs always succeed;
  they ignore your judgment on high;
  they sneer at all who oppose them.
6 They say in their hearts, "We will never fall;
  never will we see misfortune."
7 Their mouths are full of oaths, violence, and
    lies;
  discord and evil are under their tongues.*

8 They wait in ambush near towns;
  their eyes watch for the helpless,
  to murder the innocent in secret.*
9 They lurk in ambush like lions in a thicket,
  hide there to trap the poor,
  snare them and close the net.*
10 The helpless are crushed, laid low;
  they fall into the power of the wicked,
11 Who say in their hearts, "God pays no attention,
  shows no concern, never bothers to look."*

III

12 Rise up, LORD God! Raise your arm!
  Do not forget the poor!
13 Why should the wicked scorn God,
  say in their hearts, "God doesn't care"?
14 But you do see;
  you do observe this misery and sorrow;*
  you take the matter in hand.
  To you the helpless can entrust their cause;
  you are the defender of orphans.*
15 Break the arms of the wicked and depraved;
  make them account for their crimes;
  let none of them survive.

IV

16 The LORD is king forever;*
  the nations have vanished from God's
    land.
17 You listen, LORD, to the needs of the poor;
  you encourage them and hear their
    prayers.
18 You win justice for the orphaned and
    oppressed;*
  no one on earth will cause terror again.

---

† **9, 17:** *The LORD is revealed in this divine rule:* God has so made the universe that the wicked are punished by the very actions they perform.

9, 17: Sir 27, 26.
9, 19: Prv 23, 18.

10, 2: Is 32, 7.
10, 3: Ps 36, 2.

10, 4: Ps 14, 1; Jb 22, 13; Is 29, 15; Jer 5, 12; Zep 1, 12.
10, 7: Is 32, 7; Rom 3, 14.
10, 8: Ps 11, 2; Jb 24, 14.
10, 9: Ps 17, 12; Prv 1, 11; Jer 5, 26.

10, 11: Pss 44, 25; 64, 6; 73, 11; 94, 7; Ez 9, 9.
10, 14: Pss 31, 8; 56, 9; 2 Kgs 20, 5; Is 25, 8; Rv 7, 17.
10, 14: Ex 22, 21–22.
10, 16: Ps 145, 13; Jer 10, 10.
10, 18: Dt 10, 18.

PSALM 11†

Confidence in the Presence of God

¹ For the leader. Of David.

I

In the LORD I take refuge;
how can you say to me,
"Flee like a bird to the mountains!"*

² See how the wicked string their bows,
fit their arrows to the string
to shoot from the shadows at the
upright.*

³† When foundations are being destroyed,
what can the upright do?"

II

⁴ The LORD is in his holy temple;
the LORD's throne is in heaven.*
God's eyes keep careful watch;
they test all peoples.

⁵ The LORD tests the good and the bad,
hates those who love violence,

⁶† And rains upon the wicked
fiery coals and brimstone,
a scorching wind their allotted cup.*

⁷ The LORD is just and loves just deeds;
the upright shall see his face.

PSALM 12†

Prayer against Evil Tongues

¹ For the leader; "upon the eighth."
A psalm of David.

I

² Help, LORD, for no one loyal remains;
the faithful have vanished from the human
race.*

³ Those who tell lies to one another
speak with deceiving lips and a double
heart.*

II

⁴ May the LORD cut off all deceiving lips,
and every boastful tongue,

---

⁵ Those who say, "By our tongues we
prevail;
when our lips speak, who can lord it over
us?"*

III

⁶ "Because they rob the weak, and the needy
groan,
I will now arise," says the LORD;
"I will grant safety to whoever longs for it."*

IV

⁷† The promises of the LORD are sure,
silver refined in a crucible,
silver purified seven times.*

⁸ LORD, protect us always;
preserve us from this generation.

⁹ On every side the wicked strut;
the shameless are extolled by all.

PSALM 13†

Prayer in Time of Illness

¹ For the leader. A psalm of David.

I

² How long, LORD? Will you utterly forget me?
How long will you hide your face from
me?*

³ How long must I carry sorrow in my soul,
grief in my heart day after day?
How long will my enemy triumph over
me?

II

⁴ Look upon me, answer me, LORD, my God!
Give light to my eyes lest I sleep in
death,

⁵ Lest my enemy say, "I have prevailed,"
lest my foes rejoice at my downfall.*

III

⁶ I trust in your faithfulness.
Grant my heart joy in your help,
That I may sing of the LORD,
"How good our God has been to me!"*

Ps 11: A song of trust. Though friends counsel flight to the mountain country (a traditional hideout) to escape trouble (1–3), the innocent psalmist reaffirms confidence in God, who protects those who seek asylum in the temple (4–7).
11, 3: *Foundations:* usually understood of public order. Cf Ps 82, 5.
11, 6: *Their allotted cup:* the cup that God gives people to drink is a common figure for their destiny. Cf Pss 16, 5; 75, 9; Mt 20, 22; 26, 39; Rv 14, 10.
Ps 12: A lament. The psalmist, thrown into a world where lying and violent people persecute the just (2–3), prays that the wicked be punished (4–5). The prayer is not simply for vengeance but arises from a desire to see God's justice appear on earth. V 6 preserves the word of assurance spoken by the priest to the lamenter; it is not usually transmitted in such psalms. In vv 7–9 the psalmist affirms the intention to live by the word of assurance.
12, 7: *A crucible:* literally "in a crucible in the ground." The crucible was placed in the ground for support.

Ps 13: A lament in which the psalmist, seriously ill (4), expresses fear that enemies will interpret his or her death as a divine judgment. Hence the heartfelt prayer (2–3) is for healing that will signal to those enemies that the psalmist enjoys God's favor (4–5). The poem ends with a confession of trust in God and a statement of praise (6).

11, 1: Pss 55, 7; 91, 4.
11, 2: Pss 7, 13; 37, 14; 57, 5; 64, 4.
11, 4: Pss 14, 2; 102, 20; Hb 2, 20; Dt 26, 15; Is 66, 1; Mt 5, 34.
11, 6: Pss 120, 4; 140, 11; Prv 16, 27; Ez 38, 22; Rv 8, 5; 20, 10.
12, 2: Pss 14, 3; 116, 11; Is 59, 15; Mi 7, 2.
12, 3: Pss 28, 3; 55, 22; Is 59, 3–4; Jer 9, 7.
12, 5: Sir 5, 3.
12, 6: Is 33, 10.
12, 7: Pss 18, 31; 19, 8; Prv 30, 5.
13, 2: Pss 6, 4; 44, 25; 77, 8; 79, 5; 89, 47; 94, 3; Lam 5, 20.
13, 5: Ps 38, 17.
13, 6: Ps 116, 7.

PS

Believing

Angel. My LORD, the earth is filled with those who say, "There is no God!"

God. So, my messenger, what do we do with these people?

Angel. My LORD, they are fools.

God. Perhaps, but they are free. I force no one to believe in me.

Angel. Yet, the wise always seem to find you.

God. That is because they seek me. Those who seek—

Angel. Yes, I know, LORD, they shall find. But how do we get through to those others, the godless ones?

God. You must trust. My signs and wonders surround them. There is the witness of those who believe. And there are a few angels.

Angel. But they keep explaining all that away.

God. So they do. They are free, after all. Their destiny is in their hands, in the choices they make.

Angel. Including the most basic choice of all.

God. Yes. Especially that. True love is not forced. It gives and awaits a response. We must trust in love.

Angel. And hope?

God. Yes, always hope.

▶ Psalm 14

PSALM 14†

A Lament over Widespread Corruption

¹ For the leader. Of David.

I

Fools† say in their hearts,
"There is no God."*
Their deeds are loathsome and corrupt;
    not one does what is right.

2 The LORD looks down from heaven
    upon the human race,*
To see if even one is wise,*
    if even one seeks God.

3 All have gone astray;
    all alike are perverse.
Not one does what is right,
    not even one.*

II

4 Will these evildoers never learn?
    They devour my people as they devour
    bread;*

they do not call upon the LORD.*

5 They have good reason, then, to fear;
    God is with the company of the just.

6 They would crush the hopes of the poor,
    but the poor have the LORD as their refuge.

III

7† Oh, that from Zion might come
    the deliverance of Israel,
That Jacob may rejoice, and Israel be glad
    when the LORD restores his people!*

PSALM 15†

The Righteous Israelite

¹† A psalm of David.

I

LORD, who may abide in your tent?
    Who may dwell on your holy mountain?*

II

2 Whoever walks without blame,*
    doing what is right,

---

† **Ps 14:** The lament (duplicated in Ps 53) depicts the world as consisting of two types of people: "the fools" (= the wicked, 1–3) and "the company of the just" (4–6; also called "my people," and "the poor"). The wicked persecute the just, but the psalm expresses the hope that God will punish the wicked and reward the good.

14, 1: *Fools:* literally, "the fool." The singular is used typically, hence the plural translation.

14, 7: *Israel . . . Jacob . . . his people:* the righteous poor are identified with God's people.

Ps 15: The psalm records a liturgical scrutiny at the entrance to the temple court (cf Ps 24, 3–6; Is 33, 14b–16). The Israelite wishing to be admitted had to ask the temple official what conduct was ap-

propriate to God's precincts. Note the emphasis on virtues relating to one's neighbor.

15, 1: *Your tent . . . your holy mountain:* the temple could be referred to as "tent" (Ps 61, 5; Is 33, 20), a reference to the tent of the wilderness period and the tent of David (2 Sm 6, 17; 7, 2), predecessors of the temple. *Holy mountain:* a venerable designation of the divine abode (Pss 2, 6; 3, 5; 43, 3; 48, 2, etc.).

14, 1: Pss 10, 4; 36, 2; Is 32, 6; Jer 5, 12.	14, 4: Ps 27, 2; Is 9, 11.
14, 2: Pss 11, 4; 102, 20.	14, 4: Ps 79, 6.
14, 2b–3: Rom 3, 11–12.	14, 7: Ps 85, 2.
14, 3: Ps 12, 1.	15, 1: Is 56, 7.
	15, 2: Ps 119, 1.

speaking truth from the heart;

3 Who does not slander a neighbor,
   does no harm to another,
   never defames a friend;

4 Who disdains the wicked,
   but honors those who fear the LORD;
   Who keeps an oath despite the cost,

5† lends no money at interest,
   accepts no bribe against the innocent.*

III

Whoever acts like this
   shall never be shaken.

PSALM 16†

God the Supreme Good

1† A *miktam* of David.

I

Keep me safe, O God;
   in you I take refuge.*

2 I say to the LORD,
   you are my Lord,

you are my only good.

3 Worthless are all the false gods of the land.
   Accursed are all who delight in them.

4† They multiply their sorrows
   who court other gods.
   Blood libations to them I will not pour out,
   nor will I take their names upon my lips.

5 LORD, my allotted portion and my cup,
   you have made my destiny secure.*

6† Pleasant places were measured out for me;
   fair to me indeed is my inheritance.

II

7 I bless the LORD who counsels me;
   even at night my heart exhorts me.

8 I keep the LORD always before me;
   with the Lord at my right, I shall never be
   shaken.*

9 Therefore my heart is glad, my soul rejoices;
   my body also dwells secure,

10† For you will not abandon me to Sheol,
   nor let your faithful servant see the pit.*

LIVING IN YOUR TENT, ON YOUR HOLY HILL

Native Americans can appreciate the imagery of Psalm 15. Both tents and hills have a sacred meaning for them. The Lakota have the phrase *mit-a-ku-ye O-ya-sin*, which means "all my relatives." This phrase is often used at the end of a prayer, much like *amen*. It expresses the deep belief that all human beings are our brothers and sisters, and we all belong in the Holy Tent of the Great Spirit. All creatures—the two legged and the four legged, those that crawl and those that fly—are our relatives. In fact, we are related to all of creation—the sea, the rocks, the caves, the sky, the trees, the holy hills. Native Americans understand human beings as connected to all creation, and they believe that any harm we do to creation we do to ourselves.

▸ Psalm 15

---

† **15, 5:** *Lends no money at interest:* lending money in the Old Testament was often seen as assistance to the poor in their distress, not as an investment; making money off the poor by charging interest was thus forbidden (Ex 22, 24; Lv 25, 36–37; Dt 23, 20).

Ps 16: In the first section, the psalmist rejects the futile worship of false gods (2–5), preferring Israel's God (1), the giver of the land (6). The second section reflects on the wise and life-giving presence of God (7–11).

16, 1: *Miktam:* a term occurring six times in psalm superscriptions, always with "David." Its meaning is unknown.

16, 4: *Take their names:* to use the gods' names in oaths and hence to affirm them as one's own gods.

16, 6: *Pleasant places were measured out for me:* the psalmist is

pleased with the plot of land measured out to the family, which was to be passed on to succeeding generations ("my inheritance").

16, 10: *Nor let your faithful servant see the pit:* Hebrew *shahath* means here the pit, a synonym for Sheol, the underworld. The Greek translation derives the word here and elsewhere from the verb *shahath*, "to be corrupt." On the basis of the Greek, Acts 2, 25–32 and 13, 35–37 apply the verse to Christ's resurrection, "Nor will you suffer your holy one to see corruption."

*
15, 5: Ex 22, 24; 23, 8.   16, 8: Pss 73, 23; 121, 5.
16, 1: Ps 25, 20.   8–12; Acts 2, 25–28.
16, 5: Pss 23, 5; 73, 26; Nm   16, 10: Pss 28, 1; 30, 4; 49,
     18, 20; Lam 3, 24.   16; 86, 13; Jon 2, 7;
                                                     Acts 13, 35.

11 You will show me the path to life,
    abounding joy in your presence,
    the delights at your right hand forever.

PSALM 17 †

Prayer for Rescue from Persecutors

¹ A prayer of David.

I

Hear, LORD, my plea for justice;
    pay heed to my cry;
Listen to my prayer
    spoken without guile.
2 From you let my vindication come;
    your eyes see what is right.
3 You have tested my heart,
    searched it in the night.*
You have tried me by fire,
    but find no malice in me.
My mouth has not transgressed
4 as humans often do.
As your lips have instructed me,
    I have kept the way of the law.
5 My steps have kept to your paths;
    my feet have not faltered.*

II

6 I call upon you; answer me, O God.
    Turn your ear to me; hear my prayer.
7 Show your wonderful love,
    you who deliver with your right arm
    those who seek refuge from their foes.
8† Keep me as the apple of your eye;
    hide me in the shadow of your wings
9 from the violence of the wicked.*

III

My ravenous enemies press upon me;*
10† they close their hearts,
    they fill their mouths with proud roaring.
11 Their steps even now encircle me;
    they watch closely, keeping low to the
    ground,

12 Like lions eager for prey,
    like young lions lurking in ambush.
13 Rise, O LORD, confront and cast them down;
    rescue me so from the wicked.
14 Slay them with your sword;
    with your hand, LORD, slay them;
    snatch them from the world in their prime.
Their bellies are being filled with your friends;
    their children are satisfied too,
    for they share what is left with their young.
15† I am just—let me see your face;
    when I awake, let me be filled with your
    presence.*

PSALM 18 †

A King's Thanksgiving for Victory

¹ For the leader. Of David, the servant of the LORD, who
sang to the LORD the words of this song after the LORD
had rescued him from the clutches of all his enemies and
from the hand of Saul. ² He said:

I

I love you, LORD, my strength,
3† LORD, my rock, my fortress, my deliverer,*
My God, my rock of refuge,
    my shield, my saving horn, my
    stronghold!*
4 Praised be the LORD, I exclaim!
    I have been delivered from my enemies.

II

5 The breakers of death surged round about me;
    the menacing floods terrified me.
6† The cords of Sheol tightened;
    the snares of death lay in wait for me.*
7† In my distress I called out: LORD!
    I cried out to my God.*
From his temple he heard my voice;
    my cry to him reached his ears.
8† The earth rocked and shook;
    the foundations of the mountains trembled;
    they shook as his wrath flared up.*

Ps 17: A lament of an individual unjustly attacked who has taken
refuge in the temple. Confident of being found innocent, the psalmist
cries out for God's just judgment (1–5) and requests divine help
against enemies (6–9a). Those ravenous lions (9b–12) should be punished (13–14). The psalm ends with a serene statement of praise (15).
The Hebrew text of vv 3–4 and 14 is uncertain.
    17, 8: *Apple of your eye . . . shadow of your wings:* images of
God's special care. Cf Dt 32, 10; Prv 7, 2; Is 49, 2.
    17, 10–12.14: An extended metaphor: the enemies are lions.
    17, 15: *When I awake:* probably the psalmist has spent the night
in the sanctuary (cf 3) and hopes to wake to an oracle assuring God's
protective presence.
    Ps 18: A royal thanksgiving for a military victory, duplicated in
2 Sm 22. Thanksgiving psalms are in essence reports of divine rescue. The psalm has two parallel reports of rescue, the first told from
a heavenly perspective (5–20), and the second from an earthly perspective (36–46). The first report adapts old mythic language of a
cosmic battle between sea and rainstorm in order to depict God's
rescue of the Israelite king from his enemies. Each report has a short
hymnic introduction (2–4.32–35) and conclusion (21–31.47–51).

18, 3: *My saving horn:* my strong savior. The horn referred to is
the weapon of a bull and the symbol of fertility. Cf 1 Sm 2, 10; Ps
132, 17; Lk 1, 69.
    18, 6: *Cords:* hunting imagery, the cords of a snare.
    18, 7: *His temple:* his heavenly abode.
    18, 8–16: God appears in the storm, which in Palestine comes
from the west. The introduction to the theophany (vv 8–9) is probably a description of a violent, hot, and dry east-wind storm. In the
fall transition period from the rainless summer to the rainy winter,
such storms regularly precede the rains. Cf Ex 14, 21–22.

17, 3: Pss 26, 2; 139, 23.	**18, 2–51:** 2 Sm 22, 2–51.
17, 5: Ps 18, 36; Jb 23, 11–12.	**18, 3:** Pss 3, 4; 31, 3–4; 42,
17, 9: Pss 36, 8; 57, 2; 61, 5;	10; Gn 49, 24; Dt 32, 4.
63, 8; 91, 4; Dt 32, 10;	**18, 6:** Pss 88, 8; 93, 3–4;
Ru 2, 12; Zec 2, 12; Mt	116, 3–4.
23, 37.	**18, 7:** Jon 2, 3.
17, 9b–12: Pss 10, 9; 22, 14.22; 35,	**18, 8:** Pss 97, 3–4; 99, 1; Jgs
17; 58, 7; Jb 4, 10–11.	5, 4–5; Is 64, 1; Hab
17, 15: Pss 4, 7; 31, 17; 67, 2;	3, 9–11.
80, 4; Nm 6, 25; Dn 9,	
17.	

9 Smoke rose in his nostrils,
    a devouring fire poured from his mouth;
    it kindled coals into flame.
10 He parted the heavens and came down,
    a dark cloud under his feet.*
11† Mounted on a cherub he flew,
    borne along on the wings of the wind.
12 He made darkness the cover about him;
    his canopy, heavy thunderheads.
13 Before him scudded his clouds,
    hail and lightning too.*
14 The LORD thundered from heaven;
    the Most High made his voice resound.*
15† He let fly his arrows and scattered them;
    shot his lightning bolts and dispersed
    them.*
16 Then the bed of the sea appeared;
    the world's foundations lay bare,*
  At the roar of the LORD,
    at the storming breath of his nostrils.
17 He reached down from on high and seized
    me;
    drew me out of the deep waters.*
18 He rescued me from my mighty enemy,
    from foes too powerful for me.
19 They attacked me on a day of distress,
    but the LORD came to my support.
20 He set me free in the open;
    he rescued me because he loves me.

III

21 The LORD acknowledged my righteousness,
    rewarded my clean hands.*
22 For I kept the ways of the LORD;
    I was not disloyal to my God.
23 His laws were all before me,
    his decrees I did not cast aside.
24 I was honest toward him;
    I was on guard against sin.
25 So the LORD rewarded my righteousness,
    the cleanness of my hands in his sight.
26 Toward the faithful you are faithful;
    to the honest you are honest;*
27 Toward the sincere, sincere;
    but to the perverse you are devious.
28 Humble people you save;
    haughty eyes you bring low.*
29 You, LORD, give light to my lamp;
    my God brightens the darkness about me.*

30 With you I can rush an armed band,
    with my God to help I can leap a wall.
31 God's way is unerring;
    the LORD's promise is tried and true;
    he is a shield for all who trust in him.*

IV

32 Truly, who is God except the LORD?
    Who but our God is the rock?*
33 This God who girded me with might,
    kept my way unerring,
34 Who made my feet swift as a deer's,
    set me safe on the heights,*
35† Who trained my hands for war,
    my arms to bend even a bow of bronze.*

V

36 You have given me your protecting shield;
    your right hand has upheld me;
    you stooped to make me great.
37 You gave me room to stride;
    my feet never stumbled.*
38 I pursued my enemies and overtook them;
    I did not turn back till I destroyed them.
39 I struck them down; they could not rise;
    they fell dead at my feet.
40 You girded me with strength for war,
    subdued adversaries at my feet.
41 My foes you put to flight before me;
    those who hated me I destroyed.
42 They cried for help, but no one saved them;
    cried to the LORD but got no answer.
43 I ground them fine as dust in the wind;
    like mud in the streets I trampled them
    down.
44 You rescued me from the strife of peoples;
    you made me head over nations.
  A people I had not known became my slaves;
45   as soon as they heard of me they obeyed.
  Foreigners cringed before me;
46   their courage failed;
    they came trembling from their fortresses.*

VI

47 The LORD lives! Blessed be my rock!*
    Exalted be God, my savior!
48 O God who granted me vindication,
    made peoples subject to me,*
49   and preserved me from my enemies,
  Truly you have exalted me above my
    adversaries,

---

† **18, 11:** *Cherub:* a winged creature, derived from myth, in the service of the deity (Gn 3, 24; Ex 25, 18–20; 37, 6–9). Cherubim were the throne bearers of the deity (Pss 80, 2; 99, 1; 1 Kgs 6, 23–28; 8, 6–8).

18, 15: *Arrows:* lightning.

18, 35: *Bow of bronze:* hyperbole for a bow difficult to bend and therefore capable of propelling an arrow with great force.

---

* **18, 10:** Pss 104, 3; 144, 5; Is 63, 19.
18, 13: Ex 13, 21; 19, 16.
18, 14: Pss 29; 77, 19; Ex 19,
19; Jb 37, 3–4.
18, 15: Ps 144, 6; Wis 5, 21.
18, 16: Ps 77, 17; Zec 9, 14.
18, 17: Ps 144, 7.
18, 21: Ps 26; 1 Sm 26, 23.
18, 26: Ps 125, 4.
18, 28: Jb 22, 29; Prv 3, 34.
18, 29: Pss 27, 1; 36, 10; 43, 3; 119, 105; Jb 29, 3; Mi 7, 8.
18, 31: Pss 12, 6; 77, 13; Prv 30, 5.
18, 32: Is 44, 8; 45, 21.
18, 34: Hb 3, 19.
18, 35: Ps 144, 1.
18, 37: Ps 17, 5.
18, 46: Mi 7, 17.
18, 47: Ps 144, 1.
18, 48: Ps 144, 2.

from the violent you have rescued me.
50 Thus I will proclaim you, LORD, among the
nations;
I will sing the praises of your name.*
51 You have given great victories to your king,
and shown kindness to your anointed,
to David and his posterity forever.*

PSALM 19†

God's Glory in the Heavens and in the Law

1 For the leader. A psalm of David.

I

2 The heavens declare the glory of God;
the sky proclaims its builder's craft.*
3 One day to the next conveys that message;
one night to the next imparts that
knowledge.
4† There is no word or sound;
no voice is heard;
5† Yet their report goes forth through all the
earth,
their message, to the ends of the world.
God has pitched there a tent for the sun;
6 it comes forth like a bridegroom from his
chamber,
and like an athlete joyfully runs its course.
7 From one end of the heavens it comes forth;
its course runs through to the other;
nothing escapes its heat.

II

8 The law of the LORD is perfect,
refreshing the soul.
The decree of the LORD is trustworthy,
giving wisdom to the simple.*
9 The precepts of the LORD are right,
rejoicing the heart.
The command of the LORD is clear,
enlightening the eye.
10 The fear of the LORD is pure,
enduring forever.
The statutes of the LORD are true,
all of them just;
11 More desirable than gold,
than a hoard of purest gold,
Sweeter also than honey
or drippings from the comb.*

"The Heavens Declare the Glory of God"

Does that opening line of Psalm 19
sound familiar? Perhaps you've seen
it on a poster or sung it at Mass. The sky
constantly tells us how glorious and magnificent God is!

Have you ever watched the awesome show of a thunder and lightning
storm? been delighted by a rainbow?
marveled at the power behind a tornado
or a hurricane? been tickled by a gentle
spring breeze? caught snowflakes on your
tongue? had leaves dance around you in a
brisk autumn wind? lost yourself looking
up into a star-filled night? felt breathless
watching a magnificent sunset?

As amazing as the sky is, it only hints
at how amazing God is! And in the second
half of Psalm 19, the psalmist reminds us
that God's law is equally wonderful. Read
Psalm 19 as your own prayer of praise to
God for the many ways God communicates to us.

▶ Psalm 19

12† By them your servant is instructed;
obeying them brings much reward.

III

13 Who can detect heedless failings?
Cleanse me from my unknown faults.
14 But from willful sins keep your servant;
let them never control me.
Then shall I be blameless,
innocent of grave sin.
15 Let the words of my mouth meet with your
favor,
keep the thoughts of my heart before you,
LORD, my rock and my redeemer.

Ps 19: The heavenly elements of the world, now beautifully
arranged, bespeak the power and wisdom of their creator (2–7). The
creator's wisdom is available to human beings in the law (8–11), toward which the psalmist prays to be open (12–15). The themes of
light and speech unify the poem.
19, 4: *No word or sound:* the regular functioning of the heavens
and the alternation of day and night inform humans without words
of the creator's power and wisdom.
19, 5: *The sun:* in other religious literature the sun is a judge and
lawgiver since it sees all in its daily course; 5b–7 form a transition to

the law in 8–11. The six synonyms for God's revelation (8–11) are applied to the sun in comparable literature.
19, 12: *Instructed:* the Hebrew verb means both to shine and to
teach. Cf Dn 12, 3.

18, 50: Pss 7, 18; 30, 5; 57, 9;
135, 3; 146, 2; Rom
15, 9.
18, 51: Pss 89, 28–37; 144,
10; 1 Sm 2, 10.
19, 2: Pss 8, 1; 50, 6; 97, 6.
19, 8: Pss 12, 7; 119.
19, 11: Sir 24, 19.

PSALM 20†

Prayer for the King in Time of War

¹ For the leader. A psalm of David.

I

2 The LORD answer you in time of distress;
   the name of the God of Jacob defend you!

3 May God send you help from the temple,
   from Zion be your support.*

4† May God remember your every offering,
   graciously accept your holocaust,   *Selah*

5 Grant what is in your heart,
   fulfill your every plan.

6† May we shout for joy at your victory,
   raise the banners in the name of our God.
   The LORD grant your every prayer!

II

7 Now I know victory is given
   to the anointed of the LORD.*
   God will answer him from the holy heavens
   with a strong arm that brings victory.

8 Some rely on chariots, others on horses,
   but we on the name of the LORD our God.*

9 They collapse and fall,
   but we stand strong and firm.*

10 LORD, grant victory to the king;
   answer when we call upon you.

PSALM 21†

Thanksgiving and Assurances for the King

¹ For the leader. A psalm of David.

I

2 LORD, the king finds joy in your power;*
   in your victory how greatly he rejoices!

3 You have granted him his heart's desire;
   you did not refuse the prayer of his lips.
                                          Selah

4 For you welcomed him with goodly blessings;
   you placed on his head a crown of pure gold.

5 He asked life of you;
   you gave it to him,
   length of days forever.*

6 Great is his glory in your victory;
   majesty and splendor you confer upon him.

7 You make him the pattern of blessings forever,
   you gladden him with the joy of your
   presence.

8 For the king trusts in the LORD,
   stands firm through the love of the Most
   High.

II

9 Your hand will reach all your enemies;
   your right hand will reach your foes!

10 At the time of your coming
   you will drive them into a furnace.
   Then the LORD's anger will consume them,
   devour them with fire.

11 Even their descendants you will wipe out
   from the earth,
   their offspring from the human race.

12 Though they intend evil against you,
   devising plots, they will not succeed,

13 For you will put them to flight;
   you will aim at them with your bow.

III

14 Arise, LORD, in your power!*
   We will sing and chant the praise of your
   might.

PSALM 22†

The Prayer of an Innocent Person

¹† For the leader; according to "The deer of the dawn."
   A psalm of David.

I

2 My God, my God, why have you abandoned
   me?
   Why so far from my call for help,
   from my cries of anguish?*

3 My God, I call by day, but you do not
   answer;
   by night, but I have no relief.*

4 Yet you are enthroned as the Holy One;
   you are the glory of Israel.*

Ps 20: The people pray for the king before battle. The people ask for divine help (2–6) and express confidence that such help will be given (7–10). A solemn assurance of divine help may well have been given between the two sections in the liturgy, something like the promises of Pss 12, 6 and 21, 9–13. The final verse (10) echoes the opening verse.

20, 4: *Remember:* God's remembering implies readiness to act. Cf Gn 8, 1; Ex 2, 24.

20, 6: *Victory:* the Hebrew root is often translated "salvation," "to save," but in military contexts it can have the specific meaning of "victory."

Ps 21: The first part of this royal psalm is a thanksgiving (2–8), and the second is a promise that the king will triumph over his enemies (9–14). The king's confident prayer (3.5) and trust in God (8) enable him to receive the divine gifts of vitality, peace, and military success. V 14 reprises v 1. When kings ceased in Israel after the sixth century B.C., the psalm was sung of a future Davidic king.

Ps 22: A lament unusual in structure and in intensity of feeling.

The psalmist's present distress is contrasted with God's past mercy in vv 2–12. In vv 13–22 enemies surround the psalmist. The last third is an invitation to praise God (23–27), becoming a universal chorus of praise (28–32). The psalm is important in the New Testament. Its opening words occur on the lips of the crucified Jesus (Mk 15, 34; Mt 27, 46), and several other verses are quoted, or at least alluded to, in the accounts of Jesus' passion (Mt 27, 35.43; Jn 19, 24).

22, 1: *"The deer of the dawn":* apparently the title of the melody.

20, 3: Pss 128, 5; 134, 3.
20, 7: Pss 18, 51; 144, 10;
   1 Sm 2, 10.
20, 8: Ps 147, 10–11; 2 Chr
   14, 10; Prv 21, 31;
   1 Sm 17, 45; Is 31, 1;
   36, 9.
20, 9: Is 40, 30.

21, 2: Ps 63, 12.
21, 5: 1 Kgs 3, 14.
21, 14: Nm 10, 35.
22, 2: Is 49, 14; 54, 7; Mt 27,
   46; Mk 15, 34.
22, 3: Sir 2, 10.
22, 4: Is 6, 3.

5   In you our ancestors trusted;
        they trusted and you rescued them.
6   To you they cried out and they escaped;
        in you they trusted and were not
            disappointed.*
7†   But I am a worm, hardly human,
        scorned by everyone, despised by the
            people.*
8   All who see me mock me;
        they curl their lips and jeer;
        they shake their heads at me:*
9   "You relied on the LORD—let him deliver you;
        if he loves you, let him rescue you."*
10   Yet you drew me forth from the womb,
        made me safe at my mother's breast.
11   Upon you I was thrust from the womb;
        since birth you are my God.*
12   Do not stay far from me,
        for trouble is near,
        and there is no one to help.*

II

13† Many bulls surround me;
        fierce bulls of Bashan encircle me.
14   They open their mouths against me,
        lions that rend and roar.*
15   Like water my life drains away;
        all my bones grow soft.
     My heart has become like wax,
        it melts away within me.
16† As dry as a potsherd is my throat;
        my tongue sticks to my palate;
        you lay me in the dust of death.
17   Many dogs surround me;
        a pack of evildoers closes in on me.
     So wasted are my hands and feet
18   that I can count all my bones.*
     They stare at me and gloat;
19   they divide my garments among them;
        for my clothing they cast lots.*
20   But you, LORD, do not stay far off;
        my strength, come quickly to help me.
21   Deliver me from the sword,
        my forlorn life from the teeth of the dog.
22   Save me from the lion's mouth,
        my poor life from the horns of wild bulls.*

Catholic Connections

HOPE IN DESPAIR

The Gospel writers make many references to Psalm 22 in telling the story of Jesus' suffering and death. During the long Gospel readings on Palm Sunday and Good Friday, you will hear them. Try reading Mt 27, 45–50 and then reading Psalm 22. What sound like words of despair in Matthew are actually words of promise for those familiar with the psalm. This is because Psalm 22 is a hymn of hope, which ends by praising God for hearing and rescuing those who cry out. So, even in the horrible suffering of Jesus' death, there was already the promise of God's saving action.

▶ Psalm 22

III

23† Then I will proclaim your name to the
            assembly;
        in the community I will praise you:*
24   "You who fear the LORD, give praise!
        All descendants of Jacob, give honor;
        show reverence, all descendants of Israel!
25† For God has not spurned or disdained
        the misery of this poor wretch,
     Did not turn away from me,
        but heard me when I cried out.
26   I will offer praise in the great assembly;
        my vows I will fulfill before those who fear
            him.

22, 7: *I am a worm, hardly human:* the psalmist's sense of isolation and dehumanization, an important motif of Ps 22, is vividly portrayed here.
22, 13–14: *Bulls:* the enemies of the psalmist are also portrayed in less-than-human form, as wild animals (cf 17.21–22). *Bashan:* a grazing land east of the Jordan, famed for its cattle. Cf Dt 32, 14; Ez 39, 18; Am 4, 1.
22, 16: *The dust of death:* the netherworld, the domain of the dead.
22, 23: *In the community I will praise you:* the person who offered a thanksgiving sacrifice in the temple recounted to the other worshipers the favor received from God and invited them to share in the sacrificial banquet. The final section (24–32) may be a summary or a citation of the psalmist's poem of praise.

22, 25: *Turn away:* literally, "hides his face from me," an important metaphor for God withdrawing from someone, e.g., Mi 3, 4; Is 8, 17; Pss 27, 9; 69, 18; 88, 15.

*
22, 6: Ps 25, 3; Is 49, 23; Dn 3, 40.
22, 7: Is 53, 3.
22, 8: Ps 109, 25; Mt 27, 39; Mk 15, 29; Lk 23, 35.
22, 9: Ps 71, 11; Wis 2, 18–20; Mt 27, 43.
22, 11: Ps 71, 6; Is 44, 2; 46, 3.
22, 12: Pss 35, 22; 38, 22; 71, 12.

22, 14: Ps 17, 12; Jb 4, 10; 1 Pt 5, 8.
22, 18: Ps 109, 24.
22, 19: Mt 27, 35; Mk 15, 24; Lk 23, 34; Jn 19, 24.
22, 22: Pss 7, 2–3; 17, 12; 35, 17; 57, 5; 58, 7; 2 Tm 4, 17.
22, 23: Pss 26, 12; 35, 18; 40, 10; 109, 30; 149, 1; 2 Sm 22, 50; Heb 2, 12.

27† The poor will eat their fill;
  those who seek the LORD will offer praise.
  May your hearts enjoy life forever!"*

      IV

28 All the ends of the earth
  will worship and turn to the LORD;
 All the families of nations
  will bow low before you.*

29 For kingship belongs to the LORD,
  the ruler over the nations.*

30† All who sleep in the earth
  will bow low before God;
 All who have gone down into the dust
  will kneel in homage.

31 And I will live for the LORD;
  my descendants will serve you.

32 The generation to come will be told of the Lord,
  that they may proclaim to a people yet
   unborn
  the deliverance you have brought.*

PSALM 23†

The LORD, Shepherd and Host

1† A psalm of David.

      I

The LORD is my shepherd;
 there is nothing I lack.*

THE GOOD SHEPHERD LOOKS AFTER US!

The famous Psalm 23 offers two images of God: the Good Shepherd and a generous host. Both images speak of God's nearness and gentle care for us. In the New Testament, Jesus appears as the Good Shepherd who gives his life for the life of his sheep (Jn 10, 1–29). He also appears several times as a host, particularly in the stories about the multiplication of the loaves and the Last Supper.

  Similar images repeat time and again in Hispanic homes. The following traditional sayings are just some examples of the caring and generous attitudes among Hispanic families: "My home is your home" *(Mi casa es su casa);* "God help you! What can I do for you?" *(¡Dios te ampare! ¿Cómo puedo ayudarte?);* "Where two eat, three eat; where six eat, seven eat" *(Donde comen dos comen tres; donde comen seis comen siete);* "Welcome! We just add water to the beans" *(¡Bienvenidos! Le echamos más agua a los frijoles);* and "Stay with us! From wall to wall, all is mattress" *(¡Quédense con nosotros! De pared a pared todo es colchón!).*

  As a Christian, you should pray Psalm 23 feeling the nearness of Jesus, the Good Shepherd, and asking his help to be a good shepherd for people in need:

■ Pray the psalm slowly, letting God fill you with peace and security.

■ Pray the psalm again, this time thinking of friends who might be feeling like sheep without a shepherd. How can you lead them to Jesus? How can you care more for them?

▶ Psalm 23

---

† **22, 27:** *The poor:* originally the poor, who were dependent on God; the term (*'anawim*) came to include the religious sense of "humble, pious, devout."

 22, 30: Hebrew unclear. The translation assumes that all on earth (28–29) and under the earth (30) will worship God.

 Ps 23: God's loving care for the psalmist is portrayed under the figures of a shepherd for the flock (1–4) and a host's generosity toward a guest (5–6). The imagery of both sections is drawn from traditions of the exodus (Is 40, 11; 49, 10; Jer 31, 10).

 23, 1: *My shepherd:* God as good shepherd is common in both the Old Testament and the New Testament (Ez 34, 11–16 and Jn 10, 11–18).

*——
22, 27: Pss 23, 5; 69, 33.
22, 28: Ps 86, 9; Tb 13, 11; Is 45, 22; 52, 10; Zec 14, 16.
22, 29: Ps 103, 19; Ob 21; Zec 14, 9.
22, 32: Pss 48, 14–15; 71, 18; 78, 6; 102, 19; Is 53, 10.
23, 1: Pss 80, 2; 95, 7; 100, 3; Dt 2, 7.

P
S

2 In green pastures you let me graze;
    to safe waters you lead me;
3† you restore my strength.
    You guide me along the right path
    for the sake of your name.*
4† Even when I walk through a dark valley,*
    I fear no harm for you are at my side;
    your rod and staff give me courage.

II

5† You set a table before me
    as my enemies watch;
    You anoint my head with oil;*
    my cup overflows.*
6† Only goodness and love will pursue me
    all the days of my life;
    I will dwell in the house of the LORD*
    for years to come.

PSALM 24†

The Glory of God in Procession to Zion
¹ A psalm of David.

I

The earth is the LORD's and all it holds,*
    the world and those who live there.
2 For God founded it on the seas,
    established it over the rivers.*

II

3 Who may go up the mountain of the LORD?*
    Who can stand in his holy place?
4† "The clean of hand and pure of heart,
    who are not devoted to idols,
    who have not sworn falsely.
5 They will receive blessings from the LORD,
    and justice from their saving God.
6 Such are the people that love the LORD,
    that seek the face of the God of Jacob."
                                    Selah

III

7† Lift up your heads, O gates;
    rise up, you ancient portals,
    that the king of glory may enter.*
8 Who is this king of glory?
    The LORD, a mighty warrior,

? did you KNOW?

Temple Worship

When Israel was ruled by kings (1000–587 B.C.), worship in the Temple at Jerusalem was an important part of the people's religious life. Many of the psalms, like Psalm 24, refer to going up to the Temple (the "holy place" in verse 3). Although the first Temple was destroyed in 587 B.C., it was later rebuilt. Temple worship started again and continued into Jesus' time. This is what the priests did during some of the Temple ceremonies:

Daily Temple worship
- every morning, presented a burnt offering (a year-old male lamb), grain, drink, and an incense offering
- every evening, presented a second burnt offering and a cereal offering

Sabbath (weekly) Temple worship
- gave two additional burnt offerings
- replaced the twelve loaves of bread, called the showbread (1 Kgs 7, 48) or bread of offering (Mt 12, 4 & Heb 9, 2), recalling the manna with which God fed Israel in the desert
- made an incense offering

Monthly and festival Temple worship
- blew the trumpet
- presented additional burnt offerings and a sin offering (a male goat)
- on the Day of Atonement, laid their hands on a living goat while confessing the people's sins and then sent the goat away into the wilderness

---

† **23, 3:** *The right path:* connotes "right way" and "way of righteousness."
23, 4: *A dark valley:* a different division of the Hebrew consonants yields the translation "the valley of the shadow of death."
23, 5: *You set a table before me:* this expression occurs in an exodus context in Ps 78, 19. *As my enemies watch:* my enemies see that I am God's friend and guest. *Oil:* a perfumed ointment made from olive oil, used especially at banquets (Ps 104, 15; Mt 26, 7; Lk 7, 37.46; Jn 12, 2).
23, 6: *Goodness and love:* the blessings of God's covenant with Israel.
Ps 24: The psalm apparently accompanied a ceremony of the entry of God (invisibly enthroned upon the ark), followed by the people, into the temple. The temple commemorated the creation of the world (1–2). The people had to affirm their fidelity before being admitted into the sanctuary (3–6; cf Ps 15). A choir identifies the ap-

proaching God and invites the very temple gates to bow down in obeisance (7–10).
24, 4–5: Literally, "the one whose hands are clean." The singular is used for the entire class of worshipers, hence the plural translation.
24, 7.9: *Lift up your heads, O gates . . . you ancient portals:* the literal meaning is impossible since the portcullis (a gate that moves up and down) was unknown in the ancient world. Extra-biblical parallels suggest a full personification of the circle of gate towers: they are like a council of elders, bowed down and anxious, awaiting the return of the army and the Great Warrior gone to battle.

23, 3: Prv 4, 11.
23, 4: Jb 10, 21–22; Is 50, 10.
23, 5: Ps 92, 11.
23, 5: Ps 16, 5.
23, 6: Ps 27, 4.

24, 1: Pss 50, 12; 89, 12; Dt 10, 14; 1 Cor 10, 26.
24, 2: Ps 136, 6; Is 42, 5.
24, 3: Ps 15, 1.
24, 7: Ps 118, 19–20.

the LORD, mighty in battle.
9 Lift up your heads, O gates;
  rise up, you ancient portals,
    that the king of glory may enter.
10 Who is this king of glory?
  The LORD of hosts is the king of glory. *Selah*

PSALM 25†

Confident Prayer for Forgiveness and Guidance
1 Of David.

I

I wait for you, O LORD;
  I lift up my soul 2 to my God.*
In you I trust; do not let me be disgraced;*
  do not let my enemies gloat over me.
3 No one is disgraced who waits for you,*
  but only those who lightly break faith.
4 Make known to me your ways, LORD;
  teach me your paths.*
5† Guide me in your truth and teach me,
  for you are God my savior.
For you I wait all the long day,
  because of your goodness, LORD.
6 Remember your compassion and love,
    O LORD;
  for they are ages old.*
7 Remember no more the sins of my
    youth;*
  remember me only in light of your love.

II

8 Good and upright is the LORD,
  who shows sinners the way,
9 Guides the humble rightly,
  and teaches the humble the way.
10 All the paths of the LORD are faithful love
  toward those who honor the covenant
    demands.
11 For the sake of your name, LORD,
  pardon my guilt, though it is great.
12 Who are those who fear the LORD?
  God shows them the way to choose.*
13 They live well and prosper,
  and their descendants inherit the land.*

14 The counsel of the LORD belongs to the
    faithful;
  the covenant instructs them.
15 My eyes are ever upon the LORD,
  who frees my feet from the snare.*

III

16 Look upon me, have pity on me,
  for I am alone and afflicted.*
17 Relieve the troubles of my heart;
  bring me out of my distress.
18 Put an end to my affliction and suffering;
  take away all my sins.
19 See how many are my enemies,
  see how fiercely they hate me.
20 Preserve my life and rescue me;
  do not let me be disgraced, for I trust in
    you.
21 Let honesty and virtue preserve me;
  I wait for you, O LORD.
22† Redeem Israel, God,
  from all its distress!

PSALM 26†

Prayer of Innocence
1 Of David.

I

Grant me justice, LORD!
  I have walked without blame.*
In the LORD I have trusted;
  I have not faltered.
2 Test me, LORD, and try me;
  search my heart and mind.*
3 Your love is before my eyes;
  I walk guided by your faithfulness.*

II

4 I do not sit with deceivers,
  nor with hypocrites do I mingle.
5 I hate the company of evildoers;
  with the wicked I do not sit.
6† I will wash my hands in innocence*
  and walk round your altar, LORD,
7 Lifting my voice in thanks,
  recounting all your wondrous deeds.

---

† **Ps 25:** A lament. Each verse begins with a successive letter of the Hebrew alphabet. Such acrostic psalms are often a series of statements only loosely connected. The psalmist mixes ardent pleas (1–2, 16–22) with expressions of confidence in God who forgives and guides.
25, 5: *Because of your goodness, LORD:* these words have been transposed from the end of 7 to preserve the pattern of two lines per letter of the Hebrew alphabet in the acrostic poem.
25, 22: A final verse beginning with the Hebrew letter *pe* is added to the normal 22-letter alphabet. Thus the letters *aleph, lamed,* and *pe* open the first, middle (v 11), and last lines of the psalm. Together, they spell *aleph,* the first letter of the alphabet.
Ps 26: Like a priest washing before approaching the altar (Ex 30, 17–21), the psalmist seeks God's protection upon entering the temple. 1–3, matched by 11–12, remind God of past integrity while

asking for purification; 4–5, matched by 9–10, pray for inclusion among the just; 6–8, the center of the poem, express the joy in God at the heart of all ritual.
26, 6: *I will wash my hands:* the washing of hands was a liturgical act (Ex 30, 19.21; 40, 31–32), symbolic of inner as well as outer cleanness. Cf Is 1, 16.

25, 2: Pss 86, 4; 143, 8.
25, 2: Ps 71, 1.
25, 3: Ps 22, 6; Is 49, 23; Dn 3, 40.
25, 4: Pss 27, 11; 86, 11; 119, 12.35; 143, 8.10.
25, 6: Sir 51, 8.
25, 7: Jb 13, 26; Is 64, 8.
25, 12: Prv 19, 23.
25, 13: Ps 37, 9.29.
25, 15: Pss 123, 1.2; 141, 8.
25, 16: Pss 86, 16; 119, 132.
26, 1: Ps 7, 9.
26, 2: Pss 17, 3; 139, 23.
26, 3: Ps 86, 11.
26, 6: Ps 73, 13.

8 LORD, I love the house where you
        dwell,
     the tenting-place of your glory.*
                 III
9 Do not take me away with sinners,
     nor my life with the violent.*
10 Their hands carry out their schemes;
     their right hands are full of bribes.
11 But I walk without blame;*
     redeem me, be gracious to me!*
12† My foot stands on level ground;
     in assemblies I will bless the LORD.*

Integrity and Values

People with integrity know what they
value and have a commitment to being consistent in what they believe and
what they do. It is impossible for us to
have integrity if we follow one set of values in one situation and another set of
values in a different situation. The integrity of the writer of Psalm 26 comes
from following God in everything (Ps 26,
1). The psalmist even wants to be tested
by God (verse 2) to be sure of complete
faithfulness! To have the kind of integrity
that the psalmist writes about, we have to
let God be the only ruler of our life. Being
able to do that takes a lifetime of growth
and conversion.

What values are you committed to
consistently? Can you think of times when
your actions did not reflect your values
or beliefs? Pray that God will give you
strength to do what is right, even when
it is most difficult.

▶ Psalm 26

PSALM 27†

Trust in God
1 Of David

                 A
                 I
The LORD is my light and my salvation;*
     whom do I fear?
The LORD is my life's refuge;
     of whom am I afraid?
2† When evildoers come at me
     to devour my flesh,*
These my enemies and foes
     themselves stumble and fall.
3 Though an army encamp against me,
     my heart does not fear;
Though war be waged against me,
     even then do I trust.
                 II
4 One thing I ask of the LORD;
     this I seek:
To dwell in the LORD's house
     all the days of my life,
To gaze on the LORD's beauty,
     to visit his temple.*
5 For God will hide me in his shelter
     in time of trouble,*
Will conceal me in the cover of his tent;
     and set me high upon a rock.
6 Even now my head is held high
     above my enemies on every side!
I will offer in his tent
     sacrifices with shouts of joy;
     I will sing and chant praise to the LORD.

                 B
                 I
7 Hear my voice, LORD, when I call;
     have mercy on me and answer me.
8† "Come," says my heart, "seek God's face";
     your face, LORD, do I seek!*
9 Do not hide your face from me;
     do not repel your servant in anger.
You are my help; do not cast me off;
     do not forsake me, God my savior!

26, 12: *On level ground:* in safety, where there is no danger of
tripping and falling. *In assemblies:* at the temple. Having walked
around the altar, the symbol of God's presence, the psalmist
blesses God.

Ps 27: Tradition has handed down the two sections of the psalm
(1–6 and 7–14) as one psalm, though each part could be understood
as complete in itself. Asserting boundless hope that God will bring
rescue (1–3), the psalmist longs for the presence of God in the temple, protection from all enemies (4–6). In part B there is a clear shift
in tone (7–12), the climax of the poem comes with "I believe" (13),
echoing "I trust" (3).

27, 2: *To devour my flesh:* the psalmist's enemies are rapacious
beasts (Pss 7, 3; 17, 12; 22, 14.17).

27, 8: *"Seek God's face"* (literally: "to seek his face"): to commune with God in the temple. The idiom is derived from the practice of journeying to sacred places. Cf Hos 5, 15; 2 Sm 21, 1; Ps
24, 6.

26, 8: Pss 29, 9; 63, 3; Ex 24,
   16; 25, 8.
26, 9: Ps 28, 3.
26, 11: Ps 101, 6.
26, 12: Pss 22, 23; 35, 18;
   149, 1.

27, 1: Pss 18, 29; 36, 10; 43,
   3; Is 10, 17; Mi 7, 8.
27, 2: Ps 14, 4.
27, 4: Pss 23, 6; 61, 5.
27, 5: Ps 31, 21.
27, 8: Ps 24, 6; Hos 5, 15.

10 Even if my father and mother forsake me,
      the LORD will take me in.*

II

11 LORD, show me your way;
      lead me on a level path
      because of my enemies.*
12 Do not abandon me to the will of my foes;
      malicious and lying witnesses have risen
        against me.
13† But I believe I shall enjoy the LORD's goodness
      in the land of the living.*
14 Wait for the LORD, take courage;
      be stouthearted, wait for the LORD!

PSALM 28 †

Petition and Thanksgiving

1† Of David.

I

To you, LORD, I call;
   my Rock, do not be deaf to me.*
If you fail to answer me,
   I will join those who go down to
     the pit.*
2† Hear the sound of my pleading when I cry to
     you,
   lifting my hands toward your holy
     place.*
3 Do not drag me off with the wicked,
   with those who do wrong,*
Who speak peace to their neighbors
   though evil is in their hearts.*
4 Repay them for their deeds,
   for the evil that they do.
For the work of their hands repay them;
   give them what they deserve.*
5 They pay no heed to the LORD's works,
   to the deeds of God's hands.*
God will tear them down,
   never to be rebuilt.

II

6† Blessed be the LORD,
      who has heard the sound of my
        pleading.
7 The LORD is my strength and my shield,
      in whom my heart trusted and found
        help.
So my heart rejoices;
      with my song I praise my God.

III

8† LORD, you are the strength of your people,
      the saving refuge of your anointed king.
9 Save your people, bless your inheritance;
      feed and sustain them forever!

PSALM 29 †

The LORD of Majesty Acclaimed as King of the World

1 A psalm of David.

I

Give to the LORD, you heavenly beings,†
   give to the LORD glory and might;
2 Give to the LORD the glory due God's name.
   Bow down before the LORD's holy
     splendor!*

II

3† The voice of the LORD is over the waters;
   the God of glory thunders,
   the LORD, over the mighty waters.
4 The voice of the LORD is power;
   the voice of the LORD is splendor.*
5 The voice of the LORD cracks the cedars;
   the LORD splinters the cedars of Lebanon,
6† Makes Lebanon leap like a calf,
   and Sirion like a young bull.
7 The voice of the LORD strikes with fiery
     flame;
8† the voice of the LORD rocks the desert;
   the LORD rocks the desert of Kadesh.

---

† 27, 13: *In the land of the living:* or "in the land of life," an epithet of the Jerusalem temple (Pss 52, 7; 116, 9; Is 38, 11), where the faithful had access to the life-giving presence of God.

Ps 28: A lament asking that the psalmist, who has taken refuge in the temple (2), not be punished with the wicked, who are headed inevitably toward destruction (1.3–5). The statement of praise is exceptionally lengthy and vigorous (6–7). The psalm ends with a prayer (8–9).

28, 1: *The pit:* a synonym for Sheol, the shadowy place of the dead.

28, 2: *Your holy place:* the innermost part of the temple, the holy of holies, containing the ark. Cf 1 Kgs 6, 16.19–23; 8, 6–8.

28, 6: The psalmist shifts to fervent thanksgiving, probably responding to a priestly or prophetic oracle in 5cd (not usually transmitted) assuring the worshiper that the prayer has been heard.

28, 8: *Your people . . . your anointed king:* salvation is more than individual, affecting all the people and their God-given leader.

Ps 29: The hymn invites the members of the heavenly court to acknowledge God's supremacy by ascribing glory and might to God alone (1–2a.9b). Divine glory and might are dramatically visible in the storm (3–9a). The storm apparently comes from the Mediterranean onto the coast of Syria-Palestine and then moves inland. In 10

the divine beings acclaim God's eternal kingship. The psalm concludes with a prayer that God will impart the power just displayed to the Israelite king and through the king to Israel.

29, 1: *You heavenly beings:* literally "sons of God," i.e., members of the heavenly court who served Israel's God in a variety of capacities.

29, 3: *The voice of the LORD:* the sevenfold repetition of the phrase imitates the sound of crashing thunder and may allude to God's primordial slaying of Leviathan, the seven-headed sea monster of Canaanite mythology.

29, 6: *Sirion:* the Phoenician name for Mount Hermon. Cf Dt 3, 9.

29, 8: *The desert of Kadesh:* probably north of Palestine in the neighborhood of Lebanon and Hermon.

27, **10:** Is 49, 15.
27, **11:** Pss 25, 4; 86, 11.
27, **13:** Ps 116, 9; Is 38, 11.
28, **1:** Ps 18, 2.
28, **1:** Pss 30, 4; 88, 5; 143, 7; Prv 1, 12.
28, **2:** Ps 134, 2.
28, **3:** Ps 26, 9.
28, **3:** Pss 12, 2; 55, 22; 62, 5; Prv 26, 24–28.
28, **4:** 2 Sm 3, 39.
28, **5:** Is 5, 12.
29, **2:** Pss 68, 35; 96, 7–9.
29, **4:** Pss 46, 7; 77, 18–19; Jb 37, 4; Is 30, 30.

P
S

9† The voice of the LORD twists the oaks
   and strips the forests bare.
   All in his palace say, "Glory!"

III

10† The LORD sits enthroned above the flood!*
   The LORD reigns as king forever!
11† May the LORD give might to his people;
   may the LORD bless his people with peace!*

PSALM 30†

Thanksgiving for Deliverance

1† A psalm. A song for the dedication of the temple.
   Of David.

I

2   I praise you, LORD, for you raised me up
    and did not let my enemies rejoice over me.
3† O LORD, my God,
    I cried out to you and you healed me.
4† LORD, you brought me up from Sheol;
    you kept me from going down to the pit.*

II

5   Sing praise to the LORD, you faithful;
    give thanks to God's holy name.
6   For divine anger lasts but a moment;
    divine favor lasts a lifetime.
    At dusk weeping comes for the night;
    but at dawn there is rejoicing.

III

7† Complacent, I once said,
    "I shall never be shaken."
8   LORD, when you showed me favor
    I stood like the mighty mountains.
    But when you hid your face
    I was struck with terror.*
9   To you, LORD, I cried out;
    with the Lord I pleaded for mercy:
10† "What gain is there from my lifeblood,
    from my going down to the grave?
    Does dust give you thanks
    or declare your faithfulness?
11 Hear, O LORD, have mercy on me;
    LORD, be my helper."

The Eye of the Storm

Thunderstorms can be frightening. They often come up quickly and without warning. The winds and lightning that accompany them can be destructive. Children and animals (okay, lots of adults too) are often afraid at the sheer force of it all.

It would be difficult to read Psalm 29 aloud and not be expressive. Phrases such as "the God of glory thunders" (verse 3), and "the voice of the LORD cracks the cedars" (verse 5) and "strikes with fiery flame" (verse 7) evoke a divine splendor that we do not often hear about. The psalmist speaks with admiration about the power and majesty of God.

When have you experienced the awesome power of God?

▶ Psalm 29

IV

12 You changed my mourning into dancing;
    you took off my sackcloth
    and clothed me with gladness.*
13 With my whole being I sing
    endless praise to you.
    O LORD, my God,
    forever will I give you thanks.

PSALM 31†

Prayer in Distress and Thanksgiving for Escape

1 For the leader. A psalm of David.

I

2   In you, LORD, I take refuge;*
    let me never be put to shame.

29, 9b–10: Having witnessed God's supreme power (3–9a), the gods acknowledge the glory that befits the king of the divine and human world.

29, 10: *The flood:* God defeated the primordial waters and made them part of the universe. Cf Pss 89, 10–13 and 93, 3–4.

29, 11: *His people:* God's people, Israel.

Ps 30: An individual thanksgiving in four parts: praise and thanks for deliverance and restoration (2–4); an invitation to others to join in (5–6); a flashback to the time before deliverance (7–11); a return to praise and thanks (12–13). Two sets of images recur: 1) going down, death, silence; 2) coming up, life, praising. God has delivered the psalmist from one state to the other.

30, 1: *For the dedication of the temple:* a later adaptation of the psalm to celebrate the purification of the temple in 164 B.C. during the Maccabean Revolt.

30, 3: *Healed:* for God as healer, see also Pss 103, 3; 107, 20; Hos 6, 1; 7, 1; 11, 3; 14, 5.

30, 4: *Sheol . . . pit:* the shadowy underworld residence of the spirits of the dead, here a metaphor for near death.

30, 7: *Complacent:* untroubled existence is often seen as a source of temptation to forget God. Cf Dt 8, 10–18; Hos 13, 6; Prv 30, 9.

30, 10: In the stillness of Sheol no one gives you praise; let me live and be among your worshipers. Cf Pss 6, 6; 88, 11–13; 115, 17; Is 38, 18.

Ps 31: A lament (2–19) with a strong emphasis on trust (4.6.15–16), ending with an anticipatory thanksgiving (20–25). As is usual in laments, the affliction is couched in general terms. The psalmist feels overwhelmed by evil people but trusts in the "faithful God" (6).

29, 10: Bar 3, 3.
29, 11: Ps 68, 36.
30, 4: Ps 28, 1; Jon 2, 7.
30, 8: Ps 104, 29.
30, 12: Is 61, 3; Jer 31, 13.
31, 2–4: Ps 71, 1–3.

Cultural Connections

COURAGE

Psalm 31 ends "Be strong and take heart, / all you who hope in the LORD" (verse 25). Courage is an important value for many Native American peoples. For the Lakota tribe, it is one of four primary values. The Lakota word for courage is *woo-hit-i-ka*.

Leaders particularly have to be brave. It takes courage to make unpopular decisions and to go against peer pressure. It takes courage to do the right thing when the wrong thing might be easier or more enjoyable. It takes courage to protect others and to care for their needs. Because these kinds of actions take courage, practicing them will earn you honor.

What is the most courageous thing you have done for the sake of someone else?

To explore the other primary Lakota virtues, see the Cultural Connections articles for Psalms 73, 89, and 112.

▶ **Psalm 31**

In your justice deliver me;
3   incline your ear to me;
       make haste to rescue me!
   Be my rock of refuge,
       a stronghold to save me.
4 You are my rock and my fortress;*
       for your name's sake lead and guide me.
5 Free me from the net they have set for me,
       for you are my refuge.
6† Into your hands I commend my spirit;*
       you will redeem me, LORD, faithful God.
7 You hate those who serve worthless idols,
       but I trust in the LORD.
8 I will rejoice and be glad in your love,
       once you have seen my misery,
       observed my distress.*
9 You will not abandon me into enemy hands,
       but will set my feet in a free and open space.

II

10 Be gracious to me, LORD, for I am in
         distress;
      with grief my eyes are wasted,
         my soul and body spent.

11 My life is worn out by sorrow,
       my years by sighing.
   My strength fails in affliction;
       my bones are consumed.*
12 To all my foes I am a thing of scorn,
       to my neighbors, a dreaded sight,
       a horror to my friends.
   When they see me in the street,
       they quickly shy away.*
13† I am forgotten, out of mind like the
         dead;
       I am like a shattered dish.
14† I hear the whispers of the crowd;
       terrors are all around me.
   They conspire against me;
       they plot to take my life.
15 But I trust in you, LORD;
       I say, "You are my God."*
16 My times are in your hands;
       rescue me from my enemies,
       from the hands of my pursuers.
17 Let your face shine on your servant;*
       save me in your kindness.

---

† **31, 6:** *Into your hands I commend my spirit:* in Lk 23, 46 Jesus breathes his last with this psalm verse. Stephen in Acts 7, 59 alludes to these words as he is attacked by enemies. The verse is used as an antiphon in the Divine Office at Compline, the last prayer of the day.

31, 13: *Like a shattered dish:* a common comparison for something ruined and useless. Cf Is 30, 14; Jer 19, 11; 22, 28.

31, 14: *Terrors are all around:* a cry used in inescapable danger. Cf Jer 6, 25; 20, 10; 46, 5; 49, 29.

31, 4: Ps 18, 2.   31, 12: Jb 19, 13–19.
31, 6: Lk 23, 46; Acts 7, 59.   31, 15: Ps 140, 7; Is 25, 1.
31, 8: Ps 10, 14.   31, 17: Ps 67, 1; Nm 6, 24.
31, 11: Pss 32, 3; 38, 10–11.

18 Do not let me be put to shame,
    for I have called to you, LORD.
  Put the wicked to shame;
    reduce them to silence in Sheol.

19 Strike dumb their lying lips,
    proud lips that attack the just
    in contempt and scorn.*

III

20 How great is your goodness, LORD,
    stored up for those who fear you.
  You display it for those who trust you,
    in the sight of all the people.

21 You hide them in the shelter of your
      presence,
    safe from scheming enemies.
  You keep them in your abode,
    safe from plotting tongues.*

22 Blessed be the LORD,
    who has shown me wondrous love,
    and been for me a city most secure.

23 Once I said in my anguish,
    "I am shut out from your sight."*
  Yet you heard my plea,
    when I cried out to you.

24 Love the LORD, all you faithful.
    The LORD protects the loyal,
    but repays the arrogant in full.

25 Be strong and take heart,
    all you who hope in the LORD.

PSALM 32†

Remission of Sin

¹ Of David. A *maskil.*

I

Happy the sinner whose fault is removed,
  whose sin is forgiven.*

2 Happy those to whom the LORD imputes no
    guilt,
  in whose spirit is no deceit.

II

3† As long as I kept silent, my bones wasted away;
    I groaned all the day.*

4 For day and night your hand was heavy upon me;

my strength withered as in dry summer
    heat.   *Selah*

5 Then I declared my sin to you;
    my guilt I did not hide.*
  I said, "I confess my faults to the LORD,"
    and you took away the guilt of my sin.
                                            Selah

6† Thus should all your faithful pray
    in time of distress.
  Though flood waters threaten,
    they will never reach them.*

7 You are my shelter; from distress you keep me;
    with safety you ring me round.   *Selah*

III

8 I will instruct you and show you the way you
    should walk,
  give you counsel and watch over you.

9 Do not be senseless like horses or mules;
    with bit and bridle their temper is curbed,
    else they will not come to you.

IV

10 Many are the sorrows of the wicked,
    but love surrounds those who trust in the
    LORD.

11 Be glad in the LORD and rejoice, you just;
    exult, all you upright of heart.*

PSALM 33†

Praise of the LORD's Power and Providence

I

1 Rejoice, you just, in the LORD;
    praise from the upright is fitting.*

2 Give thanks to the LORD on the harp;
    on the ten-stringed lyre offer praise.*

3 Sing to God a new song;
    skillfully play with joyful chant.

4 For the LORD's word is true;
    all his works are trustworthy.

5 The LORD loves justice and right
    and fills the earth with goodness.*

II

6† By the LORD's word the heavens were made;*
    by the breath of his mouth all their host.*

Ps 32: An individual thanksgiving and the second of the seven Penitential Psalms (cf Ps 6). The opening declaration—the forgiven are blessed (1–2)—arises from the psalmist's own experience. At one time the psalmist was stubborn and closed, a victim of sin's power (3–4), and then became open to the forgiving God (5–7). Sin here, as often in the Bible, is not only the personal act of rebellion against God but also the consequences of that act—frustration and waning of vitality. Having been rescued, the psalmist can teach others the joys of justice and the folly of sin (8–11).

32, 3: *I kept silent:* did not confess the sin before God.

32, 6: *Flood waters:* the untamed waters surrounding the earth, a metaphor for danger.

Ps 33: A hymn in which the just are invited (1–3) to praise God, who by a mere word (4–5) created the three-tiered universe of the

heavens, the cosmic waters, and the earth (6–9). Human words, in contrast, effect nothing (10–11). The greatness of human beings consists in God's choosing them as a special people and their faithful response (12–22).

33, 6: *All their host:* the stars of the sky are commonly viewed as a vast army, e.g., Neh 9, 6; Is 40, 26; 45, 12; Jer 33, 22.

31, 19: Ps 12, 4.
31, 21: Ps 27, 5.
31, 23: Jon 2, 5.
32, 1: Is 1, 18; Ps 65, 3; Rom 4, 7–8.
32, 3: Ps 31, 11.
32, 5: Pss 38, 19; 51, 5.

32, 6: Ps 18, 5.
32, 11: Ps 33, 1.
33, 1: Pss 32, 11; 147, 1.
33, 2: Pss 92, 4; 144, 9.
33, 5: Ps 119, 64.
33, 6: Gn 2, 1.

7† The waters of the sea were gathered as in a
    bowl;
  in cellars the deep was confined.*

III

8 Let all the earth fear the LORD;
   let all who dwell in the world show reverence.
9 For he spoke, and it came to be,
   commanded, and it stood in place.*
10 The LORD foils the plan of nations,
   frustrates the designs of peoples.
11 But the plan of the LORD stands forever,
   wise designs through all generations.*
12 Happy the nation whose God is the LORD,
   the people chosen as his very own.*

IV

13 From heaven the LORD looks down
   and observes the whole human race,*
14 Surveying from the royal throne
   all who dwell on earth.
15 The one who fashioned the hearts of them all
   knows all their works.

V

16 A king is not saved by a mighty army,
   nor a warrior delivered by great strength.
17 Useless is the horse for safety;
   its great strength, no sure escape.
18 But the LORD's eyes are upon the reverent,
   upon those who hope for his gracious help,
19 Delivering them from death,
   keeping them alive in times of famine.

VI

20 Our soul waits for the LORD,
   who is our help and shield.*
21 For in God our hearts rejoice;
   in your holy name we trust.
22 May your kindness, LORD, be upon us;
   we have put our hope in you.

PSALM 34†

Thanksgiving to God Who Delivers the Just

1† Of David, when he feigned madness before
   Abimelech, who forced him to depart.

I

2 I will bless the LORD at all times;
  praise shall be always in my mouth.*

3 My soul will glory in the LORD
  that the poor may hear and be glad.
4 Magnify the LORD with me;
  let us exalt his name together.

II

5 I sought the LORD, who answered me,
  delivered me from all my fears.
6 Look to God that you may be radiant with joy
  and your faces may not blush for shame.
7 In my misfortune I called,
  the LORD heard and saved me from all
    distress.
8 The angel of the LORD, who encamps with them,
  delivers all who fear God.*
9 Learn to savor how good the LORD is;
  happy are those who take refuge in him.*
10 Fear the LORD, you holy ones;
   nothing is lacking to those who fear him.*
11† The powerful grow poor and hungry,
   but those who seek the LORD lack no good
     thing.

III

12† Come, children, listen to me;*
   I will teach you the fear of the LORD.
13 Who among you loves life,*
   takes delight in prosperous days?
14 Keep your tongue from evil,
   your lips from speaking lies.
15 Turn from evil and do good;*
   seek peace and pursue it.
16 The LORD has eyes for the just*
   and ears for their cry.
17 The LORD's face is against evildoers
   to wipe out their memory from the earth.
18 When the just cry out, the LORD hears
   and rescues them from all distress.
19 The LORD is close to the brokenhearted,
   saves those whose spirit is crushed.
20 Many are the troubles of the just,
   but the LORD delivers from them all.
21 God watches over all their bones;
   not a one shall be broken.*
22 Evil will slay the wicked;
   those who hate the just are condemned.
23 The LORD redeems loyal servants;
   no one is condemned whose refuge is God.

P
S

---

† **33, 7:** *The waters . . . as in a bowl:* ancients sometimes attributed
the power keeping the seas from overwhelming land to a primordial
victory of the storm-god over personified Sea. God confines the seas
as easily as one puts water in a bowl.
  Ps 34: A thanksgiving in acrostic form, each line beginning with
a successive letter of the Hebrew alphabet. In this psalm one letter is
missing and two are in reverse order. The psalmist, fresh from the experience of being rescued (5.7), can teach the "poor," those who are
defenseless, to trust in God alone (4.12). God will make them powerful (5–11) and give them protection (12–23).
  34, 1: *Abimelech:* a scribal error for Achish. In 1 Sm 21, 13–16,
David feigned madness before Achish, not Abimelech.
  34, 11: *The powerful:* literally, "lions." Fierce animals were

sometimes metaphors for influential people.
  34, 12: *Children:* the customary term for students in Wisdom literature.

33, 7: Ps 78, 13; Gn 1, 9–10;   34, 2: Ps 145, 2.
    Ex 15, 8.   34, 8: Ex 14, 19.
33, 9: Ps 148, 5; Gn 1, 3f; Jdt   34, 9: Ps 2, 12.
    16, 14.   34, 10: Prv 3, 7.
33, 11: Prv 19, 21; Is 40, 8.   34, 12: Prv 1, 8; 4, 1.
33, 12: Ps 144, 15; Ex 19, 6;   34, 13–17: 1 Pt 3, 10–12.
    Dt 7, 6.   34, 15: Ps 37, 27.
33, 13: Jb 34, 21; Sir 15, 19;   34, 16: Ps 33, 18.
    Jer 16, 17; 32, 19.   34, 21: Jn 19, 36.
33, 20: Ps 115, 9.

PSALM 35†

Prayer for Help against Unjust Enemies

¹† Of David.

I

Oppose, LORD, those who oppose me;
   war upon those who make war upon me.
² Take up the shield and buckler;
   rise up in my defense.
³ Brandish lance and battle-ax
   against my pursuers.
Say to my heart,
   "I am your salvation."
⁴ Let those who seek my life
   be put to shame and disgrace.
Let those who plot evil against me*
   be turned back and confounded.
⁵ Make them like chaff before the wind,*
   with the angel of the LORD driving them
     on.
⁶ Make their way slippery and dark,
   with the angel of the LORD pursuing
     them.

II

⁷ Without cause they set their snare for me;
   without cause they dug a pit for me.
⁸ Let ruin overtake them unawares;
   let the snare they have set catch them;
   let them fall into the pit they have dug.*
⁹ Then I will rejoice in the LORD,
   exult in God's salvation.
¹⁰ My very bones shall say,
   "O LORD, who is like you,*
Who rescue the afflicted from the
     powerful,
   the afflicted and needy from the
     despoiler?"

III

¹¹ Malicious witnesses come forward,
   accuse me of things I do not know.
¹² They repay me evil for good
   and I am all alone.*
¹³† Yet I, when they were ill, put on sackcloth,
   afflicted myself with fasting,
   sobbed my prayers upon my bosom.

¹⁴ I went about in grief as for my brother,
   bent in mourning as for my mother.
¹⁵ Yet when I stumbled they gathered with
     glee,
   they gathered against me like strangers.
They slandered me without ceasing;
¹⁶   without respect they mocked me,
   gnashed their teeth against me.

IV

¹⁷ LORD, how long will you look on?
   Save me from roaring beasts,
   my precious life from lions!*
¹⁸ Then I will thank you in the great assembly;
   I will praise you before the mighty
     throng.*
¹⁹ Do not let lying foes smirk at me,
   my undeserved enemies wink
     knowingly.*
²⁰ They speak no words of peace,
   but against the quiet in the land
   they fashion deceitful speech.*
²¹ They open wide their mouths against me.
   They say, "Aha! Good!
   Our eyes relish the sight!"*
²² You see this, LORD; do not be silent;*
   Lord, do not withdraw from me.
²³ Awake, be vigilant in my defense,
   in my cause, my God and my Lord.
²⁴ Defend me because you are just, LORD;
   my God, do not let them gloat over me.
²⁵ Do not let them say in their hearts,
   "Aha! Just what we wanted!"
Do not let them say,
   "We have devoured that one!"
²⁶ Put to shame and confound
   all who relish my misfortune.
Clothe with shame and disgrace
   those who lord it over me.
²⁷ But let those who favor my just cause
   shout for joy and be glad.
May they ever say, "Exalted be the LORD
who delights in the peace of his loyal
     servant."
²⁸ Then my tongue shall recount your justice,
   declare your praise, all the day long.*

---

† **Ps 35:** A lament of a person betrayed by friends. The psalmist prays that the evildoers be publicly exposed as unjust (1–8), and gives thanks in anticipation of vindication (9–10). Old friends are the enemies (11–16). May their punishment come quickly (17–21)! The last part (22–26) echoes the opening in praying for the destruction of the psalmist's persecutors. The psalm may appear vindictive, but one must keep in mind that the psalmist is praying for *public* redress now of a *public* injustice. There is at this time no belief in an afterlife in which justice will be redressed.

35, 1–6: The mixture of judicial, martial, and hunting images shows that the language is figurative. The actual injustice is false accusation of serious crimes (11.15.20–21). The psalmist seeks lost honor through a trial before God.

35, 13.15–17: The Hebrew is obscure.

35, 4: Pss 40, 15; 71, 13.
35, 5: Pss 1, 4; 83, 14; Jb 21, 18.
35, 8: Pss 7, 16; 9, 16; 57, 7; Prv 26, 27; Eccl 10, 8; Sir 27, 26.
35, 10: Pss 86, 8; 89, 7.9; Ex 15, 11.
35, 12: Pss 27, 12; 38, 20–21; 109, 5; Jer 18, 20.
35, 17: Pss 17, 12; 22, 22; 58, 7.
35, 18: Pss 22, 23; 26, 12; 35, 18; 40, 10; 149, 1.
35, 19: Ps 38, 17.
35, 20: Ps 120, 6–7.
35, 21: Ps 40, 16; Lam 2, 16.
35, 22: Pss 22, 12; 38, 21; 109, 1.
35, 28: Ps 71, 15–16.

PSALM 36†

Human Wickedness and Divine Providence

¹ For the leader. Of David, the servant of the LORD.

I

² Sin directs the heart of the wicked;
    their eyes are closed to the fear of God.*

³† For they live with the delusion:
    their guilt will not be known and hated.

⁴ Empty and false are the words of their mouth;
    they have ceased to be wise and do good.

⁵ In their beds they hatch plots;
    they set out on a wicked way;
    they do not reject evil.*

II

⁶† LORD, your love reaches to heaven;
    your fidelity, to the clouds.*

⁷ Your justice is like the highest mountains;
    your judgments, like the mighty deep;
    all living creatures you sustain, LORD.

⁸† How precious is your love, O God!
    We take refuge in the shadow of your wings.*

⁹ We feast on the rich food of your house;
    from your delightful stream* you give us drink.

¹⁰ For with you is the fountain of life,*
    and in your light we see light.*

¹¹ Continue your kindness toward your friends,
    your just defense of the honest heart.

¹² Do not let the foot of the proud overtake me,
    nor the hand of the wicked disturb me.

¹³ There make the evildoers fall;
    thrust them down, never to rise.

PSALM 37†

The Fate of Sinners and the Reward of the Just

¹ Of David.

ALEPH

Do not be provoked by evildoers;
    do not envy those who do wrong.*

² Like grass they wither quickly;
    like green plants they wilt away.*

BETH

³† Trust in the LORD and do good
    that you may dwell in the land and live secure.*

⁴ Find your delight in the LORD
    who will give you your heart's desire.*

GIMEL

⁵ Commit your way to the LORD;
    trust that God will act*

⁶ And make your integrity shine like the dawn,
    your vindication like noonday.*

DALETH

⁷ Be still before the LORD;
    wait for God.
Do not be provoked by the prosperous,
    nor by malicious schemers.

HE

⁸ Give up your anger, abandon your wrath;
    do not be provoked; it brings only harm.

⁹† Those who do evil will be cut off,
    but those who wait for the LORD will possess the land.*

WAW

¹⁰ Wait a little, and the wicked will be no more;
    look for them and they will not be there.

¹¹† But the poor will possess the land,*
    will delight in great prosperity.

ZAYIN

¹² The wicked plot against the just
    and grind their teeth at them;

¹³ But the LORD laughs at them,*
    knowing their day is coming.

HETH

¹⁴ The wicked draw their swords;
    they string their bows
To fell the poor and oppressed,
    to slaughter those whose way is honest.*

Ps 36: A psalm with elements of wisdom (2–5), the hymn (6–10), and the lament (11–13). The rule of sin over the wicked (2–5) is contrasted with the rule of divine love and mercy over God's friends (6–10). The psalm ends with a prayer that God's guidance never cease (11–13).

36, 3: *Hated:* punished by God.

36, 6–7: *Love . . . judgments:* God actively controls the entire world.

36, 8: *The shadow of your wings:* metaphor for divine protection. It probably refers to the winged cherubim in the holy of holies in the temple. Cf 1 Kgs 6, 23–28.32; 2 Chr 3, 10–13; Ez 1, 4–9.

Ps 37: The psalm responds to the problem of evil, which the Old Testament often expresses as a question: Why do the wicked prosper and the good suffer? The psalm answers that the situation is only temporary. God will reverse things, rewarding the good and punishing the wicked here on earth. The perspective is concrete and earthbound: people's very actions place them among the ranks of the good or wicked. Each group or "way" has its own inherent dynamism—eventual frustration for the wicked, eventual reward for the just. The psalm is an acrostic, i.e., each section begins with a suc-

cessive letter of the Hebrew alphabet. Each section has its own imagery and logic.

37, 3.9.11.22.27.29.34: *The land:* the promised land, Israel, which became for later interpreters a type or figure of heaven. Cf Heb 11, 9–10.13–16. The New Testament Beatitudes (Mt 5, 3–12; Lk 6, 20–26) have been influenced by the psalm, especially their total reversal of the present and their interpretation of the happy future as possession of the land.

36, 2: Rom 3, 18.	**37, 3:** Ps 128, 2.
36, 5: Mi 2, 1.	**37, 4:** Prv 10, 24.
36, 6: Pss 57, 11; 71, 19.	**37, 5:** Pss 55, 23; Prv 3, 5;
36, 8: Ps 17, 8.	16, 3.
36, 9: Gn 2, 8.10.	**37, 6:** Wis 5, 6; Is 58, 10.
36, 10: Is 55, 1; Jn 4, 14.	**37, 9:** Ps 25, 13; Prv 2, 21; Is
36, 10: Ps 80, 4.8.20.	57, 13.
37, 1: Prv 3, 31; 23, 17; 24,	**37, 11:** Mt 5, 4.
1.19.	**37, 13:** Pss 2, 4; 59, 9; Wis 4,
37, 2: Pss 90, 5–6; 102, 12;	18.
103, 15–16; Jb 14, 2;	**37, 14:** Pss 11, 2; 57, 5; 64, 4.
Is 40, 7.	

15   Their swords will pierce their own hearts;
        their bows will be broken.

TETH

16   Better the poverty of the just
        than the great wealth of the wicked.*
17   The arms of the wicked will be broken;
        the LORD will sustain the just.

YODH

18   The LORD watches over the days of the
        blameless;
        their heritage lasts forever.
19   They will not be disgraced when times are
        hard;
        in days of famine they will have plenty.

KAPH

20   The wicked perish,
        the enemies of the LORD;
     Like the beauty of meadows they vanish;
        like smoke they disappear.*

LAMEDH

21   The wicked borrow but do not repay;
        the just are generous in giving.
22† For those blessed by the Lord will possess the
        land,
        but those accursed will be cut off.

MEM

23   Those whose steps are guided by the
        LORD;*
        whose way God approves,
24   May stumble, but they will never fall,
        for the LORD holds their hand.

NUN

25   Neither in my youth, nor now in old age
        have I ever seen the just abandoned*
        or their children begging bread.
26   The just always lend generously,
        and their children become a blessing.

SAMEKH

27† Turn from evil and do good,
        that you may inhabit the land forever.*
28   For the LORD loves justice
        and does not abandon the faithful.

AYIN

When the unjust are destroyed,
   and the children of the wicked cut off,

29† The just will possess the land
        and live in it forever.*

PE

30   The mouths of the just utter wisdom;*
        their tongues speak what is right.
31   God's teaching is in their hearts;*
        their steps do not falter.

SADHE

32   The wicked spy on the just
        and seek to kill them.
33   But the LORD does not leave the just in their
        power,
        nor let them be condemned when tried.

QOPH

34† Wait eagerly for the LORD,
        and keep to the way;*
     God will raise you to possess the land;
        you will gloat when the wicked are
        cut off.

RESH

35   I have seen ruthless scoundrels,
        strong as flourishing cedars.*
36   When I passed by again, they were gone;
        though I searched, they could not be
        found.

SHIN

37   Observe the honest, mark the upright;
        those at peace with God have a future.*
38   But all sinners will be destroyed;
        the future of the wicked will be cut off.

TAW

39   The salvation of the just is from the LORD,
        their refuge in time of distress.*
40   The LORD helps and rescues them,
        rescues and saves them from the
        wicked,
        because in God they take refuge.

PSALM 38†

Prayer of an Afflicted Sinner

¹ A psalm of David. For remembrance.

I

2   LORD, punish me no more in your anger;
        in your wrath do not chastise me!*
3   Your arrows have sunk deep in me;*
        your hand has come down upon me.

---

†   **Ps 38:** In this lament, one of the Penitential Psalms (cf Ps 6), the psalmist acknowledges the sin that has brought physical and mental sickness and social ostracism. There is no one to turn to for help; only God can undo the past and restore the psalmist.

37, 16: Prv 15, 16; 16, 8.   37, 23: Prv 20, 24.
37, 20: Wis 5, 14.   37, 25: Jb 4, 7; Sir 2, 10.

37, 27: Ps 34, 14–15; Am 5,   37, 35: Ps 92, 8–9; Is 2, 13; Ez
   14.   31, 10–11.
37, 29: Ps 25, 13; Prv 2, 21; Is   37, 37: Prv 23, 18; 24, 14.
   57, 13.   37, 39: Ps 9, 10; Is 25, 4.
37, 30: Prv 10, 31.   38, 2: Ps 6, 2.
37, 31: Ps 40, 9; Dt 6, 6; Is 51, 38, 3: Jb 6, 4; Lam 3, 12; Pss
   7; Jer 31, 33.   31, 11; 64, 7.
37, 34: Ps 31, 24.

4 My flesh is afflicted because of your anger;
       my frame aches because of my sin.*
5 My iniquities overwhelm me,
       a burden beyond my strength.*

II

6 Foul and festering are my sores
       because of my folly.
7 I am stooped and deeply bowed;*
       all day I go about mourning.
8 My loins burn with fever;
       my flesh is afflicted.
9 I am numb and utterly crushed;
       I wail with anguish of heart.*
10 My Lord, my deepest yearning is before
       you;
       my groaning is not hidden from you.
11 My heart shudders, my strength forsakes
       me;
       the very light of my eyes has failed.*
12 Friends and companions shun my pain;
       my neighbors stand far off.
13 Those who seek my life lay snares for me;
       they seek my misfortune, they speak
           of ruin;
       they plot treachery all the day.

III

14 But I am like the deaf, hearing nothing,
       like the dumb, saying nothing,
15 Like someone who does not hear,
       who has no answer ready.
16 LORD, I wait for you;
       O Lord, my God, answer me.*
17 For I fear they will gloat,
       exult over me if I stumble.

IV

18 I am very near to falling;
       my pain is with me always.
19 I acknowledge my guilt
       and grieve over my sin.*
20 But many are my foes without cause,
       a multitude of enemies without
           reason,
21 Repaying me evil for good,
       harassing me for pursuing good.*
22 Forsake me not, O LORD;
       my God, be not far from me!*
23 Come quickly to help me,*
       my Lord and my salvation!

PSALM 39†

The Vanity of Life
1 For the leader, for Jeduthun.* A psalm of David.

I

2 I said, "I will watch my ways,
       lest I sin with my tongue;
       I will set a curb on my mouth."
3 Dumb and silent before the wicked,
       I refrained from any speech.
   But my sorrow increased;
4   my heart smoldered within me.*
   In my thoughts a fire blazed up,
       and I broke into speech:

II

5 LORD, let me know my end, the number
       of my days,
       that I may learn how frail I am.
6 You have given my days a very short
       span;
       my life is as nothing before you.
       All mortals are but a breath.*   Selah
7 Mere phantoms, we go our way;
       mere vapor, our restless pursuits;
       we heap up stores without knowing for
           whom.
8 And now, Lord, what future do I have?
       You are my only hope.
9 From all my sins deliver me;
       let me not be the taunt of fools.

III

10 I was silent and did not open my mouth
       because you were the one who did
           this.
11 Take your plague away from me;
       I am ravaged by the touch of your
           hand.
12 You rebuke our guilt and chasten us;
       you dissolve all we prize like a
           cobweb.
       All mortals are but a breath.   Selah
13 Listen to my prayer, LORD, hear my cry;
       do not be deaf to my weeping!
   I sojourn with you like a passing
       stranger,
       a guest, like all my ancestors.*
14 Turn your gaze from me, that I may find
       peace
       before I depart to be no more.

† **Ps 39:** The lament of a mortally ill person who at first had resolved to remain silently submissive (2–4). But the grief was too much and now the psalmist laments the brevity and vanity of life (5–7), yet remaining hopeful (8–10). The psalmist continues to express both acceptance of the illness and hope for healing in 11–14.

38, 4: Is 1, 5–6.
38, 5: Ps 40, 13; Ezr 9, 6.
38, 7: Ps 35, 14.
38, 9: Ps 102, 4–6.
38, 11: Pss 6, 8; 31, 10.
38, 16: Ps 13, 4.
38, 19: Pss 32, 5; 51, 5.
38, 21: Ps 109, 5.
38, 22: Pss 22, 2.12.20;
    35, 22.

38, 23: Ps 40, 14.
39, 1: 1 Chr 16, 41; Pss 62,
    1; 77, 1.
39, 4: Jer 20, 9.
39, 6: Pss 62, 10; 90, 9–10;
    144, 4; Jb 7, 6.16; 14,
    1.5; Eccl 6, 12; Wis
    2, 5.
39, 13: Ps 119, 19; Gn 23, 4;
    Heb 11, 13; 1 Pt 2, 11.

PS

PSALM 40†

Gratitude and Prayer for Help

¹ For the leader. A psalm of David.

A

I

2 I waited, waited for the LORD;
   who bent down and heard my cry,*

3 Drew me out of the pit of destruction,
   out of the mud of the swamp,*
   Set my feet upon rock,
   steadied my steps,

4† And put a new song in my mouth,*
   a hymn to our God.
   Many shall look on in awe
   and they shall trust in the LORD.

II

5 Happy those whose trust is the LORD,
   who turn not to idolatry
   or to those who stray after falsehood.*

6 How numerous, O LORD, my God,
   you have made your wondrous deeds!
   And in your plans for us
   there is none to equal you.*
   Should I wish to declare or tell them,
   too many are they to recount.*

III

7† Sacrifice and offering you do not want;*
   but ears open to obedience you gave me.
   Holocausts and sin-offerings you do not
   require;

8 so I said, "Here I am;
   your commands for me are written in the
   scroll.

9 To do your will is my delight;
   my God, your law is in my heart!"*

10 I announced your deed to a great assembly;
   I did not restrain my lips;
   you, LORD, are my witness.*

11 Your deed I did not hide within my heart;
   your loyal deliverance I have proclaimed.

I made no secret of your enduring kindness
to a great assembly.

B

I

12 LORD, do not withhold your compassion from
   me;
   may your enduring kindness ever preserve
   me.*

13 For all about me are evils beyond count;
   my sins so overcome me I cannot see.
   They are more than the hairs of my head;
   my courage fails me.*

II

14 LORD, graciously rescue me!*
   Come quickly to help me, LORD!

15 Put to shame and confound
   all who seek to take my life.
   Turn back in disgrace
   those who desire my ruin.*

16 Let those who say "Aha!"*
   know dismay and shame.

17 But may all who seek you
   rejoice and be glad in you.
   May those who long for your help
   always say, "The LORD be glorified."*

18 Though I am afflicted and poor,
   the Lord keeps me in mind.
   You are my help and deliverer;
   my God, do not delay!

PSALM 41†

Thanksgiving after Sickness

¹ For the leader. A psalm of David.

I

2† Happy those concerned for the lowly and poor;
   when misfortune strikes, the LORD delivers
   them.*

3 The LORD keeps and preserves them,
   makes them happy in the land,
   and does not betray them to their enemies.

---

† **Ps 40:** A thanksgiving (2–13) has been combined with a lament (14–18), that appears also in Ps 70. The psalmist describes the rescue in spatial terms—being raised up from the swampy underworld to firm earth where one can praise God (2–4). All who trust God will experience like protection (5–6)! The psalm stipulates the precise mode of thanksgiving: not animal sacrifice but open and enthusiastic proclamation of the salvation just experienced (7–11). A prayer for protection concludes (12–18).

40, 4: *A new song:* a song in response to the new action of God (cf Pss 33, 3; 96, 1; 144, 9; 149, 1; Is 42, 10). Giving thanks is not purely a human response but is itself a divine gift.

40, 7–9: Obedience is better than sacrifice (cf 1 Sm 15, 22; Is 1, 10–20; Hos 6, 6; Am 5, 22–25; Mi 6, 6–8; Acts 7, 42–43 [quoting Am 5, 25–26]). Heb 10, 5–9 quotes the somewhat different Greek version and interprets it as Christ's self-oblation.

Ps 41: A thanksgiving for rescue from illness (4.5.9). Many people, even friends, have interpreted the illness as a divine punishment for sin and have ostracized the psalmist (5–11). The healing shows the return of God's favor and rebukes the psalmist's detractors (12–13).

41, 2: *Happy those concerned for the lowly and poor:* other psalms use the same formula ("Happy those") for those whom God favors. Cf Pss 32, 1–2; 34, 9; 40, 5; 65, 5. The psalmist's statement about God's love of the poor is based on the experience of being rescued (1–3).

*
40, 2: Lam 3, 25.
40, 3: Pss 28, 1; 30, 4; 69, 3.
   15–16; 88, 5; Prv 1,
   12; Jon 2, 7.
40, 4: Ps 33, 3.
40, 5: Ps 1, 1; Prv 16, 20; Jer
   17, 7.
40, 6: Ps 35, 10.
40, 6: Pss 71, 15; 139,
   17–18.
40, 7–9: Heb 10, 5–7; Ps 51,
   18–19; Am 5, 22; Hos
   6, 6; Is 1, 11–15.

40, 9: Ps 37, 31.
40, 10: Pss 22, 23; 26, 12; 35,
   18; 149, 1.
40, 12: Ps 89, 34.
40, 13: Ps 38, 5.11; Ezr 9, 6.
40, 14–18: Pss 70, 2–6; 71, 12.
40, 15: Ps 35, 4.26.
40, 16: Ps 35, 21.25.
40, 17: Ps 35, 27.
41, 2: Tb 4, 7–11.

⁴ The LORD sustains them on their sickbed,
    allays the malady when they are ill.

II

⁵ Once I prayed, "LORD, have mercy on me;
    heal me, I have sinned against you.
⁶ My enemies say the worst of me:
    'When will that one die and be
        forgotten?'
⁷ When people come to visit me,
    they speak without sincerity.
  Their hearts store up malice;
    they leave and spread their vicious lies.*
⁸ My foes all whisper against me;
    they imagine the worst about me:
⁹ I have a deadly disease, they say;
    I will never rise from my sickbed.
¹⁰† Even the friend who had my trust,
    who shared my table, has scorned me.*
¹¹† But you, LORD, have mercy and raise me up
    that I may repay them as they deserve."

III

¹² By this I know you are pleased with me,
    that my enemy no longer jeers at me.
¹³ For my integrity you have supported me
    and let me stand in your presence forever.

* * *

¹⁴† Blessed be the LORD, the God of Israel,
    from all eternity and forever.
    Amen. Amen.*

SECOND BOOK — PSALMS 42–72

PSALMS 42 – 43†

Longing for God's Presence in the Temple

¹† For the leader. A *maskil* of the Korahites.

I

² As the deer longs for streams of water,*
    so my soul longs for you, O God.
³† My being thirsts for God, the living God.
    When can I go and see the face of God?*

⁴ My tears have been my food day and night,*
    as they ask daily, "Where is your God?"*
⁵ Those times I recall
    as I pour out my soul,*
  When I went in procession with the crowd,
    I went with them to the house of God,
  Amid loud cries of thanksgiving,
    with the multitude keeping festival.*
⁶ Why are you downcast, my soul;
    why do you groan within me?
  Wait for God, whom I shall praise again,
    my savior and my God.

II

⁷† My soul is downcast within me;
    therefore I will remember you
  From the land of the Jordan and Hermon,
    from the land of Mount Mizar.*
⁸† Here deep calls to deep in the roar of your
        torrents.
    All your waves and breakers sweep over me.*
⁹ At dawn may the LORD bestow faithful love

42, 2 &

42, 3: *See the face of God:* "face" designates a personal presence (Gn 33, 10; Ex 10, 28–29; 2 Sm 17, 11). The expressions "see God/God's face" occur elsewhere (Pss 11, 7; 17, 15; 63, 3; cf Ex 24, 10; 33, 7–11; Jb 33, 26) for the presence of God in the temple.
42, 7: *From the land of the Jordan:* the sources of the Jordan are in the foothills of Mount Hermon in present-day southern Lebanon. Mount Mizar is presumed to be a mountain in the same range.
42, 8: *Here deep calls to deep:* to the psalmist, the waters arising in the north are overwhelming and far from God's presence, like the waters of chaos (Pss 18, 5; 69, 2–3.15; Jon 2, 3–6).

41, 10: *Even the friend . . . has scorned me:* Jn 13, 18 cites this verse to characterize Judas as a false friend. *Scorned me:* an interpretation of the unclear Hebrew, "made great the heel against me."
41, 11: *That I may repay them as they deserve:* the healing itself is an act of judgment through which God decides for the psalmist and against the false friends. The prayer is not necessarily for strength to punish enemies.
41, 14: The doxology, not part of the psalm, marks the end of the first of the five books of the Psalter. Compare Pss 72, 18–20; 89, 53; 106, 48.
Pss 42–43: Pss 42–43 form a single lament of three sections, each section ending in an identical refrain (42, 6.12; 43, 5). The psalmist is in the extreme north of Israel, far from Jerusalem, and longs for the divine presence that Israel experienced in the temple liturgy. Despite sadness, the psalmist hopes once again to join the worshiping crowds.
42, 1: *The Korahites:* a major guild of temple singers (2 Chr 20, 19) whose name appears in the superscriptions of Pss 42; 44–49; 84–85; 87–88.

41, 7: Pss 31, 12; 38, 12–13; 88, 8; Jb 19, 13–19; Jer 20, 10.	**42, 3:** Ps 27, 4.
	42, 4: Pss 80, 6; 102, 10.
41, 10: Ps 55, 14–15; Jn 13, 18.	**42, 4:** Ps 79, 10; Jl 2, 17.
	42, 5: Ps 122, 5.
41, 14: Neh 9, 5.	**42, 7:** Ps 43, 3.
42, 2–3: Pss 63, 2; 84, 3; 143, 6; Is 26, 9.	**42, 8:** Pss 18, 5; 32, 6; 69, 2; 88, 8; Jon 2, 4.

Randy's First Day of School

Randy and his family have just moved to a new town. Randy is hopeful about this move because he didn't like his old neighborhood and school. There he was often made fun of for his size. So he figures this will be a new start for him, and just maybe the kids here will give him a chance.

The first day of school is exciting. Randy is nervous but can't wait to meet some new people. As the principal walks him down to his new homeroom, he has hopeful visions of how great it will be. When they walk into the classroom, all that changes. As the principal introduces him, someone yells from the back of the room, "Hey, hey, hey, it's Fat Albert!" Everyone laughs. Randy smiles, only to hide the pain and anger he feels inside.

Have you ever experienced painful moments like the one Randy went through? Psalms 42–43 is a good prayer to turn to during moments like these. Verse 6 says, "Wait for God, whom I shall praise again, / my savior and my God." If you follow this advice, the situation may not change, but your heart may find peace rather than anger.

▸ Psalms 42–43

that I may sing praise through the night,
    praise to the God of my life.
10 I say to God, "My rock,
    why do you forget me?*
Why must I go about mourning
    with the enemy oppressing me?"
11 It shatters my bones, when my adversaries
    reproach me.
They say to me daily: "Where is your God?"
12 Why are you downcast, my soul,

why do you groan within me?
Wait for God, whom I shall praise again,
    my savior and my God.

III

1 Grant me justice, God;
    defend me from a faithless people;
    from the deceitful and unjust rescue me.*
2 You, God, are my strength.
    Why then do you spurn me?
Why must I go about mourning,
    with the enemy oppressing me?
3† Send your light and fidelity,
    that they may be my guide*
And bring me to your holy mountain,
    to the place of your dwelling,*
4 That I may come to the altar of God,
    to God, my joy, my delight.
Then I will praise you with the harp,
    O God, my God.
5 Why are you downcast, my soul?
    Why do you groan within me?
Wait for God, whom I shall praise again,
    my savior and my God.

PSALM 44†

God's Past Favor and Israel's Present Need

1 For the leader. A *maskil* of the Korahites.

I

2 O God, we have heard with our own ears;
    our ancestors have told us*
The deeds you did in their days,
    with your own hand in days of old:
3 You rooted out nations to plant them,*
    crushed peoples to make room for them.
4 Not with their own swords did they conquer
        the land,*
    nor did their own arms bring victory;
It was your right hand, your own arm,
    the light of your face, for you favored
        them.*
5 You are my king and my God,*
    who bestows victories on Jacob.
6 Through you we batter our foes;
    through your name, trample our adversaries.
7 Not in my bow do I trust,
    nor does my sword bring me victory.
8 You have brought us victory over our enemies,
    shamed those who hate us.

---

† **43, 3:** *Your light and fidelity:* a pair of divine attributes personified as guides for the pilgrimage. The psalmist seeks divine protection for the journey to Jerusalem.

Ps 44: In this lament the community reminds God of past favors which it has always acknowledged (2–9). But now God has abandoned Israel to defeat and humiliation (10–17), though the people are not conscious of any sin against the covenant (18–23). They struggle with being God's special people amid divine silence; yet they continue to pray (24–27).

42, 10: Pss 18, 2; 31, 3–4.
43, 1: Ps 119, 154.
43, 3: Pss 18, 29; 27, 1; 36, 10; Mi 7, 8.
43, 3: Ps 122, 1.
44, 2: Ps 78, 3.
44, 3: Pss 78, 55; 80, 9f.
44, 4: Dt 8, 17f; Jos 24, 12.
44, 4: Pss 4, 7; 31, 17; 67, 2; 80, 4; Nm 6, 25; Dn 9, 17.
44, 5: Ps 145, 1.

9   In God we have boasted all the day long;
      your name we will praise forever.   *Selah*

II

10 But now you have rejected and disgraced us;*
      you do not march out with our armies.*

11† You make us retreat before the foe;
      those who hate us plunder us at will.*

12 You hand us over like sheep to be slaughtered,
      scatter us among the nations.*

13 You sell your people for nothing;
      you make no profit from their sale.*

14 You make us the reproach of our neighbors,*
      the mockery and scorn of those around us.

15 You make us a byword among the nations;
      the peoples shake their heads at us.

16 All day long my disgrace is before me;
      shame has covered my face

17 At the sound of those who taunt and revile,
      at the sight of the spiteful enemy.

III

18 All this has come upon us,
      though we have not forgotten you,
      nor been disloyal to your covenant.

19† Our hearts have not turned back,
      nor have our steps strayed from your path.

20† Yet you have left us crushed,
      desolate in a place of jackals;*
      you have covered us with darkness.

21 If we had forgotten the name of our God,
      stretched out our hands to another god,

22 Would not God have discovered this,
      God who knows the secrets of the heart?

23 For you we are slain all the day long,
      considered only as sheep to be
      slaughtered.*

IV

24 Awake! Why do you sleep, O Lord?
      Rise up! Do not reject us forever!*

25 Why do you hide your face;*
      why forget our pain and misery?

26 We are bowed down to the ground;*
      our bodies are pressed to the earth.

27 Rise up, help us!
      Redeem us as your love demands.

PSALM 45†

Song for a Royal Wedding

1 For the leader; according to "Lilies." A *maskil* of the
      Korahites. A love song.

I

2   My heart is stirred by a noble theme,
      as I sing my ode to the king.
      My tongue is the pen of a nimble scribe.

II

3   You are the most handsome of men;
      fair speech has graced your lips,
      for God has blessed you forever.*

4   Gird your sword upon your hip, mighty
      warrior!
      In splendor and majesty ride on
      triumphant!*

5   In the cause of truth and justice
      may your right hand show you wondrous
      deeds.

6   Your arrows are sharp;
      peoples will cower at your feet;
      the king's enemies will lose heart.

7† Your throne, O god, stands forever;*
      your royal scepter is a scepter for justice.

8   You love justice and hate wrongdoing;
      therefore God, your God, has anointed you
      with the oil of gladness above your fellow
      kings.

9† With myrrh, aloes, and cassia
      your robes are fragrant.
      From ivory-paneled palaces
      stringed instruments bring you joy.

10† Daughters of kings are your lovely wives;
      a princess arrayed in Ophir's gold
      comes to stand at your right hand.

PS

44, 11: *You make us retreat:* the corollary of v 4. Defeat, like victory, is God's doing; neither Israel nor its enemies can claim credit (23).

44, 19: *Our hearts have not turned back:* Israel's defeat was not caused by its lack of fidelity.

44, 20: *A place of jackals:* following Israel's defeat and exile (11–12), the land lies desolate, inhabited only by jackals. Cf Is 13, 22; Jer 9, 10; 10, 22. Others take *tannim* as "sea monster" (cf Ez 29, 3; 32, 2) and render: "you crushed us as you did the sea monster."

Ps 45: A song for the Davidic king's marriage to a foreign princess from Tyre in Phoenicia. The court poet sings (2.18) of God's choice of the king (3.8), of his role in establishing divine rule (4–8), and of his splendor as he waits for his bride (9–10). The woman is to forget her own house when she becomes wife to the king (11–13). Her majestic beauty today is a sign of the future prosperity of the royal house (14–18). The psalm was retained in the collection when there was no reigning king, and came to be applied to the king who was to come, the messiah.

45, 7: *O god:* the king, in courtly language, is called "god," i.e.,

more than human, representing God to the people. Heb 1, 8–9 applies 7–8 to Christ.

45, 9: *Ivory-paneled palaces:* literally, "palaces of ivory." Ivory paneling and furniture decoration have been found in Samaria and other ancient Near Eastern cities. Cf Am 3, 15.

45, 10: *Ophir's gold:* uncertain location, possibly a region on the coast of southern Arabia or eastern Africa, famous for its gold. Cf 1 Kgs 9, 28; 10, 11; Jb 22, 24.

44, 10–27: Ps 89, 39–52.
44, 10: Ps 60, 12.
44, 11: Lv 26, 17; Dt 28, 25.
44, 12: Lv 26, 33; Dt 28, 64.
44, 13: Dt 32, 30; Is 52, 3.
44, 14–17: Pss 79, 4; 80, 7; 123, 3–4; Jb 12, 4; Dn 9, 16.
44, 20: Jer 9, 10.
44, 23: Rom 8, 36.
44, 24: Pss 10, 1; 74, 1; 77, 8; 79, 5; 83, 2.
44, 25: Pss 10, 11; 89, 47; Jb 13, 24.
44, 26: Ps 119, 25.
45, 3: Song 5, 10–16.
45, 4: Ps 21, 5.
45, 7–8: Heb 1, 8–9.

III

11† Listen, my daughter, and understand;
    pay me careful heed.
    Forget your people and your father's house,
12   that the king might desire your beauty.
    He is your lord;
13   honor him, daughter of Tyre.
    Then the richest of the people
    will seek your favor with gifts.*
14 All glorious is the king's daughter as she
    enters,*
    her raiment threaded with gold;
15 In embroidered apparel she is led to the king.
    The maids of her train are presented to the
    king.
16 They are led in with glad and joyous acclaim;
    they enter the palace of the king.

IV

17 The throne of your fathers your sons will
    have;
    you shall make them princes through all
    the land.*
18 I will make your name renowned through all
    generations;
    thus nations shall praise you forever.*

PSALM 46†

God, the Protector of Zion

1† For the leader. A song of the Korahites.
According to *alamoth.*

I

2 God is our refuge and our strength,
    an ever-present help in distress.*
3† Thus we do not fear, though earth be shaken
    and mountains quake to the depths of the
    sea,
4† Though its waters rage and foam
    and mountains totter at its surging.*
    The LORD of hosts is with us;
    our stronghold is the God of Jacob.   *Selah*

II

5† Streams of the river gladden the city of God,
    the holy dwelling of the Most High.*
6 God is in its midst; it shall not be shaken;
    God will help it at break of day.*
7 Though nations rage and kingdoms totter,
    God's voice thunders and the earth
    trembles.*
8† The LORD of hosts is with us;
    our stronghold is the God of Jacob.   *Selah*

III

9 Come and see the works of the LORD,
    who has done fearsome deeds on earth;*
10 Who stops wars to the ends of the earth,
    breaks the bow, splinters the spear,
    and burns the shields with fire;*
11 Who says:
    "Be still and confess that I am God!
    I am exalted among the nations,
    exalted on the earth."*
12† The LORD of hosts is with us;
    our stronghold is the God of Jacob.   *Selah*

PSALM 47†

The Ruler of All the Nations

1 For the leader. A psalm of the Korahites.

I

2 All you peoples, clap your hands;
    shout to God with joyful cries.*
3 For the LORD, the Most High, inspires awe,
    the great king over all the earth,*
4 Who made people subject to us,
    brought nations under our feet,*
5† Who chose a land for our heritage,
    the glory of Jacob, the beloved.*   *Selah*

II

6† God mounts the throne amid shouts of joy;
    the LORD, amid trumpet blasts.*
7 Sing praise to God, sing praise;
    sing praise to our king, sing praise.

45, 11: *Forget your people and your father's house:* the bride should no longer consider herself a daughter of her father's house, but the wife of the king—the queen.

Ps 46: A song of confidence in God's protection of Zion with close parallels to Ps 48. The dominant note in Ps 46 is sounded by the refrain, *The LORD of hosts is with us* (4.8.12). The first strophe (2–4) sings of the security of God's presence even in utter chaos; the second (5–8), of divine protection of the city from its enemies; the third (9–12), of God's imposition of imperial peace.

46, 1: *Alamoth:* the melody of the psalm, now lost.

46, 3–4: Figurative ancient Near Eastern language to describe social and political upheavals.

46, 4b: The first line of the refrain is similar in structure and meaning to Isaiah's name for the royal child, Immanuel, With us is God (Is 7, 14; 8, 8.10).

46, 5: Jerusalem is not situated on a river. This description derives from mythological descriptions of the divine abode and symbolizes the divine presence as the source of all life (cf Is 33, 21; Ez 47, 1–12; Jl 4, 18; Zec 14, 8; Rv 22, 1–2).

Ps 47: A hymn calling on the nations to acknowledge the universal rule of Israel's God (2–5) who is enthroned as king over Israel and the nations (6–10).

47, 5: *Our heritage . . . the glory:* the land of Israel (cf Is 58, 14), which God has given Israel in an act of sovereignty.

47, 6: *God mounts the throne:* "has gone up to the throne," according to the context (9). Christian liturgical tradition has applied the verse to the ascension of Christ.

45, 13: Ps 72, 10–11; Is 60, 5f.
45, 14–16: Ez 16, 10–13.
45, 17: Gn 17, 6.
45, 18: Is 60, 15.
46, 2: Ps 48, 4; Is 33, 2.
46, 4: Ps 93, 3–4; Jb 9, 5–6; Is 24, 18–20; 54, 10.
46, 5: Pss 48, 2–3; 76, 3.
46, 6: Is 7, 14.
46, 7: Pss 2, 1–5; 48, 5–8; 76, 7–9; Is 17, 12–14.
46, 9: Ps 48, 9–10.
46, 10: Ps 76, 4.
46, 11: Ps 48, 11.
47, 2: Ps 89, 16; Zep 3, 14.
47, 3: Ps 95, 3; Ex 15, 18; Is 24, 23; 52, 7.
47, 4: Ps 2, 8.
47, 5: Is 58, 14.
47, 6: Pss 24, 8.10; 68, 18–19; 98, 6.

III

8 God is king over all the earth;*
    sing hymns of praise.
9 God rules over the nations;
    God sits upon his holy throne.
10 The princes of the peoples assemble
    with the people of the God of Abraham.
    For the rulers of the earth belong to God,
    who is enthroned on high.*

PSALM 48†

The Splendor of the Invincible City

1† A psalm of the Korahites. A song.

I

2 Great is the LORD and highly praised
    in the city of our God:*
    The holy mountain, 3† fairest of heights,
    the joy of all the earth,*
    Mount Zion, the heights of Zaphon,*
    the city of the great king.

II

4 God is its citadel,
    renowned as a stronghold.
5 See! The kings assembled,
    together they invaded.
6† When they looked they were astounded;
    terrified, they were put to flight!*
7 Trembling seized them there,
    anguish, like a woman's labor,*
8† As when the east wind wrecks
    the ships of Tarshish!

III

9† What we had heard we now see
    in the city of the LORD of hosts,
    In the city of our God,
    founded to last forever.   Selah

10 O God, within your temple
    we ponder your steadfast love.
11 Like your name, O God,
    your praise reaches the ends of the
        earth.*
    Your right hand is fully victorious.
12 Mount Zion is glad!
    The cities of Judah rejoice
    because of your saving deeds!*

IV

13 Go about Zion, walk all around it,
    note the number of its towers.
14 Consider the ramparts, examine its citadels,
    that you may tell future generations:*
15† "Yes, so mighty is God,
    our God who leads us always!"

PSALM 49†

Confidence in God rather than in Riches

1† For the leader. A psalm of the Korahites.

2 Hear this, all you peoples!
    Give ear, all who inhabit the world,
3 You of lowly birth or high estate,
    rich and poor alike.
4 My mouth shall speak wisdom,
    my heart shall offer insight.*
5† I will turn my attention to a problem,
    expound my question to the music of a lyre.

I

6 Why should I fear in evil days,
    when my wicked pursuers ring me round,
7 Those who trust in their wealth
    and boast of their abundant riches?*
8† One cannot redeem oneself,
    pay to God a ransom.*

Ps 48: A Zion hymn, praising the holy city as the invincible dwelling place of God. Unconquerable, it is an apt symbol of God who has defeated all enemies. After seven epithets describing the city (2–3), the psalm describes the victory by the Divine Warrior over hostile kings (4–8). The second half proclaims the dominion of the God of Zion over all the earth (9–12) and invites pilgrims to announce that God is eternally invincible like Zion itself (13–15).

48, 1: *Korahites:* see note on Ps 42, 1.

48, 3: *The heights of Zaphon:* the mountain abode of the Canaanite storm-god Baal in comparable texts. To speak of Zion as if it were Zaphon was to claim for Israel's God what Canaanites claimed for Baal. Though topographically speaking Zion is only a hill, viewed religiously it towers over other mountains as the home of the supreme God (cf Ps 68, 16–17).

48, 6: *When they looked:* the kings are stunned by the sight of Zion, touched by divine splendor. The language is that of holy war, in which the enemy panics and flees at the sight of divine glory.

48, 8: *The ships of Tarshish:* large ships, named after the distant land or port of Tarshish, probably ancient Tartessus in southern Spain, although other identifications have been proposed. Cf Is 2, 16; 60, 9; Jon 1, 3.

48, 9: *What we had heard we now see:* the glorious things that new pilgrims had heard about the holy city—its beauty and awesomeness—they now see with their own eyes. The seeing here contrasts with the seeing of the hostile kings in 6.

48, 15: *So mighty is God:* Israel's God is like Zion in being eternal

and invincible. The holy city is therefore a kind of "sacrament" of God.

Ps 49: The psalm affirms confidence in God (cf Pss 23; 27, 1–6; 62) in the face of the apparent good fortune of the unjust rich. Cf Pss 37; 73. Reliance on wealth is misplaced (8–10) for it is of no avail in the face of death (18–20). After inviting all to listen to this axiom of faith (2–5), the psalmist depicts the self-delusion of the ungodly (6–13), whose destiny is to die like ignorant beasts (13.18; cf Prv 7, 21–23). Their wealth should occasion no alarm, for they will come to nought, whereas God will save the just (14–21).

49, 1: *Korahites:* see note on Ps 42, 1.

49, 5: *Problem:* the psalmist's personal solution to the perennial biblical problem of the prosperity of the wicked. *Question:* parallel in meaning to *problem;* in Wisdom literature it means the mysterious way of how the world works.

49, 8: *One cannot redeem oneself:* an axiom. For the practice of redemption, cf Jb 6, 21–23. A play on the first Hebrew word of v 8 and v 16 relates the two verses.

47, 8–9: Pss 72, 11; 93, 1; 96,   48, 7: Ex 15, 14; Jer 4, 31.
    10; 97, 1; 99, 1; Jer   48, 11: Mal 1, 11.
    10, 7.   48, 12: Ps 97, 8.
47, 10: Ps 89, 19; Ex 3, 6; Is 2,   48, 14: Pss 22, 31–32; 71, 18.
    2–4.   49, 4: Ps 78, 2; Mt 13, 35.
48, 2: Pss 96, 4; 145, 3.   49, 7: Jb 31, 24.
48, 3: Ps 50, 2; Lam 2, 15.   49, 8: Prv 10, 15; 11, 4; Ez 7,
48, 3: Is 14, 13.   19; Mt 16, 26.
48, 6: Jgs 5, 19.

PS

PS

9 Too high the price to redeem a life;
   one would never have enough
10 To stay alive forever
   and never see the pit.
11 Anyone can see that the wisest die,
   the fool and the senseless pass away too,*
   and must leave their wealth to others.*
12 Tombs are their homes forever,
   their dwellings through all generations,
   though they gave their names to their lands.
13 For all their riches
   mortals do not abide;
   they perish like the beasts.*

II

14 This is the destiny of those who trust in folly,
   the end of those so pleased with their
   wealth.   *Selah*
15 Like sheep they are herded into Sheol,
   where death will be their shepherd.
   Straight to the grave they descend,
   where their form will waste away,
   Sheol will be their palace.
16† But God will redeem my life,   *Selah*
   will take me from the power of Sheol.*
17 Do not fear when others become rich,
   when the wealth of their houses grows great.
18 When they die they will take nothing with them,
   their wealth will not follow them down.*
19 When living, they congratulate themselves
   and say:
   "All praise you, you do so well."
20 But they will join the company of their
   forebears,
   never again to see the light.*
21 For all their riches,
   if mortals do not have wisdom,
   they perish like the beasts.

PSALM 50†

The Acceptable Sacrifice

¹ A psalm of Asaph.

I

The LORD, the God of gods,
   has spoken and summoned the earth
   from the rising of the sun to its setting.*
2 From Zion God shines forth,*
   perfect in beauty.

3 Our God comes and will not be silent!
   Devouring fire precedes,
   storming fiercely round about.*
4 God summons the heavens above
   and the earth to the judgment of his people:
5 "Gather my faithful ones before me,
   those who made a covenant with me by
   sacrifice."
6 The heavens proclaim divine justice,
   for God alone is the judge.*   *Selah*

II

7 "Listen, my people, I will speak;
   Israel, I will testify against you;
   God, your God, am I.
8 Not for your sacrifices do I rebuke you,
   nor for your holocausts, set before me daily.
9 I need no bullock from your house,
   no goats from your fold.*
10 For every animal of the forest is mine,
   beasts by the thousands on my mountains.
11 I know every bird of the heavens;
   the creatures of the field belong to me.
12 Were I hungry, I would not tell you,
   for mine is the world and all that fills it.*
13 Do I eat the flesh of bulls
   or drink the blood of goats?
14 Offer praise as your sacrifice to God;*
   fulfill your vows to the Most High.
15 Then call on me in time of distress;*
   I will rescue you, and you shall honor me."

III

16 But to the wicked God says:
   "Why do you recite my commandments
   and profess my covenant with your lips?
17 You hate discipline;
   you cast my words behind you!
18 When you see thieves, you befriend them;
   with adulterers you throw in your lot.
19 You give your mouth free rein for evil;
   you harness your tongue to deceit.
20 You sit maligning your own kin,
   slandering the child of your own mother.
21 When you do these things should I be silent?
   Or do you think that I am like you?
   I accuse you, I lay the charge before you.

IV

22 "Understand this, you who forget God,
   lest I attack you with no one to rescue.

---

† **49, 16:** *Will take me:* the same Hebrew verb is used of God "taking up" a favored servant: Enoch in Gn 5, 24; Elijah in 2 Kgs 2, 11–12; the righteous person in Ps 73, 24. The verse apparently states the hope that God will rescue the faithful psalmist in the same manner.

Ps 50: A covenant lawsuit stating that the sacrifice God really wants is the sacrifice of praise accompanied by genuine obedience (cf Mi 6, 1–8). It begins with a theophany and the summoning of the court (1–6). Then in direct address God explains what is required of the faithful (7–15), rebukes the hypocritical worshiper (16–21), and concludes with a threat and a promise (22–23; cf Is 1, 19–20).

* **49, 11:** Eccl 2, 16.
49, 11: Ps 39, 7; Sir 11, 18–19.
49, 13: Eccl 3, 18–21.
49, 16: Pss 16, 10; 86, 13; 103, 4; 116, 8.
49, 18: Sir 11, 18–19; Eccl 5, 15; 1 Tm 6, 7.
49, 20: Jb 10, 21–22.
50, 1: Dt 10, 17; Jos 22, 22.

50, 2: Ps 48, 2.
50, 3: Ps 97, 3; Dn 7, 10.
50, 6: Pss 19, 2; 97, 6.
50, 9: Ps 69, 32; Am 5, 21–22.
50, 12: Pss 24, 1; 89, 12; Dt 10, 14; 1 Cor 10, 26.
50, 14: Heb 13, 15.
50, 15: Ps 77, 3.

23 Those who offer praise as a sacrifice honor
     me;
   to the obedient I will show the salvation of
     God."*

PSALM 51 †

The Miserere: Prayer of Repentance

1 For the leader. A psalm of David,
2 when Nathan the prophet came to him
   after his affair with Bathsheba.*

I

3 Have mercy on me, God, in your goodness;
   in your abundant compassion blot out my
     offense.
4 Wash away all my guilt;
   from my sin cleanse me.
5 For I know my offense;
   my sin is always before me.*
6 Against you alone have I sinned;
   I have done such evil in your sight

That you are just in your sentence,
   blameless when you condemn.*
7† True, I was born guilty,
   a sinner, even as my mother conceived
     me.*
8 Still, you insist on sincerity of heart;
   in my inmost being teach me wisdom.
9† Cleanse me with hyssop, that I may be pure;
   wash me, make me whiter than snow.*
10 Let me hear sounds of joy and gladness;
   let the bones you have crushed rejoice.

II

11 Turn away your face from my sins;
   blot out all my guilt.
12 A clean heart create for me, God;
   renew in me a steadfast spirit.*
13 Do not drive me from your presence,
   nor take from me your holy spirit.*
14 Restore my joy in your salvation;
   sustain in me a willing spirit.

P
S

A Fresh Start

Psalm 51 is a beautiful prayer of sorrow and remorse. It is attributed to King David, who would have written it seeking forgiveness and a fresh start after committing adultery with Bathsheba. Take a few minutes to read this psalm prayerfully and reflect on the marvelous way it asks for God's help in starting over.

In our time too, people can fall into a sinful pattern of having sex outside of marriage. Many people experience a deep regret and sadness in losing their virginity in a short-term and uncommitted relationship. Thinking they can never regain their moral virtue, they then pursue one loveless relationship after another. The promise of Psalm 51 is that they can start fresh at any point in this cycle! Some people call this new beginning a secondary virginity—not, of course, a physical virginity, but a virginity of the heart and soul. It means a commitment not to have sex again except with the person they marry.

So, whenever you are feeling the weight of sin, whether it is premarital sex or some other sin, pray Psalm 51. Let it mark your commitment to start fresh with God's help. Ask God to show you what situations to avoid and what people you need to ask to support you. Remember, God is always ready to forgive you, and all of heaven rejoices each time you make a fresh start!

▸ Psalm 51

---

† **Ps 51:** A lament, the most famous of the seven Penitential Psalms, prays for the removal of the personal and social disorders that sin has brought. The poem has two parts of approximately equal length: 3–10 and 11–19, and a conclusion in 20–21. The two parts interlock by repetition of "blot out" in the first verse of each section (3.11), of "wash (away)" just after the first verse of each section (4) and just before the last verse (9) of the first section, and of "heart," "God," and "spirit" in 12 and 19. The first part (3–10) asks deliverance from sin, which is not just a past act but its emotional, physical, and social consequences. The second part (11–19) seeks something more profound than wiping the slate clean: nearness to God, living by the spirit of God (12–13), like the relation between God and people described in Jer 31, 33–34. Nearness to God brings joy and the authority to teach sinners (15–16). Such proclamation is better than offering sacrifice (17–19). The last two verses ask for the rebuilding of Jerusalem (20–21).

51, 7: *A sinner, even as my mother conceived me:* literally, "In iniquity was I conceived," an instance of hyperbole: at no time was the psalmist ever without sin. Cf Ps 88, 16, "I am mortally afflicted since youth," i.e., I have always been afflicted. The verse does not imply that the sexual act of conception is sinful.

51, 9: *Hyssop:* a small bush whose many woody twigs make a natural sprinkler. It was prescribed in the Mosaic law as an instrument for sprinkling sacrificial blood or lustral water for cleansing. Cf Ex 12, 22; Lv 14, 4; Nm 19, 18.

* 50, 23: Ps 91, 16.   51, 9: Jb 9, 30; Is 1, 18; Ez
51, 2: 2 Sm 12.   36, 25.
51, 5: Pss 32, 5; 38, 19; Is   51, 12: Ez 11, 19.
   59, 12.   51, 13: Wis 1, 5; 9, 17; Is 63,
51, 6: Rom 3, 4.   11; Hg 2, 5; Rom 8, 9.
51, 7: Jb 14, 4.

15 I will teach the wicked your ways,
　　that sinners may return to you.

16 Rescue me from death, God, my saving God,
　　that my tongue may praise your healing
　　　power.*

17 Lord, open my lips;
　　my mouth will proclaim your praise.

18† For you do not desire sacrifice;
　　a burnt offering you would not accept.*

19 My sacrifice, God, is a broken spirit;
　　God, do not spurn a broken, humbled
　　　heart.

III

20† Make Zion prosper in your good pleasure;
　　rebuild the walls of Jerusalem.*

21 Then you will be pleased with proper
　　　sacrifice,
　　burnt offerings and holocausts;
　　then bullocks will be offered on your altar.

PSALM 52†

The Deceitful Tongue

¹ For the leader. A *maskil* of David,
² when Doeg the Edomite went and told Saul,
"David went to the house of Ahimelech."*

I

3 Why do you glory in evil,
　　you scandalous liar?
All day long ⁴ you plot destruction;
　　your tongue is like a sharpened razor,
　　you skillful deceiver.*

5 You love evil rather than good,
　　lies rather than honest speech.*　　Selah

6 You love any word that destroys,
　　you deceitful tongue.*

II

7 Now God will strike you down,
　　leave you crushed forever,
Pluck you from your tent,
　　uproot you from the land of the living.*
　　　　　　　　　　　　　　Selah

8 The righteous will look on with awe;
　　they will jeer and say:*

9 "That one did not take God as a refuge,
　　but trusted in great wealth,
　　relied on devious plots."*

III

10† But I, like an olive tree in the house of God,*
　　trust in God's faithful love forever.

11 I will praise you always
　　for what you have done.
I will proclaim before the faithful*
　　that your name is good.

PSALM 53†

A Lament over Widespread Corruption

¹ For the leader; according to *Mahalath*.
A *maskil* of David.

I

2 Fools say in their hearts,*
　　"There is no God."*
Their deeds are loathsome and corrupt;
　　not one does what is right.

3 God looks down from heaven
　　upon the human race,*
To see if even one is wise,*
　　if even one seeks God.

4 All have gone astray;
　　all alike are perverse.
Not one does what is right, not even one.*

II

5 Will these evildoers never learn?
　　They devour my people as they devour
　　　bread;*
　　they do not call upon God.*

6 They have good reason to fear,
　　though now they do not fear.
For God will certainly scatter
　　the bones of the godless.
They will surely be put to shame,
　　for God has rejected them.

III

7 Oh, that from Zion might come
　　the deliverance of Israel,
That Jacob may rejoice and Israel be glad*
　　when God restores the people!

51, 18: *For you do not desire sacrifice:* the mere offering of the ritual sacrifice apart from good dispositions is not acceptable to God. Cf Ps 50.

51, 20–21: Most scholars think that these verses were added to the psalm some time after the destruction of the temple in 587 B.C. The verses assume that the rebuilt temple will be an ideal site for national reconciliation.

Ps 52: A condemnation of the powerful and arrogant (3–6), who bring down upon themselves God's judgment (7). The just, those who trust in God alone, are gladdened and strengthened by the downfall of their traditional enemies (8–11).

52, 10: *Like an olive tree:* the righteous will flourish in the house of God like a well-watered olive tree. Cf Pss 92, 14; 128, 3.

Ps 53: A lament of an individual, duplicated in Ps 14, except that "God" is used for "the LORD," and v 6 is different. See under Ps 14.

51, 16: Ps 30, 10.
51, 18: Pss 40, 7; 50, 8; Am 5, 21–22; Hos 6, 6; Is 1, 11–15; Heb 10, 5–7.
51, 20: Jer 31, 4; Ez 36, 33.
52, 2: 1 Sm 21, 8; 22, 6ff.
52, 4: Pss 12, 3; 59, 8; 120, 2–3; Sir 51, 3.
52, 5: Jer 4, 22; Jn 3, 19–20.
52, 6: Jer 9, 4.
52, 7: Pss 27, 13; 28, 5; 56, 14; Jb 18, 14; Prv 2, 22; Is 38, 11.
52, 8: Pss 44, 14; 64, 9.
52, 9: Jb 31, 24; Prv 11, 28.
52, 10: Pss 1, 3; 92, 12–14; Jer 11, 16; 17, 8.
52, 11: Pss 22, 23; 26, 12; 35, 18; 149, 1.
53, 2–6a: Ps 14, 1–5a.
53, 2: Pss 10, 4; 36, 2; Is 32, 6; Jer 5, 12.
53, 3: Pss 11, 4; 102, 20.
53, 2b–3: Rom 3, 11–12.
53, 4: Ps 12, 2.
53, 5: Ps 27, 2; Is 9, 11.
53, 5: Ps 79, 6.
53, 7: Ps 85, 2.

PSALM 54†

Confident Prayer in Great Peril

1 For the leader. On stringed instruments.
A *maskil* of David,
2 when the Ziphites came and said to Saul,
"David is hiding among us."*

I

3† O God, by your name save me.
  By your strength defend my cause.
4 O God, hear my prayer.
  Listen to the words of my mouth.
5 The arrogant have risen against me;
    the ruthless seek my life;
    they do not keep God before them.*   *Selah*

II

6 God is present as my helper;*
    the Lord sustains my life.
7 Turn back the evil upon my foes;
    in your faithfulness, destroy them.*
8 Then I will offer you generous sacrifice
    and praise your gracious name, LORD,
9 Because it has rescued me from every trouble,
    and my eyes look down on my foes.*

PSALM 55†

A Lament over Betrayal

1 For the leader. On stringed instruments.
A *maskil* of David.

I

2 Listen, God, to my prayer;*
    do not hide from my pleading;
3   hear me and give answer.
  I rock with grief; I groan
4   at the uproar of the enemy,
    the clamor of the wicked.
  They heap trouble upon me,
    savagely accuse me.
5 My heart pounds within me;
    death's terrors fall upon me.
6 Fear and trembling overwhelm me;
    shuddering sweeps over me.
7 I say, "If only I had wings like a dove
    that I might fly away and find rest.*

Betrayed!

Maybe you don't have enemies quite
as bad as the enemies described in
Psalm 55, but you may be able to sympathize with the psalmist when he writes
this:

> They strike out at friends
>   and go back on their promises.
>   **(Verse 21)**

When you feel betrayed by others
like the psalmist does—maybe betrayed
by a friend who didn't keep a promise or
by a parent who seemed to treat you
unfairly or by anyone else for whatever
reason—call on God, and say a prayer
like the following:

*I trust you, God; I want to believe you are
with me. Help me to know you are here
and that I am not alone. Amen.*

▶ **Psalm 55**

8   Far away I would flee;
    I would stay in the desert.*   *Selah*
9   I would soon find a shelter
      from the raging wind and storm."

II

10 Lord, check and confuse their scheming.
    I see violence and strife in the city
11   making rounds on its walls day and night.
  Within are mischief and evil;
12   treachery is there as well;
    oppression and fraud never leave its streets.*
13 If an enemy had reviled me,
    that I could bear;
  If my foe had viewed me with contempt,
    from that I could hide.
14 But it was you, my other self,
    my comrade and friend,*

---
† **Ps 54:** A lament in which the person under attack calls directly upon God for help (3–5). Refusing to despair, the psalmist hopes in God, who is active in history and just (6–7). The psalm ends with a serene promise to return thanks (8–9).

54, 3: *By your name:* one is present in one's name, hence God as revealed to humans.

Ps 55: The psalmist, betrayed by intimate friends (14–15.21–22), prays that God punish those oath breakers and thus be acknowledged as the protector of the wronged. The sufferings of the psalmist include both ostracism (4) and mental turmoil (5–6), culminating in the wish to flee society (7–9). The wish for a sudden death for one's enemies (16) occurs elsewhere in the psalms; an example of such a death is the earth opening under the wicked Dathan and Abiram (Nm 16, 31–32). The psalmist, confident of vindication, exhorts oth-

ers to a like trust in the God of justice (23–24). The psalm is not so much for personal vengeance as for a public vindication of God's righteousness now. There was no belief in an afterlife where such vindication could take place.

54, 2: 1 Sm 23, 19; 26, 1.
54, 5: Ps 86, 14.
54, 6: Ps 118, 7.
54, 7: Ps 143, 12.
54, 9: Pss 59, 11; 91, 8; 92, 12.
55, 2–3: Pss 5, 2–3; 55, 2–3; 86, 6; 130, 1–2;

Lam 3, 56; Jon 2, 3.
55, 7: Ps 11, 1.
55, 8: Jer 9, 1; Rv 12, 6.
55, 12: Jer 5, 1; 6, 6; Ez 22, 2; Hb 1, 3; Zep 3, 1.
55, 14: Ps 41, 10; Jer 9, 3; Mt 26, 21–24 par.

PS

15 You, whose company I enjoyed,
   at whose side I walked
   in procession in the house of God.

III

16 Let death take them by surprise;
   let them go down alive to Sheol,*
   for evil is in their homes and hearts.

17 But I will call upon God,
   and the LORD will save me.

18 At dusk, dawn, and noon
   I will grieve and complain,
   and my prayer will be heard.*

19 God will give me freedom and peace
   from those who war against me,
   though there are many who oppose me.

20 God, who sits enthroned forever,*
   will hear me and humble them.
   For they will not mend their ways,
   they have no fear of God.

21 They strike out at friends
   and go back on their promises.

22 Softer than butter is their speech,
   but war is in their hearts.
   Smoother than oil are their words,
   but they are unsheathed swords.*

23 Cast your care upon the LORD,
   who will give you support.
   God will never allow
   the righteous to stumble.*

24 But you, God, will bring them down
   to the pit of destruction.*
   These bloodthirsty liars
   will not live half their days,
   but I put my trust in you.*

PSALM 56†

Trust in God

1† For the director. According to *Yonath elem
rehoqim*. A *miktam* of David, when the Philistines
seized him at Gath.*

I

2 Have mercy on me, God,
   for I am treated harshly;

   attackers press me all the day.

3 My foes treat me harshly all the day;
   yes, many are my attackers.
   O Most High, 4 when I am afraid,
   in you I place my trust.

5 God, I praise your promise;
   in you I trust, I do not fear.*
   What can mere flesh do to me?*

II

6 All the day they foil my plans;
   their every thought is of evil against
   me.

7 They hide together in ambush;
   they watch my every step;
   they lie in wait for my life.*

8 They are evil; watch them, God!
   Cast the nations down in your anger!

9† My wanderings you have noted;
   are my tears not stored in your vial,
   recorded in your book?*

10 My foes turn back when I call on you.
   This I know: God is on my side.

11 God, I praise your promise;
12 in you I trust, I do not fear.
   What can mere mortals do to me?

III

13 I have made vows to you, God;
   with offerings I will fulfill them,*

14 Once you have snatched me from death,
   kept my feet from stumbling,
   That I may walk before God
   in the light of the living.

PSALM 57†

Confident Prayer for Deliverance

1† For the director. Do not destroy. A *miktam*
of David, when he fled from Saul into a cave.*

I

2† Have mercy on me, God,
   have mercy on me.
   In you I seek shelter.
   In the shadow of your wings I seek shelter
   till harm pass by.*

Ps 56: Beset physically (2–3) and psychologically (6–7), the psalmist maintains a firm confidence in God (5.9–10). Nothing will prevent the psalmist from keeping the vow to give thanks for God's gift of life (13–14). A refrain (5.11–12) divides the psalm in two equal parts.
56, 1: *Yonath elem rehoqim:* Hebrew words probably designating the melody to which the psalm was to be sung.
56, 9: *Are my tears not stored in your vial:* a unique saying in the Old Testament. The context suggests that the tears are saved because they are precious; God puts a high value on each of the psalmist's troubles.
Ps 57: Each of the two equal strophes contains a prayer for rescue from enemies, accompanied by joyful trust in God (2–5.7–11). The refrain prays that God be manifested as saving (6.12). Ps 108 is nearly identical to part of this psalm (57, 8–12 = 108, 2–6).
57, 1: *Do not destroy:* Probably the title of the melody to which the psalm was to be sung.

57, 2: *The shadow of your wings:* probably refers to the wings of the cherubim (powerful winged animals) whose wings spread over the ark in the inner chamber of the temple (1 Kgs 6, 23–28).

55, 16: Ps 49, 15; Nm 16, 33;
   Prv 1, 2; Is 5, 14.
55, 18: Dn 6, 11.
55, 20: Pss 29, 10; 93, 2; Bar
   3, 3.
55, 22: Pss 12, 3; 28, 3; 57, 5;
   62, 5; 64, 4; Prv 26,
   24–28; Jer 9, 7.
55, 23: Ps 37, 5; Prv 3, 5; 16,
   3; 1 Pt 5, 7.
55, 24: Pss 28, 1; 30, 4; 40, 3;
   88, 5; 143, 7; Prv 1,
   12; Jon 2, 7.
55, 24: Pss 25, 2; 56, 4;
   130, 5.
56, 1: 1 Sm 21, 10.
56, 5: Ps 130, 5.
56, 5: Ps 118, 6; Heb 13, 6.
56, 7: Ps 140, 5–6.
56, 9: Ps 10, 14; 2 Kgs 20, 5;
   Is 25, 8; Rv 7, 17.
56, 13: Nm 30, 3.
57, 1: 1 Sm 22, 1.
57, 2: Pss 17, 8; 36, 8.

3 I call to God Most High,
      to God who provides for me.
4 May God send help from heaven to
         save me,
      shame those who trample upon me.
      May God send fidelity and love.   *Selah*
5 I must lie down in the midst of lions
      hungry for human prey.*
   Their teeth are spears and arrows;
      their tongue, a sharpened sword.*
6 Show yourself over the heavens, God;
      may your glory appear above all the
         earth.*

II

7 They have set a trap for my feet;
      my soul is bowed down;
   They have dug a pit before me.
      May they fall into it themselves!*   *Selah*
8 My heart is steadfast, God,
      my heart is steadfast.
      I will sing and chant praise.*
9† Awake, my soul;
      awake, lyre and harp!
      I will wake the dawn.*
10 I will praise you among the peoples,
      Lord;
   I will chant your praise among the
         nations.*
11 For your love towers to the heavens;
      your faithfulness, to the skies.*
12 Show yourself over the heavens, God;
      may your glory appear above all the
         earth.

PSALM 58†

The Dethroning of Unjust Rulers

1† For the leader. Do not destroy.
A *miktam* of David.

I

2† Do you indeed pronounce justice, O gods;
      do you judge mortals fairly?*

3 No, you freely engage in crime;
      your hands dispense violence to the
         earth.

II

4 The wicked have been corrupt since birth;
      liars from the womb, they have gone
         astray.
5† Their poison is like the poison of a snake,
      like that of a serpent stopping its ears,*
6 So as not to hear the voice of the charmer
      who casts such cunning spells.

III

7 O God, smash the teeth in their mouths;
      break the jaw-teeth of these lions,
         LORD!*
8 Make them vanish like water flowing
         away;*
      trodden down, let them wither like
         grass.*
9† Let them dissolve like a snail that oozes
         away,
      like an untimely birth that never sees
         the sun.*
10 Suddenly, like brambles or thistles,
      have the whirlwind snatch them away.*
11 Then the just shall rejoice to see the
         vengeance
      and bathe their feet in the blood of the
         wicked.*
12 Then it will be said:
      "Truly there is a reward for the just;
      there is a God who is judge on earth!"

PSALM 59†

Complaint against Bloodthirsty Enemies

1† For the director. Do not destroy. A *miktam*
of David, when Saul sent people to watch his house
and kill him.*

I

2 Rescue me from my enemies, my God;
      lift me out of reach of my foes.

57, 9: *I will wake the dawn:* by a bold figure the psalmist imagines the sound of music and singing will waken a new day.

Ps 58: A lament expressing trust in God's power to dethrone all
powers obstructing divine rule of the world. First condemned are
"the gods," the powers that were popularly imagined to control human destinies (2–3), then "the wicked," the human instruments of
these forces (4–6). The psalmist prays God to prevent them from
harming the just (7–10). The manifestation of justice will gladden the
just; they will see that their God is with them (11–12). The psalm is
less concerned with personal vengeance than with public vindication of God's justice now.

58, 1: *Do not destroy:* probably the title of the melody to which
the psalm was to be sung.

58, 2: *Gods:* the Bible sometimes understands pagan gods to be
lesser divine beings who are assigned by Israel's God to rule the foreign nations. Here they are accused of injustice, permitting the human judges under their patronage to abuse the righteous. Cf Ps 82.

58, 5–6: The image is that of a poisonous snake that is controlled
by the voice or piping of its trainer.

58, 9: *A snail that oozes away:* empty shells suggested to ancients
that snails melted away as they left a slimy trail.

Ps 59: A lament in two parts (2–9.11b–17), each ending in a refrain (10.18). Both parts alternate prayer for vindication (2–3.5b–6.
11b–14) with vivid depictions of the psalmist's enemies (4–5a.7–8.
15–16). The near curse in 12–13 is not a crude desire for revenge but
a wish that God's just rule over human affairs be recognized now.

59, 1: *Do not destroy:* probably the title of the melody to which
the psalm was to be sung.

57, 5: Pss 17, 11–12; 22, 22;	58, 5: Pss 64; 4; 140, 3; Rom
58, 7.	3, 13.
57, 5: Pss 11, 2; 64, 4.	58, 7: Ps 3, 7.
57, 6: Ps 72, 19; Nm 14, 21.	58, 8: Wis 16, 29.
57, 7: Pss 7, 15; 140, 5–6.	58, 8: Ps 37, 2.
57, 8: Ps 108, 2.	58, 9: Jb 3, 16.
57, 9: Jb 38, 12.	58, 10: Jb 21, 18; Hos 13, 3;
57, 10: Pss 9, 12; 18, 50.	Na 1, 10.
57, 11: Pss 36, 6; 71, 19.	58, 11: Ps 68, 24; Is 63, 1–6.
58, 2: Ps 82, 2; Dt 16, 19.	59, 1: 1 Sm 19, 11.

PS

3 Deliver me from evildoers;
   from the bloodthirsty save me.
4 They have set an ambush for my life;
   the powerful conspire against me.
   For no offense or misdeed of mine, LORD,
5 for no fault they hurry to take up arms.
   Come near and see my plight!
6 You, LORD of hosts, are the God of Israel!
   Awake! Punish all the nations.
      Have no mercy on these worthless traitors.
                                          Selah
7 Each evening they return,
   growling like dogs, prowling the city.*
8† Their mouths pour out insult;
   sharp words are on their lips.
   They say: "Who is there to hear?"
9 You, LORD, laugh at them;
   you deride all the nations.*
10 My strength, for you I watch;
   you, God, are my fortress, 11 my loving
   God.

II

May God go before me,
   and show me my fallen foes.
12 Slay them, God,
   lest they deceive my people.
   Shake them by your power;
   Lord, our shield, bring them down.
13 For the sinful words of their mouths and lips
   let them be caught in their pride.
   For the lies they have told under oath*
14 destroy them in anger,
   destroy till they are no more.

Then people will know God rules over Jacob,
   yes, even to the ends of the earth.*   Selah
15 Each evening they return,
   growling like dogs, prowling the city.
16 They roam about as scavengers;
   if they are not filled, they howl.

III

17 But I shall sing of your strength,
   extol your love at dawn,
   For you are my fortress,
   my refuge in time of trouble.
18 My strength, your praise I will sing;
   you, God, are my fortress, my loving God.

PSALM 60†

Lament after Defeat in Battle

1 For the leader; according to "The Lily of . . . ."
   A *miktam* of David (for teaching),
2 when he fought against Aram-Naharaim and
   Aram-Zobah; and Joab, coming back, killed
twelve thousand Edomites in the Valley of Salt.*

I

3 O God, you rejected us, broke our defenses;
   you were angry but now revive us.
4 You rocked the earth, split it open;*
   repair the cracks for it totters.
5 You made your people go through hardship,
   made us stagger from the wine you gave us.*
6 Raise up a flag for those who revere you,
   a refuge for them out of bowshot.   Selah
7† Help with your right hand and answer us
   that your loved ones may escape.

The Agony of Defeat

LIVE IT!

The athletic team that has never lost does not exist. As a matter of fact, losing is
what often inspires athletic teams to get stronger or faster or score more points.
The psalmist who sang Psalm 60 knew how it felt to lose. Although this
Psalm was written after defeat in battle, its spirit has echoed through the ages by
athletic teams and all others who have competed and lost. The next time your team loses,
read verses 1–7, and think about how the psalmist calls on God as a helper.

▸ Psalm 60, 1–7

59, 8: *"Who is there to hear?":* a sample of the enemies' godless
reflection. The answer is that God hears their blasphemies.
   Ps 60: The community complains that God has let the enemy win
the battle (3–5) and asks for an assurance of victory (6–7). In the oracle God affirms ownership of the land; the invasion of other nations
is not permanent and will be reversed ultimately (8–10). With renewed confidence, the community resolves to fight again (11). The
opening lament is picked up again (12–14), but this time with new
awareness of God's power and human limitation.

60, 7–14: These verses occur again as the second half of Ps 108.

59, 7: Ps 55, 11.
59, 9: Pss 2, 4; 37, 13; Wis 4,
   18.
59, 13: Prv 12, 13; 18, 7.
59, 14: Ps 83, 18–19; Ez 5, 13.

60, 2: 2 Sm 8, 2.3.13; 1 Chr
   18, 2.3.12.
60, 4: Ps 75, 4; Is 24, 19.
60, 5: Ps 75, 9; Is 51, 17.
   21–22; Jer 25, 15.

II

8† In the sanctuary God promised:
   "I will exult, will apportion Shechem;
   the valley of Succoth I will measure out.
9† Gilead is mine, mine is Manasseh;
   Ephraim is the helmet for my head,
   Judah, my own scepter.
10† Moab is my washbowl;
   upon Edom I cast my sandal.*
   I will triumph over Philistia."

III

11† Who will bring me to the fortified city?
   Who will lead me into Edom?
12 Was it not you who rejected us, God?
   Do you no longer march with our armies?*
13 Give us aid against the foe;
   worthless is human help.
14 We will triumph with the help of God,
   who will trample down our foes.

PSALM 61†

Prayer of the King in Time of Danger

1 For the leader; with stringed instruments. Of David.

I

2 Hear my cry, O God,
   listen to my prayer!
3† From the brink of Sheol I call;
   my heart grows faint.
   Raise me up, set me on a rock,
4   for you are my refuge,
   a tower of strength against the foe.*
5 Then I will ever dwell in your tent,
   take refuge in the shelter of your wings.*
                                          Selah

II

6† O God, when you accept my vows
   and hear the plea of those
   who revere your name in prayer:
7 "Add to the days of the king's life;
   may his years be many generations;*
8 May he reign before God forever;*

may your love and fidelity preserve
   him"—*
9† Then I will sing your name forever,
   fulfill my vows day after day.

PSALM 62†

Trust in God Alone

1† For the leader; 'al Jeduthun. A psalm of David.

I

2 My soul rests in God alone,*
   from whom comes my salvation.
3 God alone is my rock and salvation,
   my secure height; I shall never fall.
4 How long will you set upon people,
   all of you beating them down,
   As though they were a sagging fence
   or a battered wall?
5 Even from my place on high
   they plot to dislodge me.
   They delight in lies;
   they bless with their mouths,
   but inwardly they curse.*   *Selah*

II

6 My soul, be at rest in God alone,
   from whom comes my hope.
7 God alone is my rock and my salvation,
   my secure height; I shall not fall.
8 My safety and glory are with God,*
   my strong rock and refuge.
9 Trust God at all times, my people!
   Pour out your hearts to God our refuge!
                                          Selah

III

10† Mortals are a mere breath,
   the powerful but an illusion;*
   On a balance they rise;
   together they are lighter than air.
11 Do not trust in extortion;
   in plunder put no empty hope.
   Though wealth increase,
   do not set your heart upon it.*

60, 8: *I. . . will apportion . . . measure out:* God lays claim to these places. *The valley of Succoth:* probably the lower stretch of the Jabbok valley.
60, 9: *Judah, my own scepter:* an allusion to the Testament of Jacob, Gn 49, 10.
60, 10: *Moab is my washbowl:* Moab borders the Dead Sea, hence a metaphor for the country. *Upon Edom I cast my sandal:* an ancient legal gesture of taking possession of land.
60, 11: *The fortified city:* perhaps Bozrah, the fortified capital of Edom. Cf Is 34, 6; 63, 1; Am 1, 12.
Ps 61: A lament of the king who feels himself at the brink of death (3) and cries out for the strong and saving presence of God (3b–5). The king cites the prayer being made for him (7–8), and promises to give thanks to God.
61, 3: *Brink of Sheol:* literally, "edge of the earth," "earth" being taken in its occasional meaning "the underworld." Cf Jon 2, 3.
61, 6: *In prayer:* added for sense. Vv 7–8 express *the plea* of v 6.
61, 9: *Then:* Hebrew "just as," i.e., in accord with the vows referred to in v 6.

Ps 62: A song of trust displaying serenity from experiencing God's power (the refrains of 2–3 and 6–7) and anger toward unjust enemies (4–5). From the experience of being rescued, the psalmist can teach others to trust in God (10–13).
62, 1: *'Al Jeduthun:* apparently the Hebrew name for the melody.
62, 10: *On a balance they rise:* precious objects were weighed by balancing two pans suspended from a beam. The lighter pan rises.

60, 10: Ru 4, 7–8.
60, 12: Ps 44, 10.
61, 4: Ps 46, 2.
61, 5: Pss 17, 8; 36, 8; 57, 2.
61, 7: Ps 21, 5.
61, 8: Pss 72, 5; 89, 5.30.37.
61, 8: Pss 85, 11; 89, 15.25;
   Prv 20, 28.
62, 2–3.6–7: Pss 18, 3; 31, 3–4; 42,
   10; 118, 8; 146, 3.
62, 5: Pss 12, 3; 28, 3; 55,
   22; Prv 26, 24–25.
62, 8: Ps 3, 3; Is 26, 4; 60,
   19.
62, 10: Pss 39, 6–7; 144, 4; Jb
   7, 16; Wis 2, 5.
62, 11: Jb 31, 25; Eccl 5, 9;
   Jer 17, 11; Mt 6,
   19–21.24.

12† One thing God has said;
　　　two things I have heard:*
　　　Power belongs to God;
13　　so too, Lord, does kindness,
　　　And you render to each of us
　　　according to our deeds.*

Decide!

Whom are you going to trust? Where will you find your power? in the right people? in the right clothes? in money? in the right job?

　　Or can you trust God to be your rock and your salvation (Ps 62, 3)? Will you let God be your refuge (61, 4; 62, 8) in times of hardship? Why is it so hard sometimes to let your soul rest in God alone (62, 2)?

God, I am weak. Help me every day to put my trust in you.

　　Help me to believe that you and I can do anything together.

▶ Psalm 62

PSALM 63†

Ardent Longing for God

1 A psalm of David, when he was in the wilderness of Judah.*

I

2　O God, you are my God—
　　for you I long!
　For you my body yearns;
　　for you my soul thirsts,
　Like a land parched, lifeless,
　　and without water.*
3　So I look to you in the sanctuary
　　to see your power and glory.

4† For your love is better than life;
　　my lips offer you worship!

II

5　I will bless you as long as I live;
　　I will lift up my hands, calling on your name.
6　My soul shall savor the rich banquet of praise,
　　with joyous lips my mouth shall honor you!
7　When I think of you upon my bed,
　　through the night watches I will recall
8　That you indeed are my help,
　　and in the shadow of your wings I shout for joy.*
9　My soul clings fast to you;
　　your right hand upholds me.

III

10　But those who seek my life will come to ruin;
　　they shall go down to the depths of the earth!
11　They shall be handed over to the sword
　　and become the prey of jackals!
12† But the king shall rejoice in God;
　　all who swear by the Lord shall exult,
　　for the mouths of liars will be shut!*

PSALM 64†

Treacherous Conspirators Punished by God

1 For the leader. A psalm of David.

I

2　O God, hear my anguished voice;
　　from the foes I dread protect my life.
3　Hide me from the malicious crowd,
　　the mob of evildoers.
4　They sharpen their tongues like swords,
　　ready their bows for arrows of poison words.*
5† They shoot at the innocent from ambush,
　　shoot without risk, catch them unawares.
6　They resolve on their wicked plan;
　　they conspire to set snares;
　　they say: "Who will see us?"
7　They devise wicked schemes,
　　conceal the schemes they devise;
　　the designs of their hearts are hidden.*

---

† **62, 12:** *One thing . . . two things:* parallelism of numbers for the sake of variation, a common device in Semitic poetry. One should not literally add up the numbers. Cf Am 1, 3; Prv 6, 16–19; 30, 15.18.21.

Ps 63: A psalm expressing the intimate relationship between God and the worshiper. Separated from God (2), the psalmist longs for the divine life given in the temple (3–6), which is based on a close relationship with God (7–9). May all my enemies be destroyed and God's true worshipers continue in giving praise (10–12)!

63, 4: *For your love is better than life:* only here in the Old Testament is anything prized above life—in this case God's love.

63, 12: *All who swear by the Lord:* to swear by a particular god meant that one was a worshiper of that god (Is 45, 23; 48, 1; Zep 1, 5).

Ps 64: A lament of a person overwhelmed by the malice of the wicked, who are depicted in the psalms as the enemies of the righteous (2–7). When people see God bringing upon the wicked the evil they intended against others, they will know who is the true ruler of the world (8–10). The final verse is a vow of praise (11).

64, 5: *Catch them unawares:* literally, "suddenly," i.e., "unexpectedly."

62, 12: Jb 40, 5.
62, 13: Pss 28, 4; 31, 24; 2 Sm
　3, 39; Jb 34, 11; Jer
　17, 10; Mt 16, 27;
　Rom 2, 6; 2 Tm 4, 14.
63, 1: 1 Sm 24.

63, 2: Pss 42, 2; 143, 6; Is
　26, 9.
63, 8: Pss 17, 8; 36, 8.
63, 12: Ps 107, 42.
64, 4: Pss 11, 2; 37, 14; 55,
　22; 57, 5.
64, 7: Ps 140, 3; Prv 6, 14.

II

8 But God will shoot arrows at them
  and strike them unawares.*
9 They will be brought down by their own
    tongues;
  all who see them will shake their heads.*
10 Then all will fear and proclaim God's deed,
  pondering what has been done.
11 The just will rejoice and take refuge in the
    LORD;
  all the upright will glory in their God.*

PSALM 65 †

Thanksgiving for God's Blessings

¹ For the leader. A psalm of David. A song.

I

2† To you we owe our hymn of praise,
  O God on Zion;
To you our vows must be fulfilled,
3† you who hear our prayers.
To you all flesh must come*
4 with its burden of wicked deeds.
We are overcome by our sins;
  only you can pardon them.*
5 Happy the chosen ones you bring
  to dwell in your courts.
May we be filled with the good things of your
    house,
  the blessings of your holy temple!

II

6† You answer us with awesome deeds of justice,
  O God our savior,
The hope of all the ends of the earth
  and of far distant islands.*
7 You are robed in power,
  you set up the mountains by your might.
8 You still the roaring of the seas,*
  the roaring of their waves,
  the tumult of the peoples.*
9 Distant peoples stand in awe of your
    marvels;

east and west you make resound with joy.
10† You visit the earth and water it,
  make it abundantly fertile.*
God's stream† is filled with water;
  with it you supply the world with grain.
Thus do you prepare the earth:
11 you drench plowed furrows,
  and level their ridges.
With showers you keep the ground soft,
  blessing its young sprouts.
12† You adorn the year with your bounty;
  your paths drip with fruitful rain.
13 The untilled meadows also drip;
  the hills are robed with joy.
14 The pastures are clothed with flocks,
  the valleys blanketed with grain;
  they cheer and sing for joy.*

PSALM 66 †

Praise of God, Israel's Deliverer

¹ For the leader. A song; a psalm.

I

Shout joyfully to God, all you on earth;
2 sing of his glorious name;
  give him glorious praise.*
3 Say to God: "How awesome your deeds!
  Before your great strength your enemies
    cringe.
4 All on earth fall in worship before you;*
  they sing of you, sing of your name!" *Selah*

II

5† Come and see the works of God,
  awesome in the deeds done for us.
6 He changed the sea to dry land;
  through the river they passed on foot.*
Therefore let us rejoice in him,
7 who rules by might forever,
Whose eyes are fixed upon the nations.
  Let no rebel rise to challenge! *Selah*
8 Bless our God, you peoples;
  loudly sound his praise,

Ps 65: The community, aware of its unworthiness (3–4), gives thanks for divine bounty (5), a bounty resulting from God's creation victory (6–9). At God's touch the earth comes alive with vegetation and flocks (10–14).

65, 2: *Vows:* the Israelites were accustomed to promising sacrifices in the temple if their prayers were heard.

65, 3: *To you all flesh must come:* all must have recourse to God's mercy.

65, 6: *Awesome deeds:* the acts of creating—installing mountains, taming seas, restraining nations (7–8)—that are visible worldwide (6.9).

65, 10–14: Apparently a description of the agricultural year, beginning with the first fall rains that soften the hard sun-baked soil (10–11).

65, 10: *God's stream:* the fertile waters of the earth derive from God's fertile waters in the heavenly world.

65, 12: *Paths:* probably the tracks of God's storm chariot dropping rain upon earth.

Ps 66: In the first part (1–12), the community praises God for powerful acts for Israel, both in the past (the exodus from Egypt and the entry into the land [6]) and in the present (deliverance from a recent but unspecified calamity [8–12]). In the second part (13–20), an individual from the rescued community fulfills a vow to offer a sacrifice of thanksgiving. As often in thanksgivings, the rescued person steps forward to teach the community what God has done (16–20).

66, 5–6: Cf the events described in Ex 14, 1—15, 21; Jos 3, 11—4, 24, and Ps 114.

64, 8: Pss 7, 13–14; 38, 3; Dt 32, 42.	38, 11; Mt 8, 26.
64, 9: Pss 5, 11; 44, 14; 52, 6.	65, 8: Is 17, 12.
	65, 10: Lv 26, 4; Is 30, 23.25; Jl 2, 22–23.
64, 11: Pss 36, 8; 57, 2.	65, 14: Is 44, 23.
65, 3: Is 66, 23.	66, 2: Ps 65, 14; Is 44, 23.
65, 4: Pss 32, 1–2; 78, 38; Is 1, 18.	66, 3–4: Ps 18, 45; Mi 7, 17.
65, 6: Is 66, 19.	66, 6: Pss 74, 15; 114, 3; Ex 14, 21f; Jos 3, 14ff; Is 44, 27; 50, 2.
65, 8: Pss 89, 10; 107, 29; Jb	

9 Who has kept us alive
   and not allowed our feet to slip.*

10 You tested us, O God,
   tried us as silver tried by fire.*

11 You led us into a snare;
   you bound us at the waist as captives.

12† You let captors set foot on our neck;
   we went through fire and water;
   then you led us out to freedom.*

III

13† I will bring holocausts to your house;
   to you I will fulfill my vows,

14 The vows my lips pronounced
   and my mouth spoke in distress.

15 Holocausts of fatlings I will offer you
   and burnt offerings of rams;
   I will sacrifice oxen and goats.   Selah

16 Come and hear, all you who fear God,
   while I recount what has been done for me.

17 I called to the Lord with my mouth;
   praise was upon my tongue.

18 Had I cherished evil in my heart,
   the Lord would not have heard.

19 But God did hear
   and listened to my voice in prayer.

20 Blessed be God, who did not refuse me
   the kindness I sought in prayer.

PSALM 67†

Harvest Thanks and Petition

1 For the leader; with stringed instruments.
   A psalm; a song.

I

2† May God be gracious to us and bless us;
   may God's face shine upon us.*   Selah

3 So shall your rule be known upon the earth,
   your saving power among all the nations.*

4 May the peoples praise you, God;
   may all the peoples praise you!

II

5 May the nations be glad and shout for joy;
   for you govern the peoples justly,
   you guide the nations upon the earth.*
                              Selah

6 May the peoples praise you, God;
   may all the peoples praise you!

III

7 The earth has yielded its harvest;
   God, our God, blesses us.*

8 May God bless us still;
   that the ends of the earth may revere our
   God.

PSALM 68†

The Exodus and Conquest, Pledge of Future Help

1 For the leader. A psalm of David, a song.

I

2† God will arise for battle;
   the enemy will be scattered;
   those who hate God will flee.*

3 The wind will disperse them like smoke;
   as wax is melted by fire,
   so the wicked will perish before God.*

4 Then the just will be glad;
   they will rejoice before God;
   they will celebrate with great joy.

II

5† Sing to God, praise the divine name;
   exalt the rider of the clouds.

66, 12: *You let captors set foot on our neck:* literally, "you let men mount our head." Conquerors placed their feet on the neck of their enemies as a sign of complete defeat. Cf Jos 10, 24. A ceremonial footstool of the Egyptian king Tutankhamen portrays bound and prostrate bodies of enemies ready for the king's feet on their heads, and one of Tutankhamen's ceremonial chariots depicts the king as a sphinx standing with paw atop the neck of an enemy.

66, 13: *Holocausts:* wholly burnt offerings. Cf Lv 1, 3–13; 6, 1–4; 22, 17–20.

Ps 67: A petition for a bountiful harvest (7), made in the awareness that Israel's prosperity will persuade the nations to worship its God.

67, 2: *May God be gracious to us:* the people's petition echoes the blessing pronounced upon them by the priests. Cf Nm 6, 22–27.

Ps 68: The psalm is extremely difficult because the Hebrew text is badly preserved and the ceremony that it describes is uncertain. The translation assumes the psalm accompanied the early autumn Feast of Tabernacles (Sukkoth), which included a procession of the tribes (25–28). Israel was being oppressed by a foreign power, perhaps Egypt (31–32)—unless Egypt stands for any oppressor. The psalm may have been composed from segments of ancient poems, which would explain why the transitions are implied rather than explicitly stated. At any rate, v 2 is based on Nm 10, 35–36, and vv 8–9 are derived from Jgs 5, 4–5.

The argument develops in nine stanzas (each of three to five poetic lines): 1) confidence that God will destroy Israel's enemies (2–4); 2) call to praise God as savior (5–7); 3) God's initial rescue of Israel from Egypt (8), the Sinai encounter (9), and the settlement in Canaan (10–11); 4) the defeat of the Canaanite kings (12–15); 5) the taking of Jerusalem, where Israel's God will rule the world (16–19); 6) praise for God's past help and for the future interventions that will be modeled on the ancient exodus-conquest (20–24); 7) procession at the Feast of Tabernacles (25–28); 8) prayer that the defeated enemies bring tribute to the temple (29–32); 9) invitation for all kingdoms to praise Israel's God (33–36).

68, 2: The opening line alluding to Nm 10, 35 makes clear that God's assistance in the period of the exodus and conquest is the model and assurance of all future divine help.

68, 5: *Exalt the rider of the clouds:* God's intervention is in the imagery of Canaanite myth in which the storm-god mounted the storm clouds to ride to battle. Such theophanies occur throughout the psalm: 2–3.8–10.12–15.18–19.22–24.29–32.34–35. See Dt 33, 26; Ps 18, 8–16; Is 19, 1.

66, 9: Pss 91, 12; 121, 3;
   1 Sm 2, 9; Prv 3, 23.
66, 10: Is 48, 10.
66, 12: Is 43, 2.
67, 2: Pss 4, 7; 31, 17; 44, 4;
   80, 4; Dn 9, 17.
67, 3: Jer 33, 9.
67, 5: Ps 98, 7.

67, 7: Ps 85, 13; Lv 26, 4; Ez
   34, 27; Hos 2, 23–24.
68, 2: Nm 10, 35.
68, 3: Ps 97, 5; Jdt 16, 15;
   Wis 5, 14; Mi 1, 4.
68, 5: Pss 18, 10; 104, 3; Dt
   33, 26; Is 19, 1.

Cultural Connections

BLACK PEOPLE PRAISE THE LORD

Psalm 68 commands us to sing praises to the LORD. We are told to praise the LORD because God is the "Father of the fatherless, defender of widows" (verse 6), "gives a home to the forsaken" and "leads prisoners out to prosperity" (verse 7), daily "carries us" (verse 20), and "will crush the skulls of the enemy" (verse 22).

Near the end of all this praise, the psalmist says, "Exact rich tribute from lower Egypt, / from upper Egypt, gold and silver; / make Ethiopia extend its hands to God" (verse 32). The psalmist's call to Egypt and Ethiopia is significant for African Americans because the Egyptians and the Ethiopians were North African black people.

Nevertheless, the message of Psalm 68 is for all people, whether they are black, brown, red, yellow, or white. All people ought to submit to the LORD, all people ought to praise the LORD, and all people ought to render their whole self and their whole substance to the LORD. It matters not who we are or where we come from; the LORD is God and worthy of all praise!

▶ Psalm 68

Rejoice before this God
   whose name is the LORD.*
6 Father of the fatherless, defender of
     widows—*
   this is the God whose abode is holy,
7† Who gives a home to the forsaken,
   who leads prisoners out to prosperity,
   while rebels live in the desert.

III
8 God, when you went forth before your people,*
   when you marched through the desert,
                         Selah
9 The earth quaked, the heavens shook,
   before God, the One of Sinai,
   before God, the God of Israel.
10 You claimed a land as your own, O God;
11 your people settled there.
   There you poured abundant rains, God,
   graciously given to the poor in their need.

IV
12a† The Lord announced the news of victory:
13a   "The kings and their armies are in desperate
     flight.*
12b All you people so numerous,
14a   will you stay by the sheepfolds?*
13b Every household will share the booty,
14b   perhaps a dove sheathed with silver,
14c   its wings covered with yellow gold."
15† When the Almighty routed the kings there,
   the spoils were scattered like snow on
   Zalmon.

V
16 You high mountains of Bashan,
   you rugged mountains of Bashan,
17† You rugged mountains, why look with envy
   at the mountain where God has chosen to
   dwell,
   where the LORD resides forever?*

---

† 68, 7: *While rebels live in the desert:* rebels must live in the arid desert, whereas God's people will live in the well-watered land (vv 8–11).

68, 12–15: The Hebrew text upon which the translation is based has apparently suffered dislocation and has been substantially re-arranged for sense. The version of the defeat of the kings differs from that in the Book of Joshua, where the people play a significant role. Here God alone is responsible for the victory (though the actual battle is not described); Israel only gathers the spoils. God alone is the source of Israel's success; human effort is not important.

68, 15: *Zalmon:* generally taken as the name of a mountain where snow is visible in winter, perhaps to be located in the Golan Heights or in the mountains of Bashan or Hauran east of the Sea of Galilee.

68, 17: *The mountain:* Mount Zion, the site of the temple.

* 68, 6–7: Pss 103, 6; 146, 7.9;
   Ex 22, 20–22; Bar 6,
   37.
68, 8–9: Pss 44, 10; 114, 4.7;
   Jgs 5, 4–5; Heb 12, 26.

68, 13: Jgs 5, 19.22.
68, 14: Jgs 5, 16.
68, 17: Ps 132, 13–14; Ez
   43, 7.

18 God's chariots were myriad, thousands upon
        thousands;
    from Sinai the Lord entered the holy place.
19 You went up to its lofty height;
        you took captives, received slaves as
            tribute.*
    No rebels can live in the presence of God.

VI

20 Blessed be the Lord day by day,
        God, our salvation, who carries us.*   Selah
21 Our God is a God who saves;
        escape from death is in the LORD God's
            hands.
22 God will crush the skulls of the enemy,
        the hairy heads of those who walk in sin.*
23† The Lord has said:
        "Even from Bashan I will fetch them,
    fetch them even from the depths of the sea.
24 You will wash your feet in your enemy's
        blood;
    the tongues of your dogs will lap it up."*

VII

25† Your procession comes into view, O God,
        your procession into the holy place, my
            God and king.
26 The singers go first, the harpists follow;
        in their midst girls sound the timbrels.*
27 In your choirs, bless God;
        bless the LORD, you from Israel's
            assemblies.
28 In the lead is Benjamin, few in number;
        there the princes of Judah, a large throng,
        the princes of Zebulun, the princes of
            Naphtali, too.*

VIII

29 Summon again, O God, your power,
        the divine power you once showed for us.
30 Show it from your temple on behalf of
        Jerusalem,
    that kings may bring you tribute.
31† Roar at the wild beast of the reeds,

the herd of mighty bulls, the lords of
    nations;
scatter the nations that delight in war.
32† Exact rich tribute from lower Egypt,*
        from upper Egypt, gold and silver;
    make Ethiopia extend its hands to God.*

IX

33 You kingdoms of the earth, sing to God;*
        chant the praises of the Lord,   Selah
34 Who rides the heights of the ancient heavens,
        whose voice is thunder, mighty
            thunder.
35 Confess the power of God,
        whose majesty protects Israel,
        whose power is in the sky.
36 Awesome is God in his holy place,
        the God of Israel,
        who gives power and strength to his people.*
    Blessed be God!

PSALM 69†

A Cry of Anguish in Great Distress

1† For the leader; according to "Lilies." Of David.

I

2† Save me, God,
        for the waters have reached my neck.*
3   I have sunk into the mire of the deep,
        where there is no foothold.
    I have gone down to the watery depths;
        the flood overwhelms me.*
4   I am weary with crying out;
        my throat is parched.
    My eyes have failed,
        looking for my God.*
5† More numerous than the hairs of my head
        are those who hate me without cause.*
    Too many for my strength
        are my treacherous enemies.
    Must I now restore
        what I did not steal?

---

†
68, 23: *Even from Bashan . . . from the depths of the sea:* the
heights and the depths, the farthest places where enemies might flee.
68, 25–28: *Your procession:* the procession renews God's original taking up of residence on Zion, described in 16–19.
68, 31: *The wild beast of the reeds:* probably the Nile crocodile,
a symbol for Egypt; see 32 and Ez 29, 2–5.
68, 32: *Lower Egypt* is the delta area north of Cairo. *Upper
Egypt* is the Nile Valley from Cairo to Aswan. *Ethiopia* is still further south.
Ps 69: A lament complaining of suffering in language both
metaphorical (2–3 and 15–16, the waters of chaos) and literal
(4.5.9.11–13, exhaustion, alienation from family and community,
false accusation). In the second part the psalmist prays with special
emphasis that the enemies are punished for all to see (23–29). Despite the pain, the psalmist does not lose hope that all be set right,
and promises public praise (30–37). The psalm, which depicts the
suffering of the innocent just person vividly, is cited often by the New
Testament especially in the passion accounts, e.g., v 5 in Jn 15, 25;
v 22 in Mk 15, 23.36 and parallels and in Jn 19, 29. The psalm prays
not so much for personal vengeance as for public vindication of

God's justice. There was, at this time, no belief in an afterlife where
such vindication could take place. Redress had to take place now, in
the sight of all.
69, 1: *"Lilies":* apparently the name of the melody.
69, 2: *Waters:* the waters of chaos from which God created the
world are a common metaphor for extreme distress. Cf Pss 18, 5;
42, 8; 88, 8; Jon 2, 3–6.
69, 5: *What I did not steal:* the psalmist, falsely accused of theft,
is being forced to make restitution.

68, 19: Ps 47, 8; Eph 4, 8–10.
68, 20: Pss 34, 2; 145, 2; Is
    46, 3–4; 63, 9.
68, 22: Dt 32, 42.
68, 24: Pss 58, 11; 1 Kgs 21,
    19; 22, 38; Is 63, 1–6.
68, 26: Pss 81, 2–3; 87, 7;
    149, 3; 150, 3–5; 2 Sm
    6, 5.
68, 28: Is 8, 23.

68, 32: Ez 29, 2ff.
68, 32: Is 18, 7; 45, 14.
68, 33: Ps 138, 4.
68, 36: Pss 28, 8; 29, 11.
69, 2: Pss 18, 5; 93, 3–4; Jb
    22, 11.
69, 3: Pss 40, 2; 124, 4–5.
69, 4: Pss 25, 15; 119, 82;
    123, 2; 141, 8; Is 38, 14.
69, 5: Ps 40, 13; Lam 3, 52;
    Jn 15, 25.

II

6 God, you know my folly;
   my faults are not hidden from you.
7 Let those who wait for you, LORD of hosts,
   not be shamed through me.
   Let those who seek you, God of Israel,*
   not be disgraced through me.
8 For your sake I bear insult,
   shame covers my face.*
9 I have become an outcast to my kin,
   a stranger to my mother's children.*
10† Because zeal for your house consumes me,
   I am scorned by those who scorn you.*
11 I have wept and fasted,*
   but this led only to scorn.
12 I clothed myself in sackcloth;
   I became a byword for them.
13 They who sit at the gate gossip about me;
   drunkards make me the butt of their songs.

III

14 But I pray to you, LORD,
   for the time of your favor.
   God, in your great kindness answer me
   with your constant help.*
15 Rescue me from the mire;*
   do not let me sink.
   Rescue me from my enemies
   and from the watery depths.
16 Do not let the floodwaters overwhelm me,
   nor the deep swallow me,
   nor the mouth of the pit close over me.
17 Answer me, LORD, in your generous love;
   in your great mercy turn to me.
18 Do not hide your face from your servant;
   in my distress hasten to answer me.*
19 Come and ransom my life;
   because of my enemies redeem me.
20 You know my reproach, my shame, my
     disgrace;
   before you stand all my foes.
21 Insult has broken my heart, and I am weak;
   I looked for compassion, but there was
     none,
   for comforters, but found none.*
22 Instead they put gall in my food;
   for my thirst they gave me vinegar.*

IV

23 Make their own table a snare for them,
   a trap for their friends.*
24 Make their eyes so dim they cannot see;
   keep their backs ever feeble.
25 Pour out your wrath upon them;
   let the fury of your anger overtake them.
26 Make their camp desolate,
   with none to dwell in their tents.*
27 For they pursued the one you struck,
   added to the pain of the one you wounded.
28 Add that to their crimes;
   let them not attain to your reward.
29 Strike them from the book of the living;
   do not count them among the just!*

V

30 But I am afflicted and in pain;
   let your saving help protect me, God,
31† That I may praise God's name in song
   and glorify it with thanksgiving.
32 My song will please the LORD more than oxen,
   more than bullocks with horns and hooves:*
33 "See, you lowly ones, and be glad;
   you who seek God, take heart!*
34 For the LORD hears the poor,
   does not spurn those in bondage.
35 Let the heavens and the earth sing praise,
   the seas and whatever moves in them!"

VI

36 God will rescue Zion,
   rebuild the cities of Judah.*
   God's servants shall dwell in the land and
     possess it;
37 it shall be the heritage of their descendants;
   those who love God's name shall dwell there.*

PSALM 70 †

Prayer for Divine Help

1 For the leader; of David. For remembrance.

2 Graciously rescue me, God!*
   Come quickly to help me, LORD!*
3 Confound and put to shame
   those who seek my life.*
   Turn back in disgrace

---

† **69, 10:** *Zeal for your house consumes me:* the psalmist's commitment to God's cause brings only opposition. Cf Jn 2, 17. *I am scorned by those who scorn you:* Rom 15, 3 uses the verse as an example of Jesus' unselfishness.
   69, 31: *That I may praise God's name in song:* the actual song is cited in 33–35, the word "praise" in 35 referring back to "praise" in 31.
   Ps 70: A lament of a poor and afflicted person (6) who has no resource except God, and who cries out to be saved from the enemy. The psalm is almost identical to Ps 40, 14–18.

69, 7: Ps 40, 17.   69, 8: Jer 15, 15.

69, 9: Jb 19, 13–15.
69, 10: Ps 119, 139; Jn 2, 17;
   Rom 15, 3.
69, 11–13: Ps 109, 24–25; Jb
   30, 9; Lam 3, 14.
69, 14: Is 49, 8.
69, 15–16: Pss 28, 1; 30, 4; 32, 6;
   40, 3; 88, 5; Prv 1, 12.
69, 18: Pss 102, 3; 143, 7.
69, 21: Lam 1, 2.
69, 22: Lam 3, 15; Mt 27, 34.
   48; Mk 15, 23.
69, 23: Rom 11, 9–10.
69, 26: Acts 1, 20.

69, 29: Ps 139, 16; Ex 32, 32;
   Is 4, 3; Dn 12, 1; Mal
   3, 16; Rv 3, 5.
69, 32: Pss 40, 7; 50, 8–9.14;
   51, 18; Is 1, 11–15;
   Hos 6, 6; Am 5,
   21–22; Heb 10, 5–8.
69, 33: Pss 22, 27; 35, 27;
   70, 5.
69, 36: Is 44, 26; Ez 36, 10.
69, 37: Ps 102, 29; Is 65, 9.
70, 2–6: Ps 40, 14–18.
70, 2: Ps 71, 12.
70, 3: Ps 35, 4.26.

those who desire my ruin.
4 Let those who say "Aha!"*
   turn back in their shame.
5 But may all who seek you
   rejoice and be glad in you.
   May those who long for your help
   always say, "God be glorified!"*
6 Here I am, afflicted and poor.
   God, come quickly!
   You are my help and deliverer.
   LORD, do not delay!

PSALM 71†

Prayer in Time of Old Age

I

1 In you, LORD, I take refuge;*
   let me never be put to shame.*
2 In your justice rescue and deliver me;
   listen to me and save me!
3 Be my rock and refuge,
   my secure stronghold;
   for you are my rock and fortress.*
4 My God, rescue me from the power of the
      wicked,
   from the clutches of the violent.*
5 You are my hope, Lord;
   my trust, GOD, from my youth.
6 On you I depend since birth;
   from my mother's womb you are my
      strength;*
   my hope in you never wavers.
7† I have become a portent to many,
   but you are my strong refuge!
8 My mouth shall be filled with your praise,
   shall sing your glory every day.

II

9 Do not cast me aside in my old age;
   as my strength fails, do not forsake me.
10 For my enemies speak against me;
   they watch and plot against me.*
11 They say, "God has abandoned that one.
   Pursue, seize the wretch!
   No one will come to the rescue!"
12 God, do not stand far from me;
   my God, hasten to help me.*

13 Bring to a shameful end
   those who attack me;
   Cover with contempt and scorn
   those who seek my ruin.*
14 I will always hope in you
   and add to all your praise.
15 My mouth shall proclaim your just deeds,
   day after day your acts of deliverance,
   though I cannot number them all.*
16 I will speak of the mighty works of the Lord;
   O GOD, I will tell of your singular justice.

III

17 God, you have taught me from my youth;
   to this day I proclaim your wondrous deeds.
18 Now that I am old and gray,*
   do not forsake me, God,
   That I may proclaim your might
   to all generations yet to come,*
   Your power 19 and justice, God,
   to the highest heaven.
   You have done great things;*
   O God, who is your equal?*
20 You have sent me many bitter afflictions,
   but once more revive me.
   From the watery depths of the earth
   once more raise me up.
21 Restore my honor;
   turn and comfort me,
22 That I may praise you with the lyre
   for your faithfulness, my God,
   And sing to you with the harp,
   O Holy One of Israel!
23 My lips will shout for joy as I sing your praise;
   my soul, too, which you have redeemed.
24 Yes, my tongue shall recount
   your justice day by day.
   For those who sought my ruin
   will have been shamed and disgraced.

PSALM 72†

A Prayer for the King
1† Of Solomon.

I

O God, give your judgment to the king;
   your justice to the son of kings;*

Ps 71: A lament of an old person (9.18) whose afflictions are interpreted by enemies as a divine judgment (11). The first part of the psalm pleads for help (1–4) on the basis of a hope learned from a lifetime's experience of God; the second part describes the menace (9–13) yet remains buoyant (14–16); the third develops the theme of hope and praise.
   71, 7: *A portent to many:* the afflictions of the sufferer are taken as a manifestation of God's anger. Cf Dt 28, 46; Ps 31, 12.
   Ps 72: A royal psalm in which the Israelite king, as the representative of God, is the instrument of divine justice (1–4.12–14) and blessing (5–7.15–17) for the whole world. The king is human, giving only what he has received from God. Hence intercession must be made for him. The extravagant language is typical of oriental royal courts.

72, 1: *The king . . . the son of kings:* the crown prince is the king's son; the prayer envisages the dynasty.

70, 4: Ps 35, 21.25.
70, 5: Ps 35, 27.
71, 1–3: Ps 31, 2–4.
71, 1: Ps 25, 2.
71, 3: Ps 31, 3.
71, 4: Ps 140, 2.
71, 6: Ps 22, 11.
71, 10: Pss 3, 2; 22, 8.
71, 12: Ps 22, 20.

71, 13: Pss 35, 4; 40, 15;
   70, 3.
71, 15: Ps 35, 28.
71, 18: Is 46, 3–4.
71, 18: Pss 22, 31–32; 48,
   14–15; 145, 4.
71, 19: Ps 72, 18.
71, 19: Ps 86, 8.
72, 1: Ps 99, 4; Jer 23, 5.

OPEN UP YOUR TREASURE

If you are black, you may have thought that you've been left out, that God doesn't need you or your talents. African Americans and other ethnic groups have often been relegated to the background. But as Eccl 3, 1 says, "There is an appointed time for everything, / and a time for every affair under the heavens." And from Psalm 72, we see there is a timing for God's call to us.

Psalm 72, 10 says the kings of Arabia and Seba shall come to pay tribute to the King of Israel. Arabia, or Seba, was an ancient kingdom, located near Ethiopia, that included black-skinned people.

In Matthew's story of Jesus' birth, God sends a message in the heavens to inform the dark-skinned wise men from the East when it is time to come and open up their treasures to the King.

God is sending a star to us now. God is talking loud to us, including blacks as a people. "Get yourself ready, and be prepared to bring your gifts to me," God says. God has opened the door for us to come, but we must be willing to fall down and worship God and open up our treasures. If we do that, we too will be wise people who acknowledge the One who is born King. Are you ready to acknowledge our real King?

▶ Psalm 72, 10–11

2 That he may govern your people with
        justice,
      your oppressed with right judgment,*
3 That the mountains may yield their bounty
        for the people,
      and the hills great abundance,*
4 That he may defend the oppressed among the
        people,
      save the poor and crush the oppressor.
                    II
5 May he live as long as the sun endures,
      like the moon, through all generations.*
6 May he be like rain coming down upon the
        fields,
      like showers watering the earth,*
7 That abundance may flourish in his days,
      great bounty, till the moon be no more.
                    III
8† May he rule from sea to sea,

      from the river to the ends of the earth.*
9 May his foes kneel before him,
      his enemies lick the dust.*
10† May the kings of Tarshish and the islands
        bring tribute,
      the kings of Arabia and Seba offer
        gifts.*
11 May all kings bow before him,
      all nations serve him.*
12 For he rescues the poor when they cry out,
      the oppressed who have no one to help.
13 He shows pity to the needy and the poor*
      and saves the lives of the poor.
14† From extortion and violence he frees them,
      for precious is their blood in his sight.
                    IV
15 Long may he live, receiving gold from Arabia,
      prayed for without cease, blessed day by
        day.

72, 8: *From sea to sea . . . the ends of the earth:* the boundaries of the civilized world known at the time: from the Mediterranean Sea (the western sea) to the Persian Gulf (the eastern sea), and from the Euphrates (the river) to the islands and lands of southwestern Europe, "the ends of the earth." The words may also have a mythic nuance—the earth surrounded by cosmic waters, hence everywhere.

72, 10: *Tarshish and the islands:* the far west (Ps 48, 6); Arabia and Seba: the far south (1 Kgs 10, 1).

72, 14: *Their blood:* cf Ps 116, 15.

72, 2: Prv 31, 8–9.
72, 3: Is 52, 7; 55, 12.
72, 5: Ps 89, 37–38; Jer 31, 35.
72, 6: Dt 32, 2; Is 45, 8; Hos
    6, 3.
72, 8: Dt 11, 24; Zec 9, 10.

72, 9: Is 49, 23; Mi 7, 17.
72, 10: Ps 68, 30; Is 60, 5–6;
    1 Kgs 10, 1ff.
72, 11: Ps 47, 8.
72, 13: Prv 31, 9.

16† May wheat abound in the land,
  flourish even on the mountain heights.
  May his fruit increase like Lebanon's,
  his wheat like the grasses of the land.*

17† May his name be blessed forever;
  as long as the sun, may his name endure.*
  May the tribes of the earth give blessings with
  his name;
  may all the nations regard him as favored.*

* * *

18† Blessed be the LORD, the God of Israel,
  who alone does wonderful deeds.*

19 Blessed be his glorious name forever;
  may all the earth be filled with the LORD's
  glory.*
  Amen and amen.

20 The end of the psalms of David, son of Jesse.

THIRD BOOK — PSALMS 73–89

PSALM 73 †

The Trial of the Just
¹ A psalm of Asaph.

How good God is to the upright,
  the Lord, to those who are clean of heart!

I

2 But, as for me, I lost my balance;
  my feet all but slipped,
3 Because I was envious of the arrogant
  when I saw the prosperity of the wicked.*
4 For they suffer no pain;
  their bodies are healthy and sleek.
5 They are free of the burdens of life;
  they are not afflicted like others.
6 Thus pride adorns them as a necklace;
  violence clothes them as a robe.
7 Out of their stupidity comes sin;
  evil thoughts flood their hearts.*

8 They scoff and spout their malice;
  from on high they utter threats.*
9† They set their mouths against the heavens,
  their tongues roam the earth.
10† So my people turn to them
  and drink deeply of their words.
11 They say, "Does God really know?"
  "Does the Most High have any
  knowledge?"*
12 Such, then, are the wicked,
  always carefree, increasing their wealth.

II

13 Is it in vain that I have kept my heart clean,
  washed my hands in innocence?*
14 For I am afflicted day after day,
  chastised every morning.
15 Had I thought, "I will speak as they do,"
  I would have betrayed your people.
16 Though I tried to understand all this,
  it was too difficult for me,
17† Till I entered the sanctuary of God
  and came to understand their end.

III

18 You set them, indeed, on a slippery road;
  you hurl them down to ruin.
19 How suddenly they are devastated;
  undone by disasters forever!
20 They are like a dream after waking, Lord,
  dismissed like shadows when you arise.*

IV

21 Since my heart was embittered
  and my soul deeply wounded,
22 I was stupid and could not understand;
  I was like a brute beast in your presence.
23 Yet I am always with you;
  you take hold of my right hand.*
24† With your counsel you guide me,
  and at the end receive me with honor.
25 Whom else have I in the heavens?
  None beside you delights me on earth.
26 Though my flesh and my heart fail,

72, 16: The translation of the difficult Hebrew is tentative.
72, 17: *May the tribes of the earth give blessings with his name:* an echo of the promise to the ancestors (Gn 12, 3; 26, 4; 28, 14), suggesting that the monarchy in Israel fulfilled the promise to Abraham, Isaac, and Jacob.
72, 18–19: A doxology marking the end of Book II of the Psalter.
Ps 73: The opening verse of this probing poem (cf Pss 37, 49) is actually the psalmist's hard-won conclusion from personal experience: God is just and good! The psalmist describes near loss of faith (2–3), occasioned by observing the wicked who blasphemed God with seeming impunity (4–12). Feeling abandoned despite personal righteousness, the psalmist could not bear the injustice until an experience of God's nearness in the temple made clear how deluded the wicked were. Their sudden destruction shows their impermanence (13–20). The just can thus be confident, for, as the psalmist now knows, their security is from God (1.23–28).
73, 9: *They set their mouths against the heavens:* in an image probably derived from mythic stories of half-divine giants, the monstrous speech of the wicked is likened to enormous jaws gaping wide, devouring everything in sight.

73, 10: The Hebrew is obscure.
73, 17: *And came to understand their end:* the psalmist receives a double revelation in the temple: 1) the end of the wicked comes unexpectedly (18–20); 2) God is with me.
73, 24: *And at the end receive me with honor:* a perhaps deliberately enigmatic verse. It is understood by some commentators as reception into heavenly glory, hence the traditional translation, "receive me into glory." The Hebrew verb can indeed refer to mysterious divine elevation of a righteous person into God's domain: Enoch in Gn 5, 24; Elijah in 2 Kgs 2, 11–12; the righteous psalmist in Ps 49, 16. Personal resurrection in the Old Testament, however, is clearly attested only in the second century B.C. The verse is perhaps best left unspecified as a reference to God's nearness and protection.

72, 16: Is 27, 6; Hos 14, 6–8;
    Am 9, 13.
72, 17: Ps 21, 7.
72, 17: Gn 12, 3; Zec 8, 13.
72, 18: Pss 41, 14; 89, 53;
    106, 48; 136, 4.
72, 19: Ps 57, 5; Nm 14, 21.

73, 3: Ps 37, 1; Jb 21, 13.
73, 7: Jb 15, 27.
73, 8: Ps 17, 10.
73, 11: Ps 10, 11; Jb 22, 13.
73, 13: Ps 26, 6; Mal 3, 14.
73, 20: Jb 20, 8.
73, 23: Ps 121, 5.

WISDOM

Psalm 73 explores the common wisdom question of why the wicked prosper (verse 3). The psalmist finally sees clearly that the wicked eventually fall to ruin (verse 17). The gift of wisdom is also an important value for many Native American peoples. For the Lakota tribe, it is one of four primary values. The Lakota word for wisdom is *wok-sa-pe*.

Wisdom is the ability to see clearly and not be taken in by illusions or outer appearances. The wise person knows that what is inside someone is more important than what is outside. The wise person also knows that we are nothing without the power of Wakan-Tanka, the Great Spirit. Because the sun helps us see things the way they really are, many Native Americans face the rising sun each day to pray to God for wisdom.

To explore the other primary Lakota virtues, see the Cultural Connections articles for Psalms 31, 89, and 112.

▸ Psalm 73

God is the rock of my heart, my portion
    forever.
27 But those who are far from you perish;
    you destroy those unfaithful to you.
28 As for me, to be near God is my good,
    to make the Lord GOD my refuge.
I shall declare all your works
    in the gates of daughter Zion.

PSALM 74†

Prayer at the Destruction of the Temple

1† A *maskil* of Asaph.

I

Why, God, have you cast us off forever?*
    Why does your anger burn against the
    sheep of your pasture?*
2 Remember your flock that you gathered of
    old,
    the tribe you redeemed as your very own.

Remember Mount Zion where you dwell.*
3 Turn your steps toward the utter ruins,
    toward the sanctuary devastated by the
    enemy.
4 Your foes roared triumphantly in your shrine;
    they set up their own tokens of victory.
5 They hacked away like foresters gathering
    boughs,
    swinging their axes in a thicket of trees.
6 They smashed all your engraved work,
    pounded it with hammer and pick.
7 They set your sanctuary on fire;
    the abode of your name they razed and
    profaned.*
8 They said in their hearts, "Destroy them all!
    Burn all the shrines of God in the land!"
9† Now we see no signs,
    we have no prophets,*
    no one who knows how long.

---

† **Ps 74:** A communal lament sung when the enemy invaded the temple; it would be especially appropriate at the destruction of Jerusalem in 587 B.C. Israel's God is urged to look upon the ruined sanctuary and remember the congregation who worshiped there (1–11). People and sanctuary are bound together; an attack on Zion is an attack on Israel. In the second half of the poem, the community brings before God the story of their origins—their creation (12–17)—in order to move God to reenact that deed of creation now. Will God allow a lesser power to destroy the divine project (18–23)?

74, 1: *Forever:* the word implies that the disaster is already of long duration. Cf 74, 9 and note.

74, 9: *Now we see no signs:* ancients often asked prophets to say for how long a divine punishment was to last. Cf 2 Sm 24, 13. Here no prophet has arisen to indicate the duration.

*

74, 1: Pss 10, 1; 44, 24;   15, 17; Jer 10, 16; 51,
    77, 8.   19.
74, 1: Ps 80, 5.   74, 7: Is 64, 10; Ps 79, 1.
74, 2: Pss 68, 17; 132, 13; Ex   74, 9: Lam 2, 9.

P
S

10 How long, O God, shall the enemy jeer?*
   Shall the foe revile your name forever?

11 Why draw back your right hand,
   why keep it idle beneath your cloak?

II

12† Yet you, God, are my king from of old,
    winning victories throughout the earth.

13 You stirred up the sea in your might;*
   you smashed the heads of the dragons on
   the waters.*

14 You crushed the heads of Leviathan,*
   tossed him for food to the sharks.

15 You opened up springs and torrents,
   brought dry land out of the primeval
   waters.

16 Yours the day and yours the night;
   you set the moon and sun in place.

17 You fixed all the limits of the earth;
   summer and winter you made.*

18 Remember how the enemy has jeered, O LORD,
   how a foolish people has reviled your name.

19 Do not surrender to beasts those who praise you;
   do not forget forever the life of your afflicted.

20 Look to your covenant,
   for the land is filled with gloom;
   the pastures, with violence.

21 Let not the oppressed turn back in shame;
   may the poor and needy praise your name.

22 Arise, God, defend your cause;
   remember the constant jeers of the fools.

23 Do not ignore the clamor of your foes,
   the unceasing uproar of your enemies.

PSALM 75†

God the Judge of the World

¹ For the leader. Do not destroy! A psalm
of Asaph; a song.

I

2† We thank you, God, we give thanks;
   we call upon your name,

declare your wonderful deeds.
You said:

3 "I will choose the time;
  I will judge fairly.

4 The earth and all its inhabitants will
  quake,
  but I have firmly set its pillars."*   Selah

II

5† So I say to the boastful: "Do not boast!"*
   to the wicked: "Do not raise your horns!

6 Do not raise your horns against heaven!
  Do not speak arrogantly against the
  Rock!"*

7 For judgment comes not from east or from
  west,
  not from the desert or from the
  mountains,*

8 But from God who decides,
  who brings some low and raises others
  high.*

9† Yes, a cup is in the LORD's hand,
   foaming wine, fully spiced.
When God pours it out,
   they will drain it even to the dregs;
   all the wicked of the earth must drink.*

10 But I will rejoice forever;
   I will sing praise to the God of Jacob,

11 Who has said:
   "I will break off all the horns of the wicked,
   but the horns of the just shall be lifted
   up."*

PSALM 76†

God Defends Zion

¹ For the leader; a psalm with stringed instruments.
A song of Asaph.

I

2 Renowned in Judah is God,*
  whose name is great in Israel.

3† On Salem is God's tent, a shelter on Zion.

74, 12–17: Comparable Canaanite literature describes the storm-god's victory over all-encompassing Sea and its allies (dragons and Leviathan) and the subsequent peaceful arrangement of the universe, sometimes through the placement of paired cosmic elements (day and night, sun and moon). Cf Ps 89, 12–13. The psalm apparently equates the enemies attacking the temple with the destructive cosmic forces already tamed by God. Why then are those forces now raging untamed against your own people?

Ps 75: The psalmist gives thanks and rejoices (2.10) for the direct intervention of God, which is promised in two oracles (3–4.11). Expecting that divine intervention, the psalmist warns evildoers to repent (5–9).

75, 2: You said: supplied for clarity here and in v 11. The translation assumes in both places that the psalmist is citing an oracle of God.

75, 5: Do not raise your horns!: the horn is the symbol of strength; to raise one's horn is to exalt one's own power as v 6 explains.

75, 9: A cup: "the cup of God's wrath" is the punishment inflicted on the wicked. Cf Is 51, 17; Jer 25, 15–29; 49, 12; Ez 23, 31–33.

Spiced: literally, "a mixed drink"; spices or drugs were added to wine. Cf Prv 9, 2.5.

Ps 76: A song glorifying Zion, the mountain of Jerusalem where God destroyed Israel's enemies. Zion is thus the appropriate site to celebrate the victory (3–4), a victory described in parallel scenes (5–7.8–11). Israel is invited to worship its powerful patron deity (12–13).

76, 3: Salem: an ancient name for Jerusalem, used here perhaps on account of its allusion to the Hebrew word for peace, shalom. Cf Gn 14, 18; Heb 7, 1–3.

74, 10: Ps 89, 47.
74, 13: Ps 89, 10.
74, 13: Is 51, 9–10.
74, 14: Jb 3, 8; 40, 25; Is
   27, 1.
74, 16–17: Gn 1.
75, 4: Pss 46, 3; 60, 4; 93, 1;
   96, 10; 104, 5; 1 Sm 2,
   8; Is 24, 19.

75, 5: 1 Sm 2, 3; Zec 2, 1–4.
75, 6: Jb 15, 25.
75, 7: Mt 24, 23–27.
75, 8: Jb 5, 11; 1 Sm 2, 7.
75, 9: Ps 60, 5; Jb 21, 20; Is
   51, 17.21–22; Jer 25,
   15ff; Hb 2, 16.
75, 11: Ps 92, 11.
76, 2: Hb 3, 2.

4　There the flashing arrows were shattered,
　　shield, sword, and weapons of war.*　　*Selah*

II

5†　Terrible and awesome are you,
　　stronger than the ancient mountains.
6　Despoiled are the bold warriors;
　　they sleep their final sleep;
　　the hands of all the mighty have failed.*
7　At your roar, O God of Jacob,
　　chariots and steeds lay still.
8　So terrible and awesome are you;
　　who can stand before you and your great
　　　anger?*
9　From the heavens you pronounced sentence;
　　the earth was terrified and reduced to silence,
10　When you arose, O God, for judgment
　　to deliver the afflicted of the land.　　*Selah*
11†　Even wrathful Edom praises you;
　　the remnant of Hamath keeps your feast.

III

12　Make and keep vows to the LORD your God.*
　　May all present bring gifts to this awesome
　　　God,
13　Who checks the pride of princes,
　　inspires awe among the kings of earth.

PSALM 77†

Confidence in God during National Distress

1　For the leader; *'al Jeduthun*. A psalm of Asaph.

I

2　I cry aloud to God,
　　cry to God to hear me.
3　On the day of my distress I seek the Lord;
　　by night my hands are raised unceasingly;*
　　I refuse to be consoled.
4　When I think of God, I groan;
　　as I ponder, my spirit grows faint.*　　*Selah*
5　My eyes cannot close in sleep;
　　I am troubled and cannot speak.
6　I consider the days of old;
　　the years long past 7 I remember.*
In the night I meditate in my heart;
　　I ponder and my spirit broods:
8　"Will the Lord reject us forever,*
　　never again show favor?

P
S

The Big Picture

Perspective is a valuable thing. It is easy for us to get caught up in the moment, overwhelmed by the urgency of school assignments, sports, and time with family and friends. As difficult as it is, we need to step back for a moment or two and try to grasp the big picture.

You've probably heard the maxim Hindsight is twenty-twenty. When we look back at our life and see where we have come from, the path often makes sense. The twists and turns that were so frustrating and confusing can now be recognized as temporary diversions on our journey. Everything we experienced—the good and the bad—contains lessons for us. The question is, How good a student are we?

The key to wisdom is reflection. Psalm 77 keeps saying this in different ways: "I ponder" (verses 4 and 7), "I consider" (verse 6), and "I will remember" (verse 12). How do you take the time to remember where you have been and to meditate on where you hope to go? Do you learn from the great teacher, life experience? Do you see the whole forest or only the trees right in front of you?

If you don't already spend some time at the end of each day reflecting on the events of that day, begin doing so. Perhaps keep a journal on how you felt or what you learned. Over time, you will see the big picture emerge and even have a greater sense of God's presence in your life.

▶ Psalm 77

---

†　**76, 5:** *Ancient mountains:* conjectural translation of a difficult Hebrew phrase on the basis of Gn 49, 26. The mountains are part of the structure of the universe (Ps 89, 12–13).

　76, 11: *Edom . . . Hamath:* conjectural translation. Israel's neighbors to the southeast and north.

　Ps 77: A community lament in which the speaker ("I") describes the anguish of Israel at God's silence when its very existence is at stake (2–11). In response the speaker recites the story of how God brought the people into existence (12–21). The question is thus posed to God: Will you allow the people you created to be destroyed?

---

*　76, 4: Pss 46, 10; 122, 6–9.
　76, 6: 2 Kgs 19, 35; Jer 51,
　　39; Na 3, 18.
　76, 8: Dt 7, 21; 1 Sm 6, 20;
　　Na 1, 6; Mal 3, 2.
　76, 12: Nm 30, 3.

　77, 3: Pss 50, 15; 88, 2.
　77, 4: Jon 2, 8.
　77, 7: Ps 143, 5; Dt 32, 7.
　77, 8–10: Pss 13, 2; 44, 24; 74,
　　1; 80, 5; 89, 47; Lam
　　3, 31.

9 Has God's love ceased forever?
   Has the promise failed for all ages?

10 Has God forgotten mercy,
   in anger withheld compassion?"   Selah

11† I conclude: "My sorrow is this,
   the right hand of the Most High has
     left us."*

II

12† I will remember the deeds of the LORD;
   yes, your wonders of old I will
     remember.*

13 I will recite all your works;
   your exploits I will tell.

14 Your way, O God, is holy;
   what god is as great as our God?*

15 You alone are the God who did wonders;
   among the peoples you revealed your
     might.*

16 With your arm you redeemed your
     people,
   the descendants of Jacob and Joseph.*
                 Selah

17 The waters saw you, God;
   the waters saw you and lashed
     about,
   trembled even to their depths.*

18 The clouds poured down their rains;
   the thunderheads rumbled;
   your arrows flashed back and forth.*

19 The thunder of your chariot wheels
     resounded;
   your lightning lit up the world;
   the earth trembled and quaked.*

20 Through the sea was your path;
   your way, through the mighty waters,
   though your footsteps were unseen.*

21 You led your people like a flock
   under the care of Moses and
     Aaron.*

PSALM 78†

A New Beginning in Zion and David

1 A *maskil* of Asaph.

I

Attend, my people, to my teaching;
   listen to the words of my mouth.

2† I will open my mouth in story,
   drawing lessons from of old.*

3 We have heard them, we know them;
   our ancestors have recited them to us.*

4 We do not keep them from our children;
   we recite them to the next generation,
The praiseworthy and mighty deeds of
     the LORD,
   the wonders that he performed.*

5 God set up a decree in Jacob,
   established a law in Israel:*
What he commanded our ancestors,
   they were to teach their children;

6 That the next generation might come
     to know,
   children yet to be born.*
In turn they were to recite them to their
     children,

7 that they too might put their trust in God,
And not forget the works of God,
   keeping his commandments.

8 They were not to be like their ancestors,
   a rebellious and defiant generation,*
A generation whose heart was not
     constant,*
   whose spirit was not faithful to God,

9† Like the ranks of Ephraimite archers,
   who retreated on the day of battle.

10 They did not keep God's covenant;
   they refused to walk by his law.

11 They forgot his works,
   the wondrous deeds he had shown them.

77, 11: *I conclude:* literally, "I said." The psalmist, after pondering the present distress and God's promises to Israel, has decided that God has forgotten the people.

77, 12: *I will remember:* the verb sometimes means to make present the great deeds of Israel's past by reciting them. Cf Pss 78, 42; 105, 5; 106, 7.

Ps 78: A recital of history to show that past generations did not respond to God's gracious deeds and were punished by God making the gift into a punishment. Will Israel now fail to appreciate God's new act—the choosing of Zion and of David? The tripartite introduction invites Israel to learn the lessons hidden in its traditions (1–4.5–7.8–11); each section ends with the mention of God's acts. There are two distinct narratives of approximately equal length: the wilderness events (12–39) and the movement from Egypt to Canaan (40–72). The structure of both is parallel: gracious act (12–16.40–55), rebellion (17–20.56–58), divine punishment (21–31.59–64), God's readiness to forgive and begin anew (32–39.65–72). The psalm may reflect the reunification program of either King Hezekiah (late eighth century) or King Josiah (late seventh century) in that the Northern Kingdom (Ephraim, Joseph) is especially invited to accept Zion and the Davidic king.

78, 2: *Story:* Hebrew *mashal* literally means "comparison" and can signify a story with a hidden meaning. Mt 13, 35 cites the verse to explain Jesus' use of parables.

78, 9: *Ephraimite archers:* Ephraim was the most important tribe of the Northern Kingdom. Its military defeat (here unspecified) demonstrates its infidelity to God, who otherwise would have protected it.

77, 11: Ex 15, 6.12; Pss 17, 7;
   18, 36.
77, 12: Ps 143, 5.
77, 14: Ps 18, 31; Ex 15, 11.
77, 15: Pss 86, 10; 89, 6.
77, 16: Gn 46, 26–27; Neh 1,
   10.
77, 17: Pss 18, 16; 114, 3; Na
   1, 4.
77, 18: Pss 18, 14–15; 29;
   144, 6; Jb 37, 3–4; Wis
   5, 21; Hb 3, 10–11;
   Zec 9, 14.
77, 19: Pss 18, 8; 97, 4; 99, 1;
   Ex 19, 16; Jgs 5, 4–5.

77, 20: Neh 9, 11; Wis 14, 3;
   Is 51, 10; Hb 3, 15.
77, 21: Ps 78, 52; Is 63,
   11–14; Hos 12, 14; Mi
   6, 4.
78, 2: Ps 49, 5; Mt 13, 35.
78, 3: Ps 44, 2.
78, 4: Ex 10, 2; Dt 4, 9; Jb
   8, 8.
78, 5: Ps 147, 19; Dt 33, 4.
78, 6: Ps 22, 31–32; Dt 4, 9;
   6, 7.
78, 8: Dt 31, 27; 32, 5.
78, 8: Ps 95, 10.

II

A

12† In the sight of their ancestors God did
    wonders,
    in the land of Egypt, the plain of Zoan.*

13 He split the sea and led them across,*
    piling up the waters rigid as walls.*

14 God led them with a cloud by day,
    all night with the light of fire.*

15 He split rock in the desert,
    gave water to drink, abounding as the
    deep.*

16 He made streams flow from crags,
    drew out rivers of water.

B

17 But they went on sinning against him,
    rebelling against the Most High in the
    desert.*

18 They tested God in their hearts,
    demanding the food they craved.*

19 They spoke against God, and said,
    "Can God spread a table in the desert?*

20 True, when he struck the rock,
    water gushed forth,
    the wadis flooded.
    But can he also provide bread,
    give meat to his people?"

C

21 The LORD heard and grew angry;*
    fire blazed up against Jacob;
    anger flared up against Israel.

22 For they did not believe in God,
    did not trust in his saving power.

23† So he commanded the skies above;
    the doors of heaven he opened.

24 God rained manna upon them for food;
    bread from heaven he gave them.*

25 All ate a meal fit for heroes;
    food he sent in abundance.

26 He stirred up the east wind in the heavens;
    by his power God brought on the south wind.

27 He rained meat upon them like dust,
    winged fowl like the sands of the sea,

28 Brought them down in the midst of the camp,
    round about their tents.

29 They ate and were well filled;
    he gave them what they had craved.

30 But while they still wanted more,
    and the food was still in their mouths,

31 God's anger attacked them,
    killed their best warriors,
    laid low the youth of Israel.*

32 In spite of all this they went on sinning,
    they did not believe in his wonders.

D

33 God ended their days abruptly,
    their years in sudden death.

34 When he slew them, they began to seek him;
    they again inquired of their God.*

35† They remembered that God was their rock,
    God Most High, their redeemer.

36 But they deceived him with their mouths,
    lied to him with their tongues.

37 Their hearts were not constant toward him;
    they were not faithful to his covenant.*

38† But God is merciful and forgave their sin;
    he did not utterly destroy them.
    Time and again he turned back his anger,
    unwilling to unleash all his rage.*

39 He was mindful that they were flesh,
    a breath that passes and does not return.

III

A

40 How often they rebelled against God in the
    desert,
    grieved him in the wasteland.

41 Again and again they tested God,
    provoked the Holy One of Israel.

42 They did not remember his power,
    the day he redeemed them from the foe,*

43† When he displayed his wonders in Egypt,
    his marvels in the plain of Zoan.*

44 God changed their rivers to blood;
    their streams they could not drink.

45 He sent insects that devoured them,*
    frogs that destroyed them.

46 He gave their harvest to the caterpillar,
    the fruits of their labor to the locust.

47 He killed their vines with hail,*
    their sycamores with frost.

48 He exposed their flocks to deadly hail,
    their cattle to lightning.*

---

† **78, 12.43:** *Zoan:* a city on the arm of the Nile, a former capital of Egypt.

78, 23–31: On the manna and the quail, see Ex 16 and Nm 11. Unlike Ex 16, here both manna and quail are instruments of punishment, showing that a divine gift can become deadly because of Israel's apostasy.

78, 35: *Remembered:* invoked God publicly in worship. Their words were insincere (36).

78, 38: God is always ready to forgive and begin anew, as in choosing Zion and David (65–72).

78, 43–55: Ex 7–12 records ten plagues. Here there are six divine attacks upon Egypt; the seventh climactic act is God's bringing Israel to the holy land.

* 78, 12: Ps 106, 7.
78, 13–14: Ex 14–15; Ps 136, 13.
78, 13: Ex 14, 22; 15, 8.
78, 14: Ps 105, 39; Ex 13, 21; Wis 18, 3.
78, 15: Pss 105, 41; 114, 8; Ex 17, 1–7; Nm 20, 2–13; Dt 8, 15; Wis 11, 4; Is 48, 21.
78, 17: Dt 9, 7; Ez 20, 13.
78, 18: Ps 106, 14; Ex 16, 2–36.
78, 19: Ps 23, 5.
78, 21f: Nm 11; Dt 32, 22.

78, 24: Ps 105, 40; Ex 16, 4.14; Dt 8, 3; Wis 16, 20; Jn 6, 31.
78, 31: Nm 14, 29.
78, 34: Dt 32, 15.18; Is 26, 16.
78, 37: Ps 95, 10; Is 29, 13.
78, 38: Ps 85, 4; Ex 32, 14; Is 48, 9; Ez 20, 22.
78, 42: Ps 106, 21.
78, 43f: Pss 105, 27–36; 135, 9; Ex 7, 14—11, 10; 12, 29–36; Wis 16–18.
78, 45: Ex 8, 17.
78, 47: Wis 16, 16.
78, 48: Ex 9, 3.

PS

⁴⁹ He unleashed against them his fiery breath,
   roar, fury, and distress,
   storming messengers of death.

⁵⁰ He cleared a path for his anger;
   he did not spare them from death;
   he delivered their beasts to the plague.

⁵¹ He struck all the firstborn of Egypt,*
   love's first child in the tents of Ham.

⁵² God led forth his people like sheep;
   he guided them through the desert like a
      flock.*

⁵³ He led them on secure and unafraid,
   but the sea enveloped their enemies.*

⁵⁴ He brought them to his holy land,
   the mountain his right hand had won.*

⁵⁵ God drove out the nations before them,
   apportioned them a heritage by lot,
   settled the tribes of Israel in their tents.

B

⁵⁶ But they tested, rebelled against God Most High,
   his decrees they did not observe.

⁵⁷ They turned back, deceitful like their ancestors;
   they proved false like a bow with no
      tension.

⁵⁸ They enraged him with their high places;
   with their idols they goaded him.*

C

⁵⁹ God heard and grew angry;
   he rejected Israel completely.

⁶⁰† He forsook the shrine at Shiloh,*
   the tent where he dwelt with humans.

⁶¹ He gave up his might into captivity,
   his glorious ark into the hands of the foe.*

⁶² God abandoned his people to the sword;
   he was enraged against his heritage.

⁶³ Fire consumed their young men;
   their young women heard no wedding
      songs.*

⁶⁴ Their priests fell by the sword;
   their widows made no lamentation.

D

⁶⁵ Then the Lord awoke as from sleep,
   like a warrior from the effects of wine.

⁶⁶ He put his enemies to flight;
   everlasting shame he dealt them.

⁶⁷ He rejected the tent of Joseph,
   chose not the tribe of Ephraim.

⁶⁸† God chose the tribe of Judah,
   Mount Zion which he favored.*

⁶⁹ He built his shrine like the heavens,
   like the earth which he founded forever.

⁷⁰ He chose David his servant,
   took him from the sheepfold.*

⁷¹ From tending sheep God brought him,
   to shepherd Jacob, his people,
   Israel, his heritage.*

⁷² He shepherded them with a pure heart;
   with skilled hands he guided them.

PSALM 79†

A Prayer for Jerusalem
¹ A psalm of Asaph.

I

O God, the nations have invaded your
      heritage;
   they have defiled your holy temple,
   have laid Jerusalem in ruins.*

² They have left the corpses of your servants
      as food for the birds of the heavens,
   the flesh of your faithful for the beasts of
      the earth.*

³ They have spilled their blood like water
      all around Jerusalem,
   and no one is left to bury them.*

⁴ We have become the reproach of our
      neighbors,
   the scorn and derision of those around us.*

II

⁵ How long, LORD? Will you be angry forever?
   Will your rage keep burning like fire?*

⁶ Pour out your wrath on nations that reject
      you,
   on kingdoms that do not call on your
      name,*

⁷ For they have devoured Jacob,
   laid waste his home.

⁸ Do not hold past iniquities against us;
   may your compassion come quickly,
   for we have been brought very low.*

---

† **78, 60:** *Shiloh:* an important shrine in the north prior to Jerusalem. Despite its holy status, it was destroyed (60–64; cf Jer 7, 12.14).

   78, 68.70: God's ultimate offer of mercy to the sinful helpless people is Zion and the Davidic king.

   Ps 79: A communal lament complaining that the nations have defiled the temple and murdered the holy people, leaving their corpses unburied (1–4). The occasion is probably the destruction of Jerusalem by the Babylonian army in 587 B.C. The people ask how long the withdrawal of divine favor will last (5), pray for action now (6–7), and admit that their own sins have brought about the catastrophe (8–9). They seek to persuade God to act for reasons of honor: the nations who do not call upon the Name are running amok (6); the divine honor is compromised (1.10.12); God's own servants suffer (2–4.11).

---

* 78, 51: Pss 105, 36; 136, 10;
   Ex 12, 29.
78, 52: Ps 77, 21.
78, 53: Ex 14, 26–28.
78, 54: Ex 15, 17.
78, 58: Dt 32, 16.21.
78, 60: Jos 18, 1; 1 Sm 1, 3;
   Jer 7, 12; 26, 6.
78, 61: 1 Sm 4, 11.22.
78, 63: Dt 32, 25; Jer 7, 34.
78, 68: Pss 48, 2; 50, 2; Lam
   2, 15.
78, 70: Ps 89, 21; Ez 34, 23;
   37, 24; 2 Chr 6, 6.

78, 71: 1 Sm 16, 11–13; 2 Sm
   7, 8.
79, 1: 2 Kgs 25, 9–10; Lam
   1, 10.
79, 2: Jer 7, 33.
79, 3: 1 Mc 7, 17; Jer 14, 16.
79, 4: Pss 44, 14; 80, 7; 123,
   3–4; Jb 12, 4; Dn 9,
   16; Zep 2, 8.
79, 5: Pss 13, 2; 44, 24; 89,
   47; Dt 4, 24.
79, 6: Ps 14, 4; Jer 10, 25.
79, 8: Ps 142, 7.

III

9 Help us, God our savior,
      for the glory of your name.
   Deliver us, pardon our sins
      for your name's sake.*
10 Why should the nations say,
      "Where is their God?"*
   Before our eyes make clear to the nations
      that you avenge the blood of your
         servants.*

IV

11 Let the groans of prisoners come before you;
      by your great power free those doomed to
         death.*
12 Lord, inflict on our neighbors sevenfold
      the disgrace they inflicted on you.*
13 Then we, your people, the sheep of your
         pasture,
      will give thanks to you forever;
   through all ages we will declare your praise.

PSALM 80†

Prayer to Restore God's Vineyard

1† For the leader; according to "Lilies." *Eduth.*
      A psalm of Asaph.

I

2 Shepherd of Israel, listen,
      guide of the flock of Joseph!
   From your throne upon the cherubim reveal
         yourself*
3   to Ephraim, Benjamin, and Manasseh.
   Stir up your power, come to save us.
4   O LORD of hosts, restore us;
   Let your face shine upon us,
      that we may be saved.*

II

5 LORD of hosts,
      how long will you burn with anger
      while your people pray?*
6 You have fed them the bread of tears,
      made them drink tears in abundance.*

7 You have left us to be fought over by our
         neighbors;
      our enemies deride us.*
8 O LORD of hosts, restore us;
      let your face shine upon us,
      that we may be saved.

III

9† You brought a vine out of Egypt;
      you drove away the nations and planted it.
10 You cleared the ground;
      it took root and filled the land.
11 The mountains were covered by its shadow,
      the cedars of God by its branches.
12† It sent out boughs as far as the sea,
      shoots as far as the river.
13 Why have you broken down the walls,
      so that all who pass by pluck its fruit?*
14 The boar from the forest strips the vine;
      the beast of the field feeds upon it.*
15 Turn again, LORD of hosts;
      look down from heaven and see;
   Attend to this vine,
16   the shoot your right hand has planted.
17 Those who would burn or cut it down—
      may they perish at your rebuke.
18† May your help be with the man at your right
         hand,
      with the one whom you once made
         strong.
19 Then we will not withdraw from you;
      revive us, and we will call on your name.
20 LORD of hosts, restore us;
      let your face shine upon us,
      that we may be saved.

PSALM 81†

An Admonition to Fidelity

1† For the leader; "upon the *gittith.*" Of Asaph.

I

2 Sing joyfully to God our strength;*
      shout in triumph to the God of Jacob!

Ps 80: A community lament in time of military defeat. Using the familiar image of Israel as a vineyard, the people complain that God has broken down the wall protecting the once splendid vine brought from Egypt (9–14). They pray that God will again turn to them and use the Davidic king to lead them to victory (15–20).

80, 1: *"Lilies"* . . . . *Eduth:* the first term is probably the title of the melody to which the psalm was to be sung; the second is unexplained.

80, 9: *A vine:* a frequent metaphor for Israel. Cf Is 5, 1–7; 27, 2–5; Jer 2, 21; Hos 10, 1; Mt 21, 33.

80, 12: *The sea:* the Mediterranean. *The river:* the Euphrates. Cf Gn 15, 18; 1 Kgs 5, 1. The terms may also have a mythic nuance—the seas that surround the earth; sea and river are sometimes paralleled in poetry.

80, 18: *The man at your right hand . . . the one:* the Davidic king who will lead the army in battle.

Ps 81: At a pilgrimage feast, probably harvest in the fall, the people assemble in the temple in accord with the Sinai ordinances (2–6a). They hear a divine word (mediated by a temple speaker)

telling how God rescued them from slavery in Egypt (7–9), gave them the fundamental commandment of fidelity (9–11), which would bring punishment if they refused to obey (12–13). But if Israel repents, God will be with them once again, bestowing protection and fertility (14–17).

81, 1: *"Upon the gittith":* probably the title of the melody to which the psalm was to be sung or a muscial instrument.

79, 9: Ez 20, 44; 36, 22.
79, 10: Pss 42, 4; 115, 2; Jl 2,
      17.
79, 10: Jl 4, 21.
79, 11: Ps 102, 21.
79, 12: Ps 89, 51–52.
80, 2: Pss 23, 1–3; 95, 7;
      100, 3; Gn 48, 15; Ex
      25, 22; 1 Sm 4, 4;
      2 Sm 6, 2; Mi 7, 14.
80, 4.8.20: Pss 4, 7; 31, 17; 67, 2;
      85, 5; Nm 6, 25; Dn 9,
      17.

80, 5: Pss 13, 2; 44, 24;
      74, 1; 79, 5; 89, 47; Dt
      4, 24.
80, 6: Pss 42, 4; 102, 10.
80, 7: Pss 44, 14; 79, 4; 123,
      3–4; Jb 12, 4; Dn 9,
      16; Zep 2, 8.
80, 13: Ps 89, 41.
80, 14: Hos 2, 14.
81, 2: Pss 43, 4; 68, 26; 149,
      3; 150, 3–4; Jdt 16, 1.

P
S

3 Take up a melody, sound the timbrel,
       the sweet-sounding harp and lyre.
4† Blow the trumpet at the new moon,
       at the full moon, on our solemn feast.*
5 For this is a law in Israel,
       an edict of the God of Jacob,*
6 Who made it a decree for Joseph
       when he came out of the land of Egypt.

II

I hear a new oracle:†
7† "I relieved their shoulders of the burden;
       their hands put down the basket.*
8† In distress you called and I rescued you;
       unseen, I spoke to you in thunder;
    At the waters of Meribah I tested you
           and said:*   *Selah*
9 'Listen, my people, I give you warning!
       If only you will obey me, Israel!*
10† There must be no foreign god among you;*
       you must not worship an alien god.
11 I, the LORD, am your God,
       who brought you up from the land of Egypt.

Open wide your mouth that I may fill it.'
12 But my people did not listen to my words;
       Israel did not obey me.
13 So I gave them over to hardness of heart;
       they followed their own designs.*
14 But even now if my people would listen,
       if Israel would walk in my paths,*
15 In a moment I would subdue their foes,
       against their enemies unleash my hand.*
16 Those who hate the LORD would tremble,
       their doom sealed forever.
17 But Israel I would feed with the finest wheat,
       satisfy them with honey from the rock."*

PSALM 82†

The Downfall of Unjust Gods

1 A psalm of Asaph.

I

God rises in the divine council,
       gives judgment in the midst of the gods.*
2 "How long will you judge unjustly
       and favor the cause of the wicked?*   *Selah*

AIDS—a Matter of Compassion

Jerry died of complications due to the AIDS virus. The paper carried an article about his life. The writer said: "His worst fears were not realized. His church did not reject him in the end. It surrounded him with love." What an awesome example of love and justice. Jerry's parish did not condemn him; it showed compassion for his life.

We are tempted, in our society, to blame the weakest and the poorest for their situation and to excuse ourselves from any need to help. We say that people who are poor are too lazy to work. That those who are hungry should get a job. That people dying of AIDS deserve it because of their choices. These attitudes portray a cold justice without mercy. They are not from the mind of God. For God, mercy and justice go hand in hand. Thank goodness, the people of Jerry's parish understood that.

Psalm 82 is a plea for God's justice, a cry to "render justice to the afflicted and needy" (verse 3). Take these words to heart, pray for those who judge without mercy, and remember the reporter's words about Jerry: "His church . . . surrounded him with love."

▶ Psalm 82

---

†
81, 4: *New moon . . . full moon:* the pilgrimage feast of harvest began with a great assembly (Lv 23, 24; Nm 29, 1), used the new moon as a sign (Nm 29, 6), and included trumpets (Lv 23, 24).
81, 6: *I hear a new oracle:* literally, "a tongue I do not know I hear." A temple official speaks the word of God (6b–17), which is authoritative and unlike merely human words (cf Nm 24, 4.16).
81, 7: *I relieved their shoulders of the burden:* literally, "his [Israel's] shoulder," hence the plural translation. A reference to the liberation of Israel from salvery in Egypt. *The basket:* for carrying clay to make bricks. Cf Ex 1, 14.
81, 8: *Meribah:* place of rebellion in the wilderness; cf Ex 17, 7; Nm 20, 13.
81, 10: *There must be no foreign god among you:* as in Pss 50 and 95, Israel is challenged to obey the first commandment of fidelity to God after the proclamation of the exodus.

Ps 82: As in Ps 58, the pagan gods are seen as subordinate divine beings to whom Israel's God had delegated oversight of the foreign countries in the beginning (Dt 32, 8–9 LXX). Now God arises in the heavenly assembly (1) to rebuke the unjust "gods" (2–4), who are stripped of divine status and reduced in rank to mortals (5–7). They are accused of misruling the earth by not upholding the poor. A short prayer for universal justice concludes the psalm (8).

81, 4: Lev 23, 24; Nm 29, 1.
81, 5: Ex 23, 14ff.
81, 6: Ex 1, 14; 6, 6.
81, 8: Ps 95, 8; Ex 2, 23ff;
   17, 7; 19, 16; Nm 20,
   13; 27, 14.
81, 9: Ex 15, 26; Is 55, 2–3.
81, 10–11: Ex 20, 2–6; Dt 5,
   6–10.
81, 13: Jer 3, 17; 7, 24.
81, 14: Is 48, 18.
81, 15: Lv 26, 7–8.
81, 17: Ps 147, 14; Dt 32,
   13–14.
82, 1: Is 3, 13–14.
82, 2: Ps 58, 2.

3 Defend the lowly and fatherless;
    render justice to the afflicted and needy.
4 Rescue the lowly and poor;
    deliver them from the hand of the wicked."*

II

5† The gods neither know nor understand,
    wandering about in darkness,
    and all the world's foundations shake.
6† I declare: "Gods though you be,
    offspring of the Most High all of you,
7 Yet like any mortal you shall die;
    like any prince you shall fall."
8† Arise, O God, judge the earth,
    for yours are all the nations.

PSALM 83†

Prayer against a Hostile Alliance
1 A song; a psalm of Asaph.

I

2 God, do not be silent;
    God, be not still and unmoved!*
3 See how your enemies rage;
    your foes proudly raise their heads.
4 They conspire against your people,
    plot against those you protect.*
5 They say, "Come, let us wipe out their nation;
    let Israel's name be mentioned no more!"
6 They scheme with one mind,
    in league against you:*
7† The tents of Ishmael and Edom,
    the people of Moab and Hagar,*
8 Gebal, Ammon, and Amalek,*
    Philistia and the inhabitants of Tyre.*
9 Assyria, too, in league with them
    gives aid to the descendants of Lot.   Selah

II

10† Deal with them as with Midian,
    as with Sisera and Jabin at the torrent
    Kishon,*

11 Those destroyed at Endor,
    who became dung for the ground.*
12 Make their nobles like Oreb and Zeeb,
    all their princes like Zebah and
    Zalmunna,
13 Who made a plan together,
    "Let us seize the pastures of God."
14 My God, turn them into withered
    grass,
    into chaff flying before the wind.*
15 As a fire raging through a forest,
    a flame setting mountains ablaze,*
16 Pursue them with your tempest;
    terrify them with your storm.*
17 Cover their faces with shame,
    till they pay you homage, LORD.
18 Let them be dismayed and shamed
    forever;
    let them perish in disgrace.
19 Show them you alone are the LORD,
    the Most High over all the earth.*

PSALM 84†

Prayer of a Pilgrim to Jerusalem
1 For the leader; "upon the *gittith*." A psalm
    of the Korahites.

I

2 How lovely your dwelling,
    O LORD of hosts!*
3 My soul yearns and pines
    for the courts of the LORD.*
    My heart and flesh cry out
    for the living God.
4† As the sparrow finds a home
    and the swallow a nest to settle her
    young,
    My home is by your altars,
    LORD of hosts, my king and my God!*

---

† 82, 5: The gods are blind and unable to declare what is right. Their misrule shakes earth's foundations (cf Pss 11, 3; 75, 4), which God made firm in creation (Ps 96, 10).

82, 6: *I declare: "Gods though you be":* in Jn 10, 34 Jesus uses the verse to prove that those to whom the word of God is addressed can fittingly be called "gods."

82, 8: *Judge the earth:* according to Dt 32, 8–9 LXX, Israel's God had originally assigned jurisdiction over the foreign nations to the subordinate deities, keeping Israel as a personal possession. Now God will directly take over the rulership of the whole world.

Ps 83: The community lament complains to God of the nations' attempts to wipe out the name of Israel (2–9). The psalmist sees all Israel's enemies throughout its history united in a conspiracy (3–9). May God destroy the current crop of enemies as the enemies of old were destroyed (10–13), and may they be pursued until they acknowledge the name of Israel's God (14–19).

83, 7–9: Apart from the Assyrians, all the nations listed here were neighbors of Israel. *The people of . . . Hagar:* a tribe of the desert regions east of *Ammon* and *Moab* (1 Chr 5, 10.19–22). *Gebal* is the Phoenician city of Byblos or perhaps a mountain region south of the Dead Sea. *The descendants of Lot* are Moab and Edom (Gn 19, 36–38 and Dt 2, 9). These nations were never united against Is-

rael in the same period; the psalm has lumped them all together.

83, 10–13: For the historical events, see Jgs 4–8.

Ps 84: Israelites celebrated three pilgrimage feasts in Jerusalem annually. The psalm expresses the sentiments of the pilgrims eager to enjoy the divine presence.

84, 4: The desire of a restless bird for a secure home is an image of the desire of a pilgrim for the secure house of God. Cf Ps 42, 2–3, where the image for the desire of the pilgrim is the thirst of the deer for water.

* 82, 4: Dt 1, 17.
83, 2: Pss 10, 1; 44, 24; 109, 1.
83, 4: Jer 11, 9.
83, 6: Ps 2, 2.
83, 7: Nm 20, 23; 1 Chr 5, 10.19.
83, 8: Ex 17, 8.
83, 8: Jos 13, 2.
83, 10: Ex 2, 15; Is 9, 3; 10, 26.
83, 11: Jer 8, 2.

83, 14: Pss 1, 4; 35, 5; 58, 10; Is 5, 24; 10, 17; 17, 13; 29, 5; Ez 21, 3.
83, 15: Ps 50, 3.
83, 16: Jb 25, 32; 27, 21.
83, 19: Ps 97, 9; Dt 4, 39; Dn 3, 45.
84, 2: Pss 43, 3–4; 122, 1.
84, 3: Pss 42, 2–3; 63, 2–3; 143, 6; Is 26, 9.
84, 4: Ps 5, 3.

P
S

5 Happy are those who dwell in your house!
   They never cease to praise you.   Selah

II

6 Happy are those who find refuge in you,
   whose hearts are set on pilgrim roads.

7† As they pass through the Baca valley,
   they find spring water to drink.
   Also from pools the Lord provides water
   for those who lose their way.

8 They pass through outer and inner wall
   and see the God of gods on Zion.

III

9 LORD of hosts, hear my prayer;
   listen, God of Jacob.   Selah

10† O God, look kindly on our shield;
   look upon the face of your anointed.*

IV

11 Better one day in your courts
   than a thousand elsewhere.
   Better the threshold of the house of my God
   than a home in the tents of the wicked.

12 For a sun and shield is the LORD God,
   bestowing all grace and glory.
   The LORD withholds no good thing
   from those who walk without reproach.

13 O LORD of hosts,
   happy are those who trust in you!

PSALM 85†

Prayer for Divine Favor

1 For the leader. A psalm of the Korahites.

I

2 You once favored, LORD, your land,
   restored the good fortune of Jacob.*

3 You forgave the guilt of your people,
   pardoned all their sins.   Selah

4 You withdrew all your wrath,
   turned back your burning anger.*

II

5 Restore us once more, God our savior;
   abandon your wrath against us.*

6 Will you be angry with us forever,
   drag out your anger for all generations?*

7 Please give us life again,
   that your people may rejoice in you.

8 Show us, LORD, your love;
   grant us your salvation.

III

9† I will listen for the word of God;
   surely the LORD will proclaim peace
   To his people, to the faithful,
   to those who trust in him.

10 Near indeed is salvation for the loyal;
   prosperity will fill our land.

11† Love and truth will meet;
   justice and peace will kiss.*

12 Truth will spring from the earth;
   justice will look down from heaven.*

13 The LORD will surely grant abundance;
   our land will yield its increase.*

14 Prosperity will march before the Lord,
   and good fortune will follow behind.

PSALM 86†

Prayer in Time of Distress

1 A prayer of David.

I

Hear me, LORD, and answer me,
   for I am poor and oppressed.

2 Preserve my life, for I am loyal;
   save your servant who trusts in you.

3 You are my God; pity me, Lord;
   to you I call all the day.

4 Gladden the soul of your servant;
   to you, Lord, I lift up my soul.*

5 Lord, you are kind and forgiving,
   most loving to all who call on you.*

6 LORD, hear my prayer;
   listen to my cry for help.*

7 In this time of trouble I call,
   for you will answer me.

II

8 None among the gods can equal you, O Lord;
   nor can their deeds compare to yours.*

9 All the nations you have made shall come
   to bow before you, Lord,
   and give honor to your name.*

---

† **84, 7:** *Baca valley:* Hebrew obscure; probably a valley on the way to Jerusalem.
   84, 10: *Our shield . . . your anointed:* the king had a role in the liturgical celebration. For the king as shield, cf Ps 89, 19.
   Ps 85: A national lament reminding God of past favors and forgiveness (2–4) and begging for forgiveness and grace now (5–8). A speaker represents the people who wait humbly with open hearts (9–10); God will be active on their behalf (11–14). The situation suggests the conditions of Judea during the early postexilic period, the fifth century B.C.; the thoughts are similar to those of postexilic prophets (Hg 1, 5–11; 2, 6–9).
   85, 9: The prophet listens to God's revelation. Cf Hb 2, 1.
   85, 11–14: Divine activity is personified as pairs of virtues.
   Ps 86: An individual lament. The psalmist, "poor and oppressed"

(1), "devoted" (2), "your servant" (2.4.16), "rescued from the depths of Sheol" (13), attacked by the ruthless (14), desires only God's protection (1–7.11–17).

*
84, 10: Ps 89, 19.   86, 4: Pss 25, 1; 143, 8.
85, 2: Pss 14, 7; 126, 4.   86, 5: Jl 2, 13.
85, 4: Ps 78, 38; Ex 32, 14; Is   86, 6: Pss 5, 2; 130, 1–2.
   48, 9.   86, 8: Pss 35, 10; 89, 9; Ex
85, 5: Ps 80, 4.   15, 11; Dt 3, 24; Jer
85, 6: Pss 79, 5; 89, 47.   10, 6.
85, 11: Pss 89, 15; 97, 2.   86, 9: Ps 22, 28; Zec 14, 16;
85, 12: Is 45, 8.   Rv 15, 4.
85, 13: Ps 67, 7; Lv 26, 4; Ez
   34, 27; Hos 2, 23–24;
   Zec 8, 12.

10 For you are great and do wondrous deeds;
       and you alone are God.

III

11 Teach me, LORD, your way
       that I may walk in your truth,*
       single-hearted and revering your name.
12 I will praise you with all my heart,
       glorify your name forever, Lord my God.
13 Your love for me is great;
       you have rescued me from the depths
          of Sheol.*
14 O God, the arrogant have risen against me;
       a ruthless band has sought my life;
       to you they pay no heed.
15 But you, Lord, are a merciful and gracious God,
       slow to anger, most loving and true.*
16 Turn to me, have pity on me;
       give your strength to your servant;
       save this child of your handmaid.*
17 Give me a sign of your favor:
       make my enemies see, to their confusion,
       that you, LORD, help and comfort me.

PSALM 87†

Zion the True Birthplace of Diaspora Pilgrims

¹ A psalm of the Korahites. A song.

I

   The LORD loves the city*
      founded on holy mountains,
2† Loves the gates of Zion
      more than any dwelling in Jacob.
3   Glorious things are said of you,
      O city of God!   *Selah*

II

4   From Babylon and Egypt I count
      those who acknowledge the LORD.
   Philistia, Ethiopia, Tyre,
      of them it can be said:
      "This one was born there."
5† But of Zion it must be said:
      "They all were born here."*
   The Most High confirms this;*
6   the LORD notes in the register of the peoples:
      "This one was born here."*   *Selah*

---

7 So all sing in their festive dance:
      "Within you is my true home."*

PSALM 88†

A Despairing Lament

¹ A song; a psalm of the Korahites. For the leader;
   according to *Mahalath*. For singing; a *maskil* of
   Heman the Ezrahite.

I

2   LORD, my God, I call out by day;
      at night I cry aloud in your presence.*
3   Let my prayer come before you;
      incline your ear to my cry.*
4† For my soul is filled with troubles;*
      my life draws near to Sheol.
5   I am reckoned with those who go down
         to the pit;
      I am weak, without strength.
6   My couch is among the dead,
      with the slain who lie in the grave.
   You remember them no more;
      they are cut off from your care.
7   You plunged me into the bottom of the
         pit,
      into the darkness of the abyss.
8   Your wrath lies heavy upon me;
      all your waves crash over me.*   *Selah*
9   Because of you my friends shun me;
      you make me loathsome to them;*
   Caged in, I cannot escape;
10   my eyes grow dim from trouble.

II

   All day I call on you, LORD;
      I stretch out my hands to you.
11† Do you work wonders for the dead?
      Do the shades arise and praise you?*

                                                   Selah

12 Is your love proclaimed in the grave,
      your fidelity in the tomb?
13 Are your marvels declared in the
         darkness,
      your righteous deeds in the land of
         oblivion?

Ps 87: A song of Zion, like Psalms 46, 48, 76, and 132. After the
exile of the sixth century B.C., diaspora Jews from all over the world
(4) made the long pilgrimage to Jerusalem, the city of God (1–3).
Such Jews may have hailed from distant lands, but the psalm sees
them as children of Zion (5–7). The original occasion may have been
Pentecost, which always attracted a large number of diaspora Jews.
  87, 2: *The gates:* the city itself, a common Hebrew idiom.
  87, 5–6: The bond between the exile and the holy city was so
strong as to override the exile's citizenship of lesser cities.
  Ps 88: A lament in which the psalmist prays for rescue from the
alienation of approaching death. Each of the three stanzas begins
with a call to God (2.10b.14) and complains of the death that separates one from God. The tone is persistently grim.
  88, 4–8: In imagination the psalmist already experiences the
alienation of Sheol.
  88, 11–13: The psalmist seeks to persuade God to act out of con-

cern for divine honor: the shades give you no worship, so keep me
alive to offer you praise.

86, 11: Pss 25, 4; 26, 3; 27,
   11; 119, 12.35; 143, 8.
   10.
86, 13: Pss 30, 4; 40, 3; Jon
   2, 7.
86, 15: Pss 103, 8; 130, 7;
   145, 8; Ex 34, 6.
86, 16: Pss 25, 16; 116, 16;
   Wis 9, 5.
87, 1–2: Pss 76, 2–3; 78, 68–69.
87, 5: Gal 4, 26.
87, 5: Ps 48, 9.
87, 6: Is 4, 3.
87, 7: Pss 68, 26; 149, 3.

88, 2: Ps 77, 3.
88, 3: Ps 119, 170.
88, 4–7: Pss 28, 1; 30, 4; 40, 3;
   86, 13; 143, 7; Nm 16,
   33; Jb 17, 1; Jon 2, 7.
88, 8: Pss 18, 5; 32, 6; 42, 8;
   69, 2; Jon 2, 4.
88, 9: Pss 38, 12; 79, 4; 80,
   7; 123, 3–4; 142, 8; Jb
   12, 4; 19, 13; Lam 3,
   7; Dn 9, 16.
88, 11: Pss 6, 6; 30, 10; 38,
   18; 115, 17.

RESPECT

Respect is an important value for many Native American peoples. For the Lakota tribe, it is one of four primary values. The Lakota word for respect is *wo-wac-in-tan-ka*.

Psalm 89, 6–9 speaks to the Lakota people of the power and the awesomeness of the Great Spirit. We owe reverence and respect not only to our God but also to all our God has created— the earth, the animals, and one another. The young respect the elders because the elders are people of history and experience. The old respect the young because they are the future of the world. When everyone lives in respect, the earth is at peace.

To explore the other primary Lakota virtues, see the Cultural Connections articles for Psalms 31, 73, and 112.

▶ **Psalm 89**

III

14 But I cry out to you, LORD;
     in the morning my prayer comes before
     you.
15 Why do you reject me, LORD?
     Why hide your face from me?
16 I am mortally afflicted since youth;
     lifeless, I suffer your terrible blows.
17 Your wrath has swept over me;
     your terrors have reduced me to silence.*
18 All the day they surge round like a flood;
     from every side they close in on me.
19 Because of you companions shun me;*
     my only friend is darkness.

PSALM 89†

A Lament over God's Promise to David

¹ A *maskil* of Ethan the Ezrahite.

I

2 The promises of the LORD I will sing forever,*
   proclaim your loyalty through all ages.

3† For you said, "My love is established forever;
     my loyalty will stand as long as the heavens.
4   I have made a covenant with my chosen one;
     I have sworn to David my servant:
5   I will make your dynasty stand forever
     and establish your throne through all
          ages."*   *Selah*

II

6   The heavens praise your marvels, LORD,
     your loyalty in the assembly of the holy
          ones.*
7† Who in the skies ranks with the LORD?
     Who is like the LORD among the gods?*
8   A God dreaded in the council of the holy ones,
     greater and more awesome than all who sit
          there!
9   LORD, God of hosts, who is like you?
     Mighty LORD, your loyalty is always present.
10 You rule the raging sea;*
     you still its swelling waves.
11† You crushed Rahab with a mortal blow;

---

†
Ps 89: The community laments the defeat of the Davidic king, to whom God promised kingship as enduring as the heavens (2–5). The psalm narrates how God became king of the divine beings (6–9) and how the Davidic king became king of earthly kings (20–38). Since the defeat of the king calls into question God's promise, the community ardently prays for God to be faithful to the original promise to David (39–52).

89, 3–5: David's dynasty is to be as long-lasting as the heavens, a statement reinforced by using the same verbs (establish, stand) both of the divine love and loyalty and of the Davidic dynasty and throne. Cf 29–30.

89, 7: *The gods:* literally, "the sons of gods," "the holy ones" and

"courtiers" of 6 and 8. These heavenly spirits are members of God's court.

89, 11: *Rahab:* a mythological sea monster whose name is used in the Bible mainly as a personification of primeval chaos. Cf Jb 9, 13; 26, 12; Ps 74, 13–14; Is 51, 9.

*
88, 17: Jb 6, 4; 20, 25.
88, 19: Jb 19, 13.
89, 2: Is 63, 7.
89, 5: Pss 61, 7–8; 132, 11;
     2 Sm 7, 8–16.
89, 6: Pss 29, 1; 82, 1; Jb 1,
     6; 5, 1.
89, 7–9: Pss 35, 10; 86, 8; 113,
     5; Ex 15, 11; Jer 10, 6.
89, 10–11: Pss 65, 8; 74, 13–15;
     107, 29; Jb 7, 12; Is
     51, 9–10.

your strong arm scattered your foes.

12 Yours are the heavens, yours the earth;
    you founded the world and everything in
      it.*

13† Zaphon and Amanus you created;
    Tabor and Hermon rejoice in your name.

14 Mighty your arm, strong your hand,
    your right hand is ever exalted.

15 Justice and judgment are the foundation of
      your throne;
    love and loyalty march before you.*

16 Happy the people who know you, LORD,
    who walk in the radiance of your face.

17 In your name they sing joyfully all the day;
    at your victory they raise the festal shout.*

18† You are their majestic strength;
    by your favor our horn is exalted.*

19 Truly the LORD is our shield,
    the Holy One of Israel, our king!*

III

20 Once you spoke in vision;*
    to your faithful ones you said:
    "I have set a leader over the warriors;
    I have raised up a hero from the army.

21 I have chosen David, my servant;
    with my holy oil I have anointed him.

22 My hand will be with him;*
    my arm will make him strong.

23 No enemy shall outwit him,
    nor shall the wicked defeat him.

24 I will crush his foes before him,
    strike down those who hate him.

25 My loyalty and love will be with him;
    through my name his horn will be exalted.

26† I will set his hand upon the sea,
    his right hand upon the rivers.

27 He shall cry to me, 'You are my father,*
    my God, the Rock that brings me victory!'

28† I myself make him firstborn,
    Most High over the kings of the earth.

29 Forever I will maintain my love for him;*
    my covenant with him stands firm.

30 I will establish his dynasty forever,
    his throne as the days of the heavens.

31 If his descendants forsake my law,*
    do not follow my decrees,

32 If they fail to observe my statutes,
    do not keep my commandments,

33 I will punish their crime with a rod
    and their guilt with lashes.

34 But I will not take my love from him,
    nor will I betray my bond of loyalty.*

35 I will not violate my covenant;
    the promise of my lips I will not alter.*

36 By my holiness I swore once for all:*
    I will never be false to David.

37† His dynasty will continue forever,*
    his throne, like the sun before me.

38 Like the moon it will stand eternal,
    forever firm like the sky!"   *Selah*

IV

39 But now you have rejected and spurned,*
    been enraged at your anointed.

40 You renounced the covenant with your
      servant,
    defiled his crown in the dust.

41 You broke down all his defenses,*
    left his strongholds in ruins.

42 All who pass through seize plunder;
    his neighbors deride him.

43 You have exalted the right hand of his foes,
    have gladdened all his enemies.*

44 You turned back his sharp sword,
    did not support him in battle.

45 You brought to an end his splendor,
    hurled his throne to the ground.

46 You cut short the days of his youth,
    covered him with shame.   *Selah*

47 How long, LORD?
    Will you stay hidden forever?
    Must your wrath smolder like fire?*

48 Remember how brief is my life,
    how frail the race you created!*

49 What mortal can live and not see death?
    Who can escape the power of Sheol?*
                      Selah

50 Where are your promises of old, Lord,
    the loyalty sworn to David?

89, 13: *Zaphon and Amanus:* two sacred mountains in northern Syria. *Tabor:* a high hill in the valley of Jezreel in northern Israel. *Hermon:* a mountain in Lebanon, forming the southern spur of the Anti-Lebanon range.

89, 18.25: *Horn:* a concrete noun for an abstract quality; horn is a symbol of strength.

89, 26: *The sea . . . the rivers:* geographically the limits of the Davidic Empire (the Mediterranean and the Euphrates); mythologically, the traditional forces of chaos. See note on v 11.

89, 28: *Most High:* a divine title, which is here extended to David as God's own king. Cf Ps 2, 7–9; Is 9, 5. As God rules over the members of the heavenly council (6–9), so David, God's surrogate, rules over earthly kings.

89, 37–38: *Like the sun before me . . . like the sky:* as enduring as the heavenly lights. Cf 2–5 and Ps 72, 5.17.

89, 12: Pss 24, 1–2; 50, 12; Dt 10, 14; 1 Cor 10, 26.
89, 15: Pss 85, 11–12; 97, 2.
89, 17: Ps 47, 2; Zep 3, 14.
89, 18: Pss 112, 9; 148, 14.
89, 19: Pss 47, 9; 96, 10; 97, 1; 99, 1; Is 6, 3.
89, 20–21: Pss 78, 70; 132, 11–12; 2 Sm 7, 4. 8–16; 1 Chr 17, 3. 7–14; Is 42, 1; Acts 13, 22.
89, 22–25: 1 Sm 2, 9–10.
89, 27–28: Pss 2, 7; 110, 2–3; 2 Sm 7, 9.14; Col 1, 15.18; Rv 1, 5.
89, 29–30: Pss 18, 51; 61, 8; 144, 10; 2 Sm 7, 11; Is 55, 3.
89, 31–33: Lv 26, 14–33.
89, 34: Ps 40, 12; Sir 47, 22.
89, 35: Jer 33, 20–21.
89, 36: Am 4, 2.
89, 37–38: Pss 61, 8; 72, 5; Sir 43, 6.
89, 39–47: Ps 44, 10–25.
89, 41–42: Ps 80, 13–14.
89, 43: Lam 1, 5.
89, 47: Pss 13, 2; 44, 25; 74, 10; 79, 5; Dt 4, 24.
89, 48: Pss 39, 5–6; 62, 10; 90, 9–10; 144, 4; Jb 7, 6.16; 14, 1.5; Eccl 6, 12; Wis 2, 5.
89, 49: Ps 90, 3.

51 Remember, Lord, the insults to your
    servants,
    how I bear all the slanders of the nations.*

52 Your enemies, LORD, insult your anointed;
    they insult my every endeavor.

* * *

53† Blessed be the LORD forever! Amen and
    amen!*

FOURTH BOOK — PSALMS 90–106

PSALM 90 †

God's Eternity and Human Frailty

[1] A prayer of Moses, the man of God.

I

Lord, you have been our refuge
    through all generations.

2 Before the mountains were born,
    the earth and the world brought forth,
    from eternity to eternity you are God.*

4† A thousand years in your eyes
    are merely a yesterday,*

3† But humans you return to dust,
    saying, "Return, you mortals!"*†

4c Before a watch passes in the night,†

5† you have brought them to their end;*
    They disappear like sleep at dawn;
    they are like grass that dies.

6† It sprouts green in the morning;
    by evening it is dry and withered.*

II

7 Truly we are consumed by your anger,
    filled with terror by your wrath.

8 You have kept our faults before you,
    our hidden sins exposed to your sight.*

9 Our life ebbs away under your wrath;*
    our years end like a sigh.

10 Seventy is the sum of our years,
    or eighty, if we are strong;
    Most of them are sorrow and toil;
    they pass quickly, we are all but gone.

11 Who comprehends your terrible anger?
    Your wrath matches the fear it inspires.

12 Teach us to count our days aright,
    that we may gain wisdom of heart.

13 Relent, O LORD! How long?
    Have pity on your servants!

14 Fill us at daybreak with your love,*
    that all our days we may sing for joy.

15 Make us glad as many days as you humbled
    us,
    for as many years as we have seen
      trouble.*

16 Show your deeds to your servants,
    your glory to their children.

17 May the favor of the Lord our God be ours.*
    Prosper the work of our hands!
    Prosper the work of our hands!

PSALM 91 †

Security Under God's Protection

I

1† You who dwell in the shelter of the Most
    High,
    who abide in the shadow of the Almighty,

2 Say to the LORD, "My refuge and fortress,
    my God in whom I trust."*

3 God will rescue you from the fowler's snare,
    from the destroying plague,

4 Will shelter you with pinions,
    spread wings that you may take refuge;*
    God's faithfulness is a protecting shield.

5 You shall not fear the terror of the night
    nor the arrow that flies by day,*

89, 53: The doxology at the end of the third book of the Psalms; it is not part of Ps 89.

Ps 90: A communal lament that describes only in general terms the cause of the community's distress. After confidently invoking God (1), the psalm turns to a complaint contrasting God's eternity with the brevity of human life (2–6) and sees in human suffering the punishment for sin (7–12). The psalm concludes with a plea for God's intervention (13–17).

90, 3: *Return:* one word of God is enough to return mortals to the dust from which they were created. Humans were created from earth in Gn 2, 7; 3, 19.

90, 4: The translation reverses the order of the difficult Hebrew verses 3 and 4 to get the probable original order. *A watch. . . in the night:* the night was divided into three sentry periods or watches. Cf Jgs 7, 19.

90, 5: *You have brought them to their end:* an interpretation of the unclear Hebrew.

90, 6: *It is dry and withered:* the transitory nature of the grass under the scorching sun was proverbial. Cf Ps 129, 6; Is 40, 6–8.

Ps 91: A prayer of someone who has taken refuge in the security of the temple (1–2). The psalmist is confident that God's presence will protect the people in every dangerous situation (3–13). The final verses are an oracle of salvation promising salvation to those who trust in God (14–16).

91, 1: *The shelter of the Most High:* basically "hiding place" but in the psalms a designation for the protected temple precincts. Cf Pss 27, 5; 31, 21; 61, 5. *The shadow of the Almighty:* literally, "the shadow of the wings of the Almighty." Cf Pss 17, 8; 36, 8; 57, 2; 63, 8. V 4 makes clear that the shadow is an image of the safety afforded by the outstretched wings of the cherubim in the holy of holies.

89, 51: Ps 79, 12.
89, 53: Pss 41, 14; 72, 18; 106, 48.
90, 2: Pss 48, 15; 55, 20; 93, 2; 102, 13; Hb 1, 12.
90, 4: 2 Pt 3, 8.
90, 3: Pss 103, 14; 104, 29; 146, 4; Gn 3, 19; 1 Mc 2, 63; Jb 34, 14–15; Eccl 3, 20; 12, 7; Sir 40, 11.
90, 5: Ps 89, 48.
90, 6: Pss 37, 2; 102, 11; 103, 15–16; Jb 14, 1–2; Is 40, 6–8.
90, 8: Ps 109, 14–15; Hos 7, 2.

90, 9–10: Pss 39, 5–7; 62, 10; 102, 24–25; 144, 4; Gn 6, 3; Jb 7, 6.16; 14, 5; Prv 10, 27; Eccl 6, 12; Wis 2, 5; Sir 18, 8; Is 65, 20.
90, 14: Ps 17, 15.
90, 15: Nm 14, 34; Jer 31, 13.
90, 17: Ps 33, 22.
91, 2: Pss 18, 3; 31, 3–4; 42, 10; 142, 6; 2 Sm 22, 3.
91, 4: Pss 17, 8; 36, 8; 57, 2; 63, 8; Dt 32, 11; Ru 2, 12; Mt 23, 37.
91, 5: Prv 3, 25; Song 3, 8.

6 Nor the pestilence that roams in darkness,
　　nor the plague that ravages at noon.*
7 Though a thousand fall at your side,
　　ten thousand at your right hand,
　　near you it shall not come.
8 You need simply watch;
　　the punishment of the wicked you will
　　　see.*
9 You have the LORD for your refuge;
　　you have made the Most High your
　　　stronghold.
10 No evil shall befall you,
　　no affliction come near your tent.*
11† For God commands the angels*
　　to guard you in all your ways.*
12 With their hands they shall support you,
　　lest you strike your foot against a stone.*
13 You shall tread upon the asp and the viper,
　　trample the lion and the dragon.*

II

14 Whoever clings to me I will deliver;
　　whoever knows my name I will set on
　　　high.*
15 All who call upon me I will answer;*
　　I will be with them in distress;*
　　I will deliver them and give them honor.
16 With length of days I will satisfy them
　　and show them my saving power.*

PSALM 92†

A Hymn of Thanksgiving for God's Fidelity
　　　　¹ A psalm. A sabbath song.

I

2 It is good to give thanks to the LORD,
　　to sing praise to your name, Most High,*
3 To proclaim your love in the morning,
　　your faithfulness in the night,
4 With the ten-stringed harp,
　　with melody upon the lyre.*
5 For you make me jubilant, LORD, by your deeds;
　　at the works of your hands I shout for joy.

II

6 How great are your works, LORD!*
　　How profound your purpose!
7 A senseless person cannot know this;
　　a fool cannot comprehend.

8 Though the wicked flourish like grass
　　and all sinners thrive,*
　　They are destined for eternal destruction;
9 　　for you, LORD, are forever on high.
10 Indeed your enemies, LORD,
　　indeed your enemies shall perish;
　　all sinners shall be scattered.*

III

11 You have given me the strength of a wild bull;*
　　you have poured rich oil upon me.*
12 My eyes look with glee on my wicked enemies;
　　my ears delight in the fall of my foes.*
13 The just shall flourish like the palm tree,
　　shall grow like a cedar of Lebanon.*
14† Planted in the house of the LORD,
　　they shall flourish in the courts of our God.

Have You Sung This Before?

Psalm 91 might sound familiar! Have you ever sung "On Eagle's Wings" or "Blest Be the Lord"? Both are based on this psalm. Both express confidence that God will protect us, no matter what. This idea was sung long before Jesus lived, and we still sing it today.

　And He will raise you up on eagle's
　　wings,
　bear you on the breath of dawn,
　make you to shine like the sun,
　and hold you in the palm of His hand.
　　(Michael Joncas, "On Eagle's Wings")

　Blest be the Lord; blest be the Lord,
　the God of mercy, the God who saves.
　I shall not fear the dark of night,
　nor the arrow that flies by day.
　　(Dan Schutte, "Blest Be the Lord")

▸ Psalm 91

P
S

---

† 91, 11–12: The words are cited in Mt 4, 6; Lk 4, 10–11, as part of Satan's challenge to Jesus in the desert.
Ps 92: A hymn of praise and thanks for God's faithful deeds (2–5). The wicked, deluded by their prosperity (6–9), are punished (10), whereas the psalmist has already experienced God's protection (11–16).
92, 14: *Planted:* the just are likened to trees growing in the sacred precincts of the temple, which is often seen as the source of life and fertility because of God's presence. Cf Ps 36, 9.10; Ez 47, 1–12.

91, 6: Dt 32, 24.
91, 8: Ps 92, 12.
91, 10: Prv 12, 21; Dt 7, 15.
91, 11–12: Mt 4, 6; Lk 4, 10f.
91, 11: Heb 1, 14.
91, 12: Ps 121, 3; Prv 3, 23.
91, 13: Is 11, 8; Lk 10, 19.
91, 14: Pss 9, 11; 119, 132.
91, 15: Jer 33, 3; Zec 13, 9.
91, 15: Is 43, 2.
91, 16: Prv 3, 2.

92, 2: Pss 33, 1; 147, 1.
92, 4: Pss 33, 2; 144, 9.
92, 6–7: Pss 131, 1; 139, 6.17; Wis 13, 1; 17, 1.
92, 8: Ps 37, 35.
92, 10: Pss 68, 1–2; 125, 5.
92, 11: Ps 23, 5.
92, 11: Ps 75, 10; Dt 33, 17.
92, 12: Ps 91, 8.
92, 13: Pss 1, 3; 52, 10; Jer 17, 8.

15 They shall bear fruit even in old age,
    always vigorous and sturdy,

16 As they proclaim: "The LORD is just;
    our rock, in whom there is no wrong."*

PSALM 93†

God is a Mighty King

1† The LORD is king, robed with majesty;
    the LORD is robed, girded with might.*
The world will surely stand in place,
    never to be moved.*

2 Your throne stands firm from of old;
    you are from everlasting, LORD.*

3† The flood has raised up, LORD;
    the flood has raised up its roar;
    the flood has raised its pounding waves.

4 More powerful than the roar of many waters,
    more powerful than the breakers of the sea,
    powerful in the heavens is the LORD.

5 Your decrees are firmly established;
    holiness belongs to your house, LORD,
    for all the length of days.

PSALM 94†

A Prayer for Deliverance from the Wicked

I

1 LORD, avenging God,
    avenging God, shine forth!*

2 Rise up, judge of the earth;
    give the proud what they deserve.*

II

3 How long, LORD, shall the wicked,
    how long shall the wicked glory?*

4 How long will they mouth haughty speeches,
    go on boasting, all these evildoers?*

5 They crush your people, LORD,
    torment your very own.

6 They kill the widow and alien;
    the fatherless they murder.*

7 They say, "The LORD does not see;
    the God of Jacob takes no notice."*

III

8 Understand, you stupid people!
    You fools, when will you be wise?*

9 Does the one who shaped the ear not hear?
    The one who formed the eye not see?*

10 Does the one who guides nations not
     rebuke?
    The one who teaches humans not have
     knowledge?

11 The LORD does know human plans;
    they are only puffs of air.*

IV

12 Happy those whom you guide, LORD,*
    whom you teach by your instruction.

13 You give them rest from evil days,
    while a pit is being dug for the wicked.

14 You, LORD, will not forsake your people,
    nor abandon your very own.*

15 Judgment shall again be just,
    and all the upright of heart will follow it.

V

16 Who will rise up for me against the wicked?
    Who will stand up for me against evildoers?

17 If the LORD were not my help,
    I would long have been silent in the grave.*

18 When I say, "My foot is slipping,"
    your love, LORD, holds me up.*

19 When cares increase within me,
    your comfort gives me joy.

VI

20 Can unjust judges be your allies,
    those who create burdens in the name of law,

21 Those who conspire against the just
    and condemn the innocent to death?

22 No, the LORD is my secure height,
    my God, the rock where I find refuge,

23 Who will turn back their evil upon them*
    and destroy them for their wickedness.
    Surely the LORD our God will destroy them!*

---

† **Ps 93:** A hymn celebrating the kingship of God, who created the world (1–2) by defeating the sea (3–4). In the ancient myth that is alluded to here, Sea completely covered the land, making it impossible for the human community to live. Sea, or Flood, roars in anger against God, who is personified in the storm. God's utterances or decrees are given authority by the victory over Sea (5).

93, 1: *The LORD is king:* literally, "the LORD reigns." This psalm, and Pss 47 and 96–99, are sometimes called enthronement psalms. They may have been used in a special liturgy during which God's ascent to the throne was ritually reenacted. They have also been interpreted eschatologically, pointing to the coming of God as king at the end-time.

93, 3: *The flood:* the primordial sea was tamed by God in the act of creation. It is a figure of chaos and rebellion. Cf Ps 46, 4.

Ps 94: A lament of an individual who is threatened by wicked people. The danger affects the whole community. Calling upon God as judge (1–2), the psalm complains about oppression of the holy community by people within (3–7). Bold declarations of faith follow:

denunciation of evildoers (8–11) and assurance to the just (12–15). The psalm continues with further lament (16–19) and ends with strong confidence in God's response (20–23).

*
92, 16: Dt 32, 4.	94, 7: Pss 10, 11; 64, 6; 73,
93, 1: Pss 47, 8; 96, 10; 97,	11; Jb 22, 13–14; Ez
1; 99, 1.	9, 9.
93, 1: Pss 75, 2–3; 104, 5.	94, 8: Prv 1, 22; 8, 5.
93, 2: Pss 55, 20; 90, 2; 102,	94, 9: Ex 4, 11; Prv 20, 12.
13; Hb 1, 12.	94, 11: Ps 33, 15; 1 Cor 3, 20.
94, 1: Na 1, 2.	94, 12: Ps 119, 71; Jb 5, 17.
94, 2: Jer 51, 56; Lam 3, 64.	94, 14: 1 Sm 12, 22; Sir
94, 3: Pss 13, 2; 75, 5; Jer	47, 22.
12, 1.	94, 17: Ps 115, 17.
94, 4: Ps 73; Mal 2, 17; 3,	94, 18: Ps 145, 14.
14.	94, 23: Pss 7, 16; 9, 16; 35, 8;
94, 6: Ex 22, 21–22; Dt 24,	57, 7; Prv 26, 27; Eccl
17–22.	10, 8; Sir 27, 26.
	94, 23: Ps 107, 42.

PSALM 95†

A Call to Praise and Obedience

I

1 Come, let us sing joyfully to the LORD;
   cry out to the rock of our salvation.*

2 Let us greet him with a song of praise,
   joyfully sing out our psalms.

3 For the LORD is the great God,
   the great king over all gods,*

4 Whose hand holds the depths of the earth;
   who owns the tops of the mountains.

5 The sea and dry land belong to God,
   who made them, formed them by hand.*

II

6 Enter, let us bow down in worship;
   let us kneel before the LORD who made us.

7 For this is our God,
   whose people we are,
   God's well-tended flock.*

III

Oh, that today you would hear his voice:*

8† Do not harden your hearts as at Meribah,
   as on the day of Massah in the desert.

9 There your ancestors tested me;
   they tried me though they had seen my
   works.*

10 Forty years I loathed that generation;
   I said: "This people's heart goes astray;
   they do not know my ways."*

11† Therefore I swore in my anger:
   "They shall never enter my rest."

LEBANESE CATHOLICS

Catholics are a celebratory people. By holding feasts, we celebrate our great God and the wondrous ways in which God has shown love for us. We also hold feasts in remembrance of the saints who have gone before us. The saints are shining examples of individuals leading lives in unity with the will of God.

In some parts of the Middle East, like Lebanon, Catholic feast days are extravagant events. Each town has a patron saint, and on the eve of his or her feast day, nearly everyone in the community comes to the church. All night long the townspeople pray, eat, and dance in the church, and some even sleep there. Feast days in Lebanon are celebrations that include great processions, festive liturgies, and the participation of the whole community.

In parts of the United States where there are congregations of Middle Eastern Catholics, similar events take place. Some occur on a large scale with overnight festivities, and some occur on a smaller scale, but all have common characteristics: great processions, festive liturgies, good food, and the participation of the whole parish community.

Consider trying to get your youth group or campus ministry team to begin a similar tradition on the feast day of your parish or school.

▶ **Psalm 96**

Ps 95: Twice the psalm calls the people to praise and worship God (1–2.6), the king of all creatures (3–5) and shepherd of the flock (7ab). The last strophe warns the people to be more faithful than were their ancestors in the journey to the promised land (7c–11). This invitation to praise God regularly opens the Church's official prayer, the Liturgy of the Hours.

95, 8: *Meribah:* literally, "contention"; the place where the Israelites quarreled with God. *Massah:* "testing," the place where they put God to the trial. Cf Ex 17, 7; Nm 20, 13.

95, 11: *My rest:* the promised land as in Dt 12, 9. Heb 4 applies the verse to the eternal rest of heaven.

95, 1: Dt 32, 15.
95, 3: Pss 47, 2; 135, 5.
95, 5: Ps 24, 1–2.
95, 7: Pss 23, 1–3; 100, 3; Mi 7, 14.
95, 7c–11: Pss 81, 8; 106, 32; Heb 3, 7–11.15; 4, 3.5.7.
95, 9: Nm 14, 22; 20, 2–13; Dt 6, 16; 33, 8.
95, 10: Ps 78, 8; Nm 14, 34; Dt 32, 5.

Sing to the LORD a new song; sing to the LORD, all the earth. Sing to the LORD, bless his name; announce his salvation day after day.

Sing to the LORD

96, 1–2

PSALM 96 †

God of the Universe

I

1 Sing to the LORD a new song;*
    sing to the LORD, all the earth.
2 Sing to the LORD, bless his name;
    announce his salvation day after day.
3 Tell God's glory among the nations;
    among all peoples, God's marvelous deeds.*

II

4† For great is the LORD and highly to be
    praised,
    to be feared above all gods.*
5 For the gods of the nations all do nothing,
    but the LORD made the heavens.*
6 Splendor and power go before him;
    power and grandeur are in his holy place.

III

7 Give to the LORD, you families of nations,
    give to the LORD glory and might;
8 give to the LORD the glory due his name!*
Bring gifts and enter his courts;
9 bow down to the LORD, splendid in
    holiness.

Tremble before God, all the earth;
10 say among the nations: The LORD is king.*
The world will surely stand fast, never to be
    moved.
God rules the peoples with fairness.

IV

11 Let the heavens be glad and the earth rejoice;
    let the sea and what fills it resound;*
12 let the plains be joyful and all that is in them.
Then let all the trees of the forest rejoice
13 before the LORD who comes,
    who comes to govern the earth,*
To govern the world with justice
    and the peoples with faithfulness.

PSALM 97 †

The Divine Ruler of All

I

1 The LORD is king; let the earth rejoice;
    let the many islands be glad.*
2 Cloud and darkness surround the Lord;
    justice and right are the foundation of his
    throne.*
3 Fire goes before him;
    everywhere it consumes the foes.
4 Lightning illumines the world;
    the earth sees and trembles.*
5 The mountains melt like wax before the LORD,
    before the Lord of all the earth.*
6 The heavens proclaim God's justice;
    all peoples see his glory.*

II

7† All who serve idols are put to shame,
    who glory in worthless things;
    all gods bow down before you.*
8 Zion hears and is glad,
    and the cities of Judah rejoice
    because of your judgments, O LORD.*
9 You, LORD, are the Most High over all the earth,*
    exalted far above all gods.
10 The LORD loves those who hate evil,
    protects the lives of the faithful,*
    rescues them from the hand of the wicked.
11 Light dawns for the just;

---

† **Ps 96:** A hymn inviting all humanity to praise the glories of Israel's God (1–3), who is the sole God (4–6). To the just ruler of all belongs worship (7–10); even inanimate creation is to offer praise (11–13). This psalm has numerous verbal and thematic contacts with Is 40–55, as does Ps 98. Another version of the psalm is 1 Chr 16, 23–33.

    96, 4: For references to other gods, see comments on Pss 58 and 82.

    Ps 97: The hymn begins with God appearing in a storm, a traditional picture of some ancient Near Eastern gods; cf Ps 18, 8–16; Mi 1, 3–4; Hb 3, 3–15. Israel rejoices in the overthrowing of idol worshipers and their gods (7–9) and the rewarding of the faithful righteous (10–12).

    97, 7: *All gods:* divine beings thoroughly subordinate to Israel's God. The Greek translates "angels," an interpretation adopted by Heb 1, 6.

* 96, 1: Ps 98, 1; Is 42, 10.
96, 3: Pss 98, 4; 105, 1.
96, 4: Pss 48, 2; 95, 3; 145, 3.
96, 5: Ps 97, 7; Is 40, 17; 1 Cor 8, 4.
96, 8: Ps 29, 2.
96, 10: Pss 75, 4; 93, 1.
96, 11: Ps 98, 7.
96, 13: Pss 98, 9.
97, 1: Pss 75, 4; 93, 1; 96, 10.
97, 2: Pss 85, 11; 89, 15; Ex 19, 6; Dt 4, 11; 5, 22; 1 Kgs 8, 12.
97, 4: Pss 18, 8; 50, 3; 77, 18; 99, 1; Jgs 5, 4–5.
97, 5: Jdt 16, 15; Mi 1, 4.
97, 6: Ps 50, 6.
97, 7: Ps 96, 5.
97, 8: Ps 48, 12.
97, 9: Ps 83, 19.
97, 10: Ps 121, 7.
97, 11: Ps 112, 4.

gladness, for the honest of heart.*

12 Rejoice in the LORD, you just,
and praise his holy name.*

PSALM 98†

The Coming of God

¹† A psalm.

I

Sing a new song to the LORD,
who has done marvelous deeds,*
Whose right hand and holy arm
have won the victory.*

2 The LORD has made his victory known;
has revealed his triumph for the nations to see,

3 Has remembered faithful love
toward the house of Israel.
All the ends of the earth have seen
the victory of our God.

II

4 Shout with joy to the LORD, all the earth;
break into song; sing praise.

5 Sing praise to the LORD with the harp,
with the harp and melodious song.

6 With trumpets and the sound of the horn
shout with joy to the King, the LORD.*

III

7 Let the sea and what fills it resound,*
the world and those who dwell there.

8 Let the rivers clap their hands,
the mountains shout with them for joy,*

9 Before the LORD who comes,
who comes to govern the earth,*
To govern the world with justice
and the peoples with fairness.*

PSALM 99†

The Holy King

I

¹† The LORD is king, the peoples tremble;
God is enthroned on the cherubim, the
earth quakes.*

2 The LORD is great on Zion,
exalted above all the peoples.

3 Let them praise your great and awesome
name:
holy is God!*

II

4 O mighty king, lover of justice,
you alone have established fairness;
you have created just rule in Jacob.*

5† Exalt the LORD, our God;
bow down before his footstool;*
holy is God!

III

6 Moses and Aaron were among his priests,
Samuel among those who called on God's
name;
they called on the LORD, who answered
them.*

7 From the pillar of cloud God spoke to
them;
they kept the decrees, the law they
received.*

8 O LORD, our God, you answered them;
you were a forgiving God,
though you punished their offenses.*

9 Exalt the LORD, our God;
bow down before his holy mountain;
holy is the LORD, our God.

PSALM 100†

Processional Hymn

¹ A psalm of thanksgiving.

Shout joyfully to the LORD, all you lands;

2 worship the LORD with cries of gladness;
come before him with joyful song.

3† Know that the LORD is God,
our maker to whom we belong,
whose people we are, God's well-tended
flock.*

4 Enter the temple gates with praise,

Ps 98: A hymn, similar to Ps 96, extolling God for Israel's victory (1–3). All nations (4–6) and even inanimate nature (7–8) are summoned to welcome God's coming to rule over the world (9).

   98, 1: *Marvelous deeds . . . victory:* the conquest of all threats to the peaceful existence of Israel, depicted in the psalms variously as a cosmic force such as sea, or nations bent on Israel's destruction, or evildoers seemingly triumphant. *Whose right hand and holy arm:* God is pictured as a powerful warrior.

   Ps 99: A hymn to God as the king whose grandeur is most clearly seen on Mount Zion (2) and in the laws given to Israel (4). Israel is special because of God's word of justice, which was mediated by the revered speakers, Moses, Aaron, and Samuel (6–8). The poem is structured by the threefold statement that God is holy (3.5.9) and by the twice-repeated command to praise (5.9).

   99, 1: *Enthroned on the cherubim:* cherubim were composite beings with animal and human features, common in ancient Near Eastern art. Two cherubim were placed on the ark (or box) of the covenant in the holy of holies. Upon them God was believed to

dwell invisibly. Cf Ex 25, 20–22; 1 Sm 4, 4; 2 Sm 6, 2; Ps 80, 2.

   99, 5: *Footstool:* a reference to the ark. Cf 1 Chr 28, 2; Ps 132, 7.

   Ps 100: A hymn inviting the people to enter the temple courts with thank offerings for the God who created them.

   100, 3: Although the people call on all the nations of the world to join in their hymn, they are conscious of being the chosen people of God.

97, 12: Ps 30, 5.	99, 3: Is 6, 3.
98, 1: Ps 96, 1; Is 42, 10.	99, 4: Pss 72, 1; 99, 4; Jer
98, 1: Is 59, 16; 63, 5.	23, 5.
98, 6: Ps 47, 6–7.	99, 5: Ps 132, 7.
98, 7: Ps 96, 11.	99, 6: Jer 15, 1.
98, 8: Is 44, 23; 55, 12.	99, 7: Ex 33, 9; Nm 12, 5.
98, 9: Ps 96, 13.	99, 8: Ex 32, 11; Nm 20, 12.
98, 9: Ps 67, 5.	100, 3: Pss 23, 1; 95, 7; Mi 7,
99, 1: Pss 18, 8–11; 80, 2;	14; Is 64, 7.
93, 1; Ex 25, 22; 1 Sm	
4, 4; 2 Sm 6, 2.	

its courts with thanksgiving.
Give thanks to God, bless his name;*
5   good indeed is the LORD,
Whose love endures forever,
  whose faithfulness lasts through every
    age.

PSALM 101†

Norm of Life for Rulers

¹ A psalm of David.

I

I sing of love and justice;
  to you, LORD, I sing praise.
²† I follow the way of integrity;*
  when will you come to me?
I act with integrity of heart
  within my royal court.*
3 I do not allow into my presence
  anyone who speaks perversely.
Whoever acts shamefully I hate;
  no such person can be my
    friend.*
4 I shun the devious of heart;
  the wicked I do not tolerate.
5 Whoever slanders another in secret
  I reduce to silence.*
Haughty eyes and arrogant hearts*
  I cannot endure.

II

⁶† I look to the faithful of the land;
  they alone can be my companions.
Those who follow the way of
    integrity,*
  they alone can enter my service.
7 No one who practices deceit
  can hold a post in my court.
No one who speaks falsely
  can be among my advisors.*
⁸† Each morning I clear the wicked from
    the land,
  and rid the LORD's city of all
    evildoers.

PSALM 102†

Prayer in Time of Distress

¹ The prayer of one afflicted and wasting away whose
  anguish is poured out before the LORD.

I

2 LORD, hear my prayer;
  let my cry come to you.
3 Do not hide your face from me
  now that I am in distress.*
Turn your ear to me;
  when I call, answer me quickly.
4 For my days vanish like smoke;*
  my bones burn away as in a furnace.
5 I am withered, dried up like grass,
  too wasted to eat my food.
6 From my loud groaning
  I become just skin and bones.
7 I am like a desert owl,
  like an owl among the ruins.
8 I lie awake and moan,
  like a lone sparrow on the roof.
⁹† All day long my enemies taunt me;
  in their rage, they make my name a
    curse.
10 I eat ashes like bread,
  mingle my drink with tears.*
11 Because of your furious wrath,
  you lifted me up just to cast me down.
12 My days are like a lengthening shadow;*
  I wither like the grass.*

II

13 But you, LORD, are enthroned forever;
  your renown is for all generations.*
14 You will again show mercy to Zion;
  now is the time for pity;
  the appointed time has come.
15 Its stones are dear to your servants;
  its dust moves them to pity.
16 The nations shall revere your name, LORD,
  all the kings of the earth, your glory,*
17 Once the LORD has rebuilt Zion
  and appeared in glory,

Ps 101: The king, grateful at being God's chosen (1), promises to be a ruler after God's own heart (2–3), allowing into the royal service only the God-fearing (3–8).

101, 2: *Within my royal court:* the king promises to make his own household a model for Israel, banning all officials who abuse their power.

101, 6: *I look to the faithful of the land:* the king seeks companions only among those faithful to God.

101, 8: *Each morning:* the normal time for the administration of justice (2 Sm 15, 2; Jer 21, 12) and for the arrival of divine aid (Pss 59, 17; 143, 8; Is 33, 2). *I clear the wicked from the land:* the king, as God's servant, is responsible for seeing that divine justice is carried out.

Ps 102: A lament, one of the Penitential Psalms. The psalmist, experiencing psychic and bodily disintegration (4–12), cries out to God (1–3). In the temple precincts where God has promised to be present, the psalmist recalls God's venerable promises to save the poor (13–23). The final part (24–29) restates the original complaint and prayer, and emphasizes God's eternity.

102, 9: *They make my name a curse:* enemies use the psalmist's name in phrases such as, "May you be as wretched as this person!"

100, 4–5: Pss 106, 1; 107, 1; 118, 1; 136, 1; 138, 8; Jer 33, 11.	**102, 4–6:** Ps 38, 7–9.
101, 2: Ps 26, 11.	**102, 10:** Pss 42, 4; 80, 6.
101, 2: 1 Kgs 9, 4; Is 33, 15.	**102, 12:** Pss 109, 23; 144, 4; Jb 8, 9; 14, 2; Eccl 6, 12; Wis 2, 5.
101, 3: Prv 11, 20.	**102, 12:** Ps 90, 5–6.
101, 5: Prv 17, 20; 30, 10.	**102, 13:** Pss 55, 20; 90, 2; 93, 2; 102, 13; 135, 13; 145, 13; Lam 5, 19; Hb 1, 12.
101, 5: Prv 21, 4.	
101, 6: Ps 26, 11; Prv 20, 7.	
101, 7: Pss 5, 5; Prv 25, 5.	
102, 3: Pss 69, 18; 143, 7.	**102, 16:** Is 59, 19; 66, 18.

18 Heeding the plea of the lowly,
    not scorning their prayer.
19 Let this be written for the next generation,
    for a people not yet born,
    that they may praise the LORD:*
20† "The LORD looked down from the holy
    heights,
    viewed the earth from heaven,*
21 To attend to the groaning of the prisoners,
    to release those doomed to die."*
22 Then the LORD's name will be declared on
    Zion,
    the praise of God in Jerusalem,
23 When all peoples and kingdoms gather
    to worship the LORD.*

III

24 God has shattered my strength in
    mid-course,
    has cut short my days.
25† I plead, O my God,
    do not take me in the midst of my days.*
    Your years last through all generations.
26 Of old you laid the earth's foundations;*
    the heavens are the work of your hands.
27 They perish, but you remain;

they all wear out like a garment;
Like clothing you change them and they are
    changed,
28 but you are the same, your years have no
    end.
29 May the children of your servants live on;
    may their descendants live in your
    presence.*

PSALM 103†

Praise of Divine Goodness
1 Of David.

I

Bless the LORD, my soul;
    all my being, bless his holy name!
2 Bless the LORD, my soul;
    do not forget all the gifts of God,
3 Who pardons all your sins,
    heals all your ills,
4 Delivers your life from the pit,*
    surrounds you with love and
    compassion,
5† Fills your days with good things;
    your youth is renewed like the eagle's.

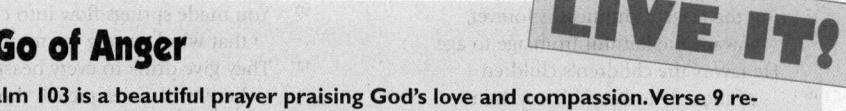

Letting Go of Anger

Psalm 103 is a beautiful prayer praising God's love and compassion. Verse 9 reminds us that God will not stay angry forever. What better lesson could we learn from our God? Anger is a natural human emotion—but in imitation of God, we should not hold on to it. When we let go of our anger, we build better relationships, because hidden anger puts other people on the defensive and destroys trust.

How do you let go of anger? Here are some suggestions:

■ Express your feelings in a letter or a journal.
■ Tell the person you are angry with how you feel and that you would like to reconcile.
■ Go for a fast walk or run, or use another form of exercise to "vent" your anger.
■ Relax with some quiet, reflective music.
■ Try to identify why you feel angry—often, anger is a symptom of another feeling such as hurt, disappointment, or even tiredness.
■ Express your anger in prayer to God, and ask for help in forgiveness.

God's way and God's goodness can be yours if you desire them. Make an effort; God does!

▶ Psalm 103

102, 20–23: Both 20–21 and 22–23 depend on 19.
    102, 25: *In the midst of my days:* when the normal span of life is but half completed. Cf Is 38, 10; Jer 17, 11.
    Ps 103: The speaker in this hymn begins by praising God for personal benefits (1–5), then moves on to God's mercy toward all the people (6–18). Even sin cannot destroy that mercy (11–13), for the eternal God is well aware of the people's human fragility (14–18). The psalmist invites the heavenly beings to join in praise (19–22).
    103, 5: *Your youth is renewed like the eagle's:* because of the ea-

gle's long life it was a symbol of perennial youth and vigor. Cf Is 40, 31.

102, 19: Ps 22, 31–32.
102, 20: Pss 11, 4; 14, 2.
102, 21: Ps 79, 11.
102, 23: Is 60, 3–4; Zec 2, 15;
    8, 22.
102, 25: Pss 39, 5; 90, 10; Jb
    14, 5.

102, 26–28:Heb 1, 10–12.
102, 29: Ps 69, 36–37.
103, 4: Pss 28, 1; 30, 4; 40, 3;
    69, 16; 88, 5; 143, 7;
    Prv 1, 12; Jon 2, 7.

II

6 The LORD does righteous deeds,
   brings justice to all the oppressed.*

7 His ways were revealed to Moses,
   mighty deeds to the people of Israel.

8 Merciful and gracious is the LORD,
   slow to anger, abounding in kindness.*

9 God does not always rebuke,
   nurses no lasting anger,

10 Has not dealt with us as our sins merit,
   nor requited us as our deeds deserve.

III

11 As the heavens tower over the earth,
   so God's love towers over the faithful.*

12 As far as the east is from the west,
   so far have our sins been removed
   from us.

13 As a father has compassion on his
   children,
   so the LORD has compassion on the
   faithful.

14 For he knows how we are formed,
   remembers that we are dust.*

15 Our days are like the grass;
   like flowers of the field we blossom.*

16 The wind sweeps over us and we are
   gone;
   our place knows us no more.

17 But the LORD's kindness is forever,
   toward the faithful from age to age.
   He favors the children's children

18 of those who keep his covenant,
   who take care to fulfill its precepts.

IV

19 The LORD's throne is established in
   heaven;
   God's royal power rules over all.

20 Bless the LORD, all you angels,*
   mighty in strength and attentive,
   obedient to every command.

21 Bless the LORD, all you hosts,
   ministers who do God's will.

22 Bless the LORD, all creatures,
   everywhere in God's domain.
   Bless the LORD, my soul!

PSALM 104†

Praise of God the Creator

I

1 Bless the LORD, my soul!
   LORD, my God, you are great indeed!
   You are clothed with majesty and glory,

2 robed in light as with a cloak.
   You spread out the heavens like a tent;*

3† you raised your palace upon the waters.
   You make the clouds your chariot;
   you travel on the wings of the wind.

4 You make the winds your messengers;
   flaming fire, your ministers.*

II

5† You fixed the earth on its foundation,
   never to be moved.

6 The ocean covered it like a garment;
   above the mountains stood the waters.

7 At your roar they took flight;
   at the sound of your thunder they fled.*

8 They rushed up the mountains, down the
   valleys
   to the place you had fixed for them.

9 You set a limit they cannot pass;
   never again will they cover the earth.*

III

10 You made springs flow into channels
   that wind among the mountains.

11 They give drink to every beast of the field;*
   here wild asses quench their thirst.

12 Beside them the birds of heaven nest;
   among the branches they sing.

13 You water the mountains from your palace;
   by your labor the earth abounds.

14 You raise grass for the cattle
   and plants for our beasts of burden.
   You bring bread from the earth,

15 and wine to gladden our hearts,
   Oil to make our faces gleam,
   food to build our strength.

16† The trees of the LORD drink their fill,
   the cedars of Lebanon, which you planted.

17 There the birds build their nests;

---

† **Ps 104:** A hymn praising God who easily and skillfully made rampaging waters and primordial night into a world vibrant with life. The psalmist describes God's splendor in the heavens (1–4), how the chaotic waters were tamed to fertilize and feed the world (5–18), and how primordial night was made into a gentle time of refreshment (19–23). The picture is like Gn 1, 1–2: a dark and watery chaos is made dry and lighted so that creatures might live. The psalmist reacts to the beauty of creation with awe (24–34). May sin not deface God's work (35)!

104, 3: *Your palace upon the waters:* God's heavenly dwelling above the upper waters of the sky. Cf Gn 1, 6–7; Ps 29, 10.

104, 5–9: God places the gigantic disk of the earth securely on its foundation and then, as a warrior, chases away the enveloping waters and confines them under, above, and around the earth.

104, 16–18: Even the exotic flora and fauna of the high mountains of the Lebanon range receive adequate water.

103, 6: Ps 146, 6–7.
103, 8: Pss 86, 15; 145, 8; Ex 34, 6–7; Nm 14, 18; Jer 3, 12; Jl 2, 13; Jon 4, 2.
103, 11: Is 55, 9.
103, 14: Ps 90, 3.
103, 15: Pss 37, 2; 90, 5–6; Is 40, 7.
103, 20: Ps 148, 2; Dn 3, 58.
104, 2: Prv 8, 27–28; Jb 9, 8; Is 40, 22; Gn 1, 6–7; Am 9, 6.
104, 4: Heb 1, 7.
104, 7: Ps 29, 3.
104, 9: Jer 5, 22; Gn 9, 11–15.
104, 11–14: Ps 147, 8–9.
104, 17: Ez 31, 6.

junipers are the home of the stork.*
¹⁸ The high mountains are for wild goats;
 the rocky cliffs, a refuge for badgers.

IV

¹⁹ You made the moon to mark the seasons,*
 the sun that knows the hour of its setting.
²⁰ You bring darkness and night falls,
 then all the beasts of the forest roam abroad.
²¹ Young lions roar for prey;
 they seek their food from God.*
²² When the sun rises, they steal away
 and rest in their dens.
²³ People go forth to their work,
 to their labor till evening falls.

V

²⁴ How varied are your works, LORD!
 In wisdom you have wrought them all;
 the earth is full of your creatures.*
²⁵ Look at the sea, great and wide!
 It teems with countless beings,
 living things both large and small.*
²⁶† Here ships ply their course;
 here Leviathan, your creature, plays.*

VI

²⁷ All of these look to you
 to give them food in due time.*
²⁸ When you give to them, they gather;
 when you open your hand, they are well
 filled.
²⁹† When you hide your face, they are lost.
 When you take away their breath, they
 perish
 and return to the dust from which they
 came.*
³⁰ When you send forth your breath, they are
 created,
 and you renew the face of the earth.

VII

³¹ May the glory of the LORD endure forever;
 may the LORD be glad in these works!
³² If God glares at the earth, it trembles;
 if God touches the mountains, they smoke!*
³³ I will sing to the LORD all my life;
 I will sing praise to my God while I live.*

³⁴ May my theme be pleasing to God;
 I will rejoice in the LORD.
³⁵† May sinners vanish from the earth,
 and the wicked be no more.
Bless the LORD, my soul! Hallelujah!

PSALM 105†

God's Fidelity to the Promise

I

¹ Give thanks to the LORD, invoke his
 name;*
 make known among the peoples his
 deeds!*
² Sing praise, play music;
 proclaim all his wondrous deeds!
³ Glory in his holy name;
 rejoice, O hearts that seek the LORD!
⁴ Rely on the mighty LORD;
 constantly seek his face.*
⁵ Recall the wondrous deeds he has done,
 his signs and his words of judgment,
⁶ You descendants of Abraham his servant,
 offspring of Jacob the chosen one!

II

⁷ The LORD is our God
 who rules the whole earth.
⁸ He remembers forever his covenant,
 the pact imposed for a thousand
 generations,
⁹ Which was made with Abraham,
 confirmed by oath to Isaac,*
¹⁰ And ratified as binding for Jacob,
 an everlasting covenant for Israel:
¹¹ "To you I give the land of Canaan,
 your own allotted heritage."*

III

¹² When they were few in number,*
 a handful, and strangers there,
¹³ Wandering from nation to nation,
 from one kingdom to another,
¹⁴† He let no one oppress them;
 for their sake he rebuked kings:

P
S

---

† **104, 26:** *Leviathan:* a sea monster symbolizing primeval chaos.
Cf Ps 74, 14; Is 27, 1; Jb 40, 25. God does not destroy chaos but
makes it part of the created order.
 104, 29–30: On one level, the spirit (or wind) of God is the fall
and winter rains that provide food for all creatures. On another, it is
the breath (or spirit) of God that makes beings live.
 104, 35: *Hallelujah:* a frequent word in the last third of the
Psalter. The word combines the plural imperative of praise (*hallelu*)
with an abbreviated form of the divine name *Yah(weh)*.
 Ps 105: A hymn to God who promised the land of Canaan to the
holy people. Cf Pss 78; 106; 136. Israel is invited to praise and seek
the presence of God (1–6), who is faithful to the promise of land to
the ancestors (7–11). In every phase of the national story—the ancestors in the land of Canaan (12–15), Joseph in Egypt (16–22), Israel
in Egypt (23–38), Israel in the desert on the way to Canaan (39–45)—

God remained faithful, reiterating the promise of the land to successive servants.
 105, 14: *Kings:* Pharaoh and Abimelech of Gerar. Cf Gn 12, 17;
20, 6–7.

*
104, 19: Sir 43, 6.	**104, 32:** Ps 144, 5.
104, 21: Jb 38, 39.	**104, 33:** Ps 146, 2.
104, 24: Ps 92, 6; Sir 39, 16.	**105, 1–15:** 1 Chr 16, 8–22.
104, 25: Sir 43, 26.	**105, 1:** Pss 18, 50; 96, 3; 145,
104, 26: Jb 3, 8; 40, 25.	5; Is 12, 4–5.
104, 27: Pss 136, 25; 145,	**105, 4:** Pss 24, 6; 27, 8.
15–16.	**105, 9:** Gn 15, 1ff; 26, 3.
104, 29: Jb 34, 14–15; Eccl 3,	**105, 11:** Gn 12, 7; 15, 18.
20; Ps 90, 3.	**105, 12–13:** Dt 4, 27; 26, 5.

15† "Do not touch my anointed,
   to my prophets do no harm."

IV

16 Then he called down a famine on the land,
   destroyed the grain that sustained them.*

17 He had sent a man ahead of them,
   Joseph, sold as a slave.*

18 They shackled his feet with chains;
   collared his neck in iron,*

19 Till his prediction came to pass,
   and the word of the LORD proved him
      true.*

20 The king sent and released him;
   the ruler of peoples set him free.*

21 He made him lord over his palace,
   ruler over all his possessions,*

22 To instruct his princes by his word,
   to teach his elders wisdom.

V

23† Then Israel entered Egypt;*
   Jacob lived in the land of Ham.

24 God greatly increased his people,
   made them too many for their foes.*

25 He turned their hearts to hate his people,
   to treat his servants unfairly.*

26 He sent his servant Moses,
   Aaron whom he had chosen.*

27† They worked his signs in Egypt*
   and wonders in the land of Ham.

28 He sent darkness and it grew dark,
   but they rebelled against his word.

29 He turned their waters into blood
   and killed all their fish.

30 Their land swarmed with frogs,
   even the chambers of their kings.

31 He spoke and there came swarms of flies,
   gnats through all their country.

32 For rain he gave them hail,
   flashes of lightning throughout their land.

33 He struck down their vines and fig trees,
   shattered the trees of their country.

34 He spoke and the locusts came,
   grasshoppers without number.*

35 They devoured every plant in the land;
   they ravaged the crops of their fields.

36 He struck down every firstborn in the land,
   the first fruits of all their vigor.

37 He brought his people out,
   laden with silver and gold;*
   no stragglers among the tribes.

38 Egypt rejoiced when they left,
   for panic had seized them.

VI

39 He spread a cloud as a cover,
   and made a fire to light up the night.*

40 They asked and he brought them quail;
   with bread from heaven he filled them.*

41 He split the rock and water gushed forth;
   it flowed through the desert like a river.*

42 For he remembered his sacred word
   to Abraham his servant.

43 He brought his people out with joy,
   his chosen ones with shouts of triumph.

44 He gave them the lands of the nations,
   the wealth of the peoples to own,*

45 That they might keep his laws
   and observe his teachings.*
Hallelujah!

PSALM 106†

Israel's Confession of Sin
1 Hallelujah!

A

Give thanks to the LORD, who is good,
   whose love endures forever.*

2 Who can tell the mighty deeds of the LORD,
   proclaim in full God's praise?

3 Happy those who do what is right,
   whose deeds are always just.*

4 Remember me, LORD, as you favor your people;

---

† **105, 15:** *My anointed . . . my prophets:* the patriarchs Abraham, Isaac, and Jacob, who were "anointed" in the sense of being consecrated and recipients of God's revelation.

105, 23.27: *The land of Ham:* a synonym for Egypt. Cf Gn 10, 6.

105, 27–38: This psalm and Ps 78, 43–51 have an account of the plagues differing in number or in order from Ex 7, 14—12, 30. Several versions of the exodus story were current.

Ps 106: Israel is invited to praise the God whose mercy has always tempered judgment of Israel (1–3). The speaker, on behalf of all, seeks solidarity with the people, who can always count on God's fidelity despite their sin (4–5). Confident of God's mercy, the speaker invites national repentance (6) by reciting from Israel's history eight instances of sin, judgment, and forgiveness. The sins are the rebellion at the Red Sea (6–12; see Ex 14–15), the craving for meat in the desert (13–15; see Nm 11), the challenge to Moses' authority (16–18; see Nm 16), the golden calf episode (19–23; see Ex 32–34), the refusal to take Canaan by the southern route (24–27; see Nm 13–14 and Dt 1–2), the rebellion at Baal-Peor (28–31; see Nm 25, 1–10), the anger of Moses (32–33; see Nm 20, 1–13), and min-

gling with the nations (34–47). The last, as suggested by its length and generalized language, may be the sin that invites the repentance of the present generation. The text gives the site of each sin: Egypt (7), the desert (14), the camp (16), Horeb (19), in their tents (25), Baal-Peor (28), the waters of Meribah (32), Canaan (38).

105, 16: Gn 41, 54.57.
105, 17: Gn 37, 28.36; 45, 5.
105, 18: Gn 39, 20.
105, 19: Gn 40–41.
105, 20: Gn 41, 14.
105, 21: Gn 41, 41–44.
105, 23: Gn 46, 1—47, 12; Acts 7, 15.
105, 24: Ex 1, 7; Acts 7, 17.
105, 25: Ex 1, 8–14.
105, 26: Ex 3, 10; 4, 27.
105, 27–36: Ps 78, 43–51; Ex 7–12.
105, 34: Jl 1, 4.
105, 37: Ex 12, 33–36.
105, 39: Ps 78, 14; Ex 13, 21–22; Wis 18, 3.
105, 40: Ps 78, 24–28; Ex 16, 13–15; Nm 11, 31ff; Wis 16, 20.
105, 41: Ps 78, 15–16; Ex 17, 1–7; Nm 20, 11.
105, 44: Dt 4, 37–40.
105, 45: Dt 6, 20–25; 7, 8–11.
106, 1: Pss 100, 5; 107, 1; 1 Chr 16, 34; Jer 33, 11; Dn 3, 89.
106, 3: Is 56, 1–2.
106, 4: Ps 25, 7; Neh 5, 19.

come to me with your saving help,*
5 That I may see the prosperity of your chosen,
rejoice in the joy of your people,
and glory with your heritage.

B
6 We have sinned like our ancestors;*
we have done wrong and are guilty.

I
7 Our ancestors in Egypt
did not attend to your wonders.
They did not remember your great love;
they defied the Most High at the Red Sea.
8 Yet he saved them for his name's sake
to make his power known.*
9 He roared at the Red Sea and it dried up.
He led them through the deep as through a
desert.*
10 He rescued them from hostile hands,
freed them from the power of the enemy.
11 The waters covered their oppressors;
not one of them survived.
12 Then they believed his words
and sang songs of praise.*

II
13 But they soon forgot all he had done;
they had no patience for his plan.
14 In the desert they gave way to their cravings,
tempted God in the wasteland.*
15 So he gave them what they asked
and sent among them a wasting disease.*

III
16 In the camp they challenged Moses*
and Aaron, the holy one of the LORD.
17 The earth opened and swallowed Dathan,
it closed on the followers of Abiram.
18 Against that company the fire blazed;
flames consumed the wicked.

IV
19 At Horeb they fashioned a calf,*
worshiped a metal statue.
20 They exchanged their glorious God
for the image of a grass-eating bull.
21 They forgot the God who saved them,

who did great deeds in Egypt,*
22 Amazing deeds in the land of Ham,
fearsome deeds at the Red Sea.
23† He would have decreed their destruction,
had not Moses, the chosen leader,
Withstood him in the breach
to turn back his destroying anger.*

V
24 Next they despised the beautiful land;*
they did not believe the promise.
25 In their tents they complained;
they did not obey the LORD.
26 So with raised hand he swore
to destroy them in the desert,
27 To scatter their descendants among the
nations,
disperse them in foreign lands.

VI
28 They joined in the rites of Baal of Peor,*
ate food sacrificed to dead gods.
29 They provoked him by their actions,
and a plague broke out among them.
30 Then Phinehas rose to intervene,
and the plague was brought to a halt.
31 This was counted for him as a righteous deed
for all generations to come.

VII
32† At the waters of Meribah they angered God,*
and Moses suffered because of them.
33 They so embittered his spirit
that rash words crossed his lips.

VIII
34 They did not destroy the peoples
as the LORD had commanded them,*
35 But mingled with the nations
and imitated their ways.*
36 They worshiped their idols
and were ensnared by them.*
37† They sacrificed to the gods
their own sons and daughters,
38 Shedding innocent blood,
the blood of their own sons and daughters,
Whom they sacrificed to the idols of Canaan,
desecrating the land with bloodshed.

† **106, 23:** *Withstood him in the breach:* the image is that of Moses standing in a narrow break made in the wall to keep anyone from entering.
   106, 32: *Moses suffered because of them:* Moses was not allowed to enter the promised land because of his rash words (Nm 20, 12). According to Dt 1, 37, Moses was not allowed to cross because of the people's sin, not his own.
   106, 37: *The gods:* Hebrew *shedim,* customarily translated "demons," occurs in parallelism with "gods" in an important inscription from Transjordan and hence is translated "gods."

106, 6–7: Ps 78, 11–17; Ex 14,
   11; Lv 26, 40; 1 Kgs 8,
   47; Bar 2, 12; Dn 9, 5.

106, 8: Ez 36, 20–22.
106, 9: Ex 14, 21–31; Is 50, 2;
   63, 11–14; Na 1, 4.

106, 12: Ex 15, 1–21.
106, 14: Ps 78, 18; Ex 15, 24;
   16, 3; Nm 11, 1–6.
106, 15: Ps 78, 26–31; Nm 11,
   33.
106, 16–18: Nm 16; Dt 11, 6; Is
   26, 11.
106, 19–20: Ex 32; Dt 9, 8–21; Jer
   2, 11; Acts 7, 41; Rom
   1, 23.
106, 21: Ps 78, 42–58; Dt 32,
   18; Jer 2, 32.
106, 23: Ex 32, 11; Dt 9, 25; Ez
   22, 30.

106, 24–27: Lv 26, 33; Nm 14; Dt
   1, 25–36; Ez 20, 15.
   23.
106, 28–31: Nm 25; Dt 26, 14; Sir
   45, 23–24.
106, 32–33: Ps 95, 8–9; Ex 17, 1–7;
   Nm 20, 2–13; Dt 6,
   16; 33, 8.
106, 34: Dt 7, 1; Jgs 2, 1–5.
106, 35: Lv 18, 3; Jgs 1, 27–35;
   3, 5.
106, 36–38: Lv 18, 21; Nm 35, 33;
   Dt 32, 17; Jgs 2,
   11–13.17.19; 2 Kgs
   16, 3; Bar 4, 7; 1 Cor
   10, 20.

39 They defiled themselves by their actions,
    became adulterers by their conduct.
40 So the LORD grew angry with his people,
    abhorred his own heritage.
41 He handed them over to the nations,
    and their adversaries ruled them.*
42 Their enemies oppressed them,
    kept them under subjection.
43 Many times did he rescue them,
    but they kept rebelling and scheming
    and were brought low by their own guilt.*
44 Still God had regard for their affliction
    when he heard their wailing.
45 For their sake he remembered his covenant
    and relented in his abundant love,*
46 Winning for them compassion
    from all who held them captive.

C

47 Save us, LORD, our God;
    gather us from among the nations
    That we may give thanks to your holy name
    and glory in praising you.*

* * *

48† Blessed be the LORD, the God of Israel,
    from everlasting to everlasting!
    Let all the people say, Amen!*
    Hallelujah!

FIFTH BOOK — PSALMS 107–150

PSALM 107†

God the Savior of Those in Distress

1 "Give thanks to the LORD who is good,
    whose love endures forever!"*
2 Let that be the prayer of the LORD's redeemed,
    those redeemed from the hand of the foe,*
3 Those gathered from foreign lands,
    from east and west, from north and south.*

I

4 Some had lost their way in a barren desert;
    found no path toward a city to live in.
5 They were hungry and thirsty;

their life was ebbing away.*
6 In their distress they cried to the LORD,
    who rescued them in their peril,
7 Guided them by a direct path*
    so they reached a city to live in.*
8 Let them thank the LORD for such kindness,
    such wondrous deeds for mere mortals.
9 For he satisfied the thirsty,
    filled the hungry with good things.*

II

10 Some lived in darkness and gloom,
    in prison, bound with chains,
11 Because they rebelled against God's word,
    scorned the counsel of the Most High,*
12 Who humbled their hearts through hardship;
    they stumbled with no one to help.*
13 In their distress they cried to the LORD,
    who saved them in their peril,
14 Led them forth from darkness and gloom
    and broke their chains asunder.*
15 Let them thank the LORD for such kindness,
    such wondrous deeds for mere mortals.
16 For he broke down the gates of bronze
    and snapped the bars of iron.

III

17 Some fell sick from their wicked ways,
    afflicted because of their sins.
18 They loathed all manner of food;*
    they were at the gates of death.
19 In their distress they cried to the LORD,
    who saved them in their peril,
20 Sent forth the word to heal them,*
    snatched them from the grave.
21 Let them thank the LORD for such kindness,
    such wondrous deeds for mere mortals.
22 Let them offer a sacrifice in thanks,
    declare his works with shouts of joy.

IV

23 Some went off to sea in ships,
    plied their trade on the deep waters.*
24 They saw the works of the LORD,
    the wonders of God in the deep.
25 He spoke and roused a storm wind;
    it tossed the waves on high.*
26 They rose up to the heavens, sank to the depths;
    their hearts trembled at the danger.

106, 48: A doxology ending Book IV of the Psalter. It is not part of the psalm.

Ps 107: A hymn inviting those who have been rescued by God to give praise (1–3). Four archetypal divine rescues are described, each ending in thanksgiving: from the sterile desert (4–9), from imprisonment in gloom (10–16), from mortal illness (17–22), and from the angry sea (23–32). The number four connotes totality, all the possible varieties of rescue. The same saving activity of God is shown in Israel's history (33–41); whenever the people were endangered God rescued them. The last verses invite people to ponder the persistent saving acts of God (42–43).

106, 41: Jgs 2, 14–23.
106, 43: Is 63, 7–9.
106, 45: Lv 26, 42.
106, 47: 1 Chr 16, 35.
106, 48: Pss 41, 14; 72, 18; 89,
    53; 1 Chr 16, 36; Neh
    9, 5.
107, 1: Pss 100, 4–5; 106, 1;
    Jer 33, 11.
107, 2: Is 63, 12.
107, 3: Is 43, 5–6; 49, 12; Zec
    8, 7.
107, 5: Dt 8, 15; 32, 10; Is 49,
    10.
107, 7: Is 35, 8; 40, 3; 43, 19.
107, 7: Dt 6, 10.
107, 9: Lk 1, 53.
107, 11: Is 42, 7.22; Jb 36, 8–9;
    Prv 1, 25.
107, 12: Ps 106, 43.
107, 14: Is 42, 7; 49, 9; 51, 14.
107, 18: Jb 6, 6–7; 33, 20.
107, 20: Ps 147, 15; Wis 16,
    12; Is 55, 11; Mt 8, 8.
107, 23: Sir 43, 25.
107, 25: Jon 1, 4.

THANKFULNESS

It's good and natural for people to express thankfulness for their blessings. Psalm 107 is an extended thanksgiving for God's love and saving power. Indonesians have a custom for offering thanks on certain special occasions, such as after a new house is built, during the seventh month of pregnancy, and thirty-five days after the birth of a child.

During a thanksgiving for a new house, the family gathers in the house and offers prayers for the people who will live, eat, work, and die there. Similar prayers are said for a mother during pregnancy and for a child after birth—in thanksgiving for their health, well-being, and happiness. After the prayers, those who are gathered share a simple traditional meal of rice, vegetables, fish or chicken, and fruit.

▶ Psalm 107

27 They reeled, staggered like drunkards;
    their skill was of no avail.*
28 In their distress they cried to the LORD,
    who brought them out of their peril,
29 Hushed the storm to a murmur;
    the waves of the sea were stilled.*
30 They rejoiced that the sea grew calm,
    that God brought them to the harbor they
    longed for.
31 Let them thank the LORD for such kindness,
    such wondrous deeds for mere mortals.
32 Let them praise him in the assembly of the
    people,
    give thanks in the council of the elders.
                      V
33† God changed rivers into desert,
    springs of water into thirsty ground,*
34 Fruitful land into a salty waste,
    because of the wickedness of its people.*
35 He changed the desert into pools of water,
    arid land into springs of water,*
36 And settled the hungry there;
    they built a city to live in.*

37 They sowed fields and planted vineyards,
    brought in an abundant harvest.*
38 God blessed them, they became very many,
    and their livestock did not decrease.*
40 But he poured out contempt on princes,
    made them wander the trackless wastes,*
39 Where they were diminished and brought low
    through misery and cruel oppression,
41 While the poor were released from their
    affliction;
    their families increased like their flocks.*
42 The upright saw this and rejoiced;*
    all wickedness shut its mouth.
43 Whoever is wise will take note of these things,*
    will ponder the merciful deeds of the LORD.

PSALM 108†

Prayer for Victory
1 A song; a psalm of David.
                      I
2 My heart is steadfast, God;*
    my heart is steadfast.

107, 33–41: God destroyed Sodom and Gomorrah in Gn 18–19, which the psalm sees as the destruction of the wicked inhabitants of Canaan to prepare the way for Israel (33–34). God then led Israel through the desert to give them a fertile land (35–38) and protected them from every danger (39–41).

Ps 108: A prayer compiled from two other psalms: 2–6 are virtually the same as Ps 57, 8–12; 7–14 are the same as Ps 60, 7–14. An old promise of salvation (8–10) is combined with a confident assurance (1–6.14) and petition (7.12–13).

107, 27: Is 29, 9.
107, 29: Pss 65, 8; 89, 10; Mt 8, 26 par.
107, 33: Is 35, 7; 42, 15; 50, 2.
107, 34: Gn 19, 23–28; Dt 29, 22; Sir 39, 23.
107, 35: Ps 114, 8; Is 41, 8.
107, 36: Ez 36, 35.
107, 37: Is 65, 21; Jer 31, 5.
107, 38: Dt 7, 13–14.
107, 40: Jb 12, 23–25.
107, 41: Ps 113, 7.
107, 42: Pss 58, 11; 63, 12.
107, 43: Hos 14, 10.
108, 2–6: Ps 57, 8–12.

I will sing and chant praise.

3 Awake, my soul; awake, lyre and harp!
  I will wake the dawn.*

4 I will praise you among the peoples, LORD;
  I will chant your praise among the nations.*

5 For your love towers to the heavens;
  your faithfulness, to the skies.*

6 Appear on high over the heavens, God;
  may your glory appear above all the earth.

7 Help with your right hand and answer us
  that your loved ones may escape.

II

8 God promised in the sanctuary:*
  "I will exult, I will apportion Shechem;
  the valley of Succoth I will measure out.

9 Gilead is mine, mine is Manasseh;
  Ephraim is the helmet for my head,
  Judah, my own scepter.

10 Moab is my washbowl;
  upon Edom I cast my sandal;*
  I will triumph over Philistia."

III

11 Who will bring me to the fortified city?
  Who will lead me into Edom?

12 Was it not you who rejected us, God?
  Do you no longer march with our armies?*

13 Give us aid against the foe;
  worthless is human help.

14 We will triumph with the help of God,
  who will trample down our foes.

PSALM 109†

Prayer of a Person Falsely Accused
1 For the leader. A psalm of David.

I

O God, whom I praise, do not be silent,*
2 for wicked and treacherous mouths attack
   me.
  They speak against me with lying tongues;
3 with hateful words they surround me,
   attacking me without cause.
4 In return for my love they slander me,
  even though I prayed for them.
5 They repay me evil for good,
  hatred for my love.*

II

My enemies say of me:
6† "Find a lying witness,
  an accuser to stand by his right hand,
7 That he may be judged and found guilty,
  that his plea may be in vain.
8 May his days be few;
  may another take his office.*
9 May his children be fatherless,
  his wife, a widow.*
10 May his children be vagrant beggars,
  driven from their hovels.
11 May the usurer snare all he owns,
  strangers plunder all he earns.
12 May no one treat him kindly
  or pity his fatherless children.
13 May his posterity be destroyed,*
  his name cease in the next generation.
14 May the LORD remember his fathers' guilt;
  his mother's sin not be canceled.*
15 May their guilt be always before the LORD,*
  till their memory is banished from the earth,*
16 For he did not remember to show kindness,
  but hounded the wretched poor
  and brought death to the brokenhearted.
17 He loved cursing; may it come upon him;
  he hated blessing; may none come to him.
18 May cursing clothe him like a robe;
  may it enter his belly like water,
  seep into his bones like oil.
19 May it be near as the clothes he wears,
  as the belt always around him."

III

20† May the LORD bring all this upon my accusers,
  upon those who speak evil against me.
21 But you, LORD, my God,
  deal kindly with me for your name's sake;
  in your great mercy rescue me.
22 For I am sorely in need;
  my heart is pierced within me.
23 Like a lengthening shadow I near my end,
  all but swept away like the locust.
24 My knees totter from fasting;*
  my flesh has wasted away.
25 I have become a mockery to them;
  when they see me, they shake their heads.

---

† **Ps 109:** A lament notable for the length and vehemence of its prayer against evildoers (6–20); the cry to God (1) and the complaint (22–25) are brief in comparison. The psalmist is apparently the victim of a slander campaign, potentially devastating in a society where reputation and honor are paramount. In the emotional perspective of the psalm, there are only two types of people: the wicked and their poor victims. The psalmist is a poor victim (22.31) and by that fact a friend of God and enemy of the wicked. The psalmist seeks vindication not on the basis of personal virtue but because of God's promise to protect the poor.

109, 6: *An accuser:* Hebrew *satan*, a word occurring in Jb 1–2 and Zec 3, 1–2. In the latter passage Satan stands at the right hand

of the high priest to bring false accusations against him before God. Here the accuser is human.

109, 20: *May the LORD bring all this:* the psalmist prays that God ratify the curses of 6–19 and bring them upon the wicked.

108, 3: Jb 38, 12.
108, 4: Pss 9, 12; 18, 50; 148, 13.
108, 5: Pss 36, 6; 71, 19.
108, 8–14: Ps 60, 8–14.
108, 10: Ru 4, 7–8.
108, 12: Ps 44, 10.
109, 1: Pss 35, 22; 83, 1.

109, 5: Pss 35, 12; 38, 21; Prv 17, 13; Jer 18, 20.
109, 8: Acts 1, 20.
109, 9: Ex 22, 23; Jer 18, 21.
109, 13: Ps 21, 11; Prv 10, 7.
109, 14: Ex 20, 5.
109, 15: Ps 90, 8.
109, 15: Ps 34, 16.
109, 24–25: Ps 69, 11–13.

26 Help me, LORD, my God;
    save me in your kindness.
27 Make them know this is your hand,
    that you, LORD, have acted.
28 Though they curse, may you bless;
    shame my foes, that your servant may
        rejoice.
29 Clothe my accusers with disgrace;
    make them wear shame like a mantle.
30 I will give fervent thanks to the LORD;
    before all I will praise my God.*
31 For God stands at the right hand of the poor
    to defend them against unjust accusers.

PSALM 110†

God Appoints the King both King and Priest

¹† A psalm of David.

The LORD says to you, my lord:
    "Take your throne at my right hand,
    while I make your enemies your
        footstool."*
2 The scepter of your sovereign might
    the LORD will extend from Zion.
    The LORD says: "Rule over your enemies!
3† Yours is princely power from the day of
        your birth.
    In holy splendor before the daystar,
    like the dew I begot you."*
4† The LORD has sworn and will not waver:
    "Like Melchizedek you are a priest
        forever."*
5 At your right hand is the Lord,
    who crushes kings on the day of wrath,*
6 Who, robed in splendor, judges nations,
    crushes heads across the wide earth,

7† Who drinks from the brook by the
        wayside
    and thus holds high his head.*

PSALM 111†

Praise of God for Goodness to Israel

¹† Hallelujah!

I will praise the LORD with all my
    heart*
    in the assembled congregation of
        the upright.
2 Great are the works of the LORD,
    to be treasured for all their delights.
3† Majestic and glorious is your work,
    your wise design endures forever.
4 You won renown for your wondrous
        deeds;
    gracious and merciful is the LORD.*
5† You gave food to those who fear you,
    mindful of your covenant forever.
6† You showed powerful deeds to your
        people,
    giving them the lands of the nations.
7 The works of your hands are right and
        true,
    reliable all your decrees,
8 Established forever and ever,
    to be observed with loyalty and care.
9 You sent deliverance to your people,
    ratified your covenant forever;
    holy and awesome is your name.
10† The fear of the LORD is the beginning
    of wisdom;*
    prudent are all who live by it.
    Your praise endures forever.

---

† **Ps 110:** A royal psalm in which a court singer recites three oracles in which God assures the king that his enemies are conquered (1–2), makes the king "son" in traditional adoption language (3), gives priestly status to the king and promises to be with him in future military ventures (4–7).

110, 1: *The LORD says to you, my lord:* literally, "The LORD says to my lord," a polite form of address of an inferior to a superior. Cf 1 Sm 25, 25; 2 Sm 1, 10. The court singer refers to the king. Jesus in the synoptic gospels (Mt 22, 41–46 and parallels) takes the psalmist to be David and hence "my lord" refers to the messiah, who must be someone greater than David. *Your footstool:* in ancient times victorious kings put their feet on the prostrate bodies of their enemies.

110, 3: *Before the daystar:* possibly an expression for before the world began (Prv 8, 22). *Like the dew I begot you:* an adoption formula as in Pss 2, 7; 89, 27–28.

110, 4: *Like Melchizedek:* Melchizedek was the ancient king of Salem (Jerusalem) who blessed Abraham (Gn 14, 18–20); like other kings of the time he performed priestly functions. Heb 7 sees in Melchizedek a type of Christ.

110, 7: *Who drinks from the brook by the wayside:* the meaning is uncertain. Some see an allusion to a rite of royal consecration at the Gihon spring (cf 1 Kgs 1, 33.38). Others find here an image of the divine warrior (or king) pursuing enemies so relentlessly that he does not stop long enough to eat and drink.

Ps 111: A temple singer (1) tells how God is revealed in Israel's

history (2–10). The deeds reveal God's very self, powerful, merciful, faithful. The poem is an acrostic, each verse beginning with a successive letter of the Hebrew alphabet.

111, 1: *In the assembled congregation of the upright:* in the temple. Cf Ps 149, 1.

111, 3: *Your:* the psalm refers to God in the third person throughout; the shift to the second person is for the sake of inclusive language.

111, 5: *Food to those who fear you:* probably a reference to the manna in the desert, which elsewhere is seen as a type of the Eucharist. Cf Jn 6, 31–33.49–51.

111, 6: *Lands:* literally, "inheritance, heritage."

111, 10: *The fear of the LORD:* reverence for God, the Hebrew term for religion.

109, 30: Ps 111, 1.
110, 1: Mt 22, 44; Acts 2,
    34–35; 1 Cor 15, 25;
    Heb 1, 13; 8, 1; 10,
    12–13; 1 Pt 3, 22.
110, 3: Pss 2, 7; 89, 27; Is
    49, 1.

110, 4: Pss 89, 35; 132, 11;
    Gn 14, 18; Heb 5, 6;
    7, 21.
110, 5: Ps 2, 9; Rv 2, 27; 12,
    5; 19, 15.
110, 7: Ps 3, 4.
111, 1: Ps 138, 1.
111, 4: Pss 103, 8; 112, 4.
111, 10: Prv 1, 7; 9, 10; Sir 1,
    16.

Cultural Connections

GENEROSITY

"All goes well for those gracious in lending, / who conduct their affairs with justice" (Ps 112, 5). Generosity is an important value for many Native American peoples. For the Lakota tribe, it is one of four primary values. The Lakota word for generosity is *wa-can-tog-na-ka*.

In this Native American culture, it is a great insult to be called selfish, and a high compliment to be called generous. You are not able to raise your social status by showing off the things that you own. You can do it only by giving things away. In fact, there is a special ceremony called the *otuhan*, or the "giveaway," in which people give away many of their possessions to honor one another. For example, young people may have a giveaway when they graduate from high school, as a way of honoring all who have helped them along the way.

To explore the other primary Lakota virtues, see the Cultural Connections articles for Psalms 31, 73, and 89.

▶ Psalm 112

PSALM 112†

The Blessings of the Just

¹† Hallelujah!

Happy are those who fear the LORD,
    who greatly delight in God's commands.*
2 Their descendants shall be mighty in the
    land,
    a generation upright and blessed.
3† Wealth and riches shall be in their homes;
    their prosperity shall endure forever.
4 They shine through the darkness, a light for
    the upright;*
    they are gracious, merciful, and just.
5 All goes well for those gracious in lending,
    who conduct their affairs with justice.
6 They shall never be shaken;
    the just shall be remembered forever.*
7 They shall not fear an ill report;

    their hearts are steadfast, trusting the LORD.
8 Their hearts are tranquil, without fear,
    till at last they look down on their foes.
9† Lavishly they give to the poor;
    their prosperity shall endure forever;*
    their horn shall be exalted in honor.
10 The wicked shall be angry to see this;
    they will gnash their teeth and waste
    away;
    the desires of the wicked come to nothing.

PSALM 113†

Praise of God's Care of the Poor

¹ Hallelujah!

I

Praise, you servants of the LORD,
    praise the name of the LORD.*
2 Blessed be the name of the LORD
    both now and forever.

---

†
  Ps 112: An acrostic poem detailing the blessings received by those who remain close to God by obedience to the commandments. Among their blessings are children (2), wealth that enables them to be magnanimous (3.5.9), and virtue by which they encourage others (4). The just person is an affront to the wicked, whose hopes remain unfulfilled (10). The logic resembles Pss 1 and 111.

  112, 1: *Happy are those:* literally, "Happy the person." "Person" is used typically, hence the plural translation.

  112, 3: *Prosperity:* literally, "justice." In the Second Temple Period the word acquired the nuance of liberality and almsgiving. Cf Sir 3, 30; 7, 10; Mt 6, 1–4.

  112, 9: *Their horn:* the symbol for vitality and honor.

  Ps 113: A hymn exhorting the congregation to praise God's name, i.e., the way in which God is present in the world; the name is mentioned three times in 1–3. The divine name is especially honored in the temple (1) but its recognition is not limited by time (2) and space (3), for God is everywhere active (4–5) especially in rescuing the lowly faithful (7–9).

112, 1: Pss 1, 1–2; 119, 1–2;   112, 6: Prv 10, 7; Wis 8, 13.
    128, 1.   112, 9: Prv 22, 9; 2 Cor 9, 9.
112, 4: Pss 37, 6; 97, 11; Prv   113, 1: Ps 135, 1.
    13, 9; Is 58, 10.

3 From the rising of the sun to its setting
   let the name of the LORD be praised.

II

4 High above all nations is the LORD;
   above the heavens God's glory.*
5 Who is like the LORD,
   our God enthroned on high,
6 looking down on heaven and earth?*
7 The LORD raises the needy from the dust,
   lifts the poor from the ash heap,*
8 Seats them with princes,
   the princes of the people,
9 Gives the childless wife a home,
   the joyful mother of children.*
   Hallelujah!

PSALM 114†

The LORD's Wonders at the Exodus

1 When Israel came forth from Egypt,
   the house of Jacob from an alien people,
2 Judah became God's holy place,
   Israel, God's domain.*
3† The sea beheld and fled;
   the Jordan turned back.*
4 The mountains skipped like rams;
   the hills, like lambs of the flock.*
5 Why was it, sea, that you fled?
   Jordan, that you turned back?

6 You mountains, that you skipped like
   rams?
   You hills, like lambs of the flock?
7 Tremble, earth, before the Lord,*
   before the God of Jacob,
8† Who turned rock into pools of water,
   stone into flowing springs.*

PSALM 115†

The Greatness of the True God

I

1 Not to us, LORD, not to us
   but to your name give glory
   because of your faithfulness and love.*
2† Why should the nations say,
   "Where is their God?"*
3 Our God is in heaven;
   whatever God wills is done.*

II

4 Their idols are silver and gold,*
   the work of human hands.*
5 They have mouths but do not speak,
   eyes but do not see.
6 They have ears but do not hear,
   noses but do not smell.
7 They have hands but do not feel,
   feet but do not walk,
   and no sound rises from their throats.

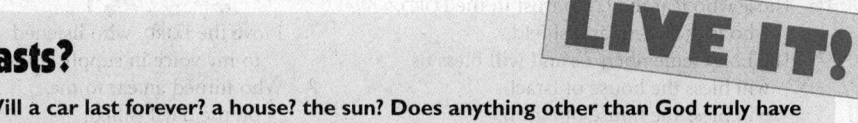

What Lasts? LIVE IT!

Will a car last forever? a house? the sun? Does anything other than God truly have no end? No matter how much you look, you won't find such a thing. So, why do we spend much of our time with what won't last, rather than what *will* last?
   Psalm 115 proclaims the greatness of God and the foolishness of idols. In the end, the things that matter most won't be how many awards you were given, how much money you made, or how many possessions you had, but rather how much you loved others, how much you served, and how much you loved God!

▸ **Psalm 115**

†
Ps 114: A hymn celebrating Israel's escape from Egypt, journey through the wilderness, and entry into the promised land, and the miracles of nature that bore witness to God's presence in their midst. In the perspective of the psalm, the people proceed directly from Egypt into the promised land (1–2). Sea and Jordan, which stood like soldiers barring the people from their land, flee before the mighty God as the earth recoils from the battle (3–4). The poet taunts the natural elements as one taunts defeated enemies (5–6).

114, 3–4: Pairs of cosmic elements such as sea and rivers, mountains and hills, are sometimes mentioned in creation accounts. Personified here as warriors, the pairs tremble in fear before the Divine Warrior. The quaking also recalls the divine appearance in the storm at Sinai (Ex 19, 16–19) and elsewhere (Jgs 5, 4–5; Ps 18, 8–16).

114, 8: The miracles of giving drink to the people in the arid desert. Cf Ex 17, 1–7; Is 41, 17–18.

Ps 115: A response to the enemy taunt, "Where is your God?"

This hymn to the glory of Israel's God (1–3) ridicules the lifeless idols of the nations (4–8), expresses in a litany the trust of the various classes of the people in God (9–11), invokes God's blessing on them as they invoke the divine name (12–15), and concludes as it began with praise of God. Ps 135, 15–18 similarly mocks the Gentile gods and has a similar litany and hymn (Ps 135, 19–21).

115, 2: "Where is their God?": implies that God cannot help them.

113, 4: Ps 148, 13.
113, 6: Ps 89, 7–9.
113, 7: Ps 107, 41; 1 Sm 2, 7–8.
113, 9: 1 Sm 2, 5; Is 54, 1.
114, 2: Ex 19, 6.
114, 3: Ex 14, 21f; Jos 3, 14ff;
   Pss 66, 6; 74, 15.
114, 4: Ps 29, 6; Wis 19, 9.
114, 7: Ps 68, 9.

114, 8: Ex 17, 6; Nm 20, 11.
115, 1: Ez 36, 22–23.
115, 2: Ps 79, 10.
115, 3: Ps 135, 6.
115, 4–10: Ps 135, 15–19; Wis
   15, 15–16; Is 44, 9f;
   Jer 10, 1–5.
115, 4: Is 40, 19.

Gratitude

Roy. Thank God, I'm feeling better.
Maria. Exactly!
Roy. Exactly what?
Maria. That's exactly what Psalm 116 is all about. Feeling better and thanking God for it.
Roy. Really? I thought the Psalms were about praising God and winning victories.
Maria. Some are. In a way, that's what Psalm 116 is about too. You can use it to praise God for your victory over illness.
Roy. I never really thought of it that way.
Maria. You prayed to get well, didn't you?
Roy. Yes, a lot.
Maria. Well, there you are. God heard your prayers. Now, how about some genuine gratitude?
Roy. You're right. Thank you, God! I'm feeling so much better!
Maria. Amen!

▶ Psalm 116

---

8 Their makers shall be like them,
   all who trust in them.

III

9† The house of Israel trusts in the LORD,*
   who is their help and shield.*
10 The house of Aaron trusts in the LORD,
   who is their help and shield.
11† Those who fear the LORD trust in the LORD,
   who is their help and shield.
12 The LORD remembers us and will bless us,
   will bless the house of Israel,
   will bless the house of Aaron,
13 Will bless those who fear the LORD,
   small and great alike.
14 May the LORD increase your number,
   you and your descendants.
15 May you be blessed by the LORD,
   who made heaven and earth.
16† The heavens belong to the LORD,
   but the earth is given to us.*
17† The dead do not praise the LORD,
   all those gone down into silence.*
18 It is we who bless the LORD,

both now and forever.
Hallelujah!

PSALM 116†

Thanksgiving to God Who Saves from Death

I

1 I love the LORD, who listened
   to my voice in supplication,
2 Who turned an ear to me
   on the day I called.
3† I was caught by the cords of death;*
   the snares of Sheol had seized me;
   I felt agony and dread.
4 Then I called on the name of the LORD,
   "O LORD, save my life!"

II

5 Gracious is the LORD and just;
   yes, our God is merciful.*
6 The LORD protects the simple;
   I was helpless, but God saved me.
7 Return, my soul, to your rest;

115, 9–11: *The house of Israel . . . the house of Aaron . . . those who fear the LORD:* the laity of Israelite birth, the priests, and the converts to Judaism. Cf Pss 118, 2–4; 135, 19–21. In the New Testament likewise "those who fear the Lord" means converts to Judaism (cf Acts 10, 2.22.35; 13, 16.26).

115, 16: *The heavens:* literally "the heaven of heavens" or "the highest heavens," i.e., above the firmament. See note on Ps 148, 4.

115, 17: See note on Ps 6, 6.

Ps 116: A thanksgiving in which the psalmist responds to divine rescue from mortal danger (3–4) and from near despair (10–11) with vows and temple sacrifices (13–14.17–19). The Greek and Latin ver-

sions divide the psalm into two parts: 1–9 and 10–19, corresponding to its two major divisions.

116, 3: *The cords of death:* death is personified here; it attempts to capture the psalmist with snares and nets. Cf Ps 18, 6.

115, 9: Ps 118, 2–4.   116, 3: Ps 18, 5; Jon 2, 3.
115, 9: Ps 33, 20.   116, 5: Ex 34, 6.
115, 16: Gn 1, 28.   116, 7: Ps 13, 6.
115, 17: Pss 6, 6; 88, 11ff; Sir
   17, 22f; Is 38, 18.

the LORD has been good to you.*
8 For my soul has been freed from
death,
my eyes from tears, my feet from
stumbling.*
9† I shall walk before the LORD
in the land of the living.*

III

10† I kept faith, even when I said,
"I am greatly afflicted!"*
11 I said in my alarm,
"No one can be trusted!"*
12 How can I repay the LORD
for all the good done for me?
13† I will raise the cup of salvation
and call on the name of the LORD.
14 I will pay my vows to the LORD
in the presence of all his people.
15† Too costly in the eyes of the LORD
is the death of his faithful.*
16 LORD, I am your servant,
your servant, the child of your
maidservant;*
you have loosed my bonds.
17 I will offer a sacrifice of thanksgiving
and call on the name of the LORD.*
18 I will pay my vows to the LORD*
in the presence of all his people,
19 In the courts of the house of the
LORD,
in your midst, O Jerusalem.
Hallelujah!

PSALM 117 †

The Nations Called to Praise

1 Praise the LORD, all you nations!
Give glory, all you peoples!*
2 The LORD's love for us is strong;
the LORD is faithful forever.
Hallelujah!

PSALM 118 †

Hymn of Thanksgiving

I

1 Give thanks to the LORD, who is good,*
whose love endures forever.
2 Let the house of Israel say:
God's love endures forever.
3 Let the house of Aaron say,
God's love endures forever.
4 Let those who fear the LORD say,*
God's love endures forever.

II

5 In danger I called on the LORD;
the LORD answered me and set me free.
6 The LORD is with me; I am not afraid;
what can mortals do against me?*
7 The LORD is with me as my helper;
I shall look in triumph on my foes.
8 Better to take refuge in the LORD*
than to put one's trust in mortals.
9 Better to take refuge in the LORD
than to put one's trust in princes.

III

10 All the nations surrounded me;
in the LORD's name I crushed them.
11 They surrounded me on every side;
in the LORD's name I crushed them.
12 They surrounded me like bees;*
they blazed like fire among thorns;
in the LORD's name I crushed them.
13 I was hard pressed and falling,
but the LORD came to my help.*
14 The LORD, my strength and might,
came to me as savior.*

IV

15 The joyful shout of deliverance
is heard in the tents of the victors:
"The LORD's right hand strikes with power;
16 the LORD's right hand is raised;
the LORD's right hand strikes with power."

P
S

116, 9: *The land of the living:* the phrase elsewhere is an epithet of the Jerusalem temple (cf Pss 27, 13; 52, 7; Is 38, 11). Hence the psalmist probably refers to being present to God in the temple.
116, 10: *I kept faith, even when I said:* even in the days of despair, the psalmist did not lose all hope.
116, 13: *The cup of salvation:* probably the libation of wine poured out in gratitude for rescue. Cf Ex 25, 29; Nm 15, 5.7.10.
116, 15: *Too costly in the eyes of the LORD:* the meaning is that the death of God's faithful is grievous to God, not that God is pleased with the death. Cf Ps 72, 14. In Wis 3, 5–6 God accepts the death of the righteous as a sacrificial burnt offering.
Ps 117: This shortest of hymns calls on the nations to acknowledge God's supremacy. The supremacy of Israel's God has been demonstrated to them by the people's secure existence, which is owed entirely to God's gracious fidelity.
Ps 118: A thanksgiving liturgy accompanying a victory procession of the king and the people into the temple precincts. After an invocation in the form of a litany (1–4), the psalmist (very likely

speaking in the name of the community) describes how the people confidently implored God's help (5–9) when hostile peoples threatened its life (10–14); vividly God's rescue is recounted (15–18). Then follows a dialogue at the temple gates between the priests and the psalmist as the latter enters to offer the thanksgiving sacrifice (19–25). Finally, the priests impart their blessing (26–27), and the psalmist sings in gratitude (28–29).

116, 8: Ps 56, 14; Is 25, 8; Rv 21, 4.
116, 9: Pss 27, 13; 56, 14; Is 38, 11.
116, 10: 2 Cor 4, 13.
116, 11: Ps 12, 2.
116, 15: Ps 72, 14; Is 43, 4.
116, 16: Pss 86, 16; 143, 12; Wis 9, 5.
116, 17: Lv 7, 12ff.
116, 18: Jon 2, 10.
117, 1: Rom 15, 11.
118, 1: Pss 100, 5; 136, 1f.
118, 4: Ps 115, 9–11.
118, 6: Ps 27, 1; Heb 13, 6.
118, 8f: Ps 146, 3.
118, 12: Dt 1, 44.
118, 13: Ps 129, 1–2.
118, 14: Ex 15, 2; Is 12, 2.

The Longest Psalm

Psalm 119 is the longest psalm. Also, it has an interesting structure that you cannot appreciate in the English translation: it consists of twenty-two sections, and all the lines of a particular section begin with the same letter of the Hebrew alphabet. All the lines of the first section begin with *Aleph*, the Hebrew equivalent of the letter *A*. All the lines of the second section begin with *Beth*, the Hebrew equivalent of the letter *B*. And so on through the whole Hebrew alphabet!

This structure is called an acrostic. An acrostic is a poem in which the beginning letters of each line form a word or a phrase or a logical sequence. You may have written a poem like this in grade school using the word *mother* or *father*.

Write your own acrostic prayer, beginning the lines of the prayer with the letters of your name or of the name of someone or something you would like to pray for.

▸ **Psalm 119**

17   I shall not die but live
     and declare the deeds of the LORD.
18   The LORD chastised me harshly,
     but did not hand me over to death.

V

19   Open the gates of victory;
     I will enter and thank the LORD.*
20†   This is the LORD's own gate,
     where the victors enter.

21   I thank you for you answered me;
     you have been my savior.
22†   The stone the builders rejected
     has become the cornerstone.*
23   By the LORD has this been done;
     it is wonderful in our eyes.
24   This is the day the LORD has made;
     let us rejoice in it and be glad.
25†   LORD, grant salvation!
     LORD, grant good fortune!

VI

26   Blessed is he
     who comes in the name of the LORD.*
     We bless you from the LORD's house.
27   The LORD is God and has given us light.
     Join in procession with leafy branches
     up to the horns of the altar.

VII

28   You are my God, I give you thanks;
     my God, I offer you praise.
29   Give thanks to the LORD, who is good,
     whose love endures forever.

PSALM 119†

A Prayer to God, the Lawgiver

ALEPH

1   Happy those whose way is blameless,
     who walk by the teaching of the LORD.*
2   Happy those who observe God's decrees,
     who seek the LORD with all their heart.*
3   They do no wrong;
     they walk in God's ways.
4   You have given them the command
     to keep your precepts with care.
5   May my ways be firm
     in the observance of your laws!
6   Then I will not be ashamed
     to ponder all your commands.
7   I will praise you with sincere heart
     as I study your just edicts.

118, 20: *Where the victors enter:* their victory has demonstrated that God favors them; they are "just" in the biblical sense.

118, 22: *The stone the builders rejected:* a proverb: what is insignificant to human beings has become great through divine election. The "stone" may originally have meant the foundation stone or capstone of the temple. The New Testament interpreted the verse as referring to the death and resurrection of Christ (Mt 21, 42; Acts 4, 11; cf Is 28, 16 and Rom 9, 33; 1 Pt 2, 7).

118, 25: *Grant salvation:* the Hebrew for this cry has come into English as "Hosanna." This cry and the words in 26 were used in the gospels to welcome Jesus entering the temple on Palm Sunday (Mk 11, 9–10).

Ps 119: This psalm, the longest by far in the psalter, praises God for giving such splendid laws and instruction for people to live by. The author glorifies and thanks God for the Torah, prays for protection from sinners enraged by others' fidelity to the law, laments the cost of obedience, delights in the law's consolations, begs for wisdom to understand the precepts, and asks for the rewards of keeping them. Several expected elements do not appear in the psalm: Mount

Sinai with its story of God's revelation and gift to Israel of instruction and commandments, the temple and other institutions related to revelation and laws (frequent in other psalms). The psalm is fascinated with God's word directing and guiding human life.

The poem is an acrostic; its twenty-two stanzas (of eight verses each) are in the order of the Hebrew alphabet. Each of the eight verses within a stanza begins with the same letter. Each verse contains one word for "instruction." The translation here given attempts to translate each Hebrew word for "instruction" with the same English word. There are, however, nine words for "instruction," not eight, so the principle of a different word for "instruction" in each verse cannot be maintained with perfect consistency. The nine words for "instruction" in the translation are: law, edict, command, precept, word, utterance, way, decree, and teaching.

118, 19: Is 26, 2.   **118, 26:** Mt 21, 9; 23, 39.
118, 22: Mt 21, 42; Lk 20, 17;   **119, 1:** Pss 1, 1–2; 15, 2;
     Acts 4, 11; Rom 9, 33;   112, 1.
     1 Pt 2, 7.   **119, 2:** Dt 4, 29.

8   I will keep your laws;
         do not leave me all alone.

BETH

9   How can the young walk without fault?
         Only by keeping your words.
10   With all my heart I seek you;
         do not let me stray from your commands.
11   In my heart I treasure your promise,
         that I may not sin against you.
12   Blessed are you, O LORD;
         teach me your laws.*
13   With my lips I recite
         all the edicts you have spoken.
14   I find joy in the way of your decrees
         more than in all riches.
15   I will ponder your precepts
         and consider your paths.
16   In your laws I take delight;
         I will never forget your word.

GIMEL

17   Be kind to your servant that I may live,
         that I may keep your word.
18   Open my eyes to see clearly
         the wonders of your teachings.
19† I am a sojourner in the land;*
         do not hide your commands from me.
20   At all times my soul is stirred
         with longing for your edicts.
21   With a curse you rebuke the proud
         who stray from your commands.
22   Free me from disgrace and contempt,
         for I observe your decrees.
23   Though princes meet and talk against me,
         your servant studies your laws.
24   Your decrees are my delight;
         they are my counselors.

DALETH

25   I lie prostrate in the dust;*
         give me life in accord with your word.
26   I disclosed my ways and you answered me;
         teach me your laws.
27   Make me understand the way of your
             precepts;
         I will ponder your wondrous deeds.
28   I weep in bitter pain;
         in accord with your word to strengthen me.
29   Lead me from the way of deceit;

favor me with your teaching.
30   The way of loyalty I have chosen;
         I have set your edicts before me.
31   I cling to your decrees, LORD;
         do not let me come to shame.
32† I will run the way of your commands,
         for you open my docile heart.

HE

33   LORD, teach me the way of your laws;
         I shall observe them with care.*
34   Give me insight to observe your teaching,
         to keep it with all my heart.
35   Lead me in the path of your commands,*
         for that is my delight.
36   Direct my heart toward your decrees
         and away from unjust gain.
37   Avert my eyes from what is worthless;
         by your way give me life.
38   For your servant fulfill your promise
         made to those who fear you.
39   Turn away from me the taunts I dread,
         for your edicts bring good.
40   See how I long for your precepts;
         in your justice give me life.

WAW

41   Let your love come to me, LORD,
         salvation in accord with your promise.
42   Let me answer my taunters with a word,
         for I trust in your word.
43   Do not take the word of truth from my
             mouth,
         for in your edicts is my hope.
44   I will keep your teachings always,
         for all time and forever.
45   I will walk freely in an open space
         because I cherish your precepts.
46   I will speak openly of your decrees
         without fear even before kings.
47   I delight in your commands,
         which I dearly love.
48† I lift up my hands to your commands;
         I study your laws, which I love.

ZAYIN

49   Remember your word to your servant
         by which you give me hope.
50   This is my comfort in affliction,
         your promise that gives me life.

119, 19: *A sojourner in the land:* like someone without the legal protection of a native inhabitant, the psalmist has a special need for the guidance of God's teaching.
    119, 32: *For you open my docile heart:* literally, "you make broad my heart."
    119, 48: *I lift up my hands to your commands:* to lift up the hands was an ancient gesture of reverence to God. Here the picture is applied to God's law.

119, 12: Pss 25, 4; 27, 11; 86, 11; 143, 8.10.
119, 19: Ps 39, 13.
119, 25: Ps 44, 26.
119, 33: Ps 19, 12.
119, 35: Pss 25, 4; 27, 11; 86, 11; 143, 8.10.

P
S

51 Though the arrogant utterly scorn me,
   I do not turn from your teaching.
52 When I recite your edicts of old
   I am comforted, LORD.
53 Rage seizes me because of the wicked;
   they forsake your teaching.
54 Your laws become my songs
   wherever I make my home.
55 Even at night I remember your name
   in observance of your teaching, LORD.
56 This is my good fortune,
   for I have observed your precepts.

HETH

57 My portion is the LORD;
   I promise to keep your words.
58 I entreat you with all my heart:
   have mercy on me in accord with your
      promise.
59 I have examined my ways
   and turned my steps to your decrees.
60 I am prompt, I do not hesitate
   in keeping your commands.
61 Though the snares of the wicked surround
      me,
   your teaching I do not forget.
62 At midnight I rise to praise you
   because your edicts are just.
63 I am the friend of all who fear you,
   of all who keep your precepts.
64 The earth, LORD, is filled with your love;*
   teach me your laws.

TETH

65 You have treated your servant well,
   according to your word, O LORD.
66 Teach me wisdom and knowledge,
   for in your commands I trust.
67 Before I was afflicted I went astray,
   but now I hold to your promise.
68 You are good and do what is good;
   teach me your laws.
69 The arrogant smear me with lies,
   but I observe your precepts with all my
      heart.
70 Their hearts are gross and fat;*
   as for me, your teaching is my delight.
71 It was good for me to be afflicted,
   in order to learn your laws.
72 Teaching from your lips is more precious
      to me
   than heaps of silver and gold.

YODH

73 Your hands made me and fashioned me;
   give me insight to learn your commands.
74 Those who fear you rejoice to see me,
   because I hope in your word.
75 I know, LORD, that your edicts are just;
   though you afflict me, you are faithful.
76 May your love comfort me
   in accord with your promise to your
      servant.
77 Show me compassion that I may live,
   for your teaching is my delight.
78 Shame the proud for oppressing me unjustly,
   that I may study your precepts.
79 Let those who fear you turn to me,
   those who acknowledge your decrees.
80 May I be wholehearted toward your laws,
   that I may not be put to shame.

KAPH

81 My soul longs for your salvation;
   I put my hope in your word.*
82 My eyes long to see your promise.*
   When will you comfort me?
83 I am like a wineskin shriveled by smoke,*
   but I have not forgotten your laws.
84 How long can your servant survive?
   When will your edict doom my foes?
85 The arrogant have dug pits for me;
   defying your teaching.
86 All your commands are steadfast.
   Help me! I am pursued without cause.
87 They have almost ended my life on earth,
   but I do not forsake your precepts.
88 In your kindness give me life,
   to keep the decrees you have spoken.

LAMEDH

89† Your word, LORD, stands forever;*
   it is firm as the heavens.
90 Through all generations your truth endures;
   fixed to stand firm like the earth.
91 By your edicts they stand firm to this day,
   for all things are your servants.
92 Had your teaching not been my delight,
   I would have perished in my affliction.
93 I will never forget your precepts;
   through them you give me life.
94 I am yours; save me,
   for I cherish your precepts.
95 The wicked hope to destroy me,
   but I pay heed to your decrees.

119, 89–91: God's word creates the world, which manifests that
word by its permanence and reliability.

119, 64: Ps 33, 5.
119, 70: Pss 17, 10; 73, 7; Jb
   15, 27.
119, 81: Ps 130, 6.
119, 82: Pss 25, 15; 123, 1–2;
   141, 8.
119, 83: Jb 30, 30.
119, 89: Is 40, 8.

96 I have seen the limits of all perfection,
   but your command is without bounds.

MEM

97 How I love your teaching, LORD!
   I study it all day long.
98 Your command makes me wiser than my foes,
   for it is always with me.
99 I have more understanding than all my teachers,
   because I ponder your decrees.
100 I have more insight than my elders,
    because I observe your precepts.*
101 I keep my steps from every evil path,
    that I may obey your word.
102 From your edicts I do not turn,
    for you have taught them to me.
103 How sweet to my tongue is your promise,
    sweeter than honey to my mouth!*
104 Through your precepts I gain insight;
    therefore I hate all false ways.

NUN

105 Your word is a lamp for my feet,
    a light for my path.*
106 I make a solemn vow
    to keep your just edicts.
107 I am very much afflicted, LORD;
    give me life in accord with your word.
108 Accept my freely offered praise;*
    LORD, teach me your decrees.
109 My life is always at risk,
    but I do not forget your teaching.
110 The wicked have set snares for me,
    but from your precepts I do not stray.
111 Your decrees are my heritage forever;
    they are the joy of my heart.
112 My heart is set on fulfilling your laws;
    they are my reward forever.

SAMEKH

113 I hate every hypocrite;
    your teaching I love.
114 You are my refuge and shield;
    in your word I hope.
115 Depart from me, you wicked,*
    that I may observe the commands of my
    God.
116 Sustain me by your promise that I may live;
    do not disappoint me in my hope.
117 Strengthen me that I may be safe,
    ever to contemplate your laws.
118 You reject all who stray from your laws,
    for vain is their deceit.

119 Like dross you regard all the wicked on
    earth;
    therefore I love your decrees.
120 My flesh shudders with dread of you;
    I hold your edicts in awe.

AYIN

121 I have fulfilled your just edict;
    do not abandon me to my oppressors.
122 Guarantee your servant's welfare;
    do not let the arrogant oppress me.
123 My eyes long to see your salvation
    and the justice of your promise.
124 Act with kindness toward your servant;
    teach me your laws.
125 I am your servant; give me discernment
    that I may know your decrees.
126 It is time for the LORD to act;
    they have disobeyed your teaching.
127 Truly I love your commands
    more than the finest gold.
128 Thus I follow all your precepts;
    every wrong way I hate.

PE

129 Wonderful are your decrees;
    therefore I observe them.
130 The revelation of your words sheds light,
    gives understanding to the simple.
131 I sigh with open mouth,
    yearning for your commands.
132 Turn to me and be gracious,*
    your edict for lovers of your name.
133 Steady my feet in accord with your promise;
    do not let iniquity lead me.
134 Free me from human oppression,
    that I may keep your precepts.
135 Let your face shine upon your servant;
    teach me your laws.
136 My eyes shed streams of tears
    because your teaching is not followed.

SADHE

137 You are righteous, LORD,
    and just are your edicts.*
138 You have issued your decrees in justice
    and in surpassing faithfulness.
139 I am consumed with rage,
    because my foes forget your words.
140 Your servant loves your promise;
    it has been proved by fire.
141 Though belittled and despised,
    I do not forget your precepts.

119, 100: Jb 32, 6; Wis 4, 8–9.   119, 108: Ps 50, 14.23; Heb 13,
119, 103: Ps 19, 11.   15.
119, 105: Ps 18, 29; Prv 6, 23.

119, 115: Pss 6, 9; 139, 19; Jb   119, 132: Pss 25, 16; 86, 16.
        21, 14.   119, 137: Tb 3, 2.

142 Your justice is forever right,
　　your teaching forever true.
143 Though distress and anguish come upon me,
　　your commands are my delight.
144 Your decrees are forever just;
　　give me discernment that I may live.

QOPH

145 I call with all my heart, O LORD;
　　answer me that I may observe your laws.
146 I call to you to save me
　　that I may keep your decrees.
147 I rise before dawn and cry out;
　　I put my hope in your words.
148 My eyes greet the night watches
　　as I meditate on your promise.*
149 Hear my voice in your love, O LORD;
　　by your edict give me life.
150 Malicious persecutors draw near me;
　　they are far from your teaching.
151 You are near, O LORD;
　　reliable are all your commands.
152 Long have I known from your decrees
　　that you have established them forever.

RESH

153 Look at my affliction and rescue me,
　　for I have not forgotten your teaching.
154 Take up my cause and redeem me;*
　　for the sake of your promise give me life.
155 Salvation is far from sinners
　　because they do not cherish your laws.
156 Your compassion is great, O LORD;
　　in accord with your edicts give me life.
157 Though my persecutors and foes are many
　　I do not turn from your decrees.
158 I view the faithless with loathing,*
　　because they do not heed your promise.
159 See how I love your precepts, LORD;
　　in your kindness give me life.
160 Your every word is enduring;
　　all your just edicts are forever.

SHIN

161 Princes persecute me without reason,
　　but my heart reveres only your word.
162 I rejoice at your promise,
　　as one who has found rich spoil.
163 Falsehood I hate and abhor;
　　your teaching I love.
164 Seven times a day I praise you
　　because your edicts are just.
165 Lovers of your teaching have much peace;*
　　for them there is no stumbling block.
166 I look for your salvation, LORD,
　　and I fulfill your commands.
167 I observe your decrees;
　　I love them very much.
168 I observe your precepts and decrees;
　　all my ways are before you.

TAW

169 Let my cry come before you, LORD;*
　　in keeping with your word give me
　　discernment.
170 Let my prayer come before you;
　　rescue me according to your promise.
171 May my lips pour forth your praise,
　　because you teach me your laws.
172 May my tongue sing of your promise,
　　for all your commands are just.
173 Keep your hand ready to help me,
　　for I have chosen your precepts.
174 I long for your salvation, LORD;
　　your teaching is my delight.
175 Let me live to praise you;
　　may your edicts give me help.
176 I have wandered like a lost sheep;
　　seek out your servant,
　　for I do not forget your
　　commands.*

PSALM 120†

Prayer of a Returned Exile

1† A song of ascents.

I

The LORD answered me
　　when I called in my distress:*
2 LORD, deliver me from lying lips,
　　from treacherous tongues.*

II

3† What will the Lord inflict on you,
　　O treacherous tongue,

---

† **Ps 120:** A thanksgiving, reporting divine rescue (1) yet with fervent prayer for further protection against lying attackers (2–4). The psalmist is acutely conscious of living away from God's own land where divine peace prevails (5–7).
　120, 1: *Song of ascents:* Pss 120–134 all begin with this superscription. Most probably these fifteen psalms once formed a collection of psalms sung when pilgrims went to Jerusalem, since one "ascended" to Jerusalem (1 Kgs 12, 28; Pss 24, 3; 122, 4; Lk 2, 42) or to the house of God or to an altar (1 Kgs 12, 33; 2 Kgs 23, 2; Ps 24, 3). Less probable is the explanation that these psalms were sung by the exiles when they "ascended" to Jerusalem from Babylonia (cf Ezr 7, 9). The idea, found in the Mishnah, that the fifteen steps on

which the Levites sang corresponded to these fifteen psalms (*Middot* 2, 5) must underlie the Vulgate translation *canticum graduum*, "song of the steps" or "gradual song."
　120, 3: *More besides:* a common curse formula in Hebrew was "May the Lord do such and such evils to you [the evils being specified], and add still more to them." Cf 1 Sm 3, 17; 14, 44; 25, 22. Here the psalmist is at a loss for a suitable malediction.

119, 148: Pss 63, 7; 77, 7.
119, 154: Ps 43, 1.
119, 158: Ps 139, 22.
119, 165: Ps 72, 7.
119, 169: Ps 88, 3.
119, 176: Is 53, 6; Jer 50, 6;
　　　Lk 15, 1–7.
120, 1: Jon 2, 3.
120, 2: Ps 12, 3–5; Sir 51, 3.

and what more besides?
4† A warrior's sharpened arrows
    and fiery coals of brushwood!*

III

5† Alas, I was an alien in Meshech,
    I lived near the tents of Kedar!
6 Too long did I live
    among those who hated peace.
7 When I spoke of peace,
    they were for war.*

PSALM 121 †

The LORD My Guardian
¹† A song of ascents.

I

I raise my eyes toward the
    mountains.
From where will my help come?*
2 My help comes from the LORD,
    the maker of heaven and earth.*

II

3 God will not allow your foot to
    slip;*
    your guardian does not sleep.
4 Truly, the guardian of Israel
    never slumbers nor sleeps.
5† The LORD is your guardian;
    the LORD is your shade
    at your right hand.*
6 By day the sun cannot harm you,
    nor the moon by night.*
7 The LORD will guard you from all
    evil,
    will always guard your life.*
8 The LORD will guard your coming
    and going
    both now and forever.*

PSALM 122 †

A Pilgrim's Prayer for Jerusalem
¹ A song of ascents. Of David.

I

I rejoiced when they said to me,
    "Let us go to the house of the LORD."*
2 And now our feet are standing
    within your gates, Jerusalem.
3† Jerusalem, built as a city,
    walled round about.*
4 Here the tribes have come,
    the tribes of the LORD,
    As it was decreed for Israel,
    to give thanks to the name of the LORD.*
5 Here are the thrones of justice,
    the thrones of the house of David.

II

6 For the peace of Jerusalem pray:
    "May those who love you prosper!
7 May peace be within your ramparts,
    prosperity within your towers."*
8 For family and friends I say,
    "May peace be yours."
9 For the house of the LORD, our God,
    I pray,
    "May blessings be yours."

PSALM 123 †

Reliance on the LORD
¹ A song of ascents.

To you I raise my eyes,
    to you enthroned in heaven.*
2 Yes, like the eyes of a servant
    on the hand of his master,
Like the eyes of a maid
    on the hand of her mistress,

120, 4: *Coals of brushwood:* coals made from the stalk of the broom plant burn with intense heat. The psalmist thinks of lighted coals cast at his enemies.
120, 5: *Meshech* was in the far north (Gn 10, 2) and *Kedar* was a tribe of the north Arabian desert (Gn 25, 13). The psalmist may be thinking generally of all aliens living among inhospitable peoples.
Ps 121: A blessing given to someone embarking on a dangerous journey, whether a soldier going on a campaign or a pilgrim returning home from the temple. People look anxiously at the wooded hills. Will God protect them on their journey (1)? The speaker declares that God is not confined to a place or a time (2), that every step is guarded (3–4); night and day (5–6) God watches over their every movement (7–8).
121, 1: *The mountains:* possibly Mount Zion, the site of the temple and hence of safety, but more probably mountains as a place of dangers, causing anxiety to the psalmist.
121, 5-6: The image of shade, a symbol of protection, is apt: God as shade protects from the harmful effects that ancients believed were caused by the sun and moon.
Ps 122: A song of Zion, sung by pilgrims obeying the law to visit Jerusalem three times on a journey. The singer anticipates joining the procession into the city (1–3). Jerusalem is a place of encounter,

where the people praise God (4) and hear the divine justice mediated by the king (5). The very buildings bespeak God's power (cf Ps 48, 13–15). May the grace of this place transform the people's lives (6–9)!
122, 3: *Walled round about:* literally, "which is joined to it," probably referring both to the density of the buildings and to the dense population.
Ps 123: A lament that begins as a prayer of an individual (1), who expresses by a touching comparison exemplary confidence in God (2). The psalm ends in prayer that God relieve the people's humiliation at the hands of the arrogant (3–4).

120, 4: Pss 11, 6; 140, 11; Prv
    16, 27.
120, 7: Pss 35, 20; 140, 3–4.
121, 1: Jer 3, 23.
121, 2: Pss 124, 8; 146, 6.
121, 3: Pss 66, 9; 91, 12; 1 Sm
    2, 9; Prv 3, 23.
121, 5: Pss 16, 8; 73, 23.
121, 6: Wis 18, 3; Is 25, 4; 49,
    10.
121, 7: Ps 97, 10.
121, 8: Dt 28, 6.
122, 1: Pss 43, 3–4; 84, 2–5.
122, 3: Ps 48, 13–14.
122, 4: Dt 16, 16.
122, 7: Ps 128, 5.
123, 1: Pss 25, 15; 119, 82;
    141, 8.

So our eyes are on the LORD our God,
    till we are shown favor.
3 Show us favor, LORD, show us favor,
    for we have our fill of contempt.*
4 We have our fill of insult from the insolent,
    of disdain from the arrogant.

PSALM 124†

God, the Rescuer of the People

¹ A song of ascents. Of David.

I

Had not the LORD been with us,
    let Israel say,*
2 Had not the LORD been with us,
    when people rose against us,
3 They would have swallowed us alive,*
    for their fury blazed against us.
4 The waters would have engulfed us,
    the torrent overwhelmed us;*
5   seething waters would have drowned
    us.

II

6 Blessed be the LORD, who did not leave us
    to be torn by their fangs.
7 We escaped with our lives
    like a bird from the fowler's snare;
    the snare was broken and we escaped.

8† Our help is the name of the LORD,
    the maker of heaven and earth.*

PSALM 125†

Israel's Protector

¹ A song of ascents.

I

Like Mount Zion are they
    who trust in the LORD,
    unshakable, forever enduring.*
2 As mountains surround Jerusalem,
    the LORD surrounds his people
    both now and forever.*

II

3† The scepter of the wicked will not
    prevail
    in the land given to the just,
Lest the just themselves
    turn their hands to evil.

III

4 Do good, LORD, to the good,
    to those who are upright of heart.*
5 But those who turn aside to crooked
    ways
    may the LORD send down with the
    wicked.*
Peace upon Israel!*

The LORD Was on Our Side

LIVE IT!

You often hear a team or group that has just played well or completed a great task say, "God was with us." The writer of Psalm 124 expressed the same sentiment in verses 1–2. What a gift it is to recognize God's help in our life. It is God who carries us when we are down, who rescues us when we are in trouble, and who gives us the talent that we have.

Are you ever afraid, or do you ever feel lost? Read Psalm 124, and be assured that others have felt the same way. Whether you are unsure about school, a job, a relationship, or your future, just remember, "Our help is in the name of the LORD, / the maker of heaven and earth" (verse 8).

▶ Psalm 124

†

Ps 124: A thanksgiving which teaches that Israel's very existence is owed to God who rescues them. In the first part Israel's enemies are compared to the mythic sea dragon (2b–3a; cf Jer 51, 34) and Flood (3b–5; cf Is 51, 9–10). The psalm heightens the malice of human enemies by linking them to the primordial enemies of God's creation. Israel is a bird freed from the trapper's snare (6–8)—freed originally from Pharaoh and now from the current danger.

124, 8: *Our help is the name:* for the idiom, see Ex 18, 4.

Ps 125: In response to exilic anxieties about the ancient promises of restoration, the psalm expresses confidence that God will surround the people as the mountains surround Zion (1–2). The just will not be contaminated by the wicked (3). May God judge between the two groups (4–5).

125, 3: *The land given to the just:* literally, "the lot of the just." The promised land was divided among the tribes of Israel by lot (Nm 26, 55; Jos 18). *The just* are the members of the people who are obedient to God. If the domination of the wicked were to continue in the land, even the just would be infected by their evil attitudes.

*
123, 3: Ps 44, 13–14; Jb 12, 4.
124, 1: Ps 129, 1.
124, 3: Prv 1, 12.
124, 4: Pss 18, 5; 69, 2.
124, 8: Pss 121, 2; 146, 6.
125, 1: Prv 10, 25.
125, 2: Dt 32, 11.
125, 4: Ps 18, 25ff.
125, 5: Prv 3, 32.
125, 5: Ps 128, 6.

PSALM 126†

The Reversal of Zion's Fortunes
¹ A song of ascents.

I

When the LORD restored the fortunes of Zion,*
  then we thought we were dreaming.
² Our mouths were filled with laughter;
  our tongues sang for joy.*
Then it was said among the nations,
  "The LORD has done great things for them."
³ The LORD had done great things for us;
  Oh, how happy we were!
⁴† Restore again our fortunes, LORD,
  like the dry stream beds of the Negeb.

II

⁵ Those who sow in tears
  will reap with cries of joy.*
⁶ Those who go forth weeping,
  carrying sacks of seed,
Will return with cries of joy,
  carrying their bundled sheaves.

PSALM 127†

The Need of God's Blessing
¹ A song of ascents. Of Solomon.

I

Unless the LORD build the house,
  they labor in vain who build.
Unless the LORD guard the city,
  in vain does the guard keep watch.
² It is vain for you to rise early
  and put off your rest at night,
To eat bread earned by hard toil—
  all this God gives to his beloved in sleep.*

II

³ Children too are a gift from the LORD,
  the fruit of the womb, a reward.*
⁴ Like arrows in the hand of a warrior
  are the children born in one's youth.
⁵† Blessed are they whose quivers are full.

They will never be shamed
  contending with foes at the gate.

PSALM 128†

The Happy Home of the Just
¹† A song of ascents.

I

Happy are all who fear the LORD,
  who walk in the ways of God.*
² What your hands provide you will enjoy;
  you will be happy and prosper:*
³ Like a fruitful vine
  your wife within your home,
Like olive plants
  your children around your table.*
⁴ Just so will they be blessed
  who fear the LORD.

II

⁵ May the LORD bless you from Zion,
  all the days of your life*
That you may share Jerusalem's joy
⁶   and live to see your children's
  children.*
Peace upon Israel!*

PSALM 129†

Against Israel's Enemies
¹ A song of ascents.

I

Much have they oppressed me from my youth,
  now let Israel say.*
² Much have they oppressed me from my youth,*
  yet they have not prevailed.
³ Upon my back the plowers plowed,
  as they traced their long furrows.*
⁴† But the just LORD cut me free
  from the ropes of the yoke of the wicked.

II

⁵ May they be scattered in disgrace,
  all who hate Zion.

Ps 126: A lament probably sung shortly after Israel's return from exile. The people rejoice that they are in Zion (1–3) but mere presence in the holy city is not enough; they must pray for the prosperity and the fertility of the land (4). The last verses are probably an oracle of promise: the painful work of sowing will be crowned with life (5–6).

126, 4: *Like the dry stream beds of the Negeb:* the psalmist prays for rain in such abundance that the dry riverbeds will run.

Ps 127: The psalm puts together two proverbs (1–2 and 3–5) on God establishing "houses" or families. The prosperity of human groups is not the work of humans but the gift of God.

127, 5: *At the gate:* the reference is not to enemies besieging the walls of a city but to adversaries in litigation. Law courts functioned in the open area near the main city gate. The more adult sons a man had, the more forceful he would appear in disputes. Cf Prv 31, 23.

Ps 128: A statement that the ever-reliable God will bless the reverent (1). God's blessing is concrete: satisfaction and prosperity, a fertile spouse and abundant children (2–4). The perspective is that of the adult male, ordinarily the ruler and representative of the house-

hold to the community. The last verses extend the blessing to all the people for generations to come (5–6).

128, 1: *All who fear the LORD:* literally, singular: "the one fearing," is used in a typical sense and so is translated by the plural.

Ps 129: A psalm giving thanks for God's many rescues of Israel over the long course of their history (1–4); the people pray that their oppressors never know the joy of harvest (5–8).

129, 4: *The ropes of the yoke of the wicked:* usually understood as the rope for yoking animals to the plow. If it is severed, the plowing (cf 3) comes to a halt.

126, 1: Ps 14, 7.
126, 2: Jb 8, 21.
126, 5: Bar 4, 23; Is 65, 19.
127, 2: Eccl 2, 24.
127, 3: Pss 115, 14; 128, 3; Dt 28, 11; Prv 17, 6.
128, 1: Ps 112, 1.
128, 2: Ps 112, 3.

128, 3: Jb 29, 5; Ps 144, 12.
128, 5: Pss 20, 3; 134, 3.
128, 6: Jb 42, 16; Prv 17, 6.
128, 6: Ps 125, 5.
129, 1: Ps 124, 1.
129, 2: Ps 118, 13.
129, 3: Is 51, 23.

6† May they be like grass on the rooftops
  withered in early growth,*
7 Never to fill the reaper's hands,
  nor the arms of the binders of sheaves,
8† With none passing by to call out:
  "The blessing of the LORD be upon you!
  We bless you in the name of the LORD!"*

PSALM 130†

Prayer for Pardon and Mercy
¹ A song of ascents.

I

Out of the depths† I call to you, LORD;
2   Lord, hear my cry!
May your ears be attentive
  to my cry for mercy.*
3 If you, LORD, mark our sins,
  Lord, who can stand?*
4† But with you is forgiveness
  and so you are revered.

II

5 I wait with longing for the LORD,
  my soul waits for his word.*
6 My soul looks for the Lord
  more than sentinels for daybreak.*
More than sentinels for daybreak,
7   let Israel look for the LORD,
For with the LORD is kindness,
  with him is full redemption,*
8 And God will redeem Israel
  from all their sins.*

PSALM 131†

Humble Trust in God
¹ A song of ascents. Of David.

LORD, my heart is not proud;
  nor are my eyes haughty.
I do not busy myself with great matters,
  with things too sublime for me.*
2 Rather, I have stilled my soul,
  hushed it like a weaned child.

Like a weaned child on its mother's lap,
  so is my soul within me.*
3 Israel, hope in the LORD,
  now and forever.

PSALM 132†

The Covenant between David and God
¹ A song of ascents.

I

LORD, remember David
  and all his anxious care;†

Hold Me, Mother God

Psalm 131 is a humble prayer of childlike trust. It gives the wonderful image of God holding us like a child in a mother's lap. Like a mother, God hugs us close and keeps us safe and warm and protected. We don't need to solve problems or be concerned about our performance. We are loved just because we are us. God created us; God loves us and cradles us.

Do you remember sitting quietly in your mother's or grandmother's lap when you were a small child? If so, do you recall her telling you stories or singing you lullabies? If you do not have such memories, have you ever seen a mother calm her child with songs and stories? How is God's love like that? In prayer, imagine being held by God, as a child is held by a mother. You might be surprised at how safe and secure you feel!

▸ Psalm 131

129, 6: *Like grass on the rooftops:* after the spring rains, grass would sprout from the coat of mud with which the flat roofs of simple houses were covered, but when the dry summer began there was no moisture in the thin roof-covering to sustain the grass.

129, 8: *The blessing of the LORD be upon you!:* harvesters greeted one another with such blessings. Cf Ru 2, 4.

Ps 130: This lament, a Penitential Psalm, is the *De profundis* used in liturgical prayers for the faithful departed. In deep sorrow the psalmist cries to God (1–2), asking for mercy (3–4). The psalmist's trust (5–6) becomes a model for the people (7–8).

130, 1: *The depths:* Sheol here is a metaphor of total misery. Deep anguish makes the psalmist feel "like those descending to the pit" (Ps 143, 7).

130, 4: *And so you are revered:* the experience of God's mercy leads one to a greater sense of God.

Ps 131: A song of trust, in which the psalmist gives up self-sufficiency (1), like a babe enjoying the comfort of its mother's lap (2), thus providing a model for Israel's faith (3).

Ps 132: A song for a liturgical ceremony in which the ark, the throne of Israel's God, was carried in procession to the temple. The singer asks that David's care for the proper housing of the ark be regarded with favor (1–5), and tells how it was brought to Jerusalem (6–10). There follows God's promise of favor to the Davidic dynasty (11–12) and to Zion (13–17). The transfer of the ark to the tent in Jerusalem is described in 2 Sm 6.

132, 1: *All his anxious care:* to build the temple. Cf 2 Sm 7, 1–17 and 1 Kgs 8, 17.

129, 6: Is 37, 27.
129, 8: Ps 118, 26.
130, 2: Pss 5, 2–3; 55, 2–3;
  86, 6; Lam 3, 55–56;
  Jon 2, 3.
130, 3: Na 1, 6.
130, 5: Ps 119, 81.

130, 6: Is 21, 11; 26, 9.
130, 7: Pss 86, 15; 100, 5;
  103, 8.
130, 8: Ps 25, 22; Mt 1, 21.
131, 1: Ps 139, 6.
131, 2: Is 66, 12–13.

2† How he swore an oath to the LORD,
   vowed to the Mighty One of Jacob:

3 "I will not enter the house where I live,*
   nor lie on the couch where I sleep;

4 I will give my eyes no sleep,
   my eyelids no rest,

5 Till I find a home for the LORD,
   a dwelling for the Mighty One of
   Jacob."

6† "We have heard of it in Ephrathah;
   we have found it in the fields of
   Jaar.

7 Let us enter God's dwelling;
   let us worship at God's footstool."*

8 "Arise, LORD, come to your resting
   place,*
   you and your majestic ark.

9 Your priests will be clothed with
   justice;
   your faithful will shout for joy."

10 For the sake of David your servant,
   do not reject your anointed.

II

11 The LORD swore an oath to David,
   a pledge never to be broken:*
   "Your own offspring* I will set upon
   your throne.

12 If your sons observe my covenant,
   the laws I shall teach them,
   Their sons, in turn,
   shall sit forever on your throne."

13 Yes, the LORD has chosen Zion,
   desired it for a dwelling:

14 "This is my resting place forever;
   here I will dwell, for I desire it.

15 I will bless Zion with meat;
   its poor I will fill with bread.

16 I will clothe its priests with blessing;
   its faithful shall shout for joy.*

17† There I will make a horn sprout for
   David's line;*
   I will set a lamp for my anointed.

18 His foes I will clothe with shame,
   but on him my crown shall
   gleam."

?did you KNOW?

Jerusalem, Zion, City of David

Jerusalem, Zion, City of David—you have probably noticed that these three names keep popping up throughout the Psalms. They all refer to the heart of Israel, the city of Jerusalem. When David became king of the united tribes of Israel, he needed a neutral place between the northern and southern tribes. He conquered Jerusalem and elevated it as the political and religious center—thus, Jerusalem was also known as the City of David. Mount Zion, located within Jerusalem, was the site of the Temple—the sacred place where God dwelt. So, Zion became another way to refer to Jerusalem.

At that time, the Israelites felt that Jerusalem was invincible because it was God's dwelling place. But eventually, Jerusalem and the Temple were destroyed. Afterward, a hope arose that one day, a messiah from David's line would renew Jerusalem and true worship of God on Zion. The New Testament portrays Jesus as the fulfillment of this hope.

▶ Psalm 132

P
S

PSALM 133†

A Vision of a Blessed Community

1† A song of ascents. Of David.

How good it is, how pleasant,
   where the people dwell as one!

---

† 132, 2.5: *Mighty One of Jacob:* one of the titles of Israel's God. Cf Gn 49, 24; Is 49, 26; 60, 16.
   132, 6: *Ephrathah:* the homeland of David. Cf Ru 4, 11. *The fields of Jaar:* poetic for Kiriath-jearim, a town west of Jerusalem, where the ark remained for several generations. Cf 1 Sm 7, 1–2; 2 Sm 6, 2; 1 Chr 13, 5–6.
   132, 17: *A horn sprout for David's line:* the image of the horn, a symbol of strength, is combined with that of a "sprout," a term used for the Davidic descendant (cf Jer 23, 5; 33, 15; Zec 3, 8; 6, 12). Early Christians referred the latter designation to Christ as son of David (Lk 1, 69).
   Ps 133: A benediction over a peaceful community, most probably the people Israel, but appropriate too for Israelite families (1). The history of Israel, whether of its ancestors in the book of Genesis or of

later periods, was a history of distinct groups struggling to live in unity. Here that unity is declared blessed, like the holy oils upon the priest Aaron or the dew of the rainless summer that waters the crops (2–3).
   133, 1: *The people:* literally, "brothers," i.e., male and female members of a kin group or people—most probably, the people Israel.

132, 3: 2 Sm 7; 1 Chr 28, 2.
132, 7: Ps 99, 5.
132, 8–10: Pss 2, 2; 89, 21; 95, 11; Nm 10, 35; 2 Chr 6, 41–42; Sir 24, 7.
132, 11: Ps 110, 4; 2 Sm 7, 12.
132, 11–14: Ps 68, 17; 1 Kgs 8, 13; Sir 24, 7.
132, 16: 2 Chr 6, 41; Is 61, 10.
132, 17: Is 11, 1; Jer 33, 15; Ez 29, 21; Zec 3, 8; Lk 1, 69.

2† Like precious ointment on the head,*
   running down upon the beard,
Upon the beard of Aaron,
   upon the collar of his robe.
3† Like dew of Hermon coming down
   upon the mountains of Zion.*
There the LORD has lavished blessings,
   life for evermore!*

PSALM 134†

Exhortation to the Night Watch to Bless God

1† A song of ascents.

Come, bless the LORD,
   all you servants of the LORD
Who stand in the house of the LORD
   through the long hours of night.*
2 Lift up your hands toward the
   sanctuary,*
   and bless the LORD.
3 May the LORD who made heaven and
   earth*
   bless you from Zion.

PSALM 135†

Praise of God, the Ruler and Benefactor of Israel

1 Hallelujah!

I

Praise the name of the LORD!
   Praise, you servants of the LORD,*
2 Who stand in the house of the LORD,
   in the courts of the house of our
   God!*
3 Praise the LORD; the LORD is good!
   Sing to God's name; it is gracious!
4† For the LORD has chosen Jacob,
   Israel as a treasured possession.*

II

5 I know that the LORD is great,
   our Lord is greater than all gods.*

6 Whatever the LORD wishes
   he does in heaven and on earth,
   in the seas and in all the deeps.*
7 He raises storm clouds from the end of the
   earth,
   makes lightning and rain,
   brings forth wind from the
   storehouse.*

III

8 He struck down Egypt's firstborn,*
   human and beast alike,
9 And sent signs and portents against you,
   Egypt,
   against Pharaoh and all his servants.
10 The Lord struck down many nations,*
   slew mighty kings—
11 Sihon, king of the Amorites,
   Og, king of Bashan,
   all the kings of Canaan—
12 And made their land a heritage,
   a heritage for Israel his people.
13 O LORD, your name is forever,
   your renown, from age to age!*
14 For the LORD defends his people,
   shows mercy to his servants.*

IV

15 The idols of the nations are silver and
   gold,*
   the work of human hands.
16 They have mouths but speak not;
   they have eyes but see not;
17 They have ears but hear not;
   no breath is in their mouths.
18 Their makers shall be like them,
   all who trust in them.

V

19 House of Israel, bless the LORD!*
   House of Aaron, bless the LORD!
20 House of Levi, bless the LORD!
   You who fear the LORD, bless the LORD!
21 Blessed from Zion be the LORD,
   who dwells in Jerusalem!
Hallelujah!

133, 2: *Ointment:* oil was used at the consecration of the high priest (Ex 30, 22–33).

133, 3: *Dew:* dew was an important source of moisture in the dry climate (Gn 27, 28; Hos 14, 6). *Hermon:* the majestic snow-capped mountain visible in the north of Palestine.

Ps 134: A brief liturgy exhorting the temple singers to acknowledge the great deeds of God at a night service (cf Is 30, 29). Mount Zion is the place from which blessings affect the lives of humans, for there Israel's God dwells.

134, 1: *Servants of the LORD:* priests and Levites. Cf Dt 10, 8; Pss 113, 1; 135, 1; Dn 3, 84–85.

Ps 135: The hymn begins and ends with an invitation to praise God (1–3.19–20) for the great act of choosing Israel (4). The story of Israel's emergence as a people is told in 5–14; God created and redeemed the people, easily conquering all opposition. God's defeat of hostile powers means that the powers themselves and their images

are useless (15–18). The last three verses appear also in Ps 115, 4–8.

135, 4: Though all nations are God's, Israel has a special status as God's "treasured" people: Ex 19, 5; Dt 7, 6; 14, 2; 26, 18; Mal 3, 17.

133, 2: Ex 30, 25.30.
133, 3: Hos 14, 6.
133, 3: Dt 28, 8; 30, 20.
134, 1: Ps 135, 1–2; 1 Chr 9, 33.
134, 2: Pss 28, 2; 141, 2.
134, 3: Pss 20, 3; 128, 5; Nm 6, 24.
135, 1: Ps 113, 1.
135, 2: Ps 134, 1.
135, 4: Pss 33, 12; 144, 15; Ex 19, 6; Dt 7, 6.
135, 5: Ps 95, 3; Ex 18, 11.
135, 6: Ps 115, 3.
135, 7: Ps 148, 8; Jer 10, 13; 51, 16; Jb 37, 9.
135, 8–9: Pss 78, 51; 105, 27.36; 136, 10; Ex 12, 29.
135, 10–12: Nm 21, 21–35; Dt 2, 24—3, 17; Ps 136, 17–22.
135, 13: Ps 102, 13; Ex 3, 15.
135, 14: Dt 32, 36.
135, 15–18: Ps 115, 4–6.8.
135, 19–20: Ps 118, 2–4.

PSALM 136†

Hymn of Thanksgiving for God's Everlasting Love

I

1 Praise the LORD, who is so good;*
      God's love endures forever;
2 Praise the God of gods;
      God's love endures forever;
3 Praise the Lord of lords;
      God's love endures forever;

II

4 Who alone has done great wonders,*
      God's love endures forever;
5 Who skillfully made the heavens,*
      God's love endures forever;
6 Who spread the earth upon the waters,*
      God's love endures forever;
7 Who made the great lights,
      God's love endures forever;
8 The sun to rule the day,
      God's love endures forever;
9 The moon and stars to rule the night,*
      God's love endures forever;

III

10 Who struck down the firstborn of Egypt,*
       God's love endures forever;
11 And led Israel from their midst,
       God's love endures forever;
12 With mighty hand and outstretched arm,*
       God's love endures forever;
13 Who split in two the Red Sea
       God's love endures forever;
14 And led Israel through,
       God's love endures forever;
15 But swept Pharaoh and his army into the Red
       Sea,*
       God's love endures forever;
16 Who led the people through the desert,*
       God's love endures forever;

IV

17 Who struck down great kings,*
       God's love endures forever;
18 Slew powerful kings,
       God's love endures forever;

---

† **Ps 136:** The hymn praises Israel's God ("the God of gods," 2), who has created the world in which Israel lives. The refrain occurring after every line suggests that a speaker and chorus sang the psalm in antiphonal fashion. A single act of God is described in 4–25: God arranges the heavens and the earth as the environment for human community, and then creates the community by freeing them and giving them land. In the final section (23–25) God, who created the people and gave them land, continues to protect and nurture them.

Catholic Connections

CALLED TO RESPOND

Have you ever been to a football game or basketball game and heard a cheerleader or fan begin a chant and suddenly everyone in the crowd is chanting along? "De-fense, de-fense, de-fense. . . ." Soon the chant becomes a rousing anthem, expressing enthusiastic support for the team.

In a similar way, Psalm 136 must have been a prayer that managed to rouse the Israelites in their praise of God. Imagine a cantor starting slowly and softly with the first part of the first verse and then building in enthusiasm and volume through the succeeding verses as the community continuously responds, "God's love endures forever." That kind of prayer and response would have been a powerful way for the community to pray.

The Psalms are prayers that lend themselves well to such call-and-response techniques. We pray one of these ancient song-prayers at every Mass. After the first reading of the Mass, the community sings the responsorial psalm. God has spoken, and the community responds to the cantor with a refrain that expresses gratitude, praise, and faith. The responsorial psalm invites us to open our hearts and to dialogue with God, who has spoken first.

This Sunday at Mass, pay close attention to the responsorial psalm. Be sure to sing the response (remember, you don't need a great voice to sing in church), and as you do, imagine that God is hanging on to your every word.

▶ **Psalm 136**

136, 1: Pss 100, 5; 118, 1.
136, 4: Ps 72, 18.
136, 5: Gn 1, 9–19.
136, 6: Ps 24, 2.
136, 9: Jer 31, 35.
136, 10: Ex 12, 29.51; 14,
      22.27; 15, 22; Pss 78,
      51–52; 135, 8.
136, 12: Dt 4, 34.
136, 15: Ex 14, 21f.
136, 16: Dt 8, 2.15.
136, 17–22: Ps 135, 10–12.

P
S

19 Sihon, king of the Amorites,
  God's love endures forever;
20 Og, king of Bashan,
  God's love endures forever;
21 And made their lands a heritage,
  God's love endures forever;
22† A heritage for Israel, God's servant,
  God's love endures forever.

V

23 The LORD remembered us in our misery,
  God's love endures forever;
24 Freed us from our foes,
  God's love endures forever;
25 And gives food to all flesh,
  God's love endures forever.

VI

26 Praise the God of heaven,
  God's love endures forever.

PSALM 137†

Sorrow and Hope in Exile

I

1 By the rivers of Babylon
  we sat mourning and weeping
  when we remembered Zion.*
2† On the poplars of that land
  we hung up our harps.*
3 There our captors asked us
  for the words of a song;
  Our tormentors, for a joyful song:
  "Sing for us a song of Zion!"
4 But how could we sing a song of the
  LORD
  in a foreign land?

II

5 If I forget you, Jerusalem,
  may my right hand wither.*
6 May my tongue stick to my palate
  if I do not remember you,
  If I do not exalt Jerusalem
  beyond all my delights.

III

7 Remember, LORD, against Edom
  that day at Jerusalem.
  They said: "Level it, level it
  down to its foundations!"*
8 Fair Babylon, you destroyer,
  happy those who pay you back
  the evil you have done us!*
9† Happy those who seize your children
  and smash them against a rock.*

PSALM 138†

Hymn of a Grateful Heart
1 Of David.

I

I thank you, LORD, with all my heart;*
 before the gods† to you I sing.
2 I bow low toward your holy temple;
  I praise your name for your fidelity and
  love.
 For you have exalted over all
  your name and your promise.
3 When I cried out, you answered;
  you strengthened my spirit.

II

4 All the kings of earth will praise you,
  LORD,
  when they hear the words of your
  mouth.
5 They will sing of the ways of the LORD:
  "How great is the glory of the LORD!"
6 The LORD is on high, but cares for the
  lowly*
  and knows the proud from afar.
7 Though I walk in the midst of dangers,
  you guard my life when my enemies
  rage.
 You stretch out your hand;
  your right hand saves me.
8 The LORD is with me to the end.
  LORD, your love endures forever.
  Never forsake the work of your hands!

---

† 136, 22: *A heritage for Israel:* the land was given to Israel by God to be handed on to future generations.

Ps 137: A temple singer refuses to sing the people's sacred songs in an alien land despite demands from Babylonian captors (1–4). The singer swears an oath by what is most dear to a musician—hands and tongue—to exalt Jerusalem always (5–6). The psalm ends with a prayer that the old enemies of Jerusalem, Edom and Babylon, be destroyed (7–9).

137, 2: *Poplars:* sometimes incorrectly translated "willow." The Euphrates poplar is a high tree common on riverbanks in the Orient.

137, 9: *Happy those who seize your children and smash them against a rock:* the infants represent the future generations, and so must be destroyed if the enemy is truly to be eradicated.

Ps 138: A thanksgiving to God, who came to the rescue of the psalmist. Divine rescue was not the result of the psalmist's virtues but of God's loving fidelity (1–3). The act is not a private transaction but a public act that stirs the surrounding nations to praise God's greatness and care for the people (4–6). The psalmist, having experienced salvation, trusts that God will always be there in moments of danger (7–8).

138, 1: *Before the gods:* i.e., heavenly beings, who were completely subordinate to Israel's God. The earthly temple represents the heavenly palace of God.

137, 1: Ez 3, 15; Lam 3, 48.
137, 2: Is 24, 8; Lam 5, 14.
137, 5: Jer 51, 50.
137, 7: Jer 49, 7; Lam 4,
 21–22; Ez 25, 12–14.
137, 8: Is 47, 1–3; Jer 50–51.
137, 9: Hos 14, 1.
138, 1: Ps 9, 1.
138, 6: Lk 1, 51–52.

PSALM 139†

The All-knowing and Ever-present God
¹ For the leader. A psalm of David.

I

LORD, you have probed me, you know me:
²†   you know when I sit and stand;*
     you understand my thoughts from afar.
³   My travels and my rest you mark;
     with all my ways you are familiar.
⁴   Even before a word is on my tongue,
     LORD, you know it all.
⁵   Behind and before you encircle me
     and rest your hand upon me.
⁶   Such knowledge is beyond me,
     far too lofty for me to reach.*

II

⁷   Where can I hide from your spirit?
     From your presence, where can I flee?
⁸   If I ascend to the heavens, you are
          there;
     if I lie down in Sheol, you are there
          too.*
⁹† If I fly with the wings of dawn
     and alight beyond the sea,
¹⁰ Even there your hand will guide me,
     your right hand hold me fast.
¹¹† If I say, "Surely darkness shall hide me,
     and night shall be my light"—
¹² Darkness is not dark for you,
     and night shines as the day.
     Darkness and light are but one.*

CELTIC TRADITIONS

Many people of the British Isles, especially the Irish, have for hundreds of years celebrated their Celtic traditions. Over the years, their Celtic traditions have become fused with their expressions of their Catholic faith. One of the central Celtic Christian themes is the presence and protection of God. Like the psalmist who wrote Psalm 139, the author of "Saint Patrick's Breastplate" illustrates how the Celts call God into their life and world:

> Christ be with me, Christ within me
>   Christ behind me, Christ before me,
> Christ beside me, Christ to win me,
>   Christ to comfort and restore me,
> Christ beneath me, Christ above me,
>   Christ in quiet, Christ in danger,
> Christ in the hearts of all that love me,
>   Christ in mouth of friend or stranger.

(Ian Bradley, *The Celtic Way*, p. 33)

The next time you want to pray for the presence of God, try praying in the Celtic tradition so beautifully expressed in "Saint Patrick's Breastplate."

▶ **Psalm 139**

---

† **Ps 139:** A hymnic meditation on God's omnipresence and omniscience. The psalmist is keenly aware of God's all-knowing gaze (1–6), of God's presence in every part of the universe (7–12), and of God's control over the psalmist's very self (13–16). Summing up 1–16.17–18 express wonder. There is only one place hostile to God's rule—wicked people. The psalmist prays to be removed from their company (19–24).
  139, 2: *When I sit and stand:* in all my physical movement.
  139, 9: *Fly with the wings of dawn:* go to the extremities of the east. *Beyond the sea:* uttermost bounds of the west; the sea is the Mediterranean.
  139, 11: *Night shall be my light:* night to me is what day is to others.

---

* 139, 2: 2 Kgs 19, 27; Jb 12, 3.   139, 8: Jb 23, 8–9; Jer 23,
139, 6: Ps 131, 1.   23–24.
                                                       139, 12: Jb 12, 22.

PS

The Sacredness of Life

"You formed my inmost being; / you knit me in my mother's womb" (Ps 139, 13). Psalm 139 speaks poetically of God's intimate care for each of us, long before we were even formed. It is perhaps the most powerful argument against abortion in the entire Bible. Who can deny that God gave us life long before we actually saw the light of day? How can we deny that every unborn child is fashioned by the hand of God?

It is easy to get caught up in arguments about individual rights and scientific terminology. But this is not about science or government or even when life begins. It is about poetry and love and the faith that God has knit together each of us in our mother's womb. God has great plans for each of us, whether we have been born, are in the womb, or have not yet even been thought of. God knows and loves us, and has through all eternity.

What else is there to say?

▸ Psalm 139

III

13 You formed my inmost being;
    you knit me in my mother's womb.*

14 I praise you, so wonderfully you made me;
    wonderful are your works!
    My very self you knew;

15†   my bones were not hidden from you,
    When I was being made in secret,
    fashioned as in the depths of the earth.

16 Your eyes foresaw my actions;
    in your book all are written down;*
    my days were shaped, before one came to
    be.

IV

17 How precious to me are your designs, O God;
    how vast the sum of them!

18 Were I to count, they would outnumber the
    sands;
    to finish, I would need eternity.*

19 If only you would destroy the wicked, O God,
    and the bloodthirsty would depart from me!*

20 Deceitfully they invoke your name;
    your foes swear faithless oaths.

21 Do I not hate, LORD, those who hate you?
    Those who rise against you, do I not loathe?*

22 With fierce hatred I hate them,
    enemies I count as my own.

V

23 Probe me, God, know my heart;
    try me, know my concerns.*

24† See if my way is crooked,
    then lead me in the ancient paths.

PSALM 140 †

Prayer for Deliverance from the Wicked

¹ For the leader. A psalm of David.

I

2 Deliver me, LORD, from the wicked;
   preserve me from the violent,*

3 From those who plan evil in their hearts,
   who stir up conflicts every day,

4† Who sharpen their tongues like serpents,
   venom of asps upon their lips.*   Selah

II

5 Keep me, LORD, from the clutches of the
   wicked;
   preserve me from the violent,
   who plot to trip me up.*

6† The arrogant have set a trap for me;
   villains have spread a net,
   laid snares for me by the wayside.   Selah

7 I say to the LORD: You are my God;*
   listen, LORD, to the words of my prayer.

139, 15: *The depths of the earth:* figurative language for the womb, stressing the hidden and mysterious operations that occur there.

139, 24: *My way . . . the ancient paths:* the manner of living of our ancestors, who were faithful to God's will. Cf Jer 6, 16.

Ps 140: A lament seeking rescue from violent and treacherous foes (2–6). The psalmist remains trusting (7–8), vigorously praying that the plans of the wicked recoil upon themselves (9–12). A serene statement of praise ends the psalm (13–14). The psalmist is content to be known as one of "the needy," "the poor," "the just," "the upright" (13–14), a class of people expecting divine protection.

140, 4: *Similar metaphors for a wicked tongue are used in Pss* 52, 4; 55, 22; 58, 5.

140, 6: *Have set a trap . . . have spread a net:* the same figure, of hunters setting traps, occurs in Pss 9, 16; 31, 5; 35, 7; 64, 6. Cf Mt 22, 15; Lk 11, 54.

139, 13: Wis 7, 1; Eccl 11, 5; Jb   139, 23: Pss 17, 3; 26, 2.
1, 21.   140, 2: Ps 71, 4.
139, 16: Mal 3, 16.   140, 4: Ps 64, 4; Rom 3, 13.
139, 18: Jb 11, 7.   140, 5: Jer 18, 22; Pss 56, 7;
139, 19: Jb 21, 14.   57, 7.
139, 21: Ps 119, 158.   140, 7: Ps 31, 15.

God Cares for those who Suffer Persecution!

Many of us like to think that persecution rarely occurs. Unfortunately, this is not true. All too frequently, people are persecuted because of their color, their ethnic origin, their political beliefs, or even their faith. Harassment can be as subtle as a rude comment or a patronizing attitude, or as aggressive as a beating or death. Young people know the feeling of persecution. They may experience it because of their origin, the way they look or talk, or what they believe.

Psalm 140 is one of several psalms (see also Psalms 35, 86) and prayers seeking God's help in times of persecution. These typically have two parts. The first part asks for God's protection against persecutors, and the second part praises God's love, justice, and mercy. This illustrates the continual tension for all believers: feeling the need for God's action while at the same time being certain that God cares for them in the midst of their persecution.

For Christians, Jesus is the perfect model of the persecuted person. He was persecuted without reason (Lk 23, 4), and he felt God's absence (Mk 15, 34), but he still put his entire faith and trust in God's will (Mt 26, 39). Following Jesus' example, Christians throughout history have bravely endured persecution, and even death, for their faith.

■ Have you or your family experienced some kind of persecution? If so, how and why? If you have ever participated in some kind of persecution of someone else, pray for forgiveness, and if possible make amends.

■ Thank God for the blessings you have, and ask God for the strength to endure whatever persecutions come your way. Pray for those who are suffering persecution, regardless of the motive.

▶ Psalm 140

---

8 My revered LORD, my strong helper,
   my helmet on the day of battle.
9 LORD, do not grant the desires of the wicked;
   do not let their plots succeed.   Selah
10 Around me they raise their proud heads;
   may the mischief they threaten overwhelm
     them.
11 May God rain burning coals upon them,*
   cast them into the grave never more to rise.
III
12 Slanderers will not survive on earth;
   evil will quickly entrap the violent.
13 For I know the LORD will secure
   justice for the needy, their rights for the poor.

14 Then the just will give thanks to your name;
   the upright will dwell in your presence.*

PSALM 141†

Prayer for Deliverance from the Wicked
¹ A psalm of David.

LORD, I call to you;
   come quickly to help me;
   listen to my plea when I call.
²† Let my prayer be incense before you;
   my uplifted hands an evening sacrifice.*
3 Set a guard, LORD, before my mouth,

---

† Ps 141: A lament of an individual (1–2) who is keenly aware that only the righteous can worship God properly and who therefore prays to be protected from the doomed wicked (3–10).

141, 2: *Incense:* literally, "smoke," i.e., the fragrant fumes arising from the altar at the burning of sacrificial animals or of aromatic spices; also used in Rv 5, 8 as a symbol of prayer. *My uplifted hands:* the gesture of supplication. Cf Pss 28, 2; 63, 5; 88, 10; 119, 48; 134, 2; 143, 6.

140, 11: Pss 11, 6; 120, 4; Gn 19, 24.   140, 14: Pss 11, 7; 16, 11; 17, 15.
141, 2: Ps 134, 2; Ex 30, 8.

a gatekeeper at my lips.*

4 Do not let my heart incline to evil,
  or yield to any sin.
I will never feast upon
  the fine food of evildoers.
5† Let the just strike me; that is kindness;
  let them rebuke me; that is oil for my
    head.*
All this I shall not refuse,
  but will pray despite these trials.
6 When their leaders are cast over the cliff,
  all will learn that my prayers were heard.
7 As when a farmer plows a field into broken
    clods,
  so their bones will be strewn at the mouth
    of Sheol.
8 My eyes are upon you, O GOD, my Lord;*
  in you I take refuge; do not strip me of
    life.
9 Guard me from the trap they have set
    for me,
  from the snares of evildoers.*
10 Into their own nets let all the wicked
    fall,
  while I make good my own escape.

PSALM 142†

A Prayer in Time of Trouble

1† A *maskil* of David, when he was in the cave.
    A prayer.

2 With full voice I cry to the LORD;
  with full voice I beseech the LORD.
3 Before God I pour out my complaint,
  lay bare my distress.
4 My spirit is faint within me,*
  but you know my path.*
Along the way I walk
  they have hidden a trap for me.*
5 I look to my right hand,*
  but no friend is there.
There is no escape for me;
  no one cares for me.

6 I cry out to you, LORD,
  I say, You are my refuge,*
  my portion in the land of the living.*
7 Listen to my cry for help,
  for I am brought very low.*
Rescue me from my pursuers,
  for they are too strong for me.
8† Lead me out of my prison,
  that I may give thanks to your
    name.
Then the just shall gather around me
  because you have been good to me.

PSALM 143†

A Prayer in Distress

1 A psalm of David.

LORD, hear my prayer;
  in your faithfulness listen to my pleading;
  answer me in your justice.
2 Do not enter into judgment with your servant;
  before you no living being can be just.*
3† The enemy has pursued me;
  they have crushed my life to the
    ground.*
They have left me in darkness
  like those long dead.*
4 My spirit is faint within me;
  my heart is dismayed.*
5 I remember the days of old;
  I ponder all your deeds;
  the works of your hands I recall.*
6 I stretch out my hands to you;
  I thirst for you like a parched land.*

                       Selah

7 Hasten to answer me, LORD;
  for my spirit fails me.
Do not hide your face from me,
  lest I become like those descending to the
    pit.*
8 At dawn let me hear of your kindness,
  for in you I trust.
Show me the path I should walk,
  for to you I entrust my life.*

141, 5–7: The Hebrew text is obscure.
Ps 142: In this lament imploring God for help (2–4b), the psalmist tells how enemies have set a trap (4c–5), and prays for rescue (6–8). The speaker feels utterly alone (5), exhausted (7), and may even be imprisoned (8a). Prison is possibly a metaphor for general distress. The last two verses are the vow of praise, made after receiving an assurance of divine help (8cd).
142, 1: *In the cave:* cf 1 Sm 22, 1; 24, 1–3; Ps 57, 1.
142, 8: *Then the just shall gather around me:* in the temple, when the psalmist offers a thanksgiving sacrifice.
Ps 143: One of the Church's seven Penitential Psalms, this lament is a prayer to be freed from death-dealing enemies. The psalmist addresses God, aware that there is no equality between God and humans; salvation is a gift (1–2). Victimized by evil people (3–4), the psalmist recites ("remembers") God's past actions on behalf of the in-

nocent (5–6). The psalm continues with fervent prayer (7–9) and a strong desire for guidance and protection (10–12).
143, 3: *They have crushed:* literally, "he crushed"; the singular is used typically, hence the plural translation.

141, 3: Sir 22, 27.
141, 5: Prv 9, 8; 25, 12.
141, 8: Pss 25, 15; 123, 1–2.
141, 9: Ps 142, 4.
142, 4: Ps 143, 4.
142, 4: Ps 141, 9.
142, 5: Pss 16, 8; 73, 23; 121, 5.
142, 6: Ps 91, 2.9.
142, 6: Pss 16, 5; 27, 13; 116, 9; Is 38, 11.
142, 7: Ps 79, 8.
143, 2: Eccl 7, 20; Jb 4, 17; Rom 3, 20.
143, 3: Ps 7, 6.
143, 3: Lam 3, 6.
143, 4: Ps 142, 4; Jb 17, 1.
143, 5: Ps 77, 6.12.
143, 6: Pss 42, 2; 63, 2.
143, 7: Pss 28, 1; 30, 4; 88, 5; Prv 1, 12.
143, 8: Pss 25, 4; 27, 11; 86, 11; 119, 12.35.

9　Rescue me, LORD, from my foes,
　　for in you I hope.
10　Teach me to do your will,
　　for you are my God.
　　May your kind spirit guide me
　　on ground that is level.
11　For your name's sake, LORD, give me
　　life;
　　in your justice lead me out of distress.
12　In your kindness put an end to my foes;
　　destroy all who attack me,
　　for I am your servant.*

PSALM 144†

A Prayer for Victory and Prosperity
¹ Of David.

I

Blessed be the LORD, my rock,†
　who trains my hands for battle,
　my fingers for war;
2　My safeguard and my fortress,
　my stronghold, my deliverer,
　My shield, in whom I trust,
　who subdues peoples under me.

II

3†　LORD, what are mortals that you notice them;
　　human beings, that you take thought of
　　them?*
4†　They are but a breath;
　　their days are like a passing shadow.*
5†　LORD, incline your heavens and come;
　　touch the mountains and make them smoke.*
6　Flash forth lightning and scatter my foes;
　　shoot your arrows and rout them.
7　Reach out your hand from on high;
　　deliver me from the many waters,
　　rescue me from the hands of foreign foes.
8†　Their mouths speak untruth;
　　their right hands are raised in lying oaths.
9　O God, a new song I will sing to you;
　　on a ten-stringed lyre I will play for you.*
10　You give victory to kings;
　　you delivered David your servant.*
　　From the menacing sword ¹¹ deliver me;

rescue me from the hands of foreign foes.
Their mouths speak untruth;
　their right hands are raised in lying oaths.

III

12　May our sons be like plants*
　　well nurtured from their youth,
　　Our daughters, like carved columns,
　　shapely as those of the temple.
13　May our barns be full
　　with every kind of store.
　　May our sheep increase by thousands,
　　by tens of thousands in our fields;
　　may our oxen be well fattened.
14　May there be no breach in the walls,
　　no exile, no outcry in our streets.*
15　Happy the people so blessed;
　　happy the people whose God is the LORD.*

A Prayer for the Young

We praise you, God, for all our nation's blessings!
We thank you for our young people, our sons and daughters who come forward to serve the people of God.
We ask you to make them strong, to call them into a trusting relationship with you, and to help them live a faithful life and be leaders and examples for others.
Happy the people whose God is the LORD!

▸ **Psalm 144**

PSALM 145†

The Greatness and Goodness of God
¹ Praise. Of David.

I will extol you, my God and king;
　I will bless your name forever.

---

† **Ps 144:** The psalm may reflect a ceremony in which the king, as leader of the army, asked God's help (1–8). In 9 the poem shifts abruptly from pleading to thanksgiving, and (except for 11) shifts again to prayer for the people. The first section (1–2) is a prayer of thanks for victory; the second (3–7a), a humble acknowledgment of human nothingness and a supplication that God show forth saving power; the third (9–11), a promise of future thanksgiving; the fourth (12–15), a wish for prosperity and peace. A prayer for deliverance from treacherous foes serves as a refrain after the second and third sections (7b–8.11). Except for its final section, the psalm is made up almost entirely of verses from other psalms.
144, 1–2: Composed of phrases from Ps 18, 3.35.47–48.
144, 3: Similar to Ps 8, 5.
144, 4: Composed of phrases from Pss 39, 6; 102, 12.
144, 5–7: Adapted in large part from Pss 18, 10.15.17; 104, 32.

144, 8b.11b: *Their right hands are raised in lying oaths:* the psalmist's enemies give false testimony.
Ps 145: A hymn in acrostic form; every verse begins with a successive letter of the Hebrew alphabet. Acrostic poems usually do not develop ideas but consist rather of loosely connected statements. The singer invites all to praise God (1–3.21). The "works of God" make God present and invite human praise (4–7); they climax in a confession (8–9). God's mighty acts show forth divine kingship (10–20), a major theme in the literature of early Judaism and in Christianity.

143, 12: Ps 116, 16.　　　　144, 9: Ps 33, 2–3.
144, 3: Jb 7, 17.　　　　　144, 10: Ps 18, 51.
144, 4: Pss 62, 10; 90, 9–10;　144, 12: Ps 128, 3.
　Jb 7, 16; Eccl 6, 12;　　144, 14: Is 65, 19.
　Wis 2, 5.　　　　　　144, 15: Ps 33, 12.
144, 5: Is 63, 19.

P
S

2 Every day I will bless you;
  I will praise your name forever.*

3 Great is the LORD and worthy of high praise;*
  God's grandeur is beyond understanding.

4 One generation praises your deeds to the next
  and proclaims your mighty works.*

5 They speak of the splendor of your majestic glory,
  tell of your wonderful deeds.*

6 They speak of your fearsome power
  and attest to your great deeds.*

7 They publish the renown of your abounding
      goodness
  and joyfully sing of your justice.

8 The LORD is gracious and merciful,
  slow to anger and abounding in love.*

9 The LORD is good to all,
  compassionate to every creature.*

10 All your works give you thanks, O LORD
  and your faithful bless you.*

11 They speak of the glory of your reign
  and tell of your great works,

12 Making known to all your power,
  the glorious splendor of your rule.

13 Your reign is a reign for all ages,
  your dominion for all generations.*
  The LORD is trustworthy in every word,
  and faithful in every work.

14 The LORD supports all who are falling
  and raises up all who are bowed down.*

15 The eyes of all look hopefully to you;
  you give them their food in due season.*

16 You open wide your hand
  and satisfy the desire of every living thing.

17 You, LORD, are just in all your ways,
  faithful in all your works.*

18 You, LORD, are near to all who call upon you,
  to all who call upon you in truth.*

19 You satisfy the desire of those who fear you;
  you hear their cry and save them.*

20 You, LORD, watch over all who love you,
  but all the wicked you destroy.*

21 My mouth will speak your praises, LORD;
  all flesh will bless your holy name forever.*

PSALM 146†

Trust in God the Creator and Redeemer

1 Hallelujah!

2 Praise the LORD, my soul;
  I shall praise the LORD all my life,
  sing praise to my God while I live.*

I

3 Put no trust in princes,
  in mere mortals powerless to save.*

4 When they breathe their last, they return to
      the earth;
  that day all their planning comes to nothing.*

II

5 Happy those whose help is Jacob's God,
  whose hope is in the LORD, their God,

6 The maker of heaven and earth,
  the seas and all that is in them,*
  Who keeps faith forever,

7   secures justice for the oppressed,*
  gives food to the hungry.
  The LORD sets prisoners free;*

8   the LORD gives sight to the blind.
  The LORD raises up those who are bowed down;*
  the LORD loves the righteous.

9 The LORD protects the stranger,
  sustains the orphan and the widow,*
  but thwarts the way of the wicked.

10 The LORD shall reign forever,
  your God, Zion, through all generations!*
  Hallelujah!

PSALM 147†

God's Word Restores Jerusalem

1 Hallelujah!

I

How good to celebrate our God in song;
  how sweet to give fitting praise.*

2 The LORD rebuilds Jerusalem,
  gathers the dispersed of Israel,*

3 Heals the brokenhearted,
  binds up their wounds,*

---

† **Ps 146:** A hymn of someone who has learned there is no other source of strength except the merciful God. Only God, not mortal humans (3–4), can help vulnerable and oppressed people (5–9). The first of the five hymns that conclude the Psalter.

Ps 147: The hymn is divided into three sections by the calls to praise in 1.7 and 12. The first section praises the powerful creator who restores exiled Judah (1–6); the second section, the creator who provides food to animals and humans; the third and climactic section exhorts the holy city to recognize it has been re-created and made the place of disclosure for God's word, a word as life-giving as water.

---

* 145, 2: Ps 34, 2.
145, 3: Pss 48, 2; 95, 3; 96, 4;
  Jb 36, 26.
145, 4: Pss 22, 31–32; 48,
  14–15; 71, 18; 78, 4;
  Ex 10, 2; Dt 4, 9.

145, 5: Pss 96, 3; 105, 2.
145, 6: Ps 66, 3.
145, 8: Pss 86, 5.15; 103, 8;
  Ex 34, 6; Sir 2, 11.
145, 9: Ps 103, 13; Wis 11, 24.
145, 10: Dn 3, 57.
145, 13: Pss 10, 16; 102, 13;
  146, 10; Lam 5, 19;
  Dn 3, 100; Rv 11, 15.
145, 14: Pss 94, 18; 146, 8.
145, 15: Pss 104, 27–28; 136,
  25; Mt 6, 25–26.
145, 17: Dt 32, 4.
145, 18: Dt 4, 7; Is 55, 6; 58, 9.
145, 19: Ps 34, 18.
145, 20: Jgs 5, 31.
145, 21: Sir 40, 35.
146, 2: Pss 103, 1; 104, 33.
146, 3: Ps 118, 8–9.

146, 4: Pss 90, 3; 104, 29;
  1 Mc 2, 63; Jb 34,
  14–15; Eccl 3, 20; 12,
  7; Sir 40, 11; Is 2, 22.
146, 6: Ex 20, 11; Pss 121, 2;
  124, 8; Acts 14, 15; Rv
  14, 7.
146, 7: Ps 103, 6.
146, 7: Ps 68, 7; Is 49, 9;
  61, 1.
146, 8: Ps 145, 14.
146, 9: Ps 68, 6; Dt 10, 18.
146, 10: Ps 145, 13; Lam 5, 19.
147, 1: Pss 33, 1; 92, 2.
147, 2: Is 11, 12; 56, 8; Jer 31,
  10.
147, 3: Jb 5, 18; Is 30, 26; 61,
  1; Jer 33, 6.

4 Numbers all the stars,
   calls each of them by name.*
5 Great is our Lord, vast in power,
   with wisdom beyond measure.*
6 The LORD sustains the poor,
   but casts the wicked to the ground.*

II

7 Sing to the LORD with thanksgiving;
   with the lyre celebrate our God,*
8† Who covers the heavens with clouds,
   provides rain for the earth,
   makes grass sprout on the mountains,*
9 Who gives animals their food
   and ravens what they cry for.*
10† God takes no delight in the strength of horses,
   no pleasure in the runner's stride.*
11 Rather the LORD takes pleasure in the devout,
   those who await his faithful care.

III

12 Glorify the LORD, Jerusalem;
   Zion, offer praise to your God,
13 Who has strengthened the bars of your gates,
   blessed your children within you,*
14 Brought peace to your borders,
   and filled you with finest wheat.*
15† The LORD sends a command to earth;
   his word runs swiftly!*
16 Thus snow is spread like wool,
   frost is scattered like ash,*

17 Hail is dispersed like crumbs;
   before such cold the waters freeze.
18 Again he sends his word and they melt;
   the wind is unleashed and the waters
   flow.
19 The LORD also proclaims his word to
   Jacob,
   decrees and laws to Israel.*
20 God has not done this for other nations;
   of such laws they know nothing.
   Hallelujah!

PSALM 148†

All Creation Summoned to Praise

1 Hallelujah!

I

Praise the LORD from the heavens;
   give praise in the heights.
2 Praise him, all you angels;
   give praise, all you hosts.*
3 Praise him, sun and moon;
   give praise, all shining stars.
4† Praise him, highest heavens,
   you waters above the heavens.
5 Let them all praise the LORD's name;
   for the LORD commanded and they
   were created,*
6 Assigned them duties forever,
   gave them tasks that will never change.

P
S

Care for God's Creation

LIVE IT!

Psalm 148 calls on all of creation to praise God. As one of the seven themes of Catholic social teaching, caring for God's creation is one way we can respond to God and the needs of others. Working to keep water clean for safe drinking and for the protection of sea life, educating ourselves and others about the effects of pollution on animal habitats and nesting sites, and protecting endangered species and all of creation are some of the ways we can fulfill our call to care for God's creation. Psalm 148 asks us to complete a cycle—God creates; we are called to care for God's creation, and all of creation continues in its praise of God.

▸ Psalm 148

147, 8–9: God clothes the fields and feeds the birds. Cf Mt 6, 26.30.

147, 10–11: Acknowledging one's dependence upon God rather than claiming self-sufficiency pleases God. Cf Pss 20, 8; 33, 16–19.

147, 15–19: God speaks through the thunder of nature and the word of revealed law. Cf Is 55, 10–11. The weather phenomena are well known in Jerusalem: a blizzard of snow and hail followed by a thunderstorm that melts the ice.

Ps 148: A hymn inviting the beings of heaven (1–6) and of earth (7–14) to praise God. The hymn does not distinguish between inanimate and animate (and rational) nature.

148, 4: *Highest heavens:* literally, "the heavens of the heavens,"

i.e., the space above the firmament, where the "upper waters" are stored. Cf Gn 1, 6–7; Dt 10, 14; 1 Kgs 8, 27; Ps 104, 3.13.

147, 4: Is 40, 26.
147, 5: Jdt 16, 13; Jer 51, 15.
147, 6: Ps 146, 9; 1 Sm 2, 7–8.
147, 7: Ps 71, 22.
147, 8: Ps 104, 13f; Jb 5, 10; Jer 14, 22; Jl 2, 23.
147, 9: Jb 38, 41; Mt 6, 26.
147, 10: Pss 20, 8; 33, 16–18.
147, 13: Ps 48, 14.
147, 14: Ps 81, 17.
147, 15: Ps 33, 9.
147, 16: Jb 6, 16; 37, 10; 38, 22.
147, 19: Ps 78, 5; Bar 3, 37; Dt 4, 7–8.
148, 2: Dn 3, 58–63; Ps 103, 20f.
148, 5: Ps 33, 9; Gn 1, 3f; Jdt 16, 14.

II

7 Praise the LORD from the earth,
  you sea monsters and all deep
    waters;*
8 You lightning and hail, snow and clouds,
  storm winds that fulfill his command;
9 You mountains and all hills,
  fruit trees and all cedars;*
10 You animals wild and tame,
  you creatures that crawl and fly;*
11 You kings of the earth and all peoples,
  princes and all who govern on earth;
12 Young men and women too,
  old and young alike.
13 Let them all praise the LORD's name,
  for his name alone is exalted,
  majestic above earth and heaven.*
14† The LORD has lifted high the horn of his people,
  to the glory of all the faithful,
  of Israel, the people near to their God.
  Hallelujah!

PSALM 149†

Praise God with Song and Sword

¹ Hallelujah!

Sing to the LORD a new song,
  a hymn in the assembly of the faithful.*
2 Let Israel be glad in their maker,
  the people of Zion rejoice in their king.
3† Let them praise his name in festive dance,
  make music with tambourine and lyre.*
4 For the LORD takes delight in his people,
  honors the poor with victory.
5† Let the faithful rejoice in their glory,
  cry out for joy at their banquet,
6 With the praise of God in their mouths,
  and a two-edged sword in their hands,*
7 To bring retribution on the nations,
  punishment on the peoples,*
8 To bind their kings with chains,
  shackle their nobles with irons,

9† To execute the judgments decreed for them—
  such is the glory of all God's faithful.
  Hallelujah!

PRAY IT

Psalm 150, Part 2

Praise God with clarinet and saxophone;
  praise God with flute and oboe!
Praise God with French horn and tuba;
  praise God with marimba and
    xylophone!
Praise God with guitar and fiddle;
  praise God with banjo and ukulele!
Praise God with bagpipe and accordion;
  praise God with piano and calliope!
Praise God with steel drum and harmonica;
  praise God with bongo and maracas!
Praise God with soaring classical music;
  praise God with mellow blues and tango!
Praise God with reggae and rap;
  praise God with jazz and rock!
Praise God with square dancing and line
    dancing;
  praise God with polka and waltz!
Let everyone who has breath and hands
    and feet and voices—
  sopranos, altos, tenors, and basses—
  praise the LORD!

▸ Psalm 150

PSALM 150†

Final Doxology

¹† Hallelujah!

Praise God in his holy sanctuary;*
  give praise in the mighty dome of heaven.

---

† ——————

148, 14: *The LORD has lifted high the horn of his people:* horn = strength, the concrete noun for the abstract. Of all peoples God has chosen Israel to return praise and thanks in a special way.

Ps 149: A hymn inviting the people of Israel to celebrate their God in song and festive dance (1–3.5) because God has chosen them and given them victory (4). The exodus and conquest are the defining acts of Israel; the people must be ready to do again those acts in the future at the divine command (6–9).

149, 3: *Make music with tambourine and lyre:* the verse recalls the great exodus hymn of Ex 15, 20.

149, 5: *At their banquet:* literally, "upon their couches." The people reclined to banquet.

149, 9: *The glory:* what brings honor to the people is their readiness to carry out the divine will, here conceived as punishing injustice done by the nations.

Ps 150: The psalm is a closing doxology both for the fifth book of

the Psalms (107–149) and for the Psalter as a whole. Temple musicians and dancers are called to lead all beings on earth and in heaven in praise of God. The psalm proclaims to whom praise shall be given, and where (1); what praise shall be given, and why (2); how praise shall be given (3–5), and by whom (6).

150, 1: *His holy sanctuary:* God's temple on earth. *The mighty dome of heaven:* literally, "[God's] strong vault"; heaven is here imagined as a giant plate separating the inhabited world from the waters of the heavens.

148, 7: Gn 1, 21; Ps 135, 6.
148, 9: Is 44, 23.
148, 10: Gn 1, 21.24f; Ps 30, 5;
  Dt 4, 7.
148, 13: Ps 30, 5; Dt 4, 7.
149, 1: Pss 22, 23; 26, 12; 35,
  18; 40, 10; Jdt 16, 1.

149, 3: Pss 68, 26; 81, 2–3;
  87, 7; 150, 3–4.
149, 6: Neh 4, 10–12; 2 Mc
  15, 27.
149, 7: Wis 3, 8.
150, 1: Dn 3, 53.

2 Give praise for his mighty deeds,*
    praise him for his great majesty.
3 Give praise with blasts upon the horn,*
    praise him with harp and lyre.
4 Give praise with tambourines and dance,
    praise him with flutes and strings.*

5 Give praise with crashing cymbals,
    praise him with sounding
      cymbals.
6 Let everything that has breath
    give praise to the LORD!*
    Hallelujah!

150, 2: Dt 3, 24.
150, 3ff: Pss 81, 3–4; 149, 3;
  2 Sm 6, 5; 1 Chr 13, 8;
  16, 5.42; 2 Chr 5,
  12–13; 7, 6.

150, 4: Ps 68, 26; Ex 15, 20.
150, 6: Rv 5, 13.

When we pick up the daily newspaper, many of us turn first to the advice columns. "My mom just doesn't understand me," we read. "Why won't she let me make my own decisions?" Or "I think my boyfriend is cheating on me. Should I show him the door?" Or "All my friends take drugs. How do I resist the pressure?" The Book of Proverbs is the advice column of the Old Testament. It covers everything from raising children to choosing friends.

In-depth

Proverbs teaches that the wise person listens to the "voices" of history: experience, intelligence, and common sense. The ancient Israelites had a long tradition of reflecting on the challenges of life. Over the centuries, a whole body of writings developed to record their reflections. These writings gave advice on common problems and questions that people faced, and directions for wise living.

Proverbs is the best-known example of this type of literature in the Old Testament. It contains two basic kinds of writings: longer instructions addressed to young people and short sayings addressed to all. With advice on matters ranging from sluggishness (6, 6–11), cheating (11, 1), pride (16, 18), and the training of children (22, 6), to laughter (14, 13), eyewinks (16, 30), visiting neighbors (25, 17), and being a good wife (31, 10–31), Proverbs is a treasure chest of advice from the ancient world. Although some of the sayings may seem outdated or funny to us today, the overall lesson is something that Jesus insists on in the Gospels: Faith is not just a matter of right believing; it is also a matter of right living.

The poetic structure of this book—a feature of most wisdom literature—reveals another basic insight of our ancestors in faith: How something is said is as important as what is said. In addition, parallelism makes the generally short sayings in this book easy to memorize. We would do well to consult Proverbs regularly for good advice, and to remember what we read. To all who care to hear, this book tells of the rewards of virtue and the dangers of vice.

At a Glance

Quick Facts

Author

King Solomon is introduced as the author, probably because of his legendary wisdom. However, the actual author is unknown, writing from the reign of King Solomon (970–931 B.C.) to sometime after the Babylonian Exile (587–538 B.C.).

Of Note

The book is made up of several collections of proverbs.

The Book of Proverbs

Proverbs

TRUST IN THE LORD WITH ALL YOUR HEART

I: Introduction: The Value of Wisdom

Purpose of the Proverbs of Solomon

1 ¹*† The proverbs of Solomon, the son of David, king of Israel:

²† That men may appreciate wisdom
and discipline,
may understand words of intelligence;

³ May receive training in wise conduct,
in what is right, just and honest;

⁴† That resourcefulness may be imparted to
the simple,
to the young man knowledge
and discretion.

⁵ A wise man by hearing them will advance
in learning,
an intelligent man will gain sound guidance,

⁶ That he may comprehend proverb and parable,
the words of the wise and their riddles.

⁷*†The fear of the LORD is the beginning
of knowledge;
wisdom and instruction fools despise.

The Path of the Wicked: Greed and Violence†

⁸ Hear, my son, your father's instruction,
and reject not your mother's teaching;

⁹ A graceful diadem will they be for your
head;
a torque for your neck.

¹⁰ My son, should sinners entice you, ¹¹ and say,
"Come along with us!
Let us lie in wait for the honest man,
let us, unprovoked, set a trap for
the innocent;

¹² Let us swallow them up, as the nether world
does, alive,
in the prime of life, like those who go
down to the pit!

¹³ All kinds of precious wealth shall we gain,
we shall fill our houses with booty;

¹⁴ Cast in your lot with us,
we shall all have one purse!"—

¹⁵ My son, walk not in the way with them,
hold back your foot from their path!

---

† **1, 1–6:** This prologue explains the purpose of the book: to educate the inexperienced in knowledge and right conduct, and to increase the learning of the wise man by proverbs, parables and riddles.

1, 2: *Discipline:* education or formation which dispels ignorance and corrects vice.

1, 4: *Simple:* immature and inexperienced, hence easily influenced for good or evil.

1, 7: *Fear of the LORD:* reverential fear and respect for God on ac-

count of his sovereignty, goodness and justice toward men. This is the foundation of religion.

1, 8–19: A warning against association with the greedy and the violent who seek to destroy the honest man and to steal his possessions (11–14). The trap which the wicked set for the innocent (11), in the end (19) takes away the life of the wicked themselves.

1, 1: Prv 10, 1; 25, 1; 1 Kgs 4, 32.

1, 7: Prv 9, 10; Jb 28, 28; Ps 111, 10; Sir 1, 16.

Media Literacy

Our society today has a powerful, persuasive tool. It is called the media. We are influenced in many ways by what we read, watch, and hear in the many forms of modern media.

We might buy things because something we read says it's the best. We might look the other way when someone is being robbed because we see so much violence at the movies that it doesn't seem to bother us. We might dance to the beat of a song and not even realize that the words are suggesting an immoral behavior.

Certainly not all the messages in the media are bad. But to resist the influence of the media's negative messages, we must educate ourselves to watch for them. In Prv 1, 10–15, we read "My son, should sinners entice you, . . . walk not in the way with them." Take time to really think about a message in the media before you choose to follow it. Verse 7 says it best: Only a fool despises wisdom!

▸ **Prv 1, 7–19**

16* [For their feet run to evil,
      they hasten to shed blood.]
17† It is in vain that a net is spread
      before the eyes of any bird—
18 These men lie in wait for their own blood,
      they set a trap for their own lives.
19 This is the fate of everyone greedy of loot:
      unlawful gain takes away the life of him
         who acquires it.

Wisdom in Person Gives Warning†

20* Wisdom cries aloud in the street,
      in the open squares she raises her voice;
21 Down the crowded ways she calls out,
      at the city gates she utters her words:
22 "How long, you simple ones, will you
      love inanity,
23 how long will you turn away at my reproof?
      Lo! I will pour out to you my spirit,
      I will acquaint you with my words.
24* "Because I called and you refused,
      I extended my hand and no one took notice;
25 Because you disdained all my counsel,
      and my reproof you ignored—
26 I, in my turn, will laugh at your doom;
      I will mock when terror overtakes you;

27 When terror comes upon you like a storm,
      and your doom approaches like
         a whirlwind;
      when distress and anguish befall you.
28† "Then they call me, but I answer not;
      they seek me, but find me not;
29 Because they hated knowledge,
      and chose not the fear of the LORD;
30 They ignored my counsel,
      they spurned all my reproof;
      And in their arrogance they
         preferred arrogance,
      and like fools they hated knowledge:
31† "Now they must eat the fruit of their own way,
      and with their own devices be glutted.
32 For the self-will of the simple kills them,
      the smugness of fools destroys them.
33* But he who obeys me dwells in security,
      in peace, without fear of harm."

The Blessings of Wisdom†

2 1† My son, if you receive my words
      and treasure my commands,
2† Turning your ear to wisdom,

---

† **1, 17:** Instructed by the wise man, the youth (of v 4) will recognize the invitation of the wicked (11–14) as a net spread before him, and he will thus, like the bird, be protected against falling into it.

1, 20–33: Wisdom is here personified: with divine authority she sets forth and proclaims the moral order, instructing and threatening (24–33) the multitudes in the streets and places of assembly.

1, 28: Overtaken by doom, the foolish seek wisdom, but in vain because they do so too late. Cf Jn 7, 34; 8, 21.

1, 31: Sinners are punished by the bad fruits which their sins produce. Cf Wis 11, 16.

2—7: These chapters form an ordered discourse in seven "columns" of twenty-two verses each. Chapter 2 introduces the four topics about which the sage instructs his pupil: the service of God (3, 1–12.25–34), the search for wisdom (3, 13–24.35; 4, 1–9), the

avoidance of evil companions among men (4, 10–27; 5, 21–23), and among women (5, 1–20; 6, 20—7, 27). The last topic is treated at a length equal to the first three because the discourse is meant especially for youths (cf Prv 1, 4).

2, 1–22: The search for wisdom (1–4) leads to the protection of God (5–8) and of wisdom herself (9ff; cf Prv 1, 20–33) and to deliverance from evil men (12–15) and evil women (16–19), and so to lasting happiness (20ff).

2, 2f: Wisdom, understanding, intelligence: various names or aspects of the same gift.

*
1, 16: Is 59, 7.	Jer 7, 13.
1, 20: Prv 8, 1–3; 9, 3.	
1, 24: Is 65, 2.12; 66, 4;	**1, 33:** Prv 8, 33f.

inclining your heart to understanding;

3 Yes, if you call to intelligence,
and to understanding raise your voice;

4 If you seek her like silver,
and like hidden treasures search her out:

5 Then will you understand the fear of
the LORD;
the knowledge of God you will find;

6* For the LORD gives wisdom,
from his mouth come knowledge
and understanding;

7 He has counsel in store for the upright,
he is the shield of those who walk honestly,

8 Guarding the paths of justice,
protecting the way of his pious ones.

9 Then you will understand rectitude
and justice,
honesty, every good path;

10 For wisdom will enter your heart,
knowledge will please your soul,

11 Discretion will watch over you,
understanding will guard you;

12 Saving you from the way of evil men,
from men of perverse speech,

13 Who leave the straight paths
to walk in ways of darkness,

14 Who delight in doing evil,
rejoice in perversity;

15 Whose ways are crooked,
and devious their paths;

16* Saving you from the wife of another,
from the adulteress with her smooth
words,

17 Who forsakes the companion of her youth
and forgets the pact with her God;

18* For her path sinks down to death,
and her footsteps lead to the shades;

19 None who enter thereon come back again,
or gain the paths of life.

20 Thus you may walk in the way of good men,
and keep to the paths of the just.

21* For the upright will dwell in the land,

the honest will remain in it;

22 But the wicked will be cut off from the land,
the faithless will be rooted out of it.

Attitude toward the Lord†

3 ¹ My son, forget not my teaching,
keep in mind my commands;

2* For many days, and years of life,
and peace, will they bring you.

3 Let not kindness and fidelity leave you;
bind them around your neck;

4 Then will you win favor and good esteem
before God and man.

5 Trust in the LORD with all your heart,
on your own intelligence rely not;

6 In all your ways be mindful of him,
and he will make straight your paths.

7* Be not wise in your own eyes,
fear the LORD and turn away from evil;

8 This will mean health for your flesh
and vigor for your bones.

9* Honor the LORD with your wealth,
with first fruits of all your produce;

10 Then will your barns be filled with grain,
with new wine your vats will overflow.

11* The discipline of the LORD, my son, disdain not;
spurn not his reproof;

12* For whom the LORD loves he reproves,
and he chastises the son he favors.

The Value of Wisdom

13*†Happy the man who finds wisdom,
the man who gains understanding!

14 For her profit is better than profit in silver,
and better than gold is her revenue;

15*†She is more precious than corals,
and none of your choice possessions can
compare with her.

16 Long life is in her right hand,
in her left are riches and honor;

17 Her ways are pleasant ways,
and all her paths are peace;

† **3, 1–12:** Many are the rewards for fidelity and trust in God, and for diffidence of self (1–8). Cf Dt 30, 20; Is 38, 19. The offering of material things for divine worship is blessed by an increase of such goods (9f). Even correction and chastisement are a mark of God's love and favor (11f).

3, 13–24: Wisdom, or understanding, is more valuable than silver and gold. Its fruit is long life, riches, honor and happiness (13–18). Even the creation of the universe and its adornment (Gn 1) were not done without wisdom (19f). It is the life of the soul and gives security in work and in repose (21–24).

3, 15: *Corals:* some precious stone may be intended.

* **2, 6:** Jb 32, 8; Wis 7, 25; Sir 1, 1; Jas 1, 5.
2, 16: Prv 5, 3.20; 6, 24; 7, 5; 22, 14.
2, 18: Prv 5, 5f; 7, 27.
2, 21f: Prv 10, 7.30; Jb 18, 17; Pss 21, 9–13; 37, 22.28.
3, 2: Prv 4, 10; 9, 11; 10, 27.
3, 7: Rom 11, 25; 12, 16.
3, 9: Ex 34, 26; Lv 27, 30; Dt 26, 2; Sir 7, 31; 35, 7.
3, 11: Heb 12, 5f.
3, 12: Jdt 8, 27; Rv 3, 19.
3, 13: Prv 8, 34f.
3, 15: Prv 8, 11.19; Wis 7, 8–11.

PRAY IT

Your Future

Read Prv 3, 5–8, and think about your plans for the future. How does God play a part in them? Do they include discernment of (prayerful listening to) God's plans for you? Here are some clues for discerning where God is calling you:

- Pray about your future, and ask for God's direction.
- Look at your talents and interests. These are gifts from God to be used for the good of others as well as yourself.
- Imagine yourself doing whatever you are considering. What feelings surface? Peace and joy are usually signs of God's presence. Excessive anxiety, fear, and shame are usually signs of God's absence.
- Talk with a trusted adult about your options. If this person is wise, she or he will not give you a direct answer but will help you sort out where God is leading.

▶ Prv 3, 5–8

18*† She is a tree of life to those who grasp her,
    and he is happy who holds her fast.

19   The LORD by wisdom founded the earth,
    established the heavens by understanding;

20† By his knowledge the depths break open,
    and the clouds drop down dew.

21   My son, let not these slip out of your sight:
    keep advice and counsel in view;

22   So will they be life to your soul,
    and an adornment for your neck.

23   Then you may securely go your way;
    your foot will never stumble;

24   When you lie down, you need not be afraid,
    when you rest, your sleep will be sweet.

35   Honor is the possession of wise men,
    but fools inherit shame.

Attitude toward Fellow Men†

25† Be not afraid of sudden terror,
    of the ruin of the wicked when it comes;

26   For the LORD will be your confidence,
    and will keep your foot from the snare.

27   Refuse no one the good on which he has
    a claim
    when it is in your power to do it for him.

28   Say not to your neighbor, "Go, and come again,
    tomorrow I will give," when you can give
    at once.

29   Plot no evil against your neighbor,
    against him who lives at peace with you.

30   Quarrel not with a man without cause,
    with one who has done you no harm.

31* Envy not the lawless man
    and choose none of his ways:

32   To the LORD the perverse man is
    an abomination,
    but with the upright is his friendship.

33   The curse of the LORD is on the house of
    the wicked,
    but the dwelling of the just he blesses;

TRUE SECURITY

We often hear: When the going gets tough, the tough get going.

But how do we know how to get going? Where do we get going to? Our faith gives us good advice and wise counsel (Prv 3, 21). Prayer keeps us close to God (verse 26). And knowing we have made the right decision is true security.

When the going gets tough, first the tough get faithful, and prayerful, and thoughtful. Then they get going.

▶ Prv 3, 21–35

---

† **3, 18:** *A tree of life:* cf Prv 11, 30; 13, 12; Gn 2, 9.

3, 20: For the Hebrews, the depths enclosed the great subterranean ocean; the rain and dew descended from the celestial ocean above the firmament; cf Gn 1, 6–10; Jb 26, 8.12; Pss 18, 16; 24, 2.

3, 25–34: Serving God with confidence in him (25f) requires serving one's neighbor through kindness (27f), peace with the good (29ff), no envy of the wicked (31), because the Lord's friendship and kindness are with the just; his curse is with the wicked.

3, 25: *The ruin of the wicked:* i.e., the ruin that comes upon the wicked.

---

*

3, 18: Prv 4, 13; 8, 35; 11, 30; Gn 2, 9; 3, 22.

3, 31: Prv 23, 17; 24, 1.19; Ps 37, 1.

34* When he is dealing with the arrogant, he
        is stern,
        but to the humble he shows kindness.

Wisdom: the Supreme Guide of Men†

4 ¹ Hear, O children, a father's instruction,
        be attentive, that you may gain
            understanding!
2   Yes, excellent advice I give you;
        my teaching do not forsake.
3   When I was my father's child,
        frail, yet the darling of my mother,
4*   He taught me, and said to me:
        "Let your heart hold fast my words:
        keep my commands, that you may live!

5   "Get wisdom, get understanding!
        Do not forget or turn aside from the words
            I utter.
6   Forsake her not, and she will preserve you;
        love her, and she will safeguard you;
7   The beginning of wisdom is: get wisdom;
        at the cost of all you have,
            get understanding.
8   Extol her, and she will exalt you;
        she will bring you honors if you
            embrace her;
9   She will put on your head a
            graceful diadem;
        a glorious crown will she bestow on you."

The Good and the Evil Way†

10* Hear, my son, and receive my words,
        and the years of your life shall be many.
11   On the way of wisdom I direct you,
        I lead you on straightforward paths.
12   When you walk, your step will not
            be impeded,
        and should you run, you will not stumble.
13   Hold fast to instruction, never let her go;
        keep her, for she is your life.

14   The path of the wicked enter not,
        walk not on the way of evil men;
15   Shun it, cross it not,
        turn aside from it, and pass on.
16   For they cannot rest unless they have done evil;

to have made no one stumble steals away
        their sleep.
17   For they eat the bread of wickedness
        and drink the wine of violence.
19   The way of the wicked is like darkness;
        they know not on what they stumble.
18† But the path of the just is like shining light,
        that grows in brilliance till perfect day.

20   My son, to my words be attentive,
        to my sayings incline your ear;
21   Let them not slip out of your sight,
        keep them within your heart;
22* For they are life to those who find them,
        to man's whole being they are health.

23   With closest custody, guard your heart,
        for in it are the sources of life.
24   Put away from you dishonest talk,
        deceitful speech put far from you.
25   Let your eyes look straight ahead
        and your glance be directly forward.
26   Survey the path for your feet,
        and let all your ways be sure.
27   Turn neither to right nor to left,
        keep your foot far from evil.

Warning against Adultery

5 ¹† My son, to my wisdom be attentive,
        to my knowledge incline your ear,
2   That discretion may watch over you,
        and understanding may guard you.
3*   The lips of an adulteress drip with honey,
        and her mouth is smoother than oil;
4   But in the end she is as bitter as wormwood,
        as sharp as a two-edged sword.
5*   Her feet go down to death,
        to the nether world her steps attain;
6   Lest you see before you the road to life,
        her paths will ramble, you know not where.

7   So now, O children, listen to me,
        go not astray from the words of my mouth.
8*   Keep your way far from her,
        approach not the door of her house,
9*† Lest you give your honor to others,
        and your years to a merciless one;

PRV

4, 1–9: The sage speaks as a father admonishing his children to
secure wisdom at any cost.
4, 10–27: The way of wisdom leads directly to life (10–13); it is a
light that grows brighter (18). The wise man is bound to shun (14–17)
the dark and violent path of the wicked (19). Singleness of purpose
and right conduct proceed from the heart of a wise man as from the
source of life (23–26); they save him from destruction on evil paths
(4, 27; 5, 21ff).
4, 18: *Till perfect day:* literally, "till the day is established"; this
may refer to full daylight or to noonday.
5, 1–20: Understanding and discretion guard a man against the
wiles of an adulteress, which lead astray and beget bitterness, blood-

shed and death (1–6). They destroy honor, waste the years of life, despoil hard-earned wealth, consume the flesh, and bring remorse in
the end (7–14). Conjugal fidelity and love for one wife only bring
happiness and security (15–20). Cf Prv 6, 20—7, 27.
5, 9: *Honor:* the words "life" and "wealth" have also been read
in this place. *A merciless one:* the offended husband; cf Prv 6, 34f.

3, 34: Prv 1, 26.   5, 5: Prv 2, 18; 7, 27.
4, 4: 1 Kgs 2, 2ff.   5, 5: Prv 2, 18; 7, 27.
4, 10: Prv 3, 2.   5, 8: Prv 7, 25.
4, 22: Prv 8, 35.   5, 9f: Sir 9, 6.

All the Days of My Life

The words "all the days of my life" have been repeated by countless couples on their wedding day, and for some of those couples, they are prophetic. The husband and wife will be together till death separates them, and then they will be reunited in heaven. Though we live in a society where divorce is frequent, many couples make it through all the trials and difficulties and are around to celebrate their twenty-fifth and fiftieth anniversaries.

The writer of Prv 5, 15–23 is warning men, in particular, against adultery, which remains, even today, a primary reason marriages break up. But the author's wish in verse 19 could easily be rephrased to address both husbands and wives: "May you always be invigorated by each other's love."

What a wonderful wedding toast!

▶ Prv 5, 15–23

10 Lest strangers have their fill of your wealth,
    your hard-won earnings go to an alien's house;
11 And you groan in the end,
    when your flesh and your body
    are consumed;
12 And you say, "Oh, why did I hate instruction,
    and my heart spurn reproof!
13 Why did I not listen to the voice of
    my teachers,
    nor to my instructors incline my ear!
14 I have all but come to utter ruin,
    condemned by the public assembly!"

15 Drink water from your own cistern,
    running water from your own well.
16 How may your water sources be
    dispersed abroad,
    streams of water in the streets?
17 Let your fountain be yours alone,
    not one shared with strangers;
18 And have joy of the wife of your youth,
19†   your lovely hind, your graceful doe.
    Her love will invigorate you always,
    through her love you will
    flourish continually,
22† When you lie down she will watch over you,
    and when you wake, she will share
    your concerns;
    wherever you turn, she will guide you.
20 Why then, my son, should you go astray for
    another's wife
    and accept the embraces of an adulteress?

21*† For each man's ways are plain to the LORD's sight;
    all their paths he surveys;
22 By his own iniquities the wicked man will
    be caught,
    in the meshes of his own sin he will be
    held fast;
23 He will die from lack of discipline,
    through the greatness of his folly he will
    be lost.

Miscellaneous Proverbs†

6 1*† My son, if you have become surety to
    your neighbor,
    given your hand in pledge to another,
2 You have been snared by the utterance of
    your lips,
    caught by the words of your mouth;
3 So do this, my son, to free yourself,
    since you have fallen into your
    neighbor's power:
    Go, hurry, stir up your neighbor!
4 Give no sleep to your eyes,
    nor slumber to your eyelids;
5 Free yourself as a gazelle from the snare,
    or as a bird from the hand of the fowler.

6* Go to the ant, O sluggard,
    study her ways and learn wisdom;
7 For though she has no chief,
    no commander or ruler,
8 She procures her food in the summer,
    stores up her provisions in the harvest.

---

† **5, 19:** *Lovely hind . . . graceful doe:* oriental symbols of feminine beauty and charm; cf Song 2, 7.9.17.

5, 22: This is transposed from chapter 6, 22.

5, 21–23: These verses are best read after Prv 4, 27.

6, 1–19: These verses interrupt the discourse of chapters 2—7, which should be read apart from them; they contain four shorter proverbs akin to those in chapter 30.

6, 1: *Given your hand in pledge:* literally, "struck your hands"; this was probably the legal method for closing a contract.

5, 21: Jb 14, 16; 31, 4; 34,   8, 13; 29, 19.
    21.   6, 6: Prv 30, 25.
6, 1f: Prv 11, 15; 22, 26; Sir

9 How long, O sluggard, will you rest?
   when will you rise from your sleep?

10† A little sleep, a little slumber,
   a little folding of the arms to rest—

11 Then will poverty come upon you like
   a highwayman,
   and want like an armed man.

12 A scoundrel, a villain, is he
   who deals in crooked talk.

13 He winks his eyes,
   shuffles his feet,
   makes signs with his fingers;

14 He has perversity in his heart,
   is always plotting evil,
   sows discord.

15 Therefore suddenly ruin comes upon him;
   in an instant he is crushed beyond cure.

16† There are six things the LORD hates,
   yes, seven are an abomination to him;

17 Haughty eyes, a lying tongue,
   and hands that shed innocent blood;

18 A heart that plots wicked schemes,
   feet that run swiftly to evil,

19 The false witness who utters lies,
   and he who sows discord among brothers.

Warning against Adultery†

20 Observe, my son, your father's bidding,
   and reject not your mother's teaching;

21 Keep them fastened over your heart always,
   put them around your neck;

23 For the bidding is a lamp, and the teaching
   a light,
   and a way to life are the reproofs
   of discipline;

24* To keep you from your neighbor's wife,
   from the smooth tongue of the adulteress.

25* Lust not in your heart after her beauty,
   let her not captivate you with her glance!

26† For the price of a loose woman
   may be scarcely a loaf of bread,
   But if she is married,
   she is a trap for your precious life.

27 Can a man take fire to his bosom,
   and his garments not be burned?

28 Or can a man walk on live coals,
   and his feet not be scorched?

29* So with him who goes in to his
   neighbor's wife—
   none who touches her shall go
   unpunished.

30 Men despise not the thief if he steals
   to satisfy his appetite when he is hungry;

31 Yet if he be caught he must pay
   back sevenfold;
   all the wealth of his house he may yield up.

32 But he who commits adultery is a fool;
   he who would destroy himself does it.

P
R
V

Leaders with Character

LIVE IT!

Look at the list of the things the LORD hates in Prv 6, 17–19. It looks like a popular description of a corrupt politician or businessperson! Now take the list and put it in the positive: humble eyes, a truthful tongue, hands that protect the innocent, a heart that plans good, feet that hurry to help, a truthful witness, and someone who brings harmony to families. That's the kind of leader everyone wants!

The author of Proverbs is constantly reminding us to be of good character. Especially when you are called to be a leader—and we all will be at some time in our life—keep the advice of Proverbs in mind. Be a leader of character by doing the things the LORD loves, not the things the LORD hates.

▸ Prv 6, 16–19

---

†
6, 10: This verse may be regarded as the sluggard's reply or as a continuation of the remonstrance.

6, 16–19: The seven vices symbolized for the most part by bodily organs are pride, lying, murder, intrigue, readiness to do evil, false witness, and the stirring up of discord.

6, 20—7, 27: Parental training and the love of wisdom are an invaluable and constant help for the young (6, 20–23; 7, 1–4). They are the best defense against adultery (6, 24; 7, 5.24f), which involves the

guilty in many dangers and punishments (6, 26–35; 7, 6–27). Cf Prv 5, 1–20.

6, 26: Some interpret the verse in a progressive sense, i.e., to satisfy the increasing demands of a courtesan a man is reduced to poverty; if the woman is married, even his very life is endangered.

6, 24: Prv 2, 16; 7, 5.   9, 8; 25, 20; Mt 5, 28.
6, 25: Ex 20, 17; Dt 5, 21; Sir   **6, 29:** Sir 9, 9.

PRV

33 A degrading beating will he get,
 and his disgrace will not be wiped away;
34 For vindictive is the husband's wrath,
 he will have no pity on the day
 of vengeance;
35 He will not consider any restitution,
 nor be satisfied with the greatest gifts.

7 1 My son, keep my words,
 and treasure my commands.
2 Keep my commands and live,
 my teaching as the apple of your eye;
3* Bind them on your fingers,
 write them on the tablet of your heart.
4 Say to Wisdom, "You are my sister!"
 call Understanding, "Friend!"
5* That they may keep you from another's wife,
 from the adulteress with her smooth
 words.
6 For at the window of my house,
 through my lattice I looked out—

7 And I saw among the simple ones,
 I observed among the young men,
 a youth with no sense,
8 Going along the street near the corner,
 then walking in the direction of
 her house—
9 In the twilight, at dusk of day,
 at the time of the dark of night.
10 And lo! the woman comes to meet him,
 robed like a harlot, with secret designs—
11 She is fickle and unruly,
 in her home her feet cannot rest;
12 Now she is in the streets, now in the
 open squares,
 and at every corner she lurks in ambush—
13 When she seizes him, she kisses him,
 and with an impudent look says to him:

14† "I owed peace offerings,
 and today I have fulfilled my vows;
15 So I came out to meet you,
 to look for you, and I have found you!
16 With coverlets I have spread my couch,
 with brocaded cloths of Egyptian linen;
17 I have sprinkled my bed with myrrh,
 with aloes, and with cinnamon.

18 "Come, let us drink our fill of love,
 until morning, let us feast on love!
19 For my husband is not at home,
 he has gone on a long journey;
20 A bag of money he took with him,
 not till the full moon will he return home."

21* She wins him over by her repeated urging,
 with her smooth lips she leads him astray;
22 He follows her stupidly,
 like an ox that is led to slaughter;
 Like a stag that minces toward the net,
23 till an arrow pierces its liver;
 Like a bird that rushes into a snare,
 unaware that its life is at stake.

24 So now, O children, listen to me,
 be attentive to the words of my mouth!
25 Let not your heart turn to her ways,
 go not astray in her paths;
26 For many are those she has struck down dead,
 numerous, those she has slain.
27* Her house is made up of ways to the
 nether world,
 leading down into the chambers of death.

The Discourse of Wisdom†

8 1* Does not Wisdom call,
 and Understanding raise her voice?
2 On the top of the heights along the road,
 at the crossroads she takes her stand;
3 By the gates at the approaches of the city,
 in the entryways she cries aloud:
4 "To you, O men, I call;
 my appeal is to the children of men.
5† You simple ones, gain resource,
 you fools, gain sense.
6 "Give heed! for noble things I speak;
 honesty opens my lips.
7† Yes, the truth my mouth recounts,
 but wickedness my lips abhor.
8 Sincere are all the words of my mouth,
 no one of them is wily or crooked;
9 All of them are plain to the man
 of intelligence,
 and right to those who attain knowledge.
10 Receive my instruction in preference to silver,
 and knowledge rather than choice gold.

7, 14: "Peace offerings . . . vows": a portion of the sacrifice reverted to the donor and had to be eaten on the same day at a family festival (Lv 7, 11–15). In this figure, the adulteress offers to share with the foolish young man the deadly feast of her sensuality.
8, 1–36: Wisdom is here personified as in Prv 1, 20–33, to confirm the words of the teacher of wisdom. She exalts her grandeur and origin, and invites all (1–11) to be attentive to her salutary influence in human society (12–21), for she was privileged to be present at the creation of the world (22–31). Finally, she promises life and the favor of God to those who find her, death to those who despise her.

8, 5: Simple ones . . . fools: see note on Prv 1, 4.
8, 7f: The truth and sincerity of wisdom are absolute because they are divine. They can neither deceive nor tolerate deception. An intelligent man understands and accepts them.

7, 3: Dt 6, 8.   7, 27: Prv 2, 18f; 5, 5.
7, 5: Prv 2, 16; 6, 24.   8, 1: Prv 1, 20f; 9, 3.
7, 21: Prv 5, 3; 6, 24.

▶ Prv 8, 1–21

The Gifts of Wisdom

To gain wisdom, you have to hunger for it, really want it, and actively seek it out. You will not find it by yourself: wisdom is found where other people are— "By the gates" where people meet (Prv 8, 3).

Wisdom's gifts described in Proverbs, chapter 8, include resource or prudence, sense or intelligence, truth, knowledge, instruction or understanding, strength, and justice. Which of these gifts do you have? Which would you like to develop? Who could help you? Write a prayer to the Holy Spirit, asking for the strength and courage to seek out these gifts.

11* [For Wisdom is better than corals,
and no choice possession can compare with her.]

12 "I, Wisdom, dwell with experience,
and judicious knowledge I attain.
13* [The fear of the LORD is to hate evil;]
Pride, arrogance, the evil way,
and the perverse mouth I hate.
14† Mine are counsel and advice;
mine is strength; I am understanding.
15 By me kings reign,
and lawgivers establish justice;
16 By me princes govern,
and nobles; all the rulers of earth.

17 "Those who love me I also love,
and those who seek me find me.
18* With me are riches and honor,
enduring wealth and prosperity.

19* My fruit is better than gold, yes, than
pure gold,
and my revenue than choice silver.
20 On the way of duty I walk,
along the paths of justice,
21 Granting wealth to those who love me,
and filling their treasuries.

22*† "The LORD begot me, the first-born of his ways,
the forerunner of his prodigies of long ago;
23*† From of old I was poured forth,
at the first, before the earth.
24† When there were no depths I was
brought forth,
when there were no fountains or springs
of water;
25 Before the mountains were settled into place,
before the hills, I was brought forth;
26 While as yet the earth and the fields were
not made,
nor the first clods of the world.

27* "When he established the heavens I was there,
when he marked out the vault over the face
of the deep;
28 When he made firm the skies above,
when he fixed fast the foundations of
the earth;
29 When he set for the sea its limit,
so that the waters should not transgress
his command;
30*† Then was I beside him as his craftsman,
and I was his delight day by day,
Playing before him all the while,
31 playing on the surface of his earth;
and I found delight in the sons of men.

32 "So now, O children, listen to me;
33 instruction and wisdom do not reject!
Happy the man who obeys me,
and happy those who keep my ways,
34 Happy the man watching daily at my gates,
waiting at my doorposts;
35* For he who finds me finds life,
and wins favor from the LORD;
36 But he who misses me harms himself;
all who hate me love death."

†
8, 14: What is here predicated of wisdom is elsewhere attributed to God (Jb 12, 13–16).
8, 22–31: Wisdom is of divine origin. It is here represented as a being which existed before all things (22–26) and concurred with God when he planned and executed the creation of the universe, adorned it with beauty and variety, and established its wonderful order (27–30). Here that plurality of divine Persons is foreshadowed which was afterward to be fully revealed when Wisdom in the Person of Jesus Christ became incarnate.
8, 23: *Poured forth:* the exact meaning of the Hebrew is uncertain; the expression must imply the equivalent of "born." The Hebrews likened the movement of air and of spirit to that of liquids.

8, 24–26: The formless mass from which God created the heavens and the earth; cf Gn 1, 1f; 2, 4ff.
8, 30: *His craftsman:* furnishing God with the plan, as it were, for the creation of all things; cf Jb 38, 1f; Wis 7, 22—8, 1. *I was his delight:* the ever-present object of God's complacency.

*
8, 11: Prv 3, 15; Wis 7, 8.
8, 13: Prv 6, 16f; 16, 5.
8, 18: Prv 3, 16.
8, 19: Prv 3, 14.
8, 22: Wis 9, 9; Sir 1, 1;
24, 9.
8, 23: Sir 1, 4.
8, 27: Prv 3, 19; Sir 24, 4f.
8, 30: Wis 9, 9.
8, 35: Prv 3, 13–18; 4, 22.

Introducing ▶ LADY WISDOM

As you read the description of wisdom in Prv 8, 1—9, 11, you might get the impression that you are reading about a goddess. But that's not the case. The wisdom writers borrowed from neighboring cultures the idea of describing wisdom as a beautiful and eternal aspect of God. They exquisitely embodied the idea of wisdom in the figure of Lady Wisdom. Lady Wisdom comes from God. She was present at the Creation of the world, and she has a special understanding of the world and its workings. For the wisdom writers, Lady Wisdom was an aspect of God that wise people would want to pursue because she reveals the right ways to live and behave.

▶ Prv 8, 1—9, 11

The Two Banquets

9 ¹† Wisdom has built her house,
    she has set up her seven columns;
² She has dressed her meat, mixed her wine,
    yes, she has spread her table.
³*†She has sent out her maidens; she calls
    from the heights out over the city:
⁴ "Let whoever is simple turn in here;
    to him who lacks understanding, I say,
⁵ Come, eat of my food,
    and drink of the wine I have mixed!
⁶ Forsake foolishness that you may live;
    advance in the way of understanding.
¹¹* For by me your days will be multiplied
    and the years of your life increased."

⁷ He who corrects an arrogant man earns insult;
    and he who reproves a wicked man
        incurs opprobrium.
⁸* Reprove not an arrogant man, lest he hate you;
    reprove a wise man, and he will love you.
⁹ Instruct a wise man, and he becomes
        still wiser;
    teach a just man, and he advances
        in learning.

¹⁰* The beginning of wisdom is the fear of
        the LORD,
    and knowledge of the Holy One
        is understanding.
¹² If you are wise, it is to your own advantage;

and if you are arrogant, you alone shall
    bear it.

¹³* The woman Folly is fickle,
    she is inane, and knows nothing.
¹⁴ She sits at the door of her house
    upon a seat on the city heights,
¹⁵ Calling to passers-by
    as they go on their straight way:
¹⁶ "Let whoever is simple turn in here,

The beginning of **wisdom** is the fear of the **LORD**, and knowledge of the **Holy One** is **understanding**

9, 10

---

† **9, 1–6.13–18:** Wisdom and folly are represented as matrons, each inviting people to her banquet. Wisdom offers the food and drink of divine doctrine and virtue which give life (1–6). Unstable and senseless folly furnishes the stolen bread and water of deceit and vice which bring death to her guests.
9, 3: *She calls:* i.e., indirectly, through her maidens; but the text

could also mean that wisdom herself publicly proclaims her invitation.

* **9, 3:** Prv 8, 1f.
9, 11: Prv 3, 2.16; 4, 10;
    10, 27.
9, 8: Sir 10, 27.

9, 10: Prv 1, 7; Jb 28, 28; Ps
    111, 10; Sir 1, 16.
9, 13–18: Prv, 7, 7–27.

or who lacks understanding; for to him I say,

17† Stolen water is sweet,
and bread gotten secretly is pleasing!"

18† Little he knows that the shades are there,
that in the depths of the nether world are
her guests!

II: First Collection of the Proverbs of Solomon†

10 1* The Proverbs of Solomon:

A wise son makes his father glad,
but a foolish son is a grief to his mother.

2* Ill-gotten treasures profit nothing,
but virtue saves from death.

3 The LORD permits not the just to hunger,
but the craving of the wicked he thwarts.

4* The slack hand impoverishes,
but the hand of the diligent enriches.

5 A son who fills the granaries in summer is
a credit;
a son who slumbers during harvest,
a disgrace.

6 Blessings are for the head of the just,
but a rod for the back of the fool.

7 The memory of the just will be blessed,
but the name of the wicked will rot.

8 A wise man heeds commands,
but a prating fool will be overthrown.

9 He who walks honestly walks securely,
but he whose ways are crooked will
fare badly.

10 He who winks at a fault causes trouble,
but he who frankly reproves promotes peace.

11 A fountain of life is the mouth of the just,
but the mouth of the wicked
conceals violence.

did you KNOW?

Live Justly

In Proverbs 10, we are given a list of the benefits of being a just person. In this chapter, a just person is one who is fair, right, moral, honest, and truthful. We read that a just person not only receives blessings, life, wisdom, and joy; he or she, by acting justly, also fulfills God's will.

Throughout the New Testament, Jesus tells his followers that his way is the just way. The parables of the Good Samaritan (see Lk 10, 29–37) and the Unforgiving Servant (see Mt 18, 21–35) are reminders of this. Living as a just person may not be easy, but it is what Christ asks of his followers.

▸ **Proverbs, chapter 10**

P R V

12*† Hatred stirs up disputes,
but love covers all offenses.

13 On the lips of the intelligent is
found wisdom,
[but the mouth of the wicked
conceals violence].

14 Wise men store up knowledge,
but the mouth of a fool is imminent ruin.

15† The rich man's wealth is his strong city;
the ruination of the lowly is their poverty.

16* The just man's recompense leads to life,
the gains of the wicked, to sin.

17* A path to life is his who heeds admonition,
but he who disregards reproof goes astray.

18 It is the lips of the liar that conceal hostility;
but he who spreads accusations is a fool.

9, 17: The secrecy implies wrongdoing.
9, 18: The banquet chamber of folly is a tomb from which no one who enters it is released.
10, 1—22, 16: The varied contents of this first collection of Solomon's proverbs apply mostly to individual life. Each of its three hundred and seventy-five proverbs is meant to be distinct from the others, developing one idea through contrasting parallelism in chapters 10—15, and a climactic treatment in 16—22.
10, 12: *Love covers all offenses:* a favorite maxim of the Apostles; cf 1 Cor 13, 7; Jas 5, 20; 1 Pt 4, 8; also Prv 17, 9.

10, 15: The inspired author reflects upon the reality of the power of money and the defeat of poverty, without approving these things.

10, 1: Prv 1, 1; 15, 20; 17, 25;
19, 13; 25, 1; 29, 15.
10, 2: Prv 11, 4.6.
10, 4: Prv 6, 11; 12, 24; 13,
4; 20, 13; 28, 19.
10, 12: 1 Cor 13, 4–7;
1 Pt 4, 8.
10, 16: Prv 11, 18f.
10, 17: Prv 15, 10.

Nothing But the Truth

"Do you swear to tell the truth, the whole truth, and nothing but the truth, so help you God?"

We have all heard these words. They are asked of every witness about to testify in a courtroom. In addition to responding positively to this crucial question, witnesses are called to place a hand on the Bible. All of this is to try to ensure that they will be honest. But despite this oath, some witnesses lie. We call that crime perjury, and it carries a severe penalty because someone's innocence or guilt may be hanging on the sworn testimony.

Proverbs 10, 18 tells us, "It is the lips of the liar that conceal hostility." Just as dishonesty is an act of hatred, so is honesty an act of love. Ultimately, our lies end up hurting others and damaging our integrity. Whether in the courtroom or in everyday life, we must always strive to tell "the truth, the whole truth, and nothing but the truth."

▸ **Prv 10, 18–21**

19* Where words are many, sin is not wanting;
    but he who restrains his lips does well.

20 Like choice silver is the just man's tongue;
    the heart of the wicked is of little worth.

21 The just man's lips nourish many,
    but fools die for want of sense.

22*†It is the LORD'S blessing that brings wealth,
    and no effort can substitute for it.

23 Crime is the entertainment of the fool;
    so is wisdom for the man of sense.

24 What the wicked man fears will befall him,
    but the desire of the just will be granted.

25 When the tempest passes, the wicked man is
    no more;
    but the just man is established forever.

26 As vinegar to the teeth, and smoke to the eyes,
    is the sluggard to those who use him as
    a messenger.

27* The fear of the LORD prolongs life,
    but the years of the wicked are brief.

28 The hope of the just brings them joy,
    but the expectation of the wicked comes
    to nought.

29 The LORD is a stronghold to him who
    walks honestly,
    but to evildoers, their downfall.

30 The just man will never be disturbed,
    but the wicked will not abide in the land.

31 The mouth of the just yields wisdom,
    but the perverse tongue will be cut off.

32 The lips of the just know how to please,
    but the mouth of the wicked, how
    to pervert.

11 1* False scales are an abomination
    to the LORD,
    but a full weight is his delight.

2 When pride comes, disgrace comes;
    but with the humble is wisdom.

3 The honesty of the upright guides them;
    the faithless are ruined by their
    duplicity.

4*†Wealth is useless on the day of wrath,
    but virtue saves from death.

5* The honest man's virtue makes his
    way straight,
    but by his wickedness the wicked man
    falls.

---

† **10, 22:** The blessing of God rather than our own industry crowns our efforts with success; cf Ps 127, 1f; Mt 6, 25–34.
11, 4: *Wealth . . . death:* not what a man is worth but what he is, counts before God.

10, 19: Prv 17, 27; Sir 20, 17;
    Jas 1, 19.
10, 22: Sir 11, 22.
10, 27: Prv 3, 2; 4, 10; 9, 11;
    14, 27.
11, 1: Prv 16, 11; 20, 10; Lv
    19, 35f.
11, 4: Prv 10, 2.
11, 5: Prv 28, 18.

6　The virtue of the upright saves them,
　　but the faithless are caught in their
　　　own intrigue.

7*　When a wicked man dies his hope perishes,
　　and what is expected from strength comes
　　　to nought.

8　The just man escapes trouble,
　　and the wicked man falls into it in
　　　his stead.

9*　With his mouth the impious man would ruin
　　　his neighbor,
　　but through their knowledge the just make
　　　their escape.

10*　When the just prosper, the city rejoices;
　　and when the wicked perish, there
　　　is jubilation.

11　Through the blessing of the righteous the city
　　　is exalted,
　　but through the mouth of the wicked it
　　　is overthrown.

Gossip

Oh, God, forgive me!
　I gossiped about someone's family
today.
I don't even know if what I said was true.
But it made me feel important to tell it to
　my friends.
Help me keep my mouth shut!
When someone tells me a secret, seal it into
　my heart,
and keep it away from my lips!
Gossip can seem like fun, but it hurts
　people.
I can't stop thinking about how the target
　of my gossip would feel
if she or he knew what I said about the
　family.
Oh, God, teach me to be trustworthy!
　Amen.

▶ Prv 11, 13

12　He who reviles his neighbor has no sense,
　　but the intelligent man keeps silent.

13*　A newsmonger reveals secrets,
　　but a trustworthy man keeps a
　　　confidence.

14*　For lack of guidance a people falls;
　　security lies in many counselors.

15*　He is in a bad way who becomes surety
　　　for another,
　　but he who hates giving pledges is safe.

16　A gracious woman wins esteem,
　　but she who hates virtue is covered
　　　with shame.

[The slothful become impoverished,
　　but the diligent gain wealth.]

17　A kindly man benefits himself,
　　but a merciless man harms himself.

18*　The wicked man makes empty profits,
　　but he who sows virtue has a sure reward.

19　Virtue directs toward life,
　　but he who pursues evil does so to
　　　his death.

20　The depraved in heart are an abomination to
　　　the LORD,
　　but those who walk blamelessly are
　　　his delight.

21　Truly the evil man shall not go unpunished,
　　but those who are just shall escape.

22　Like a golden ring in a swine's snout
　　is a beautiful woman with a
　　　rebellious disposition.

23　The desire of the just ends only in good;
　　the expectation of the wicked is wrath.

24　One man is lavish yet grows still richer;
　　another is too sparing, yet is the
　　　poorer.

25　He who confers benefits will be
　　　amply enriched,
　　and he who refreshes others will himself
　　　be refreshed.

11, 7: Prv 10, 28; Wis 3, 18.　　　11, 10: Prv 28, 12; 29, 2.
11, 9: Prv 29, 5.

11, 13: Prv 20, 19.　　　　　　　11, 15: Prv 6, 1f.
11, 14: Prv 15, 22; 20, 18; 24, 6.　　11, 18: Prv 10, 16.

PRV

26 Him who monopolizes grain, the
  people curse—
  but blessings upon the head of him who
    distributes it!

27 He who seeks the good commands favor,
  but he who pursues evil will have evil
    befall him.

28* He who trusts in his riches will fall,
  but like green leaves the just flourish.

29 He who upsets his household has empty air
  for a heritage;
  and the fool will become slave to the
    wise man.

30 The fruit of virtue is a tree of life,
  but violence takes lives away.

31* If the just man is punished on earth,
  how much more the wicked and the sinner!

12 1* He who loves correction loves
  knowledge,
  but he who hates reproof is stupid.

2 The good man wins favor from the LORD,
  but the schemer is condemned by him.

3 No man is built up by wickedness,
  but the root of the just will never
    be disturbed.

4* A worthy wife is the crown of her husband,
  but a disgraceful one is like rot in his bones.

5 The plans of the just are legitimate;
  the designs of the wicked are deceitful.

6 The words of the wicked are a deadly ambush,
  but the speech of the upright saves them.

7 The wicked are overthrown and are no more,
  but the house of the just stands firm.

8 According to his good sense a man is praised,
  but one with a warped mind is despised.

9* Better a lowly man who supports himself
  than one of assumed importance who lacks
    bread.

10 The just man takes care of his beast,
  but the heart of the wicked is merciless.

11* He who tills his own land has food in plenty,
  but he who follows idle pursuits is a fool.

12 The stronghold of evil men will
  be demolished,
  but the root of the just is enduring.

13 In the sin of his lips the evil man is ensnared,
  but the just comes free of trouble.

14*†From the fruit of his words a man has his fill
  of good things,
  and the work of his hands comes back to
    reward him.

15 The way of the fool seems right in his
  own eyes,
  but he who listens to advice is wise.

16 The fool immediately shows his anger,
  but the shrewd man passes over an
    insult.

17* He tells the truth who states what he is
  sure of,
  but a lying witness speaks deceitfully.

18 The prating of some men is like sword
  thrusts,
  but the tongue of the wise is healing.

19 Truthful lips endure forever,
  the lying tongue, for only a moment.

20 Deceit is in the hands of those who plot evil,
  but those who counsel peace have joy.

21 No harm befalls the just,
  but the wicked are overwhelmed
    with misfortune.

22* Lying lips are an abomination to the LORD,
  but those who are truthful are his delight.

23 A shrewd man conceals his knowledge,
  but the hearts of fools gush forth folly.

24* The diligent hand will govern,
  but the slothful will be enslaved.

---

† **12, 14:** Cf Mt 7, 17; Gal 6, 8.

11, 28: Ps 52, 9f.   **12, 1:** Prv 15, 5.10; 29, 1; Sir
11, 31: 1 Pt 4, 18.   19, 5; 21, 6.

12, 4: Sir 26, 1.16.   **12, 17:** Prv 14, 5.
12, 9: Sir 10, 26.   **12, 22:** Prv 6, 17.
12, 11: Prv 28, 19; Sir 20, 27.   **12, 24:** Prv 10, 4; 13, 4.
12, 14: Prv 13, 2; 18, 20.

Break the Cycle of Hopelessness

When Lucy joined the gang, she thought she had finally found a place to belong and that her new "family" would do anything for her. The gang offered many things she didn't find at home or in school. She spent a great deal of time with her new friends. Before long, they were encouraging her to do things she didn't feel comfortable doing. When they were able to sell what she had stolen, the money was good, and the gang enjoyed freely spending it. Lucy is now in prison, serving time for armed robbery.

Proverbs 13, 11 tells us that quick wealth doesn't last. Verse 20 says that the companion of fools will not do well in life. For many youth in detention centers or prisons, Lucy's story sounds familiar. That's wisdom they and many others—maybe we too—need to hear.

In the absence of caring adults, healthy role models, and detention center ministers, the cycle of hopelessness is free to continue and often results in stories like Lucy's. Find out how your parish or youth group can help at-risk youth and other young people in prison. Help them break the cycle of hopelessness.

▶ Prv 13, 11.20

P
R
V

25* Anxiety in a man's heart depresses it,
    but a kindly word makes it glad.

26 The just man surpasses his neighbor,
    but the way of the wicked leads them
        astray.

27 The slothful man catches not his prey,
    but the wealth of the diligent man is great.

28 In the path of justice there is life,
    but the abominable way leads to death.

13

1 A wise son loves correction,
    but the senseless one heeds no rebuke.

2* From the fruit of his words a man eats
        good things,
    but the treacherous one craves violence.

3* He who guards his mouth protects his life;
    to open wide one's lips brings downfall.

4 The soul of the sluggard craves in vain,
    but the diligent soul is amply satisfied.

5 Anything deceitful the just man hates,
    but the wicked brings shame and disgrace.

6* Virtue guards one who walks honestly,
    but the downfall of the wicked is sin.

7 One man pretends to be rich, yet has nothing;
    another pretends to be poor, yet has
        great wealth.

8 A man's riches serve as ransom for his life,
    but the poor man heeds no rebuke.

9*† The light of the just shines gaily,
    but the lamp of the wicked goes out.

10 The stupid man sows discord by his insolence,
    but with those who take counsel is wisdom.

11* Wealth quickly gotten dwindles away,
    but amassed little by little, it grows.

12 Hope deferred makes the heart sick,
    but a wish fulfilled is a tree of life.

13† He who despises the word must pay for it,
    but he who reveres the commandment will
        be rewarded.

14 The teaching of the wise is a fountain of life,
    that a man may avoid the snares of death.

15 Good sense brings favor,
    but the way of the faithless is their ruin.

16 The shrewd man does everything with prudence,
    but the fool peddles folly.

13, 9: *Light . . . lamp:* symbols of life and prosperity; cf Prv 4, 18f.
13, 13: *Word:* advice, or God's law.

12, 25: Prv 15, 13; 17, 22.   13, 6: Prv 11, 3.5f.
13, 2: Prv 12, 14; 18, 20.   13, 9: Prv 24, 20.
13, 3: Prv 18, 7; 21, 23.   13, 11: Prv 28, 20.22.

17   A wicked messenger brings on disaster,
    but a trustworthy envoy is a healing remedy.

18   Poverty and shame befall the man who
    disregards correction,
    but he who heeds reproof is honored.

19   Lust indulged starves the soul,
    but fools hate to turn from evil.

20* Walk with wise men and you will
    become wise,
    but the companion of fools will fare badly.

21   Misfortune pursues sinners,
    but the just shall be recompensed with good.

22   The good man leaves an inheritance to his
    children's children,
    but the wealth of the sinner is stored up for
    the just.

23   A lawsuit devours the tillage of the poor,
    but some men perish for lack of a
    law court.

24* He who spares his rod hates his son,
    but he who loves him takes care to chastise
    him.

25   When the just man eats, his hunger
    is appeased;
    but the belly of the wicked suffers want.

14

1   Wisdom builds her house,
    but Folly tears hers down with her
    own hands.

2   He who walks uprightly fears the LORD,
    but he who is devious in his ways
    spurns him.

3   In the mouth of the fool is a rod for his
    back,
    but the lips of the wise preserve them.

4   Where there are no oxen, the crib
    remains empty;
    but large crops come through the strength
    of the bull.

5* A truthful witness does not lie,
    but a false witness utters lies.

6   The senseless man seeks in vain for wisdom,
    but knowledge is easy to the man
    of intelligence.

7   To avoid the foolish man, take steps!
    But knowing lips one meets with by surprise.

8   The shrewd man's wisdom gives him
    knowledge of his way,
    but the folly of fools is their deception.

9   Guilt lodges in the tents of the arrogant,
    but favor in the house of the just.

10   The heart knows its own bitterness,
    and in its joy no one else shares.

11* The house of the wicked will be destroyed,
    but the tent of the upright will flourish.

12* Sometimes a way seems right to a man,
    but the end of it leads to death!

13   Even in laughter the heart may be sad
    and the end of joy may be sorrow.

14   The scoundrel suffers the consequences of
    his ways,
    and the good man reaps the fruit of
    his paths.

15   The simpleton believes everything,
    but the shrewd man measures his steps.

16   The wise man is cautious and shuns evil;
    the fool is reckless and sure of himself.

17   The quick-tempered man makes a fool
    of himself,
    but the prudent man is at peace.

18   The adornment of simpletons is folly,
    but shrewd men gain the crown
    of knowledge.

19   Evil men must bow down before the good,
    and the wicked, at the gates of the just.

20* Even by his neighbor the poor man is hated,
    but the friends of the rich are many.

21   He sins who despises the hungry;
    but happy is he who is kind to the poor!

13, 20: Sir 6, 34; 8, 8.17.   13f; 29, 15; Sir 30,
13, 24: Prv 19, 18; 22,15; 23,   1.8–13.

14, 5: Prv 12, 17.   14, 20: Prv 19, 4.7;
14, 11: Prv 3, 33; 12, 7; 15, 25.   Sir 6, 8.12.
14, 12: Prv 16, 25.

22 Do not those who plot evil go astray?
But those intent on good gain kindness
and constancy.

23 In all labor there is profit,
but mere talk tends only to penury.

24 The crown of the wise is resourcefulness;
the diadem of fools is folly.

25 The truthful witness saves lives,
but he who utters lies is a betrayer.

26 In the fear of the LORD is a strong defense;
even for one's children he will be a
refuge.

27 The fear of the LORD is a fountain of life,
that a man may avoid the snares of
death.

28 In many subjects lies the glory of the king;
but if his people are few, it is the
prince's ruin.

29* The patient man shows much good sense,
but the quick-tempered man displays folly
at its height.

30 A tranquil mind gives life to the body,
but jealousy rots the bones.

31* He who oppresses the poor blasphemes
his Maker,
but he who is kind to the needy
glorifies him.

32 The wicked man is overthrown by
his wickedness,
but the just man finds a refuge in
his honesty.

33 In the heart of the intelligent wisdom
abides,
but in the bosom of fools it is unknown.

34 Virtue exalts a nation,
but sin is a people's disgrace.

35 The king favors the intelligent servant,
but the worthless one incurs his wrath.

15

1* A mild answer calms wrath,
but a harsh word stirs up anger.

2 The tongue of the wise pours out knowledge,
but the mouth of fools spurts forth folly.

3 The eyes of the LORD are in every place,
keeping watch on the evil and the good.

4 A soothing tongue is a tree of life,
but a perverse one crushes the spirit.

5* The fool spurns his father's admonition,
but prudent is he who heeds reproof.

6 In the house of the just there are ample
resources,
but the earnings of the wicked are in turmoil.

7 The lips of the wise disseminate knowledge,
but the heart of fools is perverted.

8* The sacrifice of the wicked is an abomination
to the LORD,
but the prayer of the upright is his delight.

9* The way of the wicked is an abomination to
the LORD,
but he loves the man who pursues virtue.

10 Severe punishment is in store for the man
who goes astray;
he who hates reproof will die.

11† The nether world and the abyss lie open
before the LORD;
how much more the hearts of men!

12 The senseless man loves not to be reproved;
to wise men he will not go.

13* A glad heart lights up the face,
but by mental anguish the spirit is broken.

14 The mind of the intelligent man
seeks knowledge,
but the mouth of fools feeds on folly.

15 Every day is miserable for the depressed,
but a lighthearted man has a
continual feast.

15, 11: *Nether world* . . . *abyss:* the abode of the dead, signifying
the profound obscurity which is open nevertheless to the sight and
power of God.

14, 29: Prv 16, 32; 19, 11;
Jas 1, 19.
14, 31: Prv 17, 5.
15, 1: Prv 25, 15; Sir 6, 5.
15, 5: Prv 12, 1; 13, 18.

15, 8: Prv 21, 27; Eccl 4, 17;
Sir 34, 18ff; Is 1,
11–15.
15, 9: Prv 11, 20; 21, 21.
15, 13: Prv 12, 25; 17, 22; Sir
30, 22.

16† Better a little with fear of the LORD
    than a great fortune with anxiety.

17 Better a dish of herbs where love is
    than a fatted ox and hatred with it.

18* An ill-tempered man stirs up strife,
    but a patient man allays discord.

19 The way of the sluggard is hemmed in as
    with thorns,
    but the path of the diligent is a highway.

20* A wise son makes his father glad,
    but a fool of a man despises his mother.

21 Folly is joy to the senseless man,
    but the man of understanding goes the
    straight way.

22* Plans fail when there is no counsel,
    but they succeed when counselors are many.

23* There is joy for a man in his utterance;
    a word in season, how good it is!

24 The path of life leads the prudent
    man upward,
    that he may avoid the nether world below.

25 The LORD overturns the house of the proud,
    but he preserves intact the
    widow's landmark.

26* The wicked man's schemes are an
    abomination to the LORD,
    but the pure speak what is pleasing to him.

27 He who is greedy of gain brings ruin on his
    own house,
    but he who hates bribes will live.

28 The just man weighs well his utterance,
    but the mouth of the wicked pours out evil.

29 The LORD is far from the wicked,
    but the prayer of the just he hears.

30 A cheerful glance brings joy to the heart;
    good news invigorates the bones.

31* He who listens to salutary reproof
    will abide among the wise.

32 He who rejects admonition despises his
    own soul,
    but he who heeds reproof
    gains understanding.

33* The fear of the LORD is training for
    wisdom,
    and humility goes before honors.

16 ¹† Man may make plans in his heart,
    but what the tongue utters is from
    the LORD.

2* All the ways of a man may be pure in his
    own eyes,
    but it is the LORD who proves the spirit.

3 Entrust your works to the LORD,
    and your plans will succeed.

4† The LORD has made everything for his
    own ends,
    even the wicked for the evil day.

5* Every proud man is an abomination to
    the LORD;
    I assure you that he will not
    go unpunished.

Offering Your Day to God

Follow the advice of Prv 16, 3, and start each day with a prayer like this one:

Dearest LORD, today I offer you all my thoughts, deeds, and words. Let everything I do reflect your love and goodness. Amen.

▶ Prv 16, 3

15, 16f: Not the amount of temporal goods but the virtue of their possessor makes them a source of happiness.
  16, 1: Words, like actions, often produce results different from those which were planned.
  16, 4: Even the wicked, in their punishment, cannot escape glorifying God's justice.

15, 18: Prv 26, 21; 29, 22; Sir 28, 11.
15, 20: Prv 10, 1; 29, 3.
15, 22: Prv 11, 14.
15, 23: Prv 25, 11; Sir 20, 6.
15, 26: Prv 6, 18.
15, 31: Prv 25, 12.
15, 33: Prv 1, 7; Sir 1, 24.
16, 2: Prv 21, 2.
16, 5: Prv 6, 16f; 8, 13.

6 By kindness and piety guilt is expiated,
   and by the fear of the LORD man avoids evil.

7 When the LORD is pleased with a man's ways,
   he makes even his enemies be at peace
      with him.

8 Better a little with virtue,
   than a large income with injustice.

9* In his mind a man plans his course,
   but the LORD directs his steps.

10† The king's lips are an oracle;
   no judgment he pronounces is false.

11* Balance and scales belong to the LORD;
   all the weights used with them are his
      concern.

12* Kings have a horror of wrongdoing,
   for by righteousness the throne endures.

13* The king takes delight in honest lips,
   and the man who speaks what is right he
      loves.

14* The king's wrath is like messengers of death,
   but a wise man can pacify it.

15 In the light of the king's countenance is life,
   and his favor is like a rain cloud in spring.

16* How much better to acquire wisdom
      than gold!
   To acquire understanding is more desirable
      than silver.

17 The path of the upright avoids misfortune;
   he who pays attention to his way safeguards
      his life.

18 Pride goes before disaster,
   and a haughty spirit before a fall.

19* It is better to be humble with the meek
   than to share plunder with the proud.

20 He who plans a thing will be successful;
   happy is he who trusts in the LORD!

21 The wise man is esteemed for
      his discernment,
   yet pleasing speech increases
      his persuasiveness.

22 Good sense is a fountain of life to
      its possessor,
   but folly brings chastisement on fools.

23 The mind of the wise man makes
      him eloquent,
   and augments the persuasiveness of
      his lips.

24 Pleasing words are a honeycomb,
   sweet to the taste and healthful to
      the body.

25* Sometimes a way seems right to a man,
   but the end of it leads to death!

26* The laborer's appetite labors for him,
   for his mouth urges him on.

27 A scoundrel is a furnace of evil,
   and on his lips there is a scorching fire.

28* An intriguer sows discord,
   and a talebearer separates bosom friends.

29 A lawless man allures his neighbor,
   and leads him into a way that is not good.

30 He who winks his eye is plotting trickery;
   he who compresses his lips has
      mischief ready.

31* Gray hair is a crown of glory;
   it is gained by virtuous living.

32* A patient man is better than a warrior,
   and he who rules his temper, than he who
      takes a city.

33† When the lot is cast into the lap,
   its decision depends entirely on the LORD.

17 ¹ Better a dry crust with peace
      than a house full of feasting
      with strife.

16, 10: Decisions of supreme judicial authority were presumed disinterested and correct.
   16, 33: The favorable or unfavorable result of chance depends on God. Deciding strifes and doubts by lot was practiced by the ancient Hebrews; cf Ex 28, 15–30; Lv 16, 8; Jos 7, 14; 1 Sm 10, 20f.

16, 9: Prv 19, 21; 20, 24.
16, 11: Prv 11, 1.
16, 12: Prv 25, 5.
16, 13: Prv 14, 35; 22, 11.
16, 14: Prv 19, 12; 20, 2.
16, 16: Prv 8, 10f.19.
16, 19: Prv 11, 2.
16, 25: Prv 14, 12.
16, 26: Prv 10, 4.
16, 28: Prv 6, 14.19; 17, 9;
      26, 22; Sir 28, 15.
16, 31: Prv 20, 29.
16, 32: Prv 14, 29.

2† An intelligent servant will rule over a
    worthless son,
  and will share the inheritance with
    the brothers.

3 The crucible for silver, and the furnace
    for gold,
  but the tester of hearts is the LORD.

4† The evil man gives heed to wicked lips,
  and listens to falsehood from a
    mischievous tongue.

5* He who mocks the poor blasphemes
    his Maker;
  he who is glad at calamity will not
    go unpunished.

6 Grandchildren are the crown of old men,
  and the glory of children is their parentage.

7 Fine words are out of place in a fool;
  how much more, lying words in a noble!

8 A man who has a bribe to offer rates it a
    magic stone;
  at every turn it brings him success.

9 He who covers up a misdeed
    fosters friendship,

but he who gossips about it
    separates friends.

10 A single reprimand does more for a man
    of intelligence
  than a hundred lashes for a fool.

11 On rebellion alone is the wicked man bent,
  but a merciless messenger will be sent
    against him.

12 Face a bear robbed of her cubs,
  but never a fool in his folly!

13* If a man returns evil for good,
  from his house evil will not depart.

14 The start of strife is like the opening of a dam;
  therefore, check a quarrel before it begins!

15* He who condones the wicked, he who
    condemns the just,
  are both an abomination to the LORD.

16 Of what use in the fool's hand are the means
  to buy wisdom, since he has no mind
    for it?

17* He who is a friend is always a friend,
  and a brother is born for the time of stress.

LIVE IT!

Count to Ten

"The start of strife is like the opening of a dam; therefore, check a quarrel before it begins" (Prv 17, 14).

Have you ever noticed how people quickly congregate whenever a fight breaks out, especially at school? Many of the spectators seem to be in entertainment mode and are generally on one side or the other. Others want the fight to stop but lack the courage or confidence to break it up. So, everyone ends up waiting until someone in authority comes along to intervene or until one of the contenders is hurt and the fight stops.

A fight can begin so quickly. A word. A taunting phrase. A sudden turn and a punch. And there is an instant fight. Some of us have a shorter fuse than others. Some of us have a temper that flares easily or an ego that won't allow us to walk away when provoked. To paraphrase the image used in Prv 17, 14, once the water breaks through the dam, it is very hard to stop.

How do you react when you see a quarrel or a fight? How quickly do you get involved in fights or quarrels? If you have a quick temper, what can you do to control it?

▶ Prv 17, 14

17, 2: Intelligence and ability are esteemed more highly than nobility of blood.
  17, 4: To justify his own evil ways, a wicked man judges evil of
others. Cf Mt 7, 1–5.

17, 5: Prv 14, 31.   17, 15: Prv 24, 24; Is 5, 23.
17, 13: Mt 5, 39; Rom 12, 17;   17, 17: Prv 18, 24.
  1 Thes 5, 15; 1 Pt 3, 9.

18* Senseless is the man who gives his hand
       in pledge,
     who becomes surety for his neighbor.

19*†He who loves strife loves guilt;
      he who builds his gate high courts
         disaster.

20 He who is perverse in heart finds no good,
     and a double-tongued man falls
        into trouble.

21 To be a fool's parent is grief for a man;
     the father of a numskull has no joy.

22* A joyful heart is the health of the body,
      but a depressed spirit dries up the
         bones.

23 The wicked man accepts a concealed bribe
     to pervert the course of justice.

24* The man of intelligence fixes his gaze
       on wisdom,
     but the eyes of a fool are on the ends of
        the earth.

25* A foolish son is vexation to his father,
      and bitter sorrow to her who bore him.

26 It is wrong to fine an innocent man,
     but beyond reason to scourge princes.

27* He who spares his words is truly wise,
      and he who is chary of speech is a man
         of intelligence.

28 Even a fool, if he keeps silent, is
       considered wise;
     if he closes his lips, intelligent.

18 ¹ In estrangement one seeks pretexts:
        with all persistence he picks a quarrel.

2 The fool takes no delight in understanding,
     but rather in displaying what he thinks.

3 With wickedness comes contempt,
     and with disgrace comes scorn.

4* The words from a man's mouth are deep waters,
     but the source of wisdom is a flowing
        brook.

5* It is not good to be partial to the guilty,
     and so to reject a rightful claim.

6 The fool's lips lead him into strife,
     and his mouth provokes a beating.

7* The fool's mouth is his ruin;
     his lips are a snare to his life.

8* The words of a talebearer are like
       dainty morsels
     that sink into one's inmost being.

9 The man who is slack in his work
     is own brother to the man who is destructive.

10† The name of the LORD is a strong tower;
      the just man runs to it and is safe.

11* The rich man's wealth is his strong city;
      he fancies it a high wall.

12*†Before his downfall a man's heart is haughty,
      but humility goes before honors.

13*†He who answers before he hears —
      his is the folly and the shame.

14 A man's spirit sustains him in infirmity—
     but a broken spirit who can bear?

15 The mind of the intelligent gains knowledge,
     and the ear of the wise seeks knowledge.

16* A man's gift clears the way for him,
      and gains him access to great men.

17 The man who pleads his case first seems to be
       in the right;
     then his opponent comes and puts him to
        the test.

18† The lot puts an end to disputes,
      and is decisive in a controversy between
         the mighty.

P
R
V

17, 19: Builds . . . high: a symbol of arrogance.
   18, 10f: Religion is a strong support and sure refuge in the struggle of life. The rich foolishly rely on their wealth for such support.
   18, 12: Compare the Savior's words: "Whoever exalts himself
shall be humbled, but whoever humbles himself shall be exalted"
(Mt 23, 12).
   18, 13: To speak without first listening is characteristic of a fool;
cf Prv 10, 14; Sir 11, 8.
   18, 18: See note on Prv 16, 33.

17, 18: Prv 6, 1f; 11, 15.   **18, 7:** Prv 10, 14; 12, 13; 13,
17, 19: Prv 15, 18.   3; Eccl 10, 12.
17, 22: Prv 12, 25; 15, 13.   **18, 8:** Prv 26, 22.
17, 24: Eccl 8, 1.   **18, 11:** Prv 10, 15.
17, 25: Prv 10, 1; 29, 15.   **18, 12:** Prv 11, 2; 16, 18; Sir
17, 27: Prv 10, 19; Sir 1, 21;   10, 15.
   Jas 1, 19.   **18, 13:** Sir 11, 8.
18, 4: Prv 20, 5; Jn 7, 38.   **18, 16:** Prv 21, 14.
18, 5: Prv 24, 23; 28, 21.

19　A brother is a better defense than a strong city,
and a friend is like the bars of a castle.

20* †From the fruit of his mouth a man has his fill;
with the yield of his lips he sates himself.

21*　Death and life are in the power of the tongue;
those who make it a friend shall eat its fruit.

22*　He who finds a wife finds happiness;
it is a favor he receives from the LORD.

23　The poor man implores,
but the rich man answers harshly.

24*　Some friends bring ruin on us,
but a true friend is more loyal than a brother.

19 1* Better a poor man who walks in
his integrity
than he who is crooked in his ways and
rich.

2　Without knowledge even zeal is not good;
and he who acts hastily, blunders.

3　A man's own folly upsets his way,
but his heart is resentful against the LORD.

4*　Wealth adds many friends,
but the friend of the poor man deserts
him.

5*　The false witness will not go unpunished,
and he who utters lies will not escape.

6　Many curry favor with a noble;
all are friends of the man who has
something to give.

7　All the poor man's brothers hate him;
how much more do his friends shun him!

8　He who gains intelligence is his own
best friend;
he who keeps understanding will
be successful.

9　The false witness will not go unpunished,
and he who utters lies will perish.

10　Luxury is not befitting a fool;
much less should a slave rule over
princes.

11　It is good sense in a man to be slow to
anger,
and it is his glory to overlook an offense.

12*　The king's wrath is like the roaring of a lion,
but his favor, like dew on the grass.

13*　The foolish son is ruin to his father,
and the nagging of a wife is a
persistent leak.

14*　Home and possessions are an inheritance
from parents,
but a prudent wife is from the LORD.

15*　Laziness plunges a man into deep sleep,
and the sluggard must go hungry.

16*　He who keeps the precept keeps his life,
but the despiser of the word will die.

Fear of the LORD

The phrase "fear of the LORD" is used
fourteen times in Proverbs (see, for
example, 19, 23). You might ask why the
author of Proverbs keeps telling us to be
afraid of God. But in the Bible, fear of the
LORD has less to do with terror and
fright than with awe, reverence, and
respect. It's a reminder that God is far
from ordinary. To fear the LORD is to take
God very seriously.

Take some time to reflect or journal
on the question What does it mean to
fear the LORD? Describe a time when
you were awed by something about God.
Explain how you give God respect.

▶ Prv 19, 23

18, 20f: Everyone must accept the consequences, of benefit or
harm to himself, which his words produce.

18, 20: Prv 12, 14; 13, 2.　　　　**18, 21:** Sir 37, 18.

18, 22: Prv 12, 4; 19, 14; Sir
7, 26.
18, 24: Prv 17, 17.
19, 1: Prv 28, 6.
19, 4: Prv 14, 20; Sir 13,
20ff.

19, 5: Dt 19, 16–20; Dn 13,
61.
19, 12: Prv 20, 2.
19, 13: Prv 10, 1; 17, 25.
19, 14: Prv 18, 22.
19, 15: Prv 6, 9ff.
19, 16: Prv 13, 13; 16, 17.

17*†He who has compassion on the poor lends
     to the LORD,
   and he will repay him for his good
     deed.

18* Chastise your son, for in this there is
     hope;
   but do not desire his death.

19 The man of violent temper pays the
     penalty;
   even if you rescue him, you will have
     it to do again.

20 Listen to counsel and receive instruction,
   that you may eventually become wise.

21* Many are the plans in a man's heart,
   but it is the decision of the LORD that
     endures.

22 From a man's greed comes his shame;
   rather be a poor man than a liar.

23 The fear of the LORD is an aid to life;
   one eats and sleeps without being
     visited by misfortune.

24* The sluggard loses his hand in the dish;
   he will not even lift it to his mouth.

25* If you beat an arrogant man, the simple
     learn a lesson;
   if you rebuke an intelligent man, he
     gains knowledge.

26* He who mistreats his father, or drives
     away his mother,
   is a worthless and disgraceful son.

27 If a son ceases to hear instruction,
   he wanders from words of knowledge.

28 An unprincipled witness perverts justice,
   and the mouth of the wicked pours
     out iniquity.

29* Rods are prepared for the arrogant,
   and blows for the backs of fools.

20 1* Wine is arrogant, strong drink
           is riotous;
        none who goes astray for it is wise.

2* The dread of the king is as when a lion
      roars;
    he who incurs his anger forfeits his life.

3   It is honorable for a man to shun strife,
    while every fool starts a quarrel.

4   In seedtime the sluggard plows not;
    when he looks for the harvest, it is
      not there.

5* The intention in the human heart is like
      water far below the surface,
    but the man of intelligence draws it forth.

6   Many are declared to be men of virtue:
    but who can find one worthy of trust?

7   When a man walks in integrity and justice,
    happy are his children after him!

8   A king seated on the throne of judgment
    dispels all evil with his glance.

9*†Who can say, "I have made my heart clean,
    I am cleansed of my sin"?

10* Varying weights, varying measures,
    are both an abomination to the LORD.

11 Even by his manners the child betrays
    whether his conduct is innocent and right.

12 The ear that hears, and the eye that sees—
    the LORD has made them both.

13 Love not sleep, lest you be reduced to
      poverty;
    eyes wide open mean abundant food.

14† "Bad, bad!" says the buyer;
    but once he has gone his way, he boasts.

15 Like gold or a wealth of corals,
    wise lips are a precious ornament.

P
R
V

---

† **19, 17:** Cf Mt 25, 34–40.
   20, 9: Man can be free of sin only by the power of God. Cf 1 Kgs
8, 46ff; Jb 4, 17; 14, 4; Pss 51, 2ff; 130, 3f; Rom 3, 23f; 1 Jn 1, 8.
   20, 14: What one wishes to buy is valued cheaply in order that it
may be obtained at a low price; once purchased, it is deemed
more valuable.

* 19, 17: Prv 14, 21; 22, 9; 28,   20, 1: Prv 23, 29–35.
    27.   20, 2: Prv 19, 12.
19, 18: Prv 13, 24; 23, 13f.   20, 5: Prv 18, 4.
19, 21: Prv 16, 9.   20, 9: 1 Kgs 8, 46; 2 Chr
19, 24: Prv 26, 15.   6, 36; Eccl 7, 20; 1 Jn
19, 25: Prv 17, 10; 21, 11.   1, 8.
19, 26: Sir 3, 16.   20, 10: Prv 11, 1; 20, 23.
19, 29: Prv 26, 3.

16*†Take his garment who becomes surety
    for another,
    and for strangers yield it up!

17   The bread of deceit is sweet to a man,
    but afterward his mouth will be filled
    with gravel.

18   Plans made after advice succeed;
    so with wise guidance wage your war.

19   A newsmonger reveals secrets;
    so have nothing to do with a babbler!

20*†If one curses his father or mother,
    his lamp will go out at the coming
    of darkness.

21   Possessions gained hastily at the outset
    will in the end not be blessed.

22* Say not, "I will repay evil!"
    Trust in the LORD and he will help you.

23* Varying weights are an abomination to
    the LORD,
    and false scales are not good.

24*†Man's steps are from the LORD;
    how, then, can a man understand his
    way?

25† Rashly to pledge a sacred gift is a trap for
    a man,
    or to regret a vow once made.

26   A wise king winnows the wicked,
    and threshes them under the cartwheel.

27   A lamp from the LORD is the breath of man;
    it searches through all his inmost being.

28* Kindness and piety safeguard the king,
    and he upholds his throne by justice.

29* The glory of young men is their strength,
    and the dignity of old men is gray hair.

30   Evil is cleansed away by bloody lashes,
    and a scourging to the inmost being.

21

1 Like a stream is the king's heart in the
    hand of the Lord;
    wherever it pleases him, he directs it.

2* All the ways of a man may be right in his
    own eyes,
    but it is the LORD who proves hearts.

3*†To do what is right and just
    is more acceptable to the LORD
    than sacrifice.

4   Haughty eyes and a proud heart—
    the tillage of the wicked is sin.

5   The plans of the diligent are sure of profit,
    but all rash haste leads certainly to poverty.

6   He who makes a fortune by a lying tongue
    is chasing a bubble over deadly snares.

7   The oppression of the wicked will sweep
    them away,
    because they refuse to do what is right.

8   The way of the culprit is crooked,
    but the conduct of the innocent is right.

9* It is better to dwell in a corner of
    the housetop
    than in a roomy house with a quarrelsome
    woman.

10   The soul of the wicked man desires evil;
    his neighbor finds no pity in his eyes.

11* When the arrogant man is punished, the
    simple are the wiser;
    when the wise man is instructed, he gains
    knowledge.

12   The just man appraises the house of the wicked:
    there is one who brings down the wicked
    to ruin.

†————————————————————————————

20, 16: Caution is again advised in the matter of becoming surety; cf Prv 6, 1ff.

20, 20: *His lamp will go out:* misfortune, even death, awaits him; cf Prv 13, 9; Ex 21, 17.

20, 24: Man is dependent upon God and cannot fully foresee his own course.

20, 25: This verse cautions against making vows without proper reflection; cf Dt 23, 22ff; Eccl 5, 4f.

21, 3: External rites or sacrifices do not please God unless accompanied by internal worship and right moral conduct; cf Prv 15, 8; 21, 27; Is 1, 11–15; Am 5, 22; Mal 1, 12.

20, 16: Prv 27, 13.
20, 20: Prv 30, 11.17; Ex 21,
    17; Lv 20, 9; Mt 15, 4.
20, 22: Prv 24, 29; Sir 28, 1;
    Mt 5, 39; Rom 12,
    17.19; 1 Thes 5, 15;
    1 Pt 3, 9.
20, 23: Prv 11, 1; 20, 10.

20, 24: Prv 16, 9.
20, 28: Prv 16, 12.
20, 29: Prv 16, 31.
21, 2: Prv 16, 2.
21, 3: 1 Sm 15, 22; Hos 6, 6.
21, 9: Prv 21, 19; 25, 24; 27,
    15; Sir 25, 23.
21, 11: Prv 19, 25.

13 He who shuts his ear to the cry of the poor
   will himself also call and not be heard.

14 A secret gift allays anger,
   and a concealed present, violent wrath.

15* To practice justice is a joy for the just,
    but terror for evildoers.

16† The man who strays from the way of
    good sense
    will abide in the assembly of the shades.

17 He who loves pleasure will suffer want;
   he who loves wine and perfume will not
   be rich.

18*†The wicked man serves as ransom for the just,
    and the faithless man for the righteous.

19 It is better to dwell in a wilderness
   than with a quarrelsome and vexatious wife.

20 Precious treasure remains in the house of
   the wise,
   but the fool consumes it.

21 He who pursues justice and kindness
   will find life and honor.

22 The wise man storms a city of the mighty,
   and overthrows the stronghold in which
   it trusts.

23* He who guards his mouth and his tongue
    keeps himself from trouble.

24 Arrogant is the name for the man of
   overbearing pride
   who acts with scornful effrontery.

25 The sluggard's propensity slays him,
   for his hands refuse to work.

26 Some are consumed with avarice all the day,
   but the just man gives unsparingly.

27* The sacrifice of the wicked is an abomination,
    the more so when they offer it with a bad
    intention.

28* The false witness will perish,
    but he who listens will finally have his say.

29 The wicked man is brazenfaced,
   but the upright man pays heed to his ways.

30 There is no wisdom, no understanding,
   no counsel, against the LORD.

31 The horse is equipped for the day of battle,
   but victory is the LORD'S.

22

1* A good name is more desirable than
   great riches,
   and high esteem, than gold and silver.

2* Rich and poor have a common bond:
   the LORD is the maker of them all.

3* The shrewd man perceives evil and hides,
   while simpletons continue on and suffer
   the penalty.

4 The reward of humility and fear of the LORD
  is riches, honor and life.

5 Thorns and snares are on the path of
  the crooked;
  he who would safeguard his life will
  shun them.

6 Train a boy in the way he should go;
  even when he is old, he will not swerve
  from it.

7 The rich rule over the poor,
  and the borrower is the slave of the lender.

8* He who sows iniquity reaps calamity,
   and the rod destroys his labors.

9 The kindly man will be blessed,
  for he gives of his sustenance to the poor.

10 Expel the arrogant man and discord goes out;
   strife and insult cease.

11* The LORD loves the pure of heart;
    the man of winning speech has the king for
    his friend.

21, 16: *Assembly of the shades:* cf note on Jb 26, 5.
   21, 18: *Wicked . . . ransom for the just:* exemplified in the history
of God's chosen people whom he ransomed from Egypt at the cost
of the life of Pharaoh and his army (Ex 14, 23–31), and from Babylon
by giving to Cyrus, the Persian conqueror, Egypt, Ethiopia and Seba,
the richest lands of the world (Is 43, 1ff).

21, 15: Prv 10, 29.
21, 18: Prv 11, 8.
21, 23: Prv 13, 3.
21, 27: Prv 15, 8; Sir 34, 18ff.
21, 28: Prv 19, 5.9.
22, 1: Eccl 7, 1.
22, 2: Prv 29, 13.
22, 3: Prv 27, 12.
22, 8: Jb 4, 8; Sir 7, 3;
   Hos 8, 7.
22, 11: Mt 5, 8.

12 The eyes of the LORD safeguard knowledge,
    but he defeats the projects of the faithless.

13*†The sluggard says, "A lion is outside;
    in the streets I might be slain."

14* The mouth of the adulteress is a deep pit;
    he with whom the LORD is angry will fall
        into it.

15 Folly is close to the heart of a child,
    but the rod of discipline will drive it far
        from him.

16† He who oppresses the poor to enrich himself
    will yield up his gains to the rich as
        sheer loss.

III: Sayings of the Wise†

17*† The sayings of the wise:

    Incline your ear, and hear my words,
        and apply your heart to my doctrine;
18 For it will be well if you keep them in
        your bosom,
        if they all are ready on your lips.
19† That your trust may be in the LORD,
        I make known to you the words of
        Amen-em-Ope.
20 Have I not written for you the "Thirty,"
        with counsels and knowledge,
21 To teach you truly
        how to give a dependable report to one
        who sends you?

22 Injure not the poor because they are poor,
        nor crush the needy at the gate;
23* For the LORD will defend their cause,
        and will plunder the lives of those who
        plunder them.

24 Be not friendly with a hotheaded man,
        nor the companion of a wrathful man,

25 Lest you learn his ways,
        and get yourself into a snare.

26* Be not one of those who give their hand
        in pledge,
        of those who become surety for debts;
27 For if you have not the means to pay,
        your bed will be taken from under you.

28* Remove not the ancient landmark
        which your fathers set up.

29 You see a man skilled at his work?
        He will stand in the presence of kings;
        he will not stand in the presence of
        obscure men.

23 ¹ When you sit down to dine with a ruler,
        keep in mind who is before you;
2† And put a knife to your throat
        if you have a ravenous appetite.
3 Do not desire his delicacies;
        they are deceitful food.
4 Toil not to gain wealth,
        cease to be concerned about it;
5 While your glance flits to it, it is gone!
        for assuredly it grows wings,
        like the eagle that flies toward heaven.

6 Do not take food with a grudging man,
        and do not desire his dainties;
7 For in his greed he is like a storm.
    "Eat and drink," he says to you,
        though his heart is not with you;
8 The little you have eaten you will vomit up,
        and you will have wasted your
        agreeable words.
9* Speak not for the fool's hearing;
        he will despise the wisdom of your words.

10* Remove not the ancient landmark,
        nor invade the fields of orphans;
11* For their redeemer is strong;
        he will defend their cause against you.

---
†

22, 13: To avoid the effort required for doing good, the sluggard
exaggerates the difficulties that must be overcome.

22, 16: Money gained by exploiting the poor is in turn lost to
those who are more wealthy.

22, 17—24, 22: This collection of proverbs, introduced as sayings of the wise, is given in the more intimate and personal form of
an address to a pupil called the son and is arranged in strophes instead of couplets.

22, 17—23, 35: The maxims warn against: oppression of the poor
and defenseless (22, 22f), anger (24f), giving surety for debts (26f),
bad manners at a king's table (23, 1f), anxiety for riches (4f), a grudging host (6ff), intemperance in food and drink (19ff.29—35), and adultery (26ff). They exhort to: careful workmanship (22, 29), respect for
the rights of orphans (23, 10f), correction of the young (13f), filial
piety (15f.22—25), and fear of the Lord (17f).

22, 19f: *Amen-em-Ope:* an Egyptian scribe to whom is attributed
a collection of maxims in Thirty chapters (v 20) composed for the instruction of his children and addressed to a young man who wishes
to enter upon a career. The inspired editor of Proverbs does not translate these, but uses their materials in constructing a similar collection of proverbs.

23, 2: *Put a knife to your throat:* a proverbial metaphor for self-
restraint.

22, 13: Prv 26, 13.
22, 14: Prv 23, 27.
22, 17: Prv 5, 1.
22, 23: Prv 23, 11.
22, 26: Prv 6, 1f; 11, 15; 17, 18.

22, 28: Prv 23, 10; Dt 19, 14;
    27, 17.
23, 9: Prv 9, 7.
23, 10: Prv 22, 28.
23, 11: Prv 22, 23.

12 Apply your heart to instruction,
        and your ears to words of knowledge.

13* Withhold not chastisement from a boy;
        if you beat him with the rod, he will not die.
14* Beat him with the rod,
        and you will save him from the nether world.

15 My son, if your heart be wise,
        my own heart also will rejoice;
16 And my inmost being will exult,
        when your lips speak what is right.

17* Let not your heart emulate sinners,
        but be zealous for the fear of the
        LORD always;
18* For you will surely have a future,
        and your hope will not be cut off.

19 Hear, my son, and be wise,
        and guide your heart in the right way.
20 Consort not with winebibbers,
        nor with those who eat meat to excess;
21 For the drunkard and the glutton come
            to poverty,
        and torpor clothes a man in rags.

22 Listen to your father who begot you,
        and despise not your mother when she
            is old.
23 Get the truth, and sell it not—
        wisdom, instruction and understanding.
24* The father of a just man will exult with glee;
        he who begets a wise son will have joy
            in him.
25 Let your father and mother have joy;
        let her who bore you exult.

26 My son, give me your heart,
        and let your eyes keep to my ways.
27 For the harlot is a deep ditch,
        and the adulteress a narrow pit;
28* Yes, she lies in wait like a robber,
        and increases the faithless among men.

29† Who scream? Who shriek?
        Who have strife? Who have anxiety?

Who have wounds for nothing?
    Who have black eyes?
30* Those who linger long over wine,
        those who engage in trials of blended wine.
31 Look not on the wine when it is red,
        when it sparkles in the glass.
    It goes down smoothly;
32   but in the end it bites like a serpent,
        or like a poisonous adder.
33 Your eyes behold strange sights,
        and your heart utters disordered thoughts;
34 You are like one now lying in the depths of
            the sea,
        now sprawled at the top of the mast.
35† "They struck me, but it pained me not;
        they beat me, but I felt it not;
    When shall I awake
        to seek wine once again?"

24 1*† Be not emulous of evil men,
        and desire not to be with them;
2 For their hearts plot violence,
        and their lips speak of foul play.

3 By wisdom is a house built,
        by understanding is it made firm;
4 And by knowledge are its rooms filled
        with every precious and pleasing possession.
5* A wise man is more powerful than a
            strong man,
        and a man of knowledge than a man
            of might;
6* For it is by wise guidance that you wage
            your war,
        and the victory is due to a wealth of
            counselors.

7*†For a fool, to be silent is wisdom;
        not to open his mouth at the gate.
8 He who plots evil doing—
        men call him an intriguer.
9 Beyond intrigue and folly and sin,
        it is arrogance that men find
            abominable.

10† If you remain indifferent in time of adversity,
        your strength will depart from you.

P
R
V

23, 29–35: A vivid description of the evil effects, physical and psychological, of drunkenness.
23, 35: Wine makes the drunkard insensible to bodily and moral harm. His one desire is to indulge again.
24, 1–22: These verses continue an exhortation to wisdom (vv 3–7.13f), and against: violence (1f), pride and intrigue (8f), callousness (10–12), injustice (15f), joy in the failure of others (17f) or scandal at their success (19f), and rebellion against authority (21f).
24, 7: *At the gate:* of the city, where justice was administered and public affairs discussed; see note on Ru 4, 1. Cf also Pss 69, 13; 127, 5; Prv 22, 22; 31, 23.31.

24, 10: *Indifferent:* to those who suffer unjustly.

23, 13: Prv 13, 24; 19, 18;	23, 30: Prv 20, 1; Sir 19, 2;
Sir 30, 1.	Hos 4, 11.
23, 14: Prv 29, 15.17.	24, 1: Prv 3, 31; 23, 17.
23, 17: Prv 3, 31; 24, 1.19.	24, 5: Prv 21, 22.
23, 18: Prv 24, 14.	24, 6: Prv 20, 18.
23, 24: Prv 10, 1.	24, 7: Sir 6, 21.
23, 28: Prv 7, 10–27.	

WISDOM AND THE ELDERS

"By wisdom is a house built . . . / And by knowledge are its rooms filled" (Prv 24, 3–4). Becoming wise is like building and furnishing a house. It doesn't happen all at once; it takes time, experience, and work. Native American cultures understand this. Wisdom is an important value for them.

In many Native American cultures, the elders have the highest place of honor because of their wisdom. Native Americans understand that it takes an entire life to grow wise. The elders have lived through much, and their advice is always worth seeking. They are relied on to settle disagreements because they have learned to judge people by their heart and their integrity, not by their money or possessions. The others in the tribe know that through listening to the elders, they too, over time, will grow wise.

▸ **Prv 24, 3–4**

11† Rescue those who are being dragged to death,
    and from those tottering to execution
        withdraw not.

12* If you say, "I know not this man!"
    does not he who tests hearts perceive it?
He who guards your life knows it,
    and he will repay each one according to his
        deeds.

13 If you eat honey, my son, because it is good,
    if virgin honey is sweet to your taste;

14* Such, you must know, is wisdom to your soul.
    If you find it, you will have a future,
        and your hope will not be cut off.

15 Lie not in wait against the home of the just man,
    ravage not his dwelling place;

16† For the just man falls seven times and
        rises again,
    but the wicked stumble to ruin.

17 Rejoice not when your enemy falls,
    and when he stumbles, let not your
        heart exult,

18 Lest the LORD see it, be displeased with you,
    and withdraw his wrath from your enemy.

19 Be not provoked with evildoers,
    nor envious of the wicked;

20* For the evil man has no future,
    the lamp of the wicked will be put out.

21† My son, fear the LORD and the king;
    have nothing to do with those who rebel
        against them;

22 For suddenly arises the destruction they send,
    and the ruin from either one, who
        can measure?

IV: Other Sayings of the Wise†

23* These also are sayings of the wise:

To show partiality in judgment is not good.

24 He who says to the wicked man, "You
        are just"—
    men will curse him, people will
        denounce him;

---

† **24, 11:** *Rescue . . . death:* most probably refers to the legal rescue of those unjustly condemned to death.

24, 16: The just man overcomes every misfortune which oppresses him. *Seven times:* i.e., an indefinite number; cf Mt 18, 21f; Lk 17, 4.

24, 21f: One owes obedience to God and to supreme civil authority (Mt 22, 21; Rom 13, 1ff; 1 Pt 2, 13f). The punishments for failure in either duty transcend the limits of private justice.

24, 23–34: This collection of sayings continues in the same vein as the preceding: it instructs in fairness (23–26) and preparation for the future (27); and warns against vengeance (28f) and slothfulness (30–34).

24, 12: Ps 62, 13; Sir 16, 12;
    Mt 16, 27; Rom 2, 6.
24, 14: Prv 23, 18.
24, 20: Prv 13, 9.
24, 23: Prv 18, 5; 28, 21; Lv 19,
    15; Dt 1, 17; 16, 19.

25 But those who convict the evildoer will
　　fare well,
　　and on them will come the blessing
　　of prosperity.
26† He gives a kiss on the lips
　　who makes an honest reply.

27† Complete your outdoor tasks,
　　and arrange your work in the field;
　　afterward you can establish your house.

28* Be not a witness against your neighbor
　　without just cause,
　　thus committing folly with your lips.
29*†Say not, "As he did to me, so will I do to him;
　　I will repay the man according to his deeds."

30 I passed by the field of the sluggard,
　　by the vineyard of the man without sense;
31 And behold! it was all overgrown with thistles;
　　its surface was covered with nettles,
　　and its stone wall broken down.
32 And as I gazed at it, I reflected;
　　I saw and learned the lesson:
33* A little sleep, a little slumber,
　　a little folding of the arms to rest—
34 Then will poverty come upon you like
　　a highwayman,
　　and want like an armed man.

V: Second Collection of the Proverbs of Solomon

25 1*† These also are proverbs of Solomon.
　　The men of Hezekiah, king of Judah, transmitted them.

2 God has glory in what he conceals,
　　kings have glory in what they fathom.
3 As the heavens in height, and the earth
　　in depth,
　　the heart of kings is unfathomable.

4 Remove the dross from silver,
　　and it comes forth perfectly purified;
5 Remove the wicked from the presence of
　　the king,
　　and his throne is made firm
　　through righteousness.

6† Claim no honor in the king's presence,
　　nor occupy the place of great men;
7* For it is better that you be told, "Come
　　up closer!"
　　than that you be humbled before the prince.

8 What your eyes have seen
　　bring not forth hastily against an opponent;
　　For what will you do later on
　　when your neighbor puts you to shame?
9 Discuss your case with your neighbor,
　　but another man's secret do not disclose;
10 Lest, hearing it, he reproach you,
　　and your ill repute cease not.

11 Like golden apples in silver settings
　　are words spoken at the proper time.
12 Like a golden earring, or a necklace of fine gold,
　　is a wise reprover to an obedient ear.

13 Like the coolness of snow in the heat of
　　the harvest
　　is a faithful messenger for the one who
　　sends him.
　　[He refreshes the soul of his master.]

14 Like clouds and wind when no rain follows
　　is the man who boastfully promises what
　　he never gives.

15* By patience is a ruler persuaded,
　　and a soft tongue will break a bone.
16 If you find honey, eat only what you need,
　　lest you become glutted with it and vomit
　　it up.

17 Let your foot be seldom in your
　　neighbor's house,
　　lest he have more than enough of you, and
　　hate you.

18 Like a club, or a sword, or a sharp arrow,
　　is the man who bears false witness against
　　his neighbor.

19 Like an infected tooth or an unsteady foot
　　is [dependence on] a faithless man in time
　　of trouble.

24, 26: *He gives a kiss on the lips:* shows himself a true friend.
　24, 27: This verse is commonly interpreted as advocating careful and practical preparation for marriage.
　24, 29: This verse indicates great progress from the principle on the law of Talion (see note on Ex 21, 23ff) toward the teaching found in Rom 12, 17ff. Cf also Prv 25, 21ff.
　25, 1: *The men of Hezekiah:* literary men at the royal court of Hezekiah who are represented as transcribing the proverbs from

other collections. Hezekiah was a reformer of national religious life (2 Chr 29, 25–30).
　25, 6f: Compare the lesson on humility which was taught by Christ (Lk 14, 7–11).

24, 28: Prv 19, 5; 25, 18.　　　25, 1: Prv 1, 1.
24, 29: Prv 20, 22.　　　　　　25, 7: Lk 14, 8ff.
24, 33f: Prv 6, 10f.　　　　　　25, 15: Prv 15, 1.4.

20* Like a moth in clothing, or a maggot in wood,
  sorrow gnaws at the human heart.

21*†If your enemy be hungry, give him food to eat,
  if he be thirsty, give him to drink;

22 For live coals you will heap on his head,
  and the LORD will vindicate you.

23 The north wind brings rain,
  and a backbiting tongue an
   angry countenance.

24* It is better to dwell in a corner of the housetop
  than in a roomy house with a quarrelsome
   woman.

25 Like cool water to one faint from thirst
  is good news from a far country.

26 Like a troubled fountain or a polluted spring
  is a just man who gives way before
   the wicked.

27† To eat too much honey is not good;
  nor to seek honor after honor.

28 Like an open city with no defenses
  is the man with no check on his feelings.

26 ¹† Like snow in summer, or rain in
   harvest,
  honor for a fool is out of place.

2 Like the sparrow in its flitting, like the
   swallow in its flight,
  a curse uncalled-for arrives nowhere.

3* The whip for the horse, the bridle for the ass,
  and the rod for the back of fools.

4† Answer not the fool according to his folly,
  lest you too become like him.

5 Answer the fool according to his folly,
  lest he become wise in his own eyes.

6 He cuts off his feet, he drinks down violence,
  who sends messages by a fool.

7† A proverb in the mouth of a fool
  hangs limp, like crippled legs.

8 Like one who entangles the stone in the sling
  is he who gives honor to a fool.

9 Like a thorn stick brandished by the hand of
   a drunkard
  is a proverb in the mouth of fools.

10 Like an archer wounding all who pass by
  is he who hires a drunken fool.

11* As the dog returns to his vomit,
  so the fool repeats his folly.

12 You see a man wise in his own eyes?
  There is more hope for a fool than for him.

13* The sluggard says, "There is a lion in the street,
  a lion in the middle of the square!"

14 The door turns on its hinges,
  the sluggard, on his bed!

15* The sluggard loses his hand in the dish;
  he is too weary to lift it to his mouth.

16 The sluggard imagines himself wiser
  than seven men who answer with good sense.

17 Like the man who seizes a passing dog by
   the ears
  is he who meddles in a quarrel not his own.

18 Like a crazed archer
  scattering firebrands and deadly arrows

19 Is the man who deceives his neighbor,
  and then says, "I was only joking."

20 For lack of wood, the fire dies out;
  and when there is no talebearer,
   strife subsides.

21* What a bellows is to live coals, what wood is
   to fire,
  such is a contentious man in enkindling
   strife.

25, 21f: Charity is invaluable in resolving enmities and restoring peace. *Live coals:* i.e., either remorse and embarrassment for the harm done, or increased punishment for refusing reconciliation. Cf Mt 5, 44; Rom 12, 20.
25, 27: *Nor . . . honor after honor:* the text is uncertain.
26, 1–28: Concrete images describe the vices of fools (1–12), of sluggards (13–16), of meddlers (17–19), of talebearers (20ff), and of flatterers (23–28).
26, 4f: There is no contradiction between these two proverbs. In

any answer the wise man gives he must protect his own interest against the fool.
26, 7ff: The fool abuses whatever knowledge he possesses.

25, 20: Sir 30, 24.   26, 11: 2 Pt 2, 22.
25, 21: Rom 12, 20.   26, 13: Prv 22, 13.
25, 24: Prv 21, 9.   26, 15: Prv 19, 24.
26, 3: Prv 19, 29; Sir 33, 25.   26, 21: Prv 15, 18; 29, 22.

22* The words of a talebearer are like
      dainty morsels
      that sink into one's inmost being.

23   Like a glazed finish on earthenware
      are smooth lips with a wicked heart.

24   With his lips an enemy pretends,
      but in his inmost being he
      maintains deceit;

25*†When he speaks graciously, trust him not,
      for seven abominations are in his heart.

26   A man may conceal hatred
      under dissimulation,
      but his malice will be revealed in
      the assembly.

27* He who digs a pit falls into it;
      and a stone comes back upon him who
      rolls it.

28   The lying tongue is its owner's enemy,
      and the flattering mouth works ruin.

27 ¹ Boast not of tomorrow,
      for you know not what any day may
      bring forth.

2   Let another praise you—not your own
      mouth;
      someone else—not your own lips.

3*   Stone is heavy, and sand a burden,
      but a fool's provocation is heavier than
      both.

4   Anger is relentless, and wrath overwhelming—
      but before jealousy who can stand?

5   Better is an open rebuke
      than a love that remains hidden.

6   Wounds from a friend may be accepted as
      well meant,
      but the greetings of an enemy one
      prays against.

7   One who is full, tramples on virgin honey;
      but to the man who is hungry, any bitter
      thing is sweet.

8   Like a bird that is far from its nest
      is a man who is far from his home.

9   Perfume and incense gladden the heart,
      but by grief the soul is torn asunder.

10   Your own friend and your father's friend
      forsake not;
      but if ruin befalls you, enter not a
      kinsman's house.
      Better is a neighbor near at hand
      than a brother far away.

11   If you are wise, my son, you will gladden
      my heart,
      and I will be able to rebut him who
      taunts me.

12* The shrewd man perceives evil and hides;
      simpletons continue on and suffer the
      penalty.

13*†Take his garment who becomes surety
      for another,
      and for the sake of a stranger, yield it up!

14† When one greets his neighbor with a loud
      voice in the early morning,
      a curse can be laid to his charge.

15* For a persistent leak on a rainy day
      the match is a quarrelsome woman.

16   He who keeps her stores up a stormwind;
      he cannot tell north from south.

17   As iron sharpens iron,
      so man sharpens his fellow man.

26, 25: *Seven abominations:* many evil intentions.
27, 13: See note on Prv 20, 16.
27, 14: The loud voice suggests hypocrisy in the greeting.

26, 22: Prv 18, 8.
26, 25: Sir 12, 10; 27, 23.
26, 27: Eccl 10, 8; Sir 27, 25f.
27, 3: Sir 22, 14f.

27, 12: Prv 22, 3.
27, 13: Prv 20, 16.
27, 15: Prv 21, 9; 25, 24.

18 He who tends a fig tree eats its fruit,
      and he who is attentive to his master will
         be enriched.

19 As one face differs from another,
      so does one human heart from another.

20* The nether world and the abyss are
         never satisfied;
      so too the eyes of men.

21 As the crucible tests silver and the
         furnace gold,
      so a man is tested by the praise he
         receives.

22 Though you should pound the fool to bits
         with the pestle, amid the grits in a mortar,
      his folly would not go out of him.

23† Take good care of your flocks,
      give careful attention to your herds;

24 For wealth lasts not forever,
      nor even a crown from age to age.

25 When the grass is taken away and the
         aftergrowth appears,
      and the mountain greens are gathered in,

26 The lambs will provide you with clothing,
      and the goats will bring the price of a field,

27 And there will be ample goat's milk to
         supply you,
      to supply your household,
      and maintenance for your maidens.

28 ¹ The wicked man flees although no one
         pursues him;
      but the just man, like a lion, feels sure
         of himself.

2† If a land is rebellious, its princes will
         be many;
      but with a prudent man it knows security.

3   A rich man who oppresses the poor
      is like a devastating rain that leaves
         no food.

4† Those who abandon the law praise the
         wicked man,
      but those who keep the law war
         against him.

5   Evil men understand nothing of justice,
      but those who seek the LORD
         understand all.

6* Better a poor man who walks in his integrity
      than he who is crooked in his ways and
         rich.

7   He who keeps the law is a wise son,
      but the gluttons' companion disgraces
         his father.

8† He who increases his wealth by interest
         and overcharge
      gathers it for him who is kind to the
         poor.

9*† When one turns away his ear from hearing
         the law,
      even his prayer is an abomination.

Integrity

A person with integrity does the right thing, even if it doesn't lead to fame or riches. A person with integrity won't lie, steal, or cheat; won't gossip, betray, or insult, not even when everyone else seems to be doing it. A person with integrity is trustworthy, dependable, and reliable. Such a person admits making mistakes and apologizes. Such a person forgives freely and doesn't hold grudges.

LORD, I'm far from perfect. But with every word I speak, every action I take, every choice I make, may I become more aware of how I am growing into a person of integrity.

▶ Prv 28, 6

27, 23–27: The land of Palestine was very suitable for flocks and herds, which formed the principal source of wealth for their owners.
28, 2: The meaning of this poorly preserved verse seems to be that frequent changes of rulers often result from moral corruption and political disorder.
28, 4: *The law:* religious and moral teaching.
28, 8: Interest and overcharge were strictly forbidden in the old

law among Israelites because it was presumed that the borrower was in distress; cf Ex 22, 25; Lv 25, 35ff; Dt 23, 19; Ps 15, 5; Ez 18, 8. Civil and divine law will take the offender's wealth from him.
28, 9: Prayers offered in bad faith are displeasing to God.

27, 20: Prv 30, 16; Eccl 4, 8.   28, 9: Prv 21, 27.
28, 6: Prv 19, 1.

10 He who seduces the upright into an evil way
    will himself fall into his own pit.
    [And blameless men will gain prosperity.]

11 The rich man is wise in his own eyes,
    but a poor man who is intelligent sees
    through him.

12 When the just are triumphant, there is
    great jubilation;
    but when the wicked gain pre-eminence,
    people hide.

13 He who conceals his sins prospers not,
    but he who confesses and forsakes them
    obtains mercy.

14 Happy the man who is always on his
    guard;
    but he who hardens his heart will fall
    into evil.

15 Like a roaring lion or a ravenous bear
    is a wicked ruler over a poor people.

16 The less prudent the prince, the more his
    deeds oppress.
    He who hates ill-gotten gain prolongs
    his days.

17 Though a man burdened with human blood
    were to flee to the grave, none should
    support him.

18 He who walks uprightly is safe,
    but he whose ways are crooked falls into
    the pit.

19* He who cultivates his land will have plenty
    of food,
    but from idle pursuits a man has his fill of
    poverty.

20* The trustworthy man will be richly blessed;
    he who is in haste to grow rich will not go
    unpunished.

21* To show partiality is never good:
    for even a morsel of bread a man may
    do wrong.

22 The avaricious man is perturbed about
    his wealth,

and he knows not when want will come
    upon him.

23 He who rebukes a man gets more thanks in
    the end
    than one with a flattering tongue.

24* He who defrauds father or mother and calls
    it no sin,
    is a partner of the brigand.

25 The greedy man stirs up disputes,
    but he who trusts in the LORD will
    prosper.

26 He who trusts in himself is a fool,
    but he who walks in wisdom is safe.

27* He who gives to the poor suffers no want,
    but he who ignores them gets many a
    curse.

28 When the wicked gain pre-eminence, other
    men hide;
    but at their fall the just flourish.

29 1 The man who remains stiff-necked and
    hates rebuke
    will be crushed suddenly beyond cure.

2* When the just prevail, the people rejoice;
    but when the wicked rule, the people
    groan.

3* He who loves wisdom makes his father glad,
    but he who consorts with harlots squanders
    his wealth.

4 By justice a king gives stability to the land;
    but he who imposes heavy taxes ruins it.

5 The man who flatters his neighbor
    is spreading a net under his feet.

6 The wicked man steps into a snare,
    but the just man runs on joyfully.

7 The just man has a care for the rights of
    the poor;
    the wicked man has no such concern.

8* Arrogant men set the city ablaze,
    but wise men calm the fury.

28, 19: Prv 12, 11.   28, 21: Prv 24, 23.
28, 20: Prv 13, 11.   28, 24: Mk 7, 11ff.

28, 27: Prv 19, 17; Sir 4, 3–8.   29, 3: Prv 5, 10; 10, 1.
29, 2: Prv 11, 10.   29, 8: Prv 11, 11.

P
R
V

⁹ If a wise man disputes with a fool,
   he may rage or laugh but can have
      no peace.

¹⁰ Bloodthirsty men hate the honest man,
   but the upright show concern for his life.

¹¹* The fool gives vent to all his anger;
   but by biding his time, the wise man
      calms it.

¹² If a ruler listens to lying words,
   his servants all become wicked.

¹³*†The poor and the oppressor have a
      common bond:
   the Lord gives light to the eyes of both.

¹⁴ If a king is zealous for the rights of the poor,
   his throne stands firm forever.

¹⁵* The rod of correction gives wisdom,
   but a boy left to his whims disgraces his
      mother.

¹⁶ When the wicked prevail, crime increases;
   but their downfall the just will behold.

¹⁷ Correct your son, and he will bring
      you comfort,
   and give delight to your soul.

¹⁸ Without prophecy the people
      become demoralized;
   but happy is he who keeps the law.

¹⁹* By words no servant can be trained;
   for he understands what is said, but
      obeys not.

²⁰* Do you see a man hasty in his words?
   More can be hoped for from a fool!

²¹ If a man pampers his servant from childhood,
   he will turn out to be stubborn.

²²* An ill-tempered man stirs up disputes,
   and a hotheaded man is the cause of many
      sins.

²³* Man's pride causes his humiliation,
   but he who is humble of spirit obtains
      honor.

²⁴† The accomplice of a thief is his own enemy:
   he hears himself put under a curse, yet
      discloses nothing.

²⁵ The fear of man brings a snare,
   but he who trusts in the LORD is safe.

²⁶ Many curry favor with the ruler,
   but the rights of each are from the LORD.

²⁷ The evildoer is an abomination to the just,
   and he who walks uprightly is an
      abomination to the wicked.

VI: The Words of Agur

30

¹† The words of Agur, son of Jakeh the
   Massaite:

The pronouncement of mortal man: "I am
      not God;†
   I am not God, that I should prevail.
² Why, I am the most stupid of men,
   and have not even human intelligence;
³ Neither have I learned wisdom,
   nor have I the knowledge of the Holy One.
⁴ Who has gone up to heaven and come
      down again—
   who has cupped the wind in his hands?
Who has bound up the waters in a cloak—
   who has marked out all the ends of
      the earth?
What is his name, what is his son's name,
   if you know it?"
⁵* Every word of God is tested;
   he is a shield to those who take refuge
      in him.
⁶* Add nothing to his words,
   lest he reprove you, and you be exposed as
      a deceiver.

VII: Numerical Proverbs

⁷ Two things I ask of you,
   deny them not to me before I die:

---

† 29, 13: God gives life to all classes of people; cf Prv 22, 2.
29, 24: *Is his own enemy*: because he not only incurs guilt as an
accomplice but, by his silence, brings down on himself the curse invoked on the unknown guilty partner.
30, 1: *Agur*: an unknown person. *Massaite*: from Massa in northern Arabia, elsewhere referred to as an encampment of the Ishmaelites (Gn 25, 14). But the word may not be intended as a place
name; it might signify "an oracle," "a prophecy."

30, 1ff: Agur wishes to stress man's insignificance when he is
compared to God; cf Jb 38—39.

29, 11: Prv 12, 16; 25, 28; Sir   29, 20: Eccl 5, 1.
   21, 26.   29, 22: Prv 15, 18; 26, 21.
29, 13: Prv 22, 2.   29, 23: Prv 11, 2; 16, 18; 18,
29, 15: Prv 13, 24; 22, 15; 23,   12; Jb 22, 29.
   13f; Sir 22, 6; 30, 1.   30, 5: Ps 12, 7.
29, 19: Sir 33, 25f.   30, 6: Dt 4, 2.

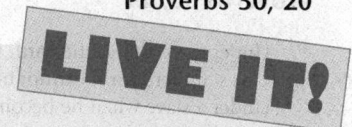

Ravens and Vultures

> The eye that mocks a father,
>   or scorns an aged mother,
> Will be plucked out by the ravens in the valley;
>   the young eagles will devour it.
>
>   (Prv 30, 17)

If this passage reflected reality, most of us would already have been eaten by those vultures hovering overhead. For who among us has not at one time mocked our parents, if not to their face, then perhaps to our friends? And is there anyone who has not disobeyed a parent?

We live in a time when families have many different forms. You might live with biological parents, stepparents, adopted parents, or foster parents. Whatever kind and number of parents you have, they need your respect, despite their weaknesses and flaws (although you must not accept verbal, physical, sexual, or other abuse).

The vast majority of us are loved by our parents. In most cases, they are trying their hardest to do what is best for us, even though it doesn't always seem that way. If we can accept this, then it might be easier to forgive them their faults and overlook some of the things they do that irritate us.

Let's keep the vultures far away!

■ What can you do to let your parents know that you love them?
■ What can you do today to show them more respect?

▶ Prv 30, 17

---

8   Put falsehood and lying far from me,
        give me neither poverty nor riches;
        [provide me only with the food I need;]
9   Lest, being full, I deny you,
        saying, "Who is the LORD?"
    Or, being in want, I steal,
        and profane the name of my God.

10 Slander not a servant to his master,
        lest he curse you, and you have to pay
        the penalty.

11*†There is a group of people that curses its father,
        and blesses not its mother.
12 There is a group that is pure in its own eyes,
        yet is not purged of its filth.
13 There is a group—how haughty their eyes!
        how overbearing their glance!
14 There is a group whose incisors are swords,
        whose teeth are knives,
    Devouring the needy from the earth,
        and the poor from among men.

15† The two daughters of the leech are,
        "Give, Give."
    Three things are never satisfied,
        four never say, "Enough!"
16* The nether world, and the barren womb;
        the earth, that is never saturated with water,
        and fire, that never says, "Enough!"
17 The eye that mocks a father,
        or scorns an aged mother,
    Will be plucked out by the ravens in the
        valley;
        the young eagles will devour it.

18† Three things are too wonderful for me,
        yes, four I cannot understand:
19 The way of an eagle in the air,
        the way of a serpent upon a rock,
    The way of a ship on the high seas,
        and the way of a man with a maiden.
20† Such is the way of an adulterous woman:
        she eats, wipes her mouth,
        and says, "I have done no wrong."

30, 11–14: Perverted people are here classified as unfilial (11), self-righteous (12), proud (13) and rapacious (14).

30, 15f: *The two daughters . . . "Give, Give":* the text is obscure but the sense seems to be that the leech is insatiable in its desire for blood, just as are the nether world for victims, the barren womb for offspring, the parched earth for water, and fire for fuel (16).

30, 18f: The soaring flight of the eagle, the mysterious movement

upon a rock of the serpent which has no feet, the path of the ship through the trackless deep, and the marvelous procreation of human life, excite great wonderment.

30, 20: This verse portrays the indifference of an adulterous woman who thinks there is no trace of her wicked act.

30, 11: Prv 20, 20.   30, 16: Prv 27, 20.

21   Under three things the earth trembles,
         yes, under four it cannot bear up:
22*   Under a slave when he becomes king,
         and a fool when he is glutted with food;
23   Under an odious woman when she is wed,
         and a maidservant when she displaces
            her mistress.

24   Four things are among the smallest on the earth,
         and yet are exceedingly wise:
25   Ants—a species not strong,
         yet they store up their food in the summer;
26†   Rock-badgers—a species not mighty,
         yet they make their home in the crags;
27   Locusts—they have no king,
         yet they migrate all in array;
28   Lizards—you can catch them with your hands,
         yet they find their way into kings' palaces.

29   Three things are stately in their stride,
         yes, four are stately in their carriage:
30   The lion, mightiest of beasts,
         who retreats before nothing;
31   The strutting cock, and the he-goat,
         and the king at the head of his people.

32†   If you have foolishly been proud
         or presumptuous—put your hand on
            your mouth;
33   For the stirring of milk brings forth curds,
         and the stirring of anger brings forth blood.

VIII: The Words of Lemuel

31   1 The words of Lemuel, king of Massa.
         The advice which his mother gave him:

2   What, my son, my first-born!
         what, O son of my womb;
         what, O son of my vows!
3*   Give not your vigor to women,
         nor your strength to those who ruin kings.
4*   It is not for kings, O Lemuel,
         not for kings to drink wine;
         strong drink is not for princes!
5   Lest in drinking they forget what the
            law decrees,
         and violate the rights of all who are in need.
6   Give strong drink to one who is perishing,
         and wine to the sorely depressed;
7   When they drink, they will forget their misery,
         and think no more of their burdens.

8   Open your mouth in behalf of the dumb,
         and for the rights of the destitute;
9   Open your mouth, decree what is just,
         defend the needy and the poor!

IX: The Ideal Wife

10*   When one finds a worthy wife,
         her value is far beyond pearls.
11   Her husband, entrusting his heart to her,
         has an unfailing prize.
12†   She brings him good, and not evil,
         all the days of her life.
13   She obtains wool and flax
         and makes cloth with skillful hands.
14†   Like merchant ships,
         she secures her provisions from afar.

? did you KNOW?

A Woman's Place

You've probably noticed that women had a much different role in biblical times than they do now. Then it was common, and expected, for women to be in the home—either their father's or their husband's—doing household chores.

Today, the Catholic church teaches that women and men share equality and that both deserve respect and mutual appreciation. It is not appropriate or just, therefore, to say that a woman's place is in the home. Women now choose where they spend their time!

Thousands of women today hold leadership positions at parish, diocesan, archdiocesan, and national levels. The church celebrates the inclusion of women in leadership positions and continues to strive for and support a more even distribution of men and women in these positions. If you are a young woman or young man interested in working for the church, ask for more information at your parish or school.

▶ Prv 31, 10–31

---

† 30, 26: *Rock-badgers*: cf note on Ps 104, 18.
   30, 32f: The anger aroused by overweening pride threatens an awesome punishment.
   31, 12: *Good, and not evil*: i.e., prosperity, not adversity.

   31, 14: *Merchant*: literally, "Canaanite" (cf v 24), probably because the merchant class had been composed chiefly of Canaanites.

30, 22: Prv 19, 10; Eccl 10, 6f.   31, 4: Prv 20, 1.
31, 3: Prv 5, 9.   31, 10–31: Sir 26, 1ff.13–18.

15 She rises while it is still night,
    and distributes food to her household.
16 She picks out a field to purchase;
    out of her earnings she plants a vineyard.
17 She is girt about with strength,
    and sturdy are her arms.
18† She enjoys the success of her dealings;
    at night her lamp is undimmed.
19 She puts her hands to the distaff,
    and her fingers ply the spindle.
20 She reaches out her hands to the poor,
    and extends her arms to the needy.
21 She fears not the snow for her household;
    all her charges are doubly clothed.
22 She makes her own coverlets;
    fine linen and purple are her clothing.
23 Her husband is prominent at the city gates
    as he sits with the elders of the land.

24 She makes garments and sells them,
    and stocks the merchants with belts.
25† She is clothed with strength and dignity,
    and she laughs at the days to come.
26 She opens her mouth in wisdom,
    and on her tongue is kindly counsel.
27 She watches the conduct of her household,
    and eats not her food in idleness.
28 Her children rise up and praise her;
    her husband, too, extols her:
29 "Many are the women of proven worth,
    but you have excelled them all."
30† Charm is deceptive and beauty fleeting;
    the woman who fears the LORD is to
    be praised.
31 Give her a reward of her labors,
    and let her works praise her at the
    city gates.

31, 18: *Her lamp is undimmed:* indicates abundance of productive work and its accompanying prosperity; cf Prv 20, 20; Jb 18, 6.
31, 25: *Laughs at the days to come:* anticipates the future with gladness free from anxiety.

31, 30: The true charm of the ideal wife is her religious spirit, for she fears the Lord; cf note on Prv 1, 7.

P
R
V

Nothing is new under the sun."
"For in much wisdom there is much sorrow, and he who stores up knowledge stores up grief."
"No one can anticipate the time of disaster."
If you saw these comments on the Internet, what would you think? That you had just found the Web site of the National Association of Pessimists? Would you be surprised to learn that all these lines come from the Bible? The author of Ecclesiastes, who was called Qoheleth (Eccl 1, 1), wrote all of them. Yet, the book is hardly a defense of pessimism. The Teacher was pointing out to the Israelites the need for a new understanding of God and life.

At a Glance

Introduction (1, 1–11).

I. Qoheleth's Investigation of Life (1, 12—6, 9).

II. Qoheleth's Conclusions (6, 10—12, 8).

Epilogue (12, 9–14).

In-depth

After a long life of careful observation, the author of Ecclesiastes was disturbed by many things:

- that wise people perished just like fools (2, 12–17)
- that those who worked hard for a living had to leave their possessions behind in death (5, 12–16)
- that sometimes bad people lived longer than good people (7, 15)
- that the most deserving did not always get what they had earned (9, 11–12)

Observing these puzzling things, the Teacher asked the obvious question: "Why should we work so hard to be wise and good?" For centuries, believers had struggled to be honest, law-abiding people in the hope of being rewarded by God. And what had they gotten? Sickness, suffering, and death—like everyone else! "Something's wrong!" the Teacher insisted. "Something's terribly wrong!"

After raising the question, the author of Ecclesiastes did not provide an answer—nor is a convincing one to be found in the writings of others in the Old Testament. However, later generations of Jews, pondering the possibility of life after death—a concept that developed late in Jewish religion—began to see things in a different light. Does God possibly reward the faithful in a life beyond the grave? For Christians, the New Testament answers that question with a resounding yes.

The Book of Ecclesiastes stands as a reminder to believers that all things change, even our understanding of God. The Teacher was not a pessimist, but a realist with a mission—to stretch the traditional understanding of faith in order to embrace the difficult questions of life.

Quick Facts

Author

Qoheleth, writing in the fourth or third century B.C.

Themes

Life is not always fair. There are no easy answers.

Of Note

Ecclesiastes is often attributed to King Solomon, although he did not write it.

Ecclesiastes

1, 3

1 ¹*† The words of David's son, Qoheleth, king in Jerusalem:

Vanity of Toil without Profit

²*†Vanity of vanities, says Qoheleth,
    vanity of vanities! All things are vanity!
³*†What profit has man from all the labor
    which he toils at under the sun?
⁴ One generation passes and another comes,
    but the world forever stays.
⁵ The sun rises and the sun goes down;
    then it presses on to the place where
      it rises.
⁶ Blowing now toward the south, then toward
      the north,
    the wind turns again and again, resuming
      its rounds.
⁷ All rivers go to the sea,
    yet never does the sea become full.
  To the place where they go,
    the rivers keep on going.
⁸*†All speech is labored;
    there is nothing man can say.

The eye is not satisfied with seeing
    nor is the ear filled with hearing.

⁹* What has been, that will be; what has been done, that will be done. Nothing is new under the sun. ¹⁰* Even the thing of which we say, "See, this is new!" has already existed in the ages that preceded us. ¹¹*† There is no remembrance of the men of old; nor of those to come will there be any remembrance among those who come after them.

I: Qoheleth's Investigation of Life

Twofold Introduction

¹² I, Qoheleth, was king over Israel in Jerusalem, ¹³* and I applied my mind to search and investigate in wisdom all things that are done under the sun.

A thankless task God has appointed
    for men to be busied about.

¹⁴*† I have seen all things that are done under the sun, and behold, all is vanity and a chase after wind.

1, 1: *Qoheleth:* see Introduction.
1, 2: *Vanity of vanities:* a Hebrew superlative expressing the supreme degree of futility and emptiness.
1, 3: *Under the sun:* used throughout this book to signify "on the earth."
1, 8: *All speech . . . man can say:* or "All things are wearisome beyond man's power to tell."
1, 11: Men remember nothing long; God, however, never forgets.
1, 14: *Chase after wind:* futility, like an attempt to corral the

winds. Cf Hos 12, 2. The ancient versions understood "affliction of spirit." These words are used to conclude sections of the discourse, as far as Eccl 6, 9.

1, 1: Eccl 7, 27; 12, 8f.
1, 2: Eccl 12, 8.
1, 3: Eccl 2, 11.22; 3, 9; 5, 15.
1, 8: Eccl 8, 17.
1, 9: Eccl 3, 15; 6, 10.
1, 10: Eccl 3, 15.
1, 11: Eccl 2, 16.
1, 13: Eccl 8, 9.
1, 14: Eccl 2, 11.17.

New and Improved!

NEW! IMPROVED! These two words are basic to many ad campaigns. No matter how good a product is, sooner or later, it will be "new and improved." The reason is simple: the advertisers want us to think the product is even better.

The writer of Ecclesiastes would not be very impressed with the claims of advertisers today. The author sounds skeptical in 1, 9: "Nothing is new under the sun." The Teacher is not going to be taken in by claims that something is new and improved. This person has seen it all before.

Advertising can get us thinking that our life isn't good enough, that we have to have more things and new things in order to be happy. In fact, we need to have a little bit of the attitude of the Teacher if we want to find contentment. Throughout the Book of Ecclesiastes, this writer invites us to enjoy what we have now.

Have you ever gotten something because of its advertising, only to be disappointed afterward? Are you enjoying the things you have right now?

▶ **Eccl 1, 1–11**

15 What is crooked cannot be made straight,
    and what is missing cannot be supplied.

16* Though I said to myself, "Behold, I have become great and stored up wisdom beyond all who were before me in Jerusalem, and my mind has broad experience of wisdom and knowledge"; 17* yet when I applied my mind to know wisdom and knowledge, madness and folly, I learned that this also is a chase after wind.

18 For in much wisdom there is much sorrow,
    and he who stores up knowledge stores
    up grief.

Study of Pleasure-seeking

2 1*† I said to myself, "Come, now, let me try you with pleasure and the enjoyment of good things." But behold, this too was vanity. 2 Of laughter I said: "Mad!" and of mirth: "What good does this do?" 3† I thought of beguiling my senses with wine, though my mind was concerned with wisdom, and of taking up folly, until I should understand what is best for men to do under the heavens during the limited days of their life. 4 I undertook great works; I built myself houses and planted vineyards; 5 I made gardens and parks, and set out in them fruit trees of all sorts. 6 And I constructed for myself reservoirs to water a flourishing woodland. 7 I acquired male and female slaves, and slaves were born in my house. I also had growing herds of cattle and flocks of sheep, more

than all who had been before me in Jerusalem. 8 I amassed for myself silver and gold, and the wealth of kings and provinces. I got for myself male and female singers and all human luxuries. 9 I became great, and I stored up more than all others before me in Jerusalem; my wisdom, too, stayed with me. 10* Nothing that my eyes desired did I deny them, nor did I deprive myself of any joy, but my heart rejoiced in the fruit of all my toil. This was my share for all my toil. 11* But when I turned to all the works that my hands had wrought, and to the toil at which I had taken such pains, behold! all was vanity and a chase after wind, with nothing gained under the sun. 12 For what will the man do who is to come after the king? What men have already done!

Study of Wisdom and Folly

I went on to the consideration of wisdom, madness and folly. 13 And I saw that wisdom has the advantage over folly as much as light has the advantage over darkness.

14* The wise man has eyes in his head,
    but the fool walks in darkness.

Yet I knew that one lot befalls both of them. 15 So I said to myself, if the fool's lot is to befall me also, why then should I be wise? Where is the profit for me? And I concluded in my heart that this too is vanity. 16* Neither of the wise man nor of the fool will there be an abiding remembrance, for in days

---

† 2, 1–11: The author here assumes the role of Solomon.
2, 3: *Though my mind . . . wisdom:* while indulging in pleasure the author hopes to discover wherein man's true happiness consists.

1, 16: Eccl 2, 9.   2, 11: Eccl 1, 17; Sir 44, 9.
1, 17: Eccl 2, 3; 7, 25.   2, 14f: Eccl 6, 8; 9, 2f.
2, 1: Wis 2, 6.   2, 16: Eccl 1, 11; Wis 2, 4.
2, 10: Eccl 3, 22; 5, 18.

to come both will have been forgotten. How is it that the wise man dies as well as the fool! [17] Therefore I loathed life, since for me the work that is done under the sun is evil; for all is vanity and a chase after wind.

Study of the Fruits of Toil

To Others the Profits

[18] And I detested all the fruits of my labor under the sun, because I must leave them to a man who is to come after me. [19] And who knows whether he will be a wise man or a fool? Yet he will have control over all the fruits of my wise labor under the sun. This also is vanity. [20] So my feelings turned to despair of all the fruits of my labor under the sun. [21] For there is a man who has labored with wisdom and knowledge and skill, and to another, who has not labored over it, he must leave his property. This also is vanity and a great misfortune. [22]* For what profit comes to a man from all the toil and anxiety of heart with which he has labored under the sun? [23] All his days sorrow and grief are his occupation; even at night his mind is not at rest. This also is vanity.

[24]*† There is nothing better for man than to eat and drink and provide himself with good things by his labors. Even this, I realized, is from the hand of God. [25] For who can eat or drink apart from him? [26]* For to whatever man he sees fit he gives wisdom and knowledge and joy; but to the sinner he gives the task of gathering possessions to be given to whatever man God sees fit. This also is vanity and a chase after wind.

Man Cannot Hit on the Right Time To Act

3 [1] There is an appointed time for everything, and a time for every affair under the heavens.

[2] A time to be born, and a time to die;
a time to plant, and a time to uproot the plant.
[3] A time to kill, and a time to heal;
a time to tear down, and a time to build.
[4] A time to weep, and a time to laugh;
a time to mourn, and a time to dance.
[5] A time to scatter stones, and a time to gather them;
a time to embrace, and a time to be far from embraces.
[6] A time to seek, and a time to lose;
a time to keep, and a time to cast away.

[7] A time to rend, and a time to sew;
a time to be silent, and a time to speak.
[8] A time to love, and a time to hate;
a time of war, and a time of peace.

[9]* What advantage has the worker from his toil? [10] I have considered the task which God has appointed for men to be busied about. [11]* He has made everything appropriate to its time, and has put the timeless into their hearts, without men's ever discovering, from beginning to end, the work which God has done. [12] I recognized that there is nothing better than to be glad and to do well during life. [13]* For every man, moreover, to eat and drink and enjoy the fruit of all his labor is a gift of God. [14] I recognized that whatever God does will endure forever; there is no adding to it, or taking

PRAY IT!

The Balance of Life

God of all seasons,
Help me to remember the sun when it is raining.
Help me to remember the rain when the sun is shining.
Teach me to respect the seniors when I am a sophomore.
Teach me to respect the sophomores when I am a senior.
When I win on the field, let me remember the times I lost.
When I lose on the field, let me remember the times I won.
Guide me to appreciate studying when I'm taking a hard test.
Guide me to appreciate hard tests when I'm studying.
During times with friends, remind me of times alone.
During times alone, remind me of times with friends.
Help me to live all moments and remember there is a balance to life.
Amen.

▸ **Eccl 3, 1–8**

ECCL

---

† **2, 24:** Unrestrained indulgence is not advocated here, but legitimate pleasure and the cheerfulness it begets.

2, 22: Eccl 1, 3.
2, 24: Eccl 3, 12f.22; 5, 17f; 8, 15.
2, 26: Prv 13, 22.
3, 9: Eccl 1, 3.
3, 11: Eccl 8, 17; 11, 5; Gn 1, 31.
3, 13: Eccl 2, 24.

A TIME FOR CONNECTIONS

The Tao te Ching (pronounced "Dow deh JING") is the ancient Chinese Book of the Way. This piece of Chinese wisdom literature was written by Lao-tzu, who probably lived about 500 B.C., close to the time of the author of Ecclesiastes. See how similar the following passage from the Tao te Ching is to Eccl 3, 1–8:

There is a time for being ahead, a time for being behind;
a time for being in motion, a time for being at rest;
a time for being vigorous, a time for being exhausted;
a time for being safe, a time for being in danger.

(Stephen Mitchell, translator, *Tao te Ching*, no. 29)

▶ Eccl 3, 1–8

ECCL

from it. Thus has God done that he may be revered. ¹⁵*† What now is has already been; what is to be, already is; and God restores what would otherwise be displaced.

The Problem of Retribution

¹⁶* And still under the sun in the judgment place I saw wickedness, and in the seat of justice, iniquity. ¹⁷* And I said to myself, both the just and the wicked God will judge, since there is a time for every affair and on every work a judgment. ¹⁸ I said to myself: As for the children of men, it is God's way of testing them and of showing that they are in themselves like beasts. ¹⁹ For the lot of man and of beast is one lot; the one dies as well as the other. Both have the same life-breath, and man has no advantage over the beast; but all is vanity. ²⁰* Both go to the same place; both were made from the dust, and to the dust they both return. ²¹* Who knows if the life-breath of the children of men goes upward and the life-breath of beasts goes earthward? ²²* And I saw that there is nothing better for a man than to rejoice in his work; for this is his lot. Who will let him see what is to come after him?

Vanity of Toil

4 ¹* Again I considered all the oppressions that take place under the sun: the tears of the victims with none to comfort them! From the hand of their oppressors comes violence, and there is none to comfort them! ²* And those now dead, I declared more fortunate in death than are the living to be still alive. ³ And better off than both is the yet unborn, who has not seen the wicked work that is done under the sun. ⁴ Then I saw that all toil and skillful work is the rivalry of one man for another. This also is vanity and a chase after wind.

⁵† "The fool folds his arms
        and consumes his own flesh"—
⁶   Better is one handful with tranquility
        than two with toil and a chase after wind!

Companions and Successors

⁷ Again I found this vanity under the sun: ⁸ a solitary man with no companion; with neither son nor brother. Yet there is no end to all his toil, and riches do not satisfy his greed. "For whom do I toil and

---

† ──────────
3, 15: *God restores:* the meaning is probably that God allows no part of his creation to drop out of existence.
4, 5: *Consumes his own flesh:* refuses to work for the necessities of life and consequently suffers hunger and impairs his bodily health.

* ──────────
3, 15: Eccl 1, 9.
3, 16: Eccl 4, 1.
3, 17: Eccl 12, 14.
3, 20: Eccl 12, 7; Gn 2, 7; 3,
    19; Ps 103, 14; Wis 2, 3;
Sir 10, 9; 17, 1; 40, 11.
3, 21: Wis 2, 2.
3, 22: Eccl 8, 7; 10, 14.
4, 1: Eccl 5, 7.
4, 2: Eccl 7, 2.

deprive myself of good things?" This also is vanity and a worthless task. ⁹ Two are better than one: they get a good wage for their labor. ¹⁰ If the one falls, the other will lift up his companion. Woe to the solitary man! For if he should fall, he has no one to lift him up. ¹¹ So also, if two sleep together, they keep each other warm. How can one alone keep warm? ¹² Where a lone man may be overcome, two together can resist. A three-ply cord is not easily broken.

¹³ Better is a poor but wise youth than an old but foolish king who no longer knows caution; ¹⁴† for from a prison house one comes forth to rule, since even in his royalty he was poor at birth. ¹⁵† Then I saw all those who are to live and move about under the sun with the heir apparent who will succeed to his place. ¹⁶ There is no end to all these people, to all over whom he takes precedence; yet the later generations will not applaud him. This also is vanity and a chase after wind.

Vanity of Many Words

¹⁷*† Guard your step when you go to the house of God. Let your approach be obedience, rather than the fools' offering of sacrifice; for they know not how to keep from doing evil.

5 ¹ Be not hasty in your utterance and let not your heart be quick to make a promise in God's presence. God is in heaven and you are on earth; therefore let your words be few.

²† For nightmares come with many cares,
    and a fool's utterance with many words.

³* When you make a vow to God, delay not its fulfillment. For God has no pleasure in fools; fulfill what you have vowed. ⁴ You had better not make a vow than make it and not fulfill it. ⁵ Let not your utterances make you guilty, and say not before his representative, "It was a mistake," lest God be angered by such words and destroy the works of your hands. ⁶* Rather, fear God!

Gain and Loss of Goods

⁷* If you see oppression of the poor, and violation of rights and justice in the realm, do not be shocked by the fact, for the high official has another higher than he watching him and above these are

---

Eat, Drink, and Be Merry

    Shirley. Do you know what the Bible says about the purpose of life?
    Brian. Well, it says a lot of things. What did you find?
    Shirley. Eat, drink, and be merry!
    Brian. What? Where did you find that?
Shirley. Ecclesiastes 3, 13.
Brian. It really says that?
Shirley. It says, "For every man, moreover, to eat and drink and enjoy the fruit of all his labor is a gift of God." So, eat, drink, and be merry!
Brian. But remember the last part of the passage: It is "a gift of God." To look on the simple pleasures of life as gifts from God changes the focus a bit.
Shirley. You're right. It adds a deeper purpose to the enjoyment. All those pleasures are gifts from a God who wants us to be happy and enjoy ourselves as long as we live, as it says in verse 12.
Brian. Yes, and verse 1 says, "There is an appointed time for everything, and a time for every affair under the heavens."
Shirley. I guess this is a time to be grateful for the simple gifts!

▸ Eccl 3, 9–15

4, 14: *Prison house:* probably his mother's womb, from which the king issues without possessions. Cf Eccl 5, 14.

4, 15: The king is no sooner dead than the people transfer their allegiance to his successor.

4, 17: *The fools'. . . sacrifice:* unacceptable to God because of their disobedience; cf 1 Sm 15, 22; Hos 6, 6.

5, 2: *Nightmares:* literally, "dreams."

4, 17: 1 Sm 15, 22; Hos 6, 6.
  5, 3: Nm 30, 3; Dt 23, 23;
    Ps 50, 14.

5, 6: Eccl 12, 13; Dt 10, 12.
5, 7: Eccl 3, 16; 4, 1.

How Much Is Enough?

How much wealth does one need? In surveys, most young people reply they want just enough money to be happy. It's an interesting answer because they are implying they don't want to be greedy, but it takes money to be happy!

According to Qoheleth, in Eccl 5, 9, those who love money will always want more. What is God trying to tell us here? Maybe that real happiness is not found in material wealth. The more we want, the less satisfied we are. Money can be an evil when it is all we want and think about.

For a week, try to do things with your family and friends that do not cost anything. Play board games, go for walks or hikes, even volunteer some time at a community organization. Consider taking the money you save and donating it to a worthy cause.

▶ Eccl 5, 9

---

others higher still—. ⁸† Yet an advantage for a country in every respect is a king for the arable land.

⁹ *The covetous man is never satisfied with money, and the lover of wealth reaps no fruit from it; so this too is vanity. ¹⁰ Where there are great riches, there are also many to devour them. Of what use are they to the owner except to feast his eyes upon? ¹¹ Sleep is sweet to the laboring man, whether he eats little or much, but the rich man's abundance allows him no sleep.

¹²* This is a grievous evil which I have seen under the sun: riches kept by their owner to his hurt. ¹³ Should the riches be lost through some misfortune, he may have a son when he is without means. ¹⁴* As he came forth from his mother's womb, so again shall he depart, naked as he came, having nothing from his labor that he can carry in his hand. ¹⁵ This too is a grievous evil, that he goes just as he came. What then does it profit him to toil for wind? ¹⁶ All the days of his life are passed in gloom and sorrow, under great vexation, sickness and wrath.

¹⁷* Here is what I recognize as good: it is well for a man to eat and drink and enjoy all the fruits of his labor under the sun during the limited days of the life which God gives him; for this is his lot. ¹⁸ Any man to whom God gives riches and property, and grants power to partake of them, so that he receives his lot and finds joy in the fruits of his toil, has a gift from God. ¹⁹† For he will hardly dwell on the shortness of his life, because God lets him busy himself with the joy of his heart.

Limited Worth of Enjoyment

6 ¹ There is another evil which I have seen under the sun, and it weighs heavily upon man: ²* there is the man to whom God gives riches and property and honor, so that he lacks none of all the things he craves; yet God does not grant him power to partake of them, but a stranger devours them. This is vanity and a dire plague. ³† Should a man have a hundred children and live many years, no matter to what great age, still if he has not the full benefit of his goods, or if he is deprived of burial, of this man I proclaim that the child born dead is more fortunate than he. ⁴ Though it came in vain and goes into darkness and its name is enveloped in darkness; ⁵ though it has not seen or known the sun, yet the dead child is at rest rather than such a man. ⁶† Should he live twice a thousand years and not enjoy his goods, do not both go to the same place?

⁷† All man's toil is for his mouth, yet his desire is not fulfilled. ⁸ For what advantage has the wise man over the fool, or what advantage has the poor man in knowing how to conduct himself in life? ⁹† "What the eyes see is better than what the desires wander after." This also is vanity and a chase after wind.

5, 8: The wording of this verse has perhaps never been adequately explained.

5, 19: The meaning is that the joys of life, though temporary, keep a man from dwelling on the ills which afflict humanity.

6, 3: A large family, a long life, an honorable burial, all were highly esteemed by the Hebrews, and it was considered a great misfortune to be deprived of them.

6, 6: *Same place:* the grave.

6, 7: *Mouth:* appetite, and therefore, body.

6, 9: *Better . . . wander after:* the good that is present to us is better than that which is absent and, perhaps, unattainable.

5, 9: Prv 28, 22.
5, 12: Jb 20, 20.
5, 14: Jb 1, 21; 1 Tm 6, 7.
5, 17f: Eccl 2, 24.
6, 2: Eccl 2, 18f.

ECCL

II: Qoheleth's Conclusions

¹⁰† Whatever is, was long ago given its name, and the nature of man is known, and that he cannot contend in judgment with one who is stronger than he. ¹¹ For though there are many sayings that multiply vanity, what profit is there for a man? ¹²* For who knows what is good for a man in life, the limited days of his vain life (which God has made like a shadow)? Because—who is there to tell a man what will come after him under the sun?

A. Man Cannot Find Out What Is Good for Him To Do

Critique of Sages on the Day of Adversity

7 ¹*† A good name is better than good
       ointment,
    and the day of death than the day of
       birth.
² * It is better to go to the house of mourning
       than to the house of feasting,
    For that is the end of every man,
    and the living should take it to heart.
³   Sorrow is better than laughter,
       because when the face is sad the heart
       grows wiser.
⁴   The heart of the wise is in the house
       of mourning,
    but the heart of fools is in the house
       of mirth.
⁵   It is better to hearken to the wise
       man's rebuke
    than to hearken to the song of fools;
⁶   For as the crackling of thorns under a pot,
       so is the fool's laughter.
       This also is vanity,
⁷   For oppression can make a fool of a
       wise man,
    and a bribe corrupts the heart.
⁸   Better is the end of speech than its
       beginning;
    better is the patient spirit than the
       lofty spirit.
⁹   Do not in spirit become quickly discontented,
    for discontent lodges in the bosom of
       a fool.

¹⁰ Do not say: How is it that former times were better than these? For it is not in wisdom that you ask about this.

¹¹   Wisdom and an inheritance are good,
       and an advantage to those that see the sun.

¹² For the protection of wisdom is as the protection of money; and the advantage of knowledge is that wisdom preserves the life of its owner. ¹³ Consider the work of God. Who can make straight what he has made crooked? ¹⁴ On a good day enjoy good things, and on an evil day consider: Both the one and the other God has made, so that man cannot find fault with him in anything.

Critique of Sages on Justice and Wickedness

¹⁵ I have seen all manner of things in my vain days: a just man perishing in his justice, and a wicked one surviving in his wickedness. ¹⁶*† "Be not just to excess, and be not overwise, lest you be ruined. ¹⁷† Be not wicked to excess, and be not foolish. Why should you die before your time?" ¹⁸† It is good to hold to this rule, and not to let that one go; but he who fears God will win through at all events.

¹⁹ Wisdom is a better defense for the wise man than would be ten princes in the city, ²⁰*† yet there is no man on earth so just as to do good and never sin. ²¹* Do not give heed to every word that is spoken lest you hear your servant speaking ill of you, ²² for you know in your heart that you have many times spoken ill of others.

²³ All these things I probed in wisdom. I said, "I will acquire wisdom"; but it was beyond me. ²⁴ What exists is far-reaching; it is deep, very deep: who can find it out? ²⁵* I turned my thoughts toward knowledge; I sought and pursued wisdom and reason, and I recognized that wickedness is foolish and folly is madness.

Critique of Sages on Women

²⁶* More bitter than death I find the woman who is a hunter's trap, whose heart is a snare and whose hands are prison bonds. He who is pleasing to God will escape her, but the sinner will be entrapped by her. ²⁷ Behold, this have I found, says Qoheleth,

---

† **6, 10:** The one who is stronger than man is God.

7, 1: *Ointment:* applied to the child at birth; a good name remains even after death.

7, 16: St. Jerome explains the warning against excessive justice in reference to the self-righteous man who is so stern that he is never willing to forgive sin in others; cf vv 20ff.

7, 17: Untimely death was traditionally recognized as a divine punishment of the wicked; cf 1 Sm 2, 31–34; Jer 17, 11; Ps 55, 24; Prv 10, 27. This warning against presumptuous wickedness is not an endorsement of any lesser degree of misconduct.

7, 18: *This rule . . . that one:* the sayings cited in vv 16f. Others

refer this and that to riches and wisdom (cf 7, 12), justice and wisdom, or justice and wickedness. This last supposition makes the author's thought hard to follow.

7, 20: This is to be understood in the sense of Rom 5, 12. See note there.

6, 12: Jb 8, 9; 14, 2; Ps 102, 12.
7, 1: Eccl 4, 2; Prv 22, 1; Sir 41, 13.
7, 2: Eccl 4, 2.
7, 16f: Eccl 8, 12ff.
7, 20: Jb 25, 4; Prv 20, 9; 1 Kgs 8, 46; Rom 3, 23; Jas 3, 2; 1 Jn 1, 8.
7, 21f: 1 Kgs 8, 46.
7, 25: Eccl 1, 17.
7, 26: Prv 5, 4.

adding one thing to another that I might discover the answer 28† which my soul still seeks and has not found: One man out of a thousand have I come upon, but a woman among them all I have not found. 29† Behold, only this have I found out: God made mankind straight, but men have had recourse to many calculations.

Critique of Sages on the Wise Man and the King

8 ¹ Who is like the wise man,
     and who knows the explanation of things?
A man's wisdom illumines his face,
     but an impudent look is resented.

² Observe the precept of the king, and in view of your oath to God, ³ be not hasty to withdraw from the king; do not join in with a base plot, for he does whatever he pleases, ⁴ because his word is sovereign, and who can say to him, "What are you doing?"

⁵ "He who keeps the commandment experiences no evil, and the wise man's heart knows times and judgments; ⁶ for there is a time and a judgment for everything."—Yet it is a great affliction for man ⁷* that he is ignorant of what is to come; for who will make known to him how it will be? ⁸ There is no man who is master of the breath of life so as to retain it, and none has mastery of the day of death. There is no exemption from the struggle, nor are the wicked saved by their wickedness. ⁹* All these things I considered and I applied my mind to every work that is done under the sun, while one man tyrannizes over another to his hurt.

The Problem of Retribution

¹⁰† Meanwhile I saw wicked men approach and enter; and as they left the sacred place, they were praised in the city for what they had done. This also is vanity. ¹¹ Because the sentence against evildoers is not promptly executed, therefore the hearts of men are filled with the desire to commit evil— ¹² because the sinner does evil a hundred times and survives. Though indeed I know that it shall be well with those who fear God, for their reverence toward him; ¹³† and that it shall not be well with the wicked man, and he shall not prolong his shadowy days, for his lack of reverence toward God.

¹⁴ This is a vanity which occurs on earth: there are just men treated as though they had done evil and wicked men treated as though they had done justly. This, too, I say is vanity. ¹⁵*† Therefore I commend mirth, because there is nothing good for man under the sun except eating and drinking and mirth: for this is the accompaniment of his toil during the limited days of the life which God gives him under the sun.

¹⁶* When I applied my heart to know wisdom and to observe what is done on earth, ¹⁷* I recognized that man is unable to find out all God's work that is done under the sun, even though neither by day nor by night do his eyes find rest in sleep. However much man toils in searching, he does not find it out; and even if the wise man says that he knows, he is unable to find it out.

B. Man Does Not Know What Is To Come

9 ¹† All this I have kept in mind and recognized: the just, the wise, and their deeds are in the hand of God. Love from hatred† man cannot tell; both appear equally vain, ² *in that there is the same lot for all, for the just and the wicked, for the good and the bad, for the clean and the unclean, for him who offers sacrifice and him who does not. As it is for the good man, so it is for the sinner; as it is

9, 7

7, 28: The author found sincerity rare among men, but among women still more rare.
7, 29: *Calculations:* the many vain attempts and schemes of men to attain happiness by their own efforts.
8, 10: The text is obscure. The Latin has "wicked men buried, who, while still alive, were in the holy place, and were praised in the city as if their works were just."
8, 13: *Shadowy:* perhaps an addition here; cf Eccl 6, 12.
8, 15: See notes on Eccl 2, 24; 5, 19.

9, 1–10: These statements are based on a very imperfect concept of life beyond the grave. With Christian revelation about the future life came the only satisfactory solution of the problem which so perplexed the author.
9, 1: *Love from hatred:* divine favor or disfavor.

8, 7: Eccl 3, 22; 10, 14.	**8, 16:** Eccl 1, 13; 3, 10.
8, 9: Eccl 1, 13f.	**8, 17:** Eccl 3, 11.
8, 15: Eccl 2, 24; 9, 7.	**9, 2:** Eccl 2, 14.

for him who swears rashly, so it is for him who fears an oath. 3 Among all the things that happen under the sun, this is the worst, that things turn out the same for all. Hence the minds of men are filled with evil, and madness is in their hearts during life; and afterward they go to the dead.

4 Indeed, for any among the living there is hope; a live dog is better off than a dead lion. 5* For the living know that they are to die, but the dead no longer know anything. There is no further recompense for them, because all memory of them is lost. 6 For them, love and hatred and rivalry have long since perished. They will never again have part in anything that is done under the sun.

7* Go, eat your bread with joy and drink your wine with a merry heart, because it is now that God favors your works. 8 At all times let your garments be white, and spare not the perfume for your head. 9 Enjoy life with the wife whom you love, all the days of the fleeting life that is granted you under the sun. This is your lot in life, for the toil of your labors under the sun. 10 Anything you can turn your hand to, do with what power you have; for there will be no work, nor reason, nor knowledge, nor wisdom in the nether world where you are going.

did you **KNOW?**

Imagine There Is No Heaven

Some people assume that the ancient Israelites believed in an afterlife as we do today. However, Ecclesiastes speaks of the end of earthly life without any hint of eternal life: "For the living know that they are to die, but the dead no longer know anything. There is no further recompense for them, because all memory of them is lost" (9, 5). The book reflects the author's belief that all life ends with death. It was not until the last two centuries before Jesus that the idea of life after death began to take root among the Jewish people.

▸ **Eccl 9, 5**

The Evil Time Not Known

11 Again I saw under the sun that the race is not won by the swift, nor the battle by the valiant, nor a livelihood by the wise, nor riches by the shrewd, nor favor by the experts; for a time of calamity comes to all alike. 12† Man no more knows his own time than fish taken in the fatal net, or birds trapped in the snare; like these the children of men are caught when the evil time falls suddenly upon them.

The Uncertain Future and the Sages

13 On the other hand I saw this wise deed under the sun, which I thought sublime. 14 Against a small city with few men in it advanced a mighty king, who surrounded it and threw up great siegeworks about it. 15 But in the city lived a man who, though poor, was wise, and he delivered it through his wisdom. Yet no one remembered this poor man. 16* Though I had said, "Wisdom is better than force," yet the wisdom of the poor man is despised and his words go unheeded.

17   "The quiet words of the wise are better heeded
        than the shout of a ruler of fools"—!

18   "A fly that dies can spoil the
        perfumer's ointment,
    and a single slip can ruin much that
        is good."

10   1 More weighty than wisdom or wealth
        is a little folly!
2† The wise man's understanding turns him to
        his right;
    the fool's understanding turns him to
        his left.

3 When the fool walks through the street, in his lack of understanding he calls everything foolish.

4 Should the anger of the ruler burst upon you, forsake not your place; for mildness abates great offenses.

5 I have seen under the sun another evil, like a mistake that proceeds from the ruler: 6 a fool put in lofty position while the rich sit in lowly places. 7 I have seen slaves on horseback, while princes walked on the ground like slaves.

8*   He who digs a pit may fall into it,
        and he who breaks through a wall may be
        bitten by a serpent.

ECCL

---

† **9, 12:** *His own time:* the time of death or sudden disaster.
  10, 2: It is doubtful whether the author is endorsing either direction; cf Prv 4, 25ff.

* **9, 5:** Eccl 1, 11.
9, 7: Eccl 2, 1.24; 8, 15; 11, 9.
9, 16: Prv 24, 5.
10, 8f: Prv 26, 27; Sir 27, 29.

9 He who moves stones may be hurt by them,
  and he who chops wood is in danger
    from it.

10 If the iron becomes dull, though at first he
made easy progress, he must increase his efforts;
but the craftsman has the advantage of his skill.

11 If the serpent bites because it has not
      been charmed,
    then there is no advantage for the
      charmer.

12* Words from the wise man's mouth win favor,
    but the fool's lips consume him.
13 The beginning of his words is folly,
    and the end of his talk is utter madness;
14* yet the fool multiplies words.
  Man knows not what is to come,
    for who can tell him what is to come
      after him?
15† When will the fool be weary of his labor,
    he who knows not the way to the city?

Man Does Not Know What Evil Will Come

16 Woe to you, O land, whose king was
      a servant,
    and whose princes dine in the morning!
17 Blessed are you, O land, whose king is of
      noble birth,
    and whose princes dine at the right time
      (for vigor and not in drinking bouts).

18 When hands are lazy, the rafters sag;
    when hands are slack, the house leaks.
19 Bread and oil call forth merriment
    and wine makes the living glad,
    but money answers for everything.
20 Even in your thoughts do not make light of
      the king,
    nor in the privacy of your bedroom revile
      the rich,
  Because the birds of the air may carry
      your voice,
    a winged creature may tell what you say.

11 1† Cast your bread upon the waters;
    after a long time you may find it again.
2† Make seven or eight portions;
    you know not what misfortune may come
      upon the earth.

Man Does Not Know What Good Will Come

3 When the clouds are full,
    they pour out rain upon the earth.
  Whether a tree falls to the south or to the
      north,
    wherever it falls, there shall it lie.
4 One who pays heed to the wind will
      not sow,
    and one who watches the clouds will
      never reap.
5* Just as you know not how the breath of life
    fashions the human frame in the
      mother's womb,

Carpe Diem—"Seize the Day"!

LIVE IT!

"Youth is wasted on the young."
  Perhaps you have heard that statement uttered by not-so-young adults struggling with growing older. There is some truth in it: many young people do not
reflect on life and do not pause to appreciate being young.
  Qoheleth says some beautiful and profound things about youthfulness. He advises
young people to "Follow the ways of your heart" (Eccl 11, 9) and to "Ward off grief from
your heart" (verse 10). Someone like Qoheleth might say today: "Follow your heart, and do
not spend so much time worrying. It is a blessing to be young, to have so much energy and so many dreams. There are many pressures and stresses on young people today, but
do not let them dominate your life. Enjoy this special time of growth and discovery."
  It is good to be young. Seize the day!

▶ Eccl 11, 7–10   Eccl 9, 5

10, 15: *He who . . . city:* perhaps a proverbial expression for supreme stupidity.
11, 1: This may refer to a spirit of adventure in business or to gen-erosity in almsgiving. *Waters:* of the ocean, which sometimes carry lost treasures to the shore.

11, 2: This verse refers either to almsgiving or to the wisdom of not putting all one's cargo into a single vessel.

10, 12: Sir 21, 19.   **11, 5:** Eccl 8, 17.
10, 14: Eccl 5, 2; 8, 7.

ECCL

So you know not the work of God
    which he is accomplishing in
      the universe.
6 In the morning sow your seed,
    and at evening let not your hand be idle:
For you know not which of the two will
      be successful,
    or whether both alike will turn out well.

Poem on Youth and Old Age

7 Light is sweet! and it is pleasant for the eyes to see the sun. 8 However many years a man may live, let him, as he enjoys them all, remember that the days of darkness will be many. All that is to come is vanity.

9   Rejoice, O young man, while you
      are young,
    and let your heart be glad in the days of
      your youth.
Follow the ways of your heart,
    the vision of your eyes;
Yet understand that as regards all this
    God will bring you to judgment.
10† Ward off grief from your heart
    and put away trouble from
      your presence,
    though the dawn of youth is fleeting.

12 ¹ Remember your Creator in the days of
    your youth,
    before the evil days come
And the years approach of which you will say,
    I have no pleasure in them;
2† Before the sun is darkened,
    and the light, and the moon, and the stars,
    while the clouds return after the rain;
3† When the guardians of the house tremble,
    and the strong men are bent,
And the grinders are idle because they are few,
    and they who look through the windows
      grow blind;
4† When the doors to the street are shut,
    and the sound of the mill is low;
When one waits for the chirp of a bird,
    but all the daughters of song
      are suppressed;
5† And one fears heights,
    and perils in the street;
When the almond tree blooms,
    and the locust grows sluggish
    and the caper berry is without effect,
Because man goes to his lasting home,
    and mourners go about the streets;
6† Before the silver cord is snapped
    and the golden bowl is broken,

Remember the Elderly

Ecclesiastes 12, 1–8 is a bittersweet poem about the difficulties of the aging process. To understand it, you need to be aware of the metaphors used, like these:
- **guardians of the house = arms and hands**
- **strong men = legs**
- **grinders = teeth**
- **windows = eyes**
- **doors = ears or lips**
- **silver cord, golden bowl = life itself**

    Aging is a natural part of life, but it is a struggle for many people. No one enjoys its accompanying loss of mobility, loss of strength, and problems with seeing and hearing. The struggle is even greater if one is alone. If you have aging grandparents, family friends, or neighbors, keep in mind how much they need to be noticed by you. Stay in touch with them so that you can learn from their wisdom and they can be strengthened by your youth!

▶ **Eccl 12, 1–8**

---

† **11, 10:** *Dawn . . . fleeting:* literally, "youth and the dawn [of life] are vanity."
  12, 2: *The sun . . . return:* the cloudy and rainy Palestinian winter, a natural symbol of old age.
  12, 3: *Guardians:* the arms; strong men: the legs; grinders: the teeth; *they who . . . windows:* the eyes.
  12, 4: *Doors:* the tightly compressed lips; *sound of the mill:* perhaps the sound of mastication; *daughters of song:* the voice.

12, 5: *The almond tree blooms:* resembling the white hair of age. *The locust . . . sluggish:* an image of the stiffness in movement of the aged. *The caper berry:* a stimulant for appetite.
  12, 6: *The golden bowl* suspended by the silver cord was a symbol of life; the snapping of the cord and the breaking of the bowl, a symbol of death. *The pitcher . . . the broken pulley:* another pair of metaphors for life and its ending.

And the pitcher is shattered at the spring,
and the broken pulley falls into the well,
7* And the dust returns to the earth as it
once was,
and the life breath returns to God who
gave it.
8* Vanity of vanities, says Qoheleth,
all things are vanity!

Epilogue

9 Besides being wise, Qoheleth taught the people
knowledge, and weighed, scrutinized and arranged

many proverbs. 10 Qoheleth sought to find pleasing
sayings, and to write down true sayings with preci-
sion. 11† The sayings of the wise are like goads; like
fixed spikes are the topics given by one collector.
12* As to more than these, my son, beware. Of the
making of many books there is no end, and in
much study there is weariness for the flesh.

13*† The last word, when all is heard: Fear God
and keep his commandments, for this is man's all;
14* because God will bring to judgment every
work, with all its hidden qualities, whether good
or bad.

12, 11: *Goads . . . one collector:* the sayings were stimulants to
thought and also spikes or centers around which to group correlated
pronouncements of the wise.
12, 13: *Man's all:* St. Jerome explains: "Unto this is every man
born, that, knowing his Maker, he may revere him in fear, honor, and
the observance of his commandments."

12, 7: Eccl 3, 20f; Jb 34, 15.   12, 13: Eccl 5, 6.
12, 8: Eccl 1, 2.   12, 14: Eccl 11, 9.
12, 12: Eccl 1, 18.

Sex sells. When we see an ad with a beautiful woman slipping out of a sports car or a bare-chested man grabbing an ice-cold soda, we sit up and take notice. Advertisers love to take advantage of our fascination with sex. Once they have our attention, they can sell us something we might not even be interested in! The Song of Songs—a collection of ancient love poems—reminds us that this powerful force is ultimately a gift from God.

At a Glance

I. The Song of Songs By Solomon

In-depth

From an advertiser's point of view, the Song of Songs is a well-kept secret. How many people are aware of its explicit sexual images? Consider these verses:

- "Let him kiss me with the kisses of his mouth!" (1, 2).
- "Your lips drip honey, my bride, / sweetmeats and milk are under your tongue" (4, 11).
- "Now let your breasts be like clusters of the vine / and the fragrance of your breath like apples" (7, 9).

Some people find these images so surprising that they wonder why the Song of Songs is found in the Bible at all.

Scholars believe that the naming of King Solomon in the Song's first verse is the main reason that this book was preserved and eventually included with the Jewish holy books. Although written long after Solomon's death, this book—like Proverbs and Ecclesiastes—was attributed to him to give it authority.

Through the centuries, some people have not been able to accept the Song of Songs as simply love poetry and have hunted for a deeper meaning. Many people believe that the lover and the beloved in this book stand for Israel and God, or for Jesus and the church. Modern-day scholars, however, begin their interpretation of the Song of Songs at the literal level, that is, as a collection of love poems. The book's inclusion among the other holy books, they insist, is an affirmation of the goodness of human sexuality: human love is holy because it is a gift from God. The passion and beauty of human sexual attraction is a reflection of the passion and beauty of God's love for us!

Quick Facts

Author
unknown, probably writing after the Jews' return from the Babylonian Exile in 538 B.C.

Theme
poetry that expresses the goodness and passion of human love

Of Note
In other translations, this book is called the Song of Solomon or the Canticle of Canticles.

The Song of Songs

Song of Songs

I. The Song Of Songs By Solomon†

Love's Desires

1

2 **B***† Let him kiss me with kisses of his mouth!

More delightful is your love than wine!

3   Your name spoken is a spreading
      perfume—
   that is why the maidens love you.

4* Draw me!—

D   We will follow you eagerly!

B Bring me, O king, to your chambers.

D With you we rejoice and exult,
we extol your love; it is beyond wine:
how rightly you are loved!

Love's Boast

5 **B**†I am as dark—but lovely,
   O daughters of Jerusalem—

As the tents of Kedar,
   as the curtains of Salma.

6† Do not stare at me because I am swarthy,
   because the sun has burned me.

My brothers have been angry with me;
   they charged me with the care of
   the vineyards:
   my own vineyard I have not cared for.

Love's Inquiry

7 **B**†Tell me, you whom my heart loves,
   where you pasture your flock,
   where you give them rest at midday,
Lest I be found wandering
   after the flocks of your companions.

8 **G** If you do not know,
   O most beautiful among women,
Follow the tracks of the flock
   and pasture the young ones
   near the shepherds' camps.

1, 1: This title is actually the first verse of chapter 1.

1, 2ff: The marginal letters indicate the speaker of the verses: B—Bride; D—Daughters of Jerusalem; G—Bridegroom. In vv 2–7 the bride and the daughters address the bridegroom who appears here as a king, but more often in the poem as a shepherd. King and shepherd are familiar figures of the Lord in the Sacred Scriptures. Cf Ps 23, 1; Is 40, 1; Jn 10, 1–16.

1, 5: *Daughters of Jerusalem:* the chorus whom the bride addresses and who ask her questions (Song 5, 9; 6, 1), thus developing action within the poem. *Kedar:* a Syrian desert region whose name

suggests blackness; tents were often made of black goat hair. *Curtains:* tent coverings of Salma, a region close to Kedar.

1, 6: *Swarthy:* tanned by the sun from working in her brothers' vineyards. *My own vineyard:* the bride herself; cf Is 5, 1–7, where Israel is designated as the vineyard and the Lord is the Lover.

1, 7: Here and elsewhere in the Song (3, 1; 5, 8; 6, 1), the bride expresses her desire to be in the company of her lover. These verses point to a certain tension in the poem. Only at the end (Song 8, 5ff) does mutual possession of the lovers become final.

1, 2f: Song 4, 10.   1, 4: Song 4, 10.

Love's Vision

⁹G†To the steeds of Pharaoh's chariots
    would I liken you, my beloved:
10 Your cheeks lovely in pendants,
    your neck in jewels.
11 We will make pendants of gold for you,
    and silver ornaments.

Love's Union

12B†For the king's banquet
    my nard gives forth its fragrance.
13† My lover is for me a sachet of myrrh
    to rest in my bosom.
14† My lover is for me a cluster of henna
    from the vineyards of Engedi.

15 G*†Ah, you are beautiful, my beloved,
    ah, you are beautiful; your eyes are doves!

16 B†Ah, you are beautiful, my lover—
    yes, you are lovely.
  Our couch, too, is verdant;
17   the beams of our house are cedars,
    our rafters, cypresses.

2 ¹† I am a flower of Sharon,
    a lily of the valley.

²G As a lily among thorns,
    so is my beloved among women.
³B As an apple tree among the trees of
    the woods,
  so is my lover among men.
  I delight to rest in his shadow,
    and his fruit is sweet to my mouth.
⁴*†He brings me into the banquet hall
    and his emblem over me is love.

BLACK AND BEAUTIFUL

> **I am as dark—but lovely,**
>   **O daughters of Jerusalem—**
> **As the tents of Kedar,**
>   **as the curtains of Salma.**
>   **(Song 1, 5)**

Who is speaking to us in this Scripture text? Who is so boldly and confidently proclaiming to us that she is black and beautiful? Some traditions say this is the bride of Solomon, the son of David and the third king of Israel.

    Many of the people in the Old Testament world were black Africans or Afro-Asiatics (Asians of black African heritage). They had various shades of dark skin. In Song 1, 5, the bride describes herself as black as the tents of Kedar; in 5, 10, she describes her lover as ruddy (reddish) in color.

    Some African Americans are ruddy; others are darker. Together, all African Americans are a rainbow of blackness. Whatever shade they are, it is good. And if you are one of them, you are black and beautiful!

▸ **Song 1, 5**

---

† 1, 9ff: The bridegroom compares the girl's beauty to the rich adornment of the royal chariot of Pharaoh.
  1, 12: *Nard:* a precious perfume, a figure of the bride; cf Song 4, 14.
  1, 13: *Myrrh:* produced from aromatic resin of balsam or roses.
  1, 14: *Henna:* a plant which bears white scented flowers.
  1, 15: *Doves:* suggesting innocence and charm.
  1, 16f: Though the meeting place of the lovers is but a shepherd's hut of green branches, it becomes a palace with beams of

cedar and rafters of cypress when adorned with their love.
  2, 1: *Flower of Sharon:* probably the narcissus, which grows in the fertile Plain of Sharon lying between Mount Carmel and Jaffa on the Mediterranean coast.
  2, 4ff: The banquet hall, the sweet things of the table, the embrace of the bride and bridegroom, express the delicacy of their affection and the intimacy of their love.

---

* 1, 15: Song 4, 1.7.   2, 4: Song 1, 4.

5* Strengthen me with raisin cakes,
    refresh me with apples,
    for I am faint with love.
6* His left hand is under my head
    and his right arm embraces me.
7*† I adjure you, daughters of Jerusalem,
    by the gazelles and hinds of the field,
    Do not arouse, do not stir up love
    before its own time.

A Tryst in the Spring

8B† Hark! my lover—here he comes
    springing across the mountains,
    leaping across the hills.
9   My lover is like a gazelle
    or a young stag.
    Here he stands behind our wall,
    gazing through the windows,
    peering through the lattices.
10   My lover speaks; he says to me,

"Arise, my beloved, my beautiful one,
    and come!
11   "For see, the winter is past,
    the rains are over and gone.
12   The flowers appear on the earth,
    the time of pruning the vines has come,
    and the song of the dove is heard in
    our land.
13   The fig tree puts forth its figs,
    and the vines, in bloom, give
    forth fragrance.
Arise, my beloved, my beautiful one,
    and come!

14† "O my dove in the clefts of the rock,
    in the secret recesses of the cliff,
Let me see you,
    let me hear your voice,
For your voice is sweet,
    and you are lovely."

ROMANTIC LOVE

God loves us passionately and seeks us with the enthusiasm of a lover who memorizes every detail and cherishes every moment (Song 1, 9–17). Romantic, playful love was created by God for us to enjoy. The way we express such love can bring joy and delight; it also can devastate and destroy if it is abused and not respected. Be careful with love. God gave us our sexuality as a gift, not as a weapon.

Hear the tender respect of this love poem from the Cherokee tradition:

You are part of me now
    You touched me.
With your kindness and love
    So enchanted.
Your soft lips are kind.
    Your eyes glow with life.
I'm glad you touched me.
    You're part of me now.

(Lloyd Carl Owle, "You Are Part of Me")

▶ **Song 1, 9–17**

---

†
2, 7: *By the gazelles and hinds:* the swiftness of these animals and the luster and soft expression of their eyes are suggestive of love; cf Prv 5, 19.
2, 8ff: In this sudden change of scene, the bride pictures her lover hastening toward her dwelling until his voice is heard bidding her come to him.

2, 14: The bride is addressed as though she were a dove in a mountain fastness out of sight and reach.

*
2, 5: Song 5, 8.   2, 7: Song 3, 5; 8, 4.
2, 6: Song 8, 3.

The Illusion of Pornography

"1-900-CALL IF YOU'RE LONELY!" Everywhere you look, it seems, you can find ads for phone sex, pornographic magazines and videos, and Internet porn sites. People are lured into the immoral world of false love through an industry that preys on those who are weak and lost, those unfortunate souls searching for love in all the wrong places.

One interpretation proposes that the Song of Songs is about passion and sexual longing between a bride and a bridegroom. Their love is committed: "My lover belongs to me and I to him" (Song 2, 16). Their love is at once both urgent ("Draw me!—We will follow you eagerly" [1, 4]) and patient ("Do not arouse, do not stir up love / before its own time" [2, 7]). This is not the kind of love offered to us in pornography, which has nothing at all to do with real love.

If you find yourself drawn to pornography, ask yourself: Is this God's purpose for human sexuality? Is this enriching to human love, or degrading? Pray for the strength to avoid the temptation and illusion of pornography.

▶ Song 2, 1–17

---

¹⁵B†Catch us the foxes, the little foxes
    that damage the vineyards; for our
      vineyards are in bloom!

¹⁶* My lover belongs to me and I to him;
    he browses among the lilies.
¹⁷*†Until the day breathes cool and the
      shadows lengthen,
    roam, my lover,
Like a gazelle or a young stag
    upon the mountains of Bether.

Loss and Discovery

3 ¹ B*† On my bed at night I sought him
    whom my heart loves—
    I sought him but I did not find him.
² I will rise then and go about the city;
    in the streets and crossings I will seek
Him whom my heart loves.
    I sought him but I did not find him.
³ The watchmen came upon me,
    as they made their rounds of the city:
Have you seen him whom my heart loves?
⁴* I had hardly left them
    when I found him whom my heart loves.
I took hold of him and would not let him go
    till I should bring him to the home of
      my mother,
    to the room of my parent.
⁵* I adjure you, daughters of Jerusalem,

by the gazelles and hinds of the field,
Do not arouse, do not stir up love
    before its own time.

Regal State of the Bridegroom

⁶D*†What is this coming up from the desert,
    like a column of smoke
Laden with myrrh, with frankincense,
    and with the perfume of every exotic dust?
⁷ Ah, it is the litter of Solomon;
    sixty valiant men surround it,
    of the valiant men of Israel:
⁸ All of them expert with the sword,
    skilled in battle,
Each with his sword at his side
    against danger in the watches of the night.

⁹ King Solomon made himself a carriage
    of wood from Lebanon.
¹⁰ He made its columns of silver,
    its roof of gold,
Its seat of purple cloth,
    its framework inlaid with ivory.
¹¹ Daughters of Jerusalem, come forth
    and look upon King Solomon
In the crown with which his mother has
      crowned him
    on the day of his marriage,
    on the day of the joy of his heart.

SONG

2, 15: A snatch of song in answer to the request of v 14; cf Song 8, 13f. *Foxes:* all who threaten to disturb the security of love symbolized by the vineyard; cf v 16.
2, 17: *Breathes cool:* in the evening when the sun is going down. Cf Gn 3, 8. *Bether:* a very obscure word; some interpret it in the sense of ruggedness; others, of spices; still others, of sacrifice (Gn 15, 10).

3, 1ff: See the parallel in Song 5, 2–8.
3, 6ff: The lover is portrayed as King Solomon, escorted by sixty armed men, coming in royal procession to meet his bride.

2, 16: Song 6, 3; 7, 10.   3, 4: Song 8, 2.
2, 17: Song 4, 6; 8, 14.   3, 5: Song 2, 7; 8, 4.
3, 1ff: Song 5, 2ff.   3, 6: Song 6, 10; 8, 5.

YOU HAVE RAVISHED MY HEART, MY SISTER, MY BRIDE; YOU HAVE RAVISHED MY HEART WITH ONE GLANCE OF YOUR

eyes

4, 9

The Charms of the Beloved

4 ¹ G* Ah, you are beautiful, my beloved,
   ah, you are beautiful!
Your eyes are doves*
   behind your veil.
Your hair is like a flock of goats
   streaming down the mountains of Gilead.
²† Your teeth are like a flock of ewes to be shorn,
   which come up from the washing,
All of them big with twins,
   none of them thin and barren.
³† Your lips are like a scarlet strand;
   your mouth is lovely.
Your cheek is like a half-pomegranate
   behind your veil.

⁴*† Your neck is like David's tower
   girt with battlements;
A thousand bucklers hang upon it,
   all the shields of valiant men.
⁵* Your breasts are like twin fawns,
   the young of a gazelle
   that browse among the lilies.
⁶*† Until the day breathes cool and the
      shadows lengthen,
   I will go to the mountain of myrrh,
   to the hill of incense.
⁷† You are all-beautiful, my beloved,
   and there is no blemish in you.

⁸† Come from Lebanon, my bride,
   come from Lebanon, come!

Descend from the top of Amana,
   from the top of Senir and Hermon,
From the haunts of lions,
   from the leopards' mountains.
⁹*† You have ravished my heart, my sister, my bride;
   you have ravished my heart with one glance
      of your eyes,
   with one bead of your necklace.
¹⁰* How beautiful is your love, my sister,
      my bride,
   how much more delightful is your love
      than wine,
   and the fragrance of your ointments than
      all spices!
¹¹† Your lips drip honey, my bride,
   sweetmeats and milk are under
      your tongue;
And the fragrance of your garments
   is the fragrance of Lebanon.

The Song of Songs

If human love is a reflection of divine love, then could parts of this love poem called the Song of Songs be understood as prayers? Could you read parts of it as your words to God, and other parts as God's words to you? Look at these sections:

■ **2, 2–6.** a prayer describing your passion for God

■ **5, 6–8.** a prayer to God when God seems absent

■ **8, 6–7.** God's words of love to you

The words may seem strange in this context, but if we are passionate about pursuing a human relationship, why can't we be passionate about pursuing our relationship with God? Some of the greatest saints expressed their love of God as a passionate, romantic love. You can do the same in your prayer with God!

---

† **4, 2:** *Teeth:* praised for whiteness and regularity.
4, 3: *Pomegranate:* a fruit somewhat like an orange, with a firm skin and deep red color. The girl's cheek is compared, in roundness and tint, to a half-pomegranate.
4, 4: The ornaments about her neck are compared to the trophies on the city walls. Cf 1 Kgs 10, 10; 14, 26ff; Ez 27, 10.
4, 6: *Mountain of myrrh . . . hill of incense:* spoken figuratively of the bride; cf Song 8, 14.
4, 7: Cf St. Paul's description of the church in Eph 5, 27. This verse is also applied to Our Lady, especially in the liturgy of the feast of the Immaculate Conception.

4, 8: *Amana . . . Senir and Hermon:* these rugged heights symbolize obstacles that would separate the lovers; cf Song 2, 14.
4, 9: *Sister:* a term of endearment; it forms part of the conventional language of love used in this canticle.
4, 11: *Honey:* sweet words. Cf Prv 5, 3.

4, 1: Song 1, 15.   4, 6: Song 2, 17.
4, 1ff: Song 6, 5ff.   4, 9: Song 6, 5.
4, 4: Song 7, 5.   4, 10: Song 1, 2f.
4, 5: Song 7, 4.

Sexuality and Dialogue

A number of the love songs included in the Song of Songs are addressed to the bridegroom and the beloved. It is as if a romantic dialogue has been recorded as lovers express the depth of feeling and desire they have for each other.

Dialogue is an essential aspect in any relationship. Open and honest communication provides the basis for maintaining and deepening the bonds of respect, friendship, and love.

Here is a time-honored test for any deep relationship: Is it possible for the two of you to speak honestly with each other about anything—especially problems and difficulties? Are you willing and able to discuss all dimensions of your love—including sexual feelings and desires?

Young couples often avoid such sensitive conversations. They fall victim to embarrassment and confusion and often leave important things unsaid. Such failure to communicate can result in hurt feelings, misunderstandings, and even behaviors that can lead to manipulation, selfishness, and sin.

Don't be afraid to discuss sexual issues. Always be ready to examine the nature of your relationships, especially when the power and passion of sexuality are present. True sexual love is rooted in dialogue, honest communication, and commitment. It finds its fullest expression in the context of marriage.

▶ Song of Songs, chapters 2—7

The Lover and His Garden

12 G*†You are an enclosed garden, my sister,
    my bride,
    an enclosed garden, a fountain sealed.
13 You are a park that puts forth pomegranates,
    with all choice fruits;
14† Nard and saffron, calamus and cinnamon,
    with all kinds of incense;
    Myrrh and aloes,
    with all the finest spices.
15 You are a garden fountain, a well of water
    flowing fresh from Lebanon.
16† Arise, north wind! Come, south wind!
    blow upon my garden
    that its perfumes may spread abroad.
    B Let my lover come to his garden
    and eat its choice fruits.

5 ¹ G*† I have come to my garden, my sister,
    my bride;
    I gather my myrrh and my spices,
    I eat my honey and my sweetmeats,
    I drink my wine and my milk.

    D Eat, friends; drink! Drink freely of love!

A Fruitless Search

2 B*†I was sleeping, but my heart kept vigil;
    I heard my lover knocking:
    "Open to me, my sister, my beloved,
    my dove, my perfect one!
    For my head is wet with dew,
    my locks with the moisture of
      the night."
3† I have taken off my robe,
    am I then to put it on?
    I have bathed my feet,
    am I then to soil them?

4 My lover put his hand through the opening;
    my heart trembled within me,
    and I grew faint when he spoke.
5 I rose to open to my lover,
    with my hands dripping myrrh:
    With my fingers dripping choice myrrh
    upon the fittings of the lock.
6 *†I opened to my lover—
    but my lover had departed, gone.
    I sought him but I did not find him;
    I called to him but he did not
      answer me.

---

† **4, 12:** *Enclosed garden . . . fountain sealed:* reserved for the bridegroom alone. The bride's fidelity is implied. Cf Prv 5, 15–19.
4, 14: These plants are all known for their sweet scent.
4, 16: The last two lines of the verse are spoken by the girl, inviting her lover to herself, the garden.
5, 1: *Eat, friends; drink!:* the lovers are encouraged to enjoy the delights of their love, symbol of Christ's union with the church.
5, 2–8: A trial similar to that in Song 3, 1ff.

5, 3f: The bride's hesitation is due, not to levity, but to strong emotion.
5, 6: The disappearance of the lover seems to be a deliberate trial and test inflicted on the girl.

4, 12: Song 6, 2.11.   5, 2ff: Song 3, 1f.
5, 1: Song 6, 2.   5, 6: Song 3, 1.

7*†The watchmen came upon me
　　as they made their rounds of the city;
They struck me, and wounded me,
　　and took my mantle from me,
　　the guardians of the walls.
8*　I adjure you, daughters of Jerusalem,
　　if you find my lover—
What shall you tell him?—
　　that I am faint with love.

The Charms of the Lost Lover

9D　How does your lover differ from any other,
　　O most beautiful among women?
How does your lover differ from any other,
　　that you adjure us so?

10　B†My lover is radiant and ruddy;
　　he stands out among thousands.
11　His head is pure gold;
　　his locks are palm fronds,
　　black as the raven.
12　His eyes are like doves
　　beside running waters,
His teeth would seem bathed in milk,
　　and are set like jewels.
13　His cheeks are like beds of spice
　　with ripening aromatic herbs.
His lips are red blossoms;
　　they drip choice myrrh.
14　His arms are rods of gold
　　adorned with chrysolites.
His body is a work of ivory
　　covered with sapphires.
15　His legs are columns of marble
　　resting on golden bases.
His stature is like the trees on Lebanon,
　　imposing as the cedars.
16　His mouth is sweetness itself;
　　he is all delight.
Such is my lover, and such my friend,
　　O daughters of Jerusalem.

Discovery

6　1 D† Where has your lover gone,
　　O most beautiful among women?
Where has your lover gone
　　that we may seek him with you?
2 B*†My lover has come down to his garden,
　　to the beds of spice,

?did you KNOW?

Sex in the Old Testament

Through its surprisingly graphic sexual content (see, for example, 7, 1–10), the Song of Songs has surprised many generations of readers. It reminds us that one of the richest images of the Old Testament is a sexual one: God as the faithful lover of Israel. In Ex 20, 5, we hear of God's jealous love of the Chosen People. By the time of the early prophets, the image of God as lover was fully developed: "On that day, says the LORD, / She shall call me 'My husband' " (Hos 2, 18).

Because of ancient Israel's conviction that human love reflects divine love—and vice versa—there was a high regard for human sexuality. This regard was reflected in Israel's sexual morality. Free-for-all sex stood in clear contradiction of the holiness of God, whose faithful love was the model for all human love. The Ten Commandments prohibit not only having sex with someone else's spouse but also desiring someone else's spouse.

Despite these high standards, some Bible stories do not comment on the morality of behavior that would be unacceptable in Christian morality. They make no comment on the many patriarchs and kings who have more than one wife, and they take for granted an inferior status of women in marriage. Because of problems like these, we must remember to read biblical passages in light of the whole Bible and the Christian tradition. In the Old Testament, we find the seeds of Christian sexual morality, not its full flower.

5, 7: The watchmen do not know the reason for the girl's appearance in the city streets; cf Song 3, 2ff.

5, 10f: In answer to the question of v 9, the girl sings her lover's praises (vv 10–16). *Gold:* indicates how precious the lover is. *Palm fronds:* his thick, luxuriant growth of hair.

6, 1: The daughters of Jerusalem are won by this description of the lover and offer their aid in seeking him.

6, 2f: Determined to share her lover with no one, the girl refuses the aid offered by the daughters in seeking him. She implies that she had never really lost him, for he has come down to his garden.

5, 7: Song 3, 3.　　　　　　6, 2: Song 4, 12; 5, 1.
5, 8: Song 2, 5.

To browse in the garden
and to gather lilies.
3* My lover belongs to me and I to him;
he browses among the lilies.

The Charms of the Beloved

4 G†You are as beautiful as Tirzah, my beloved,
as lovely as Jerusalem,
as awe-inspiring as bannered troops.
5* Turn your eyes from me,
for they torment me.
Your hair is like a flock of goats
streaming down from Gilead.
6* Your teeth are like a flock of ewes
which come up from the washing,
All of them big with twins,
none of them thin and barren.
7 Your cheek is like a half-pomegranate
behind your veil.

8 There are sixty queens, eighty concubines,
and maidens without number—
9 One alone is my dove, my perfect one,
her mother's chosen,
the dear one of her parent.
The daughters saw her and declared
her fortunate,
the queens and concubines, and they
sang her praises;
10 D*Who is this that comes forth like the dawn,
as beautiful as the moon, as resplendent
as the sun,
as awe-inspiring as bannered troops?

Love's Meeting

11B* I came down to the nut garden
to look at the fresh growth of
the valley,
To see if the vines were in bloom,
if the pomegranates had blossomed.
12† Before I knew it, my heart had made me
the blessed one of my kinswomen.

The Beauty of the Bride

7 ¹ D† Turn, turn, O Shulammite,
turn, turn, that we may look at you!

B Why would you look at the Shulammite
as at the dance of the two companies?

2D†How beautiful are your feet in sandals,
O prince's daughter!
Your rounded thighs are like jewels,
the handiwork of an artist.
3 Your navel is a round bowl
that should never lack for mixed wine.
Your body is a heap of wheat
encircled with lilies.
4* Your breasts are like twin fawns,
the young of a gazelle.
5*†Your neck is like a tower of ivory.
Your eyes are like the pools in Heshbon
by the gate of Bath-rabbim.
Your nose is like the tower on Lebanon
that looks toward Damascus.
6 Your head rises like Carmel;
your hair is like draperies of purple;
a king is held captive in its tresses.

Love's Desires

7G How beautiful you are, how pleasing,
my love, my delight!
8† Your very figure is like a palm tree,
your breasts are like clusters.
9 I said: I will climb the palm tree,
I will take hold of its branches.
Now let your breasts be like clusters of the vine
and the fragrance of your breath like apples,
10 And your mouth like an excellent wine—

Love's Union

B† that flows smoothly for my lover,
spreading over the lips and the teeth.
11*†I belong to my lover
and for me he yearns.

6, 4–9: The lover again celebrates her beauty. *Tirzah:* probably meaning "pleasant"; it was the early capital of the northern kingdom of Israel (1 Kgs 16).

6, 12: The text is obscure in Hebrew and in the ancient versions. The Vulgate reads: "I did not know; my soul disturbed me because of the chariots of Aminadab."

7, 1: *Shulammite:* so called either because the girl is considered to be from Shulam in the plain of Esdraelon (cf 1 Kgs 1, 3) or because the name may mean "the peaceful one," and thus recall the name of Solomon. *As at the dance of the two companies:* the meaning is uncertain. The question in this verse could be construed as a refusal to dance; more probably, however, the girl accedes, as the following verses suggest.

7, 2–6: A flattering description of the girl's charms. *Rounded . . . jewels:* the meaning of these Hebrew words is not certain. Wine and wheat are symbolic of fertility; they are here associated with parts of the body which have a close relation to fruitfulness.

7, 5: The comparison emphasizes the stateliness and whiteness of the neck, and the limpidity of the eyes. *Bath-rabbim:* a proper name which occurs only here; there was a city of Rabbah northeast of Heshbon in Transjordan. Cf Jer 49, 3.

7, 8f: *Palm tree:* a figure of stateliness. The bridegroom is eager to enjoy the possession of his bride.

7, 10: The bride delicately turns his compliment into an expression of the love and tenderness she feels for him.

7, 11–14: The girl's answer assures him of her affection and invites him to return with her to the rural delights which are associated with their love and which recall the meeting described in Song 6, 11f.

6, 3: Song 2, 16; 7, 11.
6, 5: Song 4, 9.
6, 6f: Song 4, 1ff.
6, 10: Song 3, 6; 8, 5.
6, 11: Song 4, 12ff; 7, 13.
7, 4: Song 4, 5.
7, 5: Song 4, 4.
7, 11: Song 2, 16; 6, 3.

12 Come, my lover, let us go forth to the fields
 and spend the night among the villages.
13* Let us go early to the vineyards, and see
 if the vines are in bloom,
 If the buds have opened,
 if the pomegranates have blossomed;
 There will I give you my love.
14† The mandrakes give forth fragrance,
 and at our doors are all choice fruits;
 Both fresh and mellowed fruits, my lover,
 I have kept in store for you.

8 1 Oh, that you were my brother,
 nursed at my mother's breasts!
 If I met you out of doors, I would kiss you
 and none would taunt me.
2* I would lead you, bring you in
 to the home of my mother.
 There you would teach me to give you
 spiced wine to drink, and pomegranate juice.
3* His left hand is under my head
 and his right arm embraces me.
4* I adjure you, daughters of Jerusalem,
 by the gazelles and hinds of the field,
 Do not arouse, do not stir up love,
 before its own time.

Homecoming

5 D*†Who is this coming up from the desert,
 leaning upon her lover?
 G Under the apple tree I awakened you;
 it was there that your mother conceived you,
 it was there that your parent conceived.

True Love

6 B†Set me as a seal on your heart,
 as a seal on your arm;
 For stern as death is love,
 relentless as the nether world is devotion;

 its flames are a blazing fire.
7 Deep waters cannot quench love,
 nor floods sweep it away.
 Were one to offer all he owns to
 purchase love,
 he would be roundly mocked.

Chastity and Its Welcome

8† "Our sister is little
 and she has no breasts as yet.
 What shall we do for our sister
 when her courtship begins?
9 If she is a wall,
 we will build upon it a silver parapet;
 If she is a door,
 we will reinforce it with a cedar plank."
10 I am a wall,
 and my breasts are like towers.
 So now in his eyes I have become
 one to be welcomed.

The Bride and Her Dowry

11B†Solomon had a vineyard at Baal-hamon;
 he gave over the vineyard to caretakers.
 For its fruit one would have to pay
 a thousand silver pieces.
12 My vineyard is at my own disposal;
 the thousand pieces are for you, O Solomon,
 and two hundred for the caretakers of
 its fruit.

Life Together

13G†O garden-dweller,
 my friends are listening for your voice,
 let me hear it!

14B*Be swift, my lover,
 like a gazelle or a young stag
 on the mountains of spices!

7, 14: *Mandrakes:* herbs believed to have power to arouse love and promote fertility; cf Gn 30, 14ff.

8, 5: The lovers are pictured walking homeward, enjoying the fulfillment of the desire which the girl expressed in vv 1f. The groom speaks of their first meeting.

8, 6f: *Seal:* this could be worn bound to the arm, as here, or suspended at the neck, or as a ring (Jer 22, 24). It was used for identification and signatures. *Stern . . . relentless:* in human experience, death and the nether world are inevitable, unrelenting; in the end they always triumph. Love, which is just as certain of its victory, matches its strength against the natural enemies of life; waters cannot extinguish it nor floods carry it away. It is more priceless than all riches.

8, 8ff: The bride affirms her chastity. In 8, 9 she quotes the course of action which her elder brothers had decided on. While she is yet immature, they will shelter her in view of eventual marriage. If she

is virtuous, she will be honored; if she is unchaste, she will be kept under strict vigilance. In reply to this she proclaims her virtue and boasts of having found welcome from her lover.

8, 11f: These enigmatic verses have been variously interpreted. In v 11 the girl alludes to a vineyard of great value which is compared to her own self in v 12. Her enormous dowry, a thousand silver pieces, is in keeping with her intrinsic worth. She has been the generous lover, giving herself and a dowry to her lover, referred to as Solomon, and also smaller gifts to her brothers, the caretakers (cf vv 8ff).

8, 13f: As in Song 2, 14f, her lover asks for a word or a song and she replies in words similar to those found in Song 2, 17.

7, 13: Song 6, 11.   8, 4: Song 2, 7; 3, 5.
8, 2: Song 3, 4.   8, 5: Song 3, 6; 6, 10.
8, 3: Song 2, 6.   8, 14: Song 2, 9.17; 4, 6.

Do you know what life was like for your great-grandparents? Were they, or other members of your family, immigrants to the United States? How much of their history do you know? Time and distance have a way of fading the memories that keep our roots alive. The same was true for the ancient Jewish people after they had settled in different countries. The Book of Wisdom was written to remind them of their roots and the wisdom of their traditions.

In-depth

The Jewish people living in Alexandria, Egypt, in the first century B.C. had long forgotten the difficult transition their ancestors had experienced in moving from Judea. In fact, they had come to feel so much at home in Alexandria that certain leaders began to fear that the Jewish faith and way of life might be lost (see "Diaspora Jews," near Est 2, 5). One of those leaders wrote the Book of Wisdom to encourage the "displaced" Jews to remain faithful to their heritage. Although incorporating new ideas into traditional arguments, the author insists that true wisdom is, in fact, very old. Its course can be traced "from the very beginning" (Wis 6, 22).

The Book of Wisdom grapples with another problem—good versus evil—in a refreshing way. The author is convinced that there will be a final judgment, in which good people will confront their oppressors "with great assurance" and their oppressors will "be shaken with dreadful fear" (5, 1.2). What is more, the just will "live forever" (5,15), whereas the evil will "be utterly laid waste" (4,19). Like Second Maccabees, the Book of Wisdom sees life after death as the answer to the troubling question Why do innocent people suffer although God is good and just?

The Book of Wisdom claims King Solomon as its honorary author, even though it was written long after his death. In this quiet way, it reminds the Jewish faithful that they must never forget their roots in their ancient faith, even though they feel at home in their new land. The book shows how people of faith take the best of their history and tradition to find new answers in new situations.

At a Glance

I. The Reward of Justice (1, 1—6, 21).

II. Praise of Wisdom by Solomon (6, 22—11, 1).

III. Special Providence of God during the Exodus (11, 2–16; 12, 23–27; 15, 18—19, 22) with digressions on God's mercy (11, 17—12, 22) and on the folly and shame of idolatry (13, 1—15, 17).

Quick Facts

Author
unknown, writing around 50 B.C., making this the latest of all Old Testament books

Theme
the reward of the righteous, the praise of wisdom, the importance of trust in God

Of Note
The book is not found in every translation of the Old Testament (see "The Case of the Missing Books," near Tb 1, 16).

The Book of Wisdom

Wisdom

I: The Reward of Justice

Exhortation to Justice, the Key to Life

1 **1*†** Love justice, you who judge the earth;
think of the LORD in goodness,
and seek him in integrity of heart;*

2* Because he is found by those who test
him not,
and he manifests himself to those who do
not disbelieve him.

3* For perverse counsels separate a man
from God,
and his power, put to the proof, rebukes
the foolhardy;

4* Because into a soul that plots evil wisdom
enters not,
nor dwells she in a body under debt of sin.

5*† For the holy spirit of discipline flees deceit
and withdraws from senseless counsels;
and when injustice occurs it is rebuked.

6* For wisdom is a kindly spirit,
yet she acquits not the blasphemer of his
guilty lips;

Because God is the witness of his inmost self
and the sure observer of his heart
and the listener to his tongue.*

7*† For the spirit of the LORD fills the world,
is all-embracing, and knows what man says.

8* Therefore no one who utters wicked things
can go unnoticed,
nor will chastising condemnation pass
him by.

9 For the devices of the wicked man shall
be scrutinized,
and the sound of his words shall reach
the LORD,
for the chastisement of his transgressions;

10* Because a jealous ear hearkens to everything,
and discordant grumblings are no secret.

11† Therefore guard against profitless grumbling,
and from calumny withhold
your tongues;
For a stealthy utterance does not
go unpunished,
and a lying mouth slays the soul.

12 Court not death by your erring way of life,

1, 1: *Justice:* not merely the cardinal virtue of that name (cf Wis 8, 7), but the universal moral quality which is the application of Wisdom to moral conduct.

1, 5: *Discipline:* here and elsewhere, another name for Wisdom; *injustice:* the opposite of the virtue in Wis 1, 1.

1, 7: This verse is applied to the holy Spirit in the liturgy at Pentecost.

1, 11: *Calumny:* speech against God and his providence is meant.

1, 1: 1 Chr 29, 17; Ps 2, 10;
    Is 26, 9.
1, 1f: Sir 1, 25.
1, 2: 1 Chr 28, 9.
1, 3: Is 59, 2.
1, 4: Sir 15, 7f; Rom 7, 14.

1, 5: Is 63, 10.
1, 6: Jer 17, 10.
1, 6f: Jer 23, 24f.
1, 7: Wis 12, 1.
1, 8: Prv 19, 5.
1, 10f: Nm 14, 27f.

God Knows Our Heart

God, you know my heart (Wis 1, 6) even better than I do. This could scare me, or it could give me peace—the peace of knowing that despite my weakness and sin, you still love me. I choose to feel peace! And knowing that you see my heart truly and still love me, I choose to do good. Give me the courage to do the right thing. Help me never to say a word meant to injure another person. Give me too the wisdom of loving justice, so that my heart might be a reflection of your own. Amen.

▶ Wis 1, 6–15

nor draw to yourselves destruction by the
   works of your hands.
13* Because God did not make death,
   nor does he rejoice in the destruction of
      the living.
14 For he fashioned all things that they might
      have being;
   and the creatures of the world
      are wholesome,
   And there is not a destructive drug
      among them
   nor any domain of the nether world
      on earth,
15* For justice is undying.

The Wicked Reject Immortality and Justice Alike

16* It was the wicked who with hands and words
      invited death,
   considered it a friend, and pined for it,
   and made a covenant with it,
   Because they deserve to be in its possession,

2 1* they who said among themselves,
      thinking not aright:
   "Brief and troublous is our lifetime;
   neither is there any remedy for
      man's dying,
   nor is anyone known to have come back
      from the nether world.

2   For haphazard were we born,
      and hereafter we shall be as though we had
         not been;
   Because the breath in our nostrils is a smoke
      and reason is a spark at the beating of
         our hearts,
3* And when this is quenched, our body will
      be ashes
   and our spirit will be poured abroad like
      unresisting air.
4   Even our name will be forgotten in time,
      and no one will recall our deeds.
   So our life will pass away like the traces of
      a cloud,
   and will be dispersed like a mist
   pursued by the sun's rays
   and overpowered by its heat.
5* For our lifetime is the passing of a shadow;
      and our dying cannot be deferred
   because it is fixed with a seal; and no
      one returns.
6* Come, therefore, let us enjoy the good things
      that are real,
   and use the freshness of creation avidly.
7   Let us have our fill of costly wine
      and perfumes,
   and let no springtime blossom pass us by;
8   let us crown ourselves with rosebuds ere
         they wither.
9*† Let no meadow be free from our
         wantonness;
   everywhere let us leave tokens of
      our rejoicing,
   for this our portion is, and this our lot.
10* Let us oppress the needy just man;
   let us neither spare the widow
   nor revere the old man for his hair grown
      white with time.
11 But let our strength be our norm of justice;
   for weakness proves itself useless.
12*†Let us beset the just one, because he is
         obnoxious to us;
   he sets himself against our doings,
   Reproaches us for transgressions of the law†
   and charges us with violations of
      our training.
13* He professes to have knowledge of God
   and styles himself a child of the LORD.
14* To us he is the censure of our thoughts;
   merely to see him is a hardship for us,

2, 9: *Let no meadow . . . wantonness:* the extant Greek Mss have
"Let none of us be without part in our wanton doings." Most Latin
Mss have both forms of this line.
   2, 12–20: Often applied to the Passion of our Lord; many have
understood these verses as a direct prophecy. Cf Mt 27, 41–44.
   2, 12: *Law:* the law of Moses; training has the same meaning.

1, 13f: Ez 18, 32; 33, 11; 2 Pt   15, 32.
   3, 9.   2, 9: Jer 13, 25.
1, 15: Is 51, 6ff.   2, 10: Ex 22, 22ff; Lv 19, 32.
1, 16: Is 28, 15.   2, 12: Hos 8, 1.
2, 1: Jb 14, 1; 7, 9.   2, 13: Mt 27, 43; Jn 8, 55;
2, 3: Jb 7, 9; Jas 4, 14.   10, 36–39.
2, 5: Ps 144, 4.   2, 14: Mt 9, 4.
2, 6: Is 22, 13; 1 Cor

W
I
S

15 Because his life is not like other men's,
  and different are his ways.

16* He judges us debased;
  he holds aloof from our paths as from
    things impure.
  He calls blest the destiny of the just
  and boasts that God is his Father.

17* Let us see whether his words be true;
  let us find out what will happen to him.

18* For if the just one be the son of God, he will
    defend him
  and deliver him from the hand of
    his foes.

19 With revilement and torture let us put him to
    the test
  that we may have proof of his gentleness
  and try his patience.

20* Let us condemn him to a shameful death;
  for according to his own words, God will
    take care of him."

21* These were their thoughts, but they erred;
  for their wickedness blinded them,

22* And they knew not the hidden counsels
    of God;
  neither did they count on a recompense
    of holiness
  nor discern the innocent souls' reward.

23* For God formed man to be imperishable;
  the image of his own nature he
    made him.

24* But by the envy of the devil, death entered
    the world,
  and they who are in his possession
    experience it.

The Hidden Counsels of God

A. On Suffering

3 ¹*† But the souls of the just are in the hand
    of God,
  and no torment shall touch them.

2 They seemed, in the view of the foolish, to
    be dead;
  and their passing away was thought
    an affliction

3 * and their going forth from us, utter
    destruction.
  But they are in peace.

BUT THE SOULS OF THE JUST ARE IN THE **God, hand of** 3, 1

AND NO TORMENT SHALL TOUCH THEM

4 For if before men, indeed, they are punished,
  yet is their hope full of immortality;

5* Chastised a little, they shall be greatly blessed,
  because God tried them
  and found them worthy of himself.

6*†As gold in the furnace, he proved them,
  and as sacrificial offerings he took them
    to himself.

7*†In the time of their visitation they shall
    shine,
  and shall dart about as sparks
    through stubble;

8* They shall judge nations and rule
    over peoples,
  and the LORD shall be their King forever.

9* Those who trust in him shall
    understand truth,
  and the faithful shall abide with him
    in love:
  Because grace and mercy are with his
    holy ones,
  and his care is with his elect.

10† But the wicked shall receive a punishment to
    match their thoughts,
  since they neglected justice and forsook
    the LORD.

11* For he who despises wisdom and instruction
    is doomed.
  Vain is their hope, fruitless are their labors,
  and worthless are their works.*

WIS

3, 1–8: Verses frequently applied to the martyrs.
3, 6: *Offerings:* the image is that of the holocaust, in which the victim is completely consumed by fire.
3, 7: *Visitation:* God's loving judgment of those who have been faithful to him; the same word is used in Wis 14, 11 for the punishment of the wicked at God's final judgment. Cf also Wis 3, 13.
3, 10: *To match their thoughts:* a fate as empty as that which they describe; cf Wis 2, 1–5.

2, 16: Jer 6, 30.
2, 17: Gn 37, 20.
2, 18: Ps 22, 9; Is 42, 1; Mt 27, 43; Jn 5, 18.
2, 20: Jas 5, 6.
2, 21: Rom 1, 21.
2, 22: Ps 18, 24f; Prv 11, 18; Mt 11, 25.
2, 23: Gn 1, 26f; Is 54, 16 LXX.
2, 24: Gn 3, 1–24; Rom 5, 12.
3, 1: Jb 12, 10; 5, 19.
3, 3: Is 57, 2.
3, 5: Tb 12, 13; 2 Cor 4, 17; 1 Pt 1, 6f.
3, 6: Ps 51, 19; Prv 17, 3; Sir 2, 5; Is 48, 10.
3, 7: Dn 12, 3; Ob 18; Mal 3, 3; Mt 13, 43.
3, 8: Wis 8, 14; Prv 8, 16; Dn 7, 22; 1 Cor 6, 2; Rv 20, 4.
3, 9: Wis 3, 9; 4, 15; Jb 10, 12; Jn 15, 10.
3, 11: Prv 1, 7.
3, 11f: Sir 41, 8.

12* Their wives are foolish and their
        children wicked;
        accursed is their brood.

B. On Childlessness

13† Yes, blessed is she who, childless and
        undefiled,
        knew not transgression of the marriage bed;
        she shall bear fruit at the visitation of souls.

14*†So also the eunuch whose hand wrought
        no misdeed,
        who held no wicked thoughts against
        the LORD—
        For he shall be given fidelity's choice reward
        and a more gratifying heritage in the
        LORD's temple.

15* For the fruit of noble struggles is a
        glorious one;
        and unfailing is the root of understanding.

16* But the children of adulterers will remain
        without issue,
        and the progeny of an unlawful bed
        will disappear.

17 For should they attain long life, they will be
        held in no esteem,
        and dishonored will their old age be at last;

18 While should they die abruptly, they have
        no hope
        nor comfort in the day of scrutiny;

19*   for dire is the end of the wicked generation.

4 1*† Better is childlessness with virtue;
        for immortal is its memory:
        because both by God is it acknowledged,
        and by men.

2 When it is present men imitate it,
        and they long for it when it is gone;
        And forever it marches crowned in triumph,
        victorious in unsullied deeds of valor.

3* But the numerous progeny of the wicked shall
        be of no avail;
        their spurious offshoots shall not strike
        deep root
        nor take firm hold.

4* For even though their branches flourish for
        a time,
        they are unsteady and shall be rocked by
        the wind

        and, by the violence of the
        winds, uprooted;

5 Their twigs shall be broken off untimely,
        and their fruit be useless, unripe
        for eating,
        and fit for nothing.

6 For children born of lawless unions
        give evidence of the wickedness of their
        parents, when they are examined.

C. On Early Death

7* But the just man, though he die early, shall be
        at rest.

8* For the age that is honorable comes not with
        the passing of time,
        nor can it be measured in terms of years.

9 Rather, understanding is the hoary crown
        for men,
        and an unsullied life, the attainment of
        old age.

10*†He who pleased God was loved;
        he who lived among sinners
        was transported—

11* Snatched away, lest wickedness pervert
        his mind
        or deceit beguile his soul;

12* For the witchery of paltry things obscures
        what is right
        and the whirl of desire transforms the
        innocent mind.

13 Having become perfect in a short while,
        he reached the fullness of a long career;

14*   for his soul was pleasing to the LORD,
        therefore he sped him out of the midst
        of wickedness.
        But the people saw and did not understand,
        nor did they take this into account.†

16* Yes, the just man dead condemns the sinful
        who live,
        and youth swiftly completed
        condemns the many years of the wicked
        man grown old.

17 For they see the death of the wise man
        and do not understand what the LORD
        intended for him,
        or why he made him secure.

18* They see, and hold him in contempt;
        but the LORD laughs them to scorn.

W
I
S

3, 13: *Visitation of souls:* that is, the last judgment. Cf Wis 3, 7–9.
3, 14: *Fidelity's choice reward:* cf Is 56, 1–8. *More gratifying:* better than sons and daughters; cf Is 56, 5.
4, 1: The Latin form of this line, "Oh, how fair is the chaste generation in its glory!" is a later adaptation, which is applied in the liturgy to the splendor of virginity.
4, 10f: There are allusions here to Enoch (Gn 5, 21–24), who was young by patriarchal standards, and to Lot (Gn 19, 10f; 2 Pt 2, 7f). Cf also Is 57, 1f.
4, 15: The verse omitted here repeats the last two lines of Wis 3, 9.

3, 12: Dt 28, 18ff.
3, 14: Is 56, 2–5.
3, 15: Sir 1, 18.
3, 16: 2 Sm 12, 14.
3, 19: Ps 34, 22.
4, 1: Sir 16, 1ff; Prv 3, 3f.
4, 3: Sir 23, 25.
4, 4: Sir 40, 15; Is 40, 24.
4, 7: Wis 3, 3.
4, 8f: Jb 12, 12; 32, 9;

Sir 25, 4ff.
4, 10: Gn 5, 24; Sir 44, 16;
Heb 11, 5.
4, 11: Is 57, 1f.
4, 12: Wis 2, 21; Dn 13, 9.
4, 14: Gn 19, 22.29;
2 Pt 2, 7.
4, 16: Mt 12, 41f.
4, 18: Ps 37, 13.

19* And they shall afterward become
  dishonored corpses
 and an unceasing mockery among
  the dead.
 For he shall strike them down speechless
  and prostrate*
 and rock them to their foundations;
 They shall be utterly laid waste
  and shall be in grief
  and their memory shall perish.

The Final Judgment of the Wicked

20† Fearful shall they come, at the counting up of
  their sins,
 and their lawless deeds shall convict them
  to their face.

5 ¹* Then shall the just one with great
  assurance confront
 his oppressors who set at nought his
  labors.*
² Seeing this, they shall be shaken with
  dreadful fear,
 and amazed at the unlooked-for salvation.
³ They shall say among themselves, rueful
 and groaning through anguish of spirit:
 "This is he whom once we held as
  a laughingstock
 and as a type for mockery, ⁴ fools that we
  were!
 His life we accounted madness,
  and his death dishonored.
⁵* See how he is accounted among the sons
  of God;
 how his lot is with the saints!
⁶* We, then, have strayed from the way of truth,
 and the light of justice did not shine for us,
 and the sun did not rise for us.*
⁷ We had our fill of the ways of mischief and
  of ruin;
 we journeyed through impassable deserts,
 but the way of the LORD we knew not.
⁸* What did our pride avail us?
 What have wealth and its boastfulness
  afforded us?
⁹* All of them passed like a shadow
 and like a fleeting rumor;
¹⁰ Like a ship traversing the heaving water,
 of which, when it has passed, no trace can
  be found,

  no path of its keel in the waves.
¹¹ Or like a bird flying through the air;
 no evidence of its course is to be found—
 But the fluid air, lashed by the beat
  of pinions,
 and cleft by the rushing force
 Of speeding wings, is traversed:
 and afterward no mark of passage can be
  found in it.
¹² Or as, when an arrow has been shot at
  a mark,
 the parted air straightway flows
  together again
 so that none discerns the way it
  went through—
¹³* Even so we, once born, abruptly came
  to nought
 and held no sign of virtue to display,
 but were consumed in our wickedness."
¹⁴* Yes, the hope of the wicked is like thistledown
  borne on the wind,
 and like fine, tempest-driven foam;
 Like smoke scattered by the wind,
 and like the passing memory of the nomad
  camping for a single day.
¹⁵* But the just live forever,
 and in the LORD is their recompense,
 and the thought of them is with the
  Most High.
¹⁶* Therefore shall they receive the
  splendid crown,
 the beauteous diadem, from the hand of
  the LORD—
 For he shall shelter them with his right hand,
 and protect them with his arm.
¹⁷* He shall take his zeal for armor
 and he shall arm creation to requite
  the enemy;
¹⁸ He shall don justice for a breastplate
 and shall wear sure judgment for
  a helmet;
¹⁹* He shall take invincible rectitude as a shield
²⁰ and whet his sudden anger for a sword,
 And the universe shall war with him against
  the foolhardy.
²¹* Well-aimed shafts of lightnings shall go forth
 and from the clouds as from a well-drawn
  bow shall leap to the mark;
²²* and as from his sling, wrathful hailstones
  shall be hurled.

---

† **4, 20:** *Counting up:* the last judgment.

4, 19: Neh 1, 10 LXX; Ps 18,
 8; Is 14, 19; Jer 23,
 39f.
4, 19: 2 Mc 3, 29.
5, 1f: 2 Thes 1, 6f.

5, 1: Col 2, 15.
5, 5: Acts 26, 18; Col 1, 12.
5, 6: Prv 4, 18f; Jn 12, 35.
5, 6f: Is 59, 6–14.
5, 8: Ps 49, 7; Prv 10, 2.

5, 9ff: 1 Chr 20, 15; Ps 144,
 4; Jb 9, 25f LXX.
5, 13: Ez 33, 10.
5, 14: Jb 21, 18; Pss 1, 4; 37,
 20; Is 17, 13.
5, 15: Is 62, 11; Ez 18, 9.

5, 16: Ex 33, 22; Is 62, 3;
 2 Tm 4, 8; 1 Pt 5, 4.
5, 17: Is 59, 16.
5, 19f: Dt 32, 40ff.
5, 21: Hb 3, 9ff.
5, 22: Dt 11, 4.

Wisdom Speaks

My name is Wisdom. In Greek, I am called Sophia. The Bible speaks of me as an aspect, or image, of God. I am sought after by many. I reveal myself to few. I appear many times in the Scriptures, yet I am elusive. What is it about me that is so attractive, so appealing? Solomon prayed for understanding, and I came to him. Indeed, wisdom is often associated with his name.

Those who seek me must desire deep in their heart to know me. That desire is the first step to finding me. The next is patience. Nothing of true and lasting importance comes quickly. I am not "fast food." In fact, you must experience a deep hunger before you can taste me. Quiet time is essential. You must be willing to simply be present, with no agenda. Imagine a "resplendent and unfading" flame (Wis 6, 12). Let that be your focus.

Soon, I will come to you. I will seek you out. I will meet you in your thoughts, and we will become friends. We will dance together, you and I. You will be changed, transformed. You will grow deeper, quieter, and peace will begin to fill your soul.

My name is Wisdom. I want to be your friend. I wait for you.

The water of the sea shall be enraged
   against them
and the streams shall abruptly overflow;
23* A mighty wind shall confront them
   and a tempest winnow them out;
Thus lawlessness shall lay the whole
   earth waste
and evildoing overturn the thrones
   of potentates.

Exhortation to Seek Wisdom

6 1* Hear, therefore, kings, and understand;
   learn, you magistrates of the earth's
   expanse!
2 Hearken, you who are in power over
   the multitude
   and lord it over throngs of peoples!
3* Because authority was given you by the LORD
   and sovereignty by the Most High,
   who shall probe your works and scrutinize
   your counsels!
4† Because, though you were ministers of his
   kingdom, you judged not rightly,
   and did not keep the law,
   nor walk according to the will of God,
5 Terribly and swiftly shall he come
   against you,
   because judgment is stern for the exalted—
6* For the lowly may be pardoned out of mercy
   but the mighty shall be mightily put to
   the test.

7* For the Lord of all shows no partiality,
   nor does he fear greatness,
   Because he himself made the great as well as
   the small,
   and he provides for all alike;
8 but for those in power a rigorous
   scrutiny impends.
9* To you, therefore, O princes, are my
   words addressed
   that you may learn wisdom and that you
   may not sin.
10† For those who keep the holy precepts
   hallowed shall be found holy,
   and those learned in them will have ready
   a response.
11 Desire therefore my words;
   long for them and you shall be
   instructed.
12* Resplendent and unfading is Wisdom,
   and she is readily perceived by those who
   love her,
   and found by those who seek her.
13* She hastens to make herself known in
   anticipation of men's desire;
14 he who watches for her at dawn shall not
   be disappointed,
   for he shall find her sitting by his gate.
15 For taking thought of her is the perfection
   of prudence,
   and he who for her sake keeps vigil shall
   quickly be free from care;

W
I
S

† 6, 4: *Law:* that of Moses; cf v 10; Wis 2, 12.
6, 10: *Response:* a suitable plea before the great Judge. Cf Prv
22, 21; Jb 31, 14; Hb 2, 1; Sir 8, 9.

* 5, 23: Wis 11, 20; Sir 10, 13f.   6, 7: Dt 1, 17; Prv 22, 2.
6, 1f: Wis 1, 1; Sir 33, 19;   6, 9ff: Dt 4, 10; Ps 2, 12; Sir
   Mi 3, 1.9.   32, 14; 1 Jn 3, 7.
6, 3: 2 Chr 36, 23; Prv 8,   6, 12: Wis 7, 10; Prv 8, 17;
   15f; Jn 19, 11; Rom   Jer 29, 13.
   13, 1ff.   6, 13ff: Prv 8, 3.17.34.
6, 6ff: Lk 12, 48.

16* Because she makes her own rounds, seeking
          those worthy of her,
     and graciously appears to them in the ways,
     and meets them with all solicitude.
17* For the first step toward discipline is a very
          earnest desire for her;
     then, care for discipline is love of her;
18   love means the keeping of her laws;
     To observe her laws is the basis
          for incorruptibility;
19   and incorruptibility makes one close
          to God;
20   thus the desire for Wisdom leads up to
          a kingdom.
21   If, then, you find pleasure in throne and
          scepter, you princes of the peoples,
     honor Wisdom, that you may reign as
          kings forever.

II: Praise of Wisdom by Solomon

Introduction

22* Now what Wisdom is, and how she came to
          be, I shall relate;
     and I shall hide no secrets from you,
     But from the very beginning I shall search out
     and bring to light knowledge of her,
          nor shall I diverge from the truth.
23* Neither shall I admit consuming jealousy to
          my company,
     because that can have no fellowship
          with Wisdom.
24* A great number of wise men is the safety of
          the world,
     and a prudent king, the stability of
          his people;
25   so take instruction from my words, to
          your profit.

Solomon Is Like All Other Men

7 1*† I too am a mortal man, the same as all
          the rest,
     and a descendant of the first man formed
          of earth.
     And in my mother's womb I was molded
          into flesh
2†   in a ten-months' period—body and blood,
     from the seed of man, and the pleasure that
          accompanies marriage.

3   And I too, when born, inhaled the
          common air,
     and fell upon the kindred earth;
     wailing, I uttered that first sound common
          to all.
4   In swaddling clothes and with constant care I
          was nurtured.
5   For no king has any different origin or birth,
6*   but one is the entry into life for all; and in
          one same way they leave it.

Solomon Prayed and Wisdom and Riches Came to Him

7*, Therefore I prayed, and prudence was
          given me;
     I pleaded, and the spirit of Wisdom came
          to me.
8*   I preferred her to scepter and throne,
     And deemed riches nothing in comparison
          with her,
9   nor did I liken any priceless gem to her;
     Because all gold, in view of her, is a
          little sand,
     and before her, silver is to be
          accounted mire.
10* Beyond health and comeliness I loved her,
     And I chose to have her rather than the light,
     because the splendor of her never yields
          to sleep.
11* Yet all good things together came to me in
          her company,
     and countless riches at her hands;
12* And I rejoiced in them all, because Wisdom is
          their leader,
     though I had not known that she is the
          mother of these.

Solomon Prays for Help To Speak of Wisdom

13* Simply I learned about her, and ungrudgingly
          do I share—
     her riches I do not hide away;
14† For to men she is an unfailing treasure;
     those who gain this treasure win the
          friendship of God,
     to whom the gifts they have from discipline
          commend them.
15   Now God grant I speak suitably
     and value these endowments at their worth:
     For he is the guide of Wisdom

7, 1: *First man formed of earth:* Adam. The author omits throughout the book the proper names of the characters in sacred history of
whom he speaks; see especially chapter 10.
7, 2: *In a ten-months' period:* thus the ancients were accustomed
to reckon the period of pregnancy.
7, 14: *Discipline:* cf note on Wis 1, 5.

6, 16: Prv 8, 20f; Sir 15, 1ff.
6, 17–21: Ps 2, 10ff; Prv 4, 4–9;

7, 1–4; 8, 15f; Dn 7,
27; Jn 14, 15.21;

1 Jn 5, 3.
6, 22: Tb 12, 7.11; Mt 13,
     11; Jn 15, 15.
6, 23: Wis 7, 13; Jas 3, 14f.
6, 24: Prv 24, 6; 29, 4; Sir
     10, 1ff.
7, 1f: Wis 10, 1; Gn 2, 7; Jb
     10, 9–12; 33, 6; 1 Cor
     15, 47ff.
7, 6: Jb 1, 21; 1 Tm 6, 7f.

7, 7: 1 Kgs 3, 5–15; Prv 2,
     3–11.
7, 8f: Wis 8, 5; 1 Kgs 10, 21;
     Prv 3, 14ff; 8, 10.18f;
     Jb 28, 15–19.
7, 10: Prv 6, 23.
7, 11: Prv 8, 21.
7, 12: Prv 8, 14f.
7, 13: Wis 6, 23.

W
I
S

THE SOURCE OF WISDOM

Solomon valued wisdom above riches, authority, health, and beauty (Wis 7, 7–10). Native American spirituality values wisdom in a similar way. The elders are seen as the people's connection to history and experience; they are a source of wisdom and sound advice. In fact, all of God's creation is seen as a potential source of wisdom. Notice how this is reflected in the following prayer from the Ojibwa (or Anishinabe) tradition:

Oh Great Spirit, whose voice I hear in the winds
And whose breath gives life to everyone,
Hear me.
I come to you as one of your many children;
I am weak . . . I am small . . . I need your wisdom and your strength.
Let me walk in beauty, and make my eyes ever behold the red and purple sunsets.
Make my hands respect the things you have made, and make my ears sharp so I may hear your
*   voice.*
Make me wise, so that I may understand what you have taught my people and
The lessons you have hidden in each leaf and each rock.
I ask for wisdom and strength,
Not to be superior to my brothers, but to be able to fight my greatest enemy, myself.
Make me ever ready to come before you with clean hands and a straight eye,
So as life fades away as a fading sunset,
My spirit may come to you without shame.

(Author unknown, "Ojibwa Prayer")

▸ **Wis 7, 7–12**

and the director of the wise.
16* For both we and our words are in his hand,
   as well as all prudence and knowledge
   of crafts.
17 For he gave me sound knowledge of
   existing things,
   that I might know the organization of the
   universe and the force of its elements,
18 The beginning and the end and the midpoint
   of times,
   the changes in the sun's course and the
   variations of the seasons,
19 Cycles of years, positions of the stars,
20 natures of animals, tempers of beasts,
   Powers of the winds and thoughts of men,
   uses of plants and virtues of roots—

21 Such things as are hidden I learned, and such
   as are plain;
22* for Wisdom, the artificer of all, taught me.

Nature and Incomparable Dignity of Wisdom

For in her is a spirit
   intelligent, holy, unique,
Manifold, subtle, agile,
   clear, unstained, certain,
Not baneful, loving the good, keen,*
   unhampered, beneficent, 23 kindly,
Firm, secure, tranquil,
   all-powerful, all-seeing,
And pervading all spirits,
   though they be intelligent, pure and
   very subtle.

W
I
S

7, 16: Wis 3, 1.   7, 22f: Heb 4, 12f; Jas 3, 17.
7, 22: Wis 14, 2; Prv 8, 30.

24* For Wisdom is mobile beyond all motion,
    and she penetrates and pervades all things
        by reason of her purity.

25 For she is an aura of the might of God
    and a pure effusion of the glory of
        the Almighty;
    therefore nought that is sullied enters
        into her.

26* For she is the refulgence of eternal light,
    the spotless mirror of the power of God,
    the image of his goodness.

27* And she, who is one, can do all things,
    and renews everything while
        herself perduring;
    And passing into holy souls from age to age,
    she produces friends of God and prophets.

28 For there is nought God loves, be it not one
    who dwells with Wisdom.

29* For she is fairer than the sun
    and surpasses every constellation of the stars.
    Compared to light, she takes precedence;

30   for that, indeed, night supplants,
    but wickedness prevails not over Wisdom.

8 ¹*† Indeed, she reaches from end to end
        mightily
    and governs all things well.

Solomon Sought Wisdom, the Source of Blessings

2* Her I loved and sought after from my youth;
    I sought to take her for my bride
    and was enamored of her beauty.

3 She adds to nobility the splendor of
        companionship with God;
    even the LORD of all loved her.

4* For she is instructress in the understanding
        of God,
    the selector of his works.

5* And if riches be a desirable possession in
        life,
    what is more rich than Wisdom, who
        produces all things?

6* And if prudence renders service,
    who in the world is a better craftsman
        than she?

7† Or if one loves justice,
    the fruits of her works are virtues;
    For she teaches moderation and prudence,
        justice and fortitude,

How Do You Image God?

Old Testament writers sometimes used attributes of God, such as spirit, word, and justice, as titles for God. Wisdom is another of these titles. Each title gives us some insight into God's nature, although no one of them, or even all of them together, can give us the whole picture. The author of the Book of Wisdom describes God's wisdom as a woman, which gives us insight into God's feminine dimension.

Read the qualities of wisdom given in Wis 7, 22—8, 1. This passage summarizes the author's understanding of God's nature. It was probably familiar to New Testament authors. Aspects of it show up in the Letter to the Hebrews (1, 1–4) and in the Gospel of John (1, 1–14).

Explore your images of God. Choose an attribute of God that is significant for you. It might be love, faithfulness, truth, or some other quality. Write a poem, like the one in Wis 8, 2–8, that describes this quality as a person.

▶ Wis 7, 22—8, 8

and nothing in life is more useful for men
    than these.

8* Or again, if one yearns for copious learning,
    she knows the things of old, and infers
        those yet to come.
She understands the turns of phrases and the
        solutions of riddles;
    signs and wonders she knows in advance
    and the outcome of times and ages.

Solomon Sought Wisdom as His Counselor and Comfort

9 So I determined to take her to live with me,
    knowing that she would be my counselor
        while all was well,
    and my comfort in care and grief.

---

† **8, 1:** *End to end:* from one end of the heavens to the other.
8, 7: *Moderation . . . fortitude:* what are now known as the cardinal virtues.

7, 24: Wis 8, 1.   **7, 26:** 2 Cor 4, 4; Col 1, 15; Heb 1, 3.

7, 27: Ex 33, 11; Jb 42, 2; Ps 104, 29; Jl 3, 1.
7, 29f: Song 6, 3.9.
8, 1: Wis 7, 24; 15, 1.
8, 2: 1 Kgs 3, 7ff; Ps 45, 12; Prv 5, 18; 8, 17.
8, 4: Prv 8, 27–31.
8, 5: Prv 8, 18f.
8, 6f: Prv 8, 14f.
8, 8: Prv 1, 6; Sir 39, 1ff; 42, 19f; Dn 2, 21.

WIS

10* For her sake I should have glory among
  the masses,
  and esteem from the elders, though I be but
  a youth.
11 I should become keen in judgment,
  and should be a marvel before rulers.
12† They would abide my silence and attend
  my utterance;
  and as I spoke on further,
  they would place their hands upon
  their mouths.
13* For her sake I should have immortality
  and leave to those after me an
  everlasting memory.
14* I should govern peoples, and nations would
  be my subjects—
15 terrible princes, hearing of me, would
  be afraid;
  in the assembly I should appear noble, and
  in war courageous.
16* Within my dwelling, I should take my repose
  beside her;
  For association with her involves no bitterness
  and living with her no grief,
  but rather joy and gladness.

Solomon Realizes That Wisdom Is a Gift of God

17* Thinking thus within myself,
  and reflecting in my heart
  That there is immortality in kinship
  with Wisdom,
18 and good pleasure in her friendship,
  and unfailing riches in the works of
  her hands,
  And that in frequenting her society there
  is prudence,
  and fair renown in sharing her discourses,
  I went about seeking to take her for my own.
19† Now, I was a well-favored child,
  and I came by a noble nature;
20 or rather, being noble, I attained an
  unsullied body.
21*† And knowing that I could not otherwise
  possess her except God gave it—

and this, too, was prudence, to know whose
  is the gift—
I went to the Lord and besought him,
  and said with all my heart:

Solomon's Prayer

9 1* God of my fathers, Lord of mercy,
  you who have made all things by
  your word*
2* And in your wisdom have established man
  to rule the creatures produced by you,
3* To govern the world in holiness and justice,
  and to render judgment in integrity of heart:
4* Give me Wisdom, the attendant at
  your throne,
  and reject me not from among your children;
5* For I am your servant, the son of
  your handmaid,
  a man weak and short-lived
  and lacking in comprehension of judgment
  and of laws.
6* Indeed, though one be perfect among the
  sons of men,
  if Wisdom, who comes from you, be not
  with him,
  he shall be held in no esteem.
7* You have chosen me king over your people
  and magistrate for your sons and daughters.
8* You have bid me build a temple on your
  holy mountain
  and an altar in the city that is your
  dwelling place,
  a copy of the holy tabernacle which you
  had established from of old.
9* Now with you is Wisdom, who knows
  your works
  and was present when you made the world;
  Who understands what is pleasing in your eyes
  and what is conformable with
  your commands.
10* Send her forth from your holy heavens
  and from your glorious throne
  dispatch her
  That she may be with me and work with me,
  that I may know what is your pleasure,

W
I
S

---

†
 8, 12: *Hands upon their mouths:* an oft-mentioned sign of respect among the ancients for unanswerable wisdom; cf Jb 40, 4.
 8, 19f: Here the sacred writer mentions first bodily, then spiritual, excellence. To make it plain that the latter is the governing factor in the harmonious development of the human person, he then reverses the order.
 8, 21: *Possess her:* in the Latin, "be continent." Though this verse has often been cited in connection with the virtue of chastity, the original must certainly mean "be possessed of Wisdom."

8, 10ff: 1 Kgs 3, 28; Jb 29, 8ff. **8, 13:** Sir 15, 6; 41, 12f; Is
21f.   56, 5.

8, 14: Wis 3, 8; Pss 18, 48; **9, 4:** 2 Chr 1, 10.
 47, 4.   **9, 5:** 1 Kgs 3, 7; Ps 116, 16.
8, 16: Prv 29, 6; Sir 15, 6;   **9, 6:** Wis 3, 17; 1 Kgs 11, 4;
 Bar 3, 38.   1 Cor 3, 18ff.
8, 17: Prv 3, 18.   **9, 7:** 1 Chr 28, 5.
8, 21: 1 Kgs 3, 9; 4, 29; Prv **9, 8:** Ex 25, 8f; 2 Sm 7, 13;
 2, 6; Jas 1, 5.   1 Chr 28, 5; 2 Chr 6,
9, 1: Ps 86, 15.   1f; 7, 7; Tb 1, 4; Pss
9, 1f: Gn 1; Ps 33, 6; Prv 3,   15, 1; 48, 2f.
 19; Jer 10, 12;   **9, 9:** Dt 6, 17f; Prv 8,
 Jn 1, 3.10.   22–31; Jn 1, 1ff.10.
9, 2: Ps 8, 7ff; Sir 17, 2ff.   **9, 10:** Wis 18, 15; Mt 5, 34;
9, 3: 1 Kgs 3, 6; 9, 4f; Ps   Jn 3, 17; 20, 21.
 9, 8f.

11* For she knows and understands all things,
   and will guide me discreetly in my affairs
   and safeguard me by her glory;

12* Thus my deeds will be acceptable,
   and I shall judge your people justly
   and be worthy of my father's throne.

13* For what man knows God's counsel,
   or who can conceive what the
      LORD intends?

14 For the deliberations of mortals are timid,
   and unsure are our plans.

15* For the corruptible body burdens the soul
   and the earthen shelter weighs down the
      mind that has many concerns.

16* And scarce do we guess the things on earth,
   and what is within our grasp we find
      with difficulty;
   but when things are in heaven, who can
      search them out?

17* Or who ever knew your counsel, except you
      had given Wisdom
   and sent your holy spirit from on high?

18* And thus were the paths of those on earth
      made straight,
   and men learned what was your pleasure,
   and were saved by Wisdom.

Wisdom Preserves Her Followers†

10 1*† She preserved the first-formed father
         of the world
      when he alone had been created;*
   And she raised him up from his fall,
2*   and gave him power to rule all things.
3*† But when the unjust man withdrew from her
      in his anger,
   he perished through his fratricidal wrath.
4*† When on his account the earth was flooded,
      Wisdom again saved it,
   piloting the just man on frailest wood.
5*† She, when the nations were sunk in
      universal wickedness,
   knew the just man, kept him blameless
      before God,

and preserved him resolute against pity for
   his child.

6*† She delivered the just man from among the
      wicked who were being destroyed,
   when he fled as fire descended
      upon Pentapolis—

7*† Where as a testimony to its wickedness,
      there yet remain a smoking desert,
   Plants bearing fruit that never ripens,
   and the tomb of a disbelieving soul, a
      standing pillar of salt.

8 For those who forsook Wisdom
      first were bereft of knowledge of the right,
   And then they left mankind a memorial of
      their folly—
   so that they could not even be hidden in
      their fall.

9* But Wisdom delivered from tribulations those
      who served her.

10*† She, when the just man fled from his
      brother's anger,
   guided him in direct ways,
   Showed him the kingdom of God
      and gave him knowledge of holy things;
   She prospered him in his labors
   and made abundant the fruit of his works,

11* Stood by him against the greed of
      his defrauders,
   and enriched him;

12*† She preserved him from foes,
   and secured him against ambush,
   And she gave him the prize for his stern struggle
      that he might know that devotion to God is
      mightier than all else.

13*† She did not abandon the just man when he
      was sold,
   but delivered him from sin.*

14 She went down with him into the dungeon,
   and did not desert him in his bonds,
   Until she brought him the scepter of royalty
      and authority over his oppressors,
   Showed those who had defamed him false,
      and gave him eternal glory.

---

† **10, 1–21:** This chapter prepares for the following section (11, 2—19, 22) on the history of Israel in the Exodus, by reviewing the dealings of Wisdom with the patriarchs. It has a parallel in Sir 44–50; cf also Wis 18, 9.

10, 1f: Adam.
10, 3: Cain.
10, 4: Noah.
10, 5: Abraham.
10, 6: Lot. *Pentapolis:* the five cities, including Sodom; cf Gn 14, 2.
10, 7: *Disbelieving soul:* Lot's wife; cf Gn 19, 26.
10, 10ff: Jacob.
10, 12: *Devotion to God:* in the Greek this signifies "piety" or "religion," and is the equivalent of the Hebrew "fear of the LORD"; cf Prv 1, 7.

10, 13f: Joseph.

---

* 9, 11: Wis 8, 8.
9, 12: 1 Kgs 3, 6–9.
9, 13: Is 40, 13; Bar 3, 31.
9, 15: Jb 4, 19.
9, 16: Sir 1, 3; Jn 3, 12.
9, 17: Jn 14, 26.
9, 18: Wis 10, 9; Prv 28, 26.
10, 1–16: Heb 11, 17–27.
10, 1: Wis 7, 1.
10, 2: Gn 1, 28.
10, 3: Gn 4, 1–16.
10, 4: Wis 14, 5f; Gn 6, 5–9.

10, 5: Gn 22, 7–10.
10, 6: Gn 18, 22–33; 19, 15–25; 2 Pt 2, 6f.
10, 7: Gn 19, 26; Lk 17, 32.
10, 9: Wis 16, 8.
10, 10: Gn 27, 43ff; 28, 12–15.
10, 11: Gn 30, 29f; 31, 5–12.
10, 12: Gn 32, 24–29; 1 Tm 4, 8.
10, 13f: Gn 37–45.
10, 13: Gn 39, 7–10.

WORDS FROM A FATHER TO HIS SON!

The following translation of a text originally written in Nahuatl is the wisdom of a native father in sixteenth-century Mexico. This spirit of wisdom still exists in many Mexican families.

My son, . . . my precious feather, you have come to life, been born, been blessed to come into the world in the land of our LORD. The One for whom we live forged your life, gave you shape. We, your mother and father, have watched over you; your aunts and uncles, all your family, have watched over you, have cried for you, have suffered for you that you might be born. (P. 49)

Love and serve others in holiness; respect and obey your mother and father, and do their hearts' desire. Your gift of service, obedience, and respect will be the recompense they deserve. (P. 53)

Push away from you all that is not good: that which is wrong, all the things that dishonor you. . . . Do no damage to the community, or the peace. Because if you do bad things, you will not come away unscathed: you must eventually suffer for such actions. (P. 79)

With these words, I encourage and strengthen you; through them, I console you. Throw away nothing I have told you, nothing you have heard. May all this be your inspiration, helping you always to remember the LORD, our God. (P. 86)

(Miguel Léon-Portilla and Librado Silva Galeana,
Huehuehtlahtolli, as translated by Richard Wood)

15* The holy people and blameless race—it
     was she
     who delivered them from the nation that
        oppressed them.
16*†She entered the soul of the LORD's servant,
     and withstood fearsome kings with signs
        and portents;
17*   she gave the holy ones the recompense of
       their labors,
     Conducted them by a wondrous road,
     and became a shelter for them by day
     and a starry flame by night.
18   She took them across the Red Sea
     and brought them through the
       deep waters—
19† But their enemies she overwhelmed,
     and cast them up from the bottom of
       the depths.

20* Therefore the just despoiled the wicked;
     and they sang, O LORD, your holy name
     and praised in unison your
       conquering hand—
21* Because Wisdom opened the mouths of
     the dumb,
     and gave ready speech to infants.

11 1* She made their affairs prosper
       through the holy prophet.

III: Special Providence of God During the Exodus

Introduction

2*†They journeyed through the
     uninhabited desert,
     and in solitudes they pitched their tents;

W
I
S

10, 16: Moses.
10, 19: *Cast them up:* their bodies, on the shore.
11, 2ff: Few verses in these later chapters can be fully understood without consulting the passages in the Mosaic books which are indicated in the cross references. The theme of this part of the book is expressed in Wis 11, 5, and is illustrated in the following chapters by five examples drawn from Exodus events.

10, 15: Ex 3, 9; 14, 30; 19, 6.
10, 16: Wis 1, 4; 7, 27; Ex 4, 10; Ps 76, 13.
10, 17ff: Wis 14, 3; 19, 7; Ex 13, 21f; 14–15; Pss 77, 20f; 78, 13.53; Is 4, 5f.
10, 20: Ex 12, 35f; 15, 1–21.

10, 21: Ex 4, 10–15; Ps 8, 3; Mt 11, 25.
11, 1: Dt 2, 7; Hos 12, 14.
11, 2ff: Ex 17, 2–6; Nm 20, 1–13; Pss 63, 2; 107, 4–7; Jer 2, 6.

3* they withstood enemies and took
vengeance on their foes.
4 When they thirsted, they called upon you,
and water was given them from the
sheer rock,
assuagement for their thirst from the
hard stone.
5* For by the things through which their foes
were punished
they in their need were benefited.

First Example: Water Punishes the Egyptians and Benefits the Israelites

6*†Instead of a spring, when the perennial
river
was troubled with impure blood
7 as a rebuke to the decree for the slaying
of infants,
You gave them abundant water in an
unhoped-for way,
8 once you had shown by the thirst they
then had
how you punished their adversaries.
9* For when they had been tried, though only
mildly chastised,
they recognized how the wicked,
condemned in anger, were
being tormented.
11* Both those afar off and those close by
were afflicted:
10 the latter you tested, admonishing them as
a father;
the former as a stern king you probed
and condemned.
12* For a twofold grief took hold of them
and a groaning at the remembrance of the
ones who had departed.
13 For when they heard that the cause of their
own torments
was a benefit to these others, they
recognized the LORD.
14* Him who of old had been cast out in
exposure they indeed mockingly rejected;
but in the end of events, they marveled
at him,
since their thirst proved unlike that of
the just.

Second Example: Animals Punish the Egyptians and Benefit the Israelites

15*†And in return for their senseless,
wicked thoughts,
which misled them into worshiping dumb
serpents and worthless insects,
You sent upon them swarms of dumb
creatures for vengeance;
16* that they might recognize that a man is
punished by the very things through
which he sins.

Digression on God's Mercy

17* For not without means was your
almighty hand,
that had fashioned the universe from
formless matter,
to send upon them a drove of bears or
fierce lions,
18 Or new-created, wrathful, unknown beasts
to breathe forth fiery breath,
Or pour out roaring smoke,
or flash terrible sparks from their eyes.
19 Not only could these attack and completely
destroy them;
even their frightful appearance itself
could slay.
20* Even without these, they could have been
killed at a single blast,
pursued by retribution
and winnowed out by your mighty spirit;
But you have disposed all things by measure
and number and weight.
21* For with you great strength abides always;
who can resist the might of your arm?
22*†Indeed, before you the whole universe is as a
grain from a balance,
or a drop of morning dew come down
upon the earth.
23* But you have mercy on all, because you can
do all things;
and you overlook the sins of men that they
may repent.
24* For you love all things that are
and loathe nothing that you have made;
for what you hated, you would not
have fashioned.

11, 6ff: *The perennial river:* the Nile; the contrast is between the first plague of Egypt (Ex 7, 17–24) and the water drawn from the rock in Horeb (Ex 17, 5–7; Nm 20, 8–11).
11, 15: *Dumb:* that is, irrational.
11, 22: *Grain from a balance:* a tiny particle used for weighing on sensitive scales.

11, 3: Ex 17, 8–16; Nm 21,
1ff.21–35; 31, 1–12;
Ps 118, 10ff.

11, 5: Wis 16, 1f.

11, 6ff: Wis 18, 5; Ex 1, 22; 7,
17–24.

11, 9ff: Wis 3, 5; 16, 3f; Dt 8,
2–5; Ps 6, 2; Prv 3, 12;
2 Mc 6, 12–16.
11, 11: Ps 6, 2.
11, 12f: Wis 16, 8; Ex 14, 4.18.
11, 14: Ex 2, 3.
11, 15: Wis 12, 23f; 15, 18—
16, 1; Ex 7, 26ff.
11, 16: Wis 12, 23.27; Ex 10,
16; Prv 1, 31f; 26, 27.

11, 17ff: Wis 12, 8f; 16, 1.5;
Gn 1, 1f; Dt 32, 24;
2 Kgs 17, 25f; Hos 13,
4–8.
11, 20: Jb 4, 9.
11, 21: Wis 12, 12; 2 Chr
20, 6.
11, 22: Hos 13, 3.
11, 23: Wis 12, 10; Dt 9, 27;
Acts 17, 30; Rom 2, 4;
11, 32; 2 Pt 3, 9.
11, 24: Ps 145, 9.

WORDS FROM A MOTHER TO HER DAUGHTER!

The following translation of a text originally written in Nahuatl is the wisdom of a native mother in sixteenth-century Mexico. This spirit of wisdom still exists in many Mexican families.

> Now, my daughter, my turtledove, little woman: you have life, you are born. You have entered the world, emerged from my womb, nourished at my breast. Our LORD forged your life, shaped you, made you within me. . . . Our LORD makes each of us earn our reputation, our honor, our warmth, our passion, our sweetness, our savor. . . .
>
> Sing well, speak well, converse deeply, respond to all, pray deeply; words are not to be bought and sold. Never allow the world to make you stupid, or silly. . . . In this way, you will live among the people, and you will be worthy of all you need . . . you will please our LORD and be worthy of our LORD's kindness and mercy. (Pp. 91–92)
>
> Be not a friend to liars, to thieves, to evil women, to meddlers, to those who are lazy. . . .
>
> And if you have belongings or property, do not waste them; do not display them when you go out to the market. . . . Then you will leave what is yours to your children and grandchildren after you.
>
> If you live in this way, as I have taught you, then in truth, you will live well among your own people, favored by all. (Pp. 95–97)
>
> **(Miguel Léon-Portilla and Librado Silva Galeana,**
> ***Huehuehtlahtolli,* as translated by Richard Wood)**

25* And how could a thing remain, unless you
willed it;
    or be preserved, had it not been called forth
    by you?
26* But you spare all things, because they are
yours, O LORD and lover of souls,

12 1* for your imperishable spirit is in
all things!
2   Therefore you rebuke offenders little by little,
warn them, and remind them of the sins
they are committing,
    that they may abandon their wickedness
    and believe in you, O LORD!
3* For, truly, the ancient inhabitants of your
holy land,
4   whom you hated for deeds most odious—
Works of witchcraft and impious sacrifices;

5† a cannibal feast of human flesh
and of blood, from the midst of . . . —
These merciless murderers of children,
6*   and parents who took with their own
hands defenseless lives,
You willed to destroy by the hands of
our fathers,
7*   that the land that is dearest of all to you
might receive a worthy colony of
God's children.
8* But even these, as they were men, you spared,
and sent wasps as forerunners of your army
that they might exterminate them
by degrees.
9* Not that you were without power to have the
wicked vanquished in battle by the just,
or wiped out at once by terrible beasts or
by one decisive word;

W
I
S

---

† **12, 5:** *And of blood, from the midst of . . .* : this line is obscure in the current Greek text and in all extant translations. Either one or two words would complete it. The horrible crimes here spoken of (cf Wis 14, 23) were not unheard of in the ancient pagan world.

11, 25: Is 41, 4.
11, 26: Wis 12, 16; Is 63, 9.
12, 1: Wis 1, 7.
12, 3ff: Wis 14, 23; Dt 18,
    9–12; Pss 5, 6; 106,
    28.34–39; Jer 19, 4f;
    Ez 16, 3.20f.36.
12, 6: Nm 33, 52.
12, 7: Dt 11, 12.
12, 8: Ex 23, 28ff; Dt 7,
    17–24.
12, 9: Wis 11, 18; 18, 15;
    Nm 16, 21.

10* But condemning them bit by bit, you gave
 them space for repentance.
 You were not unaware that their race
 was wicked
 and their malice ingrained,
 And that their dispositions would
 never change;

11* for they were a race accursed from
 the beginning.
 Neither out of fear for anyone
 did you grant amnesty for their sins.

12* For who can say to you, "What have
 you done?"
 or who can oppose your decree?
 Or when peoples perish, who can challenge
 you, their maker;
 or who can come into your presence as
 vindicator of unjust men?

13* For neither is there any god besides you who
 have the care of all,
 that you need show you have not
 unjustly condemned;

14* Nor can any king or prince confront you on
 behalf of those you have punished.

15* But as you are just, you govern all things justly;
 you regard it as unworthy of your power
 to punish one who has incurred no blame.

16* For your might is the source of justice;
 your mastery over all things makes you
 lenient to all.

17*†For you show your might when the perfection
 of your power is disbelieved;
 and in those who know you, you
 rebuke temerity.

18 But though you are master of might, you
 judge with clemency,
 and with much lenience you govern us;
 for power, whenever you will, attends you.

19* And you taught your people, by these deeds,
 that those who are just must be kind;
 And you gave your sons good ground
 for hope
 that you would permit repentance for
 their sins.

20 For these were enemies of your servants,
 doomed to death;
 yet, while you punished them with such
 solicitude and pleading,

granting time and opportunity to
 abandon wickedness,

21* With what exactitude you judged your sons,
 to whose fathers you gave the sworn
 covenants of goodly promises!

22 Us, therefore, you chastise, and our enemies
 with a thousand blows you punish,
 that we may think earnestly of your
 goodness when we judge,
 and, when being judged, may look
 for mercy.

Second Example Resumed

23* Hence those unjust also, who lived a life
 of folly,
 you tormented through their
 own abominations.

24* For they went far astray in the paths of error,
 taking for gods the worthless and disgusting
 among beasts,
 deceived like senseless infants.

25* Therefore as though upon
 unreasoning children,
 you sent your judgment on them as
 a mockery;

26 But they who took no heed of punishment
 which was but child's play
 were to experience a condemnation worthy
 of God.

27* For in the things through which they
 suffered distress,
 since they were tortured by the very things
 they deemed gods,
 They saw and recognized the true God
 whom before they had refused to know;
 with this, their final condemnation came
 upon them.

Digression on False Worship

A. NATURE WORSHIP

13 1*† For all men were by nature foolish
 who were in ignorance of God,
 and who from the good things seen did not
 succeed in knowing him who is,
 and from studying the works did not
 discern the artisan;

2*†But either fire, or wind, or the swift air,
 or the circuit of the stars, or the mighty water,

12, 17: The brunt of God's anger and vindictive justice is borne by those who know him and yet defy his authority and might. Cf Wis 1, 2; 15, 2, but also Wis 12, 27; 18, 13.
 13, 1: *Him who is:* the Hebrew sacred name of God; cf Ex 3, 14.
 13, 2: *Luminaries of heaven:* the Latin interprets, "sun and moon"; *governors:* cf Gn 1, 16.

12, 10: Wis 11, 23; Ps 55, 20; Sir 16, 9.
12, 11: Gn 9, 25.
12, 12: 2 Sm 16, 10; Eccl 8, 4; Sir 46, 19; Is 45, 9; Dn 4, 32; Rom 9, 19ff.
12, 13: Wis 6, 7; Dt 3, 24; 32, 39; Is 44, 6.8.
12, 14: Jer 49, 19; 50, 44.
12, 15: Gn 18, 23ff; Dt 32, 4.
12, 16: Wis 2, 11; 11, 26; Ps 103, 19.
12, 17: Wis 15, 2f; Ex 9, 16.
12, 19f: Wis 11, 23; Sir 17, 24.
12, 21: Wis 18, 22; Gn 50, 24;
Dt 7, 6–14; Ps 105, 8ff.
12, 23: Wis 11, 16; 16, 1.
12, 24: Dt 11, 28; Jer 5, 28; Rom 1, 23.
12, 25: Jer 4, 22.
12, 27: Wis 16, 16; Ex 14, 4.28.
13, 1: Acts 14, 17; Eph 4, 17ff.
13, 2: Gn 1, 14–19; Dt 4, 19; Jb 31, 26ff.

or the luminaries of heaven, the governors
of the world, they considered gods.

3* Now if out of joy in their beauty they thought
them gods,
let them know how far more excellent is
the Lord than these;
for the original source of beauty
fashioned them.

4* Or if they were struck by their might
and energy,
let them from these things realize how
much more powerful is he who made
them.

5 For from the greatness and the beauty of
created things
their original author, by analogy, is seen.

6† But yet, for these the blame is less;
For they indeed have gone astray perhaps,
though they seek God and wish to
find him.

7 For they search busily among his works,
but are distracted by what they see, because
the things seen are fair.

8 But again, not even these are pardonable.

9 For if they so far succeeded in knowledge
that they could speculate about
the world,
how did they not more quickly find
its LORD?

B. IDOLATRY

10* But doomed are they, and in dead things are
their hopes,
who termed gods things made by
human hands:
Gold and silver, the product of art, and
likenesses of beasts,
or useless stone, the work of an
ancient hand.

The Carpenter and Wooden Idols

11* A carpenter may saw out a suitable tree
and skillfully scrape off all its bark,
And deftly plying his art,
produce something fit for daily use,*

12 and use up the refuse from his handiwork
in preparing his food, and have his fill;

13* Then the good-for-nothing refuse from
these remnants,
crooked wood grown full of knots,

he takes and carves to occupy his spare time.
This wood he models with listless skill,
and patterns it on the image of a man

14* or makes it resemble some worthless beast.
When he has daubed it with red and
crimsoned its surface with red stain,
and daubed over every blemish in it,

15* He makes a fitting shrine for it
and puts it on the wall, fastening it with
a nail.

16* Thus lest it fall down he provides for it,
knowing that it cannot help itself;
for, truly, it is an image and needs help.

17* But when he prays about his goods or
marriage or children,
he is not ashamed to address the thing
without a soul.
And for vigor he invokes the powerless;

18 and for life he entreats the dead;
And for aid he beseeches the
wholly incompetent,
and about travel, something that cannot
even walk.

19 And for profit in business and success with
his hands
he asks facility of a thing with hands
completely inert.

14 1* Again, one preparing for a voyage and
about to traverse the wild waves
cries out to wood more unsound than the
boat that bears him.

2 For the urge for profits devised this latter,
and Wisdom the artificer produced it.

3* But your providence, O Father! guides it,
for you have furnished even in the sea
a road,
and through the waves a steady path,

4* Showing that you can save from any danger,
so that even one without skill may embark.

5* But you will that the products of your
Wisdom be not idle;
therefore men trust their lives even to
frailest wood,
and have been safe crossing the surge on
a raft.

6*†For of old, when the proud giants were
being destroyed,
the hope of the universe, who took refuge
on a raft,

---

† **13, 6:** *The blame is less:* the greater blame is incurred by those
mentioned in Wis 13, 10 and 15, 14ff.
14, 6: Noah.

* **13, 3:** Ps 8, 4.
13, 4: Jer 10, 2; Bar 6, 39.
13, 10: Wis 3, 11; 15, 5.17; Dt

4, 25–28; 7, 25; 27,
15; Ps 115, 4; Hos 14,
4; Acts 17, 29.

13, 11–19: Is 44, 9–20.
13, 11: Wis 15, 7; Bar 6, 58.
13, 13: Dt 4, 16.
13, 14: Jer 10, 9.
13, 15: Is 40, 20; 41, 7; 44, 13.
13, 16: 1 Sm 5, 3ff; Bar 6, 57.
13, 17ff: Wis 15, 15.

14, 1: Is 46, 7.
14, 3: Ps 107, 23–30; Is
43, 16.
14, 4: Wis 16, 8.
14, 5: Wis 10, 4.
14, 6: Gn 6, 4; 17, 1ff.21f.

God Is My Copilot!

Have you ever seen the bumper sticker "God is my copilot"? This seems to be the message in Wis 14, 3. The author seems to be saying, "Don't put your trust in a little idol made of wood; it is the one true God who helps you, who guides you, who sets your course!"

Your life has many challenges. One way to face those challenges is to take God along on the journey. When you feel like you can't go on, call on God. When you fail and stumble, call on God. When you succeed, call on God and celebrate. God is here to be your copilot, to help you navigate through life, so just let go and let God!

▶ Wis 14, 1–8

left to the world a future for his race, under the guidance of your hand.

7† For blest is the wood through which justice comes about;

8* but the handmade idol is accursed, and its maker as well:

he for having produced it, and it, because though corruptible, it was termed a god.

9 Equally odious to God are the evildoer and his evil deed;

10 and the thing made shall be punished with its contriver.

11* Therefore upon even the idols of the nations shall a visitation come,

since they have become abominable amid God's works,

Snares for the souls of men and a trap for the feet of the senseless.

The Origin and Evils of Idolatry

12* For the source of wantonness is the devising of idols;

and their invention was a corruption of life.

13* For in the beginning they were not, nor shall they continue forever;

14 for by the vanity of men they came into the world,

and therefore a sudden end is devised for them.

15 For a father, afflicted with untimely mourning,

made an image of the child so quickly taken from him,

And now honored as a god what was formerly a dead man

and handed down to his subjects mysteries and sacrifices.

16* Then, in time, the impious practice gained strength and was observed as law,

and graven things were worshiped by princely decrees.

17 Men who lived so far away that they could not honor him in his presence

copied the appearance of the distant king

And made a public image of him they wished to honor,

out of zeal to flatter him when absent, as though present.

18 And to promote this observance among those to whom it was strange,

the artisan's ambition provided a stimulus.

19* For he, mayhap in his determination to please the ruler,

labored over the likeness to the best of his skill;

20* And the masses, drawn by the charm of the workmanship,

soon thought he should be worshiped who shortly before was honored as a man.

21 And this became a snare for mankind,

that men enslaved to either grief or tyranny conferred the incommunicable Name on stocks and stones.

22* Then it was not enough for them to err in their knowledge of God;

but even though they live in a great war of ignorance,

they call such evils peace.*

23* For while they celebrate either child-slaying sacrifices or clandestine mysteries,

14, 7: Often applied to the Cross of our Lord.

14, 8: Rom 1, 23.
14, 11: Wis 3, 7; 23, 33; Nm 33, 4; Jos 23, 13; Ps
115, 4; Jer 6, 15; 10, 15; 46, 25; Hos 9, 15.

14, 12: Rom 1, 23ff.
14, 13: Is 2, 18.
14, 16: Dn 3, 4ff; 1 Mc 1, 47–50.
14, 19: Is 44, 12f LXX.
14, 20: Wis 15, 4.
14, 22–31: Jer 2, 20; 3, 1–25; Hos 4, 1f.9–19; Rom 1, 26–31; Gal 5, 19ff; 1 Tm 1, 9f.
14, 22: Jer 6, 14; Ez 13, 10.
14, 23: Wis 12, 4f; 14, 15; Is 57, 5.

WIS

or frenzied carousals in unheard-of rites,

24 They no longer safeguard either lives or
     pure wedlock;
     but each either waylays and kills his
        neighbor, or aggrieves him by adultery.

25* And all is confusion—blood and murder, theft
     and guile,
     corruption, faithlessness, turmoil,
     perjury,

26 Disturbance of good men, neglect
     of gratitude,
     besmirching of souls, unnatural lust,
     disorder in marriage, adultery
     and shamelessness.

27* For the worship of infamous idols
     is the reason and source and extremity of
     all evil.

28* For they either go mad with enjoyment, or
     prophesy lies,
     or live lawlessly or lightly
     forswear themselves.

29 For as their trust is in soulless idols,
     they expect no harm when they have
     sworn falsely.

30*†But on both counts shall justice
     overtake them:
     because they thought ill of God and
     devoted themselves to idols,
     and because they deliberately swore false
     oaths, despising piety.

31† For not the might of those that are sworn by
     but the retribution of sinners
     ever follows upon the transgression of
     the wicked.

15 1* But you, our God, are good and true,
     slow to anger, and governing all
     with mercy.

2* For even if we sin, we are yours, and know
     your might;
     but we will not sin, knowing that we
     belong to you.

3* For to know you well is complete justice,
     and to know your might is the root
     of immortality.

4* For neither did the evil creation of men's
     fancy deceive us,
     nor the fruitless labor of painters,
     A form smeared with varied colors,

5 the sight of which arouses yearning in the
     senseless man,
     till he longs for the inanimate form of a
     dead image.

6* Lovers of evil things, and worthy of such hopes
     are they who make them and long for them
     and worship them.

The Potter's Clay Idols

7* For truly the potter, laboriously working the
     soft earth,
     molds for our service each several article:
     Both the vessels that serve for clean purposes
     and their opposites, all alike;
     As to what shall be the use of each vessel of
     either class
     the worker in clay is the judge.

8* And with misspent toil he molds a
     meaningless god from the selfsame clay;
     though he himself shortly before was made
     from the earth
     And after a little, is to go whence he was taken,
     when the life that was lent him is
     demanded back.

9* But his concern is not that he is to die
     nor that his span of life is brief;
     Rather, he vies with goldsmiths
     and silversmiths
     and emulates molders of bronze,
     and takes pride in modeling counterfeits.

10* Ashes his heart is! more worthless than earth
     is his hope,
     and more ignoble than clay his life;

11* Because he knew not the one who
     fashioned him,
     and breathed into him a quickening soul,
     and infused a vital spirit.

12* Instead, he esteemed our life a plaything,
     and our span of life a holiday for gain;
     "For one must," says he, "make profit every
     way, be it even out of evil."

13 For this man more than any knows that he
     is sinning,
     when out of earthen stuff he creates fragile
     vessels and idols alike.

14* But all quite senseless, and worse than
     childish in mind,
     are the enemies of your people who
     enslaved them.

---

† **14, 30:** *Piety:* the sanctity of oaths.
14, 31: Perjury is a form of deceit which calls for punishment even though it be practiced in the name of a lifeless idol.

14, 25f: Jer 7, 8f; 22, 17.
14, 27: Ex 23, 13.
14, 28: Jer 5, 31; 29, 26.

14, 30: Wis 1, 1.8; 11, 20;
     Jer 5, 2.7.
15, 1: Ex 34, 6f; Pss 86, 5,
     15; 145, 8.9.14.
15, 2: Jb 10, 14f LXX.
15, 3: Wis 3, 15; Jn 17, 3.
15, 4: Wis 13, 14.
15, 6: Ps 115, 8.

15, 7: Wis 13, 11; Jer 18, 3f;
     Rom 9, 21; 2 Tm 2, 20f.
15, 8: Gn 3, 19; Eccl 12, 7.
15, 9: Bar 6, 46.
15, 10: Jb 13, 12 LXX.
15, 11: Gn 2, 7; Zec 12, 1.
15, 12: Jas 4, 13f.
15, 14: Ex 1, 13.

15* For they esteemed all the idols of the
    nations, gods,
    which have no use of the eyes for vision,
    nor nostrils to snuff the air,
Nor ears to hear,
    nor fingers on their hands for feeling;
    even their feet are useless to walk with.

16* For a man made them;
    one whose spirit has been lent him
    fashioned them.
For no man succeeds in fashioning a god
    like himself;

17   being mortal, he makes a dead thing with
    his lawless hands.
For he is better than the things he worships;
    he at least lives, but never they.

Second Example Resumed

18*†And besides, they worship the most
    loathsome beasts—
    for compared as to folly, these are worse
    than the rest,†

19* Nor for their looks are they good or
    desirable beasts,
    but they have escaped both the approval of
    God and his blessing.

16

1*† Therefore they were fittingly
    punished by similar creatures,
and were tormented by a swarm of
    insects.

2* Instead of this punishment, you benefited
    your people
    with a novel dish, the delight they craved,
    by providing quail for their food;

3* That those others, when they desired food,
    since the creatures sent to plague them were
    so loathsome,
    should be turned from even the craving
    of necessities,
While these, after a brief period of privation,
    partook of a novel dish.

4* For upon those oppressors, inexorable want
    had to come;
    but these needed only be shown how their
    enemies were being tormented.

5* For when the dire venom of beasts came
    upon them
    and they were dying from the bite of
    crooked serpents,
    your anger endured not to the end.

6† But as a warning, for a short time they
    were terrorized,
    though they had a sign of salvation, to
    remind them of the precept of your law.

7   For he who turned toward it was saved,
    not by what he saw,
    but by you, the savior of all.

8* And by this also you convinced our foes
    that you are he who delivers from all evil.

9* For the bites of locusts and of flies slew them,
    and no remedy was found to save
    their lives
    because they deserved to be punished by
    such means;

10* But not even the fangs of poisonous reptiles
    overcame your sons,
    for your mercy brought the antidote to
    heal them.

11* For as a reminder of your injunctions, they
    were stung,
    and swiftly they were saved,
Lest they should fall into deep forgetfulness
    and become unresponsive to
    your beneficence.

12* For indeed, neither herb nor application
    cured them,
    but your all-healing word, O LORD!

13* For you have dominion over life and death;
    you lead down to the gates of the nether
    world, and lead back.

14† Man, however, slays in his malice,
    but when the spirit has come away, it does
    not return,
    nor can he bring back the soul once it
    is confined.

15   But your hand none can escape.

Third Example: A Rain of Manna for Israel instead of the Plague of Storms

16* For the wicked who refused to know you
    were punished by the might of your arm,

---

†

15, 18ff: The author here returns to the main theme of chapters 11–19, which was interrupted by the digression 13, 1—15, 17.

15, 18: *For . . . rest:* this may mean that the creatures worshiped by the Egyptians (e.g., crocodiles, serpents, scarabs, etc.) were more patently lacking in intelligence than the general run of beasts; cf Wis 11, 15; 12, 24.

16, 1: *They:* the Egyptian idolaters.

16, 6: *Sign:* the brazen serpent; cf Nm 21, 9.

16, 14: *Confined:* in the nether world, in limbo.

15, 15: Wis 14, 11; Dt 4, 28;   **15, 16f:** Wis 13, 10.
    Pss 115, 4–7; 135, 15ff.   **15, 18:** Wis 11, 15; 12, 24.

15, 19: Gn 1, 25; 3, 14.   **16, 9:** Ex 8, 16–28; 10, 4–19;
16, 1: Wis 11, 15f; 12, 23.27;   Pss 78, 45f; 105, 31.
    Ex 7, 27; 8, 12.17.   34; Rv 9, 1–11.
16, 2: Wis 11, 13; 19, 11f; Ex   **16, 10:** Dt 32, 33.
    16, 13; Nm 11, 31f; Ps   **16, 11:** Ps 78, 11.
    105, 40.   **16, 12:** Ex 15, 26.
16, 3: Wis 11, 15; Ex 8, 10;   **16, 13ff:** Dt 32, 39; 1 Sm 2, 6;
    16, 3.   Tb 13, 2; Ps 78, 34.
16, 4: Wis 11, 8f.   39; Eccl 8, 8; Dn 5, 19;
16, 5f: Nm 21, 4–9; Dt 32,   2 Mc 6, 26; 7, 23.
    24; Jer 8, 7 LXX.   **16, 16:** Wis 11, 21; 12, 27; Ex
16, 8: Gn 48, 16; 2 Mc 1,   5, 2; 9, 29–34.
    24f.

W
I
S

Pursued by unwonted rains and hailstorms
    and unremitting downpours,
    and consumed by fire.
17* For against all expectation, in water which
    quenches anything,
    the fire grew more active;
    For the universe fights on behalf of
    the just.
18* For now the flame was tempered
    so that the beasts might not be burnt up
    that were sent upon the wicked,
    but that these might see and know they
    were struck by the judgment of God;
19 And again, even in the water, fire blazed
    beyond its strength
    so as to consume the produce of the
    wicked land.
20* Instead of this, you nourished your people
    with food of angels
    and furnished them bread from heaven,
    ready to hand, untoiled-for,
    endowed with all delights and conforming
    to every taste.
21* For this substance of yours revealed your
    sweetness toward your children,
    and serving the desire of him who
    received it,
    was blended to whatever flavor each
    one wished.
22*† Yet snow and ice withstood fire and were
    not melted,
    that they might know that their
    enemies' fruits
    Were consumed by a fire that blazed in
    the hail
    and flashed lightning in the rain.
23* But this fire, again, that the just might
    be nourished,
    forgot even its proper strength;
24* For your creation, serving you, its maker,
    grows tense for punishment against
    the wicked,
    but is relaxed in benefit for those who
    trust in you.
25 Therefore at that very time, transformed in
    all sorts of ways,
    it was serving your all-nourishing bounty
    according to what they needed and
    desired;
26* That your sons whom you loved might learn,
    O LORD,

---

did you KNOW?

The Exodus Pattern

The Exodus refers to all the events surrounding God's leading the formerly enslaved Israelites out of Egypt as recorded in the Books of Exodus, Leviticus, Numbers, and Deuteronomy. Because the Exodus was an important experience in the Israelites' religious history, later biblical writers began to see in it a pattern in which God rescued the just and punished the wicked.

The author of the Book of Wisdom applies the Exodus pattern to explain how the righteous will be rewarded and sinners will be punished in the author's time. Throughout chapters 11–15, the writer refers to the journey through the desert, the Egyptians, the plagues, the manna in the desert, the pillars of fire, and the Red Sea. The author even takes the liberty of adding details that were not recorded in the original books! In doing so, the writer reminds the people of that time that the pattern of the Exodus is being repeated in their life now, so they should not lose hope that God will be with them always.

▶ Wis 11, 2—19, 22

---

    that it is not the various kinds of fruits that
    nourish man,
    but it is your word that preserves those
    who believe you!
27* For what was not destroyed by fire,
    when merely warmed by a momentary
    sunbeam, melted;
28* So that men might know that one must give
    you thanks before the sunrise,
    and turn to you at daybreak.
29* For the hope of the ingrate melts like a
    wintry frost
    and runs off like useless water.

WIS

---

† **16, 22:** *Snow and ice:* the manna; cf Wis 16, 27; 19, 21.

16, 17: Wis 10, 20; 19, 20; Ex 9, 23–28; 2 Mc 8, 36; 14, 34.
16, 18f: Wis 19, 20f.
16, 20: Ex 16, 4; Nm 11, 8; Ps 78, 24f; Jn 6, 31.
16, 21: Ps 34, 9.
16, 22: Ex 9, 25–31; 10, 12; Ps 148, 8.
16, 23: Wis 19, 21.
16, 24: Wis 5, 17.20; 19, 6; Sir 39, 25ff.
16, 26: Dt 8, 3; Mt 4, 4.
16, 27: Ex 16, 21.
16, 28: Pss 57, 9f; 92, 3.
16, 29: Wis 5, 14; 2 Sm 14, 14.

Fourth Example: Darkness Afflicts the Egyptians, While the Israelites Have Light

17 1* For great are your judgments, and
hardly to be described;
therefore the unruly souls were wrong.

2* For when the lawless thought to enslave the
holy nation,
shackled with darkness, fettered by the
long night,
they lay confined beneath their own roofs
as exiles from the eternal providence.

3* For they who supposed their secret sins
were hid
under the dark veil of oblivion
Were scattered in fearful trembling,
terrified by apparitions.

4 For not even their inner chambers kept
them fearless,
for crashing sounds on all sides
terrified them,
and mute phantoms with somber
looks appeared.

5* No force, even of fire, was able to give light,
nor did the flaming brilliance of the stars
succeed in lighting up that gloomy night.

6*† But only intermittent, fearful fires
flashed through upon them;
And in their terror they thought beholding
these was worse
than the times when that sight was no
longer to be seen.

7* And mockeries of the magic art were
in readiness,
and a jeering reproof of their
vaunted shrewdness.

8 For they who undertook to banish fears and
terrors from the sick soul
themselves sickened with a ridiculous
fear.

9* For even though no monstrous thing
frightened them,
they shook at the passing of insects and the
hissing of reptiles,

10 And perished trembling,
reluctant to face even the air that they could
nowhere escape.

11* For wickedness, of its nature cowardly, testifies
in its own condemnation,
and because of a distressed conscience,
always magnifies misfortunes.

12 For fear is nought but the surrender of the
helps that come from reason;

13 and the more one's expectation is of
itself uncertain,
the more one makes of not knowing the
cause that brings on torment.

14† So they, during that night, powerless though
it was,
that had come upon them from the recesses
of a powerless nether world,
while all sleeping the same sleep,

15* Were partly smitten by fearsome apparitions
and partly stricken by their soul's surrender;
for fear came upon them, sudden
and unexpected.

16* Thus, then, whoever was there fell
into that unbarred prison and was
kept confined.

17 For whether one was a farmer, or a shepherd,
or a worker at tasks in the wasteland,
Taken unawares, he served out the
inescapable sentence;

18* for all were bound by the one bond
of darkness.
And were it only the whistling wind,
or the melodious song of birds in the
spreading branches,
Or the steady sound of rushing water,

19 or the rude crash of overthrown rocks,
Or the unseen gallop of bounding animals,
or the roaring cry of the fiercest beasts,
Or an echo resounding from the hollow of
the hills,
these sounds, inspiring terror,
paralyzed them.

20* For the whole world shone with brilliant light
and continued its works
without interruption;

21 Over them alone was spread oppressive
night,
an image of the darkness that next should
come upon them;
yet they were to themselves more
burdensome than the darkness.

18 1 But your holy ones had very great light;
And those others, who heard their
voices but did not see their forms,
since now they themselves had suffered,
called them blest;

---
† 17, 6: *Fires:* that is, lightnings.
17, 14: *Powerless:* the nether world, the home of darkness, has no power against God, nor even against such men as do not submit to it of themselves; cf Wis 1, 14ff.

17, 1: Ex 6, 6 LXX.   17, 2: Wis 18, 4; Ex 1, 13f;
19, 6; 10, 21ff.

17, 3f: Wis 1, 7f; 10, 8; 18,
17.
17, 5: Wis 10, 17; Jer 23, 24
LXX.
17, 6: Ex 9, 23f.
17, 7: Wis 12, 25f; Ex 7,
11f.22; 8, 3; 9, 11;
10, 2.

17, 9: Wis 16, 1; Jer 26, 22
LXX.
17, 11: Wis 4, 6; 10, 7; Rom 2,
15.
17, 15: Ex 11, 9f.
17, 16: Wis 18, 4; Ex 10, 23.
17, 18f: Lv 26, 36.
17, 20f: Ex 10, 23; Is 9, 1; 60,
1ff; 2 Pt 2, 17.

2† And because they who formerly had been
   wronged did not harm them, they
   thanked them,
   and pleaded with them, for the sake of the
   difference between them.

3* Instead of this, you furnished the
   flaming pillar
   which was a guide on the unknown way,
   and the mild sun for an
   honorable migration.

4* For those deserved to be deprived of light and
   imprisoned by darkness,
   who had kept your sons confined
   through whom the imperishable light of
   the law was to be given to the world.

Fifth Example: Death of the Egyptian First-born; the Israelites Are Spared

5*† When they determined to put to death the
   infants of the holy ones,
   and when a single boy had been cast forth
   but saved,
   As a reproof you carried off their multitude
   of sons
   and made them perish all at once in the
   mighty water.

6* That night was known beforehand to
   our fathers,
   that, with sure knowledge of the oaths in
   which they put their faith, they might
   have courage.

7* Your people awaited
   the salvation of the just and the destruction
   of their foes.

8* For when you punished our adversaries,
   in this you glorified us whom you
   had summoned.

9*† For in secret the holy children of the good
   were offering sacrifice
   and putting into effect with one accord the
   divine institution,
   That your holy ones should share alike the
   same good things and dangers,
   having previously sung the praises of
   the fathers.

10* But the discordant cry of their
    enemies responded,

and the piteous wail of mourning for
   children was borne to them.

11* And the slave was smitten with the same
    retribution as his master;
    even the plebeian suffered the same as
    the king.

12* And all alike by a single death
    had countless dead;
    For the living were not even sufficient for
    the burial,
    since at a single instant their nobler
    offspring were destroyed.

13*† For though they disbelieved at every turn on
    account of sorceries,
    at the destruction of the first-born they
    acknowledged that the people was
    God's son.

14 For when peaceful stillness
   compassed everything
   and the night in its swift course was
   half spent,

15* Your all-powerful word from heaven's
    royal throne
    bounded, a fierce warrior, into the
    doomed land,

16 * bearing the sharp sword of your
    inexorable decree.
    And as he alighted, he filled every place
    with death;
    he still reached to heaven, while he stood
    upon the earth.

17* Then, forthwith, visions in horrible dreams
    perturbed them
    and unexpected fears assailed them;

18 And cast half-dead, one here, another there,
   each was revealing the reason for his dying.

19 For the dreams that disturbed them had
   proclaimed this beforehand,
   lest they perish unaware of why they
   suffered ill.

20* But the trial of death touched at one time
    even the just,
    and in the desert a plague struck
    the multitude;
    Yet not for long did the anger last.

21*† For the blameless man hastened to be
    their champion,

† **18, 2:** *The difference between them:* God's distinctive manner of treating the Israelites and the Egyptians according to their respective merits.
18, 5: *Single boy:* Moses.
18, 9: *Praises of the fathers:* cf Sir 44–50; Wis 10.
18, 13: *People:* the Hebrews.
18, 21: *Blameless man:* Aaron acting according to his office of high priest and intercessor.

18, 3: Ex 13, 21.
18, 4: Wis 17, 2; Ps 119, 105; Is 2, 3.5.
18, 5: Wis 11, 7.14; Ex 1, 16.22; 2, 3.6–10; 15, 10; Neh 9, 11.
18, 6: Wis 12, 21; Ex 6, 8; 13, 5.
18, 7: Ex 14, 13.
18, 8: Wis 19, 22; Ex 3, 18; Is 43, 3f.
18, 9: Ex 12, 21–28; Sir 44–50.
18, 10: Ex 12, 30; Jer 9, 17.19.
18, 11: Ex 11, 5; 12, 29.
18, 12: Nm 33, 4.
18, 13: Wis 17, 7; Ex 4, 22f; 12, 12.29; 13, 2.13.15.
18, 15: Wis 9, 10; Ex 15, 3.
18, 16: 1 Chr 21, 16; Heb 4, 12; Rv 1, 16.
18, 17ff: Wis 17, 3f.
18, 20: Wis 16, 5; Nm 17, 9–15.
18, 21: Wis 12, 21; Ex 32, 12f; Ps 20, 8.

W
I
S

bearing the weapon of his special office,
prayer and the propitiation of incense;
He withstood the wrath and put a stop to
the calamity,
showing that he was your servant.

22*†And he overcame the bitterness
not by bodily strength, not by force of arms;
But by word he overcame the smiter,
recalling the sworn covenants with
their fathers.

23* For when corpses had already fallen one on
another in heaps,
he stood in the midst and checked the anger,
and cut off the way to the living.

24*†For on his full-length robe was the
whole world,
and the glories of the fathers were carved in
four rows upon the stones,
and your grandeur was on the crown upon
his head.

25* To these names the destroyer yielded, and
these he feared;
for the mere trial of anger was enough.

19

1*† But the wicked, merciless wrath
assailed until the end.
For he knew beforehand what they were yet
to do:

2*†That though they themselves had agreed to
the departure
and had anxiously sent them on their way,
they would regret it and pursue them.

3*†For while they were still engaged in
funeral rites
and were mourning at the burials of
the dead,
They adopted another senseless plan;
and those whom they had sent away
with entreaty,
they pursued as fugitives.

4 For a compulsion suited to this ending drew
them on,
and made them forgetful of what had
befallen them,
That they might fill out the torments of
their punishment,

5† and your people might experience a
glorious journey

while those others met an
extraordinary death.

6* For all creation, in its several kinds, was being
made over anew,
serving its natural laws,
that your children might be
preserved unharmed.

7* The cloud overshadowed their camp;
and out of what had before been water, dry
land was seen emerging:
Out of the Red Sea an unimpeded road,
and a grassy plain out of the mighty flood.

8 Over this crossed the whole nation sheltered
by your hand,
after they beheld stupendous wonders.

9* For they ranged about like horses,
and bounded about like lambs,
praising you, O Lord! their deliverer.

10* For they were still mindful of what had
happened in their sojourn:
how instead of the young of animals the
land brought forth gnats,
and instead of fishes the river swarmed
with countless frogs.

11* And later they saw also a new kind of bird
when, prompted by desire, they asked for
pleasant foods;

12 For to appease them quail came to them from
the sea.

13*†And the punishments came upon the sinners
only after forewarnings from the violence
of the thunderbolts.
For they justly suffered for their
own misdeeds,
since indeed they treated their guests with
the more grievous hatred.

14* For those others did not receive
unfamiliar visitors,
but these were enslaving beneficent
guests.

15† And not that only; but what punishment was
to be theirs
since they received strangers unwillingly!

16* Yet these, after welcoming them
with festivities,
oppressed with awful toils
those who now shared with them the
same rights.

    18, 22: *Smiter:* the destroying angel; cf v 25.
    18, 24: *Glories . . . grandeur:* the name of God and the names of the tribes were inscribed on the high priest's apparel.
    19, 1: *He:* i.e., God.
    19, 2: *Them:* the Hebrews.
    19, 3: *They:* the Egyptians.
    19, 5: *Glorious:* more precisely, "wondrous," but the word reflects glorified in Wis 18, 8 and 19, 22.
    19, 13: *More grievous:* than that of the people of Sodom; cf Gn 19.

    19, 15: *Theirs:* the people of Sodom.

18, 22: Wis 12, 21; Ex 32, 12f.	19, 7: Ex 14, 21–29.
18, 23: Nm 14, 29f.	19, 9: Wis 10, 20; 16, 8; Ex
18, 24: Ex 28, 15–21.31–38;	15, 1–18; Ps 114, 4–6.
Sir 45, 8–12; 50, 11.	19, 10: Ex 7, 27ff; 8, 12–15;
18, 25: 1 Chr 21, 15.	Ps 105, 30f.
19, 1: Ex 14, 4.	19, 11f: Wis 16, 2; Ps 78, 18.
19, 2: Ex 12, 33; 14, 5.8.	19, 13: 2 Mc 7, 18.32.
19, 3: Wis 18, 10.12; Ex 12,	19, 14f: Gn 15, 13; Ex 2, 22.
30ff.	19, 16: Gn 45, 17–20; 47, 4ff;
19, 6: Wis 5, 17; 16, 24.	Ex 1, 11.

Supernatural Resources

The Book of Wisdom ends with an inspiring statement of faith:

> For every way, O LORD! you magnified and glorified your people;
> unfailing, you stood by them in every time and circumstance.
> (19, 22)

Could you say these words? Do you have the kind of faith that is able to see the hand of God at work through everything that happens?

So many times, we pray for God's help, especially if we are struggling or someone we love is suffering. Later, when that particular crisis is over, we quickly forget how God helped us through. The Bible's message is that God is at work through all the times in our life, even in ways that we do not realize at the moment. The church's word for God's help is *grace*. Unlike most of our natural resources, the supernatural resource of grace is never in danger of being used up. In fact, the more we use it, the more of it there is!

Find a way of keeping track of how God has helped you through life. Perhaps you can maintain a journal of the difficult times you've made it through and the people who have supported you. You might be surprised by this record of how God's grace has been active!

▶ **Wis 19, 22**

17* And they were struck with blindness,
  as those others had been at the portals of
    the just—
  When, surrounded by yawning darkness,
    each sought the entrance of his own gate.
18 For the elements, in variable harmony
    among themselves,
    like strings of the harp, produce
      new melody,
    while the flow of music steadily persists.
  And this can be perceived exactly from a
    review of what took place.
19 For land creatures were changed into
    water creatures,

and those that swam went over on to
    the land.
20* Fire in water maintained its own strength,
    and water forgot its quenching nature;
21 Flames, by contrast, neither consumed
      the flesh
    of the perishable animals that went about
      in them,
    nor melted the icelike, quick-melting kind
      of ambrosial food.
22* For every way, O LORD! you magnified and
      glorified your people;
    unfailing, you stood by them in every time
      and circumstance.

19, 17: Wis 17, 2; Gn 19, 11.   19, 22: Wis 18, 8; Lv 26, 44;
19, 20f: Wis 16, 17ff.22f.27.   Ps 126, 3.

W
I
S

Sirach (Ecclesiasticus)
The Book of

Imagine that many years ago, your grandfather—
a learned and wise man—wrote a book summarizing
all his wisdom. Recently, you read the book and
discovered it has answers to many of the problems
you and your friends are struggling with. But the book
is written in your grandfather's native language, which
your friends don't understand. So, what do you do?
You translate the book! This is
exactly what the grandson of
Jesus Ben Sira did. He translated into Greek the book his
grandfather had written in
Hebrew.

In-depth

At a Glance

I. Praise of Wisdom
(chapters 1–43).

II. Praise of Israel's Great
Ancestors
(44, 1—50, 24).

III. Epilogue and Canticles
(50, 25—51, 30).

The Book of Sirach is unique in the Old Testament because it clearly identifies
its author: Jesus Ben Sira, a wise teacher who lived early in the second century
B.C. Living in Jerusalem during a time of great change, he saw many of his people—especially those who were rich—deserting traditional Jewish beliefs in
favor of more fashionable ideas coming from Greece. A book underlining the
superiority of Jewish wisdom was needed, Ben Sira thought. So, he collected his
class notes into a single volume and offered it to those who desired to learn the
ways of living well. Though full of many different kinds of writing—sayings,
hymns, prayers, and lists—the book is unified in its overall conviction: "All wisdom comes from the LORD / and with him it remains forever" (1,1).

The Book of Sirach holds fast to the long-standing belief that in this life,
good is rewarded and evil is punished. Unlike Second Maccabees and Daniel—
also written in the second century B.C.—Sirach never mentions the possibility of
life after death. But like other wisdom books, it celebrates the glories of wisdom
(chapter 1) and recalls the heroes of Jewish faith (chapters 44–50). Its view of
women is harsher than that of most of the Old Testament, though. In interpreting Sirach, you must take special care not
to conclude that women are the source of most
of men's troubles!

Sometimes called Ecclesiasticus or Ben Sira
(which is the short form for "son of Sirach"),
the Book of Sirach was well known among the
ancient Jews. It was popular in the early Christian church as well. Its influence can be found
in the New Testament, especially in the Letter
of James. Long after his death, Ben Sira continues to share the wisdom of the past and offers
us trustworthy guidance for the present.

Quick Facts

Author
Jesus Ben Sira, writing
around 180 B.C.
Theme
the superiority of Jewish
wisdom over Greek wis-
dom
Of Note
Sirach is not found in
every translation of the
Old Testament (see
"The Case of the Missing
Books," Tb 1, 16).

Sirach

FOREWORD

Many important truths have been handed down to us through the law, the prophets, and the later authors; and for these the instruction and wisdom of Israel merit praise. Now, those who are familiar with these truths must not only understand them themselves but, as lovers of wisdom, be able, in speech and in writing, to help others less familiar. Such a one was my grandfather, Jesus, who, having devoted himself for a long time to the diligent study of the law, the prophets, and the rest of the books[1] of our ancestors, and having developed a thorough familiarity with them, was moved to write something himself in the nature of instruction and wisdom, in order that those who love wisdom might, by acquainting themselves with what he too had written, make even greater progress in living in conformity with the divine law.

You therefore are now invited to read it in a spir-

---

†[1] *The law, the prophets, and the rest of the books:* the Sacred Scriptures of the Old Testament written before the time of Sirach, according to the threefold division of the present Hebrew Bible.

THE WISDOM OF SIRACH

Praise of Wisdom

1 ¹*† All wisdom† comes from the LORD
and with him it remains forever.

1, 1–8: The Lord is the source and preserver of wisdom (1); he created her from eternity, before all things else (4–7); all his works reflect wisdom (2f.8).

1, 1: *Wisdom:* here the author speaks of true wisdom, namely God's external revelation of himself. Throughout the book he describes in

---

it of attentive good will, with indulgence for any apparent failure on our part, despite earnest efforts, in the interpretation of particular passages. For words spoken originally in Hebrew are not as effective when they are translated into another language. That is true not only of this book but of the law itself, the prophets and the rest of the books, which differ no little when they are read in the original.

I arrived in Egypt in the thirty-eighth year of the reign of King Euergetes,[2] and while there, I found a reproduction[3] of our valuable teaching. I therefore considered myself in duty bound to devote some diligence and industry to the translation of this book. Many sleepless hours of close application have I devoted in the interval to finishing the book for publication, for the benefit of those living abroad who wish to acquire wisdom and are disposed to live their lives according to the standards of the law.

---

†[2] *Thirty-eighth . . . Euergetes:* 132 B.C. The reference is to Ptolemy VII, Physkon Euergetes II (170–163; 145, 117 B.C.).

†[3] *Reproduction . . . teaching:* may refer to the Septuagint (Greek) translation of Hebrew wisdom writings predating Sirach.

---

²   The sand of the seashore, the drops
        of rain,
            the days of eternity: who can number these?
³   Heaven's height, earth's breadth,
            the depths of the abyss: who can
                explore these?

---

great detail just what wisdom is; sometimes it is divine; sometimes it is a synonym for God's law; sometimes it is human. But the author makes clear that even human wisdom, properly understood, comes from God.

*
1, 1: 1 Kgs 3, 9.

---

4   Before all things else wisdom was created;
        and prudent understanding, from eternity.
5* To whom has wisdom's root been revealed?
        Who knows her subtleties?
6   There is but one, wise and truly
        awe-inspiring,
        seated upon his throne:
7* It is the LORD; he created her,
        has seen her and taken note of her.
8   He has poured her forth upon all his works,
        upon every living thing according to
        his bounty;
        he has lavished her upon his friends.
9† Fear of the LORD† is glory and splendor,
        gladness and a festive crown.
10 Fear of the LORD warms the heart,
        giving gladness and joy and length of days.
11 He who fears the LORD will have a happy end;
        even on the day of his death he will
        be blessed.
12* The beginning of wisdom is fear of the LORD,
        which is formed with the faithful in
        the womb.
13 With devoted men was she created from
        of old,
        and with their children her
        beneficence abides.
14* Fullness of wisdom is fear of the LORD;
        she inebriates men with her fruits.
15 Her entire house she fills with choice foods,
        her granaries with her harvest.
16* Wisdom's garland is fear of the LORD,
        with blossoms of peace and perfect health.
17 Knowledge and full understanding she
        showers down;
        she heightens the glory of those who
        possess her.
18 The root of wisdom is fear of the LORD;
        her branches are length of days.

19† One cannot justify unjust anger;
        anger plunges a man to his downfall.
20 A patient man need stand firm but for
        a time,
        and then contentment comes back to him.
21 For a while he holds back his words,
        then the lips of many herald his wisdom.

22 Among wisdom's treasures is the paragon
        of prudence;
        but fear of the LORD is an abomination to
        the sinner.
23 If you desire wisdom, keep the
        commandments,
        and the LORD will bestow her upon you;
24 For fear of the LORD is wisdom and culture;
        loyal humility is his delight.
25† Be not faithless to the fear of the LORD,
        nor approach it with duplicity of heart.
26 Play not the hypocrite before men;
        over your lips keep watch.
27 Exalt not yourself lest you fall
        and bring upon you dishonor;
28 For then the LORD will reveal your secrets
        and publicly cast you down,
29 Because you approached the fear of the LORD
        with your heart full of guile.

Duties toward God

2 1*† My son, when you come to serve the
        LORD,
        prepare yourself for trials.
2   Be sincere of heart and steadfast,
        undisturbed in time of adversity.
3   Cling to him, forsake him not;
        thus will your future be great.
4   Accept whatever befalls you,
        in crushing misfortune be patient;
5* For in fire gold is tested,
        and worthy men in the crucible
        of humiliation.
6   Trust God and he will help you;
        make straight your ways and hope in him.
7   You who fear the LORD, wait for his mercy,
        turn not away lest you fall.
8   You who fear the LORD, trust him,
        and your reward will not be lost.
9   You who fear the LORD, hope for good
        things,
        for lasting joy and mercy.
10* Study the generations long past
        and understand;
        has anyone hoped in the LORD and
        been disappointed?

1, 9–18: Here are described the spiritual and temporal blessings that come during the lifetime of him who fears the Lord, i.e. practice true religion.

1, 9: *Fear of the LORD:* see note on Ps 111, 10.

1, 19–22: The disciple of wisdom shuns unjust anger which brings downfall. By patience and self-control he preserves calm, re- covers contentment, and receives public praise. The sinner, on the contrary, despises the restraints which religion imposes.

1, 25–29: Infidelity to religion, or the use of it for any but the sin- gle purpose of serving God, is hypocrisy and self-exaltation, deserv- ing of public disgrace.

2, 1–11: Serving God is not without its trials (1); moreover, it must be done with sincerity, steadfastness and fidelity (2f). Misfortune and humiliation merely purify man and prove his worth (4f). Patience and unwavering trust in God are always rewarded with the benefits of God's mercy and of lasting joy (6–11).

1, 5: Bar 3, 15.
1, 7: Jb 28, 27.
1, 12: Jb 28, 28; Ps 111, 10;
    Prv 1, 7; 9, 10.
1, 14: Eccl 12, 13.

1, 16: Sir 21, 11.
2, 1: 2 Tm 3, 12.
2, 5: Prv 17, 3; Wis 3, 6;
    1 Pt 1, 7.
2, 10: Pss 31, 2; 145, 18f.

HONORING OUR PARENTS IN GOD'S WAY!

You hear Sir 3, 1–7 every year on Holy Family Sunday, the weekend after Christmas. This reading calls us to honor our parents because this is the way God established children's responsibilities toward parents. To honor our parents is to revere them (verse 6), to be kind to them (verse 14), not to dishonor them in order to feel superior (verse 10), and to take care of them and be considerate of them as they age (verses 12–13). According to Ben Sira, God assures many blessings to those who honor their parents, including safety, happiness, forgiveness of sins, the hearing of their prayers, and a long life.

Hispanics have a long tradition of being parented not only by birth parents but by the extended family, including grandparents, godparents, aunts, and uncles. Today, many young people are also parented by foster parents, stepparents, and adoptive parents.

■ Take a moment to think of the adults who have parented you. In what specific ways do you honor and show your love to them? In what ways might you have failed to do so?

■ Thank God, our heavenly parent, for the love and sacrifices of all the people who have parented you. Ask God to give you love, understanding, strength, and patience to honor them in word and deed.

▶ Sir 3, 1–16

Has anyone persevered in his fear and
  been forsaken?
    has anyone called upon him and
      been rebuffed?
11 Compassionate and merciful is the LORD;
    he forgives sins, he saves in time of trouble.

12† Woe to craven hearts and drooping hands,
    to the sinner who treads a double path!
13 Woe to the faint of heart who trust not,
    who therefore will have no shelter!
14 Woe to you who have lost hope!
    what will you do at the visitation of
      the LORD?
15* Those who fear the LORD disobey not his words;
    those who love him keep his ways.
16 Those who fear the LORD seek to please him,
    those who love him are filled with his law.
17 Those who fear the LORD prepare their hearts
    and humble themselves before him.

18* Let us fall into the hands of the LORD
    and not into the hands of men,
  For equal to his majesty
    is the mercy that he shows.

Duties toward Parents†

3 ¹ Children, pay heed to a father's right;
    do so that you may live.
2 For the LORD sets a father in honor over
    his children;
  a mother's authority he confirms over
    her sons.
3 He who honors his father atones for sins;
4   he stores up riches who reveres his mother.
5 He who honors his father is gladdened
    by children,
  and when he prays he is heard.
6 He who reveres his father will live a long life;
  he obeys the LORD who brings comfort to
    his mother.

S
I
R

---

† **2, 12–18:** A warning to those who compromise their religion in time of affliction; they fail in courage and trust and therefore have no security (12ff). But those who fear the Lord through obedience, reverence, love and humility find his mercy equal to his majesty (15–18).

3, 1–16: Besides the virtues that must characterize our conduct toward God, special duties toward our neighbor are enjoined, such

as honor and respect toward parents, with corresponding blessings (1–9). Even to old and infirm parents this respect is due (10–13); through it, the sins of children are pardoned (14f). Failure to render respect is blasphemy and merits a curse from God (16). Cf Ex 20, 12; Eph 6, 2f.

2, 15: Jn 14, 23.   **2, 18:** Sir 18, 3.

CELEBRATING FAMILIES

Ben Sira holds family relationships in high esteem. In chapter 3, he emphasizes the importance of honor and respect among family members. Many cultures have special days honoring parents and children. In the United States, we celebrate Mother's Day, Father's Day, and Grandparent's Day.

Japan also has special days honoring family members. Girls' Festival (Hinamatsuri) is celebrated on 3 March with doll displays and peach blossoms. Boys' Festival (Kodomo No Hi) is celebrated on 5 May with streamers. Respect for the Aged Day (Keiro No Hi) is celebrated on 15 September. On 15 January, the Coming of Age Festival (Seigin No Hi) takes place. This day celebrates all young people who have turned twenty during the previous year—the age when young adults are permitted to vote, drink, and smoke.

If you have Japanese friends or acquaintances, consider marking these holidays on your calendar and sending a card or note with a prayer on the appropriate day.

▶ Sir 3, 1–16

---

7   He who fears the LORD honors his father,
    and serves his parents as rulers.
8* In word and deed honor your father
    that his blessing may come upon you;
9* For a father's blessing gives a family
        firm roots,
    but a mother's curse uproots the
        growing plant.
10 Glory not in your father's shame,
    for his shame is no glory to you!
11 His father's honor is a man's glory;
    disgrace for her children, a mother's shame.
12* My son, take care of your father when he is old;
    grieve him not as long as he lives.
13 Even if his mind fail, be considerate with him;
    revile him not in the fullness of
        your strength.
14 For kindness to a father will not be forgotten,
    it will serve as a sin offering—it will take
        lasting root.
15 In time of tribulation it will be recalled to
        your advantage,
    like warmth upon frost it will melt away
        your sins.

16* A blasphemer is he who despises his father;
    accursed of his Creator, he who angers
        his mother.

Humility

17† My son, conduct your affairs with humility,
    and you will be loved more than a giver
        of gifts.
18* Humble yourself the more, the greater
        you are,
    and you will find favor with God.
19† For great is the power of God;
    by the humble he is glorified.
20* What is too sublime for you, seek not,
    into things beyond your strength
        search not.
21 What is committed to you, attend to;
    for what is hidden is not your concern.
22 With what is too much for you meddle not,
    when shown things beyond
        human understanding.
23 Their own opinion has misled many,
    and false reasoning unbalanced
        their judgment.

3, 17–27: Humility gives a true estimate of self (17ff). Through it a man performs duty, avoids what is beyond his understanding and strength (20ff). Pride, however, begets false greatness, misjudgment, stubbornness, sorrow, affliction and perdition (23–27).
3, 19: An alternate or additional line would read: "For though many have been great in the course of time, it is to the humble he reveals his secrets." Cf Mt 11, 25f; 1 Cor 1, 26–29.

3, 8: Ex 20, 12; Dt 5, 16;   3, 16: Prv 19, 26; 30,
  Mt 15, 4; Mk 7, 10;   11.14.17.
  Eph 6, 2.   3, 18: Mt 23, 12.
3, 9: Gn 27, 29; 49, 2–27.   3, 20: Ps 131, 1.
3, 12: Prv 23, 22.

24 Where the pupil of the eye is missing, there is
        no light,
    and where there is no knowledge, there is
        no wisdom.
25 A stubborn man will fare badly in the end,
    and he who loves danger will perish in it.
26 A stubborn man will be burdened
        with sorrow;
    a sinner will heap sin upon sin.
27* For the affliction of the proud man there is
        no cure;
    he is the offshoot of an evil plant.
28 The mind of a sage appreciates proverbs,
    and an attentive ear is the wise man's joy.

Alms for the Poor†

29* Water quenches a flaming fire,
    and alms atone for sins.
30 He who does a kindness is
        remembered afterward;
    when he falls, he finds a support.

4   1*† My son, rob not the poor man of his
        livelihood:
    force not the eyes of the needy to
        turn away.
2   A hungry man grieve not,
    a needy man anger not;
3   Do not exasperate the downtrodden;
    delay not to give to the needy.
4   A beggar in distress do not reject;
    avert not your face from the poor.
5   From the needy turn not your eyes,
    give no man reason to curse you;
6   For if in the bitterness of his soul he
        curse you,
    his Creator will hear his prayer.
7   Endear yourself to the assembly;
    before a ruler bow your head.
8   Give a hearing to the poor man,
    and return his greeting with courtesy;
9   Deliver the oppressed from the hand of
        the oppressor;
    let not justice be repugnant to you.
10 To the fatherless be as a father,
    and help their mother as a husband
        would;

Thus will you be like a son to the Most
    High,
and he will be more tender to you than
    a mother.

The Rewards of Wisdom†

11 Wisdom instructs her children
    and admonishes those who seek her.
12 He who loves her loves life;
    those who seek her out win her favor.
13 He who holds her fast inherits glory;
    wherever he dwells, the LORD
        bestows blessings.
14* Those who serve her serve the Holy One;
    those who love her the LORD loves.
15 He who obeys her judges nations;
    he who hearkens to her dwells in her
        inmost chambers.
16 If one trusts her, he will possess her;
    his descendants too will inherit her.
17 She walks with him as a stranger,
    and at first she puts him to the test;
    Fear and dread she brings upon him
    and tries him with her discipline;
    With her precepts she puts him to the proof,
    until his heart is fully with her.
18 Then she comes back to bring him
        happiness
    and reveal her secrets to him.
19 But if he fails her, she will abandon him
    and deliver him into the hands
        of despoilers.

Sincerity and Justice†

20 Use your time well; guard yourself from evil,
    and bring upon yourself no shame.
21 There is a sense of shame laden with guilt,
    and a shame that merits honor and
        respect.
22 Show no favoritism to your own discredit;
    let no one intimidate you to your
        own downfall.
23 Refrain not from speaking at the proper time,
    and hide not away your wisdom;
24 For it is through speech that wisdom
        becomes known,
    and knowledge through the tongue's
        rejoinder.

S
I
R

---

† **3, 29—4, 10:** Mercy and kindness toward those in misfortune
atone for sin and endear a man to God and to his fellow men.
    4, 1: *Eyes of the needy:* when they look for help; cf Sir 18, 17.
    4, 11–19: The Hebrew text presents wisdom speaking in the first
person, as in ch 24. The precious fruits of wisdom: life, favor, glory,
blessings, God's love, are intended to arouse desire for her (11–14).
Her disciples are like priests (14) and judges (15), even partners who
possess her for themselves and their descendants (16). They enjoy
happiness and penetrate her profound secrets after surviving her tests
(17f). Those who fail her are abandoned to destruction (19).

4, 20–31: Besides the interior trials of discipline and precept, the
disciple of wisdom is warned against external dangers to his sincerity and justice, namely evil, human respect (20f), compromise of liberty in speech and action (22–25), false shame, and ignorance (26).
He must fight for the truth (28), and avoid cynicism and laziness (29),
and inconsistency in his conduct (30).

3, 27: Dt 32, 32; Wis 12, 10.   **4, 1:** Tb 4, 7–11.
3, 29: Dn 4, 27.   **4, 14:** Wis 7, 28.

25 Never gainsay the truth,
    and struggle not against the rushing
    stream.

26 Be not ashamed to acknowledge your guilt,
    but of your ignorance rather be ashamed.

27 Do not abase yourself before an
    impious man,
    nor refuse to do so before rulers.

28 Even to the death fight for truth,
    and the LORD your God will battle for you.

29 Be not surly in your speech,
    nor lazy and slack in your deeds.

30 Be not a lion at home,
    nor sly and suspicious at work.

31 Let not your hand be open to receive
    and clenched when it is time to give.

Against Presumption†

5 ¹* Rely not on your wealth;
    say not: "I have the power."

2 Rely not on your strength
    in following the desires of your heart.

3 Say not: "Who can prevail against me?"
    for the LORD will exact the punishment.

4 Say not: "I have sinned, yet what has
    befallen me?"
    for the LORD bides his time.

5 Of forgiveness be not overconfident,
    adding sin upon sin.

6 Say not: "Great is his mercy;
    my many sins he will forgive."

7 For mercy and anger alike are with him;
    upon the wicked alights his wrath.

8 Delay not your conversion to the LORD,
    put it not off from day to day;

9 For suddenly his wrath flames forth;
    at the time of vengeance, you will
    be destroyed.

10* Rely not upon deceitful wealth,
    for it will be no help on the day of
    wrath.

Sincerity in Speech

11† Winnow not in every wind,
    and start not off in every direction.

12† Be consistent in your thoughts;
    steadfast be your words.

13* Be swift to hear,
    but slow to answer.

14 If you have the knowledge, answer
    your neighbor;
    if not, put your hand over your mouth.

15 Honor and dishonor through talking!
    A man's tongue can be his downfall.

16 Be not called a detractor;
    use not your tongue for calumny;

17 For shame has been created for the thief,
    and the reproach of his neighbor for
    the double-tongued.

6 ¹† Say nothing harmful, small or great;
    be not a foe instead of a friend;
    A bad name and disgrace will you acquire:
    "That for the evil man with
    double tongue!"

2* Fall not into the grip of desire,
    lest, like fire, it consume your strength;

3 Your leaves it will eat, your fruits destroy,
    and you will be left a dry tree,

4 For contumacious desire destroys its owner
    and makes him the sport of his enemies.

True Friendship†

5 A kind mouth multiplies friends,
    and gracious lips prompt friendly greetings.

6 Let your acquaintances be many,
    but one in a thousand your confidant.

7* When you gain a friend, first test him,
    and be not too ready to trust him.

8 For one sort of friend is a friend when it
    suits him,
    but he will not be with you in time
    of distress.

9 Another is a friend who becomes an enemy,
    and tells of the quarrel to your shame.

10 Another is a friend, a boon companion,
    who will not be with you when
    sorrow comes.

11 When things go well, he is your other self,
    and lords it over your servants;

12 But if you are brought low, he turns
    against you
    and avoids meeting you.

---

† 5, 1–10: The vices of the rich are pride and independence (1f), presumption (3), false security (4–7), and impenitence (8), which cannot escape the divine wrath (9f). Cf Prv 18, 23; 19, 1; 28, 6.

5, 11: A proverbial expression condemning inconstancy and advocating sincerity and honesty.

5, 12—6, 1: Proper use of the tongue requires constancy in speech (5, 12), prudence (13f), reserve (15), charity (6, 1), as well as the avoidance of detraction, calumny (16) and double talk, which bring shame and disgrace (5, 17; 6, 1).

6, 1: "That . . . double tongue!": people will say this against the man whose deceitful tongue has brought him to disgrace.

6, 5–17: True friends are discerned not by prosperity (11) but through the trials of adversity: distress, quarrels (9), sorrow (10) and misfortune (12). Such friends are rare and their value is beyond estimation, a gift from God (14–17).

*
5, 1: Lk 12, 19.   6, 2–3: Sir 9, 8; 23, 17;
5, 10: Prv 10, 2; 11, 4.28.   Jb 31, 12; Is 56, 3.
5, 13: Prv 29, 20; Jas 1, 19.   6, 7ff: Sir 12, 8f; 37, 1–5;
                                              Prv 19, 4.

Friends

God of friendship,
   Thank you for my friends, especially
for those who give me wise advice.
Thank you for my closest friends whom I see
   every day, who motivate me to grow and
   serve.
Thank you for all the good friends whom I
   used to see more often but don't see as
   much anymore.
LORD, continue to give me good friends
   throughout my life, and help me be a
   better friend to all. Amen.

▸ Sir 6, 5–17

13 Keep away from your enemies;
        be on your guard with your friends.
14 A faithful friend is a sturdy shelter;
        he who finds one finds a treasure.
15 A faithful friend is beyond price,
        no sum can balance his worth.
16 A faithful friend is a life-saving remedy,
        such as he who fears God finds;
17 For he who fears God behaves accordingly,
        and his friend will be like himself.

Blessings of Wisdom†

18 My son, from your youth
        embrace discipline;
        thus will you find wisdom with
        graying hair.
19 As though plowing and sowing, draw close
        to her;
        then await her bountiful crops.
20 For in cultivating her you will labor but little,
        and soon you will eat of her fruits.
21 How irksome she is to the unruly!
        The fool cannot abide her.
22 She will be like a burdensome stone to test him,
        and he will not delay in casting her aside.
23† For discipline is like her name,
        she is not accessible to many.

24 Listen, my son, and heed my advice;
        refuse not my counsel.
25 Put your feet into her fetters,
        and your neck under her yoke.
26 Stoop your shoulders and carry her
        and be not irked at her bonds.
27 With all your soul draw close to her;
        with all your strength keep her ways.
28 Search her out, discover her; seek her and you
        will find her.
        Then when you have her, do not let her go;
29 Thus will you afterward find rest in her,
        and she will become your joy.
30 Her fetters will be your throne of majesty;
        her bonds, your purple cord.
31*†You will wear her as your robe of glory,
        bear her as your splendid crown.

32 My son, if you wish, you can be taught;
        if you apply yourself, you will be shrewd.
33 If you are willing to listen, you will learn;
        if you give heed, you will be wise.
34 Frequent the company of the elders;
        whoever is wise, stay close to him.
35* Be eager to hear every godly discourse;
        let no wise saying escape you.
36 If you see a man of prudence, seek him out;
        let your feet wear away his doorstep!
37* Reflect on the precepts of the LORD,
        let his commandments be your
        constant meditation;
        Then he will enlighten your mind,
        and the wisdom you desire he will grant.

Conduct in Public Life†

7 ¹ Do no evil, and evil will not overtake
        you;
²   avoid wickedness, and it will turn aside
        from you.
3* Sow not in the furrows of injustice,
        lest you harvest it sevenfold.
4   Seek not from the LORD authority,
        nor from the king a place of honor.
5* Parade not your justice before the LORD,
        and before the king flaunt not your wisdom.
6   Seek not to become a judge
        if you have not strength to root out crime,
        Or you will show favor to the ruler
        and mar your integrity.

S
I
R

---

† **6, 18–37:** The various figures in each of the three strophes urge the search for wisdom through patience (19–23), docility (32–37), and perseverance in trials (25ff), promising rich rewards (28–31). Cf 4, 11–19.

6, 23: Discipline (*musar*, in the sense of wisdom) is a perfect homonym for *musar*, "removed, withdrawn"; thus the path of discipline is inaccessible to many.

6, 31: Some forms of the text speak also of the "yoke" of wisdom under the imagery of golden ornaments.

† **7, 1–17:** In the conduct of social relations wisdom forbids evil and injustice (1ff), pride (5.15ff), ambition and human respect (4, 6), public disorder (7), presumption and impatience toward God (9f), ridicule (11), mischief and deceit toward one's neighbor (8, 12f).

6, 31: Is 62, 3.
6, 35: Sir 8, 9.
6, 37: Ps 1, 2.

7, 3: Prv 22, 8.
7, 5: Jb 9, 2; Ps 143, 2;
     Prv 25, 6; 1 Cor 4, 4.

7 Be guilty of no evil before the city's populace,
nor disgrace yourself before the assembly.

8 Do not plot to repeat a sin;
not even for one will you go unpunished.

9* Say not: "He will appreciate my many gifts;
the Most High will accept my offerings."

10 Be not impatient in prayers,
and neglect not the giving of alms.

11† Laugh not at an embittered man;
be mindful of him who exalts and humbles.

12 Plot no mischief against your brother,
nor against your friend and companion.

13 Delight not in telling lie after lie,
for it never results in good.

14*†Thrust not yourself into the deliberations
of princes,
and repeat not the words of your prayer.

15* Hate not laborious tasks,
nor farming, which was ordained by the
Most High.

16 Do not esteem yourself better than your fellows;
remember, his wrath will not delay.

17* More and more, humble your pride;
what awaits man is worms.

Duties of Family Life, Religion and Charity†

18† Barter not a friend for money,
nor a dear brother for the gold of Ophir.

19 Dismiss not a sensible wife;
a gracious wife is more precious than corals.

20* Mistreat not a servant who faithfully serves,
nor a laborer who devotes himself to
his task.

21† Let a wise servant be dear to you as your
own self;
refuse him not his freedom.

22 If you have livestock, look after them;
if they are dependable, keep them.

23*†If you have sons, chastise them;
bend their necks from childhood.

24* If you have daughters, keep them chaste,
and be not indulgent to them.

25* Giving your daughter in marriage ends a
great task;
but give her to a worthy man.

26 If you have a wife, let her not seem odious
to you;
but where there is ill-feeling, trust her not.

27* With your whole heart honor your father;
your mother's birthpangs forget not.

28 Remember, of these parents you were born;
what can you give them for all they gave you?

29 With all your soul, fear God,
revere his priests.

30 With all your strength, love your Creator,
forsake not his ministers.

31*†Honor God and respect the priest;
give him his portion as you have
been commanded:
First fruits and contributions,
due sacrifices and holy offerings.

32 To the poor man also extend your hand,
that your blessing may be complete;

33† Be generous to all the living,
and withhold not your kindness from
the dead.

34* Avoid not those who weep,
but mourn with those who mourn;

35* Neglect not to visit the sick—
for these things you will be loved.

36 In whatever you do, remember your last days,
and you will never sin.

Prudence in Dealing with Other Men†

8 ¹ Contend not with an influential man,
lest you fall into his power.

2* Quarrel not with a rich man,
lest he pay out the price of your downfall;
For gold has dazzled many,
and perverts the character of princes.

3* Dispute not with a man of railing speech,
heap no wood upon his fire.

4 Be not too familiar with an unruly man,
lest he speak ill of your forebears.

7, 11: *Him who exalts and humbles:* God; cf 1 Sm 2, 7; Ps 75, 8;
Lk 1, 52.

7, 14: *Repeat not . . . prayer:* brevity of speech in dealings with
superiors and more especially with God is a sign of reverence and
respect; cf Eccl 5, 1; Mt 6, 7.

7, 18–36: The duties of respect and appreciation, justice and
kindness should characterize relations toward members of the
household (18–28), and also toward God and his priests (29ff), the
poor and afflicted, the living and the dead (32–36).

7, 18: Ophir was the port, at present unidentified, to which the
ships of Solomon sailed and from which they brought back gold and
silver; cf note on Ps 45, 10.

7, 21: After six years of service a Hebrew slave was entitled to
freedom; cf Ex 21, 2; Dt 15, 12–15.

7, 23: *Bend their necks:* keep them from rebellious pride; so with
the Greek. Cf Sir 30, 12. The present Hebrew text, which is probably
not original here, reads: "Choose wives for them while they are young."

7, 31: *First fruits . . . holy offerings:* cf Ex 29, 27; Lv 7, 31–34; Nm
18, 8–20; Dt 18, 1–5.

7, 33: This seems to refer to the observances ordained toward the
dead, that is, proper mourning and burial. Cf 2 Sm 21, 12ff; Tb 1, 20;
12, 12. When this verse is read in the light of later teaching, prayers
for the souls of the deceased would also be recommended. Cf 2 Mc
12, 43ff.

8, 1–19: A prudent man will be circumspect, avoiding conflict
with the powerful, the rich and insolent, the impious, the irascible,
and with judges (1ff.10ff.14.16). He will seek friendship not with the
undisciplined (4.12f) and the ruthless (15), nor with fools and
strangers (17ff), but with the wise and the ancients of the people (8f).

7, 9: Sir 34, 18; 35, 12.
7, 14: Sir 32, 7ff; Mt 6, 7.
7, 15: Gn 2, 15; 3, 17.
7, 17: Is 66, 24.
7, 20: Lv 19, 13; Dt 24, 14f;
    Jas 5, 4.
7, 23: Sir 30, 8–13; Prv 13,
    24.

7, 24: Sir 42, 9ff.
7, 25: 1 Cor 7, 36ff.
7, 27: Ex 20, 12.
7, 31: Lv 7, 31; Nm 18, 18.
7, 34: Rom 12, 15.
7, 35: Mt 25, 36.
8, 2: Sir 31, 6; Dt 16, 19.
8, 3: Prv 26, 20.

5*†Shame not a repentant sinner;
   remember, we all are guilty.
6 Insult no man when he is old,
   for some of us, too, will grow old.
7 Rejoice not when a man dies;
   remember, we are all to die.
8* Spurn not the discourse of the wise,
   but acquaint yourself with their proverbs;
   From them you will acquire the training
   to serve in the presence of princes.
9 Reject not the tradition of old men
   which they have learned from their fathers;
   From it you will obtain the knowledge
   how to answer in time of need.
10 Kindle not the coals of a sinner,
   lest you be consumed in his flaming fire.
11†Let not the impious man intimidate you;
   it will set him in ambush against you.
12*Lend not to one more powerful than yourself;
   and whatever you lend, count it as lost.
13 Go not surety beyond your means;
   think any pledge a debt you must pay.
14 Contend not at law with a judge,
   for he will settle it according to his whim.
15 Travel not with a ruthless man,
   lest he weigh you down with calamity;
   For he will go his own way straight,
   and through his folly you will perish
   with him.
16 Provoke no quarrel with a quick-tempered man
   nor ride with him through the desert;
   For bloodshed is nothing to him;
   when there is no one to help you, he will
   destroy you.
17 Take no counsel with a fool,
   for he can keep nothing to himself.
18*Before a stranger do nothing that should be
   kept secret,
   for you know not what it will engender.
19 Open your heart to no man,
   and banish not your happiness.

Advice concerning Women†

9 1 Be not jealous of the wife of your bosom,
   lest you teach her to do evil against you.†
2* Give no woman power over you
   to trample upon your dignity.

3 Be not intimate with a strange woman,
   lest you fall into her snares.
4 With a singing girl be not familiar,
   lest you be caught in her wiles.
5† Entertain no thoughts against a virgin,
   lest you be enmeshed in damages for
   her.
6* Give not yourself to harlots,
   lest you surrender your inheritance.
7 Gaze not about the lanes of the city
   and wander not through its squares;
8* Avert your eyes from a comely woman;
   gaze not upon the beauty of
   another's wife—
   Through woman's beauty many perish,
   for lust for it burns like fire.
9 With a married woman dine not,
   recline not at table to drink by her side,
   Lest your heart be drawn to her
   and you go down in blood to the grave.

Choice of Friends†

10 Discard not an old friend,
   for the new one cannot equal him.
   A new friend is like new wine
   which you drink with pleasure only when it
   has aged.
11 Envy not a sinner's fame,
   for you know not what disaster
   awaits him.
12 Rejoice not at a proud man's success;
   remember he will not reach
   death unpunished.
13 Keep far from the man who has power to kill,
   and you will not be filled with the dread
   of death.
   But if you approach him, offend him not,
   lest he take away your life;
   Know that you are stepping among snares
   and walking over a net.
14 As best you can, take your neighbors' measure,
   and associate with the wise.
15 With the learned be intimate;
   let all your conversation be about the law
   of the LORD.
16 Have just men for your table companions;
   in the fear of God be your glory.

8, 5: *We all are guilty:* Cf 1 Kgs 8, 46; 2 Chr 6, 36; Eccl 7, 20;
Rom 3, 9f; 1 Jn 1, 8.
8, 11: To give in to the wicked in one instance becomes an occasion of sin for the future.
9, 1–9: Prudence and reserve in dealing with women are the best
defense of morality. To preserve the liberty and dignity of his person
and the integrity of his possessions, a man must avoid jealousy toward his own wife and familiarity toward all other women. Cf Sir
25, 12—26, 18.
9, 1: Unjust suspicions often engender hatred between husband
and wife and may prompt a wife to commit those faults of which
heretofore she had been innocent.

9, 5: Cf Ex 22, 15f; Dt 22, 28f; Jb 31, 1.
9, 10–16: In social relations, adherence to the law of the Lord
should serve as a guide (15). Associate with true friends (10), with
the just and the learned (14ff); avoid the company of the mighty and
of sinners doomed to punishment (11ff). Cf Sir 8, 1–19.

8, 5: 1 Kgs 8, 46; 1 Jn 1, 8.   9, 2: Sir 25, 21.
8, 8f: Sir 6, 35.   9, 6: Prv 5, 3–11; 6, 24;
8, 12: Sir 29, 4–7; Prv 17,   29, 3.
   18.   9, 8: Sir 25, 20; 41, 21.
8, 18: Prv 25, 9f.

Friends, Old and New

Out there, somewhere, is a special person you have not yet met. He or she will eventually become a key person in your life, perhaps even a life partner. In fact, a lot of such people are out there, somewhere—including future classmates, co-workers, roommates, and friends. The challenge is in finding the particular people who will become close to you, your soul mates.

Ben Sira reminds us in Sir 9, 10 that in the excitement that accompanies making new friends, we should not forget the pleasure and comfort that an old friend brings us. A friend we have known for a long time is someone to trust, someone who knows and accepts us, warts and all. And when the circumstances of life cause separation from old friends, there is value in reconnecting occasionally to share where life has taken us or even to seek direction and support if life has become confusing or hard. We need to treasure our tried-and-true friendships, as well as welcome new ones.

Spend some time reflecting on your friends, old and new, and their value in your life.

▶ Sir 9, 10

Concerning Rulers†

17 Skilled artisans are esteemed for their deftness;
      but the ruler of his people is the skilled sage.

18 Feared in the city is the man of railing speech,
      and he who talks rashly is hated.

10

1* A wise magistrate lends stability to
      his people,
  and the government of a prudent man is
      well ordered.

2* As the people's judge, so are his ministers;
      as the head of a city, its inhabitants.

3* A wanton king destroys his people,
      but a city grows through the wisdom of
      its princes.

4 Sovereignty over the earth is in the hand of God,
      who raises up on it the man of the hour;

5 Sovereignty over every man is in the hand
      of God,
  who imparts his majesty to the ruler.

The Sin of Pride†

6* No matter the wrong, do no violence to
      your neighbor,
  and do not walk the path of arrogance.

7 Odious to the LORD and to men is arrogance,
      and the sin of oppression they both hate.

8 Dominion is transferred from one people
      to another
      because of the violence of the arrogant.

9† Why are dust and ashes proud?
      even during life man's body decays;

10 A slight illness—the doctor jests,
      a king today—tomorrow he is dead.

11* When a man dies, he inherits corruption;
      worms and gnats and maggots.

12 The beginning of pride is man's stubbornness
      in withdrawing his heart from his Maker;

13* For pride is the reservoir of sin,
      a source which runs over with vice;
  Because of it God sends unheard-of afflictions
      and brings men to utter ruin.

14 The thrones of the arrogant God overturns
      and establishes the lowly in their stead.

15 The roots of the proud God plucks up,
      to plant the humble in their place:

16 He breaks down their stem to the level of
      the ground,
  then digs their roots from the earth.

17 The traces of the proud God sweeps away
      and effaces the memory of them from
      the earth.

18 Insolence is not allotted to a man,
      nor stubborn anger to one born of woman.

9, 17—10, 5: Public office as conducted justly, or unjustly benefits or destroys the people, according to the axiom, "as the prince, so the people." Cf Is 24, 2. God, however, has sovereignty over both.

10, 6—18: Glory displayed through arrogance and pride is false and displeasing to God and men, because it is founded on dust and ashes (6–11). It is the denial of the glory due to God, and therefore the source of all sin (12f). Even the memory of the proud is destroyed and God transfers their power to the lowly (14–18).

10, 9f: The text is uncertain. Its general implication is that man deteriorates physically even while alive: a slight illness today may be followed by death tomorrow. The uncertainty of life leaves no room for pride.

10, 1: Wis 6, 24.   10, 6: Lv 19, 18.
10, 2f: Prv 29, 12.   10, 11: Jb 17, 14.
10, 3: Prv 29, 4.8.   10, 13: Prv 18, 12.

True Glory†

19 Whose offspring can be in honor? Those
      of men.
   Which offspring are in honor? Those who
      fear God.
   Whose offspring can be in disgrace? Those
      of men.
   Which offspring are in disgrace? Those who
      transgress the commandments.

20 Among brethren their leader is in honor;
   he who fears God is in honor among
      his people.

21 Be it tenant or wayfarer, alien or pauper,
   his glory is the fear of the LORD.

22* It is not just to despise a man who is wise
      but poor,
   nor proper to honor any sinner.

23 The prince, the ruler, the judge are in honor;
   but none is greater than he who fears God.

24* When free men serve a prudent slave,
   the wise man does not complain.

25 Flaunt not your wisdom in managing
      your affairs,
   and boast not in your time of need.

26* Better the worker who has plenty of everything
   than the boaster who is without bread.

27 My son, with humility have self-esteem;
   prize yourself as you deserve.

28 Who will acquit him who condemns himself?
   who will honor him who discredits himself?

29 The poor man is honored for his wisdom
   as the rich man is honored for his wealth;

30 Honored in poverty, how much more so
      in wealth!
   Dishonored in wealth, in poverty how
      much the more!

11

1 The poor man's wisdom lifts his
      head high
   and sets him among princes.

2 Praise not a man for his looks;
   despise not a man for his appearance.

3 Least is the bee among winged things,
   but she reaps the choicest of all harvests.

4 Mock not the worn cloak
   and jibe at no man's bitter day:
   For strange are the works of the LORD,
   hidden from men his deeds.

5† The oppressed often rise to a throne,
   and some that none would consider wear
      a crown.

6 The exalted often fall into utter disgrace;
   the honored are given into enemy hands.

Moderation†

7 Before investigating, find no fault;
   examine first, then criticize.

8* Before hearing, answer not,
   and interrupt no one in the middle of
      his speech.

9 Dispute not about what is not your concern;
   in the strife of the arrogant take no part.

10 My son, why increase your cares,
   since he who is avid for wealth will not
      be blameless?
   Even if you run after it, you will never
      overtake it;
   however you seek it, you will not find it.

11* One may toil and struggle and drive,
   and fall short all the more.

12 Another goes his way a weakling and
      a failure,
   with little strength and great misery—
   Yet the eyes of the LORD look favorably
      upon him;
   he raises him free of the vile dust,

13 Lifts up his head and exalts him
   to the amazement of the many.

14*† Good and evil, life and death,
   poverty and riches, are from the LORD.

15† Wisdom and understanding and knowledge
      of affairs,
   love and virtuous paths are from
      the LORD.

16 Error and darkness were formed with sinners
      from their birth,
   and evil grows old with evildoers.

17 The LORD's gift remains with the just;
   his favor brings continued success.

18 A man may become rich through a
      miser's life,
   and this is his allotted reward:

19*† When he says: "I have found rest,
      now I will feast on my possessions,"
   He does not know how long it will be
      till he dies and leaves them to others.

---

† **10, 19—11, 6:** Regardless of social barriers, genuine honor among men comes from fear of the Lord and a true estimate of self. The Lord exalts the lowly and oppressed; transgressors of the commandments merit dishonor and disgrace.
   11, 5: Cf 1 Sm 2, 8; Ps 105, 17–22; Lk 1, 52.
   11, 7–25: Discretion regulates a man's conduct toward others and their affairs (7ff); as regards his own interests, a man should avoid solicitude for the passing external benefits of life and property (10–14.18f.21.23ff), and cultivate the lasting inward gifts of wisdom and virtue (15.17.20.22).

11, 14: Divine Providence ultimately governs the lives of men. *Evil:* misfortune and calamity sent by God either in punishment or as an incentive to repentance or to greater virtue.
   11, 15f: Some ancient witnesses omit these two verses.
   11, 19: Cf the parable of the rich man, Lk 12, 16–21.

10, 22: Jas 2, 1–4.   11, 11: Ps 127, 2; Eccl 4, 8.
10, 24: Prv 17, 2.   11, 14: Jb 1, 21; 2, 10.
10, 26: Prv 12, 9.   11, 19: Eccl 4, 8; 6, 2; Lk 12,
11, 8: Prv 18, 13.   19.

20 My son, hold fast to your duty, busy yourself
with it,
    grow old while doing your task.
21 Admire not how sinners live,
    but trust in the LORD and wait for his light;
For it is easy with the LORD
    suddenly, in an instant, to make a poor
    man rich.
22 God's blessing is the lot of the just man,
    and in due time his hopes bear fruit.
23 Say not: "What do I need?
    What further pleasure can be mine?"
24 Say not: "I am independent.
    What harm can come to me now?"
25* The day of prosperity makes one
    forget adversity;
the day of adversity makes one
    forget prosperity.
26† For it is easy with the LORD on the day of death
    to repay man according to his deeds.
27 A moment's affliction brings forgetfulness of
    past delights;
when a man dies, his life is revealed.
28 Call no man happy before his death,
    for by how he ends, a man is known.

Care in Choosing Friends

29 Bring not every man into your house,
    for many are the snares of the crafty one;
30 Though he seem like a bird confined in a cage,
    yet like a spy he will pick out the weak spots.
31 The talebearer turns good into evil;
    with a spark he sets many coals afire.
32 The evil man lies in wait for blood,
    and plots against your choicest possessions.
33 Avoid a wicked man, for he breeds only evil,
    lest you incur a lasting stain.
34 Lodge a stranger with you, and he will subvert
    your course,
and make a stranger of you to your
    own household.

12 1† If you do good, know for whom you
    are doing it,
and your kindness will have its effect.
2 Do good to the just man and reward will
    be yours,
if not from him, from the LORD.
3† No good comes to him who gives comfort to
    the wicked,

nor is it an act of mercy that he does.
4* Give to the good man, refuse the sinner;
    refresh the downtrodden, give nothing to
    the proud man.
5 No arms for combat should you give him,
    lest he use them against yourself;
6 With twofold evil you will meet
    for every good deed you do for him.
7 The Most High himself hates sinners,
    and upon the wicked he takes vengeance.

8*† In our prosperity we cannot know our friends;
    in adversity an enemy will not
    remain concealed.
9* When a man is successful even his enemy
    is friendly;
in adversity even his friend disappears.
10 Never trust your enemy,
    for his wickedness is like corrosion in bronze.
11† Even though he acts humbly and peaceably
    toward you,
take care to be on your guard against him.
Rub him as one polishes a brazen mirror,
    and you will find that there is still corrosion.
12 Let him not stand near you,
    lest he oust you and take your place.
Let him not sit at your right hand,
    lest he then demand your seat,
And in the end you appreciate my advice,
    when you groan with regret, as I
    warned you.
13 Who pities a snake charmer when he
    is bitten,
or anyone who goes near a wild beast?
14 So is it with the companion of the proud man,
    who is involved in his sins:
15 While you stand firm, he makes no bold move;
    but if you slip, he cannot hold back.
16 With his lips an enemy speaks sweetly,
    but in his heart he schemes to plunge you
    into the abyss.
Though your enemy has tears in his eyes,
    if given the chance, he will never have
    enough of your blood.
17 If evil comes upon you, you will find him
    at hand;
feigning to help, he will trip you up,
18 Then he will nod his head and clap his hands
    and hiss repeatedly, and show his
    true face.

11, 26ff: Sirach, writing before Christian revelation, did not go
beyond the hour of death to find full divine retribution.
12, 1–7: The limitations to the practice of charity here reflected were
removed by Christ, who requires that good be done even to enemies
and to those who hate, persecute and calumniate us (Mt 5, 43–48).
12, 3ff: The author advises against generosity to those who would
abuse it.

12, 8–18: Through adversity friends are distinguished from enemies; to trust the latter or permit them intimacy is to invite disaster.
Cf note on Sir 6, 5–17.
12, 11: *Brazen mirror:* see note on Ex 38, 8.

11, 25: Sir 18, 25.   12, 8: Prv 17, 17.
12, 4f: Gal 6, 10.   12, 9: Prv 19, 4–7.

Caution Regarding Associates†

13 ¹ He who touches pitch blackens
his hand;
he who associates with an impious man
learns his ways.

² Bear no burden too heavy for you;
go with no one greater or wealthier
than yourself.
How can the earthen pot go with the
metal cauldron?
When they knock together, the pot will
be smashed:

³ The rich man does wrong and boasts of it,
the poor man is wronged and
begs forgiveness.

⁴ As long as the rich man can use you he will
enslave you,
but when you are exhausted, he will
abandon you.

⁵ As long as you have anything he will speak
fair words to you,
and with smiles he will win your confidence;

⁶ When he needs something from you he will
cajole you,
then without regret he will impoverish you.

⁷ While it serves his purpose he will
beguile you,
then twice or three times he will terrify you;
When later he sees you he will pass you by,
and shake his head over you.

⁸ Guard against being presumptuous;
be not as those who lack sense.

⁹ When invited by a man of influence, keep
your distance;
then he will urge you all the more.

¹⁰ Be not bold with him lest you be rebuffed,
but keep not too far away lest you
be forgotten.

¹¹ Engage not freely in discussion with him,
trust not his many words;
For by prolonged talk he will test you,
and though smiling he will probe you.

¹² Mercilessly he will make of you
a laughingstock,
and will not refrain from injury or chains.

¹³ Be on your guard and take care
never to accompany men of violence.

¹⁴ Every living thing loves its own kind,
every man a man like himself.

¹⁵ Every being is drawn to its own kind;
with his own kind every man associates.

¹⁶* Is a wolf ever allied with a lamb?
So it is with the sinner and the just.

¹⁷† Can there be peace between the hyena and
the dog?
Or between the rich and the poor can there
be peace?

¹⁸ Lion's prey are the wild asses of the desert;
so too the poor are feeding grounds for
the rich.

¹⁹ A proud man abhors lowliness;
so does the rich man abhor the poor.

²⁰ When a rich man stumbles he is supported by
a friend;
when a poor man trips he is pushed down
by a friend.

²¹ Many are the supporters for a rich man when
he speaks;
though what he says is odious, it
wins approval.
When a poor man speaks they make sport
of him;
he speaks wisely and no attention is
paid him.

²² A rich man speaks and all are silent,
his wisdom they extol to the clouds.
A poor man speaks and they say: "Who
is that?"
If he slips they cast him down.

²³ Wealth is good when there is no sin;
but poverty is evil by the standards of
the proud.

²⁴* The heart of a man changes his countenance,
either for good or for evil.

²⁵ The sign of a good heart is a
cheerful countenance;
withdrawn and perplexed is the
laborious schemer.

14 ¹* Happy the man whose mouth brings
him no grief,
who is not stung by remorse for sin.

² Happy the man whose conscience does not
reproach him,
who has not lost hope.

The Use of Wealth

³† Wealth ill becomes the mean man;
and to the miser, of what use is gold?

---

† **13, 1—14, 2:** By means of various figures Sirach indicates the practical impossibility of genuine and sincere companionship between the poor and the proud rich. He lays down the principle of associating with equals (13, 15).

13, 17: The hostility between the dogs which guard the flocks at night and the rapacious hyenas is proverbial in Palestine.

14, 3–16: The miser does no good even to himself (3–10); wealth

should be wisely used during life, for it must be left behind at death (11–16). In the light of the gospel, generosity has a higher motivation and promise of reward than the Old Testament writer could propose. Cf Mt 6, 19ff; Lk 12, 32ff.

13, 16: 2 Cor 6, 14ff.   **14, 1:** Sir 19, 15; 25, 8;
13, 24: Prv 15, 13.   Jas 3, 2.

4* What he denies himself he collects for others,
and in his possessions a stranger will revel.

5 To whom will he be generous who is stingy
with himself
and does not enjoy what is his own?

6 None is more stingy than he who is stingy
with himself;
he punishes his own miserliness.

7 If ever he is generous, it is by mistake;
and in the end he displays his greed.

8 In the miser's opinion his share is too small;

9 he refuses his neighbor and brings ruin
on himself.

10 The miser's eye is rapacious for bread,
but on his own table he sets it stale.

11* My son, use freely whatever you have
and enjoy it as best you can;

12 Remember that death does not tarry,
nor have you been told the grave's
appointed time.

13* Before you die, be good to your friend,
and give him a share in what you possess.

14 Deprive not yourself of present good things,
let no choice portion escape you.

15 Will you not leave your riches to others,
and your earnings to be divided by lot?

16 Give, take, and treat yourself well,
for in the nether world there are no joys
to seek.

17* All flesh grows old, like a garment;
the age-old law is: All must die.

18* As with the leaves that grow on a
vigorous tree:
one falls off and another sprouts—
So with the generations of flesh and blood:
one dies and another is born.

19 All man's works will perish in decay,
and his handiwork will follow after him.

The Search for Wisdom and Its Blessings†

20* Happy the man who meditates on wisdom,
and reflects on knowledge;

21 Who ponders her ways in his heart,
and understands her paths;

22 Who pursues her like a scout,
and lies in wait at her entry way;

23 Who peeps through her windows,
and listens at her doors;

24 Who encamps near her house,
and fastens his tent pegs next to her walls;

25 Who pitches his tent beside her,
and lives as her welcome neighbor;

26 Who builds his nest in her leafage,
and lodges in her branches;

27 Who takes shelter with her from the heat,
and dwells in her home.

15

1 He who fears the LORD will do this;
he who is practiced in the law will
come to wisdom.

2 Motherlike she will meet him,
like a young bride she will embrace him,

3* Nourish him with the bread of understanding,
and give him the water of learning to drink.

4 He will lean upon her and not fall,
he will trust in her and not be put to shame.

5 She will exalt him above his fellows;
in the assembly she will make
him eloquent.

6* Joy and gladness he will find,
an everlasting name inherit.

7 Worthless men will not attain to her,
haughty men will not behold her.

8 Far from the impious is she,
not to be spoken of by liars.

9 Unseemly is praise on a sinner's lips,
for it is not accorded to him by God.

10 But praise is offered by the wise man's tongue;
its rightful steward will proclaim it.

Man's Free Will

11 Say not: "It was God's doing that I fell away";
for what he hates he does not do.

12* Say not: "It was he who set me astray";
for he has no need of wicked man.

13 Abominable wickedness the LORD hates,
he does not let it befall those who fear him.

14* When God, in the beginning, created man,
he made him subject to his own free choice.

15 If you choose you can keep
the commandments;
it is loyalty to do his will.

16 There are set before you fire and water;
to whichever you choose, stretch forth
your hand.

17* Before man are life and death,
whichever he chooses shall be given him.

18 Immense is the wisdom of the LORD;
he is mighty in power, and all-seeing.

---

† **14, 20—15, 20:** From his social teaching the sage now turns to consider individual responsibility. Happiness is to be found in the pursuit and possession of wisdom (14, 20—15, 5). Joy and honor are given, not to the sinner (7ff), but to him who fears God and observes his law (1–6.10). The sinner is fully responsible for his conduct because God, who sees all things (18f), is not the author of wickedness (11ff.20): he gives to every man the liberty to choose between good and evil (14–17).

* 14, 4: Eccl 6, 2.
14, 11: Prv 3, 9.
14, 13: Sir 4, 1; Tb 4, 7.
14, 17: Ps 103, 14ff; Is 40, 6;
  Jas 1, 10; 1 Pt 1, 24.
14, 18: Eccl 1, 4.
14, 20: Ps 1, 2.
15, 3: Jn 4, 10; 6, 31ff.
15, 6: Sir 6, 29–32.
15, 12: Jas 1, 13.
15, 14: Gn 1, 27.
15, 17: Dt 30, 15.

Taking Responsibility

I t isn't my fault; she made me do it."
"He started it!" "The devil made me
do it!" We have lots of ways of blaming
others when bad things happen. Sir 15,
11 tells of one way people in Ben Sira's
time tried to put the blame on someone
else: "It was God's doing." Evidently, some
people blamed God when they fell into
sin. Ben Sira tells us it isn't God's will
when bad things happen as a result of
human choice (verses 14–17)—which is
why we need to stop the blame game and
take responsibility for our own actions.

In your prayer, take some time to
reflect or journal on the following questions:

■ **Do you tend to blame others when
bad things happen?**
■ **Have there been hurtful situations in
which you would not accept your part
of the responsibility? If so, describe one
and explain how you could have
owned up to your responsibility.**

▶ Sir 15, 11–20

19* The eyes of God see all he has made;
　　he understands man's every deed.
20　No man does he command to sin,
　　to none does he give strength for lies.

God's Punishment of Sinners†

16 ¹ Desire not a brood of worthless
　　　children,
　　nor rejoice in wicked offspring.
2　Many though they be, exult not in them
　　if they have not the fear of the LORD.
3* Count not on their length of life,
　　have no hope in their future.
　　For one can be better than a thousand;
　　rather die childless than have
　　　godless children!

4　Through one wise man can a city
　　　be peopled;
　　through a clan of rebels it
　　　becomes desolate.
5　Many such things has my eye seen,
　　even more than these has my ear heard.
6*†Against a sinful band fire is enkindled,
　　upon a godless people wrath flames out.
7*†He forgave not the leaders of old
　　who rebelled long ago in their might;
8*†He spared not the neighbors of Lot
　　whom he detested for their pride;
9†　Nor did he spare the doomed people
　　who were uprooted because of their sin;
10*†Nor the six hundred thousand foot soldiers
　　who perished for the impiety of
　　　their hearts.
11　And had there been but one stiffnecked man,
　　it were a wonder had he gone unpunished.
　　For mercy and anger alike are with him
　　who remits and forgives, though on the
　　　wicked alights his wrath.
12　Great as his mercy is his punishment;
　　he judges men, each according to his deeds.
13　A criminal does not escape with his plunder;
　　a just man's hope God does not
　　　leave unfulfilled.
14　Whoever does good has his reward,
　　which each receives according to his deeds.
15　Say not: "I am hidden from God;
　　in heaven who remembers me?
　　Among so many people I cannot be known;
　　what am I in the world of spirits?
16　Behold, the heavens, the heaven of heavens,
　　the earth and the abyss tremble at
　　　his visitation;
17　The roots of the mountains, the
　　　earth's foundations,
　　at his mere glance, quiver and quake.
18　Of me, therefore, he will take no thought;
　　with my ways who will concern himself?
19* If I sin, no eye will see me;
　　if all in secret I am disloyal, who is
　　　to know?
20　Who tells him of just deeds
　　and what could I expect for doing my duty?"
21　Such are the thoughts of senseless men,
　　which only the foolish knave will think.

---

† 16, 1–21: Sinful offspring are a great misfortune (1–4), for history
and experience show how God punishes sin (5–10). He judges
everyone according to his deeds (11ff); no one is hidden from him or
escapes retribution at his hand (15–21).

16, 6: For Korah and his band (6a), see Nm 16, 35; Ps 106, 18;
for the disgruntled Israelites (6b), Ps 78, 21f.

16, 7: *The leaders of old:* the "mighty men of old" who were destroyed by the flood: Gn 6, 4; Wis 14, 6; Bar 3, 26ff.

16, 8: The people of Sodom and Gomorrah: Gn 19, 24f; Ez
16, 49f.

16, 9: The Canaanites: Ex 23, 23f.27–31; 33, 2; Dt 7, 1; Wis
12, 3.
16, 10: The Israelites who murmured against Moses: Nm 11, 20;
14, 12.22ff.

15, 19: Pss 33, 18; 34, 16;　　16, 7: Gn 6, 4; Wis 14, 6; Bar
　Heb 4, 13.　　　　　　　　　3, 26ff.
16, 3f: Wis 4, 1f.　　　　　　16, 8: Gn 19, 24ff.
16, 6: Sir 21, 9.　　　　　　　16, 10: Nm 14, 29.
　　　　　　　　　　　　　　　16, 19: Sir 23, 18.

S
I
R

Divine Wisdom Seen in Creation†

22 Hearken to me, my son, take my advice,
   apply your mind to my words,
23 While I propose measured wisdom,
   and impart accurate knowledge.
24* When at the first God created his works
   and, as he made them, assigned their tasks,
25 He ordered for all time what they were to do
   and their domains from generation
      to generation.
   They were not to hunger, nor grow weary,
   nor ever cease from their tasks.
26 Not one should ever crowd its neighbor,
   nor should they ever disobey his word.
27* Then the LORD looked upon the earth,
   and filled it with his blessings.
28 Its surface he covered with all manner of life
   which must return into it again.

17 1* The LORD from the earth
      created man,
   and in his own image he made him.
2* Limited days of life he gives him
   and makes him return to earth again.
3 He endows man with a strength of his own,
   and with power over all things else
      on earth.
4 He puts the fear of him in all flesh,
   and gives him rule over beasts and birds.
5 He forms men's tongues and eyes and ears,
   and imparts to them an
      understanding heart.
6 With wisdom and knowledge he fills them;
   good and evil he shows them.
7 He looks with favor upon their hearts,
   and shows them his glorious works,
8 That they may describe the wonders of
      his deeds
   and praise his holy name.
9 He has set before them knowledge,
   a law of life as their inheritance;
10† An everlasting covenant he has made
      with them,
   his commandments he has revealed
      to them.

11 His majesty glory their eyes beheld,
   his glorious voice their ears heard.
12 He says to them, "Avoid all evil";
   each of them he gives precepts about his
      fellow men.
13 Their ways are ever known to him,
   they cannot be hidden from his eyes.
14*† Over every nation he places a ruler,
   but the LORD's own portion is Israel.
15 All their actions are clear as the sun to him,
   his eyes are ever upon their ways.
16 Their wickedness cannot be hidden from him;
   all of their sins are before the LORD.
17 A man's goodness God cherishes like a
      signet ring,
   a man's virtue, like the apple of his eye.
18* Later he will rise up and repay them,
   and requite each one of them as
      they deserve.

Appeal for a Return to God†

19 But to the penitent he provides a way back,
   he encourages those who are losing hope!
20 Return to the LORD and give up sin,
   pray to him and make your offenses few.
21 Turn again to the Most High and away
      from sin,
   hate intensely what he loathes;
22* Who in the nether world can glorify the
      Most High
   in place of the living who offer their praise?
23 No more can the dead give praise than those
      who have never lived;
   they glorify the LORD who are alive
      and well.
24 How great the mercy of the LORD,
   his forgiveness of those who return to him!
25 The like cannot be found in men,
   for not immortal is any son of man.
26† Is anything brighter than the sun? Yet it can
      be eclipsed.
   How obscure then the thoughts of flesh
      and blood!
27 God watches over the hosts of highest heaven,
   while all men are dust and ashes.

16, 22—17, 18: In harmony with Gn 1–2, the author describes God's wisdom in creating the universe and all things in it (22–28), endowing man with a moral nature, with wisdom and knowledge and freedom of will according to his own image (17, 1.6), so that man may govern the earth (3f), praise God's name (8), obey his law (9–12), and render to him an account of his deeds (18). Cf Pss 19; 104.

17, 10: *An everlasting covenant . . . his commandments:* the various covenants which God entered into with mankind, e.g., Gn 2, 15ff; 17, 1–22, especially on Mount Sinai where the people saw God's glory and heard his voice (Ex 19, 16—24, 18).

17, 14: *Ruler:* this may refer to civil authority or to angels placed over nations as guardians; see note on Dt 32, 8, and the cross-references above.

17, 19–27: Exhorting the sinner to return to God (19ff.24ff), the author implies that the Lord will postpone death for a repentant sinner so that he may fulfill his destiny of praising God on earth (22f). In the light of Christian teaching, the gift of final penitence extends this divine purpose into life everlasting. See note on Ps 6, 6; cf also Ez 18, 23; 33, 11–16.

17, 26: *Obscure:* literally, evil; compare Gn 6, 5. Though moral fault is not excluded, the thought here is the inability to understand the merciful designs of God. Cf Wis 9, 14–18.

16, 24: Gn 1, 4ff.   8f; Dn 10, 13–21;
16, 27: Gn 1, 20ff.   12, 1; Rom 13, 1.
17, 1: Gn 2, 7; 3, 19.
17, 2ff: Gn 1, 26ff; Ps 8, 4–8.   17, 18: Jb 19, 25; Jl 3, 4.
17, 14: Ex 19, 5; Dt 4, 19f; 32,   17, 22ff: Pss 6, 6; 115, 17; Is
                                    38, 18.

The Divine Power and Mercy†

18

1 The Eternal is the judge of all things
  without exception;
  the LORD alone is just.

2 Whom has he made equal to describing
  his works,
  and who can probe his mighty deeds?

3 Who can measure his majestic power,
  or exhaust the tale of his mercies?

4 One cannot lessen, nor increase,
  nor penetrate the wonders of the LORD.

5 When a man ends he is only beginning,
  and when he stops he is still bewildered.

6 What is man, of what worth is he? the good,
  the evil in him, what are these?

7* The sum of a man's days is great
  if it reaches a hundred years:

8 Like a drop of sea water, like a grain of sand,
  so are these few years among the days
  of eternity.

9 That is why the LORD is patient with men
  and showers upon them his mercy.

10 He sees and understands that their death
  is grievous,
  and so he forgives them all the more.

11 Man may be merciful to his fellow man,
  but the LORD'S mercy reaches all flesh,

12* Reproving, admonishing, teaching,
  as a shepherd guides his flock;

13 Merciful to those who accept his guidance,
  who are diligent in his precepts.

The Necessity of Prudence

14† My son, to your charity add no reproach,
  nor spoil any gift by harsh words.

15 Like dew that abates a burning wind,
  so does a word improve a gift.

16 Sometimes the word means more than
  the gift;
  both are offered by a kindly man.

17* Only a fool upbraids before giving;
  a grudging gift wears out the expectant
  eyes.

18 Be informed before speaking;
  before sickness prepare the cure.

19† Before you are judged, seek merit for yourself,
  and at the time of visitation you will have
  a ransom.

20 Before you have fallen, humble yourself;
  when you have sinned, show repentance.

21 Delay not to forsake sins,
  neglect it not till you are in distress.

22*† Let nothing prevent the prompt payment of
  your vows;
  wait not to fulfill them when you are
  dying.

23 Before making a vow have the means to
  fulfill it;
  be not one who tries the LORD.

24* Think of wrath and the day of death,
  the time of vengeance when he will hide
  his face.

25* Remember the time of hunger in the time
  of plenty,
  poverty and want in the day of wealth.

26 Between morning and evening the
  weather changes;
  before the LORD all things are fleeting.

27 A wise man is circumspect in all things;
  when sin is rife he keeps himself
  from wrongdoing.

28† Any learned man should make
  wisdom known,
  and he who attains to her should declare
  her praise;

29 Those trained in her words must show
  their wisdom,
  dispensing sound proverbs like
  life-giving waters.

Self-Control†

30* Go not after your lusts,
  but keep your desires in check.

31 If you satisfy your lustful appetites
  they will make you the sport of
  your enemies.

32 Have no joy in the pleasures of a moment
  which bring on poverty redoubled;

33 Become not a glutton and a winebibber
  with nothing in your purse.

18, 1–13: Not only are God's justice and power beyond man's understanding (1–5), his mercy also is boundless and surpasses all human compassion (6–13).

18, 14–27: The practice of charity is an art which avoids every offense to the recipient (14–18). Prudence directs the changing circumstances of daily life toward the attainment of its reward at the time of visitation, i.e., the day of reckoning (19–27).

18, 19: *Merit . . . ransom:* almsgiving is often portrayed in the Bible as a means of approach to the forgiving mercy of God. Cf Sir 3, 29f; 29, 11f; Tb 12, 12f; Dn 4, 24; Lk 16, 9; Acts 10, 31.

18, 22f: The usual object of a vow in Old Testament times was the offering of a bloody sacrifice.

18, 28f: A general statement on the teaching of wisdom, serving either as a conclusion to the preceding section or as an introduction

to the following one. The neighbors of the wise man are regarded as the field into which he channels the waters of wisdom to encourage growth. Cf Sir 24, 28–31.

18, 30—19, 4: Inordinate gratification of the senses makes a man unreasonable, the slave of passion, the sport of his enemies. In the end it destroys him physically and spiritually.

18, 7: Ps 90, 10.
18, 12: Jn 10, 11.
18, 17: Sir 20, 13.
18, 22: Nm 30, 3; Dt 23, 22; Ps 50, 14; Prv 20, 25;
    Eccl 5, 4.
18, 24: Sir 7, 16.
18, 25: Sir 11, 25.
18, 30: Rom 6, 12; 13, 14.

S
I
R

Don't Get Burned

It is easy to give in to temptation. Every day, we face decisions that can hurt our relationship with God. Ben Sira soundly advises us not to give in to our lusts (Sir 18, 30). These are attitudes and practices that include laziness, drunkenness, and lust, which might bring some immediate pleasure but also lead to long-term problems. Self-control is the strength to resist the lusts that lead to lifelong problems.

An old saying—If you play with matches, you might get burned—is often used by people recovering from addictions. It reminds them that risky behaviors often end up hurting them. It helps them stay focused on their long-term goal of leading a healthy and happy life. If they follow Ben Sira's advice—practice self-control—they won't end up getting burned!

What lusts tempt you the most? What do you need to do to avoid getting burned by them?

▶ **Sir 18, 30—19, 3**

19

1 He who does so grows no richer;
   he who wastes the little he has will be
      stripped bare.
2* Wine and women make the mind giddy,
   and the companion of harlots
      becomes reckless.
4 He who lightly trusts in them has no sense,
   and he who strays after them sins against
      his own life.
3 Rottenness and worms will possess him,
   for contumacious desire destroys its owner.

The Proper Use of Speech†

5 He who gloats over evil will meet with evil,
   and he who repeats an evil report has
      no sense.
6* Never repeat gossip,
   and you will not be reviled.
7* Tell nothing to friend or foe;
   if you have a fault, reveal it not,
8 For he who hears it will hold it against you,
   and in time become your enemy.
9 Let anything you hear die within you;
   be assured it will not make you burst.
10 When a fool hears something, he is in labor,
   like a woman giving birth to a child.
11 Like an arrow lodged in a man's thigh
   is gossip in the breast of a fool.
12* Admonish your friend—he may not have
      done it;
   and if he did, that he may not do it again.

13 Admonish your neighbor—he may not have
      said it;
   and if he did, that he may not say it again.
14 Admonish your friend—often it may
      be slander;
   every story you must not believe.
15* Then, too, a man can slip and not mean it;
   who has not sinned with his tongue?
16* Admonish your neighbor before you break
      with him;
   thus will you fulfill the law of the
      Most High.

How To Recognize True Wisdom†

17* All wisdom is fear of the LORD;
   perfect wisdom is the fulfillment of the law.
18 The knowledge of wickedness is not wisdom,
   nor is there prudence in the counsel
      of sinners.
19 There is a shrewdness that is detestable,
   while the simple man may be free from sin.
20 There are those with little understanding who
      fear God,
   and those of great intelligence who violate
      the law.
21 There is a shrewdness keen but dishonest,
   which by duplicity wins a judgment.
22 There is the wicked man who is bowed
      in grief,
   but is full of guile within;
23 He bows his head and feigns not to hear,

19, 5–16: An excellent commentary on the eighth commandment of the Decalogue, forbidding intemperance in speech through calumny, rash judgment, and detraction (5f), and inculcating discreet silence in defense of self and of neighbor (7–11). Justice requires that an accused neighbor be given a hearing, and charity urges fraternal correction; both together fulfill the law of the Most High (12–16); cf Mt 7, 1f; 18, 15f.
19, 17–26: True and false wisdom as here described are synony-

mous with virtue and vice, with the fulfillment of the law and the violation of it.

19, 2: Prv 20, 1; 23, 20ff.
19, 6: Prv 25, 10.
19, 7: Sir 8, 18f.
19, 12: Lv 19, 17; Mt 18, 15;
   Lk 17, 3.
19, 15: Sir 14, 1; Jas 3, 2.
19, 16: Lv 19, 17.
19, 17: Sir 1, 1.12.14; Jb 28,
   28; Ps 111, 10; Prv 1,
   7; 9, 10.

but when not observed, he will take
   advantage of you:

24 Even though his lack of strength keeps him
   from sinning,
   when he finds the opportunity, he will
   do harm.

25 One can tell a man by his appearance;
   a wise man is known as such when
   first met.

26 A man's attire, his hearty laughter and his gait,
   proclaim him for what he is.

Conduct of the Wise and the Foolish

20 ¹† An admonition can be inopportune,
   and a man may be wise to hold
   his peace.

2 It is much better to admonish than to lose
   one's temper,
   for one who admits his fault will be kept
   from disgrace.

3† Like a eunuch lusting for intimacy with
   a maiden
   is he who does right under compulsion.

4 One man is silent and is thought wise,
   another is talkative and is disliked.

5* One man is silent because he has nothing
   to say;
   another is silent, biding his time.

6 A wise man is silent till the right time comes,
   but a boasting fool ignores the proper time.

7 He who talks too much is detested;
   he who pretends to authority is hated.

8† Some misfortunes bring success;
   some things gained are a man's loss.

9† Some gifts do one no good,
   and some must be paid back double.

10 Humiliation can follow fame,
   while from obscurity a man can lift up
   his head.

11 A man may buy much for little,
   but pay for it seven times over.

12 A wise man makes himself popular by a
   few words,
   but fools pour forth their blandishments
   in vain.

13 A gift from a rogue will do you no good,

for in his eyes his one gift is equal to seven.

14 He gives little and criticizes often,
   and like a crier he shouts aloud.
   He lends today, he asks it back tomorrow;
   hateful indeed is such a man.

15 A fool has no friends,
   nor thanks for his generosity;

16 Those who eat his bread have an evil
   tongue.
   How many times they laugh him to scorn!

17† A fall to the ground is less sudden than a slip
   of the tongue;
   that is why the downfall of the wicked
   comes so quickly.

18 Insipid food is the untimely tale;
   the unruly are always ready to offer it.

19 A proverb when spoken by a fool
   is unwelcome,
   for he does not utter it at the proper time.

20 A man through want may be unable to sin,
   yet in this tranquility he cannot rest.

21 One may lose his life through shame,
   and perish through a fool's intimidation.

22 A man makes a promise to a friend out
   of shame,
   and has him for his enemy needlessly.

23 A lie is a foul blot in a man,
   yet it is constantly on the lips of the
   unruly.

24 Better a thief than an inveterate liar,
   yet both will suffer disgrace;

25 A liar's way leads to dishonor,
   his shame remains ever with him.

26† A wise man advances himself by his words,
   a prudent man pleases the great.

27 He who works his land has abundant
   crops,
   he who pleases the great is pardoned
   his faults.

28* Favors and gifts blind the eyes;
   like a muzzle over the mouth they
   silence reproof.

29 Hidden wisdom and unseen treasure—
   of what value is either?

30 Better the man who hides his folly
   than the one who hides his wisdom.

20, 1–7: Wisdom indicates the proper times for speech and silence, that is, the occasions when the most benefit can be gained from them.

20, 3: The sense is that violence or force against a person can prevent an external act of sin or compel a good deed without eliminating the internal sin or desire of wrongdoing. Cf Sir 20, 20.

20, 8–16: In a series of paradoxes the author indicates how much true and lasting values differ from apparent ones.

20, 9: *And some . . . double:* or perhaps, "but some are doubly precious."

20, 17–25: The ill-timed speech of the wicked, the unruly and a fool is repulsive (17ff); human respect exposes one to intimidation,

rash promises and enmity (21f); lies bring dishonor and lasting disgrace (23ff).

20, 26–30: Unlike the fool who invites disaster through misuse of his tongue, the sage through prudent speech gains in honor and esteem among the great (26f). He must beware, however, of accepting bribes, lest he share in evil through silence when he should reprove (28ff).

20, 5: Sir 20, 1; Prv 10, 19;   **20, 28:** Ex 23, 8; Dt 16, 19.
17, 28.

Sin Must Be Avoided†

21 ¹ My son, if you have sinned, do so
no more,
and for your past sins pray to be forgiven.

2   Flee from sin as from a serpent
that will bite you if you go near it;
Its teeth are lion's teeth,
destroying the souls of men.

3   Every offense is a two-edged sword;
when it cuts, there can be no healing.

4   Violence and arrogance wipe out wealth;
so too a proud man's home is destroyed.

5   Prayer from a poor man's lips is heard
at once,
and justice is quickly granted him.

6   He who hates correction walks the
sinner's path,
but he who fears the LORD repents in
his heart.

7   Widely known is the boastful speaker,
but the wise man knows his own faults.

8   He who builds his house with
another's money
is collecting stones for his funeral mound.

9* A band of criminals is like a bundle of tow;
they will end in a flaming fire.

10† The path of sinners is smooth stones
that end in the depths of the nether world.

The Wise and the Foolish Differ†

11 He who keeps the law controls his impulses;
he who is perfect in fear of the LORD
has wisdom.

12 He can never be taught who is not shrewd,
but one form of shrewdness is
thoroughly bitter.

13* A wise man's knowledge wells up in a flood,
and his counsel, like a living spring;

14 A fool's mind is like a broken jar—
no knowledge at all can it hold.

15 When an intelligent man hears words
of wisdom,
he approves them and adds to them;
The wanton hears them with scorn
and casts them behind his back.

16 A fool's chatter is like a load on a journey,
but there is charm to be found upon the
lips of the wise.

PRAY IT!

Examine Your Conscience

An examination of conscience is a moral inventory of one's life. When we examine our conscience, we can recognize those we have hurt, make amends where possible, and turn our life around before a pattern of sin becomes a major obstacle in our relationships with God and with others. We can also recognize the positive moral choices that we have made. Chapters 19–22 of Sirach list some of the sins from Ben Sira's time. Use them as a guide for making your own examination of conscience, as follows:

- Have you broken a confidence (19, 5–12)?
- Do you offend others with your language (20, 18–19)?
- Have you lied (20, 24–26)?
- Have you stolen from others (21, 8)?
- Have you been lazy in your use of time (22, 1–2)?
- Have you disobeyed your parents (22, 3–5)?

When you have finished this examination, read 22, 27—23, 6 as your own prayer for God's help against sinning.

▸ Sir 19, 5—23, 6

17 The views of a prudent man are sought in
an assembly,
and his words are considered with care.

18 Like a house in ruins is wisdom to a fool;
the stupid man knows it only as
inscrutable words.

19 Like fetters on the legs is learning to a fool,
like a manacle on his right hand.

20* A fool raises his voice in laughter,
but a prudent man at the most smiles gently.

21, 1–10: Under various figures the consequences of sin are described as destructive of wealth, and even of bodily life, and deserving of death and a place in the depths of the nether world (2ff.6a.8ff). Through prayer, forgiveness can be sought (1), and through fear of the Lord, repentance is achieved (1, 5.6b).

21, 10: *The path of sinners . . . nether world:* eternal retribution is not yet proposed in this reference. It became clearly revealed through the teaching of Christ; cf Mt 7, 13f; 25, 41–46; Lk 16, 19–31.

21, 11–28: The mind of the wise man is a fountain of knowledge (13.15); his will is trained to keep the law (11); his words are gra-

cious, valued, carefully weighed, sincere (16f.25f); his conduct is respectful, cultured and restrained (20.22ff). The fool's mind is devoid of knowledge and impenetrable to it (12.14.18f); his will rejects it (15); his talk is burdensome (16), his laughter unrestrained (20), his conversation shallow and meddlesome (25f); his conduct is bold and rude (22ff); his abuse of others redounds on himself (27f).

21, 9: Ps 21, 9.   21, 20: Eccl 7, 6.
21, 13: Prv 13, 14; 16, 22.

S
I
R

21 Like a chain of gold is learning to a wise man,
   like a bracelet on his right arm.

22* The fool steps boldly into a house,
   while the well-bred man remains outside;

23 A boor peeps through the doorway of a house,
   but a cultured man keeps his glance
      cast down.

24 It is rude for one to listen at a door;
   a cultured man would be overwhelmed by
      the disgrace of it.

25 The lips of the impious talk of what is not
      their concern,
   but the words of the prudent are
      carefully weighed.

26 Fools' thoughts are in their mouths,
   wise men's words are in their hearts.

27† When a godless man curses his adversary,
   he really curses himself.

28 A slanderer besmirches himself,
   and is hated by his neighbors.

On Laziness and Foolishness

22 ¹† The sluggard is like a stone in
         the mud;
      everyone hisses at his disgrace.

2 The sluggard is like a lump of dung;
   whoever touches him wipes his hands.

3* An unruly child is a disgrace to its father;
   if it be a daughter, she brings him
      to poverty.

4 A thoughtful daughter becomes a treasure to
      her husband,
   a shameless one is her father's grief.

5 A hussy shames her father and her husband;
   by both she is despised.

6† Like a song in time of mourning is
      inopportune talk,
   but lashes and discipline are at all
      times wisdom.

7* Teaching a fool is like gluing a broken pot,
   or like disturbing a man in the depths
      of sleep;

8 He talks with a slumberer who talks with
      a fool,

for when it is over, he will say, "What
      was that?"

9 Weep over the dead man, for his light has
      gone out;
   weep over the fool, for sense has left him.

10 Weep but a little over the dead man, for he is
      at rest;
   but worse than death is the life of a fool.

11* Seven days of mourning for the dead,
   but for the wicked fool a whole lifetime.

12 Speak but seldom with the stupid man,
   be not the companion of a brute;

13 Beware of him lest you have trouble
   and be spattered when he shakes himself;
   Turn away from him and you will find rest
   and not be wearied by his lack of sense.

14 What is heavier than lead,
   and what is its name but "Fool"?

15* Sand and salt and an iron mass
   are easier to bear than a stupid man.

16† Masonry bonded with wooden beams
   is not loosened by an earthquake;
   Neither is a resolve constructed with
      careful deliberation
   shaken in a moment of fear.

17 A resolve that is backed by prudent understanding
   is like the polished surface of a smooth wall.

18 Small stones lying on an open height
   will not remain when the wind blows;
   Neither can a timid resolve based on
      foolish plans
   withstand fear of any kind.

The Preservation of Friendship†

19 One who jabs the eye brings tears:
   he who pierces the heart bares its feelings.

20 He who throws stones at birds drives them away,
   and he who insults a friend breaks up
      the friendship.

21 Should you draw a sword against a friend,
   despair not, it can be undone.

22 Should you speak sharply to a friend,
   fear not, you can be reconciled.

---

† **21, 27:** *Adversary:* this can be understood in the sense that, if a man curses one who led him into sin, he implicitly curses himself for having yielded to the sin; or in the sense that the enemy is the man's own sinful nature; or even in the sense that the enemy is the devil, since the Hebrew word used here is satan. Cf 1 Chr 21, 1; Zec 3, 2; 2 Pt 2, 12f; Jude 9.
22, 1–15: To Sirach, a lazy person and an unruly child are a cause of shame and disgrace; everyone wishes to be rid of them (1–5). A wicked fool is as senseless as a man asleep or dead, but the grief he causes others lasts a lifetime (7–11). He is like a brute, troublesome and intolerable (12–15).
22, 6: *Like a song . . . is . . . talk:* some understand talk in the sense of a rebuke unheeded by the unruly as a joyful song is out of place among mourners. Corporal punishment, however, is always effective.

22, 16ff: A prudent mind firmly resolved is undisturbed by violent and conflicting thoughts, whereas a foolish person is tossed about by the winds of fear, like small stones whipped about by high winds.
22, 19–26: As disputes and violence weaken friendship, and disloyalty and abuse of confidence destroy it utterly (19–22.24.26), so kindness to a poor man in time of poverty and adversity builds up friendship and merits a share in his prosperity and inheritance (23.25).

21, 22: Prv 25, 17.   22, 11: Gn 50, 10.
22, 3: Prv 17, 21; 19, 13.   22, 15: Prv 27, 3.
22, 7–11: Prv 23, 9.

But a contemptuous insult, a
confidence broken,
or a treacherous attack will drive away
any friend.

23 Make fast friends with a man while he is poor;
thus will you enjoy his prosperity with him.
In time of trouble remain true to him,
so as to share in his inheritance when
it comes.

24 Before flames burst forth an oven smokes;
so does abuse come before bloodshed.

25 From a friend in need of support
no one need hide in shame;

26 But from him who brings harm to his friend
all will stand aloof who hear of it.

Prayer†

27* Who will set a guard over my mouth,
and upon my lips an effective seal,
That I may not fail through them,
that my tongue may not destroy me?

23 1† LORD, Father and Master of my life,
permit me not to fall by them!

2 Who will apply the lash to my thoughts,
to my mind the rod of discipline,
That my failings may not be spared,
nor the sins of my heart overlooked;

3 Lest my failings increase,
and my sins be multiplied;
Lest I succumb to my foes,
and my enemy rejoice over me?

4 LORD, Father and God of my life,
abandon me not into their control!

5 A brazen look allow me not;
ward off passion from my heart,

6 Let not the lustful cravings of the flesh
master me,
surrender me not to shameless desires.

The Proper Use of the Tongue†

7 Give heed, my children, to the instruction that
I pronounce,
for he who keeps it will not be enslaved.

8 Through his lips is the sinner ensnared;
the railer and the arrogant man fall thereby.

9* Let not your mouth form the habit
of swearing,
or becoming too familiar with the
Holy Name.

10† Just as a slave that is constantly
under scrutiny
will not be without welts,
So one who swears continually by the
Holy Name
will not remain free from sin.

11* A man who often swears heaps
up obligations;
the scourge will never be far from
his house.
If he swears in error, he incurs guilt;
if he neglects his obligation, his sin is
doubly great.
If he swears without reason he cannot be
found just,
and all his house will suffer affliction.

12 There are words which merit death;
may they never be heard among
Jacob's heirs.
For all such words are foreign to the devout,
who do not wallow in sin.

13 Let not your mouth become used to
coarse talk,
for in it lies sinful matter.

14* Keep your father and mother in mind
when you sit among the mighty,
Lest in their presence you commit a blunder
and disgrace your upbringing,
By wishing you had never been born
or cursing the day of your birth.

15 A man who has the habit of abusive language
will never mature in character as long as
he lives.

Sins of the Flesh†

16 Two types of men multiply sins,
a third† draws down wrath;
For burning passion is a blazing fire,
not to be quenched till it burns itself out:

22, 27—23, 6: The sage implores the divine assistance to preserve him through stern discipline from sins of the tongue (22, 27;
23, 1); ignorance of mind and weakness of will (2f); and inclinations
of the senses and the flesh, lest he fall into the hands of his enemies,
or become a prey of shameful desires (3–6).

23, 1: *LORD, Father and Master of my life:* these words express the
tender personal relationship between the author's soul and God, the
need of his assistance, and the truth of his providence.

23, 7–15: A warning against sins of the tongue through misuse of
the Holy Name, thoughtless swearing which involves obligation and
incurs guilt (7–11), blasphemy (12), talk that is coarse and blunder-
some (13f), and the incorrigible habit of abusive language (15).

23, 10: *As a slave . . . under scrutiny,* so is he who calls on God
to witness the truth of what he says.

23, 16–27: From sins of the tongue the author proceeds to treat
of sins of the flesh and their dire consequences. The passion of lust
tyrannizes over its victims and, like fire, consumes and utterly destroys them (16f.22–26). The false security of the adulterer serves but
to aggravate his inevitable fate (18–21). Only the fear of the Lord and
observance of his commandments can assure moral safety (27).

23, 16: *Two types . . . a third:* three kinds of sins of impurity, with
increasing degrees of gravity: solitary sins (16), fornication (17) and
adultery (18–21).

22, 27: Ps 141, 3.
23, 9: Ex 20, 7; Lv 19, 12; Dt
5, 11; Mt 5, 33ff.
23, 11: Lv 5, 4ff.
23, 14: Sir 7, 27; Ex 20, 12; Dt
5, 16.

Four-Letter Words

LIVE IT!

Four-letter words. You've heard them plenty. You have undoubtedly used them yourself. They roll off the tongue so easily. They get attention. They help you fit in with some groups of people.

You might wonder, So, what's the problem with foul language? Why does Ben Sira call it "sinful matter" (Sir 23, 13)? Well, part of the problem is that using it easily becomes a habit. You become less aware of when you are using it. You can get yourself into trouble. Ben Sira warns that you may "commit a blunder and disgrace your upbringing" (verse 14).

Maybe the worst part of the problem is that frequent use of foul language shows a lack of respect and reverence for others and certainly for God's name. Ben Sira reminds us, "For all such words are foreign to the devout" (verse 12).

Certainly, in a language with over six hundred thousand words, there are more creative ways to express emotion or frustration than relying on those all-too-familiar four-letter words. If you've developed the habit of using them, ask God and your friends to help you stop.

▶ Sir 23, 12–15

A man given to sins of the flesh,
  who never stops until the fire breaks forth;
17* The rake to whom all bread is sweet
  and who is never through till he dies;
18* And the man who dishonors his marriage
  bed
  and says to himself, "Who can see me?
Darkness surrounds me, walls hide me;
  no one sees me; why should I fear to sin?"
Of the Most High he is not mindful,
19 fearing only the eyes of men;
He does not understand that the eyes of
  the LORD,
  ten thousand times brighter than the sun,
Observe every step a man takes
  and peer into hidden corners.
20 He who knows all things before they exist
  still knows them all after they are made.
21*† Such a man will be punished in the streets of
  the city;
  when he least expects it, he will be
  apprehended.

22 So also with the woman who is unfaithful to
  her husband
  and offers as heir her son by a stranger.

23† First, she has disobeyed the law of the
  Most High;
  secondly, she has wronged her husband;
Thirdly, in her wanton adultery
  she has borne children by another man.
24† Such a woman will be dragged before
  the assembly,
  and her punishment will extend to
  her children;
25 Her children will not take root;
  her branches will not bring forth fruit.
26 She will leave an accursed memory;
  her disgrace will never be blotted out.
27* Thus all who dwell on the earth shall know,
  and all who inhabit the world
  shall understand,
That nothing is better than the fear of the LORD,
  nothing more salutary than to obey
  his commandments.

Praise of Wisdom

24 ¹† Wisdom sings her own praises,
  before her own people she proclaims
  her glory;
² In the assembly of the Most High she opens
  her mouth,

23, 21: Cf Lv 20, 19; Dt 22, 22.
23, 23: The detailed evil of adultery includes disobedience to God's law (Ex 20, 14), injustice to a partner in marriage, and disgraceful offspring.
23, 24f: The judgment of the assembly determined the illegitimacy of children born of adultery or incest and excluded them from the "community of the LORD" (Dt 23, 3). Cf Wis 3, 16–19; 4, 3–6.
24, 1–27: In this chapter Wisdom speaks in the first person, describing her origin, her dwelling place in Israel, and the reward she gives her followers. As in Prv 8, Wisdom is described as a being who

comes from God and is distinct from him. While we do not say with certainty that this description applies to a personal being, it does foreshadow the beautiful doctrine of the Word of God later developed in St. John's Gospel (Jn 1, 1–14). In the liturgy this chapter is applied to the Blessed Virgin because of her constant and intimate association with Christ, the Incarnate Wisdom.

23, 17: Prv 9, 17.   23, 27: Sir 1, 10–18.24;
23, 18: Is 29, 15.   Prv 3, 1f.
23, 21f: Lv 20, 10; Dt 22, 21.

S
I
R

in the presence of his hosts she declares
  her worth:
3* "From the mouth of the Most High I came
  forth,
  and mistlike covered the earth.
4 In the highest heavens did I dwell,
  my throne on a pillar of cloud.
5 The vault of heaven I compassed alone,
  through the deep abyss I wandered.
6 Over waves of the sea, over all the land,
  over every people and nation I held sway.
7 Among all these I sought a resting place;
  in whose inheritance should I abide?

8 "Then the Creator of all gave me
  his command,
  and he who formed me chose the spot for
  my tent,
  Saying, 'In Jacob make your dwelling,
  in Israel your inheritance.'
9 Before all ages, in the beginning, he
  created me,
  and through all ages I shall not cease to be.
10 In the holy tent I ministered before him,
  and in Zion I fixed my abode.
11 Thus in the chosen city he has given me rest,
  in Jerusalem is my domain.
12 I have struck root among the glorious people,
  in the portion of the LORD, his heritage.

13 "Like a cedar on Lebanon I am raised aloft,
  like a cypress on Mount Hermon,
14 Like a palm tree in Engedi,
  like a rosebush in Jericho,
  Like a fair olive tree in the field,
  like a plane tree growing beside the water.
15*†Like cinnamon, or fragrant balm, or
  precious myrrh,
  I give forth perfume;
  Like galbanum and onycha and sweet spices,
  like the odor of incense in the holy place.
16 I spread out my branches like a terebinth,
  my branches so bright and so graceful.
17 I bud forth delights like the vine,
  my blossoms become fruit fair and rich.
18† Come to me, all you that yearn for me,
  and be filled with my fruits;

19 You will remember me as sweeter than honey,
  better to have than the honeycomb.
20*†He who eats of me will hunger still,
  he who drinks of me will thirst for more;
21 He who obeys me will not be put to shame,
  he who serves me will never fail."

22*†All this is true of the book of the Most
  High's covenant,
  the law which Moses commanded us
  as an inheritance for the community
  of Jacob.
23* It overflows, like the Pishon, with wisdom—
  like the Tigris in the days of the new fruits.
24 It runs over, like the Euphrates,
  with understanding,
  like the Jordan at harvest time.
25† It sparkles like the Nile with knowledge,
  like the Gihon at vintage time.
26 The first man never finished
  comprehending wisdom,
  nor will the last succeed in fathoming her.
27 For deeper than the sea are her thoughts;
  her counsels, than the great abyss.

28† Now I, like a rivulet from her stream,
  channeling the waters into a garden,
29 Said to myself, "I will water my plants,
  my flower bed I will drench";
  And suddenly this rivulet of mine became
  a river,
  then this stream of mine, a sea.
30 Thus do I send my teachings forth shining like
  the dawn,
  to become known afar off.
31 Thus do I pour out instruction like prophecy
  and bestow it on generations to come.

Those Who Are Worthy of Praise†

25 ¹With three things I am delighted,
  for they are pleasing to the LORD and
  to men:
  Harmony among brethren, friendship
  among neighbors,
  and the mutual love of husband and wife.
2 Three kinds of men I hate;
  their manner of life I loathe indeed:

---

†
24, 15: These substances were associated with worship, being mentioned in Ex 30, 22f.34 as the ingredients of the anointing oil and the sacred incense. Israel was a priestly nation.
24, 18: Compare the words of the Savior in Mt 11, 28ff.
24, 20: So pleasing is wisdom to man that, far from being satiated, he will always desire more.
24, 22: Here the author begins to speak once more, Wisdom having ended her discourse in the preceding verse. Wisdom and the law of Moses are now identified.
24, 25: Gihon: understood by some to have been a name for the Nile; cf Gn 2, 13.

24, 28–31: Spoken by the author. He had at first drawn a small portion of the water of wisdom for his own private benefit, but finding it so useful, he soon began to let others share in this boon by teaching them the lessons of wisdom.
25, 1–11: While praising brotherly love, love of neighbor, and conjugal love, the sage condemns their opposites in the arrogant pauper who despises his brother, the fraudulent rich man who cheats

---

24, 3ff: Sir 1, 1; Prv 2, 6; 8,   24, 20: Is 55, 1; Jn 6, 35.
  22–36; Wis 7, 24f.   24, 22: Ex 24, 7.
24, 15: Ex 30, 22–25.   24, 23ff: Gn 2, 11–14.

A proud pauper, a rich dissembler,
   and an old man lecherous in his dotage.

3 What you have not saved in your youth,
   how will you acquire in your old age?

4 How becoming to the gray-haired
     is judgment,
   and a knowledge of counsel to those on
     in years!

5 How becoming to the aged is wisdom,
   understanding and prudence to
     the venerable!

6 The crown of old men is wide experience;
   their glory, the fear of the LORD.

7 There are nine who come to my mind
     as blessed,
   a tenth whom my tongue proclaims:
The man who finds joy in his children,
   and he who lives to see his
     enemies' downfall.

8† Happy is he who dwells with a sensible wife,
   and he who plows not like a donkey yoked
     with an ox.
Happy is he who sins not with his tongue,
   and he who serves not his inferior.

9 Happy is he who finds a friend
   and he who speaks to attentive ears.

10 He who finds wisdom is great indeed,
   but not greater than he who fears the LORD.

11 Fear of the LORD surpasses all else,
   its possessor is beyond compare.

Wicked and Virtuous Women†

12 Worst of all wounds is that of the heart,
   worst of all evils is that of a woman.

13 Worst of all sufferings is that from one's foes,
   worst of all vengeance is that of
     one's enemies:

14 No poison worse than that of a serpent,
   no venom greater than that of a woman.

15 With a dragon or a lion I would rather dwell
   than live with an evil woman.

16 Wickedness changes a woman's looks,

   and makes her sullen as a female bear.

17 When her husband sits among his neighbors,
   a bitter sigh escapes him unawares.

18 There is scarce any evil like that in a woman;
   may she fall to the lot of the sinner!

19 Like a sandy hill to aged feet
   is a railing wife to a quiet man.

20 Stumble not through woman's beauty,
   nor be greedy for her wealth;

21 The man is a slave, in disgrace and shame,
   when a wife supports her husband.

22 Depressed mind, saddened face,
   broken heart—this from an evil wife.
Feeble hands and quaking knees—
   from a wife who brings no happiness to
     her husband.

23† In woman was sin's beginning,
   and because of her we all die.

24 Allow water no outlet,
   and be not indulgent to an erring wife.

25 If she walks not by your side,
   cut her away from you.

26

1*† Happy the husband of a good wife,
   twice-lengthened are his days;

2† A worthy wife brings joy to her husband,
   peaceful and full is his life.

3* A good wife is a generous gift
   bestowed upon him who fears the LORD;

4 Be he rich or poor, his heart is content,
   and a smile is ever on his face.

5 There are three things at which my
     heart quakes,
   a fourth before which I quail:
Though false charges in public, trial before all
     the people,
   and lying testimony are harder to bear
     than death,

6† A jealous wife is heartache and mourning
   and a scourging tongue like the other three.

7 A bad wife is a chafing yoke;
   he who marries her seizes a scorpion.

---

his neighbor, and the lecherous old man unfaithful to his wife (1f).
This last, sensual from his youth, lacks the mature blessings of judgment and wisdom in old age (3–6), and the joy of a peaceful household, where honesty and dignity, friendship, wisdom and fear of God
prevail (7–11).

25, 8: *Like a donkey yoked with an ox:* incompatibility between
husband and wife.

25, 12–25: Wickedness in a woman is most grievous, painful and
bitter to her husband. Through it she becomes vengeful, dangerous
and intolerable, jealous, talkative, intemperate and unchaste. Even
her very appearance is changed (12–17). The worst of all evils, a
source of grief, a snare and a disgrace to her husband, she depresses his mind, saddens and breaks his heart, destroys his strength
(18–22). She must not be indulged but made obedient or punished (24f).

25, 23: According to the account in Gn 3, to which Ben Sirach

refers, sin, the cause of death, originated in woman: Eve, the first
human being to sin, induced Adam to follow her example. But it is
through Adam, as head of the race, that original sin and its punishment of spiritual death are presented by St. Paul (Rom 5) as having
entered the world, to become the occasion for the redemptive work
of Christ our Lord.

26, 1–4.13–18: A good wife is as a gift from God, bringing joy
and peace, happiness and contentment to her husband (1–4) through
her thoughtfulness, reserve, modesty and chastity, beauty, grace and
virtue (13–18).

26, 2: *Worthy:* gifted spiritually, mentally and physically. Cf Prv
31, 10.

26, 6–12: A repetition of the thought expressed in Sir 25, 12–25.

26, 1: Sir 25, 8; Prv 18, 22;   26, 3: Sir 36, 24.
   31, 10ff.

8 A drunken wife arouses great anger,
      for she does not hide her shame.

9 By her eyelids and her haughty stare
      an unchaste wife can be recognized.

10* Keep a strict watch over an unruly wife,
      lest, finding an opportunity, she make use
         of it;

11 Follow close if her eyes are bold,
      and be not surprised if she betrays you:

12 As a thirsty traveler with eager mouth
      drinks from any water that he finds,
   So she settles down before every tent peg
      and opens her quiver for every arrow.

13 A gracious wife delights her husband,
      her thoughtfulness puts flesh on his bones;

14 A gift from the LORD is her governed speech,
      and her firm virtue is of surpassing worth.

15 Choicest of blessings is a modest wife,
      priceless her chaste person.

16 Like the sun rising in the LORD's heavens,
      the beauty of a virtuous wife is the radiance
         of her home.

17† Like the light which shines above the
         holy lampstand,
      are her beauty of face and graceful figure.

18† Golden columns on silver bases
      are her shapely limbs and steady feet.

Dangers to Integrity and Friendship

19* These two bring grief to my heart,
      and the third arouses my horror:
   A wealthy man reduced to want;
      illustrious men held in contempt;
   And the man who passes from justice to sin,
      for whom the LORD makes ready the
         sword.

20† A merchant can hardly remain upright,
      nor a shopkeeper free from sin;

27 1* For the sake of profit many sin,
      and the struggle for wealth blinds
         the eyes.

2 Like a peg driven between fitted stones,
      between buying and selling sin is
         wedged in.

3 Unless you earnestly hold fast to the fear of
         the LORD,
      suddenly your house will be thrown down.

4 When a sieve is shaken, the husks appear;
      so do a man's faults when he speaks.

5* As the test of what the potter molds is in
         the furnace,
      so in his conversation is the test of a man.

6* The fruit of a tree shows the care it has had;
      so too does a man's speech disclose the
         bent of his mind.

7 Praise no man before he speaks,
      for it is then that men are tested.

8 If you strive after justice you will attain it,
      and put it on like a splendid robe.

9 Birds nest with their own kind,
      and fidelity comes to those who live by it.

10 As a lion crouches in wait for prey,
      so do sins for evildoers.

11 Ever wise are the discourses of the devout,
      but the godless man, like the moon,
         is inconstant.

12 Limit the time you spend among fools,
      but frequent the company of
         thoughtful men.

13 The conversation of the wicked is offensive,
      their laughter is wanton guilt.

14 Their oath-filled talk makes the hair stand
         on end,
      their brawls make one stop one's ears.

15* Wrangling among the haughty ends
         in bloodshed,
      their cursing is painful to hear.

16*†He who betrays a secret cannot be trusted,
      he will never find an intimate friend.

17 Cherish your friend, keep faith with him;
      but if you betray his confidence, follow
         him not;

18 For as an enemy might kill a man,
      you have killed your neighbor's friendship.

26, 17f: The holy lampstand and the golden columns stood in the holy place of the ancient Tabernacle (Ex 25, 31–40; 26, 32).

26, 18: Among the additions found here in some manuscripts are the following lines:

"My son, take care in the prime of life
   not to surrender your strength to strangers;
Single out from the land a goodly field
   and there with confidence sow the seed of your increase;
So shall you have your offspring around you,
   and in confidence shall they grow up.

"Though a woman for hire be thought of as a trifle,
   a married woman is a deadly snare for those who embrace her.
      [Cf Prv 6, 26.]

"A wife's complaint should be made in meekness,
   and show itself in a slight flush;
But a loud-mouthed, scolding wife
   is a trumpet signaling for battle;
Any human being who answers that challenge
   will spend his life amid the turbulence of war."

26, 20—27, 15: From proper conduct in family life, the author proceeds to social morality, warning especially against injustice in commerce (26, 20—27, 3), and perversity of speech in business (4–7). The pursuit of justice in these matters is all the more meritorious as it is difficult (8ff). The discourses of the devout are marked with wisdom, but the conversations of the wicked, with offense, swearing, cursing, quarrels and even bloodshed (11–15).

27, 16—28, 11: Betrayal of confidence through indiscretion destroys friendship and does irreparable harm (16–21); cf Sir 22, 22. False friendship based on hypocrisy and deceit is hateful to God and man (22ff); it soon becomes a victim of its own treachery (25ff). The same fate awaits the malicious and vengeful (27, 28—28, 1). They can obtain mercy and forgiveness only by first forgiving their neighbor, being mindful of death and of the commandments of the

26, 10: Sir 42, 11.
26, 19: Ez 18, 24ff.
27, 1: Sir 7, 18; 31, 6; Prv
      30, 8f.
27, 5: 1 Pt 1, 7.
27, 6: Mt 7, 20.
27, 15: Sir 23, 9–15.
27, 16: Prv 11, 13; 20, 19.

S
I
R

19 Like a bird released from the hand,
   you have let your friend go and cannot
   recapture him;

20 Follow him not, for he is far away,
   he has fled like a gazelle from the trap.

21* A wound can be bound up, and an
   insult forgiven,
   but he who betrays secrets does
   hopeless damage.

Malice, Anger and Vengeance

22 He who has shifty eyes plots mischief
   and no one can ward him off;

23* In your presence he uses honeyed talk,
   and admires your every word,
   But later he changes his tone
   and twists your words to your ruin.

24* There is nothing that I hate so much,
   and the LORD hates him as well.

25* As a stone falls back on him who throws
   it up,
   so a blow struck in treachery injures more
   than one.

26 As he who digs a pit falls into it,
   and he who lays a snare is caught in it,

27 Whoever does harm will be involved in it
   without knowing how it came upon him.

28 Mockery and abuse will be the lot of
   the proud,
   and vengeance lies in wait for them like
   a lion.

29 The trap seizes those who rejoice in pitfalls,
   and pain will consume them before
   they die;

30 Wrath and anger are hateful things,
   yet the sinner hugs them tight.

28

1* The vengeful will suffer the LORD'S
   vengeance,
   for he remembers their sins in detail.

2* Forgive your neighbor's injustice;
   then when you pray, your own sins will
   be forgiven.

3* Should a man nourish anger against
   his fellows
   and expect healing from the LORD?

4 Should a man refuse mercy to his fellows,
   yet seek pardon for his own sins?

5 If he who is but flesh cherishes wrath,
   who will forgive his sins?

6* Remember your last days, set enmity aside;
   remember death and decay, and cease
   from sin!

7 Think of the commandments, hate not
   your neighbor;
   of the Most High's covenant, and
   overlook faults.

8 Avoid strife and your sins will be fewer,
   for a quarrelsome man kindles disputes,

9* Commits the sin of disrupting friendship
   and sows discord among those at peace.

10* The more wood, the greater the fire,
   the more underlying it, the fiercer the fight;
   The greater a man's strength, the sterner
   his anger,
   the greater his power, the greater his wrath.

11 Pitch and resin make fires flare up,
   and insistent quarrels provoke bloodshed.

The Evil Tongue†

12 If you blow upon a spark, it quickens
   into flame,
   if you spit on it, it dies out;
   yet both you do with your mouth!

13* Cursed be gossips and the double-tongued,
   for they destroy the peace of many.

14 A meddlesome tongue subverts many,
   and makes them refugees among the peoples;
   It destroys walled cities,
   and overthrows powerful dynasties.

15 A meddlesome tongue can drive virtuous
   women from their homes
   and rob them of the fruit of their toil;

16 Whoever heeds it has no rest,
   nor can he dwell in peace.

17 A blow from a whip raises a welt,
   but a blow from the tongue smashes bones;

18* Many have fallen by the edge of the sword,
   but not as many as by the tongue.

19 Happy he who is sheltered from it,
   and has not endured its wrath;
   Who has not borne its yoke
   nor been fettered with its chains;

20 For its yoke is a yoke of iron
   and its chains are chains of bronze!

---

† Most High (28, 2–7). And they must avoid quarrels and strife
(8–11).

28, 12–26: Further treatment of sins of the tongue and their havoc; cf Sir 5, 12—6, 1; 19, 5–16; 20, 17–25; 23, 7–15. Gossips and
the double-tongue destroy domestic peace (12–16). The whip, the
sword, chains, even the nether world, are not so cruel as the suffering inflicted by an evil tongue (17–21). Not the just but those who
forsake the Lord are victims of their evil tongues (22f). Therefore,

guard your mouth and tongue as you would guard treasure against
an enemy (24ff).

27, 21: Sir 22, 20.   28, 2: Mt 6, 14.
27, 23: Prv 26, 24ff.   28, 3: Mt 18, 23ff.
27, 24: Prv 6, 13.16.   28, 6: Sir 7, 36; 38, 20.
27, 25f: Ps 7, 16f; Prv 26, 27;   28, 9: Prv 15, 18.
   Eccl 10, 8.   28, 10ff: Prv 26, 20f.
28, 1: Dt 32, 35; Rom   28, 13: Sir 5, 16f.
   12, 19.   28, 18: Jas 3, 5ff.

Just Walk Away

"Hey, did you hear the latest about Valerie?"
"No, what?"
"Well, last Friday night, she and Maria were at Jason's party, and—"
"Wait a minute, here comes Maria. Tell me later."

Cursed be gossips and the double-tongued,
 for they destroy the peace of many.
    (Sir 28, 13)

"Guess what I heard!"
"What?"
"Well, Teresa, who is usually so stuck-up—"
"I know. I can't stand her. She thinks she's so cool."
"Well, anyway, she went to this party and . . ."

Whoever heeds it has no rest,
 nor can he dwell in peace.
    (Verse 16)

"I can't believe what I just heard!"
"What? Tell me!"
"I heard that Juan and Sunyub went out last night, got totally trashed, and spent the night together."
"Are you kidding? Sunyub, little miss honor student? And Juan, athlete of the year? Are you sure?"
"I know. I can't believe it either, but I heard it from two different people . . ."

Many have fallen by the edge of the sword,
 but not as many as by the tongue.
    (Verse 18)

If you blow upon a spark, it quickens into flame,
 if you spit on it, it dies out;
  yet both you do with your mouth!
    (Verse 12)

The next time you hear a piece of gossip or a rumor, don't blow on it—spit on it and walk away. Someone's reputation is at stake. One of these times, it could be yours. Check out the third chapter of James in the New Testament for another version of the hazards of gossip and slander.

▶ Sir 28, 12–18

21 Dire is the death it inflicts,
 besides which even the nether world is
  a gain;
22 It will not take hold among the just
 nor scorch them in its flame,
23 But those who forsake the LORD will fall
  victims to it,
 as it burns among them
  unquenchably!
It will hurl itself against them like a lion;

 like a panther, it will tear them
  to pieces.
24* As you hedge round your vineyard
  with thorns,
 set barred doors over your mouth;
25 As you seal up your silver and gold,
 so balance and weigh your words.
26 Take care not to slip by your tongue
 and fall victim to your foe waiting
  in ambush.

28, 24: Sir 22, 27; Ps 141, 3.

Loans, Alms and Surety†

29 1* He does a kindness who lends to
his neighbor,
and he fulfills the precepts who holds out a
helping hand.

2* Lend to your neighbor in his hour of need,
and pay back your neighbor when a loan
falls due;

3 Keep your promise, be honest with him,
and you will always come by what
you need.

4 Many a man who asks for a loan
adds to the burdens of those who
help him;

5 When he borrows, he kisses the lender's hand
and speaks with respect of his
creditor's wealth;
But when payment is due he
disappoints him
and says he is helpless to meet the claim.

6 If the lender is able to recover barely half,
he considers this an achievement;
If not, he is cheated of his wealth
and acquires an enemy at no extra charge;
With curses and insults the borrower pays
him back,
with abuse instead of honor.

7 Many refuse to lend, not out of meanness,
but from fear of being cheated.

8 To a poor man, however, be generous;
keep him not waiting for your alms;

9* Because of the precept, help the needy,
and in their want, do not send them away
empty-handed.

10 Spend your money for your brother
and friend,
and hide it not under a stone to perish;

11* Dispose of your treasure as the Most
High commands,
for that will profit you more than
the gold.

12 Store up almsgiving in your treasure house,
and it will save you from every evil;

13 Better than a stout shield and a sturdy spear
it will fight for you against the foe.

14* A good man goes surety for his neighbor,
and only the shameless would play
him false;

15 Forget not the kindness of your backer,
for he offers his very life for you.

16 The wicked turn a pledge on their behalf
into misfortune,
and the ingrate abandons his protector;

17* Going surety has ruined many
prosperous men
and tossed them about like waves of
the sea,

18 Has exiled men of prominence
and sent them wandering through
foreign lands.

19 The sinner through surety comes to grief,
and he who undertakes too much falls
into lawsuits.

20 Go surety for your neighbor according to
your means,
but take care lest you fall thereby.

Frugality and Its Rewards†

21* Life's prime needs are water, bread,
and clothing,
a house, too, for decent privacy.

22* Better a poor man's fare under the shadow of
one's own roof
than sumptuous banquets among strangers.

23 Be it little or much, be content with what
you have,
and pay no heed to him who would
disparage your home;

24 A miserable life it is to go from house
to house,
for as a guest you dare not open
your mouth.

25 The visitor has no thanks for filling
the cups;
besides, you will hear these bitter words:

26 "Come here, stranger, set the table,
give me to eat the food you have!

27 Away, stranger, for one more worthy;
for my brother's visit I need the room!"

28 Painful things to a sensitive man
are abuse at home and insults from
his creditors.

---

† **29, 1–20:** Some practical maxims concerning the use of wealth.
Give to a poor man (8f), lend to a needy neighbor, but repay when
a loan falls due lest the lender's burden be increased (1–5) and his
kindness abused (6f); through charity build up defense against evil
(10–13). Go surety for your neighbor according to your means, but
take care (20) not to fall, for the shameless play false and bring their
protectors and themselves to misfortune and ruin (14–19).
29, 21–28: The man who provides his own basic needs of food,
clothing and dwelling, and is content with what he has, preserves

his freedom and self-respect (21ff). But if he lives as a guest, even
among the rich, he exposes himself to insult and abuse (24–28).

29, 1: Dt 15, 8; Ps 112, 5;   29, 11: Sir 17, 17; Tb 4, 7ff.
   Prv 19, 17.   29, 14: Sir 8, 13.
29, 2: Ex 22, 24ff; Lv 25, 36;   29, 17: Prv 6, 1f; 11, 15.
   Mt 5, 42.   29, 21: Sir 39, 26.
29, 9: Sir 4, 1ff; Lv 19, 9f; 23,   29, 22: Sir 40, 29.
   22; Dt 15, 8.

S
I
R

The Training of Children†

30 1* He who loves his son chastises
            him often,
that he may be his joy when he grows up.
2   He who disciplines his son will benefit
            from him,
      and boast of him among his intimates.
3   He who educates his son makes his
            enemy jealous,
      and shows his delight in him among
            his friends.
4   At the father's death, he will seem not dead,
      since he leaves after him one
            like himself,
5   Whom he looks upon through life with joy,
      and even in death, without regret:
6   The avenger he leaves against his foes,
      and the one to repay his friends
            with kindness.

7   He who spoils his son will have wounds
            to bandage,
      and will quake inwardly at every outcry.
8   A colt untamed turns out stubborn;
      a son left to himself grows up unruly.
9   Pamper your child and he will be a terror
            for you,
      indulge him and he will bring you grief.
10   Share not in his frivolity lest you share in
            his sorrow,
      when finally your teeth are clenched
            in remorse.
11   Give him not his own way in his youth,
      and close not your eyes to his follies.
12* Bend him to the yoke when he is young,
      thrash his sides while he is still small,
      Lest he become stubborn, disobey you,
      and leave you disconsolate.
13   Discipline your son, make heavy his yoke,
      lest his folly humiliate you.

Health of Soul and Body†

14   Better a poor man strong and robust,
      than a rich man with wasted frame.

15   More precious than gold is health and
            well-being,
      contentment of spirit than coral.
16   No treasure greater than a healthy body;
      no happiness, than a joyful heart!
17*†Preferable is death to a bitter life,
      unending sleep to constant illness.
18* Dainties set before one who cannot eat
      are like the offerings placed before a tomb.
19   What good is an offering to an idol
      that can neither taste nor smell?
20   So it is with the afflicted man
      who groans at the good things his
            eyes behold!

21* Do not give in to sadness,
      torment not yourself with brooding;
22   Gladness of heart is the very life of man,
      cheerfulness prolongs his days.
23* Distract yourself, renew your courage,
      drive resentment far away from you;
      For worry has brought death to many,
      nor is there aught to be gained
            from resentment.
24   Envy and anger shorten one's life,
      worry brings on premature old age.
25* One who is cheerful and gay while at table
      benefits from his food.

The Proper Attitude toward Riches†

31 1 Keeping watch over riches wastes
            the flesh,
      and the care of wealth drives away rest.
2†   Concern for one's livelihood
            banishes slumber;
      more than a serious illness it
            disturbs repose.
3   The rich man labors to pile up wealth,
      and his only rest is wanton pleasure;
4   The poor man toils for a meager subsistence,
      and if ever he rests, he finds himself
            in want.
5   The lover of gold will not be free from sin,
      for he who pursues wealth is led astray by it.

---

† **30, 1–13:** Sound discipline and careful education of children correct frivolity and stubbornness, prevent remorse and humiliation, and bring to parents lasting joy and delight, prestige among friends, jealousy of enemies, perpetuation and vindication of themselves through their offspring (1–6). Lack of discipline and overindulgence of children bring sorrow and disappointment, terror and grief (7–13).

30, 14–25: Health of mind and body and joy of heart are judged more precious than wealth (14ff); bitterness, constant illness and affliction more difficult to bear than death (17–20). Sadness, resentment, anxiety, envy and anger shorten . . . life; they should be dispelled by cheerfulness and gladness of heart, which help to prolong one's days (21–25).

30, 17: *Preferable is death . . . constant illness:* the true value of human suffering was revealed through the passion and death of Christ. It serves as reparation for sin, and when united with Christ's suffering, as merit for eternal life.

31, 1–11: Solicitude for acquiring wealth and anxiety over preserving it disturb repose and easily lead to sin and ruin (1–7). Cf Mt 6, 25–34. A rich man who has not sinned or been seduced by wealth is worthy of praise (8–11).

31, 2: The Hebrew adds a verse that seems out of place here: "A faithful comrade drives away reproach, and the friend who keeps secrets is as dear as life."

30, 1: Prv 13, 24; 23, 13; 29,
      15; Heb 12, 7.
30, 12: Sir 7, 23.
30, 17: Sir 41, 2.
30, 18: Tb 4, 17.

30, 21: Sir 38, 20; Prv 12, 25;
      15, 13; 17, 22.
30, 23: Sir 38, 18f.
30, 25: Prv 15, 15.

6* Many have been ensnared by gold,
    though destruction lay before their eyes;
7 It is a stumbling block to those who are avid
    for it,
    a snare for every fool.

8*†Happy the rich man found without fault,
    who turns not aside after gain!
9 Who is he, that we may praise him?
    he, of all his kindred, has done wonders,
10 For he has been tested by gold and come
    off safe,
    and this remains his glory;
   He could have sinned but did not,
    could have done evil but would not,
11* So that his possessions are secure,
    and the assembly recounts his praises.

Table Etiquette†

12 If you are dining with a great man,
    bring not a greedy gullet to his table,
   Nor cry out, "How much food there is here!"
13* Remember that gluttony is evil.
   No creature is greedier than the eye:
    therefore it weeps for any cause.
15 Recognize that your neighbor feels as
    you do,
    and keep in mind your own dislikes:
14 Toward what he eyes, do not put out a hand;
    nor reach when he does for the same dish.
16 Behave at table like a favored guest,
    and be not greedy, lest you be despised.
17* Be the first to stop, as befits good manners;
    gorge not yourself, lest you give offense.
18 If there are many with you at table,
    be not the first to reach out your hand.
19* Does not a little suffice for a well-bred man?
    When he lies down, it is without
    discomfort.
20 Distress and anguish and loss of sleep,
    and restless tossing for the glutton!
   Moderate eating ensures sound slumber
    and a clear mind next day on rising.
21† If perforce you have eaten too much,
    once you have emptied your stomach, you
    will have relief.
22 Listen to me, my son, and scorn me not;

later you will find my advice good.
   In whatever you do, be moderate,
    and no sickness will befall you.
23* On a man generous with food, blessings
    are invoked,
    and this testimony to his goodness
    is lasting;
24 He who is miserly with food is denounced
    in public,
    and this testimony to his stinginess
    is lasting.
25 Let not wine-drinking be the proof of
    your strength,
    for wine has been the ruin of many.
26 As the furnace probes the work of the smith,
    so does wine the hearts of the insolent.
27* Wine is very life to man
    if taken in moderation.
   Does he really live who lacks the wine
    which was created for his joy?
28 Joy of heart, good cheer and merriment
    are wine drunk freely at the proper time.
29 Headache, bitterness and disgrace
    is wine drunk amid anger and strife.
30 More and more wine is a snare for the fool;
    it lessens his strength and multiplies
    his wounds.
31 Rebuke not your neighbor when wine
    is served,
    nor put him to shame while he is merry;
   Use no harsh words with him
    and distress him not in the presence
    of others.

32

1 If you are chosen to preside at dinner,
    be not puffed up,
   but with the guests be as one of
    themselves;
   Take care of them first before you sit down;
2   when you have fulfilled your duty, then
    take your place,
   To share in their joy
    and win praise for your hospitality.
3 Being older, you may talk; that is only
    your right,
   but temper your wisdom, not to disturb
    the singing.

---

† **31, 8ff:** The church in her liturgy applies this passage to holy con-
fessors of the Faith.
   31, 12—32, 13: A man observing etiquette at table avoids greed
and selfishness (31, 12f), is considerate of a neighbor's likes and dislikes and generous toward him (14f.23f), observes proper manners
(16ff), is moderate in eating and drinking (19–22.25–30). A good
host makes himself one with his guests, is solicitous for them
(32, 1f), provides conversation and diversion (3–6), is modest in
speech (7f.10), is respectful of elders (9), polite in comportment and
grateful to God for his favors (11ff).

31, 21: *Emptied your stomach:* the practice of induced vomiting,
well-known among pagan Romans, and less well-known among the
Jews, seems to be referred to here.

31, 6: Sir 8, 2.	**31, 19:** Eccl 5, 11.
31, 8: Sir 5, 1.10.	**31, 23:** Prv 22, 9.
31, 11: Prv 29, 14.	**31, 27:** Ps 104, 15; 1 Tm
31, 13: Sir 37, 28ff; Prv 23, 1f.	5, 23.
31, 17: Sir 37, 29.	

A Tragic Tale

More and more wine is a snare for the fool; it lessens his strength and multiplies his wounds. (Sir 31, 30)

This is the true story of a young man we'll call Kevin. Kevin had a drinking problem. It all began when he had his first beer at age thirteen. It tasted horrible, but all his friends told him to keep drinking, and he would grow to love the feeling it gave him. He did keep drinking, and the alcohol made him feel more outgoing and more funny. This didn't seem all that bad.

Unfortunately, Kevin became an alcoholic. Weekend drinking turned into weekday drinking, and before long, he was drinking on his way to school. Kevin drank so much that he blacked out almost every other day.

One day, Kevin had drunk nearly a fifth of vodka. He was at home and was supposed to be watching his six-year-old sister, Veronica. Kevin got angry at her and slammed her across the side of the head. She fell to the ground and lay there without moving. Kevin tried calling 911 but couldn't see the numbers well enough to dial.

Veronica died as a result of Kevin's blow. Now Kevin has to live with the horror of killing his own sister. He wishes he could tell every thirteen-year-old in the world not to try that first beer.

▸ Sir 31, 25–31

4   When wine is present, do not pour
      out discourse,
      and flaunt not your wisdom at the
         wrong time.
5   Like a seal of carnelian in a setting of gold
      is a concert when wine is served.
6   Like a gold mounting with an emerald seal
      is string music with delicious wine.
7*   Young man, speak only when necessary,
      when they have asked you more
         than once;
8   Be brief, but say much in those few
         words,
      be like the wise man, taciturn.
9   When among your elders be not forward,
      and with officials be not too insistent.
10   Like the lightning that flashes before
         a storm
      is the esteem that shines on modesty.
11   When it is time to leave, tarry not;
      be off for home! There take your ease,
12   And there enjoy doing as you wish,
      but without sin or words of pride.
13   Above all, give praise to your Creator,
      who showers his favors upon you.

The Providence of God

14*†   He who would find God must
         accept discipline;
      he who seeks him obtains his request.
15*   He who studies the law masters it,
      but the hypocrite finds it a trap.
16*   His judgment is sound who fears the LORD;
      out of obscurity he draws forth a
         clear plan.
17*   The sinner turns aside reproof
      and distorts the law to suit his purpose.
18   The thoughtful man will not neglect
         direction;
      the proud and insolent man is deterred
         by nothing.
19*   Do nothing without counsel,
      and then you need have no regrets.
20   Go not on a way that is set with snares,
      and let not the same thing trip you twice.
21   Be not too sure even of smooth roads,
22   be careful on all your paths.
23   Whatever you do, be on your guard,
      for in this way you will keep
         the commandments.
24   He who keeps the law preserves himself;

---

† **32, 14—33, 4:** God is shown to reveal himself through the discipline of his law, a clear and safe plan of life for the pious Jew of old. Direction and counsel are aids in following it (14ff.18–24); 33, 1. 3f). Sinners and hypocrites, hating the law or distorting it, fail in wisdom and are devoid of security (32, 15.17f; 33, 2).

32, 7ff: Sir 7, 14.
32, 14: Sir 4, 13.
32, 15: Sir 2, 16.

32, 16: Ps 37, 6.
32, 17: Sir 21, 6; Prv 12, 1.
32, 19: Sir 37, 16; Tb 4, 18.

S
I
R

and he who trusts in the LORD shall not be
put to shame.

33

1* No evil can harm the man who fears
the LORD;
through trials, again and again he is safe.
2   He who hates the law is without wisdom,
and is tossed about like a boat in a storm.
3† The prudent man trusts in the word of the LORD,
and the law is dependable for him as a
divine oracle.
4   Prepare your words and you will be
listened to;
draw upon your training, and then give
your answer.

5† Like the wheel of a cart is the mind of a fool;
his thoughts revolve in circles.
6   A fickle friend is like the stallion
that neighs, no matter who the rider.
7   Why is one day more important than another,
when it is the sun that lights up every day?
8* It is due to the LORD'S wisdom that they differ;
it is through him the seasons and feasts
come and go.
9* Some he dignifies and sanctifies,
and others he lists as ordinary days.
10* So too, all men are of clay,
for from earth man was formed;
11 Yet with his great knowledge the LORD makes
men unlike;
in different paths he has them walk.
12 Some he blesses and makes great,
some he sanctifies and draws to himself.
Others he curses and brings low,
and expels them from their place.
13* Like clay in the hands of a potter,
to be molded according to his pleasure,
So are men in the hands of their Creator,
to be assigned by him their function.
14* As evil contrasts with good, and death with life,
so are sinners in contrast with the just;
15 See now all the works of the Most High:
they come in pairs, the one the opposite of
the other.

16† Now I am the last to keep vigil,
like a gleaner after the vintage;
17 Since by the LORD'S blessing I have
made progress
till like a vintager I have filled
my winepress,
18 I would inform you that not for myself only
have I toiled,
but for every seeker after wisdom.

Property and Servants†

19* Listen to me, O leaders of the multitude;
O rulers of the assembly, give ear!
20 Let neither son nor wife, neither brother
nor friend,
have power over you as long as you live.
21 While breath of life is still in you,
let no man have dominion over you.
Give not to another your wealth,
lest then you have to plead with him;
22 Far better that your children plead with you
than that you should look to
their generosity.
23 Keep control over all your affairs;
let no one tarnish your glory.
24 When your few days reach their limit,
at the time of death distribute
your inheritance.

25 Fodder and whip and loads for an ass;
the yoke and harness and the rod of
his master.
27 Food, correction and work for a slave;
and for a wicked slave, punishment in
the stocks.
26* Make a slave work and he will look for his rest;
let his hands be idle and he will seek to
be free.
28 Force him to work that he be not idle,
for idleness is an apt teacher of mischief.
29 Put him to work, for that is what befits him;
if he becomes unruly, load him
with chains.
30 But never lord it over any human being,
and do nothing unjust.

S
I
R

33, 3: *Oracle:* as the answer given through the Urim and Thummim to the high priest is true, so the law proves itself true to him who obeys it. Cf Ex 28, 30; Nm 27, 21.

33, 5–15: Contrasts observable in the physical universe as well as in the moral order serve the purposes of divine wisdom (5–9). All creatures are like clay . . . in the hands of their Creator—the fool and the wise man, the sinner, and the just (10–15). This does not imply that man is created to be a sinner: God is not the author of wickedness. Cf Jas 1, 13f.

33, 16ff: Here the author refers to himself as the most recent of the writers who have endeavored to present true wisdom to their readers.

33, 19–33: Public officials should reject every influence that would restrict their freedom in the management of their affairs. They must make their own household subservient to them rather than be subservient to it (19–24). Slaves are to be given food and work and correction but never to be treated unjustly (25–29). Great care should be taken of good slaves (30–33).

33, 1: Ps 91, 10.   Rom 9, 20f.
33, 8: Gn 1, 14.   33, 14: Sir 42, 25.
33, 9: Ex 20, 11.   33, 19: Wis 6, 1f.
33, 10: Gn 2, 7.   33, 26: Prv 29, 19.
33, 13: Wis 15, 7; Jer 18, 1–6;

31* If you have but one slave, treat him
    like yourself,
  for you have acquired him with your
    life's blood;

32 If you have but one slave, deal with him as
    a brother,
  for you need him as you need your life:

33 If you mistreat him and he runs away,
  in what direction will you look for him?

Trust in the LORD and Not in Dreams†

34 ¹ Empty and false are the hopes of
    the senseless,
  and fools are borne aloft by dreams.

2 Like a man who catches at shadows or chases
    the wind,
  is the one who believes in dreams.

3 What is seen in dreams is to reality
  what the reflection of a face is to the
    face itself.

4* Can the unclean produce the clean?
  can the liar ever speak the truth?

5 Divination, omens and dreams all are unreal;
  what you already expect, the mind depicts.

6 Unless it be a vision specially sent by the
    Most High,
  fix not your heart on it;

7 For dreams have led many astray,
  and those who believed in them
    have perished.

8 The law is fulfilled without fail,
  and perfect wisdom is found in the mouth
    of the faithful man.

9 A man with training gains wide knowledge;
  a man of experience speaks sense.

10 One never put to the proof knows little,
  whereas with travel a man adds to
    his resourcefulness.

11 I have seen much in my travels,
  learned more than ever I could say.

12 Often I was in danger of death,
  but by these attainments I was saved.

13 Lively is the courage of those who fear
    the LORD,
  for they put their hope in their savior;

14* He who fears the LORD is never alarmed,
  never afraid; for the LORD is his hope.

15 Happy the soul that fears the LORD!
  In whom does he trust, and who is
    his support?

16* The eyes of the LORD are upon those who
    love him;
  he is their mighty shield and
    strong support,
  A shelter from the heat, a shade from the
    noonday sun,
  a guard against stumbling, a help
    against falling.

17 He buoys up the spirits, brings a sparkle to
    the eyes,
  gives health and life and blessing.

True Worship of God†

18* Tainted his gifts who offers in sacrifice
    ill-gotten goods!
  Mock presents from the lawless win not
    God's favor.

19 The Most High approves not the gifts of
    the godless,
  nor for their many sacrifices does he forgive
    their sins.

20 Like the man who slays a son in his
    father's presence
  is he who offers sacrifice from the
    possessions of the poor.

21* The bread of charity is life itself for the needy;
  he who withholds it is a man of blood.

22 He slays his neighbor who deprives him of
    his living;
  he sheds blood who denies the laborer
    his wages.

23 If one man builds up and another
    tears down,
  what do they gain but trouble?

24 If one man prays and another curses,
  whose voice will the LORD hear?

25* If a man again touches a corpse after he
    has bathed,
  what did he gain by the purification?

26 So with a man who fasts for his sins,
  but then goes and commits them again:
  Who will hear his prayer,
  and what has he gained by
    his mortification?

34, 1–17: Confidence placed in dreams, divinations and omens is false because these are devoid of reality (1–8). True confidence is founded on knowledge and experience (9–12), and above all on the fear of the Lord, with its accompanying blessings of divine assistance and protection (13–17).

34, 18–26: To be acts of true religion, sacrifice and penance must be accompanied by the proper moral dispositions. To offer to God goods taken from the poor (18–22), or to practice penance without interior reform, is a mockery, worthless in the sight of God (23–26). Cf Mt 15, 4–7; Mk 7, 9–13.

33, 31: Sir 7, 21.
34, 4: Jb 14, 4.
34, 14: Pss 23, 4; 112, 7f; Prv 3, 23ff; 28, 1.
34, 16: Pss 33, 18; 34, 16.
34, 18: Sir 35, 11; Prv 21, 27.
34, 21f: Lv 19, 13; Dt 24, 14f; Tb 4, 14.
34, 25: Nm 19, 11f; Prv 26, 11; 2 Pt 2, 22.

35 ¹*† To keep the law is a great oblation,
and he who observes the
commandments sacrifices a
peace offering.

²† In works of charity one offers fine flour,
and when he gives alms he presents his
sacrifice of praise.

³ To refrain from evil pleases the LORD,
and to avoid injustice is an atonement.

⁴* Appear not before the LORD empty-handed,
for all that you offer is in fulfillment of
the precepts.

⁵ The just man's offering enriches the altar
and rises as a sweet odor before the
Most High.

⁶ The just man's sacrifice is most pleasing,
nor will it ever be forgotten.

⁷* In generous spirit pay homage to the LORD,
be not sparing of freewill gifts.

⁸* With each contribution show a
cheerful countenance,
and pay your tithes in a spirit of joy.

⁹ Give to the Most High as he has given to you,
generously, according to your means.

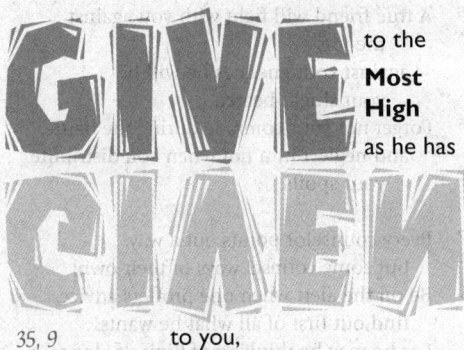

GIVE to the **Most High** as he has GIVEN

35, 9   to you,
generously,
according to your means

¹⁰* For the LORD is one who always repays,
and he will give back to you sevenfold.

¹¹* But offer no bribes, these he does not accept!

Trust not in sacrifice of the fruits
of extortion,

¹²* For he is a God of justice,
who knows no favorites.

¹³† Though not unduly partial toward the weak,
yet he hears the cry of the oppressed.

¹⁴* He is not deaf to the wail of the orphan,
nor to the widow when she pours out
her complaint;

¹⁵ Do not the tears that stream down her cheek
cry out against him that causes them
to fall?

¹⁶ He who serves God willingly is heard;
his petition reaches the heavens.

¹⁷ The prayer of the lowly pierces the clouds;
it does not rest till it reaches its goal,

¹⁸ Nor will it withdraw till the Most
High responds,
judges justly and affirms the right.

¹⁹* God indeed will not delay,
and like a warrior, will not be still

²⁰ Till he breaks the backs of the merciless
and wreaks vengeance upon the proud;

²¹ Till he destroys the haughty root and branch,
and smashes the scepter of the wicked;

²² Till he requites mankind according to
its deeds,
and repays men according to
their thoughts;

²³ Till he defends the cause of his people,
and gladdens them by his mercy.

²⁴ Welcome is his mercy in time of distress
as rain clouds in time of drought.

A Prayer for God's People†

36 ¹ Come to our aid, O God of the
universe,
and put all the nations in dread of you!

² Raise your hand against the heathen,
that they may realize your power.

³ As you have used us to show them
your holiness,
so now use them to show us your glory.

---

† **35, 1–24:** Keeping the commandments of the law and avoiding injustice constitute sacrifice pleasing and acceptable to God (1ff). Offerings also should be made to him, cheerfully and generously; these he repays . . . sevenfold (4–10). Extortion from widows and orphans is injustice, which God quickly repays (11–18). Punishing the proud and the merciless and coming to the aid of the distressed, he requites all according to their deeds (19–24).

35, 2: Fine flour, together with oil and frankincense, was a prescribed offering to God; cf Lv 2, 1ff.

35, 13: Cf Lv 19, 15.

36, 1–17: Making an act of faith and hope in the supreme Lord of the universe, the author begs God to continue manifesting his ho-

liness and mercy through Israel, his people (1ff.10–13), and his power and justice through the punishment of the nations (2.5–9), that all the earth may acknowledge him the eternal God (4.14–17).

35, 1ff: 1 Sm 15, 22; Ps 51,
  18f; Is 1, 11–18; Hos
  6, 6; Am 5, 21–24.
35, 4: Ex 23, 15; 34, 20; Dt
  16, 16.
35, 7: Sir 7, 31.
35, 8: 2 Cor 9, 7.
35, 10: Prv 19, 17.

35, 11: Sir 34, 18f; Prv 21, 27.
35, 12: Dt 10, 17; 2 Chr 19, 7;
  Jb 34, 19; Wis 6, 7;
  Acts 10, 34; Rom
  2, 11; Gal 2, 6;
  1 Pt 1, 17.
35, 14f: Ex 22, 22.
35, 19: Is 42, 13ff; 2 Pt 3, 9.

4   Thus they will know, as we know,
         that there is no God but you.

5   Give new signs and work new wonders;
         show forth the splendor of your right hand
             and arm;
6*   Rouse your anger, pour out wrath,
         humble the enemy, scatter the foe.
7   Hasten the day, bring on the time;
9   crush the heads of the hostile rulers.
8   Let raging fire consume the fugitive,
         and your people's oppressors
             meet destruction.
10   Gather all the tribes of Jacob,
         that they may inherit the land as of old.
11* Show mercy to the people called by
             your name;
         Israel, whom you named your first-born.
12* Take pity on your holy city,
         Jerusalem, your dwelling place.
13   Fill Zion with your majesty,
         your temple with your glory.

14   Give evidence of your deeds of old;
         fulfill the prophecies spoken in
             your name,
15   Reward those who have hoped in you,
         and let your prophets be proved true.
16   Hear the prayer of your servants,
         for you are ever gracious to your people;
17   Thus it will be known to the very ends of
             the earth
         that you are the eternal God.

Choice of Associates†

18   The throat can swallow any food,
         yet some foods are more agreeable
             than others;
19   As the palate tests meat by its savor,
         so does a keen mind insincere words.
20   A deceitful character causes grief,
         but an experienced man can turn the tables
             on him.
21   Though any man may be accepted as
             a husband,
         yet one girl will be more suitable
             than another:

22* A woman's beauty makes her husband's face
             light up,
         for it surpasses all else that charms the eye;
23   And if, besides, her speech is kindly,
         his lot is beyond that of mortal men.
24* A wife is her husband's richest treasure,
         a helpmate, a steadying column.
25   A vineyard with no hedge will be overrun;
         a man with no wife becomes a
             homeless wanderer.
26   Who will trust an armed band
         that shifts from city to city?
27* Or a man who has no nest,
         but lodges where night overtakes him?

37

1*   Every friend declares his friendship,
         but there are friends who are friends
             in name only.
2   Is it not a sorrow unto death
         when your bosom companion becomes
             your enemy?
3   "Alas, my companion! Why were you created
         to blanket the earth with deceit?"
4   A false friend will share your joys,
         but in time of trouble he stands afar off.
5   A true friend will fight with you against
             the foe,
         against your enemies he will be
             your shield-bearer.
6   Forget not your comrade during the battle,
         and neglect him not when you distribute
             your spoils.

7   Every counselor points out a way,
         but some counsel ways of their own;
8   Be on the alert when one proffers advice,
         find out first of all what he wants.
     For he may be thinking of himself alone;
         why should the profit fall to him?
9   He may tell you how good your way will be,
         and then stand by to watch
             your misfortune.
10   Seek no advice from one who regards you
             with hostility;
         from those who envy you, keep your
             intentions hidden.
11   Speak not to a woman about her rival,

---

† 36, 18—37, 15: In the choice of wife, friend or associate, experience is a discerner of character (18–21). Beauty and kindly speech make a woman desirable as wife (22f). The good wife becomes her husband's richest treasure, his helpmate in establishing his household (24–27). A true friend fights for his comrade and shares his spoils with him (37, 5f); a false one deceives and abandons him in time of need (1–4). A true counselor and associate should be sought among those who keep the commandments, not among those who break them and seek their own advantage (7–12). In all things pray to God for light and follow conscience (13ff).

36, 6: Ps 79, 6.   36, 22: Sir 26, 13ff.
36, 11: Ex 4, 22.   36, 24: Gn 2, 18; Prv 18, 22.
36, 12: 2 Chr 6, 41; Ps 132,   36, 27: Prv 27, 8.
    8.14; Is 2, 1ff; Mi   37, 1: Sir 6, 7ff.
    4, 1ff.

nor to a coward about war,
to a merchant about business,
to a buyer about value,
to a miser about generosity,
to a cruel man about mercy,
to a lazy man about work,
to a seasonal laborer about the harvest,
to an idle slave about a great task:
pay no attention to any advice they give.

12 Instead, associate with a religious man,
who you are sure keeps
the commandments;
Who is like-minded with yourself
and will feel for you if you fall.

13 Then, too, heed your own heart's counsel;
for what have you that you can depend
on more?

14 A man's conscience can tell him his situation
better than seven watchmen in a
lofty tower.

15 Most important of all, pray to God
to set your feet in the path of truth.

Wisdom and Temperance

16*† A word is the source of every deed;
a thought, of every act.

17 The root of all conduct is the mind;
four branches it shoots forth:

18* Good and evil, death and life,
their absolute mistress is the tongue.

19 A man may be wise and benefit many,
yet be of no use to himself.

20 Though a man may be wise, if his words
are rejected
he will be deprived of all enjoyment.

21 When a man is wise to his own advantage,
the fruits of his knowledge are seen in his
own person;

22* When a man is wise to his people's advantage,
the fruits of his knowledge are enduring:

23 Limited are the days of one man's life,
but the life of Israel is days
without number.

24 One wise for himself has full enjoyment,
and all who see him praise him;

25* One wise for his people wins a heritage
of glory,
and his name endures forever.

26† My son, while you are well, govern
your appetite
so that you allow it not what is bad for you;

27* For not every food is good for everyone,
nor is everything suited to every taste.

28* Be not drawn after every enjoyment,
neither become a glutton for choice foods,

29 For sickness comes with overeating,
and gluttony brings on biliousness.

30 Through lack of self-control many have died,
but the abstemious man prolongs his life.

Sickness and Death

38 1† Hold the physician in honor, for he
is essential to you,
and God it was who established
his profession.

2 From God the doctor has his wisdom,
and the king provides for his sustenance.

3 His knowledge makes the doctor
distinguished,
and gives him access to those in authority.

Health-Care Providers

When was the last time you went to the doctor? How often do you take medicine? Did you ever spend a night in a hospital? It's humbling to realize that the basic health care we take for granted is not available to millions of people in this country and throughout the world.

God gives the skill to heal to doctors, nurses, dentists, pharmacists, therapists, and medical technicians of every kind (Sir 38, 2). Their jobs often demand huge amounts of time and energy. Take a moment to remember in prayer the health-care providers you know personally, and ask yourself if you have a vocation in the medical profession.

▶ Sir 38, 1–15

S
I
R

37, 16–25: Thoughts determine action. Wisdom is the source of good and life; folly, of evil and death (16ff). If the fruits of a man's wisdom benefit himself, he may be praised in his own lifetime; if they benefit his people, his praise endures after him, in their lives (19–25).

37, 26–30: Temperance and self-control should govern a man's appetite for food, which is intended not to destroy but to preserve life.

38, 1–15: The profession of medicine comes from God, who makes the earth yield healing herbs and gives the physician knowl-

edge of their virtue (1–8). In illness the sick man should cleanse his soul from sin and petition God for help through an offering of sacrifice; the physician, too, does well to invoke God that he may understand the illness and apply the proper remedy (9–14). The sinner, in contrast, defies both his Maker and the doctor (15).

37, 16: Sir 32, 19.   37, 25: Sir 39, 9; 44, 13f.
37, 18: Prv 18, 21.   37, 27: 1 Cor 6, 12; 10, 23.
37, 22: Sir 15, 1ff.   37, 28f: Sir 31, 13.16ff.

4   God makes the earth yield healing herbs
     which the prudent man should not neglect;

5*   Was not the water sweetened by a twig
     that men might learn his power?

6   He endows men with the knowledge
     to glory in his mighty works,

7   Through which the doctor eases pain
     and the druggist prepares his medicines;

8   Thus God's creative work continues
     without cease
     in its efficacy on the surface of the earth.

9*   My son, when you are ill, delay not,
     but pray to God, who will heal you:

10   Flee wickedness; let your hands be just,
     cleanse your heart of every sin;

11*   Offer your sweet-smelling oblation
     and petition,
     a rich offering according to your means.

12   Then give the doctor his place
     lest he leave; for you need him too.

13   There are times that give him
     an advantage,

14   and he too beseeches God
     That his diagnosis may be correct
     and his treatment bring about a cure.

15   He who is a sinner toward his Maker
     will be defiant toward the doctor.

16*† My son, shed tears for one who is dead
     with wailing and bitter lament;
     As is only proper, prepare the body,
     absent not yourself from his burial:

17   Weeping bitterly, mourning fully,
     pay your tribute of sorrow, as he deserves,

18   One or two days, to prevent gossip;
     then compose yourself after your grief,

19*   For grief can bring on an extremity
     and heartache destroy one's health.

20*   Turn not your thoughts to him again;
     cease to recall him; think rather of the
     end.

21*   Recall him not, for there is no hope of
     his return;
     it will not help him, but will do you harm.

22*   Remember that his fate will also be yours;
     for him it was yesterday, for you today.

23   With the departed dead, let memory fade;
     rally your courage, once the soul has left.

Vocations of the Craftsman and the Scribe†

24   The scribe's profession increases his wisdom;
     whoever is free from toil can become a
     wise man.

25   How can he become learned who guides
     the plow,
     who thrills in wielding the goad like
     a lance,
     Who guides the ox and urges on the bullock,
     and whose every concern is for cattle?

26   His care is for plowing furrows,
     and he keeps a watch on the beasts in
     the stalls.

27   So with every engraver and designer
     who, laboring night and day,
     Fashions carved seals,
     and whose concern is to vary the pattern.
     His care is to produce a vivid impression,
     and he keeps watch till he finishes
     his design.

28   So with the smith standing near his anvil,
     forging crude iron.
     The heat from the fire sears his flesh,
     yet he toils away in the furnace heat.
     The clang of the hammer deafens his ears,
     his eyes are fixed on the tool he
     is shaping.
     His care is to finish his work,
     and he keeps watch till he perfects it
     in detail.

29   So with the potter sitting at his labor
     revolving the wheel with his feet.
     He is always concerned for his products,
     and he turns them out in quantity.

30   With his hands he molds the clay,
     and with his feet softens it.
     His care is for proper coloring,
     and he keeps watch on the fire of his kiln.

31   All these men are skilled with their hands,
     each one an expert at his own task;

32   Without them no city could be lived in,

---

† **38, 16–23:** A period of mourning for the deceased and care for their burial is becoming (16ff). But grief should not be excessive, for it neither helps the dead, who cannot return, nor fails to harm the living. The mourner's own end will quickly follow, and the time to prepare for it is now (19–23).

38, 24—39, 11: More excellent than the useful service of craftsmen—farmer, engraver, smith, potter (25–34)—is the profession of the scribe (24), who studies and meditates on the law of the Most High, seeks him in prayer of thanksgiving, petition and repentance for sin (39, 1.6f), explores the wisdom of the past and present, travels abroad to observe the conduct of many peoples, and attends rulers and great men. Through the spirit of understanding granted by God, he will show forth his wisdom to the glory of God's law, gaining renown for generations to come (2–5.8–11).

38, 5: Ex 15, 25.
38, 9: Is 38, 2f.
38, 11: Lv 2, 1ff.
38, 16: Sir 22, 11;
38, 19: Prv 12, 25; 15, 13;

17, 22.
38, 20: Sir 7, 36; 18, 24; 30,
    21.
38, 21: 2 Sm 12, 23; Wis 2, 1.
38, 22: Jas 4, 13ff.

and wherever they stay, they need
not hunger.

33 They do not occupy the judge's bench,
nor are they prominent in the assembly;
They set forth no decisions or judgments,
nor are they found among the rulers;

34 Yet they maintain God's ancient handiwork,
and their concern is for exercise of
their skill.

39

1 How different the man who devotes
himself
to the study of the law of the Most High!
He explores the wisdom of the men of old
and occupies himself with the prophecies;

2 He treasures the discourses of famous men,
and goes to the heart of involved sayings;

3 He studies obscure parables,
and is busied with the hidden meanings of
the sages.

4 He is in attendance on the great,
and has entrance to the ruler.

5 He travels among the peoples of foreign lands
to learn what is good and evil among men.

6 His care is to seek the LORD, his Maker,
to petition the Most High,
To open his lips in prayer,
to ask pardon for his sins.
Then, if it pleases the LORD Almighty,
he will be filled with the spirit
of understanding;
He will pour forth his words of wisdom
and in prayer give thanks to the LORD,

7 Who will direct his knowledge and
his counsel,
as he meditates upon his mysteries.

8 He will show the wisdom of what he
has learned
and glory in the law of the
LORD's covenant.

9* Many will praise his understanding;
his fame can never be effaced;
Unfading will be his memory,
through all generations his name will
live;

10 Peoples will speak of his wisdom,
and in assembly sing his praises.

11 While he lives he is one out of a thousand,
and when he dies his renown will not cease.

Praise of God the Creator†

12 Once more I will set forth my theme
to shine like the moon in its fullness!

13 Listen, my faithful children: open up
your petals,
like roses planted near running waters;

14 Send up the sweet odor of incense,
break forth in blossoms like the lily.
Send up the sweet odor of your hymn
of praise;
bless the LORD for all he has done!

15 Proclaim the greatness of his name,
loudly sing his praises,
With music on the harp and all
stringed instruments;
sing out with joy as you proclaim:

16* The works of God are all of them good;
in its own time every need is supplied.

17* At his word the waters become still as in
a flask;
he had but to speak and the reservoirs
were made.

18 He has but to command and his will is done;
nothing can limit his achievement.

19* The works of all mankind are present to him;
not a thing escapes his eye.

20 His gaze spans all the ages;
to him there is nothing unexpected.

21 No cause then to say: "What is the purpose
of this?"
Everything is chosen to satisfy a need.

22 His blessing overflows like the Nile;
like the Euphrates it enriches the surface of
the earth.

23* Again, his wrath expels the nations
and turns fertile land into a salt marsh.

24 For the virtuous his paths are level,
to the haughty they are steep;

25 Good things for the good he provided from
the beginning,
but for the wicked good things and bad.

26* Chief of all needs for human life
are water and fire, iron and salt,
The heart of the wheat, milk and honey,
the blood of the grape, and oil, and
cloth;

27 For the good all these are good,
but for the wicked they turn out evil.

39, 12–35: The sage invites his disciples to join him in joyfully proclaiming his favorite theme: The works of God are all of them good; in its own time every need is supplied (12–16.32–35). He describes God's omniscience, supreme power and wisdom, whereby all created things, good in themselves, are ever present to him, obey him, and fulfill their intended purpose (17–21), bringing blessing to

the virtuous, but evil and punishment to the wicked who misuse them (22–31). Cf similar hymns of praise, Sir 36, 1–17; 42, 15—43, 35.

39, 9: Sir 37, 25; 44, 14.   39, 19: Sir 15, 19; 42, 20.
39, 16: Gn 1, 31; Eccl 3, 11.   39, 23: Jos 1, 2–6.
39, 17: Gn 1, 6–10; Ex 14,   39, 26: Sir 29, 21.
21f; Jos 3, 16.

SIR

28 There are storm winds created to punish,
   which in their fury can dislodge mountains;
   When destruction must be, they hurl all
      their force
   and appease the anger of their Maker.

29 In his treasury also, kept for the proper time,
   are fire and hail, famine, disease,

30 Ravenous beasts, scorpions, vipers,
   and the avenging sword to exterminate
      the wicked;

31 In doing his bidding they rejoice,
   in their assignments they disobey not
      his command.

32 So from the first I took my stand,
   and wrote down as my theme:

33* The works of God are all of them good;
   every need when it comes he fills.

34 No cause then to say: "This is not as good
      as that";
   for each shows its worth at the proper time.

35 So now with full joy of heart proclaim
   and bless the name of the Holy One.

Joys and Miseries of Life

40 1*† A great anxiety has God allotted,
   and a heavy yoke, to the sons of men;
   From the day one leaves his mother's womb
   to the day he returns to the mother of all
      the living,†

2 His thoughts, the fear in his heart,
   and his troubled forebodings till the day
      he dies—

3 Whether he sits on a lofty throne
   or grovels in dust and ashes,

4 Whether he bears a splendid crown
   or is wrapped in the coarsest of cloaks—

5 Are of wrath and envy, trouble and dread,
   terror of death, fury and strife.
   Even when he lies on his bed to rest,
   his cares at night disturb his sleep.

6 So short is his rest it seems like none,
   till in his dreams he struggles as he did
      by day,
   Terrified by what his mind's eye sees,
   like a fugitive being pursued;

7 As he reaches safety, he wakes up
   astonished that there was nothing to fear.

8 So it is with all flesh, with man and
      with beast,
   but for sinners seven times more.

9* Plague and bloodshed, wrath and the sword,
   plunder and ruin, famine and death:

10 For the wicked, these were created evil,
   and it is they who bring on destruction.

11† All that is of earth returns to earth,
   and what is from above returns above.

12 All that comes from bribes or injustice will be
      wiped out,
   but loyalty remains for ages.

13 Wealth out of wickedness is like a wadi
      in spate:
   like a mighty stream with lightning
      and thunder,

14* Which, in its rising, rolls along the stones,
   but suddenly, once and for all, comes to
      an end.

15 The offshoot of violence will not flourish,
   for the root of the godless is on sheer
      rock;

16 Or they are like reeds on the riverbank,
   withered before all other plants.

17† But goodness will never be cut off,
   and justice endures forever.

   Wealth or wages can make life sweet,
   but better than either is finding a treasure.

18* A child or a city will preserve one's name,
   but better than either, attaining wisdom.

19 Sheepfolds and orchards bring
      flourishing health;
   but better than either, a devoted wife;

20* Wine and music delight the soul,
   but better than either, conjugal love.

21 The flute and the harp offer sweet melody,
   but better than either, a voice that is true.

22* Charm and beauty delight the eye,
   but better than either, the flowers of
      the field.

23 A friend, a neighbor, are timely guides,

---

† **40, 1–16:** The former idyllic description of the universe is contrasted with the picture of the evils afflicting humanity. Every man, high or low, is burdened from birth to death with fears, anxieties and troubles, by day and often by night, the time appointed for rest (1–7). For sinners, the suffering is much greater (8ff). What they gained by violence and injustice is quickly destroyed; but justice endures forever (14ff).

40, 1: *Mother of all the living:* the earth from which man was taken. Cf Gn 2, 7; 3, 19f; Jb 1, 21; Ps 139, 15.

40, 11: *All that is of earth . . . returns above:* a reference to bodily mortality and to the divine origin of life from the Spirit of God. Cf Sir 41, 10; Gn 2, 7; 3, 19; Jb 34, 14f; Pss 104, 29f; 146, 4; Eccl 12, 7.

The Greek and the Latin render the second half of the verse: "all waters shall return to the sea."

40, 17–27: Of the many treasures making life sweet, such as health, children, friends, music, vigor, the best are called true conjugal love, wisdom, and above all, fear of God; cf Sir 25, 6–11.

39, 33: Sir 39, 16; Gn 1, 31;   40, 14: Sir 23, 25; Wis 4, 3ff.
   Eccl 3, 11.   40, 18: Prv 19, 14.
40, 1: Gn 3, 17; Jb 7, 1;   40, 20: Ps 104, 15.
   14, 1; Eccl 2, 23.   40, 22: Mt 6, 28f.
40, 9: Sir 39, 28ff.

Shame on You!

"You ought to be ashamed of yourself!" How many times do we hear that while growing up? Or the simpler, more direct version: "Shame on you!" We've probably heard these and similar expressions often, but what exactly is the point of shame?

Although it is true that sometimes false shaming can be harmful to our growth and development, there are other times when we really should be ashamed of ourselves. We did something that we should not have done. Perhaps we hurt another person or broke a promise or brought dishonor to our family. These are all valid reasons for feeling ashamed, and it is often someone else who brings us to this realization.

The author of Sirach knew human nature well and gave advice about true and false shame. Think about times when you have felt ashamed of something. What caused you to feel ashamed? What role does your conscience play in feeling a sense of shame? What do you do with that sense of shame? Think about the role shame plays in the story of Adam and Eve (see Genesis 2–3) and the story of David and Bathsheba (see 2 Sm 11–12).

▶ **Sir 41, 14—42, 8**

but better than either, a prudent wife.
24 A brother, a helper, for times of stress;
     but better than either, charity that rescues.
25 Gold and silver make one's way secure,
     but better than either, sound judgment.
26 Wealth and vigor build up confidence,
     but better than either, fear of God.
Fear of the LORD leaves nothing wanting;
     he who has it need seek no other support:
27* The fear of God is a paradise of blessings;
     its canopy, all that is glorious.
28† My son, live not the life of a beggar,
     better to die than to beg;
29* When one has to look to another's table,
     his life is not really a life.
His neighbor's delicacies bring revulsion
     of spirit
to one who understands inward feelings:
30 In the mouth of the shameless man begging
     is sweet,
but within him it burns like fire.

41 ¹† O death! how bitter the thought
        of you
for the man at peace amid his possessions,
For the man unruffled and always successful,
who still can enjoy life's pleasures.

2* O death! how welcome your sentence
     to the weak man of failing strength,
Tottering and always rebuffed,
     with no more sight, with vanished hope.
3* Fear not death's decree for you;
     remember, it embraces those before you,
     and those after.
4 Thus God has ordained for all flesh;
     why then should you reject the will of the
        Most High?
Whether one has lived a thousand years, a
        hundred, or ten,
     in the nether world he has no claim on life.

5* A reprobate line are the children of sinners,
     and witless offspring are in the homes of
        the wicked.
6 Their dominion is lost to sinners' children,
     and reproach abides with their descendants.
7 Children curse their wicked father,
     for they suffer disgrace through him.
8 Woe to you, O sinful men,
     who forsake the law of the Most High.
9 If you have children, calamity will seize them;
     you will beget them only for groaning.
When you stumble, there is lasting joy;
     at death, you become a curse.

---

† **40, 28ff:** Among the Jews, beggary was considered degrading to human dignity; it was agreeable only to the shameless, who had lost their sense of honor. Cf Sir 29, 22f.

41, 1–13: Whether death seems bitter to one who enjoys peace, success and pleasure, or welcome to one who is weak and in despair, it comes to all and must be accepted as the will of God (1–4). As the human body passes away (11), so do those who have sinned through the body and their offspring alike, who, needy and accursed, pass on with their parents as if they had never been (5–10). Only the good name of the virtuous endures (11ff).

40, 27: Is 4, 5.   41, 3: Sir 38, 20ff.
40, 29: Sir 29, 24.   41, 5ff: Sir 3, 9ff; Wis 3,
41, 2: Sir 30, 17.   16–19.

10* Whatever is of nought returns to nought,
    so too the godless from void to void.
11* Man's body is a fleeting thing,
    but a virtuous name will never
    be annihilated.
12* Have a care for your name, for it will stand
    by you
    better than precious treasures in
    the thousands;
13† The boon of life is for limited days,
    but a good name, for days without
    number.

True and False Shame†

14 My children, heed my instruction
   about shame;
   judge of disgrace only according to
   my rules,
   For it is not always well to be ashamed,
   nor is it always the proper thing to blush:
15 Before father and mother be ashamed
   of immorality,
   before master and mistress, of falsehood;
16 Before prince and ruler, of flattery;
   before the public assembly, of crime;
17 Before friend and companion, of disloyalty,
   and of breaking an oath or agreement.
18 Be ashamed of theft from the people where
   you settle,
   and of stretching out your elbow when
   you dine;
19 Of refusing to give when asked,
   of defrauding another of his
   appointed share,
20 Of failing to return a greeting,
   and of rebuffing a friend;
21* Of gazing at a married woman,
    and of entertaining thoughts about
    another's wife;
    Of trifling with a servant girl you have,
    and of violating her couch;
22* Of using harsh words with friends,
    and of following up your gifts with
    insults;
23* Of repeating what you hear,
    and of betraying secrets—
24 These are the things you should rightly avoid
   as shameful

if you would be looked upon by everyone
with favor.

42 1* But of these things be not ashamed,
        lest you sin through human respect:
2 Of the law of the Most High and his precepts,
   or of the sentence to be passed upon
   the sinful;
3 Of sharing the expenses of a business or
   a journey,
   or of dividing an inheritance or property;
4* Of accuracy of scales and balances,
   or of tested measures and weights;
5* Of acquiring much or little,
   or of bargaining in dealing with
   a merchant;
   Of constant training of children,
   or of beating the sides of a disloyal
   servant;
6 Of a seal to keep an erring wife at home,
   or of a lock placed where there are
   many hands;
7 Of numbering every deposit,
   or of recording all that is given or
   received;
8 Of chastisement of the silly and the foolish,
   or of the aged and infirm answering for
   wanton conduct.
   Thus you will be truly cautious
   and recognized by all men as discreet.

A Father's Care for His Daughter†

9* A daughter is a treasure that keeps her
   father wakeful,
   and worry over her drives away rest:
   Lest she pass her prime unmarried,
   or when she is married, lest she
   be disliked;
10 While unmarried, lest she be seduced,
   or, as a wife, lest she prove unfaithful;
   Lest she conceive in her father's home,
   or be sterile in that of her husband.
11* Keep a close watch on your daughter,
    lest she make you the sport of
    your enemies,
    A byword in the city, a reproach among
    the people,
    an object of derision in public gatherings.

†
41, 13: After this verse many texts repeat Sir 20, 29f.
41, 14—42, 8: The author illustrates the subject of true and false shame with detailed and numerous examples of sin (14–24) and virtue (42, 1–8), following the norm of the commandments.
42, 9–14: The author considers a daughter to be a source of anxiety to her father, lest she fail to marry, or be seduced, or lest, marrying, she be disliked, prove unfaithful, or find herself sterile (9f). He is advised to keep a close watch on her at home, and on her companionship while abroad, lest he suffer on her account among the people (11–14).

*
41, 10: Sir 40, 11; Wis 4, 19.   42, 1: Prv 24, 23; Jas 2, 1.
41, 11: Prv 10, 7.   42, 4: Prv 11, 1.
41, 12: Prv 22, 1; Eccl 7, 1.   42, 5: Sir 30, 1–13; 33,
41, 21: Sir 9, 8; Mt 5, 28.   25–33.
41, 22: Sir 18, 14; 20, 13.   42, 9: Sir 7, 24f.
41, 23: Sir 27, 16.   42, 11: Sir 26, 10.

The Sexism of Sirach

Let's just get this right out in the open: Ben Sira was sexist by today's standards. As you read Sir 42, 9–14, you probably think it's a curse to have a daughter! Verse 14 says, "Better a man's harshness than a woman's indulgence, and a frightened daughter than any disgrace." Wow, with an attitude like that, Ben Sira wouldn't be welcomed by many modern people.

Once again, we have to remember that the Bible was written by human beings and reflects their cultural standards. Ben Sira's attitude was commonly accepted in his culture. But the cultural standards in the Bible don't always reflect God's truth. That's why we need the help of the larger church community to properly interpret the Bible. Today, the church teaches that women and men are to be treated with equal dignity and respect. Let's work together to continue making that vision a reality.

▶ Sir 42, 9–14

See that there is no lattice in her room,
    no place that overlooks the approaches to
      the house.
12* Let her not parade her charms before men,
    or spend her time with married women;
13 For just as moths come from garments,
    so harm to women comes from women:
14 Better a man's harshness than a
      woman's indulgence,
    and a frightened daughter than any disgrace.

The Works of God in Nature†

15* Now will I recall God's works;
    what I have seen, I will describe.
At God's word were his works brought
      into being;
    they do his will as he has ordained
      for them.
16 As the rising sun is clear to all,
    so the glory of the LORD fills all his works;
17 Yet even God's holy ones must fail
    in recounting the wonders of the LORD,
Though God has given these, his hosts,
      the strength
    to stand firm before his glory.
18 He plumbs the depths and penetrates the heart;
    their innermost being he understands.
The Most High possesses all knowledge,
    and sees from of old the things that are
      to come:

19 He makes known the past and the future,
    and reveals the deepest secrets.
20* No understanding does he lack;
    no single thing escapes him.
21 Perennial is his almighty wisdom;
    he is from all eternity one and the same,
22* With nothing added, nothing taken away;
    no need of a counselor for him!
23 How beautiful are all his works!
    even to the spark and fleeting vision!
24 The universe lives and abides forever;
    to meet each need, each creature
      is preserved.
25* All of them differ, one from another,
    yet none of them has he made in vain,
For each in turn, as it comes, is good;
    can one ever see enough of their splendor?

43 1* The clear vault of the sky shines forth
    like heaven itself, a vision of glory.
2 The orb of the sun, resplendent at its rising:
    what a wonderful work of the Most High!
3 At noon it seethes the surface of the earth,
    and who can bear its fiery heat?
4 Like a blazing furnace of solid metal,
    it sets the mountains aflame with its rays;
By its fiery darts the land is consumed;
    the eyes are dazzled by its light.
5 Great indeed is the LORD who made it,
    at whose orders it urges on its steeds.

S
I
R

---

† **42, 15—43, 35:** These verses comprise a new section. In them the author contemplates God's power, beauty and goodness as manifested in the mighty work of creating and preserving the universe (42, 15ff.23.25; 43, 1–27), his omniscience (42, 18ff), his perfect wisdom (21f), his eternity (24). The conclusion is a fervent hymn of praise (43, 28–35). Cf Sir 16, 22—18, 13.

* **42, 12f:** Sir 9, 1–9.
42, 15: Ps 77, 12f.
42, 20: Sir 39, 19; Wis 1, 6–10.
42, 22: Is 40, 13; Rom 11, 34.
42, 25: Sir 33, 15.
43, 1ff: Ps 19, 2f.

6* The moon, too, that marks the changing times,
  governing the seasons, their lasting sign,

7 By which we know the feast days and
    fixed dates,
  this light-giver which wanes in its course:

8 As its name says, each month it renews itself;
  how wondrous in this change!

9* The beauty, the glory, of the heavens are
    the stars
  that adorn with their sparkling the heights
    of God,

10 At whose command they keep their place
  and never relax in their vigils.
  A weapon against the flood waters stored
    on high,
  lighting up the firmament by its brilliance,

11* Behold the rainbow! Then bless its Maker,
  for majestic indeed is its splendor;

12 It spans the heavens with its glory,
  this bow bent by the mighty hand of God.

13 His rebuke marks out the path for
    the lightning,
  and speeds the arrows of his judgment to
    their goal.

14 At it the storehouse is opened,
  and like vultures the clouds hurry forth.

15 In his majesty he gives the storm its power
  and breaks off the hailstones.

16 The thunder of his voice makes the
    earth writhe;
  before his might the mountains quake.

17 A word from him drives on the south wind,
  the angry north wind, the hurricane and
    the storm.

18 He sprinkles the snow like fluttering birds;
  it comes to settle like swarms of locusts.

19 Its shining whiteness blinds the eyes,
  the mind is baffled by its steady fall.

20 He scatters frost like so much salt;
  it shines like blossoms on the thornbush.

21 Cold northern blasts he sends
  that turn the ponds to lumps of ice.
  He freezes over every body of water,
  and clothes each pool with a coat of mail.

22 When the mountain growth is scorched
    with heat,

and the flowering plains as though
    by flames,

23 The dripping clouds restore them all,
  and the scattered dew enriches the
    parched land.

24 His is the plan that calms the deep,
  and plants the islands in the sea.

25* Those who go down to the sea tell part of
    its story,
  and when we hear them we
    are thunderstruck;

26 In it are his creatures, stupendous, amazing,
  all kinds of life, and the monsters of
    the deep.

27* For him each messenger succeeds,
  and at his bidding accomplishes his will.

28† More than this we need not add;
  let the last word be, he is all in all!

29 Let us praise him the more, since we cannot
    fathom him,
  for greater is he than all his works;

30 Awful indeed is the LORD's majesty,
  and wonderful is his power.

31 Lift up your voices to glorify the LORD,
  though he is still beyond your power
    to praise;

32 Extol him with renewed strength,
  and weary not, though you cannot reach
    the end:

33* For who can see him and describe him?
  or who can praise him as he is?

34 Beyond these, many things lie hid;
  only a few of his works have we seen.

35* It is the LORD who has made all things,
  and to those who fear him he gives wisdom.

Praise of Israel's Great Ancestors

44 1† Now will I praise those godly men,
    our ancestors, each in his own time:†

2* The abounding glory of the Most High's portion,
  his own part, since the days of old.
  Subduers of the land in kingly fashion,
  men of renown for their might,

3* Or counselors in their prudence,
  or seers of all things in prophecy;

4 Resolute princes of the folk,
  and governors with their staves;

43, 28: *All in all!:* the perfections reflected in creation are found
in a transcendent way in God, who alone is their source.
  44, 1–50, 24: As in the previous section God's wisdom shone
forth in the works of nature, so in these chapters it is also revealed
through the history of God's people as seen in the lives of their patriarchs, prophets, priests and rulers. The example of these great men,
whose virtues are here recalled, constitutes a high point of the author's teaching and illustrates his belief in the canonical Scriptures.
  44, 1–15: The reader is here introduced to those men of Israel,
later mentioned by name, who through various achievements and

beneficial social activities have acquired great renown (1–8.14f);
and also to those who, though forgotten, endure through the fruit of
their virtues and through their families because of God's covenant
with them (9–13).

43, 6: Lv 23, 5; Nm
  28, 11–14; Ps 81, 4.
43, 9: Ps 8, 4.
43, 11: Gn 9, 13.
43, 25: Ps 104, 25–30.

43, 27: Ps 33, 6.
43, 33: Ps 106, 2.
43, 35: Jb 28, 28.
44, 2: Dt 32, 8f.
44, 3: Sir 39, 1.

Authors skilled in composition,
   and forgers of epigrams with their spikes;

5 Composers of melodious psalms,
   or discoursers on lyric themes;

6 Stalwart men, solidly established
   and at peace in their own estates—

7 All these were glorious in their time,
   each illustrious in his day.

8 Some of them have left behind a name
   and men recount their praiseworthy deeds;

9 But of others there is no memory,
   for when they ceased, they ceased.
And they are as though they had not lived,
   they and their children after them.

10 Yet these also were godly men
   whose virtues have not been forgotten;

11 Their wealth remains in their families,
   their heritage with their descendants;

12 Through God's covenant with them their
   family endures,
   their posterity for their sake.

13 And for all time their progeny will endure,
   their glory will never be blotted out;

14* Their bodies are peacefully laid away,
   but their name lives on and on.

15 At gatherings their wisdom is retold,
   and the assembly proclaims their praise.

The Early Patriarchs

16*†[ENOCH walked with the LORD and was
   taken up,
   that succeeding generations might learn by
   his example.]

17* NOAH, found just and perfect,
   renewed the race in the time of devastation.
Because of his worth there were survivors,
   and with a sign to him the deluge ended;

18 A lasting agreement was made with him,
   that never should all flesh be destroyed.

19* ABRAHAM, father of many peoples,
   kept his glory without stain:

20*†He observed the precepts of the Most High,
   and entered into an agreement with him;

In his own flesh he incised the ordinance,
   and when tested he was found loyal.

21† For this reason, God promised him with
   an oath
   that in his descendants the nations would
   be blessed,
That he would make him numerous as the
   grains of dust,
   and exalt his posterity like the stars;
That he would give them an inheritance from
   sea to sea,
   and from the River to the ends of the earth.

22* And for ISAAC he renewed the same promise
   because of Abraham, his father.
The covenant with all his forebears
   was confirmed,
   and the blessing rested upon the head
   of JACOB.

23 God acknowledged him as the firstborn,
   and gave him his inheritance.
He fixed the boundaries for his tribes,
   and their division into twelve.

Praise of Moses, Aaron and Phinehas

45 1*† From him was to spring the man
   who won the favor of all:
Dear to God and men,
   MOSES, whose memory is held
   in benediction.

2*†God's honor devolved upon him,
   and the Lord strengthened him with
   fearful powers;*

3* God wrought swift miracles at his words
   and sustained him in the king's presence.
He gave him the commandments for his people,
   and revealed to him his glory.

4* For his trustworthiness and meekness
   God selected him from all mankind;

5† He permitted him to hear his voice,
   and led him into the cloud,
Where, face to face, he gave him
   the commandments,
   the law of life and understanding,

44, 16: ENOCH: because of his friendship with God and also by reason of his unusual disappearance from the earth, this prophet's renown was great among the chosen people, particularly in the two centuries just before the coming of Christ; cf Gn 5, 21–24; Heb 11, 5. The present verse is an expansion of the original text; cf Sir 49, 14.

44, 20: In his own flesh . . . ordinance: the covenant of circumcision; cf Gn 17, 10–14. And when tested . . . loyal: Abraham's willingness to sacrifice his son Isaac at the Lord's command; cf Gn 22, 9–12.

44, 21: The River: the Euphrates; cf Gn 2, 14.

45, 1–5: Moses manifested God's power through miracles (1ff), God's authority through the promulgation of the commandments and the law (5), and God's mercy through the intimacy granted him by the Lord for his own faithfulness and meekness (4f). The very per-

sonification of the old covenant, Moses was also a type of Christ, the Prophet and Legislator of the new; cf Dt 18, 15.

45, 2: God's honor devolved upon him: Moses was actually God's substitute in dealing with Pharaoh, hence God entrusted his own honor to Moses.

45, 5: Face to face: on God's intimacy with Moses, see Ex 33, 11; Nm 12, 8. St. Paul alluded to this in 1 Cor 13, 12.

44, 14: Wis 3, 3.	**44, 22:** Gn 26, 3.5.24; 27, 28f;
44, 16: Sir 49, 14; Gn 5,	28, 14.
18–24; Heb 11, 5.	**45, 1:** Ex 2, 2; 11, 3; 33, 11;
44, 17: Gn 6, 8—9, 29; Heb	Nm 12, 7.
11, 7.	**45, 2:** Ex 7, 1—13, 22.
44, 19: Gn 12, 1—25, 10; Gal	**45, 2–5:** Ex 7—Dt 34.
3, 6; Heb 11, 8–19.	**45, 3:** Ex 4, 17; 7, 1.
44, 20: Gn 17, 10; 22, 1.	**45, 4:** Nm 12, 3.7.

S
I
R

That he might teach his precepts to Jacob,
    his judgments and decrees to Israel.

6*† He raised up also, like Moses in holiness,
    his brother AARON, of the tribe of Levi.

7† He made him perpetual in his office
    when he bestowed on him the priesthood
      of his people;
  He established him in honor
    and crowned him with lofty majesty;

8 He clothed him with splendid apparel,
    and adorned him with the
      glorious vestments:
  Breeches and tunic and robe
    with pomegranates around the hem,

9 And a rustle of bells round about,
    through whose pleasing sound at each step
  He would be heard within the sanctuary,
    and the children of his race would
      be remembered;

10 The sacred vestments of gold, of violet,
    and of crimson, wrought with embroidery;
  The breastpiece for decision, the ephod
    and cincture

11 with scarlet yarn, the work of the weaver;
  Precious stones with seal engravings
    in golden settings, the work of the jeweler,
  To commemorate in incised letters
    each of the tribes of Israel;

12 On his turban the diadem of gold,
    its plate wrought with the insignia
      of holiness,
  Majestic, glorious, renowned for splendor,
    a delight to the eyes, beauty supreme.

13 Before him, no one was adorned with these,
    nor may they ever be worn by any
  Except his sons and them alone,
    generation after generation, for all time.

14 His cereal offering is wholly burnt
    with the established sacrifice twice each day;

15 For Moses ordained him
    and anointed him with the holy oil,
  In a lasting covenant with him
    and with his family, as permanent as
      the heavens,
  That he should serve God in his priesthood
    and bless his people in his name.

16 He chose him from all mankind
    to offer holocausts and choice offerings,
  To burn sacrifices of sweet odor for
    a memorial,
    and to atone for the people of Israel.

17 He gave to him his laws,
    and authority to prescribe and to judge:
  To teach the precepts to his people,
    and the ritual to the descendants of Israel.

18* Men of other families were inflamed
    against him,
    were jealous of him in the desert,
  The followers of Dathan and Abiram,
    and the band of Korah in their defiance.

19 But the LORD saw this and became angry,
    he destroyed them in his burning wrath.
  He brought down upon them a miracle,
    and consumed them with his flaming fire.

20* Then he increased the glory of Aaron
    and bestowed upon him his inheritance:
  The sacred offerings he allotted to him,
    with the showbread as his portion;

21 The oblations of the LORD are his food,
    a gift to him and his descendants.

22 But he holds no land among the people
    nor shares with them their heritage;
  For the LORD himself is his portion,
    his inheritance in the midst of Israel.

23* PHINEHAS too, the son of Eleazar,
    was the courageous third of his line
  When, zealous for the God of all,
    he met the crisis of his people
  And, at the prompting of his noble heart,
    atoned for the children of Israel.

24 Therefore on him again God conferred
    the right,
    in a covenant of friendship, to provide for
    the sanctuary,
  So that he and his descendants
    should possess the high priesthood forever.

25* For even his covenant with David,
    the son of Jesse of the tribe of Judah,
  Was an individual heritage through one
    son alone;
    but the heritage of Aaron is for all his
    descendants.

45, 6–21: The author here expresses his reverence and esteem for the priesthood of the old covenant. He recalls God's choice of Aaron and his sons for this sublime office (6f), and describes in detail the beauty of the high priest's vestments (8–13). He relates the ordination of Aaron at the hands of Moses, his brother (15), and describes the priestly functions, of offering sacrifice to God (16), and of blessing (15), teaching, governing and judging the people (17); the inheritance of the high priest (20ff); the punishment of those families who were jealous of Aaron (18f); and the confirmation of the covenant of the priesthood with Aaron's descendants through Phinehas (23ff).
  45, 7: The priesthood of Aaron was superseded by the priesthood of Christ; cf Heb 7, 18–28.

45, 6ff: Ex 28f; Wis 18, 24.
45, 18: Nm 16, 1ff.
45, 20f: Nm 18, 11–21; Dt 10, 9.
45, 23: Nm 25, 7–13; Ps 106, 30f; 1 Mc 2, 26.54.
45, 25: 2 Sm 7, 12–16.

26 And now bless the LORD
     who has crowned you with glory!
   May he grant you wisdom of heart
     to govern his people in justice,
   Lest their welfare should ever be forgotten,
     or your authority, throughout all time.

Joshua, Caleb and the Judges

46 1*† Valiant leader was JOSHUA, son
           of Nun
       assistant to Moses in the prophetic office,
     Formed to be, as his name implies,
       the great savior of God's chosen ones,
     To punish the enemy
       and to win the inheritance for Israel.
2* What glory was his when he raised his arm,
     to brandish his javelin against the city!
3† And who could withstand him
     when he fought the battles of the LORD?
4* Did he not by his power stop the sun,
     so that one day became two?
5 He called upon the Most High God
     when his enemies beset him on all sides,
   And God Most High gave answer to him
     in hailstones of tremendous power,
6 Which he rained down upon the hostile army
     till on the slope he destroyed the foe;

   That all the doomed nations might know
     that the LORD was watching over his
       people's battles.
   And because he was a devoted follower
     of God
7*† and in Moses' lifetime showed
     himself loyal,
   He and CALEB, son of Jephunneh,
     when they opposed the rebel assembly,
   Averted God's anger from the people
     and suppressed the wicked complaint—
8* Because of this, they were the only
     two spared
       from the six hundred thousand
         infantry,
   To lead the people into their inheritance,
     the land flowing with milk and honey.
9* And the strength he gave to Caleb
     remained with him even in his old age
   Till he won his way onto the summits of
     the land;
       his family too received an inheritance,
10 That all the people of Jacob might know
     how good it is to be a devoted follower of
       the LORD.
11*†The JUDGES, too, each one of them,
     whose hearts were not deceived,

Heroes

Who are your heroes? Maybe they include a teacher, a coach, a friend, or a parent. What sets them apart and makes them people you look up to? Their accomplishments? A cause they represent? Or a personal trait that only someone who knows them personally would be aware of?

Whom we look to as heroes says a lot about us. If our heroes are kind and generous, then maybe we value kindness and generosity. If our heroes are wealthy, perhaps we desire wealth.

Read the last section of Sirach, starting with chapter 44, which honors many Old Testament heroes. Ben Sira considered them heroes because their hearts were fixed on the LORD (49, 3). What an awesome way to describe heroes!

Whom do you know who has his or her heart fixed on the LORD? What does your choice of heroes say about your dreams and values?

▶ Sirach, chapters 44–49

S
I
R

46, 1–6: JOSHUA: whose name means "the LORD is savior" (1), was the instrument through which God delivered his people in miraculous ways (2–6) by destroying their enemies, whose land he gave to the Israelites as an inheritance (1).

46, 3: *The battles of the LORD?:* cf Jos 6–10.

46, 7–10: Caleb, who with Joshua advised Moses and the people in the desert to conquer Canaan, despite the counsel of their companion scouts and the rebellion of the people, merited to lead the Israelites of the succeeding generation into the Promised Land. Caleb in his old age received as his inheritance a portion of land which he himself had previously conquered; cf Jos 15, 13f.

46, 11–20: Of the Judges praised and blessed for their fidelity to God in opposing idolatry, Samuel, a man of spotless integrity, was the greatest (11f.19). He was judge of the entire nation, and was also a prophet and priest who through his sacrificial offering obtained victory over the Philistines. He established the kingdom, anointed kings (13–18), and even after his death foretold the king's fate and put an end to wickedness (20).

46, 1: Ex 17, 9; Nm 27, 18;   **46, 7:** Nm 13, 30; 14, 6.
    Dt 34, 9; Jos 1, 1–4.   **46, 8:** Nm 14, 22–38.
46, 2: Jos 8, 18.   **46, 9:** Jos 14, 6; 15, 13.
46, 4: Jos 10, 13.   **46, 11:** Jgs 1, 1—16, 31.

Who did not abandon God:
may their memory be ever blessed,

12 Their bones return to life from their
resting place,
and their names receive fresh luster in
their children!

13* Beloved of his people, dear to his Maker,
dedicated from his mother's womb,
Consecrated to the LORD as a prophet,
was SAMUEL, the judge and priest.
At God's word he established the kingdom
and anointed princes to rule the people.

14 By the law of the LORD he judged the nation,
when he visited the encampments of Jacob.

15 As a trustworthy prophet he was sought out
and his words proved him true as a seer.

16* He, too, called upon God,
and offered him a suckling lamb;

17* Then the LORD thundered forth from heaven,
and the tremendous roar of his voice
was heard.

18 He brought low the rulers of the enemy
and destroyed all the lords of
the Philistines.

19* When Samuel approached the end of his life,
he testified before the LORD and his
anointed prince,
"No bribe or secret gift have I taken from
any man!"
and no one dared gainsay him.

20* Even when he lay buried, his guidance
was sought;
he made known to the king his fate,
And from the grave he raised his voice
as a prophet, to put an end to wickedness.

Nathan, David and Solomon

47 1*† After him came NATHAN
who served in the presence of David.

2* Like the choice fat of the sacred offerings,
so was DAVID in Israel.

3* He made sport of lions as though they were kids,
and of bears, like lambs of the flock.

4* As a youth he slew the giant

and wiped out the people's disgrace,
When his hand let fly the slingstone
that crushed the pride of Goliath.

5 Since he called upon the Most High God,
who gave strength to his right arm
To defeat the skilled warrior
and raise up the might of his people,

6* Therefore the women sang his praises
and ascribed to him tens of thousands.
When he assumed the royal crown, he battled

7* and subdued the enemy on every side.
He destroyed the hostile Philistines
and shattered their power till our own day.

8 With his every deed he offered thanks
to God Most High, in words of praise.
With his whole being he loved his Maker
and daily had his praises sung;

9* He added beauty to the feasts
and solemnized the seasons of each year
With string music before the altar,
providing sweet melody for the psalms

10 So that when the Holy Name was praised,
before daybreak the sanctuary would resound.

11* The LORD forgave him his sins
and exalted his strength forever;
He conferred on him the rights of royalty
and established his throne in Israel.

12*† Because of his merits he had as his successor
a wise son, who lived in security:

13* SOLOMON reigned during an era of peace,
for God made tranquil all his borders.
He built a house to the name of God,
and established a lasting sanctuary.

14* How wise you were when you were young,
overflowing with instruction, like the Nile
in flood!

15 Your understanding covered the whole earth,
and, like a sea, filled it with knowledge.

16 Your fame reached distant coasts,
and their peoples came to hear you;

17 With song and story and riddle,
and with your answers, you astounded
the nations.

47, 1–11: David, a youthful and fearless warrior, the favorite of all Israel, by defeating Goliath, the boastful Philistine giant, removed the people's disgrace and greatly strengthened their power (1–7). With his whole being he loved and praised God, and his devotion to divine worship led him to develop liturgical cult. David fell into sin, but repenting, received pardon from God and the promise of an everlasting kingdom (8–11).

47, 12–24: Solomon, son and successor of David, inherited peace through his father's conquests. He built the magnificent temple of Jerusalem (12f) and received from God the favor of unparalleled wisdom, through which he obtained great fame (14–17). Luxury and sensuality, however, brought disgrace upon him, and because of his oppressive burdens, he disposed the kingdom for divi-

sion after his death (19–21.23f). Nevertheless God did not withdraw his promise of establishing his throne in the descendants of David (22).

46, 13: 1 Sm 1, 10ff; 8, 4ff;
　　　　10, 1; 16, 13.
46, 16: 1 Sm 7, 9.
46, 17: Sir 12, 18.
46, 19: 1 Sm 12, 3.
46, 20: 1 Sm 28, 14.
47, 1: 2 Sm 7, 2.
47, 2: 1 Sm 16, 11.
47, 3: 1 Sm 17, 35.
47, 4: 1 Sm 17, 49.
47, 6: 1 Sm 18, 7.
47, 7: 2 Sm 5, 6–25.
47, 9: 1 Chr 16, 4ff; 23, 2ff;
　　　　25, 1–7.
47, 11: 2 Sm 12, 13; 7, 12–16.
47, 12: 1 Kgs 2, 12.
47, 13: 1 Kgs 5, 1.5.
47, 14–18: 1 Kgs 5, 9–14;
　　　　10, 14–28.

18† You were called by that glorious name
    which was conferred upon Israel.
Gold you gathered like so much iron,
    you heaped up silver as though it
      were lead;

19* But you abandoned yourself to women
    and gave them dominion over your body.

20 You brought dishonor upon your reputation,
    shame upon your marriage,
Wrath upon your descendants,
    and groaning upon your domain;

21* Thus two governments came into being,
    when in Ephraim kingship was usurped.

22* But God does not withdraw his mercy,
    nor permit even one of his promises to fail.
He does not uproot the posterity of his
    chosen one,
nor destroy the offspring of his friend.
So he gave to Jacob a remnant,
    to David a root from his own family.

23*† Solomon finally slept with his fathers,
    and left behind him one of his sons,
Expansive in folly, limited in sense,
    REHOBOAM, who by his policy made the
      people rebel;
Until one arose who should not
    be remembered,
    the sinner who led Israel into sin,
Who brought ruin to Ephraim

24   and caused them to be exiled from
      their land.

Elijah and Elisha

Their sinfulness grew more and more,
25†   and they lent themselves to every evil,

48

1* Till like a fire there appeared
    the prophet
whose words were as a flaming furnace.

2 Their staff of bread he shattered,
    in his zeal he reduced them to straits;

3* By God's word he shut up the heavens
    and three times brought down fire.

4 How awesome are you, ELIJAH!
    Whose glory is equal to yours?

5* You brought a dead man back to life
    from the nether world, by the will of
      the LORD.

6* You sent kings down to destruction,
    and nobles, from their beds of sickness.

7* You heard threats at Sinai,
    at Horeb avenging judgments.

8* You anointed kings who should
    inflict vengeance,
    and a prophet as your successor.

9* You were taken aloft in a whirlwind,
    in a chariot with fiery horses.

10* You are destined, it is written, in time to come
    to put an end to wrath before the day of
      the LORD,
To turn back the hearts of fathers toward
    their sons,
    and to re-establish the tribes of Jacob.

11 Blessed is he who shall have seen you before
    he dies,

12*† O Elijah, enveloped in the whirlwind!

Then ELISHA, filled with a twofold portion of
    his spirit,
    wrought many marvels by his mere word.
During his lifetime he feared no one,
    nor was any man able to intimidate
    his will.

13* Nothing was beyond his power;
    beneath him flesh was brought back
    into life.

14 In life he performed wonders,
    and after death, marvelous deeds.

15* Despite all this the people did not repent,
    nor did they give up their sins,
Until they were rooted out of their land
    and scattered all over the earth.
But Judah remained, a tiny people,
    with its rulers from the house of David.

16 Some of these did what was right,
    but others were extremely sinful.

47, 18: Cf 2 Sm 12, 25, where Solomon is called Jedidiah, "beloved of the Lord." The same term is used of Israel in Jer 11, 15.

47, 23: *Expansive:* the name Rehoboam means "the people is expansive," that is, widespread. *The sinner:* Jeroboam; cf 1 Kgs 12, 2. 20.26–32.

47, 25—48, 11: The prophetic ministry of Elijah amid widespread idolatry is here described as a judgment by fire (47, 25f). Through his preaching, miracles and vengeance against God's enemies within and without Israel, the prophet succeeded for a time in destroying idols and in restoring faith and the worship of the true God (48, 2–8). His miraculous departure from this life gave rise to the belief that he did not die but would return before the end of the world to put an end to wrath and restore the tribes of Israel (9ff). Cf Mt 17, 9–13.

48, 12–16: Elisha fearlessly continued the work of his predeces-sor by numerous miracles (12ff), but the obstinacy of the people eventually brought on the destruction of the kingdom of Israel and the dispersion of its subjects. Judah, however, survived under the rule of Davidic kings, both good and bad (15f).

47, 19: 1 Kgs 11, 1ff.
47, 21: 1 Kgs 12, 1ff.
47, 22: 2 Sm 7, 15; Ps 89, 34ff.
47, 23: 1 Kgs 11, 43; 12, 13.21; 13, 34; 2 Kgs 17, 6ff.
48, 1: 1 Kgs 17, 1.
48, 3: 1 Kgs 17, 1; 2 Kgs 1, 9–14.
48, 5: 1 Kgs 17, 22.
48, 6: 1 Kgs 21, 19; 2 Kgs 1, 17.
48, 7: 1 Kgs 19, 8ff.
48, 8: 1 Kgs 19, 15ff.
48, 9: 2 Kgs 2, 11.
48, 10: Mal 3, 23f; Mt 17, 10.
48, 12: 2 Kgs 2, 9; 3, 13.
48, 13f: 2 Kgs 13, 21.
48, 15: 2 Kgs 15, 29; 18, 11.

Hezekiah and Isaiah†

17* HEZEKIAH fortified his city
　　and had water brought into it;
　With iron tools he cut through the rock
　　and he built reservoirs for water.

18* During his reign Sennacherib led an invasion,
　　and sent his adjutant;
　He shook his fist at Zion
　　and blasphemed God in his pride.

19 The people's hearts melted within them,
　　and they were in anguish like that
　　　of childbirth.

20* But they called upon the Most High God
　　and lifted up their hands to him;
　He heard the prayer they uttered,
　　and saved them through ISAIAH.

21* God struck the camp of the Assyrians
　　and routed them with a plague.

22 For Hezekiah did what was right
　　and held fast to the paths of David,
　As ordered by the illustrious prophet
　　Isaiah, who saw the truth in visions.

23* In his lifetime he turned back the sun
　　and prolonged the life of the king.

24* By his powerful spirit he looked into
　　the future
　　and consoled the mourners of Zion;

25 He foretold what should be till the end
　　of time,
　　hidden things yet to be fulfilled.

Josiah and the Prophets†

49
1* The name Josiah is like blended
　　incense,
　　made lasting by a skilled perfumer.
　Precious is his memory, like honey to the taste,
　　like music at a banquet.

2 For he grieved over our betrayals
　　and destroyed the abominable idols.

3 He turned to God with his whole heart,
　　and, though times were evil, he
　　　practiced virtue.

4 Except for David, Hezekiah and Josiah,
　　they all were wicked;
　They abandoned the law of the Most High,
　　these kings of Judah, right to the very end.

5 So he gave over their power to others,
　　their glory to a foolish foreign nation

6* Who burned the holy city
　　and left its streets desolate,
　As JEREMIAH had foretold; 7* for they had
　　treated him badly
　who even in the womb had been made
　　a prophet,
　To root out, pull down, and destroy,
　　and then to build and to plant.

8* EZEKIEL beheld the vision
　　and described the different creatures of
　　　the chariot;

9* He also referred to JOB,
　　who always persevered in the right path.

10 Then, too, the TWELVE PROPHETS—
　　may their bones return to life from their
　　　resting place!—
　Gave new strength to Jacob
　　and saved him by their faith and hope.

The Heroes after the Exile

11*†How can we fittingly praise ZERUBBABEL,
　　who was like a signet ring on God's
　　　right hand,

12 And Jeshua, Jozadak's son?
　　In their time they built the house of God;
　They erected the holy temple,
　　destined for everlasting glory.

13* Extolled be the memory of NEHEMIAH!
　　He rebuilt our ruined walls,
　Restored our shattered defenses,
　　and set up gates and bars.

The Earliest Patriarchs

14*†Few on earth have been made the equal
　　of ENOCH,
　　for he was taken up bodily.

15* Was ever a man born like JOSEPH?
　　Even his dead body was provided for.

48, 17–25: The fidelity, trust and courage of King Hezekiah (17.
22), the zeal of the prophet Isaiah, and the prayer of the people (20)
availed with God. The Assyrian oppressors were routed (18f.21), the
king's life was prolonged, and consolations were granted the people
through Isaiah's prophecies concerning the future (23ff), especially
the coming of the Messiah and the establishment of his kingdom;
cf Is 7, 14; 9, 6f; 40—65.
　49, 1–10: The author's praise of King Josiah (1–3), of the prophets
Jeremiah and Ezekiel and likewise the minor prophets (7–10) derives
from their spirit of fidelity to the Lord and his law amid the infidelity of kings and people (4ff.10).
　49, 11ff: Zerubbabel and Jeshua, in rebuilding the temple, and
Nehemiah, the governor, in repairing the walls of the Holy City, also
restored what these constructions signify, namely, religious worship
and civil authority as prescribed in the law.

49, 14ff: The patriarchs here mentioned were glorious because of
their spirit of religion, i.e., their profound reverence for God and
obedience to him. The splendor of Adam, moreover, was due to his
direct origin from God.

48, 17: 2 Kgs 20, 20; 2 Chr
　　32, 3ff.30.
48, 18: 2 Kgs 18, 13ff; Is 36,
　　1ff.
48, 20: 2 Kgs 19, 20.
48, 21: 2 Kgs 19, 35; Is 37, 36.
48, 23: 2 Kgs 20, 11; Is 38, 8.
48, 24f: 2 Kgs 20, 17; Is 40,
　　1ff; 42, 9; 46, 10; 48,
　　6; 61, 2.
　49, 1: 2 Kgs 22, 1; 2 Chr
　　34, 1.

49, 6: 2 Kgs 25, 9; 2 Chr
　　36, 19.
49, 7: Jer 1, 5.10.
49, 8: Ez 1, 4ff.
49, 9: Ez 14, 14.20.
49, 11f: Ezr 3, 2; Hg 1, 12;
　　Zec 3, 1.
49, 13: Neh 1, 1; 3, 1.
49, 14: Sir 44, 16; Gn 5, 18–24.
49, 15: Gn 37–50; Ex 13, 19;
　　Jos 24, 32.

16* Glorious, too, were SHEM and SETH and ENOS;
　　　but beyond that of any living being
　　　was the splendor of ADAM.

Simon, Son of Jochanan

50 ¹† The greatest among his brethren, the
　　　　glory of his people,
　　was SIMON the priest, son of Jochanan,
　In whose time the house of God
　　　was renovated,
　　　in whose days the temple was reinforced.
2　In his time also the wall was built
　　　with powerful turrets for the temple precincts;
3　In his time the reservoir was dug,
　　　the pool with a vastness like the sea's.
4　He protected his people against brigands
　　　and strengthened his city against the enemy.
5　How splendid he was as he appeared from
　　　the tent,
　　　as he came from within the veil!
6　Like a star shining among the clouds,
　　　like the full moon at the holyday season;
7　Like the sun shining upon the temple,
　　　like the rainbow appearing in the cloudy sky;
8　Like the blossoms on the branches
　　　in springtime,
　　　like a lily on the banks of a stream;
　Like the trees of Lebanon in summer,
9　　like the fire of incense at the sacrifice;
　Like a vessel of beaten gold,
　　　studded with precious stones;
10　Like a luxuriant olive tree thick with fruit,
　　　like a cypress standing against the clouds;
11* Vested in his magnificent robes,
　　　and wearing his garments of splendor,
　As he ascended the glorious altar
　　　and lent majesty to the court of
　　　the sanctuary.

12　When he received the sundered victims from
　　　the priests
　　　while he stood before the sacrificial wood,
　His brethren ringed him about like a garland,
　　　like a stand of cedars on Lebanon;
13　All the sons of Aaron in their dignity
　　　clustered around him like poplars,

With the offerings to the LORD in their hands,
　　　in the presence of the whole assembly
　　　of Israel.
14　Once he had completed the services at
　　　the altar
　　with the arranging of the sacrifices for the
　　　Most High,
15* And had stretched forth his hand for the cup,
　　　to offer blood of the grape,
　And poured it out at the foot of the altar,
　　　a sweet-smelling odor to the Most High God,
16* The sons of Aaron would sound a blast,
　　　the priests, on their trumpets of
　　　beaten metal;
　A blast to resound mightily
　　　as a reminder before the Most High.
17　Then all the people with one accord
　　　would quickly fall prostrate to the ground
　In adoration before the Most High,
　　　before the Holy One of Israel.

18　Then hymns would re-echo,
　　　and over the throng sweet strains of
　　　praise resound.
19　All the people of the land would shout for joy,
　　　praying to the Merciful One,
　As the high priest completed the services at
　　　the altar
　　by presenting to God the sacrifice due;
20* Then coming down he would raise his hands
　　　over all the congregation of Israel.
　The blessing of the LORD would be upon
　　　his lips,
　　　the name of the LORD would be his glory.
21　Then again the people would lie prostrate
　　　to receive from him the blessing of the
　　　Most High.

22† And now, bless the God of all,
　　　who has done wondrous things on earth;
　Who fosters men's growth from their
　　　mother's womb,
　　　and fashions them according to his will!
23　May he grant you joy of heart
　　　and may peace abide among you;
24　May his goodness toward us endure in Israel
　　　as long as the heavens are above.

† **50, 1–21:** The son of Jochanan here mentioned was Simon II, in whose time as high priest (219–196 B.C.) great works were accomplished for the benefit of public worship and welfare (1–4). The author, a contemporary of this high priest, describes in great detail and by numerous comparisons the impression of awful majesty received, the lofty joy aroused, at sight of the high priest fully vested entering the sanctuary, ascending the altar (6–11), and, in the presence of the whole assembly of Israel, encircled by assistant priests bearing offerings, sacrificing the burnt offering on the Day of Atonement, while the trumpets blast and the people bow down in adoration of the Most High (12–17). The hymnody, the joyful shouts of the multitude, and finally the high priest's blessing, in which he pronounces—once only in the year, on this occasion—the holy name of Yahweh, climax the description of this most solemn Jewish liturgical function (18–21).

50, 22ff: Praise and thanksgiving are given to God for his wondrous works, and a blessing is invoked on man that he may enjoy peace and gladness of heart and the abiding goodness of the Most High.

49, 16: Gn 1, 27; 4, 25f.　　　50, 15f: Nm 15, 5; 28, 7.
50, 11: Sir 45, 8–12; Ex 28,　　50, 16: Nm 10, 10.
　　2–5; 39, 1–21.　　　　　　50, 20: Nm 6, 23–26.

Epilogue and Canticles

25† My whole being loathes two nations,
  the third is not even a people:†
26*†Those who live in Seir and Philistia,
  and the degenerate folk who dwell in
  Shechem.

27† Wise instruction, appropriate proverbs,
  I have written in this book,
  I, Jesus, son of Eleazar, son of Sirach,
  as they gushed forth from my
  heart's understanding.
28 Happy the man who meditates upon
  these things,
  wise the man who takes them to heart!
29 If he puts them into practice, he can cope
  with anything,
  for the fear of the LORD is his lamp.

51

1*† I give you thanks, O God of
  my father;
  I praise you, O God my savior!
  I will make known your name, refuge of
  my life;
2* you have been my helper against
  my adversaries.
  You have saved me from death,
  and kept back my body from the pit,
  From the clutches of the nether world you
  have snatched my feet;
3* you have delivered me, in your great mercy,
  From the scourge of a slanderous tongue,
  and from lips that went over to falsehood,
  From the snare of those who watched for
  my downfall,

and from the power of those who sought
  my life;
  From many a danger you have saved me,
4*   from flames that hemmed me in on
  every side;
  From the midst of unremitting fire,
5   from the deep belly of the nether world;
  From deceiving lips and painters of lies,
6*   from the arrows of dishonest tongues.
  I was at the point of death,
  my soul was nearing the depths of the
  nether world;
7* I turned every way, but there was no one to
  help me,
  I looked for one to sustain me, but could
  find no one.
8 But then I remembered the mercies of
  the LORD,
  his kindness through ages past;
  For he saves those who take refuge in him,
  and rescues them from every evil.
9 So I raised my voice from the very earth,
  from the gates of the nether world, my cry.
10* I called out: O Lord, you are my father,
  you are my champion and my savior;
  Do not abandon me in time of trouble,
  in the midst of storms and dangers.
11 I will ever praise your name
  and be constant in my prayers to you.
  Thereupon the LORD heard my voice,
  he listened to my appeal;
12† He saved me from evil of every kind
  and preserved me in time of trouble.
  For this reason I thank him and I praise him;
  I bless the name of the LORD.

---

† 50, 25f: The author's abhorrence of the pagan Edomites (Idumeans), Philistines and Samaritans can be understood in the light of Old Testament thinking, which does not always distinguish between hatred of evildoers and hatred of the evil they do.
50, 25: *Not even a people:* the Samaritans.
50, 26: *Seir:* Mount Seir in the territory of the Edomites. *Shechem:* a city in Samaria.
50, 27ff: These verses contain the subscription of the author, Jesus, son of Eleazar, son of Sirach, to his long and beautiful treatise on wisdom as applying to all of human life, integrating it under the direction of the fear of the Lord.
51, 1–12: A canticle of praise and thanks to God for delivering the author from slander, dangers, destruction, death, the nether world, and evil of every kind.
51, 12: After this verse the Hebrew text gives the litany of praise contained below. It is similar to Ps 136. Though not found in any versions, and therefore of doubtful authenticity, the litany seems from internal evidence to go back to the time of Sirach:

Give thanks to the LORD, for he is good, for his mercy endures forever;
Give thanks to the God of glory, for his mercy endures forever;
Give thanks to the guardian of Israel, for his mercy endures forever;
Give thanks to the creator of the universe, for his mercy endures forever;
Give thanks to the redeemer of Israel, for his mercy endures forever;

Give thanks to him who gathers the dispersed of Israel, for his mercy endures forever;
Give thanks to him who builds his city and his sanctuary, for his mercy endures forever;
Give thanks to him who makes a horn to sprout forth, for the house of David, for his mercy endures forever;
Give thanks to him who has chosen for his priests the sons of Zadok, for his mercy endures forever;
Give thanks to the shield of Abraham, for his mercy endures forever;
Give thanks to the rock of Isaac, for his mercy endures forever;
Give thanks to the mighty one of Jacob, for his mercy endures forever;
Give thanks to him who has chosen Zion, for his mercy endures forever;
Give thanks to the king over kings of kings, for his mercy endures forever;
He has lifted up the horn of his people, be this his praise from all his faithful ones,
From the children of Israel, the people close to him. Alleluia! (Cf Ps 148, 14.)

50, 26: 2 Kgs 17, 24; Jn 4, 9.
51, 1: Ps 138, 1.
51, 2: Ps 91, 3.
51, 3: Pss 40, 5; 91, 3.

51, 4: Ps 66, 12.
51, 6: Pss 88, 4; 94, 17.
51, 7: Pss 22, 12; 142, 5.
51, 10: Ps 89, 27.

13*†When I was young and innocent,
    I sought wisdom.
14 She came to me in her beauty,
    and until the end I will cultivate her.
15 As the blossoms yielded to ripening grapes,
    the heart's joy,
  My feet kept to the level path
    because from earliest youth I was familiar
      with her.
16 In the short time I paid heed,
    I met with great instruction.
17 Since in this way I have profited,
    I will give my teacher grateful praise.

18 I became resolutely devoted to her—
    the good I persistently strove for.
19 I burned with desire for her,
    never turning back.
  I became preoccupied with her,
    never weary of extolling her.
  My hand opened her gate
    and I came to know her secrets.
20* For her I purified my hands;
    in cleanness I attained to her.
  At first acquaintance with her, I
    gained understanding
  such that I will never forsake her.
21 My whole being was stirred as I learned
    about her;

  therefore I have made her my
    prize possession.
22 The LORD has granted me my lips as a reward,
    and my tongue will declare his praises.

23* Come aside to me, you untutored,
    and take up lodging in the house
      of instruction;
24 How long will you be deprived of
    wisdom's food,
  how long will you endure such
    bitter thirst?
25* I open my mouth and speak of her:
    gain, at no cost, wisdom for yourselves.
26* Submit your neck to her yoke,
    that your mind may accept her
      teaching.
  For she is close to those who seek her,
    and the one who is in earnest finds her.
27 See for yourselves! I have labored only
    a little,
  but have found much.
28 Acquire but a little instruction;
    you will win silver and gold through her.
29 Let your spirits rejoice in the mercy of God,
    and be not ashamed to give him praise.
30* Work at your tasks in due season,
    and in his own time God will give you
    your reward.

---

† **51, 13–30:** An alphabetic canticle describing: a) the approach to wisdom through prayer, persistent study and instruction (13–17), purification from sin, enlightenment and ardent desire; b) the possession of wisdom (18–22). The author concludes with an urgent invitation to men to receive instruction in wisdom from him, and to live by it, because wisdom gives herself to those who seek her (23–26); and for their labor. God will reward them in the end (27–30). Cf Mt 11, 28; Eccl 12, 14.

In the Greek of 13f there is an expansion introducing Solomon as the speaker. This deviates from the original author's intent. It reads, "Publicly, in my prayer, facing the temple, I asked for her."

*———————

51, 13: Sir 34, 11.   **51, 26:** Sir 6, 25.
51, 20: Prv 4, 6.   **51, 30:** Sir 2, 8; Jb 34, 11; Jn
51, 23: Prv 8, 5.   9, 4.
51, 25: Sir 6, 20.

Introduction to the

Prophets

Have you ever heard a speaker who seemed to be talking right to you? someone who could see past external appearances and into the hearts of people and events? someone committed to total honesty even if it hurt? someone who inspired you to make some needed changes and gave you hope for the future? If so, you've encountered a modern-day prophet—a person who names what God wants to say to us. In this section of books, you will meet the prophets of the Bible —unique and courageous people who did these things for ancient Israel.

In-depth

WHAT IS A PROPHET? FIRST AND FOREMOST, A prophet is a person—or sometimes a group—who speaks for God. The prophet's words spoken in God's name— usually called prophecies or oracles—are God's words. Some people think that prophets can predict the future, but this is not their role in the Bible. The biblical prophets were called by God during times of crisis to offer God's people challenge or comfort, depending on their circumstances. So, to properly understand biblical prophecies, we must try to understand the historical situation God was addressing through the prophets.

Through the prophets' inspired messages, God reminded the Israelites of the Covenant God had made with them (see "Introduction to the Pentateuch"). If the people or their leaders were not keeping their side of the Covenant, the prophets challenged them to do so. If the people were in despair that God was not keeping God's side of the Covenant, the prophets promised that God would. Here are some common Covenant themes the prophets emphasized:

■ *Warnings against idolatry.* The Israelites were constantly tempted to worship the gods of other nations and cultures. The prophets had to keep reminding the kings and people of the first law of the Ten Commandments: "I, the LORD, am your God, who brought you out of the land of Egypt, that place of slavery. You shall not have other gods besides me" (Ex 20, 2–3).

- *Warnings to act justly and to treat the poor fairly.* In their greed and struggle for power, the wealthy and the ruling class often cheated and oppressed other people. Operating as Israel's conscience, the prophets were unanimous in challenging Israel to act justly and to care for the poor and marginalized. This did not always make the prophets popular with the kings and the ruling class—they were often ridiculed and even threatened with violence.

- *Attempts to deepen the understanding of God's love and mercy.* Some Israelites felt God would not forgive them after Israel (the northern kingdom) and Judah (the southern kingdom) were conquered by foreign nations. The prophets assured them that they would receive God's forgiveness if they turned to God and kept the Covenant. In addition, some of the prophets began to teach that God was Lord over—and cared for—all nations, not just Israel.

- *Promises of hope for the future.* During these troubled and often violent times, it must have seemed to many Israelites that their world was coming to an end. The prophets responded to the people's despair with hope-filled promises that ultimately God's love and justice would prevail. These hopeful prophecies took different forms: the coming of the Ideal Ruler, the restoration of Jerusalem and the Temple, a time of judgment when good is rewarded and evil punished, and so on.

The stories of the earliest prophets—Samuel, Nathan, Elijah, and Elisha—are in the Bible's historical Books of 1 and 2 Samuel and 1 and 2 Kings. God's revelation through the later prophets is recorded in the books of this section of the Bible. The introduction to each book in this section gives background about the historical situation the prophet faced. The timeline in the back of this Bible identifies the time period for each prophet.

As you read these books, keep this in mind: the role of prophets has not died, only changed. In every age, there are people who challenge us to be faithful to God, and remind us about God's faithful love for us. In fact, Christians believe that through their Baptism, God calls them to be priest, prophet, and king. You can fulfill your prophetic calling by challenging others to live justly and reminding them of God's love. It's exciting and humbling to be called into such a proud tradition.

Other Background

- Isaiah, Jeremiah, and Ezekiel are sometimes called the major prophets because their books are long.

- Hosea, Amos, Jeremiah, First Isaiah, Obadiah, Micah, Nahum, Habakkuk, and Zephaniah prophesied before the Babylonian Exile.

- Ezekiel, Second Isaiah, and Lamentations wrote during the Exile.

- Joel, Haggai, Zechariah, Malachi, Third Isaiah, and Baruch wrote after the Exile.

- Jonah isn't a real prophet, but a fictional, reluctant prophet.

- Seven of the prophets talk about "the day of the LORD"—a final time of God's judgment when evil will be punished.

Once in a while, Hollywood releases a new movie that is actually a remake of an older film. The new movie has a new director and new actors and actresses. It keeps the same basic plot as the original but is adapted to appeal to a modern audience. This is what happened with the prophet Isaiah. The original Isaiah was such a hit that years after he died, a second and even a third person or group adapted his ideas to their situation. The stories of the original Isaiah and his two "remakes" were collected into the single Book of Isaiah that we have today.

At a Glance

A. The Book of Judgment (1, 1—39, 8).

B. The Book of Consolation (40, 1—66, 24).

In-depth

Prophets from three different periods in Israel's history contributed to the Book of Isaiah. Chapters 1–39 reflect the prophecies of the original Isaiah, called First Isaiah. His career began with his call in the Temple during the reign of Uzziah around 742 B.C. (see the timeline at the back of this Bible). First Isaiah advised the kings of Judah about the dangers of alliances with foreign nations and cautioned them to trust only in God. He cried out against the social injustices of the rich ruling class against the poor, and taught that God had a plan in which all, rich and poor, powerful and oppressed, would have a part. First Isaiah is responsible for the messianic prophecies, which tell of the coming of a perfect king.

Years later, when Israel was exiled in Babylon (587–538 B.C.), another prophet, Second Isaiah, reworked First Isaiah's prophecies to address his own people (chapters 40–55). Second Isaiah's people were struggling to understand why God allowed them to be captives in a strange land. The prophet comforted them with a hopeful message: They had been taken captive so that they would turn away from their sinful practices; now that they had learned their lesson, God would return them to rebuild Israel. Contained in this prophet's writings are the famous servant songs (see "The Servant Songs," 42, 1-7).

After the Israelites returned from exile and resettled in Judah (537–500 B.C.), they once again fell into patterns of social injustice and religious apathy. Third Isaiah responded by demanding that they practice justice toward one another, and even toward the Gentiles, non-Jews (chapters 56–66). Realizing that Israel would never be a perfect community, he spoke of "new heavens / and a new earth" (65, 17), where people would live according to God's plan.

Quick Facts

Period Covered
742–500 B.C.

Authors
the three Isaiahs or their followers

Themes
faithfulness to God, justice for the poor, hope for the future, messianic prophecies, God as lord over all nations

The Book of *Isaiah*

Isaiah

A. THE BOOK OF JUDGMENT

I: Indictment of Israel and Judah

Israel's Sinfulness

1 ¹† The vision which Isaiah, son of Amoz, had concerning Judah and Jerusalem in the days of Uzziah, Jotham, Ahaz and Hezekiah, kings of Judah.

²* Hear, O heavens, and listen, O earth,
   for the LORD speaks:
Sons have I raised and reared,
   but they have disowned me!
³† An ox knows its owner,
   and an ass, its master's manger;
But Israel does not know,
   my people has not understood.
⁴*†Ah! sinful nation, people laden with wickedness,
   evil race, corrupt children!
They have forsaken the LORD,
   spurned the Holy One of Israel,
   apostatized.

⁵† Where would you yet be struck,
   you that rebel again and again?
The whole head is sick,
   the whole heart faint.
⁶ From the sole of the foot to the head
   there is no sound spot:
Wound and welt and gaping gash,
   not drained, or bandaged,
   or eased with salve.
⁷ Your country is waste,
   your cities burnt with fire;
Your land before your eyes
   strangers devour
   [a waste, like Sodom overthrown]—
⁸† And daughter Zion is left
   like a hut in a vineyard,
Like a shed in a melon patch,
   like a city blockaded.

⁹*†Unless the LORD of hosts
   had left us a scanty remnant,
We had become as Sodom,
   we should be like Gomorrah.

God Wants Justice, Not Empty Rites!

First Isaiah denounces the hypocrisy of practicing empty religious rituals that are not grounded in justice, sincerity, and good deeds. Speaking for God, he calls the people to do good, seek justice, rescue the oppressed, and defend the orphans and the widows.

- How do you actively seek justice and take care of people in need?
- In your prayer, ask God's forgiveness for when you have not responded to God's call to practice justice or help people in need.

▶ Is 1, 10–20

---

10 Hear the word of the LORD,
    princes of Sodom!
Listen to the instruction of our God,
    people of Gomorrah!
11*† What care I for the number of your sacrifices?
    says the LORD.
I have had enough of whole-burnt rams
    and fat of fatlings;
In the blood of calves, lambs and goats
    I find no pleasure.

12 When you come in to visit me,
    who asks these things of you?
13*† Trample my courts no more!
    Bring no more worthless offerings;
    your incense is loathsome to me.
New moon and sabbath, calling
    of assemblies,
octaves with wickedness: these I cannot bear.
14 Your new moons and festivals I detest;
    they weigh me down, I tire of the load.
15*† When you spread out your hands,
    I close my eyes to you;
Though you pray the more,
    I will not listen.
Your hands are full of blood!
16   Wash yourselves clean!
Put away your misdeeds from before my eyes;

cease doing evil; 17* learn to do good.
Make justice your aim: redress the wronged,
    hear the orphan's plea, defend the widow.

18* Come now, let us set things right,
    says the LORD:
Though your sins be like scarlet,
    they may become white as snow;
Though they be crimson red,
    they may become white as wool.
19 If you are willing, and obey,
    you shall eat the good things of the land;
20 But if you refuse and resist,
    the sword shall consume you:
    for the mouth of the LORD has spoken!

21*† How has she turned adulteress,
    the faithful city, so upright!
Justice used to lodge within her,
    but now, murderers.
22 Your silver is turned to dross,
    your wine is mixed with water.
23* Your princes are rebels
    and comrades of thieves;
Each one of them loves a bribe
    and looks for gifts.
The fatherless they defend not,
    and the widow's plea does not reach them.

---

† **1, 11:** *The number of your sacrifices:* however numerous, they are not acceptable without the right dispositions on the part of the worshipers.
1, 13: *Octaves with wickedness:* the solemnity of the feasts marred by evil deeds.
1, 15: *Spread out your hands:* in prayer.
1, 21: A picture of Jerusalem, once so faithful to God. Apostasy from the covenant is often likened by the prophets to unfaithfulness to the marriage vow.

1, 11: Ps 50, 8–13; Sir 34, 19; Mi 6, 7.
1, 13: Prv 15, 8; Jer 6, 20.
1, 15: Prv 1, 28; Sir 34, 21–25.
1, 17: Ex 23, 6; Dt 24, 17; Sir 4, 9f; Jer 22, 3; Ez 22, 7; Zec 7, 9f.
1, 18: Ps 51, 9.
1, 21: Jer 3, 8; Hos 2, 7.
1, 23: Ex 23, 8; Dt 16, 19.

24* Now, therefore, says the Lord,
      the LORD of hosts, the Mighty One of Israel:
   Ah! I will take vengeance on my foes
      and fully repay my enemies!
25 I will turn my hand against you,
      and refine your dross in the furnace,
      removing all your alloy.
26* I will restore your judges as at first,
      and your counselors as in the beginning;
   After that you shall be called
      city of justice, faithful city.

27† Zion shall be redeemed by judgment,
      and her repentant ones by justice.
28 Rebels and sinners alike shall be crushed,
      those who desert the LORD shall
         be consumed.
29† You shall be ashamed of the terebinths which
         you prized,
      and blush for the groves which you chose.
30 You shall become like a tree with falling leaves,
      like a garden that has no water.
31 The strong man shall turn to tow,
      and his work shall become a spark;
   Both shall burn together,
      and there shall be none to quench
         the flames.

Zion, the Messianic Capital

2 ¹† This is what Isaiah, son of Amoz, saw concerning Judah and Jerusalem.

2*† In days to come,
   The mountain of the LORD's house
      shall be established as the highest
         mountain
      and raised above the hills.
   All nations shall stream toward it;*
3*†   many peoples shall come and say:
   "Come, let us climb the LORD's mountain,
      to the house of the God of Jacob,
   That he may instruct us in his ways,
      and we may walk in his paths."
   For from Zion shall go forth instruction,
      and the word of the LORD from Jerusalem.
4* He shall judge between the nations,
      and impose terms on many peoples.

They shall beat their swords into plowshares
   and their spears into pruning hooks;
One nation shall not raise the sword
      against another,
   nor shall they train for war again.

5 O house of Jacob, come,
      let us walk in the light of the LORD!

PRAY IT

From Violence to Love

We hear Is 2, 1-5 read every three years in church on the first Sunday of Advent. Its "swords into plowshares" theme is all about moving from violence to nonviolence and ultimately to love in our responses to conflict (see also Jl 4, 10 and Mi 4, 3).

But what exactly is a plowshare? A plowshare is a tool that helps a farmer harvest the fields. The message is that instead of tools of violence (swords), a world of peace needs only tools to feed and nourish its people (plowshares). God's reign is present when swords are turned into plowshares.

Our society often glorifies violence, weapons, battle, and war. Take a few minutes to pray, reflect, or journal on the following questions:

- Why does our society glorify violence?
- As a member of society, do you support violence or nonviolence? How?
- What nonviolent actions can you take when you find yourself in conflict situations? (For example, walking away from the situation, remaining calm, and counting to ten before responding.)
- How can we be people of love in a world that is all too often hateful?

▶ Is 2, 1–5

1, 27: This verse is the key to the whole Book of Isaiah. Zion's defiant persistence in sin has demanded a divine judgment, by which her survivors will be cleansed and will return to God in justice; cf Is 40, 2.
   1, 29: *Terebinths which you prized . . . groves which you chose:* as popular shrines for idolatrous worship.
   2, 1: An editorial addition introducing chapters 2–5.
   2, 2–4: The messianic destiny which ensures Judah's later restoration. In the messianic kingdom the prophets generally see the Lord's house as the seat of authority and the source of clear and certain doctrine; also, its rule willingly accepted by all peoples, maintained

by spiritual sanctions, and tending to universal peace. This passage is found substantially unchanged in Mi 4, 1–3; it probably, although not certainly, has Isaiah as its author.
   2, 3: *Zion . . . Jerusalem:* types of the earthly center of the messianic kingdom.

1, 24: Dt 32, 41.   2, 3: Zec 8, 20–23.
1, 26: Jer 33, 7ff; Zec 8, 3.   2, 4: Is 9, 7; 11, 4; Ps 72, 3f;
2, 2ff: Mi 4, 1ff.   Zec 9, 10.
2, 2: Is 56, 7.

The LORD's Judgment against Idols

6*†You have abandoned your people,
the house of Jacob,
Because they are filled with fortune-tellers
and soothsayers, like the Philistines;
they covenant with strangers.

7 Their land is full of silver and gold,
and there is no end to their treasures;
Their land is full of horses,
and there is no end to their chariots.

8* Their land is full of idols;
they worship the works of their hands,
that which their fingers have made.

9 But man is abased,
each one brought low.
[Do not pardon them!]

10* Get behind the rocks,
hide in the dust,
From the terror of the LORD
and the splendor of his majesty!

11† The haughty eyes of man will be lowered,
the arrogance of men will be abased,
and the LORD alone will be exalted, on
that day.

12 For the LORD of hosts will have his day
against all that is proud and arrogant,
all that is high, and it will be brought low;

13† Yes, against all the cedars of Lebanon
and all the oaks of Bashan,

14 Against all the lofty mountains
and all the high hills,

15 Against every lofty tower
and every fortified wall,

16† Against all the ships of Tarshish
and all stately vessels.

17 Human pride will be abased,
the arrogance of men brought low,
And the LORD alone will be exalted, on
that day.

18 The idols will perish forever.

19 Men will go into caves in the rocks
and into holes in the earth,
From the terror of the LORD
and the splendor of his majesty,
when he arises to overawe the earth.

20 On that day men will throw to the moles and
the bats the idols of silver and gold which they
made for worship.

21 They go into caverns in the rocks
and into crevices in the cliffs,
From the terror of the LORD
and the splendor of his majesty,
when he arises to overawe the earth.

22 As for you, let man alone,
in whose nostrils is but a breath;
for what is he worth?

Judgment of Judah and Jerusalem

3 1*† The Lord, the LORD of hosts,
shall take away from Jerusalem and
from Judah
support and prop [all supplies of bread
and water]:

2 Hero and warrior,
judge and prophet, fortune-teller and elder,

3 The captain of fifty and the nobleman,
counselor, skilled magician, and
expert charmer.

4 I will make striplings their princes;
the fickle shall govern them,

5 And the people shall oppress one another,
yes, every man his neighbor.
The child shall be bold toward the elder,
and the base toward the honorable.

6 When a man seizes his brother
in his father's house, saying,
"You have clothes! Be our ruler,
and take in hand this ruin!"—

7 Then shall he answer in that day:
"I will not undertake to cure this,
when in my own house there is no bread
or clothing!
You shall not make me ruler of the people."

8 Jerusalem is crumbling, Judah is falling;
for their speech and their deeds are before
the LORD,
a provocation in the sight of his majesty.

9 Their very look bears witness against them;
their sin like Sodom they vaunt,
They hide it not. Woe to them!
they deal out evil to themselves.

10 Happy the just, for it will be well with them,
the fruit of their works they will eat.

2, 6: *Fortune-tellers and soothsayers:* divination was strictly forbidden; cf Dt 18, 9–14.

2, 11: *That day:* the day of the Lord, a day of retribution, often referred to, especially by the minor prophets, and described in terms of natural phenomena: earthquake, fire, storm.

2, 13: *Lebanon:* Mount Lebanon in Syria, famed for its cedars. *Bashan:* the wooded uplands east of the Jordan River.

2, 16: *Tarshish:* Cf note on Ps 48, 8.

3, 1–12: Anarchy will reign in Jerusalem and Judah. In the prevailing desperation, even the most unworthy and the least qualified will be sought as rulers.

2, 6: Is 8, 19; 19, 3.   **2, 10:** 2 Thes 1, 9.
2, 8: Is 31, 1ff.   **3, 1:** Lv 26, 26; Ez 4, 16.

11 Woe to the wicked man! All goes ill,
   with the work of his hands he will
       be repaid.
12 My people—a babe in arms will be
       their tyrant,
   and women will rule them!
   O my people, your leaders mislead,
       they destroy the paths you should follow.

13 The LORD rises to accuse,
       standing to try his people.
14 The Lord enters into judgment
       with his people's elders and princes:
   It is you who have devoured the vineyard;
       the loot wrested from the poor is in
           your houses.
15* What do you mean by crushing my people,
       and grinding down the poor when they
           look to you?
   says the Lord, the GOD of hosts.
16* The LORD said:
   Because the daughters of Zion are haughty,
       and walk with necks outstretched
   Ogling and mincing as they go,
       their anklets tinkling with every step,
17† The Lord shall cover the scalps of Zion's
           daughters with scabs,
       and the LORD shall bare their heads.

18 On that day the LORD will do away with the fin-
ery of the anklets, sunbursts, and crescents; 19 the
pendants, bracelets, and veils; 20 the headdresses,
bangles, cinctures, perfume boxes, and amulets;
21† the signet rings, and the nose rings; 22 the court
dresses, wraps, cloaks, and purses; 23 the mirrors,
linen tunics, turbans, and shawls.

24 Instead of perfume there will be stench,
       instead of the girdle, a rope,
   And for the coiffure, baldness;
       for the rich gown, a sackcloth skirt.
           Then, instead of beauty:
25 Your men will fall by the sword,
       and your champions, in war;
26 Her gates will lament and mourn,
       as the city sits desolate on the ground.

4 1† Seven women will take hold of one man
       on that day, saying:
   "We will eat our own food

and wear our own clothing;
   Only let your name be given us,
       put an end to our disgrace!"

The Messianic Branch

2*† On that day,
   The branch of the LORD will be luster
       and glory,
       and the fruit of the earth will be honor
           and splendor
       for the survivors of Israel.
3*† He who remains in Zion
       and he that is left in Jerusalem
   Will be called holy:
       every one marked down for life
           in Jerusalem.
4 When the Lord washes away
       the filth of the daughters of Zion,
   And purges Jerusalem's blood from her midst
       with a blast of searing judgment,
5* Then will the LORD create,
       over the whole site of Mount Zion
       and over her place of assembly,
   A smoking cloud by day
       and a light of flaming fire by night.
6 For over all, his glory will be shelter
       and protection:
       shade from the parching heat of day,
       refuge and cover from storm and rain.

The Vineyard Song

5 1† Let me now sing of my friend,
       my friend's song concerning his vineyard.
   My friend had a vineyard
       on a fertile hillside;
2 He spaded it, cleared it of stones,
       and planted the choicest vines;
   Within it he built a watchtower,
       and hewed out a wine press.
   Then he looked for the crop of grapes,
       but what it yielded was wild grapes.

3 Now, inhabitants of Jerusalem and men
       of Judah,
       judge between me and my vineyard:
4 What more was there to do for my vineyard
       that I had not done?
   Why, when I looked for the crop of
           grapes,
       did it bring forth wild grapes?

3, 17: *Bare their heads*: a mark of social disgrace; cf Nm 5, 18.
  3, 21: *Nose rings*: of gold, a feminine ornament in the East;
cf note on Gn 24, 22.
  4, 1: *Seven women . . . one man*: the disproportion of the sexes
due to war leaves the female population almost without male partners. The women are eager to marry, not for support, but to avoid the
disgrace of being childless.

4, 2: *Branch of the LORD*: divine blessings in general, which later
culminated in the Messiah; cf Jer 23, 5; Zec 3, 8; 6, 12.
  4, 3: *Marked down for life*: in God's list of his elect; cf Ex 32, 32.
  5, 1: *My friend had a vineyard*: the Lord and his chosen people.

3, 15: Lv 25, 42.55.   4, 3: Is 6, 13; 10, 20; Ob 17.
3, 16ff: Is 32, 11f.   4, 5: Ex 13, 21.
  4, 2: Is 11, 1; Jer 23, 5; 33, 15.

IS

5 Now, I will let you know
    what I mean to do to my vineyard:
Take away its hedge, give it to grazing,
    break through its wall, let it be trampled!
6 Yes, I will make it a ruin:
    it shall not be pruned or hoed,
but overgrown with thorns and briers;
I will command the clouds
    not to send rain upon it.
7† The vineyard of the LORD of hosts is the house
    of Israel,
and the men of Judah are his cherished
    plant;
He looked for judgment, but see, bloodshed!
    for justice, but hark, the outcry!

Doom of the Unjust

8*†Woe to you who join house to house,
    who connect field with field,
Till no room remains, and you are left to dwell
    alone in the midst of the land!
9* In my hearing the LORD of hosts has sworn:
    Many houses shall be in ruins,
large ones and fine, with no one to live
    in them.
10† Ten acres of vineyard
    shall yield but one liquid measure,
And a homer of seed
    shall yield but an ephah.
17 Lambs shall graze there at pasture,
    and kids shall eat in the ruins of the rich.
11 Woe to those who demand strong drink
    as soon as they rise in the morning,
And linger into the night
    while wine inflames them!
12* With harp and lyre, timbrel and flute,
    they feast on wine;
But what the LORD does, they regard not,
    the work of his hands they see not.
13 Therefore my people go into exile,
    because they do not understand;
Their nobles die of hunger,
    and their masses are parched with thirst.
14*†Therefore the nether world enlarges its throat
    and opens its maw without limit;
Down go their nobility and their masses,
    their throngs and their revelry.
15 Men shall be abased, each one brought low,
    and the eyes of the haughty lowered,

16 But the LORD of hosts shall be exalted by
    his judgment,
and God the Holy shall be shown holy by
    his justice.

18 Woe to those who tug at guilt with cords
    of perversity,
and at sin as if with cart ropes!
19* To those who say, "Let him make haste
    and speed his work, that we may see it;
On with the plan of the Holy One of Israel!
    let it come to pass, that we may know it!"
20 Woe to those who call evil good, and
    good evil,
who change darkness into light, and light
    into darkness,
who change bitter into sweet, and sweet
    into bitter!
21* Woe to those who are wise in their own sight,
    and prudent in their own esteem!
22* Woe to the champions at drinking wine,
    the valiant at mixing strong drink!
23* To those who acquit the guilty for bribes,
    and deprive the just man of his rights!
24 Therefore, as the tongue of fire licks
    up stubble,
as dry grass shrivels in the flame,
Even so their root shall become rotten
    and their blossom scatter like dust;
For they have spurned the law of the LORD
    of hosts,
and scorned the word of the Holy One
    of Israel.
25 Therefore the wrath of the LORD blazes against
    his people,
he raises his hand to strike them;
When the mountains quake,
    their corpses shall be like refuse in the streets.
For all this, his wrath is not turned back,
    and his hand is still outstretched.

Invasion†

26 He will give a signal to a far-off nation,
    and whistle to them from the ends of
    the earth;
speedily and promptly will they come.
27 None of them will stumble with weariness,
    none will slumber and none will sleep.
None will have his waist belt loose,

5, 7: *Judgment . . . bloodshed . . . justice . . . outcry:* in Hebrew, these adversative terms constitute a play on words.
    5, 8–10: Land-grabbers who unjustly acquire property will be impoverished instead of enriched.
    5, 10: *Ten acres:* a field requiring ten days of plowing by a yoke of oxen. *Liquid measure:* in Hebrew, a "bath," i.e., about ten gallons. *Homer:* a dry measure of about ten bushels. *Ephah:* a dry measure of about one bushel.

5, 14: *Nether world:* cf note on Ps 6, 6.
    5, 26–30: A description of the invading Assyrian army, God's instrument for punishing his people.

5, 8: Mi 2, 2.   5, 19: Jer 5, 12; 2 Pt 3, 4.
5, 9: Is 6, 12.   5, 21: Prv 3, 7; Rom 12, 16.
5, 12: Am 6, 5f.   5, 22: Sir 31, 3.
5, 14: Hb 2, 5.   5, 23: Ex 23, 8; Prv 17, 15.

Introducing...
▶FIRST ISAIAH

The name Isaiah means "God is salvation" in Hebrew, and First Isaiah's preaching certainly reflects that message. Born in Jerusalem, he prophesied there during the reigns of Kings Uzziah, Jotham, Ahaz, and Hezekiah, between 742 and 701 B.C. (see 2 Kings, chapters 15–20, and 2 Chronicles, chapters 26–32). He was married to a prophet, and they had two sons whose names played a symbolic role in his prophecy: Shear-jashub, meaning "a remnant shall remain," and Maher-shalal-hash-baz, meaning "the spoil speeds, the prey hastes." In his preaching, he emphasized the role of Jerusalem (Zion) as God's dwelling place and home to King David's dynasty. For this reason, he is also called Isaiah of Jerusalem.

    First Isaiah had ready access to Judah's kings and was probably a member of an aristocratic family. His education shows in his use of language—he is responsible for some of the loftiest and most beautiful poetry in the Old Testament.

nor the thong of his sandal broken.

28   Their arrows are sharp,
     and all their bows are bent.
The hoofs of their horses seem like flint,
     and their chariot wheels like the hurricane.
29   Their roar is that of the lion,
     like the lion's whelps they roar;
They growl and seize the prey,
     they carry it off and none will rescue it.
30* [They will roar over it, on that day,
     with a roaring like that of the sea.]

II: Immanuel Prophecies

Call of Isaiah

6 1*† In the year king Uzziah died, I saw the Lord seated on a high and lofty throne, with the train of his garment filling the temple.† 2* Seraphim were stationed above; each of them had six wings: with two they veiled their faces, with two they veiled their feet, and with two they hovered aloft. 3 "Holy, holy, holy is the LORD of hosts!" they

cried one to the other. "All the earth is filled with his glory!" 4*† At the sound of that cry, the frame of the door shook and the house was filled with smoke.

5*† Then I said, "Woe is me, I am doomed! For I am a man of unclean lips, living among a people of unclean lips; yet my eyes have seen the King, the LORD of hosts!" 6 Then one of the seraphim flew to me, holding an ember which he had taken with tongs from the altar. 7*† He touched my mouth with it. "See," he said, "now that this has touched your lips, your wickedness is removed, your sin purged."

8 Then I heard the voice of the Lord saying, "Whom shall I send? Who will go for us?" "Here I am;" I said; "send me!" 9*† And he replied: Go and say to this people:

Listen carefully, but you shall not understand!
Look intently, but you shall know nothing!
10* You are to make the heart of this
     people sluggish,
to dull their ears and close their eyes;

---

† 6, 1: *In the year King Uzziah died:* 742 B.C.
  6, 1ff: *Temple:* the holy place, just in front of the holy of holies. *Seraphim:* literally "the burning ones," are celestial beings who surround the throne of God. Each has six wings. Reverence for the divine majesty causes them to veil their faces with two wings; modesty, to veil their extremities in similar fashion; alacrity in God's service, to extend two wings in preparation for flight. *Holy, holy, holy:* God's perfect interior holiness whose exterior manifestation is his glory. These words are found in the Roman liturgy just before the Canon of the Mass.
  6, 4: *Smoke:* reminiscent of the clouds which surrounded God at Mount Sinai; cf Ex 19, 16–19; Dt 4, 11f.
  6, 5: *Doomed:* it was popularly believed that to see God would lead to one's death; cf Gn 32, 31; Ex 33, 20; Jgs 13, 22.
  6, 7: *Touched your lips:* Isaiah is thus symbolically purified to be

worthy of his vocation as God's prophet. In the Roman liturgy, the celebrant at Mass makes reference to this incident just before he reads the gospel.
  6, 9f: The truth that the nation will remain impenitent is vividly foretold, as if its obstinacy would be caused, instead of merely occasioned, by the prophet's warning. Cf Mt 13, 13ff; Mk 4, 12; Lk 8, 10.

5, 30: Is 8, 22.   6, 7: Jer 1, 9; Dn 10, 16.
6, 1: Jn 12, 41.   6, 9: Mt 13, 14f; Mk 4, 12;
6, 2: Rv 4, 8.   Lk 8, 10; Acts 28, 26f.
6, 4: 1 Kgs 8, 10f; Rv 15, 8.   6, 10: Jer 5, 21; Jn 12, 40.
6, 5: Gn 32, 3; Ex 20, 19;
    33, 20; Jgs 6, 22; 13,
    22.

Here I Am, Lord!

Phrases from the sixth chapter of Isaiah may be familiar from the song "Here I Am, Lord." This chapter tells of First Isaiah's call, which follows a biblical pattern:

1. *The person has some experience of God.* Isaiah has a dramatic vision of God in the Temple.
2. *God gives the person a mission.* God sends Isaiah to speak to the people.
3. *The person may deny being worthy.* Isaiah knows he has unclean (or sinful) lips.
4. *God addresses the denial and reassures the person.* God purifies Isaiah with fire and words of forgiveness.

You can see the same pattern for Moses' call in Ex 3, 1–12, Samuel's call in 1 Sm 3, 1–14, Jeremiah's call in Jer 1, 4–10, and Mary's call in Lk 1, 26–38.

　　Christians are called by God to participate in Jesus' saving mission. They believe everyone needs to discover the way God wants them to live out that call. Do you believe that God has a mission for your life? How can you use your talents to create a more loving and just world?

▶ Is 6, 1–13

Else their eyes will see, their ears hear,
　　their heart understand,
　　and they will turn and be healed.

11 "How long, O Lord?" I asked. And he replied:

Until the cities are desolate,
　　without inhabitants,
Houses, without a man,
　　and the earth is a desolate waste.
12† Until the LORD removes men far away,
　　and the land is abandoned more
　　　and more.
13* If there be still a tenth part in it,
　　then this in turn shall be
　　　laid waste;
As with a terebinth or an oak
　　whose trunk remains when its leaves
　　　have fallen.
　　[Holy offspring is the trunk.]

Birth of Immanuel

7 1*† In the days of Ahaz, king of Judah, son of Jotham, son of Uzziah, Rezin, king of Aram, and Pekah, king of Israel, son of Remaliah, went up to attack Jerusalem, but they were not able to conquer it. 2 When word came to the house of David

that Aram was encamped in Ephraim, the heart of the king and the heart of the people trembled, as the trees of the forest tremble in the wind.

　3*† Then the LORD said to Isaiah: Go out to meet Ahaz, you and your son Shear-jashub, at the end of the conduit of the upper pool, on the highway of the fuller's field, 4 and say to him: Take care you remain tranquil and do not fear; let not your courage fail before these two stumps of smoldering brands [the blazing anger of Rezin and the Arameans, and of the son of Remaliah], 5 because of the mischief that Aram [Ephraim and the son of Remaliah] plots against you, saying, 6† "Let us go up and tear Judah asunder, make it our own by force, and appoint the son of Tabeel king there."

　7　Thus says the LORD:

　　This shall not stand, it shall not be!
8　Damascus is the capital of Aram,
　　and Rezin the head of Damascus;
　　Samaria is the capital of Ephraim,
　　and Remaliah's son the head of Samaria.
9*†But within sixty years and five,
　　Ephraim shall be crushed, no longer a nation.
　Unless your faith is firm
　　you shall not be firm!

6, 12: Several limited deportations in the time of Isaiah would later culminate in the Babylonian Exile.

7, 1: *Days of Ahaz:* who ruled from 735 to 715 B.C. This attack against Jerusalem by the kings of Aram (Syria) and Israel was occasioned by Ahaz' refusal to enter with them into an anti-Assyrian alliance; cf 2 Kgs 16.

7, 3: *Shear-jashub:* this name means "a remnant will return."

7, 6: *Son of Tabeel:* an adherent of Jerusalem's enemies. His ap-

pointment would interrupt the lawful succession from David.

　7, 9: *Within sixty years and five:* if the text is correct, its reference is unknown.

6, 13: Is 10, 22.
7, 1: 2 Kgs 16, 5; 2 Chr 28, 5–15.
7, 3: Is 36, 2; 2 Chr 32, 3.
7, 9: Is 8, 6ff.

¹⁰ Again the LORD spoke to Ahaz: ¹¹† Ask for a sign from the LORD, your God; let it be deep as the nether world, or high as the sky! ¹²† But Ahaz answered, "I will not ask! I will not tempt the LORD!" ¹³ Then he said: Listen, O house of David! Is it not enough for you to weary men, must you also weary my God? ¹⁴† Therefore the Lord himself will give you this sign: the virgin shall be with child, and bear a son, and shall name him Immanuel. ¹⁵† He shall be living on curds and honey by the time he learns to reject the bad and choose the good. ¹⁶ For before the child learns to re-ject the bad and choose the good, the land of those two kings whom you dread shall be deserted.

¹⁷ The LORD shall bring upon you and your peo-ple and your father's house days worse than any since Ephraim seceded from Judah. [This means the king of Assyria.] ¹⁸ On that day

The LORD shall whistle
  for the fly that is in the farthest streams
    of Egypt,
  and for the bee in the land of Assyria.

GOD-WITH-US!

Many Bibles refer to Isaiah, chapters 7–12, as the Book of Immanuel. In these chapters, First Isaiah announces that Israel's salvation will come from a child from the family of Jesse, the father of King David. This child will be named Immanuel (also spelled Emmanuel), which means "God-with-Us." With this message, Isaiah emphasizes that God is with the little ones who trust in God's saving power.

Biblical scholars agree that the child Isaiah is referring to is the son of King Ahaz—the fu-ture king Hezekiah. But the Gospel writers later see in this passage a reference to Jesus (Mt 1, 23), the Son of God, who is truly Immanuel, God-with-Us.

For Hispanic people, Immanuel is a constant reality. Hispanics give witness of the nearness of God in daily affairs through the following expressions, which you may hear more than a dozen times a day in their communities: "God help you" (*Dios te ayude*), "Go with God" (*Ve con Dios*), "If God wants it" (*Si Dios quiere*), "With God's permission" (*Si Dios lo permite*), "Through the pow-er of God" (*Dios mediante*), "Thanks to God" (*Gracias a Dios*), "For the love of God" (*Por el amor de Dios*), "God give you a good day" (*Buen día te dé Dios*), and "God bless you" (*Dios te bendiga*).

- **If you come from a family or community tradition where these faith expressions are common, feel the presence of God each time they are voiced, and use them boldly yourself.**
- **Think about what happened to you today. How many of these expressions could you have applied to different situations and felt God-with-You? Choose the expression that best fits the yearnings of your heart at this time, and pray with it, repeating it several times.**

▶ **Isaiah, chapters 7–12**

---

† **7, 11:** *Deep . . . sky:* an extraordinary or miraculous sign that would prove God's firm will to save the royal house of David from its oppressors.

7, 12: *Tempt the LORD:* Ahaz expresses in this hypocritical way his preference for depending upon the might of Assyria rather than upon God.

7, 14: The sign proposed by Isaiah was concerned with the preservation of Judah in the midst of distress (cf Is 7, 15.17), but more especially with the fulfillment of God's earlier promise to David (2 Sm 7, 12–16) in the coming of Immanuel (meaning, "With us is God") as the ideal king (cf Is 9, 5–6; 11, 1–5). The church has always followed St. Matthew in seeing the transcendent fulfillment of this verse in Christ and his Virgin Mother. The prophet need not have known the full force latent in his own words; and some Catholic writers have sought a preliminary and partial fulfillment in the con-ception and birth of the future King Hezekiah, whose mother, at the time Isaiah spoke, would have been a young, unmarried woman (Hebrew, *almah*). The Holy Spirit was preparing, however, for anoth-er Nativity which alone could fulfill the divinely given terms of Im-manuel's mission, and in which the perpetual virginity of the Mother of God was to fulfill also the words of this prophecy in the integral sense intended by the divine Wisdom.

7, 15: *Curds and honey:* the restricted diet of those who remain after devastation has changed the once fertile fields of Judah into grazing land; cf Is 7, 21–25.

I
S

19 All of them shall come and settle
     in the steep ravines and in the rocky clefts,
     on all thornbushes and in all pastures.

20† On that day the LORD shall shave with the razor hired from across the River [with the king of Assyria] the head, and the hair between the legs. It shall also shave off the beard.

21 On that day a man shall keep a heifer or a couple of sheep, 22 and from their abundant yield of milk he shall live on curds; curds and honey shall be the food of all who remain in the land. 23 On that day every place where there used to be a thousand vines, worth a thousand pieces of silver, shall be turned to briers and thorns. 24 Men shall go there with bow and arrows; for all the country shall be briers and thorns. 25 For fear of briers and thorns you shall not go upon any mountainside which used to be hoed with the mattock; they shall be grazing land for cattle and shall be trampled upon by sheep.

The Son of Isaiah

8 1† The LORD said to me: Take a large cylinder-seal, and inscribe on it in ordinary letters: "Belonging to Maher-shalal-hash-baz." 2† And I took reliable witnesses, Uriah the priest, and Zechariah, son of Jeberechiah. 3† Then I went to the prophetess and she conceived and bore a son. The LORD said to me: Name him Maher-shalal-hash-baz, 4 for before the child knows how to call his father or mother by name, the wealth of Damascus and the spoil of Samaria shall be carried off by the king of Assyria.

5 Again the LORD spoke to me:

6*†Because this people has rejected
     the waters of Shiloah that flow gently,
   And melts with fear before the loftiness of
          Rezin and Remaliah's son,
7 Therefore the LORD raises against them
     the waters of the River, great and mighty
     [the king of Assyria and all his power].
   It shall rise above all its channels,
     and overflow all its banks;

8 It shall pass into Judah, and flood it
     all throughout;
   up to the neck it shall reach;
   It shall spread its wings
     the full width of your land, Immanuel!
9 Know, O peoples, and be appalled!
     Give ear, all you distant lands!
     Arm, but be crushed! Arm, but be crushed!
10† Form a plan, and it shall be thwarted;
     make a resolve, and it shall not be
          carried out,
     for "With us is God!"

Disciples of Isaiah

11* For thus said the LORD to me, taking hold of me and warning me not to walk in the way of this people:

12   Call not alliance what this people calls alliance,
       and fear not, nor stand in awe of what
            they fear.
13   But with the LORD of hosts make your
          alliance—
       for him be your fear and your awe.
14* Yet he shall be a snare, an obstacle and a
          stumbling stone
       to both the houses of Israel,
     A trap and a snare
       to those who dwell in Jerusalem;
15   And many among them shall stumble and fall,
       broken, snared, and captured.

16† The record is to be folded and the sealed instruction kept among my disciples. 17 For I will trust in the LORD, who is hiding his face from the house of Jacob; yes, I will wait for him. 18† Look at me and the children whom the Lord has given me: we are signs and portents in Israel from the LORD of hosts who dwells on Mount Zion. 19*† And when they say to you, "Inquire of mediums and fortune-tellers (who chirp and mutter!); should not a people inquire of their gods, apply to the dead on behalf of the living?"— 20† then this document will furnish its instruction. That kind of thing they will surely say.

---

† **7, 20:** God will use the Assyrians from across the River (the Euphrates) as his instrument (razor) to inflict disgrace and suffering upon his people.
  8, 1: *Ordinary letters:* easily read by all. *Maher-shalal-hash-baz:* a symbolic name to be given to another son of Isaiah (v 3); it means "quick spoils; speedy plunder," and describes what the Assyrians will do.
  8, 2: *Reliable witnesses:* who would testify that Isaiah had indeed prophesied the future destruction. *Uriah the priest:* cf 2 Kgs 16, 10.
  8, 3: *The prophetess:* wife of Isaiah.
  8, 6ff: *This people:* Judah. *Waters of Shiloah:* the stream that flows into the pool of Shiloah in Jerusalem, its slow current symbolizing the silent, divine protection which Judah has rejected. God will therefore summon the mighty Assyrian army, symbolized by the River (Euphrates), to devastate Judah, which, however, will not be

entirely destroyed, because it is the land of Immanuel.
  8, 10: The plan of Israel's enemies will be thwarted because, as the name "Immanuel" signifies, With us is God.
  8, 16: *Kept among my disciples:* for preservation and transmission.
  8, 18: *Signs:* Isaiah and his sons had symbolic names.
  8, 19: *Chirp and mutter:* a mocking reference to the sounds uttered by necromancers, as if the dead were speaking; all such practices were forbidden.
  8, 21f: These verses have been transposed and placed within Is 14, 25, which affords the context in which they can be understood.

8, 6: Jn 9, 7.11.   **8, 14:** Rom 9, 33; 1 Pt 2, 8.
8, 11: Ez 3, 14.   **8, 19:** Lv 19, 31; Dt 18, 10ff.

The Prince of Peace

23† First he degraded the land of Zebulun and the land of Naphtali; but in the end he has glorified the seaward road, the land west of the Jordan, the District of the Gentiles.

Anguish has taken wing, dispelled is darkness:
   for there is no gloom where until now there
      was distress.

9 1* The people who walked in darkness
      have seen a great light;
   Upon those who dwelt in the land of gloom
      a light has shone.
2 You have brought them abundant joy
      and great rejoicing,
   As they rejoice before you as at the harvest,
      as men make merry when dividing spoils.
3 For the yoke that burdened them,
      the pole on their shoulder,
   And the rod of their taskmaster
      you have smashed, as on the day of Midian.
4* For every boot that tramped in battle,
      every cloak rolled in blood,
      will be burned as fuel for flames.
5*† For a child is born to us, a son is given us;
      upon his shoulder dominion rests.
   They name him Wonder-Counselor, God-Hero,
      Father-Forever, Prince of Peace.
6* His dominion is vast
      and forever peaceful,
   From David's throne, and over his kingdom,
      which he confirms and sustains
   By judgment and justice,
      both now and forever.
   The zeal of the LORD of hosts will do this!

Fall of the Northern Kingdom

7 The Lord has sent word against Jacob,
      it falls upon Israel;
8 And all the people know it,
      Ephraim and those who dwell in Samaria,
      those who say in arrogance and pride
         of heart,
9 "Bricks have fallen,
      but we will build with cut stone;
   Sycamores are felled,
      but we will replace them with cedars."

Christmas Light

Isaiah 9, 1–6 describes Immanuel as a wise, brave, courageous, virtuous, and righteous king. Here, First Isaiah may be referring to King Hezekiah, the reformer king of Judah (see 2 Chronicles, chapters 29–33). However, after Hezekiah's death, the passage came to be understood as predicting the coming of an ideal future savior or messiah. That's why the passage is called a messianic prophecy.

Christians see in these words a perfect description of Jesus. In fact, Catholics read these verses at Christmas during midnight Mass. On one of the longest nights of the year, they imagine Jesus' presence in the world as a light dispelling the darkness of sin.

This is the opening prayer for the Christmas Mass at midnight:

Father,
You make this holy night radiant
with the splendor of Jesus Christ our
   light.
We welcome him as Lord, the true light
   of the world.
Bring us to eternal joy in the kingdom of
   heaven,
where he lives and reigns with you and
   the Holy Spirit,
one God, for ever and ever.
                    (Sacramentary, p. 40)

▶ Is 9, 1–6

10 But the LORD raises up their foes against them
      and stirs up their enemies to action:
11† Aram on the east and the Philistines on the west
      devour Israel with open mouth,
   For all this, his wrath is not turned back,
      and his hand is still outstretched!
12 The people do not turn to him who struck them,
      nor seek the LORD of hosts.

8, 23: *Zebulun . . . Naphtali:* northern Palestine, which was first to be attacked by the Assyrians; God, however, redeems it, as he redeems all his people. *Seaward road:* from Damascus, across southern Galilee to the Mediterranean Sea. *District of the Gentiles:* northern Galilee, inhabited by pagans; cf Jos 20, 7; Is 9, 1. Mt 4, 15f refers to this, since Jesus began his public mission in Galilee.
9, 5: *A child:* the Immanuel of Is 7, 14 and 8, 8; cf Is 11, 1.2.9. In Christian tradition and liturgy, this passage is used to refer to Christ. *Upon his shoulder dominion rests:* authority. *Wonder-Counselor:*

remarkable for his wisdom and prudence. *God-Hero:* a warrior and a defender of his people, like God himself. *Father-Forever:* ever devoted to his people. *Prince of Peace:* his reign will be characterized by peace.
9, 11: *Aram:* the Syrian kingdom, with its capital at Damascus.

9, 1f: Mt 4, 15f.   9, 5: Ps 72, 7; Lk 2, 11.14.
9, 4: Sir 39, 9.   9, 6: Jer 23, 5; Lk 1, 32f.

13 So the LORD severs from Israel head and tail,
   palm branch and reed in one day.
14 [The elder and the noble are the head,
   the prophet who teaches falsehood is
   the tail.]
15* The leaders of this people mislead them
   and those to be led are engulfed.
16 For this reason, the Lord does not spare their
   young men,
   and their orphans and widows he does
   not pity;
   They are wholly profaned and sinful,
   and every mouth gives vent to folly.
   For all this, his wrath is not turned back,
   his hand is still outstretched!

17 For wickedness burns like fire,
   devouring brier and thorn;
   It kindles the forest thickets,
   which go up in columns of smoke.
18 At the wrath of the LORD of hosts the
   land quakes,
   and the people are like fuel for fire;
   No man spares his brother,
   each devours the flesh of his neighbor.
19 Though they hack on the right, they
   are hungry;
   though they eat on the left, they are
   not filled.
20† Manasseh devours Ephraim, and
   Ephraim Manasseh;
   together they turn on Judah.
   For all this, his wrath is not turned back,
   his hand is still outstretched!

Social Injustice

10

1* Woe to those who enact unjust
   statutes
   and who write oppressive decrees,
2* Depriving the needy of judgment
   and robbing my people's poor of
   their rights.
   Making widows their plunder,
   and orphans their prey!
3 What will you do on the day of punishment,
   when ruin comes from afar?
   To whom will you flee for help?
   Where will you leave your wealth,
4 Lest it sink beneath the captive
   or fall beneath the slain?
   For all this, his wrath is not turned back,
   his hand is still outstretched!

Assyria the Unconscious Instrument of God

5 Woe to Assyria! My rod in anger,
   my staff in wrath.
6† Against an impious nation I send him,
   and against a people under my wrath I
   order him
   To seize plunder, carry off loot,
   and tread them down like the mud of
   the streets.
7 But this is not what he intends,
   nor does he have this in mind;
   Rather, it is in his heart to destroy,
   to make an end of nations not a few.
8 "Are not my commanders all kings?" he says,
9*† "Is not Calno like Carchemish,
   Or Hamath like Arpad,
   or Samaria like Damascus?
10 Just as my hand reached out to
   idolatrous kingdoms
   that had more images than Jerusalem
   and Samaria,
11* Just as I treated Samaria and her idols,
   shall I not do to Jerusalem and her
   graven images?"

12† [But when the LORD has brought to an end all
his work on Mount Zion and in Jerusalem,

   I will punish the utterance
   of the king of Assyria's proud heart,
13 and the boastfulness of his haughty eyes.
   For he says:]

   "By my own power I have done it,
   and by my wisdom, for I am shrewd.
   I have moved the boundaries of peoples,
   their treasures I have pillaged,
   and, like a giant, I have put down
   the enthroned.
14 My hand has seized like a nest
   the riches of nations;
   As one takes eggs left alone,
   so I took in all the earth;
   No one fluttered a wing,
   or opened a mouth, or chirped!"

15 Will the axe boast against him who hews
   with it?
   Will the saw exalt itself above him who
   wields it?
   As if a rod could sway him who lifts it,
   or a staff him who is not wood!

9, 20: *Manasseh . . . Ephraim:* two of the leading tribes of the
northern kingdom.
10, 6f: *Impious nation:* Israel. It was God's intention to use Assyria merely to punish, not to destroy, his people.
10, 9: *Calno . . . Damascus:* cities captured by the Assyrians.

9, 15: Is 28, 7; Jer 2, 8; 5, 31;   10, 1: Jer 8, 8.
20, 6; 23, 13f; 29,   10, 2: Is 1, 23.
30ff; Ez 13, 1–7;   10, 9: Is 36, 19; Am 6, 2.
22, 28; Mi 3, 11.   10, 11: Is 36, 20.

16† Therefore the Lord, the LORD of hosts,
  will send among his fat ones leanness,
And instead of his glory there will be kindling
  like the kindling of fire.
17 The Light of Israel will become a fire,
  Israel's Holy One a flame,
That burns and consumes his briers
  and his thorns in a single day.
18 His splendid forests and orchards
  will be consumed, soul and body;
19 And the remnant of the trees in his forest
  will be so few,
Like poles set up for signals,
  that any boy can record them.
20   On that day
The remnant of Israel,
  the survivors of the house of Jacob,
will no more lean upon him who
  struck them;
But they will lean upon the LORD,
  the Holy One of Israel, in truth.
21† A remnant will return, the remnant of Jacob,
  to the mighty God.
22* For though your people, O Israel,
  were like the sand of the sea,
Only a remnant of them will return;
  their destruction is decreed
  as overwhelming justice demands.

23 Yes, the destruction he has decreed, the Lord, the GOD of hosts, will carry out within the whole land. 24 Therefore thus says the Lord, the GOD of hosts: O my people, who dwell in Zion, do not fear the Assyrian, though he strikes you with a rod, and raises his staff against you. 25 For only a brief moment more, and my anger shall be over; but them I will destroy in wrath. 26* Then the LORD of hosts will raise against them a scourge such as struck Midian at the rock of Oreb; and he will raise his staff over the sea as he did against Egypt. 27† On that day,

His burden shall be taken from your shoulder,
  and his yoke shattered from your neck.

Sennacherib's Invasion

He has come up from the direction of Rimmon,
28 he has reached Aiath, passed
    through Migron,

at Michmash his supplies are stored.
29 They cross the ravine:
  "We will spend the night at Geba."
Ramah is in terror,
  Gibeah of Saul has fled.
30 Cry and shriek, O daughter of Gallim!
  Hearken, Laishah! Answer her, Anathoth!
31 Madmenah is in flight,
  the inhabitants of Gebim seek refuge.
32† Even today he will halt at Nob,
  he will shake his fist at the mount of
    daughter Zion,
  the hill of Jerusalem!
33 Behold, the Lord, the LORD of hosts,
  lops off the boughs with terrible violence;
The tall of stature are felled,
  and the lofty ones brought low;
34 The forest thickets are felled with the axe,
  and Lebanon in its splendor falls.

The Rule of Immanuel

11 1*† But a shoot shall sprout from the
       stump of Jesse,
  and from his roots a bud shall blossom.
2*†The spirit of the LORD shall rest upon him:
  a spirit of wisdom and of understanding,
A spirit of counsel and of strength,
  a spirit of knowledge and of fear of
    the LORD,
3   and his delight shall be the fear of the LORD.
Not by appearance shall he judge,
  nor by hearsay shall he decide,
4* But he shall judge the poor with justice,
  and decide aright for the land's afflicted.
He shall strike the ruthless with the rod of
  his mouth,
  and with the breath of his lips he shall slay
    the wicked.
5   Justice shall be the band around his waist,
  and faithfulness a belt upon his hips.

6*†Then the wolf shall be a guest of
    the lamb,
  and the leopard shall lie down with
    the kid;
The calf and the young lion shall
    browse together,
  with a little child to guide them.

10, 16: *His fat ones:* the strong men of the king of Assyria.
10, 21: *A remnant will return:* in Hebrew, *shear-jashub,* an allusion to the name of Isaiah's son, Shear-jashub; cf Is 7, 3.
10, 27–32: A poetic description of the progress of the Assyrian army, advancing from the north through Judah to the gates of Jerusalem.
10, 32ff: Just when the enemy is about to capture Jerusalem, God intervenes and destroys the hostile army.
11, 1: *Shoot . . . stump:* after the Babylonian exile only a stump of the Davidic dynasty will remain; from it will arise the new shoot, the messianic King. *Jesse:* David's father.

11, 2f: The source of the traditional names of the gifts of the Holy Spirit. The Septuagint and the Vulgate read "piety" for fear of the Lord in its first occurrence, thus listing seven gifts.
11, 6–9: This picture of the idyllic harmony of paradise is a dramatic symbol of the universal peace and justice of messianic times.

10, 22: Rom 9, 27f.   11, 4: Pss 72, 2.4; 98, 9;
10, 26: Jgs 7, 25.   2 Thes 2, 8.
11, 1: Lk 3, 32.   11, 6: Is 65, 25.
11, 2: Mt 3, 16; Mk 1, 10.

Lions and Lambs

There are so many troubled spots in the world. It seems that almost every week, violence and ethnic clashes occur somewhere. How easily we forget that we are all members of the human family.

Yet, we are drawn to the image of the peaceable kingdom in Is 11, 6–9. To imagine natural predators such as wolves and lions living together in harmony with lambs and calves, their natural prey, gives us an insight into the Reign of God. Harmony. Peace. Gentleness. No wonder this scene has been the inspiration for numerous artists.

It is a vision we must all aim for, while we do our best to resist all the things that pull us apart as a human family. We are all in this together. We need to work to make the peaceable Reign of God a reality. It is God's work we do.

It is inspiring that First Isaiah also uses the image of youth to express his vision of peace. What can you as a young person do to help bring about the peaceable kingdom?

▸ **Is 11, 6–9**

7 The cow and the bear shall be neighbors,
together their young shall rest;
the lion shall eat hay like the ox.
8 The baby shall play by the cobra's den,
and the child lay his hand on the
adder's lair.
9* There shall be no harm or ruin on all my
holy mountain;
for the earth shall be filled with knowledge
of the LORD,
as water covers the sea.

Union of Ephraim and Judah

10* On that day,
The root of Jesse,
set up as a signal for the nations,
The Gentiles shall seek out,
for his dwelling shall be glorious.
11*† On that day,
The Lord shall again take it in hand
to reclaim the remnant of his people
that is left from Assyria and Egypt,
Pathros, Ethiopia, and Elam,
Shinar, Hamath, and the isles of the sea.
12 He shall raise a signal to the nations
and gather the outcasts of Israel;
The dispersed of Judah he shall assemble
from the four corners of the earth.
13* The envy of Ephraim shall pass away,
and the rivalry of Judah be removed;
Ephraim shall not be jealous of Judah,
and Judah shall not be hostile to Ephraim;
14† But they shall swoop down on the foothills
of the Philistines to the west,
together they shall plunder the Kedemites;
Edom and Moab shall be their possessions,
and the Ammonites their subjects.
15*†The LORD shall dry up the tongue of the Sea
of Egypt,
and wave his hand over the Euphrates in
his fierce anger
And shatter it into seven streamlets,
so that it can be crossed in sandals.

11, 11: *Pathros . . . sea:* where God's people lived in exile. *Pathros:* upper Egypt. *Elam:* east of Babylonia. *Shinar:* Babylonia. *Hamath:* on the Orontes River in Syria. *Isles:* or coastlands, in the Mediterranean.

11, 14: *Kedemites:* tribes in the Arabian Desert.

11, 15: *Tongue . . . Egypt:* the body of water between Egypt and Palestine.

11, 9: Hb 2, 14.
11, 10: Is 49, 22; Rom 15, 12.
11, 11: Is 27, 13; Mi 7, 12;
Zec 10, 10.
11, 13: Ex 37, 16–17.
11, 15: Ex 14, 29.

16 There shall be a highway for the remnant of
        his people
    that is left from Assyria,
    As there was for Israel
        when he came up from the land of Egypt.

Song of Thanksgiving†

12 1 On that day, you will say:
    I give you thanks, O LORD;
    though you have been angry with me,
    your anger has abated, and you have
        consoled me.
2* God indeed is my savior;
    I am confident and unafraid.
    My strength and my courage is the LORD,
        and he has been my savior.

3 With joy you will draw water
    at the fountain of salvation, 4 and say on
        that day:
    Give thanks to the LORD, acclaim his name;
        among the nations make known his deeds,
        proclaim how exalted is his name.
5* Sing praise to the LORD for his
        glorious achievement;
    let this be known throughout all the earth.
6* Shout with exultation, O city of Zion,
    for great in your midst
        is the Holy One of Israel!

III: Oracles Against the Pagan Nations

Babylon

13 1 An oracle concerning Babylon; a vision
        of Isaiah, son of Amoz.

2*†Upon the bare mountains set up a signal;
        cry out to them,
    Wave for them to enter
        the gates of the volunteers.

3† I have commanded my dedicated soldiers,
    I have summoned my warriors,
        eager and bold to carry out my anger.
4* Listen! the rumble on the mountains:
        that of an immense throng!
    Listen! the noise of kingdoms,
        nations assembled!
    The LORD of hosts is mustering
        an army for battle.
5 They come from a far-off country,
        and from the end of the heavens,
    The LORD and the instruments of his wrath,
        to destroy all the land.

6*†Howl, for the day of the LORD is near;
        as destruction from the Almighty it comes.
7* Therefore all hands fall helpless,
        the bows of the young men fall from
        their hands.

In God We Trust

In God we trust. Every piece of U.S. currency bears this statement, yet many of us never notice it. First Isaiah proclaims this same message:

> **God indeed is my savior;**
> **I am confident and unafraid.**
> **My strength and my courage is the LORD,**
> **and he has been my savior.**
>
> **(Is 12, 2)**

How often does fear keep us from trusting? How often does it keep us from being and doing what God is calling us to be and do? We need to reach out to God and to others in our life and trust that God is with us. Jesus came to tell us that love is more powerful than fear, and his life and death testified to his deep trust in his Father. Many times, he told his disciples, "Do not be afraid."

Let us truly live the words "In God we trust."

▶ Is 12, 1–6

---

† **12, 1–6:** Israel's thanksgiving to the Lord, expressed in language like that of the Psalms.

  13, 2: *To them:* the Medes (v 17) and Persians, who would destroy Babylon. *Gates of the volunteers:* the mustering places of Babylon's enemies for war against her.

  13, 3: *Dedicated soldiers:* in the sense that they will wage a "holy war" and carry out God's plan.

  13, 6ff: *Day of the LORD:* described often in prophetical writings,

it generally signified the coming of the Lord in power and majesty to destroy his enemies and inaugurate his kingdom. Here it refers to the overthrow of Babylon. The figures used convey the idea of horror and destruction. Read vv 6–8 with vv 14–16.

12, 2: Ex 15, 2; Ps 118, 14.   13, 2: Is 5, 26.
12, 5: Ex 15, 1.   13, 4: Jer 50, 9.
12, 6: Is 41, 14.16; 54, 1; Zep   13, 6: Jer 46, 10; Jl 1, 15.
  3, 14; Zec 2, 10.   13, 7: Ez 7, 17.

Every man's heart melts [8]* in terror.
  Pangs and sorrows take hold of them,
  like a woman in labor they writhe;
They look aghast at each other,
  their faces aflame.

9   Lo, the day of the LORD comes,
  cruel, with wrath and burning anger;
To lay waste the land
  and destroy the sinners within it!

10* The stars and constellations of the heavens
  send forth no light;
The sun is dark when it rises,
  and the light of the moon does not shine.

11* Thus I will punish the world for its evil
  and the wicked for their guilt.
I will put an end to the pride of the arrogant,
  the insolence of tyrants I will humble.

12† I will make mortals more rare than pure gold,
  men, than gold of Ophir.

13   For this I will make the heavens tremble
  and the earth shall be shaken from
    its place,
At the wrath of the LORD of hosts
  on the day of his burning anger.

14* Like a hunted gazelle,
  or a flock that no one gathers,
Every man shall turn to his kindred
  and flee to his own land.

15   Everyone who is caught shall be run through;
  to a man, they shall fall by the sword.

16* Their infants shall be dashed to pieces in
    their sight;
  their houses shall be plundered
  and their wives ravished.

17* I am stirring up against them the Medes,
  who think nothing of silver
  and take no delight in gold.

18   The fruit of the womb they shall not spare,
  nor shall they have eyes of pity for children.

19   And Babylon, the jewel of kingdoms,
  the glory and pride of the Chaldeans,
Shall be overthrown by God
  like Sodom and like Gomorrah.

20* She shall never be inhabited,
  nor dwelt in, from age to age;
The Arab shall not pitch his tent there,
  nor shepherds couch their flocks.

21*† But wildcats shall rest there
  and owls shall fill the houses;
There ostriches shall dwell,
  and satyrs shall dance.

22   Desert beasts shall howl in her castles,
  and jackals in her luxurious palaces.
Her time is near at hand
  and her days shall not be prolonged.

The King of Babylon

14 1* When the LORD has pity on Jacob and again chooses Israel and settles them on their own soil, the aliens will join them and be counted with the house of Jacob. 2* The house of Israel will take them and bring them along to its place, and possess them as male and female slaves on the Lord's soil, making captives of its captors and ruling over its oppressors. 3* On the day the LORD relieves you of sorrow and unrest and the hard service in which you have been enslaved, 4*† you will take up this taunt-song against the king of Babylon:

How the oppressor has reached his end!
  how the turmoil is stilled!

5   The LORD has broken the rod of the wicked,
  the staff of the tyrants

6   That struck the peoples in wrath
  relentless blows;
That beat down the nations in anger,
  with oppression unchecked.

7   The whole earth rests peacefully,
  song breaks forth;

8* The very cypresses rejoice over you,
  and the cedars of Lebanon:
"Now that you are laid to rest,
  there will be none to cut us down."

9   The nether world below is all astir
  preparing for your coming;
It awakens the shades to greet you,
  all the leaders of the earth;
It has the kings of all nations
  rise from their thrones.

10   All of them speak out
  and say to you,
"You too have become weak like us,
  you are the same as we.

11* Down to the nether world your pomp
    is brought,

---

†
13, 12: *Ophir:* cf note to Ps 45, 10.
13, 21: *Satyrs:* in the popular mind, demons of goatlike form dwelling in ruins, symbols of immorality; cf Lv 17, 7.
14, 4–21: This taunt-song, or satire, is one of the finest in the Bible.

*
13, 8: Is 21, 3; Ps 48, 7;
  Mi 4, 9.
13, 10: Is 24, 23.
13, 11: Is 2, 17; Jer 50, 32.
13, 14: Jer 50, 16.
13, 16: Na 3, 10.
13, 17: Is 21, 2; Jer 51, 11.28.
13, 20: Jer 51, 62.
13, 21: Is 34, 13f; 35, 7.

14, 1: Is 56, 3; 60, 4; Ps
  102, 14; Jer 24, 6;
  Zec 1, 17.
14, 2: Is 66, 20.
14, 3: Jer 30, 10.
14, 4: Hb 2, 6.
14, 8: Ez 31, 16.
14, 11: Sir 10, 13.

the music of your harps.
The couch beneath you is the maggot,
    your covering, the worm."

12† How have you fallen from the heavens,
    O morning star, son of the dawn!
How are you cut down to the ground,
    you who mowed down the nations!
13*†You said in your heart:
    "I will scale the heavens;
Above the stars of God
    I will set up my throne;
I will take my seat on the Mount of Assembly,
    in the recesses of the North.
14* I will ascend above the tops of the clouds;
    I will be like the Most High!"
15 Yet down to the nether world you go
    to the recesses of the pit!
16 When they see you they will stare,
    pondering over you:
    "Is this the man who made the earth tremble,
    and kingdoms quake?
17 Who made the world a desert,
    razed its cities,
    and gave his captives no release?
18 All the kings of the nations lie in glory,
    each in his own tomb;
19 But you are cast forth without burial,
    loathsome and corrupt,
Clothed as those slain at sword-point,
    a trampled corpse.
Going down to the pavement of the pit,
20   you will never be one with them in
        the grave."
For you have ruined your land,
    you have slain your people!

Let him not be named forever,
    that scion of an evil race!
21 Make ready to slaughter his sons
    for the guilt of their fathers;
Lest they rise and possess the earth,
    and fill the breadth of the world with tyrants.

22*I will rise up against them, says the LORD of
hosts, and cut off from Babylon name and remnant,
progeny and offspring, says the LORD. 23 I will make
it a haunt of hoot owls and a marshland; I will
sweep it with the broom of destruction, says the
LORD of hosts.

Assyria

24   The LORD of hosts has sworn:
As I have resolved,
    so shall it be;
As I have proposed,
    so shall it stand:
25 I will break the Assyrian in my land
    and trample him on my mountains;
21† He shall pass through it hard-pressed
        and hungry,
    and in his hunger he shall become enraged,
    and curse his king and his gods.
He shall look upward,
    but there shall be strict darkness
    without any dawn;
22 He shall gaze at the earth,
    but there shall be distress and darkness,
    with the light blacked out by its clouds.
(25) Then his yoke shall be removed from them,
    and his burden from their shoulder.
26 This is the plan proposed for the whole earth,
    and this the hand outstretched over
        all nations.
27 The LORD of hosts has planned;
    who can thwart him?
His hand is stretched out;
    who can turn it back?

Philistia

28† In the year that King Ahaz died, there came
this oracle:

29† Rejoice not, O Philistia, not a man of you,
    that the rod which smote you is broken;
For out of the serpent's root shall come
        an adder,
    its fruit shall be a flying saraph.
30 In my pastures the poor shall eat,
    and the needy lie down in safety;
But I will kill your root with famine
    that shall slay even your remnant.
31 Howl, O gate; cry out, O city!
    Philistia, all of you melts away!
For there comes a smoke from the north,
    without a straggler in the ranks.
32* What will one answer the messengers of
        the nation?
    "The LORD has established Zion,
    and in her the afflicted of his people
        find refuge."

14, 12: *Morning star:* the king of Babylon. The Vulgate has "Lu-
cifer," a name applied by the church Fathers to Satan.
14, 13: *Recesses of the North:* see note on Ps 48, 3.
14, 21f: *He . . . clouds:* the two verses have been transposed
from chap. 8.
14, 28: *The year that King Ahaz died:* 715 B.C.
14, 29: *Rod:* an Assyrian oppressor whose identity is uncertain.

Flying saraph: a poisonous serpent, distinguished by its speedy
movement; cf note on Nm 21, 6.

14, 13: Jer 51, 53; Am 9, 2.   14, 32: Pss 87, 5; 102, 17f;
14, 14: Ez 28, 2.   Zep 3, 12.
14, 22: Jer 51, 62.

?did you KNOW?

Oracles

In the ancient world, an oracle was understood as a communication of the gods. By means of oracles, First Isaiah presents God's judgment on Israel's enemies, including Egypt, Babylon, Assyria, Philistia, Moab, and Edom (Isaiah, chapters 13–23). When we read these oracles today, we can understand their angry and vengeful spirit if we recall the terrible suffering that these nations inflicted on Israel. Still, we should also keep in mind the New Testament commandment to avoid revenge in all its forms (Mt 5, 38–48). Jesus calls us to be peacemakers in spite of our suffering.

▸ Isaiah, chapters 13–23

Moab

15 1* Oracle on Moab:
Laid waste in a night,
Ar of Moab is destroyed;
Laid waste in a night,
Kir of Moab is destroyed.
2*† Up goes daughter Dibon
to the high places to weep;
Over Nebo and over Medeba
Moab wails.
Every head is shaved,
every beard sheared off.
3 In the streets they wear sackcloth,
lamenting and weeping;
On rooftops and in the squares
everyone wails.
4* Heshbon and Elealeh cry out,
they are heard as far as Jahaz.
At this the loins of Moab tremble,
his soul quivers within him;
5* The heart of Moab cries out,
his fugitives reach Zoar
[Eglath-shelishiyah].

The ascent of Luhith
they climb weeping;
On the way to Horonaim
they utter rending cries.
6 The waters of Nimrim
have become a waste;
The grass is withered,
new growth is gone,
nothing is green.
7 So now whatever they have acquired or
stored away
they carry across the Gorge of the Poplars,
8 For the cry has gone round
the land of Moab;
As far as Eglaim the wailing,
and to Beer-elim, the wail.
9† The waters of Dimon were filled with blood,
but I will bring still more upon Dimon:
Lions for those who are fleeing from Moab
and for those who remain in the land!

16 1 Send them forth, hugging the earth
like reptiles,
from Sela across the desert,
to the mount of daughter Zion.
2† Like flushed birds,
like startled nestlings,
Are the daughters of Moab
at the fords of the Arnon.
3† Offer counsel, take their part:
at high noon let your shadow be like
the night,
To hide the outcasts,
to conceal the fugitives.
4 Let the outcasts of Moab live with you,
be their shelter from the destroyer.
When the struggle is ended, the
ruin complete,
and they have done with trampling the land,
5* A throne shall be set up in mercy,
and on it shall sit in fidelity
[in David's tent]
A judge upholding right
and prompt to do justice.
6* We have heard of the pride of Moab,
how very proud he is,
With his haughty, arrogant insolence
that his empty words do not match.

---

† **15, 2:** *Every head . . . sheared off:* traditional signs of grief.
15, 9: There is in the Hebrew a play on words: Dimon and dam, the latter signifying "blood."
16, 2: *The Arnon:* principal river of Moab.
16, 3–5: Directed to Jerusalem, which should receive the suffering Moabites with mercy, as befits the city of David's family, who were partly descended from Ruth the Moabite.

---

* 15, 1: Is 16, 7.   15, 5: Is 16, 9; Jer 48, 3.
15, 2: Jer 48, 38f.   16, 5: Is 32, 1.
15, 4: Jer 48, 34.   16, 6: Jer 48, 29.

⁷*†Therefore Moab wails for Moab,
  everywhere they wail;
For the raisin cakes† of Kir-hareseth
  they sigh, stricken with grief.
⁸† The terraced slopes of Heshbon languish,
  the vines of Sibmah,
Whose clusters overpowered
  the lords of nations,
While they reached as far as Jazer
  and scattered over the desert,
And whose branches spread forth
  and extended over the sea.
⁹* Therefore I weep with Jazer
  for the vines of Sibmah;
I water you with tears,
  Heshbon and Elealeh;
For on your summer fruits and harvests
  the battle cry has fallen.
¹⁰* From the orchards are taken away
  joy and gladness,
In the vineyards there is no singing,
  no shout of joy;
In the wine presses no one treads grapes,
  the vintage shout is stilled.
¹¹* Therefore for Moab
  my breast moans like a lyre,
  and my heart for Kir-hareseth.
¹²*†When Moab grows weary on the high places,
  he shall enter his sanctuary to pray,
  but it shall avail him nothing.

¹³† This is the word the LORD spoke against Moab in times past. ¹⁴ But now the LORD has spoken: In three years, like those of a hireling, the glory of Moab shall be degraded despite all its great multitude; there shall be a remnant, very small and weak.

Damascus

17 ¹*†   Oracle on Damascus:
  Lo, Damascus shall cease to be a city
  and become a ruin;
² Her cities shall be forever abandoned,
  given over to flocks to lie in undisturbed.

³† The fortress shall be lost to Ephraim
  and the kingdom to Damascus;
The remnant of Aram shall have the
  same glory
  as the Israelites,
  says the LORD of hosts.
⁴*   On that day
The glory of Jacob shall fade,
  and his full body grow thin,
⁵† Like the reaper's mere armful of stalks
  when he gathers the standing grain;
Or as when one gleans the ears
  in the Valley of Rephaim.
⁶*†Only a scattering of grapes shall be left!
  As when an olive tree has been beaten,
Two or three olives remain at the very top,
  four or five on its fruitful branches,
  says the LORD, the God of Israel.

⁷* On that day man shall look to his maker,
  his eyes turned toward the Holy One
  of Israel.
⁸† He shall not look to the altars,
  his handiwork,
  nor shall he regard what his fingers
  have made:
  the sacred poles or the incense stands.
⁹* On that day his strong cities shall be
  like those abandoned by the Hivites
  and Amorites
When faced with the children of Israel:
  they shall be laid waste.
¹⁰*†For you have forgotten God, your savior,
  and remembered not the Rock, your strength.
Therefore, though you plant your
  pagan plants
  and set out your foreign vine slips,
¹¹ Though you make them grow the day you
  plant them
  and make your sprouts blossom on the
  next morning,
The harvest shall disappear on the day of the
  grievous blow,
  the incurable blight.

---

† **16, 7–14:** Moab had been prosperous; now it has become a desert.

16, 7: *Raisin cakes:* masses of dried compressed grapes used as food (cf 2 Sm 6, 19; 1 Chr 16, 3; Cf 2, 5), and also in pagan cult (Hos 3, 1).

16, 8: *Desert:* to the east. *Sea:* the Dead Sea.

16, 12: In vain do the Moabites appeal to their god Chemosh.

16, 13f: A prose application of the preceding poetic oracle against Moab (15, 1—16, 12); cf Jer 4, 8. *Like those of a hireling:* who fulfills his period of service according to the shortest manner of reckoning; cf Is 21, 16.

17, 1: *Damascus:* capital of Syria, destroyed in 732 B.C.

17, 3: *Ephraim:* Israel, leagued with Syria against Assyria and Judah; destroyed in 721 B.C. *Aram:* Syria.

17, 5: *Valley of Rephaim:* a fertile plain to the southwest of Jerusalem; cf Jos 15, 8; 2 Sm 5, 18.

17, 6: Olives not easily picked by hand were knocked from the tree by means of a long stick; cf Is 24, 13.

17, 8: *Sacred poles:* see note on Ex 34, 13. *Incense stands:* small altars on which incense was burned in idolatrous worship; cf Is 27, 9; Lv 26, 30.

17, 10: *Pagan plants:* literally, "plants of delights," understood by some as planted in honor of the god of fertility.

16, 7: Is 15, 3.	17, 4: Is 10, 16.
16, 9: Is 15, 5; Jer 48, 32.	17, 6: Is 24, 13.
16, 10: Is 24, 8.	17, 7: Mi 5, 12.
16, 11: Is 15, 5; Jer 48, 36.	17, 9: Is 27, 10.
16, 12: Jer 48, 13.	17, 10: Jer 2, 32; Hos 8, 14.
17, 1: Jer 49, 23.	

12† Ah! the roaring of many peoples
        that roar like the roar of the seas!
    The surging of nations
        that surge like the surging of mighty waves!
13 But God shall rebuke them,
        and they shall flee far away;
    Windswept, like chaff on the mountains,
        like tumbleweed in a storm.
14 In the evening, they spread terror,
        before morning, they are gone!
    Such is the portion of those who despoil us,
        the lot of those who plunder us.

Ethiopia

18 1† Ah, land of buzzing insects,
        beyond the rivers of Ethiopia,†
2* Sending ambassadors by sea,
        in papyrus boats on the waters!
    Go, swift messengers,
        to a nation tall and bronzed,
    To a people dreaded near and far,
        a nation strong and conquering,
        whose land is washed by rivers.
3   All you who inhabit the world,
        who dwell on earth,
    When the signal is raised on the
            mountain, look!
    When the trumpet blows, listen!
4   For thus says the LORD to me:
        I will quietly look on from where I dwell,
    Like the glowing heat of sunshine,
        like a cloud of dew at harvest time.
5   Before the vintage, when the flowering is ended,
        and the blooms are succeeded by
            ripening grapes,
    Then comes the cutting of branches with
            pruning hooks
        and the discarding of the lopped-off shoots.
6   They shall all be left to the mountain birds
            of prey,
        and to the beasts in the land;
    The birds of prey shall summer on them
        and on them all the beasts of the earth
            shall winter.

7* Then will gifts be brought to the LORD of hosts
from a people tall and bronzed, from a people
dreaded near and far, a nation strong and conquering, whose land is washed by rivers—to Mount
Zion where dwells the name of the LORD of hosts.

Egypt

19 1   Oracle on Egypt:
        See, the LORD is riding on a swift cloud
    on his way to Egypt;
    The idols of Egypt tremble before him,
        the hearts of the Egyptians melt within them.
2   I will rouse Egypt against Egypt:
        brother will war against brother,
    Neighbor against neighbor,
        city against city, kingdom against kingdom.
3* The courage of the Egyptians ebbs away
            within them,
        and I will bring to nought their counsel;
    They shall consult idols and charmers,
        ghosts and spirits.
4*† I will deliver Egypt
        into the power of a cruel master,
    A harsh king who shall rule over them,
        says the Lord, the LORD of hosts.
5* The waters shall be drained from the sea,
        the river shall shrivel and dry up;
6   Its streams shall become foul,
        and the canals of Egypt shall dwindle and
            dry up.
    Reeds and rushes shall wither away,
7   and bulrushes on the bank of the Nile;
    All the sown land along the Nile
        shall dry up and blow away, and be no more.
8   The fishermen shall mourn and lament,
        all who cast hook in the Nile;
    Those who spread their nets in the water
        shall pine away.
9* The linen-workers shall be disappointed,
        the combers and weavers shall turn pale;
10 The spinners shall be crushed,
        all the hired laborers shall be despondent.
11† Utter fools are the princes of Zoan!
        the wisest of Pharaoh's advisers give
            stupid counsel.
    How can you say to Pharaoh,
        "I am a disciple of wise men, of
            ancient kings"?
12 Where then are your wise men?
        Let them tell you and make known
    What the LORD of hosts has planned
        against Egypt.
13 The princes of Zoan have become fools,
        the princes of Memphis have been deceived.
    The chiefs of her tribes
        have led Egypt astray.

17, 12f: *Many peoples:* the hordes that accompanied the invading Assyrians, whom God repels just as he vanquished the primeval
waters of chaos; see notes on Jb 3, 8; 7, 12; Ps 89, 11.
    18, 1: *Land of buzzing insects:* the region of the Upper Nile
where these multiplied with great rapidity.
    18, 1f: *Papyrus boats:* light and serviceable vessels made of bun-
dles of papyrus stalks and sealed with pitch. Egypt, ruled by a dynasty from Ethiopia, had invited Judah to join a coalition against

Assyria, but Isaiah bade the ambassadors return to their own people.
    19, 4: *Cruel master:* the king of Assyria.
    19, 11.13: *Zoan:* later known as Tanis, and Memphis (in Hebrew
Noph) were the key cities of the Nile Delta.

18, 2: Is 18, 7.   19, 4: Ez 29, 19; 30, 10.
18, 7: Is 45, 14; Zep 3, 10;   19, 5: Ez 30, 12; 32, 2.
    Mal 1, 11.   19, 9: Ez 27, 7.
19, 3: Is 44, 25.

14 The LORD has prepared among them
    a spirit of dizziness,
And they have made Egypt stagger in whatever
      she does,
    as a drunkard staggers in his vomit.
15*† Egypt shall have no work to do
    for head or tail, palm branch or reed.

16* On that day the Egyptians shall be like
women, trembling with fear, because of the LORD of
hosts shaking his fist at them. 17* And the land of
Judah shall be a terror to the Egyptians. Every time
they remember Judah, they shall stand in dread because of the plan which the LORD of hosts has in
mind for them.

18† On that day there shall be five cities in the
land of Egypt speaking the language of Canaan and
swearing by the LORD of hosts; one shall be called
"City of the Sun."

19 On that day there shall be an altar to the LORD
in the land of Egypt, and a sacred pillar to the LORD
near the boundary. 20 It shall be a sign and a witness to the LORD of hosts in the land of Egypt, when
they cry out to the LORD against their oppressors,
and he sends them a savior to defend and deliver
them. 21* The LORD shall make himself known to
Egypt, and the Egyptians shall know the LORD in
that day; they shall offer sacrifices and oblations,
and fulfill the vows they make to the LORD. 22 Although the LORD shall smite Egypt severely, he shall
heal them; they shall turn to the LORD and he shall
be won over and heal them.

23 On that day there shall be a highway from Egypt
to Assyria; the Assyrians shall enter Egypt, and the
Egyptians enter Assyria, and Egypt shall serve Assyria.

24* On that day Israel shall be a third party with
Egypt and Assyria, a blessing in the midst of the
land, 25 when the LORD of hosts blesses it: "Blessed
be my people Egypt, and the work of my hands Assyria, and my inheritance, Israel."

Captivity of Egypt and Ethiopia

20 1 In the year the general sent by Sargon,
king of Assyria, fought against Ashdod
and captured it, 2† the LORD gave a warning
through Isaiah, the son of Amoz: Go and take off
the sackcloth from your waist, and remove the sandals from your feet. This he did, walking naked and
barefoot. 3 Then the LORD said: Just as my servant
Isaiah has gone naked and barefoot for three years
as a sign and portent against Egypt and Ethiopia,
4 so shall the king of Assyria lead away captives
from Egypt, and exiles from Ethiopia, young and
old, naked and barefoot, with buttocks uncovered
[the shame of Egypt]. 5* They shall be dismayed
and ashamed because of Ethiopia, their hope, and
because of Egypt, their boast. 6* The inhabitants of
this coastland shall say on that day, "Look at our
hope! We have fled here for help and deliverance
from the king of Assyria; where can we flee now?"

Fall of Babylon

21 1† Oracle on the wastelands by
      the sea:
Like whirlwinds sweeping in waves through
      the Negeb,
    there comes from the desert,
    from the fearful land,
2*† A cruel sight, revealed to me:
    the traitor betrays,
    the despoiler spoils.
"Go up, Elam; besiege, O Media;
    I will put an end to all groaning!"
3* Therefore my loins are filled with anguish,
    pangs have seized me like those of a
      woman in labor;
I am too bewildered to hear,
    too dismayed to look.
4   My mind reels,
    shuddering assails me;
My yearning for twilight
    has turned into dread.
5† They set the table,
    spread out the rugs;
    they eat, they drink.
Rise up, O princes,
    oil the shield!
6   For thus says my Lord to me:
    Go, station a watchman,
    let him tell what he sees.
7   If he sees a chariot,
    a pair of horses,
Someone riding an ass,
    someone riding a camel,
Then let him pay heed,
    very close heed.

† 19, 15: *Head or tail, palm branch or reed:* the leaders or the people; cf Is 9, 13f.
19, 18: *Five cities:* colonies of Jews living together and speaking
their languages, Hebrew and Aramaic; cf Jer, chap. 43. *City of the
Sun:* the meaning is uncertain, but the reference seems to be to the
city known later as Heliopolis.
20, 2–6: The symbolic act of the prophet conveyed the idea that
Assyria would lead captive the Egyptians and Ethiopians. The Judeans
and their allies would then realize the folly of having trusted in them.
21, 1: *Wastelands by the sea:* Babylonia. *Negeb:* the desert south
of Judah.

21, 2: *Elam . . . Media:* nations which, under the leadership of
Cyrus, captured Babylon in 538 B.C. *End to all groaning:* those who
were captives of Babylon shall be freed.
21, 5: Babylon is destroyed while its leaders are feasting; cf Dn
5. *Oil the shield:* shields were oiled and greased so as to divert blows
more easily.

*
19, 15: Is 9, 14.   20, 5: Is 30, 3.5.
19, 16: Na 3, 13.   20, 6: Is 31, 3; 36, 6.
19, 17: Ex 14, 25.   21, 2: Is 13, 17.
19, 21: Zec 14, 16.18.   21, 3: Ps 38, 8.
19, 24: Gn 12, 2.

8*   Then the watchman cried,
"On the watchtower, O my Lord,
    I stand constantly by day;
And I stay at my post
    through all the watches of the night.

9*   Here he comes now:
    a single chariot,
    a pair of horses;
He calls out and says,
    'Fallen, fallen is Babylon,
And all the images of her gods
    are smashed to the ground.' "

10*   O my people who have been threshed,
    beaten on my threshing floor!
What I have heard
    from the LORD of hosts,
The God of Israel,
    I have announced to you.

Edom

11†   Oracle on Edom:
They call to me from Seir,
    "Watchman, how much longer the night?
    Watchman, how much longer the night?"

12   The watchman replies,
    "Morning has come, and again night.
    If you will ask, ask; come back again."

Arabia

13†   Oracle on Arabia:
In the thicket in the nomad country spend
    the night,
    O caravans of Dedanites.

14   Meet the thirsty, bring them water;
    you who dwell in the land of Tema,
    greet the fugitives with bread.

15   They flee from the sword,
    from the whetted sword;
From the taut bow,
    from the fury of battle.

16† For thus says the Lord to me: In another year,
like those of a hireling, all the glory of Kedar shall
come to an end. 17 Few of Kedar's stalwart archers
shall remain, for the LORD, the God of Israel, has
spoken.

Jerusalem

22 ¹† Oracle of the Valley of Vision:
    What is the matter with you now, that
      you have gone up,
    all of you, to the housetops,

2*   O city full of noise and chaos,
    O wanton town!
Your slain are not slain with the sword,
    nor killed in battle.

3*   All your leaders fled away together,
    fled afar off;
All who were in you were captured together,
    captured without the use of a bow.

4*   At this I say: Turn away from me,
    let me weep bitterly;
Do not try to comfort me
    for the ruin of the daughter of my people.

5*   It is a day of panic, rout and confusion,
    from the Lord, the GOD of hosts, in the
      Valley of Vision.
Walls crash;
    they cry for help to the mountains.

6†   Elam takes up the quivers,
    Aram mounts the horses,
    and Kir uncovers the shields.

7   Your choice valleys are filled with chariots,
    and horses are posted at the gates,

8†   and shelter over Judah is removed.

On that day you looked to the weapons in the
House of the Forest; 9 you saw that the breaches in
the City of David were many; you collected the water of the lower pool. 10 You numbered the houses
of Jerusalem, tearing some down to strengthen the
wall; 11 you made a reservoir between the two walls
for the water of the old pool. But you did not look
to the city's Maker, nor did you consider him who
built it long ago.

12*   On that day the Lord,
    the GOD of hosts, called on you
To weep and mourn,
    to shave your head and put on sackcloth.

13*   But look! you feast and celebrate,
    you slaughter oxen and butcher sheep,
You eat meat and drink wine:
    "Eat and drink, for tomorrow we die!"

---

† **21, 11f:** *Seir:* another name for Edom. The Edomites ask the
prophet how much longer they must suffer (the night of suffering); he
answers ambiguously: "Liberation (morning) and further suffering
(night)," but perhaps they will later receive a more encouraging answer (ask; come back again).
   21, 13f: *Arabia:* that is, the nomad country. *Dedanites:* an Arab
tribe associated with Edom and Tema, and living east of the Red Sea;
cf Gn 10, 7; 25, 3; Jer 25, 23.
   21, 16: *Year . . . of a hireling:* see note on Is 16, 14. *Kedar:* a nomad tribe in Arabia; cf Is 42, 11; 60, 7; Ps 120, 5.
   22, 1–8: *Valley of Vision:* while the people live in revelry and disorder, the prophet foresees the impending doom of the city.

   22, 6: *Elam, Aram, Kir:* all allies of Assyria. *Kir:* perhaps the same
people referred to in Am 1, 5.
   22, 8–11: Defense measures, in which the inhabitants of
Jerusalem placed their trust instead of relying on God. *House of the
Forest:* an armory built by Solomon; its columns of wood suggested
the trees of a forest; cf 1 Kgs 7, 2; 10, 17.

21, 8: Hb 2, 1.	**22, 4:** Jer 6, 26; 9, 1; 14, 17.
21, 9: Is 46, 1; Jer 50, 2; 51,	**22, 5:** Is 37, 3.
8; Rv 14, 8.	**22, 12:** Jl 2, 17.
21, 10: Is 51, 23.	**22, 13:** Is 56, 12; Wis 2, 6;
22, 2: Is 32, 13.	1 Cor 15, 32.
22, 3: 2 Kgs 25, 4.	

Faith and Politics

Every group that we belong to has a leader. And every leader might be corrupt. Like First Isaiah, we should demand integrity from our leaders as well as practicing it ourselves.

In Is 22, 15–25, the prophet denounces the steward Shebna for his self-seeking ways. Evidently, Shebna is using his position of leadership to prepare an expensive tomb for himself (verse 16) and to acquire ornate chariots (verse 18). Isaiah prefers Eliakim to take over his position. The prophet's interest in local politics points out a biblical truth: Our faith applies to our daily life, including our political choices.

We need to search out and endorse good leaders for school, community, state, and federal governments and for organizations like school clubs, sports teams, youth groups, and Scouts. Challenge your leaders to be people of integrity by avoiding corruption and seeking the best for the people they serve.

▶ Is 22, 15–25

---

14 This reaches the ears of the LORD of hosts—
    You shall not be pardoned this wickedness
        till you die,
    says the Lord, the GOD of hosts.

Shebna and Eliakim

15† Thus says the Lord, the GOD of hosts:
    Up, go to that official,
    Shebna, master of the palace,
16 Who has hewn for himself a sepulcher on
        a height
    and carved his tomb in the rock:
    "What are you doing here, and what people
        have you here,
    that here you have hewn for yourself a tomb?"
17 The LORD shall hurl you down headlong,
        mortal man!
    He shall grip you firmly
18 And roll you up and toss you like a ball
        into an open land
    To perish there, you and the chariots you
        glory in,
    you disgrace to your master's house!
19 I will thrust you from your office
    and pull you down from your station.

20*†On that day I will summon my servant
    Eliakim, son of Hilkiah;
21 I will clothe him with your robe,
    and gird him with your sash,
    and give over to him your authority.

He shall be a father to the inhabitants
        of Jerusalem,
    and to the house of Judah.
22*†I will place the key of the House of David on
        his shoulder;
    when he opens, no one shall shut,
    when he shuts, no one shall open.
23 I will fix him like a peg in a sure spot,
    to be a place of honor for his family;
24† On him shall hang all the glory of his family:
    descendants and offspring,
    all the little dishes, from bowls to jugs.

25 On that day, says the LORD of hosts, the peg fixed in a sure spot shall give way, break off and fall, and the weight that hung on it shall be done away with; for the LORD has spoken.

Tyre and Sidon

23 1† Oracle on Tyre:
    Wail, O ships of Tarshish,
    for your port is destroyed;
    From the land of the Kittim†
        the news reaches them.
2   Silence! you who dwell on the coast,
        you merchants of Sidon,
    Whose messengers crossed the sea
3†   over the deep waters.
    The grain of Shihor, the harvest of the Nile,
        was her revenue,
        and she the merchant among nations.

---

†
22, 15: *Shebna:* referred to as the scribe in Is 36, 3.
22, 20: *Eliakim:* also referred to in Is 36, 3; he is described as loyal to God.
22, 22: *Key:* symbol of authority; cf Mt 16, 19; Rv 3, 7.
22, 24f: If Eliakim should anger God, he and his family (compared here to dishes, bowls and jugs) will suffer disaster.
23, 1–4.12ff: These verses refer to Sidon, vv 5–11 to Tyre.

23, 1: *Kittim:* Cyprus.
23, 3: *Shihor:* a synonym for the Nile.

22, 20: 2 Kgs 18, 18.37.   **22, 22:** Rv 3, 7.

4† Shame, O Sidon, fortress on the sea,
　for the sea has spoken:
"I have not been in labor, nor given birth,
　nor raised young men,
　nor reared virgins."
5　When it is heard in Egypt
　they shall be in anguish at the news of Tyre.
6　Pass over to Tarshish, wailing,
　you who dwell on the coast!
7　Is this your wanton city,
　whose origin is from of old,
Whose feet have taken her
　to dwell in distant lands?
8　Who has planned such a thing
　against Tyre, the bestower of crowns,
Whose merchants are princes,
　whose traders are the earth's honored men?
9* The LORD of hosts has planned it,
　to disgrace all pride of majesty,
　to degrade all the earth's honored men.
10　Cross to your own land,
　O ship of Tarshish;
　the harbor is no more.
11† His hand he stretches out over the sea,
　he shakes kingdoms;
The LORD has ordered the destruction
　of Canaan's strongholds.
12* You shall exult no more, he says,
　you who are now oppressed, virgin
　　daughter Sidon.
Arise, pass over to the Kittim,
　even there you shall find no rest.
13*† [This people is the land of the Chaldeans, not
Assyria.]
　She whom the impious founded,
　　setting up towers for her,
Has had her castles destroyed,
　and has been turned into a ruin.
14　Lament, O ships of Tarshish,
　for your haven is destroyed.

15*† On that day, Tyre shall be forgotten for seventy years. With the days of another king, at the end of seventy years, it shall be for Tyre as in the song about the harlot:

16　Take a harp, go about the city,
　O forgotten harlot;

Pluck the strings skillfully, sing many songs,
　that they may remember you.

17* At the end of the seventy years the LORD shall visit Tyre. She shall return to her hire and deal with all the world's kingdoms on the face of the earth. 18† But her merchandise and her hire shall be sacred to the LORD. It shall not be stored up or laid away, but from her merchandise those who dwell before the LORD shall eat their fill and clothe themselves in choice attire.

IV. Apocalypse of Isaiah†

Devastation of the World: A Remnant Saved

24 1* Lo, the LORD empties the land and
　　lays it waste;
　he turns it upside down,
　　scattering its inhabitants:
2　Layman and priest alike,
　servant and master,
The maid as her mistress,
　the buyer as the seller,
The lender as the borrower,
　the creditor as the debtor.
3　The earth is utterly laid waste, utterly stripped,
　for the LORD has decreed this thing.
4　The earth mourns and fades,
　the world languishes and fades;
　both heaven and earth languish.
5† The earth is polluted because of its inhabitants,
　who have transgressed laws,
　　violated statutes,
　broken the ancient covenant.
6　Therefore a curse devours the earth,
　and its inhabitants pay for their guilt;
Therefore they who dwell on earth turn pale,
　and few men are left.
7* The wine mourns, the vine languishes,
　all the merry-hearted groan.
8* Stilled are the cheerful timbrels,
　ended the shouts of the jubilant,
　stilled is the cheerful harp.
9　They cannot sing and drink wine;
　strong drink is bitter to those who partake
　　of it.
10*† Broken down is the city of chaos,
　shut against entry, every house.

---

† **23, 4:** The sea brings to distant coasts the news that Sidon must disown her children; her people are dispersed.
　23, 11: *Canaan's strongholds:* the fortresses of Phoenicia.
　23, 13: The gloss here identifies she whom the impious founded with the land of the Chaldeans.
　23, 15: *Seventy years:* a conventional period of time indicating simply a long disaster; cf Jer 25, 11 and 29, 10.
　23, 18: Describes the conversion of Tyre.
　24, 1—27, 13: This section, probably composed at a later date, contains oracles on the day of the Lord, combined with hymns of thanksgiving and of supplication.

24, 5: *Ancient covenant:* God's commandments to all mankind.
　24, 10: *City of chaos:* a symbol of godlessness as opposed to Jerusalem, the city of God.

* 　
23, 9: Ez 28, 7.　　　　　24, 1: Is 13, 9; Hos 4, 9.
23, 12: Ez 28, 21f.　　　　24, 7: Jl 1, 10.
23, 13: Ez 26, 7.　　　　　24, 8: Jer 7, 34; Hos 2, 13.
23, 15: Jer 25, 11.　　　　24, 10: Is 25, 2.
23, 17: Ez 27, 12.

11* In the streets they cry out for lack of wine;
    all joy has disappeared
    and cheer has left the land.
12 In the city nothing remains but ruin;
    its gates are battered and desolate.
13* Thus it is within the land,
    and among the peoples,
    As with an olive tree after it is beaten,
    as with a gleaning when the vintage
      is done.
14† These lift up their voice in acclaim;
    from the sea they proclaim the majesty of
      the LORD:
15* "For this, in the coastlands,
    give glory to the LORD!
    In the coastlands of the sea,
    to the name of the LORD, the God of Israel!"
16 From the end of the earth we hear songs:
    "Splendor to the Just One!"
    But I said, "I am wasted, wasted away.
    Woe is me! The traitors betray:
    with treachery have the traitors betrayed!
17* Terror, pit, and trap
    are upon you, inhabitant of the earth;
18 He who flees at the sound of terror
    will fall into the pit;
    He who climbs out of the pit
    will be caught in the trap.
    For the windows on high will be opened
    and the foundations of the earth will shake.
19 The earth will burst asunder,
    the earth will be shaken apart,
    the earth will be convulsed.
20* The earth will reel like a drunkard,
    and it will sway like a hut;
    Its rebellion will weigh it down,
    until it falls, never to rise again."

21*† On that day the LORD will punish
    the host of the heavens in the heavens,
    and the kings of the earth on the earth.
22 They will be gathered together
    like prisoners into a pit;
    They will be shut up in a dungeon,
    and after many days they will be punished.
23*† Then the moon will blush
    and the sun grow pale,
    For the LORD of hosts will reign
    on Mount Zion and in Jerusalem,
    glorious in the sight of his elders.

25

1*† O LORD, you are my God,
    I will extol you and praise your name;
For you have fulfilled your wonderful plans
    of old,
    faithful and true.
2* For you have made the city a heap,
    the fortified city a ruin;
The castle of the insolent is a city no more,
    nor ever to be rebuilt.
3 Therefore a strong people will honor you,
    fierce nations will fear you.
4* For you are a refuge to the poor,
    a refuge to the needy in distress;
Shelter from the rain,
    shade from the heat.
As with the cold rain,
5   as with the desert heat,
    even so you quell the uproar of the wanton.
6† On this mountain the LORD of hosts
    will provide for all peoples
A feast of rich food and choice wines,
    juicy, rich food and pure, choice wines.
7* On this mountain he will destroy
    the veil that veils all peoples,
The web that is woven over all nations;
8   he will destroy death forever.
The Lord GOD will wipe away
    the tears from all faces;
The reproach of his people he will remove
    from the whole earth; for the LORD
    has spoken.

9*   On that day it will be said:
"Behold our God, to whom we looked to
    save us!
    This is the LORD for whom we looked;
    let us rejoice and be glad that he has
    saved us!"
10*† For the hand of the LORD will rest on
    this mountain,
    but Moab will be trodden down
    as a straw is trodden down in the mire.
11* He will stretch forth his hands in Moab
    as a swimmer extends his hands to swim;
    He will bring low their pride
    as his hands sweep over them.
12* The high-walled fortress he will raze,
    and strike it down level with the earth, with
    the very dust.

24, 14: *These:* the saved.
24, 21: *Host of the heavens:* the stars, which were regarded by the pagans as gods; cf Dt 4, 19; Jer 8, 2.
24, 23: *His elders:* the heavenly courtiers surrounding the throne of God.
25, 1–8: Victory in messianic times.
25, 6: *This mountain:* Zion, symbol of the heavenly Jerusalem.
25, 10: *Moab:* symbol of God's enemies.

24, 11: Jer 48, 33; Lam 5, 14f.
24, 13: Is 17, 6; Mi 7, 1.
24, 15: Is 42, 10.12; Zep 2, 11.
24, 17f: Jer 48, 43f.
24, 20: Is 9, 14.
24, 21: Ps 76, 13.
24, 23: Is 13, 10; Jl 3, 3f; 4, 15.
25, 1: Ex 15, 2.
25, 2: Jer 9, 11.
25, 4: Is 14, 32; 32, 2; Na 1, 7.
25, 7: Is 60, 1.3; 1 Cor 15, 53ff; Rv 7, 17; 21, 4.
25, 9: Is 30, 18f.
25, 10: Zep 2, 9f.
25, 11: Is 16, 6f.14.
25, 12: Is 26, 5.

The Divine Vindicator

26 [1] On that day they will sing this song in
the land of Judah:

"A strong city have we;
    he sets up walls and ramparts to protect us.
[2]* Open up the gates
    to let in a nation that is just,
    one that keeps faith.
[3]* A nation of firm purpose you keep in peace;
    in peace, for its trust in you."

[4]* Trust in the LORD forever!
    For the LORD is an eternal Rock.
[5]* He humbles those in high places,
    and the lofty city he brings down;
He tumbles it to the ground,
    levels it with the dust.
[6] It is trampled underfoot by the needy,
    by the footsteps of the poor.
[7]* The way of the just is smooth;
    the path of the just you make level.
[8] Yes, for your way and your judgments,
    O LORD,
    we look to you;
Your name and your title
    are the desire of our souls,
[9]* My soul yearns for you in the night,
    yes, my spirit within me keeps vigil for
    you;
When your judgment dawns upon the earth,
    the world's inhabitants learn justice.
[10]* The wicked man, spared, does not
    learn justice;
    in an upright land he acts perversely,
    and sees not the majesty of the LORD.
[11] O LORD, your hand is uplifted,
    but they behold it not;
Let them be shamed when they see your zeal
    for your people:
    let the fire prepared for your enemies
    consume them.
[12]* O LORD, you mete out peace to us,
    for it is you who have accomplished all we
    have done.
[13] O LORD, our God, other lords than you have
    ruled us;
    it is from you only that we can call upon
    your name.

[14] Dead they are, they have no life,
    shades that cannot rise;
For you have punished and destroyed them,
    and wiped out all memory of them.
[15]* You have increased the nation, O LORD,
    increased the nation to your own glory,
    and extended far all the borders of
    the land.
[16]* O LORD, oppressed by your punishment,
    we cried out in anguish under
    your chastising.
[17]* As a woman about to give birth
    writhes and cries out in her pains,
    so were we in your presence, O LORD.
[18] We conceived and writhed in pain,
    giving birth to wind;
Salvation we have not achieved for the earth,
    the inhabitants of the world cannot bring
    it forth.
[19]*† But your dead shall live, their corpses
    shall rise;
    awake and sing, you who lie in the dust.
For your dew is a dew of light,
    and the land of shades gives birth.

Day of the LORD: Reward and Punishment

[20] Go, my people, enter your chambers,
    and close your doors behind you;
Hide yourselves for a brief moment,
    until the wrath is past.
[21]* See, the LORD goes forth from his place,
    to punish the wickedness of the
    earth's inhabitants;
The earth will reveal the blood upon her,
    and no longer conceal her slain.

27 [1]*† On that day,
    The LORD will punish with his sword
that is cruel, great, and strong,
Leviathan the fleeing serpent,
    Leviathan the coiled serpent;
    and he will slay the dragon that is in
    the sea.
[2]* On that day—
The pleasant vineyard, sing about it!
[3]* I, the LORD, am its keeper,
    I water it every moment;
Lest anyone harm it,
    night and day I guard it.

26, 19: This verse refers to the restoration of Israel in messianic
times under the figure of the resurrection of the dead; cf Ez, chap. 37.
    27, 1: *Leviathan . . . dragon:* symbols of the forces of evil which
God vanquishes even as he overcame primeval chaos; cf notes on Jb
3, 8; 7, 12.

26, 2: Ps 118, 19f.
26, 3: Is 32, 17f; 54, 13.
26, 4: Is 30, 29; Ps 62, 8.
26, 5: Is 25, 12; 32, 19.
26, 7: Ps 23, 3f; Prv 11, 3.5.
26, 9: Ps 94, 15.
26, 10: Is 5, 12.
26, 12: Jer 29, 11.
26, 15: Is 54, 2f; Neh 9, 23.
26, 16: Hos 6, 1.
26, 17: Mi 4, 10.
26, 19: Ez 37, 5f; Dn 12, 2;
    Hos 6, 2.
26, 21: Mi 1, 3.
27, 1: Jb 40, 25–32; Ez 32, 2.
27, 2: Is 5, 1.
27, 3: Is 5, 2ff; Ps 121, 4f.

4* I am not angry,
    but if I were to find briers and thorns,
In battle I should march against them;
    I should burn them all.
8* Expunging and expelling, I should strive
       against them,
    carrying them off with my cruel wind in
       time of storm.
6 In days to come Jacob shall take root,
    Israel shall sprout and blossom,
    covering all the world with fruit.
7† Is he to be smitten as his smiter was smitten?
    or slain as his slayer was slain?
5*†Or shall he cling to me for refuge?
    He must make peace with me;
    peace shall he make with me!
9 This, then, shall be the expiation of
     Jacob's guilt,
    this the whole fruit of the removal of
      his sin:
He shall pulverize all the stones of the altars
    like pieces of chalk;
    no sacred poles or incense altars
      shall stand.
10*† For the fortified city shall be desolate,
    an abandoned pasture, a
      forsaken wilderness,
    where calves shall browse and lie.
Its boughs shall be destroyed,
11*   its branches shall wither and be
      broken off,
and women shall come to build a fire
    with them.
This is not an understanding people;
    therefore their maker shall not spare them,
    nor shall he who formed them have mercy
      on them.
12†   On that day,
The LORD shall beat out the grain
    between the Euphrates and the Wadi
      of Egypt,
    and you shall be gleaned one by one,
      O sons of Israel.
13*†   On that day,
A great trumpet shall blow,
    and the lost in the land of Assyria
    and the outcasts in the land of Egypt

Shall come and worship the LORD
    on the holy mountain, in Jerusalem.

V: The LORD Alone, Israel's and Judah's Salvation

The Fate of Samaria

28 1*† Woe to the majestic garland
    of the drunkard Ephraim,
To the fading blooms of his glorious beauty,
    on the head of him who is stupefied
      with wine.
2*†Behold, the LORD has a strong one and
    a mighty,
    who, like a downpour of hail, a
      destructive storm,
Like a flood of water, great and overflowing,
    levels to the ground with violence;
3 With feet that will trample
    the majestic garland of the
      drunkard Ephraim.
4 The fading blooms of his glorious beauty
    on the head of the fertile valley
Will be like an early fig before summer:
    when a man sees it,
    he picks and swallows it at once.
5 On that day the LORD of hosts
    will be a glorious crown
And a brilliant diadem
    to the remnant of his people,
6 A spirit of justice
    to him who sits in judgment,
And strength to those
    who turn back the battle at the gate.

Against Judah

7* But these also stagger from wine
    and stumble from strong drink:
Priest and prophet stagger from
    strong drink,
    overpowered by wine;
Led astray by strong drink,
    staggering in their visions,
    tottering when giving judgment.
8 Yes, all the tables
    are covered with filthy vomit,
    with no place left clean.

---

† 27, 7: God's people will not be treated as sternly as were their enemies.

27, 5.9: Israel will make peace with God and destroy all signs of idolatrous worship.

27, 10f: *The fortified city:* symbol of the powers of evil; see note on Is 24, 10.

27, 12: *The Euphrates and the Wadi of Egypt:* the ideal borders of Israel; cf Gn 15, 18; 2 Kgs 24, 7.

27, 13: The triumph of God's people is described in eschatological language; they will gather in Jerusalem from Assyria and Egypt.

28, 1: *Ephraim:* the northern kingdom. Its capital, Samaria, was built upon a hill, suggestive of a majestic garland adorning the head of the drunken kingdom.

28, 2: *A strong one and a mighty:* Assyria.

27, 4: Is 10, 17.
27, 8: Jer 18, 17.
27, 5: Is 37, 31; Rom 11, 12.
27, 10: Is 6, 11.
27, 11: Jer 4, 22.

27, 13: Hos 11, 11.
28, 1: Hos 7, 5; Am 6, 6.
28, 2: Is 30, 30.
28, 7: Is 56, 10.12.

9† "To whom would he impart knowledge?
    To whom would he convey the message?
    To those just weaned from milk,
        those taken from the breast? 10For
        he says,
    'Command on command, command
        on command,
    rule on rule, rule on rule,
    here a little, there a little!' "
11*† Yes, with stammering lips and in a
        strange language
    he will speak to this people
12 to whom he said:
    This is the resting place,
        give rest to the weary;
    Here is repose—
        but they would not listen.
13 So for them the word of the LORD shall be:
    "Command on command, command
        on command,
    Rule on rule, rule on rule,
        here a little, there a little!"
    So that when they walk, they
        stumble backward,
    broken, ensnared, and captured.

14 Therefore, hear the word of the LORD,
        you arrogant,
    who rule this people in Jerusalem:
15*† Because you say, "We have made a covenant
        with death,
    and with the nether world we have made
        a pact;
    When the overwhelming scourge passes,
        it will not reach us;
    For we have made lies our refuge,
        and in falsehood we have found a
        hiding place,"—
16*† Therefore, thus says the Lord GOD:
    See, I am laying a stone in Zion,
        a stone that has been tested,
    A precious cornerstone as a sure
        foundation;

    he who puts his faith in it shall not
        be shaken.
17 I will make of right a measuring line,
        of justice a level.—
    Hail shall sweep away the refuge of lies,
        and waters shall flood the hiding place.
18 Your covenant with death shall be canceled
        and your pact with the nether world shall
        not stand.
    When the overwhelming scourge passes,
        you shall be trampled down by it.
19 Whenever it passes, it shall take you;
        morning after morning it shall pass,
    By day and by night;
        terror alone shall convey the message.
20 For the bed shall be too short to stretch
        out in,
    and the cover too narrow to wrap in.
21*† For the LORD shall rise up as on
        Mount Perazim,
    bestir himself as in the Valley of Gibeon,
    To carry out his work, his singular work,
        to perform his deed, his strange deed.
22* Now, be arrogant no more
        lest your bonds be tightened,
    For I have heard from the Lord, the GOD
        of hosts,
        the destruction decreed for the whole earth.
23† Give ear and hear my voice,
        pay attention and listen to what I say:
24 Is the plowman forever plowing,
        always loosening and harrowing his land
        for planting?
25† When he has leveled the surface,
        does he not scatter gith and sow cumin,
    Put in wheat and barley,
        with spelt as its border?
26 He has learned this rule,
        instructed by his God.
27 Gith is not threshed with a sledge,
        nor does a cartwheel roll over cumin.
    But gith is beaten out with a staff,
        and cumin crushed for food with a rod.

28, 9f: The words of those who ridicule Isaiah. The Hebrew of v 10, by its very sound, conveys the idea of mocking imitation of what the prophet says, as though he spoke like a stammering child: *SAU LASAU, SAU LASAU, CAU LACAU, CAU LACAU, ZE'ER SHAM, ZE'ER SHAM.* But in v 13 God repeats these words in deadly earnest, putting them in the mouth of the victorious pagan army.
28, 11: God will answer the mockers and defend Isaiah. *Strange language:* spoken by the invading army.
28, 15.18: *A covenant with death, and with the nether world:* an alliance with foreign powers, such as Egypt and Babylon, to prevent death and destruction. *Overwhelming scourge:* the flood of the Assyrian invasion; cf Is 8, 7f. *Have made lies . . . a hiding place:* this confidence in human aid proves to be false and deceitful, incapable of averting the dreaded disaster.
28, 16: *A stone in Zion:* the true and sure foundation of salvation promised by God to the Davidic dynasty (cf Is 7, 13–16; 9, 1–6), which the Apostles saw fulfilled in Christ the universal Savior; cf 1 Pt

2, 6–8; Rom 9, 33; 10, 9ff. *Cornerstone:* the assurance of salvation rejected by Israel in the prophet's time, is reflected by the psalmist (Ps 118, 22) and fulfilled in the Person of Christ; cf Mt 21, 42; Lk 20, 17; Acts 4, 11; Rom 9, 33; 1 Pt 2, 7.
28, 21: *Mount Perazim . . . Valley of Gibeon:* where David defeated the Philistines; cf 2 Sm 5, 20.25; 1 Chr 14, 11.16.
28, 23–29: The practical variation of the farmer's work taught him by God reflects God's dealing with his people, wisely adapted to circumstances; he does not crush their weakness altogether; cf ch 29.
28, 25: *Gith . . . cumin:* herbs used in seasoning food. *Spelt:* a variety of wheat.

28, 11: Jer 5, 15; 1 Cor 14, 21;   1 Pt 2, 6.
         Dt 28, 49; Bar 4, 15.   **28, 21:** Jos 10, 10; 2 Sm 5, 20;
28, 15: Wis 1, 16; Jer 5, 12.   1 Chr 14, 11.
28, 16: Ps 118, 22; Mt 21, 42;   **28, 22:** Is 10, 23.
         Acts 4, 11; Rom 9, 33;

28 No, he does not thresh it unendingly,
    nor does he crush it
    with his noisy cartwheels and horses.
29 This too comes from the LORD of hosts;
    wonderful is his counsel and great
    his wisdom.

The Fall of Jerusalem

29

1† Woe to Ariel, Ariel,
    the city where David encamped!
Add year to year,
    let the feasts come round.
2* But I will bring distress upon Ariel,
    with mourning and grief.
You shall be to me like Ariel,
3* I will encamp like David against you;
I will encircle you with outposts
    and set up siege works against you.
4† Prostrate you shall speak from the earth,
    and from the base dust your words
        shall come.
Your voice shall be like a ghost's from the earth,
    and your words like chirping from the dust.
5* The horde of your arrogant shall be like
        fine dust,
    the horde of the tyrants like flying chaff.
Then suddenly, in an instant,
6   you shall be visited by the LORD of hosts,
With thunder, earthquake, and great noise,
    whirlwind, storm, and the flame of
        consuming fire.

7† Then like a dream,
    a vision in the night,
Shall be the horde of all the nations
    who war against Ariel
    with all the earthworks of her besiegers.
8 As when a hungry man dreams he is eating
    and awakens with an empty stomach,
Or when a thirsty man dreams he is drinking
    and awakens faint and dry,
So shall the horde of all the nations be,
    who make war against Zion.

Blindness and Perversity

9*† Be irresolute, stupefied;
    blind yourselves and stay blind!

Be drunk, but not from wine,
    stagger, but not from strong drink!
10* For the LORD has poured out on you
    a spirit of deep sleep.
He has shut your eyes [the prophets]
    and covered your heads [the seers].

11* For you the revelation of all this has become
like the words of a sealed scroll. When it is handed
to one who can read, with the request, "Read this,"
he replies, "I cannot; it is sealed." 12 When it is
handed to one who cannot read, with the request,
"Read this," he replies, "I cannot read."

13*   The Lord said:
Since this people draws near with words only
    and honors me with their lips alone,
    though their hearts are far from me,
And their reverence for me has become
    routine observance of the precepts of men,
14* Therefore I will again deal with this people
    in surprising and wondrous fashion:
The wisdom of its wise men shall perish
    and the understanding of its prudent men
        be hid.
15* Woe to those who would hide their plans
    too deep for the LORD!
Who work in the dark, saying,
    "Who sees us, or who knows us?"
16* Your perversity is as though the potter
    were taken to be the clay:
As though what is made should say of
        its maker,
    "He made me not!"
Or the vessel should say of the potter,
    "He does not understand."

Redemption†

17* But a very little while,
    and Lebanon shall be changed into
        an orchard,
    and the orchard be regarded as a forest!
18* On that day the deaf shall hear
    the words of a book;
And out of gloom and darkness,
    the eyes of the blind shall see.
19* The lowly will ever find joy in the LORD,

29, 1f: *Ariel:* variously interpreted to mean "lion of God" or "hearth (altar) of God," a poetic name for Jerusalem; or perhaps to be read as Uru-el, "foundation of God," an archaic name for the Jebusite city of Jerusalem; like that Ariel, against which David encamped, it will be besieged by God.

29, 4: *Chirping:* see note on Is 8, 19.

29, 7f: Just when the Assyrians think their capture of Jerusalem to be certain, the Lord will snatch victory from their hands and save his city.

29, 9–12: Jerusalem in her blindness refuses to believe God's revelation that she will be saved.

29, 17–24: The prophet presents God's plan of redemption in terms of unheard-of natural phenomena as if such changes in nature took place, e. g., the change of the cedars of Lebanon into an orchard (v 17).

29, 1: 2 Sm 5, 9.	Mk 7, 6f.
29, 2: Is 33, 7.	29, 14: Jer 49, 7; 1 Cor 1, 19.
29, 3: 2 Kgs 25, 1; Ez 4, 2.	29, 15: Is 30, 1; Ez 8, 12; Jn
29, 5: Is 17, 13; Ps 18, 43; Jb	3, 19f.
21, 18.	29, 16: Is 45, 9; Jer 18, 6; Rom
29, 9: Is 19, 14; 28, 7f.	9, 20.
29, 10: Is 6, 10; Rom 11, 8.	29, 17: Is 32, 15.
29, 11: Dn 12, 4.	29, 18: Is 35, 5; 42, 6f.
29, 13: Ez 33, 31; Mt 15, 8f;	29, 19: Is 61, 1.

I
S

Preference for the Poor

Isaiah 29, 17–21 proclaims that God's power will transform society: the deaf will hear, the blind will see, the lowly will know joy, and the poor will rejoice. First Isaiah's words are reflected in Jesus' words in the Beatitudes (see Lk 6, 20–26). Both Jesus and Isaiah say that in God's Reign, the rights and needs of the lowliest and the weakest come first (see Isaiah, chapters 58, 61).

The Catholic church refers to this principle as preferential love for the poor. People who are poor and helpless have a right to a just society where they get what they need to live with dignity and where they have a voice in the structures that govern their life. One can tell how near a society is to the Reign of God by seeing how it treats the most vulnerable members of the human family. Those who are poor should never be ignored when others have the resources to share.

Write your own prayer describing God's vision for those who are poor. Use Isaiah's words and the Beatitudes for ideas. Share your prayer with your family or youth group.

▸ Is 29, 17–21

and the poor rejoice in the Holy One
    of Israel.
20* For the tyrant will be no more
    and the arrogant will have gone;
All who are alert to do evil will be cut off,
21*   those whose mere word condemns a man,
Who ensnare his defender at the gate,
    and leave the just man with an
        empty claim.
22*†Therefore thus says the LORD,
    the God of the house of Jacob,
    who redeemed Abraham:

Now Jacob shall have nothing to be
    ashamed of,
    nor shall his face grow pale.
23   When his children see
        the work of my hands in his midst,
They shall keep my name holy;
    they shall reverence the Holy One of Jacob,
    and be in awe of the God of Israel.
24   Those who err in spirit shall
        acquire understanding,
    and those who find fault shall
        receive instruction.

Futile Alliance with Egypt

30 ¹* Woe to the rebellious children,
        says the LORD,
Who carry out plans that are not mine,
    who weave webs that are not inspired
        by me,
    adding sin upon sin.
²*   They go down to Egypt,
        but my counsel they do not seek.
They find their strength in
        Pharaoh's protection
    and take refuge in Egypt's shadow;
³*   Pharaoh's protection shall be your shame,
    and refuge in Egypt's shadow your disgrace.
⁴*   When their princes are at Zoan
    and their messengers reach Hanes,
⁵*   All shall be ashamed
        of a people that gain them nothing,
Neither help nor benefit,
        but only shame and reproach.

⁶†   [Oracle on the Beasts of the Negeb]

Through the distressed and troubled land
    of the lioness and roaring lion,
    of the viper and flying saraph,
They carry their riches on the backs of asses
    and their treasures on the humps of camels
To a people good for nothing,
⁷†   to Egypt whose help is futile and vain.
Therefore I call her
    "Rahab quelled."
⁸*†Now come, write it on a tablet they can keep,
    inscribe it in a record;
That it may be in future days
    an eternal witness:

---

† **29, 22:** *Who redeemed Abraham:* by freeing him from the idolatry of his native land.

30, 6: *Flying saraph:* see note on Nm 21, 6.

30, 7: *Rahab:* Egypt, here as elsewhere (cf Ps 87, 4), is compared to the stormy, impetuous sea monster (cf Is 51, 9; Jb 26, 12; Ps 89, 11), which yet, when asked for aid by Judah, becomes silent, quelled.

30, 8: Isaiah will write down his condemnation of the people so that (vv 12–18) its fulfillment may afterward be admitted.

29, 20: Is 28, 22.
29, 21: Am 5, 10.12.
29, 22: Is 45, 17.
30, 1: Is 1, 4.
30, 2: Is 31, 1; 36, 6.
30, 3: Is 20, 5; Jer 2, 26f.
30, 4: Is 19, 11.
30, 5: Is 36, 6.
30, 8: Is 8, 1.16; Jer 36, 2; Heb 2, 2.

9* This is a rebellious people,
  deceitful children,
Children who refuse
  to obey the law of the LORD.
10* They say to the seers, "Have no visions";
  to the prophets, "Do not descry for us what
  is right;
  speak flatteries to us, conjure up illusions.
11* Out of the way! Out of our path!
  Let us hear no more
  of the Holy One of Israel."
12 Therefore, thus says the Holy One of Israel:
  Because you reject this word,
  And put your trust in what is crooked
  and devious,
  and depend on it,
13* This guilt of yours shall be
  like a descending rift
  Bulging out in a high wall
  whose crash comes suddenly, in an instant.
14* It crashes like a potter's jar
  smashed beyond rescue,
  And among its fragments cannot be found
  a sherd to scoop fire from the hearth
  or dip water from the cistern.

15* For thus said the Lord GOD,
  the Holy One of Israel:
  By waiting and by calm you shall be saved,
  in quiet and in trust your strength lies.
  But this you did not wish.
16* "No," you said,
  "Upon horses we will flee."
  —Very well, flee!
  "Upon swift steeds we will ride."
  —Not so swift as your pursuers.
17 A thousand shall tremble at the threat of one;
  if five threaten you, you shall flee,
  Until you are left like a flagstaff on
  the mountaintop,
  like a flag on the hill.
18* Yet the LORD is waiting to show you favor,
  and he rises to pity you;
  For the LORD is a God of justice:
  blessed are all who wait for him!

19* O people of Zion, who dwell in Jerusalem,
  no more will you weep;
  He will be gracious to you when you cry out,
  as soon as he hears he will answer you.
20† The Lord will give you the bread you need

and the water for which you thirst.
No longer will your Teacher hide himself,
  but with your own eyes you shall see
  your Teacher,
21* While from behind, a voice shall sound in
  your ears:
  "This is the way; walk in it,"
  when you would turn to the right or to
  the left.
22* And you shall consider unclean your
  silver-plated idols
  and your gold-covered images;
  You shall throw them away like filthy rags
  to which you say, "Begone!"

Zion's Future Prosperity

23* He will give rain for the seed
  that you sow in the ground,
  And the wheat that the soil produces
  will be rich and abundant.
  On that day your cattle will graze
  in spacious meadows;
24 The oxen and the asses that till the ground
  will eat silage tossed to them
  with shovel and pitchfork.
25* Upon every high mountain and lofty hill
  there will be streams of running water.
  On the day of the great slaughter,
  when the towers fall,
26* The light of the moon will be like that of
  the sun
  and the light of the sun will be seven
  times greater
  [like the light of seven days].
  On the day the LORD binds up the wounds of
  his people,
  he will heal the bruises left by his blows.

Divine Judgment on Assyria†

27 See the name of the LORD coming from afar
  in burning wrath, with lowering clouds!
  His lips are filled with fury,
  his tongue is like a consuming fire;
28 His breath, like a flood in a ravine
  that reaches suddenly to the neck,
  Will winnow the nations with a
  destructive winnowing,
  and with repeated winnowings will he
  battle against them
  [and a bridle on the jaws of the peoples to
  send them astray].

30, 20: *Teacher:* God, who in the past taught in a veiled manner through his prophets, will in future help them to understand his teaching clearly. This was eminently true when the Son of God became Man.

30, 27–33: God's punishment of Assyria. *The name of the LORD:* God himself; cf Ps 20, 2.

30, 9: Is 1, 4; Jer 7, 28.
30, 10: Jer 5, 31.
30, 11: Jb 21, 14f.
30, 13: Ez 13, 14.
30, 14: Jer 19, 11.
30, 15: Is 7, 4; Mi 7, 7.
30, 16: Is 31, 3.
30, 18: Ps 34, 9; Jer 17, 7.
30, 19: Is 58, 9.
30, 21: Jer 31, 33f.
30, 22: Is 31, 7.
30, 23: Lv 26, 3.5.
30, 25: Jl 4, 18.
30, 26: Jer 30, 17.

S

30 The LORD will make his glorious voice heard,
　　and let it be seen how his arm descends
In raging fury and flame of consuming fire,
　　in driving storm and hail.

31 When the LORD speaks, Assyria will
　　　be shattered,
　　as he strikes with the rod;

32 While at every sweep of the rod
　　which the LORD will bring down on him
　　　in punishment,

29† You will sing
　　as on a night when a feast is observed,
And be merry of heart,
　　as one marching along with a flute
Toward the mountain of the LORD,
　　toward the Rock of Israel,
　　accompanied by the timbrels and lyres.

33 For the pyre has long been ready,
　　prepared for the king;
Broad and deep it is piled
　　with dry grass and wood in abundance,
And the breath of the LORD, like a stream
　　of sulphur,
　　will set it afire.

Against the Egyptian Alliance

31 1* Woe to those who go down to Egypt
　　　for help,
who depend upon horses;
Who put their trust in chariots because of
　　their number,
　　and in horsemen because of their
　　　combined power,
But look not to the Holy One of Israel
　　nor seek the LORD!

2 Yet he too is wise and will bring disaster;
　　he will not turn from what he has
　　　threatened to do.
He will rise up against the house of
　　the wicked
　　and against those who help evildoers.

3* The Egyptians are men, not God,
　　their horses are flesh, not spirit;
When the LORD stretches forth his hand,
　　the helper shall stumble, the one helped
　　　shall fall,
　　and both of them shall perish together.

4 　　Thus says the LORD to me:
As a lion or a lion cub
　　growling over its prey,

With a band of shepherds
　　assembled against it,
Is neither frightened by their shouts
　　nor disturbed by their noise,
So shall the LORD of hosts come down
　　to wage war upon the mountain and hill
　　　of Zion.

5* Like hovering birds, so the LORD of hosts
　　shall shield Jerusalem,
To protect and deliver,
　　to spare and rescue it.

6* Return, O children of Israel, to him whom
you have utterly deserted. 7* On that day each one
of you shall spurn his sinful idols of silver and gold,
which he made with his hands.

Downfall of Assyria

8* Assyria shall fall by a sword not wielded
　　by man,
　　no mortal sword shall devour him;
He shall flee before the sword,
　　and his young men shall be impressed
　　　as laborers.

9† He shall rush past his crag in panic,
　　and his princes shall flee in terror from
　　　his standard,
Says the LORD who has a fire in Zion
　　and a furnace in Jerusalem.

The Kingdom of Justice

32 1* See, a king will reign justly
　　　and princes will rule rightly.

2* Each of them will be a shelter from the wind,
　　a retreat from the rain.
They will be like streams of water in a
　　dry country,
　　like the shade of a great rock in a
　　parched land.

3 The eyes of those who see will not be closed;
　　the ears of those who hear will be attentive.

4 The flighty will become wise and capable,
　　and the stutterers will speak fluently
　　and clearly.

5 No more will the fool be called noble,
　　nor the trickster be considered honorable.

6* For the fool speaks foolishly,
　　planning evil in his heart:
How to do wickedness,
　　to speak perversely against the LORD,
To let the hungry go empty

---

† **30, 29–33:** *Pyre:* on which the corpse of the king of Assyria is
burned. This is the occasion of festal rejoicing for the Israelites, who
are now free from his yoke.
31, 9: *Crag:* the king as the rallying point of the princes.

31, 1: Is 30, 2; 36, 6.
31, 3: Ps 146, 3ff.
31, 5: Ps 91, 4.
31, 6: Jer 3, 12.
31, 7: Is 30, 22.
31, 8: Is 37, 36.

32, 1: Is 16, 5; Ps 72, 2ff; Jer
　　23, 5.
32, 2: Is 4, 6; 25, 4.
32, 6: Prv 10, 32; Eccl 10,
　　12f.

and the thirsty be without drink.

7 And the trickster uses wicked trickery,
  planning crimes:
  How to ruin the poor with lies,
  and the needy when they plead their case.

8 But the noble man plans noble things,
  and by noble things he stands.

The Women of Jerusalem

9 O complacent ladies, rise up and hear my voice,
  overconfident women, give heed to
  my words.

10* In a little more than a year
  you overconfident ones will be shaken;
  The vintage will fail,
  there will be no harvest.

11* Tremble, you who are complacent!
  Shudder, you who are overconfident!
  Strip yourselves bare,
  with only a loincloth to cover you.

12 Beat your breasts
  for the pleasant fields, the fruitful vine,

13* And the soil of my people,
  overgrown with thorns and briers;
  For all the joyful houses,
  the wanton city.

14** †Yes, the castle will be forsaken,
  the noisy city deserted;

19 Down it comes, as trees come down in
  the forest!
  The city will be utterly laid low.
  Hill and tower will become wasteland forever
  for wild asses to frolic in, and flocks
  to pasture,

15* †Until the spirit from on high
  is poured out on us.
  Then will the desert become an orchard
  and the orchard be regarded as a forest.

16 Right will dwell in the desert
  and justice abide in the orchard.

17* Justice will bring about peace;
  right will produce calm and security.

18* My people will live in peaceful country,
  in secure dwellings and quiet resting places.

20* Happy are you who sow beside every stream,
  and let the ox and the ass go freely!

Overthrow of Assyria

33 ¹ Woe, O destroyer never destroyed,
  O traitor never betrayed!
  When you finish destroying, you will
  be destroyed;
  when wearied with betraying, you will
  be betrayed.

2* O LORD, have pity on us, for you we wait.
  Be our strength every morning,
  our salvation in time of trouble!

3 At the roaring sound, peoples flee;
  when you rise in your majesty, nations
  are scattered.

4* Men gather spoil as caterpillars are
  gathered up;
  they rush upon it like the onrush
  of locusts.

5* The LORD is exalted, enthroned on high;
  he fills Zion with right and justice.

6* That which makes her seasons lasting,

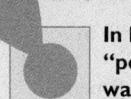

Shalom

LIVE IT!

In Israel, people greet one another by saying "Shalom." In the Bible, *shalom* means "peace" in its fullest sense (see Is 32, 16–20). Shalom is not just the absence of war and violence but also the presence of justice, righteousness, happiness, and fullness of life. What better way to greet your neighbors or friends than to wish them shalom.

In your own life, seek peace. Begin each day by praying for peace of mind and heart, and to act with justice in all that you do. The very prayer that you speak will become the way that you live. Peace can become a reality only when we become a shalom people. It begins with us. If we wait, it may never come.

▶ Is 32, 16–20

---

† **32, 14.19:** *The castle:* the citadel of Jerusalem. *Hill and tower:* the fortified hill, in Hebrew *Ophel*, with its stronghold called "the great projecting tower" in Neh 3, 27.
32, 15–18.20: Extraordinary peace and prosperity will come to Israel under just rulers.

* **32, 10:** Zep 1, 13.
32, 11: Jer 4, 8.
32, 13: Is 7, 23; 34, 13.
32, 14: Is 27, 10.
32, 15: Is 35, 1; 44, 3.
32, 17: Is 54, 13f; Ps 72, 7; Jas 3, 18.
32, 18: Mi 4, 4.
32, 20: Is 30, 23.
33, 2: Is 25, 9.
33, 4: 2 Chr 20, 25.
33, 5: Is 1, 26.
33, 6: Prv 9, 10.

IS

the riches that save her, are wisdom
and knowledge;
the fear of the LORD is her treasure.

7† See, the men of Ariel cry out in the streets,
the messengers of Shalem weep bitterly.

8* The highways are desolate,
travelers have quit the paths,
Covenants are broken, their terms are spurned;
yet no man gives it a thought.

9*†The country languishes in mourning,
Lebanon withers with shame;
Sharon is like the steppe,
Bashan and Carmel are stripped bare.

10 Now will I rise up, says the LORD,
now will I be exalted, now be lifted up.

11 You conceive dry grass, bring forth stubble;
my spirit shall consume you like fire.

12* The peoples shall be as in a limekiln,
like brushwood cut down for burning in
the fire.

13 Hear, you who are far off, what I have done;
you who are near, acknowledge my might.

14* On Zion sinners are in dread,
trembling grips the impious:
"Who of us can live with the consuming fire?
who of us can live with the
everlasting flames?"

15* He who practices virtue and speaks honestly,
who spurns what is gained by oppression,
Brushing his hands free of contact with
a bribe,
stopping his ears lest he hear of bloodshed,
closing his eyes lest he look on evil—

16 He shall dwell on the heights,
his stronghold shall be the rocky fastness,
his food and drink in steady supply.

Restoration of Zion

17† Your eyes will see a king in his splendor,
they will look upon a vast land.

18 Your mind will dwell on the terror:
"Where is he who counted, where is he
who weighed?
Where is he who counted the towers?"

19 To the people of alien tongue you will look
no more,
the people of obscure speech,
stammering in a language not understood.

20 Look to Zion, the city of our festivals;
let your eyes see Jerusalem

as a quiet abode, a tent not to be struck,
Whose pegs will never be pulled up,
nor any of its ropes severed.

22 Indeed the LORD will be there with us, majestic;
yes, the LORD our judge, the LORD
our lawgiver,
the LORD our king, he it is who will save us.

21† In a place of rivers and wide streams
on which no boat is rowed,
where no majestic ship passes,

23 The rigging hangs slack;
it cannot hold the mast in place,
nor keep the sail spread out.
Then the blind will divide great spoils
and the lame will carry off the loot.

24 No one who dwells there will say, "I am sick";
the people who live there will be forgiven
their guilt.

VI: The LORD, Zion's Avenger

Judgment upon Edom

34 1* Come near, O nations, and hear;
be attentive, O peoples!
Let the earth and what fills it listen,
the world and all it produces.

2 The LORD is angry with all the nations
and is wrathful against all their host;
he has doomed them and given them over
to slaughter.

3* Their slain shall be cast out,
their corpses shall send up a stench;
The mountains shall run with their blood,

4* and all the hills shall rot;
The heavens shall be rolled up like a scroll,
and all their host shall wither away,
As the leaf wilts on the vine,
or as the fig withers on the tree.

5* When my sword has drunk its fill in
the heavens,
lo, it shall come down in judgment
upon Edom, a people I have doomed.

6* The LORD has a sword filled with blood,
greasy with fat,
With the blood of lambs and goats,
with the fat of rams' kidneys;
For the LORD has a sacrifice in Bozrah,
a great slaughter in the land of Edom.

7 Wild oxen shall be struck down with fatlings,
and bullocks with bulls;

33, 7: *Ariel . . . Shalem:* Jerusalem; cf Is 29, 1; Gn 14, 18.
33, 9: *Sharon:* the fertile plain near the Mediterranean.
33, 17: *King:* the messianic King, or God; cf v 22.
33, 21.23: *Boat . . . majestic ship:* of a foreign oppressor.

33, 8: Jgs 5, 6.
33, 9: Na 1, 4.
33, 12: Is 10, 17.
33, 14: Na 1, 6.
33, 15: Pss 15, 2–6; 24, 4f.
34, 1: Dt 32, 1.

34, 3: Ez 32, 4.6.
34, 4: Is 13, 10; Ez 32,
7f; 4, 15.
34, 5: Jer 46, 10.
34, 6f: Jer 49, 12f.

Their land shall be soaked with blood,
and their earth greasy with fat.

8* For the LORD has a day of vengeance,
a year of requital by Zion's defender.

9 Edom's streams shall be changed into pitch
and her earth into sulphur,
and her land shall become burning pitch;

10 Night and day it shall not be quenched,
its smoke shall rise forever.
From generation to generation she shall
lie waste,
never again shall anyone pass through her.

11*† But the desert owl and hoot owl shall
possess her,
the screech owl and raven shall dwell in her.
The LORD will measure her with line
and plummet
to be an empty waste
for satyrs to dwell in.

12* Her nobles shall be no more,
nor shall kings be proclaimed there;
all her princes are gone.

13* Her castles shall be overgrown with thorns,
her fortresses with thistles and briers.
She shall become an abode for jackals
and a haunt for ostriches.

14† Wildcats shall meet with desert beasts,
satyrs shall call to one another;
There shall the lilith repose,
and find for herself a place to rest.

15 There the hoot owl shall nest and lay eggs,
hatch them out and gather them in
her shadow;
There shall the kites assemble,
none shall be missing its mate.

16*† Look in the book of the LORD and read:
No one of these shall be lacking,
For the mouth of the LORD has ordered it,
and his spirit shall gather them there.

17 It is he who casts the lot for them,
and with his hand he marks off their shares
of her;
They shall possess her forever,
and dwell there from generation
to generation.

Israel's Deliverance†

35 1* The desert and the parched land
will exult;
the steppe will rejoice and bloom.

2* They will bloom with abundant flowers,
and rejoice with joyful song.
The glory of Lebanon will be given to them,
the splendor of Carmel and Sharon;
They will see the glory of the LORD,
the splendor of our God.

3* Strengthen the hands that are feeble,
make firm the knees that are weak,

4* Say to those whose hearts are frightened:
Be strong, fear not!
Here is your God,
he comes with vindication;
With divine recompense
he comes to save you.

5* Then will the eyes of the blind be opened,
the ears of the deaf be cleared;

6* Then will the lame leap like a stag,
then the tongue of the dumb will sing.

Streams will burst forth in the desert,
and rivers in the steppe.

7 The burning sands will become pools,
and the thirsty ground, springs of water;
The abode where jackals lurk
will be a marsh for the reed and papyrus.

ADVENT REJOICING

Isaiah 35, 1–7, 10 is read at Mass on the third Sunday of Advent. The third candle of the Advent wreath and the vestments that priests wear on this Sunday are often the color rose, which is a symbol for rejoicing. Together, this passage from Isaiah and this color remind us that the coming of the Messiah is a joyful event.

▶ Is 35, 1–10

---

† 34, 11: *Satyrs:* see note on Is 13, 21; cf Is 34, 14.
34, 14: *Lilith:* a female demon thought to roam about the desert.
34, 16: *Book of the LORD:* God's list of all his creatures; cf Ps 69, 29, "the book of the living"; Ps 139, 16, "your book."
35, 1–10: Similar to the description of the return from the Exile, as found in chaps. 40–55.

* 34, 8: Is 13, 9; 63, 4.   35, 2: Is 60, 13; Ps 96, 12.
34, 11: Is 14, 23; Zep 2, 14.   35, 3: Jb 4, 3f; Heb 12, 12.
34, 12: Ob 18.   35, 4: Is 41, 10; Zec 8, 13.
34, 13: Is 13, 21; Hos 9, 6.   35, 5: Is 29, 18; 32, 3.
34, 16: Jos 18, 10; Ps 78, 55.   35, 6: Is 41, 18; 43, 10.19.
35, 1: Is 55, 12f.

I
S

8 A highway will be there,
       called the holy way;
    No one unclean may pass over it,
       nor fools go astray on it.
9* No lion will be there,
       nor beast of prey go up to be met
          upon it.
    It is for those with a journey to make,
       and on it the redeemed will walk.
10* Those whom the LORD has ransomed
          will return
       and enter Zion singing,
    crowned with everlasting joy;
    They will meet with joy and gladness,
       sorrow and mourning will flee.

VII: Historical Appendix

Invasion of Sennacherib†

36 1* In the fourteenth year of King Hezekiah, Sennacherib, king of Assyria, went
on an expedition against all the fortified cities of
Judah and captured them. 2 From Lachish the king
of Assyria sent his commander with a great army to
King Hezekiah in Jerusalem. When he stopped at
the conduit of the upper pool, on the highway of
the fuller's field, 3 there came out to him the master
of the palace, Eliakim, son of Hilkiah, and Shebna
the scribe, and the herald Joah, son of Asaph. 4 The
commander said to them, "Tell King Hezekiah:
Thus says the great king, the king of Assyria, 'On
what do you base this confidence of yours? 5 Do
you think mere words substitute for strategy and
might in war? On whom, then, do you rely, that you
rebel against me? 6* This Egypt, the staff on which
you rely, is in fact a broken reed which pierces the
hand of anyone who leans on it. That is what
Pharaoh, king of Egypt, is to all who rely on him.
7*† But if you say to me: "We rely on the LORD, our
God," is not he the one whose high places and altars Hezekiah removed, commanding Judah and
Jerusalem to worship before this altar?'

8 "Now, make a wager with my lord the king of
Assyria: 'I will give you two thousand horses, if you
can put riders on them.' 9 How then can you repulse
even one of the least servants of my lord? And yet
you rely on Egypt for chariots and horsemen!
10* 'Was it without the LORD's will that I have come

up to destroy this land? The LORD said to me, "Go
up and destroy that land!" ' "

11† Then Eliakim and Shebna and Joah said to
the commander, "Please speak to your servants in
Aramaic; we understand it. Do not speak to us in
Judean within earshot of the people who are on the
wall."

12 But the commander replied, "Was it to you
and your master that my lord sent me to speak
these words? Was it not rather to the men sitting on
the wall, who, with you, will have to eat their own
excrement and drink their own urine?" 13 Then the
commander stepped forward and cried out in a
loud voice in Judean, "Listen to the words of the
great king, the king of Assyria. 14 Thus says the king:
'Do not let Hezekiah deceive you, since he cannot
deliver you. 15 Let not Hezekiah induce you to rely
on the LORD, saying, "The LORD will surely save us;
this city will not be handed over to the king of Assyria." ' 16* Do not listen to Hezekiah, for the king
of Assyria says: 'Make peace with me and surrender!
Then each of you will eat of his own vine and of his
own fig tree, and drink the water of his own cistern,
17 until I come to take you to a land like your own,
a land of grain and wine, of bread and vineyards.
18* Do not let Hezekiah seduce you by saying, "The
LORD will save us." Has any of the gods of the nations ever rescued his land from the hand of the
king of Assyria? 19* Where are the gods of Hamath
and Arpad? Where are the gods of Sepharvaim?
Where are the gods of Samaria? Have they saved
Samaria from my hand? 20 Which of all the gods of
these lands ever rescued his land from my hand?
Will the LORD then save Jerusalem from my
hand?' " 21 But they remained silent and did not answer him one word, for the king had ordered them
not to answer him.

22 Then the master of the palace, Eliakim, son of
Hilkiah, Shebna the scribe, and the herald Joah, son
of Asaph, came to Hezekiah with their garments
torn, and reported to him what the commander
had said.

37 1 When King Hezekiah heard this, he tore
his garments, wrapped himself in sackcloth, and went into the temple of the LORD. 2 He
sent Eliakim, the master of the palace, and Shebna
the scribe, and the elders of the priests, wrapped in

---

† **36, 1—39, 8:** Except for 38, 9–20, this historical appendix describing the siege, etc., is paralleled in 2 Kgs 18, 13—20, 19, which,
however, has certain details proper to itself. The events are also
recorded in substantially the same way in the cuneiform inscriptions
of Sennacherib.

36, 7: The Assyrians pretend that Hezekiah's removal of the high
places and altars (illegal sanctuaries) was taken by the Lord as an insult. They declare to Jerusalem's emissaries that the city therefore no
longer has a right to the Lord's protection and that they are the ones
who truly carry out his will (cf v 10).

36, 11: The Jewish emissaries ask that the conversation be carried
on in Aramaic, not in Judean, for they fear the effect of the Assyrian
claims upon the morale of the people.

35, 9: Is 62, 10; Lv 26, 6.   36, 7: 2 Kgs 18, 4.
35, 10: Is 51, 11.   36, 10: Is 10, 5f.
36, 1: 2 Kgs 18, 13; 2 Chr   36, 16: 1 Kgs 4, 25; Zec 3, 10.
    32, 1.   36, 18: Is 37, 11.
36, 6: Is 30, 2.   36, 19: Is 10, 9; 37, 13.

sackcloth, to tell the prophet Isaiah, son of Amoz: ³† "Thus says Hezekiah: 'This is a day of distress, of rebuke, and of disgrace. Children are at the point of birth, but there is no strength to bring them forth. ⁴ Perhaps the LORD, your God, will hear the words of the commander, whom his master, the king of Assyria, sent to taunt the living God, and will rebuke him for the words which the LORD, your God, has heard. Send up a prayer for the remnant that is here.' "

⁵ When the servants of King Hezekiah had come to Isaiah, ⁶* he said to them: "Tell this to your master: 'Thus says the LORD: Do not be frightened by the words you have heard, with which the servants of the king of Assyria have blasphemed me. ⁷ I am about to put in him such a spirit that, when he hears a certain report, he will return to his own land, and there I will cause him to fall by the sword.' "

⁸ When the commander returned to Lachish and heard that the king of Assyria had left there, he found him besieging Libnah. ⁹† The king of Assyria heard a report that Tirhakah, king of Ethiopia, had come out to fight against him. Again he sent envoys to Hezekiah with this message: "Thus shall you say to Hezekiah, king of Judah: ¹⁰* 'Do not let your God on whom you rely deceive you by saying that Jerusalem will not be handed over to the king of Assyria. ¹¹ You yourself have heard what the kings of Assyria have done to all the countries: They doomed them! Will you, then, be saved? ¹² Did the gods of the nations whom my fathers destroyed save them? Gozen, Haran, Rezeph, and the Edenites in Telassar? ¹³ Where is the king of Hamath, the king of Arpad, or a king of the cities of Sepharvaim, Hena or Ivvah?' "

¹⁴ Hezekiah took the letter from the hand of the messengers and read it; then he went up to the temple of the LORD, and spreading it out before him, ¹⁵ he prayed to the LORD: ¹⁶† "O LORD of hosts, God of Israel, enthroned upon the cherubim! You alone are God over all the kingdoms of the earth. You have made the heavens and the earth. ¹⁷ Incline your ear, O LORD, and listen! Open your eyes, O LORD, and see! Hear all the words of the letter that Sennacherib sent to taunt the living God. ¹⁸ Truly, O LORD, the kings of Assyria have laid waste all the nations and their lands, ¹⁹* and cast their gods into the fire; they destroyed them because they were not gods but the work of human hands, wood and stone. ²⁰ Therefore, O LORD, our God, save us from his hand, that all the kingdoms of the earth may know that you, O LORD, alone are God."

Punishment of Sennacherib

²¹ Then Isaiah, son of Amoz, sent this message to Hezekiah: Thus says the LORD, the God of Israel: In answer to your prayer for help against Sennacherib, king of Assyria, ²²* this is the word the LORD has spoken concerning him:

She despises you, laughs you to scorn,
the virgin daughter Zion;
Behind you she wags her head,
daughter Jerusalem.
²³* Whom have you insulted and blasphemed,
against whom have you raised your voice
And lifted up your eyes on high?
Against the Holy One of Israel!
²⁴ Through your servants you have insulted
the Lord:
You said, "With my many chariots
I climbed the mountain heights,
the recesses of Lebanon;
I cut down its lofty cedars,
its choice cypresses;
I reached the remotest heights,
its forest park.
²⁵ I dug wells and drank water in foreign lands;
I dried up with the soles of my feet
all the rivers of Egypt."
²⁶ Have you not heard?
Long ago I prepared it,
From days of old I planned it,
now I have brought it to pass:
That you should reduce fortified cities
into heaps of ruins,
²⁷ While their inhabitants, shorn of power,
are dismayed and ashamed,
Becoming like the plants of the field,
like the green growth,
like the scorched grass on the housetops.
²⁸ I am aware whether you stand or sit;
I know whether you come or go,
and also your rage against me.
²⁹ Because of your rage against me
and your fury which has reached my ears,
I will put my hook in your nose

37, 3: A proverbial expression. In the Bible the pangs of childbirth often typify extreme anguish; cf Is 13, 8; Jer 6, 24; Mi 4, 9f. In this instance there is reference to the desperate situation of Hezekiah from which he was scarcely able to free himself.

37, 9: *Tirhakah:* may have been general of the Egyptian army in 701 B.C.; later he became king, one of the Ethiopian dynasty of Egyptian kings (c. 690–664 B.C.). Many consider that this account in Isaiah combines features of two originally distinct sieges of Jerusalem by Sennacherib.

37, 16: In contrast to the empty boasting of the Assyrians, Hezekiah proclaims the Lord as God over all the kingdoms of the earth.

37, 6: Is 41, 10–14; 51, 7.   37, 22: 2 Kgs 19, 21.
37, 10: Is 36, 14.   37, 23: Is 1, 4.
37, 19: Jer 16, 20.

and my bit in your mouth,
and make you return the way you came.

30† This shall be a sign for you:
this year you shall eat the aftergrowth,
next year, what grows of itself;
But in the third year, sow and reap,
plant vineyards and eat their fruit!

31* The remaining survivors of the house of Judah
shall again strike root below
and bear fruit above.

32 For out of Jerusalem shall come a remnant,
and from Mount Zion, survivors.
The zeal of the LORD of hosts shall do this.

33 Therefore, thus says the LORD concerning the king of Assyria: He shall not reach this city, nor shoot an arrow at it, nor come before it with a shield, nor cast up siegeworks against it. 34* He shall return by the same way he came, without entering the city, says the LORD. 35* I will shield and save this city for my own sake, and for the sake of my servant David.

36*† The angel of the LORD went forth and struck down one hundred and eighty-five thousand in the Assyrian camp. Early the next morning, there they were, all the corpses of the dead. 37* So Sennacherib, the king of Assyria, broke camp and went back home to Nineveh.

38† When he was worshiping in the temple of his god Nisroch, his sons Adrammelech and Sharezer slew him with the sword and fled into the land of Ararat. His son Esarhaddon reigned in his stead.

Sickness and Recovery of Hezekiah

38 1*† In those days,† when Hezekiah was mortally ill, the prophet Isaiah, son of Amoz, came and said to him: "Thus says the LORD: Put your house in order, for you are about to die; you shall not recover." 2 Then Hezekiah turned his face to the wall and prayed to the LORD:

3* "O LORD, remember how faithfully and wholeheartedly I conducted myself in your presence, doing what was pleasing to you!" And Hezekiah wept bitterly.

4 Then the word of the LORD came to Isaiah: 5† "Go, tell Hezekiah: Thus says the LORD, the God of your father David: I have heard your prayer and seen your tears. I will heal you: in three days you shall go up to the LORD'S temple; I will add fifteen years to your life. 6* I will rescue you and this city from the hand of the king of Assyria; I will be a shield to this city."

21 Isaiah then ordered a poultice of figs to be taken and applied to the boil, that he might recover. 22 Then Hezekiah asked, "What is the sign that I shall go up to the temple of the LORD?"

7 [Isaiah answered:] "This will be the sign for you from the LORD that he will do what he has promised: 8*† See, I will make the shadow cast by the sun on the stairway to the terrace of Ahaz go back the ten steps it has advanced." So the sun came back the ten steps it had advanced.

Hezekiah's Hymn of Thanksgiving

9 The song of Hezekiah, king of Judah, after he had been sick and had recovered from his illness:

10*† Once I said,
"In the noontime of life I must depart!
To the gates of the nether world I shall
be consigned
for the rest of my years."

11† I said, "I shall see the LORD no more
in the land of the living.
No longer shall I behold my fellow men
among those who dwell in the world."

12*† My dwelling, like a shepherd's tent,
is struck down and borne away from me;
You have folded up my life, like a weaver
who severs the last thread.
Day and night you give me over to torment;

13 I cry out until the dawn.
Like a lion he breaks all my bones;

37, 30: *A sign:* it is difficult to know the nature of this sign. Either it is merely a proverbial expression to signify that prosperity follows adversity, or it indicates that after two years the normal conditions of life will be resumed. *You:* Hezekiah.

37, 36: The destruction of Sennacherib's army is also recorded by Herodotus, a Greek historian of the fifth century B.C. It was probably due to the bubonic plague, but the sacred author attributes it to its ultimate cause, God through his angel.

37, 38: The violent death of Sennacherib (681 B.C.) is also mentioned in non-biblical sources. It occurred twenty years after his invasion of Judea.

38, 1—39, 8: The events of this section—sickness and recovery of Hezekiah, embassy of Merodach-baladan—point forward to Babylon (cc 40—66). They occurred prior to the events of Is 36, 1—37, 38, which point back to Assyria (Is 1, 1—35, 10).

38, 1: *In those days:* a time prior to the siege of Jerusalem in 701 B.C.

38, 5: Since Hezekiah died in 687 B.C. this sickness of his seems to have been in 702 B.C., that is, fifteen years before.

38, 8: *Stairway to the terrace of Ahaz:* this interpretation is based on a reading of the Hebrew text revised according to the Dead Sea Scroll of Isaiah; cf 2 Kgs 23, 12. Many translate the phrase as "steps of Ahaz" and understand this as referring to a sundial.

38, 10: *In the noontime of life:* long before the end of a full span of life; cf Pss 55, 24; 102, 25.

38, 11: *See the LORD:* go to the temple and take part in its service.

38, 12: These two metaphors emphasize the suddenness and finality of death.

37, 31: Is 27, 6.
37, 34: Is 37, 29.
37, 35: 1 Kgs 15, 4f.
37, 36: Is 10, 12; 17, 14.
37, 37: 2 Kgs 19, 35f.
37, 1: 2 Kgs 20, 1.
38, 3: 2 Kgs 18, 5f.
38, 6: Is 37, 35.
38, 8: 2 Kgs 20, 9.11.
38, 10: Jb 17, 11; Ps 102, 25.
38, 12: Jb 7, 6.

[day and night you give me over to torment].

14 Like a swallow I utter shrill cries;
　　I moan like a dove.
　My eyes grow weak, gazing heavenward:
　　O Lord, I am in straits; be my surety!

15† What am I to say or tell him?
　　He has done it!
　I shall go on through all my years
　　despite the bitterness of my soul.
16† Those live whom the LORD protects;
　　yours . . . the life of my spirit.
　You have given me health and life;
17† 　thus is my bitterness transformed
　　into peace.
　You have preserved my life
　　from the pit of destruction,
　When you cast behind your back
　　all my sins.
18*†For it is not the nether world that gives
　　you thanks,
　　nor death that praises you;
　Neither do those who go down into the pit
　　await your kindness.
19 The living, the living give you thanks,
　　as I do today.
　Fathers declare to their sons,
　　O God, your faithfulness.
20 The LORD is our savior;
　　we shall sing to stringed instruments
　In the house of the LORD
　　all the days of our life.

Embassy from Merodach-baladan

39 ¹*† At that time when Merodach-baladan, son of Baladan, king of Babylon, heard that Hezekiah had recovered from his sickness, he sent letters and gifts to him. ²* Hezekiah was pleased at this, and therefore showed the messengers his treasury, the silver and gold, the spices and fine oil, his whole armory, and everything that was in his storerooms; there was nothing in his house or in his whole realm that he did not show them. ³ Then Isaiah the prophet came to King Hezekiah and asked him, "What did these men say to you?

Where did they come from?" Hezekiah answered, "They came to me from a distant land, from Babylon." ⁴ "What did they see in your house?" he asked. Hezekiah replied, "They saw everything in my house; there is nothing in my storerooms that I did not show them."

⁵ Then Isaiah said to Hezekiah, "Hear the word of the LORD of hosts: ⁶*† Behold, the days shall come when all that is in your house, and everything that your fathers have stored up until this day, shall be carried off to Babylon; nothing shall be left, says the LORD. ⁷* Some of your own bodily descendants shall be taken and made servants in the palace of the king of Babylon." ⁸*† Hezekiah replied to Isaiah, "The word of the LORD which you have spoken is favorable." For he thought, "There will be peace and security in my lifetime."

B. THE BOOK OF CONSOLATION

I: The Lord's Glory in Israel's Liberation

Promise of Salvation

40 ¹ Comfort, give comfort to my people,
　　says your God.
²*†Speak tenderly to Jerusalem, and proclaim
　　to her
　　that her service is at an end,
　　her guilt is expiated;
　Indeed, she has received from the hand of
　　the LORD
　　double for all her sins.

3*† 　A voice cries out:
　In the desert prepare the way of the LORD!
　　Make straight in the wasteland a highway
　　for our God!
4 Every valley shall be filled in,
　　every mountain and hill shall be made low;
　The rugged land shall be made a plain,
　　the rough country, a broad valley.
5 Then the glory of the LORD shall be revealed,
　　and all mankind shall see it together;
　　for the mouth of the LORD has spoken.

38, 15: *What am I to say or tell him?:* a rhetorical question, as if the poet were at a loss in giving fitting expression to his gratitude; cf Ps 116, 12. *He has done it:* accomplished the cure. *Despite the bitterness:* even though the one praying was previously so dejected.
38, 16: *Yours . . . the life of my spirit:* the current Hebrew text is corrupt. The revised Latin psalter renders it: "You have revived my soul."
38, 17: *You cast behind your back all my sins:* figurative language to express the divine forgiveness of sins, as if God no longer saw or cared about them. This expression is ordinarily used of men forgetting God; cf 1 Kgs 14, 9; Ez 23, 35; Ps 50, 17.
38, 18f: See note on Ps 6, 6.
39, 1: *Merodach-baladan:* twice king of Babylon, probably from 721 to 710 B.C., and again for nine months, in 704–703. This visit of his messengers, certainly before 701, was in reality a political one.

Babylon hoped to lead an anti-Assyrian confederation composed of neighboring states.
39, 6: Because Judah preferred to follow a pro-Babylonian policy, instead of trusting in God, it would later be exiled to Babylon.
39, 8: *Favorable:* for the Exile would not occur in his lifetime.
40, 2: *Service:* servitude and exile.
40, 3–5: The figurative language here describes the actual return of the exiles from Babylon to Jerusalem. It is the Lord who leads them; their road is made easy for them. Mt 3, 3 and parallels see in these verses a prophecy of the Baptizer and Christ.

38, 18: Pss 6, 6; 88, 11–13.　　　39, 7: 2 Chr 33, 11; Dn 1, 2f.
39, 1–8: 2 Kgs 20, 12.　　　　　39, 8: 2 Chr 32, 26.
39, 2: 2 Chr 32, 25ff.　　　　　40, 2: Is 50, 21.
39, 6: 2 Kgs 24, 13; 25, 13ff.　　40, 3: Mt 3, 3; Jn 1, 23.

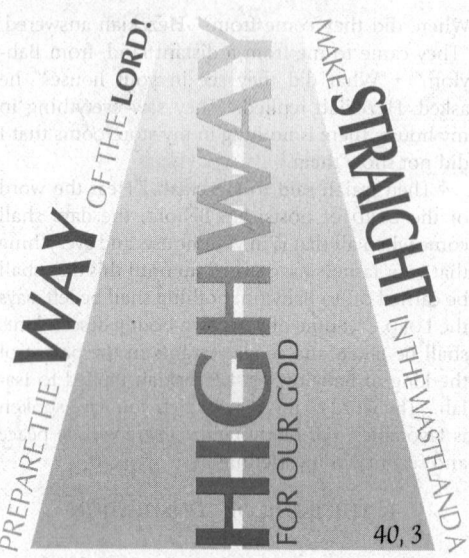

PREPARE THE WAY OF THE LORD!
MAKE STRAIGHT IN THE WASTELAND A HIGHWAY FOR OUR GOD

40, 3

6* A voice says, "Cry out!"
    I answer, "What shall I cry out?"
    "All mankind is grass,
        and all their glory like the flower of the field.
7   The grass withers, the flower wilts,
        when the breath of the LORD blows upon it.
    [So then, the people is the grass.]
8   Though the grass withers and the flower wilts,
        the word of our God stands forever."

9   Go up onto a high mountain,
        Zion, herald of glad tidings;
    Cry out at the top of your voice,
        Jerusalem, herald of good news!
    Fear not to cry out
        and say to the cities of Judah:
        Here is your God!
10 Here comes with power
        the Lord GOD,
    who rules by his strong arm;
    Here is his reward with him,
        his recompense before him.
11* Like a shepherd he feeds his flock;
        in his arms he gathers the lambs,
    Carrying them in his bosom,
        and leading the ewes with care.

Power of the Creator To Save His People

12† Who has cupped in his hand the waters of
        the sea,
    and marked off the heavens with a span?

Who has held in a measure the dust of
        the earth,
    weighed the mountains in scales
    and the hills in a balance?
13* Who has directed the spirit of the LORD,
        or has instructed him as his counselor?
14 Whom did he consult to gain knowledge?
    Who taught him the path of judgment,
        or showed him the way of understanding?
15 Behold, the nations count as a drop of
        the bucket,
        as dust on the scales;
    the coastlands weigh no more than
        powder.
16† Lebanon would not suffice for fuel,
        nor its animals be enough for holocausts.
17 Before him all the nations are as nought,
        as nothing and void he accounts them.

PRAY IT?

The Hope of Second Isaiah

Second Isaiah prophesies to the Israelites living in exile in Babylon with words full of love and hope: "Comfort, give comfort to my people, / says your God" (Is 40, 1). Isaiah promises these Israelites a new liberation and the eventual restoration of Jerusalem and the Temple (44, 26–28).

The author of the Gospel of Luke uses Is 40, 3–5 to describe the ministry of John the Baptist in announcing Jesus' arrival (Lk 3, 4–6). This writer wants to make it clear that Isaiah's promises are answered by the coming of Jesus.

In your prayer, reflect or journal on the following questions:
■ Is there hope for our society?
■ What are some things that you are hopeful for?
■ Imagine God is speaking words of hope to you. What is God saying?

▶ Is 40, 1–5

40, 12: *Span:* the distance between the extended little finger and the thumb. *Measure:* literally, "third"; here a small container.
40, 16: *Lebanon . . . fuel:* the famed cedars would not be enough to keep the fires of sacrifice burning.

40, 6: Jb 8, 12; 14, 2; Ps 37,
  2; Sir 14, 18; Jas 1, 10;
  1 Pt 1, 24.
40, 11: Is 49, 9f; 63, 11; Ez 34,
  23; 37, 24; Jn 10, 11.
40, 13: Wis 9, 13; Rom 11, 34;
  1 Cor 2, 16; Jb 38, 1ff.

Between a Rock and a Soft Place

Joe. Is God a rock or a pillow?

Valerie. A rock, I guess. God is strong and reliable. When I think of a rock, I think of something I can brace myself against when things are changing all around me.

Joe. For me, God is a pillow. God is someone I can come home to and be comfortable with. I can sit back and relax, leaning against God and feeling at ease.

Valerie. But a pillow is so ordinary and doesn't have any character. A rock is distinctive and doesn't change.

Joe. But a rock is so hard and unyielding. What kind of compassion can you get from a rock?

Valerie. What kind of strength can you draw from a pillow?

Joe. The strength that comes from relaxing and resting and being comforted. The strength that comes from being energized to go forward again.

Valerie. I'm sorry, but a pillow seems too soft to be like God.

Joe. And a rock seems much too hard.

Valerie. Isn't God both a pillow and a rock? In chapter 40 of Isaiah, it seems that the pillow image wins out. The picture of a comforting God gathering the lambs conveys a softness that is sometimes hard to find in the Old Testament.

Joe. That's true. There are times when we need a pillow to get comfortable. It is good to know that God is there waiting for us, helping us to feel at home.

Valerie. And it is also good to know that God the rock is there for the times when we need something to hold on to (see Ps 18, 3).

▶ Is 40, 1–11

18* To whom can you liken God?
   With what equal can you confront him?

19* An idol, cast by a craftsman,
   which the smith plates with gold
   and fits with silver chains?

20* Mulberry wood, the choice portion
   which a skilled craftsman picks out
      for himself,
   Choosing timber that will not rot,
   to set up an idol that will not be unsteady?

6† One man helps another,
   one says to the other, "Keep on!"

7 The craftsman encourages the goldsmith,
   the one who beats with the hammer, him
      who strikes on the anvil;
   He says the soldering is good,
   and he fastens it with nails to steady it.

21 Do you not know? Have you not heard?
   Was it not foretold you from the
      beginning?
   Have you not understood? Since the earth
      was founded

22* He sits enthroned above the vault of the earth,
   and its inhabitants are like grasshoppers;
   He stretches out the heavens like a veil,
   spreads them out like a tent to dwell in.

23 He brings princes to nought
   and makes the rulers of the earth
      as nothing.

24 Scarcely are they planted or sown,
   scarcely is their stem rooted in the earth,
   When he breathes upon them and
      they wither,
   and the stormwind carries them away
      like straw.

25 To whom can you liken me as an equal?
   says the Holy One.

26*†Lift up your eyes on high
   and see who has created these:
   He leads out their army and numbers them,
   calling them all by name.
   By his great might and the strength of
      his power
   not one of them is missing!

40, 6–7: These two verses have been transposed from chap. 41.
40, 26: *Created:* see note on Gn 1, 1. *By name:* for he is their Creator.

40, 18f: Acts 17, 29.
40, 19: Ps 115, 4–7.
40, 20: Is 44, 13.

40, 22: Ps 104, 2.
40, 26: Ps 147, 4f.

27† Why, O Jacob, do you say,
        and declare, O Israel,
    "My way is hidden from the LORD,
        and my right is disregarded by
            my God"?

28 Do you not know
        or have you not heard?
    The LORD is the eternal God,
        creator of the ends of the earth.
    He does not faint nor grow weary,
        and his knowledge is beyond scrutiny.

29 He gives strength to the fainting;
        for the weak he makes vigor abound.

30 Though young men faint
            and grow weary,
        and youths stagger and fall,

31 They that hope in the LORD will renew
            their strength,
        they will soar as with eagles' wings;
    They will run and not grow weary,
        walk and not grow faint.

The Liberator of Israel

41 ¹† Keep silence before me, O coastlands;
        you peoples, wait for my words!
    Let them draw near and speak;
        let us come together for judgment.

²† Who has stirred up from the East the
            champion of justice,
        and summoned him to be his attendant?
    To him he delivers the nations
        and subdues the kings;
    With his sword he reduces them to dust,
        with his bow, to driven straw.

3   He pursues them, passing on without loss,
        by a path his feet do not even tread.

4* Who has performed these deeds?
        He who has called forth the generations
            since the beginning.

    I, the LORD, am the first,
        and with the last I will also be.

THE TENT AND THE CIRCLE

Isaiah 40, 22–23 has significance in Native American spirituality for several reasons. First, the vault (verse 22), often depicted in the shape of a circle, is a symbol of unity and healing. In silhouette, the sun, the moon, and the earth are all circles. The poles of a teepee are arranged in a circle, and the teepees of a village are placed in a circle. The people of a nation are called the hoop or the circle, and sit in a circle for the sweat lodge ceremony (see "You Will Be Cleansed," Ez 36, 25–26) and to smoke from the sacred pipe.

Second, the tent (verse 22) is a symbol of home and family for a people that traditionally dwelled in tents.

Third, the Great Spirit is well described as the one who "sits enthroned above the [circle]" (verse 22).

Last, the insight that God, the Great Spirit, cares very little about the status of princes and rulers (verse 23) is powerful to a people that is oppressed, treated violently, scattered, and despised in its homeland. Native Americans have been subjected to such treatment by the explorers, then the colonists, then the pioneers, and now many citizens of the United States.

Pray for the circle of humanity—that we learn to celebrate the diversity of our cultures and cease oppression of any form.

▶ Is 40, 22–23

40, 27f: God's people, here called Jacob and Israel, must not give way to discouragement: their Lord is the eternal God.

41, 1–4: It is generally agreed that these verses describe the vocation and victory of Cyrus, whom the Lord used as his instrument to redeem Israel.

41, 2: Cyrus is the champion of justice and God's attendant.

41, 4: Is 44, 7; 46, 10.

5 The coastlands see, and fear;
    the ends of the earth tremble:
    these things are near, they come to pass.
8* But you, Israel, my servant,
    Jacob, whom I have chosen,
    offspring of Abraham my friend—
9 You whom I have taken from the ends of
        the earth
    and summoned from its far-off places,
    You whom I have called my servant,
    whom I have chosen and will not cast off—
10 Fear not, I am with you;
    be not dismayed; I am your God.
    I will strengthen you, and help you,
    and uphold you with my right hand
        of justice.

11 Yes, all shall be put to shame
        and disgrace
    who vent their anger against you;
    Those shall perish and come to nought
    who offer resistance.
12 You shall seek out, but shall not find,
    those who strive against you;
    They shall be as nothing at all
    who do battle with you.

13 For I am the LORD, your God,
    who grasp your right hand;
    It is I who say to you, "Fear not,
    I will help you."
14† Fear not, O worm Jacob,
    O maggot Israel;
    I will help you, says the LORD;
    your redeemer is the Holy One of Israel.
15 I will make of you a threshing sledge,
    sharp, new, and double-edged,
    To thresh the mountains and crush them,
    to make the hills like chaff.
16 When you winnow them, the wind shall
        carry them off
    and the storm shall scatter them.
    But you shall rejoice in the LORD,
    and glory in the Holy One of Israel.
17 The afflicted and the needy seek water in
        vain,
    their tongues are parched with thirst.
    I, the LORD, will answer them;
    I, the God of Israel, will not
        forsake them.
18 I will open up rivers on the bare heights,
    and fountains in the broad valleys;

I will turn the desert into a marshland,
    and the dry ground into springs
        of water.
19 I will plant in the desert the cedar,
    acacia, myrtle, and olive;
    I will set in the wasteland the cypress,
    together with the plane tree and
        the pine,
20 That all may see and know,
    observe and understand,
    That the hand of the LORD has done this,
    the Holy One of Israel has created it.

21† Present your case, says the LORD;
    bring forward your reasons, says the
        King of Jacob.
22 Let them come near and foretell to us
    what it is that shall happen!
    What are the things of long ago?
    Tell us, that we may reflect on them
    And know their outcome;
    or declare to us the things to come!
23 Foretell the things that shall come
        afterward,
    that we may know that you are gods!
    Do something, good or evil,
    that will put us in awe and in fear.
24 Why, you are nothing and your work
        is nought!
    To choose you is an abomination.
25† I have stirred up one from the north,
        and he comes;
    from the east I summon him by name;
    He shall trample the rulers down like
        red earth,
    as the potter treads the clay.
26 Who announced this from the beginning,
        that we might know;
    beforehand, that we might say it is true?
    Not one of you foretold it, not one spoke;
    no one heard you say,
27 "The first news for Zion: they are
        coming now,"
    or, "For Jerusalem I will pick out a
        bearer of the glad tidings."
28 When I look, there is not one,
    no one of them to give counsel,
    to make an answer when I
        question them.
29 Ah, all of them are nothing,
    their works are nought,
    their idols are empty wind!

41, 14: *Redeemer:* in Hebrew, *goel*, one who frees another from slavery and avenges his sufferings; cf Lv 25, 48: Dt 19, 6.12.
41, 21–24: An indictment of idols.
41, 25: *I summon him:* Cyrus.

41, 8f: Is 44, 1f.21; 45, 4.

did you KNOW?

The Servant Songs

Second Isaiah's four songs of the servant (Is 42, 1–7; 49, 1–6; 50, 4–9; 52, 13—53, 12) have had an important place in Christian theology and worship. They portray the qualities of the ideal servant leader. Through these songs, the prophet speaks of hope: the faithful Israelites, though in exile, are still God's servants (42, 1), chosen from the womb (49, 1). Through their courageous suffering (50, 7–8), Israel will be restored to bring salvation to all nations (53, 5).

It is not surprising that the early Christians saw in the servant songs a remarkable similarity to Jesus' words and actions. The fourth song in particular—which talks of a suffering servant—helped the followers of Jesus understand his suffering and humiliating death on the cross. Because of this, these passages have become part of the Catholic church's formal worship during Holy Week (the week before Easter): Isaiah 42, 1–7 on Monday, 49, 1–6 on Tuesday, 50, 4–9 on Wednesday, and 52, 13—53, 12 on Friday.

▶ Is 42, 1–7

The Servant of the Lord

42 ¹*† Here is my servant whom I uphold,
my chosen one with whom I
am pleased,
Upon whom I have put my spirit;
he shall bring forth justice to the nations,
² Not crying out, not shouting,
not making his voice heard in the street.
³† A bruised reed he shall not break,
and a smoldering wick he shall not quench,
⁴† Until he establishes justice on the earth;
the coastlands will wait for his teaching.

⁵ Thus says God, the LORD,
who created the heavens and stretched
them out,
who spreads out the earth with its crops,
Who gives breath to its people
and spirit to those who walk on it:
⁶* I, the LORD, have called you for the victory
of justice,
I have grasped you by the hand;
I formed you, and set you
as a covenant of the people,
a light for the nations,
⁷ To open the eyes of the blind,
to bring out prisoners from confinement,
and from the dungeon, those who live
in darkness.
⁸ I am the LORD, this is my name;
my glory I give to no other,
nor my praise to idols.
⁹ See, the earlier things have come to pass,
new ones I now foretell;
Before they spring into being,
I announce them to you.

The Salvation of Israel despite Its Sins

¹⁰ Sing to the LORD a new song,
his praise from the end of the earth:
Let the sea and what fills it resound,
the coastlands, and those who dwell
in them.
¹¹† Let the steppe and its cities cry out,
the villages where Kedar dwells;

PRAY IT?

The Servant's Mission

Read Is 42, 1–7 and then reflect or journal on the following questions:
■ What is the servant's mission from God?
■ How does Jesus fulfill this mission (compare Is 42, 6–7 with Lk 4, 18)?
■ How do you participate in this mission?

▶ Is 42, 1–7

---

† **42, 1–4:** *Servant:* there are three other "Servant-of-the-Lord" oracles, Is 49, 1–7; 50, 4–11; 52, 13—53, 12. Many identifications have been proposed, e.g., historical Israel, ideal Israel, an Old Testament historical character before or during the lifetime of the prophet, the prophet himself. The New Testament and Christian tradition, however, have seen a fulfillment of these prophecies in Jesus Christ.
42, 3: A reference to the mercy of Christ.

42, 4: *Coastlands:* the lands of the Mediterranean. In the Old Testament the word often refers to the pagan lands of the west.
42, 11: *Kedar:* cf footnote to Is 21, 16. *Sela:* Petra, the capital of Edom.

42, 1: Is 45, 6; 49, 6.   **42, 6:** Is 45, 13.

Let the inhabitants of Sela exult,
and shout from the top of the mountains.
12 Let them give glory to the LORD,
and utter his praise in the coastlands.
13* The LORD goes forth like a hero,
like a warrior he stirs up his ardor;
He shouts out his battle cry,
against his enemies he shows his might:
14 I have looked away, and kept silence,
I have said nothing, holding myself in;
But now, I cry out as a woman in labor,
gasping and panting.
15* I will lay waste mountains and hills,
all their herbage I will dry up;
I will turn the rivers into marshes,
and the marshes I will dry up.
16* I will lead the blind on their journey;
by paths unknown I will guide them.
I will turn darkness into light before them,
and make crooked ways straight.
These things I do for them,
and I will not forsake them.
17 They shall be turned back in utter shame
who trust in idols;
Who say to molten images,
"You are our gods."
18† You who are deaf, listen,
you who are blind, look and see!
19 Who is blind but my servant,
or deaf like the messenger I send?
20 You see many things without taking note;
your ears are open, but without hearing.
21 Though it pleased the LORD in his justice
to make his law great and glorious,
22† This is a people despoiled and plundered,
all of them trapped in holes,
hidden away in prisons.
They are taken as booty, with no one to
rescue them,
as spoil, with no one to demand their return.
23 Who of you gives ear to this?
Who listens and pays heed for the time
to come?
24† Who was it that gave Jacob to be plundered,
Israel to the despoilers?
Was it not the LORD, against whom we
have sinned?
In his ways they refused to walk,
his law they disobeyed.
25 So he poured out wrath upon them,
his anger, and the fury of battle;

It blazed round about them, yet they did
not realize,
it burned them, but they took it not
to heart.

Promises of Redemption and Restoration

43 ¹ But now, thus says the LORD,
who created you, O Jacob, and
formed you, O Israel:
Fear not, for I have redeemed you;
I have called you by name:
you are mine.
2 When you pass through the water, I will be
with you;
in the rivers you shall not drown.
When you walk through fire, you shall not
be burned;
the flames shall not consume you.
3† For I am the LORD, your God,
the Holy One of Israel, your savior.
I give Egypt as your ransom,
Ethiopia and Seba in return for you.
4* Because you are precious in my eyes
and glorious, and because I love you,
I give men in return for you
and peoples in exchange for your life.

Be Not Afraid

The words of Is 43, 1–5 might sound
familiar to you. Most of the song "Be
Not Afraid" is based on these verses.
God calls us to be disciples and leaders. God calls us from within our faith
community to serve others. How easy is
it for you to go forth and do God's work?
How easy is it to be not afraid?

Be not afraid.
I go before you always.
Come follow me,
and I will give you rest.
(From Bob Dufford, "Be Not Afraid")

▸ Is 43, 1–5

42, 18–20: Because of their unbelief, the Lord rebukes his people, whom he calls his servant, his messenger.
42, 22: *A people:* Israel in exile.
42, 24: *Despoilers:* the Assyrians and Babylonians.
43, 3f: *Egypt . . . Ethiopia and Seba:* countries which God permitted the Persians to conquer in return for having given Israel
its freedom.

42, 13: Ex 14, 3.   42, 16: Ex 13, 21.
42, 15: Ex 9, 25; 10, 15;   43, 4: Dt 4, 37; Hos 11, 1.
14, 21; Ps 105, 33ff.

5 Fear not, for I am with you;
  from the east I will bring back
    your descendants,
  from the west I will gather you.

6* I will say to the north: Give them up!
  and to the south: Hold not back!
  Bring back my sons from afar,
    and my daughters from the ends of
    the earth:

7 Everyone who is named as mine,
  whom I created for my glory,
  whom I formed and made.

8 Lead out the people who are blind though
  they have eyes,
  who are deaf though they have ears.

9† Let all the nations gather together,
  let the peoples assemble!
  Who among them could have revealed this,
  or foretold to us the earlier things?
  Let them produce witnesses to prove
    themselves right,
  that one may hear and say, "It is true!"

10 You are my witnesses, says the LORD,
  my servants whom I have chosen
  To know and believe in me
  and understand that it is I.
  Before me no god was formed,
  and after me there shall be none.

11 It is I, I the LORD;
  there is no savior but me.

12 It is I who foretold, I who saved;
  I made it known, not any strange god
    among you;
  You are my witnesses, says the LORD.
  I am God, 13* yes, from eternity I am He;
  There is none who can deliver from my hand:
  who can countermand what I do?

14† Thus says the LORD, your redeemer,
  the Holy One of Israel:
  For your sakes I send to Babylon;
  I will lower all the bars,
  and the Chaldeans shall cry out
  in lamentation.

15 I am the LORD, your Holy One,
  the creator of Israel, your King.

16* Thus says the LORD,

who opens a way in the sea
  and a path in the mighty waters,

17* Who leads out chariots and horsemen,
  a powerful army,
  Till they lie prostrate together, never to rise,
  snuffed out and quenched like a wick.

18† Remember not the events of the past,
  the things of long ago consider not;

19 See, I am doing something new!
  Now it springs forth, do you not perceive it?
  In the desert I make a way,
  in the wasteland, rivers.

20 Wild beasts honor me,
  jackals and ostriches,
  For I put water in the desert
  and rivers in the wasteland
  for my chosen people to drink,

21 The people whom I formed for myself,
  that they might announce my praise.

22† Yet you did not call upon me, O Jacob,
  for you grew weary of me, O Israel.

23* You did not bring me sheep for
    your holocausts,
  nor honor me with your sacrifices.
  I did not exact from you the service of offerings,
  nor weary you for frankincense.

24† You did not buy me sweet cane for money,
  nor fill me with the fat of your sacrifices;
  Instead, you burdened me with your sins,
  and wearied me with your crimes.

25 It is I, I, who wipe out,
  for my own sake, your offenses;
  your sins I remember no more.

26 Would you have me remember, have us come
  to trial?
  Speak up, prove your innocence!

27† Your first father sinned;
  your spokesmen rebelled against me

28 Till I repudiated the holy gates,
  put Jacob under the ban,
  and exposed Israel to scorn.

44

1 Hear then, O Jacob, my servant,
  Israel, whom I have chosen.

2† Thus says the LORD who made you,
  your help, who formed you from the womb:
  Fear not, O Jacob, my servant,
  the darling whom I have chosen.

43, 9: Only God can know and predict future events; cf Is 41, 1–5.21–29.

43, 14–17: The destruction of Babylon.

43, 18: No need to think solely of the past wonders of the exodus from Egypt; equally great is the exodus from Babylon.

43, 22–28: The reason for the liberation of the Israelites is not their fidelity but rather God's mercy.

43, 24: *Sweet cane:* a fragrant substance used in making incense and the sacred anointing oil; cf Ex 30, 23; Jer 6, 20.

43, 27: *First father:* Adam or Jacob, or collectively "early ancestors." *Spokesmen:* leaders, priests, prophets.

44, 2: *The darling:* see note on Dt 32, 15; cf also Dt 33, 5.26.

43, 6: Is 49, 22; Ez 16, 20.   43, 17: Ex 15, 4.
43, 13: Is 41, 4.   43, 23: Jer 6, 20.
43, 16: Is 51, 10f; Ex 14, 21.

3   I will pour out water upon the thirsty ground,
        and streams upon the dry land;
    I will pour out my spirit upon your offspring,
        and my blessing upon your descendants.
4* They shall spring up amid the verdure
        like poplars beside the flowing waters.
5*† One shall say, "I am the LORD'S,"
        another shall be named after Jacob,
    And this one shall write on his hand,
        "The LORD'S,"
    and Israel shall be his surname.

The True God and False Gods

6* Thus says the LORD, Israel's King
        and redeemer, the LORD of hosts:
    I am the first and I am the last;
        there is no God but me.
7   Who is like me? Let him stand up and speak,
        make it evident, and confront me with it.
    Who of old announced future events?
        Let them foretell to us the things to come.
8*† Fear not, be not troubled:
        did I not announce and foretell it long ago?
    You are my witnesses! Is there a God
        or any Rock besides me?

9*† Idol makers all amount to nothing, and their
precious works are of no avail, as they themselves
give witness. To their shame, they neither see nor
know anything; and they are more deaf than men
are. 10 Indeed, all the associates of anyone who
forms a god, or casts an idol to no purpose, will be
put to shame; 11 they will all assemble and stand
forth, to be reduced to fear and shame.

12* The smith fashions an iron image, works it
over the coals, shapes it with hammers, and forges
it with his strong arm. He is hungry and weak,
drinks no water and becomes exhausted.

13 The carpenter stretches a line and marks with a
stylus the outline of an idol. He shapes it with a
plane and measures it off with a compass, making
it like a man in appearance and dignity, to occupy a
shrine. 14 He cuts down cedars, takes a holm or an
oak, and lays hold of other trees of the forest, which
the Lord had planted and the rain made grow 15 to
serve man for fuel. With a part of their wood he
warms himself, or makes a fire for baking bread;
but with another part he makes a god which he
adores, an idol which he worships. 16 Half of it he
burns in the fire, and on its embers he roasts his
meat; he eats what he has roasted until he is full,
and then warms himself and says, "Ah! I am warm,
I feel the fire." 17 Of what remains he makes a god,
his idol, and prostrate before it in worship, he implores it, "Rescue me, for you are my god."

18 The idols have neither knowledge nor reason;
their eyes are coated so that they cannot see, and
their hearts so that they cannot understand. 19 Yet
he does not reflect, nor have the intelligence and
sense to say, "Half of the wood I burned in the fire,
and on its embers I baked bread and roasted meat
which I ate. Shall I then make an abomination out
of the rest, or worship a block of wood?" 20† He is
chasing ashes—a thing that cannot save itself when
the flame consumes it; yet he does not say, "Is not
this thing in my right hand a fraud?"

21 Remember this, O Jacob,
        you, O Israel, who are my servant!
    I formed you to be a servant to me;
        O Israel, by me you shall never be forgotten:
22 I have brushed away your offenses like a cloud,
        your sins like a mist;
        return to me, for I have redeemed you.

23 Raise a glad cry, you heavens: the LORD has
            done this;
        shout, you depths of the earth.
    Break forth, you mountains, into song,
        you forest, with all your trees.
    For the LORD has redeemed Jacob,
        and shows his glory through Israel.

Cyrus, Anointed of the Lord, Liberator of Israel

24* Thus says the LORD, your redeemer,
        who formed you from the womb:
    I am the LORD, who made all things,
        who alone stretched out the heavens;
        when I spread out the earth, who was
            with me?
25 It is I who bring to nought the omens of liars,
        who make fools of diviners;
    I turn wise men back
        and make their knowledge foolish.
26 It is I who confirm the words of my servants,
        I carry out the plan announced by
            my messengers;
    I say to Jerusalem: Be inhabited;
        to the cities of Judah: Be rebuilt;
        I will raise up their ruins.

44, 5: *Write on his hand:* an allusion to the Babylonian custom of
tatooing the owner's name on the hand of his slave; cf also Rv 13, 16.
    44, 8: *Rock:* place of refuge; said of God in Dt 32, 4.18; 1 Sm
2, 2; etc.
    44, 9–20: Satire on the makers and worshipers of idols.
    44, 20: *Chasing ashes:* exerting efforts in vain; cf Hos 12, 2; Eccl
1, 14; 2, 11.17.

44, 4: Is 54, 1ff.   44, 8: Is 43, 10.12; Dt 32, 4.
44, 5: Is 43, 7; 45, 14.   44, 9: Is 48, 5.7.
44, 6: Is 41, 44; 43, 15; 45,   44, 12: Wis 13, 11ff.
    21; 48, 3.12; 51, 15;   44, 24: Is 40, 22; Jb 9, 8.
    54, 5.

27* It is I who said to the deep: Be dry;
  I will dry up your wellsprings.
28*† I say of Cyrus: My shepherd,
  who fulfills my every wish;
He shall say of Jerusalem, "Let her be rebuilt,"
  and of the temple, "Let its foundations
    be laid."

45

1† Thus says the LORD to his
    anointed, Cyrus,
  whose right hand I grasp,
Subduing nations before him,
  and making kings run in his service,
Opening doors before him
  and leaving the gates unbarred:
2*† I will go before you
  and level the mountains;
Bronze doors I will shatter,
  and iron bars I will snap.
3 I will give you treasures out of the darkness,
  and riches that have been hidden away,
That you may know that I am the LORD,
  the God of Israel, who calls you by
    your name.
4* For the sake of Jacob, my servant,
  of Israel my chosen one,
I have called you by your name,
  giving you a title, though you knew me not.
5 I am the LORD and there is no other,
  there is no God besides me.
It is I who arm you, though you know
    me not,
6† so that toward the rising and the setting of
    the sun
  men may know that there is none
    besides me.

I am the LORD, there is no other;
7† I form the light, and create the darkness,
  I make well-being and create woe;
I, the LORD, do all these things.
8*† Let justice descend, O heavens, like dew
    from above,
  like gentle rain let the skies drop it down.
Let the earth open and salvation bud forth;

let justice also spring up!
  I, the LORD, have created this.
9*† Woe to him who contends with his Maker;
  a potsherd among potsherds of the earth!
Dare the clay say to its modeler, "What are
    you doing?"
  or, "What you are making has no hands"?
10 Woe to him who asks a father, "What are
    you begetting?"
  or a woman, "What are you giving birth to?"
11 Thus says the LORD,
  the Holy One of Israel, his maker:
You question me about my children,
  or prescribe the work of my hands for me!
12 It was I who made the earth
  and created mankind upon it;
It was my hands that stretched out
    the heavens;
  I gave the order to all their host.
13† It was I who stirred up one for the triumph
    of justice;
  all his ways I make level.
He shall rebuild my city
  and let my exiles go free
Without price or ransom,
  says the LORD of hosts.
14*† Thus says the LORD:
The earnings of Egypt, the gain of Ethiopia,
  and the Sabeans, tall of stature,
Shall come over to you and belong to you;
  they shall follow you, coming in chains.
Before you they shall fall prostrate,
  saying in prayer:
"With you only is God, and nowhere else;
  the gods are nought.
15*† Truly with you God is hidden,
  the God of Israel, the savior!
16 Those are put to shame and disgrace
  who vent their anger against him;
Those go in disgrace
  who carve images.
17 Israel, you are saved by the LORD,
  saved forever!
You shall never be put to shame or disgrace
  in future ages."

44, 28: *Cyrus:* king of Persia (559–529 B.C.) and conqueror of Babylon (538 B.C.), who liberated the Jews, permitting them to return to their native land and to rebuild Jerusalem and the Temple.

45, 1: *Anointed:* in Hebrew, *meshiah,* from which the word "Messiah" is derived; from its Greek translation, *Christos,* we have the name "Christ." Applied to kings, "anointed" originally referred only to those of Israel, but it is here given to Cyrus because he is the agent of the Lord.

45, 2: *Bronze doors:* of Babylon.

45, 6: The Gentiles will come to know the true God; cf also vv 20–25.

45, 7: *Create woe:* God permits evil for the sake of a greater good.

45, 8: The Vulgate rendering gives a more precise Messianic sense to this verse, using "just one" and "savior" in place of justice and salvation. The Advent liturgy uses the Vulgate form, *Rorate coeli desuper . . . ,* to express the world's longing for the coming of Christ.

45, 9: No one may challenge God's freedom of action, exemplified here by the selection of Cyrus as his anointed.

45, 13: *One:* Cyrus, called by God for the deliverance and restoration of Israel.

45, 14: *Egypt . . . Ethiopia . . . Sabeans:* the Egyptians and their allies who, when conquered by Cyrus, are seen as acknowledging the God of Israel to be the one true God; cf Is 43, 3.

45, 15: *God is hidden:* he dwells invisibly in the holy of holies.

44, 27: Is 42, 15; 51, 10.   45, 8: Pss 72, 6; 85, 11.
44, 28: Jer 3, 15; Ez 34, 23.   45, 9: Jer 18, 6; Rom 9, 20.
45, 2: Ps 107, 16.   45, 14: Is 43, 3.
45, 4: Is 40, 26.   45, 15: Is 55, 8; Prv 25, 2.

¹⁸†   For thus says the LORD,
The creator of the heavens,
    who is God,
The designer and maker of the earth
    who established it,
Not creating it to be a waste,
    but designing it to be lived in:
I am the LORD, and there is no other.

¹⁹   I have not spoken from hiding
    nor from some dark place of the earth,
And I have not said to the descendants of Jacob,
    "Look for me in an empty waste."
I, the LORD, promise justice,
    I foretell what is right.

²⁰† Come and assemble, gather together,
    you fugitives from among the gentiles!
They are without knowledge who bear
        wooden idols
    and pray to gods that cannot save.

²¹   Come here and declare
    in counsel together:
Who announced this from the beginning
    and foretold it from of old?
Was it not I, the LORD,
    besides whom there is no other God?
    There is no just and saving God but me.

²²   Turn to me and be safe,
    all you ends of the earth,
    for I am God; there is no other!

²³* By myself I swear,
    uttering my just decree
    and my unalterable word:
To me every knee shall bend;
    by me every tongue shall swear,

²⁴   Saying, "Only in the LORD
    are just deeds and power.
Before him in shame shall come
    all who vent their anger against him.

²⁵   In the LORD shall be the vindication and
        the glory
    of all the descendants of Israel."

The Gods of Babylon

46

¹† Bel bows down, Nebo stoops,
    their idols are upon beasts and cattle;
They must be borne up on shoulders,
    carried as burdens by the weary.

²   They stoop and bow down together;
    unable to save those who bear them,
    they too go into captivity.

³* Hear me, O house of Jacob,
    all who remain of the house of Israel,
My burden since your birth,
    whom I have carried from your infancy.

⁴   Even to your old age I am the same,
    even when your hair is gray I will bear you;
It is I who have done this, I who
        will continue,
    and I who will carry you to safety.

⁵   Whom would you compare me with, as
        an equal,
    or match me against, as though we
        were alike?

⁶   There are those who pour out gold from
        a purse
    and weigh out silver on the scales;
Then they hire a goldsmith to make it
        into a god
    before which they fall down in worship.

⁷   They lift it to their shoulders to carry;
    when they set it in place again, it stays,
    and does not move from the spot.
Although they cry out to it, it cannot answer;
    it delivers no one from distress.

⁸   Remember this and be firm,
    bear it well in mind, you rebels;
    remember the former things, those
        long ago:

⁹   I am God, there is no other;
    I am God, there is none like me.

¹⁰   At the beginning I foretell the outcome;
    in advance, things not yet done.
I say that my plan shall stand,
    I accomplish my every purpose.

¹¹† I call from the east a bird of prey,
    from a distant land, one to carry out
        my plan.
Yes, I have spoken, I will accomplish it;
    I have planned it, and I will do it.

¹²   Listen to me, you fainthearted,
    you who seem far from the victory
        of justice:

¹³   I am bringing on my justice, it is not
        far off,
    my salvation shall not tarry;
I will put salvation within Zion,
    and give to Israel my glory.

45, 18: *Waste:* an allusion to the beginning of creation, when the earth was waste and void (Gn 1, 2), the same Hebrew word, *tohu,* being used in both passages. The further reference here is to Palestine, which God wishes again to be inhabited by the returning exiles.

45, 20: *Who bear wooden idols:* in their religious processions. The gods of the pagans have feet but cannot walk; cf Ps 115, 7; Bar 6, 25.

46, 1: *Bel . . . Nebo:* gods of Babylon; their complete helplessness is here contrasted with God's omnipotence.

46, 11: *From the east a bird of prey:* Cyrus; cf Is 41, 2–4.

45, 23: Rom 14, 11; Phil 2, 10.   46, 3: Is 44, 2.

The Fall of Babylon†

47 ¹ Come down, sit in the dust,
O virgin daughter Babylon;
Sit on the ground, dethroned,
O daughter of the Chaldeans.
No longer shall you be called
dainty and delicate.

2   Take the millstone and grind flour,
remove your veil;
Strip off your train, bare your legs,
pass through the streams.

3   Your nakedness shall be uncovered
and your shame be seen;
I will take vengeance,
I will yield to no entreaty,
says our redeemer.

4   Whose name is the LORD of hosts,
the Holy One of Israel.

5   Go into darkness and sit in silence,
O daughter of the Chaldeans,
No longer shall you be called
sovereign mistress of kingdoms.

6   Angry at my people,
I profaned my inheritance,
And I gave them into your hand;
but you showed them no mercy,
And upon old men
you laid a very heavy yoke.

7*   You said, "I shall remain always,
a sovereign mistress forever!"
But you did not lay these things to heart,
you disregarded their outcome.

8*   Now hear this, voluptuous one,
enthroned securely,
Saying to yourself,
"I, and no one else!
I shall never be a widow,
or suffer the loss of my children"—

9†   Both these things shall come to you
suddenly, in a single day:
Complete bereavement and widowhood
shall come upon you
For your many sorceries
and the great number of your spells;

10   Because you felt secure in your wickedness,
and said, "No one sees me."
Your wisdom and your knowledge
led you astray,
And you said to yourself,
"I, and no one else!"

11   But upon you shall come evil
you will not know how to predict;
Disaster shall befall you
which you cannot allay.
Suddenly there shall come upon you
ruin which you will not expect.

12   Keep up, now, your spells
and your many sorceries;
Perhaps you can make them avail,
perhaps you can strike terror!

13   You wearied yourself with
many consultations,
at which you toiled from your youth;
Let the astrologers stand forth to save you,
the stargazers who forecast at each
new moon
what would happen to you.

14   Lo, they are like stubble,
fire consumes them;
They cannot save themselves
from the spreading flames.
This is no warming ember,
no fire to sit before.

15   Thus do your wizards serve you
with whom you have toiled from your youth;
Each wanders his own way,
with none to save you.

Exhortations to the Exiles

48 ¹ Hear this, O house of Jacob
called by the name Israel,
sprung from the stock of Judah,
You who swear by the name of the LORD
and invoke the God of Israel
without sincerity or justice,

2   Though you are named after the holy city
and rely on the God of Israel,
whose name is the LORD of hosts.

3   Things of the past I foretold long ago,
they went forth from my mouth, I let you
hear of them;
then suddenly I took action and they came
to be.

4   Because I know that you are stubborn
and that your neck is an iron sinew
and your forehead bronze,

5   I foretold them to you of old;
before they took place I let you hear of them,
That you might not say, "My idol did them,
my statue, my molten image
commanded them."

6*   Now that you have heard, look at all this;
must you not admit it?

---

† **47, 1–15:** A taunt-song, mocking Babylon, once queen of the nations, now made a slave girl.
47, 9.13.15: Babylon was known for its sorcery and astrology.

47, 7: Is 14, 13f.   **48, 6:** Is 42, 9.
47, 8: Zep 2, 15; Rv 18, 7.

From now on I announce new things to you,
hidden events of which you knew not.

7 Now, not long ago, they are brought
into being,
and beforetime you did not hear of them,
so that you cannot claim to have
known them;

8* You neither heard nor knew,
they did not reach your ears beforehand.
Yes, I know you are utterly treacherous,
a rebel you were called from birth.

9 For the sake of my name I restrain my anger,
for the sake of my renown I hold it back
from you,
lest I should destroy you.

10* See, I have refined you like silver,
tested you in the furnace of affliction.

11 For my sake, for my own sake, I do this;
why should I suffer profanation?
My glory I will not give to another.

12* Listen to me, Jacob,
Israel, whom I named!
I, it is I who am the first,
and also the last am I.

13* Yes, my hand laid the foundations of
the earth;
my right hand spread out the heavens.
When I call them,
they stand forth at once.

14† All of you assemble and listen:
Who among you foretold these things?
The LORD's friend shall do his will
against Babylon and the progeny
of Chaldea.

15 I myself have spoken, I have called him,
I have brought him, and his way
succeeds!

16† Come near to me and hear this!
Not from the beginning did I speak it
in secret;
At the time it comes to pass, I am present:
"Now the Lord GOD has sent me, and
his spirit."

17 Thus says the LORD, your redeemer,
the Holy One of Israel:
I, the LORD, your God,
teach you what is for your good,
and lead you on the way you should go.

18 If you would hearken to my
commandments,

your prosperity would be like a river,
and your vindication like the waves of
the sea;

19 Your descendants would be like the sand,
and those born of your stock like
its grains,
Their name never cut off
or blotted out from my presence.

20 Go forth from Babylon, flee from Chaldea!
With shouts of joy proclaim this, make
it known;
Publish it to the ends of the earth, and say,
"The LORD has redeemed his servant Jacob.

21* They did not thirst
when he led them through dry lands;
Water from the rock he set flowing for them;
he cleft the rock, and waters welled forth."

22 [There is no peace for the wicked,
says the LORD.]

II: Expiation of Sin, Spiritual Liberation of Israel

The Servant of the LORD†

49 1*† Hear me, O coastlands,
listen, O distant peoples.
The LORD called me from birth,
from my mother's womb he gave me
my name.

The Servant's Success

Isaiah 49, 1–6 is the second of the four servant songs (see "The Servant Songs," Is 42, 1–7). In this passage, the servant expresses a feeling of failure (49, 4). But God responds that the servant will be a success, a "light to the nations" (verse 6). In your prayer, reflect or journal on a time when you felt you failed, but something good happened anyway. How do you now see God's hand at work in the situation?

▸ Is 49, 1–6

48, 14: *The LORD's friend:* Cyrus, who carries out God's plans.
48, 16: *"Now the Lord . . . spirit.":* said by Cyrus; cf v 14.
49, 1–7: The second of the four "Servant-of-the-Lord" oracles.
49, 1: *Gave me my name:* designated me for a special office
(cf Jer 1, 5), or perhaps, made me renowned (cf Ps 45, 18).

48, 8: Is 43, 22ff.
48, 10: Is 1, 25; Jer 6, 29f; Zec
13, 9; Mal 3, 2.
48, 12: Is 41, 4; 44, 6; 48, 12;
Rv 1, 8.17.
48, 13: Is 40, 22.26; 45,
12.18.
48, 21: Ex 17, 6; Nm 20, 11.
49, 1: Is 41, 9; 43, 1; 44,
2.24; 46, 3.

Is

²† He made of me a sharp-edged sword
    and concealed me in the shadow of his arm.
He made me a polished arrow,
    in his quiver he hid me.
³† You are my servant, he said to me,
    Israel, through whom I show my glory.

⁴* Though I thought I had toiled in vain,
    and for nothing, uselessly, spent
        my strength,
Yet my reward is with the LORD,
    my recompense is with my God.
⁵ For now the LORD has spoken
    who formed me as his servant from
        the womb,
That Jacob may be brought back to him
    and Israel gathered to him;
And I am made glorious in the sight of
        the LORD,
    and my God is now my strength!
⁶*† It is too little, he says, for you to be
        my servant,
    to raise up the tribes of Jacob,
    and restore the survivors of Israel;
I will make you a light to the nations,
    that my salvation may reach to the ends of
        the earth.

⁷* Thus says the LORD,
    the redeemer and the Holy One of Israel,
To the one despised, whom the nations abhor,
    the slave of rulers:
When kings see you, they shall stand up,
    and princes shall prostrate themselves
Because of the LORD who is faithful,
    the Holy One of Israel who has chosen you.

The Liberation and Restoration of Zion

⁸*   Thus says the LORD:
In a time of favor I answer you,
    on the day of salvation I help you,
To restore the land
    and allot the desolate heritages,
⁹* Saying to the prisoners: Come out!
To those in darkness: Show yourselves!
Along the ways they shall find pasture,
    on every bare height shall their pastures be.
¹⁰* They shall not hunger or thirst,
    nor shall the scorching wind or the sun
        strike them;
For he who pities them leads them
    and guides them beside springs of water.
¹¹* I will cut a road through all my mountains,
    and make my highways level.
¹²† See, some shall come from afar,
    others from the north and the west,
    and some from the land of Syene.

¹³ Sing out, O heavens, and rejoice, O earth,
    break forth into song, you mountains.
For the LORD comforts his people
    and shows mercy to his afflicted.

¹⁴* But Zion said, "The LORD has forsaken me;
    my Lord has forgotten me."
¹⁵* Can a mother forget her infant,
    be without tenderness for the child of
        her womb?
Even should she forget,
    I will never forget you.
¹⁶† See, upon the palms of my hands I have
        written your name;
    your walls are ever before me.

I Will Never Forget You, My People

God is like a loving mother: forgiving, embracing, nurturing, tender, and gentle. The Hebrew root of the word *compassion* means "womb." A God of compassion and love is by definition a God of the womb, a God of motherly tenderness.
    Picture your mother figure: perhaps your birth mother, grandmother, adoptive mother, stepmother, or godmother. How do you see God's love reflected in her love?

▶ Is 49, 13–16

---

†
49, 2: The servant was made ready and fit for the preaching of God's word.
49, 3: *Israel:* the Servant is identified with the people of Israel as their ideal representative; however, since vv 5f seem to distinguish the Servant from Israel, some regard the word Israel here as a gloss.
49, 6: The Servant's vocation will be not only the restoration of Israel but the conversion of the world; cf Lk 2, 32.
49, 12: *Syene:* now called Aswan, at the first cataract of the Nile in southern Egypt.

49, 16: *Upon the palms . . . name:* for continual remembrance; cf Ex 13, 9.16; Dt 6, 6–9.

49, 4: Is 40, 27.
49, 6: Is 42, 1–6; 44, 5; 45, 14; Lk 2, 32; Acts 13, 46f.
49, 7: Is 49, 23; 55, 5.
49, 8: 2 Cor 6, 2.
49, 9: Is 42, 7.18ff.
49, 10: Is 51, 14; Rv 7, 16.
49, 11: Is 40, 3f.
49, 14: Is 40, 27.
49, 15: Is 43, 4; 44, 21; 46, 3f.

17 Your rebuilders make haste,
   as those who tore you down and laid
      you waste
   go forth from you;
18 Look about and see,
   they are all gathering and coming to you.
   As I live, says the LORD,
      you shall be arrayed with them all as
         with adornments,
      like a bride you shall fasten them on you.

19 Though you were waste and desolate,
      a land of ruins,
   Now you shall be too small for
      your inhabitants,
   while those who swallowed you up will be
      far away.
20 The children whom you had lost
      shall yet say to you,
   "This place is too small for me,
      make room for me to live in."
21* You shall ask yourself:
   "Who has borne me these?
   I was bereft and barren
      [exiled and repudiated];
   who has reared them?
   I was left all alone;
      where then do these come from?"

22*   Thus says the Lord GOD:
   See, I will lift up my hand to the nations,
      and raise my signal to the peoples;
   They shall bring your sons in their arms,
      and your daughters shall be carried on
         their shoulders.
23 Kings shall be your foster fathers,
      their princesses your nurses;
   Bowing to the ground, they shall worship you
      and lick the dust at your feet.
   Then you shall know that I am the LORD,
      and those who hope in me shall never
         be disappointed.

24   Thus says the LORD:
   Can booty be taken from a warrior?
      or captives be rescued from a tyrant?
25 Yes, captives can be taken from a warrior,
      and booty be rescued from a tyrant;
   Those who oppose you I will oppose,
      and your sons I will save.

26* I will make your oppressors eat their
      own flesh,
   and they shall be drunk with their
      own blood
   as with the juice of the grape.
   All mankind shall know
      that I, the LORD, am your savior,
      your redeemer, the mighty one
         of Jacob.

Salvation Only through the Lord's Servant

50 1*† Thus says the LORD:
   Where is the bill of divorce
   with which I dismissed your mother?
   Or to which of my creditors
      have I sold you?
   It was for your sins that you were sold,
      for your crimes that your mother was
         dismissed.

2*†Why was no one there when I came?
   Why did no one answer when I called?
   Is my hand too short to ransom?
   Have I not the strength to deliver?
   Lo, with my rebuke I dry up the sea,
      I turn rivers into a desert;
   Their fish rot for lack of water,
      and die of thirst.
3 I clothe the heavens in mourning,
   and make sackcloth their vesture.

The Servant's Strength

Isaiah 50, 4–9 is the third of the four servant songs (see "The Servant Songs," Is 42, 1–7). Read the song twice. The first time, think of how it reflects Jesus' relationship with his heavenly Father. The second time, meditate on the verses that inspire you and give you strength to be a prophet to other young people.

▶ Is 50, 4–9

---

† **50, 1:** Responding to the people's complaint of utter abandonment by God, the prophet shows that their sins were responsible for their banishment. Since there was no bill of divorce, the bond between the Lord and his people still exists and he will ultimately save them.

50, 2: Israel's faith in God is weak; she does not answer his call, nor believe in his promises of deliverance.

---

* **49, 21:** Is 54, 1ff.
  49, 22: Is 5, 26; 13, 2.
  49, 26: Is 19, 2; Ez 38, 21; Zec 14, 13.
  50, 1: Dt 24, 1–4; Mt 19, 3; Mk 10, 2ff; 54, 6ff.
  50, 2: Ex 7, 18; Ps 105, 29.

4† The Lord GOD has given me
    a well-trained tongue,
That I might know how to speak to the weary
    a word that will rouse them.
Morning after morning
    he opens my ear that I may hear;
5† And I have not rebelled,
    have not turned back.
6*†I gave my back to those who beat me,
    my cheeks to those who plucked my beard;
My face I did not shield
    from buffets and spitting.

7* The Lord GOD is my help,
    therefore I am not disgraced;
I have set my face like flint,
    knowing that I shall not be put to shame.
8 He is near who upholds my right;
    if anyone wishes to oppose me,
    let us appear together.
Who disputes my right?
    Let him confront me.
9* See, the Lord GOD is my help;
    who will prove me wrong?
Lo, they will all wear out like cloth,
    the moth will eat them up.

10*†Who among you fears the LORD,
    heeds his servant's voice,
And walks in darkness
    without any light,
Trusting in the name of the LORD
    and relying on his God?
11 All of you kindle flames
    and carry about you fiery darts;
Walk by the light of your own fire
    and by the flares you have burnt!
This is your fate from my hand:
    you shall lie down in a place of pain.

Exhortation To Trust in the Lord

51 1*† Listen to me, you who pursue
        justice,
    who seek the LORD;
Look to the rock from which you were hewn,
    to the pit from which you were quarried;

2* Look to Abraham, your father,
    and to Sarah, who gave you birth;
When he was but one I called him,
    I blessed him and made him many.
3 Yes, the LORD shall comfort Zion
    and have pity on all her ruins;
Her deserts he shall make like Eden,
    her wasteland like the garden of the LORD;
Joy and gladness shall be found in her,
    thanksgiving and the sound of song.

4*†Be attentive to me, my people;
    my folk, give ear to me.
For law shall go forth from my presence,
    and my judgment, as the light of
        the peoples.
5 I will make my justice come speedily;
    my salvation shall go forth
    [and my arm shall judge the nations];
In me shall the coastlands hope,
    and my arm they shall await.

6† Raise your eyes to the heavens,
    and look at the earth below;
Though the heavens grow thin like smoke,
    the earth wears out like a garment
    and its inhabitants die like flies,
My salvation shall remain forever
    and my justice shall never be dismayed.
7 Hear me, you who know justice,
    you people who have my teaching at heart:
Fear not the reproach of men,
    be not dismayed at their revilings.
8* They shall be like a garment eaten by moths,
    like wool consumed by grubs;
But my justice shall remain forever
    and my salvation, for all generations.

9*†Awake, awake, put on strength,
    O arm of the LORD!
Awake as in the days of old,
    in ages long ago!
Was it not you who crushed Rahab,
    you who pierced the dragon?
10† Was it not you who dried up the sea,
    the waters of the great deep,

50, 4–11: The third of the four "Servant-of-the-Lord" oracles; in vv 4–9 the Servant speaks; in vv 10f God reproves the people for not following the Servant.
50, 5: The Servant does not refuse the divine vocation.
50, 6: He willingly submits to insults and beatings. *Plucked my beard:* a grave insult.
50, 10f: Instead of trusting in the Lord and his Servant, the people rely on their own devices, to their own destruction.
51, 1: *Rock . . . pit:* your glorious ancestry.
51, 4f: The conversion of the Gentiles.
51, 6: God's salvation and justice are eternal, in contrast to the impermanence of the heavens and the earth: cf Mt 24, 35.

51, 9: *Rahab:* see note on Is 30, 7. *The dragon:* see notes on Is 27, 1; Ps 74, 13.
51, 10: *Great deep:* another reference to the primeval chaos of Gn 1, 2.

50, 6: 2 Sm 10, 4ff; Mt 26,
   67; 27, 30.
50, 7: Ez 3, 9.
50, 9: Is 51, 6–8; Ps 102, 27.
50, 10: Is 43, 1f; 44, 1f.
51, 1: Rom 9, 30f.

51, 2: Ez 33, 24; Gn 12, 2ff;
   22, 17.
51, 4: Is 2, 3.
51, 8: Is 50, 9.
51, 9: Ex 15, 16; Jb 9, 13; 26,
   12; Pss 74, 13; 89, 11.

Who made the depths of the sea into a way
　　for the redeemed to pass over?
11　Those whom the LORD has ransomed
　　　　will return
　　and enter Zion singing,
　　crowned with everlasting joy;
　　They will meet with joy and gladness,
　　　　sorrow and mourning will flee.
12　I, it is I who comfort you.
　　　　Can you then fear mortal man,
　　who is human only, to be looked upon
　　　　as grass,
13　And forget the LORD, your maker,
　　　　who stretched out the heavens
　　and laid the foundations of the earth?
　　All the day you are in constant dread
　　　　of the fury of the oppressor;
　　But when he sets himself to destroy,
　　　　what is there of the oppressor's fury?

14　The oppressed shall soon be released;
　　　　they shall not die and go down into
　　　　the pit,
　　nor shall they want for bread.
15*　For I am the LORD, your God,
　　　　who stirs up the sea so that its waves roar;
　　the LORD of hosts by name.
16　I have put my words into your mouth
　　　　and shielded you in the shadow of
　　　　my hand,
　　I, who stretched out the heavens,
　　　　who laid the foundations of the earth,
　　who say to Zion: You are my people.

The Cup of the LORD

17*　Awake, awake!
　　　　Arise, O Jerusalem,
　　You who drank at the LORD's hand
　　　　the cup of his wrath;
　　Who drained to the dregs
　　　　the bowl of staggering!
18　She has no one to guide her
　　　　of all the sons she bore;
　　She has no one to grasp her by the hand,
　　　　of all the sons she reared!—
19　Your misfortunes are double;
　　　　who is there to condole with you?
　　Desolation and destruction, famine
　　　　and sword!
　　Who is there to comfort you?
20　Your sons lie helpless
　　　　at every street corner

like antelopes in a net.
　　They are filled with the wrath of the LORD,
　　　　the rebuke of your God.

21*　But now, hear this, O afflicted one,
　　　　drunk, but not with wine,
22　Thus says the LORD, your Master,
　　　　your God, who defends his people:
　　See, I am taking from your hand
　　　　the cup of staggering;
　　The bowl of my wrath
　　　　you shall no longer drink.
23　I will put it into the hands of
　　　　your tormentors,
　　　　those who ordered you
　　　　to bow down, that they might walk
　　　　over you,
　　While you offered your back like
　　　　the ground,
　　　　like the street for them to walk on.

Let Zion Rejoice

52

¹ Awake, awake!
　　　　Put on your strength, O Zion;
　　Put on your glorious garments,
　　　　O Jerusalem, holy city.
　　No longer shall the uncircumcised
　　　　or the unclean enter you.
2　Shake off the dust,
　　　　ascend to the throne, Jerusalem;
　　Loose the bonds from your neck,
　　　　O captive daughter Zion!
3　　For thus says the LORD:
　　You were sold for nothing,
　　　　and without money you shall be redeemed.
4　　　Thus says the Lord GOD:
　　To Egypt in the beginning my people
　　　　went down,
　　　　to sojourn there;
　　　　Assyria, too, oppressed them for nought.
5　But now, what am I to do here?
　　　　says the LORD.
　　My people have been taken away
　　　　without redress;
　　　　their rulers make a boast of it,
　　　　says the LORD;
　　　　all the day my name is constantly reviled.
6　Therefore on that day my people shall know
　　　　my renown,
　　　　that it is I who have foretold it. Here I am!
7*†How beautiful upon the mountains
　　　　are the feet of him who brings glad tidings,

52, 7–10: God leads his people back from Babylon to Zion, from whose ruined walls *watchmen . . . shout for joy;* cf Rom 10, 15.

51, 15: Jer 31, 35.　　　　　**51, 21:** Is 29, 9.
51, 17: Jer 25, 15ff; Ez 23,　　**52, 7:** Is 40, 9; Rom 10, 15.
　32ff.

Announcing peace, bearing good news,
announcing salvation, and saying to Zion,
"Your God is King!"

8* Hark! Your watchmen raise a cry,
together they shout for joy,
For they see directly, before their eyes,
the LORD restoring Zion.

9 Break out together in song,
O ruins of Jerusalem!
For the LORD comforts his people,
he redeems Jerusalem.

10 The LORD has bared his holy arm
in the sight of all the nations;
All the ends of the earth will behold
the salvation of our God.

11† Depart, depart, come forth from there,
touch nothing unclean!
Out from there! Purify yourselves,
you who carry the vessels of the LORD.

12* Yet not in fearful haste will you come out,
nor leave in headlong flight,
For the LORD comes before you,
and your rear guard is the God of Israel.

Suffering and Triumph of the Servant of the LORD†

13 See, my servant shall prosper,
he shall be raised high and greatly exalted.

14* Even as many were amazed at him—
so marred was his look beyond that of man,
and his appearance beyond that of mortals—

15* So shall he startle many nations,
because of him kings shall stand speechless;
For those who have not been told shall see,
those who have not heard shall ponder it.

53

1* Who would believe what we have
heard?
To whom has the arm of the LORD
been revealed?

2*† He grew up like a sapling before him,
like a shoot from the parched earth;
There was in him no stately bearing to make
us look at him,
nor appearance that would attract us
to him.

Catholic Connections

THE SUFFERING SERVANT

Isaiah 52, 13—53, 12 is the fourth of the four servant songs (see "The Servant Songs," Is 42, 1–7). In it, the servant suffers for the salvation of others. Can you see how this description fits Jesus? Take a moment to say your own prayer of thanksgiving to Jesus for saving us from sin and death.

▶ Is 52, 13—53, 12

3*† He was spurned and avoided by men,
a man of suffering, accustomed to infirmity,
One of those from whom men hide their faces,
spurned, and we held him in no esteem.

4*† Yet it was our infirmities that he bore,
our sufferings that he endured,
While we thought of him as stricken,
as one smitten by God and afflicted.

5* But he was pierced for our offenses,
crushed for our sins,
Upon him was the chastisement that makes
us whole,
by his stripes we were healed.

6* We had all gone astray like sheep,
each following his own way;
But the LORD laid upon him
the guilt of us all.

7* Though he was harshly treated, he submitted
and opened not his mouth;
Like a lamb led to the slaughter
or a sheep before the shearers,
he was silent and opened not his mouth.

---

† 52, 11: *From there:* from Babylon. *Vessels of the LORD:* taken to Babylon by Nebuchadnezzar, now carried back by the exiled priests returning in procession to Zion; cf Ezr 1, 7.

52, 13—53, 12: The last of the four "Servant-of-the-Lord" oracles. An extraordinary description of the sinless Servant, who by his voluntary suffering atones for the sins of his people, and saves them from just punishment at the hands of God. Only in Jesus Christ is the prophecy perfectly fulfilled.

53, 2: Only God appreciated his Servant's true greatness.

53, 3: Because he suffered, he was regarded as a sinner and therefore as one to be spurned.

53, 4ff: He did indeed suffer but it was for the sins of mankind, and through his sufferings men are healed.

52, 8: Is 62, 6.
52, 12: Ex 12, 11.
52, 14: Ps 69, 8.
52, 15: Mi 7, 16.
53, 1: Is 52, 10; Jn 12, 38; Rom 10, 16.
53, 2: Is 11, 1.
53, 3: Jb 19, 18; Ps 31, 11ff; Mk 9, 11.
53, 4: Jer 10, 19; Mt 8, 17.
53, 5: 1 Cor 15, 3; 1 Pt 2, 24.
53, 6: Lv 16, 21ff.
53, 7: Mt 26, 63; Acts 8, 32.

8 Oppressed and condemned, he was
taken away,
and who would have thought any more of
his destiny?
When he was cut off from the land of
the living,
and smitten for the sin of his people,
9* A grave was assigned him among the wicked
and a burial place with evildoers,
Though he had done no wrong
nor spoken any falsehood.
10† [But the LORD was pleased
to crush him in infirmity.]

If he gives his life as an offering for sin,
he shall see his descendants in a long life,
and the will of the LORD shall be
accomplished through him.
11 Because of his affliction
he shall see the light in fullness of days;
Through his suffering, my servant shall
justify many,
and their guilt he shall bear.
12* Therefore I will give him his portion among
the great,
and he shall divide the spoils with
the mighty,
Because he surrendered himself to death
and was counted among the wicked;
And he shall take away the sins of many,
and win pardon for their offenses.

The New Zion

54 1*† Raise a glad cry, you barren one
who did not bear,
break forth in jubilant song, you who were
not in labor,
For more numerous are the children of the
deserted wife
than the children of her who has a husband,
says the LORD.
2* Enlarge the space for your tent,
spread out your tent cloths unsparingly;
lengthen your ropes and make firm
your stakes.
3 For you shall spread abroad to the right and
to the left;
your descendants shall dispossess the nations
and shall people the desolate cities.

4 Fear not, you shall not be put to shame;
you need not blush, for you shall not
be disgraced.
The shame of your youth you shall forget,
the reproach of your widowhood no
longer remember.
5† For he who has become your husband is
your Maker;
his name is the LORD of hosts;
Your redeemer is the Holy One of Israel,
called God of all the earth.
6* The LORD calls you back,
like a wife forsaken and grieved in spirit,
A wife married in youth and then cast off,
says your God.
7 For a brief moment I abandoned you,
but with great tenderness I will take
you back.
8 In an outburst of wrath, for a moment
I hid my face from you;
But with enduring love I take pity on you,
says the LORD, your redeemer.
9* This is for me like the days of Noah,
when I swore that the waters of Noah
should never again deluge the earth;
So I have sworn not to be angry with you,
or to rebuke you.
10* Though the mountains leave their place
and the hills be shaken,
My love shall never leave you
nor my covenant of peace be shaken,
says the LORD, who has mercy on you.
11*† O afflicted one, storm-battered
and unconsoled,
I lay your pavements in carnelians,
and your foundations in sapphires;
12 I will make your battlements of rubies,
your gates of carbuncles,
and all your walls of precious stones.
13 All your sons shall be taught by the LORD,
and great shall be the peace of your children.
14 In justice shall you be established,
far from the fear of oppression,
where destruction cannot come near you.
15 Should there be any attack, it shall not be of
my making;
whoever attacks you shall fall before you.

53, 10ff: Because he fulfilled the divine will by suffering for the sins of others, the Servant will be rewarded by the Lord. *See the light:* enjoy happiness. This line may originally have read, "he shall drink and eat to the full"—at the thanksgiving sacrifice at which he shall divide the spoils (v 12).
54, 1: Jerusalem, pictured as a wife who had been barren and deserted, now suddenly finds herself with innumerable children (the returning exiles); cf Gal 4, 27 for the application of this text to the church, the New Zion.

54, 5: *Redeemer:* cf note on Is 41, 14.
54, 11f: Cf Rv 21. *Afflicted one:* Jerusalem; *carnelians:* reddish quartz, hard and durable; *carbuncles:* another precious stone of red color.

53, 9: 1 Pt 2, 22f; 1 Jn 3, 5.   **54, 6:** Mal 2, 14f.
53, 12: Mk 15, 28; Lk 22, 37.   **54, 9:** Gn 9, 15.
54, 1: Gal 4, 27.   **54, 10:** Pss 46, 3; 76, 5.
54, 2: Is 49, 20.   **54, 11:** Rv 21, 18–21.

16 Lo, I have created the craftsman
    who blows on the burning coals
    and forges weapons as his work;
It is I also who have created
    the destroyer to work havoc.

17 No weapon fashioned against you
    shall prevail;
    every tongue you shall prove false
    that launches an accusation against you.
This is the lot of the servants of the LORD,
    their vindication from me, says the LORD.

An Invitation to Grace

55 1*† All you who are thirsty,
        come to the water!
You who have no money,
    come, receive grain and eat;
Come, without paying and without cost,
    drink wine and milk!

2 Why spend your money for what is not bread;
    your wages for what fails to satisfy?
Heed me, and you shall eat well,
    you shall delight in rich fare.

3* Come to me heedfully,
    listen, that you may have life.
I will renew with you the everlasting covenant,
    the benefits assured to David.

4 As I made him a witness to the peoples,
    a leader and commander of nations,

5* So shall you summon a nation you knew not,
    and nations that knew you not shall run
        to you,
Because of the LORD, your God,
    the Holy One of Israel, who has
        glorified you.

6 Seek the LORD while he may be found,
    call him while he is near.

7 Let the scoundrel forsake his way,
    and the wicked man his thoughts;
Let him turn to the LORD for mercy;
    to our God, who is generous in forgiving.

8 For my thoughts are not your thoughts,
    nor are your ways my ways, says the LORD.

9 As high as the heavens are above the earth,
    so high are my ways above your ways
    and my thoughts above your thoughts.

10 For just as from the heavens

the rain and snow come down
And do not return there
    till they have watered the earth,
    making it fertile and fruitful,
Giving seed to him who sows
    and bread to him who eats,

11 So shall my word be
    that goes forth from my mouth;
It shall not return to me void,
    but shall do my will,
    achieving the end for which I sent it.

12 Yes, in joy you shall depart,
    in peace you shall be brought back;
Mountains and hills shall break out in song
    before you,
    and all the trees of the countryside shall
        clap their hands.

13† In place of the thornbush, the cypress
        shall grow,
    instead of nettles, the myrtle.
This shall be to the LORD's renown,
    an everlasting imperishable sign.

III: Return of the First Captives

The Lord's House Open to All†

56 1   Thus says the LORD:
        Observe what is right, do what is just;
    for my salvation is about to come,
    my justice, about to be revealed.

2 Happy is the man who does this,
    the son of man who holds to it;
Who keeps the sabbath free from profanation,
    and his hand from any evildoing.

3† Let not the foreigner say,
    when he would join himself to the LORD,
    "The LORD will surely exclude me from
        his people";
Nor let the eunuch say,
    "See, I am a dry tree."

4* For thus says the LORD:
To the eunuchs who observe my sabbaths
    and choose what pleases me
    and hold fast to my covenant,

5† I will give, in my house
    and within my walls, a monument and
        a name

55, 1ff: God's salvation is freely extended to his people and to all nations; through him will the benefits assured to David be renewed; cf Is 12, 3; Jn 7, 37.

55, 13: *Thornbush . . . nettles:* suggestive of the desert and therefore symbolic of suffering and hardship; *cypress. . . myrtle:* suggestive of fertile land and therefore symbolic of joy and strength.

56, 1–8: Participation in the future messianic salvation is offered to all who believe in the Lord and keep his commandments, regardless of origin or social condition.

56, 3: Eunuchs had originally been excluded from the communi-

ty of the Lord; cf Dt 23, 2; Wis 3, 14. *Dry tree:* unable to produce the fruit of offspring.

56, 5: *A monument and a name:* a memorial inscription to prevent oblivion for one who had no children; cf 2 Sm 18, 18; Neh 7, 15; 13, 14.

55, 1: Jn 4, 10ff; 6, 35; 7,
       37ff; Rv 21, 6; 22, 17.
55, 3: 2 Sm 7, 12–16.

55, 5: Acts 13, 34.
56, 4: Wis 3, 14f.

The Optimism of Third Isaiah

The last eleven chapters of Isaiah contain the messages of several prophets known collectively as Third Isaiah. The common element of these prophecies is optimism. They proclaim the hopeful message that God's Covenant will be extended to all nations and that Jerusalem will become God's holy city, the throne of the Eternal King.

Third Isaiah, in contrast to many of the other biblical prophets, proclaims joy as a sign of God's presence. Joy is absent in the life of many people today, as it was in the time of Isaiah. Let us remember all the wonderful things God has done for us, and we too will find cause for rejoicing!

▶ **Is 56, 1—66, 24**

Better than sons and daughters;
   an eternal, imperishable name will I
     give them.

6 And the foreigners who join themselves to
   the LORD,
   ministering to him,
Loving the name of the LORD,
   and becoming his servants—
All who keep the sabbath free
   from profanation
   and hold to my covenant,
7* Them I will bring to my holy mountain
   and make joyful in my house
     of prayer;
Their holocausts and sacrifices
   will be acceptable on my altar,
For my house shall be called
   a house of prayer for all peoples.
8 Thus says the Lord GOD,
   who gathers the dispersed of Israel:
Others will I gather to him
   besides those already gathered.

Blind Leaders

9*†All you wild beasts† of the field,
   come and eat,
   all you beasts in the forest!
10 My watchmen are blind,
   all of them unaware;
They are all dumb dogs,
   they cannot bark;
Dreaming as they lie there,
   loving their sleep.

11 They are relentless dogs,
   they know not when they have enough.
These are the shepherds
   who know no discretion;
Each of them goes his own way,
   every one of them to his own gain:
12* "Come, I will fetch some wine;
   let us carouse with strong drink,
And tomorrow will be like today,
   or even greater."

57 ¹ The just man perishes,
   but no one takes it to heart;
Devout men are swept away,
   with no one giving it a thought.
Though he is taken away from the presence
   of evil,
   the just man ²enters into peace;
There is rest on his couch
   for the sincere, straightforward man.

Faithless People

3 But you, draw near,
   you sons of a sorceress,
   adulterous, wanton race!
4 Of whom do you make sport,
   at whom do you open wide your mouth,
   and put out your tongue?
Are you not rebellious children,
   a worthless race;
5* You who are in heat among the terebinths,
   under every green tree;
You who immolate children in the wadies,
   behind the crevices in the cliffs?

56, 9—57, 13: This section is apparently preexilic, written in the manner of the older prophets who condemned the pagan rites of Baal worship.
56, 9: *Wild beasts:* foreign nations, which are invited to come and ravage Israel.

56, 7: 1 Kgs 8, 29f; Mt 21,
   13.
56, 9: Ez 34, 5.

56, 12: Is 28, 7ff; Wis 2, 7.
57, 5: Jer 7, 31; 19, 5; Ez 20,
   28.31.

6† Among the smooth stones of the wadi is
    your portion,
   these are your lot;
To these you poured out libations,
   and brought offerings.
   Should I decide not to punish these things?

7* Upon a high and lofty mountain
   you made your bed,
   and there you went up to offer sacrifice.

8 Behind the door and the doorpost
   you placed your indecent symbol.
Deserting me, you spread out
   your high, wide bed;
And of those whose embraces you love
   you carved the symbol and gazed upon it

9† While you approached the king with
    scented oil,
   and multiplied your perfumes;
While you sent your ambassadors far away,
   down even to the nether world.

10 Though worn out by your many misdeeds,
   you never said, "It is hopeless";
New strength you found,
   and so you did not weaken.

11 Of whom were you afraid? Whom did
    you fear,
   that you became false
And did not remember me
   or give me any thought?
Was I to remain silent and unseeing,
   so that you would not have me to fear?

12† I will expose your justice
   and your works;

13† They shall not help you when you cry out,
   nor save you in your distress.
All these the wind shall carry off,
   the breeze shall bear away;
But he who takes refuge in me shall inherit
   the land,
   and possess my holy mountain.

Comfort for the Afflicted

14* Build up, build up, prepare the way,
   remove the stumbling blocks from my
    people's path.

15* For thus says he who is high and exalted,

living eternally, whose name is the
   Holy One:
On high I dwell, and in holiness,
   and with the crushed and dejected in spirit,
To revive the spirits of the dejected,
   to revive the hearts of the crushed.

16 I will not accuse forever,
   nor always be angry;
For their spirits would faint before me,
   the souls that I have made.

17* Because of their wicked avarice I was angry,
   and struck them, hiding myself in wrath,
   as they went their own rebellious way.

18 I saw their ways,
   but I will heal them and lead them;
I will give full comfort
   to them and to those who mourn for them,

19 I, the Creator, who gave them life.

Peace, peace to the far and the near,
   says the LORD; and I will heal them.

20 But the wicked are like the tossing sea
   which cannot be calmed,
And its waters cast up mud and filth.

21*   No peace for the wicked! says my God.

True Fasting

58 1† Cry out full-throated and
     unsparingly,
   lift up your voice like a trumpet blast;
Tell my people their wickedness,
   and the house of Jacob their sins.

2† They seek me day after day,
   and desire to know my ways,
Like a nation that has done what is just
   and not abandoned the law of their God;
They ask me to declare what is due them,
   pleased to gain access to God.

3 "Why do we fast, and you do not see it?
   afflict ourselves, and you take no note
   of it?"

Lo, on your fast day you carry out your
   own pursuits,
   and drive all your laborers.

4 Yes, your fast ends in quarreling and fighting,
   striking with wicked claw.

57, 6: *Smooth stones:* the Hebrew word for this expression has the same consonants as the word for "portion"; instead of making the Lord their portion (cf Ps 16, 5), the people adored slabs of stone which they took from the streambeds in valleys and set up as idols; cf Jer 3, 9. Therefore, it is implied, they will be swept away as by a sudden torrent of waters carrying them down the rocky-bottomed gorge to destruction and death without burial.
   57, 9: *The king:* the pagan god Moloch. *Ambassadors:* children sent to him through a sacrificial death.
   57, 12: *Justice:* here used ironically.

57, 13: *All these:* the wicked mentioned in Is 57, 3–10.
58, 1: This command is directed to the prophet.
58, 2–14: Merely external worship does not avail with God; it must be joined to internal sincerity.

57, 7: Hos 4, 13; Jer 2, 20; Ez   57, 15: Is 61, 2f.
   6, 13.   57, 17: Is 56, 11.
57, 14: Is 40, 3f.   57, 21: Is 48, 21.

Cultural Connections

"IF YOU WANT PEACE, WORK FOR JUSTICE"

"If you want peace, work for justice" is a famous quote of Pope Paul VI. We hear a similar message in Is 56, 1, and 58, 6–14 gives us clear examples of works that create justice and peace.

At the core of justice is the understanding that life—all life—is precious. All people are to be honored, protected, and celebrated. Ensuring that this happens is our responsibility, even when it seems to be a burden. The following prayer by a worker of Peace Market in Korea reflects this passion:

> *Make us keep the sputtering lantern burning*
> *and not to break a wounded reed.*
> *Make us understand*
> *the secret of eternal life*
> *from the pulse of blood in our veins*
> *and realise the worth of a life*
> *from the movement of a warm heart.*
> *Make us not discriminate*
> *the rich and the poor,*
> *the high and the low,*
> *the learned and the ignorant*
> *those we know well and those we do not know.*
> *Oh!*
> *A human life can't be exchanged for the whole world*
> *this supreme task of keeping the lives*
> *of the sons and daughters of God.*
> *Let us realise how lovely it is*
> *to feel the burdens of responsibility.*

("Our Prayer, Your Will Be Done")

▶ Is 58, 6–14

Would that today you might fast
 so as to make your voice heard on high!
5* Is this the manner of fasting I wish,
 of keeping a day of penance:
That a man bow his head like a reed,
 and lie in sackcloth and ashes?
Do you call this a fast,
 a day acceptable to the LORD?
6 This, rather, is the fasting that I wish:
 releasing those bound unjustly,
 untying the thongs of the yoke;

Setting free the oppressed,
 breaking every yoke;
7* Sharing your bread with the hungry,
 sheltering the oppressed and the homeless;
Clothing the naked when you see them,
 and not turning your back on your own.
8 Then your light shall break forth like the dawn,
 and your wound shall quickly be healed;
Your vindication shall go before you,
 and the glory of the LORD shall be your
 rear guard.

58, 5: Zec 7, 5.   58, 7: Ez 18, 7.16; Mt 25, 35.

58, 6

9 Then you shall call, and the LORD will answer,
  you shall cry for help, and he will say: Here
    I am!
  If you remove from your midst oppression,
    false accusation and malicious speech;
10 If you bestow your bread on the hungry
    and satisfy the afflicted;
  Then light shall rise for you in the darkness,
    and the gloom shall become for you
      like midday;
11* Then the LORD will guide you always
    and give you plenty even on the
      parched land.
  He will renew your strength,
    and you shall be like a watered garden,
    like a spring whose water never fails.
12* The ancient ruins shall be rebuilt for
      your sake,
    and the foundations from ages past you
      shall raise up;
  "Repairer of the breach," they shall call you,
    "Restorer of ruined homesteads."

13 If you hold back your foot on the sabbath
    from following your own pursuits on my
      holy day;
  If you call the sabbath a delight,
    and the LORD'S holy day honorable;
  If you honor it by not following your ways,

seeking your own interests, or speaking
  with malice—
14 Then you shall delight in the LORD,
    and I will make you ride on the heights of
      the earth;
  I will nourish you with the heritage of Jacob,
    your father,
    for the mouth of the LORD has spoken.

Sin and Confession

59 1* Lo, the hand of the LORD is not too
      short to save,
    nor his ear too dull to hear.
2 Rather, it is your crimes
    that separate you from your God,
  It is your sins that make him hide his face
    so that he will not hear you.
3* For your hands are stained with blood,
    your fingers with guilt;
  Your lips speak falsehood,
    and your tongue utters deceit.
4† No one brings suit justly,
    no one pleads truthfully;
  They trust in emptiness and tell lies;
    they conceive mischief and bring
      forth malice.
5*†They hatch adders' eggs,
    and weave spiders' webs:
  Whoever eats their eggs will die,
    if one of them is pressed, it will hatch as
      a viper;
6 Their webs cannot serve as clothing,
    nor can they cover themselves with
      their works.
  Their works are evil works,
    and deeds of violence come from their hands.
7* Their feet run to evil,
    and they are quick to shed innocent blood;
  Their thoughts are destructive thoughts,
    plunder and ruin are on their highways.
8 The way of peace they know not,
    and there is nothing that is right in
      their paths;
  Their ways they have made crooked,
    whoever treads them knows no peace.

9† That is why right is far from us
    and justice does not reach us.
  We look for light, and lo, darkness;
    for brightness, but we walk in gloom!

59, 4: *Emptiness:* things having no value.
59, 5f: A proverb signifying evil works—*adders' eggs*—and useless devices—*spiders' webs;* the former do positive harm to oneself
and others, the latter serve no useful purpose.
59, 9–15: Spoken by the people through the mouth of
the prophet.

58, 11: Is 51, 3; Ps 24.   59, 3: Is 1, 15.
58, 12: Is 61, 4.   59, 5: Jb 20, 12–16.
59, 1: Is 50, 2; Nm 11, 23.   59, 7: Rom 3, 15.

10 Like blind men we grope along the wall,
      like people without eyes we feel our way.
   We stumble at midday as at dusk,
      in Stygian darkness, like the dead.
11 * We all growl like bears,
      like doves we moan without ceasing.
   We look for right, but it is not there;
      for salvation, and it is far from us.
12 For our offenses before you are many,
      our sins bear witness against us.
   Yes, our offenses are present to us,
      and our crimes we know:
13 Transgressing, and denying the LORD,
      turning back from following our God,
   Threatening outrage, and apostasy,
      uttering words of falsehood the heart
        has conceived.
14 Right is repelled,
      and justice stands far off;
   For truth stumbles in the public square,
      uprightness cannot enter.
15 Honesty is lacking,
      and the man who turns from evil
        is despoiled.

The Redeemer in Zion

The LORD saw this, and was aggrieved
      that right did not exist.
16 He saw that there was no one,
      and was appalled that there was none
        to intervene;
   So his own arm brought about the victory,
      and his justice lent him its support.
17 * He put on justice as his breastplate,
      salvation, as the helmet on his head;
   He clothed himself with garments
        of vengeance,
      wrapped himself in a mantle of zeal.
18 He repays his enemies their deserts,
      and requites his foes with wrath.
19 Those in the west shall fear the name of
        the LORD,
      and those in the east, his glory;
   For it shall come like a pent-up river
      which the breath of the LORD drives on.
20 * He shall come to Zion a redeemer
      to those of Jacob who turn from sin, says
        the LORD.
21 This is the covenant with them
      which I myself have made, says the LORD:
   My spirit which is upon you

and my words that I have put into
      your mouth
Shall never leave your mouth,
      nor the mouths of your children
Nor the mouths of your children's children
      from now on and forever, says the LORD.

Glory of the New Zion

60 ¹† Rise up in splendor! Your light
        has come,
   the glory of the Lord shines upon you.
2 See, darkness covers the earth,
      and thick clouds cover the peoples;
   But upon you the LORD shines,
      and over you appears his glory.
3 * Nations shall walk by your light,
      and kings by your shining radiance.
4 * Raise your eyes and look about;
      they all gather and come to you:
   Your sons come from afar,
      and your daughters in the arms of their
        nurses.

5 Then you shall be radiant at what you see,
      your heart shall throb and overflow,
   For the riches of the sea shall be emptied out
        before you,
      the wealth of nations shall be brought
        to you.
6 Caravans of camels shall fill you,
      dromedaries from Midian and Ephah;
   All from Sheba shall come
      bearing gold and frankincense,
      and proclaiming the praises of the LORD.
7 All the flocks of Kedar shall be gathered
        for you,
      the rams of Nebaioth shall be
        your sacrifices;
   They will be acceptable offerings on my altar,
      and I will enhance the splendor of
        my house.

8† What are these that fly along like clouds,
      like doves to their cotes?
9 All the vessels of the sea are assembled,
      with the ships of Tarshish in the lead,
   To bring your children from afar
      with their silver and gold,
   In the name of the LORD, your God,
      the Holy One of Israel, who has
        glorified you.

60, 1–6: The Church makes use of these verses for the first reading of the Mass on the feast of Epiphany, for she sees in them symbols of her universality.
  60, 8f: *Like clouds, like doves:* the white sails of the ships of Tarshish; cf note on Ps 48, 8.

59, 11: Is 38, 14.
59, 17: Wis 5, 17ff; Eph 6, 14;
  1 Thes 5, 8.
59, 20: Rom 11, 26f.
60, 3: Is 42, 6; 45, 14; 49, 6.
60, 4: Is 49, 18.

IS

10 Foreigners shall rebuild your walls,
    and their kings shall be your attendants;
  Though I struck you in my wrath,
    yet in my good will I have shown
      you mercy.
11* Your gates shall stand open constantly;
    day and night they shall not be closed
  But shall admit to you the wealth of nations,
    and their kings, in the vanguard.
12 For the people or kingdom shall perish
    that does not serve you;
  those nations shall be utterly destroyed.
13*†The glory of Lebanon shall come to you:
    the cypress, the plane and the pine,
  To bring beauty to my sanctuary,
    and glory to the place where I set my feet.
14 The children of your oppressors shall come,
    bowing low before you;
  All those who despised you
    shall fall prostrate at your feet.
  They shall call you "City of the LORD,"
    "Zion of the Holy One of Israel."

15* Once you were forsaken,
    hated and unvisited,
  Now I will make you the pride of the ages,
    a joy to generation after generation.
16 You shall suck the milk of nations,
    and be nursed at royal breasts;
  You shall know that I, the LORD, am
    your savior,
    your redeemer, the mighty one of Jacob.
17 In place of bronze I will bring gold,
    instead of iron, silver;
  In place of wood, bronze,
    instead of stones, iron;
  I will appoint peace your governor,
    and justice your ruler.
18 No longer shall violence be heard of in
    your land,
    or plunder and ruin within
    your boundaries.
  You shall call your walls "Salvation"
    and your gates "Praise."
19* No longer shall the sun
    be your light by day,
  Nor the brightness of the moon
    shine upon you at night;
  The LORD shall be your light forever,
    your God shall be your glory.
20 No longer shall your sun go down,

or your moon withdraw,
  For the LORD will be your light forever,
    and the days of your mourning shall be at
      an end.
21 Your people shall all be just,
    they shall always possess the land,
  They, the bud of my planting,
    my handiwork to show my glory.
22* The smallest shall become a thousand,
    the youngest, a mighty nation;
  I, the LORD, will swiftly accomplish these things
    when their time comes.

The Mission to the Afflicted

61 1*† The spirit of the Lord GOD is
      upon me,
  because the LORD has anointed me;
  He has sent me to bring glad tidings to
    the lowly,
    to heal the brokenhearted,
  To proclaim liberty to the captives
    and release to the prisoners,
2* To announce a year of favor from the LORD
    and a day of vindication by our God,
    to comfort all who mourn;
3 To place on those who mourn in Zion
    a diadem instead of ashes,
  To give them oil of gladness in place
    of mourning,
    a glorious mantle instead of a listless spirit.
  They will be called oaks of justice,
    planted by the LORD to show his glory.

The Reward of Israel

4* They shall rebuild the ancient ruins,
    the former wastes they shall raise up
  And restore the ruined cities,
    desolate now for generations.
5 Strangers shall stand ready to pasture
    your flocks,
    foreigners shall be your farmers
    and vinedressers.
6 You yourselves shall be named priests of
    the LORD,
    ministers of our God you shall be called.
  You shall eat the wealth of the nations
    and boast of riches from them.
7* Since their shame was double
    and disgrace and spittle were
    their portion,

  60, 13: *Glory of Lebanon:* the cedars, together with the cypress, the plane and the pine, all precious, durable wood.
  61, 1f: This was spoken by the prophet in regard to the restoration of Zion, but quoted by Christ as referring to his mission; cf Lk 4, 18f. *Year of favor . . . day of vindication:* the time of God's salvation.

60, 11: Rv 21, 25.
60, 13: Is 35, 2.
60, 15: Ez 16.
60, 19: Rv 21, 23; 22, 5.
60, 22: Gn 12, 2; 17, 6.
61, 1: Is 42, 1; 48, 16; Lk 4, 18f.
61, 2: Mt 5, 5.
61, 4: Is 58, 12.
61, 7: Is 40, 2.

did you **KNOW?**

Bride and Bridegroom

In ancient Israel, the bride and bridegroom gradually became a metaphor, or symbol, for the relation between Israel and God as pictured in Is 61, 10 and 62, 5. In these passages, Israel is the bride, and God is the faithful bridegroom, who loves her, lavishes her with blessings, and continues to be faithful to her. When Israel strays from the Covenant or goes after foreign gods, she is compared to an unfaithful lover, even a prostitute who pursues other partners (for a graphic example, see Ez 16, 1–43). The prophet Hosea even marries a prostitute as a living example of God's faithfulness (Hos 1, 2)! The wonder of God's love is that through all of Israel's infidelity (and ours), God always remains willing to take her (and us) back.

▶ **Is 61, 10**

They shall have a double inheritance in
    their land,
        everlasting joy shall be theirs.
8* For I, the LORD, love what is right,
        I hate robbery and injustice;
    I will give them their recompense faithfully,
        a lasting covenant I will make with them.
9   Their descendants shall be renowned among
        the nations,
        and their offspring among the peoples;
    All who see them shall acknowledge them
        as a race the LORD has blessed.

10 I rejoice heartily in the LORD,
        in my God is the joy of my soul;
    For he has clothed me with a robe of salvation,
        and wrapped me in a mantle of justice,
    Like a bridegroom adorned with a diadem,
        like a bride bedecked with her jewels.
11 As the earth brings forth its plants,
        and a garden makes its growth spring up,
    So will the Lord GOD make justice and praise
        spring up before all the nations.

Jerusalem the Lord's Bride

62 [1] For Zion's sake I will not be silent,
        for Jerusalem's sake I will not
            be quiet,
    Until her vindication shines forth like
        the dawn
        and her victory like a burning torch.

2*† Nations shall behold your vindication,
        and all kings your glory;
    You shall be called by a new name
        pronounced by the mouth of the LORD.
3   You shall be a glorious crown in the hand of
        the LORD,
        a royal diadem held by your God.
4* No more shall men call you "Forsaken,"
        or your land "Desolate,"
    But you shall be called "My Delight,"
        and your land "Espoused."
    For the LORD delights in you,
        and makes your land his spouse.
5   As a young man marries a virgin,
        your Builder shall marry you;
    And as a bridegroom rejoices in his bride
        so shall your God rejoice in you.

Restoration of Zion

6† Upon your walls, O Jerusalem,
        I have stationed watchmen;
    Never, by day or by night,
        shall they be silent.
    O you who are to remind the LORD,
        take no rest
7   And give no rest to him,
        until he re-establishes Jerusalem
    And makes of it
        the pride of the earth.

8* The LORD has sworn by his right hand
        and by his mighty arm:
    No more will I give your grain
        as food to your enemies;
    Nor shall foreigners drink your wine,
        for which you toiled.
9* But you who harvest the grain shall
        eat it,
        and you shall praise the LORD;
    You who gather the grapes shall drink
        the wine
        in the courts of my sanctuary.

---

† **62, 2:** *New name:* figurative expression for a new state of happiness; cf Rv 2, 17; 3, 12.
   62, 6f: *Remind the LORD . . . give no rest to him:* figuratively, as though to make certain that the Lord will remember his pledge to Jerusalem. Cf Lk 11, 7f.

61, 8: Is 55, 3; 59, 21.   **62, 8:** Is 52, 10.
62, 2: Rv 2, 17; 3, 12.   **62, 9:** Dt 12, 17f; 14, 23.
62, 4: Is 49, 15f; 54, 1ff.

10*† Pass through, pass through the gates,
    prepare the way for the people;
Build up, build up the highway,
    clear it of stones,
    raise up a standard over the nations.

11* See, the LORD proclaims
    to the ends of the earth:
Say to daughter Zion,
    your savior comes!
Here is his reward with him,
    his recompense before him.

12* They shall be called the holy people,
    the redeemed of the LORD,
And you shall be called "Frequented,"
    a city that is not forsaken.

Punishment of Edom†

63 ¹ Who is this that comes from Edom,
    in crimsoned garments, from
      Bozrah—
This one arrayed in majesty,
    marching in the greatness of
      his strength?
"It is I, I who announce vindication,
    I who am mighty to save."

2* Why is your apparel red,
    and your garments like those of the
      wine presser?

3 "The wine press I have trodden alone,
    and of my people there was no one
      with me.
I trod them in my anger,
    and trampled them down in
      my wrath;
Their blood spurted on my garments;
    all my apparel I stained.

4* For the day of vengeance was in my heart,
    my year for redeeming was at hand.

5* I looked about, but there was no one
      to help,
I was appalled that there was no one to
    lend support;
So my own arm brought about the victory
    and my own wrath lent me its support.

6 I trampled down the peoples in
      my anger,
I crushed them in my wrath,
    and I let their blood run out upon
      the ground."

Prayer for the Return of God's Favor†

7* The favors of the LORD I will recall,
    the glorious deeds of the LORD,
Because of all he has done for us;
    for he is good to the house of Israel,
He has favored us according to his mercy
    and his great kindness.

8 He said: They are indeed my people,
    children who are not disloyal;
So he became their savior
9*   in their every affliction.
It was not a messenger or an angel,
    but he himself who saved them.
Because of his love and pity
    he redeemed them himself,
Lifting them and carrying them
    all the days of old.

10 But they rebelled, and grieved
    his holy spirit;
So he turned on them like an enemy,
    and fought against them.

11 Then they remembered the days of old
    and Moses, his servant;
Where is he who brought up out of the sea
    the shepherd of his flock?
Where is he who put his holy spirit
    in their midst;

12 Whose glorious arm
    was the guide at Moses' right;
Who divided the waters before them,
    winning for himself eternal renown;

13 Who led them without stumbling through
    the depths
    like horses in the open country,

14 Like cattle going down into the plain,
    the spirit of the LORD guiding them?
Thus you led your people,
    bringing glory to your name.

15* Look down from heaven and regard us
    from your holy and glorious palace!
Where is your zealous care and
    your might,
    your surge of pity and your mercy?
O Lord, hold not back,
16   for you are our father.
Were Abraham not to know us,
    nor Israel to acknowledge us,

62, 10: The command is given to the workmen to begin the reconstruction of the city.

63, 1–6: In a dramatic dialogue between God and the prophet, the Lord is portrayed as the sole avenger of justice against his enemies.

63, 7—64, 11: A prayer probably composed toward the end of the exile, in which the prophet, after recalling God's blessings on Israel in its past history (63, 7–10), especially at the exodus (11–14),

begs the Lord to come once more to the aid of his people (63, 15—64, 3), who now humbly confess their sins (4–11).

62, 10: Is 58, 14.
62, 11: Is 40, 10.
62, 12: Is 62, 4.
63, 2: Rv 19, 13.
63, 4: Is 34, 8; 61, 2.

63, 5: Is 59, 16.
63, 7: Is 26, 15.
63, 9: Dt 4, 37f.
63, 15: Dt 26, 15; Bar 2, 16.

The Master Potter

Have you ever seen a potter at work? Perhaps you have even made a pot yourself. Pot making is still practiced today much as it was at the time of Third Isaiah: The potter takes a lump of moist clay and begins to shape it by hand, with an image in mind of what the finished product will look like. The artisan then puts the piece of clay on a potter's wheel and spins the wheel, continuing to form the pot with his or her hands. Because it is designed by hand, rather than mass-produced by machine, each work of the potter is original; there is no other just like it.

The image of God as a potter and each of us as a clay pot reminds us of the second Creation story, where God scoops up clay from the earth and forms the first human being and breathes life into the being (Gn 2, 7). It also reminds us of Psalm 139's description of our being knit together in our mother's womb.

The idea of God's hands shaping us like clay is intimate and comforting. No one but the potter knows how much time and love went into the fashioning of a particular pot. The potter gives each pot its own special design and markings. The potter also knows its flaws. The potter and the pot share a bond that seems much like the one between each of us and God. Isaiah 64, 7 indeed gives us a vivid and beautiful image for God's relationship with each of us (see also Jer 18, 1–6).

In your prayer, reflect or journal on the following questions:

- How has God molded you as a unique person?
- What are your special features and markings (gifts), and what are your flaws (weaknesses)?
- How is God still molding you?

▶ Is 64, 7

You, LORD, are our father,
　　our redeemer you are named forever.
17　Why do you let us wander, O LORD, from
　　　　your ways,
　　and harden our hearts so that we fear
　　　　you not?
Return for the sake of your servants,
　　the tribes of your heritage.
18　Why have the wicked invaded your holy place,
　　why have our enemies trampled
　　　　your sanctuary?
19　Too long have we been like those you do
　　　　not rule,
　　who do not bear your name.

Oh, that you would rend the heavens and
　　come down,
　　with the mountains quaking before you,

64 ¹ As when brushwood is set ablaze,
　　　　or fire makes the water boil!
Thus your name would be made known to
　　　　your enemies
　　and the nations would tremble before you,
2　While you wrought awesome deeds we could
　　　　not hope for,
3*　such as they had not heard of from of old.
No ear has ever heard, no eye ever seen,
　　any God but you
　　doing such deeds for those who wait
　　　　for him.
4　Would that you might meet us doing right,
　　that we were mindful of you in our ways!
Behold, you are angry, and we are sinful;
5　all of us have become like unclean men,
　　all our good deeds are like polluted rags;
We have all withered like leaves,
　　and our guilt carries us away like the wind.
6　There is none who calls upon your name,
　　who rouses himself to cling to you;
For you have hidden your face from us
　　and have delivered us up to our guilt.
7　Yet, O LORD, you are our father;
　　we are the clay and you the potter:
　　we are all the work of your hands.
8　Be not so very angry, LORD,
　　keep not our guilt forever in mind;
　　look upon us, who are all your people.
9*　Your holy cities have become a desert,
　　Zion is a desert, Jerusalem a waste.
10　Our holy and glorious temple
　　in which our fathers praised you
Has been burned with fire;
　　all that was dear to us is laid waste.

11 Can you hold back, O LORD, after all this?
     Can you remain silent, and afflict us
        so severely?

Necessity of Punishment

65 1* I was ready to respond to those who
            asked me not,
        to be found by those who sought me not.
     I said: Here I am! Here I am!
        To a nation that did not call upon my name.
2* I have stretched out my hands all the day
        to a rebellious people,
     Who walk in evil paths
        and follow their own thoughts,
3 People who provoke me
        continually, to my face,
     Offering sacrifices in the groves
        and burning incense on bricks,
4 Living among the graves
        and spending the night in caverns,
     Eating swine's flesh,
        with carrion broth in their dishes,
5† Crying out, "Hold back,
        do not touch me; I am too sacred for you!"

     These things enkindle my wrath,
        a fire that burns all the day.
6 Lo, before me it stands written;
        I will not be quiet until I have
           paid in full
7 Your crimes and the crimes of your fathers
        as well,
     says the LORD.
     Since they burned incense on
        the mountains,
        and disgraced me on the hills,
     I will at once pour out in full measure
        their recompense into their laps.

Fate of the Good and the Bad in Israel

8   Thus says the LORD:
     When the juice is pressed from grapes,
        men say, "Do not discard them,
        for there is still good in them";
     Thus will I do with my servants:
        I will not discard them all;
9 From Jacob I will save offspring,
        from Judah, those who are to inherit
           my mountains;
     My chosen ones shall inherit the land,
        my servants shall dwell there.
10 Sharon shall be a pasture for the flocks

and the valley of Achor a resting place for
     the cattle
     of my people who have sought me.

11† But you who forsake the LORD,
        forgetting my holy mountain,
     You who spread a table for Fortune
        and fill cups of blended wine for Destiny,
12* You I will destine for the sword;
        you shall all go down in slaughter.
     Since I called and you did not answer,
        I spoke and you did not listen,
     But did what was evil in my sight
        and preferred things which displease me,
13   therefore thus says the Lord GOD:
     Lo, my servants shall eat,
        but you shall go hungry;
     My servants shall drink,
        but you shall be thirsty;
     My servants shall rejoice,
        but you shall be put to shame;
14 My servants shall shout
        for joy of heart,
     But you shall cry out for grief of heart
        and howl for anguish of spirit.
15 The Lord GOD shall slay you,
        and the name you leave
     Shall be used by my chosen ones for cursing;
        but my servants shall be called by
           another name
16 By which he will be blessed
        on whom a blessing is invoked in the land;
     He who takes an oath in the land
        shall swear by the God of truth;
     For the hardships of the past shall be forgotten,
        and hidden from my eyes.

The World Renewed

17* Lo, I am about to create new heavens
        and a new earth;
     The things of the past shall not be remembered
        or come to mind.
18 Instead, there shall always be rejoicing
        and happiness
        in what I create;
     For I create Jerusalem to be a joy
        and its people to be a delight;
19 I will rejoice in Jerusalem
        and exult in my people.
     No longer shall the sound of weeping be
        heard there,

65, 5: *I am too sacred for you:* the uncleanness of pork, obvious to a Semite, is what these people claim has made them sacred! The prophet ridicules them. Some translate: "I will render you sacred," and understand this as referring to the concept of sacredness as something contagious.

65, 11f: *Destiny:* the Hebrew also has a play on the words: Destiny and *destine; meni* and *manithi.*

65, 1: Rom 10, 20.   65, 12: Is 66, 4; Prv 1, 24; Jer
65, 2: Rom 10, 21.   7, 13.
                                           65, 17: Is 66, 22; Rv 21, 1.

or the sound of crying;

20 No longer shall there be in it
an infant who lives but a few days,
or an old man who does not round out his
full lifetime;
He dies a mere youth who reaches but a
hundred years,
and he who fails of a hundred shall be
thought accursed.

21 They shall live in the houses they build,
and eat the fruit of the vineyards they plant;

22 They shall not build houses for others to
live in,
or plant for others to eat.
As the years of a tree, so the years of my people;
and my chosen ones shall long enjoy
the produce of their hands.

23 They shall not toil in vain,
nor beget children for sudden destruction;
For a race blessed by the LORD
are they and their offspring.

24 Before they call, I will answer;
while they are yet speaking, I will hearken
to them.

25 *†The wolf and the lamb shall graze alike,
and the lion shall eat hay like the ox
[but the serpent's food shall be dust].
None shall hurt or destroy
on all my holy mountain, says the LORD.

True and False Worship

66 1* Thus says the LORD:
The heavens are my throne,
the earth is my footstool.
What kind of house can you build for me;
what is to be my resting place?

2 My hand made all these things
when all of them came to be, says
the LORD.
This is the one whom I approve:
the lowly and afflicted man who trembles
at my word.

3* Merely slaughtering an ox is like slaying a man;
sacrificing a lamb, like breaking a
dog's neck;
Bringing a cereal offering, like offering
swine's blood;
burning incense, like paying homage to
an idol.

Since these have chosen their own ways
and taken pleasure in their
own abominations,

4 *†I in turn will choose ruthless treatment
for them
and bring upon them what they fear.

Because, when I called, no one answered,
when I spoke, no one listened;
Because they did what was evil in
my sight,
and chose what gave me displeasure,

5 Hear the word of the LORD,
you who tremble at his word:
Your brethren who, because of my name,
hate and reject you, say,
"Let the LORD show his glory
that we may see your joy";
but they shall be put to shame.

6* A sound of roaring from the city,
a sound from the temple,
The sound of the LORD
repaying his enemies their deserts!

Mother Zion

7 *†Before she comes to labor,
she gives birth;
Before the pains come upon her,
she safely delivers a male child.

8 Who ever heard of such a thing,
or saw the like?
Can a country be brought forth in one day,
or a nation be born in a single moment?
Yet Zion is scarcely in labor
when she gives birth to her children.

9 Shall I bring a mother to the point
of birth,
and yet not let her child be born? says
the LORD;
Or shall I who allow her to conceive,
yet close her womb? says your God.

10 Rejoice with Jerusalem and be glad because
of her,
all you who love her;
Exult, exult with her,
all you who were mourning over her!

11 Oh, that you may suck fully
of the milk of her comfort,
That you may nurse with delight
at her abundant breasts!

---

† **65, 25:** See note on Is 11, 6–9.
66, 4f: Worship which is merely external is as evil as though it were idolatry.
66, 7–9: The absence of labor in Zion's childbearing is a symbol of the joyful begetting of the new people of God.

* **65, 25:** Is 11, 6–9.
66, 1: 2 Sm 7, 4ff; 1 Kgs 8, 27; Acts 7, 49; 17, 24.
66, 3: Lv 11, 7.
66, 4: Prv 1, 24; Is 65, 12; Jer 7, 13.
66, 6: Jl 4, 16; Am 1, 2.
66, 7–9: Is 49, 18–21; 54, 1.

12 For thus says the LORD:
Lo, I will spread prosperity over her like a river,
and the wealth of the nations like
an overflowing torrent.
As nurslings, you shall be carried in her arms,
and fondled in her lap;

13 As a mother comforts her son,
so will I comfort you;
in Jerusalem you shall find your comfort.

14 When you see this, your heart
shall rejoice,
and your bodies flourish like the grass;
The LORD'S power shall be known to
his servants,
but to his enemies, his wrath.

15 Lo, the LORD shall come in fire,
his chariots like the whirlwind,
To wreak his wrath with burning heat
and his punishment with fiery flames.

16 For the LORD shall judge all mankind
by fire and sword,
and many shall be slain by the LORD.

17* They who sanctify and purify themselves to go to the groves, as followers of one who stands within, they who eat swine's flesh, loathsome things and mice, shall all perish with their deeds and their thoughts, says the LORD.

Gathering of the Nations

18† I come to gather nations of every language; they shall come and see my glory. 19 I will set a sign among them; from them I will send fugitives to the nations: to Tarshish, Put and Lud, Mosoch, Tubal and Javan, to the distant coastlands that have never heard of my fame, or seen my glory; and they shall proclaim my glory among the nations. 20 They shall bring all your brethren from all the nations as an offering to the LORD, on horses and in chariots, in carts, upon mules and dromedaries, to Jerusalem, my holy mountain, says the LORD, just as the Israelites bring their offering to the house of the LORD in clean vessels. 21 Some of these I will take as priests and Levites, says the LORD.

Lasting Reward and Punishment

22* As the new heavens and the new earth
which I will make
Shall endure before me, says the LORD,
so shall your race and your name endure.

23 From one new moon to another,
and from one sabbath to another,
All mankind shall come to worship
before me, says the LORD.

24*†They shall go out and see the corpses
of the men who rebelled against me;
Their worm shall not die,
nor their fire be extinguished;
and they shall be abhorrent to all mankind.

66, 18–21: God summons the neighboring nations to Zion and from among them will send some to far distant lands to proclaim his glory. *All your brethren:* Jews in exile.
66, 24: God's enemies lie dead outside the walls of the New Jerusalem; just as in the past, corpses, filth and refuse lay in the Val-

ley of Hinnom outside the city, where huge fires were constantly burning; cf Jos 15, 8; 2 Chr 28, 3; Mk 9, 45–48.

66, 17: Lv 11, 29.   66, 24: Mk 9, 45.
66, 22: Is 65, 17; Rv 21, 1.

Imagine you're watching a movie. One of the leading characters imposes severe hardships on others and then goes off to dine in luxury. Immediately, you know the character is a villain. Another leading character calls for others to endure sacrifice and lives under the same conditions as they do. You know this is a hero, because heroes practice what they preach. Jeremiah the prophet was such a hero; he not only preached a hard message but accepted the trials that came with it.

In-depth

At the beginning of Jeremiah's prophetic ministry, King Josiah ruled the southern kingdom of Judah (2 Chronicles, chapters 34–35). He was a good king who expanded Judah's territory and started a religious reform. Jeremiah approved of Josiah and Josiah's reforms, but he was afraid they were too little, too late. Chapters 2–5 of his book contain his prophecies during Josiah's rule. In them, he speaks out against Israel's sin and corruption but hopes that things will improve if the people turn to God (4, 1–2). Unfortunately, King Josiah was suddenly killed in battle, and things went from bad to worse.

Kings Jehoiakim and Zedekiah were the main rulers who followed Josiah, and they were Josiah's complete opposite (2 Chr 36, 5–14). Both were ruthless, power hungry, and corrupt. During Jehoiakim's reign, Jeremiah had to go into hiding out of fear for his life. Chapters 7–20 of Jeremiah's book contain his prophecies during this time, when his preaching against the sins of Israel became stronger. Chapters 21–29 and 34–45 record his life and preaching during Zedekiah's reign—the last few years before the Babylonian Exile. While Zedekiah ruled, Jeremiah was imprisoned, beaten, and thrown into a well to die.

Jeremiah survived his experience in the well to see Jerusalem and the Temple destroyed by the Babylonians. To give the people hope that God was still on their side, he prophesied the destruction of all Israel's enemies, especially Babylon (see chapters 46–51).

Ultimately, Jeremiah realized that even a new king like David would not be enough to correct what was wrong. The people were unable to fulfill God's commandments because they had hearts of stone. In chapters 30–33, the Book of Consolation, Jeremiah said that the Lord would make a new Covenant with Israel in the future, and this time, the Law would be written on the people's hearts (31, 31–34).

At a Glance

I. Oracles in the Days of Josiah (1, 1—6, 30).

II. Oracles Mostly in the Days of Jehoiakim (7, 1—20, 18).

III. Oracles in the Last Years of Jerusalem (21, 1—33, 26).

IV. Fall of Jerusalem (34, 1—45, 5).

V. Oracles against the Nations (46, 1—51, 64).

VI. Historical Appendix (52, 1–34).

Quick Facts

Period Covered
626–583 B.C.

Authors
Jeremiah and his disciples, including Baruch

Themes
Israel's need for repentance, Jeremiah's struggles, the New Covenant

The Book of Jeremiah

963

Jeremiah

Before I formed you in the womb I knew you

I: Oracles in the Days of Josiah

1 ¹† The words of Jeremiah, son of Hilkiah, of a priestly family in Anathoth, in the land of Benjamin. ²* The word of the LORD first came to him in the days of Josiah, son of Amon, king of Judah, in the thirteenth year of his reign, ³*† and continued through the reign of Jehoiakim, son of Josiah, king of Judah, and until the downfall and exile of Jerusalem in the fifth month of the eleventh year of Zedekiah, son of Josiah, king of Judah.

Call of Jeremiah

4   The word of the LORD came to me thus:

⁵*†Before I formed you in the womb I knew you,
    before you were born I dedicated you,
    a prophet to the nations I appointed you.
⁶† "Ah, Lord GOD!" I said,
    "I know not how to speak; I am
        too young."

7   But the LORD answered me,

Say not, "I am too young."
    To whomever I send you, you shall go;
    whatever I command you, you shall speak.
8   Have no fear before them,
    because I am with you to deliver you, says
        the LORD.

⁹* Then the LORD extended his hand and touched my mouth, saying,

See, I place my words in your mouth!
10   This day I set you
        over nations and over kingdoms,
    To root up and to tear down,
        to destroy and to demolish,
    to build and to plant.

¹¹† The word of the LORD came to me with the question: What do you see, Jeremiah? "I see a

---

1, 1: *Anathoth:* a village about three miles northeast of Jerusalem, where Solomon exiled Abiathar (1 Kgs 2, 26f); it is probable that Jeremiah belonged to the priestly family of Abiathar.

1, 3: *Until the downfall:* these words were originally prefixed as a title to a collection of Jeremiah's prophecies which lacked chapters 40–44. The new title in Jer 40, 1 and the oracles that follow clearly show that Jeremiah continued to prophesy after the destruction of Jerusalem in 587 B.C.

1, 5: Jeremiah was destined to the office of prophet before his birth; cf Is 49, 1.5; Lk 1, 15; Gal 1, 15f. *I knew you:* I loved you and chose you. *I dedicated you:* I set you apart to be a prophet. Some Fathers and later theologians understand this to mean that Jeremiah was freed from original sin before his birth. The context does not

justify this conclusion. *The nations:* the pagan neighbors of Judah, besides the great world powers—Assyria, Babylonia, Egypt—intimately associated with Judah's destiny.

1, 6: *I am too young:* Jeremiah's youth (he was less than thirty years old) must not be an obstacle to the responsibilities of the prophetic office; God will supply for his human defects (cf vv 7f).

1, 11: *The watching-tree:* the almond tree, which is the first to blossom in the springtime as though it had not slept. The Hebrew name contains a play on words with "I am watching."

1, 2: Jer 25, 3.   **1, 5:** Jer 49, 1; Gal 1, 15f.
1, 3: Jer 25, 1.   **1, 9:** Is 6, 7.

You Are Not Too Young!

Jeremiah was a young man when God tapped him on the shoulder. In response to God, Jeremiah said, "I know not how to speak; I am too young" (verse 6). But God gave Jeremiah the words and the ability to become a hero.

When you need to do something difficult but for the good of others, remember God's response to Jeremiah: "Say not, 'I am too young' " (verse 7). God wants you to know that you too are capable of bringing about positive change in the world. God knows what you are able to do and say and be. Listen to God.

▶ Jer 1, 4–10

branch of the watching-tree," I replied. ¹² Then the LORD said to me: Well have you seen, for I am watching to fulfill my word. ¹³*† A second time the word of the LORD came to me with the question: What do you see? "I see a boiling cauldron," I replied, "that appears from the north."

¹⁴* And from the north, said the LORD to me, evil will boil over upon all who dwell in the land.

¹⁵* Lo, I am summoning
   all the kingdoms of the north, says
      the LORD;
Each king shall come and set up his throne
   at the gateways of Jerusalem,
Opposite her walls all around
   and opposite all the cities of Judah.
¹⁶* I will pronounce my sentence
      against them
   for all their wickedness in forsaking me,
And in burning incense to strange gods
   and adoring their own handiwork.

¹⁷ But do you gird your loins;
   stand up and tell them
   all that I command you.
Be not crushed on their account,
   as though I would leave you crushed
      before them;
¹⁸* For it is I this day
   who have made you a fortified city,
A pillar of iron, a wall of brass,
   against the whole land:
Against Judah's kings and princes,
   against its priests and people.

¹⁹ They will fight against you, but not prevail
      over you,
   for I am with you to deliver you, says
      the LORD.

Infidelity of Israel

2 ¹† This word of the LORD came to me: ²*† Go, cry out this message for Jerusalem to hear!

I remember the devotion of your youth,
   how you loved me as a bride,
Following me in the desert,
   in a land unsown.
³*†Sacred to the LORD was Israel,
   the first fruits of his harvest;
Should anyone presume to partake
      of them,
   evil would befall him, says the LORD.

⁴ Listen to the word of the LORD, O house
      of Jacob!
All you clans of the house of Israel,
⁵* thus says the LORD:
What fault did your fathers find in me
   that they withdrew from me,
Went after empty idols,
   and became empty themselves?
⁶* They did not ask, "Where is the LORD
   who brought us up from the land of Egypt,
Who led us through the desert,
   through a land of wastes and gullies,
Through a land of drought and darkness,
   through a land which no one crosses,
   where no man dwells?"

1, 13: *Boiling cauldron . . . the north:* symbol of an invasion from the north; cf vv 14f.
2, 1–3, 5: These verses probably contain the earliest of Jeremiah's preachings. The covenant relationship, symbolized by the figure of a marriage, was frequently broken by Israel, seen here as an unfaithful wife unworthy of reconciliation with God (Jer 3, 1–5).
2, 2: *Devotion:* Israel's gratitude, fidelity, and love for God.
2, 3: *First fruits:* an offering to God which became his exclusive

property, and could therefore not be put to profane use; cf Lv 22, 1.

1, 13: Ez 11, 3.7; 24, 3.
1, 14: Jer 4, 6; 6, 1.
1, 15: Jer 6, 22.
1, 16: Is 2, 8.
1, 18: Jer 6, 27; 15, 20; Ex
   3, 8.

2, 2: Dt 2, 7; 32, 9–12; Mi
   6, 4.
2, 3: Jer 12, 14; Ex 4, 22; Dt
   7, 6; 14, 2.
2, 5: Is 5, 4; Mi 6, 3.
2, 6: Ex 20, 2f; Dt 8, 14; Is
   63, 11ff.

7* When I brought you into the garden land
   to eat its goodly fruits,
You entered and defiled my land,
   you made my heritage loathsome.
8*†The priests asked not,
   "Where is the LORD?"
Those who dealt with the law knew me not:
   the shepherds rebelled against me.
The prophets prophesied by Baal,
   and went after useless idols.
9* Therefore will I yet accuse you, says the LORD,
   and even your children's children I
      will accuse.
10† Pass over to the coast of the Kittim and see,
   send to Kedar and carefully inquire:
   Where has the like of this been done?
11 * Does any other nation change its gods?—
   yet they are not gods at all!
But my people have changed their glory
for useless things.
12 Be amazed at this, O heavens,
   and shudder with sheer horror, says
      the LORD.
13* Two evils have my people done:
   they have forsaken me, the source of
      living waters;
They have dug themselves cisterns,
   broken cisterns, that hold no water.
14† Is Israel a slave, a bondman by birth?
   Why then has he become booty?
15* Against him lions roar
   full-throated cries.
They have made his land a waste;
   his cities are charred ruins,
      without inhabitant.
16† Yes, the people of Memphis and Tahpanhes
   shave the crown of your head.

Introducing ►JEREMIAH

Have you ever felt ridiculed for defending your values or doing a good deed? If so, then you can probably relate to Jeremiah, who once told God:

   You duped me, O LORD,
      and I let myself be duped;

   . . . .

   All the day I am an object of laughter;
      everyone mocks me.

                    (Jer 20, 7)

Jeremiah knew what it was like to be rejected for delivering God's message.
   Jeremiah was born in 645 B.C. of a priestly family from a northern Israelite tribe. He was very young when he began his prophetic career. Like Isaiah, Jeremiah was a prophet for all seasons. He was both optimistic (chapter 31) and condemning (22, 18–23). He was courageous (chapter 37), enduring beatings, imprisonment, and even being thrown into a well to die (38, 1–6) for the sake of delivering God's message. He loved his people so much that he was sometimes called the weeping prophet because of his bitter tears for them and their fast-approaching doom (8, 23; 13, 7).
   The Book of Jeremiah gives us a fascinating inside look at the prophet's relationship with God. Several passages, called the Confessions of Jeremiah, are personal accounts of his struggles with God (12, 1–6; 15, 10–21; 17, 12–18; 18, 18–23; 20, 7–18). If you take the time to read these passages, you may find that your own doubts and struggles aren't all that different.

2, 8: *Those who dealt with the law:* the priests. *The shepherds:* the kings and nobles.
2, 10: *Kittim:* a Phoenician colony in Cyprus. *Kedar:* a nomad tribe of the Syrian desert. These two names represent West and East.
2, 14: *Bondman by birth:* a perpetual slave, different from the debt-slave, who was to be freed after six years; cf Ex 21, 2.
2, 16: *Memphis:* the capital of Lower Egypt. *Tahpanhes:* a fron-tier city of Egypt, east of the Delta. *Shave the crown of your head:* the spoliation of Judah at the hands of the Egyptians.

2, 7: Lv 18, 24f; Dt 8, 7–10;   2, 11: Jer 16, 20; Ps 106, 20.
      32, 13f.   2, 13: Jer 17, 13; Ps 36, 9;
2, 8: Jer 8, 8ff; 23, 1.13.   Is 1, 4.
2, 9: Ex 20, 5.   2, 15: Jer 9, 11.

17* Has not the forsaking of the LORD, your God,
     done this to you?
18† And now, why go to Egypt,
     to drink the waters of the Nile?
   Why go to Assyria,
     to drink the waters of the Euphrates?
19* Your own wickedness chastises you,
     your own infidelities punish you.
   Know then, and see, how evil and bitter
     is your forsaking the LORD, your God,
   And showing no fear of me,
     says the Lord, the GOD of hosts.

20*†Long ago you broke your yoke,
     you tore off your bonds.
   "I will not serve," you said.
   On every high hill, under every green tree,
     you gave yourself to harlotry.
21* I had planted you, a choice vine
     of fully tested stock;
   How could you turn out obnoxious to me,
     a spurious vine?
22* Though you scour it with soap,

   and use much lye,
   The stain of your guilt is still before me,
     says the Lord GOD.
23† How can you say, "I am not defiled,
     I have not gone after the Baals"?
   Consider your conduct in the Valley,
     recall what you have done:
   A frenzied she-camel, coursing near and far,
24   breaking away toward the desert,
   Snuffing the wind in her ardor—
     who can restrain her lust?
   No beasts need tire themselves seeking her;
     in her month they will meet her.

25* Stop wearing out your shoes
     and parching your throat!
   But you say, "No use! no!
   I love these strangers,
     and after them I must go."
26* As the thief is shamed when caught,
     so shall the house of Israel be shamed:
   They, their kings and their princes,
     their priests and their prophets;

HISPANICS ASSUME THEIR MISSION AS PROPHETS!

Jeremiah and many of the other Old Testament prophets call for solidarity with the poor and oppressed. During the Third Encuentro Nacional Hispano de Pastoral, in 1985, Hispanics assumed their mission as prophets in contemporary society. They expressed their solidarity with the social groups in need of liberation and their desire to live and promote justice. The following statements are from the Encuentro:

- We, as Hispanic people, make a preferential option for and in solidarity with the poor and marginalized.
- We, as Hispanic people, make a preferential option for Hispanic youth so that they will participate at all levels of pastoral ministry.
- We, as Hispanic people, want to follow the line of a Church that promotes and exemplifies justice.
- We, as Hispanic people, wish to follow an approach of valuing and promoting women, recognizing their equality and dignity and their role in the Church, the family, and society.

(Secretariat for Hispanic Affairs, *Prophetic Voices*, p. 6)

---

† **2, 18:** Egypt and Assyria were the protecting foreign powers favored by rival parties within Judah. The desire for such foreign alliances is a further desertion of the Lord, the source of living waters (v 13), in favor of the above-named powers, symbolized by the Nile and the Euphrates rivers.

2, 20: *Harlotry:* idolatry (because Israel is the bride of God).

2, 23: *The Valley:* of Ben-hinnom, south of Jerusalem, site of the

infamous sanctuary of Topheth where children were sacrificed to Molech; cf Jer 7, 31.

2, 17: Jer 4, 18; 30, 15.
2, 19: Prv 5, 22; Hos 5, 5.
2, 20: Jer 3, 6.13; Jgs 10, 6.
2, 21: Ex 15, 17; Ps 80, 9; Is 5, 4.
2, 22: Jb 9, 30.
2, 25: Jer 18, 12.
2, 26: Jer 48, 27; Rom 6, 21.

27 They who say to a piece of wood, "You are
  my father,"
 and to a stone, "You gave me birth."
 They turn to me their backs, not their faces;
  yet, in their time of trouble they cry out,
  "Rise up and save us!"
28* Where are the gods you made for yourselves?
  Let them rise up!
 Will they save you in your time of trouble?
 For as numerous as your cities
  are your gods, O Judah!
 And as many as the streets of Jerusalem
  are the altars you have set up for Baal.

29 How dare you still plead with me?
  You have all rebelled against me, says
   the LORD.
30* In vain I struck your children;
  the correction they did not take.
 Your sword devoured your prophets
  like a ravening lion.
31 You, of this generation,
  take note of the word of the Lord:
 Have I been a desert to Israel,
  a land of darkness?
 Why do my people say, "We have moved on,
  we will come to you no more"?
32* Does a virgin forget her jewelry,
  a bride her sash?
 Yet my people have forgotten me
  days without number.

33 How well you pick your way
  when seeking love!
 You who, in your wickedness,
  have gone by ways unclean!
34 You, on whose clothing there is
  the life-blood of the innocent,
  whom you found committing no burglary;
35 Yet withal you say, "I am innocent;
  at least, his anger is turned away from me."
 Behold, I will judge you
  on that word of yours, "I have not sinned."
36* How very base you have become
  in changing your course!
 By Egypt will you be shamed,
  as you were shamed by Assyria.
37* From there also shall you go away
  with hands upon your head;
 For the LORD has rejected those in whom
   you trust,
  with them you will have no success.

3

1*† If a man sends away his wife
  and, after leaving him,
  she marries another man,
 Does the first husband come back to her?
  Would not the land be wholly defiled?
 But you have sinned with many lovers,
  and yet you would return to me! says
   the LORD.

2*†Lift your eyes to the heights, and see,
  where have men not lain with you?
 By the waysides you waited for them
  like an Arab in the desert.
 You defiled the land
  by your wicked harlotry.
3* Therefore the showers were withheld,
  the spring rain failed.
 But because you have a harlot's brow,
  you refused to blush.

4 Even now do you not call me,
  "My father,
  you who are the bridegroom of
   my youth"?
5 "Will he keep his wrath forever,
  will he hold his grudge to the end?"
 This is what you say; yet you do
  all the evil you can.

Judah and Israel

6* The LORD said to me in the days of King
Josiah: See now what rebellious Israel has done!
She has gone up every high mountain, and under
every green tree she has played the harlot. 7 And I
thought, after she has done all this she will return
to me. But she did not return. Then, even though
her traitor sister Judah saw 8* that for all the adulteries rebellious Israel had committed, I put her
away and gave her a bill of divorce, nevertheless
her traitor sister Judah was not frightened; she too
went off and played the harlot. 9* Eager to sin, she
polluted the land, committing adultery with stone
and wood. 10 With all this, the traitor sister Judah
did not return to me wholeheartedly, but insin-
cerely, says the LORD.

Restoration of Israel

11* Then the LORD said to me: Rebel Israel is
inwardly more just than traitorous Judah. 12* Go,
proclaim these words toward the north, and say:

3, 1: Such remarriage of divorced spouses was forbidden by Dt
24, 1–4. Under this figure the prophet sees the presumption of Judah,
the unfaithful spouse, who thinks she can return to the Lord after
uniting herself to other gods.
 3, 2: *An Arab:* a marauding nomad who lay in wait for caravans.

2, 28: Jer 11, 13; Dt 32, 38;
  Jgs 10, 14.
2, 30: Jer 5, 3; Neh 9, 26.
2, 32: Jer 13, 25; Dt 32, 18.
2, 36: 2 Chr 28, 16–21.
2, 37: 2 Sm 13, 19.
3, 1: Dt 24, 1–4.
3, 2: Ex 16, 24f.

3, 3: Jer 6, 15; 8, 12.
3, 6: Jer 2, 20; Dt 12, 2.
3, 8: 2 Kgs 17, 6.18–23; Ez
  23, 11.
3, 9: Jer 2, 27.
3, 11: Ez 16, 51; 23, 11.
3, 12: Dt 4, 29ff.

Return, rebel Israel, says the LORD,
   I will not remain angry with you;
For I am merciful, says the LORD,
   I will not continue my wrath forever.
13* Only know your guilt:
   how you rebelled against the LORD,
     your God,
How you ran hither and yon to strangers
   [under every green tree]
   and would not listen to my voice, says
     the LORD.
14*† Return, rebellious children, says the LORD,
   for I am your Master;
I will take you, one from a city, two from
   a clan,
   and bring you to Zion.
15* I will appoint over you shepherds after my
   own heart,
   who will shepherd you wisely and prudently.
16 When you multiply and become fruitful in
   the land,
   says the LORD,
They will in those days no longer say,
   "The ark of the covenant of the LORD!"
They will no longer think of it, or remember it,
   or miss it, or make another.

17* At that time they will call Jerusalem the LORD's throne; there all nations will be gathered together to honor the name of the LORD at Jerusalem, and they will walk no longer in their hardhearted wickedness. 18* In those days the house of Judah will join the house of Israel; together they will come from the land of the north to the land which I gave to your fathers as a heritage.

Conditions for Forgiveness

19* I had thought:
   How I should like to treat you as sons,
And give you a pleasant land,
   a heritage most beautiful among
     the nations!
You would call me, "My Father," I thought,
   and never cease following me.
20* But like a woman faithless to her lover,
   even so have you been faithless to me,
   O house of Israel, says the LORD.
21 A cry is heard on the heights!
   the plaintive weeping of Israel's children,
Because they have perverted their ways
   and forgotten the LORD, their God.

22* Return, rebellious children,
   and I will cure you of your rebelling.
"Here we are, we now come to you
   because you are the LORD, our God.
23* Deceptive indeed are the hills,
   the thronging mountains;
In the LORD, our God, alone
   is the salvation of Israel.
24† The shame-god has devoured
   our fathers' toil from our youth,
Their sheep and their cattle,
   their sons and their daughters.

Catholic Connections

CONTRITION

Jeremiah calls the people to acknowledge their sin and return to God. In Catholic Tradition, the word contrition describes sorrow for sins and the commitment not to sin again. Jeremiah is calling the people to contrition with the promise that God wants their return and is eager to welcome them back.

An act of contrition is a prayer in which you express your sorrow and hate for your sin and your resolve not to sin again. You may have learned an act of contrition to prepare to celebrate the sacrament of Reconciliation (or Penance). You can use this prayer form any time you need to acknowledge a sin and ask God's forgiveness.

Try writing your own act of contrition. Use it whenever sin has separated you from God—knowing that God is merciful and wants nothing to separate you from God's love.

▸ Jer 3, 12–14

3, 14–18: A remnant of Israel (14) will reunite with Judah (18). The elementary cult of the Lord represented by the ark of the covenant will now be replaced by a more deeply spiritual and universal alliance, symbolized by his throne in the ideal Jerusalem around which all nations will be gathered together (17).
3, 24: *Shame-god:* literally, shame, a term commonly substituted for Baal, the Canaanite god with many local shrines.

3, 13: Jer 2, 20.25; Lv 26, 40.
3, 14: Jer 23, 3; Is 10, 21f.
3, 15: Ez 34, 23; Jn 21, 15.
3, 17: Is 2, 2.
3, 18: Jer 30, 3; 31, 8.
3, 19: Jer 31, 9.20; Is 63, 16.
3, 20: Jer 5, 11.
3, 22: Hos 3, 5.
3, 23: Jer 14, 8.

25* Let us lie down in our shame,
　　　let our disgrace cover us,
　　　for we have sinned against the LORD,
　　　　our God,
　　From our youth to this day, we and our
　　　　fathers also;
　　　we listened not to the voice of the LORD,
　　　　our God."

4
1* If you wish to return, O Israel, says
　　　　the LORD,
　　　return to me.
　　If you put your detestable things out of
　　　　my sight,
　　　and do not stray,
2* †Then you can swear, "As the LORD lives,"
　　　in truth, in judgment, and in justice;
　　Then shall the nations use his name
　　　　in blessing,
　　　and glory in him.

3* For to the men of Judah and to Jerusalem,
thus says the LORD:

　　Till your untilled ground,
　　　sow not among thorns.
4* †For the sake of the LORD, be circumcised,
　　　remove the foreskins of your hearts,
　　　O men of Judah and citizens of Jerusalem;
　　Lest my anger break out like fire,
　　　and burn till none can quench it,
　　　because of your evil deeds.

The Invasion from the North

5　Proclaim it in Judah,
　　　make it heard in Jerusalem;
　　Blow the trumpet through the land,
　　　summon the recruits!
　　Say, "Fall in, let us march
　　　to the fortified cities."
6　Bear the standard to Zion,
　　　seek refuge without delay!
　　Evil I bring from the north,
　　　and great destruction.
7* Up comes the lion from his lair,
　　　the destroyer of nations has set out,
　　　has left his place,
　　To turn your land into desolation,
　　　till your cities lie waste and empty.

8* So gird yourselves with sackcloth,
　　　mourn and wail:
　　"The blazing wrath of the LORD
　　　is not turned away from us."

9　　　In that day, says the LORD,
　　The king will lose heart, and the princes;
　　　the priests will be amazed,
　　　and the prophets stunned.
10* †"Alas! Lord GOD," they will say,
　　　"You only deceived us
　　When you said: Peace shall be yours;
　　　for the sword touches our very soul."
11　At that time it will be said
　　　of this people and of Jerusalem,
　　"From the glaring heights through the desert
　　　a wind comes toward the daughter of
　　　　my people."
　　Not to winnow, not to cleanse,
12*　does this wind from the heights come at
　　　　my bidding;
　　And I myself now pronounce
　　　sentence upon them.

13　See! like storm clouds he advances,
　　　like a hurricane his chariots;
　　Swifter than eagles are his steeds:
　　　"Woe to us! we are ruined."
14　Cleanse your heart of evil, O Jerusalem,
　　　that you may be saved.
　　How long must your pernicious thoughts
　　　lodge within you?
15　Listen! They proclaim it from Dan,
　　　from Mount Ephraim they
　　　　announce destruction:
16* "Make this known to the nations,
　　　announce it to Jerusalem:
　　The besiegers are coming from the
　　　　distant land,
　　　shouting their war cry against the cities
　　　　of Judah."
17* Like watchmen of the fields they
　　　surround her,
　　　for she has rebelled against me, says
　　　　the LORD.
18* Your conduct, your misdeeds, have done this
　　　　to you;
　　　how bitter is this disaster of yours,
　　　how it reaches to your very heart!

4, 2: *As the LORD lives:* this oath, made sincerely, implies Israel's
return to God and loyal adherence to him. Thus the ancient promises are fulfilled; cf Gn 12, 3; 18, 18; 22, 18; 26, 4; Ps 72, 17.
　　4, 4: The mere external rite of circumcision avails nothing unless
accompanied by the removal of blindness and obstinacy of heart;
cf Rom 2, 25.29; 1 Cor 7, 19; Gal 5, 6; 6, 13.15.
　　4, 10: *You only deceived us:* the false prophets blame their deception on God; cf Jer 14, 13–16.

3, 25: Jer 16, 11f; 22, 21.　　　　4, 7: Jer 2, 15; 5, 6.
4, 1: Jer 25, 5.　　　　　　　　　4, 8: Jer 6, 26; Is 5, 25.
4, 2: Jer 12, 16; Dt 10, 20;　　　4, 10: Jer 6, 14.
　Is 65, 16.　　　　　　　　　　4, 12: Jer 1, 16.
4, 3: Hos 10, 12; Mt　　　　　　4, 16: Jer 5, 15.
　13, 7.22.　　　　　　　　　　4, 17: Jer 6, 3.
4, 4: Jer 9, 24.　　　　　　　　4, 18: Jer 2, 17.19.

¹⁹† My breast! my breast! how I suffer!
  The walls of my heart!
My heart beats wildly,
  I cannot be still;
For I have heard the sound of the trumpet,
  the alarm of war.
²⁰* Ruin after ruin is reported;
  the whole earth is laid waste.
In an instant my tents are ravaged;
  in a flash, my shelters.
²¹ How long must I see that signal,
  hear that trumpet sound!

²²* Fools my people are,
  they know me not;
Senseless children they are,
  having no understanding;
They are wise in evil,
  but know not how to do good.
²³* I looked at the earth, and it was waste
    and void;
  at the heavens, and their light had
    gone out!
²⁴ I looked at the mountains, and they
    were trembling,
  and all the hills were crumbling!
²⁵ I looked and behold, there was no man;
  even the birds of the air had flown
    away!
²⁶* I looked and behold, the garden land was
    a desert,
  with all its cities destroyed
before the LORD, before his
    blazing wrath.

²⁷*   For thus says the LORD:
Waste shall the whole land be;
  I will [not] wholly destroy it.
²⁸* Because of this the earth shall mourn,
  the heavens above shall darken;
I have spoken, I will not repent,
  I have resolved, I will not turn back.
²⁹ At the shout of horseman and bowman
  each city takes to flight;
They shrink into the thickets,
  they scale the rocks:
All the cities are abandoned,
  and no one dwells in them.
³⁰ You now who are doomed, what do
    you mean
  by putting on purple,
  bedecking yourself with gold,

Shading your eyes with cosmetics,
  beautifying yourself in vain?
Your lovers spurn you,
  they seek your life.
³¹* Yes, I hear the moaning, as of a woman
    in travail,
  like the anguish of a mother with her
    first child—
The cry of daughter Zion gasping,
  as she stretches forth her hands:
"Ah, woe is me! I sink exhausted
  before the slayers!"

Universal Corruption

5 ¹ Roam the streets of Jerusalem,
    look about and observe,
Search through her public places,
  to find even one
Who lives uprightly
  and seeks to be faithful,
  and I will pardon her!
² Though they say, "As the LORD lives,"
  they swear falsely.
³*   O LORD, do your eyes not look for
    honesty?
You struck them, but they did not cringe;
  you laid them low, but they
    refused correction;
They set their faces harder than stone,
  and refused to return to you.
⁴* It is only the lowly, I thought,
  who are foolish;
For they know not the way of the LORD,
  their duty to their God.
⁵* I will go to the great ones
  and speak with them;
For they know the way of the LORD,
  their duty to their God.
But, one and all, they had broken the yoke,
  torn off the harness.
⁶ Therefore lions from the forest slay them,
  wolves of the desert ravage them,
Leopards keep watch round their cities:
  all who come out are torn to pieces
For their many crimes
  and their numerous rebellions.

⁷ Why should I pardon you these things?
  Your sons have forsaken me,
  they swear by gods that are not.
I fed them, but they committed adultery;
  to the harlot's house they throng.

---

† **4, 19ff:** Probably the prophet's own anguish at the coming destruction of Judah.

4, 20: Jer 10, 20.   **4, 22:** Dt 32, 5f.28.

4, 23: Is 24, 1.3.   4, 31: Jer 6, 24.
4, 26: Lv 26, 31.   5, 3: Jer 2, 30.
4, 27: Jer 5, 18.   5, 4: Jer 8, 7.
4, 28: Is 24, 4.   5, 5: Jer 6, 13.

8* Lustful stallions they are,
    each neighs after another's wife.
9 Shall I not punish them for these things?
    says the LORD;
    On a nation such as this shall I not
        take vengeance?
10* Climb to her terraces, and ravage them,
    destroy them [not] wholly.
    Tear away her tendrils,
    they do not belong to the LORD.
11* For they have openly rebelled against me,
    both the house of Israel and the house
        of Judah,
    says the LORD,
12*†They denied the LORD,
    saying, "Not he—
    No evil shall befall us,
    neither sword nor famine shall we see.
13 The prophets have become wind,
    and the word is not in them.
    May their threats be carried out
        against themselves!"

14 Now, for this that you have said,
    says the LORD, the God of hosts—
    Behold, I make my words
    in your mouth, a fire,
    And this people is the wood
        that it shall devour!—
15* Beware, I will bring against you
    a nation from afar,
    O house of Israel, says the LORD;
    A long-lived nation, an ancient nation,
    a people whose language you know not,
    whose speech you cannot understand.
16 Their quivers are like open graves;
    all of them are warriors.
17* They will devour your harvest and your bread,
    devour your sons and your daughters,
    Devour your sheep and cattle,
    devour your vines and fig trees;
    They will beat flat with the sword
    the fortified city in which you trust.

18* Yet even in those days, says the LORD, I will not
wholly destroy you. 19 And when they ask, "Why
has the LORD done all these things to us?" say to
them, "As you have forsaken me to serve strange
gods in your own land, so shall you serve strangers
in a land not your own."

20 Announce this to the house of Jacob,
    proclaim it in Judah:
21* Pay attention to this,
    foolish and senseless people
    Who have eyes and see not,
    who have ears and hear not.
22* Should you not fear me, says the LORD,
    should you not tremble before me?
    I made the sandy shore the sea's limit,
    which by eternal decree it may not overstep.
    Toss though it may, it is to no avail;
    though its billows roar, they cannot pass.
23 But this people's heart is stubborn
        and rebellious;
    they turn and go away,
24*†And say not in their hearts,
    "Let us fear the LORD, our God,
    Who gives us rain
    early and late, in its time;
    Who watches for us
    over the appointed weeks of harvest."
25* Your crimes have prevented these things,
    your sins have turned back these blessings
        from you.
26* For there are among my people criminals;
    like fowlers they set traps,
    but it is men they catch.
27 Their houses are as full of treachery
    as a bird-cage is of birds;
    Therefore they grow powerful and rich,
28* fat and sleek.
    They go their wicked way;
    justice they do not defend
    By advancing the claim of the fatherless
    or judging the cause of the poor.
29 Shall I not punish these things? says the LORD;
    on a nation such as this shall I not
        take vengeance?
30 A shocking, horrible thing
    has happened in the land:
31* The prophets prophesy falsely,
    and the priests teach as they wish;
    Yet my people will have it so;
    what will you do when the end comes?

The Enemy at the Gates

6 1* Flee, sons of Benjamin,
    out of Jerusalem!
    Blow the trumpet in Tekoa,
    raise a signal over Beth-haccherem;

---

†
    5, 12: *They denied the LORD:* the people act as though God does
not exist and will not interfere.
    5, 24: *Rain early and late:* autumn and spring rains respectively.
Appointed weeks of harvest: the seven weeks between the Passover
(Dt 16, 9f) and Pentecost, during which it ordinarily did not rain.

*
5, 8: Jer 13, 27.
5, 10: Jer 2, 21.
5, 11: Jer 3, 20.
5, 12: Jer 14, 13; Is 28, 15.
5, 15: Dt 28, 49.
5, 17: Dt 28, 31.
5, 18: Jer 4, 27.
5, 21: Is 6, 9.
5, 22: Jb 38, 10f.
5, 24: Gn 8, 22; Dt 11, 14.
5, 25: Jer 2, 17.19.
5, 26: Prv 1, 11.
5, 28: Jer 12, 1; Is 1, 23.
5, 31: Jer 14, 14; Mi 2, 11.
6, 1: Jer 1, 14f.

For evil threatens from the north,
and mighty destruction.

2   O lovely and delicate
daughter Zion, you are ruined!

3*†Against her, shepherds come with
their flocks;
all around, they pitch their tents,
each one grazes his portion.

4   "Prepare for war against her,
Up! let us rush upon her at midday!
Alas! the day is waning,
evening shadows lengthen;

5* Up! let us rush upon her by night,
destroy her palaces!"

6*   For thus says the LORD of hosts:
Hew down her trees,
throw up a siege mound against Jerusalem.
Woe to the city marked for punishment;
nought but oppression within her!

7* As the well gushes out its waters,
so she gushes out her wickedness.
Violence and destruction resound in her;
ever before me are wounds and blows.

8   Be warned, O Jerusalem,
lest I be estranged from you;
Lest I turn you into a desert,
a land where no man dwells.

9   Thus says the LORD of hosts:
Glean, glean like a vine
the remnant of Israel;
Pass your hand, like a vintager,
repeatedly over the tendrils.

10* To whom shall I speak?
whom shall I warn, and be heard?
See! their ears are uncircumcised,
they cannot give heed;
See, the word of the LORD has become
for them
an object of scorn, which they will not have.

11* Therefore my wrath brims up within me,
I am weary of holding it in;
I will pour it out upon the child in the street,
upon the young men gathered together.
Yes, all will be taken, husband and wife,
graybeard with ancient.

12* Their houses will fall to strangers,
their fields and their wives as well;

For I will stretch forth my hand
against those who dwell in this land, says
the LORD.

13* Small and great alike, all are greedy for gain;
prophet and priest, all practice fraud.

14*†They would repair, as though it were nought,
the injury to my people:
"Peace, peace!" they say,
though there is no peace.

15* They are odious; they have done
abominable things,
yet they are not at all ashamed,
they know not how to blush.
Hence they shall be among those who fall;
in their time of punishment they shall
go down,
says the LORD.

16*†   Thus says the LORD:
Stand beside the earliest roads,
ask the pathways of old
Which is the way to good, and walk it;
thus you will find rest for your souls.
But they said, "We will not walk it."

17† When I raised up watchmen for them:
"Hearken to the sound of the trumpet!"
they said, "We will not hearken."

18 Therefore hear, O nations,
and know, O earth,
what I will do with them:

19* See, I bring evil upon this people,
the fruit of their own schemes,
Because they heeded not my words,
because they despised my law.

20* Of what use to me incense that comes
from Sheba,
or sweet cane from far-off lands?
Your holocausts find no favor with me,
your sacrifices please me not.

21*   Therefore, thus says the LORD:
See, I will place before this people
obstacles to bring them down;
Fathers and sons alike,
neighbors and friends shall perish.

22*   Thus says the LORD:
See, a people comes from the land of the north,
a great nation, roused from the ends of
the earth.

J
E
R

6, 3: *Shepherds . . . with their flocks:* foreign invaders with their armies.

6, 14: *As though it were nought:* the false assurance of well-being given by priest and prophet cannot reduce the harm which universal materialism and corruption have done to the people.

6, 16: *Earliest roads . . . pathways of old:* history and the lessons to be learned from it.

6, 17: *Watchmen:* the prophets who, like Jeremiah, had upheld God's moral law.

6, 3: Jer 4, 17.
6, 5: 2 Chr 36, 19.
6, 6: Jer 32, 24; Zep 3, 1–4.
6, 7: Is 57, 20.
6, 10: Jer 7, 26; 20, 8.
6, 11: Ez 9, 6.
6, 12: Jer 8, 10; Dt 28, 30ff.
6, 13: Jer 8, 10; 23, 11.
6, 14: Jer 8, 11.
6, 15: Jer 3, 3; 8, 12.
6, 16: Jer 7, 23f; 18, 15.
6, 19: Prv 1, 31.
6, 20: Is 1, 11; 43, 24.
6, 21: Is 8, 14f.
6, 22: Jer 1, 15; 5, 15.

23 Bow and javelin they wield;
  cruel and pitiless are they.
They sound like the roaring sea
  as they ride forth on steeds,
Each in his place, for battle
  against you, daughter Zion.
24* We hear the report of them;
  helpless fall our hands,
Anguish takes hold of us,
  throes like a mother's in childbirth.
25 Go not forth into the field,
  step not into the street,
Beware of the enemy's sword;
  terror on every side!
26* O daughter of my people, gird on
    sackcloth,
  roll in the ashes.
Mourn as for an only child
  with bitter wailing,
For sudden upon us
  comes the destroyer.

27* A tester among my people I have appointed
    you,
  to search and test their way.
28 Arch-rebels are they all,
  dealers in slander,
  all of them corrupt.
29 The bellows roars,
  the lead is consumed by the fire;
In vain has the smelter refined,
  the wicked are not drawn off.
30 "Silver rejected" they shall be
    called,
  for the LORD has rejected them.

II: Oracles Mostly in the Days of Jehoiakim

The Temple Sermon

7 ¹† The following message came to Jeremiah from the LORD: ² Stand at the gate of the house of the LORD, and there proclaim this message: Hear the word of the LORD, all you of Judah who enter these gates to worship the LORD! ³* Thus says the LORD of hosts, the God of Israel: Reform your ways and your deeds, so that I may remain

with you in this place. ⁴* Put not your trust in the deceitful words: "This is the temple of the LORD! The temple of the LORD! The temple of the LORD!" ⁵ Only if you thoroughly reform your ways and your deeds; if each of you deals justly with his neighbor; ⁶*† if you no longer oppress the resident alien, the orphan, and the widow; if you no longer shed innocent blood in this place, or follow strange gods to your own harm, ⁷* will I remain with you in this place, in the land which I gave your fathers long ago and forever.

⁸ But here you are, putting your trust in deceitful words to your own loss! ⁹* Are you to steal and murder, commit adultery and perjury, burn incense to Baal, go after strange gods that you know not, ¹⁰* and yet come to stand before me in this house which bears my name, and say: "We are safe; we can commit all these abominations again"? ¹¹* Has this house which bears my name become in your eyes a den of thieves? I too see what is being done, says the LORD. ¹²*† You may go to Shiloh, which I made the dwelling place of my name in the beginning. See what I did to it because of the wickedness of my people Israel. ¹³ And now, because you have committed all these misdeeds, says the LORD, because you did not listen, though I spoke to you untiringly; because you did not answer, though I called you, ¹⁴* I will do to this house named after me, in which you trust, and to this place which I gave to you and your fathers, just as I did to Shiloh. ¹⁵* I will cast you away from me, as I cast away all your brethren, all the offspring of Ephraim.

Abuses in Worship

¹⁶* You, now, do not intercede for this people; raise not in their behalf a pleading prayer! Do not urge me, for I will not listen to you. ¹⁷ Do you not see what they are doing in the cities of Judah, in the streets of Jerusalem? ¹⁸*† The children gather wood, their fathers light the fire, and the women knead dough to make cakes for the queen of heaven, while libations are poured out to strange gods in order to hurt me. ¹⁹* Is it I whom they hurt, says the LORD; is it not rather themselves, to their own confusion? ²⁰* See now, says the Lord GOD, my anger and my wrath will pour out upon this place, upon man and beast, upon the trees of the

---

7, 1–15: The temple of the Lord will not serve as a place of refuge for the Jews against their enemies if they fail to reform their evil ways.

7, 6: *The resident alien:* specially protected by law; cf Ex 20, 10; Nm 9, 14; 15, 14; Dt 5, 14; 28, 43.

7, 12: *Shiloh:* original place of worship from the time of Joshua to that of Samuel. The sanctuary was later rejected by God and destroyed by the Philistines; cf 1 Sm 1, 9; 4, 3f; Ps 78, 60.68f.

7, 18: *Queen of heaven:* the Assyro-Babylonian Ishtar, goddess of fertility, whose worship was introduced under King Manasseh and was revived after Josiah's death. Cakes shaped like stars (Ishtar was

identified with the planet Venus) were offered in her honor.

6, 24: Jer 4, 31.	7, 12: Jos 18, 1.
6, 26: Jer 25, 34; Am 8, 10.	7, 14: Jer 26, 9.
6, 27: Jer 1, 18.	7, 15: 1 Kgs 9, 7; 2 Kgs 17, 23.
7, 3: Jer 18, 11; 26, 13.	
7, 4: Mi 3, 11.	7, 16: Jer 11, 14; 14, 11.
7, 6: Ex 22, 21–24.	7, 18: Jer 44, 17.19.
7, 7: Dt 4, 40.	7, 19: Jb 35, 6.
7, 9: Jer 44, 17.	7, 20: Jer 36, 29; 2 Kgs 22, 17.
7, 10: Jer 32, 34.	
7, 11: Mt 21, 13.	

?did you KNOW?

The Prophet and the Temple

In ancient Israel, the Temple was considered the dwelling place of God. Most Israelites felt that as long as the Temple stood, God was keeping the Covenant promise to stay with Israel. They believed this because Jerusalem and Judea had been spared when the northern kingdom fell to Assyria (721 B.C.). The Israelites failed to remember that God's Covenant with them was a mutual one—that they in turn had to keep their commitment to worship God alone.

Speaking for God at the gates of the Temple, Jeremiah told the people the Temple would be destroyed if Israel continued to disobey the commandments of the Covenant (see how the sins he accused them of in Jer 7, 8–9 reflect the Ten Commandments). The destruction of the Temple would be a visible sign that the Covenant had been broken—not by God, but by the people.

The Temple was destroyed, and then rebuilt. Centuries later, Jesus preached to a new generation who thought that the Temple was a guarantee of God's presence and favor. He predicted the Temple would be destroyed again (Mt 24, 1–2).

▸ Jer 7, 1–15

field and the fruits of the earth; it will burn without being quenched.

21 Thus says the LORD of hosts, the God of Israel: Heap your holocausts upon your sacrifices; eat up the flesh! 22† In speaking to your fathers on the day I brought them out of the land of Egypt, I gave them no command concerning holocaust or sacrifice.

23* This rather is what I commanded them: Listen to my voice; then I will be your God and you shall be my people. Walk in all the ways that I command you, so that you may prosper.

24* But they obeyed not, nor did they pay heed. They walked in the hardness of their evil hearts and turned their backs, not their faces, to me. 25* From the day that your fathers left the land of Egypt even to this day, I have sent you untiringly all my servants the prophets. 26* Yet they have not obeyed me nor paid heed; they have stiffened their necks and done worse than their fathers. 27 When you speak all these words to them, they will not listen to you either; when you call to them, they will not answer you. 28 Say to them: This is the nation which does not listen to the voice of the LORD, its God, or take correction. Faithfulness has disappeared; the word itself is banished from their speech.

29*†Cut off your dedicated hair and throw it
    away!
  on the heights intone an elegy;
For the LORD has rejected and cast off
  the generation that draws down his
    wrath.

30* The people of Judah have done what is evil in my eyes, says the LORD. They have defiled the house which bears my name by setting up in it their abominable idols. 31 In the Valley of Ben-hinnom they have built the high place of Topheth to immolate in fire their sons and their daughters, such a thing as I never commanded or had in mind. 32* Therefore, beware! days will come, says the LORD, when Topheth and the Valley of Ben-hinnom will no longer be called such, but rather the Valley of Slaughter. For lack of space, Topheth will be a burial place. 33* The corpses of this people will be food for the birds of the sky and for the beasts of the field, which no one will drive away. 34* In the cities of Judah and in the streets of Jerusalem I will silence the cry of joy, the cry of gladness, the voice of the bridegroom and the voice of the bride; for the land will be turned to rubble.

8 1* At that time, says the LORD, the bones of the kings and princes of Judah, the bones of the priests and the prophets, and the bones of the citizens of Jerusalem will be emptied out of their

---

7, 22: *I gave them no command:* right conduct rather than mere external cult was God's will concerning his people (v 23).

7, 29: *Dedicated hair:* the unshorn hair of the nazirite, regarded as sacred because of a vow, temporary or permanent, to abstain from cutting or shaving the hair, from contact with a corpse, and from all products of the vine; cf Nm 6, 4–8. The cutting of this hair was a sign of extreme mourning.

7, 23: Jer 11, 4; Lv 26, 3.12.
7, 24: Jer 17, 23.
7, 25: 2 Chr 36, 15f;
  Bar 1, 19.
7, 26: Jer 19, 15; 2 Chr 30, 8.
7, 29: Jer 9, 17–21.
7, 30: Jer 32, 34.
7, 32: Jer 19, 6; 32, 35.
7, 33: Jer 16, 4; 34, 20.
7, 34: Jer 16, 9.
8, 1: Bar 2, 24.

graves [2]*† and spread out before the sun and the moon and the whole army of heaven, which they loved and served, which they followed, consulted, and worshiped. They will not be gathered up for burial, but will lie like dung upon the ground. [3] Death will be preferred to life by all the survivors of this wicked race who remain in any of the places to which I banish them, says the LORD of hosts.

Israel's Conduct Incomprehensible

[4]   Tell them: Thus says the LORD:
  When someone falls, does he not rise
        again?
    if he goes astray, does he not turn back?
[5]* Why do these people rebel
    with obstinate resistance?
  Why do they cling to deceptive idols,
    refuse to turn back?
[6]* I listen closely:
    they speak what is not true;
  No one repents of his wickedness,
    saying "What have I done!"
  Everyone keeps on running his course,
    like a steed dashing into battle.
[7]* Even the stork in the air
    knows its seasons;
  Turtledove, swallow and thrush
    observe their time of return,
  But my people do not know
    the ordinance of the LORD.
[8]*† How can you say, "We are wise,
    we have the law of the LORD"?
  Why, that has been changed into falsehood
    by the lying pen of the scribes!
[9]* The wise are confounded,
    dismayed and ensnared;
  Since they have rejected the word of the LORD,
    of what avail is their wisdom?

Shameless in Their Crimes

[10]* Therefore, I will give their wives to strangers,
    their fields to spoilers.
  Small and great alike, all are greedy for gain,
    prophet and priest, all practice fraud.
[11]*† They would repair, as though it were nought,
    the injury to the daughter of my people:
  "Peace, peace!" they say,
    though there is no peace.
[12]* They are odious; they have done
    abominable things,

yet they are not at all ashamed,
    they know not how to blush.
  Hence they shall be among those who fall;
    in their time of punishment they shall
        go down,
    says the LORD.

Threats of Punishment

[13] I will gather them all in, says the LORD:
    no grapes on the vine,
  No figs on the fig trees,
    foliage withered!
[14]* Why do we remain here?
    Let us form ranks and enter the walled
        cities,
    to perish there;
  For the LORD has wrought our destruction,
    he has given us poison to drink,
    because we have sinned against the LORD.
[15]* We wait for peace to no avail;
    for a time of healing, but terror
        comes instead.
[16] From Dan is heard
    the snorting of his steeds;
  The neighing of his stallions
    shakes the whole land.
  They come devouring the land and all
    it contains,
    the city and those who dwell in it.
[17]* Yes, I will send against you
    poisonous snakes,
  Against which no charm will work
    when they bite you, says the LORD.

The Prophet's Grief over the People's Suffering

[18] My grief is incurable,
    my heart within me is faint.
[19]* Listen! the cry of the daughter of
        my people,
    far and wide in the land!
  Is the LORD no longer in Zion,
    is her King no longer in her midst?
  [Why do they provoke me with their idols,
    with their foreign nonentities?]
[20] "The harvest has passed, the summer is at
        an end,
    and yet we are not safe!"
[21]* I am broken by the ruin of the daughter of
        my people.
    I am disconsolate; horror has seized me.

8, 2: *Army of heaven:* the stars, worshiped by the pagan nations and even by the inhabitants of Jerusalem during the reigns of Manasseh and Amon.
  8, 8f: *Lying pen of the scribes:* because the interpretations and ordinances of the scribes ran counter to the word of the Lord.
  8, 11: *Daughter of my people:* the people itself personified as a woman.

8, 2: Dt 4, 19.
8, 5: Jer 5, 3; 7, 24.26.
8, 6: Jb 34, 31f.
8, 7: Is 1, 3.
8, 8: Mal 2, 8; Rom 2, 17–23.
8, 9: 1 Cor 3, 20.
8, 10: Jer 6, 13; Dt 28, 30.
8, 11: Jer 6, 14.
8, 12: Jer 6, 15.
8, 14: Jer 9, 14; 23, 15.
8, 15: Jer 14, 19.
8, 17: Dt 32, 24.
8, 19: Dt 32, 21; Mi 4, 9.
8, 21: Jer 14, 17.

22*†Is there no balm in Gilead,
    no physician there?
Why grows not new flesh
    over the wound of the daughter of
        my people?
23 Oh, that my head were a spring of water,
    my eyes a fountain of tears,
That I might weep day and night
    over the slain of the daughter of
        my people!

The Corruption of the People

9 ¹ Would that I had in the desert
    a travelers' lodge!
That I might leave my people
    and depart from them.
They are all adulterers,
    a faithless band.
² They ready their tongues like a
      drawn bow;
    with lying, and not with truth,
    they hold forth in the land.
They go from evil to evil,
    but me they know not, says the LORD.
³† Be on your guard, everyone against
      his neighbor;
    put no trust in any brother.
Every brother apes Jacob, the supplanter,
    every friend is guilty of slander.
⁴* Each one deceives the other,
    no one speaks the truth.
They have accustomed their tongues
    to lying,
    and are perverse, and cannot repent.
⁵ Violence upon violence,
    deceit upon deceit:
They refuse to recognize me,
    says the LORD.

⁶   Therefore, thus says the LORD of hosts:
I will smelt them and test them;
    how else should I deal with
      their wickedness?
⁷* A murderous arrow is his tongue,
    his mouth utters deceit;
He speaks cordially with his friends,
    but in his heart he lays an ambush!
⁸* For these things, says the LORD,
    shall I not punish them?
On a nation such as this
    shall I not take vengeance?

Dirge over the Ravaged Land

⁹* Over the mountains, break out in cries
    of lamentation,
    over the pasture lands, intone a dirge:
They are scorched, and no man crosses them,
    unheard is the bleat of the flock;
Birds of the air as well as beasts,
    all have fled, and are gone.
¹⁰* I will turn Jerusalem into a heap of ruins,
    a haunt of jackals;
The cities of Judah I will make into a waste,
    where no one dwells.

¹¹* Who is so wise that he can understand this?
Let him to whom the mouth of the LORD has spoken make it known:

    Why is the land ravaged,
      scorched like a wasteland untraversed?

¹² The LORD answered: Because they have abandoned my law, which I set before them, and have
not followed it or listened to my voice, ¹³* but followed rather the hardness of their hearts and the
Baals, as their fathers had taught them; ¹⁴* therefore, thus says the LORD of hosts, the God of Israel:
See now, I will give them wormwood to eat and poison to drink. ¹⁵* I will scatter them among nations
whom neither they nor their fathers have known; I
will send the sword to pursue them until I have
completely destroyed them.

¹⁶   Thus says the LORD of hosts:
Attention! tell the wailing women to come,
    summon the best of them;
¹⁷* Let them come quickly
    and intone a dirge for us,
That our eyes may be wet with weeping,
    our cheeks run with tears.
¹⁸ The dirge is heard from Zion:
    Ruined we are, and greatly ashamed;
We must leave the land,
    give up our homes!
¹⁹ Hear, you women, the word of the LORD,
    let your ears receive his message.
Teach your daughters this dirge,
    and each other this lament.
²⁰* Death has come up through our windows,
    has entered our palaces;
It cuts down the children in the street,
    young people in the squares.

J
E
R

8, 22: *Gilead:* noted for its healing balm but unable to heal the moral wound of the people.
9, 3: *Jacob, the supplanter:* in Hebrew, a play on words. Jacob, as his name indicates ("he supplants"), deprived his brother Esau of his birthright; cf Gn 25, 26.33.

8, 22: Jer 46, 11.
9, 4: Jer 12, 6.
9, 7: Pss 28, 3; 62, 4.
9, 8: Jer 5, 9.29.
9, 9: Jer 4, 25; 12, 4.
9, 10: Is 13, 22.
9, 11: Ps 107, 43; Hos
14, 10.
9, 13: Jer 7, 24; 19, 4f.
9, 14: Jer 23, 15.
9, 15: Lv 26, 33; Dt 28,
    36.64.
9, 17: Jer 14, 17.
9, 20: Jer 14, 16.

21 The corpses of the slain
        lie like dung on a field,
    Like sheaves behind the harvester,
        with no one to gather them.

True Glory

22*   Thus says the LORD:
    Let not the wise man glory in his wisdom,
        nor the strong man glory in his strength,
        nor the rich man glory in his riches;
23 But rather, let him who glories, glory in this,
        that in his prudence he knows me,
    Knows that I, the LORD, bring about kindness,
        justice and uprightness on the earth;
    For with such am I pleased, says the LORD.

Circumcision Worthless

24* See, days are coming, says the LORD, when I
will demand an account of all those circumcised in
their flesh: 25† Egypt and Judah, Edom and the Ammonites, Moab and the desert dwellers who shave
their temples. For all these nations, like the whole
house of Israel, are uncircumcised in heart.

The Folly of Idolatry

10 ¹ Hear the word which the LORD speaks
to you, O house of Israel. ²*† Thus says
the LORD:

    Learn not the customs of the nations,
        and have no fear of the signs of the heavens,
        though the nations fear them.
3* For the cult idols of the nations are nothing,
        wood cut from the forest,
    Wrought by craftsmen with the adze,
4*   adorned with silver and gold.
    With nails and hammers they are fastened,
        that they may not totter.
5* Like a scarecrow in a cucumber field are they,
        they cannot speak;
    They must be carried about,
        for they cannot walk.
    Fear them not, they can do no harm,
        neither is it in their power to do good.
6* No one is like you, O LORD,
        great are you,
        great and mighty is your name.
7* Who would not fear you,
        King of the nations,
        for it is your due!

Among all the wisest of the nations,
    and in all their domain,
    there is none like you.
8 One and all they are dumb and senseless,
        these idols they teach about are wooden:
9 Silver strips brought from Tarshish,
        and gold from Ophir,
    The work of the craftsman
        and the handiwork of the smelter,
    Clothed with violet and purple—
        all of them the work of artisans.

11* Thus shall you say of them: Let the gods that
did not make heaven and earth perish from the
earth, and from beneath these heavens!

10* The LORD is true God,
        he is the living God, the eternal King,
    Before whose anger the earth quakes,
        whose wrath the nations cannot endure:
12* He who made the earth by his power,
        established the world by his wisdom,
        and stretched out the heavens by his skill.
13 When he thunders, the waters in the
            heavens roar,
        and he brings up clouds from the end of
            the earth;
    He makes the lightning flash in the rain,
        and releases stormwinds from
            their chambers.
14* Every man is stupid, ignorant;
        every artisan is put to shame by his idol:
    He has molded a fraud,
        without breath of life.
15 Nothingness are they, a ridiculous work;
        they will perish in their time
        of punishment.
16* Not like these is the portion of Jacob:
        he is the creator of all things;
    Israel is his very own tribe,
        LORD of hosts is his name.

Abandonment of Judah

17 Lift your bundle and leave the land,
        O city living in a state of siege!
18   For thus says the LORD:
    Behold, this time
        I will sling away the inhabitants of
            the land;

---

† 9, 25: *Desert dwellers . . . temples:* Arab tribesmen who cut off
their hair and shaved their temples in honor of the pagan god of
Dushara. This was forbidden the Israelites (Lv 19, 27).
    10, 2: *Signs of the heavens:* phenomena in the sky superstitious-
ly regarded by the pagans as dire omens.

9, 22: Prv 21, 30.
9, 24: Jer 4, 4.
10, 2: Bar 6, 6.
10, 3: Wis 13, 11; Is 44, 9.
10, 4: Is 40, 19; 41, 7.
10, 5: Ps 115, 4–8; Bar 6, 15.
10, 6: Ps 86, 8ff.
10, 7: Jer 5, 22; Ps 47, 2.8.
10, 11: Ps 96, 5.
10, 10: Ps 10, 16.
10, 12: Ps 104, 5.
10, 14: Rom 1, 22f.
10, 16: Jer 31, 35.

I will hem them in,
that they may be taken.
19 Woe is me! I am undone,
my wound is incurable;
Yet I had thought:
if I make light of my wound, I can bear it.
20* My tent is ruined,
all its cords are severed.
My sons have left me, they are no more:
no one to pitch my tent,
no one to raise its curtains.
21* Yes, the shepherds were stupid as cattle,
the LORD they sought not;
Therefore they had no success,
and all their flocks were scattered.
22 Listen! a noise! it comes closer,
a great uproar from the northern land:
To turn the cities of Judah
into a desert haunt of jackals.

Prayer of Jeremiah

23 You know, O LORD,
that man is not master of his way;
Man's course is not within his choice,
nor is it for him to direct his step.
24 Punish us, O LORD, but with equity,
not in anger, lest you have us dwindle away.
25* Pour out your wrath on the nations that know
you not,
on the tribes that call not upon your name;
For they have devoured Jacob utterly,
and laid waste his dwelling.

Plea for Fidelity to the Covenant

11 ¹The following message came to Jeremiah from the LORD: ² Speak to the men of Judah and to the citizens of Jerusalem, ³* saying to them: Thus says the LORD, the God of Israel: Cursed be the man who does not observe the terms of this covenant, ⁴* which I enjoined upon your fathers the day I brought them up out of the land of Egypt, that iron foundry, saying: Listen to my voice and do all that I command you. Then you shall be my people, and I will be your God. ⁵ Thus I will fulfill the oath which I swore to your fathers, to give them a land flowing with milk and honey: the one you have today. "Amen, LORD," I answered.

⁶ Then the LORD said to me: Proclaim all these words in the cities of Judah and in the streets of Jerusalem: Hear the words of this covenant and obey them. ⁷ Urgently and constantly I warned your fathers to obey my voice, from the day I brought them up out of the land of Egypt even to this day.

⁸* But they did not listen or give ear. Each one followed the hardness of his evil heart, till I brought upon them all the threats of this covenant which they had failed to observe as I commanded them.

⁹ A conspiracy has been found, the LORD said to me, among the men of Judah and the citizens of Jerusalem. ¹⁰* They have returned to the crimes of their forefathers who refused to obey my words. They also have followed and served strange gods; the covenant which I had made with their fathers, the house of Israel and the house of Judah have broken. ¹¹* Therefore, thus says the LORD: See, I bring upon them misfortune which they cannot escape. Though they cry out to me, I will not listen to them. ¹²* Then the cities of Judah and the citizens of Jerusalem will go and cry out to the gods to which they have been offering incense. But these gods will give them no help whatever when misfortune strikes.

¹³* For as numerous as your cities
are your gods, O Judah!
And as many as the streets of Jerusalem
are the altars for offering sacrifice to Baal.

¹⁴* Do not intercede on behalf of this people, nor utter a plea for them. I will not listen when they call to me at the time of their misfortune.

Sacrifices of No Avail

15 What right has my beloved in my house,
while she prepares her plots?
Can vows and sacred meat turn away
your misfortune from you?
Will you still be jubilant
16 when you hear the great invasion?
A spreading olive tree, goodly to behold,
the LORD has named you;
Now he sets fire to it,
its branches burn.

¹⁷* The LORD of hosts who planted you has decreed misfortune for you because of the evil done by the house of Israel and by the house of Judah, who provoked me by sacrificing to Baal.

The Plot against Jeremiah

¹⁸ I knew it because the LORD informed me; at that time you, O LORD, showed me their doings.

12 ¹* You would be in the right, O LORD,
if I should dispute with you;
even so, I must discuss the case with you.

10, 20: Jer 4, 20.
10, 21: Jer 23, 1; Ez 34, 5f.
10, 25: Ps 79, 6f.
11, 3: Dt 27, 26.
11, 4: Dt 4, 20; 1 Kgs 8, 51.
11, 8: 2 Kgs 17, 14.
11, 10: Dt 31, 16; Ez 20, 21–30.
11, 11: Jer 14, 12; Mi 3, 4.
11, 12: Dt 32, 37f.
11, 13: Jer 2, 28; Hos 10, 1.
11, 14: Jer 7, 16; 14, 11.
11, 17: Is 5, 2.
12, 1: Jb 21, 7; Mal 3, 15.

Why does the way of the godless prosper,
    why live all the treacherous
      in contentment?

2* You planted them; they have taken root,
    they keep on growing and bearing fruit.
  You are upon their lips,
    but far from their inmost thoughts.

3*†You, O Lord, know me, you see me,
    you have found that at heart I am
      with you.
  Pick them out like sheep for the slaughter,
    set them apart for the day of carnage.

4 How long must the earth mourn,
    the green of the whole countryside wither?
  For the wickedness of those who dwell in it
  beasts and birds disappear,
    because they say, "God does not see
      our ways."

5 If running against men has wearied you,
    how will you race against horses?
  And if in a land of peace you fall headlong,
    what will you do in the thickets of
      the Jordan?

6*For even your own brothers, the members of your father's house, betray you; they have recruited a force against you. Do not believe them, even if they are friendly to you in their words.

19*† Yet I, like a trusting lamb led to slaughter, had not realized that they were hatching plots against me: "Let us destroy the tree in its vigor; let us cut him off from the land of the living, so that his name will be spoken no more."

20* But, you, O LORD of hosts, O just Judge,
    searcher of mind and heart,
  Let me witness the vengeance you take
    on them,
    for to you I have entrusted my cause!

21* Therefore, thus says the LORD concerning the men of Anathoth who seek your life, saying, "Do not prophesy in the name of the LORD; else you shall die by our hand." 22* Therefore, thus says the LORD of hosts: I am going to punish them. The young men shall die by the sword; their sons and daughters shall die by famine. 23* None shall be spared among them, for I will bring misfortune upon the men of Anathoth, the year of their punishment.

?did you KNOW?

The Confessions of Jeremiah

Jeremiah 12, 1–6 is the first of five passages that are sometimes called the Confessions of Jeremiah (12, 1–6; 15, 10–21; 17, 12–18; 18, 18–23; 20, 7–18). In the confessions, Jeremiah speaks to God in a very personal, very direct way. He complains to God about the people's stubbornness, he complains about his treatment, and he accuses God of deceiving him. Some scholars believe the confessions are a private journal kept by Jeremiah that he never intended to be made public.

In 12, 1–4, Jeremiah asks God why God lets evil people prosper—why doesn't God just slaughter them like sheep? God's reply in verses 5–6 is that things are going to get worse before they get better and that even Jeremiah's own family will turn against him. God never answers Jeremiah directly in any of the confessions—although in 15, 19–21, God does promise to support Jeremiah.

If this famous prophet shared his anger, doubts, and fears with God honestly, so can we. Jeremiah's confessions are a good reminder that God wants to share everything with us—not just our happy thoughts.

▸ Jer 12, 1–6

The Lord's Complaint

7* I abandon my house,
    cast off my heritage;
  The beloved of my soul I deliver
    into the hand of her foes.

8* My heritage has turned on me
    like a lion in the jungle;
  Because she has roared against me,
    I treat her as an enemy.

---

† **12, 3:** Jeremiah does not seek private vengeance but the punishment of the wicked by the Lord; cf Jer 20, 12. Nevertheless, the prophet's reaction to persecution shows the difference between spirit of the Old Testament and the New.

11, 19–23: These verses have been transposed from ch 11.

12, 2: Is 29, 13.
12, 3: Jer 17, 18; Jb 23, 10.
12, 6: Jer 9, 4.
12, 19: Jer 18, 18; 20, 10; Wis 2, 20.
12, 20: Jer 15, 15.
12, 21: Am 7, 13.16.
12, 22: Jer 18, 21f.
12, 23: Jer 23, 12.
12, 7: Ps 78, 62; Lam 2, 1f.
12, 8: Ps 106, 40.

9 * My heritage is a prey for hyenas,
     is surrounded by vultures;
Come, gather together, all you beasts of
     the field,
     come and eat!

10 * Many shepherds have ravaged my vineyard,
     have trodden my heritage underfoot;
The portion that delighted me they
     have turned
     into a desert waste.

11 They have made it a mournful waste,
     desolate it lies before me,
Desolate, all the land,
     because no one takes it to heart.

12 * Upon every desert height
     brigands have come up.
The LORD has a sword which consumes
     the land, from end to end:
     no peace for all mankind.

13 They have sown wheat and reaped thorns,
     they have tired themselves out to
     no purpose;
They recoil before their harvest,
     the flaming anger of the LORD.

Judah's Neighbors

14 * † Thus says the LORD against all my evil neighbors who plunder the heritage which I gave my people Israel as their own: See, I will pluck them up from their land; the house of Judah I will pluck up in their midst. 15 * But after plucking them up, I will pity them again and bring them back, each to his heritage, each to his land. 16 * And if they carefully learn my people's custom of swearing by my name, "As the LORD lives," they who formerly taught my people to swear by Baal shall be built up in the midst of my people. 17 * But if they do not obey, I will uproot and destroy that nation entirely, says the LORD.

Judah's Corruption

13 1 † The LORD said to me: Go buy yourself a linen loincloth; wear it on your loins, but do not put it in water. 2 I bought the loincloth, as the LORD commanded, and put it on. 3 A second time the word of the LORD came to me thus: 4 Take the loincloth which you bought and are wearing, and go now to the Parath; there hide it in a cleft of the rock. 5 Obedient to the LORD's command, I went to the Parath and buried the loincloth. 6 After a long interval, he said to me: Go now to the Parath and fetch the loincloth which I told you to hide there. 7 Again I went to the Parath, sought out and took the loincloth from the place where I had hid it. But it was rotted, good for nothing! 8 Then the message came to me from the LORD: 9 * Thus says the LORD: So also I will allow the pride of Judah to rot, the great pride of Jerusalem. 10 * This wicked people who refuse to obey my words, who walk in the stubbornness of their hearts, and follow strange gods to serve and adore them, shall be like this loincloth which is good for nothing. 11 * For, as close as the loincloth clings to a man's loins, so had I made the whole house of Israel and the whole house of Judah cling to me, says the LORD; to be my people, my renown, my praise, my beauty. But they did not listen.

The Broken Wineflask

12 Now speak to them this word: Thus says the LORD, the God of Israel: Every wineflask is meant to be filled with wine. If they reply, "Do we not know that every wineflask is meant to be filled with wine?" 13 * say to them: Thus says the LORD: Beware! I am filling with drunkenness all the inhabitants of this land, the kings who succeed to David's throne, the priests and prophets, and all the citizens of Jerusalem. 14 * I will dash them against each other, fathers and sons together, says the LORD; I will show no compassion, I will not spare or pity, but will destroy them.

A Last Warning

15 Give ear, listen humbly,
     for the LORD speaks.

16 * Give glory to the LORD, your God,
     before it grows dark;
Before your feet stumble
     on darkening mountains;
Before the light you look for turns to
     darkness,
     changes into black clouds.

17 * If you do not listen to this in your pride,
     I will weep in secret many tears;
My eyes will run with tears
     for the LORD's flock, led away to exile.

Exile

18 * Say to the king and to the queen mother:
     come down from your throne;
From your heads fall
     your magnificent crowns.

12, 14: *My evil neighbors:* nations surrounding Israel, the land belonging to the Lord; cf Is 8, 8.

13, 1–11: This is probably a vision of the prophet symbolizing the religious corruption of Judah at the hands of the Babylonians, represented here by the river Parath, the Euphrates; though a spring of the same name, northeast of Anathoth, may be directly meant.

12, 9: 2 Kgs 24, 2; Is 56, 9.
12, 10: Jer 6, 3; Is 63, 18.
12, 12: Is 42, 25; 57, 21.
12, 14: 2 Kgs 24, 2.
12, 15: Am 9, 14.
12, 16: Dt 6, 13.
12, 17: Is 60, 12.
13, 9: Prv 16, 18.
13, 10: Jer 2, 20; 7, 24; 16, 11.
13, 11: Ex 19, 5; Dt 26, 18f.
13, 13: Jer 25, 15–18; Is 51, 17.
13, 14: Jer 19, 10f.
13, 16: Prv 4, 18f; Is 5, 30; Am 8, 9.
13, 17: Jer 14, 17; Ps 119, 136.
13, 18: Jer 22, 26; 2 Kgs 24, 12.15.

JER

19 The cities of the Negeb are besieged,
        with no one to relieve them;
    All Judah is banished
        in universal exile.

Jerusalem's Disgrace

20* Lift up your eyes and see
        men coming from the north.
    Where is the flock entrusted to you,
        the sheep that were your glory?
21* What will you say when they place as rulers
            over you
        those whom you taught to be your lovers?
    Will not pangs seize you
        like those of a woman giving birth?
22* If you ask in your heart
        why these things befall you:
    For your great guilt your skirts are
            stripped away
        and you are violated.
23* Can the Ethiopian change his skin?
        the leopard his spots?
    As easily would you be able to do good,
        accustomed to evil as you are.
24* I will scatter them like chaff that flies
        when the desert wind blows.
25* This is your lot, the portion measured out
            to you
        from me, says the LORD.
    Because you have forgotten me,
        and trusted in the lying idol,
26* I now will strip off your skirts from you,
        so that your shame will appear.
27* Your adulteries, your neighings,
        your shameless prostitutions:
    On the hills in the highlands
        I see these horrible crimes of yours.
    Woe to you, Jerusalem, how long will it yet be
        before you become clean!

The Great Drought

14 1* The word of the LORD that came to Jer-
        emiah concerning the drought:

2* Judah mourns,
        her gates are lifeless;
    Her people sink down in mourning:
        from Jerusalem ascends a cry of anguish.
3* The nobles send their servants for water,
        but when they come to the cisterns
    They find no water
        and return with empty jars.

Ashamed, despairing, they cover their heads
4*   because of the stricken soil;
    Because there is no rain in the land
        the farmers are ashamed, they cover
            their heads.
5   Even the hind in the field deserts her offspring
        because there is no grass.
6   The wild asses stand on the bare heights,
        gasping for breath like jackals;
    Their eyes grow dim,
        because there is no vegetation to be seen.
7* Even though our crimes bear witness
            against us,
        take action, O LORD, for the honor of
            your name—
    Even though our rebellions are many,
        though we have sinned against you.
8   O Hope of Israel, O LORD,
        our savior in time of need!
    Why should you be a stranger in this land,
        like a traveler who has stopped but for
            a night?
9* Why are you like a man dumbfounded,
        a champion who cannot save?
    You are in our midst, O LORD,
        your name we bear:
        do not forsake us!
10*   Thus says the LORD of this people:
    They so love to wander
        that they do not spare their feet.
    The LORD has no pleasure in them;
        now he remembers their guilt,
        and will punish their sins.

11* Then the LORD said to me: Do not intercede
for this people. 12* If they fast, I will not listen to
their supplication. If they offer holocausts or cereal
offerings, I will not accept them. Rather, I will destroy them with the sword, famine, and pestilence.

13* Ah! Lord GOD, I replied, it is the prophets
who say to them, "You shall not see the sword;
famine shall not befall you. Indeed, I will give you
lasting peace in this place."

14* Lies these prophets utter in my name, the
LORD said to me. I did not send them; I gave them
no command nor did I speak to them. Lying visions, foolish divination, dreams of their own
imagination, they prophesy to you. 15* Therefore,
thus says the LORD: Concerning the prophets who
prophesy in my name, though I did not send them;
who say, "Sword and famine shall not befall this
land": by the sword and famine shall these

13, 20: Jer 6, 22f.
13, 21: 2 Kgs 16, 7.
13, 22: Is 47, 2f.
13, 23: Ps 55, 20.
13, 24: Pss 1, 4; 83, 14.
13, 25: Jb 20, 29.
13, 26: Ez 16, 32.
13, 27: Jer 2, 20.
14, 1: Lv 26, 19f.
14, 2: Is 3, 26.

14, 3: Am 4, 8.
14, 4: Dt 28, 23.
14, 7: Dn 9, 4–14.
14, 9: Is 59, 1f; 63, 19.
14, 10: Jer 2, 25.
14, 11: Jer 11, 14; Ex 32, 10.
14, 12: Jer 6, 20; Is 1, 11.13.
14, 13: Jer 4, 10; 5, 12.
14, 14: Jer 5, 31; 23, 16.
14, 15: Jer 5, 12f.

The Empty Promises of False Prophets

In Jer 14, 13–16, Jeremiah attacks prophets who preach what the people want to hear. The people want peace and plenty, so that is what the false prophets preach. They offer false and dangerous security.

People deceive themselves when they listen only to what they want to hear. Sometimes, God tells us things that are hard to hear or asks us to do things that are hard to do.

In your prayer, reflect or journal on the following questions:

- When have you tried to ignore God's message for you?
- When have you heard and responded to God even if God's message was difficult?
- What are the hardest things for you to hear or do?

▸ Jer 14, 13–16

prophets meet their end. 16* The people to whom they prophesy shall be cast out into the streets of Jerusalem by famine and the sword. No one shall bury them, their wives, their sons, or their daughters, for I will pour out upon them their own wickedness. 17* Speak to them this word:

Let my eyes stream with tears
    day and night, without rest,
Over the great destruction which overwhelms
    the virgin daughter of my people,
    over her incurable wound.
18 If I walk out into the field,
    look! those slain by the sword;
If I enter the city,
    look! those consumed by hunger.
Even the prophet and the priest
    forage in a land they know not.

19* Have you cast Judah off completely?
    Is Zion loathsome to you?
Why have you struck us a blow

that cannot be healed?
We wait for peace, to no avail;
    for a time of healing, but terror
        comes instead.
20* We recognize, O LORD, our wickedness,
    the guilt of our fathers;
    that we have sinned against you.
21* For your name's sake spurn us not,
    disgrace not the throne of your glory;
    remember your covenant with us, and
        break it not.
22* Among the nations' idols is there any that
        gives rain?
    Or can the mere heavens send showers?
Is it not you alone, O LORD,
    our God, to whom we look?
You alone have done all these things.

15 1* The LORD said to me: Even if Moses and Samuel stood before me, my heart would not turn toward this people. Send them away from me. 2* If they ask you where they should go, tell them, Thus says the LORD: Whoever is marked for death, to death; whoever is marked for the sword, to the sword; whoever is marked for famine, to famine; whoever is marked for captivity, to captivity. 3* Four kinds of scourge I have decreed against them, says the LORD: the sword to slay them; dogs to drag them about; the birds of the sky and the beasts of the earth to devour and destroy them. 4* And I will make them an object of horror to all the kingdoms of the earth because of what Manasseh, son of Hezekiah, king of Judah, did in Jerusalem.

Scene of Tragedy

5* Who will pity you, Jerusalem,
    who will console you?
Who will stop to ask
    about your welfare?
6* You have disowned me, says the LORD,
    turned your back upon me;
And so I stretched out my hand to
    destroy you,
    I was weary of sparing you.
7* I winnowed them with the fan
    in every city gate.
I destroyed my people through bereavement;
    they returned not from their evil ways.
8 Their widows were more numerous before me
    than the sands of the sea.
I brought against the mother of youths
    the spoiler at midday;

14, 16: Jer 7, 33; 19, 7.
14, 17: Jer 9, 17.
14, 19: Jer 8, 15; 2 Chr 36, 16.
14, 20: Ps 106, 6; Dn 9, 5.8.

14, 21: Jer 14, 7; Lv 26, 44;
    Ps 25, 11.
14, 22: Jer 5, 24; Zec 10, 1.
15, 1: Ps 99, 6; Ez 14, 14.16.

15, 2: Jer 14, 12; Ez 5, 12.
15, 3: Ez 14, 21.
15, 4: Jer 24, 9; 2 Kgs 21,
    11–16; 23, 26; 24, 3f.

15, 5: Is 51, 19.
15, 6: Am 7, 8.
15, 7: Is 41, 16.

Suddenly I struck her
with anguish and terror.
9* The mother of seven swoons away,
gasping out her life;
Her sun sets in full day,
she is disgraced, despairing.
Their survivors I will give to the sword
before their enemies, says the LORD.

Jeremiah's Complaint

10* Woe to me, mother, that you gave me birth!
a man of strife and contention to all the land!
I neither borrow nor lend,
yet all curse me.
11* Tell me, LORD, have I not served you for
their good?
Have I not interceded with you
in the time of misfortune and anguish?†
15* You know I have.
Remember me, LORD, visit me,
and avenge me on my persecutors.
Because of your long-suffering banish me not;
know that for you I have borne insult.
16 When I found your words, I devoured them;
they became my joy and the happiness of
my heart,
Because I bore your name,
O LORD, God of hosts.
17* I did not sit celebrating
in the circle of merrymakers;
Under the weight of your hand I sat alone
because you filled me with indignation.
18*†Why is my pain continuous,
my wound incurable, refusing to be healed?
You have indeed become for me a
treacherous brook,
whose waters do not abide!
19 Thus the LORD answered me:
If you repent, so that I restore you,
in my presence you shall stand;
If you bring forth the precious without the vile,
you shall be my mouthpiece.
Then it shall be they who turn to you,
and you shall not turn to them;
20* And I will make you toward this people
a solid wall of brass.
Though they fight against you,
they shall not prevail,
For I am with you,
to deliver and rescue you, says the LORD.

21 I will free you from the hand of the wicked,
and rescue you from the grasp of
the violent.

Jeremiah's Life a Warning

16 [1] This message came to me from the
LORD: [2] Do not marry any woman; you
shall not have sons or daughters in this place, [3] for
thus says the LORD concerning the sons and daughters who will be born in this place, the mothers who will give them birth, the fathers who will beget them in this land: [4]* Of deadly disease they shall die. Unlamented and unburied they will lie like dung on the ground. Sword and famine will make an end of them, and their corpses will become food for the birds of the sky and the beasts of the field.

[5]* Go not into a house of mourning, the LORD continued: go not there to lament or offer sympathy. For I have withdrawn my friendship from this people, says the LORD, my kindness and my pity. [6]*† They shall die, the great and the lowly, in this land, and shall go unburied and unlamented. No one will gash himself or shave his head for them. [7]* They will not break bread with the bereaved to console them in their bereavement; they will not give them the cup of consolation to drink over the death of father or mother.

[8] Enter not a house where people are celebrating, to sit with them eating and drinking. [9]* For thus says the LORD of hosts, the God of Israel: Before your very eyes and during your lifetime I will silence from this place the cry of joy and the cry of gladness, the voice of the bridegroom and the voice of the bride.

[10]* When you proclaim all these words to this people and they ask you: "Why has the LORD pronounced all these great evils against us? What is our crime? What sin have we committed against the LORD, our God?" — [11]* you shall answer them: It is because your fathers have forsaken me, says the LORD, and followed strange gods, which they served and worshiped; but me they have forsaken, and my law they have not observed. [12]* And you have done worse than your fathers. Here you are, every one of you, walking in the hardness of his evil heart instead of listening to me. [13] I will cast you out of this land into a land that neither you nor your fathers have known; there you can serve strange gods day and night, because I will not grant you my mercy.

---

† **15, 12ff:** These verses are corruptions of the text and are therefore omitted.
15, 18: *A treacherous brook:* that dries up when its waters are needed. The prophet complains that he cannot rely on God with unfailing assurance of his assistance.
16, 6f: These verses refer to popular mourning practices, sometimes connected with pagan superstition; cf Dt 14, 1f.

* 15, 9: 1 Sm 2, 5.
15, 10: Jer 20, 14.
15, 11: Jer 39, 11–14.
15, 15: Jer 11, 20; 12, 3; Ps 69, 8.
15, 17: Ps 25, 4.
15, 18: Jer 14, 19; 30, 15.
15, 20: Jer 1, 18; 6, 27.
16, 4: Jer 7, 33; 22, 18.
16, 5: Ez 24, 16f.
16, 6: Lv 19, 28; Dt 14, 1.
16, 7: Ez 24, 17.
16, 9: Jer 7, 34; 25, 10.
16, 10: Jer 2, 35; 5, 19; 13, 22.
16, 11: Jer 22, 9; Dt 29, 25.
16, 12: Jer 7, 24ff.

Return from Exile

14* However, days will surely come, says the LORD, when it will no longer be said, "As the LORD lives, who brought the Israelites out of Egypt"; 15* but rather, "As the LORD lives, who brought the Israelites out of the land of the north and out of all the countries to which he had banished them." I will bring them back to the land which I gave their fathers.

Double Punishment

16* Look! I will send many fishermen, says the LORD, to catch them. After that, I will send many hunters to hunt them out from every mountain and hill and from the clefts of the rocks. 17* For my eyes are upon all their ways; they are not hidden from me, nor does their guilt escape my view. 18* I will at once repay them double for their crime and their sin of profaning my land with their detestable corpses of idols, and filling my heritage with their abominations.

Conversion of the Heathen

19* O LORD, my strength, my fortress,
     my refuge in the day of distress!
   To you will the nations come
       from the ends of the earth, and say,
   "Mere frauds are the heritage of our fathers,
       empty idols of no use."
20* Can man make for himself gods?
       These are not gods.
21* Look, then: I will give them knowledge;
       this time I will leave them in no doubt
   Of my strength and my power:
       they shall know that my name is LORD.

The Sin of Judah and Its Punishment

17

1* The sin of Judah is written
     with an iron stylus,
   Engraved with a diamond point
       upon the tablets of their hearts.

[And the horns of their altars, 2 when their sons remember their altars and their sacred poles, beside the green trees, on the high hills, 3 the peaks in the highland.]

   Your wealth and all your treasures
       I will give as spoil.
   In recompense for all your sins
       throughout your borders,
4* You will relinquish your hold on
       your heritage

which I have given you.
   I will enslave you to your enemies
       in a land that you know not:
   For a fire has been kindled by my wrath
       that will burn forever.

True Wisdom

5*   Thus says the LORD:
   Cursed is the man who trusts in
       human beings,
     who seeks his strength in flesh,
       whose heart turns away from the LORD.
6 He is like a barren bush in the desert
       that enjoys no change of season,
   But stands in a lava waste,
       a salt and empty earth.
7* Blessed is the man who trusts in the LORD,
       whose hope is the LORD.
8* He is like a tree planted beside the waters
       that stretches out its roots to the stream:
   It fears not the heat when it comes,
       its leaves stay green;
   In the year of drought it shows no distress,
       but still bears fruit.
9 More tortuous than all else is the human heart,
       beyond remedy; who can understand it?
10 * I, the LORD, alone probe the mind
       and test the heart,
   To reward everyone according to his ways,
       according to the merit of his deeds.
11* A partridge that mothers a brood not her own
       is the man who acquires wealth unjustly:
   In midlife it will desert him;
       in the end he is only a fool.

The Source of Life

12* A throne of glory, exalted from the beginning,
       such is our holy place.
13* O hope of Israel, O LORD!
       all who forsake you shall be in disgrace;
   The rebels in the land shall be put to shame;
       they have forsaken the source of
         living waters
       [the LORD].

Prayer for Vengeance

14 Heal me, LORD, that I may be healed;
       save me, that I may be saved,
       for it is you whom I praise.
15* See how they say to me,
       "Where is the word of the LORD?
       Let it come to pass!"

16, 14: Jer 23, 7f.
16, 15: Jer 24, 6.
16, 16: 2 Kgs 24, 2; Lam 4, 19.
16, 17: Jer 32, 19; Jb 34, 21.
16, 18: Is 40, 2.
16, 19: Jer 2, 11; Is 2, 2f.
16, 20: Jer 2, 11; Gal 4, 8.
16, 21: Am 5, 8.
17, 1: Jb 19, 24.

17, 4: Jer 5, 19; Dt 32, 22.
17, 5: Ps 146, 2f.
17, 7: Ps 1, 3.
17, 8: Is 58, 11.
17, 10: Jer 32, 19; 1 Sm 16, 7; Eccl 12, 14.
17, 11: Prv 13, 11; Lk 12, 20.
17, 12: Jer 14, 21.
17, 13: Jer 2, 13.
17, 15: Is 5, 19; 2 Pt 3, 4.

J E R

16 Yet I did not press you to send calamity;
 the day without remedy I have not desired.
 You know what passed my lips;
 it is present before you.
17* Do not be my ruin,
 you, my refuge in the day of misfortune.
18* Let my persecutors, not me, be confounded;
 let them, not me, be broken.
 Bring upon them the day of misfortune,
 crush them with repeated destruction.

Observance of the Sabbath

19*† Thus said the LORD to me: Go, stand at the Gate of Benjamin, where the kings of Judah enter

and leave, and at the other gates of Jerusalem. 20 There say to them: Hear the word of the LORD, you kings of Judah, and all Judah, and all you citizens of Jerusalem who enter these gates! 21* Thus says the LORD: As you love your lives, take care not to carry burdens on the sabbath day, to bring them in through the gates of Jerusalem. 22* Bring no burden from your homes on the sabbath. Do no work whatever, but keep holy the sabbath, as I commanded your fathers, 23* though they did not listen or give ear, but stiffened their necks so as not to hear or take correction. 24* If you obey me wholeheartedly, says the LORD, and carry no burden through the gates of this city on the sabbath,

CHILDREN AND GREEN TREES

The land is very important in Native American spirituality; trees, grass, and flowers are given reverence similar to that afforded people because all are connected. It is the greatest wish of the elders that the children learn this lesson and carry it on to their own children. Native Americans would view the loss and destruction of the land described in Jer 17, 1–3 as a horrible punishment. See how their value for the land is reflected in this prayer from the Mohawk tradition:

Oh Great Spirit, Creator of all things;
Human Beings, trees, grass, berries.
Help us, be kind to us.
Let us be happy on earth.
Let us lead our children
To a good life and old age.
These our people; give them good minds
To love one another.
Oh Great Spirit,
Be kind to us.
Give these people the favour
To see green trees,
Green grass, flowers, and berries
This next spring;
So we all meet again.
Oh Great Spirit,
We ask of you.

(Author unknown, "Mohawk Indian Prayer")

▶ Jer 17, 1–3

---

† **17, 19:** *The Gate of Benjamin:* probably the northern gate of the temple area and city wall of Jerusalem; cf Jer 20, 2; 37, 12; 38, 7.

17, 17: Jer 16, 19.
17, 18: Jer 15, 15; 18, 20–23; Ps 35, 5f.
17, 19: Jer 7, 2.
17, 21: Neh 13, 15–19.
17, 22: Ex 20, 8; 23, 12.
17, 23: Jer 5, 3; 7, 24.
17, 24: Is 58, 14.

keeping the sabbath holy and abstaining from all work on it, 25* then, through the gates of this city, kings who sit upon the throne of David will continue to enter, riding in their chariots or upon their horses, along with their princes, and the men of Judah, and the citizens of Jerusalem. This city will remain inhabited forever. 26† To it people will come from the cities of Judah and the neighborhood of Jerusalem, from the land of Benjamin and from the foothills, from the hill country and the Negeb, to bring holocausts and sacrifices, cereal offerings and incense and thank offerings to the house of the LORD. 27* But if you do not obey me and keep holy the sabbath, if you carry burdens and come through the gates of Jerusalem on the sabbath, I will set unquenchable fire to its gates, which will consume the palaces of Jerusalem.

The Potter's Vessel

18 ¹† This word came to Jeremiah from the LORD: ² Rise up, be off to the potter's house; there I will give you my message. ³ I went down to the potter's house and there he was, working at the wheel. ⁴* Whenever the object of clay which he was making turned out badly in his hand, he tried again, making of the clay another object of whatever sort he pleased. ⁵ Then the word of the Lord came to me: ⁶* Can I not do to you, house of Israel, as this potter has done? says the LORD. Indeed, like clay in the hand of the potter, so are you in my hand, house of Israel. ⁷* Sometimes I threaten to uproot and tear down and destroy a nation or a kingdom. ⁸* But if that nation which I have threatened turns from its evil, I also repent of the evil which I threatened to do. ⁹ Sometimes, again, I promise to build up and plant a nation or a kingdom. ¹⁰* But if that nation does what is evil in my eyes, refusing to obey my voice, I repent of the good with which I promised to bless it.

¹¹* And now, tell this to the men of Judah and the citizens of Jerusalem: Thus says the LORD: Take care! I am fashioning evil against you and making a plan. Return, each of you, from his evil way; reform your ways and your deeds. ¹²* But they will say, "No use! We will follow our own devices; each one of us will behave according to the stubbornness of his evil heart!"

Judah's Apostasy Unnatural

13*   Therefore thus says the LORD:
Ask among the nations—
   who has ever heard the like?
Truly horrible things
   has virgin Israel done!
14† Does the snow of Lebanon
   desert the rocky heights?
Do the gushing waters dry up
   that flow fresh down the mountains?
15* Yet my people have forgotten me:
   they burn incense to a thing that does
      not exist.
They stumble out of their ways,
   the paths of old,
To travel on bypaths,
   not the beaten track.
16* Their land shall be turned into a desert,
   an object of lasting ridicule:
All passers-by will be amazed,
   will shake their heads.
17* Like the east wind, I will scatter them
   before their enemies;
I will show them my back, not my face,
   in their day of disaster.

Another Prayer for Vengeance

18* "Come," they said, "let us contrive a plot against Jeremiah. It will not mean the loss of instruction from the priests, nor of counsel from the wise, nor of messages from the prophets. And so, let us destroy him by his own tongue; let us carefully note his every word."

19   Heed me, O LORD,
   and listen to what my adversaries say.
20* Must good be repaid with evil
   that they should dig a pit to take my life?
Remember that I stood before you
   to speak in their behalf,
   to turn away your wrath from them.
21*† So now, deliver their children to famine,
   do away with them by the sword.
Let their wives be made childless
   and widows;
   let their men die of pestilence,
   their young men be slain by the sword
      in battle.

---

† **18, 1–12:** The lesson of the potter is not that God deals arbitrarily with his people, but that he is almighty to destroy or restore, accordingly as they disobey him or fulfill his plans.

18, 14: *Lebanon:* here apparently including Mount Hermon, whose snow-capped peak can be seen from parts of Palestine all year round. The prophet contrasts the certainties of nature with Israel's unnatural desertion of the Lord for idols (v 15).

18, 21: In the Old Testament a man's family was regarded as part of his personality, to be rewarded or punished along with him; cf Jos 7, 24ff.

* 17, 25: Jer 22, 4.
17, 26: Jer 32, 44.
17, 27: Ez 22, 8.
 18, 4: Rom 9, 20f.
 18, 6: Wis 15, 7; Is 45, 9.
 18, 7: Jer 1, 10.
 18, 8: Jer 26, 3; Is 55, 7; Ez
        18, 21.27.
 18, 10: Nm 14, 22f.
 18, 11: Jer 7, 3; 25, 5; 35, 15.

 18, 12: Jer 2, 25; 7, 24.
 18, 13: Jer 2, 10f; 5, 30.
 18, 15: Jer 2, 13.32.
 18, 16: Jer 19, 8; Lv 26, 32;
        1 Kgs 9, 8.
 18, 17: Prv 1, 24–31.
 18, 18: Jer 11, 19; Ps 35, 15f.
 18, 20: Ps 35, 12.
 18, 21: Ps 109, 9f.

22 May cries be heard from their homes,
       when suddenly you send plunderers
          against them.
    For they have dug a pit to capture me,
       they have hid snares for my feet;
23* But you, O LORD, know
       all their plans to slay me.
    Forgive not their crime,
       blot not out their sin in your sight!
    Let them go down before you,
       proceed against them in the time of
          your anger.

Symbol of the Potter's Flask

19 ¹ Thus said the LORD: Go, buy a potter's earthen flask. Take along some of the elders of the people and of the priests, ²† and go out toward the Valley of Ben-hinnom, at the entrance of the Potsherd Gate; there proclaim the words which I will speak to you: ³ Listen to the word of the LORD, kings of Judah and citizens of Jerusalem: Thus says the LORD of hosts, the God of Israel: I am going to bring such evil upon this place that all who hear of it will feel their ears tingle. ⁴* This is because they have forsaken me and alienated this place by burning in it incense to strange gods which neither they nor their fathers knew; and the kings of Judah have filled this place with the blood of the innocent. ⁵* They have built high places for Baal to immolate their sons in fire as holocausts to Baal: such a thing as I neither commanded nor spoke of, nor did it ever enter my mind. ⁶* Therefore, days will come, says the LORD, when this place will no longer be called Topheth, or the Valley of Ben-hinnom, but rather, the Valley of Slaughter. ⁷* In this place I will foil the plan of Judah and Jerusalem; I will make them fall by the sword before their enemies, by the hand of those that seek their lives. Their corpses I will give as food to the birds of the sky and the beasts of the field. ⁸ I will make this city an object of amazement and derision. Because of all its wounds, every passer-by will be amazed and will catch his breath. ⁹* I will have them eat the flesh of their sons and daughters; they shall eat one another's flesh during the strict siege by which their enemies and those who seek their lives will confine them.

¹⁰ And you shall break the flask in the sight of the men who went with you, ¹¹* and say to them: Thus says the LORD of hosts: Thus will I smash this people and this city, as one smashes a clay pot so that it cannot be repaired. And Topheth shall be a burial place, for lack of place to bury elsewhere. ¹²* Thus I will do to this place and to its inhabitants, says the LORD; I will make this city like Topheth. ¹³* And the houses of Jerusalem and the palaces of the kings of Judah shall be defiled like the place of Topheth, all the houses upon whose roofs they burnt incense to the whole host of heaven and poured out libations to strange gods.

¹⁴* When Jeremiah returned from Topheth, where the LORD had sent him to prophesy, he stood in the court of the house of God and said to all the people: ¹⁵* Thus says the LORD of hosts, the God of Israel: I will surely bring upon this city all the evil with which I threatened it, because they have stiffened their necks and have not obeyed my words.

20 ¹*† Jeremiah was heard prophesying these things by the priest Pashhur, son of Immer, chief officer in the house of the LORD. ²* So he had the prophet scourged and placed in the stocks at the upper Gate of Benjamin in the house of the LORD. ³*† The next morning, after Pashhur had released Jeremiah from the stocks, the prophet said to him: Instead of Pashhur, the LORD will name you "Terror on every side." ⁴† For thus says the LORD: Indeed, I will deliver you to terror, you and all your friends. Your own eyes shall see them fall by the sword of their enemies. All Judah I will deliver to the king of Babylon, who shall take them captive to Babylon or slay them with the sword. ⁵* All the wealth of this city, all it has toiled for and holds dear, all the treasures of the kings of Judah, I will give as plunder into the hands of their foes, who shall seize it and carry it away to Babylon. ⁶* You, Pashhur, and all the members of your household shall go into exile. To Babylon you shall go, you and all your friends; there you shall die and be buried, because you have prophesied lies to them.

---

† **19, 2:** *Potsherd Gate:* in the south wall of Jerusalem, through which potsherds and other refuse were carried to the Valley of Ben-hinnom.

20, 1: *Chief officer in the house of the LORD:* head of the temple police; cf Jer 29, 26. By entering the temple court (Jer 19, 14), Jeremiah had put himself under Pashhur's jurisdiction.

20, 3: *"Terror on every side":* Pashhur will share the fate of doomed Jerusalem and will experience personally all that the people as a whole have had to endure.

20, 4: *Babylon:* mentioned here for the first time as the land of exile. The prophecy probably dates from after 605 B.C., when Neb-

uchadnezzar defeated Egypt and made the Chaldean empire dominant in Syria and Palestine.

18, 23: Neh 4, 5; Pss 35, 4; 37, 32f.	**19, 13:** Jer 32, 29.
	19, 14: Jer 26, 2.
19, 4: Jer 1, 16; 2 Kgs 21, 16; 24, 4.	**19, 15:** Jer 7, 26; Prv 29, 1.
	20, 1: Jer 21, 1.
19, 5: Jer 7, 31f; 32, 35.	**20, 2:** Jer 29, 26.
19, 6: Jer 7, 32.	**20, 3:** Jer 6, 25.
19, 7: Jer 7, 33.	**20, 5:** 2 Kgs 20, 17; 24, 12–16.
19, 9: Lv 26, 29.	
19, 11: Jer 7, 32.	**20, 6:** Jer 14, 13f; 28, 15.
19, 12: 2 Kgs 23, 10.	

J E R

Jeremiah's Interior Crisis

7† You duped me, O LORD, and I let myself
   be duped;
   you were too strong for me, and
      you triumphed.
All the day I am an object of laughter;
   everyone mocks me.
8 Whenever I speak, I must cry out,
   violence and outrage is my message;
The word of the LORD has brought me
   derision and reproach all the day.
9* I say to myself, I will not mention him,
   I will speak in his name no more.
But then it becomes like fire burning in
   my heart,
   imprisoned in my bones;
I grow weary holding it in,
   I cannot endure it.
10* Yes, I hear the whisperings of many:
   "Terror on every side!
   Denounce! let us denounce him!"
All those who were my friends
   are on the watch for any misstep of
      mine.
"Perhaps he will be trapped; then we
   can prevail,
   and take our vengeance on him."
11* But the LORD is with me, like a
   mighty champion:
   my persecutors will stumble, they will
      not triumph.
In their failure they will be put to
   utter shame,
   to lasting, unforgettable confusion.
12* O LORD of hosts, you who test the just,
   who probe mind and heart,
Let me witness the vengeance you take
   on them,
   for to you I have entrusted my cause.
13* Sing to the LORD,
   praise the LORD,
For he has rescued the life of the poor
   from the power of the wicked!

14*†Cursed be the day
   on which I was born!
May the day my mother gave me birth
   never be blessed!

15   Cursed be the man who brought the news
   to my father, saying,
   "A child, a son, has been born to you!"
      filling him with great joy.
16* Let that man be like the cities
   which the LORD relentlessly overthrew;
Let him hear war cries in the morning,
   battle alarms at noonday,
17* because he did not dispatch me in
   the womb!
Then my mother would have been
   my grave,
   her womb confining me forever.
18* Why did I come forth from the womb,
   to see sorrow and pain,
   to end my days in shame?

III: Oracles in the Last Years of Jerusalem

Fate of Zedekiah and Jerusalem

21 ¹† The message which came to Jeremiah
from the LORD when King Zedekiah sent
him Pashhur, son of Malchiah, and the priest
Zephaniah, son of Maaseiah, with this request:
² Inquire for us of the LORD, because Nebuchadnezzar, king of Babylon, is attacking us. Perhaps
the LORD will deal with us according to all his wonderful works, so that he will withdraw from us.
³ But Jeremiah answered them: This is what you
shall report to Zedekiah: ⁴* Thus says the LORD, the
God of Israel: I will turn back in your hands the
weapons with which you intend to fight the king of
Babylon and the Chaldeans who besiege you outside the walls. These weapons I will pile up in the
midst of this city, ⁵* and I myself will fight against
you with outstretched hand and mighty arm, in
anger, and wrath, and great rage! ⁶* I will strike the
inhabitants of this city, both man and beast; they
shall die in a great pestilence. ⁷* After that, says the
LORD, I will hand over Zedekiah, king of Judah,
and his ministers and the people in this city who
survive pestilence, sword, and famine, into the
hand of Nebuchadnezzar, king of Babylon, into the
hands of their enemies and those who seek their
lives. He shall strike them with the edge of the
sword, without quarter, without pity or mercy.
⁸* And to this people you shall say: Thus says the

20, 7: *You duped me:* to be understood in the light of Jeremiah's intimate dealings with God; cf Jer 15, 18.
   20, 14–18: Deception, sorrow and terror have brought the prophet close to the point of despair; nevertheless he has expressed his utmost confidence in the triumph of God's will (vv 11ff); cf Jb 3, 3–12.
   21, 1: *Zedekiah:* brother of Jehoiakim, appointed king by Neb-uchadnezzar after he had carried Jehoiachin away to captivity (2 Kgs 24, 17). *Pashhur:* different from the one in Jer 20, 1ff but also one of Jeremiah's enemies; cf Jer 38, 1.4.

20, 9: Jer 6, 11; Jb 32, 18.
20, 10: Jb 19, 19; Ps 31, 13;
   Lk 20, 20.
20, 11: Jer 1, 8; 15, 20.
20, 12: Jer 11, 20.
20, 13: Pss 35, 9f; 109, 30f.
20, 14: Jer 15, 10; Jb 3, 1–10;
   10, 18.
20, 16: Gn 19, 25; Is 13, 19.
20, 17: Jb 3, 10f; 10, 19.
20, 18: Jb 14, 1.
21, 4: Jer 37, 8ff.
21, 5: Is 63, 10; Lam 2, 4f.
21, 6: Jer 16, 4.
21, 7: Jer 24, 8ff; Dt 28, 49f.
21, 8: Jer 21, 9; Dt 30, 15.19.

JER

LORD: See, I am giving you a choice between life and death. ⁹ Whoever remains in this city shall die by the sword or famine or pestilence. But whoever leaves and surrenders to the besieging Chaldeans shall live and have his life as booty. ¹⁰† For I have turned against this city, for its woe and not for its good, says the LORD. It shall be given into the power of the king of Babylon who shall burn it with fire.

Oracles regarding the Kings

¹¹†   To the royal house of Judah:
    Hear the word of the LORD, ¹²* O house of
      David!
    Thus says the LORD:
    Each morning dispense justice,
      rescue the oppressed from the hand of
        the oppressor,
    Lest my fury break out like fire
      which burns without being quenched,
      because of the evil of your deeds.
¹³† Beware! I am against you, Valley-site,
    Rock of the Plain, says the LORD.
    You who say, "Who will attack us,
      who can penetrate our retreats?"
¹⁴*†I will punish you, says the LORD,
      as your deeds deserve!
    I will kindle a fire in its forest
      that shall devour all its surroundings.

22 ¹ The LORD told me this: Go down to the palace of the king of Judah and there deliver this message: ²* You shall say: Listen to the word of the LORD, king of Judah, who sit on the throne of David, you, your ministers, and your people that enter by these gates! ³* Thus says the LORD: Do what is right and just. Rescue the victim from the hand of his oppressor. Do not wrong or oppress the resident alien, the orphan, or the widow, and do not shed innocent blood in this place. ⁴ If you carry out these commands, kings who succeed to the throne of David will continue to enter the gates of this palace,

riding in chariots or mounted on horses, with their ministers, and their people. ⁵ But if you do not obey these commands, I swear by myself, says the LORD: this palace shall become rubble. ⁶† For thus says the LORD concerning the palace of the king of Judah:

    Though you be to me like Gilead,
      like the peak of Lebanon,
    I will turn you into a waste,
      a city uninhabited.
⁷* Against you I will send destroyers,
      each with his axe:
    They shall cut down your choice cedars,
      and cast them into the fire.

⁸* Many people will pass by this city and ask one another: "Why has the LORD done this to so great a city?" ⁹* And the answer will be given: "Because they have deserted their covenant with the LORD, their God, by worshiping and serving strange gods."

Jehoahaz

¹⁰*†Weep not for him who is dead,
      mourn not for him!
    Weep rather for him who is going away;
      never again will he see
      the land of his birth.

¹¹† Thus says the LORD concerning Shallum, son of Josiah, king of Judah, who succeeded his father as king. He has left this place never to return. ¹² Rather, he shall die in the place where they exiled him; this land he shall not see again.

Jehoiakim

¹³*†Woe to him who builds his house on wrong,
      his terraces on injustice;
    Who works his neighbor without pay,
      and gives him no wages.
¹⁴   Who says, "I will build myself a
        spacious house,
      with airy rooms,"

21, 10: Jeremiah consistently pointed out the uselessness of resistance to Babylon, since the Lord had delivered Judah to Nebuchadnezzar (Jer 27, 6). Because of this the prophet was denounced and imprisoned as a traitor (Jer 37, 13f).

21, 11—23, 8: This section contains an editor's collection of Jeremiah's oracles against the kings of Judah. They are placed in the chronological order of the kings, and are prefaced by the oracles against the kings of Judah in general (Jer 21, 11—22, 9).

21, 13: Valley-site, Rock of the Plain: Mount Zion, surrounded by valleys, was regarded by the royal house as impregnable. Despite this natural fortification, God shows derisively that it is no more than a rock rising from the plain, undefendable against the attack of his fury.

21, 14: Its forest: probably the royal palace, built of cedar wood; cf Jer 22, 14; in 1 Kgs 7, 2 the armory of Solomon's palace is called "The Forest of Lebanon."

22, 6: Gilead . . . Lebanon: both were known for their trees; cf v 7.

22, 10: Him who is dead: Josiah. His successor, Jehoahaz, who is going away, was deported by Pharaoh Neco to Egypt, where he died (2 Kgs 23, 33f).

22, 11: Shallum: Jehoahaz is called this only here. Presumably it was his name at birth, while Jehoahaz was his royal name.

22, 13: Without pay: either by forced labor in public works, or in as much as workers were defrauded of their hire. Despite the impoverishment caused in Judah by the payment of foreign tribute, Jehoiakim embarked on a program of lavish building in Jerusalem (v 14). Social injustice is the cause of much of the prophetic condemnation of the kings (v 17).

21, 12: Jer 4, 4; 22, 3; Zec 7, 9.	**22, 7:** Jer 21, 14.
	22, 8: Dt 29, 24ff.
21, 14: 2 Kgs 25, 9; 2 Chr 36, 19.	**22, 9:** Jer 19, 4; 40, 2f.
	22, 10: 2 Chr 35, 23ff.
22, 2: Jer 17, 20.	**22, 13:** Lv 19, 13; Dt 24, 14;
22, 3: Jer 21, 12; Ex 22, 21–24; Dt 24, 17.	Hb 2, 9.12.

Who cuts out windows for it,
    panels it with cedar,
    and paints it with vermillion.
¹⁵*†Must you prove your rank among kings
    by competing with them in cedar?
Did not your father eat and drink?
    He did what was right and just,
    and it went well with him.
¹⁶* Because he dispensed justice to the weak and
        the poor,
    it went well with him.
Is this not true knowledge of me?
    says the LORD.
¹⁷* But your eyes and heart are set on nothing
        except on your own gain,
On shedding innocent blood,
    on practicing oppression and extortion.

¹⁸*† Therefore, thus says the LORD concerning
Jehoiakim, son of Josiah, king of Judah:

They shall not lament him,
    "Alas! my brother"; "Alas! sister."
They shall not lament him,
    "Alas, Lord! alas, Majesty!"
¹⁹*†The burial of an ass shall he be given,
    dragged forth and cast out
    beyond the gates of Jerusalem.

Jeconiah

²⁰*†Scale Lebanon and cry out,
    in Bashan lift up your voice;
Cry out from Abarim,
    for all your lovers are crushed.
²¹   I spoke to you when you were secure,
    but you answered, "I will not listen."
This has been your way from your youth,
    not to listen to my voice.
²²   The wind shall shepherd all your shepherds,
    your lovers shall go into exile.
Surely then you shall be ashamed
    and confounded
    because of all your wickedness.

²³   You who dwell on Lebanon,
    who nest in the cedars,
How you shall groan when pains come
        upon you,
    like the pangs of a woman in travail!

²⁴† As I live, says the LORD, if you, Coniah, son of
Jehoiakim, king of Judah, are a signet ring on my
right hand, I will snatch you from it. ²⁵* I will deliver you into the hands of those who seek your life; the
hands of those whom you fear; the hands of

22, 15f: Josiah, the reforming king, prospered materially without
oppressing his people; he embodied all the ideals of kingship.
22, 18: *"Alas! my brother"; "Alas! sister":* customary cries of
mourning.
22, 19: *The burial of an ass:* no burial at all, except to be cast outside the city as refuse. This prophecy regards the popular feeling toward Jehoiakim rather than the actual circumstances of his burial.
According to 2 Kgs 24, 5 he was buried with his fathers in Jerusalem.
However, his grave may have been profaned by Nebuchadnezzar.
22, 20–23: The prophet first apostrophizes Jerusalem, which is
bidden to scale Lebanon, Bashan, and Abarim, i.e., the highest surrounding mountains to the north, northeast, and southeast, to gaze
on the ruin of its lovers, i.e., the false leaders of Judah, called its
shepherds (22); cf Jer 2, 8. The year is 597 B.C., after Nebuchadnezzar's deportation of Jehoiachin. Jerusalem still stands (23), apparently as secure as the heights of Lebanon, but destruction is to follow (cf
v 6).

22, 24: *Coniah:* a shortened form of Jeconiah, the name which
Jeremiah gives the king called elsewhere in the Bible Jehoiachin. *A
signet ring:* the seal used by important men—in a sense, their most
valuable possession—mounted in a ring worn constantly on the
hand. The Lord says that even were Jehoiachin such a precious possession, he would reject him. The words in vv 24–30 date from the
short three-month reign of Jehoiachin, before he was carried away
by Nebuchadnezzar.

22, 15: 2 Kgs 23, 25.
22, 16: Prv 31, 9.
22, 17: Ez 22, 13.27.
22, 18: Jer 16, 4ff; 1 Kgs 13, 30.
22, 19: Jer 36, 30.
22, 20: Jer 30, 14f; Dt 32, 49.
22, 25: Jer 21, 7; 34, 20.

Nebuchadnezzar, king of Babylon, and the Chaldeans. 26*† I will cast you out, you and the mother who bore you, into a different land from the one you were born in; and there you shall die. 27* Neither of them shall come back to the land for which they yearn.

28   Is this man Coniah a vessel despised, to be
            broken up,
        an instrument that no one wants?
      Why are he and his descendants cast out?
        why thrown into a land they know not?
29   O land, land, land,
        hear the word of the LORD—
30*†   Thus says the LORD:
      Write this man down as one childless,
        who will never thrive in his lifetime!
      No descendant of his shall achieve
        a seat on the throne of David
        as ruler again over Judah.

Messianic Reign

23 ¹*† Woe to the shepherds who mislead and scatter the flock of my pasture, says the LORD. ²* Therefore, thus says the LORD, the God of Israel, against the shepherds who shepherd my people: You have scattered my sheep and driven them away. You have not cared for them, but I will take care to punish your evil deeds. ³* I myself will gather the remnant of my flock from all the lands to which I have driven them and bring them back to their meadow; there they shall increase and multiply. ⁴* I will appoint shepherds for them who will shepherd them so that they need no longer fear and tremble; and none shall be missing, says the LORD.

5*   Behold, the days are coming, says the LORD,
        when I will raise up a righteous shoot
          to David;
      As king he shall reign and govern wisely,
      he shall do what is just and right in
          the land.
6*   In his days Judah shall be saved,
      Israel shall dwell in security.

This is the name they give him:
    "The LORD our justice."

7* Therefore, the days will come, says the LORD, when they shall no longer say, "As the LORD lives, who brought the Israelites out of the land of Egypt"; 8 but rather, "As the LORD lives, who brought the descendants of the house of Israel up from the land of the north"—and from all the lands to which I banished them; they shall again live on their own land.

The False Prophets†

9   Concerning the prophets:
      My heart within me is broken,
        my bones all tremble;
      I am like a man who is drunk,
        overcome by wine,
      Because of the LORD,
        because of his holy words.
10*   With adulterers the land is filled;
        on their account the land mourns,
        the pasture ranges are seared.
      Theirs is an evil course,
        theirs is unjust power.
11*   Both prophet and priest are godless!
        In my very house I find their wickedness,
        says the LORD.
12*   Hence their way shall become for them
          slippery ground.
      In the darkness they shall lose their footing,
          and fall headlong;
      Evil I will bring upon them:
        the year of their punishment, says
          the LORD.
13*   Among Samaria's prophets
        I saw unseemly deeds:
      They prophesied by Baal
        and led my people Israel astray.
14*   But among Jerusalem's prophets
        I saw deeds still more shocking:
      Adultery, living in lies,
        siding with the wicked,
      so that no one turns from evil;

22, 26: *You and the mother who bore you:* the queen mother held a special position in the monarchy of Judah, and in the Books of Kings she is invariably mentioned by name along with the king (1 Kgs 15, 2; 2 Kgs 18, 2). Jehoiachin did indeed die in Babylon.

22, 30: *Childless:* Jehoiachin is so considered because none of his descendants will be king. From the Book of Ezekiel, who dates his oracles according to Jehoiachin's fictitious regnal years, it is evident that the people expected Jehoiachin to return. The above prophecy of Jeremiah was uttered to dispel this hope (Jer 28, 4). Of the seven sons born to Jehoiachin in exile, none became king. His grandson Zerubbabel presided for a time over the Jewish community after the return from exile, but not as king.

23, 1–8: With the false rulers who have governed his people the Lord contrasts himself, the good shepherd, who will in the times of restoration appoint worthy rulers (1–4). A messianic King will arise from the line of David who will rule over Judah and Israel with the justice of the Lord, fulfilling all the kingly ideals (5f). "The LORD our

justice" is probably an ironic wordplay on the name of the weak King Zedekiah ("The Lord is justice"); the messianic King will be in reality what Zedekiah's name falsely proclaims him. The final verses, 7–8, were probably added during the exile.

23, 9–40: After the collection of oracles against the kings, the editor of the book placed this collection of oracles against the false prophets. With them are associated the priests, for both have betrayed their trust as instructors in the religion of the Lord; cf Jer 2, 8; 4, 9; 6, 13f.

22, 26: 2 Kgs 24, 15.
22, 27: Jer 44, 14.
22, 30: Jer 36, 30; 1 Chr 3,
    16f; Mt 1, 12.
23, 1: Jer 22, 22.
23, 2: Ez 34, 4ff; Zec 11, 16f.
23, 3: Jer 29, 14; 32, 37.
23, 4: Jer 3, 15; Ez 34, 11f.

23, 5: Jer 33, 14ff; Is 4, 2; 9,
    5f; 11, 1–5.
23, 6: Dn 9, 24.
23, 7f: Jer 16, 14f.
23, 10: Jer 4, 22; 5, 7f; 9, 2.10.
23, 11: Jer 6, 13.
23, 12: Ps 35, 6.
23, 13: 1 Kgs 18, 19.
23, 14: Jer 29, 21ff; Is 1, 9f.

To me they are all like Sodom,
  its citizens like Gomorrah.

15* Therefore, thus says the LORD of hosts against
the prophets:

Behold, I will give them wormwood to eat,
  and poison to drink;
For from Jerusalem's prophets
  ungodliness has gone forth into the
    whole land.
16*   Thus says the LORD of hosts:
Listen not to the words of your prophets,
  who fill you with emptiness;
Visions of their own fancy they speak,
  not from the mouth of the LORD.
17*†They say to those who despise the word of
    the LORD,
  "Peace shall be yours";
And to everyone who walks in hardness
    of heart,
  "No evil shall overtake you."
18* Now, who has stood in the council of the LORD,
  to see him and to hear his word?
  Who has heeded his word, so as to
    announce it?
19* See, the storm of the LORD!
  His wrath breaks forth
In a whirling storm
  that bursts upon the heads of the wicked.
20 The anger of the LORD shall not abate
  until he has done and fulfilled
what he has determined in his heart.
When the time comes,
  you shall fully understand.
21* I did not send these prophets,
  yet they ran;
I did not speak to them,
  yet they prophesied.
22 Had they stood in my council,
  and did they but proclaim to my people
    my words,
They would have brought them back from
    evil ways
  and from their wicked deeds.
23*†Am I a God near at hand only, says the LORD,
  and not a God far off?

24   Can a man hide in secret
    without my seeing him? says the LORD.
  Do I not fill
    both heaven and earth? says the LORD.

25 I have heard the prophets who prophesy lies in
my name say, "I had a dream! I had a dream!"
26 How long will this continue? Is my name in the
hearts of the prophets who prophesy lies and their
own deceitful fancies? 27* By their dreams which
they recount to each other, they think to make my
people forget my name, just as their fathers forgot
my name for Baal. 28*† Let the prophet who has a
dream recount his dream; let him who has my word
speak my word truthfully!

What has straw to do with the wheat?
  says the LORD.
29   Is not my word like fire, says the LORD,
    like a hammer shattering rocks?

30* Therefore I am against the prophets, says the
LORD, who steal my words from each other. 31 Yes, I
am against the prophets, says the LORD, who borrow speeches to pronounce oracles. 32* Yes, I am
against the prophets who prophesy lying dreams,
says the LORD, and who lead my people astray by
recounting their lies and by their empty boasting.
From me they have no mission or command, and
they do this people no good at all, says the LORD.

33† And when this people, or a prophet or a
priest asks you, "What is the burden of the LORD?"
you shall answer, "You are the burden, and I cast
you off, says the LORD." 34 If a prophet or a priest
or anyone else mentions "the burden of the
LORD," I will punish that man and his house.
35 Thus you shall ask, when speaking to one another, "What answer did the LORD give?" or, "What
did the LORD say?" 36 But the burden of the LORD
you shall mention no more. For each man his own
word becomes the burden so that you pervert the
words of the living God, the LORD of hosts, our
God. 37 Thus shall you ask the prophet, "What answer did the LORD give?" or, "What did the LORD
say?" 38 But if you ask about "the burden of the
LORD," then thus says the LORD: Because you use
this phrase, "the burden of the LORD," though I

---

† **23, 17–20:** Not only are the false prophets personally immoral,
but they encourage immorality by prophesying good of those who
do evil. The true prophet, on the other hand, sees the inevitable consequences of sin.
  23, 23: *Near at hand only . . . far off:* God knows not merely the
present but also the future.
  23, 28f: *Straw . . . wheat:* such is the contrast between false and
true prophecy. True prophecy is like fire (cf Jer 5, 14; 20, 9), producing violent results (v 29); Jeremiah's own life is a testimony of this.
  23, 33–40: A wordplay on massa, which means both oracle (usually of woe) and burden. In 34ff it appears that the word massa itself

is forbidden the people in the meaning of a divine oracle. Doubtless
this was because of some association unknown to us. In Hos 2, 18 it
is forbidden to call God "Baal" ("master"), because of the association
of this title with the Canaanite god.

23, 15: Jer 8, 14; 9, 14.
23, 16: Jer 14, 14.
23, 17: Jer 5, 12; Ez 13, 10; Mi
    3, 11; Zec 10, 2.
23, 18: Jb 15, 8; Is 40, 13;
    1 Cor 2, 16.
23, 19: Jer 30, 23.

23, 21: Jer 29, 9.
23, 23: Jer 16, 17; Ps 139, 8.
23, 27: Jgs 3, 7; 8, 33.
23, 28: Nm 12, 6.
23, 30: Dt 18, 20.
23, 32: Jer 28, 15ff.

forbade you to use it, ³⁹ therefore I will lift you on high and cast you from my presence, you and the city which I gave to you and your fathers. ⁴⁰* And I will bring upon you eternal reproach, eternal, unforgettable shame.

The Two Baskets of Figs

24 ¹*† The LORD showed me two baskets of figs placed before the temple of the LORD. —This was after Nebuchadnezzar, king of Babylon, had exiled from Jerusalem Jeconiah, son of Jehoiakim, king of Judah, and the princes of Judah, the artisans and the skilled workers, and brought them to Babylon.— ² One basket contained excellent figs, the early-ripening kind. But the other basket contained very bad figs, so bad they could not be eaten. ³* Then the LORD said to me: What do you see, Jeremiah? "Figs," I replied; "the good ones are very good, but the bad ones very bad, so bad they cannot be eaten." ⁴ Thereupon this word of the LORD came to me: ⁵* Thus says the LORD, the God of Israel: Like these good figs, even so will I regard with favor Judah's exiles whom I sent away from this place into the land of

did you KNOW?

Fig Trees

The fig tree was widely cultivated in the ancient Near East. Its sweet fruit was a delight to taste, and its broad leaves offered welcome shade from the scorching summer sun. In Jer 24, 5–7, ripe figs are presented as an image of the faithful exiles in Babylon. In I Kgs 5, 5, fig leaves symbolize protection and safety. Jesus tells a parable about a fig tree in Lk 13, 6–9. Think about it the next time you eat a Fig Newton!

▶ Jer 24, 1–10

the Chaldeans. ⁶* I will look after them for their good, and bring them back to this land, to build them up, not to tear them down; to plant them, not to pluck them out. ⁷* I will give them a heart with which to understand that I am the LORD. They shall be my people and I will be their God, for they shall return to me with their whole heart. ⁸* And like the figs that are bad, so bad they cannot be eaten—yes, thus says the LORD—even so will I treat Zedekiah, king of Judah, and his princes, the remnant of Jerusalem remaining in this land and those who have settled in the land of Egypt. ⁹* I will make them an object of horror to all the kingdoms of the earth, a reproach and a byword, a taunt and a curse, in all the places to which I will drive them. ¹⁰* I will send upon them the sword, famine, and pestilence, until they have disappeared from the land which I gave them and their fathers.

Seventy Years of Exile

25 ¹*† The word that came to Jeremiah concerning all the people of Judah, in the fourth year of Jehoiakim, son of Josiah, king of Judah (the first year of Nebuchadnezzar, king of Babylon). ² This word the prophet Jeremiah spoke to all the people of Judah and all the citizens of Jerusalem: ³* Since the thirteenth year of Josiah, son of Amon, king of Judah, to this day—these three and twenty years—the word of the LORD has come to me and I spoke to you untiringly, but you would not listen. ⁴* Though you refused to listen or pay heed, the LORD has sent you without fail all his servants the prophets ⁵ with this message: Turn back, each of you, from your evil way and from your evil deeds; then you shall remain in the land which the LORD gave you and your fathers, from of old and forever. ⁶* Do not follow strange gods to serve and adore them, lest you provoke me with your handiwork, and I bring evil upon you. ⁷* But you would not listen to me, says the LORD, and so you provoked me with your handiwork to your own harm. ⁸ Hence, thus says the LORD of hosts: Since you would not listen to my words, ⁹* lo! I will send for and fetch all the tribes of the north, says the LORD (and I will send to Nebuchadnezzar, king of Babylon, my servant); I will bring them

---

24, 1–10: Jeremiah, like Ezekiel, saw that no good could be expected from the people who had been left in Judah under Zedekiah or who had fled into Egypt; good was to be hoped for only from those who would pass through the purifying experience of the exile to form the new Israel.

25, 1–14: *The fourth year of Jehoiakim:* 605 B.C. Officially, the first year of Nebuchadnezzar began the following year; but as early as his victory over Egypt at Carchemish in 605, Nebuchadnezzar was the dominant power in the Near East, in whom Jeremiah now saw the fulfillment of his prophecy of the enemy to come from the north (cf Jer 1, 13; 6, 22ff). In vv 11f occurs for the first time the prophecy

of the seventy years' exile; cf Jer 29, 10. This Jeremiah intends as a round number, to signify that the present generation must die out.

23, 40: Jer 20, 11.	**24, 9:** Jer 15, 4; Dt 28, 37.
24, 1: Am 8, 1f.	**24, 10:** Jer 14, 12.
24, 3: Jer 1, 11.	**25, 1:** Jer 36, 1.
24, 5: Jer 29, 11; Lv 26, 44f.	**25, 3:** Jer 1, 2.
24, 6: Jer 12, 15; Am 9, 15.	**25, 4:** 2 Chr 36, 15.
24, 7: Jer 30, 22; 31, 1; 32,	**25, 6:** Jer 7, 6f.
37; Bar 2, 31.	**25, 7:** Jer 7, 17ff.
24, 8: Jer 29, 18.	**25, 9:** Jer 1, 15; 43, 10.

against this land, against its inhabitants, and against all these neighboring nations. I will doom them, making them an object of horror, of ridicule, of everlasting reproach. 10 Among them I will bring to an end the song of joy and the song of gladness, the voice of the bridegroom and the voice of the bride, the sound of the millstone and the light of the lamp. 11* This whole land shall be a ruin and a desert. Seventy years these nations shall be enslaved to the king of Babylon; 12* but when the seventy years have elapsed, I will punish the king of Babylon and the nation and the land of the Chaldeans for their guilt, says the LORD. Their land I will turn into everlasting desert. 13 Against that land I will fulfill all the words I have spoken against it [all that is written in this book, which Jeremiah prophesied against all the nations]. 14* They also shall be enslaved to great nations and mighty kings, and thus I will repay them according to their own deeds and according to their own handiwork.

The Cup of Judgment on the Nations

15*† For thus said the LORD, the God of Israel, to me: Take this cup of foaming wine from my hand, and have all the nations to whom I will send you drink it. 16* They shall drink, and be convulsed, and go mad, because of the sword I will send among them. 17 I took the cup from the hand of the LORD and gave drink to all the nations to which the LORD sent me: 18 [Jerusalem, the cities of Judah, her kings and her princes, to make them a ruin and a desert, an object of ridicule and cursing, as they are today;] 19 Pharaoh, king of Egypt, and his servants, his princes, all the people under him, native 20† and foreign; all the kings of the land of Uz; all the kings of the land of the Philistines: Ashkelon, Gaza, Ekron, and the remnant of Ashdod; 21 Edom, Moab, and the Ammonites; 22† all the kings of Tyre, of Sidon, and of the shores beyond the sea; 23† Dedan and Tema and Buz, all the desert dwellers who shave their temples; 24 [all the kings of Arabia;] 25 all the kings of Zimri, of Elam, of the Medes; 26† all the kings of the north, near and far, one after the other; all the kingdoms upon the face of the earth [and after them the king of Sheshach shall drink].

27* Tell them: Thus says the LORD of hosts, the God of Israel: Drink! become drunk and vomit; fall,

never to rise, before the sword that I will send among you! 28* If they refuse to take the cup from your hand and drink, say to them: Thus says the LORD of hosts: You must drink! 29 For since with this city, which is called by my name, I begin to inflict evil, how can you possibly be spared? You shall not be spared! I will call down the sword upon all who inhabit the earth, says the LORD of hosts.

30* Prophesy against them all these things and say to them:

The LORD roars from on high,
     from his holy dwelling he raises
         his voice;
Mightily he roars over the range,
     a shout like that of vintagers over
         the grapes.
31 To all who inhabit the earth to its very ends
     the uproar spreads;
For the LORD has an indictment against
     the nations,
he is to pass judgment upon all mankind:
The godless shall be given to the sword,
     says the LORD.
32   Thus says the LORD of hosts:
Lo! calamity stalks
     from nation to nation;
A great storm is unleashed
     from the ends of the earth.

33* On that day, those whom the LORD has slain will be strewn from one end of the earth to the other. None will mourn them, none will gather them for burial; they shall lie like dung on the field.

34 Howl, you shepherds, and wail!
     roll in the dust, leaders of the flock!
The time for your slaughter has come;
     like choice rams you shall fall.
35* There is no flight for the shepherds,
     no escape for the leaders of the flock.
36 Listen! Wailing from the shepherds,
     howling by the leaders of the flock!
For the LORD lays waste their grazing place,
37   desolate lie the peaceful pastures;
38* The lion leaves his lair,
     and their land is made desolate
By the sweeping sword,
     by the burning wrath of the LORD.

---

† **25, 15ff:** Jeremiah is a prophet to the nations (cf 1, 5) as well as to his own people. All the nations mentioned here appear again in the more extensive collection of Jeremiah's oracles against the nations in chapters 46–51.
25, 20: *Uz:* the homeland of Job, in Edomite or Arabian territory.
25, 22: *The shores beyond the sea:* Phoenician commercial colonies planted throughout the Mediterranean world.
25, 23: *Dedan and Tema and Buz:* North Arabian tribes.

25, 26: *Sheshach:* Babylon. The word is formed from babel by substituting letters of the Hebrew alphabet in inverse order.

25, 11: Lv 26, 32–35.	25, 27: Ob 16.
25, 12: Is 13, 20ff.	25, 28: Jer 49, 12.
25, 14: Jer 27, 7; 50, 9.41f;	25, 30: Jer 51, 14.
51, 6.24.	25, 33: Jer 8, 2; 16, 4.6.
25, 15: Rv 14, 10.	25, 35: Jer 32, 4.
25, 16: Jer 51, 7.	25, 38: Jer 4, 7.

Jeremiah Threatened with Death

26 [1]† In the beginning of the reign of Jehoiakim, son of Josiah, king of Judah, this message came from the LORD: [2]* Thus says the LORD: Stand in the court of the house of the LORD and speak to the people of all the cities of Judah who come to worship in the house of the LORD; whatever I command you, tell them, and omit nothing. [3]* Perhaps they will listen and turn back, each from his evil way, so that I may repent of the evil I have planned to inflict upon them for their evil deeds. [4] Say to them: Thus says the LORD: If you disobey me, not living according to the law I placed before you [5]* and not listening to the words of my servants the prophets, whom I send you constantly though you do not obey them, [6]* I will treat this house like Shiloh, and make this the city which all the nations of the earth shall refer to when cursing another.

[7] Now the priests, the prophets, and all the people heard Jeremiah speak these words in the house of the LORD. [8] When Jeremiah finished speaking all that the LORD bade him speak to all the people, the priests and prophets laid hold of him, crying, "You must be put to death! [9] Why do you prophesy in the name of the LORD: 'This house shall be like Shiloh,' and 'This city shall be desolate and deserted'?" And all the people gathered about Jeremiah in the house of the LORD.

[10] When the princes of Judah were informed of these things, they came up from the king's palace to the house of the LORD and held court at the New Gate of the house of the LORD. [11]* The priests and prophets said to the princes and to all the people, "This man deserves death; he has prophesied against this city, as you have heard with your own ears." [12] Jeremiah gave this answer to the princes and all the people: "It was the LORD who sent me to prophesy against this house and city all that you have heard. [13]* Now, therefore, reform your ways and your deeds; listen to the voice of the LORD your God, so that the LORD will repent of the evil with which he threatens you. [14] As for me, I am in your hands; do with me what you think good and right. [15] But mark well: if you put me to death, it is innocent blood you bring on yourselves, on this city and its citizens. For in truth it was the LORD who sent me to you, to speak all these things for you to hear."

[16] Thereupon the princes and all the people said to the priests and the prophets, "This man does not deserve death; it is in the name of the LORD, our God, that he speaks to us." [17] At this, some of the elders of the land came forward and said to all the people assembled, [18]*† "Micah of Moresheth used to prophesy in the days of Hezekiah, king of Judah, and he told all the people of Judah: Thus says the LORD of hosts:

> Zion shall become a plowed field,
> Jerusalem a heap of ruins,
> and the temple mount a forest ridge.

[19]* Did Hezekiah, king of Judah, and all Judah condemn him to death? Did they not rather fear the LORD and entreat the favor of the LORD, so that he repented of the evil with which he had threatened them? But we are on the point of committing this great evil to our own undoing."

The Fate of Uriah

[20] There was another man who prophesied in the name of the LORD, Uriah, son of Shemaiah, from Kiriath-jearim; he prophesied the same things against this city and land as Jeremiah did. [21] When King Jehoiakim and all his officers and princes were informed of his words, the king sought to kill him. But Uriah heard of it and fled in fear to Egypt. [22] Thereupon King Jehoiakim sent Elnathan, son of Achbor, and others with him into Egypt [23] to bring Uriah back to the king, who had him slain by the sword and his corpse cast into the common grave. [24]† But Ahikam, son of Shaphan, protected Jeremiah, so that he was not handed over to the people to be put to death.

Serve Babylon or Perish

27 [1]† [In the beginning of the reign of Jehoiakim, son of Josiah, king of Judah,]† . . . this message came to Jeremiah from the LORD: [2] Thus said the LORD to me: Make for yourself bands and yoke bars and put them over your shoulders. [3] Send to the kings of Edom, of Moab, of the Ammonites, of Tyre, and of Sidon, through the ambassadors who have come to Jerusalem to Zedekiah, king of Judah, [4] and charge them thus:

---

† **26, 1:** *The beginning of the reign:* a technical expression for the time between a king's accession to the throne and the beginning of his first official (calendar) year as king. Jehoiakim's first regnal year was 608 B.C.

26, 18: *Micah of Moresheth:* the prophet Micah, who appears among the canonical minor prophets (cf Mi 1, 1).

26, 24: *Ahikam, son of Shaphan:* one of Josiah's officials (2 Kgs 22, 12) and father of Gedaliah, Jeremiah's friend, who was governor of Judah after Zedekiah's deportation (cf Jer 39, 14; 40, 5ff).

27, 1—29, 32: A special collection of Jeremiah's prophecies dealing with false prophets. From stylistic peculiarities, quite evident in the Hebrew, it is plain that these three chapters once existed independently of the other prophecies of Jeremiah.

27, 1: *[In the beginning of the reign of Jehoiakim . . . Judah,]:* this gloss cannot be correct because according to Jer 28, 1 the time is the fourth year of Zedekiah, 594 B.C., the occasion of an embassy of the neighboring states (v 3), doubtless for the purpose of laying plans against Nebuchadnezzar.

26, 2: Jer 7, 2.   **26, 11:** Jer 38, 4.
26, 3: Jer 18, 3.   **26, 13:** Jer 7, 3.
26, 5: Jer 25, 4.   **26, 18:** Mi 1, 1; 3, 12.
26, 6: Jer 7, 12.14. **26, 19:** 2 Chr 32, 26.

27, 2

Tell your masters: Thus says the LORD of hosts, the God of Israel: 5* It was I who made the earth, and man and beast on the face of the earth, by my great power, with my outstretched arm; and I can give them to whomever I think fit. 6* Now I have given all these lands into the hand of Nebuchadnezzar, king of Babylon, my servant; even the beasts of the field I have given him for his use. 7* All nations shall serve him and his son and his grandson, until the time of his land, too, shall come. Then it in turn shall serve great nations and mighty kings. 8* Meanwhile, if any nation or kingdom will not serve Nebuchadnezzar, king of Babylon, or will not bend its neck under the yoke of the king of Babylon, I will punish that nation with sword, famine, and pestilence, says the LORD, until I give them into his hand.

9*† You, however, must not listen to your prophets, to your diviners and dreamers, to your soothsayers and sorcerers, who say to you, "You need not serve the king of Babylon." 10* For they prophesy lies to you, in order to drive you far from your land, to make me banish you so that you will perish. 11* The people that submits its neck to the yoke of the king of Babylon to serve him I will leave in peace on its own land, says the LORD, to till it and dwell in it.

12* To Zedekiah, king of Judah, I spoke the same words: Submit your necks to the yoke of the king of Babylon; serve him and his people, so that you may live. 13* Why should you and your people die by sword, famine, and pestilence, with which the LORD has threatened the nation that will not serve the king of Babylon? 14* Do not listen to the words of those prophets who say, "You need not serve the king of Babylon," for they prophesy lies to you. 15* I did not send them, says the LORD, but they prophesy falsely in my name, with the result that I must banish you, and you will perish, you and the prophets who are prophesying to you.

16* To the priests and to all the people I spoke as follows: Thus says the LORD: Do not listen to the words of your prophets who prophesy to you: "The vessels of the house of the LORD will be brought back from Babylon soon now," for they prophesy lies to you. 17 Do not listen to them! Serve the king of Babylon that you may live; else this city will become a heap of ruins. 18 If they were prophets, if the word of the LORD were with them, they would intercede with the LORD of hosts, that the vessels which remain in the house of the LORD and in the palace of the king of Judah and in Jerusalem might not be taken to Babylon. 19† For thus says the LORD of hosts concerning the pillars, the bronze sea, the stands, and the rest of the vessels that remain in this city, 20 which Nebuchadnezzar, king of Babylon, did not take when he exiled Jeconiah, son of Jehoiakim, king of Judah, from Jerusalem to Babylon, along with all the nobles of Judah and Jerusalem— 21* yes, thus says the LORD of hosts, the God of Israel, concerning the vessels that remain in the house of the LORD, in the palace of the king of Judah, and in Jerusalem: 22 To Babylon they shall be brought, and there they shall remain, until the day I look for them, says the LORD; then I will bring them back and restore them to this place.

The Two Yokes

28 1 That same year, in [the beginning of] the reign of Zedekiah, king of Judah, in the fifth month of the fourth year, the prophet Hananiah, son of Azzur, from Gibeon, said to me in the house of the LORD in the presence of the priests and all the people: 2 "Thus says the LORD of hosts, the God of Israel: 'I will break the yoke of the king of Babylon. 3 Within two years I will restore to this place all the vessels of the temple of the LORD which Nebuchadnezzar, king of Babylon, took away from this place to Babylon. 4 And I will bring back

---

27, 9: *Your prophets:* seers and diviners served the Gentile kings as the professional prophets served the kings of Judah.
27, 19–22: This prophecy was fulfilled after Zedekiah's disastrous defeat; cf 2 Kgs 25, 13ff.

27, 5: Jer 32, 17.   **27, 6:** Jer 25, 9; 43, 10; Ez 30, 21.25.

27, 7: Jer 25, 11; 2 Chr 36, 20.
27, 8: Jer 25, 9; Bar 2, 22.
27, 9: Jer 29, 8.
27, 10: Jer 14, 13–16.
27, 11: Bar 2, 21.
27, 12: Jer 38, 17.
27, 13: Jer 24, 8ff.
27, 14: Jer 14, 14; 23, 21.
27, 15: Jer 20, 6.
27, 16: Jer 28, 3; 2 Chr 36, 7.10.18.
27, 21f: 2 Kgs 25, 13–17; 2 Chr 36, 18.22.

to this place Jeconiah, son of Jehoiakim, king of Judah, and all the exiles of Judah who went to Babylon,' says the LORD, 'for I will break the yoke of the king of Babylon.'"

5 The prophet Jeremiah answered the prophet Hananiah in the presence of the priests and all the people assembled in house of the LORD, 6 and said: Amen! thus may the LORD do! May he fulfill the things you have prophesied by bringing the vessels of the house of the LORD and all the exiles back from Babylon to this place! 7 But now, listen to what I am about to state in your hearing and the hearing of all the people. 8 From of old, the prophets who were before you and me prophesied war, woe, and pestilence against many lands and mighty kingdoms. 9* But the prophet who prophesies peace is recognized as truly sent by the LORD only when his prophetic prediction is fulfilled.

10 Thereupon the prophet Hananiah took the yoke from the neck of the prophet Jeremiah, broke it, 11 and said in the presence of all the people: "Thus says the LORD: 'Even so, within two years I will break the yoke of Nebuchadnezzar, king of Babylon, from off the neck of all the nations.'" At that, the prophet Jeremiah went away.

12 Some time after the prophet Hananiah had broken the yoke from off the neck of the prophet Jeremiah, the word of the LORD came to Jeremiah: 13 Go tell Hananiah this: Thus says the LORD: By breaking a wooden yoke, you forge an iron yoke! 14* For thus says the LORD of hosts, the God of Israel: A yoke of iron I will place on the necks of all these nations serving Nebuchadnezzar, king of Babylon, and they shall serve him; even the beasts of the field I give him.

15 To the prophet Hananiah the prophet Jeremiah said: Hear this, Hananiah! The LORD has not sent you, and you have raised false confidence in this people. 16* For this, says the LORD, I will dispatch you from the face of the earth; this very year you shall die, because you have preached rebellion against the LORD. 17 That same year, in the seventh month, Hananiah the prophet died.

Letter to the Exiles in Babylon

29 1 This is the contents of the letter which the prophet Jeremiah sent from Jerusalem to the remaining elders among the exiles, to the priests, the prophets, and all the people who were exiled by Nebuchadnezzar from Jerusalem to Babylon. 2* This was after King Jeconiah and the queen mother, the courtiers, the princes of Judah and Jerusalem, the artisans and the skilled workmen had left Jerusalem. 3† Delivered in Babylon by Elasah, son of Shaphan, and by Gemariah, son of Hilkiah, whom Zedekiah, king of Judah, sent to the king of Babylon, the letter read:

4 Thus says the LORD of hosts, the God of Israel, to all the exiles whom I exiled from Jerusalem to Babylon: 5 Build houses to dwell in; plant gardens, and eat their fruits. 6 Take wives and beget sons and daughters; find wives for your sons and give your daughters husbands, so that they may bear sons and daughters. There you must increase in number, not decrease. 7* Promote the welfare of the city to which I have exiled you; pray for it to the LORD, for upon its welfare depends your own.

10* Thus says the LORD: Only after seventy years have elapsed for Babylon will I visit you and fulfill for you my promise to bring you back to this place. 11 For I know well the plans I have in mind for you, says the LORD, plans for your welfare, not for woe! plans to give you a future full of hope. 12* When you call me, when you go to pray to me, I will listen to you. 13 When you look for me, you will find me. Yes, when you seek me with all your heart, 14* you will find me with you, says the LORD, and I will change your lot; I will gather you together from all the nations and all the places to which I have banished you, says the LORD, and bring you back to the place from which I have exiled you.

16 Thus says the LORD concerning the king who sits on David's throne, and all the people who remain in this city, your brethren who did not go with you into exile; 17 thus says the LORD of hosts: I am sending against them sword, famine and pestilence. I will make them like rotten figs, too bad to be eaten. 18* I will pursue them with sword, famine, and pestilence, and make them an object of horror to all the kingdoms of the earth, of malediction, astonishment, ridicule, and reproach to all the nations among which I will banish them. 19* For they did not listen to my words, says the LORD, though I kept sending them my servants the prophets, only to have them go unheeded, says the LORD.

20 You, now, listen to the word of the LORD, all you exiles whom I sent away from Jerusalem to Babylon. 15 As for your saying, "The LORD has raised up for us prophets here in Babylon"— 8* thus says

29, 3: *Elasah:* possibly the brother of Ahikam (cf Jer 26, 24). Gemariah; perhaps the son of the high priest Hilkiah; cf 2 Kgs 22, 4. Zedekiah had dispatched these men to Nebuchadnezzar for some other purpose, possibly the payment of tribute, but Jeremiah took advantage of their mission to send his letter by them.

28, 9: Dt 18, 22.
28, 14: Jer 27, 6f; Dt 28, 48.
28, 16: Dt 13, 6.
29, 2: 2 Kgs 24, 15.
29, 7: 1 Tm 2, 1f.
29, 10: Jer 25, 11; 2 Chr 36, 21f; Ezr 1, 1; Dn 9, 2; Zec 1, 12; 7, 5.
29, 12: Jer 33, 3.
29, 14: Jer 23, 3.8.
29, 18: Jer 15, 4; 24, 9; 34, 17f.
29, 19: Jer 25, 4.
29, 8: Jer 27, 9.14.

the LORD of hosts, the God of Israel: Do not let yourselves be deceived by the prophets and diviners who are among you; do not listen to those among you who dream dreams. 9* For they prophesy lies to you in my name; I did not send them, says the LORD. 21 *This is what the LORD of hosts, the God of Israel, has to say about those who prophesy lies to you in my name, Ahab, son of Kolaiah, and Zedekiah, son of Maaseiah: I am handing them over to Nebuchadnezzar, king of Babylon, who will slay them before your eyes. 22 All the exiles of Judah in Babylon will pattern a curse after them: "May the LORD make you like Zedekiah and Ahab, whom the king of Babylon roasted in the flames." 23 *For they are criminals in Israel, committing adultery with their neighbors' wives, and alleging in my name things I did not command. I know, I am witness, says the LORD.

The False Prophet Shemaiah

24 Say this to Shemaiah, the Nehelamite: 25 Thus says the LORD of hosts, the God of Israel: Because you sent letters on your own authority to all the people of Jerusalem, to all the priests and to Zephaniah, the priest, son of Maaseiah, with this message: 26† "The LORD has appointed you priest in place of the priest Jehoiada, so that there may be police officers in the house of the LORD, to take action against all madmen and those who pose as prophets, by putting them into the stocks or the pillory. 27 Why, then, do you not rebuke Jeremiah of Anathoth who poses as a prophet among you? 28 For he sent us in Babylon this message: It will be a long time; build houses to live in; plant gardens and eat their fruits. . . ."

29 When the priest Zephaniah read this letter to the prophet, 30 the word of the LORD came to Jeremiah: 31 Send the message to all the exiles: Thus says the LORD concerning Shemaiah, the Nehelamite: Because Shemaiah prophesies to you without a mission from me, and raises false confidence, 32 says the LORD, I will therefore punish Shemaiah, the Nehelamite, and his offspring. None of them shall survive among this people to see the good I will do to this people, says the LORD, because he preached rebellion against the LORD.

The Restoration

30 1† The following message came to Jeremiah from the LORD: 2* Thus says the LORD, the God of Israel: Write all the words I have spoken to you in a book. 3* For behold, the days will come, says the LORD, when I will change the lot of my people (of Israel and Judah, says the LORD), and bring them back to the land which I gave to their fathers; they shall have it as their possession.

4 These are the words which the LORD spoke to Israel and to Judah: 5 thus says the LORD:

A cry of dismay we hear;
 fear reigns, not peace.
6* Inquire, and see:
 since when do men bear children?
Why, then, do I see all these men,
 with their hands on their loins
 like women in childbirth?
Why have all their faces turned deathly pale?
7* How mighty is that day—
 none like it!
A time of distress for Jacob,
 though he shall be saved from it.

8* On that day, says the LORD of hosts, "I will break his yoke from off your necks and snap your bonds." Strangers shall no longer enslave them; 9*† instead, they shall serve the LORD, their God, and David, their king, whom I will raise up for them.

10* But you, my servant Jacob, fear not, says
 the LORD,
 be not dismayed, O Israel!
Behold, I will deliver you from the far-off land,
 your descendants, from their land of exile;
Jacob shall again find rest,
 shall be tranquil and undisturbed,
11* for I am with you, says the LORD, to
 deliver you.
I will make an end of all the nations
 among which I have scattered you;
 but of you I will not make an end.
I will chastise you as you deserve,
 I will not let you go unpunished.

---

† **29, 26–29:** The words of Jeremiah to the false prophet Shemaiah are not fully preserved in the current Hebrew text, as is seen in the incomplete sentence of this translation (vv 25–28). In his letter to Zephaniah Shemaiah reminds him of his authority, as Pashhur's successor, to imprison Jeremiah. Zephaniah, however, merely reads the letter to Jeremiah but does not imprison him.

30, 1—31, 40: These two chapters do not belong chronologically to those that precede or follow. They contain mainly oracles of salvation which Jeremiah originally uttered on behalf of the conquered remnants of the northern kingdom; then, after Judah began to share Samaria's fate, the oracles were extended to include Judah. Their composition is to be placed early in Jeremiah's ministry, probably after the fall of Nineveh (612 B.C.), when Josiah assumed power over the North; cf 2 Kgs 23, 15ff.

30, 9: *David, their king:* the messianic King of the Davidic line, often called David by the prophets; cf Ez 34, 23f; 37, 24f; Hos 3, 5.

29, 9: Jer 5, 31.
29, 21: Jer 14, 14.
29, 23: Jer 23, 14.
30, 2: Jer 36, 2; Hb 2, 2; Rv 1, 11.
30, 3: Jer 29, 14; 31, 8.10.23; 32, 37.44; Ez 39, 25; Am 9, 14.
30, 6: Jer 6, 24; 50, 43.
30, 7: Am 5, 18; Zep 1, 14f.
30, 8: Is 14, 5f; Ez 34, 27.
30, 9: Ez 34, 23; 37, 24; Hos 3, 5; Lk 1, 69.
30, 10: Jer 46, 27; Is 43, 5.
30, 11: Jer 46, 28; Ez 11, 16f; Am 9, 8f.

12*   For thus says the LORD:
    Incurable is your wound,
      grievous your bruise;
13 There is none to plead your cause,
    no remedy for your running sore,
    no healing for you.
14* All your lovers have forgotten you,
    they do not seek you.
    I struck you as an enemy would strike,
    punished you cruelly;
15* Why cry out over your wound?
    your pain is without relief.
    Because of your great guilt,
    your numerous sins,
    I have done this to you.
16* Yet all who devour you shall be devoured,
    all your enemies shall go into exile.
    All who plunder you shall be plundered,
    all who pillage you I will hand over to pillage.
17* For I will restore you to health;
    of your wounds I will heal you, says the LORD.
    "The outcast" they have called you,
    "with no avenger."
18*   Thus says the LORD:
    See! I will restore the tents of Jacob,
    his dwellings I will pity;
    City shall be rebuilt upon hill,
    and palace restored as it was.
19* From them will resound songs of praise,
    the laughter of happy men.
    I will make them not few, but many;
    they will not be tiny, for I will glorify them.
20* His sons shall be as of old,
    his assembly before me shall stand firm;
    I will punish all his oppressors.
21† His leader shall be one of his own,
    and his rulers shall come from his kin.
    When I summon him, he shall approach me;
    how else should one take the deadly risk
    of approaching me? says the LORD.
22* You shall be my people,
    and I will be your God.

23* See, the storm of the LORD!
    His wrath breaks forth
    In a whirling storm
    that bursts upon the heads of the wicked.

24* The anger of the LORD will not abate
    until he has done and fulfilled
    what he has determined in his heart.
    When the time comes,
    you will fully understand.

Good News of the Return

31 1* At that time, says the LORD,
    I will be the God of all the tribes
    of Israel,
    and they shall be my people.
2†   Thus says the LORD:
    The people that escaped the sword
    have found favor in the desert.
    As Israel comes forward to be given his rest,
3*   the LORD appears to him from afar:
    With age-old love I have loved you;
    so I have kept my mercy toward you.
4 Again I will restore you, and you shall
    be rebuilt,
    O virgin Israel;
    Carrying your festive tambourines,
    you shall go forth dancing with
    the merrymakers.
5* Again you shall plant vineyards
    on the mountains of Samaria;
    those who plant them shall enjoy the fruits.
6* Yes, a day will come when the watchmen
    will call out on Mount Ephraim:
    "Rise up, let us go to Zion,
    to the LORD, our God."

The Road of Return

7*   For thus says the LORD:
    Shout with joy for Jacob,
    exult at the head of the nations;
    proclaim your praise and say:
    The LORD has delivered his people,
    the remnant of Israel.
8* Behold, I will bring them back
    from the land of the north;
    I will gather them from the ends of the world,
    with the blind and the lame in their midst,
    The mothers and those with child;
    they shall return as an immense throng.
9* They departed in tears,
    but I will console them and guide them;

30, 21: *His leader:* probably not the messianic King, but simply any one of the rulers of the restored Israel, who will no longer be foreigners, and with whom the Lord will be on terms of intimacy, as with the whole people. *The deadly risk of approaching me:* to approach God unsummoned brings death; cf Lv 16, 1f.

31, 2: *The people that escaped the sword:* the exiles who were not killed but deported; they have found favor in the desert, across which they were driven into captivity. The prophet alludes to the first desert wandering of Israel (Ex 16ff), in which the people found the Lord. *His rest:* the land of promise. The perfect fulfillment of this promised rest is found only in the New Testament (Hebrews, chapters 3 and 4).

30, 12: Jer 10, 19; 14, 17; 15, 18.
30, 14: Jer 22, 22; Lam 1, 19.
30, 15: Jer 15, 18.
30, 16: Jer 2, 3.
30, 17: Jer 33, 6.
30, 18: Jer 33, 7.11; Ezr 6, 3–15; Ez 36, 10.
30, 19: Is 35, 10; 51, 11.
30, 20: Is 49, 26.
30, 22: Jer 24, 7; 31, 1.33; 32, 38; Lv 26, 12; Ez 11, 20; 36, 28.

30, 23: Jer 23, 19.
30, 24: Jer 23, 20.
31, 1: Jer 30, 22.
31, 3: Dt 7, 8; 10, 15; Is 43, 4; 63, 9; Hos 11, 1.4.
31, 5: Is 65, 21; Am 9, 14.
31, 6: Is 2, 3; 27, 13; Mi 4, 2.
31, 7: Is 12, 6.
31, 8: Jer 3, 18; 23, 3.8; Is 35, 5f.
31, 9: Ex 4, 22.

I will lead them to brooks of water,
    on a level road, so that none shall stumble.
For I am a father to Israel,
    Ephraim is my first-born.
10 Hear the word of the LORD, O nations,
    proclaim it on distant coasts, and say:
He who scattered Israel, now gathers
      them together,
he guards them as a shepherd his flock.
11* The LORD shall ransom Jacob,
    he shall redeem him from the hand of
      his conqueror.
12* Shouting, they shall mount the heights of Zion,
    they shall come streaming to the
      LORD's blessings:
The grain, the wine, and the oil,
    the sheep and the oxen;
They themselves shall be like
      watered gardens,
    never again shall they languish.
13 Then the virgins shall make merry and dance,
    and young men and old as well.
I will turn their mourning into joy,
    I will console and gladden them after
      their sorrows.
14 I will lavish choice portions upon the priests,
    and my people shall be filled with
      my blessings,
    says the LORD.

End of Rachel's Mourning

15*†   Thus says the LORD:
In Ramah is heard the sound of moaning,
    of bitter weeping!
Rachel mourns her children,
    she refuses to be consoled
    because her children are no more.
16   Thus says the LORD:
Cease your cries of mourning,
    wipe the tears from your eyes.
The sorrow you have shown shall have
    its reward,
    says the LORD,
    they shall return from the enemy's land.
17* There is hope for your future, says the LORD;
    your sons shall return to their own borders.

18* I hear, I hear Ephraim pleading:
    You chastised me, and I am chastened;
    I was an untamed calf.
If you allow me, I will return,
    for you are the LORD, my God.

Rachel Weeps

Rachel was the "mother of Israel," the favored wife of Jacob (Gn 29, 28–30) — the patriarch whose twelve sons formed the twelve tribes of Israel. In Jer 31, 15–17, she is symbolically weeping over the death and captivity of her children—the Israelites—after the Babylonian invasion.

Rachel weeping has become an image of trauma and unrelenting grief over violence, death, and slaughter, especially when children are involved. For example, Mt 2, 16–18 quotes Jer 31, 15–17 in a story about the massacre of infants in Bethlehem. Project Rachel is an organized ministry for women who have had abortions. And Rachel Weeps is a Holocaust exhibition recalling the murder of millions of Jewish men, women, and children.

Jeremiah goes on in verses 16–17 with words of hope. God promises that the scattered children will be brought back. We can trust that God is with the victims of senseless violence and those who grieve for them. Let us pray for Rachel's grief to end.

▶ Jer 31, 15–17

19* I turn in repentance;
    I have come to myself, I strike my breast;
I blush with shame,
    I bear the disgrace of my youth.
20* Is Ephraim not my favored son,
    the child in whom I delight?
Often as I threaten him,
    I still remember him with favor;
My heart stirs for him,
    I must show him mercy, says the LORD.

Summons To Return Home

21 Set up road markers,
    put up guideposts;
Turn your attention to the highway,
    the road by which you went.

31, 15: *Ramah:* a village about five miles north of Jerusalem, where Rachel was buried (1 Sm 10, 2). *Rachel:* said to mourn for her children since she was the ancestress of Ephraim, the chief of the northern tribes. Mt 2, 18 applies this verse to the slaughter of the innocents by Herod.

31, 11: Is 44, 23; 48, 20.
31, 12: Is 58, 11.
31, 15: Mt 2, 18.
31, 17: Jer 29, 10–14.

31, 18: Lv 26, 40ff.
31, 19: Dt 30, 1ff.
31, 20: Hos 11, 8.

Turn back, O virgin Israel,
   turn back to these your cities.
22† How long will you continue to stray,
   rebellious daughter?
The LORD has created a new thing upon
   the earth:
   the woman must encompass the man
    with devotion.

23* Thus says the LORD of hosts, the God of Israel: When I change their lot in the land of Judah
and her cities, they shall again repeat this greeting:
"May the LORD bless you, holy mountain, abode
of justice!" 24 Judah and all her cities, the farmers
and those who lead the flock, shall dwell there together. 25 For I will refresh the weary soul; every
soul that languishes I will replenish. 26† Upon this
I awoke and opened my eyes; but my sleep was
sweet to me.

27 The days are coming, says the LORD, when I
will seed the house of Israel and the house of Judah
with the seed of man and the seed of beast. 28* As I
once watched over them to uproot and pull down,
to destroy, to ruin, and to harm, so I will watch over

them to build and to plant, says the LORD. 29*† In
those days they shall no longer say,

"The fathers ate unripe grapes,
   and the children's teeth are set on edge,"

30 but through his own fault only shall anyone die:
the teeth of him who eats the unripe grapes shall be
set on edge.

The New Covenant

31*† The days are coming, says the LORD, when I
will make a new covenant with the house of Israel
and the house of Judah. 32* It will not be like the
covenant I made with their fathers the day I took
them by the hand to lead them forth from the land
of Egypt; for they broke my covenant and I had to
show myself their master, says the LORD. 33* But
this is the covenant which I will make with the
house of Israel after those days, says the LORD. I will
place my law within them, and write it upon their
hearts; I will be their God, and they shall be my
people. 34* No longer will they have need to teach
their friends and kinsmen how to know the LORD.

The Heart of the Matter

LIVE IT!

The Ten Commandments. The stone tablets on which they were written are the
most famous stone tablets in the world, and yet no one knows where they are.
The ark of the Covenant, in which they were once kept, was taken during a raid
on the Temple (Jer 52, 17–23). What a find they would be today! Imagine all the
people flocking to see the original Ten Commandments.

But perhaps their absence makes Jeremiah's beautiful words about the new Covenant
in Jer 31, 31–34 even more fitting. What was etched in stone on those tablets needs to be
etched in our heart. We keep in our heart what is most valuable to us. If we keep God's law
there, we have no need for it written in stone.

When you look into your heart, what do you find written there?

▸ Jer 31, 31–34

31, 22: *The woman must encompass the man:* the words "with
devotion," not in the Hebrew, are added for the sense. No fully satisfactory explanation has been given this text. Among the more probable are these: (a) Formerly the man (the Lord) encompassed the
woman (Israel) with mercy and devotion; now in the spiritual religion of Israel which will follow on the restoration, this order will be
reversed. (b) So secure will Israel be after the restoration that women
will no longer need the natural protection of their husbands, but
even weak women can protect men. (c) St. Jerome in his commentary on this verse understood it of Mary's virginal conception of
Christ. "The Lord has created a new thing on earth; without seed of
man, without carnal union and conception, 'a woman will encompass a man' within her womb—One who, though He will later appear to advance in wisdom and age through the stages of infancy and
childhood, yet, while confined for the usual number of months in his
mother's womb, will already be perfect man."

31, 26: *I awoke . . . sweet to me:* probably said by the
prophet himself.

31, 29: *"The fathers . . . on edge":* a proverb used in Israel, expressing the idea that children suffer for the sins of their parents (cf Ez
18, 2). The Israel of the restoration will be characterized instead by
personal responsibility and retribution for one's acts (v 30; cf vv
31–34).

31, 31–34: The new covenant to be made with Israel is a common theme of the prophets, beginning with Hosea. According to Jeremiah, the qualities of the new covenant that make it different from
the old are: (a) It will not be broken, but will last forever; (b) Its law
will be written in the heart, not merely on tablets of stone; (c) The
knowledge of God will be so generally shown forth in the life of the
people that it will no longer be necessary to put it into words of instruction. In the fullest sense, this prophecy was fulfilled only
through the work of Jesus Christ; cf Lk 22, 20; 1 Cor 11, 25.

31, 23: Jer 30, 3; Ps 122, 8.
31, 28: Jer 1, 10; 18, 7.
31, 29: Dt 24, 16; Ez 18, 2.
31, 31: Jer 32, 40; Heb 9, 15.
31, 32: Ex 24, 7f; Dt 5, 2.
31, 33: Jer 32, 40; Ez 37, 26;
   Heb 10, 16.
31, 34: Is 54, 13.

All, from least to greatest, shall know me, says the LORD, for I will forgive their evildoing and remember their sin no more.

Certainty of God's Promise

35*   Thus says the LORD,
He who gives the sun to light the day,
    moon and stars to light the night;
Who stirs up the sea till its waves roar,
    whose name is LORD of hosts:
36* If ever these natural laws give way
    in spite of me, says the LORD,
Then shall the race of Israel cease
    as a nation before me forever.
37   Thus says the LORD:
If the heavens on high can be measured,
    or the foundations below the earth
    be sounded,
Then will I cast off the whole race of Israel
    because of all they have done, says
    the LORD.

Rebuilding of Jerusalem

38*† The days are coming, says the LORD, when the city shall be rebuilt as the LORD'S, from the Tower of Hananel to the Corner Gate. 39 The measuring line shall be stretched from there straight to the hill Gareb and then turn to Goah. 40† The whole valley of corpses and ashes, all the slopes toward the Kidron Valley, as far as the corner of the Horse Gate at the east, shall be holy to the LORD. Never again shall the city be rooted up or thrown down.

Pledge of Restoration†

32 ¹ This message came to Jeremiah from the LORD in the tenth year of Zedekiah,† king of Judah, the eighteenth year of Nebuchadnezzar. ²* At that time the army of the king of Babylon was besieging Jerusalem, and the prophet Jeremiah was imprisoned in the quarters of the guard, at the king's palace. ³* Zedekiah, king of Judah, had imprisoned him there, remonstrating: "How dare you

prophesy: Thus says the LORD: I am handing over this city to the king of Babylon, who will capture it. ⁴* Neither shall Zedekiah, king of Judah, escape the hands of the Chaldeans; rather shall he be handed over to the king of Babylon. They shall meet and speak face to face, ⁵* and Zedekiah shall be taken to Babylon. There he shall remain, until I attend to him, says the LORD; in fighting the Chaldeans, you cannot win!"

⁶† This message came to me from the LORD, said Jeremiah: ⁷*† Hanamel, son of your uncle Shallum, will come to you with the offer: "Buy for yourself my field in Anathoth, since you, as nearest relative, have the first right of purchase." ⁸ Then, as the LORD foretold, Hanamel, my uncle's son, came to me to the quarters of the guard and said, "Please buy my field in Anathoth, in the district of Benjamin; as nearest relative, you have the first claim to possess it; make it yours." I knew this was what the LORD meant, ⁹ so I bought the field in Anathoth from my cousin Hanamel, paying him the money, seventeen silver shekels.

¹⁰ When I had written and sealed the deed, called witnesses and weighed out the silver on the scales, ¹¹† I accepted the deed of purchase, both the sealed copy, containing title and conditions, and the open one. ¹²* This deed of purchase I gave to Baruch, son of Neriah, son of Mahseiah, in the presence of my cousin Hanamel and of the witnesses who had signed the deed, and before all the men of Judah who happened to be in the quarters of the guard.

¹³ In their presence I gave Baruch this charge: ¹⁴† Thus says the LORD of hosts, the God of Israel: Take these deeds, both the sealed and the open deed of purchase, and put them in an earthen jar, so that they can be kept there a long time. ¹⁵ For thus says the LORD of hosts, the God of Israel: Houses and fields and vineyards shall again be bought in this land.

¹⁶ After giving the deed of purchase to Baruch, son of Neriah, I prayed thus to the LORD: ¹⁷* Ah, Lord GOD, you have made heaven and earth by your great

---

31, 38: *From the Tower of Hananel to the Corner Gate:* from the northeast to the northwest.

31, 40: *Valley of corpses and ashes:* the Valley of Ben-hinnom, which joins the Kidron at the southeast of ancient Jerusalem. *The Horse Gate:* in the eastern city wall, at the southeast corner of the temple area.

32, 1–44: This chapter recounts a prophecy "in action." At the Lord's command, Jeremiah fulfills his family duty to purchase the land of his cousin, carrying out all the legal forms, including records, to testify that Judah will be restored and that the life of the past will be resumed.

32, 1: *The tenth year of Zedekiah:* 588 B.C. *The eighteenth year of Nebuchadnezzar:* dating his reign from his victory at Carchemish; see note on Jer 25, 1–14.

32, 6–9: Jeremiah's imprisonment by the weak-willed Zedekiah was a technical custody that did not deprive him of all freedom of action. The siege maintained by the Chaldeans (v 2) was only now beginning (v 24), and could be bypassed by individual persons going to and fro between Jerusalem and nearby Anathoth.

32, 7: *The first right of purchase:* the obligation of the closest relative to redeem the property of one in economic distress, so that the ancestral land might remain within the family (Lv 25, 25–28); see note on Ru 2, 20.

32, 11: *The sealed copy . . . and the open one:* the legal deed of sale was written on a scroll, which was then rolled up and sealed; about it was rolled another scroll, left unsealed, containing a copy or a summary of the first.

32, 14: *In an earthen jar:* the first of the Dead Sea Scrolls were found in such a jar.

31, 35: Gn 1, 14–18.
31, 36: Jer 33, 20f.
31, 38: Neh 12, 38; Zec 14, 10f.
32, 2: Jer 33, 1; 37, 20; 38, 6; 39, 14.
32, 3: Jer 26, 9; 34, 2; 37, 6–10.
32, 4: Jer 34, 3; 38, 18.23; 39, 4–7.
32, 5: Jer 39, 7; 52, 11.
32, 7: Lv 25, 24–34; Ru 4, 4.
32, 12: Jer 36, 4.
32, 17: 2 Kgs 19, 15; Jb 42, 2.

might, with your outstretched arm; nothing is impossible to you. ¹⁸* You continue your kindness through a thousand generations; and you repay the fathers' guilt, even into the lap of their sons who follow them. O God, great and mighty, whose name is LORD of hosts, ¹⁹* great in counsel, mighty in deed, whose eyes are open to all the ways of men, giving to each according to his ways, according to the fruit of his deeds: ²⁰* you have wrought signs and wonders in the land of Egypt and to this day, both in Israel and among all other men, until now you have gained renown. ²¹ With strong hand and outstretched arm you brought your people Israel out of the land of Egypt amid signs and wonders and great terror. ²²* This land you gave them, as you had promised their fathers under oath, a land flowing with milk and honey. ²³* They entered and took possession of it, but they did not listen to your voice; by your law they did not live, and what you commanded they failed to do. Hence you let all these evils befall them. ²⁴* See, the siegeworks have arrived at this city to breach it; the city will be handed over to the Chaldeans who are attacking it, amid sword, famine, and pestilence. What you threatened has happened, you see it yourself; ²⁵ and yet you tell me, O Lord GOD: Buy the field with money, call in witnesses. But the city has already been handed over to the Chaldeans!

²⁶ Then this word of the LORD came to Jeremiah: ²⁷ I am the LORD, the God of all mankind! Is anything impossible to me? ²⁸ This now is what the LORD says: I will hand over this city to the Chaldeans, for Nebuchadnezzar, king of Babylon, to take. ²⁹* The Chaldeans who are attacking it shall enter this city and set fire to it, burning it and its houses, on the roofs of which incense was burned to Baal and libations were poured out to strange gods as a provocation to me. ³⁰* The Israelites and the Judeans from their youth have done only what is evil in my eyes; the Israelites did nothing but provoke me with the works of their hands, says the LORD. ³¹ From the day it was built to this day, this city has excited my anger and wrath, ³²* so that I must put it out of my sight for all the wickedness the Israelites and Judeans, with their kings and their princes, their priests and their prophets, the men of Judah and the citizens of Jerusalem, have done to provoke me. ³³* They turned their backs to me, not their faces; though I kept teaching them, they would not listen to my correction. ³⁴* They defiled the house named

after me by the horrid idols they set up in it. ³⁵*† They built high places to Baal in the Valley of Ben-hinnom, and immolated their sons and daughters to Molech, bringing sin upon Judah; this I never commanded them, nor did it even enter my mind that they should practice such abominations.

³⁶ Now, therefore, thus says the LORD, the God of Israel, concerning this city, which as you say is handed over to the king of Babylon amid sword, famine, and pestilence: ³⁷* Behold, I will gather them together from all the lands to which in anger, wrath, and great rage I banish them; I will bring them back to this place and settle them here in safety. ³⁸* They shall be my people, and I will be their God. ³⁹ One heart and one way I will give them, that they may fear me always, to their own good and that of their children after them. ⁴⁰* I will make with them an eternal covenant, never to cease doing good to them; into their hearts I will put the fear of me, that they may never depart from me. ⁴¹* I will take delight in doing good to them: I will replant them firmly in this land, with all my heart and soul.

⁴²* For thus says the LORD: Just as I brought upon this people all this great evil, so I will bring upon them all the good I promise them. ⁴³* Fields shall again be bought in this land, which you call a desert, without man or beast, handed over to the Chaldeans. ⁴⁴* Fields shall be bought with money, deeds written and sealed, and witnesses shall be used in the land of Benjamin, in the suburbs of Jerusalem, in the cities of Judah and of the hill country, in the cities of the foothills and of the Negeb, when I change their lot, says the LORD.

Restoration of Jerusalem

33 ¹ The word of the LORD came to Jeremiah a second time while he was still imprisoned in the quarters of the guard: ² Thus says the LORD who made the earth and gave it form and firmness, whose name is LORD: ³* Call to me, and I will answer you; I will tell to you things great beyond reach of your knowledge. ⁴* Thus says the LORD, the God of Israel, concerning the houses of this city and the palaces of Judah's kings, which are being destroyed in the face of siegeworks and the sword: ⁵* men come to battle the Chaldeans, and these houses will be filled with the corpses of those whom I slay in my anger and wrath, when I hide my face from this city for all their wickedness.

---

† **32, 35:** *Molech:* the god to whom human sacrifice was offered in the Valley of Ben-hinnom. Here, as in Jer 19, 5, he is given the name Baal; see note on Lv 18, 21.

32, 18: Ex 20, 5f; Dt 5, 9.
32, 19: Jb 34, 21; Ps 33, 13ff.
32, 20: Ex 6, 6; Dt 4, 34; Ps 135, 9.
32, 22: Jer 11, 5; Gn 15, 18; 17, 8; 26, 3.
32, 23: Jer 7, 24ff; Dn 9, 10–14.
32, 24: Jer 21, 5; 33, 4.
32, 29: Jer 21, 10; 37, 8ff.
32, 30: Jer 3, 25; 44, 8.
32, 32: Jer 2, 26; Is 3, 8.
32, 33: Jer 7, 24.
32, 34: Jer 7, 30; 2 Kgs 21, 4f.
32, 35: Jer 7, 31; 19, 5; Ps 106, 37f.
32, 37: Jer 23, 3; 29, 14; Is 11, 12; Ez 11, 17.
32, 38: Jer 24, 7; 31, 33.
32, 40: Jer 31, 31ff.
32, 41: Dt 30, 9.
32, 42: Jer 33, 10–14; Zec 8, 13.
32, 43: Jer 33, 10.
32, 44: Jer 17, 26; 33, 7.
33, 3: Jer Is 48, 6.
33, 4: Jer 32, 24.
33, 5: Jer 21, 4ff.

⁶* Behold, I will treat and assuage the city's wounds; I will heal them, and reveal to them an abundance of lasting peace. ⁷* I will change the lot of Judah and the lot of Israel, and rebuild them as of old. ⁸* I will cleanse them of all the guilt they incurred by sinning against me; all their offenses by which they sinned and rebelled against me, I will forgive. ⁹ Then Jerusalem shall be my joy, my praise, my glory, before all the nations of the earth, as they hear of all the good I will do among them. They shall be in fear and trembling over all the peaceful benefits I will give her.

¹⁰* Thus says the LORD: In this place of which you say, "How desolate it is, without man, without beast!" and in the cities of Judah, in the streets of Jerusalem that are now deserted, without man, without citizen, without beast, there shall yet be heard ¹¹* the cry of joy, the cry of gladness, the voice of the bridegroom, the voice of the bride, the sound of those who bring thank offerings to the house of the LORD, singing, "Give thanks to the LORD of hosts, for the LORD is good; his mercy endures forever." For I will restore this country as of old, says the LORD.

¹² Thus says the LORD of hosts: In this place, now desolate, without man or beast, and in all its cities there shall again be sheepfolds for the shepherds to couch their flocks. ¹³ In the cities of the hill country, of the foothills, and of the Negeb, in the land of Benjamin and the suburbs of Jerusalem, and in the cities of Judah, flocks will again pass under the hands of the one who counts them, says the LORD.

¹⁴† The days are coming, says the LORD, when I will fulfill the promise I made to the house of Israel and Judah. ¹⁵* In those days, in that time, I will raise up for David a just shoot; he shall do what is right and just in the land. ¹⁶ In those days Judah shall be safe and Jerusalem shall dwell secure; this is what they shall call her: "The LORD our justice." ¹⁷* For thus says the LORD: Never shall David lack a successor on the throne of the house of Israel, ¹⁸* nor shall priests of Levi ever be lacking, to offer holocausts before me, to burn cereal offerings, and to sacrifice victims.

This word of the LORD also came to Jeremiah: ¹⁹ Thus says the LORD: ²⁰* If you can break my covenant with day, and my covenant with night, so

that day and night no longer alternate in sequence, ²¹ then can my covenant with my servant David also be broken, so that he will not have a son to be king upon his throne, and my covenant with the priests of Levi who minister to me. ²² Like the host of heaven which cannot be numbered, and the sands of the sea which cannot be counted, I will multiply the descendants of my servant David and the Levites who minister to me.

²³ This word of the LORD came to Jeremiah: ²⁴* Have you not noticed what these people are saying: "The LORD has rejected the two tribes which he had chosen"? They spurn my people as if it were no longer a nation in their eyes. ²⁵* Thus says the LORD: When I have no covenant with day and night, and have given no laws to heaven and earth, ²⁶ then too will I reject the descendants of Jacob and of my servant David, so as not to take from his descendants rulers for the race of Abraham, Isaac, and Jacob. For I will change their lot and show them mercy.

IV: Fall of Jerusalem

Fate of Zedekiah

34 ¹* This word came to Jeremiah from the LORD while Nebuchadnezzar, king of Babylon, and his armies and the earth's kingdoms subject to him, as well as the other peoples, were all attacking Jerusalem and all her cities: ²* Thus says the LORD, the God of Israel: Go to Zedekiah, king of Judah, and tell him: Thus says the LORD: I am handing this city over to the king of Babylon; he will destroy it with fire. ³* Neither shall you escape his hand; rather you will be captured and fall into his hands. You shall see the king of Babylon and speak to him face to face. Then you shall be taken to Babylon.

⁴ But if you obey the word of the LORD, Zedekiah, king of Judah, then, says the LORD to you, you shall not die by the sword. ⁵ You shall die in peace, and they will lament you as their lord, and burn spices for your burial as they did for your fathers, the kings who preceded you from the first; it is I who make this promise, says the LORD.

⁶ The prophet Jeremiah told all these things to Zedekiah, king of Judah, in Jerusalem, ⁷† while the

33, 14–26: This is the longest continuous passage in the Book of Jeremiah that is lacking in the Greek. It appears to be the postexilic composition of an inspired writer who used parts of the prophecies of Jeremiah—often, however, in a sense different from the prophet's. The prediction of an eternal Davidic dynasty (14–17) to fulfill the prophecy of Nathan (2 Sm 7, 11–16), and of a perpetual priesthood and sacrifice (18), was not to be realized in the restoration of the Jewish nation. It finds its fulfillment only in Jesus of Nazareth, who combined with his messianic Davidic kingship an eternal priesthood; cf Heb 6, 20; 7, 24f.

34, 7: *Lachish and Azekah:* fortress towns to the southwest of Jerusalem which Nebuchadnezzar besieged to prevent help coming to Jerusalem from Egypt. Between 1935 and 1938, archaeologists

found at Lachish several letters written on pottery fragments which date from 598 or 588 B.C., and which mention both Lachish and Azekah.

33, 6: Is 57, 18.
33, 7: Jer 30, 3; 32, 44.
33, 8: Ez 36, 25.
33, 10: Jer 32, 43.
33, 11: 1 Chr 16, 34; Ezr 3, 11; Ps 136, 1.
33, 15: Jer 23, 5; Ps 72, 1–4.12ff; Is 11, 1.

33, 17: 2 Sm 7, 16; 1 Kgs 2, 4; Ps 89, 4f.29.36f.
33, 18: Ez 44, 15f.
33, 20f: Jer 31, 36f; Ps 89, 37f.
33, 24: Rom 11, 1f.
33, 25f: Jer 31, 36f; 32, 44.
34, 1: Jer 52, 4; 2 Kgs 25, 1.
34, 2: Jer 21, 10; 32, 3.28.
34, 3: Jer 32, 4; 52, 11.

armies of the king of Babylon were attacking Jerusalem and the remaining cities of Judah, Lachish, and Azekah, since these alone were left of the fortified cities of Judah.

The Pact Broken

8† This is the word that came to Jeremiah from the LORD after King Zedekiah had made an agreement with all the people in Jerusalem to issue an edict of emancipation. 9* Everyone was to free his Hebrew slaves, male and female, so that no one should hold a man of Judah, his brother, in slavery. 10 All the princes and the others who entered the agreement consented to set free their male and female servants, so that they should be slaves no longer. But though they agreed and freed them, 11 afterward they took back their male and female slaves whom they had set free and again forced them into service.

12 Then this word of the LORD came to Jeremiah: 13 Thus says the LORD, the God of Israel: The day I brought your fathers out of the land of Egypt, out of the place where they were slaves, I made this covenant with them: 14 Every seventh year each of you shall set free his Hebrew brother who has sold himself to you; six years he shall serve you, but then you shall let him go free. Your fathers, however, did not heed me or obey me. 15 Today you indeed repented and did what is right in my eyes by proclaiming the emancipation of your brethren and making an agreement before me in the house that is named after me. 16* But then you changed your mind and profaned my name by taking back your male and female slaves to whom you had given their freedom; you forced them once more into slavery. 17 Therefore, thus says the LORD: You did not obey me by proclaiming your neighbors and kinsmen free. I now proclaim you free, says the LORD, for the sword, famine, and pestilence. I will make you an object of horror to all the kingdoms of the earth. 18† The men who violated my covenant and did not observe the terms of the agreement which they made before me, I will make like the calf which they cut in two, between whose two parts

they passed. 19 The princes of Judah and of Jerusalem, the courtiers, the priests, and the common people, who passed between the parts of the calf, 20* I will hand over, all of them, to their enemies, to those who seek their lives: their corpses shall be food for the birds of the air and the beasts of the field.

21* Zedekiah, too, king of Judah, and his princes, I will hand over to their enemies, to those who seek their lives, to the soldiers of the king of Babylon who have at present withdrawn from you. 22* I will give the command, says the LORD, and bring them back to this city. They shall attack and capture it, and destroy it with fire; the cities of Judah I will turn into a desert where no man dwells.

The Faithful Rechabites

35 1 This word came to Jeremiah from the LORD in the days of Jehoiakim, son of Josiah, king of Judah: 2† Approach the Rechabites and speak to them; bring them into the house of the LORD, to one of the rooms, and give them wine to drink. 3 So I went and brought Jaazaniah, son of Jeremiah, son of Habazziniah, his brothers and all his sons, the whole company of the Rechabites, 4† into the house of the LORD, to the room of the sons of Hanan, son of Igdaliah, the man of God, next to the princes' room, above the room of Maaseiah, son of Shallum, keeper of the doorway. 5 I set before these Rechabite men bowls full of wine and offered them cups to drink the wine.

6† "We do not drink wine," they said to me: "Jonadab, Rechab's son, our father, forbade us in these words: 'Neither you nor your children shall ever drink wine. 7 Build no house and sow no seed; neither plant nor own a vineyard. You shall dwell in tents all your life, so that you may live long on the earth where you are wayfarers.' 8 Now we have heeded Jonadab, Rechab's son, our father, in all his prohibitions. All our lives we have not drunk wine, neither we, nor our wives, nor our sons, nor our daughters. 9 We build no houses to live in; we own no vineyards or fields or crops, 10 and we live in tents; we obediently do everything our father

† **34, 8–22:** While the Chaldean siege of Jerusalem was in progress, the citizens of Jerusalem made a covenant at Zedekiah's instigation to free their brother Judeans who were in slavery. Doubtless this was both to provide additional free defenders for the city and to offer reparation for past violations of the law, according to which Hebrew slaves were to serve no longer than six years (Dt 15, 12–15). But when the siege was temporarily lifted, probably because of the help promised by Pharaoh Hophra (cf Jer 37, 5), the inhabitants of Jerusalem broke the covenant and once more pressed their brethren into slavery (v 11).

34, 18f: As the Bible (Gn 15, 10–17) and also contemporary inscriptions make clear, agreements were sometimes ratified by walking between the divided pieces of animals while the contracting parties invoked on themselves a fate similar to that of the slaughtered beast if they should fail to keep their word. *The agreement:* that mentioned in vv 10.15.

35, 2: *The Rechabites:* reactionaries who believed that the Lord could not be well served except by maintaining the original nomadic conditions of Israel's life. Without sharing their convictions, the prophet holds up their fidelity to their ideals as an example to put to shame his faithless countrymen. *In the days of Jehoiakim:* probably in 599 or 598 B.C.

35, 4: *The sons of Hanan:* probably the disciples of this man of God or prophet. *Maaseiah:* possibly the father of the priest Zephaniah (Jer 29, 25; 37, 3). *Keeper of the doorway:* a priestly function of responsibility; cf Jer 52, 24.

35, 6: *Jonadab:* a contemporary of King Jehu; cf 2 Kgs 10, 15ff.

34, 9: Ex 21, 2ff; Lv 25,　　　34, 21: Jer 37, 5.11.
　　　39.46; Dt 15, 12–15.　　34, 22: Jer 37, 8; 52, 7–13;
34, 16: Lv 19, 12.　　　　　　2 Chr 36, 17.19.
34, 20: Jer 7, 33; 16, 4; 19, 7.

Jonadab commanded us. [11]† But when Nebuchadnezzar, king of Babylon, invaded this land, we decided to come into Jerusalem to escape the army of the Chaldeans and the army of Aram; that is why we are now living in Jerusalem."

[12] Then this word of the LORD came to Jeremiah: [13]* Thus says the LORD of hosts, the God of Israel: Go, say to the men of Judah and to the citizens of Jerusalem: Will you not take correction and obey my words? says the LORD. [14]* The advice of Jonadab, Rechab's son, by which he forbade his children to drink wine, has been followed: to this day they have not drunk it; they obeyed their father's command. Me, however, you have not obeyed, although I spoke to you untiringly and insistently. [15]* I kept sending you all my servants the prophets, telling you to turn back, all of you, from your evil way; to reform your conduct, and not follow strange gods or serve them, if you would remain on the land which I gave you and your fathers; but you did not heed me or obey me. [16] Yes, the children of Jonadab, Rechab's son, observed the command which their father laid on them; but this people does not obey me! [17]* Now, therefore, says the LORD God of hosts, the God of Israel: I will bring upon Judah and all the citizens of Jerusalem every evil that I threatened; because when I spoke they did not obey, when I called they did not answer.

[18] But to the company of the Rechabites Jeremiah said: Thus says the LORD of hosts, the God of Israel: Since you have obeyed the command of Jonadab, your father, kept all his commands and done everything he commanded you, [19] thus therefore says the LORD of hosts, the God of Israel: Never shall there fail to be a descendant of Jonadab, Rechab's son, standing in my service.

Baruch Writes the Prophecies of Jeremiah

36 [1] In the fourth year of Jehoiakim, son of Josiah, king of Judah, this word came to Jeremiah from the LORD: [2] Take a scroll and write on it all the words I have spoken to you against Israel, Judah, and all the nations, from the day I first spoke to you, in the days of Josiah, until today. [3]* Perhaps, when the house of Judah hears all the evil I have in mind to do to them, they will turn back each from his evil way, so that I may forgive their wickedness and their sin. [4] So Jeremiah called Baruch, son of Neriah, who wrote down on a scroll, as Jeremiah dictated, all the words which the LORD had spoken to him.

[9] In the ninth month, in the fifth year of Jehoiakim, son of Josiah, king of Judah, a fast to placate the LORD was proclaimed for all the people of Jerusalem and all who came from Judah's cities to Jerusalem. [5]† Then Jeremiah charged Baruch: I cannot go to the house of the LORD; I am prevented from doing so. [6] Do you go on the fast day and read publicly in the LORD's house the LORD's words from the scroll you wrote at my dictation; read them also to all the men of Judah who come up from their cities. [7]* Perhaps they will lay their supplication before the LORD and will all turn back from their evil way; for great is the fury of anger with which the LORD has threatened this people.

[8] Baruch, son of Neriah, did everything the prophet Jeremiah commanded; from the book-scroll he read the LORD's words in the LORD's house. [10]† It was in the room of Gemariah, son of the scribe Shaphan, in the upper court of the LORD's house, at the entrance of the New Temple-Gate, that Baruch publicly read the words of Jeremiah from his book.

[11] Now Micaiah, son of Gemariah, son of Shaphan, heard all the words of the LORD read from the book. [12]† So he went down to the king's palace, into the scribe's chamber, where the princes were just then in session: Elishama, the scribe, Delaiah, son of Shemaiah, Elnathan, son of Achbor, Gemariah, son of Shaphan, Zedekiah, son of Hananiah, and the other princes. [13] To them Micaiah reported all that he had heard Baruch read publicly from his book. [14] Thereupon the princes sent Jehudi, son of Nethaniah, son of Shelemiah, son of Cushi, to Baruch with the order: "Come, and bring with you the scroll you read publicly to the people." Scroll in hand, Baruch, son of Neriah, went to them. [15] "Sit down," they said to him, "and read it to us." Baruch read it to them, [16] and when they heard all its words, they were frightened and said to one another, "We must certainly tell the king all these things." [17] Then they asked Baruch: "Tell us, please, how you came to write down all these words." [18] "Jeremiah dictated all these words to me," Baruch answered them, "and I wrote them down with ink in the book." [19] At this the princes said to Baruch, "Go into hiding, you and Jeremiah; let no one know where you are."

[20] Leaving the scroll in safekeeping in the room of Elishama the scribe, they entered the room where the king was. When they told him everything that

---

35, 11: The army of Aram; Nebuchadnezzar enlisted the help of Judah's foreign neighbors in his assault on Jerusalem.

36, 5: *I am prevented:* probably because of his temple sermon (Jer 7, 1–15), or because of temporary ritual uncleanness.

36, 10: *Gemariah:* member of a family friendly to Jeremiah, which had rights to a room in the fortress of the temple gateway overlooking the court of the temple; from a window in this room Bar-

uch read Jeremiah's prophetic sermon to the people.

36, 12: *The scribe's chamber:* the office of the royal secretary.

35, 13: Jer 32, 33.
35, 14: Jer 7, 13; 25, 3; 2 Chr 36, 15f.
35, 15: Jer 25, 4f.7.
35, 17: Jer 11, 8f.
36, 3: Jer 26, 3; Is 55, 6f.
36, 7: 2 Kgs 22, 13.

JER

had happened, 21 he sent Jehudi to fetch the scroll. Jehudi brought it from the room of Elishama the scribe, and read it to the king and to all the princes who were in attendance on the king. 22 Now the king was sitting in his winter house, since it was the ninth month, and fire was burning in a brazier before him. 23† Each time Jehudi finished reading three or four columns, the king would cut off the piece with a scribe's knife and cast it into the fire in the brazier, until the entire roll was consumed in the fire. 24 Hearing all these words did not frighten the king and his ministers or cause them to rend their garments. 25 And though Elnathan, Delaiah, and Gemariah urged the king not to burn the scroll, he would not listen to them, 26 but commanded Jerahmeel, a royal prince, and Seraiah, son of Azriel, and Shelemiah, son of Abdeel, to arrest Baruch, the secretary, and the prophet Jeremiah. But the LORD kept them concealed.

27 This word of the LORD came to Jeremiah, after the king burned the scroll with the text Jeremiah had dictated to Baruch: 28 Take another scroll, and write on it everything that the first scroll contained, which Jehoiakim, king of Judah, burned up. 29 And against Jehoiakim, king of Judah, say this: Thus says the LORD: You burned that scroll, saying, "Why did you write on it: Babylon's king shall surely come and lay waste this land and empty it of man and beast?" 30*† The LORD now says of Jehoiakim, king of Judah: No descendant of his shall succeed to David's throne; his corpse shall be cast out, exposed to the heat of day, to the cold of night. 31 I will punish him and his descendants and his ministers for their wickedness; against them and the citizens of Jerusalem and the men of Judah I will fulfill all the threats of evil which went unheeded.

32 Jeremiah took another scroll, and gave it to his secretary, Baruch, son of Neriah; he wrote on it at Jeremiah's dictation all the words contained in the book which Jehoiakim, king of Judah, had burned in the fire, and many others of the same kind in addition.

Jeremiah in the Dungeon

37 1* Coniah, son of Jehoiakim, was succeeded by King Zedekiah, son of Josiah; he was made king over the land of Judah by Nebuchadnezzar, king of Babylon. 2 Neither he, nor his ministers, nor the people of the land would listen to the words of the LORD spoken by Jeremiah the prophet. 3* Yet King Zedekiah sent Jehucal, son of Shelemiah, and Zephaniah, son of Maaseiah the priest, to the prophet Jeremiah with this request: "Pray to the LORD, our God, for us." 4*† At this time Jeremiah had not yet been put into prison; he still came and went freely among the people. 5*† Also, Pharaoh's army had set out from Egypt, and when the Chaldeans who were besieging Jerusalem heard this report they marched away from the city.

6 This word of the LORD then came to the prophet Jeremiah: 7* Thus says the LORD, the God of Israel: Give this answer to the king of Judah who sent you to me to consult me: Pharaoh's army

Facing Fear

You can bet Jeremiah felt fear at times. For example, in Jer 37, 17, King Zedekiah asks the prophet if he has had any word from God. Jeremiah has just been beaten and imprisoned (verse 15). Surely, he has some fear for what will happen to him if he delivers a message that angers the king. But Jeremiah courageously tells Zedekiah that he, Zedekiah, will be handed over to the king of Babylon (verse 17).

Throughout our life, when trying to do God's will, we will face situations that cause us to fear for our safety, for our reputation, or even that our friends will abandon us. This isn't the same fear we feel when watching a horror film or riding a roller coaster. It is an anxiety that can cause us to shut down and quit trying. We need to offer up that fear to God and ask the LORD to calm our heart.

Quiet your mind and pray:

LORD, give me the courage I need to be faithful to you. Let my love for you and for other people be so great that my fears will never be able to keep me from doing what is right. Amen!

▸ Jer 37, 11–21

---

† **36, 23:** *A scribe's knife:* used to sharpen the reeds which were employed as pens.
36, 30: Jehoiakim's son Jehoiachin was named king, but reigned only three months; he was known better for his thirty-seven-year exile in Babylon. *His corpse shall be cast out:* see note on Jer 22, 19.
37, 4: *Put into prison:* as described in Jer 32, 1ff. Chronologically, the present episode follows Jer 34, 1–7.

37, 5: *Pharaoh's army:* the force sent by Pharaoh Hophra which caused the Chaldeans momentarily to lift the siege of Jerusalem (cf Jer 34, 21).

36, 30: Jer 22, 19.
37, 1: Jer 52, 1; 2 Kgs 24, 17; 2 Chr 36, 10.
37, 3: Jer 21, 1.
37, 5: Ez 17, 15; 29, 6f.
37, 7: Ez 17, 17.

which has set out to help you will return to its own land, Egypt. 8* The Chaldeans shall return to the fight against this city; they shall capture it and destroy it with fire.

9 Thus says the LORD: Do not deceive yourselves with the thought that the Chaldeans will leave you for good, because they shall not leave! 10* Even if you were to defeat the whole Chaldean army now attacking you, and only the wounded remained, each in his tent, these would rise up and destroy the city with fire.

11* When the Chaldean army lifted the siege of Jerusalem at the threat of the army of Pharaoh, 12 Jeremiah set out from Jerusalem for the district of Benjamin, to take part with his family in the division of an inheritance. 13 But when he reached the Gate of Benjamin, he met the captain of the guard, a man named Irijah, son of Shelemiah, son of Hananiah; he seized the prophet Jeremiah, saying, "You are deserting to the Chaldeans!" 14 "That is a lie!" Jeremiah answered, "I am not deserting to the Chaldeans." Without listening, Irijah kept Jeremiah in custody and brought him to the princes.

15* The princes were enraged, and had Jeremiah beaten and thrown into prison in the house of Jonathan the scribe, which they were using as a jail. 16 And so Jeremiah entered the vaulted dungeon, where he remained a long time.

17* Once King Zedekiah had him brought to his palace and he asked him secretly whether there was any message from the LORD. Yes! Jeremiah answered: you shall be handed over to the king of Babylon. 18* Jeremiah then asked King Zedekiah: In what have I wronged you, or your ministers, or this people, that you should put me in prison? 19 And where are your own prophets now, 20 who prophesied to you that the king of Babylon would not attack you or this land? Hear now, my lord king, and grant my petition: do not send me back into the house of Jonathan the scribe, or I shall die there.

21* King Zedekiah ordered that Jeremiah be confined in the quarters of the guard, and given a loaf of bread each day from the bakers' shop until all the bread in the city was eaten up. Thus Jeremiah remained in the quarters of the guard.

Jeremiah in the Miry Cistern

38 1 † Shephatiah, son of Mattan, Gedaliah, son of Pashhur, Jucal, son of Shelemiah, and Pashhur, son of Malchiah, heard Jeremiah speaking these words to all the people: 2* Thus says the LORD: He who remains in this city shall die by sword, or famine, or pestilence; but he who goes out to the Chaldeans shall live; his life shall be spared him as booty, and he shall live. 3 Thus says the LORD: This city shall certainly be handed over to the army of the king of Babylon; he shall capture it.

4*† "This man ought to be put to death," the princes said to the king; "he demoralizes the soldiers who are left in this city, and all the people, by speaking such things to them; he is not interested in the welfare of our people, but in their ruin." 5 King Zedekiah answered: "He is in your power"; for the king could do nothing with them. 6* And so they took Jeremiah and threw him into the cistern of Prince Malchiah, which was in the quarters of the guard, letting him down with ropes. There was no water in the cistern, only mud, and Jeremiah sank into the mud.

7† Now Ebed-melech, a Cushite, a courtier in the king's palace, heard that they had put Jeremiah into the cistern. The king happened just then to be at the Gate of Benjamin, 8 and Ebed-melech went there from the palace and said to him, 9* "My lord king, these men have been at fault in all they have done to the prophet Jeremiah, casting him into the cistern. He will die of famine on the spot, for there is

Prayer from the Well

Almighty Creator of ups and downs, like Jeremiah, I often find myself at the bottom. Sometimes, I just fall there; other times, I am thrown there. It's cold, dark, and lonely there.

Bless me with friends like Ebed-melech to care for me and pull me out. And make me an Ebed-melech for others—a friend who is loyal enough to get the rope and tug until they are up again, who is considerate enough to get rags for their armpits so that the process won't be so painful. Amen.

▸ Jer 38, 1–13

38, 1: Jeremiah enjoyed sufficient liberty in the quarters of the guard (Jer 37, 21) to speak to the people; cf Jer 32, 6–9. *Gedaliah, son of Pashhur:* the latter is possibly the Pashhur of Jer 20, 1. *Pashhur, son of Malchiah:* mentioned in Jer 21, 1.
38, 4: *He demoralizes the soldiers:* literally, "he weakens their hands." One of the Lachish ostraca (see note on Jer 34, 7) uses the same expression of the princes in Jerusalem.

38, 7: *A Cushite:* an Ethiopian. Ebed-melech evidently held a position of some authority at court.

37, 8: Jer 34, 22.	37, 21: Jer 32, 2; 38, 28.
37, 10: Jer 21, 4.	38, 2: Jer 21, 9f; 39, 18; 45, 5.
37, 11: Zec 14, 10.	38, 4: Jer 26, 11.
37, 15: Jer 38, 6–13.	38, 6: Jer 37, 14f.
37, 17: Jer 21, 7; 32, 3; 34, 21.	38, 9: Jer 52, 6.
37, 18: Jer 26, 19.	

J
E
R

no more food in the city." [10] Then the king ordered Ebed-melech the Cushite to take three men along with him, and draw the prophet Jeremiah out of the cistern before he should die. [11] Ebed-melech took the men along with him, and went first to the linen closet in the palace, from which he took some old, tattered rags; these he sent down to Jeremiah in the cistern, with ropes. [12] Then he said to Jeremiah, "Put the old, tattered rags between your armpits and the ropes." Jeremiah did so, [13] and they drew him up with the ropes out of the cistern. But Jeremiah remained in the quarters of the guard.

[14]* Once King Zedekiah summoned the prophet Jeremiah to come to him at the third entrance to the house of the LORD. "I have a question to ask you," the king said to Jeremiah; "hide nothing from me." Jeremiah answered Zedekiah: [15]* If I tell you anything, you will have me killed, will you not? If I counsel you, you will not listen to me! [16] But King Zedekiah swore to Jeremiah secretly: "As the LORD lives who gave us the breath of life, I will not kill you; nor will I hand you over to these men who seek your life."

[17]* Thereupon Jeremiah said to Zedekiah: Thus says the LORD God of hosts, the God of Israel: If you surrender to the princes of Babylon's king, you shall save your life; this city shall not be destroyed with fire, and you and your family shall live. [18]* But if you do not surrender to the princes of Babylon's king, this city shall fall into the hands of the Chaldeans, who shall destroy it with fire, and you shall not escape their hands.

[19]* King Zedekiah, however, said to Jeremiah, "I am afraid of the men of Judah who have deserted to the Chaldeans; I may be handed over to them, and they will mistreat me." [20]* You will not be handed over, Jeremiah answered. Please obey the voice of the LORD and do as I tell you; then it shall go well with you, and your life will be spared. [21] But if you refuse to surrender, this is what the LORD shows me: [22]* All the women left in the house of Judah's king shall be brought out to the princes of Babylon's king, and they shall taunt you thus:

"They betrayed you, outdid you,
 your good friends!
Now that your feet are stuck in the mud,
 they slink away."

[23]* All your wives and sons shall be led forth to the Chaldeans, and you shall not escape their hands; you shall be handed over to the king of Babylon, and this city shall be destroyed with fire.

[24] Then Zedekiah said to Jeremiah, "Let no one know about this conversation, or you shall die. [25] If the princes hear I spoke to you, if they come and ask you, 'Tell us what you said to the king; do not hide it from us, or we will kill you,' or, 'What did the king say to you?' [26] give them this answer: 'I petitioned the king not to send me back to Jonathan's house to die there.' " [27] When all the princes came to Jeremiah, they questioned him, and he answered them in the very words the king had commanded. They said no more to him, for nothing had been heard of the earlier conversation. [28]* Thus Jeremiah stayed in the quarters of the guard till the day Jerusalem was taken.

Jeremiah and Gedaliah

39 When Jerusalem was taken. . . . [1]*† In the tenth month of the ninth year of Zedekiah, king of Judah, Nebuchadnezzar, king of Babylon, and all his army marched against Jerusalem and besieged it. [2]† On the ninth day of the fourth month, in the eleventh year of Zedekiah, a breach was made in the city's defenses. [3] All the princes of the king of Babylon came and occupied the middle gate: Nergal-sharezer, of Simmagir, the chief officer, Nebushazban, the high dignitary, and all the other princes of the king of Babylon. . . . [4]*† When Zedekiah, king of Judah, saw them, he and all his warriors fled by night, leaving the city on the Royal Garden Road through the gate between the two walls. He went in the direction of the Arabah, [5]*† but the Chaldean army pursued them, and overtook and captured Zedekiah in the desert near Jericho. He was brought to Riblah, in the land of Hamath, where Nebuchadnezzar, king of Babylon, pronounced sentence upon him. [6] *As Zedekiah looked on, his sons were slain at Riblah by order of the king of Babylon, who slew also all the nobles of Judah. [7]* He then blinded Zedekiah and bound him in chains to bring him to Babylon.

[8]* The Chaldeans set fire to the king's palace and the houses of the people, and demolished the

39, 1: *The tenth month of the ninth year:* the month Tebet (mid-December to mid-January) of the year 589/8 B.C.

39, 2: *The ninth day of the fourth month, in the eleventh year:* in July of 587 B.C.

39, 4: *The Royal Garden Road:* along the southeast side of the city; the royal garden was in the Kidron Valley. *The gate between the two walls:* the southernmost city gate, at the end of the Tyropoean Valley. *The Arabah:* the Jordan Valley. Zedekiah was attempting to escape across the Jordan when he was captured near Jericho.

39, 5: *Riblah:* Nebuchadnezzar's headquarters in Syria, which had also been used by Pharaoh Neco (2 Kgs 23, 33).

38, 14: Jer 37, 16.
38, 15: Lk 22, 67f.
38, 17: Jer 27, 12f; 2 Kgs 24, 12.
38, 18: Jer 32, 4.
38, 19: 1 Sm 31, 4.
38, 20: 2 Chr 20, 20.
38, 22: Jb 6, 15; 19, 13f.19.
38, 23: Jer 41, 10.
38, 28: Jer 39, 14.
39, 1f: Jer 52, 4–16; 2 Kgs 25, 1–12; Ez 24, 1.
39, 4: Jer 52, 7.
39, 5: Jer 32, 4f; 38, 18.
39, 6: Jer 34, 21.
39, 7: Jer 32, 4f; Ez 12, 13.
39, 8: Jer 21, 10; 34, 2; 52, 13.

RISKY BUSINESS

Ebed-melech is a biblical character we do not hear too much about. But he played a significant role in Jeremiah's life, and he has special meaning for African Americans because he was black. The Bible refers to him as the Ethiopian.

Ebed-melech is important because he was available to God and he was willing to risk his neck. Although Ebed-melech had the king's permission to rescue Jeremiah, he would have lost his life if his plan to do so had been discovered by the king's generals and counselors (Jer 38, 7–13). Ebed-melech shows us that being a servant of God is risky business. We cannot do God's will without taking risks. There is just no such thing as playing it safe and doing what God wants us to do.

Ebed-melech is also important because he was willing to help his "brother." Jeremiah was a Jew, and Ebed-melech was an Ethiopian, but still they were brothers in the LORD. Ebed-melech knew that he had to act when he saw his brother in trouble. When destruction finally came upon Jerusalem, God rewarded Ebed-melech by keeping him safe (39, 18) because he had trusted in God enough to help his brother Jeremiah.

LORD, grant me a large portion of trust in you, that I might step out at your bidding and not be afraid of the outcome. Amen.

▸ Jer 39, 15–18

---

walls of Jerusalem. 9* Nebuzaradan, chief of the bodyguard, deported to Babylon the rest of the people left in the city, those who had deserted to him, and the rest of the workmen. 10* But some of the poor who had no property were left in the land of Judah by Nebuzaradan, chief of the bodyguard, and were given at the same time vineyards and farms.

11 Concerning Jeremiah, Nebuchadnezzar, king of Babylon, gave the following orders through Nebuzaradan, chief of the bodyguard: 12* "Take him and look after him; let no harm befall him, but treat him as he himself requests." 13 Thereupon Nebuzaradan, chief of the bodyguard, and Nebushazban, the high dignitary, and Nergalsharezer, the chief officer, and all the nobles of the king of Babylon, 14* had Jeremiah taken out of the quarters of the guard, and entrusted to Gedaliah, son of Ahikam, son of Shaphan, to be brought home. And so he remained among the people.

A Word of Comfort for Ebed-melech

15 While Jeremiah was still imprisoned in the quarters of the guard, the word of the LORD came to him: 16* Go, tell this to Ebed-melech the Cushite: Thus says the LORD of hosts, the God of Israel: Behold, I am now fulfilling the words I spoke against this city, for evil and not for good; and this before your very eyes. 17 But on that day I will rescue you, says the LORD; you shall not be handed over to the men of whom you are afraid. 18* I will make certain that you escape and do not fall by the sword. Your life shall be spared as booty, because you trusted in me, says the LORD.

Jeremiah Still in Judah

40 1*† This word came to Jeremiah from the LORD, after Nebuzaradan, captain of the bodyguard, had released him in Ramah, where he had found him a prisoner in chains, among the captives of Jerusalem and Judah who were being exiled to Babylon. 2 When the captain of the bodyguard took

---

40, 1: *This word:* actually, no further word of the Lord is recorded until Jer 42, 7ff. This is a title affixed to the following chapters after they were attached to an earlier form of the book ending with chapter 39.

39, 9: 2 Kgs 25, 11.
39, 10: 2 Kgs 25, 12.22.
39, 12: Jer 40, 4.
39, 14: Jer 26, 24; 38, 28.

39, 16: Jer 21, 10; Dn 9, 12.
39, 18: Jer 45, 5; Pss 25, 3; 36, 40.
40, 1: Jer 39, 14.

charge of Jeremiah, he said to him, "The LORD, your God, foretold the ruin of this place. 3 Now he has brought about in deed what he threatened; because you sinned against the LORD and did not obey his voice, this fate has befallen you. 4* And now, I am freeing you today from the fetters that bind your hands; if it seems good to you to come with me to Babylon, you may come: I will look after you well. But if it does not please you to come to Babylon, you need not come. See, the whole land is before you; go wherever you think good and proper"; 5* and then, before he left— "or go to Gedaliah, son of Ahikam, son of Shaphan, whom the king of Babylon has appointed ruler over the cities of Judah; stay with him among the people, or go wherever you please." The captain of the bodyguard gave him food and gifts and let him go. 6*† Jeremiah went to Gedaliah, son of Ahikam, in Mizpah, and stayed with him among the people left in the land.

7 When the army leaders who were still in the field with all their men heard that the king of Babylon had given Gedaliah, son of Ahikam, charge of the land, of men, women, and children, and of those poor who had not been led captive to Babylon, 8† they came with their men to Gedaliah in Mizpah: Ishmael, son of Nethaniah; Johanan, son of Kareah; Seraiah, son of Tanhumeth; the sons of Ephai of Netophah; and Jezaniah of Beth-maacah. 9* Gedaliah, son of Ahikam, son of Shaphan, adjured them and their men not to be afraid to serve the Chaldeans: to stay in the land and submit to the king of Babylon, for their own welfare, 10 saying that he himself would remain in Mizpah, as their intermediary with the Chaldeans who should come to them. They were to collect the wine, the fruit, and the oil, to store them in jars, and to settle in the cities they occupied. 11 When the people of Judah in Moab, those among the Ammonites, those in Edom, and those in all other lands heard that the king of Babylon had left a remnant in Judah, and had appointed over them Gedaliah, son of Ahikam, son of Shaphan, 12 they all returned to the land of Judah from the places to which they had scattered. They went to Gedaliah at Mizpah and had a rich harvest of wine and fruit.

Assassination of Gedaliah

13 Now Johanan, son of Kareah, and all the leaders of the armies in the field came to Gedaliah in Mizpah 14*† and asked him whether he did not

know that Baalis, the king of the Ammonites, had sent Ishmael, son of Nethaniah, to assassinate him. 15 But Gedaliah, son of Ahikam, would not believe them. Then Johanan, son of Kareah, said secretly to Gedaliah in Mizpah: "Let me go and kill Ishmael, son of Nethaniah; no one will know it. Why should he be allowed to kill you? All the Jews who have now rallied to you will be dispersed and the remnant of Judah will perish." 16 Nevertheless, Gedaliah, son of Ahikam, answered Johanan, son of Kareah, "You shall do nothing of the kind; you have lied about Ishmael."

41 1* In the seventh month Ishmael, son of Nethaniah, son of Elishama, of royal descent, one of the king's nobles, came with ten men to Gedaliah, son of Ahikam, at Mizpah. And while they were together at table in Mizpah, 2 Ishmael, son of Nethaniah, and the ten who were with him, rose up and attacked with swords Gedaliah, son of Ahikam, son of Shaphan, whom the king of Babylon had made ruler over the land; and they killed him. 3 Ishmael also slew all the men of Judah of military age who were with Gedaliah and the Chaldean soldiers who were there.

4 The second day after the murder of Gedaliah, before anyone knew of it, 5 eighty men with beards shaved off, clothes in rags, and with gashes on their bodies came from Shechem, Shiloh, and Samaria, bringing food offerings and incense for the house of the LORD. 6 Ishmael, son of Nethaniah, went out from Mizpah to meet them, weeping as he went. 7 "Come to Gedaliah, son of Ahikam," he said as he met them. When they were once inside the city, Ishmael, son of Nethaniah, and his men slew them and threw them into the cistern. 8 But there were ten among them who pleaded with Ishmael: "Do not kill us; we have stores buried in the field: wheat and barley, oil and honey." And so he spared them and did not kill them, as he had killed their companions. 9* The cistern into which Ishmael threw all the corpses of the men he had killed was the large one made by King Asa to defend himself against Baasha, king of Israel; this cistern Ishmael, son of Nethaniah, filled with the slain.

10† Ishmael, son of Nethaniah, led away the remnant of the people left in Mizpah and the princesses, whom Nebuzaradan, captain of the bodyguard,

---

40, 6: *Mizpah:* some five miles northwest of Jerusalem, where Israel chose its first king (1 Sm 10, 17–24). Presumably Jerusalem had been damaged too much by the Chaldean conquest to remain a seat of government.

40, 8: *Jezaniah:* the seal ring of a high official of this name was discovered in 1932 at the site usually identified with Mizpah, Tell en-Nasbe.

40, 14: *The Ammonites:* they resented the survival of their ancient enemy, Judah. *Ishmael:* their willing tool, who doubtless as-

pired to rule over Judah himself, as he was of the house of David; cf Jer 41, 1.

41, 10: *The princesses:* of the royal house of Judah. They had not been deported to Babylon with the men of this house.

---
*

40, 4: Jer 39, 12.	40, 14: Jer 41, 1ff.10.
40, 5: Jer 39, 14; 2 Kgs 25, 22.	41, 1: Jer 40, 14ff; 2 Kgs 25, 25.
40, 6: Jer 39, 14.	41, 9: 1 Kgs 15, 16; 2 Chr 16, 6.
40, 9: Jer 27, 12f; 2 Kgs 25, 24.	

had confided to Gedaliah, son of Ahikam. With these captives, Ishmael, son of Nethaniah, set out to make his way to the Ammonites.

Flight to Egypt

¹¹ But when Johanan, son of Kareah, and the other army leaders with him heard of the crimes Ishmael, son of Nethaniah, had committed, ¹²† they took all their men and set out to attack Ishmael, son of Nethaniah. They overtook him at the Great Waters in Gibeon. ¹³ At the sight of Johanan, son of Kareah, and the other army leaders, the people who were Ishmael's captives rejoiced. ¹⁴ All of those whom Ishmael had brought away from Mizpah went over to Johanan, son of Kareah. ¹⁵ But Ishmael, son of Nethaniah, escaped from Johanan and fled to the Ammonites with eight men. ¹⁶ Then Johanan, son of Kareah, and all his army leaders took charge of the remnant of the people, both the soldiers and the women and children with their guardians, whom Ishmael, son of Nethaniah, had brought away from Mizpah after he killed Gedaliah, son of Ahikim. From Gibeon, ¹⁷ they retreated to the lodging place of Chimham near Bethlehem, where they stopped, intending to flee into Egypt. ¹⁸ They were afraid of the Chaldeans, because Ishmael, son of Nethaniah, had slain Gedaliah, son of Ahikam, whom the king of Babylon had made ruler in the land of Judah.

42 ¹ Then all the army leaders, Johanan, son of Kareah, Azariah, son of Hoshaiah, and all the people, high and low, approached the prophet Jeremiah ² and said, "Grant our petition; pray for us to the LORD, your God, for all this remnant. We are now few who once were many, as you well see. ³ Let the LORD, your God, show us what way we should take and what we should do." ⁴* Very well! the prophet Jeremiah answered them: I will pray to the LORD, your God, as you desire; whatever the LORD answers you, I will tell you; I will withhold nothing from you. ⁵* And they said to Jeremiah, "May the LORD be our witness: we will truly and faithfully follow all the instructions the LORD, your God, will send us. ⁶* Whether it is pleasant or difficult, we will obey the command of the LORD, our God, to whom we are sending you, so that it will go well with us for obeying the command of the LORD, our God."

⁷ Ten days passed before the word of the LORD came to Jeremiah. ⁸ Then he called Johanan, son of

Kareah, his army leaders, and all the people, high and low, ⁹ and said to them: Thus says the LORD, the God of Israel, to whom you sent me to offer your prayer: ¹⁰* If you remain quietly in this land I will build you up, and not tear you down; I will plant you, not uproot you; for I regret the evil I have done you. ¹¹* Do not fear the king of Babylon, before whom you are now afraid; do not fear him, says the LORD, for I am with you to save you, to rescue you from his power. ¹²* I will grant you mercy, so that he will be sorry for you and let you return to your land. ¹³ But if you disobey the voice of the LORD, your God, and decide not to remain in this land, ¹⁴* saying, "No, we will go to Egypt, where we will see no more of war, hear the trumpet alarm no longer, nor hunger for bread; there we will live"; ¹⁵ then listen to the word of the LORD, remnant of Judah: Thus says the LORD of hosts, the God of Israel: If you are determined to go to Egypt, when you arrive there to stay, ¹⁶* the sword you fear shall reach you in the land of Egypt; the hunger you dread shall cling to you no less in Egypt, and there you shall die. ¹⁷* All those men who determine to go to Egypt to stay, shall die by the sword, famine, and pestilence; not one shall survive or escape the evil that I will bring upon them. ¹⁸* For thus says the LORD of hosts, the God of Israel: Just as my furious anger was poured out upon the citizens of Jerusalem, so shall my anger be poured out on you when you reach Egypt. You shall become an example of malediction and horror, a curse and a reproach, and you shall never see this place again.

¹⁹ It is the LORD who has spoken to you, remnant of Judah; do not go to Egypt! You can never say that I did not warn you this day. ²⁰ At the cost of your lives you have deceived me, sending me to the LORD, your God, saying, "Pray for us to the LORD, our God; make known to us all that the LORD, our God, shall say, and we will do it." ²¹* Today I proclaim his message, but you obey the voice of the LORD, your God, in nothing that he has commissioned me to make known to you. ²²* Have no doubt of this, you shall die by the sword, famine, and pestilence in the place where you wish to go and settle.

43 ¹ When Jeremiah finished speaking to the people all these words of the LORD, their God, with which the LORD had sent him to them, ² Azariah, son of Hoshaiah, Johanan, son of

---

† **41, 12:** *Gibeon:* today called El-Jib; it is northwest of Jerusalem. The most recent excavations have revealed the extensive dimensions of the city spring and well; called here the Great Waters; cf 2 Sm 2, 12ff.

42, 4: 1 Sm 3, 18.
42, 5: Jgs 11, 10.
42, 6: Jer 7, 23; Dt 5, 33; 6, 3.
42, 10: Jer 31; 28; 32, 41.
42, 11: Jer 30, 10f.
42, 12: Ps 106, 45f; Prv 16, 7.

42, 14: Dt 28, 68.
42, 16: Jer 44, 13f.27.
42, 17: Jer 29, 17f; 44, 14.28.
42, 18: Jer 44, 12.
42, 21: Zec 7, 11f.
42, 22: Jer 44, 12; Hos 9, 6.

Kareah, and all the insolent men shouted to Jeremiah: "You lie; it was not the LORD, our God, who sent you to tell us not to go to Egypt to settle. 3* It is Baruch, son of Neriah, who stirs you up against us, to hand us over to the Chaldeans to be killed or exiled to Babylon."

4* Johanan, son of Kareah, and the rest of the leaders and the people did not obey the LORD's command to stay in the land of Judah. 5 Instead, Johanan, son of Kareah, and all the army leaders took along the whole remnant of Judah that had been dispersed among the nations and had returned thence to dwell again in the land of Judah: 6* men, women, and children, the princesses and everyone whom Nebuzaradan, captain of the bodyguard, had entrusted to Gedaliah, son of Ahikam, son of Shaphan; also Jeremiah, the prophet, and Baruch, son of Neriah. 7* Against the LORD's command they went to Egypt, and arrived at Tahpanhes.

Jeremiah in Egypt

8 This word of the LORD came to Jeremiah in Tahpanhes: 9† Take with you large stones and sink them in mortar in the brickyard at the entrance to the royal building in Tahpanhes, while the men of Judah look on, 10* and then say to them: Thus says the LORD of hosts, the God of Israel: I will send for my servant Nebuchadnezzar, king of Babylon, and bring him here. He will set his throne upon these stones which I, Jeremiah, have sunk, and stretch his canopy over them. 11* He shall come and strike the land of Egypt: with death, whoever is marked for death; with exile, everyone destined for exile; with the sword, all who are intended for the sword. 12* He shall set fire to the temples of Egypt's gods, and burn the gods or carry them off. As a shepherd delouses his cloak, he shall delouse the land of Egypt and depart victorious. 13 He shall smash the obelisks of the temple of the sun in the land of Egypt and destroy with fire the temples of the Egyptian gods.

44 1 This word came to Jeremiah for all the people of Judah who were living in Egypt, at Migdol, Tahpanhes, and Memphis, and in Upper Egypt: 2*† Thus says the LORD of hosts, the God of Israel: You have seen all the evil I brought on Jerusalem and the other cities of Judah. Today they are ruins and uninhabited, 3* because of the evil they did to provoke me, going after strange

gods, serving them and sacrificing to them, gods which neither they, nor you, nor your fathers knew. 4 Though I kept sending to you all my servants the prophets, with the plea not to commit this horrible deed which I hate, 5* they would not listen or accept the warning to turn away from the evil of sacrificing to strange gods. 6 Therefore the fury of my anger poured forth in flame over the cities of Judah and the streets of Jerusalem, so that they became the ruinous waste they are today.

7 Now thus says the LORD God of hosts, the God of Israel: Why do you inflict so great an evil upon yourselves? Will you root out from Judah man and wife, child and nursling, and not leave yourselves even a remnant? 8* Will you go on provoking me by the works of your hands, by sacrificing to strange gods here in the land of Egypt where you have come to live? Will you be rooted out and become a curse and a disgrace among all the nations of the earth? 9* Have you forgotten the evil deeds which your fathers, and the kings of Judah and their wives, and you yourselves and your wives have done in the land of Judah and the streets of Jerusalem? 10* To this day they have not been crushed; they do not fear or follow the law and the statutes which I set before you and your fathers.

11 Hence, thus says the LORD of hosts, the God of Israel: I have determined evil against you; and I will uproot all Judah. 12* I will take away the remnant of Judah who insisted on coming to dwell in Egypt, so that they shall be wholly destroyed. In the land of Egypt they shall fall by the sword or be consumed by hunger. High and low, they shall die by the sword, or by hunger, and become an example of malediction, a horror, a curse and a reproach. 13* Thus will I punish those who live in Egypt, just as I punished Jerusalem with sword, hunger, and pestilence. None of the remnant of Judah that have come to settle in the land of Egypt shall escape or survive. 14 None shall return to the land of Judah, though they yearn to return and live there. Only scattered refugees shall return.

15 From all the men who knew that their wives were burning incense to strange gods, from all the women who were present in the immense crowd, and from all the people who lived in Lower and Upper Egypt, Jeremiah received this answer: 16* "We will not listen to what you say in the name of the LORD. 17* Rather will we continue doing what we had proposed; we will burn incense to the queen of heaven and pour out libations to her, as we and our

---

† **43, 9:** *The royal building:* residence of the Egyptian governor.
44, 2–30: Chronologically, this is the last of Jeremiah's prophecies to his countrymen. The narrative leaves him an old man nearing seventy, rejected by his people. According to tradition, he was murdered in Egypt by fellow Judeans.

43, 3: Jer 38, 4.
43, 4: Jer 41, 16.
43, 6: Jer 41, 10.
43, 7: Jer 42, 13f; 44, 1.
43, 10: Jer 27, 6; Ez 29, 19.
43, 11: Jer 46, 13; Ez 30, 10.
43, 12: Jer 46, 25; Ez 30, 13f.
44, 2: Jer 34, 22; Lv 26, 32f.
44, 3: Jer 11, 17; Dt 32, 17.
44, 5: Jer 7, 24.26; 19, 4.
44, 8: Jer 25, 6f.
44, 9: 1 Kgs 11, 1.8; Ezr 9, 7.14.
44, 10: Jer 7, 24.
44, 12: Jer 42, 15.18.22.
44, 13: Jer 43, 11.
44, 16: Jer 6, 16f.
44, 17: Jer 5, 3; 7, 18.

fathers, our kings and princes have done in the cities of Judah and the streets of Jerusalem. Then we had enough food to eat and we were well off; we suffered no misfortune. [18] But since we stopped burning incense to the queen of heaven and pouring out libations to her, we are in need of everything and are being destroyed by the sword and by hunger. [19]* And when we burned incense to the queen of heaven and poured out libations to her, was it without our husbands' consent that we baked for her cakes in her image and poured out libations to her?"

[20] To all the people, men and women, who gave him this answer, Jeremiah said: [21]* Was it not this that the LORD remembered and brought to mind, that you burned incense in the cities of Judah and the streets of Jerusalem: you, your fathers, your kings and princes, and the people generally? [22]* The LORD could no longer bear your evil deeds, the horrible things which you were doing; and so your land became a waste, a desert, a thing accursed and without inhabitants, as it is today. [23]* Because you burned incense and sinned against the LORD, not obeying the voice of the LORD, not living by his law, his statutes, and his decrees, this evil has befallen you at the present day.

[24] Jeremiah said further to all the people, including the women: Hear the word of the LORD, all you Judeans in the land of Egypt: [25] Thus says the LORD of hosts, the God of Israel: You and your wives have stated your intentions, and kept them in fact: "We will continue to fulfill the vows we have made to burn incense to the queen of heaven and to pour out libations to her." Very well! keep your vows, carry out your resolutions! [26] But listen then to the word of the LORD, all you people of Judah who live in Egypt; I swear by my own great name, says the LORD, in the whole land of Egypt no man of Judah shall henceforth pronounce my name, saying, "As the Lord GOD lives." [27]* I am watching over them to do evil, not good. All the men of Judah in Egypt shall perish by the sword or famine until they are utterly destroyed. [28]* Those who escape the sword to return from the land of Egypt to the land of Judah shall be few in number. The whole remnant of Judah who came to settle in Egypt shall know whose word stands, mine or theirs.

[29] That you may know how surely my threats of punishment for you shall be fulfilled, this shall be a sign to you, says the LORD, that I will punish you in this place. [30]*† Thus says the LORD: See! I will hand over Pharaoh Hophra, king of Egypt, to his enemies, to those who seek his life, just as I handed over Zedekiah, king of Judah, to his enemy and mortal foe, Nebuchadnezzar, king of Babylon.

A Message to Baruch

45 [1]*† This is the message that the prophet Jeremiah gave to Baruch, son of Neriah, when he wrote in a book the prophecies that Jeremiah dictated in the fourth year of Jehoiakim, son of Josiah, king of Judah: [2] Thus says the LORD, God of Israel, to you, Baruch, [3]* because you said, "Alas! the LORD adds grief to my pain; I am weary from groaning, and can find no rest": [4]* say this to him, says the LORD: What I have built, I am tearing down; what I have planted, I am uprooting: even the whole land. [5]* And do you seek great things for yourself? Seek them not! I am bringing evil on all mankind, says the LORD, but your life I will leave you as booty, wherever you may go.

V: Oracles against the Nations†

46 [1] This is the word of the LORD that came to the prophet Jeremiah against the nations.

Against Egypt

[2]† Concerning Egypt. Against the army of Pharaoh Neco, king of Egypt, which was defeated at Carchemish on the Euphrates by Nebuchadnezzar, king of Babylon, in the fourth year of Jehoiakim, son of Josiah, king of Judah:

3　Prepare shield and buckler!
　　　march to battle!
4　Harness the horses,
　　　mount, charioteers!
　　Fall in with your helmets;
　　　polish your spears, put on
　　　your breastplates.

† **44, 30:** *Hophra:* killed by his own people. The ruler of Egypt at the time of its conquest by Nebuchadnezzar was Hophra's successor Amasis, who was also slain by his enemies.
45, 1–5: At the conclusion of his narrative, Baruch appends a prophecy given him personally by Jeremiah when he first wrote down Jeremiah's words (cf chap. 36). The future revealed by the prophet had depressed Baruch; this prophecy was to assure him of his personal safety, while repeating the Lord's determination to destroy Judah.
46—51: In these chapters most of Jeremiah's oracles against the foreign nations have been gathered together and placed at the end of his book; in the Greek text they appear with the other oracles against the nations, in chap. 25. In general, they are in chronologi-

cal order: 46, 1—49, 33, from the fourth year of Jehoiakim; 49, 34–39, at the beginning of Zedekiah's reign; 50, 1—51, 64, from the fourth year of Zedekiah.
46, 2: *Carchemish on the Euphrates:* the western terminus of the Mesopotamian trade route, where Nebuchadnezzar defeated Neco in 605 B.C., thus gaining undisputed control of Syria and Palestine.

44, 19: Jer 7, 18.
44, 21: Jer 11, 13.
44, 22: Jer 15, 6.
44, 23: 2 Kgs 17, 15; Dn 9, 11f.
44, 27: Ez 7, 3–7.
44, 28: Dt 28, 62; Is 10, 22.

44, 30: Jer 39, 5ff; 46, 25f; Ez 29, 3f; 30, 21.
45, 1: Jer 36, 4.18.32.
45, 3: Lam 1, 3; 5, 5.
45, 4: Jer 18, 7; Is 5, 5f.
45, 5: Jer 25, 26–29.

JER

5* What do I see?
   With broken ranks
   They fall back;
      their heroes are routed,
   They flee headlong
      without making a stand.
   Terror on every side,
      says the LORD!
6 The swift cannot flee,
      nor the hero escape:
   There in the north, on the Euphrates' bank,
      they stumble and fall.

7 Who is this that surges forward like the Nile,
      like rivers of billowing waters?
8* Egypt surges like the Nile,
      like rivers of billowing waters.
   "I will surge forward," he says, "and cover
      the earth,
      destroying the city and its people.
9 Forward, horses!
      drive madly, chariots!
   Set out, warriors,
   Cush and Put, bearing your shields,
   Men of Lud, stretching your bows!"
10* But this is the day of the Lord GOD of hosts,
      a day of vengeance, vengeance on his foes!
   The sword devours, is sated, drunk with
         their blood:
      for the Lord GOD of hosts holds a
         slaughter feast
      in the northland, on the Euphrates.

11* Go up to Gilead, and take balm,
      O virgin daughter Egypt!
   No use to multiply remedies;
      for you there is no cure.
12* The nations hear of your shame,
      your cries fill the earth.
   Warrior trips over warrior,
      both fall together.

13*† The message which the LORD gave to the
prophet Jeremiah concerning the advance of Nebuchadnezzar, king of Babylon, to attack the land of
Egypt:

14* Announce it in Egypt, publish it in Migdol,
      proclaim it in Memphis and Tahpanhes!
   Say: Take your stand, prepare yourselves,

?did you KNOW?

Oracles against the Nations

The Oracles against the Nations, in Jeremiah, chapters 46–51, resemble the oracles in chapters 13–23 of Isaiah. In both,
God's threats to destroy the enemies of
Israel, as proclaimed by a prophet, reflect
the bitterness that has welled up in the
nation's heart during its long history of
suffering.

Is God really as vengeful as the prophecies from Jeremiah suggest? We must
balance our understanding of God's vengeance with Jesus' teachings—for example, Jesus' claim that God makes the "sun
rise on the bad and the good" (Mt 5, 45).
The God whom Jesus called Abba is the
parent of all nations, who wants enemies to be reconciled with one another.
The Oracles against the Nations challenge Christians to be the first to offer
the handshake of forgiveness and break
the cycle of violence.

▶ Jeremiah, chapters 46–51

      the sword has already devoured
         your neighbors.
15† Why has Apis fled,
      your mighty one failed to stand?
   The LORD thrust him down;
16*   he stumbled repeatedly, and fell.
   They said one to another,
      "Up! let us return to our own people,
   To the land of our birth,
      away from the destroying sword."

17† Call Pharaoh, king of Egypt, by the name
      "The noise that let its time go by."
18† As I live, says the King
      whose name is LORD of hosts,

46, 13: In 601 B.C. Nebuchadnezzar advanced against Egypt and
even entered the country, but finally had to withdraw to Syria.
46, 15: *Apis:* the chief god of Memphis, venerated in the form of
a black bull.
46, 17: *"The noise . . . go by":* in Hebrew there is wordplay here
on the name Hophra, who still made a pretense of power though his
career was at an end.

46, 18: *Tabor . . . Carmel:* outstanding mountains of Palestine,
symbols of strength, to which Nebuchadnezzar is compared.

46, 5: Jer 6, 25; 49, 29.
46, 8: Ez 29, 3; 32, 2.
46, 10: Dt 32, 42; Is 13, 9; Ez
   39, 17–20.
46, 11: Jer 8, 22; 51, 8; Ez 30,
   21f.
46, 12: Ez 32, 9–12.
46, 13: Jer 43, 10f; 44, 30;
   Is 19, 1.
46, 14: Jer 44, 1.
46, 16: Lv 26, 37.

Like Tabor among the mountains he
   shall come,
   like Carmel above the sea.

19 Pack your baggage for exile,
   capital city of daughter Egypt;
Memphis shall become a desert,
   an empty ruin.

20 Egypt is a pretty heifer,
   from the north a horsefly lights upon her.

21 The mercenaries in her ranks
   are like fatted calves;
They too turn and flee together,
   stand not their ground,
When the day of their ruin comes upon them,
   the time of their punishment.

22 She sounds like a retreating reptile!
   Yes, they come in force;
   like woodchoppers, they attack her with axes.

23 They cut down her forest, says the LORD,
   impenetrable though it be;
More numerous than locusts,
   they cannot be counted.

24 Disgraced is daughter Egypt,
   handed over to the people of the north.

25*† The LORD of hosts, the God of Israel, has said: See! I will punish Amon of Thebes, and Egypt, her gods and her kings, Pharaoh, and those who trust in him. 26* I will hand them over to those who seek their lives, to Nebuchadnezzar, king of Babylon, and his ministers. But later on Egypt shall be inhabited again, as in times past, says the LORD.

27* But you, my servant Jacob, fear not;
   be not dismayed, O Israel.
Behold, I will deliver you from the far-off land,
   your descendants, from their land of exile.
Jacob shall again find rest,
   shall be tranquil and undisturbed.

28* You, my servant Jacob, never fear, says
   the LORD,
   for I am with you;
I will make an end of all the nations
   to which I have driven you,
But of you I will not make an end:
   I will chastise you as you deserve,
   I will not let you go unpunished.

Against the Philistines

47 1* This is the word that came from the LORD to the prophet Jeremiah concerning the Philistines, before Pharaoh attacked Gaza: 2† Thus says the LORD:

Behold: waters are rising from the north,
   a torrent in flood;
It shall flood the land and all that is in it,
   the cities and their people.
All the people of the land
   set up a wailing cry.

3 They hear the stamping hooves of
   his steeds,
   the rattling chariots, the rumbling wheels.
Fathers turn not to save their children;
   their hands fall helpless

4*†Because of the day which has come
   to ruin all the Philistines,
And cut off from Tyre and Sidon
   the last of their allies.
Yes, the LORD is destroying the Philistines,
   the remnant from the coasts of Caphtor.

5*†Gaza is shaved bald,
   Ashkelon is reduced to silence;
Ashdod, the remnant of their strength,
   how long will you gash yourself?

6† Alas, sword of the LORD!
   how long till you find rest?
Return into your scabbard;
   stop, be still!

7* How can it find rest
   when the LORD has commanded it?
Against Ashkelon and the seashore
   he has appointed it.

Against Moab

48 1† Concerning Moab, thus says the LORD of hosts, the God of Israel:

Woe to Nebo, it is laid waste;
   Kiriathaim is disgraced and captured,
Disgraced and overthrown is the stronghold:

2   Moab's glory is no more.
Evil they plan against Heshbon:
   "Come, let us put an end to her as
   a people."

46, 25: *Amon:* the sun-god worshiped at Thebes, in Upper Egypt.
47, 2–7: This prophecy was fulfilled in 605/4 B.C.
47, 4: *Tyre and Sidon:* Phoenician cities associated commercially with the Philistines, and enemies of Nebuchadnezzar; cf Jer 27, 1–4. Nebuchadnezzar carried out a thirteen-year siege of Tyre which was only partially successful. *Caphtor:* probably the island of Crete, the traditional place of origin of the Philistines; cf Am 9, 7.
47, 5: Of the ancient Philistine cities, neither Gath nor Ekron (Jer 25, 20) is mentioned in this period of waning independence of the seacoast.
47, 6: Words of the Philistines.

48, 1–47: Moab was one of the Israelites' bitterest enemies. According to Flavius Josephus, Moab and Ammon were conquered by Nebuchadnezzar in this twenty-third year, 582 B.C., five years after the destruction of Jerusalem.

46, 25: Ez 30, 15f.   **47, 1:** Ez 25, 15f; Zep 2, 4.
46, 26: Jer 44, 30; Ez 30, 4;   **47, 4:** Jer 25, 22; Ez 25, 16f;
   32, 11f.   Am 1, 8; 9, 7.
46, 27: Jer 30, 10; 43, 5.   **47, 5:** Am 1, 7.
46, 28: Jer 30, 11.   **47, 7:** Zep 2, 5f.

You, too, Madmen, shall be reduced to silence;
　behind you stalks the sword.
3 * Listen! a cry from Horonaim
　of ruin and great destruction!
4 　Moab is crushed,
　　their outcry is heard in Zoar.
5 　The ascent of Luhith
　　they climb weeping;
　On the descent to Horonaim
　　the cry of destruction is heard.
6 　"Flee, save your lives,
　　to survive like the wild ass in the desert!"
7 *†Because you trusted in your works and
　　　your treasures,
　　you also shall be captured.
　Chemosh shall go into exile,
　　his priests and princes with him.
8 　The destroyer comes upon every city,
　　not a city escapes;
　Ruined is the valley,
　　wasted the plain, as the LORD has said.
9 　Set up a memorial for Moab,
　　for it is an utter wasteland;
　Its cities are turned into ruins
　　where no one dwells.
10 　[Cursed be he who does the LORD's
　　　work remissly,
　　cursed he who holds back his sword
　　　from blood.]
11 * Moab has been tranquil from his youth,
　　has rested upon his lees;
　He was not poured from one flask to another,
　　he went not into exile.
　Thus he kept his taste,
　　and his scent was not lost.

12 Hence, the days shall come, says the LORD,
when I will send him coopers to turn him over;
they shall empty his flasks and break his jars.
13 * Chemosh shall disappoint Moab, as Israel was
disappointed by Bethel in which they trusted.

14 　How can you say, "We are heroes,
　　men valiant in war"?
15 　The ravager of Moab and his cities advances,
　　the flower of his youth goes down to
　　　be slaughtered,
　　says the King, the LORD of hosts by name.
16 　Near at hand is Moab's ruin,
　　his disaster hastens apace.
17 　Mourn for him, all you his neighbors,
　　all you who knew him well!

Say: How the strong staff is broken,
　the glorious rod!
18 * Come down from glory, sit on the ground,
　you that dwell in Dibon;
　Moab's ravager has come up against you,
　　he has ruined your strongholds.
19 * Stand by the wayside, watch closely,
　you that dwell in Aroer;
　Ask the man who flees, the woman who tries
　　to escape:
　say to them, "What has happened?"
20 * Moab is disgraced, yes, destroyed,
　howl and cry out;
　Publish it at the Arnon,
　　Moab is ruined!

21 *For judgment has come on the land of the
plateau: on Holon, Jahzah, and Mephaath, 22 on Dibon, Nebo, and Beth-diblathaim, 23 on Kiriathaim,
Beth-gamul, and Beth-meon, 24 on Kerioth and on
Bozrah: on all the cities of Moab, far and near.

25 　Moab's strength is broken,
　　his might is shattered, says the LORD.

26 Because he boasted against the LORD, make
Moab drunk so that he retches and vomits, and he
too becomes a laughingstock. 27 * Is Israel a laughingstock to you? Was she caught among thieves, that
you shake your head whenever you speak of her?

28 　Leave the cities, dwell in the crags,
　　you that dwell in Moab.
　Be like a dove that nests
　　out of reach on the edge of a chasm.
29 * We have heard of the pride of Moab,
　　pride beyond bounds:
　His loftiness, his pride, his scorn,
　　his insolence of heart.
30 　I know, says the LORD, his arrogance;
　　liar in boast, liar in deed.
31 * And so I wail over Moab,
　　over all Moab I cry,
　　over the men of Kir-heres I moan.
32 * More than for Jazer I weep over you,
　　vineyard of Sibmah.
　Your tendrils trailed down to the sea,
　　as far as Jazer they stretched.
　Upon your harvest, upon your vintage,
　　the ravager has fallen.
33 　Joy and jubilation are at an end
　　in the fruit gardens of the land of Moab.

---

† **48, 7:** *Chemosh:* chief god of the Moabites.

48, 3ff: Is 15, 5.　　　　　　48, 7: Nm 21, 29.

48, 11: Zep 1, 12.　　　　　48, 21: Is 15, 4.
48, 13: Is 16, 12.　　　　　48, 27: Zep 2, 8ff.
48, 18: Nm 21, 30.　　　　48, 29f: Is 16, 6.
48, 19: Dt 2, 36.　　　　　48, 31: Is 16, 7.
48, 20: Is 16, 7.　　　　　48, 32: Is 16, 8f.

THE EAGLE

Jeremiah 48, 40 portrays the punisher of Moab as an eagle. In the Bible, that is not an unusual description for this majestic bird (see also Jb 39, 27; Is 40, 31; Ez 17, 3; Dn 7, 4). Native American cultures admire the eagle as the strongest and bravest of all birds, and therefore view eagle feathers as a symbol of what is high and holy.

So, in some Native American tribes, when someone is honored for being brave, strong, and holy, an eagle feather is given to her or him. Native Americans also use eagle feathers for blessings. They hold or wave the feathers over a person's head as a prayer for peace and happiness. (Note: Native Americans are able to acquire feathers for use in their rituals. But keep in mind that it is generally illegal to hunt eagles or even to take a feather you find!)

The next time you see an eagle or a picture of an eagle, remember what its feathers symbolize, and pray about those ideals of honor, peace, protection, strength, courage, and holiness.

▶ Jer 48, 40

I drain the wine from the wine vats,
   the treader treads no more,
   the vintage shout is stilled.

34* The cry of Heshbon and Elealeh is heard as far as Jahaz; they call from Zoar to Horonaim, and to Eglath-shelishiyah, for even the waters of Nimrim turn into a desert. 35 I will leave no one in Moab, says the LORD, to offer a holocaust on the high place, or to burn incense to his gods. 36* Hence the wail of flutes for Moab is in my heart; for the men of Kir-heres the wail of flutes is in my heart: the wealth they acquired has perished. 37* Every head has been made bald, every beard shaved; every hand is gashed, and the loins of all are clothed in sackcloth. 38 On every roof of Moab and in all his squares there is mourning; I have shattered Moab like a pot that no one wants, says the LORD. 39 How terror seizes Moab, and wailing! How he turns his back in shame! Moab has become a laughingstock and a horror to all his neighbors! 40* For thus says the LORD:

Behold, like an eagle he soars,
   spreads his wings over Moab.
41* Cities are taken,
   strongholds seized:

On that day the hearts of Moab's heroes
   are like the heart of a woman in travail.
42* Moab shall be destroyed, no more
     a people,
   because he boasted against the LORD.
43* Terror, pit, and trap be upon you,
   people of Moab, says the LORD.
44 He who flees from the terror
   falls into the pit;
He who climbs from the pit
   is caught in the trap;
For I will bring these things upon Moab
   in the year of their punishment, says
     the LORD.
45* In Heshbon's shadow stop short
   the exhausted refugees;
For fire breaks forth from Heshbon,
   and a blaze from the house of Sihon:
It consumes the brow of Moab,
   the skull of the noisemakers.
46 Woe to you, O Moab,
   you are ruined, O people of Chemosh!
Your sons are taken into exile,
   your daughters into captivity.
47* But I will change the lot of Moab
   in the days to come, says the LORD.
Thus far the judgment of Moab.

48, 34: Is 15, 4f.
48, 36: Is 16, 11.

48, 37: Jer 47, 5; Is 15, 2f;
   Ez 7, 18.

48, 40: Jer 49, 22.
48, 41: Jer 6, 24; 30, 6.
48, 42: Zep 2, 9f.

48, 43: Is 24, 17f.
48, 45: Nm 21, 28f.
48, 47: Jer 49, 39.

Against the Ammonites

49

¹† Concerning the Ammonites, thus says the LORD:

Has Israel no sons?
  has he no heir?
Why then has Milcom disinherited Gad,
  why have his people settled in Gad's
    cities?
²*†But the days are coming, says the LORD,
  when against Rabbah of the Ammonites
  I will sound the battle alarm;
She shall become a mound of ruins,
  and her daughter cities shall be destroyed
    by fire.
Israel shall inherit those who disinherited her,
  says the LORD.
³* Howl, Heshbon, for the ravager approaches,
  shriek, daughters of Rabbah!
Put on sackcloth and mourn,
  run to and fro, gashing yourselves;
For Milcom goes into exile
  along with his priests and captains.
⁴ Why do you glory in your strength,
  your ebbing strength, rebellious daughter?
You who trust in your treasures, saying,
  "Who can come against me?"
⁵* I am bringing terror upon you,
  says the Lord GOD of hosts,
  from all round about you;
You shall be scattered, each man in
    headlong flight,
  with no one to rally the fugitives.
⁶ But afterward I will change the lot
  of the Ammonites, says the LORD.

Against Edom†

⁷ Concerning Edom, thus says the LORD of hosts:

Is there no more wisdom in Teman,†
  has counsel perished from the prudent,
  has their wisdom become corrupt?
⁸*†Flee, retreat, hide in deep holes,
  you who live in Dedan:
For I will bring destruction upon Esau
  when I come to punish him.

⁹* If vintagers came upon you,
  they would leave no gleanings;
If thieves by night,
  they would destroy as they pleased.
¹⁰* So I myself will strip Esau;
  I will uncover his retreats so that he
    cannot hide.
He is ruined: sons, and brothers,
  and neighbors, so that he is no more.
¹¹* Leave your orphans behind, I will keep
    them alive;
  your widows, let them trust in me.

¹²* For thus says the LORD: Even those not sentenced to drink the cup must drink it! Shall you then go unpunished? You shall not go unpunished; you shall surely drink it. ¹³*† By my own self I have sworn, says the LORD: Bozrah shall become an object of horror and a disgrace, a desolation and a curse; she and all her cities shall become ruins forever.

¹⁴ I have heard a report from the LORD,
  a herald has been sent among the nations:
Gather together, move against her,
  rise up for battle.
¹⁵* Small will I make you among the nations,
  despised among men!
¹⁶* The terror you spread beguiled you,
  and your presumption of heart;
You that live in rocky crags,
  that hold the heights of the hill:
Though you build your nest high as the eagle,
  from there I will drag you down, says
    the LORD.

¹⁷ Edom shall become an object of horror. Every passer-by shall be appalled and catch his breath at all her wounds. ¹⁸* As when Sodom, Gomorrah, and their neighbors were overthrown, says the LORD, not a man shall dwell there: no one shall visit there.

¹⁹* As when a lion comes up from the thicket
    of Jordan
  to the permanent feeding grounds,

49, 1: *Milcom:* chief god of the Ammonites. The Transjordan tribe of Gad bordered on Ammon, and after the collapse of the northern kingdom the Ammonites occupied its territory.

49, 2: *Rabbah of the Ammonites:* or Rabbath-Ammon, capital of the Ammonite kingdom. The modern Amman is the capital of the kingdom of Jordan.

49, 7–22: *Edom:* this implacable enemy from ancient times profited from Judah's downfall; cf Ob 11f.

49, 7: *Teman:* a district of Edom, used here for the whole country; it was famous for its wise men; cf Jb 2, 11.

49, 8: *Esau:* Jacob's brother, the traditional ancestor of the Edomites; cf Gn 36.

49, 13: *Bozrah:* capital of Edom, southeast of the Dead Sea.

49, 2: Am 1, 14.
49, 3: Is 15, 2ff.
49, 5: Jer 48, 47.
49, 8: Ez 25, 13.
49, 9: Ob 5.
49, 10: Mal 1, 3.
49, 11: Dt 10, 18; Ps 68, 6.
49, 12: Jer 25, 15.28; Lam 4, 21f.

49, 13: Is 34, 6; Ez 35, 3–9;
  Ob 16.
49, 15: Ob 2.
49, 16: Jer 48, 29f.
49, 18: Jer 50, 40; Dt 29, 23.
49, 19: Jer 12, 5; 25, 9; 50, 44f.

So I, in an instant, will drive men off;
   and whom I choose I will establish there!
For who is like me? who can call me
   to account?
What shepherd can stand against me?
20 Therefore, hear the counsel of the LORD,
   which he has taken against Edom;
Hear the plans he has made
   against those that live in Teman:
They shall be dragged away, even the smallest
   sheep,
   their own pasture shall be aghast because
   of them.
21 At the noise of their fall the earth quakes,
   to the Red Sea the outcry is heard!
22* See! like an eagle he soars aloft,
   and spreads his wings over Bozrah;
On that day the hearts of Edom's heroes
   shall be
   like the heart of a woman in travail.

Against Damascus

Concerning Damascus:

23*† Hamath and Arpad are covered with shame,
   they have heard bad news;
Worried, they toss like the sea
   which cannot rest.
24 Damascus is weakened, she turns to flee,
   panic has seized her.
Distress and pangs take hold of her,
   like those of a woman in travail.
25 How can the city of glory be forsaken,
   the town of delight!
26 But now her young men shall fall in her streets,
   and all her warriors shall be stilled.
     On that day, says the LORD of hosts,
27† I will set fire to the wall of Damascus,
   and it shall devour the palaces of Ben-hadad.

Against Arabia

28* Of Kedar and the kingdoms of Hazor, defeated by Nebuchadnezzar, king of Babylon, thus says the LORD:

Rise up, attack Kedar,
   ravage the Easterners.
29* Their tents and herds shall be taken away,
   their tent curtains and all their goods;
Their camels they shall carry off
   for themselves,

and shout from upon them, "Terror on
   every side!"
30 Flee! leave your homes, hide in
   deep holes,
   you that live in Hazor, says the LORD;
For counsel has been taken against you,
   a plan has been formed against you
   [Nebuchadnezzar, king of Babylon].
31 Rise up! set out against a nation that is
   at peace,
   that lives secure, says the LORD,
That has no gates or bars,
   and dwells alone.
32* Their camels shall be your booty,
   their many herds your spoil;
I will scatter to the winds those who shave
   their temples,
   from all sides I will bring ruin
   upon them,
   says the LORD.
33 Hazor shall become a haunt of jackals,
   a desert forever,
Where no man lives,
   no human being stays.

Against Elam

34† The following word of the LORD against Elam came to the prophet Jeremiah at the beginning of the reign of Zedekiah, king of Judah: 35 Thus says the LORD of hosts:

Behold, I will break the bow of Elam,
   the mainstay of their might.
36 I will bring upon Elam the four winds
   from the four ends of the heavens:
I will scatter them to all these winds,
   till there is no nation
   to which the outcasts of Elam shall
   not come.
37 I will break Elam before their foes,
   before those who seek their life;
I will bring evil upon them,
   my burning wrath, says the LORD.
I will send the sword to pursue them
   until I have completely made an end
   of them;
38 My throne I will set up in Elam
   and destroy from there king and princes,
   says the LORD.
39 But in the days to come I will change
   the lot of Elam, says the LORD.

49, 23: *Hamath and Arpad:* independent Aramean states to the north of Damascus; the invasion is conceived as coming from the north. The situation is of the eighth century B.C. Cf Is 10, 9ff.
49, 27: *The palaces of Ben-hadad:* the royal palaces in Damascus where at least three kings bore this name; cf 1 Kgs 15, 18; 20.
49, 34: *Elam:* the ancient kingdom to the east of Babylonia.

49, 22: Jer 4, 13.
49, 23: Is 36, 19; 37, 13.
49, 28: Is 21, 16.
49, 29: Jer 4, 20.
49, 32: Jer 9, 25.

The First Prophecy against Babylon

50 ¹*† The word which the LORD spoke against Babylon, against the land of the Chaldeans, through the prophet Jeremiah:

²† Announce and publish it among the nations;
   publish it, hide it not, but say:
Babylon is taken, Bel confounded,
      Merodach shattered;
   her images are put to shame, her
      idols shattered.
³* A people from the north advances against her
      to turn her land into a desert,
So that no one shall live there,
      because man and beast have fled away.
⁴* In those days, at that time, says the LORD,
   the men of Israel and of Judah shall come,
Weeping as they come, to seek the LORD,
      their God;
⁵* to their goal in Zion they shall ask the way.
   "Come, let us join ourselves to the LORD
      with covenant everlasting, never to
      be forgotten."
⁶* Lost sheep were my people,
      their shepherds misled them,
      straggling on the mountains;
From mountain to hill they wandered,
      losing the way to their fold.
⁷* Whoever came upon them devoured them,
      and their enemies said, "We incur no guilt,
Because they sinned against the LORD,
      the hope of their fathers, their abode of
      justice."

⁸* Flee from Babylon, leave the land of
      the Chaldeans,
   be like the rams at the head of the flock.
⁹* See, I am stirring up against Babylon
   a band of great nations from the north;
   from there they advance, and she shall
      be taken.
Their arrows are arrows of the skilled warrior;
   none shall return without effect.
¹⁰ Chaldea shall be their plunder,
   and all her plunderers shall be enriched,
   says the LORD.

¹¹ Yes, rejoice and exult,
      you that plunder my portion;
Frisk like calves on the green,
      snort like stallions!
¹²* Your mother shall be sorely put to shame,
      she that bore you shall be abashed;
See, the last of the nations,
      a desert, dry and waste.
¹³* Because of the LORD's wrath she shall
      be empty,
   and become a total desert;
Everyone who passes by Babylon will
      be appalled
   and catch his breath, at all her wounds.
¹⁴* Take your posts encircling Babylon,
      you who bend the bow;
Shoot at her, spare not your arrows,
¹⁵*† raise the war cry against her on all sides.
She surrenders, her bastions fall,
      her walls are torn down:
Vengeance of the LORD is this! Take revenge
      on her,
   as she has done, do to her;
   for she sinned against the LORD.
¹⁶* Cut off from Babylon the sower
      and him who wields the sickle in
         harvest time!
Before the destroying sword,
   each of them turns to his own people,
   everyone flees to his own land.
¹⁷* A stray sheep was Israel
      that lions pursued;
Formerly the king of Assyria devoured her,
      now Nebuchadnezzar of Babylon gnaws
      her bones.
¹⁸* Therefore, thus says the LORD of hosts, the
God of Israel:

I will punish the king of Babylon and his land,
      as once I punished the king of Assyria;
¹⁹* But I will bring back Israel to her fold,
      to feed on Carmel and Bashan,
And on Mount Ephraim and Gilead,
      till she has her fill.

²⁰* In those days, at that time, says the LORD:

---

† **50, 1—51, 58:** A collection of miscellaneous prophecies against Babylon which now stands as the introduction to the story in Jer 51, 59–64. The Greek text of Jer 50, 1 omits through the prophet Jeremiah, and it is in fact likely that these oracles are not Jeremiah's, but were composed by other inspired writers after the fall of Jerusalem, who may have used some of Jeremiah's texts. Babylon fell to the Persians in 538 B.C.

50, 2: *Bel:* originally the name of the god of Nippur in Mesopotamia, then identified with Merodach (Marduk), chief god of Babylon.

50, 15: *Her walls are torn down:* the prophet is not predicting the details of Babylon's downfall, but describing such a downfall in con-

ventional language. Actually, Babylon was surrendered peaceably, without destruction.

50, 1: Jer 51, 1; Is 13, 1–14; 21, 1–10.	**50, 13:** Jer 25, 12.
50, 3: Jer 51, 48; Is 13, 17.	**50, 14:** Jer 51, 11; Is 21, 2.
50, 4: Jer 3, 18; Ps 126, 6.	**50, 15:** Jer 51, 11.44.58; Ps 137, 8.
50, 5: Jer 31, 31; 32, 40.	**50, 16:** Is 13, 14.
50, 6: Is 53, 6; 1 Pt 2, 25.	**50, 17:** 2 Kgs 17, 24; 18, 14.
50, 7: Jer 31, 23.	**50, 18:** Is 10, 12; 14, 24f.
50, 8: Jer 51, 6.45; Is 48, 20.	**50, 19:** Jer 23, 3; Ez 34, 13f.
50, 9: Jer 51, 27.	**50, 20:** Jer 31, 34; Is 43, 25; Mi 7, 19.
50, 12: Jer 51, 43; Is 13, 20ff.	

They shall seek Israel's guilt, but it shall be
  no more,
  and Judah's sins, but these shall no longer
    be found;
  for I will forgive the remnant I preserve.

21† Attack the land of Merathaim,
  and those who live in Pekod;
Slaughter and doom them, says the LORD,
  do all I have commanded you.
22 Battle alarm in the land,
  dire destruction!
23* How has the hammer of the whole earth
  been broken and shattered!
What an object of horror
  Babylon has become among the nations.
24* You ensnared yourself, and were caught,
  O Babylon, before you knew it!
You were discovered and seized,
  because you challenged the LORD.
25* The LORD opens his armory
  and brings forth the weapons of his wrath;
For the Lord GOD of hosts has work to do
  in the land of the Chaldeans.

26 Come upon her from every side,
  open her granaries,
Pile up her goods in heaps and doom it,
  leave not a remnant.
27 Slay all her oxen,
  let them go down to the slaughter;
Woe to them! their day has come,
  the time of their punishment.
28* Listen! the fugitives, the escaped
  from the land of Babylon:
They announce in Zion
  the vengeance of the LORD, our God.
29* Call up against Babylon archers,
  all who bend the bow;
Encamp around her,
  let no one escape.
Repay her for her deeds;
  as she has done, do to her,
For she insulted the LORD,
  the Holy One of Israel.
30* Therefore her young men shall fall in
  her streets,
all her warriors shall perish on that day;
  says the LORD.

31 I am against you, man of insolence,
  says the Lord GOD of hosts;

For your day has come,
  the time for me to punish you.
32 Insolence stumbles and falls;
  there is no one to raise him up.
I will kindle in his cities a fire
  that shall devour everything around him.
33   Thus says the LORD of hosts:
Oppressed are the men of Israel,
  and with them the men of Judah;
All their captors hold them fast
  and refuse to let them go.
34* Strong is their avenger,
  whose name is LORD of hosts;
He will defend their cause with success,
  and give rest to the earth,
  but unrest to those who live in Babylon.

35 A sword upon the Chaldeans, says the LORD,
  upon Babylon's people, her princes and
    wise men!
36 A sword upon the soothsayers,
  that they may become fools!
A sword upon her warriors,
  that they may tremble;
37* A sword upon her motley throng,
  that they may become women!
A sword upon her treasures,
  that they may be plundered;
38* A sword upon her waters,
  that they may dry up!
For it is a land of idols,
  and they shall be made frantic by
    fearful things.
39* Hence, wildcats and desert beasts shall
    dwell there,
  and ostriches shall occupy it;
Never again shall it be peopled, or lived in,
  from age to age.
40* As when God overturned Sodom
  and Gomorrah, with their neighbors, says
    the LORD,
Not a man shall dwell there,
  no human being shall tarry there.
41* See! a people comes from the north,
  a great nation, and mighty kings
  roused from the ends of the earth.
42 Bow and javelin they wield,
  cruel and pitiless are they;
They sound like the roaring sea,
  as they ride forth on steeds,
Each in his place for battle
  against you, daughter Babylon.

---

† **50, 21:** *Merathaim,* "twice bitter," and *Pekod,* "punishment," are here symbolic terms for Babylonia, though probably they suggest also the names of regions in that country.

50, 23: Jer 51, 20; Is 14, 6.   **50, 24:** Jer 51, 57.

50, 25: Jer 51, 11; Is 13, 5.   **50, 37:** Jer 51, 30; Na 3, 13.
50, 28: Jer 51, 10f.   **50, 38:** Jer 51, 32.36.
50, 29: Jer 51, 56.   **50, 39:** Jer 51, 37; Is 13, 21f.
50, 30: Jer 49, 26; 51, 4.   **50, 40:** Jer 51, 43.
50, 34: Jer 51, 36.   **50, 41:** Jer 51, 27f.

43* The king of Babylon hears news of them,
      and helpless fall his hands;
   Anguish seizes him,
      throes like a mother's in childbirth.
44* As when a lion comes up from the
         Jordan's thicket
      to the permanent feeding grounds,
   So I, in one instant, will drive them off,
      and whom I choose I will establish there;
   For who is like me? who calls me to account?
      what shepherd can stand against me?
45* Therefore hear the counsel of the LORD
      which he has taken against Babylon;
   Hear the plans he has made
      against the land of the Chaldeans:
   They shall be dragged away, even the
         smallest sheep;
      their own pasture shall be aghast because
         of them.
46* At the cry "Babylon is captured!" the
         earth quakes;
      the outcry is heard among the nations.

The Second Prophecy against Babylon

51 ¹   Thus says the LORD:
   See! I rouse against Babylon,
   and against those who live in Chaldea,
   a destroying wind.
 2* Against Babylon I will send winnowers
      to winnow her and lay waste her land;
   They shall besiege her from all sides
      on the day of affliction.
 3* Let the bowman draw his bow,
      and flaunt his coat of mail;
   Spare not her young men,
      doom her entire army.
 4* The slain shall fall in the land of Chaldea,
      the transfixed, in her streets;
 5 For Israel and Judah are not widowed
      of their God, the LORD of hosts,
   And the Chaldean land is full of guilt
      to be punished by the Holy One of Israel.

 6* Flee out of Babylon;
      let each one save his life,
      perish not for her guilt;
   This is a time of vengeance for the LORD,
      he pays her her due.
 7* Babylon was a golden cup in the hand of
         the LORD

which made the whole earth drunk;
   The nations drank its wine,
      with this they have become mad.
 8* Babylon suddenly falls and is crushed:
      howl over her!
   Bring balm for her wounds,
      in case she can be healed.
 9* "We have tried to heal Babylon,
      but she cannot be healed.
   Leave her, let us go, each to his own land."
   Her judgment reaches heaven,
      it touches the clouds.
10* The LORD has brought to light our just cause;
      come, let us tell in Zion
      what the LORD, our God, has done.

11*†Sharpen the arrows,
      fill the quivers;
   The LORD has stirred up the spirit of
         Media's kings;
      Babylon he is resolved to destroy.
   Yes, it is the vengeance of the LORD,
      vengeance for his temple.
12 Against the walls of Babylon raise a signal,
      make strong the watch;
   Post sentries,
      arrange ambushes!
   For the LORD has planned and he will carry out
      his threat against the inhabitants of Babylon.
13* You who dwell by mighty waters,
      rich in treasure,
   Your end has come,
      the term at which you shall be cut off!
14 The LORD of hosts has sworn by himself:
      I will fill you with men as numerous
         as locusts,
      who shall raise over you the vintage shout!
15* He has sworn who made the earth by
         his power,
      and established the world by his wisdom,
      and stretched out the heavens by his skill.
16 When he thunders, the waters in the
         heavens roar,
      and he brings up clouds from the end of
         the earth;
   He makes the lightning flash in the rain,
      and releases stormwinds from
         their chambers.
17 Every man is stupid, ignorant;
      every artisan is put to shame by his idol:

51, 11: *Media's kings:* the Medes dwelt with the Persians in the
land now known as Iran. At the time these words were written the
Medes were the dominant people of the two, but within a short time
the Persians had gained the ascendancy.

50, 43: Is 13, 7.
50, 44: Jer 49, 19.
50, 45: Jer 51, 12.29.
50, 46: Jer 51, 29.
51, 2: Jer 15, 7; Is 41, 16.
51, 3: Jer 50, 14.29.
51, 4: Jer 50, 30.
51, 6: Jer 50, 8.15.29; Is 48,
  20.
51, 7: Rv 14, 8; 17, 4.
51, 8: Rv 18, 9-18.
51, 9: Is 13, 14; Rv 18, 5.
51, 10: Jer 50, 28.
51, 11: 2 Kgs 17, 6; Is 13, 17.
51, 13: Na 2, 1.
51, 15: Jer 10, 12.

He molded a fraud,
  without breath of life.
18 Nothingness are they, a ridiculous work,
   that will perish in their time of punishment.
19 Not like these is the portion of Jacob,
   he is the creator of all things;
   Israel is his very own tribe,
   LORD of hosts is his name.

20 You are my hammer,
   my weapon for war;
   With you I shatter nations,
   with you I destroy kingdoms.
21* With you I shatter horse and rider,
    with you I shatter chariot and driver.
22* With you I shatter man and wife,
    with you I shatter old and young,
    with you I shatter youth and maiden.
23 With you I shatter the shepherd and
   his flock,
   with you I shatter the farmer and
   his team,
   with you I shatter satraps and prefects.
24* Thus will I repay Babylon,
    and all who live in Chaldea
    All the evil they did to Zion,
    as you shall see with your own eyes, says
    the LORD.
25* Beware! I am against you,
    destroying mountain,
    destroyer of the entire earth, says
    the LORD;
    I will stretch forth my hand against you,
    roll you down over the cliffs,
    and make you a burnt mountain:
26* They will not take from you a cornerstone,
    or a foundation stone;
    Ruins forever shall you be,
    say the LORD.

27*† Raise a signal on the earth,
     blow the trumpet among the nations;
     Dedicate peoples to war against her,
     summon against her the kingdoms,
     Ararat, Minni, and Ashkenaz;
     Appoint recruiting officers against her,
     send up horses like bristling locusts.
28 Dedicate peoples to war against her:
   the king of Media,
   Its governors and all its prefects,
   every land in his domain.

29 The earth quakes and writhes,
   the LORD's plan against Babylon is
   carried out,
   Turning the land of Babylon
   into a desert where no one lives.
30 Babylon's warriors have ceased to fight,
   they remain in their strongholds;
   Dried up is their strength,
   they have become women.
   Burned are their homes,
   and broken their bars.
31* One runner meets another,
    herald meets herald,
    Telling the king of Babylon
    that all his city is taken.
32 The fords have been seized,
   and the fortresses set on fire,
   while warriors are in panic.
33* For thus says the LORD of hosts, the God of
Israel:

   Daughter Babylon is like a threshing floor
   at the time it is trodden;
   Yet a little while,
   and the harvest time will come for her.
34† He has consumed me, routed me,
    [Nebuchadnezzar, king of Babylon,]
    he has left me as an empty vessel;
    He has swallowed me like a dragon:
    filled his belly with my delights, and cast
    me out.
35 My torn flesh be upon Babylon,
   says the city on Zion;
   My blood upon the people of Chaldea,
   says Jerusalem.
36   But now, thus says the LORD:
   Surely I will defend your cause,
   I will avenge you;
   I will dry up her sea,
   and drain her fountain.
37* Babylon shall become a heap of ruins,
    a haunt of jackals;
    A place of horror and ridicule,
    where no one lives.
38* They all roar like lions,
    growl like lion cubs.
39 When they are parched, I will set a drink
   before them
   to make them drunk, that they may
   be overcome
   with perpetual sleep, never to awaken, says
   the LORD.

---

† 51, 27: *Ararat, Minni, and Ashkenaz:* regions or people in what is now Armenia, subject at this time to Media.
  51, 34: *Me. . . my:* refers to Jerusalem.
*

51, 21: Dn 7, 7.19.23.   51, 22: Is 13, 16.18.

51, 24: Jer 25, 14; 50, 29;   51, 31: 2 Chr 30, 6; Jb 1,
         Ps 137, 8.   14–18.
51, 25: Rv 8, 7; 18, 8f.   51, 33: Rv 14, 15.
51, 26: Jer 25, 12; Ps 118, 22.   51, 37: Is 25, 2.
51, 27: Na 3, 17.   51, 38: Na 2, 11f.

40 I will bring them down like lambs to
  the slaughter,
  like rams and goats.
41* How has she been seized, made captive,
  the glory of the whole world!
  What a horror has Babylon become
  among nations:
42 against Babylon the sea rises,
  she is overwhelmed by the roaring waves!
43 Her cities have become a desert,
  parched and arid land
  Where no man lives,
  and no one passes through.
44 I will punish Bel in Babylon,
  and make him disgorge what he
  swallowed;
  peoples shall stream to him no more.
  The wall of Babylon falls!
45 Leave her, my people, let each one
  save himself
  from the burning wrath of the LORD.

46* Be not discouraged for fear of rumors spread
in the land; this year the rumor comes, then violence in the land, tyrant against tyrant. **47** But behold, the days are coming when I will punish the
idols of Babylon; her whole land shall be put to
shame, and all her slain shall lie fallen within her.
48* Then heaven, and earth, and everything in them
shall shout over Babylon with joy, when the destroyers come against her from the north, says the
LORD. **49** Babylon, too, must fall, O slain of Israel, as
at the hands of Babylon have fallen the slain of all
the earth.

50 You who have escaped the sword,
  go on, stand not still;
  Remember the LORD from afar,
  let Jerusalem come to your minds.
51* We are ashamed because we have
  heard taunts,
  confusion covers our faces; strangers
  have entered
  the holy places of the house of the LORD.
52 But behold, the days are coming, says
  the LORD,
  when I will punish her idols,
  and in her whole land the wounded
  will groan.
53* Though Babylon scale the heavens,
  and make her strong heights
  inaccessible,
  destroyers from me shall reach her, says
  the LORD.

Whatever Happened to Babylon?

In his time, Jeremiah prophesied about
the destruction of Babylon, the powerful
empire with the most glamorous and
glittering capital in the Middle East (see
Jeremiah, chapters 50–51). Not long afterward, in 587 B.C., King Nebuchadrezzar
(also called Nebuchadnezzar) of Babylon
destroyed Jerusalem, blinded the king of
Judah, and led the leaders of Judah off to
exile. This seemed to be the end of
Jerusalem and perhaps even the
Israelites. However, the captives were
eventually released when Persia defeated
Babylon. Today, Jerusalem is a thriving
city, and Judaism—as it emerged after
the Exile—is a great religion. Babylon is
long gone, and no one worships its chief
god, Marduk.

Jeremiah saw past the immediate
destruction of Jerusalem to the eventual
doom of Babylon. He had a much broader
vision of the future. Great cities come and
go, but God is forever, and the people of
God live on through all the ebbs and flows
of history.

▶ Jeremiah, chapter 51

54 Hear! loud cries from Babylon,
  dire destruction from the land of
  the Chaldeans;
55 For the LORD lays Babylon waste,
  stills her loud cry,
  Though her waves were roaring like
  mighty waters,
  and their clamor was heard afar.
56* For the destroyer comes upon her,
  [Babylon,]
  her heroes are captured, their bows
  broken;
  The LORD is a God who requites,
  he will surely repay.

51, 41: Is 13, 19.   51, 51: Pss 44, 16f; 78, 1–4.
51, 46: Mt 24, 6f.   51, 53: Is 14, 13.
51, 48: Rv 18, 20.   51, 56: Na 1, 2.

[57] I will make her princes and her wise men drunk, her governors, her prefects, and her warriors, so that they sleep an eternal sleep, never to awaken, says the King, whose name is the LORD of hosts. [58]* Thus says the LORD of hosts:

> The walls of spacious Babylon shall be
>   leveled utterly;
>   her lofty gates shall be destroyed by fire.
> The toil of the nations is for nothing;
>   for the flames the peoples
>   weary themselves.

The Prophecy Sent to Babylon

[59]† This was the errand given by the prophet Jeremiah to Seraiah, son of Neriah, son of Mahseiah, when he went to Babylon for the king in the fourth year of the reign of Zedekiah; Seraiah was chief quartermaster. [60]† Jeremiah had written all the misfortune that was to befall Babylon in a single book: all these words that were written against Babylon. [61]* And Jeremiah said to Seraiah: When you reach Babylon, see that you read aloud all these words, [62] and then say: O LORD, you yourself threatened to destroy this place, so that neither man nor beast should dwell in it, since it would remain an everlasting desert. [63]* When you have finished reading this book, tie a stone to it and throw it in the Euphrates, [64]† and say: Thus shall Babylon sink. Never shall she rise, because of the evil I am bringing upon her. [To "weary themselves" are the words of Jeremiah.]

VI: Historical Appendix†

Capture of Jerusalem

52 [1]* Zedekiah was twenty-one years old when he became king, and he reigned eleven years in Jerusalem. His mother's name was Hamutal, daughter of Jeremiah of Libnah. [2] He did what was evil in the eyes of the LORD, just as Jehoiakim had done. [3] Indeed, what was done in Jerusalem and in Judah so angered the LORD that he cast them out from his presence.

Zedekiah rebelled against the king of Babylon. [4]*† In the tenth month of the ninth year of his reign, on the tenth day of the month, Nebuchadnezzar, king of Babylon, and his whole army advanced against Jerusalem, encamped around it, and built siege walls on every side. [5] The siege of the city continued until the eleventh year of King Zedekiah.

[6] On the ninth day of the fourth month, when famine had gripped the city and the people had no more bread, [7] the city walls were breached. Then all the soldiers took to flight and left the city by night through the gate between the two walls which was near the king's garden. With the Chaldeans surrounding the city, they went in the direction of the Arabah. [8] But the Chaldean army pursued the king and overtook Zedekiah in the desert near Jericho, while his whole army fled from him.

[9] The king, therefore, was arrested and brought to Riblah, in the land of Hamath, to the king of Babylon, who pronounced sentence on him. [10] As Zedekiah looked on, the king of Babylon slew his sons as well as all the princes of Judah at Riblah. [11] Then he blinded Zedekiah, bound him with fetters, and had him brought to Babylon and kept in prison until the day of his death.

Destruction of Jerusalem

[12]† On the tenth day of the fifth month (this was in the nineteenth year of Nebuchadnezzar, king of Babylon), Nebuzaradan, captain of the bodyguard, came to Jerusalem as the representative of the king of Babylon. [13] He burned the house of the LORD, the palace of the king, and all the houses of Jerusalem; every large building he destroyed with fire. [14] And the Chaldean troops who were with the captain of the guard tore down all the walls that surrounded Jerusalem.

[15] Then Nebuzaradan, captain of the guard, led into exile the rest of the people left in the city, and those who had deserted to the king of Babylon, and the rest of the artisans. [16] But some of the country's poor, Nebuzaradan, captain of the guard, left behind as vinedressers and farmers.

[17] The bronze pillars that belonged to the house of the LORD, and the wheeled carts and the bronze sea in the house of the LORD, the Chaldeans broke into pieces; they carried away all the bronze to Babylon. [18] They took also the pots, the shovels, the

51, 59: *Seraiah:* the brother of Baruch; cf Jer 32, 12. *The king:* Zedekiah. Perhaps Seraiah went to Babylon to explain away the presence of foreign ambassadors in Jerusalem that same year; cf Jer 27, 3.

51, 60: Jeremiah prophesied against Babylon, even as he foretold Judah's release from Babylon's power (Jer 3, 14–18; 32, 15; 33, 6–9.12f); but his book against Babylon was thrown in the Euphrates (v 63). The preceding oracles were composed by later writers; see note on Jer 50, 1—51, 58.

51, 64: *To "weary themselves" are the words of Jeremiah:* an editorial remark concerning the end of v 58.

52, 1–34: This supplement to the Book of Jeremiah was taken by the final editor from 2 Kgs 24, 18—25, 30 and placed here in order to show the fulfillment of Jeremiah's prophecies. In part this repeats the history given in Jer 39–41; the history of Gedaliah in 2 Kgs 25, 22–26, however, has not been reproduced here.

52, 4: *In the tenth month of the ninth year of his reign, on the tenth day of the month:* January 15, 588 B.C. Cf Jer 39, 1.

52, 12: *On the tenth day of the fifth month . . . nineteenth year:* the tenth of Ab—July/August in 587 B.C.

51, 58: Hb 2, 13.
51, 61: Jer 50, 1–51.
51, 63: Rv 18, 21.
52, 1–27: 2 Kgs 24, 18—25, 21.
52, 4–16: Jer 39, 1–10.

snuffers, the bowls, the pans, and all the bronze vessels used for service. 19 The basins also, the fire holders, the bowls, the pots, the lampstands, the pans, the sacrificial bowls which were of gold or silver, these too the captain of the guard carried off, 20 as well as the two pillars, the one sea, and the twelve oxen of bronze under the sea, and the wheeled carts which King Solomon had made for the house of the LORD. The bronze of all these furnishings could not be weighed.

21 Each of the pillars was eighteen cubits high and twelve cubits in diameter; each was four fingers thick, and hollow inside. 22 A bronze capital five cubits high surmounted the one pillar, and a network with pomegranates encircled the capital, all of brass; and so for the other pillar. The pomegranates . . . 23 there were ninety-six pomegranates. There were a hundred pomegranates, all around the network.

24 The captain of the guard also took Seraiah, the high priest, Zephaniah, the second priest, and the three keepers of the entry. 25 And from the city he took one courtier, a commander of soldiers, and seven men in the personal service of the king who were present in the city, and the scribe of the army commander who mustered the people of the land, and sixty of the common people who were in the city. 26 The captain of the guard, Nebuzaradan,

arrested these and brought them to the king of Babylon at Riblah, 27 who had them struck down and put to death in Riblah, in the land of Hamath.

Thus was Judah exiled from her land. 28† This is the number of the people whom Nebuchadnezzar led away captive: in his seventh year, three thousand and twenty-three people of Judah; 29 in the eighteenth year of Nebuchadnezzar, eight hundred and thirty-two persons from Jerusalem; 30 in the twenty-third year of Nebuchadnezzar, Nebuzaradan, captain of the guard, exiled seven hundred and forty-five people of Judah: four thousand six hundred persons in all.

Favor Shown to Jehoiachin

31*† In the thirty-seventh year of the exile of Jehoiachin, king of Judah, on the twenty-fifth day of the twelfth month, Evil-merodach, king of Babylon, in the inaugural year of his reign, took up the case of Jehoiachin, king of Judah, and released him from prison. 32† He spoke kindly to him and gave him a throne higher than that of the other kings who were with him in Babylon. 33 Jehoiachin took off his prison garb and ate at the king's table as long as he lived. 34 The allowance given him by the king of Babylon was a perpetual allowance, in fixed daily amounts, all the days of his life until the day of his death.

---

† **52, 28–30:** These verses are missing in the Greek text and have not been taken from 2 Kgs 25, but from some other source using a different system of chronology. Besides the deportations of 598 and 587 B.C., mention is made here of a final one that took place in the year 582/1, possibly as a sequel to the murder of Gedaliah; cf Jer 41, 2.

52, 31–34: In the year 561/0 B.C., Jehoiachin was released from

prison by Nebuchadnezzar's successor Awel-Marduk (Evil-merodach), who reigned only two years. Babylonian records confirm the fact that Jehoiachin and his family were supported at public expense.

52, 32: *The other kings:* who had also been brought as captives to Babylon.

*

52, 31–34: 2 Kgs 25, 27–30.

I f someone close to you has died, you know that the grief and sadness can be almost too much for words. At such times of deep emotion, many people resort to poetry or song to try to express their feelings. Written during the Babylonian Exile, the Book of Lamentations poetically expresses the overwhelming grief the Israelites felt over the loss of their homes, their freedom, their capital, and their Temple. Through its passages, we get an insight into how devastating and destructive those days actually were.

At a Glance

I. Jerusalem Abandoned and Disgraced (chapter 1).

II. The LORD's Wrath against Zion (chapter 2).

III. Sufferings of the Prophet and His People (chapter 3).

IV. Miseries of the Besieged City (chapter 4).

V. The Prophet's Lament and Supplication (chapter 5).

In-depth

The Book of Lamentations is a collection of five poem songs, each a separate chapter in the book. If you take a quick look, you will notice that each poem has twenty-two verses, except the third, which has sixty-six. This is not an accident. In the original Hebrew language, each verse of the first, second, fourth, and fifth poems begins with a different letter of the Hebrew alphabet, which has twenty-two letters. In the third poem, every set of three verses begins with a different letter of the alphabet. This poetic structure, called acrostic, cannot be successfully translated into English. It is found in several poetic sections of the Old Testament, including Psalm 119.

We are not sure why the Lamentation poems were written in this fashion. It may be because the structure made them easier to memorize. Some scholars believe that it may have been a mystical sign of order and completeness. Another possibility is that the poem's structure helped to give form to the people's grief, which is important because uncontrollable grief can keep people from moving on in life. Knowing that the poem had a definite end may have reminded them that their sorrow would also come to an end.

Through these beautiful poems, Israelites were able to grieve and acknowledge the sin that led to their destruction. By recalling their experience of the goodness of God in the past, they were also able to hope for the day when God would lead them back to their land to rebuild their lives in faithfulness to the Covenant.

Quick Facts

Period Covered
the Babylonian Exile, 587–538 B.C.

Authors
unknown

Theme
poems of grief over the destruction of Jerusalem and the hardships of the Exile

The Book of Lamentations

Lamentations

Jerusalem Abandoned and Disgraced†

1 [1] How lonely she is now,
    the once crowded city!
Widowed is she
    who was mistress over nations;
The princess among the provinces
    has been made a toiling slave.

[2]* Bitterly she weeps at night,
    tears upon her cheeks,
With not one to console her
    of all her dear ones;
Her friends have all betrayed her
    and become her enemies.

[3]* Judah has fled into exile
    from oppression and cruel slavery;
Yet where she lives among the nations
    she finds no place to rest:
All her persecutors come upon her
    where she is narrowly confined.

[4]* The roads to Zion mourn
    for lack of pilgrims going to her feasts;
All her gateways are deserted,
    her priests groan,
Her virgins sigh;
    she is in bitter grief.

[5] Her foes are uppermost,
    her enemies are at ease;
The LORD has punished her
    for her many sins.
Her little ones have gone away,
    captive before the foe.

[6] Gone from daughter Zion
    is all her glory:
Her princes, like rams
    that find no pasture,
Have gone off without strength
    before their captors.

[7] Jerusalem is mindful of the days
    of her wretched homelessness,
When her people fell into enemy hands,
    and she had no one to help her;
When her foes gloated over her,
    laughed at her ruin.

[8]* Through the sin of which she is
        guilty,
    Jerusalem is defiled;
All who esteemed her think her vile
    now that they see her nakedness;
She herself groans
    and turns away.

1, 1–22: In this poem the poet first describes Jerusalem's miserable state after the destruction wrought by the Chaldeans (vv 1–11a); in v 11b the city itself takes up the lament.

1, 2: Jer 30, 14; Ez 16, 37.
1, 3: Dt 28, 65; Jer 45, 3.
1, 4: Jer 14, 2.
1, 8: Is 47, 2; Jer 13, 22.26.

9   Her filth is on her skirt;
      she gave no thought how she would end.
   Astounding is her downfall,
      with no one to console her.
   Look, O LORD, upon her misery,
      for the enemy has triumphed!

10*   The foe stretched out his hand
      to all her treasures;
   She has seen those nations
      enter her sanctuary
   Whom you forbade to come
      into your assembly.

11*   All her people groan,
      searching for bread;
   They give their treasures for food,
      to retain the breath of life.
   "Look, O LORD, and see
      how worthless I have become!

12   "Come, all you who pass by the way,
      look and see
   Whether there is any suffering like
      my suffering,
      which has been dealt me
   When the LORD afflicted me
      on the day of his blazing wrath.

13*   "From on high he sent fire
      down into my very frame;
   He spread a net for my feet,
      and overthrew me.
   He left me desolate,
      in pain all the day.

14†   "He has kept watch over my sins;
      by his hand they have been plaited:
   They have settled about my neck,
      he has brought my strength to its knees;
   The Lord has delivered me into their grip,
      I am unable to rise.

15*   "All the mighty ones in my midst
      the Lord has cast away;
   He summoned an army against me
      to crush my young men;
   The LORD has trodden in the wine press
      virgin daughter Judah.

16*   "At this I weep,
      my eyes run with tears:
   Far from me are all who could console me,
      any who might revive me;
   My sons were reduced to silence
      when the enemy prevailed."

17*   Zion stretched out her hands,
      but there was no one to console her;
   The LORD gave orders against Jacob
      for his neighbors to be his foes;
   Jerusalem has become in their midst
      a thing unclean.

18*   "The LORD is just;
      I had defied his command.
   Listen, all you peoples,
      and behold my suffering:
   My maidens and my youths
      have gone into captivity.

19*†   "I cried out to my lovers,
      but they failed me.
   My priests and my elders
      perished in the city;
   Where they sought food for themselves,
      they found it not.

20*   "Look, O LORD, upon my distress:
      all within me is in ferment,
   My heart recoils within me
      from my monstrous rebellion.
   In the streets the sword bereaves,
      at home death stalks.

21   "Give heed to my groaning;
      there is no one to console me.
   All my enemies rejoice at my
      misfortune:
      it is you who have wrought it.
   Bring on the day you have proclaimed,
      that they may be even as I.

22*†   "Let all their evil come before you;
      deal with them
   As you have dealt with me
      for all my sins;
   My groans are many,
      and I am sick at heart."

L
A
M

1, 14: *They have been plaited . . . my neck:* the sins of the people have been bound together and laid as a yoke on their back; cf Mt 23, 4.
1, 19: *My lovers:* Zion's foreign allies, who failed to help her, as the prophets had warned.
1, 22: Zion fully acknowledges her guilt and the justness of divine punishment; nevertheless, she pleads that her enemies also be punished for their guilt.

1, 10: Jer 51, 51.
1, 11: Jer 52, 6.
1, 13: Ez 12, 13.
1, 15: Jer 8, 16.
1, 16: Jer 13, 17; 14, 17.
1, 17: Ps 74, 7.
1, 18: Dt 28, 41.
1, 19: Jer 30, 14.
1, 20: Lam 2, 11.
1, 22: Lam 3, 64.

The Lord's Wrath against Zion

2 ¹† How the Lord in his wrath
    has detested daughter Zion!
He has cast down from heaven to earth
    the glory of Israel,
Unmindful of his footstool
    on the day of his wrath.

²   The Lord has consumed without pity
    all the dwellings of Jacob;
He has torn down in his anger
    the fortresses of daughter Judah;
He has brought to the ground in dishonor
    her king and her princes.

³*†He broke off, in fiery wrath,
    the horn that was Israel's whole
      strength;
He withheld the support of his right hand
    when the enemy approached;
He blazed up in Jacob like a flaming fire
    devouring all about it.

⁴* Like an enemy he made taut his bow;
    with his arrows in his right hand
He took his stand as a foe, and slew
    all on whom the eye doted;
Over the tent of daughter Zion
    he poured out his wrath like fire.

⁵   The Lord has become an enemy,
    he has consumed Israel:
Consumed all her castles
    and destroyed her fortresses;
For daughter Judah he has multiplied
    moaning and groaning.

⁶* He has demolished his shelter like a
      garden booth,
    he has destroyed his dwelling;
In Zion the LORD has made
    feast and sabbath to be forgotten;
He has scorned in fierce wrath
    both king and priest.

⁷* The Lord has disowned his altar,
    rejected his sanctuary;
The walls of her towers
    he has handed over to the enemy,

Who shout in the house of the LORD
    as on a feast day.

⁸*†The LORD marked for destruction
    the wall of daughter Zion:
He stretched out the measuring line;
    his hand brought ruin, yet he did
      not relent—
He brought grief on wall and rampart
    till both succumbed.

⁹* Sunk into the ground are her gates;
    he has removed and broken her
      bars.
Her king and her princes are among
    the pagans;
    priestly instruction is wanting,
And her prophets have not received
    any vision from the LORD.

¹⁰*†On the ground in silence sit
    the old men of daughter Zion;
They strew dust on their heads
    and gird themselves with sackcloth;
The maidens of Jerusalem
    bow their heads to the ground.

¹¹*†Worn out from weeping are my eyes,
    within me all is in ferment;
My gall is poured out on the ground
    because of the downfall of the daughter of
      my people,
As child and infant faint away
    in the open spaces of the town.

¹²* They ask their mothers,
    "Where is the cereal?"—in vain,
As they faint away like the wounded
    in the streets of the city,
And breathe their last
    in their mothers' arms.

¹³* To what can I liken or compare you,
    O daughter Jerusalem?
What example can I show you for
      your comfort,
    virgin daughter Zion?
For great as the sea is your downfall;
    who can heal you?

2, 1: *The glory of Israel:* the temple. *His footstool:* the ark of the covenant (1 Chr 28, 2; Pss 99, 5; 132, 7); or again, the temple (Ez 43, 7).

2, 3: *Horn:* symbol of power and strength; cf Lam 2, 17; 1 Sm 2, 10; Lk 1, 69; etc.

2, 8: *The measuring line:* used not only in building, but in deciding what must be destroyed; cf Is 34, 11; 2 Kgs 21, 13.

2, 10: *They strew dust:* as a sign of penance; cf Jb 2, 12.

2, 11: *My gall is poured out on the ground:* I am afflicted with bitter sorrow; cf Jb 16, 13.

2, 3: Lam 1, 12.
2, 4: Jer 30, 14.
2, 6: Lam 1, 4; Is 1, 13; 5, 5.
2, 7: Ez 24, 21.
2, 8: Jer 52, 13.

2, 9: Dt 28, 36.
2, 10: Is 3, 26.
2, 11: Lam 3, 48.
2, 12: Lam 1, 11.
2, 13: Lam 1, 12.

Violence in Our City Streets

Poetic language is often used in the Bible to express the depth of human emotion that either the author feels or the author is trying to convey. When reading the Scriptures, we should be aware that poetic language often does not lend itself to a literal interpretation. Instead, we should open ourselves up to the spiritual and emotional truth this poetry contains.

The Book of Lamentations is a book of poetry that helps us reflect on the feelings and thoughts of the Jewish people in exile, who were suffering from the loss of their homes, freedom, security, and so much more. Verses 12 and 19 of the poem in chapter 2 of Lamentations both mention hunger and violence in the streets. Are things much different in our streets? In our own time, children are hungry, and people are being killed and violated. Our voice echoes the voice of this ancient prayer, calling out for God's mercy.

When will the violence stop, Lord?
How many will die today from drug over-
*   dose and domestic abuse?*
How many children will go hungry because
*   nobody took the time to care for them?*
Have mercy on your people, Lord!

▶ Lamentations, chapter 2

14* Your prophets had for you
    false and specious visions;
They did not lay bare your guilt,
    to avert your fate;
They beheld for you in vision
    false and misleading portents.

15* All who pass by
    clap their hands at you;
They hiss and wag their heads
    over daughter Jerusalem:

"Is this the all-beautiful city,
    the joy of the whole earth?"

16* All your enemies
    open their mouths against you;
They hiss and gnash their teeth.
    They say, "We have devoured her.
This at last is the day we hoped for;
    we have lived to see it!"

17* The LORD has done as he decreed:
    he has fulfilled the threat
He set forth from days of old;
    he has destroyed and had no pity,
Letting the enemy gloat over you
    and exalting the horn of your foes.

18 Cry out to the Lord;
    moan, O daughter Zion!
Let your tears flow like a torrent
    day and night;
Let there be no respite for you,
    no repose for your eyes.

19 Rise up, shrill in the night,
    at the beginning of every watch;
Pour out your heart like water
    in the presence of the Lord;
Lift up your hands to him
    for the lives of your little ones
[Who faint from hunger
    at the corner of every street].

20*† "Look, O LORD, and consider:
    whom have you ever treated thus?
Must women eat their offspring,
    their well-formed children?
Are priest and prophet to be slain
    in the sanctuary of the LORD?

21* "Dead in the dust of the streets
    lie young and old;
My maidens and young men
    have fallen by the sword;
You have slain on the day of your wrath,
    slaughtered without pity.

22* "You summoned as for a feast day
    terrors against me from all sides;
There was not, on the day of your wrath,
    either fugitive or survivor;
Those whom I bore and reared
    my enemy has utterly destroyed."

2, 20: *Must women eat their offspring:* extreme famine in a besieged city sometimes led to this form of cannibalism; cf Lam 4, 10; 2 Kgs 6, 28f; Bar 2, 3; Ez 5, 10.

2, 14: Is 58, 1; Jer 2, 8; 23, 16.
2, 15: Jer 18, 16.
2, 16: Lam 3, 46.
2, 17: Dt 28, 15.
2, 20: Lam 4, 10.
2, 21: Lam 3, 43; 2 Chr 36, 17; Jer 6, 11.
2, 22: Jer 42, 17.

Sufferings of the Prophet and His People

3

1*† I am a man who knows affliction
　　from the rod of his anger,

2 One whom he has led and forced to walk
　in darkness, not in the light;

3 Against me alone he brings back his hand
　again and again all the day.

4* He has worn away my flesh and my skin,
　he has broken my bones;

5 He has beset me round about
　with poverty and weariness;

6* He has left me to dwell in the dark
　like those long dead.

7 He has hemmed me in with no escape
　and weighed me down with chains;

8* Even when I cry out for help,
　he stops my prayer;

9 He has blocked my ways with fitted
　　stones,
　and turned my paths aside.

10* A lurking bear he has been to me,
　a lion in ambush!

11* He deranged my ways, set me astray,
　left me desolate.

12* He bent his bow, and set me up
　as the target for his arrow.

13* He pierces my sides
　with shafts from his quiver.

14* I have become a laughingstock for all nations,
　their taunt all the day long;

15* He has sated me with bitter food,
　made me drink my fill of wormwood.

16 He has broken my teeth with gravel,
　pressed my face in the dust;

17 My soul is deprived of peace,
　I have forgotten what happiness is;

18 I tell myself my future is lost,
　all that I hoped for from the LORD.

19 The thought of my homeless poverty
　is wormwood and gall;

20 Remembering it over and over
　leaves my soul downcast within me.

21 But I will call this to mind,
　as my reason to have hope:

22* The favors of the LORD are not exhausted,
　his mercies are not spent;

23 They are renewed each morning,
　so great is his faithfulness.

24* My portion is the LORD, says my soul;
　therefore will I hope in him.

25* Good is the LORD to one who waits for him,
　to the soul that seeks him;

26 It is good to hope in silence
　for the saving help of the LORD.

27† It is good for a man to bear
　the yoke from his youth.

28 Let him sit alone and in silence,
　when it is laid upon him.

Each New Day

LIVE IT!

The poems in Lamentations also have their hopeful side. They acknowledge that the favors of the LORD are not exhausted (3, 22) and that the Israelites will not experience the LORD's rejection forever (verse 31). Verse 23 reminds the people that God's favors are renewed each morning.

　Imagine that at the beginning of each day, you are given $86,400. You have the whole day to spend every last penny any way you want. Does that sound exciting? Well, God gives you 86,400 seconds every day to use however you like. Try making a one-day budget of the best ways to spend your 86,400 seconds. Remember, each day is a new gift filled with God's love. Make the most of it, and do so for God!

▶ **Lam 3, 22–33**

---

†
3, 1–21: The author identifies Zion's sufferings with his own.
3, 27: *To bear the yoke:* to do God's will; cf Jer 2, 20.

3, 1: Jer 20, 18.
3, 4: Jb 30, 30; Is 38, 13.
3, 6: Ps 143, 3.
3, 8: Ps 22, 2.

3, 10: Jb 10, 16; Hos 13, 8.
3, 11: Lam 1, 13.
3, 12: Lam 2, 4; Jb 16, 12.
3, 13: Jb 6, 4; Ps 38, 3.
3, 14: Jb 30, 9; Ps 69, 13.

3, 15: Jer 9, 14; 23, 15.
3, 22: Neh 9, 31.
3, 24: Pss 16, 5; 73, 26.
3, 25: Ps 130, 6; Is 30, 18.

29* †Let him put his mouth to the dust;
     there may yet be hope.
30* Let him offer his cheek to be struck,
     let him be filled with disgrace.

31* For the Lord's rejection
     does not last forever;
32* Though he punishes, he takes pity,
     in the abundance of his mercies;
33* He has no joy in afflicting
     or grieving the sons of men.

34 When anyone tramples underfoot
     all the prisoners in the land,
35 When he distorts men's rights
     in the very sight of the Most High,
36 When he presses a crooked claim,
     the Lord does not look on unconcerned.

37 Who commands, so that it comes to pass,
     except the Lord ordains it;
38* Except it proceeds from the mouth of the
     Most High,
     whether the thing be good or bad!
39* Why should any living man complain,
     any mortal, in the face of his sins?

40* Let us search and examine our ways
     that we may return to the LORD!
41 Let us reach out our hearts
     toward God in heaven!
42 We have sinned and rebelled;
     you have not forgiven us.

43* You veiled yourself in wrath and pursued us,
     you slew us and took no pity;
44 You wrapped yourself in a cloud
     which prayer could not pierce.
45* You have made us offscourings and refuse
     among the nations.

46 All our enemies
     have opened their mouths against us;
47* Terror and the pit have been our lot,
     desolation and destruction;
48* My eyes run with streams of water
     over the downfall of the daughter of my
     people.

49 My eyes flow without ceasing,
     there is no respite,

50 Till the LORD from heaven
     looks down and sees.
51 My eyes torment my soul
     at the sight of all the daughters of my city.

52 Those who were my enemies without
     cause
     hunted me down like a bird;
53* They struck me down alive in the pit,
     and sealed me in with a stone.
54 The waters flowed over my head,
     and I said, "I am lost!"

55* I called upon your name, O LORD,
     from the bottom of the pit;
56 You heard me call, "Let not your ear
     be deaf to my cry for help!"
57 You came to my aid when I called to you;
     you said, "Have no fear!"

58 You defended me in mortal danger,
     you redeemed my life.
59* You see, O LORD, how I am wronged;
     do me justice!
60 You see all their vindictiveness,
     all their plots against me.

61 You hear their insults, O LORD,
     [all their plots against me],
62 The whispered murmurings of my foes,
     against me all the day;
63 Whether they sit or stand,
     see, I am their taunt song.

64 Requite them as they deserve, O LORD,
     according to their deeds;
65* Give them hardness of heart,
     as your curse upon them;
66 Pursue them in wrath and destroy them
     from under your heavens!

Miseries of the Besieged City

4 ¹ How tarnished is the gold,
     how changed the noble metal;
How the sacred stones lie strewn
     at every street corner!

2* Zion's precious sons,
     fine gold their counterpart,
Now worth no more than earthen jars
     made by the hands of a potter!

---

† **3, 29:** *Let him put his mouth to the dust:* in humble submission;
cf Ps 72, 9.

3, 29: Jb 42, 6.
3, 30: Is 50, 6; Mt 5, 39.
3, 31: Ps 103, 9.
3, 32: Is 54, 8f.
3, 33: Heb 12, 10f.
3, 38: Is 45, 7.
3, 39: Prv 19, 3.
3, 40: Jl 2, 12f.
3, 43: Lam 2, 21.
3, 45: 1 Cor 4, 13.
3, 47: Is 24, 17; Jer 48, 43.
3, 48: Ps 119, 136.
3, 53: Jer 37, 16; 38, 6–9.
3, 55f: Ps 130, 1f.
3, 59: Ps 35, 23.
3, 65: Jer 11, 20; 2 Tm 4, 14.
4, 2: Jer 19, 11.

3*†Even the jackals bare their breasts
  and suckle their young;
The daughter of my people has become as
    cruel
  as the ostrich in the desert.

4 The tongue of the suckling cleaves
    to the roof of its mouth in thirst;
The babes cry for food,
    but there is no one to give it to them.

5* Those accustomed to dainty food
    perish in the streets;
Those brought up in purple
    now cling to the ash heaps.

6* The punishment of the daughter of my people
    is greater than the penalty of Sodom,
Which was overthrown in an instant
    without the turning of a hand.

7 Brighter than snow were her princes,
    whiter than milk,
More ruddy than coral,
    more precious than sapphire.

8* Now their appearance is blacker than soot,
    they are unrecognized on the streets;
Their skin shrinks on their bones,
    as dry as wood.

9 Better for those who perish by the sword
    than for those who die of hunger,
Who waste away, as though pierced through,
    lacking the fruits of the field!

10* The hands of compassionate women
    boiled their own children,
To serve them as mourners' food
    in the downfall of the daughter of my people.

11* The LORD has spent his anger,
    poured out his blazing wrath;
He has kindled a fire in Zion
    that has consumed her foundations.

12 The kings of the earth did not believe,
    nor any of the world's inhabitants,

That enemy or foe could enter
    the gates of Jerusalem.

13*†Because of the sins of her prophets
    and the crimes of her priests,
Who shed in her midst
    the blood of the just!—

14* They staggered blindly in the streets,
    soiled with blood,
So that people could not touch
    even their garments:

15 "Away, you unclean!" they cried to them,
    "Away, away, do not draw near!"
If they left and wandered among the
    nations,
    nowhere could they remain.

16 The LORD himself has dispersed them,
    he regards them no more;
He does not receive the priests with favor,
    nor show kindness to the elders.

17† Our eyes ever wasted away,
    looking in vain for aid;
From our watchtower we watched
    for a nation that could not save us.

18 Men dogged our steps
    so that we could not walk in our streets;
Our end drew near, and came;
    our time had expired.

19* Our pursuers were swifter
    than eagles in the air,
They harassed us on the mountains
    and waylaid us in the desert.

20*†The anointed one of the LORD, our breath
    of life,
    was caught in their snares,
He in whose shadow we thought
    we could live on among the nations.

21*†Though you rejoice and are glad,
    O daughter Edom,
    you who dwell in the land of Uz,

4, 3: *Cruel as the ostrich:* see note on Jb 39, 14ff. Jerusalem, in her distress, had abandoned her children.
  4, 13ff: The priests and the false prophets lulled the people into an illusory security (Jer 2, 8; 5, 31; 6, 13; etc.), condoning and entering into their crimes so that they themselves became unclean.
  4, 17: *A nation:* Egypt, which failed to give effective aid against Babylon.
  4, 20: *Our breath of life:* the king. This is a royal epithet borrowed from Egyptian usage, while the anointed one of the Lord is Israelite. After the disaster of 598 B.C. (2 Kgs 24, 1–17), Jerusalem could have hoped

to live in peace amidst her neighbors; but they (vv 21f) as well as Babylon turned against her to ensure her total devastation in 587 B.C.
  4, 21: *Uz:* see note on Jer 25, 20.

4, 3: Jb 39, 16.
4, 5: Dt 28, 56.
4, 6: Gn 19, 23–29; 2 Pt 2, 6; Jude 7.
4, 8: Lam 3, 4.
4, 10: Lam 2, 20; Dt 28, 56f; 2 Kgs 6, 29.
4, 11: Jer 7, 20; Ez 5, 13.
4, 13: Jer 6, 13.
4, 14: Is 59, 10.
4, 19: Jer 4, 13; Hb 1, 8.
4, 20: Lam 2, 9; Ez 19, 4.8.
4, 21: Lam 1, 21; Jer 25, 15.

To you also shall the cup be passed;
    you shall become drunk and naked.

22* Your chastisement is completed,
    O daughter Zion,
    he will not prolong your exile;
But your wickedness, O daughter Edom,
    he will punish,
    he will lay bare your sins.

The Prophet's Lament and Supplication

5 ¹ Remember, O LORD, what has befallen us,
    look, and see our disgrace:
2* Our inherited lands have been turned
    over to strangers,
    our homes to foreigners.
3 We have become orphans, fatherless;
    widowed are our mothers.
4 The water we drink we must buy,
    for our own wood we must pay.
5 On our necks is the yoke of those who
    drive us;
    we are worn out, but allowed no rest.

6† To Egypt we submitted,
    and to Assyria, to fill our need
    of bread.
7† Our fathers, who sinned, are no more;
    but we bear their guilt.

8† Slaves rule over us;
    there is no one to rescue us from
    their hands.
9* At the peril of our lives we bring in
    our sustenance,
    in the face of the desert heat;
10* Our skin is shriveled up, as though by
    a furnace,
    with the searing blasts of famine.

11* The wives in Zion were ravished by
    the enemy,
    the maidens in the cities of Judah;
12* Princes were gibbeted by them,
    elders shown no respect.
13 The youths carry the millstones,
    boys stagger under their loads
    of wood;
14† The old men have abandoned the gate,
    the young men their music.

15* The joy of our hearts has ceased,
    our dance has turned into
    mourning;
16 The garlands have fallen from
    our heads:
    woe to us, for we have sinned!
17 Over this our hearts are sick,
    at this our eyes grow dim:

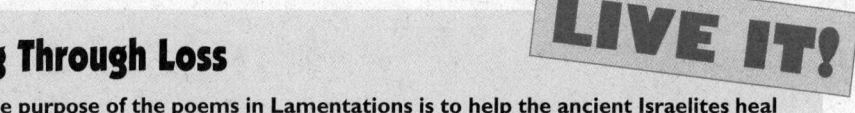

Growing Through Loss

LIVE IT!

One purpose of the poems in Lamentations is to help the ancient Israelites heal from the horrible tragedy of their loss. The poems accomplish this in three ways. First, in describing Israel's present loss and tragedy, they acknowledge that grief and mourning are needed. Second, they challenge Israel to look at its past, both to accept responsibility for its sin and to remember its great blessings from God. Finally, they encourage Israel to have hope for the future. In image after image, Israel is assured that the door to God's mercy is still open, in spite of great pain and loss.

So too must we allow ourselves to grieve when we have experienced the loss of someone we love. If we wall up our grief—and perhaps our guilt, because guilt often accompanies such a loss—we may at the same time shut out those who can help us heal. We must also reclaim our memories of the person we lost, celebrating those of good times and healing those of hurtful times. Finally, as difficult as it may seem, we must open ourselves to the future, for God's love continues to be there for us, calling us to new life.

---

† **5, 6:** In its state of abjection, Judah was forced to depend on its traditional enemies to the west and the east for subsistence. Mesopotamia is here called by the name it had long borne, Assyria, though in these times the power of the Assyrians had been superseded by that of the Chaldeans.

5, 7: *Our fathers:* collective responsibility, for good and for evil, was recognized in the Old Testament; cf Jer 31, 29. But the present generation is also personally guilty of sin (v 16).

5, 8: Administrations imposed by foreign powers were notoriously corrupt and inept. The Hebrew word for "slave" is the same as that used for an official (servant of the ruler); the author doubtless intends the double meaning here.

5, 14: *The gate:* the place of assembly, where city decisions were made and judgment given by the elders and other notables; see note on Ru 4, 1.

4, 22: Is 40, 2.
5, 2: Ps 79, 1.
5, 9: Jer 6, 25.
5, 10: Lam 4, 8.

5, 11: Zec 14, 2.
5, 12: Lam 4, 16.
5, 15: Jer 16, 9; 25, 10;
    Am 8, 10.

LAM

18 That Mount Zion should be desolate,
with jackals roaming there!

19* You, O LORD, are enthroned forever;
your throne stands from age to age.

20* Why, then, should you forget us,
abandon us so long a time?

5, 19: Pss 9, 8; 45, 7; 102,   5, 21: Ps 80, 19f.
    13.27.   5, 22: Jer 14, 19.
5, 20: Pss 13, 1; 42, 10.

21* Lead us back to you, O LORD, that we may
be restored:
give us anew such days as we had
of old.

22* For now you have indeed rejected us,
and in full measure turned your wrath
against us.

Perhaps you've seen them on the television news—long lines of refugees leaving war-torn countries. Or the camps where they set up temporary homes, waiting to return to their homeland. The sad truth is many of them can never return home. They are faced with the difficult task of building new homes in a foreign land. The Book of Baruch was written in such a situation—after many Israelites were forced to relocate following the Babylonian invasion in 587 B.C.

In-depth

In the ancient world, it was not uncommon for people to write books and letters in the name of famous ancestors or historical figures. Several Old and New Testament books, including Baruch, were written in this manner. An anonymous person collected a variety of independent writings and named them for Baruch, the famous secretary of the prophet Jeremiah, in order to emphasize their link with Jeremiah's tradition of prophecy.

The short Book of Baruch recalls the Babylonian conquest of Jerusalem in the sixth century B.C. In doing so, it points out these lessons to be learned from the painful past:

Quick Facts

Period Covered
after the Babylonian
Exile, probably 500–300
B.C.

Author
an unknown compiler
who attributed the book
to Baruch, Jeremiah's
secretary

Theme
Even in foreign lands,
God's people can live a
faithful life and find hope
in God's promises.

Of Note
Baruch is not found in
every translation of the
Old Testament (see
"The Case of the Missing
Books" near Tb 1, 16).

At a Glance

I. Prayer of the Exiles
(1, 1—3, 8).

II. Praise of Wisdom in
the Law of Moses
(3, 9—4, 4).

III. Jerusalem Bewails and
Consoles Her Captive
Children (4, 5–29).

IV. Jerusalem Consoled:
The Captivity about to
End (4, 30—5, 9).

V. The Letter of Jeremiah
against Idolatry
(6, 1–72).

- We do not gain anything when we sin. Instead, we invite suffering into our life.
- No matter how difficult life gets, we can always rely on God's goodness.
- Believers can always approach God in prayer, even when their situation seems impossibly painful.
- The traditions we have inherited from our ancestors are a reliable guide in facing life's challenges.
- We should resist all cultural pressures to act in violation of God's will.

The core truth Baruch addresses is that no matter where they are, God's people can lead a happy and holy life by admitting their sinfulness and committing themselves to the LORD. This is an important lesson for all believers to learn. Unless we learn from history, we will repeat its mistakes.

Baruch

Baruch

Chap. 6

I: Prayer of the Exiles

Meeting in Babylon

1 [1]* Now these are the words of the scroll which Baruch, son of Neriah, son of Mahseiah, son of Zedekiah, son of Hasadiah, son of Hilkiah, wrote in Babylon, [2]*† in the fifth year [on the seventh day of the month, at the time when the Chaldeans took Jerusalem and burnt it with fire]. [3]* And Baruch read the words of this scroll for Jeconiah, son of Jehoiakim, king of Judah, to hear it, as well as all the people who came to the reading:* [4]† the nobles, the kings' sons, the elders, and the whole people, small and great alike—all who lived in Babylon by the river Sud.

[5] They wept and fasted and prayed before the LORD, [6]* and collected such funds as each could furnish. [7] These they sent to Jerusalem, to Jehoiakim, son of Hilkiah, son of Shallum, the priest, and to the priests and the whole people who were with him in Jerusalem. [8]† [This was when he received the vessels of the house of the LORD that had been removed from the temple, to restore them to the land of Judah, on the tenth of Sivan. These silver vessels Zedekiah, son of Josiah, king of Judah, had had made [9] after Nebuchadnezzar, king of Babylon, carried off Jeconiah, and the princes, and the skilled workers, and the nobles, and the people of the land from Jerusalem, as captives, and brought them to Babylon.]

[10]* Their message was: "We send you funds, with which you are to procure holocausts, sin offerings, and frankincense, and to prepare cereal offerings; offer these on the altar of the LORD our God, [11]*† and pray for the life of Nebuchadnezzar, king of Babylon, and that of Belshazzar, his son, that their lifetimes may equal the duration of the heavens above the earth; [12] and that the LORD may give us strength, and light to our eyes, that we may live under the protective shadow of Nebuchadnezzar, king of Babylon, and that of Belshazzar, his son, and serve them long, finding favor in their sight.

1, 2: *In the fifth year [on the seventh day of the month:* Jerusalem fell on the seventh day of the fifth month; cf 2 Kgs 25, 8; Jer 52, 12. Either the text read originally "the fifth month," or it refers to the observance of an anniversary of the fall of Jerusalem in 587 B.C.

1, 4: *The river Sud:* one of the Babylonian canals, not otherwise identified. In ancient non-Biblical Hebrew fragments discovered in 1952, there is reference to a river "Sur" in a similar context.

1, 8f: *He:* possibly Baruch; less likely Jehoiakim . . . the priest (v 7), a member of the high-priestly family not mentioned elsewhere. The silver vessels here described are distinct from the vessels referred to in 2 Kgs 25, 14 and Ezr 1, 7ff. The author of this note may have thought of the fifth year (v 1) of Zedekiah, in view of Jer 28, 1; 29, 1ff.

A "fifth year," again with no month mentioned, is given in Ez 1, 2 for the inaugural vision of Ezekiel's prophetic career.

1, 11: *Nebuchadnezzar . . . Belshazzar, his son:* as in Dn 5, 1f. Later Jewish tradition seems to have simplified the history of the past by making the last Chaldean ruler of Babylon the son of the conqueror of Jerusalem.

*

1, 1: Jer 32, 12; 36, 4; 45, 1–5.	1, 3–4: 2 Kgs 23, 1–2.
1, 2: 2 Kgs 25, 8ff.	1, 6: Dt 16, 17.
1, 3: 2 Kgs 24, 8–17; Jer 22, 24–30; 51, 59–64.	1, 10: Jer 17, 26.
	1, 11: Dt 11, 21; Jer 29, 7; Dn 5, 1–2; 1 Tm 2, 1f.

Confession of Guilt

13 "Pray for us also to the LORD, our God; for we have sinned against the LORD, our God, and the wrath and anger of the LORD have not yet been withdrawn from us at the present day. 14* And read out publicly this scroll which we send you, in the house of the LORD, on the feast day and during the days of assembly:

15* "Justice is with the LORD, our God; and we today are flushed with shame, we men of Judah and citizens of Jerusalem, 16 that we, with our kings and rulers and priests and prophets, and with our fathers, 17 have sinned in the LORD'S sight 18 and disobeyed him. We have neither heeded the voice of the LORD, our God, nor followed the precepts which the LORD set before us. 19 From the time the LORD led our fathers out of the land of Egypt until the present day, we have been disobedient to the LORD, our God, and only too ready to disregard his voice. 20* And the evils and the curse which the LORD enjoined upon Moses, his servant, at the time he led our fathers forth from the land of Egypt to give us the land flowing with milk and honey, cling to us even today. 21 For we did not heed the voice of the LORD, our God, in all the words of the prophets whom he sent us, 22 but each one of us went off after the devices of our own wicked hearts, served other gods, and did evil in the sight of the LORD, our God.

2 1 "And the LORD fulfilled the warning he had uttered against us: against our judges, who governed Israel, against our kings and princes, and against the men of Israel and Judah. 2* He brought down upon us evils so great that there has not been done anywhere under heaven what has been done in Jerusalem, as was written in the law of Moses: 3† that one after another of us should eat the flesh of his son or of his daughter. 4* He has made us subject to all the kingdoms round about us, a reproach and a horror among all the nations round about to which the LORD has scattered us. 5 We are brought low, not raised up, because we sinned against the LORD, our God, not heeding his voice.

6* "Justice is with the LORD, our God; and we, like our fathers, are flushed with shame even today. 7 All the evils of which the LORD had warned us have come upon us; 8 and we did not plead before the LORD, or turn, each from the figments of his evil heart. 9* And the LORD kept watch over the evils, and brought them home to us; for the LORD is just in all the works he commanded us to do, 10 but we did not heed his voice, or follow the precepts of the LORD which he set before us.

Prayer for Deliverance

11* "And now, LORD, God of Israel, you who led your people out of the land of Egypt with your mighty hand, with signs and wonders and great might, and with your upraised arm, so that you have made for yourself a name till the present day: 12* we have sinned, been impious, and violated, O LORD, our God, all your statutes. 13 Let your anger be withdrawn from us, for we are left few in number among the nations to which you scattered us. 14 Hear, O LORD, our prayer of supplication, and deliver us for your own sake: grant us favor in the presence of our captors, 15* that the whole earth may know that you are the LORD, our God, and that Israel and his descendants bear your name. 16* O LORD, look down from your holy dwelling and take thought of us; turn, O LORD, your ear to hear us. 17* Look directly at us, and behold: it is not the dead in the nether world, whose spirits have been taken from within them, who will give glory and vindication to the LORD. 18* He whose soul is deeply grieved, who walks bowed and feeble, with failing eyes and famished soul, will declare your glory and justice, LORD!

19 "Not on the just deeds of our fathers and our kings do we base our plea for mercy in your sight, O LORD, our God. 20 You have brought your wrath and anger down upon us, as you had warned us through your servants the prophets: 21* 'Thus says the LORD: Bend your shoulders to the service of the king of Babylon, that you may continue in the land I gave your fathers: 22 for if you do not hear the LORD'S voice so as to serve the king of Babylon,

23* I will make to cease from the cities of Judah
   and from the streets of Jerusalem
The sounds of joy and the sounds of
   gladness,
      the voice of the bridegroom
      and the voice of the bride;
And all the land shall be deserted,
      without inhabitants.'

24* But we did not heed your voice, or serve the king of Babylon, and you fulfilled the threats you

---

† 2, 3: *One after another of us should eat:* see note on Lam 2, 20.

1, 14: Ex 23, 14ff; Lv 23, 35f;
    Hos 9, 5; Sir 50, 6.
1, 15: Bar 2, 6; 3, 8; Neh 9,
    6–37; Ezr 9, 6–15; Dn
    9, 4–19.
1, 20: Lv 26, 14–39; Dt 28,

15–68.
2, 2f: 2 Kgs 6, 28f; Jer 19, 9;
    Lam 2, 20; 4, 10; Ez 5,
    10.
2, 4: Jer 29, 18.
2, 6: Bar 1, 15.

2, 9: Jer 1, 12; 31, 28; 44,
    27.
2, 11: Dt 6, 21–22.
2, 12: Ps 106, 6.
2, 15: Sir 36, 11; Jer 14, 9.
2, 16: Dt 26, 15.

2, 17: Ps 6, 6; Is 38, 18.
2, 18: Zep 2, 3.
2, 21: Jer 27, 12.
2, 23: Jer 7, 34.
2, 24: Jer 8, 1f.

had made through your servants the prophets, to have the bones of our kings and the bones of our fathers brought out from their burial places. 25*† And indeed, they lie exposed to the heat of day and the frost of night. They died in dire anguish, by hunger and the sword and plague. 26*† And you reduced the house which bears your name to what it is today, for the wickedness of the kingdom of Israel and the kingdom of Judah.

God's Promises Recalled

27 "But with us, O Lord, our God, you have dealt in all your clemency and in all your great mercy. 28 This was your warning through your servant Moses, the day you ordered him to write down your law in the presence of the Israelites: 29 If you do not heed my voice, surely this great and numerous throng will dwindle away among the nations to which I will scatter them. 30* For I know they will not heed me, because they are a stiff-necked people. But in the land of their captivity they shall have a change of heart; 31* they shall know that I, the LORD, am their God. I will give them hearts, and heedful ears; 32* and they shall praise me in the land of their captivity, and shall invoke my name. 33* Then they shall turn back from their stiff-necked stubbornness, and from their evil deeds, because they shall remember the fate of their fathers who sinned against the LORD. 34 And I will bring them back to the land which with my oath I promised to their fathers, to Abraham, Isaac and Jacob; and they shall rule it. I will make them increase; they shall not then diminish. 35* And I will establish for them, as an eternal covenant, that I will be their God, and they shall be my people; and I will not again remove my people Israel from the land I gave them.

3 1 "LORD Almighty, God of Israel, afflicted souls and dismayed spirits call to you. 2 Hear, O LORD, for you are a God of mercy; and have mercy on us, who have sinned against you: 3* for you are enthroned forever, while we are perishing forever. 4 LORD Almighty, God of Israel, hear the prayer of Israel's few, the sons of those who sinned against you; they did not heed the voice of the LORD, their God, and the evils cling to us. 5 Remember at this time not the misdeeds of our fathers, but your own hand and name: 6 for you are the LORD our God; and you, O LORD, we will praise! 7* For this, you put into our hearts the fear of you: that we may call

upon your name, and praise you in our captivity, when we have removed from our hearts all the wickedness of our fathers who sinned against you. 8 Behold us today in our captivity, where you scattered us, a reproach, a curse, and a requital for all the misdeeds of our fathers, who withdrew from the LORD, our God."

II: Praise of Wisdom in the Law of Moses

9* Hear, O Israel, the commandments of life:
　　listen, and know prudence!
10 How is it, Israel,
　　that you are in the land of your foes,
　　grown old in a foreign land,
Defiled with the dead,
11*　accounted with those destined for the
　　　nether world?
12* You have forsaken the fountain of
　　　wisdom!
13*　Had you walked in the way of God,
　　　you would have dwelt in enduring peace.
14* Learn where prudence is,
　　where strength, where understanding;
That you may know also
　　where are length of days, and life,
　　where light of the eyes, and peace.

15* Who has found the place of wisdom,
　　who has entered into her treasuries?
16* Where are the rulers of the nations,
　　they who lorded it over the wild beasts of
　　　the earth,
17　and made sport of the birds of the heavens:
They who heaped up the silver
　　and the gold in which men trust;
　　of whose possessions there was no end?
18　They schemed anxiously for money,
　　but there is no trace of their work:
19　They have vanished down into the
　　　nether world,
　　and others have risen up in their stead.

20　Later generations have seen the light,
　　have dwelt in the land,
But the way to understanding they have
　　not known,
21　they have not perceived her paths, or
　　reached her;
　　their offspring were far from the way to her.

---

† 2, 25: *They lie exposed:* probably an allusion to Jer 36, 30; see note on Jer 22, 19.
2, 26: *The house which bears your name:* the temple of Jerusalem. *What it is today:* during the exile it lay in ruins.

*
2, 25: Jer 7, 34; 14, 12; 31,
　30.
2, 26: Jer 7, 10–15.

2, 30: Dt 30, 1f; 31, 27.
2, 31: Jer 24, 7; Ez 36, 26; Ps
　40, 7.

2, 32: Tb 13, 7.
2, 33ff: Dt 30, 1–10.
2, 35: Jer 31, 31; Lam 4, 22.
3, 3: Pss 29, 10; 102, 12f.
3, 7: Jer 31, 33.
3, 9: Prv 4, 20ff.

3, 11: Ps 88, 5.
3, 12: Jer 2, 13; Jn 4, 10.14.
3, 13: Is 48, 18.
3, 14: Prv 3, 2; 8, 14.
3, 15ff: Jb 28, 1–28.
3, 16: Jer 27, 6.

The House of God

LIVE IT!

It is a warm, clear summer night. You and a good friend are sitting outside talking about the struggles both of you have been having with parents. Suddenly, you see a shooting star. Both of you spend a few moments gazing at the sky and marveling at how many stars there are and how clear the night is. The problems you were just discussing seem to pale in significance next to the vastness of the universe. And you realize that the two of you are seeing only one corner of the universe, "the house of God" (Bar 3, 24). You both feel a connection with the stars and the sky and with the God who created it all.

The author of Bar 3, 24–37 seems to be having a similar moment. This writer describes God's wisdom as vast and endless (verse 25) and beyond any person's grasp (verse 29), but given to Israel for salvation (verse 37). The author is saying: "Be at ease. God is bigger than your problems and in control."

When struggling with life's problems, recall the beauty of the night sky in order to put them in perspective. Spend a few moments gazing at the stars, and remember who's really in control.

▶ Bar 3, 24–37

22*† She has not been heard of in Canaan,
    nor seen in Teman.
23 The sons of Hagar who seek knowledge
    on earth,
    the merchants of Midian and Teman,
    the phrasemakers seeking knowledge,
    These have not known the way to wisdom,
    nor have they her paths in mind.

24† O Israel, how vast is the house of God,
    how broad the scope of his dominion:
25 Vast and endless,
    high and immeasurable!
26* In it were born the giants,
    renowned at the first,
    stalwarts, skilled in war.
27* Not these did God choose,
    nor did he give them the way
    of understanding;
28* They perished for lack of prudence,
    perished through their folly.
29* Who has gone up to the heavens and
    taken her,
    or brought her down from the clouds?
30 Who has crossed the sea and found her,
    bearing her away rather than choice gold?
31 None knows the way to her,
    nor has any understood her paths.

32 Yet he who knows all things knows her;
    he has probed her by his knowledge—
    He who established the earth for all time,
    and filled it with four-footed beasts;
33 He who dismisses the light, and it departs,
    calls it, and it obeys him trembling;
34 Before whom the stars at their posts
    shine and rejoice;
35* When he calls them, they answer, "Here we are!"
    shining with joy for their Maker.
36 Such is our God;
    no other is to be compared to him:
37* He has traced out all the way
    of understanding,
    and has given her to Jacob, his servant,
    to Israel, his beloved son.

38* Since then she has appeared on earth,
    and moved among men.

4

1* She is the book of the precepts of God,
    the law that endures forever;
    All who cling to her will live,
    but those will die who forsake her.
2* Turn, O Jacob, and receive her:
    walk by her light toward splendor.
3 Give not your glory to another,
    your privileges to an alien race.

---

† **3, 22f:** Despite the renown for wisdom of the peoples of Canaan or Phoenicia (Ez 28, 3f), of Teman (Jer 49, 7), of the sons of Hagar or the Arabians, they did not possess true wisdom, which is found only in the law of God.
    3, 24: *The house of God:* here, the created universe.

* **3, 22:** Jer 49, 7; Ez 28, 4–5;
    Zec 9, 2; Jb 2, 11.
3, 26: Gn 6, 4; Wis 14, 6.
3, 27: 1 Sm 16, 7–10.
3, 28: Sir 10, 8.
3, 29: Dt 30, 12f; Sir 24, 4;
    Rom 10, 6f.

3, 35: Jb 38, 7; Ps 147, 4;
    Is 40, 26.
3, 37: Ps 147, 19; Sir 24,
    8–12.
3, 38: Wis 9, 18; Jn 1, 14.
4, 1: Dt 4, 6–8; Prv 8, 35f;
    Sir 24, 22.
4, 2: Prv 4, 13.19.

BAR

4* Blessed are we, O Israel;
    for what pleases God is known to us!

III: Jerusalem Bewails and Consoles Her Captive Children

5   Fear not, my people!
    Remember, Israel,
6* You were sold to the nations
    not for your destruction;
    It was because you angered God
    that you were handed over to your foes.
7* For you provoked your Maker
    with sacrifices to demons, to no-gods;
8   You forsook the Eternal God who
    nourished you,
    and you grieved Jerusalem who
    fostered you.
9   She indeed saw coming upon you
    the anger of God; and she said:

    "Hear, you neighbors of Zion!
    God has brought great mourning
    upon me,
10 For I have seen the captivity
    that the Eternal God has brought
    upon my sons and daughters.
11 With joy I fostered them;
    but with mourning and lament I let
    them go.
12* Let no one gloat over me, a widow,
    bereft of many:
    For the sins of my children I am left desolate,
    because they turned from the law of God,
13 and did not acknowledge his statutes;
    In the ways of God's commandments they did
    not walk,

    nor did they tread the disciplined paths of
    his justice.

14 "Let Zion's neighbors come,
    to take note of the captivity of my sons
    and daughters,
    brought upon them by the Eternal God.
15* He has brought against them a nation
    from afar,
    a nation ruthless and of alien speech,
    That has neither reverence for age
    nor tenderness for childhood;
16 They have led away this widow's
    cherished sons,
    have left me solitary, without daughters.
17 What can I do to help you?
18* He who has brought this evil upon you
    must himself deliver you from your
    enemies' hands.
19 Farewell, my children, farewell:
    I am left desolate.
20* I have taken off the garment of peace,
    have put on sackcloth for my prayer
    of supplication,
    and while I live I will cry out to the Eternal
    God.

21* "Fear not, my children; call upon God,
    who will deliver you from oppression at
    enemy hands.
22 I have trusted in the Eternal God for
    your welfare,
    and joy has come to me from the Holy One
    Because of the mercy that will swiftly
    reach you
    from your eternal savior.

Stand Up!

The poem that begins with Bar 4, 5 has the nation of Israel speaking to the Jews in exile. After recalling that their disobedience brought on the exile, the author of the poem calls them to conversion. Worried that they may start worshiping the false gods of their new neighbors, the writer reminds them that if they are faithful to God, God will not abandon them.

It can be said that as Christians, we too live in a culture that is in some ways foreign to our values and beliefs. How easy is it to stand up against the pressures of peers, media values, and social standards that go against Christian values and beliefs? Are you confident enough to do what's right if others do not?

▶ Bar 4, 17–19

4, 4: Dt 4, 32–37; 33, 29.
4, 6: Jgs 2, 14; Is 50, 1;
    52, 3.
4, 7–8: Dt 32, 13–18; 1 Cor
    10, 20.
4, 12: Lam 1, 1.2.7.
4, 15: Dt 28, 49f; Jer 5, 15;
    6, 22f.
4, 18: Jer 32, 42.
4, 20: Jdt 9, 1; Est 4, 16.
4, 21: Jer 51, 5.

23* With mourning and lament I sent you forth,
    but God will give you back to me
    with enduring gladness and joy.
24* As Zion's neighbors lately saw you
        taken captive,
    so shall they soon see God's salvation come
        to you,
    with great glory and the splendor of the
        Eternal God.

25*† "My children, bear patiently the anger
    that has come from God upon you;
    Your enemies have persecuted you,
    and you will soon see their destruction
    and trample upon their necks.
26* My pampered children have trodden
      rough roads,
    carried off by their enemies like sheep in
      a raid.
27* Fear not, my children; call out to God!
    He who brought this upon you will
      remember you.
28 As your hearts have been disposed to stray
      from God,
    turn now ten times the more to seek him;
29* For he who has brought disaster upon you
    will, in saving you, bring you back
      enduring joy."

IV: Jerusalem Consoled: The Captivity About to End

30* Fear not, Jerusalem!
    He who gave you your name is
      your encouragement.
31 Fearful are those who harmed you,
    who rejoiced at your downfall;
32* Fearful are the cities where your children
      were enslaved,
    fearful the city that took your sons.
33* As that city rejoiced at your collapse,
    and made merry at your downfall,
    so shall she grieve over her own desolation.
34 I will take from her the joyous throngs,
    and her exultation shall be turned
      to mourning:
35*† For fire shall come upon her
    from the Eternal God, for a long time,
    and demons shall dwell in her from that
      time on.

36* Look to the east, Jerusalem!
    behold the joy that comes to you
      from God.
37 Here come your sons whom you once let go,
    gathered in from the east and from the west
    By the word of the Holy One,
    rejoicing in the glory of God.

5 1* Jerusalem, take off your robe of mourning
      and misery;
    put on the splendor of glory from
      God forever:
2* Wrapped in the cloak of justice from God,
    bear on your head the mitre
    that displays the glory of the eternal name.
3 For God will show all the earth your splendor:
4* you will be named by God forever
    the peace of justice, the glory of God's
      worship.

5 Up, Jerusalem! stand upon the heights;
    look to the east and see your children
    Gathered from the east and the west
    at the word of the Holy One,
    rejoicing that they are remembered by God.
6* Led away on foot by their enemies they
      left you:
    but God will bring them back to you
    borne aloft in glory as on royal thrones.
7* For God has commanded
    that every lofty mountain be made low,
    And that the age-old depths and gorges
    be filled to level ground,
    that Israel may advance secure in the glory
      of God.
8* The forests and every fragrant kind of tree
    have overshadowed Israel at
      God's command;
9 For God is leading Israel in joy
    by the light of his glory,
    with his mercy and justice for company.

V: The Letter of Jeremiah Against Idolatry

6 1* A copy of the letter which Jeremiah sent to those who were being led captive to Babylon by the king of the Babylonians, to convey to them what God had commanded him:
For the sins you committed before God, you are

---

†
4, 25: *Trample upon their necks:* love of enemies was not an Old Testament ideal. The Babylonians are considered here, however, to be God's enemies as well as Israel's.
    4, 35: Deserts and desolate places were looked upon as the special habitations of demons; Tb 8, 3; Lk 11, 24.

4, 23: Jer 31, 12f.
4, 24: Is 60, 1ff.
4, 25: Is 51, 23.
4, 26: Lam 2, 22.

4, 27: Is 40, 1.
4, 29: Is 35, 10.
4, 30: Ps 46, 5; Is 60, 14.
4, 32: Jer 51, 43.
4, 33f: Is 13, 20ff; 47, 1–11;
    Jer 50, 13.
4, 35: Is 34, 9–14.
4, 36: Is 60, 4f.
5, 1: Is 52, 1.

5, 2: Ex 39, 30; Wis 18, 24;
    Is 61, 10; 62, 3.
5, 4: Is 1, 26; 32, 17; Jer 33,
    16.
5, 6: Is 49, 22.
5, 7: Is 40, 3f.
5, 8: Is 41, 19.
6, 1: Jer 29, 1.

being led captive to Babylon by Nebuchadnezzar, king of the Babylonians. ²† When you reach Babylon you will be there many years, a period seven generations long; after which I will bring you back from there in peace. ³* And now in Babylon you will see borne upon men's shoulders gods of silver and gold and wood, which cast fear upon the pagans. ⁴ Take care that you yourselves do not imitate their alien example and stand in fear of them, ⁵ when you see the crowd before them and behind worshiping them. Rather, say in your hearts, "You, O LORD, are to be worshiped!"; ⁶* for my angel is with you, and he is the custodian of your lives.

⁷* Their tongues are smoothed by woodworkers; they are covered with gold and silver—but they are a fraud, and cannot speak. ⁸ People bring gold, as to a maiden in love with ornament, ⁹ and furnish crowns for the heads of their gods. Then sometimes the priests take the silver and gold from their gods and spend it on themselves, ¹⁰† or give part of it to the harlots on the terrace. They trick them out in garments like men, these gods of silver and gold and wood; ¹¹ but though they are wrapped in purple clothing, they are not safe from corrosion or insects. ¹² They wipe their faces clean of the house dust which is thick upon them. ¹³ Each has a scepter, like the human ruler of a district; but none does away with those that offend against it. ¹⁴ Each has in its right hand an axe or dagger, but it cannot save itself from war or pillage. Thus it is known they are not gods; do not fear them.

¹⁵ As useless as one's broken tools ¹⁶ are their gods, set up in their houses; their eyes are full of dust from the feet of those who enter. ¹⁷ Their courtyards are walled in like those of a man brought to execution for a crime against the king; the priests reinforce their houses with gates and bars and bolts, lest they be carried off by robbers. ¹⁸ They light more lamps for them than for themselves, yet not one of these can they see. ¹⁹ They are like any beam in the house; it is said their hearts are eaten away. Though the insects out of the ground consume them and their garments, they do not feel it. ²⁰ Their faces are blackened by the smoke of the house. ²¹ Bats and swallows alight on their bodies and on their heads; and cats as well as birds. ²² Know, therefore, that they are not gods, and do not fear them.

²³ Despite the gold that covers them for adornment, unless someone wipes away the corrosion,

Lucky Charms?

The whole sixth chapter of Baruch points out the foolishness of people who worship statues of gods and goddesses. Some ancient peoples felt these images gave them luck or fertility or health. The author of this chapter is warning, "Just because you are in a foreign land, don't take up silly superstitions!"

Sometimes, modern people like to carry a special lucky charm in the belief that it will protect them or bring them good luck. Do you carry a rabbit's foot, wear a special piece of clothing for big events, or use some other good luck charm? If so, why?

Dear LORD, sometimes, when I feel like I can use every bit of luck I can get, a "lucky" object can be a comfort. Help me to remember, though, the true power over my life that comes from you.

▸ Baruch, chapter 6

they do not shine; nor did they feel anything when they were molded. ²⁴ They are bought at any price, and there is no spirit in them. ²⁵* Having no feet, they are carried on men's shoulders, displaying their shame to all; and those who worship them are put to confusion ²⁶ because, if they fall to the ground, the worshipers must raise them up. They neither move of themselves if one sets them upright, nor come upright if they fall; but one puts gifts beside them as beside the dead. ²⁷*† Their priests resell their sacrifices for their own advantage. Even their wives cure parts of the meat, but do not share it with the poor and the weak; ²⁸ the menstruous and women in childbed handle their sacrifices. Knowing from this that they are not gods, do not fear them.

²⁹ How can they be called gods? For women bring the offerings to these gods of silver and gold and wood; ³⁰* and in their temples the priests squat with torn tunic and with shaven hair and beard, and with

---

6, 2: *Seven generations:* possibly an indication of the date of this composition by an author writing for his contemporaries for whom the conditions of the exile were still realities. He has multiplied the seventy years of Jer 29, 10 by three or four.

6, 10: *Harlots on the terrace:* cult prostitutes, common in the idolatrous religions of the Gentiles.

6, 27–31: From the point of view of Jewish ritual law, the prac-

tices named here were grotesque and depraved; cf Lv 12, 2ff; 15, 19–23.

6, 3: Is 46, 7; Jer 10, 1–16.	6, 27: Lv 12, 4; 15, 19f; Dt
6, 6: Ex 23, 20.	14, 28f.
6, 7: Ps 135, 16.	6, 30: Lv 10, 6; 21, 5.10.
6, 25: Wis 13, 16.	

their heads uncovered. ³¹ They shout and wail before their gods as others do at a funeral banquet. ³² The priests take some of their clothing and put it on their wives and children. ³³*† Whether they are treated well or ill by anyone, they cannot requite it; they can neither set up a king nor remove him. ³⁴ Similarly, they cannot give anyone riches or coppers; if one fails to fulfill a vow to them, they cannot exact it of him. ³⁵* They neither save a man from death, nor deliver the weak from the strong. ³⁶ To no blind man do they restore his sight, nor do they save any man in an emergency. ³⁷ They neither pity the widow nor benefit the orphan. ³⁸ These gilded and silvered wooden statues are like stones from the mountains; and their worshipers will be put to shame. ³⁹ How then can it be thought or claimed that they are gods?

⁴⁰† Even the Chaldeans themselves have no respect for them; for when they see a deaf mute, incapable of speech, they bring forward Bel and ask the god to make noise, as though the man could understand; ⁴¹ and they are themselves unable to reflect and abandon these gods, for they have no sense. ⁴²*† And their women, girt with cords, sit by the roads, burning chaff for incense; ⁴³ and whenever one of them is drawn aside by some passerby who lies with her, she mocks her neighbor who has not been dignified as she has, and has not had her cord broken. ⁴⁴ All that takes place around these gods is a fraud: how then can it be thought or claimed that they are gods?

⁴⁵ They are produced by woodworkers and goldsmiths, and they are nothing else than what these craftsmen wish them to be. ⁴⁶ Even those who produce them are not long-lived; ⁴⁷ how then can what they have produced be gods? They have left frauds and opprobrium to their successors. ⁴⁸ For when war or disaster comes upon them, the priests deliberate among themselves where they can hide with them. ⁴⁹ How then can one not know that these are no-gods, which do not save themselves either from war or from disaster? ⁵⁰ They are wooden, gilded and silvered; they will later be known for frauds. To all peoples and kings it will be clear that they are not gods, but human handiwork; and that God's work is not in them.

⁵¹ Who does not know that they are not gods? ⁵² They set no king over the land, nor do they give men rain. ⁵³ They neither vindicate their own rights, nor do they recover what is unjustly taken, for they are unable; ⁵⁴ they are like crows between heaven and earth. For when fire breaks out in the temple of these wooden or gilded or silvered gods, though the priests flee and are safe, they themselves are burnt up in the fire like beams. ⁵⁵ They cannot resist a king, or enemy forces. ⁵⁶ How then can it be admitted or thought that they are gods?

They are safe from neither thieves nor bandits, these wooden and silvered and gilded gods; ⁵⁷ those who seize them strip off the gold and the silver, and go away with the clothing that was on them, and they cannot help themselves. ⁵⁸* How much better to be a king displaying his valor, or a handy tool in a house, the joy of its owner, than these false gods; or the door of a house, that keeps safe those who are within, rather than these false gods; or a wooden post in a palace, rather than these false gods! ⁵⁹ The sun and moon and stars are bright, and obedient in the service for which they are sent. ⁶⁰ Likewise the lightning, when it flashes, is a goodly sight; and the same wind blows over all the land. ⁶¹ The clouds, too, when commanded by God to proceed across the whole world, fulfill the order; ⁶² and fire, sent from on high to burn up the mountains and the forests, does what has been commanded. But these false gods are not their equal, whether in beauty or in power; ⁶³ so that it is unthinkable, and cannot be claimed, that they are gods. They can neither execute judgment, nor benefit man. ⁶⁴ Know, therefore, that they are not gods, and do not fear them.

⁶⁵ Kings they neither curse nor bless. ⁶⁶ They show the nations no signs in the heavens, nor are they brilliant like the sun, nor shining like the moon. ⁶⁷ The beasts which can help themselves by fleeing to shelter are better than they are. ⁶⁸ Thus in no way is it clear to us that they are gods; so do not fear them. ⁶⁹ For like a scarecrow in a cucumber patch, that is no protection, are their wooden, gilded, silvered gods. ⁷⁰ Just like a thornbush in a garden on which perches every kind of bird, or like a corpse hurled into darkness, are their silvered and gilded wooden gods. ⁷¹ From the rotting of the purple and the linen upon them, it can be known that they are not gods; they themselves will in the end be consumed, and be a disgrace in the land. ⁷² The better for the just man who has no idols: he shall be far from disgrace!

---

† **6, 33–39:** All that the gods cannot do, the true God does; cf 1 Sm 2, 7; Dt 23, 22; Pss 68, 6; 146, 7–9; Is 35, 4f.
6, 40: *Bel:* cf note on Jer 50, 2.
6, 42f: This seems to refer to the obligation of Babylonian women to serve once in their lives as cult prostitutes. The unbroken cord was a sign that this duty had not yet been fulfilled. *Chaff:* burnt as an aphrodisiac or for use in erotic rites.

6, 33: Dn 2, 21.   6, 42–43: Jer 3, 2.
6, 35: Pss 68, 6; 146, 7ff.   6, 58: Wis 13, 10–15; 15, 7ff.

Four-headed creatures, a strange craft made up of wheels within wheels, a being of light that appears out of the sky—the first chapter of the Book of Ezekiel sounds like a preview for a science fiction movie. Ezekiel, more than any other prophet, proclaims astonishing visions that are filled with bizarre images, symbols, and creatures.

In-depth

Ezekiel lived during the last days of Judah, just before it was destroyed by the Babylonians. He was probably among an early group of captives sent into exile in Babylon before Judah and the city of Jerusalem were demolished in 587 B.C. (see the timeline at the back of this Bible). He began his prophetic ministry in 593 B.C., when he received a fantastic vision and call, described in chapters 1–3 of his book. We know that Ezekiel came from a priestly family (1, 3) and that he was married (24, 16–18).

Ezekiel preached many of the traditional themes of the other prophets but in a unique way. Note these examples:

- *The LORD's presence in the Temple.* Possibly because of Ezekiel's priestly heritage, he gave God's presence—or lack of presence—in the Temple a more central role than did the other prophets. In his vision, the Temple will be the center of the new Israel, and a great priest will rule instead of a king.
- *The awesomeness of God.* For Ezekiel, the LORD did not appear as a parent or someone to be argued with. Rather, God was awesome and overpowering, beyond human explanations. Ezekiel often spoke of God's glory and holiness.
- *Personal responsibility.* Ezekiel did not condemn the previous generation for the destruction of Judah, but preached that every generation is responsible for its own acts. Each individual can direct his or her life according to God's will.
- *Apocalyptic prophecy.* Some of Ezekiel's prophecies take the form of symbolic images. The images are so mysterious they require special explanation by heavenly beings. The Books of Daniel and Revelation continue this type of writing, which is called apocalyptic literature.

At a Glance

I. Call of the Prophet (1, 1—3, 27).

II. Before the Siege of Jerusalem (4, 1—24, 27).

III. Prophecies against Foreign Nations (25, 1—32, 32).

IV. Salvation for Israel (33, 1—39, 29).

V. The New Israel (40, 1—48, 35).

Quick Facts

Period Covered
593–573 B.C.

Authors
Ezekiel, and the scribes who recorded his words and actions

Themes
Jerusalem is being punished for its sin. God's glory will be known to all the nations. God will restore the Temple.

Ezekiel

I: Call of the Prophet

The Vision: God on the Cherubim

1 ¹*† In the thirtieth year, on the fifth day of the fourth month, while I was among the exiles by the river Chebar, the heavens opened, and I saw divine visions. — ²† On the fifth day of the month, the fifth year, that is, of King Jehoiachin's exile, ³ the word of the LORD came to the priest Ezekiel, the son of Buzi, in the land of the Chaldeans by the river Chebar.—There the hand of the LORD came upon me.

⁴† As I looked, a stormwind came from the North, a huge cloud with flashing fire [enveloped in brightness], from the midst of which [the midst of the fire] something gleamed like electrum. ⁵† Within it were figures resembling four living creatures that looked like this: their form was human, ⁶ but each had four faces and four wings, ⁷ and their legs went straight down; the soles of their feet were round. They sparkled with a gleam like burnished bronze.

¹⁰*† Their faces were like this: each of the four had the face of a man, but on the right side was the face of a lion, and on the left side the face of an ox, and finally each had the face of an eagle. ⁹ Their faces [and their wings] looked out on all their four sides; they did not turn when they moved, but each went straight forward. ¹² [Each went straight forward; wherever the spirit wished to go, there they went; they did not turn when they moved.]

⁸ Human hands were under their wings, and the wings of one touched those of another. ¹¹ Each had two wings spread out above so that they touched one another's, while the other two wings of each covered his body. ¹³ In among the living creatures something like burning coals of fire could be seen; they seemed like torches, moving to and fro among the living creatures. The fire gleamed, and from it came forth flashes of lightning.

¹⁵ As I looked at the living creatures, I saw wheels on the ground, one beside each of the four living creatures. ¹⁶ The wheels had the sparkling appearance of chrysolite, and all four of them looked the same: they were constructed as though one wheel were within another. ¹⁷ They could move in any of the four directions they faced, without veering as they moved. ¹⁸* The four of them had rims, and I

---

† **1, 1:** The thirtieth year, which corresponds to the fifth year of exile (v 2), has never been satisfactorily explained; possibly it refers to the prophet's age. *The river Chebar:* probably a canal near Nippur, southeast of Babylon, one of the sites on which the Jewish exiles were settled.
1, 2: *The fifth day of the fourth month, the fifth year:* July 31, 593 B.C.; cf v 1.
1, 4: *The North:* the abode of God; see notes on Jb 37, 22; Ps 48, 3. *Electrum:* an alloy of gold and silver, used here for some undetermined bright metal.

1, 5: *Four living creatures:* identified as cherubim in Ez 10, 20f.
1, 10–22: Note the changed order of the verses and the omission of the textually uncertain verses 14 and 21. Such changes also occur elsewhere in this book.

*
1, 1: Ez 3, 23; 10, 20; 43, 3.   **1, 18:** Ez 10, 12; Rv 4, 6.8.
1, 10: Rv 4, 6f.

saw that their rims were full of eyes all around. ¹⁹ When the living creatures moved, the wheels moved with them; and when the living creatures were raised from the ground, the wheels also were raised. ²⁰ Wherever the spirit wished to go, there the wheels went, and they were raised together with the living creatures; for the spirit of the living creatures was in the wheels.

²²† Over the heads of the living creatures, something like a firmament could be seen, seeming like glittering crystal, stretched straight out above their heads. ²³ Beneath the firmament their wings were stretched out, one toward the other. [Each of them had two covering his body.] ²⁴ Then I heard the sound of their wings, like the roaring of mighty waters, like the voice of the Almighty. When they moved, the sound of the tumult was like the din of an army. [And when they stood still, they lowered their wings.]

²⁶† Above the firmament over their heads something like a throne could be seen, looking like sapphire. Upon it was seated, up above, one who had the appearance of a man. ²⁷ Upward from what resembled his waist I saw what gleamed like electrum; downward from what resembled his waist I saw what looked like fire; he was surrounded with splendor. ²⁸ Like the bow which appears in the clouds on a rainy day was the splendor that surrounded him. Such was the vision of the likeness of the glory of the LORD.

Eating of the Scroll

2 When I had seen it, I fell upon my face and heard a voice that said to me: ¹† Son of man, stand up! I wish to speak with you. ²† As he spoke to me, spirit entered into me and set me on my feet, and I heard the one who was speaking ³ say to me: Son of man, I am sending you to the Israelites, rebels who have rebelled against me; they and their fathers have revolted against me to this very day. ⁴ Hard of face and obstinate of heart are they to whom I am sending you. But you shall say to them: Thus says the Lord GOD! ⁵ And whether they heed or resist—for they are a rebellious house—they shall know that a prophet has been among them. ⁶† But as for you, son of man, fear neither them nor their words when they contradict you and reject you, and when you sit on scorpions. Neither fear their words nor be dismayed at their looks, for they are a rebellious house. ⁷ [But speak my words to them, whether they heed or resist, for they are rebellious.] ⁸ As for you, son of ma n, obey me when I speak to you: be not rebellious like this house of rebellion, but open your mouth and eat what I shall give you.

Introducing ►EZEKIEL

Ezekiel's name means "God strengthens." He was a complex person: priest and prophet, poet and teacher, tender and angry. He experienced God in mysterious ways, often through visions that greatly influenced his life and prophetic ministry.

Ezekiel's vision of creatures from heaven in chapters 1–3 of his book was the basis for his call and prophetic ministry. His vision of the defilement of the Temple in chapters 8–11 was a major conversion experience. He, along with most of Israel, believed that God's glory resided in the Temple and that nothing could ever change that. The vision revealed corruption in Jerusalem and that the glory of God had left the Temple and had come to Babylon. His vision of dry bones coming to life in chapter 37 helped him understand that God would breathe new life into Israel. His final visions of a new Temple in chapters 40, 43, and 47 told him that God would restore Jerusalem and the Temple.

Besides having symbolic visions, Ezekiel also performed many dramatic, symbolic actions (see "Street Theater," Ez 4, 1—5, 4). These were designed to catch people's attention and transmit God's message.

1, 22f.26: This symbolic description of God's throne is similar to that in Ex 24, 9f.

1, 26: *One who had the appearance of a man:* God appearing in human form (v 28); cf Ex 33, 18–23.

2, 1: *Son of man:* a formal way of saying simply "man"; God's habitual way of addressing the prophet throughout this book. Prob- ably the title is used to emphasize the separation of the divine and the human.

2, 2: *Spirit:* vital power, coming from God, which enables the prophet to hear the word of God; cf Ez 8, 3; 9, 24; 11, 1.

2, 6: *When you sit on scorpions:* the prophet must be prepared for the bitterest opposition.

⁹* It was then I saw a hand stretched out to me, in which was a written scroll ¹⁰ which he unrolled before me. It was covered with writing front and back, and written on it was: Lamentation and wailing and woe!

3 ¹ He said to me: Son of man, eat what is before you; eat this scroll, then go, speak to the house of Israel. ² So I opened my mouth and he gave me the scroll to eat. ³*† Son of man, he then said to me, feed your belly and fill your stomach with this scroll I am giving you. I ate it, and it was as sweet as honey in my mouth. He said: ⁴ Son of man, go now to the house of Israel, and speak my words to them.

⁵ Not to a people with difficult speech and barbarous language am I sending you, ⁶ nor to the many peoples [with difficult speech and barbarous language] whose words you cannot understand. If I were to send you to these, they would listen to you; ⁷ but the house of Israel will refuse to listen to you, since they will not listen to me. For the whole house of Israel is stubborn of brow and obstinate in heart. ⁸ But I will make your face as hard as theirs, and your brow as stubborn as theirs, ⁹ like diamond, harder than flint. Fear them not, nor be dismayed at their looks, for they are a rebellious house.

¹⁰ Son of man, he said to me, take into your heart all my words that I speak to you; hear them well. ¹¹ Now go to the exiles, to your countrymen, and say to them: Thus says the Lord GOD!—whether they heed or resist!

¹²† Then spirit lifted me up, and I heard behind me the noise of a loud rumbling as the glory of the LORD rose from its place: ¹³ the noise made by the wings of the living creatures striking one another, and by the wheels alongside them, a loud rumbling. ¹⁴ The spirit which had lifted me up seized me, and I went off spiritually stirred, while the hand of the LORD rested heavily upon me. ¹⁵† Thus I came to the exiles who lived at Tel-abib by the river Chebar, and for seven days I sat among them distraught.

The Prophet as Watchman

¹⁷*† Thus the word of the LORD came to me: Son of man, I have appointed you a watchman for the house of Israel. When you hear a word from my mouth, you shall warn them for me.

¹⁸ If I say to the wicked man, You shall surely die; and you do not warn him or speak out to dissuade him from his wicked conduct so that he may live: that wicked man shall die for his sin, but I will hold you responsible for his death. ¹⁹ If, on the other hand, you have warned the wicked man, yet he has not turned away from his evil nor from his wicked conduct, then he shall die for his sin, but you shall save your life.

²⁰ If a virtuous man turns away from virtue and does wrong when I place a stumbling block before him, he shall die. He shall die for his sin, and his virtuous deeds shall not be remembered; but I will hold you responsible for his death if you did not

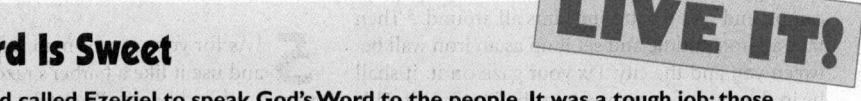

The Word Is Sweet

God called Ezekiel to speak God's Word to the people. It was a tough job; those people were rebellious. But Ezekiel opened his mouth to receive the scroll containing God's Word, and the scroll was sweet (see Ez 3, 3).

God gave Ezekiel words to eat. God nourished Ezekiel so that Ezekiel could carry out his calling. In the same way, God gives us the Word to eat and nourishes us to carry out our calling. Jesus is often called the Word of God (see "The 'Cosmic Christ,'" Jn 1, 1–18).

At the Eucharist, we receive not only the Word of God when the Scriptures are proclaimed but also the body of Christ when we come forward for Communion. With both Word and nourishment, we are called to share the Good News of our faith with others.

What are some ways we can bring this Good News to others? What are some things we might say or do to share our faith with the people we know?

▸ Ez 2, 1—3, 11

---

† **3, 3:** *As sweet as honey:* though the prophet must foretell terrible things the word of God is sweet to him who receives it.
3, 12: *The glory of the LORD:* the divine presence, manifested here in visible form.
3, 15: *Tel-abib:* one of the sites where the exiles were settled, probably near Nippur.

3, 17–21: This passage refers to one of the prophet's most characteristic qualities. It was placed here by an editor, though it properly belongs to a later stage in Ezekiel's ministry; cf chapter 33.

*
2, 9: Rv 5, 1.   3, 17: Ez 33, 7.
3, 3: Rv 10, 9f.

warn him. 21 When, on the other hand, you have warned a virtuous man not to sin, and he has in fact not sinned, he shall surely live because of the warning, and you shall save your own life.

Ezekiel's Dumbness

22† The hand of the Lord came upon me, and he said to me: Get up and go out into the plain, where I will speak with you. 23* So I got up and went out into the plain, and I saw that the glory of the LORD was in that place, like the glory I had seen by the river Chebar. I fell prone, 24 but then spirit entered into me and set me on my feet, and he spoke with me.

He said to me: Go shut yourself up in your house. 25 [As for you, son of man, they will put cords upon you and bind you with them, so that you cannot go out among them.] 26† I will make your tongue stick to your palate so that you will be dumb and unable to rebuke them for being a rebellious house. 27 Only when I speak with you and open your mouth, shall you say to them: Thus says the Lord GOD! Let him heed who will, and let him resist who will, for they are a rebellious house.

II: Before the Siege of Jerusalem

Acts Symbolic of Siege and Exile

4 16† At the end of seven days . . . . : 1 As for you, son of man, take a clay tablet; lay it in front of you, and draw on it a city [Jerusalem]. 2 Raise a siege against it: build a tower, lay out a ramp, pitch camps, and set up battering rams all around. 3 Then take an iron griddle and set it up as an iron wall between you and the city. Fix your gaze on it: it shall be in the state of siege, and you shall besiege it. This shall be a sign for the house of Israel. 4 Then you shall lie on your left side, while I place the sins of the house of Israel upon you. As many days as you lie thus, you shall bear their sins. 5† For the years of their sins I allot you the same number of days, three hundred and ninety, during which you will bear the sins of the house of Israel. 6 When you finish this, you are to lie down again, but on your right side, and bear the sins of the house of Judah forty days;

one day for each year I have allotted you. 7† Fixing your gaze on the siege of Jerusalem, with bared arm you shall prophesy against it. 8 See, I will bind you with cords so that you cannot turn from one side to the other until you have completed the days of your siege.

9† Again, take wheat and barley, and beans and lentils, and millet and spelt; put them in a single vessel and make bread out of them. Eat it for as many days as you lie upon your side, three hundred and ninety. 10 The food you eat shall be twenty shekels a day by weight; each day the same. 11 And the water you drink shall be the sixth of a hin by measure; each day the same. 16*† Then he said to me: Son of man, I am breaking the staff of bread in Jerusalem. They shall eat bread which they have weighed out anxiously, and they shall drink water which they have measured out fearfully, 17 so that, owing to the scarcity of bread and water, everyone shall be filled with terror and waste away because of his sins.

12 For your food you must bake barley loaves over human excrement in their sight, said the LORD. 13* Thus the Israelites shall eat their food unclean among the nations where I scatter them. 14 "Oh no, Lord GOD!" I protested. "Never have I been made unclean, and from my youth till now, never have I eaten carrion flesh or that torn by wild beasts: never has any unclean meat entered my mouth." 15 Very well, he replied, I allow you cow's dung in place of human excrement; bake your bread on that.

5 1 As for you, son of man, take a sharp sword and use it like a barber's razor, passing it over your head and beard. Then take a set of scales and divide the hair you have cut. 2† Burn a third in the fire, within the city, when the days of your siege are completed; place another third around the city and strike it with the sword; the final third strew in the wind, and pursue it with the sword. 3 [But of the last take a small number and tie them in the hem of your garment. 4 Then take some of these and throw them in the midst of the fire and burn them.]

Say to the whole house of Israel: 5 Thus says the

---

† ——

3, 22–27: This passage also belongs to a later period, with Ez 24, 25ff and 33, 21f, during the time of the final siege of Jerusalem, when Ezekiel's prophecies consisted mainly of symbolic actions rather than words.

3, 26: *Dumb:* unwilling to speak to the people in exile while Jerusalem was being besieged; cf Ez 24, 27.

3, 16: *At the end of seven days . . . :* the incomplete sentence probably contained some such words as "the word of the Lord came to me." For seven days, see v 15. (This verse has been transposed from ch 3.)

4, 5f: *Three hundred and ninety days . . . forty days:* symbolically representing the respective lengths of the periods of exile of northern Israelites and Judahites. Northern Israel had already fallen to Assyria in 722 B.C. The letters in the Hebrew phrase for the days of

your siege (v 8), each of which has its own numerical value, add up to three hundred and ninety. Forty years represent one generation.

4, 7: *Bared arm:* a symbol of unrestrained power.

4, 9–17: This action represents the scarcity of food during the siege of Jerusalem, and the consequent need to eat whatever is at hand. *Twenty shekels:* about nine ounces. *The sixth of a hin:* about one quart.

4, 16: *Breaking the staff of bread:* reducing the supply of bread which sustains the life of man as the walking staff sustains the traveler on his journey; cf Ez 5, 16; 14, 13; Lv 26, 26; Ps 105, 16; Is 3, 1.

5, 2: *The city:* the one drawn on the tablet.

3, 23: Ez 1, 3; 10, 15.20.22; 43, 3.   **4, 16:** Ez 5, 16; 14, 13.   **4, 13:** Hos 9, 4.

Street Theater

Look over what the prophet does in Ezekiel, chapters 3–5, to get people's attention before the fall of Jerusalem in 587 B.C. He is speechless (3, 22–27) as a sign that the people are rebellious and unwilling to hear God's word. He lies on his left side for days, and then his right (4, 4–5), as a sign of the number of years the two kingdoms Israel and Judah will be in exile. He eats small amounts of food cooked on dung (verses 10–15) as a sign of the shortage of food during the siege of the city. Ezekiel's "street theater" is a good way of making a point that everyone can understand.

Christians today need to use creative means to raise consciousness about the ways society violates human life and harms our world. Radio and television, public prayer services, and rallies all help people get the message out. What does your church do to raise consciousness and move people to change their ways? What can you do?

▶ Ez 4, 1—5, 4

Lord GOD: This is Jerusalem! In the midst of the nations I placed her, surrounded by foreign countries. ⁶ But she rebelled against my ordinances more wickedly than the nations, and against my statutes more than the foreign countries surrounding her; she has spurned my ordinances and has not lived by my statutes. ⁷ Therefore thus says the Lord GOD: Because you have been more rebellious than the nations surrounding you, not living by my statutes nor fulfilling my ordinances, but acting according to the ordinances of the surrounding nations; ⁸† therefore thus says the Lord GOD: See, I am coming at you! I will inflict punishments in your midst while the nations look on. ⁹ Because of all your abominations I will do with you what I have never done before, the like of which I will never do again. ¹⁰† This means that fathers within you shall eat sons, and sons shall eat fathers. I will inflict punishments upon you and scatter all that remain of your people in every direction.

¹¹ Therefore, as I live, says the Lord GOD, because you have defiled my sanctuary with all your detestable abominations, I swear to cut you down. I will not look upon you with pity nor have mercy. ¹² A third of your people shall die of pestilence and perish of hunger within you; another third shall fall by the sword all around you; and a third I will scatter in every direction, and I will pursue them with the sword. ¹⁶* When I loose against you the cruel, destructive arrows of hunger, I will break your staff of bread; ¹⁷ I will send famine against you, and wild beasts that shall rob you of your children. Pestilence and bloodshed shall stalk through you, and I will bring the sword upon you. I, the LORD, have spoken!

¹³ Thus shall my anger spend itself, and I will wreak my fury upon them till I am appeased; they shall know that I, the LORD, have spoken in my jealousy when I spend my fury upon them. ¹⁴ I will make you a waste and a reproach among the nations that surround you, which every passer-by may see. ¹⁵ When I execute judgment upon you in anger and fury and with furious chastisements, you shall be a reproach and an object of scorn, a terrible warning to the nations that surround you. I, the LORD, have spoken!

Against the Mountains of Israel

6 ¹ Thus the word of the LORD came to me: ² Son of man, turn toward the mountains of Israel, and prophesy against them: ³*† Mountains of Israel, hear the word of the Lord GOD. Thus says the Lord GOD [to the mountains and hills, the ravines and valleys]: See, I am bringing a sword against you, and I will destroy your high places. ⁴ Your altars shall be laid waste, your incense stands shall be broken, and I will cast down your slain ones before your idols; ⁵† I will scatter their bones all around your altars. ⁶ In all your dwelling places cities shall be made desolate and high places laid waste, so that your altars will be made desolate and laid waste, your idols broken and removed, and your incense stands smashed to bits. ⁷ [The slain shall fall in your midst, and you shall know that I am the LORD. ⁸ I have warned you.]

---

† **5, 8:** *I am coming at you:* an expression borrowed from the language of warfare in which enemies attacked one another with the sword. *You* in vv 8–17 is Jerusalem.

5, 10: *Fathers . . . shall eat sons, and sons . . . fathers:* see note on Lam 2, 20.

6, 3: *High places:* the sanctuaries on the mountaintops where illegal worship, whether of the Lord or of Canaanite deities, was performed.

6, 5: *Scatter their bones . . . altars:* dead men's bones defiled a place; cf 2 Kgs 23, 14.

5, 16: Ez 4, 16; 14, 13.   **6, 3:** Ez 36, 1.

When some of your people have escaped to other nations from the sword, and have been scattered over the foreign lands, 9 then those who have escaped will remember me among the nations to which they have been exiled, after I have broken their adulterous hearts that turned away from me [and their eyes which lusted after idols]. They shall loathe themselves because of their evil deeds, all their abominations. 10 Then they shall know that it was not in vain that I, the LORD, threatened to inflict this calamity upon them.

11† Thus says the Lord GOD: Clap your hands, stamp your feet, and cry "Alas!" because of all the abominations of the house of Israel, for which they shall fall by the sword, by famine, and by pestilence. 12 He that is far off shall die of pestilence, he that is near shall fall by the sword, and he that is besieged shall perish by famine; so will I spend my fury upon them. 13† Then shall they know that I am the LORD, when their slain shall lie amid their idols, all about their altars, on every high hill and mountaintop, beneath every green tree and leafy oak, wherever they offered appeasing odors to any of their gods. 14† I will stretch out my hand against them, and wherever they live I will make the land a desolate waste, from the desert to Riblah; thus shall they know that I am the LORD.

The End Has Come

7 1 Thus the word of the LORD came to me: 2 Son of man, now say: Thus says the Lord GOD to the land of Israel: An end! The end has come upon the four corners of the land! 3 Now the end is upon you; I will unleash my anger against you and judge you according to your conduct and lay upon you the consequences of all your abominations. 4 I will not look upon you with pity nor have mercy; I will bring your conduct down upon you, and the consequences of your abominations shall be in your midst; then shall you know that I am the LORD.

5 Thus says the Lord GOD: Disaster upon disaster! See it coming! 6 An end is coming, the end is coming upon you! See it coming! 7 The climax has come for you who dwell in the land! The time has come, near is the day: a time of consternation, not of rejoicing. 8 Soon now I will pour out my fury upon you and spend my anger upon you; I will judge you according to your conduct and lay upon you the consequences of all your abominations. 9 I will not look upon you with pity nor have mercy; I will deal with you according to your conduct, and the consequences of your abominations shall be in your midst; then shall you know that it is I, the LORD, who strike.

10 See, the day of the LORD! See, the end is coming! Lawlessness is in full bloom, insolence flourishes, 11 violence has risen to support wickedness. It shall not be long in coming, nor shall it delay. 12† The time has come, the day dawns. Let not the buyer rejoice nor the seller mourn, for wrath shall be upon all the throng. 13 The seller shall not regain what he sold as long as he lives, for wrath shall be upon all the throng. Because of his sins, no one shall preserve his life. 14 They shall sound the trumpet and make everything ready, yet no one shall go to war, for my wrath is upon all the throng.

15 The sword is outside; pestilence and hunger are within. He that is in the country shall die by the sword; pestilence and famine shall devour those in the city. 16 Even those who escape and flee to the mountains like the doves of the valleys—I will put them all to death, each one for his own sins. 17 All their hands shall be limp, and all their knees shall run with water. 18*† They shall put on sackcloth, and horror shall cover them; shame shall be on all their faces and baldness on all their heads. 19* They shall fling their silver into the streets, and their gold shall be considered refuse. Their silver and gold cannot save them on the day of the LORD'S wrath. They shall not be allowed to satisfy their craving or fill their bellies, for this has been the occasion of their sin. 20 In the beauty of their ornaments they put their pride: they made of them their abominable images [their idols]. For this reason I make them refuse. 21 I will hand them over as booty to foreigners, to be spoiled and defiled by the wicked of the earth. 22† I will turn away my face from them, and my treasure shall be profaned: robbers shall enter and profane it.

23 They shall wreak slaughter, for the land is filled with bloodshed and the city full of violence. 24 I will bring in the worst of the nations, who shall take possession of their houses. I will put an end to their proud strength, and their sanctuaries shall be profaned. 25 When anguish comes they shall seek peace, but there will be none. 26 There shall be disaster after disaster, rumor after rumor. Prophetic vision shall fade; instruction shall be lacking to the priest, and counsel to the elders, 27 while the prince

---

6, 11: *Clap your hands, stamp your feet:* here evidently signs of mourning; in Ez 25, 6, signs of joy.

6, 13: *Every green tree and leafy oak:* sacred groves had a long history in Palestine as places of worship; cf Dt 12, 2; note on Gn 12, 6.

6, 14: *From the desert to Riblah:* the whole land, from the far south to the far north.

7, 12f: Mundane affairs will cease to have any meaning in view of the disaster that is to come.

7, 18: *Baldness:* shaving the head was a sign of mourning.
7, 22: *My treasure:* the temple of Jerusalem.

7, 18: Is 15, 2; Jer 48, 37.   7, 19: Prv 11, 4; Sir 5, 10;
                                              Zep 1, 18.

shall be enveloped in terror, and the hands of the common people shall tremble. I will deal with them according to their conduct, and according to their judgments I will judge them; thus they shall know that I am the LORD.

Vision of Abominations in the Temple

8 3*† Spirit lifted me up in the air and brought me in divine visions to Jerusalem, to the entrance of the north gate, where stood the statue of jealousy which stirs up jealousy. 5† He said to me: Son of man, look toward the north! I looked toward the north and saw northward of the gate the altar of the statue of jealousy. 6 Son of man, he asked me, do you see what they are doing? Do you see the great abominations that the house of Israel is practicing here, so that I must depart from my sanctuary? But you shall see still greater abominations!

7 Then he brought me to the entrance of the court, where I saw there was a hole in the wall. 8 Son of man, he ordered, dig through the wall. I dug through the wall and saw a door. 9 Enter, he said to me, and see the abominable evils which they are doing here. 10† I entered and saw that all around upon the wall were pictured the figures of all kinds of creeping things and loathsome beasts [all the idols of the house of Israel]. 11 Before these stood seventy of the elders of the house of Israel, among whom stood Jaazaniah, son of Shaphan, each of them with his censer in his hand, and the fragrance of the incense was rising upward. 12 Then he said to me: Do you see, son of man, what each of these elders of the house of Israel is doing in his idol room? They think: "The LORD cannot see us; the LORD has forsaken the land." 13 He continued: You shall see still greater abominations that they are practicing.

14† Then he brought me to the entrance of the north gate of the temple, and I saw sitting there the women who were weeping for Tammuz. 15 Then he said to me: Do you see this, son of man? You shall see other abominations, greater than these!

16† Then he brought me into the inner court of the LORD's house, and there at the door of the LORD's temple, between the vestibule and the altar, were about twenty-five men with their backs to the LORD's temple and their faces toward the east; they were bowing down to the sun. 17† Do you see, son of man? he asked me. Is it such a trivial matter for the house of Judah to do the abominable things they have done here—for they have filled the land with violence, and again and again they have provoked me—that now they must also put the branch to my nose? 18 Therefore I in turn will act furiously: I will not look upon them with pity nor will I show mercy.

Slaughter of the Idolaters

9 1 Then he cried loud for me to hear: Come, you scourges of the city! 2 With that I saw six men coming from the direction of the upper gate which faces the north, each with a destroying weapon in his hand. In their midst was a man dressed in linen, with a writer's case at his waist. They entered and stood beside the bronze altar. 3 Then he called to the man dressed in linen with the writer's case at his waist, 4*† saying to him: Pass through the city [through Jerusalem] and mark an X on the foreheads of those who moan and groan over all the abominations that are practiced within it. 5 To the others I heard him say: Pass through the city after him and strike! Do not look on them with pity nor show any mercy! 6 Old men, youths and maidens, women and children—wipe them out! But do not touch any marked with the X; begin at my sanctuary. So they began with the men [the elders] who were in front of the temple. 7 Defile the temple, he said to them, and fill the courts with the slain; then go out and strike in the city.

8 As they began to strike, I was left alone. I fell prone, crying out, "Alas, Lord GOD! Will you destroy all that is left of Israel when you pour out your fury on Jerusalem?" 9 He answered me: The sins of the house of Israel are great beyond measure; the land is filled with bloodshed, the city with lawlessness. They think that the LORD has forsaken the

---

8, 3: *The statue of jealousy which stirs up jealousy:* the statue which provokes the Lord's jealousy for his honor. This was probably the statue of the goddess Asherah erected by the wicked King Manasseh (cf 2 Kgs 21, 7; 2 Chr 33, 7.15). Though it had been removed by King Josiah (2 Kgs 23, 6), it had no doubt been set up again in the repaganizing of Jerusalem that followed on Josiah's death.

8, 5: *He:* an angel accompanies Ezekiel in these visions and represents the voice of the Lord; cf Ez 40, 3f.

8, 10: *Creeping things and loathsome beasts:* probably Egyptian deities, which were represented in animal form. During the last days of Jerusalem King Zedekiah was allied with Egypt, trusting in it for protection against the Chaldeans.

8, 14: *Weeping for Tammuz:* the withering of trees and plants in autumn was thought to be due to the descent of Tammuz, the Babylonian god of fertility, to the nether world of the dead; this descent was bewailed by the women.

8, 16: *Bowing down to the sun:* sun worship had been made an important part of Judahite idolatry by the impious kings; cf 2 Kgs 23, 11.

8, 17: *Put the branch to my nose:* the meaning is uncertain. Perhaps it refers to an Egyptian practice imported into Judah; the Egyptian sun god Re is pictured with a vine branch at his nose, signifying the transfer of creative power (divine breath) to living things. Such rites were abominable to the Lord.

9, 4: Ezekiel is preeminently the prophet of personal retribution; the innocent inhabitants of Jerusalem are to be spared when the idolatrous are punished. *An X:* literally, the Hebrew letter taw, which had the form of a cross.

8, 3: Dn 14, 6.   9, 4: Ex 12, 7; Rv 7, 3.

land, that he does not see them. [10] I, however, will not look upon them with pity, nor show any mercy. I will bring down their conduct upon their heads.

[11] Then I saw the man dressed in linen with the writing case at his waist make his report: "I have done as you ordered."

[24]† Spirit lifted me up and brought me back to the exiles in Chaldea [in a vision, by God's spirit]. Then the vision I had seen left me, [25] and I told the exiles everything the LORD had shown me.

God's Glory Leaves Jerusalem

10 [1]† On the fifth day of the sixth month, in the sixth year,† as I was sitting in my house, and the elders of Judah sat before me, the hand of the Lord GOD fell upon me there. [2]† I looked up and saw a form that looked like a man. Downward from what seemed to be his waist, there was fire; from his waist upward there seemed to be a brightness like the sheen of electrum. He stretched out what appeared to be a hand and seized me by the hair of my head. . . .†

[4] I saw there the glory of the God of Israel, like the vision I had seen in the plain. The cherubim were stationed to the right of the temple; [20]* these were the living creatures I had seen beneath the God of Israel by the river Chebar, whom I now recognized to be cherubim. [21] Each had four faces and four wings; something like human hands were under their wings. [22] Their faces looked just like those I had seen by the river Chebar; each one went straight forward. [14]* Each had four faces: the first face was that of an ox, the second that of a man, the third that of a lion, and the fourth that of an eagle. [15] Such were the living creatures I had seen by the river Chebar.

[9]* I also saw four wheels beside them, one wheel beside each cherub; the wheels appeared to have the luster of chrysolite stone. [10] All four of them seemed to be made the same, as though there were a wheel within a wheel. [11] When they moved, they went in any one of their four directions without veering as they moved; for in whichever direction they were faced, they went straight towards it without veering as they moved. [12]* The rims of the four wheels were full of eyes all around. [13] I heard the wheels given the name "wheelwork." [16]* When the

cherubim moved, the wheels went beside them; when the cherubim lifted their wings to rise from the earth, even then the wheels did not leave their sides. [17] When they stood still, the wheels stood still; when they rose, the wheels rose with them; for the living creatures' spirit was in them.

[1] I looked and saw in the firmament above the cherubim what appeared to be sapphire stone; something like a throne could be seen upon it. [2]† He said to the man dressed in linen: Go within the wheelwork under the cherubim; fill both your hands with burning coals from among the cherubim, then scatter them over the city. As I looked on, he entered.

The glory of the God of Israel had gone up from the cherubim, upon which it had been, to the threshold of the temple. [3] As the man entered, the cloud filled the inner court, [4] and the glory of the LORD rose from over the cherubim to the threshold of the temple; the temple was filled with the cloud, and all the court was bright with the glory of the LORD. [5] The noise of the wings of the cherubim could be heard as far as the outer court; it was like the voice of God the Almighty when he speaks.

[6] When he had commanded the man dressed in linen to take fire from within the wheelwork, among the cherubim, the man entered and stood by one of the wheels. [7] Thereupon its cherub stretched out his hand toward the fire that was among the cherubim. He took up some of it and put it in the hands of the one dressed in linen, who took it and came out. [8] [Something like human hands could be seen under the wings of the cherubim.]

[18] Then the glory of the LORD left the threshold of the temple and rested upon the cherubim. [19] These lifted their wings, and I saw them rise from the earth, the wheels rising along with them. They stood at the entrance of the eastern gate of the LORD's house, and the glory of the God of Israel was up above them. [22]† Then the cherubim lifted their wings, and the wheels went along with them, while up above them was the glory of the God of Israel. [23] And the glory of the LORD rose from the city and took a stand on the mountain which is to the east of the city.

9, 24f: These verses have been transposed from ch 11.

10, 1: In chapters 8, 1—11, 25 of the current Hebrew text, several visions involving the temple of Jerusalem were combined to form a single continuous vision. The redistribution of verses in this translation is an attempt to separate the original visions. (10, 1.2.4. have been transposed from ch 8)

10, 1: *The fifth day of the sixth month, in the sixth year:* September 17, 592 B.C.

10, 2: The dots suppose the omission of some words describing the prophet's being transported in his visions to the court of the temple.

10, 2: The burning coals within the wheelwork under God's throne, a sign of the divine presence (cf Ez 28, 14; Ps 18, 13), symbolize the judgment to be visited on the city.

10, 22f: These verses have been transposed from ch 11.

---
*

10, 20: Ez 1, 1.3.	10, 12: Ez 1, 18.
10, 14: Ez 1, 10.	10, 16: Ez 1, 19.
10, 9: Ez 1, 15f.	

Judgment of the Princes

11 [1] Spirit lifted me up and brought me to the east gate of the temple. At the entrance of the gate I saw twenty-five men, among whom were Jaazaniah, son of Azzur, and Pelatiah, son of Benaiah, princes of the people. [2] The LORD said to me: Son of man, these are the men who are planning evil and giving wicked counsel in this city. [3]† "Shall we not," they say, "be building houses soon? The city is the kettle, and we are the meat." [4] Therefore prophesy against them, son of man, prophesy! [5] Then the spirit of the LORD fell upon me, and he told me to say: Thus says the LORD: This is the way you talk, house of Israel, and what you are plotting I well know. [6] You have slain many in this city and have filled its streets with your slain. [7] Therefore thus says the Lord GOD: Your slain whom you have placed within it, they are the meat, and the city is the kettle; but you I will take out of it. [8] You fear the sword, but the sword I will bring upon you, says the Lord GOD. [9] I will bring you out of the city, and hand you over to foreigners, and inflict punishments upon you. [10] By the sword you shall fall; at the boundaries of Israel I will judge you; thus you shall know that I am the LORD. [11] The city shall not be a kettle for you, nor shall you be the meat within it. At the boundaries of Israel I will judge you, [12] and you shall know that I am the LORD, by whose statutes you have not lived, and whose ordinances you have not kept; rather, you have acted according to the ordinances of the nations around you.

[13] While I was prophesying, Pelatiah, the son of Benaiah, died. I fell prone and cried out in a loud voice: "Alas, Lord GOD! will you utterly wipe out what remains of Israel?"

Restoration of the Exiles

[14] Thus the word of the LORD came to me: [15]† Son of man, it is about your kinsmen, your fellow exiles, and the whole house of Israel that the inhabitants of Jerusalem say, "They are far away from the LORD; to us the land of Israel has been given as our possession." [16] Therefore say: Thus says the Lord GOD: Though I have removed them far among the nations and scattered them over foreign countries—and was for a while their only sanctuary in the countries to which they had gone— [17] I will gather you from the nations and assemble you from the countries over which you have been scattered, and I will restore to you the land of Israel. [18] They

shall return to it and remove from it all its detestable abominations. [19]* I will give them a new heart and put a new spirit within them; I will remove the stony heart from their bodies, and replace it with a natural heart, [20] so that they will live according to my statutes, and observe and carry out my ordinances; thus they shall be my people and I will be their God. [21] But as for those whose hearts are devoted to their detestable abominations, I will bring down their conduct upon their heads, says the Lord GOD.

Acts Symbolic of the Exile

12 [1] Thus the word of the LORD came to me: [2] Son of man, you live in the midst of a rebellious house; they have eyes to see but do not see, and ears to hear but do not hear, for they are a rebellious house. [3] Now, son of man, during the day while they are looking on, prepare your baggage as though for exile, and again while they are looking on, migrate from where you live to another place; perhaps they will see that they are a rebellious house. [4] You shall bring out your baggage like

---

Have a Heart!

The Old Testament prophets are concerned about people's hearts. The ancient Israelites understood the heart as the center of intelligence, feelings, and human will. Jeremiah says the New Covenant will be written on people's hearts (Jer 31, 33), and Ezekiel says God will take away their stony hearts and give them natural hearts (Ez 11, 19).

In your prayer, reflect or journal on the following questions:

- What's the difference between having a natural, fleshy heart and a cold, stony heart?
- Why would a natural heart lead to obeying God (verse 20)?
- When does your heart feel natural? When does it feel stony?

▶ Ez 11, 19–20

11, 3: These words reflect the false confidence of the inhabitants of Jerusalem in the face of the Chaldean invasion. Jerusalem, they think, is like an iron kettle protecting the meat within it from harm; but cf Ez 24, 3–6.

11, 15–21: Like Jeremiah (cf chapter 29), Ezekiel knows that no

reform is to be expected from the men of Judah who remained in Palestine; but the exiles will be the ones to form the new Israel. The new, spiritual covenant will replace the former covenant; cf Jer 24, 7.

11, 19: Ez 36, 26; Jer 31, 33.

an exile in the daytime while they are looking on; in the evening, again while they are looking on, you shall go out like one of those driven into exile; 5† while they look on, dig a hole in the wall and pass through it; 6 while they look on, shoulder the burden and set out in the darkness; cover your face that you may not see the land, for I have made you a sign for the house of Israel.

7 I did as I was told. During the day I brought out my baggage as though it were that of an exile, and at evening I dug a hole through the wall with my hand and, while they looked on, set out in the darkness, shouldering my burden.

8 Then, in the morning, the word of the LORD came to me: 9 Son of man, did not the house of Israel, that rebellious house, ask you what you were doing? 10 Tell them: Thus says the Lord GOD: This oracle concerns Jerusalem and the whole house of Israel within it. 11 I am a sign for you: as I have done, so shall it be done to them; as captives they shall go into exile. 12 The prince who is among them shall shoulder his burden and set out in darkness, going through a hole that he has dug in the wall, and covering his face lest he be seen by anyone. 13*† But I will spread my net over him, and he shall be taken in my snare. I will bring him to Babylon, into the land of the Chaldeans—but he shall not see it—and there he shall die. 14 All his retinue, his aides, and his troops I will scatter in every direction, and pursue them with the sword. 15 Then shall they know that I am the LORD, when I disperse them among the nations and scatter them over foreign lands. 16 Yet I will leave a few of them to escape the sword, famine and pestilence, so that they may tell of all their abominations among the nations to which they will come; thus they shall know that I am the LORD.

17 Thus the word of the LORD came to me: 18 Son of man, eat your bread trembling, and drink your water shaking with anxiety. 19 Then say to the people of the land: Thus says the Lord GOD of the inhabitants of Jerusalem [to the land of Israel]: They shall eat their bread in anxiety and drink their water in horror, that their land may be emptied of the violence of all its inhabitants that now fills it. 20 Inhabited cities shall be in ruins, and the land shall be a waste; thus you shall know that I am the LORD.

Prophecy Ridiculed

21 Thus the word of the LORD came to me: 22† Son of man, what is this proverb that you have in the land of Israel: "The days drag on, and no vision ever comes to anything"? 23 Say to them therefore: Thus says the Lord GOD: I will put an end to this proverb; they shall never quote it again in Israel. Rather, say to them: The days are at hand, and also the fulfillment of every vision. 25 Whatever I speak is final, and it shall be done without further delay. In your days, rebellious house, whatever I speak I will bring about, says the Lord GOD.

24 There shall no longer be any false visions or deceitful divinations within the house of Israel, because it is I, the LORD, who will speak.

26 Thus the word of the LORD came to me: 27 Son of man, listen to the house of Israel saying, "The vision he sees is a long way off; he prophesies of the distant future!" 28 Say to them therefore: Thus says the Lord GOD: None of my words shall be delayed any longer; whatever I speak is final, and it shall be done, says the Lord GOD.

Against the Prophets of Peace

13 1 Thus the word of the LORD came to me: 2 Son of man, prophesy against the prophets of Israel, prophesy! Say to those who prophesy their own thought: Hear the word of the LORD:† 5 You did not step into the breach, nor did you build a wall about the house of Israel that would stand firm against attack on the day of the LORD. 7 Was not the vision you saw false, and your divination lying? 8 Therefore thus says the Lord GOD: Because you have spoken falsehood and have seen lying visions, therefore see! I am coming at you, says the Lord GOD.

10† For the very reason that they led my people astray, saying, "Peace!" when there was no peace, and that, as one built a wall, they would cover it with whitewash, 11 say then to the whitewashers: I will bring down a flooding rain; hailstones shall fall, and a stormwind shall break out. 12 And when the wall has fallen, will you not be asked: Where is the whitewash you spread on?

13 Therefore thus says the Lord GOD: In my fury I will let loose stormwinds; because of my anger there shall be a flooding rain, and hailstones shall fall with destructive wrath. 14 I will tear down the wall that you have whitewashed and level it to the ground, laying bare its foundations. When it falls, you shall be crushed beneath it; thus you shall know that I am the LORD. 15 When I have spent my fury on the wall and its whitewashers, I tell you there shall be no wall, nor shall there be whitewashers—

---

† **12, 5:** *Dig a hole in the wall:* the exiles are to leave Jerusalem through the broken walls of the ruined city.
12, 13: *But he shall not see it:* Zedekiah was blinded by Nebuchadnezzar before being deported to Babylonia; cf 2 Kgs 25, 7.
12, 22.27: These words used against Ezekiel because of the apparent failure of his prophecies; cf Jer 20, 7ff.
13, 3-23: These verses have been transposed according to the following order: 7-8.10-16.3-4.6.9.17.22-23.18-21.
13, 10: To the confidence which the people had in their defenses against the Chaldeans, the false prophets contributed the illusion of security by predictions of peace, like men who whitewash a wall rather than allow its defects to be seen.

12, 13: Ez 17, 20; 32, 3.   **13, 3:** Ez 14, 9; 34, 2; Jer 23, 1.

16 those prophets of Israel who prophesied to Jerusalem and saw for it visions of peace when there was no peace, says the Lord GOD.

Against False Prophets in Chaldea

3* Thus says the Lord GOD: Woe to those prophets who are fools, who follow their own spirit and have seen no vision. 4 Like foxes among ruins are your prophets, O Israel! 6 Their visions are false and their divination lying. They say, "Thus says the LORD!" though the LORD did not send them; then they wait for him to fulfill their word! 9 But I will stretch out my hand against the prophets who have false visions and who foretell lies. They shall not belong to the community of my people, nor be recorded in the register of the house of Israel, nor enter the land of Israel; thus you shall know that I am the LORD.

Against False Prophetesses

17 Now, son of man, turn toward the daughters of your people who prophesy their own thoughts; against these, prophesy: Thus says the Lord GOD: 22 Because you have disheartened the upright man with lies when I did not wish him grieved, and have encouraged the wicked man not to turn from his evil conduct and save his life; 23 therefore you shall no longer see false visions and practice divination, but I will rescue my people from your power. Thus you shall know that I am the LORD.

Against Sorceresses

18† Woe to those who sew bands for everyone's wrists and make veils for every size of head so as to entrap their owners. Do you think to entrap the lives of my people, yet keep yourselves alive? 19† You dishonor me before my people with handfuls of barley and crumbs of bread, killing those who should not die and keeping alive those who should not live, lying to my people who willingly hear lies. 20 Therefore thus says the Lord GOD: See! I am coming at those bands of yours in which you entrap men's lives: I will tear them from their arms and set free those you have caught. 21 I will tear off your veils and rescue my people from your power, so that they shall no longer be prey to your hands. Thus you shall know that I am the LORD.

Prophecy Useless for Idolaters

14 1 When certain elders of Israel came and sat down before me, 2 the word of the LORD came to me: 3 Son of man, these men have the memory of their idols fresh in their hearts, and they keep the occasion of their sin before them. Why should I allow myself to be consulted by them? 4 Therefore speak with them, and say to them: Thus says the Lord GOD: If anyone of the house of Israel, holding the memory of his idols in his heart and keeping the occasion of his sin before him, has recourse to a prophet, I, the LORD, will be his answer in person because of his many idols. 5 Thus would I bring back to their senses the house of Israel, who have become estranged from me through all their idols.

6 Therefore say to the house of Israel: Thus says the Lord GOD: Return and be converted from your idols; turn yourselves away from all your abominations. 7 For if anyone of the house of Israel or any alien resident in Israel is estranged from me, and holds the memory of his idols in his heart and keeps the occasion of his sin before him, yet asks a prophet to consult me for him, I, the LORD, will be his answer in person. 8 I will turn against that man, and make of him an example and a byword. I will cut him off from the midst of my people. Thus you shall know that I am the LORD.

9*† As for the prophet, if he is beguiled into speaking a word, I, the LORD, shall have beguiled that prophet; I will stretch out my hand against him and root him out of my people Israel. 10 Each shall receive punishment for his sin, the inquirer and the prophet shall be punished alike, 11 so that the house of Israel may no longer stray from me and may no longer be defiled by all their sins. Thus they shall be my people, and I will be their God, says the Lord GOD.

Personal Responsibility

12† Thus the word of the LORD came to me: 13* Son of man, when a land sins against me by breaking faith, I stretch out my hand against it and break its staff of bread, I let famine loose upon it and cut off from it both man and beast; 14† and even if these three men were in it, Noah, Daniel, and Job, they could save only themselves by their virtue, says the Lord GOD. 15 If I were to cause wild beasts to prowl the land, depopulating it so that it became

---

13, 18: *Sew bands . . . make veils:* magical practices believed to give to the sorceresses power over those on whom they placed these objects.

13, 19: *Handfuls of barley and crumbs of bread:* used in divination and forecasting the future.

14, 9: *I, the LORD, shall have beguiled that prophet:* the ancient Israelites attributed to God every action, good or evil; cf 1 Sm 18, 10; 2 Sm 24, 1ff. We would say, rather, that God permitted this deceit.

14, 12–23: The doctrine of personal responsibility before God

was not new (cf Ez 3, 16–21; 18; 33, 1–20); but it had not been emphasized by the prophets before the Exile, who mostly predicted national retribution and called for national repentance.

14, 14: *Noah, Daniel, and Job:* proverbially virtuous men. The Daniel named here may be the traditional just judge of the ancient past, celebrated in Canaanite literature, who is possibly reflected in Dn 13, but is not the hero of Dn 1–12.

14, 9: 1 Kgs 22, 23.   **14, 13:** Ez 4, 16.

a waste, traversed by none because of the wild beasts, ¹⁶ and these three men were in it, as I live, says the Lord GOD, I swear they could save neither sons nor daughters; they alone would be saved, and the land would be a waste. ¹⁷ Or if I brought the sword upon this country, commanding the sword to pass through the land cutting off from it man and beast, ¹⁸ and these three men were in it, as I live, says the Lord GOD, they would be unable to save either sons or daughters; they alone would be saved. ¹⁹ Or if I were to send pestilence into this land, pouring out upon it my bloodthirsty fury, cutting off from it man and beast, ²⁰ even if Noah, Daniel, and Job were in it, as I live, says the Lord GOD, I swear that they could save neither son nor daughter; they would save only themselves by their virtue.

²¹ Thus says the Lord GOD: Even though I send Jerusalem my four cruel punishments, the sword, famine, wild beasts, and pestilence, to cut off from it man and beast, ²² still some survivors shall be left in it who will bring out sons and daughters; when they come out to you, you shall see their conduct and their actions and be consoled regarding the evil I have brought on Jerusalem [all that I have brought upon it]. ²³ They shall console you when you see their conduct and actions, for you shall then know that it was not without reason that I did to it what I did, says the Lord GOD.

Parable of the Vine

15 ¹ Thus the word of the LORD came to me: ² Son of man, what makes the wood of the vine better than any other wood? That branch among the trees of the forest! ³ Can you use its wood to make anything worthwhile? Can you make even a peg from it, to hang on it any kind of vessel? ⁴ If you throw it on the fire as fuel and the fire devours both ends and even the middle is scorched, is it still good for anything? ⁵ Why, even when it was whole it was good for nothing; how much less, when the fire has devoured and scorched it, can it be used for anything! ⁶ Therefore, thus says the Lord GOD: Like the wood of the vine among the trees of the forest, which I have destined as fuel for the fire, do I make the inhabitants of Jerusalem. ⁷ I will set my face against them; they have escaped from the fire, but the fire shall devour them. Thus you shall know that I am the LORD, when I turn my face against them. ⁸ I will make the land a waste, because they have broken faith, says the Lord GOD.

The Faithless Spouse

16 ¹ Thus the word of the LORD came to me: ² Son of man, make known to Jerusalem her abominations. ³† Thus says the Lord GOD to Jerusalem: By origin and birth you are of the land of Canaan; your father was an Amorite and your mother a Hittite. ⁴ As for your birth, the day you were born your navel cord was not cut; you were neither washed with water nor anointed, nor were you rubbed with salt, nor swathed in swaddling clothes. ⁵ No one looked on you with pity or compassion to do any of these things for you. Rather, you were thrown out on the ground as something loathsome, the day you were born.

⁶ Then I passed by and saw you weltering in your blood. I said to you: Live in your blood ⁷ and grow like a plant in the field. You grew and developed, you came to the age of puberty; your breasts were formed, your hair had grown, but you were still stark naked. ⁸† Again I passed by you and saw that you were now old enough for love. So I spread the corner of my cloak over you to cover your nakedness; I swore an oath to you and entered into a covenant with you; you became mine, says the Lord GOD. ⁹ Then I bathed you with water, washed away your blood, and anointed you with oil. ¹⁰ I clothed you with an embroidered gown, put sandals of fine leather on your feet; I gave you a fine linen sash and silk robes to wear. ¹¹ I adorned you with jewelry: I put bracelets on your arms, a necklace about your neck, ¹² a ring in your nose, pendants in your ears, and a glorious diadem upon your head. ¹³ Thus you were adorned with gold and silver; your garments were of fine linen, silk, and embroidered cloth. Fine flour, honey, and oil were your food. You were exceedingly beautiful, with the dignity of a queen. ¹⁴ You were renowned among the nations for your beauty, perfect as it was, because of my splendor which I had bestowed on you, says the Lord GOD.

¹⁵ But you were captivated by your own beauty, you used your renown to make yourself a harlot, and you lavished your harlotry on every passer-by, whose own you became. ¹⁶† You took some of your gowns and made for yourself gaudy high places, where you played the harlot. . . . ¹⁷ You took the splendid gold and silver ornaments that I had given you and made for yourself male images, with which also you played the harlot. ¹⁸ You took your embroidered gowns to cover them; my oil and my incense you set before them; ¹⁹ the food that I had given you, the fine flour, the oil, and the honey with

---

16, 3f: *By origin and birth . . . Canaan . . . Amorite . . . Hittite:* the inhabitants of Jerusalem and Judah absorbed not only pre-Israelite racial strains, but also many elements of the country's pagan cult and customs.

16, 8: *I spread the corner of my cloak over you to cover your*

nakedness: and also to signify the intention of marriage; cf Ru 3, 9.
16, 16: Fine robes were used to cover a couch for harlotry; cf Prv 7, 16f. In the allegory of this chapter the viewpoint often shifts from the figure (harlotry) to the reality (idolatry).

which I fed you, you set before them as an appeasing odor, says the Lord GOD. 20*† The sons and daughters you had borne me you took and offered as sacrifices to be devoured by them! Was it not enough that you had become a harlot? 21* You slaughtered and immolated my children to them, making them pass through fire. 22 And through all your abominations and harlotries you remembered nothing of when you were a girl, stark naked and weltering in your blood.

23 Then after all your evildoing—woe, woe to you! says the Lord GOD— 24† you raised for yourself a platform and a dais in every public place. 25* At every street corner you built a dais for yourself to use your beauty obscenely, spreading your legs for every passer-by, playing the harlot countless times. 26 You played the harlot with the Egyptians, your lustful neighbors, so many times that I was provoked to anger. 27 Therefore I stretched out my hand against you, I diminished your allowance and delivered you over to the will of your enemies, the Philistines, who revolted at your lewd conduct. 28 You also played the harlot with the Assyrians, because you were not satisfied; and after playing the harlot with them, you were still not satisfied. 29 Again and again you played the harlot, now going to Chaldea, the land of the traders; but despite this, you were still not satisfied.

30 How wild your lust! says the Lord GOD, that you did all these things, acting like a shameless prostitute, 31 building your platform at every street corner and erecting your dais in every public place! Yet you were unlike a prostitute, since you disdained payment. 32 The adulterous wife receives, instead of her husband, payment. 33 All harlots receive gifts. But you rather bestowed your gifts on all your lovers, bribing them to come to you from all sides for your harlotry. 34 Thus in your harlotry you were different from all other women. No one sought you out for prostitution. Since you gave payment instead of receiving it, how different you were!

35 Therefore, harlot, hear the word of the LORD! 36 Thus says the Lord GOD: Because you poured out your lust and revealed your nakedness in your harlotry with your lovers and abominable idols, and because you sacrificed the life-blood of your children to them, 37* I will now gather together all your lovers whom you tried to please, whether you loved them or loved them not; I will gather them against you from all sides and expose you naked for them to see. 38 I will inflict on you the sentence of adulteresses and murderesses; I will wreak fury and jealousy upon you. 39 I will hand you over to them to tear down your platform and demolish your dais; they shall strip you of your garments and take away your splendid ornaments, leaving you stark naked. 40 They shall lead an assembly against you to stone you and hack you with their swords. 41* They shall burn your apartments with fire and inflict punishments on you while many women look on. Thus I will put an end to your harlotry, and you shall never again give payment. 42 When I have wreaked my fury upon you I will cease to be jealous of you, I will be quiet and no longer vexed. 43 Because you did not remember what happened when you were a girl, but enraged me with all these things, therefore in return I am bringing down your conduct upon your head, says the Lord GOD. For did you not add lewdness to the rest of your abominable deeds?

44 See, everyone who is fond of proverbs will say of you, 'Like mother, like daughter.' 45† Yes, you are the true daughter of the mother who spurned her husband and children, and you are a true sister to those who spurned their husbands and children— your mother was a Hittite and your father an Amorite. 46† Your elder sister was Samaria with her daughters, living to the north of you; and your younger sister, living to the south of you, was Sodom with her daughters. 47 Yet not only in their ways did you walk, and act as abominably as they did; in a very short time you became more corrupt in all your ways than they. 48 As I live, says the Lord GOD, I swear that your sister Sodom, with her daughters, has not done as you and your daughters have done! 49* And look at the guilt of your sister Sodom: she and her daughters were proud, sated with food, complacent in their prosperity, and they gave no help to the poor and needy. 50 Rather, they became haughty and committed abominable crimes in my presence; then, as you have seen, I removed them. 51 Samaria did not commit half your sins! You have done more abominable things than they, and have even made your sisters appear just, with all the abominable deeds you have done. 52 You, then, bear your shame; you are an argument in favor of your sisters! In view of your sinful deeds, more abominable than theirs, they appear just in

EZ

---

† **16, 20f:** Human sacrifice was introduced under Judah's impious kings; cf 2 Kgs 16, 3; 17, 17; Jer 7, 31.

16, 24: *A platform and a dais:* associated with ritual prostitution, which the Israelites borrowed from Canaanite practice.

16, 45: *True daughter of the mother:* Jerusalem has followed in the footsteps of its heathen forebears; cf v 3.

16, 46: *Your elder sister was Samaria:* Samaria can be called an elder sister in view of the relatively greater importance of the northern kingdom, Israel, during most of Old Testament history. Also, the relatively insignificant Sodom of ancient history can be called your younger sister.

*
16, 20: Ez 20, 26.31; 23, 37ff;	21, 6; 23, 10.
Lv 18, 21; 20, 2; Dt	**16, 25:** Ez 23, 8; Is 57, 7; Jer
12, 31; 18, 10; 2 Kgs	2, 20; 3, 2; 5, 7; 13,
21, 6; 23, 10; 24, 4;	27; Hos 2, 4; 4, 13.
Jer 7, 31; 19, 5; 32, 34;	**16, 37:** Ez 23, 10.
Mi 6, 7.	**16, 41:** 2 Kgs 25, 9.
16, 21: 2 Kgs 16, 3; 17, 17;	**16, 49:** Gn 19, 24.

comparison with you. Blush for shame, and bear the shame of having made your sisters appear just. 53 I will restore their fortunes, the fortune of Sodom and her daughters and of Samaria and her daughters [and I will restore your fortune along with them], 54 that you may bear your shame and be disgraced for all the comfort you brought them. 55 Yes, your sisters, Sodom and her daughters, Samaria and her daughters, shall return to their former state [you and your daughters shall return to your former state]. 56 Was not your sister Sodom kept in bad repute by you while you felt proud of yourself, 57 before your wickedness became evident? Now you are like her, reproached by the Edomites and all your neighbors, despised on all sides by the Philistines. 58 The penalty of your lewdness and your abominations—you must bear it all, says the LORD.

59 For thus speaks the Lord GOD: I will deal with you according to what you have done, you who despised your oath, breaking a covenant. 60 Yet I will remember the covenant I made with you when you were a girl, and I will set up an everlasting covenant with you. 61 Then you shall remember your conduct and be ashamed when I take your sisters, those older and younger than you, and give them to you as daughters, even though I am not bound by my covenant with you. 62 For I will re-establish my covenant with you, that you may know that I am the LORD, 63 that you may remember and be covered with confusion, and that you may be utterly silenced for shame when I pardon you for all you have done, says the Lord GOD.

The Eagles and the Vine

17 1 Thus the word of the LORD came to me: 2 Son of man, propose a riddle, and speak this proverb to the house of Israel: 3 Thus speaks the Lord GOD:

The great eagle, with great wings, with
    long pinions,
    with thick plumage, many-hued, came
    to Lebanon.
He took the crest of the cedar,
4   tearing off its topmost branch,
And brought it to a land of tradesmen,
    set it in a city of merchants.
5   Then he took some seed of the land,
    and planted it in a seedbed;
A shoot by plentiful waters,
    like a willow he placed it,

6   To sprout and grow up a vine,
    dense and low-lying,
Its branches turned toward him,
    its roots lying under him.
Thus it became a vine, produced
    branches
    and put forth shoots.
7   But there was another great eagle,
    great of wing, rich in plumage;
To him this vine bent its roots,
    sent out its branches,
That he might water it more freely
    than the bed where it was planted.
8   In a fertile field by plentiful waters it
    was planted,
    to grow branches, bear fruit,
    and become a majestic vine.

9 Say: Thus says the Lord GOD: Can it prosper? Will he not rather tear it out by the roots and strip off its fruit, so that all its green growth will wither when he pulls it up by the roots? [No need of a mighty arm or many people to do this.] 10 True, it is planted, but will it prosper? Will it not rather wither, when touched by the east wind, in the bed where it grew?

11† Thus the word of the LORD came to me: 12 Son of man, say now to the rebellious house: Do you not understand what this means? It is this: The king of Babylon came to Jerusalem and took away its king and princes with him to Babylon. 13 Then he selected a man of the royal line with whom he made a covenant, binding him under oath, while removing the nobles of the land, 14 so that the kingdom would remain a modest one, without aspirations, and would keep his covenant and obey him. 15 But this man rebelled against him, sending envoys to Egypt to obtain horses and a great army. Can he prosper? Can he who does such things escape? Can he break a covenant and still go free? 16 As I live, says the Lord GOD, in the home of the king who set him up to rule, whose oath he spurned, whose covenant with him he broke, there in Babylon I swear he shall die! 17 When ramps are cast up and siege towers are built for the destruction of many lives, he shall not be saved in the conflict by Pharaoh with a great army and numerous troops. 18 He spurned his oath, breaking his covenant. Though he gave his hand in pledge, he did all these things. He shall not escape!

19 Therefore say: Thus says the Lord GOD: As I live, my oath which he spurned, my covenant which he broke, I swear to bring down upon his

---

† **17, 11–21:** These verses explain the foregoing allegory. In 597 B.C. Nebuchadnezzar removed King Jehoiachin and took him into exile; in his place he set Zedekiah, Jehoiachin's uncle, on the throne and received from him the oath of loyalty. But Zedekiah was beguiled into rebellion by Pharaoh Hophra of Egypt, and thereby merited punishment; cf 2 Kgs 24, 10—25, 7.

head. 20* I will spread my net over him, and he shall be taken in my snare. I will bring him to Babylon and enter into judgment with him there over his breaking faith with me. 21 All the crack troops among his forces shall fall by the sword, and the survivors shall be scattered in every direction. Thus you shall know that I, the LORD, have spoken.

22† Therefore say: Thus says the Lord GOD:

I, too, will take from the crest of the cedar,
   from its topmost branches tear off a
     tender shoot,
And plant it on a high and lofty mountain;
23   on the mountain heights of Israel I will
     plant it.
It shall put forth branches and bear fruit,
   and become a majestic cedar.
Birds of every kind shall dwell beneath it,
   every winged thing in the shade of its boughs.
24 And all the trees of the field shall know
   that I, the LORD,
Bring low the high tree,
   lift high the lowly tree,
Wither up the green tree,
   and make the withered tree bloom.

As I, the LORD, have spoken, so will I do.

Personal Responsibility

18 1 Thus the word of the LORD came to me: Son of man, 2*† what is the meaning of this proverb that you recite in the land of Israel:

"Fathers have eaten green grapes,
   thus their children's teeth are on edge"?

3 As I live, says the Lord GOD: I swear that there shall no longer be anyone among you who will repeat this proverb in Israel. 4 For all lives are mine; the life of the father is like the life of the son, both are mine; only the one who sins shall die.

5 If a man is virtuous—if he does what is right and just, 6† if he does not eat on the mountains, nor raise his eyes to the idols of the house of Israel; if he does not defile his neighbor's wife, nor have relations with a woman in her menstrual period; 7* if he oppresses no one, gives back the pledge received for a debt, commits no robbery; if he gives food to the hungry and clothes the naked; 8 if he does not lend at interest nor exact usury; if he holds off from evildoing, judges fairly between a man and his opponent; 9 if he lives by my statutes and is careful to observe my ordinances, that man is virtuous—he shall surely live, says the Lord GOD.

LIVE IT!

❗ Individuals are Responsible for their Behavior!

Ezekiel, chapter 18, begins with a popular proverb from Ezekiel's time that implies that children are destined to bear the burden of their parents' actions. Ezekiel goes on to explain how this is not so. He emphasizes individual responsibility for our actions. He discourages fatalistic beliefs that we will somehow suffer for the sins of our ancestors (verse 20) and that parents are responsible for the sins of their children. Ezekiel calls the people of his time—and us—to overcome immature attitudes that blame God or others for our personal faults and sins.

- In what areas do you need to assume responsibility for your actions?
- Pray for God's help in abandoning immature attitudes that blame others and prevent you from assuming personal responsibility for your actions.

▶ Ez 18, 1–32

17, 22f: *I, too, will take from the crest of the cedar . . . plant it:* the Lord will restore Israel under a messianic King from the same Davidic dynasty.

18, 2: *Fathers . . . on edge:* a proverb by which the people claimed that they were being punished for their ancestors' sins rather than for their own; cf Jer 31, 29.

18, 6: *Eat on the mountains:* partake of ritual meals at the heathen high places.

17, 20: Ez 12, 13; 32, 3.   18, 7: Is 58, 7; Mt 25, 35.
18, 2: Jer 13, 29.

10 But if he begets a son who is a thief, a murderer, or who does any of these things 11 (though the father does none of them), a son who eats on the mountains, defiles the wife of his neighbor, 12 oppresses the poor and needy, commits robbery, does not give back a pledge, raises his eyes to idols, does abominable things, 13 lends at interest and exacts usury—this son certainly shall not live. Because he practiced all these abominations, he shall surely die; his death shall be his own fault.

14 On the other hand, if a man begets a son who, seeing all the sins his father commits, yet fears and does not imitate him; 15 a son who does not eat on the mountains, or raise his eyes to the idols of the house of Israel, or defile his neighbor's wife; 16 who does not oppress anyone, or exact a pledge, or commit robbery; who gives his food to the hungry and clothes the naked; 17 who holds off from evildoing, accepts no interest or usury, but keeps my ordinances and lives by my statutes—this one shall not die for the sins of his father, but shall surely live. 18 Only the father, since he violated rights, and robbed, and did what was not good among his people, shall in truth die for his sins. 19 You ask: "Why is not the son charged with the guilt of his father?" Because the son has done what is right and just, and has been careful to observe all my statutes, he shall surely live. 20* Only the one who sins shall die. The son shall not be charged with the guilt of his father, nor shall the father be charged with the guilt of his son. The virtuous man's virtue shall be his own, as the wicked man's wickedness shall be his.

21 But if the wicked man turns away from all the sins he committed, if he keeps all my statutes and does what is right and just, he shall surely live, he shall not die. 22 None of the crimes he committed shall be remembered against him; he shall live because of the virtue he has practiced. 23* Do I indeed derive any pleasure from the death of the wicked? says the Lord GOD. Do I not rather rejoice when he turns from his evil way that he may live?

24 And if the virtuous man turns from the path of virtue to do evil, the same kind of abominable things that the wicked man does, can he do this and still live? None of his virtuous deeds shall be remembered, because he has broken faith and committed sin; because of this, he shall die. 25* You say, "The LORD's way is not fair!" Hear now, house of Israel: Is it my way that is unfair or, rather, are not your ways unfair? 26 When a virtuous man turns away from virtue to commit iniquity, and dies, it is because of the iniquity he committed that he must

die. 27 But if a wicked man, turning from the wickedness he has committed, does what is right and just, he shall preserve his life; 28 since he has turned away from all the sins which he committed, he shall surely live, he shall not die. 29 And yet the house of Israel says, "The LORD's way is not fair!" Is it my way that is not fair, house of Israel, or rather, is it not that your ways are not fair?

30* Therefore I will judge you, house of Israel, each one according to his ways, says the Lord GOD. Turn and be converted from all your crimes, that they may be no cause of guilt for you. 31 Cast away from you all the crimes you have committed, and make for yourselves a new heart and a new spirit. Why should you die, O house of Israel? 32* For I have no pleasure in the death of anyone who dies, says the Lord GOD. Return and live!

19

1 As for you, son of man, raise a lamentation over the prince of Israel:

Allegory of the Lions†

2   What a lioness was your mother,
    a lion of lions!
  Among young lions she couched
    to rear her whelps.
3   One whelp she raised up,
    a young lion he became;
  He learned to seize prey,
    men he devoured.
4   Then nations raised cries against him,
    in their pit he was caught;
  They took him away with hooks
    to the land of Egypt.
5   Then she saw that in vain she had waited,
    her hope was destroyed.
  She took another of her whelps,
    him she made a young lion.
6   He prowled among the lions,
    a young lion he became;
  He learned to seize prey,
    men he devoured;
7   He ravaged their strongholds,
    their cities he wasted.
  The land and all in it were appalled
    at the noise of his roar.
8   Nations laid out against him
    snares all about him;
  They spread their net to take him,
    in their pit he was caught.
9   They put him in a cage and took him away
    to the king of Babylon,

---

† 19, 2–9: The meaning of this allegory is uncertain. Probably the two young lions are Jehoahaz and Zedekiah, sons of the same mother, who were deported to Egypt and Babylonia respectively. Cf 2 Kgs 23, 31–34; 24, 18ff.

* 18, 20: Dt 24, 16; 2 Kgs 14, 6; 2 Chr 25, 4.
18, 23: Ez 33, 11; 2 Pt 3, 9.
18, 25: Ez 33, 20.
18, 30: Mt 3, 2; Lk 3, 3.
18, 32: Ez 18, 23; 33, 11; 2 Pt 3, 9.

So that his voice would not be heard
  on the mountains of Israel.

Allegory of the Vine Branch

10† Your mother was like a vine
  planted by the water;
Fruitful and branchy was she
  because of the abundant water.
11 One strong branch she put out
  as a royal scepter.
Stately was her height
  amid the dense foliage;
Notably tall was she
  with her many clusters.
12* But she was torn up in fury
  and flung to the ground;
The east wind withered her up,
  her fruit was torn off;
Then her strong branch withered up,
  fire devoured it.
13 So now she is planted in the desert,
  in a land dry and parched,
14 For fire came out of the branch
  and devoured her shoots;
She is now without a strong branch,
  a ruler's scepter.

This is a lamentation and serves as a lamentation.

Israel's History of Infidelity

20 ¹† In the seventh year, on the tenth day of the fifth month, some of the elders of Israel came to consult the LORD and sat down before me. ² Then the word of the LORD came to me: ³ Son of man, speak with the elders of Israel and say to them: Thus says the Lord GOD: Have you come to consult me? As I live! I swear I will not allow myself to be consulted by you, says the Lord GOD.

⁴ Will you judge them? Will you judge, son of man? Make known to them the abominations of their ancestors ⁵ in these words: Thus speaks the Lord GOD: The day I chose Israel, I swore to the descendants of the house of Jacob; in the land of Egypt I revealed myself to them and swore: I am the LORD, your God. ⁶ That day I swore to bring them out of the land of Egypt to the land I had scouted for them, a land flowing with milk and honey, a jewel among all lands. ⁷ Then I said to them: Throw away, each of you, the detestable things that have held your eyes; do not defile yourselves with the idols of Egypt: I am the LORD, your God.

⁸ But they rebelled against me and refused to listen to me; none of them threw away the detestable things that had held their eyes, they did not abandon the idols of Egypt. Then I thought of pouring out my fury on them and spending my anger on them there in the land of Egypt; ⁹ but I acted for my name's sake, that it should not be profaned in the sight of the nations among whom they were, in whose presence I had made myself known to them, revealing that I would bring them out of the land of Egypt. ¹⁰ Therefore I led them out of the land of Egypt and brought them into the desert. ¹¹* Then I gave them my statutes and made known to them my ordinances, which everyone must keep, to have life through them. ¹²* I also gave them my sabbaths to be a sign between me and them, to show that it was I, the LORD, who made them holy.

¹³ But the house of Israel rebelled against me in the desert. They did not observe my statutes, and they despised my ordinances that bring life to those who keep them. My sabbaths, too, they desecrated grievously. Then I thought of pouring out my fury on them in the desert to put an end to them, ¹⁴ but I acted for my name's sake, that it should not be profaned in the sight of the nations in whose presence I had brought them out. ¹⁵ Nevertheless I swore to them in the desert not to bring them to the land I had given them, a land flowing with milk and honey, a jewel among all lands. ¹⁶ So much were their hearts devoted to their idols, they had not lived by my statutes, but despised my ordinances and desecrated my sabbaths. ¹⁷ But I looked on them with pity, not wanting to destroy them, so I did not put an end to them in the desert.

¹⁸ Then I said to their children in the desert: Do not observe the statutes of your parents or keep their ordinances; do not defile yourselves with their idols. ¹⁹ I am the LORD, your God: observe my statutes and be careful to keep my ordinances; ²⁰ keep holy my sabbaths, as a sign between me and you to show that I am the LORD, your God. ²¹ But their children rebelled against me: they did not observe my statutes or keep my ordinances that bring life to those who observe them, and my sabbaths they desecrated. Then I thought of pouring out my fury on them, of spending my anger on them in the desert; ²² but I stayed my hand, acting for my name's sake, lest it be profaned in the sight of the nations in whose presence I brought them out. ²³ Nevertheless I swore to them in the desert that I would disperse them among the nations and scatter them over foreign lands; ²⁴ for they did not keep my ordinances, but despised my statutes and desecrated my sabbaths with eyes only for the idols of

---

19, 10–14: *A vine:* Judah. *One strong branch:* the Davidic king.
20, 1: *The seventh year, on the tenth day of the fifth month:* August 14, 591 B.C.

19, 12: Hos 13, 15.
20, 11: Lv 18, 5; Rom 10, 5.

20, 12: Ex 20, 8; 31, 13; Dt 5, 12.

their fathers. [25]† Therefore I gave them statutes that were not good, and ordinances through which they could not live. [26] I let them become defiled by their gifts, by their immolation of every first-born, so as to make them an object of horror.

[27] Therefore speak to the house of Israel, son of man, and tell them: Thus says the Lord GOD: In this way also your fathers blasphemed me, breaking faith with me: [28] when I had brought them to the land I had sworn to give them, and they saw all its high hills and leafy trees, there they offered their sacrifices [there they brought their offensive offerings], there they sent up appeasing odors, and there they poured out their libations. [29] I asked them: To what sort of high place do you betake yourselves?—and so they call it a high place even to the present day. [30] Therefore say to the house of Israel: Thus says the Lord GOD: Will you defile yourselves like your fathers? Will you lust after their detestable idols? [31] By offering your gifts, by making your children pass through the fire, you defile yourselves with all your idols even to this day. Shall I let myself be consulted by you, house of Israel? As I live! says the Lord GOD: I swear I will not let myself be consulted by you.

[32] What you are thinking of shall never happen: "We shall be like the nations, like the peoples of foreign lands, serving wood and stone." [33] As I live, says the Lord GOD, with a mighty hand and outstretched arm, with poured-out wrath, I swear I will be king over you! [34] With a mighty hand and outstretched arm, with poured-out wrath, I will bring you out from the nations and gather you from the countries over which you are scattered; [35]† then I will lead you to the desert of the peoples, where I will enter into judgment with you face to face. [36] Just as I entered into judgment with your fathers in the desert of the land of Egypt, so will I enter into judgment with you, says the Lord GOD. [37] I will count you with the staff and bring back but a small number. [38] I will separate from you those who have rebelled and transgressed against me; from the land where they sojourned as aliens I will bring them out, but they shall not return to the land of Israel. Thus you shall know that I am the LORD.

[39] As for you, house of Israel, thus says the Lord GOD: Come, each one of you, destroy your idols! Then listen to me, and never again profane my holy name with your gifts and your idols. [40] For on my holy mountain, on the mountain height of Israel, says the Lord GOD, there the whole house of Israel without exception shall worship me; there I will

accept them, and there I will claim your tributes and the first fruits of your offerings, and all that you dedicate. [41] As a pleasing odor I will accept you, when I have brought you from among the nations and gathered you out of the countries over which you were scattered; and by means of you I will manifest my holiness in the sight of the nations. [42] Thus you shall know that I am the LORD, when I bring you back to the land of Israel, the land which I swore to give to your fathers. [43] There you shall recall your conduct and all the deeds by which you defiled yourselves; and you shall loathe yourselves because of all the evil things you did. [44] And you shall know that I am the LORD when I deal with you thus, for my name's sake, and not according to your evil conduct and corrupt actions, O house of Israel, says the Lord GOD.

The Sword of the Lord

21 [1] Thus the word of the LORD came to me: [2]† Son of man, look southward, preach toward the south, and prophesy against the forest of the southern land. [3] Hear the word of the LORD! you shall say to the southern forest. Thus says the Lord GOD: See! I am kindling a fire in you that shall devour all trees, the green as well as the dry. The blazing flame shall not be quenched, but from south to north every face shall be scorched by it. [4] Everyone shall see that I, the LORD, have kindled it, and it shall not be quenched.

[5] But I said, "Alas! Lord GOD, they say to me, 'Is not this the one who is forever spinning parables?' " [6] Then the word of the LORD came to me: [7] Son of man, look toward Jerusalem, preach against their sanctuary, and prophesy against the land of Israel, [8]† saying to the land of Israel: Thus says the LORD: See! I am coming at you; I will draw my sword from its sheath and cut off from you the virtuous and the wicked. [9] Thus my sword shall leave its sheath against everyone from south to north, [10] and everyone shall know that I, the LORD, have drawn my sword from its sheath, and it shall not be sheathed again.

Act Symbolic of the City's Fall

[11] As for you, son of man, groan! with shattered strength groan bitterly while they look on. [12]† And when they ask you, "Why are you groaning?", you shall say: Because of a report; when it comes every heart shall fail, every hand shall fall helpless, every spirit shall be daunted, and every knee shall run with water. See, it is coming, it is here! says the Lord GOD.

20, 25f: *I gave them statutes that were not good:* the Lord permitted them to adopt pagan practices, including the abominable sacrifice of their newborn infants, which could only merit their destruction. See note on Ez 14, 9.

20, 35–38: Exile in the pagan lands will serve the same purpose as the desert journey after the Exodus from Egypt: the rebel-

lious will be eliminated, and only a remnant will survive.

21, 2ff: The southern kingdom, Judah, is likened to a forest about to be burned; cf Jer 21, 14.

21, 8: *Cut off from you the virtuous and the wicked:* a more complete devastation of Jerusalem than that described in Ez 9, 6.

21, 12: *A report:* the news of the fall of Jerusalem; cf Ez 33, 21f.

Song of the Sword

13 Thus the word of the LORD came to me: 14 Son of man, prophesy! say: Thus says the LORD:

A sword, a sword has been sharpened,
  a sword, a sword has been burnished:
15 To work slaughter has it been sharpened,
  to flash lightning has it been burnished.
Why should I now withdraw it?
  You have spurned the rod and every
    judgment!
16 I have given it over to the burnisher
  that he might hold it in his hand,
A sword sharpened and burnished
  to be put in the hand of a slayer.
17† Cry out and wail, son of man,
  for it is destined for my people;
It is for all the princes of Israel,
  victims of the sword with my people.

Therefore, slap your thigh, 18 for the sword has been tested; and why should it not be so? says the Lord GOD, since you have spurned the rod.

19   As for you, son of man, prophesy,
    brushing one hand against the other:
While the sword is doubled and tripled,
  this sword of slaughter,
This great sword of slaughter
  which threatens all around,
20   That every heart may tremble;
    for many will be the fallen.
At all their gates
  I have appointed the sword for slaughter,
Fashioned to flash lightning,
  burnished for slaughter.
21   Cleave to the right! destroy!
    to the left! wherever your edge is turned.

22† Then I, too, shall brush one hand against the other and wreak my fury. I, the LORD, have spoken.

Nebuchadnezzar at the Crossroads

23 Thus the word of the LORD came to me: 24 Son of man, make for yourself two roads over which the sword of the king of Babylon can come. Both roads shall lead out from the same land. Then put a sign-post at the head of each road, 25 so that the sword can come to Rabbah of the Ammonites or to Judah's capital, Jerusalem. 26† For at the fork where the two roads divide stands the king of Babylon, divining; he has shaken the arrows, inquired of the teraphim, inspected the liver. 27† In his right hand is the divining arrow marked "Jerusalem," bidding him to give the order for slaying, to raise his voice in the battle cry, to post battering rams at the gates, to cast up a ramp, to build a siege tower. 28 In their eyes this is but a lying oracle; yet they are bound by the oaths they have sworn, and the arrow taken in hand marks their guilt.

29 Therefore thus says the Lord GOD: Because you have drawn attention to your guilt, with your crimes laid bare and your sinfulness in all your wicked deeds revealed (because attention has been drawn to you), you shall be taken in hand. 30 And as for you, depraved and wicked prince of Israel, whose day is coming when your life of crime will be ended, 31 thus says the Lord GOD: Off with the turban and away with the crown! Nothing shall be as it was! Up with the low and down with the high! 32 Twisted, twisted, twisted will I leave it; it shall not be the same until he comes who has the claim against the city; and to him I will hand it over.

Against the Ammonites

33† As for you, son of man, prophesy: Thus says the Lord GOD against the Ammonites and their insults: A sword, a sword is drawn for slaughter, burnished to consume and to flash lightning, 34 because you planned with false visions and lying divinations to lay it on the necks of depraved and wicked men whose day has come when their crimes are at an end. 35 Return it to its sheath! In the place where you were created, in the land of your origin, I will judge you. 36 I will pour out my indignation upon you, breathing my fiery wrath upon you; I will hand you over to ravaging men, artisans of destruction. 37 You shall be fuel for the fire, your blood shall flow throughout the land. You shall not be remembered, for I, the LORD, have spoken.

Crimes of Jerusalem

22 1 Thus the word of the LORD came to me: 2 You, son of man, would you judge, would you judge the bloody city? Then make known all her abominations, 3 and say: Thus says the Lord GOD: Woe to the city which sheds blood within herself so that her time has come, and which

---

21, 17: *Slap your thigh:* a gesture signifying grief and dread.
21, 22: *Brush one hand against the other:* a gesture signifying the rejection of responsibility; cf Ez 22, 13; Nm 24, 10.
21, 26: Three forms of divination are mentioned: arrow divination, consisting in the use of differently marked arrows extracted or shaken from a case at random; the consultation of the teraphim or household idols; and liver divination, scrutiny of the configurations of the livers of newly slaughtered animals, a common form of divination in Mesopotamia.

21, 27f: An arrow marked "Jerusalem" is picked out, which marks the guilt of the city's inhabitants for having broken their oath of allegiance to Nebuchadnezzar.
21, 33–37: In the preceding section Nebuchadnezzar is represented as deciding whether to attack Jerusalem or Rabbath-Ammon. As it happened, Jerusalem was chosen for attack; later, however, the Chaldeans also invaded Ammon. The present oracle against Ammon is inserted here, rather than in chapters 25–32, in order to complement the oracle against Jerusalem.

has made idols for her own defilement. ⁴ By the blood which you shed you have been made guilty, and with the idols you made you have become defiled; you have brought on your day, so that the end of your years has come. Therefore I make you an object of scorn to the nations and a laughingstock to all foreign lands. ⁵ Those near you and those far off shall deride you because of your foul reputation and your great perversity. ⁶ See! the princes of Israel, family by family, are in you only for bloodshed; ⁷ Within you, father and mother are despised; in your midst, they extort from the resident alien; within you, they oppress orphans and widows. ⁸ What is holy to me you have spurned, and my sabbaths you have desecrated. ⁹ There are those in you who slander to cause bloodshed; within you are those who feast on the mountains; in your midst are those who do lewd things. ¹⁰ In you are those who uncover the nakedness of their fathers, and in you those who coerce women in their menstrual period. ¹¹* There are those in you who do abominable things with the wives of their neighbors, men who defile their daughters-in-law by incest, men who coerce their sisters, the daughters of their own fathers. ¹² There are those in you who take bribes to shed blood. You exact interest and usury; you despoil your neighbors violently; and me you have forgotten, says the Lord GOD.

¹³ See, I am brushing one hand against the other because of the unjust profits you have made and because of the blood shed in your midst. ¹⁴ Can your heart remain firm, will your hands be strong, in the days when I deal with you? I, the LORD, have spoken, and I will act. ¹⁵ I will disperse you among the nations and scatter you over foreign lands, so that I may purge your uncleanness. ¹⁶ In you I will allow myself to be profaned in the eyes of the nations; thus you shall know that I am the LORD.

¹⁷ Thus the word of the LORD came to me: ¹⁸ Son of man, the house of Israel has become dross for me. All of them are bronze and tin, iron and lead [in the midst of a furnace]: dross from silver have they become. ¹⁹ Therefore thus says the Lord GOD: Because all of you have become dross, therefore I must gather you together within Jerusalem. ²⁰ Just as silver, bronze, iron, lead, and tin are gathered into a furnace and smelted in the roaring flames, so I will gather you together in my furious wrath, put you in, and smelt you. ²¹ When I have assembled you, I will blast you with the fire of my anger and smelt you with it. ²² You shall be smelted by it just as silver is smelted in a furnace. Thus you shall know that I, the Lord, have poured out my fury on you.

²³ Thus the word of the LORD came to me: ²⁴ Son of man, say to her: You are a land unrained on [that is, not rained on] at the time of my fury. ²⁵ Her princes are like roaring lions that tear prey; they devour people, seizing their wealth and precious things, and make widows of many within her. ²⁶ Her priests violate my law and profane what is holy to me; they do not distinguish between the sacred and the profane, nor teach the difference between the unclean and the clean; they pay no attention to my sabbaths, so that I have been profaned in their midst. ²⁷* Her nobles within her are like wolves that tear prey, shedding blood and destroying lives to get unjust gain. ²⁸ Her prophets cover them with whitewash, pretending to visions that are false and performing lying divinations, saying, "Thus says the Lord GOD," although the LORD has not spoken. ²⁹ The people of the land practice extortion and commit robbery; they afflict the poor and the needy, and oppress the resident alien without justice. ³⁰ Thus I have searched among them for someone who could build a wall or stand in the breach before me to keep me from destroying the land; but I found no one. ³¹ Therefore I have poured out my fury upon them; with my fiery wrath I have consumed them; I have brought down their conduct upon their heads, says the Lord GOD.

The Two Sisters

23 ¹ Thus the word of the LORD came to me: ² Son of man, there were two women, daughters of the same mother, ³ who even as young girls played the harlot in Egypt. There the Egyptians caressed their bosoms and fondled their virginal breasts. ⁴† Oholah was the name of the elder, and the name of her sister was Oholibah. They became mine and bore sons and daughters. [As for their names: Samaria is Oholah, and Jerusalem is Oholibah.] ⁵ Oholah became a harlot faithless to me; she lusted after her lovers, the Assyrians, warriors ⁶ dressed in purple, governors and officers, all of them attractive young men, knights mounted on horses. ⁷ Thus she gave herself as a harlot to them, to all the elite of the Assyrians, and she defiled herself with all those for whom she lusted [with all their idols]. ⁸ She did not give up the harlotry which she had begun in Egypt, when they had lain with her as a young girl, fondling her virginal breasts and pouring out their impurities on her. ⁹ Therefore I handed her over to her lovers, the Assyrians for whom she had lusted. ¹⁰* They exposed her nakedness, her sons and daughters they took away, and herself they slew with the sword.

---

† **23, 4:** *Oholah . . . Oholibah:* symbolic names. The first, standing for Samaria, may be read to mean "her own tent"; the latter, standing for Jerusalem, means "My tent is in her." The references seem to be to the schismatic temple and cult of the Lord in Samaria, as op-

posed to their authentic counterpart in Jerusalem.

* 22, 11: Jer 5, 7f.   23, 10: Ez 16, 37.
22, 27: Mi 3, 11; Zep 3, 3.

Irresponsible Children

Raising children is a demanding job. In teaching their children about life, parents try to help them be responsible—to accept the consequences of their actions. For example, a parent might say: "You threw the ball and broke the window. The wind had nothing to do with it! Now, what are you going to do about it?"

Chapters 13–24 of Ezekiel contain prophecies, allegories, fables, and symbolic actions, all intended to encourage the people of Judah to take responsibility for their sinful actions. In a graphic allegory in chapter 23, the northern and southern kingdoms are compared to promiscuous daughters who will sleep with almost anyone who comes their way. God is using just about every possible means to say, "Take responsibility for your actions, my children, and live with the consequences!"

We are all like little children in that we are often tempted to ignore the consequences of our actions. For instance, we may think of cheating on homework as just a little wrong. But that wrong will catch up with us. It will lead to more cheating, in bigger things. By then, our "little" wrong could mean losing a job or destroying a relationship. If you want to please God, be honest in looking at the consequences of your actions and choose responsibly!

▶ Ez 23, 1–21

Thus she became a byword for women, for they punished her grievously.

11 Though her sister Oholibah saw all this, her lust was more depraved than her sister's, and she outdid her in harlotry. 12 She too lusted after the Assyrians, governors and officers, warriors impeccably clothed, knights mounted on horses, all of them attractive young men. 13 I saw that she had defiled herself. Both had gone down the same path, 14 yet she went further in her harlotry. When she saw men drawn on the wall, the images of Chaldeans drawn with vermillion, 15 with sashes girded about their waists, flowing turbans on their heads, all looking like chariot warriors, the portraits of Babylonians, natives of Chaldea, 16 she lusted for them; no sooner had she set eyes on them than she sent messengers to them in Chaldea. 17 Then the Babylonians came to her, to the love couch, and defiled her with their intercourse. As soon as she was defiled by them, she became disgusted with them. 18 Her harlotry was discovered and her shame was revealed, and I became disgusted with her as I had become disgusted with her sister. 19 But she played the harlot all the more, recalling the days of her girlhood, when she had been a harlot in the land of Egypt. 20 She lusted for the lechers of Egypt, whose members are like that of an ass, and whose heat is like those of stallions. 21 You yearned for the lewdness of your girlhood, when the Egyptians fondled your breasts, caressing your bosom. 22 Therefore, Oholibah, thus says the Lord GOD: I will now stir up your lovers against you, those with whom you are disgusted, and I will bring them against you from every side: 23† the men of Babylon and all of Chaldea, Pekod, Shoa and Koa, along with all those of Assyria, attractive young men, all of them governors and officers, charioteers and warriors, all of them horsemen. 24 They shall come against you from the north with chariots and wagons and many peoples. Shields, bucklers, and helmets they shall array against you everywhere. 25 I will leave it to them to judge, and they will judge you by their own ordinances. I will let loose my jealousy against you, so that they shall deal with you in fury, cutting off your nose and ears; and what is left of you shall fall by the sword. They shall take away your sons and daughters, and what is left of you shall be devoured by fire. 26 They shall strip off your clothes and seize your splendid ornaments. 27 I will put an end to your lewdness and to the harlotry you began in Egypt; you shall no longer look toward it, nor shall you remember Egypt again.

28 For thus says the Lord GOD: I am now handing you over to those whom you hate, to those who fill you with disgust. 29 They shall deal with you in hatred, seizing all that you have worked for and leaving you stark naked, so that your indecent nakedness is exposed. Your lewdness and harlotry 30 have brought these things upon you, because you played the harlot with the nations by defiling yourself with their idols.

---

† **23, 23:** *Pekod, Shoa and Koa:* peoples living about the Tigris, part of "greater Babylonia."

31 Because you followed in the path of your sister, I will hand you her cup. 32 Thus says the Lord GOD:

The cup of your sister you shall drink,
    so wide and deep, which holds so much,
33   Filled with destruction and grief,
    a cup of dismay, the cup of your sister.

34 You shall drain it dry, and gnaw at the very sherds of the cup, and you shall tear out your breasts; for I have spoken, says the Lord GOD. 35 Therefore thus says the Lord GOD: Because you have forgotten me and cast me behind your back, it is for you to bear the penalty of your lewdness and harlotry.

36 Then the LORD said to me: Son of man, would you judge Oholah and Oholibah? Then make known to them their abominations. 37 For they committed adultery, and blood is on their hands. They committed adultery with their idols; to feed them they immolated the children they had borne me. 38 [This, too, they did to me: they defiled my sanctuary and desecrated my sabbaths. 39 On the very day they slew their children for their idols, they entered my sanctuary to desecrate it. Thus they acted within my house.] 40† Moreover, they sent for men who had to come from afar, to whom messengers were sent. And so they came—and for them you bathed yourself, painted your eyes, and put on ornaments. 41 You sat on a couch prepared for them, with a table spread before it, on which you had set my incense and oil. 42 Then was heard the shout of a carefree mob in the city, and these were men brought in from the desert, who put bracelets on the women's arms and splendid diadems on their heads. 43 So I said: "Oh, this woman jaded with adulteries! Now they will commit whoredom with her, and as for her. . . ." 44 And indeed they did come to her as men come to a harlot. Thus they came to Oholah and Oholibah, the lewd women. 45 But just men shall punish them with the sentence meted out to adulteresses and murderesses, for they have committed adultery, and blood is on their hands.

46 Thus says the Lord GOD: Summon an assembly against them, and deliver them over to terror and plunder. 47 The assembly shall stone them and hack them to pieces with their swords. They shall slay their sons and daughters, and burn their houses with fire. 48 Thus I will put an end to lewdness in the land, and all the women will be warned not to imitate your lewdness. 49 They shall inflict on you the penalty of your lewdness, and you shall pay for your sins of idolatry. Thus you shall know that I am the LORD.

Allegory of the Pot

24 1† On the tenth day of the tenth month, in the ninth year, the word of the LORD came to me: 2 Son of man, write down this date today, for this very day the king of Babylon has invested Jerusalem. 3† Propose this parable to the rebellious house: Thus says the Lord GOD:

Set up the pot, set it up,
    then pour in some water.
4   Put in it pieces of meat,
    all good pieces: thigh and shoulder;
Fill it with the choicest joints
5   taken from the pick of the flock.
Then pile the wood beneath it;
    bring to a boil these pieces
    and the joints that are in it.
6* Take out its pieces, one by one,
    without casting lots for it.

Therefore, thus says the Lord GOD: Woe to the bloody city, a pot containing rust, whose rust has not been removed. 7† For the blood she shed is in her midst; she poured it on the bare rock; she did not pour it out on the earth, to be covered with dust. 8 To work up my wrath, to excite my vengeance, she put her blood on the bare rock, not to be covered. 9 Therefore, thus says the Lord GOD:

I, too, will heap up a great bonfire,
10   piling on wood and kindling the fire,
Till the meat has been cooked,
    till the broth has boiled.

11 Then I will set the pot empty on the coals till its metal glows red hot, till the impurities in it melt, and its rust disappears. 12 Yet not even with fire will its great rust be removed. 13 Because you have sullied yourself with lewdness when I would have purified you, and you refused to be purified of your uncleanness, therefore you shall not be purified until I wreak my fury on you. 14 I, the LORD, have

---

† 23, 40: *Men who had to come from afar:* ambassadors from Assyria and Babylon. Alliances with these countries aided in the corruption of both Israel and Judah.

24, 1: *The tenth day of the tenth month, in the ninth year:* January 15, 588 B.C. The same date is given in Jer 52, 4.

24, 3ff: This present comparison of the inhabitants of Jerusalem to meat boiled in a pot symbolizes their punishment rather than their supposed protection as in Ez 11, 3.

† 24, 7: *Blood . . . to be covered with dust:* since blood was sacred to God, it had to be covered with earth (Lv 17, 13); the blood of a murdered man that was left uncovered cried to heaven for vengeance; cf Jb 16, 18; Gn 4, 10.

24, 6: Na 3, 1; Hb 2, 12.

spoken; it is coming, for I will bring it about without fail. I will not have pity nor repent. By your conduct and your deeds you shall be judged, says the Lord GOD.

Symbol of the Destruction of the Temple

15 Thus the word of the LORD came to me: 16 Son of man, by a sudden blow I am taking away from you the delight of your eyes, but do not mourn or weep or shed any tears. 17† Groan in silence, make no lament for the dead, bind on your turban, put your sandals on your feet, do not cover your beard, and do not eat the customary bread. 18 That evening my wife died, and the next morning I did as I had been commanded. 19 Then the people asked me, "Will you not tell us what all these things that you are doing mean for us?" I therefore spoke to the people that morning, 20 saying to them: Thus the word of the LORD came to me: 21 Say to the house of Israel: Thus says the Lord GOD: I will now desecrate my sanctuary, the stronghold of your pride, the delight of your eyes, the desire of your soul. The sons and daughters you left behind shall fall by the sword. 24 Ezekiel shall be a sign for you: all that he did you shall do when it happens. Thus you shall know that I am the LORD. 22† You shall do as I have done, not covering your beards nor eating the customary bread. 23 Your turbans shall remain on your heads, your sandals on your feet. You shall not mourn or weep, but you shall rot away because of your sins and groan one to another.

End of Ezekiel's Dumbness

25* As for you, son of man, truly, on the day I take away from them their bulwark, their glorious joy, the delight of their eyes, the desire of their soul, and the pride of their hearts, their sons and daughters, 26 that day the fugitive will come to you, that you may hear it for yourself; 27 that day your mouth shall be opened and you shall be dumb no longer. Thus you shall be a sign to them, and they shall know that I am the LORD.

III: Prophecies Against Foreign Nations

Against Ammon

25 1 Thus the word of the LORD came to me: 2 Son of man, turn toward the Ammonites and prophesy against them. 3* Say to the

Ammonites: Hear the word of the LORD! Thus says the Lord GOD: Because you cried out your joy over the desecration of my sanctuary, the devastation of the land of Israel, and the exile of the house of Judah, 4† therefore I will deliver you into the possession of the Easterners. They shall set up their encampments among you and pitch their tents; they shall eat your fruits and drink your milk. 5 I will make Rabbah a pasture for camels, and the villages of the Ammonites a resting place for flocks. Thus you shall know that I am the LORD.

6 For thus says the Lord GOD: Because you clapped your hands and stamped your feet, rejoicing most maliciously in your heart over the land of Israel, 7 therefore I will stretch out my hand against you. I will make you plunder for the nations, I will cut you off from the peoples, and remove you from the lands. I will destroy you, and thus you shall know that I am the LORD.

Against Moab

8* Thus says the Lord GOD: Because Moab said, "See! the house of Judah is like all other nations," 9† therefore I will clear the shoulder of Moab totally of its cities, the jewels of the land: Beth-jesimoth, Baalmeon, and Kiriathaim. 10 I will hand her over, along with the Ammonites, into the possession of the Easterners, that she may not be remembered among the peoples. 11 Thus I will execute judgment upon Moab, that they may know that I am the LORD.

Against Edom

12* Thus says the Lord GOD: Because Edom has taken vengeance on the house of Judah and has made itself grievously guilty by taking vengeance on them, 13 therefore thus says the Lord GOD: I will stretch out my hand against Edom and cut off from it man and beast. I will make it a waste from Teman to Dedan; they shall fall by the sword. 14 My vengeance upon Edom I will entrust to my people Israel, who will deal with Edom in accordance with my anger and my fury; thus they shall know my vengeance, says the Lord GOD.

Against the Philistines

15 Thus says the Lord GOD: Because the Philistines have acted revengefully, and have taken vengeance with destructive malice in their hearts,

---

24, 17: *The customary bread:* eaten as a mourning observance; cf Jer 16, 7. The other gestures here forbidden were also popular mourning customs.

24, 22f: The fall of the city will be so sudden and final that the exiles will have no time to go into mourning.

25, 4: *The Easterners:* nomadic tribes to the east of Ammon and Moab.

25, 9: *The shoulder of Moab:* the edge of the Moabite plateau.

24, 25ff: Ez 3, 22–27.
  25, 3: Jer 40, 14; 41, 10; 49, 2; Am 1, 13ff; Zep 2, 8ff.

25, 8: Sir 50, 26; Is 15, 1–9; 16, 1–14; Jer 48, 1–47; Am 2, 1ff; Zep 2, 8f.
25, 12ff: Ez 35, 1ff; Is 34, 5; Jer 49, 7–22; Jl 4, 19; Am 1, 11f; Ob 1–21.

with an undying enmity, [16]† therefore thus says the Lord GOD: See! I am stretching out my hand against the Philistines; I will cut off the Cherethites and wipe out the remnant on the seacoast. [17] I will execute great acts of vengeance on them, punishing them furiously. Thus they shall know that I am the LORD, when I wreak my vengeance on them.

Against the City of Tyre

26 [1] On the first day of the . . . month in the eleventh year, the word of the LORD came to me: [2] Son of man, because of what Tyre said of Jerusalem:

"Aha! it is broken, the gateway to the
  peoples;
now that it is ruined, its wealth reverts
  to me!"
[3]* therefore thus says the Lord GOD:
See! I am coming at you, Tyre;
  I will churn up against you many nations,
  even as the sea churns up its waves;
[4]† They shall destroy the walls of Tyre
  and raze her towers.
I will scrape the ground from her
  and leave her a bare rock;
[5] She shall be a drying place for nets
  in the midst of the sea.

I have spoken, says the Lord GOD: and she shall be booty for the nations. [6]† And her daughters on the mainland shall be slaughtered by the sword; thus they shall know that I am the LORD.

[7] For thus says the Lord GOD: I am now bringing up against Tyre from the north Nebuchadnezzar the king of Babylon, the king of kings, with horses and chariots, with cavalry and a great and mighty army.

[8] Your daughters on the mainland
  he shall slay with the sword;
He shall place a siege tower against you,
  cast up a ramp about you,
  and raise his shields against you.
[9] He shall pound your walls with battering-rams
  and break down your towers with
  his weapons.
[10] The surge of his horses shall cover you
  with dust,
  amid the noise of steeds, of wheels and
  of chariots.

Your walls shall shake as he enters your
  gates,
  even as one enters a city that is breached.
[11] With the hoofs of his horses
  he shall trample all your streets;
Your people he shall slay by the sword;
  your mighty pillars he shall pull to
  the ground.
[12] Your wealth shall be plundered,
  your merchandise pillaged;
Your walls shall be torn down,
  your precious houses demolished;
Your stones, your timber, and your clay
  shall be cast into the sea.
[13] I will put an end to the noise of your
  songs,
  and the sound of your lyres shall be heard
  no more.
[14] I will make you a bare rock;
  a drying place for nets shall you be.

Never shall you be rebuilt, for I have spoken, says the Lord GOD.

[15] Thus says the Lord GOD to Tyre: At the noise of your fall, at the groaning of the wounded, when the sword slays in your midst, shall not the isles quake? [16]† All the princes of the sea shall step down from their thrones, lay aside their robes, and strip off their embroidered garments. They shall be clothed in mourning and, sitting on the ground, they shall tremble at every moment and be horrified at you. [17] Then they shall utter a lament over you:

How have you perished, gone from the seas,
  city most prized!
Once she was mighty on the sea,
  she and her dwellers,
Who spread terror into all
  that dwelt by the sea.
[18] On this, the day of your fall,
  the islands quake!

The isles in the sea are terrified at your passing.

[19] For thus says the Lord GOD: When I make you a city desolate like cities that are no longer inhabited, when I churn up the abyss against you, and its mighty waters cover you, [20]† then I will thrust you down with those who descend into the pit, those of the bygone age; and I will make you dwell in the nether lands, in the everlasting ruins, with those

---

25, 16: *Cherethites:* a people forming part of the Philistine nation; cf Zep 2, 5.
26, 4f: *A bare rock:* the Tyre of Ezekiel's time was situated on a rocky island just off the Phoenician coast; it was not until the time of Alexander the Great that it was connected by a causeway to the mainland.
26, 6: *Her daughters:* tributary towns and villages on the mainland.

26, 16: *The princes of the sea:* the rulers of the islands and coastal cities leagued commercially with Tyre.
26, 20: *Those who descend into the pit:* the dead, pictured as dwelling in a place or cave of darkness.

26, 3: Is 26, 1–21; 47, 4; Jl 4,
  4f; Zec 9, 2ff.

who go down to the pit, so that you may never return to take your place in the land of the living. [21] I will make you a devastation, and you shall be no more; you shall be sought, but never again found, says the Lord GOD.

The Ship Tyre

27 [1] Thus the word of the LORD came to me: [2] As for you, son of man, utter a lament over Tyre, [3] and say to Tyre that is situated at the approaches of the sea, that brought the trade of the peoples to many a coastland: Thus says the Lord GOD:

> Tyre, you said, "I am a ship,
>   perfect in beauty."
[4] In the midst of the sea your builders
>   placed you,
>   perfected your beauty.
[5]† With cypress from Senir they built for you
>   all of your decks;
>   Cedar from Lebanon they took
>   to make you a mast;
[6]† From the highest oaks of Bashan
>   they made your oars;
>   Your bridge they made of cypress wood
>   from the coasts of Kittim.
[7]† Fine embroidered linen from Egypt
>   became your sail [to serve you as
>   a banner].
>   Purple and scarlet from the coasts of Elishah
>   covered your cabin.
[8]† Citizens of Sidon and Arvad
>   served as your oarsmen;
>   Skilled men of Zemer were in you
>   to be your mariners;
[9] The elders and experts of Gebal were in you
>   to caulk your seams.

Every ship and sailor on the sea came to you to carry trade. [10] Persia and Lud and Put were in your army as warriors; shield and helmet they hung upon you, increasing your splendor. [11] The men of Arvad were all about your walls, and the Gamadites were in your towers; they hung their bucklers all around on your walls, and made perfect your beauty. [12] Tarshish traded with you, so great was your wealth, exchanging silver, iron, tin, and lead for your wares. [13] Javan, Tubal, and Meshech were also traders with you, exchanging slaves and articles of bronze for your goods. [14] From Beth-togarmah horses, steeds, and mules were exchanged for your wares. [15] The Rhodanites trafficked with you; many coastlands traded with you; ivory tusks and ebony wood they gave you for payment. [16] Edom traded with you, so many were your products, exchanging garnets, purple, embroidered cloth, fine linen, coral, and rubies for your wares. [17] Judah and the land of Israel trafficked with you, exchanging Minnith wheat, figs, honey, oil, and balm for your goods. [18] Damascus traded with you, so great was your wealth, exchanging Helbon wine and Zahar wool. [19] Javan exchanged wrought iron, cassia, and aromatic cane from Uzal for your wares. [20] Dedan traded with you for riding gear. [21] The trade of Arabia and of all the sheikhs of Kedar belonged to you; they dealt in lambs, rams, and goats. [22] The merchants of Sheba and Raamah also traded with you, exchanging for your wares the very choicest spices, all kinds of precious stones, and gold. [23] Haran, Canneh, and Eden, the merchants of Sheba, Asshur, and Chilmad [24] traded with you, marketing with you rich garments, violet mantles, embroidered cloth, varicolored carpets, and firmly woven cords. [25] Ships of Tarshish journeyed for you in your merchandising.

> You were full and heavily laden
>   in the heart of the sea.
[26] Through the deep waters your oarsmen
>   brought you home,
>   But the east wind smashed you
>   in the heart of the sea.
[27] Your wealth, your goods, your wares,
>   your sailors, and your crew,

[the caulkers of your seams, those who traded for your goods, all your warriors who were in you, and all the great crowd within you]

> Sank into the heart of the sea
>   on the day of your shipwreck.
[28] Hearing the shouts of your mariners,
>   the shores begin to quake.
[29] Down from their ships
>   come all who ply the oar;
>   The sailors, all the mariners of the sea,
>   stand on the shore,
[30] Making their voice heard on your behalf,
>   shouting bitter cries,
>   Strewing dust on their heads,
>   rolling in the ashes.
[31] For you they shave their heads
>   and put on sackcloth,
>   For you they weep in anguish,
>   with bitter lament.

27, 5: *Senir:* another name for Mount Hermon; cf Dt 3, 9.
27, 6: *Bashan:* northern Transjordan, which, like Lebanon, was noted for its great forests. *Kittim:* probably Cyprus.

27, 7: *Elishah:* probably another term for Cyprus.
27, 8f: *Sidon . . . Arvad . . . Zemer . . . Gebal:* Phoenician cities in Tyre's orbit of influence; the last-named is the classical Byblos.

32 In their mourning they utter a lament
      over you;
   thus they wail over you:
   Who was ever destroyed like Tyre
      in the midst of the sea?
33 With your goods which you drew from
      the seas
      you filled many peoples;
   With your great wealth and merchandise
      you enriched the kings of the earth.
34 Now you are wrecked in the sea,
      in the watery depths;
   Your wares and all your crew
      have gone down with you.
35 All who dwell on the coastlands
      are aghast over you,
   Their kings are terrified,
      their faces convulsed.
36 The traders among the peoples
      now hiss at you;
   You have become a horror,
      and you shall be no more.

27, 34

The Prince of Tyre

28 ¹ Thus the word of the LORD came to me:
² Son of man, say to the prince of Tyre:
Thus says the Lord GOD:

   Because you are haughty of heart,
      you say, "A god am I!
   I occupy a godly throne
      in the heart of the sea!"—

And yet you are a man, and not a god,
   however you may think yourself like a god.
3† Oh yes, you are wiser than Daniel,
   there is no secret that is beyond you.
4 By your wisdom and your intelligence
   you have made riches for yourself;
   You have put gold and silver
   into your treasuries.
5 By your great wisdom applied to your trading
   you have heaped up your riches;
   your heart has grown haughty from
      your riches—
6   therefore thus says the Lord GOD:
   Because you have thought yourself
   to have the mind of a god,
7 Therefore I will bring against you
   foreigners, the most barbarous of nations.
   They shall draw their swords
   against your beauteous wisdom,
      they shall run them through your
      splendid apparel.
8 They shall thrust you down to the pit, there
      to die
   a bloodied corpse, in the heart of the sea.
9 Will you then say, "I am a god!"
      when you face your murderers?
   No, you are a man, not a god,
   handed over to those who will slay you.
10 You shall die the death of the uncircumcised
   at the hands of foreigners,
   for I have spoken,
      says the Lord GOD.

11 Thus the word of the LORD came to me:
12† Son of man, utter a lament over the king of Tyre,
saying to him: Thus says the Lord GOD:

   You were stamped with the seal of perfection,
      of complete wisdom and perfect beauty.
13 In Eden, the garden of God, you were,
      and every precious stone was your covering

[carnelian, topaz, and beryl, chrysolite, onyx, and
jasper, sapphire, garnet, and emerald];

   Of gold your pendants and jewels
      were made, on the day you were created.
14† With the Cherub I placed you;
   you were on the holy mountain of God,
   walking among the fiery stones.
15 Blameless you were in your conduct
      from the day you were created,

†
28, 3: *Wiser than Daniel:* see note on Ez 14, 14.
28, 12–19: This picture of Tyre and its fall recalls images of the earthly paradise portraying the creation of man in perfection and his fall (Gn, chapters 2–3).

28, 14: *The holy mountain of God:* the residence of God was sometimes designated as a mountain; cf Is 14, 13. *The fiery stones:* associated with the divine presence; cf Ez 1, 13; Ps 18, 13.

Until evil was found in you,
16   the result of your far-flung trade;
         violence was your business, and you sinned.
      Then I banned you from the mountain
         of God;
      the Cherub drove you from among the
         fiery stones.
17   You became haughty of heart because of
         your beauty;
      for the sake of splendor you debased
         your wisdom.
      I cast you to the earth, so great was your guilt;
      I made you a spectacle in the sight of kings.
18   Because of your guilt, your sinful trade,
      I have profaned your sanctuaries,
      And I have brought out fire from your midst
         which will devour you.
      I have reduced you to dust on the earth
         in the sight of all who should see you.
19   Among the peoples, all who knew you
         stand aghast at you;
      You have become a horror,
         you shall be no more.

Against Sidon

20* Thus the word of the LORD came to me: Son of
man, look toward Sidon, 21* and prophesy against it:
22* Thus says the Lord GOD: See! I am coming at you,
Sidon; I will be glorified in your midst. Then they
shall know that I am the LORD, when I inflict punishments upon it and use it to manifest my holiness.

23   Into it I will send pestilence,
         and blood shall flow in its streets.
      Within it shall fall those slain
         by the sword that comes against it from
            every side.

Thus they shall know that I am the LORD. 24 Sidon
shall no longer be a tearing thorn for the house of
Israel, a brier that scratches them more than all the
others about them who despise them; thus they
shall know that I am the LORD.

25 Thus says the Lord GOD: When I gather the
house of Israel from the peoples among whom they
are scattered, then I will manifest my holiness
through them in the sight of the nations. Then they
shall live on their land which I gave to my servant
Jacob; 26 they shall live on it in security, building
houses and planting vineyards. They shall dwell secure while I inflict punishments on all their

neighbors who despised them; thus they shall
know that I, the LORD, am their God.

Egypt the Crocodile

29 1† On the twelfth day of the tenth month
in the tenth year, the word of the LORD
came to me: 2† Son of man, set your face against
Pharaoh, king of Egypt, and prophesy against him
and against all Egypt. 3† Say this to him: Thus says
the Lord GOD:

      See! I am coming at you, Pharaoh,
         king of Egypt,
      Great crouching monster
         amidst your Niles:
      Who say, "The Niles are mine;
         it is I who made them!"

4 I will put hooks in your jaws and make the fish of
your Niles stick to your scales, then draw you up
from the midst of your Niles along with all the fish
of your Niles sticking to your scales.

5   I will cast you into the desert,
         you and all the fish of your Niles;
      You shall fall upon the open field,
         you shall not be taken up or buried;
      To the beasts of the earth and the birds of
            the air
         I give you as food,
6*   That all who dwell in Egypt may know
         that I am the LORD.
      Because you have been a reed staff
         for the house of Israel:
7   When they held you in hand, you splintered,
         throwing every shoulder out of joint;
      When they leaned on you, you broke,
         bringing each one of them down headlong;

8 therefore thus says the Lord GOD: See! I will bring
the sword against you, and cut off from you both
man and beast. 9 The land of Egypt shall become a
desolate waste; thus they shall know that I am the
LORD.

Because you said, "The Niles are mine; it is I who
made them," 10† therefore see! I am coming at you
and against your Niles; I will make the land of
Egypt a waste and a desolation from Migdol to
Syene, and even to the frontier of Ethiopia. 11 No
foot of man or beast shall pass through it; they shall
not pass through it, and it will be uninhabited for

29, 1: *The twelfth day of the tenth month in the tenth year:* January 7, 587 B.C. The siege of Jerusalem had begun a year earlier;
cf Ez 24, 1.

29, 2: Egypt was allied with Judah against the Chaldeans.

29, 3: *Niles:* the many rivulets of the Nile as it branches out into
the Delta.

29, 10: *From Migdol to Syene:* from the northern to the southern
extremity of Egypt. Syene is the modern Assuan.

28, 20: Is 23, 1–18.   28, 22: Jl 4, 4; Zec 9, 2ff.
28, 21: Jer 47, 4.   29, 6: Is 36, 6.

forty years. ¹² I will make the land of Egypt the most desolate of lands, and its cities shall be the most deserted of cities for forty years; and I will scatter the Egyptians among the nations and strew them over foreign lands. ¹³ Yet thus says the Lord GOD: At the end of forty years I will gather the Egyptians from the peoples among whom they are scattered, ¹⁴† and I will restore Egypt's fortune, bringing them back to the land of Pathros, the land of their origin, where it will be the lowliest ¹⁵ of kingdoms, never more to set itself above the nations. I will make them few, that they may not dominate the nations. ¹⁶ No longer shall they be for the house of Israel to trust in, but the living reminder of its guilt for having turned to follow after them. Thus they shall know that I am the LORD.

The Wages of Nebuchadnezzar

¹⁷† On the first day of the first month in the twenty-seventh year, the word of the LORD came to me: ¹⁸† Son of man, Nebuchadnezzar, the king of Babylon, has led his army in an exhausting campaign against Tyre. Their heads became bald and their shoulders were galled; but neither he nor his army received any wages from Tyre for the campaign he led against it. ¹⁹* Therefore thus says the Lord GOD: I am now giving the land of Egypt to Nebuchadnezzar, king of Babylon. He shall carry off its riches, plundering and pillaging it for the wages of his soldiers, who did it for me; ²⁰ as payment for his toil I have given him the land of Egypt, says the Lord GOD.

²¹ On that day I will make a horn sprout for the house of Israel, and I will cause you to speak out in their midst; thus they shall know that I am the LORD.

The Day of the Lord against Egypt

30 ¹ Thus the word of the LORD came to me: ² Son of man, speak this prophecy: Thus says the Lord GOD: Cry, Oh, the day! ³ for near is the day, near is the day of the Lord; a day of clouds, doomsday for the nations shall it be. ⁴ Then a sword shall come upon Egypt, and anguish shall be in Ethiopia, when the slain fall in Egypt, when her riches are seized and her foundations are overthrown.

⁵ Ethiopia, Put, Lud, all Arabia, Libya, and people of the allied territory shall fall by the sword with them. ⁶ Those who support Egypt shall fall, and down shall come her proud strength; from Migdol to Syene they shall fall there by the sword, says the Lord GOD. ⁷ She shall be the most devastated of lands, and her cities shall be the most desolate of all. ⁸ Then they shall know that I am the LORD, when I set fire to Egypt and when all who help her are broken. ⁹ On that day messengers shall hasten forth at my command to terrify unsuspecting Ethiopia; they shall be in anguish on the day of Egypt, which is surely coming.

¹⁰ Thus says the Lord GOD: I will put an end to the throngs of Egypt by the hand of Nebuchadnezzar, king of Babylon. ¹¹ He and his people with him, the most ruthless of nations, shall be brought in to devastate the land. They shall draw their swords against Egypt, and fill the land with the slain. ¹² I will turn the Niles into dry land and sell the land over to the power of the wicked. The land and everything in it I will hand over to foreigners to devastate. I, the LORD, have spoken.

¹³* Thus says the Lord GOD: I will put an end to the great ones of Memphis and the princes of the land of Egypt, that they may be no more. I will cast fear into the land of Egypt, and devastate Pathros. ¹⁴ I will set fire to Zoan, and inflict punishments on Thebes. ¹⁵ I will pour out my wrath on Pelusium, Egypt's stronghold, and cut down the crowds in Memphis. ¹⁶ I will set fire to Egypt; Syene shall writhe in anguish; Thebes shall be breached and its walls shall be demolished. ¹⁷ The young men of On and of Pibeseth shall fall by the sword, and the cities themselves shall go into captivity. ¹⁸ In Tehaphnehes the day shall be darkened when I break the scepter of Egypt. Her haughty pride shall cease from her, clouds shall cover her, and her daughters shall go into captivity. ¹⁹ Thus will I inflict punishments on Egypt, that they may know that I am the LORD.

Pharaoh's Broken Arm

²⁰† On the seventh day of the first month in the eleventh year, the word of the LORD came to me: ²¹† Son of man, I have broken the arm of Pharaoh,

---

29, 14: *Pathros, the land of their origin:* upper Egypt, that is, southern Egypt, where the Egyptians were thought to have originated; Is 11, 11; Jer 44, 1.15.

29, 17: *The first day of the first month in the twenty-seventh year:* April 26, 571 B.C. This is the latest date attached to any prophecy in Ezekiel.

29, 18f: The fulfillment of Ezekiel's prophecy against Tyre (chapters 26–28) was a thirteen-year siege of the city by Nebuchadnezzar (587–574 B.C.). Tyre seems to have been taken, but its resources were exhausted and the booty was small. Therefore Ezekiel now prophesies that Nebuchadnezzar will collect his wages as God's instrument in the punishment of Tyre, by plundering Egypt.

30, 20: *The seventh day of the first month in the eleventh year:* April 29, 587 B.C.

30, 21–26: This oracle was uttered during the siege of Jerusalem, which had now lasted more than a year (Ez 24, 1). Pharaoh Hophra went to the aid of Jerusalem, causing the Chaldeans to lift the siege temporarily; cf Jer 34, 21; 37, 6f. In the prophet's eyes, this was interfering with the divine punishment of Judah that was to be inflicted by the Chaldeans. The Egyptians were routed by the Chaldeans, and were able to offer no more help to Jerusalem; cf chapter 31.

*

29, 19: Jer 46, 2.   30, 13: Zec 13, 2.

the king of Egypt, and see, it has not been bound up with bandages and healing remedies that it may be strong enough to hold the sword. 22 Therefore thus says the Lord GOD: See! I am coming at Pharaoh, the king of Egypt. I will break his strong arm, so that the sword drops from his hand. 23 I will scatter the Egyptians among the nations and strew them over foreign lands. 24 But I will strengthen the arms of the king of Babylon, and put my sword in his hand, which he will bring against Egypt so as to plunder and pillage it. 25 [I will make the arms of the king of Babylon strong, but the arms of Pharaoh shall drop.] Then they shall know that I am the LORD, when I put my sword in the hand of the king of Babylon for him to wield against the land of Egypt. 26 [I will scatter the Egyptians among the nations and strew them over foreign lands.] Thus they shall know that I am the LORD.

Allegory of the Cypress

31 1† On the first day of the third month in the eleventh year, the word of the LORD came to me: 2 Son of man, say to Pharaoh, the king of Egypt, and to his hordes: What are you like in your greatness?

3　Behold, a cypress [cedar] in Lebanon,
　　beautiful of branch, lofty of stature,
　　amid the very clouds lifted its crest.
4　Waters made it grow, the abyss made
　　it flourish,
　　sending its rivers round where it
　　was planted,
　　turning its streams to all the trees of
　　the field.
5　Thus it grew taller than every other tree of
　　the field,
　　and longer of branch because of the
　　abundant water.
6　In its boughs nested all the birds of
　　the air,
　　under its branches all beasts of the field
　　gave birth,
　　in its shade dwelt numerous peoples of
　　every race.
7　It became beautiful and stately in its spread
　　of foliage,
　　for its roots were turned toward
　　abundant water.
8　The cedars in the garden of God were not
　　its equal,
　　nor could the fir trees match its
　　boughs,

Neither were the plane trees like it
　　for branches;
　　no tree in the garden of God matched
　　its beauty.
9　I made it beautiful, with much foliage,
　　the envy of all Eden's trees in the garden
　　of God.

10 Therefore thus says the Lord GOD: Because it became lofty in stature, raising its crest among the clouds, and because it became proud in heart at its height, 11 I have handed it over to the mightiest of the nations, which has dealt with it in keeping with its wickedness. I humiliated it. 12 Foreigners, the most ruthless of the nations, cut it down and left it on the mountains. Its foliage was brought low in all the valleys, its branches lay broken in all the ravines of the land, and all the peoples of the land withdrew from its shade, abandoning it.

13　On its fallen trunk rested all the birds of the air,
　　and by its branches were all the beasts of
　　the field.

14 Thus no tree may grow lofty in stature or raise its crest among the clouds; no tree fed by water may stand by itself in its loftiness.

For all of them are destined for death,
　　for the land below,
For the company of mortals,
　　those who go down into the pit.

15 Thus says the Lord GOD: On the day he went down to the nether world I made the abyss close up over him; I stopped its streams so that the deep waters were held back. I cast gloom over Lebanon because of him, so that all the trees in the land drooped on his account. 16 At the crash of his fall I made the nations rock, when I cast him down to the nether world with those who go down into the pit. In the land below, all Eden's trees were consoled, Lebanon's choice and best, all that were fed by water. 17 They too have come down with him to the nether world, to those slain by the sword; those who dwelt in his shade are dispersed among the nations. 18 Which was your equal in glory or size among the trees of Eden? Yet you have been brought down with the trees of Eden to the land below. You shall lie with the uncircumcised, with those slain by the sword. Such are Pharaoh and all his hordes, says the Lord GOD.

---

† **31, 1:** *The first day of the third month in the eleventh year:* June 21, 587 B.C.

Dirge over Pharaoh

32 [1]† On the first day of the twelfth month in the twelfth year, the word of the LORD came to me: [2] Son of man, utter a lament over Pharaoh, the king of Egypt, saying to him: Lion of the nations, you are destroyed.

You were like a monster in the sea,
    spouting in your streams,
Stirring the water with your feet
    and churning its streams.
[3]* Thus says the Lord GOD:
I will spread my net over you
    [with a host of many nations],
    and draw you up in my seine.
[4]   I will leave you on the land;
    on the open field I will cast you.
I will have all the birds of the air alight on you,
    and all the beasts of the earth eat their fill
    of you.
[5]   I will leave your flesh on the mountains,
    and fill the valleys with your carcass.
[6]   I will water the land with what flows from you,
    and the river beds shall be filled with
    your blood.
[7]* When I snuff you out I will cover the heavens,
    and all their stars I will darken;
The sun I will cover with clouds,
    and the moon shall not give its light.
[8]   All the shining lights in the heavens
    I will darken on your account,
And I will spread darkness over your land,
    says the Lord GOD.

[9] I will grieve the hearts of many peoples when I lead you captive among the nations, to lands which you do not know. [10] Many peoples shall be appalled at you, and their kings shall shudder over you in horror when they see me brandish my sword, and on the day of your downfall every one of them shall continuously tremble for his own life. [11] For thus says the Lord GOD: The sword of the king of Babylon shall come upon you.

[12]   I will cut down your horde with the blades
    of warriors,
    all of them the most ruthless of the nations;
They shall lay waste the glory of Egypt,
    and all her hordes shall be destroyed.
[13]   I will have all of her animals perish
    beside her abundant waters;

The foot of man shall stir them no longer,
    nor shall the hoof of beast disturb them.
[14]   Then will I make their waters clear,
    and their streams flow like oil,
    says the Lord GOD.

[15] When I turn Egypt into a waste, the land shall be devastated of all that is in it; when I strike all who live there, they shall know that I am the LORD. [16] This is a dirge, and it shall be sung: the daughters of the nations shall chant it; over Egypt and all its hordes shall they chant it, says the Lord GOD.

Dirge over Egypt

[17] On the fifteenth day of the first month in the twelfth year, the word of the LORD came to me: [18] Son of man, lament over the throngs of Egypt, for the mighty nations have thrust them down to the bottom of the earth, with those who go down into the pit. [20] In the midst of those slain by the sword shall they fall, and place shall be made with them for all their hordes. Then from the midst of the nether world, the mighty warriors shall speak to Egypt: [19] "Whom do you excel in beauty? [21] Come down, you and your allies, lie with the uncircumcised, with those slain by the sword."

[22] There is Assyria with all her company, all of them slain, [23] whose graves have been made in the recesses of the pit; her company is around Egypt's grave, all of them slain, fallen by the sword, who spread terror in the land of the living. [24] There is Elam with all her throng about Egypt's grave, all of them slain, fallen by the sword: they have gone down uncircumcised to the bottom of the earth, who spread their terror in the land of the living, and they bear their disgrace with those who go down into the pit; [25] in the midst of the slain they are placed. [26] There are Meshech and Tubal and all their throng about her grave, all of them uncircumcised, slain by the sword, for they spread their terror in the land of the living.

[27]† They do not lie with the mighty men fallen of old, who went down to the nether world with their weapons of war, whose swords were placed under their heads and whose shields were laid over their bones, though the mighty men caused terror in the land of the living. [28] But in the midst of the uncircumcised shall you lie, with those slain by the sword.

[29] There are Edom, her kings, and all her princes, who despite their might have been placed with those slain by the sword; with the uncircumcised

---

† **32, 1:** *The first day of the twelfth month in the twelfth year:* March 3, 585 B.C.

32, 27: *The mighty men fallen of old:* the semilegendary heroes of the prehistoric past, who were thought to have once dominated the world; cf Is 14, 9.

32, 3: Ez 12, 13; 17, 20.

32, 7: Is 13, 10; Jl 2, 10; 4, 15; Mt 24, 29.

they lie, and with those who go down into the pit. ³⁰ There are all the princes of the north and all the Sidonians, who have gone down with the slain, because of the terror their might inspired; they lie uncircumcised with those slain by the sword and bear their disgrace with those who go down to the pit. ³¹ When Pharaoh sees these, he shall be comforted for all his hordes slain by the sword—Pharaoh and all his army, says the Lord GOD. ³² Since he spread his terror in the land of the living, therefore is he laid to rest among the uncircumcised, with those slain by the sword—Pharaoh and all his hordes, says the Lord GOD.

IV: Salvation for Israel

The Prophet a Watchman

33 ¹ Thus the word of the LORD came to me: ² Son of man, speak thus to your countrymen: When I bring the sword against a country, and the people of this country select one of their number to be their watchman, ³ and the watchman, seeing the sword coming against the country, blows the trumpet to warn the people, ⁴ anyone hearing but not heeding the warning of the trumpet and therefore slain by the sword that comes against him, shall be responsible for his own death. ⁵ He heard the trumpet blast yet refused to take warning; he is responsible for his own death, for had he taken warning he would have escaped with his life. ⁶ But if the watchman sees the sword coming and fails to blow the warning trumpet, so that the sword comes and takes anyone, I will hold the watchman responsible for that person's death, even though that person is taken because of his own sin.

⁷* You, son of man, I have appointed watchman for the house of Israel; when you hear me say anything, you shall warn them for me. ⁸ If I tell the wicked man that he shall surely die, and you do not speak out to dissuade the wicked man from his way, he [the wicked man] shall die for his guilt, but I will hold you responsible for his death. ⁹ But if you warn the wicked man, trying to turn him from his way, and he refuses to turn from his way, he shall die for his guilt, but you shall save yourself.

Individual Retribution

¹⁰ As for you, son of man, speak to the house of Israel: You people say, "Our crimes and our sins weigh us down; we are rotting away because of

them. How can we survive?" ¹¹* Answer them: As I live, says the Lord GOD, I swear I take no pleasure in the death of the wicked man, but rather in the wicked man's conversion, that he may live. Turn, turn from your evil ways! Why should you die, O house of Israel?

¹² As for you, son of man, tell your countrymen: The virtue which a man has practiced will not save him on the day that he sins; neither will the wickedness that a man has done bring about his downfall on the day that he turns from his wickedness [nor can the virtuous man, when he sins, remain alive]. ¹³ Though I say to the virtuous man that he shall surely live, if he then presumes on his virtue and does wrong, none of his virtuous deeds shall be remembered; because of the wrong he has done, he shall die. ¹⁴ And though I say to the wicked man that he shall surely die, if he turns away from his sin and does what is right and just, ¹⁵ giving back pledges, restoring stolen goods, living by the statutes that bring life, and doing no wrong, he shall surely live, he shall not die. ¹⁶ None of the sins he committed shall be held against him; he has done what is right and just, he shall surely live.

¹⁷ Yet your countrymen say, "The way of the LORD is not fair!"; but it is their way that is not fair. ¹⁸ When a virtuous man turns away from what is right and does wrong, he shall die for it. ¹⁹ But when a wicked man turns away from wickedness and does what is right and just, because of this he shall live. ²⁰* And still you say, "The way of the LORD is not fair!"? I will judge every one of you according to his ways, O house of Israel.

The Fugitive from Jerusalem

²¹† On the fifth day of the tenth month, in the twelfth year of our exile, the fugitive came to me from Jerusalem and said, "The city is taken!" ²² The hand of the LORD had come upon me the evening before the fugitive arrived, and he opened my mouth when the fugitive reached me in the morning. My mouth was opened, and I was dumb no longer.

The Survivors in Judah

²³† Thus the word of the Lord came to me: ²⁴ Son of man, they who live in the ruins on the land of Israel reason thus: "Abraham, though but a single individual, received possession of the land; we, therefore, being many, have as permanent possession the land that has been given to us." ²⁵ Give

---

† **33, 21f:** January 8, 585 B.C. According to Jeremiah (39, 2), Jerusalem was taken in July, 587. Some MSS read "eleventh" for twelfth year (January, 586); even so, there was ample time between the fall of Jerusalem and the arrival of the fugitive from that city to journey to Babylon. However, this is the fugitive sent to fulfill the promise of Ez 24, 25.27, the eyewitness who would release Ezekiel from his dumbness; cf Ez, 2, 26f.

33, 23–29: News brought by the fugitive furnished the occasion of this prophecy. Like Jeremiah, Ezekiel rejects the idea that the survivors in Judah have any claim to the land. The new Israel is to be formed from the exiles.

* **33, 7:** Ez 3, 17.   **33, 20:** Ez 18, 25.
33, 11: Ez 18, 23–32.

them this answer: Thus says the Lord GOD: You eat on the mountains, you raise your eyes to your idols, you shed blood—yet you would keep possession of the land? 26 You rely on your sword, you do abominable things, each one of you defiles his neighbor's wife—yet you would keep possession of the land? 27 Tell them this: Thus says the Lord GOD: As I live, those who are in the ruins I swear shall fall by the sword; those who are in the open field I have given to the wild beasts for food; and those who are in fastnesses and in caves shall die by the plague. 28 I will make the land a desolate waste, so that its proud strength will come to an end, and the mountains of Israel shall be so desolate that no one will cross them. 29 Thus they shall know that I am the LORD, when I make the land a desolate waste because of all the abominable things they have done.

The Prophet's False Popularity

30† As for you, son of man, your countrymen are talking about you along the walls and in the doorways of houses. They say to one another, "Come and hear the latest word that comes from the LORD." 31 My people come to you as people always do; they sit down before you and hear your words, but they will not obey them, for lies are on their lips and their desires are fixed on dishonest gain. 32 For them you are only a ballad singer, with a pleasant voice and a clever touch. They listen to your words, but they will not obey them. 33 But when it comes—and it is surely coming!—they shall know that there was a prophet among them.

Parable of the Shepherds

34 1 Thus the word of the LORD came to me: 2*† Son of man, prophesy against the shepherds of Israel, in these words prophesy to them [to the shepherds]: Thus says the Lord GOD: Woe to the shepherds of Israel who have been pasturing themselves! Should not shepherds, rather, pasture sheep? 3 You have fed off their milk, worn their wool, and slaughtered the fatlings, but the sheep you have not pastured. 4 You did not strengthen the weak nor heal the sick nor bind up the injured. You did not bring back the strayed nor seek the lost, but you lorded it over them harshly and brutally. 5 So they were scattered for lack of a shepherd, and became food for all the wild beasts. My sheep were scattered 6 and wandered over all the mountains and high hills; my sheep were scattered over the whole earth, with no one to look after them or to search for them.

7 Therefore, shepherds, hear the word of the LORD: 8 As I live, says the Lord GOD, because my sheep have been given over to pillage, and because my sheep have become food for every wild beast, for lack of a shepherd; because my shepherds did not look after my sheep, but pastured themselves and did not pasture my sheep; 9 because of this, shepherds, hear the word of the LORD: 10 Thus says the Lord GOD: I swear I am coming against these shepherds. I will claim my sheep from them and put a stop to their shepherding my sheep so that they may no longer pasture themselves. I will save my sheep, that they may no longer be food for their mouths.

11 For thus says the Lord GOD: I myself will look after and tend my sheep. 12 As a shepherd tends his flock when he finds himself among his scattered sheep, so will I tend my sheep. I will rescue them from every place where they were scattered when it was cloudy and dark. 13 I will lead them out from among the peoples and gather them from the foreign lands; I will bring them back to their own country and pasture them upon the mountains of Israel [in the land's ravines and all its inhabited places]. 14 In good pastures will I pasture them, and on the mountain heights of Israel shall be their grazing ground. There they shall lie down on good grazing ground, and in rich pastures shall they be pastured on the mountains of Israel. 15 I myself will pasture my sheep; I myself will give them rest, says the Lord GOD. 16 The lost I will seek out, the strayed I will bring back, the injured I will bind up, the sick I will heal [but the sleek and the strong I will destroy], shepherding them rightly.

Separation of the Sheep

17 As for you, my sheep, says the Lord GOD, I will judge between one sheep and another, between rams and goats. 18 Was it not enough for you to graze on the best pasture, that you had to trample the rest of your pastures with your feet? Was it not enough for you to drink the clearest water, that you had to foul the remainder with your feet? 19 Thus my sheep had to graze on what your feet had trampled and drink what your feet had fouled. 20 Therefore thus says the Lord GOD: Now will I judge between the fat and the lean sheep. 21 Because you push with side and shoulder, and butt all the weak sheep with your horns until you have driven them out, 22 I will save my sheep so that they may no longer be despoiled, and I will judge between one sheep and another. 23*† I will appoint one

---

33, 30: The fulfillment of Ezekiel's prophecies about Jerusalem was responsible for this temporary enthusiasm among the unstable people.
34, 2: *The shepherds of Israel:* the leaders of the people.
34, 23: *One shepherd . . . my servant David:* a messianic Da-

vidic King who will rule over the restored Israel (vv 25–31) in the name of the Lord.

34, 2: Ez 13, 3; Jer 23, 1.　　　34, 23: Is 40, 21; Hos 3, 5; Jn 10, 11.14.

shepherd over them to pasture them, my servant David; he shall pasture them and be their shepherd. 24 I, the Lord, will be their God, and my servant David shall be prince among them. I, the LORD, have spoken.

25 I will make a covenant of peace with them, and rid the country of ravenous beasts, that they may dwell securely in the desert and sleep in the forests. 26 I will place them about my hill, sending rain in due season, rains that shall be a blessing to them. 27 The trees of the field shall bear their fruits, and the land its crops, and they shall dwell securely on their own soil. Thus they shall know that I am the LORD

PRAY IT!

The Good Shepherd

The theme of the good shepherd is common in the Bible. Psalm 23 compares God to a protective shepherd. Ezekiel, chapter 34, describes bad shepherds and contrasts them with God, the true shepherd, who feeds the flock with justice. In Jn 10, 1–18, Jesus compares himself to a good shepherd.

God, the true shepherd, thank you for your care and protection. Today, I will do what I can to help your work. Make me aware of the people in my life who are weak, injured, straying, or lost. With your help, I will do what I can to strengthen them, heal them, and bring them back to you. Maybe I too can be more like a shepherd than like a sheep that merely follows!

▶ Ezekiel, chapter 34

when I break the bonds of their yoke and free them from the power of those who enslaved them. 28 They shall no longer be despoiled by the nations or devoured by beasts of the earth, but shall dwell secure, with no one to frighten them. 29 I will prepare for them peaceful fields for planting; they shall no longer be carried off by famine in the land, or bear the reproaches of the nations. 30 Thus they shall know that I, the LORD, am their God, and they are my people, the house of Israel, says the Lord GOD. 31 [You, my sheep, you are the sheep of my pasture, and I am your God, says the Lord GOD.]

Against Edom

35 1*† Thus the word of the LORD came to me: 2 Son of man, set your face against Mount Seir, and prophesy against it. 3 Say to it: Thus says the Lord GOD: See! I am coming at you, Mount Seir. I will stretch out my hand against you and make you a desolate waste. 4 Your cities I will turn into ruins, and you shall be a waste; thus you shall know that I am the LORD.

5 Because you never let die your hatred for the Israelites, whom you delivered over to the power of the sword at the time of their trouble, when their crimes came to an end, 6 therefore, as I live, says the Lord GOD, you have been guilty of blood, and blood, I swear, shall pursue you. 7 I will make Mount Seir a desolate waste, and cut off from it any traveler. 8 With the slain I will fill your hills, your valleys, and all your ravines [in them the slain shall fall by the sword]: 9 desolate will I make you forever, and leave your cities without inhabitants; thus you shall know that I am the LORD.

10† Because you said: The two nations and the two lands have become mine; we shall possess them—although the LORD was there— 11 therefore, as I live, says the Lord GOD, I will deal with you according to your anger and your envy which you have exercised [in your hatred] against them. I will make myself known among you when I judge you, 12 and you shall know that I am the LORD.

I have heard all the contemptuous things you have uttered against the mountains of Israel: "They are desolate, they have been given us to devour." 13 I have heard the insolent and wild words you have spoken against me. 14 Thus says the Lord GOD: Just as you rejoiced over my land because it was desolate, so will I do to you. 15 In keeping with your glee over the devastation of the inheritance of the house of Israel, so will I treat you. A waste shall you be, Mount Seir, you and the whole of Edom. Thus they shall know that I am the LORD.

Regeneration of the Land

36 1* As for you, son of man, prophesy to the mountains of Israel: Mountains of Israel, hear the word of the LORD! 2 Thus says the Lord GOD: Because the enemy has said of you, "Ha! the everlasting heights have become our possession" 3 [therefore prophesy in these words: Thus says the Lord GOD:]; because you have been ridiculed and despised on all sides for having become a possession for the rest of the nations, and have become a byword and a popular jeer; 4 therefore, mountains

---

† 35, 1–15: After the fall of Jerusalem, Edom assisted the Chaldeans in devastating the land and subduing the population, and ended by occupying part of Judah's former territory. For this reason these oracles against Edom are found in the context of the city's fall.

35, 10: *The two nations and the two lands:* the superseded kingdoms of Israel and Judah and their territories.

* 35, 1ff: Ez 25, 12ff.   36, 1: Ez 6, 3.

of Israel, hear the word of the LORD: [Thus says the Lord GOD to the mountains and hills, the ravines and valleys, the desolate ruins and abandoned cities, which have been given over to the pillage and mockery of the remaining nations round about; 5 therefore thus says the Lord GOD:] Truly, with burning jealousy I speak against the rest of the nations [and against all of Edom] who with wholehearted joy and utter contempt have considered my land their possession to be delivered over to plunder. 6 [Therefore, prophesy concerning the land of Israel, and say to the mountains and hills, the ravines and valleys: Thus says the Lord GOD:] With jealous fury I speak, because you have borne the reproach of the nations. 7 Therefore do I solemnly swear that your neighboring nations shall bear their own reproach.

8 As for you, mountains of Israel, you shall grow branches and bear fruit for my people Israel, for they shall soon return. 9 See, I come to you, it is to you that I turn; you will be tilled and sown, 10 and I will settle crowds of men upon you, the whole house of Israel; cities shall be repeopled, and ruins rebuilt. 11 I will settle crowds of men and beasts upon you, to multiply and be fruitful. I will repeople you as in the past, and be more generous to you than in the beginning; thus you shall know that I am the LORD. 12 [My people Israel are the ones whom I will

have walk upon you; they shall take possession of you, and you shall be their heritage. Never again shall you rob them of their children.]

13† Thus says the Lord GOD: Because they have said of you, "You are a land that devours men, and you rob your people of their children"; 14 therefore, never again shall you devour men or rob your people of their children, says the Lord GOD. 15 No more will I permit you to hear the reproach of nations, or bear insults from peoples, or rob your people of their children, says the Lord GOD.

Regeneration of the People

16 Thus the word of the LORD came to me: 17 Son of man, when the house of Israel lived in their land, they defiled it by their conduct and deeds. In my sight their conduct was like the defilement of a menstruous woman. 18 Therefore I poured out my fury upon them [because of the blood which they poured out on the ground, and because they defiled it with idols]. 19 I scattered them among the nations, dispersing them over foreign lands; according to their conduct and deeds I judged them. 20* But when they came among the nations [wherever they came], they served to profane my holy name, because it was said of them: "These are the people of the LORD, yet they had to leave their

YOU WILL BE CLEANSED

The sweat lodge ceremony is a Native American tradition that is still used today. It is performed whenever there is a need to be purified in order to prepare for God's blessings or ask for God's help.

This ceremony is held in a shelter of poles and blankets that is made over a pit, with the door flap facing west, the direction the rains come from. Heated rocks fill the pit, and steam is formed when water is poured on the rocks. The ceremony consists of entering the shelter and sitting in a circle, passing a pipe, making steam, and praying toward the four directions for guidance and blessings and for maintaining an attitude of thankfulness.

This tradition ritualizes the cleansing and conversion Ezekiel proclaims in Ez 36, 25–26. It reflects a faith that the Great Spirit, or God, will cleanse us with waters and give us a new heart and spirit.

▶ Ez 36, 25–26

---

land." 21 So I have relented because of my holy name which the house of Israel profaned among the nations where they came. 22 Therefore say to the house of Israel: Thus says the Lord GOD: Not for your sakes do I act, house of Israel, but for the sake of my holy name, which you profaned among the nations to which you came. 23 I will prove the holiness of my great name, profaned among the nations, in whose midst you have profaned it. Thus the nations shall know that I am the LORD, says the Lord GOD, when in their sight I prove my holiness through you. 24 For I will take you away from among the nations, gather you from all the foreign lands, and bring you back to your own land. 25* I will sprinkle clean water upon you to cleanse you from all your impurities, and from all your idols I will cleanse you. 26* I will give you a new heart and place a new spirit within you, taking from your bodies your stony hearts and giving you natural hearts. 27* I will put my spirit within you and make you live by my statutes, careful to observe my decrees. 28 You shall live in the land I gave your fathers; you shall be my people, and I will be your God. 29 I will save you from all your impurities; I will order the grain to be abundant, and I will not send famine against you. 30 I will increase the fruit on your trees and the crops in your fields; thus you shall no longer bear among the nations the reproach of famine. 31 Then you shall remember your evil conduct, and that your deeds were not good; you shall loathe yourselves for your sins and your abominations. 32 Not for your sakes do I act, says the Lord GOD—let this be known to you! Be

ashamed and abashed because of your conduct, O house of Israel.

33 Thus says the Lord GOD: When I purify you from all your crimes, I will repeople the cities, and the ruins shall be rebuilt; 34 the desolate land shall be tilled, which was formerly a wasteland exposed to the gaze of every passer-by. 35 "This desolate land has been made into a garden of Eden," they shall say. "The cities that were in ruins, laid waste, and destroyed are now repeopled and fortified." 36 Thus the neighboring nations that remain shall know that I, the LORD, have rebuilt what was destroyed and replanted what was desolate. I, the LORD, have promised, and I will do it.

37 Thus says the Lord GOD: This also I will be persuaded to do for the house of Israel: to multiply them like sheep. 38 As with sacrificial sheep, the sheep of Jerusalem on its feast days, the cities which were in ruins shall be filled with flocks of men; thus they shall know that I am the LORD.

Vision of the Dry Bones

37 1† The hand of the LORD came upon me, and he led me out in the spirit of the LORD and set me in the center of the plain, which was now filled with bones. 2 He made me walk among them in every direction so that I saw how many they were on the surface of the plain. How dry they were! 3 He asked me: Son of man, can these bones come to life? "Lord GOD," I answered, "you alone know that." 4 Then he said to me: Prophesy over these bones, and say to them: Dry bones, hear the word of the LORD! 5 Thus says the Lord GOD to

---

Bone Dry   LIVE IT!

When have you felt dry and lifeless, like the collection of dry bones Ezekiel sees in his vision in Ez 37, 1–2? What helps you to re-energize, to put muscle and flesh back on your tired bones? What winds blow life through you to give you breath again, to make you new again?

Bones are our body's support structure, and prayer is our soul's support structure. In verse 14, God's spirit brings life. We need to pray for God's spirit—the Holy Spirit—to fill us in order to avoid shriveling up and becoming parched and lifeless. And we need to share God's spirit with others, to breathe life into the dry bones around us—the people who seem to have no energy or hope.

What are the dry bones in your life? What can you do to be re-energized by God when you feel like dry bones? How can you help to energize others who seem dry and lifeless?

▶ Ezekiel, chapter 37

---

† **37, 1–14:** This vision is a prediction of the restoration of Israel under the figure of a resurrection from the dead; it is not concerned with the doctrine of resurrection itself.

* **36, 25:** Ps 51, 4; Zec 13, 1; Jn 3, 5; Heb 10, 22.
36, 26: Jer 31, 33.
36, 27: Ez 37, 14; 39, 29; Is 42, 1; 44, 3; 59, 21; Hg 2, 5; Jl 3, 1f.

these bones: See! I will bring spirit into you, that you may come to life. 6 I will put sinews upon you, make flesh grow over you, cover you with skin, and put spirit in you so that you may come to life and know that I am the LORD. 7 I prophesied as I had been told, and even as I was prophesying I heard a noise; it was a rattling as the bones came together, bone joining bone. 8 I saw the sinews and the flesh come upon them, and the skin cover them, but there was no spirit in them. 9 Then he said to me: Prophesy to the spirit, prophesy, son of man, and say to the spirit: Thus says the Lord GOD: From the four winds come, O spirit, and breathe into these slain that they may come to life. 10 I prophesied as he told me, and the spirit came into them; they came alive and stood upright, a vast army. 11 Then he said to me: Son of man, these bones are the whole house of Israel. They have been saying, "Our bones are dried up, our hope is lost, and we are cut off." 12 Therefore, prophesy and say to them: Thus says the Lord GOD: O my people, I will open your graves and have you rise from them, and bring you back to the land of Israel. 13 Then you shall know that I am the LORD, when I open your graves and have you rise from them, O my people! 14 I will put my spirit in you that you may live, and I will settle you upon your land; thus you shall know that I am the LORD. I have promised, and I will do it, says the LORD.

The Two Sticks

15† Thus the word of the LORD came to me: 16 Now, son of man, take a single stick, and write on it: Judah and those Israelites who are associated with him. Then take another stick and write on it: Joseph [the stick of Ephraim] and all the house of Israel associated with him. 17 Then join the two sticks together, so that they form one stick in your hand. 18 When your countrymen ask you, "Will you not tell us what you mean by all this?", 19 answer them: Thus says the Lord GOD: [I will take the stick of Joseph, which is in the hand of Ephraim, and of the tribes of Israel associated with him, and I will join to it the stick of Judah, making them a single stick; they shall be one in my hand. 20 The sticks on which you write you shall hold up before them to see. 21 Tell them: Thus speaks the LORD GOD:] I will take the Israelites from among the nations to which they have come, and gather them from all sides to bring them back to their land. 22 I will make them one nation upon the land, in the mountains of Israel, and there shall be one prince for them all. Never again shall they be two nations, and never again shall they be divided into two kingdoms.

23 No longer shall they defile themselves with

their idols, their abominations, and all their transgressions. I will deliver them from all their sins of apostasy, and cleanse them so that they may be my people and I may be their God. 24* My servant David shall be prince over them, and there shall be one shepherd for them all; they shall live by my statutes and carefully observe my decrees. 25 They shall live on the land which I gave to my servant Jacob, the land where their fathers lived; they shall live on it forever, they, and their children, and their children's children, with my servant David their prince forever. 26* I will make with them a covenant of peace; it shall be an everlasting covenant with them, and I will multiply them, and put my sanctuary among them forever. 27 My dwelling shall be with them; I will be their God, and they shall be my people. 28 Thus the nations shall know that it is I, the LORD, who make Israel holy, when my sanctuary shall be set up among them forever.

---

† **37, 15–22:** The symbolic action of joining two sticks into one signifies the future union of Israel and Judah under one messianic King.

* 37, 24: Ez 34, 23; Jer 23, 5; 33, 15.   37, 26: Ps 110, 4.

First Prophecy against Gog

38 ¹† Thus the word of the LORD came to me: ²*† Son of man, turn toward Gog [the land of Magog], the chief prince of Meshech and Tubal, and prophesy against him: ³ Thus says the Lord GOD: See! I am coming at you, Gog, chief prince of Meshech and Tubal. ⁴ I will lead you forth with all your army, horses and riders all handsomely outfitted, a great horde with bucklers and shields, all of them carrying swords: ⁵ Persia, Cush, and Put with them [all with shields and helmets], ⁶ Gomer with all its troops, Beth-togarmah from the recesses of the north with all its troops, many peoples with you. ⁷ Prepare yourself, be ready, you and all your horde assembled about you, and be at my disposal. ⁸ After many days you will be mustered [in the last years you will come] against a nation which has survived the sword, which has been assembled from many peoples [on the mountains of Israel which were long a ruin], which has been brought forth from among the peoples and all of whom now dwell in security. ⁹ You shall come up like a sudden storm, advancing like a cloud to cover the earth, you and all your troops and the many peoples with you.

¹⁰ Thus says the Lord GOD: At that time thoughts shall arise in your mind, and you shall devise an evil scheme: ¹¹ "I will go up against a land of open villages and attack the peaceful people who are living in security, all of them living without walls, having neither bars nor gates, ¹²† to plunder and pillage, turning my hand against the ruins that were repeopled and against a people gathered from the nations, a people concerned with cattle and goods, who dwell at the navel of the earth." ¹³ Sheba and Dedan, the merchants of Tarshish and all her young lions shall ask you: "Is it for plunder that you have come? Is it for pillage that you have summoned your horde, to carry off silver and gold, to take away cattle and goods, to seize much plunder?"

¹⁷ Thus says the Lord GOD: It is of you that I spoke in ancient times through my servants, the prophets of Israel, who prophesied in those days that I would bring you against them. ¹⁸ But on that day, the day when Gog invades the land of Israel, says the Lord GOD, my fury shall be aroused. In my anger ¹⁹ and in my jealousy, in my fiery wrath, I swear: On that day there shall be a great shaking upon the land of Israel. ²⁰ Before me shall tremble the fish of the sea and the birds of the air, the beasts of the field and all the reptiles that crawl upon the ground, and all men who are on the land. Mountains shall be overturned, and cliffs shall tumble, and every wall shall fall to the ground. ²¹ Against him I will summon every terror, says the Lord GOD, every man's sword against his brother. I will hold judgment with him in pestilence and bloodshed; ²² flooding rain and hailstones, fire and brimstone, I will rain upon him, upon his troops, and upon the many peoples with him. ²³ I will prove my greatness and holiness and make myself known in the sight of many nations; thus they shall know that I am the LORD.

Second Prophecy against Gog

¹⁴ Therefore prophesy, son of man, and say to Gog: Thus says the Lord GOD: When my people Israel are dwelling in security, will you not bestir yourself ¹⁵ and come from your home in the recesses of the north, you and many peoples with you, all mounted on horses, a great horde and a mighty army? ¹⁶ You shall come up against my people Israel like a cloud covering the land. In the last days I will bring you against my land, that the nations may know of me, when in their sight I prove my holiness through you, O Gog.

Third Prophecy against Gog

39 ¹ Now, son of man, prophesy against Gog in these words: Thus says the Lord GOD: See! I am coming at you, Gog, chief prince of Meshech and Tubal. ² I will turn you about, I will urge you on, and I will make you come up from the recesses of the north; I will lead you against the mountains of Israel. ³ Then I will strike the bow from your left hand, and make the arrows drop from your right. ⁴ Upon the mountains of Israel you shall fall, you and all your troops and the peoples who are with you. To birds of prey of every kind and to the wild beasts I am giving you to be eaten. ⁵ On the open field you shall fall, for I have decreed it, says the Lord GOD.

⁶ I will send fire upon Magog and upon those who live securely in the coastlands; thus they shall know that I am the LORD. ⁷ I will make my holy name known among my people Israel; I will no longer allow my holy name to be profaned. Thus the nations shall know that I am the LORD, the Holy One in

---

38, 1—39, 20: These three oracles against Gog may refer either to a specific foreign invasion in the future, or to the apocalyptic struggle between good and evil at the end of time. By some they are ascribed to a later author than Ezekiel, who lived after the exile and the return to Palestine.
38, 2: *Gog:* the name is almost certainly a symbolic one taken from that of Gyges, king of Lydia, whether or not the prophet has a specific person in mind. The gloss Magog may be an Akkadian expression, mat-Gog, "the land of Gog." *Meshech and Tubal,* as well

as *Gomer* and *Beth-togarmah* (v 6), were countries around the Black Sea, the northernmost countries known to the Hebrews: the north (cf also v 15) was the traditional direction from which invasion was expected; cf Jer 1, 13ff.
38, 12: *Who dwell at the navel of the earth:* the people of Israel (cf v 18; also Ez 5, 5). Many ancient peoples spoke of their own homelands as "the navel," that is, the center of the earth.

38, 2: Rv 20, 7f.

Israel. [8] Yes, it is coming and shall be fulfilled, says the Lord GOD. This is the day I have decreed.

[9] Then shall those who live in the cities of Israel go out and burn weapons: [shields and bucklers,] bows and arrows, clubs and lances; for seven years they shall make fires with them. [10] They shall not have to bring in wood from the fields or cut it down in the forests, for they shall make fires with the weapons. Thus they shall plunder those who plundered them and pillage those who pillaged them, says the Lord GOD.

[11]† On that day I will give Gog for his tomb a well-known place in Israel, the Valley of Abarim east of the sea [it is blocked to travelers]. Gog shall be buried there with all his horde, and it shall be named "Valley of Hamon gog." [12] To purify the land, the house of Israel shall need seven months to bury them. [13] All the people of the land shall bury them and gain renown for it, when I reveal my glory, says the Lord GOD. [14] Men shall be permanently employed to pass through the land burying those who lie unburied, so as to purify the land. For seven months they shall keep searching. [15] When they pass through, should they see a human bone, let them put up a marker beside it, until others have buried it in the Valley of Hamon-gog. [16] [Also the name of the city shall be Hamonah.] Thus the land shall be purified.

[17] As for you, son of man, says the Lord GOD, say to birds of every kind and to all the wild beasts: Come together, from all sides gather for the slaughter I am about to provide for you, a great slaughter on the mountains of Israel: you shall have flesh to eat and blood to drink. [18] You shall eat the flesh of warriors and drink the blood of the princes of the land [rams, lambs, and goats, bullocks, fatlings of Bashan, all of them]. [19] From the slaughter which I will provide for you, you shall eat fat until you are filled and drink blood until you are drunk. [20] You shall be filled at my table with horses and riders, with warriors and soldiers of every kind, says the Lord GOD.

Israel's Return

[21] Thus I will display my glory among the nations, and all the nations shall see the judgment I have executed and the hand I have laid upon them. [22] From that day forward the house of Israel shall know that I am the LORD, their God. [23] The nations shall know that because of its sins the house of Israel went into exile; for they transgressed against me, and I hid my face from them and handed them over to their foes, so that all of them fell by the sword. [24] According to their uncleanness and their transgressions I dealt with them, hiding my face from them.

[25] Therefore, thus says the Lord GOD: Now I will restore the fortunes of Jacob and have pity on the whole house of Israel, and I will be jealous for my holy name. [26] They shall forget their disgrace and all the times they broke faith with me, when they live in security on their land with no one to frighten them. [27] When I bring them back from among the peoples, I will gather them from the lands of their enemies, and will prove my holiness through them in the sight of many nations. [28]* Thus they shall know that I, the LORD, am their God, since I who exiled them among the nations, will gather them back on their land, not leaving any of them behind. [29] No longer will I hide my face from them, for I have poured out my spirit upon the house of Israel, says the Lord GOD.

V: The New Israel†

The New Temple
The Man with a Measure

40 [1] On the tenth day of the month beginning the twenty-fifth year of our exile, fourteen years after the city was taken, that very day the hand of the LORD came upon me and brought me [2] in divine visions to the land of Israel, where he set me down on a very high mountain. On it there seemed to be a city being built before me. [3] When he had brought me there, all at once I saw a man whose appearance was that of bronze; he was standing in the gate, holding a linen cord and a measuring rod. [4] The man said to me, "Son of man, look carefully and listen intently, and pay strict attention to all that I will show you, for you have been brought here so that I might show it to you. Tell the house of Israel all that you see." [5]† [Then I saw an outer wall that completely surrounded the temple. The man was holding a measuring rod six cubits long, each cubit being a cubit and a handbreadth; he measured the width and the height of the structure, each of which was found to be one rod.]

39, 11: *The Valley of Abarim:* in the Abarim mountains, east of the Jordan. *Hamon-gog:* means "the horde of Gog."

40, 1—48, 35: This lengthy vision of the new Israel is dated (Ez 40, 1) April 28, 573 B.C. It is largely concerned with the new temple and the prescriptions to govern it, but other details of the restored commonwealth are included, forming a kind of program for the future. The literary form of the vision has been aptly termed "utopian": it is plain that the prophet did not expect a literal fulfillment of much of what he described. The passage doubtless underwent successive additions, both from the prophet and from later inspired writers.

40, 5: *A cubit and a handbreadth:* the ordinary cubit consisted of six handbreadths; the great cubit, of seven. In measuring the temple, a rod six great cubits long was used. The ordinary cubit was about one and a half feet, or, more exactly, 17.5 inches; the large cubit, 20.4 inches.

*

39, 28: Ez 36, 23.

The East Gate

6† Then he went to the gate which faced the east, climbed its steps, and measured the gate's threshold, which was found to be a rod wide. 7 The cells were a rod long and a rod wide, and the pilasters between the cells measured five cubits. The threshold of the gate adjoining the vestibule of the gate toward the inside measured one rod. 8 He measured the vestibule of the gate, 9 which was eight cubits, and its pilasters, which were two cubits. The vestibule of the gate was toward the inside. 10 The cells of the east gate were three on either side, of equal size, and the pilasters on either side were also of equal size. 11 He measured the gate's entrance, which was ten cubits wide, while the width of the gate's passage itself was thirteen cubits. 12 The border before each of the cells on both sides was one cubit; the cells themselves were six cubits on either side, from opening to opening. 13 He measured the gate from the back wall of one cell to the back wall of the cell on the opposite side: the width was twenty-five cubits. 14 He measured the vestibule, which was twenty-five cubits. The pilasters adjoining the court on either side were six cubits. 15 The length of the gate from the front entrance to the front of the vestibule on the inside was fifty cubits. 16 Within the gateway on both sides there were splayed windows let into the cells [and into their pilasters]; likewise, within the vestibule on both sides there were windows. The pilasters were decorated with palms.

The Outer Court

17† Then he brought me to the outer court, where there were chambers and a pavement. The pavement was laid all around the court, and the chambers, which were on the pavement, were thirty in number. 18 The pavement lay alongside the gates, as wide as the gates were long; this was the lower pavement. 19 He measured the width of the court from the front of the lower gate to the front of the inner gate; it was one hundred cubits between them.

The North Gate

Then he proceeded north, 20 where, on the outer court, there was a gate facing north, whose length and width he measured. 21 Its cells, three on either side, its pilasters, and its vestibule had the same measurements as those of the first gate; it was fifty cubits long and twenty-five cubits wide. 22 Its windows, the windows of its vestibule, and its palm

decorations were of the same proportions as those of the gate facing the east. Seven steps led up to it, and its vestibule was toward the inside. 23 The inner court had a gate opposite the north gate, just as at the east gate; he measured one hundred cubits from one gate to the other.

The South Gate

24 Then he led me south, to where there was a southern gate, whose cells, pilasters, and vestibule he measured; they were the same size as the others. 25 The gate and its vestibule had windows on both sides, like the other windows. It was fifty cubits long and twenty-five cubits wide. 26 It was ascended by seven steps; its vestibule was toward the inside; and it was decorated with palms here and there on its pilasters. 27 The inner court also had a southern gate; from gate to gate he measured one hundred cubits.

Gates of the Inner Court

28† Then he brought me to the inner court by the south gate, where he measured the south gate. Its dimensions were the same as the others; 29 its cells, its pilasters, and its vestibule were the same size as the others. The gate and its vestibule had windows on both sides; and it was fifty cubits long and twenty-five cubits wide. 31 But its vestibule was toward the outer court; palms were on its pilasters, and it had a stairway of eight steps. 32 Then he brought me to the gate facing the east, where he measured the gate, whose dimensions were found to be the same. 33 Its cells, its pilasters, and its vestibule were the same size as the others; the gate and its vestibule had windows on both sides; it was fifty cubits long and twenty-five cubits wide. 34 But its vestibule was toward the outer court; palms were on its pilasters here and there, and it had a stairway of eight steps. 35 Then he brought me to the north gate, where he measured the dimensions 36 of its cells, its pilasters, and its vestibule, and found them the same. The gate and its vestibule had windows on both sides; it was fifty cubits long and twenty-five cubits wide. 37 Its vestibule was toward the outer court; palms were on its pilasters here and there, and it had a stairway of eight steps.

Side Rooms

38 There was a chamber opening off the vestibule of the gate, where the holocausts were rinsed. 39 In

---

† **40, 6–16:** The east gate, leading into the outer court of the temple, is described more fully than the north and south gates, which, however, were of the same dimensions. On the west side of the outer court there was a large building instead of a gate (Ez 41, 12).
40, 17: *The outer court:* the court outside the temple area proper, which had its own inner court (vv 28–37).

40, 28–37: The gates leading into the inner court of the temple area correspond to the gates leading into the outer court, with the exception that their vestibules are on the outer rather than the inner side. (Verse 30, a dittography of v 29, is omitted.)

the vestibule of the gate there were two tables on either side, on which were slaughtered the sin offerings and guilt offerings. 40 Along the wall of the vestibule, but outside, near the entrance of the north gate, were two tables, and on the other side of the vestibule of the gate there were two tables. 41 There were four tables on either side of the gate [eight tables], on which the sacrifices were slaughtered. 42 There were four tables for holocausts, made of cut stone, one and a half cubits long, one and a half cubits wide, and one cubit high. 43 The ledges, a handbreadth wide, were set on the inside all around, and on them were laid the instruments with which the holocausts were slaughtered. On the tables themselves the flesh was laid. 44 He then led me to the inner court where there were two chambers, one beside the north gate, facing south, and the other beside the south gate, facing north. 45 He said to me, "This chamber which faces south is for the priests who have charge of the temple, 46† and the chamber which faces north is for the priests who have charge of the altar. These are the Zadokites, the only Levites who may come near to minister to the LORD." 47 Then he measured the court, which was a hundred cubits long and a hundred cubits wide, a perfect square. The altar stood in front of the temple.

The Temple Building

48† Then he brought me into the vestibule of the temple and measured the pilasters on each side, which were five cubits. The width of the doorway was fourteen cubits, and the side walls on either side of the door measured three cubits. 49† The vestibule was twenty cubits wide and twelve cubits deep; ten steps led up to it, and there were columns by the pilasters, one on either side.

41 1 Then he brought me to the nave and measured the pilasters, which were six cubits thick on either side. 2 The width of the entrance was ten cubits, and the walls at either side of it measured five cubits each. He measured the length of the nave, which was found to be forty cubits, while its width was twenty. 3 Then he went in beyond and measured the pilasters flanking that entrance, which were two cubits; the width of the entrance was six cubits, and the walls at either side of it extended seven cubits each. 4† He measured the space beyond the nave, twenty cubits long and twenty cubits wide, and said to me, "This is the holy of holies."

5 Then he measured the wall of the temple, which was six cubits thick; the side chambers, which extended all the way around the temple, had a width of four cubits. 6 There were thirty side chambers built one above the other in three stories, and there were offsets in the outside wall of temple that enclosed the side chambers; these served as supports, so that there were no supports in the temple wall proper. 7 There was a broad circular passageway that led upward to the side chambers, for the temple was enclosed all the way around and all the way upward; therefore the temple had a broad way running upward so that one could pass from the lowest to the middle and the highest story. 8 About the temple was a raised pavement completely enclosing it—the foundations of the side chambers—a full rod of six cubits in extent. 9 The width of the outside wall which enclosed the side chambers was five cubits. Between the side chambers of the temple 10 and the chambers of the court was an open space twenty cubits wide going all around the temple. 11 The side chambers had entrances to the open space, one entrance on the north and another on the south. The width of the wall surrounding the open space was five cubits. 12† The building fronting the free area on the west side was seventy cubits front to back; the wall of the building was five cubits thick all around, and it measured ninety cubits from side to side. 13 He measured the temple, which was one hundred cubits long. The free area, together with the building and its walls, was a hundred cubits in length. 14 The façade of the temple, along with the free area, on the east side, was one hundred cubits wide. 15 He measured the building which lay the length of the free area and behind it, and together with its walls on both sides it was one hundred cubits.

Interior of the Temple

The inner nave and the outer vestibule 16 were paneled with precious wood all around, covered from the ground to the windows. There were splayed windows with trellises about them [facing the threshold]. 17 As high as the lintel of the door, even into the interior part of the temple as well as outside, on every wall on every side in both the inner and outer rooms were carved 18 the figures of cherubim and palmtrees: a palmtree between every two cherubim. Each cherub had two faces: 19 a man's face looking at a palmtree on one side, and a lion's face looking at a palmtree on the other; thus they were figured on every side throughout the

---

† **40, 46:** *The Zadokites:* descendants of the priestly line of Zadok; cf 2 Sm 15, 24–29; 1 Kgs 1, 32ff; 2, 35.

40, 48—41, 15: The description of Ezekiel's visionary temple closely follows the description of the temple of Solomon (1 Kgs 6).

40, 49—41, 4: *Vestibule . . . nave . . . holy of holies:* the three di-

visions of the temple building in progressing order of sanctity. The last is called "the inner sanctuary" in 1 Kgs 6.

41, 12: *The building:* the function of this structure lying behind the temple is never specified.

whole temple. ²⁰ From the ground to the lintel of the door the cherubim and palmtrees were carved on the walls. ²¹ The way into the nave was a square doorframe. In front of the holy place was something that looked like ²²† a wooden altar, three cubits in height, two cubits long, and two cubits wide. It had corners, and its base and sides were of wood. He said to me, "This is the table which is before the LORD." ²³ The nave had a double door, and also the holy place had ²⁴ a double door. Each door had two movable leaves; two leaves were on one doorjamb and two on the other. ²⁵ Carved upon them [on the doors of the nave] were cherubim and palmtrees, like those carved on the walls. Before the vestibule outside was a wooden lattice. ²⁶ There were splayed windows [and palmtrees] on both side walls of the vestibule, and the side chambers of the temple. . . .

Other Structures

42 ¹ Then he led me north to the outer court, bringing me to some chambers on the north that lay across the free area and which were also across from the building. ² Their length was a hundred cubits on the north side, and they were fifty cubits wide. ³ Across the twenty cubits of the inner court and the pavement of the outer court, there were three parallel rows of them on different levels. ⁴ In front of the chambers, to the inside, was a walk ten cubits broad and a wall of one cubit; but the entrances of the chambers were on the north. ⁵† The outermost chambers were the lowest, for the

system of levels set them at a level lower than the closest chambers and those in between; ⁶ for they were in three rows and had no foundations to conform with the foundations of the courts, therefore they were on a lower terrace of the ground than the closest and the middle chambers. ⁷ On the far side there was a wall running parallel to the chambers along the outer court; its length before these chambers was fifty cubits, ⁸ for the length of the chambers belonging to the outer court was fifty cubits, but along its entire length the wall measured one hundred cubits. ⁹ Below these chambers there was the way in from the east, so that one could enter from the outer court ¹⁰ where the wall of the court began.

To the south along the side of the free area and the building there were also chambers, ¹¹ before which was a passage. These looked like the chambers to the north, just as long and just as wide, with the same exits and plan and entrances. ¹² Below the chambers to the south there was an entrance at the beginning of the way which led to the back wall, by which one could enter from the east. ¹³† He said to me, "The north and south chambers which border on the free area are the sanctuary chambers; here the priests who draw near to the LORD shall eat the most sacred meals, and here they shall keep the most sacred offerings: cereal offerings, sin offerings, and guilt offerings; for it is a holy place. ¹⁴ When the priests have once entered, they shall not leave the holy place for the outer court until they have left here the clothing in which they ministered, for it is holy. They shall put on other garments, and then approach the place destined for the people."

Measuring the Outer Court

¹⁵ When he had finished measuring the inner temple area, he brought me out by way of the gate which faces east and measured all the limits of the court. ¹⁶ He measured the east side: five hundred cubits by his measuring rod. Then he turned ¹⁷ and measured the north side: five hundred cubits by the measuring rod. He turned ¹⁸ to the south and measured five hundred cubits by the measuring rod. ¹⁹ Then he turned to the west and measured five hundred cubits by the measuring rod. ²⁰ Thus he measured it in the four directions, five hundred cubits long and five hundred cubits wide. It was surrounded by a wall, to separate the sacred from the profane.

41, 22: *A wooden altar:* the altar of incense, standing in the nave at the entrance to the holy of holies.
42, 5f: The three rows of identical chambers, since they rested on different ground levels, necessarily had roofs on correspondingly different levels.

42, 13: The function of these chambers is explained again in Ez 46, 19f.

God's Dwelling Place

Ezekiel's vision of God returning to the Temple in Ez 43, 1–5 completes the circle of his prophecy. Earlier, as described in chapter 10, he had a unique vision of God's glory leaving the Temple and coming to rest in Babylon. For Ezekiel, the Temple represents the heart of Israel's relationship with God, and it is important that God's presence will return to it. This probably explains why Ezekiel carefully records the specifics of the new Temple in the remaining chapters of his book—to help make it more real.

The early Christians learned from Jesus that God's presence isn't limited to the Temple. The good news is that God is present in every person! First Corinthians 3, 16 says, "Do you not know that you are the temple of God, and that the Spirit of God dwells in you?" The basis for our self-worth should be knowing that God's spirit dwells within us. If that doesn't make us special, what will?

▸ Ez 43, 1–5

Restoration of the Temple

The Return of the Lord

43 ¹ Then he led me to the gate which faces the east, ² and there I saw the glory of the God of Israel coming from the east. I heard a sound like the roaring of many waters, and the earth shone with his glory. ³* The vision was like that which I had seen when he came to destroy the city, and like that which I had seen by the river Chebar. I fell prone ⁴ as the glory of the LORD entered the temple by way of the gate which faces the east, ⁵ but spirit lifted me up and brought me to the inner court. And I saw that the temple was filled with the glory of the LORD. ⁶ Then I heard someone speaking to me from the temple, while the man stood beside me. ⁷ The voice said to me: Son of man, this is where my throne shall be, this is where I will set the soles of my feet; here I will dwell among the Israelites forever. Never again shall they and their kings profane my holy name with their harlotries and with the corpses of their kings [their high places]. ⁸† When they placed their threshold against my threshold and their doorpost next to mine, so that only a wall was between us, they profaned my holy name by their abominable deeds; therefore I consumed them in my wrath. ⁹ From now on they shall put far from me their harlotry and the corpses of their kings, and I will dwell in their midst forever.

The Law of the Temple

¹⁰ As for you, son of man, describe the temple to the house of Israel [that they may be ashamed of their sins], both its measurements and its design; ¹¹ [and if they are ashamed of all that they have done,] make known to them the form and design of the temple, its exits and entrances, all its statutes and laws; write these down for them to see, that they may carefully observe all its laws and statutes. ¹² This is the law of the temple: its whole surrounding area on the mountain top shall be most sacred.

The Altar

¹³† These were the measurements of the altar in cubits of one cubit plus a handbreadth. Its base was one cubit high and one cubit deep, with a rim around its edge of one span. The height of the altar itself was as follows: ¹⁴ from its base at the bottom up to the lower ledge it was two cubits high, and this ledge was one cubit deep; from the lower to the upper ledge it was four cubits high, and this ledge also was one cubit deep; ¹⁵ the hearth of the altar was four cubits high, and extending from the top of the hearth were the four horns of the altar. ¹⁶ The hearth was a square: twelve cubits long and twelve cubits wide. ¹⁷ The upper ledge was also a square: fourteen cubits long and fourteen cubits wide. The lower ledge, likewise a square, was sixteen cubits long and sixteen cubits wide, with a half-cubit rim

---

43, 8: *They placed their threshold against my threshold:* the pre-exilic temple and the royal palace belonged to the same complex of buildings, and this physical proximity was reflected in the use made of the temple by kings like Ahaz and Manasseh, who treated it as their private chapel for pagan rites. In the new Israel the temple is

free, even physically, from civil jurisdiction; cf Ez 45, 7f.
43, 13: *The altar:* of holocausts, standing in the inner court of the temple area; cf Ez 40, 47.

43, 3: Ez 1, 1.

surrounding it. And there was a base of one cubit all around. The steps of the altar face the east.

¹⁸ Then he said to me: Son of man, thus says the Lord GOD: These are the statutes for the altar when it is set up for the offering of holocausts upon it and for the sprinkling of blood against it. ¹⁹ Give a young bull as a sin offering to the priests, the Levites who are of the line of Zadok, who draw near me to minister to me, says the Lord GOD. ²⁰ Take some of its blood and put it on the four horns of the altar, and on the four corners of the ledge, and on the rim all around. Thus you shall purify it and make atonement for it. ²¹ Then take the bull of the sin offering, which is to be burnt in a designated part of the temple, outside the sanctuary. ²² On the second day present an unblemished he-goat as a sin offering, to purify the altar as was done with the bull. ²³ When you have finished the purification, bring an unblemished young bull and an unblemished ram from the flock, ²⁴ and present them before the LORD; the priests shall strew salt on them and offer them to the LORD as holocausts. ²⁵ Daily for seven days you shall offer a he-goat as a sin offering, and a young bull and a ram from the flock, all unblemished, shall be offered ²⁶ for seven days. Thus atonement shall be made for the altar, and it shall be purified and dedicated. ²⁷ And when these days are over, from the eighth day on, the priests shall offer your holocausts and peace offerings on the altar. Then I will accept you, says the Lord GOD.

The Closed Gate

44 ¹ Then he brought me back to the outer gate of the sanctuary, facing the east; but it was closed. ² He said to me: This gate is to remain closed; it is not to be opened for anyone to enter by it; since the LORD, the God of Israel, has entered by it, it shall remain closed. ³† Only the prince may sit down in it to eat his meal in the presence of the LORD. He must enter by way of the vestibule of the gate, and leave by the same way.

The New Law
Admission to the Temple

⁴ Then he brought me by way of the north gate to the façade of the temple, and when I looked I saw the glory of the LORD filling the LORD'S temple, and I fell prone. ⁵ Then he said to me: Son of man, pay strict attention, look carefully, and listen intently to

all that I will tell you about the statutes and laws of the LORD'S temple; be attentive in regard to those who are to be admitted to the temple and all those who are to be excluded from the sanctuary. ⁶ Say to that rebellious house, the house of Israel: Thus says the Lord GOD: Enough of all these abominations of yours, O house of Israel! ⁷† You have admitted foreigners, uncircumcised both in heart and flesh, to my sanctuary to profane it when you offered me food, fat, and blood; thus you have broken my covenant by all your abominations. ⁸ Instead of caring for the service of my temple, you have appointed such as these to serve me in my sanctuary in your stead. ⁹ Thus says the Lord GOD: No foreigners, uncircumcised in heart and in flesh, shall ever enter my sanctuary; none of the foreigners who live among the Israelites.

Levites

¹⁰† But as for the Levites who departed from me when Israel strayed from me to pursue their idols, they shall bear the consequences of their sin. ¹¹ They shall serve in my sanctuary as gatekeepers and temple servants; they shall slaughter the holocausts and the sacrifices for the people, and they shall stand before the people to minister for them. ¹² Because they used to minister for them before their idols, and became an occasion of sin to the house of Israel, therefore I have sworn an oath against them, says the Lord GOD: they shall bear the consequences of their sin. ¹³ They shall no longer draw near me to serve as my priests, nor shall they touch any of my sacred things, or the most sacred things. Thus they shall bear their disgrace because of all their abominable deeds. ¹⁴ But I will set them to the service of the temple, for all its work and for everything that is to be done in it.

Priests

¹⁵ As for the levitical priests, however, the Zadokites who cared for my sanctuary when the Israelites strayed from me, they shall draw near me to minister to me, and they shall stand before me to offer me fat and blood, says the Lord GOD. ¹⁶ It is they who shall enter my sanctuary, they who shall approach my table to minister to me, and they who shall carry out my service. ¹⁷ Whenever they enter the gates of the inner court, they shall wear linen garments; they shall not put on anything woolen

---

44, 3: The prince stands at the eastern gate of the inner court while his sacrifice is offered up (Ez 46, 2); he then goes to the vestibule of the outer court, there to partake of his sacrificial meal. The closed outer gate on the eastern side signifies that the Lord has entered the temple permanently, not to depart again.

44, 7ff: In the preexilic temple various menial services had been performed by foreigners; cf Jos 9, 22–27. In the new temple the Levites will perform these services (vv 10–14).

44, 10–14: Levites other than the Zadokite priesthood of Jerusalem had performed priestly functions at the various sanctuaries and high places in Israel and Judah, where the worship of the Lord had often been corrupted with pagan elements. The demotion of the Levites to menial service in the temple was enforced in the actual restoration after the exile, and explains why relatively few Levites were willing to return; cf 1 Ezr 8, 15ff.

when they minister at the gates of the inner court or within the temple. 18* They shall have linen turbans on their heads and linen drawers on their loins; they shall not gird themselves with anything that causes sweat. 19*† When they are to go out to the people in the outer court, they shall take off the garments in which they ministered and leave them in the chambers of the sanctuary, putting on other garments; thus they will not transmit holiness to the people with their garments.

20* They shall not shave their heads nor let their hair hang loose, but they shall keep their hair carefully trimmed. 21* No priest shall drink wine when he is to enter the inner court. 22* They shall not take for their wives either widows or divorced women, but only virgins of the race of Israel; however, they may marry women who are the widows of priests. 23 They shall teach my people to distinguish between the sacred and the profane, and make known to them the difference between the clean and the unclean. 24* In capital cases they shall stand as judges, judging them according to my decrees. They shall observe my laws and statutes on all my festivals, and keep my sabbaths holy.

25* They shall not make themselves unclean by coming near any dead person, unless it be their father, mother, son, daughter, brother, or maiden sister; for these they may make themselves unclean. 26 After a priest has been cleansed, he must wait an additional seven days, 27 and on the day he enters the inner court to minister in the sanctuary, he shall present his sin offering, says the Lord GOD. 28* They shall have no inheritance, for I am their inheritance; you shall give them no property in Israel, for I am their property. 29*† They shall eat the cereal offering, the sin offering, and the guilt offering; whatever is under the ban in Israel shall be theirs. 30* All the choicest first fruits of every kind, and all the best of your offerings of every kind, shall belong to the priests; likewise the best of your dough you shall give to the priests to bring a blessing down upon your house. 31* The priests shall not eat anything, whether flesh or fowl, that has died of itself or has been killed by wild beasts.

The Sacred Tract

45 ¹ When you apportion the land into inheritances, you shall set apart a sacred tract of land for the LORD, twenty-five thousand cubits long and twenty thousand wide; its whole area shall be sacred. ² Of this land a square plot, five hundred by five hundred cubits, surrounded by a free space of fifty cubits, shall be assigned to the sanctuary. ³ Also from this sector measure off a strip, twenty-five thousand cubits long and ten thousand wide, within which shall be the sanctuary, the holy of holies. ⁴ This shall be the sacred part of the land belonging to the priests, the ministers of the sanctuary, who draw near to minister to the LORD; it shall be a place for their homes and pasture land for their cattle. ⁵ Also there shall be a strip twenty-five thousand cubits long and ten thousand wide as property for the Levites, the ministers of the temple, that they may have cities to live in. ⁶ As property of the City you shall designate a strip five thousand cubits wide and twenty-five thousand long, parallel to the sacred tract; this shall belong to the whole house of Israel. ⁷ The prince shall have a section bordering on both sides of the combined sacred tract and City property, extending westward on the western side and eastward on the eastern side, corresponding in length to one of the tribal portions from the western boundary to the eastern boundary ⁸ of the land. This shall be his property in Israel, so that the princes of Israel will no longer oppress my people, but will leave the land to the house of Israel according to their tribes.

Weights and Measures

⁹† Thus says the Lord GOD: Enough, you princes of Israel! Put away violence and oppression, and do what is right and just! Stop evicting my people! says the Lord GOD. 10* You shall have honest scales, an honest ephah, and an honest liquid measure. 11 The ephah and the liquid measure shall be of the same size: the liquid measure equal to a tenth of a homer, and the ephah equal to a tenth of a homer; by the homer they shall be determined. 12* The shekel shall be twenty gerahs. Twenty shekels, twenty-five shekels, plus fifteen shekels shall be your mina.

44, 19: *Thus they will not transmit holiness to the people:* holiness was thought of as something physical, as though it were communicable, and therefore not to be brought in contact with unconsecrated persons.

44, 29: *Under the ban:* dedicated to the Lord, withdrawn from profane use.

45, 9–12: Besides the land monopoly fostered by royal greed and collusion with the wealthy (Mi 2, 2; Is 3, 12–15; 5, 8–10), one grave social evil of preexilic Israel was dishonesty in business; cf Hos 12, 8; Am 8, 5. *Ephah:* a dry measure; liquid measure: in Hebrew, a "bath," standardized according to the homer (a dry measure of about 10 bushels, or 80 gallons). In v 12 reference is made to the change in value of the mina: before the exile it was valued at 50 shekels, but afterward, in imitation of Babylonian practice, the 60-shekel mina was adopted. The shekel was a unit of weight slightly less than half an ounce. As a monetary unit, the value obviously differed greatly, depending on whether it was a gold or a silver shekel.

44, 18: Ex 28, 40.42; 29, 9; 38, 28; Lv 6, 3.	44, 29: Lv 2, 3.10; 6, 9.22; 7, 9; 10, 12; Nm 18, 9; 18, 14.
44, 19: Ez 42, 13.14.	
44, 20: Lv 21, 5.	44, 30: Ex 34, 26; Dt 18, 4.
44, 21: Lv 10, 9.	44, 31: Lv 22, 8.
44, 22: Lv 21, 7.14.	45, 10: Lv 19, 35; Dt 25, 13–16; Hos 12, 8; Am 8, 5; Mi 6, 10f.
44, 24: Dt 17, 9; 19, 17.	
44, 25: Lv 21, 1ff.11.	
44, 28: Nm 18, 20; Dt 18, 1.	45, 12: Ex 30, 13; Lv 27, 25; Nm 3, 47; 18, 16.

Offerings

13 These are the offerings you shall make: one sixth of an ephah from each homer of wheat, and one sixth of an ephah from each homer of barley. 14† The regulation for oil: for every measure of oil, a tenth of a measure, computed by the kor of ten liquid measures [or a homer, for ten liquid measures make a homer]. 15 One sheep from the flock for every two hundred from the pasturage of Israel, for sacrifice—holocausts and peace offerings and atonement sacrifices, says the Lord GOD. 16 All the people of the land shall be bound to this offering [for the prince in Israel]. 17 It shall be the duty of the prince to provide the holocausts, cereal offerings, and libations on the feasts, new moons, and sabbaths, on all the festivals of the house of Israel. He shall offer the sin offerings, cereal offerings, holocausts, and peace offerings, to make atonement on behalf of the house of Israel.

The Passover

18 Thus says the Lord GOD: On the first day of the first month you shall use an unblemished young bull as a sacrifice to purify the sanctuary. 19 Then the priest shall take some of the blood from the sin offering and put it on the doorposts of the temple, on the four corners of the ledge of the altar, and on the doorposts of the gates of the inner court. 20 You shall repeat this on the first day of the seventh month for those who have sinned through inadvertence or ignorance; thus you shall make atonement for the temple. 21* On the fourteenth day of the first month you shall observe the feast of the Passover; for seven days unleavened bread is to be eaten. 22 On that day the prince shall offer on his own behalf, and on behalf of all the people of the land, a bull as a sin offering. 23 On each of the seven days of the feast he shall offer as a holocaust to the Lord seven bulls and seven rams without blemish, and as a sin offering he shall offer one male goat each day. 24† As a cereal offering he shall offer one ephah for each bull and one ephah for each ram; and he shall offer one hin of oil for each ephah.

The Feast of Booths

25 On the fifteenth day of the seventh month, the feast day, and for seven days, he shall perform the same rites, making the same sin offerings, the same holocausts, the same cereal offerings and offerings of oil.

Sabbaths

46 1 Thus says the Lord GOD: The gate toward the east of the inner court shall remain closed throughout the six working days, but on the sabbath and on the day of the new moon it shall be open. 2 The prince shall enter from outside by way of the vestibule of the gate and remain standing at the doorpost of the gate; then while the priests offer his holocausts and peace offerings, he shall worship at the threshold of the gate and then leave; the gate shall not be closed until evening. 3 The people of the land shall worship before the LORD at the door of this gate on the sabbaths and new moons. 4* The holocausts which the prince presents to the LORD on the sabbath shall consist of six unblemished lambs and an unblemished ram, 5 together with a cereal offering of one ephah for the ram, whatever he pleases for the lambs, and a hin of oil for each ephah. 6* On the day of the new moon he shall provide an unblemished young bull, also six lambs and a ram without blemish, 7 with a cereal offering of one ephah for the bull and one for the ram, for the lambs as much as he has at hand, and for each ephah a hin of oil.

Ritual Laws

8 The prince shall always enter and depart by the vestibule of the gate. 9* When the people of the land enter the presence of the LORD to worship on the festivals, if they enter by the north gate they shall leave by the south gate, and if they enter by the south gate they shall leave by the north gate; no one shall return by the gate through which he has entered, but he shall leave by the opposite gate. 10 The prince shall be in their midst when they enter, and he shall also leave with them. 11 On the feasts and festivals the cereal offering shall be an ephah for a bull, an ephah for a ram, but for the lambs as much as one pleases, and a hin of oil with each ephah. 12 When the prince makes a freewill offering to the LORD, whether holocausts or peace offerings, the eastern gate shall be opened for him, and he shall offer his holocausts or his peace offerings as on the sabbath; then he shall leave, and the gate shall be closed after his departure. 13* He shall offer as a daily holocaust to the LORD an unblemished yearling lamb; this he shall offer every morning. 14 With it every morning he shall provide as a cereal offering one sixth of an ephah, with a third of a hin of oil to moisten the fine flour. This cereal offering to the LORD is mandatory with the established holocaust. 15* The lamb,

E
Z

---

† **45, 14:** *Kor:* both a liquid and a dry measure, corresponding to the homer.
45, 24: *Hin:* a sixth part of the liquid measure called a bath.

* **45, 21:** Ex 12, 6; Lv 23, 5; Nm 28, 16.
46, 4: Nm 28, 9f.
46, 6: Nm 28, 11–15.
46, 9: Ex 23, 17; 34, 23; Dt 16, 16.
46, 13: Ex 29, 38–42; Nm 28, 3–8.
46, 15: Ex 29, 42.

the cereal offering, and the oil are to be offered every morning as an established holocaust.

The Prince and the Land

16 Thus says the Lord GOD: If the prince makes a gift of part of his inheritance to any of his sons, it shall belong to his sons; that property is theirs by inheritance. 17† But if he makes a gift of part of his inheritance to one of his servants, it shall belong to the latter only until the year of release, when it shall revert to the prince. Only the inheritance given to his sons is permanent. 18 The prince shall not seize any part of the inheritance of the people by evicting them from their property. He shall provide an inheritance for his sons from his own property, so that none of my people will be driven from their property.

The Temple Kitchens

19 Then he brought me by the entrance which is on the side of the gate to the chambers [of the sanctuary, reserved to the priests] which face the north. There, at their west end, I saw a place, 20 concerning which he said to me, "Here the priests cook the guilt offerings and the sin offerings, and bake the cereal offerings, so that they do not have to take them into the outer court at the risk of transmitting holiness to the people." 21 Then he led me into the outer court and had me pass around the four corners of the court, and I saw that in each corner there was another court: 22 in the four corners of the court, minor courts, forty cubits long and thirty wide, all four of them the same size. 23 A wall of stones surrounded each of the four, and hearths were built beneath the stones all the way around. 24 He said to me, "These are the kitchens where the temple ministers cook the sacrifices of the people."

The Wonderful Stream

47 1*† Then he brought me back to the entrance of the temple, and I saw water flowing out from beneath the threshold of the temple toward the east, for the façade of the temple was toward the east; the water flowed down from the southern side of the temple, south of the altar. 2 He led me outside by the north gate, and around to the outer gate facing the east, where I saw water trickling from the southern side. 3 Then when he had walked off to the east with a measuring cord in his

hand, he measured off a thousand cubits and had me wade through the water, which was ankle-deep. 4 He measured off another thousand and once more had me wade through the water, which was now knee-deep. Again he measured off a thousand and had me wade; the water was up to my waist. 5 Once more he measured off a thousand, but there was now a river through which I could not wade; for the water had risen so high it had become a river that could not be crossed except by swimming. 6 He asked me, "Have you seen this, son of man?" Then he brought me to the bank of the river, where he had me sit. 7 Along the bank of the river I saw very many trees on both sides. 8 He said to me, "This water flows into the eastern district down upon the Arabah, and empties into the sea, the salt waters, which it makes fresh. 9 Wherever the river flows, every sort of living creature that can multiply shall live, and there shall be abundant fish, for wherever this water comes the sea shall be made fresh. 10† Fishermen shall be standing along it from En-gedi to En-eglaim, spreading their nets there. Its kinds of fish shall be like those of the Great Sea, very numerous. 11 Only its marshes and swamps shall not be made fresh; they shall be left for salt. 12 Along both banks of the river, fruit trees of every kind shall grow; their leaves shall not fade, nor their fruit fail. Every month they shall bear fresh fruit, for they shall be watered by the flow from the sanctuary. Their fruit shall serve for food, and their leaves for medicine."

The New Israel

Boundaries of the Land

13† Thus says the Lord GOD: These are the boundaries within which you shall apportion the land among the twelve tribes of Israel [Joseph having two portions]. 14 All of you shall have a like portion in this land which I swore to give to your fathers, that it might fall to you as your inheritance. 15* This is the boundary of the land on the north side: from the Great Sea in the direction of Hethlon, past Labo of Hamath, to Zedad, 16 Berothah, and Sibraim, along the frontiers of Hamath and Damascus, to Hazar-enon which is on the border of the Hauran. 17 Thus the border shall extend from the sea to Hazar-enon, with the frontier of Hamath and Damascus to the north. This is the northern boundary. 18 The eastern boundary: between the

---

46, 17: *The year of release:* the jubilee year; cf Lv 25, 23–55.

47, 1–12: The wonderful and superabundant stream flowing from the temple, restoring fertility traditionally arid ground, is symbolic of the return of the conditions of primeval paradise; cf Gn 2, 10–14. Water signifies great blessings, just as dryness signifies a curse; cf Ez 26, 5.14.

47, 10: *From En-gedi to En-eglaim:* the former was about halfway down the western shore of the Dead Sea, the latter may have been at its northern extremity.

47, 13–20: These boundaries of the restored Israel correspond to those of the Davidic kingdom at its fullest extent, the so-called "ideal boundaries" of the promised land; cf Nm 34, 3–12.

47, 1: Sir 24, 28f; Jl 4, 18;   **47, 15:** Nm 34, 7ff.
  Zec 13, 1; Rv 22, 1f.

Hauran—toward Damascus—and Gilead on the one side, and the land of Israel on the other side, the Jordan shall form the boundary down to the eastern sea as far as Tamar. This is the eastern boundary. ¹⁹ The southern boundary: from Tamar to the waters of Meribath-kadesh, thence to the Wadi of Egypt, and on to the Great Sea. This is the southern boundary. ²⁰ The western boundary: the Great Sea forms the boundary up to a point parallel to Labo of Hamath. This is the western boundary.

The Northern Portions

²¹ You shall distribute this land among yourselves according to the tribes of Israel. ²²* You shall allot it as inheritances for yourselves and for the aliens resident in your midst who have bred children among you. The latter shall be to you like native Israelites; along with you they shall receive inheritances among the tribes of Israel. ²³ In whatever tribe the alien may be resident, there you shall assign him his inheritance, says the Lord GOD.

48 ¹*† This is the list of the tribes. Dan: at the northern extremity, adjoining Hamath, all along from the approaches to Hethlon through Labo of Hamath to Hazar-enon, on the northerly border with Damascus, with his possession reaching from the eastern to the western boundary. ² Asher: on the frontier of Dan, from the eastern to the western boundary. ³ Naphtali: on the frontier of Asher, from the eastern to the western boundary. ⁴ Manasseh: on the frontier of Naphtali, from the eastern to the western boundary. ⁵ Ephraim: on the frontier of Manasseh, from the eastern to the western boundary. ⁶ Reuben: on the frontier of Ephraim, from the eastern to the western boundary. ⁷ Judah: on the frontier of Reuben, from the eastern to the western boundary.

The Sacred Tract

⁸ On the frontier of Judah, from the eastern to the western boundary there shall be the tract which you shall set apart, twenty-five thousand cubits from north to south, and as wide as one of the tribal portions from the eastern to the western boundary. In the center of the tract shall be the sanctuary. ⁹ The tract that you set aside for the LORD shall be twenty-five thousand cubits across by twenty thousand north and south. ¹⁰ In this sacred tract the priests shall have twenty-five thousand cubits on the north, ten thousand on the west, ten thousand on the east, and twenty-five thousand on the south; and the sanctuary of the LORD shall be in its

center. ¹¹ The consecrated priests, the Zadokites, who fulfilled my service and did not stray along with the Israelites as the Levites did, ¹² shall have within this tract of land their own most sacred domain, next to the territory of the Levites. ¹³ The Levites shall have a territory corresponding to that of the priests, twenty-five thousand cubits by ten thousand. The whole tract shall be twenty-five thousand cubits across and twenty thousand north and south. ¹⁴ They may not sell or exchange or alienate this, the best part of the land, for it is sacred to the LORD. ¹⁵ The remaining five thousand cubits along the twenty-five-thousand-cubit line are profane land, assigned to the City for dwellings and pasture; the City shall be at their center. ¹⁶ These are the dimensions of the City: the north side, forty-five hundred cubits; the south side, forty-five hundred cubits; the east side, forty-five hundred cubits; and the west side, forty-five hundred cubits. ¹⁷ The pasture lands of the City shall extend north two hundred and fifty cubits, south two hundred and fifty cubits, east two hundred and fifty cubits, and west two hundred and fifty cubits. ¹⁸ There shall remain an area along the sacred tract, ten thousand cubits to the east and ten thousand to the west, whose produce shall provide food for the workers of the City. ¹⁹ The workers in the City shall be taken from all the tribes of Israel. ²⁰ The entire tract shall be twenty-five thousand by twenty-five thousand cubits; as a perfect square you shall set apart the sacred tract together with the City property.

²¹ The remainder shall belong to the prince: the land on both sides of the sacred tract and the City property, extending along the twenty-five-thousand-cubit line eastward to the eastern boundary, and westward along the twenty-five-thousand-cubit line to the western boundary, a territory parallel with the tribal portions for the prince. The sacred tract and the sanctuary of the temple shall be in the middle. ²² Thus, except for the property of the Levites and the City property, which lie in the midst of the prince's property, the territory between the portions of Judah and of Benjamin shall belong to the prince.

The Southern Portions

²³ These are the remaining tribes. Benjamin: from the eastern to the western boundary. ²⁴ Simeon: on the frontier of Benjamin, from the eastern to the western boundary. ²⁵ Issachar: on the frontier of Simeon, from the eastern to the western boundary. ²⁶ Zebulun: on the frontier of Issachar, from the

---

48, 1–29: This distribution of the land among the tribes does not correspond to the geographical realities of Palestine. It is a description of the ideal order, like that in Ez 47, 1–12.

47, 22: Ex 12, 48; Lv 19, 34; 24, 22; Nm 9, 14; Jos 8, 33.

48, 1: Ez 47, 15ff.

eastern to the western boundary. ²⁷ Gad: on the frontier of Zebulun, from the eastern to the western boundary. ²⁸ Along the frontier of Gad shall be the southern boundary, which shall extend from Tamar to the waters of Meribath-kadesh, and from there to the Wadi of Egypt, and on to the Great Sea. ²⁹ Such is the land which you shall apportion as inheritances among the tribes of Israel, and these are their portions, says the Lord GOD.

The Gates of the City

³⁰ These are the exits of the City, the gates of which are named after the tribes of Israel. On the north side, measuring forty-five hundred cubits, ³¹ there shall be three gates: the gate of Reuben, the gate of Judah, and the gate of Levi. ³² On the east side, measuring forty-five hundred cubits, there shall be three gates: the gate of Joseph, the gate of Benjamin, and the gate of Dan. ³³ On the south side, measuring forty-five hundred cubits, there shall be three gates: the gate of Simeon, the gate of Issachar, and the gate of Zebulun. ³⁴ On the west side, measuring forty-five hundred cubits, there shall be three gates: the gate of Gad, the gate of Asher, and the gate of Naphtali. ³⁵ The perimeter of the City is eighteen thousand cubits. The name of the City shall henceforth be "The LORD is here."

Do you have a favorite superhero from television or comic books? One characteristic of these larger-than-life heroes is their commitment to their own values and to saving victims of injustice. The Book of Daniel portrays just such a hero. Daniel's powers are his courage to remain faithful to God despite the threat of punishment, and his special visions, which foresee how things will turn out good even though the present situation seems far from hopeful. These powers enable him to lead his people on the right path in a foreign land filled with persecution and idolatry.

At a Glance

I. Daniel and the Kings of Babylon (1, 1—6, 29).

II. Daniel's Visions (7, 1—12, 13).

III. Appendix (13, 1—14, 42).

In-depth

Daniel represents the ideal leader with the spiritual and prophetic insight to lead people through troubled times. Scholars question whether he was an actual person. If he was, he lived in the sixth century B.C.—but the Book of Daniel was written four hundred years later, during the reign of an evil Greek-Syrian king, Antiochus IV Epiphanes. This was also the time of the Maccabean revolt told about in 1 and 2 Maccabees (see the timeline at the back of this Bible). King Antiochus desecrated the Temple and attempted to erase many of Israel's religious practices. To many in Israel, this seemed like the end of the world.

The author of the Book of Daniel writes about the great hero Daniel to give the people hope during this persecution. Chapters 1–6 present six stories of Daniel and three friends living their faith during the Babylonian Exile. Chapters 7–12 tell of Daniel's four visions about the empires that dominated Israel after the Exile: Media, Persia, and Greece. The visions are full of strange symbols meant to be understood by the Israelites but not the Greek rulers of the author's time.

As you read the Book of Daniel, you will find themes familiar from other biblical books. Like Baruch, it describes living faithfully in a strange land. Like 1 and 2 Maccabees, the book shows the courage of Israelites willing to die for their beliefs. And it declares even more clearly than 2 Maccabees and the Book of Wisdom the belief in life after death. Daniel is shown as the ideal Jew—the embodiment of all the best of the people in exile. In the face of unjust persecution and oppression, he leads his people in faithfulness to God, even through death itself.

Quick Facts

Period Covered
before the Babylonian Exile, the sixth century B.C.

Author
unknown, writing around 164 B.C., during the persecution of Israel by Antiochus IV Epiphanes

Theme
to give hope to those experiencing oppression and persecution

The Book of Daniel

Daniel

Chap. 6

I: Daniel and the Kings of Babylon

The Food Test

1 [1]* In the third year of the reign of Jehoiakim, king of Judah, King Nebuchadnezzar of Babylon came and laid siege to Jerusalem. [2]*† The Lord handed over to him Jehoiakim, king of Judah, and some of the vessels of the temple of God, which he carried off to the land of Shinar, and placed in the temple treasury of his god.

[3] The king told Ashpenaz, his chief chamberlain, to bring in some of the Israelites of royal blood and of the nobility, [4] young men without any defect, handsome, intelligent and wise, quick to learn, and prudent in judgment, such as could take their place in the king's palace; they were to be taught the language and literature of the Chaldeans; [5] after three years' training they were to enter the king's service. The king allotted them a daily portion of food and wine from the royal table. [6] Among these were men of Judah: Daniel, Hananiah, Mishael, and Azariah. [7]† The chief chamberlain changed their names: Daniel to Belteshazzar, Hananiah to Shadrach, Mishael to Meshach, and Azariah to Abednego.

[8]† But Daniel was resolved not to defile himself with the king's food or wine; so he begged the chief chamberlain to spare him this defilement. [9] Though God had given Daniel the favor and sympathy of the chief chamberlain, [10] he nevertheless said to Daniel, "I am afraid of my lord the king; it is he who allotted your food and drink. If he sees that you look wretched by comparison with the other young men of your age, you will endanger my life with the king." [11] Then Daniel said to the steward whom the chief chamberlain had put in charge of Daniel, Hananiah, Mishael, and Azariah, [12] "Please test your servants for ten days. Give us vegetables to eat and water to drink. [13] Then see how we look in comparison with the other young men who eat from the royal table, and treat your servants according to what you see." [14] He acceded to this request, and tested them for ten days; [15] after ten days they looked healthier and better fed than any of the young men who ate from the royal table. [16] So the steward continued to take away the food and wine they were to receive, and gave them vegetables.

[17] To these four young men God gave knowledge and proficiency in all literature and science, and to Daniel the understanding of all visions and dreams. [18] At the end of the time the king had specified for

---

1, 2: *Shinar:* ancient name for Babylonia, a deliberate archaism in this text: cf Gn 10, 10; 11, 2.

1, 7: The young men are given Babylonian names as a sign of their adoption by the king.

1, 8: *This defilement:* the bread, meat, and wine of the Gentiles, which were unclean (Hos 9, 3; Tb 1, 12; Jdt 10, 5; 12, 1f) because

they might have been offered to idols or prepared over firewood taken from a sacred grove. Only raw vegetables and water were safe from this danger (v 12).

1, 1: 2 Kgs 24, 1; 2 Chr 36, 6; Jer 25, 1.
1, 2: Dn 5, 2; Gn 10, 10;

2 Kgs 24, 2; 2 Chr 36, 7.

their preparation, the chief chamberlain brought them before Nebuchadnezzar. [19] When the king had spoken with all of them, none was found equal to Daniel, Hananiah, Mishael, and Azariah; and so they entered the king's service. [20] In any question of wisdom or prudence which the king put to them, he found them ten times better than all the magicians and enchanters in his kingdom. [21]*† Daniel remained there until the first year of King Cyrus.

The King's Dream†

2 [1] In the second year of his reign, King Nebuchadnezzar had a dream which left his spirit no rest and robbed him of his sleep. [2]† So he ordered that the magicians, enchanters, sorcerers, and Chaldeans be summoned to interpret the dream for him. When they came and presented themselves to the king, [3] he said to them, "I had a dream which will allow my spirit no rest until I know what it means." [4]† The Chaldeans answered the king [Aramaic]: "O king, live forever! Tell your servants the dream and we will give its meaning." [5] The king answered the Chaldeans, "This is what I have decided: unless you tell me the dream and its meaning, you shall be cut to pieces and your houses destroyed. [6] But if you tell me the dream and its meaning, you shall receive from me gifts and presents and great honors. Now tell me the dream and its meaning."

[7] Again they answered, "Let the king tell his servants the dream and we will give its meaning." [8] But the king replied: "I know for certain that you are bargaining for time, since you know what I have decided. [9] If you do not tell me the dream, there can be but one decree for you. You have framed a false and deceitful interpretation to present me with till the crisis is past. Tell me the dream, therefore, that I may be sure that you can also give its correct interpretation."

[10] The Chaldeans answered the king: "There is not a man on earth who can do what you ask, O king; never has any king, however great and mighty, asked such a thing of any magician, enchanter, or Chaldean. [11] What you demand, O king, is too difficult; there is no one who can tell it to the king except the gods who do not dwell among men." [12] At this the king became violently angry

and ordered all the wise men of Babylon to be put to death. [13] When the decree was issued that the wise men should be slain, Daniel and his companions were also sought out.

[14] Then Daniel prudently took counsel with Arioch, the captain of the king's guard, who had set out to kill the wise men of Babylon: [15] "O officer of the king," he asked, "what is the reason for this harsh order from the king?" When Arioch told him, [16] Daniel went and asked for time from the king, that he might give him the interpretation.

[17] Daniel went home and informed his companions Hananiah, Mishael, and Azariah, [18] that they might implore the mercy of the God of heaven in regard to this mystery, so that Daniel and his companions might not perish with the rest of the wise men of Babylon. [19] During the night the mystery was revealed to Daniel in a vision, and he blessed the God of heaven:

[20]   "Blessed be the name of God forever and ever,
      for wisdom and power are his.
[21]   He causes the changes of the times and seasons,
      makes kings and unmakes them.
      He gives wisdom to the wise
      and knowledge to those who understand.
[22]* He reveals deep and hidden things
      and knows what is in the darkness,
      for the light dwells with him.
[23]   To you, O God of my fathers,
      I give thanks and praise,
      because you have given me wisdom and power.
      Now you have shown me what we asked of you,
      you have made known to us the king's dream."

[24] So Daniel went to Arioch, whom the king had appointed to destroy the wise men of Babylon, and said to him, "Do not put the wise men of Babylon to death. Bring me before the king, and I will tell him the interpretation of the dream." Arioch quickly brought Daniel to the king and said, [25] "I have found a man among the Judean captives who can give the interpretation to the king." [26] The king asked Daniel, whose name was Belteshazzar, "Can

---

† **1, 21:** *The first year of King Cyrus:* the year of this Persian king's conquest of Babylon, 539/8 B.C.

2, 1–49: The chronology of v 1 is in conflict with that of Dn 1, 5.18, and in v 25 Daniel appears to be introduced to the king for the first time. It seems that the story of this chapter was originally entirely independent of chapter 1, and later retouched slightly to fit its present setting.

2, 2: *Chaldeans:* here probably astrologers, who were so associated with the Chaldeans in the Hebrew mind that in the later language they are sometimes simply called by the name of that people.

2, 4: *Aramaic:* from Dn 2, 4 to 7, 28 the text of Daniel is in Aramaic, not Hebrew, as indicated by this gloss.

1, 21: Dn 6, 28.   1 Cor 4, 5; 1 Jn 1, 6.
2, 22: Jn 1, 9; 8, 12;

you tell me the dream that I had, and its meaning?" [27] In the king's presence Daniel made this reply:

"The mystery about which the king has inquired, the wise men, enchanters, magicians, and astrologers could not explain to the king. [28] But there is a God in heaven who reveals mysteries, and he has shown King Nebuchadnezzar what is to happen in days to come; this was the dream you saw as you lay in bed. [29] To you in your bed there came thoughts about what should happen in the future, and he who reveals mysteries showed you what is to be. [30] To me also this mystery has been revealed; not that I am wiser than any other living person, but in order that its meaning may be made known to the king, that you may understand the thoughts in your own mind.

[31] "In your vision, O king, you saw a statue, very large and exceedingly bright, terrifying in appearance as it stood before you. [32] The head of the statue was pure gold, its chest and arms were silver, its belly and thighs bronze, [33]† the legs iron, its feet partly iron and partly tile. [34] While you looked at the statue, a stone which was hewn from a mountain without a hand being put to it, struck its iron and tile feet, breaking them in pieces. [35] The iron, tile, bronze, silver, and gold all crumbled at once, fine as the chaff on the threshing floor in summer, and the wind blew them away without leaving a trace. But the stone that struck the statue became a great mountain and filled the whole earth.

[36]† "This was the dream; the interpretation we shall also give in the king's presence. [37] You, O king, are the king of kings; to you the God of heaven has given dominion and strength, power and glory; [38] men, wild beasts, and birds of the air, wherever they may dwell, he has handed over to you, making you ruler over them all; you are the head of gold. [39] Another kingdom shall take your place, inferior to yours, then a third kingdom, of bronze, which shall rule over the whole earth. [40] There shall be a fourth kingdom, strong as iron; it shall break in pieces and subdue all these others, just as iron breaks in pieces and crushes everything else. [41] The feet and toes you saw, partly of potter's tile and partly of iron, mean that it shall be a divided kingdom, but yet have some of the hardness of iron. As you saw the iron mixed with clay tile, [42] and the toes partly iron and partly tile, the kingdom shall be

partly strong and partly fragile. [43] The iron mixed with clay tile means that they shall seal their alliances by intermarriage, but they shall not stay united, any more than iron mixes with clay. [44] *In the lifetime of those kings the God of heaven will set up a kingdom that shall never be destroyed or delivered up to another people; rather, it shall break in pieces all these kingdoms and put an end to them, and it shall stand forever. [45] That is the meaning of the stone you saw hewn from the mountain without a hand being put to it, which broke in pieces the tile, iron, bronze, silver, and gold. The great God has revealed to the king what shall be in the future; this is exactly what you dreamed, and its meaning is sure."

[46] Then King Nebuchadnezzar fell down and worshiped Daniel and ordered sacrifice and incense offered to him. [47] To Daniel the king said, "Truly your God is the God of gods and Lord of kings and a revealer of mysteries; that is why you were able to reveal this mystery." [48] He advanced Daniel to a high post, gave him many generous presents, made him ruler of the whole province of Babylon and chief prefect over all the wise men of Babylon. [49] At Daniel's request the king made Shadrach, Meshach, and Abednego administrators of the province of Babylon, while Daniel himself remained at the king's court.

The Fiery Furnace

3 [1]† King Nebuchadnezzar had a golden statue made, sixty cubits high and six cubits wide, which he set up in the plain of Dura in the province of Babylon. [2]† He then ordered the satraps, prefects, and governors, the counselors, treasurers, judges, magistrates and all the officials of the provinces to be summoned to the dedication of the statue which he had set up. [3] The satraps, prefects, and governors, the counselors, treasurers, judges, and magistrates and all the officials of the provinces, all these came together for the dedication and stood before the statue which King Nebuchadnezzar had set up. [4]† A herald cried out: "Nations and peoples of every language, when you hear the sound of the trumpet, flute, lyre, harp, psaltery, bagpipe, and all the other musical instruments, [5] you are ordered to fall down and worship the golden statue which King Nebuchadnezzar has

---

†

2, 33: *Partly tile:* terra cotta tile was much in use among the Babylonians for decoration and for actual construction.

2, 36–45: The four successive kingdoms in this apocalyptic perspective are the Babylonian (gold), the Median (silver), the Persian (bronze), and the Hellenistic (iron). The last, after Alexander's death, was divided among his generals (vv 41f). The two resulting kingdoms, which most affected the Jews, were the dynasty of the Ptolemies in Egypt and that of the Seleucids in Syria, who tried in vain, by war and through intermarriage, to restore the unity of Alexander's empire (v 43). The stone hewn from the mountain is the

messianic kingdom awaited by the Jews (vv 44f). Our Lord made this image personal to himself; cf Lk 20, 17f.

3, 1: *Dura:* several places in Babylonia bore this name. Probably the present reference is to one a few miles south of Babylon. Colossi of the type mentioned here were not uncommon in antiquity; a cubit was seventeen and a half inches.

3, 2: *Satraps:* the Persian major governors.

3, 4: *Psaltery:* a harplike instrument.

2, 44: Mt 21, 44; Lk 20, 18.

Doing the Right Thing

Chapter 3 of Daniel tells us of Shadrach, Meshach, and Abednego, three companions of Daniel's who refuse to compromise their religious beliefs. Even in the face of death, they will not denounce the Lord and worship the god of Nebuchadnezzar (also called Nebuchadrezzar).

The pressure to do what we know is wrong takes many forms. Caving in to that pressure leads many people to suffering, because by definition, sin leads to unhappy and unhealthy consequences. It may offer some short-term satisfaction, but denying what we know is right is ultimately denying God and the fullness of life God has planned for us.

Follow Shadrach, Meshach, and Abednego's example and stand up for what is right, stand up for God!

▶ Dn 3, 1–24

set up. [6]† Whoever does not fall down and worship shall be instantly cast into a white-hot furnace." [7] Therefore, as soon as they heard the sound of the trumpet, flute, lyre, harp, psaltery, bagpipe, and all the other musical instruments, the nations and peoples of every language all fell down and worshiped the golden statue which King Nebuchadnezzar had set up.

[8] At that point, some of the Chaldeans came and accused the Jews [9] to King Nebuchadnezzar: "O king, live forever! [10] O king, you issued a decree that everyone who heard the sound of the trumpet, flute, lyre, harp, psaltery, bagpipe, and all the other musical instruments should fall down and worship the golden statue; [11] whoever did not was to be cast into a white-hot furnace. [12] There are certain Jews whom you have made administrators of the province of Babylon: Shadrach, Meshach, Abednego; these men, O king, have paid no attention to you; they will not serve your god or worship the golden statue which you set up."

[13] Nebuchadnezzar flew into a rage and sent for Shadrach, Meshach, and Abednego, who were promptly brought before the king. [14] King Nebuchadnezzar questioned them: "Is it true, Shadrach, Meshach, and Abednego, that you will not serve my god, or worship the golden statue that I set up? [15] Be ready now to fall down and worship the statue I had made, whenever you hear the sound of the trumpet, flute, lyre, harp, psaltery, bagpipe, and all the other musical instruments; otherwise, you shall be instantly cast into the white-hot furnace; and who is the God that can deliver you out of my hands?" [16] Shadrach, Meshach, and Abednego an-

swered King Nebuchadnezzar, "There is no need for us to defend ourselves before you in this matter. [17]† If our God, whom we serve, can save us from the white-hot furnace and from your hands, O king, may he save us! [18] But even if he will not, know, O king, that we will not serve your god or worship the golden statue which you set up."

[19] Nebuchadnezzar's face became livid with utter rage against Shadrach, Meshach, and Abednego. He ordered the furnace to be heated seven times more than usual [20] and had some of the strongest men in his army bind Shadrach, Meshach, and Abednego and cast them into the white-hot furnace. [21] They were bound and cast into the white-hot furnace with their coats, hats, shoes and other garments, [22] for the king's order was urgent. So huge a fire was kindled in the furnace that the flames devoured the men who threw Shadrach, Meshach, and Abednego into it. [23] But these three fell, bound, into the midst of the white-hot furnace.

[24]† They walked about in the flames, singing to God and blessing the Lord. [25] In the fire Azariah stood up and prayed aloud:

[26] "Blessed are you, and praiseworthy,
      O Lord, the God of our fathers,
      and glorious forever is your name.
[27] For you are just in all you have done;
      all your deeds are faultless, all your ways right,
      and all your judgments proper.
[28] You have executed proper judgments
      in all that you have brought upon us
      and upon Jerusalem, the holy city of
      our fathers.

---

† **3, 6:** Death by fire was not unknown as a punishment in Babylonia; cf Jer 29, 22.

3, 17: *If our God . . . can save us:* the youths do not question the efficacy of the divine power, but whether it will be exercised (v 18).

3, 24–90: These verses are inspired additions to the Aramaic text

of Daniel, translated from the Greek form of the book. They were originally composed in Hebrew or Aramaic, which has not been preserved. The church has always regarded them as part of the canonical Scriptures.

D N

3, 19-97

By a proper judgment you have done all this
  because of our sins;
29 For we have sinned and transgressed
  by departing from you,
  and we have done every kind of evil.
30 Your commandments we have not heeded
  or observed,
  nor have we done as you ordered us for
  our good.
31 Therefore all you have brought upon us,
  all you have done to us,
  you have done by a proper judgment.
32 You have handed us over to our enemies,
  lawless and hateful rebels;
  to an unjust king, the worst in all the world.
33 Now we cannot open our mouths;
  we, your servants, who revere you,
  have become a shame and a reproach.
34 For your name's sake, do not deliver us
  up forever,
  or make void your covenant.
35 Do not take away your mercy from us,
  for the sake of Abraham, your beloved,
  Isaac your servant, and Israel your
  holy one,
36 To whom you promised to multiply
  their offspring
  like the stars of heaven,
  or the sand on the shore of the sea.
37 For we are reduced, O Lord, beyond any
  other nation,
  brought low everywhere in the world
  this day
  because of our sins.
38 We have in our day no prince, prophet,
  or leader,
  no holocaust, sacrifice, oblation, or incense,

no place to offer first fruits, to find favor
  with you.
39 But with contrite heart and humble spirit
  let us be received;
40 As though it were holocausts of rams
  and bullocks,
  or thousands of fat lambs,
So let our sacrifice be in your presence today
  as we follow you unreservedly;
  for those who trust in you cannot be put
  to shame.
41 And now we follow you with our whole heart,
  we fear you and we pray to you.
42 Do not let us be put to shame,
  but deal with us in your kindness and
  great mercy.
43 Deliver us by your wonders,
  and bring glory to your name, O Lord:
44 Let all those be routed
  who inflict evils on your servants;
Let them be shamed and powerless,
  and their strength broken;
45 Let them know that you alone are the
  Lord God,
  glorious over the whole world."

46 Now the king's men who had thrown them in
continued to stoke the furnace with brimstone,
pitch, tow, and faggots. 47 The flames rose forty-
nine cubits above the furnace, 48 and spread out,
burning the Chaldeans nearby. 49 But the angel of
the Lord went down into the furnace with Azariah
and his companions, drove the fiery flames out of
the furnace, 50 and made the inside of the furnace
as though a dew-laden breeze were blowing
through it. The fire in no way touched them or
caused them pain or harm. 51 Then these three in
the furnace with one voice sang, glorifying and
blessing God:

52 "Blessed are you, O Lord, the God of our
  fathers,
  praiseworthy and exalted above all forever;
And blessed is your holy and glorious name,
  praiseworthy and exalted above all for
  all ages.
53 Blessed are you in the temple of your
  holy glory,
  praiseworthy and glorious above
  all forever.
54 Blessed are you on the throne of
  your kingdom,
  praiseworthy and exalted above all forever.
55 Blessed are you who look into the depths
  from your throne upon the cherubim,
  praiseworthy and exalted above all forever.
56 Blessed are you in the firmament of heaven,

praiseworthy and glorious forever.

57 Bless the Lord, all you works of the Lord,
   praise and exalt him above all forever.
58 Angels of the Lord, bless the Lord,
   praise and exalt him above all forever.
59* You heavens, bless the Lord,
   praise and exalt him above all forever.
60 All you waters above the heavens, bless
   the Lord,
   praise and exalt him above all forever.
61 All you hosts of the Lord, bless the Lord;
   praise and exalt him above all forever.
62 Sun and moon, bless the Lord;
   praise and exalt him above all forever.
63 Stars of heaven, bless the Lord;
   praise and exalt him above all forever.
64 Every shower and dew, bless the Lord;
   praise and exalt him above all forever.
65 All you winds, bless the Lord;
   praise and exalt him above all forever.
66 Fire and heat, bless the Lord;
   praise and exalt him above all forever.
67 [Cold and chill, bless the Lord;
   praise and exalt him above all forever.
68 Dew and rain, bless the Lord;
   praise and exalt him above all forever.]
69 Frost and chill, bless the Lord;
   praise and exalt him above all forever.
70 Ice and snow, bless the Lord;
   praise and exalt him above all forever.
71 Nights and days, bless the Lord;
   praise and exalt him above all forever.
72 Light and darkness, bless the Lord;
   praise and exalt him above all forever.
73 Lightnings and clouds, bless the Lord;
   praise and exalt him above all forever.
74 Let the earth bless the Lord,
   praise and exalt him above all forever.
75 Mountains and hills, bless the Lord;
   praise and exalt him above all forever.
76 Everything growing from the earth, bless
   the Lord;
   praise and exalt him above all forever.
77 You springs, bless the Lord;
   praise and exalt him above all forever.
78 Seas and rivers, bless the Lord;
   praise and exalt him above all forever.
79 You dolphins and all water creatures, bless
   the Lord;
   praise and exalt him above all forever.
80 All you birds of the air, bless the Lord;
   praise and exalt him above all forever.
81 All you beasts, wild and tame, bless the Lord;
   praise and exalt him above all forever.

82 You sons of men, bless the Lord;
   praise and exalt him above all forever.
83 O Israel, bless the Lord;
   praise and exalt him above all forever.
84 Priests of the Lord, bless the Lord;
   praise and exalt him above all forever.
85 Servants of the Lord, bless the Lord;
   praise and exalt him above all forever.
86 Spirits and souls of the just, bless the Lord;
   praise and exalt him above all forever.
87 Holy men of humble heart, bless the Lord;
   praise and exalt him above all forever.
88 Hananiah, Azariah, Mishael, bless the Lord;
   praise and exalt him above all forever.
   For he has delivered us from the nether world,
   and saved us from the power of death;
   He has freed us from the raging flame
   and delivered us from the fire.
89 Give thanks to the Lord, for he is good,
   for his mercy endures forever.
90 Bless the God of gods, all you who fear
   the Lord;
   praise him and give him thanks,
   because his mercy endures forever."

Hearing them sing, and astonished at seeing them alive, 91 King Nebuchadnezzar rose in haste and asked his nobles, "Did we not cast three men bound into the fire?" "Assuredly, O king," they answered. 92† "But," he replied, "I see four men unfettered and unhurt, walking in the fire, and the fourth looks like a son of God." 93 Then Nebuchadnezzar came to the opening of the white-hot furnace and called to Shadrach, Meshach, and Abednego: "Servants of the most high God, come out." Thereupon Shadrach, Meshach, and Abednego came out of the fire. 94 When the satraps, prefects, governors, and nobles of the king came together, they saw that the fire had had no power over the bodies of these men; not a hair of their heads had been singed, nor were their garments altered; there was not even a smell of fire about them. 95 Nebuchadnezzar exclaimed, "Blessed be the God of Shadrach, Meshach, and Abednego, who sent his angel to deliver the servants that trusted in him; they disobeyed the royal command and yielded their bodies rather than serve or worship any god except their own God. 96 Therefore I decree for nations and peoples of every language that whoever blasphemes the God of Shadrach, Meshach, and Abednego shall be cut to pieces and his house destroyed. For there is no other God who can rescue like this." 97 Then the king promoted Shadrach, Meshach, and Abednego in the province of Babylon.

DN

---

† 3, 92: *A son of God:* an angel; cf Jb 1, 6.

3, 59f: Ps 148, 4.

Vision of the Great Tree†

⁹⁸ King Nebuchadnezzar to the nations and peoples of every language, wherever they dwell on earth: abundant peace! ⁹⁹† It has seemed good to me to publish the signs and wonders which the most high God has accomplished in my regard.

¹⁰⁰* How great are his signs, how mighty
    his wonders;
his kingdom is an everlasting kingdom,
and his dominion endures through
    all generations.

4 ¹ I, Nebuchadnezzar, was at home in my palace, content and prosperous. ² I had a terrifying dream as I lay in bed, and the images and the visions of my mind frightened me. ³ So I issued a decree that all the wise men of Babylon should be brought before me to give the interpretation of the dream. ⁴ When the magicians, enchanters, Chaldeans, and astrologers had come in, I related the dream before them; but none of them could tell me its meaning. ⁵*† Finally there came before me Daniel, whose name is Belteshazzar after the name of my god, and in whom is the spirit of the holy God. I repeated the dream to him: ⁶ "Belteshazzar, chief of the magicians, I know that the spirit of the holy God is in you and no mystery is too difficult for you; tell me the meaning of the visions that I saw in my dream.

⁷ "These were the visions I saw while in bed: I saw a tree of great height at the center of the world. ⁸ It was large and strong, with its top touching the heavens, and it could be seen to the ends of the earth. ⁹ Its leaves were beautiful and its fruit abundant, providing food for all. Under it the wild beasts found shade, in its branches the birds of the air nested; all men ate of it. ¹⁰† In the vision I saw while in bed, a holy sentinel came down from heaven, ¹¹† and cried out:

  " 'Cut down the tree and lop off its branches,
    strip off its leaves and scatter its fruit;
    let the beasts flee its shade, and the birds
    its branches.
¹² But leave in the earth its stump and roots,

fettered with iron and bronze, in the grass
    of the field.
Let him be bathed with the dew of heaven;
    his lot be to eat, among beasts, the grass of
    the earth.
¹³ Let his mind be changed from the human;
    let him be given the sense of a beast,
    till seven years pass over him.
¹⁴* By decree of the sentinels is this decided,
    by order of the holy ones, this sentence;
That all who live may know
    that the Most High rules over the kingdom
    of men:
He can give it to whom he will,
    or set over it the lowliest of men.'

¹⁵ "This is the dream that I, King Nebuchadnezzar, had. Now, Belteshazzar, tell me its meaning. Although none of the wise men in my kingdom can tell me the meaning, you can, because the spirit of the holy God is in you."

¹⁶ Then Daniel, whose name was Belteshazzar, was appalled for a while, terrified by his thoughts. "Belteshazzar," the king said to him, "let not the dream or its meaning terrify you." ¹⁷† "My lord," Belteshazzar replied, "this dream should be for your enemies, and its meaning for your foes. The large, strong tree that you saw, with its top touching the heavens, that could be seen by the whole earth, ¹⁸ which had beautiful foliage and abundant fruit, providing food for all, under which the wild beasts lived, and in whose branches the birds of the air dwelt— ¹⁹ you are that tree, O king, large and strong! Your majesty has become so great as to touch the heavens, and your rule extends over the whole earth. ²⁰ As for the king's vision of a holy sentinel that came down from heaven and proclaimed: 'Cut down the tree and destroy it, but leave in the earth its stump and roots, fettered with iron and bronze in the grass of the field; let him be bathed with the dew of heaven, and let his lot be among wild beasts till seven years pass over him'— ²¹ this is its meaning, O king; this is the sentence which the Most High has passed upon my lord king: ²²*† You shall be cast out from among men and dwell with wild beasts; you shall be given grass

---

† **3, 98—4, 34:** This section has the form of a letter written by Nebuchadnezzar to his subjects.

3, 99: *The most high God:* the Jews, especially in the diaspora, used this title to distinguish their God from those of the pagans. On the lips of a polytheist (so also in v 93) it was merely the title of another god. It was an ancient divine name used in Canaan; cf Gn 14, 18.

4, 5: *After the name of my god:* Belteshazzar, the Babylonian name given to Daniel at the king's orders (Dn 1, 7), is Balatsuussur, "protect his life." In the king's intention, this would be an abbreviation for Bel-balatsu-ussur. It would thus include an appeal to the god Bel, originally the name of the city god of Nippur, and later identified with Marduk, the chief god of Babylon. Daniel's use of the name would refer the prayer rather than to the true God.

4, 10: *A holy sentinel:* an angel. This term is found in the Bible only in this chapter of Daniel, but it is common in later Jewish literature.

4, 11ff: As the tree is Nebuchadnezzar (v 19), the description passes from metaphor to the reality.

4, 17: *"This dream . . . for your foes":* Daniel speaks as a courtier.

4, 22: The description is of a form of insanity called lycanthropy, in which the patient acts like a wolf.

---

* **3, 100:** Dn 4, 31; 7, 14.   Is 62, 6.
  4, 5: Gn 41, 38.   **4, 22:** Dn 5, 21.
  4, 14: 1 Sm 2, 8; 16, 11;

to eat like an ox and be bathed with the dew of heaven; seven years shall pass over you, until you know that the Most High rules over the kingdom of men and gives it to whom he will. ²³ The command that the stump and roots of the tree are to be left means that your kingdom shall be preserved for you, once you have learned it is heaven that rules. ²⁴*† Therefore, O king, take my advice; atone for your sins by good deeds, and for your misdeeds by kindness to the poor; then your prosperity will be long."

²⁵ All this happened to King Nebuchadnezzar. ²⁶ Twelve months later, as he was walking on the roof of the royal palace in Babylon, ²⁷† the king said, "Babylon the great! Was it not I, with my great strength, who built it as a royal residence for my splendor and majesty?" ²⁸ While these words were still on the king's lips, a voice spoke from heaven, "It has been decreed for you, King Nebuchadnezzar, that your kingdom is taken from you! ²⁹ You shall be cast out from among men, and shall dwell with wild beasts; you shall be given grass to eat like an ox, and seven years shall pass over you, until you learn that the Most High rules over the kingdom of men and gives it to whom he will." ³⁰† At once this was fulfilled. Nebuchadnezzar was cast out from among men, he ate grass like an ox, and his body was bathed with the dew of heaven, until his hair grew like the feathers of an eagle, and his nails like the claws of a bird.

³¹* When this period was over, I, Nebuchadnezzar, raised my eyes to heaven; my reason was restored to me, and I blessed the Most High, I praised and glorified him who lives forever:

> His dominion is an everlasting dominion,
>   and his kingdom endures through
>   all generations.
> ³² All who live on the earth are counted
>   as nothing;
> he does as he pleases with the powers
>   of heaven
> as well as with those who live on the
>   earth.
> There is no one who can stay his hand
>   or say to him, "What have you done?"

³³ At the same time my reason returned to me, and for the glory of my kingdom, my majesty and

King Nebuchadnezzar's Conversion

Sometimes, it seems God has to go to extremes to get our attention. In Daniel, chapter 4 (written like a letter from the king to his subjects), King Nebuchadnezzar tells how he had to go through some pretty intense humiliation—acting like a wild animal (verses 29–30)—before God got his attention. Even Daniel's prior warning didn't rein in his ego and bring him to his senses (see verses 23–24). After Nebuchadnezzar's reason returned, he realized the power of God and turned to praise and honor God.

Many people go through a conversion —a turning toward God—after they have suffered the consequences of their sinful actions. For others, the catalyst might be an illness or the death of a close friend or family member. Why does it take a crisis for us to realize our need for God? Maybe because during such a time, we realize that we cannot control life and that we need God's loving presence.

In your prayer, reflect or journal on the following questions:

- Where do you recognize your need for God?
- Is a conversion toward God in a crisis only a temporary thing, or can it lead to a lifelong commitment? Why?

▶ **Daniel, chapter 4**

my splendor returned to me. My nobles and lords sought me out; I was restored to my kingdom, and became much greater than before. ³⁴ Therefore, I, Nebuchadnezzar, now praise and exalt and glorify the King of heaven, because all his works are right and his ways just; and those who walk in pride he is able to humble.

D
N

---

† **4, 24:** A classic Scriptural text for the efficacy of good works.

  4, 27: The words attributed to the king are similar to the boastings in the royal inscriptions by which the Mesopotamian kings testified to their mighty works.

  4, 30ff: There is no certainty of any such thing happening to Nebuchadnezzar as is described here. Some scholars think that the Nebuchadnezzar of this chapter is actually Nabonidus, the father of Belshazzar, who was mysteriously absent from Babylon for a number of years. The Biblical author's chief interest was not in the historicity of this popular tale, but in the object lesson it contained for the proud "divine" kings of the Seleucid dynasty.

4, 24: Sir 3, 30; 4, 8.   4, 31: Dn 3, 100; 7, 14.

The Writing on the Wall

5 ¹† King Belshazzar gave a great banquet for a thousand of his lords, with whom he drank. ²† Under the influence of the wine, he ordered the gold and silver vessels which Nebuchadnezzar, his father, had taken from the temple in Jerusalem, to be brought in so that the king, his lords, his wives and his entertainers might drink from them. ³ When the gold and silver vessels taken from the house of God in Jerusalem had been brought in, and while the king, his lords, his wives and his entertainers were drinking ⁴ wine from them, they praised their gods of gold and silver, bronze and iron, wood and stone.

⁵ Suddenly, opposite the lampstand, the fingers of a human hand appeared, writing on the plaster of the wall in the king's palace. When the king saw the wrist and hand that wrote, ⁶ his face blanched; his thoughts terrified him, his hip joints shook, and his knees knocked. ⁷ The king shouted for the enchanters, Chaldeans, and astrologers to be brought in. "Whoever reads this writing and tells me what it means," he said to the wise men of Babylon, "shall be clothed in purple, wear a golden collar about his neck, and be third in the government of the kingdom." ⁸ But though all the king's wise men came in, none of them could either read the writing or tell the king what it meant. ⁹ Then King Belshazzar was greatly terrified; his face went ashen, and his lords were thrown into confusion.

¹⁰ When the queen heard of the discussion between the king and his lords, she entered the banquet hall and said, "O king, live forever! Be not troubled in mind, nor look so pale! ¹¹ There is a man in your kingdom in whom is the spirit of the holy God; during the lifetime of your father he was seen to have brilliant knowledge and god-like wisdom. In fact, King Nebuchadnezzar, your father, made him chief of the magicians, enchanters, Chaldeans, and astrologers, ¹² because of the extraordinary mind possessed by this Daniel, whom the king named Belteshazzar. He knew and understood how to interpret dreams, explain enigmas, and solve difficulties. Now therefore, summon Daniel to tell you what this means."

¹³ Then Daniel was brought into the presence of the king. The king asked him, "Are you the Daniel, the Jewish exile, whom my father, the king, brought from Judah? ¹⁴ I have heard that the spirit of God is in you, that you possess brilliant knowledge and extraordinary wisdom. ¹⁵ Now, the wise men and enchanters were brought in to me to read this writing and tell me its meaning, but they could not say what the words meant. ¹⁶ But I have heard that you can interpret dreams and solve difficulties; if you are able to read the writing and tell me what it means, you shall be clothed in purple, wear a gold collar about your neck, and be third in the government of the kingdom."

¹⁷ Daniel answered the king: "You may keep your gifts, or give your presents to someone else; but the writing I will read for you, O king, and tell you what it means. ¹⁸ The Most High God gave your father Nebuchadnezzar a great kingdom and glorious majesty. ¹⁹ Because he made him so great, the nations and peoples of every language dreaded and feared him. Whomever he wished, he killed or let live; whomever he wished, he exalted or humbled. ²⁰ But when his heart became proud and his spirit hardened by insolence, he was put down from his royal throne and deprived of his glory; ²¹* he was cast out from among men and was made insensate as a beast; he lived with wild asses, and ate grass like an ox; his body was bathed with the dew of heaven, until he learned that the Most High God rules over the kingdom of men and appoints over it whom he will. ²² You, his son, Belshazzar, have not humbled your heart, though you knew all this; ²³ you have rebelled against the Lord of heaven. You had the vessels of his temple brought before you, so that you and your nobles, your wives and your entertainers, might drink wine from them; and you praised the gods of silver and gold, bronze and iron, wood and stone, that neither see nor hear nor have intelligence. But the God in whose hand is your life breath and the whole course of your life, you did not glorify. ²⁴ By him were the wrist and hand sent, and the writing set down.

²⁵† "This is the writing that was inscribed: MENE, TEKEL, and PERES. These words mean: ²⁶† MENE, God has numbered your kingdom and put an end to it; ²⁷ TEKEL, you have been weighed on the scales and found wanting; ²⁸ PERES, your kingdom has been divided and given to the Medes and Persians."

²⁹ Then by order of Belshazzar they clothed Daniel in purple, with a gold collar about his neck, and proclaimed him third in the government of the

---

† **5, 1:** *King Belshazzar:* Belshazzar was actually the crown prince, but he had been given royal authority in Babylon by his father Nabonidus.

5, 2: *Nebuchadnezzar, his father:* several kings of Babylon intervened between Nebuchadnezzar and Belshazzar. Either the term father is used here in the broad sense of "remote predecessor," or the name Nebuchadnezzar is used for "Nabonidus."

5, 25: MENE, TEKEL, *and* PERES: these seem to be the Aramaic names of weights and monetary values: the mina, the shekel (the sixtieth part of a mina), and the parsu (a half-mina).

5, 26ff: Daniel interprets these three terms by a play on the words: MENE, connected with the verb meaning to number; TEKEL, with the verb meaning to weigh; PERES, with the verb meaning to divide. There is also a play on the last term with the word for Persians.

---

* **5, 21:** Dn 4, 22.

kingdom. [30] The same night Belshazzar, the Chaldean king, was slain:

6

[1]† And Darius the Mede succeeded to the kingdom at the age of sixty-two.

In the Lions' Den

[2] Darius decided to appoint over his entire kingdom one hundred and twenty satraps, to safeguard his interests; [3] these were accountable to three supervisors, one of whom was Daniel. [4] Daniel outshone all the supervisors and satraps because an extraordinary spirit was in him, and the king thought of giving him authority over the entire kingdom. [5] Therefore the supervisors and satraps tried to find grounds for accusation against Daniel as regards the administration. But they could accuse him of no wrongdoing; because he was trustworthy, no fault of neglect or misconduct was to be found in him. [6] Then these men said to themselves, "We shall find no grounds for accusation against this Daniel unless by way of the law of his God." [7] So these supervisors and satraps went thronging to the king and said to him, "King Darius, live forever! [8]* All the supervisors of the kingdom, the prefects, satraps, nobles, and governors are agreed that the following prohibition ought to be put in force by royal decree: no one is to address any petition to god or man for thirty days, except to you, O king; otherwise he shall be cast into a den of lions. [9]† Now, O king, issue the prohibition over your signature, immutable and irrevocable under Mede and Persian law." [10] So King Darius signed the prohibition and made it law.

[11] Even after Daniel heard that this law had been signed, he continued his custom of going home to kneel in prayer and give thanks to his God in the upper chamber three times a day, with the windows open toward Jerusalem. [12] So these men rushed in and found Daniel praying and pleading before his God. [13] Then they went to remind the king about the prohibition: "Did you not decree, O king, that no one is to address a petition to god or man for thirty days, except to you, O king; otherwise he shall be cast into a den of lions?" The king answered them, "The decree is absolute, irrevocable under the Mede and Persian law." [14] To this they replied, "Daniel, the Jewish exile, has paid no attention to you, O king, or to the decree you issued; three times

a day he offers his prayer." [15] The king was deeply grieved at this news and he made up his mind to save Daniel; he worked till sunset to rescue him. [16] But these men insisted. "Keep in mind, O king," they said, "that under the Mede and Persian law every royal prohibition or decree is irrevocable." [17]† So the king ordered Daniel to be brought and cast into the lions' den. To Daniel he said, "May your God, whom you serve so constantly, save you." [18] To forestall any tampering, the king sealed with his own ring and the rings of the lords the stone that had been brought to block the opening of the den.

[19] Then the king returned to his palace for the night; he refused to eat and he dismissed the entertainers. Since sleep was impossible for him, [20] the king rose very early the next morning and hastened to the lions' den. [21] As he drew near, he cried out to Daniel sorrowfully, "O Daniel, servant of the living God, has the God whom you serve so constantly been able to save you from the lions?" [22]* Daniel answered the king: "O king, live forever! [23] My God has sent his angel and closed the lions' mouths so that they have not hurt me. For I have been found innocent before him; neither to you have I done any harm, O king!" [24] This gave the king great joy. At his order Daniel was removed from the den, unhurt because he trusted in his God. [25] The king then ordered the men who had accused Daniel, along with their children and their wives, to be cast into the lions' den. Before they reached the bottom of the den, the lions overpowered them and crushed all their bones.

[26] Then King Darius wrote to the nations and peoples of every language, wherever they dwell on the earth: "All peace to you! [27] I decree that throughout my royal domain the God of Daniel is to be reverenced and feared:

"For he is the living God, enduring forever;
   his kingdom shall not be destroyed,
   and his dominion shall be without end.
[28]* He is a deliverer and savior,
   working signs and wonders in heaven and
     on earth,
   and he delivered Daniel from the
     lions' power."

[29] So Daniel fared well during the reign of Darius and the reign of Cyrus the Persian.

---

† **6, 1:** *Darius the Mede:* unknown in profane history. The Median kingdom had already been conquered by Cyrus the Persian, and it was Cyrus who captured Babylon. Evidently the author of Daniel has deliberately adopted an apocalyptic view of history, derived from prophecy (cf Is 13, 17ff; Jer 51, 11.28ff), according to which the Medes formed the second of four world kingdoms preceding the messianic times; see note on Dn 2, 36–45. The character of Darius the Mede has probably been modeled on that of the Persian king Darius the Great (552–486 B.C.), the second successor of Cyrus.

6, 9: *Immutable and irrevocable:* the passages in Est 1, 19 and 8, 8 also refer to the immutability of Medo-Persian laws. The historian Diodorus Siculus indicates that such a concept existed in the time of Darius III (335–331 B.C.), the last of the Persian kings. Cf vv 13.16.

6, 17: *The lions' den:* a pit too deep to be easily scaled; its opening was blocked with a stone (v 18).

6, 8: Est 1, 19.   **6, 28:** Dn 1, 21.
6, 22: 1 Mc 2, 60.

D
N

II: Daniel's Visions

Vision of the Four Beasts

7 [1]† In the first year of King Belshazzar of Babylon, Daniel had a dream as he lay in bed, and was terrified by the visions of his mind. Then he wrote down the dream; the account began: [2]† In the vision I saw during the night, suddenly the four winds of heaven stirred up the great sea, [3] from which emerged four immense beasts, each different from the others. [4]† The first was like a lion, but with eagle's wings. While I watched, the wings were plucked; it was raised from the ground to stand on two feet like a man, and given a human mind. [5]† The second was like a bear; it was raised up on one side, and among the teeth in its mouth were three tusks. It was given the order, "Up, devour much flesh." [6]† After this I looked and saw another beast, like a leopard; on its back were four wings like those of a bird, and it had four heads. To this beast dominion was given. [7]† After this, in the visions of the night I saw the fourth beast, different from all the others, terrifying, horrible, and of extraordinary strength; it had great iron teeth with which it devoured and crushed, and what was left it trampled with its feet. [8] I was considering the ten horns it had, when suddenly another, a little horn, sprang out of their midst, and three of the previous horns were torn away to make room for it. This horn had eyes like a man, and a mouth that spoke arrogantly. [9]† As I watched,

---

7, 1–27: The significance of this vision is the same as that of Nebuchadnezzar's dream in chapter 2; see note on Dn 2, 36–45. To the four succeeding world kingdoms, Babylonian, Median, Persian, and Greek, is opposed and messianic kingdom of the people of God. The imagery of this chapter has been used extensively in the Revelation of St. John, where it is applied to the Roman empire, the persecutor of the church.

7, 2: *The great sea:* the primordial ocean beneath the earth, according to primitive cosmology (Gn 7, 11; 49, 25). This was thought to contain various monsters (Is 27, 1; Jb 7, 12), and in particular mythological monsters symbolizing the chaos which God had vanquished in ancient times (Jb 9, 13; 26, 13; etc.).

7, 4: The representation of the Babylonian empire as a winged lion, a common motif in Babylonian art, symbolizes the bestial power hostile to God. The two wings that are plucked represent Nebuchadnezzar and Belshazzar. *On two feet like a man . . . a human mind:* contrasts with what is said in Dn 4, 13.30.

7, 5: *A bear:* represents the Median empire, its three tusks symbolizing its destructive nature; hence, the command: "Up, devour much flesh."

7, 6: *A leopard:* used to symbolize the swiftness with which Cyrus the Persian established his kingdom. *Four heads:* corresponding to the four Persian kings of Dn 11, 2.

7, 7f: Alexander's empire was different from all the others in that it was Western rather than Oriental in inspiration. The ten horns represent the kings of the Seleucid dynasty, the only part of the Hellenistic empire that concerned the author. The little horn is Antiochus IV Epiphanes (175–163 B.C.), the worst of the Seleucid kings, who usurped the throne.

7, 9f: A vision of the heavenly throne of God (the Ancient One), who sits in judgment (symbolized by fire) over the nations. Some of the details of the vision, depicting the divine majesty and omnipotence, are to be found in Ez 1.

? did you KNOW?

Apocalyptic Literature

As you read chapters 7–10 of Daniel, you might ask, What's with the four beasts in chapter 7, and the goat with the horn in chapter 8, and the man with a face like lightning in chapter 10? These are all examples of apocalyptic literature. *Apocalypse* is a Greek word meaning "to uncover or reveal." Apocalyptic literature is written to sound like an attempt to foretell the future by using symbols and visions. But the symbols are often codes for people and events in the present. This type of literature frequently is produced during a time of persecution, when using real names could get a person into trouble or even killed. Apocalyptic literature developed in Israel around 200 B.C. when the country was enduring great persecution and suffering. The Book of Revelation in the New Testament is another example of apocalyptic literature.

The Book of Daniel contains some explanation of the visions it describes. But sometimes, you will have to consult a good Bible commentary (a book that gives additional background on Bible passages) to completely understand the symbols. For instance, you might need help recognizing that the four beasts in chapter 7 are symbols for Babylon, Media, Persia, and Greece—the four nations that ruled over Israel but would pass away. Or that the arrogant eleventh horn on the fourth beast's head is a symbol for Antiochus IV Epiphanes, the king who persecuted the Jews during the time Daniel was written.

Apocalyptic literature assured the people of Israel that God would triumph and the present evil would eventually pass away. It was one more way to reinforce the belief that evil would be punished and good rewarded, even when it didn't look that way at the moment.

▸ Daniel, chapters 7–10

Thrones were set up
and the Ancient One took his throne.
His clothing was snow bright,
and the hair on his head as white as wool;
His throne was flames of fire,
with wheels of burning fire.
10* A surging stream of fire
flowed out from where he sat;
Thousands upon thousands were ministering
to him,
and myriads upon myriads attended him.

The court was convened, and the books were opened. 11 I watched, then, from the first of the arrogant words which the horn spoke, until the beast was slain and its body thrown into the fire to be burnt up. 12 The other beasts, which also lost their dominion, were granted a prolongation of life for a time and a season. 13† As the visions during the night continued, I saw

One like a son of man coming,
on the clouds of heaven;
When he reached the Ancient One
and was presented before him,
14* He received dominion, glory, and kingship;
nations and peoples of every language
serve him.
His dominion is an everlasting dominion
that shall not be taken away,
his kingship shall not be destroyed.

15 I, Daniel, found my spirit anguished within its sheath of flesh, and I was terrified by the visions of my mind. 16 I approached one of those present and asked him what all this meant in truth; in answer, he made known to me the meaning of the things: 17 "These four great beasts stand for four kingdoms which shall arise on the earth. 18 But the holy ones of the Most High shall receive the kingship, to possess it forever and ever."

19 But I wished to make certain about the fourth beast, so very terrible and different from the others, devouring and crushing with its iron teeth and bronze claws, and trampling with its feet what was

left; 20 about the ten horns on its head, and the other one that sprang up, before which three horns fell; about the horn with the eyes and the mouth that spoke arrogantly, which appeared greater than its fellows. 21 For, as I watched, that horn made war against the holy ones and was victorious 22 until the Ancient One arrived; judgment was pronounced in favor of the holy ones of the Most High, and the time came when the holy ones possessed the kingdom. 23 He answered me thus:

"The fourth beast shall be a fourth kingdom
on earth,
different from all the others;
It shall devour the whole earth,
beat it down, and crush it.
24 The ten horns shall be ten kings
rising out of that kingdom;
another shall rise up after them,
Different from those before him,
who shall lay low three kings.
25† He shall speak against the Most High
and oppress the holy ones of the
Most High,
thinking to change the feast days and
the law.
They shall be handed over to him
for a year, two years, and a half-year.
26 But when the court is convened,
and his power is taken away
by final and absolute destruction,
27 Then the kingship and dominion and majesty
of all the kingdoms under the heavens
shall be given to the holy people of the
Most High,
Whose kingdom shall be everlasting:
all dominions shall serve and obey him."

28† The report concluded: I, Daniel, was greatly terrified by my thoughts, and my face blanched, but I kept the matter to myself.

Vision of the Ram and He-goat†

8 1 After this first vision, I, Daniel, had another, in the third year of the reign of King

---

† **7, 13f:** *One like a son of man:* in contrast to the wordly kingdoms opposed to God, which appear as beasts, the glorified people of God that will form his kingdom on earth is represented in human form (v 18). Just as our Lord applied the figure of the stone hewn from the mountain to himself (Dn 2, 36–45), he also made the title, "Son of Man" his most characteristic way of referring to himself, as the One in whom and through whom the salvation of God's people came to be realized.

7, 25: The reference is to the persecutions of Antiochus IV and his attempt to force the Jews to give up their customs and to adopt Hellenistic ways (1 Mc 1, 33f). *A year, two years, and a half-year:* an indefinite, evil period of time. As seven is the Jewish "perfect" number, half of it signifies great imperfection. Actually, this corresponds fairly accurately to the duration of Antiochus' persecution.

7, 28: This verse ends the Aramaic part of the Book of Daniel.
8, 1–27: This vision repeats the major part of the preceding one, though in a more explicit fashion. As explained in vv 20ff, the two-horned ram represents the combined kingdom of the Medes and Persians, destroyed by Alexander's Hellenistic empire originating in the west. Once again the author is interested only in the Seleucid dynasty, which emerged from the dissolution of Alexander's empire after his death in 323 B.C.

* **7, 10:** Rv 5, 11.
7, 14: Dn 3, 100; 4, 31; Mi

4, 7; Lk 1, 32.

Belshazzar. ²† In my vision I saw myself in the fortress of Susa in the province of Elam; I was beside the river Ulai. ³ I looked up and saw standing by the river a ram with two great horns, the one larger and newer than the other. ⁴ I saw the ram butting toward the west, north, and south. No beast could withstand it or be rescued from its power; it did what it pleased and became very powerful.

⁵ As I was reflecting, a he-goat with a prominent horn on its forehead suddenly came from the west across the whole earth without touching the ground. ⁶ It approached the two-horned ram I had seen standing by the river, and rushed toward it with savage force. ⁷ I saw it attack the ram with furious blows when they met, and break both its horns. It threw the ram, which had not the force to withstand it, to the ground, and trampled upon it; and no one could rescue it from its power.

⁸ The he-goat became very powerful, but at the height of its power the great horn was shattered, and in its place came up four others, facing the four winds of heaven. ⁹† Out of one of them came a little horn which kept growing toward the south, the east, and the glorious country. ¹⁰† Its power extended to the host of heaven, so that it cast down to earth some of the host and some of the stars and trampled on them. ¹¹ It boasted even against the prince of the host, from whom it removed the daily sacrifice, and whose sanctuary it cast down, ¹² as well as the host, while sin replaced the daily sacrifice. It cast truth to the ground, and was succeeding in its undertaking.

¹³† I heard a holy one speaking, and another said to whichever one it was that spoke, "How long shall the events of this vision last concerning the daily sacrifice, the desolating sin which is placed there, the sanctuary, and the trampled host?" ¹⁴ He answered him, "For two thousand three hundred evenings and mornings; then the sanctuary shall be purified."

¹⁵ While I, Daniel, sought the meaning of the vision I had seen, a manlike figure stood before me, ¹⁶† and on the Ulai I heard a human voice that cried out, "Gabriel, explain the vision to this man." ¹⁷† When he came near where I was standing, I fell prostrate in terror. But he said to me, "Understand, son of man, that the vision refers to the end time." ¹⁸ As he spoke to me, I fell forward in a faint; he touched me and made me stand up. ¹⁹ "I will show you," he said, "what is to happen later in the period of wrath; for at the appointed time, there will be an end.

²⁰ "The two-horned ram you saw represents the kings of the Medes and Persians. ²¹ The he-goat is the king of the Greeks, and the great horn on its forehead is the first king. ²² The four that rose in its place when it was broken are four kingdoms that will issue from his nation, but without his strength.

23   "After their reign,
        when sinners have reached their measure,
     There shall arise a king, impudent
        and skilled in intrigue.
24   He shall be strong and powerful,
        bring about fearful ruin,
        and succeed in his undertaking.
     He shall destroy powerful peoples;
25   his cunning shall be against the holy ones,
        his treacherous conduct shall succeed.
     He shall be proud of heart
        and destroy many by stealth.
     But when he rises against the prince of princes,
        he shall be broken without a hand
           being raised.
26   The vision of the evenings and the mornings
        is true, as spoken;
     Do you, however, keep this
        vision undisclosed,
        because the days are to be many."

²⁷ I, Daniel, was weak and ill for some days; then I arose and took care of the king's affairs. But I was appalled at the vision, which I could not understand.

Gabriel and the Seventy Weeks

9 ¹† It was the first year that Darius, son of Ahasuerus, of the race of the Medes, reigned over the kingdom of the Chaldeans; ²*† in the first year of his reign I, Daniel, tried to understand in the

---

8, 2: *The fortress of Susa:* the royal palace of the Persian kings in the ancient territory of Elam, east of Babylonia. *The river Ulai:* a canal along the northern side of Susa.

8, 9: The little horn, as in chapter 7, is Antiochus IV. *The glorious country:* Palestine.

8, 10ff: *The host of heaven:* ordinarily meaning the stars, here refers to the people of God; cf Dn 12, 3. *The prince of the host:* God himself, with whose holy religion Antiochus interfered (1 Mc 1, 45).

8, 13: *The desolating sin:* the Hebrew contains a wordplay (shomem) on the name Baal Shamem ("lord of the heavens," the Greek Zeus Olympios), referring to the statue with which Antiochus profaned the temple of Jerusalem (2 Mc 6, 2).

8, 16: The angel Gabriel is mentioned here for the first time in the Bible. There is wordplay in the preceding verse on geber—manlike figure.

8, 17: *The end time:* the day of the Lord, when God sits in judgment on his enemies (v 19).

9, 1: *Darius:* see the note on Dn 6, 1.

9, 2: *Seventy years:* the prophet Jeremiah (25, 11; 29, 10) prophesied a Babylonian captivity of seventy years, a round number signifying the complete passing away of the existing generation. Jeremiah's prophecy was fulfilled in the capture of Babylon by Cyrus and the subsequent return of the Jews to Palestine. However, the author of Daniel, living during the persecution of Antiochus, sees the conditions of the exile still existing; therefore in his mediation he extends Jeremiah's number to seventy weeks of years (v 24, i.e., seven times seventy years), to characterize the Jewish victory over the Seleucids as the ultimate fulfillment of the prophecy.

9, 2f: Jer 25, 11; 29, 10.

Scriptures the counting of the years of which the LORD spoke to the prophet Jeremiah: that for the ruins of Jerusalem seventy years must be fulfilled. ³ I turned to the Lord God, pleading in earnest prayer, with fasting, sackcloth, and ashes. ⁴* I prayed to the LORD, my God, and confessed, "Ah, Lord, great and awesome God, you who keep your merciful covenant toward those who love you and observe your commandments! ⁵* We have sinned, been wicked and done evil; we have rebelled and departed from your commandments and your laws. ⁶ We have not obeyed your servants the prophets, who spoke in your name to our kings, our princes, our fathers, and all the people of the land. ⁷ Justice, O Lord, is on your side; we are shamefaced even to this day: the men of Judah, the residents of Jerusalem, and all Israel, near and far, in all the countries to which you have scattered them because of their treachery toward you. ⁸ O LORD, we are shamefaced, like our kings, our princes, and our fathers, for having sinned against you. ⁹ But yours, O Lord, our God, are compassion and forgiveness! Yet we rebelled against you ¹⁰ and paid no heed to your command, O LORD, our God, to live by the law you gave us through your servants the prophets. ¹¹* Because all Israel transgressed your law and went astray, not heeding your voice, the sworn malediction, recorded in the law of Moses, the servant of God, was poured out over us for our sins. ¹² You carried out the threats you spoke against us and against those who governed us, by bringing upon us in Jerusalem the greatest calamity that has ever occurred under heaven. ¹³† As it is written in the law of Moses, this calamity came full upon us. As we did not appease the LORD, our God, by turning back from our wickedness and recognizing his constancy, ¹⁴ so the Lord kept watch over the calamity and brought it upon us. You, O LORD, our God, are just in all that you have done, for we did not listen to your voice.

¹⁵* "Now, O Lord, our God, who led your people out of the land of Egypt with a strong hand, and made a name for yourself even to this day, we have sinned, we are guilty. ¹⁶ O Lord, in keeping with all your just deeds, let your anger and your wrath be turned away from your city Jerusalem, your holy mountain. On account of our sins and the crimes of our fathers, Jerusalem and your people have become the reproach of all our neighbors. ¹⁷ Hear,

therefore, O God, the prayer and petition of your servant; and for your own sake, O Lord, let your face shine upon your desolate sanctuary. ¹⁸* Give ear, O my God, and listen; open your eyes and see our ruins and the city which bears your name. When we present our petition before you, we rely not on our just deeds, but on your great mercy. ¹⁹ O Lord, hear! O Lord, pardon! O Lord, be attentive and act without delay, for your own sake, O my God, because this city and your people bear your name!"

²⁰ I was still occupied with my prayer, confessing my sin and the sin of my people Israel, presenting my petition to the LORD, my God, on behalf of his holy mountain— ²¹*† I was still occupied with this prayer, when Gabriel, the one whom I had seen before in vision, came to me in rapid flight at the time of the evening sacrifice. ²² He instructed me in these words: "Daniel, I have now come to give you understanding. ²³ When you began your petition, an answer was given which I have come to announce, because you are beloved. Therefore, mark the answer and understand the vision.

²⁴† "Seventy weeks are decreed
        for your people and for your holy city:

A Closer Look

Let's look closely at the prayer in chapter 9 of Daniel. Here, the prophet uses four types of prayer:

- **intercession**, because he prays on behalf of the people
- **praise**, because he proclaims God to be awesome and great
- **sorrow**, because he expresses sadness for past sinfulness and asks for forgiveness
- **petition**, because he asks God for help

Try creating a personal prayer that includes three or all four of these types of prayer.

▸ **Daniel, chapter 9**

D
N

---

† **9, 13:** *As it is written:* the first time that this formula of Scriptural citation is used in the Bible. The reference (v 11) is to the sanctions of Lv 26, 14ff; Dt 28, 15ff.

9, 21: *At the time of the evening sacrifice:* between three and four in the afternoon.

9, 24: *Seventy weeks:* i. e., of years. Just as Jeremiah's seventy years was an approximation (see note on v 2), the four hundred and ninety years here is not to be taken literally. Similarly, the distribu-

tion of the "weeks" in the following verses indicates only relative proportions of the total figure. *A most holy:* an expression used almost always of an object, the altar or the temple, but once (1 Chr 23, 13) of Aaron the high priest. The author sees the definitive establishment of the kingdom of God, realized in the reconsecration of

*
9, 4: Neh 1, 5.   9, 15: Bar 2, 11; Ex 14, 22.
9, 5: Bar 1, 17.   9, 18: Jer 25, 29.
9, 11: Dt 27, 15.   9, 21: Dn 8, 16.

Then transgression will stop and sin will end,
    guilt will be expiated,
Everlasting justice will be introduced,
    vision and prophecy ratified,
    and a most holy will be anointed.
25†   Know and understand this:
From the utterance of the word
    that Jerusalem was to be rebuilt
Until one who is anointed and a leader,
    there shall be seven weeks.
During sixty-two weeks
    it shall be rebuilt,
With streets and trenches,
    in time of affliction.
26† After the sixty-two weeks
    an anointed shall be cut down
    when he does not possess the city;
And the people of a leader who will come
    shall destroy the sanctuary.
Then the end shall come like a torrent;
    until the end there shall be war,
    the desolation that is decreed.
27*†For one week he shall make
    a firm compact with the many;
Half the week
    he shall abolish sacrifice and oblation;
On the temple wing shall be the
    horrible abomination
    until the ruin that is decreed
    is poured out upon the horror."

Vision of the Hellenistic Wars†

10 ¹ In the third year of Cyrus, king of Persia, a revelation was given to Daniel, who had been named Belteshazzar. The revelation was certain: a great war; he understood it from the vision. ²† In those days, I, Daniel, mourned three full weeks. ³ I ate no savory food, I took no meat or wine, and I did not anoint myself at all until the end of the three weeks.

⁴† On the twenty-fourth day of the first month I was on the bank of the great river, the Tigris. ⁵† As I looked up, I saw a man dressed in linen with a belt of fine gold around his waist. ⁶ His body was like chrysolite, his face shone like lightning, his eyes were like fiery torches, his arms and feet looked like burnished bronze, and his voice sounded like the roar of a multitude. ⁷ I alone, Daniel, saw the vision; but great fear seized the men who were with me; they fled and hid themselves, although they did not see the vision. ⁸ So I was left alone, seeing this great vision. No strength remained in me; I turned the color of death and was powerless. ⁹ When I heard the sound of his voice, I fell face forward in a faint.

¹⁰ But then a hand touched me, raising me to my hands and knees. ¹¹ "Daniel, beloved," he said to me, "understand the words which I am speaking to you; stand up, for my mission now is to you." When he said this to me, I stood up trembling. ¹² "Fear not, Daniel," he continued; "from the first day you made up your mind to acquire understanding and humble yourself before God, your prayer was heard. Because of it I started out, ¹³† but the prince of the kingdom of Persia stood in my way for twenty-one days, until finally Michael, one of the chief princes, came to help me. I left him there with the prince of the kings of Persia, ¹⁴ and came to make you understand what shall happen to your people in the days to come; for there is yet a vision concerning those days."

¹⁵ While he was speaking thus to me, I fell forward and kept silent. ¹⁶ Then something like a man's hand touched my lips; I opened my mouth and said to the one facing me, "My lord, I was seized with pangs at the vision and I was powerless. ¹⁷ How can my lord's servant speak with you, my lord? For now no strength or even breath is left in me." ¹⁸ The one who looked like a man touched me again and strengthened me, saying, ¹⁹ "Fear not,

---

the temple after Antiochus' desecration, or personified in the holy community (like the Son of Man of chapter 7). The Fathers of the church almost unanimously understood the reference to be to Christ, the final realization of the prophecy.

9, 25: *From the utterance . . . to be rebuilt:* from the time of Jeremiah's prophecy. *One . . . anointed and a leader:* either Cyrus, who was called the anointed of the Lord to end the exile (Is 45, 1), or the high priest Joshua, who presided over the rebuilding of the altar of sacrifice after the exile (Ezr 3, 2). *Seven weeks:* forty-nine years, an approximation of the time of the exile. *During sixty-two weeks . . . rebuilt:* a period of 434 years, roughly approximating the interval between the rebuilding of Jerusalem after the exile and the beginning of the Seleucid persecution.

9, 26: *An anointed:* doubtless the high priest Onias III, murdered in 171 B.C., from which the author dates the beginning of the persecution. Onias was in exile when he was killed. *A leader:* Antiochus IV.

9, 27: *One week:* the final phase of the period in view, the time of Antiochus' persecution; he is Antiochus himself. *The many:* the faithless Jews who allied themselves with the heathen; cf 1 Mc 1, 11ff. *Half the week:* three and a half years; see note on Dn 7, 25. The temple was desecrated by Antiochus from 167 to 165 B.C. *The*

temple wing: probably the main portal. *The horrible abomination:* see note on Dn 8, 13. Perhaps an inscription was placed on the portal of the temple dedicating it to the Olympian Zeus. Our Lord referred to this passage in his own prediction of the destruction of Jerusalem (Mt 24, 15).

10, 1—12, 13: This final vision repeats some of the material contained in the others. It is concerned with history of the worldly kingdoms from the time of Cyrus to the defeat of the tyrant Antiochus.

10, 2: *Mourned:* perhaps the author intends to recall the interruption in the rebuilding of the temple, which occurred during this time (Ezr 4, 1–4).

10, 4: *The first month:* the month Nisan (mid-March to mid-April).

10, 5f: The heavenly person of the vision is probably the angel Gabriel, as in Dn 9, 21. *Chrysolite:* or topaz, a yellowish precious stone.

10, 13: *The prince of the kingdom of Persia:* the guardian angel of Persia. The later Judaism ascribed protecting angels to various groups of human society, often as little more than personifications. *Michael:* the angel who is the protector of God's people (v 21).

9, 27: Mt 24, 15; 2 Mc 6, 2.

DN

beloved, you are safe; take courage and be strong." [20] When he spoke to me, I grew strong and said, "Speak, my lord, for you have strengthened me." "Do you know," he asked, "why I have come to you? Soon I must fight the prince of Persia again. When I leave, the prince of Greece will come; [21]* but I shall tell you what is written in the truthful book. No one supports me against all these except Michael, your prince, [1]† standing as a reinforcement and a bulwark for me. [2]† Now I shall tell you the truth.

11 "Three kings of Persia are yet to come; and a fourth shall acquire the greatest riches of all. Strengthened by his riches, he shall rouse all the kingdom of Greece. [3] But a powerful king shall appear and rule with great might, doing as he pleases. [4] No sooner shall he appear than his kingdom shall be broken and divided in the four directions under heaven; but not among his descendants or in keeping with his mighty rule, for his kingdom shall be torn to pieces and belong to others than they.

[5]† "The king of the south shall grow strong, but one of his princes shall grow stronger still and govern a domain greater than his. [6] After some years they shall become allies: the daughter of the king of the south shall come to the king of the north in the interest of peace. But her bid for power shall fail: and her line shall not be recognized, and she shall be given up, together with those who brought her, her son and her husband. But later [7] a descendant of her line shall succeed to his rank, and shall come against the rampart and enter the stronghold of the king of the north, and conquer them. [8] Even their gods, with their molten images and their precious vessels of silver and gold, he shall carry away as booty into Egypt. For years he shall have nothing to do with the king of the north. [9] Then the latter shall invade the land of the king of the south, and return to his own country.

[10] "But his sons shall prepare and assemble a great armed host, which shall advance like a flood, then withdraw. When it returns and surges around the stronghold, [11] the king of the south, provoked, shall go out to fight against the king of the north, whose great host shall make a stand but shall be given into his hand [12] and be carried off. In the pride of his heart, he shall lay low tens of thousands, but he shall not triumph. [13] For the king of the north shall raise another army, greater than before; after some years he shall attack with this large army and great resources. [14]* In those times many shall resist the king of the south, and outlaws of your people shall rise up in fulfillment of vision, but they shall fail. [15] When the king of the north comes, he shall set up siegeworks and take the fortified city by storm. The power of the south shall not withstand him, and not even his picked troops shall have the strength to resist. [16] He shall attack him and do as he pleases, with no one to withstand him. He shall stop in the glorious land, dealing destruction. [17] He shall set himself to penetrate the entire strength of his kingdom. He shall conclude an agreement with him and give him a daughter in marriage in order to destroy the kingdom, but this shall not succeed in his favor. [18] He shall turn to the coastland and take many, but a leader shall put an end to his shameful conduct, so that he cannot renew it against him. [19] He shall turn to the strongholds of his own land, but shall stumble and fall, to be found no more. [20] In his stead one shall arise who will send a tax collector through the glorious kingdom, but he shall soon be destroyed, though not in conflict or in battle.

[21] "There shall rise in his place a despicable person, to whom the royal insignia shall not be given. By stealth and fraud he shall seize the kingdom. [22] Armed might shall be completely overwhelmed by him and crushed, and even the prince of the covenant. [23] After allying with him, he shall treacherously rise to power with a small party. [24] By stealth he shall enter prosperous provinces and do that which his fathers or grandfathers never did; he shall distribute spoil, booty, and riches among them and devise plots against their strongholds; but only for a time. [25] He shall call on his strength and cleverness to meet the king of the south with a great army; the king of the south shall prepare for battle with a very large and strong army, but he shall not succeed because of the plots devised against him. [26] Even his table companions shall seek to destroy him, his army shall be overwhelmed, and many shall fall slain. [27] The two kings, resolved on evil, shall sit at table together and exchange lies, but they shall have no success, because the appointed end is not yet.

11, 1f: *Standing . . . truth:* these are the first two verses of ch 11.
11, 2–4: The three kings of Persia who follow Cyrus are uncertain, since there were more than three Persian kings between Cyrus and the dissolution of the kingdom. The fourth is doubtless Xerxes I (486–465 B.C.), the great campaigner against Greece. The powerful king is Alexander the Great, who ended the Persian empire by his victory at Issus in 333 B.C.
11, 5–45: These verses describe the dynastic histories of the Ptolemies in Egypt (the king of the south) and the Seleucids in Syria (the king of the north), the two divisions of the Hellenistic empire

that were of interest to the author (v 6). In vv 10–20 is described the struggle between the two kingdoms for the control of Palestine, in which the Seleucids were eventually victorious. The reference in v 20 is to Seleucus IV, who sent Heliodorus to plunder the temple treasure in Jerusalem (2 Mc 3). Finally, vv 21–45 describe the career of Antiochus IV and his persecution, in details that have been seen above.

10, 21: Rv 12, 7.   11, 14: Is 19, 1.

28 "He shall turn back toward his land with great riches, his mind set against the holy covenant; he shall arrange matters and return to his land. 29 At the time appointed he shall come again to the south, but this time it shall not be as before. 30† When ships of the Kittim confront him, he shall lose heart and retreat. Then he shall direct his rage and energy against the holy covenant; those who forsake it he shall once more single out. 31 Armed forces shall move at his command and defile the sanctuary stronghold, abolishing the daily sacrifice and setting up the horrible abomination. 32 By his deceit he shall make some who were disloyal to the covenant apostatize; but those who remain loyal to their God shall take strong action. 33 The nation's wise men shall instruct the many; though for a time they will become victims of the sword, of flames, exile, and plunder. 34 When they fall, few people shall help them, but many shall join them out of treachery. 35 Of the wise men, some shall fall, so that the rest may be tested, refined, and purified, until the end time which is still appointed to come.

36† "The king shall do as he pleases, exalting himself and making himself greater than any god; he shall utter dreadful blasphemies against the God of gods. He shall prosper only till divine wrath is ready, for what is determined must take place. 37 He shall have no regard for the gods of his ancestors or for the one in whom women delight; for no god shall he have regard, because he shall make himself greater than all. 38 Instead, he shall give glory to the god of strongholds; a god unknown to his fathers he shall glorify with gold, silver, precious stones, and other treasures. 39 To defend the strongholds he shall station a people of a foreign god. Whoever acknowledges him he shall provide with abundant honor; he shall make them rule over the many and distribute the land as a reward.

40 "At the appointed time the king of the south shall come to grips with him, but the king of the north shall overwhelm him with chariots and horsemen and a great fleet, passing through the countries like a flood. 41 He shall enter the glorious land and many shall fall, except Edom, Moab, and the chief part of Ammon, which shall escape from his power. 42 He shall extend his power over the countries, and not even the land of Egypt shall escape. 43 He shall control the riches of gold and silver and all the treasures of Egypt; Libya and Ethiopia shall be in his train. 44 When news from the east and the north terrifies him, he shall set out with great fury to slay and to doom many. 45 He shall pitch the tents of his royal pavilion between the sea and the glorious holy mountain, but he shall come to his end with none to help him.

12

1*† "At that time there shall arise
Michael, the great prince,
guardian of your people;
It shall be a time unsurpassed in distress
since nations began until that time.
At that time your people shall escape,
everyone who is found written in the book.
2*†Many of those who sleep
in the dust of the earth shall awake;
Some shall live forever,
others shall be an everlasting horror
and disgrace.
3* But the wise shall shine brightly
like the splendor of the firmament,
And those who lead the many to justice
shall be like the stars forever.

did you KNOW?

Resurrection

Most of the Old Testament contains no indication of a belief in life after death. Daniel, however, speaks of individual resurrection, or rising to life from death. This goes beyond the less specific belief in life after death expressed in Wis 5, 15 and is similar to the belief expressed in 2 Mc 7, 23. The understanding of personal resurrection developed quite late in Israel's existence. It is described as the complete transformation of the human being, body and soul, after death. Dn 12, 3 says the resurrected will shine like stars.

▶ Dn 12, 1–3

---

† **11, 30:** *Kittim:* originally this word meant Cypriots or other island dwellers. Here it means the Romans, who forced Antiochus to withdraw from Egypt during his second campaign there.
11, 36–39: Instead of venerating Apollo, one of the gods of his ancestors, Antiochus venerated, and even identified himself with, Zeus Olympios, whom the Romans equated with the god of their fortress in Rome, Jupiter Capitolinus, the god of strongholds.
12, 1: *Written in the book:* the book of God's predestination.

12, 2: The first Israelites who have fallen (Dn 11, 33ff) shall awake, that is, rise to live forever. A resurrection of the wicked as in later, Christian teaching (Jn 5, 28f) is implied here if the others are included in the many; but cf Is 66, 24.

12, 1: Rv 12, 7.   12, 3: Wis 3, 7.
12, 2: Mt 25, 46; Jn 5, 29.

4 "As for you, Daniel, keep secret the message and seal the book until the end time; many shall fall away and evil shall increase."

5 I, Daniel, looked and saw two others, one standing on either bank of the river. 6 One of them said to the man clothed in linen, who was upstream, "How long shall it be to the end of these appalling things?" 7*† The man clothed in linen, who was upstream, lifted his right and left hands to heaven; and I heard him swear by him who lives forever that it should be for a year, two years, a half-year; and that, when the power of the destroyer of the holy people was brought to an end, all these things should end. 8 I heard, but I did not understand; so I asked, "My lord, what follows this?" 9 "Go, Daniel," he said, "because the words are to be kept secret and sealed until the end time. 10 Many shall be refined, purified, and tested, but the wicked shall prove wicked; none of them shall have understanding, but the wise shall have it. 11 From the time that the daily sacrifice is abolished and the horrible abomination is set up, there shall be one thousand two hundred and ninety days. 12 Blessed is the man who has patience and perseveres until the one thousand three hundred and thirty-five days. 13 Go, take your rest, you shall rise for your reward at the end of days."

III. Appendix†

Susanna's Virtue

13 1 In Babylon there lived a man named Joakim, 2 who married a very beautiful and God-fearing woman, Susanna, the daughter of Hilkiah; 3 her pious parents had trained their daughter according to the law of Moses. 4 Joakim was very rich; he had a garden near his house, and the Jews had recourse to him often because he was the most respected of them all.

5 That year, two elders of the people were appointed judges, of whom the Lord said, "Wickedness has come out of Babylon: from the elders who were to govern the people as judges." 6 These men, to whom all brought their cases, frequented the house of Joakim. 7 When the people left at noon, Susanna used to enter her husband's garden for a walk. 8 When the old men saw her enter every day for her walk, they began to lust for her. 9 They suppressed their consciences; they would not allow their eyes to look to heaven, and did not keep in mind just judgments. 10 Though both were enamored of her,

Susanna

Daniel is called the hero of chapter 13 of his book. But don't forget Susanna. A real hero, Susanna chooses to risk death rather than submitting to sin. Her prayer demanding God's justice causes the Holy Spirit to stir Daniel into action. Prayer can challenge and inspire us. What injustices might you pray about? Whose attention do you need to get?

▶ Daniel, chapter 13

they did not tell each other their trouble, 11 for they were ashamed to reveal their lustful desire to have her. 12 Day by day they watched eagerly for her. 13 One day they said to each other, "Let us be off for home, it is time for lunch." So they went out and parted; 14 but both turned back, and when they met again, they asked each other the reason. They admitted their lust, and then they agreed to look for an occasion when they could meet her alone.

15 One day, while they were waiting for the right moment, she entered the garden as usual, with two maids only. She decided to bathe, for the weather was warm. 16 Nobody else was there except the two elders, who had hidden themselves and were watching her. 17 "Bring me oil and soap," she said to the maids, "and shut the garden doors while I bathe." 18 They did as she said; they shut the garden doors and left by the side gate to fetch what she had ordered, unaware that the elders were hidden inside.

19 As soon as the maids had left, the two old men got up and hurried to her. 20 "Look," they said, "the garden doors are shut, and no one can see us; give in to our desire, and lie with us. 21 If you refuse, we will testify against you that you dismissed your maids because a young man was here with you."

22 "I am completely trapped," Susanna groaned. "If I yield, it will be my death; if I refuse, I cannot escape your power. 23 Yet it is better for me to fall into your power without guilt than to sin before the Lord." 24 Then Susanna shrieked, and the old men also shouted at her, 25 as one of them ran to open the garden doors. 26 When the people in the house

D
N

12, 7: *A year, two years, a half-year:* see note on Dn 7, 25. The author's perspective is the end of Antiochus, and beyond, the final consummation of all things.

13, 1—14, 42: The short stories in these two chapters may have originally been about some other Daniel or Daniels than the hero of the main part of the book. They exist now only in Greek, but prob-

ably were first composed in Hebrew or Aramaic. They are excluded from the Jewish canon of Scripture, but the church as always included them among the inspired writings.

12, 7: Rv 10, 5f.

heard the cries from the garden, they rushed in by the side gate to see what had happened to her. 27 At the accusations by the old men, the servants felt very much ashamed, for never had any such thing been said about Susanna.

28 When the people came to her husband Joakim the next day, the two wicked elders also came, fully determined to put Susanna to death. Before all the people they ordered: 29 "Send for Susanna, the daughter of Hilkiah, the wife of Joakim." When she was sent for, 30 she came with her parents, children and all her relatives. 31 Susanna, very delicate and beautiful, 32 was veiled; but those wicked men ordered her to uncover her face so as to sate themselves with her beauty. 33 All her relatives and the onlookers were weeping.

34 In the midst of the people the two elders rose up and laid their hands on her head. 35 Through her tears she looked up to heaven, for she trusted in the Lord wholeheartedly. 36 The elders made this accusation: "As we were walking in the garden alone, this woman entered with two girls and shut the doors of the garden, dismissing the girls. 37 A young man, who was hidden there, came and lay with her. 38 When we, in a corner of the garden, saw this crime, we ran toward them. 39 We saw them lying together, but the man we could not hold, because he was stronger than we; he opened the doors and ran off. 40 Then we seized this one and asked who the young man was, 41 but she refused to tell us. We testify to this." The assembly believed them, since they were elders and judges of the people, and they condemned her to death.

42 But Susanna cried aloud: "O eternal God, you know what is hidden and are aware of all things before they come to be: 43 you know that they have testified falsely against me. Here I am about to die, though I have done none of the things with which these wicked men have charged me."

44 The Lord heard her prayer. 45 As she was being led to execution, God stirred up the holy spirit of a young boy named Daniel, 46 and he cried aloud: "I will have no part in the death of this woman." 47 All the people turned and asked him, "What is this you are saying?" 48 He stood in their midst and continued, "Are you such fools, O Israelites! To condemn a woman of Israel without examination and without clear evidence? 49 Return to court, for they have testified falsely against her."

50 Then all the people returned in haste. To Daniel the elders said, "Come, sit with us and inform us, since God has given you the prestige of old age." 51 But he replied, "Separate these two far from one another that I may examine them."

52 After they were separated one from the other, he called one of them and said: "How you have grown evil with age! Now have your past sins come to term: 53* passing unjust sentences, condemning the innocent, and freeing the guilty, although the Lord says, 'The innocent and the just you shall not put to death.' 54 Now, then, if you were a witness, tell me under what tree you saw them together." 55† "Under a mastic tree," he answered. "Your fine lie has cost you your head," said Daniel; "for the angel of God shall receive the sentence from him and split you in two." 56 Putting him to one side, he ordered the other one to be brought. "Offspring of Canaan, not of Judah," Daniel said to him, "beauty has seduced you, lust has subverted your conscience. 57† This is how you acted with the daughters of Israel, and in their fear they yielded to you; but a daughter of Judah did not tolerate your wickedness. 58 Now then, tell me under what tree you surprised them together." 59 "Under an oak," he said. "Your fine lie has cost you also your head," said Daniel; "for the angel of God waits with a sword to cut you in two so as to make an end of you both."

60 The whole assembly cried aloud, blessing God who saves those that hope in him. 61* They rose up against the two elders, for by their own words Daniel had convicted them of perjury. According to the law of Moses, they inflicted on them the penalty they had plotted to impose on their neighbor: 62 they put them to death. Thus was innocent blood spared that day.

63 Hilkiah and his wife praised God for their daughter Susanna, as did Joakim her husband and all her relatives, because she was found innocent of any shameful deed. 64 And from that day onward Daniel was greatly esteemed by the people.

Bel and the Dragon

14 1† After King Astyages was laid with his fathers, Cyrus the Persian succeeded to his kingdom. 2† Daniel was the king's favorite and was held in higher esteem than any of the friends of the king. 3† The Babylonians had an idol called Bel,

---

13, 55–59: The contrast between the mastic tree, which is small, and the majestic oak emphasizes the contradiction between the statements of the two elders. In the Greek text there is a play on words between the names of these two trees and the mortal punishment decreed by Daniel for the elders.

13, 57: Besides the evident moral intent of this story, it appears to have served the purpose of contrasting the northern and the southern kingdom, Israel and Judah, in favor of the latter.

14, 1: *King Astyages:* the last of the Median kings, defeated by

Cyrus in 550 B.C. This story preserves the fiction of a successive Median and Persian rule of Babylon.

14, 2: This verse in the Septuagint Greek text reads: "There was once a priest, Daniel by name, the son of Abal, a favorite of the king of Babylon." This may represent an earlier form of the story, before it was attached to the Book of Daniel.

14, 3: *Bel:* see the note on Dn 4, 5.

13, 53: Ex 23, 7.   13, 61f: Dt 19, 18.19.

CALLED TO BE PROPHETS!

The following excerpt from *Prophetic Voices* reveals how Hispanic young people express their prophetic mission:

As Hispanic young people, as members of the Catholic Church, we wish to raise our prophetic voice in order to announce the values of the Gospel, to denounce sin, to invite all youth to struggle for the Kingdom of God.

First of all, we announce the option for peace as against violence (Mt 26, 51–52; 2 Cor 5, 18); for love as against injustice (Jn 15, 17); for good as against evil (Dt 30, 15); for the family as a fundamental value through which faith is transmitted (Eph 6, 4); and for maintaining one's own culture.

Likewise, we denounce materialism, which leads us to believe that the important thing in life is to have more and more in contrast to the teachings of the Gospel (Mt 6, 25–30; *Populorum Progressio* 19).

We denounce the injustice and oppression that Latin America suffers as a result of the cultural, economic, military, and political intervention of wealthy nations. . . .

We denounce the Melting Pot theory and make an option for learning the culture of this country without forgetting our own (*Evangelii Nuntiandi* 20). We denounce abortion, the abuse of drugs and alcohol, and the negative and manipulative influence of commercial propaganda that creates false needs.

We do not just denounce these injustices, we also feel ourselves called to struggle for peace in the world, to live a more simple life-style in solidarity with our poor brothers and sisters. . . .

Let us be aware that we can change the world with our way of life today.

(Secretariat for Hispanic Affairs, page 12)

---

and every day they provided for it six barrels of fine flour, forty sheep, and six measures of wine. 4 The king worshiped it and went every day to adore it; but Daniel adored only his God. 5 When the king asked him, "Why do you not adore Bel?" Daniel replied, "Because I worship not idols made with hands, but only the living God who made heaven and earth and has dominion over all mankind." 6 Then the king continued, "You do not think Bel is a living god? Do you not see how much he eats and drinks every day? 7 Daniel began to laugh. "Do not be deceived, O king," he said; "it is only clay inside and bronze outside; it has never taken any food or drink." 8 Enraged, the king called his priests and said to them, "Unless you tell me who it is that consumes these provisions, you shall die. 9 But if you can show that Bel consumes them, Daniel shall die for blaspheming Bel." Daniel said to the king, "Let it be as you say!" 10 There were seventy priests of Bel, besides their wives and children.

When the king went with Daniel into the temple of Bel, 11 the priests of Bel said, "See, we are going to leave. Do you, O king, set out the food and prepare the wine; then shut the door and seal it with your ring. 12 If you do not find that Bel has eaten it all when you return in the morning, we are to die; otherwise Daniel shall die for his lies against us." 13 They were not perturbed, because under the table they had made a secret entrance through which they always came in to consume the food. 14 After they departed the king set the food before Bel, while Daniel ordered his servants to bring some ashes, which they scattered through the whole temple; the king alone was present. Then they went outside, sealed the closed door with the king's ring, and departed. 15 The priests entered that night as usual, with their wives and children, and they ate and drank everything.

16 Early the next morning, the king came with Daniel. 17 "Are the seals unbroken, Daniel?" he

asked. And Daniel answered, "They are unbroken, O king." [18] As soon as he had opened the door, the king looked at the table and cried aloud, "Great you are, O Bel; there is no trickery in you." [19] But Daniel laughed and kept the king from entering. "Look at the floor," he said; "whose footprints are these?" [20] "I see the footprints of men, women, and children!" said the king. [21] The angry king arrested the priests, their wives, and their children. They showed him the secret door by which they used to enter to consume what was on the table. [22] He put them to death, and handed Bel over to Daniel, who destroyed it and its temple.

[23] There was a great dragon which the Babylonians worshiped. [24] "Look!" said the king to Daniel, "you cannot deny that this is a living god, so adore it." [25] But Daniel answered, "I adore the Lord, my God, for he is the living God. [26] Give me permission, O king, and I will kill this dragon without sword or club." "I give you permission," the king said. [27] Then Daniel took some pitch, fat, and hair; these he boiled together and made into cakes. He put them into the mouth of the dragon, and when the dragon ate them, he burst asunder. "This," he said, "is what you worshiped."

[28] When the Babylonians heard this, they were angry and turned against the king. "The king has become a Jew," they said; "he has destroyed Bel, killed the dragon, and put the priests to death." [29] They went to the king and demanded: "Hand Daniel over to us, or we will kill you and your family." [30] When he saw himself threatened with violence, the king was forced to hand Daniel over to them. [31] They threw Daniel into a lions' den, where he remained six days. [32] In the den were seven lions, and two carcasses and two sheep had been given to them daily. But now they were given nothing, so that they would devour Daniel.

[33] In Judea there was a prophet, Habakkuk; he mixed some bread in a bowl with the stew he had boiled, and was going to bring it to the reapers in the field, [34] when an angel of the Lord told him, "Take the lunch you have to Daniel in the lions' den at Babylon." [35] But Habakkuk answered, "Babylon, sir, I have never seen, and I do not know the den!" [36]* The angel of the Lord seized him by the crown of his head and carried him by the hair; with the speed of the wind, he set him down in Babylon above the den. [37] "Daniel, Daniel," cried Habakkuk, "take the lunch God has sent you." [38] "You have remembered me, O God," said Daniel; "you have not forsaken those who love you." [39] While Daniel began to eat, the angel of the Lord at once brought Habakkuk back to his own place.

[40] On the seventh day the king came to mourn for Daniel. As he came to the den and looked in, there was Daniel, sitting there! [41] The king cried aloud, "You are great, O Lord, the God of Daniel, and there is no other besides you!" [42] Daniel he took out, but those who had tried to destroy him he threw into the den, and they were devoured in a moment before his eyes.

14, 36: Ez 8, 3.

G o marry a prostitute." Say what, God? A picture is worth a thousand words, and Hosea's family life was a living picture of Israel's infidelity and God's continuing faithfulness. The Book of Hosea captures this faithful prophet's commitment to God and his loving faithfulness to his straying wife.

In-depth

Hosea preached to the northern kingdom of Israel before it was conquered by the Assyrians in 721 B.C. As we learn from Hosea's speeches, the situation in the northern kingdom was not good. Over twenty-five years, Hosea saw seven kings come and go, most of them corrupt (see the timeline at the back of this Bible, and 2 Kgs 14, 23—17, 23). Pursuing their own greedy ends and trying to play power politics, the ruling class overlooked the poor and the needy in their midst and led the people into idolatry. Through Hosea, God proclaimed, "I am the LORD, your God, / since the land of Egypt" (Hos 13, 4).

Even more powerful than Hosea's words was the living symbol of his marriage. Early in Hosea's preaching, God commanded him to marry a prostitute and have children by her. Hosea remained faithful to her, loving her even when she wandered to other men. Hosea used the image of his own marriage to preach his message to Israel. As Hosea's wife was unfaithful to him, so too was Israel unfaithful to God, wandering off in worship of other gods. However, just as Hosea was faithful to his wife and awaited her return, so too God was faithful to Israel and awaited its return from the distractions of power, wealth, and other gods.

Hosea and Amos were prophets in the northern kingdom at about the same time. But Amos had come from the southern kingdom and was more distant and cynical in describing the sins of the ruling class (see his description of well-off women in Am 4, 1-3). Hosea was from the northern kingdom—these people were his people! He took their sins personally and passionately. Initially, he had hopes that the people would repent and return to God (see Hos 2, 16–25). But after a succession of selfish and violent rulers, he prophesied against his people with all the passion of a scorned lover (see Hos 13, 7-11). Still, at the end, he hoped for Israel's return to God (14, 2-3).

At a Glance

I. **The Prophet's Marriage and Its Lesson (1, 1—3, 5).**

II. **Israel's Guilt and Punishment (4, 1—14, 10).**

Quick Facts

Period Covered
786–746 B.C.

Authors
Hosea and later scribes

Themes
God's faithful love for Israel, the image of God as a loving parent

Hosea

The Book of

Hosea

I. The Prophet's Marriage and Its Lesson†

Marriage with an Unfaithful Wife

1 ¹ The word of the LORD that came to Hosea, the son of Beeri, in the days of Uzziah, Jotham, Ahaz, Hezekiah, kings of Judah, and in the days of Jeroboam, son of Joash, king of Israel. ²† In the beginning of the LORD's speaking to Hosea, the LORD said to Hosea:

Go, take a harlot wife and harlot's children,
for the land gives itself to harlotry,
turning away from the LORD.

³ So he went and took Gomer, the daughter of Diblaim; and she conceived and bore him a son. ⁴† Then the LORD said to him:

Give him the name Jezreel,
for in a little while
I will punish the house of Jehu
for the bloodshed at Jezreel
And bring to an end the kingdom
of the house of Israel;
⁵ On that day I will break the bow of Israel
in the valley of Jezreel.

⁶† When she conceived again and bore a daughter, the LORD said to him:

Give her the name Lo-ruhama;
I no longer feel pity for the house
of Israel:
rather, I abhor them utterly.
⁷† Yet for the house of Judah I feel pity;
I will save them by the LORD, their God;

But I will not save them by war,
   by sword or bow, by horses or horsemen.

[8] After she weaned Lo-ruhama, she conceived and bore a son. [9†] Then the LORD said:

Give him the name Lo-ammi,
   for you are not my people,
   and I will not be your God.

Israel's Punishment and Restoration

2 [4†] Protest against your mother, protest!
   for she is not my wife,
   and I am not her husband.
Let her remove her harlotry from before her,
   her adultery from between her breasts,
[5†] Or I will strip her naked,
   leaving her as on the day of her birth;
I will make her like the desert,
   reduce her to an arid land,
   and slay her with thirst.
[6] I will have no pity on her children,
   for they are the children of harlotry.
[7†] Yes, their mother has played the harlot;
   she that conceived them has
     acted shamefully.
"I will go after my lovers," she said,
   "who give me my bread and my water,
   my wool and my flax, my oil and my drink."

[10] Since she has not known
   that it was I who gave her
   the grain, the wine, and the oil,
And her abundance of silver,
   and of gold, which they used for Baal,
[11] Therefore I will take back my grain in its time,
   and my wine in its season;
I will snatch away my wool and my flax,
   with which she covers her nakedness.
[12] So now I will lay bare her shame
   before the eyes of her lovers,
   and no one can deliver her out of my hand.
[13] I will bring an end to all her joy,
   her feasts, her new moons, her sabbaths,
   and all her solemnities.
[14] I will lay waste her vines and fig trees,

of which she said, "These are the hire
   my lovers have given me";
I will turn them into rank growth
   and wild beasts shall devour them.
[15†] I will punish her for the days of the Baals,
   for whom she burnt incense
While she decked herself out with her rings
     and her jewels,
   and, in going after her lovers,
   forgot me, says the LORD.
[8†] Therefore, I will hedge in her way with thorns
   and erect a wall against her,
   so that she cannot find her paths.
[9] If she runs after her lovers, she shall not
     overtake them;
   if she looks for them she shall not find them.
Then she shall say,
   "I will go back to my first husband,
   for it was better with me then than now."

[16†] So I will allure her;
   I will lead her into the desert
   and speak to her heart.
[17] From there I will give her the vineyards she had,
   and the valley of Achor as a door of hope.
She shall respond there as in the days of
     her youth,
   when she came up from the land of Egypt.

[18†]   On that day, says the LORD,
She shall call me "My husband,"
   and never again "My baal."
[19] Then will I remove from her mouth the
     names of the Baals,
   so that they shall no longer be invoked.
[20] I will make a covenant for them on that day,
   with the beasts of the field,
With the birds of the air,
   and with the things that crawl on the ground.
Bow and sword and war
   I will destroy from the land,
   and I will let them take their rest in security.

[21†] I will espouse you to me forever:
   I will espouse you in right and in justice,
   in love and in mercy;

---

†
1, 9: *Lo-ammi:* "not my people."
2, 4: The Lord speaks of Israel, still using the example of Hosea's wife.
2, 5: *I will strip her naked:* contemporary documents indicate that this was a conventional punishment for adultery.
2, 7: *My lovers:* the local fertility deities to whom, rather than to the Lord (v 10), the unfaithful Israelites attributed the produce of the land.
2, 15: *The days of the Baals:* ritual observances held in various local shrines in honor of Baal.
2, 8f: The crop failures, blight, etc., sent by the Lord (vv 11–14) have as their purpose to make Israel see the folly of her ways.
2, 16f: Israel's journey in the desert represents for Hosea the time of Israel's fidelity, before it was corrupted by the ways of Canaan;

cf Jer 2, 2–7; Am 5, 25. Thus, he pictures a restoration in terms of a new entry into the promised land.
2, 18: *My baal:* the word means "lord, master." It was commonly used by women of their husbands, but it is to be shunned as a title for the Lord because of its association with the pagan god Baal. Probably it had been so used by many Israelites, who saw little if any difference between the worship of the Lord and the worship of Baal.
2, 21f: The Lord will once more espouse Israel; the qualities ascribed to the renewed people are the bridal gift (cf Gn 24, 53) with which he will endow it. *In right and in justice:* two terms dear to Hosea, used by him especially to condemn the popular social injustice and corruption of the legal processes. Here they mean right conduct in general. *Love:* one of the most characteristic words of Hosea's

Unconditional Faithfulness

We don't know all the details of Hosea's relationship with his wife, Gomer. But most people understand Hos 3, 1–3 to mean that Hosea accepted her back after she was unfaithful to him. We can only hope that Gomer was so touched by Hosea's unconditional forgiveness that she turned her life around and was faithful to him in return.

It is hard to be faithful to someone who is unfaithful to you. The other person doesn't have to be an adulterous spouse. She or he can be a friend who starts spending time with someone else instead of you, or a family member who keeps breaking promises to be with you. A natural reaction is to return the hurt in some way. How much harder—and more Christlike—it is to keep being faithful and friendly.

Have you ever been hurt by someone's unfaithful behavior? If so, how did you react? How can you address a friend's or family member's unfaithful behavior and still remain faithful and loving yourself?

▶ Hos 3, 1–3

22 I will espouse you in fidelity,
    and you shall know the LORD.
23 On that day I will respond, says the LORD;
    I will respond to the heavens,
    and they shall respond to the earth;
24 The earth shall respond to the grain, and
    wine, and oil,
    and these shall respond to Jezreel.
25* I will sow him for myself in the land,
    and I will have pity on Lo-ruhama.
    I will say to Lo-ammi, "You are
    my people,"
    and he shall say, "My God!"

Triumph of Love

3 1† Again the LORD said to me:
    Give your love to a woman
    beloved of a paramour, an adulteress;
Even as the LORD loves the people of Israel,
    though they turn to other gods
    and are fond of raisin cakes.†

2† So I bought her for fifteen pieces of silver and a homer and a lethech of barley. 3 Then I said to her:

"Many days you shall wait for me;
    you shall not play the harlot
Or belong to any man;
    I in turn will wait for you."
4† For the people of Israel shall remain many days
    without king or prince,
Without sacrifice or sacred pillar,
    without ephod or household idols.
5*†Then the people of Israel shall turn back
    and seek the LORD, their God,
    and David, their king;
They shall come trembling to the LORD
    and to his bounty, in the last days.
1*† The number of the Israelites
    shall be like the sand of the sea,
    which can be neither measured
      nor counted.
Whereas they were called,
    "Lo-ammi,"
They shall be called,
    "Children of the living God."
2 Then the people of Judah and of Israel
    shall be gathered together;
They shall appoint for themselves one head

---

†prophecy. It means a dutiful love, based on a social relation; here it refers to the covenant between God and his people. It is a love fulfilled by the performance of mutual obligations. *Mercy:* from the same root as the word translated pity in Hos 1, 6; cf v 25. *And you shall know the Lord:* another characteristic expression of Hosea; cf Hos 4, 1; 5, 4; 6, 3.6. It means not an abstract but a practical knowledge, i.e., acknowledgment of his will, obedience to his law.

3, 1–5: Hosea is instructed to take Gomer back, redeeming her from her paramours. On condition of her amendment, she will be restored to her former position of wife. This in turn signifies God's enduring love for his people. He will put the people through a period of trial—the dissolution of the kingdom—in order that they may return to him wholeheartedly.

3, 1: *Raisin cakes:* offerings to the fertility goddess Ashera, the female counterpart of Baal; cf Jer 7, 18; 44, 19.

3, 2: *Homer:* about ten bushels. *Lethech:* a half-homer.

3, 4: *Sacred pillar:* the stone massebah, originally perhaps a phallic symbol, representing Baal. These were also used, with another signification, in Israelite worship; see notes on Gn 28, 18; Ex 34, 13. *Ephod:* an instrument used in consulting the deity; cf 1 Sm 23, 6–12; 30, 7; see notes on Ex 28, 6.15–30. *Household idols:* images regarded as the tutelary deities of the household; cf Gn 31, 19; Jgs 17, 5; 18, 14.17f.

3, 5: *David, their king:* the messianic King of the Davidic line who will restore the kingdom of God's people; cf Jer 23, 5; Ez 34, 23f. *The last days:* the messianic age.

3, 1–3: These verses (The number . . . Ruhama) (transposed from ch 2) continue the conditional promise of restoration made in Hos 3, 1–5, reversing the dire predictions of chapter 1; the symbolic names now become names of honor: *Jezreel,* "God sows"; *Ammi,* "my people"; *Ruhama,* "she is pitied."

---

*
2, 25: Rom 9, 25; 1 Pt 2, 10.   3,1: Rom 9, 26.
3, 5: Ez 34, 23.

and come up from other lands,
for great shall be the day of Jezreel.
3 Say to your brothers, "Ammi,"
and to your sisters, "Ruhama."

II: Israel's Guilt and Punishment

Crimes of Israel

4 ¹ Hear the word of the LORD, O people of
Israel,
for the LORD has a grievance
against the inhabitants of the land:
There is no fidelity, no mercy,
no knowledge of God in the land.
²* False swearing, lying, murder, stealing
and adultery!
in their lawlessness, bloodshed
follows bloodshed.
3 Therefore the land mourns,
and everything that dwells in it languishes:
The beasts of the field,
the birds of the air,
and even the fish of the sea perish.

Guilt of the Priests

4† But let no one protest, let no one complain;
with you is my grievance, O priests!
5 You shall stumble in the day,
and the prophets shall stumble with you
at night;
I will destroy your mother.
6 My people perish for want of knowledge!
Since you have rejected knowledge,
I will reject you from my priesthood;
Since you have ignored the law of your God,
I will also ignore your sons.
7 One and all they sin against me,
exchanging their glory for shame.
8 They feed on the sin of my people,
and are greedy for their guilt.
9* The priests shall fare no better than
the people:
I will punish them for their ways,
and repay them for their deeds.
10 They shall eat but not be satisfied,

they shall play the harlot but not increase,
Because they have abandoned the LORD
11 to practice harlotry.
Old wine and new
deprive my people of understanding.
12† They consult their piece of wood,
and their wand makes pronouncements
for them,
For the spirit of harlotry has led them astray;
they commit harlotry, forsaking their God.
13 On the mountaintops they offer sacrifice
and on the hills they burn incense,
Beneath oak and poplar and terebinth,
because of their pleasant shade.
That is why your daughters play the harlot,
and your daughters-in-law are adulteresses.
14† Am I then to punish your daughters for
their harlotry,
your daughters-in-law for their adultery?
You yourselves consort with harlots,
and with prostitutes you offer sacrifice!
So must a people without understanding
come to ruin.
15† Though you play the harlot, O Israel,
let not Judah become guilty!
Come not to Gilgal,
nor up to Beth-aven,
to swear, "As the Lord lives!"
16 For Israel is as stubborn as a heifer;
will the LORD now give them broad pastures
as though they were lambs?
17† Ephraim is an associate of idols,
let him alone!
18 When their carousing is over,
they give themselves to harlotry;
in their arrogance they love shame.
19† The wind has bound them up in its pinions;
they shall have only shame from
their altars.

Guilt of the Leaders

5 ¹*† Hear this, O priests,
Pay attention, O house of Israel,
O household of the king, give ear!
It is you who are called to judgment.

4, 4ff: Hosea is particularly severe with the priests in the northern kingdom, who had led the way in the general apostasy from God's law. The prophets here associated with the priests (v 5) were doubtless cult prophets, who were often unworthy of their pretended calling; cf Jer 2, 8; 4, 9f; 6, 13f; 23, 9–40.
4, 12: Wood . . . wand: an idol used in divination.
4, 14: With prostitutes you offer sacrifice: the ritual prostitution practiced at the Canaanite shrines was introduced even into sanctuaries dedicated to the Lord. In comparison, the adultery that had become common in Israel was a far less reprehensible crime.
4, 15: Gilgal: not the Gilgal of the south (Jos 4, 19f), but a sanctuary north of Bethel where there was an association of cult prophets (2 Kgs 2, 1ff; 4, 38). Beth-aven: literally, "house of iniquity," Hosea's nickname for Bethel, or a scribal substitute for Bethel, "house of god," in this context. Bethel was one of the royal shrines of Israel,

where there was a schismatic public worship of the Lord; cf 1 Kgs 12, 26–30.
4, 17: Ephraim: the heartland of the northern kingdom. During the latter part of Hosea's prophetic career, Ephraim was all that remained of Israel after the Assyrians had overrun Transjordan and Galilee.
4, 19: The Israelites shall be carried from their country as by a whirlwind. To this their idolatry has brought them.
5, 1: Mizpah: probably the Mizpah in Transjordan is meant; cf Jos 11, 8. Tabor: the mountain that dominates the valley of Jezreel.

4, 2: Ex 20, 13–17.   5, 1: Mi 3, 1.
4, 9: Is 24, 2.

For you have become a snare at Mizpah,
   and a net spread upon Tabor.
2 In their perversity they have sunk
      into wickedness,
   and I am rejected by them all.
3 I know Ephraim,
   and Israel is not hidden from me;
Now Ephraim has played the harlot,
   Israel is defiled.
4 Their deeds do not allow them
      to return to their God;
For the spirit of harlotry is in them,
   and they do not recognize the LORD.

5 The arrogance of Israel bears witness
      against him;
Ephraim stumbles in his guilt,
   and Judah stumbles with them.
6 With their flocks and their herds they shall go
   to seek the LORD, but they shall not find him:
he has withdrawn himself from them.
7 They have been untrue to the LORD,
   for they have begotten illegitimate children;
Now shall the new moon devour them
   together with their fields.

Political Upheavals†

8† Blow the horn in Gibeah,
      the trumpet in Ramah!
Sound the alarm in Beth-aven:
   "Look behind you, O Benjamin!"
9 Ephraim shall become a waste
      on the day of chastisement:
Against the tribes of Israel
   I announce what is sure to be.
10*†The princes of Judah have become
      like those that move a boundary line;
Upon them I will pour out
   my wrath like water.

11† Is Ephraim maltreated, his rights violated?
      No, he has willingly gone after filth!
12† I am like a moth for Ephraim,
      like maggots for the house of Judah.
13† When Ephraim saw his infirmity,
      and Judah his sore,

Ephraim went to Assyria,
   and Judah sent to the great king.
But he cannot heal you
   nor take away your sore.
14 For I am like a lion to Ephraim,
   like a young lion to the house of Judah;
It is I who rend the prey and depart,
   I carry it away and no one can save it
      from me.

Insincere Conversion

15† I will go back to my place
   until they pay for their guilt
   and seek my presence.

6 † In their affliction, they shall look for me:
1 "Come, let us return to the LORD,
For it is he who has rent, but he will heal us;
   he has struck us, but he will bind
      our wounds.
2*†He will revive us after two days;
   on the third day he will raise us up,
   to live in his presence.
3 Let us know, let us strive to know the LORD;
   as certain as the dawn is his coming,
   and his judgment shines forth like the light
      of day!
He will come to us like the rain,
   like spring rain that waters the earth."

4† What can I do with you, Ephraim?
      What can I do with you, Judah?
Your piety is like a morning cloud,
   like the dew that early passes away.
5 For this reason I smote them through
      the prophets,
   I slew them by the words of my mouth;
6* For it is love that I desire, not sacrifice,
      and knowledge of God rather
         than holocausts.
7 But they, in their land, violated
      the covenant;
   there they were untrue to me.
8 Gilead is a city of evildoers,
      tracked with blood.
9 As brigands ambush a man,

5, 8–14: This passage refers to the Syro-Ephraimite war of 735–734 B.C., when a coalition of Arameans and Israelites attempted to dethrone the king of Judah. Judah repulsed the attempt with the aid of Assyria, and the latter devastated both Aram and Israel; cf 2 Kgs 16, 5–9. Hosea condemns both Israel and Judah for the war.
5, 8: A vision of invasion, from Gibeah and Ramah in northern Judah, into Israel.
5, 10: Like those that move a boundary line: comparison of the invaders to a classic case of social injustice; cf Dt 19, 14; 27, 17; Prv 23, 10f.
5, 11: Gone after filth: by allying himself with Aram.
5, 12: Moth . . . maggots: internal corruption will work the Lord's punishment on both Israel and Judah.
5, 13: Ephraim went . . . the great king: in 738 B.C. the Israelite

king Manahem had to pay tribute to the Assyrian king Tiglath-pileser III, whose vassal he became (2 Kgs 15, 19f). Under the threat of the Syro-Ephraimite invasion King Ahaz of Judah also submitted himself and his country to Tiglath-pileser (2 Kgs 16, 7–9). "The great king" was the title used by the Assyrian kings.
5, 15: The Lord withdraws himself from Israel, hoping for its repentance.
6, 1: In . . . me: this is the last line of ch 5.
6, 2: After two days; on the third day: after a short lapse of time.
6, 4: Piety: the word is translated "love" in Hos 2, 21 and in v 6 below.

5, 10: Dt 19, 14; 27, 17.   6, 6: 1 Sm 15, 22; Eccl 4,
6, 2: 1 Cor 15, 4.   17; Mt 9, 13; 12, 7.

a band of priests slay on the way
    to Shechem,
committing monstrous crime.
10 In the house of Israel I have seen a
     horrible thing:
there harlotry is found in Ephraim,
Israel is defiled.
11† For you also, O Judah,
    a harvest has been appointed.

7

1 When I would bring about the restoration
    of my people,
when I would heal Israel,
The guilt of Ephraim stands out,
    the wickedness of Samaria;
They practice falsehood,
    thieves break in, bandits plunder abroad.
2 Yet they do not remind themselves
    that I remember all their wickedness.
Even now their crimes surround them,
    present to my sight.

Failure of the Monarchy †

3 In their wickedness they regale the king,
    the princes too, with their deceits.
4 They are all kindled to wrath
    like a blazing oven,
Whose fire the baker desists from stirring
    once the dough is kneaded until it has risen.
5 On the day of our king,
    the princes are overcome with the heat
     of wine.
He extends his hand among dissemblers;
6   the plotters approach with hearts like ovens.
All the night their anger sleeps;
    in the morning it flares like a blazing fire.
7 They are all heated like ovens,
    and consume their rulers.
All their kings have fallen;
    none of them calls upon me.

Foreign Alliances

8† Ephraim mingles with the nations,
    Ephraim is a hearth cake unturned.
9 Strangers have sapped his strength,
    but he takes no notice of it;

Of gray hairs, too, there is a sprinkling,
    but he takes no notice of it.
10 The arrogance of Israel bears witness
     against him;
yet they do not return to the LORD, their God,
    nor seek him, for all that.
11 Ephraim is like a dove,
    silly and senseless;
They call upon Egypt,
    they go to Assyria.
12 Even as they go I will spread my net
    around them,
like birds in the air I will bring them down.
In an instant I will send them captive from
    their land.

Perversity of Israel

13 Woe to them, they have strayed from me!
    Ruin to them, they have sinned against me!
Though I wished to redeem them,
    they spoke lies against me.
14† They have not cried to me from their hearts
    when they wailed upon their beds;
For wheat and wine they lacerated themselves,
    while they rebelled against me.
15 Though I trained and strengthened their arms,
    yet they devised evil against me.
16 They have again become useless,
    like a treacherous bow.
Their princes shall fall by the sword
    because of the insolence of their tongues;
thus they shall be mocked in the land
    of Egypt.

8

1 A trumpet to your lips,
    You who watch over the house of the LORD!
Since they have violated my covenant,
    and sinned against my law,
2 While to me they cry out,
    "O God of Israel, we know you!"
3 The men of Israel have thrown away what
    is good;
the enemy shall pursue them.
4† They made kings, but not by my authority;
    they established princes, but without
     my approval.

6, 11: *Harvest:* when the land will reap the consequences of its sins.

7, 3–7: This passage refers to the dynastic upheavals of Israel's declining days. Between the death of Jeroboam II and the fall of Samaria to the Assyrians, a matter of some twenty-five years, there were four separate dynasties on the throne and as many murdered kings. The prophet compares the Israelite nobles who were inflamed with passion to an overheated oven that consumes what it is supposed to bake; thus the land consumes its kings. *Regale:* with wine (v 3). Like fire smoldering through the night and blazing up in the morning, the sleeping anger of plotters soon breaks out in open rebellion; the succession of night and morning suggests the short reigns of the various kings of this troubled period.

7, 8: *A hearth cake unturned:* burnt on one side, half baked on the other, and therefore useless. Israel's decline in power is ascribed to its disastrous meddling in the power politics of the neighboring nations.

7, 14: *They lacerated themselves:* a common oriental practice in prayers of earnest impetration (1 Kgs 18, 28); the practice was forbidden in Israelite religion (Lv 19, 28; Dt 14, 1).

8, 4–6: Israel's monarchy and separate sanctuary are here associated, as in 1 Kgs 12, 20–33; both were the result of rebellion against the divinely approved Davidic dynasty and the Jerusalem temple with the ark of the covenant. The calf image set up by Jeroboam I in the royal shrines prevented Israel from attaining innocence (vv 5f).

With their silver and gold they made
  idols for themselves, to their
  own destruction.
5 Cast away your calf, O Samaria!
  my wrath is kindled against them;
How long will they be unable to attain
  innocence in Israel?
6 The work of an artisan,
  no god at all,
Destined for the flames—
  such is the calf of Samaria!

7 When they sow the wind,
  they shall reap the whirlwind;
The stalk of grain that forms no ear
  can yield no flour;
Even if it could,
  strangers would swallow it.
8 Israel is swallowed up;
  he is now among the nations
  a thing of no value.
9 They went up to Assyria—
  a wild ass off on its own—
  Ephraim bargained for lovers.
10 Even though they bargain with the nations,
  I will now gather an army;
King and princes shall shortly
  succumb under the burden.

11† When Ephraim made many altars to expiate sin,
  his altars became occasions of sin.
12 Though I write for him my many ordinances,
  they are considered as a stranger's.
13 Though they offer sacrifice,
  immolate flesh and eat it,
  the LORD is not pleased with them.
He shall still remember their guilt
  and punish their sins;
  they shall return to Egypt.
14* Israel has forgotten his maker
  and built palaces.
Judah, too, has fortified many cities;
  but I will send fire upon his cities,
  to devour their castles.

Exile without Worship

9 1† Rejoice not, O Israel,
  exult not like the nations!
For you have been unfaithful to your God,

Reaping the Whirlwind

Hosea uses lots of metaphors, or symbols, in describing Israel's relationship with God. Hosea 8, 7 gives one of those metaphors, saying the Israelites have sowed the wind and will reap the whirlwind. The wind is their political scheming, injustice, and idolatry; the whirlwind is violence and injustice that will destroy the whole country.

Like Israel, we are free to reject or accept God, but will have to reap the consequences of our choices.

In your prayer, reflect or journal on the following questions:
- **What significant decisions have you made recently?**
- **What consequences are likely to follow as a result of each decision?**
- **Were your choices the ones that God wanted you to make?**

▸ **Hos 8, 7**

loving a harlot's hire
  upon every threshing floor.
2 Threshing floor and wine press shall not
  nourish them,
  the new wine shall fail them.
3 They shall not dwell in the LORD's land;
  Ephraim shall return to Egypt,
  and in Assyria they shall eat unclean food.
4† They shall not pour libations of wine to
  the LORD,
  or proffer their sacrifices before him.
Theirs will be like mourners' bread,
  that makes unclean all who eat of it;
Such food as they have shall be for themselves;
  it cannot enter the house of the LORD.

5† What will you do on the festival day,
  the day of the LORD's feast?

8, 11: The very multiplicity of sanctuaries throughout the land was a danger to the purity of worship. The local shrines were speedily assimilated to the cult places used by the Canaanites, and the Lord was identified with the god Baal worshiped there. Thus the Deuteronomic writers, influenced by prophetic ideas, ended by restricting sacrificial worship to the one temple in Jerusalem.
9, 1f: Upon every threshing floor: an allusion to harvest festivals in honor of Baal, to whom the Israelites had attributed the fertility of the land; cf Hos 2, 7.

9, 4: Mourners' bread: bread eaten at funeral rites; cf Dt 26, 13f. Contact with a corpse made a person ritually unclean, together with everything he touched. Such bread could not be offered to the Lord.
9, 5: The LORD's feast: doubtless the autumn feast of Booths, the most important of the Israelite public celebrations; cf Lv 23, 34.

8, 14: Am 2, 5.

6 When they go from the ruins,
       Egypt shall gather them in, Memphis shall
         bury them.
   Weeds shall overgrow their silver treasures,
       and thorns invade their tents.

The Prophet Ridiculed

7 They have come, the days of punishment!
       they have come, the days of recompense!
   Let Israel know it!
       "The prophet is a fool,
       the man of the spirit is mad!"
   Because your iniquity is great,
       great, too, is your hostility.
8 A prophet is Ephraim's watchman with God,
       yet a fowler's snare is on all his ways,
       hostility in the house of his God.
9† They have sunk to the depths of corruption,
       as in the days of Gibeah;
   He shall remember their iniquity
       and punish their sins.

Crime of Baal-peor

10† Like grapes in the desert,
       I found Israel;
   Like the first fruits of the fig tree in its prime,
       I considered your fathers.
   When they came to Baal-peor
       and consecrated themselves to the Shame,
       they became as abhorrent as the thing
         they loved.
11 The glory of Ephraim flies away like a bird:
       no birth, no carrying in the womb,
       no conception.
   Were they to bear children,
       I would slay the darlings of their womb.
12 Even though they bring up their children,
       I will make them childless, till not one
         is left.
   Woe to them
       when I turn away from them!
13 Ephraim, as I saw, was like Tyre,
       planted in a beauteous spot;
   But Ephraim shall bring out
       his children to the slayer.
14† Give them, O LORD!
       give them what?
   Give them an unfruitful womb,
       and dry breasts!

Crime of Gilgal

15*†All their wickedness is in Gilgal;
       yes, there they incurred my hatred.
   Because of their wicked deeds
       I will drive them out of my house.
   I will love them no longer;
       all their princes are rebels.
16 Ephraim is stricken,
       their root is dried up;
       they shall bear no fruit.

17 My God will disown them
       because they have not listened to him;
       they shall be wanderers among the nations.

Punishment of Idolatry

10 ¹† Israel is a luxuriant vine
          whose fruit matches its growth.
   The more abundant his fruit,
       the more altars he built;
   The more productive his land,
       the more sacred pillars he set up.
2 Their heart is false,
       now they pay for their guilt;
   God shall break down their altars
       and destroy their sacred pillars.
3 If they would say,
       "We have no king"—
   Since they do not fear the LORD,
       what can the king do for them?
4† Nothing but make promises,
       swear false oaths, and make alliances,
   While justice grows wild
       like wormwood in a plowed field!
5† The inhabitants of Samaria fear
       for the calf of Beth-aven;
   The people mourn for it
       and its priests wail over it,
       because the glory has departed from it.
6 It too shall be carried to Assyria,
       as an offering to the great king.
   Ephraim shall be taken into captivity,
       Israel be shamed by his schemes.

7 The king of Samaria shall disappear,
       like foam upon the waters.
8* The high places of Aven shall be destroyed,
       the sin of Israel;
   thorns and thistles shall overgrow their altars.

9, 9: *The days of Gibeah:* a reference to the outrage committed at Gibeah in the days of the Judges (Jgs 19, 22–30).
9, 10: At Baal-peor (Nm 25, 1–5) the Israelites consecrated themselves to Baal, here called the Shame.
9, 14: *An unfruitful womb:* this appears to be a reversal of the ancient blessing of Joseph contained in Gn 49, 25f, in which the increase, hence fruitfulness, promised to the patriarch is even signified by the name of his son Ephraim, on whose descendants the prophet now invokes the curse of extinction.

9, 15: *Gilgal:* see note on Hos 4, 15.
10, 1: *Sacred pillars:* see note on Hos 3, 4.
10, 4: *Justice . . . like wormwood:* the administration of justice, which should have been the mainstay of the people, has in corrupt hands become another instrument of oppression; cf Am 6, 13.
10, 5: *The calf of Beth-aven:* see notes on Hos 4, 15; 8, 4ff.

9, 15: 1 Sm 8, 5.   Rv 6, 16.
10, 8: Is 2, 19; Lk 23, 30;

Then they shall cry out to the mountains,
"Cover us!"
and to the hills, "Fall upon us!"

9* Since the days of Gibeah
you have sinned, O Israel.
There they took their stand;
war was not to reach them in Gibeah.
10*† Against the wanton people I came
and I chastised them;
I gathered troops against them
when I chastised them for their two crimes.

Time To Seek the LORD

11 Ephraim was a trained heifer,
willing to thresh;
I myself laid a yoke
upon her fair neck;
Ephraim was to be harnessed, Judah was
to plow,
Jacob was to break his furrows:
12* "Sow for yourselves justice,
reap the fruit of piety;
Break up for yourselves a new field,
for it is time to seek the LORD,
till he come and rain down justice
upon you."
13 But you have cultivated wickedness,
reaped perversity,
and eaten the fruit of falsehood.

Because you have trusted in your chariots,
and in your many warriors,
14*† Turmoil shall break out among your tribes
and all your fortresses shall be ravaged
As Salman ravaged Beth-arbel in time of war,
smashing mothers and their children.
15 So shall it be done to you, Bethel,
because of your utter wickedness:
At dawn the king of Israel
shall perish utterly.

When Israel Was a Child

11 1*† When Israel was a child I loved him,
out of Egypt I called my son.
2 The more I called them,
the farther they went from me,
Sacrificing to the Baals

and burning incense to idols.
3 Yet it was I who taught Ephraim to walk,
who took them in my arms;
4† I drew them with human cords,
with bands of love;
I fostered them like one
who raises an infant to his cheeks;
Yet, though I stooped to feed my child,
they did not know that I was their healer.

5 He shall return to the land of Egypt,
and Assyria shall be his king;
6 The sword shall begin with his cities
and end by consuming his solitudes.
Because they refused to repent,
their own counsels shall devour them.
7 His people are in suspense about returning
to him;
and God, though in unison they cry out
to him,
shall not raise them up.

End of the Exile

8*† How could I give you up, O Ephraim,
or deliver you up, O Israel?

A Parent's Love

Hosea, chapter 11, describes God as a loving parent. This is one of the most touching passages of the Old Testament. Despite God's tenderness and care, Israel behaves as a rebellious child. God is heartbroken by Israel's rejection, but is compassionate in calling for its return.

God, loving father and mother, thank you for your generous and unconditional love. Let me remember that you always love me even when I have done something wrong. Help me to return your love by living in a way that is pleasing to you. Amen.

▶ Hos 11, 1–7

10, 10: *Their two crimes:* possibly the outrage described in Jgs 19 is conceived as a double crime, of adultery and murder. Or the prophet regards the proclamation of the monarchy (cf 1 Sm 10, 23f) as a crime.

10, 14: *As Salman ravaged Beth-arbel:* allusion to an invasion not otherwise mentioned in the Bible. Salman may have been the Moabite king of this name mentioned in an inscription of Tiglath-pileser III. There were several Beth-arbels in Palestine; this one was probably in Transjordan.

11, 1: *Out of Egypt:* Hosea, like most of the prophets, dates the

real beginning of Israel from the time of Moses and the Exodus. Mt 2, 15 applies this text to the return of the Christ Child from Egypt.

11, 4: *I drew them . . . with bands of love:* not forcing them like draft animals, but drawing them with kindness and affection.

11, 8: *Admah . . . Zeboiim:* cities destroyed with Sodom and Gomorrah (Dt 29, 22).

10, 9: Jgs 20, 1.
10, 10: Jer 4, 3.
10, 12: Is 45, 8.
10, 14: Jgs 8, 10ff.
11, 1: Mt 2, 15.
11, 8: Gn 19, 24f.

I THEREFORE COMMIT

This prayer from Elizabeth S. Tapia of the Philippines could have been written in response to Hosea's call to live justly, to live the spirit of being a holy people of God:

We should not oppress children, indigenous people,
women, the homeless, refugees and victims of war.
We need to live in defense of peoples and creation.
For I believe in the interwovenness of life.
Creator and Creatures. Cosmic and Individual.
West, North, East, South. Rest and Prayer.
Food and Freedom. Theology and Ecology.
I therefore commit myself, together with you,
to take care of mother earth.
To advocate for peace and justice.
To choose and celebrate life!
These things I believe. Amen.

("Earth Credo," from *A Time to Speak*)

▶ Hos 12, 3–7

How could I treat you as Admah,
   or make you like Zeboiim?
My heart is overwhelmed,
   my pity is stirred.
9   I will not give vent to my blazing anger,
   I will not destroy Ephraim again;
For I am God and not man,
   the Holy One present among you;
   I will not let the flames
      consume you.
10 They shall follow the LORD,
   who roars like a lion;
When he roars,
   his sons shall come frightened from
      the west,
11 Out of Egypt they shall come trembling,
   like sparrows,
   from the land of Assyria, like doves;
And I will resettle them in their homes,
   says the LORD.

Infidelity of Israel

12   1 Ephraim has surrounded me with lies,
   the house of Israel, with deceit;
Judah is still rebellious against God,
   against the Holy One, who is faithful.
2† Ephraim chases the wind,
   ever pursuing the gale.
His lies and falsehoods are many:
   he comes to terms with Assyria,
   and carries oil to Egypt.
3† The LORD has a grievance against Israel:
   he shall punish Jacob for his conduct,
   for his deeds he shall repay him.
4* In the womb he supplanted his brother,
   and as a man he contended with God;
5 He contended with the angel and triumphed,
   entreating him with tears.
At Bethel he met God
   and there he spoke with him:
6 The LORD, the God of hosts,
   the LORD is his name!

HOS

12, 2: *He comes . . . Egypt:* allusion to the commercial and military pacts with the great powers, consistently condemned by the prophets as derogatory to the Lord's claim on his people.

12, 3–7: Contemporary Israel and the Israel represented by its ancestor Jacob (Israel) are here alternated, a splendid example of the Hebrew concept of "corporate personality" or easy transition from

the individual to the community of which he is part. Hosea recalls the history of Jacob as it now appears in Genesis, but with some differences of detail and order.

12, 4: Gn 25, 26; 32, 25.

7   You shall return by the help of your God,
    if you remain loyal and do right
    and always hope in your God.

8   A merchant who holds a false balance,
    who loves to defraud!
9   Though Ephraim says,
    "How rich I have become;
    I have made a fortune!"
    All his gain shall not suffice him
    for the guilt of his sin.
10   I am the LORD, your God,
    since the land of Egypt;
    I will again have you live in tents,
    as in that appointed time.
11   I granted many visions
    and spoke to the prophets,
    through whom I set forth examples.
12   In Gilead is falsehood, they have come
    to nought,
    in Gilgal they sacrifice to bullocks;
    Their altars are like heaps of stones
    in the furrows of the field.

13*   When Jacob fled to the land of Aram,
    he served for a wife;
    for a wife Israel tended sheep.
14*† By a prophet the LORD brought Israel out
    of Egypt,
    and by a prophet they were protected.
15   Ephraim has exasperated his lord;
    therefore he shall cast his bloodguilt
    upon him
    and repay him for his outrage.

Furrows of the Field

13   1 Ephraim's word caused fear,
    for he was exalted in Israel;
    but he sinned through Baal and died.

Punishment for Ingratitude

2   Now they continue to sin,
    making for themselves molten images,
    Silver idols according to their fancy,
    all of them the work of artisans.
    "To these," they say, "offer sacrifice."
    Men kiss calves!
3   Therefore, they shall be like a morning cloud
    or like the dew that early passes away,

    Like chaff storm-driven from the threshing floor
    or like smoke out of the window.

4*   I am the LORD, your God,
    since the land of Egypt;
    You know no God besides me,
    and there is no savior but me.
5   I fed you in the desert,
    in the torrid land.
6   They ate their fill;
    when filled, they became proud of heart
    and forgot me.

7   Therefore, I will be like a lion to them,
    like a panther by the road I will keep watch.
8   I will attack them like a bear robbed of
    its young,
    and tear their hearts from their breasts;
    I will devour them on the spot like a lion,
    as though a wild beast were to rend them.

9   Your destruction, O Israel!
    who is there to help you?
10*   Where now is your king,
    that he may rescue you in all your cities?
    And your rulers, of whom you said,
    "Give me a king and princes"?
11†   I give you a king in my anger,
    and I take him away in my wrath.

12   The guilt of Israel is wrapped up,
    his sin is stored away.
13†   The birth pangs shall come for him,
    but he shall be an unwise child;
    For when it is time he shall not
    present himself
    where children break forth.

14*† Shall I deliver them from the power of the
    nether world?
    shall I redeem them from death?
    Where are your plagues, O death!
    where is your sting, O nether world!
    My eyes are closed to compassion.

15*   Though he be fruitful among his fellows,
    an east wind shall come, a wind from
    the LORD,
    rising from the desert,

---

† ——————

12, 14: *A prophet:* Moses.
13, 11: *I give you a king . . . in my wrath:* the Lord punishes the people of the northern kingdom by giving them incompetent kings who are soon deposed.
13, 13: Israel's sin is such as to warrant its destruction (v 12), because it refuses to do penance. It will therefore perish as surely as the unborn child which dies in its mother's body because it does not properly employ the only way to safety.
13, 14: *Shall . . . nether world:* a vigorous affirmation of the

Lord's determination to destroy Israel. St. Paul cites these words in a different sense (1 Cor 15, 54f), that of the ultimate victory of life over death in the resurrection of the body on the last day, wrought through the merits of Christ's passion and resurrection.

---

*——————

12, 13: Gn 28, 5; 29, 20.   13, 10: 1 Sm 8, 5.
12, 14: Ex 14, 21f.   13, 14: 1 Cor 15, 54.
13, 4: Is 43, 11.   13, 15: Ex 19, 12.

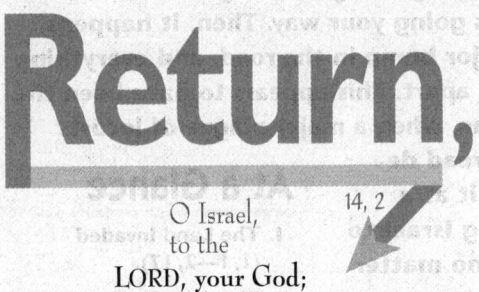

Return,

O Israel,
to the
LORD, your God;

you have

coll aPs ed

through your guilt

That shall dry up his spring,
and leave his fountain dry.
It shall loot his land
of every precious thing.

14 ¹ Samaria shall expiate her guilt,
for she has rebelled against her God.
They shall fall by the sword,
their little ones shall be dashed to pieces,
their expectant mothers shall be
ripped open.

Sincere Conversion

2 Return, O Israel, to the LORD, your God;
you have collapsed through your guilt.
3 Take with you words,
and return to the LORD;
Say to him, "Forgive all iniquity,

and receive what is good, that we
may render
as offerings the bullocks from our stalls.
4 Assyria will not save us,
nor shall we have horses to mount;
We shall say no more, 'Our god,'
to the work of our hands;
for in you the orphan finds compassion."

5 I will heal their defection,
I will love them freely;
for my wrath is turned away from them.
6 I will be like the dew for Israel:
he shall blossom like the lily;
He shall strike root like the Lebanon cedar,
and put forth his shoots.
His splendor shall be like the olive tree
and his fragrance like the Lebanon cedar.
8 Again they shall dwell in his shade
and raise grain;
They shall blossom like the vine,
and his fame shall be like the wine
of Lebanon.

9 Ephraim! What more has he to do with idols?
I have humbled him, but I will prosper him.
"I am like a verdant cypress tree"—
Because of me you bear fruit!

* * *

10† Let him who is wise understand these things;
let him who is prudent know them.
Straight are the paths of the LORD,
in them the just walk,
but sinners stumble in them.

---

† **14, 10:** A later addition in the style of the wisdom literature.

You're just cruising along, in the groove, and everything is going your way. Then, it happens. You hit a major bump in the road, and everything starts falling apart. This appears to have been the situation in Joel's time, when a major plague of locusts was causing widespread destruction. Joel took it as a wake-up sign, calling Israel to rely totally on God no matter what happened.

At a Glance

I. The Land Invaded (1, 1—2, 17).

II. Blessings for God's People (2, 18—4, 21).

In-depth

The Book of Joel does not state clearly when it was written, but it gives several clues that lead biblical scholars to believe it was written after the Babylonian Exile. During this time, Israel was ruled by the Greeks and did not have a king. The Temple and Jerusalem had been rebuilt, and Israel enjoyed relative peace, along with a growing expectancy for the coming of a messiah, a savior.

In this period, a natural disaster, perhaps a plague of locusts, occurred. In the first part of the book, Joel uses this tragedy to call Israel's attention toward God and renew its faith. He compares the plague of locusts to an invading army that brings devastation to a city. Eventually, prayer and penance end the plague and bring rain for new crops. More important, the gift of the Spirit renews the people of God (Jl 3, 1–2).

A major element of this book is a warrior-type song in which Joel speaks of the coming of the day of the LORD (2, 1–17). He describes this as the day when judgment will be delivered against the nations that have destroyed Israel. The day of the LORD is a theme that runs throughout the Bible. It is sometimes described as a joyful time of celebration (Is 9, 2), and other times as a day of punishment and destruction (Am 5, 18–24). Initially, writers of the Scriptures applied the term *day of the LORD* only to Israel; Joel applied it to all nations. Gradually, it became connected to the final judgment (Mt 25, 31–46).

The Book of Joel ends by affirming that the LORD dwells in Zion (Jerusalem) and the land will be fruitful once more. This is Joel's central message: Despite plagues and even war, God is present in Judah, and there is reason for hope.

Quick Facts

Period Covered
after the rebuilding of the Temple (515 B.C.) and before the destruction of Sidon (343 B.C.)

Authors
Joel and scribes, writing around 400 B.C.

Theme
a plague of locusts as an occasion to call for Israel to repent and turn to the LORD

The Book of Joel

Joel

The Land Invaded

1 ¹ The word of the LORD which came to Joel, the son of Pethuel.

² Hear this, you elders!
　Pay attention, all you who dwell in the land!
Has the like of this happened in your days,
　or in the days of your fathers?
³ Tell it to your children,
　and your children to their children,
　and their children to the next generation.
⁴† What the cutter left,
　the locust swarm has eaten;
What the locust swarm left,
　the grasshopper has eaten;
And what the grasshopper left,
　the devourer has eaten.

⁵ Wake up, you drunkards, and weep;
　wail, all you drinkers of wine,
Because the juice of the grape
　will be withheld from your mouths.
⁶† For a people has invaded my land,
　mighty and without number;
His teeth are the teeth of a lion,
　and his molars those of a lioness.

⁷ He has laid waste my vine,
　and blighted my fig tree;
He has stripped it, sheared off its bark;
　its branches are made white.
⁸ Lament like a virgin girt with sackcloth
　for the spouse of her youth.
⁹ Abolished are offering and libation
　from the house of the LORD;
In mourning are the priests,
　the ministers of the LORD.
¹⁰ The field is ravaged,
　the earth mourns,
Because the grain is ravaged,
　the must has failed,
　the oil languishes.

¹¹ Be appalled, you husbandmen!
　wail, you vinedressers!
Over the wheat and the barley,
　because the harvest of the field
　　has perished.
¹² The vine has dried up,
　the fig tree is withered;
The pomegranate, the date palm also, and
　　the apple,
　all the trees of the field are dried up;

---

† **1, 4:** *Cutter . . . locust . . . grasshopper . . . devourer:* these names refer to various species of locusts: they can only be approximate.

1, 6: *A people:* the locusts compared to an invading army.

1133

Yes, joy has withered away
   from among mankind.

Call to Penance

13 Gird yourselves and weep, O priests!
      wail, O ministers of the altar!
   Come, spend the night in sackcloth,
      O ministers of my God!
   The house of your God is deprived
      of offering and libation.
14* Proclaim a fast,
      call an assembly;
   Gather the elders,
      all who dwell in the land,
   Into the house of the LORD, your God,
      and cry to the LORD!

15 Alas, the day!
      for near is the day of the LORD,
      and it comes as ruin from the Almighty.
16 From before our very eyes
      has not the food been cut off;
   And from the house of our God,
      joy and gladness?
17 The seed lies shriveled under its clods;
      the stores are destroyed,
   The barns are broken down,
      for the grain has failed.
18 How the beasts groan!
      The herds of cattle are bewildered!
   Because they have no pasturage,
      even the flocks of sheep have perished.

19 To you, O LORD, I cry!
      for fire has devoured the pastures of
         the plain,
      and flame has enkindled all the trees of
         the field.
20 Even the beasts of the field
      cry out to you;
   For the streams of water are dried up,
      and fire has devoured the pastures of
         the plain.

The Day of the LORD

2 ¹ Blow the trumpet in Zion,
      sound the alarm on my holy mountain!
   Let all who dwell in the land tremble,
      for the day of the LORD is coming;
2   Yes, it is near, a day of darkness and of gloom,
      a day of clouds and somberness!
   Like dawn spreading over the mountains,
      a people numerous and mighty!

Their like has not been from of old,
   nor will it be after them,
   even to the years of distant generations.
3   Before them a fire devours,
      and after them a flame enkindles;
   Like the garden of Eden is the land before them,
      and after them a desert waste;
      from them there is no escape.

4   Their appearance is that of horses;
      like steeds they run.
5   As with the rumble of chariots
      they leap on the mountaintops;
   As with the crackling of a fiery flame
      devouring stubble;
   Like a mighty people
      arrayed for battle.
6   Before them peoples are in torment,
      every face blanches.

7   Like warriors they run,
      like soldiers they scale the wall;
   They advance, each in his own lane,
      without swerving from their paths.
8   No one crowds another,
      each advances in his own track;
   Though they fall into the ditches,
      they are not checked.
9   They assault the city,
      they run upon the wall,
      they climb into the houses;
   In at the windows
      they come like thieves.
10* Before them the earth trembles,
      the heavens shake;
   The sun and the moon are darkened,
      and the stars withhold their brightness.

11* The LORD raises his voice
      at the head of his army;
   For immense indeed is his camp,
      yes, mighty, and it does his bidding.
   For great is the day of the LORD,
      and exceedingly terrible; who can bear it?
12 Yet even now, says the LORD,
      return to me with your whole heart,
      with fasting, and weeping, and mourning;
13* Rend your hearts, not your garments,
      and return to the LORD, your God.
   For gracious and merciful is he,
      slow to anger, rich in kindness,
      and relenting in punishment.

1, 14: Jl 2, 15.   32, 7f; Mt 24, 29; Mk   2, 11: Jer 30, 7; Am 5, 18;   2, 13: Ps 86, 5; Jon 4, 2.
2, 10: Jl 4, 15; Is 13, 10; Ez   13, 24; Lk 21, 25f.   Zep 1, 15.

14* Perhaps he will again relent
     and leave behind him a blessing,
Offerings and libations
     for the LORD, your God.
15* Blow the trumpet in Zion!
     proclaim a fast,
     call an assembly;
16 Gather the people,
     notify the congregation;
Assemble the elders,
     gather the children
     and the infants at the breast;
Let the bridegroom quit his room,
     and the bride her chamber.
17† Between the porch and the altar
     let the priests, the ministers of the
          LORD, weep,
And say, "Spare, O LORD, your people,
     and make not your heritage
          a reproach,
     with the nations ruling over them!
Why should they say among the peoples,
     'Where is their God?' "

Blessings for God's People

18 Then the LORD was stirred to concern for his
land and took pity on his people. 19 The LORD answered and said to his people:

     See, I will send you
          grain, and wine, and oil,
          and you shall be filled with them;
     No more will I make you
          a reproach among the nations.
20† No, the northerner I will remove far from you,
          and drive him out into a land arid
               and waste,
     With his van toward the eastern sea,
          and his rear toward the western sea;
     And his foulness shall go up,
          and his stench shall go up.

21 Fear not, O land!
          exult and rejoice!
     for the LORD has done great things.
22 Fear not, beasts of the field!
          for the pastures of the plain are green;
     The tree bears its fruit,
          the fig tree and the vine give their yield.

23* †And do you, O children of Zion, exult
          and rejoice in the LORD, your God!
     He has given you the teacher of justice:
          he has made the rain come down for you,
          the early and the late rain as before.
24   The threshing floors shall be full of grain
          and the vats shall overflow with wine
               and oil.
25   And I will repay you for the years
          which the locust has eaten,
     The grasshopper, the devourer, and the cutter,
          my great army which I sent among you.
26   You shall eat and be filled,
          and shall praise the name of the LORD,
               your God,
     Because he has dealt wondrously with you;
          my people shall nevermore be put to shame.

2, 17: The priests stood in the open space between the outdoor
altar of holocausts and the temple building, facing the latter in order
thereby to look toward God present in the holy of holies.
2, 20: *The northerner:* the locusts, that are compared to an invading army which in Palestine came from the north; cf Jer 1, 14f;
4, 6; Ez 26, 7; 38, 6.15.
2, 23: *The teacher of justice:* the rain sent by God to show his fidelity to his promises, and to teach his people to be faithful to his

commandments; cf Dt 11, 14. There is also a play on words here between the Hebrew word *moreh* (teacher) and the Hebrew word
yoreh (the early rain). The expression likewise has a messianic connotation; cf Is 30, 20. The founder of the Essene sect of Qumran (second century B.C.) was known as "The Teacher of Justice."

2, 14: Jon 3, 9.   2, 23: Hos 10, 12.
2, 15: Jl 1, 14.

J
L

Cultural Connections

VISION QUEST

Joel 3, 1 mentions young men having visions. Vision quests are a Native American tradition. A young man with only a blanket is led by a holy person to a hill to be on his own for several days. During that time, he refrains from eating and drinking and tries to focus on being very still, believing that he will receive a personal vision. That vision will give shape to his life and help him know his place in the world. The key is in the waiting. When the young man returns from his vision quest, he is considered a man and can become the person he is destined to become. He now has a vision to live out.

Jesus went on something like a vision quest before he began his public ministry. He went into the wilderness, fasted, and wrestled with his demons.

Joel 3, 1–5 is read at Pentecost—the church feast day that celebrates the coming of the Holy Spirit. You can let the Holy Spirit help you discern the path for your life through a personal retreat, guided by a spiritual director in the Christian tradition.

▸ Jl 3, 1–5

27   And you shall know that I am in the midst
of Israel;
I am the LORD, your God, and there is
no other;
my people shall nevermore be put
to shame.

3 ¹*† Then afterward I will pour out
my spirit upon all mankind.
Your sons and daughters shall prophesy,
your old men shall dream dreams,
your young men shall see visions;
²   Even upon the servants and the handmaids,
in those days, I will pour out my spirit.

³   And I will work wonders in the heavens and
on the earth,
blood, fire, and columns of smoke;
⁴*   The sun will be turned to darkness,
and the moon to blood,
At the coming of the day of the LORD,
the great and terrible day.
⁵*   Then everyone shall be rescued
who calls on the name of the LORD;

For on Mount Zion there shall be a remnant,
as the LORD has said,
And in Jerusalem survivors
whom the LORD shall call.

Judgment upon the Nations

4 ¹ Yes, in those days, and at that time,
when I would restore the fortunes
of Judah and Jerusalem,
²†   I will assemble all the nations
and bring them down to the Valley
of Jehoshaphat,
And I will enter into judgment with them there
on behalf of my people and my
inheritance, Israel;
Because they have scattered them among
the nations,
and divided my land.
³   Over my people they have cast lots;
they gave a boy for a harlot,
and sold a girl for the wine they drank.

⁴ Moreover, what are you to me, Tyre and Sidon,
and all the regions of Philistia? Would you take

3, 1f: *I will pour out my spirit:* in the Old Testament the spirit is the gift of God bestowed on those acting as his agents. The promise of the spirit is quoted by St. Peter in Acts 2, 17–21 as fulfilled in an eminent way by the gift of the Holy Spirit, the Third Person of the Blessed Trinity, bestowed on the Apostles.
4, 2: *Valley of Jehoshaphat:* a symbolic name of the place of fi-

nal judgment (v 14). The name Jehoshaphat signifies "Yahweh judges." This place has been popularly identified with the Kidron Valley.

3, 1–5: Is 44, 3; Acts 2, 17–21.   3, 5: Rom 10, 13.
3, 4: Jl 2, 10.

vengeance upon me by some action? But if you do take action against me, swiftly, speedily, I will return your deed upon your own head. ⁵ You took my silver and my gold, and brought my precious treasures into your temples! ⁶ You sold the people of Judah and Jerusalem to the Greeks, removing them far from their own country! ⁷ See, I will rouse them from the place into which you have sold them, and I will return your deed upon your own head. ⁸† I will sell your sons and your daughters to the people of Judah, who shall sell them to the Sabeans, a nation far off. Indeed, the LORD has spoken.

9   Declare this among the nations:
          proclaim a war,
          rouse the warriors to arms!
      Let all the soldiers
          report and march!
¹⁰†   Beat your plowshares into swords,
          and your pruning hooks into spears;
      let the weak man say, "I am a warrior!"

¹¹†   Hasten and come, all you neighboring peoples,
          assemble there!
      [Bring down, O Lord, your warriors!]
¹²   Let the nations bestir themselves and come up
          to the Valley of Jehoshaphat;
      For there will I sit in judgment
          upon all the neighboring nations.

¹³*† Apply the sickle,
          for the harvest is ripe;
      Come and tread,
          for the wine press is full;
      The vats overflow,
          for great is their malice.
¹⁴   Crowd upon crowd
          in the valley of decision;

For near is the day of the LORD
    in the valley of decision.
¹⁵* Sun and moon are darkened,
        and the stars withhold
            their brightness.
¹⁶* The LORD roars from Zion,
        and from Jerusalem raises his voice;
      The heavens and the earth quake,
        but the LORD is a refuge to his
            people,
      a stronghold to the men of Israel.

Salvation for God's Elect

¹⁷   Then shall you know that I, the LORD, am
            your God,
        dwelling on Zion, my holy mountain;
      Jerusalem shall be holy,
        and strangers shall pass through her
            no more.
¹⁸*† And then, on that day,
        the mountains shall drip new wine,
        and the hills shall flow with milk;
      And the channels of Judah
        shall flow with water:
      A fountain shall issue from the house of
            the LORD,
        to water the Valley of Shittim.
¹⁹   Egypt shall be a waste,
        and Edom a desert waste,
      Because of violence done to the people
            of Judah,
        because they shed innocent blood in
            their land.
²⁰   But Judah shall abide forever,
        and Jerusalem for all generations.
²¹   I will avenge their blood,
        and not leave it unpunished.
      The LORD dwells in Zion.

4, 8: *Sabeans:* a south Arabian people known for their commerce.

4, 10: This imagery is used in the reverse sense in Is 2, 4; Mi 4, 3. Here the warlike weapons are made in response to God's summons to armies which he selected to expel forever the unlawful invaders from the land of his chosen people.

4, 11: *Warriors:* the angels; cf Zec 14, 5.

4, 13: Because of their numerous crimes, the nations are ripe for punishment. The use of warlike weapons against them is likened to the onslaught on the fields and vines at harvest time.

4, 18: *The Valley of Shittim,* or "the ravine of the acacia trees": perhaps a part of the Kidron Valley southeast of Jerusalem; the prophetic picture of a stream of water flowing from a fountain in the temple of Jerusalem is to be found in Ez 47, 1. The Shittim east of the Jordan (see note on Nm 25, 1) is hardly referred to here.

4, 13: Rv 14, 15.
4, 15: Jl 2, 10; 3, 4.
4, 16: Jer 25, 30; Am 1, 2.

4, 18: Ez 47, 1–12; Am 9, 13;
        Zec 14, 8.

you've probably run across people who bluntly state what they see going on. They don't seem to care too much about what other people think. They say, "I just tell it like it is." The prophet Amos was like that. He didn't pull any punches in describing the wealthy class's sins or the destruction that God had planned for it. He was a powerful voice calling for justice in God's plan of salvation.

At a Glance

I. Judgment of the Nations (1, 1—2, 16).

II. Words and Woes for Israel (3, 1—6, 14).

III. Symbolic Visions: Threats and Promises (7, 1—9, 8b); Epilogue: Messianic Perspective (9, 8c–15).

In-depth

Amos lived when there were two separate kingdoms of Israelites: a northern kingdom, named Israel, and a southern kingdom, named Judah. He was born in the southern kingdom and worked as a shepherd and tree trimmer (Am 7, 14). But God called him to preach to the northern kingdom. Amos was not an official prophet of the king's court, so he was free to speak against the king and the court and to be brutally honest in delivering God's message.

Among the Old Testament prophecies, Amos's are the least hopeful. Amos stresses that Israel's destruction, complete and total, is certain. He condemns Israel for its failure to be faithful to the Covenant, but he has a special anger toward the king, the priests, and the wealthy class. He accuses them of being hypocrites who lead the people of Israel astray while pretending to be faithful themselves.

What was Amos's evidence? First, the Covenant demanded special care for the poor, the outcast, and the marginalized. The king, the wealthy, and some of the priests were ignoring this demand. Instead of caring for the poor and the lowly, the wealthy were cheating them and treating them unjustly (2, 6–8).

Second, with the monies they cheated out of the poor, the ruling class and the wealthy staged lavish ceremonies to God that were modeled on ceremonies honoring foreign gods. They went through the motions of worshiping God, but they ignored the demand to care for their neighbor (5, 21–24). For Amos, this was the heart of Israel's hypocrisy—its sinful habit of separating its religious rituals from concern for its citizens. This phoniness was repulsive to God, and because of Israel's sin, God would bring it to destruction. Amos is rightly called the prophet of the LORD's justice.

Quick Facts

Period Covered
786–746 B.C.

Authors
Amos and later scribes

Theme
God's destruction of Israel because of the injustice and hypocrisy of the wealthy and the ruling class

The Book of Amos

Amos

5, 24

I: Judgment of the Nations

1 ¹*† The words of Amos, a shepherd from Tekoa, which he received in vision concerning Israel, in the days of Uzziah, king of Judah, and in the days of Jeroboam, son of Joash, king of Israel, two years before the earthquake:

² * The LORD will roar from Zion,
    and from Jerusalem raise his voice:
The pastures of the shepherds will
        languish,
    and the summit of Carmel wither.

Aram

³† Thus says the LORD:
For three crimes of Damascus, and for four,
    I will not revoke my word;
Because they threshed Gilead
    with sledges of iron,
⁴† I will send fire upon the house of Hazael,
    to devour the castles of Ben-hadad.
⁵† I will break the bar of Damascus;
    I will root out those who live in the Valley
        of Aven,
And the sceptered ruler of Beth-eden;
    the people of Aram shall be exiled to Kir,
    says the LORD.

Philistia

⁶ Thus says the LORD:
For three crimes of Gaza, and for four,
    I will not revoke my word;
Because they took captive whole groups
    to hand over to Edom,
⁷ I will send fire upon the wall of Gaza,
    to devour her castles;
⁸ I will root out those who live in Ashdod,
    and the sceptered ruler of Ashkelon;
I will turn my hand against Ekron,
    and the last of the Philistines shall perish,
    says the Lord God.

---

† **1, 1:** *The earthquake:* which according to Hebrew tradition marked the crime of Uzziah when he attempted to offer incense in the temple (2 Chr 26, 16–21). Zechariah mentions it several centuries later (Zec 14, 5).

1, 3: *For three crimes . . . four:* crime after crime, an indefinite number; cf Am 1, 6. The series of judgments on the foreign nations shows that the Lord demands the observance of the moral order everywhere; Israel and Judah, despite their privileged position, are no exception. *I will not revoke my word:* God will not withdraw his threat of punishment against each of these nations. *They threshed Gilead:* the people of Aram under King Hazael had devastated Gilead; cf 2 Kgs 10, 32f.

1, 4: *Fire:* devastation caused by the Assyrians (Am 1, 7.10.12.14; 2, 2.5); cf 1 Sm 15, 18. *Hazael* and *Ben-hadad:* kings of the Arameans whose capital was Damascus (v 5); they fought against Israel (2 Kgs 13, 3), and had long occupied the region of Gilead (v 3) in Transjordan.

1, 5: *Bar of Damascus:* the beam securing the main gate of the city against invaders, symbol of its defenses. *Valley of Aven* ("vale of wickedness") and *Beth-eden* ("house of pleasure"): Aramean territory from southwest to northeast.

1, 1: Zec 14, 5.   **1, 2:** Jer 25, 30; Jl 3, 16.

Tyre

9†   Thus says the LORD:
For three crimes of Tyre, and for four,
    I will not revoke my word;
Because they delivered whole groups captive
    to Edom,
    and did not remember the pact
    of brotherhood,
10   I will send fire upon the wall of Tyre,
    to devour her castles.

Edom

11†   Thus says the LORD:
For three crimes of Edom, and for four,
    I will not revoke my word;
Because he pursued his brother with
    the sword,
    choking up all pity;
Because he persisted in his anger
    and kept his wrath to the end,
12† I will send fire upon Teman,
    and it will devour the castles of Bozrah.

Ammon

13   Thus says the LORD:
For three crimes of the Ammonites, and
    for four,
    I will not revoke my word;
Because they ripped open expectant mothers
    in Gilead,
    while extending their territory,
14† I will kindle a fire upon the wall of Rabbah,
    and it will devour her castles
Amid clamor on the day of battle
    and stormwind in a time of tempest.
15   Their king shall go into captivity,
    he and his princes with him, says the LORD.

Moab

2 ¹†   Thus says the LORD:
For three crimes of Moab, and for four,
    I will not revoke my word;
Because he burned to ashes
    the bones of Edom's king,
2   I will send fire upon Moab,

    to devour the castles of Kerioth;
Moab shall meet death amid uproar
    and shouts and trumpet blasts.
3   I will root out the judge from her midst,
    and her princes I will slay with him, says
    the LORD.

Judah

4†   Thus says the LORD:
For three crimes of Judah, and for four,
    I will not revoke my word;
Because they spurned the law of the LORD,
    and did not keep his statutes;
Because the lies which their fathers followed
    have led them astray,
5   I will send fire upon Judah,
    to devour the castles of Jerusalem.

Israel

6†   Thus says the LORD:
For three crimes of Israel, and for four,
    I will not revoke my word;
Because they sell the just man for silver,
    and the poor man for a pair of sandals.†
7   They trample the heads of the weak
    into the dust of the earth,
    and force the lowly out of the way.
Son and father go to the same prostitute,
    profaning my holy name.
8† Upon garments taken in pledge
    they recline beside any altar;
And the wine of those who have been fined
    they drink in the house of their god.

9*   Yet it was I who destroyed the Amorites
    before them,
    who were as tall as the cedars,
    and as strong as the oak trees.
I destroyed their fruit above,
    and their roots beneath.
10* It was I who brought you up from the land
    of Egypt,
    and who led you through the desert for
    forty years,
    to occupy the land of the Amorites:

1, 9: *Pact of brotherhood:* Hiram of Tyre had made a pact with Solomon and called him brother (1 Kgs 5, 12; 9, 13).
  1, 11: *Pursued his brother:* the Edomites were descended from Esau, the brother of Jacob (Gn 25–27); nevertheless they constantly nourished enmity against Jacob's descendants, the Israelites.
  1, 12: *Teman* and *Bozrah:* two of the chief cities of Edom; cf Jer 49, 20.
  1, 14: *Rabbah:* now called Amman, the modern capital of the Hashemite Kingdom of Jordan.
  2, 1: Here the prophet stresses the gravity of Moab's violation of the Semitic custom of providing honorable burial for the dead.
  2, 4: *The lies:* false gods, who exist only in the minds of their worshipers. The crimes of Judah are infidelity and idolatry, in contrast to the sins for which the surrounding nations are judged.

2, 6–13: The detailed crimes of Israel are placed in strong contrast with the benefits with which the Lord favored his people.
  2, 6: *A pair of sandals:* indicating how cheaply the rich regarded the poor.
  2, 8: *Upon garments . . . any altar:* usurers kept the garments taken as pledges from the poor; but instead of restoring them to their owners before nightfall (Ex 22, 25; Dt 24, 12), they used them in idolatrous worship. *Wine . . . their god:* under the guise of a religious ceremony they drink the wine obtained through unjust fines.

2, 9: Nm 21, 24; Dt 2, 24.   2, 10: Ex 14, 21; Dt 8, 2.14.

11† I who raised up prophets among your sons,
and nazirites among your young men.
Is this not so, O men of Israel?
says the LORD.

12 But you gave the nazirites wine to drink,
and commanded the prophets not
to prophesy.

13 Beware, I will crush you into the ground
as a wagon crushes when laden
with sheaves.

14 Flight shall perish from the swift,
and the strong man shall not retain
his strength;
The warrior shall not save his life,

15 nor the bowman stand his ground;
The swift of foot shall not escape,
nor the horseman save his life.

16 And the most stouthearted of warriors
shall flee naked on that day, says
the LORD.

II: Words and Woes for Israel

First Word

3 ¹ Hear this word, O men of Israel, that the
LORD pronounces over you, over the whole
family that I brought up from the land of Egypt:

2† You alone have I favored,
more than all the families of the earth;
Therefore I will punish you
for all your crimes.

3 Do two walk together
unless they have agreed?

4 Does a lion roar in the forest
when it has no prey?
Does a young lion cry out from its den
unless it has seized something?

5 Is a bird brought to earth by a snare
when there is no lure for it?
Does a snare spring up from the ground
without catching anything?

6† If the trumpet sounds in a city,
will the people not be frightened?
If evil befalls a city,
has not the LORD caused it?

7 Indeed, the Lord GOD does nothing
without revealing his plan
to his servants, the prophets.

8 The lion roars—
who will not be afraid!
The Lord GOD speaks—
who will not prophesy!

9† Proclaim this in the castles of Ashdod,
in the castles of the land of Egypt:
"Gather about the mountain of Samaria,
and see the great disorders within her,
the oppression in her midst."

10 For they know not how to do what is right,
says the LORD,
Storing up in their castles
what they have extorted and robbed.

11 Therefore, thus says the Lord GOD:
An enemy shall surround the land,
and strip you of your strength,
and pillage your castles.

12 Thus says the LORD:
As the shepherd snatches from the mouth of
the lion
a pair of legs or the tip of an ear of
his sheep,

did you KNOW?

The Remnant

Does Amos feel that Israel is so corrupt that God will destroy it entirely? Apparently not, because he refers in several places to a tiny portion that will be saved (Am 3, 12). The idea that God will save a remnant—a small part—of the Jewish people gets picked up by others who prophesy after Amos (see Is 10, 20–22; Jer 23, 3; Mi 5, 7–8; Zep 3, 13).

The remnant that will be saved becomes an important biblical symbol of God's plan not to let Israel be completely destroyed. It will be known as a holy group because of its faith, repentance, purification, and willingness to be God's servant.

▸ **Am 3, 12**

---

† **2, 11:** *Nazirites:* see note on Nm 6, 1ff.
3, 2: God's choice of Israel brought its own responsibility.
3, 6: The sufferings which sinful man experiences through the permissive will of God are presented here, as elsewhere in the Old Testament, simply as caused by the Lord.

3, 9: Israel's southern neighbors, beyond Judah, are invited by the prophetic orator to witness the moral disorders of God's people.

A
M

So the Israelites who dwell in Samaria
   shall escape
   with the corner of a couch or a piece of a cot.

13 Hear and bear witness against the house of Jacob, says the Lord GOD, the God of hosts:

14   On the day when I punish Israel for
        his crimes,
      I will visit also the altars of Bethel:
      The horns of the altar shall be broken off
        and fall to the ground.
15† Then will I strike the winter house
        and the summer house;
      The ivory apartments shall be ruined,
        and their many rooms shall be no more,
      says the LORD.

Second Word

4 1† Hear this word, women of the mountain
        of Samaria,
      you cows of Bashan,
      You who oppress the weak
        and abuse the needy;
      Who say to your lords,
        "Bring drink for us!"
2   The Lord GOD has sworn by his holiness:
      Truly the days are coming upon you
      When they shall drag you away with hooks,
        the last of you with fishhooks;
3   You shall go out through the breached walls
        each by the most direct way,
      And you shall be cast into the mire,
        says the LORD.

4† Come to Bethel and sin,
        to Gilgal, and sin the more;
      Each morning bring your sacrifices,
        every third day, your tithes;
5   Burn leavened food as a thanksgiving sacrifice,
        proclaim publicly your freewill offerings,
      For so you love to do, O men of Israel,
        says the Lord GOD.

6   Though I have made your teeth
        clean of food in all your cities,
        and have made bread scarce in all
          your dwellings,
      Yet you returned not to me,
        says the LORD.

7   Though I also withheld the rain from you
        when the harvest was still three
          months away;
      I sent rain upon one city
        but not upon another;
      One field was watered by rain,
        but another without rain dried up;
8   Though two or three cities staggered to
        one city
        for water that did not quench their thirst;
      Yet you returned not to me,
        says the LORD.

9* I struck you with blight and searing wind;
        your many gardens and vineyards,
        your fig trees and olive trees the
          locust devoured;
      Yet you returned not to me,
        says the LORD.

10† I sent upon you a pestilence like that of Egypt,
        and with the sword I slew your young men;
      Your horses I let be captured,
        to your nostrils I brought the stench of
          your camps;
      Yet you returned not to me,
        says the LORD.

11* I brought upon you such upheaval
        as when God overthrew Sodom
        and Gomorrah:
        you were like a brand plucked from the fire;
      Yet you returned not to me,
        says the LORD.

12   So now I will deal with you in my own way,
        O Israel!
        and since I will deal thus with you,
        prepare to meet your God, O Israel:
13   Him who formed the mountains, and created
        the wind,
        and declares to man his thoughts;
      Who made the dawn and the darkness,
        and strides upon the heights of the earth:
      The LORD, the God of hosts by name.

Third Word

5 1 Hear this word which I utter over you,
        a lament, O house of Israel:
2   She is fallen, to rise no more,

3, 15: *Ivory apartments:* rooms containing furniture inlaid in ivory, similar to the pieces discovered in the excavations at Samaria.
4, 1: *Bashan:* the region east of the Sea of Galilee, famous for its rich pasture and fattened herds, to which Amos likens the indolent women of Samaria.
4, 4f: This invitation to the sanctuaries of the northern kingdom is ironical. Pilgrimages to the shrines of Bethel and Gilgal were the more displeasing to God because they were contrary to his will and ineffective toward improvement of morals.
4, 10: *Pestilence like that of Egypt:* plagues were well known in Egypt; cf Dt 7, 15; 28, 27.60. *Stench of your camps:* caused by the unburied bodies.

4, 9: Hg 2, 17.   4, 11: Gn 19, 24.

the virgin Israel;
She lies abandoned upon her land,
  with no one to raise her up.

3   For thus says the Lord GOD:
The city that marched out with a thousand
  shall be left with a hundred,
Another that marched out with a hundred
  shall be left with ten,
  of the house of Israel.

4 For thus says the LORD
    to the house of Israel:
Seek me, that you may live,
5   but do not seek Bethel;
Do not come to Gilgal,
  and do not cross to Beer-sheba.
For Gilgal shall be led into exile,
  and Bethel shall become nought.
6† Seek the LORD, that you may live,
  lest he come upon the house of Joseph like
    a fire
That shall consume, with none to quench it
  for the house of Israel:
8* He who made the Pleiades and Orion,
  who turns darkness into dawn,
  and darkens day into night;
Who summons the waters of the sea,
  and pours them out upon the surface of
    the earth;
9 Who flashes destruction upon the strong,
  and brings ruin upon the fortress;
  whose name is LORD.

First Woe

7 Woe to those who turn judgment
    to wormwood
    and cast justice to the ground!
10† They hate him who reproves at the gate
  and abhor him who speaks the truth.
11* Therefore, because you have trampled upon
    the weak
  and exacted of them levies of grain,
Though you have built houses of hewn stone,
  you shall not live in them!
Though you have planted choice vineyards,
  you shall not drink their wine!

12 Yes, I know how many are your crimes,
  how grievous your sins:
Oppressing the just, accepting bribes,
  repelling the needy at the gate!
13 Therefore the prudent man is silent at
    this time,
  for it is an evil time.
14 Seek good and not evil,
  that you may live;
Then truly will the LORD, the God of hosts,
  be with you as you claim!
15* Hate evil and love good,
  and let justice prevail at the gate;
Then it may be that the LORD, the God
    of hosts,
  will have pity on the remnant of Joseph.

16 Therefore, thus says the LORD,
  the God of hosts, the Lord:
In every square there shall be lamentation,
  and in every street they shall cry, Alas! Alas!
They shall summon the farmers to wail
  and professional mourners to lament,
17 And in every vineyard there shall
    be lamentation
  when I pass through your midst, says
    the LORD.

Second Woe

18*†Woe to those who yearn for the day of
    the LORD!
  What will this day of the LORD mean
    for you?
  Darkness and not light!
19 As if a man were to flee from a lion,
  and a bear should meet him;
Or as if on entering his house
  he were to rest his hand against the wall,
  and a snake should bite him.
20 Will not the day of the LORD be darkness and
    not light,
  gloom without any brightness?

21*†I hate, I spurn your feasts,
  I take no pleasure in your solemnities;
22 Your cereal offerings I will not accept,
  nor consider your stall-fed peace offerings.

5, 6: *House of Joseph:* the kingdom of Israel or northern kingdom, the chief tribes of which were descended from Ephraim and Manasseh, the sons of Joseph; cf Am 5, 15; 6, 6.
5, 10: *At the gate:* see note on Ps 127, 5.
5, 18: *Day of the LORD:* a technical expression which in earliest times referred to God's special intervention in human affairs. Through it his power and justice triumphed in his people. The present passage is the first instance in which it means a day of punishment of sinners. During the exile it assumed the meaning of a time when God would avenge Israel against her oppressors and bring about her restoration (Jer 50, 27; Ez 30, 3ff). Still later it came to mean the day of final judgment of the world when the

good will be rewarded and the wicked punished (Jl 2, 1ff; Zep 1, 14ff; Mal 3, 19ff).
5, 21–27: The Lord condemns, not ritual worship in itself, but the cult whose exterior rites and solemnity have no relation to interior morality and justice. The Israelites falsely worshiped him as neighboring nations adored Baal or Chamos, deities which were thought to protect their respective peoples against their enemies in return for ritual observances, without any relation to right conduct.

5, 8: Am 9, 6.   Zep 1, 15.
5, 11: Zep 1, 13.   **5, 21:** Is 1, 11; Jer 6, 20; Mal
5, 15: Ps 97, 10; Rom 12, 9. 1, 12.
5, 18: Jer 30, 7; Jl 2, 11;

Prayer That Does Justice

In 5, 21–24, Amos again has harsh words, this time for the people who attend lavish religious ceremonies but don't practice justice in their life. Amos says that their worship is meaningless noise to God—just so many empty words.

Amos's harsh words challenge us too. The next time you attend Mass or pray, think about the words you say and hear. How are they challenging you to act more justly? How would trying to act more justly change the way you pray?

▶ Am 5, 21–24

23 Away with your noisy songs!
   I will not listen to the melodies of
      your harps.
   But if you would offer me holocausts,
24   then let justice surge like water,
      and goodness like an unfailing stream.
25*† Did you bring me sacrifices and offerings
      for forty years in the desert, O house
         of Israel?
26† You will carry away Sakkuth, your king,
      and Kaiwan, your star god,
      the images that you have made
         for yourselves;
27 For I will exile you beyond Damascus,
      say I, the LORD, the God of hosts by name.

Third Woe

6 1*† Woe to the complacent in Zion,
      To the overconfident on the mount
         of Samaria,†
   Leaders of a nation favored from the first,
      to whom the people of Israel have recourse!
2 Pass over to Calneh and see,
      go from there to Hamath the great,
      and down to Gath of the Philistines!
   Are you better than these kingdoms,

or is your territory wider than theirs?
3 You would put off the evil day,
      yet you hasten the reign of violence!

4 Lying upon beds of ivory,
      stretched comfortably on their couches,
   They eat lambs taken from the flock,
      and calves from the stall!
5 Improvising to the music of the harp,
      like David, they devise their
         own accompaniment.
6 They drink wine from bowls
      and anoint themselves with the best oils;
      yet they are not made ill by the collapse
         of Joseph!
7 Therefore, now they shall be the first to go
         into exile,
      and their wanton revelry shall be done
         away with.

8* The Lord GOD has sworn by his very self,
      say I, the LORD, the God of hosts:
   I abhor the pride of Jacob,
      I hate his castles,
      and I give over the city with everything
         in it;
9 Should there remain ten men
      in a single house, these shall die.

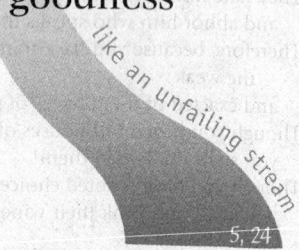

Let **Justice**
surge like water,
and
goodness
like an unfailing stream
5, 24

† 5, 25: The meaning is not certain; according to some, the idea is that during the forty years' wandering in the desert the simple, rudimentary worship of God was accompanied by the practice of justice, in contrast to the elaborate ritual unaccompanied by works of justice in the prophet's time.
5, 26: *Sakkuth . . . star god:* although the text is uncertain, it seems quite probable that reference is made to the Assyrian deities, Sakkuth, god of war and light, and Kaiwan, the planet Saturn. The people will go into exile, from which these gods have been unable to save them.

6, 1–7: The luxury of the people in Samaria will be punished by exile. They failed to learn the lesson from Calneh, Hamath and Gath at the approach of the powerful and warlike Assyrians.
6, 1: *The complacent in Zion . . . the overconfident . . . of Samaria:* the proud and self-interested rulers of Judah and Israel.

5, 25: Acts 7, 42.   6, 8: Jer 51, 14.
6, 1: Lk 6, 24.

10 Only a few shall be left
   to carry the dead out of the houses;
   If one says to a man inside a house,
      "Is anyone with you?" and he answers,
      "No one,"
   Then he shall say, "Silence!"
      for no one must mention the name of
         the LORD.
11 Indeed, the LORD has given the command
      to shatter the great house to bits,
      and reduce the small house to rubble.

12† Can horses run across a cliff?
      or can one plow the sea with oxen?
   Yet you have turned judgment into gall,
      and the fruit of justice into wormwood.
13† You rejoice in Lodebar,
      and say, "Have we not, by our own
         strength,
      seized for ourselves Karnaim?"
14† Beware, I am raising up against you, O house
         of Israel,
      say I, the LORD, the God of hosts,
   A nation that shall oppress you
      from Labo of Hamath even to the
         Wadi Arabah.

III: Symbolic Visions: Threats and Promises

Vision of Locusts

7 ¹† This is what the Lord GOD showed me: He was forming a locust swarm when the late growth began to come up (the late growth after the king's mowing). ² While they were eating all the grass in the land, I said:

   Forgive, O Lord GOD!
      How can Jacob stand?
      He is so small!

³ And the LORD repented of this. "It shall not be," said the Lord GOD.

Vision of Fire

⁴† Then the Lord GOD showed me this: he called for a judgment by fire. It had devoured the great abyss, and was consuming the land, ⁵ when I said:

   Cease, O Lord GOD!
      How can Jacob stand?
      He is so small!

⁶ The LORD repented of this. "This also shall not be," said the Lord GOD.

Vision of the Plummet

⁷† Then the Lord GOD showed me this: he was standing by a wall, plummet in hand. ⁸ The LORD asked me, "What do you see, Amos?" And when I answered, "A plummet," the LORD said:

   See, I will lay the plummet
      in the midst of my people Israel;
      I will forgive them no longer.
9   The high places of Isaac shall be laid waste,
      and the sanctuaries of Israel made desolate;
      I will attack the house of Jeroboam with
         the sword.

Amos and Amaziah

¹⁰ Amaziah, the priest of Bethel, sent word to Jeroboam, king of Israel: "Amos has conspired against you here within Israel; the country cannot endure all his words. ¹¹ For this is what Amos says:

   Jeroboam shall die by the sword,
      and Israel shall surely be exiled from
         its land."

¹² To Amos, Amaziah said: "Off with you, visionary, flee to the land of Judah! There earn your bread by prophesying, ¹³ but never again prophesy in Bethel; for it is the king's sanctuary and a royal temple." ¹⁴† Amos answered Amaziah, "I was no prophet, nor have I belonged to a company of prophets; I was a shepherd and a dresser of sycamores. ¹⁵ The LORD took me from following the flock, and said to me, Go, prophesy to my people Israel. ¹⁶ Now hear the word of the LORD!"

   You say: prophesy not against Israel,
      preach not against the house of Isaac.
17   Now thus says the LORD:
   Your wife shall be made a harlot in the city,
      and your sons and daughters shall fall by
         the sword;
   Your land shall be divided by measuring line,

---

† **6, 12:** *Can horses . . . oxen?*: one cannot change the course of nature, as the Israelites attempted to do by their sins of injustice.
6, 13: *Lodebar . . . Karnaim*: in Transjordan; they had been captured by the Israelites. Perhaps it is in irony that reference is made to these two cities, for the root of the first suggests "nothing" and that of the second, "horns" or "strength."
6, 14: *A nation*: Assyria.
7, 1: *The king's mowing*: the first mowing, a portion of which was payable to the king as a tax.

7, 4: *Fire*: understood by many as a burning drought.
7, 7: *Plummet in hand*: signifying that God is about to withdraw his mercy from his people and that the nation is to be measured for destruction.
7, 14f: Amos denies that he belonged to the class of professional prophets; his vocation is due to the personal intervention of the Lord.

and you yourself shall die in an
   unclean land;
Israel shall be exiled far from its land.

Vision of the Fruit Basket

8 ¹ This is what the Lord GOD showed me: a basket of ripe fruit. ² "What do you see, Amos?" he asked. I answered, "A basket of ripe fruit." Then the LORD said to me:

The time is ripe to have done with my
   people Israel;
I will forgive them no longer.
³ The temple songs shall become wailings on
   that day,
   says the Lord GOD.
Many shall be the corpses,
   strewn everywhere.—Silence!

Against Greed

⁴ Hear this, you who trample upon the
   needy
   and destroy the poor of the land!
⁵† "When will the new moon be over," you ask,
   "that we may sell our grain,
   and the sabbath, that we may display
   the wheat?
We will diminish the ephah,
   add to the shekel,
   and fix our scales for cheating!

⁶ We will buy the lowly man for silver,
   and the poor man for a pair of sandals;
   even the refuse of the wheat we will sell!"
⁷† The LORD has sworn by the pride of Jacob:
   Never will I forget a thing they have
   done!
⁸† Shall not the land tremble because of this,
   and all who dwell in it mourn,
While it rises up and tosses like the Nile,
   and settles back like the river of Egypt?

⁹ On that day, says the Lord GOD,
   I will make the sun set at midday
   and cover the earth with darkness in
   broad daylight.
¹⁰* I will turn your feasts into mourning
   and all your songs into lamentations.
I will cover the loins of all with sackcloth
   and make every head bald.
I will make them mourn as for an only son,
   and bring their day to bitter end.

¹¹ Yes, days are coming, says the Lord GOD,
   when I will send famine upon the land:
Not a famine of bread, or thirst for water,
   but for hearing the word of the LORD.
¹² Then shall they wander from sea to sea
   and rove from the north to the east
In search of the word of the LORD,
   but they shall not find it.

Stand Up and Be Counted!

In a small-town newspaper's opinion page, a reader complains about a low-income housing development. The reader writes: "Our town does not need more white trash. The citizens of this town have worked hard for their homes and do not deserve to have their home values brought down by a low-income development. Stand up and be counted and do not let this happen!"

Amos would have had a harsh reply for the author of that letter. Read 8, 4–10 for his words condemning the people of his time who had no care or thought for the poor. Amos says that the more we choose to think of ourselves, rather than those who are needy, the closer we come to our own destruction. Jesus later echoes Amos in teaching that God's reign of peace and justice will come through our efforts to support the weaker and less fortunate people in our world (see "Jesus' Preference for the Poor!" Lk 6, 17–49).

Let's be examples of God's care for those who are poor, until all opinion-page letters read, "Stand up and be counted—let's work to end poverty and until then welcome the people who are poor among us!"

▸ Am 8, 4–10

8, 5: *Ephah:* a standard of measure; a little more than a bushel.
8, 7: *The pride of Jacob:* the sinful pride detested by God (Am 6, 8), in contrast to God himself, who is the true Pride of Jacob.
8, 8: The figure is based on the annual flooding of the river Nile.

8, 10: Tb 2, 6; 1 Mc 1, 41.

13 On that day, fair virgins and young men
 shall faint from thirst;
14† Those who swear by the shameful idol
 of Samaria,
 "By the life of your god, O Dan!"
 "By the life of your love, O Beer-sheba!"
 those shall fall, never to rise again.

Vision of the Altar

9 ¹† I saw the Lord standing beside the altar,
and he said:

Strike the bases, so that the doorjambs totter
 till you break them off on the heads of
 them all!
Those who are left I will slay with the sword;
 not one shall flee,
 no survivor shall escape.
2* Though they break through to the
 nether world,
 even from there my hand shall bring
 them out;
Though they climb to the heavens,
 I will bring them down;
3† Though they hide on the summit of Carmel,
 there too I will hunt them out and take
 them away;
Though they hide from my gaze
 in the bottom of the sea,
 I will command the serpent there to
 bite them;
4* Though they are led into captivity by
 their enemies,
 there will I command the sword to
 slay them.
I will fix my gaze upon them
 for evil, and not for good,
5 I, the Lord GOD of hosts.
I melt the earth with my touch,
 so that all who dwell on it mourn,
While it all rises up like the Nile,
 and settles back like the river of Egypt;
6* I have built heaven, my upper chamber,
 and established my vault over the earth;
I summon the waters of the sea
 and pour them out upon the surface of
 the earth,
 I, the LORD by name.

7*† Are you not like the Ethiopians to me,
 O men of Israel, says the LORD?
Did I not bring the Israelites from the land
 of Egypt
As I brought the Philistines from Caphtor
 and the Arameans from Kir?
8 The eyes of the Lord GOD are on this
 sinful kingdom:
 I will destroy it from off the face of the earth.

Epilogue: Messianic Perspective

But I will not destroy the house of
 Jacob completely,
 says the LORD.
9 For see, I have given the command
 to sift the house of Israel among all
 the nations,
As one sifts with a sieve,
 letting no pebble fall to the ground.
10 By the sword shall all sinners among my
 people die,
 those who say, "Evil will not reach or
 overtake us."
11*† On that day I will raise up
 the fallen hut of David;
I will wall up its breaches,
 raise up its ruins,
 and rebuild it as in the days of old,
12 That they may conquer what is left of Edom
 and all the nations that shall bear my name,
 say I, the LORD, who will do this.
13* Yes, days are coming,
 says the LORD,
When the plowman shall overtake the reaper,
 and the vintager, him who sows the seed;
The juice of grapes shall drip down
 the mountains,
 and all the hills shall run with it.
14 I will bring about the restoration of my
 people Israel;
 they shall rebuild and inhabit their
 ruined cities,
Plant vineyards and drink the wine,
 set out gardens and eat the fruits.
15 I will plant them upon their own ground;
 never again shall they be plucked
From the land I have given them,
 say I, the LORD, your God.

8, 14: *Dan* and *Beer-sheba,* the extreme northern and southern limits of the country, where idolatrous worship was offered.

9, 1–8: There will be no escape from God's punishment, symbolized here by the destruction of a building, probably the schismatic temple at Bethel.

9, 3: *Serpent:* the sea monster of familiar legend, subdued by God at the time of creation and lurking still in the ocean depths; cf Ps 89, 10f.

9, 7: *The Ethiopians . . . the Philistines . . . the Arameans:* by nature Israel is not different from any other nation. It was not because

of any merit on Israel's part that God delivered them from Egypt. *Caphtor:* the island of Crete.

9, 11f: In Acts 15, 15ff St. James interprets this passage in a messianic sense. *Fallen hut:* the kingdom. *The nations that shall bear my name:* the Gentile peoples who shall be converted to the Lord, that is, conquered by him, and therefore shall bear his name.

9, 2: Ps 139, 8.   9, 7: Dt 2, 23; Jer 47, 4.
9, 4: Jer 44, 11.   9, 11: Acts 15, 16.
9, 6: Am 5, 8.   9, 13: Jl 3, 18.

A betrayal is always difficult, and a betrayal by someone who is related to you is a particularly hard pill to swallow. We can only imagine the anger during the Civil War in the United States when family members found themselves fighting on opposite sides. It has taken the country a long time to heal from that division. Similarly, the Book of Obadiah has angry words against the nation of Edom, whose people were related to the Israelites. It should remind us that when the people we expect to care for us actually take advantage of us, the wound is especially painful.

At a Glance

I. Edom Shall Perish (verses 1–9).

II. The Cause (verses 10–14).

III. Judgment upon the Nations (verses 15–21).

In-depth

The Book of Genesis records a conflict between Jacob (the father of the nation of Israel) and his brother Esau (the father of the nation of Edom, later called Idumea). Hundreds of years later, the Israelites still fought with the Edomites (see map 3, "The Kingdom Years"). In the Book of Obadiah, the bitterness deepens.

In 587 B.C., Jerusalem was destroyed by the Babylonians. Apparently, the Edomites not only did not aid their "brother" (Obadiah, verse 10) but took advantage of Israel's situation by exulting (verse 12), looting (verse 13), and raiding its territory (verse 14). Because of the Edomites' cruelty, the prophet Obadiah foretold the destruction of Edom by another country (verse 15).

Like many of the Old Testament prophets, Obadiah ultimately saw a hopeful future for Israel. All Israel's enemies would whither before the strong arm of the LORD. And there would come a day—"the day of the LORD" (verse 15)—when all Jews would unite and return to Mount Zion (the place where the Temple stood in Jerusalem). Mount Zion would "rule the mount of Esau" and that new "kingship shall be the LORD's" (verse 21).

We are given no clues about the identity or life of the prophet Obadiah. We know only that he wrote the shortest book in the Old Testament—just one chapter long.

Quick Facts

Period Covered
after the Babylonian Exile, sometime in the fifth century B.C.

Author
Obadiah

Theme
God will punish Edom for its abuse of Judah.

Of Note
Obadiah means "servant" or "worshiper of the LORD."

Obadiah

Title and Theme

1* The vision of Obadiah.
[Thus says the LORD God:]
Of Edom we have heard a message from
  the LORD,
  and a herald has been sent among
  the nations:
"Up! let us go to war against him!"

Edom Shall Perish

2* See, I make you small among the nations;
  you are held in dire contempt.
3 The pride of your heart has deceived you:
  you who dwell in the clefts of the rock,
  whose abode is in the heights,
Who say in your heart,
  "Who will bring me down to earth?"
4 Though you go as high as the eagle,
  and your nest be set among the stars,
From there will I bring you down,
  says the LORD.
5*† If thieves came to you, if robbers by night,
  how could you be thus destroyed:

would they not steal merely till they
  had enough?
If vintagers came to you,
  would they not leave some gleanings?
6 How they search Esau,
  seek out his hiding places!
7† To the border they drive you—
  all your allies;
They deceive you, they overpower you—
  those at peace with you;
Those who eat your bread
  lay snares beneath you:
  There is no understanding in him!
8*† Shall I not, says the LORD, on that day
  make the wise men disappear from Edom,
  and understanding from the mount of Esau?
9† Your warriors, O Teman, shall be crushed,
  till all on Mount Esau are destroyed.

The Cause

10*† Because of violence to your brother Jacob,
  disgrace shall cover you
  and you shall be destroyed forever.

5: Something of value may escape the robber, and the vintager always leaves something for the gleaners, but God's devastation of Edom will be complete.
7: *There is no understanding in him*: Edom's faithless allies assure one another that he does not have sense enough to be able to defend himself.
8: *The wise men*: Edom was proverbial for its wise men; cf Jer 49, 7.
9: *Teman*: one of the names used for the land southeast of Pales-

tine, here synonymous with Edom. *Esau*: here used as the name of the land.
10: *Your brother Jacob*: Esau, also called Edom, and Jacob, the father of Judah, were the sons of Isaac (Gn 25, 24ff).

1: Jer 49, 14.   8: Is 29, 14; 1 Cor 1, 19.
2ff: Jer 49, 15f.   10: Gn 27, 41f.
5: Jer 49, 9.

OB

11† On the day when you stood by,
 on the day when aliens carried off
  his possessions,
And strangers entered his gates
 and cast lots over Jerusalem,
 you too were one of them.
12 Gaze not upon the day of your brother,
 the day of his disaster;
Exult not over the children of Judah
 on the day of their ruin;
Speak not haughtily
 on the day of distress!
13 Enter not the gate of my people
 on the day of their calamity;
Gaze not, you at least, upon
 his misfortune
  on the day of his calamity;
Lay not hands upon his possessions
 on the day of his calamity!
14 Stand not at the crossroads
 to slay his refugees;
Betray not his fugitives
 on the day of distress!

Judgment upon the Nations

15* For near is the day of the LORD
 for all the nations!
As you have done, so shall it be done to you,
 your deed shall come back upon your
  own head;
16† As you have drunk upon my holy mountain,
 so shall all the nations drink continually.
Yes, they shall drink and swallow,
 and shall become as though they had
  not been.

Judah Shall Be Restored

17† But on Mount Zion there shall be a
 portion saved;
 the mountain shall be holy,
And the house of Jacob shall take possession
 of those that dispossessed them.
18 The house of Jacob shall be a fire,
 and the house of Joseph a flame;
The house of Esau shall be stubble,
 and they shall set them ablaze and
  devour them;

Then none shall survive of the house of Esau,
 for the LORD has spoken.
19 They shall occupy the Negeb, the mount
 of Esau,
 and the foothills of the Philistines;
And they shall occupy the lands of Ephraim
 and the lands of Samaria,
 and Benjamin shall occupy Gilead.
20† The captives of this host of the children
 of Israel
 shall occupy the Canaanite land as far
  as Zarephath,
And the captives of Jerusalem who are
 in Sepharad
 shall occupy the cities of the Negeb.
21† And saviors shall ascend Mount Zion
 to rule the mount of Esau,
 and the kingship shall be the LORD's.

What Goes Around

What goes around comes around.
**Have you ever heard that saying?
Isn't that exactly what Obadiah is saying
in verse 15?**

 **Whatever you do comes back to
affect you eventually. If you are honest,
people will trust you and tell you the
truth. If you lie, cheat, and steal, people
will deceive you. If you respect the earth,
it will take care of you. If you litter, pollute, and destroy, you ruin your home,
your country, and your world.**

 **Pray that all people take this lesson to
heart. Pray that we learn to respect all
living things. The results of our actions
will come back to us eventually—if not to
us personally, to other people and future
generations.**

▸ **Obadiah, verse 15**

 11: After the devastation of Judah, Edom occupied the southern part of its territory. Edomites also joined the invading Chaldean forces (13) and assisted them in capturing the people of Judah (14).
 16: *As you have drunk:* the Lord addresses the people of Judah. As the people of Jerusalem have drunk the cup of retribution, so shall the nations, and especially Edom (18), suffer punishment. This metaphorical use of drinking the cup of God's wrath is common in the Bible; cf Jb 21, 20; Is 19, 14; Jer 25, 15f.
 17ff: The Israelites shall be restored and shall occupy the lands of those who oppressed them. The survivors of Judah shall be rejoined by the returned exiles from northern Israel.

 20: *Zarephath:* a town in Phoenicia, north of Tyre; cf 1 Kgs 17, 10. Ezekiel's ideal boundaries of the new Israel (Ez 47, 13ff) extend farther north. *Sepharad:* probably Sardis in western Asia Minor. The later rabbis thought it to be Spain.
 21: *Saviors:* the victorious Israelites who will rule over their enemies after the fashion of the ancient Judges; cf Jgs 3, 9.15.31; 10, 1.

15f: Ps 137, 7ff.

You're watching a comedy show where someone dressed like a doctor starts making outrageous comments about a person's health. You laugh, not because sickness is funny, but because doctors are supposed to be sensitive and caring. That's the basis of satire—that someone or something that is supposed to act one way acts another way. You're about to read a biblical satire about Jonah the prophet. The Book of Jonah uses humor to make an important point—God is the God of all people, even those we consider our enemies.

At a Glance

I. The First Mission (1, 1—2, 2).

II. Psalm of Thanksgiving (2, 3—2, 11).

III. Conversion of Nineveh (chapter 3).

IV. Jonah's Anger: God's Reproof (chapter 4).

In-depth

This story was written after the Jews returned from their exile in Babylon. Jewish leaders encouraged Jewish people to stay away from non-Jewish people (see Ezra, chapter 9) in order to avoid falling into idolatry again. A result was a religious bigotry against other nations—a belief that God was against every nation that opposed Israel. The Book of Jonah was written to correct that narrow attitude. Through satire, this fictional short story gently pokes fun at Israel's religious self-righteousness.

How is the book funny? Well, right off the bat, Jonah is called by God and immediately takes off in the opposite direction (1, 1–3). What kind of prophet is this? When God tries to get his attention with a storm, it's the non-Jewish sailors who get the point (verse 14). Just as the reader is probably wondering how God is going to get Jonah to Nineveh, along comes a taxi in the form of a large fish's stomach (2, 1).

There's more. Readers from the author's time would have expected Jonah to be ignored at best, more likely beaten or killed by the people of Nineveh. After all, these were Israel's mortal enemies. Instead, the Ninevites immediately respond to Jonah's message and repent, even the animals (3, 8)! At this point, the reader is giggling at the goofiness of pigs and sheep in sackcloth, but getting the message about God's salvation being for all nations.

Jonah's angry and upset. He didn't expect the Ninevites to convert—he wanted them punished. He goes outside the city to mope, and his favorite tree dies. The book ends with God chiding Jonah for his bigoted anger. If Jonah is so concerned for his little tree (4, 6–8), shouldn't God be concerned for the great city of Nineveh with its thousands of people (verse 11)? The point is driven home, and the humor has helped to make a challenging message easier to accept.

Quick Facts

Period Covered
the eighth century B.C.

Author
unknown, probably writing in the fifth century B.C.

Theme
a fictional short story showing that God cares for all people, including Israel's enemies

The Book of *Jonah*

1151

Jonah

The First Mission

1 [1]*† This is the word of the LORD that came to Jonah, son of Amittai: [2]* "Set out for the great city of Nineveh, and preach against it; their wickedness has come up before me." [3]† But Jonah made ready to flee to Tarshish away from the LORD. He went down to Joppa, found a ship going to Tarshish, paid the fare, and went aboard to journey with them to Tarshish, away from the LORD.

[4] The LORD, however, hurled a violent wind upon the sea, and in the furious tempest that arose the ship was on the point of breaking up. [5] Then the mariners became frightened and each one cried to his god. To lighten the ship for themselves, they threw its cargo into the sea. Meanwhile, Jonah had gone down into the hold of the ship, and lay there fast asleep. [6] The captain came to him and said, "What are you doing asleep? Rise up, call upon your God! Perhaps God will be mindful of us so that we may not perish."

[7] Then they said to one another, "Come, let us cast lots to find out on whose account we have met with this misfortune." So they cast lots, and thus singled out Jonah. [8] "Tell us," they said, "what is your business? Where do you come from? What is your country, and to what people do you belong?" [9] "I am a Hebrew," Jonah answered them; "I worship the LORD, the God of heaven, who made the sea and the dry land."

[10] Now the men were seized with great fear and said to him, "How could you do such a thing!"—They knew that he was fleeing from the LORD, because he had told them.— [11] "What shall we do with you," they asked, "that the sea may quiet down for us?" For the sea was growing more and more turbulent. [12] Jonah said to them, "Pick me up and throw me into the sea, that it may quiet down for you; since I know it is because of me that this violent storm has come upon you."

[13] Still the men rowed hard to regain the land, but they could not, for the sea grew ever more turbulent. [14]† Then they cried to the LORD: "We beseech you, O LORD, let us not perish for taking this man's life; do not charge us with shedding innocent blood, for you, LORD, have done as you saw fit." [15] Then they took Jonah and threw him into the sea, and the sea's raging abated. [16] Struck with great fear of the LORD, the men offered sacrifice and made vows to him.

2 [1]* But the LORD sent a large fish, that swallowed Jonah; and he remained in the belly of the fish three days and three nights. [2] From the belly of the fish Jonah said this prayer to the LORD, his God:

1, 1: *Jonah, son of Amittai:* a prophet of this name lived at the time of Jeroboam II (786–746 B.C.).

1, 3: *Tarshish:* identified by many with Tartessus, an ancient Phoenician colony in southwest Spain; precise identification with any particular Phoenician center in the western Mediterranean is uncertain. To the Hebrews it stood for the far west.

1, 14: Since it has pleased the Lord to punish Jonah, the mariners ask that in ridding themselves of him they be not charged with the crime of murder.

1, 1: 2 Kgs 14, 25.   **2, 1:** Mt 12, 40; 16, 4; Lk
1, 2: Jon 3, 3; 4, 11.   11, 30; 1 Cor 15, 4.

Jesus and Jonah

Do you see any similarities between Jonah and Jesus? Jonah is in the darkness of a fish's belly for three days before the LORD commands the fish to spit him out. Jesus experiences the darkness of death for three days before he bursts from the tomb in resurrected glory. In Mt 16, 4 and Lk 11, 29, Jesus even refers to "the sign of Jonah" in relation to his own ministry.

Jonah's prayer in Jon 2, 3–10 could well have been Jesus' prayer before his death. It reminds us that salvation comes from God when we are experiencing dark times. When you are going through a difficult time, use Jonah's prayer as a model for writing your own prayer of trust. Describe your difficulties and your situation, and end by expressing your ultimate trust in God. Then say your prayer until the difficulty passes. It could make a difference!

▶ Jon 2, 3–10

Psalm of Thanksgiving

3* Out of my distress I called to the LORD,
    and he answered me;
From the midst of the nether world I cried
      for help,
    and you heard my voice.
4* For you cast me into the deep, into the heart
      of the sea,
    and the flood enveloped me;
All your breakers and your billows
      passed over me.
5* Then I said, "I am banished from your sight!
    yet would I again look upon your
      holy temple."
6* The waters swirled about me, threatening my life;
    the abyss enveloped me;
      seaweed clung about my head.
7* Down I went to the roots of the mountains;

    the bars of the nether world
      were closing behind me forever,
But you brought up my life from the pit,
    O LORD, my God.
8* When my soul fainted within me,
    I remembered the LORD;
My prayer reached you
    in your holy temple.
9* Those who worship vain idols
    forsake their source of mercy.
10* But I, with resounding praise,
    will sacrifice to you;
What I have vowed I will pay:
    deliverance is from the LORD.

11 Then the LORD commanded the fish to spew Jonah upon the shore.

Conversion of Nineveh

3 1 The word of the LORD came to Jonah a second time: 2 "Set out for the great city of Nineveh, and announce to it the message that I will tell you." 3 So Jonah made ready and went to Nineveh, according to the LORD'S bidding. Now Nineveh was an enormously large city; it took three days to go through it. 4† Jonah began his journey through the city, and had gone but a single day's walk announcing, "Forty days more and Nineveh shall be destroyed," 5* when the people of Nineveh believed God; they proclaimed a fast and all of them, great and small, put on sackcloth.

6 When the news reached the king of Nineveh, he rose from his throne, laid aside his robe, covered himself with sackcloth, and sat in the ashes. 7 Then he had this proclaimed throughout Nineveh, by decree of the king and his nobles: "Neither man nor beast, neither cattle nor sheep, shall taste anything; they shall not eat, nor shall they drink water. 8† Man and beast shall be covered with sackcloth and call loudly to God; every man shall turn from his evil way and from the violence he has in hand. 9* Who knows, God may relent and forgive, and withold his blazing wrath, so that we shall not perish." 10 When God saw by their actions how they turned from their evil way, he repented of the evil that he had threatened to do to them; he did not carry it out.

Jonah's Anger: God's Reproof

4 1† But this was greatly displeasing to Jonah, and he became angry. 2* "I beseech you,

† 3, 4: *Shall be destroyed:* the Hebrew expression reminds the reader of the "overthrowing" of the wicked cities, Sodom and Gomorrah, by a special act of God.
3, 8: *Beast . . . sackcloth:* the animals carried the signs of this repentance, as on occasions of joy they bore garlands.
4, 1: *He became angry:* because of his narrowly nationalistic vindictiveness, Jonah did not wish the Lord to forgive the Ninevites.

2, 3: Pss 18, 7; 120, 1.
2, 4: Ps 42, 8.
2, 5: Ps 31, 23; Is 38, 11.
2, 6: Pss 18, 5; 69, 2.
2, 7: Pss 16, 10; 30, 4.
2, 8: Pss 5, 8; 18, 7; 88, 3.
2, 9: Ps 31, 7.
2, 10: Ps 50, 14.
3, 5: Mt 12, 41; Lk 11, 32.
3, 9: Jl 2, 14.
4, 2: Ps 86, 5; Jl 2, 13.

Mistaken Loyalties

When God spares Nineveh, Jonah is angry! He is so angry he is willing to let his anger destroy him. And all because of mistaken loyalty. Jonah thought he was loyal to God (which is funny because at first, he tried to run away from God), and he feels that God is being disloyal to him by not destroying Nineveh. Jonah does not—or will not—understand that God's loyalty is to the whole human race, not just to Jonah's desires.

Are you ever angry with God because things don't go your way? Maybe your anger is about mistaken loyalties. If you didn't get picked for the lead part, that doesn't mean God is being disloyal to you. God is God over everyone—which sometimes means you will not get what you want so that other people can receive what they need.

The next time you are angry at God, ask yourself: Am I willing to see things from a large enough perspective? Am I expecting to receive God's favor at someone else's expense?

▸ Jon 4, 1–8

LORD," he prayed, "is not this what I said while I was still in my own country? This is why I fled at first to Tarshish. I knew that you are a gracious and merciful God, slow to anger, rich in clemency, loathe to punish. ³* And now, LORD, please take my life from me; for it is better for me to die than to live." ⁴ But the LORD asked, "Have you reason to be angry?"

⁵ Jonah then left the city for a place to the east of it, where he built himself a hut and waited under it in the shade, to see what would happen to the city. ⁶† And when the LORD God provided a gourd plant, that grew up over Jonah's head, giving shade that relieved him of any discomfort, Jonah was very happy over the plant. ⁷ But the next morning at dawn God sent a worm which attacked the plant, so that

it withered. ⁸ And when the sun arose, God sent a burning east wind; and the sun beat upon Jonah's head till he became faint. Then he asked for death, saying, "I would be better off dead than alive."

⁹ But God said to Jonah, "Have you reason to be angry over the plant?" "I have reason to be angry," Jonah answered, "angry enough to die." ¹⁰† Then the LORD said, "You are concerned over the plant which cost you no labor and which you did not raise; it came up in one night and in one night it perished. ¹¹ And should I not be concerned over Nineveh, the great city, in which there are more than a hundred and twenty thousand persons who cannot distinguish their right hand from their left, not to mention the many cattle?"

4, 6: *Gourd plant:* the Hebrew word, *kikayon*, means here a wide-leafed plant of the cucumber or castor-bean variety.

4, 10f: Jonah is selfish in bemoaning his personal loss of a shady gourd plant without any concern over the threat of loss of life to the Ninevites through the destruction of their city. If God in his kindness provided the plant for his prophet without the latter's effort or merit,

how much more is he disposed to show love and mercy toward all men, Jew and Gentile, when they repent of their sins and implore his pardon! God's providence is also shown here to extend even to animals.

4, 3: 1 Kgs 19, 4.

There is a story about a country mouse and a city mouse who visit each other on separate occasions. For each, the visit is a discovery of new experiences and a different way of life. Indeed, people who visit the places where we live often see things that we have overlooked or taken for granted. The prophet Micah was like such a visitor. His home was a small village, but he prophesied in the big capital city of Jerusalem. God uses Micah's unique perspective to communicate warnings and promises to the people of Israel and to us.

At a Glance

I. Punishment of Israel's Sins (1, 1—3, 12).

II. The New Israel (4, 1—5, 14).

III. Admonition (6, 1—7, 20).

In-depth

The Book of Micah is a collection of oracles (poemlike prophetic messages) taking different forms. Some of the oracles are harsh judgments (see 1, 8—2, 11), some are comforting promises that God will not desert the people (see chapter 4), and some are the prophet's own confessions of faith (3, 8; 7, 7). The Book of Micah shows us a God who is passionate for justice and fairness (3, 9).

Perhaps because of his rural background, the prophet Micah had a special connection to the land and the people who work it. He speaks against those who covet and seize fields and homes (2, 2). He describes the destruction of Zion (Jerusalem) as plowing a field (3, 12). He represents the Ideal Kingdom as a place where all the people have their own grapevines and fig trees (4, 4).

The Book of Micah shows signs of being extensively edited and revised to keep the prophet's message relevant during changing times. This is particularly true in chapters 4 and 5, which were added after the Babylonian Exile to give hope following the nation's great tragedy. In 4, 3, the prophet envisions a day when nations will "beat their swords into plowshares" and "One nation shall not raise the sword against another, / nor shall they train for war again."

Micah prophesied at about the same time as First Isaiah (see the timeline at the back of this Bible), during the days of Kings Jotham, Ahaz, and Hezekiah (see 2 Chr 27, 1—31, 21). But whereas Isaiah was a member of the upper class, defending the rights of the poor, Micah was a poor person, suffering with the poor. That is why he speaks so passionately about their mistreatment (see Mic 3, 1-3). Even though his message went unheeded at the time, he models for us trust in the LORD's saving power (7, 7).

Quick Facts

Period Covered
the late eighth century B.C.

Authors
Micah and later editors

Themes
warnings against injustice and idolatry, promises of a new future

The Book of Micah

Micah

I: Punishment of Israel's Sins

Divine Judgment

1 [1] The word of the LORD which came to Micah of Moresheth in the days of Jotham, Ahaz, and Hezekiah, kings of Judah: that is, the vision he received concerning Samaria and Jerusalem.

[2]*† Hear, O peoples, all of you,
  give heed, O earth, and all that fills you!
Let the Lord GOD be witness against you,
  the Lord from his holy temple!
[3]* For see, the LORD comes forth from his place,
  he descends and treads upon the heights of
    the earth.
[4] The mountains melt under him
  and the valleys split open,
Like wax before the fire,
  like water poured down a slope.

[5] For the crime of Jacob all this comes to pass,
  and for the sins of the house of Israel.
What is the crime of Jacob?
  Is it not Samaria?

And what is the sin of the house of Judah?
  Is it not Jerusalem?
[6] I will make Samaria a stone heap in the field,
  a place to plant for vineyards;
I will throw down into the valley her stones,
  and lay bare her foundations.
[7]*† All her idols shall be broken to pieces,
  all her wages shall be burned in the fire,
  and all her statues I will destroy.
As the wages of a harlot they were gathered,
  and to the wages of a harlot shall
    they return.

[8]* For this reason I lament and wail,
  I go barefoot and naked;
I utter lamentation like the jackals,
  and mourning like the ostriches.
[9] There is no remedy for the blow she has
    been struck;
  rather, it has come even to Judah,
It reaches to the gate of my people,
  even to Jerusalem.
[10]*† Publish it not in Gath,
  weep not at all;

---

† **1, 2:** *His holy temple:* God's heavenly temple; the prophet pictures a theophany (3f).

1, 7: The comparison of the unfaithful people with a prostitute, first found in Hosea, is frequent with the prophets; probably ritual prostitution is meant; cf Am 2, 7f; Hos 4, 14.

1, 10–15: The Judean cities here named were in the vicinity of Moresheth, the region with which Micah was most familiar. They

were to experience divine chastisement. In the Hebrew, wordplays on the names of these cities abound. The text is partly obscure.

1, 2: Dt 32, 1; Is 1, 2.
1, 3f: Is 26, 21; Na 1, 5; Hb 3, 10.
1, 7: Hos 9, 1.
1, 8: Jb 30, 29.
1, 10: 2 Sm 1, 20.

In Beth-leaphrah
   roll in the dust.
11 Pass by,
   you who dwell in Shaphir!
The inhabitants of Zaanan
   come not forth from their city.
The lamentation of Beth-ezel
   finds in you its grounds.
12 How can the inhabitants of Maroth
   hope for good?
For evil has come down from the LORD
   to the gate of Jerusalem.
13 Harness steeds to the chariots,
   O inhabitants of Lachish;
Lachish, the beginning of sin
   for daughter Zion,
Because there were in you
   the crimes of Israel.
14 Therefore you shall give parting gifts
   to Moresheth-gath;
Beth-achzib is a deception
   to the kings of Israel.
15 Yet must I bring to you the conqueror,
   O inhabitants of Mareshah;
Even to Adullam shall go
   the glory of Israel.

16† Make yourself bald, pluck out your hair,
   for the children whom you cherish;
Let your baldness be as the eagle's,
   because they are exiled from you.

Social Evils

2 ¹ Woe to those who plan iniquity,
   and work out evil on their couches;
In the morning light they accomplish it
   when it lies within their power.
2† They covet fields, and seize them;
   houses, and they take them;
They cheat an owner of his house,
   a man of his inheritance.
3   Therefore thus says the LORD:
Behold, I am planning against this race an evil
   from which you shall not withdraw
     your necks;
Nor shall you walk with head high,
   for it will be a time of evil.

4 On that day a satire shall be sung over you,
   and there shall be a plaintive chant:

?did you KNOW?

Micah Challenges Us to Fight Injustice

In chapter 2, the prophet Micah challenges the people to take an honest look at their behavior. In harsh images and language, he articulates how greed and injustice have destroyed the well-being of the nation. In verse 3, Micah implies that because of their injustice, the people will be like oxen whose necks are confined to yokes that hold their heads down in shame. Micah's message is that injustice forces all in the community and nation to carry a heavy burden.

This theme of examining injustices in the world has been repeated numerous times throughout the Scriptures. And to this very day, we continue to hear similar teachings coming out of the church. What are we doing in our communities and in our country to fight against modern instances of injustice, such as racism, hunger, poverty, abortion, capital punishment, violence, and destruction of the natural environment? What injustices do you see in your own actions and in your own community? What can you do to stop injustices from happening so that our communities and nation can live freely in peace?

▸ Micah, chapter 2

"Our ruin is complete,
   our fields are portioned out among
     our captors,
The fields of my people are measured out,
   and no one can get them back!"
5† Thus you shall have no one
   to mark out boundaries by lot
   in the assembly of the LORD.

---

† **1, 16:** Shaving the head was a sign of mourning; cf Is 3, 24; Am 8, 10.

2, 2: Land monopoly, also denounced by Isaiah, was a chronic vice in Judah. To protect the poor against it, a man's inheritance, his ancestral property, was supposed to be inviolate; cf 1 Kgs 21, 1–4; but the wealthy in their greed were enslaving men for their debts and depriving them of their land.

2, 5: *To mark out boundaries by lot:* an allusion to the initial distribution of the land of Palestine among the Israelites; cf Jos 13–21. The appropriate punishment of those greedy for land will be the loss of their land to their enemies (v 4), a loss that will be irrevocable.

6† "Preach not," they preach,
  "let them not preach of these things!"
  The shame will not withdraw.
7 How can it be said, O house of Jacob,
  "Is the LORD short of patience,
  or are such his deeds?"
  Do not my words promise good
  to him who walks uprightly?

8 But of late my people has risen up as
    an enemy:
  you have stripped off the mantle covering
    the tunic
  Of those who go their way in confidence,
    as though it were spoils of war.
9† The women of my people you drive out
    from their pleasant houses;
  From their children you take away
    forever the honor I gave them.
10† "Up! Be off,
    this is no place to rest";
  For any trifle you exact
    a crippling pledge.

11 If one, acting on impulse, should make the
      futile claim:
  "I pour you wine and strong drink as
      my prophecy,"
  then he would be the prophet of this people.
12† I will gather you, O Jacob, each and every one,
    I will assemble all the remnant of Israel;
  I will group them like a flock in the fold,
    like a herd in the midst of its corral;
    they shall not be thrown into panic by men.
13 With a leader to break the path
    they shall burst open the gate and go out
      through it;
  Their king shall go through before them,
    and the LORD at their head.

Downfall of Present Leaders

3 1   And I said:
  Hear, you leaders of Jacob,
    rulers of the house of Israel!
  Is it not your duty to know what is right,
2*   you who hate what is good,
      and love evil?
  You who tear their skin from them,
    and their flesh from their bones!

3 They eat the flesh of my people,
    and flay their skin from them,
    and break their bones.
  They chop them in pieces like flesh in a kettle,
    and like meat in a caldron.
4 When they cry to the LORD,
    he shall not answer them;
  Rather shall he hide his face from them at
      that time,
    because of the evil they have done.

5*†Thus says the LORD regarding the prophets
    who lead my people astray;
  Who, when their teeth have something
      to bite,
    announce peace,
  But when one fails to put something in
      their mouth,
    proclaim war against him.
6* Therefore you shall have night, not vision,
    darkness, not divination;
  The sun shall go down upon the prophets,
    and the day shall be dark for them.
7 Then shall the seers be put to shame,
    and the diviners confounded;
  They shall cover their lips, all of them,
    because there is no answer from God.
8 But as for me, I am filled with power,
    with the spirit of the LORD,
    with authority and with might;
  To declare to Jacob his crimes
    and to Israel his sins.
9 Hear this, you leaders of the house of Jacob,
    you rulers of the house of Israel!
  You who abhor what is just,
    and pervert all that is right;
10 Who build up Zion with bloodshed,
    and Jerusalem with wickedness!
11* Her leaders render judgment for a bribe,
    her priests give decisions for a salary,
    her prophets divine for money,
  While they rely on the LORD, saying,
    "Is not the LORD in the midst of us?
    No evil can come upon us!"
12* Therefore, because of you,
    Zion shall be plowed like a field,
    and Jerusalem reduced to rubble,
  And the mount of the temple
    to a forest ridge.

2, 6f: The words in quotation marks are the protestations of the people against the prophet's predictions of doom.
2, 9: *The honor I gave them:* their dignity as free Israelites.
2, 10: *A crippling pledge:* Israelite law forbade exacting pledges for loans that would work hardship on the borrower (Ex 22, 25f; Dt 24, 6.10–13.17); but the law was habitually violated.
2, 12f: This messianic passage concerning the restoration after the Babylonian exile seems out of place here and is probably a later addition.

3, 5–8: Almost all the prophetic books contain oracles against the false prophets. Here Micah accuses them of prophesying for venal motives and determining the prophecy by the price that is paid them; he contrasts his own disinterested preaching of the word of God.

3, 2: Am 2, 7.   3, 11: Ez 22, 27; Zep 3, 3.
3, 5: Ez 13, 10.   3, 12: Jer 26, 18.
3, 6: Jer 15, 9; Am 8, 9; Zec
    13, 3.

M
I

II: The New Israel

The People To Be Restored

4 ¹*† In days to come
the mount of the LORD's house
Shall be established higher than the mountains;
it shall rise high above the hills,
And peoples shall stream to it:

² Many nations shall come, and say,
"Come, let us climb the mount of the LORD,
to the house of the God of Jacob,
That he may instruct us in his ways,
that we may walk in his paths."
For from Zion shall go forth instruction,
and the word of the LORD from Jerusalem.

³ He shall judge between many peoples
and impose terms on strong and
distant nations;
They shall beat their swords into plowshares,
and their spears into pruning hooks;
One nation shall not raise the sword
against another,
nor shall they train for war again.

⁴* Every man shall sit under his own vine
or under his own fig tree, undisturbed;
for the mouth of the LORD of hosts
has spoken.

⁵ For all the peoples walk
each in the name of its god,
But we will walk in the name of the LORD,
our God, forever and ever.

⁶ On that day, says the LORD,
I will gather the lame,
And I will assemble the outcasts,
and those whom I have afflicted.

⁷* I will make of the lame a remnant,
and of those driven far off a strong nation;
And the LORD shall be king over them on
Mount Zion,
from now on forever.

⁸† And you, O Magdal-eder,
hillock of daughter Zion!
Unto you shall it come:
the former dominion shall be restored,
the kingdom of daughter Jerusalem.

⁹ Now why do you cry out so?
Are you without a king?

Or has your counselor perished,
That you are seized with pains
like a woman in travail?

¹⁰† Writhe in pain, grow faint,
O daughter Zion,
like a woman in travail;
For now shall you go forth from the city
and dwell in the fields;
To Babylon shall you go,
there shall you be rescued.
There shall the LORD redeem you
from the hand of your enemies.

¹¹ How many nations are gathered against you!
They say, "Let her be profaned,
let our eyes see Zion's downfall!"

¹² But they know not the thoughts
of the LORD,
nor understand his counsel,
When he has gathered them
like sheaves on the threshing floor.

¹³* Arise and thresh, O daughter Zion;
your horn I will make iron
And your hoofs bronze,
that you may crush many peoples;
You shall devote their spoils to the LORD,
and their riches to the Lord of the
whole earth.

Restoration through the Messiah

¹⁴† Now fence yourself in, Bat-gader!
"They have laid siege against us!"
With the rod they strike on the cheek
the ruler of Israel.

5 ¹*† But you, Bethlehem-Ephrathah,
too small to be among the clans of Judah,
From you shall come forth for me
one who is to be ruler in Israel;
Whose origin is from of old,
from ancient times.

²*†(Therefore the Lord will give them up, until
the time
when she who is to give birth has borne,
And the rest of his brethren shall return
to the children of Israel.)

³ He shall stand firm and shepherd his flock
by the strength of the LORD,
in the majestic name of the LORD, his God;

4, 1ff: See note on Is 2, 2ff.
4, 8: *Magdal-eder:* "tower of the flock," an ancient place name (cf Gn 35, 21), here used symbolically of Jerusalem.
4, 10: *For now . . . your enemies:* probably a later addition to the text, when the prediction of exile had been fulfilled in the Babylonian captivity. The prophet sees the exile as the means whereby God will purify and restore his people.
4, 14: *Bat-gader:* "fenced-in maiden," another symbolic name for Jerusalem, then under siege from the Assyrians.
5, 1: In contrast to Bat-gader (Mi 4, 14), where the ruler of Israel,

the reigning king, is in peril of his life from the Assyrians, is the tiny city and clan of Bethlehem-Ephrathah, from which comes the ancient Davidic dynasty (whose origin is from of old, from ancient times) with its messianic King, one who is to be ruler in Israel.
5, 2: *She who is to give birth:* the mother of the Messiah: cf Is 7, 14.

4, 1ff: Is 2, 2ff.   **4, 13:** Is 41, 15; Hos 10, 11.
4, 4: Hos 14, 8; Am 9, 14.   **5, 1:** Ru 1, 2; 1 Sm 17, 12;
4, 7: Is 6, 13; Dn 7, 14; Zep   Mt 2, 6; Jn 7, 42.
3, 19; Lk 1, 32.   **5, 2f:** Is 7, 14; 11, 1f.

From Humble Beginnings

As a country boy, Micah has a different vision than do some of the other prophets. He doesn't see the Ideal Ruler coming out of a big city like Jerusalem. No, he sees this great person coming from Bethlehem—a tiny, insignificant city, but also a place free from political corruption. The Gospel of Matthew shows Micah's prophecy being fulfilled in the birth of Jesus (Mt 2, 5–6).

Often in the Bible, we hear of God's accomplishing huge feats with small and humble people and things. In your prayer, reflect or journal on the following questions:

- What famous people started from humble beginnings?
- Why does God often use small and hidden people or things to accomplish God's purposes?
- What small or hidden gifts do you have to offer God to work with?

▸ Mi 5, 1–4

And they shall remain, for now his greatness
　　shall reach to the ends of the earth;
4† 　he shall be peace.

If Assyria invades our country
　　and treads upon our land,
We shall raise against it seven shepherds,
　　eight men of royal rank;
5† And they shall tend the land of Assyria with
　　　the sword,
　　and the land of Nimrod with the
　　　drawn sword;
And we shall be delivered from Assyria,
　　if it invades our land
　　and treads upon our borders.

6　The remnant of Jacob shall be
　　in the midst of many peoples,

Like dew coming from the LORD,
　　like raindrops on the grass,
Which wait for no man,
　　nor tarry for the sons of men.
7　And the remnant of Jacob shall be among
　　　the nations,
　　in the midst of many peoples,
Like a lion among beasts of the forest,
　　like a young lion among flocks
　　　of sheep;
When it passes through, it tramples
　　and tears, and there is none to deliver.
8　Your hand shall be lifted above your foes,
　　and all your enemies shall be destroyed.

9† 　　On that day, says the LORD,
　　I will destroy the horses from your midst
　　and ruin your chariots;
10　I will demolish the cities of your land
　　and tear down all your fortresses.
11　I will abolish the means of divination from
　　　your use,
　　and there shall no longer be soothsayers
　　　among you.
12*†I will abolish your carved images
　　and the sacred pillars from your midst;
And you shall no longer adore
　　the works of your hands.
13　I will tear out the sacred poles from
　　　your midst,
　　and destroy your cities.
14　I will wreak vengeance in anger and wrath
　　upon the nations that have not hearkened.

III: Admonition

Accusation and Answer

6 1* 　Hear, then, what the LORD says:
　　Arise, present your plea before the
　　　mountains,
　　and let the hills hear your voice!
2　Hear, O mountains, the plea of the LORD,
　　pay attention, O foundations of the earth!
For the LORD has a plea against his people,
　　and he enters into trial with Israel.

3* 　O my people, what have I done to you,
　　or how have I wearied you? Answer me!
4* 　For I brought you up from the land of Egypt,

5, 4f: This passage, expressing confidence in Judah's ability to deliver itself from Assyria, is in contrast with the preceding messianic oracle, which ascribes deliverance to the Lord and his agent. Some believe that here the prophet is quoting the words of the defiant men of Judah. The shepherds and men of royal rank are one and the same: warriors capable of routing Assyria. The same kind of numerical progression is used by Amos (1, 3), and elsewhere in the Bible.
5, 5: *Nimrod:* the legendary ancestor of the Mesopotamians; cf Gn 10, 10ff.

5, 9–13: Part of the messianic restoration will consist in the removal of everything that has drawn Israel away from the Lord; this includes not only the objects of false worship, but also the armaments in which the idolators had trusted.
5, 12f: *Sacred pillars . . . sacred poles:* see note on Ex 34, 13.

5, 12: Hos 3, 4; 10, 1f.　　　　6, 3: Jer 2, 5.
6, 1: Is 6, 2; Ob 1.　　　　6, 4: Ex 15, 20.

LIVE IT!

"To Love Goodness"

Perhaps you have heard the expression Perform a random act of kindness. It is a wonderful antidote to the reality of random acts of violence. Imagine what our world would be like if each day, each of us performed a random act of goodness—something nice and unexpected for someone, anyone, whether we knew the person or not. We could make someone's day. And in turn, someone could make ours. Just as violence leads to more violence, so also can goodness create more goodness. No wonder Micah includes goodness in his simple formula for doing God's will: "to do the right and to love goodness, / and to walk humbly with your God" (Mi 6, 8).

▸ Mi 6, 8

from the place of slavery I released you;
And I sent before you Moses,
    Aaron, and Miriam.
5*† My people, remember what Moab's King
    Balak planned,
and how Balaam, the son of Beor,
    answered him
. . . from Shittim to Gilgal,
that you may know the just deeds of
    the LORD.
6*† With what shall I come before the LORD,
    and bow before God most high?

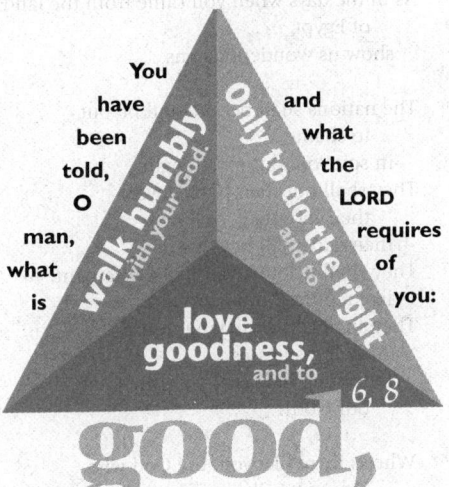

Shall I come before him with holocausts,
    with calves a year old?
7† Will the LORD be pleased with thousands
    of rams,
    with myriad streams of oil?
Shall I give my first-born for my crime,
    the fruit of my body for the sin of my soul?
8* You have been told, O man, what is good,
    and what the LORD requires of you:
Only to do the right and to love goodness,
    and to walk humbly with your God.

9† Hark! the LORD cries to the city.
    [It is wisdom to fear your name!]
    Hear, O tribe and city council,
12 You whose rich men are full of violence,
    whose inhabitants speak falsehood
    with deceitful tongues in their heads!
10 Am I to bear any longer criminal hoarding
    and the meager ephah that is accursed?
11 Shall I acquit criminal balances,
    bags of false weights?

13 Rather I will begin to strike you
    with devastation because of your sins.
15* You shall sow, yet not reap,
    tread out the olive, yet pour no oil,
    and the grapes, yet drink no wine.
14* You shall eat, without being satisfied,
    food that will leave you empty;
What you acquire, you cannot save;
    what you do save, I will deliver up to
    the sword.

6, 5: *From Shittim to Gilgal:* from the east to the west side of the Jordan; the events described in Jos 3–5 are meant. The text is defective; however, it is evident that this verse continues the remembrance of God's deeds of mercy to Israel, beginning with the Exodus (v 4) and extending to the conquest, deeds which have provoked so little response from his people.

6, 6ff: The people ask how they shall worship the Lord, proposing the various forms of sacrifice. The prophet replies that sacrifice avails nothing without the true spirit of religion. This is one of the best expressions of the prophetic teaching on religion, the preparation for such New Testament passages as Jas 1, 27.

6, 7: *Shall I give my first-born:* through Canaanite influence the abominable practice of human sacrifice had been introduced under impious kings (cf 2 Kgs 16, 3; 21, 6).

6, 9: *The city:* Jerusalem as the embodiment of the crimes of the entire land.

6, 5: Nm 22, 23.
6, 6f: Hos 6, 6; 8, 13; Am 5, 21.
6, 8: Dt 26, 16; Zec 7, 9; Mt 23, 23.
6, 15: Dt 28, 38; Am 5, 11; Hg 1, 6.
6, 14: Hos 4, 10.

16† You have kept the decrees of Omri,
   and all the works of the house of Ahab,
   and you have walked in their counsels;
Therefore I will deliver you up to ruin,
   and your citizens to derision;
   and you shall bear the reproach of
     the nations.

Condemnation and Prayer

7 ¹ Alas! I am as when the fruit is gathered,
   as when the vines have been gleaned;
There is no cluster to eat,
   no early fig that I crave.
²* The faithful are gone from the earth,
   among men the upright are no more!
They all lie in wait to shed blood,
   each one ensnares the other.
³* Their hands succeed at evil;
   the prince makes demands,
The judge is had for a price,
   the great man speaks as he pleases,
⁴ The best of them is like a brier,
   the most upright like a thorn hedge.
The day announced by your watchmen!
   your punishment has come;
   now is the time of your confusion.
⁵*†Put no trust in a friend,
   have no confidence in a companion;
Against her who lies in your bosom
   guard the portals of your mouth.
⁶* For the son dishonors his father,
   the daughter rises up against her mother,
The daughter-in-law against her
    mother-in-law,
   and a man's enemies are those of
    his household.
⁷* But as for me, I will look to the LORD,
   I will put my trust in God my savior;
   my God will hear me!

⁸† Rejoice not over me, O my enemy!
   though I have fallen, I will arise;
   though I sit in darkness, the LORD is my light.
⁹ The wrath of the LORD I will endure
   because I have sinned against him,
Until he takes up my cause,
   and establishes my right.

He will bring me forth to the light;
   I will see his justice.
¹⁰ When my enemy sees this,
   shame shall cover her:
She who said to me,
   "Where is the LORD, thy God?"
My eyes shall see her downfall;
   now shall she be trampled underfoot,
   like the mire in the streets.

¹¹† It is the day for building your walls;
   on that day the boundary shall be
    taken away.
¹²* It is the day; and they shall come to you
   from Assyria and from Egypt,
From Tyre even to the River,
   from sea to sea, and from mountain
    to mountain;
¹³ And the land shall be a waste
   because of its citizens,
   as a result of their deeds.

¹⁴† Shepherd your people with your staff,
   the flock of your inheritance,
That dwells apart in a woodland,
   in the midst of Carmel.
Let them feed in Bashan and Gilead,
   as in the days of old;
¹⁵ As in the days when you came from the land
    of Egypt,
   show us wonderful signs.

¹⁶ The nations shall behold and be put
    to shame,
   in spite of all their strength;
They shall put their hands over
    their mouths;
   their ears shall become deaf.
¹⁷ They shall lick the dust like the serpent,
   like reptiles on the ground;
They shall come quaking from
    their fastnesses,
   trembling in fear of you [the LORD,
    our God].

¹⁸* Who is there like you, the God who
    removes guilt

6, 16: Judah has followed the example of the northern kingdom epitomized in the semipaganism of Omri and his son Ahab (1 Kgs 16, 25–34), copying both the corrupted worship and the social injustice of their reigns.

7, 5f: Corresponding to the widespread civil corruption and apostasy from religion is the breakdown of normal human and family relations.

7, 8ff: The unnamed enemy of Judah mentioned in these verses may be Assyria or one of the neighboring countries, such as Edom, which stood by to profit at Judah's downfall.

7, 11ff: This prophecy of restoration and repopulation of the promised land by the Jews now in exile appears to be from the period after the destruction of Jerusalem by the Chaldeans (587 B.C.).

7, 14–17: This prayer appears to be from the time after the return from exile (537 B.C.), when the people few in number, possessed only a fragment of their former land, and were surrounded by hostile nations.

7, 2: Is 1, 21; Hos 4, 2.
7, 3: Is 1, 23.
7, 5: Jer 9, 3.
7, 6: Mt 10, 35f.
7, 7: Is 8, 17.
7, 12: Zec 14, 16.
7, 18: Jer 10, 6; Acts 10, 43.

and pardons sin for the remnant of
his inheritance;
Who does not persist in anger forever,
but delights rather in clemency,

19   And will again have compassion on us,
treading underfoot our guilt?

You will cast into the depths of the sea
all our sins;
20 * You will show faithfulness to Jacob,
and grace to Abraham,
As you have sworn to our fathers
from days of old.

7, 20: Ps 105, 6; Is 41, 8; 63,
16.

Devastation, desolation, and destruction! If the Book of Nahum were made into a movie, it would have to be rated R for graphic violence. You are about to read some angry words. They portray a vengeful God bringing destruction upon Israel's enemies. What could make the prophet Nahum so angry? What could make God so angry?

In-depth

At a Glance

I. The LORD's Coming in Judgment (1, 2—2, 1.3).

II. The Fall of Nineveh (2, 2—3, 19).

At the time Nahum was written, the Assyrian Empire had been the terror of the Middle East for several centuries. In 721 B.C., it destroyed the northern part of Israel, called Israel. In 701 B.C., it invaded the southern part of Israel, called Judah, and laid siege to Jerusalem (see the timeline and map 4, "The Assyrian Empire," at the back of this Bible). The siege broke off, and Jerusalem did not fall, but the chosen people of God got a gruesome taste of Assyria's savage cruelty.

The sole concern of the prophet Nahum is the destruction of this evil world power. In the first chapter of his book, he declares the coming wrath of God, and in chapters 2–3, he describes the destruction of Nineveh (the Assyrian capital). We shouldn't be too surprised that when Assyria falls in 612 B.C., Nahum sees the justice of God being worked out: the Assyrians are finally getting a taste of their own medicine! Nahum seems almost to be gloating in 3, 19:

> All who hear this news of you
> clap their hands over you;
> For who has not been overwhelmed,
> steadily, by your malice?

Hidden among the threats and violence against Assyria, we also find words of comfort for God's chosen people: the awesome war with which God will avenge them because their enemies are God's enemies (1, 2); good news and peace are coming for Judah (2, 1); the LORD will restore Israel to its original majesty (2, 3). We even find some wonderful reminders of God's love and protection, which balance the image of the God of vengeance and destruction: "The LORD is slow to anger, yet great in power" (1, 3); "The LORD is good" (1, 7); God is "a refuge on the day of distress" (1, 7); God "takes care of those who have recourse to him" (1, 7). Nahum reminds us that God has many sides and is always more than we can imagine.

Quick Facts

Period Covered
663–612 B.C.

Author
Nahum

Theme
God will avenge Israel and destroy its cruel enemies, the Assyrians.

The Book of *Nahum*

Nahum

1 ¹ Oracle about Nineveh. The book of the vision of Nahum of Elkosh.

The LORD's Coming in Judgment

²† A jealous and avenging God† is the LORD,
    an avenger is the LORD, and angry;
The LORD brings vengeance on his adversaries,
    and lays up wrath for his enemies;
³* The LORD is slow to anger, yet great in power,
    and the LORD never leaves the
      guilty unpunished.
In hurricane and tempest is his path,
    and clouds are the dust at his feet;
⁴*†He rebukes the sea and leaves it dry,
    and all the rivers he dries up.
Withered are Bashan and Carmel,
    and the bloom of Lebanon fades;
⁵ The mountains quake before him,
    and the hills dissolve;
The earth is laid waste before him,
    the world and all who dwell in it.
⁶*†Before his wrath, who can stand firm,
    and who can face his blazing anger?

His fury is poured out like fire,
    and the rocks are rent asunder before him.
⁷ The LORD is good,
    a refuge on the day of distress;
He takes care of those who have recourse
      to him,
⁸   when the flood rages;
He makes an end of his opponents,
    and his enemies he pursues with darkness.
⁹† What are you imputing to the LORD?
    It is he who will make an end!
    The enemy shall not rise a second time;
¹⁰ As when a tangle of thornbushes is set aflame,
    like dry stubble, they shall be
      utterly consumed.
¹²† For, says the LORD,
    be they ever so many and so vigorous,
    still they shall be mown down
      and disappear.
Though I have humbled you,
    I will humble you no more.
¹³* Now will I break his yoke from off you,
    and burst asunder your bonds.

1, 2–8: A poem written in the style of the alphabetic psalms; cf Pss 9A; 25; 111; 119. Here, however, most of the verses beginning with the letters of the second half of the alphabet are not preserved.
1, 2: *A jealous . . . God:* see note on Ex 20, 5.
1, 4: Bashan, Carmel and Lebanon were famous for their forests.
1, 6f: The coming of God in judgment has two aspects: to those who oppose him it will be unbearable; to those who have recourse to him it will bring strength and consolation.

1, 9: *What are you imputing to the LORD?:* the people of Judah are asked what they think God has in mind.
1, 12f: *They:* the enemies of Judah. *You:* Judah. *His yoke:* the dominion of the Assyrian king over Judah.

1, 3: Ex 19, 16ff.
1, 4: Is 33, 9; Hb 3, 6ff.
1, 6: Zep 1, 15; 2, 3.
1, 13: Is 9, 4; 10, 27.

11† From you he came
  who devised evil against the LORD,
  the scoundrel planner.
14† The LORD has commanded regarding you:
  no descendant shall come to bear
   your name;
 From your temple I will abolish
  the carved and the molten image;
 I will make your grave a mockery.

2 ¹* See, upon the mountains there advances
  the bearer of good news, announcing
   peace!
 Celebrate your feasts, O Judah,
  fulfill your vows!
 For nevermore shall you be invaded
  by the scoundrel; he is
   completely destroyed.
³ The LORD will restore the vine of Jacob,
  the pride of Israel,
 Though ravagers have ravaged them
  and ruined the tendrils.

The Fall of Nineveh

²† The hammer comes up against you;
  guard the rampart,
 Keep watch on the road, gird your loins,
  marshal all your strength!
⁴ The shields of his warriors are crimsoned,
  the soldiers colored in scarlet;
 Fiery steel are the chariots
  on the day of his mustering.
 The horses are frenzied;
⁵ the chariots dash madly through the streets
 And wheel in the squares,
  looking like firebrands,
  flashing like lightning bolts.
⁶† His picked troops are called,
  ranks break at their charge;
 To the wall they rush,
  the mantelet is set up.
⁷ The river gates are opened,
  the palace shudders,
⁸† Its mistress is led forth captive,
  and her handmaids, under guard,
 Moaning like doves,

Images of God

LIVE IT!

**The many slain, the heaping corpses,
the endless bodies to stumble upon!
(Na 3, 3)**

  The descriptions of God's vengeance on the Assyrians throughout chapters 2 and 3 of Nahum seem contradictory to Jesus' command to love one's enemies (Mt 5, 43–48). Was God different back in Old Testament times? Or was Nahum just mistaken? These are difficult but important questions!

  In understanding Nahum's message, it helps to keep in mind three things. First, throughout the Bible, there is a strong theme of divine hatred for all sin. In the New Testament, though, a distinction emerges that although God hates the sin, God still loves the sinner. Nahum doesn't make that distinction.

  Second, Christians today make a distinction between God's directly causing something to happen and God's allowing something to occur—usually as a result of human limitations, people's poor choices, or natural phenomena. Again, Nahum doesn't make this distinction —for Nahum, if something happens, God is its direct cause.

  Finally, we have to keep in mind that all our attempts to understand God will fall short. God is beyond human understanding. That is why the Bible's authors, including Nahum, describe God in many different—and often seemingly contradictory—ways.

  How do you see God? as a vengeful fire (Na 1, 6) or as a refuge from distress (verse 7)? Are you comfortable imagining God in different—even opposite—ways?

 ▶ Na 2, 1—3, 3

---

†
 1, 11: *From you . . . the scoundrel planner:* addressed to Nineveh, the capital city of Sennacherib, king of Assyria, who besieged Jerusalem c. 700 B.C.
 1, 14: *You:* the king of Assyria.
 2, 2: *The hammer comes up against you:* the enemy is about to crush Nineveh.

 2, 6: *Mantelet:* a movable shelter protecting the besiegers.
 2, 8: *Mistress . . . and her handmaids:* either the queen of Nineveh with the ladies of her court, or the statute of Ishtar, Nineveh's chief goddess, with her temple prostitutes.

 2, 1: Is 52, 7; Rom 10, 15.

beating their breasts.

9 Nineveh is like a pool
   whose waters escape;
"Stop! Stop!"
   but none turns back.

10 "Plunder the silver, plunder the gold!"
   There is no end to the treasure,
   to their wealth in precious things of
      every kind!

11* Emptiness, desolation, waste;
   melting hearts and trembling knees,
Writhing in every frame,
   every face blanched!

12† Where is the lions' cave,
   the young lions' den,
Where the lion went in and out,
   and the cub, with no one to disturb them?

13 The lion snatched enough for his cubs,
   and strangled for his lionesses;
He filled his dens with prey,
   and his caves with plunder.

14 I come against you,
   says the LORD of hosts;
I will consume in smoke your chariots,
   and the sword shall devour your
      young lions;
Your preying on the land I will bring to
      an end,
   the cry of your lionesses shall be heard
      no more.

Ruin Imminent and Inevitable

3 1* Woe to the bloody city, all lies,
   full of plunder, whose looting never stops!

2 The crack of the whip, the rumbling sounds
      of wheels;
   horses a-gallop, chariots bounding,

3 Cavalry charging,
The flame of the sword, the flash of the spear,
   the many slain, the heaping corpses,
   the endless bodies to stumble upon!

4* For the many debaucheries of the harlot,
   fair and charming, a mistress of witchcraft,
Who enslaved nations with her harlotries,
   and peoples by her witchcraft:

5*† I am come against you,
   and I will strip your skirt from you;
I will show your nakedness to the nations,
   to the kingdoms your shame!

6 I will cast filth upon you,
   disgrace you and put you to shame;

7 Till everyone who sees you runs from
      you, saying,
   "Nineveh is destroyed; who can pity her?
   Where can one find any to console her?"

8*† Are you better than No-amon
   that was set among the streams,
Surrounded by waters,
   with the flood for her rampart
   and water her wall?

9 Ethiopia was her strength, and Egypt,
   and others without end;
   Put and the Libyans were her auxiliaries.

10 Yet even she went captive into exile,
   even her little ones were dashed to pieces
      at the corner of every street;
For her nobles they cast lots,
   and all her great men were put into
      chains.

11* You, too, shall drink of this till you
      faint away;
   you, too, shall seek a refuge from the foe.

12 All your fortresses are but fig trees,
   bearing early figs
That fall, when shaken,
   into the hungry mouth.

13* See, the troops are women in your midst;
   to your foes the gates of your land are
      open wide,
   fire has consumed their bars.

14† Draw water for the siege,
   strengthen your fortresses;
Go down into the mud and tread the clay,
   take hold of the brick mold!

15 There the fire shall consume you,
   the sword shall cut you down.
Multiply like the grasshoppers,
   multiply like the locusts!

16 Make your couriers more numerous than
      the stars,

17 your garrisons as many as grasshoppers,
And your scribes as locust swarms
   gathered on the rubble fences on a
      cold day!
Yet when the sun warms them,
   the grasshoppers will spread their wings
      and fly,
   and vanish, no one knows where.

N
A

2, 12: *The lion:* the king of Assyria.
3, 5f: The punishment of adulteresses.
3, 8: *No-amon:* No was the Egyptian name of the capital of Upper Egypt, called Thebes by the Greeks; its tutelary deity was Amon. This great city was destroyed by the Assyrians in 663 B.C.
3, 14: An ironic exhortation to prepare the city for a futile defense. *Go down . . . brick mold:* make bricks for the city walls.

2, 11: Jl 2, 6.	Hos 2, 12.
3, 1: Hb 2, 12.	**3, 8:** Jer 46, 25.
3, 4: Mi 1, 7; Rv 17, 1f.	**3, 11:** Mi 2, 11.
3, 5: Is 47, 3; Jer 13, 26;	**3, 13:** Jer 51, 30.

18 Alas! how your shepherds slumber, O king
     of Assyria,
   your nobles have gone to rest;
Your people are scattered upon
     the mountains,
   with none to gather them.

19 There is no healing for your hurt,
     your wound is mortal.
All who hear this news of you
     clap their hands over you;
For who has not been overwhelmed,
     steadily, by your malice?

God, why aren't you answering our cries for help? How long must we endure this trial?" Most people have wondered this at times. Why does our good, all-powerful God let suffering or injustice go on? The prophet Habakkuk struggled with these same painful and disturbing questions. His hope in God's justice is a model of faith amid doubt.

At a Glance

I. The Prophet's Complaint and Its Answer (1, 1—2, 20).

II. Canticle (chapter 3).

In-depth

Habakkuk was the first prophet who dared to ask God about God's behavior. He looked around at all the terrible things that were happening to his people and cried out: "God, where are you? Do you even care about us? Why do you allow evil people to oppress us?"

We know little about Habakkuk except that he was a prophet in the southern kingdom of Judah in the late seventh century B.C. The Chaldeans (another name for the Babylonians) and the corrupt king of Judah, Jehoiakim, were causing so much trouble that Habakkuk was ready to despair. God answered him in a most surprising way, saying that the Chaldeans—as bad as they were—were chosen as God's instrument to punish the wicked all over the earth. Habakkuk was not satisfied. He asked why God was silent while the wicked destroyed the righteous. God then spoke to him in a vision (Hb 2, 2), saying that justice would come to the wicked in its own time, but "the just man, because of his faith, shall live" (verse 4). Later, Paul would use these same words to describe the Christians (Rom 1, 17; Gal 3, 11). For Habakkuk, faith in God and hope in God's justice were the same thing.

The short Book of Habakkuk is unique among the prophetic books in the variety of its writings. Its reflections about the problem of evil in the world resemble the wisdom literature. Its dialogs with God (see 1, 2) are similar to Jeremiah's confessions (see Jer 12, 6). Chapter 3 is a canticle (song).

The prophet's concluding canticle is a prayer of confidence in God's power to save the people. We too can pray in confidence because God is just and will save us in our time of need.

Quick Facts

Period Covered
probably the reign of King Jehoiakim, 605–597 B.C. (see 2 Kgs 23, 36—24, 7)

Author
Habakkuk

Theme
The answer to evil is faith in God's justice.

Habakkuk

The Book of

Habakkuk

1, 8

1

¹ The oracle which Habakkuk the prophet received in vision.

The Prophet's Complaint and Its Answer

²† How long, O LORD? I cry for help
   but you do not listen!
I cry out to you, "Violence!"
   but you do not intervene.
³ Why do you let me see ruin;
   why must I look at misery?
Destruction and violence are before me;
   there is strife, and clamorous discord.
⁴ This is why the law is benumbed,
   and judgment is never rendered:
Because the wicked circumvent the just;
   this is why judgment comes forth perverted.

⁵*† Look over the nations and see,
   and be utterly amazed!
For a work is being done in your days
   that you would not have believed, were
   it told.

⁶ For see, I am raising up Chaldea,
   that bitter and unruly people,
That marches the breadth of the land
   to take dwellings not his own.
⁷ Terrible and dreadful is he,
   from himself derive his law and
   his majesty.
⁸† Swifter than leopards are his horses,
   and keener than wolves at evening.
His horses prance,
   his horsemen come from afar:
They fly like the eagle hastening to devour;
⁹   each comes for the rapine,
Their combined onset is that of a stormwind
   that heaps up captives like sand.
¹⁰ He scoffs at kings,
   and princes are his laughingstock;
He laughs at any fortress,
   heaps up a ramp, and conquers it.
¹¹† Then he veers like the wind and is gone—
   this culprit who makes his own strength
   his god!

1, 2–4: Traditionally, these verses have been taken as the prophet's complaint against the internal evils of Judah; the language used is that employed by Amos, Isaiah, and Jeremiah to condemn the social abuses of their day. In vv 5ff the Lord answers this complaint by indicating the Chaldean empire as his instrument for punishing his people for these sins.
1, 5: *Look over the nations and see:* after Nebuchadnezzar's defeat of Egypt in 605 B.C., there could be little doubt that it was the Chaldean ambition to dominate the entire Near East.
1, 8: *Wolves at evening:* the wolf is apparently thought of as more rabid and vicious in the evening when setting out for prey (Jer 5, 6; Zep 3, 3).

1, 11: *Veers like the wind:* the conquests of the ancient Near East were mainly raiding expeditions to collect tribute. As far as administration of conquered territories was concerned, both the Assyrians and Chaldeans were usually content to install friendly rulers and then depart. *This culprit:* though the Chaldeans were used by God as the agents of his punishment, this did not diminish their own guilt as ruthless marauders.

1, 5: Acts 13, 41.

12† Are you not from eternity, O LORD,
     my holy God, immortal?
O LORD, you have marked him for judgment,
     O Rock,† you have readied him
       for punishment!
13 Too pure are your eyes to look upon evil,
     and the sight of misery you cannot endure.
Why, then, do you gaze on the faithless
       in silence
     while the wicked man devours
     one more just than himself?
14 You have made man like the fish of the sea,
     like creeping things without a ruler.
15† He brings them all up with his hook,
     he hauls them away with his net,
He gathers them in his seine;
     and so he rejoices and exults.
16† Therefore he sacrifices to his net,
     and burns incense to his seine;
For thanks to them his portion is generous,
     and his repast sumptuous.
17 Shall he, then, keep on brandishing his
       sword
     to slay peoples without mercy?

2 1* I will stand at my guard post,
     and station myself upon the rampart,
And keep watch to see what he will say to me,
     and what answer he will give to my
       complaint.
2 Then the LORD answered me and said:
     Write down the vision
Clearly upon the tablets,
     so that one can read it readily.
3 For the vision still has its time,
     presses on to fulfillment, and will
       not disappoint;
If it delays, wait for it,
     it will surely come, it will not be late.
4*†The rash man has no integrity;
     but the just man, because of his faith,
       shall live.
Wealth, too, is treacherous:
     the proud, unstable man—
5 He who opens wide his throat like the
       nether world,
     and is insatiable as death,
Who gathers to himself all the nations,

Now!   LIVE IT!

"I want it all, and I want it now!"
     That statement could sum up the ambitions of a lot of people. It is how they define success. The key word in their goal is *now*. They don't like to wait in lines; they want instant service and immediate gratification.
     There is a temptation to apply this goal to our spiritual life. We want to grow closer to God—now! But the spiritual life does not work that way. Recall these words from the Book of Ecclesiastes: "There is an appointed time for everything , and a time for every affair under the heavens" (3, 1). We have to remind ourselves that many valuable things take time. Our growth in faith will take time. We need to be open, patient, and trusting. As God reminds Habakkuk in his vision in Hb 2, 3, "If it delays, wait for it, / it will surely come, it will not be late."
     Consider these questions:
- What are your goals for your relationship with God?
- How patient are you with your spiritual growth? How do you nurture it day by day?

▶ Hb 2, 3

H
B

---

† **1, 12—2, 1:** It is generally thought that this complaint is directed against the Chaldeans and their terrible destruction. But it may well be a continuation of Hb 1, 2–4, against the wicked Judahites who have merited God's punishment.
     1, 12: *O Rock:* an ancient title celebrating the Lord's power; cf Ps 18, 32.
     1, 15: The he of this and the following verses, to whom is attributed such extensive evil and the destruction of many peoples, may be the wicked of Judah embodied in King Jehoiakim, ally of the powerful Pharaoh Neco of Egypt; the devastation wrought by Jehoiakim and Neco together is condemned.
     1, 16: *He sacrifices to his net:* in v 15 the wicked ruler in ques-

tion is represented as catching men in a net. This verse alludes to some rite involving the sacrificial veneration of the weapons of war.
     2, 4: *The just man, because of his faith, shall live:* the faith which here enables the virtuous man to survive the impending doom is both a confident belief in God's justice, and patience in awaiting its execution. St. Paul quotes these words (Rom 1, 17; Gal 3, 11; Heb 10, 38) to confirm his teaching that man receives justification and supernatural life through faith in Christ.

2, 1: Ps 85, 9.   Heb 10, 38.
2, 4: Rom 1, 17; Gal 3, 11;

and rallies to himself all the peoples—

6 Shall not all these take up a taunt
against him.
satire and epigrams about him, to say:

Woe to him who stores up what is not his:
how long can it last!
he loads himself down with debts.

7 Shall not your creditors rise suddenly?
Shall not they who make you
tremble awake?
You shall become their spoil!

8 Because you despoiled many peoples
all the rest of the nations shall despoil you;
Because of men's blood shed,
and violence done to the land,
to the city and to all who dwell in it.

9 Woe to him who pursues evil gain for
his household,
setting his nest on high
to escape the reach of misfortune!

10 You have devised shame for your
household,
cutting off many peoples, forfeiting your
own life:

11† For the stone in the wall shall cry out,
and the beam in the woodwork shall
answer it!

12* Woe to him who builds a city by bloodshed,
and establishes a town by wickedness!

13*† Is not this from the LORD of hosts:
peoples toil for the flames,
and nations grow weary for nought!

14* But the earth shall be filled
with the knowledge of the LORD's glory
as water covers the sea.

15 Woe to you who give your neighbors
a flood of your wrath to drink,
and make them drunk, till their nakedness
is seen!

16 You are filled with shame instead of glory;
drink, you too, and stagger!

On you shall revert the cup from the LORD's
right hand,
and utter shame on your glory.

17† For the violence done to Lebanon shall
cover you,
and the destruction of the beasts shall
terrify you;
Because of men's blood shed,
and violence done to the land,
to the city and to all who dwell in it.

19 Woe to him who says to wood, "Awake!"
to dumb stone, "Arise!"
Can such a thing give oracles?
See, it is overlaid with gold and silver,
but there is no life breath in it.

18† Of what avail is the carved image,
that its maker should carve it?
Or the molten image and lying oracle,
that its very maker should trust in it,
and make dumb idols?

20* But the LORD is in his holy temple;
silence before him, all the earth!

Canticle

3 ¹† **Prayer of Habakkuk, the prophet. To a
plaintive tune.**

2† O LORD, I have heard your renown,
and feared, O LORD, your work.
In the course of the years revive it,
in the course of the years make it known;
in your wrath remember compassion!

3† God comes from Teman,
the Holy One from Mount Paran.
Covered are the heavens with his glory,
and with his praise the earth is filled.

4 His splendor spreads like the light;
rays shine forth from beside him,
where his power is concealed.

5 Before him goes pestilence,
and the plague follows in his steps.

6 He pauses to survey the earth;
his look makes the nations tremble.
The eternal mountains are shattered,

2, 11f: The palaces, built at the expense of gross injustice (vv 6–10), call down vengeance on their builders. This is typical prophetic language for the condemnation of social crimes within Israel and Judah.

2, 13: *Peoples toil for the flames:* they build only to have fire consume their work, when they build contrary to God's will.

2, 17: *The violence done to Lebanon:* the spoliation of the cedar forests of Lebanon, used in lavish building projects by the great conquerors; cf Is 14, 8; 37, 24. *The destruction of the beasts:* the killing-off of the wild animals through excessive hunting by the same conquerors; cf Bar 3, 16.

2, 18–20: Idolatrous worship is here shown to be folly by contrasting man-made idols with the majesty of the one true God.

3, 1: A later liturgical rubric. So also the end of v 19.

3, 2: *In the course of the years revive it:* renew today your wondrous deeds of the past.

3, 3–15: Cf the theophanies in Dt 33, 2f; Jgs 5, 4f; Pss 18, 8–16; 68, 8f; 77, 17–21; 97, 1–5; Na 1, 3–6, etc. Conventional language is employed to describe the appearance of the Lord, as in Ex 19, 16–19.

3, 3: *Teman:* a region in Edom. *Mount Paran:* in the territory of Edom, or the northern part of the Sinaitic peninsula. The Lord is represented as coming from Sinai, where he had appeared to Moses and given Israel the covenant and the law.

2, 12: Ez 24, 9; Na 3, 1.   2, 14: Is 11, 9.
2, 13: Jer 51, 58.   2, 20: Ps 11, 4.

the age-old hills bow low
　　along his ancient ways.

7　I see the tents of Cushan collapse;
　　trembling are the pavilions of the land
　　　of Midian.

8　Is your anger against the streams, O LORD?
　　Is your wrath against the streams,
　　　your rage against the sea,
　　That you drive the steeds
　　　of your victorious chariot?

9　Bared and ready is your bow,
　　filled with arrows is your quiver.
　　Into streams you split the earth;

10　　at sight of you the mountains tremble.
　　A torrent of rain descends;
　　　the ocean gives forth its roar.
　　The sun forgets to rise,

11*　　the moon remains in its shelter,
　　At the light of your flying arrows,
　　　at the gleam of your flashing spear.

12　In wrath you bestride the earth,
　　in fury you trample the nations.

13*†You come forth to save your people,
　　to save your anointed one.
　　You crush the heads of the wicked,
　　　you lay bare their bases at the neck.

14　You pierce with your shafts the heads of
　　　their princes
　　whose boast would be of devouring
　　　the wretched in their lair.

15　You tread the sea with your steeds
　　amid the churning of the deep waters.

16　I hear, and my body trembles;
　　at the sound, my lips quiver.
　　Decay invades my bones,
　　　my legs tremble beneath me.
　　I await the day of distress
　　　that will come upon the people who
　　　　attack us.

17　For though the fig tree blossom not
　　nor fruit be on the vines,
　　Though the yield of the olive fail
　　　and the terraces produce no nourishment,
　　Though the flocks disappear from the fold
　　　and there be no herd in the stalls,

18*　Yet will I rejoice in the LORD
　　and exult in my saving God.

19　GOD, my Lord, is my strength;
　　he makes my feet swift as those of hinds
　　　and enables me to go upon the heights.

**For the leader; with stringed
instruments.**

3, 13: *Your anointed one:* the theocratic king, the head of
God's people.

3, 11: Jos 10, 12.
3, 13: Is 51, 9ff.

3, 18f: Ps 18, 32f; Mi 7, 7.

During childhood, we usually have to clean up messes, take time-outs, or lose privileges as consequences for poor choices we have made. As we get older, we learn that our wrongdoing has more personal and painful consequences: perhaps a parent's refusal to trust us, a friend's anger, or pain after hurting someone we love. The prophet Zephaniah warned the people of Judah of the severe consequences of their sin against the LORD.

In-depth

The Book of Zephaniah gives us few clues about the prophet Zephaniah's identity. We do know that he preached in the southern kingdom of Judah during the reign of King Josiah (see 2 Chronicles, chapters 34–35), around 630 B.C. He followed First Isaiah and Micah, and came a little before Habakkuk and during the time of Nahum.

Zephaniah follows the footsteps of the classical Old Testament prophets in denouncing the wrongdoing of society. His main contribution is considering pride (1, 6; 2, 10; 3, 11) as the source of problems such as smugness (1, 12), rebellion (3, 2), and treachery (3, 11). All these attitudes toward God lead to idolatry and social sin. Although all people sin, leaders have a greater responsibility, and their sins will provoke a harsh judgment during the coming day of the LORD (1, 14). Only those who worship God humbly and who seek justice will be spared. Zephaniah calls them the remnant (3, 12–13), meaning "a little piece that is left over." They are the ones who will stay faithful to God through both good times and bad.

The book ends with a song of joy reassuring the people of Jerusalem that God still loves them and will save them in the end. We are not sure whether the song is from Zephaniah himself or is the addition of a later editor. It is as if the writer knows that when people are experiencing the negative results of sinful actions, they need to be reassured that they are still loved. God's punish-ment is to teach us, not to destroy us. Therefore, God's people should not despair but keep their trust in God.

At a Glance

I. The Day of the LORD: A Day of Doom (chapter 1).

II. The Day of the LORD: A Day of Judgment (chapter 2).

III. Reproach and Promise for Jerusalem (chapter 3).

Quick Facts

Period Covered
approximately 630 B.C.

Author
Zephaniah (and perhaps a later editor)

Theme
Judah and its neighbors will experience the consequences of their sinfulness.

The Book of *Zephaniah*

Zephaniah

1 [1] The word of the LORD which came to Zephaniah, the son of Cushi, the son of Gedaliah, the son of Amariah, the son of Hezekiah, in the days of Josiah, the son of Amon, king of Judah.

The Day of the LORD: A Day of Doom

[2] I will completely sweep away all things
  from the face of the earth, says the LORD.

[3]* I will sweep away man and beast,
  I will sweep away the birds of the sky,
  and the fishes of the sea.
I will overthrow the wicked;
  I will destroy mankind
  from the face of the earth, says the LORD.

[4] I will stretch out my hand against Judah,
  and against all the inhabitants of Jerusalem;
I will destroy from this place the last vestige
    of Baal,
  the very names of his priests,

[5]*† And those who adore the host of heaven on
    the roofs,
  with those who adore the LORD
  but swear by Milcom;

[6] And those who have fallen away from
    the LORD,
  and those who do not seek the LORD.

[7]† Silence in the presence of the Lord GOD!
  for near is the day of the LORD,
Yes, the LORD has prepared a slaughter feast,
  he has consecrated his guests.

[8]   On the day of the LORD'S slaughter feast
I will punish the princes, and the king's sons,
  and all that dress in foreign apparel.

[9]† I will punish, on that day,
  all who leap over the threshold,
Who fill the house of their master
  with violence and deceit.

[10]†   On that day, says the LORD,
A cry will be heard from the Fish Gate,
  a wail from the New Quarter,
  loud crashing from the hills.

[11] Wail, O inhabitants of the Mortar!
  for all the merchants will be destroyed,
  all who weigh out silver, done away with.

[12]† At that time I will explore Jerusalem
    with lamps;

1, 5: *The host of heaven:* the stars, the worship of which was introduced into Judah by the Assyrians. *Milcom:* the god of the Ammonites; cf 1 Kgs 11, 5.7.33; 2 Kgs 23, 13.

1, 7: *He has consecrated his guests:* God has prepared those whom he has invited to share as soldiers in the booty, or as beast and bird scavengers of carrion, on the day of slaughter. Cf Jer 46, 10; Ez 39, 17.

1, 9: *Leap over the threshold:* the reference is to a superstitious custom of the pagans, witnessed to at least in regard to the worship of Dagon (1 Sm 5, 5).

1, 10f: *The New Quarter . . . the Mortar:* sections of Jerusalem (cf 2 Kgs 22, 14).

1, 12: *The men who thicken on their lees:* those who are over-confident because, like bottles of wine in which the sediment has settled to the bottom, they have remained at peace and undisturbed for a long time.

1, 3: Hos 4, 3.   **1, 5:** Jer 8, 2; 19, 13.

I will punish the men who thicken on
         their lees,
Who say in their hearts,
   "Neither good nor evil can the LORD do."
13* Their wealth shall be given to pillage
         and their houses to devastation;
They will build houses, but shall not dwell
         in them,
      plant vineyards, but not drink their wine.
14 Near is the great day of the LORD,
         near and very swiftly coming;
Hark, the day of the LORD!
      bitter, then, the warrior's cry.
15* A day of wrath is that day,
      a day of anguish and distress,
A day of destruction and desolation,
      a day of darkness and gloom,
A day of thick black clouds,
16*   a day of trumpet blasts and battle alarm
Against fortified cities,
      against battlements on high.
17 I will hem men in
      till they walk like the blind,
      because they have sinned against the LORD;
And their blood shall be poured out
         like dust,
      and their brains like dung.
18* Neither their silver nor their gold
      shall be able to save them
      on the day of the LORD's wrath,
When in the fire of his jealousy
      all the earth shall be consumed.
For he shall make an end, yes, a sudden end,
      of all who live on the earth.

The Day of the LORD: A Day of Judgment

2 1† Gather, gather yourselves together,
         O nation without shame!
2   Before you are driven away,
         like chaff that passes on;
Before there comes upon you
      the blazing anger of the LORD;
Before there comes upon you
      the day of the LORD's anger.
3   Seek the LORD, all you humble of the earth,
      who have observed his law;
Seek justice, seek humility;
      perhaps you may be sheltered
      on the day of the LORD's anger.
4*†For Gaza shall be forsaken,

and Ashkelon shall be a waste,
   Ashdod they shall drive out at midday,
   and Ekron shall be uprooted.
5† Woe to you who dwell by the seacoast,
      to the Cretan folk!
The word of the LORD is against you,
   I will humble you, land of the Philistines,
   and leave you to perish without
         an inhabitant!
6   The coastland of the Cretans shall become
      fields for shepherds, and folds for flocks.
7   The coast shall belong
      to the remnant of the house of Judah;
      by the sea they shall pasture.
In the houses of Ashkelon at evening
      they shall couch their flocks,
For the LORD their God shall visit them,
      and bring about their restoration.

8   I have heard the revilings uttered by Moab,
      and the insults of the Ammonites,
When they reviled my people
      and made boasts against their territory.
9   Therefore, as I live, says the LORD of hosts,
      the God of Israel,
Moab shall become like Sodom,
      the land of Ammon like Gomorrah:
A field of nettles and a salt pit
      and a waste forever.
The remnant of my people shall
         plunder them,
      the survivors of my nation dispossess them.
10 Such shall be the requital of their pride,
      because they reviled and boasted against
      the people of the LORD of hosts.
11 The LORD shall inspire them with fear
      when he makes all the gods of earth to
         waste away;
Then, each from its own place,
      all the coastlands of the nations shall
         adore him.

12† You too, O Cushites,
      shall be slain by the sword of the LORD.
13 He will stretch out his hand against
         the north,
      to destroy Assyria;
He will make Nineveh a waste,
      dry as the desert.
14* In her midst shall settle in droves

---

†
   2, 1: *Nation without shame:* Judah.
   2, 4: *Gaza . . . Ashkelon . . . Ashdod . . . Ekron:* four of the five
cities of the Philistine confederation. The fifth city, Gath, is not mentioned, perhaps because it was already destroyed.
   2, 5: *Cretan folk:* the Philistines, who came from Crete; see note
on Dt 2, 23.

   2, 12: *Cushites:* the Egyptians, at this time under a Cushite or
Ethiopian dynasty.

   1, 13: Am 5, 11.   **1, 18:** Zep 3, 8; Ez 7, 19.
   1, 15: Jer 30, 7; Jl 2, 11; Am   **2, 4:** Am 1, 6ff; Zec 9, 5.
   5, 18.   **2, 14:** Is 34, 11.
   1, 16: Am 2, 2.

all the wild life of the hollows;
The screech owl and the desert owl
    shall roost in her columns;
Their call shall resound from the window,
    the raven's croak from the doorway.

15† Is this the exultant city
    that dwelt secure;
That told herself,
    "There is no other than I!"
How has she become a waste,
    a lair for wild beasts?
Whoever passes by her
    hisses, and shakes his fist!

Reproach and Promise for Jerusalem

3 ¹ Woe to the city, rebellious and polluted,
    to the tyrannical city!
2* She hears no voice,
    accepts no correction;
In the LORD she has not trusted,
    to her God she has not drawn near.
3* Her princes in her midst
    are roaring lions;
Her judges are wolves of the night
    that have had no bones to gnaw
      by morning.
4* Her prophets are insolent,
    treacherous men;
Her priests profane what is holy,
    and do violence to the law.
5 The LORD within her is just,
    who does no wrong;
Morning after morning he renders judgment
    unfailingly, at dawn.

6* I have destroyed nations,
    their battlements are laid waste;
I have made their streets deserted,
    with no one passing through;
Their cities are devastated,
    with no man dwelling in them.
7 I said, "Surely now you will fear me,
    you will accept correction";
She should not fail to see
    all I have visited upon her.
Yet all the more eagerly have they done
    all their corrupt deeds.
8* Therefore, wait for me, says the LORD,
    against the day when I arise as accuser;
For it is my decision to gather together
    the nations,
    to assemble the kingdoms,

In order to pour out upon them my wrath,
    all my blazing anger;
For in the fire of my jealousy
    shall all the earth be consumed.
9 For then I will change and purify
    the lips of the peoples,
That they all may call upon the name of
    the LORD,
    to serve him with one accord;
10 From beyond the rivers of Ethiopia
    and as far as the recesses of the North,
    they shall bring me offerings.

11   On that day
You need not be ashamed
    of all your deeds,
    your rebellious actions against me;
For then will I remove from your midst
    the proud braggarts,
And you shall no longer exalt yourself
    on my holy mountain.
12* But I will leave as a remnant in your midst
    a people humble and lowly,
Who shall take refuge in the name of
    the Lord:
13*   the remnant of Israel.
They shall do no wrong
    and speak no lies;
Nor shall there be found in their mouths
    a deceitful tongue;
They shall pasture and couch their flocks
    with none to disturb them.

14* Shout for joy, O daughter Zion!
    sing joyfully, O Israel!
Be glad and exult with all your heart,
    O daughter Jerusalem!
15 The LORD has removed the judgment
      against you,
    he has turned away your enemies;
The King of Israel, the LORD, is in your midst,
    you have no further misfortune to fear.
16* On that day, it shall be said to Jerusalem:
    Fear not, O Zion, be not discouraged!
17 The LORD, your God, is in your midst,
    a mighty savior;
He will rejoice over you with gladness,
    and renew you in his love,
He will sing joyfully because of you,
18   as one sings at festivals.
I will remove disaster from among you,
    so that none may recount your disgrace.

---

† **2, 15:** *The exultant city:* Nineveh.

3, 2: Jer 2, 30; 7, 28.   **3, 4:** Jer 23, 32.
3, 3: Ez 22, 27; Mi 3, 11.   **3, 6:** Jer 2, 15.
3, 8: Zep 1, 18.   **3, 14:** Zec 9, 9.
3, 12: Hos 14, 4.   **3, 16:** Mt 14, 27.
3, 13: Mi 4, 4.

MATERIAL POVERTY AND SPIRITUAL POVERTY!

In the Bible, God is always opposed to material poverty and misery. Over and over in the Old Testament, wealth is called a blessing and poverty a curse. The laws of the Covenant assert that poverty should not exist in Israel. Rich people are commanded to periodically forgive the debts of the poor and return land taken as payment of debt to the land's original owners (see Lv 25, 8). Selfishness leads to injustice, and injustice leads to tragedy, violence, and despair.

Zephaniah gives a spiritual connotation to the word *poor* (translated as "lowly" in Zep 3, 12). He relates poverty to humility. In this sense, to be poor is to be empty of egoism and pride, and therefore open to God's action in us. Zephaniah believes a small group of spiritually poor people, known as the remnant of Israel or the poor of God, will keep the Covenant alive.

Hispanic spirituality is deeply rooted in this concept of the poor, and the Virgin Mary is the culture's supreme example of it. To be spiritually poor is to be receptive to the Holy Spirit, to be generous with others, to trust in God's providence, and to accept suffering without losing hope.

■ How will you live out the call to be spiritually poor, free of material goods beyond what is necessary to live?

■ Ask God to give you the strength to respond to this call, which is so necessary in this world of pride, injustice, and materialism.

▶ Zep 3, 11–13

19* Yes, at that time I will deal
  with all who oppress you:
  I will save the lame,
    and assemble the outcasts;
  I will give them praise and renown
    in all the earth, when I bring about
      their restoration.

20 At that time I will bring you home,
    and at that time I will gather you;
  For I will give you renown and
    praise,
    among all the peoples of the earth,
  When I bring about your restoration
    before your very eyes, says the LORD.

3, 19: Mi 4, 6.

ZEP

I magine that you've been saving for months for a new stereo system. Just when you are about to purchase it, a good friend's family has a major house fire. Unfortunately, they were not insured—so the community is taking up a collection to help them rebuild. Now, you are faced with a decision: will you buy the new stereo or help your friend's family? The Jews at the time of the prophet Haggai faced an even more difficult decision: returning to Jerusalem after the Babylonian Exile, which would they rebuild first—their homes or God's Temple?

At a Glance

I. Exhortation to Rebuild the Temple of the LORD (chapter 1).

II. Future Glory of the New Temple (2, 1–19).

III. Pledge to Zerubbabel (2, 20–23).

In-depth

When the people of ancient Judah lost their Temple in 587 B.C. and were deported to a strange land, they experienced a crisis in faith. Had God abandoned them? Were they no longer God's people? Was God punishing them for their sins? Some of them dreamed of a time when they could return to their land and rebuild God's Temple. However, when they finally were able to return in 538 B.C., things weren't as easy as they had hoped. Suffering from poverty, droughts, and crop failures (Hg 1, 10–11), they put off rebuilding the Temple. Into this scene came the prophet Haggai. He told the people that God was still with them, and life was so difficult because they didn't seem to care that God's house was in ruins (verse 9). They had to get their priorities in order!

The people heard God's word spoken through Haggai, and immediately began working on the Temple. In their minds, they knew the new Temple would never be as beautiful as the original one (2, 3). Haggai used this opportunity to prophesy about a future Temple that would be filled with God's glory (verse 7), a time when God would again bless these people and make their offerings holy. God would establish Judah as a powerful nation, and Zerubbabel (a descendant of David) would be its anointed king.

Quick Facts

Period Covered
approximately 520 B.C.

Author
Haggai

Theme
rebuilding God's Temple

Haggai

Exhortation To Rebuild the Temple of the Lord

1 ¹*† On the first day of the sixth month in the second year of King Darius, the word of the LORD came through the prophet Haggai to the governor of Judah, Zerubbabel, son of Shealtiel, and to the high priest Joshua, son of Jehozadak: ² Thus says the LORD of hosts: This people says: "Not now has the time come to rebuild the house of the LORD." ³ (Then this word of the LORD came through Haggai, the prophet:) ⁴*† Is it time for you to dwell in your own paneled houses, while this house lies in ruins?

⁵ Now thus says the LORD of hosts:
Consider your ways!
⁶* You have sown much, but have brought
in little;
you have eaten, but have not been satisfied;
You have drunk, but have not
been exhilarated;
have clothed yourselves, but not
been warmed;
And he who earned wages
earned them for a bag with holes in it.

⁷ Thus says the LORD of hosts:
Consider your ways!
⁸ Go up into the hill country;
bring timber, and build the house
That I may take pleasure in it
and receive my glory, says the LORD.
⁹* You expected much, but it came to little;
and what you brought home, I blew away.
For what cause? says the LORD of hosts.
Because my house lies in ruins,
while each of you hurries to his own house.
¹⁰* Therefore the heavens withheld from you
their dew,
and the earth her crops.
¹¹ And I called for a drought
upon the land and upon the mountains;
Upon the grain, and upon the wine, and upon
the oil,
and upon all that the ground brings forth;
Upon men and upon beasts,
and upon all that is produced by hand.

¹²† Then Zerubbabel, son of Shealtiel, and the high priest Joshua, son of Jehozadak, and all the

---

1, 1: *The sixth month in the second year:* August/September in 520 B.C.
1, 4: The luxury of the homes of the wealthy with their paneled houses contrasts sadly with the ruined state of the Lord's house.
1, 12: *The remnant of the people:* a technical term in Haggai and Zechariah for the returned exiles.

1, 1: Ezr 4, 24; 5, 1; 6, 14.
1, 4: 2 Sm 7, 2.
1, 6: Dt 28, 38ff; Mi 6, 15.

1, 9: 2 Kgs 25, 9.
1, 10: Gn 27, 28; Am 4, 6–9.

God at the Center

The people of Haggai's time felt that they did not have enough wealth to rebuild the Temple (Hg 1, 2). God told them they were poor and unsuccessful because they had not rebuilt the Temple (verse 9). They needed to trust that if they put their priorities in the right order, God would provide.

Perhaps Haggai's people had forgotten what the true riches in life are. One of the first things many poor European immigrants settling in the United States did was to build a church (and often a school). They did this at a great sacrifice of time and materials. The church was more than a building; it was a symbol of their willingness to work together and of their common faith. It is in things like this that true wealth is found.

God, help me and my family, friends, and community to put you and the building of your Reign first in our lives. Give us the true wealth that comes from working with others for the good of all. Amen.

▶ Haggai, chapter 1

Future Glory of the New Temple

2 In the second year of King Darius, ¹ on the twenty-first day of the seventh month, the word of the LORD came through the prophet Haggai: ² Tell this to the governor of Judah, Zerubbabel, son of Shealtiel, and to the high priest Joshua, son of Jehozadak, and to the remnant of the people:

³   Who is left among you
       that saw this house in its former glory?
    And how do you see it now?
       Does it not seem like nothing in your eyes?
⁴* But now take courage, Zerubbabel, says
       the LORD,
       and take courage, Joshua, high priest, son
         of Jehozadak,
    And take courage, all you people of the land,
       says the LORD, and work!
    For I am with you, says the LORD of hosts.
⁵* This is the pact that I made with you
       when you came out of Egypt,
    And my spirit continues in your midst;
       do not fear!

⁶*†   For thus says the LORD of hosts:
    One moment yet, a little while,
       and I will shake the heavens and the earth,
       the sea and the dry land.
⁷* I will shake all the nations,
       and the treasures of all the nations will
         come in,
    And I will fill this house with glory,
       says the LORD of hosts.
⁸   Mine is the silver and mine the gold,
       says the LORD of hosts.
⁹* Greater will be the future glory of this house
       than the former, says the LORD of hosts;
    And in this place I will give peace,
       says the LORD of hosts!

Offerings of the Unclean Rejected

¹⁰ On the twenty-fourth day of the ninth month, in the second year of King Darius, the word of the LORD came to the prophet Haggai: ¹¹* Thus says the LORD of hosts: Ask the priests for a decision: ¹²† If a man carries sanctified flesh in the fold of his garment and the fold touches bread, or pottage, or wine, or oil, or any other food, do they become sanctified? "No," the priests answered. ¹³* Then

remnant of the people listened to the voice of the LORD, their God, and to the words of the prophet Haggai, because the LORD, their God, had sent him, and the people feared because of the LORD. ¹³ And the LORD'S messenger, Haggai, proclaimed to the people as the message of the LORD: I am with you, says the LORD.

¹⁴ Then the LORD stirred up the spirit of the governor of Judah, Zerubbabel, son of Shealtiel, and the spirit of the high priest Joshua, son of Jehozadak, and the spirit of all the remnant of the people, so that they came and set to work on the house of the LORD of hosts, their God, ¹⁵ on the twenty-fourth day of the sixth month.

---

† **2, 6–9:** From the later period of Ezekiel's preaching onward, the temple became, as here, one of the dominant messianic themes. *Greater will be the future glory of this house than the former:* because Christ will enter it.

2, 12ff: According to the ritual concepts of the Jews, uncleanness was more contagious than sacredness. Inasmuch as the people were unclean, their offerings became unclean (Nm 19, 22).

2, 4: Zec 8, 9.   Rv 21, 26.
2, 5: Ex 29, 45; Lv 26, 45.   2, 9: Is 2, 2ff; Zec 6, 13.
2, 6: Heb 12, 26.   2, 11: Dt 17, 8–13; Zec 7, 3.
2, 7: Gn 49, 10; Is 60,   2, 13: Nm 19, 11.13.22.
     5.9.11; Mal 3, 1;

Haggai said: If a person unclean from contact with a corpse touches any of these, do they become unclean?" The priests answered, "They become unclean." 14 Then Haggai continued:

So is this people, and so is this nation
    in my sight, says the LORD:
And so are all the works of their hands;
    and what they offer there is unclean.

Promise of Immediate Blessings

15† But now, consider from this day forward. Before there was a stone laid upon a stone in the temple of the LORD, 16* how did you fare?

When one went to a heap of grain for
    twenty measures,
    it would yield but ten;
When another went to the vat to draw
    fifty measures,
    there would be but twenty.
17 I struck you in all the works of your hands
    with blight, searing wind, and hail,
    yet you did not return to me, says the LORD.

18† [Consider from this day forward: from the twenty-fourth day of the ninth month. From the day on which the temple of the LORD was founded, consider!]

19   Indeed, the seed has not sprouted,
        nor have the vine, the fig, the
            pomegranate
        and the olive tree yet borne.
    From this day, I will bless!

Pledge to Zerubbabel

20† The message of the LORD came a second time to Haggai on the twenty-fourth day of the month: 21 Tell this to Zerubbabel, the governor of Judah:

I will shake the heavens and the earth;
22*   I will overthrow the thrones of kingdoms,
        destroy the power of the kingdoms of
            the nations.
    I will overthrow the chariots and their riders,
        and the riders with their horses
        shall go down by one another's sword.
23*†   On that day, says the LORD of hosts,
    I will take you, Zerubbabel,
        son of Shealtiel, my servant, says the LORD,
    And I will set you as a signet ring;
        for I have chosen you, says the LORD
            of hosts.

2, 15–19: This prophecy is intimately linked with chapter 1, and should be read with it.
2, 18: *The ninth month:* the ordinal ninth has been copied incorrectly from Hg 2, 10. This note clearly concerns the twenty-fourth day of the sixth month, on which the temple of the Lord was founded (Hg 1, 15).
2, 20: *The month:* probably again the sixth month, as in Hg 1, 15 and 2, 18; see note on the latter.

2, 23: This promise to Zerubbabel, reversing the punishment of his grandfather (Jer 22, 24), is a continuation of the messianic hope; cf Zec 6, 11f.

2, 16: Is 5, 10.
2, 22: Ez 38, 21; Dn 2, 44;
    Zec 14, 13; Lk 1, 52.

2, 23: Song 8, 6; Sir 49, 11;
    Is 42, 1; 44, 1f.

What do you do when life is difficult and things only seem to be getting worse? Some people dream about the future. They imagine a time when all their troubles have ended and life is happy again. If their trouble is caused by certain people, they may imagine how these people eventually pay for their wrongdoing. The Book of Zechariah looks at Israel's future in exactly these two ways.

In-depth

Like the Book of Isaiah, the Book of Zechariah was written by at least two prophets. The original Zechariah—we'll call him First Zechariah—lived around the same time as Haggai, after the exiled Israelites returned to Jerusalem from Babylon (see the timeline at the back of this Bible). Second Zechariah, who may have been one or more prophets, wrote about two hundred years later.

The optimistic message of the first prophet in chapters 1–8 of Zechariah is centered on two concerns: the rebuilding of the Temple and the end of time. First Zechariah saw that a rebuilt Temple was needed to restore the people's unity, identity, and relationship with God. Through a series of visions (see "Apocalyptic Literature," Daniel, chapters 7–10), he announced his message: under the guidance of the priest Joshua and the prince Zerubbabel (a descendant of King David), Israel would be restored. It would become a nation of justice, faith, love, mercy, and truth where the LORD would dwell. Even the Gentiles (non-Jews) would come from faraway lands to worship God.

Second Zechariah wrote later, when Israel was under Greek domination (see the timeline). He preached not through visions, but through oracles (prophetic speeches) of warning, violence, and also promise. He talked about a great battle that was about to take place between the forces of good and the forces of evil. This was the final war, which would bring an end to the present-day evil and corrupt world. But Second Zechariah also proclaimed the coming of a humble king who would bring peace to all nations. Jerusalem would be purified and would become victorious as the city where God reigns as the highest power for good.

Quick Facts

Period Covered
First Zechariah around 520 B.C., Second Zechariah sometime after 333 B.C.

Authors
the original Zechariah, and an unknown prophet or prophets writing much later

Themes
a command to rebuild the Temple, the message that God will win the final victory

Of Note
The prophecies of Zechariah are quoted in the New Testament as proof that Jesus was the promised Messiah.

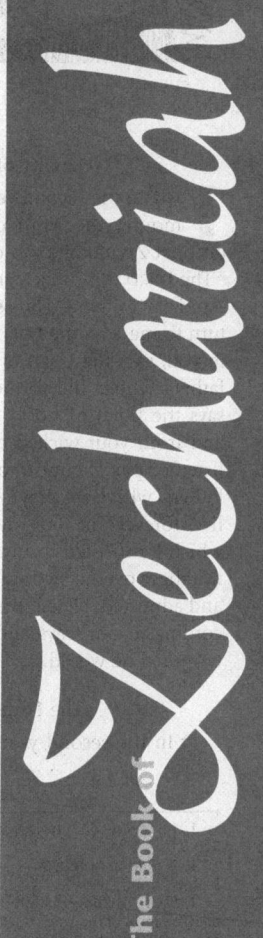

The Book of Zechariah

Zechariah

Chap. 11

Necessity of Conversion

1 ¹*† In the second year of Darius, in the eighth month, the word of the LORD came to the prophet Zechariah, son of Berechiah, son of Iddo: ² The LORD was indeed angry with your fathers . . . . ³ and say to them: Thus says the LORD of hosts: Return to me, says the LORD of hosts, and I will return to you, says the LORD of hosts. ⁴* Be not like your fathers whom the former prophets warned: Thus says the LORD of hosts: Turn from your evil ways and from your wicked deeds. But they would not listen or pay attention to me, says the LORD. ⁵ Your fathers, where are they? And the prophets, can they live forever? ⁶* But my words and my decrees, which I entrusted to my servants the prophets, did not these overtake your fathers? Then they repented and admitted: "The LORD of hosts has treated us according to our ways and deeds, just as he had determined he would."

The Four Horsemen

⁷† In the second year of Darius, on the twenty-fourth day of Shebat, the eleventh month, the word of the LORD came to the prophet Zechariah, son of Berechiah, son of Iddo, in the following way: ⁸*† I had a vision during the night. There appeared the driver of a red horse, standing among myrtle trees in a shady place, and behind him were red, sorrel, and white horses. ⁹ Then I asked, "What are these, my lord?"; and the angel who spoke with me answered me, "I will show you what these are." ¹⁰* The man who was standing among the myrtle trees spoke up and said, "These are they whom the LORD has sent to patrol the earth." ¹¹ And they answered the angel of the LORD who was standing among the myrtle trees and said, "We have patrolled the earth; see, the whole earth is tranquil and at rest!"

¹²*† Then the angel of the Lord spoke out and said, "O LORD of hosts, how long will you be without mercy for Jerusalem and the cities of Judah that have felt your anger these seventy years?" ¹³* To the angel who spoke with me, the LORD replied with comforting words.

1, 1: *The second year . . . eighth month:* October/November, 520 B.C.
1, 7: *The second year . . . eleventh month:* January/February, 519 B.C.
1, 8–11: *The driver of a red horse:* apparently distinct from the man, or angel of the Lord . . . standing among the myrtle trees, who spoke with the prophet. The four horsemen are sent by God to the four corners of the earth (Zec 2, 10), to see if the whole earth is at peace.

1, 12: *These seventy years:* see note on Jer 25, 1–14.

1, 1: Ezr 4, 24; 5, 1; 6, 14.
1, 4: Jer 25, 5; 35, 15; Mal 3, 7.
1, 6: Lv 26, 14ff; Dt 28, 15; Lam 2, 17.
1, 8: Rv 6, 4.
1, 10: Zec 6, 7.
1, 12: Zec 7, 5; Jer 25, 11; Dn 9, 2.
1, 13: Jer 29, 10.

Cultural Connections

FOUR WINDS, FOUR DIRECTIONS

To many Native American peoples, the repeated emphasis on the number four in the visions of Zechariah could have a special meaning. In these visions are four horns representing the nations that oppressed Israel (Zec 2, 1), four smiths to beat those horns down (verse 3), and four chariots sent out to the four directions of the world (6, 1–8).

Native Americans see the number four as special because it is repeated often in nature. There are four compass directions, four chambers of the human heart, four seasons, four phases of human life (child, youth, adult, and elder), and four basic elements (fire, water, rock, and air).

When Native Americans offer a formal prayer, they often do so facing the four directions, each with its own traditional color and emphasis:

- east (yellow), where the sun rises; the direction of light and wisdom
- south (white), where the warmth is; the direction of life
- west (black), where the sun sets; the direction of water and cleansing
- north (red), where the cold is; the direction of strength in hardship

Sometimes, two more directions are added: up, toward Father Sky (blue), and down, toward Mother Earth (green).

▶ Zec 2, 1–4

14* And the angel who spoke with me said to me, Proclaim: Thus says the LORD of hosts: I am deeply moved for the sake of Jerusalem and Zion, 15*† and I am exceedingly angry with the complacent nations; whereas I was but a little angry, they added to the harm. 16*† Therefore, says the LORD: I will turn to Jerusalem in mercy; my house shall be built in it, says the LORD of hosts, and a measuring line shall be stretched over Jerusalem. 17* Proclaim further: Thus says the LORD of hosts: My cities shall again overflow with prosperity; the LORD will again comfort Zion, and again choose Jerusalem.

Four Horns and Four Blacksmiths

2 1† I raised my eyes and looked: there were four horns. 2 Then I asked the angel who spoke with me what these were. He answered me,

"These are the horns that scattered Judah and Israel and Jerusalem."

3 Then the LORD showed me four blacksmiths. And I asked, "What are these coming to do?" 4 And he said, "Here are the horns that scattered Judah, so that no man raised his head any more; but these have come to terrify them: to cast down the horns of the nations that raised their horns to scatter the land of Judah."

The New Jerusalem

5* Again I raised my eyes and looked: there was a man with a measuring line in his hand. 6* "Where are you going?" I asked. "To measure Jerusalem," he answered; "to see how great is its width and how great its length."

7 Then the angel who spoke with me advanced,

---

† **1, 15:** *The complacent nations:* the neighbors of Judah, especially Edom, which enjoyed their present prosperity and security at Judah's expense.

1, 16: *Measuring line:* not for devastation, as in Is 34, 11, but for reconstruction.

2, 1–4: *Four horns:* symbolic of the hostile forces which, from the four corners of the earth, invaded and devastated the land of Judah. *Four blacksmiths:* the powers used by God to destroy these enemies of his people.

1, 14: Zec 8, 2; Jl 2, 18.   1, 17: Is 51, 3.
1, 15: Is 47, 6; Ob 10–14.   2, 5: Rv 11, 1.
1, 16: Zec 8, 3; Ezr 6, 14.   2, 6: Dt 28, 64.

and another angel came out to meet him [8]*† and said to him, "Run, tell this to that young man: People will live in Jerusalem as though in open country, because of the multitude of men and beasts in her midst. [9] But I will be for her an encircling wall of fire, says the LORD, and I will be the glory in her midst."

[10]† Up, up! Flee from the land of the north, says the LORD; for I scatter you to the four winds of heaven, says the LORD. [11] Up, escape to Zion! you who dwell in daughter Babylon. [12]* For thus said the LORD of hosts (after he had already sent me) concerning the nations that have plundered you: Whoever touches you touches the apple of my eye. [13] See, I wave my hand over them; they become plunder for their slaves. Thus you shall know that the LORD of hosts has sent me.

[14]* Sing and rejoice, O daughter Zion! See, I am coming to dwell among you, says the LORD. [15] Many nations shall join themselves to the LORD on that day, and they shall be his people, and he will dwell among you, and you shall know that the LORD of hosts has sent me to you. [16] The LORD will possess Judah as his portion in the holy land, and he will again choose Jerusalem. [17] Silence, all mankind, in the presence of the LORD! for he stirs forth from his holy dwelling.

Joshua the High Priest

3 [1]* Then he showed me Joshua the high priest standing before the angel of the LORD, while Satan stood at his right hand to accuse him. [2]* And the angel of the LORD said to Satan, "May the LORD rebuke you, Satan; may the LORD who has chosen Jerusalem rebuke you! Is not this man a brand snatched from the fire?"

[3]† Now Joshua was standing before the angel, clad in filthy garments. [4]* He spoke and said to those who were standing before him, "Take off his filthy garments, and clothe him in festal garments." [5] He also said, "Put a clean miter on his head." And they put a clean miter on his head and clothed him with the garments. Then the angel of the LORD, standing, said, "See, I have taken away your guilt."

[6] The angel of the LORD then gave Joshua this assurance: [7] "Thus says the LORD of hosts: If you walk in my ways and heed my charge, you shall judge my house and keep my courts, and I will give you access among these standing here. [8]*† Listen, O Joshua, high priest! You and your associates who sit before you are men of good omen. Yes, I will bring my servant the Shoot. [9]*† Look at the stone that I have placed before Joshua, one stone with seven facets. I will engrave its inscription, says the LORD of hosts, and I will take away the guilt of the land in one day. [10]* On that day, says the LORD of hosts, you will invite one another under your vines and fig trees."

4 [4] Then I said to the angel who spoke with me, "What are these things, my lord?" [5] And the angel who spoke with me replied, "Do you not know what these things are?" "No, my lord," I answered. [6] Then he said to me, "This is the LORD's message to Zerubbabel: Not by an army, nor by might, but by my spirit, says the LORD of hosts. [7]*† What are you, O great mountain? Before Zerubbabel you are but a plain. He shall bring out the capstone amid exclamations of 'Hail, Hail' to it."

[8] This word of the LORD then came to me: [9]* The hands of Zerubbabel have laid the foundations of this house, and his hands shall finish it; then you shall know that the LORD of hosts has sent me to you. [10]* For even they who were scornful on that day of small beginnings shall rejoice to see the select stone in the hands of Zerubbabel. These seven facets are the eyes of the LORD that range over the whole earth.

The Lampstand

[1] Then the angel who spoke with me returned and awakened me, like a man awakened from his sleep. [2]* "What do you see?" he asked me. "I see a lampstand all of gold, with a bowl at the top," I replied; "on it are seven lamps with their tubes, [3]* and beside it are two olive trees, one on the right and the other on the left." [11] I then asked him, "What are these two olive trees at each side of the lampstand?" [12] And again I asked, "What are the two olive tufts which freely pour out fresh oil through

---

2, 8: *That young man:* the angel or man with a measuring line of v 5.

2, 10: *The land of the north:* Babylonia (v 11).

3, 3: *Filthy garments:* symbolic of mourning for the dead, or of national catastrophe, and implying acknowledgment of guilt (v 5).

3, 8: *Men of good omen:* the restoration of the priesthood is a sign of the coming of the messianic times. *My servant the Shoot:* identified, in the earliest form of Zec 6, 11f as the prophet composed it, with Zerubbabel, direct descendant of King David and rebuilder of the temple; and, as such, a type of the Messiah; cf Jer 23, 5.

3, 9: *One stone with seven facets:* apparently the same as the select stone of Zec 4, 10, which seems to be a precious gem. The seven facets are explained in Zec 4, 10 as signifying the LORD's vigilance over the world. *I will engrave its inscription:* the same Hebrew verb for engrave is used in Ex 28, 9.11 in regard to the inscriptions on the twelve precious stones of the priestly breastpiece.

4, 7: *Great mountain:* figure of the obstacles confronting Zerubbabel in building the temple. *A plain:* figure of the ease with which he will overcome these obstacles.

4, 1ff.11–14: *The two anointed:* literally, "the two sons of oil," Joshua, the anointed high priest, and Zerubbabel, the anointed prince. Just as the two olive trees in this imagery supply the sacred seven-branched lampstand (Ex 25, 31–40) with oil (v 12), so these two men, in ministering to the community, stand by (serve) the Lord.

2, 8: Ez 36, 11.	33, 15.
2, 12: Dt 32, 10; Ps 17, 8.	**3, 9:** Zec 4, 10.
2, 14: Ez 37, 26.	**3, 10:** 1 Kgs 4, 25.
3, 1: 1 Chr 21, 1; Hg 1, 1.	**4, 7:** Ezr 3, 11f; Ps 118, 22.
3, 2: Rom 8, 33; Jude 9.	**4, 9:** Ezr 6, 14ff.
3, 4: Lk 15, 22.	**4, 10:** Zec 3, 9.
3, 8: Is 4, 2; 11, 1; Jer 23, 5;	**4, 2:** Rv 1, 12.

the two golden channels?" ¹³ "Do you not know what these are?" he said to me. "No, my lord," I answered him. ¹⁴† He said, "These are the two anointed who stand by the LORD of the whole earth."

The Flying Scroll

5 ¹*† Then I raised my eyes again and saw a scroll flying. ² "What do you see?" he asked me. I answered, "I see a scroll flying; it is twenty cubits long and ten cubits wide." ³ Then he said to me: "This is the curse which is to go forth over the whole earth; in accordance with it shall every thief be swept away, and in accordance with it shall every perjurer be expelled from here. ⁴* I will send it forth, says the LORD of hosts, and it shall come into the house of the thief, or into the house of him who perjures himself with my name; it shall lodge within his house, consuming it, timber and stones."

The Flying Bushel

⁵† Then the angel who spoke with me came forward and said to me, "Raise your eyes and see what this is that comes forth." ⁶ "What is it?" I asked. And he answered, "This is a bushel container coming. This is their guilt in all the land." ⁷ Then a leaden cover was lifted, and there was a woman sitting inside the bushel. ⁸ "This is Wickedness," he said; and he thrust her inside the bushel, pushing the leaden cover into the opening. ⁹ Then I raised my eyes and saw two women coming forth with a wind ruffling their wings, for they had wings like the wings of a stork. As they lifted up the bushel into the air, ¹⁰ I said to the angel who spoke with me, "Where are they taking the bushel?" ¹¹* He replied, "To build a temple for it in the land of Shinar; when the temple is ready, they will deposit it there in its place."

Four Chariots

6 ¹† Again I raised my eyes and saw four chariots coming out from between two mountains; and the mountains were of bronze. ²* The first chariot had red horses, the second chariot black horses, ³ the third chariot white horses, and the fourth chariot spotted horses—all of them strong horses. ⁴ I

6, 1

asked the angel who spoke with me, "What are these, my lord?" ⁵* The angel said to me in reply, "These are the four winds of the heavens, which are coming forth after being reviewed by the LORD of all the earth." ⁶ The chariot with the black horses was turning toward the land of the north, the red and the white horses went after them, and the spotted ones went toward the land of the south. ⁷ As these strong horses emerged, eager to set about patrolling the earth, he said, "Go, patrol the earth!" Then, as they patrolled the earth, ⁸ he called out to me and said, "See, they that go forth to the land of the north will make my spirit rest in the land of the north."

The Coronation

⁹ This word of the LORD then came to me: ¹⁰ Take from the returned captives Heldai, Tobijah, Jedaiah; and go the same day to the house of Josiah, son of Zephaniah (these had come from Babylon). ¹¹† Silver and gold you shall take, and make a crown; place it on the head of [Joshua, son of Jehozadak, the high priest] Zerubbabel. ¹²* And say to him: Thus says the LORD of hosts: Here is a man whose name is Shoot, and where he is he shall sprout, and he shall

---

5, 1–4: The enormous scroll, thirty feet by fifteen (the dimensions in length and breadth of the portico of Solomon's temple, 1 Kgs 6, 3), contains a list of maledictions on sinners, similar to that in Dt 27, 15–26. The thief and the perjurer represent all sinners, who are expelled from the holy community.

5, 5–11: The woman sealed in the bushel container is a figure of the general corruption of the people of Judah. She is removed from the Holy Land and transported to Shinar, that is, Babylonia, where a dwelling is being prepared for her; that is a symbol of the reign of Wickedness in pagan lands, contrasted with the reign of holiness in the Lord's dwelling on Mount Zion.

6, 1–8: The four chariots represent the angelic hosts sent by the Lord to the four ends of the earth. The chariot with the black horses brings the spirit, i.e., anger of the Lord against the land of the north, Babylonia.

6, 11: *Make a crown; place it on the head of [Joshua, son of Jehozadak, the high priest] Zerubbabel:* according to the current Hebrew text, Joshua the high priest is to be crowned. However, since the crown is a sign of royalty, the original text must have had the name of Zerubbabel here, not that of Joshua. In Zec 3, 8 Joshua is a different man from the one called the Shoot, and in v 12 it is upon the Shoot that the crown is to be placed.

4, 3: Rv 11, 4.	**6, 2:** Zec 1, 8; Rv 6, 4.
5, 1: Ez 2, 9.	**6, 5:** Ps 104, 4.
5, 4: Lv 19, 12.	**6, 12:** Zec 3, 8; Eph 2, 20;
5, 11: Gn 11, 2ff.	Heb 3, 3.

ZEC

build the temple of the LORD. 13* Yes, he shall build the temple of the LORD, and taking up the royal insignia, he shall sit as ruler upon his throne. The priest shall be at his right hand, and between the two of them there shall be friendly understanding. 14 The crown itself shall be a memorial offering in the temple of the LORD in favor of Heldai, Tobijah, Jedaiah, and the son of Zephaniah. 15* And they who are from afar shall come and build the temple of the LORD, and you shall know that the LORD of hosts has sent me to you. And if you heed carefully the voice of the LORD your God. . . .

True Fasting

7 1† In the fourth year of Darius the king [the word of the LORD came to Zechariah], on the fourth day of Chislev, the ninth month, 2 Bethelsarezer sent Regemmelech and his men to implore favor of the LORD 3* and to ask the priests of the house of the LORD of hosts, and the prophets, "Must I mourn and abstain in the fifth month as I have been doing these many years?" 4 Thereupon this word of the LORD of hosts came to me: 5* Say to all the people of the land and to the priests: When you fasted and mourned in the fifth and in the seventh month these seventy years, was it really for me that you fasted? 6 And when you were eating and drinking, was it not for yourselves that you ate, and for yourselves that you drank? 7* Were not these the words which the LORD spoke through the former prophets, when Jerusalem and the surrounding cities were inhabited and at peace, when the Negeb and the foothills were inhabited? 8 [This word of the LORD came to Zechariah: 9* Thus says the LORD of hosts:] Render true judgment, and show kindness and compassion toward each other. 10* Do not oppress the widow or the orphan, the alien or the poor; do not plot evil against one another in your hearts. 11* But they refused to listen; they stubbornly turned their backs and stopped their ears so as not to hear. 12* And they made their hearts diamondhard so as not to hear the teaching and the message that the LORD of hosts had sent by his spirit through the former prophets. 13* Then the LORD of hosts in his great anger said that, as they had not listened when he called, so he would not listen when they called, 14* but would scatter them with a whirlwind among all the nations that they did not know. Thus the land was left desolate after

them with no one traveling to and fro; they made the pleasant land into a desert.

In the Days of the Messiah

8 1 This word of the LORD of hosts came: Thus says the LORD of hosts:

2* I am intensely jealous for Zion,
　　stirred to jealous wrath for her.
3* 　　Thus says the LORD:
　I will return to Zion,
　　and I will dwell within Jerusalem;
　Jerusalem shall be called the faithful city,
　　and the mountain of the LORD of hosts,
　　the holy mountain.

4 Thus says the LORD of hosts: Old men and old women, each with staff in hand because of old age, shall again sit in the streets of Jerusalem. 5 The city shall be filled with boys and girls playing in her streets. 6 Thus says the LORD of hosts: Even if this should seem impossible in the eyes of the remnant of this people, shall it in those days be impossible in my eyes also, says the LORD of hosts? 7* Thus says the LORD of hosts: Lo, I will rescue my people from the land of the rising sun, and from the land of the setting sun. 8* I will bring them back to dwell within Jerusalem. They shall be my people, and I will be their God, with faithfulness and justice.

9* Thus says the LORD of hosts: Let your hands be strong, you who in these days hear these words spoken by the prophets on the day when the foundation of the house of the LORD of hosts was laid for the building of the temple. 10 For before those days there were no wages for men, or hire for beasts; those who came and went had no security from the enemy, for I set every man against his neighbor. 11 But now I will not deal with the remnant of this people as in former days, says the LORD of hosts, 12 for it is the seedtime of peace: the vine shall yield its fruit, the land shall bear its crops, and the heavens shall give their dew; all these things I will have the remnant of the people possess. 13* Just as you were a curse among the nations, O house of Judah and house of Israel, so will I save you that you may be a blessing; do not fear, but let your hands be strong.

14* Thus says the LORD of hosts: As I determined to harm you when your fathers provoked me to wrath, says the LORD of hosts, and I did not relent,

---

7, 1: *The fourth year of Darius . . . the fourth day of Chislev, the ninth month:* November, 518 B.C.

6, 13: Ps 110, 4; Heb 3, 1.
6, 15: Eph 2, 19f.
7, 3: Zec 8, 19.

7, 5: Is 58, 5; Rom 14, 6.
7, 7: Jer 17, 26.
7, 9: Is 58, 6.
7, 10: Ex 22, 21–24; Dt 24,
17; Is 1, 17; Jer 5, 28.
7, 11: Neh 9, 29; Hos 4, 16.
7, 12: Neh 9, 29; Ez 11, 19;
36, 26.
7, 13: Is 1, 15; Mi 3, 4.
7, 14: Dt 4, 27.
8, 2: Na 1, 2.

8, 3: Is 2, 2; Jer 31, 23.
8, 7: Is 11, 11; Jer 30, 18.
8, 8: Jer 4, 2.
8, 9: Ezr 5, 1; Hg 2, 18.

8, 13: Is 19, 24; Jer 42, 18;
Hg 2, 19; Zep 3, 20.

Thumbs Up!

"So will I save you that you may be a blessing; do not fear, but let your hands be strong" (Zec 8, 13). These words are a promise that God will bring the people of Israel out of hard times into good times. They are also an encouragement to us.

A young woman named Ana was in a car accident in which the driver lost control and three people were killed. Ana was severely hurt and faced months of rehabilitation. Ana, who once hoped to play college softball, now needed to learn to walk and talk again.

Ana knew that for some reason, God spared her life. She knew that it was not going to be easy and would take hard work. She was motivated by her faith and the feeling that God was there helping her. Her attitude and ambition came out every time she was asked how she was doing. She raised her hand and lifted her thumb and said faintly, "Thumbs up."

How might you say, "Thumbs up," when faced with a personal challenge?

▸ Zec 8, 9–17

---

15 so again in these days I have determined to favor Jerusalem and the house of Judah; do not fear! 16* These then are the things you should do: Speak the truth to one another; let there be honesty and peace in the judgments at your gates, 17* and let none of you plot evil against another in his heart, nor love a false oath. For all these things I hate, says the LORD.

18 This word of the LORD of hosts came to me: 19† Thus says the LORD of hosts: The fast days of the fourth, the fifth, the seventh, and the tenth months shall become occasions of joy and gladness, cheerful festivals for the house of Judah; only love faithfulness and peace. 20 Thus says the LORD of hosts: There shall yet come peoples, the inhabitants of many cities; 21* and the inhabitants of one city shall approach those of another, and say, "Come! let us go to implore the favor of the LORD"; and, "I too will go to seek the LORD." 22* Many peoples and strong nations shall come to seek the LORD of hosts in Jerusalem and to implore the favor of the LORD. 23* Thus says the LORD of hosts: In those days ten men of every nationality, speaking different tongues, shall take hold, yes, take hold of every Jew by the edge of his garment and say, "Let us go with you, for we have heard that God is with you."

Invasion by the LORD†

9
1 An oracle:
The word of the LORD is upon the land
   of Hadrach,
   and Damascus is its resting place,
For the cities of Aram are the LORD'S,
   as are all the tribes of Israel,
2* Hamath also, on its border,
   Tyre, too, and Sidon, however wise they be.
3 Tyre built herself a stronghold,
   and heaped up silver like dust,
   and gold like the mire of the streets.
4* Lo, the LORD will strip her of her
     possessions,
   and smite her power on the sea,
   and she shall be devoured by fire.
5 Ashkelon shall see it and be afraid;
   Gaza also: she shall be in great anguish;
   Ekron, too, for her hope shall come
     to nought.
The king shall disappear from Gaza,
   and Ashkelon shall not be inhabited.
6*† and the baseborn shall occupy Ashdod.
I will destroy the pride of the Philistine
7†   and take from his mouth his bloody meat,
   and his abominations from between
     his teeth:

---

† 8, 19: The fast day of the fourth month recalled the fall of Jerusalem in June, 587 B.C. (2 Kgs 25, 3f); that of the fifth month, the burning of the temple by Nebuzaradan in July of the same year (2 Kgs 25, 8f); that of the seventh month, the murder of Gedaliah in September of the same year (Jer 41, 1f); that of the tenth month, the beginning of the final siege of Jerusalem in January, 588 B.C. (2 Kgs 25, 1).

9, 1–8: Divine judgment is about to fall on the surrounding hostile peoples: Aram (Syria), including the cities of Hadrach and Damascus; Phoenicia, with its cities of Tyre and Sidon; Philistia, with its cities of Ashkelon, Gaza, Ekron, and Ashdod.

9, 6: The baseborn: people of mixed ancestry.
9, 7: Remnant: see note on Hg 1, 12. The Jebusites: the pre-Israelite inhabitants of Jerusalem, conquered by David and incorporated into Israel.

8, 14: Jer 31, 28.	8, 23: Is 66, 23.
8, 16: Zec 7, 9.	9, 2: Jer 49, 23.
8, 17: Zec 7, 10.	9, 4: Is 23, 1–18; Ez 26, 1—
8, 21: Is 2, 3.	28, 26.
8, 22: Is 60, 3.	9, 6: Am 1, 8.

He also shall become a remnant for our God,
and shall be like a family in Judah,
and Ekron shall be like the Jebusites.

8† I will encamp by my house as a guard
that none may pass to and fro;
No oppressor shall pass over them again,
for now I have regard for their affliction.

Restoration under the Messiah

9*†Rejoice heartily, O daughter Zion,
shout for joy, O daughter Jerusalem!
See, your king shall come to you;
a just savior is he,
Meek, and riding on an ass,
on a colt, the foal of an ass.

10*†He shall banish the chariot from Ephraim,
and the horse from Jerusalem;
The warrior's bow shall be banished,
and he shall proclaim peace to
the nations.
His dominion shall be from sea to sea,
and from the River to the ends of the earth.

11*†As for you, for the blood of your covenant
with me,
I will bring forth your prisoners from
the dungeon.

12*†In the return to the fortress
of the waiting prisoners,
This very day, I will return you
double for your exile.

13 For I will bend Judah as my bow,
I will arm myself with Ephraim;
I will arouse your sons, O Zion,
[against your sons, O Yavan,]
and I will use you as a warrior's sword.

14 The LORD shall appear over them,
and his arrow shall shoot forth as lightning;
The LORD God shall sound the trumpet,
and come in a storm from the south.

15 The LORD of hosts shall be a shield
over them,
they shall overcome sling stones
and trample them underfoot;
They shall drink blood like wine,
till they are filled with it like
libation bowls,
like the corners of the altar.

16* And the LORD, their God, shall save them on
that day,
his people, like a flock.
For they are the jewels in a crown
raised aloft over his land.

17 For what wealth is theirs, and what beauty!
grain that makes the youths flourish,
and new wine, the maidens!

The New Order of Things

10 1* Ask of the LORD rain in the spring
season!
It is the LORD who makes the
storm clouds,
And sends men the pouring rain;
for everyone, grassy fields.

2*†For the teraphim speak nonsense,
the diviners have false visions:
Deceitful dreams they tell,
empty comfort they offer.
This is why they wander like sheep,
wretched: they have no shepherd.

3 My wrath is kindled against the shepherds,
and I will punish the leaders;
For the LORD of hosts will visit his flock,
the house of Judah,
and make them his stately war horse.

4 From him shall come leader and chief,
from him warrior's bow and
every officer.

5 They shall all be warriors,
trampling the mire of the streets in battle;
They shall wage war because the LORD is
with them,
and shall put the horsemen to rout.

6 I will strengthen the house of Judah,
the house of Joseph I will save;
I will bring them back, because I have mercy
on them,
they shall be as though I had never cast
them off,
for I am the LORD, their God, and I will
hear them.

7 Then Ephraim shall be valiant men,
and their hearts shall be cheered as
by wine.

9, 8: *My house:* the Holy Land; cf Hos 8, 1; 9, 15; Jer 12, 7.
9, 9: The Messiah will come, not as a conquering warrior, but in lowliness and peace. Not like the last kings of Judah, who rode in chariots and on horses (Jer 17, 25; 22, 4), but like the princes of old (Gn 49, 11; Jgs 5, 10; 10, 4), the Messiah will ride on an ass. The Evangelists see a literal fulfillment of this prophecy in the Savior's triumphant entry into Jerusalem (Mt 21, 4f; Jn 12, 14f).
9, 10: *The River:* the Euphrates; see note on Ps 72, 8.
9, 11: *The blood of your covenant with me:* the covenant between the Lord and Israel sealed with sacrificial blood (Ex 24, 8).

9, 12: *The waiting prisoners:* the exiles awaiting the return to their country, where they will receive a double compensation for the double punishment they had suffered; cf Is 40, 2; 61, 7.
10, 2: *Teraphim:* household idols, used for divination; cf Gn 31, 19.34f; Jgs 17, 5; 18, 17f.20; Ez 21, 26; Hos 3, 4.

9, 9: Is 62, 11; Jer 23, 5; Mt   9, 11: Is 42, 7; Ez 24, 8.
21, 5; Jn 12, 15.   9, 12: Is 61, 7.
9, 10: Hos 1, 7.   9, 16: Is 62, 3.
   10, 1: Dt 11, 14; Jer 14, 22.

Their children shall see it and be glad,
   their hearts shall rejoice in the LORD.

8* I will whistle for them to come together,
   and when I redeem them
   they will be as numerous as before.
9 I sowed them among the nations,
   yet in distant lands they remember me;
   they shall rear their children
     and return.
10* I will bring them back from the land of Egypt,
   and gather them from Assyria.
   I will bring them into Gilead and
     into Lebanon,
   but these shall not suffice them;
11* I will cross over to Egypt
   and smite the waves of the sea
   and all the depths of the Nile shall be
     dried up.

The pride of Assyria shall be cast down,
   and the scepter of Egypt taken away.
12* I will strengthen them in the LORD,
   and they shall walk in his name, says
     the LORD.

11

1 Open your doors, O Lebanon,
   that the fire may devour
   your cedars!
2 Wail, you cypress trees,
   for the cedars are fallen,
   the mighty have been despoiled.
Wail, you oaks of Bashan,
   for the impenetrable forest is
   cut down!
3 Hark! the wailing of the shepherds,
   their glory has been ruined.
Hark! the roaring of the young lions,
   the jungle of the Jordan is laid waste.

THE PRINCIPLE OF *UMOJA*

Chapter 11 of Zechariah contains several allegorical images that represent the breakdown of the Israelite nation. In one, a shepherd's staff named Unity, or Bonds, is broken—symbolizing that the people have lost the unity that bound them together.

    Unity is vital to the success of any people. For example, African Americans rely on the Kwanzaa principle of unity, called *umoja* (see "Kwanzaa as a Way of Life," near Dt 10, 12–22). *Umoja* signifies unity in the family, community, nation, and race. This unity keeps brothers from killing brothers and sisters from killing sisters. This unity keeps families together even when the going gets tough.

    Any race or culture can and often does experience difficulty maintaining and promoting *umoja*, especially a race or culture facing injustice, racism, or prejudice. With these elements present, a race or culture can be negatively affected; positive unity can become negative as individuals, young and old, are tempted to come together in attitudes and behaviors that are selfish and destructive.

    All of us are called to live in unity. All of us are called to foster unity and to direct our efforts toward bringing our families, communities, races, and nations together.

    Keep the Kwanzaa principle of *umoja* alive! Be united in making the honor roll. Be united in respecting and protecting one another. Be united in putting an end to the problems that plague our cities and nation. Be united in being the best you can be!

▶ Zec 11, 4–17

10, 2: Jer 10, 8; Ez 34, 5.   11, 11.
10, 8: Ez 36, 37.   10, 11: Is 11, 15; Ez 30, 13.
10, 10: Is 11, 11; 49, 20; Hos   10, 12: Mi 4, 5.

Allegory of the Shepherds

4† Thus said the LORD, my God: Shepherd the flock to be slaughtered. 5* For they who buy them slay them with impunity; while those who sell them say, "Blessed be the LORD, I have become rich!" Even their own shepherds do not feel for them. 6 (Nor shall I spare the inhabitants of the earth any more, says the LORD. Yes, I will deliver each of them into the power of his neighbor, or into the power of his king; they shall crush the earth, and I will not deliver it out of their power.)

7 *So I became the shepherd of the flock to be slaughtered for the sheep merchants. I took two staffs, one of which I called "Favor," and the other, "Bonds," and I fed the flock. 8 In a single month I did away with the three shepherds. I wearied of them, and they behaved badly toward me. 9* "I will not feed you," I said. "What is to die, let it die; what is to perish, let it perish, and let those that are left devour one another's flesh."

10 Then I took my staff "Favor" and snapped it asunder, breaking off the covenant which I had made with all peoples; 11 that day it was broken off. The sheep merchants who were watching me understood that this was the word of the LORD. 12* I said to them, "If it seems good to you, give me my wages; but if not, let it go." And they counted out my wages, thirty pieces of silver. 13* But the LORD said to me, "Throw it in the treasury, the handsome price at which they valued me." So I took the thirty pieces of silver and threw them into the treasury in the house of the LORD.

14 Then I snapped asunder my other staff, "Bonds," breaking off the brotherhood between Judah and Israel. 15 The LORD said to me: This time take the gear of a foolish shepherd. 16* For I will raise up a shepherd in the land who will take no note of those that perish, nor seek the strays, nor heal the injured, nor feed what survives—he will eat the flesh of the fat ones and tear off their hoofs!

17* Woe to my foolish shepherd
who forsakes the flock!
May the sword fall upon his arm
and upon his right eye;
Let his arm wither away entirely,
and his right eye be blind forever!

?did you KNOW?

Prophecies of God's Victory

Zechariah, chapters 12–14, has several of Second Zechariah's prophecies on the final judgment, the restoration of Israel, and the Reign of God. Many of these prophecies were applied to Jesus by the first Christians.

For example: Zechariah foretells a time of mourning for "him whom they have thrust through" (Zec 12, 10); the Gospel of John applies this verse to Jesus' death on the cross (Jn 19, 37). Zechariah says the sheep will be dispersed when the shepherd is struck (Zec 13, 7); the Gospel of Matthew uses this verse to describe the disciples deserting Jesus (Mt 26, 31). And passages from Zechariah's description of the day of the LORD (Zec 14, 6–9) show up in the Book of Revelation's description of the new Jerusalem (Rv 11, 15; 21, 23)

These beautiful prophecies assured Israel's people of God's love and mercy. For Christians, they have additional meaning. They also describe Jesus Christ, whose death is our salvation and whose Resurrection is the promise of the fullness of God's Reign!

▸ Zechariah, chapters 12–14

Jerusalem God's Instrument

12 1*† An oracle: the word of the LORD concerning Israel. Thus says the LORD, who spreads out the heavens, lays the foundations of the earth, and forms the spirit of man within him: 2* See, I will make Jerusalem a bowl to stupefy all peoples round about. [Judah will be besieged, even

---

† 11, 4–17: In this allegory the prophet becomes the good shepherd of God's flock, which is being slaughtered; he is the defender of the people exploited by bad rulers. The three shepherds, rulers in general, are to destroy one another in a short time (a single month). The service of the good shepherd is contemptuously valued at thirty pieces of silver, the legal indemnity (Ex 21, 32) for a gored slave. The prophet is thus a type of Christ whose mission of salvation to his people was appraised by the Sanhedrists, the false shepherds, at the same base price (Mt 26, 14ff). In the case of the prophet as well as of Christ (Mt 27, 5), the money is thrown into the temple treasury,

i.e., paid to God, showing thereby how shamefully his divine love and care are requited.

12, 1–9: Under the image of the deliverance of Judah and Jerusalem from invading enemies, the prophet foretells the ultimate victory of God's people in the messianic age.

*
11, 5: Jer 50, 7.
11, 7: Hos 5, 6.
11, 9: Jer 15, 2.
11, 12: Ex 21, 32; Mt 26, 15.

11, 13: Mt 27, 9f.
11, 16: Ez 34, 2ff.
11, 17: Jn 10, 12.
12, 1: Is 42, 5.
12, 2: Is 51, 17; Jer 51, 7.

Jerusalem.] ³* On that day I will make Jerusalem a weighty stone for all peoples. All who attempt to lift it shall injure themselves badly, and all the nations of the earth shall be gathered against her. ⁴ On that day, says the LORD, I will strike every horse with fright, and its rider with madness. I will strike blind all the horses of the peoples, but upon the house of Judah I will open my eyes, ⁵ and the princes of Judah shall say to themselves, "The inhabitants of Jerusalem have their strength in the LORD of hosts, their God." ⁶* On that day I will make the princes of Judah like a brazier of fire in the woodland, and like a burning torch among sheaves, and they shall devour right and left all the surrounding peoples; but Jerusalem shall still abide on its own site. ⁷ The LORD shall save the tents of Judah first, that the glory of the house of David and the glory of the inhabitants of Jerusalem may not be exalted over Judah. ⁸* On that day, the LORD will shield the inhabitants of Jerusalem, and the weakling among them shall be like David on that day, and the house of David godlike, like an angel of the LORD before them. ⁹ On that day I will seek the destruction of all nations that come against Jerusalem.

Messianic Jerusalem

¹⁰*† I will pour out on the house of David and on the inhabitants of Jerusalem a spirit of grace and petition; and they shall look on him whom they have thrust through, and they shall mourn for him as one mourns for an only son, and they shall grieve over him as one grieves over a firstborn. ¹¹*† On that day the mourning in Jerusalem shall be as great as the mourning of Hadadrimmon in the plain of Megiddo. ¹² And the land shall mourn, each family apart: the family of the house of David, and their wives; the family of the house of Nathan, and their wives; ¹³ the family of the house of Levi, and their wives; the family of Shemei, and

their wives; ¹⁴ and all the rest of the families, each family apart, and the wives apart.

The End of Falsehood

13 ¹*† On that day there shall be open to the house of David and to the inhabitants of Jerusalem, a fountain to purify from sin and uncleanness. ²* On that day, says the LORD of hosts, I will destroy the names of the idols from the land, so that they shall be mentioned no more; I will also take away the prophets and the spirit of uncleanness from the land. ³* If a man still prophesies, his parents, father and mother, shall say to him, "You shall not live, because you have spoken a lie in the name of the LORD." When he prophesies, his parents, father and mother, shall thrust him through.

⁴† On that day, every prophet shall be ashamed to prophesy his vision, neither shall he assume the hairy mantle to mislead, ⁵* but he shall say, "I am no prophet, I am a tiller of the soil, for I have owned land since my youth." ⁶† And if anyone asks him, "What are these wounds on your chest?" he shall answer, "With these I was wounded in the house of my dear ones."

The Song of the Sword

⁷*† Awake, O sword, against my shepherd,
     against the man who is my associate,
     says the LORD of hosts.
   Strike the shepherd
     that the sheep may be dispersed,
     and I will turn my hand against the
       little ones.
⁸   In all the land, says the LORD,
     two thirds of them shall be cut off and perish,
     and one third shall be left.
⁹*   I will bring the one third through fire,
     and I will refine them as silver is refined,
     and I will test them as gold is tested.

---

† **12, 10:** The divine blessings (a spirit of grace and petition) will be poured out on God's people through the intervention of an unnamed sufferer (him whom they have thrust through), similar to the Servant of the Lord in Is 52, 13—53, 12. In Jn 19, 37 the Evangelist sees in this passage a prophecy fulfilled in the piercing of Christ's side.

12, 11: The mourning for the pierced victim in Jerusalem is compared to a lamentation in the plain of Megiddo apparently over a certain personage called Hadadrimmon. The reference is no longer clear. Both Hadad and Rimmon were names of the Semitic storm god, often identified with the god Baal. Some see here a reference to the annual mourning by the pagans over the death of the fertility god. According to others, Hadadrimmon is the name of a place near Megiddo, and the reference would then be to the mourning over the death of King Josiah, who was killed in battle there; cf 2 Chr 35, 22–25.

13, 1: *A fountain to purify from sin:* in contrast to the lustral water used in ritual purification; cf Nm 19, 9.13.20; 31, 23. The Lord himself is the fountain of living water (Jer 2, 13); cf Is 12, 2ff.

13, 4: *Hairy mantle:* worn by prophets as a mark of their calling; cf 2 Kgs 1, 8; Mt 3, 4.

13, 6: *Wounds on your chest:* literally "wounds between your hands." The false prophets, like the prophet of Baal (1 Kgs 13, 28), apparently inflicted wounds on themselves; to defend himself against the accusation of being a false prophet, a man will deny having inflicted wounds on himself and say instead that he received them at home, "in the house of my dear ones." In the liturgy this text is applied to Christ in an accommodated sense.

13, 7: When the shepherd is killed, the sheep are scattered. In Mt 26, 31 the Evangelist quotes from this verse, in somewhat different form, the words, I will smite the shepherd, and the sheep of the flock will be scattered, as said by Christ shortly before his arrest in the Garden of Olives and the flight of the Apostles.

12, 3: Mt 21, 44.
12, 6: Ob 18.
12, 8: Ex 32, 34.
12, 10: Jer 6, 26; Jn 19, 34; Rv 1, 7.
12, 11: 2 Chr 35, 22–25.

13, 1: Heb 9, 14; 1 Pt 1, 18f; Rv 1, 5.
13, 2: Mi 5, 12; 2 Pt 2, 1.
13, 3: Dt 18, 20; Mi 3, 5ff.
13, 5: Am 7, 14.
13, 7: Mt 26, 31.

They shall call upon my name, and I will
hear them.
I will say, "They are my people,"
and they shall say, "The LORD is my God."

The Fight for Jerusalem

14 [1]† Lo, a day shall come for the LORD
when the spoils shall be divided in your
midst. [2] And I will gather all the nations against
Jerusalem for battle: the city shall be taken, houses
plundered, women ravished; half of the city shall go
into exile, but the rest of the people shall not be removed from the city. [3] Then the LORD shall go forth
and fight against those nations, fighting as on a day
of battle. [4] That day his feet shall rest upon the
Mount of Olives, which is opposite Jerusalem to the
east. The Mount of Olives shall be cleft in two from
east to west by a very deep valley, and half of the
mountain shall move to the north and half of it to
the south. [5] And the valley of the LORD'S mountain
shall be filled up when the valley of those two
mountains reaches its edge; it shall be filled up as it
was filled up by the earthquake in the days of King
Uzziah of Judah. Then the LORD, my God, shall
come, and all his holy ones with him.

[6] On that day there shall no longer be cold or
frost. [7]* There shall be one continuous day, known
to the LORD, not day and night, for in the evening
time there shall be light.

[8]* On that day, living waters shall flow from
Jerusalem, half to the eastern sea, and half to the
western sea, and it shall be so in summer and in
winter. [9]* The LORD shall become king over the
whole earth; on that day the LORD shall be the only
one, and his name the only one.

[10]* And from Geba to Rimmon in the Negeb, all
the land shall turn into a plain; but Jerusalem shall
remain exalted in its place. From the Gate of Benjamin to the place of the First Gate, to the Corner
Gate; and from the Tower of Hananel to the king's

wine presses, [11]* they shall occupy her. Never again
shall she be doomed; Jerusalem shall abide in security.

[12] And this shall be the plague with which the
LORD shall strike all the nations that have fought
against Jerusalem: their flesh shall rot while they
stand upon their feet, and their eyes shall rot in
their sockets, and their tongues shall rot in their
mouths.

[13] On that day there shall be among them a great
tumult from the LORD: every man shall seize the
hand of his neighbor, and the hand of each shall be
raised against that of his neighbor. [14] Judah also
shall fight against Jerusalem. The riches of all the
surrounding nations shall be gathered together,
gold, silver, and garments, in great abundance.

[15] Similar to this plague shall be the plague upon
the horses, mules, camels, asses, and upon all the
beasts that are in those camps.

[16]* All who are left of all the nations that came
against Jerusalem shall come up year after year to
worship the King, the LORD of hosts, and to celebrate the feast of Booths. [17] If any of the families of
the earth does not come up to Jerusalem to worship
the King, the LORD of hosts, no rain shall fall upon
them. [18] And if the family of Egypt does not come
up, or enter, upon them shall fall the plague which
the LORD will inflict upon all the nations that do
not come up to celebrate the feast of Booths. [19] This
shall be the punishment of Egypt, and the punishment of all the nations that do not come up to celebrate the feast of Booths.

[20] On that day there shall be upon the bells of
the horses, "Holy to the LORD." The pots in the
house of the LORD shall be as the libation bowls before the altar. [21]*And every pot in Jerusalem and in
Judah shall be holy to the LORD of hosts; and all
who come to sacrifice shall take them and cook in
them. On that day there shall no longer be any merchant in the house of the LORD of hosts.

---

† **14, 1–21:** An apocalyptic description of the day of the Lord, in
which Jerusalem, the figure of God's elect, after much suffering
(siege: vv 1ff; riot: v 13; plague: vv 12, 15), is rescued by the Lord
(vv 4f) and given great blessings (vv 6–11.14.16–21).

* 13, 9: Ps 66, 10; Jer 30, 22.
14, 7: Rv 21, 23.
14, 8: Zec 13, 1; Ez 47, 1–8;
Jl 3, 18.
14, 9: Dt 6, 4; Eph 4, 5f; Rv
11, 15.
14, 10: Zec 12, 6; Neh 3, 6;
12, 38.
14, 11: Jer 31, 40; Rv 22, 3.
14, 16: Lv 23, 34.43; Neh 8,
14; Is 60, 6.9.
14, 21: Mt 21, 12; Jn 2,
13–16.

you promised me!" These three words speak volumes when they're used against us. A promise is a sacred thing, and breaking promises hurts and destroys relationships. The last book of the Old Testament, Malachi, focuses on promises with God that have been broken. At the time of its writing, priests had broken the Covenant by offering inferior sacrifices, and men had broken the Covenant by marrying foreign women and divorcing their Jewish wives. The prophet Malachi predicts that someone is coming who will purify the people, punishing the wicked and rewarding the righteous.

At a Glance

I. Israel Preferred to Edom and the Sins of the Priests (1, 1—2, 9).

II. Sins of the People (2, 10–17).

III. The Messenger of the Covenant (3, 1–24).

In-depth

The author of the Book of Malachi wrote just before the reforms of Ezra and Nehemiah, starting around 455 B.C. (see the timeline at the back of this Bible). The Temple had been rebuilt (see the Books of Haggai and Zechariah), and Temple worship had been restored, but serious violations of the covenantal law existed.

The Book of Malachi addresses two main problems. The first is the failure of Israel's priests to provide good leadership. Through a series of questions and answers, the prophet Malachi speaks harsh words against the priests of the Temple for failing to live up to their calling to honor God. They offer inferior sacrifices on the altar of the Temple, thinking that God won't notice. The prophet compares these priests with their ancestor Levi, who offered only the finest gifts to God. Levi was a good and honest man who kept God's Covenant; these priests are not.

The second problem has to do with marriage and divorce. Evidently, many men are marrying non-Jewish women and divorcing their Jewish wives. It's not clear why they are doing this, but maybe they are trying to climb the social ladder. The prophet challenges the people to be faithful to one another because their marriages are a reminder of God's Covenant with the people of Judah.

The book ends with a prophecy that forms a bridge to the New Testament and the coming of Jesus. It says that God will send a messenger, the prophet Elijah, before the day of judgment. His job will be to prepare the way for God. Those who repent will enjoy God's blessings; those who do not will be punished by God. New Testament writers saw this prophecy fulfilled by John the Baptist, who prepared the way for the coming of the Messiah, Jesus of Nazareth.

Quick Facts

Period Covered
around 455 B.C.

Author
unknown

Theme
calls for priestly reform and faithfulness in marriage

The Book of Malachi

Malachi

3, 1-5

¹ An oracle. The word of the LORD to Israel through Malachi.

Israel Preferred to Edom

²* I have loved you, says the LORD;
  but you say, "How have you loved us?"
³*†Was not Esau Jacob's brother? says the LORD:
  yet I loved Jacob, but hated Esau;
  I made his mountains a waste,
  his heritage a desert for jackals.
⁴* If Edom says, "We have been crushed
  but we will rebuild the ruins,"
  Thus says the LORD of hosts:
  They indeed may build, but I will
  tear down,
  And they shall be called the land of guilt,
  the people with whom the LORD is
  angry forever.
⁵* Your own eyes shall see it, and you will say,
  "Great is the LORD, even beyond the land
  of Israel."

Sins of the Priests and Levites

⁶ A son honors his father,
  and a servant fears his master;

If then I am a father,
  where is the honor due to me?
And if I am a master,
  where is the reverence due to me?—
So says the LORD of hosts to you, O priests,
  who despise his name.
But you ask, "How have we despised
  your name?"
⁷ By offering polluted food on my altar!
Then you ask, "How have we polluted it?"
  By saying the table of the LORD may
  be slighted!
⁸*†When you offer a blind animal for
  sacrifice,
  is this not evil?
When you offer the lame or the sick,
  is it not evil?
Present it to your governor; see if he will
  accept it,
  or welcome you, says the LORD of hosts.
⁹ So now if you implore God for mercy
  on us,
  when you have done the like
Will he welcome any of you?
  says the LORD of hosts.

1, 3ff: The thought passes from the person Esau to his descendants, Edom, and from the person Jacob to his descendants, Israel. *Loved:* preferred; *hated:* rejected; cf Gn 25, 21ff. St. Paul uses this passage as an example of God's freedom of choice in calling the Gentiles to the faith (Rom 9, 13).
1, 8: The offering in sacrifice of a lame, sick or blind animal was forbidden in the law (Lv 22, 17–25; Dt 17, 1).

1, 2: Dt 7, 6ff; Ez 16; Am 1, 11.
1, 3: Gn 25, 23; Rom 9, 13.
1, 4: Is 34, 5f; 63, 1–6; Jer
49, 7–22; Ob 21.
1, 5: Is 60.
1, 8: Lv 22, 19–25; Dt 15, 21.

10† Oh, that one among you would shut the
      temple gates
         to keep you from kindling fire on my altar
         in vain!
   I have no pleasure in you, says the LORD
      of hosts;
         neither will I accept any sacrifice from
         your hands,
11* For from the rising of the sun, even to
      its setting,
         my name is great among the nations;
   And everywhere they bring sacrifice to
      my name,
         and a pure offering;
   For great is my name among the nations,
      says the LORD of hosts.
12 But you behave profanely toward me
      by thinking
         the LORD's table and its offering may
         be polluted,
         and its food slighted.
13 You also say, "What a burden!"
         and you scorn it, says the LORD of hosts;
   You bring in what you seize, or the lame, or
      the sick;
         yes, you bring it as a sacrifice.
   Shall I accept it from your hands?
      says the LORD.
14 Cursed is the deceiver, who has in his flock
      a male,
         but under his vow sacrifices to the LORD
         a gelding;
   For a great King am I, says the LORD of hosts,
      and my name will be feared among
         the nations.

2 1 And now, O priests, this commandment is
      for you:
         If you do not listen,
2* And if you do not lay it to heart,
      to give glory to my name, says the LORD
      of hosts,
   I will send a curse upon you
      and of your blessing I will make a
         curse.
   Yes, I have already cursed it,
      because you do not lay it to heart.
3† Lo, I will deprive you of the shoulder
      and I will strew dung in your faces,
   The dung of your feasts,

Catholic Connections

A PURE OFFERING TO GOD

The prophecy of a pure offering to God,
from the sun's rising to its setting, in Mal 1,
11, is a wonderful image. It is unclear what it
meant to the writer of Malachi. However,
with the spread of Catholicism across the
globe, Catholics see this vision becoming
reality: at any moment, somewhere in the
world, people are celebrating the Mass.
   Through the celebration of the Eucharist, Catholics are linked to their sisters and
brothers in faith around the globe. At special
times, like World Youth Day, this connection
becomes a face-to-face reality. Such gatherings remind us of what a powerful experience it can be to gather together around the
LORD's table.

▸ Mal 1, 1–11

      and you will be carried off with it.
4* Then you will know that I sent you
      this commandment
         because I have a covenant with Levi,
         says the LORD of hosts.
5* My covenant with him was one of life
      and peace;
         fear I put in him, and he feared me,
         and stood in awe of my name.
6* True doctrine was in his mouth,
         and no dishonesty was found upon his
         lips;
   He walked with me in integrity
      and uprightness,
         and turned many away from evil.
7* For the lips of the priest are to
      keep knowledge,

---

† **1, 10f:** The imperfect sacrifices offered without sincerity by the
people of Judah are displeasing to the Lord. He will rather be pleased
with the offerings of the Gentile nations throughout the world (from
the rising of the sun, even to its setting), which anticipate the pure offering to be sacrificed in messianic times, the universal Sacrifice of
the Mass, as we are told by the Council of Trent.
   2, 3: *I will deprive you of the shoulder:* this part of a sacrificial

animal, allotted by the law (Dt 18, 3) to the priests, will be withheld
from them.

1, 11: Ps 113, 3; Is 59, 19.   26ff.
2, 2: Lv 26, 14–45; Dt 28,   **2, 6:** Dt 33, 8–11.
      15–68.   **2, 7:** Lv 10, 10f; Dt 17, 9f;
2, 4: Nm 25, 12f.   Jer 18, 18; Hg 2, 12.
2, 5: Nm 25, 12; Ez 37,

and instruction is to be sought from
his mouth,
because he is the messenger of the LORD
of hosts.

8 But you have turned aside from the way,
and have caused many to falter by
your instruction;
You have made void the covenant of Levi,
says the LORD of hosts.

9 I, therefore, have made you contemptible
and base before all the people,
Since you do not keep my ways,
but show partiality in your decisions.

Sins of the People

10*† Have we not all the one Father?
Has not the one God created us?
Why then do we break faith with each other,
violating the covenant of our fathers?

11* Judah has broken faith; an abominable thing
has been done in Israel and in Jerusalem.
Judah has profaned the temple which the
LORD loves,
and has married an idolatrous woman.

12 May the LORD cut off from the man who
does this
both witness and advocate out of the tents
of Jacob,
and anyone to offer sacrifice to the LORD
of hosts!

13 This also you do: the altar of the LORD
you cover
with tears, weeping and groaning,
Because he no longer regards your sacrifice
nor accepts it favorably from your hand;

14* And you say, "Why is it?"—
Because the LORD is witness
between you and the wife of your youth,
With whom you have broken faith
though she is your companion, your
betrothed wife.

15* Did he not make one being, with flesh
and spirit:
and what does that one require but
godly offspring?
You must then safeguard life that is your
own,

and not break faith with the wife of
your youth.

16 For I hate divorce,
says the LORD, the God of Israel,
And covering one's garment with injustice,
says the LORD of hosts;
You must then safeguard life that is your own,
and not break faith.

17 You have wearied the LORD with your
words,
yet you say, "How have we wearied him?"
By your saying, "Every evildoer
is good in the sight of the LORD,
And he is pleased with him";
or else, "Where is the just God?"

The Messenger of the Covenant

3 1*† Lo, I am sending my messenger
to prepare the way before me;
And suddenly there will come to the temple
the LORD whom you seek,
And the messenger of the covenant whom
you desire.
Yes, he is coming, says the LORD of hosts.

2 But who will endure the day of his coming?
And who can stand when he appears?
For he is like the refiner's fire,
or like the fuller's lye.

3* He will sit refining and purifying [silver],
and he will purify the sons of Levi,
Refining them like gold or like silver
that they may offer due sacrifice to
the LORD.

4 Then the sacrifice of Judah and Jerusalem
will please the LORD,
as in the days of old, as in years gone by.

5 I will draw near to you for judgment,
and I will be swift to bear witness
Against the sorcerers, adulterers, and
perjurers,
those who defraud the hired man of
his wages,
Against those who defraud widows
and orphans;
those who turn aside the stranger,
and those who do not fear me, says the
LORD of hosts.

---

† **2, 10–16:** Intermarriage of Israelites with foreigners was forbidden according to Dt 7, 1–4. After the exile this law was strictly enforced (Ezr 9–10). Foreign marriages are here portrayed as a violation of the covenant (v 10), which made the sacrifices offered by the offenders unacceptable to God (v 13). They were all the more reprehensible when accompanied by the divorce of Israelite wives (vv 14ff). This gradual return to the primitive ideal of the indissolubility of marriage was fully realized in New Testament times through the teaching of Christ; cf Mt 19, 3–12.

3, 1: *My messenger . . . before me:* in v 23 this messenger is

called Elijah. In Mt 11, 10 these words are quoted by Christ as referring to John the Baptizer, who prepared the way for the coming of the Savior; cf Mt 3, 1ff.11f; 17, 11ff; Mk 1, 2–8; Lk 3, 2–18; Jn 1, 31–34.

2, 10: Jb 31, 15; Mt 23, 9;
  Eph 4, 6.
2, 11: Ezr 9, 2; Neh 13, 25.
2, 14: Gn 31, 49f; Prv 5,
  18ff.

2, 15: Gn 2, 7.22ff.
3, 1: Is 40, 3; Mt 11, 10; Mk
  1, 2; Lk 1, 17; 7, 27.
3, 3: Is 1, 25; Zec 13, 9.

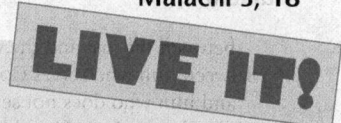

Prepare the Way

Malachi 3, 1–2 talks about the sending of a messenger to prepare for God's coming. That arrival will mark a day of purification, when anything that isn't of value will be burnt away. What does that have to do with you? Take a few moments to reflect on the following dialog:

Prophet. Prepare the way of the LORD!
Listener. Who, me?
Prophet. Yes, of course, you!
Listener. But that's John the Baptist's job.
Prophet. *Was.* That *was* John the Baptist's job. Now, it belongs to you, as a follower of Christ.
Listener. So, what do I do? Where do I start?
Prophet. Listen to Jesus. Nurture your relationship with God through prayer and the sacraments. Live a happy, holy, and healthy life in order to be a light for others. Share what you believe with others so that they can also find their way. By the way, you are not alone.
Listener. You mean there are a lot of us preparing the way?
Prophet. That's right.
Listener. Well, then, I'm on my way—or rather, we are on *God's* way.

▶ Mal 3, 1–7

⁶† Surely I, the LORD, do not change,
    nor do you cease to be sons of Jacob.
⁷* Since the days of your fathers you have
        turned aside
    from my statutes, and have not kept them.
  Return to me, and I will return to you,
    says the LORD of hosts.
  Yet you say, "How must we return?"
⁸*   Dare a man rob God? Yet you are
        robbing me!
  And you say, "How do we rob you?"
    In tithes and in offerings!
⁹ You are indeed accursed,
    for you, the whole nation, rob me.
¹⁰*†Bring the whole tithe
    into the storehouse,
  That there may be food in my house,
    and try me in this, says the LORD of
        hosts:
  Shall I not open for you the floodgates
        of heaven,
    to pour down blessing upon you
        without measure?
¹¹ For your sake I will forbid the locust
    to destroy your crops;
  And the vine in the field will not be barren,
    says the LORD of hosts.
¹² Then all nations will call you blessed,

  for you will be a delightful land,
    says the LORD of hosts.

¹³ You have defied me in word, says the LORD,
    yet you ask, "What have we spoken
        against you?"
¹⁴* You have said, "It is vain to serve God,
    and what do we profit by keeping
        his command,
  And going about in penitential dress
    in awe of the LORD of hosts?
¹⁵ Rather must we call the proud blessed;
    for indeed evildoers prosper,
    and even tempt God with impunity."
¹⁶*†Then they who fear the LORD spoke with
        one another,
    and the LORD listened attentively;
  And a record book was written before him
    of those who fear the LORD and trust in
        his name.
¹⁷* And they shall be mine, says the LORD
        of hosts,
    my own special possession, on the day I
        take action.
  And I will have compassion on them,
    as a man has compassion on his son who
        serves him.
¹⁸ Then you will again see the distinction

---

† **3, 6f:** God is faithful to his promises. He will not abandon the Israelites, who are still his people.
3, 10: *Storehouse:* the temple treasury.
3, 16: *Record book:* see note on Ex 32, 32.

* 3, 7: Zec 1, 3f; Acts 7, 51.
3, 8: Neh 13, 10–14.
3, 10: 2 Chr 31, 10f; Neh 10,
    38; 13, 12; Prv 3, 9f.
3, 14: Jb 21, 14f; 22, 17; Ps

73, 11f.
3, 16: Rv 20, 12.
3, 17: Ex 19, 5; Dt 7, 6; Pss
    103, 13; 135, 4.

MAL

between the just and the wicked;
Between him who serves God,
  and him who does not serve him.
19 * For lo, the day is coming, blazing like
    an oven,
  when all the proud and all evildoers will
    be stubble,
And the day that is coming will set them
    on fire,
  leaving them neither root nor branch,
  says the LORD of hosts.
20 But for you who fear my name, there will arise
    the sun of justice with its healing rays;
And you will gambol like calves out of
    the stall
21 *   and tread down the wicked;
They will become ashes under the soles of
    your feet,
  on the day I take action, says the LORD
    of hosts.

22 * Remember the law of Moses my servant,
    which I enjoined upon him on Horeb,
  The statutes and ordinances
    for all Israel.
23 † Lo, I will send you
    Elijah, the prophet,
  Before the day of the LORD comes,

the great and terrible day,
24 * †To turn the hearts of the fathers to
    their children,
  and the hearts of the children to
    their fathers,
Lest I come and strike
    the land with doom.

Lo, I will send you
  Elijah, the prophet,
Before the day of the LORD comes,
  the great and terrible day.

Lo,
I am
sending
my

messenger...

3, 1–2

WHO *day*
will
endure
the
of his

coming?

---

† **3, 23:** *Elijah:* described in 2 Kgs 2, 11 as taken heavenward in a fiery chariot. Here his return to earth seems to be foretold. Jewish tradition has interpreted this literally; Christ declares it to be fulfilled in the coming of John the Baptizer (Mt 17, 10–13).

3, 24: The words in fine print, a repetition of v 23a-d, have been added by the scribes so that the collection of the twelve minor prophets will not end with the threat of doom.

3, 19: Is 13, 9; 34, 8; Jl 3, 3;
  Zep 1, 18; 2 Pt 3, 7.
3, 21: Lk 1, 78f.
3, 22: Ex 20; Lv 26;

Dt 4, 1.5f.
3, 24: Mt 11, 14; 17, 10; Mk
  9, 10ff; Lk 1, 17.

THE New Testament

Preface to the New American Bible: First Edition of The New Testament

The New Testament translation has been approached with essentially the same fidelity to the thought and individual style of the biblical writers as was applied in the Old Testament. In some cases, however, the problem of marked literary peculiarities had to be met. What by any Western standard are the limited vocabularies and stylistic infelicities of the evangelists cannot be retained in the exact form in which they appear in the originals without displeasing the modern ear. A compromise is here attempted whereby some measure of the poverty of the evangelists' expression is kept and placed at the service of their message in its richness. Similarly, the syntactical shortcomings of Paul, his frequent lapses into anacoluthon, and the like, are rendered as they occur in his epistles rather than "smoothed out." Only thus, the translators suppose, will contemporary readers have some adequate idea of the kind of writing they have before them. When the prose of the original flows more smoothly, as in Luke, Acts, and Hebrews, it is reflected in the translation.

The Gospel according to John comprises a special case. Absolute fidelity to his technique of reiterated phrasing would result in an assault on the English ear, yet the softening of the vocal effect by substitution of other words and phrases would destroy the effectiveness of his poetry. Again, resort is had to compromise. This is not an easy matter when the very repetitiousness which the author deliberately employed is at the same time regarded by those who read and speak English to be a serious stylistic defect. Only those familiar with the Greek originals can know what a relentless tattoo Johannine poetry can produce. A similar observation could be made regarding other New Testament books as well. Matthew and Mark are given to identical phrasing twice and three times in the same sentence. As for the rhetorical overgrowth and mixed figures of speech in the letters of Peter, James, and Jude, the translator must resist a powerful compulsion to tidy them up if only to render these letters intelligibly.

Without seeking refuge in complaints against the inspired authors, however, the translators of *The New American Bible* here state that what they have attempted is a translation rather than a paraphrase. To be sure, all translation can be called paraphrase by definition. Any striving for complete fidelity will shortly end in infidelity. Nonetheless, it must be pointed out that the temptation to improve overladen sentences by the consolidation or elimination of multiplied adjectives, or the simplification of clumsy hendiadys, has been resisted here. For the most part, rhetorically ineffective words and phrases are retained in this translation in some form, even when it is clear that a Western contemporary writer would never have employed them.

The spelling of proper names in *The New American Bible* follows the customary forms found in most English Bibles since the Authorized Version.

Despite the arbitrary character of the divisions into numbered verses (a scheme which in its present form is only four centuries old), the translators have made a constant effort to keep within an English verse the whole verbal content of the Greek verse. At times the effort has not seemed worth the result since it often does violence to the original author's flow of expression, which preceded it by so many centuries. If this translation had been prepared for purposes of public reading only, the editors would have forgone the effort at an early stage. But since they never departed from the threefold objective of preparing a translation suitable for liturgical use, private reading, and the purposes of students, the last-named consideration prevailed. Those familiar with Greek should be able to discover how the translators of the New Testament have rendered any given original verse of scripture, if their exegetical or theological tasks require them to know this. At the same time, the fact should be set down here that the editors did not commit themselves in the synoptic gospels to rendering repeated words or phrases identically.

This leads to a final consideration: the Greek text used for the New Testament. Here, punctuation and verse division are at least as important as variant readings. In general, Nestle-Aland's *Novum Testamentum Graece* (25th edition, 1963) was followed. Additional help was derived from *The Greek New Testament*

(Aland, Black, Metzger, Wikgren), produced for the use of translators by the United Bible Societies in 1966. However, the editors did not confine themselves strictly to these texts; at times, they inclined toward readings otherwise attested. The omission of alternative translations does not mean that the translators think them without merit, but only that in every case they had to make a choice.

Poorly attested readings do not occur in this translation. Doubtful readings of some merit appear within brackets; public readers may include such words or phrases, or omit them entirely without any damage to sense. Parentheses are used, as ordinarily in English, as a punctuation device. Material they enclose is in no sense textually doubtful. It is simply thought to be parenthetical in the intention of the biblical author, even though there is no such punctuation mark in Greek. The difficulty in dealing with quotation marks is well known. Since they do not appear in any form in the original text, wherever they occur here they constitute an editorial decision.

Preface to the Revised Edition

The New Testament of *The New American Bible*, a fresh translation from the Greek text, was first published in complete form in 1970, together with the Old Testament translation that had been completed the previous year. Portions of the New Testament had appeared earlier, in somewhat different form, in the provisional Mass lectionary of 1964 and in the *Lectionary for Mass* of 1970.

Since 1970 many different printings of the New Testament have been issued by a number of publishers, both separately and in complete bibles, and the text has become widely known both in the United States and in other English-speaking countries. Most American Catholics have been influenced by it because of its widespread use in the liturgy, and it has received a generally favorable reception from many other Christians as well. It has taken its place among the standard contemporary translations of the New Testament, respected for its fidelity to the original and its attempt to render this into current American English.

Although the scriptures themselves are timeless, translations and explanations of them quickly become dated in an era marked by rapid cultural change to a degree never previously experienced. The explosion of biblical studies that has taken place in our century and the changing nature of our language itself require periodic adjustment both in translations and in the accompanying explanatory materials. The experience of actual use of the New Testament of *The New American Bible*, especially in oral proclamation, has provided a basis for further improvement. Accordingly, it was decided in 1978 to proceed with a thorough revision of the New Testament to reflect advances in scholarship and to satisfy needs identified through pastoral experience.

For this purpose a steering committee was formed to plan, organize, and direct the work of revision, to engage collaborators, and to serve as an editoral board to coordinate the work of the various revisers and to determine the final form of the text and the explanatory materials. Guidelines were drawn up and collaborators selected in 1978 and early 1979, and November of 1980 was established as the deadline for manuscripts. From December 1980 through September 1986 the editoral board met a total of fifty times and carefully reviewed and revised all the material in order to ensure accuracy and consistency of approach. The editors also worked together with the bishops' ad hoc committee that was appointed by the National Conference of Catholic Bishops in 1982 to oversee the revision.

The threefold purpose of the translation that was expressed in the preface to the first edition has been maintained in the revision: to provide a version suitable for liturgical proclamation, for private reading, and for purposes of study. Special attention has been given to the first of these purposes, since oral proclamation demands special qualities in a translation, and experience had provided insights and suggestions that could lead to improvement in this area. Efforts have also been made, however, to facilitate devotional reading by providing suitable notes and introductory materials, and to assist the student by achieving greater accuracy and consistency in the translation and supplying more abundant information in the introductions and notes.

The primary aim of the revision is to produce a version as accurate and faithful to the meaning of the Greek original as is possible for a translation. The editors have consequently moved in the direction of a formal-equivalence approach to translation, matching the vocabulary, structure, and even word order of the original as closely as possible in the receptor language. Some other contemporary biblical versions have adopted, in varying degrees, a dynamic-equivalence approach, which attempts to respect the individuality of each language by expressing the meaning of the original in a linguistic structure suited to English, even though this may be very different from the corresponding Greek structure. While this approach often results in fresh and brilliant renderings, it has the disadvantages of more or less radically abandoning traditional biblical and liturgical terminology and phraseology, of expanding the text to include what more properly belongs in notes, commentaries, or preaching, and of tending toward paraphrase. A more formal approach seems better suited to the specific purposes intended for this translation.

At the same time, the editors have wished to produce a version in English that reflects contemporary American usage and is readily understandable to ordinary educated people, but one that will be recognized as dignified speech, on the level of formal rather than colloquial usage. These aims are not in fact contradictory, for there are different levels of language in current use: the language of formal situations as not that of colloquial conversation, though people understand both and may pass from one to the other without adverting to the transition. The liturgy is a formal situation that requires a level of discourse more dignified, formal, and hieratic than the world of business, sport, or informal communication. People readily understand this more formal level even though they may not often use it; our passive vocabulary is much larger than our active vocabulary. Hence this revision, while avoiding archaisms, does not shrink from traditional biblical terms that are easily understood even though not in common use in everyday speech. The level of language consciously aimed at is one appropriate for liturgical proclamation; this may also permit the translation to serve the purposes of devotional reading and serious study.

A particular effort has been made to insure consistency of vocabulary. Always to translate a given Greek word by the same English equivalent would lead to ludicrous results and to infidelity to the meaning of the text. But in passages where a particular Greek term retains the same meaning, it has been rendered in the same way insofar as this has been feasible; this is particularly significant in the case of terms that have a specific theological meaning. The synoptic gospels have been carefully translated so as to reveal both the similarities and the differences of the Greek.

An especially sensitive problem today is the question of discrimination in language. In recent years there has been much discussion about allegations of anti-Jewish expressions in the New Testament and of language that discriminates against various minorities. Above all, however, the question of discrimination against women affects the largest number of people and arouses the greatest degree of interest and concern. At present there is little agreement about these problems or about the best way to deal with them. In all these areas the present translation attempts to display a sensitivity appropriate to the present state of the questions under discussion, which are not yet resolved and in regard to which it is impossible to please everyone, since intelligent and sincere participants in the debate hold mutually contradictory views.

The primary concern in this revision is fidelity to what the text says. When the meaning of the Greek is inclusive of both sexes, the translation seeks to reproduce such inclusivity insofar as this is possible in normal English usage, without resort to inelegant circumlocutions or neologisms that would offend against the dignity of the language. Although the generic sense of man is traditional in English, many today reject it; its use has therefore generally been avoided, though it is retained in cases where no fully satisfactory equivalent could be found. English does not possess a gender-inclusive third personal pronoun in the singular, and this translation continues to use the masculine resumptive pronoun after *everyone* or *anyone*, in the traditional way, where this cannot be avoided without infidelity to the meaning.

The translation of the Greek word *adelphos*, particularly in the plural form *adelphoi*, poses an especially delicate problem. While the term literally means *brothers* or other male blood relatives, even in profane Greek the plural can designate two persons, one of either sex, who were born of the same parents. It was adopted by the early Christians to designate, in a figurative sense, the members of the Christian community, who were conscious of a new familial relationship to one another by reason of their adoption as children of God. They are consequently addressed as *adelphoi*. This has traditionally been rendered into English by *brothers* or, more archaically, *brethren*. There has never been any doubt that this designation includes *all* the members of the Christian community, both male and female. Given the absence in English of a corresponding term that explicitly includes both sexes, this translation retains the usage of *brothers*, with the inclusive meaning that has been traditionally attached to it in this biblical context.

Since the New Testament is the product of a particular time and culture, the views expressed in it and the language in which they are expressed reflect a particular cultural conditioning, which sometimes makes them quite different from contemporary ideas and concerns. Discriminatory language should be eliminated insofar as possible whenever it is unfaithful to the meaning of the New Testament, but the text should not be altered in order to adjust it to contemporary concerns. This translation does not introduce any changes, expansions, additions to, or subtractions from the text of scripture. It further retains the traditional biblical ways of speaking about God and about Christ, including the use of masculine nouns and pronouns.

The Greek text followed in this translation is that of the third edition of *The Greek New Testament*, edited by Kurt Aland, Matthew Black, Carlo Martini, Bruce Metzger, and Allen Wikgren, and published by the United Bible Societies in 1975. The same text, with a different critical apparatus and variations in punctuation and typography, was published as the twenty-sixth edition of the Nestle-Aland *Novum Testamentum Graece* in 1979 by the Deutsche Bibelstiftung, Stuttgart. This edition has also been consulted. When variant readings occur, the translation, with few exceptions, follows the reading that was placed in the text of these Greek editions, though the occurrence of the principal variants is pointed out in the notes.

The editors of the Greek text placed square brackets around words or portions of words of which the authenticity is questionable because the evidence of textual witnesses is inconclusive. The same has been done in the translation insofar as it is possible to reproduce this convention in English. It should be possible to read the text either with or without the disputed words, but in English it is not always feasible to provide this alternative, and in some passages the bracketed words must be included to make sense. As in the first edition, parentheses do not indicate textual uncertainty, but are simply a punctuation device to indicate a passage that in the editors' judgment appears parenthetical to the thought of the author.

Citations from the Old Testament are placed within quotation marks; longer citations are set off as block quotations in a separate indented paragraph. The sources of such citations, as well as those of many more or less subtle allusions to the Old Testament, are identified in the biblical cross-reference section at the bottom of each page. Insofar as possible, the translation of such Old Testament citations agrees with that of *The New American Bible* Old Testament whenever the underlying Greek agrees with the Hebrew (or, in some cases, the Aramaic or Greek) text from which the Old Testament translation was made. But citations in the New Testament frequently follow the Septuagint or some other version, or were made from memory, hence, in many cases the translation in the New Testament passage will not agree with what appears in the Old Testament. Some of these cases are explained in the notes.

It is a further aim of the revised edition to supply explanatory materials more abundantly than in the first edition. In most cases the introductions and notes have been entirely rewritten and expanded, and the cross-references checked and revised. It is intended that these materials should reflect the present state of sound biblical scholarship and should be presented in such a form that they can be assimilated by the ordinary intelligent reader without specialized biblical training. While they have been written with the ordinary educated Christian in mind, not all technical vocabulary can be entirely dispensed with in approaching the Bible, any more than in any other field. It is the hope of the editors that these materials, even if they sometimes demand an effort, will help the reader to a fuller and more intelligent understanding of the New Testament and a fruitful appropriation of its meaning for personal spiritual growth.

The New American Bible is a Roman Catholic translation. This revision, however, like the first edition, has been accomplished with the collaboration of scholars from other Christian churches, both among the revisers and on the editorial board, in response to the encouragement of Vatican Council II (*Dei Verbum*, 22).

The editorial board expresses gratitude to all who have collaborated in the revision: to all the revisers, consultants, and bishops who contributed to it, to reviewers of the first edition, and to those who voluntarily submitted suggestions. May this translation fulfill its threefold purpose, "so that the word of the Lord may speed forward and be glorified" (2 Thes 3, 1).

September 30, 1986   *The Feast of St. Jerome*

Introduction to the

Gospels

and the Acts of the Apostles

If you have ever written a research paper for a class project, you know how important it is to have good sources. You want sources that have the most insight into your chosen topic, sources that provide inspiration. The books of the New Testament are those sources for the Christian faith. The Gospels of Matthew, Mark, Luke, and John lay the foundation for understanding the message and the mission of Jesus, the center of the Christian faith. The Acts of the Apostles continues with an inspiring account of how the earliest Christians continued Jesus' mission despite conflicts and persecution. The Good News in these books invites a response from us: to accept Jesus as the promised Messiah, the Son of God, the savior of the world.

In-depth

THE BOOKS OF THE NEW TESTAMENT CONTINUE the Old Testament's revelation of God's saving work in the world. Their focus is on Jesus Christ—the hoped-for Messiah, the savior. Jesus Christ is revealed as God's Son, being both fully human and fully divine. In Jesus, God's promises to Abraham, Moses, and David were fulfilled. In Jesus, a New Covenant is available to all people, not just the Jews. In Jesus lie the forgiveness of sins and a new life of love and freedom for anyone who believes.

The New Testament tells of this Good News through four different types of books: (1) four similar but unique views of Jesus' life and teaching in books called the Gospels, (2) stories on how the Apostles spread the Good News of Jesus in the Acts of the Apostles, (3) letters from early Christian leaders to the first Christians and Christian communities, and (4) apocalyptic writings in the Book of Revelation. This introduction is on the four Gospels and the Acts of the Apostles; another introduction will give further background on the letters and Revelation.

The Gospels of Matthew, Mark, Luke, and John tell the story of Jesus from four different perspectives. They are not historical biographies or documentaries like you might read today. They grew out of the teaching and preaching about Jesus in different early Christian communities. They reflect these early Christian communities' beliefs about Jesus, but they do not tell us exactly what

Jesus said and did in his life on earth. Inspired by God, the authors of the Gospels arranged the stories to bring out a particular understanding of Jesus that had great importance in their Christian communities. Because of God's inspiration, the Gospels are without error in teaching us the truth about Christ's message, mission, and identity.

The Gospels of Matthew, Mark, and Luke are similar in their style and share much of the same content. They are called synoptic (from a Greek word that means "seeing the whole together") Gospels. It is likely that Mark was written first and the authors of Matthew and Luke used Mark as a source in creating their own Gospels (Lk 1, 1 mentions other accounts of Jesus). The Gospel of John is quite different from the synoptic Gospels. It was written later than them and is more symbolic in its expression of who Jesus is.

The Acts of the Apostles is a continuation of Luke's Gospel (see Acts 1, 1). However, it is not itself a Gospel. It picks up where the Gospel of Luke ends, telling the story of the origins of Christianity after the death and Resurrection of Jesus, covering the period from about A.D. 30 to 64. Although Acts gives us a good deal of information about early church leaders like Peter and Paul, its purpose is not to tell us their biographies. Rather, it gives us an interpretation of the events of the beginnings of Christianity that emphasizes God's saving purpose. The Book of Acts explains how Christianity, which began as an offshoot of the Jewish faith, gradually spread beyond Judaism into the Gentile, or non-Jewish, world.

The original Greek word for *gospel* is *euangelion*, which means "big or important news" (sometimes translated as "good news"). The authors of the Gospels wanted to share with others the important news of Jesus Christ. When you read these powerful stories of faith, let God use them to inspire and strengthen your faith in Jesus.

Other Background

- The Gospel of Matthew emphasizes Jesus as the promised Messiah of the Jewish people. Jesus is portrayed as the greatest prophet, teaching the New Law and calling people to be faithful to God.

- The Gospel of Mark was probably the first of the four Gospels to be written. It portrays Jesus as an active healer and miracle worker who accepts loneliness and suffering as the cost of obedience to God's will.

- The Gospel of Luke is a clear, orderly presentation of Jesus' mission to all people, Jews and Gentiles. This Gospel emphasizes Jesus' mercy, compassion, and concern for poor people.

- The Gospel of John was the last Gospel written and seeks to show Jesus as the fully divine Son of God. This Gospel portrays Jesus as noble and powerful, fully in control of his own destiny.

- The Acts of the Apostles was written by the author of the Gospel of Luke. It shows God at work in the growth of the early Christian communities, particularly through the efforts of Peter and Paul.

Matthew

Does your family have a traditional way of celebrating a holiday? Family traditions are usually handed down from one generation to the next. They give meaning to our special celebrations and help us know where we came from. The Gospel of Matthew presents Jesus as the promised Messiah and highlights Jesus' Jewish origins. The author wanted Jewish-Christian readers to know that believing in Jesus as the Son of God was not a break with their tradition but the fulfillment of it.

In-depth

The author of Matthew was probably a Christian convert from Judaism in a community of Jewish Christians. This community was feeling the sting of being rejected by other Jews. In defense of the community's belief in Jesus, the Gospel of Matthew links Jesus to important Jewish traditions and gives them new meanings. The Gospel begins with a list of Jesus' Jewish ancestors, connecting Jesus to Abraham, the father of Judaism, and David, Israel's greatest king. Then it makes frequent references to Old Testament laws, prophecies, and events that Jesus fulfills or completes.

The author of Matthew also wanted to show how Jesus broke with certain Jewish beliefs—no doubt to help explain why his community of Jewish Christians was rejected by other Jews. So in the Sermon on the Mount (5, 1—7, 29), the Gospel has Jesus giving new interpretation to Jewish laws. And Jesus is frequently in conflict with the scribes and Pharisees over things like healing on the Sabbath (12, 9–14). Such incidents probably reflect the experience of the author's community with Jewish leaders as much as Jesus' own conflicts.

Gradually, the Gospel of Matthew paints a picture of Jesus as the promised son of David who would reign as king forever. He is the Messiah, the fulfillment of all that the Jewish people have been waiting for, the one who will bring their liberation and salvation. This good news should be proclaimed to Jews and non-Jews alike. And so the Gospel ends with the risen Jesus telling his disciples, "Go, therefore, and make disciples of all nations" (28, 19).

At a Glance

I. **The Infancy Narrative** (1, 1—2, 23).

II. **The Proclamation of the Kingdom** (3, 1—7, 29).

III. **Ministry and Mission in Galilee** (8, 1—11, 1).

IV. **Opposition from Israel** (11, 2—13, 53).

V. **Jesus, the Kingdom, and the Church** (13, 54—18, 35).

VI. **Ministry in Judea and Jerusalem** (19, 1—25, 46).

VII. **The Passion and Resurrection** (26, 1—28, 20).

Quick Facts

Author
unknown; traditionally associated with the Apostle Matthew

Date Written
approximately A.D. 85

Audience
Christian Jews

Image of Jesus
the greatest prophet, who brings the New Law

Matthew

I: The Infancy Narrative†

The Genealogy of Jesus

1 ¹* The book of the genealogy of Jesus Christ, the son of David, the son of Abraham.†

²* Abraham became the father of Isaac, Isaac the father of Jacob, Jacob the father of Judah and his brothers.* ³* Judah became the father of Perez and Zerah, whose mother was Tamar. Perez became the father of Hezron, Hezron the father of Ram, ⁴* Ram the father of Amminadab. Amminadab became the father of Nahshon, Nahshon the father of Salmon, ⁵* Salmon the father of Boaz, whose mother was Rahab. Boaz became the father of Obed, whose mother was Ruth. Obed became the father of Jesse, ⁶* Jesse the father of David the king.

David became the father of Solomon, whose mother had been the wife of Uriah. ⁷*† Solomon became the father of Rehoboam, Rehoboam the father of Abijah, Abijah the father of Asaph. ⁸ Asaph became the father of Jehoshaphat, Jehoshaphat the father of Joram, Joram the father of Uzziah. ⁹ Uzziah became the father of Jotham, Jotham the father of Ahaz, Ahaz the father of Hezekiah. ¹⁰† Hezekiah became the father of Manasseh, Manasseh the father of Amos, Amos the father of Josiah.

1, 1—2, 23: The infancy narrative forms the prologue of the gospel. Consisting of a genealogy and five stories, it presents the coming of Jesus as the climax of Israel's history, and the events of his conception, birth, and early childhood as the fulfillment of Old Testament prophecy. The genealogy is probably traditional material that Matthew edited. In its first two sections (1, 2–11) it was drawn from Ru 4, 18–22 and 1 Chr 1–3. Except for Jechoniah, Shealtiel, and Zerubbabel, none of the names in the third section (1, 12–16) is found in any Old Testament genealogy. While the genealogy shows the continuity of God's providential plan from Abraham on, discontinuity is also present. The women Tamar (1, 3), Rahab and Ruth (1, 5), and the wife of Uriah, Bathsheba (1, 6), bore their sons through unions that were in varying degrees strange and unexpected. These "irregularities" culminate in the supreme "irregularity" of the Messiah's birth of a virgin mother; the age of fulfillment is inaugurated by a creative act of God.

Drawing upon both biblical tradition and Jewish stories, Matthew portrays Jesus as reliving the Exodus experience of Israel and the persecutions of Moses. His rejection by his own people and his passion are foreshadowed by the troubled reaction of "all Jerusalem" to the question of the magi who are seeking the "newborn king of the Jews" (2, 2–3), and by Herod's attempt to have him killed. The magi who do him homage prefigure the Gentiles who will accept the preaching of the gospel. The infancy narrative proclaims who Jesus is, the savior of his people from their sins (1, 21), Emmanuel in whom "God is with us" (1, 23), and the Son of God (2, 15).

1, 1: *The Son of David, the son of Abraham:* two links of the genealogical chain are singled out. Although the later, David is placed first in order to emphasize that Jesus is the royal Messiah. The mention of Abraham may be due not only to his being the father of the nation Israel but to Matthew's interest in the universal scope of Jesus' mission; cf Gn 22, 18, ". . . in your descendants all the nations of the earth shall find blessing."

1, 7: The successor of Abijah was not Asaph but Asa (see 1 Chr 3, 10). Some textual witnesses read the latter name; however, *Asaph* is better attested. Matthew may have deliberately introduced the psalmist Asaph into the genealogy (and in v 10 the prophet Amos) in order to show that Jesus is the fulfillment not only of the promises made to David (see 2 Sm 7) but of all the Old Testament.

1, 10: *Amos:* some textual witnesses read *Amon*, who was the actual successor of Manasseh (see 1 Chr 3, 14).

1, 1: Gn 5, 1; 1 Chr 17, 11; Gn 22, 18.
1, 2–17: Lk 3, 23–38.
1, 2: Gn 21, 3; 25, 26; 29, 35; 1 Chr 2, 1.
1, 3: Gn 38, 29–30; Ru 4, 18; 1 Chr 2, 4–9.
1, 4: Ru 4, 19–20; 1 Chr 2, 10–11.
1, 5: Ru 4, 21–22; 1 Chr 2, 11–12.
1, 6: 2 Sm 12, 24; 1 Chr 2, 15; 3, 5.
1, 7–11: 2 Kgs 25, 1–21; 1 Chr 3, 10–15.

11 Josiah became the father of Jechoniah and his brothers at the time of the Babylonian exile.

12* After the Babylonian exile, Jechoniah became the father of Shealtiel, Shealtiel the father of Zerubbabel, 13 Zerubbabel the father of Abiud. Abiud became the father of Eliakim, Eliakim the father of Azor, 14 Azor the father of Zadok. Zadok became the father of Achim, Achim the father of Eliud, 15 Eliud the father of Eleazar. Eleazar became the father of Matthan, Matthan the father of Jacob, 16 Jacob the father of Joseph, the husband of Mary. Of her was born Jesus who is called the Messiah.

17† Thus the total number of generations from Abraham to David is fourteen generations; from David to the Babylonian exile, fourteen generations; from the Babylonian exile to the Messiah, fourteen generations.

The Birth of Jesus

18† Now this is how the birth of Jesus Christ came about. When his mother Mary was betrothed to Joseph,† but before they lived together, she was found with child through the holy Spirit. 19† Joseph her husband, since he was a righteous man, yet unwilling to expose her to shame, decided to divorce her quietly. 20*† Such was his intention when, behold, the angel of the Lord appeared to him in a dream and said, "Joseph, son of David, do not be afraid to take Mary your wife into your home. For it is through the holy Spirit that this child has been conceived in her. 21† She will bear a son and you are to name him Jesus, because he will save his people from their sins." 22 All this took place to fulfill what the Lord had said through the prophet:

did you KNOW?

Jesus' Family Tree

In the first two chapters of Matthew, the author begins to reveal the unique focus of the Gospel. He starts by tracing Jesus' family tree, making his case that Jesus was the Messiah who would restore the Covenant promised to Abraham, the father of the Jewish people. He also traces Jesus' ancestry back to David to show that Jesus is the fulfillment of the promises made to David (2 Samuel, chapter 7).

Things get even more interesting with a closer look at all the people mentioned in the list. There is a wide assortment of groups and social classes: patriarchs and slaves, kings and peasants, men and women, Jews and non-Jews. Matthew is planting the seed that Jesus has come for the salvation of all people.

▶ Mt 1, 1–17

23*† "Behold, the virgin shall be with child and
          bear a son,
    and they shall name him Emmanuel,"

which means "God is with us." 24 When Joseph awoke, he did as the angel of the Lord had commanded him and took his wife into his home. 25*† He had no relations with her until she bore a son, and he named him Jesus.

---

†

1, 17: Matthew is concerned with fourteen generations, probably because fourteen is the numerical value of the Hebrew letters forming the name of David. In the second section of the genealogy (6b–11), three kings of Judah, Ahaziah, Joash, and Amaziah, have been omitted (see 1 Chr 3, 11–12), so that there are fourteen generations in that section. Yet the third (12–16) apparently has only thirteen. Since Matthew here emphasizes that each section has fourteen, it is unlikely that the thirteen of the last was due to his oversight. Some scholars suggest that *Jesus who is called the Messiah* (16b) doubles the final member of the chain: *Jesus,* born within the family of David, opens up the new age as *Messiah,* so that in fact there are fourteen generations in the third section. This is perhaps too subtle, and the hypothesis of a slip not on the part of Matthew but of a later scribe seems likely. On *Messiah,* see the note on Lk 2, 11.

1, 18–25: This first story of the infancy narrative spells out what is summarily indicated in v 16. The virginal conception of Jesus is the work of the Spirit of God. Joseph's decision to divorce Mary is overcome by the heavenly command that he take her into his home and accept the child as his own. The natural genealogical line is broken but the promises to David are fulfilled; through Joseph's adoption the child belongs to the family of David. Matthew sees the virginal conception as the fulfillment of Is 7, 14.

1, 18: *Betrothed to Joseph:* betrothal was the first part of the marriage, constituting a man and a woman as husband and wife. Subsequent infidelity was considered adultery. The betrothal was followed some months later by the husband's taking his wife into his home, at which time normal married life began.

1, 19: *A righteous man:* as a devout observer of the Mosaic law, Joseph wished to break his union with someone whom he suspected of gross violation of the law. It is commonly said that the law required him to do so, but the texts usually given in support of that view, e.g., Dt 22, 20–21, do not clearly pertain to Joseph's situation. *Unwilling to expose her to shame:* the penalty for proved adultery was death by stoning; cf Dt 22, 21–23.

1, 20: *The angel of the Lord:* in the Old Testament a common designation of God in communication with a human being. *In a dream:* see 2, 13.19.22. These dreams may be meant to recall the dreams of Joseph, son of Jacob the patriarch (Gn 37, 5–11.19). A closer parallel is the dream of Amram, father of Moses, related by Josephus (*Antiquities* 2, 9, 3 §§212, 215–16).

1, 21: *Jesus:* in first-century Judaism the Hebrew name Joshua (Greek *Iēsous*) meaning "Yahweh helps" was interpreted as "Yahweh saves."

1, 23: *God is with us:* God's promise of deliverance to Judah in Isaiah's time is seen by Matthew as fulfilled in the birth of Jesus, in whom God is with his people. The name Emmanuel is alluded to at the end of the gospel where the risen Jesus assures his disciples of his continued presence, ". . . I am with you always, until the end of the age" (28, 20).

1, 25: *Until she bore a son:* the evangelist is concerned to emphasize that Joseph was not responsible for the conception of Jesus. The Greek word translated "until" does not imply normal marital conduct after Jesus' birth, nor does it exclude it.

1, 12–16: 1 Chr 3, 16–19.   **1, 23:** Is 7, 14 LXX.
1, 20: Mt 2, 13.19; Lk 1, 35.   **1, 25:** Lk 2, 7.

? did you **KNOW?**

Jesus, Emmanuel

In announcing Jesus' birth, the Gospel of Matthew quotes Is 7, 14, in which Isaiah tells King Ahaz that his young wife will conceive a son and they will name him Emmanuel, which means "God is with us" (see Mt 1, 23). This is the perfect description for Jesus, the Son of God, who fully shares our humanity. The Gospel ends with the same promise, when the risen Jesus tells his disciples, "I am with you always" (28, 20).

▸ Mt 1, 23

The Visit of the Magi

2 [1]† When Jesus was born in Bethlehem of Judea, in the days of King Herod,† behold, magi from the east arrived in Jerusalem, [2]*† saying, "Where is the newborn king of the Jews? We saw his star at its rising and have come to do him homage." [3] When King Herod heard this, he was greatly troubled, and all Jerusalem with him. [4]† Assembling all the chief priests and the scribes of the people, he inquired of them where the Messiah was to be born. [5]* They said to him, "In Bethlehem of Judea, for thus it has been written through the prophet:

6   'And you, Bethlehem, land of Judah,
          are by no means least among the rulers
              of Judah;
        since from you shall come a ruler,
          who is to shepherd my people Israel.' "

[7] Then Herod called the magi secretly and ascertained from them the time of the star's appearance.

Cultural Connections

JESUS BROUGHT THE GOOD NEWS OF SALVATION TO PEOPLE OF ALL RACES!

The Wise Men from another culture, who came to offer Jesus gifts for a royal messiah, symbolize that Jesus came as the savior of all races and cultures. Matthew 2, 1–12 is the biblical basis for the religious feast day of Epiphany, which officially is 6 January but is celebrated on the first Sunday after the New Year.

In some Latin American traditions, children receive gifts on Epiphany, in remembrance of the gifts the Wise Men offered to Jesus. The evening before, at parties celebrated in homes and offices, a special bread is shared that has a figure of the baby Jesus baked inside of it. Whoever finds the figure of the baby Jesus in a piece of bread has to sponsor a party to celebrate Jesus' presentation in the Temple (Lk 2, 22–24). The church celebrates this feast on 2 February.

■ How do you accept and celebrate people of different cultures?
■ Think of spiritual gifts that you have received from other people. Express your gratitude to God for those gifts.

▸ Mt 2, 1–12

---

† **2, 1–12:** The future rejection of Jesus by Israel and his acceptance by the Gentiles are retrojected into this scene of the narrative.
2, 1: *In the days of King Herod:* Herod reigned from 37 to 4 B.C. *Magi:* originally a designation of the Persian priestly caste, the word became used of those who were regarded as having more than human knowledge. Matthew's magi are astrologers.
2, 2: *We saw his star:* it was a common ancient belief that a new star appeared at the time of a ruler's birth. Matthew also draws upon the Old Testament story of Balaam, who had prophesied

that "A star shall advance from Jacob" (Nm 24, 17), though there the star means not an astral phenomenon but the king himself.
2, 4: Herod's consultation with the chief priests and scribes has some similarity to a Jewish legend about the child Moses in which the "sacred scribes" warn Pharaoh about the imminent birth of one who will deliver Israel from Egypt and the king makes plans to destroy him.

*
2, 2: Nm 24, 17.   2, 5–6: Mi 5, 1; 2 Sm 5, 2.

8 He sent them to Bethlehem and said, "Go and search diligently for the child. When you have found him, bring me word, that I too may go and do him homage." 9 After their audience with the king they set out. And behold, the star that they had seen at its rising preceded them, until it came and stopped over the place where the child was. 10 They were overjoyed at seeing the star, 11*† and on entering the house they saw the child with Mary his mother. They prostrated themselves and did him homage. Then they opened their treasures and offered him gifts of gold, frankincense, and myrrh. 12 And having been warned in a dream not to return to Herod, they departed for their country by another way.

The Flight to Egypt

13† When they had departed, behold, the angel of the Lord appeared to Joseph in a dream and said, "Rise, take the child and his mother, flee to Egypt,†

and stay there until I tell you. Herod is going to search for the child to destroy him." 14 Joseph rose and took the child and his mother by night and departed for Egypt. 15*† He stayed there until the death of Herod, that what the Lord had said through the prophet might be fulfilled, "Out of Egypt I called my son."

The Massacre of the Infants

16 When Herod realized that he had been deceived by the magi, he became furious. He ordered the massacre of all the boys in Bethlehem and its vicinity two years old and under, in accordance with the time he had ascertained from the magi. 17 Then was fulfilled what had been said through Jeremiah the prophet:

18*† "A voice was heard in Ramah,
     sobbing and loud lamentation;
   Rachel weeping for her children,

Jesus' Family Lives as Immigrants!

Following an angel's order and facing the massacre of all boys under two years old, Joseph takes Mary and Jesus to Egypt to protect them from Herod's threats. They become immigrants to avoid persecution.

Every year, millions of people in the world become immigrants, fleeing their countries because of hunger, poverty, or persecution. Often, they find themselves unwelcomed strangers, not able to communicate in the language of their new land and even persecuted by its inhabitants. But Christians should have a special compassion for immigrants because Jesus told us to love everyone, especially those who suffer.

- Imagine Jesus, Mary, and Joseph exiled in this country. How would you treat them?
- What is your attitude toward refugees and immigrants in our country?
- Ask God to bless legislators with the love and wisdom to welcome immigrants, and to give your generation a courageous heart to seek justice and peace in the world.

▸ Mt 2, 13

2, 11: Cf Ps 72, 10.15; Is 60, 6. These Old Testament texts led to the interpretation of the magi as kings.

2, 13–23: Biblical and nonbiblical traditions about Moses are here applied to the child Jesus, though the dominant Old Testament type is not Moses but Israel (see v 15).

2, 13: *Flee to Egypt:* Egypt was a traditional place of refuge for those fleeing from danger in Palestine (see 1 Kgs 11, 40; Jer 26, 21), but the main reason why the child is to be taken to Egypt is that he may relive the Exodus experience of Israel.

2, 15: The fulfillment citation is taken from Hos 11, 1. Israel, God's son, was called out of Egypt at the time of the Exodus; Jesus, the Son of God, will similarly be called out of that land in a new exodus. The father-son relationship between God and the nation is set in a higher key. Here

the son is not a group adopted as "son of God," but the child who, as conceived by the holy Spirit, stands in unique relation to God. He is son of David and of Abraham, of Mary and of Joseph, but, above all, of God.

2, 18: Jer 31, 15 portrays Rachel, wife of the patriarch Jacob, weeping for her children taken into exile at the time of the Assyrian invasion of the northern kingdom (722–21 B.C.). Bethlehem was traditionally identified with Ephrath, the place near which Rachel was buried (see Gn 35, 19; 48, 7), and the mourning of Rachel is here applied to her lost children of a later age. *Ramah:* about six miles north of Jerusalem. The lamentation of Rachel is so great as to be heard at a far distance.

2, 11: Ps 72, 10–11.15; Is 60, 6.	2, 15: Hos 11, 1.
	2, 18: Jer 31, 15.

The Slaughter of the Innocents

The event described in Mt 2, 16–18 is often called the Slaughter of the Innocents. In many circumstances in history, innocent people, including infants and young children, have been massacred in the name of war or convenience (see "Rachel Weeps," Jer 31, 15–17).

Today, abortion is one of those circumstances. To many people, it seems to be a simple solution to the inconvenience of an unwanted pregnancy. But what of the innocent lives that are destroyed? With abortion, "they were no more" (Mt 2, 18). Our church teaching is clear: All human life is sacred, and abortion is wrong. How might we as individuals or communities support pregnant women to ensure they do not choose abortion?

▶ Mt 2, 16–18

and she would not be consoled,
since they were no more."

The Return from Egypt

¹⁹ When Herod had died, behold, the angel of the Lord appeared in a dream to Joseph in Egypt ²⁰*† and said, "Rise, take the child and his mother and go to the land of Israel, for those who sought the child's life are dead." ²¹ He rose, took the child and his mother, and went to the land of Israel. ²²† But when he heard that Archelaus was ruling over Judea in place of his father Herod, he was afraid to go back there. And because he had been warned in a dream, he departed for the region of Galilee. ²³*† He went and dwelt in a town called Nazareth, so that what had been spoken through the prophets might be fulfilled, "He shall be called a Nazorean."

II: The Proclamation of the Kingdom

The Preaching of John the Baptist

3 ¹*† In those days John the Baptist appeared, preaching in the desert of Judea† ²*† [and] saying, "Repent, for the kingdom of heaven is at hand!" ³*† It was of him that the prophet Isaiah had spoken when he said:

"A voice of one crying out in the desert,
'Prepare the way of the Lord,
make straight his paths.'"

⁴*† John wore clothing made of camel's hair and had a leather belt around his waist. His food was locusts and wild honey. ⁵ At that time Jerusalem, all Judea, and the whole region around the Jordan

---

2, 20: *For those who sought the child's life are dead:* Moses, who had fled from Egypt because the Pharaoh sought to kill him (see Ex 2, 15), was told to return there, "for all the men who sought your life are dead" (Ex 4, 19).

2, 22: With the agreement of the emperor Augustus, Archelaus received half of his father's kingdom, including Judea, after Herod's death. He had the title "ethnarch" (i.e., "ruler of a nation") and reigned from 4 B.C. to A.D. 6.

2, 23: *Nazareth . . . He shall be called a Nazorean:* the tradition of Jesus' residence in Nazareth was firmly established, and Matthew sees it as being in accordance with the foreannounced plan of God. The town of Nazareth is not mentioned in the Old Testament, and no such prophecy can be found there. The vague expression "through the prophets" may be due to Matthew's seeing a connection between Nazareth and certain texts in which there are words with a remote similarity to the name of that town. Some such Old Testament texts are Is 11, 1 where the Davidic king of the future is called "a bud" (*nēṣer*) that shall blossom from the roots of Jesse, and Jgs 13, 5.7 where Samson, the future deliverer of Israel from the Philistines, is called one who shall be consecrated (a *nāzîr*) to God.

3, 1–12: Here Matthew takes up the order of Jesus' ministry found in the gospel of Mark, beginning with the preparatory preaching of John the Baptist.

3, 1: Unlike Luke, Matthew says nothing of the Baptist's origins and does not make him a relative of Jesus. *The desert of Judea:* the

barren region west of the Dead Sea extending up the Jordan valley.

3, 2: *Repent:* the Baptist calls for a change of heart and conduct, a turning of one's life from rebellion to obedience toward God. *The kingdom of heaven is at hand:* "heaven" (literally, "the heavens") is a substitute for the name "God" that was avoided by devout Jews of the time out of reverence. The expression "the kingdom of heaven" occurs only in the gospel of Matthew. It means the effective rule of God over his people. In its fullness it includes not only human obedience to God's word, but the triumph of God over physical evils, supremely over death. In the expectation found in Jewish apocalyptic, the kingdom was to be ushered in by a judgment in which sinners would be condemned and perish, an expectation shared by the Baptist. This was modified in Christian understanding where the kingdom was seen as being established in stages, culminating with the parousia of Jesus.

3, 3: See the note on Jn 1, 23.

3, 4: The clothing of John recalls the austere dress of the prophet Elijah (2 Kgs 1, 8). The expectation of the return of Elijah from heaven to prepare Israel for the final manifestation of God's kingdom was widespread, and according to Matthew this expectation was fulfilled in the Baptist's ministry (11, 14; 17, 11–13).

2, 20: Ex 4, 19.
2, 23: Mt 13, 54; Mk 1, 9; Lk 2, 39; 4, 34; Jn 19, 19.
3, 1–12: Mk 1, 2–8; Lk 3, 2–17.

3, 2: Mt 4, 17; 10, 7.
3, 3: Is 40, 3.
3, 4: Mt 11, 7–8; 2 Kgs 1, 8; Zec 13, 4.

did you KNOW?

Pharisees, Sadducees, and Scribes

In Jesus' day, several groups of Jews held positions of status or leadership. The *Pharisees* were devoted laymen who believed that salvation was achieved by rigorously following the Jewish Law. People looked up to them for guidance about how they should live as good Jews. The *Sadducees* were associated with the Temple and the ruling class. They did not believe in life after death. They did believe that wealth was a sign of being blessed by God. The *scribes* were skilled at reading and writing, and performed those services for the majority of the population, who were unable to read and write for themselves. Scribes probably were involved in writing some of the Old Testament books.

The negative reaction of John the Baptist to the Pharisees and Sadducees is typical in Matthew. But in general, Pharisees, Sadducees, and scribes were respected leaders during Jesus' time. The persecution later experienced by the community in which the author of Matthew lived probably affected his portrayal of them. (See "Jewish Sects," near the end of 2 Maccabees, for more information on these groups.)

▶ Mt 3, 7

were going out to him ⁶† and were being baptized by him in the Jordan River as they acknowledged their sins.

⁷*† When he saw many of the Pharisees and Sadducees coming to his baptism, he said to them, "You brood of vipers! Who warned you to flee from the coming wrath? ⁸ Produce good fruit as evidence of your repentance. ⁹*And do not presume to say to yourselves, 'We have Abraham as our father.' For I tell you, God can raise up children to Abraham from these stones. ¹⁰ Even now the ax lies at the root of the trees. Therefore every tree that does not bear good fruit will be cut down and thrown into the fire. ¹¹*† I am baptizing you with water, for repentance, but the one who is coming after me is mightier than I. I am not worthy to carry his sandals. He will baptize you with the holy Spirit and fire. ¹²*† His winnowing fan is in his hand. He will clear his threshing floor and gather his wheat into his barn, but the chaff he will burn with unquenchable fire."

The Baptism of Jesus

¹³*† Then Jesus came from Galilee to John at the Jordan to be baptized by him. ¹⁴† John tried to prevent him, saying, "I need to be baptized by you, and yet you are coming to me?" ¹⁵ Jesus said to him in reply, "Allow it now, for thus it is fitting for us to fulfill all righteousness." Then he allowed him. ¹⁶*† After Jesus was baptized, he came up from the water and behold, the heavens were opened [for him], and he saw the Spirit of God descending like a dove [and] coming upon him. ¹⁷*† And a voice came from the heavens, saying, "This is my beloved Son, with whom I am well pleased."

The *winnowing fan* was a forklike shovel with which the threshed wheat was thrown into the air. The kernels fell to the ground; the light chaff, blown off by the wind, was gathered and burned up.

3, 13–17: The baptism of Jesus is the occasion on which he is equipped for his ministry by the holy Spirit and proclaimed to be the Son of God.

3, 14–15: This dialogue, peculiar to Matthew, reveals John's awareness of Jesus' superiority to him as the mightier one who is coming and who will baptize with the holy Spirit (11). His reluctance to admit Jesus among the sinners whom he is baptizing with water is overcome by Jesus' response. *To fulfill all righteousness:* in this gospel *to fulfill* usually refers to fulfillment of prophecy, and *righteousness* to moral conduct in conformity with God's will. Here, however, as in 5, 6 and 6, 33, *righteousness* seems to mean the saving activity of God. *To fulfill all righteousness* is to submit to the plan of God for the salvation of the human race. This involves Jesus' identification with sinners; hence the propriety of his accepting John's baptism.

3, 16: The Spirit . . . coming upon him: cf Is 42, 1.

3, 17: This is my beloved Son: the Marcan address to Jesus (Mk 1, 11) is changed into a proclamation. The Father's voice speaks in terms that reflect Is 42, 1; Ps 2, 7; and Gn 22, 2.

3, 6: Ritual washing was practiced by various groups in Palestine between 150 B.C. and A.D. 250. John's baptism may have been related to the purificatory washings of the Essenes at Qumran.

3, 7: *Pharisees and Sadducees:* the former were marked by devotion to the law, written and oral, and the scribes, experts in the law, belonged predominantly to this group. The Sadducees were the priestly aristocratic party, centered in Jerusalem. They accepted as scripture only the first five books of the Old Testament, followed only the letter of the law, rejected the oral legal traditions, and were opposed to teachings not found in the Pentateuch, such as the resurrection of the dead. Matthew links both of these groups together as enemies of Jesus (16, 1.6.11.12; cf Mk 8, 11–13.15). The threatening words that follow are addressed to them rather than to "the crowds" as in Lk 3, 7. *The coming wrath:* the judgment that will bring about the destruction of unrepentant sinners.

3, 11: *Baptize you with the holy Spirit and fire:* the water baptism of John will be followed by an "immersion" of the repentant in the cleansing power of the Spirit of God, and of the unrepentant in the destroying power of God's judgment. However, some see *the holy Spirit* and *fire* as synonymous, and the effect of this "baptism" as either purification or destruction. See the note on Lk 3, 16.

3, 12: The discrimination between the good and the bad is compared to the procedure by which a farmer separates wheat and chaff.

3, 7: Mt 12, 34; 23, 33; Is 59, 5.   Jer 15, 7.
3, 9: Jn 8, 33.39; Rom 9,   3, 13–17: Mk 1, 9–11; Lk 3,
7–8; Gal 4, 21–31.   21–22; Jn 1, 31–34.
3, 11: Jn 1, 26–27.33; Acts   3, 16: Is 42, 1.
1, 5.   3, 17: Mt 12, 18; 17, 5; Gn
3, 12: Mt 13, 30; Is 41, 16;   22, 2; Ps 2, 7; Is 42, 1.

The Temptation of Jesus

4 ¹*† Then Jesus was led by the Spirit into the desert to be tempted by the devil. ²*† He fasted for forty days and forty nights, and afterwards he was hungry. ³ The tempter approached and said to him, "If you are the Son of God, command that these stones become loaves of bread." ⁴*† He said in reply, "It is written:

'One does not live by bread alone,
    but by every word that comes forth from
        the mouth of God.' "

⁵† Then the devil took him to the holy city, and made him stand on the parapet of the temple, ⁶* and said to him, "If you are the Son of God, throw yourself down. For it is written:

'He will command his angels concerning you'
    and 'with their hands they will support you,
lest you dash your foot against a stone.' "

⁷*Jesus answered him, "Again it is written, 'You shall not put the Lord, your God, to the test.' " ⁸ Then the devil took him up to a very high mountain, and showed him all the kingdoms of the world in their magnificence, ⁹† and he said to him, "All these I shall give to you, if you will prostrate yourself and worship me." ¹⁰*At this, Jesus said to him, "Get away, Satan! It is written:

'The Lord, your God, shall you worship
    and him alone shall you serve.' "

¹¹ Then the devil left him and, behold, angels came and ministered to him.

---

† **4, 1–11:** Jesus, proclaimed Son of God at his baptism, is subjected to a triple temptation. Obedience to the Father is a characteristic of true sonship, and Jesus is tempted by the devil to rebel against God, overtly in the third case, more subtly in the first two. Each refusal of Jesus is expressed in language taken from the Book of Deuteronomy (Dt 8, 3; 6, 13.16). The testings of Jesus resemble those of Israel during the wandering in the desert and later in Canaan, and the victory of Jesus, the true Israel and the true Son, contrasts with the failure of the ancient and disobedient "son," the old Israel. In the temptation account Matthew is almost identical with Luke; both seem to have drawn upon the same source.

4, 2: *Forty days and forty nights:* the same time as that during which Moses remained on Sinai (Ex 24, 18). The time reference, however, seems primarily intended to recall the forty years during which Israel was tempted in the desert (Dt 8, 2).

4, 4: Cf Dt 8, 3. Jesus refuses to use his power for his own benefit and accepts whatever God wills.

4, 5–7: The devil supports his proposal by an appeal to the scriptures, Ps 91, 11a.12. Unlike Israel (Dt 6, 16), Jesus refuses to "test" God by demanding from him an extraordinary show of power.

4, 9: The worship of Satan to which Jesus is tempted is probably intended to recall Israel's worship of false gods. His refusal is expressed in the words of Dt 6, 13.

4, 1–11: Mk 1, 12–13; Lk 4, 1–13.
4, 2: Ex 24, 18; Dt 8, 2.
4, 4: Dt 8, 3.
4, 6: Ps 91, 11–12.
4, 7: Dt 6, 16.
4, 10: Mt 16, 23; Dt 6, 13.

Catholic Connections

BAPTISM

John the Baptist was the last great prophet before Jesus. John may have belonged to a religious group that initiated new members through a rite of immersion in water (baptism). The rite used by John symbolized the moral conversion—through repentance, confession of sins, and change of heart—required for receiving God's salvation. Although Jesus was without sin, his willingness to be baptized is a sign of how fully he embraced his humanity.

Baptism is also one of the seven sacraments that Catholics celebrate. Although many Catholics are baptized as infants, some young people and adults, called catechumens, are baptized at the Easter Vigil on Holy Saturday each year. During the Baptism ritual, the baptized person is marked with chrism, a special oil. (In the Old Testament, such an oil was used to anoint priests, prophets, and kings for service.) The person then has water poured over her or him or is immersed in water. This is a sign of dying to sin and rising anew in the presence of God. The Holy Trinity is called upon, baptizing her or him in the name of the Father, the Son, and the Holy Spirit. A candle is given to the newly baptized person to symbolize the light of Christ that now burns within her or him, and a white garment or stole is put on the person to signify her or his new life in Christ.

The sacraments of Baptism, Confirmation, and the Eucharist are a person's initiation into the Christian community. They call Christians to continual conversion in following Jesus.

▶ Mt 3, 13–17

Jesus' Temptations, My Temptations

Command that these stones become loaves of bread." (Mt 4, 3)

Jesus, you trusted God to provide your material needs. Help me to avoid placing my priorities on material things.

"Throw yourself down. For it is written: . . .
'with their hands they will support you,
lest you dash your foot against a stone.' "

(Verse 6)

Jesus, you resisted using your power for vain and foolish reasons. Help me to resist doing foolish things only to impress others.

"All these I shall give to you, if you will prostrate yourself and worship me."

(Verse 9)

Jesus, you refused to cooperate with the devil to achieve status and power. Help me to refuse to cooperate with evil and injustice in achieving my life's goals.

▶ Mt 4, 1–11

The Beginning of the Galilean Ministry

12*† When he heard that John had been arrested, he withdrew to Galilee. 13* He left Nazareth and went to live in Capernaum by the sea, in the region of Zebulun and Naphtali, 14 that what had been said through Isaiah the prophet might be fulfilled:

15* "Land of Zebulun and land of Naphtali,
the way to the sea, beyond the Jordan,
Galilee of the Gentiles,
16* the people who sit in darkness
have seen a great light,
on those dwelling in a land overshadowed
by death
light has arisen."

17*† From that time on, Jesus began to preach and say, "Repent, for the kingdom of heaven is at hand."

Follow Me

As the first disciples chose to follow Jesus, what did they leave behind? Nets, boats, even parents. The very things they depended on for life and security! Knowing what you know of Jesus, what are you ready to "leave behind" in order to follow him and continue his mission?

▶ Mt 4, 18–22

The Call of the First Disciples

18*† As he was walking by the Sea of Galilee, he saw two brothers, Simon who is called Peter, and his brother Andrew, casting a net into the sea; they were fishermen. 19 He said to them, "Come after me, and I will make you fishers of men." 20† At once they left their nets and followed him. 21 He walked along from there and saw two other brothers, James, the son of Zebedee, and his brother John. They were in a boat, with their father Zebedee, mending their nets. He called them, 22 and immediately they left their boat and their father and followed him.

Ministering to a Great Multitude

23*† He went around all of Galilee, teaching in their synagogues,† proclaiming the gospel of the

---

4, 12–17: Isaiah's prophecy of the light rising upon Zebulun and Naphtali (Is 8, 23—9, 1) is fulfilled in Jesus' residence at Capernaum. The territory of these two tribes was the first to be devastated (733–32 B.C.) at the time of the Assyrian invasion. In order to accommodate Jesus' move to Capernaum to the prophecy, Matthew speaks of that town as being "in the region of Zebulun and Naphtali" (13), whereas it was only in the territory of the latter, and he understands the sea of the prophecy, the Mediterranean, as the sea of Galilee.
4, 17: At the beginning of his preaching Jesus takes up the words of John the Baptist (3, 2) although with a different meaning; in his ministry the kingdom of heaven has already begun to be present (12, 28).
4, 18–22: The call of the first disciples promises them a share in Jesus' work and entails abandonment of family and former way of life. Three of the four, Simon, James, and John, are distinguished among the disciples by a closer relation with Jesus (17, 1; 26, 37).
4, 20: Here and in v 22, as in Mark (1, 16–20) and unlike the

Lucan account (5, 1–11), the disciples' response is motivated only by Jesus' invitation, an element that emphasizes his mysterious power.
4, 23–25: This summary of Jesus' ministry concludes the narrative part of the first book of Matthew's gospel (chs 3–4). The activities of his ministry are teaching, proclaiming the gospel, and healing; cf 9, 35.
4, 23: Their synagogues: Matthew usually designates the Jewish synagogues as their synagogue(s) (9, 35; 10, 17; 12, 9; 13, 54) or, in address to Jews, your synagogues (23, 34), an indication that he wrote after the break between church and synagogue.

4, 12–13: Mk 1, 14–15; Lk 4, 14.31.   4, 18–22: Mk 1, 16–20; Lk 5,
  4, 13: Jn 2, 12.   1–11.
4, 15–16: Is 8, 23 LXX; 9, 1.   4, 23: Mt 9, 35; Mk 1, 39;
  4, 16: Lk 1, 79.   Lk 4, 15.44.
  4, 17: Mt 3, 2.

An Upside-Down Kingdom

Read Mt 5, 1–12. These familiar words of Jesus, called the Beatitudes, begin what is called the Sermon on the Mount. In chapters 5–7, Jesus speaks about life in a way that startled his listeners. Many thought it was a sign of God's blessing to be rich, powerful, and content. They thought it was justified to respond to violence and oppression with violence and oppression.

Jesus' words continue to challenge us today. Pay attention to these hard words of Jesus. Christianity is not always easy, but it is the only way for all people to live as sons and daughters of God. The challenge for us is to see life more and more the way God does, and then to live that vision!

▸ **Mt 5, 1–12**

kingdom, and curing every disease and illness among the people. 24† His fame spread to all of Syria, and they brought to him all who were sick with various diseases and racked with pain, those who were possessed, lunatics, and paralytics, and he cured them. 25*† And great crowds from Galilee, the Decapolis, Jerusalem, and Judea, and from beyond the Jordan followed him.

The Sermon on the Mount

5 1† When he saw the crowds,† he went up the mountain, and after he had sat down, his disciples came to him. 2 He began to teach them, saying:

The Beatitudes†

3* "Blessed are the poor in spirit,†
　　for theirs is the kingdom of heaven.
4*†Blessed are they who mourn,
　　for they will be comforted.
5*†Blessed are the meek,
　　for they will inherit the land.
6† Blessed are they who hunger and thirst
　　　for righteousness,
　　for they will be satisfied.
7* Blessed are the merciful,
　　for they will be shown mercy.
8*†Blessed are the clean of heart,
　　for they will see God.
9 Blessed are the peacemakers,
　　for they will be called children
　　　of God.
10*† Blessed are they who are persecuted
　　　for the sake of righteousness,
　　for theirs is the kingdom of heaven.

11*Blessed are you when they insult you and persecute you and utter every kind of evil against

---

4, 24: *Syria:* the Roman province to which Palestine belonged.

4, 25: *The Decapolis:* a federation of Greek cities in Palestine, originally ten in number, all but one east of the Jordan.

5, 1—7, 29: The first of the five discourses that are a central part of the structure of this gospel. It is the discourse section of the first book and contains sayings of Jesus derived from Q and from M. The Lucan parallel is in that gospel's "Sermon on the Plain" (Lk 6, 20–49), although some of the sayings in Matthew's "Sermon on the Mount" have their parallels in other parts of Luke. The careful arrangement of the sermon is probably not due only to Matthew's editing; he seems to have had a structured discourse of Jesus as one of his sources. The form of that source may have been as follows: four beatitudes (5, 3–4.6.11–12), a section on the new righteousness with illustrations (5, 17.20–24.27–28.33–48), a section on good works (6, 1–6.16–18), and three warnings (7, 1–2.15–21.24–27).

5, 1–2: Unlike Luke's sermon, this is addressed not only to the disciples but to the crowds (see 7, 28).

5, 3–12: The form *Blessed are (is)* occurs frequently in the Old Testament in the Wisdom literature and in the psalms. Although modified by Matthew, the first, second, fourth, and ninth beatitudes have Lucan parallels (5, 3 // Lk 6, 20; 5, 4 // Lk 6, 21b; 5, 6 // Lk 6, 21a; 5, 11–12 // Lk 5, 22–23). The others were added by the evangelist and are probably his own composition. A few manuscripts, Western and Alexandrian, and many versions and patristic quotations give the second and third beatitudes in inverted order.

5, 3: *The poor in spirit:* in the Old Testament, the *poor* (*'anāwîm*) are those who are without material possessions and whose confi-

dence is in God (see Is 61, 1; Zep 2, 3; in the NAB the word is translated *lowly* and *humble*, respectively, in those texts). Matthew added *in spirit* in order either to indicate that only the devout poor were meant or to extend the beatitude to all, of whatever social rank, who recognized their complete dependence on God. The same phrase *poor in spirit* is found in the Qumran literature (1QM 14, 7).

5, 4: Cf Is 61, 2, "(The Lord has sent me) . . . to comfort all who mourn." *They will be comforted:* here the passive is a "theological passive" equivalent to the active "God will comfort them"; so also in vv 6 and 7.

5, 5: Cf Ps 37, 11, ". . . the poor will possess the land." In the psalm "the land" means the land of Palestine; here it means the kingdom.

5, 6: *For righteousness:* a Matthean addition. For the meaning of *righteousness* here, see the note on 3, 14–15.

5, 8: Cf Ps 24, 4. Only one "pure of heart" can take part in the temple worship. To be with God in the temple is described in Ps 42, 3 as "see[ing] the face of God," but here the promise to the *clean of heart* is that they will *see God* not in the temple but in the coming kingdom.

5, 10: *Righteousness* here, as usually in Matthew, means conduct in conformity with God's will.

4, 25: Mk 3, 7–8; Lk 6, 17–19.　　　5, 8: Pss 24, 4–5; 73, 1.
5, 3–12: Lk 6, 20–23.　　　　　　　　5, 10: 1 Pt 2, 20; 3, 14;
　5, 4: Is 61, 2–3; Rv 21, 4.　　　　　　　　4, 14.
　5, 5: Gn 13, 15; Ps 37, 11.　　　　5, 11: Mt 10, 22; Acts 5, 41.
　5, 7: Mt 18, 33; Jas 2, 13.

you [falsely] because of me. [12]*† Rejoice and be glad, for your reward will be great in heaven. Thus they persecuted the prophets who were before you.

The Similes of Salt and Light†

[13]* "You are the salt of the earth. But if salt loses its taste, with what can it be seasoned? It is no longer good for anything but to be thrown out and trampled underfoot.† [14]* You are the light of the world. A city set on a mountain cannot be hidden. [15]* Nor do they light a lamp and then put it under a bushel basket; it is set on a lampstand, where it gives light to all in the house. [16]* Just so, your light must shine before others, that they may see your good deeds and glorify your heavenly Father.

Teaching about the Law

[17]† "Do not think that I have come to abolish the law or the prophets. I have come not to abolish but to fulfill. [18]* Amen, I say to you, until heaven and earth pass away, not the smallest letter or the smallest part of a letter will pass from the law, until all things have taken place. [19]† Therefore, whoever breaks one of the least of these commandments and teaches others to do so will be called least in the kingdom of heaven. But whoever obeys and teaches these commandments will be called greatest in the kingdom of heaven. [20] I tell you, unless your righteousness surpasses that of the scribes and Pharisees, you will not enter into the kingdom of heaven.

Teaching about Anger

[21]*† "You have heard that it was said to your ancestors, 'You shall not kill; and whoever kills will be liable to judgment.'† [22]*† But I say to you, whoever is angry with his brother will be liable to judgment, and whoever says to his brother, 'Raqa,' will be answerable to the Sanhedrin, and whoever says, 'You fool,' will be liable to fiery Gehenna.† [23]* Therefore, if you bring your gift to the altar, and there recall that your brother has anything against you, [24] leave your gift there at the altar, go first and be reconciled with your brother, and then come and offer your gift. [25]* Settle with your opponent quickly while on the way to court with him. Otherwise your opponent will hand you over to the judge, and the judge will hand you over to the guard, and you will be thrown into prison. [26] Amen, I say to you, you will not be released until you have paid the last penny.

Teaching about Adultery

[27]*† "You have heard that it was said, 'You shall not commit adultery.' [28] But I say to you, everyone who looks at a woman with lust has already committed adultery with her in his heart. [29]*† If your right eye causes you to sin, tear it out and throw it away. It is better for you to lose one of your

---

5, 12: *The prophets who were before you:* the disciples of Jesus stand in the line of the persecuted prophets of Israel. Some would see the expression as indicating also that Matthew considered all Christian disciples as prophets.

5, 13–16: By their deeds the disciples are to influence the world for good. They can no more escape notice than a *city set on a mountain.* If they fail in good works, they are as useless as flavorless salt or as a lamp whose light is concealed.

5, 13: The unusual supposition of salt losing its flavor has led some to suppose that the saying refers to the salt of the Dead Sea that, because chemically impure, could lose its taste.

5, 17–20: This statement of Jesus' position concerning the Mosaic law is composed of traditional material from Matthew's sermon documentation (see the note on 5, 1—7, 29), other Q material (cf 18 and Lk 16, 17), and the evangelist's own editorial touches. *To fulfill* the law appears at first to mean a literal enforcement of the law in the least detail: *until heaven and earth pass away* nothing of the law *will pass* (18). Yet the "passing away" of heaven and earth is not necessarily the end of the world understood, as in much apocalyptic literature, the dissolution of the existing universe. The "turning of the ages" comes with the apocalyptic event of Jesus' death and resurrection, and those to whom this gospel is addressed are living in the new and final age, prophesied by Isaiah as the time of "new heavens and a new earth" (Is 65, 17; 66, 22). Meanwhile, during Jesus' ministry when the kingdom is already breaking in, his mission remains within the framework of the law, though with significant anticipation of the age to come, as the following antitheses (vv 21–48) show.

5, 19: Probably *these commandments* means those of the Mosaic law. But this is an interim ethic "until heaven and earth pass away."

5, 21–48: Six examples of the conduct demanded of the Christian disciple. Each deals with a commandment of the law, introduced by *You have heard that it was said to your ancestors* or an equivalent formula, followed by Jesus' teaching in respect to that commandment, *But I say to you;* thus their designation as "antitheses." Three of them accept the Mosaic law but extend or deepen it (21–22; 27–28; 43–44); three reject

it as a standard of conduct for the disciples (31–32; 33–37; 38–39).

5, 21: Cf Ex 20, 13; Dt 5, 17. The second part of the verse is not an exact quotation from the Old Testament, but cf Ex 21, 12.

5, 22: Anger is the motive behind murder, as the insulting epithets are steps that may lead to it. They, as well as the deed, are all forbidden. *Raqa:* an Aramaic word *rēqā'* or *rēqâ* probably meaning "imbecile," "blockhead," a term of abuse. The ascending order of punishment, *judgment* (by a local council?), trial before *the Sanhedrin,* condemnation to *Gehenna,* points to a higher degree of seriousness in each of the offenses. *Sanhedrin:* the highest judicial body of Judaism. *Gehenna:* in Hebrew *gê-hinnōm,* "Valley of Hinnom," or *gê ben-hinnōm,* "Valley of the son of Hinnom," southwest of Jerusalem, the center of an idolatrous cult during the monarchy in which children were offered in sacrifice (see 2 Kgs 23, 10; Jer 7, 31). In Jos 18, 16 (Septuagint, Codex Vaticanus) the Hebrew is transliterated into Greek as *gaienna,* which appears in the New Testament as *geenna.* The concept of punishment of sinners by fire either after death or after the final judgment is found in Jewish apocalyptic literature (e.g., Enoch 90, 26) but the name *geenna* is first given to the place of punishment in the New Testament.

5, 22–26: Reconciliation with an offended brother is urged in the admonition of vv 23–24 and the parable of vv 25–26 (// Lk 12, 58–59). The severity of the judge in the parable is a warning of the fate of unrepentant sinners in the coming judgment by God.

5, 27: See Ex 20, 14; Dt 5, 18.

5, 29–30: No sacrifice is too great to avoid total destruction in *Gehenna.*

5, 12: 2 Chr 36, 16; Heb 11, 32–38; Jas 5, 10.
5, 13: Mk 9, 50; Lk 14, 34–35.
5, 14: Jn 8, 12.
5, 15: Mk 4, 21; Lk 8, 16; 11, 33.
5, 16: Jn 3, 21.
5, 18: Lk 16, 17.
5, 21: Ex 20, 13; Dt 5, 17.
5, 22: Jas 1, 19–20.
5, 23: Mk 11, 25.
5, 25–26: Mt 18, 34–35; Lk 12, 58–59.
5, 27: Ex 20, 14; Dt 5, 18.
5, 29–30: Mt 18, 8–9; Mk 9, 43–47.

members than to have your whole body thrown into Gehenna. 30 And if your right hand causes you to sin, cut it off and throw it away. It is better for you to lose one of your members than to have your whole body go into Gehenna.

Teaching about Divorce

31*† "It was also said, 'Whoever divorces his wife must give her a bill of divorce.' 32* But I say to you, whoever divorces his wife (unless the marriage is unlawful) causes her to commit adultery, and whoever marries a divorced woman commits adultery.

Teaching about Oaths

33*† "Again you have heard that it was said to your ancestors, 'Do not take a false oath, but make good to the Lord all that you vow.' 34*† But I say to you, do not swear at all; not by heaven, for it is God's throne; 35 nor by the earth, for it is his footstool; nor by Jerusalem, for it is the city of the great King. 36 Do not swear by your head, for you cannot make a single hair white or black. 37† Let your 'Yes' mean 'Yes,' and your 'No' mean 'No.' Anything more is from the evil one.

Teaching about Retaliation

38*† "You have heard that it was said, 'An eye for an eye and a tooth for a tooth.' 39* But I say to you, offer no resistance to one who is evil. When someone strikes you on [your] right cheek, turn the other one to him as well. 40 If anyone wants to go to law with you over your tunic, hand him your cloak as well. 41*† Should anyone press you into service for one mile, go with him for two miles. 42* Give to the one who asks of you, and do not turn your back on one who wants to borrow.

Christians and Revenge

For Jesus, one way to love our enemies is to refuse to take revenge on those who have wronged us. Is this really possible to do?

Consider the case of a young woman named Julie Welch who was killed by a terrorist bombing in Oklahoma City. Julie's father worked unceasingly against the death penalty for the man responsible for the bombing. He knew that revenge would not bring his daughter back or make him feel better. He believed that Christians are obligated to always assume that for even the most heinous criminal, reconciliation and remorse are possible. Although his stance was not easy or popular, it illustrates what this passage teaches.

In your prayer, reflect or journal on the following questions:
- Who are your enemies?
- When they or someone else hurts you, what is your usual reaction?
- What is the greatest challenge for you in living out this teaching from Jesus?

▶ Mt 5, 38–48

MT

---

† **5, 31–32:** See Dt 24, 1–5. The Old Testament commandment that a bill of divorce be given to the woman assumes the legitimacy of divorce itself. It is this that Jesus denies. *(Unless the marriage is unlawful):* this "exceptive clause," as it is often called, occurs also in 19, 9, where the Greek is slightly different. There are other sayings of Jesus about divorce that prohibit it absolutely (see Mk 10, 11–12; Lk 16, 18; cf 1 Cor 7, 10.11b), and most scholars agree that they represent the stand of Jesus. Matthew's "exceptive clauses" are understood by some as a modification of the absolute prohibition. It seems, however, that the unlawfulness that Matthew gives as a reason why a marriage must be broken refers to a situation peculiar to his community: the violation of Mosaic law forbidding marriage between persons of certain blood and/or legal relationship (Lv 18, 6–18). Marriages of that sort were regarded as incest *(porneia),* but some rabbis allowed Gentile converts to Judaism who had contracted such marriages to remain in them. Matthew's "exceptive clause" is against such permissiveness for Gentile converts to Christianity; cf the similar prohibition of *porneia* in Acts 15, 20.29. In this interpretation, the clause constitutes no exception to the absolute prohibition of divorce when the marriage is lawful.

5, 33: This is not an exact quotation of any Old Testament text, but see Ex 20, 7, Dt 5, 11, and Lv 19, 12. The purpose of an oath was to guarantee truthfulness by one's calling on God as witness.

5, 34–36: The use of these oath formularies that avoid the divine name is in fact equivalent to swearing by it, for all the things sworn by are related to God.

5, 37: *Let your 'Yes' mean 'Yes,' and your 'No' mean 'No':* literally, "let your speech be 'Yes, yes,' 'No, no.' " Some have understood this as a milder form of oath, permitted by Jesus. In view of v 34, "Do not swear at all," that is unlikely. *From the evil one:* i.e., from the devil. Oath-taking presupposes a sinful weakness of the human race, namely, the tendency to lie. Jesus demands of his disciples a truthfulness that makes oaths unnecessary.

5, 38–42: See Lv 24, 20. The Old Testament commandment was meant to moderate vengeance; the punishment should not exceed the injury done. Jesus forbids even this proportionate retaliation. Of the five examples that follow, only the first deals directly with retaliation for evil; the others speak of liberality.

5, 41: Roman garrisons in Palestine had the right to requisition the property and services of the native population.

5, 31: Mt 19, 3–9; Dt 24, 1.
5, 32: Lk 16, 18; 1 Cor 7, 10–11.
5, 33: Lv 19, 12; Nm 30, 3.
5, 34–37: Ps 48, 3; Sir 23, 9; Is 66, 1; Jas 5, 12.
5, 38: Ex 21, 24; Lv 24, 19–20.
5, 39–42: Lk 6, 29–30.
5, 41: Lam 3, 30.
5, 42: Dt 15, 7–8.

Love of Enemies

43*† "You have heard that it was said, 'You shall love your neighbor and hate your enemy.'* 44 But I say to you, love your enemies, and pray for those who persecute you, 45 that you may be children of your heavenly Father, for he makes his sun rise on the bad and the good, and causes rain to fall on the just and the unjust. 46† For if you love those who love you, what recompense will you have? Do not the tax collectors do the same? 47† And if you greet your brothers only, what is unusual about that? Do not the pagans do the same? 48*† So be perfect, just as your heavenly Father is perfect.

Teaching about Almsgiving

6 1*† "[But] take care not to perform righteous deeds in order that people may see them; otherwise, you will have no recompense from your heavenly Father. 2*† When you give alms, do not blow a trumpet before you, as the hypocrites do in the synagogues and in the streets to win the praise of others. Amen, I say to you, they have received their reward. 3 But when you give alms, do not let your left hand know what your right is doing, 4 so that your almsgiving may be secret. And your Father who sees in secret will repay you.

Teaching about Prayer

5 "When you pray, do not be like the hypocrites, who love to stand and pray in the synagogues and on street corners so that others may see them. Amen, I say to you, they have received their reward. 6 But when you pray, go to your inner room, close the door, and pray to your Father in secret. And your Father who sees in secret will repay you. 7† In praying, do not babble like the

PRAY IT!

Ash Wednesday

Matthew 6, 1–18 is read on Ash Wednesday, the beginning of Lent. Lent is traditionally a forty-day period to examine and renew our spiritual life. It is a time of prayer, service, and fasting. The forty days recall the forty years that the people of Israel wandered in the wilderness before arriving at the Promised Land and the forty days that Jesus spent in the wilderness after being baptized.

On Ash Wednesday, we receive ashes that remind us of our nature as created beings (Gn 3, 19). This practice echoes the Old Testament tradition of wearing ashes as a sign of anguish and repentance. As the ash cross is made on our forehead, we hear words that echo John the Baptist's call to conversion, "Turn away from sin and be faithful to the gospel" (*Sacramentary*, p. 77). We respond "Amen," meaning "So be it."

When Lent begins again, how will you use the forty days to strengthen your spiritual life? Make a special commitment, and ask God for the grace to grow from it.

▶ Mt 6, 1–18

5, 43–48: See Lv 19, 18. There is no Old Testament commandment demanding hatred of one's enemy, but the "neighbor" of the love commandment was understood as one's fellow countryman. Both in the Old Testament (Ps 139, 19–22) and at Qumran (1QS 9, 21) hatred of evil persons is assumed to be right. Jesus extends the love commandment to the enemy and the persecutor. His disciples, as children of God, must imitate the example of their Father, who grants his gifts of sun and rain to both the good and the bad.

5, 46: *Tax collectors:* Jews who were engaged in the collection of indirect taxes such as tolls and customs. See the note on Mk 2, 14.

5, 47: Jesus' disciples must not be content with merely usual standards of conduct; see v 20 where the verb "surpass" (Greek *perisseuō*) is cognate with the *unusual* (*perisson*) of this verse.

5, 48: *Perfect:* in the gospels this word occurs only in Matthew, here and in 19, 21. The Lucan parallel (6, 36) demands that the disciples be *merciful.*

6, 1–18: The sermon continues with a warning against doing good in order to be seen and gives three examples, almsgiving (2–4), prayer (5, 15), and fasting (16–18). In each, the conduct of *the hypocrites* (2) is contrasted with that demanded of the disciples. The sayings about *reward* found here and elsewhere (5, 12.46; 10, 41–42) show that this is a genuine element of Christian moral exhortation. Possibly to underline the difference between the Christian idea of *reward* and that of *the hypocrites,* the evangelist uses two different

Greek verbs to express the rewarding of the disciples and that of *the hypocrites;* in the latter case it is the verb *apechō,* a commercial term for giving a receipt for what has been paid in full (2.5.16).

6, 2: *The hypocrites:* the scribes and Pharisees, see 23, 13.15.23.25.27.29. The designation reflects an attitude resulting not only from the controversies at the time of Jesus' ministry but from the opposition between Pharisaic Judaism and the church of Matthew. *They have received their reward:* they desire praise and have received what they were looking for.

6, 7–15: Matthew inserts into his basic traditional material an expansion of the material on prayer that includes the model prayer, the "Our Father." That prayer is found in Lk 11, 2–4 in a different context and in a different form.

6, 7: The example of what Christian prayer should be like contrasts it now not with the prayer of the hypocrites but with that of *the pagans.* Their babbling probably means their reciting a long list of divine names, hoping that one of them will force a response from the deity.

5, 43–48: Lk 6, 27.32–36. 6, 1: Mt 23, 5.
5, 43: Lv 19, 18. 6, 2: Jn 12, 43.
5, 48: Lv 11, 44; 19, 2;
  Dt 18, 13; Jas 1, 4;
  1 Pt 1, 16; 1 Jn 3, 3.

pagans, who think that they will be heard because of their many words.† ⁸ Do not be like them. Your Father knows what you need before you ask him.

The Lord's Prayer

⁹*† "This is how you are to pray:

> Our Father in heaven,
>   hallowed be your name,†
> ¹⁰*†   your kingdom come,
>   your will be done,
>   on earth as in heaven.
> ¹¹*†   Give us today our daily bread;
> ¹²*†   and forgive us our debts,
>   as we forgive our debtors;
> ¹³*†   and do not subject us to the final test,
>   but deliver us from the evil one.

¹⁴*† If you forgive others their transgressions, your heavenly Father will forgive you. ¹⁵*But if you do not forgive others, neither will your Father forgive your transgressions.

---

† **6, 9–13:** Matthew's form of the "Our Father" follows the liturgical tradition of his church. Luke's less developed form also represents the liturgical tradition known to him, but it is probably closer than Matthew's to the original words of Jesus.

6, 9: *Our Father in heaven:* this invocation is found in many rabbinic prayers of the post-New Testament period. *Hallowed be your name:* though the "hallowing" of the divine name could be understood as reverence done to God by human praise and by obedience to his will, this is more probably a petition that God hallow his own name, i.e., that he manifest his glory by an act of power (cf Ez 36, 23), in this case, by the establishment of his kingdom in its fullness.

6, 10: *Your kingdom come:* this petition sets the tone of the prayer, and inclines the balance toward divine rather than human action in the petitions that immediately precede and follow it. *Your will be done, on earth as in heaven:* a petition that the divine purpose to establish the kingdom, a purpose present now *in heaven*, be executed *on earth*.

6, 11: *Give us today our daily bread:* the rare Greek word *epiousios*, here *daily*, occurs in the New Testament only here and in Lk 11, 3. A single occurrence of the word outside of these texts and of literature dependent on them has been claimed, but the claim is highly doubtful. The word may mean *daily* or "future" (other meanings have also been proposed). The latter would conform better to the eschatological tone of the whole prayer. So understood, the petition would be for a speedy coming of the kingdom (*today*), which is often portrayed in both the Old Testament and the New under the image of a feast (Is 25, 6; Mt 8, 11; 22, 1–10; Lk 13, 29; 14, 15–24).

6, 12: *Forgive us our debts:* the word *debts* is used metaphorically of sins, "debts" owed to God (see Lk 11, 4). The request is probably for forgiveness at the final judgment.

6, 13: Jewish apocalyptic writings speak of a period of severe trial before the end of the age, sometimes called the "messianic woes." This petition asks that the disciples be spared that *final test*.

6, 14–15: These verses reflect a set pattern called "Principles of Holy Law." Human action now will be met by a corresponding action of God at the final judgment.

6, 9–13: Lk 11, 2–4.
6, 10: Mt 26, 42.
6, 11: Prv 30, 8–9.
6, 12: Mt 18, 21–22; Sir 28, 2.
6, 13: Jn 17, 15; 2 Thes 3, 3.
6, 14: Mt 18, 35; Sir 28, 1–5; Mk 11, 25.
6, 15: Jas 2, 13.

A Lord's Prayer Reflection

In Matthew, Jesus teaches his followers the Lord's Prayer as an alternative to hypocritical and empty prayer. Most of us have memorized the Lord's Prayer. But although we know it by heart, we do not always pray it from the heart. It can easily become "babble" (6, 7). Let this reflection help you to pray the Lord's Prayer thoughtfully:

> Our Father in heaven,
>   hallowed be your name,
>   (Verse 9)

How do I honor God as creator of all things? How do I honor God in my thoughts, my words, and my actions?

> your kingdom come,
>   your will be done,
>   on earth as in heaven.
>   (Verse 10)

How does my life reflect God's reign of love, justice, and peace? Am I putting too much emphasis on the material things I have?

> Give us today our daily bread;
>   (Verse 11)

Can I trust God to provide for my daily physical, emotional, and spiritual needs?

> and forgive us our debts,
>   as we forgive our debtors;
>   (Verse 12)

When I have sinned, do I admit my wrong, ask God's forgiveness, and start anew? When people have wronged me, do I hold a grudge? Am I able to forgive them as God forgives me?

> and do not subject us to the final test,
>   but deliver us from the evil one.
>   (Verse 13)

What are the temptations I face in life? How do I rely on God for the strength to resist them?

▶ Mt 6, 5–15

Teaching about Fasting

¹⁶† "When you fast, do not look gloomy like the hypocrites. They neglect their appearance, so that they may appear to others to be fasting. Amen, I say to you, they have received their reward. ¹⁷ But when you fast, anoint your head and wash your face, ¹⁸ so that you may not appear to others to be fasting, except to your Father who is hidden. And your Father who sees what is hidden will repay you.

Treasure in Heaven

¹⁹*† "Do not store up for yourselves treasures on earth, where moth and decay destroy, and thieves break in and steal. ²⁰* But store up treasures in heaven, where neither moth nor decay destroy, nor thieves break in and steal. ²¹ For where your treasure is, there also will your heart be.

The Light of the Body

²²*† "The lamp of the body is the eye. If your eye is sound, your whole body will be filled with light; ²³ but if your eye is bad, your whole body will be in darkness. And if the light in you is darkness, how great will the darkness be.

God and Money

²⁴*† "No one can serve two masters. He will either hate one and love the other, or be devoted to one and despise the other. You cannot serve God and mammon.

Dependence on God

²⁵*† "Therefore I tell you, do not worry about your life, what you will eat [or drink], or about your body, what you will wear. Is not life more than food and the body more than clothing? ²⁶* Look at the birds in the sky; they do not sow or reap, they gather nothing into barns, yet your heavenly Father feeds them. Are not you more important than they? ²⁷† Can any of you by worrying add a single moment to your life-span? ²⁸ Why are you anxious about clothes? Learn from the way the wild flowers grow. They do not work or spin. ²⁹ But I tell you that not even Solomon in all his splendor was clothed like one of them. ³⁰† If God so clothes the grass of the field, which grows today and is thrown into the oven tomorrow, will he not much more provide for you, O you of little faith? ³¹ So do not worry and say, 'What are we to eat?' or 'What are we to drink?' or 'What are we to wear?' ³² All these things the pagans seek. Your heavenly Father knows that you need them all. ³³† But seek first the kingdom [of God] and his righteousness, and all these things will be given you besides. ³⁴ Do not worry about tomorrow; tomorrow will take care of itself. Sufficient for a day is its own evil.

Judging Others

7 ¹*† "Stop judging,† that you may not be judged.* ²* For as you judge, so will you be judged, and the measure with which you measure will be measured out to you. ³ Why do you notice the splinter in your brother's eye, but do not perceive the wooden beam in your own eye? ⁴ How can you say to your brother, 'Let me remove that splinter from your eye,' while the wooden beam is in your eye? ⁵† You hypocrite, remove the wooden beam from your eye first; then you will see clearly to remove the splinter from your brother's eye.

Pearls before Swine

⁶*† "Do not give what is holy to dogs, or throw your pearls before swine, lest they trample them underfoot, and turn and tear you to pieces.

6, 16: The only fast prescribed in the Mosaic law was that of the Day of Atonement (Lv 16, 31), but the practice of regular fasting was common in later Judaism; cf *Didache* 9, 1.

6, 19–34: The remaining material of this chapter is taken almost entirely from Q. It deals principally with worldly possessions, and the controlling thought is summed up in v 24: the disciple can serve only one master and must choose between God and wealth (*mammon*). See further the note on Lk 16, 9.

6, 22–23: In this context the parable probably points to the need for the disciple to be enlightened by Jesus' teaching on the transitory nature of earthly riches.

6, 24: *Mammon:* an Aramaic word meaning wealth or property.

6, 25–34: Jesus does not deny the reality of human needs (32), but forbids making them the object of anxious care and, in effect, becoming their slave.

6, 27: *Life-span:* the Greek word can also mean "stature." If it is taken in that sense, the word here translated *moment* (literally, "cubit") must be translated literally as a unit not of time but of spatial measure. The cubit is about eighteen inches.

6, 30: *Of little faith:* except for the parallel in Lk 12, 28, the word translated *of little faith* is found in the New Testament only in Matthew. It is used by him of those who are disciples of Jesus but whose faith in him is not as deep as it should be (see Mt 8, 26; 14, 31; 16, 8 and the cognate noun in 17, 20).

6, 33: *Righteousness:* see the note on 3, 14–15.

7, 1–12: In v 1 Matthew returns to the basic traditional material of the sermon (Lk 6, 37–38.41–42). The governing thought is the correspondence between conduct toward one's fellows and God's conduct toward the one so acting.

7, 1: This is not a prohibition against recognizing the faults of others, which would be hardly compatible with vv 5 and 6, but against passing judgment in a spirit of arrogance, forgetful of one's own faults.

7, 5: *Hypocrite:* the designation previously given to the scribes and Pharisees is here given to the Christian disciple who is concerned with the faults of another and ignores his own more serious offenses.

7, 6: *Dogs* and *swine* were Jewish terms of contempt for Gentiles. This saying may originally have derived from a Jewish Christian community opposed to preaching the gospel (*what is holy . . . pearls*) to Gentiles. In the light of 28, 19 that can hardly be Matthew's meaning. He may have taken the saying as applying to a Christian dealing with an obstinately impenitent fellow Christian (18, 17).

6, 19: Jas 5, 2–3.
6, 20–21: Lk 12, 33–34.
6, 22–23: Lk 11, 34–36.
6, 24: Lk 16, 13.
6, 25–33: Lk 12, 22–31.
6, 26: Pss 145, 15–16; 147, 9.

7, 1–5: Lk 6, 37–38.41–42.
7, 1: Rom 2, 1–2; 1 Cor 4, 5.
7, 2: Wis 12, 22; Mk 4, 24.
7, 6: Prv 23, 9.

The Answer to Prayers

7* "Ask and it will be given to you; seek and you will find; knock and the door will be opened to you.* 8* For everyone who asks, receives; and the one who seeks, finds; and to the one who knocks, the door will be opened. 9† Which one of you would hand his son a stone when he asks for a loaf of bread, 10 or a snake when he asks for a fish? 11* If you then, who are wicked, know how to give good gifts to your children, how much more will your heavenly Father give good things to those who ask him.

The Golden Rule

12*† "Do to others whatever you would have them do to you. This is the law and the prophets.

The Narrow Gate

13*† "Enter through the narrow gate;† for the gate is wide and the road broad that leads to destruction, and those who enter through it are many. 14 How narrow the gate and constricted the road that leads to life. And those who find it are few.

False Prophets

15*† "Beware of false prophets, who come to you in sheep's clothing, but underneath are ravenous wolves. 16* By their fruits you will know them. Do people pick grapes from thornbushes, or figs from thistles? 17 Just so, every good tree bears good fruit, and a rotten tree bears bad fruit. 18 A good tree cannot bear bad fruit, nor can a rotten tree bear good fruit. 19* Every tree that does not bear good fruit will be cut down and thrown into the fire. 20 So by their fruits you will know them.

The True Disciple

21*† "Not everyone who says to me, 'Lord, Lord,' will enter the kingdom of heaven, but only the one who does the will of my Father in heaven. 22* Many will say to me on that day, 'Lord, Lord, did we not prophesy in your name? Did we not drive out

The Gospel Call to Conversion

In closing the Sermon on the Mount, Jesus calls people to conversion. It is not enough to talk the talk; you must also walk the walk. As part of our conversion, Jesus asks the following:

■ **Rich people need to share their wealth with poor people.**
■ **Powerful people need to serve those without power.**
■ **Priests need to serve all people without prejudice.**
■ **Politicians need to govern with justice, taking into account the needs of people, especially people in want.**
■ **Wise people need to express their knowledge in ways everyone can understand.**
■ **Pharisees need to leave their hypocrisy behind and remove the weight of the Law through which they oppressed the people.**

In your prayer, reflect or journal on the following questions:
■ **In the above list, what are some of the most needed areas of conversion in society today? in your local community? in your life?**
■ **List some concrete ways you can make those conversions real.**

▶ **Mt 7, 21–27**

---

† 7, 9–10: There is a resemblance between a stone and a round loaf of bread and between a serpent and the scaleless fish called *bar-but*.

7, 12: See Lk 6, 31. This saying, known since the eighteenth century as the "Golden Rule," is found in both positive and negative form in pagan and Jewish sources, both earlier and later than the gospel. *This is the law and the prophets* is an addition probably due to the evangelist.

7, 13–28: The final section of the discourse is composed of a series of antitheses, contrasting two kinds of life within the Christian community, that of those who obey the words of Jesus and that of those who do not. Most of the sayings are from Q and are found also in Luke.

7, 13–14: The metaphor of the "two ways" was common in pagan philosophy and in the Old Testament. In Christian literature it is found also in the *Didache* (1–6) and the *Epistle of Barnabas* (18–20).

7, 15–20: Christian disciples who claimed to speak in the name of God are called *prophets* (15) in 10, 41 and in 23, 34. They were

presumably an important group within the church of Matthew. As in the case of the Old Testament prophets, there were both true and false ones, and for Matthew the difference could be recognized by the quality of their deeds, the *fruits* (16). The mention of *fruits* leads to the comparison with trees, some producing good fruit, others bad.

7, 21–23: The attack on the false prophets is continued, but is broadened to include those disciples who perform works of healing and exorcism in the name of Jesus (*Lord*) but live evil lives. Entrance into the kingdom is only for those who do the will of the Father. On the day of judgment (*on that day*) the morally corrupt prophets and miracle workers will be rejected by Jesus.

---

*
7, 7–11: Mk 11, 24; Lk 11, 9–13.	7, 15: 2 Pt 2, 1.
7, 7: Mt 18, 19.	7, 16–17: Mt 12, 33; Lk 6, 43–44.
7, 8: Lk 18, 1–8; Jn 14, 13.	7, 19: Mt 3, 10.
7, 11: 1 Jn 5, 14–15.	7, 21: Is 29, 13; Lk 6, 46.
7, 12: Lk 6, 31.	7, 22–23: Lk 13, 26–27.
7, 13: Lk 13, 24.	7, 22: Mt 25, 11–12.

MT

demons in your name? Did we not do mighty deeds in your name?'* 23*† Then I will declare to them solemnly, 'I never knew you. Depart from me, you evildoers.'

The Two Foundations

24*† "Everyone who listens to these words of mine and acts on them will be like a wise man who built his house on rock. 25* The rain fell, the floods came, and the winds blew and buffeted the house. But it did not collapse; it had been set solidly on rock. 26 And everyone who listens to these words of mine but does not act on them will be like a fool who built his house on sand. 27 The rain fell, the floods came, and the winds blew and buffeted the house. And it collapsed and was completely ruined."

28† When Jesus finished these words, the crowds were astonished at his teaching, 29*† for he taught them as one having authority, and not as their scribes.

III: Ministry and Mission in Galilee

The Cleansing of a Leper

8 1*† When Jesus came down from the mountain, great crowds followed him. 2† And then a leper approached, did him homage, and said, "Lord, if you wish, you can make me clean." 3 He stretched out his hand, touched him, and said, "I will do it. Be made clean." His leprosy was cleansed immediately. 4*† Then Jesus said to him, "See that you tell no one, but go show yourself to the priest, and offer the gift that Moses prescribed; that will be proof for them."

The Healing of a Centurion's Servant†

5* When he entered Capernaum, a centurion† approached him and appealed to him, 6 saying,

"Lord, my servant is lying at home paralyzed, suffering dreadfully." 7 He said to him, "I will come and cure him." 8† The centurion said in reply, "Lord, I am not worthy to have you enter under my roof; only say the word and my servant will be healed. 9 For I too am a person subject to authority, with soldiers subject to me. And I say to one, 'Go,' and he goes; and to another, 'Come here,' and he comes; and to my slave, 'Do this,' and he does it."

Catholic Connections

LORD, I AM NOT WORTHY

Those words of the centurion are similar to the ones Catholics say at Mass just before receiving the body and blood of Christ. We say these words not to emphasize our sinfulness but in humble recognition of God's awesome gift of Jesus, whom we are about to receive in the bread and wine of the Eucharist. The next time you receive the Eucharist, think about these words, and pray for the faith it takes to believe in what you are saying.

▸ **Mt 8, 8**

---

† 7, 23: *I never knew you:* cf 10, 33. *Depart from me, you evildoers:* cf Ps 6, 9.

7, 24–27: The conclusion of the discourse (cf Lk 6, 47–49). Here the relation is not between saying and doing as in vv 15–23 but between hearing and doing, and the words of Jesus are applied to every Christian (*everyone who listens*).

7, 28–29: *When Jesus finished these words:* this or a similar formula is used by Matthew to conclude each of the five great discourses of Jesus (cf 11, 1; 13, 53; 19, 1; 26, 1).

7, 29: *Not as their scribes:* scribal instruction was a faithful handing down of the traditions of earlier teachers; Jesus' teaching is based on his own authority. *Their scribes:* for the implications of *their,* see the note on 4, 23.

8, 1—9, 38: This narrative section of the second book of the gospel is composed of nine miracle stories, most of which are found in Mark, although Matthew does not follow the Marcan order and abbreviates the stories radically. The stories are arranged in three groups of three, each group followed by a section composed principally of sayings of Jesus about discipleship. Verse 9, 35 is an almost verbatim repetition of 4, 23. Each deals with Jesus' teaching, preaching, and healing. The teaching and preaching form the content of chs 5–7; the healing, that of chs 8–9. Some scholars speak of a portrayal of Jesus as "Messiah of the Word" in 5–7 and "Messiah of the Deed" in 8–9. That is accurate so far as it goes, but there is also a strong emphasis on discipleship in 8–9; these chapters have not only christological but ecclesiological import.

8, 2: *A leper:* see the note on Mk 1, 40.

8, 4: Cf Lv 14, 2–9. *That will be proof for them:* the Greek can also mean "that will be proof against them." It is not clear whether *them* refers to the priests or the people.

8, 5–13: This story comes from Q (see Lk 7, 1–10) and is also reflected in Jn 4, 46–54. The similarity between the Q story and the Johannine is due to a common oral tradition, not to a common literary source. As in the later story of the daughter of the Canaanite woman (15, 21–28) Jesus here breaks with his usual procedure of ministering only to Israelites and anticipates the mission to the Gentiles.

8, 5: *A centurion:* a military officer commanding a hundred men. He was probably in the service of Herod Antipas, tetrarch of Galilee; see the note on 14, 1.

8, 8–9: Acquainted by his position with the force of a command, the centurion expresses faith in the power of Jesus' mere word.

7, 23: Pss 5, 5; 6, 9.
7, 24–27: Lk 6, 47–49.
7, 25–26: Prv 10, 25.
7, 29: Mk 1, 22; Lk 4, 32.
8, 1–4: Mk 1, 40–44; Lk 5, 12–14.
8, 4: Lv 14, 2–32; Lk 17, 14.
8, 5–13: Lk 7, 1–10; Jn 4, 46–53.

did you KNOW?

Miracles and the Reign of God

Matthew, chapters 8–9, describes ten miracles of Jesus intended as signs of the coming of the Reign of God. Most of Jesus' miracles are healings, but some also show his power over demons and nature. The Gospel of Mark records the most miracles, twenty-one, and the Gospel of John, the least, eight.

People today tend to view reports of miracles with suspicion. That's because our scientific mind wants to believe everything has a rational explanation. Because of this, we miss the point. People in Jesus' time were more concerned about what the miracle revealed than in the miracle itself or even the miracle worker. Other people besides Jesus were known to perform miracles. In fact, Jesus' healing miracles were not taken as proof of his divinity (although this seemed to be the purpose of his nature miracles).

In curing people of their illnesses and driving out demons, Jesus was revealing that the Reign of God is a place where suffering and evil are banished. By curing sinners, women, and foreigners, he showed that the Reign of God is also open to all, especially outcasts.

Miracles—then and now—point to God. Whether they are easily explained or beyond reasonable explanation does not matter. What matters is that they make us aware of God's loving presence in our life. If we look at the events in our life and ask: "What do they point to? What do they tell us about God's presence in the world?" we might find ourselves utterly surrounded by miracles.

▶ Mt 8, 1—9, 34

¹⁰† When Jesus heard this, he was amazed and said to those following him, "Amen, I say to you, in no one in Israel have I found such faith. ¹¹*† I say to you, many will come from the east and the west, and will recline with Abraham, Isaac, and Jacob at the banquet in the kingdom of heaven, ¹² but the children of the kingdom will be driven out into the outer darkness, where there will be wailing and grinding of teeth." ¹³ And Jesus said to the centurion, "You may go; as you have believed, let it be done for you." And at that very hour [his] servant was healed.

The Cure of Peter's Mother-in-Law

¹⁴*† Jesus entered the house of Peter, and saw his mother-in-law lying in bed with a fever. ¹⁵* He touched her hand, the fever left her, and she rose and waited on him.

Other Healings

¹⁶† When it was evening, they brought him many who were possessed by demons, and he drove out the spirits by a word and cured all the sick, ¹⁷*† to fulfill what had been said by Isaiah the prophet:

"He took away our infirmities
    and bore our diseases."

The Would-be Followers of Jesus†

¹⁸* When Jesus saw a crowd around him, he gave orders to cross to the other side.† ¹⁹*† A scribe approached and said to him, "Teacher, I will follow you wherever you go." ²⁰† Jesus answered him,

is found elsewhere in the New Testament only in Lk 13, 28.

8, 14–15: Cf Mk 1, 29–31. Unlike Mark, Matthew has no implied request by others for the woman's cure. Jesus acts on his own initiative, and the cured woman rises and waits not on "them" (Mk 1, 31) but on *him.*

8, 16: *By a word:* a Matthean addition to Mk 1, 34; cf 8, 8.

8, 17: This fulfillment citation from Is 53, 4 follows the MT, not the LXX. The prophet speaks of the Servant of the Lord who suffers vicariously for the sins ("infirmities") of others; Matthew takes the *infirmities* as physical afflictions.

8, 18–22: This passage between the first and second series of miracles about following Jesus is taken from Q (see Lk 9, 57–62). The third of the three sayings found in the source is absent from Matthew.

8, 18: *The other side:* i.e., of the Sea of Galilee.

8, 19: *Teacher:* for Matthew, this designation of Jesus is true, for he has Jesus using it of himself (10, 24.25; 23, 8; 26, 18), yet when it is used of him by others they are either his opponents (9, 11; 12, 38; 17, 24; 22, 16.24.36) or, as here and in 19, 16, well-disposed persons who cannot see more deeply. Thus it reveals an inadequate recognition of who Jesus is.

8, 20: *Son of Man:* see the note on Mk 8, 31. This is the first occurrence in Matthew of a term that appears in the New Testament only in sayings of Jesus, except for Acts 7, 56 and possibly 9, 6 (// Mk 2, 10; Lk 5, 24). In Matthew it refers to Jesus in his ministry (seven times, as here), in his passion and resurrection (nine times, e.g., 17, 22), and in his glorious coming at the end of the age (thirteen times, e.g., 24, 30).

8, 10: *In no one in Israel:* there is good textual attestation (e.g., Codex Sinaiticus) for a reading identical with that of Lk 7, 9, "not even in Israel." But that seems to be due to a harmonization of Matthew with Luke.

8, 11–12: Matthew inserts into the story a Q saying (see Lk 13, 28–29) about the entrance of Gentiles into the kingdom and the exclusion of those Israelites who, though descended from the patriarchs and members of the chosen nation (*the children of the kingdom*), refused to believe in Jesus. *There will be wailing and grinding of teeth:* the first occurrence of a phrase used frequently in this gospel to describe final condemnation (13, 42.50; 22, 13; 24, 51; 25, 30). It

---

8, 11–12: Mt 13, 42.50; 22, 13; 24, 51; 25, 30; Lk 13, 28–29.	**8, 15:** Mt 9, 25.
	8, 17: Is 53, 4.
	8, 18: Mk 4, 35.
8, 14–16: Mk 1, 29–34; Lk 4, 38–41.	**8, 19–22:** Lk 9, 57–60.

"Foxes have dens and birds of the sky have nests, but the Son of Man has nowhere to rest his head." 21 Another of [his] disciples said to him, "Lord, let me go first and bury my father." 22† But Jesus answered him, "Follow me, and let the dead bury their dead."

The Calming of the Storm at Sea

23*† He got into a boat and his disciples followed him. 24† Suddenly a violent storm came up on the sea, so that the boat was being swamped by waves; but he was asleep. 25*† They came and woke him, saying, "Lord, save us! We are perishing!" 26† He said to them, "Why are you terrified, O you of little faith?" Then he got up, rebuked the winds and the sea, and there was great calm. 27 The men were amazed and said, "What sort of man is this, whom even the winds and the sea obey?"

The Healing of the Gadarene Demoniacs

28*† When he came to the other side, to the territory of the Gadarenes, two demoniacs who were coming from the tombs met him. They were so savage that no one could travel by that road. 29† They cried out, "What have you to do with us, Son of God? Have you come here to torment us before the appointed time?" 30† Some distance away a herd of many swine was feeding. 31* The demons pleaded with him, "If you drive us out, send us into the herd of swine." 32 And he said to them, "Go then!" They came out and entered the swine, and the whole herd rushed down the steep bank into the sea where they drowned. 33 The swineherds ran away, and when they came to the town they reported everything, including what had happened to the demoniacs. 34 Thereupon the whole town came out to meet Jesus, and when they saw him they begged him to leave their district.

The Healing of a Paralytic

9 1*† He entered a boat, made the crossing, and came into his own town. 2* And there people brought to him a paralytic lying on a stretcher. When Jesus saw their faith, he said to the paralytic, "Courage, child, your sins are forgiven." 3† At that, some of the scribes said to themselves, "This man is blaspheming." 4 Jesus knew what they were

Spiritual Paralysis

Jesus, healer, like the man you healed spiritually and physically, I too have experienced paralysis. Not a physical paralysis, but a spiritual paralysis that keeps me from walking with you.

This paralysis happens at times in school and in my neighborhood when I know what the right thing to do is, but I am afraid to do it. I see someone discriminating against or abusing another person, but I stand by and do nothing. By my silence, I give my approval, but I am afraid to risk ridicule and rejection.

Forgive me of my sin of silence, Lord. Help me to overcome my fears so that I can stand up for what is right. Heal me of my spiritual paralysis so that I may walk with you. Amen.

▶ Mt 9, 1–8

8, 22: *Let the dead bury their dead:* the demand of Jesus overrides what both the Jewish and the Hellenistic world regarded as a filial obligation of the highest importance. See the note on Lk 9, 60.
8, 23: *His disciples followed him:* the first miracle in the second group (8, 23—9, 8) is introduced by a verse that links it with the preceding sayings by the catchword "follow." In Mark the initiative in entering the boat is taken by the disciples (Mk 4, 35–41); here, Jesus enters first and the disciples follow.
8, 24: *Storm:* literally, "earthquake," a word commonly used in apocalyptic literature for the shaking of the old world when God brings in his kingdom. All the synoptics use it in depicting the events preceding the parousia of the Son of Man (24, 7; Mk 13, 8; Lk 21, 11). Matthew has introduced it here and in his account of the death and resurrection of Jesus (27, 51–54; 28, 2).
8, 25: The reverent plea of the disciples contrasts sharply with their reproach of Jesus in Mk 4, 38.
8, 26: *You of little faith:* see the note on 6, 30. *Great calm:* Jesus' calming the sea may be meant to recall the Old Testament theme of God's control over the chaotic waters (Pss 65, 8; 89, 10; 93, 3–4; 107, 29).
8, 28: *Gadarenes:* this is the reading of Codex Vaticanus, supported by other important textual witnesses. The original reading of Codex Sinaiticus was Gazarenes, later changed to Gergesenes, and a few versions have Gerasenes. Each of these readings points to a dif-

ferent territory connected, respectively, with the cities Gadara, Gergesa, and Gerasa (modern Jerash). There is the same confusion of readings in the parallel texts, Mk 5, 1 and Lk 8, 26; there the best reading seems to be "Gerasenes," whereas "Gadarenes" is probably the original reading in Matthew. The town of Gadara was about five miles southeast of the Sea of Galilee, and Josephus (*Life* 9 §42) refers to it as possessing territory that lay on that sea. *Two demoniacs:* Mark (5, 1–20) has one.
8, 29: *What have you to do with us?:* see the note on Jn 2, 4. *Before the appointed time:* the notion that evil spirits were allowed by God to afflict human beings until the time of the final judgment is found in Enoch 16, 1 and Jubilees 10, 7–10.
8, 30: The tending of pigs, animals considered unclean by Mosaic law (Lv 11, 6–7), indicates that the population was Gentile.
9, 1: *His own town:* Capernaum; see 4, 13.
9, 3: *Scribes:* see the note on Mk 2, 6. Matthew omits the reason given in the Marcan story for the charge of blasphemy: "Who but God alone can forgive sins?" (Mk 2, 7).

8, 23–27: Mk 4, 35–40; Lk 8, 22–25.
8, 25–26: Ps 107, 28–29.
8, 28–34: Mk 5, 1–17; Lk 8, 26–37.
8, 31: Lk 4, 34.41.
9, 1–8: Mk 2, 3–12; Lk 5, 18–26.
9, 2: Lk 7, 48.

thinking, and said, "Why do you harbor evil thoughts? [5] Which is easier, to say, 'Your sins are forgiven,' or to say, 'Rise and walk'? [6]*† But that you may know that the Son of Man has authority on earth to forgive sins"—he then said to the paralytic, "Rise, pick up your stretcher, and go home." [7] He rose and went home. [8]† When the crowds saw this they were struck with awe and glorified God who had given such authority to human beings.

The Call of Matthew

[9]*† As Jesus passed on from there, he saw a man named Matthew† sitting at the customs post. He said to him, "Follow me." And he got up and followed him. [10]*† While he was at table in his house, many tax collectors and sinners came and sat with Jesus and his disciples. [11]† The Pharisees saw this and said to his disciples, "Why does your teacher eat with tax collectors and sinners?" [12]† He heard this and said, "Those who are well do not need a physician, but the sick do. [13]*† Go and learn the meaning of the words, 'I desire mercy, not sacrifice.' I did not come to call the righteous but sinners."

The Question about Fasting

[14]* Then the disciples of John approached him and said, "Why do we and the Pharisees fast [much], but your disciples do not fast?" [15]† Jesus answered them, "Can the wedding guests mourn as long as the bridegroom is with them? The days will come when the bridegroom is taken away from them, and then they will fast. [16]† No one patches an old cloak with a piece of unshrunken cloth, for its fullness pulls away from the cloak and the tear gets worse. [17] People do not put new wine into old wineskins. Otherwise the skins burst, the wine spills out, and the skins are ruined. Rather, they pour new wine into fresh wineskins, and both are preserved."

The Official's Daughter and the Woman with a Hemorrhage

[18]*† While he was saying these things to them, an official† came forward, knelt down before him, and said, "My daughter has just died. But come, lay your hand on her, and she will live." [19] Jesus rose and followed him, and so did his disciples. [20]† A woman suffering hemorrhages for twelve years came up behind him and touched the tassel on his cloak. [21]* She said to herself, "If only I can touch his cloak, I shall be cured." [22] Jesus turned around and saw her, and said, "Courage, daughter! Your faith has saved you." And from that hour the woman was cured.

[23] When Jesus arrived at the official's house and saw the flute players and the crowd who were making a commotion, [24]† he said, "Go away! The girl is not dead but sleeping." And they ridiculed him. [25] When the crowd was put out, he came and took her by the hand, and the little girl arose. [26] And news of this spread throughout all that land.

9, 6: It is not clear whether *"But that you may know . . . to forgive sins"* is intended to be a continuation of the words of Jesus or a parenthetical comment of the evangelist to those who would hear or read this gospel. In any case, Matthew here follows the Marcan text.

9, 8: *Who had given such authority to human beings:* a significant difference from Mk 2, 12 ("They . . . glorified God saying, 'We have never seen anything like this.' "). Matthew's extension to *human beings* of the authority to forgive sins points to the belief that such authority was being claimed by Matthew's church.

9, 9–17: In this section the order is the same as that of Mk 2, 13–22.

9, 9: *A man named Matthew:* Mark names this tax collector Levi (2, 14). No such name appears in the four lists of the twelve who were the closest companions of Jesus (10, 2–4; Mk 3, 16–19; Lk 6, 14–16; Acts 1, 13 [eleven, because of the defection of Judas Iscariot]), whereas all four list a Matthew, designated in 10, 3 as "the tax collector." The evangelist may have changed the "Levi" of his source to *Matthew* so that this man, whose call is given special notice, like that of the first four disciples (4, 18–22), might be included among the twelve. Another reason for the change may be that the disciple Matthew was the source of traditions peculiar to the church for which the evangelist was writing.

9, 10: *His house:* it is not clear whether *his* refers to Jesus or Matthew. *Tax collectors:* see the note on 5, 46. Table association with such persons would cause ritual impurity.

9, 11: *Teacher:* see the note on 8, 19.

9, 12: See the note on Mk 2, 17.

9, 13: *Go and learn . . . not sacrifice:* Matthew adds the prophetic statement of Hos 6, 6 to the Marcan account (see also 12, 7). If mercy is superior to the temple sacrifices, how much more to the laws of ritual impurity.

9, 15: Fasting is a sign of mourning and would be as inappropriate at this time of joy, when Jesus is proclaiming the kingdom, as it would be at a marriage feast. Yet the saying looks forward to the time when Jesus will no longer be with the disciples visibly, the time of Matthew's church. *Then they will fast:* see Didache 8, 1.

9, 16–17: Each of these parables speaks of the unsuitability of attempting to combine the old and the new. Jesus' teaching is not a patching up of Judaism, nor can the gospel be contained within the limits of Mosaic law.

9, 18–34: In this third group of miracles, the first (18–26) is clearly dependent on Mark (Mk 5, 21–43). Though it tells of two miracles, the cure of the woman had already been included within the story of the raising of the official's daughter, so that the two were probably regarded as a single unit. The other miracles seem to have been derived from Mark and Q respectively, though there Matthew's own editing is much more evident.

9, 18: *Official:* literally, "ruler." Mark calls him "one of the synagogue officials" (Mk 5, 22). *My daughter has just died:* Matthew heightens the Marcan "my daughter is at the point of death" (Mk 5, 23).

9, 20: *Tassel:* possibly "fringe." The Mosaic law prescribed that tassels be worn on the corners of one's garment as a reminder to keep the commandments (see Nm 15, 37–39; Dt 22, 12).

9, 24: *Sleeping:* sleep is a biblical metaphor for death (see Ps 87, 6 LXX; Dn 12, 2; 1 Thes 5, 10). Jesus' statement is not a denial of the child's real death, but an assurance that she will be roused from her sleep of death.

9, 6: Jn 5, 27.
9, 9–13: Mk 2, 14–17; Lk 5, 27–32.
9, 10: Mt 11, 19; Lk 15, 1–2.
9, 13: Mt 12, 7; Hos 6, 6.
9, 14–17: Mk 2, 18–22; Lk 5, 33–39.
9, 18–26: Mk 5, 22–43; Lk 8, 41–56.
9, 21: Mt 14, 36; Nm 15, 37.

9, 25

The Healing of Two Blind Men

27*† And as Jesus passed on from there, two blind men followed [him], crying out, "Son of David,† have pity on us!"* 28 When he entered the house, the blind men approached him and Jesus said to them, "Do you believe that I can do this?" "Yes, Lord," they said to him. 29 Then he touched their eyes and said, "Let it be done for you according to your faith." 30 And their eyes were opened. Jesus warned them sternly, "See that no one knows about this." 31 But they went out and spread word of him through all that land.

The Healing of a Mute Person

32*† As they were going out, a demoniac who could not speak was brought to him, 33* and when the demon was driven out the mute person spoke. The crowds were amazed and said, "Nothing like this has ever been seen in Israel." 34*† But the Pharisees said, "He drives out demons by the prince of demons."

The Compassion of Jesus

35*† Jesus went around to all the towns and villages, teaching in their synagogues, proclaiming the gospel of the kingdom, and curing every disease and illness. 36*† At the sight of the crowds, his heart was moved with pity for them because they were troubled and abandoned, like sheep without a shepherd. 37*† Then he said to his disciples, "The harvest is abundant but the laborers are few; 38 so ask the master of the harvest to send out laborers for his harvest."

The Mission of the Twelve

10 1*† Then he summoned his twelve disciples† and gave them authority over unclean spirits to drive them out and to cure every disease and every illness. 2† The names of the twelve apostles are these: first, Simon called Peter, and his brother Andrew; James, the son of Zebedee, and his brother John; 3 Philip and Bartholomew, Thomas and Matthew the tax collector; James, the son of Alphaeus, and Thaddeus; 4 Simon the Cananean, and Judas Iscariot who betrayed him.

9, 27–31: This story was probably composed by Matthew out of Mark's story of the healing of a blind man named Bartimaeus (Mk 10, 46–52). Mark places the event late in Jesus' ministry, just before his entrance into Jerusalem, and Matthew has followed his Marcan source at that point in his gospel also (see 20, 29–34). In each of the Matthean stories the single blind man of Mark becomes two. The reason why Matthew would have given a double version of the Marcan story and placed the earlier one here may be that he wished to add a story of Jesus' curing the blind at this point in order to prepare for Jesus' answer to the emissaries of the Baptist (11, 4–6) in which Jesus, recounting his works, begins with his giving sight to the blind.

9, 27: *Son of David:* this messianic title is connected once with the healing power of Jesus in Mark (10, 47–48) and Luke (18, 38–39) but more frequently in Matthew (see also 12, 23; 15, 22; 20, 30–31).

9, 32–34: The source of this story seems to be Q (see Lk 11, 14–15). As in the preceding healing of the blind, Matthew has two versions of this healing, the later in 12, 22–24 and the earlier here.

9, 34: This spiteful accusation foreshadows the growing opposition to Jesus in chs 11 and 12.

9, 35: See the notes on 4, 23–25 and 8, 1—9, 38.

9, 36: See Mk 6, 34; Nm 27, 17; 1 Kgs 22, 17.

9, 37–38: This Q saying (see Lk 10, 2) is only imperfectly related to this context. It presupposes that only God (*the master of the harvest*) can take the initiative in sending out preachers of the gospel, whereas in Matthew's setting it leads into ch 10, where Jesus does so.

10, 1—11, 1: After an introductory narrative (10, 1–4), the second of the discourses of the gospel. It deals with the mission now to be undertaken by the disciples (5–15), but the perspective broadens and includes the missionary activity of the church between the time of the resurrection and the parousia.

10, 1: *His twelve disciples:* although, unlike Mark (3, 13–14) and Luke (6, 12–16), Matthew has no story of Jesus' choosing the Twelve, he assumes that the group is known to the reader. The earliest New Testament text to speak of it is 1 Cor 15, 5. The number probably is meant to recall the twelve tribes of Israel and implies Jesus' authority to call all Israel into the kingdom. While Luke (6, 13) and probably Mark (4, 10.34) distinguish between the Twelve and a larger group also termed disciples, Matthew tends to identify the disciples and the Twelve. *Authority . . . every illness:* activities the same as those of Jesus; see 4, 23; 9, 35; 10, 8. The Twelve also share in his proclamation of the kingdom (10, 7). But although he teaches (4, 23; 7, 28; 9, 35), they do not. Their commission to teach comes only after Jesus' resurrection, when they have been fully instructed by him (28, 20).

10, 2–4: Here, for the only time in Matthew, the Twelve are designated *apostles.* The word "apostle" means "one who is sent," and therefore fits the situation here described. In the Pauline letters, the place where the term occurs most frequently in the New Testament, it means primarily one who has seen the risen Lord and has been commissioned to proclaim the resurrection. With slight variants in Luke and Acts, the names of those who belong to this group are the same in the four lists given in the New Testament (see the note on 9, 9). *Cananean:* this represents an Aramaic word meaning "zealot." The meaning of that designation is unclear (see the note on Lk 6, 15).

9, 27–31: Mt 20, 29–34.
9, 27: Mt 15, 22.
9, 32–34: Mt 12, 22–24; Lk 11, 14–15.
9, 33: Mk 2, 12; 7, 37.
9, 34: Mk 10, 25; Mk 3, 22.
9, 35: Mt 4, 23; Lk 8, 1.
9, 36: Nm 27, 17; 1 Kgs 22, 17; Jer 50, 6; Ez 34, 5; Mk 6, 34.
9, 37–38: Lk 10, 2; Jn 4, 35.
10, 1–4: Mk 3, 14–19; Lk 6, 13–16; Acts 1, 13.

The Commissioning of the Twelve

5*† Jesus sent out these twelve after instructing them thus, "Do not go into pagan territory or enter a Samaritan town. 6* Go rather to the lost sheep of the house of Israel. 7* As you go, make this proclamation: 'The kingdom of heaven is at hand.' 8† Cure the sick, raise the dead, cleanse lepers, drive out demons. Without cost you have received; without cost you are to give. 9* Do not take gold or silver or copper for your belts; 10* no sack for the journey, or a second tunic, or sandals, or walking stick. The laborer deserves his keep. 11* Whatever town or village you enter, look for a worthy person in it, and stay there until you leave. 12 As you enter a house, wish it peace. 13† If the house is worthy, let your peace come upon it; if not, let your peace return to you. 14*† Whoever will not receive you or listen to your words—go outside that house or town and shake the dust from your feet. 15* Amen, I say to you, it will be more tolerable for the land of Sodom and Gomorrah on the day of judgment than for that town.

Coming Persecutions

16* "Behold, I am sending you like sheep in the midst of wolves; so be shrewd as serpents and simple as doves. 17*† But beware of people, for they will hand you over to courts and scourge you in their synagogues,* 18 and you will be led before governors and kings for my sake as a witness before them and the pagans. 19* When they hand you over, do not worry about how you are to speak or what you are to say. You will be given at that moment what you are to say. 20 For it will not be you who speak but the Spirit of your Father speaking through you. 21*† Brother will hand over brother to

death, and the father his child; children will rise up against parents and have them put to death. 22† You will be hated by all because of my name, but whoever endures to the end will be saved. 23† When they persecute you in one town, flee to another. Amen, I say to you, you will not finish the towns of Israel before the Son of Man comes. 24* No disciple is above his teacher, no slave above his master. 25† It is enough for the disciple that he become like his teacher, for the slave that he become like his master. If they have called the master of the house Beelzebul, how much more those of his household!

Courage under Persecution

26*† "Therefore do not be afraid of them. Nothing is concealed that will not be revealed, nor secret that will not be known.* 27 What I say to you in the darkness, speak in the light; what you hear whispered, proclaim on the housetops. 28* And do not be afraid of those who kill the body but cannot kill the soul; rather, be afraid of the one who can destroy both soul and body in Gehenna. 29 Are not two sparrows sold for a small coin? Yet not one of them falls to the ground without your Father's knowledge. 30 Even all the hairs of your head are counted. 31 So do not be afraid; you are worth more than many sparrows. 32† Everyone who acknowledges me before others I will acknowledge before my heavenly Father. 33* But whoever denies me before others, I will deny before my heavenly Father.

Jesus: A Cause of Division

34* "Do not think that I have come to bring peace upon the earth. I have come to bring not peace but the sword. 35 For I have come to set

---

† **10, 5–6:** Like Jesus (15, 24), the Twelve are sent only to Israel. This saying may reflect an original Jewish Christian refusal of the mission to the Gentiles, but for Matthew it expresses rather the limitation that Jesus himself observed during his ministry.

10, 8–11: The Twelve have received their own call and mission through God's gift, and the benefits they confer are likewise to be given freely. They are not to take with them money, provisions, or unnecessary clothing; their lodging and food will be provided by those who receive them.

10, 13: The greeting of peace is conceived of not merely as a salutation but as an effective word. If it finds no worthy recipient, it will return to the speaker.

10, 14: Shake the dust from your feet: this gesture indicates a complete disassociation from such unbelievers.

10, 17: The persecutions attendant upon the post-resurrection mission now begin to be spoken of. Here Matthew brings into the discourse sayings found in Mk 13, which deals with events preceding the parousia.

10, 21: See Mi 7, 6, which is cited in vv 35.36.

10, 22: To the end: the original meaning was probably "until the parousia." But it is not likely that Matthew expected no missionary disciples to suffer death before then, since he envisages the martyrdom of other Christians (21). For him, the end is probably that of the individual's life (see 28).

10, 23: Before the Son of Man comes: since the coming of the Son of Man at the end of the age had not taken place when this gospel was written, much less during the mission of the Twelve during Jesus' ministry, Matthew cannot have meant the coming to refer to the parousia.

It is difficult to know what he understood it to be: perhaps the "proleptic parousia" of 28, 16–20, or the destruction of the temple in A.D. 70, viewed as a coming of Jesus in judgment on unbelieving Israel.

10, 25: Beelzebul: see 9, 34 for the charge linking Jesus with "the prince of demons," who is named Beelzebul in 12, 24. The meaning of the name is uncertain; possibly, "lord of the house."

10, 26: The concealed and secret coming of the kingdom is to be proclaimed by them, and no fear must be allowed to deter them from that proclamation.

10, 32–33: In the Q parallel (Lk 12, 8–9), the Son of Man will acknowledge those who have acknowledged Jesus, and those who deny him will be denied (by the Son of Man) before the angels of God at the judgment. Here Jesus and the Son of Man are identified, and the acknowledgment or denial will be before his heavenly Father.

10, 5–15: Mk 6, 7–13; Lk 9, 1–6.
  10, 6: Mt 15, 24.
  10, 7: Mt 3, 2; 4, 17.
10, 9–10: Mk 6, 8–9; Lk 9, 3;
    10, 4.
  10, 10: Lk 10, 7; 1 Cor 9, 14;
    2 Tm 5, 18.
10, 11–15: Mk 6, 10–11; Lk 9,
    4–5; 10, 5–12.
  10, 14: Acts 13, 51; 18, 6.
  10, 15: Mt 11, 24; Gn 19,
    1–29; Jude 7.
  10, 16: Lk 10, 3.
10, 17–22: Mk 13, 9–13; Lk 21,
    12–19.

  10, 17: Acts 5, 40.
  10, 19: Ex 4, 11–12; Jer 1,
    6–10; Lk 12, 11–12.
10, 21–22: Mt 24, 9.13.
10, 24–25: Lk 6, 40; Jn 13, 16;
    15, 20.
10, 26–33: Lk 12, 2–9.
  10, 26: Mk 4, 22; Lk 8, 17;
    1 Tm 5, 25.
  10, 28: Jas 4, 12.
  10, 33: Mk 8, 38; Lk 9, 26;
    2 Tm 2, 12; Rv 3, 5.
10, 34–35: Lk 12, 51–53.

A Violent Jesus?

Jesus says a curious thing as he prepares the Twelve for their mission, "I have come to bring not peace but the sword" (Mt 10, 34). This is one of the many hard sayings attributed to Jesus in the Gospels. Jesus is speaking metaphorically to emphasize the extreme demands of discipleship. He is not advocating violence but simply predicting how people will react to the new values and way of life of his followers. The author of Matthew lived in a community that knew living as Jesus' disciples is not always simple or easy. The people wished for peace, but living by Jesus' words brought them hatred and conflict with people in power. At the time Matthew was written, Christians needed to be able to give up everything, including family attachments, in order to follow Jesus. Is it any different today? Are you up to the challenge?

▶ Mt 10, 34–39

---

a man 'against his father,
a daughter against her mother,
and a daughter-in-law against her
mother-in-law;
36 and one's enemies will be those of
his household.'

The Conditions of Discipleship

37* "Whoever loves father or mother more than me is not worthy of me, and whoever loves son or daughter more than me is not worthy of me; 38† and whoever does not take up his cross and follow after me is not worthy of me. 39*† Whoever finds his life will lose it, and whoever loses his life for my sake will find it.

Rewards

40*† "Whoever receives you receives me, and whoever receives me receives the one who sent me. 41† Whoever receives a prophet because he is a prophet will receive a prophet's reward, and whoever receives a righteous man because he is righteous will receive a righteous man's reward. 42* And

whoever gives only a cup of cold water to one of these little ones to drink because he is a disciple—amen, I say to you, he will surely not lose his reward."

11 1† When Jesus finished giving these commands to his twelve disciples, he went away from that place to teach and to preach in their towns.

IV: Opposition from Israel

The Messengers from John the Baptist

2*† When John heard in prison† of the works of the Messiah, he sent his disciples to him 3† with this question, "Are you the one who is to come, or should we look for another?" 4 Jesus said to them in reply, "Go and tell John what you hear and see: 5*† the blind regain their sight, the lame walk, lepers are cleansed, the deaf hear, the dead are raised, and the poor have the good news proclaimed to them. 6 And blessed is the one who takes no offense at me."

---

†
10, 38: The first mention of the cross in Matthew, explicitly that of the disciple, but implicitly that of Jesus (and follow after me). Crucifixion was a form of capital punishment used by the Romans for offenders who were not Roman citizens.
10, 39: One who denies Jesus in order to save one's earthly life will be condemned to everlasting destruction; loss of earthly life for Jesus' sake will be rewarded by everlasting life in the kingdom.
10, 40–42: All who receive the disciples of Jesus receive him, and God who sent him, and will be rewarded accordingly.
10, 41: A prophet: one who speaks in the name of God; here, the Christian prophets who proclaim the gospel. Righteous man: since righteousness is demanded of all the disciples, it is difficult to take the righteous man of this verse and one of these little ones (42) as indicating different groups within the followers of Jesus. Probably all three designations are used here of Christian missionaries as such.
11, 1: The closing formula of the discourse refers back to the original addressees, the Twelve.
11, 2—12, 50: The narrative section of the third book deals with the growing opposition to Jesus. It is largely devoted to disputes and attacks relating to faith and discipleship and thus contains much sayings-material, drawn in large part from Q.

11, 2: In prison: see 4, 12; 14, 1–12. The works of the Messiah: the deeds of chs 8–9.
11, 3: The question probably expresses a doubt of the Baptist that Jesus is the one who is to come (cf Mal 3, 1) because his mission has not been one of fiery judgment as John had expected (3, 2).
11, 5–6: Jesus' response is taken from passages of Isaiah (26, 19; 29, 18–19; 35, 5–6; 61, 1) that picture the time of salvation as marked by deeds such as those that Jesus is doing. The beatitude is a warning to the Baptist not to disbelieve because his expectations have not been met.

10, 37–39: Mt 16, 24–25; Lk 14,
    26–27.
10, 39: Mk 8, 35; Lk 9, 24;
    Jn 12, 25.
10, 40: Lk 10, 16; Jn 12, 44;
    13, 20.
10, 42: Mt 25, 40; Mk 9, 41.
11, 2–11: Lk 7, 18–28.
11, 5: Is 26, 19; 29, 18–19;
    35, 5–6; 61, 1.

Jesus' Testimony to John

7*† As they were going off, Jesus began to speak to the crowds about John, "What did you go out to the desert to see? A reed swayed by the wind? 8 Then what did you go out to see? Someone dressed in fine clothing? Those who wear fine clothing are in royal palaces. 9† Then why did you go out? To see a prophet? Yes, I tell you, and more than a prophet. 10* This is the one about whom it is written:

'Behold, I am sending my messenger ahead
     of you;
he will prepare your way before you.'

11† Amen, I say to you, among those born of women there has been none greater than John the Baptist; yet the least in the kingdom of heaven is greater than he. 12*† From the days of John the Baptist until now, the kingdom of heaven suffers violence, and the violent are taking it by force. 13† All the prophets and the law prophesied up to the time of John. 14*And if you are willing to accept it, he is Elijah, the one who is to come. 15 Whoever has ears ought to hear.

16*† "To what shall I compare this generation? It is like children who sit in marketplaces and call to one another, 17 'We played the flute for you, but you did not dance, we sang a dirge but you did not mourn.' 18*For John came neither eating nor drinking, and they said, 'He is possessed by a demon.' 19* The Son of Man came eating and drinking and they said, 'Look, he is a glutton and a drunkard, a friend of tax collectors and sinners.' But wisdom is vindicated by her works."

Reproaches to Unrepentant Towns

20* Then he began to reproach the towns where most of his mighty deeds had been done, since they had not repented. 21*† "Woe to you, Chorazin! Woe to you, Bethsaida! For if the mighty deeds done in your midst had been done in Tyre and Sidon, they would long ago have repented in sackcloth and ashes. 22 But I tell you, it will be more tolerable for Tyre and Sidon on the day of judgment than for you. 23*† And as for you, Capernaum:

'Will you be exalted to heaven?
You will go down to the netherworld.'

For if the mighty deeds done in your midst had been done in Sodom, it would have remained until this day. 24*But I tell you, it will be more tolerable for the land of Sodom on the day of judgment than for you."

The Praise of the Father

25*† At that time Jesus said in reply, "I give praise to you, Father, Lord of heaven and earth, for although you have hidden these things from the wise and the learned you have revealed them to the childlike. 26 Yes, Father, such has been your gracious

---

11, 7–19: Jesus' rebuke of John is counterbalanced by a reminder of the greatness of the Baptist's function (7–15) that is followed by a complaint about those who have heeded neither John nor Jesus (16–19).

11, 9–10: In common Jewish belief there had been no prophecy in Israel since the last of the Old Testament prophets, Malachi. The coming of a new prophet was eagerly awaited, and Jesus agrees that John was such. Yet he was *more than a prophet*, for he was the precursor of the one who would bring in the new and final age. The Old Testament quotation is a combination of Mal 3, 1 and Ex 23, 20, with the significant change that the *before me* of Malachi becomes *before you*. The messenger now precedes not God, as in the original, but Jesus.

11, 11: John's preeminent greatness lies in his function of announcing the imminence of the kingdom (3, 1). But to be in the kingdom is so great a privilege that the least who has it is greater than the Baptist.

11, 12: The meaning of this difficult saying is probably that the opponents of Jesus are trying to prevent people from accepting the kingdom and to snatch it away from those who have received it.

11, 13: *All the prophets and the law:* Matthew inverts the usual order, "law and prophets," and says that both *prophesied.* This emphasis on the prophetic character of the law points to its fulfillment in the teaching of Jesus and to the transitory nature of some of its commandments (see the note on 5, 17–20).

11, 16–19: See Lk 7, 31–35. The meaning of the parable (16–17) and its explanation (18–19b) is much disputed. A plausible view is that the *children* of the parable are two groups, one of which proposes different entertainments to the other that will not agree with either proposal. The first represents John, Jesus, and their disciples; the second those who reject John for his asceticism and Jesus for his table association with those despised by the religiously observant.

Verse 19c (*her works*) forms an inclusion with v 2 ("the works of the Messiah"). The original form of the saying is better preserved in Lk 7, 35, ". . . wisdom is vindicated by all her children." There John and Jesus are the children of Wisdom; here the works of Jesus the Messiah are those of divine Wisdom, of which he is the embodiment. Some important textual witnesses, however, have essentially the same reading as in Luke.

11, 21: Tyre and Sidon were pagan cities denounced for their wickedness in the Old Testament; cf Jl 4, 4–7.

11, 23: Capernaum's pride and punishment are described in language taken from the taunt song against the king of Babylon (Is 14, 13–15).

11, 25–27: This Q saying, identical with Lk 10, 21–22 except for minor variations, introduces a joyous note into this section, so dominated by the theme of unbelief. While the *wise and the learned,* the scribes and Pharisees, have rejected Jesus' preaching and the significance of his mighty deeds, *the childlike* have accepted them. Acceptance depends upon the Father's revelation, but this is granted to those who are open to receive it and refused to the arrogant. Jesus can speak of all mysteries because he is *the Son* and there is perfect reciprocity of knowledge between him and the Father; what has been *handed over* to him is revealed only to those whom he wishes.

11, 7: Mt 3, 3.5.   **11, 18:** Lk 1, 15.
11, 10: Ex 23, 20; Mal 3, 1;   **11, 19:** Mt 9, 10–11.
    Mk 1, 2; Lk 1, 76.   **11, 20–24:** Lk 10, 12–15.
11, 12: Lk 16, 16.   **11, 21:** Jl 4, 4–7.
11, 14: Mt 17, 10–13; Mal 3,   **11, 23:** Is 14, 13–15.
    23; Lk 1, 17.   **11, 24:** Mt 10, 15.
11, 16–19: Lk 7, 31–35.   **11, 25–27:** Lk 10, 21–22.

will. 27* All things have been handed over to me by my Father. No one knows the Son except the Father, and no one knows the Father except the Son and anyone to whom the Son wishes to reveal him.

The Gentle Mastery of Christ

28† "Come to me, all you who labor and are burdened,† and I will give you rest. 29*† Take my yoke upon you and learn from me, for I am meek and humble of heart; and you will find rest for yourselves. 30 For my yoke is easy, and my burden light."

Picking Grain on the Sabbath

12 1*† At that time Jesus was going through a field of grain on the sabbath. His disciples were hungry and began to pick the heads of grain and eat them.*† 2 When the Pharisees saw this, they said to him, "See, your disciples are doing what is unlawful to do on the sabbath." 3*† He said to them, "Have you not read what David did when he and his companions were hungry, 4* how he went into the house of God and ate the bread of offering, which neither he nor his companions but only the priests could lawfully eat? 5*† Or have you not read in the law that on the sabbath the priests serving in the temple violate the sabbath and are innocent? 6 I say to you, something greater than the temple is here. 7*† If you knew what this meant, 'I desire mercy, not sacrifice,' you would not have condemned these innocent men. 8*† For the Son of Man is Lord of the sabbath."

The Man with a Withered Hand

9* Moving on from there, he went into their synagogue. 10† And behold, there was a man there who had a withered hand. They questioned him, "Is it lawful to cure on the sabbath?" so that they might accuse him. 11† He said to them, "Which one of you who has a sheep that falls into a pit on the sabbath will not take hold of it and lift it out? 12 How much more valuable a person is than a sheep. So it is lawful to do good on the sabbath." 13 Then he said to the man, "Stretch out your hand." He stretched it out, and it was restored as sound as the other. 14*† But the Pharisees went out and took counsel against him to put him to death.

The Chosen Servant†

15 When Jesus realized this, he withdrew from that place. Many [people] followed him, and he cured them all,† 16 but he warned them not to make him known. 17 This was to fulfill what had been spoken through Isaiah the prophet:

18* "Behold, my servant whom I have chosen,
    my beloved in whom I delight;
I shall place my spirit upon him,
    and he will proclaim justice to the Gentiles.
19† He will not contend or cry out,
    nor will anyone hear his voice in the streets.
20   A bruised reed he will not break,
    a smoldering wick he will not quench,
    until he brings justice to victory.
21†   And in his name the Gentiles will hope."

11, 28–29: These verses are peculiar to Matthew and are similar to Ben Sirach's invitation to learn wisdom and submit to her yoke (Sir 51, 23.26).

11, 28: *Who labor and are burdened:* burdened by the law as expounded by the scribes and Pharisees (23, 4).

11, 29: In place of the yoke of the law, complicated by scribal interpretation, Jesus invites the burdened to take the yoke of obedience to his word, under which they *will find rest;* cf Jer 6, 16.

12, 1–14: Matthew here returns to the Marcan order that he left in 9, 18. The two stories depend on Mk 2, 23–28 and 3, 1–6, respectively, and are the only places in either gospel that deal explicitly with Jesus' attitude toward sabbath observance.

12, 1–2: The picking of the heads of grain is here equated with reaping, which was forbidden on the sabbath (Ex 34, 21).

12, 3–4: See 1 Sm 21, 2–7. In the Marcan parallel (2, 25–26) the high priest is called Abiathar, although in 1 Samuel this action is attributed to Ahimelech. The Old Testament story is not about a violation of the sabbath rest; its pertinence to this dispute is that a violation of the law was permissible because of David's men being without food.

12, 5–6: This and the following argument (7) are peculiar to Matthew. The temple service seems to be the changing of the showbread on the sabbath (Lv 24, 8) and the doubling on the sabbath of the usual daily holocausts (Nm 28, 9–10). The argument is that the law itself requires work that breaks the sabbath rest, because of the higher duty of temple service. If temple duties outweigh the sabbath law, how much more does the presence of Jesus, with his proclamation of the kingdom (*something greater than the temple*), justify the conduct of his disciples.

12, 7: See the note on 9, 13.

12, 8: The ultimate justification for the disciples' violation of the sabbath rest is that Jesus, the Son of Man, has supreme authority over the law.

12, 10: Rabbinic tradition later than the gospels allowed relief to be given to a sufferer on the sabbath if life was in danger. This may also have been the view of Jesus' Pharisaic contemporaries. But the case here is not about one in danger of death.

12, 11: Matthew omits the question posed by Jesus in Mk 3, 4 and substitutes one about rescuing a sheep on the sabbath, similar to that in Lk 14, 5.

12, 14: Matthew follows Mk 3, 6. Here the plan to bring about Jesus' death is attributed to the Pharisees only. This is probably due to the situation of Matthew's church, when the sole opponents were the Pharisees.

12, 15–21: Matthew follows Mk 3, 7–12 but summarizes his source in two verses (15.16) that pick up the withdrawal, the healings, and the command for silence. To this he adds a fulfillment citation from the first Servant Song (Is 42, 1–4) that does not correspond exactly to either the Hebrew or the LXX of that passage. It is the longest Old Testament citation in this gospel, emphasizing the meekness of Jesus, the Servant of the Lord, and foretelling the extension of his mission to the Gentiles.

12, 15: Jesus' knowledge of the Pharisees' plot and his healing *all* are peculiar to Matthew.

12, 19: The servant's not contending is seen as fulfilled in Jesus' withdrawal from the disputes narrated in 1–14.

12, 21: Except for a minor detail, Matthew here follows the LXX, although the meaning of the Hebrew ("the coastlands will wait for his teaching") is similar.

11, 27: Jn 3, 35; 6, 46; 7, 28;
    10, 15.
11, 29: Sir 51, 26; Jer 6, 16.
12, 1–8: Mk 2, 23–28; Lk 6,
    1–5.
12, 1: Dt 23, 26.
12, 3–4: 1 Sm 21, 2–7.

12, 4: Lv 24, 5–9.
12, 5: Lv 24, 8; Nm 28, 9–10.
12, 7: Hos 6, 6.
12, 8: Jn 5, 16–17.
12, 9–15: Mk 3, 1–6; Lk 6, 6–11.
12, 14: Jn 5, 18.
12, 18–21: Is 42, 1–4.

Jesus and Beelzebul

22*† Then they brought to him a demoniac who was blind and mute. He cured the mute person so that he could speak and see. 23*† All the crowd was astounded, and said, "Could this perhaps be the Son of David?" 24*† But when the Pharisees heard this, they said, "This man drives out demons only by the power of Beelzebul, the prince of demons." 25*† But he knew what they were thinking and said to them, "Every kingdom divided against itself will be laid waste, and no town or house divided against itself will stand. 26 And if Satan drives out Satan, he is divided against himself; how, then, will his kingdom stand? 27† And if I drive out demons by Beelzebul, by whom do your own people drive them out? Therefore they will be your judges. 28*† But if it is by the Spirit of God that I drive out demons, then the kingdom of God has come upon you. 29† How can anyone enter a strong man's house and steal his property, unless he first ties up the strong man? Then he can plunder his house. 30*† Whoever is not with me is against me, and whoever does not gather with me scatters. 31*† Therefore, I say to you, every sin and blasphemy will be forgiven people, but blasphemy against the Spirit will not be forgiven. 32 And whoever speaks a word against the Son of Man will be forgiven; but whoever speaks against the holy Spirit will not be forgiven, either in this age or in the age to come.

A Tree and Its Fruits

33*† "Either declare the tree good and its fruit is good, or declare the tree rotten and its fruit is rotten, for a tree is known by its fruit. 34*† You brood of vipers, how can you say good things when you are evil? For from the fullness of the heart the mouth speaks. 35 A good person brings forth good out of a store of goodness, but an evil person brings forth evil out of a store of evil. 36*† I tell you, on the day of judgment people will render an account for every careless word they speak. 37 By your words you will be acquitted, and by your words you will be condemned."

12, 22–32: For the exorcism, see the note on 9, 32–34. The long discussion combines Marcan and Q material (Mk 3, 22–30; Lk 11, 19–20.23; 12, 10). Mk 3, 20–21 is omitted, with a consequent lessening of the sharpness of 12, 48.

12, 23: See the note on 9, 27.

12, 24: See the note on 10, 25.

12, 25–26: Jesus' first response to the Pharisees' charge is that if it were true, Satan would be destroying his own kingdom.

12, 27: Besides pointing out the absurdity of the charge, Jesus asks how the work of Jewish exorcists (*your own people*) is to be interpreted. Are they, too, to be charged with collusion with Beelzebul? For an example of Jewish exorcism see Josephus, *Antiquities* 8, 2, 5 §§42–49.

12, 28: The Q parallel (Lk 11, 20) speaks of the "finger" rather than the "spirit" of God. While the difference is probably due to Matthew's editing, he retains *the kingdom of God* rather than changing it to his usual "kingdom of heaven." *Has come upon you:* see 4, 17.

12, 29: A short parable illustrates what Jesus is doing. The *strong man* is Satan, whom Jesus has tied up and whose *house* he is plundering. Jewish expectation was that Satan would be chained up in the last days (Rv 20, 2); Jesus' exorcisms indicate that those days have begun.

12, 30: This saying, already attached to the preceding verses in Q (see Lk 11, 23), warns that there can be no neutrality where Jesus is concerned. Its pertinence in a context where Jesus is addressing not

the neutral but the bitterly opposed is not clear. The accusation of scattering, however, does fit the situation. Jesus is the shepherd of God's people (2, 6), his mission is to the lost sheep of Israel (15, 24); the Pharisees, who oppose him, are guilty of scattering the sheep.

12, 31: *Blasphemy against the Spirit:* the sin of attributing to Satan (24) what is the work of the Spirit of God (28).

12, 33: *Declare:* literally, "make." The meaning of this verse is obscure. Possibly it is a challenge to the Pharisees either to declare Jesus and his exorcisms good or both of them bad. A tree is known by its fruit; if the fruit is good, so must the tree be. If the driving out of demons is good, so must its source be.

12, 34: The admission of Jesus' goodness cannot be made by the Pharisees, for they are evil, and the words that proceed from their evil hearts cannot be good.

12, 36–37: If on the day of judgment people will be held accountable for even their *careless* words, the vicious accusations of the Pharisees will surely lead to their condemnation.

12, 22–24: Mt 9, 32–34; Lk 11,   12, 30: Lk 11, 23.
            14–15.   12, 31–32: Mk 3, 28–30; Lk
12, 23: Mt 9, 27.   12, 10.
12, 24: Mt 10, 25; Mk 3, 22.   12, 33–35: Lk 6, 43–45.
12, 25–29: Mk 3, 23–27; Lk 11,   12, 34: Mt 3, 7; 23, 33; 15,
            17–22.   11–12; Lk 3, 7.
12, 28: Lk 11, 20.   12, 36–37: Jas 3, 1–2.

The Demand for a Sign†

38* Then some of the scribes and Pharisees said to him, "Teacher,† we wish to see a sign from you." 39† He said to them in reply, "An evil and unfaithful generation seeks a sign, but no sign will be given it except the sign of Jonah the prophet. 40† Just as Jonah was in the belly of the whale three days and three nights, so will the Son of Man be in the heart of the earth three days and three nights. 41† At the judgment, the men of Nineveh will arise with this generation and condemn it, because they repented at the preaching of Jonah; and there is something greater than Jonah here. 42* At the judgment the queen of the south will arise with this generation and condemn it, because she came from the ends of the earth to hear the wisdom of Solomon; and there is something greater than Solomon here.

The Return of the Unclean Spirit

43*† "When an unclean spirit goes out of a person it roams through arid regions searching for rest but finds none. 44 Then it says, 'I will return to my home from which I came.' But upon returning, it finds it empty, swept clean, and put in order. 45 Then it goes and brings back with itself seven other spirits more evil than itself, and they move in and dwell there; and the last condition of that person is worse than the first. Thus it will be with this evil generation."

The True Family of Jesus

46*† While he was still speaking to the crowds, his mother and his brothers appeared outside, wishing to speak with him. [47† Someone told him, "Your mother and your brothers are standing outside, asking to speak with you."] 48 But he said in reply to the one who told him, "Who is my mother? Who are my brothers?" 49 And stretching out his hand toward his disciples, he said, "Here are my mother and my brothers. 50 For whoever does the will of my heavenly Father is my brother, and sister, and mother."

---

did you KNOW?

Parables

The Gospels frequently describe Jesus teaching in parables. A parable is a literary form that uses a fictional story to make a point.

Many of Jesus' parables are like riddles. They have surprising or shocking endings designed to tease the people of his time into examining certain beliefs they took for granted. Unfortunately, the surprise of Jesus' parables is hard for some of us to understand today because we may be unfamiliar with the examples he used: baking bread, planting crops, herding sheep, or fishing for our supper.

Jesus also used parables to teach about God's Reign. These were often in the form of analogies comparing God's Reign to common things or events: "The kingdom of heaven is like . . .". Using parables, Jesus challenged powerful and educated people but was also understood by common people.

▶ Mt 13, 10

12, 38–42: This section is mainly from Q (see Lk 11, 29–32). Mk 8, 11–12, which Matthew has followed in 16, 1–4, has a similar demand for a sign. The scribes and Pharisees refuse to accept the exorcisms of Jesus as authentication of his claims and demand a sign that will end all possibility of doubt. Jesus' response is that no such sign will be given. Because his opponents are evil and see him as an agent of Satan, nothing will convince them.

12, 38: *Teacher:* see the note on 8, 19. In 16, 1 the request is for a sign "from heaven" (Mk 8, 11).

12, 39: *Unfaithful:* literally, "adulterous." The covenant between God and Israel was portrayed as a marriage bond, and unfaithfulness to the covenant as adultery; cf Hos 2, 4–15; Jer 3, 6–10.

12, 40: See Jon 2, 1. While in Q the sign was simply Jonah's preaching to the Ninevites (Lk 11, 30.32), Matthew here adds Jonah's sojourn *in the belly of the whale* for *three days and three nights,* a prefigurement of Jesus' sojourn in the abode of the dead and, implicitly, of his resurrection.

12, 41–42: The Ninevites who *repented* (see Jon 3, 1–10) and the *queen of the south* (i.e., of Sheba; see 1 Kgs 10, 1–13) were pagans who responded to lesser opportunities than have been offered to Israel in the ministry of Jesus, *something greater than Jonah* or

Solomon. At the final judgment they will condemn the faithless *generation* that has rejected him.

12, 43–45: Another Q passage; cf 11, 24–26. Jesus' ministry has broken Satan's hold over Israel, but the refusal of *this evil generation* to accept him will lead to a worse situation than what preceded his coming.

12, 46–50: See Mk 3, 31–35. Matthew has omitted Mk 3, 20–21, which is taken up in Mk 3, 31 (see the note on 12, 22–32), yet the point of the story is the same in both gospels: natural kinship with Jesus counts for nothing; only one who *does the will of* his *heavenly Father* belongs to his true family.

12, 47: This verse is omitted in some important textual witnesses, including Codex Sinaiticus (original reading) and Codex Vaticanus.

12, 38–42: Mt 16, 1–4; Jon 2, 1; 3, 1–10; Mk 8, 11–12; Lk 11, 29–32.
12, 42: 1 Kgs 10, 1–10.

12, 43–45: Lk 11, 24–26.
12, 46–50: Mk 3, 31–35; Lk 8, 19–21.

The Parable of the Sower

13 [1]*† On that day, Jesus went out of the house and sat down by the sea. [2] Such large crowds gathered around him that he got into a boat and sat down, and the whole crowd stood along the shore. [3]† And he spoke to them at length in parables, saying: "A sower went out to sow.† [4] And as he sowed, some seed fell on the path, and birds came and ate it up. [5] Some fell on rocky ground, where it had little soil. It sprang up at once because the soil was not deep, [6] and when the sun rose it was scorched, and it withered for lack of roots. [7] Some seed fell among thorns, and the thorns grew up and choked it. [8] But some seed fell on rich soil, and produced fruit, a hundred or sixty or thirtyfold. [9] Whoever has ears ought to hear."

The Purpose of Parables

[10] The disciples approached him and said, "Why do you speak to them in parables?" [11]† He said to them in reply, "Because knowledge of the mysteries of the kingdom of heaven has been granted to you, but to them it has not been granted. [12]*† To anyone who has, more will be given and he will grow rich; from anyone who has not, even what he has will be taken away. [13]*† This is why I speak to them in parables, because 'they look but do not see and hear but do not listen or understand.' [14]* Isaiah's prophecy is fulfilled in them, which says:

'You shall indeed hear but not understand,
　　you shall indeed look but never see.
[15]　Gross is the heart of this people,
　　they will hardly hear with their ears,
　　　they have closed their eyes,
　　lest they see with their eyes
　　and hear with their ears
　　and understand with their heart and
　　　　be converted,
　　and I heal them.'

The Privilege of Discipleship

[16]*† "But blessed are your eyes, because they see, and your ears, because they hear. [17] Amen, I say to you, many prophets and righteous people longed to see what you see but did not see it, and to hear what you hear but did not hear it.

The Explanation of the Parable of the Sower

[18]*† "Hear then the parable of the sower. [19] The seed sown on the path is the one who hears the word of the kingdom without understanding it, and

---

13, 1–53: The discourse in parables is the third great discourse of Jesus in Matthew and constitutes the second part of the third book of the gospel. Matthew follows the Marcan outline (Mk 4, 1–35) but has only two of Mark's parables, the five others being from Q and M. In addition to the seven parables, the discourse gives the reason why Jesus uses this type of speech (10–15), declares the blessedness of those who understand his teaching (16–17), explains the parable of the sower (18–23) and of the weeds (36–43), and ends with a concluding statement to the disciples (51–52).

13, 3: In parables: the word "parable" (Greek parabolē) is used in the LXX to translate the Hebrew māshāl, a designation covering a wide variety of literary forms such as axioms, proverbs, similitudes, and allegories. In the New Testament the same breadth of meaning of the word is found, but there it primarily designates stories that are illustrative comparisons between Christian truths and events of everyday life. Sometimes the event has a strange element that is quite different from usual experience (e.g., in v 33, the enormous amount of dough in the parable of the yeast); this is meant to sharpen the curiosity of the hearer. If each detail of such a story is given a figurative meaning, the story is an allegory. Those who maintain a sharp distinction between parable and allegory insist that a parable has only one point of comparison, and that while parables were characteristic of Jesus' teaching, to see allegorical details in them is to introduce meanings that go beyond their original intention and even falsify it. However, to exclude any allegorical elements from a parable is an excessively rigid mode of interpretation, now abandoned by many scholars.

13, 3–8: Since in Palestine sowing often preceded plowing, much of the seed is scattered on ground that is unsuitable. Yet while much is wasted, the seed that falls on good ground bears fruit in extraordinarily large measure. The point of the parable is that, in spite of some failure because of opposition and indifference, the message of Jesus about the coming of the kingdom will have enormous success.

13, 11: Since a parable is figurative speech that demands reflection for understanding, only those who are prepared to explore its meaning can come to know it. To understand is a gift of God, granted to the disciples but not to the crowds. In Semitic fashion, both the disciples' understanding and the crowd's obtuseness are attributed to God. The question of human responsibility for the obtuseness is not dealt with, although it is asserted in v 13. The mysteries: as in Lk 8, 10; Mk 4, 11 has "the mystery." The word is used in Dn 2, 18.19.27 and in the Qumran literature (1QpHab 7, 8; 1QS

3, 23; 1QM 3, 9) to designate a divine plan or decree affecting the course of history that can be known only when revealed. Knowledge of the mysteries of the kingdom of heaven means recognition that the kingdom has become present in the ministry of Jesus.

13, 12: In the New Testament use of this axiom of practical "wisdom" (see 25, 29; Mk 4, 25; Lk 8, 18; 19, 26), the reference transcends the original level. God gives further understanding to one who accepts the revealed mystery; from the one who does not, he will take it away (note the "theological passive," more will be given, what he has will be taken away).

13, 13: Because 'they look . . . or understand': Matthew softens his Marcan source, which states that Jesus speaks in parables so that the crowds may not understand (Mk 4, 12), and makes such speaking a punishment given because they have not accepted his previous clear teaching. However, his citation of Is 6, 9–10 in v 14 supports the harsher Marcan view.

13, 16–17: Unlike the unbelieving crowds, the disciples have seen that which the prophets and the righteous of the Old Testament longed to see without having their longing fulfilled.

13, 18–23: See Mk 4, 14–20; Lk 8, 11–15. In this explanation of the parable the emphasis is on the various types of soil on which the seed falls, i.e., on the dispositions with which the preaching of Jesus is received. The second and third types particularly are explained in such a way as to support the view held by many scholars that the explanation derives not from Jesus but from early Christian reflection upon apostasy from the faith that was the consequence of persecution and worldliness respectively. Others, however, hold that the explanation may come basically from Jesus even though it was developed in the light of later Christian experience. The four types of persons envisaged are (1) those who never accept the word of the kingdom (19); (2) those who believe for a while but fall away because of persecution (20–21); (3) those who believe, but in whom the word is choked by worldly anxiety and the seduction of riches (22); (4) those who respond to the word and produce fruit abundantly (23).

13, 1–15: Mk 4, 1–12; Lk 8, 4–10.
13, 12: Mt 24, 29; Mk 4, 25; Lk 8, 18; 19, 26.
13, 13: Jn 9, 39.
13, 14–15: Is 6, 9–10; Jn 12, 40; Acts 28, 26–27; Rom 11, 8.
13, 16–17: Lk 10, 23–24; 1 Pt 1, 10–12.
13, 18–23: Mk 4, 13–20; Lk 8, 11–15.

the evil one comes and steals away what was sown in his heart. 20 The seed sown on rocky ground is the one who hears the word and receives it at once with joy. 21 But he has no root and lasts only for a time. When some tribulation or persecution comes because of the word, he immediately falls away. 22 The seed sown among thorns is the one who hears the word, but then worldly anxiety and the lure of riches choke the word and it bears no fruit. 23 But the seed sown on rich soil is the one who hears the word and understands it, who indeed bears fruit and yields a hundred or sixty or thirtyfold."

The Parable of the Weeds among the Wheat

24† He proposed another parable to them. "The kingdom of heaven may be likened to a man who sowed good seed in his field. 25† While everyone was asleep his enemy came and sowed weeds all through the wheat, and then went off. 26 When the crop grew and bore fruit, the weeds appeared as well. 27 The slaves of the householder came to him and said, 'Master, did you not sow good seed in your field? Where have the weeds come from?' 28 He answered, 'An enemy has done this.' His slaves said to him, 'Do you want us to go and pull them up?' 29 He replied, 'No, if you pull up the weeds you might uproot the wheat along with them. 30*† Let them grow together until harvest; then at harvest time I will say to the harvesters, "First collect the weeds and tie them in bundles for burning; but gather the wheat into my barn." ' "

The Parable of the Mustard Seed

31*† He proposed another parable to them. "The kingdom of heaven is like a mustard seed that a person took and sowed in a field. 32*† It is the smallest of all the seeds, yet when full-grown it is the largest of plants. It becomes a large bush, and the 'birds of the sky come and dwell in its branches.' "

The Parable of the Yeast

33*† He spoke to them another parable. "The kingdom of heaven is like yeast that a woman took and mixed with three measures of wheat flour until the whole batch was leavened."

The Use of Parables

34*† All these things Jesus spoke to the crowds in parables. He spoke to them only in parables, 35*† to fulfill what had been said through the prophet:

"I will open my mouth in parables,
    I will announce what has lain hidden from
      the foundation [of the world]."

The Explanation of the Parable of the Weeds

36† Then, dismissing the crowds, he went into the house. His disciples approached him and said, "Explain to us the parable of the weeds in the field." 37† He said in reply, "He who sows good seed is the Son of Man, 38† the field is the world, the good seed the children of the kingdom. The weeds are the children of the evil one, 39† and the enemy who sows them is the devil. The harvest is the end of the age, and the harvesters are angels. 40 Just as weeds are collected and burned [up] with fire, so will it be at the end of the age. 41† The Son of Man will send his angels, and they will collect out of his kingdom all who cause others to sin and all evildoers. 42* They will throw them into the fiery furnace, where there

---

† **13, 24–30:** This parable is peculiar to Matthew. The comparison in v 24 does not mean that *the kingdom of heaven may be likened* simply to the person in question but to the situation narrated in the whole story. The refusal of *the householder* to allow his *slaves* to separate *the wheat* from *the weeds* while they are still growing is a warning to the disciples not to attempt to anticipate the final judgment of God by a definitive exclusion of sinners from the kingdom. In its present stage it is composed of the good and the bad. The judgment of God alone will eliminate the sinful. Until then there must be patience and the preaching of repentance.

13, 25: *Weeds:* darnel, a poisonous weed that in its first stage of growth resembles wheat.

13, 30: *Harvest:* a common biblical metaphor for the time of God's judgment; cf Jer 51, 33; Jl 4, 13; Hos 6, 11.

13, 31–33: See Mk 4, 30–32; Lk 13, 18–21. The parables of the mustard seed and the yeast illustrate the same point: the amazing contrast between the small beginnings of the kingdom and its marvelous expansion.

13, 32: See Dn 4, 7–9.17–19, where the birds nesting in the tree represent the people of Nebuchadnezzar's kingdom. See also Ez 17, 23 and 31, 6.

13, 33: Except in this Q parable and in 16, 12, *yeast* (or "leaven") is, in New Testament usage, a symbol of corruption (see 16, 6.11–12; Mk 8, 15; Lk 12, 1; 1 Cor 5, 6–8; Gal 5, 9). *Three measures:* an enormous amount, enough to feed a hundred people. The exaggeration of this element of the parable points to the greatness of the kingdom's effect.

13, 34: *Only in parables:* see vv 10–15.

13, 35: *The prophet:* some textual witnesses read "Isaiah the

prophet." The quotation is actually from Ps 78, 2; the first line corresponds to the LXX text of the psalm. The psalm's title ascribes it to Asaph, the founder of one of the guilds of temple musicians. He is called "the prophet" (NAB "the seer") in 2 Chr 29, 30, but it is doubtful that Matthew averted to that; for him, any Old Testament text that could be seen as fulfilled in Jesus was prophetic.

13, 36: *Dismissing the crowds:* the return of Jesus to the house marks a break with the crowds, who represent unbelieving Israel. From now on his attention is directed more and more to his disciples and to their instruction. The rest of the discourse is addressed to them alone.

13, 37–43: In the explanation of the parable of the weeds emphasis lies on the fearful end of the wicked, whereas the parable itself concentrates on patience with them until judgment time.

13, 38: *The field is the world:* this presupposes the resurrection of Jesus and the granting to him of "all power in heaven and on earth" (28, 18).

13, 39: *The end of the age:* this phrase is found only in Matthew (13, 40.49; 24, 3; 28, 20).

13, 41: *His kingdom:* the *kingdom of the Son of Man* is distinguished from that of the Father (43); see 1 Cor 15, 24–25. The church is the place where Jesus' kingdom is manifested, but his royal authority embraces the entire world; see the note on 13, 38.

---

* 13, 30: Mt 3, 12.
13, 31–32: Mk 4, 30–32; Lk 13, 18–19.
13, 32: Ez 17, 23; 31, 6; Dn 4, 7–9.17–19.
13, 33: Lk 13, 20–21.
13, 34–35: Mk 4, 33–34.
13, 35: Ps 78, 2.
13, 42: Mt 8, 12; Rv 21, 8.

will be wailing and grinding of teeth. ⁴³*† Then the righteous will shine like the sun in the kingdom of their Father. Whoever has ears ought to hear.

More Parables†

⁴⁴* "The kingdom of heaven is like a treasure buried in a field,† which a person finds and hides again, and out of joy goes and sells all that he has and buys that field. ⁴⁵ Again, the kingdom of heaven is like a merchant searching for fine pearls. ⁴⁶ When he finds a pearl of great price, he goes and sells all that he has and buys it. ⁴⁷ Again, the kingdom of heaven is like a net thrown into the sea, which collects fish of every kind. ⁴⁸ When it is full they haul it ashore and sit down to put what is good into buckets. What is bad they throw away. ⁴⁹ Thus it will be at the end of the age. The angels will go out and separate the wicked from the righteous ⁵⁰ and throw them into the fiery furnace, where there will be wailing and grinding of teeth.

Treasures New and Old

⁵¹† "Do you understand all these things?" They answered, "Yes." ⁵²† And he replied, "Then every scribe who has been instructed in the kingdom of heaven is like the head of a household who brings from his storeroom both the new and the old." ⁵³ When Jesus finished these parables, he went away from there.

V: Jesus, the Kingdom, and the Church

The Rejection at Nazareth

⁵⁴*† He came to his native place and taught the people in their synagogue. They were astonished† and said, "Where did this man get such wisdom and mighty deeds?* ⁵⁵* Is he not the carpenter's son? Is not his mother named Mary and his brothers James, Joseph, Simon, and Judas? ⁵⁶ Are not his

sisters all with us? Where did this man get all this?" ⁵⁷* And they took offense at him. But Jesus said to them, "A prophet is not without honor except in his

---

PRAY IT!

The Kingdom Is Like . . .

In trying to get people to understand something as mystifying and overwhelming as the kingdom of heaven, Jesus used ordinary objects like seeds and light, salt and yeast. He chose everyday actions like farming, fishing, and baking. And in doing so, he helped the people of his time understand the new life that comes with the kingdom of heaven.

What is the kingdom like to you? Take a walk outside, or look around the room you are in right now. Pick any object that catches your attention. Try to imagine how Jesus, the master teacher, would use that object to describe the kingdom of heaven. For example, he might say: "The kingdom of heaven is like this telephone. It connects you to everyone else in the world no matter who or where they are."

End your meditation with a prayer that your life will be a living sign to help others understand what the kingdom of heaven is all about.

▶ Mt 13, 10–53

---

†

13, 43: See Dn 12, 3.

13, 44–50: The first two of the last three parables of the discourse have the same point. The *person* who *finds* a buried *treasure* and the *merchant* who finds *a pearl of great price* sell *all* that they have to acquire these finds; similarly, the one who understands the supreme value of the kingdom gives up whatever he must to obtain it. The *joy* with which this is done is made explicit in the first parable, but it may be presumed in the second also. The concluding parable of the fishnet resembles the explanation of the parable of the weeds with its stress upon the final exclusion of evil persons from the kingdom.

13, 44: In the unsettled conditions of Palestine in Jesus' time, it was not unusual to guard valuables by burying them in the ground.

13, 51: Matthew typically speaks of the understanding of the disciples.

13, 52: Since Matthew tends to identify the disciples and the Twelve (see the note on 10, 1), this saying about the Christian *scribe* cannot be taken as applicable to all who accept the message of Jesus. While the Twelve are in many ways representative of all who believe in him, they are also distinguished from them in certain respects. The church of Matthew has leaders among whom are a group designated as "scribes" (23, 34). Like the scribes of Israel, they are teachers. It is the Twelve and these their later counterparts to

whom this verse applies. The *scribe . . . instructed in the kingdom of heaven* knows both the teaching of Jesus (*the new*) and the law and prophets (*the old*) and provides in his own teaching *both the new and the old* as interpreted and fulfilled by *the new*. On the translation *head of a household* (for the same Greek word translated *householder* in v 27), see the note on 24, 45–51.

13, 54—17, 27: This section is the narrative part of the fourth book of the gospel.

13, 54–58: After the Sermon on the Mount the crowds are in admiring astonishment at Jesus' teaching (7, 28); here the astonishment is of those who take *offense at him.* Familiarity with his background and family leads them to regard him as pretentious. Matthew modifies his Marcan source (6, 1–6). Jesus is not the carpenter but *the carpenter's son* (55), "and among his own kin" is omitted (57), *he did not work many mighty deeds* in face of such unbelief (58) rather than the Marcan ". . . he was not able to perform any mighty deed there" (6, 5), and there is no mention of his amazement at his townspeople's lack of faith.

*

13, 43: Dn 12, 3.
13, 44–45: Prv 2, 4; 4, 7.
13, 54–58: Mk 6, 1–6; Lk 4, 16–30.

13, 54: Mt 2, 23; Jn 1, 46; 7, 15.
13, 55: Mt 12, 46; 27, 56; Jn 6, 42.
13, 57: Jn 4, 44.

MT

THE CARPENTER'S SON

In Mt 13, 55, Jesus is called the carpenter's son. The carpenter is Saint Joseph, who has two feast days attributed to him—May 1 and March 19. In Sicily, there is a custom called Saint Joseph's Altar. The custom began during a time of severe drought and famine in the Middle Ages. The Sicilian people offered intercessory prayers to Saint Joseph for rain so that their crops would grow. Eventually, their prayers were answered, the crops grew, and they harvested grains, fruits, and vegetables in abundance. In thanksgiving to Saint Joseph, the people gathered to share their harvest with the poor people of the area. Bread, wine, vegetables, fruits, eggs, and fish were placed on an altar and then distributed to those in need. The altar filled with the harvest came to be known as Saint Joseph's Altar.

This event is now celebrated annually in Sicily on March 19. Throughout the year, Sicilians also direct many other intercessions toward Saint Joseph, their patron saint. The Sicilians pray not only for good weather and crops but also for health, for family members and friends, and for all kinds of other personal intentions. On March 19, they show their gratitude to Saint Joseph by preparing a Saint Joseph's Altar and by celebrating their good fortune with one another and the community.

▶ Mt 13, 55

---

native place and in his own house." 58 And he did not work many mighty deeds there because of their lack of faith.

Herod's Opinion of Jesus

14 1*† At that time Herod the tetrarch† *heard of the reputation of Jesus* 2 and said to his servants, "This man is John the Baptist. He has been raised from the dead; that is why mighty powers are at work in him."

The Death of John the Baptist

3*† Now Herod had arrested John, bound [him], and put him in prison on account of Herodias, the wife of his brother Philip, 4* for John had said to him, "It is not lawful for you to have her." 5* Although he wanted to kill him, he feared the people, for they regarded him as a prophet. 6 But at a birthday celebration for Herod, the daughter of Herodias performed a dance before the guests and delighted Herod 7 so much that he swore to give her whatever she might ask for. 8 Prompted by her mother, she said, "Give me here on a platter the head of John the Baptist." 9 The king was distressed, but because of his oaths and the guests who were present, he ordered that it be given, 10 and he had John beheaded in the prison. 11 His head was brought in on a platter and given to the girl, who took it to her mother. 12 His disciples came and took away the corpse and buried him; and they went and told Jesus.

---

† **14, 1–12:** The murder of the Baptist by Herod Antipas prefigures the death of Jesus (see 17, 12). The Marcan source (6, 14–29) is much reduced and in some points changed. In Mark Herod reveres John as a holy man and the desire to kill him is attributed to Herodias (6, 19.20), whereas here that desire is Herod's from the beginning (5).

14, 1: *Herod the tetrarch:* Herod Antipas, son of Herod the Great. When the latter died, his territory was divided among three of his surviving sons, Archelaus who received half of it (2, 23), Herod Antipas who became ruler of Galilee and Perea, and Philip who became ruler of northern Transjordan. Since he received a quarter of his father's domain, Antipas is accurately designated *tetrarch* ("ruler of a fourth [part]"), although in v 9 Matthew repeats the "king" of his Marcan source (6, 26).

14, 3: Herodias was not the wife of Herod's half-brother Philip but of another half-brother, Herod Boethus. The union was prohibited by Lv 18, 16; 20, 21. According to Josephus (*Antiquities* 18, 5, 2 §§116–19), Herod imprisoned and then executed John because he feared that the Baptist's influence over the people might enable him to lead a rebellion.

14, 1–12: Mk 6, 14–29.
　14, 1: Lk 3, 1.
14, 1–2: Lk 9, 7–9.

14, 3–4: Lk 3, 19–20.
14, 4: Lv 18, 16; 20, 21.
14, 5: Mt 21, 26.

The Return of the Twelve and the Feeding of the Five Thousand

13*† When Jesus heard of it, he withdrew in a boat to a deserted place by himself. The crowds heard of this and followed him on foot from their towns. 14 When he disembarked and saw the vast crowd, his heart was moved with pity for them, and he cured their sick. 15 When it was evening, the disciples approached him and said, "This is a deserted place and it is already late; dismiss the crowds so that they can go to the villages and buy food for themselves." 16 [Jesus] said to them, "There is no need for them to go away; give them some food yourselves." 17 But they said to him, "Five loaves and two fish are all we have here." 18 Then he said, "Bring them here to me," 19† and he ordered the crowds to sit down on the grass. Taking the five loaves and the two fish, and looking up to heaven, he said the blessing, broke the loaves, and gave them to the disciples, who in turn gave them to the crowds. 20† They all ate and were satisfied, and they picked up the fragments left over—twelve wicker baskets full. 21 Those who ate were about five thousand men, not counting women and children.

The Walking on the Water

22*† Then he made the disciples get into the boat and precede him to the other side, while he dismissed the crowds. 23* After doing so, he went up on the mountain by himself to pray. When it was evening he was there alone. 24 Meanwhile the boat, already a few miles offshore, was being tossed about by the waves, for the wind was against it. 25† During the fourth watch of the night, he came toward them, walking on the sea. 26 When the disciples saw him walking on the sea they were terrified. "It is a ghost," they said, and they cried out in fear. 27† At once [Jesus] spoke to them, "Take

Do You Trust Jesus?

At this point in the Gospel of Matthew, different groups are beginning to line up for or against Jesus. The Pharisees, Sadducees, and scribes do not trust him. The disciples still follow Jesus, but they do not yet understand who he really is. In chapters 14–17, through several signs and wonders, the true identity of Jesus is revealed to the disciples. Peter in particular is being prepared for his role as leader.

Of the four Gospels, only Matthew includes the story of Peter walking on the water. If you have gotten acquainted with Peter (see "Peter the Rock," Mt 16, 13–20), it will not surprise you that he was willing to take the risk. But why does Peter start to sink? When he is focused on Jesus, everything is fine. It is when he takes his eyes off Jesus, noticing the fierce wind, that he begins to sink.

Jesus invites you to risk a relationship with him. You have to step out in faith, maybe leaving some old ways of life behind. Learn from Peter to keep your focus on Jesus. As the disciples learned, this is no ordinary man but the Son of God! Following Jesus might get scary or difficult at times, but all great adventures involve some risks.

▶ Mt 14, 22–33

---

† **14, 13–21:** The feeding of the five thousand is the only miracle of Jesus that is recounted in all four gospels. The principal reason for that may be that it was seen as anticipating the Eucharist and the final banquet in the kingdom (8, 11; 26, 29), but it looks not only forward but backward, to the feeding of Israel with manna in the desert at the time of the Exodus (Ex 16), a miracle that in some contemporary Jewish expectation would be repeated in the messianic age (2 Baruch 29, 8). It may also be meant to recall Elisha's feeding a hundred men with small provisions (2 Kgs 4, 42–44).

14, 19: The *taking*, saying the blessing, *breaking*, and *giving* to the disciples correspond to the actions of Jesus over the bread at the Last Supper (26, 26). Since they were usual at any Jewish meal, that correspondence does not necessarily indicate a eucharistic reference here. Matthew's silence about Jesus' dividing the fish among the people (Mk 6, 41) is perhaps more significant in that regard.

14, 20: The *fragments left over:* as in Elisha's miracle, food was *left over* after all had been fed. The word *fragments* (Greek *klasmata*) is used, in the singular, of the broken bread of the Eucharist in *Didache* 9, 3–4.

14, 22–33: The disciples, laboring against the turbulent sea, are saved by Jesus. For his power over the waters, see the note on 8, 26. Here that power is expressed also by his *walking on the sea* (25; cf Ps 77, 20; Jb 9, 8). Matthew has inserted into the Marcan story (Mk 6, 45–52) material that belongs to his special traditions on Peter (28–31).

14, 25: *The fourth watch of the night:* between 3 a.m. and 6 a.m. The Romans divided the twelve hours between 6 p.m. and 6 a.m. into four equal parts called "watches."

14, 27: *It is I:* see the note on Mk 6, 50.

* 14, 13–21: Mt 15, 32–38; Mk 6, 32–44; Lk 9, 10–17; Jn 6, 1–13.

14, 22–33: Mk 6, 45–52; Jn 6, 16–21.
14, 23: Mk 1, 35; Lk 5, 16; 6, 12.

MT

courage, it is I; do not be afraid." 28 Peter said to him in reply, "Lord, if it is you, command me to come to you on the water." 29 He said, "Come." Peter got out of the boat and began to walk on the water toward Jesus. 30* But when he saw how [strong] the wind was he became frightened; and, beginning to sink, he cried out, "Lord, save me!" 31† Immediately Jesus stretched out his hand and caught him, and said to him, "O you of little faith, why did you doubt?" 32 After they got into the boat, the wind died down. 33*† Those who were in the boat did him homage, saying, "Truly, you are the Son of God."

The Healings at Gennesaret

34* After making the crossing, they came to land at Gennesaret. 35 When the men of that place recognized him, they sent word to all the surrounding country. People brought to him all those who were sick 36* and begged him that they might touch only the tassel on his cloak, and as many as touched it were healed.

The Tradition of the Elders

15 1*† Then Pharisees and scribes came to Jesus from Jerusalem and said, 2*† "Why do your disciples break the tradition of the elders? They do not wash [their] hands when they eat a meal." 3† He said to them in reply, "And why do you break the commandment of God for the sake of your tradition? 4* For God said, 'Honor your father and your mother,' and 'Whoever curses father or mother shall die.' 5† But you say, 'Whoever says to father or mother, "Any support you might have had from me is dedicated to God," 6 need not honor his father.' You have nullified the word of God for the sake of your tradition. 7 Hypocrites, well did Isaiah prophesy about you when he said:

8*†   'This people honors me with their lips,
    but their hearts are far from me;
9*   in vain do they worship me,
    teaching as doctrines human precepts.' "

10* He summoned the crowd and said to them, "Hear and understand. 11 It is not what enters one's mouth that defiles that person; but what comes out of the mouth is what defiles one." 12 Then his disciples approached and said to him, "Do you know that the Pharisees took offense when they heard what you said?" 13† He said in reply, "Every plant that my heavenly Father has not planted will be uprooted. 14* Let them alone; they are blind guides [of the blind]. If a blind person leads a blind person, both will fall into a pit." 15† Then Peter said to him in reply, "Explain [this] parable to us." 16 He said to them, "Are even you still without understanding? 17 Do you not realize that everything that enters the mouth passes into the stomach and is expelled into the latrine? 18* But the things that come out of the mouth come from the heart, and they defile. 19† For from the heart come evil thoughts, murder, adultery, unchastity, theft, false witness, blasphemy. 20 These are what defile a person, but to eat with unwashed hands does not defile."

The Canaanite Woman's Faith

21*† Then Jesus went from that place and withdrew to the region of Tyre and Sidon. 22 And behold, a Canaanite woman of that district came and called

---

14, 31: *You of little faith:* see the note on 6, 30. *Why did you doubt?:* the verb is peculiar to Matthew and occurs elsewhere only in 28, 17.

14, 33: This confession is in striking contrast to the Marcan parallel (6, 51) where the disciples are "completely astounded."

15, 1–20: This dispute begins with the question of the Pharisees and scribes who charge Jesus' disciples are breaking the *tradition of the elders* about washing one's hands before eating (2). Jesus' counterquestion accuses his opponents of breaking *the commandment of God for the sake of their tradition* (3) and illustrates this by their interpretation of the commandment of the Decalogue concerning parents (4–6). Denouncing them as hypocrites, he applies to them a derogatory prophecy of Isaiah (7–8). Then with a wider audience (*the crowd*, 10) he goes beyond the violation of tradition with which the dispute has started. The parable (11) is an attack on the Mosaic law concerning clean and unclean foods, similar to those antitheses that abrogate the law (5, 31–32.33–34.38–39). After a warning to his disciples not to follow the moral guidance of the Pharisees (13–14), he explains the *parable* (15) to them, saying that defilement comes not from what *enters the mouth* (17) but from the evil thoughts and deeds that rise from within, *from the heart* (18–20). The last verse returns to the starting point of the dispute (eating *with unwashed hands*). Because of Matthew's omission of Mk 7, 19b, some scholars think that Matthew has weakened the Marcan repudiation of the Mosaic food laws. But that half verse is ambiguous in the Greek, which may be the reason for its omission here.

15, 2: *The tradition of the elders:* see the note on Mk 7, 5. The purpose of the handwashing was to remove defilement caused by contact with what was ritually unclean.

15, 3–4: For the commandment see Ex 20, 12 (// Dt 5, 16); 21, 17. The honoring of one's parents had to do with supporting them in their needs.

15, 5: See the note on Mk 7, 11.

15, 8: The text of Is 29, 13 is quoted approximately according to the Septuagint.

15, 13–14: Jesus leads his disciples away from the teaching authority of the Pharisees.

15, 15: Matthew specifies *Peter* as the questioner, unlike Mk 7, 17. Given his tendency to present the disciples as more understanding than in his Marcan source, it is noteworthy that here he retains the Marcan rebuke, although in a somewhat milder form. This may be due to his wish to correct the Jewish Christians within his church who still held to the food laws and thus separated themselves from Gentile Christians who did not observe them.

15, 19: The Marcan list of thirteen things that defile (7, 21–22) is here reduced to seven that partially cover the content of the Decalogue.

15, 21–28: See the note on 8, 5–13.

14, 30–31: Mt 8, 25–26.
14, 33: Mt 16, 16.
14, 34–36: Mk 6, 53–56.
14, 36: Mk 9, 20–22.
15, 1–20: Mk 7, 1–23.
15, 2: Lk 11, 38.
15, 4: Ex 20, 12; 21, 17; Lv 20, 9; Dt 5, 16; Prv 20, 20.
15, 8: Is 29, 13 LXX.
15, 9: Col 2, 23.
15, 10: Mk 7, 14.
15, 14: Mt 23, 16.19.24; Lk 6, 39; Jn 9, 40.
15, 18: Mt 12, 34.
15, 21–28: Mk 7, 24–30.

A PRAYER FOR HEALING HUMANKIND

In Mt 15, 1–20, Jesus addresses the hypocrisy of the Jewish leaders who manipulate the Law to their own good. They and the people who follow them are blind to the results. In this prayer, the Ojibwa (or Anishinabe) recognize the need for humans to overcome their blindness to the results of evil intentions:

> Grandfather,
> Look at our brokenness.
> We know that in all creation
> Only the human family
> Has strayed from the Sacred Way.
> We know that we are the ones
> Who must come back together
> To walk in the Sacred Way.
> Grandfather,
> Sacred One,
> Teach us love, compassion, and honor
> That we may heal the earth
> And heal each other.

(David Schiller, editor, The Little Book of Prayers, pp. 328–329)

▶ Mt 15, 1–20

---

out, "Have pity on me, Lord, Son of David! My daughter is tormented by a demon." 23 But he did not say a word in answer to her. His disciples came and asked him, "Send her away, for she keeps calling out after us." 24† He said in reply, "I was sent only to the lost sheep of the house of Israel." 25* But the woman came and did him homage, saying, "Lord, help me." 26† He said in reply, "It is not right to take the food of the children and throw it to the dogs." 27 She said, "Please, Lord, for even the dogs eat the scraps that fall from the table of their masters." 28*† Then Jesus said to her in reply, "O woman, great is your faith! Let it be done for you as you wish." And her daughter was healed from that hour.

The Healing of Many People

29 Moving on from there Jesus walked by the Sea of Galilee, went up on the mountain, and sat down there. 30* Great crowds came to him, having with them the lame, the blind, the deformed, the mute, and many others. They placed them at his feet, and he cured them. 31 The crowds were amazed when they saw the mute speaking, the deformed made whole, the lame walking, and the blind able to see, and they glorified the God of Israel.

The Feeding of the Four Thousand

32*† Jesus summoned his disciples and said, "My heart is moved with pity for the crowd, for

---

15, 24: See the note on 10, 5–6.
15, 26: *The children:* the people of Israel. *Dogs:* see the note on 7, 6.
15, 28: As in the case of the cure of the centurion's servant (8, 10), Matthew ascribes Jesus' granting the request to the woman's *great faith*, a point not made equally explicit in the Marcan parallel (7, 24–30).
15, 32–39: Most probably this story is a doublet of that of the feeding of the five thousand (14, 13–21). It differs from it notably

only in that Jesus takes the initiative, not the disciples (32), and in the numbers: the crowd has been with Jesus *three days* (32), *seven loaves* are multiplied (36), *seven baskets* of fragments remain after the feeding (37), and *four thousand* men are fed (38).

15, 25: Mt 10, 6.   15, 30: Is 35, 5–6.
15, 28: Mt 8, 10.   15, 32–39: Mk 8, 1–10.

they have been with me now for three days and have nothing to eat. I do not want to send them away hungry, for fear they may collapse on the way." 33 The disciples said to him, "Where could we ever get enough bread in this deserted place to satisfy such a crowd?" 34 Jesus said to them, "How many loaves do you have?" "Seven," they replied, "and a few fish." 35 He ordered the crowd to sit down on the ground. 36† Then he took the seven loaves and the fish, gave thanks, broke the loaves, and gave them to the disciples, who in turn gave them to the crowds. 37* They all ate and were satisfied. They picked up the fragments left over—seven baskets full. 38 Those who ate were four thousand men, not counting women and children. 39 And when he had dismissed the crowds, he got into the boat and came to the district of Magadan.

The Demand for a Sign

16 1*† The Pharisees and Sadducees came and, to test him, asked him to show them a sign from heaven. 2† He said to them in reply, "[In the evening you say, 'Tomorrow will be fair, for the sky is red'; 3* and, in the morning, 'Today will be stormy, for the sky is red and threatening.' You know how to judge the appearance of the sky, but you cannot judge the signs of the times.] 4*† An evil and unfaithful generation seeks a sign, but no sign will be given it except the sign of Jonah." Then he left them and went away.

The Leaven of the Pharisees and Sadducees

5*† In coming to the other side of the sea, the disciples had forgotten to bring bread. 6*† Jesus said to them, "Look out, and beware of the leaven of the Pharisees and Sadducees." 7† They concluded among themselves, saying, "It is because we have brought no bread." 8 When Jesus became aware of this he said, "You of little faith, why do you conclude among yourselves that it is because you have no bread? 9* Do you not yet understand, and do you not remember the five loaves for the five thousand, and how many wicker baskets you took up? 10* Or the seven loaves for the four thousand, and how many baskets you took up? 11 How do you not comprehend that I was not speaking to you about bread? Beware of the leaven of the Pharisees and Sadducees." 12† Then they understood that he was not telling them to beware of the leaven of bread, but of the teaching of the Pharisees and Sadducees.

Peter's Confession about Jesus†

13* When Jesus went into the region of Caesarea Philippi† he asked his disciples, "Who do people say that the Son of Man is?" 14*† They replied, "Some say John the Baptist, others Elijah, still others Jeremiah or one of the prophets." 15 He said to them, "But who do you say that I am?" 16*† Simon Peter said in reply, "You are the Messiah, the Son of the living God." 17† Jesus said to him in reply, "Blessed are you, Simon son of Jonah. For flesh and

---

15, 36: *Gave thanks:* see 14, 19, "said the blessing." There is no difference in meaning. The thanksgiving was a blessing of God for his benefits.

16, 1: *A sign from heaven:* see the note on 12, 38–42.

16, 2–3: The answer of Jesus in these verses is omitted in many important textual witnesses, and it is very uncertain that it is an original part of this gospel. It resembles Lk 12, 54–56 and may have been inserted from there. It rebukes the Pharisees and Sadducees who are able to read indications of coming weather but not the indications of the coming kingdom in the signs that Jesus does offer, his mighty deeds and teaching.

16, 4: See the notes on 12, 39.40.

16, 5–12: Jesus' warning his disciples against *the teaching of the Pharisees and Sadducees* comes immediately before his promise to confer on Peter the authority to bind and to loose on earth (19), an authority that will be confirmed in heaven. Such authority most probably has to do, at least in part, with teaching. The rejection of the teaching authority of the Pharisees (see also 12, 12–14) prepares for a new one derived from Jesus.

16, 6: *Leaven:* see the note on 13, 33. *Sadducees:* Matthew's Marcan source speaks rather of "the leaven of Herod" (8, 15).

16, 7–11: The disciples, men *of little faith,* misunderstand Jesus' metaphorical use of *leaven,* forgetting that, as the feeding of the crowds shows, he is not at a loss to provide them with bread.

16, 12: After his rebuke, the disciples understand that by *leaven* he meant the corrupting influence of *the teaching of the Pharisees and Sadducees.* The evangelist probably understands this *teaching* as common to both groups. Since at the time of Jesus' ministry the two differed widely on points of teaching, e.g., the resurrection of the dead, and at the time of the evangelist the Sadducee party was no longer a force in Judaism, the supposed common *teaching* fits neither period. The disciples' eventual understanding of Jesus' warning contrasts with their continuing obtuseness in the Marcan parallel (8, 14–21).

16, 13–20: The Marcan confession of Jesus as Messiah, made by Peter as spokesman for the other disciples (8, 27–29; cf also Lk 9, 18–20), is modified significantly here. The confession is of Jesus both as *Messi-*

ah and as *Son of the living God* (16). Jesus' response, drawn principally from material peculiar to Matthew, attributes the confession to a divine revelation granted to Peter alone (17) and makes him the *rock* on which Jesus *will build* his *church* (18) and the disciple whose authority in the church *on earth* will be confirmed *in heaven,* i.e., by God (19).

16, 13: *Caesarea Philippi:* situated about twenty miles north of the Sea of Galilee in the territory ruled by Philip, a son of Herod the Great, tetrarch from 4 B.C. until his death in A.D. 34 (see the note on 14, 1). He rebuilt the town of Paneas, naming it *Caesarea* in honor of the emperor, and *Philippi* ("of Philip") to distinguish it from the seaport in Samaria that was also called Caesarea. *Who do people say that the Son of Man is?:* although the question differs from the Marcan parallel (8, 27: "Who . . . that I am?"), the meaning is the same, for Jesus here refers to himself as the *Son of Man* (cf 15).

16, 14: *John the Baptist:* see 14, 2. *Elijah:* cf Mal 3, 23–24; Sir 48, 10; and see the note on 3, 4. *Jeremiah:* an addition of Matthew to the Marcan source.

16, 16: *The Son of the living God:* see 2, 15; 3, 17. The addition of this exalted title to the Marcan confession eliminates whatever ambiguity was attached to the title Messiah. This, among other things, supports the view proposed by many scholars that Matthew has here combined his source's confession with a post-resurrectional confession of faith in Jesus as *Son of the living God* that belonged to the appearance of the risen Jesus to Peter; cf 1 Cor 15, 5; Lk 24, 34.

16, 17: *Flesh and blood:* a Semitic expression for human beings, especially in their weakness. *Has not revealed this . . . but my heavenly Father:* that Peter's faith is spoken of as coming not through human means but through a revelation from God is similar to Paul's description of his recognition of who Jesus was; see Gal 1, 15–16, ". . . when [God] . . . was pleased to reveal his Son to me. . . ."

15, 37: Mt 16, 10.
16, 1–10: Mk 8, 11–21.
16, 3: Lk 12, 54–56.
16, 4: Mt 12, 39; Jon 2, 1.
16, 5–12: Mk 8, 14–21.
16, 6: Lk 12, 1.

16, 9: Mt 14, 17–21; Jn 6, 9.
16, 10: Mt 15, 34–38.
16, 13–16: Mk 8, 27–29; Lk 9, 18–20.
16, 14: Mt 14, 2.
16, 16: Jn 6, 69.

Introducing...

▶ PETER THE ROCK

What images does the name Saint Peter bring to your mind? The simple fisherman named Simon who was among the first disciples called by Jesus (Mt 4, 18; Mk 1, 16; Lk 5, 10)? The hopeful believer who first recognized Jesus as the Messiah (Mt 16, 16; Mk 8, 29; Lk 9, 20)? The fearful friend who denied Jesus three times (Mt 26, 69–74; Mk 14, 66–72; Lk 22, 54–62; Jn 18, 15–27)? The leader of the early church whom we recognize as the first pope (Jn 21, 15; Acts 2, 14)? Peter is all these things and more. The Bible paints a picture of a very human leader with sins and weaknesses along with many gifts and great faith.

The author of Matthew uses a play on words to make a statement about Peter as the foundation of the church. The new name that Jesus gives him—Peter—means "rock." So Jesus is saying, "You are [a rock], and upon this rock I will build my church" (Mt 16, 18). The Catholic church uses this Scripture passage as support for its teaching on the pope's position as the spiritual leader and highest authority of the church. Peter's primacy as the first of Jesus' Apostles is understood to be passed on to the current pope, through the succession of popes who go back to the beginnings of the church at Rome.

▶ Mt 16, 13–20

---

blood has not revealed this to you, but my heavenly Father. [18]*† And so I say to you, you are Peter, and upon this rock I will build my church, and the gates of the netherworld shall not prevail against it. [19]*† I will give you the keys to the kingdom of heaven. Whatever you bind on earth shall be bound in heaven; and whatever you loose on earth shall be loosed in heaven." [20]*† Then he strictly ordered his disciples to tell no one that he was the Messiah.

The First Prediction of the Passion†

[21]* From that time on, Jesus began to show his disciples that he† must go to Jerusalem and suffer

---

16, 18: *You are Peter, and upon this rock I will build my church:* the Aramaic word *kēpā'* meaning *rock* and transliterated into Greek as *Kēphas* is the name by which Peter is called in the Pauline letters (1 Cor 1, 12; 3, 22; 9, 5; 15, 4; Gal 1, 18; 2, 9.11.14) except in Gal 2, 7–8 ("Peter"). It is translated as *Petros* ("Peter") in Jn 1, 42. The presumed original Aramaic of Jesus' statement would have been, in English, "You are the Rock (*Kēpā'*) and upon this rock (*kēpā'*) I will build my church." The Greek text probably means the same, for the difference in gender between the masculine noun *petros*, the disciple's new name, and the feminine noun *petra* (rock) may be due simply to the unsuitability of using a feminine noun as the proper name of a male. Although the two words were generally used with slightly different nuances, they were also used interchangeably with the same meaning, "rock." *Church:* this word (Greek *ekklēsia*) occurs in the gospels only here and in 18, 17 (twice). There are several possibilities for an Aramaic original. Jesus' *church* means the community that he *will* gather and that, like a building, will have Peter as its solid foundation. That function of Peter consists in his being witness to Jesus as *the Messiah, the Son of the living God. The gates of the netherworld shall not prevail against it:* the netherworld (Greek *Hadēs*, the abode of the dead) is conceived of as a walled city whose *gates* will not close in upon the church of Jesus, i.e., it will not be overcome by the power of death.

16, 19: *The keys to the kingdom of heaven:* the image of the *keys* is probably drawn from Is 22, 15–25, where Eliakim, who succeeds Shebna as master of the palace, is given "the key of the House of David," which he authoritatively "opens" and "shuts" (22, 22). *Whatever you bind . . . loosed in heaven:* there are many instances in rabbinic literature of the binding-loosing imagery. Of the several meanings given there to the metaphor, two are of special importance here: the giving of authoritative teaching, and the lifting or imposing of the ban of excommunication. It is disputed whether the image of *the keys* and that of binding and loosing are different metaphors meaning the same thing. In any case, the promise of the keys is given to Peter alone. In 18, 18 all the disciples are given the power of binding and loosing, but the context of that verse suggests that there the power of excommunication

alone is intended. That *the keys* are those to the *kingdom of heaven* and that Peter's exercise of authority in the church on earth will be confirmed *in heaven* show an intimate connection between, but not an identification of, the church and the *kingdom of heaven.*

16, 20: Cf Mk 8, 30. Matthew makes explicit that the prohibition has to do with speaking of Jesus as *the Messiah;* see the note on Mk 8, 27–30.

16, 21–23: This first prediction of the passion follows Mk 8, 31–33 in the main and serves as a corrective to an understanding of Jesus' messiahship as solely one of glory and triumph. By his addition of *from that time on* (21) Matthew has emphasized that Jesus' revelation of his coming suffering and death marks a new phase of the gospel. Neither this nor the two later passion predictions (17, 22–23; 20, 17–19) can be taken as sayings that, as they stand, go back to Jesus himself. However, it is probable that he foresaw that his mission would entail suffering and perhaps death, but was confident that he would ultimately be vindicated by God (see 26, 29).

16, 21: *He:* the Marcan parallel (8, 31) has "the Son of Man." Since Matthew has already designated Jesus by that title (13), its omission here is not significant. The Matthean prediction is equally about the sufferings of the Son of Man. *Must:* this necessity is part of the tradition of all the synoptics; cf Mk 8, 31; Lk 9, 21. *The elders, the chief priests, and the scribes:* see the note on Mk 8, 31. *On the third day:* so also Lk 9, 22, against the Marcan "after three days" (8, 31). Matthew's formulation is, in the Greek, almost identical with the pre-Pauline fragment of the kerygma in 1 Cor 15, 4, and also with Hos 6, 2, which many take to be the Old Testament background to the confession that Jesus was raised *on the third day.* Josephus uses "after three days" and "on the third day" interchangeably (*Antiquities* 7, 11, 6 §§280–81; 8, 8, 1–2 §§214, 218) and there is probably no difference in meaning between the two phrases.

16, 18: Jn 1, 42.
16, 19: Is 22, 22; Rv 3, 7.
16, 20: Mk 8, 30; Lk 9, 21.

16, 21–28: Mk 8, 31–9, 1; Lk 9, 22–27.
16, 21: Mt 17, 22–23; 20, 17–19.

MT

greatly from the elders, the chief priests, and the scribes, and be killed and on the third day be raised.* 22† Then Peter took him aside and began to rebuke him, "God forbid, Lord! No such thing shall ever happen to you." 23* He turned and said to Peter, "Get behind me, Satan! You are an obstacle to me. You are thinking not as God does, but as human beings do."

The Conditions of Discipleship†

24* Then Jesus said to his disciples, "Whoever wishes to come after me must deny himself,† take up his cross, and follow me. 25*† For whoever wishes to save his life will lose it, but whoever los-es his life for my sake will find it. 26 What profit would there be for one to gain the whole world and forfeit his life? Or what can one give in exchange for his life? 27*† For the Son of Man will come with his angels in his Father's glory, and then he will repay everyone according to his conduct. 28† Amen, I say to you, there are some standing here who will not taste death until they see the Son of Man coming in his kingdom."

The Transfiguration of Jesus†

17 1* After six days Jesus took Peter, James, and John his brother, and led

THE PRINCIPLE OF *UJAMAA*

A man who won't die for something is not fit to live. (Martin Luther King Jr.)

Jesus tells us that we need to leave behind our old life of selfishness and embrace a new way of life marked by caring about the needs of others. Only then can the spirit of the Lord abound. Martin Luther King Jr. practiced this new way of life in his dream for a better day for African Americans—a dream he was willing to work and die for.

The Kwanzaa principle of *ujamaa*, or cooperative economics, requires this kind of selfless love for others. To practice *ujamaa* means sharing resources with our brothers and sisters, supporting one another's businesses, and living so that everybody receives what they need to prosper. Jesus' words challenge us to build up our communities, preserving the gains we have made and laying foundations for the success of those who come after us. The cost is our me-first attitudes, but the reward is a new life of justice and freedom.

Dear God, my humanness wants to hoard myself; my spirit wants to give!

▶ Mt 16, 25

---

† 16, 22–23: Peter's refusal to accept Jesus' predicted suffering and death is seen as a satanic attempt to deflect Jesus from his God-appointed course, and the disciple is addressed in terms that recall Jesus' dismissal of the devil in the temptation account (4, 10: "Get away, Satan!"). Peter's satanic purpose is emphasized by Matthew's addition to the Marcan source of the words *You are an obstacle to me.*

16, 24–28: A readiness to follow Jesus even to giving up one's life for him is the condition for true discipleship; this will be repaid by him at the final judgment.

16, 24: *Deny himself:* to deny someone is to disown him (see 10, 33; 26, 34–35) and to deny oneself is to disown oneself as the center of one's existence.

16, 25: See the notes on 10, 38.39.

16, 27: The parousia and final judgment are described in 25, 31 in terms almost identical with these.

16, 28: *Coming in his kingdom:* since the *kingdom* of the *Son of Man* has been described as "the world" and Jesus' sovereignty pre-cedes his final coming in glory (13, 38.41), the *coming* in this verse is not the parousia as in the preceding but the manifestation of Jesus' rule after his resurrection; see the notes on 13, 38.41.

17, 1–8: The account of the transfiguration confirms that Jesus is the *Son* of *God* (5) and points to fulfillment of the prediction that he will come *in his Father's glory* at the end of the age (16, 27). It has been explained by some as a resurrection appearance retrojected into the time of Jesus' ministry, but that is not probable since the account lacks many of the usual elements of the resurrection-appearance narratives. It draws upon motifs from the Old Testament and noncanonical Jewish apocalyptic literature that express the presence of the heavenly and the divine, e.g., brilliant light, white garments, and the overshadowing cloud.

16, 23: Mt 4, 10.
16, 24: Lk 14, 27.
16, 25: Lk 17, 33; Jn 12, 25.

16, 27: Mt 25, 31–33; Jb 34, 11; Ps 62, 13; Jer 17, 10; 2 Thes 1, 7–8.
17, 1–8: Mk 9, 2–8; Lk 9, 28–36.

them up a high mountain by themselves.† ²*† And he was transfigured before them; his face shone like the sun and his clothes became white as light. ³† And behold, Moses and Elijah appeared to them, conversing with him. ⁴† Then Peter said to Jesus in reply, "Lord, it is good that we are here. If you wish, I will make three tents here, one for you, one for Moses, and one for Elijah." ⁵*† While he was still speaking, behold, a bright cloud cast a shadow over them, then from the cloud came a voice that said, "This is my beloved Son, with whom I am well pleased; listen to him." ⁶† When the disciples heard this, they fell prostrate and were very much afraid. ⁷ But Jesus came and touched them, saying, "Rise, and do not be afraid." ⁸ And when the disciples raised their eyes, they saw no one else but Jesus alone.

The Coming of Elijah†

⁹* As they were coming down from the mountain, Jesus charged them, "Do not tell the vision† to anyone until the Son of Man has been raised from the dead." ¹⁰*† Then the disciples asked him, "Why do the scribes say that Elijah must come first?" ¹¹*† He said in reply, "Elijah will indeed come and restore all things; ¹²* but I tell you that Elijah has already come, and they did not recognize him but did to him whatever they pleased. So also will the Son of Man suffer at their hands." ¹³† Then the disciples understood that he was speaking to them of John the Baptist.

The Healing of a Boy with a Demon

¹⁴*† When they came to the crowd a man

THE TRANSFIGURATION

The Gospels of Matthew, Mark, and Luke each include the story in Mt 17, 1–13, called the Transfiguration. Jesus goes up a mountain with his select disciples, who get to see him in his full glory, as brilliant as the sun. In the Old Testament, mountains are sacred places where people encounter God. The same is true here. God's voice comes from a cloud overshadowing the mountain, and God reveals to the disciples that Jesus is God's beloved Son. Moses (see "Moses," Ex 2, 1), representing the Law, and Elijah (see "Elijah and Elisha," 1 Kgs 17, 1), representing the prophets, also appear with Jesus. The appearance of these two Old Testament heroes confirms that Jesus is the fulfillment of both the Law and the prophets—a key point for the author of Matthew.

The Catholic church celebrates the Transfiguration of Jesus in its liturgical year on 6 August.

▶ Mt 17, 1–13

---

† **17, 1:** These three disciples are also taken apart from the others by Jesus in Gethsemane (26, 37). *A high mountain:* this has been identified with Tabor or Hermon, but probably no specific mountain was intended by the evangelist or by his Marcan source (9, 2). Its meaning is theological rather than geographical, possibly recalling the revelation to Moses on Mount Sinai (Ex 24, 12–18) and to Elijah at the same place (1 Kgs 19, 8–18; Horeb Sinai).

17, 2: *His face shone like the sun:* this is a Matthean addition; cf Dn 10, 6. *His clothes became white as light:* cf Dn 7, 9, where the clothing of God appears "snow bright." For the *white* garments of other heavenly beings, see Rv 4, 4; 7, 9; 19, 14.

17, 3: See the note on Mk 9, 5.

17, 4: *Three tents:* the booths in which the Israelites lived during the feast of Tabernacles (cf Jn 7, 2) were meant to recall their ancestors' dwelling in booths during the journey from Egypt to the promised land (Lv 23, 39–42). The same Greek word, *skēnē,* here translated *tents,* is used in the LXX for the booths of that feast, and some scholars have suggested that there is an allusion here to that liturgical custom.

17, 5: *Cloud cast a shadow over them:* see the note on Mk 9, 7. *This is my beloved Son . . . listen to him:* cf 3, 17. The voice repeats the baptismal proclamation about Jesus, with the addition of the command *listen to him.* The latter is a reference to Dt 18, 15 in which the Israelites are commanded to *listen* to the prophet like Moses whom God will raise up for them. The command to *listen* to Jesus is general, but in this context it probably applies particularly to the preceding predictions of his passion and resurrection (16, 21)

and of his coming (16, 27.28).

17, 6–7: A Matthean addition; cf Dn 10, 9–10.18–19.

17, 9–13: In response to the disciples' question about the expected return of Elijah, Jesus interprets the mission of the Baptist as the fulfillment of that expectation. But that was not suspected by those who opposed and finally killed him, and Jesus predicts a similar fate for himself.

17, 9: *The vision:* Matthew alone uses this word to describe the transfiguration. *Until the Son of Man has been raised from the dead:* only in the light of Jesus' resurrection can the meaning of his life and mission be truly understood; until then no testimony to *the vision* will lead people to faith.

17, 10: See the notes on 3, 4; 16, 14.

17, 11–12: The preceding question and this answer may reflect later controversy with Jews who objected to the Christian claims for Jesus that Elijah had not yet come.

17, 13: See 11, 14.

17, 14–20: Matthew has greatly shortened the Marcan story (9, 14–29). Leaving aside several details of the boy's illness, he concentrates on the need for faith, not so much on the part of the boy's father (as does Mark, for Matthew omits Mk 9, 22b–24) but on that of his own disciples whose inability to drive out the demon is ascribed to their *little faith* (20).

17, 2: Mt 28, 3; Dn 7, 9; 10,	**17, 10:** Mal 3, 23–24.
6; Rv 4, 4; 7, 9; 19, 14.	**17, 11:** Lk 1, 17.
17, 5: Mt 3, 17; Dt 18, 15;	**17, 12–13:** Mt 11, 14.
2 Pt 1, 17.	**17, 14–21:** Mk 9, 14–29; Lk 9,
17, 9–13: Mk 9, 9–13.	37–43.

M
T

approached, knelt down before him, ¹⁵† and said, "Lord, have pity on my son, for he is a lunatic and suffers severely; often he falls into fire, and often into water. ¹⁶ I brought him to your disciples, but they could not cure him." ¹⁷*† Jesus said in reply, "O faithless and perverse generation, how long will I be with you? How long will I endure you? Bring him here to me." ¹⁸† Jesus rebuked him and the demon came out of him, and from that hour the boy was cured. ¹⁹ Then the disciples approached Jesus in private and said, "Why could we not drive it out?" ²⁰*† He said to them, "Because of your little faith. Amen, I say to you, if you have faith the size of a mustard seed, you will say to this mountain, 'Move from here to there,' and it will move. Nothing will be impossible for you." [²¹]†

The Second Prediction of the Passion

²²*† As they were gathering in Galilee, Jesus said to them, "The Son of Man is to be handed over to men, ²³ and they will kill him, and he will be raised on the third day." And they were overwhelmed with grief.

Payment of the Temple Tax†

²⁴* When they came to Capernaum, the collectors of the temple tax† approached Peter and said, "Doesn't your teacher pay the temple tax?" ²⁵† "Yes," he said. When he came into the house, before he had time to speak, Jesus asked him, "What is your opinion, Simon? From whom do the kings of the earth take tolls or census tax? From their subjects or from foreigners?" ²⁶† When he said, "From foreigners," Jesus said to him, "Then the subjects are exempt. ²⁷† But that we may not offend them, go to the sea, drop in a hook, and take the first fish that comes up. Open its mouth and you will find a coin worth twice the temple tax. Give that to them for me and for you."

The Greatest in the Kingdom

18 ¹*† At that time the disciples† approached Jesus and said, "Who is the

---

[†]
17, 15: *A lunatic:* this description of the boy is peculiar to Matthew. The word occurs in the New Testament only here and in 4, 24 and means one affected or struck by the moon. The symptoms of the boy's illness point to epilepsy, and attacks of this were thought to be caused by phases of the moon.

17, 17: *Faithless and perverse:* so Matthew and Luke (9, 41) against Mark's *faithless* (9, 19). The Greek word here translated *perverse* is the same as that in Dt 32, 5 LXX, where Moses speaks to his people. There is a problem in knowing to whom the reproach is addressed. Since the Matthean Jesus normally chides his disciples for their *little faith* (as in 20), it would appear that the charge of lack of faith could not be made against them and that the reproach is addressed to unbelievers among the Jews. However in v 20b (*if you have faith the size of a mustard seed*), which is certainly addressed to the disciples, they appear to have not even the smallest faith; if they had, they would have been able to cure the boy. In the light of v 20b the reproach of v 17 could have applied to the disciples. There seems to be an inconsistency between the charge of *little faith* in v 20a and that of not even a little in v 20b.

17, 18: *The demon came out of him:* not until this verse does Matthew indicate that the boy's illness is a case of demoniacal possession.

17, 20: The entire verse is an addition of Matthew who (according to the better attested text) omits the reason given for the disciples' inability in Mk 9, 29. *Little faith:* see the note on 6, 30. *Faith the size of a mustard seed . . . and it will move:* a combination of a Q saying (cf Lk 17, 6) with a Marcan saying (cf Mk 11, 23).

17, 21: Some manuscripts add, "But this kind does not come out except by prayer and fasting"; this is a variant of the better reading of Mk 9, 29.

17, 22–23: The second passion prediction (cf 16, 21–23) is the least detailed of the three and may be the earliest. In the Marcan parallel the disciples do not understand (9, 32); here they understand and are *overwhelmed with grief* at the prospect of Jesus' death (23).

17, 24–27: Like 14, 28–31 and 16, 16b–19, this episode comes from Matthew's special material on Peter. Although the question of *the collectors* concerns Jesus' payment of *the temple tax*, it is put to *Peter.* It is he who receives instruction from Jesus about freedom from the obligation of payment and yet why it should be made. The means of doing so is provided miraculously. The pericope deals with a problem of Matthew's church, whether its members should pay the temple tax, and the answer is given through a word of Jesus conveyed to Peter. Some scholars see here an example of the teaching authority of Peter exercised in the name of Jesus (see 16, 19). The specific problem was a Jewish Christian one and may have arisen when the Matthean church was composed largely of that group.

17, 24: *The temple tax:* before the destruction of the Jerusalem temple in A.D. 70 every male Jew above nineteen years of age was obliged to make an annual contribution to its upkeep (cf Ex 30, 11–16; Neh 10, 33). After the destruction the Romans imposed upon Jews the obligation of paying that tax for the temple of Jupiter Capitolinus. There is disagreement about which period the story deals with.

17, 25: *From their subjects or from foreigners?:* the Greek word here translated *subjects* literally means "sons."

17, 26: *Then the subjects are exempt:* just as *subjects* are not bound by laws applying to *foreigners,* neither are Jesus and his disciples, who belong to the kingdom of heaven, bound by the duty of paying the temple tax imposed on those who are not of the kingdom. If the Greek is translated "sons," the freedom of Jesus, the Son of God, and of his disciples, children ("sons") of the kingdom (cf 13, 38), is even more clear.

17, 27: *That we may not offend them:* though they are *exempt* (26), Jesus and his disciples are to avoid giving offense; therefore the tax is to be paid. *A coin worth twice the temple tax:* literally, "a stater," a Greek coin worth two double drachmas. Two double drachmas were equal to the Jewish shekel and the tax was a half-shekel. *For me and for you:* not only Jesus but Peter pays the tax, and this example serves as a standard for the conduct of all the disciples.

18, 1–35: This discourse of the fourth book of the gospel is often called the "church order" discourse, but it lacks most of the considerations usually connected with church order, such as various offices in the church and the duties of each, and deals principally with the relations that must obtain among the members of the church. Beginning with the warning that greatness in *the kingdom of heaven* is measured not by rank or power but by childlikeness (1–5), it deals with the care that the disciples must take not to cause the *little ones to sin* or to neglect them if they stray from the community (6–14), the correction of members who sin (15–18), the efficacy of the prayer of the disciples because of the presence of Jesus (19–20), and the forgiveness that must be repeatedly extended to sinful members who repent (21–35).

18, 1: The initiative is taken not by Jesus as in the Marcan parallel (9, 33–34) but by the disciples. *Kingdom of heaven:* this may mean *the kingdom* in its fullness, i.e., after the parousia and the final judgment. But what follows about causes of sin, church discipline, and forgiveness, all dealing with the present age, suggests that the question has to do with rank also in the church, where *the kingdom* is manifested here and now, although only partially and by anticipation; see the notes on 3, 2; 4, 17.

---

*
17, 17: Dt 32, 5 LXX;
17, 20: Mt 21, 21; Lk 17, 6;
   1 Cor 13, 2.
17, 22–23: Mt 16, 21; 20, 18–19.

17, 24: Ex 30, 11–16;
   Neh 10, 33.
18, 1–5: Mk 9, 36–37; Lk 9,
   46–48.

SANTO NINO

The feast of Santo Nino, which means "Holy Child," is celebrated in the Philippines on the Sunday after the feast of the baptism of the Lord. The beginning of chapter 18 of Matthew is one of the readings you might hear at Mass that day. The feast of Santo Nino celebrates Jesus as a child and is associated with a special statue. The statue portrays the child Jesus wearing a crown, red pants, and a white robe with a large triangular red collar flaring out from the shoulders. The statue can be found in many Philippine churches and car windows.

The original Santo Nino statue was made in Belgium and sent to a girl in the Philippines as a gift for her Baptism. Then it was lost for twenty-four years, until, during a battle, a soldier found it unharmed in the flaming ruins of a house. Folklore says that the statue once hid the island of Cebu from English invaders and that when the statue was placed in the sea during a drought, it miraculously began to rain.

The devotion to Santo Nino can help us remember that Jesus was once a child who was taught and cared for by loving parents. In the spirit of Santo Nino, why not surprise a parent or grandparent with a love letter thanking him or her for all he or she has done for you?

▶ Mt 18, 1–11

---

greatest in the kingdom of heaven?"† ² He called a child over, placed it in their midst, ³*† and said, "Amen, I say to you, unless you turn and become like children, you will not enter the kingdom of heaven. ⁴* Whoever humbles himself like this child is the greatest in the kingdom of heaven. ⁵† And whoever receives one child such as this in my name receives me.

Temptations to Sin

⁶*† "Whoever causes one of these little ones who believe in me to sin, it would be better for him to have a great millstone hung around his neck and to be drowned in the depths of the sea. ⁷† Woe to the world because of things that cause sin! Such things must come, but woe to the one through whom they come! ⁸*† If your hand or foot causes you to sin, cut it off and throw it away. It is better for you to enter into life maimed or crippled than with two hands or two feet to be thrown into eternal fire. ⁹ And if your eye causes you to sin, tear it out and throw it away. It is better for you to enter into life with one eye than with two eyes to be thrown into fiery Gehenna.

---

† **18, 3:** *Become like children:* the child is held up as a model for the disciples not because of any supposed innocence of children but because of their complete dependence on, and trust in, their parents. So must the disciples be, in respect to God.

18, 5: Cf 10, 40.

18, 6: *One of these little ones:* the thought passes from the child of vv 2–4 to the disciples, *little ones* because of their becoming *like children.* It is difficult to know whether this is a designation of all who are disciples or of those who are insignificant in contrast to others, e.g., the leaders of the community. Since apart from this chapter the designation *little ones* occurs in Matthew only in 10, 42 where it means disciples as such, that is its more likely meaning here. *Who believe in me:* since discipleship is impossible without at least some degree of faith, this further specification seems superfluous. However, it serves to indicate that the warning against causing a *little one* to sin is principally directed against whatever would lead such a one to a weakening or loss of faith. The Greek verb *skandalizein,* here translated *causes . . . to sin,* means literally "causes to stumble"; what the stumbling is depends on the context. It is used of falling

away from faith in 13, 21. According to the better reading of Mk 9, 42, *in me* is a Matthean addition to the Marcan source. *It would be better . . . depths of the sea:* cf Mk 9, 42.

18, 7: This is a Q saying; cf Lk 17, 1. The inevitability of *things that cause sin* (literally, "scandals") does not take away the responsibility of *the one through whom they come.*

18, 8–9: These verses are a doublet of 5, 29–30. In that context they have to do with causes of sexual sin. As in the Marcan source from which they have been drawn (Mk 9, 42–48), they differ from the first warning about scandal, which deals with causing another person to sin, for they concern *what causes* oneself *to sin* and they do not seem to be related to another's loss of faith, as the first warning is. It is difficult to know how Matthew understood the logical connection between these verses and vv 6–7.

18, 3: Mt 19, 14; Mk 10, 15;   **18, 6–7:** Mk 9, 42; Lk 17,
   Lk 18, 17.   1–2.
18, 4: Mt 23, 12.   **18, 8–9:** Mt 5, 29–30;
                                   Mk 9, 43–47.

The Parable of the Lost Sheep†

10* "See that you do not despise one of these little ones, for I say to you that their angels in heaven always look upon the face of my heavenly Father.† [11]*† 12 What is your opinion? If a man has a hundred sheep and one of them goes astray, will he not leave the ninety-nine in the hills and go in search of the stray? 13 And if he finds it, amen, I say to you, he rejoices more over it than over the ninety-nine that did not stray. 14 In just the same way, it is not the will of your heavenly Father that one of these little ones be lost.

A Brother Who Sins†

15* "If your brother† sins [against you], go and tell him his fault between you and him alone. If he listens to you, you have won over your brother. 16*† If he does not listen, take one or two others along with you, so that 'every fact may be established on the testimony of two or three witnesses.' 17*† If he refuses to listen to them, tell the church. If he refuses to listen even to the church, then treat him as you would a Gentile or a tax collector. 18*† Amen, I say to you, whatever you bind on earth shall be bound in heaven, and whatever you loose on earth shall be loosed in heaven. 19*† Again, [amen,] I say to you, if two of you agree on earth about anything for which they are to pray, it shall be granted to them by my heavenly Father. 20*† For where two or three are gathered together in my name, there am I in the midst of them."

The Parable of the Unforgiving Servant

21*† Then Peter approaching asked him, "Lord, if my brother sins against me, how often must I forgive him? As many as seven times?" 22† Jesus answered, "I say to you, not seven times but seventy-seven times. 23* That is why the kingdom of heaven may be likened to a king who decided to settle accounts with his servants. 24† When he began the

---

18, 10–14: The first and last verses are peculiar to Matthew The parable itself comes from Q; see Lk 15, 3–7. In Luke it serves as justification for Jesus' table-companionship with sinners; here, it is an exhortation for the disciples to seek out fellow disciples who have gone astray. Not only must no one cause a fellow disciple to sin, but those who have strayed must be sought out and, if possible, brought back to the community. The joy of the shepherd on finding the sheep, though not absent in Matthew (13), is more emphasized in Luke. By his addition of vv 10 and 14, Matthew has drawn out explicitly the application of the parable to the care of the *little ones*.

18, 10: *Their angels in heaven . . . my heavenly Father:* for the Jewish belief in angels as guardians of nations and individuals, see Dn 10, 13.20–21; Tb 5, 4–7; 1QH 5, 20–22; as intercessors who present the prayers of human beings to God, see Tb 13, 12.15. The high worth of the *little ones* is indicated by their being represented before God by these heavenly beings.

18, 11: Some manuscripts add, "For the Son of Man has come to save what was lost"; cf 9, 13. This is practically identical with Lk 19, 10 and is probably a copyist's addition from that source.

18, 15–20: Passing from the duty of Christian disciples toward those who have strayed from their number, the discourse now turns to how they are to deal with one who sins and yet remains within the community. First there is to be private correction (15); if this is unsuccessful, further correction before *two or three witnesses* (16); if this fails, the matter is to be brought before the assembled community (*the church*), and if the sinner refuses to attend to the correction of *the church*, he is to be expelled (17). The church's judgment will be ratified *in heaven*, i.e., by God (18). This three-step process of correction corresponds, though not exactly, to the procedure of the Qumran community; see 1QS 5, 25–6, 1; 6, 24—7, 25; CD 9, 2–8. The section ends with a saying about the favorable response of God to prayer, even to that of a very small number, for Jesus is in the midst of any gathering of his disciples, however small (19–20). Whether this prayer has anything to do with the preceding judgment is uncertain.

18, 15: *Your brother:* a fellow disciple; see 23, 8. The bracketed words, *against you,* are widely attested but they are not in the important codices Sinaiticus and Vaticanus or in some other textual witnesses. Their omission broadens the type of sin in question. *Won over:* literally, "gained."

18, 16: Cf Dt 19, 15.

18, 17: *The church:* the second of the only two instances of this word in the gospels; see the note on 16, 18. Here it refers not to the entire *church* of Jesus, as in 16, 18, but to the local congregation. *Treat him . . . a Gentile or a tax collector:* just as the observant Jew avoided the company of Gentiles and tax collectors, so must the congregation of Christian disciples separate itself from the arrogantly sinful member who refuses to repent even when convicted of his sin by the whole *church*. Such a one is to be set outside the fellowship of the community. The harsh language about *Gentile* and *tax*

collector probably reflects a stage of the Matthean *church* when it was principally composed of Jewish Christians. That time had long since passed, but the principle of exclusion for such a sinner remained. Paul makes a similar demand for excommunication in 1 Cor 5, 1–13.

18, 18: Except for the plural of the verbs *bind* and *loose,* this verse is practically identical with 16, 19b, and many scholars understand it as granting to all the disciples what was previously given to Peter alone. For a different view, based on the different contexts of the two verses, see the note on 16, 19.

18, 19–20: Some take these verses as applying to prayer on the occasion of the church's gathering to deal with the sinner of v 17. Unless an *a fortiori* argument is supposed, this seems unlikely. God's answer to the prayer of *two or three* envisages a different situation from one that involves the entire congregation. In addition, the object of this prayer is expressed in most general terms as *anything for which they are to pray.*

18, 20: *For where two or three . . . midst of them:* the presence of Jesus guarantees the efficacy of the prayer. This saying is similar to one attributed to a rabbi executed in A.D. 135 at the time of the second Jewish revolt: ". . . When two sit and there are between them the words of the Torah, the divine presence (*Shekinah*) rests upon them" (*Pirqê 'Abôt* 3, 3).

18, 21–35: The final section of the discourse deals with the forgiveness that the disciples are to give to their fellow disciples who sin against them. To the question of Peter how often forgiveness is to be granted (21), Jesus answers that it is to be given without limit (22) and illustrates this with the parable of the unmerciful servant (23–34), warning that his *heavenly Father* will give those who do not forgive the same treatment as that given to the unmerciful servant (35). Verses 21–22 correspond to Lk 17, 4; the parable and the final warning are peculiar to Matthew. That the parable did not originally belong to this context is suggested by the fact that it really does not deal with repeated forgiveness, which is the point of Peter's question and Jesus' reply.

18, 22: *Seventy-seven times:* the Greek corresponds exactly to the LXX of Gn 4, 24. There is probably an allusion, by contrast, to the limitless vengeance of Lamech in the Genesis text. In any case, what is demanded of the disciples is limitless forgiveness.

18, 24: *A huge amount:* literally, "ten thousand talents." The talent was a unit of coinage of high but varying value depending on its metal (gold, silver, copper) and its place of origin. It is mentioned in the New Testament only here and in 25, 14–30.

18, 10–14: Ez 34, 1–3.16; Lk 15, 3–7.
18, 11: Lk 19, 10.
18, 15: Lv 19, 17; Sir 19, 13; Gal 6, 1.
18, 16: Dt 19, 15; Jn 8, 17; 1 Tm 5, 19.
18, 17: 1 Cor 5, 1–13.
18, 18: Mt 16, 19; Jn 20, 23.
18, 19: Mt 7, 7–8; Jn 15, 7.
18, 20: 1 Cor 5, 4.
18, 21–22: Mt 6, 12; Lk 17, 4.
18, 23: Mt 25, 19.

Forgive Us Our Debts

The parable of the unforgiving servant spells out clearly (and a bit harshly) what it means to ask God to "forgive us our debts, / as we forgive our debtors" (Mt 6, 12).

Bring to mind a person who has hurt you or made you angry lately. Hold this person's image in your thoughts, and realize that Jesus is calling you to forgive her or him. Now, tell this person in your thoughts how she or he has hurt you. Finally, offer your forgiveness to the person so that you can let go of the burden of your hurt.

When you are done, imagine Jesus in your prayer, and share with him something you have done that has hurt another person. Let Jesus forgive you in the same way you just forgave.

▶ Mt 18, 21–35

accounting, a debtor was brought before him who owed him a huge amount. 25 Since he had no way of paying it back, his master ordered him to be sold, along with his wife, his children, and all his prop-

erty, in payment of the debt. 26† At that, the servant fell down, did him homage, and said, 'Be patient with me, and I will pay you back in full.' 27 Moved with compassion the master of that servant let him go and forgave him the loan. 28† When that servant had left, he found one of his fellow servants who owed him a much smaller amount. He seized him and started to choke him, demanding, 'Pay back what you owe.' 29 Falling to his knees, his fellow servant begged him, 'Be patient with me, and I will pay you back.' 30 But he refused. Instead, he had him put in prison until he paid back the debt. 31 Now when his fellow servants saw what had happened, they were deeply disturbed, and went to their master and reported the whole affair. 32 His master summoned him and said to him, 'You wicked servant! I forgave you your entire debt because you begged me to. 33* Should you not have had pity on your fellow servant, as I had pity on you?' 34† Then in anger his master handed him over to the torturers until he should pay back the whole debt. 35*† So will my heavenly Father do to you, unless each of you forgives his brother from his heart."

VI: Ministry in Judea and Jerusalem

Marriage and Divorce

19 1† When Jesus† finished these words,† he left Galilee and went to the district of Judea across the Jordan. 2 Great crowds followed him, and he cured them there. 3*† Some Pharisees approached him, and tested him, saying, "Is it lawful for a man to divorce his wife for any cause whatever?"

18, 26: *Pay you back in full:* an empty promise, given the size of the debt.

18, 28: *A much smaller amount:* literally, "a hundred denarii." A denarius was the normal daily wage of a laborer. The difference between the two debts is enormous and brings out the absurdity of the conduct of the Christian who has received the great forgiveness of God and yet refuses to forgive the relatively minor offenses done to him.

18, 34: Since the debt is so great as to be unpayable, the punishment will be endless.

18, 35: The Father's forgiveness, already given, will be withdrawn at the final judgment for those who have not imitated his forgiveness by their own.

19, 1—23, 39: The narrative section of the fifth book of the gospel. The first part (19, 1—20, 34) has for its setting the journey of Jesus from Galilee to Jerusalem; the second (21, 1—23, 39) deals with Jesus' ministry in Jerusalem up to the final great discourse of the gospel (chs 24–25). Matthew follows the Marcan sequence of events, though adding material both special to this gospel and drawn from Q. The second part ends with the denunciation of the scribes and Pharisees (23, 1–36) followed by Jesus' lament over Jerusalem (37–39). This long and important speech raises a problem for the view that Matthew is structured around five other discourses of Jesus (see Introduction) and that this one has no such function in the gospel. However, it is to be noted that this speech lacks the customary concluding formula that follows the five discourses (see the note on 7, 28), and that those discourses are all addressed either exclusively (chs 10, 18, 24–25) or primarily (chs 5–7, 13) to the disciples, whereas this is addressed primarily to the scribes and Pharisees (13–36). Consequently, it seems plausible to maintain that the evangelist did not intend to give it the structural importance of the five other discourses,

and that, in spite of its being composed of sayings-material, it belongs to the narrative section of this book. In that regard, it is similar to the sayings-material of 11, 7–30. Some have proposed that Matthew wished to regard it as part of the final discourse of chs 24–25, but the intervening material (24, 1–4) and the change in matter and style of those chapters do not support that view.

19, 1–12: In giving Jesus' teaching on divorce (3–9), Matthew here follows his Marcan source (10, 2–12) as he does Q in 5, 31–32 (cf Lk 16, 18). Verses 10–12 are peculiar to Matthew.

19, 1: *When Jesus finished these words:* see the note on 7, 28–29. *The district of Judea across the Jordan:* an inexact designation of the territory. Judea did not extend *across the Jordan;* the territory east of the river was Perea. The route to Jerusalem by way of Perea avoided passage through Samaria.

19, 3: *Tested him:* the verb is used of attempts of Jesus' opponents to embarrass him by challenging him to do something they think impossible (16, 1; Mk 8, 11; Lk 11, 16) or by having him say something that they can use against him (22, 18.35; Mk 10, 2; 12, 15). *For any cause whatever:* this is peculiar to Matthew and has been interpreted by some as meaning that Jesus was being asked to take sides in the dispute between the schools of Hillel and Shammai on the reasons for divorce, the latter holding a stricter position than the former. It is unlikely, however, that to ask Jesus' opinion about the differing views of two Jewish schools, both highly respected, could be described as "testing" him, for the reason indicated above.

18, 33: Sir 28, 4.   19, 3–9: Mk 10, 2–12.
18, 35: Mt 6, 15; Jas 2, 13.

4*† He said in reply, "Have you not read that from the beginning the Creator 'made them male and female' 5* and said, 'For this reason a man shall leave his father and mother and be joined to his wife, and the two shall become one flesh'? 6 So they are no longer two, but one flesh. Therefore, what God has joined together, no human being must separate." 7*† They said to him, "Then why did Moses command that the man give the woman a bill of divorce and dismiss [her]?" 8 He said to them, "Because of the hardness of your hearts Moses allowed you to divorce your wives, but from the beginning it was not so. 9*† I say to you, whoever divorces his wife (unless the marriage is unlawful) and marries another commits adultery." 10 [His] disciples said to him, "If that is the case of a man with his wife, it is better not to marry." 11† He answered, "Not all can accept [this] word, but only those to whom that is granted. 12† Some are incapable of marriage because they were born so; some, because they were made so by others; some, because they have renounced marriage for the sake of the kingdom of heaven. Whoever can accept this ought to accept it."

Blessing of the Children

13*† Then children were brought to him that he might lay his hands on them and pray. The disciples rebuked them, 14* but Jesus said, "Let the children come to me, and do not prevent them; for the kingdom of heaven belongs to such as these." 15 After he placed his hands on them, he went away.

The Rich Young Man†

16* Now someone approached him and said, "Teacher, what good must I do to gain eternal life?"†

Catholic Connections

MARRIAGE

When the Pharisees try to test Jesus with a question about divorce, Jesus speaks about marriage. Rather than focus on the negative, Jesus turns everyone's attention to the positive—the beauty of two people who "are no longer two, but one flesh" (Mt 19, 6). Catholics celebrate Jesus' positive view in the sacrament of Marriage, one of the seven official sacraments of the church. The church believes that in a Christian marriage, God's love and grace are present in a special way (see Eph 5, 21–33).

The vows exchanged by the bride and groom and received by the church's official witness are the sacramental experience of marriage. It is the married couple's love, commitment, and faith that make God's love real and present to the community.

▶ Mt 19, 1–9

19, 4–6: Matthew recasts his Marcan source, omitting Jesus' question about Moses' command (Mk 10, 3) and having him recall at once two Genesis texts that show the will and purpose of *the Creator* in making human beings *male and female* (Gn 1, 27), namely, that a *man may be joined to his wife* in marriage in the intimacy of *one flesh* (Gn 2, 24). *What God has* thus *joined* must not be separated by any *human being*. (The NAB translation of the Hebrew *bāsār* of Gn 2, 24 as "body" rather than "flesh" obscures the reference of Matthew to that text.)

19, 7: See Dt 24, 1–4.

19, 9: Moses' concession to human sinfulness (*the hardness of your hearts,* 8) is repudiated by Jesus, and the original will of the Creator is reaffirmed against that concession. (*Unless the marriage is unlawful*): see the note on 5, 31–32. There is some evidence suggesting that Jesus' absolute prohibition of divorce was paralleled in the Qumran community (see 11QTemple 57, 17–19; CD 4, 12b—5, 14). Matthew removes Mark's setting of this verse as spoken to the disciples alone "in the house" (Mk 10, 10) and also his extension of the divorce prohibition to the case of a woman's divorcing her husband (10, 12), probably because in Palestine, unlike the places where Roman and Greek law prevailed, the woman was not allowed to initiate the divorce.

19, 11: [*This*] *word:* probably the disciples' *it is better not to marry* (10). Jesus agrees but says that celibacy is not for all but only for those *to whom that is granted* by God.

19, 12: *Incapable of marriage:* literally, "eunuchs." Three classes are mentioned, eunuchs from birth, eunuchs by castration, and those who have voluntarily *renounced marriage* (literally, "have made themselves eunuchs") *for the sake of the kingdom,* i.e., to devote themselves entirely to its service. Some scholars take the last class to be those who have been divorced by their spouses and have refused to enter another marriage. But it is more likely that it is rather those who have chosen never to marry, since that suits better the optional

nature of the decision: *Whoever can . . . ought to accept it.*

19, 13–15: This account is understood by some as intended to justify the practice of infant baptism. That interpretation is based principally on the command not to *prevent* the children from coming, since that word sometimes has a baptismal connotation in the New Testament; see Acts 8, 36.

19, 16–30: Cf Mk 10, 17–31. This story does not set up a "two-tier" morality, that of those who seek (only) *eternal life* (16) and that of those who *wish to be perfect* (21). It speaks rather of the obstacle that riches constitute for the following of Jesus and of the impossibility, humanly speaking, for one who has *many possessions* (22) *to enter the kingdom* (24). Actual renunciation of riches is not demanded of all; Matthew counts the rich Joseph of Arimathea as a disciple of Jesus (27, 57). But only the poor in spirit (5, 3) can *enter the kingdom* and, as here, such poverty may entail the sacrifice of one's *possessions.* The Twelve, who *have given up everything* (27) to follow Jesus, will have as their reward a share in Jesus' (the Son of Man's) *judging the twelve tribes of Israel* (28), and all who have similarly sacrificed family or property for his sake *will inherit eternal life* (29).

19, 16: *Gain eternal life:* this is equivalent to "entering into life" (17) and "being saved" (25); the *life* is that of the new age after the final judgment (see 25, 46). It probably is also equivalent here to "entering the kingdom of heaven" (23) or "the kingdom of God" (24), but see the notes on 3, 2; 4, 17; 18, 1 for the wider reference of *the kingdom* in Matthew.

19, 4: Gn 1, 27.
19, 5: Gn 2, 24; 1 Cor 6, 16;
   Eph 5, 31.
19, 7: Dt 24, 1–4.
19, 9: Mt 5, 32; Lk 16, 18;
   1 Cor 7, 10–11.
19, 13–15: Mk 10, 13–16; Lk 18,
   15–17.
19, 14: Mt 18, 3; Acts 8, 36.
19, 16–30: Mk 10, 17–31; Lk 18,
   18–30.

[17]† He answered him, "Why do you ask me about the good? There is only One who is good. If you wish to enter into life, keep the commandments." [18]*† He asked him, "Which ones?" And Jesus replied, " 'You shall not kill; you shall not commit adultery; you shall not steal; you shall not bear false witness; [19] honor your father and your mother'; and 'you shall love your neighbor as yourself.' " [20]† The young man said to him, "All of these I have observed. What do I still lack?" [21]*† Jesus said to him, "If you wish to be perfect, go, sell what you have and give to [the] poor, and you will have treasure in heaven. Then come, follow me." [22] When the young man heard this statement, he went away sad, for he had many possessions. [23]† Then Jesus said to his disciples, "Amen, I say to you, it will be hard for one who is rich to enter the kingdom of heaven. [24]* Again I say to you, it is easier for a camel to pass through the eye of a needle than for one who is rich to enter the kingdom of God." [25]† When the disciples heard this, they were greatly astonished and said, "Who then can be saved?" [26]* Jesus looked at them and said, "For human beings this is impossible, but for God all things are possible." [27]* Then Peter said to him in reply, "We have given up everything and followed you. What will there be for us?" [28]*† Jesus said to them, "Amen, I say to you that you who have followed me, in the new age, when the Son of Man is seated on his throne of glory, will yourselves sit on twelve thrones, judging the twelve tribes of Israel. [29] And everyone who has given up houses or brothers or sisters or father or mother or children or lands for the sake of my name will receive a hundred times more, and will inherit eternal life. [30]*† But many who are first will be last, and the last will be first.

The Workers in the Vineyard

20 [1]† "The kingdom of heaven is like a landowner who went out at dawn to hire laborers for his vineyard. [2] After agreeing with them for the usual daily wage, he sent them into his vineyard. [3] Going out about nine o'clock, he saw others standing idle in the marketplace, [4]† and he said to them, 'You too go into my vineyard, and I will give you what is just.' [5] So they went off. [And] he went out again around noon, and around three o'clock, and did likewise. [6] Going out about five o'clock, he found others standing around, and said to them, 'Why do you stand here idle all day?' [7] They answered, 'Because no one has hired us.' He said to them, 'You too go into my vineyard.' [8]*† When it was evening the owner of the vineyard said to his foreman, 'Summon the laborers and give them their pay, beginning with the last and ending with the first.' [9] When those who had started about five o'clock came, each received the usual daily wage. [10] So when the first came, they thought that they would receive more, but each of them also got the usual wage. [11] And on receiving it they grumbled against the landowner, [12] saying, 'These last ones worked only one hour, and you have made them equal to us, who bore the day's burden and the heat.' [13]† He said to one of them in reply, 'My friend, I am not cheating you. Did you not agree

---

19, 17: By Matthew's reformulation of the Marcan question and reply (Mk 10, 17–18) Jesus' repudiation of the term "good" for himself has been softened. Yet the Marcan assertion that "no one is good but God alone" stands, with only unimportant verbal modification.

19, 18–19: The first five commandments cited are from the Decalogue (see Ex 20, 12–16; Dt 5, 16–20). Matthew omits Mark's "you shall not defraud" (10, 19; see Dt 24, 14) and adds Lv 19, 18. This combination of commandments of the Decalogue with Lv 19, 18 is partially the same as Paul's enumeration of the demands of Christian morality in Rom 13, 9.

19, 20: *Young man:* in Matthew alone of the synoptics the questioner is said to be a *young man;* thus the Marcan "from my youth" (10, 20) is omitted.

19, 21: *If you wish to be perfect: to be perfect* is demanded of all Christians; see 5, 48. In the case of this man, it involves selling his possessions and giving to the poor; only so can he *follow* Jesus.

19, 23–24: Riches are an obstacle to entering the *kingdom* that cannot be overcome by human power. The comparison with the impossibility of a camel's passing *through the eye of a needle* should not be mitigated by such suppositions as that *the eye of a needle* means a low or narrow gate. *The kingdom of God:* as in 12, 28; 21, 31.43, instead of Matthew's usual *kingdom of heaven.*

19, 25–26: See the note on Mk 10, 23–27.

19, 28: This saying, directed to the Twelve, is from Q; see Lk 22, 29–30. *The new age:* the Greek word here translated "new age" occurs in the New Testament only here and in Ti 3, 5. Literally, it means "rebirth" or "regeneration," and is used in Titus of spiritual rebirth through baptism. Here it means the "rebirth" effected by the coming of the kingdom. Since that coming has various stages (see the notes on 3, 2; 4, 17), *the new age* could be taken as referring to the time after the resurrection when the Twelve will govern the true Israel, i.e., the church of Jesus. (For "judge" in the sense of "govern," cf Jgs 12, 8.9.11; 15, 20; 16, 31; Ps 2, 10). But since it is connected here with the time when *the Son of Man* will be *seated on his throne of glory,* language that Matthew uses in 25, 31 for the time of final judgment, it is more likely that what the Twelve are promised is that they will be joined with Jesus then in judging the people of Israel.

19, 30: Different interpretations have been given to this saying, which comes from Mk 10, 31. In view of Matthew's associating it with the following parable (20, 1–15) and substantially repeating it (in reverse order) at the end of that parable (20, 16), it may be that his meaning is that all who respond to the call of Jesus, at whatever time (*first* or *last*), will be the same in respect to inheriting the benefits of the kingdom, which is the gift of God.

20, 1–16: This parable is peculiar to Matthew. It is difficult to know whether the evangelist composed it or received it as part of his traditional material and, if the latter is the case, what its original reference was. In its present context its close association with 19, 30 suggests that its teaching is the equality of all the disciples in the reward of inheriting eternal life.

20, 4: *What is just:* although the wage is not stipulated as in the case of those first hired, it will be fair.

20, 8: *Beginning with the last . . . the first:* this element of the parable has no other purpose than to show how *the first* knew what *the last* were given (12).

20, 13: *I am not cheating you:* literally, "I am not treating you unjustly."

19, 18–19: Ex 20, 12–16; Dt 5,
　　　　　　16–20; Lv 19, 18; Rom
　　　　　　13, 9.
　19, 21: Mt 5, 48; 6, 20.
　19, 24: Mt 7, 14.
　19, 26: Gn 18, 14; Jb 42, 2; Lk
　　　　　1, 37.
19, 27: Mt 4, 20.22.
19, 28: Mt 25, 31; Dn 7, 9.22;
　　　　Lk 22, 30; Rv 3, 21;
　　　　20, 4.
19, 30: Mt 20, 16.
20, 8: Lv 19, 13; Dt 24, 15.

Are You for Real?

Read Mt 20, 1–16 as an introduction to this prayer:

Lord, could you really be such a generous God? I have heard that you offer the same welcome to the sinner as to the saint. That you walk with the angry as well as the joyful, and can embrace the hurtful as well as the helpful. That you even offer the exact same love for the last to turn to you as you do for the first.

That's just not the way it is done around here, God, so excuse me if I have a hard time believing. But then, I've heard it said that you are as patient with the doubtful as you are with the faithful.

If you are this type of God, then please be with me right now. I need to talk to someone who understands and loves me in spite of my doubts and sin. I need a God who breaks the rules to let me know how much I am loved.

If you are indeed this kind of God, thanks! Thanks for being so crazy with your love that you would allow someone like me to hang around you. Promise to stay with me as I learn to trust in you and your acceptance of all people. Amen.

▸ *Mt 20, 1–16*

with me for the usual daily wage? [14]† Take what is yours and go. What if I wish to give this last one the same as you? [15] [Or] am I not free to do as I wish with my own money? Are you envious because I am generous?' [16]† Thus, the last will be first, and the first will be last."

The Third Prediction of the Passion

[17]*† As Jesus was going up to Jerusalem, he took the twelve [disciples] aside by themselves, and said to them on the way, [18] "Behold, we are going up to Jerusalem, and the Son of Man will be handed over to the chief priests and the scribes, and they will condemn him to death, [19] and hand him over to the Gentiles to be mocked and scourged and crucified, and he will be raised on the third day."

The Request of James and John†

[20]* Then the mother† of the sons of Zebedee approached him with her sons and did him homage, wishing to ask him for something. [21] He said to her, "What do you wish?" She answered him, "Command that these two sons of mine sit, one at your right and the other at your left, in your kingdom." [22]† Jesus said in reply, "You do not know what you are asking. Can you drink the cup that I am going to drink?" They said to him, "We can." [23] He replied, "My cup you will indeed drink, but to sit at my right and at my left [,this] is not mine to give but is for those for whom it has been prepared by my Father." [24]* When the ten heard this, they became indignant at the two brothers. [25] But Jesus summoned them and said, "You know that the rulers of the Gentiles lord it over them, and the great ones make their authority over them felt. [26] But it shall not be so among you. Rather, whoever wishes to be great among you shall be your servant; [27]* whoever wishes to be first among you shall be your slave. [28]*† Just so, the Son of Man did

---

20, 14–15: The owner's conduct involves no violation of justice (4.13), and that all the workers receive the same wage is due only to his generosity to the latest arrivals; the resentment of the first comes from envy.

20, 16: See the note on 19, 30.

20, 17–19: Cf Mk 10, 32–34. This is the third and the most detailed of the passion predictions (16, 21–23; 17, 22–23). It speaks of Jesus' being *handed over to the Gentiles* (27, 2), his being *mocked* (27, 27–30), *scourged* (27, 26), and *crucified* (27, 31.35). In all but the last of these points Matthew agrees with his Marcan source, but whereas Mark speaks of Jesus' being killed (10, 34), Matthew has the specific *to be . . . crucified*.

20, 20–28: Cf Mk 10, 35–45. The request of the sons of Zebedee, made through their mother, for the highest places of honor in the *kingdom*, and the indignation of *the* other *ten* disciples at this request, show that neither *the two brothers* nor the others have understood that what makes for greatness in the kingdom is not lordly power but humble service. Jesus gives the example, and his ministry of service will reach its highest point when he gives his life for the deliverance of the human race from sin.

20, 20–21: The reason for Matthew's making *the mother* the petitioner (cf Mk 10, 35) is not clear. Possibly he intends an allusion to

Bathsheba's seeking the kingdom for Solomon; see 1 Kgs 1, 11–21. *Your kingdom:* see the note on 16, 28.

20, 22: *You do not know what you are asking:* the Greek verbs are plural and, with the rest of the verse, indicate that the answer is addressed not to the woman but to her sons. *Drink the cup:* see the note on Mk 10, 38–40. Matthew omits the Marcan "or be baptized with the baptism with which I am baptized" (10, 38).

20, 28: *Ransom:* this noun, which occurs in the New Testament only here and in the Marcan parallel (10, 45), does not necessarily express the idea of liberation by payment of some price. The cognate verb is used frequently in the LXX of God's liberating Israel from Egypt or from Babylonia after the Exile; see Ex 6, 6; 15, 13; Ps 77 (76 LXX), 16; Is 43, 1; 44, 22. The liberation brought by Jesus' death will be *for many;* cf Is 53, 12. *Many* does not mean that some are excluded, but is a Semitism designating the collectivity who benefit from the service of the one, and is equivalent to "all." While there are few verbal contacts between this saying and the fourth Servant Song (Is 52, 13—53, 12), the ideas of that passage are reflected here.

20, 17–19: Mt 16, 21; 17, 22–23;   20, 24–27: Lk 22, 25–27.
           Mk 10, 32–34; Lk 18,   20, 27: Mk 9, 35.
           31–33.   20, 28: Mt 26, 28; Is 53, 12;
20, 20–28: Mk 10, 35–45.   Rom 5, 6; 1 Tm 2, 6.

not come to be served but to serve and to give his life as a ransom for many."

The Healing of Two Blind Men

²⁹*† As they left Jericho, a great crowd followed him. ³⁰*† Two blind men were sitting by the roadside, and when they heard that Jesus was passing by, they cried out, "[Lord,] Son of David, have pity on us!" ³¹ The crowd warned them to be silent, but they called out all the more, "Lord, Son of David, have pity on us!" ³² Jesus stopped and called them and said, "What do you want me to do for you?" ³³ They answered him, "Lord, let our eyes be opened." ³⁴ Moved with pity, Jesus touched their eyes. Immediately they received their sight, and followed him.

The Entry into Jerusalem†

21 ¹* When they drew near Jerusalem and came to Bethphage† on the Mount of Olives, Jesus sent two disciples, ²† saying to them, "Go into the village opposite you, and immediately you will find an ass tethered, and a colt with her. Untie them and bring them here to me. ³ And if anyone should say anything to you, reply, 'The master has need of them.' Then he will send them at once." ⁴† This happened so that what had been spoken through the prophet might be fulfilled:

⁵* "Say to daughter Zion,
'Behold, your king comes to you,
　meek and riding on an ass,
　and on a colt, the foal of a beast of burden.'"

True Greatness

What good parent does not want his or her son or daughter to find success in life? Like most people at the time of Jesus, the mother of James and John is confused about the Kingdom that Jesus had come to establish. She lobbies for her sons (see verse 21), hoping they might be made "senior vice presidents" of the new "firm."

The resulting confusion and anger among the disciples allows Jesus the opportunity to remind them of how God defined true greatness. Jesus turns the tables on them by asking in a veiled way, "Can you drink the cup that I am going to drink?" (verse 22). He reminds them—and reminds us today—that true greatness is gained in serving others (see verses 26–27).

When you are in a position of leadership, do you see it as a chance to control others in order to gain power or social status, or do you see it as a chance to serve others and help them obtain what they need to live full and healthy lives? Why is it that wanting power for ourselves so often gets in the way of our wanting to serve the needs of others?

▸ **Mt 20, 20–28**

---

† 20, 29–34: The cure of the blind men is probably symbolic of what will happen to the disciples, now blind to the meaning of Jesus' passion and to the necessity of their sharing his suffering. As the men are given sight, so, after the resurrection, will the disciples come to see that to which they are now blind. Matthew has abbreviated his Marcan source (10, 46–52) and has made Mark's one man two. Such doubling is characteristic of this gospel; see 8, 28–34 (// Mk 5, 1–20) and the note on 9, 27–31.

20, 30: [Lord,]: some important textual witnesses omit this, but that may be because copyists assimilated this verse to 9, 27. Son of David: see the note on 9, 27.

21, 1–11: Jesus' coming to Jerusalem is in accordance with the divine will that he must go there (cf 16, 21) to suffer, die, and be raised. He prepares for his entry into the city in such a way as to make it a fulfillment of the prophecy of Zec 9, 9 (2) that emphasizes the humility of the king who comes (5). That prophecy, absent from the Marcan parallel account (11, 1–11) although found also in the Johannine account of the entry (12, 15), is the center of the Matthean story. During the procession from Bethphage to Jerusalem, Jesus is acclaimed as the Davidic messianic king by the crowds who accompany him (9). On his arrival the whole city was shaken, and to the inquiry of the amazed populace about Jesus' identity the crowds with him reply that he is the prophet, from Nazareth in Galilee (10.11).

21, 1: Bethphage: a village that can no longer be certainly identified. Mark mentions it before Bethany (11, 1), which suggests that it lay to the east of the latter. The Mount of Olives: the hill east of Jerusalem that is spoken of in Zec 14, 4 as the place where the Lord will come to rescue Jerusalem from the enemy nations.

21, 2: An ass tethered, and a colt with her: instead of the one animal of Mk 11, 2, Matthew has two, as demanded by his understanding of Zec 9, 9.

21, 4–5: The prophet: this fulfillment citation is actually composed of two distinct Old Testament texts, Is 62, 11 (Say to daughter Zion) and Zec 9, 9. The ass and the colt are the same animal in the prophecy, mentioned twice in different ways, the common Hebrew literary device of poetic parallelism. That Matthew takes them as two is one of the reasons why some scholars think that he was a Gentile rather than a Jewish Christian who would presumably not make that mistake (see Introduction).

20, 29–34: Mk 10, 46–52; Lk 18, 35–43.
20, 30: Mt 9, 27.
21, 1–11: Mk 11, 1–11; Lk 19, 28–38; Jn 12, 12–15.
21, 5: Is 62, 11; Zec 9, 9.

21, 8

⁶ The disciples went and did as Jesus had ordered them. ⁷† They brought the ass and the colt and laid their cloaks over them, and he sat upon them. ⁸*† The very large crowd spread their cloaks on the road, while others cut branches from the trees and strewed them on the road. ⁹*† The crowds preceding him and those following kept crying out and saying:

"Hosanna to the Son of David;
　　blessed is he who comes in the name of
　　　　the Lord;
　　hosanna in the highest."

¹⁰† And when he entered Jerusalem the whole city was shaken and asked, "Who is this?" ¹¹† And the crowds replied, "This is Jesus the prophet, from Nazareth in Galilee."

The Cleansing of the Temple†

¹²* Jesus entered the temple area and drove out all those engaged in selling and buying there.* He overturned the tables of the money changers and the seats of those who were selling doves.† ¹³*† And he said to them, "It is written:

'My house shall be a house of prayer,'
　　but you are making it a den of thieves.'

¹⁴*† The blind and the lame approached him in the temple area, and he cured them. ¹⁵† When the chief priests and the scribes saw the wondrous things he was doing, and the children crying out in the temple area, "Hosanna to the Son of David," they were indignant ¹⁶*† and said to him, "Do you hear what they are saying?" Jesus said to them, "Yes; and have you never read the text, 'Out of the mouths of infants and nurslings you have brought forth praise'?" ¹⁷ And leaving them, he went out of the city to Bethany, and there he spent the night.

The Cursing of the Fig Tree

¹⁸*† When he was going back to the city in the morning, he was hungry. ¹⁹* Seeing a fig tree by the road, he went over to it, but found nothing on it

---

21, 7: *Upon them:* upon the two animals; an awkward picture resulting from Matthew's misunderstanding of the prophecy.

21, 8: *Spread . . . on the road:* cf 2 Kgs 9, 13. There is a similarity between the cutting and strewing of the *branches* and the festivities of Tabernacles (Lv 23, 39–40); see also 2 Mc 10, 5–8 where the celebration of the rededication of the temple is compared to that of Tabernacles.

21, 9: *Hosanna:* the Hebrew means "(O LORD) grant salvation"; see Ps 118, 25, but that invocation had become an acclamation of jubilation and welcome. *Blessed is he . . . in the name of the Lord:* see Ps 118, 26 and the note on Jn 12, 13. *In the highest:* probably only an intensification of the acclamation, although *Hosanna in the highest* could be taken as a prayer, "May God save (him)."

21, 10: *Was shaken:* in the gospels this verb is peculiar to Matthew where it is used also of the earthquake at the time of the crucifixion (27, 51) and of the terror of the guards of Jesus' tomb at the appearance of the angel (28, 4). For Matthew's use of the cognate noun, see the note on 8, 24.

21, 11: *The prophet:* see 16, 14 ("one of the prophets") and 21, 46.

21, 12–17: Matthew changes the order of Mark (11, 11.12.15) and places the cleansing of the temple on the same day as the entry into Jerusalem, immediately after it. The activities going on *in the temple area* were not secular but connected with the temple worship. Thus Jesus' attack on those so engaged and his charge that they were *making* God's *house of prayer a den of thieves* (12–13) constituted a claim to authority over the religious practices of Israel and were a challenge to the priestly authorities. Verses 14–17 are peculiar to Matthew. Jesus' healings and his countenancing the children's cries of praise rouse the indignation of *the chief priests and the scribes* (15). These two groups appear in the infancy narrative (2, 4) and have been mentioned in the first and third passion predictions (16, 21; 20, 18). Now, as the passion approaches, they come on the scene again, exhibiting their hostility to Jesus.

21, 12: These activities were carried on in the court of the Gentiles, the outermost court of *the temple area*. Animals for sacrifice were sold; the *doves* were for those who could not afford a more expensive offering; see Lv 5, 7. *Tables of the money changers:* only the coinage of Tyre could be used for the purchases; other money had to be exchanged for that.

21, 13: *'My house . . . prayer':* cf Is 56, 7. Matthew omits the final words of the quotation, "for all peoples" ("all nations"), possibly because for him the worship of the God of Israel by all nations belongs to the time after the resurrection; see 28, 19. *A den of thieves:* the phrase is taken from Jer 7, 11.

21, 14: *The blind and the lame:* according to 2 Sm 5, 8 (LXX) *the blind and the lame* were forbidden to enter "the house of the Lord," the temple. These are the last of Jesus' healings in Matthew.

21, 15: *The wondrous things:* the healings.

21, 16: *'Out of the mouths . . . praise':* cf Ps 8, 3 (LXX).

21, 18–22: In Mark the effect of Jesus' cursing the fig tree is not immediate; see 11, 14.20. By making it so, Matthew has heightened the miracle. Jesus' act seems arbitrary and ill-tempered, but it is a prophetic action similar to those of Old Testament prophets that vividly symbolize some part of their preaching; see, e.g., Ez 12, 1–20. It is a sign of the judgment that is to come upon the Israel that with all its apparent piety lacks the fruit of good deeds (3, 10) and will soon bear the punishment of its fruitlessness (43). Some scholars propose that this story is the development in tradition of a parable of Jesus about the destiny of a fruitless tree, such as Lk 13, 6–9. Jesus' answer to the question of the amazed disciples (20) makes the miracle an example of the power of prayer made with unwavering *faith* (21–22).

21, 8: 2 Kgs 9, 13.
21, 9: Ps 118, 25–26.
21, 12–17: Mk 11, 15–19; Lk 19,
　　45–48; Jn 2, 14–22.
21, 12: Lv 5, 7.
21, 13: Is 56, 7; Jer 7, 11.
21, 14: 2 Sm 5, 8 LXX.
21, 16: Ps 8, 2 LXX; Wis
　　10, 21.
21, 18–22: Mk 11, 12–14.20–24.
21, 19: Jer 8, 13; Lk 13, 6–9.

except leaves. And he said to it, "May no fruit ever come from you again." And immediately the fig tree withered. 20 When the disciples saw this, they were amazed and said, "How was it that the fig tree withered immediately?" 21*† Jesus said to them in reply, "Amen, I say to you, if you have faith and do not waver, not only will you do what has been done to the fig tree, but even if you say to this mountain, 'Be lifted up and thrown into the sea,' it will be done. 22* Whatever you ask for in prayer with faith, you will receive."

The Authority of Jesus Questioned†

23* When he had come into the temple area, the chief priests and the elders of the people approached him as he was teaching and said, "By what authority are you doing these things?† And who gave you this authority?"* 24† Jesus said to them in reply, "I shall ask you one question, and if you answer it for me, then I shall tell you by what authority I do these things. 25 Where was John's baptism from? Was it of heavenly or of human origin?" They discussed this among themselves and said, "If we say 'Of heavenly origin,' he will say to us, 'Then why did you not believe him?' 26*† But if we say, 'Of human origin,' we fear the crowd, for they all regard John as a prophet." 27† So they said to Jesus in reply, "We do not know." He himself said to them, "Neither shall I tell you by what authority I do these things.

The Parable of the Two Sons

28† "What is your opinion? A man had two sons. He came to the first and said, 'Son, go out and work in the vineyard today.' 29 He said in reply, 'I will not,' but afterwards he changed his mind and went. 30 The man came to the other son and gave the same order. He said in reply, 'Yes, sir,' but did not

---

did you KNOW?

Jesus and Civil Disobedience

The cleansing of the Temple is one of the few stories that occur in all four Gospels. To fully understand Jesus' anger in this situation, we need to remember that the Jews were required to offer sacrificial animals as part of their religious obligation. Herod the Great had turned the sale of sacrificial animals into a money-making enterprise. Money changers were needed because Roman coins had images of pagan gods on them and could not be used to purchase animals for this religious purpose; therefore, religious and civil leaders were becoming wealthy, charging people a fee for this necessary exchange of coins. Because this was not an appropriate Temple activity, it upset many people, including Jesus.

Jesus' clearing of the Temple was an act of religious and civil disobedience, challenging the highest members of Jewish society. The Gospels of Luke and Mark both say that immediately after this event, Jewish leaders began looking for a way to kill Jesus. They waited because Jesus was so popular with the people (see Mk 11, 18–19 and Lk 19, 47–48). Jesus knew that his actions and teachings made these corrupt leaders angry and would ultimately lead to his death (see Mt 20, 17–19).

▶ Mt 21, 12–13

21, 21: See 17, 20.

21, 23–27: Cf Mk 11, 27–33. This is the first of five controversies between Jesus and the religious authorities of Judaism in 21, 23—22, 46, presented in the form of questions and answers.

21, 23: *These things:* probably his entry into the city, his cleansing of the temple, and his healings there.

21, 24: To reply by counterquestion was common in rabbinical debate.

21, 26: *We fear . . . as a prophet:* cf 14, 5.

21, 27: Since through embarrassment on the one hand and fear on the other the religious authorities claim ignorance of the origin of John's baptism, they show themselves incapable of speaking with authority; hence Jesus refuses to discuss with them the grounds of his authority.

21, 28–32: The series of controversies is interrupted by three parables on the judgment of Israel (21, 28—22, 14) of which this, peculiar to Matthew, is the first. The second (21, 33–46) comes from Mark (12, 1–12), and the third (22, 1–14) from Q; see Lk 14, 15–24. This interruption of the controversies is similar to that in Mark, although Mark has only one parable between the first and second controversy. As regards Matthew's first parable, vv 28–30 if taken by themselves could point simply to the difference between saying and doing, a theme of much importance in this gospel (cf 7, 21; 12, 50); that may have been the parable's original reference. However, it is given a more specific ap-

plication by the addition of vv 31–32. The two sons represent, respectively, the religious leaders and the religious outcasts who followed John's call to repentance. By the answer they give to Jesus' question (31) the leaders condemn themselves. There is much confusion in the textual tradition of the parable. Of the three different forms of the text given by important textual witnesses, one has the leaders answer that the son who agreed to go but did not was the one who did the father's will. Although some scholars accept that as the original reading, their arguments in favor of it seem unconvincing. The choice probably lies only between a reading that puts the son who agrees and then disobeys before the son who at first refuses and then obeys, and the reading followed in the present translation. The witnesses to the latter reading are slightly better than those that support the other.

21, 21: Mt 17, 20; Lk 17, 6.   21, 23: Jn 2, 18.
21, 22: Mt 7, 7; 1 Jn 3, 22.   21, 26: Mt 14, 5.
21, 23–27: Mk 11, 27–33; Lk 20, 1–8.

MT

go. [31]† Which of the two did his father's will?" They answered, "The first." Jesus said to them, "Amen, I say to you, tax collectors and prostitutes are entering the kingdom of God before you. [32]*† When John came to you in the way of righteousness, you did not believe him; but tax collectors and prostitutes did. Yet even when you saw that, you did not later change your minds and believe him.

The Parable of the Tenants†

[33]* "Hear another parable. There was a landowner who planted a vineyard,* put a hedge around it, dug a wine press in it, and built a tower.† Then he leased it to tenants and went on a journey. [34]† When vintage time drew near, he sent his servants to the tenants to obtain his produce. [35] But the tenants seized the servants and one they beat, another they killed, and a third they stoned. [36] Again he sent other servants, more numerous than the first ones, but they treated them in the same way. [37] Finally, he sent his son to them, thinking, 'They will respect my son.' [38]† But when the tenants saw the son, they said to one another, 'This is the heir. Come, let us kill him and acquire his inheritance.' [39]*† They seized him, threw him out of the vineyard, and killed him. [40] What will the owner of the vineyard do to those tenants when he

comes?" [41]† They answered him, "He will put those wretched men to a wretched death and lease his vineyard to other tenants who will give him the produce at the proper times." [42]*† Jesus said to them, "Did you never read in the scriptures:

'The stone that the builders rejected
    has become the cornerstone;
by the Lord has this been done,
    and it is wonderful in our eyes'?

[43]† Therefore, I say to you, the kingdom of God will be taken away from you and given to a people that will produce its fruit. [[44]† The one who falls on this stone will be dashed to pieces; and it will crush anyone on whom it falls.]" [45]† When the chief priests and the Pharisees heard his parables, they knew that he was speaking about them. [46] And although they were attempting to arrest him, they feared the crowds, for they regarded him as a prophet.

The Parable of the Wedding Feast

22 [1]*† Jesus again in reply spoke to them in parables, saying, [2]† "The kingdom of heaven may be likened to a king who gave a wedding feast for his son. [3]† He dispatched his servants to summon the invited guests to the feast, but they

---

† **21, 31:** *Entering . . . before you:* this probably means "they enter; you do not."

21, 32: Cf Lk 7, 29–30. Although the thought is similar to that of the Lucan text, the formulation is so different that it is improbable that the saying comes from Q. *Came to you . . . way of righteousness:* several meanings are possible: that John himself was righteous, that he taught righteousness to others, or that he had an important place in God's plan of salvation. For the last, see the note on 3, 14–15.

21, 33–46: Cf Mk 12, 1–12. In this parable there is a close correspondence between most of the details of the story and the situation that it illustrates, the dealings of God with his people. Because of that heavy allegorizing, some scholars think that it does not in any way go back to Jesus, but represents the theology of the later church. That judgment applies to the Marcan parallel as well, although the allegorizing has gone farther in Matthew. There are others who believe that while many of the allegorical elements are due to church sources, they have been added to a basic parable spoken by Jesus. This view is now supported by the Gospel of Thomas, 65, where a less allegorized and probably more primitive form of the parable is found.

21, 33: *Planted a vineyard . . . a tower:* cf Is 5, 1–2. The *vineyard* is defined in Is 5, 7 as "the house of Israel."

21, 34–35: *His servants:* Matthew has two sendings of *servants* as against Mark's three sendings of a single servant (11, 2–5a) followed by a statement about the sending of "many others" (11, 2.5b). That these *servants* stand for the prophets sent by God to Israel is clearly implied but not made explicit here, but see 23, 37. *His produce:* cf Mk 12, 2, "some of the produce." The *produce* is the good works demanded by God, and his claim to them is total.

21, 38: *Acquire his inheritance:* if a Jewish proselyte died without heir, the tenants of his land would have final claim on it.

21, 39: *Threw him out . . . and killed him:* the change in the Marcan order where the son is killed and his corpse then thrown out (12, 8) was probably made because of the tradition that Jesus died outside the city of Jerusalem; see Jn 19, 17; Heb 13, 12.

21, 41: *They answered:* in Mk 12, 9 the question is answered by Jesus himself; here the leaders answer and so condemn themselves; cf v 31. Matthew adds that the new *tenants* to whom the vineyard will be transferred *will give the owner the produce at the proper times.*

21, 42: Cf Ps 118, 22–23. The psalm was used in the early church as a prophecy of Jesus' resurrection; see Acts 4, 11; 1 Pt 2, 7. If, as some think, the original parable ended at v 39, it was thought necessary to complete it by a reference to Jesus' vindication by God.

21, 43: Peculiar to Matthew. *Kingdom of God:* see the note on 19, 23–24. Its presence here instead of Matthew's usual "kingdom of heaven" may indicate that the saying came from Matthew's own traditional material. *A people that will produce its fruit:* believing Israelites and Gentiles, the church of Jesus.

21, 44: The majority of textual witnesses omit this verse. It is probably an early addition to Matthew from Lk 20, 18 with which it is practically identical.

21, 45: *The Pharisees:* Matthew inserts into the group of Jewish leaders (23) those who represented the Judaism of his own time.

22, 1–14: This parable is from Q; see Lk 14, 15–24. It has been given many allegorical traits by Matthew, e.g., the burning of the *city* of the guests who refused the invitation (7), which corresponds to the destruction of Jerusalem by the Romans in A.D. 70. It has similarities with the preceding parable of the tenants: the sending of two groups of *servants* (3.4), the murder of the *servants* (6), the punishment of the *murderers* (7), and the entrance of a new group into a privileged situation of which the others had proved themselves unworthy (8–10). The parable ends with a section that is peculiar to Matthew (11–14), which some take as a distinct parable. Matthew presents the *kingdom* in its double aspect, already present and something that can be entered here and now (1–10), and something that will be possessed only by those present members who can stand the scrutiny of the final judgment (11–14). The parable is not only a statement of God's judgment on Israel but a warning to Matthew's church.

22, 2: *Wedding feast:* the Old Testament's portrayal of final salvation under the image of a banquet (Is 25, 6) is taken up also in 8, 11; cf Lk 13, 15.

22, 3–4: *Servants . . . other servants:* probably Christian missionaries in both instances; cf 23, 34.

---

* **21, 32:** Lk 7, 29–30.
21, 33–46: Mk 12, 1–12; Lk 20, 9–19.
21, 33: Is 5, 1–27.
21, 39: Heb 13, 12.
21, 42: Ps 118, 22–23; Is 28, 16; Acts 4, 11; 1 Pt 2, 7.
22, 1–14: Lk 14, 15–24.

refused to come. [4] A second time he sent other servants, saying, 'Tell those invited: "Behold, I have prepared my banquet, my calves and fattened cattle are killed, and everything is ready; come to the feast."' [5] Some ignored the invitation and went away, one to his farm, another to his business. [6]* The rest laid hold of his servants, mistreated them, and killed them. [7]† The king was enraged and sent his troops, destroyed those murderers, and burned their city. [8] Then he said to his servants, 'The feast is ready, but those who were invited were not worthy to come. [9] Go out, therefore, into the main roads and invite to the feast whomever you find.' [10]† The servants went out into the streets and gathered all they found, bad and good alike, and the hall was filled with guests. [11]† But when the king came in to meet the guests he saw a man there not dressed in a wedding garment. [12] He said to him, 'My friend, how is it that you came in here without a wedding garment?' But he was reduced to silence. [13]*† Then the king said to his attendants, 'Bind his hands and feet, and cast him into the darkness outside, where there will be wailing and grinding of teeth.' [14] Many are invited, but few are chosen."

Paying Taxes to the Emperor†

[15]* Then the Pharisees† went off and plotted how they might entrap him in speech. [16]† They sent their disciples to him, with the Herodians, saying, "Teacher, we know that you are a truthful man and that you teach the way of God in accordance with the truth. And yo[...]cerned with anyone's opinion, for[...]gard a person's status. [17]† Tell us[...]your opinion: Is it lawful to pay t[...]Caesar or not?" [18] Knowing thei[...]said, "Why are you testing me, you hypocrites? [19]† Show me the coin that pays the census tax." Then they handed him the Roman coin. [20] He said to them, "Whose image is this and whose inscription?" [21]*† They replied, "Caesar's." At that he said to them, "Then repay to Caesar what belongs to Caesar and to God what belongs to God." [22] When they heard this they were amazed, and leaving him they went away.

The Question about the Resurrection†

[23]* On that day Sadducees approached him, saying that there is no resurrection.† They put this question to him, [24]*† saying, "Teacher, Moses said, 'If a man dies without children, his brother shall marry his wife and raise up descendants for his brother.' [25] Now there were seven brothers among us. The first married and died and, having no descendants, left his wife to his brother. [26] The same happened with the second and the third, through all seven. [27] Finally the woman died. [28] Now at the resurrection, of the seven, whose wife will she be? For they all had been married to her." [29]† Jesus said to them in reply, "You are misled because you do not know the scriptures or the power of God. [30] At the resurrection they neither

---

22, 7: See the note on vv 1–14.

22, 10: *Bad and good alike:* cf 13, 47.

22, 11: *A wedding garment:* the repentance, change of heart and mind, that is the condition for entrance into the kingdom (3, 2; 4, 17) must be continued in a life of good deeds (7, 21–23).

22, 13: *Wailing and grinding of teeth:* the Christian who lacks the wedding garment of good deeds will suffer the same fate as those Jews who have rejected Jesus; see the note on 8, 11–12.

22, 15–22: The series of controversies between Jesus and the representatives of Judaism (see the note on 21, 23–27) is resumed. As in the first (21, 23–27), here and in the following disputes Matthew follows his Marcan source with few modifications.

22, 15: *The Pharisees:* while Matthew retains the Marcan union of Pharisees and Herodians in this account, he clearly emphasizes the Pharisees' part. They alone are mentioned here, and the Herodians are joined with them only in a prepositional phrase of v 16. *Entrap him in speech:* the question that they will pose is intended to force Jesus to take either a position contrary to that held by the majority of the people or one that will bring him into conflict with the Roman authorities.

22, 16: *Herodians:* see the note on Mk 3, 6. They would favor payment of the tax; the Pharisees did not.

22, 17: *Is it lawful:* the law to which they refer is the law of God.

22, 19: *They handed him the Roman coin:* their readiness in producing the money implies their use of it and their acceptance of the financial advantages of the Roman administration in Palestine.

22, 21: *Caesar's:* the emperor Tiberius (A.D. 14–37). *Repay to Caesar what belongs to Caesar:* those who willingly use the coin that is Caesar's should *repay* him in kind. The answer avoids taking sides in the question of the lawfulness of the tax. *To God what belongs to God:* Jesus raises the debate to a new level. Those who have hypocritically asked about tax in respect to its relation to the law of God should be concerned rather with repaying *God* with the good deeds that are his due; cf 21, 41.43.

22, 23–33: Here Jesus' opponents are the *Sadducees,* members of the powerful priestly party of his time; see the note on 3, 7. Denying the resurrection of the dead, a teaching of relatively late origin in Judaism (cf Dn 12, 2), they appeal to a law of the Pentateuch (Dt 25, 5–10) and present a case based on it that would make resurrection from the dead ridiculous (24–28). Jesus chides them for knowing neither *the scriptures* nor *the power of God* (29). His argument in respect to God's *power* contradicts the notion, held even by many proponents as well as by opponents of the teaching, that the life of those raised from the dead would be essentially a continuation of the type of life they had had before death (30). His argument based on the scriptures (31–32) is of a sort that was accepted as valid among Jews of the time.

22, 23: *Saying that there is no resurrection:* in the Marcan parallel (12, 18) the Sadducees are correctly defined as those "who say there is no resurrection"; see also Lk 20, 27. Matthew's rewording of Mark can mean that these particular Sadducees deny the resurrection, which would imply that he was not aware that the denial was characteristic of the party. For some scholars this is an indication of his being a Gentile Christian; see the note on 21, 4–5.

22, 24: *'If a man dies . . . his brother':* this is known as the "law of the levirate," from the Latin *levir,* "brother-in-law." Its purpose was to continue the family line of the deceased *brother* (Dt 25, 6).

22, 29: The sexual relationships of this world will be transcended; the risen body will be the work of the creative *power of God.*

22, 6: Mt 21, 35.　　　　　　**22, 21:** Rom 13, 7.
22, 13: Mt 8, 12; 25, 30.　　**22, 23–33:** Mk 12, 18–27;
22, 15–22: Mk 12, 13–17; Lk 20,　　　　　Lk 20, 27–40.
　　　20–26.　　　　　　　　**22, 24:** Gn 38, 8; Dt 25, 5–6.

The Miniature Gospel

Can you imagine a world where every person lives according to the two commandments Jesus gives in Mt 22, 34–40? Where every word, thought, and action are motivated by a deep love for God and by a desire for the well-being of others? Sounds a bit like the Garden of Eden! Libraries are filled with volumes describing philosophies for achieving the ideal human society, yet Jesus articulates the perfect plan in a few short sentences. These two great commandments remain for us as a kind of miniature Gospel.

Why not take the time to memorize verses 37–39? Let this miniature Gospel become such a part of you that you become a living, breathing example for others.

▶ **Mt 22, 34–40**

---

marry nor are given in marriage but are like the angels in heaven. 31† And concerning the resurrection of the dead, have you not read what was said to you by God, 32* 'I am the God of Abraham, the God of Isaac, and the God of Jacob'? He is not the God of the dead but of the living." 33 When the crowds heard this, they were astonished at his teaching.

The Greatest Commandment

34*† When the Pharisees heard that he had silenced the Sadducees, they gathered together, 35† and one of them [a scholar of the law] tested him by asking, 36† "Teacher, which commandment in the law is the greatest?" 37*† He said to him, "You shall love the Lord, your God, with all your heart, with all your soul, and with all your mind.

38 This is the greatest and the first commandment. 39*† The second is like it: You shall love your neighbor as yourself. 40*† The whole law and the prophets depend on these two commandments."

The Question about David's Son†

41* While the Pharisees were gathered together, Jesus questioned them,† 42† saying, "What is your opinion about the Messiah? Whose son is he?" They replied, "David's." 43 He said to them, "How, then, does David, inspired by the Spirit, call him 'lord,' saying:

44* 'The Lord said to my lord,
   "Sit at my right hand
      until I place your enemies under
         your feet" '?

---

† **22, 31–32:** Cf Ex 3, 6. In the Pentateuch, which the Sadducees accepted as normative for Jewish belief and practice, God speaks even now (to you) of himself as the God of the patriarchs who died centuries ago. He identifies himself in relation to them, and because of their relation to him, the living God, they too are alive. This might appear no argument for the resurrection, but simply for life after death as conceived in Wis 3, 1–3. But the general thought of early first-century Judaism was not influenced by that conception; for it human immortality was connected with the existence of the body.

22, 34–40: The Marcan parallel (12, 28–34) is an exchange between Jesus and a scribe who is impressed by the way in which Jesus has conducted himself in the previous controversy (12, 28), who compliments him for the answer he gives him (12, 32), and who is said by Jesus to be "not far from the kingdom of God" (12, 34). Matthew has sharpened that scene. The questioner, as the representative of other Pharisees, tests Jesus by his question (34–35), and both his reaction to Jesus' reply and Jesus' commendation of him are lacking.

22, 35: [A scholar of the law]: meaning "scribe." Although this reading is supported by the vast majority of textual witnesses, it is the only time that the Greek word so translated occurs in Matthew. It is relatively frequent in Luke, and there is reason to think that it may have been added here by a copyist since it occurs in the Lucan parallel (10, 25–28). Tested: see the note on 19, 3.

22, 36: For the devout Jew all the commandments were to be kept with equal care, but there is evidence of preoccupation in Jewish sources with the question put to Jesus.

22, 37–38: Cf Dt 6, 5. Matthew omits the first part of Mark's fuller quotation (12, 29; Dt 6, 4–5), probably because he considered its monotheistic emphasis needless for his church. The love of God must engage the total person (heart, soul, mind).

22, 39: Jesus goes beyond the extent of the question put to him and joins to the greatest and the first commandment a second, that of love of neighbor, Lv 19, 18; see the note on 19, 18–19. This combination of the two commandments may already have been made in Judaism.

22, 40: The double commandment is the source from which the whole law and the prophets are derived.

22, 41–46: Having answered the questions of his opponents in the preceding three controversies, Jesus now puts a question to them about the sonship of the Messiah. Their easy response (43a) is countered by his quoting a verse of Ps 110 that raises a problem for their response (43b–45). They are unable to solve it and from that day on their questioning of him is ended.

22, 41: The Pharisees . . . questioned them: Mark is not specific about who are questioned (12, 35).

22, 42–44: David's: this view of the Pharisees was based on such Old Testament texts as Is 11, 1–9; Jer 23, 5; and Ez 34, 23; see also the extrabiblical Psalms of Solomon 17, 21. How, then . . . saying: Jesus cites Ps 110, 1, accepting the Davidic authorship of the psalm, a common view of his time. The psalm was probably composed for the enthronement of a Davidic king of Judah. Matthew assumes that the Pharisees interpret it as referring to the Messiah, although there is no clear evidence that it was so interpreted in the Judaism of Jesus' time. It was widely used in the early church as referring to the exaltation of the risen Jesus. My lord: understood as the Messiah.

22, 32: Ex 3, 6.
22, 34–40: Mk 12, 28–34; Lk 10, 25–28.
22, 37: Dt 6, 5.
22, 39: Lv 19, 18; Jas 2, 8.

22, 40: Rom 13, 8–10; Gal 5, 14.
22, 41–46: Mk 12, 35–37; Lk 20, 41–44.
22, 44: Ps 110, 1; Acts 2, 35; Heb 1, 13.

45† If David calls him 'lord,' how can he be his son?" 46* No one was able to answer him a word, nor from that day on did anyone dare to ask him any more questions.

Denunciation of the Scribes and Pharisees

23 1*† Then Jesus spoke to the crowds and to his disciples, 2† saying, "The scribes and the Pharisees have taken their seat on the chair of Moses. 3 Therefore, do and observe all things whatsoever they tell you, but do not follow their example. For they preach but they do not practice. 4*† They tie up heavy burdens [hard to carry] and lay them on people's shoulders, but they will not lift a finger to move them. 5*† All their works are performed to be seen. They widen their phylacteries and lengthen their tassels. 6*† They love places of honor at banquets, seats of honor in synagogues, 7 greetings in marketplaces, and the salutation 'Rabbi.' 8† As for you, do not be called 'Rabbi.' You have but one teacher, and you are all brothers. 9 Call no one on earth your father; you have but one Father in heaven. 10 Do not be called 'Master'; you have but one master, the Messiah. 11* The greatest among you must be your servant. 12* Whoever exalts himself will be humbled; but whoever humbles himself will be exalted.

13*† "Woe to you, scribes and Pharisees, you hypocrites. You lock the kingdom of heaven† before human beings. You do not enter yourselves, nor do you allow entrance to those trying to enter. [14]†

15† "Woe to you, scribes and Pharisees, you hypocrites. You traverse sea and land to make one convert, and when that happens you make him a child of Gehenna twice as much as yourselves.

22, 45: Since Matthew presents Jesus both as Messiah (16, 16) and as Son of David (1, 1; see also the note on 9, 27), the question is not meant to imply Jesus' denial of Davidic sonship. It probably means that although he is the Son of David, he is someone greater, Son of Man and Son of God, and recognized as greater by David who calls him my *'lord.'*

23, 1–39: The final section of the narrative part of the fifth book of the gospel is a denunciation by Jesus of the scribes and the Pharisees (see the note on 3, 7). It depends in part on Mark and Q (cf Mk 12, 38–39; Lk 11, 37–52; 13, 34–35), but in the main it is peculiar to Matthew. (For the reasons against considering this extensive body of sayings-material either as one of the structural discourses of this gospel or as part of the one that follows in chs 24–25, see the note on 19, 1—23, 39.) While the tradition of a deep opposition between Jesus and the Pharisees is well founded, this speech reflects an opposition that goes beyond that of Jesus' ministry and must be seen as expressing the bitter conflict between Pharisaic Judaism and the church of Matthew at the time when the gospel was composed. The complaint often made that the speech ignores the positive qualities of Pharisaism and of its better representatives is true, but the complaint overlooks the circumstances that gave rise to the invective. Nor is the speech purely anti-Pharisaic. The evangelist discerns in his church many of the same faults that he finds in its opponents and warns his fellow Christians to look to their own conduct and attitudes.

23, 2–3: *Have taken their seat . . . Moses:* it is uncertain whether this is simply a metaphor for Mosaic teaching authority or refers to an actual *chair* on which the teacher sat. It has been proved that there was a seat so designated in synagogues of a later period than that of this gospel. *Do and observe . . . they tell you:* since the Matthean Jesus abrogates Mosaic law (5, 31–42), warns his disciples against the teaching of the Pharisees (14, 1–12), and, in this speech, denounces the Pharisees as blind guides in respect to their teaching on oaths (16–22), this commandment *to observe all things whatsoever they* (the scribes and Pharisees) *tell you* cannot be taken as the evangelist's understanding of the proper standard of conduct for his church. The saying may reflect a period when the Matthean community was largely Jewish Christian and was still seeking to avoid a complete break with the synagogue. Matthew has incorporated this traditional material into the speech in accordance with his view of the course of salvation history, in which he portrays the time of Jesus' ministry as marked by the fidelity to the law, although with significant pointers to the new situation that would exist after his death and resurrection. The crowds and the disciples (1) are exhorted not to *follow* the *example* of the Jewish leaders, whose deeds do not conform to their teaching (3).

23, 4: *Tie up heavy burdens:* see the note on 11, 28.

23, 5: To the charge of preaching but not practicing (3), Jesus adds that of acting in order to earn praise. The disciples have already been warned against this same fault (see the note on 6, 1–18). *Phylacteries:* the Mosaic law required that during prayer small boxes containing parchments on which verses of scripture were written be worn on the left forearm and the forehead (see Ex 13, 9.16; Dt 6, 8; 11, 18). *Tassels:* see the note on 9, 20. The widening of *phylacteries* and the lengthening of *tassels* were for the purpose of making these evidences of piety more noticeable.

23, 6–7: Cf Mk 12, 38–39. *'Rabbi':* literally, "my great one," a title of respect for teachers and leaders.

23, 8–12: These verses, warning against the use of various titles, are addressed to the disciples alone. While only the title *'Rabbi'* has been said to be used in addressing the scribes and Pharisees (7), the implication is that *Father* and *'Master'* also were. The prohibition of these titles to the disciples suggests that their use was present in Matthew's church. The Matthean Jesus forbids not only the titles but the spirit of superiority and pride that is shown by their acceptance. *Whoever exalts . . . will be exalted:* cf Lk 14, 11.

23, 13–36: This series of seven "woes," directed against the *scribes and Pharisees* and addressed to them, is the heart of the speech. The phrase *woe to* occurs often in the prophetic and apocalyptic literature, expressing horror of a sin and punishment for those who commit it. *Hypocrites:* see the note on 6, 2. The hypocrisy of the *scribes and Pharisees* consists in the difference between their speech and action (3) and in demonstrations of piety that have no other purpose than to enhance their reputation as religious persons (5).

23, 13: *You lock the kingdom of heaven:* cf 16, 19 where Jesus tells Peter that he will give him the keys to *the kingdom of heaven.* The purpose of the authority expressed by that metaphor is to give entrance into the kingdom (the kingdom is closed only to those who reject the authority); here the charge is made that the authority of the *scribes and Pharisees* is exercised in such a way as to be an obstacle to entrance. Cf Lk 11, 52 where the accusation against the "scholars of the law" (Matthew's *scribes*) is that they "have taken away the key of knowledge."

23, 14: Some manuscripts add a verse here or after v 12, "Woe to you, scribes and Pharisees, you hypocrites. You devour the houses of widows and, as a pretext, recite lengthy prayers. Because of this, you will receive a very severe condemnation." Cf Mk 12, 40; Lk 20, 47. This "woe" is almost identical with Mk 12, 40 and seems to be an interpolation derived from that text.

23, 15: In the first century A.D. until the First Jewish Revolt against Rome (A.D. 66–70), many Pharisees conducted a vigorous missionary campaign among Gentiles. *Convert:* literally, "proselyte," a Gentile who accepted Judaism fully by submitting to circumcision and all other requirements of Mosaic law. *Child of Gehenna:* worthy of everlasting punishment; for *Gehenna*, see the note on 5, 22. *Twice as much as yourselves:* possibly this refers simply to the zeal of the *convert*, surpassing that of the one who converted him.

22, 46: Lk 20, 40.
23, 1–39: Mk 12, 38–39; Lk 11, 37–52; 13, 34–35.
23, 4: Lk 11, 46.
23, 5: Mt 6, 1–6; Ex 13, 9.16; Nm 15, 38–39; Dt 6, 8; 11, 18.
23, 6–7: Mk 12, 38–39; Lk 11, 43; 20, 46.
23, 11: Mt 20, 26.
23, 12: Lk 14, 11; 18, 14.
23, 13: Lk 11, 52.

No Respect

The "woe" statements of Jesus in Mt 23, 1–24 are his harshest words in all the Gospels. The community in which the author of Matthew lived had negative experiences with Jewish leaders (see "Pharisees, Sadducees, and Scribes," Mt 3, 7), and their hard feelings are reflected in Jesus' words. We should take Mt 23, 3–4 not as a condemnation of Jewish people but as a call to do the following:

- practice what we preach (verse 3)
- show compassion; don't burden others (verse 4)
- practice religion not to look important but as an expression of faith (verses 8–15)
- humbly respect the people who follow us (verses 8–15)
- be guided by mercy and justice in our understanding of law (verses 23–24)

Jesus' sharpest criticism here and in many other places in the Gospels is directed towards hypocrisy—the act of pretending to be holy and just while actually doing sinful things. In your prayer, reflect or journal on the following questions:

- How have I expressed my faith in my spoken words as well as in my inner thoughts?
- When has my life demonstrated what my faith is all about?
- When have I asked others to do something that I was not willing to do myself? Why did I do that?
- When have I used any power or influence I might have in a way that was humble and served the needs of others? How did I do that?

Try looking at these same questions each week or month, and see if your answers change over time.

▶ Mt 23, 1–36

16*† "Woe to you, blind guides, who say, 'If one swears by the temple, it means nothing, but if one swears by the gold of the temple, one is obligated.' 17 Blind fools, which is greater, the gold, or the temple that made the gold sacred? 18 And you say, 'If one swears by the altar, it means nothing, but if one swears by the gift on the altar, one is obligated.' 19 You blind ones, which is greater, the gift, or the altar that makes the gift sacred? 20* One who swears by the altar swears by it and all that is upon it; 21 one who swears by the temple swears by it and by him who dwells in it; 22 one who swears by heaven swears by the throne of God and by him who is seated on it.

23*† "Woe to you, scribes and Pharisees, you hypocrites. You pay tithes of mint and dill and cummin, and have neglected the weightier things of the law: judgment and mercy and fidelity. [But] these you should have done, without neglecting the others. 24*† Blind guides, who strain out the gnat and swallow the camel!

25*† "Woe to you, scribes and Pharisees, you hypocrites. You cleanse the outside of cup and dish, but inside they are full of plunder and self-indulgence. 26 Blind Pharisee, cleanse first the inside of the cup, so that the outside also may be clean.

27† "Woe to you, scribes and Pharisees, you hypocrites. You are like whitewashed tombs, which appear beautiful on the outside, but inside are full of dead men's bones and every kind of filth. 28* Even

of values, reveals the teachers to be *blind guides;* cf 15, 14. Since the Matthean Jesus forbids all oaths to his disciples (5, 33–37), this *woe* does not set up a standard for Christian moral conduct, but ridicules the Pharisees on their own terms.

23, 23: The Mosaic law ordered tithing of the produce of the land (Lv 27, 30; Dt 14, 22–23), and the scribal tradition is said here to have extended this law to even the smallest herbs. The practice is criticized not in itself but because it shows the Pharisees' preoccupation with matters of less importance while they neglect *the weightier things of the law.*

23, 24: Cf Lv 11, 41–45 that forbids the eating of any "swarming creature." The Pharisees' scrupulosity about minor matters and neglect of greater ones (23) is further brought out by this contrast between straining liquids that might contain a tiny "swarming creature" and yet swallowing *the camel.* The latter was one of the unclean animals forbidden by the law (Lv 11, 4), but it is hardly possible that the scribes and Pharisees are being denounced as guilty of so gross a violation of the food laws. To *swallow the camel* is only a hyperbolic way of speaking of their neglect of what is important.

23, 25–26: The ritual washing of utensils for dining (cf Mk 7, 4) is turned into a metaphor illustrating a concern for appearances while inner purity is ignored. The *scribes and Pharisees* are compared to cups carefully washed on the outside but filthy within. *Self-indulgence:* the Greek word here translated means lack of self-control, whether in drinking or in sexual conduct.

23, 27–28: The sixth *woe,* like the preceding one, deals with concern for externals and neglect of what is *inside.* Since contact with dead bodies, even when one was unaware of it, caused ritual impurity (Nm 19, 11–22), tombs were whitewashed so that no one would contract such impurity inadvertently.

---

† **23, 16–22:** An attack on the casuistry that declared some oaths binding (*one is obligated*) and others not (*it means nothing*) and held the binding oath to be the one made by something of lesser value (*the gold; the gift on the altar*). Such teaching, which inverts the order

23, 16: Mt 15, 14.   **23, 24:** Lv 11, 41–45.
23, 20–22: Mt 5, 34–35.   **23, 25–26:** Mk 7, 4; Lk 11, 39.
   23, 23: Lv 27, 30; Dt 14, 22;   **23, 28:** Lk 16, 15; 18, 9.
        Lk 11, 42.

so, on the outside you appear righteous, but inside you are filled with hypocrisy and evildoing.

29† "Woe to you, scribes and Pharisees,† you hypocrites. You build the tombs of the prophets and adorn the memorials of the righteous, 30* and you say, 'If we had lived in the days of our ancestors, we would not have joined them in shedding the prophets' blood.' 31* Thus you bear witness against yourselves that you are the children of those who murdered the prophets; 32 now fill up what your ancestors measured out! 33* You serpents, you brood of vipers, how can you flee from the judgment of Gehenna? 34*† Therefore, behold, I send to you prophets and wise men and scribes; some of them you will kill and crucify, some of them you will scourge in your synagogues and pursue from town to town, 35 so that there may come upon you all the righteous blood shed upon earth, from the righteous blood of Abel to the blood of Zechariah, the son of Barachiah, whom you murdered between the sanctuary and the altar. 36 Amen, I say to you, all these things will come upon this generation.

The Lament over Jerusalem

37*† "Jerusalem, Jerusalem, you who kill the prophets and stone those sent to you, how many times I yearned to gather your children together, as a hen gathers her young under her wings, but you were unwilling!* 38* Behold, your house will be abandoned, desolate. 39* I tell you, you will not see me again until you say, 'Blessed is he who comes in the name of the Lord.' "

The Destruction of the Temple Foretold

24 1*† Jesus left the temple area and was going away, when his disciples approached him to point out the temple buildings. 2† He said to them in reply, "You see all these things, do you not? Amen, I say to you, there will not be left here a stone upon another stone that will not be thrown down."

The Beginning of Calamities

3† As he was sitting on the Mount of Olives, the disciples approached him privately and said, "Tell us, when will this happen, and what sign will there be of your coming, and of the end of the

---

† **23, 29–36:** The final *woe* is the most serious indictment of all. It portrays the *scribes and Pharisees* as standing in the same line as their *ancestors* who murdered *the prophets* and *the righteous*.
23, 29–32: In spite of honoring the slain dead by building their *tombs* and adorning their *memorials,* and claiming that they would not have joined in their ancestors' crimes if they *had lived in their days,* the *scribes and Pharisees* are true *children* of their ancestors and are defiantly ordered by Jesus to *fill up* what those *ancestors measured out.* This order reflects the Jewish notion that there was an allotted measure of suffering that had to be completed before God's final judgment would take place.
23, 34–36: There are important differences between the Matthean and the Lucan form of this Q material; cf Lk 11, 49–51. In Luke the one who sends the emissaries is the "wisdom of God." If, as many scholars think, that is the original wording of Q, Matthew, by making Jesus the sender, has presented him as the personified divine wisdom. In Luke, wisdom's emissaries are the Old Testament "prophets" and the Christian "apostles." Matthew's *prophets and wise men and scribes* are probably Christian disciples alone; cf 10, 41 and see the note on 13, 52. *You will kill:* see 24, 9. *Scourge in your synagogues . . . town to town:* see 10, 17.23 and the note on 10, 17. *All the righteous blood shed upon the earth:* the slaying of the disciples is in continuity with all the shedding of *righteous blood* beginning with that *of Abel.* The persecution of Jesus' disciples by *this generation* involves the persecutors in the guilt of their murderous ancestors. *The blood of Zechariah:* see the note on Lk 11, 51. By identifying him as *the son of Barachiah* Matthew understands him to be Zechariah the Old Testament minor prophet; see Zec 1, 1.
23, 37–39: Cf Lk 13, 34–35. The denunciation of Pharisaic Judaism ends with this lament over *Jerusalem,* which has repeatedly rejected and murdered those whom God has *sent* to her. *How many times:* this may refer to various visits of Jesus to the city, an aspect of his ministry found in John but otherwise not in the synoptics. *As a hen . . . under her wings:* for imagery similar to this, see Pss 17, 8; 91, 4. *Your house . . . desolate:* probably an allusion to the destruction of the temple in A.D. 70. *You will not see me . . . in the name of the Lord:* Israel will not see Jesus again until he comes in glory for the final judgment. The acclamation has been interpreted in contrasting ways, as an indication that Israel will at last accept Jesus at that time, and as its troubled recognition of him as its dreaded judge who will pronounce its condemnation; in support of the latter view see 24, 30.
24, 1–25, 46: The discourse of the fifth book, the last of the five around which the gospel is structured. It is called the "eschatological" discourse since it deals with the coming of the new age (the

eschaton) in its fullness, with events that will precede it, and with how the disciples are to conduct themselves while awaiting an event that is as certain as its exact time is unknown to all but the Father (24, 36). The discourse may be divided into two parts, 24, 1–44 and 24, 45–25, 46. In the first, Matthew follows his Marcan source (13, 1–37) closely. The second is drawn from Q and from the evangelist's own traditional material. Both parts show Matthew's editing of his sources by deletions, additions, and modifications. The vigilant waiting that is emphasized in the second part does not mean a cessation of ordinary activity and concentration only on what is to come, but a faithful accomplishment of duties at hand, with awareness that the end, for which the disciples must always be ready, will entail the great judgment by which the everlasting destiny of all will be determined.
24, 2: As in Mark, Jesus predicts the destruction of the temple. By omitting the Marcan story of the widow's contribution (12, 41–44) that immediately precedes the prediction in that gospel, Matthew has established a close connection between it and 23, 38, ". . . your house will be abandoned desolate."
24, 3: *The Mount of Olives:* see the note on 21, 1. *The disciples:* cf Mk 13, 3–4 where only Peter, James, John, and Andrew put the question that is answered by the discourse. In both gospels, however, the question is put *privately:* the ensuing discourse is only for those who are *disciples* of Jesus. *When will this happen . . . end of the age?:* Matthew distinguishes carefully between the destruction of the temple (*this*) and the *coming* of Jesus that will bring *the end of the age.* In Mark the two events are more closely connected, a fact that may be explained by Mark's believing that the one would immediately succeed the other. *Coming:* this translates the Greek word *parousia,* which is used in the gospels only here and in vv 27, 37, and 39. It designated the official visit of a ruler to a city or the manifestation of a saving deity, and it was used by Christians to refer to the final coming of Jesus in glory, a term first found in the New Testament with that meaning in 1 Thes 2, 19. *The end of the age:* see the note on 13, 39.

23, 30: Lk 11, 47.
23, 31: Acts 7, 52.
23, 33: Mt 3, 7; 12, 34.
23, 34–36: Mt 5, 12; Gn 4, 8; 2 Chr 24, 20–22; Zec 1, 1; Lk 11, 49–51; Rv 18, 24.
23, 37–39: Lk 13, 34–35; 19, 41–44.
23, 37: Mt 21, 35.
23, 38: Jer 12, 7.
23, 39: Ps 118, 26.
24, 1–44: Mk 13, 1–37; Lk 21, 5–36.

MT

age?" ⁴† Jesus said to them in reply, "See that no one deceives you. ⁵ For many will come in my name, saying, 'I am the Messiah,' and they will deceive many. ⁶*† You will hear of wars and reports of wars; see that you are not alarmed, for these things must happen, but it will not yet be the end. ⁷* Nation will rise against nation, and kingdom against kingdom; there will be famines and earthquakes from place to place. ⁸† All these are the beginning of the labor pains. ⁹*† Then they will hand you over to persecution, and they will kill you. You will be hated by all nations because of my name. ¹⁰ And then many will be led into sin; they will betray and hate one another. ¹¹ Many false prophets will arise and deceive many; ¹² and because of the increase of evildoing, the love of many will grow cold. ¹³* But the one who perseveres to the end will be saved. ¹⁴*† And this gospel of the kingdom will be preached throughout the world as a witness to all nations, and then the end will come.

The Great Tribulation†

¹⁵* "When you see the desolating abomination† spoken of through Daniel the prophet standing in the holy place (let the reader understand), ¹⁶† then those in Judea must flee to the mountains, ¹⁷*† a person on the housetop must not go down to get things out of his house, ¹⁸ a person in the field must not return to get his cloak. ¹⁹ Woe to pregnant women and nursing mothers in those days. ²⁰† Pray that your flight not be in winter or on the sabbath, ²¹*† for at that time there will be great tribulation, such as has not been since the beginning of the world until now, nor ever will be. ²² And if those days had not been shortened, no one would be saved; but for the sake of the elect they will be shortened. ²³* If anyone says to you then, 'Look, here is the Messiah!' or, 'There he is!' do not believe it. ²⁴ False messiahs and false prophets will arise, and they will perform signs and wonders so great as to deceive, if that were possible, even the elect. ²⁵ Behold, I have told it to you beforehand. ²⁶† So

---

24, 4–14: This section of the discourse deals with calamities in the world (6–7) and in the church (9–12). The former *must happen before the end* comes (6), but they are only *the beginning of the labor pains* (8). (It may be noted that the Greek word translated *the end* in v 6 and in vv 13–14 is not the same as the phrase "the end of the age" in v 3, although the meaning is the same.) The latter are sufferings of the church, both from within and without, that will last until the *gospel is preached . . . to all nations. Then the end will come* and those who have endured the sufferings with fidelity *will be saved* (13–14).

24, 6–7: The disturbances mentioned here are a commonplace of apocalyptic language, as is the assurance that they *must happen* (see Dn 2, 28 LXX), for that is the plan of God. *Kingdom against kingdom:* see Is 19, 2.

24, 8: *The labor pains:* the tribulations leading up to the end of the age are compared to the pains of a woman about to give birth. There is much attestation for rabbinic use of the phrase "the woes (or birth pains) of the Messiah" after the New Testament period, but in at least one instance it is attributed to a rabbi who lived in the late first century A.D. In this Jewish usage it meant the distress of the time preceding the coming of the Messiah; here, the *labor pains* precede the coming of the Son of Man in glory.

24, 9–12: Matthew has used Mk 13, 9–12 in his missionary discourse (10, 17–21) and omits it here. Besides the sufferings, including death, and the hatred of *all nations* that the disciples will have to endure, there will be worse affliction within the church itself. This is described in vv 10–12, which are peculiar to Matthew. *Will be led into sin:* literally, "will be scandalized," probably meaning that they will become apostates; see 13, 21 where "fall away" translates the same Greek word as here. *Betray:* in the Greek this is the same word as the *hand over* of v 9. The handing over to persecution and hatred from outside will have their counterpart within the church. *False prophets:* these are Christians; see the note on 7, 15–20. *Evildoing:* see 7, 23. Because of the apocalyptic nature of much of this discourse, the literal meaning of this description of the church should not be pressed too hard. However, there is reason to think that Matthew's addition of these verses reflects in some measure the condition of his community.

24, 14: Except for the last part (*and then the end will come*), this verse substantially repeats Mk 13, 10. The Matthean addition raises a problem since what follows in vv 15–23 refers to the horrors of the First Jewish Revolt including the destruction of the temple, and Matthew, writing after that time, knew that the parousia of Jesus was still in the future. A solution may be that the evangelist saw the events of those verses as foreshadowing the cosmic disturbances that he associates with the parousia (29) so that the period in which the former took place could be understood as belonging to *the end*.

24, 15–28: Cf Mk 13, 14–23; Lk 17, 23–24.37. A further stage in the tribulations that will precede the coming of the Son of Man, and an answer to the question of v 3a, "when will this (the destruction of the temple) happen?"

24, 15: *The desolating abomination:* in 167 B.C. the Syrian king Antiochus IV Epiphanes desecrated the temple by setting up in it a statue of Zeus Olympios (see 1 Mc 1, 54). That event is referred to in Dn 12, 11 LXX as the "desolating abomination" (NAB "horrible abomination") and the same Greek term is used here; cf also Dn 9, 27; 11, 31. Although the desecration had taken place before Daniel was written, it is presented there as a future event, and Matthew sees that "prophecy" fulfilled in the desecration of the temple by the Romans. *In the holy place:* the temple; more precise than Mark's *where he should not* (13, 14). *Let the reader understand:* this parenthetical remark, taken from Mk 13, 14, invites the *reader* to realize the meaning of Daniel's "prophecy."

24, 16: The tradition that the Christians of Jerusalem fled from that city to Pella, a city of Transjordan, at the time of the First Jewish Revolt is found in Eusebius (*Ecclesiastical History,* 3, 5, 3), who attributes the flight to "a certain oracle given by revelation before the war." The tradition is not improbable but the Matthean command, derived from its Marcan source, is vague in respect to the place of flight (*to the mountains*), although some scholars see it as applicable to the flight to Pella.

24, 17–19: Haste is essential, and the journey will be particularly difficult for women who are burdened with unborn or infant children.

24, 20: *On the sabbath:* this addition to *in winter* (cf Mk 13, 18) has been understood as an indication that Matthew was addressed to a church still observing the Mosaic law of sabbath rest and the scribal limitations upon the length of journeys that might lawfully be made on that day. That interpretation conflicts with Matthew's view on sabbath observance (cf 12, 1–14). The meaning of the addition may be that those undertaking on the sabbath a journey such as the one here ordered would be offending the sensibilities of law-observant Jews and would incur their hostility.

24, 21: For the unparalleled distress of that time, see Dn 12, 1.

24, 26–28: Claims that the Messiah is to be found in some distant or secret place must be ignored. *The coming of the Son of Man* will be as clear as *lightning* is to all and as *the corpse* of an animal is to *vultures;* cf Lk 17, 24.37. Here there is clear identification of *the Son of Man* and the Messiah; cf v 23.

24, 6: Dn 2, 28 LXX.
24, 7: Is 19, 2.
24, 9: Mt 10, 17.
24, 13: Mt 10, 22.
24, 14: Mt 28, 19; Rom 10, 18.
24, 15: Dn 9, 27; 11, 31; 12, 11; Mk 13, 14.
24, 17: Lk 17, 31.
24, 21: Dn 12, 1.
24, 23: Lk 17, 23.

if they say to you, 'He is in the desert,' do not go out there; if they say, 'He is in the inner rooms,' do not believe it. 27* For just as lightning comes from the east and is seen as far as the west, so will the coming of the Son of Man be. 28 Wherever the corpse is, there the vultures will gather.

The Coming of the Son of Man

29*† "Immediately after the tribulation of those days,

the sun will be darkened,
and the moon will not give its light,
and the stars will fall from the sky,
and the powers of the heavens will
be shaken.

30*† And then the sign of the Son of Man will appear in heaven, and all the tribes of the earth will mourn, and they will see the Son of Man coming upon the clouds of heaven with power and great glory.

31*† And he will send out his angels with a trumpet blast, and they will gather his elect from the four winds, from one end of the heavens to the other.

The Lesson of the Fig Tree

32† "Learn a lesson from the fig tree. When its branch becomes tender and sprouts leaves, you know that summer is near. 33 In the same way, when you see all these things, know that he is near, at the gates. 34† Amen, I say to you, this generation will not pass away until all these things have taken place. 35* Heaven and earth will pass away, but my words will not pass away.

The Unknown Day and Hour†

36* "But of that day and hour no one knows, neither the angels of heaven, nor the Son,† but the Father alone. 37*† For as it was in the days of Noah, so it will be at the coming of the Son of Man. 38 In [those] days before the flood, they were eating and drinking, marrying and giving in marriage, up to

Be Ready

LIVE IT!

Have you ever been asked questions like these: If you knew you only had one week to live, what would you do in that time? If you knew you were going to see a loved one for the last time, what would you say to him or her? Faced with those scenarios, many people imagine themselves acting more lovingly and generously than they ordinarily do.

Jesus sets up a similar scenario when he warns his followers to stay awake (Mt 24, 42). In this final teaching in Matthew, Jesus is speaking of the final coming of God. The Gospel reminds us that no one knows when Christ will come for us. It is foolish and dangerous to put off living a life committed to Christ.

If you knew you were to stand before God tomorrow, how would you live your life today?

▶ Mt 24, 36–44

24, 29: The answer to the question of v 3b, "What sign will there be of your coming?" *Immediately after . . . those days:* the shortening of time between the preceding *tribulation* and the parousia has been explained as Matthew's use of a supposed device of Old Testament prophecy whereby certainty that a predicted event will occur is expressed by depicting it as imminent. While it is questionable that that is an acceptable understanding of the Old Testament predictions, it may be applicable here, for Matthew knew that the parousia had not come *immediately after* the fall of Jerusalem, and it is unlikely that he is attributing a mistaken calculation of time to Jesus. *The sun . . . be shaken:* cf Is 13, 10.13.
24, 30: *The sign of the Son of Man:* perhaps this means *the sign* that is the glorious appearance *of the Son of Man;* cf 12, 39–40 where "the sign of Jonah" is Jonah's being in the "belly of the whale." *Tribes of the earth will mourn:* peculiar to Matthew; cf Zec 12, 12–14. *Coming upon the clouds . . . glory:* cf Dn 7, 13, although there the "one like a son of man" comes to God to receive kingship; here *the Son of Man* comes from heaven for judgment.
24, 31: *Send out his angels:* cf 13, 41 where they are sent out to collect the wicked for punishment. *Trumpet blast:* cf Is 27, 13; 1 Thes 4, 16.
24, 32–35: Cf Mk 13, 28–31.
24, 34: The difficulty raised by this verse cannot be satisfactorily

removed by the supposition that *this generation* means the Jewish people throughout the course of their history, much less the entire human race. Perhaps for Matthew it means the *generation* to which he and his community belonged.
24, 36–44: The statement of v 34 is now counterbalanced by one that declares that the exact time of the parousia is known only to *the Father* (36), and the disciples are warned to be always ready for it. This section is drawn from Mark and Q (cf Lk 17, 26–27.34–35; 12, 39–40).
24, 36: Many textual witnesses omit *nor the Son,* which follows Mk 13, 32. Since its omission can be explained by reluctance to attribute this ignorance to *the Son,* the reading that includes it is probably original.
24, 37–39: Cf Lk 17, 26–27. *In the days of Noah:* the Old Testament account of the flood lays no emphasis upon what is central for Matthew, i.e., the unexpected coming of the flood upon those who were unprepared for it.

24, 27–28: Lk 17, 24.37.
24, 29: Is 13, 10.13; Ez 32, 7; Am 8, 9.
24, 30: Dn 7, 13; Zec 12, 12–14; Rv 1, 7.
24, 31: Is 27, 13; 1 Cor 15, 52; 1 Thes 4, 16.
24, 35: Is 40, 8.
24, 36: Acts 1, 7.
24, 37–39: Gn 6, 5—7, 23; Lk 17, 26–27; 2 Pt 3, 6.

MT

the day that Noah entered the ark. [39] They did not know until the flood came and carried them all away. So will it be [also] at the coming of the Son of Man. [40]*† Two men will be out in the field; one will be taken, and one will be left. [41] Two women will be grinding at the mill; one will be taken, and one will be left. [42]*† Therefore, stay awake! For you do not know on which day your Lord will come. [43]* Be sure of this: if the master of the house had known the hour of night when the thief was coming, he would have stayed awake and not let his house be broken into. [44] So too, you also must be prepared, for at an hour you do not expect, the Son of Man will come.

The Faithful or the Unfaithful Servant†

[45]* "Who, then, is the faithful and prudent servant, whom the master has put in charge of his household to distribute to them their food at the proper time?† [46] Blessed is that servant whom his master on his arrival finds doing so. [47] Amen, I say to you, he will put him in charge of all his property. [48]† But if that wicked servant says to himself, 'My master is long delayed,' [49] and begins to beat his fellow servants, and eat and drink with drunkards, [50] the servant's master will come on an unexpected day and at an unknown hour [51]*† and will punish him severely and assign him a place with the hypocrites, where there will be wailing and grinding of teeth.

The Parable of the Ten Virgins†

25 [1] "Then† the kingdom of heaven will be like ten virgins who took their lamps and went out to meet the bridegroom. [2]† Five of them were foolish and five were wise. [3] The foolish ones, when taking their lamps, brought no oil with them, [4] but the wise brought flasks of oil with their lamps.

When Are You Coming?

I have accepted your invitation, Lord.
　But when are you coming?
I need to be ready, Lord.
　But when are you coming?
I want to share your love with others, Lord.
　But when are you coming?
I will be prepared, Lord.
　No matter when you are coming.

▶ **Mt 25, 1–13**

---

[5] Since the bridegroom was long delayed, they all became drowsy and fell asleep. [6] At midnight, there was a cry, 'Behold, the bridegroom! Come out to meet him!' [7] Then all those virgins got up and trimmed their lamps. [8] The foolish ones said to the wise, 'Give us some of your oil, for our lamps are going out.' [9] But the wise ones replied, 'No, for there may not be enough for us and you. Go instead to the merchants and buy some for yourselves.' [10] While they went off to buy it, the bridegroom came and those who were ready went into the wedding feast with him. Then the door was locked. [11]*† Afterwards the other virgins came and said, 'Lord, Lord, open the door for us!' [12] But he said in reply, 'Amen, I say to you, I do not know you.' [13]*† Therefore, stay awake, for you know neither the day nor the hour.

The Parable of the Talents†

[14]* "It will be as when a man who was going on a journey† called in his servants and entrusted his

---

† **24, 40–41:** Cf Lk 17, 34–35. *Taken . . . left:* the former probably means *taken* into the kingdom; the latter, *left* for destruction. People in the same situation will be dealt with in opposite ways. In this context, the discrimination between them will be based on their readiness for the coming of the Son of Man.

24, 42–44: Cf Lk 12, 39–40. The theme of vigilance and readiness is continued with the bold comparison of the Son of Man to a thief who comes to break into a house.

24, 45–51: The second part of the discourse (see the note on 24, 1–25, 46) begins with this parable of *the faithful* or unfaithful *servant;* cf Lk 12, 41–46. It is addressed to the leaders of Matthew's church; *the servant* has been *put in charge* of his master's *household* (45) even though that *household* is composed of those who are his *fellow servants* (49).

24, 45: *To distribute . . . proper time:* readiness for the master's return means a vigilance that is accompanied by faithful performance of the duty assigned.

24, 48: *My master . . . delayed:* the note of delay is found also in the other parables of this section; cf 25, 5.19.

24, 51: *Punish him severely:* the Greek verb, found in the New Testament only here and in the Lucan parallel (12, 46), means, literally, "cut in two." *With the hypocrites:* see the note on 6, 2. Matthew classes the unfaithful Christian leader with the unbelieving leaders of Judaism. *Wailing and grinding of teeth:* see the note on 8, 11–12.

25, 1–13: Peculiar to Matthew.

25, 1: *Then:* at the time of the parousia. *Kingdom . . . will be like:* see the note on 13, 24–30.

25, 2–4: *Foolish . . . wise:* cf the contrasted "wise man" and "fool" of 7, 24.26, where the two are distinguished by good deeds and lack of them, and such deeds may be signified by the *oil* of this parable.

25, 11–12: *Lord, Lord:* cf 7, 21. *I do not know you:* cf 7, 23, where the Greek verb is different but synonymous.

25, 13: *Stay awake:* some scholars see this command as an addition to the original parable of Matthew's traditional material, since in v 5 all the virgins, wise and foolish, fall asleep. But the wise virgins are adequately equipped for their task, and *stay awake* may mean no more than to be prepared; cf 24, 42.44.

25, 14–30: Cf Lk 19, 12–27.

25, 14: *It will be as when . . . . journey:* literally, "For just as a man who was going on a journey." Although the comparison is not completed, the sense is clear; the kingdom of heaven is like the situation here described. Faithful use of one's gifts will lead to participation in the fullness of the kingdom, lazy inactivity to exclusion from it.

24, 40–41: Lk 17, 34–35.
24, 42–44: Mt 25, 13; Lk 12, 39–40.
24, 43: 1 Thes 5, 2.
24, 45–51: Lk 12, 41–46.
24, 51: Mt 13, 42; 25, 30.
25, 11–12: Mt 7, 21.23; Lk 13, 25.27.
25, 13: Mt 24, 42; Mk 13, 33.
25, 14–30: Lk 19, 12–27.

THE PRINCIPLE OF *KUUMBA*

Sometimes I wish I had a great singing voice. I often daydream about belting out songs with the vocal power of the sister of soul, Aretha Franklin. Sure, I have other gifts, but more than anything else, I wish I could sing. Here I go again, neglecting what I do have as I yearn for what I lack. Why do I do that?

This attitude sounds a bit like that of the ungrateful servant Jesus speaks of in Mt 25, 14–30, the parable of the talents, doesn't it? In the parable, the master gives the third servant a talent, but the servant keeps it hidden. And precisely because he keeps it hidden, the timid servant loses the one talent he does have.

God has given us our talents and abilities. The Kwanzaa principle of *kuumba* (creativity) calls us to use our talents creatively and boldly in the service of God. Don't second-guess the Lord by wanting something you do not have. Trust that God has blessed you with the gifts you need, and use them!

Dear God, thank you for what I have. Help me use it to your glory. Amen.

▸ Mt 25, 14–30

possessions to them. ¹⁵† To one he gave five talents; to another, two; to a third, one—to each according to his ability. Then he went away. Immediately ¹⁶ the one who received five talents went and traded with them, and made another five. ¹⁷ Likewise, the one who received two made another two. ¹⁸† But the man who received one went off and dug a hole in the ground and buried his master's money. ¹⁹ After a long time the master of those servants came back and settled accounts with them. ²⁰† The one who had received five talents came forward bringing the additional five. He said, 'Master, you gave me five talents. See, I have made five more.' ²¹* His master said to him, 'Well done, my good and faithful servant. Since you were faithful in small matters, I will give you great responsibilities. Come, share your master's joy.' ²² [Then] the one who had received two talents also came forward and said, 'Master, you gave me two talents. See, I have made two more.' ²³ His master said to him, 'Well done,

my good and faithful servant. Since you were faithful in small matters, I will give you great responsibilities. Come, share your master's joy.' ²⁴ Then the one who had received the one talent came forward and said, 'Master, I knew you were a demanding person, harvesting where you did not plant and gathering where you did not scatter; ²⁵ so out of fear I went off and buried your talent in the ground. Here it is back.' ²⁶† His master said to him in reply, 'You wicked, lazy servant! So you knew that I harvest where I did not plant and gather where I did not scatter? ²⁷ Should you not then have put my money in the bank so that I could have got it back with interest on my return? ²⁸ Now then! Take the talent from him and give it to the one with ten. ²⁹*† For to everyone who has, more will be given and he will grow rich; but from the one who has not, even what he has will be taken away. ³⁰† And throw this useless servant into the darkness outside, where there will be wailing and grinding of teeth.'

† **25, 15:** *Talents:* see the note on 18, 24.
  25, 18: *Buried his master's money:* see the note on 13, 44.
  25, 20–23: Although the first two servants have received and doubled large sums, their faithful trading is regarded by the master as fidelity *in small matters* only, compared with the *great responsibilities* now to be given to them. The latter are unspecified. *Share your master's joy:* probably the joy of the banquet of the kingdom; cf 8, 11.
  25, 26–28: *Wicked, lazy servant:* this man's inactivity is not neg-

ligible but seriously culpable. As punishment, he loses the gift he had received, that is now given to the first servant, whose possessions are already great.
  25, 29: See the note on 13, 12 where there is a similar application of this maxim.
  25, 30: See the note on 8, 11–12.

─────

25, 21: Lk 16, 10.   **25, 29:** Mt 13, 12; Mk 4, 25; Lk 8, 18; 19, 26.

The Judgment of the Nations†

31* "When the Son of Man comes in his glory, and all the angels with him, he will sit upon his glorious throne,† 32*† and all the nations will be assembled before him. And he will separate them one from another, as a shepherd separates the sheep from the goats. 33 He will place the sheep on his right and the goats on his left. 34 Then the king will say to those on his right, 'Come, you who are blessed by my Father. Inherit the kingdom prepared for you from the foundation of the world. 35* For I was hungry and you gave me food, I was thirsty and you gave me drink, a stranger and you welcomed me, 36 naked and you clothed me, ill and you cared for me, in prison and you visited me.' 37† Then the righteous will answer him and say, 'Lord, when did

we see you hungry and feed you, or thirsty and give you drink? 38 When did we see you a stranger and welcome you, or naked and clothe you? 39 When did we see you ill or in prison, and visit you?' 40* And the king will say to them in reply, 'Amen, I say to you, whatever you did for one of these least brothers of mine, you did for me.' 41*† Then he will say to those on his left, 'Depart from me, you accursed, into the eternal fire prepared for the devil and his angels. 42* For I was hungry and you gave me no food, I was thirsty and you gave me no drink, 43 a stranger and you gave me no welcome, naked and you gave me no clothing, ill and in prison, and you did not care for me.' 44† Then they will answer and say, 'Lord, when did we see you hungry or thirsty or a stranger or naked or ill or in prison, and

"You Did for Me"

LIVE IT!

"If the poor would only get out and find work, they would not be poor!" This common misconception pacifies the conscience of many people. Instead, Jesus says that we shouldn't let people suffer; we must reach out to them. He is neither suggesting that we respond nor encouraging us to; he is demanding that we do. He also states quite clearly that we will be judged by God as to how well we care for those who are disadvantaged.

How does your local community respond to Jesus' call? Can hungry people get a free meal somewhere? Does your school or parish have food or clothing drives? How are shut-ins and terminally ill people cared for? Who visits or writes to the prisoners in the county jail? How does your community, school, or parish respond to refugees or immigrants? Who are the hungry, the thirsty, the strangers, the naked, the sick, or the imprisoned in your neighborhood or community? What can you do to help minister to them?

Many opportunities exist for young people to do such ministry. For example, every spring break, young people from all over the country help build homes for poor people. Every weekend, teenagers in major cities serve food in soup kitchens. Many teenagers staff day-care centers for children of people who live in homeless shelters. Many young people are responding! Are you?

▶ Mt 25, 31–46

25, 31–46: The conclusion of the discourse, which is peculiar to Matthew, portrays the final judgment that will accompany the parousia. Although often called a "parable," it is not really such, for the only parabolic elements are the depiction of *the Son of Man* as a *shepherd* and of *the righteous* and the wicked as *sheep* and *goats* respectively (32–33). The criterion of judgment will be the deeds of mercy that have been done for the *least* of Jesus' *brothers* (40). A difficult and important question is the identification of these *least brothers.* Are they all people who have suffered hunger, thirst, etc. (35.36) or a particular group of such sufferers? Scholars are divided in their response and arguments can be made for either side. But leaving aside the problem of what the traditional material that Matthew edited may have meant, it seems that a stronger case can be made for the view that in the evangelist's sense the sufferers are Christians, probably Christian missionaries whose sufferings were brought upon them by their preaching of the gospel. The criterion of judgment for *all the nations* is their treatment of those who have borne to the world the message of Jesus, and this means ultimately their acceptance or rejection of Jesus himself; cf 10, 40, "Whoever receives you, receives me."

25, 31: See the note on 16, 27.

25, 32: *All the nations:* before the end the gospel will have been preached throughout the world (24, 14); thus the Gentiles will be judged on their response to it. But the phrase *all the nations* includes the Jews also, for at the judgment "the Son of Man . . . will repay everyone according to his conduct" (16, 27).

25, 37–40: *The righteous* will be astonished that in caring for the needs of the sufferers they were ministering to the *Lord* himself. *One of these least brothers of mine:* cf 10, 42.

25, 41: *Fire prepared . . . his angels:* cf 1 Enoch 10, 13 where it is said of the evil angels and Semyaza, their leader, "In those days they will lead them into the bottom of the fire—and in torment—in the prison (where) they will be locked up forever."

25, 44–45: The *accursed* (41) will be likewise astonished that their neglect of the sufferers was neglect of the *Lord* and will receive from him a similar answer.

25, 31: Mt 16, 27; Dt 33, 2 LXX.
25, 32: Ez 34, 17.
25, 35–36: Is 58, 7; Ez 18, 7.
25, 40: Mt 10, 40.42.
25, 41: Mt 7, 23; Lk 13, 27.
25, 42–43: Jb 22, 7; Jas 2, 15–16.

not minister to your needs?' ⁴⁵ He will answer them, 'Amen, I say to you, what you did not do for one of these least ones, you did not do for me.' ⁴⁶* And these will go off to eternal punishment, but the righteous to eternal life."

VII: The Passion and Resurrection

The Conspiracy against Jesus

26 ¹† When Jesus finished all these words,† he said to his disciples, ²* "You know that in two days' time it will be Passover, and the Son of Man will be handed over to be crucified." ³† Then the chief priests and the elders of the people assembled in the palace of the high priest, who was called Caiaphas, ⁴* and they consulted together to arrest Jesus by treachery and put him to death. ⁵† But they said, "Not during the festival, that there may not be a riot among the people."

The Anointing at Bethany

⁶*† Now when Jesus was in Bethany in the house of Simon the leper, ⁷ a woman came up to him with an alabaster jar of costly perfumed oil, and poured it on his head while he was reclining at table. ⁸ When the disciples saw this, they were indignant and said, "Why this waste? ⁹ It could have been sold for much, and the money given to the poor." ¹⁰ Since Jesus knew this, he said to them, "Why do you make trouble for the woman? She has done a good thing for me. ¹¹* The poor you will always have with you; but you will not always have me. ¹²† In pouring this perfumed oil upon my body, she did it to prepare me for burial. ¹³ Amen, I say to

you, wherever this gospel is proclaimed in the whole world, what she has done will be spoken of, in memory of her."

The Betrayal by Judas

¹⁴*† Then one of the Twelve, who was called Judas Iscariot, went to the chief priests ¹⁵*† and said, "What are you willing to give me if I hand him over to you?" They paid him thirty pieces of silver, ¹⁶ and from that time on he looked for an opportunity to hand him over.

Preparations for the Passover

¹⁷*† On the first day of the Feast of Unleavened Bread, the disciples approached Jesus and said, "Where do you want us to prepare for you to eat the Passover?"* ¹⁸† He said, "Go into the city to a certain man and tell him, 'The teacher says, "My appointed time draws near; in your house I shall celebrate the Passover with my disciples."'" ¹⁹ The disciples then did as Jesus had ordered, and prepared the Passover.

The Betrayer

²⁰ When it was evening, he reclined at table with the Twelve. ²¹† And while they were eating, he said, "Amen, I say to you, one of you will betray me." ²² Deeply distressed at this, they began to say to him one after another, "Surely it is not I, Lord?" ²³ He said in reply, "He who has dipped his hand into the dish with me is the one who will betray me. ²⁴*† The Son of Man indeed goes, as it is written of him, but woe to that man by whom the Son of Man is betrayed. It would be better for that man if he had

---

26, 1—28, 20: The five books with alternating narrative and discourse (3, 1–25, 46) that give this gospel its distinctive structure lead up to the climactic events that are the center of Christian belief and the origin of the Christian church, the passion and resurrection of Jesus. In his passion narrative (chs 26–27) Matthew follows his Marcan source closely but with omissions (e.g., Mk 14, 51–52) and additions (e.g., 27, 3–10.19). Some of the additions indicate that he utilized traditions that he had received from elsewhere; others are due to his own theological insight (e.g., 26, 28, ". . . for the forgiveness of sins"; 27, 52). In his editing Matthew also altered Mark in some minor details. But there is no need to suppose that he knew any passion narrative other than Mark's.
26, 1–2: *When Jesus finished all these words:* see the note on 7, 28–29. *"You know . . . crucified":* Matthew turns Mark's statement of the time (14, 1) into Jesus' final prediction of his passion. *Passover:* see the note on Mk 14, 1.
26, 3: *Caiaphas* was high priest from A.D. 18 to 36.
26, 5: *Not during the festival:* the plan to delay Jesus' arrest and execution until after *the festival* was not carried out, for according to the synoptics he was arrested on the night of Nisan 14 and put to death the following day. No reason is given why the plan was changed.
26, 6–13: See the notes on Mk 14, 3–9 and Jn 12, 1–8.
26, 12: *To prepare me for burial:* cf Mk 14, 8. In accordance with the interpretation of this act as Jesus' *burial* anointing, Matthew, more consistent than Mark, changes the purpose of the visit of the women to Jesus' tomb; they do not go to anoint him (Mk 16, 1) but "to see the tomb" (28, 1).
26, 14: *Iscariot:* see the note on Lk 6, 16.
26, 15: The motive of avarice is introduced by Judas's question about the price for betrayal, which is absent in the Marcan source

(14, 10–11). *Hand him over:* the same Greek verb is used to express the saving purpose of God by which Jesus is handed over to death (cf 17, 22; 20, 18; 26, 2) and the human malice that hands him over. *Thirty pieces of silver:* the price of the betrayal is found only in Matthew. It is derived from Zec 11, 12 where it is the wages paid to the rejected shepherd, a cheap price (Zec 11, 13). That amount is also the compensation paid to one whose slave has been gored by an ox (Ex 21, 32).
26, 17: *The first day of the Feast of Unleavened Bread:* see the note on Mk 14, 1. Matthew omits Mark's "when they sacrificed the Passover lamb."
26, 18: By omitting much of Mk 14, 13–15, adding *My appointed time draws near,* and turning the question into a statement, *in your house I shall celebrate the Passover,* Matthew has given this passage a solemnity and majesty greater than that of his source.
26, 21: Given Matthew's interest in the fulfillment of the Old Testament, it is curious that he omits the Marcan designation of Jesus' betrayer as "one who is eating with me" (14, 18), since that is probably an allusion to Ps 41, 10. However, the shocking fact that the betrayer is one who shares table fellowship with Jesus is emphasized in v 23.
26, 24: *It would be better . . . born:* the enormity of the deed is such that it would be better not to exist than to do it.

---
*
25, 46: Dn 12, 2.   26, 14–16: Mk 14, 10–11; Lk 22,
   26, 2–5: Mk 14, 1–2; Lk 22,   3–6.
      1–2.   26, 15: Zec 11, 12.
    26, 4: Jn 11, 47–53.   26, 17–25: Mk 14, 12–21;
26, 6–13: Mk 14, 3–9; Jn 12, 1–8.   Lk 22, 7–23.
   26, 11: Dt 15, 11.   26, 17: Ex 12, 14–20.
                         26, 24: Is 53, 8–10.

MT

never been born." 25† Then Judas, his betrayer, said in reply, "Surely it is not I, Rabbi?" He answered, "You have said so."

26, 26

The Lord's Supper

26*† While they were eating,* Jesus took bread, said the blessing, broke it, and giving it to his disciples said, "Take and eat; this is my body."† 27† Then he took a cup, gave thanks, and gave it to them, saying, "Drink from it, all of you, 28* for this is my blood of the covenant, which will be shed on behalf of many for the forgiveness of sins. 29† I tell you, from now on I shall not drink this fruit of the vine until the day when I drink it with you new in the kingdom of my Father." 30† Then, after singing a hymn, they went out to the Mount of Olives.

Peter's Denial Foretold

31*† Then Jesus said to them, "This night all of you will have your faith in me shaken, for it is written:

'I will strike the shepherd,
    and the sheep of the flock will
        be dispersed';*

32 but after I have been raised up, I shall go before you to Galilee." 33 Peter said to him in reply, "Though all may have their faith in you shaken, mine will never be." 34*† Jesus said to him, "Amen, I say to you, this very night before the cock crows, you will deny me three times."* 35 Peter said to him, "Even though I should have to die with you, I will not deny you." And all the disciples spoke likewise.

The Agony in the Garden

36*† Then Jesus came with them to a place called Gethsemane,† and he said to his disciples,* "Sit here while I go over there and pray." 37*† He took along Peter and the two sons of Zebedee, and began to

---

26, 25: Peculiar to Matthew. *You have said so:* cf 26, 64; 27, 11. This is a half-affirmative. Emphasis is laid on the pronoun and the answer implies that the statement would not have been made if the question had not been asked.

26, 26–29: See the note on Mk 14, 22–24. The Marcan-Matthean is one of the two major New Testament traditions of the words of Jesus when instituting the Eucharist. The other (and earlier) is the Pauline-Lucan (1 Cor 11, 23–25; Lk 22, 19–20). Each shows the influence of Christian liturgical usage, but the Marcan-Matthean is more developed in that regard than the Pauline-Lucan. The words over the bread and cup succeed each other without the intervening meal mentioned in 1 Cor 11, 25; Lk 22, 20; and there is parallelism between the consecratory words (*this is my body . . . this is my blood*). Matthew follows Mark closely but with some changes.

26, 26: See the note on 14, 19. *Said the blessing:* a prayer blessing God. *Take and eat:* literally, *Take, eat. Eat* is an addition to Mark's "take it" (literally, "take"; 14, 22). *This is my body:* the bread is identified with Jesus himself.

26, 27–28: *Gave thanks:* see the note on 15, 36. *Gave it to them . . . all of you:* cf Mk 14, 23–24. In the Marcan sequence the disciples drink and then Jesus says the interpretative words. Matthew has changed this into a command to *drink* followed by those words. *My blood:* see Lv 17, 11 for the concept that the *blood* is "the seat of life" and that when placed on the altar it "makes atonement." *Which will be shed:* the present participle, "being shed" or "going to be shed," is future in relation to the Last Supper. *On behalf of:* Greek *peri;* see the note on Mk 14, 24. *Many:* see the note on 20, 28. *For the forgiveness of sins:* a Matthean addition. The same phrase occurs in Mk 1, 4 in connection with John's baptism but Matthew avoids it there (3, 11). He places it here probably because he wishes to emphasize that it is the sacrificial death of Jesus that brings *forgiveness of sins.*

26, 29: Although his death will interrupt the table fellowship he has had with the disciples, Jesus confidently predicts his vindication by God and a new table fellowship with them at the banquet of the kingdom.

26, 30: See the note on Mk 14, 26.

26, 31: *Will have . . . shaken:* literally, "will be scandalized in me"; see the note on 24, 9–12. *I will strike . . . dispersed:* cf Zec 13, 7.

26, 34: *Before the cock crows:* see the note on 14, 25. The third watch of the night was called "cockcrow." *Deny me:* see the note on 16, 24.

26, 36–56: Cf Mk 14, 32–52. The account of Jesus in Gethsemane is divided between that of his agony (36–46) and that of his betrayal and arrest (47–56). Jesus' *sorrow and distress* (37) in face of death is unrelieved by the presence of his three disciples who, though urged to *watch with* him (38.41), fall asleep (40.43). He prays that *if . . . possible* his death may be avoided (39) but that his Father's will be done (39.42.44). Knowing then that his death must take place, he announces to his companions that *the hour* for his being *handed over* has come (45). Judas arrives with an armed band provided by the Sanhedrin and greets Jesus with a kiss, the prearranged sign for his identification (47–49). After his arrest, he rebukes a disciple who has attacked the *high priest's servant* with a *sword* (51–54), and chides those who have come out to seize him with *swords and clubs* as if he were a *robber* (55–56). In both rebukes Jesus declares that the treatment he is now receiving is the fulfillment of the scriptures (55.56). The subsequent flight of *all the disciples* is itself the fulfillment of his own prediction (cf 31). In this episode, Matthew follows Mark with a few alterations.

26, 36: *Gethsemane:* the Hebrew name means "oil press" and designates an olive orchard on the western slope of the Mount of Olives; see the note on 21, 1. The name appears only in Matthew and Mark. The place is called a "garden" in Jn 18, 1.

26, 37: *Peter and the two sons of Zebedee:* cf 17, 1.

26, 26–30: Mk 14, 22–26; Lk 22,
            14–23; 1 Cor 11,
            23–25.
26, 26–27: 1 Cor 10, 16.
26, 28: Ex 24, 8; Is 53, 12.
26, 31–35: Mk 14, 7–31.
26, 31: Zec 13, 7; Jn 16, 32.

26, 34–35: Lk 22, 33–34;
            Jn 13, 37–38.
26, 34: Mt 26, 69–75.
26, 36–46: Mk 14, 32–42; Lk 22,
            39–46.
26, 36: Jn 18, 1.
26, 37–39: Heb 5, 7.

feel sorrow and distress. 38*† Then he said to them, "My soul is sorrowful even to death. Remain here and keep watch with me." 39*† He advanced a little and fell prostrate in prayer, saying, "My Father, if it is possible, let this cup pass from me; yet, not as I will, but as you will." 40 When he returned to his disciples he found them asleep. He said to Peter, "So you could not keep watch with me for one hour? 41† Watch and pray that you may not undergo the test. The spirit is willing, but the flesh is weak." 42*† Withdrawing a second time, he prayed again, "My Father, if it is not possible that this cup pass without my drinking it, your will be done!" 43 Then he returned once more and found them asleep, for they could not keep their eyes open. 44 He left them and withdrew again and prayed a third time, saying the same thing again. 45* Then he returned to his disciples and said to them, "Are you still sleeping and taking your rest? Behold, the hour is at hand when the Son of Man is to be handed over to sinners. 46 Get up, let us go. Look, my betrayer is at hand."

The Betrayal and Arrest of Jesus

47* While he was still speaking, Judas, one of the Twelve, arrived, accompanied by a large crowd, with swords and clubs, who had come from the chief priests and the elders of the people. 48 His betrayer had arranged a sign with them, saying, "The man I shall kiss is the one; arrest him." 49† Immediately he went over to Jesus and said, "Hail, Rabbi!" and he kissed him. 50 Jesus answered him, "Friend, do what you have come for." Then stepping forward they laid hands on Jesus and arrested him. 51 And behold, one of those who accompanied Jesus put his hand to his sword, drew it, and struck the high priest's servant, cutting off his ear. 52 Then Jesus said to him, "Put your sword back into its sheath, for all who take the sword will perish by the sword. 53 Do you think that I cannot call upon my Father and he will not provide me at this moment with more than twelve legions of angels? 54 But then how would the scriptures be fulfilled which say that it must come to pass in this way?" 55† At that hour Jesus said to

THE NEW COVENANT

In the Old Testament, the word covenant is used to express the special relationship between God and the people of Israel. Covenant relationships are rooted in mutual and freely made promises. The laws and worship practices in the Old Testament were signs of this special relationship. But during the Last Supper, Jesus establishes a New Covenant, one sealed with his blood, his very life.

Christians believe that through the paschal mystery—Jesus' life, death, and Resurrection—the New Covenant is established and the Old Covenant is fulfilled. We enter into this new and eternal Covenant through our Baptism. We keep the Covenant by remaining faithful to Christ. The Holy Spirit, God's loving presence in our life, gives us power to live the New Covenant.

In the Eucharist, as we share in the Body and Blood of Christ, it is the New Covenant that we celebrate and renew. So the next time you respond "Amen" at a Eucharistic celebration, know that you are saying "Yes!" to a special and life-giving relationship with God.

For more on the Eucharist, see the articles for Mk 14, 22–25; Lk 22, 14–20; Jn 13, 1–17.

▸ Mt 26, 26–29

26, 38: Cf Ps 42, 6.12. In the Septuagint (Ps 41, 5.12) the same Greek word for sorrowful is used as here. To death: i.e., "enough to die"; cf Jon 4, 9.

26, 39: My Father: see the note on Mk 14, 36. Matthew omits the Aramaic 'abbā' and adds the qualifier my. This cup: see the note on Mk 10, 38–40.

26, 41: Undergo the test: see the note on 6, 13. In that verse "the final test" translates the same Greek word as is here translated test, and these are the only instances of the use of that word in Matthew. It is possible that the passion of Jesus is seen here as an anticipation of the great tribulation that will precede the parousia (see the notes on 24, 8; 24, 21) to which 6, 13 refers, and that just as Jesus prays to be delivered from death (39), so he exhorts the disciples to pray that they will not have to undergo the great test that his passion would be for them. Some scholars, however, understand not undergo (literally, "not enter") the test as meaning not that the disci-

ples may be spared the test but that they may not yield to the temptation of falling away from Jesus because of his passion even though they will have to endure it.

26, 42: Your will be done: cf 6, 10.

26, 49: Rabbi: see the note on 23, 6–7. Jesus is so addressed twice in Matthew (cf 25), both times by Judas. For the significance of the closely related address "teacher" in Matthew, see the note on 8, 19.

26, 55: Day after day . . . arrest me: cf Mk 14, 49. This suggests that Jesus had taught for a relatively long period in Jerusalem, whereas 21, 1–11 puts his coming to the city for the first time only a few days before.

26, 38: Ps 42, 6.12; Jon 4, 9.
26, 39: Jn 4, 34; 6, 38; Phil 2, 8.
26, 42: Mt 6, 10; Heb 10, 9.

26, 45: Jn 12, 23; 13, 1; 17, 1.
26, 47–56: Mk 14, 43–50; Lk 22, 47–53; Jn 18, 3–11.

Jesus' Imperfect Friends

Imagine that you are in the middle of a crisis and ask your best friends to stay with you while you prepare to face the situation. They all promise to be there for you. But one friend after another fails to come through, and you are left to face the trauma alone.

The friends of Jesus were no different. They were well-intentioned and meant to stay awake with him. But in their tiredness, they let him down.

We recognize that the friends of Jesus, the Apostles in particular, were special and holy, but they were also human and had their own weaknesses. Even Peter, one of the greatest heroes of Christianity, lacked the courage to admit he knew Jesus, as we read in Mt 26, 69–75. Yet Jesus loved them despite their failings and even when they were disloyal.

Is it easy for you to stay friends with those who let you down? Can you follow the example of Jesus?

▶ Mt 26, 36–45

the crowds, "Have you come out as against a robber, with swords and clubs to seize me? Day after day I sat teaching in the temple area, yet you did not arrest me. 56* But all this has come to pass that the writings of the prophets may be fulfilled." Then all the disciples left him and fled.

Jesus before the Sanhedrin†

57* Those who had arrested Jesus led him away to Caiaphas† the high priest, where the scribes and the elders were assembled. 58 Peter was following him at a distance as far as the high priest's courtyard, and going inside he sat down with the servants to see the outcome. 59† The chief priests and the entire Sanhedrin kept trying to obtain false testimony against Jesus in order to put him to death, 60*† but they found none, though many false

witnesses came forward. Finally two came forward 61 who stated, "This man said, 'I can destroy the temple of God and within three days rebuild it.' " 62 The high priest rose and addressed him, "Have you no answer? What are these men testifying against you?" 63*† But Jesus was silent. Then the high priest said to him, "I order you to tell us under oath before the living God whether you are the Messiah, the Son of God." 64*† Jesus said to him in reply, "You have said so. But I tell you:

From now on you will see 'the Son of Man
    seated at the right hand of the Power'
    and 'coming on the clouds of heaven.' "

65† Then the high priest tore his robes and said, "He has blasphemed! What further need have we of

---

26, 57–68: Following Mk 14, 53–65, Matthew presents the nighttime appearance of Jesus before the Sanhedrin as a real trial. After many false witnesses bring charges against him that do not suffice for the death sentence (60), two came forward who charge him with claiming to be able to destroy the temple . . . and within three days to rebuild it (60–61). Jesus makes no answer even when challenged to do so by the high priest, who then orders him to declare under oath . . . whether he is the Messiah, the Son of God (62–63). Matthew changes Mark's clear affirmative response (14, 62) to the same one as that given to Judas (cf 25), but follows Mark almost verbatim in Jesus' predicting that his judges will see him (the Son of Man) seated at the right hand of God and coming on the clouds of heaven (64). The high priest then charges him with blasphemy (65), a charge with which the other members of the Sanhedrin agree by declaring that he deserves to die (66). They then attack him (67) and mockingly demand that he prophesy (68). This account contains elements that are contrary to the judicial procedures prescribed in the Mishnah, the Jewish code of law that dates in written form from ca. A.D. 200, e.g., trial on a feast day, a night session of the court, pronouncement of a verdict of condemnation at the same session at which testimony was received. Consequently, some scholars regard the account entirely as a creation of the early Christians without historical value. However, it is disputable whether the norms found in the Mishnah were in force at the time of Jesus. More to the point is the question whether the Matthean-Marcan night trial derives from a combination of two separate incidents, a nighttime preliminary investigation (cf Jn 18, 13.19–24) and a formal trial on the following morning (cf Lk 22, 66–71).

26, 57: Caiaphas: see the note on 26, 3.

26, 59: Sanhedrin: see the note on Lk 22, 66.

26, 60–61: Two: cf Dt 19, 15. I can destroy . . . rebuild it: there are significant differences from the Marcan parallel (14, 58). Matthew omits "made with hands" and "not made with hands" and changes Mark's "will destroy" and "will build another" to can destroy and (can) rebuild. The charge is probably based on Jesus' prediction of the temple's destruction; see the notes on 23, 37–39; 24, 2; and Jn 2, 19. A similar prediction by Jeremiah was considered as deserving death; cf Jer 7, 1–15; 26, 1–8.

26, 63: Silent: possibly an allusion to Is 53, 7. I order you . . . living God: peculiar to Matthew; cf Mk 14, 61.

26, 64: You have said so: see the note on 26, 25. From now on . . . heaven: the Son of Man who is to be crucified (cf 20, 19) will be seen in glorious majesty (cf Ps 110, 1) and coming on the clouds of heaven (cf Dn 7, 13). The Power: see the note on Mk 14, 61–62.

26, 65: Blasphemed: the punishment for blasphemy was death by stoning (see Lv 24, 10–16). According to the Mishnah, to be guilty of blasphemy one had to pronounce "the Name itself," i.e. Yahweh; cf Sanhedrin 7, 4.5. Those who judge the gospel accounts of Jesus' trial by the later Mishnah standards point out that Jesus uses the surrogate "the Power," and hence no Jewish court would have regarded him as guilty of blasphemy; others hold that the Mishnah's narrow understanding of blasphemy was a later development.

26, 56: Mt 26, 31.
26, 57–68: Mk 14, 53–65; Lk 22,
    54–55.63–71; Jn 18,
    12–14.19–24.
26, 60–61: Dt 19, 15; Jn 2, 19;
    Acts 6, 14.
26, 63: Is 53, 7.
26, 64: Ps 110, 1; Dn 7, 13.

witnesses? You have now heard the blasphemy; 66 what is your opinion?" They said in reply, "He deserves to die!" 67*† Then they spat in his face and struck him, while some slapped him, 68 saying, "Prophesy for us, Messiah: who is it that struck you?"

Peter's Denial of Jesus

69* Now Peter was sitting outside in the courtyard. One of the maids came over to him and said, "You too were with Jesus the Galilean." 70† But he denied it in front of everyone, saying, "I do not know what you are talking about!" 71 As he went out to the gate, another girl saw him and said to those who were there, "This man was with Jesus the Nazorean." 72 Again he denied it with an oath, "I do not know the man!" 73† A little later the bystanders came over and said to Peter, "Surely you too are one of them; even your speech gives you away." 74 At that he began to curse and to swear, "I do not know the man." And immediately a cock crowed. 75* Then Peter remembered the word that Jesus had spoken: "Before the cock crows you will deny me three times." He went out and began to weep bitterly.

Jesus before Pilate

27 1*† When it was morning, all the chief priests and the elders of the people took counsel† against Jesus to put him to death. 2 They bound him, led him away, and handed him over to Pilate, the governor.

The Death of Judas

3*† Then Judas, his betrayer, seeing that Jesus had been condemned, deeply regretted what he had done. He returned the thirty pieces of silver to the chief priests and elders,* 4 saying, "I have sinned in betraying innocent blood." They said, "What is that to us? Look to it yourself." 5† Flinging the money into the temple, he departed and went off and hanged himself. 6 The chief priests

---

?did you KNOW?

Judas's Suicide

The Gospel of Matthew presents Judas's suicide as the fulfillment of an Old Testament prophecy from Jeremiah, but it does not tell us why Judas killed himself. Did he kill himself because he felt guilty and could not face the other disciples? Did he feel that the only way he could pay for his sin was with his own life? Whatever his reason, Judas did not believe that he could make up for his mistake—but suicide didn't solve his problem.

Some teenagers think suicide will end their pain, and use it as a way out. Unfortunately, suicide ends everything; not just the current pain but future possibilities for healing, for growth, for new relationships and good times. Consider that both Judas and Peter betrayed Jesus. But whereas Judas ended his life, Peter trusted in God's love and forgiveness and went on to become a great hero. Nothing you can do is so terrible that your only option is taking your life.

Do you ever have thoughts of suicide? If so, talk about them with someone you trust. Speak with a priest, a parent, a youth minister, a school counselor, a coach, or a trusted friend. Caring people will help you. Seeking their help is a better way out.

For more on suicide, see "Suicide Is Not an Answer," 1 Sm 31, 1–6.

▸ Mt 27, 3–10

---

†   **26, 67–68:** The physical abuse, apparently done to Jesus by the members of the Sanhedrin themselves, recalls the sufferings of the Isaian Servant of the Lord; cf Is 50, 6. The mocking challenge to *prophesy* is probably motivated by Jesus' prediction of his future glory (64).

26, 70: *Denied it in front of everyone:* see 10, 33. Peter's repentance (75) saves him from the fearful destiny of which Jesus speaks there.

26, 73: *Your speech . . . away:* Matthew explicates Mark's "you too are a Galilean" (14, 70).

27, 1–31: Cf Mk 15, 1–20. Matthew's account of the Roman trial before *Pilate* is introduced by a consultation of the Sanhedrin after which Jesus is *handed over to . . . the governor* (1–2). Matthew follows his Marcan source closely but adds some material that is peculiar to him, the death of *Judas* (3–10), possibly the name *Jesus* as the name of *Barabbas* also (16–17), the intervention of Pilate's *wife* (19), Pilate's washing *his hands* in token of his disclaiming responsibility for Jesus' death (24), and the assuming of that responsibility by *the whole people* (25).

27, 1–2: There is scholarly disagreement about the meaning of the Sanhedrin's taking *counsel* (*symboulion elabon;* cf 12, 14; 22, 15; 27, 7; 28, 12); see the note on Mk 15, 1. Some understand it

as a discussion about the strategy for putting their death sentence against Jesus into effect since they lacked the right to do so themselves. Others see it as the occasion for their passing that sentence, holding that Matthew, unlike Mark (14, 64), does not consider that it had been passed in the night session (26, 66). Even in the latter interpretation, their handing *him over to Pilate* is best explained on the hypothesis that they did not have competence to put their sentence into effect, as is stated in Jn 18, 31.

27, 3: *The thirty pieces of silver:* see 26, 15.

27, 5–8: For another tradition about the death of Judas, cf Acts 1, 18–19. The two traditions agree only in the purchase of a *field* with *the money* paid to Judas for his betrayal of Jesus and the name given to the *field,* the Field of Blood. In Acts Judas himself buys the field and its name comes from his own blood shed in his fatal accident on it. *The potter's field:* this designation of the field is based on the fulfillment citation in v 10.

26, 67: Wis 2, 19; Is 50, 6.
26, 69–75: Mk 14, 66–72; Lk 22, 56–62; Jn 18, 17–18.25–27.
26, 75: Mt 26, 34.

27, 1–2: Mk 15, 1; Lk 23, 1; Jn 18, 28.
27, 3–10: Acts 1, 18–19.
27, 3: Mt 26, 15.

gathered up the money, but said, "It is not lawful to deposit this in the temple treasury, for it is the price of blood." [7] After consultation, they used it to buy the potter's field as a burial place for foreigners. [8] That is why that field even today is called the Field of Blood. [9]† Then was fulfilled what had been said through Jeremiah the prophet, "And they took the thirty pieces of silver, the value of a man with a price on his head, a price set by some of the Israelites, [10]* and they paid it out for the potter's field just as the Lord had commanded me."

Jesus Questioned by Pilate

[11]*† Now Jesus stood before the governor, and he questioned him, "Are you the king of the Jews?" Jesus said, "You say so." [12]*† And when he was accused by the chief priests and elders, he made no answer. [13] Then Pilate said to him, "Do you not hear how many things they are testifying against you?" [14] But he did not answer him one word, so that the governor was greatly amazed.

The Sentence of Death

[15]*† Now on the occasion of the feast the governor was accustomed to release to the crowd one prisoner whom they wished. [16]† And at that time they had a notorious prisoner called [Jesus] Barabbas.

[17] So when they had assembled, Pilate said to them, "Which one do you want me to release to you, [Jesus] Barabbas, or Jesus called Messiah?" [18]† For he knew that it was out of envy that they had handed him over. [19]† While he was still seated on the bench, his wife sent him a message, "Have nothing to do with that righteous man. I suffered much in a dream today because of him." [20]* The chief priests and the elders persuaded the crowds to ask for Barabbas but to destroy Jesus. [21] The governor said to them in reply, "Which of the two do you want me to release to you?" They answered, "Barabbas!" [22]† Pilate said to them, "Then what shall I do with Jesus called Messiah?" They all said, "Let him be crucified!" [23] But he said, "Why? What evil has he done?" They only shouted the louder, "Let him be crucified!" [24]*† When Pilate saw that he was not succeeding at all, but that a riot was breaking out instead, he took water and washed his hands in the sight of the crowd, saying, "I am innocent of this man's blood. Look to it yourselves." [25] And the whole people said in reply, "His blood be upon us and upon our children." [26]† Then he released Barabbas to them, but after he had Jesus scourged, he handed him over to be crucified.

Mockery by the Soldiers

[27]*† Then the soldiers of the governor took Jesus

27, 9–10: Cf 26, 15. Matthew's attributing this text to Jeremiah is puzzling, for there is no such text in that book, and *the thirty pieces of silver* thrown by Judas "into the temple" (5) recall rather Zec 11, 12–13. It is usually said that the attribution of the text to Jeremiah is due to Matthew's combining the Zechariah text with texts from Jeremiah that speak of a *potter* (18, 2–3), the buying of a *field* (32, 6–9), or the breaking of a potter's flask at Topheth in the valley of Ben-Hinnom with the prediction that it will become a burial place (19, 1–13).

27, 11: *King of the Jews:* this title is used of Jesus only by pagans. The Matthean instances are, besides this verse, 2, 2; 27, 29.37. Matthew equates it with "Messiah"; cf 2, 2.4 and 27, 17.22 where he has changed "the king of the Jews" of his Marcan source (15, 9.12) to "(Jesus) called Messiah." The normal political connotation of both titles would be of concern to the Roman *governor. You say so:* see the note on 26, 25. An unqualified affirmative response is not made because Jesus' kingship is not what Pilate would understand it to be.

27, 12–14: Cf 26, 62–63. As in the trial before the Sanhedrin, Jesus' silence may be meant to recall Is 53, 7. *Greatly amazed:* possibly an allusion to Is 52, 14–15.

27, 15–26: The choice that Pilate offers *the crowd* between *Barabbas* and *Jesus* is said to be in accordance with a custom of releasing at the Passover feast *one prisoner* chosen *by the crowd* (15). This custom is mentioned also in Mk 15, 6 and Jn 18, 39 but not in Luke; see the note on Lk 23, 17. Outside of the gospels there is no direct attestation of it, and scholars are divided in their judgment of the historical reliability of the claim that there was such a practice.

27, 16–17: *Jesus Barabbas:* it is possible that the double name is the original reading; *Jesus* was a common Jewish name; see the note on 1, 21. This reading is found in only a few textual witnesses, although its absence in the majority can be explained as an omission of *Jesus* made for reverential reasons. That name is bracketed because of its uncertain textual attestation. The Aramaic name *Barabbas* means "son of the father"; the irony of the choice offered between him and Jesus, the true son of the Father, would be evident to those addressees of Matthew who knew that.

27, 18: Cf Mk 14, 10. This is an example of the tendency, found in varying degree in all the gospels, to present Pilate in a relatively favorable light and emphasize the hostility of the Jewish authorities and eventually of the people.

27, 19: Jesus' innocence is declared by a Gentile woman. *In a dream:* in Matthew's infancy narrative, dreams are the means of divine communication; cf 1, 20; 2, 12.13.19.22.

27, 22: *Let him be crucified:* incited by the chief priests and elders (20), the crowds demand that Jesus be executed by crucifixion, a peculiarly horrible form of Roman capital punishment. The Marcan parallel, "Crucify him" (15, 3), addressed to Pilate, is changed by Matthew to the passive, probably to emphasize the responsibility of the crowds.

27, 24–25: Peculiar to Matthew. *Took water . . . blood:* cf Dt 21, 1–8, the handwashing prescribed in the case of a murder when the killer is unknown. The elders of the city nearest to where the corpse is found must wash their hands, declaring, "Our hands did not shed this blood." *Look to it yourselves:* cf v 4. *The whole people:* Matthew sees in those who speak these words the entire *people* (Greek *laos*) of Israel. *His blood . . . and upon our children:* cf Jer 26, 15. The responsibility for Jesus' death is accepted by the nation that was God's special possession (Ex 19, 5), his own *people* (Hos 2, 25), and they thereby lose that high privilege; see 21, 43 and the note on that verse. The controversy between Matthew's church and Pharisaic Judaism about which was the true people of God is reflected here. As the Second Vatican Council has pointed out, guilt for Jesus' death is not attributable to all the Jews of his time or to any Jews of later times.

27, 26: *He had Jesus scourged:* the usual preliminary to crucifixion.

27, 27: *The praetorium:* the residence of the Roman *governor.* His usual place of residence was at Caesarea Maritima on the Mediterranean coast, but he went to Jerusalem during the great feasts, when the influx of pilgrims posed the danger of a nationalistic riot. It is disputed whether *the praetorium* in Jerusalem was the old palace of Herod in the west of the city or the fortress of Antonia northwest of the temple area. *The whole cohort:* normally six hundred soldiers.

27, 10: Zec 11, 12–13.
27, 11–14: Mk 15, 2–5; Lk 23, 2–3; Jn 18, 29–38.
27, 12: Is 53, 7.
27, 15–26: Mk 15, 6–15; 23, 17–25; Jn 18, 39—19, 16.
27, 20: Acts 3, 14.
27, 24: Dt 21, 1–8.
27, 27–31: Mk 15, 16–20; Jn 19, 2–3.

PRAY IT

Suffering Prayer

Jesus, anointed one, everyone endures some suffering in their life. Some suffer in silence. Some loudly complain, making it known to all. Some bitterly blame everyone around them. You suffered ridicule, betrayal, persecution, crucifixion, and death. Your burden was so great, yet you endured. Glorifying God, your sacrifice gives us the hope of eternal life.

Strengthen me to withstand the suffering I must face in my life. When I feel that I have more than I can take, fortify me with the endurance of Job. Give me the patience to suffer injustices without lashing out at others. Fill me with mercy to forgive those who persecute me. Fill me with your loving presence to be a faithful witness to the glory of God and to the promise of eternal life. Amen.

▶ Mt 27, 27–44

inside the praetorium and gathered the whole cohort around him. 28† They stripped off his clothes and threw a scarlet military cloak about him. 29*† Weaving a crown out of thorns, they placed it on his head, and a reed in his right hand. And kneeling before him, they mocked him, saying, "Hail, King of the Jews!" 30*† They spat upon him and took the reed and kept striking him on the head. 31 And when they had mocked him, they stripped him of the cloak, dressed him in his own clothes, and led him off to crucify him.

The Way of the Cross

32*† As they were going out, they met a Cyrenian named Simon; this man they pressed into service to carry his cross.

The Crucifixion

33* And when they came to a place called Golgotha (which means Place of the Skull), 34*† they gave Jesus wine to drink mixed with gall. But when he had tasted it, he refused to drink. 35*† After they had crucified him, they divided his garments by casting lots; 36 then they sat down and kept watch over him there. 37† And they placed over his head the written charge against him: This is Jesus, the King of the Jews. 38† Two revolutionaries were crucified with him, one on his right and the other on his left. 39*† Those passing by reviled him, shaking their heads 40* and saying, "You who would destroy the temple and rebuild it in three days, save yourself, if you are the Son of God, [and] come down from the cross!" 41 Likewise the chief priests with the scribes and elders mocked him and said, 42† "He saved others; he cannot save himself. So he is the king of Israel! Let him come down from the cross now, and we will believe in him. 43*† He trusted in God; let him deliver him now if he wants him. For he said, 'I am the Son of God.'" 44 The revolutionaries who were crucified with him also kept abusing him in the same way.

The Death of Jesus

45*† From noon onward,* darkness came over the whole land until three in the afternoon. 46*† And

---

27, 28: *Scarlet military cloak:* so Matthew as against the royal purple of Mk 15, 17 and Jn 19, 2.

27, 29: *Crown out of thorns:* probably of long *thorns* that stood upright so that it resembled the "radiant" *crown*, a diadem with spikes worn by Hellenistic kings. The soldiers' purpose was mockery, not torture. *A reed:* peculiar to Matthew; a mock scepter.

27, 30: *Spat upon him:* cf 26, 67 where there also is a possible allusion to Is 50, 6.

27, 32: See the note on Mk 15, 21. *Cyrenian named Simon:* Cyrenaica was a Roman province on the north coast of Africa and Cyrene was its capital city. The city had a large population of Greek-speaking Jews. *Simon* may have been living in Palestine or have come there for the Passover as a pilgrim. *Pressed into service:* see the note on 5, 41.

27, 34: *Wine . . . mixed with gall:* cf Mk 15, 23 where the drink is "wine drugged with myrrh," a narcotic. Matthew's text is probably an inexact allusion to Ps 69, 22. That psalm belongs to the class called the individual lament, in which a persecuted just man prays for deliverance in the midst of great suffering and also expresses confidence that his prayer will be heard. That theme of the suffering Just One is frequently applied to the sufferings of Jesus in the passion narratives.

27, 35: The clothing of an executed criminal went to his executioner(s), but the description of that procedure in the case of Jesus, found in all the gospels, is plainly inspired by Ps 22, 19. However, that psalm verse is quoted only in Jn 19, 24.

27, 37: The offense of a person condemned to death by crucifixion was written on a tablet that was displayed on his cross. The

charge against Jesus was that he had claimed to be the *King of the Jews* (cf 11), i.e., the Messiah (cf 17.22).

27, 38: *Revolutionaries:* see the note on Jn 18, 40 where the same Greek word as that found here is used for Barabbas.

27, 39–40: *Reviled him . . . heads:* cf Ps 22, 8. *You who would destroy . . . three days:* cf 26, 61. *If you are the Son of God:* the same words as those of the devil in the temptation of Jesus; cf 4, 3.6.

27, 42: *King of Israel:* in their mocking of Jesus the members of the Sanhedrin call themselves and their people not "the Jews" but *Israel*.

27, 43: Peculiar to Matthew. *He trusted in God . . . wants him:* cf Ps 22, 9. *He said . . . of God:* probably an allusion to Wis 2, 12–20 where the theme of the suffering Just One appears.

27, 45: Cf Amos 8, 9 where on the day of the Lord "the sun will set at midday."

27, 46: *Eli, Eli, lema sabachthani?:* Jesus cries out in the words of Ps 22, 2a, a psalm of lament that is the Old Testament passage most frequently drawn upon in this narrative. In Mark the verse is cited entirely in Aramaic, which Matthew partially retains but changes the invocation of God to the Hebrew *Eli*, possibly because that is more easily related to the statement of the following verse about Jesus' calling for Elijah.

27, 29: Mt 27, 11.
27, 30: Is 50, 6.
27, 32: Mk 15, 21; Lk 23, 26.
27, 33–44: Mk 15, 22–32; Lk 23, 32–38; Jn 19, 17–19.23–24.
27, 34: Ps 69, 21.
27, 35: Ps 22, 19.

27, 39: Ps 22, 8.
27, 40: Mt 4, 3.6; 26, 61.
27, 43: Ps 22, 9; Wis 2, 12–20.
27, 45–46: Mk 15, 33–41; Lk 23, 44–49; Jn 19, 28–30.
27, 45: Am 8, 9.
27, 46: Ps 22, 2.

?did you KNOW?

Jesus Prays Psalm 22

The Gospel writer tells us that before Jesus gave up his spirit and breathed his last breath, he cried out, "My God, my God, why have you abandoned me?" Jesus was actually reciting and praying the opening lines to Psalm 22. This Psalm begins in despair but ends in triumph and confidence through God's saving help. With this prayer to God, Jesus invites all people gathered at the crucifixion to pray the entire psalm, not just the first words of despair but also the concluding words of hope.

Read also "Hope in Despair," Psalm 22.

▸ **Mt 27, 46**

about three o'clock Jesus cried out in a loud voice, *"Eli, Eli, lema sabachthani?"* which means, "My God, my God, why have you forsaken me?" [47]† Some of the bystanders who heard it said, "This one is calling for Elijah." [48]* Immediately one of them ran to get a sponge; he soaked it in wine, and putting it on a reed, gave it to him to drink. [49] But the rest said, "Wait, let us see if Elijah comes to save him." [50]† But Jesus cried out again in a loud voice, and gave up his spirit. [51]*† And behold, the veil of the sanctuary was torn in two from top to bottom. The earth quaked, rocks were split, [52]* tombs were opened, and the bodies of many saints who had fallen asleep were raised. [53] And coming forth from

their tombs after his resurrection, they entered the holy city and appeared to many. [54]† The centurion and the men with him who were keeping watch over Jesus feared greatly when they saw the earthquake and all that was happening, and they said, "Truly, this was the Son of God!" [55]† There were many women there, looking on from a distance, who had followed Jesus from Galilee, ministering

?did you KNOW?

The Dawn of a New Age

According to the Gospel of Matthew, some strange things happened when Jesus died. Each event tells us something about Jesus. The darkness that covered the land (27, 45) and the earthquake (verse 51) show that all creation was aware that something significant had happened, a new age was dawning. The splitting of the sanctuary veil (verse 51), which is the barrier that separated the holiest part of the Temple (where God was thought to dwell) from the rest of the Temple area, symbolizes that now God would be directly accessible to the people. And what do the dead saints who came out of their tombs to walk in the city symbolize? They are the fulfillment of Ezekiel's vision (Ezekiel, chapter 37). The dried bones had come to life—God had triumphed over death!

▸ **Mt 27, 45–54**

27, 47: *Elijah:* see the note on 3, 4. This prophet, taken up into heaven (2 Kgs 2, 11), was believed to come to the help of those in distress, but the evidences of that belief are all later than the gospels.

27, 50: *Gave up his spirit:* cf the Marcan parallel (15, 37), "breathed his last." Matthew's alteration expresses both Jesus' control over his destiny and his obedient giving up of his life to God.

27, 51–53: *Veil of the sanctuary . . . bottom:* cf Mk 15, 38; Lk 23, 45. Luke puts this event immediately before the death of Jesus. There were two veils in the Mosaic tabernacle on the model of which the temple was constructed, the outer one before the entrance of the Holy Place and the inner one before the Holy of Holies (see Ex 26, 31–36). Only the high priest could pass through the latter and that only on the Day of Atonement (see Lv 16, 1–18). Probably the *torn veil* of the gospels is the inner one. The meaning of the scene may be that now, because of Jesus' death, all people have access to the presence of God, or that the temple, its holiest part standing exposed, is now profaned and will soon be destroyed. *The earth quaked . . . appeared to many:* peculiar to Matthew. The earthquake, the splitting of the *rocks,* and especially the resurrection of the dead *saints* indicate the coming of the final age. In the Old Testament the coming of God is frequently portrayed with the imagery of an earthquake (see Pss 68, 9; 77, 19), and Jesus speaks of the earthquakes

that will accompany the "labor pains" that signify the beginning of the dissolution of the old world (24, 7–8). For the expectation of the resurrection of the dead at the coming of the new and final age, see Dn 12, 1–3. Matthew knows that the end of the old age has not yet come (28, 20), but the new age has broken in with the death (and resurrection; cf the earthquake in 28, 2) of Jesus; see the note on 16, 28. *After his resurrection:* this qualification seems to be due to Matthew's wish to assert the primacy of Jesus' *resurrection* even though he has placed the resurrection of the dead *saints* immediately after Jesus' death.

27, 54: Cf Mk 15, 39. The Christian confession of faith is made by Gentiles, not only *the centurion,* as in Mark, but the other soldiers *who were keeping watch over Jesus* (cf 36).

27, 55–56: *Looking on from a distance:* cf Ps 38, 12. *Mary Magdalene . . . Joseph:* these two women are mentioned again in v 61 and 28, 1 and are important as witnesses of the reality of the empty tomb. A *James* and *Joseph* are referred to in 13, 55 as brothers of Jesus.

27, 48: Ps 69, 21.   **27, 52:** Dn 12, 1–3.
27, 51: Ex 26, 31–36; Pss 68, 9; 77, 19.

JESUS DIED ON THE CROSS BECAUSE HE LOVES US!

Hispanics often identify more with the suffering and crucified Christ than with the risen Christ. In the cross, Hispanics find God's immense love for them. It is a redemptive love, one that brings peace and the strength to accept what cannot be changed and to continue the struggle out of poverty and oppression.

Hispanic young people learn from their families and culture that there is always suffering in life. When this suffering is not accepted, it is even worse. In contrast, when we accept suffering, it is bearable, and we have the inner peace needed to continue living and working for a better life. Suffering achieves its highest meaning when it is accepted out of love. That Jesus is capable of suffering gives witness to God's special love for those who suffer.

Finding God's life in the midst of suffering leads to generous sacrifices that are a source of life for those we love. Let's pray:

Jesus, help us to always remember that your commitment to your mission led to your death. Help us to understand that true life is always achieved through love. Help us to have love at the core of all we think and do. And help us to share your love, especially with those who need it the most, the poor and marginalized people. Amen.

▸ Mt 27, 24–56

---

to him. ⁵⁶* Among them were Mary Magdalene and Mary the mother of James and Joseph, and the mother of the sons of Zebedee.

The Burial of Jesus

⁵⁷*† When it was evening, there came a rich man from Arimathea named Joseph, who was himself a disciple of Jesus.* ⁵⁸ He went to Pilate and asked for the body of Jesus; then Pilate ordered it to be handed over. ⁵⁹ Taking the body, Joseph wrapped it [in] clean linen ⁶⁰ and laid it in his new tomb that he had hewn in the rock. Then he rolled a huge stone across the entrance to the tomb and departed.

⁶¹ But Mary Magdalene and the other Mary remained sitting there, facing the tomb.

The Guard at the Tomb†

⁶² The next day, the one following the day of preparation,† the chief priests and the Pharisees gathered before Pilate ⁶³* and said, "Sir, we remember that this impostor while still alive said, 'After three days I will be raised up.' ⁶⁴† Give orders, then, that the grave be secured until the third day, lest his disciples come and steal him and say to the people, 'He has been raised from the dead.' This last imposture would be worse than the first." ⁶⁵† Pilate

---

† **27, 57–61:** Cf Mk 15, 42–47. Matthew drops Mark's designation of *Joseph of Arimathea* as "a distinguished member of the council" (the Sanhedrin), and makes him *a rich man* and *a disciple of Jesus.* The former may be an allusion to Is 53, 9 (the Hebrew reading of that text is disputed and the one followed in the NAB OT has nothing about the rich, but they are mentioned in the LXX version). That the tomb was the *new tomb* of a *rich man* and that it was seen by the women are indications of an apologetic intent of Matthew; there could be no question about the identity of Jesus' burial place. *The other Mary:* the mother of James and Joseph (56).

27, 62–66: Peculiar to Matthew. The story prepares for 28, 11–15 and the Jewish charge that the tomb was empty because the *disciples* had stolen the body of Jesus (28, 13.15).

27, 62: *The next day . . . preparation:* the sabbath. According to the synoptic chronology, in that year the *day of preparation* (for the sabbath) was the Passover; cf Mk 15, 42. *The Pharisees:* the principal opponents of Jesus during his ministry and, in Matthew's time, of

the Christian church, join with *the chief priests* to guarantee against a possible attempt of Jesus' *disciples* to steal his body.

27, 64: *This last imposture . . . the first:* the claim that Jesus *has been raised from the dead* is clearly the *last imposture* (63); the *first* may be either his claim that he would *be raised up* (63) or his claim that he was the one with whose ministry the kingdom of God had come (see 12, 28).

27, 65: *The guard is yours:* literally, "have a guard" or "you have a guard." Either the imperative or the indicative could mean that Pilate granted the petitioners some Roman soldiers as guards, which is the sense of the present translation. However, if the verb is taken as an indicative it could also mean that Pilate told them to use their own Jewish guards.

27, 56: Mt 13, 55.   27, 57: Is 53, 9.
27, 57–61: Mk 15, 42–47; Lk 23,   27, 63: Mt 12, 40; 16, 21; 17,
50–56; Jn 19, 38–42.   23; 20, 19.

said to them, "The guard is yours; go secure it as best you can." ⁶⁶ So they went and secured the tomb by fixing a seal to the stone and setting the guard.

The Resurrection of Jesus

28 ¹*† After the sabbath, as the first day of the week was dawning,† Mary Magdalene and the other Mary came to see the tomb. ²*† And behold, there was a great earthquake; for an angel of the Lord descended from heaven, approached, rolled back the stone, and sat upon it. ³* His appearance was like lightning and his clothing was white as snow. ⁴ The guards were shaken with fear of him and became like dead men. ⁵ Then the angel said to the women in reply, "Do not be afraid! I know that you are seeking Jesus the crucified. ⁶† He is not here, for he has been raised just as he said. Come and see the place where he lay. ⁷* Then go quickly and tell his disciples, 'He has been raised from the dead, and he is going before you to Galilee; there you will see him.' Behold, I have told you." ⁸† Then they went away quickly from the tomb, fearful yet overjoyed, and ran to announce this to his disciples. ⁹*† And behold, Jesus met them on their way and greeted them. They approached, embraced his feet, and did him homage. ¹⁰ Then Jesus said to them, "Do not be afraid. Go tell my brothers to go to Galilee, and there they will see me."

The Report of the Guard

¹¹† While they were going, some of the guard went into the city and told the chief priests all

---

PRAY IT!

I Will Follow

If you lead me to travel to other nations,
I will follow, Lord.
If you lead me to write to glorify your name,
I will follow, Lord.
If you lead me to preach of your heavenly
Kingdom,
I will follow, Lord.
If you lead me to show others your way,
I will follow, Lord.
If you lead me to use my actions to declare
your Gospel,
I will follow, Lord.
Because you are always with me,
so I will follow, Lord.

▸ Mt 28, 16–20

28, 1–20: Except for vv 1–8, based on Mk 16, 1–8, the material of this final chapter is peculiar to Matthew. Even where he follows Mark, Matthew has altered his source so greatly that a very different impression is given from that of the Marcan account. The two points that are common to the resurrection testimony of all the gospels are that the tomb of Jesus had been found empty and that the risen Jesus had appeared to certain persons, or, in the original form of Mark, that such an appearance was promised as soon to take place (see Mk 16, 7). On this central and all-important basis, Matthew has constructed an account that interprets the resurrection as the turning of the ages (2–4), shows the Jewish opposition to Jesus as continuing *to the present* in the claim that the resurrection is a deception perpetrated by the *disciples* who stole his body from the tomb (11–15), and marks a new stage in the mission of *the disciples* once limited to Israel (10, 5–6); now they are to *make disciples of all nations*. In this work they will be strengthened by the presence of the exalted Son of Man, who will be with them *until* the kingdom comes in fullness at *the end of the age* (16–20).

28, 1: *After the sabbath . . . dawning:* since the sabbath ended at sunset, this could mean in the early evening, for *dawning* can refer to the appearance of the evening star; cf Lk 23, 54. However, it is probable that Matthew means the morning dawn of the day after the sabbath, as in the similar though slightly different text of Mark, "when the sun had risen" (16, 2). *Mary Magdalene and the other Mary:* see the notes on 27, 55–56; 57–61. *To see the tomb:* cf Mk 16, 1–2 where the purpose of the women's visit is to anoint Jesus' body.

28, 2–4: Peculiar to Matthew. *A great earthquake:* see the note on 27, 51–53. *Descended from heaven:* this trait is peculiar to Matthew, although his interpretation of the "young man" of his Marcan source (16, 5) as an *angel* is probably true to Mark's intention; cf Lk 24, 23 where the "two men" of 24, 4 are said to be "angels." *Rolled back the stone . . . upon it:* not to allow the risen Jesus to leave the tomb but to make evident that the tomb is empty (see 6). Unlike the apocryphal Gospel of Peter (9, 35—11, 44), the New Testament does not describe the resurrection of Jesus, nor is there

anyone who sees it. *His appearance was like lightning . . . snow:* see the note on 17, 2.

28, 6–7: Cf Mk 16, 6–7. *Just as he said:* a Matthean addition referring to Jesus' predictions of his resurrection, e.g., 16, 21; 17, 23; 20, 19. *Tell his disciples:* like the angel of the Lord of the infancy narrative, the angel interprets a fact and gives a commandment about what is to be done; cf 1, 20–21. Matthew omits Mark's "and Peter" (16, 7); considering his interest in Peter, this omission is curious. Perhaps the reason is that the Marcan text may allude to a first appearance of Jesus to Peter alone (cf 1 Cor 15, 5; Lk 24, 34) which Matthew has already incorporated into his account of Peter's confession at Caesarea Philippi; see the note on 16, 16. *He is going . . . Galilee:* like Mk 16, 7, a reference to Jesus' prediction at the Last Supper (26, 32; Mk 14, 28). Matthew changes Mark's "as he told you" to a declaration of the angel.

28, 8: Contrast Mk 16, 8 where the women in their fear "said nothing to anyone."

28, 9–10: Although these verses are peculiar to Matthew, there are similarities between them and Jn's account of the appearance of Jesus to Mary Magdalene (20, 17). In both there is a touching of Jesus' body, and a command of Jesus to bear a message to his disciples, designated as his *brothers.* Matthew may have drawn upon a tradition that appears in a different form in John. Jesus' words to the women are mainly a repetition of those of the angel (5a; 7b).

28, 11–15: This account indicates that the dispute between Christians and Jews about the empty tomb was not whether the tomb was empty but why.

28, 1–10: Mk 16, 1–8; Lk 24, 1–12; Jn 20, 1–10.   28, 3: Mt 17, 2.
28, 2: Mt 25, 51.   28, 7: Mt 26, 32.
    28, 9–10: Jn 20, 17.

that had happened. 12 They assembled with the elders and took counsel; then they gave a large sum of money to the soldiers, 13 telling them, "You are to say, 'His disciples came by night and stole him while we were asleep.' 14 And if this gets to the ears of the governor, we will satisfy [him] and keep you out of trouble." 15 The soldiers took the money and did as they were instructed. And this story has circulated among the Jews to the present [day].

The Commissioning of the Disciples†

16* The eleven† disciples went to Galilee, to the mountain to which Jesus had ordered them. 17† When they saw him, they worshiped, but they doubted. 18*† Then Jesus approached and said to them, "All power in heaven and on earth has been given to me. 19*† Go, therefore, and make disciples of all nations, baptizing them in the name of the Father, and of the Son, and of the holy Spirit, 20*† teaching them to observe all that I have commanded you. And behold, I am with you always, until the end of the age."

TRINITY SUNDAY

On the first Sunday after Pentecost Sunday, the Catholic church celebrates Trinity Sunday. The Gospel of Matthew ends with Jesus' only specific reference to the Holy Trinity that appears in all four Gospels, instructing the disciples to go out and baptize "in the name of the Father and of the Son and of the Holy Spirit" (28, 19).

▸ Mt 28, 16–20

28, 16–20: This climactic scene has been called a "proleptic parousia," for it gives a foretaste of the final glorious coming of the Son of Man (26, 64). Then his triumph will be manifest to all; now it is revealed only to *the disciples*, who are commissioned to announce it to *all nations* and bring them to belief in Jesus and obedience to his commandments.

28, 16: *The eleven:* the number recalls the tragic defection of Judas Iscariot. *To the mountain . . . ordered them:* since the message to *the disciples* was simply that they were to go to Galilee (10), some think that *the mountain* comes from a tradition of the message known to Matthew and alluded to here. For the significance of *the mountain*, see the note on 17, 1.

28, 17: *But they doubted:* the Greek can also be translated, "but some doubted." The verb occurs elsewhere in the New Testament only in 14, 31 where it is associated with Peter's being of "little faith." For the meaning of that designation, see the note on 6, 30.

28, 18: *All power . . . me:* the Greek word here translated *power* is the same as that found in the LXX translation of Dn 7, 13–14 where one "like a son of man" is given *power* and an everlasting kingdom by God. The risen Jesus here claims universal power, i.e., in *heaven and on earth*.

28, 19: *Therefore:* since universal power belongs to the risen Jesus (18), he gives the eleven a mission that is universal. They are to

make disciples of all nations. While *all nations* is understood by some scholars as referring only *to all* Gentiles, it is probable that it included the Jews as well. *Baptizing them:* baptism is the means of entrance into the community of the risen one, the Church. *In the name of the Father . . . holy Spirit:* this is perhaps the clearest expression in the New Testament of trinitarian belief. It may have been the baptismal formula of Matthew's church, but primarily it designates the effect of baptism, the union of the one baptized with the Father, Son, and holy Spirit.

28, 20: *All that I have commanded you:* the moral teaching found in this gospel, preeminently that of the Sermon on the Mount (chs 5–7). The commandments of Jesus are the standard of Christian conduct, not the Mosaic law as such, even though some of the Mosaic commandments have now been invested with the authority of Jesus. *Behold, I am with you always:* the promise of Jesus' real though invisible presence echoes the name Emmanuel given to him in the infancy narrative; see the note on 1, 23. *End of the age:* see the notes on 13, 39 and 24, 3.

28, 16–20: Mk 16, 14–16; Lk 24,   28, 19: Acts 1, 8.
     36–49; Jn 20, 19–23.   28, 20: Mt 1, 23; 13, 39;
   28, 18: Dn 7, 14 LXX.   24, 3.

Have you ever been ridiculed or rejected by others—maybe even your friends—for trying to do something good? Jesus would understand your feelings. In the Gospel of Mark, Jesus is misunderstood and abandoned by those closest to him. This Gospel was written for early Christians experiencing persecution or death for their faith. The author is reminding them and us to put our total trust in God as Jesus did, despite whatever difficulties we encounter in being a Christian.

At a Glance

I. The Preparation for the Public Ministry of Jesus (1, 1–13).

II. The Mystery of Jesus (1, 14—8, 26).

III. The Mystery Begins to Be Revealed (8, 27—9, 32).

IV. The Full Revelation of the Mystery (9, 33—16, 8). The Longer Ending (16, 9–20) The Shorter Ending The Freer Logion (in the note on 16, 9–20).

In-depth

The Gospel of Mark is the shortest of the four Gospels and can be easily read in one sitting. It portrays Jesus as a man of action—human in his feelings, and always on the move fulfilling his mission. This Gospel answers two fundamental questions: Who is this Jesus called the Christ? and What does it mean to be his disciple? Because the people hearing this Gospel were in danger of losing their life for what they believed, those questions were a matter of life and death.

To answer the first question, the Gospel of Mark tells stories about Jesus' power to heal and about his compassion for suffering people. It tells about his conflicts with demons and with religious and civil authorities and how he was misunderstood by his own disciples. Through these stories comes the realization that Jesus is the Messiah, the promised savior. But he did not come as the victorious king many Jews expected. Instead, he accepted the suffering that comes with doing God's will. His painful and shameful death was needed before his glory could be seen. Can we believe in a very human, suffering Messiah?

Mark answers the second question in surprising ways. The disciples Jesus called were initially fearful and hard-hearted. They wanted to be powerful and important, and they wanted the approval of their peers. But gradually, they came to believe that Jesus was the Messiah, and to understand his mission. The Gospel of Mark also tells stories about a blind man, a leper, and Gentiles (non-Jews), all of whom were Jesus' disciples because they placed their total trust in him. Whether gradually or quickly, can we place our complete faith in Jesus, becoming his disciples?

Quick Facts

Author
a Gentile Christian, possibly a disciple of Peter's named John Mark

Date Written
approximately A.D. 65 to 70; this was the first written Gospel

Audience
non-Jewish Christians (in Rome?) who were experiencing persecution because of their belief in Jesus

Image of Jesus
healer and miracle worker who accepts suffering as the cost for following God's will

Mark

1, 9

I: The Preparation for the Public Ministry of Jesus†

1 ¹ The beginning of the gospel of Jesus Christ [the Son of God].†

The Preaching of John the Baptist

²*† As it is written in Isaiah the prophet:

"Behold, I am sending my messenger ahead
    of you;
  he will prepare your way.*
³* A voice of one crying out in the desert:
  'Prepare the way of the Lord,
    make straight his paths.' "

⁴ John [the] Baptist appeared in the desert proclaiming a baptism of repentance for the forgiveness of sins. ⁵ People of the whole Judean countryside and all the inhabitants of Jerusalem were going out to him and were being baptized by him in the Jordan River as they acknowledged their sins. ⁶† John was clothed in camel's hair, with a leather belt around his waist. He fed on locusts and wild honey. ⁷ And this is what he proclaimed: "One mightier than I is coming after me. I am not worthy to stoop and loosen the thongs of his sandals. ⁸*† I have baptized you with water; he will baptize you with the holy Spirit."

The Baptism of Jesus

⁹* It happened in those days that Jesus came from Nazareth of Galilee and was baptized in the Jordan by John. ¹⁰† On coming up out of the water he saw the heavens being torn open and the Spirit,

---

† **1, 1–13:** The prologue of the Gospel according to Mark begins with the title (1) followed by three events preparatory to Jesus' preaching: (1) the appearance in the Judean wilderness of John, baptizer, preacher of repentance, and precursor of Jesus (2–8); (2) the baptism of Jesus, at which a voice from heaven acknowledges Jesus to be God's Son, and the holy Spirit descends on him (9–11); (3) the temptation of Jesus by Satan (12–13).

1, 1: *The gospel of Jesus Christ [the Son of God]:* the "good news" of salvation in and through Jesus, crucified and risen, acknowledged by the Christian community as Messiah (8, 29; 14, 61–62) and Son of God (Mk 1, 11; 9, 7; 15, 39), although some important manuscripts here omit *the Son of God.*

1, 2–3: Although Mark attributes the prophecy to Isaiah, the text is a combination of Mal 3, 1; Is 40, 3; and Ex 23, 20; cf Mt 11, 10; Lk 7, 27. John's ministry is seen as God's prelude to the saving mission of his Son. *The way of the Lord:* this prophecy of Deutero-Isaiah concerning the end of the Babylonian exile is here applied to the coming of Jesus; John the Baptist is to prepare the way for him.

1, 6: *Clothed in camel's hair . . . waist:* the Baptist's garb recalls that of Elijah in 2 Kgs 1, 8. Jesus speaks of the Baptist as Elijah who has already come (9, 11–13; Mt 17, 10–12; cf Mal 3, 23–24; Lk 1, 17).

1, 8–9: Through the life-giving baptism with the holy Spirit (8), Jesus will create a new people of God. But first he identifies himself with the people of Israel in submitting to John's baptism of repentance and in bearing on their behalf the burden of God's decisive judgment (9; cf 4). As in the desert of Sinai, so here in the wilderness of Judea, Israel's sonship with God is to be renewed.

1, 10–11: *He saw the heavens . . . and the Spirit . . . upon him:* indicating divine intervention in fulfillment of promise. Here the descent of the Spirit on Jesus is meant, anointing him for his ministry; cf Is 11, 2; 42, 1; 61, 1; 63, 9. *A voice . . . with you I am well pleased:* God's acknowledgment of Jesus as his unique Son, the object of his love. His approval of Jesus is the assurance that Jesus will fulfill his messianic mission of salvation.

1, 2–8: Mt 3, 1–11; Lk 3, 2–16.
1, 2: Mal 3, 1.
1, 3: Is 40, 3; Jn 1, 23.
1, 8: Jn 1, 27; Acts 1, 5; 11, 16.
1, 9–11: Mt 3, 13–17; Lk 3, 21–23; Jn 1, 32–33.

like a dove, descending upon him. ¹¹* And a voice came from the heavens, "You are my beloved Son; with you I am well pleased."

The Temptation of Jesus

¹²*† At once the Spirit drove him out into the desert, ¹³ and he remained in the desert for forty days, tempted by Satan. He was among wild beasts, and the angels ministered to him.

II: The Mystery of Jesus

The Beginning of the Galilean Ministry

¹⁴*† After John had been arrested, Jesus came to Galilee proclaiming the gospel of God: ¹⁵* "This is the time of fulfillment. The kingdom of God is at hand. Repent, and believe in the gospel."

The Call of the First Disciples

¹⁶*† As he passed by the Sea of Galilee, he saw Simon and his brother Andrew casting their nets into the sea; they were fishermen. ¹⁷ Jesus said to them, "Come after me, and I will make you fishers of men." ¹⁸ Then they abandoned their nets and followed him. ¹⁹ He walked along a little farther and saw James, the son of Zebedee, and his brother John. They too were in a boat mending their nets. ²⁰ Then he called them. So they left their father Zebedee in the boat along with the hired men and followed him.

The Cure of a Demoniac

²¹*† Then they came to Capernaum, and on the sabbath he entered the synagogue and taught. ²²* The people were astonished at his teaching, for he taught them as one having authority and not as

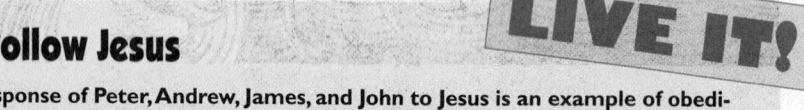

Called to Follow Jesus

LIVE IT!

The response of Peter, Andrew, James, and John to Jesus is an example of obedience to God's call. Jesus calls them because he loves them and trusts them to share in his mission.

The Catholic church believes that through Baptism, all Christians are called to be Jesus' disciples (followers) in whatever path their life takes. Most people are called to mission as a layperson. A few are called to serve through the priesthood, diaconate, or religious life. So whether you end up a priest or a plumber, married or single, poor or rich, faithfulness to God's call is the most important loyalty you can have.

It might be hard to imagine how school or a fast-food job is part of your call to follow Jesus. But attitude is everything! Do you see school as a necessary evil to get a job that makes lots of money? Or do you see it as preparation for a career that will allow you to serve others and contribute to society? If you work, do you approach your job halfheartedly, or are you enthusiastic, always giving your best effort? Do you treat coworkers and customers with warmth and respect? Jesus is calling you to be his disciple wherever you are and whatever you might be doing.

▸ Mk 1, 16–20

---

†

1, 12–13: The same Spirit who descended on Jesus in his baptism now drives him into the desert for forty days. The result is radical confrontation and temptation by Satan who attempts to frustrate the work of God. The presence of wild beasts may indicate the horror and danger of the desert regarded as the abode of demons or may reflect the paradise motif of harmony among all creatures; cf Is 11, 6–9. The presence of ministering angels to sustain Jesus recalls the angel who guided the Israelites in the desert in the first Exodus (14, 19; 23, 20) and the angel who supplied nourishment to Elijah in the wilderness (1 Kgs 19, 5–7). The combined forces of good and evil were present to Jesus in the desert. His sustained obedience brings forth the new Israel of God there where Israel's rebellion had brought death and alienation.

1, 14–15: *After John had been arrested:* in the plan of God, Jesus was not to proclaim the good news of salvation prior to the termination of the Baptist's active mission. *Galilee:* in the Marcan account, scene of the major part of Jesus' public ministry before his arrest and condemnation. *The gospel of God:* not only the good news from God but about God at work in Jesus Christ. *This is the time of fulfillment:* i.e., of God's promises. *The kingdom of God . . . Repent:* see the note on Mt 3, 2.

1, 16–20: These verses narrate the call of the first disciples. See the notes on Mt 4, 18–22 and 4, 20.

1, 21–45: The account of a single day's ministry of Jesus on a sabbath in and outside the synagogue of Capernaum (21–31) combines teaching and miracles of exorcism and healing. Mention is not made of the content of the teaching but of the effect of astonishment and alarm on the people. Jesus' teaching with authority, making an absolute claim on the hearer, was in the best tradition of the ancient prophets, not of the scribes. The narrative continues with events that evening (32–34); see the notes on Mt 8, 14–17) and the next day (35–39). The cleansing in vv 40–45 stands as an isolated story.

1, 11: Ps 2, 7.
1, 12–13: Mt 4, 1–11; Lk 4, 1–13.
1, 14–15: Mt 4, 12–17; Lk 4, 14–15.

1, 15: Mt 3, 2.
1, 16–20: Mt 4, 18–22; Lk 5, 2–11.
1, 21–28: Lk 4, 31–37.
1, 22: Mt 7, 28–29.

SPIRITS

Most Native American peoples would not be surprised by all the angels and spirits in the first chapter of Mark. Many Native American cultures believe in the presence of good and bad spirits in the world. They view good spirits as personal helpers and message bearers, like the angels who attend Jesus in verse 13. They believe that spirits often appear as animals, much as the Holy Spirit appears as a dove in verse 10. And many believe that bad spirits influence and control people, just as the unclean spirit does in verse 23.

Isn't it interesting that different cultures can develop such parallel religious beliefs? Whether we call them angels and demons or good and bad spirits, we share a common understanding about unseen powers influencing our life. It is an understanding of the world that is often rejected in our scientific, technology-filled culture.

▶ **Mk 1, 9–39**

the scribes. 23† In their synagogue was a man with an unclean spirit; 24† he cried out, "What have you to do with us, Jesus of Nazareth? Have you come to destroy us? I know who you are—the Holy One of God!"† 25 Jesus rebuked him and said, "Quiet! Come out of him!" 26 The unclean spirit convulsed him and with a loud cry came out of him. 27 All were amazed and asked one another, "What is this? A new teaching with authority. He commands even the unclean spirits and they obey him." 28 His fame spread everywhere throughout the whole region of Galilee.

The Cure of Simon's Mother-in-Law

29* On leaving the synagogue he entered the house of Simon and Andrew with James and John. 30 Simon's mother-in-law lay sick with a fever. They immediately told him about her. 31 He approached, grasped her hand, and helped her up. Then the fever left her and she waited on them.

Other Healings

32 When it was evening, after sunset, they brought to him all who were ill or possessed by demons. 33 The whole town was gathered at the door. 34 He cured many who were sick with various diseases, and he drove out many demons, not permitting them to speak because they knew him.

Jesus Leaves Capernaum

35* Rising very early before dawn, he left and went off to a deserted place, where he prayed. 36 Simon and those who were with him pursued him 37 and on finding him said, "Everyone is looking for you." 38 He told them, "Let us go on to the nearby villages that I may preach there also. For this purpose have I come." 39 So he went into their synagogues, preaching and driving out demons throughout the whole of Galilee.

The Cleansing of a Leper

40*† A leper came to him [and kneeling down] begged him and said, "If you wish, you can make me clean." 41* Moved with pity, he stretched out his hand, touched him, and said to him, "I do will it. Be made clean." 42* The leprosy left him immediately, and he was made clean. 43 Then, warning

---

† **1, 23:** *An unclean spirit:* so called because of the spirit's resistance to the holiness of God. The spirit knows and fears the power of Jesus to destroy his influence; cf 32.34; 3, 11; 6, 13.

1, 24: *What have you to do with us?:* see the note on Jn 2, 4.

1, 24–25: *The Holy One of God:* not a confession but an attempt to ward off Jesus' power, reflecting the notion that use of the precise name of an opposing spirit would guarantee mastery over him. Jesus silenced the cry of the unclean spirit and drove him out of the man.

1, 40: *A leper:* for the various forms of skin disease, see Lv

13, 1–50 and the note on Lv 13, 2–4. There are only two instances in the Old Testament in which God is shown to have cured a leper (Nm 12, 10–15 and 2 Kgs 5, 1–14). The law of Moses provided for the ritual purification of a leper. In curing the leper, Jesus assumes that the priests will reinstate the cured man into the religious community. See also the note on Lk 5, 14.

1, 29–34: Mt 8, 14–16; Lk 4,   **1, 40–44:** Mt 8, 2–4;
    38–41.   Lk 5, 12–14.
1, 35–39: Lk 4, 42–44.   **1, 41:** Mk 5, 30.
                                                        1, 42: Lk 17, 14.

him sternly, he dismissed him at once. ⁴⁴* Then he said to him, "See that you tell no one anything, but go, show yourself to the priest and offer for your cleansing what Moses prescribed; that will be proof for them." ⁴⁵ The man went away and began to publicize the whole matter. He spread the report abroad so that it was impossible for Jesus to enter a town openly. He remained outside in deserted places, and people kept coming to him from everywhere.

The Healing of a Paralytic

2 ¹*† When Jesus returned to Capernaum after some days, it became known that he was at home.† ² Many gathered together so that there was no longer room for them, not even around the door, and he preached the word to them. ³ They came bringing to him a paralytic carried by four men. ⁴ Unable to get near Jesus because of the crowd, they opened up the roof above him. After they had broken through, they let down the mat on which the paralytic was lying. ⁵† When Jesus saw their faith, he said to the paralytic, "Child, your sins are forgiven."

⁶† Now some of the scribes were sitting there asking themselves, ⁷*† "Why does this man speak that way? He is blaspheming. Who but God alone can forgive sins?" ⁸ Jesus immediately knew in his mind what they were thinking to themselves, so he said, "Why are you thinking such things in your hearts? ⁹ Which is easier, to say to the paralytic, 'Your sins are forgiven,' or to say, 'Rise, pick up your mat and walk'? ¹⁰† But that you may know that the Son of Man has authority to forgive sins on earth"— ¹¹ he said to the paralytic, "I say to you, rise, pick up your mat, and go home." ¹² He rose, picked up his mat at once, and went away in the sight of everyone. They were all astounded and glorified God, saying, "We have never seen anything like this."

The Call of Levi

¹³*† Once again he went out along the sea. All the crowd came to him and he taught them. ¹⁴*† As he passed by, he saw Levi, son of Alphaeus, sitting at the customs post. He said to him, "Follow me." And he got up and followed him. ¹⁵† While he was at table in his house, many tax collectors and sinners

Faithful Friends
LIVE IT!

We are not given many details about the paralyzed man in the story in Mk 2, 1–12, but we might conclude one thing: he had at least four good friends! The main point of this story is that Jesus has the authority to forgive sins, a power that belongs only to God. But what can be said about the four friends who carried the paralyzed man to Jesus?

First, their actions show that they were convinced that Jesus could do something for their paralyzed friend. Second, they were committed to their friend. And last, they didn't let a seemingly insurmountable obstacle—the crowded doorway—prevent them from getting their friend to the feet of Jesus.

What faithful people in your life have helped you come to know Jesus? For whom might you currently have the opportunity to be that kind of faithful friend?

▶ Mk 2, 1–12

---

†
2, 1—3, 6: This section relates a series of conflicts between Jesus and the scribes and Pharisees in which the growing opposition of the latter leads to their plot to put Jesus to death (3, 6).

2, 1–2: *He was at home:* to the crowds that gathered in and outside the house Jesus *preached the word,* i.e., the gospel concerning the nearness of the kingdom and the necessity of repentance and faith (1, 14).

2, 5: It was the faith of the paralytic and those who carried him that moved Jesus to heal the sick man. Accounts of other miracles of Jesus reveal more and more his emphasis on faith as the requisite for exercising his healing powers (5, 34; 9, 23–24; 10, 52).

2, 6: *Scribes:* trained in oral interpretation of the written law; in Mark's gospel, adversaries of Jesus, with one exception (12, 28.34).

2, 7: *He is blaspheming:* an accusation made here and repeated during the trial of Jesus (14, 60–64).

2, 10: *But that you may know that the Son of Man . . . on earth:* although vv 8–9 are addressed to the scribes, the sudden interruption of thought and structure in v 10 seems not addressed to them nor to the paralytic. Moreover, the early public use of the designa-

tion "Son of Man" to unbelieving scribes is most unlikely. The most probable explanation is that Mark's insertion of v 10 is a commentary addressed to Christians for whom he recalls this miracle and who already accept in faith that Jesus is Messiah and Son of God.

2, 13: *He taught them:* see the note on 1, 21–45.

2, 14: *As he passed by:* see the note on 1, 16–20. *Levi, son of Alphaeus:* see the note on Mt 9, 9. *Customs post:* such tax collectors paid a fixed sum for the right to collect customs duties within their districts. Since whatever they could collect above this amount constituted their profit, the abuse of extortion was widespread among them. Hence, Jewish customs officials were regarded as sinners (16), outcasts of society, and disgraced along with their families. *He got up and followed him:* i.e., became a disciple of Jesus.

2, 15: *In his house:* cf v 1; Mt 9, 10. Lk 5, 29 clearly calls it Levi's house.

1, 44: Lv 14, 2–32.	2, 7: Is 43, 25.
2, 1–12: Mt 9, 2–8; Lk 5,	2, 13: Mk 4, 1.
18–26.	2, 14–17: Mt 9, 9–13; Lk 5,
	27–32.

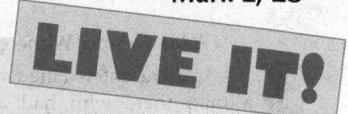

Getting Personal

It is one thing to be seen hanging out with certain groups of people, but it is another to be seen eating with them. Jesus was often criticized for eating with the wrong kind of people, a charge he answers in Mk 2, 13–17. He knew that the only way to help someone grow was to get to know him or her—personally.

It did not matter to Jesus whether the person was rich or poor, well known or unknown, regarded as a saint or as a sinner. It did not matter to him whether the person was black or white, male or female, young or old. What did matter to Jesus was whether the person he approached was interested in getting to know him—and his heavenly Father—personally.

Are you ready to get to know Jesus personally? If so, take a few minutes to close your eyes and think about what it says in this passage. Talk to Jesus about what is going on in your life and in your family's life. When you are done talking, spend some time quietly listening for what Jesus has to say to you—personally.

▸ Mk 2, 13–17

MK

---

sat with Jesus and his disciples; for there were many who followed him. [16]† Some scribes who were Pharisees saw that he was eating with sinners and tax collectors and said to his disciples, "Why does he eat with tax collectors and sinners?" [17]† Jesus heard this and said to them [that], "Those who are well do not need a physician, but the sick do. I did not come to call the righteous but sinners."

The Question about Fasting

[18]*† The disciples of John and of the Pharisees were accustomed to fast. People came to him and objected, "Why do the disciples of John and the disciples of the Pharisees fast, but your disciples do not fast?" [19]† Jesus answered them, "Can the wedding guests fast while the bridegroom is with them? As long as they have the bridegroom with them they cannot fast. [20] But the days will come when the bridegroom is taken away from them, and then they will fast on that day. [21] No one sews a piece of unshrunken cloth on an old cloak. If he does, its fullness pulls away, the new from the old, and the tear gets worse. [22] Likewise, no one pours new wine into old wineskins. Otherwise, the wine will burst the skins, and both the wine and the skins are ruined. Rather, new wine is poured into fresh wineskins."

The Disciples and the Sabbath

[23]*† As he was passing through a field of grain on the sabbath, his disciples began to make a path while picking the heads of grain. [24]* At this the Pharisees said to him, "Look, why are they doing what is unlawful on the sabbath?" [25]† He said to them, "Have you never read what David did when he was in need and he and his companions were hungry? [26]* How he went into the house of God when Abiathar was high priest and ate the bread of offering that only the priests could lawfully eat, and shared it with his companions?" [27]*† Then he said to them, "The sabbath was made for man, not man for the sabbath. [28]† That is why the Son of Man is lord even of the sabbath."

2, 16–17: This and the following conflict stories reflect a similar pattern: a statement of fact, a question of protest, and a reply by Jesus.

2, 17: *Do not need a physician:* this maxim of Jesus with its implied irony was uttered to silence his adversaries who objected that he ate with *tax collectors and sinners* (16). Because the scribes and Pharisees were self-righteous, they were not capable of responding to Jesus' call to repentance and faith in the gospel.

2, 18–22: This conflict over the question of fasting has the same pattern as vv 16–17; see the notes on Mt 9, 15 and 9, 16–17.

2, 19: *Can the wedding guests fast?:* the bridal metaphor expresses a new relationship of love between God and his people in the person and mission of Jesus to his disciples. It is the inauguration of the new and joyful messianic time of fulfillment and the passing of the old. Any attempt at assimilating the Pharisaic practice of fasting, or of extending the preparatory discipline of John's disciples beyond the arrival of the bridegroom, would be as futile as sewing *a piece of unshrunken cloth on an old cloak* or pouring *new wine into old wineskins* with the resulting destruction of both cloth and wine (21–22). Fasting is rendered superfluous during the earthly ministry of Jesus; cf v 20.

2, 23–28: This conflict regarding the sabbath follows the same pattern as in vv 18–22.

2, 25–26: *Have you never read what David did?:* Jesus defends the action of his disciples on the basis of 1 Sm 21, 2–7 in which an exception is made to the regulation of Lv 24, 9 because of the extreme hunger of David and his men. According to 1 Samuel, the priest who gave the bread to David was Ahimelech, father of Abiathar.

2, 27: *The sabbath was made for man:* a reaffirmation of the divine intent of the sabbath to benefit Israel as contrasted with the restrictive Pharisaic tradition added to the law.

2, 28: *The Son of Man is lord even of the sabbath:* Mark's comment on the theological meaning of the incident is to benefit his Christian readers; see the note on 2, 10.

2, 18–22: Mt 9, 14–17; Lk 5, 33–39.
2, 23–28: Mt 12, 1–8; Lk 6, 1–5.
2, 24: Dt 23, 25.
2, 26: 1 Sm 21, 2–7; Lv 24, 5–9.
2, 27: 2 Mc 5, 19.

A Man with a Withered Hand

3 ¹*† Again he entered the synagogue. There was a man there who had a withered hand. ² They watched him closely to see if he would cure him on the sabbath so that they might accuse him. ³ He said to the man with the withered hand, "Come up here before us." ⁴ Then he said to them, "Is it lawful to do good on the sabbath rather than to do evil, to save life rather than to destroy it?" But they remained silent. ⁵* Looking around at them with anger and grieved at their hardness of heart, he said to the man, "Stretch out your hand." He stretched it out and his hand was restored. ⁶† The Pharisees went out and immediately took counsel with the Herodians against him to put him to death.

The Mercy of Jesus

⁷*† Jesus withdrew toward the sea with his disciples. A large number of people [followed] from Galilee and from Judea. ⁸ Hearing what he was doing, a large number of people came to him also from Jerusalem, from Idumea, from beyond the Jordan, and from the neighborhood of Tyre and Sidon. ⁹ He told his disciples to have a boat ready for him because of the crowd, so that they would not crush him. ¹⁰* He had cured many and, as a result, those who had diseases were pressing upon him to touch him. ¹¹*† And whenever unclean spirits saw him they would fall down before him and shout, "You are the Son of God." ¹² He warned them sternly not to make him known.

The Mission of the Twelve

¹³*† He went up the mountain and summoned those whom he wanted and they came to him. ¹⁴*† He appointed twelve [whom he also named apostles] that they might be with him and he might send them forth to preach ¹⁵ and to have au-

Trusting God   **LIVE IT!**

Have you ever read the book *Johnny Tremain*? Its main character is a boy whose hand is severely burned, and the story is about how he learns to live with a disfigured limb. At many points in the story, Johnny hides his hand from others to avoid feeling embarrassed.

In Mk 3, 1–6, among those gathered in the synagogue is a man with a "withered hand." There is no indication that he is seeking out Jesus or that he commands any special attention. Jesus notices him and invites him to come forward. Jesus then asks the man to stretch out his disfigured hand for all to see.

Like Johnny Tremain, the man, we might guess, probably did not feel proud of his hand. It certainly would be understandable if, when invited by Jesus to stretch out his hand for all to see, the man had stormed out of the synagogue in anger and shame. Instead, he did what Jesus asked, and through his trust in Jesus, his hand was restored to wholeness.

Whether physically, emotionally, or spiritually, we are all "disfigured" in some ways. What source of pain or shame in your own life might Jesus be inviting you to share with him? Can you risk becoming vulnerable and trusting him with it?

▶ Mk 3, 1–6

---

†

3, 1–5: Here Jesus is again depicted in conflict with his adversaries over the question of sabbath-day observance. His opponents were already ill disposed toward him because they regarded Jesus as a violator of the sabbath. Jesus' question *Is it lawful to do good on the sabbath rather than to do evil?* places the matter in the broader theological context outside the casuistry of the scribes. The answer is obvious. Jesus heals the man with the withered hand in the sight of all and reduces his opponents to silence; cf Jn 5, 17–18.

3, 6: In reporting the plot of the Pharisees and Herodians to put Jesus to death after this series of conflicts in Galilee, Mark uses a pattern that recurs in his account of later controversies in Jerusalem (11, 17–18; 12, 13–17). The help of the Herodians, supporters of Herod Antipas, tetrarch of Galilee and Perea, is needed to take action against Jesus. Both series of conflicts point to their gravity and to the impending passion of Jesus.

3, 7–19: This overview of the Galilean ministry manifests the power of Jesus to draw people to himself through his teaching and deeds of power. The crowds of Jews from many regions surround Jesus

(7–12). This phenomenon prepares the way for creating a new people of Israel. The choice and mission of the Twelve is the prelude (13–19).

3, 11–12: See the note on 1, 24–25.

3, 13: *He went up the mountain:* here and elsewhere the mountain is associated with solemn moments and acts in the mission and self-revelation of Jesus (6, 46; 9, 2–8; 13, 3). Jesus acts with authority as he *summoned those whom he wanted and they came to him.*

3, 14–15: *He appointed twelve [whom he also named apostles] that they might be with him:* literally "he made," i.e., instituted them as apostles to extend his messianic mission through them (6, 7–13). See the notes on Mt 10, 1 and 10, 2–4.

3, 1–6: Mt 12, 9–14; Lk 6, 6–11.
3, 5: Lk 14, 4.
3, 7–12: Mt 4, 23–25; 12, 15; Lk 6, 17–19.
3, 10: Mk 5, 30.
3, 11: Mk 1, 34; Lk 4, 41.
3, 13–19: Mt 10, 1–4; Lk 6, 12–16.
3, 14: Mk 6, 7.

thority to drive out demons: ¹⁶† [he appointed the twelve:] Simon, whom he named Peter; ¹⁷* James, son of Zebedee, and John the brother of James, whom he named Boanerges, that is, sons of thunder; ¹⁸ Andrew, Philip, Bartholomew, Matthew, Thomas, James the son of Alphaeus; Thaddeus, Simon the Cananean, ¹⁹ and Judas Iscariot who betrayed him.

Blasphemy of the Scribes

²⁰*† He came home.† Again [the] crowd gathered, making it impossible for them even to eat. ²¹* When his relatives heard of this they set out to seize him, for they said, "He is out of his mind." ²²*† The scribes who had come from Jerusalem said, "He is possessed by Beelzebul," and "By the prince of demons he drives out demons."

Jesus and Beelzebul

²³ Summoning them, he began to speak to them in parables, "How can Satan drive out Satan? ²⁴ If a kingdom is divided against itself, that kingdom cannot stand. ²⁵ And if a house is divided against itself, that house will not be able to stand. ²⁶ And if Satan has risen up against himself and is divided, he cannot stand; that is the end of him. ²⁷ But no one can enter a strong man's house to plunder his property unless he first ties up the strong man. Then he can plunder his house. ²⁸* Amen, I say to you, all sins and all blasphemies that people utter will be forgiven them. ²⁹† But whoever blasphemes against the holy Spirit will never have forgiveness, but is guilty of an everlasting sin." ³⁰ For they had said, "He has an unclean spirit."

Jesus and His Family

³¹* His mother and his brothers arrived. Standing outside they sent word to him and called him. ³²† A crowd seated around him told him, "Your mother and your brothers [and your sisters] are outside asking for you." ³³ But he said to them in reply, "Who are my mother and [my] brothers?" ³⁴ And looking around at those seated in the circle he said,

Catholic Connections

HOLY ORDERS

Jesus appoints twelve men as the Apostles (the word *apostle* means "sent out"). Their mission—to preach the Good News, drive out demons, and cure the sick—is an extension of Jesus' mission. The Catholic church considers bishops as the successors of the Apostles. Bishops are responsible for the church's mission, for its organization, and for seeing that Jesus' message is taught and lived faithfully from generation to generation.

Bishops are ordained by other bishops as a sign of their unbroken connection with the first Apostles. Bishops also ordain priests and deacons for service in the church, especially for sacramental ministry. These ordinations happen in the sacrament of Holy Orders, one of the seven sacraments of the church. In the sacrament of Holy Orders, the bishop places his hands on the head of the man being ordained and prays for a special outpouring of the Holy Spirit.

▶ Mk 3, 13–19

"Here are my mother and my brothers. ³⁵ [For] whoever does the will of God is my brother and sister and mother."

---

† **3, 16:** *Simon, whom he named Peter:* Mark indicates that Simon's name was changed on this occasion. Peter is first in all lists of the apostles (Mt 10, 2; Lk 6, 14; Acts 1, 13; cf 1 Cor 15, 5–8).

3, 20–35: Within the narrative of the coming of Jesus' relatives (20–21) is inserted the account of the unbelieving scribes from Jerusalem who attributed Jesus' power over demons to Beelzebul (22–30); see the note on 5, 21–43. There were those even among the relatives of Jesus who disbelieved and regarded Jesus as *out of his mind* (21). Against this background, Jesus is informed of the arrival of his mother and brothers [and sisters] (32). He responds by showing that not family ties but doing God's will (35) is decisive in the kingdom; cf the note on Mt 12, 46–50.

3, 20: *He came home:* cf 2, 1–2 and see the note on 2, 15.

3, 22: *By Beelzebul:* see the note on Mt 10, 25. Two accusations

are leveled against Jesus: (1) that *he is possessed* by an unclean spirit, and (2) *by the prince of demons he drives out demons.* Jesus answers the second charge by a parable (24–27) and responds to the first charge in vv 28–29.

3, 29: *Whoever blasphemes against the holy Spirit:* this sin is called *an everlasting sin* because it attributes to Satan, who is the power of evil, what is actually the work of the holy Spirit, namely, victory over the demons.

3, 32: *Your brothers:* see the note on 6, 3.

3, 17: Mt 16, 18; Jn 1, 42.   3, 28: Lk 12, 10.
3, 20: Mk 2, 2.   3, 31–35: Mt 12, 46–50;
3, 21: Jn 10, 20.   Lk 8, 19–21.
3, 22–30: Mt 12, 24–32; Lk 11,
    15–22; 12, 10.

JESUS TEACHES US THROUGH STORIES!

In Mark, chapter 4, Jesus teaches about God's Reign through parables (see "Parables," Mt 13, 10). In some Hispanic families, it is customary for young people to hear their *abuelita* (grandmother) tell stories about their family history, traditions, and faith. Many of the stories are true; others may be created to give a moral teaching, like the parables. Here is a true story:

A little girl's father died, leaving her family in extreme poverty. Her mother never lost faith in God, daily prayed to the Divine Providence, and asked other people to pray with her. Her prayers were always answered: food appeared miraculously in front of the family's door, and her six children were accepted free in Catholic schools.

Eventually, the mother married a creative businessman. When the business prospered, she remembered the way God had moved the hearts of people so that her family could have food and education, and with great confidence in God, she started a boarding school for boys. Whenever there was not enough food, she prayed and invited other people to pray. The Divine Providence always responded. The school has sheltered and educated two hundred boys each year for the last seventy years.

■ Which stories of faith, love, and service have marked the history of your family?
■ How are you honoring your family's tradition of bringing the Gospel to people in need?

▶ Mk 4, 1–34

The Parable of the Sower

4 **1***† On another occasion he began to teach by the sea.† A very large crowd gathered around him so that he got into a boat on the sea and sat down. And the whole crowd was beside the sea on land.* **2** And he taught them at length in parables, and in the course of his instruction he said to them, **3**† "Hear this! A sower went out to sow. **4** And as he sowed, some seed fell on the path, and the birds came and ate it up. **5** Other seed fell on rocky ground where it had little soil. It sprang up at once because the soil was not deep. **6** And when the sun rose, it was scorched and it withered for lack of roots. **7** Some seed fell among thorns, and the thorns grew up and choked it and it produced no grain. **8** And some seed fell on rich soil and produced fruit. It came up and grew and yielded thirty, sixty, and a hundredfold." **9** He added, "Whoever has ears to hear ought to hear."

The Purpose of the Parables

10 And when he was alone, those present along with the Twelve questioned him about the parables. **11**† He answered them, "The mystery of the kingdom of God has been granted to you. But to those outside everything comes in parables, **12*** so that

'they may look and see but not perceive,
and hear and listen but not understand,
in order that they may not be converted and
be forgiven.' "

4, 1–34: *In parables* (2): see the note on Mt 13, 3. The use of parables is typical of Jesus' enigmatic method of teaching the crowds (2–9.12) as compared with the interpretation of the parables he gives to his disciples (10–25.33–34), to each group according to its capacity to understand (9–11). The key feature of the parable at hand is the sowing of the seed (3), representing the breakthrough of the kingdom of God into the world. The various types of soil refer to the diversity of response accorded the word of God (4–7). The climax of the parable is the harvest of thirty, sixty, and a hundredfold, indicating the consummation of the kingdom (8). Thus both the present and the future action of God, from the initiation to the fulfillment of the kingdom, is presented through this and other parables (26–29.30–32).
4, 1: *By the sea:* the shore of the Sea of Galilee or a boat near the shore (2, 13; 3, 7–8) is the place where Mark depicts Jesus teaching the crowds. By contrast the mountain is the scene of Jesus at prayer (6, 46) or in the process of forming his disciples (3, 13; 9, 2).
4, 3–8: See the note on Mt 13, 3–8.
4, 11–12: These verses are to be viewed against their background in 3, 6.22 concerning the unbelief and opposition Jesus encountered in his ministry. It is against this background that the distinction in Jesus' method becomes clear of presenting the kingdom to the disbelieving crowd in one manner and to the disciples in another. To the former it is presented in parables and the truth remains hidden; for the latter the parable is interpreted and the mystery is partially revealed because of their faith; see the notes on Mt 13, 11 and 13, 13.

4, 1–12: Mt 13, 1–13; Lk 8, 4–10.   **4, 1:** Mk 2, 13; Lk 5, 1.   **4, 12:** Is 6, 9; Jn 12, 40; Acts 28, 26; Rom 11, 8.

¹³*† Jesus said to them, "Do you not understand this parable? Then how will you understand any of the parables? ¹⁴ The sower sows the word. ¹⁵ These are the ones on the path where the word is sown. As soon as they hear, Satan comes at once and takes away the word sown in them. ¹⁶ And these are the ones sown on rocky ground who, when they hear the word, receive it at once with joy. ¹⁷ But they have no root; they last only for a time. Then when tribulation or persecution comes because of the word, they quickly fall away. ¹⁸ Those sown among thorns are another sort. They are the people who hear the word, ¹⁹ but worldly anxiety, the lure of riches, and the craving for other things intrude and choke the word, and it bears no fruit. ²⁰ But those sown on rich soil are the ones who hear the word and accept it and bear fruit thirty and sixty and a hundredfold."

Parable of the Lamp

²¹* He said to them, "Is a lamp brought in to be placed under a bushel basket or under a bed, and not to be placed on a lampstand?* ²²* For there is nothing hidden except to be made visible; nothing is secret except to come to light. ²³ Anyone who has ears to hear ought to hear." ²⁴* He also told them, "Take care what you hear. The measure with which you measure will be measured out to you, and still more will be given to you. ²⁵* To the one who has, more will be given; from the one who has not, even what he has will be taken away."

Seed Grows of Itself

²⁶*† He said, "This is how it is with the kingdom of God; it is as if a man were to scatter seed on the land ²⁷ and would sleep and rise night and day and the seed would sprout and grow, he knows not how. ²⁸ Of its own accord the land yields fruit, first the blade, then the ear, then the full grain in the ear. ²⁹ And when the grain is ripe, he wields the sickle at once, for the harvest has come."

The Mustard Seed

³⁰* He said, "To what shall we compare the kingdom of God, or what parable can we use for it? ³¹ It is like a mustard seed that, when it is sown in the ground, is the smallest of all the seeds on the earth. ³²† But once it is sown, it springs up and becomes the largest of plants and puts forth large branches,

so that the birds of the sky can dwell in its shade." ³³* With many such parables he spoke the word to them as they were able to understand it. ³⁴ Without parables he did not speak to them, but to his own disciples he explained everything in private.

The Calming of a Storm at Sea

³⁵*† On that day, as evening drew on, he said to them, "Let us cross to the other side." ³⁶ Leaving the crowd, they took him with them in the boat just as

Life's Storms

Storms on the Sea of Galilee are a common occurrence. They are a fisher's nightmare, and the one described in Mk 4, 35–41 was really bad! It is no wonder the Apostles felt fearful and powerless. As part of your prayer, try this meditation:

Begin by closing your eyes and relaxing. Then visualize yourself standing on the beach with Jesus and the disciples. Join them as they board the boat. When the squall comes, experience the rocking of the boat, the waves crashing on deck, and the winds blowing. Feel the disciples' anxiety and fear as the boat is tossed and water pours into the boat. Go with the disciples to wake Jesus, and watch as Jesus calms the storm. Now, experience the peacefulness and tranquility of the miracle you have witnessed.

All of us have storms we must face, that is, parts of our life that are filled with anxiety or fear. Think about your life. What are the storms that batter and rock your world? Who in your family or in your community can calm your fears? How would you respond to Jesus' question, "Do you not yet have faith?" (Mk 4, 40).

▶ Mk 4, 35–41

4, 13–20: See the note on Mt 13, 18–23.
4, 26–29: Only Mark records the parable of the seed's growth. Sower and harvester are the same. The emphasis is on the power of the seed to grow of itself without human intervention (27). Mysteriously it produces *blade* and *ear* and *full grain* (28). Thus the kingdom of God initiated by Jesus in proclaiming the word develops quietly yet powerfully until it is fully established by him at the final judgment (29); cf Rv 14, 15.
4, 32: The universality of the kingdom of God is indicated here; cf Ez 17, 23; 31, 6; Dn 4, 17–19.

4, 35—5, 43: After the chapter on parables, Mark narrates four miracle stories: 4, 35–41; 5, 1–20; and two joined together in 5, 21–43. See also the notes on Mt 8, 23–34 and 9, 8–26.

4, 13–20: Mt 13, 18–23; Lk 8, 11–15.	4, 26–29: Jas 5, 7.
4, 21–25: Lk 8, 16–18.	4, 30–32: Mt 13, 31–32; Lk 13, 18–19.
4, 21: Mt 5, 15; Lk 11, 33.	4, 33–34: Mt 13, 34.
4, 22: Mt 10, 26; Lk 12, 2.	4, 35–40: Mt 8, 18.23–37; Lk 8, 22–25.
4, 24: Mt 7, 2; Lk 6, 38.	
4, 25: Mt 13, 12; Lk 19, 26.	

he was. And other boats were with him. [37] A violent squall came up and waves were breaking over the boat, so that it was already filling up. [38] Jesus was in the stern, asleep on a cushion. They woke him and said to him, "Teacher, do you not care that we are perishing?" [39]† He woke up, rebuked the wind, and said to the sea, "Quiet! Be still!" The wind ceased and there was great calm. [40] Then he asked them, "Why are you terrified? Do you not yet have faith?" [41]*† They were filled with great awe and said to one another, "Who then is this whom even wind and sea obey?"

The Healing of the Gerasene Demoniac

5 [1]*† They came to the other side of the sea, to the territory of the Gerasenes. [2]† When he got out of the boat, at once a man from the tombs who had an unclean spirit met him. [3] The man had been dwelling among the tombs, and no one could restrain him any longer, even with a chain. [4] In fact, he had frequently been bound with shackles and chains, but the chains had been pulled apart by him and the shackles smashed, and no one was strong enough to subdue him. [5] Night and day among the tombs and on the hillsides he was always crying out and bruising himself with stones. [6] Catching sight of Jesus from a distance, he ran up and prostrated himself before him, [7]† crying out in a loud voice, "What have you to do with me, Jesus, Son of the Most High God? I adjure you by God, do not torment me!" [8] (He had been saying to it, "Unclean spirit, come out of the man!") [9]*† He asked him, "What is your name?" He replied, "Legion is my name. There are many of us." [10] And he pleaded earnestly with him not to drive them away from that territory.

[11]† Now a large herd of swine was feeding there on the hillside. [12] And they pleaded with him, "Send us into the swine. Let us enter them." [13] And he let them, and the unclean spirits came out and entered the swine. The herd of about two thousand rushed down a steep bank into the sea, where they were drowned. [14] The swineherds ran away and reported the incident in the town and throughout the countryside. And people came out to see what had

happened. [15] As they approached Jesus, they caught sight of the man who had been possessed by Legion, sitting there clothed and in his right mind. And they were seized with fear. [16] Those who witnessed the incident explained to them what had happened to the possessed man and to the swine. [17] Then they began to beg him to leave their district. [18] As he was getting into the boat, the man who had been possessed pleaded to remain with him. [19]† But he would not permit him but told him instead, "Go home to your family and announce to them all that the Lord in his pity has done for you." [20] Then the man went off and began to proclaim in the Decapolis what Jesus had done for him; and all were amazed.

Everyone's Welcome!

In Mark, chapters 5–8, Jesus expands his mission into Gentile territory, the region on the eastern side of the Sea of Galilee. Three miraculous healings of Gentiles—the Gerasene demoniac (5, 1–13), the Syrophoenician's daughter (7, 24–30), and the deaf man from Tyre (7, 31–37)—extend the promises of the Reign of God to all who have faith in Jesus. In arranging these stories, the author of the Gospel emphasizes that God's salvation is available to everyone, not just to the Jews.

In your prayer, reflect or journal on the following questions:

- How do you treat people from a different race, culture, or religion?
- How could you be more welcoming toward them, more like Jesus?

Write a prayer expressing your desire.

▶ Mk 5, 1—8, 26

4, 39: *Quiet! Be still!:* as in the case of silencing a demon (1, 25), Jesus rebukes the wind and subdues the turbulence of the sea by a mere word; see the note on Mt 8, 26.

4, 41: Jesus is here depicted as exercising power over wind and sea. In the Christian community this event was seen as a sign of Jesus' saving presence amid persecutions that threatened its existence.

5, 1: *The territory of the Gerasenes:* the reference is to pagan territory; cf Is 65, 1. Another reading is "Gadarenes"; see the note on Mt 8, 28.

5, 2–6: The man was an outcast from society, dominated by unclean spirits (8.13), living among the tombs. The prostration before Jesus (6) indicates Jesus' power over evil spirits.

5, 7: *What have you to do with me?:* cf 1, 24 and see the note on Jn 2, 4.

5, 9: *Legion is my name:* the demons were numerous and the condition of the possessed man was extremely serious; cf Mt 12, 45.

5, 11: *Herd of swine:* see the note on Mt 8, 30.

5, 19: *Go home:* Jesus did not accept the man's request *to remain with him* as a disciple (18), yet invited him to announce to his own people what the Lord had done for him, i.e., proclaim the gospel message to his pagan family; cf 1, 14.39; 3, 14; 13, 10.

4, 41: Mk 1, 27.   **5, 9:** Mt 12, 45; Lk 8, 2;
5, 1–20: Mt 8, 28–34; Lk 8,   11, 26.
26–39.

did **KNOW?**
you

Demon Possession

The Gospels of Matthew, Mark, and Luke all have stories about Jesus curing people of unclean spirits, or demons. Many cultures believe in spirits, both good and bad (see "Spirits," Mk 1, 9–39), which can influence or even control people's decisions and actions. In the Bible, a demon is first mentioned in the Book of Tobit, which was written about two hundred years before Jesus' birth. Demons represented evil— mysterious powers hostile to God, health, and goodness. Jesus' ability to free people of demonic influence was a sign of the arrival of the Reign of God (see "Miracles and the Reign of God," Mt 8, 1—9, 34).

Over time, the explanation for evil or illness shifted from unclean spirits to Satan (see "Satan," Jb 1, 6—2, 10), the leader of all demonic forces. The Gospel of John does not mention unclean spirits at all but instead refers to Satan's influence in the evil leading to Jesus' death (see Jn 13, 2).

What the Bible calls demon possession might, at times, have been mental or physical illness. But many people are becoming aware of what the ancient people already knew: that illness and evil are part of the spiritual reality that can affect our life.

▸ Mk 1, 23–34; 5, 1–20

Jairus's Daughter and the Woman with a Hemorrhage

21*† When Jesus had crossed again [in the boat] to the other side, a large crowd gathered around him, and he stayed close to the sea. 22* One of the synagogue officials, named Jairus, came forward. Seeing him he fell at his feet 23† and pleaded earnestly with him, saying, "My daughter is at the point of death. Please, come lay your hands on her that she may get well and live." 24 He went off with him, and a large crowd followed him and pressed upon him.

25 There was a woman afflicted with hemorrhages for twelve years. 26 She had suffered greatly at the hands of many doctors and had spent all that she had. Yet she was not helped but only grew worse. 27 She had heard about Jesus and came up behind him in the crowd and touched his cloak. 28† She said, "If I but touch his clothes, I shall be cured." 29 Immediately her flow of blood dried up. She felt in her body that she was healed of her affliction. 30 Jesus, aware at once that power had gone out from him, turned around in the crowd and asked, "Who has touched my clothes?" 31 But his disciples said to him, "You see how the crowd is pressing upon you, and yet you ask, 'Who touched me?'" 32 And he looked around to see who had done it. 33 The woman, realizing what had happened to her, approached in fear and trembling. She fell down before Jesus and told him the whole truth. 34* He said to her, "Daughter, your faith has saved you. Go in peace and be cured of your affliction."

35† While he was still speaking, people from the synagogue official's house arrived and said, "Your daughter has died; why trouble the teacher any longer?" 36 Disregarding the message that was reported, Jesus said to the synagogue official, "Do not be afraid; just have faith." 37 He did not allow anyone to accompany him inside except Peter, James, and John, the brother of James. 38 When they arrived at the house of the synagogue official, he caught sight of a commotion, people weeping and wailing loudly. 39*† So he went in and said to them, "Why this commotion and weeping? The child is not dead but asleep." 40 And they ridiculed him. Then he put them all out. He took along the child's father and mother and those who were with him and entered the room where the child was. 41† He took the child by the hand and said to her,

---

5, 21–43: The story of the raising to life of Jairus's daughter is divided into two parts: vv 21–24 and 35–43. Between these two separated parts the account of the cure of the hemorrhage victim (25–34) is interposed. This technique of intercalating or sandwiching one story within another occurs several times in Mark: 3, 19b-21 (22–30) 31–35; 6, 6b-13 (14–29) 30; 11, 12–14 (15–19) 20–25; 14, 53 (54) 55–65 (66–73).

5, 23: *Lay your hands on her:* this act for the purpose of healing is frequent in Mark (6, 5; 7, 32–35; 8, 23–25; 16, 18) and is also found in Mt 9, 18; Lk 4, 40; 13, 13; Acts 9, 17; 28, 8.

5, 28: Both in the case of Jairus and his daughter (23) and in the case of the hemorrhage victim, the inner conviction that physical contact (30) accompanied by faith in Jesus' saving power could effect a cure was rewarded.

5, 35: The faith of Jairus was put to a twofold test: (1) that his daughter might be cured and, now that she had died, (2) that she might be restored to life. His faith contrasts with the lack of faith of the crowd.

5, 39: *Not dead but asleep:* the New Testament often refers to death as sleep (Mt 27, 52; Jn 11, 11; 1 Cor 15, 6; 1 Thes 4, 13–15); see the note on Mt 9, 24.

5, 41: *Arise:* the Greek verb *egeirein* is the verb generally used to express resurrection from death (6, 14.16; Mt 11, 5; Lk 7, 14) and Jesus' own resurrection (16, 6; Mt 28, 6; Lk 24, 6).

5, 21: Mk 2, 13.   5, 34: Lk 7, 30.
5, 22–43: Mt 9, 18–26;   5, 39–40: Acts 9, 40.
         Lk 8, 41–56.

MK

"Talitha koum," which means, "Little girl, I say to you, arise!" [42] The girl, a child of twelve, arose immediately and walked around. [At that] they were utterly astounded. [43] He gave strict orders that no one should know this and said that she should be given something to eat.

The Rejection at Nazareth

6 [1]*† He departed from there and came to his native place, accompanied by his disciples. [2]† When the sabbath came he began to teach in the synagogue, and many who heard him were astonished. They said, "Where did this man get all this? What kind of wisdom has been given him? What mighty deeds are wrought by his hands! [3]*† Is he not the carpenter, the son of Mary, and the brother of James and Joses and Judas and Simon? And are not his sisters here with us?" And they took offense at him. [4]*† Jesus said to them, "A prophet is not without honor except in his native place and among his own kin and in his own house." [5]† So he was not able to perform any mighty deed there, apart from curing a few sick people by laying his hands on them. [6] He was amazed at their lack of faith.

The Mission of the Twelve

He went around to the villages in the vicinity teaching. [7]*† He summoned the Twelve and began to send them out two by two and gave them authority over unclean spirits. [8]† He instructed them to take nothing for the journey but a walking stick—no food, no sack, no money in their belts. [9] They were, however, to wear sandals but not a second tunic. [10]† He said to them, "Wherever you

When the Good News Comes Calling

We often can choose whether to allow into our life the people bearing the Good News of Jesus, just as the people to whom the disciples were sent in Mk 6, 6–13 could. Why might we turn away such guests? Perhaps their message is too challenging or upsetting to our lifestyle. Maybe we are not ready to accept what God is offering to us through them. Maybe we are too busy to realize that they have something to offer us.

Open your hands as if to receive a gift, and offer a prayer to God for the openness to welcome God's messengers and to receive the Good News they bring.

▸ Mk 6, 6–13

enter a house, stay there until you leave from there. [11] Whatever place does not welcome you or listen to you, leave there and shake the dust off your feet in testimony against them." [12] So they went off and preached repentance. [13]*† They drove out many demons, and they anointed with oil many who were sick and cured them.

6, 1: *His native place:* the Greek word *patris* here refers to Nazareth (cf 1, 9; Lk 4, 16.23–24), though it can also mean native land.

6, 2–6: See the note on Mt 13, 54–58.

6, 3: *Is he not the carpenter?:* no other gospel calls Jesus a carpenter. Some witnesses have "the carpenter's son," as in Mt 13, 55. *Son of Mary:* contrary to Jewish custom, which calls a man the son of his father, this expression may reflect Mark's own faith that God is the Father of Jesus (1, 1.11; 8, 38; 13, 32; 14, 36). *The brother of James . . . Simon:* in Semitic usage, the terms 'brother,' 'sister' are applied not only to children of the same parents, but to nephews, nieces, cousins, half-brothers, and half-sisters; cf Gn 14, 16; 29, 15; Lv 10, 4. While one cannot suppose that the meaning of a Greek word should be sought in the first place from Semitic usage, the Septuagint often translates the Hebrew *'āh* by the Greek word *adelphos*, "brother," as in the cited passages, a fact that may argue for a similar breadth of meaning in some New Testament passages. For instance, there is no doubt that in v 17, "brother" is used of Philip, who was actually the half-brother of Herod Antipas. On the other hand, Mark may have understood the terms literally; see also Mt 3, 31–32; 12, 46; 13, 55–56; Lk 8, 19; Jn 7, 3.5. The question of meaning here would not have arisen but for the faith of the church in Mary's perpetual virginity.

6, 4: *A prophet is not without honor except . . . in his own house:* a saying that finds parallels in other literatures, especially Jewish and Greek, but without reference to a prophet. Comparing himself to previous Hebrew prophets whom the people rejected, Jesus intimates his own eventual rejection by the nation especially in view of the dishonor his own relatives had shown him (3, 21) and now his townspeople as well.

6, 5: *He was not able to perform any mighty deed there:* according to Mark, Jesus' power could not take effect because of a person's lack of faith.

6, 7–13: The preparation for the mission of the Twelve is seen in the call (1) of the first disciples to be fishers of men (1, 16–20), (2) then of the Twelve set apart to be with Jesus and to receive authority to preach and expel demons (3, 13–19). Now they are given the specific mission to exercise that authority in word and power as representatives of Jesus during the time of their formation.

6, 8–9: In Mark the use of a *walking stick* (8) and *sandals* (9) is permitted, but not in Mt 10, 10 nor in Lk 10, 4. Mark does not mention any prohibition to visit pagan territory and to enter Samaritan towns. These differences indicate a certain adaptation to conditions in and outside of Palestine and suggest in Mark's account a later activity in the church. For the rest, Jesus required of his apostles a total dependence on God for food and shelter; cf vv 35–44; 8, 1–9.

6, 10–11: Remaining in the same house as a guest (10) rather than moving to another offering greater comfort avoided any impression of seeking advantage for oneself and prevented dishonor to one's host. Shaking the dust off one's feet served as testimony against those who rejected the call to repentance.

6, 13: *Anointed with oil . . . cured them:* a common medicinal remedy, but seen here as a vehicle of divine power for healing.

6, 1–6: Mt 13, 54–58; Lk 4, 16–30.
6, 3: Mk 15, 40; Mt 12, 46; Jn 6, 42.
6, 4: Jn 4, 44.
6, 7–11: Mt 10, 1.9–14; Lk 9, 15; 10, 4–11.
6, 13: Jas 5, 14.

Herod's Opinion of Jesus†

14* King Herod† heard about it, for his fame had become widespread, and people were saying, "John the Baptist has been raised from the dead; that is why mighty powers are at work in him."* 15* Others were saying, "He is Elijah"; still others, "He is a prophet like any of the prophets." 16 But when Herod learned of it, he said, "It is John whom I beheaded. He has been raised up."

The Death of John the Baptist

17*† Herod was the one who had John arrested and bound in prison on account of Herodias, the wife of his brother Philip, whom he had married. 18* John had said to Herod, "It is not lawful for you to have your brother's wife." 19† Herodias harbored a grudge against him and wanted to kill him but was unable to do so. 20 Herod feared John, knowing him to be a righteous and holy man, and kept him in custody. When he heard him speak he was very much perplexed, yet he liked to listen to him. 21 She had an opportunity one day when Herod, on his birthday, gave a banquet for his courtiers, his military officers, and the leading men of Galilee. 22 Herodias's own daughter came in and performed a dance that delighted Herod and his guests. The king said to the girl, "Ask of me whatever you wish and I will grant it to you." 23* He even swore [many things] to her, "I will grant you whatever you ask of me, even to half of my kingdom." 24 She went out and said to her mother, "What shall I ask for?" She replied, "The head of John the Baptist." 25 The girl hurried back to the king's presence and made her request, "I want you to give me at once on a platter the head of John the Baptist." 26 The king was deeply distressed, but because of his oaths and the guests he did not wish to break his word to her. 27* So he promptly dispatched an executioner with orders to bring back his head. He went off and beheaded him in the prison. 28 He brought in the head on a platter and gave it to the girl. The girl in turn gave it to her mother. 29 When his disciples heard about it, they came and took his body and laid it in a tomb.

The Return of the Twelve

30*† The apostles gathered together with Jesus and reported all they had done and taught. 31*† He said to them, "Come away by yourselves to a deserted place and rest a while." People were coming and going in great numbers, and they had no opportunity even to eat. 32* So they went off in the boat by themselves to a deserted place. 33 People saw them leaving and many came to know about it. They hastened there on foot from all the towns and arrived at the place before them.

The Feeding of the Five Thousand

34 When he disembarked and saw the vast crowd, his heart was moved with pity for them, for they were like sheep without a shepherd; and he began to teach them many things. 35† By now it was already late and his disciples approached him and said, "This is a deserted place and it is already very late. 36 Dismiss them so that they can go to the surrounding farms and villages and buy themselves something to eat." 37 He said to them in reply, "Give them some food yourselves." But they said to him, "Are we to buy two hundred days' wages worth of food and give it to them to eat?" 38 He asked them, "How many loaves do you have? Go and see." And when they had found out they said, "Five loaves and two fish." 39 So he gave orders to have them sit down in groups on the green grass. 40† The people took their places in rows by hundreds and by fifties. 41† Then, taking the five loaves and the

---

6, 14–16: The various opinions about Jesus anticipate the theme of his identity that reaches its climax in 8, 27–30.

6, 14: *King Herod:* see the note on Mt 14, 1.

6, 17–29: Similarities are to be noted between Mark's account of the imprisonment and death of John the Baptist in this pericope, and that of the passion of Jesus (15, 1–47). Herod and Pilate, each in turn, acknowledges the holiness of life of one over whom he unjustly exercises the power of condemnation and death (26–27; 15, 9–10.14–15). The hatred of Herodias toward John parallels that of the Jewish leaders toward Jesus. After the deaths of John and of Jesus, well-disposed persons request the bodies of the victims of Herod and of Pilate in turn to give them respectful burial (29; 15, 45–46).

6, 19: *Herodias:* see the note on Mt 14, 3.

6, 30: *Apostles:* here, and in some manuscripts at 3, 14, Mark calls apostles (i.e., those sent forth) the Twelve whom Jesus sends as his emissaries, empowering them to preach, to expel demons, and to cure the sick (13). Only after Pentecost is the title used in the technical sense.

6, 31–34: The withdrawal of Jesus with his disciples to a desert place to rest attracts a great number of people to follow them. Toward this people of the new exodus Jesus is moved with pity; he satisfies their spiritual hunger by teaching them many things, thus gradually showing himself the faithful shepherd of a new Israel; cf Nm 27, 17; Ez 34, 15.

6, 35–44: See the note on Mt 14, 13–21. Compare this section with 8, 1–9. The various accounts of the multiplication of loaves and fishes, two each in Mark and in Matthew and one each in Luke and in John, indicate the wide interest of the early church in their eucharistic gatherings; see, e.g., v 41; 8, 6; 14, 22; and recall also the sign of bread in Ex 16; Dt 8, 3–16; Pss 78, 24–25; 105, 40; Wis 16, 20–21.

6, 40: *The people . . . in rows by hundreds and by fifties:* reminiscent of the groupings of Israelites encamped in the desert (Ex 18, 21–25) and of the wilderness tradition of the prophets depicting the transformation of the wasteland into pastures where the true shepherd feeds his flock (Ez 34, 25–26) and makes his people beneficiaries of messianic grace.

6, 41: On the language of this verse as eucharistic (cf 14, 22), see the notes on Mt 14, 19.20. Jesus observed the Jewish table ritual of blessing God before partaking of food.

6, 14–16: Lk 9, 7–8.
6, 14–29: Mt 14, 1–12.
6, 15: Mt 16, 14.
6, 17: Lk 3, 19–20.
6, 18: Lv 18, 16.
6, 23: Est 5, 3.

6, 27–28: Lk 9, 9.
6, 30: Lk 9, 10.
6, 31: Mk 3, 20; Mt 14, 13; Lk 9, 10.
6, 32–44: Mt 14, 13–21; Lk 9, 10–17; Jn 6, 1–13.

did **you KNOW?**

Those Thickheaded Disciples

The disciples in the Gospel of Mark seem unable to do anything right. During a storm at sea, they fail to put their trust in Jesus (4, 35–41). Then they cannot understand about the miracle of the bread because their hearts are hardened (6, 52). When Jesus gives them private tutoring sessions, they still fail to understand his teachings. Later, Peter proclaims that Jesus is the Messiah, but he ends up arguing with him after Jesus predicts that he will be a suffering Messiah (8, 27–33). Finally, when Jesus is arrested, the disciples all desert him (14, 50).

The author of Mark intentionally emphasizes the lack of faith of the original disciples in order to contrast it with the unexpected faith of people like the Syrophoenician woman in 7, 24–30. The Gospel makes the point that Jesus' true disciples are the ones who hear Jesus and place their faith in him. But don't count out the original disciples. Their journey is like most of ours, a lifelong experience of growing in faith and understanding. The Acts of the Apostles tells how they fearlessly preached the news about the risen Christ. Despite their human weakness, God works through them. That goes for us too!

▶ Mk 6, 30–52

two fish and looking up to heaven, he said the blessing, broke the loaves, and gave them to [his] disciples to set before the people; he also divided the two fish among them all. ⁴² They all ate and were satisfied. ⁴³ And they picked up twelve wicker baskets full of fragments and what was left of the fish. ⁴⁴ Those who ate [of the loaves] were five thousand men.

The Walking on the Water†

⁴⁵* Then he made his disciples get into the boat and precede him to the other side toward Bethsaida,† while he dismissed the crowd. ⁴⁶† And when he had taken leave of them, he went off to the mountain to pray. ⁴⁷ When it was evening, the boat was far out on the sea and he was alone on shore. ⁴⁸† Then he saw that they were tossed about while rowing, for the wind was against them. About the fourth watch of the night, he came towards them walking on the sea. He meant to pass by them. ⁴⁹ But when they saw him walking on the sea, they thought it was a ghost and cried out. ⁵⁰† They had all seen him and were terrified. But at once he spoke with them, "Take courage, it is I, do not be afraid!" ⁵¹ He got into the boat with them and the wind died down. They were [completely] astounded. ⁵²*† They had not understood the incident of the loaves. On the contrary, their hearts were hardened.

The Healings at Gennesaret

⁵³* After making the crossing, they came to land at Gennesaret and tied up there. ⁵⁴ As they were leaving the boat, people immediately recognized him. ⁵⁵ They scurried about the surrounding country and began to bring in the sick on mats to wherever they heard he was. ⁵⁶* Whatever villages or towns or countryside he entered, they laid the sick in the marketplaces and begged him that they might touch only the tassel on his cloak; and as many as touched it were healed.

The Tradition of the Elders

7 ¹*† Now when the Pharisees with some scribes who had come from Jerusalem gathered around

---

6, 45–52: See the note on Mt 14, 22–33.

6, 45: *To the other side toward Bethsaida:* a village at the northeastern shore of the Sea of Galilee.

6, 46: *He went off to the mountain to pray:* see 1, 35–38. In Jn 6, 15 Jesus withdrew to evade any involvement in the false messianic hopes of the multitude.

6, 48: *Walking on the sea:* see the notes on Mt 14, 22–33 and on Jn 6, 19.

6, 50: *It is I, do not be afraid!:* literally, "I am." This may reflect the divine revelatory formula of Ex 3, 14; Is 41, 4.10.14; 43, 1–3.10.13. Mark implies the hidden identity of Jesus as Son of God.

6, 52: *They had not understood . . . the loaves:* the revelatory character of this sign and that of the walking on the sea completely escaped the disciples. *Their hearts were hardened:* in 3, 5–6 hardness of heart was attributed to those who did not accept Jesus and plotted his death. Here the same disposition prevents the disciples

from comprehending Jesus' self-revelation through signs; cf 8, 17.

7, 1–23: See the note on Mt 15, 1–20. Against the Pharisees' narrow, legalistic, and external practices of piety in matters of purification (2–5), external worship (6–7), and observance of commandments, Jesus sets in opposition the true moral intent of the divine law (8–13). But he goes beyond contrasting the law and Pharisaic interpretation of it. The parable of vv 14–15 in effect sets aside the law itself in respect to clean and unclean food. He thereby opens the way for unity between Jew and Gentile in the kingdom of God, intimated by Jesus' departure for pagan territory beyond Galilee. For similar contrast see 2, 1–3, 6; 3, 20–35; 6, 1–6.

6, 45–51: Mt 14, 22–32; Jn 6,   **6, 56:** Mk 5, 27–28;
    15–21.   Acts 5, 15.
6, 52: Mk 4, 13.   **7, 1–23:** Mt 15, 1–20.
6, 53–56: Mt 14, 34–36.

him, ² they observed that some of his disciples ate their meals with unclean, that is, unwashed, hands. ³† (For the Pharisees and, in fact, all Jews, do not eat without carefully washing their hands, keeping the tradition of the elders. ⁴ And on coming from the marketplace they do not eat without purifying themselves. And there are many other things that they have traditionally observed, the purification of cups and jugs and kettles [and beds].) ⁵† So the Pharisees and scribes questioned him, "Why do your disciples not follow the tradition of the elders but instead eat a meal with unclean hands?" ⁶* He responded, "Well did Isaiah prophesy about you hypocrites, as it is written:

'This people honors me with their lips,
    but their hearts are far from me;
⁷ In vain do they worship me,
    teaching as doctrines human precepts.'

⁸ You disregard God's commandment but cling to human tradition." ⁹ He went on to say, "How well you have set aside the commandment of God in order to uphold your tradition! ¹⁰* For Moses said, 'Honor your father and your mother,' and 'Whoever curses father or mother shall die.' ¹¹† Yet you say, 'If a person says to father or mother, "Any support you might have had from me is qorban"' (meaning, dedicated to God), ¹² you allow him to do nothing more for his father or mother. ¹³ You nullify the word of God in favor of your tradition that you have handed on. And you do many such things."
¹⁴* He summoned the crowd again and said to them, "Hear me, all of you, and understand. ¹⁵ Nothing that enters one from outside can defile that person; but the things that come out from within are what defile." [¹⁶]†

¹⁷*† When he got home away from the crowd his disciples questioned him about the parable. ¹⁸ He said to them, "Are even you likewise without understanding? Do you not realize that everything that goes into a person from outside cannot defile, ¹⁹*† since it enters not the heart but the stomach and passes out into the latrine?" (Thus he declared all foods clean.) ²⁰ "But what comes out of a person, that is what defiles. ²¹* From within people, from their hearts, come evil thoughts, unchastity, theft, murder, ²² adultery, greed, malice, deceit, licentiousness, envy, blasphemy, arrogance, folly. ²³ All these evils come from within and they defile."

The Syrophoenician Woman's Faith

²⁴*† From that place he went off to the district of Tyre. He entered a house and wanted no one to know about it, but he could not escape notice. ²⁵ Soon a woman whose daughter had an unclean spirit heard about him. She came and fell at his feet. ²⁶* The woman was a Greek, a Syrophoenician by birth, and she begged him to drive the demon out of her daughter. ²⁷† He said to her, "Let the children

Sin's Source

LIVE IT!

Some people believe that spiritual depth is measured by how well certain rules or religious practices are followed. Jesus reminds us in Mk 7, 14–15 that our greater concern ought to be with what is in our heart. What is in our heart should have a greater effect on our spiritual life than do outside sources.

▶ Mk 7, 14–23

---

†——

7, 3: *Carefully washing their hands:* refers to ritual purification.
7, 5: *Tradition of the elders:* the body of detailed, unwritten, human laws regarded by the scribes and Pharisees to have the same binding force as that of the Mosaic law; cf Gal 1, 14.
7, 11: *Qorban:* a formula for a gift to God, dedicating the offering to the temple, so that the giver might continue to use it for himself but not give it to others, even needy parents.
7, 16: Verse 16, "Anyone who has ears to hear ought to hear," is omitted because it is lacking in some of the best Greek manuscripts and was probably transferred here by scribes from 4, (9).23.
7, 17: *Away from the crowd . . . the parable:* in this context of privacy the term *parable* refers to something hidden, about to be revealed to the disciples; cf 4, 10—11.34. Jesus sets the Mosaic food laws in the context of the kingdom of God where they are abrogated, and he declares moral defilement the only cause of uncleanness.
7, 19: *(Thus he declared all foods clean.):* if this bold declaration goes back to Jesus, its force was not realized among Jewish Christians in the early church; cf Acts 10, 1—11, 18.
7, 24–37: The withdrawal of Jesus to the district of Tyre may

have been for a respite (24), but he soon moved onward to Sidon and, by way of the Sea of Galilee, to the Decapolis. These districts provided a Gentile setting for the extension of his ministry of healing because the people there acknowledged his power (29.37). The actions attributed to Jesus (33–35) were also used by healers of the time.
7, 27–28: The figure of a household in which children at table are fed first and then their leftover food is given to the dogs under the table is used effectively to acknowledge the prior claim of the Jews to the ministry of Jesus; however, Jesus accedes to the Gentile woman's plea for the cure of her afflicted daughter because of her faith.

*——
7, 6: Is 29, 13.
7, 10: Ex 21, 17; Lv 20, 9; Dt
    5, 16; Eph 6, 2.
7, 14–23: Mt 15, 10–20.
7, 17: Mk 4, 10.13.

7, 19: Acts 10, 15.
7, 21: Jer 17, 9.
7, 24–30: Mt 15, 21–28.
7, 26: Mt 8, 29.

be fed first. For it is not right to take the food of the children and throw it to the dogs." 28 She replied and said to him, "Lord, even the dogs under the table eat the children's scraps." 29 Then he said to her, "For saying this, you may go. The demon has gone out of your daughter." 30 When the woman went home, she found the child lying in bed and the demon gone.

The Healing of a Deaf Man

31* Again he left the district of Tyre and went by way of Sidon to the Sea of Galilee, into the district of the Decapolis. 32 And people brought to him a deaf man who had a speech impediment and begged him to lay his hand on him. 33 He took him off by himself away from the crowd. He put his finger into the man's ears and, spitting, touched his tongue; 34 then he looked up to heaven and groaned, and said to him, "*Ephphatha!*" (that is, "Be opened!") 35 And [immediately] the man's ears were opened, his speech impediment was removed, and he spoke plainly. 36† He ordered them not to tell anyone. But the more he ordered them not to, the more they proclaimed it. 37* They were exceedingly astonished and they said,

"He has done all things well. He makes the deaf hear and [the] mute speak."

The Feeding of the Four Thousand

8 1*† In those days when there again was a great crowd without anything to eat, he summoned the disciples and said, 2 "My heart is moved with pity for the crowd, because they have been with me now for three days and have nothing to eat. 3 If I send them away hungry to their homes, they will collapse on the way, and some of them have come a great distance." 4 His disciples answered him, "Where can anyone get enough bread to satisfy them here in this deserted place?" 5 Still he asked them, "How many loaves do you have?" "Seven," they replied. 6† He ordered the crowd to sit down on the ground. Then, taking the seven loaves he gave thanks, broke them, and gave them to his disciples to distribute, and they distributed them to the crowd. 7 They also had a few fish. He said the blessing over them and ordered them distributed also. 8 They ate and were satisfied. They picked up the fragments left over—seven baskets. 9 There were about four thousand people.

He dismissed them 10 and got into the boat with his disciples and came to the region of Dalmanutha.

The Demand for a Sign

11*† The Pharisees came forward and began to argue with him, seeking from him a sign from heaven to test him.* 12 He sighed from the depth of his spirit and said, "Why does this generation seek a sign? Amen, I say to you, no sign will be given to this generation." 13 Then he left them, got into the boat again, and went off to the other shore.

The Leaven of the Pharisees

14* They had forgotten to bring bread, and they had only one loaf with them in the boat. 15† He enjoined them, "Watch out, guard against the leaven of the Pharisees and the leaven of Herod." 16 They concluded among themselves that it was because they had no bread. 17* When he became aware of this he said to them, "Why do you conclude that it is because

---

†
7, 36: *The more they proclaimed it:* the same verb *proclaim* attributed here to the crowd in relation to the miracles of Jesus is elsewhere used in Mark for the preaching of the gospel on the part of Jesus, of his disciples, and of the Christian community (1, 14; 13, 10; 14, 9). Implied in the action of the crowd is a recognition of the salvific mission of Jesus; see the note on Mt 11, 5–6.

8, 1–10: The two accounts of the multiplication of loaves and fishes (8, 1–10 and 6, 31–44) have eucharistic significance. Their similarity of structure and themes but dissimilarity of detail are considered by many to refer to a single event that, however, developed in two distinct traditions, one Jewish Christian and the other Gentile Christian, since Jesus in Mark's presentation (7, 24–37) has extended his saving mission to the Gentiles.

8, 6: See the note on 6, 41.

8, 11–12: The objection of the Pharisees that Jesus' miracles are

unsatisfactory for proving the arrival of God's kingdom is comparable to the request of the crowd for a sign in Jn 6, 30–31. Jesus' response shows that a sign originating in human demand will not be provided; cf Nm 14, 11.22.

8, 15: *The leaven of the Pharisees . . . of Herod:* the corruptive action of leaven (1 Cor 5, 6–8; Gal 5, 9) was an apt symbol of the evil dispositions both of the Pharisees (11–13; 7, 5–13) and of Herod (6, 14–29) toward Jesus. The disciples of Jesus are warned against sharing such rebellious attitudes toward Jesus; cf vv 17, 21.

*
7, 31–37: Mt 15, 29–31.
7, 37: Mt 15, 31.
8, 1–10: Mk 6, 34–44; Mt 15, 32–39.

8, 11–13: Mt 12, 38–39; 16, 1–4.
8, 11: Lk 11, 16.
8, 14–21: Mt 16, 5–12; Lk 12, 1.
8, 17: Mk 4, 13.

you have no bread? Do you not yet understand or comprehend? Are your hearts hardened? [18]* Do you have eyes and not see, ears and not hear? And do you not remember, [19] when I broke the five loaves for the five thousand, how many wicker baskets full of fragments you picked up?" They answered him, "Twelve." [20] "When I broke the seven loaves for the four thousand, how many full baskets of fragments did you pick up?" They answered [him], "Seven." [21] He said to them, "Do you still not understand?"

The Blind Man of Bethsaida

[22]† When they arrived at Bethsaida, they brought to him a blind man and begged him to touch him. [23]* He took the blind man by the hand and led him outside the village. Putting spittle on his eyes he laid his hands on him and asked, "Do you see anything?" [24] Looking up he replied, "I see people looking like trees and walking." [25] Then he laid hands on his eyes a second time and he saw clearly;

his sight was restored and he could see everything distinctly. [26] Then he sent him home and said, "Do not even go into the village."

III: The Mystery Begins to Be Revealed

Peter's Confession about Jesus

[27]*† Now Jesus and his disciples set out for the villages of Caesarea Philippi. Along the way he asked his disciples, "Who do people say that I am?" [28] They said in reply, "John the Baptist, others Elijah, still others one of the prophets." [29] And he asked them, "But who do you say that I am?" Peter said to him in reply, "You are the Messiah." [30] Then he warned them not to tell anyone about him.

The First Prediction of the Passion

[31]*† He began to teach them that the Son of Man must suffer greatly and be rejected by the elders, the chief priests, and the scribes, and be killed, and rise

M
K

Total Commitment

LIVE IT!

In Mk 8, 34–38, Jesus calls for a total commitment requiring great sacrifice. He tells the disciples that to be truly alive, they must be willing to deny themselves and take up their own crosses. The cross symbolizes denying the way of the world and embracing the way of Jesus. It means tough self-sacrifice and, at times, a willingness to suffer for what is right.

But what does it mean to deny ourselves and take up our own crosses?

When we deny ourselves, it means that we cannot be fooled by what the world says about being truly alive. The world tells us to buy our happiness with wealth, power, prestige, or selfish pleasure. But those things actually make us feel less alive and more anxious.

Taking up our own crosses means that we need to be willing to cling to the right things—forgiveness, justice, service, and compassion for the poor and unpopular—even if it brings us suffering and pain. Being committed to Jesus and these virtues or "right things" will bring us real life, true freedom, joy, and inner peace.

The way of the cross is the path to resurrection and eternal life.

▸ Mk 8, 34–38

---

† **8, 22–26:** Jesus' actions and the gradual cure of the blind man probably have the same purpose as in the case of the deaf man (7, 31–37). Some commentators regard the cure as an intended symbol of the gradual enlightenment of the disciples concerning Jesus' messiahship.

8, 27–30: This episode is the turning point in Mark's account of Jesus in his public ministry. Popular opinions concur in regarding him as a prophet. The disciples by contrast believe him to be the Messiah. Jesus acknowledges this identification but prohibits them from making his messianic office known to avoid confusing it with ambiguous contemporary ideas on the nature of that office. See further the notes on Mt 16, 13–20.

8, 31: *Son of Man:* an enigmatic title. It is used in Dn 7, 13–14 as a symbol of "the saints of the Most High," the faithful Israelites who receive the everlasting kingdom from the Ancient One (God). They are represented by a human figure that contrasts with the various beasts who represent the previous kingdoms of the earth. In the Jewish apocryphal books of 1 Enoch and 4 Ezra the "Son of Man" is not, as in Daniel, a group, but a unique figure of extraordinary spir-

itual endowments, who will be revealed as the one through whom the everlasting kingdom decreed by God will be established. It is possible though doubtful that this individualization of the Son of Man figure had been made in Jesus' time, and therefore his use of the title in that sense is questionable. Of itself, this expression means simply a human being, or, indefinitely, someone, and there are evidences of this use in pre-Christian times. Its use in the New Testament is probably due to Jesus' speaking of himself in that way, "a human being," and the later church's taking this in the sense of the Jewish apocrypha and applying it to him with that meaning. *Rejected by the elders, the chief priests, and the scribes:* the supreme council called the Sanhedrin was made up of seventy-one members of these three groups and presided over by the high priest. It exercised authority over the Jews in religious matters. See the note on Mt 8, 20.

* 8, 18: Jer 5, 21; Ez 12, 2.   8, 31–38: Mt 16, 21–27; Lk 9,
  8, 23: Mk 7, 33; Jn 9, 6.   22–26.
8, 27–30: Mt 16, 13–20; Lk 9,
  18–21.

MK

after three days. ³² He spoke this openly. Then Peter took him aside and began to rebuke him. ³³ At this he turned around and, looking at his disciples, rebuked Peter and said, "Get behind me, Satan. You are thinking not as God does, but as human beings do."

The Conditions of Discipleship

³⁴*† He summoned the crowd with his disciples and said to them, "Whoever wishes to come after me must deny himself, take up his cross, and follow me. ³⁵*† For whoever wishes to save his life will lose it, but whoever loses his life for my sake and that of the gospel will save it. ³⁶ What profit is there for one to gain the whole world and forfeit his life? ³⁷ What could one give in exchange for his life? ³⁸* Whoever is ashamed of me and of my words in this faithless and sinful generation, the Son of Man will be ashamed of when he comes in his Father's glory with the holy angels."

9 ¹*† He also said to them, "Amen, I say to you, there are some standing here who will not taste death until they see that the kingdom of God has come in power."

The Transfiguration of Jesus

²*† After six days Jesus took Peter, James, and John and led them up a high mountain apart by themselves. And he was transfigured before them, ³ and his clothes became dazzling white, such as no fuller on earth could bleach them. ⁴ Then Elijah appeared to them along with Moses, and they were conversing with Jesus. ⁵† Then Peter said to Jesus in reply, "Rabbi, it is good that we are here! Let us make three tents: one for you, one for Moses, and one for Elijah." ⁶ He hardly knew what to say, they were so terrified. ⁷† Then a cloud came, casting a shadow over them; then from the cloud came a voice, "This is my beloved Son. Listen to him." ⁸ Suddenly, looking around, they no longer saw anyone but Jesus alone with them.

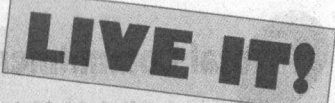

The Transfiguration: On Top of the World

The story of the Transfiguration takes place after Jesus tells his disciples about his coming suffering, death, and Resurrection (Mk 8, 31). They need hope and a boost of faith. Jesus takes three disciples to a mountaintop to see the Kingdom of God coming in power. The three disciples see Jesus in a glorious state talking with Moses and Elijah.

God revealed the secret about Jesus to three of his disciples. The two Old Testament figures are key symbols: Moses represents the Law, and Elijah, the prophets. The message is clear: Jesus is the person who fulfills the Law and who realizes God's promises to the prophets. It was a profound religious experience. The disciples glimpsed Jesus' glory, but they could not understand it. Understanding came only after Jesus' Resurrection.

It is understandable to want to found our faith on mountaintop experiences (see "Spiritual Highs," Lk 9, 28–36). But though profound religious experiences enliven our faith, listening and following Jesus' words daily are what really fortify our faith and give us a new life.

▶ Mk 9, 2–8

8, 34–35: This utterance of Jesus challenges all believers to authentic discipleship and total commitment to himself through self-renunciation and acceptance of the cross of suffering, even to the sacrifice of life itself. *Whoever wishes to save his life will lose it . . . will save it:* an expression of the ambivalence of life and its contrasting destiny. Life seen as mere self-centered earthly existence and lived in denial of Christ ends in destruction, but when lived in loyalty to Christ, despite earthly death, it arrives at fullness of life.

8, 35: *For my sake and that of the gospel:* Mark here, as at 10, 29, equates Jesus with the gospel.

9, 1: *There are some standing . . . come in power:* understood by some to refer to the establishment by God's power of his kingdom on earth in and through the church; more likely, as understood by others, a reference to the imminent parousia.

9, 2–8: Mark and Mt 17, 1 place the transfiguration of Jesus six days after the first prediction of his passion and death and his instruction to the disciples on the doctrine of the cross; Lk 9, 28 has "about eight days." Thus the transfiguration counterbalances the prediction of the passion by affording certain of the disciples insight into the divine glory that Jesus possessed. His glory will overcome his death and that of his disciples; cf 2 Cor 3, 18; 2 Pt 1, 16–19. The heavenly voice (7) prepares the disciples to understand that in the divine plan Jesus must die ignominiously before his messianic glory is made manifest; cf Lk 24, 25–27. See further the note on Mt 17, 1–8.

9, 5: Moses and Elijah represent respectively law and prophecy in the Old Testament and are linked to Mt. Sinai; cf Ex 19, 16—20, 17; 1 Kgs 19, 2.8–14. They now appear with Jesus as witnesses to the fulfillment of the law and the prophets taking place in the person of Jesus as he appears in glory.

9, 7: *A cloud came, casting a shadow over them:* even the disciples enter into the mystery of his glorification. In the Old Testament the cloud covered the meeting tent, indicating the Lord's presence in the midst of his people (Ex 40, 34–35) and came to rest upon the temple in Jerusalem at the time of its dedication (1 Kgs 8, 10).

8, 34: Mt 10, 38–39; 16, 24–27; Lk 14, 26–27.
8, 35: Jn 12, 25.
8, 38: Mt 10, 33; Lk 12, 8.

9, 1: Mt 16, 28; Lk 9, 27.
9, 2–13: Mt 17, 1–13; Lk 9, 28–36.

The Coming of Elijah

⁹*† As they were coming down from the mountain, he charged them not to relate what they had seen to anyone, except when the Son of Man had risen from the dead. ¹⁰ So they kept the matter to themselves, questioning what rising from the dead meant. ¹¹* Then they asked him, "Why do the scribes say that Elijah must come first?" ¹² He told them, "Elijah will indeed come first and restore all things, yet how is it written regarding the Son of Man that he must suffer greatly and be treated with contempt? ¹³* But I tell you that Elijah has come and they did to him whatever they pleased, as it is written of him."

The Healing of a Boy with a Demon

¹⁴*† When they came to the disciples, they saw a large crowd around them and scribes arguing with them. ¹⁵ Immediately on seeing him, the whole crowd was utterly amazed. They ran up to him and greeted him. ¹⁶ He asked them, "What are you arguing about with them?" ¹⁷ Someone from the crowd answered him, "Teacher, I have brought to you my son possessed by a mute spirit. ¹⁸ Wherever it seizes him, it throws him down; he foams at the mouth, grinds his teeth, and becomes rigid. I asked your disciples to drive it out, but they were unable to do so." ¹⁹ He said to them in reply, "O faithless generation, how long will I be with you? How long will I endure you? Bring him to me." ²⁰ They brought the boy to him. And when he saw him, the spirit immediately threw the boy into convulsions. As he fell to the ground, he began to roll around and foam at the mouth. ²¹ Then he questioned his father, "How long has this been happening to him?" He replied, "Since childhood. ²² It has often thrown him into fire and into water to kill him. But if you can do anything, have compassion on us and help us." ²³ Jesus said to him, " 'If you can!' Everything is possible to one who has faith." ²⁴ Then the boy's father cried out, "I do believe, help my unbelief!" ²⁵ Jesus, on seeing a crowd rapidly gathering, rebuked the unclean spirit and said to it, "Mute and deaf spirit, I command you: come out of him and never enter him again!" ²⁶ Shouting and throwing the boy into convulsions, it came out. He became like a corpse, which caused many to say, "He is dead!" ²⁷ But Jesus took him by the hand, raised him, and he stood up. ²⁸ When he entered the house, his disciples asked him in private, "Why could we not drive it out?" ²⁹† He said to them, "This kind can only come out through prayer."

"I Do Believe, Help My Unbelief!"

Saying that we believe in something may not be enough to prove that we truly believe. Faith in God means knowing that God is totally with us even when it doesn't seem that way!

When we have nagging doubts whether even God can help us in a particular situation—like the father in Mk 9, 24—we can turn to God by praying for faith. We don't have to have our faith or our life perfectly together before we ask God for help. The test of faith is trusting that God cares for us and provides what we need, even when our prayers are not answered in the way we desire.

▸ Mk 9, 14–29

The Second Prediction of the Passion

³⁰* They left from there and began a journey through Galilee, but he did not wish anyone to know about it.* ³¹ He was teaching his disciples and telling them, "The Son of Man is to be handed over to men and they will kill him, and three days after his death he will rise." ³² But they did not understand the saying, and they were afraid to question him.

IV: The Full Revelation of the Mystery

The Greatest in the Kingdom

³³*† They came to Capernaum and, once inside the house, he began to ask them, "What were you

---

† **9, 9–13:** At the transfiguration of Jesus his disciples had seen Elijah. They were perplexed because, according to the rabbinical interpretation of Mal 3, 23–24, Elijah was to come first. Jesus' response shows that Elijah has come, in the person of John the Baptist, to prepare for the day of the Lord. Jesus *must suffer greatly and be treated with contempt* (12) like the Baptist (13); cf 6, 17–29.

9, 14–29: The disciples' failure to effect a cure seems to reflect unfavorably on Jesus (14–18.22). In response Jesus exposes their lack of trust in God (19) and scores their lack of prayer (29), i.e., of conscious reliance on God's power when acting in Jesus' name. For Matthew, see the note on 17, 14–20. Lk 9, 37–43 centers attention on Jesus' sovereign power.

9, 29: *This kind can only come out through prayer:* a variant reading adds "and through fasting."

9, 33–37: Mark probably intends this incident and the sayings that follow as commentary on the disciples' lack of understanding (32). Their role in Jesus' work is one of service, especially to the poor and lowly. Children were the symbol Jesus used for the *anawim*, the poor in spirit, the lowly in the Christian community.

9, 9: Mk 8, 31.
9, 11–12: Is 53, 3; Mal 3, 23.
9, 13: 1 Kgs 19, 2–10.
9, 14–29: Mt 17, 14–21; Lk 9, 37–43.
9, 30: Jn 7, 1.
9, 30–32: Mk 8, 31; Mt 17, 22–23; Lk 9, 43–45.
9, 33–37: Mt 18, 1–5; Lk 9, 46–48.

arguing about on the way?" 34 But they remained silent. They had been discussing among themselves on the way who was the greatest. 35* Then he sat down, called the Twelve, and said to them, "If anyone wishes to be first, he shall be the last of all and the servant of all." 36 Taking a child he placed it in their midst, and putting his arms around it he said to them, 37* "Whoever receives one child such as this in my name, receives me; and whoever receives me, receives not me but the One who sent me."

Another Exorcist

38*† John said to him, "Teacher, we saw someone driving out demons in your name, and we tried to prevent him because he does not follow us." 39 Jesus replied, "Do not prevent him. There is no one who performs a mighty deed in my name who can at the same time speak ill of me. 40* For whoever is not against us is for us. 41* Anyone who gives you a cup of water to drink because you belong to Christ, amen, I say to you, will surely not lose his reward.

Temptations to Sin

42* "Whoever causes one of these little ones who believe [in me] to sin, it would be better for him if a great millstone were put around his neck and he were thrown into the sea. 43† If your hand causes you to sin, cut it off. It is better for you to enter into life maimed than with two hands to go into Gehenna, into the unquenchable fire. [44]† 45 And if your foot causes you to sin, cut if off. It is better for you to enter into life crippled than with two feet to be thrown into Gehenna. [46]† 47 And if your eye causes you to sin, pluck it out. Better for you to enter into the kingdom of God with one eye than with two eyes to be thrown into Gehenna, 48* where 'their worm does not die, and the fire is not quenched.'

The Simile of Salt

49† "Everyone will be salted with fire. 50* Salt is good, but if salt becomes insipid, with what will you restore its flavor? Keep salt in yourselves and you will have peace with one another."

Marriage and Divorce

10 1 He set out from there and went into the district of Judea [and] across the Jordan. Again crowds gathered around him and, as was his custom, he again taught them. 2*† The Pharisees approached and asked, "Is it lawful for a husband to divorce his wife?" They were testing him. 3 He said to them in reply, "What did Moses command you?" 4* They replied, "Moses permitted him to write a bill of divorce and dismiss her." 5 But Jesus told them, "Because of the hardness of your hearts he wrote you this commandment. 6* But from the beginning of creation, 'God made them male and female. 7* For this reason a man shall leave his father and mother [and be joined to his wife], 8 and the two shall become one flesh.' So they are no longer two but one flesh. 9 Therefore what God has joined together, no human being must separate." 10 In the house the disciples again questioned him about this. 11* He said to them, "Whoever divorces his wife and marries another commits adultery against her; 12 and if she divorces her husband and marries another, she commits adultery."

Blessing of the Children

13* And people were bringing children to him that he might touch them, but the disciples rebuked them.* 14 When Jesus saw this he became indignant and said to them, "Let the children come to me; do not prevent them, for the kingdom of God belongs to such as these. 15*† Amen, I say to you, whoever does not accept the kingdom of God like a child will not enter it." 16 Then he embraced them and blessed them, placing his hands on them.

9, 38–41: Jesus warns against jealousy and intolerance toward others, such as exorcists who do *not follow us.* The saying in v 40 is a broad principle of the divine tolerance. Even the smallest courtesies shown to those who teach in Jesus' name do not go unrewarded.

9, 43.45.47: *Gehenna:* see the note on Mt 5, 22.

9, 44.46: These verses, lacking in some important early manuscripts, are here omitted as scribal additions. They simply repeat v 48, itself a modified citation of Is 66, 24.

9, 49: *Everyone will be salted with fire:* so the better manuscripts. Some add "every sacrifice will be salted with salt." The purifying and preservative use of salt in food (Lv 2, 13) and the refinement effected through fire refer here to comparable effects in the spiritual life of the disciples of Jesus.

10, 2–9: In the dialogue between Jesus and the Pharisees on the subject of divorce, Jesus declares that the law of Moses permitted divorce (Dt 24, 1) only *because of the hardness of your hearts* (4–5). In citing Gn 1, 27 and 2, 24, Jesus proclaims permanence to be the divine intent from the beginning concerning human marriage (6–8). He reaffirms this with the declaration that *what God has joined*

together, no human being must separate (9). See further the notes on Mt 5, 31–32 and 19, 3–9.

10, 15: *Whoever does not accept the kingdom of God like a child:* i.e., in total dependence upon and obedience to the gospel; cf Mt 18, 3–4.

9, 35: Mt 20, 27.
9, 37: Mt 10, 40; 18, 5; Jn 13, 20.
9, 38–41: Nm 11, 28; Lk 9, 49–50; 1 Cor 12, 3.
9, 40: Mt 12, 30.
9, 41: Mt 10, 42; 1 Cor 3, 23.
9, 42–47: Mt 5, 29–30; 18, 6–9; Lk 17, 1–2.
9, 48: Is 66, 24.
9, 50: Lv 2, 13; Mt 5, 13; Lk 14, 34–35; Col 4, 6.

10, 2–12: Mt 19, 3–9.
10, 4: Dt 24, 1–4.
10, 6: Gn 1, 27.
10, 7–8: Gn 2, 24; 1 Cor 6, 16; Eph 5, 31.
10, 11–12: Mt 5, 32; Lk 16, 18; 1 Cor 7, 10–11.
10, 13–16: Mt 19, 13–15; Lk 18, 15–17.
10, 13: Lk 9, 47.
10, 15: Mt 18, 3.

The Rich Man

17* As he was setting out on a journey, a man ran up, knelt down before him, and asked him, "Good teacher, what must I do to inherit eternal life?" 18† Jesus answered him, "Why do you call me good? No one is good but God alone. 19* You know the commandments: 'You shall not kill; you shall not commit adultery; you shall not steal; you shall not bear false witness; you shall not defraud; honor your father and your mother.' " 20 He replied and said to him, "Teacher, all of these I have observed from my youth." 21 Jesus, looking at him, loved him and said to him, "You are lacking in one thing. Go, sell what you have, and give to [the] poor and you will have treasure in heaven; then come, follow me." 22 At that statement his face fell, and he went away sad, for he had many possessions.

23*† Jesus looked around and said to his disciples, "How hard it is for those who have wealth to enter the kingdom of God!" 24 The disciples were amazed at his words. So Jesus again said to them in reply, "Children, how hard it is to enter the kingdom of God! 25 It is easier for a camel to pass through [the] eye of [a] needle than for one who is rich to enter the kingdom of God." 26 They were exceedingly astonished and said among themselves, "Then who can be saved?" 27 Jesus looked at them and said, "For human beings it is impossible, but not for God. All things are possible for God." 28 Peter began to say to him, "We have given up everything and followed you." 29 Jesus said, "Amen, I say to you, there is no one who has given up house or brothers or sisters or mother or father or children or lands for my sake and for the sake of the gospel 30 who will not receive a hundred times more now in this present age: houses and brothers and sisters and mothers and children and lands, with persecutions, and eternal life in the age to come. 31* But many that are first will be last, and [the] last will be first."

The Third Prediction of the Passion

32* They were on the way, going up to Jerusalem, and Jesus went ahead of them. They were amazed, and those who followed were afraid. Taking the Twelve aside again, he began to tell them what was going to happen to him. 33 "Behold, we are going up to Jerusalem, and the Son of Man will be handed over to the chief priests and the scribes, and they will condemn him to death and hand him over to the Gentiles 34 who will mock him, spit upon him, scourge him, and put him to death, but after three days he will rise."

Ambition of James and John

35* Then James and John, the sons of Zebedee, came to him and said to him, "Teacher, we want you to do for us whatever we ask of you." 36 He replied, "What do you wish [me] to do for you?" 37 They answered him, "Grant that in your glory we may sit one at your right and the other at your left." 38*† Jesus said to them, "You do not know what you are asking. Can you drink the cup that I drink or be baptized with the baptism with which I am baptized?" 39 They said to him, "We can." Jesus said to them, "The cup that I drink, you will drink, and

Catholic Connections

TRUE GREATNESS

The disciples think that Jesus is going to be a great king, and they want to share in his power and glory. Instead, Jesus tells them that they must be servants. Servanthood is the true mark of greatness. That is why the pope is sometimes called the servant of the servants of God. Jesus not only taught true servanthood but lived it by giving up his life as a ransom for all.

▸ Mk 10, 35–45

10, 18: *Why do you call me good?*: Jesus repudiates the term "good" for himself and directs it to God, the source of all goodness who alone can grant the gift of eternal life; cf Mt 19, 16–17.

10, 23–27: In the Old Testament wealth and material goods are considered a sign of God's favor (Jb 1, 10; Ps 128, 1–2; Is 3, 10). The words of Jesus in 23–25 provoke astonishment among the disciples because of their apparent contradiction of the Old Testament concept (24.26). Since wealth, power, and merit generate false security, Jesus rejects them utterly as a claim to enter the kingdom. Achievement of salvation is beyond human capability and depends solely on the goodness of God who offers it as a gift (27).

10, 38–40: *Can you drink the cup . . . I am baptized?*: the metaphor of drinking the cup is used in the Old Testament to refer to acceptance of the destiny assigned by God; see the note on Ps 11, 6.

In Jesus' case, this involves divine judgment on sin that Jesus the innocent one is to expiate on behalf of the guilty (14, 24; Is 53, 5). His baptism is to be his crucifixion and death for the salvation of the human race; cf Lk 12, 50. The request of James and John for a share in the glory (35–37) must of necessity involve a share in Jesus' sufferings, the endurance of tribulation and suffering for the gospel (39). The authority of assigning places of honor in the kingdom is reserved to God (40).

10, 17–31: Mt 19, 16–30; Lk 18, 18–30.
10, 19: Ex 20, 12–16; Dt 5, 16–21.
10, 23: Prv 11, 28.
10, 31: Mt 19, 30; Lk 13, 30.
10, 32–34: Mk 8, 31; Mt 20, 17–19; Lk 18, 31–33.
10, 35–45: Mt 20, 20–28.
10, 38: Lk 12, 50.

with the baptism with which I am baptized, you will be baptized; 40 but to sit at my right or at my left is not mine to give but is for those for whom it has been prepared." 41 When the ten heard this, they became indignant at James and John. 42*† Jesus summoned them and said to them, "You know that those who are recognized as rulers over the Gentiles lord it over them, and their great ones make their authority over them felt. 43 But it shall not be so among you. Rather, whoever wishes to be great among you will be your servant; 44 whoever wishes to be first among you will be the slave of all. 45 For the Son of Man did not come to be served but to serve and to give his life as a ransom for many."

The Blind Bartimaeus

46*† They came to Jericho. And as he was leaving Jericho with his disciples and a sizable crowd, Bartimaeus, a blind man, the son of Timaeus, sat by the roadside begging. 47 On hearing that it was Jesus of Nazareth, he began to cry out and say, "Jesus, son of David, have pity on me." 48 And many rebuked him, telling him to be silent. But he kept calling out all the more, "Son of David, have pity on me." 49 Jesus stopped and said, "Call him." So they called the blind man, saying to him, "Take courage; get up, he is calling you." 50 He threw aside his cloak, sprang up, and came to Jesus. 51 Jesus said to him in reply, "What do you want me to do for you?" The blind man replied to him, "Master, I want to see." 52 Jesus told him, "Go your way; your faith has saved you." Immediately he received his sight and followed him on the way.

The Entry into Jerusalem

11 1*† When they drew near to Jerusalem, to Bethphage and Bethany at the Mount of Olives, he sent two of his disciples 2 and said to them, "Go into the village opposite you, and immediately on entering it, you will find a colt tethered on which no one has ever sat. Untie it and bring it here. 3 If anyone should say to you, 'Why are you doing this?' reply, 'The Master has need of it and will send it back here at once.' " 4 So they went off and found a colt tethered at a gate outside on the street, and they untied it. 5 Some of the bystanders said

to them, "What are you doing, untying the colt?" 6 They answered them just as Jesus had told them to, and they permitted them to do it. 7 So they brought the colt to Jesus and put their cloaks over it. And he sat on it. 8 Many people spread their cloaks on the road, and others spread leafy branches that they had cut from the fields. 9* Those preceding him as well as those following kept crying out:

"Hosanna!
Blessed is he who comes in the name of
the Lord!
10 Blessed is the kingdom of our father David
that is to come!
Hosanna in the highest!"

11* He entered Jerusalem and went into the temple area. He looked around at everything and, since it was already late, went out to Bethany with the Twelve.

Jesus Curses a Fig Tree

12*† The next day as they were leaving Bethany he was hungry. 13 Seeing from a distance a fig tree in leaf, he went over to see if he could find anything on it. When he reached it he found nothing but leaves; it was not the time for figs. 14 And he said to it in reply, "May no one ever eat of your fruit again!" And his disciples heard it.

Cleansing of the Temple

15*† They came to Jerusalem, and on entering the temple area he began to drive out those selling and buying there. He overturned the tables of the money changers and the seats of those who were selling doves. 16 He did not permit anyone to carry anything through the temple area. 17* Then he taught them saying, "Is it not written:

'My house shall be called a house of prayer
for all peoples'?
But you have made it a den of thieves."

18 The chief priests and the scribes came to hear of it and were seeking a way to put him to death, yet they feared him because the whole crowd was

---

†
10, 42–45: Whatever authority is to be exercised by the disciples must, like that of Jesus, be rendered as service to others (45) rather than for personal aggrandizement (42–44). The service of Jesus is his passion and death for the sins of the human race (45); cf 14, 24; Lk 53, 11–12; Mt 26, 28; Lk 22, 19–20.

10, 46–52: See the notes on Mt 9, 27–31 and 20, 29–34.

11, 1–11: In Mark's account Jesus takes the initiative in ordering the preparation for his entry into Jerusalem (1–6) even as he later orders the preparation of his last Passover Supper (14, 12–16). In vv 9–10 the greeting Jesus receives stops short of proclaiming him Messiah. He is greeted rather as the prophet of the coming messianic kingdom. Contrast Mt 21, 9.

11, 12–14: Jesus' search for fruit on the fig tree recalls the

prophets' earlier use of this image to designate Israel; cf Jer 8, 13; 29, 17; Jl 1, 7; Hos 9, 10.16. Cursing the fig tree is a parable in action representing Jesus' judgment (20) on barren Israel and the fate of Jerusalem for failing to receive his teaching; cf Is 34, 4; Hos 2, 14; Lk 13, 6–9.

11, 15–19: See the note on Mt 21, 12–17.

---

*
10, 42–45: Lk 22, 25–27.
10, 46–52: Mt 20, 29–34; Lk 18, 35–43.
11, 1–10: Mt 21, 1–9; Lk 19, 29–38; Jn 12, 12–15.
11, 9–10: 2 Sm 7, 16; Ps 118, 26.

11, 11: Mt 21, 10.17.
11, 12–14: Mt 21, 18–20; Lk 13, 6–9.
11, 15–18: Mt 21, 12–13; Lk 19, 45–46; Jn 2, 14–16.
11, 17: Is 56, 7; Jer 7, 11.

Unanswered Prayer

Did you ever want something so badly that you prayed for it?

Sometimes when things turn out the way we want, we say that God has answered our prayers. But when things don't turn out the way we want, we say that God didn't answer our prayers.

In Mk 11, 24, it seems that we have the power to obtain what we want from God—just by stating our wishes. This is a dangerous thought, though, especially when someone else might be praying for the exact opposite of what we're praying for. Why should God answer our prayers and not someone else's? In addition, when something horrible happens, despite all our prayers, it is dangerous to think that God willed such pain and suffering. For example, sometimes we hear people saying, "God must have wanted me to learn some lesson from this tragedy." God never causes tragedy. Tragedy just happens.

People often ask, and we may be asking ourselves, "Why pray at all if it isn't going to change anything?"

Here's a good response: "Prayer doesn't change things. Prayer changes people, and people change things."

▸ **Mk 11, 24**

---

astonished at his teaching. 19* When evening came, they went out of the city.

The Withered Fig Tree

20* Early in the morning, as they were walking along, they saw the fig tree withered to its roots. 21 Peter remembered and said to him, "Rabbi, look! The fig tree that you cursed has withered."

22 Jesus said to them in reply, "Have faith in God. 23* Amen, I say to you, whoever says to this mountain, 'Be lifted up and thrown into the sea,' and does not doubt in his heart but believes that what he says will happen, it shall be done for him. 24* Therefore I tell you, all that you ask for in prayer, believe that you will receive it and it shall be yours. 25* When you stand to pray, forgive anyone against whom you have a grievance, so that your heavenly Father may in turn forgive you your transgressions. [26]† "

The Authority of Jesus Questioned

27*† They returned once more to Jerusalem. As he was walking in the temple area, the chief priests, the scribes, and the elders approached him 28 and said to him, "By what authority are you doing these things? Or who gave you this authority to do them?" 29 Jesus said to them, "I shall ask you one question. Answer me, and I will tell you by what authority I do these things. 30 Was John's baptism of heavenly or of human origin? Answer me." 31 They discussed this among themselves and said, "If we say, 'Of heavenly origin,' he will say, '[Then] why did you not believe him?' 32 But shall we say, 'Of human origin'?"—they feared the crowd, for they all thought John really was a prophet. 33 So they said to Jesus in reply, "We do not know." Then Jesus said to them, "Neither shall I tell you by what authority I do these things."

Parable of the Tenants

12 1*† He began to speak to them in parables. "A man planted a vineyard, put a hedge around it, dug a wine press, and built a tower. Then he leased it to tenant farmers and left on a journey.* 2 At the proper time he sent a servant to the tenants to obtain from them some of the produce of the vineyard. 3 But they seized him, beat him, and sent him away empty-handed. 4 Again he sent them another servant. And that one they beat over the head and treated shamefully. 5 He sent yet another whom they killed. So, too, many others; some they beat, others they killed. 6 He had one other to send, a beloved son. He sent him to them last of all, thinking, 'They will respect my son.' 7 But those tenants said to one another, 'This is the heir.

---

† **11, 26:** This verse, which reads, "But if you do not forgive, neither will your heavenly Father forgive your transgressions," is omitted in the best manuscripts. It was probably added by copyists under the influence of Mt 6, 15.

11, 27–33: The mounting hostility toward Jesus came from the chief priests, the scribes, and the elders (27); the Herodians and the Pharisees (12, 13); and the Sadducees (12, 18). By their rejection of God's messengers, John the Baptist and Jesus, they incurred the divine judgment implied in vv 27–33 and confirmed in the parable of the vineyard tenants (12, 1–12).

12, 1–12: The vineyard denotes Israel (Is 5, 1–7). The tenant farmers are the religious leaders of Israel. God is the owner of the

vineyard. His servants are his messengers, the prophets. The beloved son is Jesus (1, 11; 9, 7; Mt 3, 17; 17, 5; Lk 3, 22; 9, 35). The punishment of the tenants refers to the religious leaders, and the transfer of the vineyard to others refers to the people of the new Israel.

11, 19: Lk 21, 37.	11, 25: Mt 6, 14; 18, 35.
11, 20–24: Mt 21, 20–22.	11, 27–33: Mt 21, 23–27; Lk 20,
11, 23: Mt 21, 20–21;	1–8.
Lk 17, 6.	12, 1–12: Mt 21, 33–46; Lk 20,
11, 24: Mt 7, 7; Jn 11, 22;	9–19.
14, 13.	12, 1: Is 5, 1–7; Jer 2, 21.

MK

What Do You Want from Me?

Dear God, Jesus tells us to give to you what is yours. What do you want from me, God? What can I give to you?

As a young person still growing and developing, I don't have much to offer financially. I can make a small financial contribution to the church, to poor people, . . . but is it enough, Lord? What more can I give?

I can offer my time and talents to serve my faith community. I can sing, play an instrument, draw posters, greet visitors, clean, decorate, organize, cook, bake, and telephone. I can help teach children, lector, or usher, . . . but is it enough, Lord? What more can I give?

I can reach out to serve and share your love at home, in my neighborhood, my school, my community, . . . but is it enough, Lord? What more can I give?

I want to serve you better, Lord. Speak to me, and I will listen. Amen.

▶ Mk 12, 13–17

Come, let us kill him, and the inheritance will be ours.' 8 So they seized him and killed him, and threw him out of the vineyard. 9 What [then] will the owner of the vineyard do? He will come, put the tenants to death, and give the vineyard to others. 10* Have you not read this scripture passage:

'The stone that the builders rejected
        has become the cornerstone;
11   by the Lord has this been done,
        and it is wonderful in our eyes'?"

12 They were seeking to arrest him, but they feared the crowd, for they realized that he had addressed the parable to them. So they left him and went away.

Paying Taxes to the Emperor

13*† They sent some Pharisees and Herodians to him to ensnare him* in his speech.† 14 They came and said to him, "Teacher, we know that you are a truthful man and that you are not concerned with anyone's opinion. You do not regard a person's status but teach the way of God in accordance with the truth. Is it lawful to pay the census tax to Caesar or not? Should we pay or should we not pay?" 15 Knowing their hypocrisy he said to them, "Why are you testing me? Bring me a denarius to look at." 16 They brought one to him and he said to them, "Whose image and inscription is this?" They replied to him, "Caesar's." 17* So Jesus said to them, "Repay to Caesar what belongs to Caesar and to God what belongs to God." They were utterly amazed at him.

The Question about the Resurrection

18† Some Sadducees, who say there is no resurrection, came to him and put this question to him, 19* saying, "Teacher, Moses wrote for us, 'If someone's brother dies, leaving a wife but no child, his brother must take the wife and raise up descendants for his brother.' 20 Now there were seven brothers. The first married a woman and died, leaving no descendants. 21 So the second married her and died, leaving no descendants, and the third likewise. 22 And the seven left no descendants. Last of all the woman also died. 23 At the resurrection [when they arise] whose wife will she be? For all seven had been married to her." 24 Jesus said to them, "Are you not misled because you do not know the scriptures or the power of God? 25 When they rise from the dead, they neither marry nor are given in marriage, but they are like the angels in heaven. 26* As for the dead being raised, have you not read in the Book of Moses, in the passage about the bush, how God told him, 'I am the God of Abraham, [the] God of Isaac, and [the] God of Jacob'? 27 He is not God of the dead but of the living. You are greatly misled."

The Greatest Commandment

28*† One of the scribes, when he came forward and heard them disputing and saw how well he had answered them, asked him, "Which is the first of all the commandments?" 29 Jesus replied, "The first is this: 'Hear, O Israel! The Lord our God is Lord alone! 30* You shall love the Lord your God with all your

---

12, 13–34: In the ensuing conflicts (cf also 2, 1—3, 6) Jesus vanquishes his adversaries by his responses to their questions and reduces them to silence (34).

12, 13–17: See the note on Mt 22, 15–22.
12, 18–27: See the note on Mt 22, 23–33.
12, 28–34: See the note on Mt 22, 34–40.

12, 10–11: Ps 118, 22–23; Is 28, 16.
12, 13–27: Mt 22, 15–33; Lk 20, 20–39.
12, 13: Mk 3, 6.
12, 17: Rom 13, 7.
12, 19: Dt 25, 5.
12, 26: Ex 3, 6.
12, 28–34: Mt 22, 34–40; Lk 10, 25–28.
12, 30: Dt 6, 4–5.

heart, with all your soul, with all your mind, and with all your strength.' 31* The second is this: 'You shall love your neighbor as yourself.' There is no other commandment greater than these." 32 The scribe said to him, "Well said, teacher. You are right in saying, 'He is One and there is no other than he.' 33* And 'to love him with all your heart, with all your understanding, with all your strength, and to love your neighbor as yourself' is worth more than all burnt offerings and sacrifices." 34* And when Jesus saw that [he] answered with understanding, he said to him, "You are not far from the kingdom of God." And no one dared to ask him any more questions.

The Question about David's Son

35*† As Jesus was teaching in the temple area he said, "How do the scribes claim that the Messiah is the son of David? 36* David himself, inspired by the holy Spirit, said:

'The Lord said to my lord,
"Sit at my right hand
    until I place your enemies under
        your feet." '

37 David himself calls him 'lord'; so how is he his son?" [The] great crowd heard this with delight.

Denunciation of the Scribes

38*† In the course of his teaching he said, "Beware of the scribes, who like to go around in long robes and accept greetings in the marketplaces, 39 seats of honor in synagogues, and places of honor at banquets. 40 They devour the houses of widows and, as a pretext, recite lengthy prayers. They will receive a very severe condemnation."

The Poor Widow's Contribution

41*† He sat down opposite the treasury and observed how the crowd put money into the treasury. Many rich people put in large sums. 42 A poor widow also came and put in two small coins worth a few cents. 43 Calling his disciples to himself, he said to them, "Amen, I say to you, this poor widow put in more than all the other contributors to the treasury. 44 For they have all contributed from their surplus wealth, but she, from her poverty, has contributed all she had, her whole livelihood."

SACRIFICIAL GIVING

Native Americans can appreciate the widow's offering in Mk 12, 41–44. For example, the Lakota tribe has a custom called *otuhan*, or "giveaway." During important occasions, a person honors the other members of the tribe by giving away much of what he or she has. Sometimes, everything is given away. To be called stingy is the worst insult.

Think about your own circumstances. How easy would it be to share or give away your favorite possessions? Could you give away something you really value? Why or why not?

Many Native Americans believe that all we have belongs to the Great Spirit and is a gift to be shared with others. Make a decision! Follow the example of the widow, and be generous to others to the point of sacrifice.

▸ Mk 12, 41–44

---

†
  12, 35–37: Jesus questions the claim of the scribes about the Davidic descent of the Messiah, not to deny it (Mt 1, 1; Acts 2, 20.34; Rom 1, 3; 2 Tm 2, 8) but to imply that he is more than this. His superiority derives from his transcendent origin, to which David himself attested when he spoke of the Messiah with the name "Lord" (Ps 110, 1). See also the note on Mt 22, 41–46.
  12, 38–40: See the notes on 7, 1–23 and Mt 23, 1–39.
  12, 41–44: See the note on Lk 21, 1–4.

*
12, 31: Lv 19, 18; Rom 13, 9; Gal 5, 14; Jas 2, 8.
12, 33: Dt 6, 4; Ps 40, 7–9.
12, 34: Mt 22, 46; Lk 20, 40.
12, 35–37: Mt 22, 41–45; Lk 20, 41–44.
12, 36: Ps 110, 1.
12, 38–40: Mt 23, 1–7; Lk 11, 43; 20, 45–47.
12, 41–44: Lk 21, 1–4.

The Destruction of the Temple Foretold

13 ¹*† As he was making his way out of the temple area one of his disciples said to him, "Look, teacher, what stones and what buildings!" ² Jesus said to him, "Do you see these great buildings? There will not be one stone left upon another that will not be thrown down."

The Signs of the End

³*† As he was sitting on the Mount of Olives opposite the temple area, Peter, James, John, and Andrew asked him privately, ⁴ "Tell us, when will this happen, and what sign will there be when all these things are about to come to an end?" ⁵* Jesus began to say to them, "See that no one deceives you. ⁶ Many will come in my name saying, 'I am he,' and they will deceive many. ⁷ When you hear of wars and reports of wars do not be alarmed; such things must happen, but it will not yet be the end. ⁸ Nation will rise against nation and kingdom against kingdom. There will be earthquakes from place to place and there will be famines. These are the beginnings of the labor pains.

The Coming Persecution

⁹* "Watch out for yourselves. They will hand you over to the courts. You will be beaten in synagogues. You will be arraigned before governors and kings because of me, as a witness before them. ¹⁰† But the gospel must first be preached to all nations. ¹¹* When they lead you away and hand you over, do not worry beforehand about what you are to say. But say whatever will be given to you at that hour. For it will not be you who are speaking but the holy Spirit. ¹² Brother will hand over brother to death, and the father his child; children will rise up against parents and have them put to death. ¹³ You will be hated by all because of my name. But the one who perseveres to the end will be saved.

The Great Tribulation

¹⁴*† "When you see the desolating abomination standing where he should not (let the reader understand), then those in Judea must flee to the mountains,* ¹⁵* [and] a person on a housetop must not go down or enter to get anything out of his house, ¹⁶ and a person in a field must not return to get his cloak. ¹⁷ Woe to pregnant women and nursing mothers in those days. ¹⁸ Pray that this does not happen in winter. ¹⁹* For those times will have tribulation such as has not been since the beginning of God's creation until now, nor ever will be. ²⁰ If the Lord had not shortened those days, no one would be saved; but for the sake of the elect whom he chose, he did

did you KNOW?

Signs and Omens

The community for which the author of Mark's Gospel wrote saw its sufferings as part of the troubles that would come with the end time. However, the author didn't intend that his readers take Jesus' signs and omens of wars and earthquakes literally to mean that the end of the world was at hand. Rather, these descriptions were used symbolically (see "Apocalyptic Literature," Daniel, chapters 7–10) to help the community make sense of its persecutions. The message of this Gospel is that Christians who were getting beaten up and thrown in jail would be saved by God. And ultimately, human history would climax in the perfect Reign of God. It was their job to hang on and endure to the end. All they had to worry about was spreading the Good News of Jesus Christ, and God would take care of the rest.

▸ Mark, chapter 13

---

†
13, 1–2: The reconstructed temple with its precincts, begun under Herod the Great ca. 20 B.C., was completed only some seven years before it was destroyed by fire in A.D. 70 at the hands of the Romans; cf Jer 26, 18; Mt 24, 1–2. For the dating of the reconstruction of the temple, see further the note on Jn 2, 20.

13, 3–37: Jesus' prediction of the destruction of the temple (2) provoked questions that the four named disciples put to him in private regarding the time and the sign when all *these things are about to come to an end* (3–4). The response to their questions was Jesus' eschatological discourse prior to his imminent death. It contained instruction and consolation exhorting the disciples and the church to faith and obedience through the trials that would confront them (5–13). The sign is the presence of *the desolating abomination* (14; see Dn 9, 27), i.e., of the Roman power profaning the temple. Flight from Jerusalem is urged rather than defense of the city through misguided messianic hope (14–23). Intervention will occur only after destruction (24–27), which will happen before the end of the first Christian gen-

eration (28–31). No one but the Father knows the precise time, or that of the parousia (32); hence the necessity of constant vigilance (33–37). Luke sets the parousia at a later date, after "the time of the Gentiles" (Lk 21, 24). See also the notes on Mt 24, 1—25, 46.

13, 10: *The gospel . . . to all nations:* the period of the Christian mission.

13, 14: The participle *standing* is masculine, in contrast to the neuter at Mt 24, 15.

13, 1–2: Mt 24, 1–2; Lk 21, 5–6.
13, 3–8: Mt 24, 3–8; Lk 21, 7–11.
13, 5: Eph 5, 6; 2 Thes 2, 3.
13, 9–13: Mt 24, 9–14; Lk 21, 12–19.
13, 11–12: Mt 10, 19–22; Lk 12, 11–12.
13, 14–23: Mt 24, 15–22; Lk 21, 20–24.
13, 14: Dn 9, 27; Mt 24, 15.
13, 15: Lk 17, 31.
13, 19: Dn 12, 1.

MK

shorten the days. ²¹ If anyone says to you then, 'Look, here is the Messiah! Look, there he is!' do not believe it. ²² False messiahs and false prophets will arise and will perform signs and wonders in order to mislead, if that were possible, the elect. ²³ Be watchful! I have told it all to you beforehand.

The Coming of the Son of Man

²⁴* "But in those days after that tribulation

the sun will be darkened,
   and the moon will not give its light,*
²⁵   and the stars will be falling from the sky,
   and the powers in the heavens will
      be shaken.

²⁶*† And then they will see 'the Son of Man coming in the clouds' with great power and glory, ²⁷ and then he will send out the angels and gather [his] elect from the four winds, from the end of the earth to the end of the sky.

The Lesson of the Fig Tree

²⁸* "Learn a lesson from the fig tree. When its branch becomes tender and sprouts leaves, you know that summer is near. ²⁹ In the same way, when you see these things happening, know that he is near, at the gates. ³⁰ Amen, I say to you, this generation will not pass away until all these things have taken place. ³¹ Heaven and earth will pass away, but my words will not pass away.

Need for Watchfulness

³² "But of that day or hour, no one knows, neither the angels in heaven, nor the Son, but only the Father. ³³* Be watchful! Be alert! You do not know when the time will come. ³⁴* It is like a man traveling abroad. He leaves home and places his servants in charge, each with his work, and orders the gatekeeper to be on the watch. ³⁵ Watch, therefore; you do not know when the lord of the house is coming, whether in the evening, or at midnight, or at cockcrow, or in the morning. ³⁶ May he not come suddenly and find you sleeping. ³⁷ What I say to you, I say to all: 'Watch!' "

The Conspiracy against Jesus

14 ¹*† The Passover and the Feast of Unleavened Bread† were to take place in two days' time. So the chief priests and the scribes were seeking a way to arrest him by treachery and put him to death. ² They said, "Not during the festival, for fear that there may be a riot among the people."

The Anointing at Bethany

³*† When he was in Bethany reclining at table in the house of Simon the leper, a woman came with an alabaster jar of perfumed oil, costly genuine spikenard. She broke the alabaster jar and poured it on his head. ⁴ There were some who were indignant. "Why has there been this waste of perfumed oil? ⁵ It could have been sold for more than three hundred days' wages and the money given to the poor." They were infuriated with her. ⁶ Jesus said, "Let her alone. Why do you make trouble for her? She has done a good thing for me. ⁷ The poor you will always have with you, and whenever you wish you can do good to them, but you will not always have me. ⁸ She has done what she could. She has anticipated anointing my body for burial. ⁹ Amen, I say to you, wherever the gospel is proclaimed to the whole world, what she has done will be told in memory of her."

The Betrayal by Judas

¹⁰* Then Judas Iscariot, one of the Twelve, went off to the chief priests to hand him over to them. ¹¹ When they heard him they were pleased and promised to pay him money. Then he looked for an opportunity to hand him over.

M
K

13, 26: *Son of Man . . . with great power and glory:* Jesus cites this text from Dn 7, 13 in his response to the high priest, *Are you the Messiah?* (14, 61). In Ex 34, 5; Lv 16, 2; and Nm 11, 25 the clouds indicate the presence of the divinity. Thus in his role of Son of Man, Jesus is a heavenly being who will come in power and glory.

14, 1—16, 8: In the movement of Mark's gospel the cross is depicted as Jesus' way to glory in accordance with the divine will. Thus the passion narrative is seen as the climax of Jesus' ministry.

14, 1: *The Passover and the Feast of Unleavened Bread:* the connection between the two festivals is reflected in Ex 12, 3–20; 34, 18; Lv 23, 4–8; Nm 9, 2–14; 28, 16–17; Dt 16, 1–8. The Passover commemorated the redemption from slavery and the departure of the Israelites from Egypt by night. It began at sundown after the Passover lamb was sacrificed in the temple in the afternoon of the fourteenth day of the month of Nisan. With the Passover supper on the same evening was associated the eating of unleavened bread. The latter was continued through Nisan 21, a reminder of the affliction of the Israelites and of the haste surrounding their departure. Praise and thanks to God for his goodness in the past were combined at this dual festival with the hope of future salvation. *The chief*

priests . . . to death: the intent to put Jesus to death was plotted for a long time but delayed for fear of the crowd (3, 6; 11, 18; 12, 12).

14, 3–9: At Bethany on the Mount of Olives, a few miles from Jerusalem, *in the house of Simon the leper,* Jesus defends a woman's loving action of anointing his head with perfumed oil in view of his impending death and burial as a criminal, in which case his body would not be anointed. See further the note on Jn 12, 7. He assures the woman of the remembrance of her deed in the worldwide preaching of the good news.

13, 24–27: Mt 24, 29–31; Lk 21, 25–27.
   13, 24: Is 13, 10; Ez 32, 7; Jl 2, 10.
   13, 26: Mk 14, 62; Dn 7, 13–14.
13, 28–32: Mt 24, 32–36; Lk 21, 29–33.
13, 33–37: Mt 24, 42; 25, 13–15.

   13, 34: Mt 25, 14–30; Lk 19, 12–27.
   14, 1–2: Mt 26, 2–5; Lk 22, 1–2; Jn 11, 45–53.
   14, 3–9: Mt 26, 6–13; Jn 12, 1–8.
   14, 10–11: Mt 26, 14–16; Lk 22, 3–6.

MK

Preparations for the Passover

12*† On the first day of the Feast of Unleavened Bread, when they sacrificed the Passover lamb, his disciples said to him, "Where do you want us to go and prepare for you to eat the Passover?" 13† He sent two of his disciples and said to them, "Go into the city and a man will meet you, carrying a jar of water. Follow him. 14 Wherever he enters, say to the master of the house, 'The Teacher says, "Where is my guest room where I may eat the Passover with my disciples?" ' 15 Then he will show you a large upper room furnished and ready. Make the preparations for us there." 16 The disciples then went off, entered the city, and found it just as he had told them; and they prepared the Passover.

The Betrayer

17* When it was evening, he came with the Twelve. 18† And as they reclined at table and were eating, Jesus said, "Amen, I say to you, one of you will betray me, one who is eating with me." 19 They began to be distressed and to say to him, one by one, "Surely it is not I?" 20 He said to them, "One of the Twelve, the one who dips with me into the dish. 21† For the Son of Man indeed goes, as it is written of him, but woe to that man by whom the Son of Man is betrayed. It would be better for that man if he had never been born."

The Lord's Supper

22*† While they were eating, he took bread, said the blessing, broke it, and gave it to them, and said, "Take it; this is my body." 23 Then he took a cup, gave thanks, and gave it to them, and they all drank from it. 24† He said to them, "This is my blood of the covenant, which will be shed for many. 25 Amen, I say to you, I shall not drink again the fruit of the vine until the day when I drink it new in the kingdom of God." 26*† Then, after singing a hymn, they went out to the Mount of Olives.

Peter's Denial Foretold

27*† Then Jesus said to them, "All of you will have your faith shaken, for it is written:

'I will strike the shepherd,
    and the sheep will be dispersed.'

PRAY IT

Mass Prayer

Dear Jesus, "Take it; this is my body. . . . This is my blood." Those words make me feel guilty because I should be hearing them at Mass. And you know I often find excuses not to go to Mass. The church pews are uncomfortable; I'd rather sleep late; I don't like the music or the homily; it is too nice outside; it's boring. My parents have even quit trying to get me to go.

Why is it so easy to forget that you gave us this special invitation to share in the eucharistic meal? It is a way of participating in your death and Resurrection and strengthening our faith and renewing our hope until you come again in glory. It is a privilege to be invited to the eucharistic table and to connect with both the present church and all the saints of the past who have shared this sacred meal.

Thank you for your invitation, Lord. Help me to value the Eucharist more, and give me the desire to meet you there. Amen.

For more on the Eucharist, see the articles for Mt 26, 26–29; Lk 22, 14–20; Jn 13, 1–20.

▶ Mk 14, 22–25

---

†

14, 12: *The first day of the Feast of Unleavened Bread . . . the Passover lamb:* a less precise designation of the day for sacrificing the Passover lamb as evidenced by some rabbinical literature. For a more exact designation, see the note on 14, 1. It was actually Nisan 14.

14, 13: *A man . . . carrying a jar of water:* perhaps a prearranged signal, for only women ordinarily carried water in jars. The Greek word used here, however, implies simply a person and not necessarily a male.

14, 18: *One of you will betray me, one who is eating with me:* contrasts the intimacy of table fellowship at the Passover meal with the treachery of the traitor; cf Ps 41, 10.

14, 21: *The Son of Man indeed goes, as it is written of him:* a reference to Ps 41, 10 cited by Jesus concerning Judas at the Last Supper; cf Jn 13, 18–19.

14, 22–24: The actions and words of Jesus express within the framework of the Passover meal and the transition to a new covenant the sacrifice of himself through the offering of his body and blood in anticipation of his passion and death. *His blood of the covenant* both alludes to the ancient rite of Ex 24, 4–8 and indicates the new community that the sacrifice of Jesus will bring into being (Mt 26–28; Lk 22, 19–20; 1 Cor 11, 23–25).

14, 24: *Which will be shed:* see the note on Mt 26, 27–28. For *many:* the Greek preposition *hyper* is a different one from that at Mt 26, 28 but the same as that found at Lk 22, 19.20 and 1 Cor 11, 24. The sense of both words is vicarious, and it is difficult in Hellenistic Greek to distinguish between them. For *many* in the sense of "all," see the note on Mt 20, 28.

14, 26: *After singing a hymn:* Pss 114–118, thanksgiving songs concluding the Passover meal.

14, 27–31: Jesus predicted that the Twelve would waver in their faith, even abandon him, despite their protestations to the contrary. Yet he reassured them that after his resurrection he would regather them in Galilee (16, 7; cf Mt 26, 32; 28, 7.10.16; Jn 21), where he first summoned them to be his followers as he began to preach the good news (1, 14–20).

14, 12–16: Mt 26, 17–19; Lk 22, 7–13.
14, 17–21: Mt 26, 20–24; Lk 22, 21–23; Jn 13, 21–26.
14, 22–25: Mt 26, 26–30; Lk 22, 19–20; 1 Cor 11, 23–25.
14, 26–31: Mt 26, 30–35; Lk 22, 34.39; Jn 13, 36–38.
14, 27: Zec 13, 7; Jn 16, 32.

28 But after I have been raised up, I shall go before you to Galilee." 29 Peter said to him, "Even though all should have their faith shaken, mine will not be." 30 Then Jesus said to him, "Amen, I say to you, this very night before the cock crows twice you will deny me three times." 31 But he vehemently replied, "Even though I should have to die with you, I will not deny you." And they all spoke similarly.

The Agony in the Garden

32*† Then they came to a place named Gethsemane, and he said to his disciples, "Sit here while I pray."* 33 He took with him Peter, James, and John, and began to be troubled and distressed. 34 Then he said to them, "My soul is sorrowful even to death. Remain here and keep watch." 35 He advanced a little and fell to the ground and prayed that if it were possible the hour might pass by him; 36† he said, "Abba, Father, all things are possible to you. Take this cup away from me, but not what I will but what you will." 37 When he returned he found them asleep. He said to Peter, "Simon, are you asleep? Could you not keep watch for one hour? 38*† Watch and pray that you may not undergo the test. The spirit is willing but the flesh is weak." 39 Withdrawing again, he prayed, saying the same thing. 40 Then he returned once more and found them asleep, for they could not keep their eyes open and did not know what to answer him. 41 He returned a third time and said to them, "Are you still sleeping and taking your rest? It is enough. The hour has come. Behold, the Son of Man is to be handed over to sinners. 42 Get up, let us go. See, my betrayer is at hand."

The Betrayal and Arrest of Jesus

43* Then, while he was still speaking, Judas, one of the Twelve, arrived, accompanied by a crowd with swords and clubs who had come from the chief priests, the scribes, and the elders. 44 His betrayer had arranged a signal with them, saying, "The man I shall kiss is the one; arrest him and lead him away securely." 45 He came and immediately went over to him and said, "Rabbi." And he kissed him. 46 At this they laid hands on him and arrested him. 47 One of the bystanders drew his sword, struck the high priest's servant, and cut off his ear. 48 Jesus said to them in reply, "Have you come out as against a robber, with swords and clubs, to seize me? 49 Day after day I was with you teaching in the temple area, yet you did not arrest me; but that the scriptures may be fulfilled." 50 And they all left him and fled. 51 Now a young man followed him wearing nothing but a linen cloth about his body. They seized him, 52 but he left the cloth behind and ran off naked.

Jesus before the Sanhedrin

53*† They led Jesus away to the high priest, and all the chief priests and the elders and the scribes came together. 54 Peter followed him at a distance into the high priest's courtyard and was seated with the guards, warming himself at the fire. 55 The chief priests and the entire Sanhedrin kept trying to obtain testimony against Jesus in order to put him to death, but they found none. 56 Many gave false witness against him, but their testimony did not agree. 57† Some took the stand and testified falsely against him, alleging, 58* "We heard him say, 'I will destroy this temple made with hands and within three days I will build another not made with hands.' " 59 Even so their testimony did not agree. 60 The high priest rose before the assembly and questioned Jesus, saying, "Have you no answer? What are these men testifying against you?" 61† But he was silent and answered nothing. Again the high priest asked him and said to him, "Are you the Messiah, the son of the Blessed One?" 62* Then Jesus answered, "I am;

and 'you will see the Son of Man
seated at the right hand of the Power
and coming with the clouds of heaven.' "

---

† **14, 32–34:** The disciples who had witnessed the raising to life of the daughter of Jairus (5, 37) and the transfiguration of their Master (9, 2) were now invited to witness his degradation and agony and to watch and pray with him.

14, 36: *Abba, Father:* an Aramaic term, here also translated by Mark, Jesus' special way of addressing God with filial intimacy. The word *'abbā'* seems not to have been used in earlier or contemporaneous Jewish sources to address God without some qualifier. Cf Rom 8, 15; Gal 4, 6 for other occurrences of the Aramaic word in the Greek New Testament. *Not what I will but what you will:* note the complete obedient surrender of the human will of Jesus to the divine will of the Father; cf Jn 4, 34; 8, 29; Rom 5, 19; Phil 2, 8; Heb 5, 8.

14, 38: *The spirit is willing but the flesh is weak:* the spirit is drawn to what is good yet found in conflict with the flesh, inclined to sin; cf Ps 51, 7.12. Everyone is faced with this struggle, the full force of which Jesus accepted on our behalf and, through his bitter passion and death, achieved the victory.

14, 53: *They led Jesus away . . . came together:* Mark presents a

formal assembly of the whole Sanhedrin (chief priests, elders, and scribes) at night, leading to the condemnation of Jesus (64), in contrast to Lk 22, 66.71, where Jesus is condemned in a daytime meeting of the council; see also Jn 18, 13.19–24.

14, 57–58: See the notes on Mt 26, 60–61 and Jn 2, 19.

14, 61–62: *The Blessed One:* a surrogate for the divine name, which Jews did not pronounce. *I am:* indicates Jesus' acknowledgment that he is the Messiah and Son of God; cf 1, 1. Contrast Mt 26, 64 and Lk 22, 67–70, in which Jesus leaves his interrogators to answer their own question. *You will see the Son of Man . . . with the clouds of heaven:* an allusion to Dn 7, 13 and Ps 110, 1, portending the enthronement of Jesus as judge in the transcendent glory of God's kingdom. *The Power:* another surrogate for the name of God.

14, 32–42: Mt 26, 36–46; Lk 22, 40–46.
14, 32: Jn 18, 1.
14, 38: Rom 7, 5.
14, 43–50: Mt 26, 47–56; Lk 22, 47–53; Jn 18, 3–11.

14, 53–65: Mt 26, 57–68; Lk 22, 54–55.63–65.67–71; Jn 18, 12–13.
14, 58: Mk 15, 29; 2 Cor 5, 1.
14, 62: Mk 13, 26; Ps 110, 1; Dn 7, 13; Mt 24, 30.

MK

63 At that the high priest tore his garments and said, "What further need have we of witnesses? 64 You have heard the blasphemy. What do you think?" They all condemned him as deserving to die. 65* Some began to spit on him. They blindfolded him and struck him and said to him, "Prophesy!" And the guards greeted him with blows.

Peter's Denial of Jesus

66* While Peter was below in the courtyard, one of the high priest's maids came along. 67 Seeing Peter warming himself, she looked intently at him and said, "You too were with the Nazarene, Jesus." 68† But he denied it saying, "I neither know nor understand what you are talking about." So he went out into the outer court. [Then the cock crowed.] 69 The maid saw him and began again to say to the bystanders, "This man is one of them." 70 Once again he denied it. A little later the bystanders said to Peter once more, "Surely you are one of them; for you too are a Galilean." 71 He began to curse and to swear, "I do not know this man about whom you are talking." 72* And immediately a cock crowed a second time. Then Peter remembered the word

that Jesus had said to him, "Before the cock crows twice you will deny me three times." He broke down and wept.

Jesus before Pilate

15 1*† As soon as morning came,* the chief priests with the elders and the scribes, that is, the whole Sanhedrin, held a council. They bound Jesus, led him away, and handed him over to Pilate. 2† Pilate questioned him, "Are you the king of the Jews?" He said to him in reply, "You say so." 3 The chief priests accused him of many things. 4 Again Pilate questioned him, "Have you no answer? See how many things they accuse you of." 5 Jesus gave him no further answer, so that Pilate was amazed.

The Sentence of Death

6*† Now on the occasion of the feast he used to release to them one prisoner whom they requested. 7† A man called Barabbas was then in prison along with the rebels who had committed murder in a rebellion. 8 The crowd came forward and began to ask him to do for them as he was accustomed. 9 Pilate answered, "Do you want me to

A Friend's Betrayal

LIVE IT!

Imagine that you are facing a difficult time. Your best friend promises to be with you no matter what. This is the one person you rely on, who has been there for you and has been the most loyal and faithful of all your friends. You have spent the last three years together . . . working, studying, enjoying holidays, traveling, and sharing countless meals and discussions. Now, imagine that this friend completely lets you down.

Peter was one of Jesus' best friends. As the story is told in the Gospel of Mark, the relationship has its difficult times, but Jesus continuously tries to reach Peter. Knowing Peter is going to deny him, Jesus even tries warning Peter that things would happen this way (14, 30).

Probably just like some of your friends, Peter had good intentions but could not follow through with his assurances to Jesus (verses 66–72). But Jesus did not give up on Peter (Jn 21, 15–19), and Peter became one of the greatest heroes of our church. Don't give up on your friends either.

▶ Mk 14, 66–72

---

† **14, 68:** [*Then the cock crowed*]: found in most manuscripts, perhaps in view of vv 30 and 72, but omitted in others.
15, 1: *Held a council:* the verb here, *poieō*, can mean either "convene a council" or "take counsel." This reading is preferred to a variant "reached a decision" (cf 3, 6), which 14, 64 describes as having happened at the night trial; see the note on Mt 27, 1–2. *Handed him over to Pilate:* lacking authority to execute their sentence of condemnation (14, 64), the Sanhedrin had recourse to Pilate to have Jesus tried and put to death (15); cf Jn 18, 31.
15, 2: *The king of the Jews:* in the accounts of the evangelists a certain irony surrounds the use of this title as an accusation against Jesus (see the note on 15, 26). While Pilate uses this term (2.9.12),

he is aware of the evil motivation of the chief priests who handed Jesus over for trial and condemnation (10; Lk 23, 14–16.20; Mt 27, 18.24; Jn 18, 38; 19, 4.6.12).
15, 6–15: See the note on Mt 27, 15–26.
15, 7: *Barabbas:* see the note on Mt 27, 16–17.

14, 65: Lk 22, 63–65.
14, 66–72: Mt 26, 69–75; Lk 22, 56–62; Jn 18, 16–18.25–27.
14, 72: Jn 13, 38.
15, 1–5: Mt 27, 1–2.11–14; Lk 23, 1–3.
15, 1: Jn 18, 28.
15, 6–15: Mt 27, 15–26; Lk 23, 17–25; Jn 18, 39–40.

release to you the king of the Jews?" 10 For he knew that it was out of envy that the chief priests had handed him over. 11 But the chief priests stirred up the crowd to have him release Barabbas for them instead. 12 Pilate again said to them in reply, "Then what [do you want] me to do with [the man you call] the king of the Jews?" 13† They shouted again, "Crucify him." 14 Pilate said to them, "Why? What evil has he done?" They only shouted the louder, "Crucify him." 15† So Pilate, wishing to satisfy the crowd, released Barabbas to them and, after he had Jesus scourged, handed him over to be crucified.

Mockery by the Soldiers

16*† The soldiers led him away inside the palace, that is, the praetorium, and assembled the whole cohort. 17 They clothed him in purple and, weaving a crown of thorns, placed it on him. 18 They began to salute him with, "Hail, King of the Jews!" 19 and kept striking his head with a reed and spitting upon him. They knelt before him in homage. 20 And when they had mocked him, they stripped him of the purple cloak, dressed him in his own clothes, and led him out to crucify him.

The Way of the Cross

21*† They pressed into service a passer-by, Simon, a Cyrenian, who was coming in from the country, the father of Alexander and Rufus, to carry his cross.

The Crucifixion

22* They brought him to the place of Golgotha (which is translated Place of the Skull). 23 They gave him wine drugged with myrrh, but he did not take it. 24*† Then they crucified him and divided his garments by casting lots for them to see what each should take. 25† It was nine o'clock in the morning when they crucified him. 26† The inscription of the charge against him read, "The King of the Jews." 27* With him they crucified

Facing the Hard Times

Lord, you really do know what it is like to be beaten, teased, pushed around, and rejected.

If you could put up with this torment, then maybe there is hope for others who feel the same way at times. Like when we are made fun of or rejected because of the way we look or act or for what we believe in. Or when we feel all alone or that no one understands what we are feeling.

But now, I know that you understand, Lord. You took these difficult steps even before we did. You have been there. You show us a way through these tough times.

Teach me to pray as you did: "Abba, Father, all things are possible to you. Take this cup away from me, but not what I will but what you will" (Mk 14, 36). Give me the strength to overcome my despair. Give me faith to abandon myself in God's hands as you did. Give me hope to see a new life beyond these moments of pain and hopelessness. Amen.

▸ Mk 15, 16–20

two revolutionaries, one on his right and one on his left. [28]† 29*† Those passing by reviled him, shaking their heads and saying, "Aha! You who would destroy the temple and rebuild it in three days, 30 save yourself by coming down from the cross." 31 Likewise the chief priests, with the scribes, mocked him among themselves and said, "He saved others; he cannot save himself. 32* Let the Messiah, the King of Israel, come down now

---

15, 13: Crucify him: see the note on Mt 27, 22.
15, 15: See the note on Mt 27, 26.
15, 16: Praetorium: see the note on Mt 27, 27.
15, 21: They pressed into service . . . Simon, a Cyrenian: a condemned person was constrained to bear his own instrument of torture, at least the crossbeam. The precise naming of Simon and his sons is probably due to their being known among early Christian believers to whom Mark addressed his gospel. See also the notes on Mt 27, 32 and Lk 23, 26–32.
15, 24: See the notes on Mt 27, 35 and Jn 19, 23–25a.
15, 25: It was nine o'clock in the morning: literally, "the third hour," thus between 9 a.m. and 12 noon. Cf vv 33.34.42 for Mark's chronological sequence, which may reflect liturgical or catechetical considerations rather than the precise historical sequence of events; contrast the different chronologies in the other gospels, especially Jn 19, 14.

15, 26: The inscription . . . the King of the Jews: the political reason for the death penalty falsely charged by the enemies of Jesus. See further the notes on Mt 27, 37 and Jn 19, 19.
15, 28: This verse, "And the scripture was fulfilled that says, 'And he was counted among the wicked,' " is omitted in the earliest and best manuscripts. It contains a citation from Is 53, 12, and was probably introduced from Lk 22, 37.
15, 29: See the note on Mt 27, 39–40.

15, 16–20: Mt 27, 27–31; Jn 19, 2–3.
15, 21: Mt 27, 32; Lk 23, 26.
15, 22–38: Mt 27, 33–51; Lk 23, 32–46; Jn 19, 17–30.
15, 24: Ps 22, 18.
15, 27: Lk 23, 33.
15, 29: Jn 2, 19.
15, 32: Lk 23, 39.

WE WERE THERE

According to Mk 15, 21, the Roman soldiers compelled a North African black man from Cyrene by the name of Simon, a passerby, to carry the cross of Jesus. We do not know anything more about Simon of Cyrene, except that Mark identifies him as the father of Alexander and Rufus. The reference to Simon's sons by name and the possibility that Rufus is the same person Paul greets in Rom 16, 13 indicate that they were known among the early Christians. This is significant for African Americans because it is evidence of the prominence and influence of African people in the early Christian church.

African people were there from the beginning of Christianity (see also Acts 8, 26–40). They were not latecomers to the Christian faith. Thank God, somebody always remembers! African Americans and other people who have experienced oppression are in danger of forgetting who they are and where they come from. Not because they are forgetful peoples, but because the oppressors have tried to erase their culture and identity in order to cripple and control them. Yet despite all of this, somebody always remembers.

We praise you, God, for having African people there from the beginning of your plan of salvation. We praise you in knowing that people of all races will be with you at the end. Hallelujah. Amen!

▶ Mk 15, 21

Chap. 15

from the cross that we may see and believe." Those who were crucified with him also kept abusing him.

The Death of Jesus

33 At noon darkness came over the whole land until three in the afternoon. 34*† And at three o'clock Jesus cried out in a loud voice, *"Eloi, Eloi, lema sabachthani?"* which is translated, "My God, my God, why have you forsaken me?" 35† Some of the bystanders who heard it said, "Look, he is calling Elijah." 36 One of them ran, soaked a sponge with wine, put it on a reed, and gave it to him to drink, saying, "Wait, let us see if Elijah comes to take him down." 37 Jesus gave a loud cry and breathed his last. 38† The veil of the sanctuary was torn in two from top to bottom. 39*† When the centurion who stood facing him saw how he breathed his last he said, "Truly this man was the

---

15, 34: An Aramaic rendering of Ps 22, 2. See also the note on Mt 27, 46.

15, 35: *Elijah:* a verbal link with *Eloi* (34). See the note on 9, 9–13; cf Mal 3, 23–24. See also the note on Mt 27, 47.

15, 38: See the note on Mt 27, 51–53.

15, 39: The closing portion of Mark's gospel returns to the theme of its beginning in the Gentile centurion's climactic declaration of

belief that Jesus *was the Son of God.* It indicates the fulfillment of the good news announced in the prologue (1, 1) and may be regarded as the firstfruit of the passion and death of Jesus.

15, 34: Ps 22, 2.   15, 39–41: Mt 27, 54–56; Lk 23, 47–49.

Son of God!" [40]*† There were also women looking on from a distance. Among them were Mary Magdalene, Mary the mother of the younger James and of Joses, and Salome. [41] These women had followed him when he was in Galilee and ministered to him. There were also many other women who had come up with him to Jerusalem.

The Burial of Jesus

[42]* When it was already evening, since it was the day of preparation, the day before the sabbath, [43]† Joseph of Arimathea, a distinguished member of the council, who was himself awaiting the kingdom of God, came and courageously went to Pilate and asked for the body of Jesus. [44] Pilate was amazed that he was already dead. He summoned the centurion and asked him if Jesus had already died. [45] And when he learned of it from the centurion, he gave the body to Joseph. [46] Having bought a linen cloth, he took him down, wrapped him in the linen cloth and laid him in a tomb that had been hewn out of the rock. Then he rolled a stone against the entrance to the tomb. [47] Mary Magdalene

and Mary the mother of Joses watched where he was laid.

The Resurrection of Jesus

16 [1]*† When the sabbath was over, Mary Magdalene, Mary, the mother of James, and Salome bought spices so that they might go and anoint him.* [2] Very early when the sun had risen, on the first day of the week, they came to the tomb. [3] They were saying to one another, "Who will roll back the stone for us from the entrance to the tomb?" [4] When they looked up, they saw that the stone had been rolled back; it was very large. [5]* On entering the tomb they saw a young man sitting on the right side, clothed in a white robe, and they were utterly amazed. [6] He said to them, "Do not be amazed! You seek Jesus of Nazareth, the crucified. He has been raised; he is not here. Behold, the place where they laid him. [7]* But go and tell his disciples and Peter, 'He is going before you to Galilee; there you will see him, as he told you.' " [8] Then they went out and fled from the tomb, seized with trembling and bewilderment. They said nothing to anyone, for they were afraid.

M
K

Alone!

One summer weekend several years ago, eight teenagers went on a hiking trip to the high country in the mountains of New Mexico. After an argument, one of the girls wandered off by herself and became separated from the group. When her absence was discovered, a search party quickly formed. Everyone was worried and anxious.

Afraid! Vulnerable! Lost and alone! She later described her feelings as the worst she had ever had in her life. She had no way of changing the situation. She even screamed at the sky and begged God to save her! All she could do was just pray and wait and hope.

Jesus may have had similar feelings. He may have felt lost, and he may have felt completely abandoned by his friends and even by God. He had to face his death alone. Can you imagine anything more lonely? His prayers did not change his circumstances but gave him a way to lament, to cry out to God to express his distress.

What makes you the most lonely and afraid? Have you ever felt abandoned? It is always okay to lament. When do you most feel the need to do so? Crying out does not always change our circumstances, but it can help remind us that we are not truly alone—God is with us.

▶ Mk 15, 33–34

---

† **15, 40–41:** See the note on Mt 27, 55–56.
15, 43: *Joseph of Arimathea:* see the note on Mt 27, 57–61.
16, 1–8: The purpose of this narrative is to show that the tomb is empty and that Jesus *has been raised* (6) and *is going before you to Galilee* (7) in fulfillment of 14, 28. The women find the tomb empty, and an angel stationed there announces to them what has happened. They are told to proclaim the news to Peter and the disciples in order to prepare them for a reunion with him. Mark's composition of the gospel ends at v 8 with the women telling no one, because they

were afraid. This abrupt termination causes some to believe that the original ending of this gospel may have been lost. See the following note.

15, 40: Mk 6, 3; Lk 8, 2–3.
15, 42–47: Mt 27, 57–61; Lk 23,
    50–56; Jn 19, 38–42.
16, 1–8: Mt 28, 1–8; Lk 24,
    1–10; Jn 20, 1–10.

16, 1–2: Mt 28, 1; Lk 23, 56.
16, 5: Jn 20, 12.
16, 7: Mk 14, 28.

Jesus Strengthens Our Faith

A group of faithful women accompany Jesus from afar when he dies on the cross, and they look to see where he is buried (Mk 15, 40–47). They are witnesses to the terrible violence of Jesus' death. Two days later, after the Sabbath, three of the women go to the tomb to anoint Jesus' body, giving him a proper burial. When they receive the good news that Jesus is alive, they flee from the tomb terrified and amazed.

This is where the original Gospel of Mark ends. Immediately, we want to ask lots of questions. What happened to the disciples? Did they go to Galilee? How did the word get out that Jesus had risen from the dead? Apparently, early Christians found this abrupt ending troublesome, and so they added other endings similar to those of the other Gospels.

These additions, starting at Mk 16, 9, emphasize the surprise of the disciples. It seems as if they are paralyzed. Only a strong scolding by Jesus and being commissioned to proclaim the Good News to the whole creation brings them around.

How do doubts and confusion paralyze you in living your faith? Pay attention to Jesus! Hear his voice! He is telling you to carry his message of love to other people. By doing so, you will strengthen your faith, and your life will be full of joy!

▶ Mk 16, 1–20

The Longer Ending

The Appearance to Mary Magdalene

[9*† When he had risen, early on the first day of the week, he appeared first to Mary Magdalene, out of whom he had driven seven demons. 10 *She went and told his companions who were mourning and weeping. 11 When they heard that he was alive and had been seen by her, they did not believe.

The Appearance to Two Disciples

12* After this he appeared in another form to two of them walking along on their way to the country. 13 They returned and told the others; but they did not believe them either.

The Commissioning of the Eleven

14* [But] later, as the eleven were at table, he appeared to them and rebuked them for their unbelief and hardness of heart because they had not believed those who saw him after he had been raised. 15* He said to them, "Go into the whole world and proclaim the gospel to every creature. 16 Whoever believes and is baptized will be saved; whoever does not believe will be condemned. 17 These signs will accompany those who believe: in my name they will drive out demons, they will speak new languages. 18* They will pick up serpents [with their hands], and if they drink any deadly thing, it will not harm them. They will lay hands on the sick, and they will recover."

The Ascension of Jesus

19* So then the Lord Jesus, after he spoke to them, was taken up into heaven and took his seat at the right hand of God. 20* But they went forth and preached everywhere, while the Lord worked with them and confirmed the word through accompanying signs.]

The Shorter Ending

[And they reported all the instructions briefly to Peter's companions. Afterwards Jesus himself, through them, sent forth from east to west the sacred and imperishable proclamation of eternal salvation. Amen.]

---

† **16, 9–20:** This passage, termed the Longer Ending to the Marcan gospel by comparison with a much briefer conclusion found in some less important manuscripts, has traditionally been accepted as a canonical part of the gospel and was defined as such by the Council of Trent. Early citations of it by the Fathers indicate that it was composed by the second century, although vocabulary and style indicate that it was written by someone other than Mark. It is a general resume of the material concerning the appearances of the risen Jesus, reflecting, in particular, traditions found in Luke (24) and John (20).

The Shorter Ending: Found after v 8 before the Longer Ending in four seventh-to-ninth-century Greek manuscripts as well as in one Old Latin version, where it appears alone without the Longer Ending.

The Freer Logion: Found after v 14 in a fourth-fifth century manuscript preserved in the Freer Gallery of Art, Washington, DC, this ending was known to Jerome in the fourth century. It reads: "And they excused themselves, saying, 'This age of lawlessness and unbelief is under Satan, who does not allow the truth and power of God to prevail over the unclean things dominated by the spirits [or, does not allow the unclean things dominated by the spirits] to grasp the truth and power of God]. Therefore reveal your righteousness now.' They spoke to Christ. And Christ responded to them, 'The limit of the years of Satan's power is completed, but other terrible things draw near. And for those who sinned I was handed over to death, that they might return to the truth and no longer sin, in order that they might inherit the spiritual and incorruptible heavenly glory of righteousness. But . . . !'"

16, 9–20: Mt 28, 1–10; Jn 20, 11–18.
16, 10–11: Lk 24, 10–11; Jn 20, 18.
16, 12–14: Lk 24, 13–35.
16, 14: Lk 24, 36–49; 1 Cor 15, 5.
16, 15–16: Mk 13, 10; Mt 28, 18–20; Lk 24, 47; Jn 20, 21.
16, 18: Mt 10, 1; Lk 10, 19; Acts 28, 3–6.
16, 19: Lk 24, 50–53.
16, 20: 1 Tm 3, 16.

Perhaps one of the most discouraging moments in life is the first time you realize that you are in the "out"-group. Children, youth, and adults all have ways of marking who's "in" and who's "out." For people who find themselves frequently in the out-group, life can be painful. The good news in the Gospel of Luke is that there is no out-group anymore. In the Reign of God, everyone is part of the in-group.

In-depth

The author of the Gospel of Luke was a Gentile (non-Jewish) convert to Christianity. So one of Luke's important concerns is to show that both Gentiles and Jews are seen as part of Jesus' in-group. In Luke, Jesus praises the faith of a centurion (7, 1–10), who is a Gentile and a hated symbol of the Roman occupation. Jesus also makes a Samaritan (Samaritans were considered foreigners by other Jews) the hero of a parable (10, 25–37).

Other in-groups for Jesus in Luke's Gospel are women and poor people. Women had little status in society at the time. But Luke includes many stories about women, including Mary's visit to her cousin Elizabeth before the births of their sons, Jesus and John the Baptist (1, 39–66). This Gospel also shows how Jesus loved the poor and scolded the rich for their lack of concern for the poor. For example, it includes a story about a poor man named Lazarus, who begged for food at a rich man's door. God honored Lazarus with a special place in Abraham's bosom (heaven) when he died (16, 19–31), whereas the rich man suffered in Hades.

Finally, Luke's Gospel shows Jesus' compassion and forgiveness for outcasts and sinners. It includes stories about the tax collector Zacchaeus, who climbs a tree to see Jesus (19, 1–10), the good Samaritan (10, 25–37), and the penitent sinner who was crucified beside Jesus (23, 39–43). The Gospel presents a vivid picture of how Jesus made the Reign of God present, inspiring his disciples to take the Gospel message to other lands and cultures.

At a Glance

I. The Prologue (1, 1–4).

II. The Infancy Narrative (1, 5—2, 52).

III. The Preparation for the Public Ministry (3, 1—4, 13).

IV. The Ministry in Galilee (4, 14—9, 50).

V. The Journey to Jerusalem: Luke's Travel Narrative (9, 51—19, 27).

VI. The Teaching Ministry in Jerusalem (19, 28—21, 38).

VII. The Passion Narrative (22, 1—23, 56).

VIII. The Resurrection Narrative (24, 1–53).

Quick Facts

Author
a Gentile Christian named Luke, who may have been a disciple of Paul (Col 4, 14)

Date Written
Approximately A.D. 80 to 90

Audience
Gentile (Greek) Christians represented by Theophilus (see Lk 1, 3)

Of Note
Luke also wrote the Acts of the Apostles.

Image of Jesus
merciful, compassionate, with a special concern for poor people, women, and non-Jews

Luke

I: The Prologue

1 ¹*† Since many have undertaken to compile a narrative of the events that have been fulfilled among us, ²* just as those who were eyewitnesses from the beginning and ministers of the word have handed them down to us, ³ I too have decided, after investigating everything accurately anew, to write it down in an orderly sequence for you, most excellent Theophilus, ⁴ so that you may realize the certainty of the teachings you have received.

II: The Infancy Narrative†

Announcement of the Birth of John

⁵* In the days of Herod, King of Judea,† there was a priest named Zechariah of the priestly division of Abijah; his wife was from the daughters of Aaron, and her name was Elizabeth. ⁶ Both were righteous in the eyes of God, observing all the commandments and ordinances of the Lord blamelessly. ⁷*† But they had no child, because Elizabeth was barren and both

---

1, 1–4: The Gospel according to Luke is the only one of the synoptic gospels to begin with a literary prologue. Making use of a formal, literary construction and vocabulary, the author writes the prologue in imitation of Hellenistic Greek writers and, in so doing, relates his story about Jesus to contemporaneous Greek and Roman literature. Luke is not only interested in the words and deeds of Jesus, but also in the larger context of the birth, ministry, death, and resurrection of Jesus as the fulfillment of the promises of God in the Old Testament. As a second- or third-generation Christian, Luke acknowledges his debt to earlier *eyewitnesses* and *ministers of the word*, but claims that his contribution to this developing tradition is a complete and accurate account, told in an orderly manner, and intended to provide *Theophilus* ("friend of God," literally) and other readers with certainty about earlier teachings they have received.

1, 5—2, 52: Like the Gospel according to Matthew, this gospel opens with an infancy narrative, a collection of stories about the birth and childhood of Jesus. The narrative uses early Christian traditions about the birth of Jesus, traditions about the birth and circumcision of John the Baptist, and canticles such as the Magnificat (1, 46–55) and Benedictus (1, 67–79), composed of phrases drawn from the Greek Old Testament. It is largely, however, the composition of Luke who writes in imitation of Old Testament birth stories, combining historical and legendary details, literary ornamentation and interpretation of scripture, to answer in advance the question, "Who is Jesus Christ?" The focus of the narrative, therefore, is primarily christological. In this section Luke announces many of the themes that will become prominent in the rest of the gospel: the centrality of Jerusalem and the temple, the journey motif, the universality of salvation, joy and peace, concern for the lowly, the importance

of women, the presentation of Jesus as savior, Spirit-guided revelation and prophecy, and the fulfillment of Old Testament promises. The account presents parallel scenes (diptychs) of angelic announcements of the birth of John the Baptist and of Jesus, and of the birth, circumcision, and presentation of John and Jesus. In this parallelism, the ascendency of Jesus over John is stressed: John is prophet of the Most High (1, 76); Jesus is Son of the Most High (1, 32). John is great in the sight of the Lord (1, 15); Jesus will be Great (a LXX attribute, used absolutely, of God) (1, 32). John will go before the Lord (1, 16–17); Jesus is Lord (1, 43; 2, 11).

1, 5: *In the days of Herod, King of Judea:* Luke relates the story of salvation history to events in contemporary world history. Here and in 3, 1–2, he connects his narrative with events in Palestinian history; in 2, 1–2 and 3, 1, he casts the Jesus story in the light of events of Roman history. Herod the Great, the son of the Idumean Antipater, was declared "King of Judea" by the Roman Senate in 40 B.C., but became the undisputed ruler of Palestine only in 37 B.C. He continued as king until his death in 4 B.C. *Priestly division of Abijah:* a reference to the eighth of the twenty-four divisions of priests who, for a week at a time, twice a year, served in the Jerusalem temple.

1, 7: *They had no child:* though childlessness was looked upon in contemporaneous Judaism as a curse or punishment for sin, it is intended here to present Elizabeth in a situation similar to that of some of the great mothers of important Old Testament figures: Sarah (Gn 15, 3; 16, 1); Rebekah (Gn 25, 21); Rachel (Gn 29, 31; 30, 1);

1, 1–4: Acts 1, 1; 1 Cor 15, 3.
1, 2: Lk 24, 48; Jn 15, 27; Acts 1, 21–22.
1, 5: 1 Chr 24, 10.
1, 7: Gn 18, 11; Jgs 13, 2–5; 1 Sm 1, 5–6.

were advanced in years. [8] Once when he was serving as priest in his division's turn before God, [9]* according to the practice of the priestly service, he was chosen by lot to enter the sanctuary of the Lord to burn incense. [10] Then, when the whole assembly of the people was praying outside at the hour of the incense offering, [11] the angel of the Lord appeared to him, standing at the right of the altar of incense. [12] Zechariah was troubled by what he saw, and fear came upon him. [13]*† But the angel said to him, "Do not be afraid, Zechariah, because your prayer has been heard. Your wife Elizabeth will bear you a son, and you shall name him John. [14] And you will have joy and gladness, and many will rejoice at his birth,

[15]*† for he will be great in the sight of [the] Lord. He will drink neither wine nor strong drink. He will be filled with the holy Spirit even from his mother's womb, [16] and he will turn many of the children of Israel to the Lord their God. [17]*† He will go before him in the spirit and power of Elijah to turn the hearts of fathers toward children and the disobedient to the understanding of the righteous, to prepare a people fit for the Lord." [18] Then Zechariah said to the angel, "How shall I know this? For I am an old man, and my wife is advanced in years." [19]*† And the angel said to him in reply, "I am Gabriel, who stand before God. I was sent to speak to you and to announce to you this good news. [20]*† But now you will be

Introducing
►MARY OF NAZARETH

Luke's Gospel makes it clear that Mary of Nazareth has a special place in God's plan of salvation. Beginning with Mary's humble acceptance of God's will revealed by the angel Gabriel (1, 26–38), Mary is presented as the true, first disciple who does the will of God. Her yes to God leads to Jesus' presence among us. She follows Jesus to the cross and is with the disciples in the upper room during the coming of the Holy Spirit (Acts 1, 14). Mary reveals to us the meaning of true faith—a willingness to accept God's call and to gradually discover the full meaning of God's will.

In choosing Mary to be the mother of Jesus, God selected not a rich queen, but a poor young girl open to the action of the Holy Spirit in her life. In Mary, Luke emphasizes God's preference for the poor and the little ones (see "The Magnificat, the Prayer of the Poor!" Lk 1, 39–56).

Besides being the mother of Jesus, Mary is presented in the Bible as the mother of the church (Jn 19, 25–27). For this reason, Catholic Christians have a special devotion to Mary. They celebrate her virginal conception of Jesus on the feast of the Annunciation (25 March). They believe that Mary was born free from original sin, and celebrate this on the feast of the Immaculate Conception (8 December). They also believe that she was taken into heaven, body and soul, at the end of her life, and celebrate this on the feast of the Assumption (15 August). Catholics also have a special prayer form honoring Mary, called the rosary.

▶ **Lk 1, 26–56**

---

† the mother of Samson and wife of Manoah (Jgs 13, 2–3); Hannah (1 Sm 1, 2).

1, 13: *Do not be afraid:* a stereotyped Old Testament phrase spoken to reassure the recipient of a heavenly vision (Gn 15, 1; Jos 1, 9; Dn 10, 12.19 and elsewhere in 1, 30; 2, 10). *You shall name him John:* the name means "Yahweh has shown favor," an indication of John's role in salvation history.

1, 15: *He will drink neither wine nor strong drink:* like Samson (Jgs 13, 4–5) and Samuel (1 Sm 1, 11 LXX and 4QSamª), John is to be consecrated by Nazirite vow and set apart for the Lord's service.

1, 17: *He will go before him in the spirit and power of Elijah:* John is to be the messenger sent before Yahweh, as described in Mal 3, 1–2. He is cast, moreover, in the role of the Old Testament fiery reformer, the prophet Elijah, who according to Mal 3, 23 (4, 5) is sent before "the great and terrible day of the Lord comes."

1, 19: *I am Gabriel:* "the angel of the Lord" is identified as

Gabriel, the angel who in Dn 9, 20–25 announces the seventy weeks of years and the coming of an anointed one, a prince. By alluding to Old Testament themes in vv 17 and 19, such as the coming of the day of the Lord and the dawning of the messianic era, Luke is presenting his interpretation of the significance of the births of John and Jesus.

1, 20: *You will be speechless and unable to talk:* Zechariah's becoming mute is the sign given in response to his question in v 18. When Mary asks a similar question in 1, 34, unlike Zechariah who was punished for his doubt, she, in spite of her doubt, is praised and reassured (35–37).

1, 9: Ex 30, 7.
1, 13: Lk 1, 57.60.63; Mt 1, 20–21.
1, 15: Lk 7, 23; Nm 6, 1–21; Jgs 13, 4; 1 Sm 1, 11 LXX.
1, 17: Sir 48, 10; Mal 3, 1; 3, 23–24; Mt 11, 14; 17, 11–13.
1, 19: Dn 8, 16; 9, 21.
1, 20: Lk 1, 45.

speechless and unable to talk until the day these things take place, because you did not believe my words, which will be fulfilled at their proper time."

21 Meanwhile the people were waiting for Zechariah and were amazed that he stayed so long in the sanctuary. 22 But when he came out, he was unable to speak to them, and they realized that he had seen a vision in the sanctuary. He was gesturing to them but remained mute. 23 Then, when his days of ministry were completed, he went home. 24 After this time his wife Elizabeth conceived, and she went into seclusion for five months, saying, 25* "So has the Lord done for me at a time when he has seen fit to take away my disgrace before others."

Announcement of the Birth of Jesus

26† In the sixth month, the angel Gabriel was sent from God to a town of Galilee called Nazareth, 27* to a virgin betrothed to a man named Joseph, of the house of David, and the virgin's name was Mary. 28* And coming to her, he said, "Hail, favored one! The Lord is with you." 29 But she was greatly troubled at what was said and pondered what sort of greeting this might be. 30 Then the angel said to her, "Do not be afraid, Mary, for you have found favor with God. 31* Behold, you will conceive in your womb and bear a son, and you shall name him Jesus. 32*† He will be great and will be called Son of the Most High, and the Lord God will give him the throne of David his father, 33* and he will rule over the house of Jacob forever, and of his kingdom there will be no end." 34† But Mary said to the angel, "How can this be, since I have no relations with a man?" 35* And the angel said to her in reply, "The holy Spirit will come upon you, and the power of the Most High will overshadow you. Therefore the child to be born will be called holy, the Son of God. 36† And behold, Elizabeth, your relative, has also conceived a son in her old age, and this is the sixth month for her who was called barren; 37* for nothing will be impossible for God." 38 Mary said, "Behold, I am the handmaid of the Lord. May it be done to me according to your word." Then the angel departed from her.

Mary Visits Elizabeth

39 During those days Mary set out and traveled to the hill country in haste to a town of Judah, 40 where she entered the house of Zechariah and greeted Elizabeth. 41* When Elizabeth heard Mary's greeting, the infant leaped in her womb, and Elizabeth, filled with the holy Spirit, 42* cried out in a loud voice and said, "Most blessed are you among women, and blessed is the fruit of your womb. 43† And how does this happen to me, that the mother of my Lord should come to me? 44 For at the moment the sound of your greeting reached my ears, the infant in my womb leaped for joy. 45*† Blessed are you who believed that what was spoken to you by the Lord would be fulfilled."

The Canticle of Mary

46*† And Mary said:

"My soul proclaims the greatness of the Lord;*
47*   my spirit rejoices in God my savior.
48* For he has looked upon his
    handmaid's lowliness;
    behold, from now on will all ages call
    me blessed.

1, 26–38: The announcement to Mary of the birth of Jesus is parallel to the announcement to Zechariah of the birth of John. In both the angel Gabriel appears to the parent who is troubled by the vision (11–12.26–29) and then told by the angel not to fear (13.30). After the announcement is made (14–17.31–33) the parent objects (18.34) and a sign is given to confirm the announcement (20.36). The particular focus of the announcement of the birth of Jesus is on his identity as Son of David (32–33) and Son of God (32.35).

1, 32: *Son of the Most High:* cf 1, 76 where John is described as "prophet of the Most High." "Most High" is a title for God commonly used by Luke (35.76; 6, 35; 8, 28; Acts 7, 48; 16, 17).

1, 34: Mary's questioning response is a denial of sexual relations and is used by Luke to lead to the angel's declaration about the Spirit's role in the conception of this child (35). According to Luke, the virginal conception of Jesus takes place through the holy Spirit, the power of God, and therefore Jesus has a unique relationship to Yahweh: he is Son of God.

1, 36–37: The sign given to Mary in confirmation of the angel's announcement to her is the pregnancy of her aged relative Elizabeth. If a woman past the childbearing age could become pregnant, why, the angel implies, should there be doubt about Mary's pregnancy, for *nothing will be impossible for God.*

1, 43: Even before his birth, Jesus is identified in Luke as the Lord.

1, 45: *Blessed are you who believed:* Luke portrays Mary as a believer whose faith stands in contrast to the disbelief of Zechariah (20). Mary's role as believer in the infancy narrative should be seen in connection with the explicit mention of her presence among "those who believed" after the resurrection at the beginning of the Acts of the Apostles (1, 14).

1, 46–55: Although Mary is praised for being the mother of the Lord and because of her belief, she reacts as the servant in a psalm of praise, the Magnificat. Because there is no specific connection of the canticle to the context of Mary's pregnancy and her visit to Elizabeth, the Magnificat (with the possible exception of v 48) may have been a Jewish Christian hymn that Luke found appropriate at this point in his story. Even if not composed by Luke, it fits in well with themes found elsewhere in Luke: joy and exultation in the Lord; the lowly being singled out for God's favor; the reversal of human fortunes; the fulfillment of Old Testament promises. The loose connection between the hymn and the context is further seen in the fact that a few Old Latin manuscripts identify the speaker of the hymn as Elizabeth, even though the overwhelming textual evidence makes Mary the speaker.

1, 25: Gn 30, 23.
1, 27: Lk 2, 5; Mt 1, 16.18.
1, 28: Jgs 6, 12; Ru 2, 4; Jdt 13, 18.
1, 31: Gn 16, 11; Jgs 13, 3; Is 7, 14; Mt 1, 21–23.
1, 32–33: 2 Sm 7, 12.13.16; Is 9, 7.
1, 33: Dn 2, 44; 7, 14; Mi 4, 7; Mt 28, 18.
1, 35: Mt 1, 20.
1, 37: Gn 18, 14; Jer 32, 27; Mt 19, 26.

1, 41: Lk 1, 15; Gn 25, 22 LXX.
1, 42: Lk 11, 27–28; Jgs 5, 24; Jdt 13, 18; Dt 28, 4.
1, 45: Lk 1, 20.
1, 46–55: 1 Sm 2, 1–10.
1, 46: Ps 35, 9; Is 61, 10; Hb 3, 18.
1, 47: Ti 3, 4; Jude 25.
1, 48: Lk 11, 27; 1 Sm 1, 11; 2 Sm 16, 12; 2 Kgs 14, 26; Ps 113, 7.

THE MAGNIFICAT, THE PRAYER OF THE POOR!

Mary gives a testimony of her faith right after she receives the news that she will be the mother of God. During her visit to her cousin Elizabeth, she sings of God's salvation in a song known as the Magnificat, which means "[my soul] praises." This prayer is mainly made up of verses taken from the Psalms and the Prophets. Mary first sings of her salvation; then she sings of God's salvation brought to the humble, the poor, and the hungry; and she finishes by singing of the salvation brought to all the people of God as promised to Abraham.

The Magnificat is an important prayer for Hispanic people. It is the song of the poor of God, those who expected salvation from God, not from people in power or through wars and conquests. The social consequences of God's salvation are clearly revealed in Mary's song. The Magnificat is like a summary of Jesus' life on earth, which raised up the lowly and brought down the powerful to build the Reign of God.

- In a world marked by huge gaps between rich people and poor people, is it clear that Christians are in solidarity with the poor?
- How are you helping the poor now, and how are you planning to do so as an adult?
- Pray the Magnificat slowly, savoring what it says, letting it move to the core of your heart.

▸ Lk 1, 39–56

49* The Mighty One has done great things
        for me,
    and holy is his name.
50* His mercy is from age to age
    to those who fear him.
51* He has shown might with his arm,
    dispersed the arrogant of mind and heart.
52* He has thrown down the rulers from
        their thrones
    but lifted up the lowly.
53* The hungry he has filled with good things;
    the rich he has sent away empty.
54* He has helped Israel his servant,
    remembering his mercy,
55* according to his promise to our fathers,

to Abraham and to his
    descendants forever."

56 Mary remained with her about three months and then returned to her home.

The Birth of John

57† When the time arrived for Elizabeth to have her child she gave birth to a son. 58* Her neighbors and relatives heard that the Lord had shown his great mercy toward her, and they rejoiced with her. 59*† When they came on the eighth day to circumcise the child, they were going to call him Zechariah after his father, 60* but his mother said in reply, "No. He will be called John." 61 But they answered

---

† **1, 57–66:** The birth and circumcision of John above all emphasize John's incorporation into the people of Israel by the sign of the covenant (Gn 17, 1–12). The narrative of John's circumcision also prepares the way for the subsequent description of the circumcision of Jesus in 2, 21. At the beginning of his two-volume work Luke shows those who play crucial roles in the inauguration of Christianity to be wholly a part of the people of Israel. At the end of the Acts of the Apostles (21, 20; 22, 3; 23, 6–9; 24, 14–16; 26, 2–8.22–23) he will argue that Christianity is the direct descendant of Pharisaic Judaism.

1, 59: The practice of Palestinian Judaism at this time was to name the child at birth; moreover, though naming a male child after the father is not completely unknown, the usual practice was to name the child after the grandfather (see 61). The naming of the child

John and Zechariah's recovery from his loss of speech should be understood as fulfilling the angel's announcement to Zechariah in 1, 13 and 20.

1, 49: Dt 10, 21; Pss 71, 19; 111, 9; 126, 2–3.
1, 50: Pss 89, 2; 103, 13.17.
1, 51: Pss 89, 10; 118, 15; Jer 32, 17 (39, 17 LXX).
1, 52: 1 Sm 2, 7; 2 Sm 22, 28; Jb 5, 11; 12, 19; Ps 147, 6; Sir 10, 14; Jas 4, 6; 1 Pt 5, 5.
1, 53: 1 Sm 2, 5; Ps 107, 9.
1, 54: Ps 98, 3; Is 41, 8–9.
1, 55: Gn 13, 15; 17, 7; 18, 18; 22, 17–18; Mi 7, 20.
1, 58: Lk 1, 14.
1, 59: Lk 2, 21; Gn 17, 10.12; Lv 12, 3.
1, 60: Lk 1, 13.

her, "There is no one among your relatives who has this name." 62 So they made signs, asking his father what he wished him to be called. 63 He asked for a tablet and wrote, "John is his name," and all were amazed. 64* Immediately his mouth was opened, his tongue freed, and he spoke blessing God. 65 Then fear came upon all their neighbors, and all these matters were discussed throughout the hill country of Judea. 66 All who heard these things took them to heart, saying, "What, then, will this child be?" For surely the hand of the Lord was with him.

The Canticle of Zechariah

67 Then Zechariah his father, filled with the holy Spirit, prophesied, saying:

68*† "Blessed be the Lord, the God of Israel,
    for he has visited and brought redemption
        to his people.
69*† He has raised up a horn for our salvation
    within the house of David his servant,
70   even as he promised through the mouth of
        his holy prophets from of old:
71*   salvation from our enemies and from
        the hand of all who hate us,
72*   to show mercy to our fathers
        and to be mindful of his holy covenant*
73*   and of the oath he swore to Abraham
        our father,
        and to grant us that, 74 rescued from the
        hand of enemies,
        without fear we might worship him 75* in
        holiness and righteousness
        before him all our days.
76*† And you, child, will be called prophet of the
        Most High,
        for you will go before the Lord to prepare
        his ways,
77   to give his people knowledge of salvation
        through the forgiveness of their sins,
78*† because of the tender mercy of our God
        by which the daybreak from on high will
        visit us*

THE BENEDICTUS

Zechariah's prayer in Lk 1, 68–79 is called the Benedictus (which means "blessed") or the Canticle of Zechariah. After Zechariah regains his voice, he praises God for sending a savior from the line of David. The savior he sings of is not a warrior king but someone bringing salvation through the forgiveness of sins and leading people into the way of peace.

The Benedictus is recited during morning prayer, and the Magnificat (see Lk 1, 46–55) is recited during evening prayer in the Liturgy of the Hours. Why not make the Magnificat and the Benedictus part of your prayer life too? Place a bookmark in this chapter, and turn to it when you want to praise God and express your faith in God's saving power.

▶ Lk 1, 46–80

79   to shine on those who sit in darkness and
        death's shadow,
        to guide our feet into the path of peace."

80* The child grew and became strong in spirit, and he was in the desert until the day of his manifestation to Israel.

---

†
1, 68–79: Like the canticle of Mary (46–55) the canticle of Zechariah is only loosely connected with its context. Apart from vv 76–77, the hymn in speaking of *a horn for our salvation* (69) and the *daybreak from on high* (78) applies more closely to Jesus and his work than to John. Again like Mary's canticle, it is largely composed of phrases taken from the Greek Old Testament and may have been a Jewish Christian hymn of praise that Luke adapted to fit the present context by inserting vv 76–77 to give Zechariah's reply to the question asked in v 66.
1, 69: *A horn for our salvation:* the horn is a common Old Testament figure for strength (Pss 18, 3; 75, 5–6; 89, 18; 112, 9; 148, 14). This description is applied to God in Ps 18, 3 and is here transferred to Jesus. The connection of the phrase with *the house of David* gives the title messianic overtones and may indicate an allusion to a phrase in Hannah's song of praise (1 Sm 2, 10), "the horn of his anointed."

1, 76: *You will go before the Lord:* here *the Lord* is most likely a reference to Jesus (contrast 15–17 where *Yahweh* is meant) and John is presented as the precursor of Jesus.
1, 78: *The daybreak from on high:* three times in the LXX (Jer 23, 5; Zec 3, 8; 6, 12), the Greek word used here for *daybreak* translates the Hebrew word for "scion, branch," an Old Testament messianic title.

*
1, 64: Lk 1, 20.	**1, 73–74:** Gn 22, 16–17.
1, 68: Lk 7, 16; Pss 41, 13; 72, 18; 106, 48; 111, 9.	**1, 75:** Ti 2, 12.
1, 69: Ps 18, 3.	**1, 76:** Is 40, 3; Mal 3, 1; Mt 3, 3; 11, 10.
1, 71: Ps 106, 10.	**1, 78:** Mal 3, 20.
1, 72: Ps 106, 45–46.	**1, 78–79:** Is 60, 1–2.
1, 72–73: Gn 17, 7; Lv 26, 42; Ps 105, 8–9; Mi 7, 20.	**1, 80:** Lk 2, 40; Mt 3, 1.

The Birth of Jesus

2 ¹† In those days a decree went out from Caesar Augustus† that the whole world should be enrolled. ² This was the first enrollment, when Quirinius was governor of Syria. ³ So all went to be enrolled, each to his own town. ⁴* And Joseph too went up from Galilee from the town of Nazareth to Judea, to the city of David that is called Bethlehem, because he was of the house and family of David, ⁵* to be enrolled with Mary, his betrothed, who was with child. ⁶ While they were there, the time came for her to have her child, ⁷*† and she gave birth to her firstborn son. She wrapped him in swaddling clothes and laid him in a manger, because there was no room for them in the inn.

⁸† Now there were shepherds in that region living in the fields and keeping the night watch over their flock. ⁹* The angel of the Lord appeared to them and the glory of the Lord shone around them, and they were struck with great fear. ¹⁰ The angel said to them, "Do not be afraid; for behold, I proclaim to you good news of great joy that will be for all the people. ¹¹*† For today in the city of David a savior has been born for you who is Messiah and Lord. ¹² And this

Jesus' Birth: Good News to the Poor

On 25 December, we celebrate Christmas, the birth of Jesus. We recall the moment of God's entering our world—a defining moment in the history of salvation. As Luke records the moment of the birth of the Messiah, who are the stars of the show? To whom do the angels appear to announce this remarkable event, this "good news of great joy that will be for all the people"? the high priest? the rich and important residents of Bethlehem? No. The announcement is made to shepherds, poor workers living in the fields nearby.

Like Mary, the shepherds are people of little power and significance. Luke makes the point that sometimes what the world sees as unimportant, God honors. This is the justice of God. It is the same today. The poorest in our world, the most hidden people who have no power, hold a special place in the heart of God. And, like the shepherds, poor people often know God better than those who are rich or powerful by this world's standards.

This truth is a challenge but also good news for all of us, rich and poor alike. How do your attitudes and actions—even the way you celebrate Christmas—reflect God's special attention to poor people?

▶ Lk 2, 8–20

---

† **2, 1–2:** Although universal registrations of Roman citizens are attested in 28 B.C., 8 B.C., and A.D. 14 and enrollments in individual provinces of those who are not Roman citizens are also attested, such a universal census of the Roman world under Caesar Augustus is unknown outside the New Testament. Moreover, there are notorious historical problems connected with Luke's dating the census *when Quirinius was governor of Syria*, and the various attempts to resolve the difficulties have proved unsuccessful. P. Sulpicius Quirinius became legate of the province of Syria in A.D. 6–7 when Judea was annexed to the province of Syria. At that time, a provincial census of Judea was taken up. If Quirinius had been legate of Syria previously, it would have to have been before 10 B.C. because the various legates of Syria from 10 B.C. to 4 B.C. (the death of Herod) are known, and such a dating for an earlier census under Quirinius would create additional problems for dating the beginning of Jesus' ministry (3, 1.23). A previous legateship after 4 B.C. (and before A.D. 6) would not fit with the dating of Jesus' birth in the days of Herod (1, 5; Mt 2, 1). Luke may simply be combining Jesus' birth in Bethlehem with his vague recollection of a census under Quirinius (see also Acts 5, 37) to underline the significance of this birth for the whole Roman world: through this child born in Bethlehem peace and salvation come to the empire.

2, 1: *Caesar Augustus:* the reign of the Roman emperor Caesar Augustus is usually dated from 27 B.C. to his death in A.D. 14. According to Greek inscriptions, Augustus was regarded in the Roman Empire as "savior" and "god," and he was credited with establishing a time of peace, the *pax Augusta*, throughout the Roman world during his long reign. It is not by chance that Luke relates the birth of Jesus to the time of Caesar Augustus: the real savior (11) and peace-bearer (14; see also 19, 38) is the child born in Bethlehem. The great emperor is simply God's agent (like the Persian king Cyrus in Is 44, 28 –45, 1) who provides the occasion for God's purposes to be accomplished. *The whole world:* that is, the whole Roman world: Rome, Italy, and the Roman provinces.

2, 7: *Firstborn son:* the description of Jesus as *firstborn son* does not necessarily mean that Mary had other sons. It is a legal description indicating that Jesus possessed the rights and privileges of the firstborn son (Gn 27; Ex 13, 2; Nm 3, 12–13; 18, 15–16; Dt 21, 15–17). See the notes on Mt 1, 25 and Mk 6, 3. *Wrapped him in swaddling clothes:* there may be an allusion here to the birth of another descendant of David, his son Solomon, who though a great king was wrapped in swaddling clothes like any other infant (Wis 7, 4–6). *Laid him in a manger:* a feeding trough for animals. A possible allusion to Is 1, 3 LXX.

2, 8–20: The annoucement of Jesus' birth to the shepherds is in keeping with Luke's theme that the lowly are singled out as the recipients of God's favors and blessings (see also 1, 48.52).

2, 11: The basic message of the infancy narrative is contained in the angel's announcement: this child is *savior, Messiah,* and *Lord.* Luke is the only synoptic gospel writer to use the title *savior* for Jesus (11; Acts 5, 31; 13, 23; see also 1, 69; 19, 9; Acts 4, 12). As savior, Jesus is looked upon by Luke as the one who rescues humanity from sin and delivers humanity from the condition of alienation from God. The title *christos,* "Christ," is the Greek equivalent of the Hebrew *māšah,* "Messiah," "anointed one." Among certain groups in first-century Palestinian Judaism, the title was applied to an expected royal leader from the line of David who would restore the kingdom to Israel (see Acts 1, 6). The political overtones of the title are played down in Luke and instead the Messiah of the Lord (26) or the Lord's anointed is the one who now brings salvation to all humanity, Jew and Gentile (29–32). *Lord* is the most frequently used title for Jesus in Luke and Acts. In the New Testament it is also applied to Yahweh, as it is in the Old Testament. When used of Jesus it points to his transcendence and dominion over humanity.

*

2, 4: Mi 5, 2; Mt 2, 6.
2, 5: Lk 1, 27; Mt 1, 18.
2, 7: Mt 1, 25.
2, 9: Lk 1, 11.26.

2, 11: Mt 1, 21; 16, 16; Jn 4, 42; Acts 2, 36; 5, 31; Phil 2, 11.

O CHRISTMAS TREE!

Did you ever wonder where the tradition of the Christmas tree came from? It began in Germany, the country that also gave us the beautiful song "Silent Night." For hundreds of years, the Christmas tree has been the focal point and symbol of the Christmas season for the people of Germany.

In the year A.D. 350, Pope Julius declared December 25, which had been the day of the pagan feast of the sun god, a feast day in observance of the birth of the Son of God. Prior to A.D. 350, the German people had a tradition of keeping evergreen branches in the house to ward off evil spirits. This pagan tradition was exchanged for a Christian tradition of having branches in the house to symbolize the life that Jesus brought to the world. After some time, the branches themselves were exchanged for entire trees, which were brought into homes and decorated with candles. As the German people immigrated into North America, especially to the U.S. and Canada, they brought the lovely tradition of the Christmas tree with them.

Today, the Christmas tree is a central symbol of Christmas in the United States. Adding lights and decorations helps us to celebrate the birth of Jesus, the light of the world.

▶ Lk 2, 1–14

will be a sign for you: you will find an infant wrapped in swaddling clothes and lying in a manger." 13 And suddenly there was a multitude of the heavenly host with the angel, praising God and saying:

14*† "Glory to God in the highest
   and on earth peace to those on whom his
      favor rests."

The Visit of the Shepherds

15 When the angels went away from them to heaven, the shepherds said to one another, "Let us go, then, to Bethlehem to see this thing that has taken place, which the Lord has made known to us." 16 So they went in haste and found Mary and Joseph, and the infant lying in the manger. 17 When they saw this,

they made known the message that had been told them about this child. 18 All who heard it were amazed by what had been told them by the shepherds. 19 And Mary kept all these things, reflecting on them in her heart. 20 Then the shepherds returned, glorifying and praising God for all they had heard and seen, just as it had been told to them.

The Circumcision and Naming of Jesus

21*† When eight days were completed for his circumcision, he was named Jesus, the name given him by the angel before he was conceived in the womb.

The Presentation in the Temple

22*† When the days were completed for their purification† according to the law of Moses, they took

---

2, 14: *On earth peace to those on whom his favor rests:* the peace that results from the Christ event is for those whom God has favored with his grace. This reading is found in the oldest representatives of the Western and Alexandrian text traditions and is the preferred one; the Byzantine text tradition, on the other hand, reads: "on earth peace, good will toward men." The peace of which Luke's gospel speaks (14; 7, 50; 8, 48; 10, 5–6; 19, 38.42; 24, 36) is more than the absence of war of the *pax Augusta*; it also includes the security and well-being characteristic of peace in the Old Testament.

2, 21: Just as John before him had been incorporated into the people of Israel through his circumcision, so too this child (see the note on 1, 57–66).

2, 22–40: The presentation of Jesus in the temple depicts the parents of Jesus as devout Jews, faithful observers of the law of the Lord (23.24.39), i.e., the law of Moses. In this respect, they are described in a fashion similar to the parents of John (1, 6) and Simeon (25) and Anna (36–37).

2, 22: *Their purification:* syntactically, *their* must refer to Mary and Joseph, even though the Mosaic law never mentions the purification of the husband. Recognizing the problem, some Western scribes have altered the text to read "his purification," understanding the presentation of Jesus in the temple as a form of purification; the Vulgate version has a Latin form that could be either "his" or "her." According to the Mosaic law (Lv 12, 2–8), the woman who gives birth to a boy is unable for forty days to touch anything sacred or to enter the temple area by reason of her legal impurity. At the end of this period she is required to offer a year-old lamb as a burnt offering and a turtledove or young pigeon as an expiation of sin. The woman who could not afford a lamb offered instead two turtledoves or two young pigeons, as Mary does here. *They took him up to Jerusalem to present him to the Lord:* as the firstborn son (7) Jesus

2, 14: Lk 19, 38.   2, 22–24: Lv 12, 2–8.
2, 21: Lk 1, 31; Gn 17, 12;
      Mt 1, 21.

him up to Jerusalem to present him to the Lord, 23* just as it is written in the law of the Lord, "Every male that opens the womb shall be consecrated to the Lord," 24 and to offer the sacrifice of "a pair of turtledoves or two young pigeons," in accordance with the dictate in the law of the Lord.

25† Now there was a man in Jerusalem whose name was Simeon. This man was righteous and devout, awaiting the consolation of Israel, and the holy Spirit was upon him. 26 It had been revealed to him by the holy Spirit that he should not see death before he had seen the Messiah of the Lord. 27 He came in the Spirit into the temple; and when the parents brought in the child Jesus to perform the custom of the law in regard to him, 28 he took him into his arms and blessed God, saying:

29 "Now, Master, you may let your servant go
        in peace, according to your word,
30*   for my eyes have seen your salvation,
31   which you prepared in sight of all
            the peoples,
32*   a light for revelation to the Gentiles,
            and glory for your people Israel."

33 The child's father and mother were amazed at what was said about him; 34* and Simeon blessed them and said to Mary his mother, "Behold, this child is destined for the fall and rise of many in Israel, and to be a sign that will be contradicted 35† (and you yourself a sword will pierce) so that the thoughts of many hearts may be revealed."

36 There was also a prophetess, Anna, the daughter of Phanuel, of the tribe of Asher. She was advanced in years, having lived seven years with her husband after her marriage, 37 and then as a widow until she was eighty-four. She never left the temple, but worshiped night and day with fasting and prayer. 38* And coming forward at that very time, she gave

Introducing ▶ THE HOLY FAMILY

On the first Sunday after Christmas, the Catholic church celebrates the feast of the Holy Family: Jesus, Mary, and Joseph. The Bible does not tell us a lot about the Holy Family. We know that Joseph was a kind and compassionate man, eager to do God's will. He raised Jesus as his own son, even though he was not Jesus' biological father. Jesus was raised in a home in which love and faith were the norm.

We can be sure that the Holy Family had their moments of conflict and crisis—all families do. Luke's story of Jesus' getting separated from his parents demonstrates that. But we can also be sure that their love and faith helped them to survive such conflicts and grow stronger because of them. The church holds the Holy Family up as a model of respect, compassion, love, and faith in family life.

How does your family express love and respect for one another? What crises and conflicts have you and your family survived? What can you do to bring the qualities of the Holy Family more fully into your family's life?

▶ Lk 2, 41–52

---

was consecrated to the Lord as the law required (Ex 13, 2.12), but there was no requirement that this be done at the temple. The concept of a presentation at the temple is probably derived from 1 Sm 1, 24–28, where Hannah offers the child Samuel for sanctuary services. The law further stipulated (Nm 3, 47–48) that the firstborn son should be redeemed by the parents through their payment of five shekels to a member of a priestly family. About this legal requirement Luke is silent.

2, 25: *Awaiting the consolation of Israel:* Simeon here and later Anna who speak about the child to all who were awaiting the redemption of Jerusalem represent the hopes and expectations of faithful and devout Jews who at this time were looking forward to the restoration of God's rule in Israel. The birth of Jesus brings these hopes to fulfillment.

2, 35: *(And you yourself a sword will pierce):* Mary herself will not be untouched by the various reactions to the role of Jesus (34). Her blessedness as mother of the Lord will be challenged by her son who describes true blessedness as "hearing the word of God and observing it" (8, 20–21 and 11, 27–28).

2, 23: Ex 13, 2.12.
2, 30–31: Lk 3, 6; Is 40, 5 LXX;
    52, 10.
2, 32: Is 42, 6; 46, 13; 49, 6;
    Acts 13, 47; 26, 23.
2, 34: Lk 12, 51; Is 8, 14; Jn
    9, 39; Rom 9, 33;
    1 Cor 1, 23; 1 Pt 2,
    7–8.
2, 38: Is 52, 9.

Jesus Grows in Age and Wisdom

LIVE IT!

Luke is the only Gospel that has any stories of Jesus' childhood. When Jesus was twelve, he left his family to stay in the Temple in Jerusalem. At the Temple, Jesus listened to and questioned the teachers, trying to understand his faith better. His questions and his understanding—and we can presume his sincerity—amazed all who heard him.

Adolescence is an important time for exploring life's questions—including life's religious questions. Sometimes, young people are led to believe that they shouldn't have any questions—which is a sad statement about adult leaders and teachers. Wise teachers—like those the boy Jesus met in the Temple—welcome and encourage your questions, even your religious questions. So ask yourself: How well do I know my faith? What are my main questions? Who are the wise teachers I can go to for help in searching out the answers?

▶ Lk 2, 41–52

thanks to God and spoke about the child to all who were awaiting the redemption of Jerusalem.

The Return to Nazareth

39* When they had fulfilled all the prescriptions of the law of the Lord, they returned to Galilee, to their own town of Nazareth. 40* The child grew and became strong, filled with wisdom; and the favor of God was upon him.

The Boy Jesus in the Temple

41*† Each year his parents went to Jerusalem for the feast of Passover, 42 and when he was twelve years old, they went up according to festival custom. 43 After they had completed its days, as they were returning, the boy Jesus remained behind in Jerusalem, but his parents did not know it. 44 Thinking that he was in the caravan, they journeyed for a day and looked for him among their relatives and acquaintances, 45 but not finding him, they returned to Jerusalem to look for him. 46 After three days they found him in the temple, sitting in the midst of the teachers, listening to them and asking them questions, 47 and all who heard him were astounded at his understanding and his answers. 48 When his parents saw him, they were astonished, and his mother said to him, "Son, why have you done this to us? Your father and I have been looking for you with great anxiety." 49† And he said to them, "Why were you looking for me? Did you not know that I must be in my Father's house?" 50 But they did not understand what he said to them. 51* He went down with them and came to Nazareth, and was obedient to them; and his mother kept all these things in her heart. 52* And Jesus advanced [in] wisdom and age and favor before God and man.

III: The Preparation for the Public Ministry

The Preaching of John the Baptist†

3 1* In the fifteenth year of the reign of Tiberius Caesar,† when Pontius Pilate was governor of

---

2, 41–52: This story's concern with an incident from Jesus' youth is unique in the canonical gospel tradition. It presents Jesus in the role of the faithful Jewish boy, raised in the traditions of Israel, and fulfilling all that the law requires. With this episode, the infancy narrative ends just as it began, in the setting of the Jerusalem temple.

2, 49: *I must be in my Father's house:* this phrase can also be translated, "I must be about my Father's work." In either translation, Jesus refers to God as his Father. His divine sonship, and his obedience to his heavenly Father's will, take precedence over his ties to his family.

3, 1–20: Although Luke is indebted in this section to his sources, the Gospel of Mark and a collection of sayings of John the Baptist, he has clearly marked this introduction to the ministry of Jesus with his own individual style. Just as the gospel began with a long periodic sentence (1, 1–4), so too this section (1–2). He casts the call of John the Baptist in the form of an Old Testament prophetic call (2) and extends the quotation from Isaiah found in Mk 1, 3 (Is 40, 3) by the addition of Is 40, 4–5 in vv 5–6. In doing so, he presents his theme of the universality of salvation, which he has announced earlier in the words of Simeon (2, 30–32). Moreover, in describing the expectation of the people (15), Luke is characterizing the time of John's preaching in the same way as he had earlier described the situation of other devout Israelites in the infancy narrative (2, 25–26.37–38). In vv 7–18 Luke presents the preaching of John the Baptist who urges the crowds to re-form in view of the coming wrath (7.9: eschatological preaching), and who offers the crowds certain standards for reforming social conduct (10–14: ethical preaching), and who announces to the crowds the coming of *one mightier than* he (15–18: messianic preaching).

3, 1: *Tiberius Caesar:* Tiberius succeeded Augustus as emperor in A.D. 14 and reigned until A.D. 37. The fifteenth year of his reign, depending on the method of calculating his first regnal year, would have fallen between A.D. 27 and 29. *Pontius Pilate:* prefect of Judea from A.D. 26 to 36. The Jewish historian Josephus describes him as a greedy and ruthless prefect who had little regard for the local Jewish population and their religious practices (see 13, 1). *Herod:* i.e., Herod Antipas, the son of Herod the Great. He ruled over Galilee and Perea from 4 B.C. to A.D. 39. His official title *tetrarch* means literally, "ruler of a quarter," but came to designate any subordinate prince. *Philip:* also a son of Herod the Great, tetrarch of the territory to the north and east of the Sea of Galilee from 4 B.C. to A.D. 34. Only two small areas of this territory are mentioned by Luke. *Lysanias:* nothing is known about this Lysanias who is said here to have been tetrarch of Abilene, a territory northwest of Damascus.

2, 39: Mt 2, 23.
2, 40: Lk 1, 80; 2, 52.
2, 41: Ex 12, 24–27; 23, 15;
    Dt 16, 1–8.
2, 51: Lk 2, 19.
2, 52: Lk 1, 80; 2, 40; 1 Sm
    2, 26.
3, 1–20: Mt 3, 1–12; Mk 1,
    1–8; Jn 1, 19–28.

Judea, and Herod was tetrarch of Galilee, and his brother Philip tetrarch of the region of Ituraea and Trachonitis, and Lysanias was tetrarch of Abilene, [2]*† during the high priesthood of Annas and Caiaphas, the word of God came to John the son of Zechariah in the desert. [3]*† He went throughout [the] whole region of the Jordan, proclaiming a baptism of repentance for the forgiveness of sins, [4]*† as it is written in the book of the words of the prophet Isaiah:

"A voice of one crying out in the desert:
'Prepare the way of the Lord,
   make straight his paths.
[5] Every valley shall be filled
   and every mountain and hill shall be
     made low.

The winding roads shall be made straight,
   and the rough ways made smooth,
[6]* and all flesh shall see the salvation of God.' "

[7]* He said to the crowds who came out to be baptized by him, "You brood of vipers! Who warned you to flee from the coming wrath? [8]* Produce good fruits as evidence of your repentance; and do not begin to say to yourselves, 'We have Abraham as our father,' for I tell you, God can raise up children to Abraham from these stones. [9]* Even now the ax lies at the root of the trees. Therefore every tree that does not produce good fruit will be cut down and thrown into the fire."

[10] And the crowds asked him, "What then should we do?" [11] He said to them in reply, "Whoever has two cloaks should share with the person who has none. And whoever has food should do likewise."

Introducing...
► JOHN THE BAPTIST

Picture a man living in the desert, eating grasshoppers and wild honey, and wearing a camel hair coat. Does this sound like the person Jesus described as "among those born of women, no one is greater than John" (Lk 7, 28)? The person Jesus is talking about is John the Baptist, and he plays an important role in all four Gospels. John is portrayed like an Old Testament prophet, calling people to repentance for their sins. Indeed, his ministry was so similar to Jesus' ministry that after Herod had John killed (Mt 14, 1–12), he thought that Jesus might have been John raised from the dead (Lk 9, 7–9). The power of John's preaching is demonstrated by Jesus' disciples' still encountering John's followers years after John's death (Acts 19, 1–7).

John the Baptist was Jesus' cousin, and the Gospel of Luke presents many parallels between the two men. John's preaching gives us a preview into Jesus' message. John was preparing the way for Jesus. He was a humble servant "not worthy to loosen the thongs of [Jesus'] sandals" (Lk 3, 16). He described his baptism as a baptism of water in contrast with Jesus' baptism with "the holy Spirit and fire" (verse 16).

John the Baptist is the model of how Christians should perform their prophetic mission, pointing others toward Jesus with passion and humility.

► Lk 3, 1–20

†
   3, 2: *During the high priesthood of Annas and Caiaphas:* after situating the call of John the Baptist in terms of the civil rulers of the period, Luke now mentions the religious leadership of Palestine (see the note on 1, 5). Annas had been high priest A.D. 6–15. After being deposed by the Romans in A.D. 15 he was succeeded by various members of his family and eventually by his son-in-law, Caiaphas, who was high priest A.D. 18–36. Luke refers to Annas as high priest at this time (but see Jn 18, 13.19), possibly because of the continuing influence of Annas or because the title continued to be used for the ex-high priest. *The word of God came to John:* Luke is alone among the New Testament writers in associating the preaching of John with a call from God. Luke is thereby identifying John with the prophets whose ministries began with similar calls. In 7, 26 John will

be described as "more than a prophet"; he is also the precursor of Jesus (7, 27), a transitional figure inaugurating the period of the fulfillment of prophecy and promise.
   3, 3: See the note on Mt 3, 2.
   3, 4: The Essenes from Qumran used the same passage to explain why their community was in the desert studying and observing the law and the prophets (1QS 8, 12–15).

*
3, 2: Lk 1, 80.	**3, 6:** Lk 2, 30–31.
3, 3: Acts 13, 24; 19, 4.	**3, 7:** Mt 12, 34.
3, 4–6: Is 40, 3–5.	**3, 8:** Jn 8, 39.
3, 4: Jn 1, 23.	**3, 9:** Mt 7, 19; Jn 15, 6.

?did you KNOW?

The Liturgical Year

The story of Jesus' baptism is one of the readings for the feast of the Baptism of the Lord. The feast days and holy days celebrated by Catholics and other Christians follow a yearly pattern. This pattern is called the liturgical year; it is not the same as the calendar year. You can read more about church feast days and see a diagram of the liturgical calendar in the introductory material of this Bible.

▶ Lk 3, 15–22

12* Even tax collectors came to be baptized and they said to him, "Teacher, what should we do?" 13 He answered them, "Stop collecting more than what is prescribed." 14 Soldiers also asked him, "And what is it that we should do?" He told them, "Do not practice extortion, do not falsely accuse anyone, and be satisfied with your wages."

15* Now the people were filled with expectation, and all were asking in their hearts whether John might be the Messiah. 16*† John answered them all, saying, "I am baptizing you with water, but one mightier than I is coming. I am not worthy to loosen the thongs of his sandals. He will baptize you with the holy Spirit and fire. 17*† His winnowing fan is in his hand to clear his threshing floor and to gather the wheat into his barn, but the chaff he will burn with unquenchable fire." 18 Exhorting them in many other ways, he preached good news to the people. 19*† Now Herod the tetrarch, who had been censured by him because of Herodias, his brother's wife, and because of all the evil deeds Herod had committed, 20 added still another to these by [also] putting John in prison.

The Baptism of Jesus

21*† After all the people had been baptized and Jesus also had been baptized and was praying,† heaven was opened 22*† and the holy Spirit descended upon him in bodily form like a dove. And a voice came from heaven, "You are my beloved Son; with you I am well pleased."

The Genealogy of Jesus

23*† When Jesus began his ministry he was about thirty years of age. He was the son, as was thought, of Joseph, the son of Heli,* 24 the son of Matthat, the son of Levi, the son of Melchi, the son of Jannai, the son of Joseph, 25 the son of Mattathias, the son of Amos, the son of Nahum, the son of Esli, the son of Naggai, 26 the son of Maath, the son of Mattathias, the son of Semein, the son of Josech, the son of Joda, 27* the son of Joanan, the son of Rhesa, the son of Zerubbabel, the son of Shealtiel, the son of Neri, 28 the son of Melchi, the son of Addi, the son of Cosam, the son of Elmadam, the son of Er, 29 the son of Joshua, the son of Eliezer, the son of Jorim, the son of Matthat, the son of Levi, 30 the son of Simeon, the son of Judah, the son of Joseph, the son of Jonam, the son of Eliakim, 31*† the son of Melea, the son of Menna, the son of

---

† 3, 16: He will baptize you with the holy Spirit and fire: in contrast to John's baptism with water, Jesus is said to baptize with the holy Spirit and with fire. From the point of view of the early Christian community, the Spirit and fire must have been understood in the light of the fire symbolism of the pouring out of the Spirit at Pentecost (Acts 2, 1–4); but as part of John's preaching, the Spirit and fire should be related to their purifying and refining characteristics (Ez 36, 25–27; Mal 3, 2–3). See the note on Mt 3, 11.

3, 17: Winnowing fan: see the note on Mt 3, 12.

3, 19–20: Luke separates the ministry of John the Baptist from that of Jesus by reporting the imprisonment of John before the baptism of Jesus (21–22). Luke uses this literary device to serve his understanding of the periods of salvation history. With John the Baptist, the time of promise, the period of Israel, comes to an end; with the baptism of Jesus and the descent of the Spirit upon him, the time of fulfillment, the period of Jesus, begins. In his second volume, the Acts of the Apostles, Luke will introduce the third epoch in salvation history, the period of the church.

3, 21–22: This episode in Luke focuses on the heavenly message identifying Jesus as Son and, through the allusion to Is 42, 1, as Servant of Yahweh. The relationship of Jesus to the Father has already been announced in the infancy narrative (1, 32.35; 2, 49); it occurs here at the beginning of Jesus' Galilean ministry and will reappear in 9, 35 before another major section of Luke's gospel, the travel narrative (9, 51—19, 27). Elsewhere in Luke's writings (4, 18; Acts 10, 38), this incident will be interpreted as a type of anointing of Jesus.

3, 21: Was praying: Luke regularly presents Jesus at prayer at im-

portant points in his ministry: here at his baptism; at the choice of the Twelve (6, 12); before Peter's confession (9, 18); at the transfiguration (9, 28); when he teaches his disciples to pray (11, 1); at the Last Supper (22, 32); on the Mount of Olives (22, 41); on the cross (23, 46).

3, 22: You are my beloved Son; with you I am well pleased: this is the best attested reading in the Greek manuscripts. The Western reading, "You are my Son, this day I have begotten you," is derived from Ps 2, 7.

3, 23–38: Whereas Mt 1, 2 begins the genealogy of Jesus with Abraham to emphasize Jesus' bonds with the people of Israel, Luke's universalism leads him to trace the descent of Jesus beyond Israel to Adam and beyond that to God (38) to stress again Jesus' divine sonship.

3, 31: The son of Nathan, the son of David: in keeping with Jesus' prophetic role in Luke and Acts (e.g., 7, 16.39; 9, 8; 13, 33; 24, 19; Acts 3, 22–23; 7, 37) Luke traces Jesus' Davidic ancestry through the prophet Nathan (see 2 Sm 7, 2) rather than through King Solomon, as Mt 1, 6–7.

---

* 3, 12: Lk 7, 29.
3, 15–16: Acts 13, 25.
3, 16: Lk 7, 19–20; Jn 1, 27;
Acts 1, 5; 11, 16.
3, 17: Mt 3, 12.
3, 19–20: Mt 14, 3–4; Mk 6,
17–18.
3, 21–22: Mt 3, 13–17; Mk 1,
9–11.
3, 22: Lk 9, 35; Ps 2, 7; Is 42,

1; Mt 12, 18; 17, 5;
Mk 9, 7; Jn 1, 32; 2 Pt
1, 17.
3, 23–38: Mt 1, 1–17.
3, 23: Lk 4, 22; Jn 6, 42.
3, 27: 1 Chr 3, 17; Ez 3, 2.
3, 31: 2 Sm 5, 14.
3, 31–32: 1 Sm 16, 1.18.
3, 31–33: Ru 4, 17–22; 1 Chr 2,
1–15.

Mattatha, the son of Nathan,* the son of David,* [32] the son of Jesse, the son of Obed, the son of Boaz, the son of Sala, the son of Nahshon, [33]* the son of Amminadab, the son of Admin, the son of Arni, the son of Hezron, the son of Perez, the son of Judah,* [34]* the son of Jacob, the son of Isaac, the son of Abraham, the son of Terah, the son of Nahor, [35] the son of Serug, the son of Reu, the son of Peleg, the son of Eber, the son of Shelah, [36]* the son of Cainan, the son of Arphaxad, the son of Shem, the son of Noah, the son of Lamech, [37] the son of Methuselah, the son of Enoch, the son of Jared, the son of Mahalaleel, the son of Cainan, [38]* the son of Enos, the son of Seth, the son of Adam, the son of God.

The Temptation of Jesus†

4 [1]* Filled with the holy Spirit,† Jesus returned from the Jordan and was led by the Spirit into the desert [2]*† for forty days, to be tempted by the devil. He ate nothing during those days, and when they were over he was hungry. [3] The devil said to him, "If you are the Son of God, command this stone to become bread." [4]* Jesus answered him, "It is written, 'One does not live by bread alone.'" [5] Then he took him up and showed him all the kingdoms of the world in a single instant. [6]* The devil said to him, "I shall give to you all this power and their glory; for it has been handed over to me, and I may give it to whomever I wish. [7] All this will be yours, if you worship me." [8]* Jesus said to him in reply, "It is written:

'You shall worship the Lord, your God,
and him alone shall you serve.'"

[9]† Then he led him to Jerusalem, made him stand on the parapet of the temple, and said to him, "If you are the Son of God, throw yourself down from here, [10]* for it is written:

'He will command his angels concerning you,
to guard you,'

[11]* and:

'With their hands they will support you,
lest you dash your foot against a stone.'"

THE BIBLE, TRADITION, AND THE MAGISTERIUM

Notice that each time Jesus is tempted, he uses phrases from the Bible as a defense against the devil (Lk 4, 4.8.12). But also notice that the devil knows the Scriptures and uses them to try to tempt Jesus (verses 10–11)!

We should always be careful about misinterpreting the Bible. That is why the Catholic church teaches that our faith is based on both the Bible and the sacred Tradition handed down by the Apostles. The apostolic Tradition provides direction for understanding the Bible, and the Bible provides background for understanding the Tradition. The Magisterium—the pope and bishops—ensures that the Bible and Tradition are correctly taught and misinterpretations are corrected. That is why the Bible, Tradition, and the Magisterium are considered the three pillars of the Catholic church.

The Bible is a reliable guide and companion as long as we take care not to misuse it!

▶ Lk 4, 1–13

[12]* Jesus said to him in reply, "It also says, 'You shall not put the Lord, your God, to the test.'" [13]*† When the devil had finished every temptation, he departed from him for a time.

---

† **4, 1–13:** See the note on Mt 4, 1–11.

4, 1: *Filled with the holy Spirit:* as a result of the descent of the Spirit upon him at his baptism (3, 21–22), Jesus is now equipped to overcome the devil. Just as the Spirit is prominent at this early stage of Jesus' ministry (1.14.18), so too it will be at the beginning of the period of the church in Acts (Acts 1, 4; 2, 4.17).

4, 2: *For forty days:* the mention of forty days recalls the forty years of the wilderness wanderings of the Israelites during the Exodus (Dt 8, 2).

4, 9: *To Jerusalem:* the Lucan order of the temptations concludes on the parapet of the temple in Jerusalem, the city of destiny in Luke-Acts. It is in Jerusalem that Jesus will ultimately face his destiny (9, 51; 13, 33).

4, 13: *For a time:* the devil's opportune time will occur before the passion and death of Jesus (Lk 22, 3.31–32.53).

3, 33: Gn 29, 35; 38, 29.	**4, 2:** Heb 4, 15.
3, 34: Gn 21, 3; 25, 26;	**4, 4:** Dt 8, 3.
1 Chr 1, 34; 28, 34.	**4, 6:** Jer 27, 5; Mt 28, 18.
3, 34–36: Gn 11, 10–26; 1 Chr	**4, 8:** Dt 6, 13.
1, 24–27.	**4, 10:** Ps 91, 11.
3, 36–38: Gn 4, 25—5, 32;	**4, 11:** Ps 91, 12.
1 Chr 1, 1–4.	**4, 12:** Dt 6, 16; 1 Cor 10, 9.
4, 1–13: Mt 4, 1–11; Mk 1,	**4, 13:** Lk 22, 3; Jn 13, 2.27;
12–13.	Heb 4, 15.

FREE . . . TO BE TEMPTED

Black people have been struggling for freedom for a long time. They have sung about freedom. They have written poems about it. And they have had demonstrations over it. For most black people, freedom is the promised land, a place overflowing with milk and honey, a place like heaven where everything is pleasant.

After Jesus' baptism, he went out into the wilderness to be alone in order to plan his life. While he was out there, he realized that he could still be tempted to make selfish choices. Read Lk 4, 1–13. Imagine how tempting it might have been for Jesus to use his power to prove to the world how great he was, instead of how great and loving God is.

Many people throughout history have faced the choice of using their newly won freedom for their own selfish interests or for the good of others. After securing their freedom, some slaves, like Harriet Tubman, decided to spend their lives helping others become free—often at great risk and sacrifice to themselves. You can be sure that they were tempted to choose an easier and safer life.

If we want to be free, we must face temptation. And if we want to remain free, we must resist the temptation to choose selfishly. Because once we give in to selfishness, we become less free to resist it the next time around. And before long, we will become slaves again—slaves to our own desires.

▶ Lk 4, 1–13

IV: The Ministry in Galilee

The Beginning of the Galilean Ministry

14*† Jesus returned to Galilee in the power of the Spirit, and news of him spread throughout the whole region.* 15 He taught in their synagogues and was praised by all.

The Rejection at Nazareth†

16* He came to Nazareth, where he had grown up, and went according to his custom† into the synagogue on the sabbath day. He stood up to read 17 and was handed a scroll of the prophet Isaiah. He unrolled the scroll and found the passage where it was written:

18*† "The Spirit of the Lord is upon me,
　　because he has anointed me
　　　to bring glad tidings to the poor.
He has sent me to proclaim liberty
　　to captives
　　and recovery of sight to the blind,
　　　to let the oppressed go free,
19　and to proclaim a year acceptable to
　　　the Lord."

20 Rolling up the scroll, he handed it back to the attendant and sat down, and the eyes of all in the synagogue looked intently at him. 21† He said to them, "Today this scripture passage is fulfilled in your

---

† **4, 14:** News of him spread: a Lucan theme; see v 37; 5, 15; 7, 17.

4, 16–30: Luke has transposed to the beginning of Jesus' ministry an incident from his Marcan source, which situated it near the end of the Galilean ministry (Mk 6, 1–6a). In doing so, Luke turns the initial admiration (22) and subsequent rejection of Jesus (28–29) into a foreshadowing of the whole future ministry of Jesus. Moreover, the rejection of Jesus in his own hometown hints at the greater rejection of him by Israel (Acts 13, 46).

4, 16: According to his custom: Jesus' practice of regularly attending synagogue is carried on by the early Christians' practice of meeting in the temple (Acts 2, 46; 3, 1; 5, 12).

4, 18: The Spirit of the Lord is upon me, because he has anointed me: see the note on 3, 21–22. As this incident develops, Jesus is portrayed as a prophet whose ministry is compared to that of the prophets Elijah and Elisha. Prophetic anointings are known in first-century Palestinian Judaism from the Qumran literature that speaks

of prophets as God's anointed ones. To bring glad tidings to the poor: more than any other gospel writer Luke is concerned with Jesus' attitude toward the economically and socially poor (see 6, 20.24; 12, 16–21; 14, 12–14; 16, 19–26; 19, 8). At times, the poor in Luke's gospel are associated with the downtrodden, the oppressed and afflicted, the forgotten and the neglected (18; 6, 20–22; 7, 22; 14, 12–14), and it is they who accept Jesus' message of salvation.

4, 21: Today this scripture passage is fulfilled in your hearing: this sermon inaugurates the time of fulfillment of Old Testament prophecy. Luke presents the ministry of Jesus as fulfilling Old Testament hopes and expectations (7, 22); for Luke, even Jesus' suffering, death, and resurrection are done in fulfillment of the scriptures (24, 25–27.44–46; Acts 3, 18).

4, 14–15: Mt 4, 12–17; Mk 1,　　**4, 16–30:** Mt 13, 53–58; Mk 6,
　　14–15.　　　　　　　　　　　1–6.
4, 14: Lk 5, 15; Mt 3, 16.　　　**4, 18–19:** Is 61, 1–2; 58, 6.

Jesus Liberates People from Oppression!

In Luke, Jesus begins his mission by referring to Isaiah's prophecy (Is 61, 1). In the Gospel, we see Jesus fulfilling this prophecy by acting in the following ways:

- **healing the sick**, whose sickness is viewed as God's punishment for their sinfulness
- **touching and curing lepers**, who are separated from the rest of society
- **speaking and spending time with Samaritans**, who are looked down upon and rejected by the Jews
- **accepting as disciples women**, who are generally not accepted as equals, socially and religiously
- **responding to the request of the Roman centurion**, a foreigner who represents social domination
- **forgiving and eating with sinners**, who are put down and discriminated against by leaders of the Temple
- **liberating those possessed by demons**, whom all avoid because they are believed to be under the power of Satan

Consider these questions:

- **What types of oppression in society do Christians need to respond to today?**
- **Are you suffering from oppression? If so, how and from whom?**

Ask God for help in responding to oppression in your life and in society with truth and love.

▶ Lk 4, 14–30

---

hearing." ²²* And all spoke highly of him and were amazed at the gracious words that came from his mouth. They also asked, "Isn't this the son of Joseph?" ²³† He said to them, "Surely you will quote me this proverb, 'Physician, cure yourself,' and say, 'Do here in your native place the things that we heard were done in Capernaum.' " ²⁴ And he said, "Amen, I say to you, no prophet is accepted in his own native place. ²⁵*† Indeed, I tell you, there were many widows in Israel in the days of Elijah when the sky was closed for three and a half years and a severe famine spread over the entire land. ²⁶*† It was to none of these that Elijah was sent, but only to a widow in Zarephath in the land

of Sidon. ²⁷* Again, there were many lepers in Israel during the time of Elisha the prophet; yet not one of them was cleansed, but only Naaman the Syrian." ²⁸ When the people in the synagogue heard this, they were all filled with fury. ²⁹ They rose up, drove him out of the town, and led him to the brow of the hill on which their town had been built, to hurl him down headlong. ³⁰ But he passed through the midst of them and went away.

The Cure of a Demoniac

³¹*† Jesus then went down to Capernaum, a town of Galilee.* He taught them on the sabbath, ³²* and they were astonished at his teaching

---

4, 23: *The things that we heard were done in Capernaum:* Luke's source for this incident reveals an awareness of an earlier ministry of Jesus in Capernaum that Luke has not yet made use of because of his transposition of this Nazareth episode to the beginning of Jesus' Galilean ministry. It is possible that by use of the future tense *you will quote me. . . ,* Jesus is being portrayed as a prophet.

4, 25–26: The references to Elijah and Elisha serve several purposes in this episode: they emphasize Luke's portrait of Jesus as a prophet like Elijah and Elisha; they help to explain why the initial admiration of the people turns to rejection; and they provide the scriptural justification for the future Christian mission to the Gentiles.

4, 26: *A widow in Zarephath in the land of Sidon:* like Naaman

the Syrian in v 27, a non-Israelite becomes the object of the prophet's ministry.

4, 31–44: The next several incidents in Jesus' ministry take place in Capernaum and are based on Luke's source, Mk 1, 21–39. To the previous portrait of Jesus as prophet (16–30) they now add a presentation of him as teacher (31–32), exorcist (32–37.41), healer (38–40), and proclaimer of God's kingdom (43).

4, 22: Lk 3, 23; Jn 6, 42.   4, 27: 2 Kgs 5, 1–14.
4, 25: 1 Kgs 17, 1–7; 18, 1;   4, 31–37: Mk 1, 21–28.
    Jas 5, 17.   4, 31: Mt 4, 13; Jn 2, 12.
4, 26: 1 Kgs 17, 9.   4, 32: Mt 7, 28–29.

because he spoke with authority. ³³* In the synagogue there was a man with the spirit of an unclean demon, and he cried out in a loud voice, ³⁴*† "Ha! What have you to do with us, Jesus of Nazareth? Have you come to destroy us? I know who you are—the Holy One of God!" ³⁵ Jesus rebuked him and said, "Be quiet! Come out of him!" Then the demon threw the man down in front of them and came out of him without doing him any harm. ³⁶ They were all amazed and said to one another, "What is there about his word? For with authority and power he commands the unclean spirits, and they come out." ³⁷ And news of him spread everywhere in the surrounding region.

The Cure of Simon's Mother-in-Law

³⁸*† After he left the synagogue, he entered the house of Simon. Simon's mother-in-law was afflicted with a severe fever, and they interceded with him about her. ³⁹ He stood over her, rebuked the fever, and it left her. She got up immediately and waited on them.

Other Healings

⁴⁰* At sunset, all who had people sick with various diseases brought them to him. He laid his hands on each of them and cured them. ⁴¹*† And demons also came out from many, shouting, "You are the Son of God." But he rebuked them and did not allow them to speak because they knew that he was the Messiah.

Jesus Leaves Capernaum

⁴²*† At daybreak, Jesus left and went to a deserted place. The crowds went looking for him, and when they came to him, they tried to prevent him

from leaving them. ⁴³* But he said to them, "To the other towns also I must proclaim the good news of the kingdom of God, because for this purpose I have been sent." ⁴⁴† And he was preaching in the synagogues of Judea.

The Call of Simon the Fisherman*†

5 ¹* While the crowd was pressing in on Jesus and listening to the word of God, he was standing by the Lake of Gennesaret. ² He saw two boats there alongside the lake; the fishermen had disembarked and were washing their nets. ³ Getting into one of the boats, the one belonging to Simon, he asked him to put out a short distance from the shore. Then he sat down and taught the crowds from the boat. ⁴* After he had finished speaking, he said to Simon, "Put out into deep water and lower your nets for a catch." ⁵ Simon said in reply, "Master, we have worked hard all night and have caught nothing, but at your command I will lower the nets." ⁶ When they had done this, they caught a great number of fish and their nets were tearing. ⁷ They signaled to their partners in the other boat to come to help them. They came and filled both boats so that they were in danger of sinking. ⁸ When Simon Peter saw this, he fell at the knees of Jesus and said, "Depart from me, Lord, for I am a sinful man." ⁹ For astonishment at the catch of fish they had made seized him and all those with him, ¹⁰* and likewise James and John, the sons of Zebedee, who were partners of Simon. Jesus said to Simon, "Do not be afraid; from now on you will be catching men." ¹¹*† When they brought their boats to the shore, they left everything and followed him.

4, 34: *What have you to do with us?:* see the note on Jn 2, 4. *Have you come to destroy us?:* the question reflects the current belief that before the day of the Lord control over humanity would be wrested from the evil spirits, evil destroyed, and God's authority over humanity reestablished. The synoptic gospel tradition presents Jesus carrying out this task.

4, 38: *The house of Simon:* because of Luke's arrangement of material, the reader has not yet been introduced to Simon (cf Mk 1, 16–18.29–31). Situated as it is before the call of Simon (5, 1–11), it helps the reader to understand Simon's eagerness to do what Jesus says (5, 5) and to follow him (5, 11).

4, 41: *They knew that he was the Messiah:* that is, the Christ (see the note on 2, 11).

4, 42: *They tried to prevent him from leaving them:* the reaction of these strangers in Capernaum is presented in contrast to the reactions of those in his hometown who rejected him (28–30).

4, 44: *In the synagogues of Judea:* instead of *Judea,* which is the best reading of the manuscript tradition, the Byzantine text tradition and other manuscripts read "Galilee," a reading that harmonizes Luke with Mt 4, 23 and Mk 1, 39. Up to this point Luke has spoken only of a ministry of Jesus in Galilee. Luke may be using *Judea* to refer to the land of Israel, the territory of the Jews, and not to a specific portion of it.

5, 1–11: This incident has been transposed from his source, Mk 1, 16–20, which places it immediately after Jesus makes his appearance in Galilee. By this transposition Luke uses this example of Simon's acceptance of Jesus to counter the earlier rejection of him by his hometown people, and since several incidents dealing with Je-

sus' power and authority have already been narrated, Luke creates a plausible context for the acceptance of Jesus by Simon and his partners. Many commentators have noted the similarity between the wondrous catch of fish reported here (4–9) and the post-resurrectional appearance of Jesus in Jn 21, 1–11. There are traces in Luke's story that the post-resurrectional context is the original one: in v 8 Simon addresses Jesus as *Lord* (a post-resurrectional title for Jesus—see 24, 34; Acts 2, 36—that has been read back into the historical ministry of Jesus) and recognizes himself as a sinner (an appropriate recognition for one who has denied knowing Jesus—22, 54–62). As used by Luke, the incident looks forward to Peter's leadership in Luke-Acts (6, 14; 9, 20; 22, 31–32; 24, 34; Acts 1, 15; 2, 14–40; 10, 11–18; 15, 7–12) and symbolizes the future success of Peter as fisherman (Acts 2, 41).

5, 11: *They left everything:* in Mk 1, 16–20 and Mt 4, 18–22 the fishermen who follow Jesus leave their nets and their father; in Luke, they leave *everything* (see also 28; 12, 33; 14, 33; 18, 22), an indication of Luke's theme of complete detachment from material possessions.

4, 33–34: Lk 8, 28; Mt 8, 29; Mk 1, 23–24; 5, 7.
4, 34: Lk 4, 41; Jn 6, 69.
4, 38–39: Mt 8, 14–15; Mk 1, 29–31.
4, 40–41: Mt 8, 16; Mk 1, 32–34.
4, 41: Lk 4, 34; Mt 8, 29; Mk 3, 11–12.

4, 42–44: Mk 1, 35–39.
4, 43: Lk 8, 1; Mk 1, 14–15.
5, 1–11: Mt 4, 18–22; Mk 1, 16–20.
5, 1–3: Mt 13, 1–2; Mk 2, 13; 3, 9–10; 4, 1–2.
5, 4–9: Jn 21, 1–11.
5, 10: Jer 16, 16.
5, 11: Mt 19, 27.

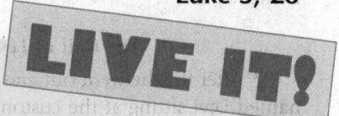

Do Not Be Afraid

How would you respond if someone walked into the room right now and announced that God wanted to see you in the next room in five minutes? As astonishing as that would be, few of us would probably be anxious to run right in to see God. We would probably want a little more time to get some things in our life "straightened out"!

The Gospel of Luke reveals something interesting when it describes a miraculous catch of fish and the call of the first disciples. Upon seeing the miraculous catch, Peter knows he is in the presence of a holy person and asks Jesus to leave because he is overwhelmed by his own sinfulness and feels unworthy in Jesus' presence (5, 8).

If we found ourselves in a boat with God, we might respond the same way. Jesus reassures Peter, uttering words so important that they are repeated six times in Luke: "Do not be afraid." God knows we are sinners too. Jesus came not to condemn us but to save us and to make God's love known to us. Jesus is also saying to us: "Do not be afraid. Come, follow me!"

▸ Lk 5, 1–11

LK

The Cleansing of a Leper

12*† Now there was a man full of leprosy in one of the towns where he was; and when he saw Jesus, he fell prostrate, pleaded with him, and said, "Lord, if you wish, you can make me clean." 13 Jesus stretched out his hand, touched him, and said, "I do will it. Be made clean." And the leprosy left him immediately. 14*† Then he ordered him not to tell anyone, but "Go, show yourself to the priest and offer for your cleansing what Moses prescribed; that will be proof for them." 15 The report about him spread all the more, and great crowds assembled to listen to him and to be cured of their ailments, 16* but he would withdraw to deserted places to pray.

The Healing of a Paralytic

17*† One day as Jesus was teaching, Pharisees† and teachers of the law were sitting there who had come from every village of Galilee and Judea and Jerusalem, and the power of the Lord was with him for healing. 18 And some men brought on a stretcher a man who was paralyzed; they were trying to bring him in and set [him] in his presence. 19† But not finding a way to bring him in because of the crowd, they went up on the roof and lowered him on the stretcher through the tiles into the middle in front of Jesus. 20† When he saw their faith, he said, "As for you, your sins are forgiven." 21*† Then the scribes and Pharisees began to ask themselves, "Who is this who speaks blasphemies? Who but God alone can forgive sins?" 22* Jesus knew their thoughts and said to them in reply, "What are you thinking in your hearts? 23 Which is easier, to say, 'Your sins are forgiven,' or to say, 'Rise and walk'? 24*† But that you may know that the Son of Man has authority on earth to forgive sins"—he said to the man who was paralyzed, "I say to you, rise, pick up your stretcher, and go home." 25 He stood up immediately before them, picked up what he had been lying on, and went home, glorifying God. 26 Then astonishment seized them all and they glorified God, and, struck with awe, they said, "We have seen incredible things today."

†
5, 12: *Full of leprosy:* see the note on Mk 1, 40.
5, 14: *Show yourself to the priest . . . what Moses prescribed:* this is a reference to Lv 14, 2–9 that gives detailed instructions for the purification of one who had been a victim of leprosy and thereby excluded from contact with others (see Lv 13, 45–46.49; Nm 5, 2–3). *That will be proof for them:* see the note on Mt 8, 4.
5, 17—6, 11: From his Marcan source, Luke now introduces a series of controversies with Pharisees: controversy over Jesus' power to forgive sins (17–26); controversy over his eating and drinking with tax collectors and sinners (27–32); controversy over not fasting (33–36); and finally two episodes narrating controversies over observance of the sabbath (1–11).
5, 17: *Pharisees:* see the note on Mt 3, 7.
5, 19: *Through the tiles:* Luke has adapted the story found in Mark to his non-Palestinian audience by changing "opened up the roof" (Mk 2, 4, a reference to Palestinian straw and clay roofs) to *through the tiles,* a detail that reflects the Hellenistic Greco-Roman house with tiled roof.
5, 20: *As for you, your sins are forgiven:* literally, "O man, your sins are forgiven you." The connection between the forgiveness of sins and the cure of the paralytic reflects the belief of first-century Palestine (based on the Old Testament: Ex 20, 5; Dt 5, 9) that sickness and infirmity are the result of sin, one's own or that of one's ancestors (see also 13, 2; Jn 5, 14; 9, 2).
5, 21: *The scribes:* see the note on Mk 2, 6.
5, 24: See the notes on Mt 9, 6 and Mk 2, 10.

*
5, 12–16: Mt 8, 2–4; Mk 1, 40–45.
5, 14: Lk 8, 56; Lv 14, 2–32; Mk 7, 36.
5, 16: Mk 1, 35.
5, 17–26: Mt 9, 1–8; Mk 2, 1–12.
5, 21: Lk 7, 49; Is 43, 25.
5, 22: Lk 6, 8; 9, 47.
5, 24–25: Jn 5, 8–9.27.

The Call of Levi

27* After this he went out and saw a tax collector named Levi sitting at the customs post. He said to him, "Follow me." 28† And leaving everything behind, he got up and followed him. 29* Then Levi gave a great banquet for him in his house, and a large crowd of tax collectors and others were at table with them. 30 The Pharisees and their scribes complained to his disciples, saying, "Why do you eat and drink with tax collectors and sinners?" 31 Jesus said to them in reply, "Those who are healthy do not need a physician, but the sick do. 32 I have not come to call the righteous to repentance but sinners."

The Question about Fasting

33* And they said to him, "The disciples of John fast often and offer prayers, and the disciples of the Pharisees do the same; but yours eat and drink." 34† Jesus answered them, "Can you make the wedding guests† fast while the bridegroom is with them? 35 But the days will come, and when the bridegroom is taken away from them, then they will fast in those days." 36† And he also told them a parable. "No one tears a piece from a new cloak to patch an old one. Otherwise, he will tear the new and the piece from it will not match the old cloak. 37 Likewise, no one pours new wine into old wineskins. Otherwise, the new wine will burst the skins, and it will be spilled, and the skins will be ruined. 38 Rather, new wine must be poured into fresh wineskins. 39† [And] no one who has been drinking old wine desires new, for he says, 'The old is good.'"

Debates about the Sabbath

6 1*† While he was going through a field of grain on a sabbath, his disciples were picking the heads of grain, rubbing them in their hands, and eating them.* 2 Some Pharisees said, "Why are you doing what is unlawful on the sabbath?" 3* Jesus said to them in reply, "Have you not read what David did when he and those [who were] with him were hungry? 4*† [How] he went into the house of God, took the bread of offering, which only the priests could lawfully eat, ate of it, and shared it with his companions." 5 Then he said to them, "The Son of Man is lord of the sabbath."

6* On another sabbath he went into the synagogue and taught, and there was a man there whose right hand was withered. 7* The scribes and the Pharisees watched him closely to see if he would cure on the sabbath so that they might discover a reason to accuse him. 8* But he realized their intentions and said to the man with the withered hand, "Come up and stand before us." And he rose and stood there. 9 Then Jesus said to them, "I ask you, is it lawful to do good on the sabbath rather than to do evil, to save life rather than to destroy it?" 10 Looking around at them all, he then said to him, "Stretch out your hand." He did so and his hand was restored. 11 But they became enraged and discussed together what they might do to Jesus.

The Mission of the Twelve†

12* In those days he departed to the mountain to pray, and he spent the night in prayer† to God.

---

† **5, 28:** *Leaving everything behind:* see the note on 5, 11.
5, 34–35: See the notes on Mt 9, 15 and Mk 2, 19.
5, 34: *Wedding guests:* literally, "sons of the bridal chamber."
5, 36–39: See the notes on Mt 9, 16–17 and Mk 2, 19.
5, 39: *The old is good:* this saying is meant to be ironic and offers an explanation for the rejection by some of the new wine that Jesus offers: satisfaction with old forms will prevent one from sampling the new.
6, 1–11: The two episodes recounted here deal with gathering grain and healing, both of which were forbidden on the sabbath. In his defense of his disciples' conduct and his own charitable deed, Jesus argues that satisfying human needs such as hunger and performing works of mercy take precedence even over the

sacred sabbath rest. See also the notes on Mt 12, 1–14 and Mk 2, 25–26.
6, 4: *The bread of offering:* see the note on Mt 12, 5–6.
6, 12–16: See the notes on Mt 10, 1–11, 1 and Mk 3, 14–15.
6, 12: *Spent the night in prayer:* see the note on 3, 21.

5, 27–32: Mt 9, 9–13; Mk 2, 13–17.	6, 3–4: 1 Sm 21, 1–6.
5, 29–30: Lk 15, 1–2.	6, 4: Lv 24, 5–9.
5, 33–39: Mt 9, 14–17; Mk 2, 18–22.	6, 6–11: Mt 12, 9–14; Mk 3, 1–6.
6, 1–5: Mt 12, 1–8; Mk 2, 23–28.	6, 7: Lk 14, 1.
6, 1: Dt 23, 26.	6, 8: Lk 5, 22; 9, 47.
	6, 12–16: Mt 10, 1–4; Mk 3, 13–19.

PRAY IT!

Jesus' Preference for the Poor

In the Gospel of Luke, Jesus gives the Sermon on the Plain, which parallels the Sermon on the Mount in Matthew. Even more clearly than Matthew, Luke makes the point that God's justice has a preference for the poor and the little ones. So it's not surprising that the four beatitudes (blessings) in Luke are balanced by four woes ("Woe!" is like saying, "Trouble ahead!"). For example, "Blessed are you who are poor" (6, 20) is countered by "Woe to you who are rich" (verse 24). Jesus shows his care for both rich people and poor people by calling the rich to practice justice and the poor to have hope.

Unlike Matthew, Luke does not "spiritualize" the Beatitudes. Matthew says, "Blessed are the poor in spirit" (5, 3), but Luke simply says, "Blessed are you who are poor" (6, 20), meaning materially poor. Matthew is concerned for people's salvation; Luke is concerned about their salvation and their material needs.

How do you show special concern for poor people? Pray that God helps us to share God's love with those caught in the struggles of life.

▶ Lk 6, 17–49

13† When day came, he called his disciples to himself, and from them he chose Twelve, whom he also named apostles: 14*† Simon, whom he named Peter, and his brother Andrew, James, John, Philip, Bartholomew, 15† Matthew, Thomas, James the son of Alphaeus, Simon who was called a Zealot, 16† and Judas the son of James, and Judas Iscariot, who became a traitor.

Ministering to a Great Multitude

17*† And he came down with them and stood on a stretch of level ground. A great crowd of his disciples and a large number of the people from all Judea and Jerusalem and the coastal region of Tyre and Sidon, 18 came to hear him and to be healed of their diseases; and even those who were tormented by unclean spirits were cured. 19 Everyone in the crowd sought to touch him because power came forth from him and healed them all.

Sermon on the Plain

20*† And raising his eyes toward his disciples he said:

"Blessed are you who are poor,†
　　for the kingdom of God is yours.

66–70. Because the existence of the Zealots as a distinct group during the lifetime of Jesus is the subject of debate, the meaning of the identification of Simon as a Zealot is unclear.

6, 16: *Judas Iscariot:* the name *Iscariot* may mean "man from Kerioth."

6, 17: *The coastal region of Tyre and Sidon:* not only Jews from Judea and Jerusalem, but even Gentiles from outside Palestine come to hear Jesus (see 2, 31–32; 3, 6; 4, 24–27).

6, 20–49: Luke's "Sermon on the Plain" is the counterpart to Matthew's "Sermon on the Mount" (Mt 5, 1—7, 27). It is addressed to the disciples of Jesus, and, like the sermon in Matthew, it begins with beatitudes (20–22) and ends with the parable of the two houses (46–49). Almost all the words of Jesus reported by Luke are found in Matthew's version, but because Matthew includes sayings that were related to specifically Jewish Christian problems (e.g., Mt 5, 17–20; 6, 1–8.16–18) that Luke did not find appropriate for his predominantly Gentile Christian audience, the "Sermon on the Mount" is considerably longer. Luke's sermon may be outlined as follows: an introduction consisting of blessings and woes (20–26); the love of one's enemies (27–36); the demands of loving one's neighbor (37–42); good deeds as proof of one's goodness (43–45); a parable illustrating the result of listening to and acting on the words of Jesus (46–49). At the core of the sermon is Jesus' teaching on the love of one's enemies (27–36) that has as its source of motivation God's graciousness and compassion for all humanity (35–36) and Jesus' teaching on the love of one's neighbor (37–42) that is characterized by forgiveness and generosity.

6, 20–26: The introductory portion of the sermon consists of blessings and woes that address the real economic and social conditions of humanity (the poor—the rich; the hungry—the satisfied; those grieving—those laughing; the outcast—the socially acceptable). By contrast, Matthew emphasizes the religious and spiritual values of disciples in the kingdom inaugurated by Jesus ("poor in spirit," Mt 5, 5; "hunger and thirst for righteousness" 5, 6). In the sermon, *blessed* extols the fortunate condition of persons who are favored with the blessings of God; the woes, addressed as they are to the disciples of Jesus, threaten God's profound displeasure on those so blinded by their present fortunate situation that they do not recognize and appreciate the real values of God's kingdom. In all the blessings and woes, the present condition of the persons addressed will be reversed in the future.

6, 13: *He chose Twelve:* the identification of this group as the *Twelve* is a part of early Christian tradition (see 1 Cor 15, 5), and in Matthew and Luke, the Twelve are associated with the twelve tribes of Israel (22, 29–30; Mt 19, 28). After the fall of Judas from his position among the Twelve, the need is felt on the part of the early community to reconstitute this group before the Christian mission begins at Pentecost (Acts 1, 15–26). From Luke's perspective, they are an important group who because of their association with Jesus from the time of his baptism to his ascension (Acts 1, 21–22) provide the continuity between the historical Jesus and the church of Luke's day and who as the original eyewitnesses guarantee the fidelity of the church's beliefs and practices to the teachings of Jesus (1, 1–4). *Whom he also named apostles:* only Luke among the gospel writers attributes to Jesus the bestowal of the name *apostles* upon the Twelve. See the note on Mt 10, 2–4. "Apostle" becomes a technical term in early Christianity for a missionary sent out to preach the word of God. Although Luke seems to want to restrict the title to the Twelve (only in Acts 4, 4.14 are Paul and Barnabas termed apostles), other places in the New Testament show an awareness that the term was more widely applied (1 Cor 15, 5–7; Gal 1, 19; 1 Cor 1, 1; 9, 1; Rom 16, 7).

6, 14: *Simon, whom he named Peter:* see the note on Mk 3, 16.

6, 15: *Simon who was called a Zealot:* the Zealots were the instigators of the First Revolt of Palestinian Jews against Rome in A.D.

6, 14–16: Acts 1, 13.　　　　　　6, 20–26: Mt 5, 1–12.
6, 17–19: Mt 4, 23–25; Mk 3,
　　7–10.

21* Blessed are you who are now hungry,
     for you will be satisfied.
   Blessed are you who are now weeping,
     for you will laugh.
22* Blessed are you when people hate you,
     and when they exclude and
       insult you,
     and denounce your name as evil
     on account of the Son of Man.

23* Rejoice and leap for joy on that day! Behold, your reward will be great in heaven. For their ancestors treated the prophets in the same way.

24* But woe to you who are rich,
     for you have received your
       consolation.
25* But woe to you who are filled now,
     for you will be hungry.
   Woe to you who laugh now,
     for you will grieve and weep.
26* Woe to you when all speak well
       of you,
     for their ancestors treated the
       false prophets in this way.

Love of Enemies

27*† "But to you who hear I say, love your enemies, do good to those who hate you,* 28* bless those who curse you, pray for those who mistreat you. 29 To the person who strikes you on one cheek, offer the other one as well, and from the person who takes your cloak, do not withhold even your tunic. 30 Give to everyone who asks of you, and from the one who takes what is yours do not demand it back. 31* Do to others as you would have them do to you. 32 For if you love those who love you, what credit is that to you? Even sinners love those who love them. 33 And if you do good to those who do good to you, what credit is that to you? Even sinners do the same. 34* If you lend money to those from whom you expect repayment, what credit [is] that to you? Even sinners lend to sinners, and get back the same amount. 35* But rather, love your enemies and do good to them, and lend expecting nothing back; then your reward will be great and you will be children of the Most High, for he himself is kind to the ungrateful and the wicked. 36 Be merciful, just as [also] your Father is merciful.

Judging Others†

37* "Stop judging and you will not be judged. Stop condemning and you will not be condemned. Forgive and you will be forgiven.* 38* Give and gifts will be given to you; a good measure, packed together, shaken down, and overflowing, will be poured into your lap. For the measure with which you measure will in return be measured out to you." 39* And he told them a parable, "Can a blind person guide a blind person? Will not both fall into a pit? 40* No disciple is superior to the teacher; but when fully trained, every disciple will be like his teacher. 41 Why do you notice the splinter in your brother's eye, but do not perceive the wooden beam in your own? 42 How can you say to your brother, 'Brother, let me remove that splinter in your eye,' when you do not even notice the wooden beam in your own eye? You hypocrite! Remove the wooden beam from your eye first; then you will see clearly to remove the splinter in your brother's eye.

A Tree Known by Its Fruit

43*† "A good tree does not bear rotten fruit, nor does a rotten tree bear good fruit. 44 For every tree is known by its own fruit. For people do not pick figs from thornbushes, nor do they gather grapes from brambles. 45 A good person out of the store of goodness in his heart produces good, but an evil person out of a store of evil produces evil; for from the fullness of the heart the mouth speaks.

The Two Foundations

46* "Why do you call me, 'Lord, Lord,' but not do what I command? 47*† I will show you what someone is like who comes to me, listens to my words, and acts on them. 48 That one is like a person building a house, who dug deeply and laid the foundation on rock; when the flood came, the river burst against that house but could not shake it because it had been well built. 49 But the one who listens and does not act is like a person who built a house on the ground without a foundation. When the river burst against it, it collapsed at once and was completely destroyed."

---

† **6, 27–36:** See the notes on Mt 5, 43–48 and 5, 48.
6, 37–42: See the notes on Mt 7, 1–12; 7, 1; 7, 5.
6, 43–46: See the notes on Mt 7, 15–20 and 12, 33.
6, 47–49: See the note on Mt 7, 24–27.

* **6, 21:** Ps 126, 5–6; Is 61, 3; Jer 31, 25; Rv 7, 16–17.   **6, 23:** Lk 11, 47–48; 2 Chr 36, 16; Mt 23, 30–31.   **6, 24:** Jas 5, 1.   **6, 25:** Is 65, 13–14.   **6, 22:** Jn 15, 19; 16, 2; 1 Pt 4, 14.   **6, 26:** Jas 4, 4.

6, 27–36: Mt 5, 38–48.   **6, 27:** Prv 25, 21; Rom 12, 20–21.   **6, 28:** Rom 12, 14; 1 Pt 3, 9.   **6, 31:** Mt 7, 12.   **6, 34:** Dt 15, 7–8.   **6, 35:** Lv 25, 35–36.   **6, 37–42:** Mt 7, 1–5.   **6, 37:** Mt 6, 14; Jas 2, 13.   **6, 38:** Mk 4, 24.   **6, 39:** Mt 15, 14; 23, 16–17.24.   **6, 40:** Mt 10, 24–25; Jn 13, 16; 15, 20.   **6, 43–45:** Mt 7, 16–20; 12, 33.35.   **6, 46:** Mt 7, 21; Rom 2, 13; Jas 1, 22.   **6, 47–49:** Mt 7, 24–27.

The Healing of a Centurion's Slave

7 ¹*† When he had finished all his words to the people, he entered Capernaum.† ²† A centurion there had a slave who was ill and about to die, and he was valuable to him. ³ When he heard about Jesus, he sent elders of the Jews to him, asking him to come and save the life of his slave. ⁴ They approached Jesus and strongly urged him to come, saying, "He deserves to have you do this for him, ⁵ for he loves our nation and he built the synagogue for us." ⁶† And Jesus went with them, but when he was only a short distance from the house, the centurion sent friends to tell him, "Lord, do not trouble yourself, for I am not worthy to have you enter under my roof. ⁷ Therefore, I did not consider myself worthy to come to you; but say the word and let my servant be healed. ⁸ For I too am a person subject to authority, with soldiers subject to me. And I say to one, 'Go,' and he goes; and to another, 'Come here,' and he comes; and to my slave, 'Do this,' and he does it." ⁹ When Jesus heard this he was amazed at him and, turning, said to the crowd following him, "I tell you, not even in Israel have I found such faith." ¹⁰ When the messengers returned to the house, they found the slave in good health.

Raising of the Widow's Son

¹¹*† Soon afterward he journeyed to a city called Nain, and his disciples and a large crowd accompanied him. ¹²* As he drew near to the gate of the city, a man who had died was being carried out, the only son of his mother, and she was a widow. A large crowd from the city was with her. ¹³ When the Lord saw her, he was moved with pity for her and said to her, "Do not weep." ¹⁴ He stepped forward and touched the coffin; at this the bearers halted, and he said, "Young man, I tell you, arise!" ¹⁵* The dead man sat up and began to speak, and Jesus

THE REUNION DINNER

The words of the centurion in Lk 7, 6–7 are the basis for the words Catholics say before receiving the Holy Eucharist, "Lord, I am not worthy to receive you, but only say the word and I shall be healed." These words indicate our humility and our willingness to accept God's forgiveness and healing in our life. They remind us to receive Jesus in a state of peace with God and one another, especially by seeking reconciliation with family and friends.

The Chinese New Year's celebration includes a "reunion dinner." The whole family gathers at the home of the eldest family member. People travel from faraway cities, and even from other countries, to be together. The meal is not eaten until everyone is present, and no one eats until any disagreement or hurt is forgiven, and the family is at peace.

▶ **Lk 7, 1–10**

---

† **7, 1—8, 3:** The episodes in this section present a series of reactions to the Galilean ministry of Jesus and reflect some of Luke's particular interests: the faith of a Gentile (1–10); the prophet Jesus' concern for a widowed mother (11–17); the ministry of Jesus directed to the afflicted and unfortunate of Is 61, 1 (18–23); the relation between John and Jesus and their role in God's plan for salvation (24–35); a forgiven sinner's manifestation of love (36–50); the association of women with the ministry of Jesus (8, 1–3).

7, 1–10: This story about the faith of the centurion, a Gentile who cherishes the Jewish nation (5), prepares for the story in Acts of the conversion by Peter of the Roman centurion Cornelius who is similarly described as one who is generous to the Jewish nation (Acts 10, 2). See also Acts 10, 34–35 in the speech of Peter: "God shows no partiality . . . whoever fears him and acts uprightly is acceptable to him." See also the notes on Mt 8, 5–13 and Jn 4, 43–54.

7, 2: *A centurion:* see the note on Mt 8, 5.

7, 6: *I am not worthy to have you enter under my roof:* to enter the house of a Gentile was considered unclean for a Jew; cf Acts 10, 28.

7, 11–17: In the previous incident Jesus' power was displayed for a Gentile whose servant was dying; in this episode it is displayed toward a widowed mother whose only son has already died. Jesus' power over death prepares for his reply to John's disciples in v 22: "the dead are raised." This resuscitation in alluding to the prophet Elijah's resurrection of the only son of a widow of Zarephath (1 Kgs 7, 18–24) leads to the reaction of the crowd: "A great prophet has arisen in our midst" (16).

7, 1–10: Mt 8, 5–13; Jn 4, 43–54.
7, 11–17: Lk 4, 25–26; 1 Kgs 17, 17–24.

7, 12: Lk 8, 42; 1 Kgs 17, 17.
7, 15: 1 Kgs 17, 23; 2 Kgs 4, 36.

gave him to his mother. [16]* Fear seized them all, and they glorified God, exclaiming, "A great prophet has arisen in our midst," and "God has visited his people." [17] This report about him spread through the whole of Judea and in all the surrounding region.

The Messengers from John the Baptist

[18]*† The disciples of John told him about all these things. John summoned two of his disciples [19]* and sent them to the Lord to ask, "Are you the one who is to come, or should we look for another?" [20] When the men came to him, they said, "John the Baptist has sent us to you to ask, 'Are you the one who is to come, or should we look for another?'" [21] At that time he cured many of their diseases, sufferings, and evil spirits; he also granted sight to many who were blind. [22]* And he said to them in reply, "Go and tell John what you have seen and heard: the blind regain their sight, the lame walk, lepers are cleansed, the deaf hear, the dead are raised, the poor have the good news proclaimed to them. [23]† And blessed is the one who takes no offense at me."

Jesus' Testimony to John

[24]*† When the messengers of John had left, Jesus began to speak to the crowds about John. "What did you go out to the desert to see—a reed swayed by the wind? [25] Then what did you go out to see? Someone dressed in fine garments? Those who dress luxuriously and live sumptuously are found in royal palaces. [26]* Then what did you go out to see? A prophet? Yes, I tell you, and more than a prophet. [27]* This is the one about whom scripture says:

'Behold, I am sending my messenger ahead
  of you,
 he will prepare your way before you.'

[28] I tell you, among those born of women, no one is greater than John; yet the least in the kingdom of God is greater than he." [29]* (All the people who listened, including the tax collectors, and who were baptized with the baptism of John, acknowledged the righteousness of God; [30] but the Pharisees and scholars of the law, who were not baptized by him, rejected the plan of God for themselves.)

[31]*† "Then to what shall I compare the people of this generation? What are they like? [32] They are like children who sit in the marketplace and call to one another,

'We played the flute for you, but you did
  not dance.
 We sang a dirge, but you did not weep.'

[33] For John the Baptist came neither eating food nor drinking wine, and you said, 'He is possessed by a demon.' [34]* The Son of Man came eating and drinking and you said, 'Look, he is a glutton and a drunkard, a friend of tax collectors and sinners.' [35] But wisdom is vindicated by all her children."

The Pardon of the Sinful Woman†

[36]* A Pharisee invited him to dine with him, and he entered the Pharisee's house and reclined at table.† [37]* Now there was a sinful woman in the city who learned that he was at table in the house of the Pharisee. Bringing an alabaster flask of ointment,* [38] she stood behind him at his feet weeping and began to bathe his feet with her tears. Then she wiped them with her hair, kissed them, and anointed them with the ointment. [39] When the Pharisee who had invited him saw this he said to himself, "If this man were a prophet, he would know who and what sort of woman this is who is touching him, that she is a sinner." [40] Jesus said to him in reply, "Simon, I have something to say to you." "Tell me, teacher," he said. [41]† "Two people were in debt to a certain creditor;

---

† **7, 18–23:** In answer to John's question, *Are you the one who is to come?*—a probable reference to the return of the fiery prophet of reform, Elijah, "before the day of the LORD comes, the great and terrible day" (Mal 3, 23)—Jesus responds that his role is rather to bring the blessings spoken of in Is 61, 1 to the oppressed and neglected of society (22; cf 4, 18).

7, 23: *Blessed is the one who takes no offense at me:* this beatitude is pronounced on the person who recognizes Jesus' true identity in spite of previous expectations of what "the one who is to come" would be like.

7, 24–30: In his testimony to John, Jesus reveals his understanding of the relationship between them: John is the precursor of Jesus (27); John is the messenger spoken of in Mal 3, 1 who in Mal 3, 23 is identified as Elijah. Taken with the previous episode, it can be seen that Jesus identifies John as precisely the person John envisioned Jesus to be: the Elijah who prepares the way for the coming of the day of the Lord.

7, 31–35: See the note on Mt 11, 16–19.

7, 36–50: In this story of the pardoning of the sinful woman Luke presents two different reactions to the ministry of Jesus. A Pharisee, suspecting Jesus to be a prophet, invites Jesus to a festive banquet in

his house, but the Pharisee's self-righteousness leads to little forgiveness by God and consequently little love shown toward Jesus. The sinful woman, on the other hand, manifests a faith in God (50) that has led her to seek forgiveness for her sins, and because so much was forgiven, she now overwhelms Jesus with her display of love; cf the similar contrast in attitudes in 18, 9–14. The whole episode is a powerful lesson on the relation between forgiveness and love.

7, 36: *Reclined at table:* the normal posture of guests at a banquet. Other oriental banquet customs alluded to in this story include the reception by the host with a kiss (45), washing the feet of the guests (44), and the anointing of the guests' heads (46).

7, 41: *Days' wages:* one denarius is the normal daily wage of a laborer.

7, 16: Lk 1, 68; 19, 44.	**7, 27:** Mal 3, 1 / Is 40, 3.
7, 18–23: Mt 11, 2–6.	**7, 29–30:** Lk 3, 7.12; Mt 21, 32.
7, 19: Mal 3, 1; Rv 1, 4.8;	**7, 31–35:** Mt 11, 16–19.
4, 8.	**7, 34:** Lk 15, 2.
7, 22: Lk 4, 18; Is 35, 5–6;	**7, 36:** Lk 11, 37; 14, 1.
61, 1.	**7, 37:** Mt 26, 7; Mk 14, 3.
7, 24–30: Mt 11, 7–15.	**7, 37–38:** Jn 12, 3.
7, 26: Lk 1, 76.	

one owed five hundred days' wages and the other owed fifty. 42 Since they were unable to repay the debt, he forgave it for both. Which of them will love him more?" 43 Simon said in reply, "The one, I suppose, whose larger debt was forgiven." He said to him, "You have judged rightly." 44 Then he turned to the woman and said to Simon, "Do you see this woman? When I entered your house, you did not give me water for my feet, but she has bathed them with her tears and wiped them with her hair. 45 You did not give me a kiss, but she has not ceased kissing my feet since the time I entered. 46 You did not anoint my head with oil, but she anointed my feet with ointment. 47† So I tell you, her many sins have been forgiven; hence, she has shown great love. But the one to whom little is forgiven, loves little." 48* He said to her, "Your sins are forgiven." 49* The others at table said to themselves, "Who is this who even forgives sins?" 50 But he said to the woman, "Your faith has saved you; go in peace."

Galilean Women Follow Jesus

8 1*† Afterward he journeyed from one town and village to another, preaching and proclaiming the good news of the kingdom of God. Accompanying him were the Twelve 2* and some women who had been cured of evil spirits and infirmities, Mary, called Magdalene, from whom seven demons had gone out, 3 Joanna, the wife of Herod's steward Chuza, Susanna, and many others who provided for them out of their resources.

The Parable of the Sower

4*† When a large crowd gathered, with people from one town after another journeying to him, he spoke in a parable.† 5 "A sower went out to sow his seed. And as he sowed, some seed fell on the path and was trampled, and the birds of the sky ate it up. 6 Some seed fell on rocky ground, and when it grew, it withered for lack of moisture. 7 Some seed fell among thorns, and the thorns grew with it and choked it. 8* And some seed fell on good soil, and when it grew, it produced fruit a hundredfold." After saying this, he called out, "Whoever has ears to hear ought to hear."

The Purpose of the Parables

9* Then his disciples asked him what the meaning of this parable might be. 10* He answered, "Knowledge of the mysteries of the kingdom of God has been granted to you; but to the rest, they are made known through parables so that 'they may look but not see, and hear but not understand.'

The Parable of the Sower Explained

11*† "This is the meaning of the parable. The seed is the word of God.* 12 Those on the path are the ones who have heard, but the devil comes and takes away the word from their hearts that they may not believe and be saved. 13 Those on rocky ground are the ones who, when they hear, receive the word with joy, but they have no root; they believe only for a time and fall away in time of trial. 14 As for the seed that fell among thorns, they are the ones who have heard, but as they go along, they are choked by the anxieties and riches and pleasures of life, and they fail to produce mature fruit. 15 But as for the seed that fell on rich soil, they are the ones who, when they have heard the word, embrace it with a generous and good heart, and bear fruit through perseverance.

The Parable of the Lamp

16*† "No one who lights a lamp conceals it with a vessel or sets it under a bed; rather, he places it on a lampstand so that those who enter may see the light.* 17* For there is nothing hidden that will not become visible, and nothing secret that will not be known and come to light. 18* Take care, then, how you hear. To anyone who has, more will be given, and from the one who has not, even what he seems to have will be taken away."

L
K

---

† **7, 47:** *Her many sins have been forgiven; hence, she has shown great love:* literally, "her many sins have been forgiven, seeing that she has loved much." That the woman's sins have been forgiven is attested by the great love she shows toward Jesus. Her love is the consequence of her forgiveness. This is also the meaning demanded by the parable in vv 41–43.

8, 1–3: Luke presents Jesus as an itinerant preacher traveling in the company of the Twelve and of the Galilean women who are sustaining them out of their means. These Galilean women will later accompany Jesus on his journey to Jerusalem and become witnesses to his death (23, 49) and resurrection (24, 9–11, where Mary Magdalene and Joanna are specifically mentioned; cf also Acts 1, 14). The association of women with the ministry of Jesus is most unusual in the light of the attitude of first-century Palestinian Judaism toward women. The more common attitude is expressed in Jn 4, 27, and early rabbinic documents caution against speaking with women in public.

8, 4–21: The focus in this section is on how one should hear the word of God and act on it. It includes the parable of the sower and its explanation (4–15), a collection of sayings on how one should act on the word that is heard (16–18), and the identification of the mother and brothers of Jesus as the ones who hear the word and act on it

(19–21). See also the notes on Mt 13, 1–53 and Mk 4, 1–34.
8, 4–8: See the note on Mt 13, 3–8.
8, 11–15: On the interpretation of the parable of the sower, see the note on Mt 13, 18–23.
8, 16–18: These sayings continue the theme of responding to the word of God. Those who hear the word must become a light to others (16); even the mysteries of the kingdom that have been made known to the disciples (9–10) must come to light (17); a generous and persevering response to the word of God leads to a still more perfect response to the word.

7, 48: Lk 5, 20; Mt 9, 20; Mk 2, 5.	8, 9–10: Mt 13, 10–13; Mk 4, 10–12.
7, 49: Lk 5, 21.	8, 10: Is 6, 9.
8, 1: Lk 4, 43.	8, 11–15: Mt 13, 18–23; Mk 4, 13–20.
8, 2–3: Lk 23, 49; 24, 10; Mt 27, 55–56; Mk 15, 40–41; Jn 19, 5.	8, 11: 1 Pt 1, 23.
8, 4–8: Mt 13, 1–9; Mk 4, 1–9.	8, 16–18: Mk 4, 21–25.
8, 8: Lk 14, 35; Mt 11, 15; 13, 43; Mk 4, 23.	8, 16: Lk 11, 33; Mt 5, 15.
	8, 17: Lk 12, 2; Mt 10, 26.
	8, 18: Lk 19, 26; Mt 13, 12; 25, 29.

Jesus and His Family

19*† Then his mother and his brothers came to him but were unable to join him because of the crowd. 20* He was told, "Your mother and your brothers are standing outside and they wish to see you." 21† He said to them in reply, "My mother and my brothers are those who hear the word of God and act on it."

The Calming of a Storm at Sea

22*† One day he got into a boat with his disciples and said to them, "Let us cross to the other side of the lake." So they set sail, 23 and while they were sailing he fell asleep. A squall blew over the lake, and they were taking in water and were in danger. 24 They came and woke him saying, "Master, master, we are perishing!" He awakened, rebuked the wind and the waves, and they subsided and there was a calm. 25 Then he asked them, "Where is your faith?" But they were filled with awe and amazed and said to one another, "Who then is this, who commands even the winds and the sea, and they obey him?"

The Healing of the Gerasene Demoniac

26*† Then they sailed to the territory of the Gerasenes, which is opposite Galilee. 27 When he came ashore a man from the town who was possessed by demons met him. For a long time he had not worn clothes; he did not live in a house, but lived among the tombs. 28* When he saw Jesus, he cried out and fell down before him; in a loud voice he shouted, "What have you to do with me, Jesus, son of the Most High God? I beg you, do not torment me!" 29 For he had ordered the unclean spirit to come out of the man. (It had taken hold of him many times, and he used to be bound with chains and shackles as a restraint, but he would break his bonds and be driven by the demon into deserted places.) 30† Then Jesus asked him, "What is your name?" He replied, "Legion," because many demons had entered him. 31† And they pleaded with him not to order them to depart to the abyss.

32 A herd of many swine was feeding there on the hillside, and they pleaded with him to allow them to enter those swine; and he let them. 33 The demons came out of the man and entered the swine, and the herd rushed down the steep bank into the lake and was drowned. 34 When the swineherds saw what had happened, they ran away and reported the incident in the town and throughout the countryside. 35† People came out to see what had happened and, when they approached Jesus, they discovered the man from whom the demons had come out sitting at his feet. He was clothed and in his right mind, and they were seized with fear. 36 Those who witnessed it told them how the possessed man had been saved. 37 The entire population of the region of the Gerasenes asked Jesus to leave them because they were seized with great fear. So he got into a boat and returned. 38 The man from whom the demons had come out begged to remain with him, but he sent him away, saying, 39 "Return home and recount what God has done for you." The man went off and proclaimed throughout the whole town what Jesus had done for him.

Jairus's Daughter and the Woman with a Hemorrhage

40*† When Jesus returned, the crowd welcomed him, for they were all waiting for him. 41 And a man named Jairus, an official of the synagogue, came forward. He fell at the feet of Jesus and begged him to come to his house, 42† because he had an only daughter, about twelve years old, and she was dying. As he went, the crowds almost crushed him. 43† And a woman afflicted with hemorrhages for

---

† **8, 19:** *His brothers:* see the note on Mk 6, 3.

8, 21: The family of Jesus is not constituted by physical relationship with him but by obedience to the word of God. In this, Luke agrees with the Marcan parallel (3, 31–35), although by omitting Mk 3, 33 and especially Mk 3, 20–21 Luke has softened the Marcan picture of Jesus' natural family. Probably he did this because Mary has already been presented in 1, 38 as the obedient handmaid of the Lord who fulfills the requirement for belonging to the eschatological family of Jesus; cf also 11, 27–28.

8, 22–56: This section records four miracles of Jesus that manifest his power and authority: (1) the calming of a storm on the lake (22–25); (2) the exorcism of a demoniac (26–39); (3) the cure of a hemorrhaging woman (40–48); (4) the raising of Jairus's daughter to life (49–56). They parallel the same sequence of stories at Mk 4, 35–5, 43.

8, 26: *Gerasenes:* other manuscripts read Gadarenes or Gergesenes. See also the note on Mt 8, 28. *Opposite Galilee:* probably Gentile territory (note the presence in the area of pigs—unclean animals to Jews) and an indication that the person who receives salvation (36) is a Gentile.

8, 30: *What is your name?:* the question reflects the popular belief that knowledge of the spirit's name brought control over the spirit. *Legion:* to Jesus' question the demon replies with a Latin word

transliterated into Greek. The Roman legion at this period consisted of 5,000 to 6,000 foot soldiers; hence the name implies a very large number of demons.

8, 31: *Abyss:* the place of the dead (Rom 10, 7) or the prison of Satan (Rv 20, 3) or the subterranean "watery deep" that symbolizes the chaos before the order imposed by creation (Gn 1, 2).

8, 35: *Sitting at his feet:* the former demoniac takes the position of a disciple before the master (10, 39; Acts 22, 3).

8, 40–56: Two interwoven miracle stories, one a healing and the other a resuscitation, present Jesus as master over sickness and death. In the Lucan account, faith in Jesus is responsible for the cure (48) and for the raising to life (50).

8, 42: *An only daughter:* cf the son of the widow of Nain whom Luke describes as an "only" son (7, 12; see also 9, 38).

8, 43: *Afflicted with hemorrhages for twelve years:* according to the Mosaic law (Lv 15, 25–30) this condition would render the woman unclean and unfit for contact with other people.

*

8, 19–21: Mt 12, 46–50; Mk 3, 31–35.
8, 20–21: Lk 11, 27–28.
8, 22–25: Mt 8, 18.23–27; Mk 4, 35–41.
8, 26–39: Mt 8, 28–34; Mk 5, 1–20.
8, 28–29: Lk 4, 33–35; Mt 8, 29; Mk 1, 23–24.
8, 40–56: Mt 9, 18–26; Mk 5, 21–43.

twelve years, who [had spent her whole livelihood on doctors and] was unable to be cured by anyone, 44 came up behind him and touched the tassel on his cloak. Immediately her bleeding stopped. 45 Jesus then asked, "Who touched me?" While all were denying it, Peter said, "Master, the crowds are pushing and pressing in upon you." 46* But Jesus said, "Someone has touched me; for I know that power has gone out from me." 47 When the woman realized that she had not escaped notice, she came forward trembling. Falling down before him, she explained in the presence of all the people why she had touched him and how she had been healed immediately. 48* He said to her, "Daughter, your faith has saved you; go in peace."

49 While he was still speaking, someone from the synagogue official's house arrived and said, "Your daughter is dead; do not trouble the teacher any longer." 50 On hearing this, Jesus answered him, "Do not be afraid; just have faith and she will be saved." 51 When he arrived at the house he allowed no one to enter with him except Peter and John and James, and the child's father and mother. 52*† All were weeping and mourning for her, when he said, "Do not weep any longer, for she is not dead, but sleeping." 53 And they ridiculed him, because they knew that she was dead. 54 But he took her by the hand and called to her, "Child, arise!" 55 Her breath returned and she immediately arose. He then directed that she should be given something to eat. 56 Her parents were astounded, and he instructed them to tell no one what had happened.

The Mission of the Twelve

9 1*† He summoned the Twelve and gave them power and authority over all demons and to cure diseases, 2 and he sent them to proclaim the kingdom of God and to heal [the sick]. 3† He said to them, "Take nothing for the journey, neither walking stick, nor sack, nor food, nor money, and let no one take a second tunic. 4* Whatever house you enter, stay there and leave from there. 5*† And as for those who do not welcome you, when you leave that town, shake the dust from your feet in testimony against them." 6 Then they set out and went from village to village proclaiming the good news and curing diseases everywhere.

Herod's Opinion of Jesus

7*† Herod the tetrarch† heard about all that was happening, and he was greatly perplexed because some were saying, "John has been raised from the

L
K

Mission Possible

LIVE IT!

Just like the director of operations from the classic television show *Mission Impossible*, Jesus in Lk 9, 1–6 seems to say to the disciples, "Your mission, should you choose to accept it . . ." But whereas the director in the television show labeled his missions as impossible, Jesus knew his missions were possible—though not always popular.

We too are asked to share in Jesus' mission. Sound easy? We know it is not. Doing what Jesus would do may mean sticking our neck out rather than following the crowd. The hardest part? Letting people know that the reason for our actions is our faith in Jesus Christ. It's not impossible, but it's certainly a challenge! Are you up to it? If you trust in God, you will be!

▸ Lk 9, 1–6

8, 52: *Sleeping:* her death is a temporary condition; cf Jn 11, 11–14.

9, 1–6: Armed with the power and authority that Jesus himself has been displaying in the previous episodes, the Twelve are now sent out to continue the work that Jesus has been performing throughout his Galilean ministry: (1) proclaiming the kingdom (4, 43; 8, 1); (2) exorcising demons (4, 33–37.41; 8, 26–39) and (3) healing the sick (4, 38–40; 5, 12–16.17–26; 6, 6–10; 7, 1–10.17.22; 8, 40–56).

9, 3: *Take nothing for the journey:* the absolute detachment required of the disciple (14, 33) leads to complete reliance on God (12, 22–31).

9, 5: *Shake the dust from your feet:* see the note on Mt 10, 14.

9, 7–56: This section in which Luke gathers together incidents that focus on the identity of Jesus is introduced by a question that

Herod is made to ask in this gospel: *"Who then is this about whom I hear such things?"* (9). In subsequent episodes, Luke reveals to the reader various answers to Herod's question: Jesus is one in whom God's power is present and who provides for the needs of God's people (10–17); Peter declares Jesus to be "the Messiah of God" (18–21); Jesus says he is the suffering Son of Man (22.43–45); Jesus is the Master to be followed, even to death (23–27); Jesus is God's Son, his Chosen One (28–36).

9, 7: *Herod the tetrarch:* see the note on 3, 1.

8, 46: Lk 6, 19.
8, 48: Lk 7, 50; 17, 19; 18, 42.
8, 52: Lk 7, 13.
9, 1–6: Mt 10, 1.5–15; Mk 6, 7–13.
9, 4: Lk 10, 5–7.
9, 5: Lk 10, 10–11; Acts 13, 51.
9, 7–9: Mt 14, 1–12; Mk 6, 14–29.

dead";* [8] others were saying, "Elijah has appeared"; still others, "One of the ancient prophets has arisen." [9]*† But Herod said, "John I beheaded. Who then is this about whom I hear such things?" And he kept trying to see him.

The Return of the Twelve and the Feeding of the Five Thousand

[10]* When the apostles returned, they explained to him what they had done. He took them and withdrew in private to a town called Bethsaida. [11] The crowds, meanwhile, learned of this and followed him. He received them and spoke to them about the kingdom of God, and he healed those who needed to be cured. [12] As the day was drawing to a close, the Twelve approached him and said, "Dismiss the crowd so that they can go to the surrounding villages and farms and find lodging and provisions; for we are in a deserted place here." [13]* He said to them, "Give them some food yourselves." They replied, "Five loaves and two fish are all we have, unless we ourselves go and buy food for all these people." [14] Now the men there numbered about five thousand. Then he said to his disciples, "Have them sit down in groups of [about] fifty." [15] They did so and made them all sit down. [16]*† Then taking the five loaves and the two fish, and looking up to heaven, he said the blessing over them, broke them, and gave them to the disciples to set before the crowd. [17] They all ate and were satisfied. And when the leftover fragments were picked up, they filled twelve wicker baskets.

Peter's Confession about Jesus

[18]*† Once when Jesus was praying in solitude,† and the disciples were with him, he asked them, "Who do the crowds say that I am?" [19]* They said

in reply, "John the Baptist; others, Elijah; still others, 'One of the ancient prophets has arisen.'" [20]† Then he said to them, "But who do you say that I am?" Peter said in reply, "The Messiah of God." [21] He rebuked them and directed them not to tell this to anyone.

The First Prediction of the Passion

[22]* He said, "The Son of Man must suffer greatly and be rejected by the elders, the chief priests, and the scribes, and be killed and on the third day be raised."

The Conditions of Discipleship

[23]*† Then he said to all, "If anyone wishes to come after me, he must deny himself and take up his cross daily and follow me.* [24]* For whoever wishes to save his life will lose it, but whoever loses his life for my sake will save it. [25] What profit is there for one to gain the whole world yet lose or forfeit himself? [26]* Whoever is ashamed of me and of my words, the Son of Man will be ashamed of when he comes in his glory and in the glory of the Father and of the holy angels. [27] Truly I say to you, there are some standing here who will not taste death until they see the kingdom of God."

The Transfiguration of Jesus†

[28]* About eight days after he said this, he took Peter, John, and James and went up the mountain to pray.† [29] While he was praying his face changed in appearance and his clothing became dazzling white. [30]† And behold, two men were conversing with him, Moses and Elijah, [31]*† who appeared in glory and spoke of his exodus that he was going to accomplish in Jerusalem. [32]*† Peter and his companions had been overcome by sleep, but becoming fully awake, they saw his glory and the two men

---

9, 9: *And he kept trying to see him:* this indication of Herod's interest in Jesus prepares for 13, 31–33 and for 23, 8–12 where Herod's curiosity about Jesus' power to perform miracles remains unsatisfied.

9, 16: *Then taking . . . :* the actions of Jesus recall the institution of the Eucharist in 22, 19; see also the note on Mt 14, 19.

9, 18–22: This incident is based on Mk 8, 27–33, but Luke has eliminated Peter's refusal to accept Jesus as suffering Son of Man (Mk 8, 32) and the rebuke of Peter by Jesus (Mk 8, 33). Elsewhere in the gospel, Luke softens the harsh portrait of Peter and the other apostles found in his Marcan source (cf 22, 39–46, which similarly lacks a rebuke of Peter that occurs in the source, Mk 14, 37–38).

9, 18: *When Jesus was praying in solitude:* see the note on 3, 21.

9, 20: *The Messiah of God:* on the meaning of this title in first-century Palestinian Judaism, see the notes on 2, 11 and on Mt 16, 13–20 and Mk 8, 27–30.

9, 23: *Daily:* this is a Lucan addition to a saying of Jesus, removing the saying from a context that envisioned the imminent suffering and death of the disciple of Jesus (as does the saying in Mk 8, 34–35) to one that focuses on the demands of daily Christian existence.

9, 28–36: Situated shortly after the first announcement of the passion, death, and resurrection, this scene of Jesus' transfiguration provides the heavenly confirmation to Jesus' declaration that his suffering will end in glory (32); see also the notes on Mt 17, 1–8 and Mk 9, 2–8.

9, 28: *Up the mountain to pray:* the "mountain" is the regular place of prayer in Luke (see 6, 12; 22, 39–41).

9, 30: *Moses and Elijah:* the two figures represent the Old Testament law and the prophets. At the end of this episode, the heavenly voice will identify Jesus as the one to be listened to now (35). See also the note on Mk 9, 5.

9, 31: *His exodus that he was going to accomplish in Jerusalem:* Luke identifies the subject of the conversation as the *exodus* of Jesus, a reference to the death, resurrection, and ascension of Jesus that will take place in Jerusalem, the city of destiny (see 9, 51). The mention of *exodus,* however, also calls to mind the Israelite Exodus from Egypt to the promised land.

9, 32: *They saw his glory:* the *glory* that is proper to God is here attributed to Jesus (see 24, 26).

9, 7–8: Lk 9, 19; Mt 16, 14; Mk 8, 28.	20, 18–19; Mk 8, 31; 10, 33–34.
9, 9: Lk 23, 8.	9, 23–27: Mt 16, 24–28; Mk 8, 34—9, 1.
9, 10–17: Mt 14, 13–21; Mk 6, 30–44; Jn 6, 1–14.	9, 23: Lk 14, 27; Mt 10, 38.
9, 13–17: 2 Kgs 4, 42–44.	9, 24: Lk 17, 33; Mt 10, 39; Jn 12, 25.
9, 16: Lk 22, 19; 24, 30–31; Acts 2, 42; 20, 11; 27, 35.	9, 26: Lk 12, 9; Mt 10, 33; 2 Tm 2, 12.
9, 18–21: Mt 16, 13–20; Mk 8, 27–30.	9, 28–36: Mt 17, 1–8; Mk 9, 2–8.
9, 19: Lk 9, 7–8.	9, 31: Lk 9, 22; 13, 33.
9, 22: Lk 24, 7.26; Mt 16, 21;	9, 32: Jn 1, 14; 2 Pt 1, 16.

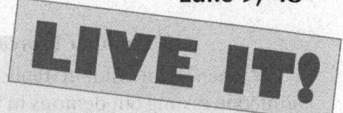

Spiritual Highs

Have you ever been on a great retreat, camp, or service trip? If so, you may have felt really close to God and to others who shared that experience with you. You may have even wished the experience did not have to end.

Peter, James, and John must have felt that way when they saw Jesus in his glory talking with Moses and Elijah on the mountaintop. Peter wanted to stay up on the mountain, but it quickly became clear that he could not do so.

Faith has its high moments as well as its low moments. It is unrealistic to think that we can maintain some kind of spiritual high all the time—doing so may even be dangerous. The faith of those who depend on mountaintop experiences often fizzles out. The better challenge is to learn what it means to live as a Christian down in the thick of life. Remember: Our faith is more than feelings. God's love and mercy do not depend on our ability to feel "warm fuzzies," as nice as those can be.

Recall a special time in your life when you felt on top of the world. Relive the moment in your mind, this time looking for how God was present in that experience. What direction was God inviting you to go after it was over? Are you there yet?

▶ Lk 9, 28–36

L
K

standing with him. [33]† As they were about to part from him, Peter said to Jesus, "Master, it is good that we are here; let us make three tents, one for you, one for Moses, and one for Elijah." But he did not know what he was saying. [34]† While he was still speaking, a cloud came and cast a shadow over them, and they became frightened when they entered the cloud. [35]*† Then from the cloud came a voice that said, "This is my chosen Son; listen to him." [36]† After the voice had spoken, Jesus was found alone. They fell silent and did not at that time tell anyone what they had seen.

The Healing of a Boy with a Demon

[37]*† On the next day, when they came down from the mountain, a large crowd met him. [38] There was a man in the crowd who cried out, "Teacher, I beg you, look at my son; he is my only child. [39] For a spirit seizes him and he suddenly screams and it convulses him until he foams at the mouth; it releases him only with difficulty, wearing him out. [40] I begged your disciples to cast it out but they could not." [41] Jesus said in reply, "O faithless and perverse generation, how long will I be with you and endure

you? Bring your son here." [42] As he was coming forward, the demon threw him to the ground in a convulsion; but Jesus rebuked the unclean spirit, healed the boy, and returned him to his father. [43]* And all were astonished by the majesty of God.

The Second Prediction of the Passion

While they were all amazed at his every deed, he said to his disciples, [44] "Pay attention to what I am telling you. The Son of Man is to be handed over to men." [45] But they did not understand this saying; its meaning was hidden from them so that they should not understand it, and they were afraid to ask him about this saying.

The Greatest in the Kingdom

[46]*† An argument arose among the disciples about which of them was the greatest.* [47] Jesus realized the intention of their hearts and took a child and placed it by his side [48]* and said to them, "Whoever receives this child in my name receives me, and whoever receives me receives the one who sent me. For the one who is least among all of you is the one who is the greatest."

---

† **9, 33:** *Let us make three tents:* in a possible allusion to the feast of Tabernacles, Peter may be likening his joy on the occasion of the transfiguration to the joyful celebration of this harvest festival.
9, 34: *Over them:* it is not clear whether *them* refers to Jesus, Moses, and Elijah, or to the disciples. For the cloud casting its shadow, see the note on Mk 9, 7.
9, 35: Like the heavenly voice that identified Jesus at his baptism prior to his undertaking the Galilean ministry (3, 22), so too here before the journey to the city of destiny is begun (51) the heavenly voice again identifies Jesus as Son. *Listen to him:* the two representatives of Israel of old depart (33) and Jesus is left alone (36) as the teacher whose words must be heeded (see also Acts 3, 22).

9, 36: *At that time:* i.e., before the resurrection.
9, 37–43a: See the note on Mk 9, 14–29.
9, 46–50: These two incidents focus on attitudes that are opposed to Christian discipleship: rivalry and intolerance of outsiders.

9, 35: Lk 3, 22; Dt 18, 15; Ps 2, 7; Is 42, 1; Mt 3, 17; 12, 18; Mk 1, 11; 2 Pt 1, 17–18.
9, 37–43: Mt 17, 14–18; Mk 9, 14–27.
9, 43–45: Lk 18, 32–34; Mt 17, 22–23; Mk 9, 30–32.
9, 46–48: Mt 18, 1–5; Mk 9, 33–37.
9, 46: Lk 22, 24.
9, 48: Lk 10, 16; Mt 10, 40; Jn 13, 20.

Another Exorcist

49* Then John said in reply, "Master, we saw someone casting out demons in your name and we tried to prevent him because he does not follow in our company." 50 Jesus said to him, "Do not prevent him, for whoever is not against you is for you."

V: The Journey to Jerusalem: Luke's Travel Narrative†

Departure for Jerusalem; Samaritan Inhospitality

51*† When the days for his being taken up† were fulfilled, he resolutely determined to journey to Jerusalem, 52*† and he sent messengers ahead of him. On the way they entered a Samaritan village to prepare for his reception there, 53 but they would not welcome him because the destination of his journey was Jerusalem. 54* When the disciples James and John saw this they asked, "Lord, do you want us to call down fire from heaven to consume them?" 55 Jesus turned and rebuked them, 56 and they journeyed to another village.

The Would-be Followers of Jesus

57*† As they were proceeding on their journey someone said to him, "I will follow you wherever you go." 58 Jesus answered him, "Foxes have dens and birds of the sky have nests, but the Son of Man has nowhere to rest his head." 59 And to another he said, "Follow me." But he replied, "[Lord,] let me go first and bury my father." 60† But he answered him, "Let the dead bury their dead. But you, go and proclaim the kingdom of God." 61* And another said, "I will follow you, Lord, but first let me say farewell to my family at home." 62 [To him] Jesus said, "No one who sets a hand to the plow and looks to what was left behind is fit for the kingdom of God."

The Mission of the Seventy-two†

10 1* After this the Lord appointed seventy [-two]† others whom he sent ahead of him in pairs to every town and place he intended to visit. 2* He said to them, "The harvest is abundant but the laborers are few; so ask the master of the harvest to send out laborers for his harvest. 3* Go on your way; behold, I am sending you like lambs among wolves. 4*† Carry no money bag, no sack, no sandals;* and greet no one along the way. 5† Into whatever house you enter, first say, 'Peace to this household.' 6† If a peaceful person lives there, your peace will rest on him; but if not, it will return to you. 7* Stay in the same house and eat and drink what is offered to you, for the laborer deserves his payment. Do not move about from one house to another. 8* Whatever town you enter and they welcome you, eat what is set before you, 9* cure the

---

9, 51—18, 14: The Galilean ministry of Jesus finishes with the previous episode and a new section of Luke's gospel begins, the journey to Jerusalem. This journey is based on Mk 10, 1–52, but Luke uses his Marcan source only in 18, 15—19, 27. Before that point he has inserted into his gospel a distinctive collection of sayings of Jesus and stories about him that he has drawn from Q, a collection of sayings of Jesus used also by Matthew, and from his own special traditions. All of the material collected in this section is loosely organized within the framework of a journey of Jesus to Jerusalem, the city of destiny, where his exodus (suffering, death, resurrection, ascension) is to take place (9, 31), where salvation is accomplished, and from where the proclamation of God's saving word is to go forth (24, 47; Acts 1, 8). Much of the material in the Lucan travel narrative is teaching for the disciples. During the course of this journey Jesus is preparing his chosen Galilean witnesses for the role they will play after his exodus (9, 31): they are to be his witnesses to the people (Acts 10, 39; 13, 31) and thereby provide certainty to the readers of Luke's gospel that the teachings they have received are rooted in the teachings of Jesus (1, 1–4).

9, 51–55: Just as the Galilean ministry began with a rejection of Jesus in his hometown, so too the travel narrative begins with the rejection of him by Samaritans. In this episode Jesus disassociates himself from the attitude expressed by his disciples that those who reject him are to be punished severely. The story alludes to 2 Kgs 1, 10.12, where the prophet Elijah takes the course of action Jesus rejects, and Jesus thereby rejects the identification of himself with Elijah.

9, 51: Days for his being taken up: like the reference to his exodus in v 31, this is probably a reference to all the events (suffering, death, resurrection, ascension) of his last days in Jerusalem. He resolutely determined: literally, "he set his face."

9, 52: Samaritan: Samaria was the territory between Judea and Galilee west of the Jordan river. For ethnic and religious reasons, the Samaritans and the Jews were bitterly opposed to one another (see Jn 4, 9).

9, 57–62: In these sayings Jesus speaks of the severity and the unconditional nature of Christian discipleship. Even family ties and filial obligations, such as burying one's parents, cannot distract one

no matter how briefly from proclaiming the kingdom of God. The first two sayings are paralleled in Mt 8, 19–22; see also the notes there.

9, 60: Let the dead bury their dead: i.e., let the spiritually dead (those who do not follow) bury their physically dead. See also the note on Mt 8, 22.

10, 1–12: Only the Gospel of Luke contains two episodes in which Jesus sends out his followers on a mission: the first (9, 1–6) is based on the mission in Mk 6, 6b-13 and recounts the sending out of the Twelve; here in vv 1–12 a similar report based on Q becomes the sending out of seventy-two in this gospel. The episode continues the theme of Jesus preparing witnesses to himself and his ministry. These witnesses include not only the Twelve but also the seventy-two who may represent the Christian mission in Luke's own day. Note that the instructions given to the Twelve and to the seventy-two are similar and that what is said to the seventy-two in v 4 is directed to the Twelve in 22, 35.

10, 1: Seventy[-two:] important representatives of the Alexandrian and Caesarean text types read "seventy," while other important Alexandrian texts and Western readings have "seventy-two."

10, 4: Carry no money bag . . . greet no one along the way: because of the urgency of the mission and the singlemindedness required of missionaries, attachment to material possessions should be avoided and even customary greetings should not distract from the fulfillment of the task.

10, 5: First say, 'Peace to this household': see the notes on 2, 14 and Mt 10, 13.

10, 6: A peaceful person: literally, "a son of peace."

9, 49–50: Mk 9, 38–40.
  9, 51: Lk 9, 53; 13, 22.33;
    17, 11; 18, 31; 19, 28;
    24, 51; Acts 1,
    2.9–11.22.
  9, 52: Mal 3, 1.
  9, 54: 2 Kgs 1, 10.12.
9, 57–60: Mt 8, 19–22.
9, 61–62: 1 Kgs 19, 20.

10, 1: Mk 6, 7.
10, 2: Mt 9, 37–38; Jn 4, 35.
10, 3: Mt 10, 16.
10, 4: Lk 9, 3; 2 Kgs 4, 29.
10, 4–11: Mt 10, 7–14.
10, 7: Lk 9, 4; Mt 10, 10; 1 Cor
    9, 6–14; 1 Tm 5, 18.
10, 8: 1 Cor 10, 27.
10, 9: Mt 3, 2; 4, 17; Mk 1, 15.

sick in it and say to them, 'The kingdom of God is at hand for you.' ¹⁰* Whatever town you enter and they do not receive you, go out into the streets and say, ¹¹* 'The dust of your town that clings to our feet, even that we shake off against you.' Yet know this: the kingdom of God is at hand. ¹²* I tell you, it will be more tolerable for Sodom on that day than for that town.

Reproaches to Unrepentant Towns

¹³*† "Woe to you, Chorazin! Woe to you, Bethsaida!* For if the mighty deeds done in your midst had been done in Tyre and Sidon, they would long ago have repented, sitting in sackcloth and ashes. ¹⁴ But it will be more tolerable for Tyre and Sidon at the judgment than for you. ¹⁵*† And as for you, Capernaum, 'Will you be exalted to heaven? You will go down to the netherworld.' " ¹⁶* Whoever listens to you listens to me. Whoever rejects you rejects me. And whoever rejects me rejects the one who sent me."

Return of the Seventy-two

¹⁷ The seventy[-two] returned rejoicing, and said, "Lord, even the demons are subject to us because of your name." ¹⁸*† Jesus said, "I have observed Satan fall like lightning from the sky. ¹⁹* Behold, I have given you the power 'to tread upon serpents' and scorpions and upon the full force of the enemy and nothing will harm you. ²⁰* Nevertheless, do not rejoice because the spirits are subject to you, but rejoice because your names are written in heaven."

Praise of the Father

²¹*† At that very moment he rejoiced [in] the holy Spirit and said, "I give you praise, Father, Lord of heaven and earth, for although you have hidden these things from the wise and the learned you have revealed them to the childlike. Yes, Father, such has been your gracious will.* ²² All things have been handed over to me by my Father. No one knows who the Son is except the Father, and who the Father is except the Son and anyone to whom the Son wishes to reveal him."

The Privileges of Discipleship

²³* Turning to the disciples in private he said, "Blessed are the eyes that see what you see. ²⁴ For I say to you, many prophets and kings desired to see

Discrimination in Jesus' Time

LIVE IT!

The good Samaritan is a popular Bible story with an obvious message: We must help others. But did you know it is also a story about prejudice and discrimination? In Jesus' day, the Samaritans were despised by Jews, even though Abraham was the father of faith for both groups. Jesus' making a Samaritan the hero of the story would have given the lawyer and other people listening to Jesus something to think about.

Imagine that this story takes place in your community. Who are the Samaritans, that is, the culture or race that other people judge and reject? How does this reflection affect your understanding of discrimination and racism?

It seems that when we have a real relationship with others—even with those who are different from us—we are less likely to be prejudiced or to discriminate. Maybe we should work in our communities to invite all people to get to know one another better so that all "Samaritans" are regarded as good. What do you think?

▶ Lk 10, 25–37

L
K

10, 13–16: The call to repentance that is a part of the proclamation of the kingdom brings with it a severe judgment for those who hear it and reject it.

10, 15: *The netherworld:* the underworld, the place of the dead (Acts 2, 27.31), here contrasted with heaven; see also the note on Mt 11, 23.

10, 18: *I have observed Satan fall like lightning:* the effect of the mission of the seventy-two is characterized by the Lucan Jesus as a symbolic fall of Satan. As the kingdom of God is gradually being established, evil in all its forms is being defeated; the dominion of Satan over humanity is at an end.

10, 21: *Revealed them to the childlike:* a restatement of the theme announced in 8, 10: the mysteries of the kingdom are revealed to the disciples. See also the note on Mt 11, 25–27.

10, 10–11: Lk 9, 5.
  10, 11: Acts 13, 51; 18, 6.
  10, 12: Mt 10, 15; 11, 24.
10, 13–15: Mt 11, 20–24.
10, 13–14: Is 23; Ez 26–28; Jl 3, 4–8; Am 1, 1–10; Zec 9, 2–4.
  10, 15: Is 14, 13–15.
  10, 16: Mt 10, 40; Jn 5, 23; 13, 20; 15, 23.

10, 18: Is 14, 12; Jn 12, 31; Rv 12, 7–12.
  10, 19: Ps 19, 13; Mk 16, 18.
  10, 20: Ex 32, 32; Dn 12, 1; Mt 7, 22; Phil 4, 3; Heb 12, 23; Rv 3, 5; 21, 27.
10, 21–22: Mt 11, 25–27.
  10, 21: 1 Cor 1, 26–28.
  10, 22: Jn 3, 35; 10, 15.
  10, 23–24: Mt 13, 16–17.

what you see, but did not see it, and to hear what you hear, but did not hear it."

The Greatest Commandment

25*† There was a scholar of the law† who stood up to test him and said, "Teacher, what must I do to inherit eternal life?"* 26 Jesus said to him, "What is written in the law? How do you read it?" 27* He said in reply, "You shall love the Lord, your God, with all your heart, with all your being, with all your strength, and with all your mind, and your neighbor as yourself." 28* He replied to him, "You have answered correctly; do this and you will live."

The Parable of the Good Samaritan

29 But because he wished to justify himself, he said to Jesus, "And who is my neighbor?" 30 Jesus replied, "A man fell victim to robbers as he went down from Jerusalem to Jericho. They stripped and beat him and went off leaving him half-dead. 31† A priest happened to be going down that road, but when he saw him, he passed by on the opposite side. 32 Likewise a Levite came to the place, and when he saw him, he passed by on the opposite side. 33 But a Samaritan traveler who came upon him was moved with compassion at the sight. 34 He approached the victim, poured oil and wine over his wounds and bandaged them. Then he lifted him up on his own animal, took him to an inn and cared for him. 35 The next day he took out two silver coins and gave them to the innkeeper with the instruction, 'Take care of him. If you spend more than what I have given you, I shall repay you on my way back.' 36 Which of these three, in your opinion, was neighbor to the robbers' victim?" 37 He answered, "The one who treated him with mercy." Jesus said to him, "Go and do likewise."

Martha and Mary

38*† As they continued their journey he entered a village where a woman whose name was Martha welcomed him. 39† She had a sister named Mary [who] sat beside the Lord at his feet listening to him speak. 40 Martha, burdened with much serving, came to him and said, "Lord, do you not care that my sister has left me by myself to do the serving? Tell her to help me." 41 The Lord said to her in reply, "Martha, Martha, you are anxious and worried about many things. 42† There is need of only one thing. Mary has chosen the better part and it will not be taken from her."

Too Busy to Be Still

Help me slow down, Lord, right now, before I think of something else that I should be doing—as if it really is more important than you. Let me sit in the quiet peace of your presence and soak up all that you have to say to me. Give me the patience and perception to do nothing else for these next few moments except to be totally, completely, and wonderfully centered on you!

▶ Lk 10, 38–42

The Lord's Prayer

11 1*† He was praying in a certain place, and when he had finished, one of his disciples said to him, "Lord, teach us to pray just as John

---

10, 25–37: In response to a question from a Jewish legal expert about inheriting eternal life, Jesus illustrates the superiority of love over legalism through the story of the good Samaritan. The law of love proclaimed in the "Sermon on the Plain" (6, 27–36) is exemplified by one whom the legal expert would have considered ritually impure (see Jn 4, 9). Moreover, the identity of the "neighbor" requested by the legal expert (29) turns out to be a Samaritan, the enemy of the Jew (see the note on 9, 52).

10, 25: *Scholar of the law:* an expert in the Mosaic law, and probably a member of the group elsewhere identified as the scribes (5, 21).

10, 31–32: *Priest . . . Levite:* those religious representatives of Judaism who would have been expected to be models of "neighbor" to the victim pass him by.

10, 38–42: The story of Martha and Mary further illustrates the importance of hearing the words of the teacher and the concern with women in Luke.

10, 39: *Sat beside the Lord at his feet:* it is remarkable for first-century Palestinian Judaism that a woman would assume the posture of a disciple at the master's feet (see also 8, 35; Acts 22, 3), and it reveals a characteristic attitude of Jesus toward women in this gospel (see 8, 2–3).

10, 42: *There is need of only one thing:* some ancient versions read, "there is need of few things"; another important, although

probably inferior, reading found in some manuscripts is, "there is need of few things, or of one."

11, 1–13: Luke presents three episodes concerned with prayer. The first (1–4) recounts Jesus teaching his disciples the Christian communal prayer, the "Our Father"; the second (5–8), the importance of persistence in prayer; the third (9–13), the effectiveness of prayer.

11, 1–4: The Matthean form of the "Our Father" occurs in the "Sermon on the Mount" (Mt 6, 9–15); the shorter Lucan version is presented while Jesus is at prayer (see the note on 3, 21) and his disciples ask him to teach them to pray just as John taught his disciples to pray. In answer to their question, Jesus presents them with an example of a Christian communal prayer that stresses the fatherhood of God and acknowledges him as the one to whom the Christian disciple owes daily sustenance (3), forgiveness (4), and deliverance from the final trial (4). See also the notes on Mt 6, 9–13.

10, 25–28: Mt 22, 34–40; Mk 12, 28–34.
10, 25: Lk 18, 18; Mt 19, 16; Mk 10, 17.
10, 27: Lv 19, 18; Dt 6, 5; 10, 12; Jos 22, 5; Mt 19, 19; 22, 37–39; Rom
13, 9; Gal 5, 14; Jas 2, 8.
10, 28: Lv 18, 5; Prv 19, 16; Rom 10, 5; Gal 3, 12.
10, 38–39: Jn 11, 1; 12, 2–3.
11, 1–4: Mt 6, 9–15.

taught his disciples."† ²† He said to them, "When you pray, say:

> Father, hallowed be your name,
> your kingdom come.
> ³† Give us each day our daily bread
> ⁴ and forgive us our sins
> for we ourselves forgive everyone in debt
> to us,
> and do not subject us to the final test."

Further Teachings on Prayer

⁵* And he said to them, "Suppose one of you has a friend to whom he goes at midnight and says, 'Friend, lend me three loaves of bread, ⁶ for a friend of mine has arrived at my house from a journey and I have nothing to offer him,' ⁷ and he says in reply from within, 'Do not bother me; the door has already been locked and my children and I are already in bed. I cannot get up to give you anything.' ⁸ I tell you, if he does not get up to give him the loaves because of their friendship, he will get up to give him whatever he needs because of his persistence.

The Answer to Prayer

⁹* "And I tell you, ask and you will receive; seek and you will find; knock and the door will be opened to you.* ¹⁰ For everyone who asks, receives; and the one who seeks, finds; and to the one who knocks, the door will be opened. ¹¹ What father among you would hand his son a snake when he asks for a fish? ¹² Or hand him a scorpion when he asks for an egg? ¹³† If you then, who are wicked, know how to give good gifts to your children, how much more will the Father in heaven give the holy Spirit to those who ask him?"

Jesus and Beelzebul

¹⁴* He was driving out a demon [that was] mute, and when the demon had gone out, the mute person spoke and the crowds were amazed. ¹⁵* Some of them said, "By the power of Beelzebul, the prince of demons, he drives out demons." ¹⁶* Others, to test him, asked him for a sign from heaven. ¹⁷ But he knew their thoughts and said to them, "Every kingdom divided against itself will be laid waste and house will fall against house. ¹⁸ And if Satan is divided against himself, how will his kingdom stand? For you say that it is by Beelzebul that I drive out demons. ¹⁹† If I, then, drive out demons by Beelzebul, by whom do your own people drive them out? Therefore they will be your judges. ²⁰* But if it is by the finger of God that I drive out demons, then the kingdom of God has come upon you. ²¹ When a strong man fully armed guards his palace, his possessions are safe. ²²† But when one stronger than he attacks and overcomes him, he takes away the armor on which he relied and distributes the spoils.

LK

LIVE IT!

Nagging God

Have you ever nagged your parents for something? They may have replied, "Will you stop nagging me?!"

This is one response you will never hear from God. In fact, Jesus tells us to be persistent with God, to nag God. God wants to be nagged by us! Too often we hesitate to bring everything inside of us to God. We sort through what we think God wants to hear. Don't be selective! Bring it all to God—the big stuff as well as the little stuff. Be a nag. God doesn't mind at all.

Go ahead, nag God right now!

▶ Lk 11, 5–13

---

† **11, 2:** *Your kingdom come:* in place of this petition, some early church Fathers record: "May your holy Spirit come upon us and cleanse us," a petition that may reflect the use of the "Our Father" in a baptismal liturgy.
11, 3–4: *Daily bread:* see the note on Mt 6, 11. *The final test:* see the note on Mt 6, 13.
11, 13: *The holy Spirit:* this is a Lucan editorial alteration of a traditional saying of Jesus (see Mt 7, 11). Luke presents the gift of the holy Spirit as the response of the Father to the prayer of the Christian disciple.
11, 19: *Your own people:* the Greek reads "your sons." Other Jewish exorcists (see Acts 19, 13–20), who recognize that the power of God is active in the exorcism, would themselves convict the accusers of Jesus. See also the note on Mt 12, 27.
11, 22: *One stronger:* i.e., Jesus. Cf 3, 16 where John the Baptist identifies Jesus as "mightier than I."

11, 5–8: Lk 18, 1–5.
11, 9–13: Mt 7, 7–11.
11, 9: Mt 21, 22; Mk 11, 24; Jn 14, 13; 15, 7; 1 Jn 5, 14–15.
11, 14–23: Mt 12, 22–30; Mk 3, 20–27.
11, 15: Mt 9, 34.
11, 16: Mt 12, 38; 16, 1; Mk 8, 11; 1 Cor 1, 22.
11, 20: Ex 8, 19.

23* Whoever is not with me is against me, and whoever does not gather with me scatters.

The Return of the Unclean Spirit

24* "When an unclean spirit goes out of someone, it roams through arid regions searching for rest but, finding none, it says, 'I shall return to my home from which I came.' 25 But upon returning, it finds it swept clean and put in order. 26* Then it goes and brings back seven other spirits more wicked than itself who move in and dwell there, and the last condition of that person is worse than the first."

True Blessedness

27*† While he was speaking, a woman from the crowd called out and said to him, "Blessed is the womb that carried you and the breasts at which you nursed." 28 He replied, "Rather, blessed are those who hear the word of God and observe it."

The Demand for a Sign

29*† While still more people gathered in the crowd, he said to them, "This generation is an evil generation; it seeks a sign, but no sign will be given it, except the sign of Jonah.* 30 Just as Jonah became a sign to the Ninevites, so will the Son of Man be to this generation. 31* At the judgment the queen of the south will rise with the men of this generation and she will condemn them, because she came from the ends of the earth to hear the wisdom of Solomon, and there is something greater than Solomon here. 32* At the judgment the men of Nineveh will arise with this generation and condemn it, because at the preaching of Jonah they repented, and there is something greater than Jonah here.

The Simile of Light

33* "No one who lights a lamp hides it away or places it [under a bushel basket], but on a lampstand so that those who enter might see the light. 34* The lamp of the body is your eye. When your eye is sound, then your whole body is filled with light, but when it is bad, then your body is in darkness. 35 Take care, then, that the light in you not become darkness. 36 If your whole body is full of light, and no part of it is in darkness, then it will be as full of light as a lamp illuminating you with its brightness."

Denunciation of the Pharisees and Scholars of the Law

37*† After he had spoken, a Pharisee invited him to dine at his home. He entered and reclined at table to eat.* 38* The Pharisee was amazed to see that he did not observe the prescribed washing before the meal. 39* The Lord said to him, "Oh you Pharisees! Although you cleanse the outside of the cup and the dish, inside you are filled with plunder and evil. 40 You fools! Did not the maker of the outside also make the inside? 41 But as to what is within, give alms, and behold, everything will be clean for you. 42* Woe to you Pharisees! You pay tithes of mint and of rue and of every garden herb, but you pay no attention to judgment and to love for God. These you should have done, without overlooking the others. 43* Woe to you Pharisees! You love the seat of honor in synagogues and greetings in marketplaces. 44*† Woe to you! You are like unseen graves over which people unknowingly walk."

45*† Then one of the scholars of the law said to him in reply, "Teacher, by saying this you are insulting us too." 46 And he said, "Woe also to you scholars of the law! You impose on people burdens hard to carry, but you yourselves do not lift one finger to touch them. 47* Woe to you! You build the memorials of the prophets whom your ancestors killed. 48 Consequently, you bear witness and give consent to the deeds of your ancestors, for they killed them and you do the building. 49*† Therefore, the wisdom of God said, 'I will send to them prophets and apostles; some of them they will kill and persecute' 50 in order that this generation might be charged with the blood of all

---

11, 27–28: The beatitude in v 28 should not be interpreted as a rebuke of the mother of Jesus; see the note on 8, 21. Rather, it emphasizes (like 2, 35) that attentiveness to God's word is more important than biological relationship to Jesus.

11, 29–32: The "sign of Jonah" in Luke is the preaching of the need for repentance by a prophet who comes from afar. Cf Mt 12, 38–42 (and see the notes there) where the "sign of Jonah" is interpreted by Jesus as his death and resurrection.

11, 37–54: This denunciation of the Pharisees (39–44) and the scholars of the law (45–52) is set by Luke in the context of Jesus' dining at the home of a Pharisee. Controversies with or reprimands of Pharisees are regularly set by Luke within the context of Jesus' eating with Pharisees (see 5, 29–39; 7, 36–50; 14, 1–24). A different compilation of similar sayings is found in Mt 23 (see also the notes there).

11, 44: Unseen graves: contact with the dead or with human bones or graves (see Nm 19, 16) brought ritual impurity. Jesus presents the Pharisees as those who insidiously lead others astray through their seeming attention to the law.

11, 45: Scholars of the law: see the note on 10, 25.
11, 49: I will send to them prophets and apostles: Jesus connects the mission of the church (apostles) with the mission of the Old Testament prophets who often suffered the rebuke of their contemporaries.

11, 23: Lk 9, 50; Mk 9, 40.
11, 24–26: Mt 12, 43–45.
11, 26: Jn 5, 14.
11, 27: Lk 1, 28.42.48.
11, 29–32: Mt 12, 38–42; Mk 8, 12.
11, 29: Mt 16, 1.4; Jn 6, 30; 1 Cor 1, 22.
11, 31: 1 Kgs 10, 1–10; 2 Chr 9, 1–12.
11, 32: Jon 3, 8.10.
11, 33: Lk 8, 16; Mt 5, 15; Mk 4, 21.
11, 34–36: Mt 6, 22–23.
11, 37–54: Lk 20, 45–47; Mt 23, 1–36; Mk 12, 38–40.
11, 37: Lk 7, 36; 14, 1.
11, 38: Mt 15, 2; Mk 7, 2–5.
11, 39–41: Mt 23, 25–26.
11, 42: Lv 27, 30; Mt 23, 23.
11, 43: Lk 20, 46; Mt 23, 6; Mk 12, 38–39.
11, 44: Mt 23, 27.
11, 45: Mt 23, 4.
11, 47–48: Mt 23, 29–32.
11, 49–51: Mt 23, 34–36.

the prophets shed since the foundation of the world, 51*† from the blood of Abel to the blood of Zechariah who died between the altar and the temple building. Yes, I tell you, this generation will be charged with their blood! 52* Woe to you, scholars of the law! You have taken away the key of knowledge. You yourselves did not enter and you stopped those trying to enter." 53* When he left, the scribes and Pharisees began to act with hostility toward him and to interrogate him about many things, 54* for they were plotting to catch him at something he might say.

The Leaven of the Pharisees

12 1*† Meanwhile, so many people were crowding together that they were trampling one another underfoot. He began to speak, first to his disciples, "Beware of the leaven—that is, the hypocrisy—of the Pharisees.

Courage under Persecution

2*† "There is nothing concealed that will not be revealed, nor secret that will not be known.* 3 Therefore whatever you have said in the darkness will be heard in the light, and what you have whispered behind closed doors will be proclaimed on the housetops. 4 I tell you, my friends, do not be afraid of those who kill the body but after that can do no more. 5† I shall show you whom to fear. Be afraid of the one who after killing has the power to cast into Gehenna; yes, I tell you, be afraid of that one. 6† Are not five sparrows sold for two small coins? Yet not one of them has escaped the notice of God. 7* Even the hairs of your head have all been counted. Do not be afraid. You are worth more than many sparrows. 8 I tell you, everyone who acknowledges me before others the Son of Man will acknowledge before the angels of God. 9* But whoever denies me before others will be denied before the angels of God.

Sayings about the holy Spirit

10*† "Everyone who speaks a word against the Son of Man will be forgiven, but the one who blasphemes against the holy Spirit will not be forgiven. 11* When they take you before synagogues and before rulers and authorities, do not worry about how or what your defense will be or about what you are to say. 12 For the holy Spirit will teach you at that moment what you should say."

Saying against Greed

13† Someone in the crowd said to him, "Teacher, tell my brother to share the inheritance with me." 14* He replied to him, "Friend, who appointed me as your judge and arbitrator?" 15* Then he said to the crowd, "Take care to guard against all greed, for though one may be rich, one's life does not consist of possessions."

Parable of the Rich Fool

16 Then he told them a parable. "There was a rich man whose land produced a bountiful harvest. 17 He asked himself, 'What shall I do, for I do not have space to store my harvest?' 18 And he said, 'This is what I shall do: I shall tear down my barns and build larger ones. There I shall store all my grain and other goods 19* and I shall say to myself, "Now as for you, you have so many good things stored up for many years, rest, eat, drink, be merry!"'* 20 But God said to him, 'You fool, this night your life will be demanded of you; and the things you have prepared, to whom will they belong?' 21† Thus will it be for the one who stores up treasure for himself but is not rich in what matters to God."

Dependence on God

22* He said to [his] disciples, "Therefore I tell you, do not worry about your life and what you will eat, or about your body and what you will wear. 23 For life is more than food and the body more than clothing. 24* Notice the ravens: they do not sow or reap; they have neither storehouse nor barn, yet God feeds them. How much more important are you than birds! 25 Can any of you by worrying add a moment to your life-span? 26 If even the smallest things

L
K

11, 51: *From the blood of Abel to the blood of Zechariah:* the murder of Abel is the first murder recounted in the Old Testament (Gn 4, 8). The Zechariah mentioned here may be the Zechariah whose murder is recounted in 2 Chr 24, 20–22, the last murder presented in the Hebrew canon of the Old Testament.

12, 1: See the notes on Mk 8, 15 and Mt 16, 5–12.

12, 2–9: Luke presents a collection of sayings of Jesus exhorting his followers to acknowledge him and his mission fearlessly and assuring them of God's protection even in times of persecution. They are paralleled in Mt 10, 26–33.

12, 5: *Gehenna:* see the note on Mt 5, 22.

12, 6: *Two small coins:* the Roman copper coin, the assarion (Latin *as*), was worth about one-sixteenth of a denarius (see the note on 7, 41).

12, 10–12: The sayings about the holy Spirit are set in the context of fearlessness in the face of persecution (2–9; cf Mt 12, 31–32). The holy Spirit will be presented in Luke's second volume, the Acts of the Apostles, as the power responsible for the guidance of the Christian mission and the source of courage in the face of persecution.

12, 13–34: Luke has joined together sayings contrasting those whose focus and trust in life is on material possessions, symbolized here by the rich fool of the parable (16–21), with those who recognize their complete dependence on God (21), those whose radical detachment from material possessions symbolizes their heavenly treasure (33–34).

12, 21: *Rich in what matters to God:* literally, "rich for God."

11, 51: Gn 4, 8; 2 Chr 24, 20–22.	2 Tm 2, 12.
11, 52: Mt 23, 13.	**12, 10:** Mt 12, 31–32; Mk 3, 28–29.
11, 53: Lk 6, 11; Mt 22, 15–22.	**12, 11–12:** Lk 21, 12–15; Mt 10, 17–20; Mk 13, 11.
11, 54: Lk 20, 20.	**12, 14:** Ex 2, 14; Acts 7, 27.
12, 1: Mt 16, 6; Mk 8, 15.	**12, 15:** 1 Tm 6, 9–10.
12, 2–9: Mt 10, 26–33.	**12, 19–21:** Mt 6, 19–21;
12, 2: Lk 8, 17; Mk 4, 22.	1 Tm 6, 17.
12, 7: Lk 12, 24; 21, 18; Acts 27, 34.	**12, 19–20:** Sir 11, 19.
12, 9: Lk 9, 26; Mk 8, 38;	**12, 22–32:** Mt 6, 25–34.
	12, 24: Lk 12, 7.

The Greed Trap

It is easy to regard possessions as treasures and to find so much pleasure in them that we want more and more. This is the greed trap Jesus warns against in Lk 12, 13–21. How do we let ourselves fall into this trap? Certainly, advertisements play a role in convincing us that we need to own everything that is new and improved (see "New and Improved!" Eccl 1, 1–11). Our own insecurities also play a role—the more we possess, the more important we tend to think we are. But as Lk 12, 18 indicates, greed is a sin that is addictive. Instead of feeling fulfilled by attaining the thing we crave, we feel that what we have still isn't enough. It is a vicious cycle.

The solution to greed is simple. It's sharing—that value that we learned when we were very small. Sharing our time and possessions makes us "rich in what matters to God" (verse 21). Where do you see the sin of greed at work in your world? Where and when could you, your friends, and your family share more? Don't fall into the greed trap. Share!

▶ Lk 12, 13–21

are beyond your control, why are you anxious about the rest? 27* Notice how the flowers grow. They do not toil or spin. But I tell you, not even Solomon in all his splendor was dressed like one of them. 28 If God so clothes the grass in the field that grows today and is thrown into the oven tomorrow, will he not much more provide for you, O you of little faith? 29 As for you, do not seek what you are to eat and what you are to drink, and do not worry anymore. 30 All the nations of the world seek for these things, and your Father knows that you need them. 31 Instead, seek his kingdom, and these other things will be given you besides. 32* Do not be afraid any longer, little flock, for your Father is pleased to give you the kingdom. 33* Sell your belongings and give alms. Provide money bags for yourselves that do not wear out, an inexhaustible treasure in heaven that no thief can reach nor moth destroy. 34 For where your treasure is, there also will your heart be.

Vigilant and Faithful Servants

35*† "Gird your loins and light your lamps 36* and be like servants who await their master's return from a wedding, ready to open immediately when he comes and knocks. 37 Blessed are those servants whom the master finds vigilant on his arrival. Amen, I say to you, he will gird himself, have them recline at table, and proceed to wait on them. 38 And should he come in the second or third watch and find them prepared in this way, blessed are those servants. 39* Be sure of this: if the master of the house had known the hour when the thief was coming, he would not have let his house be broken into. 40 You also must be prepared, for at an hour you do not expect, the Son of Man will come."

41 Then Peter said, "Lord, is this parable meant for us or for everyone?" 42 And the Lord replied, "Who, then, is the faithful and prudent steward whom the master will put in charge of his servants to distribute [the] food allowance at the proper time? 43 Blessed is that servant whom his master on arrival finds doing so. 44 Truly, I say to you, he will put him in charge of all his property. 45† But if that servant says to himself, 'My master is delayed in coming,' and begins to beat the menservants and the maidservants, to eat and drink and get drunk, 46 then that servant's master will come on an unexpected day and at an unknown hour and will punish him severely and assign him a place with the unfaithful. 47* That servant who knew his master's will but did not make preparations nor act in accord with his will shall be beaten severely; 48 and the servant who was ignorant of his master's will but acted in a way deserving of a severe beating shall be beaten only lightly. Much will be required of the person entrusted with much, and still more will be demanded of the person entrusted with more.

---

† **12, 35–48:** This collection of sayings relates to Luke's understanding of the end time and the return of Jesus. Luke emphasizes for his readers the importance of being faithful to the instructions of Jesus in the period before the parousia.

12, 45: *My master is delayed in coming:* this statement indicates that early Christian expectations for the imminent return of Jesus had undergone some modification. Luke cautions his readers against counting on such a delay and acting irresponsibly. Cf the similar warning in Mt 24, 48.

12, 27: 1 Kgs 10, 4–7; 2 Chr 9, 3–6.
12, 32: Lk 22, 29; Rv 1, 6.
12, 33: Lk 18, 22; Mt 6, 20–21; Mk 10, 21.
12, 35–46: Mt 24, 45–51.
12, 36: Mt 25, 1–13; Mk 13, 35–37.
12, 39–40: Mt 24, 43–44; 1 Thes 5, 2.
12, 47: Jas 4, 17.

The Anxiety Trap

Doesn't it seem a little naive to assume that if we just trust God, we will get what we need; that we shouldn't worry about the everyday things like clothing, food, and shelter? Seems pretty risky and yet . . .

Lakeesha and Miguel were best friends. Miguel had a big problem. He worried all the time. He sometimes made himself sick with worrying. He worried that his parents would lose their jobs. He worried that he wouldn't find a job. He worried about doing poorly in school. When it was stormy out, he worried about tornadoes. He drove his friends crazy with his worrying.

Lakeesha, on the other hand, never worried. One day, Miguel asked her for her secret to staying calm. She told him: "Miguel, if you keep focused on the negative things that could happen and worry about them, you will not see all the good things happening around you. Did you know that your mom just got a raise? You didn't notice that our band teacher said you had the best fingering technique he had ever seen. And I bet you didn't even look at the want ads for new summer jobs. Right? You spend too much time worrying and not enough time noticing."

Jesus says the same thing. Don't worry so much about everyday needs. Look for the simple signs that God cares for you. Some people even keep a journal of the good things that happen to them every day. Life will be so much calmer and less stressful if you heed Jesus' message. Try it!

▶ Lk 12, 22–34

L
K

Jesus: A Cause of Division

49† "I have come to set the earth on fire, and how I wish it were already blazing! 50*† There is a baptism with which I must be baptized, and how great is my anguish until it is accomplished! 51* Do you think that I have come to establish peace on the earth? No, I tell you, but rather division.* 52 From now on a household of five will be divided, three against two and two against three; 53* a father will be divided against his son and a son against his father, a mother against her daughter and a daughter against her mother, a mother-in-law against her daughter-in-law and a daughter-in-law against her mother-in-law."

Signs of the Times

54* He also said to the crowds, "When you see [a] cloud rising in the west you say immediately that it is going to rain—and so it does; 55 and when you notice that the wind is blowing from the south you say that it is going to be hot—and so it is. 56 You hypocrites! You know how to interpret the appearance of the earth and the sky; why do you not know how to interpret the present time?

Settlement with an Opponent

57* "Why do you not judge for yourselves what is right? 58 If you are to go with your opponent before a magistrate, make an effort to settle the matter on the way; otherwise your opponent will turn you over to the judge, and the judge hand you over to the constable, and the constable throw you into prison. 59† I say to you, you will not be released until you have paid the last penny."

A Call to Repentance†

13 1 At that time some people who were present there told him about the Galileans whose blood Pilate† had mingled with the blood of their sacrifices. 2* He said to them in reply, "Do you think that because these Galileans suffered

---

† **12, 49–53:** Jesus' proclamation of the kingdom is a refining and purifying fire. His message that meets with acceptance or rejection will be a source of conflict and dissension even within families.
12, 50: *Baptism:* i.e., his death.
12, 59: *The last penny:* Greek, *lepton,* a very small amount. Mt 5, 26 has for "the last penny" the Greek word *kodrantēs* (Latin *quadrans,* "farthing").
13, 1–5: The death of the Galileans at the hands of Pilate (1) and the accidental death of those on whom the tower fell (4) are presented by the Lucan Jesus as timely reminders of the need for all to repent, for the victims of these tragedies should not be considered outstanding sinners who were singled out for punishment.
13, 1: The slaughter of the Galileans by Pilate is unknown outside

Luke; but from what is known about Pilate from the Jewish historian Josephus, such a slaughter would be in keeping with the character of Pilate. Josephus reports that Pilate had disrupted a religious gathering of the Samaritans on Mt. Gerizim with a slaughter of the participants (*Antiquities* 18, 4, 1 §§86–87), and that on another occasion Pilate had killed many Jews who had opposed him when he appropriated money from the temple treasury to build an aqueduct in Jerusalem (*Jewish War* 2, 9, 4 §§175–77; *Antiquities* 18, 3, 2 §§60–62).

12, 50: Mk 10, 38–39.   **12, 54–56:** Mt 16, 2–3.
12, 51–53: Mt 10, 34–35.   **12, 57–59:** Mt 5, 25–26.
12, 51: Lk 2, 14.   **13, 2:** Jn 9, 2.
12, 53: Mi 7, 6.

in this way they were greater sinners than all other Galileans? ³* By no means! But I tell you, if you do not repent, you will all perish as they did! ⁴† Or those eighteen people who were killed when the tower at Siloam fell on them—do you think they were more guilty than everyone else who lived in Jerusalem? ⁵ By no means! But I tell you, if you do not repent, you will all perish as they did!"

The Parable of the Barren Fig Tree

⁶*† And he told them this parable: "There once was a person who had a fig tree planted in his orchard, and when he came in search of fruit on it but found none, ⁷ he said to the gardener, 'For three years now I have come in search of fruit on this fig tree but have found none. [So] cut it down. Why should it exhaust the soil?' ⁸ He said to him in reply, 'Sir, leave it for this year also, and I shall cultivate the ground around it and fertilize it; ⁹ it may bear fruit in the future. If not you can cut it down.' "

Cure of a Crippled Woman on the Sabbath

¹⁰† He was teaching in a synagogue on the sabbath. ¹¹ And a woman was there who for eighteen years had been crippled by a spirit; she was bent over, completely incapable of standing erect. ¹² When Jesus saw her, he called to her and said, "Woman, you are set free of your infirmity." ¹³ He laid his hands on her, and she at once stood up straight and glorified God. ¹⁴* But the leader of the synagogue, indignant that Jesus had cured on the sabbath, said to the crowd in reply, "There are six days when work should be done. Come on those days to be cured, not on the sabbath day." ¹⁵*† The Lord said to him in reply, "Hypocrites! Does not each one of you on the sabbath untie his ox or his ass from the manger and lead it out for watering? ¹⁶*† This daughter of Abraham, whom Satan has bound for eighteen years now, ought she not to have been set free on the sabbath day from this bondage?" ¹⁷ When he said this, all his adversaries were humiliated; and the whole crowd rejoiced at all the splendid deeds done by him.

ANOINTING OF THE SICK

The crippled woman in Lk 13, 10–17 is just one of many people Jesus heals in Luke. Much of Jesus' ministry was spent healing people with a variety of illnesses. Through the sacrament of Anointing, one of the seven sacraments of the Catholic church, Jesus' ministry of extending God's healing love is continued.

In this sacrament, people young and old are anointed with sacred oil and prayed over by a priest. The sacrament is often given to people who are struggling with a serious illness, going into surgery, or dying. The sacrament is not a guarantee of physical healing but a way of receiving in a special way God's love and strength during those times of trial.

▶ Lk 13, 10–17

The Parable of the Mustard Seed

¹⁸*† Then he said, "What is the kingdom of God like? To what can I compare it? ¹⁹* It is like a mustard seed that a person took and planted in the garden. When it was fully grown, it became a large bush and 'the birds of the sky dwelt in its branches.' "

The Parable of the Yeast

²⁰* Again he said, "To what shall I compare the

13, 4: Like the incident mentioned in v 1, nothing of this accident in Jerusalem is known outside Luke and the New Testament.

13, 6–9: Following on the call to repentance in vv 1–5, the parable of the barren fig tree presents a story about the continuing patience of God with those who have not yet given evidence of their repentance (see 3, 8). The parable may also be alluding to the delay of the end time, when punishment will be meted out, and the importance of preparing for the end of the age because the delay will not be permanent (8–9).

13, 10–17: The cure of the crippled woman on the sabbath and the controversy that results furnishes a parallel to an incident that will be reported by Luke in 14, 1–6, the cure of the man with dropsy on the sabbath. A characteristic of Luke's style is the juxtaposition of an incident that reveals Jesus' concern for a man with an incident that reveals his concern for a woman; cf, e.g., 7, 11–17 and 8, 49–56.

13, 15–16: If the law as interpreted by Jewish tradition allowed for the untying of bound animals on the sabbath, how much more

should this woman who has been bound by Satan's power be freed on the sabbath from her affliction.

13, 16: *Whom Satan has bound:* affliction and infirmity are taken as evidence of Satan's hold on humanity. The healing ministry of Jesus reveals the gradual wresting from Satan of control over humanity and the establishment of God's kingdom.

13, 18–21: Two parables are used to illustrate the future proportions of the kingdom of God that will result from its deceptively small beginning in the preaching and healing ministry of Jesus. They are paralleled in Mt 13, 31–33 and Mk 4, 30–32.

13, 3–5: Jn 8, 24.
13, 6–9: Jer 8, 13; Hb 3, 17; Mt 21, 19; Mk 11, 13.
13, 14: Lk 6, 7; 14, 3; Ex 20, 8–11; Dt 5, 12–15; Mt 12, 10; Mk 3, 2–4; Jn 5, 16; 7, 23; 9, 14.16.
13, 15: Lk 14, 5; Dt 22, 4; Mt 12, 11.
13, 16: Lk 19, 9.
13, 18–19: Mt 13, 31–32; Mk 4, 30–32.
13, 19: Ez 17, 23–24; 31, 6.
13, 20–21: Mt 13, 33.

kingdom of God? [21] It is like yeast that a woman took and mixed [in] with three measures of wheat flour until the whole batch of dough was leavened."

The Narrow Door; Salvation and Rejection

[22]† He passed through towns and villages, teaching as he went and making his way to Jerusalem. [23] Someone asked him, "Lord, will only a few people be saved?" He answered them, [24]* "Strive to enter through the narrow gate, for many, I tell you, will attempt to enter but will not be strong enough.* [25]* After the master of the house has arisen and locked the door, then will you stand outside knocking and saying, 'Lord, open the door for us.' He will say to you in reply, 'I do not know where you are from.' [26] And you will say, 'We ate and drank in your company and you taught in our streets.' [27]* Then he will say to you, 'I do not know where [you] are from. Depart from me, all you evildoers!' [28]* And there will be wailing and grinding of teeth when you see Abraham, Isaac, and Jacob and all the prophets in the kingdom of God and you yourselves cast out. [29]* And people will come from the east and the west and from the north and the south and will recline at table in the kingdom of God. [30]* For behold, some are last who will be first, and some are first who will be last."

Herod's Desire to Kill Jesus

[31] At that time some Pharisees came to him and said, "Go away, leave this area because Herod wants to kill you." [32]† He replied, "Go and tell that fox, 'Behold, I cast out demons and I perform healings today and tomorrow, and on the third day I accomplish my purpose. [33]*† Yet I must continue on my way today, tomorrow, and the following day, for it is impossible that a prophet should die outside of Jerusalem.'

The Lament over Jerusalem

[34]* "Jerusalem, Jerusalem, you who kill the prophets and stone those sent to you, how many times I yearned to gather your children together as a hen gathers her brood under her wings, but you were unwilling! [35]* Behold, your house will be abandoned. [But] I tell you, you will not see me until [the time comes when] you say, 'Blessed is he who comes in the name of the Lord.' "

Healing of the Man with Dropsy on the Sabbath

14 [1]*† On a sabbath he went to dine at the home of one of the leading Pharisees, and the people there were observing him carefully.* [2]† In front of him there was a man suffering from dropsy. [3]* Jesus spoke to the scholars of the law and Pharisees in reply, asking, "Is it lawful to cure on the sabbath or not?" [4] But they kept silent; so he took the man and, after he had healed him, dismissed him. [5]*† Then he said to them, "Who among you, if your son or ox falls into a cistern, would not immediately pull him out on the sabbath day?" [6]* But they were unable to answer his question.

Conduct of Invited Guests and Hosts

[7]*† He told a parable to those who had been invited, noticing how they were choosing the places of honor at the table. [8]* "When you are invited by someone to a wedding banquet, do not recline at table in the place of honor. A more distinguished guest than you may have been invited by him, [9] and the host who invited both of you may approach you and say, 'Give your place to this man,' and then you would proceed with embarrassment to take the lowest place. [10] Rather, when you are invited, go and take the lowest place so that when the host comes to you he may say, 'My friend, move up to a higher position.' Then you will enjoy the esteem of your companions at the table. [11]* For everyone who exalts himself will be humbled, but the one who humbles himself will be exalted." [12]* Then he said to the host who invited him, "When you hold a lunch or a dinner, do not invite your friends or your

---

13, 22–30: These sayings of Jesus follow in Luke upon the parables of the kingdom (18–21) and stress that great effort is required for entrance into the kingdom (24) and that there is an urgency to accept the present opportunity to enter because the narrow door will not remain open indefinitely (25). Lying behind the sayings is the rejection of Jesus and his message by his Jewish contemporaries (26) whose places at table in the kingdom will be taken by Gentiles from the four corners of the world (29). Those called last (the Gentiles) will precede those to whom the invitation to enter was first extended (the Jews). See also 14, 15–24.

13, 32: Nothing, not even Herod's desire to kill Jesus, stands in the way of Jesus' role in fulfilling God's will and in establishing the kingdom through his exorcisms and healings.

13, 33: *It is impossible that a prophet should die outside of Jerusalem:* Jerusalem is the city of destiny and the goal of the journey of the prophet Jesus. Only when he reaches the holy city will his work be accomplished.

14, 1–6: See the note on 13, 10–17.

14, 2: *Dropsy:* an abnormal swelling of the body because of the retention and accumulation of fluid.

14, 5: *Your son or ox:* this is the reading of many of the oldest and most important New Testament manuscripts. Because of the strange collocation of *son* and *ox*, some copyists have altered it to "your ass or ox," on the model of the saying in 13, 15.

14, 7–14: The banquet scene found only in Luke provides the opportunity for these teachings of Jesus on humility and presents a setting to display Luke's interest in Jesus' attitude toward the rich and the poor (see the notes on 4, 18; 6, 20–26; 12, 13–34).

13, 24–30: Mt 7, 13–14.21–23.
  13, 24: Mk 10, 25.
  13, 25: Mt 25, 10–12.
  13, 27: Ps 6, 9; Mt 7, 23; 25, 41.
13, 28–29: Mt 8, 11–12.
  13, 29: Ps 107, 2–3.
  13, 30: Mt 19, 20; 20, 16; Mk 10, 31.
  13, 33: Lk 2, 38; Jn 6, 30; 8, 20.
13, 34–35: Lk 19, 41–44; Mt 23, 37–39.
  13, 35: Lk 19, 38; 1 Kgs 9,

    7–8; Ps 118, 26; Jer 7, 4–7.13–15; 12, 7; 22, 5.
14, 1–6: Lk 6, 6–11; 13, 10–17.
  14, 1: Lk 11, 37.
  14, 3: Lk 6, 9; Mk 3, 4.
  14, 5: Lk 13, 15; Dt 22, 4; Mt 12, 11.
  14, 6: Mt 22, 46.
  14, 7: Lk 11, 43; Mt 23, 6; Mk 12, 38–39.
14, 8–10: Prv 25, 6–7.
  14, 11: Lk 18, 14.
  14, 12: Lk 6, 32–35.

brothers or your relatives or your wealthy neighbors, in case they may invite you back and you have repayment. 13 Rather, when you hold a banquet, invite the poor, the crippled, the lame, the blind; 14* blessed indeed will you be because of their inability to repay you. For you will be repaid at the resurrection of the righteous."

God's Invitation List

Jesus uses the image of a banquet to describe the Reign of God. Jesus' point is not about what is on the menu but who is on the invitation list: the weak, the poor, and the little ones. Who is on your "invitation list"—who are the people you reach out to and serve?

▶ Lk 14, 7–24

The Parable of the Great Feast

15† One of his fellow guests on hearing this said to him, "Blessed is the one who will dine in the kingdom of God." 16* He replied to him, "A man gave a great dinner to which he invited many. 17 When the time for the dinner came, he dispatched his servant to say to those invited, 'Come, everything is now ready.' 18 But one by one, they all began to excuse themselves. The first said to him, 'I have purchased a field and must go to examine it; I ask you, consider me excused.' 19 And another said, 'I have purchased five yoke of oxen and am on my way to evaluate them; I ask you, consider me excused.' 20 And another said, 'I have just married a woman, and therefore I cannot come.' 21 The servant went and reported this to his master. Then the master of the house in a rage commanded his servant, 'Go out quickly into the streets and alleys of the town and bring in here the poor and the crippled, the blind and the lame.' 22 The servant reported, 'Sir, your orders have been carried out and still there is room.' 23 The master then ordered the servant, 'Go out to the highways and hedgerows and make people come in that my home may be filled. 24 For, I tell you, none of those men who were invited will taste my dinner.' "

Sayings on Discipleship

25† Great crowds were traveling with him, and he turned and addressed them, 26*† "If anyone comes to me without hating his father and mother, wife and children, brothers and sisters, and even his own life, he cannot be my disciple.* 27* Whoever does not carry his own cross and come after me cannot be my disciple. 28 Which of you wishing to construct a tower does not first sit down and calculate the cost to see if there is enough for its completion? 29 Otherwise, after laying the foundation and finding himself unable to finish the work the onlookers should laugh at him 30 and say, 'This one began to build but did not have the resources to finish.' 31 Or what king marching into battle would not first sit down and decide whether with ten thousand troops he can successfully oppose another king advancing upon him with twenty thousand troops? 32 But if not, while he is still far away, he will send a delegation to ask for peace terms. 33* In the same way, everyone of you who does not renounce all his possessions cannot be my disciple.

Spice Me Up, Lord

Lord, I want to be where I can make a difference, where I can spice up another person's life by bringing him or her the good news of your love and justice.

Help me discover all the gifts you have graced me with so that I can help turn this world around—starting with my own life! Show me how to keep fresh in my commitment to serve you each day. Amen.

▶ Lk 14, 34–35

14, 15–24: The parable of the great dinner is a further illustration of the rejection by Israel, God's chosen people, of Jesus' invitation to share in the banquet in the kingdom and the extension of the invitation to other Jews whose identification as the poor, crippled, blind, and lame (21) classifies them among those who recognize their need for salvation, and to Gentiles (23). A similar parable is found in Mt 22, 1–10.

14, 25–33: This collection of sayings, most of which are peculiar to Luke, focuses on the total dedication necessary for the disciple of Jesus. No attachment to family (26) or possessions (33) can stand in the way of the total commitment demanded of the disciple. Also, acceptance of the call to be a disciple demands readiness to accept persecution and suffering (27) and a realistic assessment of the hardships and costs (28–32).

14, 26: Hating his father . . . : cf the similar saying in Mt 10, 37. The disciple's family must take second place to the absolute dedication involved in following Jesus (see also 9, 59–62).

14, 14: Jn 5, 29.
14, 16–24: Mt 22, 2–10.
14, 26–27: Mt 10, 37–38.
14, 26: Lk 9, 57–62; 18, 29; Jn 12, 25.
14, 27: Lk 9, 23; Mt 16, 24; Mk 8, 34.
14, 33: Lk 5, 11.

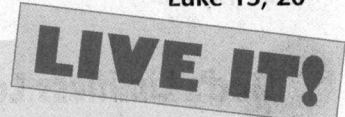

Lost and Found

Who hasn't been lost at some point in life? Everyone can identify with the frustration, fear, and loneliness that come with being lost. Which means that everyone can also identify with being found! What a wonderful feeling it is to finally see the familiar landmark or to make the right turn to the main road or to have someone help you get your life back on track.

If you identify with that lone sheep who strayed from the flock (Lk 15, 1–7), remember that God never stops looking for you. Maybe all you need to do is stop and listen for God's call so that God can embrace you and celebrate your return.

Talk to God now about the recent experiences that have led you astray and have made you feel lost. Let God hold you tight and lift you high as the divine shepherd celebrates your return.

▶ Lk 15, 1–7

The Simile of Salt

34*† "Salt is good, but if salt itself loses its taste, with what can its flavor be restored? 35* It is fit neither for the soil nor for the manure pile; it is thrown out. Whoever has ears to hear ought to hear."

The Parable of the Lost Sheep

15 1*† The tax collectors and sinners were all drawing near to listen to him, 2* but the Pharisees and scribes began to complain, saying, "This man welcomes sinners and eats with them." 3 So to them he addressed this parable. 4* "What man among you having a hundred sheep and losing one of them would not leave the ninety-nine in the desert and go after the lost one* until he finds it?* 5 And when he does find it, he sets it on his shoulders with great joy 6 and, upon his arrival home, he calls together his friends and neighbors and says to them, 'Rejoice with me because I have found my lost sheep.' 7* I tell you, in just the same way there will be more joy in heaven over one sinner who repents than over ninety-nine righteous people who have no need of repentance.

The Parable of the Lost Coin

8† "Or what woman having ten coins and losing one would not light a lamp and sweep the house, searching carefully until she finds it? 9 And when she does find it, she calls together her friends and neighbors and says to them, 'Rejoice with me be-

cause I have found the coin that I lost.' 10 In just the same way, I tell you, there will be rejoicing among the angels of God over one sinner who repents."

The Parable of the Lost Son

11 Then he said, "A man had two sons, 12 and the younger son said to his father, 'Father, give me the share of your estate that should come to me.' So the father divided the property between them. 13* After a few days, the younger son collected all his belongings and set off to a distant country where he squandered his inheritance on a life of dissipation. 14 When he had freely spent everything, a severe famine struck that country, and he found himself in dire need. 15 So he hired himself out to one of the local citizens who sent him to his farm to tend the swine. 16 And he longed to eat his fill of the pods on which the swine fed, but nobody gave him any. 17 Coming to his senses he thought, 'How many of my father's hired workers have more than enough food to eat, but here am I, dying from hunger. 18 I shall get up and go to my father and I shall say to him, "Father, I have sinned against heaven and against you. 19 I no longer deserve to be called your son; treat me as you would treat one of your hired workers." ' 20 So he got up and went back to his father. While he was still a long way off, his father caught sight of him, and was filled with compassion. He ran to his son, embraced him and

---

14, 34–35: The simile of salt follows the sayings of Jesus that demanded of the disciple total dedication and detachment from family and possessions and illustrates the condition of one who does not display this total commitment. The halfhearted disciple is like salt that cannot serve its intended purpose. See the simile of salt in Mt 5, 13 and the note there.
15, 1–32: To the parable of the lost sheep (1–7) that Luke shares with Matthew (Mt 18, 12–14), Luke adds two parables (the lost coin, 8–10; the prodigal son, 11–32) from his own special tradition to il-

lustrate Jesus' particular concern for the lost and God's love for the repentant sinner.
15, 8: *Ten coins:* literally, "ten drachmas." A drachma was a Greek silver coin.

14, 34: Mt 5, 13; Mk 9, 50.   15, 4–7: Mt 18, 12–14.
14, 35: Lk 8, 8; Mt 11, 15;   15, 4–6: Lk 19, 10.
        13, 9; Mk 4, 9.23.   15, 4: Ez 34, 11–12.16.
15, 1–7: Mt 9, 10–13.   15, 7: Ez 18, 23.
15, 2: Lk 5, 30; 19, 7.   15, 13: Prv 29, 3.

God's Limitless Love

We have all heard the story of the lost son (prodigal son). We have all heard about the older brother's envious reaction to his father's generosity. And it seems clear that the forgiving father represents God and that the sons represent each of us at different points in our life.

On second thought, perhaps there is more to this familiar parable than meets the eye. Think about the story for a moment. What does it really say about God? Not only is the father not upset about his son wasting all his money, but the father is incredibly happy to see his son return home. He runs to meet him! Picture it—this man so eager to welcome his son that he runs down the road toward him and then hugs and kisses him. Doesn't this seem a bit excessive?

But it doesn't end there. Despite the son's apology, which the father ignores, the father tells his servants to throw a huge party, to go all out for his son. This seems almost too much to believe, doesn't it? Music, dancing, expensive robes and rings, and a feast for everyone! What's going on here?

Luke is trying to show us, in the most visual way possible, that there is simply no limit to God's love for us. It is not a conditional love. It is an extravagant, outrageous love. God doesn't hold back. How can we refuse such boundless love? How can we hold back from such divine eagerness? The next time you think you have separated yourself from God's love, picture yourself walking down a road and God running toward you with open arms. What is your response?

▶ Lk 15, 11–32

---

kissed him. 21 His son said to him, 'Father, I have sinned against heaven and against you; I no longer deserve to be called your son.' 22 But his father ordered his servants, 'Quickly bring the finest robe and put it on him; put a ring on his finger and sandals on his feet. 23 Take the fattened calf and slaughter it. Then let us celebrate with a feast, 24 because this son of mine was dead, and has come to life again; he was lost, and has been found.' Then the celebration began. 25 Now the older son had been out in the field and, on his way back, as he neared the house, he heard the sound of music and dancing. 26 He called one of the servants and asked what this might mean. 27 The servant said to him, 'Your brother has returned and your father has slaughtered the fattened calf because he has him back safe and sound.' 28 He became angry, and when he refused to enter the house, his father came out and pleaded with him. 29 He said to his father in reply, 'Look, all these years I served you and not once did I disobey your orders; yet you never gave me even a young goat to feast on with my friends. 30 But when your son returns who swallowed up your property with prostitutes, for him you slaughter the fattened calf.' 31 He said to him, 'My son, you are here with me always; everything I have is yours. 32 But now we must celebrate and rejoice,

because your brother was dead and has come to life again; he was lost and has been found.' "

The Parable of the Dishonest Steward

16 1† Then he also said to his disciples, "A rich man had a steward who was

((15, 20))

---

† **16, 1–8a:** The parable of the dishonest steward has to be understood in the light of the Palestinian custom of agents acting on behalf of their masters and the usurious practices common to such agents. The dishonesty of the steward consisted in the squandering of his master's property (1) and not in any subsequent graft. The master commends the dishonest steward who has forgone his own usurious commission on the business transaction by having the debtors write new notes that reflected only the real amount owed the master (i.e., minus the steward's profit). The dishonest steward acts in this way in order to ingratiate himself with the debtors because he knows he is being dismissed from his position (3). The parable, then, teaches the prudent use of one's material goods in light of an imminent crisis.

reported to him for squandering his property. ² He summoned him and said, 'What is this I hear about you? Prepare a full account of your stewardship, because you can no longer be my steward.' ³ The steward said to himself, 'What shall I do, now that my master is taking the position of steward away from me? I am not strong enough to dig and I am ashamed to beg. ⁴ I know what I shall do so that, when I am removed from the stewardship, they may welcome me into their homes.' ⁵ He called in his master's debtors one by one. To the first he said, 'How much do you owe my master?' ⁶† He replied, 'One hundred measures of olive oil.' He said to him, 'Here is your promissory note. Sit down and quickly write one for fifty.' ⁷† Then to another he said, 'And you, how much do you owe?' He replied, 'One hundred kors of wheat.' He said to him, 'Here is your promissory note; write one for eighty.' ⁸* And the master commended that dishonest steward for acting prudently.

Application of the Parable†

"For the children of this world are more prudent in dealing with their own generation than are the children of light.† ⁹*† I tell you, make friends for yourselves with dishonest wealth, so that when it fails, you will be welcomed into eternal dwellings. ¹⁰*† The person who is trustworthy in very small matters is also trustworthy in great ones; and the person who is dishonest in very small matters is also dishonest in great ones. ¹¹ If, therefore, you are not trustworthy with dishonest wealth, who will trust you with true wealth? ¹² If you are not trustworthy with what belongs to another, who will give you what is yours? ¹³*† No servant can serve two masters. He will either hate one and love the other, or be devoted to one and despise the other. You cannot serve God and mammon."

A Saying against the Pharisees

¹⁴† The Pharisees, who loved money,† heard all these things and sneered at him. ¹⁵* And he said to them, "You justify yourselves in the sight of others, but God knows your hearts; for what is of human esteem is an abomination in the sight of God.

Sayings about the Law

¹⁶*† "The law and the prophets lasted until John;

?did you KNOW?
Understanding Parables

In some of Jesus' parables, the characters represent someone else. For example, in the parable of the prodigal son (Lk 15, 11–32), the forgiving father represents God. In other parables, the characters are examples for us to follow, as in the parable of the good Samaritan (10, 29–37). However, in some parables, the characters neither represent God nor are role models for us.

For example, in the parable of the dishonest steward (16, 1–13), the master doesn't represent God. And Jesus is not encouraging us to be dishonest like the manager. Jesus is simply saying that we need to be even more clever than dishonest people in using our money and talents for the sake of the Gospel.

For more on understanding the parables, see "Parables," Mt 13, 10.

▶ Lk 16, 1–13

16, 10–12: The second conclusion recommends constant fidelity to those in positions of responsibility.

16, 13: The third conclusion is a general statement about the incompatibility of serving God and being a slave to riches. To be dependent upon wealth is opposed to the teachings of Jesus who counseled complete dependence on the Father as one of the characteristics of the Christian disciple (12, 22–39). *God and mammon:* see the note on 16, 9. Mammon is used here as if it were itself a god.

16, 14–18: The two parables about the use of riches in ch 16 are separated by several isolated sayings of Jesus on the hypocrisy of the Pharisees (14–15), on the law (16–17), and on divorce (18).

16, 14–15: The Pharisees are here presented as examples of those who are slaves to wealth (see 16, 13) and, consequently, are unable to serve God.

16, 16: John the Baptist is presented in Luke's gospel as a transitional figure between the period of Israel, the time of promise, and the period of Jesus, the time of fulfillment. With John, the fulfillment of the Old Testament promises has begun.

---

† 16, 6: *One hundred measures:* literally, "one hundred baths." A bath is a Hebrew unit of liquid measurement equivalent to eight or nine gallons.

16, 7: *One hundred kors:* a *kor* is a Hebrew unit of dry measure for grain or wheat equivalent to ten or twelve bushels.

16, 8b–13: Several originally independent sayings of Jesus are gathered here by Luke to form the concluding application of the parable by the dishonest steward.

16, 8b–9: The first conclusion recommends the prudent use of one's wealth (in the light of the coming of the end of the age) after the manner of the children of this world, represented in the parable by the dishonest steward.

16, 9: *Dishonest wealth:* literally, "mammon of iniquity." *Mammon* is the Greek transliteration of a Hebrew or Aramaic word that is usually explained as meaning "that in which one trusts." The characterization of this wealth as *dishonest* expresses a tendency of wealth to lead one to dishonesty. *Eternal dwellings:* or, "eternal tents," i.e., heaven.

16, 8: Eph 5, 8; 1 Thes 5, 5.   16, 13: Mt 6, 24.
16, 9: Lk 12, 33.   16, 15: Lk 18, 9–14.
16, 10: Lk 19, 17; Mt 25,   16, 16: Mt 11, 12–13.
  20–23.

L
K

but from then on the kingdom of God is proclaimed, and everyone who enters does so with violence. 17* It is easier for heaven and earth to pass away than for the smallest part of a letter of the law to become invalid.

Sayings about Divorce

18* "Everyone who divorces his wife and marries another commits adultery, and the one who marries a woman divorced from her husband commits adultery.

The Parable of the Rich Man and Lazarus†

19 "There was a rich man† who dressed in purple garments and fine linen and dined sumptuously each day. 20 And lying at his door was a poor man named Lazarus, covered with sores, 21* who would gladly have eaten his fill of the scraps that fell from the rich man's table. Dogs even used to come and lick his sores. 22 When the poor man died, he was carried away by angels to the bosom of Abraham. The rich man also died and was buried, 23† and from the netherworld, where he was in torment, he raised his eyes and saw Abraham far off and Lazarus at his side. 24 And he cried out, 'Father Abraham, have pity on me. Send Lazarus to dip the tip of

his finger in water and cool my tongue, for I am suffering torment in these flames.' 25* Abraham replied, 'My child, remember that you received what was good during your lifetime while Lazarus likewise received what was bad; but now he is comforted here, whereas you are tormented. 26 Moreover, between us and you a great chasm is established to prevent anyone from crossing who might wish to go from our side to yours or from your side to ours.' 27 He said, 'Then I beg you, father, send him to my father's house, 28 for I have five brothers, so that he may warn them, lest they too come to this place of torment.' 29 But Abraham replied, 'They have Moses and the prophets. Let them listen to them.' 30† He said, 'Oh no, father Abraham, but if someone from the dead goes to them, they will repent.' 31* Then Abraham said, 'If they will not listen to Moses and the prophets, neither will they be persuaded if someone should rise from the dead.' "

Temptations to Sin

17 1* He said to his disciples, "Things that cause sin will inevitably occur, but woe to the person through whom they occur. 2 It would be better for him if a millstone were put around his neck and he be thrown into the sea than for him to

The Great Chasm

LIVE IT!

In this famous parable about the rich man and poor Lazarus, Luke puts the following words in the mouth of Abraham: "Between us and you a great chasm is established to prevent anyone from crossing who might wish to go from our side to yours or from your side to ours" (verse 26). Abraham is speaking metaphorically about heaven and hell, but he could just as easily be speaking about the gap between the "haves" and the "have-nots."

In our society and across the globe, the gap between those who are wealthy and those who are poor is indeed becoming a great chasm. It grows more and more difficult for those who are poor and destitute to improve their lot in life. And yet, we hear about millionaires becoming billionaires, many of whom seem to have little or no regard for the millions of people who go without in the world.

This parable speaks volumes to the inequities in our world and to our responsibility to be concerned for all the Lazaruses at our door. What are we doing now for those who are poor? What more could we be doing? How can we become more sensitive to the needs of those who are poor?

▸ Lk 16, 19–31

---

† **16, 19–31:** The parable of the rich man and Lazarus again illustrates Luke's concern with Jesus' attitude toward the rich and the poor. The reversal of the fates of the rich man and Lazarus (22–23) illustrates the teachings of Jesus in Luke's "Sermon on the Plain" (6, 20–21.24–25).

16, 19: The oldest Greek manuscript of Luke dating from ca. A.D. 175–225 records the name of the rich man as an abbreviated form of "Nineveh," but there is very little textual support in other manuscripts for this reading. "Dives" of popular tradition is the Latin Vulgate's translation for "rich man."

16, 23: *The netherworld:* see the note on 10, 15.
16, 30–31: A foreshadowing in Luke's gospel of the rejection of the call to repentance even after Jesus' resurrection.

16, 17: Mt 5, 18.
16, 18: Mt 5, 32; 19, 9; Mk 10, 11–12; 1 Cor 7, 10–11.
16, 21: Mt 15, 27; Mk 7, 28.
16, 25: Lk 6, 24–25.
16, 31: Jn 5, 46–47; 11, 44–48.
17, 1–2: Mt 18, 6–7.

cause one of these little ones to sin. 3*† Be on your guard! If your brother sins, rebuke him; and if he repents, forgive him. 4* And if he wrongs you seven times in one day and returns to you seven times saying, 'I am sorry,' you should forgive him."

Saying of Faith

5 And the apostles said to the Lord, "Increase our faith." 6* The Lord replied, "If you have faith the size of a mustard seed, you would say to [this] mulberry tree, 'Be uprooted and planted in the sea,' and it would obey you.

Attitude of a Servant

7† "Who among you would say to your servant who has just come in from plowing or tending sheep in the field, 'Come here immediately and take your place at table'? 8 Would he not rather say to him, 'Prepare something for me to eat. Put on your apron and wait on me while I eat and drink. You may eat and drink when I am finished'? 9 Is he grateful to that servant because he did what was commanded? 10 So should it be with you. When you have done all you have been commanded, say, 'We are unprofitable servants; we have done what we were obliged to do.' "

The Cleansing of Ten Lepers†

11* As he continued his journey to Jerusalem, he traveled through Samaria and Galilee.† 12 As he was entering a village, ten lepers met [him]. They stood at a distance from him 13* and raised their voice, saying, "Jesus, Master! Have pity on us!" 14*† And when he saw them, he said, "Go show yourselves to the priests." As they were going they were cleansed. 15 And one of them, realizing he had been healed, returned, glorifying God in a loud voice; 16 and he fell at the feet of Jesus and thanked him. He was a Samaritan. 17 Jesus said in reply, "Ten were cleansed, were they not? Where are the other nine? 18 Has none but this foreigner returned to give thanks to God?" 19* Then he said to him, "Stand up and go; your faith has saved you."

The Coming of the Kingdom of God

20*† Asked by the Pharisees when the kingdom of God would come, he said in reply, "The coming of the kingdom of God cannot be observed, 21*† and no one will announce, 'Look, here it is,' or, 'There it is.' For behold, the kingdom of God is among you."

The Day of the Son of Man

22 Then he said to his disciples, "The days will come when you will long to see one of the days of the Son of Man, but you will not see it. 23* There will be those who will say to you, 'Look, there he is,' [or] 'Look, here he is.' Do not go off, do not run in pursuit. 24* For just as lightning flashes and lights up the sky from one side to the other, so will the Son of Man be [in his day]. 25* But first he must suffer greatly and be rejected by this generation. 26* As it was in the days of Noah, so it will be in the days of the Son of Man; 27 they were eating and drinking, marrying and giving in marriage up to the day that Noah entered the ark, and the flood came and destroyed them all. 28* Similarly, as it was in the days of Lot: they were eating, drinking, buying, selling, planting, building; 29 on the day when Lot left Sodom, fire and brimstone rained from the sky to destroy them all. 30 So it will be on the day the Son of Man is revealed. 31* On that day, a person who is on the housetop and whose belongings are in the house must not go down to get them, and likewise a person in the field must not return to what was left behind.* 32 Remember the wife of

---

17, 3a: *Be on your guard:* the translation takes v 3a as the conclusion to the saying on scandal in vv 1–2. It is not impossible that it should be taken as the beginning of the saying on forgiveness in vv 3b–4.

17, 7–10: These sayings of Jesus, peculiar to Luke, which continue his response to the apostles' request to increase their faith (5–6), remind them that Christian disciples can make no claim on God's graciousness; in fulfilling the exacting demands of discipleship, they are only doing their duty.

17, 11–19: This incident recounting the thankfulness of the cleansed Samaritan leper is narrated only in Luke's gospel and provides an instance of Jesus holding up a non-Jew (18) as an example to his Jewish contemporaries (cf 10, 33 where a similar purpose is achieved in the story of the good Samaritan). Moreover, it is the faith in Jesus manifested by the foreigner that has brought him salvation (19; cf the similar relationship between faith and salvation in 7, 50; 8, 48.50).

17, 11: *Through Samaria and Galilee:* or, "between Samaria and Galilee."

17, 14: See the note on 5, 14.

17, 20–37: To the question of the Pharisees about the time of the coming of God's kingdom, Jesus replies that the kingdom is *among you* (20–21). The emphasis has thus been shifted from an imminent observable coming of the kingdom to something that is already pres-ent in Jesus' preaching and healing ministry. Luke has also appended further traditional sayings of Jesus about the unpredictable suddenness of the day of the Son of Man, and assures his readers that in spite of the delay of that day (12, 45), it will bring judgment unexpectedly on those who do not continue to be vigilant.

17, 21: *Among you:* the Greek preposition translated as *among* can also be translated as "within." In the light of other statements in Luke's gospel about the presence of the kingdom (see 10, 9.11; 11, 20) "among" is to be preferred.

17, 3: Mt 18, 15.
17, 4: Mt 6, 14; 18, 21–22.35; Mk 11, 25.
17, 6: Mt 17, 20; 21, 21; Mk 11, 23.
17, 11: Lk 9, 51–53; 13, 22.33; 18, 31; 19, 28; Jn 4, 4.
17, 13: Lk 18, 38; Mt 9, 27; 15, 22.
17, 14: Lk 5, 14; Lv 14, 2–32; Mt 8, 4; Mk 1, 44.
17, 19: Lk 7, 50; 18, 42.
17, 20: Jn 3, 3.
17, 21: Lk 17, 23; Mt 24, 23; Mk 13, 21.

17, 23: Lk 17, 21; Mt 24, 23.26; Mk 13, 21.
17, 24: Mt 24, 27.
17, 25: Lk 9, 22; 18, 32–33; Mt 16, 21; 17, 22–23; 20, 18–19; Mk 8, 31; 9, 31; 10, 33–34.
17, 26–27: Gn 6–8; Mt 24, 37–39.
17, 28–29: Gn 18, 20–21; 19, 1–29.
17, 31: Mt 24, 17–18; Mk 13, 15–16.
17, 31–32: Gn 19, 17.26.

Lot. 33* Whoever seeks to preserve his life will lose it, but whoever loses it will save it. 34 I tell you, on that night there will be two people in one bed; one will be taken, the other left. 35* And there will be two women grinding meal together; one will be taken, the other left. [36]† 37* They said to him in reply, "Where, Lord?" He said to them, "Where the body is, there also the vultures will gather."

The Parable of the Persistent Widow

18 1*† Then he told them a parable about the necessity for them to pray always without becoming weary. He said, 2 "There was a judge in a certain town who neither feared God nor respected any human being. 3 And a widow in that town used to come to him and say, 'Render a just decision for me against my adversary.' 4 For a long time the judge was unwilling, but eventually he thought, 'While it is true that I neither fear God nor respect any human being, 5*† because this widow

Can You Hear Me, Lord?

Dear God, Jesus had to remind people to pray always and not to lose hope when faced with injustice. I need to hear that too. Sometimes it seems like I pray and pray, but you are not answering.

I know that I have to be willing to look and listen for your response. I know that I have to pray always, not just in times of need. I know I need to share my daily life with you. Help me to do these things I know I need to do. Help me to pray, Lord. Amen.

▶ Lk 18, 1–8

keeps bothering me I shall deliver a just decision for her lest she finally come and strike me.' " 6 The Lord said, "Pay attention to what the dishonest judge says. 7 Will not God then secure the rights of his chosen ones who call out to him day and night? Will he be slow to answer them? 8 I tell you, he will see to it that justice is done for them speedily. But when the Son of Man comes, will he find faith on earth?"

The Parable of the Pharisee and the Tax Collector

9* He then addressed this parable to those who were convinced of their own righteousness and despised everyone else. 10 "Two people went up to the temple area to pray; one was a Pharisee and the other was a tax collector. 11 The Pharisee took up his position and spoke this prayer to himself, 'O God, I thank you that I am not like the rest of humanity—greedy, dishonest, adulterous—or even like this tax collector. 12* I fast twice a week, and I pay tithes on my whole income.' 13* But the tax collector stood off at a distance and would not even raise his eyes to heaven but beat his breast and prayed, 'O God, be merciful to me a sinner.' 14* I tell you, the latter went home justified, not the former; for everyone who exalts himself will be humbled, and the one who humbles himself will be exalted."

Saying on Children and the Kingdom

15*† People were bringing even infants to him that he might touch them,† and when the disciples saw this, they rebuked them. 16 Jesus, however, called the children to himself and said, "Let the children come to me and do not prevent them; for the kingdom of God belongs to such as these. 17* Amen, I say to you, whoever does not accept the kingdom of God like a child will not enter it."

The Rich Official

18* An official asked him this question, "Good teacher, what must I do to inherit eternal life?"*

17, 36: The inclusion of v 36, "There will be two men in the field; one will be taken, the other left behind," in some Western manuscripts appears to be a scribal assimilation to Mt 24, 40.

18, 1–14: The particularly Lucan material in the travel narrative concludes with two parables on prayer. The first (1–8) teaches the disciples the need of persistent prayer so that they not fall victims to apostasy (8). The second (9–14) condemns the self-righteous, critical attitude of the Pharisee and teaches that the fundamental attitude of the Christian disciple must be the recognition of sinfulness and complete dependence on God's graciousness. The second parable recalls the story of the pardoning of the sinful woman (7, 36–50) where a similar contrast is presented between the critical attitude of the Pharisee Simon and the love shown by the pardoned sinner.

18, 5: *Strike me:* the Greek verb translated as strike means "to strike under the eye" and suggests the extreme situation to which the persistence of the widow might lead. It may, however, be used here in the much weaker sense of "to wear one out."

18, 15—19, 27: Luke here includes much of the material about the journey to Jerusalem found in his Marcan source (10, 1–52) and

adds to it the story of Zacchaeus (19, 1–10) from his own particular tradition and the parable of the gold coins *(minas)* (19, 11–27) from Q, the source common to Luke and Matthew.

18, 15–17: The sayings on children furnish a contrast to the attitude of the Pharisee in the preceding episode (9–14) and that of the wealthy official in the following one (18–23) who think that they can lay claim to God's favor by their own merit. The attitude of the disciple should be marked by the receptivity and trustful dependence characteristic of the child.

17, 33: Lk 9, 24; Mt 10, 39; 16, 25; Mk 8, 35; Jn 12, 25.	18, 12: Mt 23, 23.
	18, 13: Ps 51, 3.
17, 35: Mt 24, 40–41.	18, 14: Lk 14, 11; Mt 23, 12.
17, 37: Jb 39, 30; Mt 24, 28.	18, 15–17: Mt 19, 13–15; Mk 10, 13–16.
18, 1: Rom 12, 12; Col 4, 2; 1 Thes 5, 17.	18, 17: Mt 18, 3.
18, 5: Lk 11, 8.	18, 18–30: Mt 19, 16–30; Mk 10, 17–31.
18, 9: Lk 16, 5; Mt 23, 25–28.	18, 18: Lk 10, 25.

¹⁹ Jesus answered him, "Why do you call me good? No one is good but God alone. ²⁰* You know the commandments, 'You shall not commit adultery; you shall not kill; you shall not steal; you shall not bear false witness; honor your father and your mother.' " ²¹ And he replied, "All of these I have observed from my youth." ²²*† When Jesus heard this he said to him, "There is still one thing left for you: sell all that you have and distribute it to the poor, and you will have a treasure in heaven. Then come, follow me." ²³ But when he heard this he became quite sad, for he was very rich.

On Riches and Renunciation

²⁴ Jesus looked at him [now sad] and said, "How hard it is for those who have wealth to enter the kingdom of God! ²⁵ For it is easier for a camel to pass through the eye of a needle than for a rich person to enter the kingdom of God." ²⁶ Those who heard this said, "Then who can be saved?" ²⁷* And he said, "What is impossible for human beings is possible for God." ²⁸ Then Peter said, "We have given up our possessions and followed you." ²⁹* He said to them,

"Amen, I say to you, there is no one who has given up house or wife or brothers or parents or children for the sake of the kingdom of God ³⁰ who will not receive [back] an overabundant return in this present age and eternal life in the age to come."

The Third Prediction of the Passion

³¹*† Then he took the Twelve aside and said to them, "Behold, we are going up to Jerusalem and everything written by the prophets about the Son of Man will be fulfilled.† ³²* He will be handed over to the Gentiles and he will be mocked and insulted and spat upon; ³³ and after they have scourged him they will kill him, but on the third day he will rise." ³⁴* But they understood nothing of this; the word remained hidden from them and they failed to comprehend what he said.

The Healing of the Blind Beggar

³⁵* Now as he approached Jericho a blind man was sitting by the roadside begging, ³⁶ and hearing a crowd going by, he inquired what was happening. ³⁷ They told him, "Jesus of Nazareth is passing by." ³⁸*† He shouted, "Jesus, Son of David, have pity on

L
K

The Loaded Question

LIVE IT!

If you ask a loaded question, you should expect a loaded answer, especially if you're asking God! Picture the rich ruler in Lk 18, 18–30, proud that he has closely and devoutly followed the Commandments all his life. Is it eagerness or conceit that makes him ask Jesus, "What must I do?"

Jesus' answer, "Sell all that you have and distribute it to the poor," must have been like a blow. Jesus asked a radical commitment from this rich ruler, just as Jesus asks a radical commitment from us. As often happens in Luke's portrayal of Jesus, that radical commitment has something to do with wealth and the poor (verse 22). If we dare to ask the loaded question, "What must I do?" we must be prepared to *unload* something too. Our human tendency is to hoard our money and our material goods. But with God's help (verse 27), we can become generous with those in need.

▶ Lk 18, 18–30

† **18, 22:** Detachment from material possessions results in the total dependence on God demanded of one who would inherit eternal life. *Sell all that you have:* the original saying (cf Mk 10, 21) has characteristically been made more demanding by Luke's addition of "all."

18, 31–33: The details included in this third announcement of Jesus' suffering and death suggest that the literary formulation of the announcement has been directed by the knowledge of the historical passion and death of Jesus.

18, 31: *Everything written by the prophets . . . will be fulfilled:* this is a Lucan addition to the words of Jesus found in the Marcan source (Mk 10, 32–34). Luke understands the events of Jesus' last days in Jerusalem to be the fulfillment of Old Testament prophecy, but, as is usually the case in Luke-Acts, the author does not specify which Old Testament prophets he has in mind; cf 24, 25.27.44; Acts 3, 8; 13, 27; 26, 22–23.

18, 38: *Son of David:* the blind beggar identifies Jesus with a title that is related to Jesus' role as Messiah (see the note on 2, 11). Through this Son of David, salvation comes to the blind man. Note the connection between salvation and house of David mentioned earlier in Zechariah's canticle (1, 69). See also the note on Mt 9, 27.

18, 20: Ex 20, 12–16; Dt 5, 16–20.	32–34; Acts 3, 18.
18, 22: Lk 12, 33; Sir 29, 11; Mt 6, 20.	**18, 32–33:** Lk 9, 22.44.
	18, 34: Mk 9, 32.
18, 27: Mk 14, 36.	**18, 35–43:** Mt 20, 29–34; Mk 10, 46–52.
18, 29–30: Lk 14, 26.	
18, 31–34: Lk 24, 25–27.44; Mt 20, 17–19; Mk 10,	**18, 38–39:** Lk 17, 13; Mt 9, 27; 15, 22.

me!" 39 The people walking in front rebuked him, telling him to be silent, but he kept calling out all the more, "Son of David, have pity on me!" 40 Then Jesus stopped and ordered that he be brought to him; and when he came near, Jesus asked him, 41* "What do you want me to do for you?" He replied, "Lord, please let me see." 42* Jesus told him, "Have sight; your faith has saved you." 43 He immediately received his sight and followed him, giving glory to God. When they saw this, all the people gave praise to God.

Zacchaeus the Tax Collector

19 1† He came to Jericho and intended to pass through the town. 2 Now a man there named Zacchaeus, who was a chief tax collector and also a wealthy man, 3 was seeking to see who Jesus was; but he could not see him because of the crowd, for he was short in stature. 4 So he ran ahead and climbed a sycamore tree in order to see Jesus, who was about to pass that way. 5 When he reached the place, Jesus looked

up and said to him, "Zacchaeus, come down quickly, for today I must stay at your house." 6 And he came down quickly and received him with joy. 7* When they all saw this, they began to grumble, saying, "He has gone to stay at the house of a sinner." 8* But Zacchaeus stood there and said to the Lord, "Behold, half of my possessions, Lord, I shall give to the poor, and if I have extorted anything from anyone I shall repay it four times over." 9*† And Jesus said to him, "Today salvation has come to this house because this man too is a descendant of Abraham. 10*† For the Son of Man has come to seek and to save what was lost."

The Parable of the Ten Gold Coins

11*† While they were listening to him speak, he proceeded to tell a parable because he was near Jerusalem and they thought that the kingdom of God would appear there immediately. 12* So he said, "A nobleman went off to a distant country to obtain the kingship for himself and then to return.

Noticed by Jesus   LIVE IT!

Why would Jesus choose Zacchaeus, who was hated and despised as a tax collector, to become a disciple? Besides that, he was pretty short and did not stand out in a crowd. Perhaps Luke is trying to tell us that our physical attributes, our past history, and other people's perceptions do not figure into God's equation. This is good news to the 98 percent of us who do not qualify as Ms. or Mr. Popularity.

When Jesus notices Zacchaeus, Zacchaeus ends up not only believing in Jesus but also doing something surprising. He gives away half of his money and possessions, perhaps to make up for all the times he cheated people. This is what conversion is—a change of heart and behavior. Conversion calls us to act in ways we would not have acted before.

Jesus has been with you from the moment of your conception. How have you tried to know him better? How do you feel knowing that he sees past externals and loves you for who you truly are?

▶ Lk 19, 1–10

19, 1–10: The story of the tax collector Zacchaeus is unique to this gospel. While a rich man (2), Zacchaeus provides a contrast to the rich man of 18, 18–23 who cannot detach himself from his material possessions to become a follower of Jesus. Zacchaeus, according to Luke, exemplifies the proper attitude toward wealth: he promises to give half of his possessions to the poor (8) and consequently is the recipient of salvation (9–10).

19, 9: A descendant of Abraham: literally, "a son of Abraham." The tax collector Zacchaeus, whose repentance is attested by his determination to amend his former ways, shows himself to be a true descendant of Abraham, the true heir to the promises of God in the Old Testament. Underlying Luke's depiction of Zacchaeus as a descendant of Abraham, the father of the Jews (1, 73; 16, 22–31), is his recognition of the central place occupied by Israel in the plan of salvation.

19, 10: This verse sums up for Luke his depiction of the role of Jesus as savior in this gospel.

19, 11–27: In this parable Luke has combined two originally distinct parables: (1) a parable about the conduct of faithful and pro-

ductive servants (13.15b–26) and (2) a parable about a rejected king (12.14–15a.27). The story about the conduct of servants occurs in another form in Mt 25, 14–20. The story about the rejected king may have originated with a contemporary historical event. After the death of Herod the Great, his son Archelaus traveled to Rome to receive the title of king. A delegation of Jews appeared in Rome before Caesar Augustus to oppose the request of Archelaus. Although not given the title of king, Archelaus was made ruler over Judea and Samaria. As the story is used by Luke, however, it furnishes a correction to the expectation of the imminent end of the age and of the establishment of the kingdom in Jerusalem (11). Jesus is not on his way to Jerusalem to receive the kingly power; for that, he must go away and only after returning from the distant country (a reference to the parousia) will reward and judgment take place.

18, 41: Mk 10, 36.
18, 42: Lk 7, 50; 17, 19.
19, 7: Lk 5, 30; 15, 2.
19, 8: Ex 21, 37; Nm 5, 6–7; 2 Sm 12, 6.
19, 9: Lk 13, 16; Mt 21, 31.
19, 10: Lk 15, 4–10; Ez 34, 16.
19, 11–27: Mt 25, 14–30.
19, 12: Mk 13, 34.

13† He called ten of his servants and gave them ten gold coins and told them, 'Engage in trade with these until I return.' 14 His fellow citizens, however, despised him and sent a delegation after him to announce, 'We do not want this man to be our king.' 15 But when he returned after obtaining the kingship, he had the servants called, to whom he had given the money, to learn what they had gained by trading. 16 The first came forward and said, 'Sir, your gold coin has earned ten additional ones.' 17* He replied, 'Well done, good servant! You have been faithful in this very small matter; take charge of ten cities.' 18 Then the second came and reported, 'Your gold coin, sir, has earned five more.' 19 And to this servant too he said, 'You, take charge of five cities.' 20 Then the other servant came and said, 'Sir, here is your gold coin; I kept it stored away in a handkerchief, 21 for I was afraid of you, because you are a demanding person; you take up what you did not lay down and you harvest what you did not plant.' 22 He said to him, 'With your own words I shall condemn you, you wicked servant. You knew I was a demanding person, taking up what I did not lay down and harvesting what I did not plant; 23 why did you not put my money in a bank? Then on my return I would have collected it with interest.' 24 And to those standing by he said, 'Take the gold coin from him and give it to the servant who has ten.' 25 But they said to him, 'Sir, he has ten gold coins.' 26* 'I tell you, to everyone who has, more will be given, but from the one who has not, even what he has will be taken away. 27 Now as for those enemies of mine who did not want me as their king, bring them here and slay them before me.' "

VI: The Teaching Ministry in Jerusalem

The Entry into Jerusalem

28*† After he had said this, he proceeded on his journey up to Jerusalem. 29* As he drew near to Bethphage and Bethany at the place called the

JESUS GOES TO JERUSALEM AS THE MESSIAH!

As Jesus enters Jerusalem to celebrate the Passover, the crowd joyfully hails him as the king and Messiah returning to the City of David. He is the prophet who brings new hope and calls people to conversion.

On Palm Sunday—also known as Passion Sunday—we begin our preparation for Holy Week. At Mass, we receive blessed branches of palms to symbolize our profession of Jesus as the Messiah, king of peace. In some Hispanic communities, the palms are woven into beautiful braids, crosses, and flowers. In others, people receive a small donkey made of palm leaves, as a remembrance of Jesus' riding the donkey into Jerusalem. Often, his entrance into Jerusalem is re-enacted. Hispanics use art, song, and drama to celebrate and express their faith.

■ **Picture yourself in the crowd welcoming Jesus. Does Jesus' coming fill you with joy and hope?**
■ **Next Palm Sunday, find a special place for your palm. Think of a concrete way you will live out your calling as a disciple of Jesus in the coming year. Each time you see the palm, remember your call, and pray for help to respond to it.**

▶ **Lk 19, 28—40**

---

† **19, 13:** *Ten gold coins:* literally, "ten minas." A mina was a monetary unit that in ancient Greece was the equivalent of one hundred drachmas.
19, 28—21, 38: With the royal entry of Jesus into Jerusalem, a new section of Luke's gospel begins, the ministry of Jesus in Jerusalem before his death and resurrection. Luke suggests that this was a lengthy ministry in Jerusalem (19, 47; 20, 1; 21, 37–38; 22, 53)

and it is characterized by Jesus' daily teaching in the temple (21, 37–38). For the story of the entry of Jesus into Jerusalem, see also Mt 21, 1–11; Mk 11, 1–10; Jn 12, 12–19 and the notes there.

*
19, 17: Lk 16, 10.   **19, 28–40:** Mt 21, 1–11; Mk 11,
19, 26: Lk 8, 18; Mt 13, 12;   1–11; Jn 12, 12–19.
      Mk 4, 25.   **19, 29:** Zec 14, 4.

Mount of Olives, he sent two of his disciples. 30* He said, "Go into the village opposite you, and as you enter it you will find a colt tethered on which no one has ever sat. Untie it and bring it here. 31 And if anyone should ask you, 'Why are you untying it?' you will answer, 'The Master has need of it.' " 32* So those who had been sent went off and found everything just as he had told them. 33 And as they were untying the colt, its owners said to them, "Why are you untying this colt?" 34 They answered, "The Master has need of it." 35* So they brought it to Jesus, threw their cloaks over the colt, and helped Jesus to mount. 36 As he rode along, the people were spreading their cloaks on the road; 37 and now as he was approaching the slope of the Mount of Olives, the whole multitude of his disciples began to praise God aloud with joy for all the mighty deeds they had seen. 38*† They proclaimed:

"Blessed is the king who comes
    in the name of the Lord.
Peace in heaven
    and glory in the highest."

39† Some of the Pharisees in the crowd said to him, "Teacher, rebuke your disciples." 40 He said in reply, "I tell you, if they keep silent, the stones will cry out!"

The Lament for Jerusalem

41*† As he drew near, he saw the city and wept over it,* 42* saying, "If this day you only knew what makes for peace—but now it is hidden from your eyes. 43*† For the days are coming upon you when your enemies will raise a palisade against you; they will encircle you and hem you in on all sides. 44* They will smash you to the ground and your children within you, and they will not leave one stone upon another within you because you did not recognize the time of your visitation."

did you KNOW?

The Human Jesus

Have you ever been so disappointed in something that you just sat down and wept? That's what happened to Jesus. In Lk 19, 41–42, we hear of his great disappointment and frustration that he cannot help Jerusalem and its people. The people of Jerusalem do not accept his message of justice and peace, so the Temple and Jerusalem are to be destroyed again. Jesus is so upset that he weeps.

We often forget that although Jesus is fully God, he is also fully human and experienced all the things that normal people experience. He enjoyed excitement, laughter, and fun times with friends. He also experienced fear, sadness, and frustration. He was completely human in all things but sin.

What does it mean to you that Jesus shares our humanity? Why is Jesus' humanity an important part of the Christian message?

▸ Lk 19, 41–42

The Cleansing of the Temple

45*† Then Jesus entered the temple area and proceeded to drive out those who were selling things,* 46* saying to them, "It is written, 'My house shall be a house of prayer, but you have made it a den of thieves.' " 47* And every day he was teaching in the temple area. The chief priests, the scribes, and the leaders of the people, meanwhile, were seeking to put him to death,* 48 but they could find no way to accomplish their purpose because all the people were hanging on his words.

19, 38: *Blessed is the king who comes in the name of the Lord:* only in Luke is Jesus explicitly given the title *king* when he enters Jerusalem in triumph. Luke has inserted this title into the words of Ps 118, 26 that heralded the arrival of the pilgrims coming to the holy city and to the temple. Jesus is thereby acclaimed as *king* (see 1, 32) and as the one *who comes* (see Mal 3, 1; Lk 7, 19). *Peace in heaven . . . :* the acclamation of the disciples of Jesus in Luke echoes the announcement of the angels at the birth of Jesus (2, 14). The peace Jesus brings is associated with the salvation to be accomplished here in Jerusalem.

19, 39: *Rebuke your disciples:* this command, found only in Luke, was given so that the Roman authorities would not interpret the acclamation of Jesus as king as an uprising against them; cf 23, 2–3.

19, 41–44: The lament for Jerusalem is found only in Luke. By not accepting Jesus (the one who mediates peace), Jerusalem will not find peace but will become the victim of devastation.

19, 43–44: Luke may be describing the actual disaster that befell Jerusalem in A.D. 70 when it was destroyed by the Romans during the First Revolt.

19, 45–46: Immediately upon entering the holy city, Jesus in a display of his authority enters the temple (see Mal 3, 1–3) and lays claim to it after cleansing it that it might become a proper place for his teaching ministry in Jerusalem (19, 47; 20, 1; 21, 37; 22, 53). See Mt 21, 12–17; Mk 11, 15–19; Jn 2, 13–17 and the notes there.

19, 30: Nm 19, 2; Dt 21, 3; 1 Sm 6, 7; Zec 9, 9.
19, 32: Lk 22, 13.
19, 35–36: 2 Kgs 9, 13.
19, 38: Lk 2, 14; Ps 118, 26.
19, 41–44: Lk 13, 34–35.
19, 41: 2 Kgs 8, 11–12; Jer 14, 17; 15, 5.
19, 42: Lk 8, 10; Is 6, 9–10; Mt 13, 14; Mk 4, 12; Acts 28, 26–27; Rom 11, 8.10.
19, 43: Is 29, 3.
19, 44: Lk 1, 68; 21, 6; Ps 137, 9; Mt 24, 2; Mk 13, 2.
19, 45–46: Mt 21, 12–13; Mk 11, 15–17; Jn 2, 13–17.
19, 45: Lk 3, 1 / Hos 9, 15.
19, 46: Is 56, 7; Jer 7, 11.
19, 47–48: Lk 20, 19; 22, 2; Mt 21, 46; Mk 11, 18; 12, 12; 14, 1–2; Jn 5, 18; 7, 30.
19, 47: Lk 21, 37; 22, 53; Jn 18, 20.

LIVE IT!

Sit and Stand Against Injustice

Jesus not only claimed to be God's son but also took an active stand against injustice, greed, and religious hypocrisy. This outraged the leaders of his time and put his life in danger.

Despite the risks, other people have followed Jesus' example of civil disobedi-ence. On 1 February 1960, in Greensboro, North Carolina, four first-year college students began a sit-in at a diner that did not allow black people. These students' actions against injustice sparked similar sit-ins across the country. Thousands of courageous people pro-tested against unfair and cruel policies that granted white people privileges that were denied to black people.

Another example of uncommon bravery occurred on 1 December 1955, in Selma, Alabama. Rosa Parks, a black woman, boarded a public bus and sat in one of the seats toward the front, where only white people were allowed to sit. For her bravery, she was arrested, jailed, and fined. This event triggered a bus boycott that lasted for months and finally put an end to that policy.

These brave actions were part of the Civil Rights movement, which ended many racist laws in the United States. As a result, many people were beaten or thrown in jail, and some were even killed.

Civil disobedience continues today. Every year, busloads of people travel to Fort Ben-ning, Georgia, to protest a U.S. military facility nicknamed The School of the Assassins. This school teaches methods of torture and terrorism. Over the years, peaceful protesters have poured water on the grounds of the military base, held candles, sung songs, and sprawled themselves on the school grounds to re-enact scenes of death inflicted upon victims of the school's graduates. The protestors often end up in jail.

Not every Christian is called to participate in acts of civil disobedience, but, for other reasons, we are all called to be aware of situations that are racist, sexist, or unjust.

▶ Lk 19, 45–48

L
K

The Authority of Jesus Questioned

20 ¹*† One day as he was teaching the peo-ple in the temple area and proclaiming the good news, the chief priests and scribes, togeth-er with the elders, approached him ²* and said to him, "Tell us, by what authority are you doing these things? Or who is the one who gave you this au-thority?" ³ He said to them in reply, "I shall ask you a question. Tell me, ⁴* was John's baptism of heav-enly or of human origin?" ⁵* They discussed this among themselves, and said, "If we say, 'Of heaven-ly origin,' he will say, 'Why did you not believe him?' ⁶ But if we say, 'Of human origin,' then all the people will stone us, for they are convinced that John was a prophet." ⁷ So they answered that they

did not know from where it came. ⁸ Then Jesus said to them, "Neither shall I tell you by what authority I do these things."

The Parable of the Tenant Farmers

⁹*† Then he proceeded to tell the people this parable. "[A] man planted a vineyard, leased it to tenant farmers, and then went on a journey for a long time.* ¹⁰* At harvest time he sent a servant to the tenant farmers to receive some of the produce of the vineyard. But they beat the servant and sent him away empty-handed. ¹¹ So he proceeded to send an-other servant, but him also they beat and insulted and sent away empty-handed. ¹² Then he proceeded to send a third, but this one too they wounded and

---

† **20, 1–47:** The Jerusalem religious leaders or their representatives, in an attempt to incriminate Jesus with the Romans and to discredit him with the people, pose a number of questions to Jesus (about his authority, 2; about payment of taxes, 22; about the resurrec-tion, 28–33).

20, 9–19: This parable about an absentee landlord and a tenant farmers' revolt reflects the social and economic conditions of rural Palestine in the first century. The synoptic gospel writers use the para-ble to describe how the rejection of the landlord's son becomes the

occasion for the vineyard to be taken away from those to whom it was entrusted (the religious leadership of Judaism that rejects the teaching and preaching of Jesus; 19).

---

*
20, 1–8: Mt 21, 23–27; Mk 11,   20, 9–19: Mt 21, 33–46; Mk 12,
  27–33.   1–12.
20, 2: Acts 4, 7.   20, 9: ls 5, 1–7.
20, 4: Lk 3, 3.16.   20, 10–12: 2 Chr 36, 15–16.
20, 5: Mt 21, 32.

threw out. ¹³* The owner of the vineyard said, 'What shall I do? I shall send my beloved son; maybe they will respect him.' ¹⁴ But when the tenant farmers saw him they said to one another, 'This is the heir. Let us kill him that the inheritance may become ours.' ¹⁵† So they threw him out of the vineyard and killed him. What will the owner of the vineyard do to them? ¹⁶ He will come and put those tenant farmers to death and turn over the vineyard to others." When the people heard this, they exclaimed, "Let it not be so!" ¹⁷* But he looked at them and asked, "What then does this scripture passage mean:

'The stone which the builders rejected
    has become the cornerstone'?

¹⁸ Everyone who falls on that stone will be dashed to pieces; and it will crush anyone on whom it falls." ¹⁹* The scribes and chief priests sought to lay their hands on him at that very hour, but they feared the people, for they knew that he had addressed this parable to them.

Paying Taxes to the Emperor

²⁰*† They watched him closely and sent agents pretending to be righteous who were to trap him in speech,* in order to hand him over to the authority and power of the governor. ²¹* They posed this question to him, "Teacher, we know that what you say and teach is correct, and you show no partiality, but teach the way of God in accordance with the truth. ²²† Is it lawful for us to pay tribute to Caesar or not?" ²³ Recognizing their craftiness he said to them, ²⁴† "Show me a denarius; whose image and name does it bear?" They replied, "Caesar's." ²⁵* So he said to them, "Then repay to Caesar what belongs to Caesar and to God what belongs to God." ²⁶ They were unable to trap him by something he might say before the people, and so amazed were they at his reply that they fell silent.

The Question about the Resurrection

²⁷*† Some Sadducees, those who deny that there is a resurrection, came forward and put this question to him,* ²⁸*† saying, "Teacher, Moses wrote for us, 'If someone's brother dies leaving a wife but no child, his brother must take the wife and raise up descendants for his brother.' ²⁹ Now there were seven brothers; the first married a woman but died childless. ³⁰ Then the second ³¹ and the third married her, and likewise all the seven died childless. ³² Finally the woman also died. ³³ Now at the resurrection whose wife will that woman be? For all seven had been married to her." ³⁴ Jesus said to them, "The children of this age marry and are given in marriage; ³⁵ but those who are deemed worthy to attain to the coming age and to the resurrection of the dead neither marry nor are given in marriage. ³⁶† They can no longer die, for they are like angels; and they are the children of God because they are the ones who will rise. ³⁷* That the dead will rise even Moses made known in the passage about the bush, when he called 'Lord' the God of Abraham, the God of Isaac, and the God of Jacob; ³⁸* and he is not God of the dead, but of the living, for to him all are alive." ³⁹ Some of the scribes said in reply, "Teacher, you have answered well." ⁴⁰* And they no longer dared to ask him anything.

The Question about David's Son

⁴¹*† Then he said to them, "How do they claim that the Messiah is the Son of David? ⁴²* For David himself in the Book of Psalms says:

'The Lord said to my lord,
  "Sit at my right hand
⁴³   till I make your enemies your footstool." '

⁴⁴ Now if David calls him 'lord,' how can he be his son?"

†
20, 15: *They threw him out of the vineyard and killed him:* cf Mk 12, 8. Luke has altered his Marcan source and reports that the murder of the son takes place outside the vineyard to reflect the tradition of Jesus' death outside the walls of the city of Jerusalem (see Heb 13, 12).

20, 20: *The governor:* i.e., Pontius Pilate, the Roman administrator responsible for the collection of taxes and maintenance of order in Palestine.

20, 22: Through their question the agents of the Jerusalem religious leadership hope to force Jesus to take sides on one of the sensitive political issues of first-century Palestine. The issue of nonpayment of taxes to Rome becomes one of the focal points of the First Jewish Revolt (A.D. 66–70) that resulted in the Roman destruction of Jerusalem and the temple. See also the note on Mt 22, 15–22.

20, 24: *Denarius:* a Roman silver coin (see the note on 7, 41).

20, 27: *Sadducees:* see the note on Mt 3, 7.

20, 28–33: The Sadducees' question, based on the law of levirate marriage recorded in Dt 25, 5–10, ridicules the idea of the resurrection. Jesus rejects their naive understanding of the resurrection (35–36) and then argues on behalf of the resurrection of the dead on the basis of the written law (37–38) that the Sadducees accept. See

also the notes on Mt 22, 23–33.

20, 36: *Because they are the ones who will rise:* literally, "being sons of the resurrection."

20, 41–44: After successfully answering the three questions of his opponents, Jesus now asks them a question. Their inability to respond implies that they have forfeited their position and authority as the religious leaders of the people because they do not understand the scriptures. This series of controversies between the religious leadership of Jerusalem and Jesus reveals Jesus as the authoritative teacher whose words are to be listened to (see 9, 35). See also the notes on Mt 22, 41–46.

* —
20, 13: Lk 3, 22.
20, 17: Ps 118, 22; Is 28, 16.
20, 19: Lk 19, 47–48; 22, 2;
    Mt 21, 46; Mk 11, 18;
    12, 12; 14, 1–2; Jn 5,
    18; 7, 30.
20, 20–26: Mt 22, 15–22; Mk 12,
    13–17.
20, 20: Lk 11, 54.
20, 21: Jn 3, 2.
20, 25: Rom 13, 6–7.

20, 27–40: Mt 22, 23–33; Mk 12,
    18–27.
20, 27: Acts 23, 8.
20, 28: Gn 38, 8; Dt 25, 5.
20, 37: Ex 3, 2.6.15–16.
20, 38: Rom 14, 8–9.
20, 40: Mt 22, 46; Mk 12, 34.
20, 41–44: Mt 22, 41–45; Mk 12,
    35–37.
20, 42–43: Ps 110, 1.

Denunciation of the Scribes

45* Then, within the hearing of all the people, he said to [his] disciples, 46* "Be on guard against the scribes, who like to go around in long robes and love greetings in marketplaces, seats of honor in synagogues, and places of honor at banquets. 47 They devour the houses of widows and, as a pretext, recite lengthy prayers. They will receive a very severe condemnation."

The Poor Widow's Contribution

21 1*† When he looked up he saw some wealthy people putting their offerings into the treasury 2 and he noticed a poor widow putting in two small coins. 3 He said, "I tell you truly, this poor widow put in more than all the rest; 4 for those others have all made offerings from their surplus wealth, but she, from her poverty, has offered her whole livelihood."

The Destruction of the Temple Foretold

5*† While some people were speaking about how the temple was adorned with costly stones and votive offerings, he said, 6* "All that you see here—the days will come when there will not be left a stone upon another stone that will not be thrown down."

The Signs of the End

7* Then they asked him, "Teacher, when will this happen? And what sign will there be when all these things are about to happen?" 8*† He answered, "See that you not be deceived, for many will come in my name, saying, 'I am he,' and 'The time has come.' Do not follow them! 9 When you hear of wars and insurrections, do not be terrified; for such things must happen first, but it will not immediately be the end." 10* Then he said to them, "Nation will rise against nation, and kingdom against kingdom. 11 There will be powerful earthquakes, famines, and plagues from place to place; and awesome sights and mighty signs will come from the sky.

The Coming Persecution

12*† "Before all this happens, however, they will seize and persecute you, they will hand you

Stewardship: Making a Contribution

In Lk 21, 1–4, Jesus notices that the rich people gave from their excess wealth, but the widow gave from her limited budget. She actually contributed more meaningfully because she gave from what little she had.

God calls us to be contributing members of the faith community and the human family—even to the point of sacrifice. We are called to stewardship, which means giving our time, talents, and treasure to support the church's mission to spread the Good News of Jesus Christ. We should also support other organizations that contribute to the positive welfare of all people in need.

How are you responding to God's call to give? Pray for the generosity of the poor widow as you discern how much of your time, talents, and treasure you are being called to give.

▶ Lk 21, 1–4

---

† **21, 1–4:** The widow is another example of the poor ones in this gospel whose detachment from material possessions and dependence on God leads to their blessedness (6, 20). Her simple offering provides a striking contrast to the pride and pretentiousness of the scribes denounced in the preceding section (20, 45–47). The story is taken from Mk 12, 41–44.

21, 5–36: Jesus' eschatological discourse in Luke is inspired by Mk 13, but Luke has made some significant alterations to the words of Jesus found there. Luke maintains, though in a modified form, the belief in the early expectation of the end of the age (see 27.28.31.32.36), but, by focusing attention throughout the gospel on the importance of the day-to-day following of Jesus and by reinterpreting the meaning of some of the signs of the end from Mk 13, he has come to terms with what seemed to the early Christian community to be a delay of the parousia. Mark, for example, described the desecration of the Jerusalem temple by the Romans (Mk 13, 14) as the apocalyptic symbol (see Dn 9, 27; 12, 11) accompanying the end of the age and the coming of the Son of Man. Luke (21, 20–24), however, removes the apocalyptic setting and sepa-rates the historical destruction of Jerusalem from the signs of the coming of the Son of Man by a period that he refers to as "the times of the Gentiles" (21, 24). See also the notes on Mt 24, 1–36 and Mk 13, 1–37.

21, 8: *The time has come:* in Luke, the proclamation of the imminent end of the age has itself become a false teaching.

21, 12: *Before all this happens . . . :* to Luke and his community, some of the signs of the end just described (10–11) still lie in the future. Now in dealing with the persecution of the disciples (12–19) and the destruction of Jerusalem (20–24) Luke is pointing to eschatological signs that have already been fulfilled.

*—
20, 45–47: Lk 11, 37–54; Mt 23, 1–36; Mk 12, 38–40.
20, 46: Lk 14, 7–11.
21, 1–4: Mk 12, 41–44.
21, 5–6: Mt 24, 1–2; Mk 13, 1–2.
21, 6: Lk 19, 44.
21, 7–19: Mt 24, 3–14; Mk 13, 3–13.
21, 8: Lk 17, 23; Mk 13, 5.6.21; 1 Jn 2, 18.
21, 10: 2 Chr 15, 6; Is 19, 2.
21, 12–15: Lk 12, 11–12; Mt 10, 17–20; Mk 13, 9–11.

over to the synagogues and to prisons, and they will have you led before kings and governors because of my name.* 13 It will lead to your giving testimony. 14 Remember, you are not to prepare your defense beforehand, 15*† for I myself shall give you a wisdom in speaking that all your adversaries will be powerless to resist or refute. 16* You will even be handed over by parents, brothers, relatives, and friends, and they will put some of you to death.* 17 You will be hated by all because of my name, 18* but not a hair on your head will be destroyed. 19* By your perseverance you will secure your lives.

The Great Tribulation

20*† "When you see Jerusalem surrounded by armies, know that its desolation is at hand.* 21* Then those in Judea must flee to the mountains. Let those within the city escape from it, and let those in the countryside not enter the city, 22 for these days are the time of punishment when all the scriptures are fulfilled. 23* Woe to pregnant women and nursing mothers in those days, for a terrible calamity will come upon the earth and a wrathful judgment upon this people. 24*† They will fall by the edge of the sword and be taken as captives to all the Gentiles; and Jerusalem will be trampled underfoot by the Gentiles until the times of the Gentiles are fulfilled.

The Coming of the Son of Man

25* "There will be signs in the sun, the moon, and the stars, and on earth nations will be in dismay, perplexed by the roaring of the sea and the waves.* 26*† People will die of fright in anticipation of what is coming upon the world, for the powers of the heavens will be shaken. 27* And then they will see the Son of Man coming in a cloud with power and great glory. 28* But when these signs begin to happen, stand erect and raise your heads because your redemption is at hand."

The Lesson of the Fig Tree

29* He taught them a lesson. "Consider the fig tree and all the other trees. 30 When their buds burst open, you see for yourselves and know that summer is now near; 31 in the same way, when you see these things happening, know that the kingdom of God is near. 32* Amen, I say to you, this generation will not pass away until all these things have taken place. 33* Heaven and earth will pass away, but my words will not pass away.

Exhortation to be Vigilant

34* "Beware that your hearts do not become drowsy from carousing and drunkenness and the anxieties of daily life, and that day catch you by surprise 35 like a trap. For that day will assault everyone who lives on the face of the earth. 36* Be vigilant at all times and pray that you have the strength to escape the tribulations that are imminent and to stand before the Son of Man."

Ministry in Jerusalem

37* During the day, Jesus was teaching in the temple area, but at night he would leave and stay at the place called the Mount of Olives. 38 And all the people would get up early each morning to listen to him in the temple area.

VII: The Passion Narrative†

The Conspiracy against Jesus

22 1* Now the feast of Unleavened Bread, called the Passover,† was drawing near, 2* and the chief priests and the scribes were seeking

---

† **21, 15:** *A wisdom in speaking:* literally, "a mouth and wisdom."
21, 20–24: The actual destruction of Jerusalem by Rome in A.D. 70 upon which Luke and his community look back provides the assurance that, just as Jesus' prediction of Jerusalem's destruction was fulfilled, so too will be his announcement of their final redemption (27–28).
21, 24: *The times of the Gentiles:* a period of indeterminate length separating the destruction of Jerusalem from the cosmic signs accompanying the coming of the Son of Man.
21, 26: *The powers of the heavens:* the heavenly bodies mentioned in v 25 and thought of as cosmic armies.
22, 1—23, 56a: The passion narrative. Luke is still dependent upon Mark for the composition of his own passion narrative but has incorporated much of his own special tradition into the narrative. Among the distinctive sections in Luke are: (1) the tradition of the institution of the Eucharist (22, 15–20); (2) Jesus' farewell discourse (22, 21–38); (3) the mistreatment and interrogation of Jesus (22, 63–71); (4) Jesus before Herod and his second appearance before Pilate (23, 6–16); (5) words addressed to the women followers on the way to the crucifixion (23, 27–32); (6) words to the penitent thief (23, 39–41); (7) the death of Jesus (23, 46.47b–49). Luke stresses the innocence of Jesus (23, 4.14–15.22) who is the victim of the powers of evil (22, 3.31.53) and who goes to his death in fulfillment of his

Father's will (22, 42.46). Throughout the narrative Luke emphasizes the mercy, compassion, and healing power of Jesus (22, 51; 23, 43) who does not go to death lonely and deserted, but is accompanied by others who follow him on the way of the cross (23, 26–31.49).
22, 1: *Feast of Unleavened Bread, called the Passover:* see the note on Mk 14, 1.

21, 12: Jn 16, 2; Acts 25, 24.
21, 15: Acts 6, 10.
21, 16–18: Mt 10, 21–22.
21, 16: Lk 12, 52–53.
21, 18: Lk 12, 7; 1 Sm 14, 45;
   Mt 10, 30; Acts 27, 34.
21, 19: Lk 8, 15.
21, 20–24: Mt 24, 15–21; Mk 13,
   14–19.
21, 20–22: Lk 19, 41–44.
21, 21: Lk 17, 31.
21, 23: 1 Cor 7, 26.
21, 24: Tb 14, 5; Ps 79, 1; Is
   63, 18; Jer 21, 7; Rom
   11, 25; Rv 11, 2.
21, 25–28: Mt 24, 29–31; Mk 13,
   24–27.
21, 25: Wis 5, 22; Is 13, 10; Ez
   32, 7; Jl 2, 10; 3, 3–4;

   4, 15; Rv 6, 12–14.
21, 26: Hg 2, 6.21.
21, 27: Dn 7, 13–14; Mt 26,
   64; Rv 1, 7.
21, 28: Lk 2, 38.
21, 29–33: Mt 24, 32–35; Mk 13,
   28–31.
21, 32: Lk 9, 27; Mt 16, 28.
21, 33: Lk 16, 17.
21, 34: Lk 12, 45–46; Mt 24,
   48–50; 1 Thes 5, 3.6–7.
21, 36: Mk 13, 33.
21, 37: Lk 19, 47; 22, 39.
22, 1–2: Mt 26, 1–5; Mk 14,
   1–2; Jn 11, 47–53.
22, 2: Lk 19, 47–48; 20, 19;
   Mt 21, 46; Mk 12, 12;
   Jn 5, 18; 7, 30.

a way to put him to death, for they were afraid of the people. [3]*† Then Satan entered into Judas, the one surnamed Iscariot, who was counted among the Twelve,* [4] and he went to the chief priests and temple guards to discuss a plan for handing him over to them. [5] They were pleased and agreed to pay him money. [6] He accepted their offer and sought a favorable opportunity to hand him over to them in the absence of a crowd.

Preparations for the Passover

[7]* When the day of the feast of Unleavened Bread arrived, the day for sacrificing the Passover lamb,* [8] he sent out Peter and John, instructing them, "Go and make preparations for us to eat the Passover." [9] They asked him, "Where do you want us to make the preparations?" [10]† And he answered them, "When you go into the city, a man will meet you carrying a jar of water. Follow him into the house that he enters [11] and say to the master of the house, 'The teacher says to you, "Where is the guest room where I may eat the Passover with my disciples?" ' [12] He will show you a large upper room that is furnished. Make the preparations there." [13]* Then they went off and found everything exactly as he had told them, and there they prepared the Passover.

The Last Supper

[14]* When the hour came, he took his place at table with the apostles. [15]† He said to them, "I have eagerly desired to eat this Passover with you before I suffer, [16]* for, I tell you, I shall not eat it [again] until there is fulfillment in the kingdom of God." [17]† Then he took a cup, gave thanks, and said, "Take this and share it among yourselves; [18] for I tell you [that] from this time on I shall not drink of the fruit of the vine until the kingdom of God comes." [19]*† Then he took the bread, said the blessing, broke it, and gave it to them, saying, "This is my body, which will be given for you; do this in memory of me." [20]* And likewise the cup after they had eaten, saying, "This cup is the new covenant in my blood, which will be shed for you.

THE EUCHARIST

Catholic Connections

In Luke's account of the Last Supper, Jesus asks his disciples to remember him and all that he did, as they share the loaf of bread that he identified as his body given for us and the cup of wine that he identified with the New Covenant sealed by his blood. The celebration of this great mystery, along with its awesome meaning, is at the center of the Eucharistic celebration.

The Eucharist is one of the seven Catholic sacraments, and it is the heart and soul of what it means to be Catholic. It serves as the common celebration of our faith, and it brings together all Catholics— young and old, rich and poor, male and female, and people of all colors, nationalities, and walks of life—to participate in the death and Resurrection of Jesus. In the Eucharist, we are all members of the one Body of Christ. No matter where you go in the world, you can join in celebrating the Eucharist as a member of the Catholic church.

For more on the Eucharist, see the articles for Mt 26, 26–29; Mk 14, 22–25; Jn 13, 1–17.

▶ Lk 22, 14–20

22, 3: *Satan entered into Judas:* see the note on 4, 13.

22, 10: *A man will meet you carrying a jar of water:* see the note on Mk 14, 13.

22, 15: *This Passover:* Luke clearly identifies this last supper of Jesus with the apostles as a Passover meal that commemorated the deliverance of the Israelites from slavery in Egypt. Jesus reinterprets the significance of the Passover by setting it in the context of the kingdom of God (16). The "deliverance" associated with the Passover finds its new meaning in the blood that will be shed (20).

22, 17: Because of a textual problem in vv 19 and 20, some commentators interpret this cup as the eucharistic cup.

22, 19c–20: *Which will be given . . . do this in memory of me:* these words are omitted in some important Western text manuscripts and a few Syriac manuscripts. Other ancient text types, including the

oldest papyrus manuscript of Luke dating from the late second or early third century, contain the longer reading presented here. The Lucan account of the words of institution of the Eucharist bears a close resemblance to the words of institution in the Pauline tradition (see 1 Cor 11, 23–26). See also the notes on Mt 26, 26–29; 26, 27–28; and Mk 14, 22–24.

22, 3–6: Mt 26, 14–16; Mk 14, 10–11; Jn 13, 2.27.	22, 14–20: Mt 26, 20.26–30; Mk 14, 17.22–26; 1 Cor 11, 23–25.
22, 3: Acts 1, 17.	22, 16: Lk 13, 29.
22, 7–13: Mt 26, 17–19; Mk 14, 12–16.	22, 19: Lk 24, 30; Acts 27, 35.
22, 7: Ex 12, 6.14–20.	22, 20: Ex 24, 8; Jer 31, 31; 32, 40; Zec 9, 11.
22, 13: Lk 19, 32.	

The Betrayal Foretold

21* "And yet behold, the hand of the one who is to betray me is with me on the table; 22 for the Son of Man indeed goes as it has been determined; but woe to that man by whom he is betrayed." 23 And they began to debate among themselves who among them would do such a deed.

Prayer of a Servant Leader

Dear Jesus, you made it clear that those who are greatest are the ones who serve, not the ones who have fame, fortune, or authority. Help me adjust my priorities to put others first. Place within me a genuine desire to serve. Enable me to recognize the daily opportunities I have to reach out to those in need in my family, in my school, and in my community. Guide me as I strive to follow your example to become a servant leader. Amen.

▸ Lk 22, 24–27

The Role of the Disciples

24*† Then an argument broke out among them about which of them should be regarded as the greatest. 25*† He said to them, "The kings of the Gentiles lord it over them and those in authority over them are addressed as 'Benefactors'; 26* but among you it shall not be so. Rather, let the greatest among you be as the youngest, and the leader as the servant. 27 For who is greater: the one seated at table or the one who serves? Is it not the one seated at table? I am among you as the one who serves. 28 It is you who have stood by me in my trials; 29* and I confer a kingdom on you, just as my Father has conferred one on me, 30* that you may eat and drink at my table in my kingdom; and you will sit on thrones judging the twelve tribes of Israel.

Peter's Denial Foretold

31*† "Simon, Simon, behold Satan has demanded to sift all of you like wheat,*† 32 but I have prayed† that your own faith may not fail; and once you have turned back, you must strengthen your brothers." 33* He said to him, "Lord, I am prepared to go to prison and to die with you." 34* But he replied, "I tell you, Peter, before the cock crows this day, you will deny three times that you know me."

Instructions for the Time of Crisis

35* He said to them, "When I sent you forth without a money bag or a sack or sandals, were you in need of anything?" "No, nothing," they replied. 36*† He said to them, "But now one who has a money bag should take it, and likewise a sack, and one who does not have a sword should sell his cloak and buy one. 37* For I tell you that this scripture must be fulfilled in me, namely, 'He was counted among the wicked'; and indeed what is written about me is coming to fulfillment." 38† Then they said, "Lord, look, there are two swords here." But he replied, "It is enough!"

The Agony in the Garden

39* Then going out he went, as was his custom, to the Mount of Olives, and the disciples followed him. 40* When he arrived at the place he said to them, "Pray that you may not undergo the test." 41* After withdrawing about a stone's throw from them and kneeling, he prayed, 42* saying, "Father, if you are willing, take this cup away from me; still, not my will but yours be done." [43† And to

---

† 22, 24–38: The Gospel of Luke presents a brief farewell discourse of Jesus; compare the lengthy farewell discourses and prayer in John, chs 13–17.

22, 25: 'Benefactors': this word occurs as a title of rulers in the Hellenistic world.

22, 31: All of you: literally, "you." The translation reflects the meaning of the Greek text that uses a second person plural pronoun here.

22, 31–32: Jesus' prayer for Simon's faith and the commission to strengthen his brothers anticipates the post-resurrectional prominence of Peter in the first half of Acts, where he appears as the spokesman for the Christian community and the one who begins the mission to the Gentiles (Acts 10–11).

22, 36: In contrast to the ministry of the Twelve and of the seventy-two during the period of Jesus (9, 3; 10, 4), in the future period of the church the missionaries must be prepared for the opposition they will face in a world hostile to their preaching.

22, 38: It is enough!: the farewell discourse ends abruptly with these words of Jesus spoken to the disciples when they take literally what was intended as figurative language about being prepared to face the world's hostility.

22, 43–44: These verses, though very ancient, were probably not part of the original text of Luke. They are absent from the oldest papyrus manuscripts of Luke and from manuscripts of wide geographical distribution.

22, 21–23: Ps 41, 10; Mt 26, 21–25; Mk 14, 18–21; Jn 13, 21–30.
22, 24: Lk 9, 46; Mt 18, 1; Mk 9, 34.
22, 25–27: Mt 20, 25–27; Mk 10, 42–44; Jn 13, 3–16.
22, 26: Mt 23, 11; Mk 9, 35.
22, 29: Lk 12, 32.
22, 30: Mt 19, 28.
22, 31–34: Mt 26, 33–35; Mk 14, 29–31; Jn 13, 37–38.
22, 31: Jb 1, 6–12; Am 9, 9.
22, 33: Lk 22, 54.
22, 34: Lk 22, 54–62.
22, 35: Lk 9, 3; 10, 4; Mt 10, 9–10; Mk 6, 7–9.
22, 36: Lk 22, 49.
22, 37: Is 53, 12.
22, 39–46: Mt 26, 30.36–46; Mk 14, 26.32–42; Jn 18, 1–2.
22, 40: Lk 22, 46.
22, 41: Heb 5, 7–8.
22, 42: Mt 6, 10.

strengthen him an angel from heaven appeared to him. 44 He was in such agony and he prayed so fervently that his sweat became like drops of blood falling on the ground.] 45 When he rose from prayer and returned to his disciples, he found them sleeping from grief. 46* He said to them, "Why are you sleeping? Get up and pray that you may not undergo the test."

22, 39

The Betrayal and Arrest of Jesus

47* While he was still speaking, a crowd approached and in front was one of the Twelve, a man named Judas. He went up to Jesus to kiss him. 48 Jesus said to him, "Judas, are you betraying the Son of Man with a kiss?" 49* His disciples realized what was about to happen, and they asked, "Lord, shall we strike with a sword?" 50* And one of them struck the high priest's servant and cut off his right ear. 51† But Jesus said in reply, "Stop, no more of this!" Then he touched the servant's ear and healed him. 52* And Jesus said to the chief priests and temple guards and elders who had come for him, "Have you come out as against a robber, with swords and clubs? 53* Day after day

I was with you in the temple area, and you did not seize me; but this is your hour, the time for the power of darkness."

Peter's Denial of Jesus

54* After arresting him they led him away and took him into the house of the high priest; Peter was following at a distance.* 55 They lit a fire in the middle of the courtyard and sat around it, and Peter sat down with them. 56 When a maid saw him seated in the light, she looked intently at him and said, "This man too was with him." 57 But he denied it saying, "Woman, I do not know him." 58 A short while later someone else saw him and said, "You too are one of them"; but Peter answered, "My friend, I am not." 59 About an hour later, still another insisted, "Assuredly, this man too was with him, for he also is a Galilean." 60 But Peter said, "My friend, I do not know what you are talking about." Just as he was saying this, the cock crowed, 61*† and the Lord turned and looked at Peter; and Peter remembered the word of the Lord, how he had said to him, "Before the cock crows today, you will deny me three times." 62 He went out and began to weep bitterly. 63* The men who held Jesus in custody were ridiculing and beating him. 64 They blindfolded him and questioned him, saying, "Prophesy! Who is it that struck you?" 65 And they reviled him in saying many other things against him.

Jesus before the Sanhedrin†

66* When day came the council of elders of the people met, both chief priests and scribes,* and they brought him before their Sanhedrin.† 67* They said, "If you are the Messiah, tell us," but he replied to them, "If I tell you, you will not believe, 68 and if I question, you will not respond. 69* But from this time on the Son of Man will be seated at the right hand of the power of God." 70 They all asked, "Are you then the Son of God?" He replied to them, "You say that I am." 71 Then they said, "What further need have we for testimony? We have heard it from his own mouth."

22, 51: *And healed him:* only Luke recounts this healing of the injured servant.

22, 61: Only Luke recounts that *the Lord turned and looked at Peter.* This look of Jesus leads to Peter's weeping bitterly over his denial (62).

22, 66–71: Luke recounts one daytime trial of Jesus (66–71) and hints at some type of preliminary nighttime investigation (54–65). Mark (and Matthew who follows Mark) has transferred incidents of this day into the nighttime interrogation with the result that there appear to be two Sanhedrin trials of Jesus in Mark (and Matthew); see the note on Mk 14, 53.

22, 66: *Sanhedrin:* the word is a Hebraized form of a Greek word meaning a "council," and refers to the elders, chief priests, and scribes who met under the high priest's leadership to decide religious

and legal questions that did not pertain to Rome's interests. Jewish sources are not clear on the competence of the Sanhedrin to sentence and to execute during this period.

22, 46: Lk 22, 40.
22, 47–53: Mt 26, 47–56; Mk 14, 43–50; Jn 18, 3–4.
22, 49: Lk 22, 36.
22, 50: Jn 18, 26.
22, 52: Lk 22, 37.
22, 53: Lk 19, 47; 21, 37; Jn 7, 30; 8, 20; Col 1, 13.
22, 54–62: Mt 26, 57–58.69–75; Mk 14, 53–54.66–72; Jn 18, 12–18.25–27.
22, 54: Lk 22, 33.
22, 61: Lk 22, 34.
22, 63–65: Mt 26, 67–68; Mk 14, 65.
22, 66–71: Mt 26, 59–66; Mk 14, 55–64.
22, 66: Mt 27, 1; Mk 15, 1.
22, 67: Jn 3, 12; 8, 45; 10, 24.
22, 69: Ps 110, 1; Dn 7, 13–14; Acts 7, 56.

?did you KNOW?

Luke's Account of Jesus' Death

The stories of Jesus' Passion—the name Christians use to describe his suffering and death—differ in all four Gospels. By comparing these stories, we get insight into the authors' portrayal of Jesus. Let's take a closer look at the perspective in the Gospel of Luke.

First, in Jesus' Passion, Luke describes the openness of Gentiles to Jesus' message of salvation. For example, Pilate finds Jesus innocent three times in Luke (23, 4.14.22) and hands him over to be crucified only at the insistence of the Jewish leaders (verse 24). Later, it is a Roman centurion who praises God at the moment of Jesus' death (verse 47).

Second, Luke emphasizes Jesus' compassion and forgiveness, even during his greatest suffering. While carrying the cross, Jesus shows his concern for the women who are following him (verses 28–31). As he is nailed to the cross, he forgives those responsible (verse 34). And when one of the criminals asks for Jesus to remember him, Jesus goes beyond that to promise him the first place in Paradise (verse 43).

Third, Luke emphasizes Jesus' glory and divinity. Whereas Mark portrays Jesus abandoned in his Passion (Mk 15, 34), Luke surrounds Jesus with sympathetic people: a crowd including the women of Jerusalem (Lk 23, 27), the good thief (verses 40–41), and the centurion (verse 47). In Mark, Jesus feels God's absence (Mk 15, 34), but Luke presents Jesus in control even at his death, handing his spirit over to God (Lk 23, 46). Luke is making it clear in his portrayal of Jesus' Passion that Jesus is the loving, forgiving savior of all humankind.

▶ Lk 22, 47—23, 56

Jesus before Pilate

23 1*† Then the whole assembly of them arose and brought him before Pilate. 2* They brought charges against him, saying, "We found this man misleading our people; he opposes the payment of taxes to Caesar and maintains that he is the Messiah, a king." 3* Pilate asked him, "Are you the king of the Jews?" He said to him in reply, "You say so." 4* Pilate then addressed the chief priests and the crowds, "I find this man not guilty." 5 But they were adamant and said, "He is inciting the people with his teaching throughout all Judea, from Galilee where he began even to here."

Jesus before Herod

6† On hearing this Pilate asked if the man was a Galilean; 7* and upon learning that he was under Herod's jurisdiction, he sent him to Herod who was in Jerusalem at that time. 8* Herod was very glad to see Jesus; he had been wanting to see him for a long time, for he had heard about him and had been hoping to see him perform some sign. 9* He questioned him at length, but he gave him no answer. 10* The chief priests and scribes, meanwhile, stood by accusing him harshly. 11* [Even] Herod and his soldiers treated him contemptuously and mocked him, and after clothing him in resplendent garb, he sent him back to Pilate. 12 Herod and Pilate became friends that very day, even though they had been enemies formerly. 13 Pilate then summoned the chief priests, the rulers, and the people 14* and said to them, "You brought this man to me and accused him of inciting the people to revolt. I have conducted my investigation in your presence and have not found this man guilty of the charges you have brought against him, 15 nor did Herod, for he sent him back to us. So no capital crime has been committed by him. 16* Therefore I shall have him flogged and then release him." [17]†

23, 6–12: The appearance of Jesus before Herod is found only in this gospel. Herod has been an important figure in Luke (9, 7–9; 13, 31–33) and has been presented as someone who has been curious about Jesus for a long time. His curiosity goes unrewarded. It is faith in Jesus, not curiosity, that is rewarded (7, 50; 8, 48.50; 17, 19).

23, 17: This verse, "He was obliged to release one prisoner for them at the festival," is not part of the original text of Luke. It is an explanatory gloss from Mk 15, 6 (also Mt 27, 15) and is not found in many early and important Greek manuscripts. On its historical background, see the notes on Mt 27, 15–26.

†
23, 1–5.13–25: Twice Jesus is brought before Pilate in Luke's account, and each time Pilate explicitly declares Jesus innocent of any wrongdoing (4.14.22). This stress on the innocence of Jesus before the Roman authorities is also characteristic of John's gospel (Jn 18, 38; 19, 4.6). Luke presents the Jerusalem Jewish leaders as the ones who force the hand of the Roman authorities (1–2.5.10.13. 18.21.23–25).

23, 1–5: Mt 27, 1–2.11–14; Mk 15, 1–5; Jn 18, 28–38.
23, 2: Lk 20, 22–25; Acts 17, 7; 24, 5.
23, 3: Lk 22, 70; 1 Tm 6, 13.
23, 4: Lk 23, 14.22.41; Mt 27, 24; Jn 19, 4.6; Acts 13, 28.
23, 7: Lk 3, 1; 9, 7.
23, 8: Lk 9, 9; Acts 4, 27–28.
23, 9: Mk 15, 5.
23, 10: Mt 27, 12; Mk 15, 3.
23, 11: Mt 27, 28–30; Mk 15, 17–19; Jn 19, 2–3.
23, 14: Lk 23, 4.22.41.
23, 16: Lk 23, 22; Jn 19, 12–14.

The Sentence of Death

18* But all together they shouted out, "Away with this man! Release Barabbas to us." 19 (Now Barabbas had been imprisoned for a rebellion that had taken place in the city and for murder.) 20 Again Pilate addressed them, still wishing to release Jesus, 21 but they continued their shouting, "Crucify him! Crucify him!" 22 Pilate addressed them a third time, "What evil has this man done? I found him guilty of no capital crime. Therefore I shall have him flogged and then release him." 23 With loud shouts, however, they persisted in calling for his crucifixion, and their voices prevailed. 24 The verdict of Pilate was that their demand should be granted. 25 So he released the man who had been imprisoned for rebellion and murder, for whom they asked, and he handed Jesus over to them to deal with as they wished.

The Way of the Cross

26*† As they led him away they took hold of a certain Simon, a Cyrenian, who was coming in from the country; and after laying the cross on him, they made him carry it behind Jesus. 27 A large crowd of people followed Jesus, including many women who mourned and lamented him. 28* Jesus turned to them and said, "Daughters of Jerusalem, do not weep for me; weep instead for yourselves and for your children, 29 for indeed, the days are coming when people will say, 'Blessed are the barren, the wombs that never bore and the breasts that never nursed.' 30* At that time people will say to the mountains, 'Fall upon us!' and to the hills, 'Cover us!' 31 for if these things are done when the wood is green what will happen when it is dry?" 32 Now two others, both criminals, were led away with him to be executed.

The Crucifixion

33* When they came to the place called the Skull, they crucified him and the criminals there, one on his right, the other on his left.* 34*† [Then Jesus said, "Father, forgive them, they know not what they do."] They divided his garments by casting lots. 35* The people stood by and watched; the rulers, meanwhile, sneered at him and said, "He saved others, let him save himself if he is the chosen one, the

SALUBONG

In the Philippines, Catholics celebrate the Salubong—meaning the encounter between the risen Jesus and his sorrowful mother on Easter morning. This is based on a tradition that Mary was with the women mentioned in Lk 23, 27.

On the day of Salubong, at dawn, two groups of worshipers begin walking in two different directions. One group carries a statue of Jesus, and the other group, a statue of Mary. Both statues are draped in black capes. The people walk through the town and meet on a main street, usually under an arch. A little robed "angel" (a small girl or boy) then removes the sorrowful black capes to reveal joyful white or golden robes on each statue, symbolizing the joy and glory of the Resurrection. Then the entire assembly returns to the church, and Easter Mass begins.

▶ Lk 23, 26–31

†   **23, 26–32:** An important Lucan theme throughout the gospel has been the need for the Christian disciple to follow in the footsteps of Jesus. Here this theme comes to the fore with the story of Simon of Cyrene who takes up the cross and follows Jesus (see 9, 23; 14, 27) and with the large crowd who likewise follow Jesus on the way of the cross. See also the note on Mk 15, 21.

23, 34a: [*Then Jesus said, "Father, forgive them, they know not what they do."*]: this portion of v 34 does not occur in the oldest papyrus manuscript of Luke and in other early Greek manuscripts and ancient versions of wide geographical distribution.

23, 18–25: Mt 27, 20–26; Mk 15, 6–7.11–15; Jn 18, 38b–40; 19, 14–16; Acts 3, 13–14.
23, 26–32: Mt 27, 32.38; Mk 15, 21.27; Jn 19, 17.
23, 28–31: Lk 19, 41–44; 21, 23–24.
23, 30: Hos 10, 8; Rv 6, 16.
23, 33–43: Mt 27, 33–44; Mk 15, 22–32; Jn 19, 17–24.
23, 33: Lk 22, 37; Is 53, 12.
23, 34: Nm 15, 27–31; Ps 22, 19; Mt 5, 44; Acts 7, 60.
23, 35–36: Ps 22, 8–9.

Messiah of God."* ³⁶* Even the soldiers jeered at him. As they approached to offer him wine ³⁷ they called out, "If you are King of the Jews, save yourself." ³⁸ Above him there was an inscription that read, "This is the King of the Jews."

³⁹† Now one of the criminals hanging there reviled Jesus, saying, "Are you not the Messiah? Save yourself and us." ⁴⁰ The other, however, rebuking him, said in reply, "Have you no fear of God, for you are subject to the same condemnation? ⁴¹* And indeed, we have been condemned justly, for the sentence we received corresponds to our crimes, but this man has done nothing criminal." ⁴²* Then he said, "Jesus, remember me when you come into your kingdom." ⁴³* He replied to him, "Amen, I say to you, today you will be with me in Paradise."

The Death of Jesus

⁴⁴*† It was now about noon* and darkness came over the whole land until three in the afternoon ⁴⁵* because of an eclipse of the sun. Then the veil of the temple was torn down the middle. ⁴⁶* Jesus cried out in a loud voice, "Father, into your hands I commend my spirit"; and when he had said this he breathed his last. ⁴⁷† The centurion who witnessed what had happened glorified God and said, "This man was innocent beyond doubt." ⁴⁸* When all the people who had gathered for this spectacle saw what had happened, they returned home beating their breasts; ⁴⁹* but all his acquaintances stood at a distance, including the women who had followed him from Galilee and saw these events.

The Burial of Jesus

⁵⁰* Now there was a virtuous and righteous man named Joseph who, though he was a member of the council, ⁵¹* had not consented to their plan of action. He came from the Jewish town of Arimathea and was awaiting the kingdom of God. ⁵² He went to Pilate and asked for the body of Jesus. ⁵³* After he had taken the body down, he wrapped it in a

WAITING IN DARKNESS

The darkness before Jesus died symbolizes the coming of the day of the Lord (see the introduction to Joel). This Iroquois prayer expresses the feeling of that moment:

We wait in the darkness!
Come, all ye who listen,
Help in our night journey:
Now no sun is shining;
Now no star is glowing;
Come show us the pathway:
The night is not friendly;
The moon has forgot us,
We wait in the darkness!

(David Schiller, editor, The Little Book of Prayers, p. 322)

▶ Lk 23, 44–46

23, 39–43: This episode is recounted only in this gospel. The penitent sinner receives salvation through the crucified Jesus. Jesus' words to the penitent thief reveal Luke's understanding that the destiny of the Christian is "to be with Jesus."

23, 44: *Noon . . . three in the afternoon:* literally, the sixth and ninth hours. See the note on Mk 15, 25.

23, 47: *This man was innocent:* or, "This man was righteous."

23, 35: Lk 4, 23.
23, 36: Ps 69, 22; Mt 27, 48; Mk 15, 36.
23, 41: Lk 23, 4.14.22.
23, 42: Lk 9, 27; 23, 2.3.38.
23, 43: 2 Cor 12, 3; Rv 2, 7.
23, 44–49: Mt 27, 45–56; Mk 15, 33–41; Jn 19, 25–30.
23, 44–45: Am 8, 9.
23, 45: Ex 26, 31–33; 36, 35.
23, 46: Ps 31, 6; Acts 7, 59.
23, 48: Lk 18, 13; Zec 12, 10.
23, 49: Lk 8, 1–3; 23, 55–56; 24, 10; Ps 38, 12.
23, 50–56: Mt 27, 57–61; Mk 15, 42–47; Jn 19, 38–42; Acts 13, 29.
23, 51: Lk 2, 25.38.
23, 53: Lk 19, 30; Acts 13, 29.

linen cloth and laid him in a rock-hewn tomb in which no one had yet been buried. ⁵⁴ It was the day of preparation, and the sabbath was about to begin. ⁵⁵* The women who had come from Galilee with him followed behind, and when they had seen the tomb and the way in which his body was laid in it, ⁵⁶* they returned and prepared spices and perfumed oils. Then they rested on the sabbath according to the commandment.

VIII: The Resurrection Narrative

The Resurrection of Jesus

24 ¹*† But at daybreak on the first day of the week they took the spices they had prepared and went to the tomb. ² They found the stone rolled away from the tomb; ³ but when they entered, they did not find the body of the Lord Jesus. ⁴* While they were puzzling over this, behold, two men in dazzling garments appeared to them. ⁵* They were terrified and bowed their faces to the ground. They said to them, "Why do you seek the living one among the dead? ⁶† He is not here, but he has been raised. Remember what he said to you while he was still in Galilee, ⁷* that the Son of Man must be handed over to sinners and be crucified, and rise on the third day." ⁸* And they remembered his words. ⁹*† Then they returned from the tomb and announced all these things to the eleven and to all the others. ¹⁰* The women were Mary Magdalene, Joanna, and Mary the mother of James; the others who accompanied them also told this to the apostles, ¹¹ but their story seemed like nonsense and they did not believe them. ¹²*† But Peter got up and ran to the tomb, bent down, and saw the burial cloths alone; then he went home amazed at what had happened.

The Appearance on the Road to Emmaus

¹³*† Now that very day two of them were going to a village seven miles† from Jerusalem called Emmaus, ¹⁴ and they were conversing about all the things that had occurred. ¹⁵ And it happened that while they were conversing and debating, Jesus

did you KNOW?

Resurrection Hope

Think about a time when you felt hopeless. Were you depressed? lonely? angry? afraid? These were probably some of the feelings of the women who approached Jesus' tomb on the Sunday morning after his death. Their leader, their teacher, their Lord had just been horribly executed before a huge crowd, and his wonderful vision of love, justice, and forgiveness had been shattered.

But what they encountered in that tomb changed their lives forever. The tomb was empty. Two dazzling men appeared and spoke to them. Jesus had indeed risen!

When you think that a situation is hopeless, that no end is in sight, that evil is winning out, remember this story. Along with the Resurrection stories in the other three Gospels, this story is proof that despair and death do not win, that God is at work in the most hopeless situations!

▸ Lk 24, 1–12

24, 1–53: The resurrection narrative in Luke consists of five sections: (1) the women at the empty tomb (23, 56b–24, 12); (2) the appearance to the two disciples on the way to Emmaus (24, 13–35); (3) the appearance to the disciples in Jerusalem (24, 36–43); (4) Jesus' final instructions (24, 44–49); (5) the ascension (24, 50–53). In Luke, all the resurrection appearances take place around Jerusalem; moreover, they are all recounted as having taken place on Easter Sunday. A consistent theme throughout the narrative is that the suffering, death, and resurrection of Jesus were accomplished in fulfillment of Old Testament promises and of Jewish hopes (19a.21.26–27.44.46). In his second volume, Acts, Luke will argue that Christianity is the fulfillment of the hopes of Pharisaic Judaism and its logical development (see Acts 24, 10–21).

24, 6a: *He is not here, but he has been raised:* this part of the verse is omitted in important representatives of the Western text tradition, but its presence in other text types and the slight difference in wording from Mt 28, 6 and Mk 16, 6 argue for its retention.

24, 9: The women in this gospel do not flee from the tomb and tell no one, as in Mk 16, 8, but return and tell the disciples about their experience. The initial reaction to the testimony of the women is disbelief (11).

24, 12: This verse is missing from the Western textual tradition but is found in the best and oldest manuscripts of other text types.

24, 13–35: This episode focuses on the interpretation of scripture by the risen Jesus and the recognition of him in the breaking of the bread. The references to the quotations of scripture and explanation of it (25–27), the kerygmatic proclamation (34), and the liturgical gesture (30) suggest that the episode is primarily catechetical and liturgical rather than apologetic.

24, 13: *Seven miles:* literally, "sixty stades." A stade was 607 feet. Some manuscripts read "160 stades" or more than eighteen miles. The exact location of Emmaus is disputed.

23, 55: Lk 8, 2; 23, 49; 24, 10.
23, 56: Ex 12, 16; 20, 10; Dt 5, 14.
24, 1–8: Mt 28, 1–8; Mk 16, 1–8; Jn 20, 1–17.
24, 4: 2 Mc 3, 26; Acts 1, 10.
24, 5: Acts 2, 9.
24, 7: Lk 9, 22.44; 17, 25; 18, 32–33; Mt 16, 21;
17, 22–23; Mk 9, 31; Acts 17, 3.
24, 8: Jn 2, 22.
24, 9–11: Mk 16, 10–11; Jn 20, 18.
24, 10: Lk 8, 2–3; Mk 16, 9.
24, 12: Jn 20, 3–7.
24, 13: Mk 16, 12–13.

Jesus Is with Us!

Tim was at Mass when he heard Lk 24, 13–35. "Pretty strange!" he thought. "Those two guys did not recognize Jesus after they had been with him for three years. I wonder if he looked different after the Resurrection. If I had been walking on the road to Emmaus, I wonder if I would have recognized him. I wonder if people would recognize him today if he came among us." Tim continued to ponder these thoughts as the Mass continued. He remembered his mother saying that Jesus is present among us every day—in the people we meet, when we gather to pray, and in the Eucharist.

Suddenly, Tim was aware of what the priest was saying: "This is my body which will be given up for you. This is the cup of my blood . . . it will be shed for you and for all. Do this in memory of me."

Tim looked around the church, noticing people he had not paid attention to before: the Amouri family, who were refugees from a war-torn country; the little Tucker baby, who had been born with severe disabilities; Mrs. Murphy, who lived alone at ninety-six years old; some other teenagers who were sitting together in the front of church. Somehow, all these different people found love and acceptance in the parish family. "I think I understand now," Tim thought. "Jesus does look different, but he is here!"

When Jesus joined the disciples at their table and broke the bread, they recognized him. It was at the Eucharist that Tim recognized the presence of Jesus alive today. How about you? When and where do you recognize Jesus? Who in your community reminds you of him the most? Why?

▶ Lk 24, 13–35

---

himself drew near and walked with them, [16]*† but their eyes were prevented from recognizing him. [17] He asked them, "What are you discussing as you walk along?" They stopped, looking downcast. [18] One of them, named Cleopas, said to him in reply, "Are you the only visitor to Jerusalem who does not know of the things that have taken place there in these days?" [19]* And he replied to them, "What sort of things?" They said to him, "The things that happened to Jesus the Nazarene, who was a prophet mighty in deed and word before God and all the people, [20] how our chief priests and rulers both handed him over to a sentence of death and crucified him. [21]* But we were hoping that he would be the one to redeem Israel; and besides all this, it is now the third day since this took place. [22]* Some women from our group, however, have astounded us: they were at the tomb early in the morning [23] and did not find his body; they came back and reported that they had indeed seen a vision of angels who announced that he was alive. [24]* Then some of those with us went to the tomb and found things just as the women had described, but him they did not see." [25]* And he said to them, "Oh, how foolish you are! How slow of heart to believe all that the prophets spoke! [26]† Was it not necessary that the Messiah should suffer these things and enter into his glory?" [27]* Then beginning with Moses and all the prophets, he interpreted to them what referred to him in all the scriptures. [28] As they approached the village to which they were going, he gave the impression that he was going on farther. [29] But they urged him, "Stay with us, for it is nearly evening and the day is almost over." So he went in to stay with them. [30] And it happened that, while he was with them at table, he took bread, said the blessing, broke it, and gave it to them. [31] With that their eyes were opened and they recognized him, but he vanished from their sight. [32] Then they said to each other, "Were not our hearts burning [within

---

† **24, 16:** A consistent feature of the resurrection stories is that the risen Jesus was different and initially unrecognizable (37; Mk 16, 12; Jn 20, 14; 21, 4).

24, 26: *That the Messiah should suffer . . . :* Luke is the only New Testament writer to speak explicitly of a suffering Messiah (26.46; Acts 3, 18; 17, 3; 26, 23). The idea of a suffering Messiah is not found in the Old Testament or in other Jewish literature prior to the New Testament period, although the idea is hinted at in Mk 8, 31–33. See the notes on Mt 26, 63 and 26, 67–68.

24, 16: Jn 20, 14; 21, 4.
24, 19: Mt 2, 23; 21, 11; Acts 2, 22.
24, 21: Lk 1, 54.68; 2, 38.
24, 22–23: Lk 24, 1–11; Mt 28, 1–8; Mk 16, 1–8.
24, 24: Jn 20, 3–10.
24, 25–26: Lk 9, 22; 18, 31; 24, 44; Acts 3, 24; 17, 3.
24, 27: Lk 24, 44; Dt 18, 25; Ps 22, 1–18; Is 53; 1 Pt 1, 10–11.

us] while he spoke to us on the way and opened the scriptures to us?" 33 So they set out at once and returned to Jerusalem where they found gathered together the eleven and those with them 34* who were saying, "The Lord has truly been raised and has appeared to Simon!" 35 Then the two recounted what had taken place on the way and how he was made known to them in the breaking of the bread.

The Appearance to the Disciples in Jerusalem

36*† While they were still speaking about this, he stood in their midst and said to them, "Peace be with you."* 37* But they were startled and terrified and thought that they were seeing a ghost. 38 Then he said to them, "Why are you troubled? And why do questions arise in your hearts? 39† Look at my hands and my feet, that it is I myself. Touch me and see, because a ghost does not have flesh and bones as you can see I have." 40* And as he said this, he showed them his hands and his feet. 41 While they were still incredulous for joy and were amazed, he asked them, "Have you anything here to eat?" 42* They gave him a piece

of baked fish; 43 he took it and ate it in front of them.

44* He said to them, "These are my words that I spoke to you while I was still with you, that everything written about me in the law of Moses and in the prophets and psalms must be fulfilled." 45* Then he opened their minds to understand the scriptures. 46*† And he said to them, "Thus it is written that the Messiah would suffer and rise from the dead on the third day 47* and that repentance, for the forgiveness of sins, would be preached in his name to all the nations, beginning from Jerusalem. 48* You are witnesses of these things. 49*† And [behold] I am sending the promise of my Father upon you; but stay in the city until you are clothed with power from on high."

The Ascension

50*† Then he led them [out] as far as Bethany, raised his hands, and blessed them. 51 As he blessed them he parted from them and was taken up to heaven. 52* They did him homage and then returned to Jerusalem with great joy, 53† and they were continually in the temple praising God.

---

† **24, 36–43.44–49:** The Gospel of Luke, like each of the other gospels (Mt 28, 16–20; Mk 16, 14–15; Jn 20, 19–23), focuses on an important appearance of Jesus to the Twelve in which they are commissioned for their future ministry. As in vv 6 and 12, so in vv 36 and 40 there are omissions in the Western text.

24, 39–42: The apologetic purpose of this story is evident in the concern with the physical details and the report that Jesus ate food.

24, 46: See the note on 24, 26.

24, 49: *The promise of my Father:* i.e., the gift of the holy Spirit.

24, 50–53: Luke brings his story about the time of Jesus to a close with the report of the ascension. He will also begin the story of the time of the church with a recounting of the ascension. In the gospel, Luke recounts the ascension of Jesus on Easter Sunday night, thereby closely associating it with the resurrection. In Acts (1, 3.9–11; 13, 31) he historicizes the ascension by speaking of a forty-day peri-

od between the resurrection and the ascension. The Western text omits some phrases in vv 51 and 52, perhaps to avoid any chronological conflict with Acts 1 about the time of the ascension.

24, 53: The Gospel of Luke ends as it began (1, 9), in the Jerusalem temple.

24, 34: 1 Cor 15, 4–5.	**24, 46:** Lk 9, 22; Is 53; Hos
24, 36–53: Mk 16, 14–19; Jn 20,	6, 2.
19–20.	**24, 47:** Mt 3, 2; 28, 19–20;
24, 36: 1 Cor 15, 5.	Mk 16, 15–16; Acts
24, 37: Mt 14, 26.	10, 41.
24, 40–41: Jn 21, 5.9–10.13.	**24, 48:** Acts 1, 8.
24, 42: Acts 10, 41.	**24, 49:** Jn 14, 26; Acts 1, 4;
24, 44: Lk 18, 31; 24, 27; Mt	2, 3–4.
16, 21; Jn 5, 39.46.	**24, 50–51:** Mk 16, 19; Acts 1,
24, 45: Jn 20, 9.	9–11.
	24, 52: Acts 1, 12.

We're both cut from the same cloth." "Lately, it seems like we're two ships passing in the night." People often use analogies or symbolic images in describing their closest relationships. The author of the Gospel of John does this. Throughout the Gospel, symbolic imagery is used to describe the Christian believer's relationship with Jesus. Very different in style from the other Gospels, John also gives us the clearest picture of the divinity of Jesus.

At a Glance

I. Prologue (1, 1–18).

II. The Book of Signs (1, 19—12, 50).

III. The Book of Glory (13, 1—20, 31).

IV. Epilogue: The Resurrection Appearance in Galilee (21, 1–25).

In-depth

The Gospel of John begins with symbolic language describing Jesus as the Word, who was with God in the beginning of creation and who became flesh to live among us. The author goes on to describe Jesus as the light that overcomes darkness. Those who believe in Jesus walk in the light—their lives have meaning and direction. Those who do not believe stumble in the darkness of confusion and sin. John is clear that Jesus is the divine Son of God and that to belong to God, we have to follow Jesus.

In addition to its symbolic language and stress on Jesus' divinity, John's Gospel differs from the synoptic Gospels—Matthew, Mark, and Luke—in other ways:

■ In the synoptic Gospels, Jesus' teaching focuses on the Kingdom (or Reign) of God. In John, Jesus' teaching stresses relationships: Jesus' relationship with God the Father and our relationship with Jesus.

■ In the synoptic Gospels, Jesus teaches with parables and performs many healings and miracles. In John, Jesus does not teach by parables. Instead, Jesus performs seven miraculous signs and explains their meaning.

■ John has several passages about the role of the Holy Spirit. The synoptic Gospels hardly mention the Holy Spirit.

John's story of Jesus climaxes with the coming of Jesus' "hour," a symbol for Jesus' death. But in John, Jesus' death is not tragic at all—it is his glorious return to the Father. This Gospel assures us that trust in God will pay off in the end. "I will come back again and take you to myself, so that where I am you also may be" (14, 3).

Quick Facts

Author
a member of a Christian community possibly founded by the Beloved Disciple

Date Written
most likely from A.D. 90 to 100

Audience
all the Christians of the world

Image of Jesus
noble, powerful, and divine; fully in control of his destiny

John

The Gospel According to

John

I: Prologue†

1 ¹*† In the beginning was the Word,
 and the Word was with God,
 and the Word was God.
² He was in the beginning with God.
³*†All things came to be through him,
 and without him nothing came to be.
What came to be ⁴* through him was life,
 and this life was the light of the
 human race;
⁵*†the light shines in the darkness,
 and the darkness has not overcome it.

⁶*† A man named John was sent from God. ⁷*† He came for testimony, to testify to the light, so that all might believe through him. ⁸* He was not the light, but came to testify to the light. ⁹* The true light, which enlightens everyone, was coming into the world.

¹⁰ He was in the world,
 and the world came to be
 through him,
 but the world did not know him.
¹¹† He came to what was his own,
 but his own people did not accept him.

1, 1–18: The prologue states the main themes of the gospel: life, light, truth, the world, testimony, and the preexistence of Jesus Christ, the incarnate *Logos*, who reveals God the Father. In origin, it was probably an early Christian hymn. Its closest parallel is in other christological hymns, Col 1, 15–20 and Phil 2, 6–11. Its core (1–5.10–11.14) is poetic in structure, with short phrases linked by "staircase parallelism," in which the last word of one phrase becomes the first word of the next. Prose inserts (at least 6–8 and 15) deal with John the Baptist.
 1, 1: *In the beginning:* also the first words of the Old Testament (Gn 1, 1). *Was:* this verb is used three times with different meanings in this verse: existence, relationship, and predication. *The Word* (Greek *logos*): this term combines God's dynamic, creative word (Genesis), personified preexistent Wisdom as the instrument of God's creative activity (Proverbs), and the ultimate intelligibility of reality (Hellenistic philosophy). *With God:* the Greek preposition here connotes communication with another. *Was God:* lack of a definite article with "God" in Greek signifies predication rather than identification.
 1, 3: *What came to be:* while the oldest manuscripts have no punctuation here, the corrector of Bodmer Papyrus P⁷⁵, some manuscripts, and the Ante-Nicene Fathers take this phrase with what follows, as staircase parallelism. Connection with v 3 reflects fourth-century anti-Arianism.

1, 5: The ethical dualism of light and darkness is paralleled in intertestamental literature and in the Dead Sea Scrolls. *Overcome:* "comprehend" is another possible translation, but cf 12, 35; Wis 7, 29–30.
 1, 6: John was *sent* just as Jesus was "sent" (4, 34) in divine mission. Other references to John the Baptist in this gospel emphasize the differences between them and John's subordinate role.
 1, 7: *Testimony:* the testimony theme of John is introduced, which portrays Jesus as if on trial throughout his ministry. All testify to Jesus: John the Baptist, the Samaritan woman, scripture, his works, the crowds, the Spirit, and his disciples.
 1, 11: *What was his own . . . his own people:* first a neuter, literally, "his own property/possession" (probably=Israel), then a masculine, "his own people" (the Israelites).

1, 1: Jn 10, 30; Gn 1, 1–5; Jb 28, 12–27; Prv 8, 22–25; Wis 9, 1–2; 1 Jn 1, 1–2; Col 1, 1.15; Rv 3, 14; 19, 13.
1, 3: Ps 33, 9; Wis 9, 1; Sir 42, 15; 1 Cor 8, 6; Col 1, 16; Heb 1, 2; Rv 3, 14.
1, 4: Jn 5, 26; 8, 12; 1 Jn 1, 2.
1, 5: Jn 3, 19; 8, 12; 9, 5; 12, 35.46; Wis 7, 29–30; 1 Thes 5, 4; 1 Jn 2, 8.
1, 6: Mt 3, 1; Mk 1, 4; Lk 3, 2–3.
1, 7: Jn 1, 19–34; 5, 33.
1, 8: Jn 5, 35.
1, 9: Jn 3, 19; 8, 12; 9, 39; 12, 46.

12* But to those who did accept him he gave power to become children of God, to those who believe in his name, 13*† who were born not by natural generation nor by human choice nor by a man's decision but of God.

14*†And the Word became flesh
and made his dwelling among us,
and we saw his glory,
the glory as of the Father's only Son,
full of grace and truth.

15*† John testified to him and cried out, saying, "This was he of whom I said, 'The one who is coming after me ranks ahead of me because he existed before me.' " 16† From his fullness we have all received, grace in place of grace, 17* because while the law was given through Moses, grace and truth came through Jesus Christ. 18*† No one has ever seen God. The only Son, God, who is at the Father's side, has revealed him.

II: The Book of Signs

John the Baptist's Testimony to Himself

19† And this is the testimony of John. When the Jews† from Jerusalem sent priests and Levites [to him] to ask him, "Who are you?" 20*† he admitted

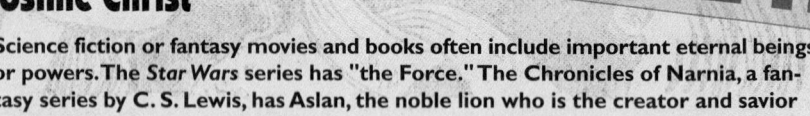

The "Cosmic Christ"

LIVE IT!

Science fiction or fantasy movies and books often include important eternal beings or powers. The *Star Wars* series has "the Force." The Chronicles of Narnia, a fantasy series by C. S. Lewis, has Aslan, the noble lion who is the creator and savior of Narnia.

The poem that begins the Gospel of John reads like something from a great science fiction classic. Only, in this case, the story is not fiction but God's revelation! The poem presents Jesus as the Word, who has existed from all time, the one through whom all things came into being. The Scriptures tell us a great mystery here: the man named Jesus, who lived in Nazareth some two thousand years ago, is the eternal God, who "became flesh / and made his dwelling among us" (Jn 1, 14). No one has ever seen God. But Jesus, the perfect image of God, "has revealed him" (verse 18) in flesh and blood.

Many people in the Gospel of John do not recognize or accept Jesus, and many people still do not today. What does it mean for you to accept Jesus?

▶ Jn 1, 1–18

---

†

1, 13: Believers in Jesus become children of God not through any of the three natural causes mentioned but through God who is the immediate cause of the new spiritual life. *Were born:* the Greek verb can mean "begotten" (by a male) or "born" (from a female or of parents). The variant "he who was begotten," asserting Jesus' virginal conception, is weakly attested in Old Latin and Syriac versions.

1, 14: *Flesh:* the whole person, used probably against docetic tendencies (cf 1 Jn 4, 2; 2 Jn 7). *Made his dwelling:* literally, "pitched his tent/tabernacle." Cf the tabernacle or tent of meeting that was the place of God's presence among his people (Ex 25, 8–9). The incarnate Word is the new mode of God's presence among his people. The Greek verb has the same consonants as the Aramaic word for God's presence (Shekinah). *Glory:* God's visible manifestation of majesty in power, which once filled the tabernacle (Ex 40, 34) and the temple (1 Kgs 8, 10–11.27), is now centered in Jesus. *Only Son:* Greek, *monogenēs,* but see the note on 1, 18. *Grace and truth:* these words may represent two Old Testament terms describing Yahweh in covenant relationship with Israel (cf Ex 34, 6), thus God's "love" and "fidelity." The Word shares Yahweh's covenant qualities.

1, 15: This verse, interrupting vv 14 and 16, seems drawn from v 30.

1, 16: *Grace in place of grace:* replacement of the Old Covenant with the New (cf 17). Other possible translations are "grace upon grace" (accumulation) and "grace for grace" (correspondence).

1, 18: *The only Son, God:* while the vast majority of later textual witnesses have another reading, "the Son, the only one" or "the only Son," the translation above follows the best and earliest manuscripts, *monogenēs theos,* but takes the first term to mean not just "Only

One" but to include a filial relationship with the Father, as at Lk 9, 38 ("only child") or Heb 11, 17 ("only son") and as translated at Jn 1, 14. The Logos is thus "only Son" and God but not Father/God.

1, 19–51: The testimony of John the Baptist about the Messiah and Jesus' self-revelation to the first disciples. This section constitutes the introduction to the gospel proper and is connected with the prose inserts in the prologue. It develops the major theme of testimony in four scenes: John's negative testimony about himself; his positive testimony about Jesus; the revelation of Jesus to Andrew and Peter; the revelation of Jesus to Philip and Nathanael.

1, 19: *The Jews:* throughout most of the gospel, the "Jews" does not refer to the Jewish people as such but to the hostile authorities, both Pharisees and Sadducees, particularly in Jerusalem, who refuse to believe in Jesus. The usage reflects the atmosphere, at the end of the first century, of polemics between church and synagogue, or possibly it refers to Jews as representative of a hostile world (10–11).

1, 20: *Messiah:* the anointed agent of Yahweh, usually considered to be of Davidic descent. See further the note on 1, 41.

1, 12: Jn 3, 11–12; 5, 43–44;
12, 46–50; Gal 3, 26;
4, 6–7; Eph 1, 5; 1 Jn
3, 2.
1, 13: Jn 3, 5–6.
1, 14: Ex 16, 10; 24, 17; 25,
8–9; 33, 22; 34, 6; Sir
24, 4.8; Is 60,1; Ez 43,
7; Jl 4, 17; Hb 2, 14;

1 Jn 1, 2; 4, 2; 2 Jn 7.
1, 15: Jn 1, 30; 3, 27–30.
1, 17: Jn 7, 19; Ex 31, 18; 34,
28.
1, 18: Jn 5, 37; 6, 46; Ex 33,
20; Jgs 13, 21–22;
1 Tm 6, 16; 1 Jn 4, 12.
1, 20: Jn 3, 28; Lk 3, 15; Acts
13, 25.

and did not deny it, but admitted, "I am not the Messiah." [21]*† So they asked him, "What are you then? Are you Elijah?" And he said, "I am not." "Are you the Prophet?" He answered, "No." [22] So they said to him, "Who are you, so we can give an answer to those who sent us? What do you have to say for yourself?" [23]*† He said:

"I am 'the voice of one crying out in the desert,
"Make straight the way of the Lord,"'

as Isaiah the prophet said." [24]† Some Pharisees were also sent. [25]* They asked him, "Why then do you baptize if you are not the Messiah or Elijah or the Prophet?" [26]*† John answered them, "I baptize with water; but there is one among you whom you do not recognize, [27] the one who is coming after me, whose sandal strap I am not worthy to untie." [28]† This happened in Bethany across the Jordan, where John was baptizing.

John the Baptist's Testimony to Jesus

[29]*† The next day he saw Jesus coming toward him and said, "Behold, the Lamb of God, who takes away the sin of the world. [30]*† He is the one of whom I said, 'A man is coming after me who ranks ahead of me because he existed before me.' [31]† I did not know him, but the reason why I came baptizing with water was that he might be made known to Is-

rael." [32]*† John testified further, saying, "I saw the Spirit come down like a dove from the sky and remain upon him. [33]* I did not know him, but the one who sent me to baptize with water told me, 'On whomever you see the Spirit come down and remain, he is the one who will baptize with the holy Spirit.' [34]*† Now I have seen and testified that he is the Son of God."

The First Disciples

[35]* The next day John was there again with two of his disciples, [36]† and as he watched Jesus walk by, he said, "Behold, the Lamb of God." [37]† The two disciples heard what he said and followed Jesus. [38] Jesus turned and saw them following him and said to them, "What are you looking for?" They said to him, "Rabbi" (which translated means Teacher), "where are you staying?" [39]† He said to them, "Come, and you will see." So they went and saw where he was staying, and they stayed with him that day. It was about four in the afternoon. [40] Andrew, the brother of Simon Peter, was one of the two who heard John and followed Jesus. [41]*† He first found his own brother Simon and told him, "We have found the Messiah" (which is translated Anointed). [42]*† Then he brought him to Jesus. Jesus looked at him and said, "You are Simon the son of John; you will be called Cephas" (which is translated Peter).

[43]† The next day he decided to go to Galilee, and

---

† **1, 21:** *Elijah:* the Baptist did not claim to be Elijah returned to earth (cf Mal 3, 23; Mt 11, 14). *The Prophet:* probably the prophet like Moses (Dt 18, 15; cf Acts 3, 22).

1, 23: This is a repunctuation and reinterpretation (as in the synoptic gospels and Septuagint) of the Hebrew text of Is 40, 3, which reads, "A voice cries out: In the desert prepare the way of the LORD."

1, 24: *Some Pharisees:* other translations, such as "Now they had been sent from the Pharisees," misunderstand the grammatical construction. This is a different group from that in v 19; the priests and Levites would have been Sadducees, not Pharisees.

1, 26: *I baptize with water:* the synoptics add "but he will baptize you with the holy Spirit" (Mk 1, 8) or ". . . holy Spirit and fire" (Mt 3, 11; Lk 3, 16). John's emphasis is on purification and preparation for a better baptism.

1, 28: *Bethany across the Jordan:* site unknown. Another reading is "Bethabara."

1, 29: *The Lamb of God:* the background for this title may be the victorious apocalyptic lamb who would destroy evil in the world (Rv 5–7; 17, 14); the paschal lamb, whose blood saved Israel (Ex 12); and/or the suffering servant led like a lamb to the slaughter as a sin-offering (Is 53, 7.10).

1, 30: *He existed before me:* possibly as Elijah (to come, 27); for the evangelist and his audience, Jesus' preexistence would be implied (see the note on 1, 1).

1, 31: *I did not know him:* this gospel shows no knowledge of the tradition (Lk 1) about the kinship of Jesus and John the Baptist. *The reason why I came baptizing with water:* in this gospel, John's baptism is not connected with forgiveness of sins; its purpose is revelatory, that Jesus may be made known to Israel.

1, 32: *Like a dove:* a symbol of the new creation (Gn 8, 8) or the community of Israel (Hos 11, 11). *Remain:* the first use of a favorite verb in John, emphasizing the permanency of the relationship between Father and Son (as here) and between the Son and the Christian. Jesus is the permanent bearer of the Spirit.

1, 34: *The Son of God:* this reading is supported by good Greek manuscripts, including the Chester Beatty and Bodmer Papyri and the Vatican Codex, but is suspect because it harmonizes this passage

with the synoptic version: "This is my beloved Son" (Mt 3, 17; Mk 1, 11; Lk 3, 22). The poorly attested alternate reading, "God's chosen One," is probably a reference to the Servant of Yahweh (Is 42, 1).

1, 36: John the Baptist's testimony makes his disciples' following of Jesus plausible.

1, 37: *The two disciples:* Andrew (40) and, traditionally, John, son of Zebedee (see the note on 13, 23).

1, 39: *Four in the afternoon:* literally, the tenth hour, from sunrise, in the Roman calculation of time. Some suggest that the next day, beginning at sunset, was the sabbath; they would have stayed with Jesus to avoid travel on it.

1, 41: *Messiah:* the Hebrew word *māšîah,* "anointed one" (see the note on Lk 2, 11), appears in Greek as the transliterated *messias* only here and in 4, 25. Elsewhere the Greek translation *christos* is used.

1, 42: *Simon, the son of John:* in Mt 16, 17, Simon is called *Bar-iōna,* "son of Jonah," a different tradition for the name of Simon's father. *Cephas:* in Aramaic = the Rock; cf Mt 16, 18. Neither the Greek equivalent *Petros* nor, with one isolated exception, *Cephas* is attested as a personal name before Christian times.

1, 43: *He:* grammatically, could be Peter, but logically is probably Jesus.

1, 21: Dt 18, 15.18; 2 Kgs 2, 11; Sir 48, 10; Mal 3, 1.23; Mt 11, 14; 17, 11–13; Mk 9, 13; Acts 3, 22.	**1, 30:** Jn 1, 15; Mt 3, 11; Mk 1, 7; Lk 3, 16.
	1, 32: Sg 5, 2; Is 11, 2; Hos 11, 11; Mt 3, 16; Mk 1, 10; Lk 3, 21–22.
1, 23: Is 40, 3; Mt 3, 3; Mk 1, 2; Lk 3, 4.	**1, 33:** Is 42, 1; Mt 3, 11; Mk 1, 8; Lk 3, 16.
1, 25: Ez 36, 25; Zec 13, 1; Mt 16, 14.	**1, 34:** Is 42, 1; Mt 3, 17; Mk 1, 11; Lk 9, 35.
1, 26: Mt 3, 11; Mk 1, 7–8; Lk 3, 16; Acts 13, 25.	**1, 35–51:** Mt 4, 18–22; Mk 1, 16–20; Lk 5, 1–11.
1, 29: Jn 1, 36; Ex 12, 53; 7; Rv 5–7; 17, 14.	**1, 41:** Jn 4, 25.
	1, 42: Mt 16, 18; Mk 3, 16.

he found Philip. And Jesus said to him, "Follow me." 44 Now Philip was from Bethsaida, the town of Andrew and Peter. 45* Philip found Nathanael and told him, "We have found the one about whom Moses wrote in the law, and also the prophets, Jesus son of Joseph, from Nazareth." 46 But Nathanael said to him, "Can anything good come from Nazareth?" Philip said to him, "Come and see." 47† Jesus saw Nathanael coming toward him and said of him, "Here is a true Israelite. There is no duplicity in him." 48*† Nathanael said to him, "How do you know me?" Jesus answered and said to him, "Before Philip called you, I saw you under the fig tree." 49*† Nathanael answered him, "Rabbi, you are the Son of God; you are the King of Israel."

50† Jesus answered and said to him, "Do you believe because I told you that I saw you under the fig tree? You will see greater things than this." 51*† And he said to him, "Amen, amen, I say to you, you will see the sky opened and the angels of God ascending and descending on the Son of Man."

The Wedding at Cana

2 1*† On the third day there was a wedding† in Cana† in Galilee, and the mother of Jesus was there. 2 Jesus and his disciples were also invited to the wedding. 3 When the wine ran short, the mother of Jesus said to him, "They have no wine." 4*† [And] Jesus said to her, "Woman, how does your concern affect me? My hour has not yet

The First Sign

If there is one day that people want to go exactly as planned, it's usually a wedding day. Months of planning, and usually lots of money, go into ensuring that the big day will go smoothly. Imagine if there wasn't enough food to feed everyone! How embarrassing! Imagine if the cake never arrived, or if there wasn't enough wine for all the guests!

This is exactly what happens at the wedding at Cana. Jesus is there, along with his followers and his mother, Mary. Mary mentions to Jesus that they are running out of wine. Take a moment to study Jesus' reaction to his mother's comment. Does it seem a bit strange? Why do you think Jesus hesitates? Why does Mary persist?

In the Gospel of John, this is the first of seven miracles, or, as John calls them, signs, that Jesus performs. How is this miracle different from all the others that Jesus performs? Why do you think this one is first? What happens because of this miracle? What might it be a sign of? Take a few moments to ponder these questions about this intriguing incident in the life of Jesus.

▶ Jn 2, 1–11

1, 47: *A true Israelite. There is no duplicity in him:* Jacob was the first to bear the name "Israel" (Gn 32, 29), but Jacob was a man of duplicity (Gn 27, 35–36).

1, 48: *Under the fig tree:* a symbol of messianic peace (cf Mi 4, 4; Zec 3, 10).

1, 49: *Son of God:* this title is used in the Old Testament, among other ways, as a title of adoption for the Davidic king (2 Sm 7, 14; Pss 2, 7; 89, 27), and thus here, with *King of Israel,* in a messianic sense. For the evangelist, *Son of God* also points to Jesus' divinity (cf 20, 28).

1, 50: Possibly a statement: "You [singular] believe because I saw you under the fig tree."

1, 51: The double "Amen" is characteristic of John. *You* is plural in Greek. The allusion is to Jacob's ladder (Gn 28, 12).

2, 1—6, 71: Signs revealing Jesus as the Messiah to all Israel. "Sign" (*sēmeion*) is John's symbolic term for Jesus' wondrous deeds (see Introduction). The Old Testament background lies in the Exodus story (cf Dt 11, 3; 29, 2). John is interested primarily in what the *sēmeia* signify: God's intervention in human history in a new way through Jesus.

2, 1–11: The first sign. This story of replacement of Jewish ceremonial washings (6) presents the initial revelation about Jesus at the outset of his ministry. He manifests his glory; the disciples believe. There is no synoptic parallel.

2, 1: *Cana:* unknown from the Old Testament. *The mother of Jesus:* she is never named in John.

2, 4: This verse may seek to show that Jesus did not work miracles to help his family and friends, as in the apocryphal gospels. *Woman:* a normal, polite form of address, but unattested in reference to one's mother. Cf also 19, 26. *How does your concern affect me?:* literally, "What is this to me and to you?"—a Hebrew expression of either hostility (Jgs 11, 12; 2 Chr 35, 21; 1 Kgs 17, 18) or denial of common interest (Hos 14, 9; 2 Kgs 3, 13). Cf Mk 1, 24; 5, 7, used by demons to Jesus. *My hour has not yet come:* the translation as a question ("Has not my hour now come?"), while preferable grammatically and supported by Greek Fathers, seems unlikely from a comparison with 7, 6.30. "The hour" is that of Jesus' passion, death, resurrection, and ascension (13, 1).

1, 45: Jn 21, 2.
1, 48: Mi 4, 4; Zec 3, 10.
1, 49: Jn 12, 13; Ex 4, 22; Dt 14, 1; 2 Sm 7, 14; Jb 1, 6; 2, 1; 38, 7; Pss 2, 7; 29, 1; 89, 27; Wis 2, 18; Sir 4, 10; Dn 3, 25; Hos 11, 1; Mt 14, 33; 16, 16; Mk 13, 32.

1, 51: Gn 28, 10–17; Dn 7, 13.
2, 1: Jn 4, 46; Jgs 14, 12; Tb 11, 8.
2, 4: Jn 7, 30; 8, 20; 12, 23; 13, 1; Jgs 11, 12; 1 Kgs 17, 18; 2 Kgs 3, 13; 2 Chr 35, 21; Hos 14, 9; Mk 1, 24; 5, 7; 7, 30; 8, 20; 12, 23; 13, 1.

come." ⁵* His mother said to the servers, "Do whatever he tells you." ⁶*† Now there were six stone water jars there for Jewish ceremonial washings, each holding twenty to thirty gallons. ⁷ Jesus told them, "Fill the jars with water." So they filled them to the brim. ⁸† Then he told them, "Draw some out now and take it to the headwaiter." So they took it. ⁹ And when the headwaiter tasted the water that had become wine, without knowing where it came from (although the servers who had drawn the water knew), the headwaiter called the bridegroom ¹⁰ and said to him, "Everyone serves good wine first, and then when people have drunk freely, an inferior one; but you have kept the good wine until now." ¹¹*† Jesus did this as the beginning of his signs in Cana in Galilee and so revealed his glory, and his disciples began to believe in him.

¹²† After this, he and his mother, [his] brothers, and his disciples went down to Capernaum and stayed there only a few days.†

Cleansing of the Temple

¹³*† Since the Passover† of the Jews was near, Jesus went up to Jerusalem. ¹⁴*† He found in the temple area those who sold oxen, sheep, and doves,† as well as the money-changers seated there. ¹⁵ He made a whip out of cords and drove them all out of the temple area, with the sheep and oxen, and spilled the coins of the money-changers and overturned their tables, ¹⁶* and to those who sold doves he said, "Take these out of here, and stop making my Father's house a marketplace." ¹⁷*† His disciples recalled the words of scripture, "Zeal for your house will consume me." ¹⁸* At this the Jews answered and said to him, "What sign can you show us for doing this?" ¹⁹*† Jesus answered and said to

did you KNOW?

Righteous Anger

Shouting! Tipping over tables! These are signs of anger. Some people might even label this behavior as out of control. But Jesus does not strike anyone with the whip; he only drives out the animals. He is not out of control, but he certainly is angry!

Even though we are often told that we should not show anger, sometimes it is appropriate to do so. Righteous anger is a reaction to an injustice or something that is not right. Jesus is upset because the greedy merchants and Temple officials have made the Temple a marketplace and have defiled the sacred space. He controls his righteous anger and channels it in a civil and religious challenge against the corrupt and greedy leaders (see "Jesus and Civil Disobedience," Mt 21, 12–13). Righteous anger should be expressed in ways that challenge evil and unjust situations but never in ways that cause violence or injury to another person.

What situations in your life or in the world might call for a response of righteous anger? How might you express your anger without going out of control?

▸ Jn 2, 13–17

2, 6: *Twenty to thirty gallons:* literally, "two or three measures"; the Attic liquid measure contained 39.39 liters. The vast quantity recalls prophecies of abundance in the last days; cf Am 9, 13–14; Hos 14, 7; Jer 31, 12.

2, 8: *Headwaiter:* used of the official who managed a banquet, but there is no evidence of such a functionary in Palestine. Perhaps here a friend of the family acted as master of ceremonies; cf Sir 32, 1.

2, 11: *The beginning of his signs:* the first of seven (see Introduction).

2, 12—3, 21: The next three episodes take place in Jerusalem. Only the first is paralleled in the synoptic gospels.

2, 12: This transitional verse may be a harmonization with the synoptic tradition in Lk 4, 31 and Mt 4, 13. There are many textual variants. John depicts no extended ministry in Capernaum as do the synoptics.

2, 13–22: This episode indicates the post-resurrectional replacement of the temple by the person of Jesus.

2, 13: *Passover:* this is the first Passover mentioned in John; a second is mentioned in 6, 4, a third in 13, 1. Taken literally, they point to a ministry of at least two years.

2, 14–22: The other gospels place the cleansing of the temple in the last days of Jesus' life (Matthew, on the day Jesus entered Jerusalem; Mark, on the next day). The order of events in the gospel narratives is often determined by theological motives rather than by chronological data.

2, 14: *Oxen, sheep, and doves:* intended for sacrifice. The doves were the offerings of the poor (Lv 5, 7). *Money-changers:* for a temple tax paid by every male Jew more than nineteen years of age, with a half-shekel coin (Ex 30, 11–16), in Tyrian currency. See the note on Mt 17, 24.

2, 17: Ps 69, 10, changed to future tense to apply to Jesus.

2, 19: This saying about the destruction of the temple occurs in various forms (Mt 24, 2; 27, 40; Mk 13, 2; 15, 29; Lk 21, 6; cf Acts 6, 14). Mt 26, 61 has: "I *can* destroy the temple of God . . ."; see the note there. In Mk 14, 58, there is a metaphorical contrast with a new temple: "I will destroy this temple *made with hands* and within three days I will build another *not made with hands.*" Here it is symbolic of Jesus' resurrection and the resulting community (see 21 and Rv 21, 2). *In three days:* an Old Testament expression for a short, indefinite period of time; cf Hos 6, 2.

2, 5: Gn 41, 55.
2, 6: Jn 3, 25; Lv 11, 33;
    Am 9, 13–14; Mt 15,
    2; 23, 25–26; Mk 7,
    2–4; Lk 11, 38.
2, 11: Jn 4, 54.
2, 13–22: Mt 21, 12–13; Mk 11,
    15–17; Lk 19, 45–46.

2, 14: Ex 30, 11–16; Lv 5, 7.
2, 16: Zec 14, 21.
2, 17: Ps 69, 9.
2, 18: Jn 6, 30.
2, 19: Mt 24, 2; 26, 61; 27,
    40; Mk 13, 2; 14, 58;
    15, 29; Lk 21, 6; Acts
    6, 14.

?did you KNOW?

"The Jews" in the Gospel of John

When you read the Gospel of John, you may notice that the Gospel writer often makes references to "the Jews." They are often portrayed questioning (2, 18) or challenging Jesus. Around the time John was written, Christian Jews were being forcibly removed from Jewish synagogues (see 16,1–4). With this rivalry in the background, the Gospel writer sometimes lumps all Jews together, portraying them as the "bad guys." Christian churches teach that we should not take John's references to "the Jews" as a basis for prejudice or anger against Jewish people.

▸ Jn 2, 18–20

them, "Destroy this temple and in three days I will raise it up." 20† The Jews said, "This temple has been under construction for forty-six years, and you will raise it up in three days?" 21 But he was speaking about the temple of his body. 22* Therefore, when he was raised from the dead, his disciples remembered that he had said this, and they came to believe the scripture and the word Jesus had spoken.

23* While he was in Jerusalem for the feast of Passover, many began to believe in his name when they saw the signs he was doing. 24 But Jesus would not trust himself to them because he knew them all, 25* and did not need anyone to testify about human nature. He himself understood it well.

Nicodemus†

3 1* Now there was a Pharisee named Nicodemus, a ruler of the Jews. 2* He came to Jesus at night and said to him, "Rabbi, we know that you are a teacher who has come from God, for no one can do these signs that you are doing unless God is with him." 3† Jesus answered and said to him, "Amen, amen, I say to you, no one can see the kingdom of God without being born from above." 4* Nicodemus said to him, "How can a person

LIVE IT!

Nic at Night

Nicodemus, a Jewish teacher with a high position of leadership, is meeting secretly with Jesus. Nicodemus has been waiting for a sign that God's promise of salvation through a savior will happen in his lifetime. He senses that maybe Jesus is this savior. But he does not yet believe in Jesus, as is emphasized by his coming to Jesus "at night" (Jn 3, 2). Speaking symbolically, Jesus outlines what it takes for salvation: to believe in Jesus as the one sent by God and to be born again through Baptism and the Holy Spirit. The same is true for people today.

Nicodemus knew that to accept Jesus publicly would put him in bad standing with the other Jewish leaders. Sometimes we must make choices that might make us look foolish to others. How hard would it be for you to express belief in Jesus publicly? Will you be a believer in the night or in the light?

▸ Jn 3, 1–21

2, 20: *Forty-six years:* based on references in Josephus (*Jewish Wars* 1, 21, 1 »»401; *Antiquities* 15, 11, 1 §380), possibly the spring of A.D. 28. Cf the note on Lk 3, 1.

3, 1–21: Jesus instructs Nicodemus on the necessity of a new birth from above. This scene in Jerusalem at Passover exemplifies the faith engendered by signs (2, 23). It continues the self-manifestation of Jesus in Jerusalem begun in ch 2. This is the first of the Johannine discourses, shifting from dialogue to monologue (11–15) to reflection of the evangelist (16–21). The shift from singular through v 10 to plural in v 11 may reflect the early church's controversy with the Jews.

3, 1: *A ruler of the Jews:* most likely a member of the Jewish council, the Sanhedrin; see the note on Mk 8, 31.

3, 3: *Born:* see the note on 1, 13. *From above:* the Greek adverb *anóthen* means both "from above" and "again." Jesus means "from above" (see 31), but Nicodemus misunderstands it as "again." This misunderstanding serves as a springboard for further instruction.

2, 22: Jn 5, 39; 12, 16; 14, 26; 20, 9; Mt 12, 6; Lk 24, 6–8; Rv 21, 22.
2, 23: Jn 4, 45.
2, 25: 1 Kgs 8, 39; Pss 33, 15; 94, 11; Sir 42, 18; Jer 17, 10; 20, 12.
3, 1: Jn 7, 50–51; 19, 39.
3, 2: Jn 9, 4.16.33; 10, 21; 11, 10; 13, 30; Mt 22, 16; Mk 12, 14; Lk 20, 21.
3, 4: Jn 1, 13.

once grown old be born again? Surely he cannot reenter his mother's womb and be born again, can he?" 5* Jesus answered, "Amen, amen, I say to you, no one can enter the kingdom of God without being born of water and Spirit. 6* What is born of flesh is flesh and what is born of spirit is spirit. 7 Do not be amazed that I told you, 'You must be born from above.' 8*† The wind blows where it wills, and you can hear the sound it makes, but you do not know where it comes from or where it goes; so it is with everyone who is born of the Spirit." 9 Nicodemus answered and said to him, "How can this happen?" 10 Jesus answered and said to him, "You are the teacher of Israel and you do not understand this? 11* Amen, amen, I say to you, we speak of what we know and we testify to what we have seen, but you people do not accept our testimony. 12* If I tell you about earthly things and you do not believe, how will you believe if I tell you about heavenly things? 13* No one has gone up to heaven except the one who has come down from heaven, the Son of Man. 14*† And just as Moses lifted up the serpent in the desert, so must the Son of Man be lifted up, 15† so that everyone who believes in him may have eternal life."

16*† For God so loved the world that he gave his only Son, so that everyone who believes in him might not perish but might have eternal life. 17*† For God did not send his Son into the world to condemn the world, but that the world might be saved through him. 18* Whoever believes in him will not be condemned, but whoever does not believe has already been condemned, because he has not believed in the name of the only Son of God. 19*† And this is the verdict, that the light came into

---

† **3, 8:** *Wind:* the Greek word *pneuma* (as well as the Hebrew *rûah*) means both "wind" and "spirit." In the play on the double meaning, "wind" is primary.

3, 14: *Lifted up:* in Nm 21, 9, Moses simply "mounted" a serpent upon a pole. John here substitutes a verb implying glorification. Jesus, exalted to glory at his cross and resurrection, represents healing for all.

3, 15: *Eternal life:* used here for the first time in John, this term stresses quality of life rather than duration.

3, 16: *Gave:* as a gift in the incarnation, and also "over to death" in the crucifixion; cf Rom 8, 32.

3, 17–19: *Condemn:* the Greek root means both judgment and condemnation. Jesus' purpose is to save, but his coming provokes judgment; some condemn themselves by turning from the light.

3, 19: Judgment is not only future but is partially realized here and now.

---

* **3, 5:** Jn 1, 32; 7, 39; 19, 30.34–35; Is 32, 15; 44, 3; Ez 36, 25–27; Jl 3, 1–2.
3, 6: Jn 6, 63; 1 Cor 15, 44–50.
3, 8: Eccl 11, 4–5; Acts 2, 2–4.
3, 11: Jn 3, 32.34; 8, 14; Mt 11, 27.
3, 12: Jn 6, 62–65; Wis 9, 16–17; 1 Cor 15, 40; 2 Cor 5, 1; Phil 2, 10;

3, 19–20.
3, 13: Jn 1, 18; 6, 62; Dn 7, 13; Rom 10, 6; Eph 4, 9.
3, 14: Jn 8, 28; 12, 32.34; Nm 21, 4–9; Wis 16, 5–7.
3, 16: 1 Jn 4, 9.
3, 17: Jn 5, 22.30; 8, 15–18; 12, 47.
3, 18: Jn 5, 24; Mk 16, 16.
3, 19: Jn 1, 5.9–11; 8, 12; 9, 5.

Catholic Connections

ARE YOU BORN AGAIN?

Rani was confused. Some of her Christian friends from school had approached her and asked if she had been saved and born again. She told them that she was Catholic and went to Mass every Sunday. Her friends told her that in order to be saved, she had to claim Jesus as her personal Lord and Savior and be baptized in the Holy Spirit. Her friends' claims caused her to worry that she might somehow not be okay with God.

In the Gospel of John, chapter 3, Jesus tells Nicodemus that no one can enter the kingdom of God unless born of water and the Holy Spirit. Some Christian churches interpret this passage to mean that one must make a conscious decision to be baptized (Baptism as an infant doesn't count) and make a public witness, or altar call, acknowledging the lordship of Jesus in one's life.

The Catholic church teaches that Baptism is a sacrament that brings us into special relationship with God. Through Baptism, we become temples of the Holy Spirit, members of the church, and God's adopted daughters and sons, through Christ. We may not have asked to be baptized, but each day we choose to be in relationship with Jesus. We renew our baptismal grace every day of our life when we live as Jesus calls us to live. And when, as disciples of Jesus, we celebrate the Eucharist and Penance and Reconciliation, we proclaim that Jesus is our Lord and Savior, whose saving death and Resurrection have brought us new life.

So how should Rani and the rest of us respond the next time someone asks if we are born again? We should say: "Yes—every day! I was baptized in the name of the Father and the Son and the Holy Spirit, and I try to live in the Spirit of Christ each and every day."

▸ Jn 3, 3–8

the world, but people preferred darkness to light, because their works were evil. ²⁰* For everyone who does wicked things hates the light and does not come toward the light, so that his works might not be exposed. ²¹* But whoever lives the truth comes to the light, so that his works may be clearly seen as done in God.

Final Witness of the Baptist

²²*† After this, Jesus and his disciples went into the region of Judea, where he spent some time with them baptizing. ²³† John was also baptizing in Aenon near Salim, because there was an abundance of water there, and people came to be baptized, ²⁴*† for John had not yet been imprisoned. ²⁵† Now a dispute arose between the disciples of John and a Jew about ceremonial washings.

²⁶* So they came to John and said to him, "Rabbi, the one who was with you across the Jordan, to whom you testified, here he is baptizing and everyone is coming to him." ²⁷* John answered and said, "No one can receive anything except what has been given him from heaven. ²⁸* You yourselves can testify that I said [that] I am not the Messiah, but that I was sent before him. ²⁹*† The one who has the bride is the bridegroom; the best man, who stands and listens for him, rejoices greatly at the bridegroom's voice. So this joy of mine has been made complete. ³⁰* He must increase; I must decrease."

The One from Heaven

³¹*† The one who comes from above is above all. The one who is of the earth is earthly and speaks of

THIS IS CHRISTMAS

This poem, by Masao and Fumiko Takenaka of Japan, is a reflection on Jesus as "living water" (Jn 4, 10):

One who said I am the eternal water
Dwelt among us
Living with us
Sustaining us
This is Christmas.

To receive a cup of living water
Is not only to cleanse ourselves
But also to cleanse all the waters.
River and well, lake and ocean,
And to share them with all.
This is Christmas.

(From Maren C. Tirabassi and
Kathy Wonson Eddy, editors,
Gifts of Many Cultures, p. 144)

▶ Jn 4, 1–15

3, 22–26: Jesus' ministry in Judea is only loosely connected with 2, 13—3, 21; cf 1, 19–36. Perhaps John the Baptist's further testimony was transposed here to give meaning to "water" in v 5. Jesus is depicted as baptizing (22); contrast 4, 2.

3, 23: *Aenon near Salim:* site uncertain, either in the upper Jordan valley or in Samaria.

3, 24: A remark probably intended to avoid objections based on a chronology like that of the synoptics (Mt 4, 12; Mk 1, 14).

3, 25: *A Jew:* some think Jesus is meant. Many manuscripts read "Jews."

3, 29: *The best man:* literally, "the friend of the groom," the *shoshben* of Jewish tradition, who arranged the wedding. Competition between him and the groom would be unthinkable.

3, 31–36: It is uncertain whether these are words by the Baptist, Jesus, or the evangelist. They are reflections on the two preceding scenes.

3, 20: Jb 24, 13–17.
3, 21: Gn 47, 29 LXX; Jos 2,
14 LXX; 2 Sm 2, 6
LXX; 15, 20 LXX; Tb 4,
6 LXX; 13, 6; Is 26, 10
LXX; Mt 5, 14–16.
3, 22–23: Jn 4, 1–2.
3, 24: Mt 4, 12; 14, 3; Mk 1,
14; 6, 17; Lk 3, 20.
3, 26: Jn 1, 26.32–34.36.
3, 27: Jn 19, 11; 1 Cor 4, 7;
2 Cor 3, 5; Heb 5, 4.
3, 28: Jn 1, 20–23; Lk 3, 15.
3, 29: Jn 15, 11; 17, 13; Mt
9, 15.
3, 30: 2 Sm 3, 1.
3, 31: Jn 8, 23.

earthly things. But the one who comes from heaven [is above all]. [32]* He testifies to what he has seen and heard, but no one accepts his testimony. [33]* Whoever does accept his testimony certifies that God is trustworthy. [34]† For the one whom God sent speaks the words of God. He does not ration his gift of the Spirit. [35]* The Father loves the Son and has given everything over to him. [36]* Whoever believes in the Son has eternal life, but whoever disobeys the Son will not see life, but the wrath of God remains upon him.

4 [1]† Now when Jesus learned that the Pharisees had heard that Jesus was making and baptizing more disciples than John [2]† (although Jesus himself was not baptizing, just his disciples), [3] he left Judea and returned to Galilee.

The Samaritan Woman

[4]† He had to pass through Samaria. [5]*† So he came to a town of Samaria called Sychar, near the plot of land that Jacob had given to his son Joseph. [6] Jacob's well was there. Jesus, tired from his journey, sat down there at the well. It was about noon.

[7] A woman of Samaria came to draw water. Jesus said to her, "Give me a drink." [8] His disciples had gone into the town to buy food. [9]*† The Samaritan woman said to him, "How can you, a Jew, ask me, a Samaritan woman, for a drink?" (For Jews use nothing in common with Samaritans.) [10]*† Jesus answered and said to her, "If you knew the gift of God and who is saying to you, 'Give me a drink,' you would have asked him and he would have given you living water." [11]† [The woman] said to him, "Sir, you do not even have a bucket and the cistern is deep; where then can you get this living water? [12]* Are you greater than our father Jacob, who gave us this cistern and drank from it himself with his children and his flocks?" [13] Jesus answered and said to her, "Everyone who drinks this water will be thirsty again; [14]* but whoever drinks the water I shall give will never

did you KNOW?

Why Are the Disciples Surprised?

The disciples "were amazed that he [Jesus] was talking with a woman" (Jn 4, 27). For several reasons, it was unusual for Jesus to be talking to her. First, in first-century Israel, men did not talk to women, especially strangers, in public places. Second, Jews did not talk to Samaritans (see "Who Belongs, and Who Does Not?" Ezra, chapters 9–10, and "Discrimination in Jesus' Time," Lk 10, 25–37), who were considered guilty of false worship (Jn 4, 20). And finally, the woman with whom Jesus was speaking was a known sinner, having married far too many times.

This episode is one more example in the Gospel of John that shows Jesus is not bound by customs and stereotypes when the message of the Gospel is at stake.

▸ Jn 4, 1–42

thirst; the water I shall give will become in him a spring of water welling up to eternal life." [15] The woman said to him, "Sir, give me this water, so that I may not be thirsty or have to keep coming here to draw water."

[16] Jesus said to her, "Go call your husband and come back." [17] The woman answered and said to him, "I do not have a husband." Jesus answered her, "You are right in saying, 'I do not have a husband.' [18]* For you have had five husbands, and the one you have now is not your husband. What you

---

3, 34: *His gift:* of God or to Jesus, perhaps both. This verse echoes vv 5 and 8.

4, 1–42: Jesus in Samaria. The self-revelation of Jesus continues with his second discourse, on his mission to "half-Jews." It continues the theme of replacement, here with regard to cult (21). Water (7–15) serves as a symbol (as at Cana and in the Nicodemus episode).

4, 2: An editorial refinement of 3, 22, perhaps directed against followers of John the Baptist who claimed that Jesus imitated him.

4, 4: *He had to:* a theological necessity; geographically, Jews often bypassed Samaria by taking a route across the Jordan.

4, 5: *Sychar:* Jerome identifies this with Shechem, a reading found in Syriac manuscripts.

4, 9: *Samaritan* women were regarded by Jews as ritually impure, and therefore Jews were forbidden to drink from any vessel they had handled.

4, 10: *Living water:* the water of life, i.e., the revelation that Jesus brings; the woman thinks of "flowing water," so much more desirable

than stagnant cistern water. On John's device of such misunderstanding, cf the note on 3, 3.

4, 11: *Sir:* the Greek *kyrios* means "master" or "lord," as a respectful mode of address for a human being or a deity; cf 4, 19. It is also the word used in the Septuagint for the Hebrew *a'dônai*, substituted for the tetragrammaton YHWH.

3, 32: Jn 3, 11.
3, 33–34: Jn 8, 26; 12, 44–50; 1 Jn 5, 10.
3, 35: Jn 13, 3; Mt 11, 27; 28, 18; Lk 10, 22.
3, 36: Jn 3, 16; 1 Jn 5, 13.
4, 5: Gn 33, 18–19; 48, 22; Jos 24, 32.
4, 9: Sir 50, 25–26; Mt 10, 5.
4, 10: Sir 24, 20–21; Is 55, 1; Jer 2, 13.
4, 12: Jn 8, 53; Mt 12, 41.
4, 14: Jn 6, 35.58; 7, 37–39; Is 44, 3; 49, 10; Jl 4, 18; Rv 7, 16; 21, 6.
4, 18: 2 Kgs 17, 24–34.

have said is true." ¹⁹* The woman said to him, "Sir, I can see that you are a prophet. ²⁰*† Our ancestors worshiped on this mountain; but you people say that the place to worship is in Jerusalem." ²¹ Jesus said to her, "Believe me, woman, the hour is coming when you will worship the Father neither on this mountain nor in Jerusalem. ²²* You people worship what you do not understand; we worship what we understand, because salvation is from the Jews. ²³† But the hour is coming, and is now here, when true worshipers will worship the Father in Spirit and truth; and indeed the Father seeks such people to worship him. ²⁴* God is Spirit, and those who worship him must worship in Spirit and truth." ²⁵*† The woman said to him, "I know that the Messiah is coming, the one called the Anointed; when he comes, he will tell us everything." ²⁶*† Jesus said to her, "I am he, the one who is speaking with you."

²⁷† At that moment his disciples returned, and were amazed that he was talking with a woman, but still no one said, "What are you looking for?" or "Why are you talking with her?" ²⁸ The woman left her water jar and went into the town and said to the people, ²⁹ "Come see a man who told me everything I have done. Could he possibly be the Messiah?" ³⁰ They went out of the town and came to him. ³¹ Meanwhile, the disciples urged him, "Rabbi, eat." ³² But he said to them, "I have food to eat of which you do not know." ³³ So the disciples said to one another, "Could someone have brought him something to eat?" ³⁴* Jesus said to them, "My food is to do the will of the one who sent me and to finish his work. ³⁵*† Do you not say, 'In four months the harvest will be here'? I tell you, look up and see the fields ripe for the harvest. ³⁶*† The reaper is already receiving his payment and gathering crops for eternal life, so that the sower and reaper can rejoice together. ³⁷* For here the saying is verified that 'One sows and another reaps.' ³⁸ I sent you to reap what you have not worked for; others have done the work, and you are sharing the fruits of their work."

³⁹† Many of the Samaritans of that town began to believe in him because of the word of the woman who testified, "He told me everything I have done." ⁴⁰ When the Samaritans came to him, they invited him to stay with them; and he stayed there two days. ⁴¹ Many more began to believe in him because of his word, ⁴²* and they said to the woman, "We no longer believe because of your word; for we have heard for ourselves, and we know that this is truly the savior of the world."

Return to Galilee

⁴³† After the two days, he left there for Galilee. ⁴⁴*† For Jesus himself testified that a prophet has

How Deep Is Your Well?

In Jn 4, 1–42, Jesus engages a Samaritan woman in conversation. She has no idea who Jesus is and what living water he is referring to, but she stands and listens. She is changed as a result. She comes to believe in Jesus and goes to tell others about the Messiah. John uses her as a role model for those who believe.

Look inside the well of faith within you. How deep is that well? Do you thirst for a deeper relationship with Jesus? Are you ready to share the Good News with others? Jesus invites each of us to join with him in a personal relationship. All we have to do is ask. Begin your relationship with Jesus by praying:

Jesus, you are the Messiah, the anointed one. I am thirsty. . . . Quench my thirst.

▸ Jn 4, 1–42

4, 20: *This mountain:* Gerizim, on which a temple was erected in the fourth century B.C. by Samaritans to rival Mt. Zion in Jerusalem; cf Dt 27, 4 (Mt. Ebal = the Jews' term for Gerizim).

4, 23: *In Spirit and truth:* not a reference to an interior worship within one's own spirit. The Spirit is the spirit given by God that reveals truth and enables one to worship God appropriately (14, 16–17). Cf "born of water and Spirit" (3, 5).

4, 25: The expectations of the Samaritans are expressed here in Jewish terminology. They did not expect a messianic king of the house of David but a prophet like Moses (Dt 18, 15).

4, 26: *I am he:* it could also be translated "I am," an Old Testament self-designation of Yahweh (Is 43, 3, etc.); cf 6, 20; 8, 24.28.58; 13, 19; 18, 5.6.8. See the note on Mk 6, 50.

4, 27: *Talking with a woman:* a religious and social restriction that Jesus is pictured treating as unimportant.

4, 35: *'In four months . . .':* probably a proverb; cf Mt 9, 37–38.

4, 36: *Already:* this word may go with the preceding verse rather than with 36.

4, 39: The woman is presented as a missionary, described in virtually the same words as the disciples are in Jesus' prayer (17, 20).

4, 43–54: Jesus' arrival in Cana in Galilee; the second sign. This section introduces another theme, that of the life-giving word of Jesus. It is explicitly linked to the first sign (2, 11). The royal official believes (50). The natural life given his son is a sign of eternal life.

4, 44: Probably a reminiscence of a tradition as in Mk 6, 4. Cf Gospel of Thomas 31: "No prophet is acceptable in his village, no physician heals those who know him."

4, 19: Jn 9, 17; Hos 1, 3.
4, 20: Dt 11, 29; 27, 4; Jos 8, 33; Ps 122, 1–5.
4, 22: 2 Kgs 17, 27; Ps 76, 2–3.
4, 24: 2 Cor 3, 17.
4, 25: Jn 1, 41.
4, 26: Jn 9, 37.
4, 34: Jn 5, 30.36; 6, 38; 9, 4; 17, 4.
4, 35: Mt 9, 37–38; Lk 10, 2; Rv 14, 15.
4, 36: Ps 126, 5–6; Am 9, 13–14.
4, 37: Dt 20, 6; 28, 30; Jb 31, 8; Mi 6, 15.
4, 42: 1 Jn 4, 14.
4, 44: Mt 13, 57; Mk 6, 4; Lk 4, 24.

no honor in his native place. [45] When he came into Galilee, the Galileans welcomed him, since they had seen all he had done in Jerusalem at the feast; for they themselves had gone to the feast.

Second Sign at Cana

[46]*† Then he returned to Cana in Galilee, where he had made the water wine. Now there was a royal official whose son was ill in Capernaum. [47] When he heard that Jesus had arrived in Galilee from Judea, he went to him and asked him to come down and heal his son, who was near death. [48]* Jesus said to him, "Unless you people see signs and wonders, you will not believe." [49] The royal official said to him, "Sir, come down before my child dies." [50]* Jesus said to him, "You may go; your son will live." The man believed what Jesus said to him and left. [51] While he was on his way back, his slaves met him and told him that his boy would live. [52] He asked them when he began to recover. They told him, "The fever left him yesterday, about one in the afternoon." [53] The father realized that just at that time Jesus had said to him, "Your son will live," and he and his whole household came to believe. [54]* [Now] this was the second sign Jesus did when he came to Galilee from Judea.

Cure on a Sabbath

5 [1]*† After this, there was a feast† of the Jews, and Jesus went up to Jerusalem. [2]*† Now there is in Jerusalem at the Sheep [Gate] a pool called in Hebrew Bethesda, with five porticoes. [3]† In these lay a large number of ill, blind, lame, and crippled. [4]† [5] One man was there who had been ill for thirty-eight years. [6] When Jesus saw him lying there and knew that he had been ill for a long time, he said to him, "Do you want to be well?" [7] The sick man answered him, "Sir, I have no one to put me into the pool when the water is stirred up; while I am on my way, someone else gets down there before me." [8]* Jesus said to him, "Rise, take up your mat, and walk." [9]* Immediately the man became well, took up his mat, and walked.

Now that day was a sabbath. [10] *So the Jews said to the man who was cured, "It is the sabbath, and it is not lawful for you to carry your mat." [11] He answered them, "The man who made me well told me, 'Take up your mat and walk.' " [12] They asked him, "Who is the man who told you, 'Take it up and walk'?" [13] *The man who was healed did not know who it was, for Jesus had slipped away, since there was a crowd there. [14]*† After this Jesus found him in the temple area and said to him, "Look, you are well; do not sin any more, so that nothing worse may happen to you." [15] The man went and told the Jews that Jesus was the one who had made him well. [16] *Therefore, the Jews began to persecute Jesus because he did this on a sabbath. [17]*† But Jesus answered them, "My Father is at work until now, so I am at work." [18] *For this reason the Jews tried all the more to kill him, because he not only broke the sabbath but he also called God his own father, making himself equal to God.

The Work of the Son

[19]*† Jesus answered and said to them, "Amen, amen, I say to you, a son cannot do anything on

---

† **4, 46–54:** The story of the cure of the royal official's son may be a third version of the cure of the centurion's son (Mt 8, 5–13) or servant (Lk 7, 1–10). Cf also Mt 15, 21–28 // Mk 7, 24–30.

5, 1–47: The self-revelation of Jesus continues in Jerusalem at a feast. The third sign (cf 2, 11; 4, 54) is performed, the cure of a paralytic by Jesus' life-giving word. The water of the pool fails to bring life; Jesus' word does.

5, 1: The reference in vv 45–46 to Moses suggests that the feast was Pentecost. The connection of that feast with the giving of the law to Moses on Sinai, attested in later Judaism, may already have been made in the first century. The feast could also be Passover (cf 6, 4). John stresses that the day was a sabbath (9).

5, 2: There is no noun with *Sheep*. "Gate" is supplied on the grounds that there must have been a gate in the NE wall of the temple area where animals for sacrifice were brought in; cf Neh 3, 1.32; 12, 39. *Hebrew:* more precisely, Aramaic. *Bethesda:* preferred to variants "Be(th)zatha" and "Bethsaida"; *bêt-eśdatayîn* is given as the name of a double pool northeast of the temple area in the Qumran Copper Roll. *Five porticoes:* a pool excavated in Jerusalem actually has five porticoes.

5, 3: The Caesarean and Western recensions, followed by the Vulgate, add "waiting for the movement of the water." Apparently an intermittent spring in the pool bubbled up occasionally (see 7). This turbulence was believed to cure.

5, 4: Toward the end of the second century in the West and among the fourth-century Greek Fathers, an additional verse was known: "For from time to time an angel of the Lord used to come down into the pool; and the water was stirred up, so the first one to get in after the stirring of the water was healed of whatever disease afflicted him." The angel was a popular explanation of the turbulence and the healing powers attributed to it. This verse is missing from all early Greek manuscripts and the earliest versions, including

the original Vulgate. Its vocabulary is markedly non-Johannine.

5, 14: While the cure of the paralytic in Mk 2, 1–12 is associated with the forgiveness of sins, Jesus never drew a one-to-one connection between sin and suffering (cf 9, 3; Lk 12, 1–5), as did Ez 18, 20.

5, 17: Sabbath observance (10) was based on God's resting on the seventh day (cf Gn 2, 2–3; Ex 20, 11). Philo and some rabbis insisted that God's providence remains active on the sabbath, keeping all things in existence, giving life in birth and taking it away in death. Other rabbis taught that God rested from creating, but not from judging (= ruling, governing). Jesus here claims the same authority to work as the Father, and, in the discourse that follows, the same divine prerogatives: power over life and death (21.24–26) and judgment (22.27).

5, 19: This proverb or parable is taken from apprenticeship in a trade: the activity of a son is modeled on that of his father. Jesus' dependence on the Father is justification for doing what the Father does.

4, 46–54: Jn 2, 1–11; Mt 8, 5–13; 15, 21–28; Mk 7, 24–30; Lk 7, 1–10.	**5, 10:** Ex 20, 8; Jer 17, 21–27; Mk 3, 2; Lk 13, 10; 14, 1.
4, 48: Jn 2, 18.23; Wis 8, 8; Mt 12, 38; 1 Cor 1, 22.	**5, 13:** Jn 8, 18; 13, 36; Mk 4, 36; 7, 17.
4, 50: 1 Kgs 17, 23.	**5, 14:** Jn 8, 11; 9, 2; Ez 18, 20.
4, 54: Jn 2, 11.	**5, 16:** Jn 7, 23; Mt 12, 8.
5, 1: Jn 6, 4.	**5, 17:** Ex 20, 11.
5, 2: Neh 3, 1.32; 12, 39.	**5, 18:** Jn 7, 1.25; 8, 37.40; 10, 33.36; 14, 28; Gn 3, 5–6; Wis 2, 16; Mt 26, 4; 2 Thes 2, 4.
5, 8: Mt 9, 6; Mk 2, 11; Lk 5, 24; Acts 3, 6.	
5, 9: Mk 2, 12; Lk 5, 25; 9, 14.	**5, 19:** Jn 3, 34; 8, 26; 9, 4; 10, 30; 12, 49.

did you KNOW?

"I Am" Sayings of Jesus

The Gospel of John contains a whole series of "I am" sayings as a way for Jesus to explain his role as the Messiah. For example:

- "I am the bread of life" (6, 35).
- "I am the light of the world" (8, 12).
- "I am the gate for the sheep" (10, 7).
- "I am the good shepherd" (10, 11).
- "I am the resurrection and the life" (11, 25).
- "I am the way and the truth and the life" (14, 6).
- "I am the vine, you are the branches" (15, 5).

The "I am" sayings are also a means of establishing the divine nature of Jesus. Jesus' use of "I am" is similar to the revelation of God's name to Moses at the burning bush (Ex 3, 14). Ironically, in John, the Jewish leaders are correct in thinking that Jesus is equating himself with God (5, 18). But they are wrong in not recognizing that Jesus is right!

▸ Jn 5, 16–18

his own, but only what he sees his father doing; for what he does, his son will do also. 20* For the Father loves his Son and shows him everything that he himself does, and he will show him greater works than these, so that you may be amazed. 21*† For just as the Father raises the dead and gives life, so also does the Son give life to whomever he

wishes. 22*† Nor does the Father judge anyone, but he has given all judgment to his Son, 23 so that all may honor the Son just as they honor the Father. Whoever does not honor the Son does not honor the Father who sent him. 24* Amen, amen, I say to you, whoever hears my word and believes in the one who sent me has eternal life and will not come to condemnation, but has passed from death to life. 25* Amen, amen, I say to you, the hour is coming and is now here when the dead will hear the voice of the Son of God, and those who hear will live. 26* For just as the Father has life in himself, so also he gave to his Son the possession of life in himself. 27* And he gave him power to exercise judgment, because he is the Son of Man. 28*† Do not be amazed at this, because the hour is coming in which all who are in the tombs will hear his voice 29* and will come out, those who have done good deeds to the resurrection of life, but those who have done wicked deeds to the resurrection of condemnation.

30* "I cannot do anything on my own; I judge as I hear, and my judgment is just, because I do not seek my own will but the will of the one who sent me.

Witnesses to Jesus

31* "If I testify on my own behalf, my testimony cannot be verified. 32† But there is another who testifies on my behalf, and I know that the testimony he gives on my behalf is true. 33* You sent emissaries to John, and he testified to the truth. 34* I do not accept testimony from a human being, but I say this so that you may be saved. 35*† He was a burning and shining lamp, and for a while you were content to rejoice in his light. 36* But I have testimony greater than John's. The works that the Father gave me to accomplish, these works that I perform testify on my behalf that the Father has sent me. 37* Moreover, the Father who sent me has testified on my behalf. But you have never heard his voice nor seen his form, 38* and you do not have his word remaining in you, because you do not believe in the one whom he has sent. 39*† You

---

5, 21: *Gives life:* in the Old Testament, a divine prerogative (Dt 32, 39; 1 Sm 2, 6; 2 Kgs 5, 7; Tb 13, 2; Is 26, 19; Dan 12, 2).

5, 22: *Judgment:* another divine prerogative, often expressed as acquittal or condemnation (Dt 32, 36; Ps 43, 1).

5, 28–29: While vv 19–27 present realized eschatology, vv 28–29 are future eschatology; cf Dn 12, 2.

5, 32: *Another:* likely the Father, who in four different ways gives testimony to Jesus, as indicated in the verse groupings 33–34, 36, 37–38, 39–40.

5, 35: *Lamp:* cf Ps 132, 17: "I will place a lamp for my anointed (= David)," and possibly the description of Elijah in Sir 48, 1. But only *for a while,* indicating the temporary and subordinate nature of John's mission.

5, 39: *You search:* this may be an imperative: "Search the scriptures, because you think that you have eternal life through them."

5, 20: Jn 3, 35.
5, 21: Jn 11, 25; Dt 32, 39; 1 Sm 2, 6; 2 Kgs 5, 7; Tb 13, 2; Wis 16, 13; Is 26, 19; Dn 7, 10.13; 12, 2; Rom 4, 17; 2 Cor 1, 9.
5, 22: Acts 10, 42; 17, 31.
5, 24: Jn 3, 18; 8, 51; 1 Jn 3, 14.
5, 25: Jn 5, 28; 8, 51; 11, 25–26; Eph 2, 1; 5, 14; Rv 3, 1.
5, 26: Jn 1, 4; 1 Jn 5, 11.
5, 27: Jn 5, 22; Dn 7, 13.22; Mt 25, 31; Lk 21, 36.

5, 28: Jn 11, 43.
5, 29: Dn 12, 2; Mt 16, 27; 25, 46; Acts 24, 15; 2 Cor 5, 10.
5, 30: Jn 6, 38.
5, 31–32: Jn 8, 13–14.18.
5, 33: Jn 1, 19–27; Mt 11, 10–11.
5, 34: 1 Jn 5, 9.
5, 35: Jn 1, 8; Ps 132, 17; Sir 48, 1.
5, 36: Jn 10, 25.
5, 37: Jn 8, 18; Dt 4, 12.15; 1 Jn 5, 9.
5, 38: 1 Jn 2, 14.
5, 39: Jn 12, 16; 19, 28; 20, 9; Lk 24, 27.44; 1 Pt 1, 10.

search the scriptures, because you think you have eternal life through them; even they testify on my behalf. ⁴⁰ But you do not want to come to me to have life.

Unbelief of Jesus' Hearers

⁴¹† "I do not accept human praise; ⁴²* moreover, I know that you do not have the love of God in you. ⁴³* I came in the name of my Father, but you do not accept me; yet if another comes in his own name, you will accept him. ⁴⁴* How can you believe, when you accept praise from one another and do not seek the praise that comes from the only God? ⁴⁵* Do not think that I will accuse you before the Father: the one who will accuse you is Moses, in whom you have placed your hope. ⁴⁶* For if you had believed Moses, you would have believed me, because he wrote about me. ⁴⁷ But if you do not believe his writings, how will you believe my words?"

Multiplication of the Loaves†

6 ¹* After this, Jesus went across the Sea of Galilee [of Tiberias].† ² A large crowd followed him, because they saw the signs he was performing on the sick. ³ Jesus went up on the mountain, and there he sat down with his disciples. ⁴* The Jewish feast of Passover was near. ⁵*† When Jesus raised his eyes and saw that a large crowd was coming to him, he said to Philip, "Where can we buy enough food for them to eat?" ⁶† He said this to test him, because he himself knew what he was going to do. ⁷*† Philip answered him, "Two hundred days' wages worth of food would not be enough for each of them to have a little [bit]." ⁸ One of his disciples, Andrew, the brother of Simon Peter, said to him, ⁹*† "There is a boy here who has five barley loaves and two fish; but what good are these for so many?" ¹⁰*† Jesus said, "Have the people recline." Now there was a great deal of grass in that place. So the men reclined, about five thousand in number. ¹¹* Then Jesus took the loaves, gave thanks, and distributed them to those who were reclining, and

also as much of the fish as they wanted. ¹² When they had had their fill, he said to his disciples, "Gather the fragments left over, so that nothing will be wasted." ¹³† So they collected them, and filled twelve wicker baskets with fragments from the five barley loaves that had been more than they could

A Little Gift Goes a Long Way

God, could you use me like the boy who helped feed the five thousand? Out of the thousands of people gathered to see you, you chose a young person, took his five loaves and two fish, and made sure thousands had more than their fill to eat (Jn 6, 1–13).

I wonder how those people felt when that little bit of food was offered by a youth? Were they embarrassed by the boy's foolishness? Or did they feel guilty that they had not offered their own food? Regardless, you accepted the gift and did fantastic things with it.

Could you do the same with me? Could you take my simple gifts and do wondrous things with them? I'm just afraid that my gifts will be rejected. It is risky, Lord, and I do not do well with risks, remember?

Help me to take the risk and let you use the gifts I have, trusting that it doesn't matter what other people think. Even if things don't work out as I plan, I'll trust that you are in charge and know better than I do. Thanks, God—and wish me luck! Amen.

▸ Jn 6, 1–14

[†]
5, 41: *Praise:* the same Greek word means "praise" or "honor" (from others) and "glory" (from God). There is a play on this in v 44.

6, 1–15: This story of the multiplication of the loaves is the fourth sign (cf the note on 5, 1–47). It is the only miracle story found in all four gospels (occurring twice in Mark and Matthew). See the notes on Mt 14, 13–21 and 15, 32–39. John differs on the roles of Philip and Andrew, the proximity of Passover (4), and the allusion to Elisha (see 9). The story here symbolizes the food that is really available through Jesus. It connotes a new exodus and has eucharistic overtones.

6, 1: *[Of Tiberias]:* the awkward apposition represents a later name of the Sea of Galilee. It was probably originally a marginal gloss.

6, 5: Jesus takes the initiative (in the synoptics, the disciples do), possibly pictured as (cf 14) the new Moses (cf Nm 11, 13).

6, 6: Probably the evangelist's comment; in this gospel Jesus is never portrayed as ignorant of anything.

6, 7: *Days' wages:* literally, "denarii"; a Roman denarius is a day's wage in Mt 20, 2.

6, 9: *Barley loaves:* the food of the poor. There seems an allusion to the story of Elisha multiplying the barley bread in 2 Kgs 4, 42–44.

6, 10: *Grass:* implies springtime, and therefore Passover. *Five thousand:* so Mk 6, 39.44 and parallels.

6, 13: *Baskets:* the word describes the typically Palestinian wicker basket, as in Mk 6, 43 and parallels.

5, 42: 1 Jn 2, 15.
5, 43: Mt 24, 5.24.
5, 44: Jn 12, 43.
5, 45: Dt 31, 26.
5, 46: Jn 5, 39; Dt 18, 15; Lk 16, 31; 24, 44.
6, 1–13: Mt 14, 13–21; Mk 6, 32–44; Lk 9, 10–17.

6, 4: Jn 2, 13; 11, 55.
6, 5: Nm 11, 13.
6, 7: Mt 20, 2.
6, 9: 2 Kgs 4, 42–44.
6, 10: Mt 14, 21; Mk 6, 44.
6, 11: Jn 21, 13.

The Eucharist

Jesus calls himself the "bread of life" (Jn 6, 35). Some type of bread is part of the basic diet of almost every culture. Thus, in a symbolic way, Jesus is telling us that he is part of the basic diet for spiritual life. And just as bread is shared and valued in every culture, Jesus shares himself with all people who are willing to believe.

Many of Jesus' early followers were troubled when he taught that they must eat his flesh and drink his blood in order to have true life (verses 56–60). The confusion and arguing among his listeners are understandable; his words must have sounded strange. Yet this teaching about the body and blood of Christ (which is portrayed in the Last Supper in Matthew, Mark, and Luke) is central to the Catholic faith. Catholics believe that Jesus is really present with us and nourishes us when we celebrate the Eucharist together, the bread and wine being changed into the body and blood of Christ.

In your prayer, reflect or journal on the following questions:

- How is Jesus a source of nourishment for you?
- How does celebrating the Eucharist help you recognize more clearly Jesus' presence?
- How are you called to be the body and blood of Christ to the world around you?

▸ John, chapter 6

eat. ¹⁴*† When the people saw the sign he had done, they said, "This is truly the Prophet, the one who is to come into the world." ¹⁵* Since Jesus knew that they were going to come and carry him off to make him king, he withdrew again to the mountain alone.

Walking on the Water

¹⁶*† When it was evening, his disciples went down to the sea, ¹⁷ embarked in a boat, and went across the sea to Capernaum. It had already grown dark, and Jesus had not yet come to them. ¹⁸ The sea was stirred up because a strong wind was blowing. ¹⁹*† When they had rowed about three or four miles, they saw Jesus walking on the sea and coming near the boat, and they began to be afraid. ²⁰† But he said to them, "It is I. Do not be afraid." ²¹ They wanted to take him into the boat, but the boat immediately arrived at the shore to which they were heading.

The Bread of Life Discourse

²²† The next day, the crowd that remained across the sea saw that there had been only one boat there, and that Jesus had not gone along with his disciples in the boat, but only his disciples had left. ²³† Other boats came from Tiberias near the place where they had eaten the bread when the Lord gave thanks. ²⁴ When the crowd saw that neither Jesus nor his disciples were there, they themselves got into boats and came to Capernaum looking for Jesus. ²⁵ And when they found him across the sea they said to him, "Rabbi, when did you get here?" ²⁶ Jesus answered them and said, "Amen, amen, I say to you, you are looking for me not because you saw signs but because you ate the loaves and were filled. ²⁷*† Do not work for food that perishes but for the food that endures for eternal life, which the Son of Man will give you. For on him the Father, God, has set his seal." ²⁸ So they said to him, "What can we do to accomplish the works of God?" ²⁹ Jesus answered and said to them, "This is the work of God, that you believe in the one he sent." ³⁰* So they said to him, "What sign can you do, that we may see and

---

† **6, 14:** *The Prophet:* probably the prophet like Moses (see the note on 1, 21). *The one who is to come into the world:* probably Elijah; cf Mal 3, 1.23.

6, 16–21: The fifth sign is a nature miracle, portraying Jesus sharing Yahweh's power. Cf the parallel stories following the multiplication of the loaves in Mk 6, 45–52 and Mt 14, 22–33.

6, 19: *Walking on the sea:* although the Greek (cf 16) could mean "on the seashore" or "by the sea" (cf 21, 1), the parallels, especially Mt 14, 25, make clear that Jesus walked upon the water. John may allude to Job 9, 8: God "treads upon the crests of the sea."

6, 20: *It is I:* literally, "I am." See also the notes on 4, 26 and Mk 6, 50.

6, 22–71: Discourse on the bread of life; replacement of the man-

na. Verses 22–34 serve as an introduction, vv 35–59 constitute the discourse proper, vv 60–71 portray the reaction of the disciples and Peter's confession.

6, 23: Possibly a later interpolation, to explain how the crowd got to Capernaum.

6, 27: *The food that endures for eternal life:* cf 4, 14, on water "springing up to eternal life."

6, 14: Dt 18, 15.18; Mal 3, 1.23; Acts 3, 22.
6, 15: Jn 18, 36.
6, 16–21: Mt 14, 22–27; Mk 6, 45–52.
6, 19: Jb 9, 8; Pss 29, 3–4; 77, 20; Is 43, 16.
6, 27: Jn 6, 50.51.54.58.
6, 30: Mt 16, 1–4; Lk 11, 29–30.

believe in you? What can you do? [31]*† Our ancestors ate manna in the desert, as it is written:

'He gave them bread from heaven to eat.' "

[32]* So Jesus said to them, "Amen, amen, I say to you, it was not Moses who gave the bread from heaven; my Father gives you the true bread from heaven. [33] For the bread of God is that which comes down from heaven and gives life to the world."

[34]* So they said to him, "Sir, give us this bread always." [35]*† Jesus said to them, "I am the bread of life; whoever comes to me will never hunger, and whoever believes in me will never thirst. [36]* But I told you that although you have seen [me], you do not believe. [37] Everything that the Father gives me will come to me, and I will not reject anyone who comes to me, [38]* because I came down from heaven not to do my own will but the will of the one who sent me. [39]* And this is the will of the one who sent me, that I should not lose anything of what he gave me, but that I should raise it [on] the last day. [40]* For this is the will of my Father, that everyone who sees the Son and believes in him may have eternal life, and I shall raise him [on] the last day."

[41] The Jews murmured about him because he said, "I am the bread that came down from heaven," [42]* and they said, "Is this not Jesus, the son of Joseph? Do we not know his father and mother? Then how can he say, 'I have come down from heaven'?" [43]*† Jesus answered and said to them, "Stop murmuring among yourselves. [44] No one can come to me unless the Father who sent me draw him, and I will raise him on the last day. [45]* It is written in the prophets:

'They shall all be taught by God.'

Everyone who listens to my Father and learns from him comes to me. [46] *Not that anyone has seen the Father except the one who is from God; he has seen the Father. [47] Amen, amen, I say to you, whoever believes has eternal life. [48] I am the bread of life. [49]* Your ancestors ate the manna in the desert, but they died; [50] this is the bread that comes down from heaven so that one may eat it and not die. [51]* I am the living bread that came down from heaven; whoever eats this bread will live forever; and the bread that I will give is my flesh for the life of the world."

[52] The Jews quarreled among themselves, saying, "How can this man give us [his] flesh to eat?" [53] Jesus said to them, "Amen, amen, I say to you, unless you eat the flesh of the Son of Man and drink his blood, you do not have life within you. [54]† Whoever eats my flesh and drinks my blood has eternal life, and I will raise him on the last day. [55] For my flesh is true food, and my blood is true drink. [56] Whoever eats my flesh and drinks my blood remains in me and I in him. [57]* Just as the living Father sent me and I have life because of the Father, so also the one who feeds on me will have life because of me. [58] This is the bread that came down from heaven. Unlike your ancestors who ate and still died, whoever eats this bread will live forever." [59] These things he said while teaching in the synagogue in Capernaum.

The Words of Eternal Life

[60]† Then many of his disciples who were listening said, "This saying is hard; who can accept it?" [61] Since Jesus knew that his disciples were murmuring about this, he said to them, "Does this shock you? [62]† What if you were to see the Son of Man ascending to where he was before? [63]† It is the spirit that gives life, while the flesh is of no avail. The words I have spoken to you are spirit and life. [64]* But there are some of you who do not believe." Jesus knew from the beginning the ones who would not believe and the one who would betray him. [65] And he said, "For this reason I have told you that no one can come to me unless it is granted him by my Father."

6, 31: *Bread from heaven:* cf Ex 16, 4.15.32–34 and the notes there; Ps 78, 24. The manna, thought to have been hidden by Jeremiah (2 Mc 2, 5–8), was expected to reappear miraculously at Passover, in the last days.

6, 35–59: Up to v 50, "bread of life" is a figure for God's revelation in Jesus; in vv 51–58, the eucharistic theme comes to the fore. There may thus be a break between vv 50 and 51.

6, 43: *Murmuring:* the word may reflect the Greek of Ex 16, 2.7.8.

6, 54–58: *Eats:* the verb used in these verses is not the classical Greek verb used of human eating, but that of animal eating: "munch," "gnaw." This may be part of John's emphasis on the reality of the flesh and blood of Jesus (cf 55), but the same verb eventually became the ordinary verb in Greek meaning "eat."

6, 60–71: These verses refer more to themes of vv 35–50 than to those of 51–58 and seem to be addressed to members of the Johannine community who found it difficult to accept the high christology reflected in the bread of life discourse.

6, 62: This unfinished conditional sentence is obscure. Probably there is a reference to vv 49–51. Jesus claims to be *the bread that*

comes down from heaven (50); this claim provokes incredulity (60); and so Jesus is pictured as asking what his disciples will say when he goes up to heaven.

6, 63: *Spirit . . . flesh:* probably not a reference to the eucharistic body of Jesus but to the supernatural and the natural, as in 3, 6. *Spirit and life:* all Jesus said about the bread of life is the revelation of the Spirit.

6, 31: Ex 16, 4–5; Nm 11, 7–9; Ps 78, 24.
6, 32: Mt 6, 11.
6, 34: Jn 4, 15.
6, 35: Is 55, 1–3; Am 8, 11–13.
6, 36: Jn 20, 29.
6, 38: Jn 4, 34; Mt 26, 39; Heb 10, 9.
6, 39: Jn 10, 28–29; 17, 12; 18, 9.
6, 40: 1 Jn 2, 25.
6, 42: Mt 13, 54–57; Mk 6, 1–4; Lk 4, 22.
6, 43: Ex 16, 2.7.8; Lk 4, 22.
6, 45: Is 54, 13; Jer 31, 33–34.
6, 46: Jn 1, 18; 7, 29; Ex 33, 20.
6, 49: 1 Cor 10, 3.5.
6, 51: Mt 26, 26–27; Lk 22, 19.
6, 57: Jn 5, 26.
6, 64: Jn 13, 11.

⁶⁶ As a result of this, many [of] his disciples returned to their former way of life and no longer accompanied him. ⁶⁷ Jesus then said to the Twelve, "Do you also want to leave?" ⁶⁸ Simon Peter answered him, "Master, to whom shall we go? You have the words of eternal life. ⁶⁹* We have come to believe and are convinced that you are the Holy One of God." ⁷⁰ Jesus answered them, "Did I not choose you twelve? Yet is not one of you a devil?" ⁷¹* He was referring to Judas, son of Simon the Iscariot; it was he who would betray him, one of the Twelve.

The Feast of Tabernacles

7 ¹* After this, Jesus moved about within Galilee; but he did not wish to travel in Judea, because the Jews were trying to kill him. ²* But the Jewish feast of Tabernacles was near. ³† So his brothers said to him, "Leave here and go to Judea, so that your disciples also may see the works you are doing. ⁴* No one works in secret if he wants to be known publicly. If you do these things, manifest yourself to the world." ⁵ For his brothers did not believe in him. ⁶† So Jesus said to them, "My time is not yet here, but the time is always right for you. ⁷* The world cannot hate you, but it hates me, because I testify to it that its works are evil. ⁸† You go up to the feast. I am not going up to this feast, because my time has not yet been fulfilled." ⁹ After he had said this, he stayed on in Galilee.

¹⁰ But when his brothers had gone up to the feast, he himself also went up, not openly but [as it were] in secret. ¹¹ The Jews were looking for him at the feast and saying, "Where is he?" ¹² And there was considerable murmuring about him in the crowds. Some said, "He is a good man," [while] others said, "No; on the contrary, he misleads the crowd." ¹³* Still, no one spoke openly about him because they were afraid of the Jews.

---

† **7–8:** These chapters contain events about the feast of Tabernacles (Sukkoth, Ingathering: Ex 23, 16; Tents, Booths: Dt 16, 13–16), with its symbols of booths (originally built to shelter harvesters), rain (water from Siloam poured on the temple altar), and lights (illumination of the four torches in the Court of the Women). They continue the theme of the replacement of feasts (Passover, 2, 13; 6, 4; Hanukkah, 10, 22; Pentecost, 5, 1), here accomplished by Jesus as the Living Water. These chapters comprise seven miscellaneous controversies and dialogues. There is a literary inclusion with Jesus in hiding in 7, 4.10 and 8, 59. There are frequent references to attempts on his life: 7, 1.13.19.25.30.32.44; 8, 37.40.59.

7, 3: *Brothers:* these relatives (cf 2, 12 and see the note on Mk 6, 3) are never portrayed as disciples until after the resurrection (Acts 1, 14). Mt 13, 55 and Mk 6, 3 give the names of four of them. Jesus has already performed works/signs in Judea; cf 2, 23; 3, 2; 4, 45; 5, 8.

7, 6: *Time:* the Greek word means "opportune time," here a synonym for Jesus' "hour" (see the note on 2, 4), his death and resurrection. In the wordplay, any time is suitable for Jesus' brothers, because they are not dependent on God's will.

7, 8: *I am not going up:* an early attested reading "not yet" seems a correction, since Jesus in the story does go up to the feast. "Go up,"

? did you KNOW?

Jesus Fulfills Jewish Feasts

In John, chapters 5–10, several references are made to four Old Testament feasts, which are also called festivals. On each feast, the author of John has Jesus say or do something that cleverly indicates he is the fulfillment of the feast's intent.

In chapter 5, after healing on the *Sabbath,* Jesus says, "My Father is at work until now, so I am at work" (verse 17). Essentially, he is declaring himself equal to God. In chapter 6, near the feast of the *Passover* (see "The Passover," Ex 12, 14–28), Jesus feeds five thousand people and teaches that he is the bread of life. The implication is that the Eucharist, symbolizing Jesus' own sacrifice, has taken over the Passover meal and the sacrifice of the lamb.

Chapters 7–9 of John refer to the *feast of booths,* also called tabernacles. This is a harvest festival that lasts for a whole week. Two of the main symbols of the feast of booths are water and light. Jesus proclaims himself living water (7, 38) and the light of the world (8, 12).

Finally, the *feast of the dedication,* sometimes called Hanukkah (see "Hanukkah," 1 Mc 4, 52–59), is mentioned in chapter 10. During this festival, which celebrates the dedication of the Temple, Jesus claims to be the one who is consecrated and sent into the world (verse 26). In fulfilling these feasts, Jesus' divinity and his saving mission are made clear. But his actions also lead to continued conflicts with the Jewish leaders.

▶ **John, chapters 5–10**

---

in a play on words, refers not only to going up to Jerusalem but also to exaltation at the cross, resurrection, and ascension; cf 3, 14; 6, 62; 20, 17.

6, 69: Jn 11, 27; Mt 16, 16; Mk 1, 24; Lk 4, 34.
6, 71: Jn 12, 4; 13, 2.27.
7, 1: Jn 5, 18; 8, 37.40.
7, 2: Ex 23, 16; Lv 23, 34; Nm 29, 12; Dt 16, 13–16; Zec 14, 16–19.
7, 4: Jn 14, 22.
7, 7: Jn 15, 18.
7, 13: Jn 9, 22; 19, 38; 20, 19.

The First Dialogue

14† When the feast was already half over, Jesus went up into the temple area and began to teach. 15*† The Jews were amazed and said, "How does he know scripture without having studied?" 16 Jesus answered them and said, "My teaching is not my own but is from the one who sent me. 17*† Whoever chooses to do his will shall know whether my teaching is from God or whether I speak on my own. 18 Whoever speaks on his own seeks his own glory, but whoever seeks the glory of the one who sent him is truthful, and there is no wrong in him. 19* Did not Moses give you the law? Yet none of you keeps the law. Why are you trying to kill me?" 20*† The crowd answered, "You are possessed! Who is trying to kill you?" 21*† Jesus answered and said to them, "I performed one work and all of you are amazed 22* because of it. Moses gave you circumcision—not that it came from Moses but rather from the patriarchs—and you circumcise a man on the sabbath. 23* If a man can receive circumcision on a sabbath so that the law of Moses may not be broken, are you angry with me because I made a whole person well on a sabbath? 24* Stop judging by appearances, but judge justly."

25 So some of the inhabitants of Jerusalem said, "Is he not the one they are trying to kill? 26† And look, he is speaking openly and they say nothing to him. Could the authorities have realized that he is the Messiah? 27* But we know where he is from. When the Messiah comes, no one will know where he is from." 28* So Jesus cried out in the temple area as he was teaching and said, "You know me and also know where I am from. Yet I did not come on my own, but the one who sent me, whom you do not know, is true. 29* I know him, because I am from him, and he sent me." 30* So they tried to arrest him, but no one laid a hand upon him, because his hour had not yet come. 31* But many of the crowd began to believe in him, and said, "When the Messiah comes, will he perform more signs than this man has done?"

Officers Sent to Arrest Jesus

32† The Pharisees heard the crowd murmuring about him to this effect, and the chief priests and the Pharisees sent guards to arrest him. 33* So Jesus said, "I will be with you only a little while longer, and then I will go to the one who sent me. 34* You will look for me but not find [me], and where I am you cannot come." 35† So the Jews said to one another, "Where is he going that we will not find him? Surely he is not going to the dispersion among the Greeks to teach the Greeks, is he? 36 What is the meaning of his saying, 'You will look for me and not find [me], and where I am you cannot come'?"

Rivers of Living Water

37*† On the last and greatest day of the feast, Jesus stood up and exclaimed, "Let anyone who thirsts come to me and drink. 38*† Whoever believes in me, as scripture says:

'Rivers of living water will flow from
        within him.' "

39*† He said this in reference to the Spirit that those who came to believe in him were to receive. There was, of course, no Spirit yet, because Jesus had not yet been glorified.

Discussion about the Origins of the Messiah

40*† Some in the crowd who heard these words said, "This is truly the Prophet." 41 Others said, "This is the Messiah." But others said, "The Messiah will not come from Galilee, will he? 42* Does not scripture say that the Messiah will be of David's family and come from Bethlehem, the village where

---

7, 14–31: Jesus teaches in the temple; debate with the Jews.

7, 15: *Without having studied:* literally, "How does he know letters without having learned?" Children were taught to read and write by means of the scriptures. But here more than Jesus' literacy is being discussed; the people are wondering how he can teach like a rabbi. Rabbis were trained by other rabbis and traditionally quoted their teachers.

7, 17: *To do his will:* presumably a reference back to the "work" of 6, 29: belief in the one whom God has sent.

7, 20: *You are possessed:* literally, "You have a demon." The insane were thought to be possessed by a demoniacal spirit.

7, 21: *One work:* the cure of the paralytic (5, 1–9) because of the reference to the sabbath (22; 5, 9–10).

7, 26: *The authorities:* the members of the Sanhedrin (same term as 3, 1).

7, 32–36: Jesus announces his approaching departure (cf also 8, 21; 12, 36; 13, 33) and complete control over his destiny.

7, 35: *Dispersion:* or "diaspora": Jews living outside Palestine. *Greeks:* probably refers to the Gentiles in the Mediterranean area; cf 12, 20.

7, 37–39: Promise of living water through the Spirit.

7, 38: *Living water:* not an exact quotation from any Old Testament passage; in the gospel context the gift of the Spirit is meant;

cf 3, 5. *From within him:* either Jesus or the believer; if Jesus, it continues the Jesus-Moses motif (water from the rock, Ex 17, 6; Nm 20, 11) as well as Jesus as the new temple (cf Ez 47, 1). Grammatically, it goes better with the believer.

7, 39: *No Spirit yet:* Codex Vaticanus and early Latin, Syriac, and Coptic versions add "given." In this gospel, the sending of the Spirit cannot take place until Jesus' glorification through his death, resurrection, and ascension; cf 20, 22.

7, 40–53: Discussion of the Davidic lineage of the Messiah.

7, 15: Lk 2, 47.
7, 17: Jn 6, 29.
7, 19: Acts 7, 53.
7, 20: Jn 8, 48–49; 10, 20.
7, 21: Jn 5, 1–9.
7, 22: Gn 17, 10; Lv 12, 3.
7, 23: Jn 5, 2–9.16; Mt 12, 11–12; Lk 14, 5.
7, 24: Jn 8, 15; Lv 19, 15; Is 11, 3–4.
7, 27: Heb 7, 3.
7, 28: Jn 8, 19.
7, 29: Jn 6, 46; 8, 55.
7, 30: Jn 7, 44; 8, 20; Lk 4, 29–30.
7, 31: Jn 2, 11; 10, 42; 11, 45.
7, 33: Jn 13, 33; 16, 16.
7, 34: Jn 8, 21; 12, 36; 13, 33.36; 16, 5; Dt 4, 29; Prv 1, 28; Is 55, 6; Hos 5, 6.
7, 37: Rv 21, 6.
7, 38: Jn 4, 10.14; 19, 34; Is 12, 3; Ez 47, 1.
7, 39: Jn 16, 7.
7, 40: Dt 18, 15.18.
7, 42: 2 Sm 7, 12–14; Pss 89, 3–4; 132, 11; Mi 5, 1; Mt 2, 5–6.

David lived?" [43] So a division occurred in the crowd because of him. [44] Some of them even wanted to arrest him, but no one laid hands on him.

[45] So the guards went to the chief priests and Pharisees, who asked them, "Why did you not bring him?" [46] The guards answered, "Never before has anyone spoken like this one." [47] So the Pharisees answered them, "Have you also been deceived? [48]* Have any of the authorities or the Pharisees believed in him? [49] But this crowd, which does not know the law, is accursed." [50]* Nicodemus, one of their members who had come to him earlier, said to them, [51]* "Does our law condemn a person before it first hears him and finds out what he is doing?" [52] They answered and said to him, "You are not from Galilee also, are you? Look and see that no prophet arises from Galilee."

A Woman Caught in Adultery

8 [53]† Then each went to his own house, [1]*† while Jesus went to the Mount of Olives. [2] But early in the morning he arrived again in the temple area, and all the people started coming to him, and he sat down and taught them. [3] Then the scribes and the Pharisees brought a woman who had been caught in adultery and made her stand in the middle. [4] They said to him, "Teacher, this woman was caught in the very act of committing adultery. [5]*† Now in the law, Moses commanded us to stone such women. So what do you say?" [6]† They said this to test him, so that they could have some charge to bring against him. Jesus bent down and began to write on the ground with his finger. [7]*† But when they continued asking him, he straightened up and said to them, "Let the one among you who is without sin be the first to throw a stone at her." [8] Again he bent down and wrote on the ground. [9] And in response, they went away one by one, beginning with the elders. So he was left alone with the woman before him. [10]* Then Jesus straightened up and said to her, "Woman, where are they? Has no one condemned you?" [11]* She replied, "No one, sir." Then Jesus said, "Neither do I condemn you. Go, [and] from now on do not sin any more."]

The Light of the World

[12]*† Jesus spoke to them again, saying, "I am the light of the world. Whoever follows me will not walk in darkness, but will have the light of life."

Divine Compassion   LIVE IT!

Jesus was great at turning the tables on his enemies. In Jn 8, 2–11, the scribes and Pharisees think they have come up with a perfect trap. He will have to either abandon his teaching on forgiveness and have a woman caught in adultery stoned to death according to the Law of Moses, or set himself up as being above the law. Either way, it will make him unpopular with the people. They know they have him!

With one amazing sentence, Jesus redefines the game. The focus moves away from the woman and onto the accusers, who cannot deny that they too are guilty of sin. The trap fails miserably, and the humbled religious leaders leave in silence.

We are often quick to notice the sinfulness of others while minimizing our own guilt. Jesus reminds us to be compassionate toward the sins of others. And notice how tenderly Christ dealt with the woman, whose dignity and reputation had been trampled upon. When you recognize your own guilt and stand exposed and shamed before God and others, remember that God is just as tender and compassionate toward you.

▶ Jn 8, 2–11

---

†

7, 53—8, 11: The story of the woman caught in adultery is a later insertion here, missing from all early Greek manuscripts. A Western text-type insertion, attested mainly in Old Latin translations, it is found in different places in different manuscripts: here, or after 7, 36, or at the end of this gospel, or after Lk 21, 38, or at the end of that gospel. There are many non-Johannine features in the language, and there are also many doubtful readings within the passage. The style and motifs are similar to those of Luke, and it fits better with the general situation at the end of Lk 21, but it was probably inserted here because of the allusion to Jer 17, 13 (cf the note on 8, 6) and the statement, "I do not judge anyone," in 8, 15. The Catholic Church accepts this passage as canonical scripture.

8, 1: *Mount of Olives:* not mentioned elsewhere in the gospel tradition outside of passion week.

8, 5: Lv 20, 10 and Dt 22, 22 mention only death, but Dt 22, 23–24 prescribes stoning for a betrothed virgin.

8, 6: Cf Jer 17, 13 (RSV): "Those who turn away from thee shall be written in the earth, for they have forsaken the LORD, the fountain of living water"; cf 7, 38.

8, 7: The first stones were to be thrown by the witnesses (Dt 17, 7).

8, 12–20: Jesus the light of the world. Jesus replaces the four torches of the illumination of the temple as the light of joy.

7, 48: Jn 12, 42.
7, 50: Jn 3, 1; 19, 39.
7, 51: Dt 1, 16–17.
8, 1–2: Lk 21, 37–38.
8, 5: Lv 20, 10; Dt 22, 22–29.

8, 7: Dt 17, 7.
8, 10: Ez 33, 11.
8, 11: Jn 5, 14.
8, 12: Jn 1, 4–5.9; 12, 46; Ex 13, 22; Is 42, 6; Zec 14, 8.

THE SUN GIVES LIFE

The Sun, the Light of the world,
I hear Him coming,
I see His Face as He comes.
He makes the beings on earth happy,
And they rejoice.
O Wakan-Tanka, I offer to You this world of light . . .
I offer all to You. . . .
May all be attentive and behold! . . . that they may live.

(Black Elk, "The Sun Dance")

For many Native Americans, the sun is a symbol of the Great Spirit, or Wakan-Tanka. Black Elk's poem prayer has a strong parallel in the Gospel of John, when Jesus reveals his divinity by saying, "I am the light of the world" (8, 12). In Christian spirituality, Jesus is sometimes called the Sun (or Son) of Righteousness.

► Jn 8, 12–20

13 So the Pharisees said to him, "You testify on your own behalf, so your testimony cannot be verified." ¹⁴*† Jesus answered and said to them, "Even if I do testify on my own behalf, my testimony can be verified, because I know where I came from and where I am going. But you do not know where I come from or where I am going. ¹⁵*† You judge by appearances, but I do not judge anyone. ¹⁶* And even if I should judge, my judgment is valid, because I am not alone, but it is I and the Father who sent me. ¹⁷*† Even in your law it is written that the testimony of two men can be verified. ¹⁸* I testify on my behalf and so does the Father who sent me." ¹⁹* So they said to him, "Where is your father?" Jesus answered, "You know neither me nor my Father. If you knew me, you would know my Father also." ²⁰* He

spoke these words while teaching in the treasury in the temple area. But no one arrested him, because his hour had not yet come.

Jesus, the Father's Ambassador†

²¹* He said to them again, "I am going away and you will look for me, but you will die in your sin.† Where I am going you cannot come." ²²† So the Jews said, "He is not going to kill himself, is he, because he said, 'Where I am going you cannot come'?" ²³* He said to them, "You belong to what is below, I belong to what is above. You belong to this world, but I do not belong to this world. ²⁴*† That is why I told you that you will die in your sins. For if you do not believe that I AM, you will die in your sins." ²⁵*† So they said to him, "Who

---

† **8, 14:** *My testimony can be verified:* this seems to contradict 5, 31, but the emphasis here is on Jesus' origin from the Father and his divine destiny. *Where I am going:* indicates Jesus' passion and glorification.

8, 15: *By appearances:* literally, "according to the flesh." *I do not judge anyone:* superficial contradiction of 5, 22.27.30; here the emphasis is that the judgment is not by material standards.

8, 17: *Your law:* a reflection of later controversy between church and synagogue.

8, 21–30: He whose ambassador I am is with me. Jesus' origin is from God; he can reveal God.

8, 21: *You will die in your sin:* i.e., of disbelief; cf v 24. *Where I am going you cannot come:* except through faith in Jesus' passion-resurrection.

8, 22: The Jews suspect that he is referring to his death. Johannine irony is apparent here; Jesus' death will not be self-inflicted but destined by God.

8, 24.28: *I AM:* an expression that late Jewish tradition understood as Yahweh's own self-designation (Is 43, 10); see the note on 4, 26. Jesus is here placed on a par with Yahweh.

8, 25: *What I told you from the beginning:* this verse seems textually corrupt, with several other possible translations: "(I am) what I say to you"; "Why do I speak to you at all?" The earliest attested reading (Bodmer Papyrus P⁶⁶) has (in a second hand), "I told you at the beginning what I am also telling you (now)." The answer here (cf Prv 8, 22) seems to hinge on a misunderstanding of v 24 "that I AM" as "what I am."

8, 14: Jn 5, 31.
8, 15: Jn 12, 47; 1 Sm 16, 7.
8, 16: Jn 5, 30.
8, 17: Dt 17, 6; 19, 15; Nm 35, 30.
8, 18: Jn 5, 23.37.
8, 19: Jn 7, 28; 14, 7; 15, 21.

8, 20: Jn 7, 30.
8, 21: Jn 7, 34; 13, 33.
8, 23: Jn 3, 31; 17, 14; 18, 36.
8, 24: Ex 3, 14; Dt 32, 39; Is 43, 10.
8, 25: Jn 10, 24.

are you?" Jesus said to them, "What I told you from the beginning. 26* I have much to say about you in condemnation. But the one who sent me is true, and what I heard from him I tell the world." 27 They did not realize that he was speaking to them of the Father. 28* So Jesus said [to them], "When you lift up the Son of Man, then you will realize that I AM, and that I do nothing on my own, but I say only what the Father taught me. 29 The one who sent me is with me. He has not left me alone, because I always do what is pleasing to him." 30 Because he spoke this way, many came to believe in him.

Jesus and Abraham†

31 Jesus then said to those Jews who believed in him,† "If you remain in my word, you will truly be my disciples, 32* and you will know the truth, and the truth will set you free." 33*† They answered

him, "We are descendants of Abraham and have never been enslaved to anyone. How can you say, 'You will become free'?" 34* Jesus answered them, "Amen, amen, I say to you, everyone who commits sin is a slave of sin. 35*† A slave does not remain in a household forever, but a son always remains. 36 So if a son frees you, then you will truly be free. 37 I know that you are descendants of Abraham. But you are trying to kill me, because my word has no room among you. 38† I tell you what I have seen in the Father's presence; then do what you have heard from the Father."

39*† They answered and said to him, "Our father is Abraham." Jesus said to them, "If you were Abraham's children, you would be doing the works of Abraham. 40 But now you are trying to kill me, a man who has told you the truth that I heard from God; Abraham did not do this. 41* You are doing

JESUS IS THE LIGHT OF LIFE!

Once again, the Gospel of John creates a sharp distinction between light and darkness, good and evil. Those who follow Jesus will never walk in darkness but will have the light of life. Light is a symbol of life, happiness, justice, and the joy of salvation and liberation in Christ. Darkness is a symbol of death, disgrace, tears, and imprisonment.

Hispanics have a long tradition of lighting candles in church, at home, and at their job site. The candles symbolize the light that comes from Christ and guides us to true life.

We need the light of Christ to live with wholeness and integrity, and to give a proper value and place to material things and human activities. The light of Christ can direct us in our journey to God. Religious symbols and rituals are privileged means to help us remember the Gospel, give witness of the Gospel with our own life, and radiate God's love to those around us.

■ How do you transmit the light of Christ to others today?
■ Where in your life do you need the light of Christ?
■ Give thanks to Jesus for inviting you to share in the life of God.

▶ Jn 8, 12–59

8, 31–59: Jesus' origin ("before Abraham") and destiny are developed; the truth will free them from sin (34) and death (51).

8, 31: *Those Jews who believed in him:* a rough editorial suture, since in v 37 they are described as trying to kill Jesus.

8, 33: *Have never been enslaved to anyone:* since, historically, the Jews were enslaved almost continuously, this verse is probably Johannine irony, about slavery to sin.

8, 35: *A slave . . . a son:* an allusion to Ishmael and Isaac (Gn 16 and 21), or to the release of a slave after six years (Ex 21, 2; Dt 15, 12).

8, 38: *The Father:* i.e., God. It is also possible, however, to un-

derstand the second part of the verse as a sarcastic reference to descent of the Jews from the devil (44), "You do what you have heard from [your] father."

8, 39: *The works of Abraham:* Abraham believed; cf Rom 4, 11–17; Jas 2, 21–23.

8, 26: Jn 12, 44–50.
8, 28: Jn 3, 14; 12, 32.34.
8, 32: Is 42, 7; Gal 4, 31.
8, 33: Mt 3, 9.
8, 34: Rom 6, 16–17.
8, 35: Gn 21, 10; Gal 4, 30; Heb 3, 5–6.
8, 39: Gn 26, 5; Rom 4, 11–17; Jas 2, 21–23.
8, 41: Mal 2, 10.

the works of your father!" [So] they said to him, "We are not illegitimate. We have one Father, God." ⁴²* Jesus said to them, "If God were your Father, you would love me, for I came from God and am here; I did not come on my own, but he sent me. ⁴³ Why do you not understand what I am saying? Because you cannot bear to hear my word. ⁴⁴* You belong to your father the devil and you willingly carry out your father's desires. He was a murderer from the beginning and does not stand in truth, because there is no truth in him. When he tells a lie, he speaks in character, because he is a liar and the father of lies. ⁴⁵ But because I speak the truth, you do not believe me. ⁴⁶* Can any of you charge me with sin? If I am telling the truth, why do you not believe me? ⁴⁷* Whoever belongs to God hears the words of God; for this reason you do not listen, because you do not belong to God."

⁴⁸† The Jews answered and said to him, "Are we not right in saying that you are a Samaritan and are possessed?" ⁴⁹ Jesus answered, "I am not possessed; I honor my Father, but you dishonor me. ⁵⁰* I do not seek my own glory; there is one who seeks it and he is the one who judges. ⁵¹* Amen, amen, I say to you, whoever keeps my word will never see death." ⁵² [So] the Jews said to him, "Now we are sure that you are possessed. Abraham died, as did the prophets, yet you say, 'Whoever keeps my word will never taste death.' ⁵³*† Are you greater than our father Abraham, who died? Or the prophets, who died? Who do you make yourself out to be?" ⁵⁴ Jesus answered, "If I glorify myself, my glory is worth nothing; but it is my Father who glorifies me, of whom you say, 'He is our God.' ⁵⁵* You do not know him, but I know him. And if I should say that I do not know him, I would be like you a liar. But I do know him and I keep his word. ⁵⁶*† Abraham your father rejoiced to see my day; he saw it and was glad. ⁵⁷† So the Jews said to him, "You are not yet

fifty years old and you have seen Abraham?" ⁵⁸*† Jesus said to them, "Amen, amen, I say to you, before Abraham came to be, I AM." ⁵⁹* So they picked up stones to throw at him; but Jesus hid and went out of the temple area.

The Man Born Blind

9 ¹*† As he passed by he saw a man blind from birth. ²*† His disciples asked him, "Rabbi, who sinned, this man or his parents, that he was born blind?" ³* Jesus answered, "Neither he nor his parents sinned; it is so that the works of God might be made visible through him. ⁴* We have to do the works of the one who sent me while it is day. Night is coming when no one can work. ⁵* While I am in the world, I am the light of the world." ⁶* When he had said this, he spat on the ground and made clay with the saliva, and smeared the clay on his eyes, ⁷*† and said to him, "Go wash in the Pool of Siloam" (which means Sent). So he went and washed, and came back able to see.

⁸ His neighbors and those who had seen him earlier as a beggar said, "Isn't this the one who used to sit and beg?" ⁹ Some said, "It is," but others said, "No, he just looks like him." He said, "I am." ¹⁰ So they said to him, "[So] how were your eyes opened?" ¹¹ He replied, "The man called Jesus made clay and anointed my eyes and told me, 'Go to Siloam and wash.' So I went there and washed and was able to see." ¹² And they said to him, "Where is he?" He said, "I don't know."

¹³ They brought the one who was once blind to the Pharisees. ¹⁴*† Now Jesus had made clay and opened his eyes on a sabbath. ¹⁵ So then the Pharisees also asked him how he was able to see. He said to them, "He put clay on my eyes, and I washed, and now I can see." ¹⁶* So some of the Pharisees said, "This man is not from God, because he does not keep the sabbath." [But] others said, "How can

---

† **8, 48:** *Samaritan:* therefore interested in magical powers; cf Acts 7, 14–24.

8, 53: *Are you greater than our father Abraham?:* cf 4, 12.

8, 56: *He saw it:* this seems a reference to the birth of Isaac (Gn 17, 7; 21, 6), the beginning of the fulfillment of promises about Abraham's seed.

8, 57: The evidence of the third-century Bodmer Papyrus P⁷⁵ and the first hand of Codex Sinaiticus indicates that the text originally read: "How can Abraham have seen you?"

8, 58: *Came to be, I AM:* the Greek word used for "came to be" is the one used of all creation in the prologue, while the word used for "am" is the one reserved for the Logos.

9, 1–10, 21: Sabbath healing of the man born blind. This fifth sign is introduced to illustrate the saying, "I am the light of the world" (8, 12; 9, 5). The narrative of conflict about Jesus contrasts Jesus (light) with the Jews (blindness, 39–41). The theme of water is reintroduced in the reference to the pool of Siloam. Ironically, Jesus is being judged by the Jews, yet the Jews are judged by the Light of the world; cf 3, 19–21.

9, 2: See the note on 5, 14, and Ex 20, 5, that parents' sins were visited upon their children. Jesus denies such a cause and emphasizes the purpose: the infirmity was providential.

9, 7: *Go wash:* perhaps a test of faith; cf 2 Kgs 5, 10–14. The water tunnel Siloam (= Sent) is used as a symbol of Jesus, sent by his Father.

9, 14: In using spittle, kneading clay, and healing, Jesus had broken the sabbath rules laid down by Jewish tradition.

8, 42: 1 Jn 5, 1.

8, 44: Gn 3, 4; Wis 1, 13; 2, 24; Acts 13, 10; 1 Jn 3, 8–15.

8, 46: Heb 4, 15; 1 Pt 2, 22; 1 Jn 3, 5.

8, 47: Jn 10, 26; 1 Jn 4, 6.

8, 50: Jn 7, 18.

8, 51: Jn 5, 24–29; 6, 40.47; 11, 25–26.

8, 53: Jn 4, 12.

8, 55: Jn 7, 28–29.

8, 56: Gn 17, 17; Mt 13, 17; Lk 17, 22.

8, 58: Jn 1, 30; 17, 5.

8, 59: Jn 10, 31.39; 11, 8; Lk 4, 29–30.

9, 1–2: Is 42, 7.

9, 2: Ex 20, 5; Ez 18, 20; Lk 13, 2.

9, 3: Jn 5, 14; 11, 4.

9, 4: Jn 11, 9–10; 12, 35–36.

9, 5: Jn 8, 12.

9, 6: Jn 5, 11; Mk 7, 33; 8, 23.

9, 7: 2 Kgs 5, 10–14.

9, 14: Jn 5, 9.

9, 16: Jn 3, 2; Mt 12, 10–11; Lk 13, 10–11; 14, 1–4.

Seeing with God's Eyes

Lord, can you fix my eyesight like you did for the blind man?

I want to see with your eyes those who are teased for being different at school.

I want to see with your eyes the homeless person on a park bench.

I want to see with your eyes people from other races and cultures.

I want to see more than people who think that being thinner or stronger makes you more lovable.

I want to see more than people who look at wealth and think that's what life is all about.

Help me to see with your eyes, Lord! Blind me to the way the world sees so that I won't give in to judging people on their looks or skin color or possessions or personality.

Help me to see, and to love, as you love, Lord—with eyes so wide open that they see past the outside and right into the heart of another.

▸ John, chapter 9

a sinful man do such signs?" And there was a division among them. 17* So they said to the blind man again, "What do you have to say about him, since he opened your eyes?" He said, "He is a prophet."

18 Now the Jews did not believe that he had been blind and gained his sight until they summoned the parents of the one who had gained his sight. 19 They asked them, "Is this your son, who you say was born blind? How does he now see?" 20 His parents answered and said, "We know that this is our son and that he was born blind. 21 We do not know how he sees now, nor do we know who opened his eyes. Ask him, he is of age; he can speak for himself." 22*† His parents said this because they were afraid of the Jews, for the Jews had already agreed that if anyone acknowledged him as the Messiah, he would be expelled from the synagogue. 23* For this reason his parents said, "He is of age; question him."

24*† So a second time they called the man who had been blind and said to him, "Give God the praise! We know that this man is a sinner." 25 He replied, "If he is a sinner, I do not know. One thing I do know is that I was blind and now I see." 26 So they said to him, "What did he do to you? How did he open your eyes?" 27 He answered them, "I told you already and you did not listen. Why do you want to hear it again? Do you want to become his disciples, too?" 28 They ridiculed him and said, "You are that man's disciple; we are disciples of Moses! 29* We know that God spoke to Moses, but we do not know where this one is from." 30 The man answered and said to them, "This is what is so amazing, that you do not know where he is from, yet he opened my eyes. 31* We know that God does not listen to sinners, but if one is devout and does his will, he listens to him. 32† It is unheard of that anyone ever opened the eyes of a person born blind. 33* If this man were not from God, he would not be able to do anything." 34 They answered and said to him, "You were born totally in sin, and are you trying to teach us?" Then they threw him out.

35 When Jesus heard that they had thrown him out, he found him and said, "Do you believe in the Son of Man?" 36 He answered and said, "Who is he, sir, that I may believe in him?" 37* Jesus said to him, "You have seen him and the one speaking with you is he." 38 He said, "I do believe, Lord," and he worshiped him. 39*† Then Jesus said, "I came into this world for judgment, so that those who do not see might see, and those who do see might become blind."

40* Some of the Pharisees who were with him heard this and said to him, "Surely we are not also blind, are we?" 41* Jesus said to them, "If you were blind, you would have no sin; but now you are saying, 'We see,' so your sin remains."

† 9, 22: This comment of the evangelist (in terms used again in 12, 42 and 16, 2) envisages a situation after Jesus' ministry. Rejection/excommunication from the synagogue of Jews who confessed Jesus as Messiah seems to have begun ca. A.D. 85, when the curse against the *mínim* or heretics was introduced into the "Eighteen Benedictions."

9, 24: *Give God the praise!*: an Old Testament formula of adjuration to tell the truth; cf Jos 7, 19; 1 Sm 6, 5 LXX. Cf 5, 41.

9, 32: *A person born blind*: the only Old Testament cure from blindness is found in Tobit (cf Tb 7, 7; 11, 7–13; 14, 1–2), but Tobit was not born blind.

9, 39–41: These verses spell out the symbolic meaning of the cure; the Pharisees are not the innocent blind, willing to accept the testimony of others.

9, 17: Jn 4, 19.
9, 22: Jn 7, 13; 12, 42; 16, 2; 19, 38.
9, 23: Jn 12, 42.
9, 24: Jos 7, 19; 1 Sm 6, 5 LXX.
9, 29: Ex 33, 11.
9, 31: Jn 10, 21; Pss 34, 16; 66, 18; Prv 15, 29; Is 1, 15.
9, 33: Jn 3, 2.
9, 37: Jn 4, 26; Dn 7, 13.
9, 39: Mt 13, 33–35.
9, 40: Mt 15, 14; 23, 26; Rom 2, 19.
9, 41: Jn 15, 22.

The Good Shepherd

10 ¹*† "Amen, amen, I say to you, whoever does not enter a sheepfold† through the gate but climbs over elsewhere is a thief and a robber. ² But whoever enters through the gate is the shepherd of the sheep. ³ The gatekeeper opens it for him, and the sheep hear his voice, as he calls his own sheep by name and leads them out. ⁴*† When he has driven out all his own, he walks ahead of them, and the sheep follow him, because they recognize his voice. ⁵ But they will not follow a stranger; they will run away from him, because they do not recognize the voice of strangers." ⁶† Although Jesus used this figure of speech, they did not realize what he was trying to tell them.

⁷† So Jesus said again, "Amen, amen, I say to you, I am the gate for the sheep. ⁸† All who came [before me] are thieves and robbers, but the sheep did not listen to them. ⁹ I am the gate. Whoever enters through me will be saved, and will come in and go out and find pasture. ¹⁰ A thief comes only to steal and slaughter and destroy; I came so that they might have life and have it more abundantly. ¹¹* I am the good shepherd. A good shepherd lays down his life for the sheep. ¹²* A hired man, who is not a shepherd and whose sheep are not his own, sees a wolf coming and leaves the sheep and runs away, and the wolf catches and scatters them. ¹³ This is because he works for pay and has no concern for the sheep. ¹⁴ I am the good shepherd, and I know mine and mine know me, ¹⁵* just as the Father knows me and I know the Father; and I will lay down my life for the sheep. ¹⁶*† I have other sheep that do not belong to this fold. These also I must lead, and they will hear my voice, and there will be one flock, one shepherd. ¹⁷* This is why the Father loves me, because I lay down my life in order to take it up again. ¹⁸*† No one takes it from me, but I lay it down on my own. I have power to lay it down, and power to take it up again. This command I have received from my Father."

PRAY IT?

Jesus, the Good Shepherd

The theme of shepherds and sheep is a recurring one in the Bible. In the Old Testament, God is often portrayed as a shepherd. For example, see Psalm 23 and Ezekiel, chapter 34. David, the greatest king of Israel, is also portrayed as a shepherd in Ps 78, 70–72. In passages like Jer 23, 1–6, God promises to raise up new shepherds who will follow in David's legacy. So it is natural that Jesus compares himself to a shepherd in Jn 10, 1–18.

Being a shepherd is not an easy job. Sheep are pretty defenseless creatures, and shepherds have to protect them from predators like lions and wolves. Sheep also have a tendency to stray from the flock, making them especially vulnerable. Shepherds endure the hardships of being away from their homes and putting up with simple food and harsh weather while pasturing sheep. Their lives can be endangered when confronted by desperate predators. Sheep learn to recognize their shepherd's voice, which makes it easier to separate different flocks when flocks are mixed together for grazing or protection.

In your prayer, reflect or journal on the following questions:

- How do you relate to Jesus as the good shepherd?
- When is it reassuring to know that Jesus is watching out for you? How do you see yourself helping to "shepherd" other people as a follower of Jesus?

▶ Jn 10, 1–18

J
N

---

† **10, 1–21:** The good shepherd discourse continues the theme of attack on the Pharisees that ends ch 9. The figure is allegorical: the hired hands are the Pharisees who excommunicated the cured blind man. It serves as a commentary on ch 9. For the shepherd motif, used of Yahweh in the Old Testament, cf Ex 34; Gn 48, 15; 49, 24; Mi 7, 14; Pss 23, 1–4; 80, 1.

10, 1: *Sheepfold:* a low stone wall open to the sky.

10, 4: *Recognize his voice:* the Pharisees do not recognize Jesus, but the people of God, symbolized by the blind man, do.

10, 6: *Figure of speech:* John uses a different word for illustrative speech than the "parable" of the synoptics, but the idea is similar.

10, 7–10: In vv 7–8, the figure is of a gate for the shepherd to come to the sheep; in vv 9–10, the figure is of a gate for the sheep to *come in and go out.*

10, 8: *[Before me]:* these words are omitted in many good early manuscripts and versions.

10, 16: *Other sheep:* the Gentiles, possibly a reference to "God's dispersed children" of 11, 52 destined to be gathered into one, or "apostolic Christians" at odds with the community of the beloved disciple.

10, 18: *Power to take it up again:* contrast the role of the Father as the efficient cause of the resurrection in Acts 2, 24; 4, 10; etc.; Rom 1, 4; 24. Yet even here is added: *This command I have received from my Father.*

10, 1–5: Gn 48, 15; 49, 24; Pss 23, 1–4; 80, 2; Jer 23, 1–4; Ez 34, 1–31; Mi 7, 14.
10, 4: Mi 2, 12–13.
10, 11: Ps 23, 1–4; Is 40, 11; 49, 9–10; Heb 13, 20; Rv 7, 17.
10, 12: Zec 11, 17.
10, 15: Jn 15, 13; 1 Jn 3, 16.
10, 16: Jn 11, 52; Is 56, 8; Jer 24; Mi 2, 12.
10, 17: Heb 10, 10.
10, 18: Jn 19, 11.

19* Again there was a division among the Jews because of these words. 20* Many of them said, "He is possessed and out of his mind; why listen to him?" 21* Others said, "These are not the words of one possessed; surely a demon cannot open the eyes of the blind, can he?"

Feast of the Dedication

22*† The feast of the Dedication was then taking place in Jerusalem. It was winter. 23† And Jesus walked about in the temple area on the Portico of Solomon. 24*† So the Jews gathered around him and said to him, "How long are you going to keep us in suspense? If you are the Messiah, tell us plainly." 25*† Jesus answered them, "I told you and you do not believe. The works I do in my Father's name testify to me. 26* But you do not believe, because you are not among my sheep. 27 My sheep hear my voice; I know them, and they follow me. 28* I give them eternal life, and they shall never perish. No one can take them out of my hand. 29*† My Father, who has given them to me, is greater than all, and no one can take them out of the Father's hand. 30*† The Father and I are one."

31* The Jews again picked up rocks to stone him. 32 Jesus answered them, "I have shown you many good works from my Father. For which of these are you trying to stone me?" 33* The Jews answered him, "We are not stoning you for a good work but for blasphemy. You, a man, are making yourself God." 34*† Jesus answered them, "Is it not written in your law, 'I said, "You are gods"'? 35 If it calls them gods to whom the word of God came, and scripture cannot be set aside, 36*† can you say that the one whom the Father has consecrated and sent

into the world blasphemes because I said, 'I am the Son of God'? 37 If I do not perform my Father's works, do not believe me; 38* but if I perform them, even if you do not believe me, believe the works, so that you may realize [and understand] that the Father is in me and I am in the Father." 39 [Then] they tried again to arrest him; but he escaped from their power.

40* He went back across the Jordan to the place where John first baptized, and there he remained. 41† Many came to him and said, "John performed no sign, but everything John said about this man was true." 42* And many there began to believe in him.

The Raising of Lazarus

11 1*† Now a man was ill, Lazarus from Bethany, the village of Mary and her sister Martha. 2 Mary was the one who had anointed the Lord with perfumed oil and dried his feet with her hair; it was her brother Lazarus who was ill. 3 So the sisters sent word to him, saying, "Master, the one you love is ill." 4*† When Jesus heard this he said, "This illness is not to end in death, but is for the glory of God, that the Son of God may be glorified through it." 5 Now Jesus loved Martha and her sister and Lazarus. 6 So when he heard that he was ill, he remained for two days in the place where he was. 7 Then after this he said to his disciples, "Let us go back to Judea." 8* The disciples said to him, "Rabbi, the Jews were just trying to stone you, and you want to go back there?" 9* Jesus answered, "Are there not twelve hours in a day? If one walks during the day, he does not stumble, because he sees the light of this world. * 10† But if one

---

10, 22: *Feast of the Dedication:* an eight-day festival of lights (Hebrew, Hanukkah) held in December, three months after the feast of Tabernacles (7, 2), to celebrate the Maccabees' rededication of the altar and reconsecration of the temple in 164 B.C., after their desecration by Antiochus IV Epiphanes (Dn 8, 13; 9, 27; cf 1 Mc 4, 36–59; 2 Mc 1, 18—2, 19; 10, 1–8).

10, 23: *Portico of Solomon:* on the east side of the temple area, offering protection against the cold winds from the desert.

10, 24: *Keep us in suspense:* literally, "How long will you take away our life?" Cf 11, 48–50. *If you are the Messiah, tell us plainly:* cf Lk 22, 67. This is the climax of Jesus' encounters with the Jewish authorities. There has never yet been an open confession before them.

10, 25: *I told you:* probably at 8, 25, which was an evasive answer.

10, 29: The textual evidence for the first clause is very divided; it may also be translated: "As for the Father, what he has given me is greater than all," or "My Father is greater than all, in what he has given me."

10, 30: This is justification for v 29; it asserts unity of power and reveals that the words and deeds of Jesus are the words and deeds of God.

10, 34: This is a reference to the judges of Israel who, since they exercised the divine prerogative to judge (Dt 1, 17), were called "gods"; cf Ex 21, 6, besides Ps 82, 6, from which the quotation comes.

10, 36: *Consecrated:* this may be a reference to the rededicated altar at the Hanukkah feast; see the note on 10, 22.

10, 41: *Performed no sign:* this is to stress the inferior role of John the Baptist. The Transjordan topography recalls the great witness of John the Baptist to Jesus, as opposed to the hostility of the authorities in Jerusalem.

11, 1–44: The raising of Lazarus, the longest continuous narrative in John outside of the Passion account, is the climax of the signs. It leads directly to the decision of the Sanhedrin to kill Jesus. The theme of life predominates. Lazarus is a token of the real life that Jesus dead and raised will give to all who believe in him. Johannine irony is found in the fact that Jesus' gift of life leads to his own death. The story is not found in the synoptics, but cf Mk 5, 21 and parallels; Lk 7, 11–17. There are also parallels between this story and Luke's parable of the rich man and poor Lazarus (Lk 16, 19–31). In both a man named Lazarus dies; in Luke, there is a request that he return to convince his contemporaries of the need for faith and repentance, while in John, Lazarus does return and some believe but others do not.

11, 4: *Not to end in death:* this is misunderstood by the disciples as referring to physical death, but it is meant as spiritual death.

11, 10: *The light is not in him:* the ancients apparently did not grasp clearly the entry of light *through* the eye; they seem to have thought of it as being *in* the eye; cf Lk 11, 34; Mt 6, 23.

---

*

10, 19: Jn 7, 43; 9, 16.	**10, 33:** Jn 5, 18; 19, 7; Lv 24, 16.
10, 20: Jn 7, 20; 8, 48.	
10, 21: Jn 3, 2.	**10, 34:** Ps 82, 6.
10, 22: 1 Mc 4, 54.59.	**10, 36:** Jn 5, 18.
10, 24: Lk 22, 67.	**10, 38:** Jn 14, 10–11.20.
10, 25: Jn 8, 25 / Jn 5, 36; 10, 38.	**10, 40:** Jn 1, 28.
	10, 42: Jn 2, 23; 7, 31; 8, 30.
10, 26: Jn 8, 45.47.	**11, 1–2:** Jn 12, 1–8; Lk 10, 38–42; 16, 19–31.
10, 28: Dt 32, 39.	
10, 29: Wis 3, 1; Is 43, 13.	**11, 4:** Jn 9, 3.24.
10, 30: Jn 1, 1; 12, 45; 14, 9; 17, 21.	**11, 8:** Jn 8, 59; 10, 31.
	11, 9: Jn 8, 12; 9, 4.
10, 31: Jn 8, 59.	**11, 9–10:** Jn 12, 35; 1 Jn 2, 10.

walks at night, he stumbles, because the light is not in him." 11 He said this, and then told them, "Our friend Lazarus is asleep, but I am going to awaken him." 12 So the disciples said to him, "Master, if he is asleep, he will be saved." 13* But Jesus was talking about his death, while they thought that he meant ordinary sleep. 14 So then Jesus said to them clearly, "Lazarus has died. 15 And I am glad for you that I was not there, that you may believe. Let us go to him." 16*† So Thomas, called Didymus, said to his fellow disciples, "Let us also go to die with him."

17 When Jesus arrived, he found that Lazarus had already been in the tomb for four days. 18† Now Bethany was near Jerusalem, only about two miles away. 19* And many of the Jews had come to Martha and Mary to comfort them about their brother. 20 When Martha heard that Jesus was coming, she went to meet him; but Mary sat at home. 21* Martha said to Jesus, "Lord, if you had been here, my brother would not have died. 22 [But] even now I know that whatever you ask of God, God will give you." 23 Jesus said to her, "Your brother will rise." 24* Martha said to him, "I know

he will rise, in the resurrection on the last day." 25* Jesus told her, "I am the resurrection and the life; whoever believes in me, even if he dies, will live, 26 and everyone who lives and believes in me will never die. Do you believe this?" 27*† She said to him, "Yes, Lord. I have come to believe that you are the Messiah, the Son of God, the one who is coming into the world."

28 When she had said this, she went and called her sister Mary secretly, saying, "The teacher is here and is asking for you." 29 As soon as she heard this, she rose quickly and went to him. 30 For Jesus had not yet come into the village, but was still where Martha had met him. 31 So when the Jews who were with her in the house comforting her saw Mary get up quickly and go out, they followed her, presuming that she was going to the tomb to weep there. 32 When Mary came to where Jesus was and saw him, she fell at his feet and said to him, "Lord, if you had been here, my brother would not have died." 33† When Jesus saw her weeping and the Jews who had come with her weeping, he became perturbed and deeply troubled, 34 and said, "Where have you laid him?" They said to him, "Sir, come

LIVE IT!

Alive Again!

"And Jesus wept" (Jn 11, 35). This is the shortest verse in the Bible and also the most telling. Why does Jesus weep? He sees his dear friend Mary crying because of the death of her brother Lazarus, and Jesus cannot help himself. He cries too, expressing both compassion for Mary and his own grief at the loss of his friend Lazarus. What a beautiful, powerful expression of Jesus' humanity!

What follows next is a powerful expression of the divinity of Jesus. It is the seventh and final sign in John's Gospel. What a dramatic moment, as Jesus steps into the tomb of a man who has been dead for four days. He says three words—"Lazarus, come out!"—and Lazarus, bound in burial cloth, indeed comes out! He is alive again. Imagine how astonished the onlookers must have been and how grateful Martha and Mary would have been to have their brother alive again.

It does make one wonder what it would feel like to be alive again after being in the grave for four days. How do people react to this man who is alive once again? Why do you think John chose this as the last sign of Jesus' power? Notice that this event occurs about a week before the last days of Jesus' life. Why is this sign such a threat to the ruling officials of Jerusalem?

▶ Jn 11, 1–44

---

†
11, 16: *Called Didymus: Didymus* is the Greek word for twin. Thomas is derived from the Aramaic word for twin; in an ancient Syriac version and in the Gospel of Thomas (80, 11–12) his given name, Judas, is supplied.

11, 18: *About two miles:* literally, "about fifteen stades"; a stade was 607 feet.

11, 27: The titles here are a summary of titles given to Jesus earlier in the gospel.

11, 33: *Became perturbed:* a startling phrase in Greek, literally,

"He snorted in spirit," perhaps in anger at the presence of evil (death).

11, 13: Mt 9, 24.
11, 16: Jn 14, 5.22.
11, 19: Jn 12, 9.17–18.
11, 21: Jn 11, 32.
11, 24: Jn 5, 29; 6, 39–40.
44.54; 12, 48; Is 2, 2;

Mi 4, 1; Acts 23, 8; 24, 15.
11, 25: Jn 5, 24; 8, 51; 14, 6; Dn 12, 2.
11, 27: Jn 1, 9; 6, 69.

and see." 35* And Jesus wept. 36 So the Jews said, "See how he loved him." 37 But some of them said, "Could not the one who opened the eyes of the blind man have done something so that this man would not have died?"

A God Who Cries

Lord, have I ever made you cry? angry enough to yell? tickled enough to laugh? proud enough to burst? I hope so. I hope you know me so well that my every movement, my every breath, is noticed by you. I want to believe that about you, Jesus, because that is the image of you I can talk to, a God who can relate to me and accept me in all that I do. Amen.

▶ Jn 11, 35

38 So Jesus, perturbed again, came to the tomb. It was a cave, and a stone lay across it. 39 Jesus said, "Take away the stone." Martha, the dead man's sister, said to him, "Lord, by now there will be a stench; he has been dead for four days." 40 Jesus said to her, "Did I not tell you that if you believe you will see the glory of God?" 41† So they took away the stone. And Jesus raised his eyes and said, "Father, I thank you for hearing me. 42* I know that you always hear me; but because of the crowd here I have said this, that they may believe that you sent me." 43† And when he had said this, he cried out in a loud voice, "Lazarus, come out!" 44 The dead man came out, tied hand and foot with burial bands, and his face was wrapped in a cloth. So Jesus said to them, "Untie him and let him go."

Session of the Sanhedrin

45* Now many of the Jews who had come to Mary and seen what he had done began to believe in him. 46 But some of them went to the Pharisees and told them what Jesus had done. 47* So the chief priests and the Pharisees convened the Sanhedrin and said, "What are we going to do? This man is performing many signs. 48† If we leave him alone, all will believe in him, and the Romans will come and take away both our land and our nation." 49*† But one of them, Caiaphas, who was high priest that year, said to them, "You know nothing, 50 nor do you consider that it is better for you that one man should die instead of the people, so that the whole nation may not perish." 51 He did not say this on his own, but since he was high priest for that year, he prophesied that Jesus was going to die for the nation, 52† and not only for the nation, but also to gather into one the dispersed children of God. 53* So from that day on they planned to kill him.

54† So Jesus no longer walked about in public among the Jews, but he left for the region near the desert, to a town called Ephraim, and there he remained with his disciples.

The Last Passover

55*† Now the Passover of the Jews was near, and many went up from the country to Jerusalem before Passover to purify themselves. 56 They looked for Jesus and said to one another as they were in the temple area, "What do you think? That he will not come to the feast?" 57 For the chief priests and the Pharisees had given orders that if anyone knew where he was, he should inform them, so that they might arrest him.

The Anointing at Bethany

12 1*† Six days before Passover Jesus came to Bethany, where Lazarus was, whom Jesus had raised from the dead.* 2* They gave a dinner for him there, and Martha served, while Lazarus was one of those reclining at table with him. 3*† Mary took a liter of costly perfumed oil made from genuine aromatic nard and anointed the feet of Jesus and dried them with her hair; the house was filled with the fragrance of the oil. 4 Then Judas the Iscariot, one [of] his disciples, and the one who would

---

† **11, 41:** *Father:* in Aramaic, *'abbā.'* See the note on Mk 14, 36.

11, 43: *Cried out in a loud voice:* a dramatization of 5, 28: "the hour is coming when all who are in the tombs will hear his voice."

11, 48: *The Romans will come:* Johannine irony; this is precisely what happened after Jesus' death.

11, 49: *That year:* emphasizes the conjunction of the office and the year. Actually, Caiaphas was high priest A.D. 18–36. The Jews attributed a gift of prophecy, sometimes unconscious, to the high priest.

11, 52: *Dispersed children of God:* perhaps the "other sheep" of 10, 16.

11, 54: *Ephraim* is usually located about twelve miles northeast of Jerusalem, where the mountains descend into the Jordan valley.

11, 55: *Purify:* prescriptions for purity were based on Ex 19, 10–11.15; Nm 9, 6–14; 2 Chr 30, 1–3.15–18.

12, 1–8: This is probably the same scene of anointing found in Mk 14, 3–9 (see the note there) and Mt 26, 6–13. The anointing by a penitent woman in Lk 7, 36–38 is different. Details from these various episodes have become interchanged.

12, 3: *The feet of Jesus:* so Mk 14, 3; but in Mt 26, 6, Mary anoints Jesus' head as a sign of regal, messianic anointing.

11, 35: Lk 19, 41.
11, 42: Jn 12, 30.
11, 45: Lk 16, 31.
11, 47: Jn 12, 19; Mt 26, 3–5; Lk 22, 2; Acts 4, 16.
11, 49–50: Jn 18, 13–14.
11, 53: Jn 5, 18; 7, 1; Mt 12, 14.

11, 55: Jn 2, 13; 5, 1; 6, 4; 18, 28; Ex 19, 10–11.15; Nm 9, 6–14; 19, 12; Dt 16, 6; 2 Chr 30, 1–3.15–18.
12, 1–11: Mt 26, 6–13; Mk 14, 3–9.
12, 1–2: Jn 11, 1.
12, 2: Lk 10, 38–42.
12, 3: Jn 11, 2.

betray him, said, ⁵† "Why was this oil not sold for three hundred days' wages and given to the poor?" ⁶* He said this not because he cared about the poor but because he was a thief and held the money bag and used to steal the contributions. ⁷† So Jesus said, "Leave her alone. Let her keep this for the day of my burial. ⁸* You always have the poor with you, but you do not always have me."

⁹* [The] large crowd of the Jews found out that he was there and came, not only because of Jesus, but also to see Lazarus, whom he had raised from the dead. ¹⁰ And the chief priests plotted to kill Lazarus too, ¹¹* because many of the Jews were turning away and believing in Jesus because of him.

The Entry into Jerusalem

¹²*† On the next day, when the great crowd that had come to the feast heard that Jesus was coming to Jerusalem, ¹³*† they took palm branches and went out to meet him, and cried out:

"Hosanna!
Blessed is he who comes in the name of
    the Lord,
[even] the king of Israel."

¹⁴ Jesus found an ass and sat upon it, as is written:

¹⁵*†"Fear no more, O daughter Zion;
    see, your king comes, seated upon an
        ass's colt."

¹⁶*† His disciples did not understand this at first,

but when Jesus had been glorified they remembered that these things were written about him and that they had done this for him. ¹⁷† So the crowd that was with him when he called Lazarus from the tomb and raised him from death continued to testify. ¹⁸ This was [also] why the crowd went to meet him, because they heard that he had done this sign. ¹⁹*† So the Pharisees said to one another, "You see that you are gaining nothing. Look, the whole world has gone after him."

The Coming of Jesus' Hour†

²⁰* Now there were some Greeks† among those who had come up to worship at the feast. ²¹*† They came to Philip, who was from Bethsaida in Galilee, and asked him, "Sir, we would like to see Jesus." ²²* Philip went and told Andrew; then Andrew and Philip went and told Jesus. ²³*† Jesus answered them, "The hour has come for the Son of Man to be glorified. ²⁴*† Amen, amen, I say to you, unless a grain of wheat falls to the ground and dies, it remains just a grain of wheat; but if it dies, it produces much fruit. ²⁵*† Whoever loves his life loses it, and whoever hates his life in this world will preserve it for eternal life. ²⁶* Whoever serves me must follow me, and where I am, there also will my servant be. The Father will honor whoever serves me.

²⁷*† "I am troubled now. Yet what should I say? 'Father, save me from this hour'? But it was for this purpose that I came to this hour. ²⁸* Father, glorify your name." Then a voice

J
N

12, 5: *Days' wages:* literally, "denarii." A denarius is a day's wage in Mt 20, 2; see the note on 6, 7.

12, 7: Jesus' response reflects the rabbinical discussion of what was the greatest act of mercy, almsgiving or burying the dead. Those who favored proper burial of the dead thought it an essential condition for sharing in the resurrection.

12, 12–19: In John, the entry into Jerusalem follows the anointing whereas in the synoptics it precedes. In John, the crowd, not the disciples, are responsible for the triumphal procession.

12, 13: *Palm branches:* used to welcome great conquerors; cf 1 Mc 13, 51; 2 Mc 10, 7. They may be related to the *lûlāb*, the twig bundles used at the feast of Tabernacles. *Hosanna:* see Ps 118, 25–26. The Hebrew word means: "(O Lord), grant salvation." *He who comes in the name of the Lord:* referred in Ps 118, 26 to a pilgrim entering the temple gates, but here a title for Jesus (see the notes on Mt 11, 3 and Jn 6, 14; 11, 27). *The king of Israel:* perhaps from Zep 3, 14–15, in connection with the next quotation from Zec 9, 9.

12, 15: *Daughter Zion:* Jerusalem. *Ass's colt:* symbol of peace, as opposed to the war-horse.

12, 16: *They had done this:* the antecedent of *they* is ambiguous.

12, 17–18: There seem to be two different crowds in these verses. There are some good witnesses to the text that have another reading for v 17: "Then the crowd that was with him began to testify that he had called Lazarus out of the tomb and raised him from the dead."

12, 19: *The whole world:* the sense is that everyone is following Jesus, but John has an ironic play on *world;* he alludes to the universality of salvation (3, 17; 4, 42).

12, 20–36: This announcement of glorification by death is an illustration of "the whole world" (19) going after him.

12, 20: *Greeks:* not used here in a nationalistic sense. These are

probably Gentile proselytes to Judaism; cf 7, 35.

12, 21–22: *Philip . . . Andrew:* the approach is made through disciples who have distinctly Greek names, suggesting that access to Jesus was mediated to the Greek world through his disciples. Philip and Andrew were from Bethsaida (1, 44); Galileans were mostly bilingual. *See:* here seems to mean "have an interview with."

12, 23: Jesus' response suggests that only after the crucifixion could the gospel encompass both Jew and Gentile.

12, 24: This verse implies that through his death Jesus will be accessible to all. *It remains just a grain of wheat:* this saying is found in the synoptic triple and double traditions (Mk 8, 35 // Mt 16, 25 // Lk 9, 24; Mt 10, 39 // Lk 17, 33). John adds the phrases (25) *in this world* and *for eternal life.*

12, 25: *His life:* the Greek word *psychē* refers to a person's natural life. It does not mean "soul," for Hebrew anthropology did not postulate body/soul dualism in the way that is familiar to us.

12, 27: *I am troubled:* perhaps an allusion to the Gethsemane agony scene of the synoptics.

12, 6: Jn 13, 29.	**12, 23:** Jn 2, 4.
12, 8: Dt 15, 11.	**12, 24:** Is 53, 10–12; 1 Cor
12, 9: Jn 11, 19.	15, 36.
12, 11: Jn 11, 45.	**12, 25:** Mt 10, 39; 16, 25; Mk
12, 12–19: Mt 21, 1–16; Mk 11,	8, 35; Lk 9, 24; 17, 33.
1–10; Lk 19, 28–40.	**12, 26:** Jn 14, 3; 17, 24; Mt
12, 13: Jn 1, 49; Lv 23, 40;	16, 24; Mk 8, 34;
1 Mc 13, 51; 2 Mc 10,	Lk 9, 23.
7; Rv 7, 9.	**12, 27:** Jn 6, 38; 18, 11; Mt
12, 15: Is 40, 9; Zec 9, 9.	26, 38–39; Mk 14,
12, 16: Jn 2, 22.	34–36; Lk 22, 42; Heb
12, 19: Jn 11, 47–48.	5, 7–8.
12, 20: Acts 10, 2.	**12, 28:** Jn 2, 11; 17, 5; Dn 4,
12, 21: Jn 1, 44.	31.34.
12, 22: Jn 1, 40.	

Dying for New Life

In Jn 12, 24–26, Jesus is describing what Christians call the *paschal mystery*. It is the belief that God brings new life out of suffering and death. The first and ultimate expression of the paschal mystery is Jesus' own death and Resurrection. God used Christ's sacrifice to free us from the bonds of sin, and Christ's Resurrection to open the path to new life. It is a mystery that no one can fully explain, but the Gospels and experience tell us it is so.

Like the grain of wheat in this Gospel passage, in death we bear the fruit of new life. The path to new life is through sacrifice and death. By dying to our selfishness and focusing on loving others, we experience the fullness of life in Christ Jesus.

In your prayer, reflect or journal on the following questions:
- What does the paschal mystery mean to you?
- What kinds of attitudes, desires, or actions must you "die to"?

Write a prayer asking God to give you the courage to let go of the things that keep you from fullness of life.

▶ Jn 12, 24–26

came from heaven, "I have glorified it and will glorify it again." 29* The crowd there heard it and said it was thunder; but others said, "An angel has spoken to him." 30* Jesus answered and said, "This voice did not come for my sake but for yours. 31*† Now is the time of judgment on this world; now the ruler of this world will be driven out. 32* And when I am lifted up from the earth, I will draw everyone to myself." 33 He said this indicating the kind of death he would die. 34*† So the crowd answered him, "We have heard from the law that the Messiah

remains forever. Then how can you say that the Son of Man must be lifted up? Who is this Son of Man?" 35* Jesus said to them, "The light will be among you only a little while. Walk while you have the light, so that darkness may not overcome you. Whoever walks in the dark does not know where he is going. 36* While you have the light, believe in the light, so that you may become children of the light."

Unbelief and Belief among the Jews

After he had said this, Jesus left and hid from them. 37*† Although he had performed so many signs in their presence they did not believe in him, 38*† in order that the word which Isaiah the prophet spoke might be fulfilled:

"Lord, who has believed our preaching,
to whom has the might of the Lord
been revealed?"

39 For this reason they could not believe, because again Isaiah said:

40* "He blinded their eyes
and hardened their heart,
so that they might not see with their eyes

13, 5

12, 31: *Ruler of this world:* Satan.

12, 34: There is no passage in the Old Testament that states precisely that *the Messiah remains forever.* Perhaps the closest is Ps 89, 37.

12, 37–50: These verses, on unbelief of the Jews, provide an epilogue to the Book of Signs.

12, 38–41: John gives a historical explanation of the disbelief of the Jewish people, not a psychological one. The Old Testament had to be fulfilled; the disbelief that met Isaiah's message was a foreshadowing of the disbelief that Jesus encountered. In v 42 and also in 3, 20, we see that there is no negation of freedom.

12, 29: Ex 9, 28; 2 Sm 22, 14; Jb 37, 4; Ps 29, 3; Lk 22, 43; Acts 23, 9.
12, 30: Jn 11, 42.
12, 31: Jn 16, 11; Lk 10, 18; Rv 12, 9.
12, 32: Jn 3, 14; 8, 28; Is 52, 13.
12, 34: Pss 89, 5; 110, 4; Is 9, 7; Dn 7, 13–14; Rv 20, 1–6.
12, 35: Jn 9, 4; 11, 10; Jb 5, 14.
12, 36: Eph 5, 8.
12, 37–43: Dt 29, 2–4; Mk 4, 11–12; Rom 9–11.
12, 38: Is 53, 1; Rom 10, 16.
12, 40: Is 6, 9–10; Mt 13, 13–15; Mk 4, 12.

JN

and understand with their heart and
be converted,
and I would heal them."

41*† Isaiah said this because he saw his glory and spoke about him. 42* Nevertheless, many, even among the authorities, believed in him, but because of the Pharisees they did not acknowledge it openly in order not to be expelled from the synagogue. 43* For they preferred human praise to the glory of God.

Recapitulation

44* Jesus cried out and said, "Whoever believes in me believes not only in me but also in the one who sent me, 45* and whoever sees me sees the one who sent me. 46* I came into the world as light, so that everyone who believes in me might not remain in darkness. 47* And if anyone hears my words and does not observe them, I do not condemn him, for I did not come to condemn the world but to save the world. 48* Whoever rejects me and does not accept my words has something to judge him: the word that I spoke, it will condemn him on the last day, 49* because I did not speak on my own, but the Father who sent me commanded me what to say and speak. 50 And I know that his commandment is eternal life. So what I say, I say as the Father told me."

III: The Book of Glory†

The Washing of the Disciples' Feet†

13 1* Before the feast of Passover,† Jesus knew that his hour had come to pass from this world to the Father. He loved his own in the world and he loved them to the end. 2*† The devil had already induced Judas, son of Simon the Iscariot, to hand him over. So, during supper, 3* fully aware that the Father had put everything into his power and that he had come from God and was returning to God, 4 he rose from supper and took off his outer garments. He took a towel and tied it around his waist. 5*† Then he poured water into a

did you KNOW?

Feast of the Passover

Chapter 13 is the beginning of the second part of the Gospel of John, sometimes called the Book of Glory. Its central theme is how Jesus is glorified through his Passion, death, and Resurrection. It begins with Jesus' washing the disciples' feet at the Last Supper, before the Passover.

The Jewish feast of Passover, also called the feast of Unleavened Bread, reminds us of how God rescued the Israelites from slavery in Egypt by killing the firstborn Egyptians and "passing over" the homes of the Israelites (about 1250 B.C.). The feast was traditionally celebrated with a meal of lamb, bitter herbs, and unleavened bread (see "The Passover," Ex 12, 14–28). It was the blood of a lamb, smeared on the doorposts of the Israelites' houses, that signaled the angel of death to spare the firstborn of God's people.

In the other Gospels, the last meal that Jesus shares with his disciples is the Passover meal. However, in the Gospel of John, Jesus is arrested before Passover. He is crucified on the preparation day of the feast of Unleavened Bread, at the same time that the lambs are being sacrificed in the Temple. The symbolism would not be missed by the readers of John: Jesus is the new and perfect Passover lamb.

▸ Jn 13, 1–20

J
N

12, 41: *His glory:* Isaiah saw the glory of Yahweh enthroned in the heavenly temple, but in John the antecedent of *his* is Jesus.
13, 1—19, 42: The Book of Glory. There is a major break here; the word "sign" is used again only in 20, 30. In this phase of Jesus' return to the Father, the discourses (chs 13–17) precede the traditional narrative of the passion (chs 18–20) to interpret them for the Christian reader. This is the only extended example of esoteric teaching of disciples in John.
13, 1—20: Washing of the disciples' feet. This episode occurs in John at the place of the narration of the institution of the Eucharist in the synoptics. It may be a dramatization of Lk 22, 27: "I am your servant." It is presented as a "model" ("pattern") of the crucifixion. It symbolizes cleansing from sin by sacrificial death.
13, 1: *Before the feast of Passover:* this would be Thursday evening, before the day of preparation; in the synoptics, the Last Supper is a Passover meal taking place, in John's chronology, on Friday evening. *To the end:* or, "completely."

13, 2: *Induced:* literally, "The devil put into the heart that Judas should hand him over."
13, 5: The act of washing another's feet was one that could not be required of the lowliest Jewish slave. It is an allusion to the humiliating death of the crucifixion.

12, 41: Jn 5, 39; Is 6, 1.4.
12, 42: Jn 9, 22.
12, 43: Jn 5, 44.
12, 44: Jn 13, 20; 14, 1.
12, 45: Jn 14, 7–9.
12, 46: Jn 1, 9; 8, 12.
12, 47: Jn 3, 17.
12, 48: Lk 10, 16; Heb 4, 12.
12, 49: Jn 14, 10.31; Dt 18, 18–19.

13, 1: Jn 2, 4; 7, 30; 8, 20; Mt 26, 17.45; Mk 14, 12.41; Lk 22, 7.
13, 2: Jn 6, 71; 17, 12; Mt 26, 20–21; Mk 14, 17–18; Lk 22, 3.
13, 3: Jn 3, 35.
13, 5: 1 Sm 25, 41.

THE *INDRIAPPAM*

In the province of Kerala, in India, about 80 percent of the population is Catholic and celebrates the Lord's Passion with special time-honored customs. One such custom takes place on Holy Thursday. On that day, nearly all the villagers or townspeople attend morning Mass. During the Eucharist, the ritual of foot washing occurs, the priest washing the feet of twelve children chosen from among those who are poor. Then, after dinner that evening, the people gather again for the stations of the cross and prayers. They return home around nine or ten o'clock for a special Passover meal.

The Passover meal consists of bread baked only on Holy Thursday and a special drink of coconut milk mixed with brown sugar and spices. This Passover bread, or *indriappam*, is baked with a cross of palm on top, which is placed there by the oldest woman of the family. At the meal, the oldest man cuts the bread and passes a piece to each person, beginning with the oldest and working down to the youngest. Often families visit one another and share this tradition throughout the evening. And if a death has occurred in any family that year, the other households of the village provide the *indriappam* for them.

On Good Friday, which is a national holiday in India despite the fact that it is a primarily Hindu country, the leftover bread and milk are served to the servants and those of the village who are poor and needy. This custom of *indriappam* combines devotion to Christ in the Eucharist with a reminder of the service we are obliged to offer to those who are needy and poor.

What customs and traditions does your family or parish take part in to commemorate the gift of the Eucharist given at the Last Supper?

▸ Jn 13, 1–17

basin and began to wash the disciples' feet and dry them with the towel around his waist. 6 He came to Simon Peter, who said to him, "Master, are you going to wash my feet?" 7 Jesus answered and said to him, "What I am doing, you do not understand now, but you will understand later." 8* Peter said to him, "You will never wash my feet." Jesus answered him, "Unless I wash you, you will have no inheritance with me." 9 Simon Peter said to him, "Master, then not only my feet, but my hands and head as well."

Jesus Models Service to Others

In Matthew, Mark, and Luke, the focus of the Last Supper is on the institution of the Eucharist. But in John, the focus is on Jesus' cleaning his disciples' feet (13, 1–17). John makes the point that serving others is at the heart of being a follower of Jesus. In Holy Thursday Mass, we celebrate both traditions, indicating that service is a necessary part of living the paschal mystery that we celebrate in the Eucharist.

■ The washing of the feet is a symbol of service, humility, and purification. Have you ever felt honored and humbled at the same time?

■ Read Jn 13, 1–17. Reflect on and listen to Jesus' message to you.

For more on the Eucharist, see the articles for Mt 26, 26–29; Mk 14, 22–25; Lk 22, 14–20.

▸ Jn 13, 1–13

13, 8: 2 Sm 20, 1.

Introducing
▶ THE BELOVED DISCIPLE

In the Last Supper scene, we are introduced to a mysterious character found only in the Gospel of John, described as the disciple "whom Jesus loved" (13, 23). He is mentioned several more times in John: at the foot of the cross with Jesus' mother (19, 25–27), on Easter morning when he enters the empty tomb with Peter (20, 2–10), and after the Resurrection when he identifies Jesus from the boat (21, 7). He is always with Peter or where Peter should be (at the cross).

So who is the mystery man? Traditionally, he has been identified as John, the son of Zebedee and one of the twelve Apostles, and as the writer of the Gospel of John. But if that is true, why does he refer to himself so strangely? Many scholars today believe that the Beloved Disciple was a lesser-known follower of Jesus who was the founder of the Christian community that ultimately produced the Gospel of John. They think that his eyewitness accounts (see 21, 24) were passed on and are the basis for the Gospel we have today.

▶ Jn 13, 23–25

10*† Jesus said to him, "Whoever has bathed has no need except to have his feet washed, for he is clean all over; so you are clean, but not all." 11* For he knew who would betray him; for this reason, he said, "Not all of you are clean."

12 So when he had washed their feet [and] put his garments back on and reclined at table again, he said to them, "Do you realize what I have done for you? 13* You call me 'teacher' and 'master,' and rightly so, for indeed I am. 14 If I, therefore, the master and teacher, have washed your feet, you ought to wash one another's feet. 15* I have given you a model to follow, so that as I have done for you, you should also do. 16*† Amen, amen, I say to you, no slave is greater than his master nor any messenger greater than the one who sent him. 17 If you understand this, blessed are you if you do it. 18* I am not speaking of all of you. I know those whom I have chosen. But so that the scripture might be fulfilled, 'The one who ate my food has raised his heel against me.' 19 From now on I am telling you before it happens, so that when it happens you may believe that I AM. 20* Amen, amen,

I say to you, whoever receives the one I send receives me, and whoever receives me receives the one who sent me."

Announcement of Judas's Betrayal

21* When he had said this, Jesus was deeply troubled and testified, "Amen, amen, I say to you, one of you will betray me." 22 The disciples looked at one another, at a loss as to whom he meant. 23*† One of his disciples, the one whom Jesus loved, was reclining at Jesus' side. 24 So Simon Peter nodded to him to find out whom he meant. 25* He leaned back against Jesus' chest and said to him, "Master, who is it?" 26† Jesus answered, "It is the one to whom I hand the morsel after I have dipped it." So he dipped the morsel and [took it and] handed it to Judas, son of Simon the Iscariot. 27* After he took the morsel, Satan entered him. So Jesus said to him, "What you are going to do, do quickly." 28 [Now] none of those reclining at table realized why he said this to him. 29* Some thought that since Judas kept the money bag, Jesus had told him, "Buy what we need for the feast," or to give

---

13, 10: *Bathed:* many have suggested that this passage is a symbolic reference to baptism. The Greek root involved is used in baptismal contexts in 1 Cor 6, 11; Eph 5, 26; Ti 3, 5; Heb 10, 22.

13, 16: *Messenger:* the Greek has *apostolos,* the only occurrence of the term in John. It is not used in the technical sense here.

13, 23: *The one whom Jesus loved:* also mentioned in 19, 26; 20, 2; 21, 7. A disciple, called "another disciple" or "the other disciple," is mentioned in 18, 15 and 20, 2; in the latter reference he is identified with the disciple whom Jesus loved. There is also an unnamed disciple in 1, 35–40; see the note on 1, 37.

13, 26: *Morsel:* probably the bitter herb dipped in salt water.

13, 10: Jn 15, 3.
13, 11: Jn 6, 70.
13, 13: Mt 23, 8.10.
13, 15: Lk 22, 27; 1 Pt 2, 21.
13, 16: Jn 15, 20; Mt 10, 24; Lk 6, 40.
13, 18: Ps 41, 10.
13, 20: Mt 10, 40; Mk 9, 37; Lk 9, 48.
13, 21–30: Mt 26, 21–25; Mk 14, 18–21; Lk 22, 21–23.
13, 23: Jn 19, 26; 20, 2; 21, 7.20; Mt 10, 37.
13, 25: Jn 21, 20.
13, 27: Jn 13, 2; Lk 22, 3.
13, 29: Jn 12, 5–6.

Cultural Connections

THE WAY AND THE TRUTH AND THE LIFE

Laotian Catholics often point to Jn 14, 6 as a significant connection between the Buddhist faith and their Catholic faith. There is a Buddhist tradition of honoring the way and the truth. Becoming a Catholic and knowing the risen Christ bring a deeper appreciation of everlasting life. This completes the triangle of "the way and the truth and the life."

▶ Jn 14, 6–7

something to the poor. ³⁰ So he took the morsel and left at once. And it was night.

The New Commandment

³¹† When he had left, Jesus said,† "Now is the Son of Man glorified, and God is glorified in him. ³²* [If God is glorified in him,] God will also glorify him in himself, and he will glorify him at once. ³³* My children, I will be with you only a little while longer. You will look for me, and as I told the Jews, 'Where I go you cannot come,' so now I say it to you. ³⁴*† I give you a new commandment: love one another. As I have loved you, so you also should love one another. ³⁵ This is how all will know that you are my disciples, if you have love for one another."

Peter's Denial Predicted

³⁶* Simon Peter said to him, "Master, where are you going?" Jesus answered [him], "Where I am going, you cannot follow me now, though you will follow later." ³⁷ Peter said to him, "Master, why can't I follow you now? I will lay down my life for

you." ³⁸* Jesus answered, "Will you lay down your life for me? Amen, amen, I say to you, the cock will not crow before you deny me three times."

Last Supper Discourses

14 ¹† "Do not let your hearts be troubled. You have faith† in God; have faith also in me. ² In my Father's house there are many dwelling places. If there were not, would I have told you that I am going to prepare a place for you? ³*† And if I go and prepare a place for you, I will come back again and take you to myself, so that where I am you also may be. ⁴† Where [I] am going you know the way." ⁵ Thomas said to him, "Master, we do not know where you are going; how can we know the way?" ⁶*† Jesus said to him, "I am the way and the truth and the life. No one comes to the Father except through me. ⁷*† If you know me, then you will also know my Father. From now on you do know him and have seen him." ⁸*† Philip said to him, "Master, show us the Father, and that will be enough for us." ⁹* Jesus said to him, "Have I been with you for so long a time and

---

13, 31—17, 26: Two farewell discourses and a prayer. These seem to be Johannine compositions, including sayings of Jesus at the Last Supper and on other occasions, modeled on similar farewell discourses in Greek literature and the Old Testament (of Moses, Joshua, David).

13, 31–38: Introduction: departure and return. Terms of coming and going predominate. These verses form an introduction to the last discourse of Jesus, which extends through chs 14 to 17. In it John has collected Jesus' words to *his own* (13, 1). There are indications that several speeches have been fused together, e.g., in 14, 31 and 17, 1.

13, 34: *I give you a new commandment:* this puts Jesus on a par with Yahweh. The commandment itself is not new; cf Lv 19, 18 and the note there.

14, 1–31: Jesus' departure and return. This section is a dialogue marked off by a literary inclusion in vv 1 and 27: "Do not let your hearts be troubled."

14, 1: *You have faith:* could also be imperative: "Have faith."

14, 3: *Come back again:* a rare Johannine reference to the parousia; cf 1 Jn 2, 28.

14, 4: *The way:* here, of Jesus himself; also a designation of Christianity in Acts 9, 2; 19, 9.23; 22, 4; 24, 14.22.

14, 6: *The truth:* in John, the divinely revealed reality of the Father manifested in the person and works of Jesus. The possession of truth confers knowledge and liberation from sin (8, 32).

14, 7: An alternative reading, "If you knew me, then you would have known my Father also," would be a rebuke, as in 8, 19.

14, 8: *Show us the Father:* Philip is pictured asking for a theophany like Ex 24, 9–10; 33, 18.

13, 32: Jn 17, 1–5.
13, 33: Jn 7, 33; 8, 21.
13, 34: Jn 15, 12–13.17; Lv 19, 18; 1 Thes 4, 9; 1 Jn 2, 7–10; 3, 23; 2 Jn 5.
13, 36: Mk 14, 27; Lk 22, 23.
13, 38: Jn 18, 27; Mt 26, 33–35; Mk 14, 29–31; Lk 22, 33–34.
14, 3: Jn 12, 26; 17, 24; 1 Jn 2, 28.
14, 6: Jn 8, 31–47.
14, 7: Jn 8, 19; 12, 45.
14, 8: Ex 24, 9–10; 33, 18.
14, 9: Jn 1, 18; 10, 30; 12, 45; 2 Cor 4, 4; Col 1, 15; Heb 1, 3.

you still do not know me, Philip? Whoever has seen me has seen the Father. How can you say, 'Show us the Father'? 10* Do you not believe that I am in the Father and the Father is in me? The words that I speak to you I do not speak on my own. The Father who dwells in me is doing his works. 11* Believe me that I am in the Father and the Father is in me, or else, believe because of the works themselves. 12* Amen, amen, I say to you, whoever believes in me will do the works that I do, and will do greater ones than these, because I am going to the Father. 13* And whatever you ask in my name, I will do, so that the Father may be glorified in the Son. 14 If you ask anything of me in my name, I will do it.

The Advocate

15* "If you love me, you will keep my commandments. 16*† And I will ask the Father, and he will give you another Advocate to be with you always, 17*† the Spirit of truth, which the world cannot accept, because it neither sees nor knows it. But you know it, because it remains with you, and will be in you. 18† I will not leave you orphans; I will come to you. 19* In a little while the world will no longer see me, but you will see me, because I live and you will live. 20* On that day you will realize that I am in my Father and you are in me and I in you. 21* Whoever has my commandments and observes them is the one who loves me. And whoever loves me will be loved by my Father, and I will love him and reveal myself to him." 22*† Judas, not the Iscariot, said to him, "Master, [then] what happened that you will reveal yourself to us and not to the world?" 23* Jesus answered and said to him, "Whoever loves me will keep my word, and my Father will love him, and we will come to him and make our dwelling with him. 24 Whoever does not love me does not keep my words; yet the word you hear is not mine but that of the Father who sent me.

25 "I have told you this while I am with you. 26* The Advocate, the holy Spirit that the Father will send in my name—he will teach you everything and remind you of all that I told you. 27*† Peace I leave with you; my peace I give to you. Not as the world gives do I give it to you. Do not let your hearts be troubled or afraid. 28*† You heard me tell you, 'I am

The Holy Spirit Guides Us into All Truth!

Jesus told his disciples that after his death, God would send the Spirit of Truth to be with them forever. Jesus calls the Holy Spirit the Advocate (Jn 16, 7), the one who defends us from evil and sin. The Holy Spirit also guides us into all Truth, by helping us to grasp the meaning of Jesus' words, actions, and miracles.

■ Jesus promises his followers that the Holy Spirit will abide in us (14, 17). How are you aware of the Holy Spirit's presence in your life?

■ Place yourself in the hands of the Most Holy Trinity and call upon the Holy Spirit to protect you from all sin and evil and to bring you peace.

▶ Jn 14, 15–31; 16, 5–15

14, 16: *Another Advocate:* Jesus is the first advocate (paraclete); see 1 Jn 2, 1, where Jesus is an advocate in the sense of intercessor in heaven. The Greek term derives from legal terminology for an advocate or defense attorney, and can mean spokesman, mediator, intercessor, comforter, consoler, although no one of these terms encompasses the meaning in John. The Paraclete in John is a teacher, a witness to Jesus, and a prosecutor of the world, who represents the continued presence on earth of the Jesus who has returned to the Father.

14, 17: *The Spirit of truth:* this term is also used at Qumran, where it is a moral force put into a person by God, as opposed to the spirit of perversity. It is more personal in John; it will teach the realities of the new order (26), and testify to the truth (6). While it has been customary to use masculine personal pronouns in English for the Advocate, the Greek word for "spirit" is neuter, and the Greek text and manuscript variants fluctuate between masculine and neuter pronouns.

14, 18: *I will come to you:* indwelling, not parousia.

14, 22: *Judas, not the Iscariot:* probably not the brother of Jesus in Mk 6, 3 // Mt 13, 55 or the apostle named Jude in Lk 6, 16, but Thomas (see the note on 11, 16), although other readings have "Judas the Cananean."

14, 27: *Peace:* the traditional Hebrew salutation *šālôm;* but Jesus' "Shalom" is a gift of salvation, connoting the bounty of messianic blessing.

14, 28: *The Father is greater than I:* because he sent, gave, etc., and Jesus is "a man who has told you the truth that I heard from God" (8, 40).

14, 10: Jn 1, 1; 10, 37–38; 12, 49.
14, 11: Jn 10, 38.
14, 12: Jn 1, 50; 5, 20.
14, 13: Jn 15, 7.16; 16, 23–24; Mt 7, 7–11.
14, 15: Jn 15, 10; Dt 6, 4–9; Ps 119; Wis 6, 18; 1 Jn 5, 3; 2 Jn 6.
14, 16: Jn 15, 26; Lk 24, 49; 1 Jn 2, 1.
14, 17: Jn 16, 13; Mt 28, 20; 2 Jn 1–2.

14, 19: Jn 16, 16.
14, 20: Jn 10, 38; 17, 21; Is 2, 17; 4, 2–3.
14, 21: Jn 16, 27; 1 Jn 2, 5; 3, 24.
14, 22: Jn 7, 4; Acts 10, 40–41.
14, 23: Rv 3, 20.
14, 26: Jn 15, 26; 16, 7.13–14; Ps 51, 13; Is 63, 10.
14, 27: Jn 16, 33; Eph 2, 14–18.
14, 28: Jn 8, 40.

going away and I will come back to you.' If you loved me, you would rejoice that I am going to the Father; for the Father is greater than I. [29]* And now I have told you this before it happens, so that when it happens you may believe. [30]† I will no longer speak much with you, for the ruler of the world is coming. He has no power over me, [31]* but the world must know that I love the Father and that I do just as the Father has commanded me. Get up, let us go.

The Vine and the Branches

15 [1]*† "I am the true vine,† and my Father is the vine grower. [2]† He takes away every branch in me that does not bear fruit, and every one that does he prunes so that it bears more fruit. [3]* You are already pruned because of the word that I spoke to you. [4] Remain in me, as I remain in you. Just as a branch cannot bear fruit on its own unless it remains on the vine, so neither can you unless you remain in me. [5] I am the vine, you are the branches. Whoever remains in me and I in him will bear much fruit, because without me you can do nothing. [6]*† Anyone who does not remain in me will be thrown out like a branch and wither; people will gather them and throw them into a fire and they will be burned. [7]* If you remain in me and my words remain in you, ask for whatever you want and it will be done for you. [8]* By this is my Father glorified, that you bear much fruit and become my disciples. [9]* As the Father loves me, so I also love you. Remain in my love. [10]* If you keep my commandments, you will remain in my love, just as I have kept my Father's commandments and remain in his love.

[11]* "I have told you this so that my joy might be in you and your joy might be complete. [12]* This is my commandment: love one another as I love you. [13]*† No one has greater love than this, to lay down one's life for one's friends. [14] You are my friends if you do what I command you. [15]*† I no longer call you slaves, because a slave does not know what his

THE PEACE OF CHRIST

John 14, 27 is the passage the priest recites during Mass just before he invites the community to share a sign of peace. This is no ordinary peace, however. It is the peace of Christ. It is a peace that is not of this world. It has allowed Christians to endure hardships, oppression, war, sickness, and death with dignity and hope. The next time you are at Mass, think about the awesome power in the peace of Christ that you are extending to the people around you.

▸ Jn 14, 27

master is doing. I have called you friends, because I have told you everything I have heard from my Father. [16]* It was not you who chose me, but I who chose you and appointed you to go and bear fruit that will remain, so that whatever you ask the Father in my name he may give you. [17]* This I command you: love one another.

The World's Hatred

[18]*† "If the world hates you, realize that it hated me first. [19]* If you belonged to the world, the world would love its own; but because you do not belong to the world, and I have chosen you out of the

---

14, 30: *The ruler of the world:* Satan; cf 12, 31; 16, 11.

15, 1—16, 4: Discourse on the union of Jesus with his disciples. His words become a monologue and go beyond the immediate crisis of the departure of Jesus.

15, 1–16, 4: Like 10, 1–5, this passage resembles a parable. Israel is spoken of as a vineyard at Is 5, 1–7; Mt 21, 33–46 and as a vine at Ps 80, 9–17; Jer 2, 21; Ez 15, 2; 17, 5–10; 19, 10; Hos 10, 1. The identification of the vine as the Son of Man in Ps 80, 16, and Wisdom's description of herself as a vine in Sir 24, 17, are further background for portrayal of Jesus by this figure. There may be secondary eucharistic symbolism here; cf Mk 14, 25, "the fruit of the vine."

15, 2: *Takes away . . . prunes:* in Greek there is a play on two related verbs.

15, 6: Branches were cut off and dried on the wall of the vineyard for later use as fuel.

15, 13: *For one's friends:* or: "those whom one loves." In 9–13a, the words for love are related to the Greek *agapaō.* In 13b–15, the words for love are related to the Greek *phileō.* For John, the two roots seem synonymous and mean "to love"; cf also 21, 15–17. The word *philos* is used here.

15, 15: *Slaves . . . friends:* in the Old Testament, Moses (Dt 34, 5), Joshua (Jos 24, 29), and David (Ps 89, 21) were called "servants" or "slaves of Yahweh"; only Abraham (Is 41, 8; 2 Chr 20, 7; cf Jas 2, 23) was called a "friend of God."

15, 18—16, 4: The hostile reaction of the world. There are synoptic parallels, predicting persecution, especially at Mt 10, 17–25; 24, 9–10.

14, 29: Jn 13, 19; 16, 4.
14, 31: Jn 6, 38.
15, 1: Ps 80, 9–17; Is 5, 1–7; Jer 2, 21; Ez 15, 2; 17, 5–10; 19, 10.
15, 3: Jn 13, 10.
15, 6: Ez 15, 6–7; 19, 10–14.
15, 7: Jn 14, 13; Mt 7, 7; Mk 11, 24; 1 Jn 5, 14.
15, 8: Mt 5, 16.
15, 9: Jn 17, 23.
15, 10: Jn 8, 29; 14, 15.
15, 11: Jn 16, 22; 17, 13.

15, 12: Jn 13, 34.
15, 13: Rom 5, 6–8; 1 Jn 3, 16.
15, 15: Dt 34, 5; Jos 24, 29; 2 Chr 20, 7; Ps 89, 21; Is 41, 8; Rom 8, 15; Gal 4, 7; Jas 2, 23.
15, 16: Jn 14, 13; Dt 7, 6.
15, 17: Jn 13, 34; 1 Jn 3, 23; 4, 21.
15, 18: Jn 7, 7; 14, 17; Mt 10, 22; 24, 9; Mk 13, 13; Lk 6, 22; 1 Jn 3, 13.
15, 19: Jn 17, 14–16; 1 Jn 4, 5.

world, the world hates you. 20*† Remember the word I spoke to you, 'No slave is greater than his master.' If they persecuted me, they will also persecute you. If they kept my word, they will also keep yours. 21*† And they will do all these things to you on account of my name, because they do not know the one who sent me. 22*† If I had not come and spoken to them, they would have no sin; but as it is they have no excuse for their sin. 23* Whoever hates me also hates my Father. 24* If I had not done works among them that no one else ever did, they would not have sin; but as it is, they have seen and hated both me and my Father. 25*† But in order that the word written in their law might be fulfilled, 'They hated me without cause.'

26*† "When the Advocate comes whom I will send you from the Father, the Spirit of truth that proceeds from the Father, he will testify to me. 27* And you also testify, because you have been with me from the beginning.

MAKE YOUR HOME WITH JESUS

Jesus calls himself the true vine, and us the branches (Jn 15, 5). What does this mean for us? First, it means that apart from Jesus, we can produce no fruit. That is, we have nothing of ultimate value to offer others. It also means that to stay alive, we must "remain" in Jesus (verse 4). To remain, in this sense, means to stay or make our home with. How at home are you with Jesus?

▶ Jn 15, 1–11

PRAY IT!
Not of This World

It is easy to get caught up in the pressures put on us by our society. It seems that we have to dress a certain way, have certain possessions, and live in a certain kind of house just to be considered average. People who resist those pressures are often labeled weird or different. They often feel out of place, not of this world.

The community from which the Gospel of John emerged did not feel at home in the world either. Their message of the divine Jesus had been rejected by Jews, Gentiles, and perhaps even other early Christians. No wonder the author has Jesus emphasize, "because you do not belong to the world, . . . the world hates you" (15, 19).

In your prayer, reflect or journal on the following questions:
- How might Christians today be considered not of this world?
- What societal pressures do you need to resist?
- How does Jesus' warning to his disciples about the world's hatred (verses 18–25) apply to Christians today?

▶ Jn 15, 18–25

16 1 "I have told you this so that you may not fall away. 2*† They will expel you from the synagogues; in fact, the hour is coming when everyone who kills you will think he is offering worship to God. 3* They will do this because they have not known either the Father or me. 4*† I have told you this so that when their hour comes you may remember that I told you.

J
N

15, 20: *The word I spoke to you:* a reference to 13, 16.

15, 21: *On account of my name:* the idea of persecution for Jesus' name is frequent in the New Testament (Mt 10, 22; 24, 9; Acts 9, 14). For John, association with Jesus' name implies union with Jesus.

15, 22.24: Jesus' words (*spoken*) and deeds (*works*) are the great motives of credibility. *They have seen and hated:* probably means that they have seen his works and still have hated; but the Greek can be read: "have seen both me and my Father and still have hated both me and my Father." *Works . . . that no one else ever did:* so Yahweh in Dt 4, 32–33.

15, 25: *In their law:* law is here used as a larger concept than the Pentateuch, for the reference is to Ps 35, 19 or 69, 5. See the notes on 10, 34; 12, 34. *Their law* reflects the argument of the church with the synagogue.

15, 26: *Whom I will send:* in 14, 16.26, the Paraclete is to be sent

by the Father, at the request of Jesus. Here the Spirit comes from both Jesus and the Father in mission; there is no reference here to the eternal procession of the Spirit.

16, 2: *Hour:* of persecution, not Jesus' "hour" (see the note on 2, 4).

16, 4b–33: A duplicate of 14, 1–31 on departure and return.

15, 20: Jn 13, 16; Mt 10, 24.	**15, 26:** Jn 14, 16.26; Mt 10, 19–20.
15, 21: Jn 8, 19; 16, 3.	
15, 22: Jn 8, 21.24; 9, 41.	**15, 27:** Lk 1, 2; Acts 1, 8.
15, 23: Jn 5, 23; Lk 10, 16; 1 Jn 2, 23.	**16, 2:** Jn 9, 22; 12, 42; Mt 10, 17; Lk 21, 12; Acts 26, 11.
15, 24: Jn 3, 2; 9, 32; Dt 4, 32–33.	**16, 3:** Jn 15, 21.
15, 25: Pss 35, 19; 69, 4.	**16, 4:** Jn 13, 19; 14, 29.

Jesus' Departure; Coming of the Advocate

"I did not tell you this from the beginning, because I was with you. [5]*† But now I am going to the one who sent me, and not one of you asks me, 'Where are you going?' [6] But because I told you this, grief has filled your hearts. [7]* But I tell you the truth, it is better for you that I go. For if I do not go, the Advocate will not come to you. But if I go, I will send him to you. [8]† And when he comes he will convict the world in regard to sin and righteousness and condemnation: [9]* sin, because they do not believe in me; [10] righteousness, because I am going to the Father and you will no longer see me; [11]* condemnation, because the ruler of this world has been condemned.

[12] "I have much more to tell you, but you cannot bear it now. [13]*† But when he comes, the Spirit of truth, he will guide you to all truth. He will not speak on his own, but he will speak what he hears, and will declare to you the things that are coming. [14] He will glorify me, because he will take from what is mine and declare it to you. [15] Everything that the Father has is mine; for this reason I told you that he will take from what is mine and declare it to you.

[16]* "A little while and you will no longer see me, and again a little while later and you will see me." [17] So some of his disciples said to one another, "What does this mean that he is saying to us, 'A little while and you will not see me, and again a little while and you will see me,' and 'Because I am going to the Father'?" [18] So they said, "What is this 'little while' [of which he speaks]? We do not know what he means." [19] Jesus knew

CHRIST LIVES IN US THROUGH THE HOLY SPIRIT!

In his farewell speech to his Apostles, Jesus tells them that he will return to the Father, but will not leave them orphaned (Jn 14, 18). The Father will give them another Advocate—the Holy Spirit. We also receive the Holy Spirit, through our Baptism and our Confirmation. Hispanic spirituality emphasizes the Spirit's gifts of love, freedom, truth, life, and hope.

- *Love* lets us find joy in the midst of suffering and pain. Christ did not end human suffering; instead, he showed how suffering for those we love can bring new life to them.
- *Freedom* from material goods, false gratification, and addictions nurtures the lifestyle we adopt as disciples of Jesus.
- *Truth* about God, us, and history can be achieved only through God's revelation. The Spirit gives us the light to discover this truth and the strength to direct our life by it.
- *God's life* in us helps us overcome prejudices, promote reconciliation, foster unity in diversity, and work for justice and peace.
- *Hope* in being forever with God and the people we love is continuously nourished by the Spirit, who gives us a glimpse of the glory to come despite our earthly limitations.

▶ Jn 14, 12–21; 16, 12–15

16, 5: *Not one of you asks me:* the difficulty of reconciling this with Simon Peter's question in 13, 36 and Thomas' words in 14, 5 strengthens the supposition that the last discourse has been made up of several collections of Johannine material.

16, 8–11: These verses illustrate the forensic character of the Paraclete's role: in the forum of the disciples' conscience he prosecutes the world. He leads believers to see (a) that the basic sin was and is refusal to believe in Jesus; (b) that, although Jesus was found guilty and apparently died in disgrace, in reality righteousness has triumphed, for Jesus has returned to his Father; (c) finally, that it is the *ruler of this world,* Satan, who has been condemned through Jesus' death (12, 32).

16, 13: *Declare to you the things that are coming:* not a reference to new predictions about the future, but interpretation of what has already occurred or been said.

16, 5: Jn 7, 33; 13, 36; 14, 5.
16, 7: Jn 7, 39; 14, 16–17.26; 15, 26.
16, 9: Jn 8, 21–24; 15, 22.
16, 11: Jn 12, 31.

16, 13: Jn 14, 17.26; 15, 26; Pss 25, 5; 143, 10; 1 Jn 2, 27; Rv 7, 17.
16, 16: Jn 7, 33; 14, 19.

that they wanted to ask him, so he said to them, "Are you discussing with one another what I said, 'A little while and you will not see me, and again a little while and you will see me'? 20* Amen, amen, I say to you, you will weep and mourn, while the world rejoices; you will grieve, but your grief will become joy. 21* When a woman is in labor, she is in anguish because her hour has arrived; but when she has given birth to a child, she no longer remembers the pain because of her joy that a child has been born into the world. 22* So you also are now in anguish. But I will see you again, and your hearts will rejoice, and no one will take your joy away from you. 23* On that day you will not question me about anything. Amen, amen, I say to you, whatever you ask the Father in my name he will give you. 24 Until now you have not asked anything in my name; ask and you will receive, so that your joy may be complete.

25*† "I have told you this in figures of speech. The hour is coming when I will no longer speak to you in figures but I will tell you clearly about the Father. 26* On that day you will ask in my name, and I do not tell you that I will ask the Father for you. 27 For the Father himself loves you, because you have loved me and have come to believe that I came from God. 28* I came from the Father and have come into the world. Now I am leaving the world and going back to the Father." 29 His disciples said, "Now you are talking plainly, and not in any figure of speech. 30† Now we realize that you know everything and that you do not need to have anyone question you. Because of this we believe that you came from God." 31 Jesus answered them, "Do you believe now? 32*† Behold, the hour is coming and has arrived when each of you will be scattered to his own home and you will leave me alone. But I am not alone, because the Father is with me. 33* I have told you this so that you might have peace in me. In the world you will have

trouble, but take courage, I have conquered the world."

The Prayer of Jesus†

17 1* When Jesus had said this, he raised his eyes to heaven† and said, "Father, the hour has come. Give glory to your son, so that your son may glorify you, 2*† just as you gave him authority over all people, so that he may give eternal life to all you gave him. 3*† Now this is eternal life, that they should know you, the only true God, and the one whom you sent, Jesus Christ. 4 I glorified you on earth by accomplishing the work that you gave me to do. 5* Now glorify me, Father, with you, with the glory that I had with you before the world began.

6† "I revealed your name to those whom you gave me out of the world. They belonged to you, and you gave them to me, and they have kept your word. 7 Now they know that everything you gave me is from you, 8 because the words you gave to me I have given to them, and they accepted them and truly understood that I came from you, and they have believed that you sent me. 9* I pray for them. I do not pray for the world but for the ones you have given me, because they are yours, 10* and everything of mine is yours and everything of yours is mine, and I have been glorified in them. 11 And now I will no longer be in the world, but they are in the world, while I am coming to you. Holy Father, keep them in your name that you have given me, so that they may be one just as we are. 12* When I was with them I protected them in your name that you gave me, and I guarded them, and none of them was lost except the son of destruction, in order that the scripture might be fulfilled. 13* But now I am coming to you. I speak this in the world so that they may share my joy completely. 14* I gave them your word, and the world hated them, because they do not belong to the world any more than I belong to the world.

J
N

16, 25: See the note on 10, 6. Here, possibly a reference to 15, 1–16 or 16, 21.

16, 30: The reference is seemingly to the fact that Jesus could anticipate their question in v 19. The disciples naively think they have the full understanding that is the climax of "the hour" of Jesus' death, resurrection, and ascension (25), but the only part of the hour that is at hand for them is their share in the passion (32).

16, 32: *You will be scattered:* cf Mk 14, 27 and Mt 26, 31, where both cite Zec 13, 7 about the sheep being dispersed.

17, 1–26: Climax of the last discourse(s). Since the sixteenth century, this chapter has been called the "high priestly prayer" of Jesus. He speaks as intercessor, with words addressed directly to the Father and not to the disciples, who supposedly only overhear. Yet the prayer is one of petition, for immediate (6–19) and future (20–21) disciples. Many phrases reminiscent of the Lord's Prayer occur. Although still in the world (13), Jesus looks on his earthly ministry as a thing of the past (4.12). Whereas Jesus has up to this time stated that the disciples could follow him (13, 33.36), now he wishes them to be with him in union with the Father (12–14).

17, 1: The action of looking up to heaven and the address *Father* are typical of Jesus at prayer; cf 11, 41 and Lk 11, 2.

17, 2: Another possible interpretation is to treat the first line of the verse as parenthetical and the second as an appositive to the clause that ends v 1: *so that your son may glorify you (just as . . . all people), so that he may give eternal life. . . .*

17, 3: This verse was clearly added in the editing of the gospel as a reflection on the preceding verse; Jesus nowhere else refers to himself as Jesus Christ.

17, 6: *I revealed your name:* perhaps the name *I AM;* cf 8, 24.28.58; 13, 19.

16, 20: Ps 126, 6.	**17, 2:** Jn 3, 35; Mt 28, 18.
16, 21: Is 26, 17–18; Jer 31, 13; Mic 4, 9.	**17, 3:** Jn 1, 17; Wis 14, 7; 15, 3; 1 Jn 5, 20.
16, 22: Jn 14, 19; 15, 11; 20, 20.	**17, 5:** Jn 1, 1.2; 12, 28; Phil 2, 6.9–11.
16, 23: Jn 14, 13.	**17, 9:** Jn 17, 20.
16, 25: Mt 13, 34–35.	**17, 10:** Jn 16, 15; 2 Thes 1, 10.12.
16, 26: Jn 14, 13.	
16, 28: Jn 1, 1.	**17, 12:** Jn 13, 18; 18, 9; Ps 41, 10; Mt 26, 24; Acts 1, 16.
16, 32: Jn 8, 29; Zec 13, 7; Mt 26, 31; Mk 14, 27.	**17, 13:** Jn 15, 11.
16, 33: Jn 14, 27.	**17, 14:** Jn 15, 19.
17, 1: Jn 13, 31.	

15*† I do not ask that you take them out of the world but that you keep them from the evil one. 16 They do not belong to the world any more than I belong to the world. 17* Consecrate them in the truth. Your word is truth. 18* As you sent me into the world, so I sent them into the world. 19 And I consecrate myself for them, so that they also may be consecrated in truth.

20 "I pray not only for them, but also for those who will believe in me through their word, 21* so that they may all be one, as you, Father, are in me and I in you, that they also may be in us, that the world may believe that you sent me. 22 And I have given them the glory you gave me, so that they may be one, as we are one, 23 I in them and you in me, that they may be brought to perfection as one, that the world may know that you sent me, and that you loved them even as you loved me. 24*† Father, they are your gift to me. I wish that where I am they also may be with me, that they may see my glory that you gave me, because you

JN

A Prayer for Friends

In John, chapter 17, Jesus prays for his friends, the disciples. And he also prays for us, his future disciples (verse 20)! Here is a prayer you can say for your friends:

Dear Jesus, thank you for my true friends. They accept me for who I am. With them, I don't have to pretend to be someone else. They support me when I feel that the world is crumbling around me. They are honest with me even if what they say is not what I want to hear. They offer their sense of humor so that we can laugh together.

Spirit of Jesus, watch over these friends just as you watch over me. Show them your loving acceptance and support. Help them to honestly look at themselves and the decisions they are making. If they experience pain, frustration, or failure, give them strength to lean on you. Fill their days with laughter and love. Protect them and keep them safe all the days of their lives. Amen.

▸ John, chapter 17

Catholic Connections

THE WORK OF THE TRINITY

Have you ever wondered who forgives us when we confess our sins? Sometimes you hear that it is Jesus who forgives, like in the sacrament of Penance and Reconciliation; other times you may hear it is God the Father who forgives sin. Whose job is it anyway?

There is a bit of confusion about how the three persons of the Trinity work in our lives, in general, and in the sacraments, in particular. The answer is simple: God forgives our sins, and that means the Father, and the Son, and the Holy Spirit together forgive our sins in one divine action. Together, as one God, they are responsible for all the things that bring us grace and salvation.

In Jn 14, 9–11, Jesus says to Philip: "Whoever has seen me has seen the Father. How can you say, 'Show us the Father'?" In fact, throughout chapters 14–17, Jesus alludes to the unity of the Father, the Son, and the Holy Spirit (see Jn 15, 18–27 and 17, 10–11, 21–23a). When the Father or the Son or the Holy Spirit acts, the whole Trinity acts. The three persons of the Holy Trinity are inseparable in who they are and in what they do.

So what is the best way to deal with the Holy Trinity? Again, the answer is rather simple—pray. Pray to the one God, the Father and the Son and the Holy Spirit, who will draw you ever closer to the one Divine Presence.

O Blessed Trinity, one and three, fill me with your presence that I may live and love with you, Father, Son, and Holy Spirit, forever and ever. Amen

▸ Jn 17, 21–23

17, 15: Note the resemblance to the petition of the Lord's Prayer, "deliver us from the evil one." Both probably refer to the devil rather than to abstract evil.

17, 24: *Where I am:* Jesus prays for the believers ultimately to join him in heaven. Then they will not see his glory as in a mirror but clearly (2 Cor 3, 18; 1 Jn 3, 2).

17, 15: Mt 6, 13; 2 Thes 3, 3; 1 Jn 5, 18.
17, 17: 1 Pt 1, 22
17, 18: Jn 20, 21–22.
17, 21: Jn 10, 30; 14, 10–11.20.
17, 24: Jn 14, 3; 1 Thes 4, 17.

Cultural Connections

RACE RELATIONS

On 4 April 2001, the thirty-third anniversary of the death of Martin Luther King Jr., Cardinal George of the Archdiocese of Chicago published a letter to the faithful titled "Dwell in My Love." In it, Cardinal George challenges us to look at Jn 17, 7-10, in which Jesus invites us to dwell in his love. Cardinal George makes the point that all people, races, cultures, and nationalities are part of the human family and that Jesus invites us to be unified in his love.

Race is a gift from God that underscores our uniqueness. It is important for us to celebrate our differences in a way that brings us together as followers of Jesus. The bottom line of Cardinal George's letter is that our diversity enriches us, making life more full and interesting.

Think of all the ways in which people of different races, cultures, and nationalities have brought richness to your community, family, parish, and school.

▶ Jn 17, 7–10

---

loved me before the foundation of the world. 25* Righteous Father, the world also does not know you, but I know you, and they know that you sent me. 26† I made known to them your name and I will make it known, that the love with which you loved me may be in them and I in them."

Jesus Arrested†

18 1* When he had said this, Jesus went out† with his disciples across the Kidron valley to where there was a garden, into which he and his disciples entered. 2 Judas his betrayer also knew the place, because Jesus had often met there with his disciples. 3*† So Judas got a band of soldiers and guards from the chief priests and the Pharisees and went there with lanterns, torches, and weapons. 4 Jesus, knowing everything that was going to happen to him, went out and said to them, "Whom are you looking for?" 5† They answered

him, "Jesus the Nazorean." He said to them, "I AM." Judas his betrayer was also with them. 6 When he said to them, "I AM," they turned away and fell to the ground. 7 So he again asked them, "Whom are you looking for?" They said, "Jesus the Nazorean." 8 Jesus answered, "I told you that I AM. So if you are looking for me, let these men go." 9*† This was to fulfill what he had said, "I have not lost any of those you gave me." 10† Then Simon Peter, who had a sword, drew it, struck the high priest's slave, and cut off his right ear. The slave's name was Malchus. 11*† Jesus said to Peter, "Put your sword into its scabbard. Shall I not drink the cup that the Father gave me?"

12* So the band of soldiers, the tribune, and the Jewish guards seized Jesus, bound him, 13*† and brought him to Annas first. He was the father-in-law of Caiaphas, who was high priest that year. 14* It was Caiaphas who had counseled the Jews

---

17, 26: *I will make it known:* through the Advocate.

18, 1–14: John does not mention the agony in the garden and the kiss of Judas, nor does he identify the place as Gethsemane or the Mount of Olives.

18, 1: *Jesus went out:* see 14, 31, where it seems he is leaving the supper room. *Kidron valley:* literally, "the winter-flowing Kidron"; this wadi has water only during the winter rains.

18, 3: *Band of soldiers:* seems to refer to Roman troops, either the full cohort of 600 men (1/10 of a legion), or more likely the maniple of 200 under their tribune (12). In this case, John is hinting at Roman collusion in the action against Jesus before he was brought to Pilate. The *lanterns* and *torches* may be symbolic of the hour of darkness.

18, 5: *Nazorean:* the form found in Mt 26, 71 (see the note on Mt 2, 23) is here used, not *Nazarene* of Mark. *I AM:* or "I am he," but probably intended by the evangelist as an expression of divinity (cf their appropriate response in 6); see the note on 8, 24. John sets the confusion of the arresting party against the background of Jesus' divine majesty.

18, 9: The citation may refer to 6, 39; 10, 28; or 17, 12.

18, 10: Only John gives the names of the two antagonists; both John and Luke mention the right ear.

18, 11: The theme of the cup is found in the synoptic account of the agony (Mk 14, 36 and parallels).

18, 13: *Annas:* only John mentions an inquiry before Annas; cf 16.19–24; see the note on Lk 3, 2. It is unlikely that this nighttime interrogation before Annas is the same as the trial before Caiaphas placed by Matthew and Mark at night and by Luke in the morning.

17, 25: Jn 1, 10.
18, 1: 2 Sm 15, 23; Mt 26, 30.36; Mk 14, 26.32; Lk 22, 39.
18, 3: Mt 26, 47–51; Mk 14, 43–44; Lk 22, 47.
18, 9: Jn 6, 39; 10, 28; 17, 12.

18, 11: Mt 20, 22; 26, 39; Mk 10, 38; Lk 22, 42.
18, 12–14: Mt 26, 57–58; Mk 14, 53–54; Lk 22, 54–55.
18, 13: Lk 3, 2.
18, 14: Jn 11, 49–50.

that it was better that one man should die rather than the people.

Peter's First Denial

¹⁵*† Simon Peter and another disciple followed Jesus. Now the other disciple was known to the high priest, and he entered the courtyard of the high priest with Jesus. ¹⁶ But Peter stood at the gate outside. So the other disciple, the acquaintance of the high priest, went out and spoke to the gatekeeper and brought Peter in. ¹⁷ Then the maid who was the gatekeeper said to Peter, "You are not one of this man's disciples, are you?" He said, "I am not." ¹⁸ Now the slaves and the guards were standing around a charcoal fire that they had made, because it was cold, and were warming themselves. Peter was also standing there keeping warm.

The Inquiry before Annas

¹⁹* The high priest questioned Jesus about his disciples and about his doctrine. ²⁰*† Jesus answered him, "I have spoken publicly to the world. I have always taught in a synagogue or in the temple area where all the Jews gather, and in secret I have said nothing. ²¹ Why ask me? Ask those who heard me what I said to them. They know what I said." ²²* When he had said this, one of the temple guards standing there struck Jesus and said, "Is this the way you answer the high priest?" ²³ Jesus answered him, "If I have spoken wrongly, testify to the wrong; but if I have spoken rightly, why do you strike me?" ²⁴*† Then Annas sent him bound to Caiaphas the high priest.

Peter Denies Jesus Again

²⁵* Now Simon Peter was standing there keeping warm. And they said to him, "You are not one of his disciples, are you?" He denied it and said, "I am not." ²⁶ One of the slaves of the high priest, a relative of the one whose ear Peter had cut off, said, "Didn't I see you in the garden with him?" ²⁷† Again Peter denied it. And immediately the cock crowed.

The Trial before Pilate

²⁸*† Then they brought Jesus from Caiaphas to the praetorium. It was morning. And they

Catholic Connections

EASTER TRIDUUM

For Catholics, the center of the liturgical year is the Easter Triduum, the three holy days that celebrate Jesus' death and Resurrection. The Triduum begins on Holy Thursday, the Thursday before Easter. The reading for the day, Jn 13, 1–15, recounts the Last Supper and Christ's humility when washing the feet of the disciples.

Holy Thursday is followed by Good Friday, during which John's account of Jesus' Passion (chapters 18–19) is read. During the service, Catholics venerate (honor) the cross, recalling Jesus' painful sacrifice that God used for our salvation.

The climax to the Triduum is the Easter Vigil held on Saturday evening, beginning after nightfall. This celebration incorporates a dramatic ceremony of light in which the Easter fire is lit, followed by the lighting of the paschal (Jesus) candle and of a candle for every person in the church. Then those who have been preparing to join the church are baptized, confirmed, and welcomed to receive the Eucharist.

The Easter Triduum, although celebrated over three days, is actually one celebration, from the opening song on Holy Thursday to the closing song of the Easter Vigil.

▶ Jn 13, 1—20, 18

18, 15–16: *Another disciple . . . the other disciple:* see the note on 13, 23.

18, 20: *I have always taught . . . in the temple area:* cf Mk 14, 49 for a similar statement.

18, 24: *Caiaphas:* see Mt 26, 3.57; Lk 3, 2; and the notes there. John may leave room here for the trial before Caiaphas described in the synoptic gospels.

18, 27: Cockcrow was the third Roman division of the night, lasting from midnight to 3 a.m.

18, 28: *Praetorium:* see the note on Mt 27, 27. *Morning:* literally, "the early hour," or fourth Roman division of the night, 3 to 6 a.m. *The Passover:* the synoptic gospels give the impression that the Thursday night supper was the Passover meal (Mk 14, 12); for John that meal is still to be eaten Friday night.

18, 15–18: Mt 26, 58.69–70; Mk 14, 54.66–68; Lk 22, 54–57.
18, 19–24: Mt 26, 59–66; Mk 14, 55–64; Lk 22, 66–71.
18, 20: Jn 6, 59; 7, 14.26; Is 48, 16; Mt 26, 55; Mk 4, 23; Lk 19, 47; 22, 53.
18, 22: Acts 23, 2.
18, 24: Mt 26, 57.
18, 25–27: Mt 26, 71–75; Mk 14, 69–72; Lk 22, 58–62.
18, 28–38a: Mt 27, 1–2.11–25; Mk 15, 1–5; Lk 23, 1–5.

?did you KNOW?

The Triumph of Jesus

The Gospel of John most closely resembles the other three Gospels in its stories of Jesus' trial, death, and Resurrection. But even here, John's unique portrayal of Jesus is seen. The most obvious difference is that in John, Jesus is clearly in charge and in his glory from the moment he is arrested. There is no agony in the garden. When the soldiers and police come to arrest Jesus, they fall to the ground as he speaks (18, 6). He teaches Pilate about his identity and mission, in essence putting Pilate on trial (verses 33–38). Jesus brings together his mother and the Beloved Disciple (19, 26–27). Jesus is not killed but decides the moment of his death when he gives up his spirit (verse 30).

John is also careful to show in detail the ways Jesus' Crucifixion fulfills Old Testament prophecies of the Messiah. He identifies Jesus with the just man who was persecuted in Psalms 22 and 69. He does this by connecting the gambling for Jesus' seamless tunic (Jn 19, 24) with Ps 22, 19, and the offering of sour wine (Jn 19, 29) with Ps 69, 22. Jesus' unbroken legs (Jn 19, 33) are a reference to the paschal lamb in Ex 12, 46, and his pierced side (Jn 19, 34) is seen as the fulfillment of Zec 12, 10.

John wants us to know that these events are the central "Hour" in the world's history and the time of Jesus' triumph. For the author of John, Jesus is clearly the divine Son of God, and by Jesus' self-sacrifice, God brings salvation to the entire world. The author of John wants to focus us not on the tragedy but on God's power at work in Jesus.

▸ John, chapters 18–19

themselves did not enter the praetorium, in order not to be defiled so that they could eat the Passover. [29] So Pilate came out to them and said, "What charge do you bring [against] this man?" [30] They answered and said to him, "If he were not a criminal, we would not have handed him over to you." [31]† At this, Pilate said to them, "Take him yourselves, and judge him according to your law." The Jews answered him, "We do not have the right to execute anyone," [32]*† in order that the word of Jesus might be fulfilled that he said indicating the kind of death he would die. [33] So Pilate went back into the praetorium and summoned Jesus and said to him, "Are you the King of the Jews?" [34] Jesus answered, "Do you say this on your own or have others told you about me?" [35]* Pilate answered, "I am not a Jew, am I? Your own nation and the chief priests handed you over to me. What have you done?" [36]* Jesus answered, "My kingdom does not belong to this world. If my kingdom did belong to this world, my attendants [would] be fighting to keep me from being handed over to the Jews. But as it is, my kingdom is not here." [37]*† So Pilate said to him, "Then you are a king?" Jesus answered, "You say I am a king. For this I was born and for this I came into the world, to testify to the truth. Everyone who belongs to the truth listens to my voice." [38]* Pilate said to him, "What is truth?"

When he had said this, he again went out to the Jews and said to them, "I find no guilt in him. [39]† But you have a custom that I release one prisoner to you at Passover. Do you want me to release to you the King of the Jews?" [40]† They cried out again, "Not this one but Barabbas!" Now Barabbas was a revolutionary.

19 [1]*† Then Pilate took Jesus and had him scourged. [2] And the soldiers wove a crown out of thorns and placed it on his head, and clothed him in a purple cloak, [3] and they came to him and said, "Hail, King of the Jews!" And they struck him repeatedly. [4]* Once more Pilate went out and said to them, "Look, I am bringing him out to you, so that you may know that I find no guilt in him." [5]* So

to the high priest. It is at best a reluctant affirmative.

18, 39: See the note on Mt 27, 15.

18, 40: *Barabbas:* see the note on Mt 27, 16–17. *Revolutionary:* a guerrilla warrior fighting for nationalistic aims, though the term can also denote a robber. See the note on Mt 27, 38.

19, 1: Luke places the mockery of Jesus at the midpoint in the trial when Jesus was sent to Herod. Mark and Matthew place the scourging and mockery at the end of the trial after the sentence of death. Scourging was an integral part of the crucifixion penalty.

18, 31: *We do not have the right to execute anyone:* only John gives this reason for their bringing Jesus to Pilate. Jewish sources are not clear on the competence of the Sanhedrin at this period to sentence and to execute for political crimes.

18, 32: The Jewish punishment for blasphemy was stoning (Lv 24, 16). In coming to the Romans to ensure that Jesus would be crucified, the Jewish authorities fulfilled his prophecy that he would be *exalted* (3, 14; 12, 32–33). There is some historical evidence, however, for Jews crucifying Jews.

18, 37: *You say I am a king:* see Mt 26, 64 for a similar response

18, 32: Jn 3, 14; 8, 28; 12, 32–33.
18, 35: Jn 1, 11.
18, 36: Jn 1, 10; 8, 23.
18, 37: Jn 8, 47; 1 Tm 6,
 · 13.18, 38b–40, Mt
 27, 15–26; Mk 15,

 6–15; Lk 23, 18–25;
 Acts 3, 14.
19, 1–16: Mt 27, 27–31; Mk 15,
 16–20; Lk 23, 13–25.
19, 4: Jn 18, 38.
19, 5: Is 52, 14.

Jesus came out, wearing the crown of thorns and the purple cloak. And he said to them, "Behold, the man!" 6* When the chief priests and the guards saw him they cried out, "Crucify him, crucify him!" Pilate said to them, "Take him yourselves and crucify him. I find no guilt in him." 7*† The Jews answered, "We have a law, and according to that law he ought to die, because he made himself the Son of God." 8 Now when Pilate heard this statement, he became even more afraid, 9* and went back into the praetorium and said to Jesus, "Where are you from?" Jesus did not answer him. 10 So Pilate said to him, "Do you not speak to me? Do you not know that I have power to release you and I have power to crucify you?" 11* Jesus answered [him], "You would have no power over me if it had not been given to you from above. For this reason the one who handed me over to you has the greater sin." 12*† Consequently, Pilate tried to release him; but the Jews cried out, "If you release him, you are not a Friend of Caesar. Everyone who makes himself a king opposes Caesar."

13† When Pilate heard these words he brought Jesus out and seated him on the judge's bench in the place called Stone Pavement, in Hebrew, Gabbatha. 14† It was preparation day for Passover, and it was about noon. And he said to the Jews, "Behold, your king!" 15 They cried out, "Take him away, take him away! Crucify him!" Pilate said to them, "Shall I crucify your king?" The chief priests answered, "We have no king but Caesar." 16† Then he handed him over to them to be crucified.

The Crucifixion of Jesus

So they took Jesus, 17*† and carrying the cross himself he went out to what is called the Place of the Skull, in Hebrew, Golgotha. 18 There they crucified him, and with him two others, one on either side, with Jesus in the middle. 19† Pilate also had an inscription written and put on the

---

19, 7: *Made himself the Son of God:* this question was not raised in John's account of the Jewish interrogations of Jesus as it was in the synoptic accounts. Nevertheless, see 5, 18; 8, 53; 10, 36.

19, 12: *Friend of Caesar:* a Roman honorific title bestowed upon high-ranking officials for merit.

19, 13: *Seated him:* others translate "(Pilate) sat down." In John's thought, Jesus is the real judge of the world, and John may here be portraying him seated on the judgment bench. *Stone Pavement:* in Greek *lithostrotos;* under the fortress Antonia, one of the conjectured locations of the praetorium, a massive stone pavement has been excavated. *Gabbatha* (Aramaic rather than Hebrew) probably means "ridge, elevation."

19, 14: *Noon:* Mk 15, 25 has Jesus crucified "at the third hour," which means either 9 a.m. or the period from 9 to 12. Noon, the time when, according to John, Jesus was sentenced to death, was the hour at which the priests began to slaughter Passover lambs in the temple; see Jn 1, 29.

19, 16: *He handed him over to them to be crucified:* in context this would seem to mean "handed him over to the chief priests." Lk 23, 25 has a similar ambiguity. There is a polemic tendency in the gospels to place the guilt of the crucifixion on the Jewish authorities

---

did you KNOW?

The Words on the Cross

In the Gospel of John, Pontius Pilate acts as a mediator between two worlds—the outside world of darkness and unbelief and the inner world of light and truth. During Jesus' trial, Pilate goes back and forth between the Jewish religious authorities who are outside (in the dark) and Jesus, who is inside Pilate's headquarters (in the light).

Does Pilate know the truth about Jesus? When he writes out the charges to be placed on the cross, "the Jews" (see "'The Jews' in the Gospel of John," Jn 2, 18–20) argue with him about the wording. He answers by saying, "What I have written, I have written" (19, 22), that is, "These words are the truth about Jesus." The words he writes are "Jesus the Nazorean, the King of the Jews" (verse 19). In Latin, they read, "*Iesus Nazarenus Rex Iudaeorum.*" When artists draw or sculpt the Crucifixion scene, they often include this Latin phrase in abbreviated form above the cross—*INRI.*

In another of the Gospel's ironies, Pilate recognizes what the Jewish leaders rejected—Jesus Christ is a king. Christians believe a deeper truth—Christ is king not only of the Jews but of all creation! On the last Sunday of the liturgical year, the Catholic church celebrates this in the feast of Christ the King.

▶ Jn 19, 19–22

---

and to exonerate the Romans from blame. But John later mentions the Roman soldiers (23), and it was to these soldiers that Pilate handed Jesus over.

19, 17: *Carrying the cross himself:* a different picture from that of the synoptics, especially Lk 23, 26, where Simon of Cyrene is made to carry the cross, walking behind Jesus. In John's theology, Jesus remained in complete control and master of his destiny (cf 10, 18). *Place of the Skull:* the Latin word for skull is *Calvaria;* hence "Calvary." *Golgotha* is actually an Aramaic rather than a Hebrew word.

19, 19: The inscription differs with slightly different words in each of the four gospels. John's form is fullest and gives the equivalent of the Latin *INRI = Jesus Nazarenus Rex Iudaeorum.* Only John mentions its polyglot character (20) and Pilate's role in keeping the title unchanged (21–22).

19, 6: Jn 18, 31; 19, 15.
19, 7: Jn 10, 33–36; Lv 24, 16.
19, 9: Jn 7, 28.

19, 11: Jn 3, 27; 10, 18; Rom 13, 1.
19, 12: Acts 17, 7.
19, 17–22: Mt 27, 32–37; Mk 15, 21–26; Lk 23, 26–35.

cross. It read, "Jesus the Nazorean, the King of the Jews." 20 Now many of the Jews read this inscription, because the place where Jesus was crucified was near the city; and it was written in Hebrew, Latin, and Greek. 21* So the chief priests of the Jews said to Pilate, "Do not write 'The King of the Jews,' but that he said, 'I am the King of the Jews.' " 22 Pilate answered, "What I have written, I have written."

23*† When the soldiers had crucified Jesus, they took his clothes and divided them into four shares, a share for each soldier.* They also took his tunic,

but the tunic was seamless, woven in one piece from the top down. 24 So they said to one another, "Let's not tear it, but cast lots for it to see whose it will be," in order that the passage of scripture might be fulfilled [that says]:

> "They divided my garments among them,
>   and for my vesture they cast lots."

This is what the soldiers did. 25*† Standing by the cross of Jesus were his mother and his mother's sister, Mary the wife of Clopas, and Mary of

OUR MOTHER OF GUADALUPE, A GIFT FROM GOD!

Devotion to Mary as mother of God and mother of the church has been a consistent dimension of Christian faith. From Jesus' words on the cross in Jn 19, 25–27, Christians have identified with the Beloved Disciple and seen Mary as their mother. This experience has led Catholics of many countries to name Mary as their patroness (advocate, protector, supporter, mother): for instance, they call her Virgin of the Immaculate Conception in the United States and Chile, Virgin of Lourdes in France, and Virgin of Fátima in Portugal. The strong devotion of Latin American countries to Mary as a mother who protects and assists her children is revealed in their titles for her: Our Lady of Mercy in the Dominican Republic, Our Lady of Caridad del Cobre (charity) in Cuba, Our Lady of Divine Providence in Puerto Rico, and Our Lady of Help in Guatemala, to name a few.

But Mexico developed the strongest devotion to Mary as mother of a nation. The Virgin of Guadalupe appeared to Saint Juan Diego, a humble native from Tenochtitlán, near Mexico City. She had the face of the mestizo people (the descendants of native and Spanish peoples), and her words to Juan Diego were those of a caring mother, especially for her children who are suffering, poor, or oppressed:

> **Here I wish to hear and help you, and all who dwell in this land and all those who love me, and invoke and place their confidence in me; and to hear your complaints and remedy all your sorrows, hardships, and suffering. . . .**
>
> **Listen and understand well my son, smallest of all, that you have no cause to be frightened. . . . Is this not your mother here next to you? Are you not here in the shelter of my loving shadow? . . . Let nothing worry or afflict you further. . . . (Office of Religious Education, *A Handbook on Guadalupe*, pp. 148, 152)**

▸ **Jn 19, 25–27**

19, 23–25a: While all four gospels describe the soldiers casting lots to divide Jesus' garments (see the note on Mt 27, 35), only John quotes the underlying passage from Ps 22, 19, and only John sees each line of the poetic parallelism literally carried out in two separate actions (23a; 23b-24).

19, 25: It is not clear whether four women are meant, or three (i.e., *Mary the wife of Cl[e]opas* [cf Lk 24, 18] is in apposition with *his mother's sister*) or two (his mother and his mother's sister, i.e.,

Mary of Cl[e]opas and Mary of Magdala). Only John mentions the mother of Jesus here. The synoptics have a group of women looking on from a distance at the cross (Mk 15, 40).

19, 21: Jn 18, 33; Lk 19, 14.   19, 23–24: Ps 22, 19; Mt 27, 35;
19, 23–27: Mt 27, 38–44; Mk 15,   Mk 15, 24; Lk 23, 34.
    27–32; Lk 23, 36–43.   19, 25: Mt 27, 55; Mk 15,
                                       40–41; Lk 8, 2; 23, 49.

Magdala. 26*† When Jesus saw his mother and the disciple there whom he loved, he said to his mother, "Woman, behold, your son." 27 Then he said to the disciple, "Behold, your mother." And from that hour the disciple took her into his home.

28*† After this, aware that everything was now finished, in order that the scripture might be fulfilled, Jesus said, "I thirst."* 29† There was a vessel filled with common wine. So they put a sponge soaked in wine on a sprig of hyssop and put it up to his mouth. 30*† When Jesus had taken the wine, he said, "It is finished." And bowing his head, he handed over the spirit.

The Blood and Water

31* Now since it was preparation day, in order that the bodies might not remain on the cross on the sabbath, for the sabbath day of that week was a solemn one, the Jews asked Pilate that their legs be broken and they be taken down. 32 So the soldiers came and broke the legs of the first and then of the other one who was crucified with Jesus. 33 But when they came to Jesus and saw that he was already dead, they did not break his legs, 34*† but one soldier thrust his lance into his side, and immediately blood and water flowed out. 35*† An eyewitness has testified, and his testimony is true; he knows that he is speaking the truth, so that you also may [come to] believe. 36* For this happened so that the scripture passage might be fulfilled:

"Not a bone of it will be broken."

37* And again another passage says:

"They will look upon him whom they
    have pierced."

Introducing

▶MARY MAGDALENE

Like the Samaritan woman, who is the first to spread the word that Jesus is the Messiah (Jn 4, 1–42), Mary Magdalene is the first to announce that Jesus has been raised from the dead. She comes to the tomb while it is still dark (symbolizing unbelief). Later, she encounters the risen Jesus and begins to see with eyes of faith. Belief prompts her to action, and so she goes to tell the others, "I have seen the Lord" (verse 18).

Mary Magdalene is first in every listing of Jesus' female disciples (Mt 27, 55–56; Mk 15, 40–41; Lk 8, 2–3). She seems to have been the leader of a group of women who followed Jesus from the beginning of his ministry, through his death and beyond. Luke indicates that Jesus cured her of seven demons (8, 2). All four Gospels name her as one of the first eyewitnesses of Jesus' Resurrection. From all this, we can presume that she was a special friend and disciple of Jesus and an important leader among the first Christians.

▶ Jn 20, 1–18

19, 26–27: This scene has been interpreted literally, of Jesus' concern for his mother; and symbolically, e.g., in the light of the Cana story in ch 2 (the presence of the mother of Jesus, the address woman, and the mention of the hour) and of the upper room in ch 13 (the presence of the beloved disciple; the hour). Now that the hour has come (28), Mary (a symbol of the church?) is given a role as the mother of Christians (personified by the beloved disciple); or, as a representative of those seeking salvation, she is supported by the disciple who interprets Jesus' revelation; or Jewish and Gentile Christianity (or Israel and the Christian community) are reconciled.

19, 28: The scripture . . . fulfilled: either in the scene of vv 25–27, or in the I thirst of v 28. If the latter, Pss 22, 16 and 69, 22 deserve consideration.

19, 29: Wine: John does not mention the drugged wine, a narcotic that Jesus refused as the crucifixion began (Mk 15, 23), but only this final gesture of kindness at the end (Mk 15, 36). Hyssop, a small plant, is scarcely suitable for carrying a sponge (Mark mentions a reed) and may be a symbolic reference to the hyssop used to daub the blood of the paschal lamb on the doorpost of the Hebrews (Ex 12, 22).

19, 30: Handed over the spirit: there is a double nuance of dying (giving up the last breath or spirit) and that of passing on the holy Spirit; see 7, 39, which connects the giving of the Spirit with Jesus' glorious return to the Father, and 20, 22, where the author portrays the conferral of the Spirit.

19, 34–35: John probably emphasizes these verses to show the reality of Jesus' death, against the docetic heretics. In the blood and water there may also be a symbolic reference to the Eucharist and baptism.

19, 35: He knows: it is not certain from the Greek that this he is the eyewitness of the first part of the sentence. May [come to] believe: see the note on 20, 31.

19, 26: Jn 13, 23.
19, 28–30: Mt 27, 45–56; Mk 15, 33–41; Lk 23, 44–49.
19, 28: Pss 22, 16; 69, 22.
19, 30: Jn 4, 34; 10, 18; 17, 4; Lk 23, 46.
19, 31: Ex 12, 16; Dt 21, 23.
19, 34: Nm 20, 11; 1 Jn 5, 6.
19, 35: Jn 7, 37–39; 21, 24.
19, 36: Ex 12, 46; Nm 9, 12; Ps 34, 21.
19, 37: Nm 21, 9; Zec 12, 10; Rv 1, 7.

The Burial of Jesus

38*† After this, Joseph of Arimathea, secretly a disciple of Jesus for fear of the Jews, asked Pilate if he could remove the body of Jesus. And Pilate permitted it. So he came and took his body. 39* Nicodemus, the one who had first come to him at night, also came bringing a mixture of myrrh and aloes weighing about one hundred pounds. 40 They took the body of Jesus and bound it with burial cloths along with the spices, according to the Jewish burial custom. 41 Now in the place where he had been crucified there was a garden, and in the garden a new tomb, in which no one had yet been buried. 42 So they laid Jesus there because of the Jewish preparation day; for the tomb was close by.

The Empty Tomb†

20 1*† On the first day of the week, Mary of Magdala came to the tomb early in the morning, while it was still dark,† and saw the stone removed from the tomb.* 2† So she ran and went to Simon Peter and to the other disciple whom Jesus loved, and told them, "They have taken the Lord from the tomb, and we don't know where they put him." 3† So Peter and the other disciple went out and came to the tomb. 4 They both ran, but the other disciple ran faster than Peter and arrived at the tomb first; 5 he bent down and saw the burial cloths there, but did not go in. 6*† When Simon Peter arrived after him, he went into the tomb and saw the burial cloths there, 7* and the cloth that had covered his head, not with the burial cloths but rolled up in a separate place. 8 Then the other disciple also went in, the one who had arrived at the tomb first, and he saw and believed. 9*† For they did not yet understand the scripture that he had to rise from the dead. 10 Then the disciples returned home.

The Appearance to Mary of Magdala

11*† But Mary stayed outside the tomb weeping. And as she wept, she bent over into the tomb 12 and

Catholic Connections

RECONCILIATION

In Jn 20, 21–23, Jesus empowers his disciples to forgive the sins of others in his name. This is one of the Bible passages that the Catholic church teaches is the basis for the sacrament of Reconciliation (or Penance). Some may know this sacrament by the term confession, because we confess our sins to a priest. The priest serves as a representative of both God and the community in the sacrament. But confessing our sins is only one step in the reconciliation process. We must also be truly sorry and attempt to repair the damage our sin has done. By seeking true reconciliation through the sacrament, we restore the peace of the risen Christ.

▶ Jn 20, 21–23

saw two angels in white sitting there, one at the head and one at the feet where the body of Jesus had been. 13 And they said to her, "Woman, why are you weeping?" She said to them, "They have taken my Lord, and I don't know where they laid him." 14* When she had said this, she turned around and saw Jesus there, but did not know it was Jesus. 15* Jesus said to her, "Woman, why are you weeping? Whom are you looking for?" She thought it was the gardener and said to him, "Sir, if you

---

19, 38–42: In the first three gospels there is no anointing on Friday. In Matthew and Luke, the women come to the tomb on Sunday morning precisely to anoint Jesus.

20, 1–31: The risen Jesus reveals his glory and confers the Spirit. This story fulfills the basic need for testimony to the resurrection. What we have here is not a record but a series of single stories.

20, 1–10: The story of the empty tomb is found in both the Matthean and the Lucan traditions; John's version seems to be a fusion of the two.

20, 1: *Still dark:* according to Mark the sun had risen, Matthew describes it as "dawning," and Luke refers to early dawn. Mary sees the stone removed, not the empty tomb.

20, 2: Mary runs away, not directed by an angel/young man as in the synoptic accounts. The plural "we" in the second part of her statement might reflect a tradition of more women going to the tomb.

20, 3–10: The basic narrative is told of Peter alone in Lk 24, 12, a verse missing in important manuscripts and which may be borrowed from tradition similar to John. Cf also Lk 24, 24.

20, 6–8: Some special feature about the state of the burial cloths caused the beloved disciple to believe. Perhaps the details emphasized that the grave had not been robbed.

20, 9: Probably a general reference to the scriptures is intended, as in Lk 24, 26 and 1 Cor 15, 4. Some individual Old Testament passages suggested are Ps 16, 10; Hos 6, 2; Jon 2, 1.2.11.

20, 11–18: This appearance to Mary is found only in John, but cf Mt 28, 8–10 and Mk 16, 9–11.

19, 38–42: Mt 27, 57–60; Mk 15, 42–46; Lk 34, 50–54.
  19, 39: Jn 3, 1–2; 7, 50; Ps 45, 9.
20, 1–10: Mt 28, 1–10; Mk 16, 1–11; Lk 24, 1–12.
  20, 1: Jn 19, 25.
  20, 6: Lk 24, 12.
20, 7: Jn 11, 44; 19, 40.
20, 9: Acts 2, 26–27; 1 Cor 15, 4.
20, 11–18: Mk 16, 9–11.
20, 14: Jn 21, 4; Mk 16, 12; Lk 24, 16; 1 Cor 15, 43–44.
20, 15–17: Mt 28, 9–10.

THE BLESSING OF BASKETS

It's early Holy Saturday morning, and the priest of the parish arrives to open the church for a special event. As he draws near the front door, the smell of eggs, sausages, freshly baked bread, and other breakfast foods wafts from the baskets of those already gathered. As people enter the church, they place their baskets on a table before the altar. The priest begins Mass with a prayer and then blesses the baskets of food with holy water and the sign of the cross:

"Blessed are you, O God! In your bounty you provide for your people. As we prepare to celebrate the Resurrection of your Son, bless these Easter foods, and strengthen your people that they may be true witnesses to the new life offered in Christ Jesus, our Lord. Amen."

This custom originated in Eastern Europe and can be found today in many churches around the world. The blessing of baskets reminds us that Jesus' death and Resurrection should touch every aspect of the life of the faithful. Especially after a long Lent of fasting and self-denial, the rich foods of the Easter table call to mind that Good Friday's sacrifice culminated in Easter glory— a time for celebration and feasting.

▶ Jn 21, 1–14

carried him away, tell me where you laid him, and I will take him." 16† Jesus said to her, "Mary!" She turned and said to him in Hebrew, "Rabbouni," which means Teacher. 17*† Jesus said to her, "Stop holding on to me, for I have not yet ascended to the Father. But go to my brothers and tell them, 'I am going to my Father and your Father, to my God and your God.' " 18 Mary of Magdala went and announced to the disciples, "I have seen the Lord," and what he told her.

Appearance to the Disciples

19*† On the evening of that first day of the week, when the doors were locked, where the disciples† were, for fear of the Jews, Jesus came and stood in their midst and said to them, "Peace be with you." 20*† When he had said this, he showed them his hands and his side. The disciples rejoiced when they saw the Lord. 21*† [Jesus] said to them again, "Peace be with you. As the Father has sent me, so I send you." 22*† And when he had said this, he

---

20, 16: *Rabbouni:* Hebrew or Aramaic for "my master."

20, 17: *Stop holding on to me:* see Mt 28, 9, where the women take hold of his feet. *I have not yet ascended:* for John and many of the New Testament writers, the ascension in the theological sense of going to the Father to be glorified took place with the resurrection as one action. This scene in John dramatizes such an understanding, for by Easter night Jesus is glorified and can give the Spirit. Therefore his ascension takes place immediately after he has talked to Mary. In such a view, the ascension after forty days described in Acts 1, 1–11 would be simply a termination of earthly appearances or, perhaps better, an introduction to the conferral of the Spirit upon the early church, modeled on Elisha's being able to have a (double) share in the spirit of Elijah if he saw him being taken up (same verb as ascending) into heaven (2 Kgs 2, 9–12). *To my Father and your Father, to my God and your God:* this echoes Ru 1, 16: "Your people shall be my people, and your God my God." The Father of Jesus will now become the Father of the disciples because, once ascended, Jesus can give them the Spirit that comes from the Father and they can be reborn as God's children (3, 5). That is why he calls them *my brothers.*

20, 19–29: The appearances to the disciples, without or with Thomas (cf 11, 16; 14, 5), have rough parallels in the other gospels only for vv 19–23; cf Lk 24, 36–39; Mk 16, 14–18.

20, 19: *The disciples:* by implication from v 24, this means ten of the Twelve, presumably in Jerusalem. *Peace be with you:* although this could be an ordinary greeting, John intends here to echo 14, 27. The theme of rejoicing in v 20 echoes 16, 22.

20, 20: *Hands and . . . side:* Lk 24, 39–40 mentions "hands and feet," based on Ps 22, 17.

20, 21: By means of this sending, the Eleven were made apostles, that is, "those sent" (cf 17, 18), though John does not use the noun in reference to them (see the note on 13, 16). A solemn mission or "sending" is also the subject of the post-resurrection appearances to the Eleven in Mt 28, 19; Lk 24, 47; Mk 16, 15.

20, 22: This action recalls Gn 2, 7, where God breathed on the first man and gave him life; just as Adam's life came from God, so now the disciples' new spiritual life comes from Jesus. Cf also the re-vivification of the dry bones in Ez 37. This is the author's version of Pentecost. Cf also the note on 19, 30.

20, 17: Acts 1, 9.	**20, 21:** Jn 17, 18; Mt 28, 19;
20, 19–23: Mt 28, 16–20; Mk 16,	Mk 16, 15; Lk 24,
14–18; Lk 24, 36–44.	47–48.
20, 20: Jn 14, 27.	**20, 22:** Gn 2, 7; Ez 37, 9;
	1 Cor 15, 45.

breathed on them and said to them, "Receive the holy Spirit. ²³*† Whose sins you forgive are forgiven them, and whose sins you retain are retained."

Thomas

²⁴ Thomas, called Didymus, one of the Twelve, was not with them when Jesus came. ²⁵* So the other disciples said to him, "We have seen the Lord." But he said to them, "Unless I see the mark of the nails in his hands and put my finger into the nailmarks and put my hand into his side, I will not believe." ²⁶* Now a week later his disciples were again inside and Thomas was with them. Jesus came, although the doors were locked, and stood in their midst and said, "Peace be with you." ²⁷ Then he said to Thomas, "Put your finger here and see my hands, and bring your hand and put it into my side, and do not be unbelieving, but believe." ²⁸*† Thomas answered and said to him, "My Lord and my God!" ²⁹*† Jesus said to him, "Have you come to believe because you have seen me? Blessed are those who have not seen and have believed."

Conclusion

³⁰*† Now Jesus did many other signs in the presence of [his] disciples that are not written in this book. ³¹* But these are written that you may [come to] believe that Jesus is the Messiah, the Son of God, and that through this belief you may have life in his name.

IV: Epilogue

The Resurrection Appearance in Galilee

The Appearance to the Seven Disciples

21 ¹*† After this, Jesus revealed himself again to his disciples at the Sea of Tiberias. He revealed himself in this way. ²† Together were Simon Peter, Thomas called Didymus, Nathanael from Cana in Galilee, Zebedee's sons, and two others of his disciples. ³*† Simon Peter said to them, "I

am going fishing." They said to him, "We also will come with you." So they went out and got into the boat, but that night they caught nothing. ⁴* When it was already dawn, Jesus was standing on the shore; but the disciples did not realize that it was Jesus. ⁵* Jesus said to them, "Children, have you caught anything to eat?" They answered him, "No." ⁶ So he said to them, "Cast the net over the right side of the boat and you will find something." So they cast it, and were not able to pull it in because

THE HUMBLE CHURCH

Peter must have felt terribly guilty about denying Jesus three times. When the risen Jesus appears to Peter, Jesus offers him three opportunities to reaffirm his love and be reconciled.

The Catholic church also believes that this passage establishes Peter as the leader of the early church and as the first pope, indicated by Jesus' commands to Peter to "feed my lambs," "tend my sheep," and "feed my sheep." By linking Peter's reconciliation to Peter's authority, John seems to be reminding the church to be humble and forgiving.

▶ Jn 21, 15–19

20, 23: The Council of Trent defined that this power to forgive sins is exercised in the sacrament of penance. See Mt 16, 19 and 18, 18.

20, 28: *My Lord and my God:* this forms a literary inclusion with the first verse of the gospel: "and the Word was God."

20, 29: This verse is a beatitude on future generations; faith, not sight, matters.

20, 30–31: These verses are clearly a conclusion to the gospel and express its purpose. While many manuscripts read *come to believe,* possibly implying a missionary purpose for John's gospel, a small number of quite early ones read "continue to believe," suggesting that the audience consists of Christians whose faith is to be deepened by the book; cf 19, 35.

21, 1–23: There are many non-Johannine peculiarities in this chapter, some suggesting Lucan Greek style; yet this passage is closer to John than 7, 53–8, 11. There are many Johannine features as well. Its closest parallels in the synoptic gospels are found in Lk 5, 1–11 and Mt 14, 28–31. Perhaps the tradition was ultimately derived from John but preserved by some disciple other than the writer

of the rest of the gospel. The appearances narrated seem to be independent of those in ch 20. Even if a later addition, the chapter was added before publication of the gospel, for it appears in all manuscripts.

21, 2: *Zebedee's sons:* the only reference to James and John in this gospel (but see the note on 1, 37). Perhaps the phrase was originally a gloss to identify, among the five, the *two others of his disciples.* The anonymity of the latter phrase is more Johannine (1, 35). The total of seven may suggest the community of the disciples in its fullness.

21, 3–6: This may be a variant of Luke's account of the catch of fish; see the note on Lk 5, 1–11.

20, 23: Mt 16, 19; 18, 18.
20, 25: 1 Jn 1, 1.
20, 26: Jn 21, 14.
20, 28: Jn 1, 1.
20, 29: Jn 4, 48; Lk 1, 45; 1 Pt 1, 8.
20, 30: Jn 21, 25.
20, 31: Jn 3, 14.15; 1 Jn 5, 13.
21, 1: Mt 26, 32; 28, 7.
21, 3: Mt 4, 18; Lk 5, 4–10.
21, 4: Jn 20, 14; Mt 28, 17; Lk 24, 16.
21, 5: Lk 24, 41.

?did you KNOW?

Resurrection Stories

There are fourteen stories about Jesus' Resurrection in the four Gospels. None of the stories describes the actual Resurrection or the physical appearance of the resurrected Christ. Matthew emphasizes God's power with dramatic symbols like earthquakes and lightning (see 28, 2–3). Mark, in its original ending, focuses on the empty tomb (see 16, 1–8). Luke emphasizes the living presence of Jesus in the Scriptures and the Eucharist (see 24, 13–35). John brings out the authority of the leaders of the early church, especially Peter's role as head of the Apostles (see Jn 20, 19–23; 21, 15–19).

Together, all these stories convey the faith of the disciples that Jesus is alive. Through God's power, life has triumphed over death. The disciples' mission is to communicate this Good News. And that's our mission too!

▶ Jn 21, 15–19

said to them, "Come, have breakfast." And none of the disciples dared to ask him, "Who are you?" because they realized it was the Lord. [13]* Jesus came over and took the bread and gave it to them, and in like manner the fish. [14]*† This was now the third time Jesus was revealed to his disciples after being raised from the dead.

Jesus and Peter

[15]† When they had finished breakfast, Jesus said to Simon Peter, "Simon, son of John, do you love me more than these?" †He said to him, "Yes, Lord,

THE GOSPEL ACCORDING TO . . .

The Gospel of John ends by saying that if everything Jesus did were to be written down, the entire world could not contain it. Sounds like a challenge, doesn't it? Perhaps the author was thinking of all the things the risen Christ continues to do in the lives of believers. If you were to write your own Gospel story, one based on the risen Jesus at work in your life, what marvelous stories would it hold? What messages and teachings would you offer to the people of today? How has your life revealed and reflected the Good News of Jesus?

As you think about these things, why not take out some paper and a pen and begin to write your Gospel story? Keep your paper near this Bible so that you can add more good news each time you read it and reflect on where the risen Christ is alive in your life and in the world.

▶ Jn 21, 24–25

of the number of fish. [7] So the disciple whom Jesus loved said to Peter, "It is the Lord." When Simon Peter heard that it was the Lord, he tucked in his garment, for he was lightly clad, and jumped into the sea. [8] The other disciples came in the boat, for they were not far from shore, only about a hundred yards, dragging the net with the fish. [9]*† When they climbed out on shore, they saw a charcoal fire with fish on it and bread. [10] Jesus said to them, "Bring some of the fish you just caught." [11]*† So Simon Peter went over and dragged the net ashore full of one hundred fifty-three large fish. Even though there were so many, the net was not torn. [12]† Jesus

---

† **21, 9.12–13:** It is strange that Jesus already has fish since none have yet been brought ashore. This meal may have had eucharistic significance for early Christians since v 13 recalls Jn 6, 11, which uses the vocabulary of Jesus' action at the Last Supper; but see also the note on Mt 14, 19.

21, 11: The exact number 153 is probably meant to have a symbolic meaning in relation to the apostles' universal mission; Jerome claims that Greek zoologists catalogued 153 species of fish. Or 153 is the sum of the numbers from 1 to 17. Others invoke Ez 47, 10.

21, 12: *None . . . dared to ask him:* is Jesus' appearance strange to them? Cf Lk 24, 16; Mk 16, 12; Jn 20, 14. The disciples do, however, recognize Jesus before the breaking of the bread (opposed to Lk 24, 35).

21, 14: This verse connects chs 20 and 21; cf 20, 19.26.

21, 15–23: This section constitutes Peter's rehabilitation and emphasizes his role in the church.

21, 15–17: In these three verses there is a remarkable variety of synonyms: two different Greek verbs for *love* (see the note on 15, 13); two verbs for *feed/tend;* two nouns for *sheep;* two verbs for *know.* But apparently there is no difference of meaning. The threefold confession of Peter is meant to counteract his earlier threefold denial (18, 17.25.27). The First Vatican Council cited these verses in defining that Jesus after his resurrection gave Peter the jurisdiction of supreme shepherd and ruler over the whole flock.

21, 15: *More than these:* probably "more than these disciples do" rather than "more than you love them" or "more than you love these things [fishing, etc.]."

21, 9: Lk 24, 41–43.   21, 13: Lk 24, 42.
21, 11: 2 Chr 2, 16.   21, 14: Jn 20, 19.26.

JN

you know that I love you." He said to him, "Feed my lambs."† 16 He then said to him a second time, "Simon, son of John, do you love me?" He said to him, "Yes, Lord, you know that I love you." He said to him, "Tend my sheep." 17* He said to him the third time, "Simon, son of John, do you love me?" Peter was distressed that he had said to him a third time, "Do you love me?" and he said to him, "Lord, you know everything; you know that I love you." [Jesus] said to him, "Feed my sheep. 18*† Amen, amen, I say to you, when you were younger, you used to dress yourself and go where you wanted; but when you grow old, you will stretch out your hands, and someone else will dress you and lead you where you do not want to go." 19* He said this signifying by what kind of death he would glorify God. And when he had said this, he said to him, "Follow me."

The Beloved Disciple

20* Peter turned and saw the disciple following whom Jesus loved, the one who had also reclined upon his chest during the supper and had said, "Master, who is the one who will betray you?" 21 When Peter saw him, he said to Jesus, "Lord, what about him?" 22*† Jesus said to him, "What if I want him to remain until I come? What concern is it of yours? You follow me." 23† So the word spread among the brothers that that disciple would not die. But Jesus had not told him that he would not die, just "What if I want him to remain until I come? [What concern is it of yours?]"

Conclusion

24*† It is this disciple who testifies to these things and has written them, and we know that his testimony is true. 25* There are also many other things that Jesus did, but if these were to be described individually, I do not think the whole world would contain the books that would be written.

21, 18: Originally probably a proverb about old age, now used as a figurative reference to the crucifixion of Peter.

21, 22: *Until I come:* a reference to the parousia.

21, 23: This whole scene takes on more significance if the disciple is already dead. The death of the apostolic generation caused problems in the church because of a belief that Jesus was to have returned first. Loss of faith sometimes resulted; cf 2 Pt 3, 4.

21, 24: *Who . . . has written them:* this does not necessarily mean he wrote them with his own hand. The same expression is used in 19, 22 of Pilate, who certainly would not have written the inscription himself. *We know:* i.e., the Christian community; cf 1, 14.16.

21, 17: Jn 13, 37–38; 18, 15–18.25–27; Mt 26, 69–75; Mk 14, 66–72; Lk 22, 55–62.
21, 18: Acts 21, 11.14; 2 Pt 1, 14.
21, 19: Jn 13, 36.
21, 20: Jn 13, 25.
21, 22: Mt 16, 28.
21, 24: Jn 19, 35.
21, 25: Jn 20, 30.

The Acts of the Apostles

In your history classes in school, you probably studied stories about the heroic men and women who helped create the United States: George Washington, Benjamin Franklin, Harriet Tubman, Susan B. Anthony, and Harry S. Truman, to name a few. The stories about these famous people are an important part of our national identity. The Acts of the Apostles is a book containing stories like these. It continues the account of salvation history by telling about the beginnings of the Christian movement, primarily through stories about two of its most important missionaries, Peter and Paul.

In-depth

The Acts of the Apostles—sometimes simply called Acts—was written by the same author as the Gospel of Luke. So Acts is really the second volume of a two-volume history. Like the Gospels, it is not a history in the sense of an eyewitness account of the beginnings of Christianity. Rather, it is an interpretation of this history, explaining how Christianity spread outside of Judaism to the Gentile world under the direction of the Holy Spirit.

Lots of great stories are in the Acts of the Apostles. We read about the descent of the Holy Spirit on the Apostles (2, 1–41), Paul's conversion to the Christian way (9, 1–19), and some miraculous escapes from prison and riots (12, 6–11; 16, 16–40). We learn about the first church council in Jerusalem, where a decision was made to accept Gentiles (non-Jews) as Christians without requiring that they also become practicing Jews (15, 1–35). Acts continuously emphasizes how faith in Christ is shared and supported through Christian community.

The Acts of the Apostles gives us information about how Christians lived in the years after Jesus' Resurrection and Ascension. We learn how the believers celebrated the Eucharist together and shared their belongings (2, 42–47). We learn how the Gospel message was preached, first to Jews in the synagogues and later to Gentiles. We learn how traveling missionaries like Paul went on long journeys and suffered many hardships to form new groups of believers across the Roman Empire. Under the guidance of the Holy Spirit, the church miraculously went from a small group of disciples in Jerusalem to a movement spreading across the entire Roman Empire, even to Rome itself.

At a Glance

I. The Preparation for the Christian Mission (1, 1—2, 13).

II. The Mission in Jerusalem (2, 14—8, 3).

III. The Mission in Judea and Samaria (8, 4—9, 43).

IV. The Inauguration of the Gentile Mission (10, 1—15, 35).

V. The Mission of Paul to the Ends of the Earth (15, 36—28, 31).

Quick Facts

Author
often identified as Luke, who also wrote the Gospel of Luke

Date Written
approximately A.D. 80

Audience
Gentile (Greek) Christians represented by Theophilus (see Acts 1, 1)

Acts

I: The Preparation for the Christian Mission

The Promise of the Spirit

1 [1]* † In the first book, Theophilus, I dealt with all that Jesus did and taught [2]* until the day he was taken up, after giving instructions through the holy Spirit to the apostles whom he had chosen. [3]* † He presented himself alive to them by many proofs after he had suffered, appearing to them during forty days and speaking about the kingdom of God. [4]* † While meeting with them, he enjoined them not to depart from Jerusalem, but to wait for "the promise of the Father about which you have heard me speak; [5]* for John baptized with water, but in a few days you will be baptized with the holy Spirit."

The Ascension of Jesus

[6]† When they had gathered together they asked him, "Lord, are you at this time going to restore the kingdom to Israel?" [7]* † He answered them, "It is not for you to know the times or seasons that the Father has established by his own authority. [8]* † But you will receive power when the holy Spirit comes upon you, and you will be my witnesses in Jerusalem,

---

1, 1–26: This introductory material (1–2) connects Acts with the Gospel of Luke, shows that the apostles were instructed by the risen Jesus (3–5), points out that the parousia or second coming in glory of Jesus will occur as certainly as his ascension occurred (6–11), and lists the members of the Twelve, stressing their role as a body of divinely mandated witnesses to his life, teaching, and resurrection (12–26).

1, 3: *Appearing to them during forty days:* Luke considered especially sacred the interval in which the appearances and instructions of the risen Jesus occurred and expressed it therefore in terms of the sacred number forty (cf Dt 8, 2). In his gospel, however, Luke connects the ascension of Jesus with the resurrection by describing the ascension on Easter Sunday evening (Lk 24, 50–53). What should probably be understood as one event (resurrection, glorification, ascension, sending of the Spirit—the paschal mystery) has been historicized by Luke when he writes of a visible ascension of Jesus after forty days and the descent of the Spirit at Pentecost. For Luke, the ascension marks the end of the appearances of Jesus except for the extraordinary appearance to Paul. With regard to Luke's understanding of salvation history, the ascension also marks the end of the time of Jesus (Lk 24, 50–53) and signals the beginning of the time of the church.

1, 4: *The promise of the Father:* the holy Spirit, as is clear from the next verse. This gift of the Spirit was first promised in Jesus' final instructions to his chosen witnesses in Luke's gospel (Lk 24, 49) and formed part of the continuing instructions of the risen Jesus on the kingdom of God, of which Luke speaks in v 3.

1, 6: The question of the disciples implies that in believing Jesus to be the Christ (see the note on Lk 2, 11) they had expected him to be a political leader who would restore self-rule to Israel during his historical ministry. When this had not taken place, they ask if it is to take place at this time, the period of the church.

1, 7: This verse echoes the tradition that the precise time of the parousia is not revealed to human beings; cf Mk 13, 32; 1 Thes 5, 1–3.

1, 8: Just as Jerusalem was the city of destiny in the Gospel of Luke (the place where salvation was accomplished), so here at the beginning of Acts, Jerusalem occupies a central position. It is the starting point for the mission of the Christian disciples to "the ends of the earth," the place where the apostles were situated and the doctrinal focal point in the early days of the community (15, 2.6). *The ends of the earth:* for Luke, this means Rome.

1, 1: Lk 1, 1–4.
1, 2: Mt 28, 19–20; Lk 24, 44–49; Jn 20, 22; 1 Tm 3, 16.
1, 3: Acts 10, 41; 13, 31.
1, 4: Jn 14, 16.17.26.
1, 5: Acts 11, 16; Mt 3, 11;

Mk 1, 8; Lk 3, 16; Jn 1, 26; Eph 1, 13.
1, 7: Mt 24, 36; 1 Thes 5, 1–2.
1, 8: Acts 2, 1–13; 10, 39; Is 43, 10; Mt 28, 19; Lk 24, 47–48.

Send us Your Spirit!

After Jesus was taken up to heaven, the Apostles, Mary, and other women and men gathered to pray together. They knew that they needed the Holy Spirit, promised by Jesus, to begin the difficult task of giving witness to the Reign of God. Today, we continue to pray:

Jesus, send us your Spirit, and renew the face of the earth. You know our strengths and weaknesses. Transform us into messengers of your Gospel for those who yearn for you.

Jesus, send us your Spirit, and renew the face of the earth. You know our history, with its beautiful and painful experiences. Help us to be untiring promoters of a society based on love, justice, and peace.

Jesus, send us your Spirit, and renew the face of the earth. You know our longing for love and community. Make us instruments of unity and service, especially for those who are weak and those who are lonely. Amen.

▸ **Acts 1, 1–11**

ACTS

throughout Judea and Samaria, and to the ends of the earth." 9* When he had said this, as they were looking on, he was lifted up, and a cloud took him from their sight. 10* While they were looking intently at the sky as he was going, suddenly two men dressed in white garments stood beside them. 11* They said, "Men of Galilee, why are you standing there looking at the sky? This Jesus who has been taken up from you into heaven will return in the same way as you have seen him going into heaven." 12* Then they returned to Jerusalem from the mount called Olivet, which is near Jerusalem, a sabbath day's journey away.

The First Community in Jerusalem

13 When they entered the city they went to the upper room where they were staying, Peter and John and James and Andrew, Philip and Thomas, Bartholomew and Matthew, James son of Alphaeus, Simon the Zealot, and Judas son of James. 14* All these devoted themselves with one accord to prayer, together with some women, and Mary the mother of Jesus, and his brothers.

The Choice of Judas's Successor

15 During those days Peter stood up in the midst of the brothers (there was a group of about one hundred and twenty persons in the one place). He said, 16* "My brothers, the scripture had to be fulfilled which the holy Spirit spoke beforehand through the mouth of David, concerning Judas, who was the guide for those who arrested Jesus. 17 He was numbered among us and was allotted a share in this ministry. 18*† He bought a parcel of land with the wages of his iniquity, and falling headlong, he burst open in the middle, and all his insides spilled out. 19 This became known to everyone who lived in Jerusalem, so that the parcel of land was called in their language 'Akeldama,' that is, Field of Blood. 20* For it is written in the Book of Psalms:

'Let his encampment become desolate,
    and may no one dwell in it.'

And:

'May another take his office.'

21 Therefore, it is necessary that one of the men who accompanied us the whole time the Lord Jesus came and went among us, 22* beginning from the baptism of John until the day on which he was taken up from us, become with us a witness to his resurrection." 23 So they proposed two, Joseph called Barsabbas,

---

† **1, 18:** Luke records a popular tradition about the death of Judas that differs from the one in Mt 27, 5, according to which Judas hanged himself. Here, although the text is not certain, Judas is depicted as purchasing a piece of property with the betrayal money and being killed on it in a fall.

1, 9: 2 Kgs 2, 11; Mk 16, 19; Lk 24, 51.
1, 10: Jn 20, 17.
1, 11: Lk 24, 51; Eph 4, 8–10; 1 Pt 3, 22; Rv 1, 7.
1, 12–14: Lk 6, 14–16.
1, 14: Lk 23, 49.
1, 16: Ps 41, 10; Lk 22, 47.
1, 18: Mt 27, 3–10.
1, 20: Pss 69, 26; 109, 8; Jn 17, 12.
1, 22: Acts 1, 8–9; 10, 39.

who was also known as Justus, and Matthias. [24] Then they prayed, "You, Lord, who know the hearts of all, show which one of these two you have chosen [25] to take the place in this apostolic ministry from which Judas turned away to go to his own place." [26]*† Then they gave lots to them, and the lot fell upon Matthias, and he was counted with the eleven apostles.

The Coming of the Spirit

2 [1]*† When the time for Pentecost was fulfilled, they were all in one place together. [2]*† And suddenly there came from the sky a noise like a strong driving wind, and it filled the entire house in which they were. [3]*† Then there appeared to them tongues as of fire, which parted and came to rest on each one of them. [4]*† And they were all filled with the holy Spirit and began to speak in different tongues, as the Spirit enabled them to proclaim.

[5] Now there were devout Jews from every nation under heaven staying in Jerusalem. [6] At this sound, they gathered in a large crowd, but they were confused because each one heard them speaking in his own language. [7]* They were astounded, and in amazement they asked, "Are not all these people who are speaking Galileans? [8] Then how does each of us hear them in his own native language? [9] We are Parthians, Medes, and Elamites, inhabitants of Mesopotamia, Judea and Cappadocia, Pontus and Asia, [10] Phrygia and Pamphylia, Egypt and the districts of Libya near Cyrene, as well as travelers from Rome, [11]* both Jews and converts to Judaism, Cretans and Arabs, yet we hear them speaking in our own tongues of the mighty acts of God." [12] They were all astounded and bewildered, and said to one another, "What does this mean?" [13]* But others said, scoffing, "They have had too much new wine."

II: The Mission in Jerusalem

Peter's Speech at Pentecost

[14]† Then Peter stood up with the Eleven, raised his voice, and proclaimed to them, "You who are

Catholic Connections

CONFIRMATION

The first verses of the Acts of the Apostles, chapter 2, are a biblical story associated with the sacrament of Confirmation, one of the seven sacraments celebrated within the Catholic church. As one of the three sacraments of initiation—along with Baptism and the Eucharist—Confirmation celebrates a person's membership in the church. But in a special way, Confirmation is associated with the gift of the Holy Spirit.

During the Confirmation ceremony, the bishop or priest anoints with blessed oil, called chrism, the foreheads of those being confirmed and signs them with the gift of the Holy Spirit. We pray that the Holy Spirit strengthen those who have been confirmed to live the Gospel and share the Good News of Jesus Christ, just as the Apostles did at the first Pentecost.

If you have been confirmed, what was your experience of receiving the sacrament? How are you aware of the presence and guidance of the Holy Spirit? How do you participate in the life of your church community? If you have not been confirmed, what would you hope for in Confirmation?

▶ Acts 2, 1–13

1, 26: The need to replace Judas was probably dictated by the symbolism of the number twelve, recalling the twelve tribes of Israel. This symbolism also indicates that for Luke (see Lk 22, 30) the Christian church is a reconstituted Israel.

2, 1–41: Luke's pentecostal narrative consists of an introduction (1–13), a speech ascribed to Peter declaring the resurrection of Jesus and its messianic significance (14–36), and a favorable response from the audience (37–41). It is likely that the narrative telescopes events that took place over a period of time and on a less dramatic scale. The Twelve were not originally in a position to proclaim publicly the messianic office of Jesus without incurring immediate reprisal from those religious authorities in Jerusalem who had brought about Jesus' death precisely to stem the rising tide in his favor.

2, 2: *There came from the sky a noise like a strong driving wind:* wind and spirit are associated in Jn 3, 8. The sound of a great rush of wind would herald a new action of God in the history of salvation.

2, 3: *Tongues as of fire:* see Ex 19, 18 where fire symbolizes the presence of God to initiate the covenant on Sinai. Here the holy

Spirit acts upon the apostles, preparing them to proclaim the new covenant with its unique gift of the Spirit (38).

2, 4: *To speak in different tongues:* ecstatic prayer in praise of God, interpreted in vv 6 and 11 as speaking in foreign languages, symbolizing the worldwide mission of the church.

2, 14–36: The first of six discourses in Acts (along with 3, 12–26; 4, 8–12; 5, 29–32; 10, 34–43; 13, 16–41) dealing with the resurrection of Jesus and its messianic import. Five of these are attributed to Peter, the final one to Paul. Modern scholars term these discourses in Acts the "kerygma," the Greek word for proclamation (cf 1 Cor 15, 11).

1, 26: Prv 16, 33.	2, 4: Acts 1, 5; 4, 31; 8,
2, 1: Lv 23, 15–21; Dt 16,	15.17; 10, 44; 11,
9–11.	15–16; 15, 8; 19, 6; Ps
2, 2–3: Jn 3, 8.	104, 30; Jn 20, 33.
2, 3: Lk 3, 16.	2, 7: Acts 1, 11.
	2, 11: Acts 10, 46.
	2, 13: 1 Cor 14, 23.

Jews, indeed all of you staying in Jerusalem. Let this be known to you, and listen to my words. ¹⁵ These people are not drunk, as you suppose, for it is only nine o'clock in the morning. ¹⁶ No, this is what was spoken through the prophet Joel:

¹⁷* 'It will come to pass in the last days,' God says,
     'that I will pour out a portion of my spirit
          upon all flesh.
     Your sons and your daughters shall prophesy,
          your young men shall see visions,
          your old men shall dream dreams.
¹⁸   Indeed, upon my servants and my handmaids
          I will pour out a portion of my spirit in
               those days,
          and they shall prophesy.
¹⁹   And I will work wonders in the heavens above
          and signs on the earth below:
               blood, fire, and a cloud of smoke.
²⁰   The sun shall be turned to darkness,
          and the moon to blood,
               before the coming of the great and
                    splendid day of the Lord,
²¹*   and it shall be that everyone shall be saved
          who calls on the name of the Lord.'

²²* You who are Israelites, hear these words. Jesus the Nazorean was a man commended to you by God with mighty deeds, wonders, and signs, which God worked through him in your midst, as you yourselves know. ²³* This man, delivered up by the set plan and foreknowledge of God, you killed, using lawless men to crucify him. ²⁴* But God raised him up, releasing him from the throes of death, because it was impossible for him to be held by it. ²⁵* For David says of him:

     'I saw the Lord ever before me,
          with him at my right hand I shall not
               be disturbed.
²⁶   Therefore my heart has been glad and my
               tongue has exulted;
          my flesh, too, will dwell in hope,
²⁷*   because you will not abandon my soul to the
               nether world,
          nor will you suffer your holy one to
               see corruption.
²⁸   You have made known to me the paths of life;
          you will fill me with joy in your presence.'

²⁹ My brothers, one can confidently say to you about the patriarch David that he died and was

PENTECOST

Genesis, chapter 11, is the story of arrogant workers who tried to build the tower of Babel to reach up to heaven. God confused their languages so they couldn't understand one another. Building was impossible. Pentecost was just the reverse! Heaven came down as the Holy Spirit descended upon the Apostles. The Jewish feast of Pentecost had celebrated the wheat harvest. Now the Apostles received the harvest of the Holy Spirit: the courage, confidence, and zeal to go out into the world and proclaim God's salvation in Jesus Christ. No matter what their language, everyone present could understand the Apostles' message. It was a holy day. It was a day to build God's people up.

Pentecost is considered the birthday of the Christian church. The Catholic church traditionally celebrates the feast of Pentecost on the second Sunday after Ascension Thursday, which is approximately fifty days after Easter (the term pente means "fifty"). It continues to be an important feast to celebrate the unity of all Christians. In the United States alone, the Gospel is preached in more than a hundred languages to people of many different cultures.

▶ Acts 2, 1–13

buried, and his tomb is in our midst to this day. ³⁰* But since he was a prophet and knew that God had sworn an oath to him that he would set one of his descendants upon his throne, ³¹* he foresaw and spoke of the resurrection of the Messiah, that neither was he abandoned to the netherworld nor did his flesh see corruption. ³² God raised this Jesus; of this we are all witnesses. ³³*† Exalted at

---

† **2, 33:** *At the right hand of God:* or "by the right hand of God."

2, 17: Is 2, 2; 44, 3; Jl 3, 1–5.
2, 21: Rom 10, 13.

2, 22: Acts 10, 38; Lk 24, 19.
2, 23: 1 Thes 2, 15.

2, 24: Acts 13, 34.
2, 25–28: Ps 16, 8–11.
2, 27: Acts 13, 35.

2, 30: 2 Sm 7, 12; Ps 132, 11.
2, 31: Acts 13, 35; Ps 16, 10.
2, 33: Acts 1, 4–5.

the right hand of God, he received the promise of the holy Spirit from the Father and poured it forth, as you [both] see and hear. 34* For David did not go up into heaven, but he himself said:

'The Lord said to my Lord,
  "Sit at my right hand
35   until I make your enemies
         your footstool." '

36* Therefore let the whole house of Israel know for certain that God has made him both Lord and Messiah, this Jesus whom you crucified."

37* Now when they heard this, they were cut to the heart, and they asked Peter and the other apostles, "What are we to do, my brothers?" 38*† Peter [said] to them, "Repent and be baptized, every one of you, in the name of Jesus Christ for the forgiveness of your sins; and you will receive the gift of the holy Spirit. 39* For the promise is made to you and to your children and to all those far off, whomever the Lord our God will call." 40* He

testified with many other arguments, and was exhorting them, "Save yourselves from this corrupt generation." 41* Those who accepted his message were baptized, and about three thousand persons were added that day.

Communal Life

42*† They devoted themselves to the teaching of the apostles and to the communal life, to the breaking of the bread and to the prayers.* 43* Awe came upon everyone, and many wonders and signs were done through the apostles. 44* All who believed were together and had all things in common; 45 they would sell their property and possessions and divide them among all according to each one's need. 46 Every day they devoted themselves to meeting together in the temple area and to breaking bread in their homes. They ate their meals with exultation and sincerity of heart, 47 praising God and enjoying favor with all the people. And every day the Lord added to their number those who were being saved.

Christian Community

LIVE IT!

In the famous passage of Acts 2, 42–47, the ideal Christian community is portrayed as open to the Holy Spirit. They shared everything in common, including prayer, meals, and possessions. No one went in need. Sound impossible?

Across the world, groups of people live together in intentional Christian communities similar to that among the believers described in Acts. Some of them pool their finances and possessions to provide for their food and housing. They commit themselves to building caring relationships of trust and respect with one another. They spend time praying together. They perform works of service together in the community. Many Christian families strive for this vision in their life together.

Is living like this attractive to you? What would be hard for you in living like this? What do you think society would be like today if this were everyone's lifestyle? Intentional Christian communities are attractive to many Christians today. As you grow older, you might look for such a community when you leave home—or even start one yourself. It is a wonderful experience of the Christian way of life.

▶ Acts 2, 42–47

A
C
T
S

---

† **2, 38:** *Repent and be baptized:* repentance is a positive concept, a change of mind and heart toward God reflected in the actual goodness of one's life. It is in accord with the apostolic teaching derived from Jesus (42) and ultimately recorded in the four gospels. Luke presents baptism in Acts as the expected response to the apostolic preaching about Jesus and associates it with the conferring of the Spirit (1, 5; 10, 44–48; 11, 16).
2, 42–47: The first of three summary passages (along with 4, 32–37 and 5, 12–16) that outline, somewhat idyllically, the chief characteristics of the Jerusalem community: adherence to the teachings of the Twelve and the centering of its religious life in the eucharistic liturgy (42); a system of distribution of goods that led wealthier Christians to sell their possessions when the needs of the

community's poor required it (44 and the note on 4, 32–37); and continued attendance at the temple, since in this initial stage there was little or no thought of any dividing line between Christianity and Judaism (46).

* 2, 34–35: Ps 110, 1.   2, 40: Dt 32, 5; Ps 78, 8; Lk
  2, 36: Acts 9, 22; Rom 10, 9;   9, 41; Phil 2, 15.
      Phil 2, 11.   2, 41: Acts 2, 47; 4, 4; 5, 14;
  2, 37: Lk 3, 10.   6, 7; 11, 21.24; 21, 20.
  2, 38: Acts 3, 19; 16, 31; Lk   2, 42–47: Acts 4, 32–35.
      3, 3.   2, 42: Acts 1, 14; 6, 4.
  2, 39: Is 57, 19; Jl 3, 5; Eph   2, 43: Acts 5, 12–16.
      2, 17.   2, 44: Acts 4, 32.34–35.

Cure of a Crippled Beggar

3 ¹† Now Peter and John were going up to the temple area for the three o'clock hour of prayer.† ²* And a man crippled from birth was carried and placed at the gate of the temple called "the Beautiful Gate" every day to beg for alms from the people who entered the temple. ³ When he saw Peter and John about to go into the temple, he asked for alms. ⁴ But Peter looked intently at him, as did John, and said, "Look at us." ⁵ He paid attention to them, expecting to receive something from them. ⁶*† Peter said, "I have neither silver nor gold, but what I do have I give you: in the name of Jesus Christ the Nazorean, [rise and] walk." ⁷ Then Peter took him by the right hand and raised him up, and immediately his feet and ankles grew strong. ⁸* He leaped up, stood, and walked around, and went into the temple with them, walking and jumping and praising God. ⁹ When all the people saw him walking and praising God, ¹⁰ they recognized him as the one who used to sit begging at the Beautiful Gate of the temple, and they were filled with amazement and astonishment at what had happened to him.

Peter's Speech

¹¹* As he clung to Peter and John, all the people hurried in amazement toward them in the portico called "Solomon's Portico." ¹²* When Peter saw this, he addressed the people, "You Israelites, why are you amazed at this, and why do you look so intently at us as if we had made him walk by our own power or piety? ¹³*† The God of Abraham, [the God] of Isaac, and [the God] of Jacob, the God of our ancestors, has glorified his servant Jesus whom you handed over and denied in Pilate's presence, when he had decided to release him. ¹⁴*† You denied the Holy and Righteous One and asked that a murderer be released to you. ¹⁵*† The author of life you put to death, but God raised him from the dead; of this we are witnesses. ¹⁶ And by faith in his

Share Christ

LIVE IT!

As is true in our own cities today, in Jerusalem during the first century, it was not uncommon to encounter beggars on the streets. And probably, like today, some people averted their eyes and walked by while others stopped to offer a few coins.

When Peter and John encounter a beggar in Acts 3, 3, they don't have a whole lot of money to share with him, but they stop just the same. Looking him in the eye, Peter offers the lame man the one thing of value he does have: the powerful gift of healing found in the name of Jesus Christ.

You may not have the gift of healing or lots of extra money to give to those in need. But Peter and John remind us that knowing Jesus is the greatest treasure one can acquire in life, and that this treasure has been given to us freely. Don't forget to share it with others!

▸ Acts 3, 1–10

---

† **3, 1—4, 31:** This section presents a series of related events: the dramatic cure of a lame beggar (3, 1–10) produces a large audience for the kerygmatic discourse of Peter (3, 11–26). The Sadducees, taking exception to the doctrine of resurrection, have Peter, John, and apparently the beggar as well, arrested (4, 1–4) and brought to trial before the Sanhedrin. The issue concerns the authority by which Peter and John publicly teach religious doctrine in the name of Jesus (4, 5–7). Peter replies with a brief summary of the kerygma, implying that his authority is prophetic (4, 8–12). The court warns the apostles to abandon their practice of invoking prophetic authority in the name of Jesus (4, 13–18). When Peter and John reply that the prophetic role cannot be abandoned to satisfy human objections, the court nevertheless releases them, afraid to do otherwise since the beggar, lame from birth and over forty years old, is a well-known figure in Jerusalem and the facts of his cure are common property (4, 19–22). The narrative concludes with a prayer of the Christian community imploring divine aid against threats of persecution (4, 23–31).

3, 1: *For the three o'clock hour of prayer:* literally, "at the ninth hour of prayer." With the day beginning at 6 a.m., the ninth hour would be 3 p.m.

3, 6–10: The miracle has a dramatic cast; it symbolizes the saving power of Christ and leads the beggar to enter the temple, where he hears Peter's proclamation of salvation through Jesus.

3, 13: *Has glorified:* through the resurrection and ascension of Jesus, God reversed the judgment against him on the occasion of his trial. *Servant:* the Greek word can also be rendered as "son" or even "child" here and also in 3, 26; 4, 25 (applied to David); 4, 27; and 4, 30. Scholars are of the opinion, however, that the original concept reflected in the words identified Jesus with the suffering Servant of the Lord of Is 52, 13—53, 12.

3, 14: *The Holy and Righteous One:* so designating Jesus emphasizes his special relationship to the Father (see Lk 1, 35; 4, 34) and emphasizes his sinlessness and religious dignity that are placed in sharp contrast with the guilt of those who rejected him in favor of Barabbas.

3, 15: *The author of life:* other possible translations of the Greek title are "leader of life" or "pioneer of life." The title clearly points to Jesus as the source and originator of salvation.

3, 2–8: Acts 14, 8–10.
3, 6: Acts 4, 10.
3, 8: Is 35, 6; Lk 7, 22.
3, 11: Acts 5, 12; Jn 10, 23.
3, 12: Acts 14, 15.
3, 13: Ex 3, 6.15; Is 52, 13;
          Lk 23, 14–25.
3, 14: Mt 27, 20–21; Mk 15,
          11; Lk 23, 18;
          Jn 18, 40.
3, 15: Acts 4, 10; 5, 31 / Acts
          1, 8; 2, 32.

name, this man, whom you see and know, his name has made strong, and the faith that comes through it has given him this perfect health, in the presence of all of you. ¹⁷*† Now I know, brothers, that you acted out of ignorance, just as your leaders did; ¹⁸*† but God has thus brought to fulfillment what he had announced beforehand through the mouth of all the prophets, that his Messiah would suffer. ¹⁹* Repent, therefore, and be converted, that your sins may be wiped away, ²⁰† and that the Lord may grant you times of refreshment and send you the Messiah already appointed for you, Jesus, ²¹† whom heaven must receive until the times of universal restoration of which God spoke through the mouth of his holy prophets from of old. ²²*† For Moses said:

'A prophet like me will the Lord, your God,
    raise up for you
    from among your own kinsmen;
to him you shall listen in all that he may say
    to you.
²³* Everyone who does not listen to that prophet
    will be cut off from the people.'

²⁴ Moreover, all the prophets who spoke, from Samuel and those afterwards, also announced these days. ²⁵* You are the children of the prophets and of the covenant that God made with your ancestors when he said to Abraham, 'In your offspring all the families of the earth shall be blessed.' ²⁶* For you first, God raised up his servant and sent him to bless you by turning each of you from your evil ways."

4 ¹† While they were still speaking to the people, the priests, the captain of the temple guard, and the Sadducees confronted them, ²* disturbed that they were teaching the people and proclaiming in Jesus the resurrection of the dead. ³ They laid hands on them and put them in custody until the next day, since it was already evening. ⁴ But many of those who heard the word came to believe and [the] number of men grew to [about] five thousand.

Before the Sanhedrin

⁵ On the next day, their leaders, elders, and scribes were assembled in Jerusalem, ⁶ with Annas the high priest, Caiaphas, John, Alexander, and all who were of the high-priestly class. ⁷ They brought them into their presence and questioned them, "By what power or by what name have you done this?" ⁸* Then Peter, filled with the holy Spirit, answered them, "Leaders of the people and elders: ⁹ If we are being examined today about a good deed done to a cripple, namely, by what means he was saved, ¹⁰ then all of you and all the people of Israel should know that it was in the name of Jesus Christ the Nazorean whom you crucified, whom God raised from the dead; in his name this man stands before you healed. ¹¹*† He is 'the stone rejected by you, the builders, which has become the cornerstone.' ¹²*† There is no salvation through anyone else, nor is there any other name under heaven given to the human race by which we are to be saved."

¹³ Observing the boldness of Peter and John and perceiving them to be uneducated, ordinary men, they were amazed, and they recognized them as the

A
C
T
S

3, 17: *Ignorance:* a Lucan motif, explaining away the actions not only of the people but also of their leaders in crucifying Jesus. On this basis the presbyters in Acts could continue to appeal to the Jews in Jerusalem to believe in Jesus, even while affirming their involvement in his death because they were unaware of his messianic dignity. See also 13, 27 and Lk 23, 34.

3, 18: *Through the mouth of all the prophets:* Christian prophetic insight into the Old Testament saw the crucifixion and death of Jesus as the main import of messianic prophecy. The Jews themselves did not anticipate a suffering Messiah; they usually understood the Servant Song in Is 52, 13—53, 12 to signify their own suffering as a people. In his typical fashion (cf Lk 18, 31; 24, 25.27.44), Luke does not specify the particular Old Testament prophecies that were fulfilled by Jesus. See also the note on Lk 24, 26.

3, 20: *The Lord . . . and send you the Messiah already appointed for you, Jesus:* an allusion to the parousia or second coming of Christ, judged to be imminent in the apostolic age. This reference to its nearness is the only explicit one in Acts. Some scholars believe that this verse preserves a very early christology, in which the title "Messiah" (Greek "Christ") is applied to him as of his parousia, his second coming (contrast 2, 36). This view of a future messiahship of Jesus is not found elsewhere in the New Testament.

3, 21: *The times of universal restoration:* like "the times of refreshment" (20), an apocalyptic designation of the messianic age, fitting in with the christology of v 20 that associates the messiahship of Jesus with his future coming.

3, 22: A loose citation of Dt 18, 15, which teaches that the Israelites are to learn the will of Yahweh from no one but their

prophets. At the time of Jesus, some Jews expected a unique prophet to come in fulfillment of this text. Early Christianity applied this tradition and text to Jesus and used them especially in defense of the divergence of Christian teaching from traditional Judaism.

4, 1: *The priests, the captain of the temple guard, and the Sadducees:* the priests performed the temple liturgy; the temple guard was composed of Levites, whose captain ranked next after the high priest. The Sadducees, a party within Judaism at this time, rejected those doctrines, including bodily resurrection, which they believed alien to the ancient Mosaic religion. The Sadducees were drawn from priestly families and from the lay aristocracy.

4, 11: Early Christianity applied this citation from Ps 118, 22 to Jesus; cf Mk 12, 10; 1 Pt 2, 7.

4, 12: In the Roman world of Luke's day, salvation was often attributed to the emperor who was hailed as "savior" and "god." Luke, in the words of Peter, denies that deliverance comes through anyone other than Jesus.

3, 17: Acts 13, 27; Lk 23, 34;
    1 Cor 2, 8; 1 Tm 1, 13.
3, 18: Lk 18, 31.
3, 19: Acts 2, 38.
3, 22: Acts 7, 37; Dt 18,
    15.18.
3, 23: Lv 23, 29; Dt 18, 19.
3, 25: Gn 12, 3; 18, 18; 22,
    18; Sir 44, 19–21; Gal
    3, 8–9.

3, 26: Acts 13, 46; Rom 1,
    16.
4, 2: Acts 23, 6–8; 24, 21.
4, 8: Mt 10, 20.
4, 11: Ps 118, 22; Is 28, 16;
    Mt 21, 42; Mk 12, 10;
    Lk 20, 17; Rom 9, 33;
    1 Pt 2, 7.
4, 12: Mt 1, 21; 1 Cor 3, 11.

I Believe!
The Apostles' Creed

In Acts 4, 5–12, Peter stands up before the unbelieving rulers and elders and boldly proclaims his faith in Jesus as healer and Messiah. Every Sunday at Mass, Catholic Christians profess the same faith when they pray the Nicene Creed. (A creed is a type of prayer that expresses faith beliefs.) Did you know there is also a shorter creed called the Apostles' Creed? The Apostles' Creed is based on the teachings and beliefs of the earliest Christians.

Take a moment to pray the Apostles' Creed:

I believe in God, the Father almighty, creator of heaven and earth. I believe in Jesus Christ, his only Son, our Lord. He was conceived by the power of the Holy Spirit and born of the Virgin Mary. He suffered under Pontius Pilate, was crucified, died, and was buried. He descended into hell. On the third day he rose again. He ascended into heaven and is seated at the right hand of the Father. He will come again to judge the living and the dead. I believe in the Holy Spirit, the holy catholic Church, the communion of saints, the forgiveness of sins, the resurrection of the body, and the life everlasting. Amen. (Catechism of the Catholic Church, pp. 49–50)

Then reflect or journal on the following questions:

- Which statements of the creed do you have questions about?
- How hard would it be for you to express your faith beliefs to people who don't believe in Jesus?

▶ Acts 4, 5–12

---

companions of Jesus. [14] Then when they saw the man who had been cured standing there with them, they could say nothing in reply. [15] So they ordered them to leave the Sanhedrin, and conferred with one another, saying, [16] "What are we to do with these men? Everyone living in Jerusalem knows that a remarkable sign was done through them, and we cannot deny it. [17]* But so that it may not be spread any further among the people, let us give them a stern warning never again to speak to anyone in this name."

[18] So they called them back and ordered them not to speak or teach at all in the name of Jesus. [19]* Peter and John, however, said to them in reply, "Whether it is right in the sight of God for us to obey you rather than God, you be the judges. [20] It is impossible for us not to speak about what we have seen and heard." [21] After threatening them further, they released them, finding no way to punish them, on account of the people who were all praising God for what had happened. [22] For the man on whom this sign of healing had been done was over forty years old.

Prayer of the Community

[23] After their release they went back to their own people and reported what the chief priests and elders had told them. [24] And when they heard it, they raised their voices to God with one accord and said, "Sovereign Lord, maker of heaven and earth and the sea and all that is in them, [25]* you said by the holy Spirit through the mouth of our father David, your servant:

'Why did the Gentiles rage
     and the peoples entertain folly?
[26]   The kings of the earth took their stand
     and the princes gathered together
          against the Lord and against his anointed.'

[27]*† Indeed they gathered in this city against your holy servant Jesus whom you anointed, Herod and Pontius Pilate, together with the Gentiles and the peoples of Israel, [28] to do what your hand and [your] will had long ago planned to take place. [29] And now, Lord, take note of their threats, and enable your servants to speak your word with all boldness, [30] as you stretch forth [your] hand to heal, and signs and wonders are done through the name of your holy servant Jesus." [31]*† As they prayed, the place where they were gathered shook, and they were all filled with the holy Spirit and continued to speak the word of God with boldness.

---

† **4, 27:** *Herod:* Herod Antipas, ruler of Galilee and Perea from 4 B.C. to A.D. 39, who executed John the Baptist and before whom Jesus was arraigned; cf Lk 23, 6–12.

4, 31: *The place . . . shook:* the earthquake is used as a sign of the divine presence in Ex 19, 18; Is 6, 4. Here the shaking of the building symbolizes God's favorable response to the prayer. Luke

may have had as an additional reason for using the symbol in this sense the fact that it was familiar in the Hellenistic world. Ovid and Virgil also employ it.

4, 17: Acts 5, 28.   **4, 27:** Lk 23, 12–13.
4, 19: Acts 5, 29–32.   **4, 31:** Acts 2, 4.
4, 25–26: Ps 2, 1–2.

ACTS

?did you KNOW?

Stewardship

Acts 4, 32–37 describes a Christian behavior called stewardship. Stewardship involves sharing the gifts of time, talent, and treasure that God has placed in your care (see "Stewardship: Making a Contribution," Lk 21, 1–4). It is key to the life of any Christian community.

Sharing our treasure and giving money are the most obvious ways of sharing. Consider the disciple named in the passage, Joseph Barnabas. How did he share? Can you think of things you spend money on—a CD, new jeans, a movie—and make a commitment to give some of that money to a charitable organization?

But giving money isn't the only way to share with others. Think about your own gifts. What are you good at that you could share with your parish, school, or community? Do not discount even the simplest ability. For example, maybe you are persistent; this talent can help any project to be successful. Or perhaps you love children and can baby-sit for overwhelmed parents.

How are you a good steward of your time, talent, and treasure? Think about it!

▸ Acts 4, 32–37

Life in the Christian Community

32† The community of believers was of one heart and mind, and no one claimed that any of his possessions was his own, but they had everything in common. 33 With great power the apostles bore witness to the resurrection of the Lord Jesus, and great favor was accorded them all. 34* There was no needy person among them, for those who owned property or houses would sell them, bring the proceeds of the sale, 35 and put them at the feet of the apostles, and they were distributed to each according to need.

36* Thus Joseph, also named by the apostles Barnabas (which is translated "son of encouragement"), a Levite, a Cypriot by birth, 37 sold a piece of property that he owned, then brought the money and put it at the feet of the apostles.

Ananias and Sapphira

5 1† A man named Ananias, however, with his wife Sapphira, sold a piece of property. 2 He retained for himself, with his wife's knowledge, some of the purchase price, took the remainder, and put it at the feet of the apostles. 3* But Peter said, "Ananias, why has Satan filled your heart so that you lied to the holy Spirit and retained part of the price of the land? 4 While it remained unsold, did it not remain yours? And when it was sold, was it not still under your control? Why did you contrive this deed? You have lied not to human beings, but to God." 5 When Ananias heard these words, he fell down and breathed his last, and great fear came upon all who heard of it. 6 The young men came and wrapped him up, then carried him out and buried him.

7 After an interval of about three hours, his wife came in, unaware of what had happened. 8 Peter said to her, "Tell me, did you sell the land for this amount?" She answered, "Yes, for that amount." 9 Then Peter said to her, "Why did you agree to test the Spirit of the Lord? Listen, the footsteps of those who have buried your husband are at the door, and they will carry you out." 10 At once, she fell down at his feet and breathed her last. When the young men entered they found her dead, so they carried her out and buried her beside her husband. 11* And great fear came upon the whole church and upon all who heard of these things.

Signs and Wonders of the Apostles

12*† Many signs and wonders were done among the people at the hands of the apostles. They were all together in Solomon's portico. 13 None of the others dared to join them, but the people esteemed

---

4, 32–37: This is the second summary characterizing the Jerusalem community (see the note on 2, 42–47). It emphasizes the system of the distribution of goods and introduces Barnabas, who appears later in Acts as the friend and companion of Paul, and who, as noted here (37), endeared himself to the community by a donation of money through the sale of property. This sharing of material possessions continues a practice that Luke describes during the historical ministry of Jesus (Lk 8, 3) and is in accord with the sayings of Jesus in Luke's gospel (Lk 12, 33; 16, 9.11.13).

5, 1–11: The sin of Ananias and Sapphira did not consist in the withholding of part of the money but in their deception of the community. Their deaths are ascribed to a lie to the holy Spirit (3.9), i.e.,

they accepted the honor accorded them by the community for their generosity, but in reality they were not deserving of it.

5, 12–16: This, the third summary portraying the Jerusalem community, underscores the Twelve as its bulwark, especially because of their charismatic power to heal the sick; cf 2, 42–47; 4, 32–37.

4, 34–35: Acts 2, 44–45.
4, 36–37: Acts 9, 27; 11, 22.30; 12, 25; 13, 15; 1 Cor 9, 6; Gal 2, 1.9.13; Col 4, 10.
5, 3: Lk 22, 3; Jn 13, 2.
5, 11: Acts 2, 43; 5, 5; 19, 17.
5, 12: Acts 2, 43; 6, 8; 14, 3; 15, 12.

them. ¹⁴ Yet more than ever, believers in the Lord, great numbers of men and women, were added to them. ¹⁵* Thus they even carried the sick out into the streets and laid them on cots and mats so that when Peter came by, at least his shadow might fall on one or another of them. ¹⁶ A large number of people from the towns in the vicinity of Jerusalem also gathered, bringing the sick and those disturbed by unclean spirits, and they were all cured.

Trial before the Sanhedrin

¹⁷*† Then the high priest rose up and all his companions, that is, the party of the Sadducees, and, filled with jealousy, ¹⁸ laid hands upon the apostles and put them in the public jail. ¹⁹* But during the night, the angel of the Lord opened the doors of the prison, led them out, and said, ²⁰ "Go and take your place in the temple area, and tell the people everything about this life." ²¹ When they heard this, they went to the temple early in the morning and taught. When the high priest and his companions arrived, they convened the Sanhedrin, the full senate of the Israelites, and sent to the jail

to have them brought in. ²² But the court officers who went did not find them in the prison, so they came back and reported, ²³ "We found the jail securely locked and the guards stationed outside the doors, but when we opened them, we found no one inside." ²⁴ When they heard this report, the captain of the temple guard and the chief priests were at a loss about them, as to what this would come to. ²⁵ Then someone came in and reported to them, "The men whom you put in prison are in the temple area and are teaching the people." ²⁶* Then the captain and the court officers went and brought them in, but without force, because they were afraid of being stoned by the people.

²⁷ When they had brought them in and made them stand before the Sanhedrin, the high priest questioned them, ²⁸* "We gave you strict orders [did we not?] to stop teaching in that name. Yet you have filled Jerusalem with your teaching and want to bring this man's blood upon us." ²⁹* But Peter and the apostles said in reply, "We must obey God rather than men. ³⁰*† The God of our ancestors raised Jesus, though you had him killed by hanging him on a tree. ³¹*† God exalted him at his right

Pop Quiz

The scene. The disciples, who are spreading the Good News of Jesus Christ, are taken before the Jewish council to explain their motives and reasons for this work.

The test. Gamaliel, a wise Jewish leader, talks the rest of the council out of killing the disciples, by using the following reasoning: If the disciples' mission is from God, it will succeed despite anything the council does. But if it is not of God's design, it will fail, and the Christians will eventually disappear anyway.

The question. If you were brought before a similar council, would your life's mission pass or fail this test? That is, would your words and actions in the past week reflect Jesus' attitudes, actions, and mission?

Your answer.

▶ Acts 5, 27–39

---

†
5, 17–42: A second action against the community is taken by the Sanhedrin in the arrest and trial of the Twelve; cf 4, 1–3. The motive is the jealousy of the religious authorities over the popularity of the apostles (17) who are now charged with the defiance of the Sanhedrin's previous order to them to abandon their prophetic role (28; cf 4, 18). In this crisis the apostles are favored by a miraculous release from prison (18–24). (For similar incidents involving Peter and Paul, see 12, 6–11; 16, 25–29.) The real significance of such an event, however, would be manifest only to people of faith, not to unbelievers; since the Sanhedrin already judged the Twelve to be inauthentic prophets, it could disregard reports of their miracles. When the Twelve immediately resumed public teaching, the Sanhedrin determined to invoke upon them the penalty of death (33) prescribed

in Dt 13, 6–10. Gamaliel's advice against this course finally prevailed, but it did not save the Twelve from the punishment of scourging (40) in a last endeavor to shake their conviction of their prophetic mission.
5, 30: *Hanging him on a tree:* that is, crucifying him (cf also Gal 3, 13).
5, 31: *At his right hand:* see the note on 2, 33.

5, 15: Acts 19, 11–12; Mk 6,   5, 26: Lk 20, 19.
56.   5, 28: Mt 27, 25.
5, 17: Acts 4, 1–3.6.   5, 29: Acts 4, 19.
5, 19: Acts 12, 7–10; 16,   5, 30: Acts 2, 23–24.
25–26.   5, 31: Acts 2, 38.

hand as leader and savior to grant Israel repentance and forgiveness of sins. 32* We are witnesses of these things, as is the holy Spirit that God has given to those who obey him."

33 When they heard this, they became infuriated and wanted to put them to death. 34*† But a Pharisee in the Sanhedrin named Gamaliel, a teacher of the law, respected by all the people, stood up, ordered the men to be put outside for a short time, 35 and said to them, "Fellow Israelites, be careful what you are about to do to these men. 36† Some time ago, Theudas appeared, claiming to be someone important, and about four hundred men joined him, but he was killed, and all those who were loyal to him were disbanded and came to nothing. 37 After him came Judas the Galilean at the time of the census. He also drew people after him, but he too perished and all who were loyal to him were scattered. 38 So now I tell you, have nothing to do with these men, and let them go. For if this endeavor or this activity is of human origin, it will destroy itself. 39 But if it comes from God, you will not be able to destroy them; you may even find yourselves fighting against God." They were persuaded by him. 40* After recalling the apostles, they had them flogged, ordered them to stop speaking in the name of Jesus, and dismissed them. 41* So they left the presence of the Sanhedrin, rejoicing that they had been found worthy to suffer dishonor for the sake of the name. 42* And all day long, both at the temple and in their homes, they did not stop teaching and proclaiming the Messiah, Jesus.

The Need for Assistants

6 1*† At that time, as the number of disciples continued to grow, the Hellenists complained against the Hebrews because their widows were being neglected in the daily distribution. 2† So the Twelve called together the community of the disciples and said, "It is not right for us to neglect the word of God to serve at table.† 3 Brothers, select from among you seven reputable men, filled with the Spirit and wisdom, whom we shall appoint to this task, 4 whereas we shall devote ourselves to prayer and to the ministry of the word." 5 The proposal was acceptable to the whole community, so they chose Stephen, a man filled with faith and the holy Spirit, also Philip, Prochorus, Nicanor, Timon, Parmenas, and Nicholas of Antioch, a convert to Judaism. 6*† They presented these men to the apostles who prayed and laid hands on them. 7* The word of God continued to spread, and the number of the disciples in Jerusalem increased greatly; even a large group of priests were becoming obedient to the faith.

Accusation against Stephen

8† Now Stephen, filled with grace and power, was working great wonders and signs among the people. 9 Certain members of the so-called Synagogue of Freedmen, Cyrenians, and Alexandrians, and people from Cilicia and Asia, came forward and debated with Stephen, 10* but they could not withstand the wisdom and the spirit with which he spoke. 11* Then they instigated some men to say, "We have heard him speaking blasphemous words

5, 34: Gamaliel: in 22, 3, Paul identifies himself as a disciple of this Rabbi Gamaliel I who flourished in Jerusalem between A.D. 25 and 50.

5, 36–37: Gamaliel offers examples of unsuccessful contemporary movements to argue that if God is not the origin of this movement preached by the apostles it will perish by itself. The movement initiated by Theudas actually occurred when C. Cuspius Fadus was governor, A.D. 44–46. Luke's placing of Judas the Galilean after Theudas and at the time of the census (see the note on Lk 2, 1–2) is an indication of the vagueness of his knowledge of these events.

6, 1–7: The Hellenists . . . the Hebrews: the Hellenists were not necessarily Jews from the diaspora, but were more probably Palestinian Jews who spoke only Greek. The Hebrews were Palestinian Jews who spoke Hebrew or Aramaic and who may also have spoken Greek. Both groups belong to the Jerusalem Jewish Christian community. The conflict between them leads to a restructuring of the community that will better serve the community's needs. The real purpose of the whole episode, however, is to introduce Stephen as a prominent figure in the community whose long speech and martyrdom will be recounted in ch 7.

6, 2–4: The essential function of the Twelve is the "service of the word," including development of the kerygma by formulation of the teachings of Jesus.

6, 2: To serve at table: some commentators think that it is not the serving of food that is described here but rather the keeping of the accounts that recorded the distribution of food to the needy members of the community. In any case, after Stephen and the others are chosen, they are never presented carrying out the task for which they were appointed (2–3). Rather, two of their number, Stephen and Philip, are presented as preachers of the Christian message. They, the Hellenist counterpart of the Twelve, are active in the ministry of the word.

6, 6: They . . . laid hands on them: the customary Jewish way of designating persons for a task and invoking upon them the divine blessing and power to perform it.

6, 8—8, 1: The summary (6, 7) on the progress of the Jerusalem community, illustrated by the conversion of the priests, is followed by a lengthy narrative regarding Stephen. Stephen's defense is not a response to the charges made against him but takes the form of a discourse that reviews the fortunes of God's word to Israel and leads to a prophetic declaration: a plea for the hearing of that word as announced by Christ and now possessed by the Christian community.

The charges that Stephen depreciated the importance of the temple and the Mosaic law and elevated Jesus to a stature above Moses (6, 13–14) were in fact true. Before the Sanhedrin, no defense against them was possible. With Stephen, who thus perceived the fuller implications of the teachings of Jesus, the differences between Judaism and Christianity began to appear. Luke's account of Stephen's martyrdom and its aftermath shows how the major impetus behind the Christian movement passed from Jerusalem, where the temple and law prevailed, to Antioch in Syria, where these influences were less pressing.

5, 32: Lk 24, 48; Jn 15, 26.
5, 34: Acts 22, 3.
5, 40: Mt 10, 17; Acts 4, 17–18.
5, 41: Mt 5, 10–11; 1 Pt 4, 13.
5, 42: Acts 2, 46; 5, 20–21.25; 8, 35; 17, 3; 18, 5.28; 19, 4–5.
6, 1: Acts 2, 45; 4, 34–35.
6, 6: Acts 1, 24; 13, 3; 14, 23.
6, 7: Acts 9, 31; 12, 24; 16, 5; 19, 20; 28, 30–31.
6, 10: Lk 21, 15.
6, 11: Mt 26, 59–61; Mk 14, 55–58; Acts 21, 21.

DON'T FORGET THE SHOULDERS YOU STAND ON

Take a few minutes to read about the martyrdom of Stephen, Acts 6, 8—7, 60. There is perhaps no more touching story in the New Testament than this young man's brave defense of his faith as he followed in his Lord's footsteps. He knew his history and his ancestors, and they gave him divine courage in the face of death.

People of all ages and cultures need to respect and honor the faith and sacrifices of their ancestors. For example, the video series *Eyes on the Prize* is a reminder for all Americans of the debt owed to African Americans of a previous generation. This documentation of the civil rights movement immortalizes the faith of countless people who were brave enough to protest the injustice of racism.

Today is a gift from them. Somebody died so that all Americans might live freely. Somebody suffered so that all Americans could enjoy civil rights. Somebody accepted persecution to call all Americans to respect God's justice.

How many youth today would be willing to make similar sacrifices in the struggle for freedom and equality—signs of the Reign of God?

Dear God, help me to treasure my ancestors' sacrifice and bravery. Help me to follow their example in working for justice with love and courage. Amen.

▶ **Acts 6, 8—7, 60**

ACTS

against Moses and God." ¹² They stirred up the people, the elders, and the scribes, accosted him, seized him, and brought him before the Sanhedrin. ¹³† They presented false witnesses who testified, "This man never stops saying things against [this] holy place and the law. ¹⁴* For we have heard him claim that this Jesus the Nazorean will destroy this place and change the customs that Moses handed down to us." ¹⁵ All those who sat in the Sanhedrin looked intently at him and saw that his face was like the face of an angel.

Stephen's Discourses

7 ¹ Then the high priest asked, "Is this so?" ²*† And he replied, "My brothers and fathers, listen. The God of glory appeared to our father Abraham while he was in Mesopotamia,† before he had settled in Haran, ³* and said to him, 'Go forth from your land and [from] your kinsfolk to the land that I will show you.' ⁴* So he went forth from the land of the Chaldeans and settled in Haran. And from there, after his father died, he made him migrate to this land where you now dwell. ⁵* Yet he gave him no inheritance in it, not even a foot's length, but he did promise to give it to him and his descendants as a possession, even though he was childless. ⁶* And God spoke thus, 'His descendants shall be aliens in a land not their own, where they shall be enslaved and oppressed for four hundred years; ⁷* but I will bring judgment on the nation

---

6, 13: *False witnesses:* here, and in his account of Stephen's execution (7, 54–60), Luke parallels the martyrdom of Stephen with the death of Jesus.

7, 2–53: Stephen's speech represents Luke's description of Christianity's break from its Jewish matrix. Two motifs become prominent in the speech: (1) Israel's reaction to God's chosen leaders in the past reveals that the people have consistently rejected them; and (2) Israel has misunderstood God's choice of the Jerusalem temple as the place where he is to be worshiped.

7, 2: *God . . . appeared to our father Abraham . . . in Mesopotamia:* the first of a number of minor discrepancies between the data of the Old Testament and the data of Stephen's discourse. According to

Gn 12, 1, God first spoke to Abraham in Haran. The main discrepancies are these: in v 16 it is said that Jacob was buried in Shechem, whereas Gn 50, 13 says he was buried at Hebron; in the same verse it is said that the tomb was purchased by Abraham, but in Gn 33, 19 and Jos 24, 32 the purchase is attributed to Jacob himself.

6, 14: Mt 26, 59–61; 27, 40;   7, 4: Gn 12, 5; 15, 7.
   Jn 2, 19.   7, 5: Gn 12, 7; 13, 15; 15,
7, 2: Gn 11, 31; 12, 1; Ps   2; 16, 1; Dt 2, 5.
   29, 3.   7, 6–7: Gn 15, 13–14.
7, 3: Gn 12, 1.   7, 7: Ex 3, 12.

they serve,' God said, 'and after that they will come out and worship me in this place.' 8* Then he gave him the covenant of circumcision, and so he became the father of Isaac, and circumcised him on the eighth day, as Isaac did Jacob, and Jacob the twelve patriarchs.

9* "And the patriarchs, jealous of Joseph, sold him into slavery in Egypt; but God was with him 10* and rescued him from all his afflictions. He granted him favor and wisdom before Pharaoh, the king of Egypt, who put him in charge of Egypt and [of] his entire household. 11* Then a famine and great affliction struck all Egypt and Canaan, and our ancestors could find no food; 12* but when Jacob heard that there was grain in Egypt, he sent our ancestors there a first time. 13* The second time, Joseph made himself known to his brothers, and Joseph's family became known to Pharaoh. 14* Then Joseph sent for his father Jacob, inviting him and his whole clan, seventy-five persons; 15* and Jacob went down to Egypt. And he and our ancestors died 16* and were brought back to Shechem and placed in the tomb that Abraham had purchased for a sum of money from the sons of Hamor at Shechem.

17* "When the time drew near for the fulfillment of the promise that God pledged to Abraham, the people had increased and become very numerous in Egypt, 18* until another king who knew nothing of Joseph came to power [in Egypt]. 19 He dealt shrewdly with our people and oppressed [our] ancestors by forcing them to expose their infants, that they might not survive. 20* At this time Moses was born, and he was extremely beautiful. For three months he was nursed in his father's house; 21* but when he was exposed, Pharaoh's daughter adopted him and brought him up as her own son. 22 Moses was educated [in] all the wisdom of the Egyptians and was powerful in his words and deeds.

23* "When he was forty years old, he decided to visit his kinsfolk, the Israelites. 24 When he saw one of them treated unjustly, he defended and avenged the oppressed man by striking down the Egyptian. 25 He assumed [his] kinsfolk would understand that God was offering them deliverance through him, but they did not understand. 26* The next day he appeared to them as they were fighting and tried to reconcile them peacefully, saying, 'Men, you are brothers. Why are you harming one another?' 27 Then the one who was harming his neighbor pushed him aside, saying, 'Who appointed you ruler

did you KNOW?

Martyrs

The stoning of Stephen is a turning point in Luke's account of the first Christians. Stephen was the first Christian martyr— someone who dies for his or her faith. His death marked the beginning of a period of persecution of the early Christians. Up to then, Christians had been imprisoned but not put to death. Would the Christian movement fall apart now that the stakes were higher? Luke makes it clear that Stephen's death actually strengthened the church. His heroic sacrifice is even presented as a model for Christians—notice all the similarities between his death and Jesus'.

It is easy for North Americans to assume that religious persecution does not exist today. We do not normally hear stories of people being killed for their beliefs in Jesus or Christianity. Not so for people on other continents. All around the world, including places close to home, people are mistreated, and even killed, because of their religious beliefs.

For example, Archbishop Oscar Romero of El Salvador was shot to death because he challenged the wealthy and powerful people in his country to change their ways so the poor people could have a better quality of life. Archbishop Romero, like Stephen, was killed for being a faithful Christian.

Stephen was young just like you. He was convinced that following the teachings of Jesus was the most important way to live. He died for his beliefs, and the church became stronger because of his faith and heroism. What would you die for?

▶ Acts 6, 8—8, 1

7, 8: Gn 17, 10–14; 21, 2–4.
7, 9: Gn 37, 11.28; 39, 2.3.21.23.
7, 10: Gn 41, 37–43; Ps 105, 21; Wis 10, 13–14.
7, 11: Gn 41, 54–57; 42, 5.
7, 12: Gn 42, 1–2.
7, 13: Gn 45, 3–4.16.
7, 14: Gn 45, 9–11.18–19; 46, 27; Ex 1, 5 LXX; Dt 10, 22.
7, 15: Gn 46, 5–6; 49, 33.
7, 16: Gn 23, 3–20; 33, 19; 49, 29–30; 50, 13; Jos 24, 32.
7, 17: Ex 1, 7.
7, 18: Ex 1, 8.
7, 20: Ex 2, 2; Heb 11, 23.
7, 21: Ex 2, 3–10.
7, 23–24: Ex 2, 11–12.
7, 26–28: Ex 2, 13–14.

and judge over us? 28 Are you thinking of killing me as you killed the Egyptian yesterday?' 29* Moses fled when he heard this and settled as an alien in the land of Midian, where he became the father of two sons.

30* "Forty years later, an angel appeared to him in the desert near Mount Sinai in the flame of a burning bush. 31 When Moses saw it, he was amazed at the sight, and as he drew near to look at it, the voice of the Lord came, 32 'I am the God of your fathers, the God of Abraham, of Isaac, and of Jacob.' Then Moses, trembling, did not dare to look at it. 33 But the Lord said to him, 'Remove the sandals from your feet, for the place where you stand is holy ground. 34 I have witnessed the affliction of my people in Egypt and have heard their groaning, and I have come down to rescue them. Come now, I will send you to Egypt.' 35* This Moses, whom they had rejected with the words, 'Who appointed you ruler and judge?' God sent as [both] ruler and deliverer, through the angel who appeared to him in the bush. 36* This man led them out, performing wonders and signs in the land of Egypt, at the Red Sea, and in the desert for forty years. 37* It was this Moses who said to the Israelites, 'God will raise up for you, from among your own kinsfolk, a prophet like me.' 38* It was he who, in the assembly in the desert, was with the angel who spoke to him on Mount Sinai and with our ancestors, and he received living utterances to hand on to us.

39* "Our ancestors were unwilling to obey him; instead, they pushed him aside and in their hearts turned back to Egypt, 40* saying to Aaron, 'Make us gods who will be our leaders. As for that Moses who led us out of the land of Egypt, we do not know what has happened to him.' 41* So they made a calf in those days, offered sacrifice to the idol, and reveled in the works of their hands. 42* Then God turned and handed them over to worship the host of heaven, as it is written in the book of the prophets:

'Did you bring me sacrifices and offerings
   for forty years in the desert, O house
      of Israel?*
43   No, you took up the tent of Moloch
   and the star of [your] god Rephan,
      the images that you made to worship.
So I shall take you into exile beyond Babylon.'

44* Our ancestors had the tent of testimony in the desert just as the One who spoke to Moses directed him to make it according to the pattern he had seen. 45* Our ancestors who inherited it brought it with Joshua when they dispossessed the nations that God drove out from before our ancestors, up to the time of David, 46* who found favor in the sight of God and asked that he might find a dwelling place for the house of Jacob. 47* But Solomon built a house for him. 48* Yet the Most High does not dwell in houses made by human hands. As the prophet says:

49* 'The heavens are my throne,
        the earth is my footstool.
   What kind of house can you build for me?
        says the Lord,
   or what is to be my resting place?
50   Did not my hand make all these things?'

Conclusion

51 "You stiff-necked people, uncircumcised in heart and ears, you always oppose the holy Spirit; you are just like your ancestors. 52* Which of the prophets did your ancestors not persecute? They put to death those who foretold the coming of the righteous one, whose betrayers and murderers you have now become. 53* You received the law as transmitted by angels, but you did not observe it."

Stephen's Martyrdom

54 When they heard this, they were infuriated, and they ground their teeth at him. 55*† But he, filled with the holy Spirit, looked up intently to heaven and saw the glory of God and Jesus standing at the right hand of God, 56 and he said, "Behold, I see the heavens opened and the Son of Man standing at the right hand of God." 57† But they cried out in a loud voice, covered their ears, and rushed upon him together. 58* They threw him out of the city, and began to stone him. The witnesses laid down their cloaks at the feet of a young man named Saul. 59*† As they were stoning Stephen, he called out, "Lord Jesus, receive my spirit." 60* Then he fell to his knees and cried out in a loud voice, "Lord, do not hold this sin against them"; and when he said this, he fell asleep.

† 7, 55: He . . . saw . . . Jesus standing at the right hand of God: Stephen affirms to the Sanhedrin that the prophecy Jesus made before them has been fulfilled (Mk 14, 62).

7, 57: Covered their ears: Stephen's declaration, like that of Jesus, is a scandal to the court, which regards it as blasphemy.

7, 59: Compare Lk 23, [34].46.

7, 29: Ex 2, 15.21–22; 18,
   3–4.
7, 30–34: Ex 3, 2–3.
7, 35: Ex 2, 14.
7, 36: Ex 7, 3.10; 14, 21; Nm
   14, 33.
7, 37: Dt 18, 15; Acts 3, 22.
7, 38: Ex 19, 3; 20, 1–17; Dt
   5, 4–22; 6, 4–25.
7, 39: Nm 14, 3.
7, 40: Ex 32, 1.23.
7, 41: Ex 32, 4–6.
7, 42–43: Am 5, 25–27.
7, 42: Jer 7, 18; 8, 2; 19, 13.
7, 44: Ex 25, 9.40.
7, 45: Jos 3, 14–17; 18, 1;
   2 Sm 7, 5–7.
7, 46: 2 Sm 7, 1–2; 1 Kgs 8,
   17; Ps 132, 1–5.
7, 47: 1 Kgs 6, 1; 1 Chr 17,
   12.
7, 48: Acts 17, 24.
7, 49: Is 66, 1–2.
7, 52: 2 Chr 36, 16; Mt 23,
   31.34.
7, 53: Gal 3, 19; Heb 2, 2.
7, 55–56: Mt 26, 64; Mk 14, 62;
   Lk 22, 69; Acts 2, 34.
7, 58: Acts 22, 20.
7, 59: Ps 31, 6; Lk 23, 46.
7, 60: Mt 27, 46.50; Mk 15,
   34; Lk 23, 46.

A
C
T
S

8 ¹*† Now Saul was consenting to his execution.

Persecution of the Church

On that day, there broke out a severe persecution of the church in Jerusalem, and all were scattered throughout the countryside of Judea and Samaria, except the apostles.† ² Devout men buried Stephen and made a loud lament over him. ³*† Saul, meanwhile, was trying to destroy the church; entering house after house and dragging out men and women, he handed them over for imprisonment.

III: The Mission in Judea and Samaria

Philip in Samaria

⁴* Now those who had been scattered went about preaching the word. ⁵* Thus Philip went down to [the] city of Samaria and proclaimed the Messiah to them. ⁶ With one accord, the crowds paid attention to what was said by Philip when they heard it and saw the signs he was doing. ⁷* For unclean spirits, crying out in a loud voice, came out of many possessed people, and many paralyzed and crippled people were cured. ⁸ There was great joy in that city.

Introducing........
► SAINT PAUL

As Stephen is stoned to death, Acts introduces a person who will become the major character in the second half of the book, Saul of Tarsus, also known as Paul. Paul begins as a persecutor of the early Christians. He is a member of the Pharisees, a group that holds to a rigid interpretation of Jewish Law (26, 4–5). He probably sees the Christians as a threat to the Jewish faith. But after a profound experience of the risen Christ, Paul is converted to the Christian faith. Paul is initially distrusted by other Christians who remember his persecution of them. However, another early Christian leader, Barnabas, becomes Paul's companion and advocate (9, 27).

Paul's major insight is that God has made salvation available to everyone, Jews and Gentiles alike. He also knows that God's offer of salvation is a free gift, that no one could do anything to actually earn it. But many of the early Christians, who are former Jews, disagree with him. This conflict comes to a head at the Council of Jerusalem (Acts of the Apostles, chapter 15), where Paul stands toe-to-toe with Peter and James (Gal 2, 1–10) and argues that the Gentiles can become Christians without following Jewish laws and customs, including circumcision.

Paul took it upon himself to spread the good news of God's salvation in Jesus to the Gentiles. During three different missionary journeys, he was instrumental in founding new Christian communities in what is now the Middle East and western Europe. He stayed in touch with those communities through letters, some of which are included as books in the New Testament. Paul's impact in spreading Christianity was so great that he is sometimes called the second founder of Christianity.

► Acts 8, 1–3

A
C
T
S

---

† **8, 1–40:** Some idea of the severity of the persecution that now breaks out against the Jerusalem community can be gathered from 22, 4 and 26, 9–11. Luke, however, concentrates on the fortunes of the word of God among people, indicating how the dispersal of the Jewish community resulted in the conversion of the Samaritans (4–17.25). His narrative is further expanded to include the account of Philip's acceptance of an Ethiopian (26–39).

8, 1: *All were scattered . . . except the apostles:* this observation leads some modern scholars to conclude that the persecution was limited to the Hellenist Christians and that the Hebrew Christians were not molested, perhaps because their attitude toward the law and temple was still more in line with that of their fellow Jews (see the charge leveled against the Hellenist Stephen in 6, 13–14). Whatever the facts, it appears that the Twelve took no public stand regarding Stephen's position, choosing, instead, to await the development of events.

8, 3: *Saul . . . was trying to destroy the church:* like Stephen, Saul was able to perceive that the Christian movement contained the seeds of doctrinal divergence from Judaism. A pupil of Gamaliel, according to 22, 3, and totally dedicated to the law as the way of salvation (Gal 1, 13–14), Saul accepted the task of crushing the Christian movement, at least insofar as it detracted from the importance of the temple and the law. His vehement opposition to Christianity reveals how difficult it was for a Jew of his time to accept a messianism that differed so greatly from the general expectation.

8, 1: Acts 22, 20.
8, 3: Acts 9, 1.13; 22, 4; 26,
    9–11; 1 Cor 5, 9; Gal
    1, 13.
8, 4: Acts 11, 19.
8, 5: Acts 6, 5; 21, 8–9.
8, 7: Mk 16, 17.

Simon the Magician

[9]† A man named Simon used to practice magic in the city and astounded the people of Samaria, claiming to be someone great. [10] All of them, from the least to the greatest, paid attention to him, saying, "This man is the 'Power of God' that is called 'Great.' " [11] They paid attention to him because he had astounded them by his magic for a long time, [12]* but once they began to believe Philip as he preached the good news about the kingdom of God and the name of Jesus Christ, men and women alike were baptized. [13] Even Simon himself believed and, after being baptized, became devoted to Philip; and when he saw the signs and mighty deeds that were occurring, he was astounded.

[14] Now when the apostles in Jerusalem heard that Samaria had accepted the word of God, they sent them Peter and John, [15] who went down and prayed for them, that they might receive the holy Spirit, [16]† for it had not yet fallen upon any of them; they had only been baptized in the name of the Lord Jesus. [17]* Then they laid hands on them and they received the holy Spirit.

[18]† When Simon saw that the Spirit was conferred by the laying on of the apostles' hands, he offered them money [19] and said, "Give me this power too, so that anyone upon whom I lay my hands may receive the holy Spirit." [20] But Peter said to him, "May your money perish with you, because you thought that you could buy the gift of God with money. [21] You have no share or lot in this matter, for your heart is not upright before God. [22] Repent of this wickedness of yours and pray to the Lord that, if possible, your intention may be forgiven. [23] For I see that you are filled with bitter gall and are in the bonds of iniquity." [24] Simon said in reply, "Pray for me to the Lord, that nothing of what you have said may come upon me." [25] So when they had testified and proclaimed the word of the Lord, they returned to Jerusalem and preached the good news to many Samaritan villages.

Bearing Good News

Acts 8, 26–40 tells the story of an Ethiopian (African) eunuch. A eunuch is a man who has been castrated, either by accident or by design. Eunuchs often served as guards of the harems of kings. This eunuch was reading a text from Isaiah while returning from a visit to Jerusalem. The Holy Spirit moved the missionary Philip to explain to him how Isaiah's prophecies pointed to Jesus. And the eunuch believed and was baptized. His baptism signals the beginning acceptance of Gentile believers.

The eunuch's faith was dependent on the interaction of three characters: himself, the searching eunuch; Philip, bearing the Good News; and the Holy Spirit, who brought them together. Reflect for a moment on the following questions:

- How are you like the Ethiopian? What are you searching for in your faith?
- How are you like Philip? How do you share the Good News with others?
- How can you share in the work of the Holy Spirit? How can you motivate other young people to become bearers of the Good News?

As Philip baptized the eunuch, geographical, ethnic, and legal barriers were washed away. Praise God for the salvation brought by Jesus to all people!

▶ Acts 8, 26–40

---

† 8, 9–13.18–24: Sorcerers were well known in the ancient world. Probably the incident involving Simon and his altercation with Peter is introduced to show that the miraculous charisms possessed by members of the Christian community (6–7) were not to be confused with the magic of sorcerers.

8, 16: Here and in 10, 44–48 and 19, 1–6, Luke distinguishes between baptism in the name of the Lord Jesus and the reception of the Spirit. In each case, the Spirit is conferred through members of the Twelve (Peter and John) or their representative (Paul). This may be Luke's way of describing the role of the church in the bestowal of the Spirit. Elsewhere in Acts, baptism and the Spirit are more closely related (1, 5; 11, 16).

8, 18–20: Simon attempts to buy the gift of God (20) with money. Peter's cursing of Simon's attempt so to use his money expresses a typically Lucan attitude toward material wealth (cf Lk 6, 24; 12, 16–21; 16, 13).

8, 12: Acts 1, 3; 19, 8; 28, 23.31.   44–47; 15, 8–9; 19, 2.6.
8, 17: Acts 2, 4; 4, 31; 10,

Philip and the Ethiopian

26† Then the angel of the Lord spoke to Philip, "Get up and head south on the road that goes down from Jerusalem to Gaza, the desert route." 27*† So he got up and set out. Now there was an Ethiopian eunuch, a court official of the Candace, that is, the queen of the Ethiopians, in charge of her entire treasury, who had come to Jerusalem to worship, 28 and was returning home. Seated in his chariot, he was reading the prophet Isaiah. 29 The Spirit said to Philip, "Go and join up with that chariot." 30† Philip ran up and heard him reading Isaiah the prophet and said, "Do you understand what you are reading?" 31* He replied, "How can I, unless someone instructs me?" So he invited Philip to get in and sit with him. 32* This was the scripture passage he was reading:

"Like a sheep he was led to the slaughter,
  and as a lamb before its shearer is silent,
    so he opened not his mouth.
33 In [his] humiliation justice was denied
    him.
  Who will tell of his posterity?
    For his life is taken from the earth."

34 Then the eunuch said to Philip in reply, "I beg you, about whom is the prophet saying this? About himself, or about someone else?" 35 Then Philip opened his mouth and, beginning with this scripture passage, he proclaimed Jesus to him. 36* As they traveled along the road they came to some water, and the eunuch said, "Look, there is water. What is to prevent my being baptized?" [37]† 38 Then he ordered the chariot to stop, and Philip and the eunuch both went down into the water, and he baptized him. 39* When they came out of the water, the Spirit of the Lord snatched Philip away, and the eunuch saw him no more, but continued on his way rejoicing. 40* Philip came to Azotus, and went about proclaiming the good news to all the towns until he reached Caesarea.

Saul's Conversion

9 1*† Now Saul, still breathing murderous threats against the disciples of the Lord, went to the high priest* 2† and asked him for letters to the synagogues in Damascus, that, if he should find any men or women who belonged to the Way, he might bring them back to Jerusalem in chains. 3* On his journey, as he was nearing Damascus, a light from the sky suddenly flashed around him. 4* He fell to the ground and heard a voice saying to him, "Saul, Saul, why are you persecuting me?"

9, 4
"Saul
Saul
why"

---

† **8, 26–40:** In the account of the conversion of the Ethiopian eunuch, Luke adduces additional evidence to show that the spread of Christianity outside the confines of Judaism itself was in accord with the plan of God. He does not make clear whether the Ethiopian was originally a convert to Judaism or, as is more probable, a "God-fearer" (10, 1), i.e., one who accepted Jewish monotheism and ethic and attended the synagogue but did not consider himself bound by other regulations such as circumcision and observance of the dietary laws. The story of his conversion to Christianity is given a strong supernatural cast by the introduction of an angel (26), instruction from the holy Spirit (29), and the strange removal of Philip from the scene (39).

8, 27: *The Candace:* Candace is not a proper name here but the title of a Nubian queen.

8, 30–34: Philip is brought alongside the carriage at the very moment when the eunuch is pondering the meaning of Is 53, 7–8, a passage that Christianity, from its earliest origins, has applied to Jesus; cf the note on 3, 13.

8, 37: The oldest and best manuscripts of Acts omit this verse, which is a Western text reading: "And Philip said, 'If you believe with all your heart, you may.' And he said in reply, 'I believe that Jesus Christ is the Son of God.' "

9, 1–19: This is the first of three accounts of Paul's conversion (with 22, 3–16 and 26, 2–18) with some differences of detail owing to Luke's use of different sources. Paul's experience was not visionary but was precipitated by the appearance of Jesus, as he insists in 1 Cor 15, 8. The words of Jesus, "Saul, Saul, why are you persecuting me?" related by Luke with no variation in all three accounts, exerted a profound and lasting influence on the thought of Paul. Under the influence of this experience he gradually developed his understanding of justification by faith (see the letters to the Galatians and Romans) and of the identification of the Christian community with Jesus Christ (see 1 Cor 12, 27). That Luke would narrate this conversion three times is testimony to the importance he attaches to it. This first account occurs when the word is first spread to the Gentiles. At this point, the conversion of the hero of the Gentile mission is recounted. The emphasis in the account is on Paul as a divinely chosen instrument (15).

9, 2: *The Way:* a name used by the early Christian community for itself (18, 26; 19, 9.23; 22, 4; 24, 14.22). The Essene community at Qumran used the same designation to describe its mode of life.

8, 27: Is 56, 3–5.
8, 31: Jn 16, 13.
8, 32–33: Is 53, 7–8 LXX.
8, 36: Acts 10, 47.
8, 39: 1 Kgs 18, 12.
8, 40: Acts 21, 8.

9, 1: Acts 8, 3; 9, 13; 22, 4;
  1 Cor 15, 9; Gal 1,
  13–14.
9, 1–2: Acts 9, 14; 26, 10.
9, 3: 1 Cor 9, 1; 15, 8; Gal
  1, 16.
9, 4: Acts 22, 6; 26, 14.

5* He said, "Who are you, sir?" The reply came, "I am Jesus, whom you are persecuting. 6* Now get up and go into the city and you will be told what you must do." 7* The men who were traveling with him stood speechless, for they heard the voice but could see no one. 8*† Saul got up from the ground, but when he opened his eyes he could see nothing; so they led him by the hand and brought him to Damascus. 9 For three days he was unable to see, and he neither ate nor drank.

Saul's Baptism

10* There was a disciple in Damascus named Ananias, and the Lord said to him in a vision, "Ananias." He answered, "Here I am, Lord." 11* The Lord said to him, "Get up and go to the street called Straight and ask at the house of Judas for a man from Tarsus named Saul. He is there praying, 12 and [in a vision] he has seen a man named Ananias come in and lay [his] hands on him, that he may regain his sight." 13*† But Ananias replied, "Lord, I have heard from many sources about this man, what evil things he has done to your holy ones in Jerusalem. 14* And here he has authority from the chief priests to imprison all who call upon your name." 15* But the Lord said to him, "Go, for this man is a chosen instrument of mine to carry my name before Gentiles, kings, and Israelites, 16 and I will show him what he will have to suffer for my name." 17 So Ananias went and entered the house; laying his hands on him, he said, "Saul, my brother, the Lord has sent me, Jesus who appeared to you on the way by which you came, that you may regain your sight and be filled with the holy Spirit." 18 Immediately things like scales fell from his eyes and he regained his sight. He got up and was baptized, 19† and when he had eaten, he recovered his strength.

Saul Preaches in Damascus

He stayed some days with the disciples in Damascus, 20† and he began at once to proclaim Jesus in the synagogues, that he is the Son of God. 21 All who heard him were astounded and said, "Is not this the man who in Jerusalem ravaged those who call upon this name, and came here expressly to take them back in chains to the chief priests?" 22 But Saul grew all the stronger and confounded [the] Jews who lived in Damascus, proving that this is the Messiah.

Conversion

Saul (or Paul) experienced some dramatic events that converted him from a persecutor of Christians to a believer in Jesus Christ. He had a powerful experience of the risen Christ during which he was blinded. His physical blindness is symbolic of his previous spiritual blindness. For three days, Paul was practically lifeless—not seeing, not eating, not drinking. This period reminds us of Jesus' three days in the tomb. In many ways, going through a conversion is like dying—dying to old ways of thinking and acting. But after three days, Paul's blindness was lifted, and he was filled with the Holy Spirit, as the other Apostles were at Pentecost.

No longer a persecutor of Christians, Paul was a new person. He now felt compelled to learn more about Jesus and to share the Good News with other people. Paul's conversion told the early Christians that even the most hard-hearted person can be called by God and radically changed.

In your prayer, reflect or journal on the following questions:
- Have you ever been suddenly aware of God's presence and calling in your life?
- What mission is God calling you for?
- How will you respond?

Then close with these words:

Dear Jesus, following you is an unending journey in which we must turn our back to sin and focus on living out Christ's message. Sometimes, it is an easy journey; sometimes, it is a struggle. Help me to find your light in the Scriptures, in others, and within myself. Amen.

▶ Acts 9, 1–19

9, 8: *He could see nothing:* a temporary blindness (18) symbolizing the religious blindness of Saul as persecutor (cf 26, 18).

9, 13: *Your holy ones:* literally, "your saints."

9, 19–30: This is a brief resume of Paul's initial experience as an apostolic preacher. At first he found himself in the position of being regarded as an apostate by the Jews and suspect by the Christian community of Jerusalem. His acceptance by the latter was finally brought about through his friendship with Barnabas (27).

9, 20: *Son of God:* the title "Son of God" occurs in Acts only

here, but cf the citation of Ps 2, 7 in Paul's speech at Antioch in Pisidia (13, 33).

9, 5: Acts 22, 8; 26, 15; Mt 25, 40.
9, 6: Acts 22, 10; 26, 16.
9, 7: Acts 22, 9; 26, 13–14.
9, 8: Acts 22, 11.
9, 10–19: Acts 22, 12–16.
9, 11: Acts 21, 39.
9, 13: Acts 8, 3; 9, 1.
9, 14: Acts 9, 1–2; 26, 10; 1 Cor 1, 2; 2 Tm 2, 22.
9, 15: Acts 22, 15; 26, 1; 27, 24.

ACTS

Saul Visits Jerusalem

23 After a long time had passed, the Jews conspired to kill him, 24* but their plot became known to Saul. Now they were keeping watch on the gates day and night so as to kill him, 25 but his disciples took him one night and let him down through an opening in the wall, lowering him in a basket.

26*† When he arrived in Jerusalem he tried to join the disciples, but they were all afraid of him, not believing that he was a disciple. 27 Then Barnabas took charge of him and brought him to the apostles, and he reported to them how on the way he had seen the Lord and that he had spoken to him, and how in Damascus he had spoken out boldly in the name of Jesus. 28 He moved about freely with them in Jerusalem, and spoke out boldly in the name of the Lord. 29† He also spoke and debated with the Hellenists, but they tried to kill him. 30* And when the brothers learned of this, they took him down to Caesarea and sent him on his way to Tarsus.

The Church at Peace

31† The church throughout all Judea, Galilee, and Samaria was at peace. It was being built up and walked in the fear of the Lord, and with the consolation of the holy Spirit it grew in numbers.

Peter Heals Aeneas at Lydda

32 As Peter was passing through every region, he went down to the holy ones living in Lydda. 33 There he found a man named Aeneas, who had been confined to bed for eight years, for he was paralyzed. 34 Peter said to him, "Aeneas, Jesus Christ heals you. Get up and make your bed." He got up at once. 35 And all the inhabitants of Lydda and Sharon saw him, and they turned to the Lord.

Peter Restores Tabitha to Life

36† Now in Joppa there was a disciple named Tabitha (which translated means Dorcas). She was completely occupied with good deeds and almsgiving. 37 Now during those days she fell sick and died, so after washing her, they laid [her] out in a room upstairs. 38 Since Lydda was near Joppa, the disciples, hearing that Peter was there, sent two men to him with the request, "Please come to us without delay." 39 So Peter got up and went with them. When he arrived, they took him to the room upstairs where all the widows came to him weeping and showing him the tunics and cloaks that Dorcas had made while she was with them. 40* Peter sent them all out and knelt down and prayed. Then he turned to her body and said, "Tabitha, rise up." She opened her eyes, saw Peter, and sat up. 41 He gave her his hand and raised her up, and when he had called the holy ones and the widows, he presented her alive. 42 This became known all over Joppa, and many came to believe in the Lord. 43*† And he stayed a long time in Joppa with Simon, a tanner.

IV: The Inauguration of the Gentile Mission

The Vision of Cornelius

10 1*† Now in Caesarea there was a man named Cornelius, a centurion of the Cohort called the Italica,† 2† devout and God-fearing along with his whole household, who used to give alms generously to the Jewish people and pray to God constantly. 3† One afternoon about three o'clock, he saw plainly in a vision an angel of God come in to him and say to him, "Cornelius." 4 He looked intently at him and, seized with fear, said, "What is it, sir?" He said to him, "Your prayers and almsgiving have ascended as a memorial offering before God. 5 Now send some men to Joppa and summon one Simon who is called Peter. 6* He is staying with another Simon, a tanner, who has a house by the sea." 7† When the angel who spoke to him had left, he called two of his servants and a

† **9, 26:** This visit of Paul to Jerusalem is mentioned by Paul in Gal 1, 18.

9, 29: *Hellenists:* see the note on 6, 1–7.

9, 31–43: In the context of the period of peace enjoyed by the community through the cessation of Paul's activities against it, Luke introduces two traditions concerning the miraculous power exercised by Peter as he was making a tour of places where the Christian message had already been preached. The towns of Lydda, Sharon, and Joppa were populated by both Jews and Gentiles and their Christian communities may well have been mixed.

9, 36: *Tabitha (Dorcas),* respectively the Aramaic and Greek words for "gazelle," exemplifies the right attitude toward material possessions expressed by Jesus in the Lucan Gospel (Lk 6, 30; 11, 41; 12, 33; 18, 22; 19, 8).

9, 43: The fact that Peter lodged with a tanner would have been significant to both the Gentile and Jewish Christians, for Judaism considered the tanning occupation unclean.

10, 1–48: The narrative centers on the conversion of Cornelius, a Gentile and a "God-fearer" (see the note on 8, 26–40). Luke considers the event of great importance, as is evident from his long treatment of

it. The incident is again related in 11, 1–18 where Peter is forced to justify his actions before the Jerusalem community and alluded to in 15, 7–11 where at the Jerusalem "Council" Peter supports Paul's missionary activity among the Gentiles. The narrative divides itself into a series of distinct episodes, concluding with Peter's presentation of the Christian kerygma (34–43) and a pentecostal experience undergone by Cornelius' household preceding their reception of baptism (44–48).

10, 1: *The Cohort called the Italica:* this battalion was an auxiliary unit of archers formed originally in Italy but transferred to Syria shortly before A.D. 69.

10, 2: *Used to give alms generously:* like Tabitha (9, 36), Cornelius exemplifies the proper attitude toward wealth (see the note on 9, 36).

10, 3: *About three o'clock:* literally, "about the ninth hour." See the note on 3, 1.

10, 7: *A devout soldier:* by using this adjective, Luke probably intends to classify him as a "God-fearer" (see the note on 8, 26–40).

9, 24–25: 2 Cor 11, 32–33.   9, 43: Acts 10, 6.
9, 26–27: Gal 1, 18.   10, 1–8: Acts 10, 30–33.
   9, 30: Acts 11, 25.   10, 6: Acts 9, 43.
   9, 40: Mk 5, 40–41.

devout soldier from his staff, [8] explained everything to them, and sent them to Joppa.

The Vision of Peter

[9]† The next day, while they were on their way and nearing the city, Peter went up to the roof terrace to pray at about noontime.† [10] He was hungry and wished to eat, and while they were making preparations he fell into a trance. [11]* He saw heaven opened and something resembling a large sheet coming down, lowered to the ground by its four corners. [12] In it were all the earth's four-legged animals and reptiles and the birds of the sky. [13] A voice said to him, "Get up, Peter. Slaughter and eat." [14]* But Peter said, "Certainly not, sir. For never have I eaten anything profane and unclean." [15]* The voice spoke to him again, a second time, "What God has made clean, you are not to call profane." [16] This happened three times, and then the object was taken up into the sky.

[17]† While Peter was in doubt about the meaning of the vision he had seen, the men sent by Cornelius asked for Simon's house and arrived at the entrance. [18] They called out inquiring whether Simon, who is called Peter, was staying there. [19]* As Peter was pondering the vision, the Spirit said [to him], "There are three men here looking for you. [20] So get up, go downstairs, and accompany them without hesitation, because I have sent them." [21] Then Peter went down to the men and said, "I am the one you are looking for. What is the reason for your being here?" [22]* They answered, "Cornelius, a centurion, an upright and God-fearing man, respected by the whole Jewish nation, was directed by a holy angel to summon you to his house and to hear what you have to say." [23] So he invited them in and showed them hospitality.

The next day he got up and went with them, and some of the brothers from Joppa went with him. [24]† On the following day he entered Caesarea. Cornelius was expecting them and had called together his relatives and close friends. [25] *When Peter entered, Cornelius met him and, falling at his feet, paid him homage. [26] Peter, however, raised him up, saying, "Get up. I myself am also a human being." [27] While he conversed with him, he went in and found many people gathered together [28]*† and said to them, "You know that it is unlawful for a Jewish man to associate with, or visit, a Gentile, but God has shown me that I should not call any person profane or unclean. [29] And that is why I came without objection when sent for. May I ask, then, why you summoned me?"

[30]† Cornelius replied, "Four days ago at this hour, three o'clock in the afternoon, I was at prayer in my house when suddenly a man in dazzling robes stood before me and said, [31] 'Cornelius, your prayer has been heard and your almsgiving remembered before God. [32] Send therefore to Joppa and summon Simon, who is called Peter. He is a guest in the house of Simon, a tanner, by the sea.' [33] So I sent for you immediately, and you were kind enough to come. Now therefore we are all here in the presence of God to listen to all that you have been commanded by the Lord."

Peter's Speech†

[34]* Then Peter proceeded to speak and said,† "In truth, I see that God shows no partiality. [35] Rather, in every nation whoever fears him and acts uprightly is acceptable to him. [36]*† You know the word [that] he sent to the Israelites† as he proclaimed peace through Jesus Christ, who is Lord of all, [37]* what has happened all over Judea, beginning in Galilee after the baptism that John preached, [38]*† how God anointed Jesus of Nazareth with the holy Spirit and

---

10, 9–16: The vision is intended to prepare Peter to share the food of Cornelius' household without qualms of conscience (48). The necessity of such instructions to Peter reveals that at first not even the apostles fully grasped the implications of Jesus' teaching on the law. In Acts, the initial insight belongs to Stephen.

10, 9: *At about noontime:* literally, "about the sixth hour."

10, 17–23: The arrival of the Gentile emissaries with their account of the angelic apparition illuminates Peter's vision: he is to be prepared to admit Gentiles, who were considered unclean like the animals of his vision, into the Christian community.

10, 24–27: So impressed is Cornelius with the apparition that he invites close personal friends to join him in his meeting with Peter. But his understanding of the person he is about to meet is not devoid of superstition, suggested by his falling down before him. For a similar experience of Paul and Barnabas, see 14, 11–18.

10, 28: Peter now fully understands the meaning of his vision; see the note on 10, 17–23.

10, 30: *Four days ago:* literally, "from the fourth day up to this hour."

10, 34–43: Peter's speech to the household of Cornelius typifies early Christian preaching to Gentiles.

10, 34–35: The revelation of God's choice of Israel to be the people of God did not mean he withheld the divine favor from other people.

10, 36–43: These words are more directed to Luke's Christian readers than to the household of Cornelius, as indicated by the opening words, "You know." They trace the continuity between the preaching and teaching of Jesus of Nazareth and the proclamation of Jesus by the early community. The emphasis on this divinely ordained continuity (41) is meant to assure Luke's readers of the fidelity of Christian tradition to the words and deeds of Jesus.

10, 36: *To the Israelites:* Luke, in the words of Peter, speaks of the prominent position occupied by Israel in the history of salvation.

10, 38: *Jesus of Nazareth:* God's revelation of his plan for the destiny of humanity through Israel culminated in Jesus of Nazareth. Consequently, the ministry of Jesus is an integral part of God's revelation. This viewpoint explains why the early Christian communities were interested in conserving the historical substance of the ministry of Jesus, a tradition leading to the production of the four gospels.

10, 11–20: Acts 11, 5–12.
10, 14: Lv 11, 1–47; Ez 4, 14.
10, 15: Mk 7, 15–19; Gal 2, 12.
10, 19: Acts 13, 2.
10, 22: Lk 7, 4–5.
10, 25–26: Acts 14, 13–15; Rv 19, 10.

10, 28: Gal 2, 11–16.
10, 34: Dt 17, 2; 2 Chr 19, 7; Jb 34, 19; Wis 6, 7; Rom 2, 11; Gal 2, 6; Eph 6, 9; 1 Pt 1, 17.
10, 36: Is 52, 7; Na 2, 1.
10, 37: Mt 4, 12; Mk 1, 14; Lk 4, 14.
10, 38: Is 61, 1; Lk 4, 18.

HERE COMES EVERYBODY

The word *catholic* means "universal." Someone once described being Catholic as, "Here comes everybody!"

In Acts 10, 34–36, we hear that because God shows no partiality, neither should we. Even so, it is sometimes easier to stick with people who are similar to us. They understand us and know where we are coming from. There's less explaining to do. Right?

But being catholic means reaching out of our familiar circle of friends and including in our group people of different cultures and religions.

Have you ever seen a Native American blanket? Threads of various colors are woven together to form an intricate, new pattern. Each blanket is completely different from every other blanket. By building relationships with people of different cultures and embracing their diversity, we become like one of the threads in such a blanket, weaving our uniquenesses in a new and beautiful pattern. The result is different and enriching, and then we become truly catholic.

▶ Acts 10, 34–36

---

power. He went about doing good and healing all those oppressed by the devil, for God was with him. [39]† We are witnesses of all that he did both in the country of the Jews and [in] Jerusalem. They put him to death by hanging him on a tree. [40] This man God raised [on] the third day and granted that he be visible, [41]* not to all the people, but to us, the witnesses chosen by God in advance, who ate and drank with him after he rose from the dead. [42]*† He commissioned us to preach to the people and testify that he is the one appointed by God as judge of the living and the dead. [43] To him all the prophets bear witness, that everyone who believes in him will receive forgiveness of sins through his name."

The Baptism of Cornelius

[44]*† While Peter was still speaking these things, the holy Spirit fell upon all who were listening to the word. [45] The circumcised believers who had accompanied Peter were astounded that the gift of the holy Spirit should have been poured out on the Gentiles also, [46] for they could hear them speaking in tongues and glorifying God. Then Peter responded, [47]* "Can anyone withhold the water for baptizing these people, who have received the holy Spirit even as we have?" [48] He ordered them to be baptized in the name of Jesus Christ. [49] Then they invited him to stay for a few days.

The Baptism of the Gentiles Explained

11 [1]† Now the apostles and the brothers who were in Judea heard that the Gentiles too had accepted the word of God. [2] So when Peter went up to Jerusalem the circumcised believers confronted him, [3]† saying, "You entered the house of uncircumcised people and ate with them." [4] Peter began and

---

10, 39: *We are witnesses:* the apostolic testimony was not restricted to the resurrection of Jesus but also included his historical ministry. This witness, however, was theological in character; the Twelve, divinely mandated as prophets, were empowered to interpret his sayings and deeds in the light of his redemptive death and resurrection. The meaning of these words and deeds was to be made clear to the developing Christian community as the bearer of the word of salvation (cf 1, 21–26). *Hanging him on a tree:* see the note on 5, 30.

10, 42: *As judge of the living and the dead:* the apostolic preaching to the Jews appealed to their messianic hope, while the preaching to Gentiles stressed the coming divine judgment; cf 1 Thes 1, 10.

10, 44: Just as the Jewish Christians received the gift of the Spirit, so too do the Gentiles.

11, 1–18: The Jewish Christians of Jerusalem were scandalized to learn of Peter's sojourn in the house of the Gentile Cornelius. Nonetheless, they had to accept the divine directions given to both Peter and Cornelius. They concluded that the setting aside of the legal barriers between Jew and Gentile was an exceptional ordinance of God to indicate that the apostolic kerygma was also to be directed to the Gentiles. Only in ch 15 at the "Council" in Jerusalem does the evangelization of the Gentiles become the official position of the church leadership in Jerusalem.

11, 3: *You entered . . . :* alternatively, this could be punctuated as a question.

10, 41: Lk 24, 41–43.   10, 44: Acts 11, 15; 15, 8.
10, 42: Acts 1, 8; 3, 15; 17, 31;   10, 47: Acts 8, 36.
          Lk 24, 48; Rom 14, 9;
          2 Tm 4, 1.

explained it to them step by step, saying, 5* "I was at prayer in the city of Joppa when in a trance I had a vision, something resembling a large sheet coming down, lowered from the sky by its four corners, and it came to me. 6 Looking intently into it, I observed and saw the four-legged animals of the earth, the wild beasts, the reptiles, and the birds of the sky. 7 I also heard a voice say to me, 'Get up, Peter. Slaughter and eat.' 8 But I said, 'Certainly not, sir, because nothing profane or unclean has ever entered my mouth.' 9 But a second time a voice from heaven answered, 'What God has made clean, you are not to call profane.' 10 This happened three times, and then everything was drawn up again into the sky. 11 Just then three men appeared at the house where we were, who had been sent to me from Caesarea. 12† The Spirit told me to accompany them without discriminating. These six brothers also went with me, and we entered the man's house. 13* He related to us how he had seen [the] angel standing in his house, saying, 'Send someone to Joppa and summon Simon, who is called Peter, 14 who will speak words to you by which you and all your household will be saved.' 15* As I began to speak, the holy Spirit fell upon them as it had upon us at the beginning, 16* and I remembered the word of the Lord, how he had said, 'John baptized with water but you will be baptized with the holy Spirit.' 17* If then God gave them the same gift he gave to us when we came to believe in the Lord Jesus Christ, who was I to be able to hinder God?" 18 When they heard this, they stopped objecting and glorified God, saying, "God has then granted life-giving repentance to the Gentiles too."

The Church at Antioch

19*† Now those who had been scattered by the persecution that arose because of Stephen went as far as Phoenicia, Cyprus, and Antioch, preaching the word to no one but Jews. 20 There were some Cypriots and Cyrenians among them, however, who came to Antioch and began to speak to the Greeks as well, proclaiming the Lord Jesus. 21 The hand of the Lord was with them and a great number who believed turned to the Lord. 22 The news about them reached the ears of the church in Jerusalem, and they sent Barnabas [to go] to Antioch. 23 When he arrived and saw the grace of God, he rejoiced and encouraged them all to remain faithful to the Lord in firmness of heart, 24 for he was a good man, filled with the holy Spirit and faith. And a large number of people was added to the Lord. 25 Then he went to Tarsus to look for Saul, 26† and when he had found him he brought him to Antioch. For a whole year they met with the church and taught a large number of

Introducing ►BARNABAS

We first met Barnabas defending Paul after Paul's conversion in Acts of the Apostles, chapter 9. Now, in chapter 11, we are told that Barnabas "was a good man, filled with the holy Spirit and faith." Barnabas's name literally means "son of encouragement." And encouraging others seemed to be Barnabas's gift. He recognized Paul's gifts and brought Paul to Antioch to minister to the new Christians there when no one else trusted Paul. Later, Barnabas reached out to Mark, disagreeing with Paul on whether to give Mark a second chance to travel with them (15, 36–41). Barnabas sounds like the friend we would all like to have, someone who would believe in us through good times and bad.

Have you had a Barnabas in your life, someone who encouraged you and believed in you even after you made mistakes? Can you be that kind of encouraging friend to others?

► Acts 11, 19–26

---

† **11, 12:** *These six brothers:* companions from the Christian community of Joppa (see 10, 23).

11, 19–26: The Jewish Christian antipathy to the mixed community was reflected by the early missionaries generally. The few among them who entertained a different view succeeded in introducing Gentiles into the community at Antioch (in Syria). When the disconcerted Jerusalem community sent Barnabas to investigate, he was so favorably impressed by what he observed that he persuaded his friend Saul to participate in the Antioch mission.

11, 26: *Christians:* "Christians" is first applied to the members of the community at Antioch because the Gentile members of the community enable it to stand out clearly from Judaism.

* **11, 5–12:** Acts 10, 11–20.
11, 13: Acts 10, 3–5.22.30–32.
11, 15: Acts 10, 44.
11, 16: Acts 1, 5; 19, 4; Lk 3, 16.
11, 17: Acts 15, 8–9.
11, 19: Acts 8, 1–4.

people, and it was in Antioch that the disciples were first called Christians.

The Prediction of Agabus

27† At that time some prophets came down from Jerusalem to Antioch, 28* and one of them named Agabus stood up and predicted by the Spirit that there would be a severe famine all over the world, and it happened under Claudius. 29* So the disciples determined that, according to ability, each should send relief to the brothers who lived in Judea. 30† This they did, sending it to the presbyters in care of Barnabas and Saul.

Herod's Persecution of the Christians

12 1† About that time King Herod laid hands upon some members of the church to harm them. 2† He had James, the brother of John, killed by the sword, 3† and when he saw that this was pleasing to the Jews he proceeded to arrest Peter also. (It was [the] feast of Unleavened Bread.) 4 He had him taken into custody and put in prison under the guard of four squads of four soldiers each. He intended to bring him before the

What Imprisons You?

*H*oly Spirit, come! Open my mind to seek the truth. Break down the barriers that imprison me. Empower me to overcome any guilt by asking for forgiveness. Enable me to forgive others and release my past hurt and anger. Open my eyes to vices, habits, and attitudes that are destructive to me and to others. Guide me to true freedom with your Word. Amen.

▸ Acts 12, 6–19

people after Passover. 5* Peter thus was being kept in prison, but prayer by the church was fervently being made to God on his behalf.

6 On the very night before Herod was to bring him to trial, Peter, secured by double chains, was sleeping between two soldiers, while outside the door guards kept watch on the prison. 7 Suddenly the angel of the Lord stood by him and a light shone in the cell. He tapped Peter on the side and awakened him, saying, "Get up quickly." The chains fell from his wrists. 8 The angel said to him, "Put on your belt and your sandals." He did so. Then he said to him, "Put on your cloak and follow me." 9 So he followed him out, not realizing that what was happening through the angel was real; he thought he was seeing a vision. 10 They passed the first guard, then the second, and came to the iron gate leading out to the city, which opened for them by itself. They emerged and made their way down an alley, and suddenly the angel left him. 11 Then Peter recovered his senses and said, "Now I know for certain that [the] Lord sent his angel and rescued me from the hand of Herod and from all that the Jewish people had been expecting." 12* When he realized this, he went to the house of Mary, the mother of John who is called Mark, where there were many people gathered in prayer. 13 When he knocked on the gateway door, a maid named Rhoda came to answer it. 14 She was so overjoyed when she recognized Peter's voice that, instead of opening the gate, she ran in and announced that Peter was standing at the gate. 15 They told her, "You are out of your mind," but she insisted that it was so. But they kept saying, "It is his angel." 16 But Peter continued to knock, and when they opened it, they saw him and were astounded. 17† He motioned to them with his hand to be quiet and explained [to them] how the Lord had led him out of the prison, and said, "Report this to James and the brothers." Then he left and went to another place. 18* At daybreak there was no small commotion among the soldiers over what had become of Peter. 19 Herod, after instituting a search but not finding him, ordered the guards tried and executed. Then he left Judea to spend some time in Caesarea.

11, 27–30: It is not clear whether the prophets from Jerusalem came to Antioch to request help in view of the coming famine or whether they received this insight during their visit there. The former supposition seems more likely. Suetonius and Tacitus speak of famines during the reign of Claudius (A.D. 41–54), while the Jewish historian Josephus mentions a famine in Judea in A.D. 46–48. Luke is interested, rather, in showing the charity of the Antiochene community toward the Jewish Christians of Jerusalem despite their differences on mixed communities.

11, 30: *Presbyters:* this is the same Greek word that elsewhere is translated "elders," primarily in reference to the Jewish community.

12, 1–19: Herod Agrippa ruled Judea A.D. 41–44. While Luke does not assign a motive for his execution of James and his intended execution of Peter, the broad background lies in Herod's support of Pharisaic Judaism. The Jewish Christians had lost the popularity they had had in Jerusalem (2, 47), perhaps because of suspicions against them traceable to the teaching of Stephen.

12, 2: *James, the brother of John:* this James, the son of Zebedee, was beheaded by Herod Agrippa ca. A.D. 44.

12, 3.4: *Feast of Unleavened Bread . . . , Passover:* see the note on Lk 22, 1.

12, 17: *To James:* this James is not the son of Zebedee mentioned in v 2, but is James, the "brother of the Lord" (Gal 1, 19), who in chs 15 and 21 is presented as leader of the Jerusalem Christian community. *He left and went to another place:* the conjecture that Peter left for Rome at this time has nothing to recommend it. His chief responsibility was still the leadership of the Jewish Christian community in Palestine (see Gal 2, 7). The concept of the great missionary effort of the church was yet to come (see 13, 1–3).

11, 28: Acts 21, 10.   12, 12: Acts 12, 25; 15, 37.
11, 29–30: Acts 12, 25.   12, 18: Acts 5, 22–24.
12, 5: Jas 5, 16.

Herod's Death

20† He had long been very angry with the people of Tyre and Sidon, who now came to him in a body. After winning over Blastus, the king's chamberlain, they sued for peace because their country was supplied with food from the king's territory. **21** On an appointed day, Herod, attired in royal robes, [and] seated on the rostrum, addressed them publicly. **22** The assembled crowd cried out, "This is the voice of a god, not of a man." **23** At once the angel of the Lord struck him down because he did not ascribe the honor to God, and he was eaten by worms and breathed his last. **24*** But the word of God continued to spread and grow.

Mission of Barnabas and Saul

25*† After Barnabas and Saul completed their relief mission, they returned to Jerusalem, taking with them John, who is called Mark.

13 **1†** Now there were in the church at Antioch prophets and teachers: Barnabas, Symeon who was called Niger, Lucius of Cyrene, Manaen who was a close friend of Herod the tetrarch, and Saul. **2** While they were worshiping the Lord and fasting, the holy Spirit said, "Set apart for me Barnabas and Saul for the work to which I have called them." **3** Then, completing their fasting and prayer, they laid hands on them and sent them off.

First Mission Begins in Cyprus

4† So they, sent forth by the holy Spirit, went down to Seleucia and from there sailed to Cyprus. **5†** When they arrived in Salamis, they proclaimed the word of God in the Jewish synagogues. They had John also as their assistant. **6†** When they had traveled through the whole island as far as Paphos, they met a magician named Bar-Jesus who was a Jewish false prophet. **7** He was with the proconsul Sergius Paulus, a man of intelligence, who had summoned Barnabas and Saul and wanted to hear the word of God. **8** But Elymas the magician (for

that is what his name means) opposed them in an attempt to turn the proconsul away from the faith. **9†** But Saul, also known as Paul, filled with the holy Spirit, looked intently at him **10** and said, "You son of the devil, you enemy of all that is right, full of

did you KNOW?

The Journeys of Paul

According to most interpretations of Acts, Paul made three missionary journeys over a ten-year period to spread the Gospel message. The details of his first journey are covered in chapters 13–14. The second journey is reported in chapters 16–18. The third journey is described in chapters 19–21. Paul himself may have seen these not as three separate journeys but as one continuous missionary activity. On these journeys, Paul made converts and started Christian communities. On the second and third journeys, he also visited established communities to give them guidance and support. See maps 7 and 8 for the routes of Paul's journeys.

Paul's third journey landed him back in Jerusalem, where some Jews had him arrested. On the basis of his Roman citizenship, Paul appealed to the emperor. So he was transported to Rome (this trip is referred to as his fourth journey). He probably died there as a martyr around A.D. 65. Some traditions say that Paul wasn't martyred there but went on to evangelize in Spain.

▸ **Acts of the Apostles, chapters 13–21**

12, 20–23: Josephus gives a similar account of Herod's death that occurred in A.D. 44. Early Christian tradition considered the manner of it to be a divine punishment upon his evil life. See 2 Kgs 19, 35 for the figure of the angel of the Lord in such a context.

12, 25: *They returned to Jerusalem:* many manuscripts read "from Jerusalem," since 11, 30 implies that Paul and Barnabas are already in Jerusalem. This present verse could refer to a return visit or subsequent relief mission.

13, 1–3: The impulse for the first missionary effort in Asia Minor is ascribed to the prophets of the Antiochene community, under the inspiration of the holy Spirit. Just as the Jerusalem community had earlier been the center of missionary activity, so too Antioch becomes the center from which the missionaries Barnabas and Saul are sent out.

13, 4–14.27: The key event in Luke's account of the first missionary journey is the experience of Paul and Barnabas at Pisidian Antioch (13, 14–52). The Christian kerygma proclaimed by Paul in the synagogue was favorably received. Some Jews and "God-fearers"

(see the note on 8, 26–40) became interested and invited the missionaries to speak again on the following sabbath (13, 42). By that time, however, the appearance of a large number of Gentiles from the city had so disconcerted the Jews that they became hostile toward the apostles (13, 44–50). This hostility of theirs appears in all three accounts of Paul's missionary journeys in Acts, the Jews of Iconium (14, 1–2) and Beroea (17, 11) being notable exceptions.

13, 5: *John:* that is, John Mark (see 12, 12.25).

13, 6: *A magician named Bar-Jesus who was a Jewish false prophet:* that is, he posed as a prophet. Again Luke takes the opportunity to dissociate Christianity from the magical acts of the time (7–11); see also 8, 18–24.

13, 9: *Saul, also known as Paul:* there is no reason to believe that his name was changed from Saul to Paul upon his conversion. The use of a double name, one Semitic (Saul), the other Greco-Roman (Paul), is well attested (cf 1, 23, Joseph Justus; 12, 12.25, John Mark).

12, 24: Acts 6, 7.   12, 25: Acts 11, 29–30.

every sort of deceit and fraud. Will you not stop twisting the straight paths of [the] Lord? [11] Even now the hand of the Lord is upon you. You will be blind, and unable to see the sun for a time." Immediately a dark mist fell upon him, and he went about seeking people to lead him by the hand. [12] When the proconsul saw what had happened, he came to believe, for he was astonished by the teaching about the Lord.

Paul's Arrival at Antioch in Pisidia

[13]* From Paphos, Paul and his companions set sail and arrived at Perga in Pamphylia. But John left them and returned to Jerusalem. [14] They continued on from Perga and reached Antioch in Pisidia. On the sabbath they entered [into] the synagogue and took their seats. [15] After the reading of the law and the prophets, the synagogue officials sent word to them, "My brothers, if one of you has a word of exhortation for the people, please speak."

Paul's Address in the Synagogue

[16]† So Paul got up, motioned with his hand, and said, "Fellow Israelites and you others who are God-fearing,† listen. [17]* The God of this people Israel chose our ancestors and exalted the people during their sojourn in the land of Egypt. With uplifted arms he led them out of it [18]*† and for about forty years he put up with them in the desert. [19]* When he had destroyed seven nations in the land of Canaan, he gave them their land as an inheritance [20]*† at the end of about four hundred and fifty years. After these things he provided judges up to Samuel [the] prophet. [21]* Then they asked for a king. God gave them Saul, son of Kish, a man from the tribe of Benjamin, for forty years. [22]* Then he removed him and raised up David as their king; of him he testified, 'I have found David, son of Jesse, a man after my own heart; he will carry out my

every wish.' [23]* From this man's descendants God, according to his promise, has brought to Israel a savior, Jesus. [24]* John heralded his coming by proclaiming a baptism of repentance to all the people of Israel; [25]* and as John was completing his course, he would say, 'What do you suppose that I am? I am not he. Behold, one is coming after me; I am not worthy to unfasten the sandals of his feet.'

[26] "My brothers, children of the family of Abraham, and those others among you who are God-fearing, to us this word of salvation has been sent. [27] The inhabitants of Jerusalem and their leaders failed to recognize him, and by condemning him they fulfilled the oracles of the prophets that are read sabbath after sabbath. [28]* For even though they found no grounds for a death sentence, they asked Pilate to have him put to death, [29]* and when they had accomplished all that was written about him, they took him down from the tree and placed him in a tomb. [30]* But God raised him from the dead, [31]*† and for many days he appeared to those who had come up with him from Galilee to Jerusalem. These are [now] his witnesses before the people. [32] We ourselves are proclaiming this good news to you that what God promised our ancestors [33]* he has brought to fulfillment for us, [their] children, by raising up Jesus, as it is written in the second psalm, 'You are my son; this day I have begotten you.' [34]* And that he raised him from the dead never to return to corruption he declared in this way, 'I shall give you the benefits assured to David.' [35]* That is why he also says in another psalm, 'You will not suffer your holy one to see corruption.' [36]* Now David, after he had served the will of God in his lifetime, fell asleep, was gathered to his ancestors, and did see corruption. [37] But the one whom God raised up did not see corruption. [38]† You must know, my brothers, that through him forgiveness of sins is being proclaimed to you, [and] in regard to everything from which you could

---

† **13, 16–41:** This is the first of several speeches of Paul to Jews proclaiming that the Christian church is the logical development of Pharisaic Judaism (see also 24, 10–21; 26, 2–23).

13, 16: *Who are God-fearing:* see the note on 8, 26–40.

13, 18: *Put up with:* some manuscripts read "sustained."

13, 20: *At the end of about four hundred and fifty years:* the manuscript tradition makes it uncertain whether the mention of four hundred and fifty years refers to the sojourn in Egypt before the Exodus, the wilderness period and the time of the conquest (see Ex 12, 40–41), as the translation here suggests, or to the time between the conquest and the time of Samuel, the period of the judges, if the text is read, "After these things, for about four hundred and fifty years, he provided judges."

13, 31: The theme of the Galilean witnesses is a major one in the Gospel of Luke and in Acts and is used to signify the continuity between the teachings of Jesus and the teachings of the church and to guarantee the fidelity of the church's teachings to the words of Jesus.

13, 38–39: *Justified:* the verb is the same as that used in Paul's letters to speak of the experience of justification and, as in Paul, is here connected with the term "to have faith" ("every believer"). But this seems the only passage about Paul in Acts where justification is men-

tioned. In Lucan fashion it is paralleled with "forgiveness of sins" (a theme at 2, 38; 3, 19; 5, 31; 10, 43) based on Jesus' resurrection (37) rather than his cross, and is put negatively (38). Therefore, some would translate, "in regard to everything from which you could not be acquitted . . . every believer is acquitted."

13, 13: Acts 15, 38.
13, 17: Ex 6, 1.6; 12, 51.
13, 18: Ex 16, 1.35; Nm 14, 34.
13, 19: Dt 7, 1; Jos 14, 1–2.
13, 20: Jgs 2, 16; 1 Sm 3, 20.
13, 21: 1 Sm 8, 5.19; 9, 16; 10, 1.20–21.24; 11, 15.
13, 22: 1 Sm 13, 14; 16, 12–13; Ps 89, 20–21.
13, 23: Is 11, 1.
13, 24: Mt 3, 1–2; Mk 1, 4–5; Lk 3, 2–3.
13, 25: Mt 3, 11; Mk 1, 7; Lk 3, 16; Jn 1, 20.27.
13, 28: Mt 27, 20.22–23; Mk 15, 13–14; Lk 23, 4.14–15.21–23; Jn 19, 4–6.15.
13, 29: Mt 27, 59–60; Mk 15, 46; Lk 23, 53; Jn 19, 38.41–42.
13, 30: Acts 2, 24.32; 3, 15; 4, 10; 17, 31.
13, 31: Acts 1, 3.8; 10, 39.41; Mt 28, 8–10.16–20; Mk 16, 9.12–20; Lk 24, 13–53; Jn 20, 11–29; 21, 1–23.
13, 33: Ps 2, 7.
13, 34: Is 55, 3.
13, 35: Ps 16, 10.
13, 36: Acts 2, 29; 1 Kgs 2, 10.

not be justified under the law of Moses, 39* in him every believer is justified. 40 Be careful, then, that what was said in the prophets not come about:

41* 'Look on, you scoffers,
    be amazed and disappear.
 For I am doing a work in your days,
    a work that you will never believe even
        if someone tells you.' "

42 As they were leaving, they invited them to speak on these subjects the following sabbath. 43 After the congregation had dispersed, many Jews and worshipers who were converts to Judaism followed Paul and Barnabas, who spoke to them and urged them to remain faithful to the grace of God.

Address to the Gentiles

44 On the following sabbath almost the whole city gathered to hear the word of the Lord. 45 When the Jews saw the crowds, they were filled with jealousy and with violent abuse contradicted what Paul said. 46*† Both Paul and Barnabas spoke out boldly and said, "It was necessary that the word of God be spoken to you first, but since you reject it and condemn yourselves as unworthy of eternal life, we now turn to the Gentiles. 47* For so the Lord has commanded us, 'I have made you a light to the Gentiles, that you may be an instrument of salvation to the ends of the earth.' "

48 The Gentiles were delighted when they heard this and glorified the word of the Lord. All who were destined for eternal life came to believe, 49 and the word of the Lord continued to spread through the whole region. 50 The Jews, however, incited the women of prominence who were worshipers and the leading men of the city, stirred up a persecution against Paul and Barnabas, and expelled them from their territory. 51*† So they shook the dust from their feet in protest against them and went to Iconium. 52 The disciples were filled with joy and the holy Spirit.

Paul and Barnabas at Iconium

14 1 In Iconium they entered the Jewish synagogue together and spoke in such a way that a great number of both Jews and Greeks came to believe, 2 although the disbelieving Jews stirred up and poisoned the minds of the Gentiles against the brothers. 3* So they stayed for a considerable period, speaking out boldly for the Lord, who confirmed the word about his grace by granting signs and wonders to occur through their hands. 4 The people of the city were divided: some were with the Jews; others, with the apostles. 5* When there was an attempt by both the Gentiles and the Jews, together with their leaders, to attack and stone them, 6 they realized it and fled to the Lycaonian cities of Lystra and Derbe and to the surrounding countryside, 7 where they continued to proclaim the good news.

Paul and Barnabas at Lystra

8† At Lystra there was a crippled man, lame from birth, who had never walked. 9 He listened to Paul

A Courageous Stance

LIVE IT!

One thing is clear about taking a stand and spreading the Gospel—it takes great courage. The story of Paul and Barnabas in Iconium is further evidence of how the early disciples risked their own lives in order to preach the Good News. It seems the Good News is not easy for some people to hear or accept.

In your prayer, reflect or journal on the following questions:

■ In what ways is God inviting you to live a little more courageously in order to spread the Good News in your school? your home? your neighborhood and community?

■ What keeps you from responding?

▶ Acts 14, 1–7

---

† **13, 46:** The refusal to believe frustrates God's plan for his chosen people; however, no adverse judgment is made here concerning their ultimate destiny. Again, Luke, in the words of Paul, speaks of the priority of Israel in the plan for salvation (see 10, 36).

13, 51: See the note on Lk 9, 5.

14, 8–18: In an effort to convince his hearers that the divine power works through his word, Paul cures the cripple. However, the pagan tradition of the occasional appearance of gods among human beings leads the people astray in interpreting the miracle. The incident reveals the cultural difficulties with which the church had to cope. Note the similarity of the miracle worked here by Paul to the one performed by Peter in 3, 2–10.

13, 39: Rom 3, 20.
13, 41: Hb 1, 5.
13, 46: Acts 3, 26; Rom 1, 16.
13, 47: Is 49, 6.
13, 51: Mt 10, 14; Mk 6, 11;
    Lk 9, 5; 10, 11.
14, 3: Mk 16, 17–20.
14, 5: 2 Tm 3, 11.

speaking, who looked intently at him, saw that he had the faith to be healed, 10 and called out in a loud voice, "Stand up straight on your feet." He jumped up and began to walk about. 11* When the crowds saw what Paul had done, they cried out in Lycaonian, "The gods have come down to us in human form." 12† They called Barnabas "Zeus" and Paul "Hermes," because he was the chief speaker. 13 And the priest of Zeus, whose temple was at the entrance to the city, brought oxen and garlands to the gates, for he together with the people intended to offer sacrifice.

14† The apostles Barnabas and Paul tore their garments when they heard this and rushed out into the crowd, shouting, 15*† "Men, why are you doing this? We are of the same nature as you, human beings. We proclaim to you good news that you should turn from these idols to the living God, 'who made heaven and earth and sea and all that is in them.' 16* In past generations he allowed all Gentiles to go their own ways; 17* yet, in bestowing his goodness, he did not leave himself without witness, for he gave you rains from heaven and fruitful seasons, and filled you with nourishment and gladness for your hearts." 18 Even with these words, they scarcely restrained the crowds from offering sacrifice to them.

19* However, some Jews from Antioch and Iconium arrived and won over the crowds. They stoned Paul and dragged him out of the city, supposing that he was dead. 20 But when the disciples gathered around him, he got up and entered the city. On the following day he left with Barnabas for Derbe.

End of the First Mission

21 After they had proclaimed the good news to that city and made a considerable number of disciples, they returned to Lystra and to Iconium and to Antioch. 22* They strengthened the spirits of the disciples and exhorted them to persevere in the faith, saying, "It is necessary for us to undergo many hardships to enter the kingdom of God." 23† They appointed presbyters for them in each church and, with prayer and fasting, commended them to the Lord in whom they had put their faith. 24 Then they traveled through Pisidia and reached Pamphylia. 25 After proclaiming the word at Perga they went down to Attalia. 26* From there they sailed to

Antioch, where they had been commended to the grace of God for the work they had now accomplished. [...] And when they arrived, [...] the church together and reported what God had done with them, and how he had opened the door of faith to the Gentiles. [...]

Catholic Connections

MINISTRY IN THE CHURCH

The Acts of the Apostles gives us some clues about how positions of ministry developed in the first Christian communities. One of the first ministries that developed was the ministry of service. Acts 6, 1–7 tells how seven people were chosen for a special ministry of service. Eventually, people with special roles of service were called deacons (see 1 Tm 3, 8–13). Today, deacons continue to have service to the community as their primary goal.

Acts 14, 21–28 tells how Paul and Barnabas appointed leaders, or "presbyters," in the communities they formed. These leaders watched over the community and guarded against those who would distort the true faith (20, 28–32). Over time, the chief leaders in this role became known as bishops (see 1 Tm 3, 1–7) and were recognized as the successors of the Apostles. The leaders who assisted the bishops became known as priests, or presbyters.

Many other ministries are listed in the New Testament, including the ministries of evangelization, of teaching, of interpreting the Scriptures, of prophecy, and of healing (see 1 Cor 12, 7–11 for one list). Many of these ministries required no special office. Today, parish ministers, such as youth ministers, religious educators, liturgical ministers, outreach ministers, and many others, continue this practice of sharing their gifts with the Christian community.

14, 12: *"Zeus" . . . "Hermes":* in Greek religion, Zeus was the chief of the Olympian gods, the "father of gods and men"; Hermes was a son of Zeus and was usually identified as the herald and messenger of the gods.

14, 14: *Tore their garments:* a gesture of protest.

14, 15–17: This is the first speech of Paul to Gentiles recorded by Luke in Acts (cf 17, 22–31). Rather than showing how Christianity is the logical outgrowth of Judaism, as he does in speeches before Jews, Luke says that God excuses past Gentile ignorance and then presents a natural theology arguing for the recognition of God's existence and

presence through his activity in natural phenomena.

14, 23: *They appointed presbyters:* the communities are given their own religious leaders by the traveling missionaries. The structure in these churches is patterned on the model of the Jerusalem community (11, 30; 15, 2.5.22; 21, 18).

14, 11: Acts 28, 6.
14, 15: Acts 3, 12; 10, 26; Ex 20, 11; Ps 146, 6.
14, 16: Acts 17, 30.
14, 17: Wis 13, 1.
14, 19–20: 2 Cor 11, 25; 2 Tm 3, 11.
14, 22: 1 Thes 3, 3.
14, 26: Acts 13, 1–3.

Antioch, where they had been commended to the grace of God for the work they had now accomplished. 27 And when they arrived, they called the church together and reported what God had done with them and how he had opened the door of faith to the Gentiles. 28 Then they spent no little time with the disciples.

Council of Jerusalem

15 1*† Some who had come down from Judea were instructing the brothers, "Unless you are circumcised according to the Mosaic practice,* you cannot be saved."† 2 Because there arose no little dissension and debate by Paul and Barnabas with them, it was decided that Paul, Barnabas, and some of the others should go up to Jerusalem to the apostles and presbyters about this question. 3 They were sent on their journey by the church, and passed through Phoenicia and Samaria telling of the conversion of the Gentiles, and brought great joy to all the brothers. 4 When they

arrived in Jerusalem, they were welcomed by the church, as well as by the apostles and the presbyters, and they reported what God had done with them. 5 But some from the party of the Pharisees who had become believers stood up and said, "It is necessary to circumcise them and direct them to observe the Mosaic law."

6† The apostles and the presbyters met together to see about this matter. 7*† After much debate had taken place, Peter got up and said to them, "My brothers, you are well aware that from early days God made his choice among you that through my mouth the Gentiles would hear the word of the gospel and believe. 8* And God, who knows the heart, bore witness by granting them the holy Spirit just as he did us. 9* He made no distinction between us and them, for by faith he purified their hearts. 10* Why, then, are you now putting God to the test by placing on the shoulders of the disciples a yoke that neither our ancestors nor we have been able to bear? 11*† On the contrary, we believe that

LIVE IT!

Unity in Faith and Love

When Paul and Barnabas were in Antioch, a controversy arose regarding the need for Gentiles to be circumcised and to follow certain Jewish laws and holidays. The earliest Christians were Jews. They believed in Jesus and continued to follow the rules of the Jewish faith as a sign that they were a Covenant people. But with Gentiles becoming Christians, new questions were raised, like: Do Gentiles have to follow all the Jewish rules? Do Gentiles need to be circumcised as a sign of the Covenant? Circumcision is the surgical removal of the foreskin from a penis, and the Gentile converts did not see the need for it.

Paul and Barnabas insisted that Christians were free from such Jewish laws; they went to Jerusalem to meet with the other Apostles to defend their position. With Peter's support, Paul and Barnabas's view won the day. This meeting of the Apostles is called the Council of Jerusalem and was a pivotal point in the history of the church. At it the Apostles decided that the center of the Christian faith was believing in the risen Christ, not conforming to a Jewish ritual.

How does your youth group or parish handle conflict? Does it handle it better when members remind themselves that they are united by their faith in Jesus?

▶ **Acts 15, 1–35**

15, 1–35: The Jerusalem "Council" marks the official rejection of the rigid view that Gentile converts were obliged to observe the Mosaic law completely. From here to the end of Acts, Paul and the Gentile mission become the focus of Luke's writing.

15, 1–5: When some of the converted Pharisees of Jerusalem discover the results of the first missionary journey of Paul, they urge that the Gentiles be taught to follow the Mosaic law. Recognizing the authority of the Jerusalem church, Paul and Barnabas go there to settle the question of whether Gentiles can embrace a form of Christianity that does not include this obligation.

15, 6–12: The gathering is possibly the same as that recalled by Paul in Gal 2, 1–10. Note that in v 2 it is only the apostles and presbyters, a small group, with whom Paul and Barnabas are to meet. Here Luke gives the meeting a public character because he wishes

to emphasize its doctrinal significance (see 22).

15, 7–11: Paul's refusal to impose the Mosaic law on the Gentile Christians is supported by Peter on the ground that within his own experience God bestowed the holy Spirit upon Cornelius and his household without preconditions concerning the adoption of the Mosaic law (see 10, 44–47).

15, 11: In support of Paul, Peter formulates the fundamental meaning of the gospel: that all are invited to be saved through faith in the power of Christ.

15, 1–4: Gal 2, 1–9.
15, 1: Lv 12, 3; Gal 5, 2.
15, 7: Acts 10, 27–43.
15, 8: Acts 10, 44–48.
15, 9: Acts 10, 34–35.
15, 10: Mt 23, 4; Gal 5, 1.
15, 11: Gal 2, 16; 3, 11; Eph 2, 5–8.

we are saved through the grace of the Lord Jesus, in the same way as they." 12 The whole assembly fell silent, and they listened while Paul and Barnabas described the signs and wonders God had worked among the Gentiles through them.

James on Dietary Law

13† After they had fallen silent, James responded, "My brothers, listen to me. 14† Symeon has described how God first concerned himself with acquiring from among the Gentiles a people for his name. 15 The words of the prophets agree with this, as is written:

16* 'After this I shall return
        and rebuild the fallen hut of David;
    from its ruins I shall rebuild it
        and raise it up again,
17 so that the rest of humanity may seek out
        the Lord,
    even all the Gentiles on whom my name
        is invoked.
    Thus says the Lord who accomplishes
        these things,
18   known from of old.'

19* It is my judgment, therefore, that we ought to stop troubling the Gentiles who turn to God, 20* but tell them by letter to avoid pollution from idols, unlawful marriage, the meat of strangled animals, and blood. 21 For Moses, for generations now, has had those who proclaim him in every town, as he has been read in the synagogues every sabbath."

Letter of the Apostles

22 Then the apostles and presbyters, in agreement with the whole church, decided to choose representatives and to send them to Antioch with Paul and Barnabas. The ones chosen were Judas, who was called Barsabbas, and Silas, leaders

among the brothers. 23 This is the letter delivered by them: "The apostles and the presbyters, your brothers, to the brothers in Antioch, Syria, and Cilicia of Gentile origin: greetings. 24 Since we have heard that some of our number [who went out] without any mandate from us have upset you with their teachings and disturbed your peace of mind, 25 we have with one accord decided to choose representatives and to send them to you along with our beloved Barnabas and Paul, 26 who have dedicated their lives to the name of our Lord Jesus Christ. 27 So we are sending Judas and Silas who will also convey this same message by word of mouth: 28* 'It is the decision of the holy Spirit and of us not to place on you any burden beyond these necessities, 29* namely, to abstain from meat sacrificed to idols, from blood, from meats of strangled animals, and from unlawful marriage. If you keep free of these, you will be doing what is right. Farewell.' "

Delegates at Antioch

30 And so they were sent on their journey. Upon their arrival in Antioch they called the assembly together and delivered the letter. 31 When the people read it, they were delighted with the exhortation. 32 Judas and Silas, who were themselves prophets, exhorted and strengthened the brothers with many words. 33 After they had spent some time there, they were sent off with greetings of peace from the brothers to those who had commissioned them. [34]† 35 But Paul and Barnabas remained in Antioch, teaching and proclaiming with many others the word of the Lord.

V: The Mission of Paul to the Ends of the Earth

Paul and Barnabas Separate

36† After some time, Paul said to Barnabas, "Come, let us make a return visit to see how the

---

† **15, 13–35:** Some scholars think that this apostolic decree suggested by James, the immediate leader of the Jerusalem community, derives from another historical occasion than the meeting in question. This seems to be the case if the meeting is the same as the one related in Gal 2, 1–10. According to that account, nothing was imposed upon Gentile Christians in respect to Mosaic law; whereas the decree instructs Gentile Christians of mixed communities to abstain from meats sacrificed to idols and from blood-meats, and to avoid marriage within forbidden degrees of consanguinity and affinity (Lv 18), all of which practices were especially abhorrent to Jews. Luke seems to have telescoped two originally independent incidents here: the first a Jerusalem "Council" that dealt with the question of circumcision, and the second a Jerusalem decree dealing mainly with Gentile observance of dietary laws (see 21, 25 where Paul seems to be learning of the decree for the first time).

15, 14: *Symeon:* elsewhere in Acts he is called either Peter or Simon. The presence of the name Symeon here suggests that, in the source Luke is using for this part of the Jerusalem "Council" incident, the name may have originally referred to someone other than Peter (see 13, 1 where the Antiochene Symeon Niger is mentioned). As the text

now stands, however, it is undoubtedly a reference to Simon Peter (7).

15, 34: Some manuscripts add, in various wordings, "But Silas decided to remain there."

15, 36—18, 22: This continuous narrative recounts Paul's second missionary journey. On the internal evidence of the Lucan account, it lasted about three years. Paul first visited the communities he had established on his first journey (16, 1–5), then pushed on into Macedonia, where he established communities at Philippi, Thessalonica, and Beroea (16, 7—17, 5). To escape the hostility of the Jews of Thessalonica, he left for Greece and while resident in Athens attempted, without success, to establish an effective Christian community there. From Athens he proceeded to Corinth and, after a stay of a year and a half, returned to Antioch by way of Ephesus and Jerusalem (17, 16—18, 22). Luke does not concern himself with the structure or statistics of the communities but aims to show the general progress of the gospel in the Gentile world as well as its continued failure to take root in the Jewish community.

15, 16–17: Am 9, 11–12.
15, 19–20: Acts 15, 28–29; 21, 25.
15, 20: Gn 9, 4; Lv 3, 17; 17,

10–14.
15, 28–29: Acts 15, 19–20.
15, 29: Gn 9, 4; Lv 3, 17; 17, 10–14.

brothers are getting on in all the cities where we proclaimed the word of the Lord." 37 Barnabas wanted to take with them also John, who was called Mark, 38* but Paul insisted that they should not take with them someone who had deserted them at Pamphylia and who had not continued with them in their work. 39 So sharp was their disagreement that they separated. Barnabas took Mark and sailed to Cyprus. 40 But Paul chose Silas and departed after being commended by the brothers to the grace of the Lord. 41 He traveled through Syria and Cilicia bringing strength to the churches.

Paul in Lycaonia: Timothy

16 1* He reached [also] Derbe and Lystra where there was a disciple named Timothy, the son of a Jewish woman who was a believer, but his father was a Greek. 2* The brothers in Lystra and Iconium spoke highly of him, 3† and Paul wanted him to come along with him. On account of the Jews of that region, Paul had him circumcised, for they all knew that his father was a Greek. 4 As they traveled from city to city, they handed on to the people for observance the decisions reached

by the apostles and presbyters in Jerusalem. 5 Day after day the churches grew stronger in faith and increased in number.

Through Asia Minor

6 They traveled through the Phrygian and Galatian territory because they had been prevented by the holy Spirit from preaching the message in the province of Asia. 7† When they came to Mysia, they tried to go on into Bithynia, but the Spirit of Jesus did not allow them, 8 so they crossed through Mysia and came down to Troas. 9 During [the] night Paul had a vision. A Macedonian stood before him and implored him with these words, "Come over to Macedonia and help us." 10† When he had seen the vision, we sought passage to Macedonia at once, concluding that God had called us to proclaim the good news to them.

Into Europe

11† We set sail from Troas, making a straight run for Samothrace, and on the next day to Neapolis, 12 and from there to Philippi, a leading city in that district of Macedonia and a Roman colony. We spent some time in that city. 13 On the sabbath we went

Introducing
▶LYDIA AND PRISCILLA

Women were a crucial part of Christianity from its beginnings. The Acts of the Apostles names two women who were instrumental in Paul's missionary journeys: Lydia and Priscilla. Lydia (16, 11–15) was Paul's first convert in Philippi, which is part of modern-day Europe. She was a textile merchant and was wealthy enough to support a household and open her home to Paul and Silas to stay for an extended time.

In chapter 18, we meet Priscilla and her husband, Aquila. This family hosted Paul in Corinth. Later, they accompanied him from Corinth to Antioch. While there, they instructed Apollos in the "Way of God" (18, 26). Luke's inclusion of these women indicates that women were active in the early church, not only supporting the missionary work of Paul but also leading and teaching. For more on the women in the Bible, see the chapter titled "Suggested Reading Plans," near the beginning of this Bible.

▶ **Acts 16, 14–15; 18, 1–26**

---

† **16, 3:** *Paul had him circumcised:* he did this in order that Timothy might be able to associate with the Jews and so perform a ministry among them. Paul did not object to the Jewish Christians' adherence to the law. But he insisted that the law could not be imposed on the Gentiles. Paul himself lived in accordance with the law, or as exempt from the law, according to particular circumstances (see 1 Cor 9, 19–23).

16, 7: *The Spirit of Jesus:* this is an unusual formulation in Luke's writings. The parallelism with v 6 indicates its meaning, the holy Spirit.

16, 10–17: This is the first of the so-called "we-sections" in Acts, where Luke writes as one of Paul's companions. The other passages

are 20, 5–15; 21, 1–18; 27, 1–28, 16. Scholars debate whether Luke may not have used the first person plural simply as a literary device to lend color to the narrative. The realism of the narrative, however, lends weight to the argument that the "we" includes Luke or another companion of Paul whose data Luke used as a source.

16, 11–40: The church at Philippi became a flourishing community to which Paul addressed one of his letters (see Introduction to the Letter to the Philippians).

15, 38: Acts 13, 13.   16; 2: Phil 2, 20.
16, 1: 1 Tm 1, 2; 2 Tm 1, 5.

outside the city gate along the river where we thought there would be a place of prayer. We sat and spoke with the women who had gathered there. 14† One of them, a woman named Lydia, a dealer in purple cloth, from the city of Thyatira, a worshiper of God, listened, and the Lord opened her heart to pay attention to what Paul was saying. 15 After she and her household had been baptized, she offered us an invitation, "If you consider me a believer in the Lord, come and stay at my home," and she prevailed on us.

Imprisonment at Philippi

16† As we were going to the place of prayer, we met a slave girl with an oracular spirit, who used to bring a large profit to her owners through her fortune-telling. 17 She began to follow Paul and us, shouting, "These people are slaves of the Most High God, who proclaim to you a way of salvation." 18 She did this for many days. Paul became annoyed, turned, and said to the spirit, "I command you in the name of Jesus Christ to come out of her." Then it came out at that moment.

19 When her owners saw that their hope of profit was gone, they seized Paul and Silas and dragged them to the public square before the local authorities. 20† They brought them before the magistrates and said, "These people are Jews and are disturbing our city 21 and are advocating customs that are not lawful for us Romans to adopt or practice." 22* The crowd joined in the attack on them, and the magistrates had them stripped and ordered them to be beaten with rods. 23 After inflicting many blows on them, they threw them into prison and instructed the jailer to guard them securely. 24 When he received these instructions, he put them in the innermost cell and secured their feet to a stake.

Deliverance from Prison

25 About midnight, while Paul and Silas were praying and singing hymns to God as the prisoners listened, 26 there was suddenly such a severe earthquake that the foundations of the jail shook; all the doors flew open, and the chains of all were pulled loose. 27 When the jailer woke up and saw the prison doors wide open, he drew [his] sword and was about to kill himself, thinking that the prisoners had escaped. 28 But Paul shouted out in a loud voice, "Do no harm to yourself; we are all here."

29 He asked for a light and rushed in and, trembling with fear, he fell down before Paul and Silas. 30 Then he brought them out and said, "Sirs, what must I do to be saved?" 31 And they said, "Believe in the Lord Jesus and you and your household will be saved." 32 So they spoke the word of the Lord to him and to everyone in his house. 33 He took them in at that hour of the night and bathed their wounds; then he and all his family were baptized at once. 34 He brought them up into his house and provided a meal and with his household rejoiced at having come to faith in God.

35† But when it was day, the magistrates sent the lictors with the order, "Release those men." 36 The jailer reported the[se] words to Paul, "The magistrates have sent orders that you be released. Now, then, come out and go in peace." 37*† But Paul said to them, "They have beaten us publicly, even though we are Roman citizens and have not been tried, and have thrown us into prison. And now, are they going to release us secretly? By no means. Let them come themselves and lead us out." 38* The lictors reported these words to the magistrates, and they became alarmed when they heard that they were Roman citizens. 39 So they came and placated them, and led them out and asked that they leave the city. 40 When they had come out of the prison, they went to Lydia's house where they saw and encouraged the brothers, and then they left.

Paul in Thessalonica

17 1* When they took the road through Amphipolis and Apollonia, they reached Thessalonica, where there was a synagogue of the Jews. 2 Following his usual custom, Paul joined them, and for three sabbaths he entered into discussions with them from the scriptures, 3* expounding and demonstrating that the Messiah had to suffer and rise from the dead, and that "This is the Messiah, Jesus, whom I proclaim to you." 4 Some of them were convinced and joined Paul and Silas; so, too, a great number of Greeks who were worshipers, and not a few of the prominent women. 5* But the Jews became jealous and recruited some worthless men loitering in the public square, formed a mob, and set the city in turmoil. They marched on the house of Jason, intending to

A
C
T
S

---

† **16, 14:** *A worshiper of God:* a "God-fearer." See the note on 8, 26–40.

16, 16: *With an oracular spirit:* literally, "with a Python spirit." The Python was the serpent or dragon that guarded the Delphic oracle. It later came to designate a "spirit that pronounced oracles" and also a ventriloquist who, it was thought, had such a spirit in the belly.

16, 20: *Magistrates:* in Greek, *stratēgoi,* the popular designation of the *duoviri,* the highest officials of the Roman colony of Philippi.

16, 35: *The lictors:* the equivalent of police officers, among

whose duties were the apprehension and punishment of criminals.

16, 37: Paul's Roman citizenship granted him special privileges in regard to criminal process. Roman law forbade under severe penalty the beating of Roman citizens (see also 22, 25).

16, 22–23: 2 Cor 11, 25; Phil 1,
    30; 1 Thes 2, 2.
16, 37: Acts 22, 25.
16, 38: Acts 22, 29.

17, 1: 1 Thes 2, 1–2.
17, 3: Acts 3, 18; Lk 24,
    25–26.46.
17, 5: Rom 16, 21.

Help Us Evangelize

Paul was wonderfully gifted for his work as an evangelist. He had the ability to communicate with both common people and intellectuals. He was familiar with three cultures—Jewish, Greek, and Roman—and proclaimed the Gospel message in ways all three could understand. He was skilled at building Christian communities. And he was absolutely fearless in preaching about Jesus Christ. Let's pray for these gifts in ourselves so that we can continue the church's mission of evangelization, particularly to young people.

O God, how I admire Paul! I too want to share your Good News with my generation. So let your Holy Spirit bless me with the gift of evangelization. Help me reach out to other young people no matter what clique or group they belong to. Help me to bring out the best in our culture and to challenge that which is wrong or misleading. Give me courage to speak fearlessly about my faith in Jesus when it is right to do so. And let me be your instrument in building communities of faith, hope, and love. Amen.

▶ **Acts of the Apostles, chapter 17**

bring them before the people's assembly. 6† When they could not find them, they dragged Jason and some of the brothers before the city magistrates, shouting, "These people who have been creating a disturbance all over the world have now come here, 7*† and Jason has welcomed them. They all act in opposition to the decrees of Caesar and claim

instead that there is another king, Jesus." 8 They stirred up the crowd and the city magistrates who, upon hearing these charges, 9 took a surety payment from Jason and the others before releasing them.

Paul in Beroea

10 The brothers immediately sent Paul and Silas to Beroea during the night. Upon arrival they went to the synagogue of the Jews. 11* These Jews were more fair-minded than those in Thessalonica, for they received the word with all willingness and examined the scriptures daily to determine whether these things were so. 12 Many of them became believers, as did not a few of the influential Greek women and men. 13 But when the Jews of Thessalonica learned that the word of God had now been proclaimed by Paul in Beroea also, they came there too to cause a commotion and stir up the crowds. 14* So the brothers at once sent Paul on his way to the seacoast, while Silas and Timothy remained behind. 15 After Paul's escorts had taken him to Athens, they came away with instructions for Silas and Timothy to join him as soon as possible.

Paul in Athens

16† While Paul was waiting for them in Athens, he grew exasperated at the sight of the city full of idols. 17 So he debated in the synagogue with the Jews and with the worshipers, and daily in the public square with whoever happened to be there. 18† Even some of the Epicurean and Stoic philosophers engaged him in discussion. Some asked, "What is this scavenger trying to say?" Others said, "He sounds like a promoter of foreign deities," because he was preaching about 'Jesus' and 'Resurrection.' 19*† They took him and led him to the Areopagus and said, "May we learn what this new teaching is that you speak of? 20 For you bring some strange notions to our ears; we should like to know what these things mean." 21 Now all the Athenians as well as the foreigners residing there used their time for nothing else but telling or hearing something new.

17, 6–7: The accusations against Paul and his companions echo the charges brought against Jesus in Lk 23, 2.

17, 7: *There is another king, Jesus:* a distortion into a political sense of the apostolic proclamation of Jesus and the kingdom of God (see 8, 12).

17, 16–21: Paul's presence in Athens sets the stage for the great discourse before a Gentile audience in vv 22–31. Although Athens was a politically insignificant city at this period, it still lived on the glories of its past and represented the center of Greek culture. The setting describes the conflict between Christian preaching and Hellenistic philosophy.

17, 18: *Epicurean and Stoic philosophers:* for the followers of Epicurus (342–271 B.C.), the goal of life was happiness attained through sober reasoning and the searching out of motives for all choice and avoidance. The Stoics were followers of Zeno, a younger contemporary of Alexander the Great. Zeno and his followers believed in a type of pantheism that held that the spark of divinity was

present in all reality and that, in order to be free, each person must live "according to nature." *This scavenger:* literally, "seed-picker," as of a bird that picks up grain. The word is later used of scrap collectors and of people who take other people's ideas and propagate them as if they were their own. *Promoter of foreign deities:* according to Xenophon, Socrates was accused of promoting new deities. The accusation against Paul echoes the charge against Socrates. *'Jesus' and 'Resurrection':* the Athenians are presented as misunderstanding Paul from the outset; they think he is preaching about Jesus and a goddess named *Anastasis,* i.e., Resurrection.

17, 19: *To the Areopagus:* the "Areopagus" refers either to the Hill of Ares west of the Acropolis or to the Council of Athens, which at one time met on the hill but which at this time assembled in the Royal Colonnade (*Stoa Basileios*).

17, 7: Lk 23, 2; Jn 19, 12–15.   17, 14: 1 Thes 3, 1–2.
17, 11: Jn 5, 39.   17, 19: 1 Cor 1, 22.

ACTS

Paul's Speech at the Areopagus

²²† Then Paul stood up at the Areopagus and said:

"You Athenians, I see that in every respect you are very religious. ²³† For as I walked around looking carefully at your shrines, I even discovered an altar inscribed, 'To an Unknown God.' What therefore you unknowingly worship, I proclaim to you. ²⁴* The God who made the world and all that is in it, the Lord of heaven and earth, does not dwell in sanctuaries made by human hands, ²⁵ nor is he served by human hands because he needs anything. Rather it is he who gives to everyone life and breath and everything. ²⁶† He made from one the whole human race to dwell on the entire surface of the earth, and he fixed the ordered seasons and the boundaries of their regions, ²⁷* so that people might seek God, even perhaps grope for him and find him, though indeed he is not far from any one of us. ²⁸† For 'In him we live and move and have our being,' as even some of your poets have said, 'For we too are his offspring.' ²⁹* Since therefore we are the offspring of God, we ought not to think that the divinity is like an image fashioned from gold, silver, or stone by human art and imagination. ³⁰ God has overlooked the times of ignorance, but now he demands that all people everywhere repent ³¹* because he has established a day on which he will 'judge the world with justice' through a man he has appointed, and he has provided confirmation for all by raising him from the dead."

³² When they heard about resurrection of the dead, some began to scoff, but others said, "We should like to hear you on this some other time." ³³ And so Paul left them. ³⁴ But some did join him, and became believers. Among them were Dionysius, a member of the Court of the Areopagus, a woman named Damaris, and others with them.

Paul in Corinth

18 ¹ After this he left Athens and went to Corinth. ²*† There he met a Jew named Aquila, a native of Pontus, who had recently come from Italy with his wife Priscilla because Claudius had ordered all the Jews to leave Rome. He went to visit them ³ and, because he practiced the same trade, stayed with them and worked, for they were tentmakers by trade. ⁴ Every sabbath, he entered into discussions in the synagogue, attempting to convince both Jews and Greeks.

⁵ When Silas and Timothy came down from Macedonia, Paul began to occupy himself totally with preaching the word, testifying to the Jews that the Messiah was Jesus. ⁶*† When they opposed him and reviled him, he shook out his garments and said to them, "Your blood be on your heads! I am clear of responsibility. From now on I will go to the Gentiles." ⁷*† So he left there and went to a house belonging to a man named Titus Justus, a worshiper of God; his house was next to a synagogue. ⁸*† Crispus, the synagogue official, came to believe in the Lord along with his entire household, and many of the Corinthians who heard believed and were baptized. ⁹* One night in a vision the Lord said to Paul, "Do not be afraid. Go on speaking, and do not be silent, ¹⁰ for I am with you. No one will attack and harm you, for I have many people in this city." ¹¹ He settled there for a year and a half and taught the word of God among them.

Accusations before Gallio

¹²† But when Gallio was proconsul of Achaia, the Jews rose up together against Paul and brought him to the tribunal, ¹³† saying, "This man is inducing people to worship God contrary to the law." ¹⁴ When Paul was about to reply, Gallio spoke to

---

17, 22–31: In Paul's appearance at the Areopagus he preaches his climactic speech to Gentiles in the cultural center of the ancient world. The speech is more theological than christological. Paul's discourse appeals to the Greek world's belief in divinity as responsible for the origin and existence of the universe. It contests the common belief in a multiplicity of gods supposedly exerting their powers through their images. It acknowledges that the attempt to find God is a constant human endeavor. It declares, further, that God is the judge of the human race, that the time of the judgment has been determined, and that it will be executed through a man whom God raised from the dead. The speech reflects sympathy with pagan religiosity, handles the subject of idol worship gently, and appeals for a new examination of divinity, not from the standpoint of creation but from the standpoint of judgment.

17, 23: 'To an Unknown God': ancient authors such as Pausanias, Philostratus, and Tertullian speak of Athenian altars with no specific dedication as altars of "unknown gods" or "nameless altars."

17, 26: From one: many manuscripts read "from one blood." Fixed . . . seasons: or "fixed limits to the epochs."

17, 28: 'In him we live and move and have our being': some scholars understand this saying to be based on an earlier saying of Epimenides of Knossos (6th century B.C.). 'For we too are his offspring': here Paul is quoting Aratus of Soli, a third-century B.C. poet from Cilicia.

18, 2: Aquila . . . Priscilla: both may already have been Christians at the time of their arrival in Corinth (see 26). According to 1 Cor

16, 19, their home became a meeting place for Christians. Claudius: the Emperor Claudius expelled the Jews from Rome ca. A.D. 49. The Roman historian Suetonius gives as reason for the expulsion disturbances among the Jews "at the instigation of Chrestos," probably meaning disputes about the messiahship of Jesus.

18, 6: Shook out his garments: a gesture indicating Paul's repudiation of his mission to the Jews there; cf 28, 17–31.

18, 7: A worshiper of God: see the note on 8, 26–40.

18, 8: Crispus: in 1 Cor 1, 14, Paul mentions that Crispus was one of the few he himself baptized at Corinth.

18, 12: When Gallio was proconsul of Achaia: Gallio's proconsulship in Achaia is dated to A.D. 51–52 from an inscription discovered at Delphi. This has become an important date in establishing a chronology of the life and missionary work of Paul.

18, 13: Contrary to the law: Gallio (15) understands this to be a problem of Jewish, not Roman, law.

17, 24: Acts 7, 48–50; Gn 1, 1;
    1 Kgs 8, 27; Is 42, 5.
17, 27: Jer 23, 23; Wis 13, 6;
    Rom 1, 19.
17, 29: Acts 19, 26; Is 40,
    18–20; 44, 10–17;
    Rom 1, 22–23.
17, 31: Acts 10, 42.

18, 2: Rom 16, 3.
18, 6: Acts 13, 51; Mt 10, 14;
    27, 24–25; Mk 6, 11;
    Lk 9, 5; 10, 10–11.
18, 7: Acts 13, 46–47; 28,
    28.
18, 8: 1 Cor 1, 14.
18, 9–10: Jer 1, 8.

the Jews, "If it were a matter of some crime or malicious fraud, I should with reason hear the complaint of you Jews; 15 but since it is a question of arguments over doctrine and titles and your own law, see to it yourselves. I do not wish to be a judge of such matters." 16 And he drove them away from the tribunal. 17 They all seized Sosthenes, the synagogue official, and beat him in full view of the tribunal. But none of this was of concern to Gallio.

Return to Syrian Antioch

18*† Paul remained for quite some time, and after saying farewell to the brothers he sailed for Syria, together with Priscilla and Aquila. At Cenchreae he had his hair cut because he had taken a vow. 19 When they reached Ephesus, he left them there, while he entered the synagogue and held discussions with the Jews. 20 Although they asked him to stay for a longer time, he did not consent, 21 but as he said farewell he promised, "I shall come back to you again, God willing." Then he set sail from Ephesus. 22† Upon landing at Caesarea, he went up and greeted the church and then went down to Antioch. 23† After staying there some time, he left and traveled in orderly sequence through the Galatian country and Phrygia, bringing strength to all the disciples.

18, 18

Apollos

24*† A Jew named Apollos, a native of Alexandria, an eloquent speaker, arrived in Ephesus. He was an authority on the scriptures. 25 He had been instructed in the Way of the Lord and, with ardent spirit, spoke and taught accurately about Jesus, although he knew only the baptism of John. 26† He began to speak boldly in the synagogue; but when Priscilla and Aquila heard him, they took him aside and explained to him the Way [of God] more accurately. 27 And when he wanted to cross to Achaia, the brothers encouraged him and wrote to the disciples there to welcome him. After his arrival he gave great assistance to those who had come to believe through grace. 28 He vigorously refuted the Jews in public, establishing from the scriptures that the Messiah is Jesus.

Paul in Ephesus

19 1† While Apollos was in Corinth, Paul traveled through the interior of the country and came [down] to Ephesus where he found some disciples. 2 He said to them, "Did you receive the holy Spirit when you became believers?" They answered him, "We have never even heard that there is a holy Spirit." 3 He said, "How were you baptized?" They replied, "With the baptism of John." 4* Paul then said, "John baptized with a baptism of repentance, telling the people to believe in the one who was to come after him, that is, in Jesus." 5 When they heard this, they were baptized in the name of the Lord Jesus. 6* And when Paul laid [his] hands on them, the holy Spirit came upon them, and they spoke in tongues and prophesied. 7 Altogether there were about twelve men.

8 He entered the synagogue, and for three months debated boldly with persuasive arguments about the kingdom of God. 9 But when some in their obstinacy and disbelief disparaged the Way before the assembly, he withdrew and took his disciples with him and began to hold daily discussions in the lecture hall of Tyrannus. 10 This continued for two years with the result that all the inhabitants of the province of Asia heard the word of the Lord, Jews and Greeks alike. 11 So extraordinary were the mighty deeds God accomplished at the hands of Paul 12* that when face cloths or aprons that

†

18, 18: *He had his hair cut because he had taken a vow:* a reference to a Nazirite vow (see Nm 6, 1–21, especially, 6, 18) taken by Paul (see also 21, 23–27).

18, 22: *He went up and greeted the church:* "going up" suggests a visit to the church in Jerusalem.

18, 23—21, 16: Luke's account of Paul's third missionary journey devotes itself mainly to his work at Ephesus (19, 1—20, 1). There is a certain restiveness on Paul's part and a growing conviction that the Spirit bids him return to Jerusalem and prepare to go to Rome (19, 21).

18, 24–25: Apollos appears as a preacher who knows the teaching of Jesus in the context of John's baptism of repentance. Aquila and Priscilla instruct him more fully. He is referred to in 1 Cor 1, 12; 3, 5–6.22.

18, 26: *The Way [of God]:* for the Way, see the note on 9, 2. Other manuscripts here read "the Way of the Lord," "the word of the Lord," or simply "the Way."

19, 1–6: Upon his arrival in Ephesus, Paul discovers other people at the same religious stage as Apollos, though they seem to have considered themselves followers of Christ, not of the Baptist. On the relation between baptism and the reception of the Spirit, see the note on 8, 16.

18, 18: Acts 21, 24; Nm 6, 18.   19, 6: Acts 8, 15–17; 10,
18, 24: 1 Cor 1, 12.   44.46.
19, 4: Acts 1, 5; 11, 16; 13,   19, 12: Acts 5, 15–16; Lk 8,
24–25; Mt 3, 11; Mk   44–47.
1, 8; Lk 3, 16.

touched his skin were applied to the sick, their diseases left them and the evil spirits came out of them.

The Jewish Exorcists

13 Then some itinerant Jewish exorcists tried to invoke the name of the Lord Jesus over those with evil spirits, saying, "I adjure you by the Jesus whom Paul preaches." 14 When the seven sons of Sceva, a Jewish high priest, tried to do this, 15 the evil spirit said to them in reply, "Jesus I recognize, Paul I know, but who are you?" 16 The person with the evil spirit then sprang at them and subdued them all. He so overpowered them that they fled naked and wounded from that house. 17 When this became known to all the Jews and Greeks who lived in Ephesus, fear fell upon them all, and the name of the Lord Jesus was held in great esteem. 18 Many of those who had become believers came forward and openly acknowledged their former practices. 19 Moreover, a large number of those who had practiced magic collected their books and burned them in public. They calculated their value and found it to be fifty thousand silver pieces. 20 Thus did the word of the Lord continue to spread with influence and power.

Paul's Plans

21* When this was concluded, Paul made up his mind to travel through Macedonia and Achaia, and then to go on to Jerusalem, saying, "After I have been there, I must visit Rome also." 22 Then he sent to Macedonia two of his assistants, Timothy and Erastus, while he himself stayed for a while in the province of Asia.

The Riot of the Silversmiths

23 About that time a serious disturbance broke out concerning the Way. 24† There was a silversmith named Demetrius who made miniature silver shrines of Artemis and provided no little work for the craftsmen. 25 He called a meeting of these and other workers in related crafts and said, "Men, you know well that our prosperity derives from this work. 26* As you can now see and hear, not only in Ephesus but throughout most of the province of Asia this Paul has persuaded and misled a great number of people by saying that gods made by hands are not gods at all.

27 The danger grows, not only that our business will be discredited, but also that the temple of the great goddess Artemis will be of no account, and that she whom the whole province of Asia and all the world worship will be stripped of her magnificence." 28 When they heard this, they were filled with fury and began to shout, "Great is Artemis of the Ephesians!" 29* The city was filled with confusion, and the people rushed with one accord into the theater, seizing Gaius and Aristarchus, the Macedonians, Paul's traveling companions. 30 Paul wanted to go before the crowd, but the disciples would not let him, 31† and even some of the Asiarchs who were friends of his sent word to him advising him not to venture into the theater. 32 Meanwhile, some were shouting one thing, others something else; the assembly was in chaos, and most of the people had no idea why they had come together. 33 Some of the crowd prompted Alexander, as the Jews pushed him forward, and Alexander signaled with his hand that he wished to explain something to the gathering. 34 But when they recognized that he was a Jew, they all shouted in unison, for about two hours, "Great is Artemis of the Ephesians!" 35† Finally the town clerk restrained the crowd and said, "You Ephesians, what person is there who does not know that the city of the Ephesians is the guardian of the temple of the great Artemis and of her image that fell from the sky? 36 Since these things are undeniable, you must calm yourselves and not do anything rash. 37 The men you brought here are not temple robbers, nor have they insulted our goddess. 38 If Demetrius and his fellow craftsmen have a complaint against anyone, courts are in session, and there are proconsuls. Let them bring charges against one another. 39 If you have anything further to investigate, let the matter be settled in the lawful assembly, 40† for, as it is, we are in danger of being charged with rioting because of today's conduct. There is no cause for it. We shall [not] be able to give a reason for this demonstration." With these words he dismissed the assembly.

Journey to Macedonia and Greece

20 1* When the disturbance was over, Paul had the disciples summoned and, after encouraging them, he bade them farewell and set

---

† **19, 24:** *Miniature silver shrines of Artemis:* the temple of Artemis at Ephesus was one of the seven wonders of the ancient world. Artemis, originally the Olympian virgin hunter, moon goddess, and goddess of wild nature, was worshiped at Ephesus as an Asian mother goddess and goddess of fertility. She was one of the most widely worshiped female deities in the Hellenistic world (see 18, 27).
19, 31: *Asiarchs:* the precise status and role of the Asiarchs is disputed. They appear to have been people of wealth and influence who promoted the Roman imperial cult and who may also have been political representatives in a league of cities in the Roman province of Asia.
19, 35: *Guardian of the temple:* this title was accorded by Rome to cities that provided a temple for the imperial cult. Inscriptional ev-

idence indicates that Ephesus was acknowledged as the temple keeper of Artemis and of the imperial cult. *That fell from the sky:* many scholars think that this refers to a meteorite that was worshiped as an image of the goddess.
19, 40: Some manuscripts omit the negative in [not] *be able,* making the meaning, "There is no cause for which we shall be able to give a reason for this demonstration."

19, 21: Acts 23, 11; Rom 1,   **19, 29:** Col 4, 10.
    13; 15, 22–32.   **20, 1:** 1 Cor 16, 1.
19, 26: Acts 17, 29.

out on his journey to Macedonia. ² As he traveled throughout those regions, he provided many words of encouragement for them. Then he arrived in Greece, ³ where he stayed for three months. But when a plot was made against him by the Jews as he was about to set sail for Syria, he decided to return by way of Macedonia.

Return to Troas

⁴* Sopater, the son of Pyrrhus, from Beroea, accompanied him, as did Aristarchus and Secundus from Thessalonica, Gaius from Derbe, Timothy, and Tychicus and Trophimus from Asia ⁵*† who went on ahead and waited for us at Troas. ⁶† We sailed from Philippi after the feast of Unleavened Bread, and rejoined them five days later in Troas, where we spent a week.

Eutychus Restored to Life

⁷† On the first day of the week when we gathered to break bread, Paul spoke to them because he was going to leave on the next day, and he kept on speaking until midnight. ⁸ There were many lamps in the upstairs room where we were gathered, ⁹ and a young man named Eutychus who was sitting on the window sill was sinking into a deep sleep as Paul talked on and on. Once overcome by sleep, he fell down from the third story and when he was picked up, he was dead. ¹⁰*† Paul went down, threw himself upon him, and said as he embraced him, "Don't be alarmed; there is life in him." ¹¹ Then he returned upstairs, broke the bread, and ate; after a long conversation that lasted until daybreak, he departed. ¹² And they took the boy away alive and were immeasurably comforted.

Journey to Miletus

¹³ We went ahead to the ship and set sail for Assos where we were to take Paul on board, as he had arranged, since he was going overland. ¹⁴ When he met us in Assos, we took him aboard and went on to Mitylene. ¹⁵ We sailed away from there on the next day and reached a point off Chios, and a day later we reached Samos, and on the following day we arrived at Miletus. ¹⁶† Paul had decided to sail past Ephesus in order not to lose time in the province of Asia, for he was hurrying to be in Jerusalem, if at all possible, for the day of Pentecost.

Paul's Farewell Speech at Miletus

¹⁷ From Miletus he had the presbyters of the church at Ephesus summoned. ¹⁸ When they came to him, he addressed them, "You know how I lived among you the whole time from the day I first came to the province of Asia. ¹⁹ I served the Lord with all humility and with the tears and trials that came to me because of the plots of the Jews, ²⁰ and I did not at all shrink from telling you what was for your benefit, or from teaching you in public or in your homes. ²¹ I earnestly bore witness for both Jews and Greeks to repentance before God and to faith in our Lord Jesus. ²² But now, compelled by the Spirit, I am going to Jerusalem. What will happen to me there I do not know, ²³* except that in one city after another the holy Spirit has been warning me that imprisonment and hardships await me. ²⁴* Yet I consider life of no importance to me, if only I may finish my course and the ministry that I received from the Lord Jesus, to bear witness to the gospel of God's grace.

²⁵ "But now I know that none of you to whom I preached the kingdom during my travels will ever see my face again. ²⁶ And so I solemnly declare to you this day that I am not responsible for the blood of any of you, ²⁷ for I did not shrink from proclaiming to you the entire plan of God. ²⁸*† Keep watch over yourselves and over the whole flock of which the holy Spirit has appointed you overseers, in which you tend the church of God that he acquired with his own blood. ²⁹* I know that after my departure savage wolves will come among you, and they will not spare the flock. ³⁰* And from your own group, men will come forward perverting the truth to draw the disciples away after them. ³¹* So be vigilant and remember that for three years, night and day, I unceasingly admonished each of you with tears. ³² And now I commend you to God and to

---

20, 5: The second "we-section" of Acts begins here. See the note on 16, 10–17.

20, 6: *Feast of Unleavened Bread:* see the note on Lk 22, 1.

20, 7: *The first day of the week:* the day after the sabbath and the first day of the Jewish week, apparently chosen originally by the Jerusalem community for the celebration of the liturgy of the Eucharist in order to relate it to the resurrection of Christ.

20, 10: The action of Paul in throwing himself upon the dead boy recalls that of Elijah in 1 Kgs 17, 21 where the son of the widow of Zarephath is revived and that of Elisha in 2 Kgs 4, 34 where the Shunamite woman's son is restored to life.

20, 16–35: Apparently aware of difficulties at Ephesus and neighboring areas, Paul calls the presbyters together at Miletus, about thirty miles from Ephesus. He reminds them of his dedication to the gospel (18–21), speaks of what he is about to suffer for the gospel (22–27), and admonishes them to guard the community against false prophets, sure to arise upon his departure (28–31). He concludes by citing a saying of Jesus (35) not recorded in the gospel tradition. Luke presents this farewell to the Ephesian presbyters as Paul's last will and testament.

20, 28: *Overseers:* see the note on Phil 1, 1. *The church of God:* because the clause "that he acquired with his own blood" following "the church of God" suggests that "his own blood" refers to God's blood, some early copyists changed "the church of God" to "the church of the Lord." Some prefer the translation "acquired with the blood of his own," i.e., Christ.

20, 4: Rom 16, 21.
20, 5: Acts 21, 29; 2 Tm 4, 20.
20, 10: 1 Kgs 17, 17–24; 2 Kgs 4, 30–37; Mt 9, 24; Mk 5, 39; Lk 8, 52.
20, 23: Acts 9, 16.
20, 24: 2 Tm 4, 7.
20, 28: Jn 21, 15–17; 1 Pt 5, 2.
20, 29: Jn 10, 12.
20, 30: Mt 7, 15; 2 Pt 2, 1–3; 1 Jn 2, 18–19.
20, 31: 1 Thes 2, 11.

that gracious word of his that can build you up and give you the inheritance among all who are consecrated. 33 I have never wanted anyone's silver or gold or clothing. 34* You know well that these very hands have served my needs and my companions. 35* In every way I have shown you that by hard work of that sort we must help the weak, and keep in mind the words of the Lord Jesus who himself said, 'It is more blessed to give than to receive.' "

36 When he had finished speaking he knelt down and prayed with them all. 37 They were all weeping loudly as they threw their arms around Paul and kissed him, 38 for they were deeply distressed that he had said that they would never see his face again. Then they escorted him to the ship.

Good-bye to a Friend

A s Paul sadly says good-bye in Acts 20, 36–38, we hear that the Christian community is experiencing similar feelings as they prepare to say good-bye to Paul. He has been an important person in their lives, and they have come to depend on him. Their grief overwhelms them, and they all experience great pain over his departure.

When we have to say good-bye to someone we care for deeply, we go through a grieving process. We feel sad and mad at the same time. Even after our friend has been gone for a long time, our heart has an empty space that our friend used to fill.

Lord, it is so difficult to say good-bye to my friend. We have shared so much together. I thank you for blessing me with this friendship. As we depart in separate directions, be our constant guardian and companion. Guide each of us safely to our destination. And until our paths cross again, surround my dear friend in your loving and protective embrace. Amen.

▸ Acts 20, 36–38

Arrival at Tyre

21 1† When we had taken leave of them we set sail, made a straight run for Cos, and on the next day for Rhodes, and from there to Patara. 2 Finding a ship crossing to Phoenicia, we went on board and put out to sea. 3 We caught sight of Cyprus but passed by it on our left and sailed on toward Syria and put in at Tyre where the ship was to unload cargo. 4 There we sought out the disciples and stayed for a week. They kept telling Paul through the Spirit not to embark for Jerusalem. 5 At the end of our stay we left and resumed our journey. All of them, women and children included, escorted us out of the city, and after kneeling on the beach to pray, 6 we bade farewell to one another. Then we boarded the ship, and they returned home.

Arrival at Ptolemais and Caesarea

7 We continued the voyage and came from Tyre to Ptolemais, where we greeted the brothers and stayed a day with them. 8*† On the next day we resumed the trip and came to Caesarea, where we went to the house of Philip the evangelist, who was one of the Seven, and stayed with him. 9 He had four virgin daughters gifted with prophecy. 10† We had been there several days when a prophet named Agabus came down from Judea. 11*† He came up to us, took Paul's belt, bound his own feet and hands with it, and said, "Thus says the holy Spirit: This is the way the Jews will bind the owner of this belt in Jerusalem, and they will hand him over to the Gentiles." 12 When we heard this, we and the local residents begged him not to go up to Jerusalem. 13* Then Paul replied, "What are you doing, weeping and breaking my heart? I am prepared not only to be bound but even to die in Jerusalem for the name of the Lord Jesus." 14*† Since he would not be dissuaded we let the matter rest, saying, "The Lord's will be done."

Paul and James in Jerusalem

15 After these days we made preparations for our journey, then went up to Jerusalem. 16 Some of the disciples from Caesarea came along to lead us to the house of Mnason, a Cypriot, a disciple of long standing, with whom we were to stay. 17† When we reached Jerusalem the brothers welcomed us warmly. 18 The next day, Paul accompanied us on a visit

---

21, 1–18: The third "we-section" of Acts (see the note on 16, 10–17).

21, 8: *One of the Seven:* see the note on 6, 2–4.

21, 10: *Agabus:* mentioned in 11, 28 as the prophet who predicted the famine that occurred when Claudius was emperor.

21, 11: The symbolic act of Agabus recalls those of Old Testament prophets. Compare Is 20, 2; Ez 4, 1; Jer 13, 1.

21, 14: The Christian disciples' attitude reflects that of Jesus (see Lk 22, 42).

21, 17–26: The leaders of the Jewish Christians of Jerusalem in-

form Paul that the Jews there believe he has encouraged the Jews of the diaspora to abandon the Mosaic law. According to Acts, Paul had no objection to the retention of the law by the Jewish Christians of Jerusalem and left the Jews of the diaspora who accepted Christianity free to follow the same practice.

20, 34: 1 Cor 4, 12; 1 Thes 2, 9; 2 Thes 3, 8.
20, 35: Sir 4, 31.
21, 8: Acts 6, 5; 8, 5–6.
21, 11: Acts 11, 28; 20, 23.
21, 13: Acts 19, 15–16.
21, 14: Mt 6, 10; 26, 39; Mk 14, 36; Lk 22, 42.

to James, and all the presbyters were present. [19] He greeted them, then proceeded to tell them in detail what God had accomplished among the Gentiles through his ministry. [20] They praised God when they heard it but said to him, "Brother, you see how many thousands of believers there are from among the Jews, and they are all zealous observers of the law. [21] They have been informed that you are teaching all the Jews who live among the Gentiles to abandon Moses and that you are telling them not to circumcise their children or to observe their customary practices. [22] What is to be done? They will surely hear that you have arrived. [23]*† So do what we tell you. We have four men who have taken a vow. [24]† Take these men and purify yourself with them, and pay their expenses that they may have their heads shaved. In this way everyone will know that there is nothing to the reports they have been given about you but that you yourself live in observance of the law. [25]*† As for the Gentiles who have come to believe, we sent them our decision that they abstain from meat sacrificed to idols, from blood, from the meat of strangled animals, and from unlawful marriage." [26]* So Paul took the men, and on the next day after purifying himself together with them entered the temple to give notice of the day when the purification would be completed and the offering made for each of them.

Paul's Arrest

[27] When the seven days were nearly completed, the Jews from the province of Asia noticed him in the temple, stirred up the whole crowd, and laid hands on him, [28]*† shouting, "Fellow Israelites, help us. This is the man who is teaching everyone everywhere against the people and the law and this place, and what is more, he has even brought Greeks

into the temple and defiled this sacred place." [29] For they had previously seen Trophimus the Ephesian in the city with him and supposed that Paul had brought him into the temple. [30] The whole city was

?did you KNOW?

Who Are Paul's Opponents?

As you read about Paul's return to Jerusalem, it may become confusing keeping track of the main characters. To help you keep it straight, here are some clues:

- One group is the Jewish Christians, represented by James and the elders (Acts 21, 17–26). Although the Jewish Christians might be suspicious of Paul's defense of the Gentile Christians, they support Paul and come up with a plan for him to try to prove his Jewish loyalty.
- Another group is the Jews who don't believe in Jesus. These Jews see the rise of the Christian faith as a threat to Judaism, and Paul as the most well-known representative of Christians. They attempt to arrest him and have him killed in a mob scene (verses 27–36).
- The third group is the Roman rulers. The Romans probably have no interest in this conflict except to keep the peace. The Roman tribune (governor) thinks he can keep the Jews happy by having Paul flogged (22, 22–29). But surprise! Paul is a Roman citizen and has civil rights that the tribune must honor.

So who are Paul's—and Christianity's—opponents? Luke tells us that at first they are the Jewish Christians. Later, they are the Jews who don't believe in Jesus. Still later—after this story occurs—they will be the Romans. Luke knows all this in hindsight and brings all three opponents into play in describing Paul's arrest and imprisonment.

▶ Acts 21, 17–26

---

†
21, 23–26: The leaders of the community suggest that Paul, on behalf of four members of the Jerusalem community, make the customary payment for the sacrifices offered at the termination of the Nazirite vow (see Nm 6, 1–24) in order to impress favorably the Jewish Christians in Jerusalem with his high regard for the Mosaic law. Since Paul himself had once made this vow (18, 18), his respect for the law would be on public record.

21, 24: *Pay their expenses:* according to Nm 6, 14–15 the Nazirite had to present a yearling lamb for a holocaust, a yearling ewe lamb for a sin offering, and a ram for a peace offering, along with food and drink offerings, upon completion of the period of the vow.

21, 25: Paul is informed about the apostolic decree, seemingly for the first time (see the note on 15, 13–35). The allusion to the decree was probably introduced here by Luke to remind his readers that the Gentile Christians themselves were asked to respect certain Jewish practices deriving from the law.

21, 28: The charges against Paul by the diaspora Jews are identical to the charges brought against Stephen by diaspora Jews in 6, 13. *Brought Greeks into the temple:* non-Jews were forbidden, under penalty of death, to go beyond the Court of the Gentiles. Inscriptions in Greek and Latin on a stone ballustrade marked off the prohibited area.

21, 23–27: Acts 18, 18; Nm 6,   21, 26: 1 Cor 9, 20.
    1–21.   21, 28: Rom 15, 31.
21, 25: Acts 15, 19–20.28–29.

A
C
T
S

in turmoil with people rushing together. They seized Paul and dragged him out of the temple, and immediately the gates were closed. ³¹† While they were trying to kill him, a report reached the cohort commander that all Jerusalem was rioting. ³² He immediately took soldiers and centurions and charged down on them. When they saw the commander and the soldiers they stopped beating Paul. ³³ The cohort commander came forward, arrested him, and ordered him to be secured with two chains; he tried to find out who he might be and what he had done. ³⁴ Some in the mob shouted one thing, others something else; so, since he was unable to ascertain the truth because of the uproar, he ordered Paul to be brought into the compound. ³⁵ When he reached the steps, he was carried by the soldiers because of the violence of the mob, ³⁶*† for a crowd of people followed and shouted, "Away with him!"

³⁷ Just as Paul was about to be taken into the compound, he said to the cohort commander, "May I say something to you?" He replied, "Do you speak Greek? ³⁸*† So then you are not the Egyptian who started a revolt some time ago and led the four thousand assassins into the desert?" ³⁹ Paul answered, "I am a Jew, of Tarsus in Cilicia, a citizen of no mean city; I request you to permit me to speak

to the people." ⁴⁰† When he had given his permission, Paul stood on the steps and motioned with his hand to the people; and when all was quiet he addressed them in Hebrew.

Paul's Defense before the Jerusalem Jews

22 ¹† "My brothers and fathers, listen to what I am about to say to you in my defense." ² When they heard him addressing them in Hebrew they became all the more quiet. And he continued, ³* "I am a Jew, born in Tarsus in Cilicia, but brought up in this city. At the feet of Gamaliel I was educated strictly in our ancestral law and was zealous for God, just as all of you are today. ⁴* I persecuted this Way to death, binding both men and women and delivering them to prison. ⁵ Even the high priest and the whole council of elders can testify on my behalf. For from them I even received letters to the brothers and set out for Damascus to bring back to Jerusalem in chains for punishment those there as well.

⁶* "On that journey as I drew near to Damascus, about noon a great light from the sky suddenly shone around me. ⁷* I fell to the ground and heard a voice saying to me, 'Saul, Saul, why are you persecuting me?' ⁸* I replied, 'Who are you, sir?' And he said to me, 'I am Jesus the Nazorean whom you are

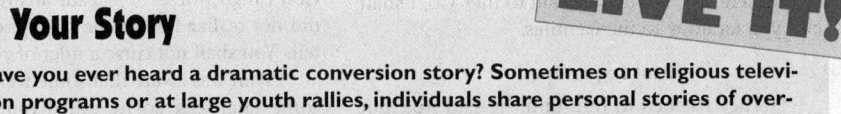

Sharing Your Story

Have you ever heard a dramatic conversion story? Sometimes on religious television programs or at large youth rallies, individuals share personal stories of overcoming addictions, terrible problems, or a great sin by believing in God. Or they tell of how they came to recognize and accept God in their life as a result of a serious illness or the death of a close friend or family member. Listening to these dramatic stories may make us feel that our own journey as a follower of Jesus—our own story—does not quite measure up. Nothing could be further from the truth in God's eyes.

We all have our own conversion stories—those moments of turning to God, of receiving a special call to serve others. And though our personal story might not be as dramatic as other people's stories, God will use it to encourage others to put their faith in Christ and dedicate their life to his mission. Are you willing to share your story of faith with others?

▸ Acts 22, 6–16

21, 31: *Cohort commander:* literally, "the leader of a thousand in a cohort." At this period the Roman cohort commander usually led six hundred soldiers, a tenth of a legion; but the number in a cohort varied.

21, 36: *"Away with him!":* at the trial of Jesus before Pilate in Lk 23, 18, the people similarly shout, "Away with this man."

21, 38: *The Egyptian:* according to the Jewish historian Josephus, an Egyptian gathered a large crowd on the Mount of Olives to witness the destruction of the walls of Jerusalem that would fall at the Egyptian "prophet's" word. The commotion was put down by the Roman authorities and the Egyptian escaped, but only after thousands had been killed. *Four thousand assassins:* literally, *sicarii.* According to Josephus, these were political nationalists who removed their opponents by assassination with a short dagger, called in Latin a *sica.*

21, 40: *In Hebrew:* meaning, perhaps, in Aramaic, which at this time was the Semitic tongue in common use.

22, 1–21: Paul's first defense speech is presented to the Jerusalem crowds. Luke here presents Paul as a devout Jew (3) and zealous persecutor of the Christian community (4–5), and then recounts the conversion of Paul for the second time in Acts (see the note on 9, 1–19).

---
* 21, 36: Lk 23, 18; Jn 19, 15;   19; 26, 9–11; Phil
    Acts 22, 22.   3, 6.
21, 38: Acts 5, 36–37.   22, 6: Acts 9, 3; 26, 13;
  22, 3: Acts 5, 34; 26, 4–5;   1 Cor 15, 8.
    2 Cor 11, 22; Gal 1,   22, 7: Acts 9, 4; 26, 14.
    13–14; Phil 3, 5–6.   22, 8: Mt 25, 40; Acts 9, 5;
  22, 4: Acts 8, 3; 9, 1–2; 22,   26, 15.

persecuting.' 9* My companions saw the light but did not hear the voice of the one who spoke to me. 10* I asked, 'What shall I do, sir?' The Lord answered me, 'Get up and go into Damascus, and there you will be told about everything appointed for you to do.' 11* Since I could see nothing because of the brightness of that light, I was led by hand by my companions and entered Damascus.

12* "A certain Ananias, a devout observer of the law, and highly spoken of by all the Jews who lived there, 13 came to me and stood there and said, 'Saul, my brother, regain your sight.' And at that very moment I regained my sight and saw him. 14 Then he said, 'The God of our ancestors designated you to know his will, to see the Righteous One, and to hear the sound of his voice; 15† for you will be his witness before all to what you have seen and heard. 16 Now, why delay? Get up and have yourself baptized and your sins washed away, calling upon his name.'

17 "After I had returned to Jerusalem and while I was praying in the temple, I fell into a trance 18 and saw the Lord saying to me, 'Hurry, leave Jerusalem at once, because they will not accept your testimony about me.' 19* But I replied, 'Lord, they themselves know that from synagogue to synagogue I used to imprison and beat those who believed in you. 20* And when the blood of your witness Stephen was being shed, I myself stood by giving my approval and keeping guard over the cloaks of his murderers.' 21*† Then he said to me, 'Go, I shall send you far away to the Gentiles.' "

Paul Imprisoned

22*† They listened to him until he said this, but then they raised their voices and shouted, "Take such a one as this away from the earth. It is not right that he should live." 23 And as they were yelling and throwing off their cloaks and flinging dust into the air, 24 the cohort commander ordered him to be brought into the compound and gave instruction that he be interrogated under the lash to determine the reason why they were making such an outcry against him. 25*† But when they had stretched him out for the whips, Paul said to the centurion on duty, "Is it lawful for you to scourge a man who is a

Roman citizen and has not been tried?" 26 When the centurion heard this, he went to the cohort commander and reported it, saying, "What are you going to do? This man is a Roman citizen." 27 Then the commander came and said to him, "Tell me, are you a Roman citizen?" "Yes," he answered. 28 The commander replied, "I acquired this citizenship for a large sum of money." Paul said, "But I was born one." 29 At once those who were going to interrogate him backed away from him, and the commander became alarmed when he realized that he was a Roman citizen and that he had had him bound.

Paul before the Sanhedrin

30 The next day, wishing to determine the truth about why he was being accused by the Jews, he freed him and ordered the chief priests and the whole Sanhedrin to convene. Then he brought Paul down and made him stand before them.

23 1* Paul looked intently at the Sanhedrin and said, "My brothers, I have conducted myself with a perfectly clear conscience before God to this day." 2† The high priest Ananias ordered his attendants to strike his mouth. 3*† Then Paul said to him, "God will strike you, you whitewashed wall. Do you indeed sit in judgment upon me according to the law and yet in violation of the law order me to be struck?" 4 The attendants said, "Would you revile God's high priest?" 5*† Paul answered, "Brothers, I did not realize he was the high priest. For it is written, 'You shall not curse a ruler of your people.' "

6* Paul was aware that some were Sadducees and some Pharisees, so he called out before the Sanhedrin, "My brothers, I am a Pharisee, the son of Pharisees; I am on trial for hope in the resurrection of the dead." 7 When he said this, a dispute broke out between the Pharisees and Sadducees, and the group became divided. 8* For the Sadducees say that there is no resurrection or angels or spirits, while the Pharisees acknowledge all three. 9 A great uproar occurred, and some scribes belonging to the Pharisee party stood up and sharply argued, "We find nothing wrong with this man. Suppose a spirit or an angel has spoken to him?" 10 The dispute was so

---

22, 15: *His witness:* like the Galilean followers during the historical ministry of Jesus, Paul too, through his experience of the risen Christ, is to be a witness to the resurrection (compare 1, 8; 10, 39–41; Lk 24, 48).

22, 21: Paul endeavors to explain that his position on the law has not been identical with that of his audience because it has been his prophetic mission to preach to the Gentiles to whom the law was not addressed and who had no faith in it as a way of salvation.

22, 22: Paul's suggestion that his prophetic mission to the Gentiles did not involve his imposing the law on them provokes the same opposition as occurred in Pisidian Antioch (13, 45).

22, 25: *"Is it lawful for you to scourge a man who is a Roman citizen and has not been tried?":* see the note on 16, 37.

23, 2: *The high priest Ananias:* Ananias, son of Nedebaeus, was high priest from A.D. 47 to 59.

23, 3: *God will strike you:* Josephus reports that Ananias was later assassinated in A.D. 66 at the beginning of the First Revolt.

23, 5: Luke portrays Paul as a model of one who is obedient to the Mosaic law. Paul, because of his reverence for the law (Ex 22, 27), withdraws his accusation of hypocrisy, "whitewashed wall" (cf Mt 23, 27), when he is told Ananias is the high priest.

22, 9: Acts 9, 7; 26, 13–14.
22, 10: Acts 9, 6; 26, 16.
22, 11: Acts 9, 8.
22, 12–16: Acts 9, 10–19.
22, 19: Acts 8, 3; 9, 1–2; 22, 4–5; 26, 9–11.
22, 20: Acts 7, 58; 8, 1.
22, 21: Acts 9, 15; Gal 2, 7–9.
22, 22: Acts 21, 36; Lk 23, 18; Jn 19, 15.
22, 25: Acts 16, 37.
23, 1: Acts 24, 16.
23, 3: Ez 13, 10–15; Mt 23, 27.
23, 5: Ex 22, 27.
23, 6: Acts 24, 15.21; 26, 5; Phil 3, 5.
23, 8: Mt 22, 23; Lk 20, 27.

serious that the commander, afraid that Paul would be torn to pieces by them, ordered his troops to go down and rescue him from their midst and take him into the compound. [11]*† The following night the Lord stood by him and said, "Take courage. For just as you have borne witness to my cause in Jerusalem, so you must also bear witness in Rome."

Transfer to Caesarea

[12] When day came, the Jews made a plot and bound themselves by oath not to eat or drink until they had killed Paul. [13] There were more than forty who formed this conspiracy. [14] They went to the chief priests and elders and said, "We have bound ourselves by a solemn oath to taste nothing until we have killed Paul. [15] You, together with the Sanhedrin, must now make an official request to the commander to have him bring him down to you, as though you meant to investigate his case more thoroughly. We on our part are prepared to kill him before he arrives." [16] The son of Paul's sister, however, heard about the ambush; so he went and entered the compound and reported it to Paul. [17]† Paul then called one of the centurions and requested, "Take this young man to the commander; he has something to report to him." [18] So he took him and brought him to the commander and explained, "The prisoner Paul called me and asked that I bring this young man to you; he has something to say to you." [19] The commander took him by the hand, drew him aside, and asked him privately, "What is it you have to report to me?" [20] He replied, "The Jews have conspired to ask you to bring Paul down to the Sanhedrin tomorrow, as though they meant to inquire about him more thoroughly, [21] but do not believe them. More than forty of them are lying in wait for him; they have bound themselves by oath not to eat or drink until they have killed him. They are now ready and only wait for your consent." [22] As the commander dismissed the young man he directed him, "Tell no one that you gave me this information."

[23]† Then he summoned two of the centurions and said, "Get two hundred soldiers ready to go to Caesarea by nine o'clock tonight, along with seventy horsemen and two hundred auxiliaries. [24] Provide mounts for Paul to ride and give him safe conduct to Felix the governor." [25] Then he wrote a letter with this content: [26]† "Claudius Lysias to his excellency the governor Felix, greetings.† [27]* This man, seized by the Jews and about to be murdered by them, I rescued after intervening with my troops when I learned that he was a Roman citizen. [28] I wanted to learn the reason for their accusations against him so I brought him down to their Sanhedrin. [29]* I discovered that he was accused in matters of controversial questions of their law and not of any charge deserving death or imprisonment. [30] Since it was brought to my attention that there will be a plot against the man, I am sending him to you at once, and have also notified his accusers to state [their case] against him before you."

[31] So the soldiers, according to their orders, took Paul and escorted him by night to Antipatris. [32] The next day they returned to the compound, leaving the horsemen to complete the journey with him. [33] When they arrived in Caesarea they delivered the letter to the governor and presented Paul to him. [34] When he had read it and asked to what province he belonged, and learned that he was from Cilicia, [35] he said, "I shall hear your case when your accusers arrive." Then he ordered that he be held in custody in Herod's praetorium.

Trial before Felix

24 [1] Five days later the high priest Ananias came down with some elders and an advocate, a certain Tertullus, and they presented formal charges against Paul to the governor. [2] When he was called, Tertullus began to accuse him, saying, "Since we have attained much peace through you, and reforms have been accomplished in this nation through your provident care, [3] we acknowledge this in every way and everywhere, most excellent Felix, with all gratitude. [4] But in order not to detain you further, I ask you to give us a brief hearing with your customary graciousness. [5]*† We found this man to be a pest; he creates dissension among Jews all over the world and is a ringleader of the sect of the Nazoreans. [6]* He even tried to desecrate our temple, but we arrested him. [[7]†] [8] If you examine him you will be able to learn from him for yourself

---

† **23, 11:** The occurrence of the vision of Christ consoling Paul and assuring him that he will be his witness in Rome prepares the reader for the final section of Acts: the journey of Paul and the word he preaches to Rome under the protection of the Romans.

23, 17: *Centurions:* a centurion was a military officer in charge of one hundred soldiers.

23, 23: *By nine o'clock tonight:* literally, "by the third hour of the night." The night hours began at 6 p.m. *Two hundred auxiliaries:* the meaning of the Greek is not certain. It seems to refer to spearmen from the local police force and not from the cohort of soldiers, which would have numbered only 500–1000 men.

23, 26–30: The letter emphasizes the fact that Paul is a Roman citizen and asserts the lack of evidence that he is guilty of a crime against the empire. The tone of the letter implies that the commander became initially involved in Paul's case because of his Roman cit-

izenship, but this is not an exact description of what really happened (see 21, 31–33; 22, 25–29).

23, 26: M. Antonius Felix was procurator of Judea from A.D. 52 to 60. His procuratorship was marked by cruelty toward and oppression of his Jewish subjects.

24, 5: *Nazoreans:* that is, followers of Jesus of Nazareth.

24, 7: The Western text has added here a verse (really 6b–8a) that is not found in the best Greek manuscripts. It reads, "and would have judged him according to our own law, but the cohort commander Lysias came and violently took him out of our hands and ordered his accusers to come before you."

23, 11: Acts 19, 21.
23, 27: Acts 21, 30–34; 22, 27.
23, 29: Acts 18, 14–15; 25,

18–19.
24, 5: Acts 24, 14; Lk 23, 2.
24, 6: Acts 21, 28.

about everything of which we are accusing him." [9] The Jews also joined in the attack and asserted that these things were so.

[10]† Then the governor motioned to him to speak and Paul replied, "I know that you have been a judge over this nation for many years and so I am pleased to make my defense before you. [11] As you can verify, not more than twelve days have passed since I went up to Jerusalem to worship. [12] Neither in the temple, nor in the synagogues, nor anywhere in the city did they find me arguing with anyone or instigating a riot among the people. [13] Nor can they prove to you the accusations they are now making against me. [14]* But this I do admit to you, that according to the Way, which they call a sect, I worship the God of our ancestors and I believe everything that is in accordance with the law and written in the prophets. [15]* I have the same hope in God as they themselves have that there will be a resurrection of the righteous and the unrighteous. [16]* Because of this, I always strive to keep my conscience clear before God and man. [17]* After many years, I came to bring alms for my nation and offerings. [18]* While I was so engaged, they found me, after my purification, in the temple without a crowd or disturbance. [19] But some Jews from the province of Asia, who should be here before you to make whatever accusation they might have against me— [20] or let these men themselves state what crime they discovered when I stood before the Sanhedrin, [21]* unless it was my one outcry as I stood among them, that 'I am on trial before you today for the resurrection of the dead.' "

[22] Then Felix, who was accurately informed about the Way, postponed the trial, saying, "When Lysias the commander comes down, I shall decide your case." [23] He gave orders to the centurion that he should be kept in custody but have some liberty, and that he should not prevent any of his friends from caring for his needs.

Captivity in Caesarea

[24]† Several days later Felix came with his wife Drusilla, who was Jewish. He had Paul summoned and listened to him speak about faith in Christ Jesus. [25] But as he spoke about righteousness and self-restraint and the coming judgment, Felix became frightened and said, "You may go for now; when I find an opportunity I shall summon you again." [26] At the same time he hoped that a bribe would be offered him by Paul, and so he sent for him very often and conversed with him.

[27]† Two years passed and Felix was succeeded by Porcius Festus. Wishing to ingratiate himself with the Jews, Felix left Paul in prison.

Appeal to Caesar

25 [1] Three days after his arrival in the province, Festus went up from Caesarea to Jerusalem [2]† where the chief priests and Jewish leaders presented him their formal charges against Paul. They asked him [3] as a favor to have him sent to Jerusalem, for they were plotting to kill him along the way. [4] Festus replied that Paul was being held in custody in Caesarea and that he himself would be returning there shortly. [5] He said, "Let your authorities come down with me, and if this man has done something improper, let them accuse him."

[6] After spending no more than eight or ten days with them, he went down to Caesarea, and on the following day took his seat on the tribunal and ordered that Paul be brought in. [7] When he appeared, the Jews who had come down from Jerusalem surrounded him and brought many serious charges against him, which they were unable to prove. [8] In defending himself Paul said, "I have committed no crime either against the Jewish law or against the temple or against Caesar." [9]† Then Festus, wishing to ingratiate himself with the Jews, said to Paul in reply, "Are you willing to go up to Jerusalem and there stand trial before me on these charges?" [10] Paul answered, "I am standing before the tribunal of Caesar; this is where I should be tried. I have committed no crime against the Jews, as you very well know. [11] If I have committed a crime or done anything deserving death, I do not seek to escape the death penalty; but if there is no substance to the charges they are bringing against me, then no one has the right to hand me over to them. I appeal to Caesar." [12] Then Festus, after conferring with his council, replied, "You have appealed to Caesar. To Caesar you will go."

†

24, 10–21: Whereas the advocate Tertullus referred to Paul's activities on his missionary journeys, the apostle narrowed the charges down to the riot connected with the incident in the temple (see 21, 27–30; 24, 17–20). In his defense, Paul stresses the continuity between Christianity and Judaism.

24, 24–25: The way of Christian discipleship greatly disquiets Felix, who has entered into an adulterous marriage with Drusilla, daughter of Herod Agrippa I. This marriage provides the background for the topics Paul speaks about and about which Felix does not want to hear.

24, 27: Very little is known of Porcius Festus who was a procurator of Judea from A.D. 60 to 62.

25, 2: Even after two years the animosity toward Paul in Jerusalem

had not subsided (see 24, 27).

25, 9–12: Paul refuses to acknowledge that the Sanhedrin in Jerusalem has any jurisdiction over him now (11). Paul uses his right as a Roman citizen to appeal his case to the jurisdiction of the Emperor (Nero, ca. A.D. 60) (12). This move broke the deadlock between Roman protective custody of Paul and the plan of his enemies to kill him (3).

*

24, 14: Acts 24, 5.	24, 17: Rom 15, 25–26; Gal 2,
24, 15: Dn 12, 2; Jn 5, 28–29.	10.
24, 16: Acts 23, 1.	24, 18–19: Acts 21, 26–30.
	24, 21: Acts 23, 6; 24, 15.

Paul before King Agrippa

13† When a few days had passed, King Agrippa and Bernice arrived in Caesarea on a visit to Festus. 14* Since they spent several days there, Festus referred Paul's case to the king, saying, "There is a man here left in custody by Felix. 15 When I was in Jerusalem the chief priests and the elders of the Jews brought charges against him and demanded his condemnation. 16 I answered them that it was not Roman practice to hand over an accused person before he has faced his accusers and had the opportunity to defend himself against their charge. 17 So when [they] came together here, I made no delay; the next day I took my seat on the tribunal and ordered the man to be brought in. 18* His accusers stood around him, but did not charge him with any of the crimes I suspected. 19 Instead they had some issues with him about their own religion and about a certain Jesus who had died but who Paul claimed was alive. 20 Since I was at a loss how to investigate this controversy, I asked if he were willing to go to Jerusalem and there stand trial on these charges. 21 And when Paul appealed that he be held in custody for the Emperor's decision, I ordered him held until I could send him to Caesar." 22 Agrippa said to Festus, "I too should like to hear this man." He replied, "Tomorrow you will hear him."

23 The next day Agrippa and Bernice came with great ceremony and entered the audience hall in the company of cohort commanders and the prominent men of the city and, by command of Festus, Paul was brought in. 24 And Festus said, "King Agrippa and all you here present with us, look at this man about whom the whole Jewish populace petitioned me here and in Jerusalem, clamoring that he should live no longer. 25 I found, however, that he had done nothing deserving death, and so when he appealed to the Emperor, I decided to send him. 26 But I have nothing definite to write about him to our sovereign; therefore I have brought him before all of you, and particularly before you, King Agrippa, so that I may have something to write as a result of this investigation. 27 For it seems senseless to me to send up a prisoner without indicating the charges against him."

King Agrippa Hears Paul

26 1 Then Agrippa said to Paul, "You may now speak on your own behalf." So Paul stretched out his hand and began his defense. 2† "I

did you KNOW?

What About the Jews?

The earliest Christians were Jews. It was agonizing to them that so many of their Jewish friends wouldn't believe in Jesus. Indeed, not only did those friends not believe in Jesus, but many tried to stop the spread of Christianity. Acts of the Apostles, chapters 22–28, tells of Jewish attacks against Paul, which ultimately end with Paul traveling to Rome to make his case before the emperor.

But the questions remain: If the Jews are God's people, why don't they believe? Couldn't God make it easier for them to believe? Does God cause their lack of faith in Jesus? Who is ultimately responsible for anyone's faith? If you are interested, read Romans, chapter 9, where Paul tries to answer those questions.

▶ Acts 22, 30—28, 31

count myself fortunate, King Agrippa, that I am to defend myself before you today against all the charges made against me by the Jews, 3 especially since you are an expert in all the Jewish customs and controversies. And therefore I beg you to listen patiently. 4† My manner of living from my youth, a life spent from the beginning among my people and in Jerusalem, all [the] Jews know. 5* They have known about me from the start, if they are willing to testify, that I have lived my life as a Pharisee, the strictest party of our religion. 6* But now I am standing trial because of my hope in the promise made by God to our ancestors. 7 Our twelve tribes hope to attain to that promise as they fervently worship God day and night; and on account of this hope I am accused by Jews, O king. 8 Why is it thought unbelievable among you that God raises the dead? 9* I myself once thought that I had to do many things against the name of Jesus the Nazorean, 10* and I did so in Jerusalem. I imprisoned many of the holy ones with

---

25, 13: *King Agrippa and Bernice:* brother and sister, children of Herod Agrippa I whose activities against the Jerusalem community are mentioned in 12, 1–19. Agrippa II was a petty ruler over small areas in northern Palestine and some villages in Perea. His influence on the Jewish population of Palestine was insignificant.

26, 2–23: Paul's final defense speech in Acts is now made before a king (see 9, 15). In the speech Paul presents himself as a zealous Pharisee and Christianity as the logical development of Pharisaic Ju-

daism. The story of his conversion is recounted for the third time in Acts in this speech (see the note on 9, 1–19).

26, 4: *Among my people:* that is, among the Jews.

25, 14: Acts 24, 27.   26, 6–8: Acts 23, 6; 24, 15.21;
25, 18–19: Acts 18, 14–15; 23, 29.   28, 20.
26, 5: Phil 3, 5–6; Gal 1,   26, 9–11: Acts 9, 8; 3; 9, 1–2; 22,
13–14; 2 Cor 11, 22.   19; Phil 3, 6.
26, 10: Acts 9, 14.

PAUL TEACHES US HOW TO LIVE OUR FAITH!

Reporters Marisa and Ricardo. [Speaking into their microphones] We're here, live, in Caesarea, where Paul of Tarsus has just spoken with King Agrippa and Governor Festus. Here comes Paul now. Let's see what he has to say. Paul, why has your message caused so much controversy?

Paul. It was never my intention to cause strife or conflict. But I must speak the truth, and the truth is that God has revealed his salvation for us in Jesus Christ. In Jesus, salvation is available to everyone—Jews and Gentiles, slaves and free people, men and women—and we are all equal as sons and daughters of God. Unfortunately, this truth is upsetting to some people, and they have gone to great lengths to try to get rid of me.

Marisa and Ricardo. But hasn't your message been well received by many people—including many different types of people?

Paul. Yes it has. I think this is because Jesus taught us always to respect every person as a son or daughter of God regardless of his or her culture or social class. Under the guidance of the Holy Spirit, Christian communities allow for diversity while keeping a common unity in Jesus Christ. I think people are hungry for this.

Marisa and Ricardo. Soon you will be heading for Rome, where you will be on trial for alleged crimes against the empire. Are you worried?

Paul. [Smiling] Why be worried? No one has ultimate power over me except my Lord Jesus Christ. I only need to be faithful to my calling, and I will receive my prize—eternal life with God. Plus I have the prayers and support of many close friends. But thank you for your concern. God's grace and peace be with you.

Marisa and Ricardo. And thank you, Paul.

▸ **Acts of the Apostles, chapter 26**

the authorization I received from the chief priests, and when they were to be put to death I cast my vote against them. [11] Many times, in synagogue after synagogue, I punished them in an attempt to force them to blaspheme; I was so enraged against them that I pursued them even to foreign cities.

[12] "On one such occasion I was traveling to Damascus with the authorization and commission of the chief priests. [13]* At midday, along the way, O king, I saw a light from the sky, brighter than the sun, shining around me and my traveling companions.* [14]*† We all fell to the ground and I heard a voice saying to me in Hebrew, 'Saul, Saul, why are you persecuting me? It is hard for you to kick

against the goad.' [15]* And I said, 'Who are you, sir?' And the Lord replied, 'I am Jesus whom you are persecuting. [16]*† Get up now, and stand on your feet. I have appeared to you for this purpose, to appoint you as a servant and witness of what you have seen [of me] and what you will be shown. [17]* I shall deliver you from this people and from the Gentiles to whom I send you, [18]*† to open their eyes that they may turn from darkness to light and from the power of Satan to God, so that they may obtain forgiveness of sins and an inheritance among those who have been consecrated by faith in me.'

[19] "And so, King Agrippa, I was not disobedient to the heavenly vision. [20] On the contrary, first to those

---

† **26, 14:** *In Hebrew:* see the note on 21, 40. *It is hard for you to kick against the goad:* this proverb is commonly found in Greek literature and in this context signifies the senselessness and ineffectiveness of any opposition to the divine influence in his life.

26, 16: The words of Jesus directed to Paul here reflect the dialogues between Christ and Ananias (9, 15) and between Ananias and Paul (22, 14–15) in the two previous accounts of Paul's conversion.

26, 18: *To open their eyes:* though no mention is made of Paul's blindness in this account (cf 9, 8–9.12.18; 22, 11–13), the task he is

commissioned to perform is the removal of other people's spiritual blindness.

26, 13–14: Acts 9, 7.
  26, 13: Acts 9, 3; 22, 6.
  26, 14: Acts 9, 4; 22, 7.
  26, 15: Mt 25, 40; Acts 9, 5;
    22, 8.
26, 16: Ez 2, 1; Acts 9, 6; 22,
    10.
26, 17: Jer 1, 7.
26, 18: Is 42, 7.16; 61, 1 LXX;
    Col 1, 13.

A
C
T
S

in Damascus and in Jerusalem and throughout the whole country of Judea, and then to the Gentiles, I preached the need to repent and turn to God, and to do works giving evidence of repentance. [21]* That is why the Jews seized me [when I was] in the temple and tried to kill me. [22]*† But I have enjoyed God's help to this very day, and so I stand here testifying to small and great alike, saying nothing different from what the prophets and Moses foretold, [23]*† that the Messiah must suffer and that, as the first to rise from the dead, he would proclaim light both to our people and to the Gentiles."

Reactions to Paul's Speech

[24] While Paul was so speaking in his defense, Festus said in a loud voice, "You are mad, Paul; much learning is driving you mad." [25] But Paul replied, "I am not mad, most excellent Festus; I am speaking words of truth and reason. [26]† The king knows about these matters and to him I speak boldly, for I cannot believe that [any] of this has escaped his notice; this was not done in a corner. [27]† King Agrippa, do you believe the prophets? I know you believe." [28] Then Agrippa said to Paul, "You will soon persuade me to play the Christian." [29] Paul replied, "I would pray to God that sooner or later not only you but all who listen to me today might become as I am except for these chains."

[30] Then the king rose, and with him the governor and Bernice and the others who sat with them. [31]† And after they had withdrawn they said to one another, "This man is doing nothing [at all] that deserves death or imprisonment." [32]* And Agrippa said to Festus, "This man could have been set free if he had not appealed to Caesar."

Departure for Rome

27 [1]† When it was decided that we should sail to Italy, they handed Paul and some other prisoners over to a centurion named Julius of the Cohort Augusta.† [2]* We went on board a ship from Adramyttium bound for ports in the province of Asia and set sail. Aristarchus, a Macedonian from Thessalonica, was with us. [3] On the following day we put in at Sidon where Julius was kind enough to allow Paul to visit his friends who took care of him. [4] From there we put out to sea and sailed around the sheltered side of Cyprus because of the headwinds, [5] and crossing the open sea off the coast of Cilicia and Pamphylia we came to Myra in Lycia.

Storm and Shipwreck

[6] There the centurion found an Alexandrian ship that was sailing to Italy and put us on board. [7] For many days we made little headway, arriving at Cnidus only with difficulty, and because the wind would not permit us to continue our course we sailed for the sheltered side of Crete off Salmone. [8] We sailed past it with difficulty and reached a place called Fair Havens, near which was the city of Lasea.

[9]*† Much time had now passed and sailing had become hazardous because the time of the fast had already gone by, so Paul warned them, [10] "Men, I can see that this voyage will result in severe damage and heavy loss not only to the cargo and the ship, but also to our lives." [11] The centurion, however, paid more attention to the pilot and to the owner of the ship than to what Paul said. [12] Since the harbor was unfavorably situated for spending the winter, the majority planned to put out to sea from there in the hope of reaching Phoenix, a port in Crete facing west-northwest, there to spend the winter.

[13] A south wind blew gently, and thinking they had attained their objective, they weighed anchor and sailed along close to the coast of Crete. [14] Before long an offshore wind of hurricane force called a "Northeaster" struck. [15] Since the ship was caught up in it and could not head into the wind we gave way and let ourselves be driven. [16] We passed along the sheltered side of an island named Cauda and managed only with difficulty to get the dinghy under control. [17] They hoisted it aboard, then used cables to undergird the ship. Because of their fear that they would run aground on the shoal of Syrtis, they

A
C
T
S

---

† **26, 22:** *Saying nothing different from what the prophets and Moses foretold:* see the note on Lk 18, 31.

26, 23: *That the Messiah must suffer:* see the note on Lk 24, 26.

26, 26: *Not done in a corner:* for Luke, this Greek proverb expresses his belief that he is presenting a story about Jesus and the church that is already well known. As such, the entire history of Christianity is public knowledge and incontestable. Luke presents his story in this way to provide "certainty" to his readers about the instructions they have received (Lk 1, 4).

26, 27–28: If the Christian missionaries proclaim nothing different from what the Old Testament prophets had proclaimed (22–23), then the logical outcome for the believing Jew, according to Luke, is to become a Christian.

26, 31–32: In recording the episode of Paul's appearance before Agrippa, Luke wishes to show that, when Paul's case was judged impartially, no grounds for legal action against him were found (see 23, 29; 25, 25).

27, 1—28, 16: Here Luke has written a stirring account of adventure on the high seas, incidental to his main purpose of showing how well Paul got along with his captors and how his prophetic influence saved the lives of all on board. The recital also establishes the existence of Christian communities in Puteoli and Rome. This account of the voyage and shipwreck also constitutes the final "we-section" in Acts (see the note on 16, 10–17).

27, 1: *Cohort Augusta:* the presence of a Cohort Augusta in Syria during the first century A.D. is attested in inscriptions. Whatever the historical background to this information given by Luke may be, the name Augusta serves to increase the prominence and prestige of the prisoner Paul whose custodians bear so important a Roman name.

27, 9: *The time of the fast:* the fast kept on the occasion of the Day of Atonement (Lv 16, 29–31), which occurred in late September or early October.

26, 21: Acts 21, 31.
26, 22–23: Acts 3, 18; Lk 24, 26–27.44–47.
26, 23: Is 42, 6; 49, 6; Lk 2,

32; 1 Cor 15, 20–23.
26, 32: Acts 25, 11–12.
27, 2: Acts 19, 29; 20, 4.
27, 9: Lv 16, 29–31.

lowered the drift anchor and were carried along in this way. [18] We were being pounded by the storm so violently that the next day they jettisoned some cargo, [19] and on the third day with their own hands they threw even the ship's tackle overboard. [20] Neither the sun nor the stars were visible for many days, and no small storm raged. Finally, all hope of our surviving was taken away.

[21] When many would no longer eat, Paul stood among them and said, "Men, you should have taken my advice and not have set sail from Crete and you would have avoided this disastrous loss. [22] I urge you now to keep up your courage; not one of you will be lost, only the ship. [23] For last night an angel of the God to whom I belong and whom I serve stood by me [24]* and said, 'Do not be afraid, Paul. You are destined to stand before Caesar; and behold, for your sake, God has granted safety to all who are sailing with you.' [25] Therefore, keep up your courage, men; I

When the Waves Get Too Rough

It is not easy to be courageous when you face danger. When you find yourself in situations where things are beyond your control, like the storm that endangered the ship Paul was on, turn to God. After all, isn't faith for the times when you feel the most helpless and out of control?

Help, Lord, I'm lost at sea! When I started this journey of life, I thought I knew where I was headed, but then a few waves started to rock the boat, and I became frightened.

Next, the wind picked up, and my fear turned into confusion. Then the night fell, and my confusion turned into despair. And now, I am lost and need you to help calm the waves in my life and stand beside me until the night turns into day.

Help me to find my bearings again, Lord. And when this storm is over, gift me with the wisdom to learn from this experience—to go back and make right what was wrong, not to lose hope at the first sign of trouble, and to hang on to you, my anchor, when life gets rough. Amen.

▶ Acts 27, 21–25

trust in God that it will turn out as I have been told. [26] We are destined to run aground on some island."

[27] On the fourteenth night, as we were still being driven about on the Adriatic Sea, toward midnight the sailors began to suspect that they were nearing land. [28] They took soundings and found twenty fathoms; a little farther on, they again took soundings and found fifteen fathoms. [29] Fearing that we would run aground on a rocky coast, they dropped four anchors from the stern and prayed for day to come. [30] The sailors then tried to abandon ship; they lowered the dinghy to the sea on the pretext of going to lay out anchors from the bow. [31] But Paul said to the centurion and the soldiers, "Unless these men stay with the ship, you cannot be saved." [32] So the soldiers cut the ropes of the dinghy and set it adrift.

[33] Until the day began to dawn, Paul kept urging all to take some food. He said, "Today is the fourteenth day that you have been waiting, going hungry and eating nothing. [34] I urge you, therefore, to take some food; it will help you survive. Not a hair of the head of anyone of you will be lost." [35]*† When he said this, he took bread, gave thanks to God in front of them all, broke it, and began to eat. [36] They were all encouraged, and took some food themselves. [37] In all, there were two hundred seventy-six of us on the ship. [38] After they had eaten enough, they lightened the ship by throwing the wheat into the sea.

[39] When day came they did not recognize the land, but made out a bay with a beach. They planned to run the ship ashore on it, if they could. [40] So they cast off the anchors and abandoned them to the sea, and at the same time they unfastened the lines of the rudders, and hoisting the foresail into the wind, they made for the beach. [41] But they struck a sandbar and ran the ship aground. The bow was wedged in and could not be moved, but the stern began to break up under the pounding [of the waves]. [42] The soldiers planned to kill the prisoners so that none might swim away and escape, [43] but the centurion wanted to save Paul and so kept them from carrying out their plan. He ordered those who could swim to jump overboard first and get to the shore, [44] and then the rest, some on planks, others on debris from the ship. In this way, all reached shore safely.

Winter in Malta

28 [1] Once we had reached safety we learned that the island was called Malta. [2] The natives showed us extraordinary hospitality; they lit a fire and welcomed all of us because it had begun to rain and was cold. [3] Paul had gathered a bundle of brushwood and was putting it on the fire when a viper, escaping from the heat, fastened on his hand.

27, 35: *He took bread . . . :* the words recall the traditional language of the celebration of the Eucharist (see Lk 22, 19).

27, 24: Acts 23, 11.
27, 35: Mt 15, 36; Mk 6, 41;   8, 6; Lk 22, 19; 1 Cor 11, 23–24.

⁴† When the natives saw the snake hanging from his hand, they said to one another, "This man must certainly be a murderer; though he escaped the sea, Justice has not let him remain alive." ⁵ But he shook the snake off into the fire and suffered no harm. ⁶* They were expecting him to swell up or suddenly to fall down dead but, after waiting a long time and seeing nothing unusual happen to him, they changed their minds and began to say that he was a god. ⁷ In the vicinity of that place were lands belonging to a man named Publius, the chief of the island. He welcomed us and received us cordially as his guests for three days. ⁸ It so happened that the father of Publius was sick with a fever and dysentery. Paul visited him and, after praying, laid his hands on him and healed him. ⁹ After this had taken place, the rest of the sick on the island came to Paul and were cured. ¹⁰ They paid us great honor and when we eventually set sail they brought us the provisions we needed.

Arrival in Rome

¹¹† Three months later we set sail on a ship that had wintered at the island. It was an Alexandrian ship with the Dioscuri as its figurehead. ¹² We put in at Syracuse and stayed there three days, ¹³ and from there we sailed round the coast and arrived at Rhegium. After a day, a south wind came up and in two days we reached Puteoli. ¹⁴ There we found some brothers and were urged to stay with them for seven days. And thus we came to Rome. ¹⁵ The brothers from there heard about us and came as far as the Forum of Appius and Three Taverns to meet us. On seeing them, Paul gave thanks to God and took courage. ¹⁶† When he entered Rome, Paul was allowed to live by himself, with the soldier who was guarding him.

Testimony to Jews in Rome

¹⁷*† Three days later he called together the leaders of the Jews. When they had gathered he said to them, "My brothers, although I had done nothing against our people or our ancestral customs, I was handed over to the Romans as a prisoner from Jerusalem. ¹⁸* After trying my case the Romans wanted to release me, because they found nothing against me deserving the death penalty. ¹⁹* But when the Jews objected, I was obliged to appeal to Caesar, even though I had no accusation to make against my own nation. ²⁰*† This is the reason, then, I have requested to see you and to speak with you, for it is on account of the hope of Israel that I wear these chains." ²¹ They answered him, "We have received no letters from Judea about you, nor has any of the brothers arrived with a damaging report or rumor about you. ²²* But we should like to hear you present your views, for we know that this sect is denounced everywhere."

²³ So they arranged a day with him and came to his lodgings in great numbers. From early morning until evening, he expounded his position to them, bearing witness to the kingdom of God and trying to convince them about Jesus from the law of Moses and the prophets. ²⁴ Some were convinced by what he had said, while others did not believe. ²⁵† Without reaching any agreement among themselves they began to leave; then Paul made one final statement. "Well did the holy Spirit speak to your ancestors through the prophet Isaiah, saying:

²⁶*   'Go to this people and say:
> You shall indeed hear but not understand.
> You shall indeed look but never see.
²⁷   Gross is the heart of this people;
>> they will not hear with their ears;
>>> they have closed their eyes,
>> so they may not see with their eyes
>> and hear with their ears
> and understand with their heart and
>>> be converted,
>> and I heal them.'

²⁸* Let it be known to you that this salvation of God has been sent to the Gentiles; they will listen." [²⁹]†

³⁰† He remained for two full years in his lodgings. He received all who came to him, ³¹ and with complete assurance and without hindrance he proclaimed the kingdom of God and taught about the Lord Jesus Christ.

28, 4: *Justice:* in Greek mythology, the pursuing goddess of vengeance and justice.

28, 11: *Dioscuri:* that is, the Twin Brothers, Castor and Pollux, the sons of Zeus and the patrons of the sailors.

28, 16: With Paul's arrival in Rome, the programmatic spread of the word of the Lord to "the ends of the earth" (1, 8) is accomplished. In Rome, Paul is placed under house arrest, and under this mild form of custody he is allowed to proclaim the word in the capital of the civilized world of his day.

28, 17–22: Paul's first act in Rome is to learn from the leaders of the Jewish community whether the Jews of Jerusalem plan to pursue their case against him before the Roman jurisdiction. He is informed that no such plan is afoot, but that the Jews of Rome have heard the Christian teaching denounced. Paul's offer to explain it to them is readily accepted.

28, 20: *The hope of Israel:* in the words of Paul (23, 6), Luke has identified this hope as hope in the resurrection of the dead.

28, 25–28: Paul's final words in Acts reflect a major concern of Luke's writings: how the salvation promised in the Old Testament, accomplished by Jesus, and offered first to Israel (13, 26), has now been offered to and accepted by the Gentiles. Quoting Is 6, 9–10,

Paul presents the scriptural support for his indictment of his fellow Jews who refuse to accept the message he proclaims. Their rejection leads to its proclamation among the Gentiles.

28, 29: The Western text has added here a verse that is not found in the best Greek manuscripts: "And when he had said this, the Jews left, seriously arguing among themselves."

28, 30–31: Although the ending of Acts may seem to be abrupt, Luke has now completed his story with the establishment of Paul and the proclamation of Christianity in Rome. Paul's confident and unhindered proclamation of the gospel in Rome forms the climax to the story whose outline was provided in 1, 8: "You will be my witnesses in Jerusalem . . . and to the ends of the earth."

28, 6: Acts 14, 11.
28, 17: Acts 24, 12–13; 25, 8.
28, 18: Acts 23, 29; 25, 25; 26, 31–32.
28, 19: Acts 25, 11.
28, 20: Acts 23, 6; 24, 15.21; 26, 6–8.
28, 22: Acts 24, 5.14.
28, 26: Is 6, 9–10; Mt 13, 14–15; Mk 4, 12; Lk 8, 10; Jn 12, 40; Rom 11, 8.
28, 28: Acts 13, 46; 18, 6; Ps 67, 2; Is 40, 5 LXX; Lk 3, 6.

A
C
T
S

Introduction to the

Letters

and Revelation

Despite the popularity of e-mailing, writing letters with pen and paper is still alive today. In letters, people often express themselves more clearly than they do in person, and say things that are difficult to say face-to-face. Perhaps you've been lucky enough to receive some special letters. Letters between parents and children, engaged couples, and even pen pals are often saved to be read again and again. They are treasured for their stories, their advice, and their expressions of love. The next twenty-one books of the New Testament are also treasured letters. Their stories, their advice, and their confidence in God's loving guidance have inspired generations of Christians.

In-depth

WHEN YOU READ SOMEONE ELSE'S MAIL, YOU see only one side of the conversation. So you have to do some reading between the lines to understand the issues being addressed. This is also true of the New Testament letters. But when you do this, they give you a firsthand look at the first Christian communities and what they believed. In fact, the letters written by Paul are the oldest Christian documents that we have, written even before the four Gospels. Paul's earliest letter, 1 Thessalonians, was probably written around A.D. 50. That's just a little over twenty years after the death and Resurrection of Jesus!

These letters follow a common pattern. They usually begin with (1) a greeting from the sender to the receiver or receivers. Next is (2) a prayer, most often of thanksgiving. This is followed by (3) the body of the letter, which addresses whatever issues the author wants to discuss; often, it includes general advice about Christian living. The letters close with (4) greetings and instructions to specific people and a final blessing.

There are exceptions to this pattern. Hebrews and 1 John do not have all four of these features, and are more like essays about faith. James has more of the features, but reads like a good sermon rather than a letter.

Saint Paul was the most prolific writer of the letters. At one time, it was thought that he produced thirteen of the twenty-one. However, modern scholars believe that some of the letters traditionally attributed to Paul were actually written by associates or later followers. Scholars have reached this conclusion because of differences in writing style, vocabulary, and thought. Those associates or followers of Paul applied his teaching to new situations faced by the early Christian communities. Similarly, the letters bearing the names of James, Peter, and John were probably written by associates or later followers of those men.

To a modern person, that might seem like forgery. But in the ancient world, it was not uncommon for followers of an important person to write in the person's name after her or his death. It was a way of honoring the person and keeping her or his traditions alive.

Although the Book of Revelation is grouped together with the letters in this introduction, it really is not a letter at all. Revelation was written as a series of visions to a disciple named John. The visions are filled with dramatic imagery and events. Some people interpret them as prophecies about the way the world will end, but for the most part, they are really coded messages about events happening in John's own time. Ultimately, the Book of Revelation is a hopeful message to persecuted Christians that God is in control and that goodness and justice will triumph.

As you explore these letters and the Book of Revelation, you'll see the church at its best: the miraculous growth, the Spirit-filled enthusiasm, and the deep love the early Christians had for one another and for Jesus. You'll also see how the early church was threatened by intense disagreements, jealousy, and scandals. Through it all, the authors reveal a deep faith and missionary spirit. They focus again and again on the death and Resurrection of Jesus and on the mystery of the church as the living Body of Christ acting in the world through the power of the Holy Spirit. These letters had a specific audience in the first century A.D., but because God inspired them, their words are for you too!

Other Background

- **There are nine letters by Paul or his followers named for the communities in which the recipient churches were located: Romans, 1 and 2 Corinthians, Galatians, Ephesians (called a captivity letter because it is attributed to Paul writing from jail), Philippians (also a captivity letter), Colossians (also a captivity letter), and 1 and 2 Thessalonians.**

- **There are four letters by Paul or his followers named for the individuals to whom they were sent: 1 and 2 Timothy and Titus (called pastoral letters), and Philemon (a captivity letter).**

- **Hebrews is named for the Christian Jews for whom it was intended.**

- **There are seven catholic letters named after their stated authors: James; 1 and 2 Peter; 1, 2, and 3 John; and Jude. They are called catholic because they are general letters to all Christians.**

- **The Book of Revelation is not a letter. It is a collection of the prophecies and visions of John of Patmos, a Christian prophet.**

Romans
The Letter to the

Have you ever wondered if you're good enough to deserve someone's unconditional love? Has it ever puzzled you that sometimes it is easier to do the wrong thing than the right thing? If you have, you're not alone. Saint Paul felt the same way. In his Letter to the Romans, he addresses some important questions of life and faith. But at its core, the message of the letter is simple: We are justified—made right with God—by faith in Jesus Christ.

At a Glance

I. Address (1, 1–15).

II. Humanity Lost without the Gospel (1, 16—3, 20).

III. Justification through Faith in Christ (3, 21—5, 21).

IV. Justification and the Christian Life (6, 1—8, 39).

V. Jews and Gentiles in God's Plan (9, 1—11, 36).

VI. The Duties of Christians (12, 1—15, 13).

VII. Conclusion (15, 14—16, 27).

In-depth

Many people consider the Letter to the Romans to be the deepest expression of Paul's thinking. This was the only letter Paul wrote to a community he had not yet visited. At the time, he was planning to go to Rome and was trying to prepare the way by explaining his teaching on salvation and faith. His ideas are summed up in a verse from the first chapter: "I am not ashamed of the gospel. It is the power of God for the salvation of everyone who believes" (verse 16).

Romans is not easy reading. Paul often makes his case by using arguments that might seem strange to us today. Some of his main points are these:

- Salvation is available to both Jews and Gentiles (non-Jews).
- Because all people have sinned, no one has "earned" salvation.
- Salvation comes through faith in Jesus Christ, not through following the Jewish religious Law.
- Even though salvation has come to the Gentiles, God has not abandoned the Jews.

The Letter to the Romans contains many wonderfully comforting words. It tells us that when we don't know how to pray, God prays for us "with inexpressible groanings" (8, 26)! And it says that "all things work for good for those who love God" (verse 28). And it asks, "If God is for us, who can be against us?" (verse 31).

So as you read this powerful letter, let go of your fears. Even though you're not perfect, God will never leave you. As Paul says, "I am convinced that neither death, nor life, nor angels, nor principalities, nor present things, nor future things, nor powers, nor height, nor depth, nor any other creature will be able to separate us from the love of God in Christ Jesus our Lord" (verses 38–39).

Quick Facts

Author
Paul

Date Written
A.D. 56–58

Audience
Jewish and Gentile Christians in Rome

Romans

6, 4

I: Address

Greeting†

1 ¹* Paul, a slave of Christ Jesus,† called to be an apostle and set apart for the gospel of God, ²* which he promised previously through his prophets in the holy scriptures, ³*† the gospel about his Son, descended from David according to the flesh, ⁴* but established as Son of God in power according to the spirit of holiness through resurrection from the dead, Jesus Christ our Lord.

⁵*† Through him we have received the grace of apostleship, to bring about the obedience of faith, for the sake of his name, among all the Gentiles, ⁶* among whom are you also, who are called to belong to Jesus Christ; ⁷*† to all the beloved of God in Rome, called to be holy. Grace to you and peace from God our Father and the Lord Jesus Christ.

Thanksgiving

⁸*† First, I give thanks to my God through Jesus Christ for all of you, because your faith is heralded

---

1, 1–7: In Paul's letters the greeting or *praescriptio* follows a standard form, though with variations. It is based upon the common Greco-Roman epistolary practice, but with the addition of Semitic and specifically Christian elements. The three basic components are: name of sender; name of addressee; greeting. In identifying himself, Paul often adds phrases to describe his apostolic mission; this element is more developed in Romans than in any other letter. Elsewhere he associates co-workers with himself in the greeting: Sosthenes (1 Corinthians), Timothy (2 Corinthians; Philippians; Philemon), Silvanus (1–2 Thessalonians). The standard secular greeting was the infinitive *chairein*, "greetings." Paul uses instead the similar-sounding *charis*, "grace," together with the Semitic greeting *šālôm* (Greek *eirēnē*), "peace." These gifts, foreshadowed in God's dealings with Israel (see Nm 6, 24–26), have been poured out abundantly in Christ, and Paul wishes them to his readers. In Romans the Pauline *praescriptio* is expanded and expressed in a formal tone; it emphasizes Paul's office as apostle to the Gentiles. Verses 3–4 stress the gospel or kerygma, v 2 the fulfillment of God's promise, and vv 1 and 5 Paul's office. On his call, see Gal 1, 15–16; 1 Cor 9, 1; 15, 8–10; Acts 9, 1–22; 22, 3–16; 26, 4–18.

1, 1: *Slave of Christ Jesus:* Paul applies the term slave to himself in order to express his undivided allegiance to the Lord of the church, the Master of all, including slaves and masters. "No one can serve (i.e., be a slave to) two masters," said Jesus (Mt 6, 24). It is this aspect of the slave-master relationship rather than its degrading implications that Paul emphasizes when he discusses Christian commitment.

1, 3–4: Paul here cites an early confession that proclaims Jesus' sonship as messianic descendant of David (cf Mt 22, 42; 2 Tm 2, 8;

Rv 22, 16) and as Son of God by the resurrection. As "life-giving spirit" (1 Cor 15, 45), Jesus Christ is able to communicate the Spirit to those who believe in him.

1, 5: Paul recalls his apostolic office, implying that the Romans know something of his history. *The obedience of faith:* as Paul will show at length in chs 6–8 and 12–15, faith in God's justifying action in Jesus Christ relates one to God's gift of the new life that is made possible through the death and resurrection of Jesus Christ and the activity of the holy Spirit (see especially 8, 1–11).

1, 7: *Called to be holy:* Paul often refers to Christians as "the holy ones" or "the saints." The Israelite community was called a "holy assembly" because they had been separated for the worship and service of the Lord (see Lv 11, 44; 23, 1–44). The Christian community regarded its members as sanctified by baptism (6, 22; 15, 16; 1 Cor 6, 11; Eph 5, 26–27). Christians are called to holiness (1 Cor 1, 2; 1 Thes 4, 7), that is, they are called to make their lives conform to the gift they have already received.

1, 8: In Greco-Roman letters, the greeting was customarily followed by a prayer. The Pauline letters usually include this element

1, 1: Gal 1, 10; Phil 1, 1; Jas 1, 1 / Acts 9, 15; 13, 2; 1 Cor 1, 1; Gal 1, 15; Ti 1, 1.	33; Phil 3, 10.
1, 2: Rom 16, 25–26; Ti 1, 2.	**1, 5:** Rom 15, 15; Gal 2, 7.9 / Rom 15, 18; Acts 9, 15; 26, 16–18; Gal 1, 16; 2, 7.9.
1, 3: Rom 9, 5; 2 Sm 7, 12; Mt 1, 1; Mk 12, 35; Jn 7, 42; Acts 13, 22–23; 2 Tm 2, 8; Rv 22, 16.	**1, 6:** 1 Cor 1, 9.
1, 4: Rom 10, 9; Acts 13,	**1, 7:** Nm 6, 25–26; 1 Cor 1, 2–3; 2 Cor 1, 1–2.
	1, 8: Rom 16, 19; 1 Thes 1, 8.

throughout the world. [9]* God is my witness, whom I serve with my spirit in proclaiming the gospel of his Son, that I remember you constantly, [10]*† always asking in my prayers that somehow by God's will I may at last find my way clear to come to you. [11]* For I long to see you, that I may share with you some spiritual gift so that you may be strengthened, [12] that is, that you and I may be mutually encouraged by one another's faith, yours and mine. [13]*† I do not want you to be unaware, brothers, that I often planned to come to you, though I was prevented until now, that I might harvest some fruit among you, too, as among the rest of the Gentiles. [14]† To Greeks and non-Greeks alike, to the wise and the ignorant, I am under obligation; [15]* that is why I am eager to preach the gospel also to you in Rome.

II: Humanity Lost Without the Gospel

God's Power for Salvation

[16]*† For I am not ashamed of the gospel. It is the power of God for the salvation of everyone who believes: for Jew first, and then Greek. [17]*† For in it is revealed the righteousness of God from faith to faith; as it is written, "The one who is righteous by faith will live."

Punishment of Idolators

[18]*† The wrath† of God† is indeed being revealed from heaven against every impiety and wickedness

---

(except Galatians and Titus), expressed in Christian thanksgiving formulas and usually stating the principal theme of the letter. In 2 Corinthians the thanksgiving becomes a blessing, and in Ephesians it is preceded by a lengthy blessing. Sometimes the thanksgiving is blended into the body of the letter, especially in 1 Thessalonians. In Romans it is stated briefly.

1, 10–12: Paul lays the groundwork for his more detailed statement in 15, 22–24 about his projected visit to Rome.

1, 13: *Brothers* is idiomatic for all Paul's "kin in Christ," all those who believe in the gospel; it includes women as well as men (cf 4, 3).

1, 14: *Greeks and non-Greeks:* literally, "Greeks and barbarians." As a result of Alexander's conquests, Greek became the standard international language of the Mediterranean world. *Greeks* in Paul's statement therefore means people who know Greek or who have been influenced by Greek culture. *Non-Greeks* were people whose cultures remained substantially unaffected by Greek influences. Greeks called such people "barbarians" (cf Acts 28, 2), meaning people whose speech was foreign. Roman citizens would scarcely classify themselves as such, and Nero, who was reigning when Paul wrote this letter, prided himself on his admiration for Greek culture. *Under obligation:* Paul will expand on the theme of obligation in 13, 8; 15, 1.27.

1, 16–17: The principal theme of the letter is salvation through faith. *I am not ashamed of the gospel:* Paul is not ashamed to proclaim the gospel, despite the criticism that Jews and Gentiles leveled against the proclamation of the crucified savior; cf 1 Cor 1, 23–24. Paul affirms, however, that it is precisely through the crucifixion and resurrection of Jesus that God's saving will and power become manifest. *Jew first* (cf 2, 9–10) means that Jews especially, in view of the example of Abraham (ch 4), ought to be the leaders in the response of faith.

1, 17: *In it is revealed the righteousness of God from faith to faith:* the gospel centers in Jesus Christ, in whom God's saving presence and righteousness in history have been made known. Faith is affirmation of the basic purpose and meaning of the Old Testament as proclamation of divine promise (2; 4, 13) and exposure of the inability of humanity to effect its salvation even through covenant law. Faith is the gift of the holy Spirit and denotes acceptance of salvation as God's righteousness, that is, God's gift of a renewed relationship in forgiveness and power for a new life. Faith is response to God's total claim on people and their destiny. *The one who is righteous by faith will live:* see the note on Hb 2, 4.

1, 18—3, 20: Paul aims to show that all humanity is in a desperate plight and requires God's special intervention if it is to be saved.

1, 18–32: In this passage Paul uses themes and rhetoric common in Jewish-Hellenistic mission proclamation (cf Wis 13, 1—14, 31) to indict especially the non-Jewish world. The close association of idolatry and immorality is basic, but the generalization needs in all

did you KNOW?

The Many Meanings of Gospel

The word *gospel* is the best translation of the Greek word *euangelion*, which was used in Rom 1, 16. *Gospel* comes from the old English word *godspel*, which means "good news." From *euangelion*, we get the word *evangelize*, which means "to share the good news."

In the New Testament, the meaning of the word *Gospel* goes through an evolution. For Paul, whose writings are the earliest in the New Testament, *Gospel* referred to the good news of salvation for all who believe. Paul associated the Gospel directly with Jesus himself, centering on his death and Resurrection.

As Christian faith developed, the understanding of *Gospel* expanded to include the Reign (Kingdom) of God that Jesus preached. The Gospel was not just associated with Jesus' saving death and Resurrection, but included all his teachings, miracles, promises, and demands. After the original Apostles died or were killed, Christian communities desired a record of their teachings about Jesus, and the Gospel message was written down. So *Gospel* came also to refer to the writings named for Matthew, Mark, Luke, and John.

▶ Rom 1, 16

1, 9: 2 Cor 1, 23; Eph 1, 16; Phil 1, 8; 1 Thes 1, 2; 2, 5.10; 2 Tm 1, 3.
1, 10: Rom 15, 23.32; Acts 18, 21; 1 Cor 4, 19; 1 Thes 2, 17.
1, 11: 1 Thes 2, 17; 3, 10.
1, 13: Rom 15, 22; Jn 15, 16; Acts 19, 21.
1, 15: Acts 28, 30–31.
1, 16: Ps 119, 46; 1 Cor 1, 18.24 / Rom 2, 9; Acts 3, 26; 13, 46.
1, 17: Rom 3, 21–22; Hb 2, 4; Gal 3, 11; Heb 10, 38.
1, 18: Rom 2, 5.8–9; Is 66, 15; Eph 5, 6; Col 3, 6.

ROM

of those who suppress the truth by their wickedness. [19]* For what can be known about God is evident to them, because God made it evident to them. [20]* Ever since the creation of the world, his invisible attributes of eternal power and divinity have been able to be understood and perceived in what he has made. As a result, they have no excuse; [21]* for although they knew God they did not accord him glory as God or give him thanks. Instead, they became vain in their reasoning, and their senseless minds were darkened. [22]* While claiming to be wise, they became fools [23]* and exchanged the glory of the immortal God for the likeness of an image of mortal man or of birds or of four-legged animals or of snakes.

[24]*† Therefore, God handed them over to impurity through the lusts of their hearts for the mutual degradation of their bodies. [25]* They exchanged the truth of God for a lie and revered and worshiped the creature rather than the creator, who is blessed forever. Amen. [26] Therefore, God handed them over to degrading passions. Their females exchanged natural relations for unnatural, [27]* and the males likewise gave up natural relations with females and burned with lust for one another. Males did shameful things with males and thus received in their own persons the due penalty for their perversity. [28] And since they did not see fit to acknowledge God, God handed them over to their undiscerning mind to do what is improper. [29]* They are filled with every form of wickedness, evil, greed, and malice; full of envy, murder, rivalry, treachery, and spite. They are gossips [30] and scandalmongers and they hate God. They are insolent, haughty, boastful, ingenious in their wickedness, and rebellious toward their parents. [31] They are senseless, faithless, heartless, ruthless. [32]* Although they know the just decree of God that all who practice such things deserve death, they not only do them but give approval to those who practice them.

did you KNOW?

Homosexuality and AIDS

In making his case that all people are in need of salvation, Paul talks about the sinfulness of humankind in Rom 1, 18–32. As a specific example of what happens when people turn from God's truth, he discusses homosexual activity in verses 26–27.

Some people interpret these verses to mean Paul is condemning homosexual persons. But this is a serious misinterpretation of Paul's words. Why? First, look at the context. After this specific example in verses 26–27, Paul lists all kinds of sinful behaviors in verses 28–32. He is not picking on homosexuals—rather, he is showing that all people are guilty of sin.

Most important, notice that Paul never condemns people; he condemns sinful behavior. The Catholic church does the same. The church teaches that homosexual orientation is not sinful, but it also states that any sexual activity outside of marriage is wrong.

Romans 1, 18–32 has also been used wrongly against AIDS victims. Some of them have been told that their horrible disease is a result of God's vengeance against homosexual behavior. Our loving God would never use AIDS, or any other disease, to punish people.

▶ Rom 1, 18–32

R
O
M

---

† fairness to be balanced against the fact that non-Jewish Christian society on many levels displayed moral attitudes and performance whose quality would challenge much of contemporary Christian culture. Romans themselves expressed abhorrence over devotion accorded to animals in Egypt. Paul's main point is that the wrath of God does not await the end of the world but goes into action at each present moment in humanity's history when misdirected piety serves as a facade for self-interest.

1, 18: *The wrath of God:* God's reaction to human sinfulness, an Old Testament phrase that expresses the irreconcilable opposition between God and evil (see Is 9, 11.16.18.20; 10, 4; 30, 27). It is not contrary to God's universal love for his creatures, but condemns Israel's turning aside from the covenant obligations. Hosea depicts Yahweh as suffering intensely at the thought of having to punish Israel (Hos 11, 8–9). God's wrath was to be poured forth especially on the "Day of Yahweh" and thus took on an eschatological connotation (see Zep 1, 15).

1, 24: In order to expose the depth of humanity's rebellion against the Creator, *God handed them over to impurity through the lusts of their hearts.* Instead of curbing people's evil interests, God abandoned them to self-indulgence, thereby removing the facade of

apparent conformity to the divine will. Subsequently Paul will show that the Mosaic law produces the same effect; cf 5, 20; 7, 13–24. The divine judgment expressed here is related to the theme of hardness of heart described in 9, 17–18.

1, 19–32: Wis 13–19; Acts 14, 15–17; 17, 23–29.	1, 24: Wis 12, 25; 14, 22–31; Acts 7, 41–42; Eph 4, 19.
1, 20: Jb 12, 7–9; Pss 8, 4; 19, 2; Sir 17, 7–9; Is 40, 26; Acts 14, 17;17, 25–28.	1, 25: Rom 9, 5; Jer 13, 25–27.
1, 21: Eph 4, 17–18.	1, 27: Lv 18, 22; 20, 13; Wis 14, 26; 1 Cor 6, 9; 1 Tm 1, 10.
1, 22: Wis 13, 1–9; Is 5, 21; Jer 10, 14; Acts 17, 29–30; 1 Cor 1, 19–21.	1, 29–31: Rom 13, 13; Mt 15, 19; Mk 7, 21–22; Gal 5, 19–21; 2 Tm 3, 2–4.
1, 23: Dt 4, 15–19; Ps 106, 20; Wis 11, 15; 12, 24; 13, 10–19; Jer 2, 11.	1, 32: Acts 8, 1; 2 Thes 2, 12.

God's Just Judgment

2 [1]*† Therefore, you are without excuse, every one of you who passes judgment.† For by the standard by which you judge another you condemn yourself, since you, the judge, do the very same things. [2] We know that the judgment of God on those who do such things is true. [3]* Do you suppose, then, you who judge those who engage in such things and yet do them yourself, that you will escape the judgment of God? [4]* Or do you hold his priceless kindness, forbearance, and patience in low esteem, unaware that the kindness of God would lead you to repentance? [5]* By your stubbornness and impenitent heart, you are storing up wrath for yourself for the day of wrath and revelation of the just judgment of God, [6]*† who will repay everyone according to his works: [7] eternal life to those who seek glory, honor, and immortality through perseverance in good works, [8]* but wrath and fury to those who selfishly disobey the truth and obey wickedness. [9] Yes, affliction and distress will come upon every human being who does evil, Jew first and then Greek. [10]* But there will be glory, honor, and peace for everyone who does good, Jew first and then Greek. [11]*† There is no partiality with God.

Judgment by the Interior Law

[12]*† All who sin outside the law will also perish without reference to it, and all who sin under the law will be judged in accordance with it. [13]* For it is not those who hear the law who are just in the sight of God; rather, those who observe the law will be justified. [14]* For when the Gentiles who do not have the law by nature observe the prescriptions of the law, they are a law for themselves even though they do not have the law. [15]† They show that the demands of the law are written in their hearts, while their conscience also bears witness and their conflicting

thoughts accuse or even defend them [16]* on the day when, according to my gospel, God will judge people's hidden works through Christ Jesus.

Judgment by the Mosaic Law

[17]*† Now if you call yourself a Jew and rely on the law and boast of God [18]* and know his will and are able to discern what is important since you are

---

Examination of Conscience

Lord, knock me off my pedestal whenever I begin to think I've earned the right to judge others. Paul reminds us that we are all guilty of sin. I have no right to judge others.

　　Direct me to turn my attention to examining my own conscience:

　　Have I been patient with those around me?

　　Have I offered forgiveness to those who have hurt me?

　　Have I had the courage to admit when I am wrong?

　　Have I treated my parents and siblings with respect?

　　Have I been sensitive to the feelings and needs of those around me?

　　Forgive me, God, for I have sinned. Bathe me in your mercy and love. Deliver me from evil as I continue to grow in Christ. Amen.

▶ Rom 2, 1–4

2, 1–3, 20: After his general indictment of the Gentile, Paul shows that in spite of special revelation Jews enjoy no advantage in moral status before God (3, 1–8). With the entire human race now declared guilty before God (3, 9–20), Paul will then be able to display the solution for the total problem: salvation through God's redemptive work that is revealed in Christ Jesus for all who believe (3, 21–31).

2, 1–11: As a first step in his demonstration that Jews enjoy no real moral supremacy over Gentiles, Paul explains that the final judgment will be a review of performance, not of privilege. From this perspective Gentiles stand on an equal footing with Jews, and Jews cannot condemn the sins of Gentiles without condemning themselves.

2, 6: *Will repay everyone according to his works:* Paul reproduces the Septuagint text of Ps 62, 12 and Prv 24, 12.

2, 11: *No partiality with God:* this sentence is not at variance with the statements in vv 9–10. Since Jews are the first to go under indictment, it is only fair that they be given first consideration in the distribution of blessings. Basic, of course, is the understanding that God accepts no bribes (Dt 10, 17).

2, 12–16: Jews cannot reasonably demand from Gentiles the standard of conduct inculcated in the Old Testament since God did not address its revelation to them. Rather, God made it possible for

Gentiles to know instinctively the difference between right and wrong. But, as Paul explained in 1, 18–32, humanity misread the evidence of God's existence, power, and divinity, and "while claiming to be wise, they became fools" (1, 22).

2, 15: Paul expands on the thought of Jer 31, 33; Wis 17, 11.

2, 17–29: Mere possession of laws is no evidence of virtue. By eliminating circumcision as an elitist moral sign, Paul clears away the last obstacle to his presentation of justification through faith without claims based on the receipt of circumcision and its attendant legal obligations.

2, 1: Mt 7, 1–2.	Sir 35, 12–13; Acts 10,
2, 3: Wis 16, 15–16.	34; Gal 2, 6; Eph 6, 9;
2, 4: Rom 3, 25–26; 9, 22;	Col 3, 25; 1 Pt 1, 17.
Wis 11, 23; 15, 1; 2 Pt	**2, 12:** Rom 3, 19.
3, 9.15.	**2, 13:** Mt 7, 21; Lk 6, 46–49;
2, 5: Ex 33, 3; Acts 7, 51; Rv	8, 21; Jas 1, 22–25;
6, 17; 11, 18.	1 Jn 3, 7.
2, 6: Ps 62, 12; Prv 24, 12;	**2, 14:** Acts 10, 35.
Sir 16, 14; Mt 16, 27;	**2, 16:** Acts 10, 42; 17, 31.
Jn 5, 29; 2 Cor 5, 10.	**2, 17:** Is 48, 1–2; Mi 3, 11;
2, 8: 2 Thes 1, 8.	Phil 3, 4–6.
2, 10: Rom 1, 16; 3, 9.	**2, 18:** Phil 1, 10.
2, 11: Dt 10, 17; 2 Chr 19, 7;	

instructed from the law, [19]* and if you are confident that you are a guide for the blind and a light for those in darkness, [20]* that you are a trainer of the foolish and teacher of the simple, because in the law you have the formulation of knowledge and truth— [21]* then you who teach another, are you failing to teach yourself? You who preach against stealing, do you steal? [22] You who forbid adultery, do you commit adultery? You who detest idols, do you rob temples? [23] You who boast of the law, do you dishonor God by breaking the law? [24]*† For, as it is written, "Because of you the name of God is reviled among the Gentiles."

[25]* Circumcision, to be sure, has value if you observe the law; but if you break the law, your circumcision has become uncircumcision.* [26]* Again, if an uncircumcised man keeps the precepts of the law, will he not be considered circumcised? [27] Indeed, those who are physically uncircumcised but carry out the law will pass judgment on you, with your written law and circumcision, who break the law. [28]* One is not a Jew outwardly. True circumcision is not outward, in the flesh. [29]* Rather, one is a Jew inwardly, and circumcision is of the heart, in the spirit, not the letter; his praise is not from human beings but from God.

Answers to Objections

3 [1]† What advantage is there then in being a Jew? Or what is the value of circumcision? [2]* Much, in every respect. [For] in the first place, they were entrusted with the utterances of God. [3]* What if some were unfaithful? Will their infidelity nullify the fidelity of God? [4]*† Of course not! God must be true, though every human being is a liar, as it is written:

> "That you may be justified in your words,
> and conquer when you are judged."

[5]* But if our wickedness provides proof of God's righteousness, what can we say? Is God unjust, humanly speaking, to inflict his wrath? [6] Of course not! For how else is God to judge the world? [7] But if God's truth redounds to his glory through my

---

?did you KNOW?

Circumcision, the Law, and Faith

Circumcision is the surgical removal of the foreskin from a male's penis. It was the sign of the Covenant (agreement) between Israel and God (Gn 17, 2). As Gentiles became Christians, many Jewish Christians claimed they had to live by Jewish religious laws, including circumcision.

Paul consistently insists that such rituals are not necessary. He says that "circumcision is of the heart" (Rom 2, 29), which leads to "faith working through love" (Gal 5, 6). In Romans, chapter 4, Paul sheds further light on this by considering the case of Abraham. Abraham was considered the father of the Jewish faith. He was made righteous by God before he was circumcised (verse 10). Why? Because of his strong and heroic faith in God. Christians are called to this kind of faith in God, whose plan of salvation is now fully revealed in Jesus Christ.

▶ Rom 2, 25–29

---

falsehood, why am I still being condemned as a sinner? [8]* And why not say—as we are accused and as some claim we say—that we should do evil that good may come of it? Their penalty is what they deserve.

Universal Bondage to Sin

[9]*† Well, then, are we better off? Not entirely, for we have already brought the charge against Jews

---

2, 24: According to Is 52, 5 the suffering of Israel prompts her enemies to revile God. Paul uses the passage in support of his point that the present immorality of Israelites is the cause of such defamation.

3, 1–4: In keeping with the popular style of diatribe, Paul responds to the objection that his teaching on the sinfulness of all humanity detracts from the religious prerogatives of Israel. He stresses that Jews have remained the vehicle of God's revelation despite their sins, though this depends on the fidelity of God.

3, 4: *Though every human being is a liar:* these words reproduce the Greek text of Ps 116, 11. The rest of the verse is from Ps 51, 6.

3, 9–20: *Well, then, are we better off?:* this phrase can also be translated "Are we at a disadvantage?" but the latter version does not substantially change the overall meaning of the passage. Having explained that Israel's privileged status is guaranteed by God's fidelity, Paul now demonstrates the infidelity of the Jews by a catena of cita-

tions from scripture, possibly derived from an existing collection of *testimonia.* These texts show that all human beings share the common burden of sin. They are linked together by mention of organs of the body: throat, tongue, lips, mouth, feet, eyes.

2, 19: Mt 15, 14; Lk 6, 39.	**4, 5;** 2 Cor 10, 18.
2, 20: 2 Tm 3, 15.	**3, 2:** Rom 9, 4; Dt 4, 7–8;
2, 21: Ps 50, 16–21; Mt 23,	Pss 103; 7; 147,
3–4.	19–20.
2, 24: Is 52, 5; Ez 36, 20;	**3, 3:** Rom 9, 6; 11, 1.29; Ps
2 Pt 2, 2.	89, 30–37; 2 Tm 2, 13.
2, 25–29: Jer 4, 4; 9, 24–25.	**3, 4:** Ps 116, 11 / Ps 51, 6.
2, 25: 1 Cor 7, 19; Gal 5, 3.	**3, 5:** Rom 9, 14; Jb 34,
2, 26: Gal 5, 6.	12–17.
2, 28: Jn 7, 24; 8, 15.39.	**3, 8:** Rom 6, 1.
2, 29: Dt 30, 6; Jer 4, 4; 9,	**3, 9:** Rom 1, 18–2, 25; 3,
25; Col 2, 11 / 1 Cor	23; Sir 8, 5.

and Greeks alike that they are all under the domination of sin, 10* as it is written:

> "There is no one just, not one,
> 11   there is no one who understands,
>   there is no one who seeks God.
> 12 All have gone astray; all alike are worthless;
>   there is not one who does good,
>   [there is not] even one.
> 13* Their throats are open graves;
>   they deceive with their tongues;
>   the venom of asps is on their lips;
> 14*   their mouths are full of bitter cursing.
> 15* Their feet are quick to shed blood;
> 16   ruin and misery are in their ways,
> 17 and the way of peace they know not.
> 18*   There is no fear of God before their eyes."

19*† Now we know that what the law says is addressed to those under the law, so that every mouth may be silenced and the whole world stand accountable to God, 20*† since no human being will be justified in his sight by observing the law; for through the law comes consciousness of sin.

III: Justification Through Faith in Christ

Justification apart from the Law†

21* But now† the righteousness of God has been manifested apart from the law, though testified to by the law and the prophets, 22* the righteousness of God through faith in Jesus Christ for all who believe. For there is no distinction; 23* all have sinned and are deprived of the glory of God. 24* They are

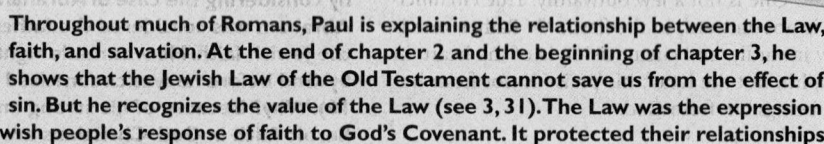

The Law, Faith, and Salvation

Throughout much of Romans, Paul is explaining the relationship between the Law, faith, and salvation. At the end of chapter 2 and the beginning of chapter 3, he shows that the Jewish Law of the Old Testament cannot save us from the effect of sin. But he recognizes the value of the Law (see 3, 31). The Law was the expression of the Jewish people's response of faith to God's Covenant. It protected their relationships with God and one another.

We often think of sin as breaking God's law. But at its core, sin is really breaking our relationship with God and distancing ourselves from God. Remember what Adam and Eve did after their first sin? They hid from God, ashamed of their action. Paul is clear that we are all guilty of sin. Separated from God, the source of all life, we would eventually perish without God's help. But God is always seeking us out. In the ultimate act of love, God sent Jesus to restore the break in our relationship caused by sin. Jesus' death and Resurrection show us that God's great love is far more powerful than any sin we can commit.

Paul uses two key words to explain all of this. He talks about *justification*, which is the process that brings us back into a good relationship with God. And he talks about *righteousness* as the state of being right with God, of not being separated from God.

How are we justified? How are we considered righteous? Not by our ability to keep any laws but by our faith in Jesus Christ. And the effect of faith is opposite that of sin. Where sin creates distance, faith draws us close. Where sin kills, faith gives life. Where sin shrivels in hate, faith is active in love.

▸ Rom 3, 21–31

---

†
3, 19: *The law:* Paul here uses the term in its broadest sense to mean all of the scriptures; none of the preceding texts is from the Torah or Pentateuch.

3, 20: *No human being will be justified in his sight:* these words are freely cited from Ps 143, 2. In place of the psalmist's "no living person," Paul substitutes "no human being" (literally "no flesh," a Hebraism), and he adds "by observing the law."

3, 21–31: These verses provide a clear statement of Paul's "gospel," i.e., the principle of justification by faith in Christ. God has found a means of rescuing humanity from its desperate plight: Paul's general term for this divine initiative is the righteousness of God (21). Divine mercy declares the guilty innocent and makes them so. God does this not as a result of the law but apart from it (21), and not because of any merit in human beings but through forgiveness of their sins (24), in virtue of the redemption wrought in Christ Jesus for all

who believe (22.24–25). God has manifested his righteousness in the coming of Jesus Christ, whose saving activity inaugurates a new era in human history.

3, 21: *But now:* Paul adopts a common phrase used by Greek authors to describe movement from disaster to prosperity. The expressions indicate that vv 21–26 are the consolatory answer to vv 9–20.

*

3, 10–11: Pss 14, 1–3; 53, 2–4;	Rom 7, 7.
Eccl 7, 20.	**3, 21:** Is 51, 6–8; Acts 10, 43.
3, 13: Pss 5, 10; 140, 4.	**3, 22:** Rom 1, 17; Gal 2, 16;
3, 14: Ps 10, 7.	Phil 3, 9.
3, 15–17: Prv 1, 16; Is 59, 7–8.	**3, 23:** Rom 3, 9; 5, 12.
3, 18: Ps 36, 2.	**3, 24:** Eph 2, 8; Ti 3, 7 /
3, 19: Rom 7, 7.	Rom 5, 1–2; Eph 1, 7.
3, 20: Ps 143, 2; Gal 2, 16 /	

justified freely by his grace through the redemption in Christ Jesus, 25*† whom God set forth as an expiation, through faith, by his blood, to prove his righteousness because of the forgiveness of sins previously committed, 26 through the forbearance of God—to prove his righteousness in the present time, that he might be righteous and justify the one who has faith in Jesus.

27*† What occasion is there then for boasting? It is ruled out. On what principle, that of works? No, rather on the principle of faith.† 28* For we consider that a person is justified by faith apart from works of the law. 29* Does God belong to Jews alone? Does he not belong to Gentiles, too? Yes, also to Gentiles, 30* for God is one and will justify the circumcised on the basis of faith and the uncircumcised through faith. 31*† Are we then annulling the law by this faith? Of course not! On the contrary, we are supporting the law.

Abraham Justified by Faith

4 1*† What then can we say that Abraham found, our ancestor according to the flesh? 2† Indeed, if Abraham was justified on the basis of his works, he has reason to boast; but this was not so in the sight of God. 3*† For what does the scripture say? "Abraham believed God, and it was credited to him as righteousness." 4* A worker's wage is credited not as a gift, but as something due. 5 But when one does not work, yet believes in the one who justifies the ungodly, his faith is credited as righteousness. 6 So also David declares the blessedness of the person to whom God credits righteousness apart from works:

7* "Blessed are they whose iniquities are forgiven and whose sins are covered.
8 Blessed is the man whose sin the Lord does not record."

9*† Does this blessedness apply only to the circumcised, or to the uncircumcised as well? Now we assert that "faith was credited to Abraham as righteousness." 10 Under what circumstances was it credited? Was he circumcised or not? He was not circumcised, but uncircumcised. 11* And he received the sign of circumcision as a seal on the righteousness received through faith while he was uncircumcised. Thus he was to be the father of all the uncircumcised who believe, so that to them [also] righteousness might be credited, 12 as well as the father of the circumcised who not only are circumcised but also follow the path of faith that our father Abraham walked while still uncircumcised.

Inheritance through Faith

13* It was not through the law that the promise was made to Abraham and his descendants that he would inherit the world, but through the righteousness that comes from faith. 14* For if those who adhere to the law are the heirs, faith is null and the promise is void. 15*† For the law produces wrath; but where there is no law, neither is there violation. 16* For this reason, it depends on faith, so that it may be a gift, and the promise may be guaranteed to all his descendants, not to those who only adhere to the law but to those who follow the faith of Abraham, who is the father of all of us, 17* as it is written, "I have made you father of many nations."

3, 25: *Expiation:* this rendering is preferable to "propitiation," which suggests hostility on the part of God toward sinners. As Paul will be at pains to point out (5, 8–10), it is humanity that is hostile to God.

3, 27–31: People cannot boast of their own holiness, since it is God's free gift (27), both to the Jew who practices circumcision out of faith and to the Gentile who accepts faith without the Old Testament religious culture symbolized by circumcision (29–30).

3, 27: *Principle of faith:* literally, "law of faith." Paul is fond of wordplay involving the term "law"; cf 7, 21.23; 8, 2. Since "law" in Greek may also connote "custom" or "principle," his readers and hearers would have sensed no contradiction in the use of the term after the negative statement concerning law in v 20.

3, 31: *We are supporting the law:* giving priority to God's intentions. God is the ultimate source of law, and the essence of law is fairness. On the basis of the Mosaic covenant, God's justice is in question if those who sinned against the law are permitted to go free (see 23–26). In order to rescue all humanity rather than condemn it, God thinks of an alternative: the law or "principle" of faith (27). What can be more fair than to admit everyone into the divine presence on the basis of forgiveness grasped by faith? Indeed, this principle of faith antedates the Mosaic law, as Paul will demonstrate in ch 4, and does not therefore mark a change in divine policy.

4, 1–25: This is an expanded treatment of the significance of Abraham's faith, which Paul discusses in Gal 3, 6–18; see the notes there.

4, 2–5: Verse 2 corresponds to v 4, and v 3 to v 5. The Greek term here rendered *credited* means "made an entry." The context determines whether it is credit or debit. Verse 8 speaks of "recording sin" as a debit. Paul's repeated use of accountants' terminology in this

and other passages can be traced both to the Old Testament texts he quotes and to his business activity as a tentmaker. The commercial term in Gn 15, 6, "credited it to him," reminds Paul in vv 7–8 of Ps 32, 2, in which the same term is used and applied to forgiveness of sins. Thus Paul is able to argue that Abraham's faith involved receipt of forgiveness of sins and that all believers benefit as he did through faith.

4, 3: Jas 2, 24 appears to conflict with Paul's statement. However, James combats the error of extremists who used the doctrine of justification through faith as a screen for moral self-determination. Paul discusses the subject of holiness in greater detail than does James and beginning with ch 6 shows how justification through faith introduces one to the gift of a new life in Christ through the power of the holy Spirit.

4, 9: *Blessedness:* evidence of divine favor.

4, 15: Law has the negative function of bringing the deep-seated rebellion against God to the surface in specific sins; see the note on 1, 18–32.

3, 25: Lv 16, 12–15; Acts 17, 31; 1 Jn 4, 10.	**4, 7–8:** Ps 32, 1–2.
	4, 9: Rom 4, 3.
3, 27: Rom 8, 2; 1 Cor 1, 29–31.	**4, 11:** Gn 17, 10–11; Gal 3, 6–8.
3, 28: Rom 5, 1; Gal 2, 16.	**4, 13:** Gn 12, 7; 18, 18; 22, 17–18; Sir 44, 21; Gal 3, 16–18.29.
3, 29: Rom 10, 12.	
3, 30: Dt 6, 4; Gal 3, 20; Jas 2, 19 / Rom 4, 11–12.	**4, 14:** Gal 3, 18.
3, 31: Rom 8, 4; Mt 5, 17.	**4, 15:** Rom 3, 20; 5, 13; 7, 8; Gal 3, 19.
4, 1: Gal 3, 6–9.	
4, 3: Gn 15, 6; Gal 3, 6; Jas 2, 14.20–24.	**4, 16:** Sir 44, 19; Gal 3, 7–9.
4, 4: Rom 11, 6.	**4, 17:** Gn 17, 5; Heb 11, 19 / Is 48, 13.

R
O
M

He is our father in the sight of God, in whom he believed, who gives life to the dead and calls into being what does not exist. 18* He believed, hoping against hope, that he would become "the father of many nations," according to what was said, "Thus shall your descendants be." 19* He did not weaken in faith when he considered his own body as [already] dead (for he was almost a hundred years old) and the dead womb of Sarah. 20† He did not doubt God's promise in unbelief; rather, he was empowered by faith and gave glory to God 21* and was fully convinced that what he had promised he was also able to do. 22* That is why "it was credited to him as righteousness." 23 But it was not for him alone that it was written that "it was credited to him"; 24* it was also for us, to whom it will be credited, who believe in the one who raised Jesus our Lord from the dead, 25* who was handed over for our transgressions and was raised for our justification.

Faith, Hope, and Love†

5 1* Therefore, since we have been justified by faith, we have peace† with God through our Lord Jesus Christ, 2* through whom we have gained access [by faith] to this grace in which we stand, and we boast in hope of the glory of God. 3 Not only that, but we even boast of our afflictions, knowing that affliction produces endurance, 4* and endurance, proven character, and proven character, hope, 5* and hope does not disappoint, because the love of God has been poured out into our hearts through the holy Spirit that has been given to us. 6 For Christ, while we were still helpless, yet died at the appointed time for the ungodly. 7† Indeed, only with difficulty does one die for a just person, though perhaps for a good person one might even find courage to die. 8* But God proves his love for us in that while we were still sinners Christ died for us. 9* How much more then, since we are now justified by his blood, will be be saved through him from the wrath. 10* Indeed, if, while we were enemies, we were reconciled to God through the death of his Son, how much more, once reconciled, will be be saved by his life. 11 Not only that, but we also boast of God through our Lord Jesus Christ,

Trusting the Grace of God

A grandmother pushes her grandson out of the path of a speeding car, and is hit by the car and dies. A stranger jumps into a surging river to save a young girl, and loses his own life. A firefighter is killed battling a blaze to rescue three trapped people. Their concern for others leads these real-life heroes to make the ultimate sacrifice.

Like the grandson, the young girl, and the three trapped people, we too have been saved from death at a great cost—Jesus' loving sacrifice in obedience to God's will. Paul reminds us that our justification—our reconciliation and peace with God—is not a reward we deserve for being good. It is God's free gift of love and salvation despite our weakness and sin. And that is grace. Put your faith not in your own ability to please God, but in God's abundant grace.

▶ Rom 5, 1–11

4, 20: *He did not doubt God's promise in unbelief:* any doubts Abraham might have had were resolved in commitment to God's promise. Heb 11, 8–12 emphasizes the faith of Abraham and Sarah.

5, 1–11: Popular piety frequently construed reverses and troubles as punishment for sin; cf Jn 9, 2. Paul therefore assures believers that God's justifying action in Jesus Christ is a declaration of peace. The crucifixion of Jesus Christ displays God's initiative in certifying humanity for unimpeded access into the divine presence. Reconciliation is God's gift of pardon to the entire human race. Through faith one benefits personally from this pardon or, in Paul's term, is justified. The ultimate aim of God is to liberate believers from the pre-Christian self as described in chs 1–3. Since this liberation will first find completion in the believer's resurrection, salvation is described as future in 5, 10. Because this fullness of salvation belongs to the future it is called the Christian hope. Paul's Greek term for hope does not, however, suggest a note of uncertainty, to the effect: "I wonder whether God really means it." Rather, God's promise in the gospel fills believers with expectation and anticipation for the climactic gift of unalloyed commitment in the holy Spirit to the performance of the will of God. The persecutions that attend Christian commitment are to teach believers patience and to strengthen this hope, which will not disappoint them because the holy Spirit dwells in their hearts and imbues them with God's love (5).

5, 1: *We have peace:* a number of manuscripts, versions, and church Fathers read "Let us have peace"; cf 14, 19.

5, 7: In the world of Paul's time the *good person* is especially one who is magnanimous to others.

4, 18: Gn 15, 5.
4, 19–20: Gn 17, 17; Heb 11,
   11.
4, 21: Gn 18, 14; Lk 1, 37.
4, 22: Gn 15, 6.
4, 24: Rom 10, 9; 1 Pt 1, 21.
4, 25: Is 53, 4–5.12; 1 Cor
   15, 17; 1 Pt 1, 3 / Rom
   8, 11.
5, 1: Rom 3, 24–28; Gal 2,
   16.

5, 2: Eph 2, 18; 3, 12.
5, 4: 2 Cor 12, 9–10; Jas 1,
   2–4; 1 Pt 1, 5–7; 4,
   12–14.
5, 5: Rom 8, 14–16; Pss 22,
   5–6; 25, 20.
5, 8: Jn 3, 16; 1 Jn 4, 10.19.
5, 9: Rom 1, 18; 1 Thes 1,
   10.
5, 10: Rom 8, 7–8; 2 Cor 5,
   18; Col 1, 21–22.

through whom we have now received reconciliation.

Humanity's Sin through Adam

12*† Therefore, just as through one person sin entered the world, and through sin, death, and thus death came to all, inasmuch as all sinned†— 13* for up to the time of the law, sin was in the world, though sin is not accounted when there is no law. 14* But death reigned from Adam to Moses, even over those who did not sin after the pattern of the trespass of Adam, who is the type of the one who was to come.

Grace and Life through Christ

15 But the gift is not like the transgression. For if by that one person's transgression the many died, how much more did the grace of God and the gracious gift of the one person Jesus Christ overflow for the many. 16 And the gift is not like the result of the one person's sinning. For after one sin there was the judgment that brought condemnation; but the gift, after many transgressions, brought acquittal. 17 For if, by the transgression of one person, death came to reign through that one, how much more will those who receive the abundance of grace and of the gift of justification come to reign in life through the one person Jesus Christ. 18* In conclusion, just as through one transgression condemnation came upon all, so through one righteous act acquittal and life came to all. 19* For just as through the disobedience of one person the many were made sinners, so through the obedience of one the many will be made righteous. 20*† The law entered in so that transgression might increase but, where sin increased, grace overflowed all the more, 21* so that, as sin reigned in death, grace also might reign through justification for eternal life through Jesus Christ our Lord.

IV: Justification and the Christian Life

Freedom from Sin; Life in God

6 1*† What then shall we say? Shall we persist in sin that grace may abound? Of course not! 2* How can we who died to sin yet live in it? 3* Or are you unaware that we who were baptized into Christ Jesus were baptized into his death? 4* We were indeed buried with him through baptism into

In Christ, We Receive New Life!

In chapter 6 of Romans, Paul tells us that we die to sin and receive a new life in Jesus Christ—who died for the forgiveness of all sin and overcame death with his Resurrection. By participating in the paschal mystery (see "Dying for New Life," Jn 12, 24–26) through Baptism, we are no longer enslaved to sin.

"Its end is eternal life. For the wages of sin is death, but the gift of God is eternal life in Christ Jesus our Lord" (Rom 6, 22–23). Let the message of this passage fill you. Feel God's liberating grace in you. Never forget that Christ has already saved you, and God's mercy is there for you as soon as you repent, pray for forgiveness, and are willing to sin no more.

▶ Rom 6, 1–23

5, 12–21: Paul reflects on the sin of Adam (Gn 3, 1–13) in the light of the redemptive mystery of Christ. Sin, as used in the singular by Paul, refers to the dreadful power that has gripped humanity, which is now in revolt against the Creator and engaged in the exaltation of its own desires and interests. But no one has a right to say, "Adam made me do it," for all are culpable (12): Gentiles under the demands of the law written in their hearts (2, 14–15), and Jews under the Mosaic covenant. Through the Old Testament law, the sinfulness of humanity that was operative from the beginning (13) found further stimulation, with the result that sins were generated in even greater abundance. According to vv 15–21, God's act in Christ is in total contrast to the disastrous effects of the virus of sin that invaded humanity through Adam's crime.

5, 12: *Inasmuch as all sinned:* others translate "because all sinned," and understand v 13 as a parenthetical remark. Unlike Wis 2, 24, Paul does not ascribe the entry of death to the devil.

5, 20: *The law entered in:* sin had made its entrance (12); now the law comes in alongside sin. See the notes on 1, 18–32; 5, 12–21. *Where sin increased, grace overflowed all the more:* Paul declares that grace outmatches the productivity of sin.

6, 1–11: To defend the gospel against the charge that it promotes moral laxity (cf 3, 5–8), Paul expresses himself in the typical style of spirited diatribe. God's display of generosity or grace is not evoked by sin but, as stated in 5, 8, is the expression of God's love, and this love pledges eternal life to all believers (5, 21). Paul views the present conduct of the believers from the perspective of God's completed salvation when the body is resurrected and directed totally by the holy Spirit. Through baptism believers share the death of Christ and thereby escape the grip of sin. Through the resurrection of Christ the power to live anew becomes reality for them, but the fullness of participation in Christ's resurrection still lies in the future. But life that is lived in dedication to God now is part and parcel of that future. Hence anyone who sincerely claims to be interested in that future will scarcely be able to say, "Let us sin so that grace may prosper" (cf 1).

5, 12: Gn 2, 17; 3, 1–19; Wis   Gal 3, 19.
   2, 24 / Rom 3, 19.23.   5, 21: Rom 6, 23.
5, 13: Rom 4, 15.   6, 1: Rom 3, 5–8.
5, 14: 1 Cor 15, 21.   6, 2: 1 Pt 4, 1.
5, 18: 1 Cor 15, 21–22.   6, 3: Gal 3, 27.
5, 19: Is 53, 11; Phil 2, 8–9.   6, 4: Col 2, 12; 1 Pt 3,
5, 20: Rom 4, 15; 7, 7–8;   21–22.

death, so that, just as Christ was raised from the dead by the glory of the Father, we too might live in newness of life.

5* For if we have grown into union with him through a death like his, we shall also be united with him in the resurrection. 6* We know that our old self was crucified with him, so that our sinful body might be done away with, that we might no longer be in slavery to sin. 7 For a dead person has been absolved from sin. 8* If, then, we have died with Christ, we believe that we shall also live with him. 9* We know that Christ, raised from the dead, dies no more; death no longer has power over him. 10* As to his death, he died to sin once and for all; as to his life, he lives for God. 11* Consequently, you too must think of yourselves as [being] dead to sin and living for God in Christ Jesus.

12*† Therefore, sin must not reign over your mortal bodies so that you obey their desires. 13* And do not present the parts of your bodies to sin as weapons for wickedness, but present yourselves to God as raised from the dead to life and the parts of your bodies to God as weapons for righteousness. 14* For sin is not to have any power over you, since you are not under the law but under grace.

15* What then? Shall we sin because we are not under the law but under grace? Of course not! 16* Do you not know that if you present yourselves to someone as obedient slaves, you are slaves of the one you obey, either of sin, which leads to death, or of obedience, which leads to righteousness?* 17† But thanks be to God that, although you were once slaves of sin, you have become obedient from the heart to the pattern of teaching to which you were entrusted. 18 Freed from sin, you have become slaves of righteousness. 19 I am speaking in human terms because of the weakness of your nature. For just as you presented the parts of your bodies as slaves to impurity and to lawlessness for lawlessness, so now present them as slaves to righteousness for sanctification. 20*† For when you were slaves of sin, you were free from righteousness. 21* But what profit did you get then from the things of which you are now ashamed? For the end of

those things is death. 22*† But now that you have been freed from sin and have become slaves of God, the benefit that you have leads to sanctification, and its end is eternal life. 23* For the wages of sin is death, but the gift of God is eternal life in Christ Jesus our Lord.

I'm Not Perfect

Some people today think, "If God is always willing to forgive me, why should I be concerned about sinning?" Evidently, some people in Paul's time thought that too (see Rom 6, 15). Paul reminds them, and us, that faith in Christ should be a matter of the heart, not simply a mechanical commitment. Like a married couple's love calls them to commit to each other (7, 2), so our love for Christ should make us want to live in the light, free from sin. Why would we want to return to the things that bring death to the soul (6, 21)?

But even when we commit to follow Christ, sin is a constant challenge. Paul encourages us, in the face of temptation, to maintain our focus on God and refrain from sin.

Jesus, you experienced temptation throughout your ministry. Yet you always made the decision to avoid sin and live in the light.

I have made the commitment to follow you. Give me the strength to overcome temptations and avoid sin. If in my weaknesses I allow my sin and passions to steer me in the wrong direction, please forgive me and help me regain control. Amen.

▸ Rom 6, 15—7, 6

6, 12–19: Christians have been released from the grip of sin, but sin endeavors to reclaim its victims. The antidote is constant remembrance that divine grace has claimed them and identifies them as people who are alive only for God's interests.

6, 17: In contrast to humanity, which was handed over to self-indulgence (1, 24–32), believers are *entrusted* ("handed over") to God's *pattern of teaching*, that is, the new life God aims to develop in Christians through the productivity of the holy Spirit. Throughout this passage Paul uses the slave-master model in order to emphasize the fact that one cannot give allegiance to both God and sin.

6, 20: *You were free from righteousness:* expressed ironically, for such freedom is really tyranny. The commercial metaphors in vv 21–23 add up only one way: sin is a bad bargain.

6, 22: *Sanctification:* or holiness.

6, 5: Phil 3, 10–11; 2 Tm 2, 11.
6, 6: Gal 5, 24; 6, 14; Eph 4, 22–23.
6, 8: 1 Thes 4, 17.
6, 9: Acts 13, 34; 1 Cor 15, 26; 2 Tm 1, 10; Rv 1, 18.
6, 10: Heb 9, 26–28; 1 Pt 3, 18.
6, 11: 2 Cor 5, 15; 1 Pt 2, 24.
6, 12: Gn 4, 7.
6, 13: Rom 12, 1; Eph 2, 5;

5, 14 / Col 3, 5.
6, 14: Gal 5, 18; 1 Jn 3, 6.
6, 15: Rom 5, 17.21.
6, 16: Jn 8, 31–34; 2 Pt 2, 19.
6, 16–18: Jn 8, 32–36.
6, 20: Jn 8, 34.
6, 21: Rom 8, 6.13; Prv 12, 28; Ez 16, 61.63.
6, 22: 1 Pt 1, 9.
6, 23: Gn 2, 17; Gal 6, 7–9; Jas 1, 15.

Freedom from the Law

7 ¹† Are you unaware, brothers (for I am speaking to people who know the law), that the law has jurisdiction over one as long as one lives? ²* Thus a married woman is bound by law to her living husband; but if her husband dies, she is released from the law in respect to her husband. ³ Consequently, while her husband is alive she will be called an adulteress if she consorts with another man. But if her husband dies she is free from that law, and she is not an adulteress if she consorts with another man.

⁴ In the same way, my brothers, you also were put to death to the law through the body of Christ, so that you might belong to another, to the one who was raised from the dead in order that we might bear fruit for God. ⁵* For when we were in the flesh, our sinful passions, awakened by the law, worked in our members to bear fruit for death. ⁶* But now we are released from the law, dead to what held us captive, so that we may serve in the newness of the spirit and not under the obsolete letter.

Acquaintance with Sin through the Law

⁷*† What then can we say? That the law is sin? Of course not!† Yet I did not know sin except through the law, and I did not know what it is to covet except that the law said, "You shall not covet." ⁸* But sin, finding an opportunity in the commandment, produced in me every kind of covetousness. Apart from the law sin is dead. ⁹ I once lived outside the law, but when the commandment came, sin became alive; ¹⁰* then I died, and the commandment that was for life turned out to be death for me. ¹¹* For sin, seizing an opportunity in the commandment, deceived me and through it put me to death. ¹²* So then the law is holy, and the commandment is holy and righteous and good.

Sin and Death

¹³*† Did the good, then, become death for me? Of course not! Sin, in order that it might be shown to be sin, worked death in me through the good, so that sin might become sinful beyond measure through the commandment. ¹⁴* We know that the law is spiritual;

Our Inner Struggle

In Rom 7, 15–16, Paul reveals his own struggle to do what is right. It seems there's a part of us that wants to do right, and another part that wants to do wrong. Even when we try to be good, "evil is at hand" (verse 21), ready to have its way.

Paul uses the words *spiritual* and *carnal* to describe this struggle. In his time, people thought passions and strong emotions originated in the body. So Paul says our flesh tempts us to do wrong, and our spirit wants us to do right. Paul does not mean that our physical bodies are evil and the source of sin. He means that we are all at war with ourselves.

Sin is hard to resist at times. To do what is right requires us to stop and think clearly about our choices and actively select good over sin. The good news is that God, the understanding forgiver, is on our side in the struggle. Thanks be to God!

▸ **Rom 7, 13–25**

---

† **7, 1–6:** Paul reflects on the fact that Christians have a different understanding of the law because of their faith in Christ. Law binds the living, not the dead, as exemplified in marriage, which binds in life but is dissolved through death. Similarly, Christians who through baptism have died with Christ to sin (cf 6, 2–4) are freed from the law that occasioned transgressions, which in turn were productive of death. Now that Christians are joined to Christ, the power of Christ's resurrection makes it possible for them to bear the fruit of newness of life for God.

7, 7–25: In this passage Paul uses the first person singular in the style of diatribe for the sake of argument. He aims to depict the disastrous consequences when a Christian reintroduces the law as a means to attain the objective of holiness pronounced in 6, 22.

7, 7–12: The apostle defends himself against the charge of identifying the law with sin. Sin does not exist in law but in human beings, whose sinful inclinations are not overcome by the proclamation of law.

7, 13–25: Far from improving the sinner, law encourages sin to

expose itself in transgressions or violations of specific commandments (see 1, 24; 5, 20). Thus persons who do not experience the justifying grace of God, and Christians who revert to dependence on law as the criterion for their relationship with God, will recognize a rift between their reasoned desire for the goodness of the law and their actual performance that is contrary to the law. Unable to free themselves from the slavery of sin and the power of death, they can only be rescued from defeat in the conflict by the power of God's grace working through Jesus Christ.

7, 2: 1 Cor 7, 39.	15, 56 / Rom 4, 15.
7, 5: Rom 6, 21; 8, 6.13.	**7, 10:** Lv 18, 5.
7, 6: Rom 8, 2; 2 Cor 3, 6.	**7, 11:** Gn 3, 13; Heb 3, 13.
7, 7: Rom 3, 20; Ex 20, 17;	**7, 12:** 1 Tm 1, 8.
Dt 5, 21.	**7, 13:** Rom 4, 15; 5, 20.
7, 8: Rom 5, 13.20; 1 Cor	**7, 14:** Rom 8, 7–8; Ps 51, 7.

but I am carnal, sold into slavery to sin. ¹⁵ What I do, I do not understand. For I do not do what I want, but I do what I hate. ¹⁶ Now if I do what I do not want, I concur that the law is good. ¹⁷ So now it is no longer I who do it, but sin that dwells in me. ¹⁸* For I know that good does not dwell in me, that is, in my flesh. The willing is ready at hand, but doing the good is not. ¹⁹ For I do not do the good I want, but I do the evil I do not want. ²⁰ Now if [I] do what I do not want, it is no longer I who do it, but sin that dwells in me. ²¹ So, then, I discover the principle that when I want to do right, evil is at hand. ²² For I take delight in the law of God, in my inner self, ²³*† but I see in my members another principle at war with the law of my mind, taking me captive to the law of sin that dwells in my members. ²⁴ Miserable one that I am! Who will deliver me from this mortal body? ²⁵* Thanks be to God through Jesus Christ our Lord. Therefore, I myself, with my mind, serve the law of God but, with my flesh, the law of sin.

The Flesh and the Spirit

8 ¹† Hence, now there is no condemnation for those who are in Christ Jesus. ²* For the law of the spirit of life in Christ Jesus has freed you from the law of sin and death. ³* For what the law, weakened by the flesh, was powerless to do, this God has done: by sending his own Son in the likeness of sinful flesh and for the sake of sin, he condemned sin in the flesh, ⁴* so that the righteous decree of the law might be fulfilled in us, who live not according to the flesh but according to the spirit. ⁵ For those who live according to the flesh are concerned with the things of the flesh, but those who live according to the spirit with the things of the spirit. ⁶* The concern of the flesh is death, but the concern of the spirit is life and peace. ⁷* For the concern of the flesh is hostility toward God; it does not submit to the law of God, nor can it; ⁸* and those who are in the flesh cannot please God. ⁹* But you are not in the flesh; on the contrary, you are in the spirit, if only the Spirit of God dwells in you. Whoever does not have the Spirit of Christ does not belong to him. ¹⁰* But if Christ is in you, although the body is dead because

Catholic Connections

LED BY THE SPIRIT

Do we allow the Spirit of God to lead us through life?

At Baptism, we receive the Holy Spirit and become temples, or homes, for that Spirit. As a result, we are God's adopted daughters and sons, and Jesus is our brother! The life of Christ has been given to us, as daughters and sons, and to all those who are baptized.

Jesus lived in the Spirit of compassion, justice, and love. His disciples, who heard his words and witnessed his deeds, discovered that they were encountering God's Holy Presence—God's Spirit.

Do our friends and family recognize and experience the Spirit of Christ in us? If we were to take an honest look at the kind of spirit we manifest every day, what would we see? Do we see justice and compassion guiding our hearts? Are our daily activities directed by faith in Christ and Christian values? Do we face opposition, even unpopularity, as we make choices to do the right thing?

▶ Rom 8, 1–17

of sin, the spirit is alive because of righteousness. ¹¹ If the Spirit of the one who raised Jesus from the dead dwells in you, the one who raised Christ from

---

† **7, 23:** As in 3, 27, Paul plays on the term *law*, which in Greek can connote custom, system, or *principle*.

8, 1–13: After his warning in ch 7 against the wrong route to fulfillment of the objective of holiness expressed in 6, 22, Paul points his addressees to the correct way. Through the redemptive work of Christ, Christians have been liberated from the terrible forces of sin and death. Holiness was impossible so long as the *flesh* (or our "old self"), that is, self-interested hostility toward God (7), frustrated the divine objectives expressed in the law. What is worse, sin used the law to break forth into all manner of lawlessness (8). All this is now changed. At the cross God broke the power of sin and pronounced sentence on it (3). Christians still retain the flesh, but it is alien to their new being, which is life in the spirit, namely the new self, governed by the holy Spirit. Under the direction of the holy Spirit Chris-

tians are able to fulfill the divine will that formerly found expression in the law (4). The same Spirit who enlivens Christians for holiness will also resurrect their bodies at the last day (11). Christian life is therefore the experience of a constant challenge to put to death the evil deeds of the body through life of the spirit (13).

---

*

7, 18: Gn 6, 5; 8, 21; Phil 2, 13.	7; Col 1, 22; Heb 2, 17; 4, 15; 1 Jn 4, 9.
7, 23: Gal 5, 17; 1 Pt 2, 11.	**8, 4:** Gal 5, 16–25.
7, 25: 1 Cor 15, 57.	**8, 6:** Rom 6, 21; 7, 5; 8, 13; Gal 6, 8.
8, 2: Rom 7, 23–24; 2 Cor 3, 17.	**8, 7:** Rom 5, 10; Jas 4, 4.
8, 3: Acts 13, 38; 15, 10 / Jn 3, 16–17; 2 Cor 5, 21; Gal 3, 13; 4, 4; Phil 2,	**8, 8:** 1 Jn 2, 16.
	8, 9: 1 Cor 3, 16.
	8, 10: Gal 2, 20; 1 Pt 4, 6.

the dead will give life to your mortal bodies also, through his Spirit that dwells in you. 12 Consequently, brothers, we are not debtors to the flesh, to live according to the flesh. 13* For if you live according to the flesh, you will die, but if by the spirit you put to death the deeds of the body, you will live.

Children of God through Adoption

14*† For those who are led by the Spirit of God are children of God. 15*† For you did not receive a spirit of slavery to fall back into fear, but you received a spirit of adoption, through which we cry, "Abba, Father!" 16* The Spirit itself bears witness with our spirit that we are children of God, 17* and if children, then heirs, heirs of God and joint heirs with Christ, if only we suffer with him so that we may also be glorified with him.

Destiny of Glory

18*† I consider that the sufferings of this present time are as nothing compared with the glory to be revealed for us. 19 For creation awaits with eager expectation the revelation of the children of God; 20* for creation was made subject to futility, not of its own accord but because of the one who subjected it, in hope 21* that creation itself would be set free from slavery to corruption and share in the glorious freedom of the children of God. 22* We know that all creation is groaning in labor pains even until now; 23* and not only that, but we ourselves, who have the firstfruits of the Spirit, we also groan within ourselves as we wait for adoption, the redemption of our bodies. 24* For in hope we were saved. Now hope that sees for itself is not hope. For who hopes for what one sees? 25 But if we hope for what we do not see, we wait with endurance.

26 In the same way, the Spirit too comes to the aid of our weakness; for we do not know how to pray as we ought, but the Spirit itself intercedes with inexpressible groanings. 27* And the one who searches hearts knows what is the intention of the Spirit, because it intercedes for the holy ones according to God's will.

God's Indomitable Love in Christ

28*† We know that all things work for good for those who love God,† who are called according to his purpose. 29*† For those he foreknew he also predestined to be conformed to the image of his Son, so that he might be the firstborn among many brothers. 30* And those he predestined he also called; and those he called he also justified; and those he justified he also glorified.

31*† What then shall we say to this? If God is for us, who can be against us? 32* He who did not spare his own Son but handed him over for us all, how will he not also give us everything else along with him? 33* Who will bring a charge against

We know that all things work for good for those who love God, who are called according to his purpose

8, 28

8, 14–17: Christians, by reason of the Spirit's presence within them, enjoy not only new life but also a new relationship to God, that of adopted children and heirs through Christ, whose sufferings and glory they share.

8, 15: Abba: see the note on Mk 14, 36.

8, 18–27: The glory that believers are destined to share with Christ far exceeds the sufferings of the present life. Paul considers the destiny of the created world to be linked with the future that belongs to the believers. As it shares in the penalty of corruption brought about by sin, so also will it share in the benefits of redemption and future glory that comprise the ultimate liberation of God's people (19–22). After patient endurance in steadfast expectation, the full harvest of the Spirit's presence will be realized. On earth believers enjoy the firstfruits, i.e., the Spirit, as a guarantee of the total liberation of their bodies from the influence of the rebellious old self (23).

8, 28–30: These verses outline the Christian vocation as it was designed by God: to be conformed to the image of his Son, who is to be the firstborn among many brothers (29). God's redemptive action on behalf of the believers has been in process before the beginning of the world. Those whom God chooses are those he foreknew (29) or elected. Those who are called (30) are predestined or predetermined. These expressions do not mean that God is arbitrary. Rather, Paul uses them to emphasize the thought and care that God has taken for the Christian's salvation.

8, 28: We know that all things work for good for those who love God: a few ancient authorities have God as the subject of the verb, and some translators render: "We know that God makes everything work for good for those who love God . . . ."

8, 29: Image: while man and woman were originally created in God's image (Gn 1, 26–27), it is through baptism into Christ, the image of God (2 Cor 4, 4; Col 1, 15), that we are renewed according to the image of the Creator (Col 3, 10).

8, 31–39: The all-conquering power of God's love has overcome every obstacle to Christians' salvation and every threat to separate them from God. That power manifested itself fully when God's own Son was delivered up to death for their salvation. Through him Christians can overcome all their afflictions and trials.

8, 13: Gal 5, 24; 6, 8; Eph 4, 22–24.	8, 22: 2 Cor 5, 2–5.
8, 14: Gal 5, 18.	8, 23: 2 Cor 1, 22; Gal 5, 5.
8, 15: Mk 14, 36; Gal 4, 5–6; 2 Tm 1, 7.	8, 24: 2 Cor 5, 7; Heb 11, 1.
	8, 27: Ps 139, 1; 1 Cor 4, 5.
8, 16: Jn 1, 12; Gal 3, 26–29.	8, 28–29: Eph 1, 4–14; 3, 11.
8, 17: Gal 4, 7; 1 Pt 4, 13; 5, 1.	8, 29: Eph 1, 5; 1 Pt 1, 2.
8, 18: 2 Cor 4, 17.	8, 30: Is 45, 25; 2 Thes 2, 13–14.
8, 20: Gn 3, 17–19.	8, 31: Ps 118, 6; Heb 13, 6.
8, 21: 2 Pt 3, 12–13; Rv 21, 1.	8, 32: Jn 3, 16.
	8, 33–34: Is 50, 8.

God's chosen ones? It is God who acquits us. 34* Who will condemn? It is Christ [Jesus] who died, rather, was raised, who also is at the right hand of God, who indeed intercedes for us. 35 What will separate us from the love of Christ? Will anguish, or distress, or persecution, or famine, or nakedness, or peril, or the sword? 36* As it is written:

> "For your sake we are being slain all the day;
> we are looked upon as sheep to
> be slaughtered."

37* No, in all these things we conquer overwhelmingly through him who loved us. 38*† For I am convinced that neither death, nor life, nor angels, nor principalities, nor present things, nor future things, nor powers, 39† nor height, nor depth, nor any other creature will be able to separate us from the love of God in Christ Jesus our Lord.

V: Jews and Gentiles in God's Plan†

Paul's Love for Israel†

9 1* I speak the truth in Christ, I do not lie; my conscience joins with the holy Spirit in bearing me witness 2 that I have great sorrow and constant anguish in my heart. 3* For I could wish that I myself were accursed and separated from Christ for the sake of my brothers, my kin according to the flesh. 4* They are Israelites; theirs the adoption, the glory, the covenants, the giving of the law, the worship, and the promises; 5*† theirs the patriarchs, and from them, according to the flesh, is the Messiah. God who is over all be blessed forever. Amen.

God's Free Choice

6* But it is not that the word of God has failed. For not all who are of Israel are Israel, 7* nor are they all children of Abraham because they are his descendants; but "It is through Isaac that

Absolutely Nothing!

God, what could separate me from your love?

Not a failed test, or a broken promise, or a hurtful word.

What could tear you from me?

Not the lure of power, or immediate gratification, or unnatural highs.

If you, God, are on my side, who could be against me?

Not a vengeful peer, or an uncaring date, or someone whose relationship with me has gone sour.

What situation could divide you and me, God?

Not depression over a loss, or anger over being laughed at, or guilt from being caught red-handed.

No, in all these things, I know that I am never alone, because you, God, conquered sin, despair, and even death itself through your endless love, a love that showed itself through your Son. I am convinced, Lord, that nothing, absolutely nothing, will ever separate me from your love . . . ever! Amen.

▶ **Rom 8, 31–39**

descendants shall bear your name." 8* This means that it is not the children of the flesh who are the children of God, but the children of the promise are counted as descendants. 9* For this is the wording of the promise, "About this time I shall return and

---

8, 38: *Present things* and *future things* may refer to astrological data. Paul appears to be saying that the gospel liberates believers from dependence on astrologers.

8, 39: *Height, depth* may refer to positions in the zodiac, positions of heavenly bodies relative to the horizon. In astrological documents the term for "height" means "exaltation" or the position of greatest influence exerted by a planet. Since hostile spirits were associated with the planets and stars, Paul includes *powers* (38) in his list of malevolent forces.

9, 1—11, 36: Israel's unbelief and its rejection of Jesus as savior astonished and puzzled Christians. It constituted a serious problem for them in view of God's specific preparation of Israel for the advent of the Messiah. Paul addresses himself here to the essential question of how the divine plan could be frustrated by Israel's unbelief. At the same time, he discourages both complacency and anxiety on the part of Gentiles. To those who might boast of their superior advantage over Jews, he warns that their enjoyment of the blessings assigned to Israel can be terminated. To those who might anxiously ask, "How can we be sure that Israel's fate will not be ours?" he replies that only unbelief can deprive one of salvation.

9, 1–5: The apostle speaks in strong terms of the depth of his grief over the unbelief of his own people. He would willingly undergo a curse himself for the sake of their coming to the knowledge of Christ (3; cf Lv 27, 28–29). His love for them derives from God's continuing choice of them and from the spiritual benefits that God bestows on them and through them on all of humanity (4–5).

9, 5: Some editors punctuate this verse differently and prefer the translation, "Of whom is Christ according to the flesh, who is God over all." However, Paul's point is that *God who is over all* aimed to use Israel, which had been entrusted with every privilege, in outreach to the entire world through the Messiah.

8, 34: Ps 110, 1; Heb 7, 25;	**9, 3:** Ex 32, 32.
1 Jn 2, 1.	**9, 4–5:** Rom 3, 2; Ex 4, 22; Dt
8, 36: Ps 44, 23; 1 Cor 4, 9;	7, 6; 14, 1–2.
15, 30; 2 Cor 4, 11;	**9, 5:** Mt 1, 1–16; Lk 3,
2 Tm 3, 12.	23–38 / Rom 1, 25; Ps
8, 37: 1 Jn 5, 4.	41, 14.
8, 38–39: 1 Cor 3, 22; Eph 1, 21;	**9, 6:** Nm 23, 19 / Mt 3, 9.
1 Pt 3, 22.	**9, 7:** Gn 21, 12; Gal 3, 29.
9, 1: 2 Cor 11, 31;	**9, 8:** Gal 4, 23.28.
1 Tm 2, 7.	**9, 9:** Gn 18, 10.14.

Sarah will have a son." [10]† And not only that, but also when Rebecca had conceived children by one husband, our father Isaac— [11] before they had yet been born or had done anything, good or bad, in order that God's elective plan might continue, [12]* not by works but by his call—she was told, "The older shall serve the younger." [13]*† As it is written:

> "I loved Jacob
>   but hated Esau."

[14]*† What then are we to say? Is there injustice on the part of God? Of course not! [15]* For he says to Moses:

> "I will show mercy to whom I will,
>   I will take pity on whom I will."

[16]* So it depends not upon a person's will or exertion, but upon God, who shows mercy. [17]* For the scripture says to Pharaoh, "This is why I have raised you up, to show my power through you that my name may be proclaimed throughout the earth." [18]*† Consequently, he has mercy upon whom he wills, and he hardens whom he wills.

[19]*† You will say to me then, "Why [then] does he still find fault? For who can oppose his will?" [20]* But who indeed are you, a human being, to talk back to God? Will what is made say to its maker, "Why have you created me so?" [21] Or does not the potter have a right over the clay, to make out of the same lump one vessel for a noble purpose and another for an ignoble one? [22]* What if God, wishing

---

9, 10: *Children by one husband, our father Isaac:* Abraham had two children, Ishmael and Isaac, by two wives, Hagar and Sarah, respectively. In that instance Isaac, although born later than Ishmael, became the bearer of the messianic promise. In the case of twins born to Rebecca, God's elective procedure is seen even more dramatically, and again the younger, contrary to Semitic custom, is given the preference.

9, 13: The literal rendering, *"Jacob I loved, but Esau I hated,"* suggests an attitude of divine hostility that is not implied in Paul's statement. In Semitic usage "hate" means to love less; cf Lk 14, 26 with Mt 10, 37. Israel's unbelief reflects the mystery of the divine election that is always operative within it. Mere natural descent from Abraham does not ensure the full possession of the divine gifts; it is God's sovereign prerogative to bestow this fullness upon, or to withhold it from, whomsoever he wishes; cf Mt 3, 9; Jn 8, 39. The choice of Jacob over Esau is a case in point.

9, 14–18: The principle of divine election does not invite Christians to theoretical inquiry concerning the nonelected, nor does this principle mean that God is unfair in his dealings with humanity. The instruction concerning divine election is a part of the gospel and reveals that the gift of faith is the enactment of God's mercy (16). God raised up Moses to display that mercy, and Pharaoh to display divine severity in punishing those who obstinately oppose their Creator.

9, 18: The basic biblical principle is: those who will not see or hear *shall* not see or hear. On the other hand, the same God who thus makes stubborn or hardens the heart can reconstruct it through the work of the holy Spirit.

9, 19–29: The apostle responds to the objection that if God rules over faith through the principle of divine election, God cannot then accuse unbelievers of sin (19). For Paul, this objection is in the last analysis a manifestation of human insolence, and his "answer" is less an explanation of God's ways than the rejection of an argument that places humanity on a level with God. At the same time, Paul shows that God is far less arbitrary than appearances suggest, for God endures *with much patience* (22) a person like the Pharaoh of the Exodus.

9, 10: Gn 25, 21.
9, 12: Rom 11, 5–6 / Gn 25, 23–24.
9, 13: Mal 1, 3.
9, 14: Dt 32, 4.
9, 15: Ex 33, 19.
9, 16: Eph 2, 8; Ti 3, 5.
9, 17: Ex 9, 16.
9, 18: Rom 11, 30–32; Ex 4, 21; 7, 3.
9, 19: Rom 3, 7; Wis 12, 12.
9, 20–21: Wis 15, 7; Is 29, 16; 45, 9; Jer 18, 6.
9, 22: Rom 2, 4; Wis 12, 20–21; Jer 50, 25.

---

did you KNOW?

The Fate of Israel

In Romans, chapters 9–11, Paul takes on a difficult question: What will happen to Israel (the Jews), God's chosen people, if they reject Jesus? For the early Jewish Christians, who probably had friends and maybe had family members who didn't believe in Jesus, this was an important question.

To respond, Paul makes several points. In the beginning of chapter 9, he affirms Israel's special place in God's plan of salvation. But the people's righteousness (see "The Law, Faith, and Salvation," Rom 3, 21–31) is based on faith, not on fulfilling the Law. In chapter 10, Paul notes that salvation is available for all. The Jewish people are not left out if they call on the name of the Lord. But Israel's rejection of Jesus is good news for the Gentiles who have come to believe.

In chapter 11, Paul uses the analogy of grafting branches onto a tree. The Gentiles were grafted onto the original tree, which is Israel. Paul says the Jews can be grafted back onto that tree (verse 23). In fact, he ends with the hopeful promise that after the salvation of the Gentiles, all Israel will be saved (verse 26)!

Christians recognize Jewish people as their spiritual ancestors. Christians have inherited from the Jews part of their Scriptures and a rich spiritual tradition. They respect the Jews' faith and their relationship with God. They pray for the Jews' salvation and their own, in the hope that Paul's promise will come to pass.

▶ **Romans, chapters 9–11**

to show his wrath and make known his power, has endured with much patience the vessels of wrath made for destruction? [23] This was to make known the riches of his glory to the vessels of mercy, which he has prepared previously for glory, [24] namely, us whom he has called, not only from the Jews but also from the Gentiles.

Witness of the Prophets

[25]*† As indeed he says in Hosea:

"Those who were not my people I will call
    'my people,'
and her who was not beloved I will
    call 'beloved.'
[26]* And in the very place where it was said to
    them, 'You are not my people,'
there they shall be called children of the
    living God."

[27]* And Isaiah cries out concerning Israel, "Though the number of the Israelites were like the sand of the sea, only a remnant will be saved; [28] for decisively and quickly will the Lord execute sentence upon the earth." [29]* And as Isaiah predicted:

"Unless the Lord of hosts had left
    us descendants,
we would have become like Sodom
and have been made like Gomorrah."

Righteousness Based on Faith

[30]*† What then shall we say? That Gentiles, who did not pursue righteousness, have achieved it, that is, righteousness that comes from faith; [31]* but that Israel, who pursued the law of righteousness, did not attain to that law? [32]*† Why not? Because they

did it not by faith, but as if it could be done by works. They stumbled over the stone that causes stumbling, [33]* as it is written:

"Behold, I am laying a stone in Zion
    that will make people stumble
    and a rock that will make them fall,
and whoever believes in him shall not be put
    to shame."

10

[1]*† Brothers, my heart's desire and prayer to God on their behalf is for salvation. [2]* I testify with regard to them that they have zeal for God, but it is not discerning. [3]* For, in their unawareness of the righteousness that comes from God and their attempt to establish their own [righteousness], they did not submit to the righteousness of God. [4]*† For Christ is the end of the law for the justification of everyone who has faith.

[5]*† Moses writes about the righteousness that comes from [the] law, "The one who does these things will live by them." [6]* But the righteousness that comes from faith says, "Do not say in your heart, 'Who will go up into heaven?' (that is, to bring Christ down) [7]*† or 'Who will go down into the abyss?' (that is, to bring Christ up from the dead)." [8]* But what does it say?

"The word is near you,
    in your mouth and in your heart"

(that is, the word of faith that we preach), [9]*† for, if you confess with your mouth that Jesus is Lord and believe in your heart that God raised him from the dead, you will be saved. [10] For one believes with the heart and so is justified, and one confesses with the mouth and so is saved. [11] *For the

---

9, 25: *Beloved:* in Semitic discourse means "preferred" or "favorite" (cf 13). See Hos 2, 1, which is transposed after Hos 3, 5 in the NAB.

9, 30–33: In the conversion of the Gentiles and, by contrast, of relatively few Jews, the Old Testament prophecies are seen to be fulfilled; cf 25–29. Israel feared that the doctrine of justification through faith would jeopardize the validity of the Mosaic law, and so they never reached their goal of righteousness that they had sought to attain through meticulous observance of the law (31). Since Gentiles, including especially Greeks and Romans, had a great regard for righteousness, Paul's statement concerning Gentiles in v 30 is to be understood from a Jewish perspective: quite evidently they had not been interested in "God's" righteousness, for it had not been revealed to them; but now in response to the proclamation of the gospel they respond in faith.

9, 32: Paul discusses Israel as a whole from the perspective of contemporary Jewish rejection of Jesus as Messiah. The Old Testament and much of Jewish noncanonical literature in fact reflect a fervent faith in divine mercy.

10, 1–13: Despite Israel's lack of faith in God's act in Christ, Paul does not abandon hope for her salvation (1). However, Israel must recognize that the Messiah's arrival in the person of Jesus Christ means the termination of the Mosaic law as the criterion for understanding oneself in a valid relationship to God. Faith in God's saving action in Jesus Christ takes precedence over any such legal claim (6).

10, 4: The Mosaic legislation has been superseded by God's ac-

tion in Jesus Christ. Others understand *end* here in the sense that Christ is the goal of the law, i.e., the true meaning of the Mosaic law, which cannot be correctly understood apart from him. Still others believe that both meanings are intended.

10, 5–6: The subject of the verb *says* (6) is *righteousness* personified. Both of the statements in vv 5 and 6 derive from Moses, but Paul wishes to contrast the language of law and the language of faith.

10, 7: Here Paul blends Dt 30, 13 and Ps 107, 26.

10, 9–11: To confess Jesus as Lord was frequently quite hazardous in the first century (cf Mt 10, 18; 1 Thes 2, 2; 1 Pt 2, 18–21; 3, 14). For a Jew it could mean disruption of normal familial and other social relationships, including great economic sacrifice. In the face of penalties imposed by the secular world, Christians are assured that *no one who believes in* Jesus *will be put to shame* (11).

9, 25: Hos 2, 25.	10, 3: Rom 9, 31–32; Phil
9, 26: Hos 2, 1.	3, 9.
9, 27–28: Is 10, 22–23; Hos 2, 1	10, 4: Acts 13, 38–39; 2 Cor
/ Rom 11, 5 / Is 28, 22.	3, 14; Heb 8, 13.
9, 29: Is 1, 9; Mt 10, 15.	10, 5: Lv 18, 5; Gal 3, 12.
9, 30: Rom 10, 4.20.	10, 6: Dt 9, 4; 30, 12.
9, 31: Rom 10, 3.	10, 7: Dt 30, 13; 1 Pt 3, 19.
9, 32: Is 8, 14.	10, 8: Dt 30, 14.
9, 33: Is 28, 16; 1 Pt 2, 6–8.	10, 9: 1 Cor 12, 3.
10, 1: Rom 9, 1.3.	10, 11: Rom 9, 33; Is 28, 16.
10, 2: Acts 22, 3.	

scripture says, "No one who believes in him will be put to shame." 12* For there is no distinction between Jew and Greek; the same Lord is Lord of all, enriching all who call upon him. 13* For "everyone who calls on the name of the Lord will be saved."

14*† But how can they call on him in whom they have not believed? And how can they believe in him of whom they have not heard? And how can they hear without someone to preach? 15*† And how can people preach unless they are sent? As it is written, "How beautiful are the feet of those who bring [the] good news!" 16* But not everyone has heeded the good news; for Isaiah says, "Lord, who has believed what was heard from us?" 17* Thus faith comes from what is heard, and what is heard comes through the word of Christ. 18* But I ask, did they not hear? Certainly they did; for

"Their voice has gone forth to all the
      earth,
   and their words to the ends of the world."

19* But I ask, did not Israel understand? First Moses says:

"I will make you jealous of those who are not
      a nation;
   with a senseless nation I will make
      you angry."

20* Then Isaiah speaks boldly and says:

"I was found [by] those who were not
      seeking me;
   I revealed myself to those who were not
      asking for me."

21 But regarding Israel he says, "All day long I stretched out my hands to a disobedient and contentious people."

The Remnant of Israel

11 1*† I ask, then, has God rejected his people? Of course not! For I too am an Israelite, a descendant of Abraham, of the tribe of Benjamin.* 2 God has not rejected his people whom he foreknew. Do you not know what the scripture

---

Are Your Feet Beautiful?

Spread the word!" "Attention all shoppers!" "Special announcement!" Companies trying to sell a product and organizations trying to attract new members go to great lengths and expense to get their message out. Without this effort, they will reach few people and fail in their mission.

The church has undoubtedly the most important mission of all—to share with others the saving power that comes from faith in Jesus Christ. The promise in Rom 10, 11-15 is that all who know and call on the name of Jesus will be saved. God is great!

How do others hear about this Good News? Paul says only through us. And he adds, "How beautiful are the feet of those who bring [the] good news!" (verse 15). In your prayer, reflect or journal on the following questions:
- **Who brought the Good News to you? What made you trust what they had to tell you about Jesus?**
- **Which of your friends need to hear this Good News about Jesus? How can you share your faith with them, perhaps through a message of hope, forgiveness, healing, or encouragement?**

▸ **Rom 10, 11-15**

ROM

says about Elijah, how he pleads with God against Israel? 3* "Lord, they have killed your prophets, they have torn down your altars, and I alone am left, and they are seeking my life." 4* But what is God's response to him? "I have left for myself seven thousand men who have not knelt to Baal." 5* So also at the present time there is a remnant, chosen

---

10, 14–21: The gospel has been sufficiently proclaimed to Israel, and Israel has adequately understood God's plan for the messianic age, which would see the gospel brought to the uttermost parts of the earth. As often in the past, Israel has not accepted the prophetic message; cf Acts 7, 51–53.

10, 15: *How beautiful are the feet of those who bring [the] good news:* in Semitic fashion, the parts of the body that bring the messenger with welcome news are praised; cf Lk 11, 27.

11, 1–10: Although Israel has been unfaithful to the prophetic message of the gospel (10, 14–21), God remains faithful to Israel. Proof of the divine fidelity lies in the existence of Jewish Christians

like Paul himself. The unbelieving Jews, says Paul, have been blinded by the Christian teaching concerning the Messiah.

10, 12: Rom 1, 16; 3, 22.29; Acts 10, 34; 15, 9.11; Gal 3, 28; Eph 2, 14.
10, 13: Jl 3, 5; Acts 2, 21.
10, 14: Acts 8, 31.
10, 15: Is 52, 7; Na 2, 1; Eph 6, 15.
10, 16: Is 53, 1; Jn 12, 38.
10, 17: Jn 17, 20.
10, 18: Ps 19, 5; Mt 24, 14.
10, 19: Rom 11, 11.14; Dt 32, 21.
10, 20–21: Rom 9, 30; Is 65, 1–2.
11, 1: 2 Cor 11, 22; Phil 3, 5.
11, 1–2: 1 Sm 12, 22; Ps 94, 14.
11, 3: 1 Kgs 19, 10.14.
11, 4: 1 Kgs 19, 18.
11, 5: Rom 9, 27.

by grace. ⁶* But if by grace, it is no longer because of works; otherwise grace would no longer be grace. ⁷* What then? What Israel was seeking it did not attain, but the elect attained it; the rest were hardened, ⁸* as it is written:

> "God gave them a spirit of deep sleep,
>   eyes that should not see
>   and ears that should not hear,
> down to this very day."

⁹* And David says:

> "Let their table become a snare and a trap,
>   a stumbling block and a retribution
>   for them;
> ¹⁰ let their eyes grow dim so that they may
>   not see,
>   and keep their backs bent forever."

The Gentiles' Salvation

¹¹*† Hence I ask, did they stumble so as to fall? Of course not! But through their transgression salvation has come to the Gentiles, so as to make them jealous. ¹² Now if their transgression is enrichment for the world, and if their diminished number is enrichment for the Gentiles, how much more their full number.

¹³* Now I am speaking to you Gentiles. Inasmuch then as I am the apostle to the Gentiles, I glory in my ministry ¹⁴ in order to make my race jealous and thus save some of them. ¹⁵ For if their rejection is the reconciliation of the world, what will their acceptance be but life from the dead? ¹⁶*† If the firstfruits are holy, so is the whole batch of dough; and if the root is holy, so are the branches.

¹⁷* But if some of the branches were broken off, and you, a wild olive shoot, were grafted in their place and have come to share in the rich root of the olive tree, ¹⁸* do not boast against the branches. If

you do boast, consider that you do not support the root; the root supports you. ¹⁹ Indeed you will say, "Branches were broken off so that I might be grafted in." ²⁰* That is so. They were broken off because of unbelief, but you are there because of faith. So do not become haughty, but stand in awe. ²¹* For if God did not spare the natural branches, [perhaps] he will not spare you either. ²²* See, then, the kindness and severity of God: severity toward those who fell, but God's kindness to you, provided you remain in his kindness; otherwise you too will be cut off. ²³* And they also, if they do not remain in unbelief, will be grafted in, for God is able to graft them in again. ²⁴ For if you were cut from what is by nature a wild olive tree, and grafted, contrary to nature, into a cultivated one, how much more will they who belong to it by nature be grafted back into their own olive tree.

God's Irrevocable Call

²⁵*† I do not want you to be unaware of this mystery, brothers, so that you will not become wise [in] your own estimation: a hardening has come upon Israel in part, until the full number of the Gentiles comes in, ²⁶* and thus all Israel will be saved, as it is written:*

> "The deliverer will come out of Zion,
>   he will turn away godlessness from
>   Jacob;
> ²⁷* and this is my covenant with them
>   when I take away their sins."

²⁸* In respect to the gospel, they are enemies on your account; but in respect to election, they are beloved because of the patriarchs. ²⁹* For the gifts and the call of God are irrevocable.

Triumph of God's Mercy

³⁰† Just as you once disobeyed God but have now received mercy because of their disobedience,

---

11, 11–15: The unbelief of the Jews has paved the way for the preaching of the gospel to the Gentiles and for their easier acceptance of it outside the context of Jewish culture. Through his mission to the Gentiles Paul also hopes to fill his fellow Jews with jealousy. Hence he hastens to fill the entire Mediterranean world with the gospel. Once all the Gentile nations have heard the gospel, Israel as a whole is expected to embrace it. This will be tantamount to resurrection of the dead, that is, the reappearance of Jesus Christ with all the believers at the end of time.

11, 16–24: Israel remains holy in the eyes of God and stands as a witness to the faith described in the Old Testament because of *the firstfruits* (or the first piece baked) (16), that is, the converted remnant, and *the root* that *is holy*, that is, the patriarchs (16). The Jews' failure to believe in Christ is a warning to Gentile Christians to be on guard against any semblance of anti-Jewish arrogance, that is, failure to recognize their total dependence on divine grace.

11, 25–29: In God's design, Israel's unbelief is being used to grant the light of faith to the Gentiles. Meanwhile, Israel remains dear to God (cf 9, 13), still the object of special providence, the mystery of which will one day be revealed.

11, 30–32: Israel, together with the Gentiles who have been handed over to all manner of vices (ch 1), has been *delivered . . . to disobedience*. The conclusion of v 32 repeats the thought of 5, 20, "Where sin increased, grace overflowed all the more."

11, 6: Rom 4, 4; Gal 3, 18.	**11, 20:** Rom 12, 16.
11, 7: Rom 9, 31.	**11, 21:** 1 Cor 10, 12.
11, 8: Dt 29, 3; Is 29, 10; Mt 13, 13–15; Acts 28, 26–27.	**11, 22:** Jn 15, 2.4; Heb 3, 14.
	11, 23: 2 Cor 3, 16.
11, 9–10: Pss 69, 23–24; 35, 8.	**11, 25:** Prv 3, 7 / Rom 12, 16; Mk 13, 10; Lk 21, 24; Jn 10, 16.
11, 11: Acts 13, 46; 18, 6; 28, 28 / Rom 10, 19; Dt 32, 21.	
	11, 26: Mt 23, 39.
11, 13: Rom 1, 5.	**11, 26–27:** Ps 14, 7; Is 59, 20–21.
11, 16: Nm 15, 17–21; Ez 44, 30; Neh 10, 36–38.	**11, 27:** Is 27, 9; Jer 31, 33–34.
	11, 28: Rom 15, 8; 1 Thes 2, 14–16.
11, 17: Eph 2, 11–19.	**11, 29:** Rom 9, 6; Nm 23, 19; Is 54, 10.
11, 18: 1 Cor 1, 31.	

31 so they have now disobeyed in order that, by virtue of the mercy shown to you, they too may [now] receive mercy. 32* For God delivered all to disobedience, that he might have mercy upon all.

33*† Oh, the depth of the riches and wisdom and knowledge of God! How inscrutable are his judgments and how unsearchable his ways!

34*† "For who has known the mind of
    the Lord
    or who has been his
      counselor?"
35*† "Or who has given him anything
    that he may be repaid?"

36* For from him and through him and for him are all things. To him be glory forever. Amen.

VI: The Duties of Christians

Sacrifice of Body and Mind

12 1*† I urge you therefore, brothers, by the mercies of God, to offer your bodies as a living sacrifice,† holy and pleasing to God, your spiritual worship. 2* Do not conform yourself to this age but be transformed by the renewal of your mind, that you may discern what is the will of God, what is good and pleasing and perfect.

Many Parts in One Body

3* For by the grace given to me I tell everyone among you not to think of himself more highly than one ought to think, but to think soberly, each according to the measure of faith that God has apportioned. 4* For as in one body we have many parts, and all the parts do not have the same function, 5† so we, though many, are one body in Christ and individually parts

A Great Team

Tracy comes up to the mound and tries to ignore the banter of the players on the opposing bench. This is it! One more out, and her team will be the new state champions!

The batter taps the dirt beside the box and glares at Tracy. Tracy focuses on her catcher's signals and hurls her best pitch. A hit! It bounces toward third, and Tracy holds her breath as Ginny twists sideways to scoop it up. Ginny turns and throws to first. Everyone can see that the ball is high. But Carrie jumps, catches it, and stretches to tag the base before the runner gets there. A cheer erupts as the fans realize that Tracy's team has won! It is the best team in the state!

A good team has talented players. A great team has players who work together so well that they respond automatically. In Rom 12, 1–8, Paul is challenging the Romans to work together to become a great team. (See also 1 Cor 12, 12–13.) What kind of teamwork do you find in your family, your parish, or your school?

▶ **Rom 12, 1–8**

---

†
11, 33–36: This final reflection celebrates the wisdom of God's plan of salvation. As Paul has indicated throughout these chapters, both Jew and Gentile, despite the religious recalcitrance of each, have received the gift of faith. The methods used by God in making this outreach to the world stagger human comprehension but are at the same time a dazzling invitation to abiding faith.

11, 34: The citation is from the Greek text of Is 40, 13. Paul does not explicitly mention Isaiah in this verse, nor Job in v 35.

11, 35: Paul quotes from an old Greek version of Jb 41, 3a, which differs from the Hebrew text (Jb 41, 11a).

12, 1—13, 14: Since Christ marks the termination of the Mosaic law as the primary source of guidance for God's people (10, 4), the apostle explains how Christians can function, in the light of the gift of justification through faith, in their relation to one another and the state.

12, 1–8: The Mosaic code included elaborate directions on sacrifices and other cultic observances. The gospel, however, invites believers to present their *bodies as a living sacrifice* (1). Instead of being limited by specific legal maxims, Christians are liberated for the exercise of good judgment as they are confronted with the many and varied decisions required in the course of daily life. To assist them, God distributes a variety of gifts to the fellowship of believers, including those of prophecy, teaching, and exhortation (6–8). Prophets assist the community to understand the will of God as it applies to the present situation (6). Teachers help people to understand themselves and their responsibilities in relation to others (7). One who ex-*horts* offers encouragement to the community to exercise their faith in the performance of all that is pleasing to God (8). Indeed, this very section, beginning with v 1, is a specimen of Paul's own style of exhortation.

12, 5: *One body in Christ:* on the church as the body of Christ, see 1 Cor 12, 12–27.

11, 32: Gal 3, 22; 1 Tm 2, 4.
11, 33: Jb 11, 7–8; Ps 139, 6.17–18; Wis 17, 1; Is 55, 8–9.
11, 34: Jb 15, 8; Wis 9, 13; Is 40, 13; Jer 23, 18; 1 Cor 2, 11–16.
11, 35: Jb 41, 3; Is 40, 14.
11, 36: 1 Cor 8, 6; Col 1, 16–17.

12, 1: 2 Cor 1, 3 / Rom 6, 13; 1 Pt 2, 5.
12, 2: Eph 4, 17.22–23; 1 Pt 1, 14 / Eph 5, 10.17; Phil 1, 10.
12, 3: Rom 15, 15 / Phil 2, 3 / 1 Cor 12, 11; Eph 4, 7.
12, 4–5: 1 Cor 12, 12.27; Eph 4, 25.

We Are the Body of Christ!

According to Rom 12, 1–8, we are the Body of Christ! Just thinking about this beautiful and powerful belief fills us with energy. Imagine the power if all Christians really behaved as the living Body of Christ in their home, church, neighborhood, country, and planet.

In verse 1, Paul calls us to present our body to God as a living, holy, and acceptable sacrifice. The best thing that we can offer to God is our whole life—all we are and all we do. When we worship God by doing this, our prayer and rituals are real and meaningful.

In verse 2, Paul calls us not to be conformed to this world but to be transformed. We are transformed by renewing our mind. We are intelligent people. God gave us the power to discern what is good and evil, true and false, in agreement with or against God's loving plan for humanity.

We must think and act according to the measure of faith and the different gifts that we have received for the service of others (charisms). So we, who are many, may become one Body in Christ and be better collaborators in Jesus' mission.

▶ Rom 12, 1–8

---

of one another. ⁶*† Since we have gifts that differ according to the grace given to us, let us exercise them: if prophecy, in proportion to the faith; ⁷ if ministry, in ministering; if one is a teacher, in teaching; ⁸† if one exhorts, in exhortation; if one contributes, in generosity; if one is over others, with diligence; if one does acts of mercy, with cheerfulness.

Mutual Love

⁹* Let love be sincere; hate what is evil, hold on to what is good; ¹⁰* love one another with mutual affection; anticipate one another in showing honor. ¹¹* Do not grow slack in zeal, be fervent in spirit, serve the Lord. ¹²* Rejoice in hope, endure in affliction, persevere in prayer. ¹³* Contribute to the needs of the holy ones, exercise hospitality. ¹⁴*† Bless those who persecute [you], bless and do not curse

them.* ¹⁵* Rejoice with those who rejoice, weep with those who weep. ¹⁶* Have the same regard for one another; do not be haughty but associate with the lowly; do not be wise in your own estimation. ¹⁷* Do not repay anyone evil for evil; be concerned for what is noble in the sight of all. ¹⁸* If possible, on your part, live at peace with all. ¹⁹* Beloved, do not look for revenge but leave room for the wrath; for it is written, "Vengeance is mine, I will repay, says the Lord." ²⁰* Rather, "if your enemy is hungry, feed him; if he is thirsty, give him something to drink; for by so doing you will heap burning coals upon his head." ²¹ Do not be conquered by evil but conquer evil with good.

Obedience to Authority

13 ¹*† Let every person be subordinate to the higher authorities, for there is no au-

---

12, 6: Everyone has some gift that can be used for the benefit of the community. When the instruction on justification through faith is correctly grasped, the possessor of a gift will understand that it is not an instrument of self-aggrandizement. Possession of a gift is not an index to quality of faith. Rather, the gift is a challenge to faithful use.

12, 8: *Over others:* usually taken to mean "rule over" but possibly "serve as a patron." Wealthier members in Greco-Roman communities were frequently asked to assist in public service projects. In view of the references to contributing *in generosity* and to *acts of mercy,* Paul may have in mind people like Phoebe (16, 1–2), who is called a *benefactor* (or "patron") because of the services she rendered to many Christians, including Paul.

12, 14–21: Since God has justified the believers, it is not necessary for them to take justice into their own hands by taking vengeance. God will ultimately deal justly with all, including those who inflict injury on the believers. This question of personal rights as a matter of justice prepares the way for more detailed consideration of the state as adjudicator.

13, 1–7: Paul must come to grips with the problem raised by a message that declares people free from the law. How are they to

---

12, 6–8: 1 Cor 12, 4–11.28–31;
  Eph 4, 7–12; 1 Pt 4,
  10–11 / 2 Cor 9, 7.
12, 9: 2 Cor 6, 6; 1 Tm 1, 5;
  1 Pt 1, 22 / Am 5, 15.
12, 10: Jn 13, 34; 1 Thes 4, 9;
  1 Pt 2, 17; 2 Pt 1, 7 /
  Phil 2, 3.
12, 11: Acts 18, 25.
12, 12: Rom 5, 2–3; Col 4, 2;
  1 Thes 5, 17.
12, 13: Heb 13, 2; 1 Pt 4, 9.
12, 14–21: Mt 5, 38–48; 1 Cor 4,
  12; 1 Pt 3, 9.
12, 14: Lk 6, 27–28.

12, 15: Ps 35, 13; Sir 7, 34;
  1 Cor 12, 26.
12, 16: Rom 15, 5; Phil 2, 2–3
  / Rom 11, 20; Prv 3, 7;
  Is 5, 21.
12, 17: Prv 3, 4; 1 Thes 5, 15;
  1 Pt 3, 9.
12, 18: Heb 12, 14.
12, 19: Lv 19, 18; Dt 32,
  35.41; Mt 5, 39; 1 Cor
  6, 6–7; Heb 10, 30.
12, 20: Prv 25, 21–22; Mt 5, 44.
13, 1: Prv 8, 15–16; Wis 6, 3;
  Jn 19, 11; 1 Pt 2,
  13–17; Ti 3, 1.

Becoming a Peacemaker

A common response when someone mistreats us is to seek revenge. But in Rom 12, 17–19, Paul tells us that only God should be the avenger. He goes on to remind us of Jesus' teaching to treat our enemies with kindness. That is certainly easier said than done! It is difficult to respond with goodwill when we are hurt.

Nevertheless, real people have tried to live by this teaching—Martin Luther King Jr., Mohandas Gandhi, Mother Teresa, and Dorothy Day, to name a few. Perhaps you know people who have made similar commitments in your own community.

Think of the people you know. Who is a peacemaker in your life? What can you do to be a peacemaker in your family, school, or community?

▶ Rom 12, 17–19

thority except from God, and those that exist have been established by God. ² Therefore, whoever resists authority opposes what God has appointed, and those who oppose it will bring judgment upon themselves. ³* For rulers are not a cause of fear to good conduct, but to evil. Do you wish to have no fear of authority? Then do what is good and you will receive approval from it, ⁴* for it is a servant of God for your good. But if you do evil, be afraid, for it does not bear the sword without purpose; it is the servant of God to inflict wrath on the evildoer. ⁵* Therefore, it is necessary to be subject not only because of the wrath but also because of conscience. ⁶ This is why you also pay taxes, for the authorities are ministers of God, devoting themselves to this very thing. ⁷* Pay to all their dues, taxes to whom taxes are due, toll to whom toll is due, respect to whom respect is due, honor to whom honor is due.

Love Fulfills the Law

⁸*† Owe nothing to anyone, except to love one another; for the one who loves another has fulfilled the law. ⁹* The commandments, "You shall not commit adultery; you shall not kill; you shall not steal; you shall not covet," and whatever other commandment there may be, are summed up in this saying, [namely] "You shall love your

neighbor as yourself." ¹⁰* Love does no evil to the neighbor; hence, love is the fulfillment of the law.

Awareness of the End of Time

¹¹*† And do this because you know the time; it is the hour now for you to awake from sleep. For our

A Real Love

Lord, why is it so hard to love? Love is mentioned so much in the Bible that it makes me wonder why we don't get it. It seems that we do a good job of talking love and a poor job of doing love. We can point out where there is no love, but it sure is hard to bring love to where it is needed.

Jesus, fill me with your love to share with others. The kind of love that changes people forever. The kind of love that breaks down barriers and overcomes fears. The love that gives without counting the costs. Amen.

▶ Rom 13, 8–10

R
O
M

---

† relate to Roman authority? The problem was exacerbated by the fact that imperial protocol was interwoven with devotion to various deities. Paul builds on the traditional instruction exhibited in Wis 6, 1–3, according to which kings and magistrates rule by consent of God. From this perspective, then, believers who render obedience to the governing authorities are obeying the one who is highest in command. At the same time, it is recognized that Caesar has the responsibility to make just ordinances and to commend uprightness; cf Wis 6, 4–21. That Caesar is not entitled to obedience when such obedience would nullify God's prior claim to the believers' moral decision becomes clear in the light of the following verses.

13, 8–10: When love directs the Christian's moral decisions, the interest of law in basic concerns, such as familial relationships, sanctity of life, and security of property, is safeguarded (9). Indeed, says Paul, the same applies to any *other commandment* (9), whether one

in the Mosaic code or one drawn up by local magistrates under imperial authority. Love anticipates the purpose of public legislation, namely, to secure the best interests of the citizenry. Since Caesar's obligation is to punish the wrongdoer (4), the Christian who acts in love is free from all legitimate indictment.

13, 11–14: These verses provide the motivation for the love that is encouraged in vv 8–10.

*

13, 3: 1 Pt 2, 13–14; 3, 13.
13, 4: Rom 12, 19.
13, 5: 1 Pt 2, 19.
13, 7: Mt 22, 21; Mk 12, 17; Lk 20, 25.
13, 8: Jn 13, 34; Gal 5, 14.
13, 9: Ex 20, 13–17 / Lv 19, 18; Dt 5, 17–21; Mt 5,

43–44; 19, 18–19; 22, 39; Mk 12, 31; Lk 10, 27; Gal 5, 14; Jas 2, 8.
13, 10: Mt 22, 40; 1 Cor 13, 4–7.
13, 11: Eph 5, 8–16; 1 Thes 5, 5–7.

salvation is nearer now than when we first believed; [12]* the night is advanced, the day is at hand. Let us then throw off the works of darkness [and] put on the armor of light; [13]*† let us conduct ourselves properly as in the day, not in orgies and drunkenness, not in promiscuity and licentiousness, not in rivalry and jealousy. [14]* But put on the Lord Jesus Christ, and make no provision for the desires of the flesh.

To Live and Die for Christ

14 [1]*† Welcome anyone who is weak in faith, but not for disputes over opinions.* [2]* One person believes that one may eat anything, while the weak person eats only vegetables. [3]* The one who eats must not despise the one who abstains, and the one who abstains must not pass judgment on the one who eats; for God has welcomed him. [4]* Who are you to pass judgment on someone else's servant? Before his own master he stands or falls. And he will be upheld, for the Lord

is able to make him stand. [5]*† [For] one person considers one day more important than another, while another person considers all days alike. Let everyone be fully persuaded in his own mind. [6] Whoever observes the day, observes it for the Lord. Also whoever eats, eats for the Lord, since he gives thanks to God; while whoever abstains, abstains for the Lord and gives thanks to God. [7] None of us lives for oneself, and no one dies for oneself. [8]*† For if we live, we live for the Lord, and if we die, we die for the Lord; so then, whether we live or die, we are the Lord's. [9]* For this is why Christ died and came to life, that he might be Lord of both the dead and the living. [10]* Why then do you judge your brother? Or you, why do you look down on your brother? For we shall all stand before the judgment seat of God; [11]* for it is written:

> "As I live, says the Lord, every knee shall bend
> before me,
> and every tongue shall give praise to God."

Respecting Differences

LIVE IT!

What is a regular coffee in your part of the country? In the Boston area, it has sugar and cream in it. In many other parts of the country, it comes without cream and sugar.

In the same way that people from different parts of the United States have different ideas about coffee, Christians have different ideas about what to believe and how to act. It seems Paul has heard that the Christians in Rome disagree about what to eat (Rom 14, 2) and what days to hold holy (verse 5). He tells them not to quarrel over these differences. Whatever they do, they should do it "for the Lord" (verse 6). The church would be shamed if these minor differences became a stumbling block to someone's faith.

The fullness of God's truth exists in a unique way in the Catholic Church, but we respect God's truth where it is found in other Christian Churches. Christians of all denominations should rejoice in their common faith, respect and learn from their differences, and work together "for the Lord."

▶ Rom 14, 1–23

---

†
13, 13: *Let us conduct ourselves properly as in the day:* the behavior described in 1, 29–30 is now to be reversed. Secular moralists were fond of making references to people who could not wait for nightfall to do their carousing. Paul says that Christians claim to be people of the new day that will dawn with the return of Christ. Instead of planning for nighttime behavior they should be concentrating on conduct that is consonant with avowed interest in the Lord's return.

14, 1—15, 6: Since Christ spells termination of the law, which included observance of specific days and festivals as well as dietary instruction, the jettisoning of long-practiced customs was traumatic for many Christians brought up under the Mosaic code. Although Paul acknowledges that in principle no food is a source of moral contamination (14), he recommends that the consciences of Christians who are scrupulous in this regard be respected by other Christians (21). On the other hand, those who have scruples are not to sit in judgment on those who know that the gospel has liberated them from such ordinances (10). See 1 Cor 8 and 10.

14, 5: Since the problem to be overcome was humanity's per-

verted mind or judgment (1, 28), Paul indicates that the *mind* of the Christian is now able to function with appropriate discrimination (cf 12, 2).

14, 8: *The Lord:* Jesus, our Master. The same Greek word, *kyrios,* was applied to both rulers and holders of slaves. Throughout the Letter to the Romans Paul emphasizes God's total claim on the believer; see the note on 1, 1.

*

13, 12: Jn 8, 12; 1 Thes 5, 4–8; 1 Jn 2, 8 / 2 Cor 6, 7; 10, 4; Eph 5, 11; 6, 13–17.
13, 13: Lk 21, 34; Eph 5, 18.
13, 14: Gal 3, 27; 5, 16; Eph 4, 24; 6, 11.
14, 1–23: 1 Cor 8, 1–13.
14, 1: Rom 15, 1.7; 1 Cor 9, 22.
14, 2: Gn 1, 29; 9, 3; 1 Cor 8, 1–13; 10, 14–33.

14, 3: Col 2, 16.
14, 4: Rom 2, 1; Mt 7, 11; Jas 4, 11–12.
14, 5: Gal 4, 10.
14, 8: Lk 20, 38; 2 Cor 5, 15; Gal 2, 20; 1 Thes 5, 10.
14, 9: Acts 10, 42.
14, 10: Acts 17, 31; 2 Cor 5, 10.
14, 11: Is 49, 18 / Is 45, 23; Phil 2, 10–11.

12* So [then] each of us shall give an account of himself [to God].

Consideration for the Weak Conscience

13* Then let us no longer judge one another, but rather resolve never to put a stumbling block or hindrance in the way of a brother. 14* I know and am convinced in the Lord Jesus that nothing is unclean in itself; still, it is unclean for someone who thinks it unclean. 15* If your brother is being hurt by what you eat, your conduct is no longer in accord with love. Do not because of your food destroy him for whom Christ died. 16* So do not let your good be reviled. 17* For the kingdom of God is not a matter of food and drink, but of righteousness, peace, and joy in the holy Spirit; 18 whoever serves Christ in this way is pleasing to God and approved by others. 19*† Let us then pursue what leads to peace and to building up one another. 20* For the sake of food, do not destroy the work of God. Everything is indeed clean, but it is wrong for anyone to become a stumbling block by eating; 21 it is good not to eat meat or drink wine or do anything that causes your brother to stumble. 22 Keep the faith [that] you have to yourself in the presence of God; blessed is the one who does not condemn himself for what he approves. 23*† But whoever has doubts is condemned if he eats, because this is not from faith; for whatever is not from faith is sin.

Patience and Self-Denial

15 1* We who are strong ought to put up with the failings of the weak and not to please ourselves; 2* let each of us please our neighbor for the good, for building up. 3*† For Christ did not please himself; but, as it is written, "The insults of those who insult you fall upon me." 4* For whatever was written previously was written for our instruction, that by endurance and by the encouragement of the scriptures we might have hope. 5*† May the God of endurance and encouragement

grant you to think in harmony with one another, in keeping with Christ Jesus, 6 that with one accord you may with one voice glorify the God and Father of our Lord Jesus Christ.

God's Fidelity and Mercy

7*† Welcome one another, then, as Christ welcomed you, for the glory of God. 8* For I say that Christ became a minister of the circumcised to show God's truthfulness, to confirm the promises to the patriarchs, 9* but so that the Gentiles might glorify God for his mercy. As it is written:

"Therefore, I will praise you among
    the Gentiles
    and sing praises to your name."

10*† And again it says:

"Rejoice, O Gentiles, with his people."

11* And again:

"Praise the Lord, all you Gentiles,
    and let all the peoples praise him."

12* And again Isaiah says:

"The root of Jesse shall come,
    raised up to rule the Gentiles;
    in him shall the Gentiles hope."

13* May the God of hope fill you with all joy and peace in believing, so that you may abound in hope by the power of the holy Spirit.

VII: Conclusion

Apostle to the Gentiles

14† I myself am convinced about you, my brothers, that you yourselves are full of goodness,† filled

---

14, 19: Some manuscripts, versions, and church Fathers read, "We then pursue . . ."; cf 5, 1.
14, 23: *Whatever is not from faith is sin:* Paul does not mean that all the actions of unbelievers are sinful. He addresses himself to the question of intracommunity living. *Sin* in the singular is the dreadful power described in 5, 12–14.
15, 3: Liberation from the law of Moses does not make the scriptures of the old covenant irrelevant. Much consolation and motivation for Christian living can be derived from the Old Testament, as in the citation from Ps 69, 10. Because this psalm is quoted several times in the New Testament, it has been called indirectly messianic.
15, 5: *Think in harmony:* a Greco-Roman ideal. Not rigid uniformity of thought and expression but thoughtful consideration of other people's views finds expression here.
15, 7–13: True oneness of mind is found in pondering the ultimate mission of the church: to bring it about that God's name be glorified throughout the world and that Jesus Christ be universally recognized as God's gift to all humanity. Paul here prepares his addressees for the climactic appeal he is about to make.
15, 10: Paul's citation of Dt 32, 43 follows the Greek version.

15, 14–33: Paul sees himself as apostle and benefactor in the priestly service of the gospel and so sketches plans for a mission in Spain, supported by those in Rome.
15, 14: *Full of goodness:* the opposite of what humanity was filled with according to 1, 29–30.

14, 12: Gal 6, 5.	15, 3: Ps 69, 10.
14, 13: 1 Cor 8, 9.13.	15, 4: Rom 4, 23–24; 1 Mc
14, 14: Mk 7, 5.20; Acts 10,	12, 9; 1 Cor 10, 11;
15; 1 Cor 10, 25–27;	2 Tm 3, 16.
1 Tm 4, 4.	15, 5: Rom 12, 16; Phil 2, 2;
14, 15: 1 Cor 8, 11–13.	4, 2.
14, 16: Rom 2, 24; Ti 2, 5.	15, 7: Rom 14, 1.
14, 17: 1 Cor 8, 8.	15, 8: Mt 15, 24 / Mi 7, 20;
14, 19: Rom 12, 18 / Rom	Acts 3, 25.
15, 2.	15, 9: Rom 11, 30 / 2 Sm 22,
14, 20–21: 1 Cor 8, 11–13; 10,	50; Ps 18, 50.
28–29; Ti 1, 15.	15, 10: Dt 32, 43.
14, 23: Ti 1, 15; Jas 4, 17.	15, 11: Ps 117, 1.
15, 1: Rom 14, 1–2.	15, 12: Is 11, 10; Rv 5, 5; 22,
15, 2: Rom 14, 1.19; 1 Cor	16.
9, 19; 10, 24.33.	15, 13: Rom 5, 1–2.

with all knowledge, and able to admonish one another. [15]* But I have written to you rather boldly in some respects to remind you, because of the grace given me by God [16]* to be a minister of Christ Jesus to the Gentiles in performing the priestly service of the gospel of God, so that the offering up of the Gentiles may be acceptable, sanctified by the holy Spirit. [17] In Christ Jesus, then, I have reason to boast in what pertains to God. [18]* For I will not dare to speak of anything except what Christ has accomplished through me to lead the Gentiles to obedience by word and deed, [19]† by the power of signs and wonders, by the power of the Spirit [of God], so that from Jerusalem all the way around to Illyricum I have finished preaching the gospel of Christ. [20]*† Thus I aspire to proclaim the gospel not where Christ has already been named, so that I do not build on another's foundation, [21]*† but as it is written:

> "Those who have never been told of him
>   shall see,
> and those who have never heard of him
>   shall understand."

Paul's Plans; Need for Prayers

[22] That is why I have so often been prevented from coming to you. [23]* But now, since I no longer have any opportunity in these regions and since I have desired to come to you for many years, [24]* I hope to see you in passing as I go to Spain and to be sent on my way there by you, after I have enjoyed being with you for a time. [25]*† Now, however, I am going to Jerusalem to minister to the holy ones.

[26]*† For Macedonia and Achaia have decided to make some contribution for the poor among the holy ones in Jerusalem; [27]* they decided to do it, and in fact they are indebted to them, for if the Gentiles have come to share in their spiritual blessings, they ought also to serve them in material blessings. [28] So when I have completed this and safely handed over this contribution to them, I shall set out by way of you to Spain; [29] and I know that in coming to you I shall come in the fullness of Christ's blessing.

[30] *I urge you, [brothers,] by our Lord Jesus Christ and by the love of the Spirit, to join me in the struggle by your prayers to God on my behalf, [31] that I may be delivered from the disobedient in Judea, and that my ministry for Jerusalem may be acceptable to the holy ones, [32] so that I may come to you with joy by the will of God and be refreshed together with you. [33]* The God of peace be with all of you. Amen.

Phoebe Commended

16 [1]*† I commend to you Phoebe our sister, who is [also] a minister† of the church at Cenchreae, [2] that you may receive her in the Lord in a manner worthy of the holy ones, and help her in whatever she may need from you, for she has been a benefactor to many and to me as well.

Paul's Greetings

[3]*† Greet Prisca and Aquila, my co-workers in Christ Jesus, [4] who risked their necks for my life, to whom not only I am grateful but also all the churches of the Gentiles; [5]*† greet also the church

---

15, 19: *Illyricum:* Roman province northwest of Greece on the eastern shore of the Adriatic.

15, 20: *I aspire:* Paul uses terminology customarily applied to philanthropists. Unlike some philanthropists of his time, Paul does not engage in cheap competition for public acclaim. This explanation of his missionary policy is to assure the Christians in Rome that he is also not planning to remain in that city and build on other people's foundations (cf 2 Cor 10, 12–18). However, he does solicit their help in sending him on his way to Spain, which was considered the limit of the western world. Thus Paul's addressees realize that evangelization may be understood in the broader sense of mission or, as in Rom 1, 15, of instruction within the Christian community that derives from the gospel.

15, 21: The citation from Is 52, 15 concerns the Servant of the Lord. According to Isaiah, the Servant is first of all Israel, which was to bring the knowledge of Yahweh to the nations. In chs 9–11 Paul showed how Israel failed in this mission. Therefore, he himself undertakes almost singlehandedly Israel's responsibility as the Servant and moves as quickly as possible with the gospel through the Roman empire.

15, 25–27: Paul may have viewed the contribution he was gathering from Gentile Christians for the poor in Jerusalem (cf 2 Cor 8 and 9) as a fulfillment of the vision of Is 60, 5–6. In confidence that the messianic fulfillment was taking place, Paul stresses in chs 14–16 the importance of harmonious relationships between Jews and Gentiles.

15, 26: *Achaia:* the Roman province of southern Greece.

16, 1–23: Some authorities regard these verses as a later addition to the letter, but in general the evidence favors the view that they

were included in the original. Paul endeavors through the long list of greetings (3–16; 21–23) to establish strong personal contact with congregations that he has not personally encountered before. The combination of Jewish and Gentile names dramatically attests the unity in the gospel that transcends previous barriers of nationality, religious ceremony, or racial status.

16, 1: *Minister:* in Greek, *diakonos;* see the note on Phil 1, 1.

16, 3: *Prisca and Aquila:* presumably the couple mentioned at Acts 18, 2; 1 Cor 16, 19; 2 Tm 4, 19.

16, 5: *The church at their house:* i.e., that meets there. Such local assemblies (cf 1 Cor 16, 19; Col 4, 15; Phlm 2) might consist of only one or two dozen Christians each. It is understandable, therefore, that such smaller groups might experience difficulty in relating to one another on certain issues. *Firstfruits:* cf 8, 23; 11, 16; 1 Cor 16, 15.

15, 15: Rom 1, 5; 12, 3.
15, 16: Rom 11, 13; Phil 2, 17.
15, 18: Acts 15, 12; 2 Cor 12, 12.
15, 20: 2 Cor 10, 13–18.
15, 21: Is 52, 15.
15, 23: Rom 1, 10–13; Acts 19, 21–22.
15, 24: 1 Cor 16, 6.
15, 25: Acts 19, 21; 20, 22.
15, 26: 1 Cor 16, 1; 2 Cor 8, 1–4; 9, 2.12.
15, 27: Rom 9, 4 / 1 Cor 9, 11.
15, 30: 2 Cor 1, 11; Phil 1, 27; Col 4, 3; 2 Thes 3, 1.
15, 33: Rom 16, 20; 2 Cor 13, 11; Phil 4, 9; 1 Thes 5, 23; 2 Thes 3, 16; Heb 13, 20.
16, 1: Acts 18, 18.
16, 3: Acts 18, 2.18–26; 1 Cor 16, 19; 2 Tm 4, 19.
16, 5: 1 Cor 16, 19; Col 4, 15; Phlm 2 / 1 Cor 16, 15.

ROM

at their house. Greet my beloved Epaenetus, who was the firstfruits in Asia for Christ. 6 Greet Mary, who has worked hard for you. 7† Greet Androni- cus and Junia, my relatives and my fellow prison- ers; they are prominent among the apostles and they were in Christ before me. 8 Greet Ampliatus, my beloved in the Lord. 9 Greet Urbanus, our co- worker in Christ, and my beloved Stachys. 10 Greet Apelles, who is approved in Christ. Greet those who belong to the family of Aristobulus. 11 Greet my relative Herodion. Greet those in the Lord who belong to the family of Narcissus. 12 Greet those workers in the Lord, Tryphaena and Tryphosa. Greet the beloved Persis, who has worked hard in the Lord. 13*† Greet Rufus, chosen in the Lord, and his mother and mine. 14 Greet Asyncritus, Phlegon, Hermes, Patrobas, Hermas, and the brothers who are with them. 15 Greet Philologus, Julia, Nereus and his sister, and Olympas, and all the holy ones who are with them. 16* Greet one another with a holy kiss. All the churches of Christ greet you.

Against Factions

17*† I urge you, brothers, to watch out for those who create dissensions and obstacles, in opposition to the teaching that you learned; avoid them. 18* For such people do not serve our Lord Christ but their own appetites, and by fair and flattering speech they deceive the hearts of the innocent. 19* For while your obedience is known to all, so that I rejoice over you, I want you to be wise as to what is good, and simple as to what is evil; 20*† then the God of peace will quickly crush Satan under your feet. The grace of our Lord Jesus be with you.

Greetings from Corinth

21* Timothy, my co-worker, greets you; so do Lu- cius and Jason and Sosipater, my relatives. 22 I, Ter- tius, the writer of this letter, greet you in the Lord. 23*† Gaius, who is host to me and to the whole church, greets you. Erastus, the city treasurer, and our brother Quartus greet you. [24]†

Introducing ▶PHOEBE AND JUNIA

In Rom 16, 1–16, Paul greets almost thirty people and their families in Rome—more peo- ple than he greets in any of his other letters. It is thought that perhaps he is trying to es- tablish a connection among the Christians in Rome by mentioning mutual acquaintances. About a third of the people he greets are women, highlighting the important role women played in Paul's ministry and in the leadership of the early church.

Of particular interest are Paul's comments about Phoebe, whom he calls a deacon, and Junia (also called Julia), whom he declares "prominent among the apostles" (verse 7). In Paul's time, deacons were usually associated with a ministry of service, and apostles with a ministry of leadership. Even though women were not allowed to fill official positions in government or society, the early church recognized them as being as important as men in service, leadership, and bringing the Gospel to others.

▶ Rom 16, 1–16

---

† 16, 7: The name Junia is a woman's name. One ancient Greek manuscript and a number of ancient versions read the name "Julia." Most editors have interpreted it as a man's name, Junias.

16, 13: This Rufus cannot be identified to any degree of certain- ty with the Rufus of Mk 15, 21.

16, 17–18: Paul displays genuine concern for the congregations in Rome by warning them against self-seeking teachers. It would be a great loss, he intimates, if their obedience, which is known to all (cf 1, 8), would be diluted.

16, 20: This verse contains the only mention of Satan in Romans.

16, 23: This Erastus is not necessarily to be identified with the Erastus of Acts 19, 22 or of 2 Tm 4, 20.

16, 24: Some manuscripts add, similarly to v 20, "The grace of our Lord Jesus Christ be with you all. Amen."

16, 13: Mk 15, 21.
16, 16: 1 Cor 16, 20; 2 Cor 13, 12; 1 Thes 5, 26; 1 Pt 5, 14.
16, 17: Mt 7, 15; Ti 3, 10.
16, 18: Phil 3, 18–19 / Col 2, 4; 2 Pt 2, 3.
16, 19: Rom 1, 8; Mt 10, 16; 1 Cor 14, 20.
16, 20: Rom 15, 33; Gn 3, 15,

Lk 10, 19 / 1 Cor 16, 23; 1 Thes 5, 28; 2 Thes 3, 18.
16, 21: Acts 16, 1–2; 19, 22; 20, 4; 1 Cor 4, 17; 16, 10; Phil 2, 19–22; Heb 13, 23.
16, 23: Acts 19, 29; 1 Cor 1, 14 / 2 Tm 4, 20.

Doxology†

[25* Now to him who can strengthen you, according to my gospel and the proclamation of Jesus Christ, according to the revelation of the mystery kept secret for long ages† 26* but now manifested through the prophetic writings and, according to the command of the eternal God, made known to all nations to bring about the obedience of faith, 27* to the only wise God, through Jesus Christ be glory forever and ever. Amen.]

16, 25–27: This doxology is assigned variously to the end of chs 14, 15, and 16 in the manuscript tradition. Some manuscripts omit it entirely. Whether written by Paul or not, it forms an admirable conclusion to the letter at this point.

16, 25: Paul's gospel reveals *the mystery kept secret for long ages:* justification and salvation through faith, with all the implications for Jews and Gentiles that Paul has developed in the letter.

16, 25: 1 Cor 2, 7; Eph 1, 9; 3, 3–9; Col 1, 26.
16, 26: 2 Tm 1, 10 / Rom 1, 5; Eph 3, 4–5.9; 1 Pt 1, 20.
16, 27: Rom 11, 36; Gal 1, 5;
Eph 3, 20–21; Phil 4, 20; 1 Tm 1, 17; 2 Tm 4, 18; Heb 13, 21; 1 Pt 4, 11; 2 Pt 3, 18; Jude 25, Rv 1, 6.

Churches have problems. Sometimes, parishes harbor power struggles, sex scandals, troubled marriages, bitter disagreements, alcohol abuse, and even disorderly worship. Maybe you know Christian communities that have had some of these difficulties. The early church in Corinth had them all. In his first letter to the Corinthians, Paul gave them guidance and encouragement. This letter can teach churches in all times to more faithfully follow Christ.

At a Glance

I. Address (1, 1–9).

II. Disorders in the Corinthian Community (1, 10—6, 20).

III. Answers to the Corinthians' Questions (7, 1—11, 1).

IV. Problems in Liturgical Assemblies (11, 2—14, 40).

V. The Resurrection (15, 1–58).

VI. Conclusion (16, 1–24).

In-depth

Corinth was an important seaport city in what is now southern Greece. It was a center of commerce for people from many cultures. It also had quite a reputation for sexual immorality. Paul established the Christian church there around A.D. 51 and spent about eighteen months with its converts. After Paul left, a man named Apollos came to help the young church grow.

Later, when Paul was in Ephesus, he got a letter (1 Cor 7, 1) and visitors (1, 11; 16, 17) from Corinth. The church there was having problems. The problems were natural in a young Christian community whose members included both Jewish Christians and Gentile (non-Jewish) converts. The community was divided into groups with different leaders. There were some disagreements on how to worship properly. And there were different opinions about eating meat that had been sacrificed to pagan idols. In addition, some of the wealthy Christians were ignoring those who were poorer. And those with certain spiritual gifts were claiming to be more important than other people.

In response to all these divisions and various questions, Paul gives the Corinthians good, practical advice. At the same time, he reminds them of what is truly important for Christian believers: the Resurrection is central to faith; human wisdom is foolish when measured against God's wisdom; others' needs and concerns must always be put before their own; and love should be the primary focus in everything they do and say.

To this divided, confused community, Paul offers a picture of unity: we are all different parts of the same Body of Christ (12, 12–26). Paul celebrates our diversity and insists on our unity. The advice and teaching he gives in this letter are good for Christians of any time or place to take to heart.

Quick Facts

Author
Paul

Date Written
A.D. 56

Audience
the mainly Gentile church at Corinth

1 Corinthians

I: Address†

Greeting

1 [1]* Paul, called to be an apostle of Christ Jesus by the will of God,† and Sosthenes our brother, [2]* to the church of God that is in Corinth, to you who have been sanctified in Christ Jesus, called to be holy, with all those everywhere who call upon the name of our Lord Jesus Christ, their Lord and ours. [3] Grace to you and peace from God our Father and the Lord Jesus Christ.

Thanksgiving

[4] I give thanks to my God always on your account for the grace of God bestowed on you in Christ Jesus, [5] that in him you were enriched in every way, with all discourse and all knowledge, [6]† as the testimony to Christ was confirmed among you, [7]* so that you are not lacking in any spiritual gift as you wait for the revelation of our Lord Jesus Christ. [8]* He will keep you firm to the end, irreproachable on the day of our Lord Jesus [Christ.] [9]* God is faithful, and by him you were called to fellowship with his Son, Jesus Christ our Lord.

II: Disorders in the Corinthian Community

A. Divisions in the Church

Groups and Slogans

[10]*† I urge you, brothers, in the name of our Lord Jesus Christ, that all of you agree in what you say, and that there be no divisions among you, but that you be united in the same mind and in the same purpose. [11] For it has been reported to me about you, my brothers, by Chloe's people, that there are rivalries among you. [12]*† I mean that each

---

1, 1–9: Paul follows the conventional form for the opening of a Hellenistic letter (cf Rom 1, 1–7), but expands the opening with details carefully chosen to remind the readers of their situation and to suggest some of the issues the letter will discuss.

1, 1: *Called . . . by the will of God:* Paul's mission and the church's existence are grounded in God's initiative. God's call, grace, and fidelity are central ideas in this introduction, emphasized by repetition and wordplays in the Greek.

1, 6: *The testimony:* this defines the purpose of Paul's mission (see also 15, 15 and the note on 2, 1). The forms of his testimony include oral preaching and instruction, his letters, and the life he leads as an apostle.

1, 10—4, 21: The first problem Paul addresses is that of divisions within the community. Although we are unable to reconstruct the situation in Corinth completely, Paul clearly traces the divisions back

to a false self-image on the part of the Corinthians, coupled with a false understanding of the apostles who preached to them (cf 4, 6.9; 9, 1–5) and of the Christian message itself. In these chapters he attempts to deal with those underlying factors and to bring the Corinthians back to a more correct perspective.

1, 12: *I belong to:* the activities of Paul and Apollos in Corinth are described in Acts 18. *Cephas* (i.e., "the Rock," a name by which Paul designates Peter also in 3, 22; 9, 5; 15, 5 and in Gal 1, 18; 2, 9.11.14) may well have passed through Corinth; he could have baptized some members of the community either there or elsewhere. The reference to *Christ* may be intended ironically here.

* ——————————————
1, 1: Rom 1, 1.
1, 2: Acts 18, 1–11.
1, 7: Ti 2, 13.
1, 8: Phil 1, 6.
1, 9: 1 Jn 1, 3.
1, 10: Phil 2, 2.
1, 12: 1 Cor 3, 4.22; 16, 12; Acts 18, 24–28.

Divisions in the Church

At a family reunion to honor his grandfather's eighty-fifth birthday, Tyrone brags about his school's victory over his cousin Martin's school in a recent football game. Martin counters that the referees overlooked a crucial penalty. Before long, the entire gathering is fighting about which team was the best. The birthday party is ruined.

This is what happened to the Christians in Corinth. They held a common belief in Jesus but spent useless energy arguing over which leaders to follow. Paul challenges them to get over this foolish division and focus on the important thing they share—the love of God and their salvation through the cross of Christ.

Christians today continue to struggle with Paul's challenge to be united. Catholics are called to see other Christians as brothers and sisters in Christ. The Catholic Church traces its origin directly back to Jesus Christ and the Apostles. Because of that, the fullness of God's revealed truth can be found only in the Catholic Church. Other Christian Churches share in this truth to a greater or lesser degree. Knowing this, we look for those shared beliefs and practices that unite us, while respectfully talking about the sometimes significant differences that exist between different Christian Churches. In this way, all Catholics seek to build unity and communion with other Christians.

▶ 1 Cor 1, 10–17

---

of you is saying, "I belong to Paul," or "I belong to Apollos," or "I belong to Cephas," or "I belong to Christ." [13]† Is Christ divided? Was Paul crucified for you? Or were you baptized in the name of Paul? [14]* I give thanks [to God] that I baptized none of you except Crispus and Gaius, [15] so that no one can say you were baptized in my name. [16]* (I baptized the household of Stephanas also; beyond that I do not know whether I baptized anyone else.) [17]*† For Christ did not send me to baptize but to preach the gospel, and not with the wisdom of human eloquence,† so that the cross of Christ might not be emptied of its meaning.

Paradox of the Cross

[18]* The message of the cross is foolishness to those who are perishing, but to us who are being saved it is the power of God. [19]* For it is written:

"I will destroy the wisdom of the wise,
    and the learning of the learned I will
    set aside."

[20]* Where is the wise one? Where is the scribe? Where is the debater of this age? Has not God made the wisdom of the world foolish? [21]† For since in the wisdom of God the world did not come to know God through wisdom, it was the will of God through the foolishness of the proclamation to save those who have faith. [22]* For Jews demand signs and Greeks look for wisdom, [23]* but we proclaim Christ crucified, a stumbling block to Jews and foolishness to Gentiles, [24] but to those who are called, Jews and Greeks alike, Christ the power of God and the wisdom of God. [25] For the foolishness of God is wiser than human wisdom, and the weakness of God is stronger than human strength.

1, 13–17: The reference to baptism and the contrast with preaching the gospel in v 17a suggest that some Corinthians were paying special allegiance to the individuals who initiated them into the community.

1, 17b–18: The basic theme of chs 1–4 is announced. Adherence to individual leaders has something to do with differences in rhetorical ability and also with certain presuppositions regarding wisdom, eloquence, and effectiveness (power), which Paul judges to be in conflict with the gospel and the cross.

1, 17b: *Not with the wisdom of human eloquence:* both of the nouns employed here involve several levels of meaning, on which Paul deliberately plays as his thought unfolds. *Wisdom (sophia)* may be philosophical and speculative, but in biblical usage the term primarily denotes practical knowledge such as is demonstrated in the choice and effective application of means to achieve an end. The same term can designate the arts of building (cf 3, 10) or of persuasive speaking (cf 2, 4) or effectiveness in achieving salvation. *Eloquence (logos):* this translation emphasizes one possible meaning of the term *logos* (cf the references to rhetorical style and persuasiveness in 2, 1.4). But the term itself may denote an internal reasoning

process, plan, or intention, as well as an external word, speech, or message. So by his expression *ouk en sophia logou* in the context of gospel preaching, Paul may intend to exclude both human ways of reasoning or thinking about things and human rhetorical technique. *Human:* this adjective does not stand in the Greek text but is supplied from the context. Paul will begin immediately to distinguish between *sophia* and *logos* from their divine counterparts and play them off against each other.

1, 21–25: True wisdom and power are to be found paradoxically where one would least expect them, in the place of their apparent negation. To human eyes the crucified Christ symbolizes impotence and absurdity.

1, 14: Acts 18, 8 / Rom 16, 23.
1, 16: 1 Cor 16, 15–17.
1, 17: 1 Cor 2, 1.4.
1, 18: 1 Cor 2, 14 / Rom 1, 16.
1, 19: Is 29, 14.
1, 20: Is 19, 12.
1, 22: Mt 12, 38; 16, 1 / Acts 17, 18–21.
1, 23: 1 Cor 2, 2; Gal 3, 1 / Gal 5, 11.

1
C
O
R

God's Wisdom and Ours

What is the difference between a smart person and a wise person? Many smart people excel in a subject in school or a skill at work. You have to be very smart to run an illegal drug ring or to make a nuclear bomb. But being smart in these ways does not make a person wise in the ways of God.

Paul reminds the Corinthians that the central Christian message—that Christ was crucified for our salvation—seems foolish to many wise people of their time. The Jews and Greeks of this period pride themselves on their wisdom. But the Jews hope for a kingly messiah who will make the nation strong. And the Greeks believe that their gods are strong. Both Jews and Greeks think the idea of a crucified messiah, or a god who can suffer and die, is foolish.

There is great mystery here: the foolishness of God is wiser than the greatest wisdom of the world. Our ways are not God's ways. Christ hanging on a cross turns upside down the world's ideas of success and failure, of victory and defeat, of power and weakness. Many people in Paul's time—and many people in our time—are not able to accept this "foolish" way of seeing the world as God sees it.

▶ 1 Cor 1, 18–31

The Corinthians and Paul

26† Consider your own calling, brothers. Not many of you were wise by human standards, not many were powerful, not many were of noble birth. 27* Rather, God chose the foolish of the world to shame the wise, and God chose the weak of the world to shame the strong, 28 and God chose the lowly and despised of the world, those who count for nothing, to reduce to nothing those who are something, 29*† so that no human being might boast before God. 30* It is due to him that you are in Christ Jesus, who became for us wisdom from God, as well as righteousness, sanctification, and redemption, 31* so that, as it is written, "Whoever boasts, should boast in the Lord."

1*† When I came to you, brothers, proclaiming the mystery of God, I did not come with sublimity of words or of wisdom. 2* For I resolved to know nothing while I was with you except Jesus Christ, and him crucified. 3† I came to you in weakness and fear and much trembling, 4*† and my message and my proclamation were not with persuasive [words of] wisdom, but with a demonstration of spirit and power, 5* so that your faith might rest not on human wisdom but on the power of God.

The True Wisdom

6† Yet we do speak a wisdom to those who are mature, but not a wisdom of this age, nor of the rulers of this age who are passing away. 7† Rather,

---

† **1, 26—2, 5:** The pattern of God's wisdom and power is exemplified in their own experience, if they interpret it rightly (1, 26–31), and can also be read in their experience of Paul as he first appeared among them preaching the gospel (2, 1–5).

1, 29–31: "Boasting (about oneself)" is a Pauline expression for the radical sin, the claim to autonomy on the part of a creature, the illusion that we live and are saved by our own resources. "Boasting in the Lord" (31), on the other hand, is the acknowledgment that we live only from God and for God.

2, 1: The mystery of God: God's secret, known only to himself, is his plan for the salvation of his people; it is clear from 1, 18–25; 2, 2.8–10 that this secret involves Jesus and the cross. In place of mystery, other good manuscripts read "testimony" (cf 1, 6).

2, 3: The weakness of the crucified Jesus is reflected in Paul's own bearing (cf 2 Cor 10–13). Fear and much trembling: reverential fear based on a sense of God's transcendence permeates Paul's existence and preaching. Compare his advice to the Philippians to work out their salvation with "fear and trembling" (Phil 2, 12), because God is at work in them just as his exalting power was paradoxically at work in the emptying, humiliation, and obedience of Jesus to death on the cross (Phil 2, 6–11).

2, 4: Among many manuscript readings here the best is either "not with the persuasion of wisdom" or "not with persuasive words of wisdom," which differ only by a nuance. Whichever reading is ac-

cepted, the inefficacy of human wisdom for salvation is contrasted with the power of the cross.

2, 6—3, 4: Paul now asserts paradoxically what he has previously been denying. To the Greeks who "are looking for wisdom" (1, 22), he does indeed bring a wisdom, but of a higher order and an entirely different quality, the only wisdom really worthy of the name. The Corinthians would be able to grasp Paul's preaching as wisdom and enter into a wisdom-conversation with him if they were more open to the Spirit and receptive to the new insight and language that the Spirit teaches.

2, 7–10a: God's wisdom: his plan for our salvation. This was his own eternal secret that no one else could fathom, but in this new age of salvation he has graciously revealed it to us. For the pattern of God's secret, hidden to others and now revealed to the Church, cf also Rom 11, 25–36; 16, 25–27; Eph 1, 3–10; 3, 3–11; Col 1, 25–28.

*
1, 27: Jas 2, 5.	**1, 31:** Jer 9, 23; 2 Cor 10, 17.
1, 29: Eph 2, 9.	**2, 1:** 1 Cor 1, 17.
1, 30: Rom 4, 17 / 1 Cor 6, 11; Rom 3, 24–26; 2 Cor 5, 21 / Eph 1, 7; Col 1, 14; 1 Thes 5, 23.	**2, 2:** 1 Cor 1, 23; Gal 6, 14.
	2, 4: 1 Cor 4, 20; Rom 15, 19; 1 Thes 1, 5.
	2, 5: 2 Cor 4, 7.

we speak God's wisdom, mysterious, hidden, which God predetermined before the ages for our glory, ⁸† and which none of the rulers of this age knew; for if they had known it, they would not have crucified the Lord of glory. ⁹* But as it is written:

"What eye has not seen, and ear has not heard,
     and what has not entered the human heart,
     what God has prepared for those who
          love him,"

¹⁰* this God has revealed to us through the Spirit.

For the Spirit scrutinizes everything, even the depths of God. ¹¹ Among human beings, who knows what pertains to a person except the spirit of the person that is within? Similarly, no one knows what pertains to God except the Spirit of God.

¹² We have not received the spirit of the world but the Spirit that is from God, so that we may understand the things freely given us by God. ¹³† And we speak about them not with words taught by human wisdom, but with words taught by the Spirit, describing spiritual realities in spiritual terms.

¹⁴† Now the natural person does not accept what pertains to the Spirit of God, for to him it is foolishness, and he cannot understand it, because it is judged spiritually. ¹⁵† The spiritual person, however, can judge everything but is not subject to judgment by anyone.

¹⁶* For "who has known the mind of the Lord, so as to counsel him?" But we have the mind of Christ.

3 ¹† Brothers, I could not talk to you as spiritual people, but as fleshly people,† as infants in

We are God's Servants, Who Share a Common Mission!

LIVE IT!

Sometimes, Christians engage in destructive competition or are motivated by personal pride. Paul says clearly that all Christians are God's servants, should work together, and should have a common purpose. Whatever we do for the Gospel is part of Jesus' mission and has the same value for God. Paul uses two images to tell us this: "Therefore, neither the one who plants nor the one who waters is anything, but only God, who causes the growth" (3, 7) and "like a wise master builder I laid a foundation, and another is building upon it. . . . for no one can lay a foundation other than the one that is there, namely, Jesus Christ" (verses 10–11).

■ As a young person, how can you work cooperatively with other young people and with the adult community?

■ Express your gratitude for the building of the church done by previous generations of Christians. Pray that young Christians will embrace Jesus' mission with passion and with the global perspective needed at this time in history.

▶ I Cor 3, 1–15

---

† **2, 8:** *The rulers of this age:* this suggests not only the political leaders of the Jews and Romans under whom Jesus was crucified (cf Acts 4, 25–28) but also the cosmic powers behind them (cf Eph 1, 20–23; 3, 10). *They would not have crucified the Lord of glory:* they became the unwitting executors of God's plan, which will paradoxically bring about their own conquest and submission (15, 24–28).
2, 13: *In spiritual terms:* the Spirit teaches spiritual people a new mode of perception (12) and an appropriate language by which they can share their self-understanding, their knowledge about what God has done in them. The final phrase in v 13 can also be translated "describing spiritual realities to spiritual people," in which case it prepares for vv 14–16.
2, 14: *The natural person:* see the note on 3, 1.
2, 15: *The spiritual person . . . is not subject to judgment:* since spiritual persons have been given knowledge of what pertains to God

(11–12), they share in God's own capacity to judge. One to whom the mind of the Lord (and of Christ) is revealed (16) can be said to share in some sense in God's exemption from counseling and criticism.
3, 1–4: The Corinthians desire a sort of wisdom dialogue or colloquy with Paul; they are looking for solid, adult food, and he appears to disappoint their expectations. Paul counters: if such a dialogue has not yet taken place, the reason is that they are still at an immature stage of development (cf 2, 6).
3, 1: *Spiritual people . . . fleshly people:* Paul employs two clusters of concepts and terms to distinguish what later theology will call

2, 9: Is 64, 3.
2, 10: Mt 11, 25; 13, 11; 16, 17.
2, 16: Wis 9, 13; Is 40, 13; Rom 11, 34.

Christ. ²* I fed you milk, not solid food, because you were unable to take it. Indeed, you are still not able, even now, ³*† for you are still of the flesh. While there is jealousy and rivalry among you, are you not of the flesh and behaving in an ordinary human way? ⁴* Whenever someone says, "I belong to Paul," and another, "I belong to Apollos," are you not merely human?

The Role of God's Ministers†

⁵ What is Apollos, after all, and what is Paul? Ministers† through whom you became believers, just as the Lord assigned each one. ⁶* I planted, Apollos watered, but God caused the growth. ⁷ Therefore, neither the one who plants nor the one who waters is anything, but only God, who causes the growth. ⁸ The one who plants and the one who waters are equal, and each will receive wages in proportion to his labor. ⁹* For we are God's co-workers; you are God's field, God's building.

¹⁰† According to the grace of God given to me, like a wise master builder I laid a foundation, and another is building upon it. But each one must be careful how he builds upon it, ¹¹ for no one can lay a foundation other than the one that is there, namely, Jesus Christ. ¹² If anyone builds on this foundation with gold, silver, precious stones, wood, hay, or straw, ¹³*† the work of each will come to light, for the Day will disclose it. It will be revealed with fire, and the fire [itself] will test the quality of each one's work. ¹⁴ If the work stands that someone built upon the foundation, that person will receive a wage. ¹⁵† But if someone's work is burned up, that one will suffer loss; the person will be saved, but only as through fire. ¹⁶* Do you not know that you are the temple of God, and that the Spirit of God dwells in you? ¹⁷† If anyone destroys God's temple, God will destroy that

From the Bottom Up

The most important part of a building is its foundation. If the foundation is built well and with care, what is placed on it will last. And so it is with people. We all have before us a wide variety of construction materials—values, beliefs, and principles—to use in building the foundation of our life. Initially, our foundation is built through our family, using the values taught in schools and churches. In our adolescent years, most of us discover that other materials are available and that we must choose which ones to add to our foundation.

In 1 Cor 3, 10–17, Paul tells the people of Corinth that whatever they choose to use in building their foundation will show itself in the end. A poor foundation will lead to a poor end. He also reminds them that they are living temples of God, to be filled with the holy Spirit.

In your prayer, reflect or journal on the following questions:

- On what foundation do you want to build your life?
- What kind of person do you want to be remembered as when you are gone?
- What qualities, values, and virtues do you want to have? How can these be a sign of the Holy Spirit living within you?

▸ 1 Cor 3, 10–17

---

† the "natural" and the "supernatural." (1) The natural person (2, 14) is one whose existence, perceptions, and behavior are determined by purely natural principles, the *psyché* (2, 14) and the *sarx* (flesh, a biblical term that connotes creatureliness, 1.3). Such persons are only infants (1); they remain on a purely human level (*anthrōpoi*, 4). (2) On the other hand, they are called to be animated by a higher principle, the *pneuma*, God's spirit. They are to become spiritual (*pneumatikoi*, 1) and mature (2, 6) in their perceptions and behavior (cf Gal 5, 16–26). The culmination of existence in the Spirit is described in 15, 44–49.

3, 3–4: Jealousy, rivalry, and divisions in the community are symptoms of their arrested development; they reveal the immaturity both of their self-understanding (4) and of the judgments about their apostles (21).

3, 5—4, 5: The Corinthians tend to evaluate their leaders by the criteria of human wisdom and to exaggerate their importance. Paul views the role of the apostles in the light of his theology of spiritual gifts (cf chs 12–14, where the charism of the apostle heads the lists). The essential aspects of all spiritual gifts (12, 4–6 presents them as gifts of grace, as services, and as modes of activity) are exemplified by the apostolate, which is a gift of grace (3, 10) through which God works (3, 9) and a form of service (3, 5) for the common good (elsewhere expressed by the verb "build up," suggested here by the image of the building, 3, 9). The apostles serve the church, but their accountability is to God and to Christ (4, 1–5).

3, 5: *Ministers:* for other expressions of Paul's understanding of himself as minister or steward to the church, cf 4, 1; 9, 17.19–27; 2 Cor 3, 6–9; 4, 1; 5, 18; 6, 3–4; and 11, 23 (the climax of Paul's defense).

3, 10–11: There are diverse functions in the service of the community, but each individual's task is serious, and each will stand accountable for the quality of his contribution.

3, 13: *The Day:* the great day of Yahweh, the day of judgment, which can be a time of either gloom or joy. *Fire* both destroys and purifies.

3, 15: *Will be saved:* although Paul can envision very harsh divine punishment (cf 17), he appears optimistic about the success of divine corrective means both here and elsewhere (cf 5, 5; 11, 32 [discipline]). The text of v 15 has sometimes been used to support the notion of purgatory, though it does not envisage this.

3, 17: *Holy:* i.e., "belonging to God." The cultic sanctity of the community is a fundamental theological reality to which Paul frequently alludes (cf 1, 2.30; 6, 11; 7, 14).

3, 2: Heb 5, 12–14.
3, 3: Jas 3, 13–16.
3, 4: 1 Cor 1, 12.
3, 6: Acts 18, 1–11.24–28.
3, 9: Eph 2, 20–22; 1 Pt 2, 5.
3, 13: Mt 3, 11–12; 2 Thes 1, 7–10.
3, 16: 1 Cor 6, 19; 2 Cor 6, 16; Eph 2, 20–22.

person; for the temple of God, which you are, is holy.

18* Let no one deceive himself. If anyone among you considers himself wise in this age, let him become a fool so as to become wise. 19* For the wisdom of this world is foolishness in the eyes of God, for it is written:

"He catches the wise in their own ruses,"

20* and again:

"The Lord knows the thoughts of the wise, that they are vain."

We Are God's Temple

We are God's temple.
   We are rich, we are poor,
We are young, we are old,
We are male, we are female,
We are disabled, we are sick, we are healthy,
We are unborn,
We are all races and cultures.
O God,
Fill us with your spirit of unity.
Abolish the destructive forces of hate:
   prejudice, racism, physical and verbal
   abuse, abortion, murder, and euthanasia.
Break down the barriers that divide us.
Fill us with your loving spirit and an
   appreciation for the value of each and
   every life. Amen.

▶ 1 Cor 3, 16–17

21*† So let no one boast about human beings, for everything belongs to you, 22 Paul or Apollos or Cephas, or the world or life or death, or the present or the future: all belong to you, 23 and you to Christ, and Christ to God.

4 1* Thus should one regard us: as servants of Christ and stewards of the mysteries of God. 2 Now it is of course required of stewards that they be found trustworthy. 3 It does not concern me in the least that I be judged by you or any human tribunal; I do not even pass judgment on myself; 4* I am not conscious of anything against me, but I do not thereby stand acquitted; the one who judges me is the Lord. 5 Therefore, do not make any judgment before the appointed time, until the Lord comes, for he will bring to light what is hidden in darkness and will manifest the motives of our hearts, and then everyone will receive praise from God.

Paul's Life as Pattern†

6 I have applied these things to myself and Apollos for your benefit, brothers, so that you may learn from us not to go beyond what is written,† so that none of you will be inflated with pride in favor of one person over against another. 7 Who confers distinction upon you? What do you possess that you have not received? But if you have received it, why are you boasting as if you did not receive it? 8† You are already satisfied; you have already grown rich; you have become kings without us! Indeed, I wish that you had become kings, so that we also might become kings with you.

9*† For as I see it, God has exhibited us apostles as the last of all, like people sentenced to death, since we have become a spectacle to the world, to angels and human beings alike. 10* We are fools on

---

3, 21–23: These verses pick up the line of thought of 1, 10–13. If the Corinthians were genuinely wise (18–20), their perceptions would be reversed, and they would see everything in the world and all those with whom they exist in the church in their true relations with one another. Paul assigns all the persons involved in the theological universe a position on a scale: God, Christ, church members, church leaders. Read from top to bottom, the scale expresses ownership; read from bottom to top, the obligation to serve. This picture should be complemented by similar statements such as those in 8, 6 and 15, 20–28.
4, 6–21: This is an emotionally charged peroration to the discussion about divisions. It contains several exhortations and statements of Paul's purpose in writing (cf 6.14–17.21) that counterbalance the initial exhortation at 1, 10.
4, 6: That you may learn from us not to go beyond what is written: the words "to go" are not in the Greek, but have here been added as the minimum necessary to elicit sense from this difficult passage. It probably means that the Corinthians should avoid the false wisdom of vain speculation, contenting themselves with Paul's proclamation of the cross, which is the fulfillment of God's promises in the Old Testament (what is written). Inflated with pride: literally, "puffed up," i.e., arrogant, filled with a sense of self-importance. The term is particularly Pauline, found in the New Testament only in 1 Cor 4, 6.18–19; 5, 2; 8, 1; 13, 4; Col 2, 18 (cf the related noun at 2 Cor 12, 20). It sometimes occurs in conjunction with the theme of "boasting," as in vv 6–7 here.
4, 8: Satisfied . . . rich . . . kings: these three statements could also be punctuated as questions continuing the series begun in v 7.

In any case these expressions reflect a tendency at Corinth toward an overrealized eschatology, a form of self-deception that draws Paul's irony. The underlying attitude has implications for the Corinthians' thinking about other issues, notably morality and the resurrection, that Paul will address later in the letter.
4, 9–13: A rhetorically effective catalogue of the circumstances of apostolic existence, in the course of which Paul ironically contrasts his own sufferings with the Corinthians' illusion that they have passed beyond the folly of the passion and have already reached the condition of glory. His language echoes that of the beatitudes and woes, which assert a future reversal of present conditions. Their present sufferings ("to this very hour," 11) place the apostles in the class of those to whom the beatitudes promise future relief (Mt 5, 3–11; Lk 6, 20–23); whereas the Corinthians' image of themselves as "already" filled, rich, ruling (8), as wise, strong, and honored (10) places them paradoxically in the position of those whom the woes threaten with future undoing (Lk 6, 24–26). They have lost sight of the fact that the reversal is predicted for the future.

3, 18: 1 Cor 8, 2; Is 5, 21;
   Gal 6, 3.
3, 19: 1 Cor 1, 20 / Jb 5, 13.
3, 20: Ps 94, 11.
3, 21: 1 Cor 4, 6 / Rom 8, 32.
4, 1: Ti 1, 7; 1 Pt 4, 10.
4, 4: 2 Cor 1, 12 / Rom 2,

16; 2 Cor 5, 10.
4, 9: 1 Cor 15, 31; Rom 8,
   36; 2 Cor 4, 8–12; 11,
   23 / Heb 10, 33.
4, 10: 1 Cor 1, 18; 3, 18;
   2 Cor 11, 19 / 1 Cor 2,
   3; 2 Cor 13, 9.

1
C
O
R

Christ's account, but you are wise in Christ; we are weak, but you are strong; you are held in honor, but we in disrepute. [11]* To this very hour we go hungry and thirsty, we are poorly clad and roughly treated, we wander about homeless [12]* and we toil, working with our own hands. When ridiculed, we bless; when persecuted, we endure; [13] when slandered, we respond gently. We have become like the world's rubbish, the scum of all, to this very moment.

[14]† I am writing you this not to shame you, but to admonish you as my beloved children. [15]* Even if you should have countless guides to Christ, yet you do not have many fathers, for I became your father in Christ Jesus through the gospel. [16]* Therefore, I urge you, be imitators of me. [17]* For this reason I am sending you Timothy, who is my beloved and faithful son in the Lord; he will remind you of my ways in Christ [Jesus], just as I teach them everywhere in every church.

[18]† Some have become inflated with pride, as if I were not coming to you. [19] But I will come to you soon, if the Lord is willing, and I shall ascertain not the talk of these inflated people but their power. [20]* For the kingdom of God is not a matter of talk but of power. [21]* Which do you prefer? Shall I come to you with a rod, or with love and a gentle spirit?

B. Moral Disorders†

A Case of Incest†

5 [1]* It is widely reported that there is immorality among you, and immorality of a kind not found even among pagans—a man living with his father's wife. [2]† And you are inflated with pride. Should you not rather have been sorrowful? The one who did this deed should be expelled from your midst. [3]* I, for my part, although absent in body but present in spirit, have already, as if present, pronounced judgment on the one who has committed this deed, [4] in the name of [our] Lord Jesus: when you have gathered together and I am with you in spirit with the power of the Lord Jesus, [5]*† you are to deliver this man to Satan for the destruction of his flesh, so that his spirit may be saved on the day of the Lord.

[6]† Your boasting is not appropriate. Do you not know that a little yeast leavens all the dough? [7]*† Clear out the old yeast, so that you may become a fresh batch of dough, inasmuch as you are unleavened. For our paschal lamb, Christ, has been sacrificed. [8]* Therefore, let us celebrate the feast, not with the old yeast, the yeast of malice and wickedness, but with the unleavened bread of sincerity and truth.

[9]† I wrote you in my letter not to associate with immoral people, [10]* not at all referring to the immoral of this world or the greedy and robbers or idolaters; for you would then have to leave the world. [11]* But I now write to you not to associate with anyone named a brother, if he is immoral, greedy, an idolater, a slanderer, a drunkard, or a robber, not even to eat with such a person. [12] For why should I be judging outsiders? Is it not your business to judge those within? [13]* God will judge

---

4, 14–17: *My beloved children:* the close of the argument is dominated by the tender metaphor of the father who not only gives his children life but also educates them. Once he has begotten them through his preaching, Paul continues to present the gospel to them existentially, by his life as well as by his word, and they are to learn, as children do, by imitating their parents (16). The reference to the *rod* in v 21 belongs to the same image-complex. So does the image of the *ways* in v 17: the ways that Paul teaches everywhere, "his ways in Christ Jesus," mean a behavior pattern quite different from the human ways along which the Corinthians are walking (3, 3).

4, 18–21: Verse 20 picks up the contrast between a certain kind of talk (*logos*) and true power (*dynamis*) from 1, 17–18 and 2, 4–5. The kingdom, which many of them imagine to be fully present in their lives (8), will be rather unexpectedly disclosed in the strength of Paul's encounter with them, if they make a powerful intervention on his part necessary. Compare the similar ending to an argument in 2 Cor 13, 1–4.10.

5, 1—6, 20: Paul now takes up a number of other matters that require regulation. These have come to his attention by hearsay (5, 1), probably in reports brought by "Chloe's people" (1, 11).

5, 1–13: Paul first deals with the incestuous union of a man with his stepmother (1–8) and then attempts to clarify general admonitions he has given about associating with fellow Christians guilty of immorality (9–13). Each of these three brief paragraphs expresses the same idea: the need of separation between the holy and the unholy.

5, 2: *Inflated with pride:* this remark and the reference to *boasting* in v 6 suggest that they are proud of themselves despite the infection in their midst, tolerating and possibly even approving the situation. The attitude expressed in 6, 2.13 may be influencing their thinking in this case.

5, 5: *Deliver this man to Satan:* once the sinner is expelled from the church, the sphere of Jesus' lordship and victory over sin, he will be in the region outside over which Satan is still master. *For the destruction of his flesh:* the purpose of the penalty is medicinal:

through affliction, sin's grip over him may be destroyed and the path to repentance and reunion laid open. With Paul's instructions for an excommunication ceremony here, contrast his recommendations for the reconciliation of a sinner in 2 Cor 2, 5–11.

5, 6: *A little yeast:* yeast, which induces fermentation, is a natural symbol for a source of corruption that becomes all-pervasive. The expression is proverbial.

5, 7–8: In the Jewish calendar, Passover was followed immediately by the festival of Unleavened Bread. In preparation for this feast all traces of old bread were removed from the house, and during the festival only unleavened bread was eaten. The sequence of these two feasts provides Paul with an image of Christian existence: Christ's death (the Jewish Passover celebration) is followed by the life of the Christian community, marked by newness, purity, and integrity (a perpetual feast of unleavened bread). Paul may have been writing around Passover time (cf 16, 5); this is a little Easter homily, the earliest in Christian literature.

5, 9–13: Paul here corrects a misunderstanding of his earlier directives against associating with immoral fellow Christians. He concedes the impossibility of avoiding contact with sinners in society at large but urges the Corinthians to maintain the inner purity of their own community.

4, 11: Rom 8, 35; 2 Cor 11, 23–27.	**5, 1:** Lv 18, 7–8; 20, 11; Dt 27, 20.
4, 12: Acts 9, 6–14; 18, 3; 20, 34; 1 Thes 2, 9 / 1 Pt 3, 9.	**5, 3:** Col 2, 5.
	5, 5: 1 Tm 1, 20.
	5, 6: Gal 5, 9.
4, 15: Gal 4, 19; Phlm 10.	**5, 7:** Ex 12, 1–13; Dt 16, 1–2; 1 Pt 1, 19.
4, 16: 1 Cor 11, 1; Phil 3, 17; 4, 9; 1 Thes 1, 6; 2 Thes 3, 7.9.	**5, 8:** Ex 12, 15–20; 13, 7; Dt 16, 3.
4, 17: 1 Cor 16, 10; Acts 19, 22.	**5, 10:** 1 Cor 10, 27; Jn 17, 15.
4, 20: 1 Cor 2, 4; 1 Thes 1, 5.	**5, 11:** Mt 18, 17; 2 Thes 3, 6.14; 2 Jn 10.
4, 21: 2 Cor 1, 23; 10, 2.	**5, 13:** Dt 13, 6; 17, 7; 22, 24.

those outside. "Purge the evil person from your midst."

Lawsuits before Unbelievers

6 [1]† How can any one of you with a case against another dare to bring it to the unjust for judgment instead of to the holy ones? [2]*† Do you not know that the holy ones will judge the world? If the world is to be judged by you, are you unqualified for the lowest law courts? [3] Do you not know that we will judge angels? Then why not everyday matters? [4] If, therefore, you have courts for everyday matters, do you seat as judges people of no standing in the church? [5] I say this to shame you. Can it be that there is not one among you wise enough to be able to settle a case between brothers? [6] But rather brother goes to court against brother, and that before unbelievers?

[7]* Now indeed [then] it is, in any case, a failure on your part that you have lawsuits against one another. Why not rather put up with injustice? Why not rather let yourselves be cheated? [8] Instead, you inflict injustice and cheat, and this to brothers. [9]*† Do you not know that the unjust will not inherit the kingdom of God? Do not be deceived; neither fornicators nor idolaters nor adulterers nor boy prostitutes† nor sodomites [10] nor thieves nor the greedy nor drunkards nor slanderers nor robbers will inherit the kingdom of God. [11]* That is what some of you used to be; but now you have had yourselves washed, you were sanctified, you were justified in the name of the Lord Jesus Christ and in the Spirit of our God.

Sexual Immorality†

[12]* "Everything is lawful for me," †but not everything is beneficial. "Everything is lawful for me," but I will not let myself be dominated by anything.

Living Well

Some people think that God or the Christian religion is primarily interested in preventing us from doing fun things. They imagine the Bible as a book of thou-shalt-nots, and the church as a place where they are told to avoid enjoying themselves!

Paul helps us understand that God's desire is for us to live well. All good gifts from God, including food and sexuality, are meant to be enjoyed to the fullest. But they also can be misused, and if they are, we miss out on the joy and purpose intended by God.

For example, in 1 Cor 6, 12–20, Paul affirms that sexual intercourse is meant to bond a man and a woman for life. Fornication—sexual intercourse between people who are not married—defeats its true purpose. Fornication diminishes the full joy and beauty of sexual intimacy as intended by God.

God created our sexuality. Our sexual desires—felt keenly during adolescence!—are not sinful but a normal part of being human. As the author of our sexuality, God wants us not to be hurt by this gift but instead to experience its fullness in marriage.

▶ 1 Cor 6, 12–20

6, 1–11: Christians at Corinth are suing one another before pagan judges in Roman courts. A barrage of rhetorical questions (1–9) betrays Paul's indignation over this practice, which he sees as an infringement upon the holiness of the Christian community.

6, 2–3: The principle to which Paul appeals is an eschatological prerogative promised to Christians: they are to share with Christ the judgment of the world (cf Dn 7, 22.27). Hence they ought to be able to settle minor disputes within the community.

6, 9–10: A catalogue of typical vices that exclude from the kingdom of God and that should be excluded from God's church. Such lists (cf 5, 10) reflect the common moral sensibility of the New Testament period.

6, 9: The Greek word translated as *boy prostitutes* may refer to catamites, i.e., boys or young men who were kept for purposes of prostitution, a practice not uncommon in the Greco-Roman world. In Greek mythology this was the function of Ganymede, the "cup-bearer of the gods," whose Latin name was Catamitus. The term translated *sodomites* refers to adult males who indulged in homosexual practices with such boys. See similar condemnations of such practices in Rom 1, 26–27; 1 Tm 1, 10.

6, 12–20: Paul now turns to the opinion of some Corinthians that sexuality is a morally indifferent area (12–13). This leads him to explain the mutual relation between the Lord Jesus and our bodies (13b) in a densely packed paragraph that contains elements of a profound theology of sexuality (15–20).

6, 12–13: *Everything is lawful for me:* the Corinthians may have derived this slogan from Paul's preaching about Christian freedom, but they mean something different by it: they consider sexual satisfaction a matter as indifferent as food, and they attribute no lasting significance to bodily functions (13a). Paul begins to deal with the slogan by two qualifications, which suggest principles for judging sexual activity. *Not everything is beneficial:* cf 10, 23, and the whole argument of chs 8–10 on the finality of freedom and moral activity. *Not let myself be dominated:* certain apparently free actions may involve in fact a secret servitude in conflict with the lordship of Jesus.

6, 2: Wis 3, 8; Mt 19, 28; Rv 20, 4.
6, 7: Mt 5, 38–42; Rom 12, 17–21; 1 Thes 5, 15.
6, 9: 1 Cor 15, 50; Gal 5, 19–21; Eph 5, 5.
6, 11: Ti 3, 3–7.
6, 12: 1 Cor 10, 23.

13 "Food for the stomach and the stomach for food," but God will do away with both the one and the other. The body, however, is not for immorality, but for the Lord, and the Lord is for the body; 14* God raised the Lord and will also raise us by his power.

15*† Do you not know that your bodies are members of Christ? Shall I then take Christ's members and make them the members of a prostitute? Of course not! 16* [Or] do you not know that anyone who joins himself to a prostitute becomes one body with her? For "the two," it says, "will become one flesh." 17* But whoever is joined to the Lord becomes one spirit with him. 18† Avoid immorality. Every other sin a person commits is outside the body, but the immoral person sins against his own body. 19*† Do you not know that your body is a temple of the holy Spirit within you, whom you have from God, and that you are not your own? 20* For you have been purchased at a price. Therefore glorify God in your body.

III: Answers to the Corinthians' Questions

A. Marriage and Virginity†

Advice to the Married†

7 ¹† Now in regard to the matters about which you wrote: "It is a good thing for a man not to touch a woman," ² but because of cases of immorality every man should have his own wife, and every woman her own husband. ³ The husband should fulfill his duty toward his wife, and likewise the wife toward her husband. ⁴ A wife does not have authority over her own body, but rather her husband, and similarly a husband does not have authority over his own body, but rather his

wife. ⁵ Do not deprive each other, except perhaps by mutual consent for a time, to be free for prayer, but then return to one another, so that Satan may not tempt you through your lack of self-control.

?did you KNOW?

Strange Advice!?

First Corinthians, chapter 7, says people shouldn't marry, uncircumcised people shouldn't get circumcised, and slaves should remain slaves.

Why is Paul giving such strange advice? Because Paul thinks that Jesus will be returning soon to establish God's Reign for all time (verse 31). So he advises the Corinthians to remain in whatever condition they were called, in order to avoid the confusion that comes when making big life changes.

But Jesus didn't come back during Paul's time. In fact, we are still waiting for his return. When is Jesus going to come again? Don't try to figure it out. Jesus told us we will never know (Mt 24, 36–44). But whatever our state of life is or will become, we would be wise to follow Paul's intent, which is to promote "propriety and adherence to the Lord without distraction" (1 Cor 7, 35).

▸ 1 Corinthians, chapter 7

6, 15b–16: *A prostitute:* the reference may be specifically to religious prostitution, an accepted part of pagan culture at Corinth and elsewhere; but the prostitute also serves as a symbol for any sexual relationship that conflicts with Christ's claim over us individually. *The two . . . will become one flesh:* the text of Gn 2, 24 is applied positively to human marriage in Matthew and Mark, and in Eph 5, 29–32: love of husband and wife reflect the love of Christ for his church. The application of the text to union with a prostitute is jarring, for such a union is a parody, an antitype of marriage, which does conflict with Christ's claim over us. This explains the horror expressed in 15b.

6, 18: *Against his own body:* expresses the intimacy and depth of sexual disorder, which violates the very orientation of our bodies.

6, 19–20: Paul's vision becomes trinitarian. *A temple:* sacred by reason of God's gift, his indwelling Spirit. *Not your own:* but "for the Lord," who acquires ownership by the act of redemption. *Glorify God in your body:* the argument concludes with a positive imperative to supplement the negative "avoid immorality" of v 18. Far from being a terrain that is morally indifferent, the area of sexuality is one in which our relationship with God (and his Christ and his Spirit) is very intimately expressed: he is either highly glorified or deeply offended.

7, 1–40: Paul now begins to answer questions addressed to him by the Corinthians (7, 1—11, 1). The first of these concerns marriage. This chapter contains advice both to the married (1–16) and to the unmarried (25–38) or widowed (39–40); these two parts are separat-

ed by vv 17–24, which enunciate a principle applicable to both.

7, 1–16: It seems that some Christians in Corinth were advocating asceticism in sexual matters. The pattern *it is a good thing . . . , but* occurs twice (1–2.8–9; cf 26), suggesting that in this matter as in others the Corinthians have seized upon a genuine value but are exaggerating or distorting it in some way. Once again Paul calls them to a more correct perspective and a better sense of their own limitations. The phrase *it is a good thing* (1) may have been the slogan of the ascetic party at Corinth.

7, 1–7: References to Paul's own behavior (7–8) suggest that his celibate way of life and his preaching to the unmarried (cf 25–35) have given some the impression that asceticism within marriage, i.e., suspension of normal sexual relations, would be a laudable ideal. Paul points to their experience of widespread immorality to caution them against overestimating their own strength (2); as individuals they may not have the particular gift that makes such asceticism feasible (7) and hence are to abide by the principle to be explained in vv 17–24.

6, 14: Rom 8, 11; 2 Cor 4, 14.
6, 15: 1 Cor 12, 27; Rom 6, 12–13; 12, 5; Eph 5, 30.
6, 16: Gn 2, 24; Mt 19, 5; Mk 10, 8; Eph 5, 31.
6, 17: Rom 8, 9–10; 2 Cor 3, 17.
6, 19: 1 Cor 3, 16–17; Rom 5, 5.
6, 20: 1 Cor 3, 23; 7, 23; Acts 20, 28 / Rom 12, 1; Phil 1, 20.

6† This I say by way of concession, however, not as a command. 7*† Indeed, I wish everyone to be as I am, but each has a particular gift from God, one of one kind and one of another.

8*† Now to the unmarried and to widows I say: It is a good thing for them to remain as they are, as I do, 9 but if they cannot exercise self-control they should marry, for it is better to marry than to be on fire. 10*† To the married, however, I give this instruction (not I, but the Lord): a wife should not separate from her husband 11 —and if she does separate she must either remain single or become reconciled to her husband—and a husband should not divorce his wife.

12† To the rest I say (not the Lord): if any brother has a wife who is an unbeliever, and she is willing to go on living with him, he should not divorce her; 13 and if any woman has a husband who is an unbeliever, and he is willing to go on living with her, she should not divorce her husband. 14* For the unbelieving husband is made holy through his wife, and the unbelieving wife is made holy through the brother. Otherwise your children would be unclean, whereas in fact they are holy.

15† If the unbeliever separates, however, let him separate. The brother or sister is not bound in such cases; God has called you to peace. 16 For how do you know, wife, whether you will save your husband; or how do you know, husband, whether you will save your wife?

The Life That the Lord Has Assigned

17† Only, everyone should live as the Lord has assigned, just as God called each one. I give this order in all the churches. 18* Was someone called after he had been circumcised? He should not try to undo his circumcision. Was an uncircumcised person called? He should not be circumcised. 19* Circumcision means nothing, and uncircumcision means nothing; what matters is keeping God's commandments. 20 Everyone should remain in the state in which he was called.

21 Were you a slave when you were called? Do not be concerned but, even if you can gain your freedom, make the most of it. 22* For the slave called in the Lord is a freed person in the Lord, just as the free person who has been called is a slave of Christ. 23* You have been purchased at a price. Do not become slaves to human beings. 24 Brothers, everyone should continue before God in the state in which he was called.

Advice to Virgins and Widows

25† Now in regard to virgins I have no commandment from the Lord, but I give my opinion as one who by the Lord's mercy is trustworthy. 26* So this is what I think best because of the present distress: that it is a good thing for a person to remain as he is. 27 Are you bound to a wife? Do not seek a separation. Are you free of a wife? Then do not look for a wife. 28 If you marry, however, you do not sin, nor does an unmarried woman sin if she marries; but such people will experience affliction in their earthly life, and I would like to spare you that.

29*† I tell you, brothers, the time is running out. From now on, let those having wives act as not having them, 30 those weeping as not weeping, those rejoicing as not rejoicing, those buying as not owning, 31 those using the world as not using it fully. For the world in its present form is passing away.

32 I should like you to be free of anxieties. An unmarried man is anxious about the things of the Lord, how he may please the Lord. 33* But a married man is anxious about the things of the world, how he may please his wife, 34* and he is divided. An unmarried woman or a virgin is anxious about the things of the Lord, so that she may be holy in

---

7, 6: *By way of concession:* this refers most likely to the concession mentioned in v 5a: temporary interruption of relations for a legitimate purpose.

7, 7: *A particular gift from God:* use of the term *charisma* suggests that marriage and celibacy may be viewed in the light of Paul's theology of spiritual gifts (chs 12–14).

7, 8: Paul was obviously unmarried when he wrote this verse. Some interpreters believe that he had previously been married and widowed; there is no clear evidence either for or against this view, which was expressed already at the end of the second century by Clement of Alexandria.

7, 10–11: *(Not I, but the Lord):* Paul reminds the married of Jesus' principle of nonseparation (Mk 10, 9). This is one of his rare specific references to the teaching of Jesus.

7, 12–14: *To the rest:* marriages in which only one partner is a baptized Christian. Jesus' prohibition against divorce is not addressed to them, but Paul extends the principle of nonseparation to such unions, provided they are marked by peacefulness and shared sanctification.

7, 15–16: *If the unbeliever separates:* the basis of the "Pauline privilege" in Catholic marriage legislation.

7, 17–24: On the ground that distinct human conditions are less significant than the whole new existence opened up by God's call, Paul urges them to be less concerned with changing their states of life than with answering God's call where it finds them. The principle applies both to the married state (1–16) and to the unmarried (25–38).

7, 25–28: Paul is careful to explain that the principle of v 17 does not bind under sin but that present earthly conditions make it advantageous for the unmarried to remain as they are (28). These remarks must be complemented by the statement about "particular gifts" from v 7.

7, 29–31: *The world . . . is passing away:* Paul advises Christians to go about the ordinary activities of life in a manner different from those who are totally immersed in them and unaware of their transitoriness.

7, 7: Mt 19, 11–12.	6; 6, 15.
7, 8: 1 Tm 5, 11–16 / 1 Cor 9, 5.	7, 22: Eph 6, 5–9; Col 3, 11; Phlm 16.
7, 10–11: Mt 5, 32; 19, 9.	7, 23: 1 Cor 6, 20.
7, 14: Rom 11, 16.	7, 26: 1 Cor 7, 8.
7, 18: 1 Mc 1, 15 / Acts 15, 1–2.	7, 29: Rom 13, 11.
7, 19: Rom 2, 25.29; Gal 5,	7, 33: Lk 14, 20.
	7, 34: 1 Tm 5, 5.

1
C
O
R

both body and spirit. A married woman, on the other hand, is anxious about the things of the world, how she may please her husband. ³⁵* I am telling you this for your own benefit, not to impose a restraint upon you, but for the sake of propriety and adherence to the Lord without distraction.

³⁶† If anyone thinks he is behaving improperly toward his virgin, and if a critical moment has come† and so it has to be, let him do as he wishes. He is committing no sin; let them get married. ³⁷ The one who stands firm in his resolve, however, who is not under compulsion but has power over his own will, and has made up his mind to keep his virgin, will be doing well. ³⁸ So then, the one who marries his virgin does well; the one who does not marry her will do better.

³⁹*† A wife is bound to her husband as long as he lives. But if her husband dies, she is free to be married to whomever she wishes, provided that it be in the Lord. ⁴⁰* She is more blessed, though, in my opinion, if she remains as she is, and I think that I too have the Spirit of God.

B. Offerings to Idols†

Knowledge Insufficient

8 ¹* Now in regard to meat sacrificed to idols:† we realize that "all of us have knowledge"; knowledge inflates with pride, but love builds up. ² If anyone supposes he knows something, he does not yet know as he ought to know. ³* But if one loves God, one is known by him.

⁴* So about the eating of meat sacrificed to idols: we know that "there is no idol in the world," and that "there is no God but one." ⁵ Indeed, even though there are so-called gods in heaven and on

Restrain Your Ego!

LIVE IT!

Maria's parents have stopped drinking alcohol. Not that they ever drank to excess. But for months, Maria bugged them, "If I can't drink, then why do you?" Because she accepted none of their arguments, they agreed that they would stop until she reached legal age.

Crazy? Not according to Paul. He recommends something similar. Paul recognizes that it is not necessarily wrong for the community of Christians in Corinth to eat meat sacrificed to idols, or pagan gods, because they don't believe in those gods. Still, he recommends that they not do it because some members of the community find it upsetting. For Paul, keeping unity is more important than always "being right."

Do you ever do things that aren't necessarily wrong just because it's your right? like whistle around a sibling who cannot stand it? or pick a sweater for the family picture that doesn't match anyone else's? or, when your younger brothers and sisters are around, watch a television show that's okay for you but not for them? When you find yourself doing something like this, think about Paul's advice. Are you making your ego more important than other people's feelings?

▶ I Cor 8, 1–13

---

† **7, 36–38:** The passage is difficult to interpret, because it is unclear whether Paul is thinking of a father and his unmarried daughter (or slave), or of a couple engaged in a betrothal or spiritual marriage. The general principles already enunciated apply: there is no question of sin, even if they should marry, but staying as they are is "better" (for the reasons mentioned in 28–35). Once again the *charisma* of v 7, which applies also to the unmarried (8–9), is to be presupposed.

7, 36: *A critical moment has come:* either because the woman will soon be beyond marriageable age, or because their passions are becoming uncontrollable (cf 9).

7, 39–40: Application of the principles to the case of widows. If they do choose to remarry, they ought to prefer Christian husbands.

8, 1—11, 1: The Corinthians' second question concerns meat that has been sacrificed to idols; in this area they were exhibiting a disordered sense of liberation that Paul here tries to rectify. These chapters contain a sustained and unified argument that illustrates Paul's method of theological reflection on a moral dilemma. Although the problem with which he is dealing is dated, the guidelines for moral decisions that he offers are of lasting validity.

Essentially Paul urges them to take a communitarian rather than an individualistic view of their Christian freedom. Many decisions that they consider pertinent only to their private relationship with God have, in fact, social consequences. Nor can moral decisions be determined by merely theoretical considerations; they must be based on concrete circumstances, specifically on the value and needs of other individuals and on mutual responsibility within the community. Paul here introduces the theme of "building up" (*oikodomē*), i.e., of contributing by individual action to the welfare and growth of the community. This theme will be further developed in ch 14; see the note on 14, 3b-5. Several years later Paul would again deal with the problem of meat sacrificed to idols in Rom 14, 1—15, 6.

8, 1a: *Meat sacrificed to idols:* much of the food consumed in the city could have passed through pagan religious ceremonies before finding its way into markets and homes. *"All of us have knowledge":* a slogan, similar to 6, 12, which reveals the self-image of the Corinthians. Verse 4 will specify the content of this knowledge.

7, 35: Lk 10, 39–42.
7, 39: Rom 7, 2.
7, 40: 1 Cor 7, 25.
8, 1: Rom 15, 14 / 1 Cor 13,

1–13; Rom 14, 15.19.
8, 3: Rom 8, 29; Gal 4, 9.
8, 4: 1 Cor 10, 19; Dt 6, 4.

earth (there are, to be sure, many "gods" and many "lords"), [6]*† yet for us there is

one God, the Father,
from whom all things are and for whom
we exist,
and one Lord, Jesus Christ,
through whom all things are and through
whom we exist.

Practical Rules

[7]* But not all have this knowledge. There are some who have been so used to idolatry up until now that, when they eat meat sacrificed to idols, their conscience, which is weak, is defiled. [8]*† Now food will not bring us closer to God. We are no worse off if we do not eat, nor are we better off if we do. [9]* But make sure that this liberty of yours in no way becomes a stumbling block to the weak. [10] If someone sees you, with your knowledge, reclining at table in the temple of an idol, may not his conscience too, weak as it is, be "built up" to eat the meat sacrificed to idols? [11]* Thus through your knowledge, the weak person is brought to destruction, the brother for whom Christ died. [12] When you sin in this way against your brothers and wound their consciences, weak as they are, you are sinning against Christ. [13]*† Therefore, if food causes my brother to sin, I will never eat meat again, so that I may not cause my brother to sin.

Paul's Rights as an Apostle

9 [1]*† Am I not free? Am I not an apostle? Have I not seen Jesus our Lord? Are you not my work in the Lord? [2] Although I may not be an apostle for others, certainly I am for you, for you are the seal of my apostleship in the Lord.

[3]† My defense against those who would pass judgment on me is this. [4]† Do we not have the right to eat and drink? [5] Do we not have the right to take along a Christian wife, as do the rest of the apostles, and the brothers of the Lord, and Cephas? [6]* Or is it only myself and Barnabas who do not have the right not to work? [7]* Who ever serves as a soldier at his own expense? Who plants a vineyard without eating its produce? Or who shepherds a flock without using some of the milk from the flock? [8] Am I saying this on human authority, or does not the law also speak of these things? [9]* It is written in the law of Moses, "You shall not muzzle an ox while it is treading out the grain." Is God concerned about oxen, [10]* or is he not really speaking for our sake? It was written for our sake, because the plowman should plow in hope, and the thresher in hope of receiving a share. [11]* If we have sown spiritual seed for you, is it a great thing that we reap a material harvest from you? [12]*† If others share this rightful claim on you, do not we still more?

Reason for Not Using His Rights

Yet we have not used this right. On the contrary, we endure everything so as not to place an obstacle to the gospel of Christ. [13]*† Do you not know that those who perform the temple services eat [what] belongs to the temple, and those who minister at the altar share in the sacrificial offerings? [14]* In the same way, the Lord ordered that those who preach

---

8, 6: This verse rephrases the monotheistic confession of v 4 in such a way as to contrast it with polytheism (5) and to express our relationship with the one God in concrete, i.e., in personal and Christian terms. *And for whom we exist:* since the Greek contains no verb here and the action intended must be inferred from the preposition *eis,* another translation is equally possible: "toward whom we return." *Through whom all things:* the earliest reference in the New Testament to Jesus' role in creation.

8, 8–9: Although the food in itself is morally neutral, extrinsic circumstances may make the eating of it harmful. *A stumbling block:* the image is that of tripping or causing someone to fall (cf 13; 9, 12; 10, 12.32; 2 Cor 6, 3; Rom 14, 13.20–21). This is a basic moral imperative for Paul, a counterpart to the positive imperative to "build one another up"; compare the expression "giving offense" as opposed to "pleasing" in 10, 32–33.

8, 13: His own course is clear: he will avoid any action that might harm another Christian. This statement prepares for the paradigmatic development in ch 9.

9, 1–27: This chapter is an emotionally charged expansion of Paul's appeal to his own example in 8, 13; its purpose is to reinforce the exhortation of 8, 9. The two opening questions introduce the themes of Paul's freedom and his apostleship (1), themes that the chapter will develop in reverse order, vv 1–18 treating the question of his apostleship and the rights that flow from it, and vv 19–27 exploring dialectically the nature of Paul's freedom. The language is highly rhetorical, abounding in questions, wordplays, paradoxes, images, and appeals to authority and experience. The argument is unified by repetitions; its articulations are highlighted by inclusions and transitional verses.

9, 3: *My defense against those who would pass judgment on me:* the reference to a defense (*apologia*) is surprising, and suggests that

Paul is incorporating some material here that he has previously used in another context. The defense will touch on two points: the fact of Paul's rights as an apostle (4–12a and 13–14) and his nonuse of those rights (12b and 15–18).

9, 4–12a: Apparently some believe that Paul is not equal to the other apostles and therefore does not enjoy equal privileges. His defense on this point (here and in 13–14) reinforces the assertion of his apostolic character in v 2. It consists of a series of analogies from natural equity (7) and religious custom (13) designed to establish his equal right to support from the churches (4—6.11–12a); these analogies are confirmed by the authority of the law (8–10) and of Jesus himself (14).

9, 12b: It appears, too, that suspicion or misunderstanding has been created by Paul's practice of not living from his preaching. The first reason he asserts in defense of this practice is an entirely apostolic one; it anticipates the developments to follow in vv 19–22. He will give a second reason in vv 15–18.

9, 13–14: The position of these verses produces an interlocking

8, 6: Mal 2, 10 / Rom 11, 36; Eph 4, 5–6 / 1 Cor 1, 2–3 / Jn 1, 3; Col 1, 16.	9, 6: Acts 4, 36–37; 13, 1–2; Gal 2, 1.9.13; Col 4, 10.
8, 7: 1 Cor 10, 28; Rom 14, 23 / Rom 14, 1; 15, 1.	9, 7: 2 Tm 2, 3–4.
8, 8: Rom 14, 17.	9, 9: Dt 25, 4; 1 Tm 5, 18.
8, 9: Rom 14, 13.20–21.	9, 10: 2 Tm 2, 6.
8, 11: Rom 14, 15.20.	9, 11: Rom 15, 27.
8, 13: Mt 18, 6; Rom 14, 20–21.	9, 12: 2 Cor 11, 7–12; 12, 13–18; 2 Thes 3, 6–12.
9, 1: 1 Cor 9, 19 / 2 Cor 12, 12 / 1 Cor 15, 8–9; Acts 9, 17; 26, 16.	9, 13: Nm 18, 8.31; Dt 18, 1–5.
	9, 14: Mt 10, 10; Lk 10, 7–8.

the gospel should live by the gospel.

¹⁵*† I have not used any of these rights, however, nor do I write this that it be done so in my case. I would rather die. Certainly no one is going to nullify my boast. ¹⁶* If I preach the gospel, this is no reason for me to boast, for an obligation has been imposed on me, and woe to me if I do not preach it! ¹⁷* If I do so willingly, I have a recompense, but if unwillingly, then I have been entrusted with a stewardship. ¹⁸* What then is my recompense? That, when I preach, I offer the gospel free of charge so as not to make full use of my right in the gospel.

All Things to All

¹⁹*† Although I am free in regard to all, I have made myself a slave to all so as to win over as many as possible. ²⁰ To the Jews I became like a Jew to win over Jews; to those under the law I became like one under the law—though I myself am not under the law—to win over those under the law. ²¹ To those outside the law I became like one outside the law—

though I am not outside God's law but within the law of Christ—to win over those outside the law. ²²* To the weak I became weak, to win over the weak. I have become all things to all, to save at least some. ²³ All this I do for the sake of the gospel, so that I too may have a share in it.

²⁴*† Do you not know that the runners in the stadium all run in the race, but only one wins the prize? Run so as to win. ²⁵* Every athlete exercises discipline in every way. They do it to win a perishable crown, but we an imperishable one. ²⁶ Thus I do not run aimlessly; I do not fight as if I were shadowboxing. ²⁷† No, I drive my body and train it, for fear that, after having preached to others, I myself should be disqualified.

Warning against Overconfidence

10 ¹*† I do not want you to be unaware, brothers, that our ancestors were all under the cloud and all passed through the sea, ²* and all of them were baptized into Moses in the cloud and in

Spiritual Perseverance

LIVE IT!

Did you know that Michael Jordan—once the points leader of the record-setting Chicago Bulls—had difficulty making his high school varsity basketball team the first year he tried out? He could have quit trying, but he set a goal for himself and made practicing over and over a priority for his daily life. Not only did he finally make the team, he broke state scoring records and was named all-state. And that was just the beginning!

Persevering means setting priorities, sticking to them even when you get discouraged, and trying over and over to accomplish your goals. For the next six months, set yourself a goal that will help you grow closer to God. What will you have to do to accomplish it? What priorities must you establish? As 1 Cor 9, 24–27 says, run your race by staying focused on your goal!

▶ 1 Cor 9, 24–27

† of the two points of Paul's defense. These arguments by analogy (13) and from authority (14) belong with those of vv 7–10 and ground the first point. But Paul defers them until he has had a chance to mention "the gospel of Christ" (12b), after which it is more appropriate to mention Jesus' injunction to his preachers and to argue by analogy from the sacred temple service to his own liturgical service, the preaching of the gospel (cf Rom 1, 9; 15, 16).

9, 15–18: Paul now assigns a more personal motive to his nonuse of his right to support. His preaching is not a service spontaneously undertaken on his part but a stewardship imposed by a sort of divine compulsion. Yet to merit any reward he must bring some spontaneous quality to his service, and this he does by freely renouncing his right to support. The material here is quite similar to that contained in Paul's "defense" at 2 Cor 11, 5–12; 12, 11–18.

9, 19–23: In a rhetorically balanced series of statements Paul expands and generalizes the picture of his behavior and explores the paradox of apostolic freedom. It is not essentially freedom *from* restraint but freedom *for* service—a possibility of constructive activity.

9, 24–27: A series of miniparables from sports, appealing to readers familiar with Greek gymnasia and the nearby Isthmian games.

9, 27: *For fear that . . . I myself should be disqualified:* a final paradoxical turn to the argument: what appears at first a free, sponta-

neous renunciation of rights (12–18) seems subsequently to be required for fulfillment of Paul's stewardship (to preach effectively he must reach his hearers wherever they are, 19–22), and finally is seen to be necessary for his own salvation (23–27). Mention of the possibility of disqualification provides a transition to ch 10.

10, 1–5: Paul embarks unexpectedly upon a panoramic survey of the events of the Exodus period. The privileges of Israel in the wilderness are described in terms that apply strictly only to the realities of the new covenant ("baptism," "spiritual food and drink"); interpreted in this way they point forward to the Christian experience (1–4). But those privileges did not guarantee God's permanent pleasure (5).

*
9, 15: 2 Cor 11, 9–10.	9, 25: 2 Tm 2, 5 / 2 Tm 4,
9, 16: Acts 26, 14–18.	7–8; Jas 1, 12; 1 Pt
9, 17: 1 Cor 4, 1; Gal 2, 7.	5, 4.
9, 18: 2 Cor 11, 7–12.	10, 1: Ex 13, 21–22; 14,
9, 19: Mt 20, 26–27.	19–20 / Ex 14,
9, 22: 1 Cor 10, 33; Rom 15,	21–22.26–30.
1; 2 Cor 11, 29.	10, 2: Rom 6, 3; Gal 3, 27 /
9, 24: Heb 12, 1.	Ex 16, 4–35.

the sea. ³ All ate the same spiritual food, ⁴*† and all drank the same spiritual drink, for they drank from a spiritual rock that followed them, and the rock was the Christ. ⁵* Yet God was not pleased with most of them, for they were struck down in the desert.

⁶*† These things happened as examples for us, so that we might not desire evil things, as they did. ⁷* And do not become idolaters, as some of them did, as it is written, "The people sat down to eat and drink, and rose up to revel." ⁸* Let us not indulge in immorality as some of them did, and twenty-three thousand fell within a single day. ⁹*† Let us not test Christ as some of them did, and suffered death by serpents. ¹⁰* Do not grumble as some of them did, and suffered death by the destroyer. ¹¹† These things happened to them as an example, and they have been written down as a warning to us, upon whom the end of the ages has come. ¹²† Therefore, whoever thinks he is standing secure should take care not to fall. ¹³* No trial has come to you but what is human. God is faithful and will not let you be tried beyond your strength; but with the trial he will also provide a way out, so that you may be able to bear it.

Warning against Idolatry

¹⁴*† Therefore, my beloved, avoid idolatry. ¹⁵ I am speaking as to sensible people; judge for yourselves what I am saying. ¹⁶* The cup of blessing that we bless, is it not a participation in the blood of Christ? The bread that we break, is it not a participation in the body of Christ? ¹⁷* Because the loaf of bread is one, we, though many, are one body, for we all partake of the one loaf.

¹⁸* Look at Israel according to the flesh; are not

Addictive Behavior

How do you spend the bulk of your free time? talking with your friends on the phone? playing video games? listening to your favorite music? If you discover that you have become obsessed with that activity, maybe it has become addictive. Although perhaps your obsession is not a true addiction—like those caused by drugs, alcohol, gambling, or eating disorders—it still might have more control over your life than it should have.

Paul reminds the Corinthians that they should put God at the center of their life. He points out that they will always be tempted to replace God with something else—which is called idolatry—like the ancient Israelites were tempted.

How about us today? We may not worship foreign gods or eat meat sacrificed to idols. But in many ways, our addictive behaviors are like idolatry. They consume our thoughts and time and can even lead us away from God.

Addictive behaviors are hard to break. And true addictions are very difficult to control. But you have the promise that God "will not let you be tried beyond your strength" (1 Cor 10, 13). If you think you may have an addiction, talk to a parent or school counselor or minister.

▶ 1 Cor 10, 6–14

10, 4: *A spiritual rock that followed them:* the Torah speaks only about a rock from which water issued, but rabbinic legend amplified this into a spring that followed the Israelites throughout their migration. Paul uses this legend as a literary type: he makes the rock itself accompany the Israelites, and he gives it a spiritual sense. *The rock was the Christ:* in the Old Testament, Yahweh is the Rock of his people (cf Dt 32, Moses' song to Yahweh the Rock). Paul now applies this image to the Christ, the source of the living water, the true Rock that accompanied Israel, guiding their experiences in the desert.

10, 6–13: This section explicitates the typological value of these Old Testament events: the desert experiences of the Israelites are examples, meant as warnings, to deter us from similar sins (idolatry, immorality, etc.) and from a similar fate.

10, 9: *Christ:* to avoid Paul's concept of Christ present in the wilderness events, some manuscripts read "the Lord."

10, 11: *Upon whom the end of the ages has come:* it is our period in time toward which past ages have been moving and in which they arrive at their goal.

10, 12–13: *Take care not to fall:* the point of the whole comparison with Israel is to caution against overconfidence, a sense of complete security (12). This warning is immediately balanced by a reassurance, based, however, on God (13).

10, 14–22: The warning against idolatry from v 7 is now repeated (14) and explained in terms of the effect of sacrifices: all sacrifices, Christian (16–17), Jewish (18), or pagan (20), establish communion. But communion with Christ is exclusive, incompatible with any other such communion (21). Compare the line of reasoning at 6, 15.

10, 4: Ex 17, 1–7; Nm 20, 7–11; Dt 8, 15.
10, 5: Nm 14, 28–38; Jude 5.
10, 6: Nm 11, 4.34.
10, 7: Ex 32, 6.
10, 8: Nm 25, 1–9.
10, 9: Nm 21, 5–9.
10, 10: Nm 14, 2–37;
16, 1–35.
10, 13: Mt 6, 13; Jas 1, 13–14 / 1 Cor 1, 9.
10, 14: 1 Jn 5, 21.
10, 16: Mt 26, 26–29; Acts 2, 42.
10, 17: Rom 12, 5; Eph 4, 4.
10, 18: Lv 7, 6.

FOOD AND GRATITUDE

Have you ever considered eating and drinking for the glory of God? Paul tells the Corinthians that it is more important to respect the conscience of their dining partners than to worry about where the meat came from. By appreciating what they have been given to eat, they show respect for the people who have prepared the food.

Native Americans have that same sense of appreciation—not just for the people they share meals with but for the animals and plants that provide the food. When they kill an animal to eat, they pray to its spirit for forgiveness. Everything from the animal is put to good use because wasting any part of it would be an insult to its honor.

This Native American meal blessing is an expression of thanks:

Now that I am about to eat, O great Spirit, give my thanks to the beasts and birds whom You have provided for my hunger, and pray deliver my sorrow that living things must make a sacrifice for my comfort and well-being. Let the feather of corn spring up in its time and let it not wither but make full grains for the fires of our cooking pots, now that I am about to eat. (From the Lama Foundation, San Cristobal, New Mexico)

▶ I Cor 10, 23–33

those who eat the sacrifices participants in the altar? 19 So what am I saying? That meat sacrificed to idols is anything? Or that an idol is anything? 20*† No, I mean that what they sacrifice, [they sacrifice] to demons, not to God, and I do not want you to become participants with demons. 21* You cannot drink the cup of the Lord and also the cup of demons. You cannot partake of the table of the Lord and of the table of demons. 22* Or are we provoking the Lord to jealous anger? Are we stronger than he?

Seek the Good of Others†

23* "Everything is lawful," but not everything is beneficial.† "Everything is lawful," but not everything builds up. 24* No one should seek his own advantage, but that of his neighbor. 25† Eat anything sold in the market, without raising questions on grounds of conscience, 26* for "the earth and its fullness are the Lord's." 27 If an unbeliever invites you and you want to go, eat whatever is placed before you, without raising questions on grounds of conscience. 28 But if someone says to you, "This was offered in sacrifice," do not eat it on account of the one who called attention to it and on account of conscience; 29 I mean not your own conscience, but the other's. For why should my freedom be determined by someone else's conscience? 30* If I partake thankfully, why am I reviled for that over which I give thanks?

---

†

10, 20: *To demons:* although Jews denied divinity to pagan gods, they often believed that there was some nondivine reality behind the idols, such as the dead, or angels, or demons. The explanation Paul offers in v 20 is drawn from Dt 32, 7: the power behind the idols, with which the pagans commune, consists of demonic powers hostile to God.

10, 23—11, 1: By way of peroration Paul returns to the opening situation (ch 8) and draws conclusions based on the intervening considerations (chs 9–10).

10, 23–24: He repeats in the context of this new problem the slogans of liberty from 6, 12, with similar qualifications. Liberty is not merely an individual perfection, nor an end in itself, but is to be used for the common good. The language of v 24 recalls the descriptions of Jesus' self-emptying in Phil 2.

10, 25–30: A summary of specific situations in which the eating of meat sacrificed to idols could present problems of conscience. Three cases are considered. In the first (the marketplace, 25–26) and the second (at table, 27), there is no need to be concerned with whether food has passed through a pagan sacrifice or not, for the principle of 8, 4–6 still stands, and the whole creation belongs to the one God. But in the third case (28), the situation changes if someone present explicitly raises the question of the sacrificial origin of the food; eating in such circumstances may be subject to various interpretations, some of which could be harmful to individuals. Paul is at pains to insist that the enlightened Christian conscience need not change its judgment about the neutrality, even the goodness, of the food in itself (29–30); yet the total situation is altered to the extent that others are potentially endangered, and this calls for a different response, for the sake of others.

*

10, 20: Dt 32, 17.
10, 21: 2 Cor 6, 14–18.
10, 22: Dt 32, 21 / Eccl 6, 10.
10, 23: 1 Cor 6, 12.
10, 24: Rom 15, 2; Phil 2, 4.21.
10, 26: Pss 24, 1; 50, 12.
10, 30: Rom 14, 6; 1 Tm 4, 3–4.

³¹ So whether you eat or drink, or whatever you do, do everything for the glory of God. ³²† Avoid giving offense, whether to Jews or Greeks or the church of God, ³³* just as I try to please everyone in every way, not seeking my own benefit but that of the many, that they may be saved.

11

¹* Be imitators of me, as I am of Christ.

IV: Problems in Liturgical Assemblies

²*† I praise you because you remember me in everything and hold fast to the traditions, just as I handed them on to you.

A. Women's Headdresses†

Man and Woman

³* But I want you to know that Christ is the head of every man, and a husband the head of his wife,† and God the head of Christ. ⁴† Any man who prays or prophesies with his head covered brings shame upon his head. ⁵ But any woman who prays or prophesies with her head unveiled brings shame upon her head, for it is one and the same thing as if she had had her head shaved. ⁶ For if a woman does not have her head veiled, she may as well have her hair cut off. But if it is shameful for a woman to have her hair cut off or her head shaved, then she should wear a veil.

Whatever you do, do everything

for the glory of God
10, 31

⁷*† A man, on the other hand, should not cover his head, because he is the image and glory of God, but woman is the glory of man. ⁸* For man did not come from woman, but woman from man; ⁹* nor was man created for woman, but woman for man; ¹⁰† for this reason a woman should have a sign of authority on her head, because of the angels. ¹¹*† Woman is not independent of man or man of woman in the Lord. ¹²* For just as woman came from man, so man is born of woman; but all things are from God.

10, 32—11, 1: In summary, the general rule of mutually responsible use of their Christian freedom is enjoined first negatively (32), then positively, as exemplified in Paul (33), and finally grounded in Christ, the pattern for Paul's behavior and theirs (11, 1; cf Rom 15, 1—3).

11, 2—14, 40: This section of the letter is devoted to regulation of conduct at the liturgy. The problems Paul handles have to do with the dress of women in the assembly (11, 3–16), improprieties in the celebration of community meals (11, 17–34), and the use of charisms or spiritual gifts (12, 1—14, 40). The statement in 11, 2 introduces all of these discussions, but applies more appropriately to the second (cf the mention of praise in 11, 17 and of tradition in 11, 23).

11, 3–16: Women have been participating in worship at Corinth without the head-covering normal in Greek society of the period. Paul's stated goal is to bring them back into conformity with contemporary practice and propriety. In his desire to convince, he reaches for arguments from a variety of sources, though he has space to develop them only sketchily and is perhaps aware that they differ greatly in persuasiveness.

11, 3: *A husband the head of his wife:* the specific problem suggests to Paul the model of the head as a device for clarifying relations within a hierarchical structure. The model is similar to that developed later in greater detail and nuance in Eph 5, 21–33. It is a hybrid model, for it grafts onto a strictly theological scale of existence (cf 3, 21–23) the hierarchy of sociosexual relations prevalent in the ancient world: men, dominant, reflect the active function of Christ in relation to his church; women, submissive, reflect the passive role of the church with respect to its savior. This gives us the functional scale: God, Christ, man, woman.

11, 4–6: From man's direct relation to Christ, Paul infers that his head should not be covered. But woman, related not directly to Christ on the scale but to her husband, requires a covering as a sign of that relationship. *Shameful . . . to have her hair cut off:* certain less honored classes in society, such as lesbians and prostitutes, are thought to have worn their hair close-cropped.

11, 7–9: The hierarchy of v 3 is now expressed in other metaphors: the image (*eikōn*) and the reflected glory (*doxa*). Paul is alluding basically to the text of Gn 1, 27, in which mankind as a whole, the male-female couple, is created in God's image and given the command to multiply and together dominate the lower creation. But Gn 1, 24 is interpreted here in the light of the second creation narrative in Gn 2, in which each of the sexes is created separately (first the man and then the woman *from* man and *for* him, to be his helpmate, Gn 2, 20–23), and under the influence of the story of the fall, as a result of which the husband rules over the woman (Gn 3, 16). This interpretation splits the single image of God into two, at different degrees of closeness.

11, 10: *A sign of authority:* "authority" (*exousia*) may possibly be due to mistranslation of an Aramaic word for "veil"; in any case, the connection with v 9 indicates that the covering is a sign of woman's subordination. *Because of the angels:* a surprising additional reason, which the context does not clarify. Presumably the reference is to cosmic powers who might inflict harm on women or whose function is to watch over women or the cult.

11, 11–12: These parenthetical remarks relativize the argument from Gn 2–3. *In the Lord:* in the Christian economy the relation between the sexes is characterized by a mutual dependence, which is not further specified. And even in the natural order conditions have changed: the mode of origin described in Gn 2 has been reversed (12a). But the ultimately significant fact is the origin that all things have in common (12b).

10, 33: 1 Cor 9, 22; Rom 15, 2.
11, 1: 1 Cor 4, 16; Phil 3, 17.
11, 2: 1 Cor 15, 3; 2 Thes 2, 15.
11, 3: Eph 5, 23.
11, 7: Gn 1, 26–27; 5, 1.

11, 8: Gn 2, 21–23.
11, 9: Gn 2, 18.
11, 11: Gal 3, 27–28.
11, 12: 1 Cor 8, 6; Rom 11, 36.

13† Judge for yourselves: is it proper for a woman to pray to God with her head unveiled? 14 Does not nature itself teach you that if a man wears his hair long it is a disgrace to him, 15 whereas if a woman has long hair it is her glory, because long hair has been given [her] for a covering? 16 But if anyone is inclined to be argumentative, we do not have such a custom, nor do the churches of God.

B. The Lord's Supper

An Abuse at Corinth

17† In giving this instruction, I do not praise the fact that your meetings are doing more harm than good. 18* First of all, I hear that when you meet as a church there are divisions among you, and to a degree I believe it; 19† there have to be factions among you in order that [also] those who are approved among you may become known. 20 When you meet in one place, then, it is not to eat the Lord's supper, 21 for in eating, each one goes ahead with his own supper, and one goes hungry while another gets drunk. 22* Do you not have houses in which you can eat and drink? Or do you show contempt for the church of God and make those who have nothing feel ashamed? What can I say to you? Shall I praise you? In this matter I do not praise you.

Tradition of the Institution

23*† For I received from the Lord what I also handed on to you, that the Lord Jesus, on the night he was handed over, took bread, 24 and, after he had given thanks, broke it and said, "This is my body that is for you. Do this in remembrance of me." 25* In the same way also the cup, after supper, saying, "This cup is the new covenant in my blood. Do this, as often as you drink it, in remembrance of me." 26 For as often as you eat this bread and drink the cup, you

Catholic Connections

THE CONSECRATION

First Corinthians 11, 23–26 contains the earliest recorded words of the Christian celebration of the Last Supper. These words are at the heart of the celebration of the Catholic Mass, or Eucharist. They are known as the words of consecration and are said by the priest just before he holds up the bread and wine. Catholics believe that the bread and wine are changed (or transubstantiated) into the real body and blood of Jesus Christ.

▸ 1 Cor 11, 23–26

proclaim the death of the Lord until he comes.

27† Therefore whoever eats the bread or drinks the cup of the Lord unworthily will have to answer for the body and blood of the Lord. 28† A person should examine himself, and so eat the bread and drink the cup. 29† For anyone who eats and drinks without discerning the body, eats and drinks judgment on himself. 30 That is why many among you are ill and infirm, and a considerable number are dying. 31 If we discerned ourselves, we would not be under judgment; 32* but since we are judged by

---

11, 13–16: The argument for conformity to common church practice is summed up and pressed home. Verses 14–15 contain a final appeal to the sense of propriety that contemporary Greek society would consider "natural" (cf 5–6).

11, 17–34: Paul turns to another abuse connected with the liturgy, and a more serious one, for it involves neglect of basic Christian tradition concerning the meaning of the Lord's Supper. Paul recalls that tradition for them and reminds them of its implications.

11, 19: That . . . those who are approved among you may become known: Paul situates their divisions within the context of the eschatological separation of the authentic from the inauthentic until the final revelation of the difference. The notion of authenticity-testing recurs in the injunction to self-examination in view of present and future judgment (28–32).

11, 23–25: This is the earliest written account of the institution of the Lord's Supper in the New Testament. The narrative emphasizes Jesus' action of self-giving (expressed in the words over the bread and the cup) and his double command to repeat his own action.

11, 27: It follows that the only proper way to celebrate the Eucharist is one that corresponds to Jesus' intention, which fits with the meaning of his command to reproduce his action in the proper spirit. If the Corinthians eat and drink unworthily, i.e., without having grasped and internalized the meaning of his death for them, they will have to answer for the body and blood, i.e., will be guilty of a sin against the Lord himself (cf 8, 12).

11, 28: Examine himself: the Greek word is similar to that for "approved" in v 19, which means "having been tested and found true." The self-testing required for proper eating involves discerning the body (29), which, from the context, must mean understanding the sense of Jesus' death (26), perceiving the imperative to unity that follows from the fact that Jesus gives himself to all and requires us to repeat his sacrifice in the same spirit (18–25).

11, 29–32: Judgment: there is a series of wordplays in these verses that would be awkward to translate literally into English; it includes all the references to judgment (krima, 29.34; krinō, 31.32), discernment (diakrinō, 29.31), and condemnation (katakrinō, 32). The judgment is concretely described as the illness, infirmity, and death that have visited the community. These are signs that the power of Jesus' death is not yet completely recognized and experienced. Yet even the judgment incurred is an expression of God's concern; it is a medicinal measure meant to rescue us from condemnation with God's enemies.

11, 18: 1 Cor 1, 10–12; Gal 5, 20.
11, 22: Jas 2, 1–7.
11, 23: 1 Cor 11, 2; 15, 3 / 1 Cor 10, 16–17; Mt
26, 26–29; Mk 14, 22–25; Lk 22, 14–20.
11, 25: Ex 24, 8; 2 Cor 3, 6; Heb 8, 6–13.
11, 32: Dt 8, 5; Heb 12, 5–11.

[the] Lord, we are being disciplined so that we may not be condemned along with the world.

33 Therefore, my brothers, when you come together to eat, wait for one another. 34 If anyone is hungry, he should eat at home, so that your meetings may not result in judgment. The other matters I shall set in order when I come.

C. Spiritual Gifts

Unity and Variety

12 1† Now in regard to spiritual gifts, brothers, I do not want you to be unaware. 2*† You know how, when you were pagans, you were constantly attracted and led away to mute idols.

3* Therefore, I tell you that nobody speaking by the spirit of God says, "Jesus be accursed." And no one can say, "Jesus is Lord," except by the holy Spirit.

4*† There are different kinds of spiritual gifts but the same Spirit; 5 there are different forms of service but the same Lord; 6 there are different workings but the same God who produces all of them in everyone. 7 To each individual the manifestation of the Spirit is given for some benefit. 8* To one is given through the Spirit the expression of wisdom; to another the expression of knowledge according to the same Spirit; 9 to another faith by the same Spirit; to another gifts of healing by the one Spirit; 10* to another mighty deeds; to another prophecy; to another discernment of spirits; to another

CALLED TO SHARE

In China and Singapore, when people meet up with friends, they ask whether the friends have eaten a meal yet. This custom dates back to the great famine of China in the 1950s, when there was so little food that people were starving and a friend's last meal might have been a day or two ago. So whatever food someone had was shared with their friends. Such generosity is truly a sign of God's love and justice.

   Paul had to remind the Corinthians about God's love and justice when they gathered in their homes to talk about their faith, share a meal, and celebrate the Eucharist. In 1 Cor 11, 17–22, Paul tells the Corinthians that when the wealthy humiliate the poor by not inviting them to share the meal, they are abusing the purpose of the Lord's Supper. To celebrate the Lord's Supper is to partake in the body and blood of Christ, and it is impossible to do this if they do not live out the values of Christ.

   In your prayer, journal or reflect on the following questions:
- What might Paul say to your church community if he sat with you during Sunday Mass?
- How do you share with people who have little or nothing?
- What can you do in your community so that the celebration of the Lord's Supper is more truly a sign of generosity, justice, and love?

▶ 1 Cor 11, 17–33

---

† **12, 1—14, 40:** Ecstatic and charismatic activity were common in early Christian experience, as they were in other ancient religions. But the Corinthians seem to have developed a disproportionate esteem for certain phenomena, especially tongues, to the detriment of order in the liturgy. Paul's response to this development provides us with the fullest exposition we have of his theology of the charisms.

12, 2–3: There is an experience of the Spirit and an understanding of ecstatic phenomena that are specifically Christian and that differ, despite apparent similarities, from those of the pagans. It is necessary to discern which spirit is leading one; ecstatic phenomena must be judged by their effect (2). Verse 3 illustrates this by an example: power to confess Jesus as Lord can come only from the Spirit,

and it is inconceivable that the Spirit would move anyone to curse the Lord.

12, 4–6: There are some features common to all charisms, despite their diversity: all are *gifts* (*charismata*), grace from outside ourselves; all are *forms of service* (*diakoniai*), an expression of their purpose and effect; and all are *workings* (*energēmata*), in which God is at work. Paul associates each of these aspects with what later theology will call one of the persons of the Trinity, an early example of "appropriation."

12, 2: Eph 2, 11–18.
12, 3: Rom 10, 9; 1 Jn 4,
        2–3.
12, 4: Rom 12, 6; Eph 4,

7.11.
12, 8: 1 Cor 2, 6–13.
12, 10: 1 Cor 14, 5.26.39; Acts
        2, 4.

varieties of tongues; to another interpretation of tongues. 11* But one and the same Spirit produces all of these, distributing them individually to each person as he wishes.

One Body, Many Parts

12*† As a body is one though it has many parts, and all the parts of the body, though many, are one body, so also Christ. 13* For in one Spirit we were all baptized into one body, whether Jews or Greeks, slaves or free persons, and we were all given to drink of one Spirit.

14 Now the body is not a single part, but many. 15 If a foot should say, "Because I am not a hand I do not belong to the body," it does not for this reason belong any less to the body. 16 Or if an ear should say, "Because I am not an eye I do not belong to the body," it does not for this reason belong any less to the body. 17 If the whole body were an eye, where would the hearing be? If the whole body were hearing, where would the sense of smell be? 18 But as it is, God placed the parts, each one of them, in the body as he intended. 19 If they were all one part, where would the body be? 20 But as it is, there are many parts, yet one body. 21 The eye cannot say to the hand, "I do not need you," nor again the head to the feet, "I do not need you." 22 Indeed, the parts of the body that seem to be weaker are all the more necessary, 23 and those parts of the body that we consider less honorable we surround with greater honor, and our less presentable parts are treated with greater propriety, 24 whereas our more presentable parts do not need this. But God has so constructed the body as to give greater honor to a part that is without it, 25 so that there may be no division in the body, but that the parts may have the same concern for one another. 26 If [one] part suffers, all the parts suffer with it; if one part is honored, all the parts share its joy.

THE BODY OF CHRIST

As Christians, we are called to work together within the Body of Christ. Read 1 Cor 12, 12–31. Here, Paul says that God has given us different gifts precisely so that we need one another.

A long time ago, Booker T. Washington realized that everyone can make a contribution to the world, regardless of their status or possessions. He wrote, "No race can prosper till it learns that there is as much dignity in tilling a field as in writing a poem." This is the Kwanzaa principle of *umoja*, or unity (see "Kwanzaa as a Way of Life," Dt 10, 12–22).

Paul proclaims that each part of the Body of Christ—not only each person, but each diverse culture and race—is needed for the church to function properly. Many look at the most visible people in the church and conclude that they are more important than others. Remember that God sees differently. Often, important things are done by quiet people with little fanfare, but God always notices.

Can you focus on the success of the whole, rather than on what you have or do not have?

Dear God, free me from excessive worry about what someone else has or is able to do. Place my mind on unity and community. Amen.

▶ 1 Cor 12, 12–31

12, 12–26: The image of *a body* is introduced to explain Christ's relationship with believers (12). Verse 13 applies this model to the church: by baptism all, despite diversity of ethnic or social origins, are integrated into one organism. Verses 14–26 then develop the need for diversity of function among the parts of a body without threat to its unity.

12, 11: 1 Cor 7, 7; Eph 4, 7.
12, 12: 1 Cor 10, 17; Rom 12, 4–5; Eph 2, 16; Col 3, 15.
12, 13: Gal 3, 28; Eph 2, 13–18; Col 3, 11 / Jn 7, 37–39.

Application to Christ

27*† Now you are Christ's body, and individually parts of it. 28*† Some people God has designated in the church to be, first, apostles; second, prophets; third, teachers; then, mighty deeds; then gifts of healing, assistance, administration, and varieties of tongues. 29 Are all apostles? Are all prophets? Are all teachers? Do all work mighty deeds? 30 Do all have gifts of healing? Do all speak in tongues? Do all interpret? 31 Strive eagerly for the greatest spiritual gifts.

The Way of Love

But I shall show you a still more excellent way.

13 1*† If I speak in human and angelic tongues† but do not have love, I am a resounding gong or a clashing cymbal. 2* And if I have the gift of prophecy and comprehend all mysteries and all knowledge; if I have all faith so as to move mountains, but do not have love, I am nothing. 3* If I give away everything I own, and if I hand my body over so that I may boast but do not have love, I gain nothing.

4*† Love is patient, love is kind. It is not jealous, [love] is not pompous, it is not inflated, 5* it is not rude, it does not seek its own interests, it is not quick-tempered, it does not brood over injury, 6 it does not rejoice over wrongdoing but rejoices with

---

† **12, 27–30:** Paul now applies the image again to the church as a whole and its members (27). The lists in vv 28–30 spell out the parallelism by specifying the diversity of functions found in the church (cf Rom 12, 6–8; Eph 4, 11).

12, 28: *First, apostles:* apostleship was not mentioned in vv 8–10, nor is it at issue in these chapters, but Paul gives it pride of place in his listing. It is not just one gift among others but a prior and fuller gift that includes the others. They are all demonstrated in Paul's apostolate, but he may have developed his theology of charisms by reflecting first of all on his own grace of apostleship (cf 3, 5–4, 14; 9, 1–27; 2 Cor 2, 14–6, 13; 10, 1–13, 30, esp. 11, 23 and 12, 12).

13, 1–13: This chapter involves a shift of perspective and a new point. All or part of the material may once have been an independent piece in the style of Hellenistic eulogies of virtues, but it is now integrated, by editing, into the context of chs 12–14 (cf the reference to tongues and prophecy) and into the letter as a whole (cf the references to knowledge and to behavior). The function of ch 13 within the discussion of spiritual gifts is to relativize all the charisms by contrasting them with the more basic, pervasive, and enduring value that gives them their purpose and their effectiveness. The rhetoric of this chapter is striking.

13, 1–3: An inventory of gifts, arranged in careful gradation: neither tongues (on the lowest rung), nor prophecy, knowledge, or faith, nor even self-sacrifice has value unless informed by love.

13, 4–7: This paragraph is developed by personification and enumeration, defining love by what it does or does not do. The Greek contains fifteen verbs; it is natural to translate many of them by adjectives in English.

12, 27: Rom 12, 5–8; Eph 1, 23; 4, 12; 5, 30; Col 1, 18.24.
12, 28: Eph 2, 20; 3, 5; 4, 11.
13, 1: 1 Cor 8, 1; 16, 14; Rom 12, 9–10; 13, 8–10.
13, 2: 1 Cor 4, 1; 14, 2 /

1 Cor 1, 5; 8, 1–3; 12, 8 / Mt 17, 20; 21, 21; Col 2, 3.
13, 3: Mt 6, 2.
13, 4: Eph 4, 2 / 1 Cor 4, 6.18; 5, 2; 8, 1.
13, 5: 1 Cor 10, 24.33; Phil 2, 4.21; 1 Thes 5, 15.

Loving Others

Read 1 Cor 13, 1–13. It is a beautiful description of how the love we receive from God translates into multiple and delicate details for the people we love.

The following statements can help you see how to express God's love to others. Think about that love as you complete the statements. Repeat each statement as many times as necessary to include all the people and situations it applies to in your life. You might want to record your responses on a sheet of paper or in your journal.

1. I show love to _____ by being patient when _____.
2. I need to show kindness to _____, especially when _____.
3. I should not envy _____, especially about _____.
4. I should not act arrogantly with _____ when _____.
5. I should not be rude with _____, especially when _____.
6. I must not force my way on _____, particularly in regard to _____.
7. When _____ does _____ to me, I should not become irritated or resentful.
8. When _____ does _____ to me, I should forgive and seek reconciliation.
9. When _____ suffers or experiences something bad, I should show empathy.
10. I should rejoice in the truth whenever _____.
11. I must bear the behaviors that bother me, especially _____.
12. I must believe when I am told _____.
13. I must hope that my relationship with _____ will be _____.
14. I would endure hard times with _____ even though _____.

Now, pray to God to give you enough love to share in the ways you have described.

▶ **1 Corinthians, chapter 13**

?did you KNOW?

God's Love

Greek, the language of the New Testament, has several words for love. There are words for parental love, romantic love, and love between friends or relatives. The rare Greek word Paul uses in First Corinthians, chapter 13—*agape*—is reserved for a special kind of love.

Agape (ah-GAH-pay) is love without conditions or motivations. It is there no matter who you are or what you do. It willingly chooses to serve without expectation of service in return. The Bible tells us that God is agape (1 Jn 4, 16). The source of agape is the unconditional love of God. God's agape is revealed to us in Jesus Christ. Through our faith in Christ, we become a channel for communicating this wonderful love to others.

We are created in God's image. God wants us to love one another with the agape that Paul describes in chapter 13. It's a wonderful challenge!

▶ 1 Corinthians, chapter 13

the truth. 7* It bears all things, believes all things, hopes all things, endures all things.

8† Love never fails. If there are prophecies, they will be brought to nothing; if tongues, they will cease; if knowledge, it will be brought to nothing. 9 For we know partially and we prophesy partially, 10 but when the perfect comes, the partial will pass away. 11 When I was a child, I used to talk as a child, think as a child, reason as a child; when I became a man, I put aside childish things. 12* At present we see indistinctly, as in a mirror, but then face to face. At present I know partially; then I shall know fully, as I am fully known. 13*† So faith, hope, love remain, these three; but the greatest of these is love.

Prophecy Greater than Tongues

14 1*† Pursue love, but strive eagerly for the spiritual gifts, above all that you may prophesy. 2† For one who speaks in a tongue does not speak to human beings but to God, for no one listens; he utters mysteries in spirit. 3*† On the other hand, one who prophesies does speak to human beings, for their building up, encouragement, and solace. 4 Whoever speaks in a tongue builds himself up, but whoever prophesies builds up the church. 5 Now I should like all of you to speak in tongues, but even more to prophesy. One who prophesies is greater than one who speaks in tongues, unless he interprets, so that the church may be built up.

6† Now, brothers, if I should come to you speaking in tongues, what good will I do you if I do not speak to you by way of revelation, or knowledge, or prophecy, or instruction? 7 Likewise, if inanimate things that produce sound, such as flute or harp, do not give out the tones distinctly, how will what is being played on flute or harp be recognized? 8 And if the bugle gives an indistinct sound, who will get ready for battle? 9 Similarly, if you, because of speaking in tongues, do not utter intelligible speech, how will anyone know what is being said? For you will be talking to the air. 10 It happens that there are many different languages in the world, and none is meaningless; 11 but if I do not know the meaning of a lan-

---

†

13, 8–13: The final paragraph announces its topic, *Love never fails* (8), then develops the permanence of love in contrast to the charisms (9–12), and finally asserts love's superiority even over the other "theological virtues" (13).

13, 13: In speaking of love, Paul is led by spontaneous association to mention faith and hope as well. They are already a well-known triad (cf 1 Thes 1, 3), three interrelated (cf 7) features of Christian life, more fundamental than any particular charism. *The greatest . . . is love:* love is operative even within the other members of the triad (7), so that it has a certain primacy among them. Or, if the perspective is temporal, love will remain (cf "never fails," 8) even when faith has yielded to sight and hope to possession.

14, 1–5: Verse 1b returns to the thought of 12, 31a and reveals Paul's primary concern. The series of contrasts in vv 2–5 discloses the problem at Corinth: a disproportionate interest in tongues, with a corresponding failure to appreciate the worth of prophecy. Paul attempts to clarify the relative values of these gifts by indicating the kind of communication achieved in each and the kind of effect each produces.

14, 2–3a: They involve two kinds of communication: tongues, private speech toward God in inarticulate terms that need interpre-

tation to be intelligible to others (see 27–28); prophecy, communication with others in the community.

14, 3b-5: They produce two kinds of effect. One who speaks in tongues *builds himself up;* it is a matter of individual experience and personal perfection, which inevitably recalls Paul's previous remarks about being inflated, seeking one's own good, pleasing oneself. But a prophet *builds up the church:* the theme of "building up" or "edifying" others, the main theme of the letter, comes to clearest expression in this chapter (3.4.5.12.17). It has been anticipated at 8, 1 and 10, 23, and by the related concept of "the beneficial" in 6, 12; 10, 23; 12, 7; etc.

14, 6–12: Sound, in order to be useful, must be intelligible. This principle is illustrated by a series of analogies from music (7–8) and from ordinary human speech (10–11); it is applied to the case at hand in v 9 and v 12.

*

13, 7: Prv 10, 12; 1 Pt 4, 8.	**14, 1:** 1 Cor 14, 5.12.39.
13, 12: 2 Cor 5, 7; Heb 11, 1 / 2 Tm 2, 19; 1 Jn 3, 2.	**14, 3:** 1 Cor 14, 4–5.12.17. 26; 3, 9; 8, 1.10; 10, 23.
13, 13: Col 1, 4; 1 Thes 1, 3; 5, 8.	

guage, I shall be a foreigner to one who speaks it, and one who speaks it a foreigner to me. 12 So with yourselves: since you strive eagerly for spirits, seek to have an abundance of them for building up the church.

Need for Interpretation

13† Therefore, one who speaks in a tongue should pray to be able to interpret. 14† [For] if I pray in a tongue, my spirit is at prayer but my mind is unproductive. 15* So what is to be done? I will pray with the spirit, but I will also pray with the mind. I will sing praise with the spirit, but I will also sing praise with the mind. 16 Otherwise, if you pronounce a blessing [with] the spirit, how shall one who holds the place of the uninstructed say the "Amen" to your thanksgiving, since he does not know what you are saying? 17 For you may be giving thanks very well, but the other is not built up. 18 I give thanks to God that I speak in tongues more than any of you, 19 but in the church I would rather speak five words with my mind, so as to instruct others also, than ten thousand words in a tongue.

Functions of These Gifts

20*† Brothers, stop being childish in your thinking. In respect to evil be like infants, but in your thinking be mature. 21* It is written in the law:

> "By people speaking strange tongues
>   and by the lips of foreigners
>   I will speak to this people,
>   and even so they will not listen to me,

says the Lord." 22 Thus, tongues are a sign not for those who believe but for unbelievers, whereas prophecy is not for unbelievers but for those who believe.

23*† So if the whole church meets in one place and everyone speaks in tongues, and then uninstructed people or unbelievers should come in, will they not say that you are out of your minds? 24 But if everyone is prophesying, and an unbeliever or uninstructed person should come in, he will be convinced by everyone and judged by everyone, 25* and the secrets of his heart will be disclosed, and so he will fall down and worship God, declaring, "God is really in your midst."

Rules of Order

26*† So what is to be done, brothers? When you assemble, one has a psalm, another an instruction, a revelation, a tongue, or an interpretation. Everything should be done for building up. 27 If anyone speaks in a tongue, let it be two or at most three, and each in turn, and one should interpret. 28 But if there is no interpreter, the person should keep silent in the church and speak to himself and to God.

29 Two or three prophets should speak, and the others discern. 30 But if a revelation is given to another person sitting there, the first one should be silent. 31 For you can all prophesy one by one, so that all may learn and all be encouraged. 32 Indeed, the spirits of prophets are under the prophets' control, 33† since he is not the God of disorder but of peace.

As in all the churches of the holy ones, 34* women should keep silent in the churches, for they are not allowed to speak, but should be subordinate, as even the law says. 35 But if they want to

---

14, 13–19: The charism of interpretation lifts tongues to the level of intelligibility, enabling them to produce the same effect as prophecy (cf 5.26–28).

14, 14–15: *My spirit:* Paul emphasizes the exclusively ecstatic, nonrational quality of tongues. The tongues at Pentecost are also described as an ecstatic experience (Acts 2, 4.12–13), though Luke superimposes further interpretations of his own. *My mind:* the ecstatic element, dominant in earliest Old Testament prophecy as depicted in 1 Sm 10, 5–13; 19, 20–24, seems entirely absent from Paul's notion of prophecy and completely relegated to tongues. He emphasizes the role of reason when he specifies instruction as a function of prophecy (6.19.31). But he does not exclude intuition and emotion; cf references to encouragement and consolation (3.31) and the scene describing the ideal exercise of prophecy (24–25).

14, 20–22: The Corinthians pride themselves on tongues as a sign of God's favor, a means of direct communication with him (2.28). To challenge them to a more mature appraisal, Paul draws from scripture a less flattering explanation of what speaking in tongues may signify. Isaiah threatened the people that if they failed to listen to their prophets, the Lord would speak to them (in punishment) through the lips of Assyrian conquerors (Is 28, 11–12). Paul compresses Isaiah's text and makes God address his people directly. Equating tongues with foreign languages (cf 10–11), Paul concludes from Isaiah that *tongues are a sign not for those who believe,* i.e., not a mark of God's pleasure for those who listen to him but a mark of his displeasure with those in the community who are faithless, who have not heeded the message that he has sent through the prophets.

14, 23–25: Paul projects the possible missionary effect of two hypothetical liturgical experiences, one consisting wholly of tongues, the other entirely of prophecy. *Uninstructed (idiōtai):* the term may simply mean people who do not speak or understand tongues, as in v 16, where it seems to designate Christians. But coupled with the term "unbelievers" it may be another way of designating those who have not been initiated into the community of faith; some believe it denotes a special class of non-Christians who are close to the community, such as catechumens. *Unbelievers (apistoi):* he has shifted from the inner-community perspective of v 22; the term here designates non-Christians (cf 6, 6; 7, 15; 10, 27).

14, 26–33a: Paul concludes with specific directives regarding exercise of the gifts in their assemblies. Verse 26 enunciates the basic criterion in the use of any gift: it must contribute to "building up."

14, 33b–36: Verse 33b may belong with what precedes, so that the new paragraph would begin only with v 34. Verses 34–35 change the subject. These two verses have the theme of submission in common with ch 11, despite differences in vocabulary, and a concern with what is or is not becoming; but it is difficult to harmonize the injunction to silence here with ch 11, which appears to take it for granted that women do pray and prophesy aloud in the assembly (cf 11, 5.13). Hence the verses are often considered an interpolation, reflecting the discipline of later churches; such an interpolation would have to have antedated our manuscripts, all of which contain them, though some transpose them to the very end of the chapter.

14, 15: Eph 5, 19; Col 3, 16.
14, 20: Mt 10, 16; Rom 16, 19; Eph 4, 14.
14, 21: Is 28, 11–12; Dt 28, 49.
14, 23: Acts 2, 6.13.
14, 25: 1 Cor 4, 5 / Is 45, 14; Zec 8, 23.
14, 26: Eph 4, 12.
14, 34: 1 Tm 2, 11–15; 1 Pt 3, 1.

1
C
O
R

?did you KNOW?

What's Going On?

In I Cor 14, 34, Paul says women should be silent in church. Yet, in 11, 5, he implies that women can pray and prophesy in church, and throughout his life, he supported and worked closely with many different women (see "Lydia and Priscilla," Acts 16, 14–15; 18, 1–26 and "Phoebe and Junia," Rom 16, 1–16).

What explains Paul's turnaround? It appears that I Cor 14, 34–36, was added to Paul's original letter by a later writer (see footnote 14, 33b–36). Perhaps someone copying Paul's letters needed to show that Christianity was not a movement that would disrupt the social order by allowing women to speak in public.

Like Paul, the Catholic church today values women's participation in worship. Women are cantors, musicians, lectors, and eucharistic ministers. But like the later editor of I Corinthians, chapter 14, the church insists on a certain order in worship. Only those who are ordained can read the Gospel during Mass and preach the homily.

▶ I Cor 14, 34–36

learn anything, they should ask their husbands at home. For it is improper for a woman to speak in the church. 36 Did the word of God go forth from you? Or has it come to you alone?

37 If anyone thinks that he is a prophet or a spiritual person, he should recognize that what I am writing to you is a commandment of the Lord. 38 If anyone does not acknowledge this, he is not acknowledged. 39 So, [my] brothers, strive eagerly to prophesy, and do not forbid speaking in tongues, 40 but everything must be done properly and in order.

V: The Resurrection†

A. The Resurrection of Christ

The Gospel Teaching

15 1† Now I am reminding you, brothers, of the gospel I preached to you, which you indeed received and in which you also stand. 2 Through it you are also being saved, if you hold fast to the word I preached to you, unless you believed in vain. 3*† For I handed on to you as of first importance what I also received: that Christ died for our sins in accordance with the scriptures; 4* that he was buried; that he was raised on the third day in accordance with the scriptures; 5* that he appeared to Cephas, then to the Twelve. 6 After that, he appeared to more than five hundred brothers at once, most of whom are still living, though some have fallen asleep. 7 After that he appeared to James, then to all the apostles. 8* Last of all, as to one born abnormally, he appeared to me. 9*† For I am the least of the apostles, not fit to be called an apostle, because I persecuted the church of God. 10 But by the grace of God I am what I am, and his grace to me has not been ineffective. Indeed, I have toiled harder than all of them; not I, however, but the grace of God [that

---

15, 1–58: Some consider this chapter an earlier Pauline composition inserted into the present letter. The problem that Paul treats is clear to a degree: some of the Corinthians are denying the resurrection of the dead (12), apparently because of their inability to imagine how any kind of bodily existence could be possible after death (35). It is plausibly supposed that their attitude stems from Greek anthropology, which looks with contempt upon matter and would be content with the survival of the soul, and perhaps also from an overrealized eschatology of gnostic coloration, such as that reflected in 2 Tm 2, 18, which considers the resurrection a purely spiritual experience already achieved in baptism and in the forgiveness of sins. Paul, on the other hand, will affirm both the essential corporeity of the resurrection and its futurity.

His response moves through three steps: a recall of the basic kerygma about Jesus' resurrection (1–11), an assertion of the logical inconsistencies involved in denial of the resurrection (12–34), and an attempt to perceive theologically what the properties of the resurrected body must be (35–58).

15, 1–11: Paul recalls the tradition (3–7), which he can presuppose as common ground and which provides a starting point for his argument. This is the fundamental content of all Christian preaching and belief (1–2.11).

15, 3–7: The language by which Paul expresses the essence of the "gospel" (1) is not his own but is drawn from older credal formulas.

This credo highlights Jesus' death for our sins (confirmed by his burial) and Jesus' resurrection (confirmed by his appearances) and presents both of them as fulfillment of prophecy. *In accordance with the scriptures:* conformity of Jesus' passion with the scriptures is asserted in Mt 16, 1; Lk 24, 25–27.32.44–46. Application of some Old Testament texts (Pss 2, 7; 16, 8–11) to his resurrection is illustrated by Acts 2, 27–31; 13, 29–39; and Is 52, 13–53, 12 and Hos 6, 2 may also have been envisaged.

15, 9–11: A persecutor may have appeared disqualified (*ouk . . . hikanos*) from apostleship, but in fact God's grace has qualified him. Cf the remarks in 2 Corinthians about his qualifications (2, 16; 3, 5) and his greater labors (11, 23). These verses are parenthetical, but a nerve has been touched (the references to his abnormal birth and his activity as a persecutor may echo taunts from Paul's opponents), and he is instinctively moved to self-defense.

15, 3: 1 Cor 11, 23 / 1 Pt 2, 24; 3, 18 / Is 53, 4–12.
15, 4: Acts 2, 23–24 / Ps 16, 8–11; Hos 6, 1–2; Jon 2, 1.
15, 5: Mk 16, 14; Mt 28, 16–17; Lk 24, 36; Jn 20, 19.
15, 8: 1 Cor 9, 1; Acts 9, 3–6; Gal 1, 16.
15, 9: Acts 8, 3; 9, 1–2; Gal 1, 23; Eph 3, 8; 1 Tm 1, 15.

THE FIRST CREED AND A CONTEMPORARY CREED!

First Corinthians 15, 3–11 contains the first creed written in the Scriptures. It expresses the fundamental aspects of the Christian faith and is made up of historic facts and faith statements such as the following. (See also "I Believe! The Apostles' Creed," Acts 4, 5–12.)

- Christ died for our sins, according to the Scriptures (see Isaiah, chapter 53).
- Christ was buried.
- Christ rose on the third day.

Although all Christians adhere to the beliefs of our common creeds (see also "I Believe! The Apostles' Creed," Acts 4, 5–12), some Christian communities create their own particular creedal statements based on the foundations of the Christian faith and their experience of God. Here are some extracts from a credo created by Hispanics during their Third Encuentro Nacional de Pastoral, in 1985:

> We believe in the most holy Trinity, God the Father, Son, and Holy Spirit. We sense God's powerful work in our people, and we see it as a model to be followed. . . .
>
> We believe in our identification with Christ, as the suffering people we are. We believe, . . . as he did, in the dignity of all human beings and in their liberation through love. . . .
>
> We believe in the Catholic Church, which is integrated in Christ by means of the communion we, as laity, share with bishops, priests, deacons, and men and women religious. . . .
>
> We have faith in our people because we know that God, who abides in a special manner and forever among us, has raised it [our people] up. . . .
>
> We believe in the gift of being a prophetic voice as something given by God to our people and as a means of promoting the unity and love that are necessary for the building of the Kingdom. . . .
>
> We believe in Mary, our Mother, who has taken our Hispanic culture under her protection, and who has accompanied us and will accompany us always in our journey as she works to carry the message of Jesus to the whole world. . . .
>
> Amen.

(Secretariat for Hispanic Affairs, *Prophetic Voices*, pp. 17–18)

▸ 1 Cor 15, 3–11

---

is] with me. [11] Therefore, whether it be I or they, so we preach and so you believed.

B. The Resurrection of the Dead

Results of Denial

[12][†] But if Christ is preached as raised from the dead, how can some among you say there is no resurrection of the dead? [13][*] If there is no resurrection of the dead, then neither has Christ been raised. [14] And if Christ has not been raised, then empty [too] is our preaching; empty, too, your faith. [15][*] Then we are also false witnesses to God, because we testified against God that he raised Christ, whom he did not raise if in fact the dead are not raised. [16] For if the dead are not raised, neither

---

[†] **15, 12–19:** Denial of the resurrection (12) involves logical inconsistencies. The basic one, stated twice (13.16), is that if there is no such thing as (bodily) resurrection, then it has not taken place even in Christ's case.

15, 13: 1 Thes 4, 14.   **15, 15:** Acts 5, 32.

Life After Death

During childhood, reality and fantasy are often confused. We might believe in Santa Claus, the Easter Bunny, the Tooth Fairy, even a monster living under our bed. We may imagine heaven as having pearly gates, golden streets, and angels flying with harps. As we grow older, some of us exchange this fantastic image for a more mature belief in the mystery of the Resurrection. But many adult Christians simply do not know what to believe about life after death.

Christians from Corinth also had problems with the concept of human resurrection. Common ideas influenced by Greek philosophy made it difficult for them to think of a body returning to life after death. For them, the body and soul were separate. The soul was immortal and continued living after the body died.

In contrast, the Hebrews saw a unity between the spiritual and material aspects of the human person. When the prophets, such as Daniel, envisaged a blessed life after death they did not think in terms of a soul freed from the body but in terms of a body filled once more with life. (See "Resurrection," Dn 12, 1–3.)

Believing in the Resurrection is essential in the Christian faith. The Gospel writers describe the risen Jesus as different from the Jesus who died on the cross; the disciples did not recognize him at first sight; they knew him only through their faith.

Paul gets right to the point: our faith depends on the fact that Christ was raised from death. He explains that in the resurrection our earthly body will be transformed—it will become a glorious, imperishable, and immortal body. We will not be disembodied spirits or souls when we have eternal life in communion with God. And we will be made alive in Christ, whether our mind can comprehend that idea or not. Our end is not death, but eternal life with Christ!

▶ I Cor 15, 35–58

---

has Christ been raised, [17]† and if Christ has not been raised, your faith is vain; you are still in your sins. [18] Then those who have fallen asleep in Christ have perished. [19] If for this life only we have hoped in Christ, we are the most pitiable people of all.

Christ the Firstfruits†

[20]* But now Christ has been raised from the dead, the firstfruits† of those who have fallen asleep. [21]† For since death came through a human being,

the resurrection of the dead came also through a human being. [22]* For just as in Adam all die, so too in Christ shall all be brought to life, [23]* but each one in proper order: Christ the firstfruits; then, at his coming, those who belong to Christ; [24]*† then comes the end, when he hands over the kingdom to his God and Father, when he has destroyed every sovereignty and every authority and power. [25]* For he must reign until he has put all his enemies under his feet. [26]*† The last enemy to be destroyed is

---

15, 17–18: The consequences for the Corinthians are grave: both forgiveness of sins and salvation are an illusion, despite their strong convictions about both. Unless Christ is risen, their faith does not save.

15, 20–28: After a triumphant assertion of the reality of Christ's resurrection (20a), Paul explains its positive implications and consequences. As a soteriological event of both human (20–23) and cosmic (24–28) dimensions, Jesus' resurrection logically and necessarily involves ours as well.

15, 20: *The firstfruits:* the portion of the harvest offered in thanksgiving to God implies the consecration of the entire harvest to come. Christ's resurrection is not an end in itself; its finality lies in the whole harvest, ourselves.

15, 21–22: Our human existence, both natural and supernatural, is corporate, involves solidarity. *In Adam . . . in Christ:* the Hebrew word *'adām* in Genesis is both a common noun for mankind and a proper noun for the first man. Paul here presents Adam as at least a literary type of Christ; the parallelism and contrast between them will be developed further in vv 45–49 and in Rom 5, 12–21.

15, 24–28: Paul's perspective expands to cosmic dimensions, as he describes the climax of history, *the end*. His viewpoint is still

christological, as in vv 20–23. Verses 24 and 28 describe Christ's final relations to his enemies and his Father in language that is both royal and military; vv 25–28 insert a proof from scripture (Pss 110, 1; 8, 7) into this description. But the viewpoint is also theological, for God is the ultimate agent and end, and likewise soteriological, for we are the beneficiaries of all the action.

15, 26: *The last enemy . . . is death:* a parenthesis that specifies the final fulfillment of the two Old Testament texts just referred to, Ps 110, 1 and Ps 8, 7. Death is not just one cosmic power among many, but the ultimate effect of sin in the universe (cf 56; Rom 5, 12). Christ defeats death where it prevails, in our bodies. The destruction of the last enemy is concretely the "coming to life" (22) of "those who belong to Christ" (23).

15, 20: Rom 8, 11; Col 1, 18;
   1 Thes 4, 14.
15, 22: Gn 3, 17–19; Rom 5,
   12–19.
15, 23: 1 Thes 4, 15–17.

15, 24: Eph 1, 22.
15, 25: Ps 110, 1.
15, 26: Rom 6, 9; 2 Tm 1, 10;
   Rv 20, 14; 21, 4.

death, ²⁷*† for "he subjected everything under his feet." But when it says that everything has been subjected, it is clear that it excludes the one who subjected everything to him. ²⁸* When everything is subjected to him, then the Son himself will [also] be subjected to the one who subjected everything to him, so that God may be all in all.

Practical Arguments†

²⁹† Otherwise, what will people accomplish by having themselves baptized for the dead? If the dead are not raised at all, then why are they having themselves baptized for them?

³⁰*† Moreover, why are we endangering ourselves all the time? ³¹* Every day I face death; I swear it by the pride in you [brothers] that I have in Christ Jesus our Lord. ³²* If at Ephesus I fought with beasts, so to speak, what benefit was it to me? If the dead are not raised:

"Let us eat and drink,
    for tomorrow we die."

³³ Do not be led astray:

"Bad company corrupts good morals."

³⁴* Become sober as you ought and stop sinning. For some have no knowledge of God; I say this to your shame.

C. The Manner of the Resurrection†

³⁵† But someone may say, "How are the dead raised? With what kind of body will they come back?"

The Resurrection Body

³⁶*† You fool! What you sow is not brought to life unless it dies. ³⁷ And what you sow is not the body that is to be but a bare kernel of wheat, perhaps, or of some other kind; ³⁸* but God gives it a body as he chooses, and to each of the seeds its own body. ³⁹† Not all flesh is the same, but there is one kind for human beings, another kind of flesh for animals, another kind of flesh for birds, and another for fish. ⁴⁰ There are both heavenly bodies and earthly bodies, but the brightness of the heavenly is one kind and that of the earthly another. ⁴¹ The brightness of the sun is one kind, the brightness of the moon another, and the brightness of the stars another. For star differs from star in brightness.

⁴²† So also is the resurrection of the dead. It is sown corruptible; it is raised incorruptible. ⁴³* It is sown dishonorable; it is raised glorious. It is sown weak; it is raised powerful. ⁴⁴ It is sown a natural body; it is raised a spiritual body. If there is a natural body, there is also a spiritual one.

⁴⁵*† So, too, it is written, "The first man, Adam, became a living being," the last Adam a life-giving

---

15, 27b-28: *The one who subjected everything to him:* the Father is the ultimate agent in the drama, and the final end of the process, to whom the Son and everything else is ordered (24.28). *That God may be all in all:* his reign is a dynamic exercise of creative power, an outpouring of life and energy through the universe, with no further resistance. This is the supremely positive meaning of "subjection": that God may fully be God.

15, 29-34: Paul concludes his treatment of logical inconsistencies with a listing of miscellaneous Christian practices that would be meaningless if the resurrection were not a fact.

15, 29: *Baptized for the dead:* this practice is not further explained here, nor is it necessarily mentioned with approval, but Paul cites it as something in their experience that attests in one more way to belief in the resurrection.

15, 30-34: A life of sacrifice, such as Paul describes in 4, 9-13 and 2 Cor, would be pointless without the prospect of resurrection; a life of pleasure, such as that expressed in the Epicurean slogan of v 32, would be far more consistent. *I fought with beasts:* since Paul does not elsewhere mention a combat with beasts at Ephesus, he may be speaking figuratively about struggles with adversaries.

15, 35-58: Paul imagines two objections that the Corinthians could raise: one concerning the manner of the resurrection (*how?*), the other pertaining to the qualities of the risen body (*what kind?*). These questions probably lie behind their denial of the resurrection (12), and seem to reflect the presumption that no kind of body other than the one we now possess would be possible. Paul deals with these objections in inverse order, in vv 36-49 and vv 50-58. His argument is fundamentally theological and its appeal is to the understanding.

15, 35-49: Paul approaches the question of the nature of the risen body (*what kind of body?*) by means of two analogies: the seed (36-44) and the first man, Adam (45-49).

15, 36-38: The analogy of the seed: there is a change of attributes

from seed to plant; the old life-form must be lost for the new to emerge. By speaking about the seed as a *body* that dies and comes to life, Paul keeps the point of the analogy before the reader's mind.

15, 39-41: The expression "its own body" (38) leads to a development on the marvelous diversity evident in bodily life.

15, 42-44: The principles of qualitative difference before and after death (36-38) and of diversity on different levels of creation (39-41) are now applied to the human body. Before: a body animated by a lower, natural life-principle (*psychē*) and endowed with the properties of natural existence (corruptibility, lack of glory, weakness). After: a body animated by a higher life-principle (*pneuma;* cf 45) and endowed with other qualities (incorruptibility, glory, power, spirituality), which are properties of God himself.

15, 45: The analogy of *the first man, Adam,* is introduced by a citation from Gn 2, 7. Paul alters the text slightly, adding the adjective *first,* and translating the Hebrew *'adām* twice, so as to give it its value both as a common noun (*man*) and as a proper name (*Adam*). Verse 45b then specifies similarities and differences between the two Adams. *The last Adam,* Christ (cf 21-22) has become a . . . *spirit* (*pneuma*), a life-principle transcendent with respect to the natural soul (*psychē*) of the first Adam (on the terminology here, cf the note on 3, 1). Further, he is not just alive, but *life-giving,* a source of life for others.

15, 27: Ps 8, 7; Eph 1, 22; Phil 3, 21.
15, 28: Eph 4, 6; Col 3, 11.
15, 30: 2 Cor 4, 8-12; 11, 23-27.
15, 31: Ps 44, 23; Rom 8, 36.
15, 32: 1 Cor 4, 9; 2 Cor 4, 10-11 / Wis 2, 5-7; Is 22, 13.
15, 34: Mt 22, 29; Mk 12, 24.
15, 36: Jn 12, 24.
15, 38: Gn 1, 11.
15, 43: Phil 3, 20-21; Col 3, 4.
15, 45: Gn 2, 7 / Jn 5, 21-29; 2 Cor 3, 6.17.

spirit. 46 But the spiritual was not first; rather the natural and then the spiritual. 47 The first man was from the earth, earthly; the second man, from heaven. 48 As was the earthly one, so also are the earthly, and as is the heavenly one, so also are the heavenly. 49*† Just as we have borne the image of the earthly one, we shall also bear the image of the heavenly one.

The Resurrection Event

50*† This I declare, brothers: flesh and blood cannot inherit the kingdom of God, nor does corruption† inherit incorruption. 51*† Behold, I tell you a mystery. We shall not all fall asleep, but we will all be changed, 52* in an instant, in the blink of an eye, at the last trumpet. For the trumpet will sound, the dead will be raised incorruptible, and we shall be changed. 53* For that which is corruptible must clothe itself with incorruptibility, and that which is mortal must clothe itself with immortality. 54*† And when this which is corruptible clothes itself with incorruptibility and this which is mortal clothes itself with immortality, then the word that is written shall come about:

"Death is swallowed up in victory.
55* Where, O death, is your victory?
Where, O death, is your sting?"

56*† The sting of death is sin, and the power of sin is the law. 57* But thanks be to God who gives us the victory through our Lord Jesus Christ.

58 Therefore, my beloved brothers, be firm, steadfast, always fully devoted to the work of the Lord, knowing that in the Lord your labor is not in vain.

VI: Conclusion

The Collection†

16 1* Now in regard to the collection† for the holy ones, you also should do as I ordered the churches of Galatia. 2 On the first day of the week each of you should set aside and save whatever he can afford, so that collections will not be going on when I come. 3 And when I arrive, I shall send those whom you have approved with letters of recommendation to take your gracious gift to Jerusalem. 4† If it seems fitting that I should go also, they will go with me.

Paul's Travel Plans

5*† I shall come to you after I pass through Macedonia (for I am going to pass through Macedonia), 6 and perhaps I shall stay or even spend the winter with you, so that you may send me on my way wherever I may go. 7* For I do not wish to see you now just in passing, but I hope to spend some time with you, if the Lord permits. 8*† I shall stay in Ephesus until Pentecost, 9* because a door has opened for me wide and productive for work, but there are many opponents.

10* If Timothy comes, see that he is without fear in your company, for he is doing the work of the Lord just as I am. 11 Therefore, no one should disdain him. Rather, send him on his way in peace that he may come to me, for I am expecting him with the brothers. 12* Now in regard to our brother Apollos, I urged him strongly to go to you with the brothers, but it was not at all his

---

15, 49: *We shall also bear the image:* although it has less manuscript support, this reading better fits the context's emphasis on futurity and the transforming action of God; on future transformation as conformity to the image of the Son, cf Rom 8, 29; Phil 3, 21. The majority reading, "let us bear the image," suggests that the image of the heavenly man is already present and exhorts us to conform to it.

15, 50–57: These verses, an answer to the first question of v 35, explain theologically how the change of properties from one image to another will take place: God has the power to transform, and he will exercise it.

15, 50–53: *Flesh and blood . . . corruption:* living persons and the corpses of the dead, respectively. In both cases, the gulf between creatures and God is too wide to be bridged unless God himself transforms us.

15, 51–52: *A mystery:* the last moment in God's plan is disclosed; cf the notes on 2, 1.7–10a. The final trumpet and the awakening of the dead are stock details of the apocalyptic scenario. *We shall not all fall asleep:* Paul expected that some of his contemporaries might still be alive at Christ's return; after the death of Paul and his whole generation, copyists altered this statement in various ways. *We will all be changed:* the statement extends to all Christians, for Paul is not directly speaking about anyone else. Whether they have died before the end or happen still to be alive, all must be transformed.

15, 54–55: *Death is swallowed up in victory:* scripture itself predicts death's overthrow. *O death:* in his prophetic vision Paul may be making Hosea's words his own, or imagining this cry of triumph on the lips of the risen church.

15, 56: *The sting of death is sin:* an explanation of Hosea's metaphor. Death, scorpion-like, is equipped with a sting, sin, by which it injects its poison. Christ defeats sin, the cause of death (Gn 3, 19; Rom 5, 12).

16, 1–4: This paragraph contains our earliest evidence for a project that became a major undertaking of Paul's ministry. The collection for the church at Jerusalem was a symbol in his mind for the unity of Jewish and Gentile Christianity. Cf Gal 2, 10; Rom 15, 25–29; 2 Cor 8–9 and the notes to this last passage.

16, 1: *In regard to the collection:* it has already begun in Galatia and Macedonia (cf 2 Cor 8), and presumably he has already instructed the Corinthians about its purpose.

16, 4: *That I should go also:* presumably Paul delivered the collection on his final visit to Jerusalem; cf Rom 15, 25–32; Acts 24, 14.

16, 5–12: The travel plans outlined here may not have materialized precisely as Paul intended; cf 2 Cor 1, 8–2, 13; 7, 4–16.

16, 8: *In Ephesus until Pentecost:* this tells us the place from which he wrote the letter and suggests he may have composed it about Easter time (cf 5, 7–8).

15, 49: Gn 5, 3 / Rom 8, 29; Phil 3, 21.
15, 50: Jn 3, 3–6.
15, 51: 1 Thes 4, 14–17.
15, 52: Jl 2, 1; Zec 9, 14; Mt 24, 31; Rv 11, 15–18.
15, 53: 2 Cor 5, 2–4.
15, 54: Is 25, 8; 2 Cor 5, 4; 2 Tm 1, 10; Heb 2, 14–15.
15, 55: Hos 13, 14.
15, 56: Rom 4, 15; 7, 7.13.
15, 57: Jn 16, 33; 1 Jn 5, 4.

16, 1: Acts 24, 17; Rom 15, 25–32; 2 Cor 8–9; Gal 2, 10.
16, 5: Acts 19, 21; Rom 15, 26; 2 Cor 1, 15–16.
16, 7: Acts 18, 21.
16, 8: 1 Cor 15, 32; Acts 18, 19; 19, 1–10.
16, 9: Acts 14, 27; 2 Cor 2, 12.
16, 10: 1 Cor 4, 17; Acts 16, 1; 19, 22; Phil 2, 19–23.
16, 12: 1 Cor 1, 12; 3, 4–6.22; Acts 18, 24–28.

1
C
O
R

will that he go now. He will go when he has an opportunity.

Exhortation and Greetings

13 Be on your guard, stand firm in the faith, be courageous, be strong. 14 Your every act should be done with love.

15* I urge you, brothers—you know that the household of Stephanas is the firstfruits of Achaia and that they have devoted themselves to the service of the holy ones— 16 be subordinate to such people and to everyone who works and toils with them. 17 I rejoice in the arrival of Stephanas,

Fortunatus, and Achaicus, because they made up for your absence, 18* for they refreshed my spirit as well as yours. So give recognition to such people.

19*† The churches of Asia send you greetings. Aquila and Prisca together with the church at their house send you many greetings in the Lord. 20* All the brothers greet you. Greet one another with a holy kiss.

21* I, Paul, write you this greeting in my own hand. 22*† If anyone does not love the Lord, let him be accursed. *Marana tha.* 23* The grace of the Lord Jesus be with you. 24 My love to all of you in Christ Jesus.

---

† **16, 19–24:** These paragraphs conform to the normal epistolary conclusion, but their language is overlaid with liturgical coloration as well. The *greetings* of the Asian churches are probably to be read, along with the letter, in the liturgy at Corinth, and the union of the church is to be expressed by a *holy kiss* (19–20). Paul adds to this his own greeting (21) and blessings (23–24).

16, 22: *Accursed:* literally, "anathema." This expression (cf 12, 3) is a formula for exclusion from the community; it may imply here a call to self-examination before celebration of the Eucharist, in preparation for the Lord's coming and judgment (cf 11, 17–34). *Marana tha:* an Aramaic expression, probably used in the early Christian liturgy. As understood here ("O Lord, come!"), it is a prayer for the

early return of Christ. If the Aramaic words are divided differently (*Maran atha*, "Our Lord has come"), it becomes a credal declaration. The former interpretation is supported by what appears to be a Greek equivalent of this acclamation in Rv 22, 20: "Amen. Come, Lord Jesus!"

---

* 16, 15: 1 Cor 1, 16.
16, 18: 1 Thes 5, 12–13.
16, 19: Acts 18, 2.18.26; Rom 16, 3–5.
16, 20: Rom 16, 16; 2 Cor 13, 12; 1 Thes 5, 26; 1 Pt 5, 14.

16, 21: Gal 6, 11; Col 4, 18; 2 Thes 3, 17.
16, 22: 1 Cor 12, 3; Rom 9, 3; Gal 1, 8–9; Rv 22, 20.
16, 23: Rom 16, 20.

Corinthians

Unfortunately, you probably know all too well what it's like to be criticized. It's no fun to be under attack. Our instinct is to get defensive and strike back. But in his Second Letter to the Corinthians, Paul shows us how God helps us rise above our instincts. Paul responds to personal attacks with directness and honesty. He demonstrates how to witness to Jesus—even when we are in the middle of conflict.

At a Glance

I. Address (1, 1–11).

II. The Crisis between Paul and the Corinthians (1, 12—7, 16).

III. The Collection for Jerusalem (8, 1—9, 15).

IV. Paul's Defense of His Ministry (10, 1—13, 10).

V. Conclusion (13, 11–13).

In-depth

The relationship between Paul and the Corinthians deteriorated after he wrote 1 Corinthians. Apparently, some other traveling missionaries came to Corinth and undermined Paul's credibility. They attacked him as a person (2 Cor 10, 10), implied that he was mentally imbalanced (5, 13), and criticized him as a speaker (10, 10). They even suggested that Paul was not trustworthy about money (8, 20–21).

As part of these attacks, some people claimed that Paul couldn't make up his mind about returning to visit Corinth; they said he kept changing between yes and no. In defending himself, Paul skillfully changes the focus and says that in Jesus, we always find a yes. For in Jesus, every one of God's promises is a yes (1, 19–20). And whereas Paul's opponents make boastful claims for themselves, Paul realizes that God's grace is all he needs. In fact, he says, "I will rather boast most gladly of my weaknesses, in order that the power of Christ may dwell with me" (12, 9).

With breathtaking insight, Paul puts all the conflict into perspective. "From now on we regard no one according to the flesh; . . . So whoever is in Christ is a new creation" (5, 16–17). Knowing Christ changes everything! Through Christ, we are reconciled with God—meaning, God overcomes the sin and weakness that separate us from God's love. We should also become ambassadors for Christ, reconciling with one another and announcing to all that they are reconciled with God.

Scholars see evidence that several original letters were combined to form 2 Corinthians. For example, Paul's concerns seem to be resolved in chapter 7, but then, chapters 10–13 pick up those concerns again. And chapters 8 and 9 each describe a collection being taken up for the Christians in Jerusalem without making any connection between the two collections. Despite its uneven flow, the letter reveals a very personal look into Paul's life and ministry.

Quick Facts

Author
Paul

Date Written
around A.D. 57

Audience
the mainly Gentile (non-Jewish) church in Corinth

2 Corinthians

I: Address

Greeting

1 ¹*† Paul, an apostle of Christ Jesus by the will of God, and Timothy our brother, to the church of God that is in Corinth, with all the holy ones throughout Achaia: ² grace to you and peace from God our Father and the Lord Jesus Christ.

Thanksgiving

³*† Blessed be the God and Father of our Lord Jesus Christ, the Father of compassion and God of all encouragement, ⁴* who encourages us in our every affliction, so that we may be able to encourage those who are in any affliction with the encouragement with which we ourselves are encouraged by God. ⁵† For as Christ's sufferings overflow to us, so through Christ does our encouragement also overflow. ⁶ If we are afflicted, it is for your encouragement and salvation; if we are encouraged, it is for your encouragement, which enables you to endure the same sufferings that we suffer. ⁷† Our hope for you is firm, for we know that as you share in the sufferings, you also share in the encouragement.

⁸*† We do not want you to be unaware, brothers, of the affliction that came to us in the province of Asia; we were utterly weighed down beyond our strength, so that we despaired even of life. ⁹*† Indeed, we had accepted within ourselves the sentence of death, that we might trust not in ourselves but in God who raises the dead. ¹⁰* He rescued us from such great danger of death, and he will continue to rescue us; in him we have put our hope [that] he will also rescue us again, ¹¹* as you help us with prayer, so that thanks may be given by many on our behalf for the gift granted us through the prayers of many.

---

† **1, 1–11:** The opening follows the usual Pauline form, except that the thanksgiving takes the form of a doxology or glorification of God (3). This introduces a meditation on the experience of suffering and encouragement shared by Paul and the Corinthians (4–7), drawn, at least in part, from Paul's reflections on a recent affliction (8–10). The section ends with a modified and delayed allusion to thanksgiving (11).

1, 3: *God of all encouragement:* Paul expands a standard Jewish blessing so as to state the theme of the paragraph. The theme of "encouragement" or "consolation" (*paraklēsis*) occurs ten times in this opening, against a background formed by multiple references to "affliction" and "suffering."

1, 5: *Through Christ:* the Father of compassion is the Father of our Lord Jesus (3); Paul's sufferings and encouragement (or "consolation") are experienced in union with Christ. Cf Lk 2, 25: the "consolation of Israel" is Jesus himself.

1, 7: *You also share in the encouragement:* the eschatological

reversal of affliction and encouragement that Christians expect (cf Mt 5, 4; Lk 6, 24) permits some present experience of reversal in the Corinthians' case, as in Paul's.

1, 8: *Asia:* a Roman province in western Asia Minor, the capital of which was Ephesus.

1, 9–10: *The sentence of death:* it is unclear whether Paul is alluding to a physical illness or to an external threat to life. The result of the situation was to produce an attitude of faith in God alone. *God who raises the dead:* rescue is the constant pattern of God's activity; his final act of encouragement is the resurrection.

1, 1: Eph 1, 1; Col 1, 1 / 2 Cor 1, 19; Acts 16 / Rom 1, 7; 1 Cor 1, 2.	2, 16.
1, 3: 1 Cor 15, 24; Eph 1, 3; 1 Pt 1, 3 / Rom 15, 5.	**1, 8:** Acts 20, 18–19; 1 Cor 15, 32.
1, 4: 2 Cor 7, 6–7.13; 1 Thes 3, 6–8; 2 Thes	**1, 9:** 2 Cor 4, 7–11; Rom 4, 17.
	1, 10: 2 Tm 4, 18.
	1, 11: 2 Cor 4, 15; 9, 12.

II: The Crisis between Paul and the Corinthians

A. Past Relationships†

Paul's Sincerity and Constancy

¹²† For our boast is this, the testimony of our conscience that we have conducted ourselves in the world, and especially toward you, with the simplicity and sincerity of God, [and] not by human wisdom but by the grace of God. ¹³ For we write you nothing but what you can read and understand, and I hope that you will understand completely, ¹⁴* as you have come to understand us partially, that we are your boast as you also are ours, on the day of [our] Lord Jesus.

¹⁵† With this confidence I formerly intended to come to you so that you might receive a double favor, ¹⁶* namely, to go by way of you to Macedonia, and then to come to you again on my return from Macedonia, and have you send me on my way to Judea. ¹⁷*† So when I intended this, did I act lightly? Or do I make my plans according to human considerations, so that with me it is "yes, yes" and "no, no"? ¹⁸† As God is faithful, our word to you is not "yes" and "no." ¹⁹* For the Son of God, Jesus Christ, who was proclaimed to you by us, Silvanus and Timothy and me, was not "yes" and "no," but "yes" has been in him. ²⁰* For however many are the promises of God, their Yes is in him; therefore, the Amen from us also goes through him to God

The Presence of God

The POWs (prisoners of war) are cold, and it takes every bit of their energy to stay warm. The conversation this night centers on the discouragement the men feel and their frustration about being abandoned and being left alone. Captain Valdez listens to the conversation for a long time, and then he interrupts: "We are not alone, and we have not been abandoned. God has been with us every minute through this ordeal. I pray every morning and every night in thanksgiving for that presence. It is on the worst days that I most strongly feel the presence of God."

When we are suffering, we often feel alone and abandoned—sometimes even by God. But Paul indicates that God is present, consoling us in our affliction. It is sometimes difficult to feel this presence because we are caught up in the pain and hurt of the situation, as are the POWs in this story. How do you experience God's presence or absence during times of pain and suffering?

Paul also says that the support of the Christian community can help us get through our pain. The comfort of friends and relatives during difficult times can help us recognize the action of God. Is there someone you can comfort who is going through a hard time?

▶ 2 Cor 1, 3–11

1, 12—2, 13: The autobiographical remarks about the crisis in Asia Minor lead into consideration of a crisis that has arisen between Paul and the Corinthians. Paul will return to this question, after a long digression, in 7, 5–16. Both of these sections deal with travel plans Paul had made, changes in the plans, alternative measures adopted, a breach that opened between him and the community, and finally a reconciliation between them.

1, 12–14: Since Paul's own conduct will be under discussion here, he prefaces the section with a statement about his habitual behavior and attitude toward the community. He protests his openness, single-mindedness, and conformity to God's grace; he hopes that his relationship with them will be marked by mutual understanding and pride, which will constantly increase until it reaches its climax at the judgment. Two references to boasting frame this paragraph (12.14), the first appearances of a theme that will be important in the letter, especially in chs 10–13; the term is used in a positive sense here (cf the note on 1 Cor 1, 29–31).

1, 15: *I formerly intended to come:* this plan reads like a revision of the one mentioned in 1 Cor 16, 5. Not until 1, 23—2, 1 will Paul tell us something his original readers already knew, that he has canceled one or the other of these projected visits.

1, 17: *Did I act lightly?:* the subsequent change of plans casts suspicion on the original intention, creating the impression that Paul is

vacillating and inconsistent or that *human considerations* keep dictating shifts in his goals and projects (cf the counterclaim of 12). *"Yes, yes" and "no, no":* stating something and denying it in the same or the next breath; being of two minds at once, or from one moment to the next.

1, 18–22: *As God is faithful:* unable to deny the change in plans, Paul nonetheless asserts the firmness of the original plan and claims a profound constancy in his life and work. He grounds his defense in God himself, who is firm and reliable; this quality can also be predicated in various ways of those who are associated with him. Christ, Paul, and the Corinthians all participate in analogous ways in the constancy of God. A number of the terms here, which appear related only conceptually in Greek or English, would be variations of the same root, *'mn,* in a Semitic language, and thus naturally associated in a Semitic mind, such as Paul's. These include the words *yes* (17–20), *faithful* (18), *Amen* (20), *gives us security* (21), *faith, stand firm* (24).

1, 14: Phil 2, 16; 1 Thes 2, 19–20.
1, 16: 1 Cor 16, 5–9; Acts 19, 21.
1, 17: Mt 5, 37; Jas 5, 12.
1, 19: Acts 16, 1–3; 1 Thes 1, 1; 2 Thes 1, 1.
1, 20: 1 Cor 14, 16; Rv 3, 14.

YES, YES, MAY WE NOT FAIL

Paul ensures the people of Corinth that he has not wavered in his commitment to them. In a similar manner, Saint Andrew Dung-Lac and the Vietnamese martyrs were unwavering in their commitment to the Gospels. These martyrs consisted of 117 people who died for their faith in nineteenth-century Vietnam. Saint Andrew was a priest in Vietnam, and many of the other 117 martyrs were Catholic laypeople. Pope John Paul II made them all saints of the church on 19 June 1988.

Vietnam is a country that has been rocked by many bloody wars, run by ruthless dictators, and overrun by rampant violence through many of the years of its history as a country. Despite such extreme social conditions, and in the midst of such horrible violence, these martyrs and many like them had the courage to preach the Gospel and live as disciples of Christ.

Take a few moments to reflect on the life of these martyrs.

▶ **2 Cor 1, 15–22**

for glory. ²¹*† But the one who gives us security with you in Christ and who anointed us is God; ²²* he has also put his seal upon us and given the Spirit in our hearts as a first installment.

Paul's Change of Plan

²³*† But I call upon God as witness, on my life, that it is to spare you that I have not yet gone to Corinth. ²⁴ Not that we lord it over your faith; rather, we work together for your joy, for you stand firm in the faith.

2 ¹ For I decided not to come to you again in painful circumstances. ² For if I inflict pain

upon you, then who is there to cheer me except the one pained by me? ³† And I wrote as I did so that when I came I might not be pained by those in whom I should have rejoiced, confident about all of you that my joy is that of all of you. ⁴ For out of much affliction and anguish of heart I wrote to you with many tears, not that you might be pained but that you might know the abundant love I have for you.

The Offender

⁵† If anyone has caused pain, he has caused it not to me, but in some measure (not to exaggerate) to all of you. ⁶ This punishment by the majority is enough for such a person, ⁷* so that on the contrary

---

1, 21–22: The commercial terms *gives us security, seal, first installment* are here used analogously to refer to the process of initiation into the Christian life, perhaps specifically to baptism. The passage is clearly trinitarian. The Spirit is the *first installment* or "down payment" of the full messianic benefits that God guarantees to Christians. Cf Eph 1, 13–14.

1, 23–24: *I have not yet gone to Corinth:* some suppose that Paul received word of some affair in Corinth, which he decided to regulate by letter even before the first of his projected visits (cf 16). Others conjecture that he did pay the first visit, was offended there (cf 2, 5), returned to Ephesus, and sent a letter (2, 3–9) in place of the second visit. The expressions *to spare you* (23) and *work together for your joy* (24) introduce the major themes of the next two paragraphs, which are remarkable for insistent repetition of key words and ideas. These form two clusters of terms in the English translation: (1) cheer, rejoice, encourage, joy; (2) pain, affliction, anguish. These clusters reappear when Paul resumes treatment of this subject in 7, 5–16.

2, 3–4: *I wrote as I did:* we learn for the first time about the sending of a letter in place of the proposed visit. Paul mentions the letter in passing, but emphasizes his motivation in sending it: to avoid being saddened by them (cf 1), and to help them realize the depth of

his love. Another motive will be added in 7, 12: to bring to light their own concern for him. *With many tears:* it has been suggested that we may have all or part of this "tearful letter" somewhere in the Corinthian correspondence, either in 1 Cor 5 (the case of the incestuous man), or in 1 Corinthians as a whole, or in 2 Cor 10–13. None of these hypotheses is entirely convincing. See the note on 13, 1.

2, 5–11: The nature of the *pain* (5) is unclear, though some believe an individual at Corinth rejected Paul's authority, thereby scandalizing many in the community. In any case, action has been taken, and Paul judges the measures adequate to right the situation (6). The follow-up directives he now gives are entirely positive: forgive, encourage, love. *Overwhelmed* (7): a vivid metaphor (literally "swallowed") that Paul employs positively at 5, 4 and in 1 Cor 15, 54 (7). It is often used to describe satanic activity (cf 1 Pt 5, 8); note the reference to Satan here in v 11.

1, 21: 1 Jn 2, 20.27.　　**1, 23:** 2 Cor 13, 2.
1, 22: Eph 1, 13–14; 4, 30 /　　**2, 7:** Col 3, 13.
　　2 Cor 5, 5; Rom 5, 5;
　　8, 16.23.

you should forgive and encourage him instead, or else the person may be overwhelmed by excessive pain. ⁸ Therefore, I urge you to reaffirm your love for him. ⁹* For this is why I wrote, to know your proven character, whether you were obedient in everything. ¹⁰ Whomever you forgive anything, so do I. For indeed what I have forgiven, if I have forgiven anything, has been for you in the presence of Christ, ¹¹* so that we might not be taken advantage of by Satan, for we are not unaware of his purposes.

Paul's Anxiety

¹²*† When I went to Troas for the gospel of Christ, although a door was opened for me in the Lord, ¹³*† I had no relief in my spirit because I did not find my brother Titus. So I took leave of them and went on to Macedonia.

B. Paul's Ministry†

Ministers of a New Covenant

¹⁴† But thanks be to God,† who always leads us in triumph in Christ† and manifests through us the odor of the knowledge of him† in every place. ¹⁵* For we are the aroma of Christ for God among those who are being saved and among those who are perishing, ¹⁶† to the latter an odor of death that leads to death, to the former an odor of life that

Ministers of the New Covenant

Sometimes we get caught up in the notion that faith is all about following the rules. We want so badly to win the "great prize" that we structure our life as a list of do's and don'ts.

Paul recalls God's words from Jer 31, 33, "I will place my law within them, and write it upon their hearts" to emphasize that Christ enables us to be ministers of this new covenant—not of the old written law but of the law of the New Covenant, "for the letter [of the law] brings death, but the Spirit gives life" (2 Cor 3,6). Because Paul's ministry comes from the Spirit, the Spirit is the only letter of recommendation he needs.

The same is true for us. With the law of the New Covenant written on our hearts we give witness to it in our lifestyle. In promoting reconciliation, fostering peace and hope, and passing Christ on to others, we are a living letter of recommendation for the Gospel, to be known and read by all people.

Think of the great honor of having been called by God to be a minister of the New Covenant. How are you doing your job? How can you do it better?

▶ 2 Cor 3, 1–11

2, 12–13: *I had no relief:* Paul does not explain the reason for his anxiety until he resumes the thread of his narrative at 7, 5: he was waiting to hear how the Corinthians would respond to his letter. Since 7, 5–16 describes their response in entirely positive terms, we never learn in detail why he found it necessary to defend and justify his change of plans, as in 1, 15–24. Was this portion of the letter written before the arrival of Titus with his good news (7, 6–7)?

2, 13: *Macedonia:* a Roman province in northern Greece.

2, 14—7, 4: This section constitutes a digression within the narrative of the crisis and its resolution (1, 12—2, 13 and 7, 5–16). The main component (2, 14—6, 10) treats the nature of Paul's ministry and his qualifications for it; this material bears some similarity to the defense of his ministry in chs 10–13, but it may well come from a period close to the crisis. This is followed by a supplementary block of material quite different in character and tone (6, 14—7, 1). These materials may have been brought together into their present position during final editing of the letter; appeals to the Corinthians link them to one another (6, 11–13) and lead back to the interrupted narrative (7, 2–4).

2, 14—6, 10: The question of Paul's adequacy (16; cf 3, 5) and his credentials (3, 1–2) has been raised. Paul responds by an extended treatment of the nature of his ministry. It is a ministry of glory (3, 7—4, 6), of life (4, 7—5, 10), of reconciliation (5, 11—6, 10).

2, 14–16a: The initial statement plunges us abruptly into another train of thought. Paul describes his personal existence and his function as a preacher in two powerful images (14) that constitute a prelude to the development to follow.

2, 14a: *Leads us in triumph in Christ:* this metaphor of a festive parade in honor of a conquering military hero can suggest either a positive sharing in Christ's triumph or an experience of defeat, being led in captivity and submission (cf 4, 8–11; 1 Cor 4, 9). Paul is probably aware of the ambiguity, as he is in the case of the next metaphor.

2, 14b–16a: *The odor of the knowledge of him:* incense was commonly used in triumphal processions. The metaphor suggests the gradual diffusion of the knowledge of God through the apostolic preaching. *The aroma of Christ:* the image shifts from the fragrance Paul diffuses to the aroma that he is. Paul is probably thinking of the "sweet odor" of the sacrifices in the Old Testament (e.g., Gn 8, 21; Ex 29, 18) and perhaps of the metaphor of wisdom as a sweet odor (Sir 24, 15). *Death . . . life:* the aroma of Christ that comes to them through Paul is perceived differently by various classes of people. To some his preaching and his life (cf 1 Cor 1, 17—2, 6) are perceived as *death,* and the effect is death for them; others perceive him, despite appearances, as *life,* and the effect is life for them. This fragrance thus produces a separation and a judgment (cf the function of the "light" in John's gospel).

2, 16b–17: *Qualified:* Paul may be echoing either the self-satisfied claims of other preachers or their charges about Paul's deficiencies. No one is really qualified; the apostle contrasts himself with those who dilute or falsify the preaching for personal advantage and insists on his totally good conscience: his ministry is from God, and he has exercised it with fidelity and integrity (cf 3, 5–6).

*

2, 9: 2 Cor 7, 15.
2, 11: Eph 4, 27.
2, 12: Acts 16, 8.
2, 13: 2 Cor 7, 6; 1 Tm 1, 3.
2, 15: 2 Cor 4, 3; 1 Cor 1, 18.

leads to life. Who is qualified for this? [17]* For we are not like the many who trade on the word of God; but as out of sincerity, indeed as from God and in the presence of God, we speak in Christ.

3 [1]*† Are we beginning to commend ourselves again? Or do we need, as some do, letters of recommendation to you or from you? [2]† You are our letter, written on our hearts, known and read by all, [3]*† shown to be a letter of Christ administered by us, written not in ink but by the Spirit of the living God, not on tablets of stone but on tablets that are hearts of flesh.

[4]† Such confidence we have through Christ toward God. [5]* Not that of ourselves we are qualified to take credit for anything as coming from us; rather, our qualification comes from God, [6]*† who has indeed qualified us as ministers of a new covenant, not of letter but of spirit; for the letter brings death, but the Spirit gives life.

Contrast with the Old Covenant

[7]*† Now if the ministry of death,† carved in letters on stone, was so glorious that the Israelites could not look intently at the face of Moses because of its glory that was going to fade, [8]† how much more will the ministry of the Spirit be glorious? [9] For if the ministry of condemnation was glorious, the ministry of righteousness will abound much more in glory. [10] Indeed, what was endowed with glory has come to have no glory in this respect because of the glory that surpasses it. [11] For if what was going to fade was glorious, how much more will what endures be glorious.

[12]† Therefore, since we have such hope, we act very boldly [13]† and not like Moses, who put a veil over his face so that the Israelites could not look intently at the cessation of what was fading. [14]† Rather, their thoughts were rendered dull, for to this present day the same veil remains unlifted when they read the old covenant, because through Christ it is taken away. [15]* To this day, in fact, whenever Moses is read, a veil lies over their hearts, [16]* but whenever a person turns to the Lord the veil is removed. [17]† Now the Lord is the Spirit, and where the Spirit of the Lord is, there is freedom.

3, 1: Paul seems to allude to certain preachers who pride themselves on their written credentials. Presumably they reproach him for not possessing similar credentials and compel him to spell out his own qualifications (4, 2; 5, 12; 6, 4). The Corinthians themselves should have performed this function for Paul (5, 12; cf 12, 11). Since he is forced to find something that can recommend him, he points to them: their very existence constitutes his *letter* of recommendation (1–2). Others who engage in self-commendation will also be mentioned in 10, 12–18.

3, 2–3: Mention of "letters of recommendation" generates a series of metaphors in which Paul plays on the word "letter": (1) the community is Paul's letter of recommendation (2a); (2) they are a letter engraved on his affections for all to see and read (2b); (3) they are a letter from Christ that Paul merely delivers (3a); (4) they are a letter written by the Spirit on the tablets of human hearts (3b). One image dissolves into another.

3, 3b: This verse contrasts Paul's letter with those *written . . . in ink* (like the credentials of other preachers) and those *written . . . on tablets of stone* (like the law of Moses). These contrasts suggest that the other preachers may have claimed special relationship with Moses. If they were Judaizers zealous for the Mosaic law, that would explain the detailed contrast between the old and the new covenants (6; 4, 7—6, 10). If they were charismatics who claimed Moses as their model, that would explain the extended treatment of Moses himself and his glory (3, 7—4, 6). *Hearts of flesh:* cf Ezekiel's contrast between the heart of flesh that the Spirit gives and the heart of stone that it replaces (Ez 36, 26); the context is covenant renewal and purification that makes observance of the law possible.

3, 4–6: These verses resume 2, 1—3, 3. Paul's confidence (4) is grounded in his sense of God-given mission (2, 17), the specifics of which are described in vv 1–3. Verses 5–6 return to the question of his qualifications (2, 16), attributing them entirely to God. Verse 6 further spells out the situation described in v 3b and "names" it: Paul is living within a *new covenant,* characterized by the Spirit, which *gives life.* The usage of a *new covenant* is derived from Jer 31, 31–33, a passage that also speaks of writing on the heart; cf 2.

3, 6b: This verse serves as a topic sentence for 3, 7—6, 10. For the contrast between *letter* and *spirit,* cf Rom 2, 29; 7, 5–6.

3, 7—4, 6: Paul now develops the contrast enunciated in 3, 6b in terms of the relative glory of the two covenants, insisting on the greater glory of the new. His polemic seems directed against individuals who appeal to the glorious Moses and fail to perceive any comparable glory either in Paul's life as an apostle or in the gospel he preaches. He asserts in response that Christians have a glory of their own that far surpasses that of Moses.

3, 7: The *ministry of death:* from his very first words, Paul describes the Mosaic covenant and ministry from the viewpoint of their limitations. They lead to *death* rather than life (6–7; cf 4, 7—5, 10),

to *condemnation* rather than reconciliation (9; cf 5, 11—6, 10). *Was so glorious:* the basic text to which Paul alludes is Ex 34, 29–35, to which his opponents have undoubtedly laid claim. *Going to fade:* Paul concedes the glory of Moses' covenant and ministry, but grants them only temporary significance.

3, 8–11: *How much more:* the argument "from the less to the greater" is repeated three times (8.9.11). Verse 10 expresses another point of view: the difference in glory is so great that only the new covenant and ministry can properly be called "glorious" at all.

3, 12: *Such hope:* the glory is not yet an object of experience, but that does not lessen Paul's confidence. *Boldly:* the term *parrēsia* expresses outspoken declaration of Christian conviction (cf 4, 1–2). Paul has nothing to hide and no reason for timidity.

3, 13–14a: *Not like Moses:* in Exodus Moses veiled his face to protect the Israelites from God's reflected glory. Without impugning Moses' sincerity, Paul attributes another effect to the veil. Since it lies between God's glory and the Israelites, it explains how they could fail to notice the glory disappearing. *Their thoughts were rendered dull:* the problem lay with their understanding. This will be expressed in vv 14b-16 by a shift in the place of the veil: it is no longer over Moses' face but over their perception.

3, 14b-16: The parallelism in these verses makes it necessary to interpret corresponding parts in relation to one another. *To this present day:* this signals the shift of Paul's attention to his contemporaries; his argument is typological, as in 1 Cor 10. The Israelites of Moses' time typify the Jews of Paul's time, and perhaps also Christians of Jewish origin or mentality who may not recognize the temporary character of Moses' glory. *When they read the old covenant:* the lasting dullness prevents proper appraisal of Moses' person and covenant. When his writings are read in the synagogue, a veil still impedes their understanding. *Through Christ:* i.e., in the new covenant. *Whenever a person turns to the Lord:* Moses in Exodus appeared before God without the veil and gazed on his face unprotected. Paul applies that passage to converts to Christianity: when they turn to the Lord fully and authentically, the impediment to their understanding is removed.

3, 17: *The Lord is the Spirit:* the "Lord" to whom the Christian turns (16) is the Spirit of whom Paul has been speaking, the lifegiving Spirit of the living God (6.8), the inaugurator of the new covenant and ministry, who is also the Spirit of Christ. *The Spirit of the Lord:* the Lord here is the living God (3), but there may also be an allusion to Christ as Lord (14.16). *Freedom:* i.e., from the ministry of death (7) and the covenant that condemned (9).

2, 17: 2 Cor 4, 2; 1 Cor 5, 8.
3, 1: Acts 18, 27; Rom 16, 1; 1 Cor 16, 3.
3, 3: Ex 24, 12; 31, 18; 32, 15–19 / Jer 31, 33; Ez 11, 19; 36, 26–27.
3, 5: Jn 3, 27.
3, 6: Eph 3, 7 / Jer 31, 31–34.
3, 7: Ex 34, 29–35.
3, 15: Rom 11, 7–10.
3, 16: Ex 34, 34.

18*† All of us, gazing with unveiled face on the glory of the Lord, are being transformed into the same image from glory to glory, as from the Lord who is the Spirit.

Integrity in the Ministry

4 1† Therefore, since we have this ministry through the mercy shown us, we are not discouraged. 2* Rather, we have renounced shameful, hidden things; not acting deceitfully or falsifying the word of God, but by the open declaration of the truth we commend ourselves to everyone's conscience in the sight of God. 3*† And even though our gospel is veiled, it is veiled for those who are perishing, 4* in whose case the god of this age has blinded the minds of the unbelievers, so that they may not see the light of the gospel of the glory of Christ, who is the image of God. 5† For we do not preach ourselves but Jesus Christ as Lord, and ourselves as your slaves for the sake of Jesus. 6*† For God who said, "Let light shine out of darkness," has shone in our hearts to bring to light the knowledge of the glory of God on the face of [Jesus] Christ.

The Paradox of the Ministry

7† But we hold this treasure in earthen vessels,† that the surpassing power may be of God and not from us. 8*† We are afflicted in every way, but not constrained; perplexed, but not driven to despair; 9 persecuted, but not abandoned; struck down, but

Christ in Us

It is sometimes tempting to take ourselves a bit too seriously, to feel too self-important. When given a particular responsibility at school, home, or church, we may begin to act as though we are what is important, rather than the task.

The same is true when we accept our calling as a disciple of Christ. Feelings of self-righteousness or pride can creep in, leading to what friends might call a holier-than-thou attitude. Paul reminds us that "we do not preach ourselves but Jesus Christ as Lord" (2 Cor 4, 5). We are simply ordinary clay jars that hold a great treasure to be shared with all. What a wonderful and awesome responsibility we have been given: to share, with our life and our words, what Jesus has done in us, giving him the glory and not seeking it for ourselves.

▸ 2 Cor 4, 5–10

3, 18: Another application of the veil image. *All of us . . . with unveiled face:* Christians (Israelites from whom the veil has been removed) are like Moses, standing in God's presence, beholding and reflecting his glory. *Gazing:* the verb may also be translated "contemplating as in a mirror"; 4, 6 would suggest that the mirror is Christ himself. *Are being transformed:* elsewhere Paul speaks of transformation, conformity to Jesus, God's image, as a reality of the end time, and even v 12 speaks of the glory as an object of hope. But the life-giving Spirit, the distinctive gift of the new covenant, is already present in the community (cf 1, 22, the "first installment"), and the process of transformation has already begun. *Into the same image:* into the image of God, which is Christ (4, 4).

4, 1–2: A ministry of this sort generates confidence and forthrightness; cf 1, 12–14; 2, 17.

4, 3–4: *Though our gospel is veiled:* the final application of the image. Paul has been reproached either for obscurity in his preaching or for his manner of presenting the gospel. But he confidently asserts that there is no veil over his gospel. If some fail to perceive its light, that is because of unbelief. The veil lies over their eyes (3, 14), a blindness induced by Satan, and a sign that they are headed for destruction (cf 2, 15).

4, 5: *We do not preach ourselves:* the light seen in his gospel is the glory of Christ (4). Far from preaching himself, the preacher should be a transparent medium through whom Jesus is perceived (cf 10–11). *Your slaves:* Paul draws attention away from individuals as such and toward their role in relation to God, Christ, and the community; cf 1 Cor 3, 5; 4, 1.

4, 6: Autobiographical allusion to the episode at Damascus clarifies the origin and purpose of Paul's service; cf Acts 9, 1–19; 22, 3–16; 26, 2–18. *"let light shine out of darkness":* Paul seems to be thinking of Gn 1, 3 and presenting his apostolic ministry as a new creation. There may also be an allusion to Is 9, 1, suggesting his prophetic calling as servant of the Lord and light to the nations; cf Is 42, 6.16; 49, 6; 60, 1–2, and the use of light imagery in Acts 26, 13–23. *To bring to light the knowledge:* Paul's role in the process of revelation, expressed at the beginning under the image of the odor and aroma (2, 14–15), is restated now, at the end of this first moment of the development, in the imagery of light and glory (3–6).

4, 7—5, 10: Paul now confronts the difficulty that his present existence does not appear glorious at all; it is marked instead by suffering and death. He deals with this by developing the topic already announced in 3, 3.6, asserting his faith in the presence and ultimate triumph of life, in his own and every Christian existence, despite the experience of death.

4, 7: *This treasure:* the glory that he preaches and into which they are being transformed. *In earthen vessels:* the instruments God uses are human and fragile; some imagine small terracotta lamps in which light is carried.

4, 8–9: A catalogue of his apostolic trials and afflictions. Yet in these the negative never completely prevails; there is always some experience of rescue, of salvation.

3, 18: Rom 8, 29–30; 12, 2; Gal 4, 19; Phil 3, 10.20–21 / 2 Cor 4, 4–6; 1 Cor 15, 49; Col 1, 15; 3, 9–11; 1 Jn 3, 2.

4, 2: 2 Cor 2, 17; 1 Thes 2, 4–7.

4, 3: 2 Cor 2, 15–16; 2 Thes 2, 10.

4, 4: Jn 12, 31–36 / 1 Tm 1, 11.

4, 6: Gn 1, 3; Is 9, 1; Acts 26, 13–23; Gal 1, 15–16 / Jn 8, 12; Heb 1, 3.

4, 8: 2 Cor 6, 4–10; 1 Cor 4, 9–13.

Hopeless and Hurting

Sometimes life can be filled with despair and discouragement. We can get down in the dumps and feel like everything is a waste of our time and energy. Paul encourages us not to lose hope but to keep our hearts and minds very much alive. Paul connects our moments of despair to Jesus' suffering on the cross. Jesus never lost hope. He believed to the end and then was raised from the dead to new life to show the world that his suffering and death had a hopeful outcome. God promises us this same hopeful outcome of being raised up.

Try this exercise: Re-read 2 Cor 4, 7–18 in a prayerful way, perhaps with some reflective music in the background. Then write a few thoughts of your own in a journal, or write your own prayer about suffering and despair. Don't forget to mention hope at the end of your prayer because, ultimately, that was Jesus' message.

▸ 2 Cor 4, 7–18

not destroyed; [10]*† always carrying about in the body the dying of Jesus, so that the life of Jesus may also be manifested in our body. [11]* For we who live are constantly being given up to death for the sake of Jesus, so that the life of Jesus may be manifested in our mortal flesh.

[12]† So death is at work in us, but life in you. [13]*† Since, then, we have the same spirit of faith, according to what is written, "I believed, therefore I spoke," we too believe and therefore speak, [14]* knowing that the one who raised the Lord Jesus will raise us also with Jesus and place us with you in his presence. [15]* Everything indeed is for you, so that the grace bestowed in abundance on more and more people may cause the thanksgiving to overflow for the glory of God.

[16]*† Therefore, we are not discouraged;† rather, although our outer self is wasting away, our inner self is being renewed day by day. [17]* For this momentary light affliction is producing for us an eternal weight of glory beyond all comparison, [18]* as we look not to what is seen but to what is unseen; for what is seen is transitory, but what is unseen is eternal.

Our Future Destiny

5 [1]*† For we know that if our earthly dwelling, a tent, should be destroyed, we have a building from God, a dwelling not made with hands, eternal in heaven. [2]*† For in this tent we groan, longing to be further clothed with our heavenly habitation [3]† if indeed, when we have taken it off,

---

†
4, 10–11: Both the negative and the positive sides of the experience are grounded christologically. The logic is similar to that of 1, 3–11. His sufferings are connected with Christ's, and his deliverance is a sign that he is to share in Jesus' resurrection.

4, 12–15: His experience does not terminate in himself, but in others (12.15; cf 1, 4–5). Ultimately, everything is ordered even beyond the community, toward God (15; cf 1, 11).

4, 13–14: Like the Psalmist, Paul clearly proclaims his faith, affirming life within himself despite death (10–11) and the life-giving effect of his experience upon the church (12.14–15). *And place us with you in his presence:* Paul imagines God presenting him and them to Jesus at the parousia and the judgment; cf 11, 2; Rom 14, 10.

4, 16–18: In a series of contrasts Paul explains the extent of his faith in life. Life is not only already present and revealing itself (8–11.16) but will outlast his experience of affliction and dying: it is eternal (17–18).

4, 16: *Not discouraged:* i.e., despite the experience of death. Paul is still speaking of himself personally, but he assumes his faith and attitude will be shared by all Christians. *Our outer self:* the individual subject of ordinary perception and observation, in contrast to the interior and hidden self, which undergoes renewal. *Is being renewed day by day:* this suggests a process that has already begun; cf 3, 18. The renewal already taking place even in Paul's dying is a share in the life of Jesus, but this is recognized only by faith (13.18; 5, 7).

5, 1: *Our earthly dwelling:* the same contrast is restated in the imagery of a dwelling. The language recalls Jesus' saying about the destruction of the temple and the construction of another building *not made with hands* (Mk 14, 58), a prediction later applied to Jesus' own body (Jn 2, 20).

5, 2–5: Verses 2–3 and 4 are largely parallel in structure. *We groan, longing:* see the note on 5, 5. *Clothed with our heavenly habitation:* Paul mixes his metaphors, adding the image of the garment to

that of the building. *Further clothed:* the verb means strictly "to put one garment on over another." Paul may desire to put the resurrection body on over his mortal body, without dying; vv 2 and 4 permit this meaning but do not impose it. Or perhaps he imagines the resurrection body as a garment put on over the Christ-garment first received in baptism (Gal 3, 27) and preserved by moral behavior (Rom 13, 12–14; Col 3, 12; cf Mt 22, 11–13). Some support for this interpretation may be found in the context; cf the references to baptism (5), to judgment according to works (10), and to present renewal (4, 16), an idea elsewhere combined with the image of "putting on" a new nature (Eph 4, 22–24; Col 3, 1–5.9–10).

5, 3: *When we have taken it off:* the majority of witnesses read "when we have put it on," i.e., when we have been clothed (in the resurrection body), then we shall not be without a body (naked). This seems mere tautology, though some understand it to mean: whether we are "found" (by God at the judgment) clothed or naked depends upon whether we have preserved or lost our original investiture in Christ (cf the previous note). In this case to "put it on" does not refer to the resurrection body, but to keeping intact the Christ-garment of baptism. The translation follows the western reading (Codex Bezae, Tertullian), the sense of which is clear: to "take it off" is to shed our mortal body in death, after which we shall be clothed in the resurrection body and hence not "naked" (cf 1 Cor 15, 51–53).

4, 10: Col 1, 24.	**4, 17:** Mt 5, 11–12; Rom 8, 18.
4, 11: Rom 8, 36; 1 Cor 15, 31.	**4, 18:** Rom 8, 24–25; Heb 11, 1.
4, 13: Ps 116, 10.	**5, 1:** Is 38, 12 / Col 3, 1–4 / Mk 14, 58; Col 2, 11; Heb 9, 11.24.
4, 14: Rom 4, 24–25; 8, 11; 1 Cor 6, 14; 1 Thes 4, 14.	**5, 2:** Rom 8, 23 / 1 Cor 15, 51–54.
4, 15: 2 Cor 1, 11.	
4, 16: 2 Cor 4, 1.1.	

It's What's Inside That Counts

Television, magazines, and advertising show the ideal person as skinny, well developed, muscular, clear complexioned, tall, and with perfect features. Very few people fit that image. Many of those who don't fit that image feel insecure and inadequate. Some people try desperately to measure up to that standard with crash diets, workouts at fitness centers, weight training, steroids, or plastic surgery. Some people even end up with eating disorders like bulimia and anorexia.

In 2 Cor 5, 1–5, Paul reminds us that our earthly body is a temporary dwelling. It is important for us to take care of this earthly "tent" with a healthy diet and regular exercise. But our desire for our heavenly dwelling should cause us to focus on our inner appearance more than our outer appearance.

In your prayer, reflect on the following questions:

- Are you satisfied with your physical appearance? Why or why not?
- Do you spend as much time working on your inner appearance—by developing virtues like compassion, generosity, mercy, and patience—as you do on your outer appearance?

Write a prayer asking God for the grace (gift) to feel secure in your outward appearance. Listen for God's response.

▸ 2 Cor 5, 1–5

we shall not be found naked. ⁴*† For while we are in this tent we groan and are weighed down, because we do not wish to be unclothed but to be further clothed, so that what is mortal may be swallowed up by life. ⁵*† Now the one who has prepared us for this very thing is God, who has given us the Spirit as a first installment.

⁶† So we are always courageous, although we know that while we are at home in the body we are away from the Lord, ⁷ for we walk by faith, not by sight. ⁸* Yet we are courageous, and we would rather leave the body and go home to the Lord. ⁹ Therefore, we aspire to please him, whether we are at home or away. ¹⁰*† For we must all appear before the judgment seat of Christ, so that each one may receive recompense, according to what he did in the body, whether good or evil.

The Ministry of Reconciliation

¹¹*† Therefore, since we know the fear of the Lord, we try to persuade others; but we are clearly apparent to God, and I hope we are also apparent to your consciousness. ¹²* We are not commending ourselves to you again but giving you an opportunity to boast of us, so that you may have something to say to those who boast of external appearance rather than of the heart. ¹³† For if we are out of our

So whoever is in Christ is a new creation

5, 17

5, 4: *We do not wish to be unclothed:* a clear allusion to physical death (4, 16; 5, 1). Unlike the Greeks, who found dissolution of the body desirable (cf Socrates), Paul has a Jewish horror of it. He seems to be thinking of the "intermediate period," an interval between death and resurrection. *Swallowed up by life:* cf 1 Cor 15, 54.

5, 5: God has created us for resurrected bodily life and already prepares us for it by the gift of the Spirit in baptism. *The Spirit as a first installment:* the striking parallel to 5, 1–5 in Rom 8, 17–30 describes Christians who have received the "firstfruits" (cf "first installment" here) of the Spirit as "groaning" (cf 2.4 here) for the resurrection, the complete redemption of their bodies. In place of clothing and building, Rom 8 uses other images for the resurrection: adoption and conformity to the image of the Son.

5, 6–9: Tension between present and future is expressed by another spatial image, the metaphor of the country and its citizens. At present we are like citizens in exile or far away from home. The Lord is the distant homeland, believed in but unseen (7).

5, 10: *We must all appear:* the verb is ambiguous: we are sched-
uled to "appear" for judgment, at which we will be "revealed" as we are (cf 11; 2, 14; 4, 10–11).

5, 11–15: This paragraph is transitional. Paul sums up much that has gone before. Still playing on the term "appearance," he reasserts his transparency before God and the Corinthians, in contrast to the self-commendation, boasting, and preoccupation with externals that characterize some others (cf 1, 12–14; 2, 14; 3, 1; 3, 7—4, 6). Verse 14 recalls 3, 7—4, 6, and sums up 4, 7—5, 10.

5, 13: *Out of our minds:* this verse confirms that a concern for ecstasy and charismatic experience may lie behind the discussion about "glory" in 3, 7—4, 6. Paul also enjoys such experiences but, unlike others, does not make a public display of them or consider them ends in themselves. *Rational:* the Greek virtue *sōphrosynē*, to which Paul alludes, implies reasonableness, moderation, good judgment, self-control.

5, 4: Is 25, 8; 1 Cor 15, 54.	Rom 2, 16; 14, 10–11.
5, 5: 2 Cor 1, 22.	**5, 11:** 2 Cor 1, 12–14.
5, 8: Phil 1, 21–23.	**5, 12:** 2 Cor 3, 1 / 2 Cor 1,
5, 10: Mt 16, 27; 25, 31–46;	14; Phil 1, 26.

Ambassadors for Christ

The title ambassador is usually used by people who are authorized to represent their country while living as a resident in a foreign nation. For example, the U.S. ambassador to Mexico is an official representative of the United States who lives in Mexico and speaks for the U.S. government in Mexico.

Paul tells us that we are reconciled—that is, united—with God through Christ, and that God has now entrusted us with the ministry of helping others to be reconciled through Christ. Imagine that; we are called ambassadors for Christ! Of all the ways God could be made known in the world, God chooses to use us. We are "authorized representatives." We are God's messengers.

That might sound a bit intimidating! We might naturally wonder how we, broken and imperfect people, are supposed to represent God, who is completely holy and just. The reality is that God wants to use us, flaws and all. God does not need perfect people—just willing people! Spend some time in prayer, and share with God your thoughts, feelings, and fears about being invited to take on this great role of ambassador for Christ.

▶ 2 Cor 5, 17–21

---

minds, it is for God; if we are rational, it is for you. [14]*† For the love of Christ impels us, once we have come to the conviction that one died for all; therefore, all have died. [15]* He indeed died for all, so that those who live might no longer live for themselves but for him who for their sake died and was raised.

[16]† Consequently, from now on we regard no one according to the flesh; even if we once knew Christ according to the flesh, yet now we know him so no longer. [17]* So whoever is in Christ is a new creation: the old things have passed away; behold, new things have come. [18]† And all this is from God, who has reconciled us to himself through Christ and given us the ministry of reconciliation, [19]* namely, God was reconciling the world to himself in Christ, not counting their trespasses against them and entrusting to us the message of reconciliation. [20]* So we are ambassadors for Christ, as if God were appealing through us. We implore you on behalf of Christ, be reconciled to God. [21]*† For our sake he made him to be sin who did not know sin, so that we might become the righteousness of God in him.

The Experience of the Ministry

6 [1]*† Working together, then, we appeal to you not to receive the grace of God in vain.† [2]*† For he says:

"In an acceptable time I heard you,
and on the day of salvation I helped you."

5, 14–15: These verses echo 4, 14 and resume the treatment of "life despite death" from 4, 7—5, 10.

5, 16–17: *Consequently:* the death of Christ described in vv 14–15 produces a whole new order (17) and a new mode of perception (16). *According to the flesh:* the natural mode of perception, characterized as "fleshly," is replaced by a mode of perception proper to the Spirit. Elsewhere Paul contrasts what Christ looks like according to the old criteria (weakness, powerlessness, folly, death) and according to the new (wisdom, power, life); cf vv 15.21; 1 Cor 1, 17—3, 3. Similarly, he describes the paradoxical nature of Christian existence, e.g., in 4, 10–11.14. *A new creation:* rabbis used this expression to describe the effect of the entrance of a proselyte or convert into Judaism or of the remission of sins on the Day of Atonement. The new order created *in Christ* is the new covenant (3, 6).

5, 18–21: Paul attempts to explain the meaning of God's action by a variety of different categories; his attention keeps moving rapidly back and forth from God's act to his own ministry as well. *Who has reconciled us to himself:* i.e., he has brought all into oneness. *Not counting their trespasses:* the reconciliation is described as an act of justification (cf "righteousness," 21); this contrasts with the covenant that condemned (3, 8). *The ministry of reconciliation:* Paul's role in the wider picture is described: entrusted with the message of reconciliation (19), he is Christ's ambassador, through whom God appeals (20a). In v 20b Paul acts in the capacity just described.

5, 21: This is a statement of God's purpose, expressed paradoxically in terms of sharing and exchange of attributes. As Christ became our righteousness (1 Cor 1, 30), we become God's righteousness (cf vv 14–15).

6, 1–10: This paragraph is a single long sentence in the Greek, interrupted by the parenthesis of v 2. The one main verb is "we appeal." In this paragraph Paul both exercises his ministry of reconciliation (cf 5, 20) and describes how his ministry is exercised: the "message of reconciliation" (5, 19) is lived existentially in his apostolic experience.

6, 1: *Not to receive . . . in vain:* i.e., conform to the gift of justification and new creation. The context indicates how this can be done concretely: become God's righteousness (5, 21), not live for oneself (5, 15), be reconciled with Paul (6, 11–13; 7, 2–3).

6, 2: *In an acceptable time:* Paul cites the Septuagint text of Is 49, 8; the Hebrew reads "in a time of favor"; it is parallel to "on the day of salvation." *Now:* God is bestowing favor and salvation at this very moment, as Paul is addressing his letter to them.

5, 14: Rom 6, 1–6.
5, 15: Rom 4, 25; 6, 4–11; 14, 9; Col 3, 3–4.
5, 17: Gal 6, 15; Eph 2, 15 / Is 43, 18–21; Rv 21, 5.
5, 19: Rom 5, 10–11; Col 1, 20.
5, 20: Eph 6, 20; Phlm 9.

5, 21: Is 53, 6–9; Gal 3, 13 / Rom 3, 24–26; 1 Cor 1, 30; 1 Pt 2, 24;1 Jn 3, 5–8.
6, 1: 1 Cor 3, 9; 1 Thes 3, 2.
6, 2: Is 49, 8.

Behold, now is a very acceptable time; behold, now is the day of salvation. ³*† We cause no one to stumble in anything, in order that no fault may be found with our ministry; ⁴*† on the contrary, in everything we commend ourselves as ministers of God, through much endurance,† in afflictions, hardships, constraints, ⁵ *beatings, imprisonments, riots, labors, vigils, fasts; ⁶*† by purity, knowledge, patience, kindness, in a holy spirit, in unfeigned love, ⁷ *in truthful speech, in the power of God; with weapons of righteousness at the right and at the left; ⁸† through glory and dishonor, insult and praise. We are treated as deceivers and yet are truthful; ⁹ *as unrecognized

and yet acknowledged; as dying and behold we live; as chastised and yet not put to death; ¹⁰ *as sorrowful yet always rejoicing; as poor yet enriching many; as having nothing and yet possessing all things.

¹¹† We have spoken frankly to you, Corinthians; our heart is open wide. ¹²* You are not constrained by us; you are constrained by your own affections. ¹³* As recompense in kind (I speak as to my children), be open yourselves.

Call to Holiness

¹⁴† Do not be yoked with those who are different, with unbelievers.† For what partnership do

AN "ANYWAY" GOD

We serve an "anyway" God. Impediments, hurdles, and obstacles are part of our inheritance, yet we excel anyway. Some of us were kidnapped from Africa, enslaved and shackled, stripped of our culture, robbed of our native language, and torn from our family, yet today, we thrive anyway.

Surely, the Lord was in the midst of the African Americans' past, ushering them on to a better day. The evidence that the Lord walked with them through horrific conditions is simply too great to deny. Yet, as a people, they can identify with Paul's words in 2 Cor 6, 1–10—their struggles have only made them stronger.

Even today, life for most of us is no cakewalk, but our ability to walk at all comes from God, who conquers all. Can you recognize God's grace and mercy and celebrate the presence of God in your good and bad times?

Dear God, no matter how high the odds are stacked against me, I can overcome them with your grace and mercy, and survive. Amen.

▶ 2 Cor 6, 1–10

6, 3: *Cause no one to stumble:* the language echoes that of 1 Cor 8–10, as does the expression "no longer live for themselves" in 5, 15. *That no fault may be found:* i.e., at the eschatological judgment (cf 1 Cor 4, 2–5).

6, 4a: This is the central assertion, the topic statement for the catalogue that follows. *We commend ourselves:* Paul's self-commendation is ironical (with an eye on the charges mentioned in 3, 1–3) and paradoxical (pointing mostly to experiences that would not normally be considered points of pride but are perceived as such by faith). Cf also the self-commendation in 11, 23–29. *As ministers of God:* the same Greek word, *diakonos,* means "minister" and "servant"; cf 11, 23, the central assertion in a similar context, and 1 Cor 3, 5.

6, 4b-5: *Through much endurance:* this phrase functions as a subtitle; it is followed by an enumeration of nine specific types of trials endured.

6, 6–7a: A list of virtuous qualities in two groups of four, the second fuller than the first.

6, 8b–10: A series of seven rhetorically effective antitheses, contrasting negative external impressions with positive inner reality. Paul perceives his existence as a reflection of Jesus' own and affirms an inner reversal that escapes outward observation. The final two members illustrate two distinct kinds of paradox or apparent contradiction that are characteristic of apostolic experience.

6, 11–13: Paul's tone becomes quieter, but his appeal for acceptance and affection is emotionally charged. References to the heart and their mutual relations bring the development begun in 2, 14—3, 3 to an effective conclusion.

6, 14—7, 1: Language and thought shift noticeably here. Suddenly we are in a different atmosphere, dealing with a quite different problem. Both the vocabulary and the thought, with their contrast between good and evil, are more characteristic of Qumran documents or the Book of Revelation than they are of Paul. Hence, critics suspect that this section was inserted by another hand.

6, 14–16a: The opening injunction to separate from unbelievers is reinforced by five rhetorical questions to make the point that Christianity is not compatible with paganism. Their opposition is emphasized also by the accumulation of five distinct designations for each group. These verses are a powerful statement of God's holiness and the exclusiveness of his claims.

6, 3: 1 Cor 9, 12; 10, 32 / 2 Cor 8, 20–21.
6, 4: 2 Cor 4, 8–11; 11, 23–27; 1 Cor 4, 9–13.
6, 5: Acts 16, 23.
6, 6: Gal 5, 22–23.
6, 7: 2 Cor 10, 4; Rom 13,

12; Eph 6, 11–17.
6, 9: 2 Cor 4, 10–11; Rom 8, 36.
6, 10: Rom 8, 32; 1 Cor 3, 21.
6, 12: 2 Cor 7, 3.
6, 13: Gal 4, 19.

Shine Like a Star

Second Corinthians 6, 14 makes a sudden transition; 6, 14—7, 1 may even be a fragment from another letter. We are not sure what kind of behavior or problem Paul is talking about here. But it does seem clear that Paul is cautioning the Corinthians against being too closely influenced by non-Christians—unbelievers. Paul doesn't want the Corinthians to return to sinful behaviors.

Christians in the United States are also surrounded by many unhealthy and unholy choices. Our words and behaviors should show that "we are the temple of the living God" (6, 16). We must be careful of friendships and media influences that might tempt us to start thinking that wrong is right. This doesn't mean we should be arrogant and separate ourselves from others. Remember that Jesus sometimes hung around with sinners. But he didn't share in their sins. He was a light for them.

As Paul says in Phil 2, 15, we are "children of God" in a "perverse generation," where we shine "like lights in the world."

▸ 2 Cor 6, 14–18

---

righteousness and lawlessness have? Or what fellowship does light have with darkness? ¹⁵ What accord has Christ with Beliar? Or what has a believer in common with an unbeliever? ¹⁶*† What agreement has the temple of God with idols? For we are the temple of the living God; as God said:

"I will live with them and move among
them,
and I will be their God
and they shall be my people.
¹⁷* Therefore, come forth from them
and be separate," says the Lord,
"and touch nothing unclean;
then I will receive you
¹⁸* and I will be a father to you,
and you shall be sons and daughters
to me,
says the Lord Almighty."

¹ Since we have these promises, beloved, let us cleanse ourselves from every defilement of flesh and spirit, making holiness perfect in the fear of God.

²† Make room for us; we have not wronged anyone, or ruined anyone, or taken advantage of anyone. ³* I do not say this in condemnation, for I have already said that you are in our hearts, that we may die together and live together. ⁴ I have great confidence in you, I have great pride in you; I am filled with encouragement, I am overflowing with joy all the more because of all our affliction.

C. Resolution of the Crisis†

Paul's Joy in Macedonia

⁵*† For even when we came into Macedonia,† our flesh had no rest, but we were afflicted in every

---

6, 16c–18: This is a chain of scriptural citations carefully woven together. God's covenant relation to his people and his presence among them (16) is seen as conditioned on cultic separation from the profane and cultically impure (17); that relation is translated into the personal language of the parent-child relationship, an extension to the community of the language of 2 Sm 7, 14 (18). Some remarkable parallels to this chain are found in the final chapters of Revelation. God's presence among his people (21, 22) is expressed there, too, by applying 2 Sm 7, 14 to the community (21, 7). There is a call to separation (18, 4) and exclusion of the unclean from the community and its liturgy (21, 27). The title "Lord Almighty" (*Pantokratōr*) occurs in the New Testament only here in 18 and nine times in Revelation.

7, 2–4: These verses continue the thought of 6, 11–13, before the interruption of 6, 14—7, 1. Verse 4 serves as a transition to the next section: the four themes it introduces (confidence; pride or "boasting"; encouragement; joy in affliction) are developed in vv 5–16. All have appeared previously in the letter.

7, 5–16: This section functions as a peroration or formal summing up of the whole first part of the letter, chs 1–7. It deals with the restoration of right relations between Paul and the Corinthians, and it is marked by fullness and intensity of emotion.

7, 5–7: Paul picks up the thread of the narrative interrupted at 2, 13 (5) and describes the resolution of the tense situation there depicted (6–7). Finally Titus arrives and his coming puts an end to Paul's restlessness (2, 13; 7, 5), casts out his fears, and reverses his mood. The theme of encouragement and affliction is reintroduced (cf 1, 3–11); here, too, encouragement is traced back to God and is described as contagious (6). The language of joy and sorrow also reappears in v 7 (cf 1, 23—2, 1 and the note on 1, 23–24).

7, 5: *Macedonia:* see the note on 2, 13.

6, 16: 1 Cor 10, 20–21 / 1 Cor 3, 16–17; 6, 19 / Ex 25, 8; 29, 45; Lv 26, 12; Jer 31, 1; 32, 38; Ez 37, 27.
6, 17: Is 52, 11; Ez 20, 34.41; Rv 18, 4; 21, 27.
6, 18: 2 Sm 7, 14; Ps 2, 7; Is 43, 6; Jer 31, 9; Rv 21, 7 / Rv 4, 8; 11, 17; 15, 3; 21, 22.
7, 3: 2 Cor 6, 11–13.
7, 5: 2 Cor 2, 13.

way—external conflicts, internal fears. 6* But God, who encourages the downcast, encouraged us by the arrival of Titus, 7 and not only by his arrival but also by the encouragement with which he was encouraged in regard to you, as he told us of your yearning, your lament, your zeal for me, so that I rejoiced even more. 8*† For even if I saddened you by my letter, I do not regret it; and if I did regret it ([for] I see that that letter saddened you, if only for a while), 9 I rejoice now, not because you were saddened, but because you were saddened into repentance; for you were saddened in a godly way, so that you did not suffer loss in anything because of us. 10 For godly sorrow produces a salutary repentance without regret, but worldly sorrow produces death. 11 For behold what earnestness this godly sorrow has produced for you, as well as readiness for a defense, and indignation, and fear, and yearning, and zeal, and punishment. In every way you have shown yourselves to be innocent in the matter. 12* So then even though I wrote to you, it was not on account of the one who did the wrong, or on account of the one who suffered the wrong, but in order that your concern for us might be made plain to you in the sight of God. 13† For this reason we are encouraged.

And besides our encouragement, we rejoice even more because of the joy of Titus, since his spirit has been refreshed by all of you. 14 For if I have boasted to him about you, I was not put to shame. No, just as everything we said to you was true, so our boasting before Titus proved to be the truth. 15* And his heart goes out to you all the more, as he remembers the obedience of all of you, when you received him with fear and trembling. 16 I rejoice, because I have confidence in you in every respect.

III: The Collection for Jerusalem†

Generosity in Giving

8 1*† We want you to know, brothers,† of the grace of God† that has been given to the churches of Macedonia, 2† for in a severe test of affliction, the abundance of their joy and their profound poverty overflowed in a wealth of generosity on their part. 3† For according to their means, I can testify, and beyond their means, spontaneously, 4* they begged us insistently for the favor of taking part in the service to the holy ones, 5† and this, not as we expected, but they gave themselves first to the Lord and to us through the will of God, 6*† so that we urged Titus that, as he had already begun, he should also complete for you this gracious act also. 7*† Now as you excel in every respect, in faith, discourse, knowledge, all earnestness, and in the love we

---

7, 8–12: Paul looks back on the episode from the viewpoint of its ending. The goal of their common activity, promotion of their joy (1, 24), has been achieved, despite and because of the sorrow they felt. That sorrow was God-given. Its salutary effects are enumerated fully and impressively in vv 10–11; not the least important of these is that it has revealed to them the attachment they have to Paul.

7, 13–16: Paul summarizes the effect of the experience on Titus: encouragement, joy, love, relief. Finally, he describes its effects on himself: encouragement, joy, confidence, pride or "boasting" (i.e., the satisfaction resulting from a boast that proves well-founded; cf 4; 1, 12.14).

8, 1—9, 15: Paul turns to a new topic, the collection for the church in Jerusalem. There is an early precedent for this project in the agreement mentioned in Gal 2, 6–10. According to Acts, the church at Antioch had sent Saul and Barnabas to Jerusalem with relief (Acts 11, 27–30). Subsequently Paul organized a project of relief for Jerusalem among his own churches. Our earliest evidence for it comes in 1 Cor 16, 1–4, after it had already begun (see the notes there); by the time Paul wrote Rom 15, 25–28 the collection was completed and ready for delivery. Chapters 8 and 9 contain what appear to be two letters on the subject. In them Paul gives us his fullest exposition of the meaning he sees in the enterprise, presenting it as an act of Christian charity and as an expression of the unity of the church, both present and eschatological. These chapters are especially rich in the recurrence of key words, on which Paul plays; it is usually impossible to do justice to these wordplays in the translation.

8, 1–24: This is a letter of recommendation for Titus and two unnamed companions, written from Macedonia probably at least a year later than 1 Cor 16. The recommendation proper is prefaced by remarks about the ideals of sharing and equality within the Christian community (1–15). Phil 4, 10–20 shows that Paul has reflected on his personal experience of need and relief in his relations with the community at Philippi; he now develops his reflections on the larger scale of relations between his Gentile churches and the mother church in Jerusalem.

8, 1–5: The example of the Macedonians, a model of what ought to be happening at Corinth, provides Paul with the occasion for expounding his theology of "giving."

8, 1: The grace of God: the fundamental theme is expressed by the Greek noun charis, which will be variously translated throughout these chapters as "grace" (8, 1; 9, 8.14), "favor" (8, 4), "gracious act"

(8, 6.7.9) or "gracious work" (8, 19), to be compared to "gracious gift" (1 Cor 16, 3). The related term, eucharistia, "thanksgiving," also occurs at 9, 11.12. The wordplay is not superficial; various mutations of the same root signal inner connection between aspects of a single reality, and Paul consciously exploits the similarities in vocabulary to highlight that connection.

8, 2: Three more terms are now introduced. Test (dokimē): the same root is translated as "to test" and "evidence" (9, 13); it means to be tried and found genuine. Abundance: variations on the same root lie behind "overflow" (8, 2; 9, 12), "excel" (8, 7), "surplus" (8, 14), "superfluous" (9, 1), "make abundant" and "have an abundance" (9, 8). These expressions of fullness contrast with references to need (8, 14; 9, 12). Generosity: the word haplotēs has nuances of both simplicity and sincerity; here and in 9, 11.13 it designates the singleness of purpose that manifests itself in generous giving.

8, 3–4: Paul emphasizes the spontaneity of the Macedonians and the nature of their action. They begged us insistently: the same root is translated as "urge," "appeal," "encourage" (8, 6.17; 9, 5). Taking part: the same word is translated "contribution" in 9, 13 and a related term as "partner" in 8, 23. Service (diakonia): this word occurs also in 9, 1.13 as "service"; in 9, 12 it is translated "administration," and in 8, 19.20 the corresponding verb is rendered "administer."

8, 5: They gave themselves . . . to the Lord and to us: on its deepest level their attitude is one of self-giving.

8, 6: Titus: 1 Cor 16 seemed to leave the organization up to the Corinthians, but apparently Paul has sent Titus to initiate the collection as well; 8, 16–17 will describe Titus' attitude as one of shared concern and cooperation.

8, 7: The charitable service Paul is promoting is seen briefly and in passing within the perspective of Paul's theology of the charisms. Earnestness (spoudē): this or related terms occur also in v 22 ("earnest") and 8, 8.16.17 ("concern").

7, 6: 2 Cor 7, 13–14; 1 Thes 3, 6–8.

7, 8: 2 Cor 2, 2–4; Heb 12, 11.

7, 12: 2 Cor 2, 3.9; 7, 8.

7, 15: 2 Cor 2, 9.

8, 1: 2 Cor 11, 9; Rom 15, 26.

8, 4: Acts 24, 17; Rom 15, 31.

8, 6: 2 Cor 2, 13; 7, 6–7.13–14; 8, 16.23; 12, 18.

8, 7: 1 Cor 1, 5.

have for you, may you excel in this gracious act also.

⁸ I say this not by way of command, but to test the genuineness of your love by your concern for others. ⁹*† For you know the gracious act of our Lord Jesus Christ, that for your sake he became poor although he was rich, so that by his poverty you might become rich. ¹⁰* And I am giving counsel in this matter, for it is appropriate for you who began not only to act but to act willingly last year: ¹¹† complete it now, so that your eager willingness may be matched by your completion of it out of what you have. ¹²† For if the eagerness is there, it is acceptable according to what one has, not according to what one does not have; ¹³ not that others should have relief while you are burdened, but that

as a matter of equality ¹⁴ your surplus at the present time should supply their needs, so that their surplus may also supply your needs, that there may be equality. ¹⁵* As it is written:

> "Whoever had much did not have more,
> and whoever had little did not have less."

Titus and His Collaborators

¹⁶† But thanks be to God who put the same concern for you into the heart of Titus, ¹⁷ for he not only welcomed our appeal but, since he is very concerned, he has gone to you of his own accord. ¹⁸*† With him we have sent the brother who is praised in all the churches for his preaching of the

CHRISTIANS SHARE THEIR MONEY OUT OF SOLIDARITY!

In chapters 8–9 of 2 Corinthians, Paul encourages the Corinthians to give generously to a collection for the poor Christians of Jerusalem. In a similar way, Hispanics in the United States often generously collect and share the money they earn with their families in Latin America.

"I cannot fail my mother," Anita said. "I always try to send her at least a hundred dollars a month because she depends on me." Anita, who lives in Minneapolis with her husband and children, has been sending money to her mother in central Mexico since Anita came to the United States eight years ago. Anita and other Hispanics share the money they make in the United States with their families in Latin America in the spirit of solidarity. "It is something that we have to do," a Central American immigrant tells us. "It is part of our culture. It is the responsibility of all adult children to help our families, even if we don't make much money."

How are you generous with your money? What financial sacrifices can you make this week for the sake of family members or others you know who are poor or poorer than you?

Ask the Holy Spirit for the gift of generosity for yourself and for other young Catholics. Pray that a willingness to share the resources God has blessed you with becomes a lifelong habit.

▶ 2 Corinthians, chapters 8–9

8, 9: The dialectic of Jesus' experience, expressed earlier in terms of life and death (5, 15), sin and righteousness (5, 21), is now rephrased in terms of poverty and wealth. Many scholars think this is a reference to Jesus' preexistence with God (his "wealth") and to his incarnation and death (his "poverty"), and they point to the similarity between this verse and Phil 2, 6–8. Others interpret the wealth and poverty as succeeding phases of Jesus' earthly existence, e.g., his sense of intimacy with God and then the desolation and the feeling of abandonment by God in his death (cf Mk 15, 34).

8, 11: *Eager:* the word *prothymia* also occurs in 8, 12.19; 9, 2.

8, 12–15: Paul introduces the principle of *equality* into the discussion. The goal is not impoverishment but sharing of resources; balance is achieved at least over the course of time. In v 15 Paul grounds his argument unexpectedly in the experience of Israel gathering manna in the desert: equality was achieved, independently of personal exertion, by God, who gave with an even hand according to need. Paul touches briefly here on the theme of "living from God."

8, 16–24: In recommending Titus and his companions, Paul stresses their personal and apostolic qualities, their good dispositions toward the Corinthians, and their authority as messengers of the churches and representatives of Christ.

8, 18: *The brother:* we do not know the identity of this co-worker of Paul, nor of the third companion mentioned below in v 22.

8, 9: 2 Cor 6, 10; Phil 2, 6–8.
8, 10: 2 Cor 9, 2; 1 Cor 16, 1–4.
8, 15: Ex 16, 18.
8, 18: 2 Cor 12, 18.

gospel. [19]* And not only that, but he has also been appointed our traveling companion by the churches in this gracious work administered by us for the glory of the Lord [himself] and for the expression of our eagerness. [20]† This we desire to avoid, that anyone blame us about this lavish gift administered by us, [21]* for we are concerned for what is honorable not only in the sight of the Lord but also in the sight of others. [22] And with them we have sent our brother whom we often tested in many ways and found earnest, but who is now much more earnest because of his great confidence in you. [23] As for Titus, he is my partner and co-worker for you; as for our brothers, they are apostles of the churches, the glory of Christ. [24]† So give proof before the churches of your love and of our boasting about you to them.

God's Indescribable Gift

9 [1]† Now about the service to the holy ones, it is superfluous for me to write to you, [2]*† for I know your eagerness, about which I boast of you to the Macedonians, that Achaia has been ready since last year; and your zeal has stirred up most of them. [3]† Nonetheless, I sent the brothers so that our boast about you might not prove empty in this case, so that you might be ready, as I said, [4] for fear that if any Macedonians come with me and find you not ready we might be put to shame (to say nothing of you) in this conviction. [5] So I thought it necessary to encourage the brothers to go on ahead to you and arrange in advance for your promised gift, so that in this way it might be ready as a bountiful gift and not as an exaction.

[6]* Consider this: whoever sows sparingly will also reap sparingly, and whoever sows bountifully will also reap bountifully. [7]* Each must do as already determined, without sadness or compulsion, for God loves a cheerful giver. [8]† Moreover, God is able to make every grace abundant for you, so that in all things, always having all you need, you may have an abundance for every good work. [9]* As it is written:

"He scatters abroad, he gives to the poor;
    his righteousness endures forever."

[10]* The one who supplies seed to the sower and bread for food will supply and multiply your seed and increase the harvest of your righteousness.

[11]† You are being enriched in every way for all generosity, which through us produces thanksgiving to God, [12] for the administration of this public service is not only supplying the needs of the holy ones but is also overflowing in many acts of thanksgiving to God. [13]* Through the evidence of this service, you are glorifying God for your obedient confession of the gospel of Christ and the generosity of your contribution to them and to all others, [14] while in prayer on your behalf they long for you, because of the surpassing grace of God upon you. [15]* Thanks be to God for his indescribable gift!

IV: Paul's Defense of His Ministry†

Accusation of Weakness†

10 [1]† Now I myself, Paul, urge you through the gentleness and clemency of Christ, I who am humble when face to face with you, but

---

8, 20–22: *That anyone blame us:* 12, 16–18 suggests that misunderstandings may indeed have arisen concerning Paul's management of the collection through the messengers mentioned here, but those same verses seem to imply that the Corinthians by and large would recognize the honesty of Paul's conduct in this area as in others (cf 6, 3).

8, 24: As Paul began by holding up the Macedonians as examples to be imitated, he closes by exhorting the Corinthians to show their love (by accepting the envoys and by cooperating as the Macedonians do), thus justifying the pride Paul demonstrates because of them before other churches.

9, 1–15: Quite possibly this was originally an independent letter, though it deals with the same subject and continues many of the same themes. In that case, it may have been written a few weeks later than ch 8, while the delegation there mentioned was still on its way.

9, 2: *Achaia:* see the note on Rom 15, 26.

9, 3: *I sent the brothers:* the Greek aorist tense here could be epistolary, referring to the present; in that case Paul would be sending them now, and ch 9 would merely conclude the letter of recommendation begun in ch 8. But the aorist may also refer to a sending that is past as Paul writes; then ch 9, with its apparently fresh beginning, is a follow-up message entrusted to another carrier.

9, 8–10: The behavior to which he exhorts them is grounded in God's own pattern of behavior. God is capable of overwhelming generosity, as scripture itself attests (9), so that they need not fear being short. He will provide in abundance, both supplying their natural needs and increasing their righteousness. Paul challenges them to godlike generosity and reminds them of the fundamental motive for encouragement: God himself cannot be outdone.

9, 11–15: Paul's vision broadens to take in all the interested parties in one dynamic picture. His language becomes liturgically colored and conveys a sense of fullness. With a final play on the words *charis* and *eucharistia* (see the note on 8, 1), he describes a circle that closes on itself: the movement of grace overflowing from God to them and handed on from them through Paul to others is completed by the prayer of praise and thanksgiving raised on their behalf to God.

10, 1—13, 10: These final chapters have their own unity of structure and theme and could well have formed the body of a separate letter. They constitute an *apologia* on Paul's part, i.e., a legal defense of his ministry and his ministry; the writing is emotionally charged and highly rhetorical. In the central section (11, 16—12, 10), the *apologia* takes the form of a boast. This section is prepared for by a prologue (11, 1–15) and followed by an epilogue (12, 11–18), which are similar in content and structure. These sections, in turn, are framed by an introduction (10, 1–18) and a conclusion (12, 19—13, 10), both of which assert Paul's apostolic authority and confidence and define the purpose of the letter. The structure that results from this disposition of the material is chiastic, i.e., the first element corresponds to the last, the second to the second last, etc., following the pattern a b c b¹ a¹.

10, 1–18: Paul asserts his apostolic authority and expresses the confidence this generates in him. He writes in response to certain opinions that have arisen in the community and certain charges raised against him and in preparation for a forthcoming visit in which he in

---

8, 19: 1 Cor 16, 3–4.
8, 21: Rom 12, 17.
9, 2: 2 Cor 8, 10; Rom 15, 26.
9, 6: Prv 11, 24–25.
9, 7: Prv 22, 8 LXX.
9, 9: Ps 112, 9.
9, 10: Is 55, 10.
9, 13: 2 Cor 8, 4; Rom 15, 31.
9, 15: Rom 5, 15–16.

brave toward you when absent, [2*†] I beg you that, when present, I may not have to be brave with that confidence with which I intend to act boldly against some who consider us as acting according to the flesh. [3†] For, although we are in the flesh, we do not battle according to the flesh, [4*] for the weapons of our battle are not of flesh but are enormously powerful, capable of destroying fortresses. We destroy arguments [5] and every pretension raising itself against the knowledge of God, and take every thought captive in obedience to Christ, [6*] and we are ready to punish every disobedience, once your obedience is complete.

[7*†] Look at what confronts you. Whoever is confident of belonging to Christ should consider that as he belongs to Christ, so do we. [8*] And even if I should boast a little too much of our authority, which the Lord gave for building you up and not for tearing you down, I shall not be put to shame. [9†] May I not seem as one frightening you through letters. [10*] For someone will say, "His letters are severe and forceful, but his bodily presence is weak, and his speech contemptible." [11*] Such a person must understand that what we are in word through letters when absent, that we also are in action when present.

[12*†] Not that we dare to class or compare ourselves with some of those who recommend themselves. But when they measure themselves by one another and compare themselves with one another, they are without understanding. [13†] But we will not boast beyond measure but will keep to the limits God has apportioned us, namely, to reach even to you. [14] For we are not overreaching ourselves, as though we did not reach you; we indeed first came to you with the gospel of Christ. [15] We are not boasting beyond measure, in other people's labors; yet our hope is that, as your faith increases, our influence among you may be greatly enlarged, within our proper limits, [16*] so that we may preach the gospel even beyond you, not boasting of work already done in another's sphere. [17*†] "Whoever boasts, should boast in the Lord." [18*†] For it is not the one who recommends himself who is approved, but the one whom the Lord recommends.

Preaching without Charge†

11 [1*†] If only you would put up with a little foolishness from me! Please put up with me. [2*†] For I am jealous of you with the jealousy of

---

tends to set things in order. This section gives us an initial glimpse of the situation in Corinth that Paul must address; much of its thematic material will be taken up again in the finale (12, 19—13, 10).

10, 1–2: A strong opening plunges us straight into the conflict. Contrasts dominate here: presence versus absence, gentleness-clemency-humility versus boldness-confidence-bravery. *Through the gentleness and clemency of Christ:* the figure of the gentle Christ, presented in a significant position before any specifics of the situation are suggested, forms a striking contrast to the picture of the bold and militant Paul (2–6); this tension is finally resolved in 13, 3–4. *Absent . . . present:* this same contrast, with a restatement of the purpose of the letter, recurs in 13, 10, which forms an inclusion with 10, 1–2.

10, 2b-4a: *Flesh:* the Greek word *sarx* can express both the physical life of the body without any pejorative overtones (as in "we are in the flesh," 3) and also our natural life insofar as it is marked by limitation and weakness (as in the other expressions) in contrast to the higher life and power conferred by the Spirit; cf the note on 1 Cor 3, 1. The wordplay is intended to express the paradoxical situation of a life already taken over by the Spirit but not yet seen as such except by faith. Lack of empirical evidence of the Spirit permits misunderstanding and misjudgment, but Paul resolutely denies that his behavior and effectiveness are as limited as some suppose.

10, 3b-6: Paul is involved in combat. The strong military language and imagery are both an assertion of his confidence in the divine power at his disposal and a declaration of war against those who underestimate his resources. The threat is echoed in 13, 2–3.

10, 7–8: *Belonging to Christ . . . so do we:* these phrases already announce the pattern of Paul's boast in 11, 21b-29, especially 11, 22–23. *For building you up and not for tearing you down:* Paul draws on the language by which Jeremiah described the purpose of the prophetic power the Lord gave to him (Jer 1, 9–10; 12, 16–17; 24, 6). Though Paul's power may have destructive effects on others (2–6), its intended effect on the community is entirely constructive (cf 13, 10). *I shall not be put to shame:* his assertions will not be refuted; they will be revealed as true at the judgment.

10, 9–10: Paul cites the complaints of some who find him lacking in personal forcefulness and holds out the threat of a personal *parousia* (both "return" and "presence") that will be forceful, indeed will be a demonstration of Christ's own power (cf 13, 2–4).

10, 12–18: Paul now qualifies his claim to boldness, indicating its limits. He distinguishes his own behavior from that of others, revealing those "others" as they appear to him: as self-recommending, immoderately boastful, encroaching on territory not assigned to them, and claiming credit not due to them.

10, 13: *Will keep to the limits:* the notion of proper limits is expressed here by two terms with overlapping meanings, *metron* and *kanōn,* which are played off against several expressions denoting overreaching or expansion beyond a legitimate sphere.

10, 17: *Boast in the Lord:* there is a legitimate boasting, in contrast to the immoderate boasting to which vv 13 and 15 allude. God's work through Paul in the community is the object of his boast (13–16; 1, 12–14) and constitutes his recommendation (3, 1–3). Cf the notes on 1, 12–14 and 1 Cor 1, 29–31.

10, 18: *Approved:* to be approved is to come successfully through the process of testing for authenticity (cf 13, 3–7 and the note on 8, 2). *Whom the Lord recommends:* self-commendation is a premature and unwarranted anticipation of the final judgment, which the Lord alone will pass (cf 1 Cor 4, 3–5). Paul alludes to this judgment throughout chs 10–13, frequently in final or transitional positions; cf 11, 15; 12, 19a; 13, 3–7.

11, 1–15: Although these verses continue to reveal information about Paul's opponents and the differences he perceives between them and himself, 11, 1 signals a turn in Paul's thought. This section constitutes a prologue to the boasting that he will undertake in 11, 16—12, 10, and it bears remarkable similarities to the section that follows the central boast, 12, 11–18.

11, 1: *Put up with a little foolishness from me:* this verse indicates more clearly than the general statement of intent in 10, 13 the nature of the project Paul is about to undertake. He alludes ironically to the Corinthians' toleration for others. *Foolishness:* Paul qualifies his project as folly from beginning to end; see the note on 11, 16—12, 10.

11, 2: Paul gives us a sudden glimpse of the theological values that are at stake. *The jealousy of God:* the perspective is that of the covenant, described in imagery of love and marriage, as in the prophets; cf 1 Cor 10, 22. *I betrothed you:* Paul, like a father (cf 12, 14), betroths the community to Christ as his bride (cf Eph 5, 21–33) and will present her to him at his second coming. Cf Mt 25, 1–13 and the nuptial imagery in Rv 21.

10, 2: 2 Cor 13, 2.10; 1 Cor 4, 21.
10, 4: 2 Cor 6, 7; 13, 2–3; 1 Cor 1, 25; Eph 6, 10–14.
10, 6: 2 Cor 2, 9.
10, 7: 1 Cor 1, 12.
10, 8: 2 Cor 13, 10.
10, 10: 1 Cor 2, 3.
10, 11: 2 Cor 13, 1–2.

10, 12: 2 Cor 3, 1–2; 4, 2; 5, 12; 6, 4; 10, 18; 12, 11.
10, 16: Rom 15, 20–21.
10, 17: Jer 9, 22–23; 1 Cor 1, 31.
10, 18: 2 Cor 13, 3–9.
11, 1: 2 Cor 11, 21; 12, 11.
11, 2: Hos 2, 21–22; Eph 5, 26–27.

God, since I betrothed you to one husband to present you as a chaste virgin to Christ. ³*† But I am afraid that, as the serpent deceived Eve by his cunning, your thoughts may be corrupted from a sincere [and pure] commitment to Christ. ⁴*† For if someone comes and preaches another Jesus than the one we preached, or if you receive a different spirit from the one you received or a different gospel from the one you accepted, you put up with it well enough. ⁵*† For I think that I am not in any way inferior to these "superapostles." ⁶*† Even if I am untrained in speaking, I am not so in knowledge; in every way we have made this plain to you in all things.

⁷*† Did I make a mistake when I humbled myself so that you might be exalted, because I preached the gospel of God to you without charge? ⁸ I plundered other churches by accepting from them in order to minister to you. ⁹* And when I was with you and in need, I did not burden anyone, for the brothers who came from Macedonia supplied my needs. So I refrained and will refrain from burdening you in any way. ¹⁰* By the truth of Christ in me, this boast of mine shall not be silenced in the regions of Achaia. ¹¹*† And why? Because I do not love you? God knows I do!

¹² And what I do I will continue to do, in order to end this pretext of those who seek a pretext for being regarded as we are in the mission of which they boast. ¹³† For such people are false apostles, deceitful workers, who masquerade as apostles of Christ. ¹⁴ And no wonder, for even Satan masquerades as an angel of light. ¹⁵ So it is not strange that his ministers also masquerade as ministers of righteousness. Their end will correspond to their deeds.

Paul's Boast: His Labors

¹⁶† I repeat, no one should consider me foolish;† but if you do, accept me as a fool, so that I too may boast a little.† ¹⁷ What I am saying I am not saying according to the Lord but as in foolishness, in this boastful state. ¹⁸ Since many boast according to the flesh, I too will boast. ¹⁹ For you gladly put up with fools, since you are wise yourselves. ²⁰† For you put up with it if someone enslaves you, or devours you, or gets the better of you, or puts on airs, or slaps you in the face. ²¹† To my shame I say that we were too weak!

---

† **11, 3:** *As the serpent deceived Eve:* before Christ can return for the community Paul fears a repetition of the primal drama of seduction. Corruption of minds is satanic activity (see 2, 11; 4, 4). Satanic imagery recurs in 11, 13–15.20; 12, 7b.16–17; see the notes on these passages.

11, 4: *Preaches another Jesus:* the danger is specified, and Paul's opponents are identified with the cunning serpent. The battle for minds has to do with the understanding of Jesus, the Spirit, the gospel; the Corinthians have flirted with another understanding than the one that Paul handed on to them as traditional and normative.

11, 5: *These "superapostles":* this term, employed again in 12, 11b, designates the opponents of whom Paul has spoken in ch 10 and again in 11, 4. They appear to be intruders at Corinth. Their preaching is marked at least by a different emphasis and style, and they do not hesitate to accept support from the community. Perhaps these itinerants appeal to the authority of church leaders in Jerusalem and even carry letters of recommendation from them. But it is not those distant leaders whom Paul is attacking here. The intruders are "superapostles" not in the sense of the "pillars" at Jerusalem (Gal 2), but in their own estimation. They consider themselves superior to Paul as apostles and ministers of Christ, and they are obviously enjoying some success among the Corinthians. Paul rejects their claim to be apostles in any superlative sense (*hyperlian*), judging them bluntly as "false apostles," ministers of Satan masquerading as apostles of Christ (13–15). On the contrary, he himself will claim to be a superminister of Christ (*hyper egō*, 23).

11, 6: Apparently found deficient in both rhetorical ability (cf 10, 10) and knowledge (cf 10, 5), Paul concedes the former charge but not the latter. *In every way:* in all their contacts with him revelation has been taking place. Paul, through whom God reveals the knowledge of himself (2, 14), and in whom the death and life of Jesus are revealed (4, 10–11; cf 6, 4), also demonstrates his own role as the bearer of true knowledge. Cf 1 Cor 1, 18—2, 16.

11, 7–10: Abruptly Paul passes to another reason for complaints: his practice of preaching without remuneration (cf 1 Cor 9, 3–18). He deftly defends his practice by situating it from the start within the pattern of Christ's own self-humiliation (cf 10, 1) and reduces objections to absurdity by rhetorical questions (cf 12, 13).

11, 11–12: Paul rejects lack of affection as his motive (possibly imputed to him by his opponents) and states his real motive, a desire to emphasize the disparity between himself and the others (cf 19–21). The topic of his gratuitous service will be taken up once more in 12, 13–18. 1 Cor 9, 15–18 gives a different but complementary explanation of his motivation.

11, 13–15: Paul picks up again the imagery of v 3 and applies it to the opponents: they are false apostles of Christ, really serving another master. *Deceitful . . . masquerade:* deception and simulation, like cunning (3), are marks of the satanic. *Angel of light:* recalls the contrast between light and darkness, Christ and Beliar at 6, 14–15. *Ministers of righteousness:* recalls the earlier contrast between the ministry of condemnation and that of righteousness (3, 9). *Their end:* the section closes with another allusion to the judgment, when all participants in the final conflict will be revealed or unmasked and dealt with as they deserve.

11, 16—12, 10: Paul now accepts the challenge of his opponents and indulges in boasting similar to theirs, but with differences that he has already signaled in 10, 12–18 and that become clearer as he proceeds. He defines the nature of his project and unmistakably labels it as folly at the beginning and the end (11, 16–23; 12, 11). Yet his boast does not spring from ignorance (11, 21; 12, 6) nor is it concerned merely with human distinctions (11, 18). Paul boasts "in moderation" (10, 13.15) and "in the Lord" (10, 17).

11, 16–29: The first part of Paul's boast focuses on labors and afflictions, in which authentic service of Christ consists.

11, 16–21: These verses recapitulate remarks already made about the foolishness of boasting and the excessive toleration of the Corinthians. They form a prelude to the boast proper.

11, 20: Paul describes the activities of the "others" in terms that fill out the picture drawn in vv 3–4.13–15. Much of the vocabulary suggests fleshly or even satanic activity. *Enslaves:* cf Gal 2, 4. *Devours:* cf 1 Pt 5, 8. *Gets the better:* the verb *lambanō* means "to take," but is used in a variety of senses; here it may imply financial advantage, as in the English colloquialism "to take someone." It is similarly used at 12, 16 and is there connected with cunning and deceit. *Puts on airs:* the same verb is rendered "raise oneself" (10, 5) and "be too elated" (12, 7).

11, 21: Paul ironically concedes the charge of personal weakness from 10, 1–18 but will refute the other charge there mentioned, that of lack of boldness, accepting the challenge to demonstrate it by his boast.

---

*

11, 3: Gn 3, 1–6.	**11, 7:** 2 Cor 12, 13–18; Acts
11, 4: Gal 1, 6–9.	18, 3; 1 Cor 9, 6–18.
11, 5: 2 Cor 12, 11.	**11, 9:** Phil 4, 15.18.
11, 6: 1 Cor 1, 5.17; 2, 1–5.	**11, 10:** 1 Cor 9, 15.
	11, 11: 2 Cor 12, 15.

But what anyone dares to boast of (I am speaking in foolishness) I also dare. 22*† Are they Hebrews? So am I. Are they Israelites? So am I. Are they descendants of Abraham? So am I. 23*† Are they ministers of Christ? (I am talking like an insane person.)† I am still more, with far greater labors, far more imprisonments, far worse beatings, and numerous brushes with death. 24* Five times at the hands of the Jews I received forty lashes minus one. 25* Three times I was beaten with rods, once I was stoned, three times I was shipwrecked, I passed a night and a day on the deep; 26 on frequent journeys, in dangers from rivers, dangers from robbers, dangers from my own race, dangers from Gentiles, dangers in the city, dangers in the wilderness, dangers at sea, dangers among false brothers; 27* in toil and hardship, through many sleepless nights, through hunger and thirst, through frequent fastings, through cold and exposure. 28 And apart from these things, there is the daily pressure upon me of my anxiety for all the churches. 29* Who is weak, and I am not weak? Who is led to sin, and I am not indignant?

Paul's Boast: His Weakness

30† If I must boast, I will boast of the things that show my weakness. 31† The God and Father of the Lord Jesus knows, he who is blessed forever, that I do not lie. 32 At Damascus, the governor under King Aretas guarded the city of Damascus, in order to seize me, 33* but I was lowered in a basket through a window in the wall and escaped his hands.

12 1† I must boast; not that it is profitable, but I will go on to visions and revelations of the Lord. 2 I know someone in Christ who, fourteen years ago (whether in the body or out of the body I do not know, God knows), was caught up to the third heaven. 3 And I know that this person (whether in the body or out of the body I do not know, God knows) 4* was caught up into Paradise

When I Am Weak, Then I Am Strong!

Sensible people go to a physician when they are suffering from an illness or injury. Smart students seek help from a teacher when they are stumped by an assigned project. Honest people admit when they have failed. Humble people are not afraid to apologize. Admitting that we are sick, or need help with a problem, or have failed or been wrong is a sign not of weakness but of wisdom and maturity.

Paul mentions a mysterious affliction he had to suffer—a "thorn in the flesh" (2 Cor 12, 7)—and how desperately he wanted to be rid of it. When he asked God to remove the "thorn," God chose to let it remain in Paul's life.

Paul wanted to be strong on his own, but his experience of struggling with this thorn reminded him that he needed to depend completely on the grace of God. Recognizing that we need God, admitting that we cannot make it on our own—that is a sign of true strength!

▶ 2 Cor 12, 1–10

11, 22: The opponents apparently pride themselves on their "Jewishness." Paul, too, can claim to be a Jew by race, religion, and promise. *Descendants of Abraham:* elsewhere Paul distinguishes authentic from inauthentic heirs of Abraham and the promise (Rom 4, 13–18; 9, 7–13; 11, 1; Gal 3, 9.27–29; cf Jn 8, 33–47). Here he grants his opponents this title in order to concentrate on the principal claim that follows.

11, 23a: *Ministers of Christ . . . I am still more:* the central point of the boast (cf the note on 11, 5). *Like an insane person:* the climax of his folly.

11, 23b–29: Service of the humiliated and crucified Christ is demonstrated by trials endured for him. This rhetorically impressive catalogue enumerates many of the labors and perils Paul encountered on his missionary journeys.

11, 30—12, 10: The second part of Paul's boast, marked by a change of style and a shift in focus. After recalling the project in which he is engaged, he states a new topic: his weaknesses as matter for boasting. Everything in this section, even the discussion of privileges and distinctions, will be integrated into this perspective.

11, 31–32: The episode at Damascus is symbolic. It aptly illustrates Paul's weakness but ends in deliverance (cf 4, 7–11).

12, 1–4: *In the body or out of the body:* he seemed no longer confined to bodily conditions, but he does not claim to understand the mechanics of the experience. *Caught up:* i.e., in ecstasy. *The third heaven . . . Paradise:* ancient cosmologies depicted a multitiered universe. Jewish intertestamental literature contains much speculation about the number of heavens. Seven is the number usually mentioned, but the Testament of Levi (2, 7–10; 3, 1–4) speaks of three; God himself dwelt in the third of these. Without giving us any clear picture of the cosmos, Paul indicates a mental journey to a nonearthly space, set apart by God, in which secrets were revealed to him. *Ineffable things:* i.e., privileged knowledge, which it was not possible or permitted to divulge.

11, 22: Acts 22, 3 / Rom 11, 1;
    Phil 3, 5–6.
11, 23: 2 Cor 6, 5; Acts 16,
    22–24; 1 Cor 15,
    31–32.
11, 24: Dt 25, 2–3.

11, 25: Acts 14, 19; 27,
    43–44.
11, 27: 1 Cor 4, 11.
11, 29: 1 Cor 9, 22.
11, 33: Acts 9, 23–25.
12, 4: Lk 23, 43; Rv 2, 7.

and heard ineffable things, which no one may utter. [5]† About this person I will boast, but about myself I will not boast, except about my weaknesses. [6] Although if I should wish to boast, I would not be foolish, for I would be telling the truth. But I refrain, so that no one may think more of me than what he sees in me or hears from me [7]*† because of the abundance of the revelations. Therefore, that I might not become too elated, a thorn in the flesh was given to me, an angel of Satan, to beat me, to keep me from being too elated. [8]*† Three times I begged the Lord about this, that it might leave me, [9]*† but he said to me, "My grace is sufficient for you, for power is made perfect in weakness." I will rather boast most gladly of my weaknesses,† in order that the power of Christ may dwell with me. [10]*† Therefore, I am content with weaknesses, insults, hardships, persecutions, and constraints, for the sake of Christ; for when I am weak, then I am strong.

Selfless Concern for the Church

[11]*† I have been foolish. You compelled me, for I ought to have been commended by you. For I am in no way inferior to these "superapostles," even though I am nothing. [12]*† The signs of an apostle were performed among you with all endurance, signs and wonders, and mighty deeds. [13]*† In what way were you less privileged than the rest of the churches, except that on my part I did not burden you? Forgive me this wrong!

[14] Now I am ready to come to you this third time. And I will not be a burden, for I want not what is yours, but you. Children ought not to save for their parents, but parents for their children. [15] I will most gladly spend and be utterly spent for your sakes. If I love you more, am I to be loved less? [16]* But granted that I myself did not burden you, yet I was crafty and got the better of you by deceit. [17] Did I take advantage of you through any of those I sent to you? [18]* I urged Titus to go and sent the brother with him. Did Titus take advantage of you? Did we not walk in the same spirit? And in the same steps?

Final Warnings and Appeals†

[19]† Have you been thinking all along that we are defending ourselves before you? In the sight of God we are speaking in Christ, and all for building you up, beloved. [20]*† For I fear that when I come I may find you not such as I wish, and that you may find me not as you wish; that there may be rivalry,

---

12, 5–7: *This person:* the indirect way of referring to himself has the effect of emphasizing the distance between that experience and his everyday life, just as the indirect *someone in Christ* (2) and all the passive verbs emphasize his passivity and receptivity in the experience. The revelations were not a personal achievement, nor were they meant to draw attention to any quality of his own.

12, 7b: *That I might not become too elated:* God assures that there is a negative component to his experience, so that he cannot lose proper perspective; cf 1, 9; 4, 7–11. *A thorn in the flesh:* variously interpreted as a sickness or physical disability, a temptation, or a handicap connected with his apostolic activity. But since Hebrew "thorn in the flesh," like English "thorn in my side," refers to persons (cf Nm 33, 55; Ez 28, 24), Paul may be referring to some especially persistent and obnoxious opponent. The language of vv 7–8 permits this interpretation. If this is correct, the frequent appearance of singular pronouns in depicting the opposition may not be merely a stylistic variation; the singular may be provoked and accompanied by the image of one individual in whom criticism of Paul's preaching, way of life, and apostolic consciousness is concentrated, and who embodies all the qualities Paul attributes to the group. *An angel of Satan:* a personal messenger from Satan; cf the satanic language already applied to the opponents in 11, 3.13–15.20.

12, 8: *Three times:* his prayer was insistent, like that of Jesus in Gethsemane, a sign of how intolerable he felt the thorn to be.

12, 9: *But he said to me:* Paul's petition is denied; release and healing are withheld for a higher purpose. The Greek perfect tense indicates that Jesus' earlier response still holds at the time of writing. *My grace is sufficient for you:* this is not a statement about the sufficiency of grace in general. Jesus speaks directly to Paul's situation. *Is made perfect:* i.e., is given most fully and manifests itself fully.

12, 9b–10a: Paul draws the conclusion from the autobiographical anecdote and integrates it into the subject of this part of the boast. *Weaknesses:* the apostolic hardships he must endure, including active personal hostility, as specified in a final catalogue (10a). *That the power of Christ may dwell with me:* Paul pinpoints the ground for the paradoxical strategy he has adopted in his self-defense.

12, 10b: *When I am weak, then I am strong:* Paul recognizes a twofold pattern in the resolution of the weakness-power (and death-life) dialectic, of which looks to Jesus as the model and is experienced in him. The first is personal, involving a reversal in oneself (Jesus, 13, 4a; Paul, 1, 9–10; 4, 10–11; 6, 9). The second is apostolic, involving an effect on others (Jesus, 5, 14–15; Paul, 1, 6; 4, 12; 13, 9). The specific kind of "effectiveness in ministry" that Paul promises to demonstrate on his arrival (13, 4b; cf 10, 1–11) involves ele-

ments of both; this, too, will be modeled on Jesus' experience and a participation in that experience (9; 13, 3b).

12, 11–18: This brief section forms an epilogue or concluding observation to Paul's boast, corresponding to the prologue in 11, 1–15. A four-step sequence of ideas is common to these two sections: Paul qualifies his boast as folly (11, 1; 12, 11a), asserts his noninferiority to the "superapostles" (11, 5; 12, 11b), exemplifies this by allusion to charismatic endowments (11, 6; 12, 12), and finally denies that he has been a financial burden to the community (11, 7–12; 12, 13–18).

12, 12: Despite weakness and affliction (suggested by the mention of *endurance*), his ministry has been accompanied by demonstrations of power (cf 1 Cor 2, 3–4). *Signs of an apostle:* visible proof of belonging to Christ and of mediating Christ's power, which the opponents require as touchstones of apostleship (11; cf 13, 3).

12, 13–18: Paul insists on his intention to continue refusing support from the community (cf 11, 8–12). In defending his practice and his motivation, he once more protests his love (cf 11, 11) and rejects the suggestion of secret self-enrichment. He has recourse here again to language applied to his opponents earlier: "cunning" (11, 3), "deceit" (11, 13), "got the better of you" (see the note on 11, 20), "take advantage" (2, 11).

12, 19—13, 10: This concludes the development begun in ch 10. In the chiastic arrangement of the material (see the note on 10, 1—13, 10), this final part corresponds to the opening; there are important similarities of content between the two sections as well.

12, 19: This verse looks back at the previous chapters and calls them by their proper name, a defense, an *apologia* (cf 1 Cor 9, 3). Yet Paul insists on an important distinction: he has indeed been speaking for their benefit, but the ultimate judgment to which he submits is God's (cf 1 Cor 4, 3–5). This verse also leads into the final section, announcing two of its themes: judgment and building up.

12, 20: *I fear that . . . :* earlier Paul expressed fear that the Corinthians were being victimized, exploited, seduced from right thinking by his opponents (11, 3–4.19–21). Here he alludes unexpectedly to moral disorders among the Corinthians themselves. The catalogue suggests the effects of factions that have grown up around rival apostles.

12, 7: Nm 33, 55; Jos 23, 13; Ez 28, 24.		**12, 12:** Rom 15, 19; 1 Thes 1, 5.
12, 8: Mt 26, 39–44.		**12, 13:** 2 Cor 11, 9–12.
12, 9: 2 Cor 4, 7.		**12, 16:** 2 Cor 11, 3.13.
12, 10: 2 Cor 6, 4–5; Rom 5, 3 / Phil 4, 13.		**12, 18:** 2 Cor 2, 13; 8, 16.23.
12, 11: 2 Cor 11, 5.		**12, 20:** 1 Cor 1, 11; 3, 3.

jealousy, fury, selfishness, slander, gossip, conceit, and disorder. ²¹† I fear that when I come again my God may humiliate me before you, and I may have to mourn over many of those who sinned earlier and have not repented of the impurity, immorality, and licentiousness they practiced.

13 ¹*† This third time I am coming to you. "On the testimony of two or three witnesses a fact shall be established." ²† I warned those who sinned earlier and all the others, and I warn them now while absent, as I did when present on my second visit, that if I come again I will not be lenient, ³† since you are looking for proof of Christ speaking in me. He is not weak toward you but powerful in you. ⁴ For indeed he was crucified out of weakness, but he lives by the power of God. So also we are weak in him, but toward you we shall live with him by the power of God.

⁵† Examine yourselves to see whether you are living in faith. Test yourselves. Do you not realize that Jesus Christ is in you?—unless, of course, you fail the test. ⁶ I hope you will discover that we have not failed. ⁷ But we pray to God that you may not

---

A Spiritual Checkup

LIVE IT!

STOP!

How often do you take a break from all the activities in your life to do a spiritual checkup on your relationships with God, other people, and yourself? In 2 Cor 13, 5–7, Paul suggests that the Corinthians give themselves a spiritual self-check. This is good advice for us today as well.

A STOP sign is a good guiding image for a spiritual checkup. It signals you to interrupt the motion of life and look at what's going on around you. Each letter of the sign can be a reminder to check a different area of your spiritual life:

- *S* can stand for "seek." Do you seek information, counsel, and help when facing difficult or confusing situations and choices?
- *T* can stand for "think." Do you honestly think about how your actions and behaviors affect you, others, and your relationship with God?
- *O* can stand for "others." Do you make it a priority to reach out and support others—particularly those in great need? Are you there for your family and friends?
- *P* can stand for "pray." Do you turn to God for guidance in your life? for the strength to do what is right? Do you thank God for your blessings and the struggles that make you stronger?

▶ 2 Cor 13, 5–7

---

†
12, 21: *Again:* one can also translate, "I fear that when I come my God may again humiliate me." Paul's allusion to the humiliation and mourning that may await him recall the mood he described in 2, 1–4, but there is no reference here to any individual such as there is in 2, 5–11. The crisis of ch 2 has happily been resolved by integration of the offender and repentance (7, 4–16), whereas 12, 21 is preoccupied with still unrepentant sinners. The sexual sins recall 1 Cor 5–7.

13, 1: *This third time I am coming:* designation of the forthcoming visit as the "third" (cf 12, 14) may indicate that, in addition to his founding sojourn in Corinth, Paul had already made the first of two visits mentioned as planned in 1, 15, and the next visit will be the long-postponed second of these. If so, the materials in 1, 12—2, 13 plus 7, 4–16 and chs 10–13 may date from the same period of time, presumably of some duration, between Paul's second and third visit, though it is not clear that they are addressing the same crisis. The chronology is too unsure and the relations between sections of 2 Corinthians too unclear to yield any certainty. The hypothesis that chs 10–13 are themselves the "tearful letter" mentioned at 2, 3–4 creates more problems than it solves.

13, 2: *I warned those who sinned earlier:* mention of unrepentant sinners (12, 21 and here) and of an oral admonition given them on an earlier visit complicates the picture at the very end of Paul's development. It provides, in fact, a second explanation for the show of power that has been threatened from the beginning (10, 1–6), but a different reason for it, quite unsuspected until now. It is not clear whether Paul is merely alluding to a dimension of the situation that he has not previously had occasion to mention, or whether some other community crisis, not directly connected with that behind chs 10–13, has influenced the final editing. *I will not be lenient:* contrast Paul's hesitation and reluctance to inflict pain in 1, 23 and 2, 1–4. The next visit will bring the showdown.

13, 3–4: Paul now gives another motive for severity when he comes, the charge of weakness leveled against him as an apostle. The motive echoes more closely the opening section (10, 1–18) and the intervening development (especially 11, 30—12, 10). *Proof of Christ speaking in me:* the threat of 10, 1–2 is reworded to recall Paul's conformity with the pattern of Christ, his insertion into the interplay of death and life, weakness and power (cf the note on 12, 10b).

13, 5–9: Paul turns the challenge mentioned in v 3 on them: they are to put themselves to the test to demonstrate whether Christ is in them. These verses involve a complicated series of plays on the theme of *dokimē* (testing, proof, passing and failing a test). Behind this stands the familiar distinction between present human judgment and final divine judgment. This is the final appearance of the theme (cf 10, 18; 11, 15; 12, 19).

---
*
13, 1: Dt 19, 15; Mt 18, 16;
Jn 8, 17; Heb 10, 28.

do evil, not that we may appear to have passed the test but that you may do what is right, even though we may seem to have failed. [8] For we cannot do anything against the truth, but only for the truth. [9] For we rejoice when we are weak but you are strong. What we pray for is your improvement.

[10]*† I am writing this while I am away, so that when I come I may not have to be severe in virtue of the authority that the Lord has given me to build up and not to tear down.

V: Conclusion

[11]† Finally, brothers, rejoice. Mend your ways, encourage one another, agree with one another, live in peace, and the God of love and peace will be with you. [12]* Greet one another with a holy kiss. All the holy ones greet you.

[13]* The grace of the Lord Jesus Christ and the love of God and the fellowship of the holy Spirit be with all of you.

13, 10: *Authority . . . to build up and not to tear down:* Paul restates the purpose of his letter in language that echoes 10, 2.8, emphasizing the positive purpose of his authority in their regard. This verse forms an inclusion with the topic sentence of the section (12, 19), as well as with the opening of this entire portion of the letter (10, 1–2).

13, 11–13: These verses may have originally concluded chs 10–13, but they have nothing specifically to do with the material of that section. It is also possible to consider them a conclusion to the

whole of 2 Corinthians in its present edited form. The exhortations are general, including a final appeal for peace in the community. The letter ends calmly, after its many storms, with the prospect of ecclesial unity and divine blessing. The final verse is one of the clearest trinitarian passages in the New Testament.

13, 10: 2 Cor 10, 8.
13, 12: Rom 16, 16; 1 Cor 16, 20 / Phil 4, 22; 1 Thes 5, 26; 1 Pt 5, 14.
13, 13: Rom 16, 20; 1 Cor 16, 23.

Do you ever scan a letter before you start to read, to see what mood the writer was in? Try it with Galatians. Notice that Paul is angry and upset. He was weak and sick when he founded the church in Galatia. Now, everything is falling apart. He feels like a mother who has to give birth to her children all over again (4, 12–20). Why? Paul is afraid the Galatians are trading in the true Gospel, based on faith in Jesus, for a false gospel based on Jewish rules and customs.

At a Glance

I. Address (1, 1–5).

II. Loyalty to the Gospel (1, 6–10).

III. Paul's Defense of His Gospel and His Authority (1, 11—2, 21).

IV. Faith and Liberty (3, 1—4, 31).

V. Exhortation to Christian Living (5, 1—6, 10).

VI. Conclusion (6, 11–18).

In-depth

Jesus, the disciples, and most of the first Christians were Jewish. When Gentiles (non-Jews) started to become Christians, a question came up that almost split the early Christian community: Do Gentiles have to become Jewish before they can become Christian? The whole debate soon centered around the Jewish law of circumcision. (Circumcision is the surgical removal of the foreskin of a male's penis.)

Paul insisted that circumcision—and all the other Jewish ceremonial laws— had nothing to do with faith in Jesus and was unnecessary for Gentile Christians. At the Council of Jerusalem (see Acts of the Apostles, chapter 15), the other Apostles reluctantly agreed with Paul. But the argument wasn't over. Other Christian missionaries came to Galatia after Paul left the Christian community there. They implied that faith in Christ wasn't enough and insisted that Gentile Christians must be circumcised. They attacked Paul's credibility by saying he wasn't a true Apostle.

When Paul heard of this, he was mad! In his Letter to the Galatians, he doesn't even include his typical thanksgiving at the end of his greeting but launches right into his concern. He starts by defending his apostlehood. He goes on to tell how the other Apostles at the Council of Jerusalem had agreed with him that the Gentiles do not need to be circumcised. He states how he later challenged Peter personally when Peter allowed himself to be influenced by missionaries preaching something else.

In his passion, Paul confronts the Galatians: "I am afraid on your account that perhaps I have labored for you in vain" (4, 11). He condemns the false missionaries: "If anyone preaches to you a gospel other than the one that you received, let that one be accursed!" (1, 9). Paul is defending the freedom of Christians from the old Jewish religious laws. He is writing the Christians' declaration of independence: "Christ set us free" (5, 1).

Quick Facts

Author
Paul

Date
A.D. 54–55

Audience
Gentile Christian churches in northern Galatia

Galatians

I: Address

Greeting†

1 ¹*† Paul, an apostle not from human beings nor through a human being but through Jesus Christ and God the Father who raised him from the dead,* ²† and all the brothers who are with me, to the churches of Galatia: ³ grace to you and peace from God our Father and the Lord Jesus Christ, ⁴*† who gave himself for our sins that he might rescue us from the present evil age in accord with the will of our God and Father, ⁵* to whom be glory forever and ever. Amen.

II: Loyalty to the Gospel†

⁶*† I am amazed that you are so quickly forsaking the one who called you by [the] grace [of Christ] for a different gospel ⁷ (not that there is another). But there are some who are disturbing you and wish to pervert the gospel of Christ. ⁸*† But even if we or an angel from heaven should preach [to you] a gospel other than the one that we preached to you, let that one be accursed! ⁹ As we have said before, and now I say again, if anyone preaches to you a gospel other than the one that you received, let that one be accursed!

¹⁰*† Am I now currying favor with human beings

1, 1–5: See the note on Rom 1, 1–7, concerning the greeting.

1, 1: *Apostle:* because of attacks on his authority in Galatia, Paul defends his apostleship. He is not an apostle commissioned by a congregation (Phil 2, 25; 2 Cor 8, 23) or even by prophets (1 Tm 1, 18 and 4, 14) but *through Jesus Christ and God the Father.*

1, 2: *All the brothers:* fellow believers in Christ, male and female; cf 3, 27–28. Paul usually mentions the co-sender(s) at the start of a letter, but the use of *all* is unique, adding weight to the letter. *Galatia:* central Turkey more likely than the Roman province of Galatia; see Introduction.

1, 4: The greeting in v 3 is expanded by a christological formula that stresses deliverance through the Lord Jesus from a world dominated by Satan; cf 2 Cor 4, 4; Eph 2, 2; 6, 12.

1, 6–10: In place of the usual thanksgiving (see the note on Rom 1, 8), Paul, with little to be thankful for in the Galatian situation, expresses amazement at the way his converts are deserting the gospel of Christ for a perverted message. He reasserts the one gospel he has preached (7–9) and begins to defend himself (10).

1, 6: *The one who called you:* God or Christ, though in actuality Paul was the divine instrument to call the Galatians.

1, 8: *Accursed:* in Greek, *anathema;* cf Rom 9, 3; 1 Cor 12, 3; 16, 22.

1, 10: This charge by Paul's opponents, that he sought to conciliate people with flattery and to curry favor with God, might refer to his mission practices (cf 1 Cor 9, 19–23) but the word *still* suggests it refers to his pre-Christian days (cf 14; Phil 3, 6). The self-description *slave of Christ* is one Paul often uses in a greeting (Rom 1, 1).

1, 1–3: Rom 1, 1–7; 1 Cor 1, 1–3.
1, 1: Gal 1, 11–12.
1, 4: Gal 2, 20; Eph 5, 2; 1 Tm 2, 6 / 1 Jn 5, 19 / Rom 12, 2; Eph 5, 16; Heb 10, 10.
1, 5: Rom 16, 27; 2 Tm 4, 18.
1, 6–7: Gal 5, 8.10; Acts 15, 1.24; 2 Cor 11, 4.
1, 8–9: 1 Cor 16, 22 / Gal 5, 3.21; 2 Cor 13, 2.
1, 10: 2 Cor 5, 11 / 1 Thes 2, 4.

or God? Or am I seeking to please people? If I were still trying to please people, I would not be a slave of Christ.

III: Paul's Defense of His Gospel and His Authority

His Call by Christ

11*† Now I want you to know, brothers, that the gospel preached by me is not of human origin. 12† For I did not receive it from a human being, nor was I taught it, but it came through a revelation of Jesus Christ.

13*† For you heard of my former way of life in Judaism, how I persecuted the church of God beyond measure and tried to destroy it, 14* and progressed in Judaism beyond many of my contemporaries among my race, since I was even more a zealot for my ancestral traditions. 15* But when [God], who from my mother's womb had set me apart and called me through his grace, was pleased 16*† to reveal his Son to me, so that I might proclaim him to the Gentiles, I did not immediately consult flesh and blood, 17† nor did I go up to Jerusalem to those who were apostles before me; rather, I went into Arabia and then returned to Damascus.

18*† Then after three years† I went up to Jerusalem to confer with Cephas and remained with him for fifteen days. 19*† But I did not see any other of the apostles, only James the brother of the Lord. 20* (As to what I am writing to you, behold, before God, I am not lying.) 21* Then I went into the regions of Syria and Cilicia. 22 And I was unknown personally to the churches of Judea that are in Christ; 23* they only kept hearing that "the one who once was persecuting us is now preaching the faith he once tried to destroy." 24 So they glorified God because of me.

The Council of Jerusalem†

2 1* Then after fourteen years† I again went up to Jerusalem with Barnabas, taking Titus along also. 2*† I went up in accord with a revelation, and I presented to them the gospel that I preach to the Gentiles—but privately to those of repute—so that I might not be running, or have run, in vain. 3*† Moreover, not even Titus, who was with me, although he was a Greek, was compelled to be

---

† **1, 11—2, 21:** Paul's presentation on behalf of his message and of his apostleship reflects rhetorical forms of his day: he first narrates the facts about certain past events (1, 12—2, 14) and then states his contention regarding justification by faith as the gospel message (2, 15–21). Further arguments follow from both experience and scripture in chs 3 and 4, before he draws out the ethical consequences (5, 1—6, 10). The specific facts that he takes up here to show that his gospel is not a human invention (1, 11) but *came through a revelation of Jesus Christ* (1, 12) deal with his own calling as a Christian missionary (1, 13–17), his initial relations with the apostles in Jerusalem (1, 18–24), a later journey to Jerusalem (2, 1–10), and an incident in Antioch involving Cephas and persons from James (2, 11–14). The content of Paul's revealed gospel is then set forth in the heart of the letter (2, 15–21).

1, 12: Although Paul received his gospel *through a revelation* from Christ, this did not exclude his use of early Christian confessional formulations. See the note on 1, 4.

1, 13–17: Along with Phil 3, 4–11, which also moves from autobiography to its climax in a discussion on justification by faith (cf Gal 2, 15–21), this passage is Paul's chief account of the change from his *former way of life* (13) to service as a Christian missionary (16); cf Acts 9, 1–22; 22, 4–16; 26, 9–18. Paul himself does not use the term "conversion" but stresses revelation (12.16). In v 15 his language echoes the Old Testament prophetic call of Jeremiah. Unlike the account in Acts (cf 22, 4–16), the calling of Paul here includes the mission to proclaim Christ *to the Gentiles* (16).

1, 16: *Flesh and blood:* human authorities (cf Mt 16, 17; 1 Cor 15, 50). Paul's apostleship comes from God (1).

1, 17: *Arabia:* probably the region of the Nabataean Arabs, east and south of Damascus.

1, 18–24: Paul's first journey to Jerusalem as a Christian, according to Galatians (cf Acts 9, 23–31 and the note on Acts 12, 25). He is quite explicit about contacts there, testifying under oath (20). On returning to *Syria* (perhaps specifically Damascus, cf v 17) *and Cilicia* (including his home town Tarsus, cf Acts 9, 30; 22, 3), Paul most likely engaged in missionary work. He underscores the fact that Christians in Judea knew of him only by reputation.

1, 18: *After three years:* two years and more, since Paul's call. To *confer with* Cephas may mean simply "pay a visit" or more specifically "get information from" him about Jesus, over a two-week period. *Cephas:* Aramaic name of Simon (Peter); cf Mt 16, 16–18 and the notes there.

1, 19: *James the brother of the Lord:* not one of the Twelve, but a brother of Jesus (see the note on Mk 6, 3). He played an important role in the Jerusalem church (see the note on Gal 2, 9), the leadership of which he took over from Peter (Acts 12, 17). Paul may have regarded James as an apostle.

2, 1–10: Paul's second journey to Jerusalem, according to Galatians, involved a private meeting with *those of repute* (2). At issue was a Gentile, Titus, and the question of circumcision, which *false brothers* (4) evidently demanded for him. Paul insists that the gospel he preaches (2; cf 1, 9.11) remained intact with no addition by those of repute (6); that *Titus* was not *compelled* to accept circumcision (3); and that he and the reputed *pillars* in Jerusalem agreed on how each would advance the missionary task (7–10). Usually, 1–10 is equated with the "Council of Jerusalem," as it is called, described in Acts 15. See the notes on Acts 15, 6–12 and 15, 13–35, the latter concerning the "decree" that Paul does not mention.

2, 1: *After fourteen years:* thirteen or more years, probably reckoned from the return to Syria and Cilicia (1, 21), though possibly from Paul's calling as a Christian (1, 15). *Barnabas:* cf 9.13; 1 Cor 9, 6. A Jewish Christian missionary, with whom Paul worked (Acts 4, 36–37; 11, 22.25.30; 12, 25; 13, 1–3; 15, 2). *Titus:* a missionary companion of Paul (2 Cor 2, 13; 7, 6.13–15; 8, 6.16.23; 12, 18), non-Jewish (Gal 2, 3), never mentioned in Acts.

2, 2: *A revelation:* cf 1, 1.12. Paul emphasizes it was God's will, not Jerusalem authority, that led to the journey. Acts 15, 2 states that the church in Antioch appointed Paul and Barnabas for the task. *Those of repute:* leaders of the Jerusalem church; the term, while positive, may be slightly ironic (cf 6.9). *Run, in vain:* while Paul presents a positive picture in what follows, his missionary work in Galatia would have been to no purpose if his opponents were correct that circumcision was needed for complete faith in Christ.

2, 3: *Not even* a Gentile Christian like Titus was compelled to receive the rite of circumcision. The Greek text could be interpreted that he voluntarily accepted circumcision, but this is unlikely in the overall argument.

1, 11–12: 1 Cor 15, 1 / Gal 1, 1;　　**1, 19:** Gal 2, 9; Mt 13, 55;
Eph 3, 3.　　　　　　　　　　　　　　Acts 12, 17.
1, 13: Acts 8, 1–3; 9, 1–2;　　　　**1, 20:** Rom 9, 1; 2 Cor 11,
1 Cor 15, 9.　　　　　　　　　　　　31.
1, 14: Acts 26, 4–5.　　　　　　　**1, 21:** Acts 9, 30.
1, 15: Is 49, 1; Jer 1, 4.　　　　　**1, 23:** Gal 1, 13.
1, 16: Gal 1, 11–12; Rom 1,　　　**2, 1:** Acts 15, 2.
5; 1 Cor 15, 10; Acts 9,　　　　　　**2, 2:** Gal 1, 11–12.16 / Gal
3–9 / Gal 2, 2.7 / Mt　　　　　　　1, 16 / Phil 2, 16.
16, 17.　　　　　　　　　　　　　　**2, 3:** 2 Cor 2, 13; 7, 6–7; 8,
1, 18: Acts 9, 26–30 / Jn 1,　　　16–17; 12, 18; Ti 1, 4
42.　　　　　　　　　　　　　　　　/ Gal 2, 14; 6, 12.

Consistent and Trustworthy

At the beginning of Galatians, chapter 2, Paul describes what went on at the Council of Jerusalem. The Council established that freedom from the Jewish Law is at the core of Christian beliefs and identity. Faith in Christ is enough to save people from sin and human weakness. Paul pleads with the Galatians not to fall back into the legalism and empty rituals being taught by some Jewish Christian leaders.

So when Peter stops eating with Gentile Christians under pressure from some Jewish Christians, Paul challenges him. He points out that Peter's behavior is not consistent with the truth of the Gospel and that this inconsistency is misleading and confusing to the Christian community.

To be a credible Christian demands that you stay consistent in your words and actions. Remember, your actions speak louder than your words. Furthermore, when your actions do not match your words, people lose their trust in you. And you begin to feel like a hypocrite and lose your self-esteem.

Take some time to reflect on how consistently your actions reflect your words. Consider ways you can improve. When your actions match your words, people will recognize you as a person of integrity and place their trust in you.

▶ **Gal 2, 11–14**

---

circumcised, [4]*† but because of the false brothers secretly brought in, who slipped in to spy on our freedom that we have in Christ Jesus, that they might enslave us— [5]*† to them we did not submit even for a moment, so that the truth of the gospel might remain intact for you. [6]* But from those who were reputed to be important (what they once were makes no difference to me; God shows no partiality)—those of repute made me add nothing. [7]*† On the contrary, when they saw that I had been entrusted with the gospel to the uncircumcised, just as Peter to the circumcised, [8] for the one who worked in Peter for an apostolate to the circumcised worked also in me for the Gentiles, [9]*† and when they recognized the grace bestowed upon me, James and

Cephas and John, who were reputed to be pillars, gave me and Barnabas their right hands in partnership, that we should go to the Gentiles and they to the circumcised. [10]*† Only, we were to be mindful of the poor, which is the very thing I was eager to do.

Peter's Inconsistency at Antioch†

[11]*† And when Cephas came to Antioch, I opposed him to his face because he clearly was wrong. [12]*† For, until some people came from James, he used to eat with the Gentiles; but when they came, he began to draw back and separated himself, because he was afraid of the circumcised. [13]*† And the rest of the Jews [also] acted hypocritically along

---

†
2, 4: *False brothers:* Jewish Christians who took the position that Gentile Christians must first become Jews through circumcision and observance of the Mosaic law in order to become Christians; cf Acts 15, 1.

2, 5: *The truth of the gospel:* the true gospel, in contrast to the false one of the opponents (1, 6–9); the gospel of grace, used as a norm (14).

2, 7–9: Some think that actual "minutes" of the meeting are here quoted. Paul's apostleship to the Gentiles (1, 16) is recognized alongside that of Peter to the Jews. Moreover, the right to proclaim the gospel without requiring circumcision and the Jewish law is sealed by a handshake. That Paul and colleagues *should go to the Gentiles* did not exclude his preaching to the Jews as well (Rom 1, 13–16) or Cephas to Gentile areas.

2, 9: *James and Cephas and John:* see the notes on 1, 18 and 19; on Peter and John as leaders in the Jerusalem church, cf Acts 3, 1 and 8, 14. The order here, with James first, may reflect his prominence in Jerusalem after Peter (Cephas) departed (Acts 12, 17).

2, 10: *The poor:* Jerusalem Christians or a group within the church there (cf Rom 15, 26). The collection for them was extremely important in Paul's thought and labor (cf Rom 15, 25–28; 1 Cor 16, 1–4; 2 Cor 8 and 9).

2, 11–14: The decision reached in Jerusalem (3–7) recognized the freedom of Gentile Christians from the Jewish law. But the problem of table fellowship between Jewish Christians, who possibly still kept

kosher food regulations, and Gentile believers was not yet settled. When Cephas first came to the racially mixed community of Jewish and Gentile Christians in Antioch (12), he ate with non-Jews. Pressure from persons arriving later from Jerusalem caused him and Barnabas to draw back. Paul therefore publicly rebuked Peter's inconsistency toward the gospel (14). Some think that what Paul said on that occasion extends through v 16 or v 21.

2, 11: *Clearly was wrong:* literally, "stood condemned," by himself and also by Paul. His action in breaking table fellowship was especially grievous if the eating involved the meal at the Lord's supper (cf 1 Cor 11, 17–25).

2, 12: *Some people came from James:* strict Jewish Christians (cf Acts 15, 1.5; 21, 20–21), either sent by James (1, 19; 2, 9) or claiming to be from the leader of the Jerusalem church. *The circumcised:* presumably Jewish Christians, not Jews.

2, 13: *The Jews:* Jewish Christians, like Barnabas. *Hypocrisy:* literally, "pretense," "play-acting"; moral insincerity.

*
2, 4: Gal 5, 1; Acts 15, 1.24.

2, 5: Gal 2, 14; 4, 16.

2, 6: Dt 10, 17; Rom 2, 11.

2, 7: Gal 1, 15–16; Acts 9, 15; 15, 12; 22, 21; Rom 1, 5.

2, 9: Rom 15, 15 / Gal 1, 18–19; Jn 1, 42; Acts

12, 17 / Gal 2, 1.

2, 10: Acts 11, 29–30; Rom 15, 25–28; 1 Cor 16, 1–4; 2 Cor 8, 9.

2, 11: Gal 1, 18 / Acts 11, 19–30; 15, 1–2.

2, 12: Acts 10, 15.28; 11, 3.

2, 13: Gal 2, 1.9.

with him, with the result that even Barnabas was carried away by their hypocrisy. 14*† But when I saw that they were not on the right road in line with the truth of the gospel, I said to Cephas in front of all, "If you, though a Jew, are living like a Gentile and not like a Jew, how can you compel the Gentiles to live like Jews?"

Faith and Works

15† We, who are Jews by nature and not sinners from among the Gentiles, 16*† [yet] who know that a person is not justified by works of the law but through faith in Jesus Christ, even we have believed in Christ Jesus that we may be justified by faith in Christ and not by works of the law, because by works of the law no one will be justified. 17† But if, in seeking to be justified in Christ, we ourselves are found to be sinners, is Christ then a minister of sin? Of course not! 18† But if I am building up again those things that I tore down, then I show myself to be a transgressor. 19*† For through the law I died to the law, that I might live for God. I have been crucified with Christ; 20* yet I live, no longer I, but Christ lives in me; insofar as I now live in the flesh, I live by faith in the Son of God who has loved me and given himself up for me. 21* I do not nullify the grace of God; for if justification comes through the law, then Christ died for nothing.

IV: Faith and Liberty

Justification by Faith†

3 1*† O stupid Galatians! Who has bewitched you, before whose eyes Jesus Christ was publicly portrayed as crucified? 2*† I want to learn only this from you: did you receive the Spirit from works of the law, or from faith in what you heard? 3*† Are you so stupid? After beginning with the Spirit, are you now ending with the flesh? 4† Did you experience so many things in vain?—if indeed it was in vain. 5* Does, then, the one who supplies the Spirit to you and works mighty deeds among you do so from works of the law or from faith in what you heard? 6*† Thus Abraham "believed God, and it was credited to him as righteousness."

did you KNOW?

Saved by Christ

Throughout Galatians, Paul speaks about the difference between being saved by faith and being saved through the Law. Christians believe that they are justified—made right with God—not through a perfect keeping of religious laws, but through faith in Christ. Christ's saving sacrifice alone will set them free from their sin. Their trust must be in him and not in their own ability to please God.

▸ **Gal 3, 1—4, 7**

2, 14: *Compel the Gentiles to live like Jews:* that is, conform to Jewish practices, such as circumcision (3–5) or regulations about food (12).

2, 15–21: Following on the series of incidents cited above, Paul's argument, whether spoken to Cephas at Antioch or only now articulated, is pertinent to the Galatian situation, where believers were having themselves circumcised (6, 12–13) and obeying other aspects of Jewish law (4, 9–10; 5, 1–4). He insists that salvation is by faith in Christ, not by works of the law. His teaching on the gospel concerns justification by faith (16) in relation to sin (17), law (19), life in Christ (19–20), and grace (21).

2, 16: *No one will be justified:* Ps 143, 2 is reflected.

2, 17: *A minister of sin:* literally, "a servant of sin" (cf Rom 15, 8), an agent of sin, one who promotes it. This is possibly a claim by opponents that justification on the basis of faith in Christ makes Christ an abettor of sin when Christians *are found to be sinners.* Paul denies the conclusion (cf Rom 6, 1–4).

2, 18: To return to observance of the law as the means to salvation would entangle one not only in inevitable transgressions of it but also in the admission that it was wrong to have abandoned the law in the first place.

2, 19: *Through the law I died to the law:* this is variously explained: the law revealed sin (Rom 7, 7–9) and led to death and then to belief in Christ; or, the law itself brought the insight that law cannot justify (16; Ps 143, 2); or, the "law of Christ" (6, 2) led to abandoning the Mosaic law; or, the law put Christ to death (cf 3, 13) and so provided a way to our salvation, through baptism into Christ, through which we die (*crucified with Christ;* see Rom 6, 6). Cf also 3, 19–25 on the role of the law in reference to salvation.

3, 1–14: Paul's contention that justification comes not through the law or the works of the law but by faith in Christ and in his death (2, 16.21) is supported by appeals to Christian experience (1–5) and to scripture (6–14). The gift of God's Spirit to the Galatians came from the gospel received in faith, not from doing what the law enjoins. The story of Abraham shows that faith in God brings *righteousness* (6; Gn 15, 6). The promise to Abraham (8; Gn 12, 3) extends to the Gentiles (14).

3, 1: *Stupid:* not just senseless, for they were in danger of deserting their salvation.

3, 2: *Faith in what you heard:* Paul's message received with faith. The Greek can also mean "the proclamation of the faith" or "a hearing that comes from faith."

3, 3: On the contrast of *Spirit* and *flesh,* cf Rom 8, 1–11. Having received the Spirit, they need not be circumcised now.

3, 4: *Experience so many things:* probably the *mighty deeds* of v 5 but possibly the experience of sufferings.

3, 6: *Abraham . . . righteousness:* see Gn 15, 6; Rom 4, 3. The Galatians like Abraham heard with faith and experienced justification. This first argument forms the basis for the further scriptural evidence that follows.

2, 14: Gal 2, 5 / Gal 1, 18; 2, 9 / Gal 2, 3.	10–11; Col 3, 3–4.
2, 16: Gal 3, 2.11; Ps 143, 1–2; Rom 3, 20.28; 4, 5; 11, 6; Eph 2, 8–9; Phil 3, 9.	**2, 21:** Gal 5, 2. **3, 1:** Gal 5, 7; 1 Cor 1, 23. **3, 2:** Gal 2, 16 / Gal 3, 14; Rom 10, 17. **3, 3:** Gal 5, 16–18.
2, 19: Gal 6, 14; Rom 6, 6.8.10; 7, 6.	**3, 5:** Gal 2, 16.
2, 20: Gal 1, 4; Rom 8,	**3, 6:** Gn 15, 6; Rom 4, 3; Jas 2, 23.

7*† Realize then that it is those who have faith who are children of Abraham. 8* Scripture, which saw in advance that God would justify the Gentiles by faith, foretold the good news to Abraham, saying, "Through you shall all the nations be blessed." 9* Consequently, those who have faith are blessed along with Abraham who had faith. 10*† For all who depend on works of the law are under a curse; for it is written, "Cursed be everyone who does not persevere in doing all the things written in the book of the law." 11* And that no one is justified before God by the law is clear, for "the one who is righteous by faith will live." 12* But the law does not depend on faith; rather, "the one who does these things will live by them." 13* Christ ransomed us from the curse of the law by becoming a curse for us, for it is written, "Cursed be everyone who hangs on a tree," 14* that the blessing of Abraham might be extended to the Gentiles through Christ Jesus, so that we might receive the promise of the Spirit through faith.

The Law Did Not Nullify the Promise

15*† Brothers, in human terms I say that no one can annul or amend even a human will once ratified. 16*† Now the promises were made to Abraham and to his descendant. It does not say, "And to descendants," as referring to many, but as referring to one, "And to your descendant," who is Christ. 17*† This is what I mean: the law, which came four hundred and thirty years afterward, does not annul a covenant previously ratified by God, so as to cancel the promise. 18*† For if the inheritance comes from the law, it is no longer from a promise; but God bestowed it on Abraham through a promise.

19*† Why, then, the law? It was added for transgressions, until the descendant† came to whom the promise had been made; it was promulgated by angels at the hand of a mediator. 20* Now there is no mediator when only one party is involved, and God is one. 21* Is the law then opposed to the promises [of God]? Of course not! For if a law had been given that could bring life, then righteousness would in reality come from the law. 22* But scripture confined all things under the power of sin, that through faith in Jesus Christ the promise might be given to those who believe.

What Faith Has Brought Us

23*† Before faith came, we were held in custody under law, confined for the faith that was to be re-

There is neither
Jew nor Greek,
there is neither
slave *nor free person*,
there is not
male and female;
for you are all one in
Christ Jesus
3, 28

3, 7–9: *Faith* is what matters, for *Abraham* and the *children of Abraham,* in contrast to the claims of the opponents that circumcision and observance of the law are needed to bring the promised blessing of Gn 12, 3; cf Gn 18, 18; Sir 44, 21; Acts 3, 25.

3, 10–14: *Those who depend* not on promise and faith but *on works of the law are under a curse* because they do *not persevere in doing all the things written in the book of the law* (10; Dt 27, 26) in order to gain life (12; Lv 18, 5; cf Rom 10, 5). But scripture teaches that *no one is justified before God by the law* (11; Hb 2, 4, adapted from the Greek version of Habakkuk; cf Rom 1, 17; Heb 10, 38). Salvation, then, depends on faith in Christ who died on the cross (13), taking upon himself a curse found in Dt 21, 23 (about executed criminals hanged in public view), to free us from *the curse of the law* (13). That the Gentile Galatians have received the promised Spirit (14) by faith and in no other way returns the argument to the experience cited in vv 1–5.

3, 15–18: A third argument to support Paul's position that salvation is not through the law but by promise (1–14) comes from legal practice and scriptural history. A legal agreement or *human will,* duly *ratified,* is unalterable (15). God's *covenant* with *Abraham* and its repeated promises (Gn 12, 2–3.7; 13, 15; 17, 7–8; 22, 16–18; 24, 7) is not superseded by *the law,* which came much later, in the time of Moses. *The inheritance* (of the Spirit and the blessings) is by promise, not by law (18). Paul's argument hinges on the fact that the same Greek word, *diathēkē,* can be rendered as *will* or *testament* (15) and as *covenant* (17).

3, 16: *Descendant:* literally, "and to his seed." The Hebrew, as in Gn 12, 7; 15, 18; 22, 17–18, is a collective singular, traditionally rendered as a plural, *descendants,* but taken by Paul in its literal number to refer to *Christ* as descendant of Abraham.

3, 17: *Four hundred and thirty years afterward:* follows Ex 12, 40

in the Greek (Septuagint) version, in contrast to Gn 15, 13 and Acts 7, 6, for chronology.

3, 18: This refutes the opponents' contention that the promises of God are fulfilled only as a reward for human observance of the law.

3, 19–22: A digression: if the Mosaic law, then, does not save or bring life, why was it given? Elsewhere, Paul says the law served to show what sin is (Rom 3, 20; 7, 7–8). Here the further implication is that the law in effect served to produce transgressions. Moreover, it was received at second hand *by angels,* through a *mediator,* not directly from God (19). The law does not, however, oppose God's purposes, for it carries out its function (22), so that *righteousness* comes by *faith* and *promise,* not by human works of the law.

3, 19: *The descendant:* Christ (16). *By angels:* Dt 33, 2–4 stressed their presence as enhancing the importance of the law; Paul uses their role to diminish its significance (cf Acts 7, 38.53). *A mediator:* Moses. But in a covenant of promise, where all depends on the one God, no mediator is needed (20).

3, 23–29: Paul adds a further argument in support of righteousness or justification by faith and through God's promise rather than

3, 7: Gal 3, 29; Rom 4, 11–12 / Sir 44, 19–21.	**3, 15:** Rom 3, 5 / Heb 9, 16–17.
3, 8: Gn 12, 3; 18, 17–19; Acts 3, 25.	**3, 16:** Gn 12, 7; 13, 15; 17, 8; 22, 17; 24, 7; Mt 1, 1.
3, 9: Rom 4, 16.	**3, 17:** Ex 12, 40.
3, 10: Dt 27, 26; Jas 2, 10.	**3, 18:** Rom 4, 16; 11, 6.
3, 11: Gal 2, 16; Hb 2, 4; Rom 1, 17.	**3, 19:** Rom 4, 15; 5, 20; 7, 7.13 / Acts 7, 38.53.
3, 12: Lv 18, 5; Rom 10, 5.	**3, 20:** Dt 6, 4.
3, 13: Dt 21, 23; Rom 8, 3; 2 Cor 5, 21.	**3, 21:** Rom 7, 7.10; 8, 2–4.
3, 14: Gal 3, 2–3.5; Is 44, 3; Jl 3, 1–2; Acts 2, 33.	**3, 22:** Rom 3, 9–20.23; 11, 32.
	3, 23: Gal 4, 3–5; 5, 18.

Radical Equality

Galatians 3, 28 may have been an early baptismal formula. In it, Paul makes a radical statement: The source of our equality as humans is Jesus Christ! (Note that the word _radical_ means both "root" and "extreme"—and that Paul's statement is both fundamental to Christian belief and a great expression of that belief.)

Think about what Paul says: Everyone is equal! But is this the reality in the world around you? Are all the people in your school regarded as equally valuable? Consider the equality of women in work, church, and society. What about those who are poor, how are they regarded? It is clear that we still need to work toward Paul's vision!

▶ **Gal 3, 28**

---

vealed. [24]*† Consequently, the law was our disciplinarian for Christ, that we might be justified by faith. [25]* But now that faith has come, we are no longer under a disciplinarian. [26]*† For through faith you are all children of God in Christ Jesus. [27]*† For all of you who were baptized into Christ have clothed yourselves with Christ.† [28]* There is neither Jew nor Greek, there is neither slave nor free person, there is not male and female; for you are all one in Christ Jesus. [29]* And if you belong to Christ, then you are Abraham's descendant, heirs according to the promise.

God's Free Children in Christ†

4 [1]† I mean that as long as the heir is not of age, he is no different from a slave, although he is the owner of everything, [2] but he is under the supervision of guardians and administrators until the date set by his father. [3]*† In the same way we also, when we were not of age, were enslaved to the elemental powers of the world. [4]* But when the fullness of time had come, God sent his Son, born of a woman, born under the law, [5]* to ransom those under the law, so that we might receive adoption. [6]*† As proof that you are children, God sent the spirit of his Son into our hearts, crying out, "Abba, Father!" [7]* So you are no longer a slave but a child, and if a child then also an heir, through God.

Do Not Throw This Freedom Away†

[8]*† At a time when you did not know God, you became slaves to things that by nature are not gods; [9]* but now that you have come to know God, or rather to be known by God, how can you turn back again to the weak and destitute elemental powers? Do you want to be slaves to them all over again? [10]*† You are observing days, months, seasons, and

---

by works of the law (2, 16; 3, 22): as _children of God, baptized into Christ,_ the Galatians are all _Abraham's descendant_ and _heirs_ of the _promise_ to Abraham (8.14.16–18.29). The teaching in 23–25, that since _faith_ (Christianity) _has come, we are no longer under_ the law, could be taken with the previous paragraph on the role of the Mosaic law, but it also fits here as a contrast between the situation _before faith_ (23) and the results after faith has come (25–29).

3, 24–25: _Disciplinarian:_ the Greek _paidagōgos_ referred to a slave who escorted a child to school but did not teach or tutor; hence, a guardian or monitor. Applying this to the law fits the role of the law described in vv 19–25.

3, 26: _Children of God:_ literally "sons," in contrast to the young child under the disciplinarian in vv 24–25. The term includes males and females (28).

3, 27–28: Likely a formula used at baptism that expresses racial, social-economic, and sexual equality in Christ (cf Col 3, 11).

3, 27: _Clothed yourselves with Christ:_ literally, "have put on Christ"; cf Rom 13, 14; Eph 4, 24; Col 3, 10. Baptismal imagery, traceable to the Old Testament (Jb 29, 14; Is 59, 17) but also found in pagan mystery cults.

4, 1–7: What Paul has argued in 3, 26–29 is now elaborated in terms of the Christian as _the heir_ (1.7; cf 3, 18.29) freed from control by others. Again, as in 3, 2–5, the proof that Christians are children of God is the gift of the Spirit of Christ relating them intimately to God.

4, 1.3: _Not of age:_ an infant or minor.

4, 3: _The elemental powers of the world:_ while the term can refer to the "elements" like earth, air, fire, and water or to elementary forms of religion, the sense here is more likely that of celestial beings

that were thought in pagan circles to control the world; cf 8; Col 2, 8.20.

4, 6: _Children:_ see the note on 3, 26; here in contrast to the infant or young person _not of age_ (1.3). _Abba:_ cf Mk 14, 36 and the note; Rom 8, 15.

4, 8–11: On the basis of the arguments advanced from 3, 1 through 4, 7, Paul now launches his appeal to the Galatians with the question, _how can you turn back_ to the slavery of the law (9)? The question is posed with reference to bondage to the _elemental powers_ (see the note on 4, 3) because the Galatians had originally been converted to Christianity from paganism, not Judaism (8). The use of the direct question is like 3, 3–5.

4, 8: _Things that by nature are not gods:_ or "gods that by nature do not exist."

4, 10: This is likely a reference to ritual observances from the Old Testament, promoted by opponents: sabbaths or Yom Kippur, new moon, Passover or Pentecost, sabbatical years.

3, 24: Gal 2, 16.	12; Jas 2, 5.
3, 25: Rom 10, 4.	4, 3: Gal 3, 23 / Gal 4, 9;
3, 26: Gal 4, 5–7; Jn 1, 12;	Col 2, 20.
Rom 8, 14–17.	4, 4: Mk 1, 15.
3, 27: Rom 6, 3; 13, 14; Eph	4, 5: Gal 3, 13.26.
4, 24.	4, 6: Gal 3, 26; Rom 8, 15.
3, 28: Rom 10, 12; 1 Cor 12,	4, 7: Gal 3, 29; Rom 8,
13; Col 3, 11.	16–17.
3, 29: Gal 3, 7.14.16.18;	4, 8: 1 Cor 12, 2.
Rom 4, 16–17; 9, 7 /	4, 9: Gal 4, 3; Col 2, 20.
Gal 4, 1.7; Rom 4,	4, 10: Col 2, 16–20.
13–14; 8, 17; Heb 6,	

years. [11]† I am afraid on your account that perhaps I have labored for you in vain.

Appeal to Former Loyalty†

[12]*† I implore you, brothers, be as I am, because I have also become as you are. You did me no wrong; [13]† you know that it was because of a physical illness that I originally preached the gospel to you, [14] and you did not show disdain or contempt because of the trial caused you by my physical condition, but rather you received me as an angel of God, as Christ Jesus. [15]† Where now is that blessedness of yours? Indeed, I can testify to you that, if it had been possible, you would have torn out your eyes and given them to me. [16] So now have I become your enemy by telling you the truth? [17]*† They show interest in you, but not in a good way; they want to isolate you, so that you may show interest in them. [18] Now it is good to be shown interest for good reason at all times, and not only when I am with you. [19]* My children, for whom I am again in labor until Christ be formed in you! [20] I would like to be with you now and to change my tone, for I am perplexed because of you.

An Allegory on Christian Freedom

[21]† Tell me, you who want to be under the law, do you not listen to the law? [22]* For it is written that Abraham had two sons, one by the slave woman and the other by the freeborn woman. [23]* The son of the slave woman was born naturally, the son of the freeborn through a promise. [24]* Now this is an allegory. These women represent two covenants. One was from Mount Sinai, bearing children for slavery; this is Hagar. [25]† Hagar represents Sinai, a mountain in Arabia; it corresponds to the present Jerusalem, for she is in slavery along with her children. [26]* But the Jerusalem above is freeborn, and she is our mother. [27]*† For it is written:

"Rejoice, you barren one who bore
    no children;
break forth and shout, you who were not
    in labor;
for more numerous are the children of the
    deserted one
    than of her who has a husband."

[28]* Now you, brothers, like Isaac, are children of the promise. [29] But just as then the child of the flesh persecuted the child of the spirit, it is the same now. [30]* But what does the scripture say?

"Drive out the slave woman and her son!
    For the son of the slave woman shall not
        share the inheritance with the son"

of the freeborn. [31]* Therefore, brothers, we are children not of the slave woman but of the freeborn woman.

V: Exhortation to Christian Living

The Importance of Faith†

5 [1]*† For freedom Christ set us free; so stand firm and do not submit again to the yoke of slavery.

[2]* It is I, Paul, who am telling you that if you

4, 11: Cf 2, 2. If the Galatians become *slaves . . . all over again* to the law (9), Paul will have worked in vain among them.

4, 12–20: A strongly personal section. Paul appeals to past ties between the Galatians and himself. He speaks sharply of the opponents (17–18) and pastorally to the Galatians (19–20).

4, 12: *Because I have also become as you are:* a terse phrase in Greek, meaning "Be as I, Paul, am," i.e., living by faith, independent of the law, for, in spite of my background in Judaism (1, 13), I have become as you Galatians are now, a brother in Christ.

4, 13: *Physical illness:* because its nature is not described, some assume an eye disease (15); others, epilepsy; some relate it to 2 Cor 12, 7–9. *Originally:* this may also be translated "formerly" or "on the first (of two) visit(s)"; cf Acts 16, 6; 18, 23.

4, 15: *That blessedness of yours:* possibly a reference to the Galatians' initial happy reception of Paul (14) and of his gospel (1, 6; 3, 1–4) and their felicitation at such blessedness, but the phrase could also refer ironically to earlier praise by Paul of the Galatians, no longer possible when they turn from the gospel to the claims of the opponents (17–18; 1, 7). If the word is a more literal reference to a beatitude, Gal 3, 26–28 may be in view.

4, 17: *Isolate you:* that is, from the blessings of the gospel and/or from Paul.

4, 21–31: Paul supports his appeal for the gospel (9; 1, 6–9; 2, 16; 3, 2) by a further argument from scripture (cf 3, 6–18). It involves the relationship of *Abraham* (3, 6–16) to his wife, Sarah, the *freeborn woman,* and to Hagar, *the slave woman,* and the contrast between the sons born to each, *Isaac,* child of promise, and Ishmael, son of Hagar (Gn 16 and 21). Only through Isaac is the promise of God preserved. This *allegory* (24), with its equation of the Sinai covenant and

Mosaic law with slavery and of the promise of God with freedom, Paul uses only in light of previous arguments. His quotation of Gn 21, 10 at v 30 suggests on a scriptural basis that the Galatians should expel those who are troubling them (1, 7).

4, 25: *Hagar represents Sinai . . . :* some manuscripts have what seems a geographical note, "For Sinai is a mountain in Arabia."

4, 27: Is 54, 1 in the Septuagint translation is applied to Sarah as the *barren one* (in Gn 15) who ultimately becomes the mother not only of Isaac but now of numerous children, i.e., of all those who believe, the *children of the promise* (28).

5, 1–6: Paul begins the exhortations, continuing through 6, 10, with an appeal to the Galatians to side with freedom instead of slavery (1). He reiterates his message of justification or righteousness by faith instead of law and circumcision (2–5); cf 2, 16; 3, 3. Faith, not circumcision, is what counts (6).

5, 1: *Freedom:* Paul stresses as the conclusion from the allegory in 4, 21–31 this result of Christ's work for us. It is a principle previously mentioned (2, 4), the responsible use of which v 13 will emphasize.

4, 12: 1 Cor 11, 1.
4, 17: Gal 1, 7; 6, 12; Acts 20, 30.
4, 19: 1 Cor 4, 14–15; 2 Cor 6, 13; 1 Thes 2, 7–8.
4, 22: Gn 16, 15; 21, 2–3.
4, 23: Gn 17, 16; Rom 4, 19–20; 9, 7–9.
4, 24: Gal 3, 17 / Ex 19, 20 / Gn 16, 1.
4, 26: Heb 12, 22; Rv 21, 2.
4, 27: Is 54, 1.
4, 28: Rom 9, 8.
4, 30: Gn 21, 10.
4, 31: Gal 3, 29; Jn 8, 35.
5, 1: Gal 2, 4; 4, 5.9; Jn 8, 32.36.
5, 2: Gal 2, 21; Acts 15, 1–29.

have yourselves circumcised, Christ will be of no benefit to you. ³*† Once again I declare to every man who has himself circumcised that he is bound to observe the entire law. ⁴ You are separated from Christ, you who are trying to be justified by law; you have fallen from grace. ⁵* For through the Spirit, by faith, we await the hope of righteousness. ⁶*† For in Christ Jesus, neither circumcision nor uncircumcision counts for anything, but only faith working through love.

Be Not Misled†

⁷† You were running well; who hindered you from following [the] truth? ⁸*† That enticement does not come from the one who called you. ⁹* A little yeast leavens the whole batch of dough. ¹⁰* I am confident of you in the Lord that you will not take a different view, and that the one who is troubling you will bear the condemnation, whoever he may be. ¹¹*† As for me, brothers, if I am still preaching circumcision, why am I still being persecuted? In that case, the stumbling block of the cross has been abolished. ¹²† Would that those who are upsetting you might also castrate themselves!

Freedom for Service†

¹³* For you were called for freedom, brothers. But do not use this freedom as an opportunity for the flesh; rather, serve one another through love.† ¹⁴*† For the whole law is fulfilled in one statement, namely, "You shall love your neighbor as yourself." ¹⁵ But if you go on biting and devouring one another, beware that you are not consumed by one another.

¹⁶*† I say, then: live by the Spirit and you will certainly not gratify the desire of the flesh. ¹⁷* For the flesh has desires against the Spirit, and the Spirit against the flesh; these are opposed to each other, so that you may not do what you want. ¹⁸* But if you are guided by the Spirit, you are not under the law. ¹⁹*† Now the works of the flesh are obvious:

PRAY IT

Fill Me, Lord

*F*ill me with the fruits of your Spirit, Lord.

Fill me with love, so that I seek to understand and appreciate the rich variety and diversity of life that surrounds me.

Fill me with joy, so that I celebrate your presence in each and every moment I am on this earth.

Fill me with peace, so that I know how to ease those angry and sometimes violent urges that well up inside of me.

Fill me with patience, so that I stop rushing long enough to witness your miraculous work taking place all around me (and within me!).

Fill me with kindness, so that I take the extra time to help the one in need, even when it isn't convenient for me.

Fill me with faithfulness, so that I place my mind, heart, and all that I do in the service of your Gospel.

Fill me with gentleness, so that others know that I believe in a God who loves and cares for all people.

Fill me with self-control, so that I act not on my impulses and urges, but rather on my beliefs and values, which are rooted in you.

Fill me with these fruits of your spirit, Lord! Amen.

▶ **Gal 5, 22–26**

5, 3: Cf 3, 10–12. Just as those who seek to live by the law must carry out all its contents, so those who have faith and live by promise must stand firm in their freedom (1.13).

5, 6: Cf Rom 2, 25–26; 1 Cor 7, 19; Gal 6, 15. The Greek for *faith working through love* or "faith expressing itself through love" can also be rendered as "faith energized by (God's) love."

5, 7–12: Paul addresses the Galatians directly: with questions (7.11), a proverb (9), a statement (8), and biting sarcasm (12), seeking to persuade the Galatians to break with those trying to add law and circumcision to Christ as a basis for salvation.

5, 7: *Running well:* as in an athletic contest; cf 2, 2; 1 Cor 9, 24–26; Phil 2, 16; 3, 14.

5, 8: *The one who called you:* see the note on 1, 6.

5, 11: *Preaching circumcision:* this could refer to Paul's pre-Christian period (possibly as a missionary for Judaism); more probably it arose as a charge from opponents, based perhaps on the story in Acts 16, 1–3 that Paul had circumcised Timothy "on account of the Jews." Unlike the Gentile Titus in Gal 2, 3, Timothy was the son of a Jewish mother. *The stumbling block of the cross:* cf 1 Cor 1, 23.

5, 12: A sarcastic half-wish that their knife would go beyond mere circumcision; cf Phil 3, 2 and the note there.

5, 13–26: In light of another reminder of the freedom of the gospel (13; cf 1), Paul elaborates on what believers are called to do and be: they fulfill the law by love of neighbor (14–15), walking in the Spirit (16–26), as is illustrated by concrete *fruit of the Spirit* in their lives.

5, 13: *Serve . . . through love:* cf v 6.

5, 14: Lv 19, 18, emphasized by Jesus (Mt 22, 39; Lk 10, 27); cf Rom 13, 8–10.

5, 16–25: *Spirit . . . flesh:* cf 3, 3 and the note on Rom 8, 1–13.

5, 19–23: Such lists of vices and virtues (cf Rom 1, 29–31; 1 Cor 6, 9–10) were common in the ancient world. Paul contrasts *works of the flesh* (19) with *fruit* (not "works") *of the Spirit* (22). Not law, but the Spirit, leads to such traits.

5, 3: Gal 3, 10; Rom 2, 25; Jas 2, 10.	**5, 13:** Gal 5, 1 / Rom 6, 18; 1 Cor 8, 9; 1 Pt 2, 16.
5, 5: Rom 8, 23.25.	**5, 14:** Lv 19, 18; Mt 22, 39; Rom 13, 8–10.
5, 6: Gal 3, 28; 6, 15; 1 Cor 7, 19.	**5, 16:** Gal 5, 24–25; Rom 8, 5.
5, 8: Gal 1, 6.	**5, 17:** Rom 7, 15.23; 8, 6.
5, 9: 1 Cor 5, 6.	**5, 18:** Rom 6, 14; 8, 14.
5, 10: Gal 1, 7.	**5, 19–21:** Rom 1, 29–31; 1 Cor 6, 9–10; Col 3, 5–6.8.
5, 11: Gal 6, 12.14; 1 Cor 1, 23.	

THE PRINCIPLE OF *IMANI*

Be not discouraged. There is a future for you. . . . The resistance encountered now predicates hope. . . . Only as we rise . . . do we encounter opposition.

These words by Frederick Douglass in 1892 encouraged African Americans not to abandon their struggle for equality. It seemed that the more they struggled, the more pain was inflicted on them. In the face of certain suffering, Douglass urged them to look toward the promise of living as equals under the law.

They knew that God was their liberator and justice giver. God made them brave in the face of danger and capable of dying for the cause they embraced. They looked to God and saw their future. They took the words of Gal 6, 9 seriously: "Let us not grow tired of doing good."

Today, we don't face slave masters and live on plantations as servants in fetters, but we do endure other situations equally as perilous. Let us not grow weary or lose heart. We must practice the Kwanzaa principle of *imani*, or "faith" (see "Kwanzaa as a Way of Life," Dt 10, 12–22). Our God is still in the saving business.

Dear God, my future is in your hands. Lead me to it with your power. Amen.

▶ Gal 6, 9

---

immorality, impurity, licentiousness, ²⁰* idolatry, sorcery, hatreds, rivalry, jealousy, outbursts of fury, acts of selfishness, dissensions, factions, ²¹† occasions of envy, drinking bouts, orgies, and the like. I warn you, as I warned you before, that those who do such things will not inherit the kingdom of God. ²²* In contrast, the fruit of the Spirit is love, joy, peace, patience, kindness, generosity, faithfulness, ²³* gentleness, self-control. Against such there is no law. ²⁴* Now those who belong to Christ [Jesus] have crucified their flesh with its passions and desires. ²⁵* If we live in the Spirit, let us also follow the Spirit. ²⁶* Let us not be conceited, provoking one another, envious of one another.

Life in the Community of Christ

6 ¹*† Brothers, even if a person is caught in some transgression, you who are spiritual should correct that one in a gentle spirit, looking to yourself, so that you also may not be tempted. ²*† Bear one another's burdens, and so you will fulfill the law of Christ. ³* For if anyone thinks he is something when he is nothing, he is deluding himself. ⁴† Each one must examine his own work, and then he will have reason to boast with regard to himself alone, and not with regard to someone else; ⁵* for each will bear his own load.

⁶*† One who is being instructed in the word

---

† **5, 21:** *Occasions of envy:* after the Greek word *phthonoi,* "envies," some manuscripts add a similar sounding one, *phonoi,* "murders."

6, 1–10: The ethical exhortations begun at 5, 1 continue with a variety of admonitions to the community (*brothers:* see the note on 1, 2). Nearly every sentence contains a separate item of practical advice; the faith and freedom of the gospel underlie each maxim. Tensions and temptation within communal life have previously been addressed in 5, 15.26, and v 1 continues in which *a person is caught in some transgression* such as those in 5, 19–21; cf 2, 17.

6, 2: *The law of Christ:* cf Rom 8, 2; 1 Cor 9, 21; Gal 5, 14. The principle of love for others is meant. To *bear one another's burdens* is to "serve one another through love" (5, 13).

6, 4–5: Self-examination is the cure for self-deception. Compare what you are with what you were before, and give the glory to God; cf Rom 6, 19–22. *Load:* used elsewhere of a soldier's pack. Correcting one's own conduct avoids burdening others with it.

6, 6: Implies oral instruction in the faith by catechists; these are to be remunerated for their service; cf Rom 15, 27.

---

*

5, 20: Rv 22, 15.
5, 22: Eph 5, 9 / 1 Cor 13, 4–7; 2 Cor 6, 6; 1 Tm 4, 12; 2 Pt 1, 6.
5, 23: 1 Tm 1, 9.
5, 24: Gal 2, 19; Rom 6, 6; 8, 13.
5, 25: Gal 5, 16.
5, 26: Phil 2, 3.

6, 1: Mt 18, 15; Jas 5, 19 / 1 Cor 10, 12–13.
6, 2: Col 3, 13 / 1 Cor 9, 21.
6, 3–4: 1 Cor 3, 18; 8, 2; 2 Cor 12, 11.
6, 5: Rom 14, 12.
6, 6: 1 Cor 9, 14.

should share all good things with his instructor. [7] Make no mistake: God is not mocked, for a person will reap only what he sows, [8]* because the one who sows for his flesh will reap corruption from the flesh, but the one who sows for the spirit will reap eternal life from the spirit. [9]* Let us not grow tired of doing good, for in due time we shall reap our harvest, if we do not give up. [10]*† So then, while we have the opportunity, let us do good to all, but especially to those who belong to the family of the faith.

VI: Conclusion

Final Appeal†

[11]*† See with what large letters I am writing to you in my own hand! [12]*† It is those who want to make a good appearance in the flesh who are trying to compel you to have yourselves circumcised, only that they may not be persecuted for the cross of Christ. [13]† Not even those having themselves circumcised observe the law themselves; they only want you to be circumcised so that they may boast of your flesh. [14]*† But may I never boast except in the cross of our Lord Jesus Christ, through which the world has been crucified to me, and I to the world. [15]*† For neither does circumcision mean anything, nor does uncircumcision, but only a new creation. [16]*† Peace and mercy be to all who follow this rule and to the Israel of God.

[17]*† From now on, let no one make troubles for me; for I bear the marks of Jesus on my body.

[18]* The grace of our Lord Jesus Christ be with your spirit, brothers. Amen.

6, 10: *The family of the faith:* the Christian household or church. Doing good has a universal object (*to all*), but the local community makes specific the reality of those to be served.

6, 11–18: A postscript in Paul's own hand, as was his practice (see 1 Cor 16, 21; 2 Thes 3, 17). Paul summarizes his appeal against his opponents (12–13), then returns to his message of glorying in the cross, not in circumcision, as the means of salvation (14–15; cf 5, 11). A benediction follows at v 16. In the polemical spirit that the attack on his apostleship called forth (1, 11—2, 21), Paul reasserts his missionary credentials (17) before giving a final benediction (18).

6, 11: *Large letters:* in contrast to the finer hand of the scribe who wrote the letter up to this point. The larger Greek letters make Paul's message even more emphatic. Some find a hint of poor eyesight on Paul's part. See the note on 4, 13.

6, 12–15: The Jewish Christian opponents wished *not to be persecuted,* possibly by Jews. But since Judaism seems to have had a privileged status as a religion in the Roman empire, circumcised Christians might, if taken as Jews, thereby avoid persecution from the Romans. In any case, Paul instead stresses conformity with *the cross of our Lord Jesus Christ;* cf 2, 19–21; 5, 11.

6, 13: *Those having themselves circumcised:* other manuscripts read, "those who have had themselves circumcised."

6, 14: *Through which:* or "through whom."

6, 15: *New creation:* or "new creature"; cf 2 Cor 5, 17.

6, 16: *This rule:* the principle in vv 14 and 15. *The Israel of God:* while the church may be meant (the phrase can be translated "to all who follow this rule, even the Israel of God"; cf 10; 1 Cor 10, 18), the reference may also be to God's ancient people, Israel; cf Pss 125, 5; 128, 6.

6, 17: *The marks of Jesus:* slaves were often branded by marks (*stigmata*) burned into their flesh to show to whom they belonged; so also were devotees of pagan gods. Paul implies that instead of outdated circumcision, his body bears the scars of his apostolic labors (2 Cor 11, 22–31), such as floggings (Acts 16, 22; 2 Cor 11, 25) and stonings (Acts 14, 19), that mark him as belonging to the Christ who suffered (cf Rom 6, 3; 2 Cor 4, 10; Col 1, 24) and will protect his own.

6, 8: Prv 11, 18; Rom 8, 6.13.
6, 9: 2 Thes 3, 13; Heb 12, 1–3.
6, 10: 1 Thes 5, 15.
6, 11: 1 Cor 16, 21.
6, 12: Gal 5, 2.11.
6, 14: Gal 2, 20; 1 Cor 2, 2.
6, 15: Gal 5, 6; 1 Cor 7, 19 / 2 Cor 5, 17.
6, 16: Pss 125, 5; 128, 6.
6, 17: 2 Cor 4, 10.
6, 18: Phil 4, 23; 2 Tm 4, 22; Phlm 25.

What's the purpose to life? Why am I alive? What's the point of it all anyway? You may have asked questions like these out of simple curiosity, or during a time when life wasn't going so well. In either case, God has an answer for you tucked away inside the Letter to the Ephesians. This letter talks about God's plan to save us for a life in union with God and one another, both now and for all eternity!

At a Glance

I. Address (1, 1–14).

II. Unity of the Church in Christ (1, 15—2, 22).

III. World Mission of the Church (3, 1—4, 24).

IV. Daily Conduct, an Expression of Unity (4, 25—6, 20).

V. Conclusion (6, 21–24).

In-depth

Three times in the poetic opening chapter, the writer of Ephesians tells us that we are here because we have been chosen by God! In this beautiful trinity of praise for the Father (verses 3–6), the Son (verse 12), and the Holy Spirit (verses 13–14), we are told that that's why we're alive!

This letter has hardly any of the personal greeting you'd expect in a communication to a specific group of people. Also, the reference to the saints in the first verse doesn't appear in many of the earliest copies we have of the letter. For these reasons, most scholars believe that this letter was intended to be read by several Christian communities and has a universal message for the early church.

Ephesians emphasizes unity among Christians. It especially emphasizes that Gentile (non-Jewish) Christians are one with Jewish Christians, for Christ "made both one and broke down the dividing wall" (2, 14). It explains that it is the early Christians' job—as it is our job—to treat one another with love, "striving to preserve the unity" (4, 3). The image of the body is used here, as it is in 1 Corinthians, chapter 12, to emphasize our unity (4, 15–16).

Ephesians also talks about the place of good works in the life of a Christian. Good works can be thought of as living a moral life, or as following moral rules, such as the Jewish Law. Paul has made clear that we are not saved by the Law. So, what is the point of living a moral life? The letter explains that we are saved not *by doing* good works but *in order to do* good works.

The letter ends with some practical advice for living out the faith on a daily basis. There are rules for moral living. There are instructions for Christian family life. There is an analogy for putting on the "armor of God" to resist evil in all its forms. If we keep in mind that this letter is written for a culture that was different from ours, the advice will serve us well too!

Quick Facts

Author
a follower of Paul (see "Introduction to the Letters and Revelation")

Date Written
after Paul's death, A.D. 70–95

Audience
Gentile churches, possibly in Asia Minor

Ephesians

2, 20

I: Address

Greeting†

1 ¹*† Paul, an apostle of Christ Jesus by the will of God, to the holy ones who are [in Ephesus] faithful in Christ Jesus: ²* grace to you and peace from God our Father and the Lord Jesus Christ.

The Father's Plan of Salvation

³*† Blessed be the God and Father of our Lord Jesus Christ, who has blessed us in Christ with every spiritual blessing in the heavens,† ⁴* as he chose us in him, before the foundation of the world, to be holy and without blemish before him. In love ⁵* he destined us for adoption to himself through Jesus Christ, in accord with the favor of his will, ⁶* for the praise of the glory of his grace that he granted us in the beloved.

Fulfillment through Christ

⁷* In him we have redemption by his blood, the forgiveness of transgressions, in accord with the riches of his grace ⁸* that he lavished upon us. In all wisdom and insight, ⁹*† he has made known to us

1, 1–2: For the epistolary form used at the beginning of letters, see the note on Rom 1, 1–7. Twenty-two of the thirty Greek words in vv 1–2 also occur in Col 1, 1–2.

1, 1: *[In Ephesus:]* the phrase is lacking in important early witnesses such as P⁴⁶ (3rd cent.), and Sinaiticus and Vaticanus (4th cent.), appearing in the latter two as a fifth-century addition. Basil and Origen mention its absence from manuscripts. See Introduction. Without the phrase, the Greek can be rendered, as in Col 1, 2, "to the holy ones and faithful brothers in Christ."

1, 3–14: While a Pauline letter usually continues after the greeting with a prayer of thanksgiving, as in 15–23 below, Ephesians first inserts a blessing of God for the blessings Christians have experienced, as in 2 Cor 1, 3–4 and 1 Pt 1, 3–12. The blessing here, akin to a Jewish *berakah*, is rich in images almost certainly drawn from hymns and liturgy. Many ideas here are also found in Col 1, 3–23. Certain phrases are frequently repeated, such as *in Christ* (3.10.12) or *in him* (4.7.9.11.13) or *in the beloved* (6) and *(for) the praise of (his) glory* (6.12.14). Some terms like *chose* (4) and *destined* (5) reflect Old Testament theology (Dt 7, 7; 9, 4–6; 23, 5) or Pauline themes (*redemption*, 7.14; *grace*, 6.7) or specific emphases in Colossians (*forgiveness*, Col 1, 14).

A triadic structure is discernible in vv 3–14: *God the Father* (3–6.8.11), *Christ* (3.5.7–10.12), and the *Spirit* (13–14). The spiritual blessings Christians have received through Christ (3) are gratefully enumerated: the call to holiness (4; cf Col 1, 22); the gift of divine *adoption* establishing a unique spiritual relationship with God the Father through Christ (5; cf Gal 4, 5); liberation from sin through Christ's sacrificial death (7); revelation of God's plan of salvation in Christ (9; cf 3, 3–4; Rom 16, 25); the gift of election and faith in Christ bestowed upon Jewish Christians (see the note on 12, *we who first hoped in Christ*); and finally, the same gift granted to Gentiles (13, *you also*). In the Christ-centered faith and existence of the Christian communities the apostle sees the predetermined *plan* of God to bring all creation under the final rule of Christ (4–5.9–10) being *made known* (9) and carried through, to God's *glory* (6.12.14).

1, 3: *In the heavens:* literally, "in the heavenlies" or "in the heavenly places," a term in Ephesians for the divine realm.

1, 9: *Mystery:* as in Rom 16, 25; Col 1, 26.27 and elsewhere, a secret of God now revealed in the *plan* to save and *sum up all things in Christ* (10); cf 3, 3–6.

1, 1: Rom 1, 7; 1 Cor 1, 1–2; Col 1, 1.
1, 2: Col 1, 2.
1, 3: Eph 2, 6; 2 Cor 1, 3.
1, 4: Eph 5, 27; Jn 15, 16; 17, 24; Rom 8, 29; 2 Thes 2, 13.
1, 5: Jn 1, 12; 1 Jn 3, 1.
1, 6: Mt 3, 17; Col 1, 13.
1, 7: Eph 2, 7–13; Rom 3, 24; Col 1, 14.20.
1, 8: Col 1, 9.
1, 9: Eph 3, 3.9; Rom 16, 25.

the mystery of his will in accord with his favor that he set forth in him [10]* as a plan for the fullness of times, to sum up all things in Christ, in heaven and on earth.

Inheritance through the Spirit

[11]* In him we were also chosen, destined in accord with the purpose of the One who accomplishes all things according to the intention of his will, [12]† so that we might exist for the praise of his glory, we who first hoped in Christ. [13]*† In him you also, who have heard the word of truth, the gospel of your salvation, and have believed in him, were sealed with the promised holy Spirit, [14]*† which is the first installment of our inheritance toward redemption as God's possession, to the praise of his glory.

II: Unity of the Church in Christ

The Church as Christ's Body†

[15]*† Therefore, I, too, hearing of your faith in the Lord Jesus and of your love for all the holy ones, [16]* do not cease giving thanks for you, remembering you in my prayers, [17]* that the God of our Lord Jesus Christ, the Father of glory, may give you a spirit of wisdom and revelation resulting in knowledge of him. [18]* May the eyes of [your] hearts be enlightened, that you may know what is the hope that belongs to his call, what are the riches of glory in his inheritance among the holy ones, [19]* and what is the surpassing greatness of his power for us who believe, in accord with the exercise of his great might, [20]* which he worked in Christ, raising him from the dead and seating him at his right hand in the heavens, [21]* far above every principality,

authority, power, and dominion, and every name that is named not only in this age but also in the one to come. [22]* And he put all things beneath his feet and gave him as head over all things to the church, [23]*† which is his body, the fullness of the one who fills all things in every way.

Generosity of God's Plan†

2 [1]*† You were dead in your transgressions and sins† [2]*† in which you once lived following the

I Give God Thanks for You!

Think of people in your family, community, school, and church who are living out the Gospel message. Who is honestly striving to live her or his Christian faith? a parent or guardian? a friend? a neighbor? a teacher? a minister?

Hold this person in your heart as you read Eph 1, 15–23. Meditate on how this person has influenced you as a Christian. How has he or she helped you on your faith journey? Consider writing your own prayer of thanks to God for this person's example. If it seems appropriate, share your prayer with this person.

▸ Eph 1, 15–23

1, 12: *We who first hoped:* probably Jewish Christians (contrast 13, *you,* the Gentiles); possibly the people of Israel, "we who already enjoyed the hope of Christ," or perhaps present hope in contrast to future redemption (cf 14).

1, 13: *Sealed:* by God, in baptism; cf 4, 30; 2 Cor 1, 22.

1, 14: *First installment:* down payment by God on full salvation, as at 2 Cor 1, 22.

1, 15–23: See the note on Rom 1, 8 for the thanksgiving form in a letter. Much of the content parallels thoughts in Col 1, 3–20. The prayer moves from God and Christ (17.20–21) to the Ephesians (17–19) and the church (22–23). Paul asks that the blessing imparted by God the Father (3) to the Ephesians will be strengthened in them through the message of the gospel (13.17–19). Those blessings are seen in the context of God's *might* in establishing the sovereignty of Christ over all other creatures (19–21) and in appointing him *head* of the church (22–23). For the allusion to angelic spirits in v 21, see Rom 8, 38 and Col 1, 16. Here, as in 1 Cor 15, 24–25 and Col 2, 15, every such *principality* and *power* is made subject to Christ.

1, 15: *Your faith . . . your love:* some manuscripts omit the latter phrase, but cf Col 1, 4.

1, 23: *His body:* the church (22); cf the note on Col 1, 18. Only in Ephesians and Colossians is Christ the *head* of the *body,* in contrast to the view in 1 Cor 12 and Rom 12, 4–8 where Christ is equated with the entire body or community. *Fullness:* see the note on Col 1, 19. Some take *the one who fills* as God, others as Christ (cf 4, 10). If Christ "dwells the fullness of the deity bodily" (Col 2, 9), then, as God "fills" Christ, Christ in turn fills the church and the believer (3, 19; 5, 18). But the difficult phrases here may also allow the church to be

viewed as the "complement" of Christ who is "being filled" as God's plan for the universe is carried out through the church (cf 3, 9–10).

2, 1–22: The gospel of *salvation* (1, 13) that God *worked in Christ* (1, 20) is reiterated in terms of what God's *great love* (4), expressed in Christ, means for us. The passage sometimes addresses *you,* Gentiles (1–2.8.11–13.19.22), but other times speaks of *all of us* who believe (3–7.10.14.18). In urging people to *remember* their grim past when they were *dead* in sins (1–3.11–12) and what they are *now* in Christ (4–10.13), the author sees both Jew and Gentile reconciled with God, now *one new person,* a new humanity, *one body, the household of God, a temple* and *dwelling place* of God's Spirit (15–16.19–22). The presentation falls into two parts, the second stressing more the meaning for the church.

2, 1–10: The recipients of Paul's letter have experienced, in their redemption from *transgressions and sins,* the effect of Christ's supremacy over the power of the devil (1–2; cf 6, 11–12), who rules not from the netherworld but from the *air* between God in heaven

1, 10: Gal 4, 4; Col 1, 16.20.	2, 12.
1, 11: Is 46, 10; Rom 8, 28; Col 1, 12; Rv 4, 11.	**1, 20:** Ps 110, 1; Heb 1, 3. 1 Pt 3, 22.
1, 13: Eph 4, 30; Acts 2, 33; Col 1, 5–6.	**1, 21:** Phil 2, 9; Col 1, 16;
1, 14: 2 Cor 1, 22; 5, 5.	**1, 22:** Eph 4, 15; Ps 8, 7; Mt 28, 18; Col 1, 18.
1, 15: Col 1, 3–4; Phlm 4–5.	**1, 23:** Eph 4, 10.12; Rom 12, 5; 1 Cor 12, 27; Col 1, 19.
1, 16: Col 1, 3.9.	
1, 17: Eph 3, 14.16; Col 1, 9–10; 1 Jn 5, 20.	**2, 1:** Col 1, 21; 2, 13.
1, 18: Eph 4, 4; Col 1, 12.27.	**2, 2:** Eph 6, 12; Jn 12, 31; Col 1, 13.
1, 19: 2 Cor 13, 4; Col 1, 11;	

EPH

age of this world, following the ruler of the power of the air, the spirit that is now at work in the disobedient. ³* All of us once lived among them in the desires of our flesh, following the wishes of the flesh and the impulses, and we were by nature children of wrath, like the rest. ⁴ But God, who is rich in mercy, because of the great love he had for us, ⁵*† even when we were dead in our transgressions, brought us to life with Christ (by grace you have been saved), ⁶* raised us up with him, and seated us with him in the heavens in Christ Jesus, ⁷* that in the ages to come he might show the immeasurable riches of his grace in his kindness to us in Christ Jesus. ⁸* For by grace you have been saved through faith, and this is not from you; it is the gift of God; ⁹* it is not from works, so no one may boast. ¹⁰* For we are his handiwork, created in Christ Jesus for the good works that God has prepared in advance, that we should live in them.

One in Christ

¹¹† Therefore, remember that at one time you, Gentiles in the flesh, called the uncircumcision by those called the circumcision, which is done in the flesh by human hands, ¹²*† were at that time without Christ, alienated from the community of Israel and strangers to the covenants of promise, without hope and without God in the world. ¹³* But now in Christ Jesus you who once were far off have become near by the blood of Christ.

¹⁴*† For he is our peace, he who made both one and broke down the dividing wall of enmity, through his flesh, ¹⁵*† abolishing the law with its commandments and legal claims, that he might create in himself one new person in place of the two, thus establishing peace, ¹⁶* and might

reconcile both with God, in one body, through the cross, putting that enmity to death by it. ¹⁷* He came and preached peace to you who were far off and peace to those who were near, ¹⁸* for through him we both have access in one Spirit to the Father.

?did you KNOW?

Faith Versus Good Works

Ephesians 2, 1–10 deals with the question of faith versus good works (good works are moral living and Gospel-motivated works of service, justice, courage, and so on). This issue has divided Christians since the early church and was a major issue at the time of the Protestant Reformation. Some say that we are saved by our good works. Others say that good works are irrelevant and that we are saved only through our faith in Christ.

The writer of Ephesians makes it clear that both those statements are incomplete. The core Christian belief is this: We are saved by God's grace through faith in Jesus Christ. We are saved not by doing good works but in order to do good works. Our salvation is God's gift to us; how we live is our gift to God.

▶ **Eph 2, 1–10**

---

and human beings on earth. Both Jew and Gentile have experienced, through Christ, God's free gift of salvation that already marks them for a future heavenly destiny (3–7). The language *dead, raised us up,* and *seated us . . . in the heavens* closely parallels Jesus' own passion and Easter experience. The terms in vv 8–9 describe salvation in the way Paul elsewhere speaks of justification: by grace, through faith, the gift of God, not from works; cf Gal 2, 16–21; Rom 3, 24–28. Christians are a newly created people in Christ, fashioned by God for a life of goodness (10).

2, 1–7: These verses comprise one long sentence in Greek, the main verb coming in v 5, God *brought us to life,* the object you/us *dead in . . . transgressions* being repeated in 1 and 5; cf Col 2, 13.

2, 2: *Age of this world:* or "aeon," a term found in gnostic thought, possibly synonymous with *the rulers of this world,* but also reflecting the Jewish idea of "two ages," this present evil age and "the age to come"; cf 1 Cor 3, 19; 5, 10; 7, 31; Gal 1, 4; Ti 2, 12. *The disobedient:* literally, "the sons of disobedience," a Semitism as at Is 30, 9.

2, 5: Our relation through baptism *with Christ,* the risen Lord, is depicted in terms of realized eschatology, as already exaltation, though v 7 brings in the future aspect too.

2, 11–22: The Gentiles lacked Israel's messianic expectation, lacked the various *covenants* God made with *Israel,* lacked *hope* of salvation and knowledge of the true *God* (11–12); but through Christ all these religious barriers between Jew and Gentile have been transcended (13–14) by the abolition of the Mosaic covenant-law (15) for the sake of uniting Jew and Gentile into a single religious community (15–16), imbued with the same holy *Spirit* and worshiping

the same *Father* (18). The Gentiles are now included in God's *household* (19) as it arises upon the *foundation* of *apostles* assisted by those endowed with the prophetic gift (3, 5), the preachers of Christ (20; cf 1 Cor 12, 28). With Christ as the *capstone* (20; cf Is 28, 16; Mt 21, 42), they are being built into the holy *temple* of God's people where the divine presence dwells (21–22).

2, 12: *The community of Israel:* or "commonwealth"; cf 4, 18. *The covenants:* cf Rom 9, 4: with Abraham, with Moses, with David.

2, 14–16: The elaborate imagery here combines pictures of Christ as *our peace* (Is 9, 5), his crucifixion, the ending of the Mosaic law (cf Col 2, 14), reconciliation (2 Cor 5, 18–21), and the destruction of *the dividing wall* such as kept people from God in the temple or a barrier in the heavens.

2, 15: *One new person:* a corporate body, the Christian community, made up of Jews and Gentiles, replacing ancient divisions; cf Rom 1; 16.

2, 3: Col 3, 6–7.	2, 12: Rom 9, 4; Col 1,
2, 5: Rom 5, 8; 6, 13; Col 2,	21.27.
13.	2, 13: Eph 2, 17; Is 57, 19;
2, 6: Rom 8, 10–11; Phil 3,	Col 1, 20.
20; Col 2, 12.	2, 14: Gal 3, 28.
2, 7: Eph 1, 7.	2, 15: 2 Cor 5, 17; Col 2, 14.
2, 8: Rom 3, 24; Gal 2, 16.	2, 16: Col 1, 20.22.
2, 9: 1 Cor 1, 29.	2, 17: Is 57, 19; Zec 9, 10.
2, 10: Eph 4, 24; Ti 2, 14.	2, 18: Eph 3, 12.

ROOTED IN LOVE

Read the prayer in Eph 3, 14–21. Then reflect on the prayer below from the Philippines, which also talks about roots and love.

> Lord,
> make us realise that our Christianity is like a rice field:
> when it is newly planted the paddies are prominent,
> but as the plants take root and grow taller,
> these divided paddies gradually vanish,
> and soon there appears only one vast continuous field.
> So give us roots that love,
> and help us grow in Christian fellowship and service,
> that thy will be done in our lives,
> through our Savior, Jesus Christ.

(From *Your Will Be Done*)

Finally, personalize the prayer in 3, 14–21 by changing *you* to *I* or *we*, and *your* to *my* or *our*. Kneel and pray this prayer, knowing that God is indeed listening to you at this very moment.

▸ **Eph 3, 14–21**

---

¹⁹* So then you are no longer strangers and sojourners, but you are fellow citizens with the holy ones and members of the household of God, ²⁰*† built upon the foundation of the apostles and prophets, with Christ Jesus himself as the capstone. ²¹* Through him the whole structure is held together and grows into a temple sacred in the Lord; ²²* in him you also are being built together into a dwelling place of God in the Spirit.

III: World Mission of the Church

Commission to Preach God's Plan†

3 ¹*† Because of this, I, Paul, a prisoner of Christ [Jesus] for you Gentiles— ²*† if, as I suppose, you have heard of the stewardship of God's grace that was given to me for your benefit, ³*† [namely, that] the mystery was made known to me by revelation, as I have written briefly earlier. ⁴ When you read this you can understand my insight into the mystery of Christ, ⁵* which was not made known to human beings in other generations as it has now been revealed to his holy apostles and prophets by the Spirit, ⁶* that the Gentiles are coheirs, members of the same body, and copartners in the promise in Christ Jesus through the gospel.

⁷* Of this I became a minister by the gift of God's grace that was granted me in accord with the exercise of his power. ⁸* To me, the very least of all the holy ones, this grace was given, to preach to the

---

2, 20: *Capstone:* the Greek can also mean cornerstone or keystone.

3, 1–13: Paul reflects on his mission to the Gentiles. He alludes to his call and appointment to the apostolic office (2–3) and how his *insight* through revelation, as well as that of the other apostles and charismatic prophets in the church (4–5), has deepened understanding of God's plan of salvation in Christ. Paul is the special herald (7) of a new *promise* to the *Gentiles* (6): that the divine plan includes them in the spiritual benefits promised to Israel. Not only is this unique apostolic role his; Paul also has been given the task of explaining to all the divine *plan* of salvation (8–9), once *hidden.* Through the *church,* God's plan to save through Christ is becoming manifest to angelic beings (10; cf 1, 21), in accord with God's *purpose* (11). The fulfillment of the plan in Christ gives the whole church more *confidence* through *faith* in God (12). The readers of this letter are also thereby encouraged to greater confidence despite Paul's imprisonment (13).

3, 1: *A prisoner of Christ:* see Introduction. Paul abruptly departs from his train of thought at the end of v 1, leaving an incomplete sentence.

3, 2: *Stewardship:* the Greek is the same term employed at 1, 10 for the *plan* that God administers (Col 1, 25) and in which Paul plays a key role.

3, 3–4: *The mystery:* God's resolve to deliver Gentiles along with Israel through Christ; cf the notes on 1, 10; 3, 9.

2, 19: Heb 12, 22–23.
2, 20: Is 28, 16; Rv 21, 14.
2, 21: 1 Cor 3, 16; Col 2, 19.
2, 22: 1 Pt 2, 5.
3, 1: Phil 1, 7.13; Col 1, 24–29; 4, 18; Phlm 9; 2 Tm 2, 9.
3, 2: Col 1, 25.
3, 3: Eph 1, 9–10; Col 1, 26.
3, 5: Col 1, 26.
3, 6: Eph 2, 13.18–19.
3, 7: Rom 15, 15; Col 1, 25.29.
3, 8: 1 Cor 15, 8–10; Gal 1, 16; 2, 7–9.

Gentiles the inscrutable riches of Christ, [9]*† and to bring to light [for all] what is the plan of the mystery hidden from ages past in God who created all things, [10]*† so that the manifold wisdom of God might now be made known through the church to the principalities and authorities in the heavens. [11] This was according to the eternal purpose that he accomplished in Christ Jesus our Lord, [12]* in whom we have boldness of speech and confidence of access through faith in him. [13]* So I ask you not to lose heart over my afflictions for you; this is your glory.

Prayer for the Readers†

[14]† For this reason I kneel before the Father, [15] from whom every family in heaven and on earth is named, [16]* that he may grant you in accord with the riches of his glory to be strengthened with power through his Spirit in the inner self, [17]* and that Christ may dwell in your hearts through faith; that you, rooted and grounded in love, [18]* may have strength to comprehend with all the holy ones what is the breadth and length and height and depth, [19]* and to know the love of Christ that surpasses knowledge, so that you may be filled with all the fullness of God.

[20]* Now to him who is able to accomplish far more than all we ask or imagine, by the power at work within us, [21] to him be glory in the church and in Christ Jesus to all generations, forever and ever. Amen.

Unity in the Body

4 [1]*† I, then, a prisoner for the Lord, urge you to live in a manner worthy of the call you have received, [2]* with all humility and gentleness, with patience, bearing with one another through love, [3]* striving to preserve the unity of the spirit through

the bond of peace: [4]*† one body and one Spirit, as you were also called to the one hope of your call; [5]* one Lord, one faith, one baptism; [6]* one God and Father of all, who is over all and through all and in all.

Diversity of Gifts

[7]* But grace was given to each of us according to the measure of Christ's gift. [8]*† Therefore, it says:

One body and one Spirit, as you were also called to the one hope of your call; one Lord, one faith, one baptism; one God and Father of all, who is over all and through all and in all

4, 4–6

---

† **3, 9:** *[For all]:* while some think this phrase was added so as to yield the sense "to enlighten all about the plan . . . ," it is more likely that some manuscripts and Fathers omitted it accidentally or to avoid the idea that *all* conflicted with Paul's assignment to preach to *the Gentiles* (8) specifically.

3, 10: *Principalities and authorities:* see the note on 1, 15–23 regarding v 21.

3, 14–21: The apostle prays that those he is addressing may, like the rest of the church, deepen their understanding of God's plan of salvation in Christ. It is a plan that affects the whole universe (15) with *the breadth and length and height and depth* of God's love in Christ (18) or possibly the universe in all its dimensions. The apostle prays that they may perceive the redemptive love of Christ for them and be completely immersed in the fullness of God (19). The prayer concludes with a doxology to God (20–21).

3, 14–15: *Every family:* in the Greek there is wordplay on the word for *the Father* (*patria, patēr*). The phrase could also mean "God's whole family" (cf 2, 21).

4, 1–16: A general plea for unity in the church. Christians have been fashioned through the *Spirit* into a single harmonious religious community (*one body,* 4.12; cf 16), belonging to a single *Lord* (in contrast to the many gods of the pagan world), and by one way of salvation through *faith,* brought out especially by the significance of *baptism* (1–6; cf Rom 6, 1–11). But Christian unity is more than adherence to a common belief. It is manifested in the exalted Christ's gifts to individuals to serve so as to make the community more Christlike

(11–16). This teaching on Christ as the source of the gifts is introduced in v 8 by a citation of Ps 68, 18, which depicts Yahweh triumphantly leading Israel to salvation in Jerusalem. It is here understood of Christ, ascending *above all the heavens,* the *head* of the church; through his redemptive death, resurrection, and ascension he has become the source of the church's spiritual gifts. The "descent" of Christ (9–10) refers more probably to the incarnation (cf Phil 2, 6–8) than to Christ's presence after his death in the world of the dead (cf 1 Pt 3, 19).

4, 4–6: The "seven unities" (church, *Spirit, hope; Lord, faith* in Christ [Eph 1, 13], *baptism; one God*) reflect the triune structure of later creeds in reverse.

4, 8–10: While the emphasis is on an ascension and gift-giving by Christ, there is also a reference in taking *prisoners captive* to the aeons and powers mentioned at 1, 21; 2, 2; 3, 10; and 6, 12.

3, 9: Rom 16, 25; Col 1, 26–27.	**3, 20:** Rom 16, 25–27; Col 1, 29.
3, 10: 1 Pt 1, 12.	**4, 1:** Eph 3, 1; Col 1, 10.
3, 12: Rom 5, 1–2; Heb 4, 16.	**4, 2:** Col 3, 12–13.
3, 13: Col 1, 22.24; 2 Tm 2, 10.	**4, 3:** Col 3, 14–15.
3, 16: Eph 6, 10; Rom 7, 22; 2 Cor 4, 16; Col 1, 11.	**4, 4:** Rom 12, 5; 1 Cor 10, 17; 12, 12–13.
3, 17: Jn 14, 23; Col 1, 23; 2, 7.	**4, 5:** 1 Cor 8, 6.
3, 18: Col 2, 2.	**4, 6:** 1 Cor 12, 6.
3, 19: Col 2, 3.9.	**4, 7:** Rom 12, 3.6; 1 Cor 12, 28.
	4, 8: Ps 68, 19; Col 2, 15.

EPH

WEAVE FOR US A GARMENT

The prayer in Eph 4, 1–6 is a prayer of unity, a prayer for us to live as one—one faith, one baptism, one God, one body, one Spirit, one hope. This Native American prayer is also a prayer of unity, a prayer for us to live in a world where all people, all creation, are woven into one garment. May we walk in such a world. May we be part of creating such a world.

> *Weave for us a garment of brightness;*
> *May the warp be the white light of morning,*
> *May the weft be the red light of evening,*
> *May the fringes be the falling rain,*
> *May the border be the standing rainbow.*
> *Thus weave for us a garment of brightness,*
> *That we may walk fittingly where birds sing,*
> *That we may walk fittingly where grass is green,*
> *O our Mother the Earth, O our Father the Sky.*

(From Suzanne Slesin and Emily Gwathmey, compilers, Amen, n.p.)

▸ Eph 4, 1–6

"He ascended on high and took
    prisoners captive;
    he gave gifts to men."

[9] What does "he ascended" mean except that he also descended into the lower [regions] of the earth? [10] The one who descended is also the one who ascended far above all the heavens, that he might fill all things.

[11]*† And he gave some as apostles, others as prophets, others as evangelists, others as pastors and teachers, [12]† to equip the holy ones for the work of ministry, for building up the body of Christ, [13]*† until we all attain to the unity of faith and knowledge of the Son of God, to mature manhood, to the extent

of the full stature of Christ, [14]* so that we may no longer be infants, tossed by waves and swept along by every wind of teaching arising from human trickery, from their cunning in the interests of deceitful scheming. [15]*† Rather, living the truth in love, we should grow in every way into him who is the head, Christ, [16]* from whom the whole body, joined and held together by every supporting ligament, with the proper functioning of each part, brings about the body's growth and builds itself up in love.

Renewal in Christ

[17]*† So I declare and testify in the Lord that you must no longer live as the Gentiles do, in the futility of their minds; [18]* darkened in understanding,

---

4, 11: Concerning this list of ministers, cf 1 Cor 12, 28 and Rom 12, 6–8. *Evangelists:* missionary preachers (cf Acts 21, 8 and 2 Tm 4, 5), not those who wrote gospels. *Pastors and teachers:* a single group in the Greek, shepherding congregations.

4, 12: The ministerial leaders in v 11 are to equip the whole people of God for their *work of ministry.*

4, 13: *Mature manhood:* literally, "a perfect man" (cf Col 1, 28), possibly the "one new person" of 2, 15, though there *anthrōpos* suggests humanity, while here *anēr* is the term for male. This personage becomes visible in the church's growing to its fullness in the unity of those who believe in Christ.

4, 15–16: *The head, Christ:* cf Col 1, 18 and contrast 1 Cor 12, 12–27 and Rom 12, 4–5 where Christ is identified with the whole body, including the head. The imagery may derive from ancient views in medicine, the *head* coordinating and caring for the

body, each *ligament* (perhaps the ministers of v 11) supporting the whole. But as at 2, 19–22, where the temple is depicted as a growing organism, there may also be the idea here of growing toward the capstone, Christ.

4, 17–24: Paul begins to indicate how the new life in Christ contrasts with the Gentiles' old way of existence. Literally, *the old self* (22) and *the new self* (24) are "the old man" and "the new man" (*anthrōpos*, person), as at 2, 15; cf the note on 4, 13.

4, 11: 1 Cor 12, 28.
4, 13: Col 1, 28.
4, 14: 1 Cor 14, 20; Col 2, 4.8; Heb 13, 9; Jas 1, 6.
4, 15: 1 Cor 11, 3; Col 1, 18; 2, 19.
4, 16: Col 2, 19.
4, 17: Rom 1, 21.
4, 18: Col 1, 21; 1 Pt 1, 14.

alienated from the life of God because of their ignorance, because of their hardness of heart, ¹⁹* they
have become callous and have handed themselves
over to licentiousness for the practice of every kind
of impurity to excess. ²⁰ That is not how you
learned Christ, ²¹ assuming that you have heard of
him and were taught in him, as truth is in Jesus,
²²* that you should put away the old self of your
former way of life, corrupted through deceitful
desires, ²³* and be renewed in the spirit of your

minds, ²⁴*† and put on the new self, created in
God's way in righteousness and holiness of truth.

IV: Daily Conduct, an Expression of Unity

Rules for the New Life

²⁵*† Therefore, putting away falsehood, speak
the truth, each one to his neighbor, for we are members one of another. ²⁶*† Be angry but do not sin;

PROPHETS OF HOPE, YOUTH ON A MISSION!

Ephesians 4, 17–32 has some teachings that were probably used in the preparation for Baptism.
Some Hispanic young people have been baptized as Catholics but have not had an opportunity to
live their faith in a vital church community. Those who are trying to follow Jesus want to be
prophets of hope, as expressed in this song:

> We're Prophets of Hope, youth on a mission,
> spreading the Gospel of Christ.
> We're Prophets of Hope, issuing the challenge:
> to build the Reign of God.

> Pilgrims on a journey, marching towards our goal.
> Led by the Spirit, strengthened by the Lord.
> We bear each other's burdens and give each other hope.
> Following our savior we press on towards our goal.

> We come from towns and cities.
> We are immigrants and natives,
> laborers and students who want a better life.
> We want to be successful, but not at any cost.
> Unless we work for justice humanity is lost.

> We face discrimination, poverty and drugs.
> The values of our culture are all under attack.
> But we have faith in Jesus; he will give us strength.
> Together we will struggle to build a better world.

> The Gospel is our road map, the Church is our guide.
> We're Catholic Latinos, youth who take a stand.
> Leaders in our churches, reflecting as we go.
> Learning from our set-backs, we never give up hope.

(Jose Antonio Rubio)

▶ Eph 4, 17–32

---

†

4, 24: *Put on:* in baptism. See the note on Gal 3, 27.

4, 25—6, 20: For similar exhortations to a morally good life in response to God's gift of faith, see the notes on Rom 12, 1—13, 14 and
Gal 5, 13–26.

4, 26: If angry, seek reconciliation that day, not giving the devil
(6, 11) opportunity to lead into sin.

*

4, 19: Col 3, 5.
4, 22: Rom 8, 13; Gal 6, 8;
   Col 3, 9.
4, 23: Rom 12, 2.

4, 24: Gn 1, 26–27; Col 3,
   10.
4, 25: Zec 8, 16.
4, 26: Ps 4, 5 LXX; Mt 5, 22.

EPH

do not let the sun set on your anger, 27* and do not leave room for the devil. 28*† The thief must no longer steal, but rather labor, doing honest work with his [own] hands, so that he may have something to share with one in need. 29* No foul language should come out of your mouths, but only such as is good for needed edification, that it may impart grace to those who hear. 30† And do not grieve the holy Spirit of God, with which you were sealed for the day of redemption. 31* All bitterness, fury, anger, shouting, and reviling must be removed from you, along with all malice. 32* [And] be kind to one another, compassionate, forgiving one another as God has forgiven you in Christ.

5 1*† So be imitators of God, as beloved children, 2* and live in love, as Christ loved us and handed himself over for us as a sacrificial offering to God for a fragrant aroma. 3* Immorality or any impurity or greed must not even be mentioned among you, as is fitting among holy ones, 4* no obscenity or silly or suggestive talk, which is out of place, but instead, thanksgiving. 5* Be sure of this, that no immoral or impure or greedy person, that is, an idolater, has any inheritance in the kingdom of Christ and of God.

Duty to Live in the Light

6*† Let no one deceive you with empty arguments, for because of these things the wrath of God is coming upon the disobedient. 7 So do not be associated with them. 8* For you were once darkness, but now you are light in the Lord. Live as children of light, 9* for light produces every kind of goodness and righteousness and truth. 10* Try to learn what is pleasing to the Lord. 11* Take no part in the fruitless works of darkness; rather expose them, 12 for it is shameful even to mention the things done by them in secret; 13* but everything exposed by the light becomes visible, 14*† for everything that becomes visible is light. Therefore, it says:

"Awake, O sleeper,
    and arise from the dead,
    and Christ will give you light."

15*† Watch carefully then how you live, not as foolish persons but as wise, 16 making the most of the opportunity, because the days are evil. 17 Therefore, do not continue in ignorance, but try to understand what is the will of the Lord. 18* And do not get drunk on wine, in which lies debauchery, but be

Alcohol

LIVE IT!

The author of Eph 5, 10–20 does not mince words. This passage encourages the early Christians, and us, to wake up and find out what pleases God. It calls them to avoid participating in actions they would be ashamed of if the actions were exposed in the light. Its tone is not of scolding but rather of passionate encouragement, wanting the best for each of us.

Although the use of alcohol is singled out in this passage, drinking is not the only substance abuse issue young people face during adolescence. Many young people have to choose whether to participate in drinking, smoking, and using drugs. Abuse of these substances prevents us from being filled with the Spirit. As the author of Ephesians advises, making wise choices about these substances is important.

Take some time to reflect on your own life. What temptations do you face in this regard? What choices can you make that would please God and allow you to enjoy the fullness of life in the Spirit? Who can help you make the correct decisions and help you stick to them?

▶ Eph 5, 10–20

---

†

4, 28: *Honest work:* literally, "the good." *His [own] hands:* some manuscripts have the full phrase as in 1 Cor 4, 12.

4, 30: See the note on 1, 13.

5, 1: *Imitators of God:* in forgiving (4, 32) and in loving (as exhibited in how *Christ loved us*).

5, 6: See the note on 2, 2.

5, 14: An early Christian hymn, possibly from a baptismal liturgy. For the content compare 2, 5–6; 3, 9 and Is 60, 1.

5, 15–16.19–20: The wording is similar to Col 4, 5 and 3, 16–17.

*

4, 27: 2 Cor 2, 11.
4, 28: 1 Thes 4, 11.
4, 29: Eph 5, 4; Col 3, 16; 4, 6.
4, 31: Col 3, 8.
4, 32: Mt 6, 14; Col 3, 12–13.
5, 1: Mt 5, 45.48.
5, 2: Ex 29, 18; Ps 40, 7; Gal 2, 20; 1 Jn 3, 16.
5, 3: Gal 5, 19; Col 3, 5.
5, 4: Eph 4, 29; Col 3, 8.
5, 5: 1 Cor 6, 9–10; Gal 5,

21; Col 3, 5.
5, 6: Rom 1, 18; Col 2, 4.8.
5, 8: Eph 2, 11–13; Jn 12, 36; Col 1, 12–13.
5, 9: Gal 5, 22.
5, 10: Rom 12, 2.
5, 11: Rom 13, 12.
5, 13: Jn 3, 20–21.
5, 14: Is 26, 19; 60, 1.
5, 15–16: Col 4, 5.
5, 18: Prv 23, 31 LXX; Lk 21, 34.

Family Relationships

When Eph 5, 21—6, 4 comes up in the Sunday readings, it sometimes causes confusion. People ask, "How can the Bible teach that a wife should be subject to her husband?" This is another case where we must take into account the cultural context in order to properly interpret the passage. At the time the Letter to the Ephesians was written, the male gender was dominant in society. Wives and children were considered men's property. The letter's challenge to a man to love his wife and to treat his children respectfully was probably viewed as a radical statement by people at the time.

Our culture is different. Just as we should not interpret 6, 5–9 as giving permission to own slaves, we should not interpret 5, 21—6, 4 as commanding submissive behavior of married women today. Understanding this, we can appreciate the passage as it was intended: a practical guide for a family life where love is the rule (see "The Christian Family," Col 3, 18—4, 1).

Read Eph 5, 21—6, 4 and then reflect on these questions:
- How does 6, 1–4 indicate that honoring is a two-way street?
- What does it mean to live in a family where love is the rule?
- How do you love and honor your parents and siblings?

▶ Eph 5, 21—6, 4

---

filled with the Spirit, [19]* addressing one another [in] psalms and hymns and spiritual songs, singing and playing to the Lord in your hearts, [20]* giving thanks always and for everything in the name of our Lord Jesus Christ to God the Father.

Wives and Husbands

[21]*† Be subordinate to one another out of reverence for Christ.† [22]* Wives should be subordinate to their husbands as to the Lord. [23]* For the husband is head of his wife just as Christ is head of the church, he himself the savior of the body. [24] As the church is subordinate to Christ, so wives should be subordinate to their husbands in everything. [25]* Husbands, love your wives, even as Christ loved the church and handed himself over for her [26]* to sanctify her, cleansing her by the bath of water with the word, [27]* that he might present to himself the church in splendor, without spot or wrinkle or any such thing, that she might be holy and without blemish. [28] So [also] husbands should love their wives as their own bodies. He who loves his wife loves himself. [29] For no one hates his own flesh but rather nourishes and cherishes it, even as Christ does the church, [30]* because we are members of his body.

[31]* "For this reason a man shall leave [his] father
            and [his] mother
        and be joined to his wife,
    and the two shall become one flesh."

[32]* This is a great mystery, but I speak in reference to Christ and the church. [33] In any case, each one of you should love his wife as himself, and the wife should respect her husband.

Children and Parents

[1]* Children, obey your parents [in the Lord], for this is right. [2]* "Honor your father and mother." This is the first commandment with a promise, [3] "that it may go well with you and that you may have a long life on earth." [4]* Fathers, do not provoke your children to anger, but bring them up with the training and instruction of the Lord.

---

† 5, 21—6, 9: Cf the notes on Col 3, 18—4, 1 and 1 Pt 2, 18—3, 7 for a similar listing of household duties where the inferior is admonished first (wives, 5, 22; children, 6, 1; slaves, 6, 5), then the superior (husbands, 5, 25; fathers, 6, 4; masters, 6, 9). Paul varies this pattern by an emphasis on mutuality (see 5, 20); use of Old Testament material about father and mother in 6, 2; the judgment to come for slave-owners (you have a Master in heaven, 6, 9); and above all the initial principle of subordination to one another under Christ, thus effectively undermining exclusive claims to domination by one party. Into the section on wives and husbands an elaborate teaching on Christ and the church has been woven (5, 22–33).

5, 21–33: The apostle exhorts married Christians to a strong mutual love. Holding with Gn 2, 24 that marriage is a divine institution (31), Paul sees Christian marriage as taking on a new meaning symbolic of the intimate relationship of love between Christ and the church. The wife should serve her husband in the same spirit as that of the church's service to Christ (22.24), and the husband should care for his wife with the devotion of Christ to the church (25–30). Paul gives to the Genesis passage its highest meaning in the light of the union of Christ and the church, of which Christlike loyalty and devotion in Christian marriage are a clear reflection (31–33).

5, 19: Ps 33, 2–3; Col 3, 16.
5, 20: Col 3, 17.
5, 21: 1 Pt 5, 5.
5, 22: Col 3, 18—4, 1; 1 Pt 3, 1–7.
5, 23: 1 Cor 11, 3; Col 1, 18.
5, 25: Col 3, 19; 1 Tm 2, 6.
5, 26: Rom 6, 4; Ti 3, 5–7.
5, 27: 2 Cor 11, 2; Col 1, 22.
5, 30: Rom 12, 5; 1 Cor 6, 15.
5, 31: Gn 2, 24; Mt 19, 5; Mk 10, 7–8.
5, 32: Rv 19, 7.
6, 1: Prv 6, 20; Sir 3, 1–6; Col 3, 20.
6, 2–3: Ex 20, 12; Dt 5, 16.
6, 4: Col 3, 21–22.

E P H

Slaves and Masters

5* Slaves, be obedient to your human masters with fear and trembling, in sincerity of heart, as to Christ, 6* not only when being watched, as currying favor, but as slaves of Christ, doing the will of God from the heart, 7 willingly serving the Lord and not human beings, 8 knowing that each will be requited from the Lord for whatever good he does, whether he is slave or free. 9* Masters, act in the same way toward them, and stop bullying, knowing that both they and you have a Master in heaven and that with him there is no partiality.

Battle against Evil

10† Finally, draw your strength from the Lord and from his mighty power. 11* Put on the armor of God so that you may be able to stand firm against the tactics of the devil. 12* For our struggle is not with flesh and blood but with the principalities, with the powers, with the world rulers of this present darkness, with the evil spirits in the heavens. 13* Therefore, put on the armor of God, that you may be able to resist on the evil day and, having done everything, to hold your ground. 14* So stand fast with your loins girded in truth, clothed with righteousness as a breastplate, 15* and your feet shod in readiness for the gospel of peace. 16* In all circumstances, hold faith as a shield, to quench all [the] flaming arrows of the evil one. 17* And take the helmet of salvation and the sword of the Spirit, which is the word of God.

Constant Prayer

18* With all prayer and supplication, pray at every opportunity in the Spirit. To that end, be watchful with all perseverance and supplication for all the holy ones 19* and also for me, that speech may be given me to open my mouth, to make known with boldness the mystery of the gospel 20* for which I am an ambassador in chains, so that I may have the courage to speak as I must.

V: Conclusion

A Final Message

21*† So that you also may have news of me and of what I am doing, Tychicus, my beloved brother

The Peace Prayer of Saint Francis of Assisi

Ephesians 6, 10–17 is a poetic passage encouraging us to resist evil. The Peace Prayer of Saint Francis of Assisi tells us how to do this—without using the imagery of warfare. After you read each line of this powerful prayer, close your eyes to meditate on its meaning for your life. What is one way you can live out each line of this prayer?

Lord, make me an instrument of your peace;
where there is hatred, let me sow love;
where there is injury, pardon;
where there is doubt, faith;
where there is despair, hope;
where there is darkness, light;
and where there is sadness, joy.
Grant that I may not so much seek
to be consoled as to console;
to be understood as to understand,
to be loved as to love;
for it is in giving that we receive,
it is in pardoning that we are pardoned,
and it is in dying that we are born to eternal life.

▶ **Eph 6, 10–17**

and trustworthy minister in the Lord, will tell you everything. 22* I am sending him to you for this very purpose, so that you may know about us and that he may encourage your hearts.

23 Peace be to the brothers, and love with faith, from God the Father and the Lord Jesus Christ. 24* Grace be with all who love our Lord Jesus Christ in immortality.

6, 10–20: A general exhortation to courage and prayer. Drawing upon the imagery and ideas of Is 11, 5; 59, 16–17; and Wis 5, 17–23, Paul describes the Christian in terms of the dress and equipment of Roman soldiers. He observes, however, that the Christian's readiness for combat is not directed against human beings but against the spiritual powers of evil (10–17; cf 1, 21; 2, 2; 3, 10). Unique importance is placed upon prayer (18–20).

6, 21–24: Tychicus: the bearer of the letter; see the note on Col 4, 7. Verses 21–22 parallel Col 4, 7–8, often word for word. If Ephesians is addressed to several Christian communities (see Introduction), it is understandable that no greetings to individual members of these communities should have been included in it.

6, 5: Col 3, 22–25; 1 Tm 6, 1–2; Ti 2, 9–10.
6, 6: 1 Pt 2, 18.
6, 9: Col 4, 1.
6, 11: Rom 13, 12; 2 Cor 6, 7; 10, 4; Jas 4, 7.
6, 12: Eph 1, 21; 2, 2; Col 1, 13.
6, 13: Rom 13, 12.
6, 14: Wis 5, 17–20; Is 11, 5; Lk 12, 35; 1 Thes 5, 8.
6, 15: Is 52, 7.
6, 16: 1 Pt 5, 9.
6, 17: Is 59, 17; 1 Thes 5, 8.
6, 18: Mt 26, 41; Col 4, 2–3.
6, 19: Acts 4, 29; Col 4, 3; 2 Thes 3, 1.
6, 20: 2 Cor 5, 20; Col 4, 4.
6, 21: Acts 20, 4; Col 4, 7; 2 Tm 4, 12.
6, 22: Col 4, 8.
6, 24: 1 Pt 1, 8.

"To be, or not to be: that is the question." In this line from Shakespeare's play *Hamlet,* Hamlet wonders which is better for him—to live or to die. He doesn't want to live and suffer, but he's afraid the "sleep of death" may be worse. Either way, he loses. In the Letter to the Philippians, Paul struggles with a similar question.

In-depth

When Paul wrote this letter, he was imprisoned facing a charge that might end in his death. He wrote it either near the end of his life when he was under house arrest in Rome or, more likely, during an earlier imprisonment in Ephesus (see 1 Cor 15, 32; 2 Cor 1, 8).

Like Hamlet, Paul is torn: "I am caught between" life and death (Phil 1, 23). But unlike Hamlet, Paul feels he'll win either way: "For to me living is Christ, and death is gain" (verse 21). In addition, Paul believes that this imprisonment will not end with his death, because he is still needed to support the new churches he helped start.

Incredibly, even in prison, Paul exhibits a spirit of hope and encouragement. In this short letter, he uses the words *rejoice* and *joy* fifteen times! Living in Christ doesn't mean everything will always go wonderfully. But it does mean that God can get you through the good times and the difficult times with joy.

In this letter, Paul asks the Philippians—and us—to imitate Christ. Imitating Christ is the way to keep a positive attitude even when things aren't going our way. Paul quotes an early Christian song (2, 6–11) to the Philippians to show what imitating Christ means. The song praises our Lord Jesus, who chose to humble himself, chose to become a servant, and was "obedient to death" (verse 8).

It is clear from this letter that Paul had a close relationship with the Philippians. No doubt, they were upset for him. Paul wanted them to rejoice and stop worrying (4, 4–6). He encouraged them to present their concerns—all of them—to God in prayer. And he pointed out that if they did so, "the peace of God that surpasses all understanding will guard your hearts and minds in Christ Jesus" (verse 7). What marvelous advice and comfort for people of all times and ages.

At a Glance

I. Address (1, 1–11).

II. Progress of the Gospel (1, 12–26).

III. Instructions for the Community (1, 27—2, 18).

IV. Travel Plans of Paul and His Assistants (2, 19—3, 1).

V. Polemic: Righteousness and the Goal in Christ (3, 2–21).

VI. Instructions for the Community (4, 1–9).

VII. Gratitude for the Philippians' Generosity (4, 10–20).

VIII. Farewell (4, 21–23).

Quick Facts

Author
Paul

Date Written
A.D. 55 if from Ephesus,
A.D. 59–63 if from Rome

Audience
the church in Philippi

The Letter to the Philippians

Philippians

I: Address

Greeting†

1 ¹* Paul and Timothy, slaves† of Christ Jesus, to all the holy ones in Christ Jesus who are in Philippi, with the overseers and ministers: ²*† grace to you and peace from God our Father and the Lord Jesus Christ.

Thanksgiving

³*† I give thanks to my God at every remembrance of you, ⁴ praying always with joy in my every prayer for all of you, ⁵ because of your partnership for the gospel from the first day until now. ⁶*† I am confident of this, that the one who began a good work in you will continue to complete it until the day of Christ Jesus. ⁷ It is right that I should think this way about all of you, because I hold you in my heart, you who are all partners with me in grace, both in my imprisonment and in the defense and confirmation of the gospel. ⁸* For God is my witness, how I long for all of you with the affection of Christ Jesus. ⁹* And this is my prayer: that your love may increase ever more and more in knowledge

---

1, 1–2: See the note on Rom 1, 1–7, concerning the greeting.

1, 1: *Slaves:* Paul usually refers to himself at the start of a letter as an apostle. Here he substitutes a term suggesting the unconditional obligation of himself and Timothy to the service of Christ, probably because, in view of the good relationship with the Philippians, he wishes to stress his status as a co-servant rather than emphasize his apostolic authority. Reference to Timothy is a courtesy: Paul alone writes the letter, as the singular verb throughout shows (3–26), and the reference (2, 19–24) to Timothy in the third person. *Overseers:* the Greek term *episkopos* literally means "one who oversees" or "one who supervises," but since the second century it has come to designate the "bishop," the official who heads a local church. In New Testament times this office had not yet developed into the form that it later assumed, though it seems to be well on the way to such development in the Pastorals; see 1 Tm 3, 2 and Ti 1, 7, where it is translated *bishop.* At Philippi, however (and at Ephesus, according to Acts 20, 28), there was more than one *episkopos,* and the precise function of these officials is uncertain. In order to distinguish this office from the later stages into which it developed, the term is here translated as *overseers. Ministers:* the Greek term *diakonoi* is used frequently in the New Testament to designate "servants," "attendants," or "ministers." Paul refers to himself and to other apostles as "ministers of God" (2 Cor 6, 4) or "ministers of Christ" (2 Cor 11, 23), In the Pastorals (1 Tm 3, 8.12) the *diakonos* has become an established official in the local church; hence the term is there translated

as *deacon.* The *diakonoi* at Philippi seem to represent an earlier stage of development of the office; we are uncertain about their precise functions. Hence the term is here translated as *ministers.* See Rom 16, 1, where Phoebe is described as a *diakonos (minister)* of the church of Cenchreae.

1, 2: The gifts come *from* Christ the Lord, not simply through him from the Father; compare the christology in 2, 6–11.

1, 3–11: As in Rom 1, 8–15 and all the Pauline letters except Galatians, a thanksgiving follows, including a direct prayer for the Philippians (9–11); see the note on Rom 1, 8. On their *partnership for the gospel* (5), cf 29–30; 4, 10–20. Their devotion to the faith and to Paul made them his pride and joy (4, 1). The characteristics thus manifested are evidence of the community's continuing preparation for the Lord's parousia (6.10). Paul's especially warm relationship with the Philippians is suggested here (7.8) as elsewhere in the letter. The eschatology serves to underscore a concern for ethical growth (9–11), which appears throughout the letter.

1, 6: *The day of Christ Jesus:* the parousia or triumphant return of

1, 1: Rom 1, 1; 2 Cor 1, 1;
1 Thes 1, 1; Phlm 1 /
1 Tm 3, 1–13.
1, 2: Rom 1, 7; Gal 1, 3;
Phlm 3.
1, 3: Rom 1, 8; 1 Cor 1, 4;
1 Thes 1, 2.

1, 6: Phil 2, 13 / Phil 1, 10;
2, 16; 1 Cor 1, 8.
1, 8: Rom 1, 9; 2 Cor 1, 23;
1 Thes 2, 5.
1, 9: Eph 3, 14–19; Col 1,
9–10; Phlm 6.

FRIENDSHIP

In Phil 1, 3–11, Paul writes beautifully of his love for and friendship with the people living in Philippi. We need to remember that Paul— and the other people who wrote the inspired words of the Scriptures—was a real person with problems and needs. He had some dear friends in Philippi, and his words to them provide a great model of true friendship: sharing the ups and downs, being committed to one another, being thankful for one another, and wanting the best for one another. Friendship in Christ is like that!

Who are true friends for you? How can you keep Christ at the center of your friendships?

▶ Phil 1, 3–11

and every kind of perception, [10]* to discern what is of value, so that you may be pure and blameless for the day of Christ, [11]* filled with the fruit of righteousness that comes through Jesus Christ for the glory and praise of God.

II: Progress of the Gospel

[12]*† I want you to know, brothers, that my situation has turned out rather to advance the gospel, [13]*† so that my imprisonment has become well known in Christ throughout the whole praetorium and to all the rest, [14]† and so that the majority of the brothers, having taken encouragement in the Lord from my imprisonment, dare more than ever to proclaim the word fearlessly.

[15] Of course, some preach Christ from envy and rivalry, others from good will. [16] The latter act out

of love, aware that I am here for the defense of the gospel; [17] the former proclaim Christ out of selfish ambition, not from pure motives, thinking that they will cause me trouble in my imprisonment. [18]*† What difference does it make, as long as in every way, whether in pretense or in truth, Christ is being proclaimed? And in that I rejoice.

Indeed I shall continue to rejoice, [19]*† for I know that this will result in deliverance for me† through your prayers and support from the Spirit of Jesus Christ. [20]* My eager expectation and hope is that I shall not be put to shame in any way, but that with all boldness, now as always, Christ will be magnified in my body, whether by life or by death. [21]* For to me life is Christ, and death is gain. [22]* If I go on living in the flesh, that means fruitful labor for me. And I do not know which I shall choose. [23]* I am caught between the two. I long to depart this life and be with Christ, [for] that is far better. [24] Yet that I remain [in] the flesh is more necessary for your benefit. [25] And this I know with confidence, that I shall remain and continue in the service of all of you for your progress and joy in the faith, [26] so that your boasting in Christ Jesus may abound on account of me when I come to you again.

III: Instructions for the Community

Steadfastness in Faith

[27]*† Only, conduct yourselves in a way worthy of the gospel of Christ, so that, whether I come and see you or am absent, I may hear news of you, that you are standing firm in one spirit, with one mind struggling together for the faith of the gospel, [28] not intimidated in any way by your opponents. This is proof to them of destruction, but of your salvation. And this is God's doing. [29]* For to you has been granted, for the sake of Christ, not only to believe

† Christ, when those loyal to him will be with him and share in his eternal glory; cf 10; 2, 16; 3, 20–21; 1 Thes 4, 17; 5, 10; 2 Thes 1, 10; 1 Cor 1, 8.
1, 12–26: The body of the letter begins with an account of Paul's present *situation*, i.e., his *imprisonment* (12–13; see Introduction), and then goes on with advice for the Philippians (1, 27–2, 18). The *advance of the gospel* (12) and the *progress* of the Philippians *in the faith* (25) frame what is said.
1, 13: *Praetorium:* either the praetorian guard in the city where Paul was imprisoned or the governor's official residence in a Roman province (cf Mk 15, 16; Acts 23, 35). See Introduction on possible sites.
1, 14–18: Although Paul is imprisoned, Christians there nonetheless go on preaching Christ. But they do so with varied motives, *some* with personal hostility toward Paul, others out of personal ambition.
1, 18: *Rejoice:* a major theme in the letter; see Introduction.
1, 19–25: Paul earnestly debates his prospects of martyrdom or continued missionary labor. While he may *long to depart this life* and thus *be with Christ* (23), his overall and final expectation is that he will be delivered from this imprisonment and *continue in the service* of the Philippians and of others (19.25; 2, 24). In either case, Christ is central (20.21); if to live means Christ for Paul, death means to be united with Christ in a deeper sense.

1, 19: *Result in deliverance for me:* an echo of Jb 13, 16, hoping that God will turn suffering to ultimate good and deliverance from evil.
1, 27–30: Ethical admonition begins at this early point in the letter, emphasizing steadfastness and congregational unity in the face of possible suffering. The *opponents* (28) are those in Philippi, probably pagans, who oppose the gospel cause. *This is proof . . .* (28) may refer to the whole outlook and conduct of the Philippians, turning out for their salvation but to the judgment of the opponents (cf 2 Cor 2, 15–16), or possibly the sentence refers to the opinion of the opponents, who hold that the obstinacy of the Christians points to the destruction of such people as defy Roman authority (though in reality, Paul holds, such faithfulness leads to salvation).

1, 10: Rom 2, 18; 12, 2 / Phil 1, 6.
1, 11: Jn 15, 8.
1, 12–13: Eph 3, 1; 6, 20; 2 Tm 2, 9; Phlm 9.
1, 13: Phil 4, 22.
1, 18: Phil 4, 10.
1, 19: Jb 13, 16 / 2 Cor 1, 11.
1, 20: 1 Cor 6, 20; 1 Pt 4, 16.
1, 21: Gal 2, 20.
1, 22: Rom 1, 13.
1, 23: 2 Cor 5, 8.
1, 27: Eph 4, 1; Col 1, 10; 1 Thes 2, 12 / Phil 4, 3.
1, 29: Mt 5, 10; 10, 38; Mk 8, 34; Acts 5, 41.

in him but also to suffer for him. ³⁰*† Yours is the same struggle as you saw in me and now hear about me.

Plea for Unity and Humility

2 ¹† If there is any encouragement in Christ, any solace in love, any participation in the Spirit, any compassion and mercy, ²* complete my joy by being of the same mind, with the same love, united in heart, thinking one thing. ³* Do nothing out of selfishness or out of vainglory; rather, humbly regard others as more important than yourselves, ⁴* each looking out not for his own interests, but [also] everyone for those of others.

⁵† Have among yourselves the same attitude that is also yours in Christ Jesus,

⁶*†Who, though he was in the form of God,
did not regard equality with God
something to be grasped.†
⁷*† Rather, he emptied himself,
taking the form of a slave,
coming in human likeness;
and found human in appearance,
⁸*† he humbled himself,
becoming obedient to death,
even death on a cross.
⁹*†Because of this, God greatly exalted him
and bestowed on him the name

Divine Humility, Cosmic Glory

LIVE IT!

Mention the name Jesus, or the title Christ, and many images spring to mind. That is good, because no single image can capture Jesus' true nature completely. In Phil 2, 6–11, borrowing from a hymn sung in the earliest days of the church, Paul describes the mystery of Jesus Christ. Jesus willingly gave up the right to remain "in the form of God" (verse 6) and entered our world as a human being. He lived in utter humility, from his simple birth to his Crucifixion. Because of his humility and obedience, Jesus' name is exalted by God so that Jesus Christ is now Lord of all creation. Because of Jesus' humility, creation achieves cosmic harmony!

To be the loving people God calls us to be, we must imitate Christ's humility in our love for one another. Most of us are used to seeing those who are "powerful" in this world being served by others. But Paul reminds us it is the nature of Jesus to serve. Christians are called to be powerful in a radically different way—to see humble service as their basic call and the path to true glory—with the "same attitude that is also yours in Christ Jesus" (verse 5).

▶ **Phil 2, 1–11**

1, 30: A reference to Paul's earlier imprisonment in Philippi (Acts 16, 19–24; 1 Thes 2, 2) and to his present confinement.

2, 1–11: The admonition to likemindedness and unity (2–5) is based on the believers' threefold experience with Christ, God's love, and the Spirit. The appeal to humility (3) and to obedience (12) is rooted in christology, specifically in a statement about Christ Jesus (6–11) and his humbling of self and obedience to the point of death (8).

2, 5: Have . . . the same attitude that is also yours in Christ Jesus: or, "that also Christ Jesus had." While it is often held that Christ here functions as a model for moral imitation, it is not the historical Jesus but the entire Christ event that vv 6–11 depict. Therefore, the appeal is to have in relations among yourselves that same relationship you have in Jesus Christ, i.e., serving one another as you serve Christ (4).

2, 6–11: Perhaps an early Christian hymn quoted here by Paul. The short rhythmic lines fall into two parts, vv 6–8 where the subject of every verb is Christ, and vv 9–11 where the subject is God. The general pattern is thus of Christ's humiliation and then exaltation. More precise analyses propose a division into six three-line stanzas (6; 7abc; 7d–8; 9; 10; 11) or into three stanzas (6–7ab; 7cd–8; 9–11). Phrases such as even death on a cross (8c) are considered by some to be additions (by Paul) to the hymn, as are vv 10c and 11c.

2, 6: Either a reference to Christ's preexistence and those aspects of divinity that he was willing to give up in order to serve in human form, or to what the man Jesus refused to grasp at to attain divinity. Many see an allusion to the Genesis story: unlike Adam, Jesus,

though . . . in the form of God (Gn 1, 26–27), did not reach out for equality with God, in contrast with the first Adam in Gn 3, 5–6.

2, 7: Taking the form of a slave, coming in human likeness: or ". . . taking the form of a slave. // Coming in human likeness, and found human in appearance." While it is common to take vv 6 and 7 as dealing with Christ's preexistence and v 8 with his incarnate life, so that lines 7b and c are parallel, it is also possible to interpret so as to exclude any reference to preexistence (see the note on 2, 6) and to take vv 6–8 as presenting two parallel stanzas about Jesus' human state (6–7b; 7cd–8); in the latter alternative, coming in human likeness begins the second stanza and parallels 6a to some extent.

2, 8: There may be reflected here language about the servant of the Lord, Is 52, 13—53, 12, especially 53, 12.

2, 9: The name: "Lord" (11), revealing the true nature of the one who is named.

1, 30: Phil 1, 13; Acts 16, 22–24.
2, 2: Rom 15, 5; 1 Cor 1, 10.
2, 3: Rom 12, 3.10; Gal 5, 26.
2, 4: 1 Cor 10, 24.33; 13, 5.
2, 6: Jn 1, 1–2; 17, 5; Col 2, 9; Heb 1, 3.

2, 7: Is 53, 3.11; Jn 1, 14; Rom 8, 3; 2 Cor 8, 9; Gal 4, 4; Heb 2, 14.17.
2, 8: Mt 26, 39; Jn 10, 17; Heb 5, 8; 12, 2.
2, 9: Acts 2, 33; Mt 23, 12; Eph 1, 20–21; Heb 1, 3–4.

that is above every name,
10*†   that at the name of Jesus
every knee should bend,
of those in heaven and on earth and under
the earth,
11*†   and every tongue confess that
Jesus Christ is Lord,
to the glory of God the Father.

Obedience and Service in the World†

12* So then, my beloved, obedient as you have always been, not only when I am present but all the more now when I am absent, work out your salvation with fear and trembling.† **13*** For God is the one who, for his good purpose, works in you both to desire and to work. **14*** Do everything without grumbling or questioning, **15*†** that you may be blameless and innocent, children of God without blemish in the midst of a crooked and perverse generation, among whom you shine like lights in the world, **16*** as you hold on to the word of life, so that my boast for the day of Christ may be that I did not run in vain or labor in vain. **17*†** But, even if I am poured out as a libation upon the sacrificial service of your faith, I rejoice and share my joy with all of you. **18*** In the same way you also should rejoice and share your joy with me.

IV: Travel Plans of Paul and His Assistants†

Timothy and Paul

19*† I hope, in the Lord Jesus, to send Timothy to you soon, so that I too may be heartened by hear-

ing news of you. **20** For I have no one comparable to him for genuine interest in whatever concerns you. **21*** For they all seek their own interests, not those of Jesus Christ. **22** But you know his worth, how as a child with a father he served along with me in the cause of the gospel. **23** He it is, then, whom I hope to send as soon as I see how things go with me, **24†** but I am confident in the Lord that I myself will also come soon.

Epaphroditus

25*† With regard to Epaphroditus, my brother and co-worker and fellow soldier, your messenger and minister in my need, I consider it necessary to send him to you. **26** For he has been longing for all of you and was distressed because you heard that he was ill. **27** He was indeed ill, close to death; but God had mercy on him, not just on him but also on me, so that I might not have sorrow upon sorrow. **28** I send him therefore with the greater eagerness, so that, on seeing him, you may rejoice again, and I may have less anxiety. **29*** Welcome him then in the Lord with all joy and hold such people in esteem, **30** because for the sake of the work of Christ he came close to death, risking his life to make up for those services to me that you could not perform.

Concluding Admonitions

3 **1*†** Finally, my brothers, rejoice in the Lord. Writing the same things to you is no burden for me but is a safeguard for you.

---

† **2, 10–11:** *Every knee should bend . . . every tongue confess:* into this language of Is 45, 23 there has been inserted a reference to the three levels in the universe, according to ancient thought, *heaven, earth, under the earth.*

2, 11: *Jesus Christ is Lord:* a common early Christian acclamation; cf 1 Cor 12, 3; Rom 10, 9. But doxology to God the Father is not overlooked here (11c) in the final version of the hymn.

2, 12–18: Paul goes on to draw out further ethical implications for daily life (14–18) from the salvation God works in Christ.

2, 12: *Fear and trembling:* a common Old Testament expression indicating awe and seriousness in the service of God (cf Ex 15, 16; Jdt 2, 28; Ps 2, 11; Is 19, 16).

2, 15–16: *Generation . . . as you hold on to . . . :* or ". . . generation. Among them shine like lights in the world because you hold the word of life . . . ."

2, 17: *Libation:* in ancient religious ritual, the pouring out on the ground of a liquid offering as a sacrifice. Paul means that he may be facing death.

2, 19—3, 1: The plans of Paul and his assistants for future travel are regularly a part of a Pauline letter near its conclusion; cf Rom 15, 22–29; 1 Cor 16, 5–12.

2, 19: *Timothy:* already known to the Philippians (Acts 16, 1–15; cf 1 Cor 4, 17; 16, 10).

2, 24: *I myself will also come soon:* cf 1, 19–25 for the significance of this statement.

2, 25: *Epaphroditus:* sent by the Philippians as their *messenger* (literally, "apostle") to aid Paul in his imprisonment, he had fallen seriously ill; Paul commends him as he sends him back to Philippi.

3, 1: *Finally . . . rejoice:* the adverb often signals the close of a let-

ter; cf 4, 8; 2 Cor 13, 11. While the verb could also be translated "good-bye" or "farewell," although it is never so used in Greek epistolography, the theme of joy has been frequent in the letter (1, 18; 2, 2.18); note also 4, 4 and the addition of "always" there as evidence for the meaning "rejoice." To write *the same things* may refer to what Paul has previously taught in Philippi or to what he has just written or to what follows.

2, 10: Is 45, 23; Jn 5, 23;	65, 23; Gal 2, 2.
Rom 14, 11; Rv 5, 13.	**2, 17:** Rom 15, 16; 2 Tm
2, 11: Acts 2, 36; Rom 10, 9;	4, 6.
1 Cor 12, 3.	**2, 18:** Phil 3, 1; 4, 4.
2, 12: Ps 2, 11; 1 Cor 2, 3;	**2, 19:** Acts 16, 1–3; 17,
2 Cor 7, 15.	14–15; 1 Cor 4, 17;
2, 13: Phil 1, 6; 1 Cor 12, 6;	16, 10.
15, 10; 2 Cor 3, 5.	**2, 21:** 1 Cor 13, 5; 2 Tm
2, 14: 1 Cor 10, 10; 1 Pt 4, 9.	4, 10.
2, 15: 1 Thes 3, 13 / Dt 32,	**2, 25:** Phil 4, 10–11.15–
5; Mt 10, 16; Acts 2,	16.18.
40 / Dn 12, 3; Mt 5,	**2, 29:** 1 Cor 16, 18.
14.16; Eph 5, 8.	**3, 1:** Phil 2, 18; 4, 4.
2, 16: 1 Thes 2, 19 / Is 49, 4;	

V: Polemic: Righteousness and the Goal in Christ†

Against Legalistic Teachers

2*† Beware of the dogs! Beware of the evil-workers! Beware of the mutilation!† 3*† For we are the circumcision, we who worship through the Spirit of God, who boast in Christ Jesus and do not put our confidence in flesh, 4* although I myself have grounds for confidence even in the flesh.

Paul's Autobiography

If anyone else thinks he can be confident in flesh, all the more can I. 5*† Circumcised on the eighth day, of the race of Israel, of the tribe of Benjamin, a Hebrew of Hebrew parentage, in observance of the law a Pharisee, 6* in zeal I persecuted the church, in righteousness based on the law I was blameless.

Righteousness from God

7*† [But] whatever gains I had, these I have come to consider a loss because of Christ. 8 More than

that, I even consider everything as a loss because of the supreme good of knowing Christ Jesus my Lord. For his sake I have accepted the loss of all things and I consider them so much rubbish, that I may gain Christ 9* and be found in him, not having any righteousness of my own based on the law but that which comes through faith in Christ, the righteousness from God, depending on faith 10* to know him and the power of his resurrection and [the] sharing of his sufferings by being conformed to his death, 11* if somehow I may attain the resurrection from the dead.

Forward in Christ†

12*† It is not that I have already taken hold of it or have already attained perfect maturity, but I continue my pursuit in hope that I may possess it, since I have indeed been taken possession of by Christ [Jesus]. 13 Brothers, I for my part do not consider myself to have taken possession. Just one thing: forgetting what lies behind but straining forward to what lies ahead, 14* I continue my pursuit toward the goal, the

Commitment to Your Goal

In what ways have you become more mature in the last five years? How do other people recognize that you are maturing?

In Phil 3, 12–16, Paul describes one measure of maturity—the ability to keep a commitment to an ultimate goal. Mature people—whether sixteen or sixty—are always striving to perfect themselves in pursuit of their goals.

Paul says the goal that guides his life is "to know [Christ] and the power of his resurrection" (verse 10). What is the goal that guides your life? How hard is it for you to stay focused on your goal?

▶ Phil 3, 12–16

†
3, 2–21: An abrupt change in content and tone, either because Paul at this point responds to disturbing news he has just heard about a threat to the faith of the Philippians in the form of false teachers, or because part of another Pauline letter was inserted here; see Introduction. The chapter describes these teachers in strong terms as *dogs*. The persons meant are evidently different from the rival preachers of 1, 14–18 and the opponents of 1, 28. Since vv 2–4 emphasize Jewish terms like *circumcision* (2–3.5), some relate them to the "Judaizers" of the Letter to the Galatians. Other phrases make them appear more like the false teachers of 2 Cor 11, 12–15, the *evilworkers*. The latter part of the chapter depicts the *many* who are *enemies* of Christ's cross in terms that may sound more Gentile or even "gnostic" than Jewish (18–19). Accordingly, some see two groups of false teachers in ch 3, others one group characterized by a claim of having attained "perfect maturity" (12–15).

3, 2–11: Paul sets forth the Christian claim, especially using personal, autobiographical terms that are appropriate to the situation. He presents his own experience in coming to know Christ Jesus in terms of *righteousness* or *justification* (cf Rom 1, 16–17; 3, 21–5, 11; Gal 2, 5–11), contrasting the *righteousness from God* through faith and that of one's own *based on the law* as two exclusive ways of pleasing God.

3, 2: *Beware of the mutilation:* literally, "incision," an ironic wordplay on "circumcision"; cf Gal 5, 12. There may be an association with the self-inflicted mutilations of the prophets of Baal (1 Kgs

18, 28) and of devotees of Cybele who slashed themselves in religious frenzy.

3, 3: *We are the circumcision:* the true people of God, seed and offspring of Abraham (Gal 3, 7.29; 6, 15). *Spirit of God:* some manuscripts read "worship God by the Spirit."

3, 5: *Circumcised on the eighth day:* as the law required (Gn 17, 12; Lv 12, 3).

3, 7: *Loss:* his knowledge of Christ led Paul to reassess the ways of truly pleasing and serving God. His reevaluation indicates the profound and lasting effect of his experience of the meaning of Christ on the way to Damascus some twenty years before (Gal 1, 15–16; Acts 9, 1–22).

3, 12–16: To be *taken possession of by Christ* does not mean that one has already arrived at perfect spiritual maturity. Paul and the Philippians instead press on, trusting in God.

3, 12: *Attained perfect maturity:* possibly an echo of the concept in the mystery religions of being an initiate, admitted to divine secrets.
*

3, 2: Ps 22, 17.21; Rv 22, 15 / 2 Cor 11, 13 / Gal 5, 6.12.	**3, 7:** Mt 13, 44.46; Lk 14, 33.
3, 3: Rom 2, 28–29; Col 2, 11.	**3, 9:** Rom 3, 21–22.
3, 4: 2 Cor 11, 18.21–23.	**3, 10:** Rom 6, 3–5; 8, 17; Gal 6, 17.
3, 5: Lk 1, 59; 2, 21 / Acts 22, 3; 23, 6; 26, 5.	**3, 11:** Jn 11, 23–26; Acts 2; Rv 20, 5–6.
3, 6: Acts 8, 3; 22, 4; 26, 9–11.	**3, 12:** 1 Tm 6, 12.19.
	3, 14: 1 Cor 9, 24–25; 2 Tm 4, 7.

P
H
I
L

prize of God's upward calling, in Christ Jesus. [15] Let us, then, who are "perfectly mature" adopt this attitude. And if you have a different attitude, this too God will reveal to you. [16]† Only, with regard to what we have attained, continue on the same course.

Wrong Conduct and Our Goal†

[17]*† Join with others in being imitators of me, brothers, and observe those who thus conduct themselves according to the model you have in us. [18]* For many, as I have often told you and now tell you even in tears, conduct themselves as enemies of the cross of Christ. [19]* Their end is destruction. Their God is their stomach; their glory is in their "shame." Their minds are occupied with earthly things. [20]*† But our citizenship is in heaven, and from it we also await a savior, the Lord Jesus Christ. [21]* He will change our lowly body to conform with his glorified body by the power that enables him also to bring all things into subjection to himself.

VI: Instructions for the Community

Live in Concord

4 [1]*† Therefore, my brothers, whom I love and long for, my joy and crown, in this way stand firm in the Lord, beloved.

[2]† I urge Euodia and I urge Syntyche to come to a mutual understanding in the Lord. [3]*† Yes, and I ask you also, my true yokemate, to help them, for they have struggled at my side in promoting the gospel, along with Clement and my other co-workers, whose names are in the book of life.

Joy and Peace

[4]*† Rejoice in the Lord always. I shall say it again: rejoice! [5]*† Your kindness should be known to all. The Lord is near. [6]* Have no anxiety at all, but in

Rejoice in the Lord always; I shall say it again: rejoice! 4, 4

everything, by prayer and petition, with thanksgiving, make your requests known to God. [7]* Then the peace of God that surpasses all understanding will guard your hearts and minds in Christ Jesus.

[8]*† Finally, brothers, whatever is true, whatever is honorable, whatever is just, whatever is pure, whatever is lovely, whatever is gracious, if there is any excellence and if there is anything worthy of praise, think about these things. [9]*† Keep on doing what you have learned and received and heard and seen in me. Then the God of peace will be with you.

VII: Gratitude for the Philippians' Generosity

[10]*† I rejoice greatly in the Lord that now at last you revived your concern for me. You were, of course, concerned about me but lacked an opportunity.

---

† **3, 16:** Some manuscripts add, probably to explain Paul's cryptic phrase, "thinking alike."

3, 17–21: Paul and those who live a life centered in Christ, envisaging both his suffering and resurrection, provide a model that is the opposite of opponents who reject Christ's cross (cf 1 Cor 1, 23).

3, 17: *Being imitators of me:* not arrogance, but humble simplicity, since all his converts know that Paul is wholly dedicated to imitating Christ (1 Cor 11, 1; cf also Phil 4, 9; 1 Thes 1, 6; 2 Thes 3, 7.9; 1 Cor 4, 6).

3, 20: *Citizenship:* Christians constitute a colony of heaven, as Philippi was a *colonia* of Rome (Acts 16, 12). The hope Paul expresses involves the final coming of Christ, not a status already attained, such as the opponents claim.

4, 1–9: This series of ethical admonitions rests especially on the view of Christ and his coming (cf 5) in 3, 20–21. Paul's instructions touch on unity within the congregation, joy, prayer, and the Christian outlook on life.

4, 2: *Euodia . . . Syntyche:* two otherwise unknown women in the Philippian congregation; on the advice to them cf 2, 2–4.

4, 3: *Yokemate:* or "comrade," although the Greek *syzygos* could also be a proper name. *Clement:* otherwise unknown, although later writers sought to identify him with Clement, bishop of Rome (Eusebius, *Ecclesiastical History* 3.15.1).

4, 4: *Rejoice:* see the note on 3, 1.

4, 5: *Kindness:* considerateness, forbearance, fairness. *The Lord is*

near: most likely a reference to Christ's parousia (1, 6.10; 3, 20–21; 1 Cor 16, 22), although some sense an echo of Ps 119, 151 and the perpetual presence of the Lord.

4, 8: The language employs terms from Roman Stoic thought.

4, 9: Cf the note on 3, 17.

4, 10–20: Paul, more directly than anywhere else in the letter (cf 1, 3–5), here thanks the Philippians for their gift of money sent through Epaphroditus (2, 25). Paul's own policy was *to be self-sufficient* as a missionary, supporting himself by his own labor (1 Thes 2, 5–9; 1 Cor 9, 15–18; cf Acts 18, 2–3). In spite of this reliance on self and on God to provide (11–13), Paul accepted gifts from the Philippians *not only once but more than once* (16) when he

3, 17: 1 Cor 4, 16; 11, 1; 1 Thes 1, 7; 1 Pt 5, 3.

3, 18: 1 Cor 1, 17.23; Gal 6, 12.

3, 19: Rom 8, 5–6; 16, 18.

3, 20: Eph 2, 6.19; Col 3, 1–3; Heb 12, 22.

3, 21: Rom 8, 23.29; 1 Cor 15, 42–57; 2 Cor 3, 18; 5, 1–5 / 1 Cor 15, 27–28.

4, 1: 1 Thes 2, 19–20.

4, 3: Ex 32, 32–33; Ps 69, 29; Dn 12, 1; Lk 10, 20; Rv 3, 5; 13, 8; 17, 8; 20, 12.15; 21, 27.

4, 4: Phil 2, 18; 3, 1.

4, 5: Ti 3, 2 / Ps 145, 18; Heb 10, 37; Jas 5, 8–9.

4, 6: Mt 6, 25–34; 1 Pt 5, 7 / Col 4, 2.

4, 7: Jn 14, 27; Col 3, 15.

4, 8: Rom 12, 17.

4, 9: 1 Thes 4, 1 / Rom 15, 33; 16, 20; 1 Cor 14, 33; 1 Thes 5, 23.

4, 10: Phil 1, 18; 2, 25; 1 Cor 9, 11; 2 Cor 11, 9.

11* Not that I say this because of need, for I have learned, in whatever situation I find myself, to be self-sufficient. 12 I know indeed how to live in humble circumstances; I know also how to live with abundance. In every circumstance and in all things I have learned the secret of being well fed and of going hungry, of living in abundance and of being in need. 13* I have the strength for everything through him who empowers me. 14 Still, it was kind of you to share in my distress.

15† You Philippians indeed know that at the beginning of the gospel, when I left Macedonia, not a single church shared with me in an account of giving and receiving, except you alone. 16 For even when I was at Thessalonica you sent me something for my needs, not only once but more than once.

17 It is not that I am eager for the gift; rather, I am eager for the profit that accrues to your account. 18*† I have received full payment and I abound. I am very well supplied because of what I received from you through Epaphroditus, "a fragrant aroma," an acceptable sacrifice, pleasing to God. 19* My God will fully supply whatever you need, in accord with his glorious riches in Christ Jesus. 20* To our God and Father, glory forever and ever. Amen.

VIII: Farewell

21† Give my greetings to every holy one in Christ Jesus. The brothers who are with me send you their greetings; 22*† all the holy ones send you their greetings, especially those of Caesar's household. 23 The grace of the Lord Jesus Christ be with your spirit.

THE BEAUTY OF CREATION

Paul ends his message to the Philippians by encouraging them to keep their minds on anything that is of excellence and worthy of praise. This would certainly include the wonder and beauty of creation, something Native Americans are deeply aware of. Let this Navaho prayer in praise of creation inspire you to keep focused on the beauty God has provided in the world around us:

I walk with beauty before me
I walk with beauty behind me
I walk with beauty above me
I walk with beauty below me
Beauty has been restored from the East
Beauty has been restored from the South
Beauty has been restored from the West
Beauty has been restored from the North
Beauty has been restored from the sky-top
Beauty has been restored from the earth-bottom
Beauty has been restored from all around me

(From Michael F. Steltenkamp,
The Sacred Vision, p. 92)

▶ Phil 4, 8–9

---

† was in Thessalonica (Acts 17, 1–9), as he does now, in prison (*my distress*, 14). While commercial terms appear in the passage, like *an account of giving and receiving* (15) and *received full payment* (18), Paul is most concerned about the spiritual growth of the Philippians (10.17.19); he emphasizes that God will care for their needs, through Christ.

4, 15: *The beginning of the gospel:* it was at Philippi that Paul first preached Christ in Europe, going on from there to Thessalonica and Beroea (Acts 16, 9—17, 14).

4, 18: *Aroma . . . sacrifice:* Old Testament cultic language (cf Gn 8, 21; Ex 29, 18.25.41; Lv 1, 9.13; Ez 20, 41) applied to the Philippians' gift; cf Eph 5, 2; 2 Cor 2, 14–16.

4, 21–23: On the usual greetings at the conclusion of a letter, see the note on 1 Cor 16, 19–24. Inclusion of greetings from *all the holy ones* in the place from which Paul writes would involve even the Christians of 1, 14–18 who had their differences with Paul.

4, 22: *Those of Caesar's household:* minor officials or even slaves and freedmen, found in Ephesus or Rome, among other places.

4, 11–12: 1 Cor 4, 11; 2 Cor 6,   Eph 5, 2; Heb 13, 16.
    10; 11, 27 / 2 Cor 12,   **4, 19:** 1 Thes 3, 11.13.
    9–10.   **4, 20:** Rom 16, 27; Eph 5,
4, 13: Col 1, 29; 2 Tm 4, 17.   20.
4, 18: Gn 8, 21; Ex 29, 18;   **4, 22:** Phil 1, 13.

Every now and then, we hear about some cult on the news. All cults tend to have the same characteristics: strict rules, strange ideas, and total obedience to the leader. Cults have been around a long time. In fact, some strange things that sounded pretty cultish were going on in the early Christian community at Colossae. The author's advice in the Letter to the Colossians is pretty direct: Let Christ be the one and only ruler in your heart!

In-depth

This letter attacks a group that was teaching a weird mixture of ideas. It insisted on rituals (2, 16), plenty of precepts and teachings (verse 22), severe treatment of one's own body (verse 23), special festivals (verse 16), and a fancy philosophy that included "the elemental powers of the world" (verse 8). This strange group might have had Jewish roots, because it observed the sabbath (verse 16). The biggest concern was that it was teaching that faith in Christ's death and Resurrection was not enough for salvation.

Against the backdrop of all this mysterious thinking, the author—who may not have been Paul but a disciple of Paul—declares the supreme mystery of Christ. Quoting a Christian hymn (1, 15–20), the writer says Christ is lifted up not only as the firstborn of creation, but also as the one through whom everything was created and who holds everything together. Christ is all we need!

Christians believe that Jesus is more than just a great teacher; they believe Jesus is God, who chose to become human and live with us. This letter gives us an early statement of that belief: "In [Christ] dwells the whole fullness of the deity bodily" (2, 9).

The Letter to the Colossians also offers comforting words about our God. God has given us life and forgiveness. God erased the record of our sins, and set it aside, "nailing it to the cross" (verse 14). Unlike cults that burden their followers with guilt and impossible rules, our God frees us from guilt and gives us life! As you read this letter, you will find these and many other words to live by: "God's chosen ones . . . forgiving one another . . . put on love . . . And let the peace of Christ control your hearts" (3, 12–15).

At a Glance

I. Address (1, 1–14).

II. The Preeminence of Christ (1, 15—2, 3).

III. Warnings against False Teachers (2, 4–23).

IV. The Ideal Christian Life in the World (3, 1—4, 6).

V. Conclusion (4, 7–18).

Quick Facts

Author
Paul or equally likely a follower of Paul (see "Introduction to the Letters and Revelation")

Date Written
around A.D. 61 if by Paul, after A.D. 61 if by a follower

Audience
the Christian community at Colossae

Colossians

The Letter to the

Colossians

I: Address

Greeting

1 [1]*† Paul, an apostle of Christ Jesus by the will of God, and Timothy our brother, [2] to the holy ones and faithful brothers in Christ in Colossae: grace to you and peace from God our Father.

Thanksgiving

[3]*† We always give thanks to God, the Father of our Lord Jesus Christ, when we pray for you, [4] for we have heard of your faith in Christ Jesus and the love that you have for all the holy ones [5]* because of the hope reserved for you in heaven. Of this you have already heard through the word of truth, the gospel, [6] that has come to you. Just as in the whole world it is bearing fruit and growing, so also among you, from the day you heard it and came to know the grace of God in truth, [7]*† as you learned it from Epaphras our beloved fellow slave, who is a trustworthy minister of Christ on your behalf [8] and who also told us of your love in the Spirit.

Prayer for Continued Progress

[9]*† Therefore, from the day we heard this, we do not cease praying for you and asking that you may be filled with the knowledge of his will through all spiritual wisdom and understanding [10] to live in a manner worthy of the Lord, so as to be fully pleasing, in every good work bearing fruit and growing in the knowledge of God, [11] strengthened with every power, in accord with his glorious might, for all endurance and patience, with joy [12]*† giving thanks to the Father, who has made you fit to share

---

1, 1–2: For the epistolary form used by Paul at the beginning of his letters, see the note on Rom 1, 1–7. On *holy ones* or "God's people," see the note on Rom 1, 7. Awareness of their calling helps this group to be *faithful brothers* and sisters *in Christ*, i.e., dedicated to the tasks implied in their calling.

1, 3–8: On thanksgiving at the start of a letter, see the note on Rom 1, 8. The apostle, recalling his own prayers for them and the good report about them he has received (3–4), congratulates the Colossians upon their acceptance of Christ and their faithful efforts to live the gospel (3, 6–8). To encourage them he mentions the success of the gospel elsewhere (6) and assures them that his knowledge of their community is accurate, since he has been in personal contact with Epaphras (7–8), who likely had evangelized Colossae and other cities in the Lycus Valley of Asia Minor (cf 4, 12.13; Phlm 23). On *faith, love,* and *hope* (4.5.8), see the note on 1 Cor 13, 13; cf 1 Thes 1, 3; 5, 8.

1, 7: *Epaphras:* now with Paul but a Colossian, founder of the church there.

1, 9–14: Moved by Epaphras' account, the apostle has prayed and continues to pray fervently for the Colossians that, in their response to the gospel, they *may be filled with the knowledge of* God's *will* (9; cf 3, 10). Paul expects a mutual interaction between their life according to the gospel and this knowledge (10), yielding results (*fruit;* 10; cf 6) *in every good work:* growth, strength, *endurance, patience,* with *joy* (11), and the further giving of thanks (12).

1, 12–14: A summary about *redemption* by *the Father* precedes the statement in vv 15–20 about the *beloved Son* who is God's love in person (13). Christians share *the inheritance . . . in light* with the *holy ones,* here probably the angels (12). The imagery reflects the Exodus (*delivered . . . transferred*) and Jesus' theme of the *kingdom. Redemption* is explained as *forgiveness of sins* (cf Acts 2, 38; Rom 3, 24–25; Eph 1, 7).

1, 1: Eph 1, 1.
1, 3: Eph 1, 15–16; Phlm 4–5.
1, 5: Eph 1, 13.18; 1 Pt 1, 4.
1, 7: Phlm 23.
1, 9: Eph 1, 15–17; 5, 17; Phil 1, 9.
1, 12: Col 3, 17; Jn 8, 12; Acts 26, 18; 1 Tm 6, 16; 1 Pt 2, 9.

The Image of God

It is possible to describe God by naming certain characteristics. We can say God is all-powerful, all-knowing, and eternal. But knowing about God is not the same as knowing God. So how can we really understand the mysterious, invisible, eternal God?

The author of Colossians gives us a clue. This writer calls Jesus "the image of the invisible God" (Col 1, 15). If we want to know about God, who is hidden from us in mystery, we look at Christ. God has existed for all eternity; through God, all things were created; and in God, all things continue to "hold together." But God also appeared on our earth as a real human being, Jesus.

Is there still mystery? Yes. We still cannot comprehend God completely. But we can understand more about God by getting to know more about Jesus Christ.

▸ Col 1, 15–20

in the inheritance of the holy ones in light. [13] He delivered us from the power of darkness and transferred us to the kingdom of his beloved Son, [14]* in whom we have redemption, the forgiveness of sins.

II: The Preeminence of Christ

His Person and Work

[15]*†He is the image† of the invisible God,
the firstborn of all creation.
[16]*†For in him were created all things in heaven
and on earth,
the visible and the invisible,
whether thrones or dominions or
principalities or powers;
all things were created through him and
for him.
[17] He is before all things,
and in him all things hold together.

[18]*†He is the head of the body, the church.
He is the beginning, the firstborn from
the dead,
that in all things he himself might
be preeminent.
[19]† For in him all the fullness was pleased
to dwell,
[20]*† and through him to reconcile all things
for him,
making peace by the blood of his cross
[through him], whether those on earth or
those in heaven.

[21]*† And you who once were alienated and hostile in mind because of evil deeds [22] he has now reconciled in his fleshly body through his death, to present you holy, without blemish, and irreproachable before him, [23] provided that you persevere in the faith, firmly grounded, stable, and not shifting from

1, 15–20: As the poetic arrangement indicates, these lines are probably an early Christian hymn, known to the Colossians and taken up into the letter from liturgical use (cf Phil 2, 6–11; 1 Tm 3, 16). They present Christ as the mediator of creation (15–18a) and of redemption (18b–20). There is a parallelism between *firstborn of all creation* (15) and *firstborn from the dead* (18). While many of the phrases were at home in Greek philosophical use and even in gnosticism, the basic ideas also reflect Old Testament themes about Wisdom found in Prv 8, 22–31; Wis 7, 22—8, 1; and Sir 1, 4. See also the notes on what is possibly a hymn in Jn 1, 1–18.

1, 15: *Image:* cf Gn 1, 27. Whereas the man and the woman were originally created in the image and likeness of God (see also Gn 1, 26), Christ as image (2 Cor 4, 4) *of the invisible God* (Jn 1, 18) now shares this new nature in baptism with those redeemed (cf 3, 10–11).

1, 16–17: Christ (though not mentioned by name) is preeminent and supreme as God's agent in the creation of *all things* (cf Jn 1, 3), as prior to *all things* (17; cf Heb 1, 3).

1, 18: *Church:* such a reference seemingly belongs under "redemption" in the following lines, not under the "creation" section of the hymn. Stoic thought sometimes referred to the world as "the body of Zeus." Pauline usage is to speak of the church as the body of Christ (1 Cor 12, 12–27; Rom 12, 4–5). Some think that the author of Colossians has inserted the reference to the church here so as to define "head of the body" in Paul's customary way. See v 24. *Preeminent:* when Christ was raised by God as *firstborn from the dead* (cf Acts 26, 23; Rv 1, 5), he was placed over the community, the

church, that he had brought into being, but he is also indicated as crown of the whole new creation, over *all things*. His further role is to *reconcile all things* (20) for God or possibly "to himself."

1, 19: *Fullness:* in gnostic usage this term referred to a spiritual world of beings above, between God and the world; many later interpreters take it to refer to *the fullness of the deity* (2, 9); the reference could also be to the fullness of grace (cf Jn 1, 16).

1, 20: *The blood of his cross:* the most specific reference in the hymn to redemption through Christ's death, a central theme in Paul; cf 2, 14–15; 1 Cor 1, 17.18.23. *[Through him]:* the phrase, lacking in some manuscripts, seems superfluous but parallels the reference to reconciliation through Christ earlier in the verse.

1, 21–23: Paul, in applying this hymn to the Colossians, reminds them that they have experienced the reconciling effect of Christ's death. He sees the effects of the cross in the redemption of human beings, not of cosmic powers such as those referred to in vv 16 and 20 (all things). Paul also urges adherence to Christ in faith and begins to point to his own role as minister (23), sufferer (24), and proclaimer (27–28) of this gospel.

1, 14: Eph 1, 7.	15, 20; Eph 1, 22–23;
1, 15: Ps 89, 28; Jn 1, 3.18;	Rv 1, 5.
2 Cor 4, 4.	**1, 20:** 2 Cor 5, 18–19; Eph 1,
1, 16: 1 Cor 8, 6; Eph 1,	10.
10.21.	**1, 21:** Eph 2, 14–16.
1, 18: 1 Cor 11, 3; 12, 12.27;	

the hope of the gospel that you heard, which has been preached to every creature under heaven, of which I, Paul, am a minister.

Christ in Us†

24† Now I rejoice in my sufferings for your sake, and in my flesh I am filling up what is lacking in the afflictions of Christ on behalf of his body, which is the church, 25 of which I am a minister in accordance with God's stewardship given to me to bring to completion for you the word of God, 26* the mystery hidden from ages and from generations past. But now it has been manifested to his holy ones, 27* to whom God chose to make known the riches of the glory of this mystery among the Gentiles; it is Christ in you, the hope for glory. 28* It is he whom we proclaim, admonishing everyone and teaching everyone with all wisdom, that we may present everyone perfect in Christ. 29* For this I labor and struggle, in accord with the exercise of his power working within me.

2 1† For I want you to know how great a struggle I am having for you and for those in Laodicea and all who have not seen me face to face, 2* that their hearts may be encouraged as they are brought together in love, to have all the richness of fully assured understanding, for the knowledge of the mystery of God, Christ, 3* in whom are hidden all the treasures of wisdom and knowledge.

III: Warnings against False Teachers

A General Admonition

4*† I say this so that no one may deceive you by specious arguments. 5* For even if I am absent in the flesh, yet I am with you in spirit, rejoicing as I observe your good order and the firmness of your faith in Christ. 6 So, as you received Christ Jesus the Lord, walk in him, 7* rooted in him and built upon him and established in the faith as you were taught, abounding in thanksgiving. 8*† See to it that no one captivate you with an empty, seductive philosophy according to human tradition, according to

Where Are Your Roots?

What is one thing that motivates you, that keeps you going? Is it a special friendship or a close family? the drive to succeed or to be the best? Maybe it's having a car or holding down a job.

Colossians 2, 7 says that we should be "rooted in [Christ] and built upon him." Where you have your roots is where you get your nourishment to keep going. Think again about what motivates you. Is it enough to nourish a full, rich life?

In your prayer, journal or reflect on the following questions:

- What things are most important in your life right now? Where is God in each of those things?
- What do you need to reorder so that God "might be preeminent" (1, 18)?

▶ Col 2, 6–7

---

† **1, 24—2, 3:** As the community at Colossae was not personally known to Paul (see Introduction), he here invests his teaching with greater authority by presenting a brief sketch of his apostolic ministry and sufferings as they reflect those of Christ on behalf of the church (24). The preaching of God's word (25) carries out the divine plan (the mystery, 26) to make Christ known to the Gentiles (27). It teaches the God-given wisdom about Christ (28), whose power works mightily in the apostle (29). Even in those communities that do not know him personally (2, 1), he can increase the perception of God in Christ, unite the faithful more firmly in love, and so bring encouragement to them (2). He hopes that his apostolic authority will make the Colossians perceive more readily the defects in the teaching of others who have sought to delude them, the next concern in the letter.

1, 24: What is lacking: although variously interpreted, this phrase does not imply that Christ's atoning death on the cross was defective. It may refer to the apocalyptic concept of a quota of "messianic woes" to be endured before the end comes; cf Mk 13, 8.19–20.24 and the note on Mt 23, 29–32. Others suggest that Paul's mystical unity with Christ allowed him to call his own sufferings the afflictions of Christ.

2, 1: Laodicea: chief city in Phrygia, northwest of Colossae; cf 4, 13.16; Rv 3, 14–22.

2, 4–23: In face of the threat posed by false teachers (4), the Colossians are admonished to adhere to the gospel as it was first preached to them (6), steeping themselves in it with grateful hearts (7). They must reject religious teachings originating in any source except the gospel (8) because in Christ alone will they have access

to God, the deity (9). So fully has Christ enlightened them that they need no other source of religious knowledge or virtue (10). They do not require circumcision (11), for in baptism their whole being has been affected by Christ (12) through forgiveness of sin and resurrection to a new life (13; cf 3, 1 and Rom 6, 1–11).

On the cross Christ canceled the record of the debt that stood against us with all its claims (14), i.e., he eliminated the law (cf Eph 2, 15) that human beings could not observe—and that could not save them. He forgave sins against the law (14) and exposed as false and misleading (15) all other powers (cf 1, 16) that purport to offer salvation. Therefore, the Colossians are not to accept judgments from such teachers on food and drink or to keep certain religious festivals or engage in certain cultic practices (16), for the Colossians would thereby risk severing themselves from Christ (19). If, when they accepted the gospel, they believed in Christ as their savior, they must be convinced that their salvation cannot be achieved by appeasing ruling spirits through dietary practices or through a wisdom gained simply by means of harsh asceticism (20–23).

2, 8: Elemental powers of the world: see the note on Gal 4, 3.

1, 26: Rom 16, 25–26; 1 Cor 2, 7; Eph 3, 3.9.
1, 27: Col 3, 4; Rom 8, 10.
1, 28: Eph 4, 13.
1, 29: Col 2, 1; 4, 12; Phil 4, 13.
2, 2: Col 1, 26–27; Eph 3, 18–19.

2, 3: Prv 2, 4–5; Is 45, 3; Rom 11, 33; 1 Cor 1, 30.
2, 4: Eph 4, 14.
2, 5: 1 Cor 5, 3; Phil 1, 27.
2, 7: Eph 2, 20–22; 3, 17.
2, 8: Gal 4, 3; Eph 5, 6.

the elemental powers of the world and not according to Christ.

Sovereign Role of Christ

⁹*† For in him dwells the whole fullness of the deity bodily, ¹⁰ and you share in this fullness in him, who is the head of every principality and power. ¹¹*† In him you were also circumcised with a circumcision not administered by hand, by stripping off the carnal body, with the circumcision of Christ. ¹²* You were buried with him in baptism, in which you were also raised with him through faith in the power of God, who raised him from the dead. ¹³* And even when you were dead [in] transgressions and the uncircumcision of your flesh, he brought you to life along with him, having forgiven us all our transgressions; ¹⁴*† obliterating the bond against us, with its legal claims, which was opposed to us, he also removed it from our midst, nailing it to the cross; ¹⁵*† despoiling the principalities and the powers, he made a public spectacle of them, leading them away in triumph by it.

Practices Contrary to Faith

¹⁶*† Let no one, then, pass judgment on you in matters of food and drink or with regard to a festival or new moon or sabbath. ¹⁷* These are shadows of things to come; the reality belongs to Christ. ¹⁸*† Let no one disqualify you, delighting in self-abasement and worship of angels, taking his stand on visions, inflated without reason by his fleshly mind, ¹⁹* and not holding closely to the head, from whom the whole body, supported and held together by its ligaments and bonds, achieves the growth that comes from God.

²⁰ If you died with Christ to the elemental powers of the world, why do you submit to regulations as if you were still living in the world? ²¹ "Do not handle! Do not taste! Do not touch!" ²²* These are all things destined to perish with use; they accord with human precepts and teachings. ²³ While they have a semblance of wisdom in rigor of devotion and self-abasement [and] severity to the body, they are of no value against gratification of the flesh.

LIVE IT!

COL

A Top-Shelf Life

In stores, the best product is often put on the top shelf, for all to see. It is also usually priced higher than other products, and therefore is not purchased by everyone. Colossians 3, 1 calls us to "seek what is above, where Christ is seated at the right hand of God"—in other words, a top-shelf life.

Living a top-shelf life means living a moral life, free from sin. It means ridding ourselves of "anger, fury, malice, slander, and obscene language out of your mouths" (verse 8). It means avoiding "immorality, impurity, licentiousness, idolatry, sorcery, hatreds, rivalry, jealousy, outbursts of fury, acts of selfishness, dissensions, factions, occasions of envy, drinking bouts, orgies, and the like" (Gal 5, 19–21). It also means living with "compassion, kindness, humility, gentleness, and patience," and forgiving one another and clothing ourselves with love (Col 3, 12–14). Paul and the other authors of the letters focus on moral living because it is what God wants for us. How could we claim to have faith in Jesus Christ and choose to live in sin?

Living a moral life, a top-shelf life, isn't always easy. But it is the way to true happiness, holiness, and health. This is the witness of the church and generations of Christian believers. Why settle for less?

▶ Col 3, 1–4

2, 9: *Fullness of the deity:* the divine nature, not just attributes; see the note on 1, 19.

2, 11: A description of baptism (12) in symbolic terms of the Old Testament rite for entry into the community. The false teachers may have demanded physical circumcision of the Colossians.

2, 14: The elaborate metaphor here about how God canceled the legal claims against us through Christ's cross depicts not Christ being nailed to the cross by men but *the bond . . . with its legal claims* being nailed to the cross by God.

2, 15: The picture derives from the *public spectacle* and *triumph* of a Roman emperor's victory parade, where captives marched in subjection. *The principalities and the powers* are here conquered, not reconciled (cf 1, 16.20). An alternate rendering for *by it* (the cross) is "by him" (Christ).

2, 16: *Festival or new moon or sabbath:* yearly, monthly, and weekly observances determined by religious powers associated with a calendar set by the heavenly bodies, sun, moon, and stars (cf 8).

2, 18: Ascetic practices encouraged by the false teachers included subjection of self humbly to their rules, worship of angels, and cultivation of visions, though exact details are unclear.

2, 9: Col 1, 19; Eph 3, 19.
2, 11: Col 1, 22; Jer 4, 4; Rom 2, 25–29; Phil 3, 3.
2, 12: Rom 6, 3–4.
2, 13: Eph 2, 1.5.
2, 14: Eph 2, 14–15.
2, 15: Col 1, 16.20; 2 Cor 2, 14; Eph 1, 21.
2, 16: Rom 14, 3–4; 1 Tm 4, 3.
2, 17: Heb 8, 5; 10, 1.
2, 18: Col 2, 23; Mt 24, 4.
2, 19: Eph 2, 21–22; 4, 16.
2, 22: Is 29, 13.

IV: The Ideal Christian Life in the World

Mystical Death and Resurrection

3 ¹*† If then you were raised with Christ, seek what is above, where Christ is seated at the right hand of God. ² Think of what is above, not of what is on earth. ³* For you have died, and your life is hidden with Christ in God. ⁴ When Christ your life appears, then you too will appear with him in glory.

Renunciation of Vice†

⁵*† Put to death, then, the parts of you that are earthly: immorality, impurity, passion, evil desire, and the greed that is idolatry. ⁶*† Because of these the wrath of God is coming [upon the disobedient]. ⁷ By these you too once conducted yourselves, when you lived in that way. ⁸*† But now you must put them all away: anger, fury, malice, slander, and obscene language out of your mouths. ⁹* Stop lying to one another, since you have taken off the old self with its practices ¹⁰*† and have put on the new self, which is being renewed, for knowledge, in the image of its creator. ¹¹*† Here there is not Greek and Jew, circumcision and uncircumcision, barbarian, Scythian, slave, free; but Christ is all and in all.

¹²* Put on then, as God's chosen ones, holy and beloved, heartfelt compassion, kindness, humility, gentleness, and patience, ¹³* bearing with one another and forgiving one another, if one has a grievance against another; as the Lord has forgiven you, so must you also do. ¹⁴* And over all these put on love, that is, the bond of perfection. ¹⁵* And let the peace of Christ control your hearts, the peace into which you were also called in one body. And be thankful. ¹⁶* Let the word of Christ dwell in you richly, as in all wisdom you teach and admonish one another, singing psalms, hymns, and spiritual songs with gratitude in your hearts to God. ¹⁷* And whatever you do, in word or in deed, do everything in the name of the Lord Jesus, giving thanks to God the Father through him.

The Christian Family

¹⁸*† Wives, be subordinate to your husbands, as is proper in the Lord. ¹⁹ Husbands, love your wives, and avoid any bitterness toward them. ²⁰* Children, obey your parents in everything, for this is pleasing to the Lord. ²¹* Fathers, do not provoke your children, so they may not become discouraged.

Slaves and Masters

²²*† Slaves, obey your human masters in everything, not only when being watched, as currying favor, but in simplicity of heart, fearing the Lord. ²³ Whatever you do, do from the heart, as for the Lord and not for others, ²⁴ knowing that you will receive from the Lord the due payment of the inheritance; be slaves of the Lord Christ. ²⁵* For the wrongdoer will receive recompense for the wrong he committed, and there is no partiality.

4 ¹ Masters, treat your slaves justly and fairly, realizing that you too have a Master in heaven.

Prayer and Apostolic Spirit

²* Persevere in prayer, being watchful in it with thanksgiving; ³* at the same time, pray for us, too, that God may open a door to us for the word, to speak of the mystery of Christ, for which I am in prison, ⁴ that I may make it clear, as I must speak. ⁵* Conduct yourselves wisely toward outsiders, making the most of the opportunity. ⁶ Let your speech always be gracious, seasoned with salt, so that you know how you should respond to each one.

3, 1–4: By retaining the message of the gospel that the risen, living Christ is the source of their salvation, the Colossians will be free from false religious evaluations of the things of the world (1–2). They have died to these; but one day *when Christ . . . appears*, they will live with Christ in the presence of God (3–4).

3, 5–17: In lieu of false asceticism and superstitious festivals, the apostle reminds the Colossians of the moral life that is to characterize their response to God through Christ. He urges their participation in the liturgical hymns and prayers that center upon God's plan of salvation in Christ (16).

3, 5.8: The two lists of five vices each are similar to enumerations at Rom 1, 29–31 and Gal 5, 19–21.

3, 6: *The wrath of God:* see the note on Rom 1, 18. Many manuscripts add, as at Eph 5, 6, "upon the disobedient."

3, 8–10: *Put . . . away; have taken off; have put on:* the terms may reflect baptismal practice, taking off garments and putting on new ones after being united with Christ, here translated into ethical terms.

3, 10: *Image:* see the note on 1, 15.

3, 11: *Scythian:* a barbarous people from north of the Black Sea.

3, 18—4, 6: After general recommendations that connect family life and the social condition of slavery with the service of Christ (3, 18—4, 1), Paul requests prayers for himself, especially in view of his imprisonment (2–3), and recommends friendly relations and meaningful discussions of Christian teaching with *outsiders*, i.e., non-Christians (5–6). See the note on Eph 5, 21—6, 9.

3, 22–25: *Slaves:* within this table of duties in family and societal relations, involving wives and husbands, children and parents (18–21), such as also appears in Eph 5, 22—6, 9, slaves here receive special attention because of the case of Onesimus the slave returning to his master (4, 9; Phlm 10–12).

3, 1: Col 2, 12; Ps 110, 1; Phil 3, 20; Eph 2, 6.	**3, 15:** Rom 12, 5; 1 Cor 12, 12; Eph 2, 16; 4, 3–4; Phil 4, 7.
3, 3: Rom 6, 2–5.	**3, 16:** Eph 5, 19–20.
3, 5: Mt 15, 19; Rom 1, 29–30; Gal 5, 19–21; Eph 5, 3.5.	**3, 17:** 1 Cor 10, 31.
	3, 18: Eph 5, 22; Ti 2, 5; 1 Pt 3, 1.
3, 6: Rom 1, 18.	**3, 20:** Eph 6, 1.
3, 8: Eph 4, 22.25.31.	**3, 21:** Eph 6, 4.
3, 9: Rom 6, 4.6; Eph 4, 22–25; Heb 12, 1; 1 Pt 2, 1; 4, 2.	**3, 22:** Eph 6, 5; 1 Tm 6, 1; Ti 2, 9–10; 1 Pt 2, 18.
3, 10: Gn 1, 26–27.	**3, 25:** Rom 2, 11.
3, 11: 1 Cor 12, 13; Gal 3, 27–28.	**4, 2:** Lk 18, 1; Rom 12, 12; Eph 6, 18–20; 1 Thes 5, 17.
3, 12: Eph 4, 1–2.32; 1 Thes 5, 15.	**4, 3:** Rom 15, 30; 1 Cor 16, 9; Eph 6, 19; 2 Thes 3, 1.
3, 13: Mt 6, 14; 18, 21–35; Eph 4, 32.	
3, 14: Rom 13, 8–10.	**4, 5:** Eph 5, 15–16.

The Christian Family

LIVE IT!

The rules for Christian families in chapter 3 of Colossians seem a little strange in our culture. But Colossians is simply calling families to be rooted in loving relationships (see also "Family Relationships," Eph 5, 21—6, 4). A family is God's gift. It is a community where we are loved and accepted simply for who we are, and where we can freely love in return, a community we can turn to for comfort and support. The Catholic church calls families the domestic church, meaning that they are the primary place where people learn about God and God's love.

Being the domestic church doesn't just happen. Every member of a family must make an effort. That means taking time to listen to one another, to help one another out, and to respect each person in the family. Sometimes, selfishness gets in the way of making God's love real. At those times, family members must try even harder. Taking time to pray together, and to read and talk about the Bible together, can help a family focus on God's presence in its life.

How is your family life? Is love the guiding rule? Does everyone take time to pray together? Do you support family activities willingly? Are you generous in helping with family chores? Are you your best self around your family?

▶ Col 3, 18—4, 1

V: Conclusion†

Tychicus and Onesimus

[7]*† Tychicus, my beloved brother, trustworthy minister, and fellow slave in the Lord, will tell you all the news of me. [8] I am sending him to you for this very purpose, so that you may know about us and that he may encourage your hearts, [9]* together with Onesimus, a trustworthy and beloved brother, who is one of you. They will tell you about everything here.

From Paul's Co-Workers

[10]*† Aristarchus, my fellow prisoner, sends you greetings, as does Mark the cousin of Barnabas (concerning whom you have received instructions; if he comes to you, receive him), [11]† and Jesus, who is called Justus, who are of the circumcision; these alone are my co-workers for the kingdom of God,

and they have been a comfort to me. [12]*† Epaphras sends you greetings; he is one of you, a slave of Christ [Jesus], always striving for you in his prayers so that you may be perfect and fully assured in all the will of God. [13]† For I can testify that he works very hard for you and for those in Laodicea and those in Hierapolis. [14]*† Luke the beloved physician sends greetings, as does Demas.

A Message for the Laodiceans

[15]† Give greetings to the brothers in Laodicea and to Nympha and to the church in her house. [16]† And when this letter is read before you, have it read also in the church of the Laodiceans, and you yourselves read the one from Laodicea. [17]*† And tell Archippus, "See that you fulfill the ministry that you received in the Lord."

[18]*† The greeting is in my own hand, Paul's. Remember my chains. Grace be with you.

---

†

4, 7–18: Paul concludes with greetings and information concerning various Christians known to the Colossians.

4, 7: *Tychicus:* Acts 20, 4 mentions his role in the collection for Jerusalem; Eph 6, 21 repeats what is said here; see also 2 Tm 4, 12; Ti 3, 12.

4, 10: *Aristarchus:* a Thessalonian who was with Paul at Ephesus and Caesarea and on the voyage to Rome (Acts 19, 29; 20, 4; 27, 2). *Mark:* also referred to at Phlm 24 and 2 Tm 4, 11 and, as "John Mark," in Acts (12, 12.25; 13, 13; 15, 37–40). See also 1 Pt 5, 13 and the note there. Traditionally the author of the second gospel.

4, 11: *Jesus:* a then common Jewish name, the Greek form of Joshua.

4, 12: *Epaphras:* see the notes on 1, 3–8 and 1, 7.

4, 13: *Laodicea:* see the note on 2, 1. *Hierapolis:* a city northeast of Laodicea and northwest of Colosse.

4, 14: *Luke:* only here described as a medical doctor; cf Phlm 24 and 2 Tm 4, 11. Traditionally the author of the third gospel. *Demas:* cf Phlm 24; he later deserted Paul (2 Tm 4, 10).

4, 15: *Nympha and . . . her house:* some manuscripts read a mas-

culine for the house-church leader, "Nymphas and . . . his house."

4, 16: *The one from Laodicea:* either a letter by Paul that has been lost or the Letter to the Ephesians (cf the note on Eph 1, 1, *in Ephesus*).

4, 17: *Fulfill the ministry:* usually taken to mean that *Archippus,* the son of Philemon and Apphia (Phlm 1–2), is "pastor" at Colosse. An alternate interpretation is that Archippus, not Philemon, is the owner of the slave Onesimus and that Paul is asking Archippus to complete the service he has received in the Lord by sending Onesimus back to minister to Paul in his captivity (cf Phlm 20).

4, 18: *My own hand:* a postscript in Paul's own hand was his custom; cf Gal 6, 11–18 and 2 Thes 3, 17–18.

*

4, 7: Acts 20, 4; Eph 6, 21–22; Phil 1, 12.
4, 9: Phlm 10–11.
4, 10: Acts 19, 29; 20, 4; 27, 2 / Acts 12, 12.25; 13, 13; 15, 37.40; 2 Tm 4, 11; Phlm 24;
1 Pt 5, 13.
4, 12: Col 1, 7; Rom 15, 30.
4, 14: Phlm 24; 2 Tm 4, 10–11.
4, 17: Phlm 2.
4, 18: 1 Cor 16, 21; Gal 6, 11; Eph 3, 1; 2 Thes 3, 17.

COL

you're about to read what is probably the oldest book in the New Testament. It was written a little over twenty years after Jesus' death and Resurrection, by a man named Paul. It is the very first Christian letter that we still have! In it, Paul answers some questions that were on people's minds back then. Even though it was written so long ago, you might have some of the same questions.

At a Glance

I. Address (1, 1–10).

II. Previous Relations with the Thessalonians (2, 1—3, 13).

III. Specific Exhortations (4, 1—5, 25).

IV. Final Greeting (5, 26–28).

In-depth

Thessalonica was the capital of a Roman province called Macedonia. Today, that area is in northern Greece (see map 7, "Paul's First and Second Journeys"). Acts of the Apostles, chapter 17, tells us that Paul spent three weeks in Thessalonica preaching about Jesus Christ. Because of his preaching, many people, mainly Gentiles (non-Jews), became Christians. Paul was forced to leave the city by the non-Christians there. After he left, he worried about the new Christian community, so he sent his co-worker Timothy back to check things out. When Timothy rejoined Paul, he had some great news. Even though the Thessalonians were being persecuted, they were staying strong in their "faith and love" (1 Thes 3, 6).

When you read this letter, you can tell that Paul is thankful that the church is thriving! Four different times he expresses his gratitude. But he also apparently feels the need to defend himself against some critics. So he reminds everyone that he has been genuine and "as a nursing mother cares for her children" (2, 7).

After reassuring the Thessalonians that the persecution they are suffering is to be expected (3, 3–4), Paul takes the time to answer some questions about the coming of the Lord at the end of time. Apparently, some of the Thessalonians are concerned about their friends who have already died. Will they join the living when Christ returns again?

Paul tells them that they don't have to worry about those who die before Jesus returns; the dead will be raised first and join the living, to "be with the Lord" (4, 17). When will that happen? they ask. No one knows, Paul says, but Christians don't have to be afraid of that day. Their job is to stay alert and clothe themselves with "faith and love and . . . hope" (5, 8).

Quick Facts

Author
Paul

Date Written
A.D. 51

Audience
the mainly Gentile church in Thessalonica

1 Thessalonians

5, 4–6

I: Address

Greeting

1 ¹*† Paul, Silvanus, and Timothy to the church of the Thessalonians in God the Father and the Lord Jesus Christ: grace to you and peace.

Thanksgiving for Their Faith

²* We give thanks to God always for all of you, remembering you in our prayers, unceasingly ³† calling to mind your work of faith and labor of love and endurance in hope of our Lord Jesus Christ, before our God and Father, ⁴* knowing, brothers loved by God, how you were chosen. ⁵* For our gospel did not come to you in word alone, but also in power and in the holy Spirit and [with] much conviction. You know what sort of people we were [among] you for your sake. ⁶† And you became imitators of us and of the Lord, receiving the word in great affliction, with joy from the holy Spirit, ⁷* so that you became a model for all the believers in Macedonia and in Achaia. ⁸* For from you the word of the Lord has sounded forth not only in Macedonia and [in] Achaia, but in every place your faith in God has gone forth, so that we have no need to say anything. ⁹* For they themselves openly declare about us what sort of reception we had among you, and how you turned to God from idols to serve the living and true God ¹⁰* and to await his Son from heaven, whom he raised from [the] dead, Jesus, who delivers us from the coming wrath.

II: Previous Relations with the Thessalonians

Paul's Ministry Among Them

2 ¹ For you yourselves know, brothers, that our reception among you was not without effect. ²* Rather, after we had suffered and been insolently treated, as you know, in Philippi, we drew courage through our God to speak to you the gospel of God with much struggle. ³ Our exhortation was not from delusion or impure motives, nor did it work through deception. ⁴*† But as we were judged worthy by God to be entrusted with the gospel, that is

---

† **1, 1:** On the address, see the note on Rom 1, 1–7.

1, 3: *Faith . . . love . . . hope:* this, along with 5, 8, is the earliest mention in Christian literature of the three "theological virtues" (see 1 Cor 13, 13). The order here stresses eschatological hope, in line with the letter's emphasis on the Lord's second, triumphal coming, or parousia (10; 2, 12.19; 3, 13; 4, 13—5, 11; 5, 23).

1, 6: *Imitators:* the Pauline theme of "imitation" (see 2, 14; 1 Cor 4, 16; 11, 1; 2 Thes 3, 9) is rooted in Paul's view of solidarity in Christ through sharing in Jesus' cross and in the Spirit of the risen Lord.

2, 4: *Judged worthy:* Paul regards "worthiness" not as grounded in one's own talent or moral self-righteousness but in God's discernment of genuinely selfless attitudes and actions (see 2 Cor 10, 17–18).

1, 1: Acts 15, 40; 16, 1–3.19; 17, 14–15; 2 Thes 1, 1–2.
1, 2: 2 Thes 1, 3.
1, 4: 2 Thes 2, 13.
1, 5: Acts 13, 52; 17, 1–9.
1, 7: 2 Thes 1, 4; 1 Cor 4, 16; 11, 1 / 1 Thes 2,
14; Phil 3, 17.
1, 8: Rom 1, 8.
1, 9: Acts 14, 15; Gal 4, 8 / 1 Thes 4, 5.
1, 10: Rom 2, 1–16; 5, 9; 13, 4 / 1 Thes 5, 9.
2, 2: Acts 16, 19–17, 10.
2, 4: Gal 1, 10.

Doing the Right Thing

Angela normally keeps to herself. But the three girls teasing Nicole have her almost in tears. Angela hesitates to say anything. But then, she looks at her WWJD ("What would Jesus do?") bracelet and speaks up: "Stop it, you guys. Can't you see you are hurting Nicole's feelings?" The three girls are quiet for a second. Then, they start in on Angela. "Hey, this isn't your business. Who do you think you are telling us what to do?" The comments sting, but despite them, Angela experiences a growing sense of peace, almost as if she can feel Jesus smiling at her.

Lord, make me stronger. Stronger to do the right thing—the Christlike thing—the next time I'm in a hurtful situation. Stronger to declare my faith in you as the reason for my actions. Stronger even to forgive those who insult me.

Jesus, give me the courage to live out what I believe in my heart, and allow me the wisdom to know that it comes from you. Amen.

▸ 1 Thes 2, 1–2

how we speak, not as trying to please human beings, but rather God, who judges our hearts. 5 Nor, indeed, did we ever appear with flattering speech, as you know, or with a pretext for greed—God is witness— 6* nor did we seek praise from human beings, either from you or from others, 7† although we were able to impose our weight as apostles of Christ. Rather, we were gentle among you, as a nursing mother cares for her children. 8 With such affection for you, we were determined to share with you not only the gospel of God, but our very selves as well, so dearly beloved had you become to us. 9* You recall, brothers, our toil and drudgery. Working night and day in order not to burden any of you, we proclaimed to you the gospel of God. 10 You are witnesses, and so is God, how devoutly and justly and blamelessly we behaved toward you believers. 11* As you know, we treated each one of you as a father treats his children, 12* exhorting and encouraging you and insisting that you conduct yourselves as worthy of the God who calls you into his kingdom and glory.

Further Thanksgiving

13 And for this reason we too give thanks to God unceasingly, that, in receiving the word of God from hearing us, you received not a human word but, as it truly is, the word of God, which is now at work in you who believe. 14† For you, brothers, have become imitators of the churches of God that

Encouragement

Sometimes, we feel alone in our faith. We wonder if anyone feels, thinks, or prays the way we do. As a first missionary of the faith, Paul must have experienced his share of dark days when he wondered if the people would really accept the Good News. He must have been so encouraged when Timothy returned to tell him of the "faith and love" of the Thessalonians (1 Thes 3, 6).

The Christian faith is never meant to be held privately. We don't grow in our faith, hope, and love by being isolated from other people. Like Paul, we need the encouragement and challenge of other people: our family, friends, and the entire Christian community.

In your prayer, reflect or journal on the following questions:
■ How do you encourage others to grow in Christ?
■ How do others encourage or challenge you to grow in faith, hope, and love?

▸ 1 Thes 3, 6–13

2, 7: *Gentle:* many excellent manuscripts read "infants" (*nēpioi*), but "gentle" (*ēpioi*) better suits the context here.

2, 14: Luke's picture of the persecutions at Philippi (by Gentiles) and in Thessalonica and Beroea (by Jews) seems to be considerably schematized (Acts 16, 11–40; 17, 1–15). Paul pictures the Thessalonian community as composed of converts from paganism (1, 9) and speaks here of persecution by their (pagan) compatriots rather than by Jews.

2, 6: Jn 5, 41.44; 1 Cor 10, 31; 2 Cor 4, 17.
2, 9: Acts 20, 34; 1 Cor 4, 12; 9, 3–18; 2 Thes 3, 7–9.
2, 11: Acts 20, 31.
2, 12: 1 Pt 5, 10 / 1 Thes 4, 7; 2 Thes 2, 14.

are in Judea in Christ Jesus. For you suffer the same things from your compatriots as they did from the Jews, [15]*† who killed both the Lord Jesus and the prophets and persecuted us; they do not please God, and are opposed to everyone, [16]* trying to prevent us from speaking to the Gentiles that they may be saved, thus constantly filling up the measure of their sins. But the wrath of God has finally begun to come upon them.

Paul's Recent Travel Plans

[17]* Brothers, when we were bereft of you for a short time, in person, not in heart, we were all the more eager in our great desire to see you in person. [18]* We decided to go to you—I, Paul, not only once but more than once—yet Satan thwarted us. [19]* For what is our hope or joy or crown to boast of in the presence of our Lord Jesus at his coming if not you yourselves? [20] For you are our glory and joy.

3 [1]* That is why, when we could bear it no longer, we decided to remain alone in Athens [2]* and sent Timothy, our brother and co-worker for God in the gospel of Christ, to strengthen and encourage you in your faith, [3]† so that no one be disturbed in these afflictions. For you yourselves know that we are destined for this. [4]* For even when we were among you, we used to warn you in advance that we would undergo affliction, just as has happened, as you know. [5] For this reason, when I too could bear it no longer, I sent to learn about your faith, for fear that somehow the tempter had put you to the test and our toil might come to nothing.

[6] But just now Timothy has returned to us from you, bringing us the good news of your faith and love, and that you always think kindly of us and long to see us as we long to see you. [7] Because of this, we have been reassured about you, brothers, in our every distress and affliction, through your faith. [8] For we now live, if you stand firm in the Lord.

Concluding Thanksgiving and Prayer

[9]† What thanksgiving, then, can we render to God for you, for all the joy we feel on your account before our God? [10] Night and day we pray beyond measure to see you in person and to remedy the deficiencies of your faith. [11] Now may God himself, our Father, and our Lord Jesus direct our way to you, [12]* and may the Lord make you increase and abound in love for one another and for all, just as

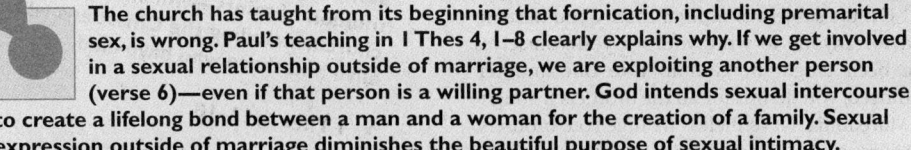

True Love Waits

LIVE IT!

The church has taught from its beginning that fornication, including premarital sex, is wrong. Paul's teaching in 1 Thes 4, 1–8 clearly explains why. If we get involved in a sexual relationship outside of marriage, we are exploiting another person (verse 6)—even if that person is a willing partner. God intends sexual intercourse to create a lifelong bond between a man and a woman for the creation of a family. Sexual expression outside of marriage diminishes the beautiful purpose of sexual intimacy.

Paul reminds the Thessalonians to live in ways pleasing to God. To behave contrary to God's purpose is to say no to the gift of the Holy Spirit and to the holiness God wants for us. In our culture, sex is often portrayed as a recreational activity, violating the gift of sexuality God created within us! God's message in the Bible and the church calls us to take a stand that is unpopular with some people—to support sexual abstinence until marriage.

Valuing our gift of sexuality and expressing it as God intended is not always easy. However, this old idea has a new slogan and campaign today: True love waits. Think about it!

▶ 1 Thes 4, 1–8

1 T H E S

---

† **2, 15–16:** Paul is speaking of historical opposition on the part of Palestinian Jews in particular and does so only some twenty years after Jesus' crucifixion. Even so, he quickly proceeds to depict the persecutors typologically, in apocalyptic terms. His remarks give no grounds for anti-Semitism to those willing to understand him, especially in view of Paul's pride in his own ethnic and religious background (Rom 9, 1–5; 10, 1; 11, 1–3; Phil 3, 4–6). Sinful conduct (16) is itself an anticipation of the ultimate wrath or judgment of God (Rom 1, 18—2, 5), whether or not it is perceived as such.

3, 3: *We are destined:* the Greek phraseology and the context suggest Paul's concern to alert his readers to difficulties he knew they would necessarily face and to enable them to see their present experience in the light of what he warned them would happen in the future. This line of thought is followed in 2 Thes 2, 1–15.

3, 9–10: The tension between Paul's optimism concerning the Thessalonians' faith and his worries about their perseverance remains unresolved. Perhaps this is accounted for not only by the continuing harassment but also by the shortness of his own stay in Thessalonica (even if that were over twice as long as the conventional three weeks that Luke assigns to it, Acts 17, 2).

2, 15: Acts 2, 23; 7, 52.
2, 16: Gn 15, 16; 2 Mc 6, 14 / Rom 1, 18; 2, 5–6.
2, 17: 1 Thes 3, 10; Rom 1, 10–11.
2, 18: Rom 15, 22.
2, 19: 2 Cor 1, 14; Phil 2, 16; 4, 1.

3, 1: Acts 17, 14.
3, 2: Acts 16, 1–2; 1 Cor 3, 5–9.
3, 4: Acts 14, 22; 2 Thes 2, 5–7; 2 Tm 3, 12.
3, 12: 1 Thes 4, 9–10; 2 Thes 1, 3.

we have for you, [13]* so as to strengthen your hearts, to be blameless in holiness before our God and Father at the coming of our Lord Jesus with all his holy ones. [Amen.]

III: Specific Exhortations

General Exhortations

4 [1] Finally, brothers, we earnestly ask and exhort you in the Lord Jesus that, as you received from us how you should conduct yourselves to please God—and as you are conducting yourselves—you do so even more. [2]† For you know what instructions we gave you through the Lord Jesus.

Holiness in Sexual Conduct

[3]† This is the will of God, your holiness: that you refrain from immorality, [4] that each of you know how to acquire a wife for himself in holiness and honor, [5]* not in lustful passion as do the Gentiles who do not know God; [6] not to take advantage of or exploit a brother in this matter, for the Lord is an avenger in all these things, as we told you before and solemnly affirmed. [7] For God did not call us to impurity but to holiness. [8]* Therefore, whoever disregards this, disregards not a human being but God, who [also] gives his holy Spirit to you.

Mutual Charity

[9]* On the subject of mutual charity you have no need for anyone to write you, for you yourselves have been taught by God to love one another. [10]* Indeed, you do this for all the brothers throughout Macedonia. Nevertheless we urge you, brothers, to progress even more, [11] and to aspire to live a tranquil life, to mind your own affairs, and to work with your [own] hands, as we instructed you, [12] that you may conduct yourselves properly toward outsiders and not depend on anyone.

Hope for the Christian Dead

[13] We do not want you to be unaware, brothers, about those who have fallen asleep, so that you may

Catholic Connections

THE COMMUNION OF SAINTS

Many early Christians thought the world would end during their lifetime. So when people started to die before Jesus returned and the world was made new, they were concerned. Paul didn't want his Thessalonian friends to worry about their dead friends and family. He assured them that just as Jesus died and rose again, so the "dead in Christ will rise" (1 Thes 4, 16). A time would come when those who were alive would meet the Lord along with the risen dead.

Grief always comes with the death of someone we love. But for Christians, there is also the joy of knowing that the person will rise again to be with God. Those who believe have God's promise that they will someday be together again in the communion of saints—which is the whole church, including the Christians who are alive and those who have died.

▶ 1 Thes 4, 13–18

not grieve like the rest, who have no hope. [14]* For if we believe that Jesus died and rose, so too will God, through Jesus, bring with him those who have fallen asleep. [15]*† Indeed, we tell you this, on the word of the Lord, that we who are alive, who are left until the coming of the Lord, will surely not precede those who have fallen asleep. [16]* For the Lord himself, with a

---

4, 2: *Instructions:* these include specific guidelines on the basis of the Lord's authority, not necessarily sayings Jesus actually uttered. More profoundly, as v 8 implies, the instructions are practical principles that Paul worked out in accordance with his understanding of the role of the Spirit.

4, 3–8: Many think that this passage deals with a variety of moral regulations (fornication, adultery, sharp business practices). It can be more specifically interpreted as bringing general norms to bear on a specific problem, namely, marriage within degrees of consanguinity (as between uncle and niece) forbidden in Jewish law but allowed according to a Greek heiress law, which would insure retention of an inheritance within the family and perhaps thereby occasion divorce. In that case, "immorality" (3) should be rendered as "unlawful marriage" and "this matter" (6) as "a lawsuit." The phrase in v 4, "acquire a wife for himself," has often been interpreted to mean "control one's body."

4, 15: *Coming of the Lord:* Paul here assumes that the second coming, or parousia, will occur within his own lifetime but insists that the time or season is unknown (5, 1–2). Nevertheless, the most important aspect of the parousia for him was the fulfillment of union with Christ. His pastoral exhortation focuses first on hope for the departed faithful, then on (5, 1–3) the need of preparedness for those who have to achieve their goal.

3, 13: 1 Thes 5, 23; 1 Cor 1, 8.
4, 5: Ps 79, 6; Jer 10, 25; 2 Thes 1, 8; 1 Pt 3, 7.
4, 8: Lk 10, 16.
4, 9: Jn 6, 45; 13, 34; 1 Jn 2, 20–21.27; 4, 7.
4, 10: 2 Thes 3, 6–12.
4, 14: 1 Cor 15, 3–4.12.20.
4, 15: 1 Cor 15, 51; Rv 14, 13; 20, 4–6.
4, 16: Mt 24, 31; 1 Cor 15, 23.52.

Cultural Connections

IROQUOIS PRAYER OF THANKSGIVING

This Iroquois prayer—although clearly not addressed to the one God who is creator of all—is still a beautiful expression of thankfulness for the wonders of the natural world. It can remind us of Paul's instruction to the Thessalonians (5, 16–24) to give thanks without ceasing.

We return thanks to our mother,
   the earth, which sustains us.
We return thanks to the rivers and streams,
   which supply us with water.
We return thanks to all herbs,
   which furnish medicines for the cure to our diseases.
We return thanks to the corn, and to her sisters,
   the beans and squashes,
   which give us life.
We return thanks to the bushes and trees,
   which provide us with fruit.
We return thanks to the wind,
   which, moving in the air, has banished diseases.
We return thanks to the moon and stars,
   which have given to us their light
   when the sun was gone.
We return thanks to our grandfather Hé-no,
   that he has protected his grandchildren
   from witches and reptiles,
   and has given to us his rain.
We return thanks to the sun,
   that he has looked upon the earth
   with a beneficent eye.
Lastly, we return thanks to the Great Spirit,
   in whom is embodied all goodness,
   and who directs all things
   for the good of his children.

(From David Schiller, editor,
The Little Book of Prayers, pp. 154–155)

▶ I Thes 5, 16–24

---

word of command, with the voice of an archangel and with the trumpet of God, will come down from heaven, and the dead in Christ will rise first. [17]† Then we who are alive, who are left, will be caught up together with them in the clouds to meet the Lord in the air. Thus we shall always be with the Lord. [18] Therefore, console one another with these words.

Vigilance

5 [1]* Concerning times and seasons, brothers, you have no need for anything to be written to you. [2]* For you yourselves know very well that the day of the Lord will come like a thief at night. [3] When people are saying, "Peace and security," then sudden disaster comes upon them, like labor

---

4, 17: *Will be caught up together:* literally, snatched up, carried off; cf 2 Cor 12, 2; Rv 12, 5. From the Latin verb here used, *rapiemur,* has come the idea of "the rapture," when believers will be transported away from the woes of the world; this construction combines this

verse with Mt 24, 40–41 (see the note there) // Lk 17, 34–35 and passages from Revelation in a scheme of millennial dispensationalism.

5, 1: Mt 24, 36–45.   5, 2: 2 Pt 3, 10.

pains upon a pregnant woman, and they will not escape.

4* But you, brothers, are not in darkness, for that day to overtake you like a thief. 5† For all of you are children of the light and children of the day. We are not of the night or of darkness. 6* Therefore, let us not sleep as the rest do, but let us stay alert and sober. 7 Those who sleep go to sleep at night, and those who are drunk get drunk at night. 8* But since we are of the day, let us be sober, putting on the breastplate of faith and love and the helmet that is hope for salvation. 9 For God did not destine us for wrath, but to gain salvation through our Lord Jesus Christ, 10† who died for us, so that whether we are awake or asleep we may live together with him. 11* Therefore, encourage one another and build one another up, as indeed you do.

Church Order

12 We ask you, brothers, to respect those who are laboring among you and who are over you in the Lord and who admonish you, 13 and to show esteem for them with special love on account of their work. Be at peace among yourselves.

14 We urge you, brothers, admonish the idle, cheer the fainthearted, support the weak, be patient with all. 15* See that no one returns evil for evil; rather, always seek what is good [both] for each other and for all. 16 Rejoice always. 17 Pray without ceasing. 18* In all circumstances give thanks, for this is the will of God for you in Christ Jesus. 19† Do not quench the Spirit. 20 Do not despise prophetic utterances. 21 Test everything; retain what is good. 22 Refrain from every kind of evil.

GIVE THANKS AT ALL TIMES!

Gratitude is an essential element of the Christian faith for Hispanic people. We turn to the Scriptures and Tradition for examples of gratitude in all things. Mary, the mother of Jesus, personified this gratitude when she accepted the responsibility of bearing the Son of God in her womb. Paul continually promoted gratitude in his letters to the first Christians.

To be grateful, we must humbly open up to receiving and acknowledging God's many gifts to us. When we do this, we express our gratitude for God's gifts by loving God and neighbor. Expressing love is an automatic response for someone who is grateful.

Juan Diego, a sixteenth-century Mexican man, opened up to the love and message of Our Lady of Guadalupe, who appeared to him on Tepeyac Hill, today located within Mexico City. In the spirit of gratitude, Juan Diego wanted to share the news of this loving appearance. After persistently speaking about it and eventually providing proof of the appearance to his local bishop, he was finally listened to and believed. For hundreds of years, a church, which is now a basilica, has stood on Tepeyac Hill. Mary had asked Juan Diego to see that a church was built there.

Juan Diego's message and Mary's message to him continue to be spread today in the lives of Mexicans and Mexican Americans. Because Juan Diego's gratitude was so great and because he shared his gratitude with so many others, Pope John Paul II declared him a saint on 31 July 2002.

▶ I Thes 5, 18

5, 5: *Children of the light:* that is, belonging to the daylight of God's personal revelation and expected to achieve it (an analogous development of imagery that appears in Jn 12, 36).

5, 10: Characteristically, Paul plays on words suggesting ultimate and anticipated death and life. Union with the crucified and risen Lord at his parousia is anticipated in some measure in contrasted states of our temporal life. The essential element he urges is our indestructible personal union in Christ's own life (see Rom 5, 1–10).

5, 19–21: Paul's buoyant encouragement of charismatic freedom

sometimes occasioned excesses that he or others had to remedy (see 1 Cor 14; 2 Thes 2, 1–15; 2 Pt 3, 1–16).

5, 4: Eph 5, 8–9.
5, 6: Mt 24, 42; Rom 13, 12–13; 1 Pt 5, 8.
5, 8: Is 59, 17; Rom 13, 11–14; Eph 6, 11.14–17.
5, 11: Rom 15, 2; 1 Cor 8, 1; 14, 12.26; Eph 4, 29.
5, 15: Prv 20, 22; Mt 5, 38–42; Rom 12, 17.
5, 18: Eph 5, 20.

> ## Test everything;
>
> ☑ retain   ☑ Refrain from
> what is   every kind
> good.   of evil.
>
> 5, 21–22

Concluding Prayer

23*† May the God of peace himself make you perfectly holy and may you entirely, spirit, soul, and body, be preserved blameless for the coming of our Lord Jesus Christ. 24 The one who calls you is faithful, and he will also accomplish it. 25 Brothers, pray for us [too].

IV: Final Greeting

26† Greet all the brothers with a holy kiss. 27 I adjure you by the Lord that this letter be read to all the brothers. 28 The grace of our Lord Jesus Christ be with you.

---

† **5, 23:** Another possible translation is, "May the God of peace himself make you perfectly holy and sanctify your spirit fully, and may both soul and body be preserved blameless for the coming of our Lord Jesus Christ." In either case, Paul is not offering an anthropological or philosophical analysis of human nature. Rather, he looks to the wholeness of what may be called the supernatural and natural aspects of a person's service of God.

5, 26: *Kiss:* the holy embrace (see Rom 16, 16; 1 Cor 16, 20; 2 Cor 13, 12; 1 Pt 5, 14) was a greeting of respect and affection, perhaps given during a liturgy at which Paul's letter would have been read.

---

* 5, 23: 2 Thes 3, 16.

Has a parent or another adult ever said to you, "You know, when I was your age," and launched into some story about how hard it was in the "good old days"? It seems all past generations, including those who lived in biblical times, had their struggles and challenges. When the Thessalonians were going through some really tough times, Paul's second letter to them promised that if they continued to trust God, everything would come out right.

At a Glance

I. Address (1, 1–12).

II. Warning against Deception Concerning the Parousia (2, 1–17).

III. Concluding Exhortations (3, 1–16).

IV. Final Greetings (3, 17–18).

In-depth

From the short Second Letter to the Thessalonians, it appears the Thessalonians were experiencing two problems. First, they were being persecuted by non-Christians. Second, some of them were becoming confused over "the coming of our Lord Jesus Christ" (2, 1), sometimes called the Second Coming. Word was being spread that Jesus had already come again (verse 2)! And some believers may have been using that as an excuse not to work and earn their keep (3, 6).

This letter speaks to the Thessalonians, using apocalyptic language (see "Apocalyptic Literature," Daniel, chapters 7–10, and the introduction to Revelation). It tells the Thessalonians to have peace and not let themselves be deceived, "For unless the apostasy comes first and the lawless one is revealed, the one doomed to perdition" (2, 3). It also tells them to have hope because at the end time, Christ will overcome all evil and will destroy the lawless one.

This letter is not as warm and personal as 1 Thessalonians. Perhaps that's because it's filled with the sobering awareness that persecution is here to stay, and that evil and deception are all around. In such an environment, the letter advises the Thessalonians—and us—to "stand firm and hold fast to the traditions that you were taught" (verse 15).

Quick Facts

Author
possibly Paul, but more likely a disciple of Paul

Date Written
around A.D. 51 if by Paul, A.D. 70–90 if by a disciple

Audience
the mainly Gentile (non-Jewish) church in Thessalonica

2 Thessalonians

I: Address

Greeting

1 ¹*† Paul, Silvanus, and Timothy to the church of the Thessalonians in God our Father and the Lord Jesus Christ: ² grace to you and peace from God [our] Father and the Lord Jesus Christ.

Thanksgiving

³*† We ought to thank God always for you, brothers, as is fitting, because your faith flourishes ever more, and the love of every one of you for one another grows ever greater. ⁴ Accordingly, we ourselves boast of you in the churches of God regarding your endurance and faith in all your persecutions and the afflictions you endure.

⁵* This is evidence of the just judgment of God, so that you may be considered worthy of the kingdom of God for which you are suffering. ⁶ For it is surely just on God's part to repay with afflictions those who are afflicting you, ⁷ and to grant rest along with us to you who are undergoing afflictions, at the revelation of the Lord Jesus from heaven with his mighty angels, ⁸* in blazing fire, inflicting punishment on those who do not acknowledge God and on those who do not obey the gospel of our Lord Jesus. ⁹* These will pay the penalty of eternal ruin, separated from the presence of the Lord and from the glory of his power, ¹⁰*† when he comes to be glorified among his holy ones and to be marveled at on that day among all who have believed, for our testimony to you was believed.

Prayer

¹¹* To this end, we always pray for you, that our God may make you worthy of his calling and powerfully bring to fulfillment every good purpose and every effort of faith, ¹²*† that the name of our Lord Jesus may be glorified in you, and you in him, in accord with the grace of our God and Lord Jesus Christ.

---

† **1, 1–2:** On the address, see the note on Rom 1, 1–7 and cf 1 Thes 1, 1.

1, 3–12: On the thanksgiving, see the note on Rom 1, 8 and cf 1 Thes 1, 2–10. Paul's gratitude to God for the faith and love of the Thessalonians (3) and his Christian pride in their faithful endurance (4–5) contrast with the condemnation announced for those who afflict them, a judgment to be carried out at the parousia (6–10), which is described in vivid language drawn from Old Testament apocalyptic. A prayer for the fulfillment of God's purpose in the Thessalonians (11–12) completes the section, as is customary in a Pauline letter (cf 1 Thes 1, 2–3).

1, 10: *Among his holy ones:* in the Old Testament, this term can

refer to an angelic throng (cf also Jude 14), but here, in parallel with *among all who have believed,* it can refer to the triumphant people of God.

1, 12: *The grace of our God and Lord Jesus Christ:* the Greek can also be translated, "the grace of our God and of the Lord Jesus Christ."

1, 1: 1 Thes 1, 1.
1, 3: 1 Cor 1, 4; 1 Thes 1, 2; 3, 12.
1, 5: Phil 1, 28; 1 Thes 2, 12.
1, 8: Ps 79, 5–6; Is 66, 15; Jer 10, 25.
1, 9: Is 2, 10.19.21.
1, 10: Ps 89, 8; Dn 7, 18–22.27; 1 Thes 3, 13.
1, 11: 1 Thes 1, 2–3.
1, 12: Is 66, 5.

II: Warning against Deception Concerning the Parousia

Christct and the Lawless One

2 ¹*† We ask you, brothers, with regard to the coming of our Lord Jesus Christ and our assembling with him, ²*† not to be shaken out of your minds suddenly, or to be alarmed either by a "spirit," or by an oral statement, or by a letter allegedly from us to the effect that the day of the Lord is at hand. ³† Let no one deceive you in any way. For unless the apostasy comes first and the lawless one is revealed, the one doomed to perdition, ⁴*† who opposes and exalts himself above every so-called god and object of worship, so as to seat himself in the temple of God, claiming that he is a god— ⁵ do you not recall that while I was still with you I told you these things? ⁶† And now you know what is restraining, that he may be revealed in his time. ⁷*† For the mystery of lawlessness is already at

?did you KNOW?

The Parousia

After Jesus' death and Resurrection, the early Christians start to wait for his Second Coming, also called the Parousia. They think Jesus will return soon in glory to judge the living and the dead and to bring to complete fulfillment the Reign of God. They even see some signs of his imminent arrival and express an urgent call to be prepared. Paul seems to expect Christ's return in the near future but insists that nobody can predict when. He emphasizes the importance of living the Gospel and always being prepared for "our assembling with him" (2 Thes 2, 1).

The important message for us today is that our history has meaning and purpose and that Christ ultimately triumphs over sin and death. The various descriptions of the signs preceding the end time are intended not to predict the future but rather to encourage us to live the Gospel as we wait in hope for Christ's glorious return.

▶ 2 Thes 1, 5—2, 17

2, 1–17: The Thessalonians have been *shaken* by a message purporting to come from Paul himself that *the day of the Lord* is already present. He warns against this deception in eschatology by citing a scenario of events that must first occur (3–12) before the end will come. The overall point Paul makes is the need to reject such lies as Satan sends; he also reaffirms the Thessalonians in their calling (13–14). They are to uphold what Paul himself has taught (15). There is a concluding prayer for their strengthening (16–17). As in 1, 8–10, the Old Testament provides a good deal of coloring; cf especially Is 14, 13–14; 66, 15.18–21; Ez 28, 2–9; Dn 11, 36–37. The contents of 2, 3b–8 may come from a previously existing apocalypse. The details have been variously interpreted.

An alternative to the possibilities noted below understands that an oracular utterance, supposedly coming from a prophetic spirit (2–3a), has so disrupted the community's thinking that its effects may be compared to those of the mania connected with the worship of the Greek god Dionysus. On this view, the writer seems to allude in vv 6–8 to Dionysiac "seizure," although, of course, ironically, somewhat as Paul alludes to witchcraft ("an evil eye") in Gal 3, 1 in speaking of the threat to faith posed by those disturbing the Galatians (Gal 1, 6–7; 5, 10b). On this view of 2 Thes 2, the Greek participles *katechon* (rendered above as *what is restraining*) and *katechōn* (*the one who restrains*) are to be translated "the seizing power" in v 6 and "the seizer" in v 7. They then allude to a pseudocharismatic force or spirit of Dionysiac character that has suddenly taken hold of the Thessalonian community (see 2). The addressees *know* (6) this force or spirit because of the problem it is causing. This pseudocharismatic force or spirit is a kind of anticipation and advance proof of the ultimate, climactic figure (*the lawless one* or the rebel, 3), of which the community has been warned (see the note on 1 Thes 3, 3). It is, however, only the beginning of the end that the latter's manifestation entails; the end is not yet. For in the course of *the mystery of lawlessness* (7), false prophetism, after it ceases in the Thessalonian community, will be manifested in the world at large (8–12), where it will also be eliminated in turn by the Lord Jesus.

2, 2: *"Spirit":* a Spirit-inspired utterance or ecstatic revelation. *An oral statement:* literally, a "word" or pronouncement, not necessarily of ecstatic origin. *A letter allegedly from us:* possibly a forged letter, so that Paul calls attention in 3, 17 to his practice of concluding a genuine letter with a summary note or greeting in his own hand, as at Gal 6, 11–18 and elsewhere.

2, 3b–5: This incomplete sentence (anacoluthon, 4) recalls what the Thessalonians had already been taught, an apocalyptic scenario depicting, in terms borrowed especially from Dn 11, 36–37 and related verses, human self-assertiveness against God in *the temple of God* itself. *The lawless one* represents the climax of such activity in this account.

2, 4: *Seat himself in the temple of God:* a reflection of the language in Dn 7, 23–25; 8, 9–12; 9, 27; 11, 36–37; and 12, 11 about the attempt of Antiochus IV Epiphanes to set up a statue of Zeus in the Jerusalem temple and possibly of the Roman emperor Caligula to do a similar thing (Mk 13, 14). Here the imagery suggests an attempt to install someone in the place of God, *claiming that he is a god* (cf Ez 28, 2). Usually, it is the Jerusalem temple that is assumed to be meant; on the alternative view sketched above (see the note on 2, 1–17), *the temple* refers to the Christian community.

2, 6–7: *What is restraining . . . the one who restrains:* neuter and masculine, respectively, of a force and person holding back the lawless one. The Thessalonians know what is meant (6), but the terms, seemingly found only in this passage and in writings dependent on it, have been variously interpreted. Traditionally, v 6 has been applied to the Roman empire and v 7 to the Roman emperor (in Paul's day, Nero) as bulwarks holding back chaos (cf Rom 13, 1–7). A second interpretation suggests that cosmic or angelic powers are binding Satan (9) and so restraining him; some relate this to an anti-Christ figure (1 Jn 2, 18) or to Michael the archangel (Rv 12, 7–9; 20, 1–3). A more recent view suggests that it is the preaching of the Christian gospel that restrains the end, for in God's plan the end cannot come until the gospel is preached to all nations (Mk 13, 10); in that case, Paul as missionary preacher par excellence is "the one who restrains," whose removal (death) will bring the end (7). On the alternative view (see the note on 2, 1–17), the phrases should be referred to that which and to him who seizes (a prophet) in ecstasy so as to have him speak pseudo-oracles.

2, 7–12: *The lawless one* and *the one who restrains* are involved in an activity or process, *the mystery of lawlessness*, behind which Satan stands (9). The action of the *Lord [Jesus]* in overcoming the lawless one is described in Old Testament language (*with the breath of*

2, 1: 1 Thes 4, 13–17.
2, 2: Mt 24, 6; 1 Cor 14, 26.32–33; 1 Thes 5, 1–2.
2, 4: Dn 11, 36–37; Ez 28, 2.
2, 7: Mt 13, 36–43; Acts 20, 29; Gal 5, 10; 2 Pt 2, 1; Rv 22, 11.

work. But the one who restrains is to do so only for the present, until he is removed from the scene. 8* And then the lawless one will be revealed, whom the Lord [Jesus] will kill with the breath of his mouth and render powerless by the manifestation of his coming, 9* the one whose coming springs from the power of Satan in every mighty deed and in signs and wonders that lie, 10 and in every wicked deceit for those who are perishing because they have not accepted the love of truth so that they may be saved. 11 Therefore, God is sending them a deceiving power so that they may believe the lie, 12 that all who have not believed the truth but have approved wrongdoing may be condemned.

13*† But we ought to give thanks to God for you always, brothers loved by the Lord, because God chose you as the firstfruits for salvation through sanctification by the Spirit and belief in truth. 14* To this end he has [also] called you through our gospel to possess the glory of our Lord Jesus Christ. 15† Therefore, brothers, stand firm and hold fast to the traditions that you were taught, either by an oral statement or by a letter of ours.

16 May our Lord Jesus Christ himself and God our Father, who has loved us and given us everlasting encouragement and good hope through his grace, 17 encourage your hearts and strengthen them in every good deed and word.

III: Concluding Exhortations

Request for Prayers

3 1*† Finally, brothers, pray for us, so that the word of the Lord may speed forward and be glorified, as it did among you, 2 and that we may be delivered from perverse and wicked people, for not all have faith. 3* But the Lord is faithful; he will strengthen you and guard you from the evil one. 4* We are confident of you in the Lord that what we instruct you, you [both] are doing and will continue to do. 5 May the Lord direct your hearts to the love of God and to the endurance of Christ.

Catholic Connections

TRADITIONS

Second Thessalonians 2, 15 directs the Thessalonians to "stand firm and hold fast to the traditions that" they were taught (this message is repeated somewhat differently in 3, 6). Traditions are an important part of the Catholic church. They give Catholics their identity and also keep them faithful to the mission and teachings of Jesus Christ.

It's important to understand the difference between traditions with a small t and Tradition with a large T. Large-T Tradition is the core truths of the Christian faith as taught by the Apostles (see "The Bible, Tradition, and the Magisterium," Lk 4, 1–13). Like the Bible, it is a primary source of God's revelation for us. The truths of Tradition are unchanging and the same for every age.

Small-t traditions are the customs and rituals that help Catholics and other Christians live out their faith. These traditions are influenced by history and culture. They can differ between cultures and times, and they account for the rich variety of faith expressions in the universal church. These traditions are also important, and they are good as long as they help us live out the mission and teachings of Jesus embodied in the Scriptures and Tradition. But Jesus condemns the exaggerated importance of small-t traditions when they present obstacles to living God's revealed commandments (Mk 7, 1–15).

Answer this question: What from the Tradition or traditions of the church has been important to you? Then ask the same question of a parent, a grandparent, or another person from a previous generation, and compare the answers.

▸ 2 Thes 2, 15

---

his mouth; cf Is 11, 4; Jb 4, 9; Rv 19, 15). *His coming* is literally the Lord's "parousia." The biblical concept of the "holy war," eschatologically conceived, may underlie the imagery.

2, 13: *As the firstfruits:* there is also strong manuscript evidence for the reading, "God chose you from the beginning," thus providing a focus on God's activity from beginning to end; *firstfruits* is a Pauline term, however; cf Rom 8, 23; 11, 16; 16, 5, among other references.

2, 15: Reference to *an oral statement* and a *letter* (2) and the content here, including a formula of conclusion (cf 1 Cor 16, 13; Gal 5, 1), suggest that vv 1–15 or even 1–17 are to be taken as a literary unit, notwithstanding the incidental thanksgiving formula in v 13.

3, 1–18: The final chapter urges the Thessalonians to pray for Paul and his colleagues (1–2) and reiterates confidence in the Thessalonians (3–5), while admonishing them about a specific problem in their community that has grown out of the intense eschatological speculation, namely, not to work but to become instead disorderly busybodies (6–15). A benediction (16) and postscript in Paul's own hand round out the letter. On vv 17–18, cf the note on 2, 2.

2, 8: Is 11, 4; Rv 19, 15.
2, 9: Mt 24, 24; Rv 13, 13.
2, 13: 1 Thes 2, 13; 5, 9.
2, 14: Rom 5, 1–10; 8, 29–30; 1 Thes 4, 7; 5, 9.
3, 1: Eph 6, 19; Col 4, 3.
3, 3: 1 Thes 5, 24 / 1 Cor 16, 13 / Mt 6, 13.
3, 4: 2 Cor 7, 16; 1 Thes 4, 1–2.

Laziness

How well do you balance work—the things you are expected to do in your home, school, job, or community—with leisure? Workaholics find it hard to relax and just do nothing. Others find it easy to loosen up and recreate, and need a little push to get back to their responsibilities.

Evidently, some of the early Thessalonians are determined to avoid work altogether (2 Thes 3, 6), presuming they can depend on the Christian community to feed and take care of them. Perhaps they feel that if the Second Coming is close, there is no need to work. The author of 2 Thessalonians sees this idleness as destructive for the church. His answer is simple: no work, no food (verse 10).

Christ invites us not to a life of laziness, where we take advantage of the kindness of others, but to an active life. Our work ought to be an expression of who we are and should contribute something meaningful and positive to the world.

▶ 2 Thes 3, 6–13

Neglect of Work

6† We instruct you, brothers, in the name of [our] Lord Jesus Christ, to shun any brother who conducts himself in a disorderly way and not according to the tradition they received from us. 7 For you know how one must imitate us. For we did not act in a disorderly way among you, 8* nor did we eat food received free from anyone. On the contrary, in toil and drudgery, night and day we worked, so as not to burden any of you. 9* Not that we do not have the right. Rather, we wanted to present ourselves as a model for you, so that you might imitate us. 10* In fact, when we were with you, we instructed you that if anyone was unwilling to work, neither should that one eat. 11* We hear that some are conducting themselves among you in a disorderly way, by not keeping busy but minding the business of others. 12 Such people we instruct and urge in the Lord Jesus Christ to work quietly and to eat their own food. 13 But you, brothers, do not be remiss in doing good. 14 If anyone does not obey our word as expressed in this letter, take note of this person not to associate with him, that he may be put to shame. 15* Do not regard him as an enemy but admonish him as a brother. 16* May the Lord of peace himself give you peace at all times and in every way. The Lord be with all of you.

IV: Final Greetings

17* This greeting is in my own hand, Paul's. This is the sign in every letter; this is how I write. 18 The grace of our Lord Jesus Christ be with all of you.

3, 6: Some members of the community, probably because they regarded the parousia as imminent or the new age of the Lord to be already here (2, 2), had apparently ceased to work for a living. The disciplinary problem they posed could be rooted in distorted thinking about Paul's own teaching (cf 1 Thes 2, 16; 3, 3–4; 5, 4–5) or, more likely, in a forged letter (2, 2) and the type of teaching dealt with in 2, 1–15. The apostle's own moral teaching, reflected in his selfless labors for others, was rooted in a deep doctrinal concern for the gospel message (cf 1 Thes 2, 3–10).

3, 8: 1 Thes 2, 9.
3, 9: Mt 10, 10; Phil 3, 17.
3, 10: 1 Thes 4, 11.
3, 11: 1 Thes 5, 14.

3, 15: 2 Cor 2, 7; Gal 6, 1.
3, 16: Jn 14, 27; Rom 15, 33.
3, 17: 1 Cor 16, 21; Gal 6, 11.

I magine you are a bishop writing a letter to the new priests, deacons, and lay ministers in your diocese. How do you encourage them? What do you warn them about? The two Letters to Timothy and the Letter to Titus are such letters, written to give good, practical advice to the leaders of the early church.

In-depth

The Letters to Timothy and Titus are called the pastoral letters because they were written to church leaders, or pastors. These letters sound as if they were written by Paul. But a great deal of evidence suggests they may have been written by later disciples of Paul, adapting Paul's teaching and advice to the situation of the churches a generation later.

The First Letter to Timothy addresses practical issues the churches needed to deal with in order to achieve stability and respond to new challenges as Christianity became more visible in society: How should the churches deal with people teaching false beliefs? What qualities should church leaders have? Who deserves financial help from the community? How should Christians view success?

The Second Letter to Timothy presents Paul as being close to his execution. As you read this letter, you will experience his sadness at death, hear his reflections on his life and ministry, and see a man who feels deserted by many. This letter tells Timothy—who stands for all faithful Christians—that he needs to endure suffering. Doing the right thing often means more pain than popularity. But even when other people desert us, God "remains faithful, / for he cannot deny himself" (2, 13).

The Letter to Titus gives advice for elders, bishops, older men, older women, slaves, younger men, and younger women. It also offers repeated warnings to guard against temptations and false teachings and to be self-controlled.

The pastoral letters give us a picture of the church moving into a new phase. The church seems to have more structure, leadership roles are becoming more defined, and the people are more concerned about its public appearance. Like Christians today, the early Christians struggled to be faithful in applying the Gospel of Jesus Christ to their culture and time.

At a Glance

I. Address (1 Tm 1, 1–2).

II. Sound Teaching (1 Tm 1, 3–20).

III. Problems of Discipline (1 Tm 2, 1—4, 16).

IV. Duties toward Others (1 Tm 5, 1—6, 2a).

V. False Teaching and True Wealth (1 Tm 6, 2b–19).

VI. Final Recommendation and Warning (1 Tm 6, 20–21).

I. Address (2 Tm 1, 1–5).

II. Exhortations to Timothy (2 Tm 1, 6—2, 13).

III. Instructions Concerning False Teaching (2 Tm 2, 14—4, 8).

IV. Personal Requests and Final Greetings (2 Tm 4, 9–22).

I. Address (Ti 1, 1–4).

II. Pastoral Charge (Ti 1, 5–16).

III. Teaching the Christian Life (Ti 2, 1—3, 15).

Quick Facts

Author
Paul or followers of Paul (see "Introduction to the Letters and Revelation")

Date Written
around A.D. 65 if by Paul, A.D. 90–100 if by followers

Audience
leaders of the early churches

The Pastoral Letters

1 Timothy

I: Address

Greeting

1 [1]*† Paul, an apostle of Christ Jesus by command of God our savior and of Christ Jesus our hope, [2]* to Timothy, my true child in faith: grace, mercy, and peace from God the Father and Christ Jesus our Lord.

II: Sound Teaching

Warning against False Doctrine

[3]*† I repeat the request I made of you when I was on my way to Macedonia, that you stay in Ephesus to instruct certain people not to teach false doctrines [4]*† or to concern themselves with myths and endless genealogies, which promote speculations rather than the plan of God that is to be received by faith. [5]* The aim of this instruction is love from a pure heart, a good conscience, and a sincere faith.

[6]* Some people have deviated from these and turned to meaningless talk, [7] wanting to be teachers of the law, but without understanding either what they are saying or what they assert with such assurance.

[8]*† We know that the law is good, provided that one uses it as law, [9] with the understanding that law is meant not for a righteous person but for the lawless and unruly, the godless and sinful, the unholy and profane, those who kill their fathers or mothers, murderers, [10]*† the unchaste, sodomites, kidnappers, liars, perjurers, and whatever else is opposed to sound teaching, [11]* according to the glorious gospel of the blessed God, with which I have been entrusted.

Gratitude for God's Mercy

[12]*† I am grateful to him who has strengthened me, Christ Jesus our Lord, because he considered me trustworthy in appointing me to the ministry.

---

† **1, 1–2:** For the Pauline use of the conventional epistolary form, see the note on Rom 1, 1–7.

1, 3–7: Here Timothy's initial task *in Ephesus* (cf Acts 20, 17–35) is outlined: to suppress the idle religious speculations, probably about Old Testament figures (3–4), but see the note on 6, 20–21), which do not contribute to the development of love within the community (5) but rather encourage similar useless conjectures (6–7).

1, 4: The *plan of God that is to be received by faith:* the Greek may also possibly mean "God's trustworthy plan" or "the training in faith that God requires."

1, 8–11: Those responsible for the speculations that are to be suppressed by Timothy do not present the Old Testament from the Christian viewpoint. The Christian values the Old Testament not as a

system of law but as the first stage in God's revelation of his saving plan, which is brought to fulfillment in the good news of salvation through faith in Jesus Christ.

1, 10: *Sodomites:* see 1 Cor 6, 9 and the note there.

1, 12–17: Present gratitude for the Christian apostleship leads Paul to recall an earlier time when he had been a fierce persecutor

---

† **1, 1:** 1 Tm 2, 3; Lk 1, 47; Ti 1, 3; 2, 10 / Col 1, 27.
1, 2: 2 Tm 1, 2; Ti 1, 4.
1, 3: Acts 20, 1.
1, 4: 1 Tm 4, 7; Ti 1, 14; 3, 9; 2 Pt 1, 16.
1, 5: Rom 13, 10.

1, 6: 1 Tm 6, 4.20; Ti 1, 10.
1, 8: Rom 7, 12.16.
1, 10: 1 Tm 4, 6; 6, 3; 2 Tm 4, 3; Ti 1, 9; 2, 1.
1, 11: Ti 1, 3.
1, 12: Phil 4, 13 / Acts 9, 15; Gal 1, 15–16.

13* I was once a blasphemer and a persecutor and an arrogant man, but I have been mercifully treated because I acted out of ignorance in my unbelief. 14* Indeed, the grace of our Lord has been abundant, along with the faith and love that are in Christ Jesus. 15*† This saying is trustworthy and deserves full acceptance: Christ Jesus came into the world to save sinners. Of these I am the foremost. 16 But for that reason I was mercifully treated, so that in me, as the foremost, Christ Jesus might display all his patience as an example for those who would come to believe in him for everlasting life. 17*† To the king of ages, incorruptible, invisible, the only God, honor and glory forever and ever. Amen.

Responsibility of Timothy†

18* I entrust this charge to you, Timothy, my child, in accordance with the prophetic words once spoken about you.† Through them may you fight a good fight 19* by having faith and a good conscience. Some, by rejecting conscience, have made a shipwreck of their faith, 20*† among them Hymenaeus and Alexander, whom I have handed over to Satan to be taught not to blaspheme.

III: Problems of Discipline

Prayer and Conduct

2 1*† First of all, then, I ask that supplications, prayers, petitions, and thanksgivings be

Conscience: God in the Gut

LIVE IT!

Do you ever wonder where God is during those really difficult moments of decision? Like when you're with some friends and someone proposes you all do something exciting but dangerous, and you feel caught in the middle. Or when an entire group is taking advantage of a teacher who has left the room during a test, or when a new kid trips and falls in the cafeteria and no one makes a move to help.

One of the best places to look for God's direction is that feeling in the center of your stomach when you are faced with life's dilemmas. That feeling may be a sign of your conscience prompting you to act.

In I Tm I, 19, Timothy is told to have "faith and a good conscience." A good conscience is based on reason and love and is developed through a commitment to make good and thoughtful moral decisions. Take time to develop your conscience by studying moral issues and the church's teaching on them. The more you develop your conscience, the more you will experience God speaking to you through those gut feelings.

▶ I Tm I, 18–19

of the Christian communities (cf Acts 26, 9–11) until his conversion by intervention of divine mercy through the appearance of Jesus. This and his subsequent apostolic experience testify to the saving purpose of Jesus' incarnation. The fact of his former ignorance of the truth has not kept the apostle from regarding himself as having been the worst of sinners (15). Yet he was chosen to be an apostle, that God might manifest his firm will to save sinful humanity through Jesus Christ (16). The recounting of so great a mystery leads to a spontaneous outpouring of adoration (17).

1, 15: *This saying is trustworthy:* this phrase regularly introduces in the Pastorals a basic truth of early Christian faith; cf 3, 1; 4, 9; 2 Tm 2, 11; Ti 3, 8.

1, 17: *King of ages:* through Semitic influence, the Greek expression could mean "everlasting king"; it could also mean "king of the universe."

1, 18–20: Timothy is to be mindful of his calling, which is here compared to the way Barnabas and Saul were designated by Christ as prophets for missionary service; cf Acts 13, 1–3. Such is probably the sense of the allusion to the prophetic words (18). His task is not to yield, whether in doctrine or in conduct, to erroneous opinions, taking warning from what has already happened at Ephesus in the case of Hymenaeus and Alexander (19–20).

1, 18: *The prophetic words once spoken about you:* the Greek may also be translated, "the prophecies that led (me) to you." It probably refers to testimonies given by charismatic figures in the Christian communities. *Fight a good fight:* this translation preserves the play on words in Greek. The Greek terms imply a lengthy engagement in battle and might well be translated "wage a good campaign."

1, 20: *Hymenaeus:* mentioned in 2 Tm 2, 17 as saying that the resurrection has already taken place (in baptism). *Alexander:* probably the Alexander mentioned in 2 Tm 4, 14 as the coppersmith who "did me a great deal of harm." *Whom I have handed over to Satan:* the same terms are used in the condemnation of the incestuous man in 1 Cor 5, 5.

2, 1–7: This marked insistence that the liturgical prayer of the community concern itself with the needs of all, whether Christian or not, and especially of those in authority, may imply that a disposition existed at Ephesus to refuse prayer for pagans. In actuality, such prayer aids the community to achieve peaceful relationships with non-Christians (2) and contributes to salvation, since it derives its value from the presence within the community of Christ, who is the one and only savior of all (3–6). The vital apostolic mission to the Gentiles (7) reflects Christ's purpose of universal salvation.

Verse 5 contains what may well have been a very primitive creed. Some interpreters have called it a Christian version of the Jewish *shema:* "Hear, O Israel, the LORD is our God, the LORD alone . . ." (Dt 6, 4–5). The assertion in v 7, "I am speaking the truth, I am not lying," reminds one of similar affirmations in Rom 9, 1; 2 Cor 11, 31; and Gal 1, 20.

1, 13: Acts 8, 3; 9, 1–2; 1 Cor 15, 9; Gal 1, 13.
1, 14: Rom 5, 20; 2 Tm 1, 13.
1, 15: Lk 15, 2; 19, 10.
1, 17: Rom 16, 27.

1, 18: 1 Tm 4, 14 / 1 Tm 6, 12; 2 Tm 4, 7; Jude 3.
1, 19: 1 Tm 3, 9.
1, 20: 2 Tm 2, 17; 4, 14 / 1 Cor 5, 5.
2, 1: Eph 6, 18; Phil 4, 6.

offered for everyone, ² for kings and for all in authority, that we may lead a quiet and tranquil life in all devotion and dignity. ³* This is good and pleasing to God our savior, ⁴* who wills everyone to be saved and to come to knowledge of the truth.

⁵* For there is one God.
    There is also one mediator between God and
        the human race,
    Christ Jesus, himself human,
⁶*†who gave himself as ransom for all.

This was the testimony at the proper time. ⁷* For this I was appointed preacher and apostle (I am speaking the truth, I am not lying), teacher of the Gentiles in faith and truth.

⁸† It is my wish, then, that in every place the men should pray, lifting up holy hands, without anger or argument. ⁹* Similarly, [too], women should adorn themselves with proper conduct, with modesty and self-control, not with braided hairstyles and gold ornaments, or pearls, or expensive clothes, ¹⁰* but rather, as befits women who profess reverence for God, with good deeds. ¹¹* A woman must receive instruction silently and under complete control. ¹²† I do not permit a woman to teach or to have authority over a man. She must be quiet. ¹³* For Adam was formed first, then Eve. ¹⁴* Further, Adam was not deceived, but the woman was deceived and transgressed. ¹⁵* But she will be saved through

---

2, 6: *The testimony:* to make sense of this overly concise phrase, many manuscripts supply "to which" (or "to whom"); two others add "was given." The translation has supplied "this was."

2, 8–15: The prayer of the community should be unmarred by internal dissension (8); cf Mt 5, 21–26; 6, 14; Mk 11, 25. At the liturgical assembly the dress of women should be appropriate to the occasion (9); their chief adornment is to be reputation for good works (10). Women are not to take part in the charismatic activity of the assembly (11–12; cf 1 Cor 14, 34) or exercise authority; their conduct there should reflect the role of man's helpmate (13; cf Gn 2, 18) and not the later relationship of Eve to Adam (14; cf Gn 3, 6–7). As long as women perform their role as wives and mothers in faith and love, their salvation is assured (15).

2, 12: *A man:* this could also mean "her husband."

3, 1–7: The passage begins by commending those who aspire to the office of bishop (*episkopos;* see the note on Phil 1, 1) within the community, but this first sentence (1) may also imply a warning about the great responsibilities involved. The writer proceeds to list the qualifications required: personal stability and graciousness; talent for teaching (2); moderation in habits and temperament (3); managerial ability (4); and experience in Christian living (5–6). Moreover, the candidate's previous life should provide no grounds for the charge that he did not previously practice what he now preaches. No list of qualifications for presbyters appears in 1 Timothy. The presbyter-bishops here and in Titus (see the note on Ti 1, 5–9) lack certain functions reserved here for Paul and Timothy.

3, 1: *This saying is trustworthy:* the saying introduced is so unlike others after this phrase that some later Western manuscripts read,

---

2, 3: 1 Tm 1, 1; 4, 10.
2, 4: 2 Tm 3, 7; 2 Pt 3, 9.
2, 5: 1 Cor 8, 6; Heb 8, 6;
    9, 15; 12, 24 / Rom 5,
    15.
2, 6: Mk 10, 45; Gal 1, 4; 2,
    20; Eph 5, 25; Ti 2, 14.
2, 7: Acts 9, 15; 1 Cor 9, 1;
    Gal 2, 7–8.

2, 9: 1 Pt 3, 3–5.
2, 10: 1 Tm 5, 10; 1 Pt 3, 1.
2, 11–12: 1 Cor 14, 34–35.
2, 13: Gn 1, 27; 2, 7.22;
    1 Cor 11, 8–9.
2, 14: Gn 3, 6.13; 2 Cor
    11, 3.
2, 15: 1 Tm 5, 14.
3, 1–7: Ti 1, 6–9.

---

motherhood, provided women persevere in faith and love and holiness, with self-control.

Qualifications of Various Ministers

3 ¹*† This saying is trustworthy:† whoever aspires to the office of bishop desires a noble

did you KNOW?

Women and Cultural Roles

A modern person reading 1 Tm 2, 8–15 may be shocked by the teaching there. A passage like this can be easily misunderstood and even misused against women. It is very important to realize that it is a reflection of women's roles in the ancient world. Whatever her religious background—Jewish, Christian, or pagan—a woman's place was in the home. Women generally married young, had no education, and were not allowed to hold a position of public authority.

The earliest Christian communities gathered in members' homes. In this less public arena, women taught and performed other ministries. As Christianity became more widely accepted, concern for how the church appeared to outsiders grew—including concern about drunken bishops, immodest dress, and women teaching in public. That is probably why the author of First Timothy says, "I do not permit a woman to teach" (2, 12).

Are things different for women in contemporary Christianity? Yes! Society has changed. Today, people in the United States are not scandalized if a woman manages a business, runs for public office, or leads a private foundation. Today, if you ask people to name influential church leaders, Mother Teresa almost always comes up. Think of women you know who are involved in church life. In your own parish or community, for example, there are probably women who are religious education directors, coordinators of youth ministry, or pastoral ministers.

▸ 1 Tm 2, 8–15

task. [2] Therefore, a bishop must be irreproachable, married only once, temperate, self-controlled, decent, hospitable, able to teach, [3]* not a drunkard, not aggressive, but gentle, not contentious, not a lover of money. [4] He must manage his own household well, keeping his children under control with perfect dignity; [5] for if a man does not know how to manage his own household, how can he take care of the church of God? [6]† He should not be a recent convert, so that he may not become conceited and thus incur the devil's punishment. [7]* He must also have a good reputation among outsiders, so that he may not fall into disgrace, the devil's trap.

[8]† Similarly, deacons must be dignified, not deceitful, not addicted to drink, not greedy for sordid gain, [9] holding fast to the mystery of the faith with a clear conscience. [10] Moreover, they should be tested first; then, if there is nothing against them, let them serve as deacons. [11]*† Women, similarly, should be dignified, not slanderers, but temperate and faithful in everything. [12] Deacons may be married only once and must manage their children and their households well. [13] Thus those who serve well as deacons gain good standing and much confidence in their faith in Christ Jesus.

The Mystery of Our Religion

[14]† I am writing you about these matters, although I hope to visit you soon. [15]* But if I should be delayed, you should know how to behave in the household of God, which is the church of the living God, the pillar and foundation of truth. [16]*† Undeniably great is the mystery of devotion,

Who was manifested in the flesh,
vindicated in the spirit,
seen by angels,
proclaimed to the Gentiles,
believed in throughout the world,
taken up in glory.

False Asceticism

4 [1]*† Now the Spirit explicitly says that in the last times some will turn away from the faith by paying attention to deceitful spirits and demonic instructions [2] through the hypocrisy of liars with branded consciences. [3]* They forbid marriage and require abstinence from foods that God created to be received with thanksgiving by those who believe and know the truth. [4]* For everything created by God is good, and nothing is to be rejected when received with thanksgiving, [5]† for it is made holy by the invocation of God in prayer.

Counsel to Timothy

[6]† If you will give these instructions to the brothers, you will be a good minister of Christ Jesus, nourished on the words of the faith and of the sound teaching you have followed. [7]* Avoid profane and silly myths. Train yourself for devotion, [8]* for, while physical training is of limited value, devotion is valuable in every respect, since it holds a promise of life both for the present and for the future. [9]* This saying is trustworthy and deserves full acceptance. [10]*† For this we toil and struggle, because we have set our hope on the living God, who is the savior of all, especially of those who believe.

"This saying is popular." It is understood by some interpreters as concluding the preceding section (2, 8–15). *Bishop:* literally, "overseer"; see the note on Phil 1, 1.

3, 6: *The devil's punishment:* this phrase could mean the punishment once incurred by the devil (objective genitive) or a punishment brought about by the devil (subjective genitive).

3, 8–13: Deacons, besides possessing the virtue of moderation (8), are to be outstanding for their faith (9) and well respected within the community (10). Women in the same role, although some interpreters take them to mean wives of deacons, must be dignified, temperate, dedicated, and not given to malicious talebearing (11). Deacons must have shown stability in marriage and have a good record with their families (12), for such experience prepares them well for the exercise of their ministry on behalf of the community (13). See further the note on Phil 1, 1.

3, 11: *Women:* this seems to refer to women deacons but may possibly mean wives of deacons. The former is preferred because the word is used absolutely; if deacons' wives were meant, a possessive "their" would be expected. Moreover, they are also introduced by the word "similarly," as in v 8; this parallel suggests that they too exercised ecclesiastical functions.

3, 14–16: In case there is some delay in the visit to Timothy at Ephesus planned for the near future, the present letter is being sent on ahead to arm and enlighten him in his task of preserving sound Christian conduct in the Ephesian church. The care he must exercise over this community is required by the profound nature of Christianity. It centers in Christ, appearing in human flesh, vindicated by the holy Spirit; the mystery of his person was revealed to the angels, announced to the Gentiles, and accepted by them in faith. He himself was taken up (through his resurrection and ascension) to the divine glory (16). This passage apparently includes part of a liturgical hymn used among the Christian communities in and around

Ephesus. It consists of three couplets in typical Hebrew balance: flesh-spirit (contrast), seen-proclaimed (complementary), world-glory (contrast).

3, 16: *Who:* the reference is to Christ, who is himself "the mystery of our devotion." Some predominantly Western manuscripts read "which," harmonizing the gender of the pronoun with that of the Greek word for mystery; many later (eighth/ninth century on), predominantly Byzantine manuscripts read "God," possibly for theological reasons.

4, 1–5: Doctrinal deviations from the true Christian message within the church have been prophesied, though the origin of the prophecy is not specified (1–2); cf Acts 20, 29–30. The letter warns against a false asceticism that prohibits marriage and regards certain foods as forbidden, though they are part of God's good creation (3).

4, 5: *The invocation of God in prayer:* literally, "the word of God and petition." The use of "word of God" without an article in Greek suggests that it refers to the name of God being invoked in blessing rather than to the "word of God" proclaimed to the community.

4, 6–10: Timothy is urged to be faithful, both in his teaching and in his own life, as he looks only to God for salvation.

4, 10: *Struggle:* other manuscripts and patristic witnesses read "suffer reproach."

3, 3: Heb 13, 5.
3, 7: 2 Cor 8, 21; 2 Tm 2, 26.
3, 11: Ti 2, 3.
3, 15: Eph 2, 19–22.
3, 16: Jn 1, 14; Rom 1, 3–4.
4, 1: 2 Tm 3, 1; 4, 3; 2 Pt 3, 3; Jude 18.
4, 3: Gn 9, 3; Rom 14, 6; 1 Cor 10, 30–31.
4, 4: Gn 1, 31; Acts 10, 15.
4, 7: 1 Tm 1, 4; 2 Tm 2, 16; Ti 1, 14.
4, 8: 1 Tm 6, 6.
4, 9: 1 Tm 1, 15; 2 Tm 2, 11; Ti 3, 8.
4, 10: 1 Tm 2, 4; Ti 2, 11.

Training for Christ

We spend countless hours in training to become better athletes, musicians, scientists, teachers, electricians; you name it, we train for it if we want to be good at it. Paul says the soul needs that same kind of training.

In your journal or on a piece of paper, make two columns, one to list the ways you train for your sporting event or other activity and the other to list ways you might train your soul to become a more loving person, in the image of Jesus. Once you have completed your lists, put them in a place where you can see them every day. Use them as a guide and as a reminder to continue in your efforts to train for Christ. You may also find that you need to keep adding to your soul-training list as your training starts to pay off!

▸ I Tm 4, 7–10

11† Command and teach these things. 12*† Let no one have contempt for your youth, but set an example for those who believe, in speech, conduct, love, faith, and purity. 13† Until I arrive, attend to the reading, exhortation, and teaching. 14*† Do not neglect the gift you have, which was conferred on you through the prophetic word with the imposition of hands of the presbyterate. 15 Be diligent in these matters, be absorbed in them, so that your progress may be evident to everyone. 16 Attend to yourself and to your teaching; persevere in both tasks, for by doing so you will save both yourself and those who listen to you.

IV: Duties toward Others

5 1*† Do not rebuke an older man, but appeal to him as a father. Treat younger men as brothers, 2 older women as mothers, and younger women as sisters with complete purity.

Rules for Widows

3 Honor widows who are truly widows. 4 But if a widow has children or grandchildren, let these first learn to perform their religious duty to their own family and to make recompense to their parents, for this is pleasing to God. 5* The real widow, who is all alone, has set her hope on God and continues in supplications and prayers night and day. 6 But the one who is self-indulgent is dead while she lives. 7 Command this, so that they may be irreproachable. 8 And whoever does not provide for relatives and especially family members has denied the faith and is worse than an unbeliever.

9 Let a widow be enrolled if she is not less than sixty years old, married only once, 10* with a reputation for good works, namely, that she has raised children, practiced hospitality, washed the feet of the holy ones, helped those in distress, involved herself in every good work. 11 But exclude younger widows, for when their sensuality estranges them from Christ, they want to marry 12 and will incur condemnation for breaking their first pledge. 13* And furthermore, they learn to be idlers, going about from house to house, and not only idlers but gossips and busybodies as well, talking about

---

4, 11–16: Timothy is urged to preach and teach with confidence, relying on the gifts and the mission that God has bestowed on him.

4, 12: *Youth:* some commentators find this reference a sign of pseudepigraphy. Timothy had joined Paul as a missionary already in A.D. 49, some fifteen years before the earliest supposed date of composition.

4, 13: *Reading:* the Greek word refers to private or public reading. Here, it probably designates the public reading of scripture in the Christian assembly.

4, 14: *Prophetic word:* this may mean the utterance of a Christian prophet designating the candidate or a prayer of blessing accompanying the rite. *Imposition of hands:* this gesture was used in the Old Testament to signify the transmission of authority from Moses to Joshua (Nm 27, 18–23; Dt 34, 9). The early Christian community used it as a symbol of installation into an office: the Seven (Acts 6, 6) and Paul and Barnabas (Acts 13, 3). *Of the presbyterate:* this would mean that each member of the college of presbyters imposed hands and appears to contradict 2 Tm 1, 6, in which Paul says that he imposed hands on Timothy. This latter text, however, does not exclude participation by others in the rite. Some prefer to translate "for the presbyterate," and thus understand it to designate the office

into which Timothy was installed rather than the agents who installed him.

5, 1–16: After a few words of general advice based on common sense (1–2), the letter takes up, in its several aspects, the subject of widows. The first responsibility for their care belongs to the family circle, not to the Christian community as such (3–4.16). The widow left without the aid of relatives may benefit the community by her prayer, and the community should consider her material sustenance its responsibility (5–8). Widows who wish to work directly for the Christian community should not be accepted unless they are well beyond the probability of marriage, i.e., sixty years of age, married only once, and with a reputation for good works (9–10). Younger widows are apt to be troublesome and should be encouraged to remarry (11–15).

4, 12: 1 Cor 16, 11; Ti 2, 15 / Phil 3, 17.
4, 14: 1 Tm 5, 22; Acts 6, 6; 8, 17; 2 Tm 1, 6.
5, 1: Lv 19, 32; Ti 2, 2.
5, 5: Jer 49, 11; Lk 2, 37; 18, 7.
5, 10: Jn 13, 14; Heb 13, 2.
5, 13: 2 Thes 3, 11.

things that ought not to be mentioned. [14]* So I would like younger widows to marry, have children, and manage a home, so as to give the adversary no pretext for maligning us. [15] For some have already turned away to follow Satan. [16]† If any woman believer has widowed relatives, she must assist them; the church is not to be burdened, so that it will be able to help those who are truly widows.

Rules for Presbyters

[17]*† Presbyters who preside well deserve double honor, especially those who toil in preaching and teaching. [18]* For the scripture says, "You shall not muzzle an ox when it is threshing," and, "A worker deserves his pay." [19]* Do not accept an accusation against a presbyter unless it is supported by two or three witnesses. [20]* Reprimand publicly those who

Let no one have contempt for your **youth,** but set an example for those who believe, in speech, conduct, love, faith, and purity

4, 12

do sin, so that the rest also will be afraid. [21] I charge you before God and Christ Jesus and the elect angels to keep these rules without prejudice, doing nothing out of favoritism. [22]* Do not lay hands too readily on anyone, and do not share in another's sins. Keep yourself pure. [23] Stop drinking only water, but have a little wine for the sake of your stomach and your frequent illnesses.

[24] Some people's sins are public, preceding them to judgment; but other people are followed by their sins. [25] Similarly, good works are also public; and even those that are not cannot remain hidden.

Rules for Slaves

6 [1]*† Those who are under the yoke of slavery must regard their masters as worthy of full respect, so that the name of God and our teaching† may not suffer abuse. [2]*† Those whose masters are believers must not take advantage of them because they are brothers but must give better service because those who will profit from their work are believers and are beloved.

V: False Teaching and True Wealth

Teach and urge these things. [3]* Whoever teaches something different and does not agree with the sound words of our Lord Jesus Christ and the religious teaching [4] is conceited, understanding nothing, and has a morbid disposition for arguments and verbal disputes. From these come envy, rivalry, insults, evil suspicions, [5]* and mutual friction among people with corrupted minds, who are deprived of the truth, supposing religion to be a means of gain. [6]*† Indeed, religion with contentment is a great gain. [7]* For we brought nothing into the world, just as we shall not be able to take

---

5, 16: *Woman believer:* some early Latin manuscripts and Fathers have a masculine here, while most later manuscripts and patristic quotations conflate the two readings, perhaps to avoid unfair restriction to women.

5, 17–25: The function of presbyters is not exactly the same as that of the *episkopos,* "bishop" (3, 1); in fact, the relation of the two at the time of this letter is obscure (but cf the note on Ti 1, 5–9). The Pastorals seem to reflect a transitional stage that developed in many regions of the church into the monarchical episcopate of the second and third centuries. The presbyters possess the responsibility of preaching and teaching, for which functions they are supported by the community (17–18). The realization that their position subjects them to adverse criticism is implied in the direction to Timothy (19–20) to make sure of the truth of any accusation against them before public reproof is given. He must be as objective as possible in weighing charges against presbyters (21), learning from his experience to take care in selecting them (22). Some scholars take v 22 as a reference not to ordination of presbyters but to reconciliation of public sinners. The letter now sounds an informal note of personal concern in its advice to Timothy not to be so ascetic that he even avoids wine (23). Judgment concerning the fitness of candidates to serve as presbyters is easy with persons of open conduct, more difficult and prolonged with those of greater reserve (24–25).

6, 1–2: Compare the tables for household duties, such as that of Col 3, 18—4, 1. Domestic relationships derive new meaning from the Christian faith.

6, 1: *Our teaching:* this refers to the teaching of the Christian community.

6, 2b–10: Timothy is exhorted to maintain steadfastly the position outlined in this letter, not allowing himself to be pressured into any other course. He must realize that false teachers can be discerned by their pride, envy, quarrelsomeness, and greed for material gain. Verse 6 is rather obscure and is interpreted, and therefore translated, variously. The suggestion seems to be that the important gain that religion brings is spiritual, but that there is material gain, too, up to the point of what is needed for physical sustenance (cf 17–19).

6, 6: *Contentment:* the word *autarkeia* is a technical Greek philosophical term for the virtue of independence from material goods (Aristotle, Cynics, Stoics).

5, 14: 1 Cor 7, 9.	**6, 1:** Eph 6, 5; Ti 2, 9–10.
5, 17: 1 Cor 16, 18; Phil 2, 29.	**6, 2:** Phlm 16.
5, 18: Dt 25, 4; 1 Cor 9, 8 / Mt 10, 10; Lk 10, 7.	**6, 3:** Gal 1, 6–9; 2 Tm 1, 13; Ti 1, 1.
5, 19: Dt 17, 6; 19, 15; Mt 18, 16; 2 Cor 13, 1.	**6, 5:** 2 Tm 3, 8; 4, 4; Ti 1, 14.
5, 20: Gal 2, 14; Eph 5, 11; 2 Tm 4, 2; Ti 1, 9.13.	**6, 6:** 1 Tm 4, 8; Phil 4, 11–12; Heb 13, 5.
5, 22: 1 Tm 4, 14; 2 Tm 1, 6.	**6, 7:** Jb 1, 21; Eccl 5, 14.

Dangers of Money

We live in a culture that glorifies material things, money, and consumption. People are generally thought to be successful if they have great riches and all the luxury items to prove it to their neighbors. There is a bumper sticker that reads, The one who dies with the most toys wins! Even when individuals or families have the essential things to live comfortably, many are driven to acquire more.

An important truth found many places in the Scriptures (see, for example, Lk 12, 20) is repeated here: You can't take it with you. The Scriptures warn about something that most of us know deep down but often ignore: "The love of money is the root of all evils," and in our eagerness to become financially rich, we usually lose sight of God and become entangled in all kinds of senseless distractions (1 Tm 6, 10).

All of us need the basic stuff of life: food, clothing, and shelter. God wants us to have these things—and more! Ultimately, real riches or success will not be measured by bank accounts or material things, but by the love and generosity with which we have lived. How rich are you becoming in these things?

▸ 1 Tm 6, 6–10

anything out of it. [8]* If we have food and clothing, we shall be content with that. [9]* Those who want to be rich are falling into temptation and into a trap and into many foolish and harmful desires, which plunge them into ruin and destruction. [10] For the love of money is the root of all evils, and some people in their desire for it have strayed from the faith and have pierced themselves with many pains.

Exhortations to Timothy†

[11]* But you, man of God,† avoid all this. Instead, pursue righteousness, devotion, faith, love, patience, and gentleness. [12]* Compete well for the faith. Lay hold of eternal life, to which you were called when you made the noble confession in the presence of many witnesses. [13]* I charge [you] before God, who gives life to all things, and before Christ Jesus, who gave testimony under Pontius Pilate for the noble confession, [14] to keep the commandment without stain or reproach until the appearance of our Lord Jesus Christ [15]* that the blessed and only ruler will make manifest at the proper time, the King of kings and Lord of lords,

[16]* who alone has immortality, who dwells in unapproachable light, and whom no human being has seen or can see. To him be honor and eternal power. Amen.

Right Use of Wealth

[17]*† Tell the rich in the present age not to be proud and not to rely on so uncertain a thing as wealth but rather on God, who richly provides us with all things for our enjoyment. [18] Tell them to do good, to be rich in good works, to be generous, ready to share, [19]* thus accumulating as treasure a good foundation for the future, so as to win the life that is true life.

VI: Final Recommendation and Warning

[20]*† O Timothy, guard what has been entrusted to you. Avoid profane babbling and the absurdities of so-called knowledge. [21]* By professing it, some people have deviated from the faith.

Grace be with all of you.

---

†

6, 11–16: Timothy's position demands total dedication to God and faultless witness to Christ (11–14) operating from an awareness, through faith, of the coming revelation of Jesus of the invisible God (15–16).

6, 11: *Man of God:* a title applied to Moses and the prophets (Dt 33, 1; 1 Sm 2, 27; 1 Kgs 12, 22; 13, 1; etc.).

6, 17–19: Timothy is directed to instruct the rich, advising them to make good use of their wealth by aiding the poor.

6, 20–21: A final solemn warning against the heretical teachers, with what seems to be a specific reference to gnosticism, the great rival and enemy of the church for two centuries and more (the Greek word for "knowledge" is *gnōsis*). If gnosticism is being referred to here, it is probable that the warnings against "speculations" and "myths and genealogies" (cf especially 1, 4; Ti 3, 9) involve allusions

to that same kind of heresy. Characteristic of the various gnostic systems of speculation was an elaborate mythology of innumerable superhuman intermediaries, on a descending scale ("genealogies"), between God and the world. Thus would be explained the emphasis upon Christ's being the *one* mediator (as in 2, 5). Although fully developed gnosticism belonged to the second and later centuries, there are signs that incipient forms of it belonged to Paul's own period.

6, 8: Prv 30, 8.
6, 9: Prv 23, 4; 28, 22.
6, 11: 2 Tm 2, 22.
6, 12: 1 Cor 9, 26; 2 Tm 4, 7.
6, 13: Jn 18, 36–37; 19, 11.
6, 15: 2 Mc 13, 4; Rv 17, 14.
6, 16: Ex 33, 20; Ps 104, 2.
6, 17: Ps 62, 11; Lk 12, 20.
6, 19: Mt 6, 20.
6, 20: 2 Tm 1, 14 / 1 Tm 4, 7.
6, 21: 1 Tm 1, 6; 2 Tm 2, 18.

2 Timothy

For background on this letter, see the introduction to the pastoral letters, before 1 Timothy.

I: Address

Greeting†

1 ¹* Paul, an apostle of Christ Jesus by the will of God for the promise of life in Christ Jesus,† ² to Timothy, my dear child: grace, mercy, and peace from God the Father and Christ Jesus our Lord.

Thanksgiving

³*† I am grateful to God, whom I worship with a clear conscience as my ancestors did, as I remember you constantly in my prayers, night and day. ⁴† I yearn to see you again, recalling your tears, so that I may be filled with joy, ⁵* as I recall your sincere faith that first lived in your grandmother Lois and in your mother Eunice and that I am confident lives also in you.

II: Exhortations to Timothy

The Gifts Timothy Has Received

⁶*† For this reason, I remind you to stir into flame the gift of God that you have through the imposition of my hands. ⁷* For God did not give us a spirit of cowardice but rather of power and love and self-control. ⁸*† So do not be ashamed of your testimony to our Lord, nor of me, a prisoner for his sake; but bear your share of hardship for the gospel with the strength that comes from God.

⁹*† He saved us and called us to a holy life, not according to our works but according to his own design and the grace bestowed on us in Christ Jesus before time began, ¹⁰* but now made manifest through the appearance of our savior Christ Jesus, who destroyed death and brought life and immortality to light

---

† **1, 1–2:** For the formula of address and greeting, see the note on Rom 1, 1–7.

1, 1: *The promise of life in Christ Jesus:* that God grants through union with Christ in faith and love; cf Col 3, 4; 1 Tm 4, 8.

1, 3: *As my ancestors did:* this emphasizes the continuity of Judaism and Christianity; for a similar view, see Rom 9, 3–5; Phil 3, 4–6.

1, 4–5: Purportedly written from prison in Rome (8.17; 4, 6–8) shortly before the writer's death, the letter recalls the earlier sorrowful parting from Timothy, commending him for his faith and expressing the longing to see him again.

1, 6: *The gift of God:* the grace resulting from the conferral of an ecclesiastical office. *The imposition of my hands:* see the note on 1 Tm 4, 14.

1, 8: *Do not be ashamed of your testimony to our Lord:* i.e., of preaching and suffering for the sake of the gospel.

1, 9–10: Redemption from sin and the call to holiness of life are not won by personal deeds but are freely and graciously bestowed according to God's eternal plan; cf Eph 1, 4.

*
1, 1: 1 Tm 4, 8.	**1, 9:** Eph 2, 8–9; Ti 3, 5 /
1, 3: 1 Tm 3, 9 / Phil 3, 5.	Eph 1, 4; Ti 1, 2.
1, 5: 1 Tm 1, 5 / Acts 16, 1.	**1, 10:** Rom 16, 26; 1 Pt 1, 20
1, 6: 1 Tm 4, 14; 5, 22 /	/ 1 Tm 6, 14 / Phil 3,
Acts 6, 2; 8, 17.	20; Ti 1, 4; 2, 13; 2 Pt
1, 7: Rom 5, 5; 8, 15; 1 Cor	1, 11 / 1 Cor 15,
2, 4.	54–55; Heb 2, 14 /
1, 8: 2 Tm 2, 3.15; Rom 1,	1 Cor 15, 53–54.
16.	

Do Not Be Ashamed

Terry is a popular guy in the senior class. He is on the basketball and track teams and served on student council. He is extremely friendly and never says anything bad about anyone. Everyone likes him.

Terry is also very active in his church's youth group. He is not afraid to let others know that church is important to him. He never preaches religion, but he lets people know that church and Jesus are central to his life.

The author of 2 Timothy encourages readers, "So do not be ashamed of your testimony to our Lord" (1, 8). You do not have to announce your faith from mountaintops or from street corners, but like Terry, you should not be afraid to admit that God is important to you. You will likely discover that others admire you for your faith and commitment.

▶ 2 Tm 1, 6–18

---

through the gospel, ¹¹*† for which I was appointed preacher and apostle and teacher. ¹²*† On this account I am suffering these things; but I am not ashamed, for I know him in whom I have believed and am confident that he is able to guard what has been entrusted to me until that day. ¹³* Take as your norm the sound words that you heard from me, in the faith and love that are in Christ Jesus. ¹⁴* Guard this rich trust with the help of the holy Spirit that dwells within us.

Paul's Suffering

¹⁵*† You know that everyone in Asia deserted me, including Phygelus and Hermogenes. ¹⁶*† May the Lord grant mercy to the family of Onesiphorus because he often gave me new heart and was not ashamed of my chains. ¹⁷ But when he came to Rome, he promptly searched for me and found me. ¹⁸*† May the Lord grant him to find mercy from the Lord on that day. And you know very well the services he rendered in Ephesus.

Timothy's Conduct

2 ¹† So you, my child, be strong in the grace that is in Christ Jesus. ² And what you heard from me through many witnesses entrust to faithful people who will have the ability to teach others as well. ³* Bear your share of hardship along with me like a good soldier of Christ Jesus. ⁴* To satisfy the one who recruited him, a soldier does not become entangled in the business affairs of life. ⁵* Similarly, an athlete cannot receive the winner's crown except by competing according to the rules. ⁶* The hardworking farmer ought to have the first share of the crop. ⁷* Reflect on what I am saying, for the Lord will give you understanding in everything.

⁸*† Remember Jesus Christ, raised from the dead, a descendant of David: such is my gospel,

---

1, 11: *Teacher:* the overwhelming majority of manuscripts and Fathers read "teacher of the nations," undoubtedly a harmonization with 1 Tm 2, 7.

1, 12: *He is able to guard . . . until that day:* the intervening words can also be translated "what I have entrusted to him" (i.e., the fruit of his ministry) as well as "what has been entrusted to me" (i.e., the faith). The same difficult term occurs in v 14, where it is modified by the adjective "rich" and used without a possessive.

1, 15: Keen disappointment is expressed, here and later (4, 16), that the Christians of the province of Asia, especially Phygelus and Hermogenes, should have abandoned the writer and done nothing to defend his case in court.

1, 16–18: *The family of Onesiphorus because he . . . of my chains:* Onesiphorus seems to have died before this letter was written. His family is mentioned twice (here and in 4, 19), though it was Onesiphorus himself who was helpful to Paul in prison and rendered much service to the community of Ephesus. Because the apostle complains of abandonment by all in Asia during his second imprisonment and trial, the assistance of Onesiphorus seems to have been given to Paul during his first Roman imprisonment (A.D. 61–63).

1, 18: *Lord . . . Lord:* the first "Lord" here seems to refer to Christ, the second "Lord" to the Father.

2, 1–7: This passage manifests a characteristic deep concern for safeguarding the faith and faithfully transmitting it through trustworthy people (1–2; cf 1, 14; 1 Tm 6, 20; Ti 1, 9). Comparisons to the soldier's detachment, the athlete's sportsmanship, and the farmer's arduous work as the price of recompense (4–6) emphasize the need of singleness of purpose in preaching the word, even at the cost of hardship, for the sake of Christ (3).

2, 8–13: The section begins with a sloganlike summary of Paul's gospel about Christ (8) and concludes with what may be part of an early Christian hymn (11b–12a; most exegetes include the rest of v 12 and all of v 13 as part of the quotation). The poetic lines suggest that through baptism Christians die spiritually with Christ and hope to live with him and reign with him forever, but the Christian life includes endurance, witness, and even suffering, as the final judgment will show and as Paul's own case makes clear; while he is imprisoned for preaching the gospel (9), his sufferings are helpful to the elect for obtaining the salvation and glory available in Christ (10), who will be true to those who are faithful and will disown those who deny him (12–13).

1, 11: 1 Tm 2, 7.
1, 12: 1 Pt 4, 16 / 1 Tm 1, 10–11.
1, 13: 1 Tm 1, 14.
1, 14: 1 Tm 6, 20 / Rom 8, 11.
1, 15: 2 Tm 4, 16.
1, 16: 2 Tm 4, 19.
1, 18: Jude 21.

2, 3: 2 Tm 1, 8; 4, 5; Phlm 2.
2, 4: 1 Cor 9, 6.
2, 5: 1 Cor 9, 25.
2, 6: 1 Cor 9, 7–10.
2, 7: Prv 2, 6.
2, 8: Rom 1, 3; 1 Cor 15, 4.20 / Rom 2, 16; Gal 1, 11; 2, 2.

9* for which I am suffering, even to the point of chains, like a criminal. But the word of God is not chained. 10* Therefore, I bear with everything for the sake of those who are chosen, so that they too may obtain the salvation that is in Christ Jesus, together with eternal glory. 11* This saying is trustworthy:

If we have died with him
we shall also live with him;
12* if we persevere
we shall also reign with him.
But if we deny him
he will deny us.
13* If we are unfaithful
he remains faithful,
for he cannot deny himself.

III: Instructions Concerning False Teaching

Warning against Useless Disputes

14*† Remind people of these things and charge them before God† to stop disputing about words. This serves no useful purpose since it harms those who listen. 15* Be eager to present yourself as acceptable to God, a workman who causes no disgrace, imparting the word of truth without deviation. 16* Avoid profane, idle talk, for such people will become more and more godless, 17* and their teaching will spread like gangrene. Among them are Hymenaeus and Philetus, 18* who have deviated from the truth by saying that [the] resurrection has already taken place and are upsetting the faith of some. 19* Nevertheless, God's solid foundation stands, bearing this inscription, "The Lord knows those who are his"; and, "Let everyone who calls upon the name of the Lord avoid evil."

20 In a large household there are vessels not only of gold and silver but also of wood and clay, some for lofty and others for humble use. 21* If anyone cleanses himself of these things, he will be a vessel for lofty use, dedicated, beneficial to the master of the house, ready for every good work. 22*† So turn from youthful desires and pursue righteousness, faith, love, and peace, along with those who call on the Lord with purity of heart. 23* Avoid foolish and ignorant debates, for you know that they breed quarrels. 24* A slave of the Lord should not quarrel, but should be gentle with everyone, able to teach, tolerant, 25* correcting opponents with kindness. It may be that God will grant them repentance that leads to knowledge of the truth, 26*† and that they may return to their senses out of the devil's snare, where they are entrapped by him, for his will.

Teaching Others   LIVE IT!

Have you ever tried to explain to someone something about your faith? That can be challenging. Second Timothy 2, 22–26 contains some tips on sharing faith with others: Avoid senseless controversies. Be kind, patient, and gentle. And be an apt teacher, that is, someone who is qualified or prepared.

Imagine that you are helping to teach a group of younger people about their faith. What do you want to say about God? How do you explain Jesus' love? How do you show your patience and gentleness? If you can answer these questions, maybe you should volunteer to help with your church's religious education program!

▸ 2 Tm 2, 22–26

---

† 2, 14–19: For those who dispute about mere words (cf 23–24) and indulge in irreligious talk to the detriment of their listeners (16–19), see the notes on 1 Tm 1, 3–7; 6, 20–21. Hymenaeus and Philetus (17), while accepting the Christian's mystical death and resurrection in Christ through baptism, claimed that baptized Christians are already risen with Christ in this life and thus that there is no future bodily resurrection or eternal glory to come. The first quotation in v 19 is from Nm 16, 5; the other quotation is from some unidentified Jewish or Christian writing.

2, 14: *Before God:* many ancient manuscripts read "before the Lord."

2, 22: *Those who call on the Lord:* those who believe in Christ and worship him as Lord, i.e., Christians (Acts 9, 14–16.20–21; Rom 10, 12–13; cf 19, literally, "Everyone who names the name of the Lord").

2, 26: Some interpreters would render this passage, "Thus they may come to their senses and, forced to do his (i.e., God's) will, may escape the devil's trap." This interpretation of the Greek is possible, but the one accepted in the text seems more likely.

* 2, 9: Phil 1, 12–14.
2, 10: Col 1, 24; 1 Tm 1, 15.
2, 11: Rom 6, 8.
2, 12: Mt 10, 22.33; Lk 12, 9.
2, 13: Nm 23, 19; Rom 3, 3–4; 1 Cor 10, 13; Ti 1, 2.
2, 14: 1 Tm 6, 4.
2, 15: 2 Tm 1, 8; 2 Cor 6, 7; Eph 1, 13; Col 1, 5.
2, 16: 1 Tm 4, 7.
2, 17: 1 Tm 1, 20.
2, 18: 2 Thes 2, 2.
2, 19: Is 28, 16; 1 Cor 3, 10–15 / Nm 16, 5; Jn 10, 14.
2, 21: 2 Tm 3, 17.
2, 22: Gal 5, 22; 1 Tm 6, 11 / Rom 10, 13; 1 Cor 1, 2.
2, 23: 1 Tm 1, 4; 4, 7; 6, 4; Ti 3, 9.
2, 24: 1 Tm 3, 2–3.
2, 25: 2 Tm 3, 7; 1 Tm 2, 4.
2, 26: 1 Tm 3, 7.

2
T
M

The Dangers of the Last Days

3 ¹*† But understand this: there will be terrifying times in the last days. ²* People will be self-centered and lovers of money, proud, haughty, abusive, disobedient to their parents, ungrateful, irreligious, ³ callous, implacable, slanderous, licentious, brutal, hating what is good, ⁴ traitors, reckless, conceited, lovers of pleasure rather than lovers of God, ⁵* as they make a pretense of religion but deny its power. Reject them. ⁶* For some of these slip into homes and make captives of women weighed down by sins, led by various desires, ⁷* always trying to learn but never able to reach a knowledge of the truth. ⁸* Just as Jannes and Jambres opposed Moses, so they also oppose the truth—people of depraved mind, unqualified in the faith. ⁹ But they will not make further progress, for their foolishness will be plain to all, as it was with those two.

Paul's Example and Teaching

¹⁰† You have followed my teaching, way of life, purpose, faith, patience, love, endurance, ¹¹* persecutions, and sufferings, such as happened to me in Antioch, Iconium, and Lystra, persecutions that I endured. Yet from all these things the Lord delivered me. ¹²* In fact, all who want to live religiously in Christ Jesus will be persecuted. ¹³ But wicked people and charlatans will go from bad to worse, deceivers and deceived. ¹⁴* But you, remain faithful to what you have learned and believed, because you know from whom you learned it, ¹⁵* and that from infancy you have known [the] sacred scriptures, which are capable of giving you wisdom for salvation through faith in Christ Jesus. ¹⁶*† All scripture is inspired by God and is useful for teaching, for refutation, for correction, and for training in righteousness,† ¹⁷* so that one who belongs to God may be competent, equipped for every good work.

For Those Who Walk with Us

We pray, Lord, for those who formed us in our faith.
We pray for our families who first spoke your name to us and shared our journey of faith from the beginning.
We pray for our friends who shared their faith and continue to walk with us in our journey.
We pray for the teachers, priests, youth ministers, and other members of our church who took the time to recognize us as individuals and who showed us that faith can be both fun and challenging.
Thank you, God, for sending these people into our lives and for their gifts of faith, love, and patience. May we honor them by sharing our faith with a new generation of believers. We pray this in Jesus' name. Amen.

▸ 2 Tm 3, 12–14

Solemn Charge

4 ¹*† I charge you in the presence of God and of Christ Jesus, who will judge the living and the dead, and by his appearing and his kingly power: ²* proclaim the word; be persistent whether it is convenient or inconvenient; convince, reprimand, encourage through all patience and teaching. ³*† For the time will come when people will not tolerate sound doctrine but, following their own

---

† **3, 1–9:** The moral depravity and false teaching that will be rampant in the last days are already at work (1–5). The frivolous and superficial, too, devoid of the true spirit of religion, will be easy victims of those who pervert them by falsifying the truth (6–8), just as Jannes and Jambres, Pharaoh's magicians of Egypt (Ex 7, 11–12.22), discredited the truth in Moses' time. Exodus does not name the magicians, but the two names are widely found in much later Jewish, Christian, and even pagan writings. Their origins are legendary.

3, 10–17: Paul's example for Timothy includes persecution, a frequent emphasis in the Pastorals. Timothy is to be steadfast to what he has been taught and to scripture. The scriptures are the source of wisdom, i.e., of belief in and loving fulfillment of God's word revealed in Christ, through whom salvation is given.

3, 16: *All scripture is inspired by God:* this could possibly also be translated, "All scripture inspired by God is useful for . . . ." In this classic reference to inspiration, God is its principal author, with the writer as the human collaborator. Thus the scriptures are the word of God in human language. See also 2 Pt 1, 20–21.

3, 16–17: *Useful for teaching . . . every good work:* because as God's word the scriptures share his divine authority. It is exercised through those who are ministers of the word.

4, 1–5: The gravity of the obligation incumbent on Timothy to preach the word can be gauged from the solemn adjuration: in the presence of God, and of Christ coming as universal judge, and by his appearance and *his kingly power* (1). Patience, courage, constancy, and endurance are required despite the opposition, hostility, indifference, and defection of many to whom the truth has been preached (2–5).

4, 3: *Insatiable curiosity:* literally, "with itching ears."

*
3, 1: 1 Tm 4, 1; 2 Pt 3, 3; Jude 18.
3, 2–4: Rom 1, 29–31.
3, 5: Rom 2, 20–22; Ti 1, 16.
3, 6: Ti 1, 11.
3, 7: 2 Tm 2, 25.
3, 8: Ex 7, 11.22; 1 Tm 6, 5.
3, 11: Acts 13, 50; 14, 5.19 / Ps 34, 20.
3, 12: Jn 15, 20; Acts 14, 22.
3, 14: 2 Tm 2, 2.
3, 15: Jn 5, 39.
3, 16: Rom 15, 4; 2 Pt 1, 19–21.
3, 17: 2 Tm 2, 21.
4, 1: 1 Tm 5, 21; 6, 14 / Acts 10, 42; Rom 14, 9–10; 1 Pt 4, 5.
4, 2: Acts 20, 30.31; 1 Tm 5, 20.
4, 3: 1 Tm 4, 1.

All scripture is (inspired) by God and is useful for teaching, for refutation, for correction, and for training in righteousness

3, 16

Reward for Fidelity

⁶*† For I am already being poured out like a libation, and the time of my departure is at hand. ⁷*† I have competed well; I have finished the race; I have kept the faith. ⁸*† From now on the crown of righteousness awaits me, which the Lord, the just judge, will award to me on that day, and not only to me, but to all who have longed for his appearance.

IV: Personal Requests and Final Greetings

Paul's Loneliness

⁹† Try to join me soon, ¹⁰*† for Demas, enamored of the present world, deserted me and went to Thessalonica, Crescens to Galatia, and Titus to Dalmatia. ¹¹* Luke is the only one with me. Get Mark and bring him with you, for he is helpful to me in the ministry. ¹²* I have sent Tychicus to Ephesus. ¹³* When you come, bring the cloak I left with Carpus in Troas, the papyrus rolls, and especially the parchments.

¹⁴*† Alexander the coppersmith did me a great

desires and insatiable curiosity, will accumulate teachers ⁴* and will stop listening to the truth and will be diverted to myths. ⁵ But you, be self-possessed in all circumstances; put up with hardship; perform the work of an evangelist; fulfill your ministry.

Misleading Messages

LIVE IT!

Sticking with something can be difficult. When things get tough, many people are tempted to quit or walk away. If swim practice is boring, they drop off the team. If personalities on a committee are difficult, they drop out. If marriage loses its spark, they leave. We are surrounded by messages like "If it feels good, do it," and "You should have whatever your heart desires," and "Life will be great if you wear these clothes" or "drink this beverage" or "hang out with these people."

But reaching a worthy goal often requires hard choices and hard work. Second Timothy 4, 1–5 warns us against being taken in by deceptive teachers or messages—like cultural teachings that life should always be easy and pleasurable. Such teachings water down the real challenge of living as a follower of Jesus Christ! If we are not finding life to be challenging, maybe we have tuned in to these misleading messages.

▶ 2 Tm 4, 1–5

---

†

4, 6: The apostle recognizes his death through martyrdom to be imminent. He regards it as an act of worship in which his blood will be poured out in sacrifice; cf Ex 29, 38–40; Phil 2, 17.

4, 7: At the close of his life Paul could testify to the accomplishment of what Christ himself foretold concerning him at the time of his conversion, "I will show him what he will have to suffer for my name" (Acts 9, 16).

4, 8: When the world is judged at the parousia, all who have eagerly looked for the Lord's appearing and have sought to live according to his teachings will be rewarded. The crown is a reference to the laurel wreath placed on the heads of victorious athletes and conquerors in war; cf 2, 5; 1 Cor 9, 25.

4, 9–13: Demas either abandoned the work of the ministry for worldly affairs or, perhaps, gave up the faith itself (10). Luke (11) may have accompanied Paul on parts of his second and third missionary journeys (Acts 16, 10–12; 20, 5–7). Notice the presence of the first person pronoun "we" in these Acts passages, suggesting to some that Luke (or at least some traveling companion of Paul's) was the author of Acts. Mark, once rejected by Paul (Acts 13, 13; 15, 39), is

now to render him a great service (11); cf Col 4, 10; Phlm 24. For Tychicus, see Eph 6, 21; cf also Acts 20, 4; Col 4, 7.

4, 10: *Galatia:* some manuscripts read "Gaul" or "Gallia."

4, 14–18: *Alexander:* an opponent of Paul's preaching (14–15), perhaps the one who is mentioned in 1 Tm 1, 20. Despite Paul's abandonment by his friends in the province of Asia (cf 1, 15–16), the divine assistance brought this first trial to a successful issue, even to the point of making the gospel message known to those who participated in or witnessed the trial (16–17).

*

4, 4: 1 Tm 1, 4; 4, 7; Ti 1, 14.
4, 6: Phil 2, 17.
4, 7: 1 Tm 1, 18; 6, 12; Jude 3 / Acts 20, 24; 1 Cor 9, 24; Heb 12, 1.
4, 8: 2 Tm 2, 5; Wis 5, 16; 1 Cor 9, 25; Phil 3, 14; Jas 1, 12; 1 Pt 5, 4; Rv 2, 10.
4, 10: Col 4, 14; Phlm 24 /

2 Cor 2, 13; 7, 6–7; 8, 23; Gal 2, 3; Ti 1, 4.
4, 11: Col 4, 14; Phlm 24 / Col 4, 10; Phlm 24.
4, 12: Acts 20, 4; Eph 6, 21; Col 4, 7.
4, 13: Acts 16, 8; 20, 6.
4, 14: 1 Tm 1, 20 / 2 Sm 3, 39; Pss 28, 4; 62, 12; Prv 24, 12; Rom 2, 6.

deal of harm; the Lord will repay him according to his deeds. 15 You too be on guard against him, for he has strongly resisted our preaching.

16* At my first defense no one appeared on my behalf, but everyone deserted me. May it not be held against them! 17* But the Lord stood by me and gave me strength, so that through me the proclamation might be completed and all the Gentiles might hear it. And I was rescued from the lion's mouth. 18* The Lord will rescue me from every evil threat and will bring me safe to his heavenly kingdom. To him be glory forever and ever. Amen.

Final Greeting

19*† Greet Prisca and Aquila and the family of Onesiphorus. 20*† Erastus remained in Corinth, while I left Trophimus sick at Miletus. 21† Try to get here before winter. Eubulus, Pudens, Linus, Claudia, and all the brothers send greetings.

22* The Lord be with your spirit. Grace be with all of you.

4, 19: *Prisca and Aquila:* they assisted Paul in his ministry in Corinth (Acts 18, 2–3) and Ephesus (Acts 18, 19.26; 1 Cor 16, 19). They risked death to save his life, and all the Gentile communities are indebted to them (Rom 16, 3–5).

4, 20: *Erastus:* he was the treasurer of the city of Corinth (Rom 16, 24); cf also Acts 19, 22. *Trophimus:* from the province of Asia, he accompanied Paul from Greece to Troas (Acts 20, 4–5).

4, 21: *Linus:* Western tradition sometimes identified this Linus with the supposed successor of Peter as bishop of Rome, and Claudia as the mother of Linus (*Apostolic Constitutions,* fourth century).

4, 16: 2 Tm 1, 15.
4, 17: Acts 23, 11; 27, 23;
  Phil 4, 13 / 1 Mc 2,
  60; Ps 22, 22; Dn 6,
  23.
4, 18: 2 Cor 1, 10 / Rom 16,
  27.
4, 19: Acts 18, 2; Rom 16, 3;

1 Cor 16, 19 / 2 Tm 1,
  16.
4, 20: Acts 19, 22; Rom 16,
  24 / Acts 20, 4; 21, 29.
4, 22: Gal 6, 18; Phil 4, 23;
  Col 4, 18; 1 Tm 6, 21;
  Ti 3, 15.

For background on this letter, see the introduction
to the pastoral letters, before I Timothy.

I: Address

Greeting

1 [1]*† Paul, a slave of God and apostle of Jesus
Christ for the sake of the faith of God's chosen
ones and the recognition of religious truth, [2]* in
the hope of eternal life that God, who does not lie,
promised before time began, [3]* who indeed at the
proper time revealed his word in the proclamation
with which I was entrusted by the command of God
our savior, [4]* to Titus, my true child in our common faith: grace and peace from God the Father
and Christ Jesus our savior.

II: Pastoral Charge

Titus in Crete

[5]† For this reason I left you in Crete so that you
might set right what remains to be done and ap-

point presbyters in every town, as I directed you,
[6]* on condition that a man be blameless, married
only once, with believing children who are not accused of licentiousness or rebellious. [7] For a bishop
as God's steward must be blameless, not arrogant,
not irritable, not a drunkard, not aggressive, not
greedy for sordid gain, [8] but hospitable, a lover of
goodness, temperate, just, holy, and self-controlled,
[9]* holding fast to the true message as taught so that
he will be able both to exhort with sound doctrine
and to refute opponents. [10]† For there are also
many rebels, idle talkers and deceivers, especially
the Jewish Christians.† [11] It is imperative to silence
them, as they are upsetting whole families by teaching for sordid gain what they should not. [12]† One
of them, a prophet of their own, once said, "Cretans
have always been liars, vicious beasts, and lazy gluttons." [13]* That testimony is true. Therefore, admonish them sharply, so that they may be sound in the

---

† **1, 1–4:** On the epistolary form, see the note on Rom 1, 1–7. The
apostolate is the divinely appointed mission to lead others to the true
faith and through it to eternal salvation (1–3).
   1, 5–9: This instruction on the selection and appointment of
presbyters, substantially identical with that in 1 Tm 3, 1–7 on a bishop (see the note there), was aimed at strengthening the authority of
Titus by apostolic mandate; cf 2, 15. In vv 5.7 and Acts 20, 17.28,
the terms *episkopos* and *presbyteros* ("bishop" and "presbyter") refer
to the same persons. Deacons are not mentioned in Titus. See also
the note on Phil 1, 1.
   1, 10–16: This adverse criticism of the defects within the community is directed especially against certain Jewish Christians, who
busy themselves with useless speculations over persons mentioned
in the Old Testament, insist on the observance of Jewish ritual purity

regulations, and thus upset whole families by teaching things they
have no right to teach; cf 3, 9; 1 Tm 1, 3–10.
   1, 10: *Jewish Christians:* literally, "those of the circumcision."
   1, 12: *Cretans . . . gluttons:* quoted from Epimenides, a Cretan
poet of the sixth century B.C.

1, 1: 1 Tm 2, 4; 4, 3; 2 Tm
   2, 25; 3, 7; Heb 10,
   26.
1, 2: Ti 3, 7; 2 Tm 1, 1; 1 Jn
   2, 25.
1, 3: Ti 2, 10; 3, 4; Ps 24, 5;
   1 Tm 1, 1; 2, 3; 4, 10;
   Jude 25.
1, 4: Ti 2, 13; 3, 6; Phil 3,

20; 2 Tm 1, 10; 2 Pt 1,
   1.11; 2, 20; 3, 2.18.
1, 6–7: 1 Tm 3, 2–7; 2 Tm 2,
   24–26.
1, 9: Ti 1, 13; 2, 1–2.8;
   1 Tm 1, 10; 6, 3; 2 Tm
   1, 13; 4, 3.
1, 13: Ti 1, 9.

Christian Leadership

Leadership is an esteemed but difficult calling. Church leaders in particular must earn the respect of others through the integrity of their lifestyle and their commitment and service to the values of Jesus Christ. Good leaders also know how to motivate others to grow and to serve.

Maybe you too possess leadership qualities and wish to pursue a leadership position in the church or in another field. Make a list of the values you think a leader should have. How closely does your list match the characteristics of a good leader in verses 5–9? When you are ready to lead, review the list from verses 5–9, and remember the importance of living a life of character and leading others to positions of leadership.

As you discern your own leadership potential, look to others who you feel possess good leadership qualities. Which leaders in your school or youth program do you admire the most? What qualities make them good leaders? How do these leaders stack up against the good-leader characteristics you listed?

▶ Ti 1, 5–9

faith, ¹⁴* instead of paying attention to Jewish myths and regulations of people who have repudiated the truth. ¹⁵* To the clean all things are clean, but to those who are defiled and unbelieving nothing is clean; in fact, both their minds and their consciences are tainted. ¹⁶ They claim to know God, but by their deeds they deny him. They are vile and disobedient and unqualified for any good deed.

III: Teaching the Christian Life

Christian Behavior

2 ¹*† As for yourself, you must say what is consistent with sound doctrine, namely, ² that older men should be temperate, dignified, self-controlled, sound in faith, love, and endurance. ³ Similarly, older women should be reverent in their behavior, not slanderers, not addicted to drink, teaching what is good, ⁴ so that they may train younger women to love their husbands and children, ⁵* to be self-controlled, chaste, good homemakers, under the control of their husbands, so that the word of God may not be discredited.

⁶ Urge the younger men, similarly, to control themselves, ⁷ showing yourself as a model of good deeds in every respect, with integrity in your teaching, dignity, ⁸ and sound speech that cannot be criticized, so that the opponent will be put to shame without anything bad to say about us.

⁹* Slaves are to be under the control of their masters in all respects, giving them satisfaction, not talking back to them ¹⁰* or stealing from them, but exhibiting complete good faith, so as to adorn the doctrine of God our savior in every way.

Transformation of Life

¹¹*† For the grace of God has appeared, saving all ¹² and training us to reject godless ways and worldly desires and to live temperately, justly, and devoutly in this age, ¹³*† as we await the blessed hope, the appearance of the glory of the great God and of our savior Jesus Christ, ¹⁴* who gave himself for us to deliver us from all lawlessness and to cleanse for himself a people as his own, eager to do what is good.

¹⁵* Say these things. Exhort and correct with all authority. Let no one look down on you.

2, 1–10: One of Titus' main tasks in Crete is to become acquainted with the character of the Cretans and thereby learn to cope with its deficiencies (see 1, 12). The counsel is not only for Titus himself but for various classes of people with whom he must deal: older men and women (2–4), younger women and men (4–7), and slaves (9–10); cf Eph 6, 1–9; Col 3, 18—4, 1.

2, 11–15: Underlying the admonitions for moral improvement in 1–10 as the moving force is the constant appeal to God's revelation of salvation in Christ, with its demand for transformation of life.

2, 13: *The blessed hope, the appearance:* literally, "the blessed hope and appearance," but the use of a single article in Greek strongly suggests an epexegetical, i.e., explanatory sense. *Of the great God and of our savior Jesus Christ:* another possible translation is "of our great God and savior Jesus Christ."

1, 14: Ti 3, 9; 1 Tm 1, 4; 4, 7;
    2 Tm 4, 4; 2 Pt 1, 16.
1, 15: Mk 7, 18–23; Acts 10,
    15; Rom 14, 14–23.
2, 1: Ti 1, 9.13; 2, 8; 1 Tm
    1, 10; 6, 3; 2 Tm 1, 13;
    4, 3.
2, 5: 1 Cor 11, 3; 14, 34;
    Eph 5, 22–24; Col 3,
    18; 1 Tm 2, 11–15;
    1 Pt 3, 1–6.
2, 9: 1 Cor 7, 21–22; Eph 6,
    5–8; Col 3, 22–25;
    1 Tm 6, 1–2; 1 Pt 2, 18.

2, 10: Ti 1, 3; 3, 4; Ps 24, 5;
    Jude 25.
2, 11: 1 Tm 2, 4; 4, 10.
2, 13: 1 Cor 1, 7; Phil 3, 20;
    1 Thes 1, 10 / 2 Tm 1,
    10 / Ti 1, 4; 3, 6; 2 Pt
    11.11; 2, 20; 3, 2.18.
2, 14: Gal 1, 4; 2, 20; Eph 5,
    2.25; 1 Tm 2, 6; 1 Pt
    1, 18–19 / Ps 130, 8.
2, 15: 1 Tm 4, 12.

3 ¹*† Remind them to be under the control of magistrates and authorities,† to be obedient, to be open to every good enterprise. ² They are to slander no one, to be peaceable, considerate, exercising all graciousness toward everyone. ³* For we ourselves were once foolish, disobedient, deluded, slaves to various desires and pleasures, living in malice and envy, hateful ourselves and hating one another.

⁴* But when the kindness and generous love
    of God our savior appeared,
⁵* not because of any righteous deeds we
        had done
    but because of his mercy,
    he saved us through the bath of rebirth
        and renewal by the holy Spirit,
⁶* whom he richly poured out on us
        through Jesus Christ our savior,

⁷* so that we might be justified by his grace
    and become heirs in hope of
        eternal life.

⁸*† This saying is trustworthy.

Advice to Titus

I want you to insist on these points, that those who have believed in God be careful to devote themselves to good works; these are excellent and beneficial to others. ⁹*† Avoid foolish arguments, genealogies, rivalries, and quarrels about the law, for they are useless and futile. ¹⁰* After a first and second warning, break off contact with a heretic, ¹¹ realizing that such a person is perverted and sinful and stands self-condemned.

Directives, Greetings, and Blessing

¹²*† When I send Artemas to you, or Tychicus,

SIOUX PRAYER FOR TRANSFORMATION

I come before thee as one of thy many children. See, I am small and weak; I need thy strength and wisdom.
Grant me to walk in beauty and that my eyes may ever behold the crimson sunset. May my hands treat with respect the things which thou hast created, may my ears hear thy voice!
Make me wise, that I may understand the things which thou hast taught my people, which thou hast hidden in every leaf and every rock.
I long for strength, not in order that I may overreach my brother but to fight my greatest enemy— myself.
Make me ever ready to come to thee with pure hands and candid eyes, so that my spirit, when life disappears like the setting sun, may stand unashamed before thee.

(From David Schiller, editor,
The Little Book of Prayers, *pp. 280–281)*

▶ Ti 3, 3–7

3, 1–8: The list of Christian duties continues from 2, 9–10, undergirded again as in 2, 11–13 by appeal to what God in Christ has done (4–7; cf 2, 11–14). The spiritual renewal of the Cretans, signified in God's merciful gift of baptism (4–7), should be reflected in their improved attitude toward civil authority and in their Christian relationship with all (1–3).
3, 1: *Magistrates and authorities:* some interpreters understand these terms as referring to the principalities and powers of the heavenly hierarchy. *To be open to every good enterprise:* this implies being good citizens. It could also be translated "ready to do every sort of good work" (as Christians); cf 14.
3, 8–11: In matters of good conduct and religious doctrine, Titus is to stand firm.
3, 9: See the note on 1 Tm 6, 20–21.
3, 12–15: *Artemas* or *Tychicus* (2 Tm 4, 12) is to replace Titus,

who will join Paul in his winter sojourn at Nicopolis in Epirus, on the western coast of Greece.

3, 1: Rom 13, 1–7; 1 Tm 2, 1–2; 1 Pt 2, 13–14.
3, 3: 1 Cor 6, 9–11; Eph 2, 1–3; 5, 8; Col 3, 5–7; 1 Pt 4, 3.
3, 4: Ti 1, 3; 2, 10; Ps 24, 5; 1 Tm 1, 1; 2, 3; 4, 10; Jude 25.
3, 5: Dt 9, 5; Eph 2, 4–5.8–9; 2 Tm 1, 9.
3, 6: Ti 1, 4; 2, 13; Phil 3, 20; 2 Tm 1, 10; 2 Pt 1, 1.11; 2, 20; 3,
2.18.
3, 7: Ti 1, 2; 2 Tm 1, 1; 1 Jn 2, 25.
3, 8: 1 Tm 1, 15; 3, 1; 4, 9; 2 Tm 2, 11.
3, 9: 1 Tm 1, 4; 4, 7; 2 Tm 2, 23.
3, 10: Mt 18, 15–18; Rom 16, 17; 1 Cor 5, 11; 2 Thes 3, 6.14–15.
3, 12: Acts 20, 4; Eph 6, 21; Col 4, 7; 2 Tm 4, 12.

try to join me at Nicopolis, where I have decided to spend the winter. 13* Send Zenas the lawyer and Apollos on their journey soon, and see to it that they have everything they need. 14* But let our people, too, learn to devote themselves to good works to supply urgent needs, so that they may not be unproductive.

15* All who are with me send you greetings. Greet those who love us in the faith.

Grace be with all of you.

3, 13: Acts 18, 24–26; 1 Cor 1, 12; 3, 4–6.22; 4, 6; 16, 12.

3, 14: Ti 2, 14; 3, 8; Heb 10, 24; 1 Pt 3, 13.

3, 15: Heb 13, 25.

The brief Letter to Philemon is about slavery. It may surprise you that it doesn't condemn slavery outright. In fact, other parts of the Bible take the idea of human slavery for granted! How can the Bible not challenge something we think is wrong? Seeking to understand this puzzling question gives us a key to understanding God's revelation in the Bible.

In-depth

One key to understanding God's message in the Bible is to understand the beliefs of the authors and the first readers. The Letter to Philemon is addressed to a slave owner named Philemon, a woman named Apphia, and a soldier named Archippus, who all lived in Colossae. Philemon's slave, Onesimus, ran away, wound up in prison with Paul, and became a Christian. Now, Paul is sending him back to Philemon, as the law requires. That same law gives Philemon the right to punish Onesimus for escaping. But Paul asks—indirectly, but clearly enough—for Onesimus's freedom. Paul also asks for something far more challenging—that Philemon, Apphia, and Archippus accept Onesimus as "a brother" (verse 16) in Christ.

It is safe to believe that Paul did not agree with slavery. Recall his basic statement on Christian freedom in Gal 3, 28: "There is neither Jew nor Greek, there is neither slave nor free person, there is not male and female; for you are all one in Christ Jesus." However, Paul expected slavery would pass away very soon with the Second Coming of Jesus Christ (see "Strange Advice!?" 1 Corinthians, chapter 7). This is probably why he never directly challenged the institution of slavery.

Although Paul may not have been a social revolutionary by our standards, he consistently challenged social institutions to reflect Gospel values. This letter is a masterpiece of persuasion as it urges the church community in Colossae to accept Onesimus as a beloved brother in Christ. It uses flattery (verses 4–7), a veiled reference to Paul's authority (verses 8–9), Paul's personal relationship with everyone involved (verses 12–17), and maybe even a little guilt in Paul's offer to pay for anything Onesimus stole (verses 18–19). Paul's message to the household of Philemon and to us is this: We must get beyond whatever cultural boundaries prevent us from treating one another as equals in Christ!

At a Glance

I. Greeting and Thanksgiving (verses 1–7).

II. Plea for Onesimus (verses 8–22).

III. Final Greetings (verses 23–25).

Quick Facts

Author
Paul

Date Written
A.D. 61–63 if from Rome

Audience
Philemon and his household

The Letter to Philemon

Philemon

Address and Greeting

[1]*† Paul, a prisoner for Christ Jesus, and Timothy our brother, to Philemon, our beloved and our co-worker, [2]*† to Apphia our sister, to Archippus our fellow soldier, and to the church at your house. [3]*† Grace to you and peace from God our Father and the Lord Jesus Christ.

Thanksgiving

[4]*† I give thanks to my God always, remembering you in my prayers, [5]† as I hear of the love and the faith you have in the Lord Jesus and for all the holy ones, [6]*† so that your partnership in the faith may become effective in recognizing every good there is in us that leads to Christ.

Plea for Onesimus

[7]*† For I have experienced much joy and encouragement from your love, because the hearts of the holy ones have been refreshed by you, brother. [8]† Therefore, although I have the full right in Christ to order you to do what is proper, [9]*† I rather urge you out of love, being as I am, Paul, an old man, and now also a prisoner for Christ Jesus. [10]* I urge you on behalf of my child Onesimus, whose father I have become in my imprisonment, [11]† who was

---

1: *Prisoner:* as often elsewhere (cf Romans, 1 Corinthians, Galatians especially), the second word in Greek enunciates the theme and sets the tone of the letter. Here it is the prisoner appealing rather than the apostle commanding.

2: *Apphia our sister:* sister is here used (like brother) to indicate a fellow Christian. *The church at your house: your* here is singular. It more likely refers to Philemon than to the last one named, Archippus; Philemon is then the owner of the slave Onesimus (10). An alternate view is that the actual master of the slave is Archippus and that the one to whom the letter is addressed, Philemon, is the most prominent Christian there; see the note on Col 4, 17.

3: *Grace . . . and peace:* for this greeting, which may be a combination of Greek and Aramaic epistolary formulae, see the note on Rom 1, 1–7.

4: *In my prayers:* literally, "at the time of my prayers."

5: *Holy ones:* a common term for members of the Christian community (so also 7).

6: *In us:* some good ancient manuscripts have *in you* (plural). *That leads to Christ: leads to* translates the Greek preposition *eis,* indicating direction or purpose.

7: *Encouragement:* the Greek word *paraklēsis* is cognate with the verb translated "urge" in vv 9.10, and serves as an introduction to

Paul's plea. *Hearts:* literally, "bowels," expressing in Semitic fashion the seat of the emotions, one's "inmost self." The same Greek word is used in v 12 and again in v 20, where it forms a literary inclusion marking off the body of the letter.

8: *Full right:* often translated "boldness," the Greek word *parrēsia* connotes the full franchise of speech, as the right of a citizen to speak before the body politic, claimed by the Athenians as their privilege (Euripides).

9: *Old man:* some editors conjecture that Paul here used a similar Greek word meaning "ambassador" (cf Eph 6, 20). This conjecture heightens the contrast with "prisoner" but is totally without manuscript support.

11: *Useless . . . useful:* here Paul plays on the name Onesimus, which means "useful" or "beneficial." The verb translated "profit" in v 20 is cognate.

1: Phlm 9; Eph 3, 1; 4, 1; Phil 1, 7.13.
2: Col 4, 17.
3: Rom 1, 7; Gal 1, 3; Phil 1, 2.
4–5: Rom 1, 8–9; Eph 1, 15–16.
6: Phil 1, 9; Col 1, 9.
7: 2 Cor 7, 4.
9: Phlm 1; Eph 3, 1; 4, 1; Phil 1, 7.13.
10: 1 Cor 4, 14–15; Gal 4, 19; Col 4, 9.

Rethinking Social Structures

In sending Onesimus back to Philemon, Paul asked Philemon not only to forgive his runaway slave but to rethink his relationship with him. Paul's plea to Philemon and the church in Colossae to look on Onesimus as a brother in Christ was radical for the time. People expected runaway slaves to be punished severely. Accepting Onesimus as a Christian would be a sign that the church truly believed in baptismal forgiveness and new life.

What commonly accepted social structures in our day might need a fresh look? Might any privileges that we take for granted actually prevent true equality in Christ?

▶ Philemon, verses 8–21

once useless to you but is now useful to [both] you and me. ¹² I am sending him, that is, my own heart, back to you. ¹³*† I should have liked to retain him for myself, so that he might serve me on your behalf in my imprisonment for the gospel, ¹⁴* but I did not want to do anything without your consent, so that the good you do might not be forced but voluntary. ¹⁵† Perhaps this is why he was away from you for a while, that you might have him back forever, ¹⁶*† no longer as a slave but more than a slave, a brother, beloved especially to me, but even more so to you, as a man and in the Lord. ¹⁷ So if you regard me as a partner, welcome him as you would me. ¹⁸† And if he has done you any injustice or owes you anything, charge it to me. ¹⁹* I, Paul, write this in my own hand: I will pay. May I not tell you that you owe me your very self. ²⁰ Yes, brother, may I profit from you in the Lord. Refresh my heart in Christ.

²¹ With trust in your compliance I write to you, knowing that you will do even more than I say. ²²* At the same time prepare a guest room for me, for I hope to be granted to you through your prayers.

Final Greetings

²³*† Epaphras, my fellow prisoner in Christ Jesus, greets you, ²⁴* as well as Mark, Aristarchus, Demas, and Luke, my co-workers. ²⁵ The grace of the Lord Jesus Christ be with your spirit.

13: *Serve:* the Greek *diakoneō* could connote a ministry.

15: *Was away from:* literally, "was separated from," but the same verb means simply "left" in Acts 18, 1. It is a euphemism for his running away.

16: *As a man:* literally, "in the flesh." With this and the following phrase, Paul describes the natural and spiritual orders.

18–19: *Charge it to me . . . I will pay:* technical legal and commercial terms in account keeping and acknowledgment of indebtedness.

23–24: *Epaphras:* a Collosian who founded the church there (Col 1, 7) and perhaps also in Laodicea and Hierapolis (Col 2, 1; 4, 12–13). *Aristarchus:* a native of Thessalonica and fellow worker of Paul (Acts 19, 29; 20, 4; 27, 2). For Mark, Demas, and Luke, see 2 Tm 4, 9–13 and the note there.

13: Phil 2, 30.
14: 2 Cor 9, 7; 1 Pt 5, 2.
16: 1 Tm 6, 2.
19: Gal 6, 11; 2 Thes 3, 17.
22: Heb 13, 19.
23: Col 1, 7; 4, 12–13.
24: Acts 12, 12.15; 13, 13; 15, 37–39; 19, 29; 20, 4; 27, 2; Col 4, 10.14; 2 Tm 4, 10–13.

Have you ever wondered why it makes sense to believe that Jesus is the savior of all humanity? It's an honest question. Evidently, some early Christians asked it. The Letter to the Hebrews is a sermon—to them and to us— to strengthen our faith and belief in Jesus Christ, the Son of God and our "great high priest" (4, 14).

In-depth

The Letter to the Hebrews gives us almost no information about its author and the community it is addressed to. But it appears that some members of the community are in danger of giving up their faith—and this is happening after the group has already survived a period of persecution. The letter encourages them to be strong in their faith and seeks to give a sound foundation for believing in Jesus Christ. It is a statement on Christ's divinity and the saving power of Christ's sacrificial death.

The letter presents Christ as the divine Son of God, through whom the world was created, superior to any angel, and the culmination of all the promises and expectations of the Old Testament. In explaining Christ's importance, the letter uses a type of argument called "from the lesser to the greater." This type of argument is based on the idea that if you accept something as true in a lesser situation, then it is certainly true in a greater situation. The author uses it to show that Christ's sacrifice is far greater than the sacrifices offered by the priests in the Temple. As the perfect high priest, Christ offers the perfect sacrifice—his death on the cross—through which God saves us once and for all from sin.

This letter reads like one long sermon made up of interconnecting parts. Begin by reading the whole thing out loud to truly appreciate its power and wording. Then, look up some of its references to people and events in the Old Testament to better appreciate its inspired explanation of Christ's nature and mission.

At a Glance

I. Introduction (1, 1–4).

II. The Son Higher than the Angels (1, 5—2, 18).

III. Jesus, Faithful and Compassionate High Priest (3, 1—5, 10).

IV. Jesus' Eternal Priesthood and Eternal Sacrifice (5, 11—10, 39).

V. Examples, Discipline, Disobedience (11, 1—12, 29).

VI. Final Exhortation, Blessing, Greetings (13, 1–25).

Quick Facts

Author
unknown

Date Written
approximately A.D. 80–90

Audience
Hellenistic (Greek-speaking) Christians and possibly Jewish Christians

The Letter to the Hebrews

Hebrews

I: Introduction

1 ¹† In times past, God spoke in partial and various ways to our ancestors through the prophets; ²* in these last days, he spoke to us through a son, whom he made heir of all things and through whom he created the universe,

³* who is the refulgence of his glory,
  the very imprint of his being,
and who sustains all things by his
  mighty word.
When he had accomplished purification
  from sins,

he took his seat at the right hand of the
  Majesty on high,
⁴* as far superior to the angels
as the name he has inherited is more excellent
  than theirs.

II: The Son Higher Than the Angels

Messianic Enthronement

⁵*† For to which of the angels did God ever say:

"You are my son; this day I have
  begotten you"?

1, 1–4: The letter opens with an introduction consisting of a reflection on the climax of God's revelation to the human race in his Son. The divine communication was initiated and maintained during Old Testament times in fragmentary and varied ways through *the prophets* (1), including Abraham, Moses, and all through whom God spoke. But now *in these last days* (2), the final age, God's revelation of his saving purpose is achieved *through a son*, i.e., one who is Son, whose role is redeemer and mediator of creation. He was made *heir of all things* through his death and exaltation to glory, yet he existed before he appeared as man; through him God *created the universe*. Verses 3–4, which may be based upon a liturgical hymn, assimilate the Son to the personified Wisdom of the Old Testament as *refulgence* of God's *glory* and *imprint of his being* (3; cf Wis 7, 26). These same terms are used of the Logos in Philo. The author now turns from the cosmological role of the preexistent Son to the redemptive work of Jesus: he brought about purification from sins and has been exalted to the right hand of God (see Ps 110, 1). The once-humiliated and crucified Jesus has been declared God's Son, and this name shows his superiority to the angels. The reason for the author's insistence on that superiority is, among other things, that in some Jewish traditions angels were mediators of the old covenant (see Acts 7, 53; Gal 3, 19). Finally, Jesus' superiority to the angels emphasizes the superiority of the new covenant to the old because of the heavenly priesthood of Jesus.

1, 5–14: Jesus' superiority to the angels is now demonstrated by a series of seven Old Testament texts. Some scholars see in the stages of Jesus' exaltation an order corresponding to that of enthronement ceremonies in the ancient Near East, especially in Egypt, namely, elevation to divine status (5–6); presentation to the angels and proclamation of everlasting lordship (7–12); enthronement and conferral of royal power (13). The citations from the Psalms in vv 5 and 13 were traditionally used of Jesus' messianic sonship (cf Acts 13, 33) through his resurrection and exaltation (cf Acts 2, 33–35); those in vv 8 and 10–12 are concerned with his divine kingship and his creative function. The central quotation in v 7 serves to contrast the angels with the Son. The author quotes it according to the Septuagint translation, which is quite different in meaning from that of the Hebrew ("You make the winds your messengers, and flaming fire your ministers"). The angels are only *sent to serve . . . those who are to inherit salvation* (14).

1, 2: Is 2, 2; Jer 23, 20; Ez 38, 16; Dn 10, 14 / Jn 3, 17; Rom 8, 3; Gal 4, 4 / Prv 8, 30; Wis 7, 22; Jn 1, 3; 1 Cor 8, 6; Col 1, 16.
1, 3: Wis 7, 26; 2 Cor 4, 4; Col 1, 15 / Heb 8, 1;

10, 12; 12, 2; Mk 16, 19; Acts 2, 33; 7, 55–56; Rom 8, 34; Eph 1, 20; Col 3, 1; 1 Pt 3, 22.
1, 4: Eph 1, 21; Phil 2, 9–11.
1, 5: Ps 2, 7 / 2 Sm 7, 14.

Or again:

"I will be a father to him, and he shall be a
    son to me"?

6*† And again, when he leads the first-born into the
world, he says:

"Let all the angels of God worship him."

7*Of the angels he says:

"He makes his angels winds
    and his ministers a fiery flame";

8*† but of the Son:

"Your throne, O God, stands forever and ever;
    and a righteous scepter is the scepter of
    your kingdom.
9   You loved justice and hated wickedness;
    therefore God, your God, anointed you
    with the oil of gladness above
    your companions";

10* and:

"At the beginning, O Lord, you established
    the earth,

and the heavens are the works of
    your hands.
11   They will perish, but you remain;
    and they will all grow old like a garment.
12   You will roll them up like a cloak,
    and like a garment they will be changed.
But you are the same, and your years will have
    no end."

13* But to which of the angels has he ever said:

"Sit at my right hand
    until I make your enemies your footstool"?

14* Are they not all ministering spirits sent to serve,
for the sake of those who are to inherit salvation?

Exhortation to Faithfulness

2 ¹† Therefore, we must attend all the more to
what we have heard, so that we may not be
carried away. ²* For if the word announced through
angels proved firm, and every transgression and
disobedience received its just recompense, ³* how
shall we escape if we ignore so great a salvation?
Announced originally through the Lord, it was
confirmed for us by those who had heard. ⁴* God
added his testimony by signs, wonders, various acts
of power, and distribution of the gifts of the holy
Spirit according to his will.

"The Very Imprint"

LIVE IT!

Throughout history, there have been many opinions about who Jesus of Nazareth
was. Some have called him a great teacher, some a prophet, some a charismatic
preacher, and others a worker of miracles. Christians believe Jesus was all of these
and more—much more.

The New Testament makes a bold claim about Jesus. It says the historical human being
from Nazareth named Jesus is the perfect human image of God. Jesus reflects God's glory
and is "the very imprint of [God's] being" (1, 3). In other words, although a human being like
us, Jesus is God.

This astonishing claim is central to the Christian faith. If you accept it as true, it will
change your life. And if you are to believe it, you need to know the whole story behind it and
all the evidence that supports it. The best place to start is with the book in your hands right
now. Read on!

▶ Heb 1, 1–14

---

†
1, 6: *And again, when he leads:* the Greek could also be translated "And when he again leads" in reference to the *parousia.*
1, 8–12: *O God:* the application of the name "God" to the Son
derives from the preexistence mentioned in vv 2–3; the psalmist had
already used it of the Hebrew king in the court style of the original.
See the note on Ps 45, 7. It is also important for the author's christology that in vv 10–12 an Old Testament passage addressed to God
is redirected to Jesus.
2, 1–4: The author now makes a transition into exhortation, using

an a fortiori argument (as at 7, 21–22; 9, 13–14; 10, 28–29; 12, 25).
The *word announced through angels* (2), the Mosaic law, is contrasted with the more powerful word that Christians have received

*
1, 6: Dt 32, 43 LXX; Ps 97, 7.
1, 7: Ps 104, 4 LXX.
1, 8: Ps 45, 7–8.
1, 10–12: Ps 102, 26–28.
1, 13: Ps 110, 1.
1, 14: Ps 91, 11; Dn 7, 10.
2, 2: Acts 7, 38.53; Gal 3, 19.
2, 3: Heb 10, 29; 12, 25.
2, 4: Mk 16, 20; Acts 14, 3;
    19, 11.

Exaltation through Abasement

5† For it was not to angels that he subjected the world to come, of which we are speaking. 6* Instead, someone has testified somewhere:

So Great a Salvation!

It is easy for us humans to rationalize why we do certain things. Even if our actions hurt other people and separate us from God, we can come up with a way to justify them. Though this way of thinking may seem to work for us, Heb 2, 1–4 says quite clearly that it never works with God.

We cannot hide from our "just recompense" (verse 2). But the good news is that God offers us salvation from our sins through Jesus Christ. In your prayer, journal or reflect on the following questions:

- **Do you believe that you will receive a just penalty for the things you have done wrong?**
- **If we can be saved from our just penalty by placing our faith in Jesus Christ, why would anyone want to "ignore so great a salvation" (verse 3)?**
- **How can you avoid being carried away (verse 1) from the good news of salvation?**

▸ Heb 2, 1–4

"What is man that you are mindful of him,
or the son of man that you care for him?
7 You made him for a little while lower than
the angels;
you crowned him with glory and honor,
8* subjecting all things under his feet."

In "subjecting" all things [to him], he left nothing not "subject to him." Yet at present we do not see "all things subject to him," 9* but we do see Jesus "crowned with glory and honor" because he suffered death, he who "for a little while" was made "lower than the angels," that by the grace of God he might taste death for everyone.

10* For it was fitting that he, for whom and through whom all things exist, in bringing many children to glory, should make the leader to their salvation perfect through suffering. 11 He who consecrates and those who are being consecrated all have one origin. Therefore, he is not ashamed to call them "brothers," 12* saying:

"I will proclaim your name to my brothers,
in the midst of the assembly I will
praise you";

13* and again:

"I will put my trust in him";

and again:

"Behold, I and the children God has
given me."

14* Now since the children share in blood and flesh, he likewise shared in them, that through death he might destroy the one who has the power

H
E
B

(3–4). Christ's supremacy strengthens Christians against being *carried away* from their faith.

2, 5–18: The humanity and the suffering of Jesus do not constitute a valid reason for relinquishing the Christian faith. Ps 8 (6–7) is also applied to Jesus in 1 Cor 15, 27; Eph 1, 22; and probably 1 Pt 3, 22. This christological interpretation, therefore, probably reflects a common early Christian tradition, which may have originated in the expression *the son of man* (6). The psalm contrasts God's greatness with man's relative insignificance but also stresses the superiority of man to the rest of creation, of which he is lord. Hebrews applies this christologically: Jesus lived a truly human existence, *lower than the angels*, in the days of his earthly life, particularly in his suffering and death; now, *crowned . . . with glory and honor*, he is raised above all creation. The author considers all things as already *subject to him* because of his exaltation (8–9), though *we do not see* this yet. The reference to Jesus as *leader* (10) sounds the first note of an important leitmotif in Hebrews: the journey of the people of God to the sabbath rest (4, 9), the heavenly sanctuary, following Jesus, their "forerunner" (6, 20). It was fitting that God should make him *perfect through suffering*, consecrated by obedient suffering. Because he is perfected as high priest, Jesus is then able to consecrate his people (11); access to God is made possible by each of these two consecrations. If Jesus is able to help human beings, it is because he has become one of us; we are his "brothers." The author then cites three Old Testament texts as proofs of this unity between ourselves and the

Son. Psalm 22, 23 is interpreted so as to make Jesus the singer of this lament, which ends with joyful praise of the Lord in the assembly of "brothers." The other two texts are from Is 8, 17.18. The first of these seems intended to display in Jesus an example of the trust in God that his followers should emulate. The second curiously calls these followers "children"; probably this is to be understood to mean children of Adam, but the point is our solidarity with Jesus. By sharing human nature, including the ban of death, Jesus broke the power of the devil over death (14); the author shares the view of Hellenistic Judaism that death was not intended by God and that it had been introduced into the world by the devil. The *fear of death* (15) is a religious fear based on the false conception that death marks the end of a person's relations with God (cf Ps 115, 17–18; Is 38, 18). Jesus deliberately allied himself with the *descendants of Abraham* (16) in order to be a *merciful and faithful high priest*. This is the first appearance of the central theme of Hebrews, Jesus the great high priest expiating the *sins of the people* (17), as one who experienced the same tests as they (18).

2, 6: Ps 8, 5–7.
2, 8: Mt 28, 18; 1 Cor 15,
25–28; Eph 1, 20–23;
Phil 3, 21; 1 Pt 3, 22.
2, 9: Phil 2, 6–11.
2, 10: Heb 12, 2; Is 53,
4 / Rom 11, 36;

1 Cor 8, 6.
2, 12: Ps 22, 23.
2, 13: Is 8, 17.18.
2, 14: Is 25, 8; Hos 13, 14;
Jn 12, 31; Rom 6, 9;
1 Cor 15, 54–55; 2 Tm
1, 10; Rv 12, 10.

of death, that is, the devil, [15] and free those who through fear of death had been subject to slavery all their life. [16] Surely he did not help angels but rather the descendants of Abraham; [17]* therefore, he had to become like his brothers in every way, that he might be a merciful and faithful high priest before God to expiate the sins of the people. [18] Because he himself was tested through what he suffered, he is able to help those who are being tested.

III: Jesus, Faithful and Compassionate High Priest

Jesus, Superior to Moses

3 [1]† Therefore, holy "brothers," sharing in a heavenly calling, reflect on Jesus, the apostle and high priest of our confession, [2]* who was faithful to the one who appointed him, just as Moses was "faithful in [all] his house." [3]* But he is worthy of more "glory" than Moses, as the founder of a house has more "honor" than the house itself. [4] Every house is founded by someone, but the founder of all is God. [5] Moses was "faithful in all his house" as a "servant" to testify to what would be spoken, [6]*† but Christ was faithful as a son placed over his house. We are his house, if [only] we hold fast to our confidence and pride in our hope.

Israel's Infidelity a Warning

[7]*† Therefore, as the holy Spirit says:

"Oh, that today you would hear his voice,
[8]   'Harden not your hearts as at the rebellion
    in the day of testing in the desert,
[9]*   where your ancestors tested and tried me

and saw my works [10] for forty years.
Because of this I was provoked with that generation
    and I said, "They have always been of erring heart,
    and they do not know my ways."
[11]   As I swore in my wrath,
    "They shall not enter into my rest." ' "

[12] Take care, brothers, that none of you may have an evil and unfaithful heart, so as to forsake the living God. [13] Encourage yourselves daily while it is still "today," so that none of you may grow hardened by the deceit of sin. [14]* We have become partners of Christ if only we hold the beginning of the reality firm until the end, [15]* for it is said:

"Oh, that today you would hear his voice:
'Harden not your hearts as at the rebellion.' "

[16]* Who were those who rebelled when they heard? Was it not all those who came out of Egypt under Moses? [17]* With whom was he "provoked for forty years"? Was it not those who had sinned, whose corpses fell in the desert? [18]* And to whom did he "swear that they should not enter into his rest," if not to those who were disobedient? [19] And we see that they could not enter for lack of faith.

The Sabbath Rest

4 [1] Therefore, let us be on our guard while the promise of entering into his rest remains, that none of you seem to have failed. [2] For in fact we have received the good news just as they did. But the word that they heard did not profit them, for

---

3, 1–6: The author now takes up the two qualities of Jesus mentioned in 2, 17, but in inverse order: faithfulness (3, 1—4, 13) and mercy (4, 14—5, 10). Christians are called *holy "brothers"* because of their common relation to him (2, 11), the *apostle*, a designation for Jesus used only here in the New Testament (cf Jn 13, 16; 17, 3), meaning one sent as God's final word to us (1, 2). He is compared with Moses probably because he is seen as mediator of the new covenant (9, 15) just as Moses was of the old (9, 19–22, including his sacrifice). But when the author of Hebrews speaks of Jesus' sacrifice, he does not consider Moses as the Old Testament antitype, but rather the high priest on the Day of Atonement (9, 6–15). Moses' faithfulness *"in [all] his house"* refers back to Nm 12, 7, on which this section is a midrashic commentary. In vv 3–6, the author does not indicate that he thinks of either Moses or Christ as the founder of the household. *His house* (2.5.6) means God's house, not that of Moses or Christ; in the case of Christ, compare v 6 with 10, 21. The *house* of v 6 is the Christian community; the author suggests its continuity with Israel by speaking not of two houses but of only one. Verse 6 brings out the reason why Jesus is superior to Moses: the latter was the faithful *servant* laboring *in* the house founded by God, but Jesus is God's *son*, placed *over* the house.

3, 6: The majority of manuscripts add "firm to the end," but these words are not found in the three earliest and best witnesses and are probably an interpolation derived from v 14.

3, 7—4, 13: The author appeals for steadfastness of faith in Jesus, basing his warning on the experience of Israel during the Exodus. In the Old Testament the Exodus had been invoked as a symbol of the return of Israel from the Babylonian exile (Is 42, 9; 43, 16–21; 51, 9–11). In the New Testament the redemption was similarly understood as a new exodus, both in the experience of Jesus himself (Lk

9, 31) and in that of his followers (1 Cor 10, 1–4). The author cites Ps 95, 7–11, a salutary example of hardness of heart, as a warning against the danger of growing weary and giving up the journey. To call God *living* (12) means that he reveals himself in his works (cf Jos 3, 10; Jer 10, 10). The *rest* (11) into which Israel was to enter was only a foreshadowing of that rest to which Christians are called. They are to remember the example of Israel's revolt in the desert that cost a whole generation the loss of the promised land (15–19; cf Nm 14, 20–29). In 4, 1–11, the symbol of *rest* is seen in deeper dimension: because the promise to the ancient Hebrews foreshadowed that given to Christians, it is *good news*; and because the promised land was the place of rest that God provided for his people, it was a share in his own rest, which he enjoyed after he had finished his creative work (3–4; cf Gn 2, 2). The author attempts to read this meaning of God's rest into Ps 95, 7–11 (6–9). The Greek form of the name of Joshua, who led Israel into the promised land, is Jesus (8). The author plays upon the name but stresses the superiority of Jesus, who leads his followers into heavenly rest. Verses 12 and 13 are meant as a continuation of the warning, for the word of God brings judgment as well as salvation. Some would capitalize *the word of God* and see it as a personal title of Jesus, comparable to that of Jn 1, 1–18.

2, 17: Heb 4, 15; 5, 1–3.   3, 14: Rom 8, 17.
  3, 2: Nm 12, 7.   3, 15: Ps 95, 7–8.
  3, 3: 2 Cor 3, 7–8.   3, 16–19: Nm 14, 1–38; Dt 1,
  3, 6: Heb 10, 21; Eph 2, 19;   19–40.
    1 Tm 3, 15; 1 Pt 4, 17.   3, 17: Nm 14, 29.
3, 7–11: Ps 95, 7–11.   3, 18: Nm 14, 22–23; Dt 1,
  3, 9: Ex 17, 7; Nm 20, 2–5.   35.

they were not united in faith with those who listened. ³* For we who believed enter into [that] rest, just as he has said:

"As I swore in my wrath,
'They shall not enter into my rest,' "

and yet his works were accomplished at the foundation of the world. ⁴* For he has spoken somewhere about the seventh day in this manner, "And God rested on the seventh day from all his works"; ⁵* and again, in the previously mentioned place, "They shall not enter into my rest." ⁶ Therefore, since it remains that some will enter into it, and those who formerly received the good news did not enter because of disobedience, ⁷* he once more set a day, "today," when long afterwards he spoke through David, as already quoted:

"Oh, that today you would hear his voice:
'Harden not your hearts.' "

⁸* Now if Joshua had given them rest, he would not have spoken afterwards of another day. ⁹ Therefore, a sabbath rest still remains for the people of God. ¹⁰ And whoever enters into God's rest, rests from his own works as God did from his. ¹¹ Therefore, let us strive to enter into that rest, so that no one may fall after the same example of disobedience.

¹²* Indeed, the word of God is living and effec-

Indeed, the **word** of **God** is *living* and *effective*, sharper than any two-edged **sword**

4, 12

tive, sharper than any two-edged sword, penetrating even between soul and spirit, joints and marrow, and able to discern reflections and thoughts of the heart. ¹³* No creature is concealed from him, but everything is naked and exposed to the eyes of him to whom we must render an account.

Jesus, Compassionate High Priest

¹⁴*† Therefore, since we have a great high priest who has passed through the heavens, Jesus, the Son of God, let us hold fast to our confession. ¹⁵* For we do not have a high priest who is unable to sympathize with our weaknesses, but one who has similarly been

H
E
B

LIVE IT!

Approach God Boldly!

Have you ever believed that you did something that God could never forgive? Or do you ever have thoughts that make you feel so ashamed that you do not dare talk with God about them?

Hebrews 4, 14–16 reminds us of a remarkable truth: Jesus, while fully divine, was also fully human. And though he never sinned, this Scripture passage tells us that he was tempted as we are in every respect. Think about that! Jesus was once fourteen years old. He was once seventeen. He was once twenty-two. There is no temptation that you have considered that Jesus cannot understand. And that is why you can approach him in any circumstance—even your deepest trouble—and find compassion and grace.

Remember: (1) you cannot hide from God, and (2) you don't have to!

▸ Heb 4, 14–16

---

† **4, 14–16:** These verses, which return to the theme first sounded in 2, 16—3, 1, serve as an introduction to the section that follows. The author here alone calls Jesus *a great high priest* (14), a designation used by Philo for the Logos; perhaps he does so in order to emphasize Jesus' superiority over the Jewish high priest. He has *been tested in every way, yet without sin* (15); this indicates an acquaintance with the tradition of Jesus' temptations, not only at the beginning (as in Mk 1, 13) but throughout his public life (cf Lk 22, 28). Although the reign of the exalted Jesus is a theme that occurs elsewhere in Hebrews, and Jesus' throne is mentioned in 1, 8, *the throne*

of grace (16) refers to the throne of God. The similarity of v 16 to 10, 19–22 indicates that the author is thinking of our confident access to God, made possible by the priestly work of Jesus.

4, 3: Heb 3, 11; Ps 95, 11.
4, 4: Gn 2, 2.
4, 5: Ps 95, 11.
4, 7: Heb 3, 7–8.15; Ps 95, 7–8.
4, 8: Dt 31, 7; Jos 22, 4.
4, 12: Wis 18, 15–16; Is 49,

2; Eph 6, 17; Rv 1, 16; 2, 12.
4, 13: Jb 34, 21–22; Pss 90, 8; 139, 2–4.
4, 14: Heb 9, 11.24.
4, 15: Heb 2, 17–18; 5, 2.

tested in every way, yet without sin. ¹⁶* So let us confidently approach the throne of grace to receive mercy and to find grace for timely help.

?did you KNOW?

The Priesthood and Christ's Sacrifice

In the Old Testament, the priesthood evolved after Israel became a nation, and it underwent a long process of development. Priests were not ordained; the priesthood was considered hereditary within the tribe of Levi. After the Exile, three classes of clergy emerged: high priests, priests, and Levites. Priestly functions included maintaining religion as the center of Israel's life, taking care of the Temple of Jerusalem, and interpreting and teaching the Scriptures. In a special way, the priests of Israel represented the people before God by offering prayer and sacrifices for the forgiveness of sin. Their sacrifices foreshadowed the sacrifice of Jesus, the only sacrifice truly capable of reconciling a broken relationship with God caused by sin.

In the New Testament, Christ made the Apostles co-ministers in his saving mission, including a special participation in his high priesthood—the high priesthood described in Heb 4, 14—5, 10. Today, the bishops, as successors of the Apostles, continue the apostolic tradition. They ordain priests to assist in their responsibilities as pastors of the faithful, preachers of God's word, and celebrants of Christian worship (see "Holy Orders," Mk 3, 13–19).

Catholic bishops and priests exercise their special participation in Christ's priesthood while presiding at the Eucharist. Acting in Christ's name and in communion with the assembly, they celebrate a memorial of Jesus' life, death, and Resurrection. In the celebration of the Eucharist, Christ's sacrifice on the cross is "re-presented," that is, Jesus' sacrifice for the forgiveness of sins is made real and present.

▸ Heb 4, 14—5, 10

5 ¹† Every high priest is taken from among men and made their representative before God, to offer gifts and sacrifices for sins.† ²† He is able to deal patiently with the ignorant and erring, for he himself is beset by weakness ³* and so, for this reason, must make sin offerings for himself as well as for the people. ⁴* No one takes this honor upon himself but only when called by God, just as Aaron was. ⁵* In the same way, it was not Christ who glorified himself in becoming high priest, but rather the one who said to him:

"You are my son;
    this day I have begotten you";

⁶*† just as he says in another place:

"You are a priest forever
    according to the order of Melchizedek."

⁷*† In the days when he was in the flesh, he offered prayers and supplications with loud cries and tears to the one who was able to save him from death, and he was heard because of his reverence. ⁸*† Son though he was, he learned obedience from what he suffered; ⁹* and when he was made perfect, he became the source of eternal salvation for all who

---

5, 1–10: The true humanity of Jesus (see the note on 2, 5–18) makes him a more rather than a less effective high priest to the Christian community. In Old Testament tradition, the high priest was identified with the people, guilty of personal sin just as they were (1–3). Even so, the office was of divine appointment (4), as was also the case with the sinless Christ (5). For v 6, see the note on Ps 110, 4. Although Jesus was Son of God, he was destined as a human being to learn obedience by accepting the suffering he had to endure (8). Because of his perfection through this experience of human suffering, he is the cause of salvation for all (9), a *high priest according to the order of Melchizedek* (10; cf 6 and 7, 3).

5, 1: *To offer gifts and sacrifices for sins:* the author is thinking principally of the Day of Atonement rite, as is clear from 9, 7. This ritual was celebrated to atone for "all the sins of the Israelites" (Lv 16, 34).

5, 2: *Deal patiently:* the Greek word *metriopathein* occurs only here in the Bible; this term was used by the Stoics to designate the golden mean between excess and defect of passion. Here it means rather the ability to sympathize.

5, 6–8: The author of Hebrews is the only New Testament writer to cite v 4 of Ps 110, here and in 7, 17.21, to show that Jesus has been called by God in his role as priest. Verses 7–8 deal with his ability to sympathize with sinners, because of his own experience of the trials and weakness of human nature, especially fear of death. In his present exalted state, weakness is foreign to him, but he understands what we suffer because of his previous earthly experience.

5, 7: *He offered prayers . . . to the one who was able to save him from death:* at Gethsemane (cf Mk 14, 35), though some see a broader reference (see the note on Jn 12, 27).

5, 8: *Son though he was:* two different though not incompatible views of Jesus' sonship coexist in Hebrews, one associating it with his exaltation, the other with his preexistence. The former view is the older one (cf Rom 1, 4).

4, 16: Heb 8, 1; 10,
    19.22.35; 12, 2;
    Eph 3, 12.
5, 3: Lv 9, 7; 16,
    15–17.30.34.
5, 4: Ex 28, 1.
5, 5: Ps 2, 7.

5, 6: Ps 110, 4.
5, 7: Mt 26, 38–44; Mk 14,
    34–40; Lk 22, 41–46;
    Jn 12, 27.
5, 8: Rom 5, 19; Phil 2, 8.
5, 9: Heb 7, 24–25.28.

obey him, [10]* declared by God high priest according to the order of Melchizedek.

IV: Jesus' Eternal Priesthood and Eternal Sacrifice

Exhortation to Spiritual Renewal

[11]† About this we have much to say, and it is difficult to explain, for you have become sluggish in hearing. [12]* Although you should be teachers by this time, you need to have someone teach you again the basic elements of the utterances of God. You need milk, [and] not solid food. [13] Everyone who lives on milk lacks experience of the word of righteousness, for he is a child. [14] But solid food is for the mature, for those whose faculties are trained by practice to discern good and evil.

6 [1]* Therefore, let us leave behind the basic teaching about Christ and advance to maturity, without laying the foundation all over again: repentance from dead works and faith in God, [2]*† instruction about baptisms and laying on of hands, resurrection of the dead and eternal judgment. [3] And we shall do this, if only God permits. [4]*† For it is impossible in the case of those who have once been enlightened and tasted the heavenly gift and shared in the holy Spirit [5]† and tasted the good word of God and the powers of the age to come, [6]*† and then have fallen away, to bring them to repentance again, since they are recrucifying the Son of God for themselves and holding him up to contempt. [7]* Ground

that has absorbed the rain falling upon it repeatedly and brings forth crops useful to those for whom it is cultivated receives a blessing from God. [8]* But if it produces thorns and thistles, it is rejected; it will soon be cursed and finally burned.

[9] But we are sure in your regard, beloved, of better things related to salvation, even though we speak in this way. [10] For God is not unjust so as to overlook your work and the love you have demonstrated for his name by having served and continuing to serve the holy ones. [11]* We earnestly desire each of you to demonstrate the same eagerness for the fulfillment of hope until the end, [12]*† so that you may not become sluggish, but imitators of those who, through faith and patience, are inheriting the promises.

God's Promise Immutable

[13]*† When God made the promise to Abraham, since he had no one greater by whom to swear, "he swore by himself," [14]* and said, "I will indeed bless you and multiply" you. [15]*† And so, after patient waiting, he obtained the promise. [16] Human beings swear by someone greater than themselves; for them an oath serves as a guarantee and puts an end to all argument. [17]* So when God wanted to give the heirs of his promise an even clearer demonstration of the immutability of his purpose, he intervened with an oath, [18]*† so that by two immutable things, in which it was impossible for God to lie, we who have taken refuge might be strongly encouraged to hold fast to the hope that lies before us. [19]*† This we have as an

5, 11—6, 20: The central section of Hebrews (5, 11—10, 39) opens with a reprimand and an appeal. Those to whom the author directs his teaching about Jesus' priesthood, which is *difficult to explain*, have become *sluggish in hearing* and forgetful of even *the basic elements* (5, 12). But rather than treating of basic teachings, the author apparently believes that the challenge of more advanced ones may shake them out of their inertia (*therefore*, 6, 1). The six examples of *basic teaching* in 6, 1–3 are probably derived from a traditional catechetical list. No effort is made to address apostates, for their very hostility to the Christian message cuts them off completely from Christ (6, 4–8). This harsh statement seems to rule out repentance after apostasy, but perhaps the author deliberately uses hyperbole in order to stress the seriousness of abandoning Christ. With 6, 9 a milder tone is introduced, and the criticism of the community (6, 1–3.9) is now balanced by an expression of confidence that its members are living truly Christian lives, and that God will justly reward their efforts (10). The author is concerned especially about their persevering (11–12), citing in this regard the achievement of Abraham, who relied on God's promise and on God's oath (13–18; cf Gn 22, 16), and proposes to them as a firm anchor of Christian hope the high priesthood of Christ, who is now living with God (19–20).

6, 2: *Instruction about baptisms:* not simply about Christian baptism but about the difference between it and similar Jewish rites, such as proselyte baptism, John's baptism, and the washings of the Qumran sectaries. *Laying on of hands:* in Acts 8, 17; 19, 6 this rite effects the infusion of the holy Spirit; in Acts 6, 6; 13, 3; 1 Tm 4, 14; 5, 22; 2 Tm 1, 6 it is a means of conferring some ministry or mission in the early Christian community.

6, 4: *Enlightened and tasted the heavenly gift:* this may refer to baptism and the Eucharist, respectively, but more probably means the neophytes' enlightenment by faith and their experience of salvation.

6, 5: *Tasted the good word of God and the powers of the age to*

come: the proclamation of the *word of God* was accompanied by signs of the Spirit's power (1 Thes 1, 5; 1 Cor 2, 4).

6, 6: *They are recrucifying the Son of God for themselves:* a colorful description of the malice of apostasy, which is portrayed as again crucifying and deriding the Son of God.

6, 12: *Imitators of those . . . inheriting the promises:* the author urges the addressees to imitate the faith of the holy people of the Old Testament, who now possess the promised goods of which they lived in hope. This theme will be treated fully in ch 11.

6, 13: *He swore by himself:* God's promise to Abraham, which he confirmed by an oath ("I swear by myself," Gn 22, 16) was the basis for the hope of all Abraham's descendants.

6, 15: *He obtained the promise:* this probably refers not to Abraham's temporary possession of the land but to the eschatological blessings that Abraham and the other patriarchs have now come to possess.

6, 18: *Two immutable things:* the promise and the oath, both made by God.

6, 19: *Anchor . . . into the interior behind the veil:* a mixed metaphor. The Holy of Holies, beyond the veil that separates it from the Holy Place (Ex 26, 31–33), is seen as the earthly counterpart of the heavenly abode of God. This theme will be developed in ch 9.

5, 10: Heb 6, 20; Ps 110, 4.	13, 7; Mk 4, 7; Lk 8, 7,
5, 12: 1 Cor 3, 1–3.	**6, 11:** Heb 3, 14.
6, 1: Heb 9, 14.	**6, 12:** Heb 5, 11; Gal 3, 14;
6, 2: Heb 9, 10; Mk 7, 4 /	Eph 1, 13–14.
Acts 6, 6; 8, 17; 13, 3;	**6, 13:** Gn 22, 16.
19, 6; 1 Tm 4, 14; 5,	**6, 14:** Gn 22, 17.
22; 2 Tm 1, 6.	**6, 15:** Heb 6, 12; Rom 4, 20.
6, 4: Heb 10, 26.32; Ps 34,	**6, 17:** Heb 6, 12.
6; 2 Cor 4, 6.	**6, 18:** Nm 23, 19; 1 Sm 15,
6, 6: 2 Pt 2, 21.	29; Jn 8, 17; 2 Tm 2, 13.
6, 7: Gn 1, 11–12; Dt 11, 11.	**6, 19:** Heb 10, 20; Ex 26,
6, 8: Gn 3, 17–18; Mt 7, 16;	31–33; Lv 16, 2.

HEB

ANCHOR OF THE SOUL

Something mighty powerful kept a smile on my mother's face every day when I was a little girl. I never knew she was in pain. All I saw was a woman with a demeanor of hope and a purpose in life.

I did not know it back then, but she was enduring racial harassment on her job. There was unceasing verbal hate toward African Americans. As I have matured, I have learned that her harassment was not unique. It was a common experience for many African Americans in this country.

When faced with oppressive situations, let us be thankful for a God who continuously fills us with hope. Without hope, oppression is lethal. Hope keeps us moving forward when we'd just as soon give up. Hope makes us smile at tomorrow, even though today is a bitter pill.

Hope is "an anchor of the soul, sure and firm" (Heb 6, 19). A hopeless soul is a major threat to the body. Is your hope anchored in the Lord?

Dear God, give me hope when I face oppression. Amen.

▶ Heb 6, 19–20

HEB

anchor of the soul, sure and firm, which reaches into the interior behind the veil, [20]* where Jesus has entered on our behalf as forerunner, becoming high priest forever according to the order of Melchizedek.

Melchizedek, a Type of Christ

7 [1]*† This "Melchizedek, king of Salem and priest of God Most High,"† "met Abraham as he returned from his defeat of the kings" and "blessed him." [2]† And Abraham apportioned to him "a tenth of everything." His name first means righteous king, and he was also "king of Salem," that is, king of peace. [3]*† Without father, mother,

or ancestry, without beginning of days or end of life, thus made to resemble the Son of God, he remains a priest forever.

[4]*† See how great he is to whom the patriarch "Abraham [indeed] gave a tenth" of his spoils. [5]* The descendants of Levi who receive the office of priesthood have a commandment according to the law to exact tithes from the people, that is, from their brothers, although they also have come from the loins of Abraham. [6] But he who was not of their ancestry received tithes from Abraham and blessed him who had received the promises. [7]† Unquestionably, a lesser person is blessed by a greater. [8] In

---

7, 1–3: Recalling the meeting between Melchizedek and Abraham described in Gn 14, 17–20, the author enhances the significance of this priest by providing the popular etymological meaning of his name and that of the city over which he ruled (2). Since Genesis gives no information on the parentage or the death of Melchizedek, he is seen here as a type of Christ, representing a priesthood that is unique and eternal (3).

7, 1: The author here assumes that Melchizedek was a priest of the God of Israel (cf Gn 14, 22 and the note there).

7, 2: In Gn 14, the Hebrew text does not state explicitly who gave tithes to whom. The author of Hebrews supplies Abraham as the subject, according to a contemporary interpretation of the passage. This supports the argument of the midrash and makes it possible to see in Melchizedek a type of Jesus. The messianic blessings of righteousness and peace are foreshadowed in the names "Melchizedek" and "Salem."

7, 3: *Without father, mother, or ancestry, without beginning of days or end of life:* this is perhaps a quotation from a hymn about Melchizedek. The rabbis maintained that anything not mentioned in the Torah does not exist. Consequently, since the Old Testament

nowhere mentions Melchizedek's ancestry, birth, or death, the conclusion can be drawn that he *remains . . . forever.*

7, 4–10: The tithe that Abraham gave to Melchizedek (4), a practice later followed by the levitical priesthood (5), was a gift (6) acknowledging a certain superiority in Melchizedek, the foreign priest (7). This is further indicated by the fact that the institution of the levitical priesthood was sustained by hereditary succession in the tribe of Levi, whereas the absence of any mention of Melchizedek's death in Genesis implies that his personal priesthood is permanent (8). The levitical priesthood itself, through Abraham, its ancestor, paid tithes to Melchizedek, thus acknowledging the superiority of his priesthood over its own (9–10).

7, 7: *A lesser person is blessed by a greater:* though this sounds like a principle, there are some examples in the Old Testament that do not support it (cf 2 Sm 14, 22; Jb 31, 20). The author may intend it as a statement of a liturgical rule.

6, 20: Heb 5, 10; Ps 110, 4.
7, 1: Gn 14, 17–20.
7, 3: Heb 4, 14; 6, 6; 10, 29.
7, 4: Gn 14, 20.
7, 5: Nm 18, 21 / Gn 35, 11.

the one case, mortal men receive tithes; in the other, a man of whom it is testified that he lives on. 9† One might even say that Levi himself, who receives tithes, was tithed through Abraham, 10 for he was still in his father's loins when Melchizedek met him.

11*† If, then, perfection came through the levitical priesthood, on the basis of which the people received the law, what need would there still have been for another priest to arise according to the order of Melchizedek, and not reckoned according to the order of Aaron? 12 When there is a change of priesthood, there is necessarily a change of law as well. 13† Now he of whom these things are said belonged to a different tribe, of which no member ever officiated at the altar. 14*† It is clear that our Lord arose from Judah, and in regard to that tribe Moses said nothing about priests. 15† It is even more obvious if another priest is raised up after the likeness of Melchizedek, 16† who has become so, not by a law expressed in a commandment concerning physical descent but by the power of a life that cannot be destroyed. 17* For it is testified:

> "You are a priest forever
>   according to the order of Melchizedek."

18* On the one hand, a former commandment is annulled because of its weakness and uselessness, 19† for the law brought nothing to perfection; on the other hand, a better hope is introduced, through which we draw near to God. 20† And to the degree that this happened not without the taking of an oath†— for others became priests without an oath, 21* but he with an oath, through the one who said to him:

> "The Lord has sworn, and he will not repent:
>   'You are a priest forever' "—

Catholic Connections

MELCHIZEDEK

Look with favor on these offerings
and accept them as once you accepted
the gifts of your servant Abel,
the sacrifice of Abraham, our father in
faith,
and the bread and wine offered by your
priest Melchisedech.
(Sacramentary, p. 546)

This quote is from the first Eucharistic prayer in the Catholic Mass. Who is Melchisedech (also spelled Melchizedek)? In the Book of Genesis, after Abraham successfully conquers the enemies of his nephew Lot, Melchizedek, a priest and king, offers a sacrifice of bread and wine to God on Abraham's behalf (14, 17–20). In this way, he becomes Abraham's priest. Early Christians saw parallels to Jesus in the story of Melchizedek, and even in his name, which means "king of righteousness." Thus, Melchizedek's life came to be viewed as an early but incomplete example of Jesus' high priesthood.

▶ Heb 7, 1–10

(18) by leading them into direct communication with God (19).
7, 16: A life that cannot be destroyed: the life to which Jesus has attained by virtue of his resurrection; it is his exaltation rather than his divine nature that makes him priest. The Old Testament speaks of the Aaronic priesthood as eternal (see Ex 40, 15); our author does not explicitly consider this possible objection to his argument but implicitly refutes it in vv 23–24.
7, 19: A better hope: this hope depends upon the sacrifice of the Son of God; through it we "approach the throne of grace" (4, 16); cf 6, 19.20.
7, 20–25: As was the case with the promise to Abraham (6, 13), though not with the levitical priesthood, the eternal priesthood of the order of Melchizedek was confirmed by God's oath (20–21); cf Ps 110, 4. Thus Jesus becomes the guarantee of a permanent covenant (22) that does not require a succession of priests as did the levitical priesthood (23) because his high priesthood is eternal and unchangeable (24). Consequently, Jesus is able to save all who draw near to God through him since he is their ever-living intercessor (25).
7, 20: An oath: God's oath in Ps 110, 4.

7, 9: Levi: for the author this name designates not only the son of Jacob mentioned in Genesis but the priestly tribe that was thought to be descended from him.
7, 11–14: The levitical priesthood was not typified by the priesthood of Melchizedek, for Ps 110, 4 speaks of a priesthood of a new order, the order of Melchizedek, to arise in messianic times (11). Since the levitical priesthood served the Mosaic law, a new priesthood (12) would not come into being without a change in the law itself. Thus Jesus was not associated with the Old Testament priesthood, for he was a descendant of the tribe of Judah, which had never exercised the priesthood (13–14).
7, 13: He of whom these things are said: Jesus, the priest "according to the order of Melchizedek." According to the author's interpretation, Ps 110 spoke prophetically of Jesus.
7, 14: Judah: the author accepts the early Christian tradition that Jesus was descended from the family of David (cf Mt 1, 1–2.16.20; Lk 1, 27; 2, 4; Rom 1, 3). The Qumran community expected two Messiahs, one descended from Aaron and one from David; Hebrews shows no awareness of this view or at least does not accept it. Our author's view is not attested in contemporaneous Judaism.
7, 15–19: Jesus does not exercise a priesthood through family lineage but through his immortal existence (15–16), fulfilling Ps 110, 4 (17; cf 3). Thus he abolishes forever both the levitical priesthood and the law it serves, because neither could effectively sanctify people

7, 11: Heb 5, 6; Ps 110, 4.
7, 14: Gn 49, 10; Is 11, 1; Mt 1, 1–2.16.20; 2, 6; Lk 1, 27; 2, 4; Rom 1, 3; Rv 5, 5.
7, 17: Heb 5, 6; Ps 110, 4.
7, 18: Heb 10, 1.
7, 21: Ps 110, 4.

22*† to that same degree has Jesus [also] become the guarantee of an [even] better covenant. 23 Those priests were many because they were prevented by death from remaining in office, 24* but he, because he remains forever, has a priesthood that does not pass away. 25*† Therefore, he is always able to save those who approach God through him, since he lives forever to make intercession for them.

26*† It was fitting that we should have such a high priest: holy, innocent, undefiled, separated from sinners, higher than the heavens.† 27*† He has no need, as did the high priests, to offer sacrifice day after day, first for his own sins and then for those of the people; he did that once for all when he offered himself. 28* For the law appoints men subject to weakness to be high priests, but the word of the oath, which was taken after the law, appoints a son, who has been made perfect forever.

Heavenly Priesthood of Jesus

8 1*† The main point of what has been said is this: we have such a high priest, who has taken his seat at the right hand of the throne of the Majesty in heaven, 2*† a minister of the sanctuary and of the true tabernacle that the Lord, not man, set up. 3* Now every high priest is appointed to offer gifts and sacrifices; thus the necessity for this one also to have something to offer. 4* If then he were on earth, he would not be a priest, since there are those who offer gifts according to the law. 5* They worship in a copy and shadow of the heavenly sanctuary, as Moses was warned when he was about to erect the tabernacle. For he says, "See that you make everything according to the pattern shown you on the mountain." 6* Now he has obtained so much more excellent a ministry as he is mediator of a better covenant, enacted on better promises.

Old and New Covenants

7† For if that first covenant had been faultless, no place would have been sought for a second one. 8*† But he finds fault with them and says:

"Behold, the days are coming, says
   the Lord,
when I will conclude a new covenant with
   the house of Israel and the house
   of Judah.
9 It will not be like the covenant I made with
   their fathers
   the day I took them by the hand to lead
   them forth from the land of Egypt;
for they did not stand by my covenant
   and I ignored them, says the Lord.
10* But this is the covenant I will establish with
   the house of Israel
   after those days, says the Lord:
I will put my laws in their minds
   and I will write them upon their hearts.
I will be their God,
   and they shall be my people.
11 And they shall not teach, each one his
   fellow citizen
   and kinsman, saying, 'Know the Lord,'
for all shall know me,
   from least to greatest.
12 For I will forgive their evildoing
   and remember their sins no more."

7, 22: An [even] better covenant: better than the Mosaic covenant because it will be eternal, like the priesthood of Jesus upon which it is based. Verse 12 argued that a change of priesthood involves a change of law; since "law" and "covenant" are used correlatively, a new covenant is likewise instituted.

7, 25: To make intercession: the intercession of the exalted Jesus, not the sequel to his completed sacrifice but its eternal presence in heaven; cf Rom 8, 34.

7, 26–28: Jesus is precisely the high priest whom the human race requires, holy and sinless, installed far above humanity (26); one having no need to offer sacrifice daily for sins but making a single offering of himself (27) once for all. The law could only appoint high priests with human limitations, but the fulfillment of God's oath regarding the priesthood of Melchizedek (Ps 110, 4) makes the Son of God the perfect priest forever (28).

7, 26: This verse with its list of attributes is reminiscent of v 3 and is perhaps a hymnic counterpart to it, contrasting the exalted Jesus with Melchizedek.

7, 27: Such daily sacrifice is nowhere mentioned in the Mosaic law; only on the Day of Atonement is it prescribed that the high priest must offer sacrifice . . . for his own sins and then for those of the people (Lv 16, 11–19). Once for all: this translates the Greek words ephapax/hapax that occur eleven times in Hebrews.

8, 1–6: The Christian community has in Jesus the kind of high priest described in 7, 26–28. In virtue of his ascension Jesus has taken his place at God's right hand in accordance with Ps 110, 1 (1), where he presides over the heavenly sanctuary established by God himself (2). Like every high priest, he has his offering to make (3; cf 9, 12.14), but it differs from that of the levitical priesthood in which he had no share (4) and which was in any case but a shadowy reflection of the true offering in the heavenly sanctuary (5). But Jesus' ministry in the heavenly sanctuary is that of mediator of a superior covenant that accomplishes what it signifies (6).

8, 2: The sanctuary: the Greek term could also mean "holy things" but bears the meaning "sanctuary" elsewhere in Hebrews (9, 8.12.24.25; 10, 19; 13, 11). The true tabernacle: the heavenly tabernacle that the Lord . . . set up is contrasted with the earthly tabernacle that Moses set up in the desert. True means "real" in contradistinction to a mere "copy and shadow" (5); compare the Johannine usage (e.g., Jn 1, 9; 6, 32; 15, 1). The idea that the earthly sanctuary is a reflection of a heavenly model may be based upon Ex 25, 9, but probably also derives from the Platonic concept of a real world of which our observable world is merely a shadow.

8, 7–13: Since the first covenant was deficient in accomplishing what it signified, it had to be replaced (7), as Jeremiah (31, 31–34) had prophesied (8–12). Even in the time of Jeremiah, the first covenant was antiquated (13). In 7, 22–24, the superiority of the new covenant was seen in the permanence of its priesthood; here the superiority is based on better promises, made explicit in the citation of Jer 31 (LXX: 38), 31–34, namely, in the immediacy of the people's knowledge of God (11) and in the forgiveness of sin (12).

8, 8–12: In citing Jeremiah the author follows the Septuagint; some apparent departures from it may be the result of a different Septuagintal text rather than changes deliberately introduced.

7, 22: Heb 8, 6–10; 9, 15–20; 10, 29; 12, 24; 13, 20.	7, 28: Heb 5, 1.2.9.
7, 24: Heb 5, 6; 13, 8.	8, 1: Heb 1, 3; 4, 14; 7, 26–28.
7, 25: Rom 8, 34; 1 Jn 2, 1; Rv 1, 18.	8, 2: Heb 9, 11; Ex 33, 7; Nm 24, 6 LXX.
7, 26: Heb 4, 14.15.	8, 3: Heb 5, 1.
7, 27: Heb 5, 3; 9, 12.25–28; 10, 11–14; Ex 29, 38–39; Lv 16, 6.11.15–17; Nm 28, 3–4; Is 53, 10; Rom 6, 10.	8, 4: Heb 7, 13.
	8, 5: Heb 9, 23; Ex 25, 40; Acts 7, 44; Col 2, 17.
	8, 6: Heb 7, 22; 9, 15.
	8, 8: Jer 31, 31–34.
	8, 10: Heb 10, 16–17.

13*† When he speaks of a "new" covenant, he declares the first one obsolete. And what has become obsolete and has grown old is close to disappearing.

The Worship of the First Covenant

9 [1†] Now [even] the first covenant had regulations for worship and an earthly sanctuary. 2*† For a tabernacle was constructed, the outer one, in which were the lampstand, the table, and the bread of offering; this is called the Holy Place. 3*† Behind the second veil was the tabernacle called the Holy of Holies, 4*† in which were the gold altar of incense and the ark of the covenant entirely covered with gold. In it were the gold jar containing the manna, the staff of Aaron that had sprouted, and the tablets of the covenant. 5*† Above it were the cherubim of glory overshadowing the place of expiation. Now is not the time to speak of these in detail.

6*† With these arrangements for worship, the priests, in performing their service, go into the outer tabernacle repeatedly, 7*† but the high priest alone goes into the inner one once a year, not without blood that he offers for himself and for the sins of the people. 8 In this way the holy Spirit shows that the way into the sanctuary had not yet been revealed while the outer tabernacle still had its place. 9† This is a symbol of the present time, in which gifts and sacrifices are offered that cannot perfect the worshiper in conscience 10* but only in matters of food and drink and various ritual washings: regulations concerning the flesh, imposed until the time of the new order.

Sacrifice of Jesus

11*† But when Christ came as high priest of the good things that have come to be,† passing through the greater and more perfect tabernacle not made by hands, that is, not belonging to this creation, 12* he entered once for all into the sanctuary, not with the blood of goats and calves but with his own blood, thus obtaining eternal redemption. 13*† For if the blood of goats and bulls and the sprinkling of a heifer's ashes can sanctify those who are defiled so that their flesh is cleansed, 14*† how much more will the blood of Christ, who through the eternal spirit offered himself unblemished to God, cleanse our consciences from dead works to worship the living God.

15*† For this reason he is mediator of a new

8, 13: *Close to disappearing:* from the prophet's perspective, not that of the author of Hebrews.

9, 1–10: The regulations for worship under the old covenant permitted all the priests to enter the Holy Place (2, 6), but only the high priest to enter the Holy of Holies and then only once a year (3–5.7). The description of the sanctuary and its furnishings is taken essentially from Ex 25–26. This exclusion of the people from the Holy of Holies signified that they were not allowed to stand in God's presence (8) because their offerings and sacrifices, which were merely symbols of their need of spiritual renewal (10), could not obtain forgiveness of sins (9).

9, 2: *The outer one:* the author speaks of *the outer tabernacle* (6) and *the inner one* (7) rather than of one Mosaic tabernacle divided into two parts or sections.

9, 3: *The second veil:* what is meant is the veil that divided the Holy Place from the Holy of Holies. It is here called *the second,* because there was another veil at the entrance to the Holy Place, or "outer tabernacle" (Ex 26, 36).

9, 4: *The gold altar of incense:* Ex 30, 6 locates this altar in the Holy Place, i.e., the first tabernacle, rather than in the Holy of Holies. Neither is there any Old Testament support for the assertion that the jar of manna and the staff of Aaron were in the ark of the covenant. For the tablets of the covenant, see Ex 25, 16.

9, 5: *The place of expiation:* the gold "mercy seat" (Greek *hilastērion,* as in Rom 3, 25), where the blood of the sacrificial animals was sprinkled on the Day of Atonement (Lv 16, 14–15). This rite achieved "expiation" or atonement for the sins of the preceding year.

9, 6: *In performing their service:* the priestly services that had to be performed regularly in the Holy Place or *outer tabernacle* included burning incense on the incense altar twice each day (Ex 30, 7), replacing the loaves on the table of the bread of offering once each week (Lv 24, 8), and constantly caring for the lamps on the lampstand (Ex 27, 21).

9, 7: *Not without blood:* blood was essential to Old Testament sacrifice because it was believed that life was located in the blood. Hence blood was especially sacred, and its outpouring functioned as a meaningful symbol of cleansing from sin and reconciliation with God. Unlike Hebrews, the Old Testament never says that the blood is "offered." The author is perhaps retrojecting into his description of Mosaic ritual a concept that belongs to the New Testament antitype, as Paul does when he speaks of the Israelites' passage through the sea as a "baptism" (1 Cor 10, 2).

9, 9: *The present time:* this expression is equivalent to the "present age," used in contradistinction to the "age to come."

9, 11–14: Christ, the high priest of the spiritual blessings foreshadowed in the Old Testament sanctuary, has actually entered the true sanctuary of heaven that is not of human making (11). His place there is permanent, and his offering is his own blood that won eternal redemption (12). If the sacrifice of animals could bestow legal purification (13), how much more effective is the blood of the sinless, divine Christ who spontaneously offered himself to purge the human race of sin and render it fit for the service of God (14).

9, 11: *The good things that have come to be:* the majority of later manuscripts here read "the good things to come"; cf 10, 1.

9, 13: *A heifer's ashes:* ashes from a red heifer that had been burned were mixed with water and used for the cleansing of those who had become ritually defiled by touching a corpse; see Nm 19, 9.14–21.

9, 14: *Through the eternal spirit:* this expression does not refer either to the holy Spirit or to the divine nature of Jesus but to the life of the risen Christ, "a life that cannot be destroyed" (7, 16).

9, 15–22: Jesus' role as *mediator of a new covenant* is based upon his sacrificial *death* (cf 8, 6). His death has effected *deliverance from transgressions,* i.e., deliverance from sins committed under the old covenant, which the Mosaic sacrifices were incapable of effacing. Until this happened, the *eternal inheritance* promised by God could not be obtained (15). This effect of his work follows the human pattern by which a last will and testament becomes effective only with the death of the testator (16–17). The Mosaic covenant was also associated with death, for Moses made use of blood to seal the pact between God and the people (18–21). In Old Testament tradition, guilt could normally not be remitted without the use of blood (22; cf Lv 17, 11).

8, 13: Rom 10, 4.
9, 2: Ex 25, 23–30.
9, 3: Ex 26, 31–34.
9, 4: Ex 16, 32–34; 25, 10.16.21; 30, 1–10; Lv 16, 12–13; Nm 17, 2–7.16–26.
9, 5: Ex 25, 16–22; 26, 34; Lv 16, 14–15.
9, 6: Ex 27, 21; 30, 7; Lv 24, 8.
9, 7: Ex 30, 10; Lv 16, 1–14.

9, 10: Heb 13, 9; Lv 11; 14, 8; Nm 19, 11–21; Col 2, 16.
9, 11: Heb 4, 14; 10, 1.20.
9, 12: Heb 7, 27; Mt 26, 28.
9, 13: Heb 10, 4; Lv 16, 6–16; Nm, 19, 9.14–21.
9, 14: Heb 10, 10; Rom 5, 9; 1 Tm 3, 9; Ti 2, 14; 1 Pt 1, 18–19; 1 Jn 1, 7; Rv 1, 5.
9, 15: 1 Tm 2, 5.

H
E
B

covenant: since a death has taken place for deliverance from transgressions under the first covenant, those who are called may receive the promised eternal inheritance. [16]† Now where there is a will, the death of the testator must be established. [17] For a will takes effect only at death; it has no force while the testator is alive. [18] Thus not even the first covenant was inaugurated without blood. [19]*† When every commandment had been proclaimed by Moses to all the people according to the law, he took the blood of calves [and goats], together with water and crimson wool and hyssop, and sprinkled both the book itself and all the people, [20]* saying, "This is 'the blood of the covenant which God has enjoined upon you.'" [21]*† In the same way, he sprinkled also the tabernacle and all the vessels of worship with blood. [22]*† According to the law almost everything is purified by blood, and without the shedding of blood there is no forgiveness.

[23]*† Therefore, it was necessary for the copies of the heavenly things to be purified by these rites, but the heavenly things themselves by better sacrifices than these. [24]* For Christ did not enter into a sanctuary made by hands, a copy of the true one, but heaven itself, that he might now appear before God on our behalf. [25] Not that he might offer himself repeatedly, as the high priest enters each year into the sanctuary with blood that is not his own; [26]*† if that were so, he would have had to suffer repeatedly from the foundation of the world. But now once for all he has appeared at the end of the ages to take away sin by his sacrifice. [27]* Just as it is appointed that human beings die once, and after this the judgment, [28]*† so also Christ, offered once to take away the sins of many, will appear a second time, not to take away sin but to bring salvation to those who eagerly await him.

One Sacrifice instead of Many

10 [1]*† Since the law has only a shadow of the good things to come,† and not the very image of them, it can never make perfect those who come to worship by the same sacrifices that they offer continually each year. [2] Otherwise, would not the sacrifices have ceased to be offered, since the worshipers, once cleansed, would no longer have had any consciousness of sins? [3]* But in those sacrifices there is only a yearly remembrance of sins, [4]* for it is impossible that the blood of bulls and goats take away sins. [5]*† For this reason, when he came into the world, he said:

9, 16–17: *A will . . . death of the testator:* the same Greek word *diathēkē,* meaning "covenant" in vv 15 and 18, is used here with the meaning *will.* The new covenant, unlike the old, is at the same time a will that requires the *death of the testator.* Jesus as eternal Son is the one who established the new covenant together with his Father, author of both covenants; at the same time he is the testator whose death puts his *will* into effect.

9, 19–20: A number of details here are different from the description of this covenant rite in Ex 24, 5–8. Exodus mentions only calves ("young bulls," NAB), not goats (but this addition in Hebrews is of doubtful authenticity), says nothing of the use of *water and crimson wool and hyssop* (these features probably came from a different rite; cf Lv 14, 3–7; Nm 19, 6–18), and describes Moses as splashing blood on the altar, whereas Hebrews says he sprinkled it on the book (but both book and altar are meant to symbolize the agreement of God). The words of Moses are also slightly different from those in Exodus and are closer to the words of Jesus at the Last Supper in Mk 14, 24 // Mt 26, 28.

9, 21: According to Exodus, the tabernacle did not yet exist at the time of the covenant rite. Moreover, nothing is said of sprinkling it with blood at its subsequent dedication (Ex 40, 9–11).

9, 22: *Without the shedding of blood there is no forgiveness:* in fact, ancient Israel did envisage other means of obtaining forgiveness; the Old Testament mentions contrition of heart (Ps 51, 19), fasting (Jl 2, 12), and almsgiving (Sir 3, 29). The author is limiting his horizon to the sacrificial cult, which did always involve the shedding of blood for its expiatory and unitive value.

9, 23–28: Since the blood of animals became a cleansing symbol among Old Testament prefigurations, it was necessary that the realities foreshadowed be brought into being by a shedding of blood that was infinitely more effective by reason of its worth (23). Christ did not simply prefigure the heavenly realities (24) by performing an annual sacrifice with a blood not his own (25); he offered the single sacrifice of himself as the final annulment of sin (26). Just as death is the unrepeatable act that ends a person's life, so Christ's offering of himself for all is the unrepeatable sacrifice that has once for all achieved redemption (27–28).

9, 26: *At the end of the ages:* the use of expressions such as this shows that the author of Hebrews, despite his interest in the Platonic concept of an eternal world above superior to temporal reality here below, nevertheless still clings to the Jewish Christian eschatology with its sequence of "the present age" and "the age to come."

9, 28: *To take away the sins of many:* the reference is to Is 53, 12. Since the Greek verb *anapherō* can mean both "to take away" and "to bear," the author no doubt intended to play upon both senses: Jesus took away sin by bearing it himself. See the similar wordplay in Jn 1, 29. *Many* is used in the Semitic meaning of "all" in the inclusive sense, as in Mk 14, 24. *To those who eagerly await him:* Jesus will appear *a second time* at the parousia, as the high priest reappeared on the Day of Atonement, emerging from the Holy of Holies, which he had entered *to take away sin.* This dramatic scene is described in Sir 50, 5–11.

10, 1–10: Christian faith now realizes that the Old Testament sacrifices did not effect the spiritual benefits to come but only prefigured them (1). For if the sacrifices had actually effected the forgiveness of sin, there would have been no reason for their constant repetition (2). They were rather a continual reminder of the people's sins (3). It is not reasonable to suppose that human sins could be removed by the blood of animal sacrifices (4). Christ, therefore, is here shown to understand his mission in terms of Ps 40, 6–8, cited according to the Septuagint (5–7). Jesus acknowledged that the Old Testament sacrifices did not remit the sins of the people and so, perceiving the will of God, offered his own body for this purpose (8–10).

10, 1: *A shadow of the good things to come:* the term *shadow* was used in 8, 5 to signify the earthly counterpart of the Platonic heavenly reality. But here it means a prefiguration of what is to come in Christ, as it is used in the Pauline literature; cf Col 2, 17.

10, 5–7: A passage from Ps 40, 7–9a is placed in the mouth of the Son at his incarnation. As usual, the author follows the Septuagint text. There is a notable difference in v 5 (Ps 40, 7b), where the Masoretic text reads "ears you have dug for me" ("ears open to obedience you gave me," NAB), but most Septuagint manuscripts have "a body you prepared for me," a reading obviously more suited to the interpretation of Hebrews.

9, 19: Heb 9, 12–13.
9, 20: Ex 24, 3–8; Mt 26, 28; Mk 14, 24.
9, 21: Ex 40, 9; Lv 8, 15.19.
9, 22: Lv 17, 11.
9, 23: Jb 15, 15.
9, 24: Heb 7, 25; Rom 8, 34; 1 Jn 2, 1–2.
9, 26: Heb 7, 27; Jn 1, 29; Gal 4, 4.
9, 27: Gn 3, 19.
9, 28: Heb 10, 10; Is 53, 12.
10, 1: Heb 8, 5; Col 2, 17.
10, 3: Lv 16, 21; Nm 5, 15 LXX.
10, 4: Is 1, 11; Mi 6, 6–8.
10, 5–7: Ps 40, 7–9.

did you **KNOW?**

The Perfect Sacrifice

The author of the Letter to the Hebrews uses the "from the lesser to the greater" argument again to explain that Christ's sacrifice on the cross is greater than any sacrifice that could ever be offered in the Temple. Even though perfect animals are offered over and over, they never take away sins (10, 1–4). The sacrifice of Christ takes away sins because it is the perfect sacrifice, offered only once for the sins of all (verses 12–14). After Christ's death, there is no longer any need for anyone else to offer a sacrifice for the forgiveness of sins.

▸ Heb 10, 1–18

"Sacrifice and offering you did not desire,
　　but a body you prepared for me;
6　holocausts and sin offerings you took no
　　　delight in.
7　Then I said, 'As is written of me in the scroll,
　　Behold, I come to do your will, O God.' "

8*† First he says, "Sacrifices and offerings, holocausts and sin offerings, you neither desired nor delighted in." These are offered according to the law. 9* Then he says, "Behold, I come to do your will." He takes away the first to establish the second. 10* By this "will," we have been consecrated through the offering of the body of Jesus Christ once for all.

11*† Every priest stands daily at his ministry, offering frequently those same sacrifices that can never take away sins. 12* But this one offered one sacrifice for sins, and took his seat forever at the right hand of God; 13† now he waits until his enemies are made his footstool. 14* For by one offering he has made perfect forever those who are being consecrated. 15† The holy Spirit also testifies to us, for after saying:

16* "This is the covenant I will establish with
　　　them after those days, says the Lord:
'I will put my laws in their hearts,
　　and I will write them upon their minds,' "

17*† he also says:

"Their sins and their evildoing
　　I will remember no more."

18 Where there is forgiveness of these, there is no longer offering for sin.

Recalling the Past

19*† Therefore, brothers, since through the blood of Jesus we have confidence of entrance into the sanctuary 20*† by the new and living way he

---

† **10, 8:** *Sacrifices and offerings, holocausts and sin offerings:* these four terms taken from the preceding passage of Ps 40 (with the first two changed to plural forms) are probably intended as equivalents to the four principal types of Old Testament sacrifices: peace offerings (Lv 3, here called *sacrifices*); cereal offerings (Lv 2, here called *offerings*); holocausts (Lv 1); and *sin offerings* (Lv 4–5). This last category includes the guilt offerings of Lv 5, 14–26.

10, 11–18: Whereas the levitical priesthood offered daily sacrifices that were ineffectual in remitting sin (11), Jesus offered a single sacrifice that won him a permanent place at God's right hand. There he has only to await the final outcome of his work (12–13; cf Ps 110, 1). Thus he has brought into being in his own person the new covenant prophesied by Jeremiah (31, 33–34) that has rendered meaningless all other offerings for sin (14–18).

10, 13: *Until his enemies are made his footstool:* Ps 110, 1 is again used; the reference here is to the period of time between the enthronement of Jesus and his second coming. The identity of the *enemies* is not specified; cf 1 Cor 15, 25–27.

10, 15–17: The testimony of the scriptures is now invoked to support what has just preceded. The passage cited is a portion of the new covenant prophecy of Jer 31, 31–34, which the author previously used in 8, 8–12.

10, 17: *He also says:* these words are not in the Greek text, which has only *kai,* "also," but the expression *after saying* in v 15 seems to require such a phrase to divide the Jeremiah text into two sayings. Others understand "the Lord says" of v 16 (here rendered *says the Lord*) as outside the quotation and consider v 16b as part of the second saying. Two ancient versions and a number of minuscules introduce the words "then he said" or a similar expression at the beginning of v 17.

10, 19–39: Practical consequences from these reflections on the priesthood and the sacrifice of Christ should make it clear that Chris-

tians may now have direct and confident access to God through the person of Jesus (19–20), who rules God's house as high priest (21). They should approach God with sincerity and faith, in the knowledge that through baptism their sins have been remitted (22), reminding themselves of the hope they expressed in Christ at that event (23). They are to encourage one another to Christian love and activity (24), not refusing, no matter what the reason, to participate in the community's assembly, especially in view of the parousia (25; cf 1 Thes 4, 13–18). If refusal to participate in the assembly indicates rejection of Christ, no sacrifice exists to obtain forgiveness for so great a sin (26); only the dreadful judgment of God remains (27). For if violation of the Mosaic law could be punished by death, how much worse will be the punishment of those who have turned their backs on Christ by despising his sacrifice and disregarding the gifts of the holy Spirit (28–29). Judgment belongs to the Lord, and he enacts it by his living presence (30–31). There was a time when the spirit of their community caused them to welcome and share their sufferings (32–34). To revitalize that spirit is to share in the courage of the Old Testament prophets (cf Is 26, 20; Hb 2, 3–4), the kind of courage that must distinguish the faith of the Christian (35–39).

10, 20: *Through the veil, that is, his flesh:* the term *flesh* is used pejoratively. As the temple veil kept people from entering the Holy of Holies (it was rent at Christ's death, Mk 15, 38), so the flesh of Jesus constituted an obstacle to approaching God.

---

*

10, 8: Heb 10, 5–6; Ps 40, 7.	**10, 14:** Heb 9, 28.
10, 9: Heb 7; Ps 40, 8; Mt 26, 39; Mk 14, 36; Lk 22, 42; Jn 6, 38.	**10, 16:** Heb 8, 10; Jer 31, 33. **10, 17:** Heb 8, 12; Jer 31, 34. **10, 19:** Heb 3, 6; 4, 16; 6, 19–20; Eph 1, 7; 3, 12.
10, 10: Heb 9, 12.14.	
10, 11: Heb 7, 27; Dt 10, 8; 18, 7.	**10, 20:** Jn 14, 6 / Heb 6, 19–20; 9, 8.11–12; Mt 27, 51; Mk 15, 38; Lk 23, 45.
10, 12–13: Ps 110, 1.	

H
E
B

opened for us through the veil, that is, his flesh, 21*† and since we have "a great priest over the house of God," 22*† let us approach with a sincere heart and in absolute trust, with our hearts sprinkled clean from an evil conscience and our bodies washed in pure water. 23* Let us hold unwaveringly to our confession that gives us hope, for he who made the promise is trustworthy. 24 We must consider how to rouse one another to love and good works. 25*† We should not stay away from our assembly, as is the custom of some, but encourage one another, and this all the more as you see the day drawing near.

26*† If we sin deliberately after receiving knowledge of the truth, there no longer remains sacrifice for sins 27* but a fearful prospect of judgment and a flaming fire that is going to consume the adversaries. 28*† Anyone who rejects the law of Moses is put to death without pity on the testimony of two or three witnesses. 29* Do you not think that a much worse punishment is due the one who has contempt for the Son of God, considers unclean the covenant-blood by which he was consecrated, and insults the spirit of grace? 30* We know the one who said:

"Vengeance is mine; I will repay,"

and again:

"The Lord will judge his people."

31* It is a fearful thing to fall into the hands of the living God.

32*† Remember the days past when, after you had been enlightened, you endured a great contest of suffering. 33* At times you were publicly exposed to abuse and affliction; at other times you associated yourselves with those so treated. 34* You even joined in the sufferings of those in prison and joyfully accepted the confiscation of your property, knowing that you had a better and lasting possession. 35* Therefore, do not throw away your confidence; it will have great recompense. 36* You need endurance to do the will of God and receive what he has promised.

37*† "For, after just a brief moment,
    he who is to come shall come;
    he shall not delay.
38* But my just one shall live by faith,
    and if he draws back I take no pleasure
    in him."

39 We are not among those who draw back and perish, but among those who have faith and will possess life.

V: Examples, Discipline, Disobedience

Faith of the Ancients†

11 1* Faith is the realization of what is hoped for and evidence† of things not seen. 2 Because of it the ancients were well attested.

---

† **10, 21:** *The house of God:* this refers back to 3, 6, "we are his house."

10, 22: *With our hearts sprinkled clean from an evil conscience:* as in 9, 13 (see the note there), the sprinkling motif refers to the Mosaic rite of cleansing from ritual impurity. This could produce only an external purification, whereas sprinkling with the blood of Christ (9, 14) cleanses the *conscience. Washed in pure water:* baptism is elsewhere referred to as a washing; cf 1 Cor 6, 11; Eph 5, 26.

10, 25: *Our assembly:* the liturgical *assembly* of the Christian community, probably for the celebration of the Eucharist. *The day:* this designation for the parousia also occurs in the Pauline letters, e.g., Rom 2, 16; 1 Cor 3, 13; 1 Thes 5, 2.

10, 26: *If we sin deliberately:* verse 29 indicates that the author is here thinking of apostasy; cf 3, 12; 6, 4–8.

10, 28: *Rejects the law of Moses:* evidently not any sin against the law, but idolatry. Dt 17, 2–7 prescribed capital punishment for idolaters who were convicted on the testimony of two or three witnesses.

10, 32: *After you had been enlightened:* "enlightenment" is an ancient metaphor for baptism (cf Eph 5, 14; Jn 9, 11), but see 6, 4 and the note there.

10, 37–38: In support of his argument, the author uses Hb 2, 3–4 in a wording almost identical with the text of the Codex Alexandrinus of the Septuagint but with the first and second lines of v 4 inverted. He introduces it with a few words from Is 26, 20: *after just a brief moment.* Note the Pauline usage of Hb 2, 4 in Rom 1, 17; Gal 3, 11.

11, 1–40: This chapter draws upon the people and events of the Old Testament to paint an inspiring portrait of religious faith, firm and unyielding in the face of any obstacles that confront it. These pages rank among the most eloquent and lofty to be found in the Bible. They expand the theme announced in 6, 12, to which the author now returns (10, 39). The material of this chapter is developed chronologically. Verses 3–7 draw upon the first nine chapters of Genesis; vv 8–22, upon the period of the patriarchs; vv 23–31, upon the time of Moses; vv 32–38, upon the history of the judges, the prophets, and the Maccabean martyrs. The author gives the most ex-

tensive description of faith provided in the New Testament, though his interest does not lie in a technical, theological definition. In view of the needs of his audience he describes what authentic faith does, not what it is in itself. Through faith God guarantees the blessings to be hoped for from him, providing evidence in the gift of faith that what he promises will eventually come to pass (1). Because they accepted in faith God's guarantee of the future, the biblical personages discussed in vv 3–38 were themselves commended by God (2). Christians have even greater reason to remain firm in faith since they, unlike the Old Testament men and women of faith, have perceived the beginning of God's fulfillment of his messianic promises (39–40).

11, 1: *Faith is the realization . . . evidence:* the author is not attempting a precise definition. There is dispute about the meaning of the Greek words *hypostasis* and *elenchos,* here translated *realization* and *evidence,* respectively. *Hypostasis* usually means "substance," "being" (as translated in 1, 3), or "reality" (as translated in 3, 14); here it connotes something more subjective, and so *realization* has been chosen rather than "assurance" (RSV). *Elenchos,* usually "proof," is used here in an objective sense and so translated *evidence* rather than the transferred sense of "(inner) conviction" (RSV).

10, 21: Heb 3, 6.
10, 22: Heb 9, 13–14; Ez 36, 25; 1 Cor 6, 11; Ti 3, 5; 1 Pt 3, 21.
10, 23: Heb 3, 1.6; 4, 14; 1 Cor 10, 13.
10, 25: Rom 13, 12; 1 Cor 3, 13.
10, 26: Heb 3, 12; 6, 4–8.
10, 27: Heb 10, 31; 9, 27; Is 26, 11 LXX; Zep 1, 18.
10, 28: Dt 17, 6.
10, 29: Heb 6, 6.
10, 30: Dt 32, 35.36; Rom 12, 19.

10, 31: Heb 10, 27; Mt 10, 28; Lk 12, 4–5.
10, 32: Heb 6, 4.
10, 33: 1 Cor 4, 9.
10, 34: Heb 13, 3; Mt 6, 19–20; Lk 12, 33–34.
10, 35: Heb 4, 16.
10, 36: Lk 21, 19.
10, 37: Is 26, 20; Hb 2, 3.
10, 38: Hb 2, 4; Rom 1, 17; Gal 3, 11.
11, 1: Heb 1, 3; 3, 14; Rom 8, 24; 2 Cor 4, 18.

3*† By faith we understand that the universe was ordered by the word of God, so that what is visible came into being through the invisible. 4*† By faith Abel offered to God a sacrifice greater than Cain's. Through this he was attested to be righteous, God bearing witness to his gifts, and through this, though dead, he still speaks. 5* By faith Enoch was taken up so that he should not see death, and "he was found no more because God had taken him." Before he was taken up, he was attested to have pleased God. 6*† But without faith it is impossible to please him, for anyone who approaches God must believe that he exists and that he rewards those who seek him. 7* By faith Noah, warned about what was not yet seen, with reverence built an ark for the salvation of his household. Through this he condemned the world and inherited the righteousness that comes through faith.

8* By faith Abraham obeyed when he was called to go out to a place that he was to receive as an inheritance; he went out, not knowing where he was to go. 9* By faith he sojourned in the promised land as in a foreign country, dwelling in tents with Isaac and Jacob, heirs of the same promise; 10* for he was looking forward to the city with foundations, whose architect and maker is God. 11* By faith he received power to generate, even though he was past the normal age—and Sarah herself was sterile—for he thought that the one who had made the promise was trustworthy. 12* So it was that there came forth from one man, himself as good as dead, descendants as numerous as the stars in the sky and as countless as the sands on the seashore.

13* All these died in faith. They did not receive what had been promised but saw it and greeted it from afar and acknowledged themselves to be strangers and aliens on earth, 14 for those who speak thus show that they are seeking a homeland. 15 If they had been thinking of the land from which they had come, they would have had opportunity to return. 16* But now they desire a better homeland, a heavenly one. Therefore, God is not ashamed to be called their God, for he has prepared a city for them.

17* By faith Abraham, when put to the test, offered up Isaac, and he who had received the

Catholic Connections

THE CLOUD OF WITNESSES

In chapters 11 and 12 of The Letter to the Hebrews, the author reminds his audience of the great legacy of men and women who have served as examples of faith and virtue. Their faith in God and their fidelity to the Covenant stand as compelling witnesses to those who seek to follow Christ. From Abel to Abraham and Sarah and from Moses up through the ages, the word of God attests to how women and men have lived their lives for God.

Jesus, however, is the one upon whom we are urged to "fix" our eyes so that we see the leader and perfecter of such faith. Christ and his sacrifice stand as the ultimate example of faith and fidelity.

The cloud of witnesses has grown as Christ has called people of all ages to holiness. From Mary, his mother, to Peter and the Apostles and martyrs, from Augustine and Aquinas to Francis and Theresa, men and women of every age, in every corner of the earth, have lived their lives for God. The cloud grows ever larger as these saints continue to forge a legacy, a witness to God's love and salvation offered in Jesus the Son.

We too are called to resist sin and offer our lives to God, even if it means facing the discipline of suffering. We are called to be the new generation of witnesses—the saints of our day whose example calls and strengthens others on the journey.

▸ Hebrews, chapters 11 and 12

11, 3: By faith . . . God: this verse does not speak of the faith of the Old Testament men and women but is in the first person plural. Hence it seems out of place in the sequence of thought.

11, 4: The "Praise of the Ancestors" in Sir 44, 1–50, 21 gives a similar list of heroes. The Cain and Abel narrative in Gn 4, 1–16 does not mention Abel's faith. It says, however, that God "looked with favor on Abel and his offering" (Gn 4, 4); in view of v 6 the author probably understood God's favor to have been activated by Abel's faith. Though dead, he still speaks: possibly because his blood "cries out to me from the soil" (Gn 4, 10), but more probably a way of saying that the repeated story of Abel provides ongoing witness to faith.

11, 6: One must believe not only that God exists but that he is concerned about human conduct; the Old Testament defines folly as the denial of this truth; cf Ps 52, 2.

11, 3: Gn 1, 3; Ps 33, 6; Wis 9, 1; Jn 1, 3.
11, 4: Heb 12, 24; Gn 4, 4.10.
11, 5: Gn 5, 24; Sir 44, 16.
11, 6: Wis 4, 10.
11, 7: Gn 6, 8–22; Sir 44, 17–18; Mt 24, 37–39; Lk 17, 26–27; 1 Pt 3, 20; 2 Pt 2, 5.
11, 8: Gn 12, 1–4; 15, 7–21; Sir 44, 19–22; Acts 7, 2–8; Rom 4, 16–22.
11, 9: Gn 12, 8; 13, 12; 23,

4; 26, 3; 35, 27.
11, 10: Heb 12, 22; 13, 14; Rv 21, 10–22.
11, 11: Gn 17, 19; 21, 2; Rom 4, 19–21 / 1 Cor 10, 13.
11, 12: Gn 15, 5; 22, 17; 32, 13; Ex 32, 13; Dt 10, 22; Dn 3, 36 LXX.
11, 13: Gn 23, 4; Ps 39, 13.
11, 16: Heb 13, 14; Ex 3, 6.
11, 17: Gn 22, 1–10; Sir 44, 20; 1 Mc 2, 52; Jas 2, 21.

HEB

promises was ready to offer his only son, [18]* of whom it was said, "Through Isaac descendants shall bear your name." [19]*† He reasoned that God was able to raise even from the dead, and he received Isaac back as a symbol. [20]*† By faith regarding things still to come Isaac blessed Jacob and Esau. [21]* By faith Jacob, when dying, blessed each of the sons of Joseph and "bowed in worship, leaning on the top of his staff." [22]* By faith Joseph, near the end of his life, spoke of the Exodus of the Israelites and gave instructions about his bones.

[23]* By faith Moses was hidden by his parents for three months after his birth, because they saw that he was a beautiful child, and they were not afraid of the king's edict. [24]*† By faith Moses, when he had grown up, refused to be known as the son of Pharaoh's daughter; [25] he chose to be ill-treated along with the people of God rather than enjoy the fleeting pleasure of sin. [26] He considered the reproach of the Anointed greater wealth than the treasures of Egypt, for he was looking to the recompense. [27]* By faith he left Egypt, not fearing the king's fury, for he persevered as if seeing the one who is invisible. [28]* By faith he kept the Passover and sprinkled the blood, that the Destroyer of the firstborn might not touch them. [29]* By faith they crossed the Red Sea as if it were dry land, but when the Egyptians attempted it they were drowned. [30]* By faith the walls of Jericho fell after being encircled for seven days. [31]* By faith Rahab the harlot did not perish with the disobedient, for she had received the spies in peace.

[32]* What more shall I say? I have not time to tell of Gideon, Barak, Samson, Jephthah, of David and Samuel and the prophets, [33]* who by faith conquered kingdoms, did what was righteous, obtained the promises; they closed the mouths of lions, [34]* put out raging fires, escaped the devouring sword; out of weakness they were made powerful, became strong in battle, and turned back foreign invaders. [35]* Women received back their dead through resurrection. Some were tortured and would not accept deliverance, in order to obtain a better resurrection. [36]* Others endured mockery, scourging, even chains and imprisonment. [37]* They were stoned, sawed in two, put to death at sword's point; they went about in skins of sheep or goats, needy, afflicted, tormented. [38]* The world was not worthy of them. They wandered about in deserts and on mountains, in caves and in crevices in the earth.

[39] Yet all these, though approved because of their faith, did not receive what had been promised. [40]† God had foreseen something better for us, so that without us they should not be made perfect.

God our Father

12 [1]† Therefore, since we are surrounded by so great a cloud of witnesses, let us rid ourselves of every burden and sin that clings to us† and persevere in running the race that lies before us [2]* while keeping our eyes fixed on Jesus, the leader and perfecter of faith. For the sake of the joy that lay before him he endured the cross, despising its shame, and has taken his seat at the right of the throne of God. [3] Consider how he endured such opposition from sinners, in order that you may not grow weary and lose heart. [4] In your struggle against sin you have not yet resisted to the point of shedding blood. [5]* You have also forgotten the exhortation addressed to you as sons:

"My son, do not disdain the discipline of
    the Lord
  or lose heart when reproved by him;
[6] for whom the Lord loves, he disciplines;
    he scourges every son he acknowledges."

11, 19: *As a symbol:* Isaac's "return from death" is seen as a symbol of Christ's resurrection. Others understand the words *en parabolē* to mean "in figure," i.e., the word *dead* is used figuratively of Isaac, since he did not really die. But in the one other place that *parabolē* occurs in Hebrews, it means symbol (9, 9).

11, 20–22: Each of these three patriarchs, Isaac, Jacob, and Joseph, had faith in the future fulfillment of God's promise and renewed this faith when near death.

11, 24–27: The reason given for Moses' departure from Egypt differs from the account in Ex 2, 11–15. The author also gives a christological interpretation of his decision to share the trials of his people.

11, 40: *So that without us they should not be made perfect:* the heroes of the Old Testament obtained their recompense only after the saving work of Christ had been accomplished. Thus they already enjoy what Christians who are still struggling do not yet possess in its fullness.

12, 1–13: Christian life is to be inspired not only by the Old Testament men and women of faith (1) but above all by Jesus. As the architect of Christian faith, he had himself to endure the cross before receiving the glory of his triumph (2). Reflection on his sufferings should give his followers courage to continue the struggle, if necessary even to the shedding of blood (3–4). Christians should regard their own sufferings as the affectionate correction of the Lord, who loves them as a father loves his children.

12, 1: *That clings to us:* the meaning is uncertain, since the Greek word *euperistatos,* translated *cling,* occurs only here. The papyrus P[46] and one minuscule read *euperispastos,* "easily distracting," which also makes good sense.

11, 18: Gn 21, 12 LXX; Rom 9, 7.
11, 19: Rom 4, 16–22.
11, 20: Gn 27, 27–40.
11, 21: Gn 27, 38–40; 47, 31 LXX; 48, 15–16.
11, 22: Gn 50, 24–25.
11, 23: Ex 2, 2; Acts 7, 20.
11, 24–25: Ex 2, 10–15; Acts 7, 23–29.
11, 27: Ex 2, 15; Acts 7, 29.
11, 28: Ex 12, 21–23; Wis 18, 25; 1 Cor 10, 10.
11, 29: Ex 14, 22–28.
11, 30: Jos 6, 12–21.
11, 31: Jos 2, 1–21; 6, 22–25; Jas 2, 25.
11, 32: Jgs 4, 6–22; 6, 11–8, 32; 11, 1–12, 7.
11, 33: Dn 6, 23.
11, 34: Dn 3, 22–25.49–50.
11, 35: 1 Kgs 17, 17–24; 2 Kgs 4, 18–37; 2 Mc 6, 18–7, 42.
11, 36: 2 Chr 36, 16; Jer 20, 2; 37, 15.
11, 37: 2 Chr 24, 21.
11, 38: 1 Mc 2, 28–30.
12, 2: Heb 2, 10; Ps 110, 1; Phil 2, 6–8.
12, 5–6: Prv 3, 11–12 / Dt 8, 5; 1 Cor 11, 32.

⁷* Endure your trials as "discipline"; God treats you as sons. For what "son" is there whom his father does not discipline? ⁸ If you are without discipline, in which all have shared, you are not sons but bastards. ⁹* Besides this, we have had our earthly fathers to discipline us, and we respected them. Should we not [then] submit all the more to the Father of spirits and live? ¹⁰ They disciplined us for a short time as seemed right to them, but he does so for our benefit, in order that we may share his holiness. ¹¹* At the time, all discipline seems a cause not for joy but for pain, yet later it brings the peaceful fruit of righteousness to those who are trained by it.

¹²* So strengthen your drooping hands and your weak knees. ¹³* Make straight paths for your feet, that what is lame may not be dislocated but healed.

Penalties of Disobedience

¹⁴* Strive for peace with everyone, and for that holiness without which no one will see the Lord. ¹⁵*† See to it that no one be deprived of the grace of God, that no bitter root spring up and cause trouble, through which many may become defiled, ¹⁶* that no one be an immoral or profane person like Esau, who sold his birthright for a single meal. ¹⁷* For you know that later, when he wanted to inherit his father's blessing, he was rejected because he found no opportunity to change his mind, even though he sought the blessing with tears.

¹⁸*† You have not approached that which could be touched and a blazing fire and gloomy darkness and storm† ¹⁹* and a trumpet blast and a voice speaking words such that those who heard begged that no message be further addressed to them, ²⁰* for they could not bear to hear the command:

"If even an animal touches the mountain, it shall be stoned." ²¹* Indeed, so fearful was the spectacle that Moses said, "I am terrified and trembling." ²²* No, you have approached Mount Zion and the city of the living God, the heavenly Jerusalem, and countless angels in festal gathering, ²³*† and the assembly of the firstborn enrolled in heaven, and God the judge of all, and the spirits of the just made perfect, ²⁴*† and Jesus, the mediator of a new covenant, and the sprinkled blood that speaks more eloquently than that of Abel.

²⁵* See that you do not reject the one who speaks. For if they did not escape when they refused the one who warned them on earth, how much more in our case if we turn away from the one who warns from heaven. ²⁶* His voice shook the earth at that time, but now he has promised, "I will once more shake not only earth but heaven." ²⁷* That phrase, "once more," points to [the] removal of shaken, created things, so that what is unshaken may remain. ²⁸* Therefore, we who are receiving the unshakable kingdom should have gratitude, with which we should offer worship pleasing to God in reverence and awe. ²⁹* For our God is a consuming fire.

VI: Final Exhortation, Blessing, Greetings

13 ¹† Let mutual love continue. ²* Do not neglect hospitality, for through it some have unknowingly entertained angels. ³* Be mindful of prisoners as if sharing their imprisonment, and of the ill-treated as of yourselves, for you also are in the body. ⁴* Let marriage be honored among all and the marriage bed be kept undefiled, for God will judge the immoral and adulterers. ⁵* Let your life be free

H
E
B

12, 15–17: Esau serves as an example in two ways: his *profane* attitude illustrates the danger of apostasy, and his inability to secure a blessing afterward illustrates the impossibility of repenting after falling away (see 6, 4–6).

12, 18–29: As a final appeal for adherence to Christian teaching, the two covenants, of Moses and of Christ, are compared. The Mosaic covenant, the author argues, is shown to have originated in fear of God and threats of divine punishment (18–21). The covenant in Christ gives us direct access to God (22), makes us members of the Christian community, God's children, a sanctified people (23), who have Jesus as mediator to speak for us (24). Not to heed the voice of the risen Christ is a graver sin than the rejection of the word of Moses (25–26). Though Christians fall away, God's kingdom in Christ will remain and his justice will punish those guilty of deserting it (28–29).

12, 18–24: This remarkably beautiful passage contrasts two great assemblies of people: that of the Israelites gathered at Mount Sinai for the sealing of the old covenant and the promulgation of the Mosaic law, and that of the followers of Jesus gathered at *Mount Zion, the heavenly Jerusalem,* the assembly of the *new covenant.* This latter scene, marked by the presence of *countless angels* and of *Jesus* with his redeeming *blood,* is reminiscent of the celestial liturgies of the Book of Revelation.

12, 23: *The assembly of the firstborn enrolled in heaven:* this expression may refer to the angels of v 22, or to the heroes of the Old Testament (see ch 11), or to the entire assembly of the new covenant.

12, 24: *Speaks more eloquently:* the blood of Abel, the first human blood to be shed, is contrasted with that of Jesus. Abel's blood cried out from the earth for vengeance, but the blood of Jesus has opened

the way for everyone, providing cleansing and access to God (10, 19).

13, 1–16: After recommendations on social and moral matters (1–6), the letter turns to doctrinal issues. The fact that the original leaders are dead should not cause the recipients of this letter to lose their faith (7), for Christ still lives and he remains always the same (8). They must not rely for their personal sanctification on regulations concerning foods (9), nor should they entertain the notion that Judaism and Christianity can be intermingled (10; cf the notes on Gal 2, 11–14 and 2, 15–21). As Jesus died separated from his own people, so must the Christian community remain apart from the religious doctrines of Judaism (11–14). Christ must be the heart and center of the community (15–16).

12, 7: Prv 13, 24; Sir 30, 1.
12, 9: Nm 16, 22; 27, 16 LXX.
12, 11: 2 Cor 4, 17; Phil 1, 11; Jas 3, 18.
12, 12: Is 35, 3; Sir 25, 23; Jb 4, 3–4.
12, 13: Prv 4, 26 LXX.
12, 14: Rom 12, 18; 14, 19.
12, 15: Dt 29, 18 (17 LXX).
12, 16: Gn 25, 33.
12, 17: Gn 27, 34–38.
12, 18: Ex 19, 12–14; Dt 4, 11; 5, 22–23.
12, 19: Ex 19, 16.19; 20, 18–19.
12, 20: Ex 19, 12–13.
12, 21: Dt 9, 19.

12, 22: Gal 4, 26; Rv 21, 2.
12, 23: Lk 10, 20; Rv 5, 11.
12, 24: Heb 7, 22; 8, 6; 9, 15 / Heb 11, 4; Gn 4, 10.
12, 25: Ex 20, 19.
12, 26: Ex 19, 18; Jgs 5, 4–5; Ps 68, 9; Hg 2, 6.
12, 27: Is 66, 22; Mt 24, 35; Mk 13, 31; Lk 21, 33.
12, 28: Dn 7, 14.18 / Rom 1, 9.
12, 29: Dt 4, 24; Is 33, 14.
13, 2: Gn 18, 3; 19, 2–3; Jgs 6, 11–22; Tb 5, 4.
13, 3: Mt 25, 36.
13, 4: 1 Cor 5, 13; Eph 5, 5.
13, 5: Dt 31, 6.8; Jos 1, 5.

Entertaining Angels

The subject of angels has always fascinated the media, especially filmmakers and television show producers. They often develop stories around the idea from the Letter to the Hebrews that people sometimes encounter angels and that angels are sent to rescue people caught in dire or tragic circumstances.

We know that God has created a category of beings that is made up of pure spirits without bodies. These beings act as God's messengers and serve as spiritual guardians for humans. Their mission is to bring God's word to those who are open to hear it and respond to it with faith and humility.

Will we ever be "touched by an angel" or have the opportunity to entertain angels in human disguise? We may never know the answer to these questions, but we should entertain this truth in our hearts and minds: God guides the world and has sent messengers and guardians, angels, whose mysterious presence offers support, protection, and intercession for those who believe in God and seek the face of God.

▸ Heb 13, 1–5

from love of money but be content with what you have, for he has said, "I will never forsake you or abandon you." 6* Thus we may say with confidence:

"The Lord is my helper,
[and] I will not be afraid.
What can anyone do to me?"

7 Remember your leaders who spoke the word of God to you. Consider the outcome of their way of life and imitate their faith. 8* Jesus Christ is the same yesterday, today, and forever.

9*† Do not be carried away by all kinds of strange teaching. It is good to have our hearts strengthened by grace and not by foods, which do not benefit those who live by them. 10† We have an altar from which those who serve the tabernacle have no right to eat. 11* The bodies of the animals whose blood the high priest brings into the sanctuary as a sin offering are burned outside the camp. 12* Therefore, Jesus also suffered outside the gate, to consecrate the people by his own blood. 13 Let us then go to him outside the camp, bearing the reproach that he bore. 14* For here we have no lasting city, but we seek the one that is to come. 15* Through him [then] let us

continually offer God a sacrifice of praise, that is, the fruit of lips that confess his name. 16* Do not neglect to do good and to share what you have; God is pleased by sacrifices of that kind.

17† Obey your leaders and defer to them, for they keep watch over you and will have to give an account, that they may fulfill their task with joy and not with sorrow, for that would be of no advantage to you.

18 Pray for us, for we are confident that we have a clear conscience, wishing to act rightly in every respect. 19 I especially ask for your prayers that I may be restored to you very soon.

20*† May the God of peace, who brought up from the dead the great shepherd of the sheep by the blood of the eternal covenant, Jesus our Lord, 21 furnish you with all that is good, that you may do his will. May he carry out in you what is pleasing to him through Jesus Christ, to whom be glory forever [and ever]. Amen.

22 Brothers, I ask you to bear with this message of encouragement, for I have written to you rather briefly. 23* I must let you know that our brother Timothy has been set free. If he comes soon, I shall see you together with him. 24 Greetings to all your leaders and to all the holy ones. Those from Italy send you greetings. 25* Grace be with all of you.

13, 9: *Strange teaching:* this doctrine about *foods* probably refers to the Jewish food laws; in view of v 10, however, the author may be thinking of the Mosaic sacrificial banquets.
13, 10: *We have an altar:* this does not refer to the Eucharist, which is never clearly mentioned in Hebrews, but to the sacrifice of Christ.
13, 17–25: Recommending obedience to the leaders of the community, the author asks for prayers (17–19). The letter concludes with a blessing (20–21), a final request for the acceptance of its message (22), information regarding Timothy (23), and general greetings (24–25).
13, 20–21: These verses constitute one of the most beautiful blessings in the New Testament. The resurrection of Jesus is presup-

posed throughout Hebrews, since it is included in the author's frequently expressed idea of his exaltation, but this is the only place where it is explicitly mentioned.

13, 6: Pss 27, 1–3; 118, 6.	13, 14: Heb 11, 10.14.
13, 8: Heb 1, 12; 7, 24; Rv 1, 17.	13, 15: Hos 14, 3.
13, 16: Phil 4, 18.	
13, 9: Rom 14, 17; 1 Cor 8, 8; Eph 4, 14; Col 2, 16.	13, 20: Is 63, 11; Zec 9, 11; Jn 10, 11; Acts 2, 24; Rom 15, 33.
13, 11: Ex 29, 14; Lv 16, 27.	13, 23: Acts 16, 1.
13, 12: Mt 21, 39; Mk 12, 8; Lk 20, 15; Jn 19, 17.	13, 25: Ti 3, 15.

Have you ever noticed how a kite strains at the string as it soars in the sky? It seems to want to be free of the string that ties it down, free to fly on its own. But if that string does break, the kite flounders and crashes. The kite only has the freedom to fly as long as it's tied to something. That's the way we are under the New Covenant in Christ. We may think we're free to do whatever we want. But if we break from a faithful response to God's love for us, we flounder and crash. The Letter of James provides guidance for living "the perfect law of freedom" (1, 25), which leads to real freedom.

At a Glance

I. Address (1, 1).

II. The Value of Trials and Temptation (1, 2–18).

III. Exhortations and Warnings (1, 19—5, 12).

IV. The Power of Prayer (5, 13–20).

In-depth

Defining the literary style of James is a little difficult. It opens like the other letters but lacks the typical closing. In some ways, it is similar to the wisdom literature of the Old Testament. It provides practical advice for how wise people ought to live. It is also similar to Greek moral teaching, which used famous people as models for how we ought to live. This has led scholars to think the book might have been written by an educated Jewish Christian, possibly living in Jerusalem. The author could have been an admirer of James, the first leader of the early church in Jerusalem.

The letter addresses several issues in Christian living. It warns that rich people should not discriminate against poor people. It insists that Christians' actions must reflect their beliefs. It cautions against careless speech and a poorly controlled tongue. It encourages believers to patiently endure suffering.

James also addresses a misunderstanding of Paul's teaching that "a person is justified by faith apart from works of the law" (Rom 3, 28). Using Abraham and Rahab as examples, the author of James declares, "A person is justified by works and not by faith alone" (Jas 2, 24). After all, "faith of itself, if it does not have works, is dead" (verse 17). To say you love Jesus, and then do unloving things, makes no sense; it's just plain hypocritical.

So here is God's message of freedom for you: Soar like a kite by staying connected to the law of liberty!

Quick Facts

Author
possibly James the relative of Jesus, but more likely a later admirer of James

Date Written
A.D. 57–62 if by James, A.D. 70–150 if by a later admirer

Audience
Christians in Palestine, Syria, or Rome

The Letter of James

James

I: Address

1 ¹*† James, a slave of God and of the Lord Jesus Christ, to the twelve tribes in the dispersion, greetings.

II: The Value of Trials and Temptation

Perseverance in Trial

²*† Consider it all joy, my brothers, when you encounter various trials, ³† for you know that the testing of your faith produces perseverance. ⁴ And let perseverance be perfect, so that you may be perfect and complete, lacking in nothing. ⁵*† But if any of you lacks wisdom, he should ask God who gives to all generously and ungrudgingly, and he will be given it. ⁶* But he should ask in faith, not

doubting, for the one who doubts is like a wave of the sea that is driven and tossed about by the wind. ⁷ For that person must not suppose that he will receive anything from the Lord, ⁸ since he is a man of two minds, unstable in all his ways.

⁹*† The brother in lowly circumstances should take pride in his high standing, ¹⁰* and the rich one in his lowliness, for he will pass away "like the flower of the field." ¹¹ For the sun comes up with its scorching heat and dries up the grass, its flower droops, and the beauty of its appearance vanishes. So will the rich person fade away in the midst of his pursuits.

Temptation

¹²*† Blessed is the man who perseveres in temptation, for when he has been proved he will receive the crown of life that he promised to those who

---

1, 1: *James, a slave of God and of the Lord Jesus Christ:* a declaration of the writer's authority for instructing the Christian communities; cf Rom 1, 1. Regarding the identity of the author, see Introduction. *Dispersion:* see Introduction.

1, 2: *Consider it all joy . . . various trials:* a frequent teaching of the New Testament derived from the words and sufferings of Jesus (Mt 5, 10–12; Jn 10, 11; Acts 5, 41).

1, 3–8: The sequence of testing, perseverance, and being perfect and complete indicates the manner of attaining spiritual maturity and full preparedness for the coming of Christ (5, 7–12; cf 1 Pt 1, 6–7; Rom 5, 3–5). These steps require wisdom (5).

1, 5: *Wisdom:* a gift that God readily grants to all who ask in faith and that sustains the Christian in times of trial. It is a kind of knowledge or understanding not accessible to the unbeliever or those who doubt, which gives the recipient an understanding of the real importance of events. In this way a Christian can deal with adversity with great calm and hope (cf 1 Cor 2, 6–12).

1, 9–11: Throughout his letter (see 2, 5; 4, 10.13–16; 5, 1–6), the author reaffirms the teaching of Jesus that worldly prosperity is not necessarily a sign of God's favor but can even be a hindrance to proper humility before God (cf Lk 6, 20–25; 12, 16–21; 16, 19–31).

1, 12: *Temptation:* the Greek word used here is the same one used for "trials" in v 2. *The crown of life:* in ancient Palestine, crowns or wreaths of flowers were worn at festive occasions as signs of joy and honor. In the Hellenistic world, wreaths were given as a reward to great statesmen, soldiers, athletes. *Life:* here means eternal life. *He promised:* some manuscripts read "God" or "the Lord," while the best witnesses do not specify the subject of "promised."

1, 1: Jn 7, 35; 1 Pt 1, 1.
1, 2: Rom 5, 3–5; 1 Pt 1, 6; 4, 13–16.
1, 5: Prv 2, 2–6; Wis 9, 4.9–12.
1, 6: Mt 7, 7; Mk 11, 24.
1, 9: Jas 2, 5.
1, 10: Is 40, 6–7.
1, 12: 1 Cor 9, 25; 2 Tm 4, 8; 1 Pt 5, 4; Rv 2, 10.

Meditation on the Walk of Faith

Relax. Clear your mind. Read and reflect on this meditation:

Imagine yourself on your favorite stretch of road. Look back along the road as if it represents your life so far. You have traveled this road all your life to get to where you are standing right now. What obstacles and temptations to your faith have you encountered? Which ones have you stumbled over? Which ones have you overcome?

You see a figure approaching. You strain to see who it is. It gets close enough to recognize. It is Jesus! Jesus sits down with you and asks about the trials you have encountered on your journey. Talk to Jesus about how they have given you the opportunity to grow. Talk to him about the many choices you have made, the good and the bad.

Leave with Jesus to continue forward on the journey. With Jesus, you can joyfully accept the tests of faith that lie ahead, knowing that each is an opportunity to build endurance "so that you may be perfect and complete, lacking in nothing" (Jas 1, 4).

▶ Jas 1, 2–18

---

love him. ¹³*† No one experiencing temptation should say, "I am being tempted by God"; for God is not subject to temptation to evil, and he himself tempts no one. ¹⁴ Rather, each person is tempted when he is lured and enticed by his own desire. ¹⁵ Then desire conceives and brings forth sin, and when sin reaches maturity it gives birth to death.

¹⁶† Do not be deceived, my beloved brothers: ¹⁷† all good giving and every perfect gift is from above, coming down from the Father of lights, with whom there is no alteration or shadow caused by change. ¹⁸*† He willed to give us birth by the word of truth that we may be a kind of firstfruits of his creatures.

III: Exhortations and Warnings

Doers of the Word

¹⁹*† Know this, my dear brothers: everyone should be quick to hear, slow to speak, slow to wrath, ²⁰* for the wrath of a man does not accomplish the righteousness of God. ²¹* Therefore, put away all filth and evil excess and humbly welcome the word that has been planted in you and is able to save your souls.

²²* Be doers of the word and not hearers only, deluding yourselves. ²³ For if anyone is a hearer of the word and not a doer, he is like a man who looks at his own face in a mirror. ²⁴ He sees himself, then goes off and promptly forgets what he looked like. ²⁵*† But the one who peers into the perfect law of freedom and perseveres, and is not a hearer who forgets but a doer who acts, such a one shall be blessed in what he does.

²⁶*† If anyone thinks he is religious and does not bridle his tongue but deceives his heart,† his religion is vain. ²⁷*† Religion that is pure and undefiled before God and the Father is this: to care for orphans and widows in their affliction and to keep oneself unstained by the world.

Sin of Partiality

2 ¹† My brothers, show no partiality as you adhere to the faith in our glorious Lord Jesus Christ. ² For if a man with gold rings on his fingers

JAS

---

† **1, 13–15:** It is contrary to what we know of God for God to be the author of human temptation (13). In the commission of a sinful act, one is first beguiled by passion (14), then consent is given, which in turn causes the sinful act. When sin permeates the entire person, it incurs the ultimate penalty of death (15).

1, 16–18: The author here stresses that God is the source of all good and of good alone, and the evil of temptation does not come from him.

1, 17: *All good giving and every perfect gift* may be a proverb written in hexameter. *Father of lights:* God is here called the Father of the heavenly luminaries, i.e., the stars, sun, and moon that he created (Gn 1, 14–18). Unlike orbs moving from nadir to zenith, he never changes or diminishes in brightness.

1, 18: Acceptance of the gospel message, *the word of truth,* constitutes new birth (Jn 3, 5–6) and makes the recipient the *firstfruits* (i.e., the cultic offering of the earliest grains, symbolizing the beginning of an abundant harvest) of a new creation; cf 1 Cor 15, 20; Rom 8, 23.

1, 19–25: *To be quick to hear* the gospel is to accept it readily and to act in conformity with it, removing from one's soul whatever

is opposed to it, so that it may take root and effect salvation (19–21). To listen to the gospel message but not practice it is failure to improve oneself (22–24). Only conformity of life to the perfect law of true freedom brings happiness (25).

1, 25: *Peers into the perfect law:* the image of a person doing this is paralleled to that of hearing God's word. The *perfect law* applies the Old Testament description of the Mosaic law to the gospel of Jesus Christ that brings freedom.

1, 26–27: A practical application of v 22 is now made.

1, 26: For control of the tongue, see the note on 3, 1–12.

1, 27: In the Old Testament, orphans and widows are classical examples of the defenseless and oppressed.

2, 1–13: In the Christian community there must be no discrimination or favoritism based on status or wealth (2–4; cf Mt 5, 3; 11, 5;

1, 13: Sir 15, 11–20; 1 Cor 10, 13.	**1, 21:** Col 3, 8.
1, 18: Jn 1, 12–13; 1 Pt 1, 23.	**1, 22:** Mt 7, 26; Rom 2, 13.
1, 19: Prv 14, 17; Sir 5, 11.	**1, 25:** Jas 2, 12; Ps 19, 8; Rom 8, 2.
1, 20: Eph 4, 26.	**1, 26:** Jas 3, 2; Ps 34, 14.
	1, 27: Ex 22, 21.

The Favorite

We all know people we label as "the favorite." We also call these people teacher's pet, brown nose, and so on. Whatever name we use, when we raise a person or a group above others because of money, personality, or power, it seems unfair; yet we all play favorites. We often want to hang out with the most popular students at school, and we usually don't want the most unpopular students to become our friends. We play favorites so that we might become the favorite. And we hate it when others—and not us!—are the favorites.

This is the situation in Jas 2, 1–13. The author clearly spells out where God stands on the issue of favoritism and partiality. God's response is to turn things upside down by raising up the poor and the lowly (verse 5). The Catholic church refers to this response as preferential love for the poor, which means always keeping in mind the needs of those who are poor when setting policies, providing benefits, and so on.

In our world, there is a big difference between rich and poor, top and bottom, included and excluded. God needs us to carry out the divine response to this injustice. If we do not give poor people real opportunities to rise up, and if we do not challenge the people in power to live according to God's justice, who will? And if we don't reach out to those students at school who seem to be the least popular or least favorite, who will?

▶ Jas 2, 1–13

and in fine clothes comes into your assembly, and a poor person in shabby clothes also comes in, ³ and you pay attention to the one wearing the fine clothes and say, "Sit here, please," while you say to the poor one, "Stand there," or "Sit at my feet," ⁴† have you not made distinctions among yourselves and become judges with evil designs?

⁵*† Listen, my beloved brothers. Did not God choose those who are poor in the world to be rich in faith and heirs of the kingdom that he promised to those who love him? ⁶ But you dishonored the poor person. Are not the rich oppressing you? And do they themselves not haul you off to court? ⁷* Is it not they who blaspheme the noble name that was invoked over you? ⁸*† However, if you fulfill the royal law according to the scripture, "You shall love your neighbor as yourself," you are doing well.

⁹* But if you show partiality, you commit sin, and are convicted by the law as transgressors. ¹⁰* For whoever keeps the whole law, but falls short in one particular, has become guilty in respect to all of it. ¹¹* For he who said, "You shall not commit adultery," also said, "You shall not kill." Even if you do not commit adultery but kill, you have become a transgressor of the law. ¹²*† So speak and so act as people who will be judged by the law of freedom. ¹³* For the judgment is merciless to one who has not shown mercy; mercy triumphs over judgment.

Faith and Works

¹⁴*† What good is it, my brothers, if someone says he has faith but does not have works? Can that faith save him? ¹⁵ If a brother or sister has nothing to wear and has no food for the day, ¹⁶* and one of

23, 6; 1 Cor 1, 27–29). Divine favor rather consists in God's election and promises (5). The rich who oppress the poor blaspheme the name of Christ (6–7). By violating one law of love of neighbor, they offend against the whole law (8–11). On the other hand, conscious awareness of the final judgment helps the faithful to fulfill the whole law (12).

2, 4: When Christians show favoritism to the rich they are guilty of the worst kind of prejudice and discrimination. The author says that such Christians set themselves up as judges who judge not by divine law but by the basest, self-serving motives.

2, 5: The poor, "God's poor" of the Old Testament, were seen by Jesus as particularly open to God for belief in and reliance on him alone (Lk 6, 20). God's law cannot tolerate their oppression in any way (9).

2, 8: *Royal:* literally, "kingly"; because the Mosaic law came from God, the universal king. There may be an allusion to Jesus' uses of this commandment in his preaching of the kingdom of God (Mt 22, 39; Mk 12, 31; Lk 10, 27).

2, 12–13: The law upon which the last judgment will be based is the law of freedom. As Jesus taught, mercy (which participates in God's own loving mercy) includes forgiveness of those who wrong us (see Mt 6, 12.14–15).

2, 14–26: The theme of these verses is the relationship of faith and works (deeds). It has been argued that the teaching here contradicts that of Paul (see especially Rom 4, 5–6). The problem can only be understood if the different viewpoints of the two authors are seen. Paul argues against those who claim to participate in God's salvation because of their good deeds as well as because they have committed themselves to trust in God through Jesus Christ (Paul's concept of faith). Paul certainly understands, however, the implications of true faith for a life of love and generosity (see Gal 5, 13–15). The author of James is well aware that proper conduct can only come about with an authentic commitment to God in faith (18.26). Many think he was seeking to correct a misunderstanding of Paul's view.

2, 5: 1 Cor 1, 26–28; Rv 2, 9.
2, 7: 1 Pt 4, 4.
2, 8: Lv 19, 18; Mt 22, 39; Rom 13, 9.
2, 9: Dt 1, 17.
2, 10: Gal 3, 10.
2, 11: Ex 20, 13–14; Dt 5, 17–18.
2, 12: Jas 1, 25; Rom 8, 2.
2, 13: Mt 5, 7; 6, 14–15; 18, 32–33.
2, 14: Mt 25, 31–46; Gal 5, 6.
2, 16: 1 Jn 3, 17.

you says to them, "Go in peace, keep warm, and eat well," but you do not give them the necessities of the body, what good is it? ¹⁷ So also faith of itself, if it does not have works, is dead.

¹⁸ Indeed someone may say, "You have faith and I have works." Demonstrate your faith to me without works, and I will demonstrate my faith to you from my works. ¹⁹ You believe that God is one. You do well. Even the demons believe that and tremble. ²⁰ Do you want proof, you ignoramus, that faith without works is useless? ²¹* Was not Abraham our father justified by works when he offered his son Isaac upon the altar? ²² You see that faith was active along with his works, and faith was completed by the works. ²³* Thus the scripture was fulfilled that says, "Abraham believed God, and it was credited to him as righteousness," and he was called "the friend of God." ²⁴ See how a person is justified by works and not by faith alone. ²⁵* And in the same way, was not Rahab the harlot also justified by works when she welcomed the messengers and sent them out by a different route? ²⁶ For just as a body without a spirit is dead, so also faith without works is dead.

Power of the Tongue

3 ¹† Not many of you should become teachers, my brothers, for you realize that we will be judged more strictly, ²* for we all fall short in many respects. If anyone does not fall short in speech, he is a perfect man, able to bridle his whole body also. ³ If we put bits into the mouths of horses to make them obey us, we also guide their whole bodies. ⁴ It is the same with ships: even though they are so large and driven by fierce winds, they are steered by a very small rudder wherever the pilot's inclination wishes. ⁵ In the same way the tongue is a small member and yet has great pretensions.

Consider how small a fire can set a huge forest ablaze. ⁶ The tongue is also a fire. It exists among our members as a world of malice, defiling the whole body and setting the entire course of our lives on fire, itself set on fire by Gehenna. ⁷ For every kind of beast and bird, of reptile and sea creature, can be tamed and has been tamed by the human species, ⁸* but no human being can tame the tongue. It is a restless evil, full of deadly poison. ⁹ With it we bless the Lord and Father, and with it we curse human beings who are made in the likeness of God. ¹⁰ From the same mouth come blessing and cursing. This need not be so, my brothers. ¹¹ Does a spring gush forth from the same opening both pure and brackish water? ¹²* Can a fig tree, my brothers, produce olives, or a grapevine figs? Neither can salt water yield fresh.

True Wisdom

¹³*† Who among you is wise and understanding? Let him show his works by a good life in the humility that comes from wisdom. ¹⁴ But if you have

Faith and Works

A person who insists that faith alone is necessary for our salvation might think: "I don't have to demonstrate my faith with action at all. I just have to believe in Jesus, and then I can do anything I want." Such an attitude isn't very faithful, mature, or helpful.

Yet a person who insists that particular actions alone are necessary for our salvation might think: "I don't have to really believe in what I'm doing. I'll just go through the motions of faith, and that way I'll play it safe." This attitude is not very faithful, mature, or helpful either.

James is nearly saying the same thing—show me a person who has real faith, and I will show you a person doing good works.

Faith and works are discussed at length in two other letters from Paul: Rom 3, 21–31 (see also "Law, Faith, and Salvation," Rom 3, 21–31) and Gal 2, 15—3, 14 (see also "Saved by Christ," Gal 3, 1—4, 7).

▶ Jas 2, 14–26

3, 1–12: The use and abuse of the important role of teaching in the church (1) are here related to the good and bad use of the tongue (9–12), the instrument through which teaching was chiefly conveyed (see Sir 5, 11—6, 1; 28, 12–26).

3, 13–18: This discussion of true wisdom is related to the previous reflection on the role of the teacher as one who is in control of his speech. The qualities of the wise man endowed from above are

detailed (17–18; cf Gal 5, 22–23), in contrast to the qualities of earthbound wisdom (14–16; cf 2 Cor 12, 20).

2, 21: Gn 22, 9–12; Heb 11, 17.
2, 23: Gn 15, 6; Rom 4, 3; Gal 3, 6 / 2 Chr 20, 7; Is 41, 8.
2, 25: Jos 2, 1–21.
3, 2: Jas 1, 26; Prv 13, 3; Sir 28, 12–26.
3, 8: Ps 140, 4.
3, 12: Mt 7, 16–17.
3, 13: Eph 4, 1–2.

The Tongue: Friend or Foe?

Sometimes, we are advised to hold it. Other times, we are ordered to bite it. Try as we might to keep this counsel, our tongue often proves to be much stronger than our will to control it.

All of us have said things that we later regretted. Frequently against our better judgment, we find ourselves speaking in ways that hurt or offend others and God. People are injured by what others say to—or about—them far more often than by physical attack. The scars left by hurtful words can last a lifetime, destroying families and ruining friendships.

How have you used your tongue lately? Have you spoken words that are hurtful to another person, directly or behind the person's back? How might you use your tongue to begin to heal someone's hurts? Apologies, compliments, and affirmations—the tongue can utter these things too! It is a mark of maturity and confidence when we are able to ask forgiveness or affirm others. Christians are called to this kind of courage and maturity.

Put your tongue to good use today!

▶ Jas 3, 1–12

bitter jealousy and selfish ambition in your hearts, do not boast and be false to the truth. 15 Wisdom of this kind does not come down from above but is earthly, unspiritual, demonic. 16 For where jealousy and selfish ambition exist, there is disorder and every foul practice. 17* But the wisdom from above is first of all pure, then peaceable, gentle, compliant, full of mercy and good fruits, without inconstancy or insincerity. 18* And the fruit of righteousness is sown in peace for those who cultivate peace.

Causes of Division

4 1*† Where do the wars and where do the conflicts among you come from? Is it not from your passions† that make war within your members? 2 You covet but do not possess. You kill and envy but you cannot obtain; you fight and wage war. You do not possess because you do not ask. 3 You ask but do not receive, because you ask wrongly, to spend it on your passions. 4*† Adulterers! Do you not know that to be a lover of the world means enmity with God? Therefore, whoever wants to be a lover of the world makes himself an enemy of God. 5† Or do you suppose that the scripture speaks without meaning when it says, "The spirit that he

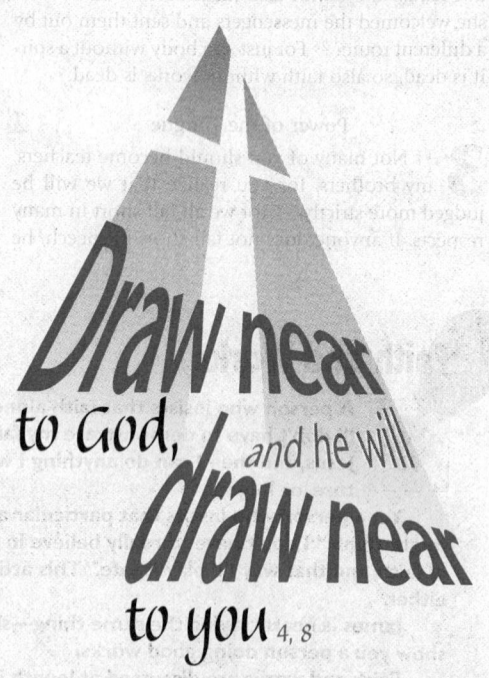

Draw near to God, and he will draw near to you 4, 8

---

† **4, 1–12:** The concern here is with the origin of conflicts in the Christian community. These are occasioned by love *of the world*, which *means enmity with God* (4). Further, the conflicts are bound up with failure to pray properly (cf Mt 7, 7–11; Jn 14, 13; 15, 7; 16, 23), that is, not asking God at all or using God's kindness only for one's pleasure (2–3). In contrast, the proper dispositions are submission to God, repentance, humility, and resistance to evil (7–10).

4, 1: *Passions:* the Greek word here (literally, "pleasures") does not indicate that pleasure is evil. Rather, as the text points out (2–3), it is the manner in which one deals with needs and desires that determines good or bad. The motivation for any action can be wrong, especially if one does not pray properly but seeks only selfish enjoyment (3).

4, 4: *Adulterers:* a common biblical image for the covenant be-

tween God and his people is the marriage bond. In this image, breaking the covenant with God is likened to the unfaithfulness of adultery.

4, 5: The meaning of this saying is difficult because the author of James cites, probably from memory, a passage that is not in any extant manuscript of the Bible. Other translations of the text with a completely different meaning are possible: "The Spirit that he (God) made to dwell in us yearns (for us) jealously," or, "He (God) yearns jealously for the spirit that he has made to dwell in us." If this last translation is correct, the author perhaps had in mind an apocryphal religious text that echoes the idea that God is zealous for his creatures; cf Ex 20, 5; Dt 4, 24; Zec 8, 2.

3, 17: Jas 1, 17; Wis 7, 22–23.
3, 18: Mt 5, 9.
4, 1: Rom 7, 23; 1 Pt 2, 11.
4, 4: Mt 6, 24; Lk 16, 13; Rom 8, 7; 1 Jn 2, 15–16.

has made to dwell in us tends toward jealousy"? 6*† But he bestows a greater grace; therefore, it says:

"God resists the proud,
    but gives grace to the humble."

7* So submit yourselves to God. Resist the devil, and he will flee from you. 8* Draw near to God, and he will draw near to you. Cleanse your hands, you sinners, and purify your hearts, you of two minds. 9 Begin to lament, to mourn, to weep. Let your laughter be turned into mourning and your joy into dejection. 10* Humble yourselves before the Lord and he will exalt you.

11† Do not speak evil of one another, brothers. Whoever speaks evil of a brother or judges his brother speaks evil of the law and judges the law. If you judge the law, you are not a doer of the law but a judge. 12* There is one lawgiver and judge who is able to save or to destroy. Who then are you to judge your neighbor?

Warning against Presumption

13† Come now, you who say, "Today or tomorrow we shall go into such and such a town, spend a year there doing business, and make a profit"— 14*† you have no idea what your life will be like tomorrow. You are a puff of smoke that appears briefly and then disappears. 15† Instead you should say, "If the Lord wills it, we shall live to do this or that." 16 But now you are boasting in your arrogance. All such boasting is evil. 17*† So for one who knows the right thing to do and does not do it, it is a sin.

Warning to the Rich

5 1*† Come now, you rich, weep and wail over your impending miseries. 2* Your wealth has rotted away, your clothes have become moth-eaten, 3* your gold and silver have corroded, and that corrosion will be a testimony against you; it will devour your flesh like a fire. You have stored up treasure for the last days. 4* Behold, the wages you

Justice for Those Who Are Poor

Warnings to the rich are common in the Bible, and should be of concern for Christians living in a wealthy nation like the United States. Here are two tough questions to consider: First, in what do we put our trust—the comfort and pleasure that can be had in wealth and material possessions, or God? And second, how does our lifestyle—including the way we spend money, the choices we make about our future work, and the way we use our time—affect the poor people of this world?

God's justice requires that Christians care about the abuse of poor people for the benefit of rich people. God does not want us to become paralyzed with guilt because we are wealthy compared with the poorest of the earth. But the Scriptures remind us that the life choices we make matter, and that those choices may either contribute to a more just world, or support a status quo that keeps rich people comfortable and poor people down. To make good life choices, we must educate ourselves about the situations that cause poverty, and examine how our own lifestyle or beliefs might unintentionally contribute to the misery of those who are poor. That is hard work—perhaps work we would rather avoid. But ignoring the plight of poor people is exactly what the Scriptures warn us against!

▶ Jas 5, 1–6

4, 6: The point of this whole argument is that God wants the happiness of all, but that selfishness and pride can make that impossible. We must work with him in humility (10).

4, 11: Slander of a fellow Christian does not break just one commandment but makes mockery of the authority of law in general and therefore of God.

4, 13–17: The uncertainty of life (14), its complete dependence on God, and the necessity of submitting to God's will (15) all help one know and do what is right (17). To disregard this is to live in pride and arrogance (16); failure to do what is right is a sin (17).

4, 14: Some important Greek manuscripts here have, "You who have no idea what tomorrow will bring. Why, what is your life?"

4, 15: If the Lord wills it: often in piety referred to as the "conditio Jacobaea," the condition James says we should employ to qualify all our plans.

4, 17: It is a sin: those who live arrogantly, forgetting the contingency of life and our dependence on God (13–16), are guilty of sin.

5, 1–6: Continuing with the theme of the transitory character of life on earth, the author points out the impending ruin of the godless. He denounces the unjust rich, whose victims cry to heaven for judgment on their exploiters (4–6). The decay and corrosion of the costly garments and metals, which symbolize wealth, prove them worthless and portend the destruction of their possessors (2–3).

4, 6: Jb 22, 29; Prv 3, 34;
    Mt 23, 12; 1 Pt 5, 5.
4, 7: 1 Pt 5, 8–9.
4, 8: Zec 1, 3; Mal 3, 7.
4, 10: Jb 5, 11; Mt 23, 12; Lk
    14, 11; 18, 14; 1 Pt 5, 6.
4, 12: Mt 7, 1; Rom 2, 1; 14, 4.
4, 14: Prv 27, 1 / Ps 39, 6–7.

4, 17: Lk 12, 47.
5, 1: Lk 6, 24.
5, 2: Mt 6, 19.
5, 3: Ps 21, 10; Prv 11, 4;
    Jdt 16, 17.
5, 4: Lv 19, 13; Dt 24,
    14–15; Mal 3, 5.

The Making of a Prayer

Have you ever been in a prayer rut? It happens when you get stuck on saying the same prayer every time, no matter what the situation. It becomes a habit, and like all habits, after a while, you may stop thinking about why you are even doing it.

James offers some advice in 5, 13 that can help you to get out of such a rut and back on track with your prayer life. This passage says to think about the needs and feelings you have at any given moment of the day and turn them into a prayer. Feeling down? Tell God about it. Just had the best day of your life? Share it with God. Want to get even with a person who hurt you? Let God know about it. In fact, there is nothing you can't tell God—even if you are mad and God is the one you are mad at.

Get in touch with what is occupying your mind the most right now—good, bad, or ordinary—and turn it into a prayer by sharing it with the God who is always ready to hear what you have to say.

▶ Jas 5, 13

---

withheld from the workers who harvested your fields are crying aloud, and the cries of the harvesters have reached the ears of the Lord of hosts. ⁵* You have lived on earth in luxury and pleasure; you have fattened your hearts for the day of slaughter. ⁶*† You have condemned; you have murdered the righteous one; he offers you no resistance.

Patience and Oaths

⁷† Be patient, therefore, brothers, until the coming of the Lord. See how the farmer waits for the precious fruit of the earth, being patient with it until it receives the early and the late rains.† ⁸* You too must be patient. Make your hearts firm, because the coming of the Lord is at hand. ⁹ Do not complain, brothers, about one another, that you may not be judged. Behold, the Judge is standing before the gates. ¹⁰ Take as an example of hardship and patience, brothers, the prophets who spoke in the name of the Lord. ¹¹* Indeed we call blessed those who have persevered. You have heard of the perseverance of Job, and you have seen the purpose of the Lord, because "the Lord is compassionate and merciful."

¹²*† But above all, my brothers, do not swear, either by heaven or by earth or with any other oath, but let your "Yes" mean "Yes" and your "No" mean "No," that you may not incur condemnation.

IV: The Power of Prayer

Anointing of the Sick

¹³ Is anyone among you suffering? He should pray. Is anyone in good spirits? He should sing praise. ¹⁴*† Is anyone among you sick? He should summon the presbyters of the church, and they should pray over him and anoint [him] with oil in the name of the Lord, ¹⁵† and the prayer of faith will save the sick person, and the Lord will raise him up. If he has committed any sins, he will be forgiven.

Confession and Intercession

¹⁶ Therefore, confess your sins to one another and pray for one another, that you may be healed. The fervent prayer of a righteous person is very powerful. ¹⁷* Elijah was a human being like us; yet he prayed earnestly that it might not rain, and for three years and six months it did not rain upon the land. ¹⁸* Then he prayed again, and the sky gave rain and the earth produced its fruit.

Conversion of Sinners

¹⁹* My brothers, if anyone among you should stray from the truth and someone bring him back, ²⁰*† he should know that whoever brings back a sinner from the error of his way will save his soul from death and will cover a multitude of sins.

5, 6: The author does not have in mind any specific crime in his readers' communities but rather echoes the Old Testament theme of the harsh oppression of the righteous poor (see Prv 1, 11; Wis 2, 10.12.20).

5, 7–11: Those oppressed by the unjust rich are reminded of the need for patience, both in bearing the sufferings of human life (9) and in their expectation of the coming of the Lord. It is then that they will receive their reward (7–8.10–11; cf Heb 10, 25; 1 Jn 2, 18).

5, 7: *The early and the late rains:* an expression related to the agricultural season in ancient Palestine (see Dt 11, 14; Jer 5, 24; Jl 2, 23).

5, 12: This is the threat of condemnation for the abuse of swearing oaths (cf Mt 5, 33–37). *By heaven or by earth:* these words were substitutes for the original form of an oath, to circumvent its binding force and to avoid pronouncing the holy name of God (see Ex 22, 10).

5, 14: In case of sickness a Christian should ask for the presbyters of the church, i.e., those who have authority in the church (cf Acts 15, 2.22–23; 1 Tm 5, 17; Ti 1, 5). They are to pray over the person and anoint with oil; oil was used for medicinal purposes in the an-

cient world (see Is 1, 6; Lk 10, 34). In Mk 6, 13, the Twelve anoint the sick with oil on their missionary journey. *In the name of the Lord:* by the power of Jesus Christ.

5, 15: The results of the prayer and anointing are physical health and forgiveness of sins. The Roman Catholic Church (Council of Trent, Session 14) declared that this anointing of the sick is a sacrament "instituted by Christ and promulgated by blessed James the apostle."

5, 20: When a Christian is instrumental in the conversion of a sinner, the result is forgiveness of sins and a reinstatement of the sinner to the life of grace.

5, 5: Jer 12, 3; Lk 16, 19–25.	5, 12: Mt 5, 34–37.
5, 6: Wis 2, 10–20.	5, 14: Mk 6, 13.
5, 8: Lk 21, 19; Heb 10, 36 / Heb 10, 25; 1 Pt 4, 7.	5, 17: 1 Kgs 17, 1; Lk 4, 25.
5, 11: Ex 34, 6; Ps 103, 8.	5, 18: 1 Kgs 18, 45.
	5, 19: Mt 18, 15; Gal 6, 1.
	5, 20: Prv 10, 12; 1 Pt 4, 8.

Close friends refuse to speak to you after you challenge them about shoplifting. Students make fun of classmates who are trying to start a prayer group before school. Citizens break windows in the homes of Christian leaders who have spoken out publicly against racist attitudes. It's enough to make some Christians ask, Is living our faith worth this persecution and separation? This is a major concern addressed by the First Letter of Peter.

In-depth

The First Letter of Peter was written to a Christian community that was alienated and persecuted because of its Christian lifestyle. Its members were ridiculed, treated as evildoers, and insulted by unbelieving neighbors who did not understand their faith or their moral code of behavior. The author—who may have been Peter but was more likely a later disciple of his—wants to console them and help them make sense of what they're going through.

The author of Peter says that Christ suffered, and therefore we should expect to suffer too. The writer also says that suffering purifies our faith and makes it more genuine (1 Pt 1, 7). When we suffer, we are united with all the world's people who are suffering (5, 9). And no matter how great our suffering is, we should be hopeful, and we should be willing to witness to our hope. Then, our persecutors will be ashamed and will repent of their wrongdoing (3, 14-16). We cannot avoid suffering, but when we follow in the footsteps of Jesus, we can make it result in something good.

Despite all this attention to suffering, 1 Peter is a hope-filled letter. It offers constant reminders of the wonderful things God has done—and will do—for us. When you are going through a hard time, turn to this letter for hope and encouragement. "The God of all grace who called you to his eternal glory through Christ [Jesus] will himself restore, confirm, strengthen, and establish you after you have suffered a little" (5, 10).

At a Glance

I. Address (1, 1–2).

II. The Gift and Call of God in Baptism (1, 3—2, 10).

III. The Christian in a Hostile World (2, 11—4, 11).

IV. Advice to the Persecuted (4, 12—5, 11).

V. Conclusion (5, 12–14).

Quick Facts

Author
possibly Peter, but most likely a later disciple of Peter

Date Written
A.D. 60–63 if by Peter, A.D. 70–90 if by a later disciple

Audience
a Gentile (non-Jewish) Christian community

The First Letter of Peter

1 Peter

2, 25

I: Address

Greeting

1 1*† Peter, an apostle of Jesus Christ, to the chosen sojourners of the dispersion† in Pontus, Galatia, Cappadocia, Asia, and Bithynia, 2* in the foreknowledge of God the Father, through sanctification by the Spirit, for obedience and sprinkling with the blood of Jesus Christ: may grace and peace be yours in abundance.

II: The Gift and Call of God in Baptism

Blessing

3*† Blessed be the God and Father of our Lord Jesus Christ, who in his great mercy gave us a new birth to a living hope through the resurrection of Jesus Christ from the dead, 4* to an inheritance that is imperishable, undefiled, and unfading, kept in heaven for you 5 who by the power of God are safeguarded through faith, to a salvation that is ready to be revealed in the final time. 6*† In this you rejoice, although now for a little while you may have to suffer through various trials, 7* so that the genuineness of your faith, more precious than gold that is perishable even though tested by fire, may prove to be for praise, glory, and honor at the revelation of Jesus Christ. 8* Although you have not seen him you love him; even though you do not see him now yet believe in him, you rejoice with an indescribable and glorious joy, 9 as you attain the goal of [your] faith, the salvation of your souls.

10† Concerning this salvation, prophets who

---

† **1, 1–2:** The introductory formula names *Peter* as the writer (but see Introduction). In his comments to the presbyters (5, 1), the author calls himself a "fellow presbyter." He addresses himself to the Gentile converts of Asia Minor. Their privileged status as a *chosen* and *sanctified* people makes them worthy of God's *grace* and *peace*. In contrast is their actual existence as aliens and *sojourners*, scattered among pagans, far from their true country.

1, 1: *Dispersion:* literally, *diaspora;* see Jas 1, 1 and Introduction to that letter. *Pontus . . . Bithynia:* five provinces in Asia Minor, listed in clockwise order from the north, perhaps in the sequence in which a messenger might deliver the letter.

1, 3–5: A prayer of praise and thanksgiving to God who bestows the gift of new life and hope in baptism (*new birth,* 3) *through the resurrection of Jesus Christ from the dead.* The new birth is a sign of an *imperishable inheritance* (4), of *salvation* that is still in the future (*to be revealed in the final time,* 5).

1, 6–9: As the glory of Christ's resurrection was preceded by his sufferings and death, the new life of faith that it bestows is to be subjected to many *trials* (6) while achieving its goal: the glory of the fullness of *salvation* (9) at the coming of Christ (7).

1, 10–12: The *Spirit of Christ* (11) is here shown to have been present in the prophets, moving them to search, investigate, and prophesy about the *grace* of *salvation* that was to come (10), and in the apostles impelling them to preach the fulfillment of salvation in the message of Christ's sufferings and glory (12).

---
*

1, 1: Jas 1, 1.
1, 2: Rom 8, 29.
1, 3: Ti 3, 5.
1, 4: Mt 6, 19–20.

1, 6: Jas 1, 2–3.
1, 7: 1 Cor 3, 13.
1, 8: 2 Cor 5, 6–7.

SAINT LUCY

December 13 marks the feast day of Saint Lucy. Little is known about Saint Lucy except that she was martyred in Sicily early in the fourth century.

In Scandinavia, however, Saint Lucy is a very important part of the Christmas celebration. By tradition, the feast of Santa Lucia marks the longest night of the year. And keep in mind that winter nights are very long there because of the northern location.

The tradition goes that the oldest daughter in each home dresses in white with a red ribbon tied around her waist and wears on her head a wreath with candles. She then rises early in the morning to serve the family hot chocolate and cinnamon rolls. This is done in commemoration of the legend that Saint Lucy brought food and water to the early Christians who were hiding from their Roman persecutors.

This Scandinavian tradition is a beautiful reminder of how, even in the midst of darkness, Christians can bring the light of hope and nourishment to one another. To whom can you bring the light of hope today?

▶ 1 Pt 1, 3–9

---

prophesied about the grace that was to be yours searched and investigated it, [11]* investigating the time and circumstances that the Spirit of Christ within them indicated when it testified in advance to the sufferings destined for Christ and the glories to follow them. [12] It was revealed to them that they were serving not themselves but you with regard to the things that have now been announced to you by those who preached the good news to you [through] the holy Spirit sent from heaven, things into which angels longed to look.

Obedience

[13]† Therefore, gird up the loins of your mind,† live soberly, and set your hopes completely on the grace to be brought to you at the revelation of Jesus Christ. [14]† Like obedient children, do not act in compliance with the desires of your former ignorance [15]* but, as he who called you is holy, be holy yourselves in every aspect of your conduct, [16]* for it

is written, "Be holy because I [am] holy."

Reverence

[17]* Now if you invoke as Father him who judges impartially according to each one's works, conduct yourselves with reverence during the time of your sojourning, [18]* realizing that you were ransomed from your futile conduct, handed on by your ancestors, not with perishable things like silver or gold [19]*† but with the precious blood of Christ as of a spotless unblemished lamb. [20] He was known before the foundation of the world but revealed in the final time for you, [21] who through him believe in God who raised him from the dead and gave him glory, so that your faith and hope are in God.

Mutual Love

[22]*† Since you have purified yourselves by obedience to the truth for sincere mutual love, love one another intensely from a [pure] heart. [23]*† You

---

† ──────────────

1, 13–25: These verses are concerned with the call of God's people to holiness and to mutual love by reason of their redemption through the blood of Christ (18–21).

1, 13: *Gird up the loins of your mind:* a figure reminiscent of the rite of Passover when the Israelites were in flight from their oppressors (Ex 12, 11), and also suggesting the vigilance of the Christian people in expectation of the parousia of Christ (Lk 12, 35).

1, 14–16: The *ignorance* here referred to (14) was their former lack of knowledge of God, leading inevitably to godless conduct. Holiness (15–16), on the contrary, is the result of their call to the knowledge and love of God.

1, 19: Christians have received the redemption prophesied by Isaiah (52, 3), through the blood (Jewish symbol of life) of the spotless

lamb (Is 53, 7.10; Jn 1, 29; Rom 3, 24–25; cf 1 Cor 6, 20).

1, 22–25: The new birth of Christians (23) derives from Christ, the *imperishable seed* or sowing that produces a new and lasting existence in those who accept the gospel (24–25), with the consequent duty of loving *one another* (22).

1, 23: *The living and abiding word of God:* or, "the word of the living and abiding God."

* ──────────────

1, 11: Is 52, 13—53, 12; Dn 9, 24.	**1, 18:** Is 52, 3; 1 Cor 6, 20.
1, 15: Mt 5, 48; 1 Jn 3, 3.	**1, 19:** Ex 12, 5; Jn 1, 29; Heb 9, 14.
1, 16: Lv 11, 44; 19, 2.	**1, 22:** Rom 12, 10.
1, 17: 1 Pt 2, 11.	**1, 23:** 1 Jn 3, 9.

1
P
T

PRAY IT

Live the Belief

Holy God,
You invite me to live the Gospel
message, not just hear and accept it. It
is not enough to say I believe. I need to
live that belief.
I need to lovingly serve you, God, and all my
brothers and sisters.
I need to seek knowledge of your word and
follow it faithfully.
I need to exercise self-control and avoid
temptations.
I need to build endurance to stand firm
against life's trials.
I need to value truth and goodness.
Provide me with the fruits of your Spirit to
sustain me for my journey, as I work to
imitate your Son, Jesus Christ. Amen.

▶ 1 Pt 1, 13–25

have been born anew, not from perishable but from
imperishable seed, through the living and abiding
word of God, 24* for:

"All flesh is like grass,
  and all its glory like the flower of
    the field;
the grass withers,
  and the flower wilts;
25   but the word of the Lord remains forever."

This is the word that has been proclaimed to you.

God's House and People

2 1*† Rid yourselves of all malice and all deceit,
insincerity, envy, and all slander; 2 like newborn infants, long for pure spiritual milk so that
through it you may grow into salvation, 3*† for you
have tasted that the Lord is good. 4*† Come to him,
a living stone, rejected by human beings but chosen
and precious in the sight of God, 5*† and, like

?did you KNOW?

The Priesthood of the Faithful

In the New Testament, the only person,
other than the Jewish priests, who is actually called a priest is Jesus. In The Letter to
the Hebrews, the efficacy, or effectiveness,
of Jesus as High Priest is proclaimed—a
new priesthood has been born in Christ,
one that surpasses the priesthood of the
Old Testament. The church has always
understood that Christ also commissioned
the Apostles to share his priesthood and to
ordain other men to do the same.

But did you know that every baptized
Christian shares in Christ's priesthood as
well? Although it is different from hierarchical or ordained priesthood, the priesthood
of each baptized person is recognized in
their participating in the priestly work of
offering sacrifice to God. Every Christian is
to offer his or her life as a living sacrifice
and to intercede on behalf of the church
and the world with the Father.

The priesthood of the faithful is part
of our baptismal responsibility to proclaim what God has done for his people
and to live a life consecrated by faith and
hope in Christ crucified and risen. Because
we share in the priesthood of the Son
through Baptism, we have access to the
divine through him. We are consecrated,
put aside for the work of salvation.

We live this priesthood by offering
ourselves to God. When we do so, we align
ourselves to the way of Christ and live as
lights for the world. We live for others and
thus become instruments in the hand of
God. Remember the words of 1 Pt 2, 9:
"You are 'a chosen race, a royal priesthood, a holy nation, a people of his own.'"

▶ 1 Pet 2, 1–10

2, 1–3: Growth toward salvation is seen here as two steps: first, stripping away all that is contrary to the new life in Christ; second, the nourishment (pure spiritual milk) that the newly baptized have received.
2, 3: Tasted that the Lord is good: cf Ps 34, 9.
2, 4–8: Christ is the cornerstone (cf Is 28, 16) that is the foundation of the spiritual edifice of the Christian community (5). To unbelievers, Christ is an obstacle and a stumbling block on which they are
destined to fall (8); cf Rom 11, 11.

2, 5: Let yourselves be built: the form of the Greek word could
also be indicative passive, "you are being built" (cf 9).

1, 24: Is 40, 6–8.	2, 4: Ps 118, 22; Mt 21, 42;
2, 1–2: Jas 1, 21.	Acts 4, 11.
2, 3: Ps 34, 9.	2, 5: Eph 2, 21–22.

living stones, let yourselves be built into a spiritual house to be a holy priesthood to offer spiritual sacrifices acceptable to God through Jesus Christ. ⁶* For it says in scripture:

"Behold, I am laying a stone in Zion,
    a cornerstone, chosen and precious,
    and whoever believes in it shall not be put
        to shame."

⁷* Therefore, its value is for you who have faith, but for those without faith:

"The stone which the builders rejected
    has become the cornerstone,"

⁸* and

"A stone that will make people stumble,
    and a rock that will make them fall."

They stumble by disobeying the word, as is their destiny.

⁹*† But you are "a chosen race, a royal priesthood, a holy nation, a people of his own, so that you may announce the praises" of him who called you out of darkness into his wonderful light.

¹⁰* Once you were "no people"
    but now you are God's people;
    you "had not received mercy"
    but now you have received mercy.

PRAY IT!

Part of the Family

All of us come from and belong to a family. Some families are large and some small, some have two parents and others one, and some include aunts, uncles, or grandparents. Every family is unique.

Christians belong to a family that extends well beyond the relationships of blood or adoption. As followers of Christ, they make up a "royal priesthood" and a "holy nation," and are called "a people of [God's] own" (1 Pt 2, 9). That is pretty lofty language! What does it mean?

First, it means that our faith is not just between us and God but also shared with others. Yes, there is something personal about our relationship with the Lord, but in addition, we are called by God into a community of disciples who share a common faith. Second, God has chosen us to live together in such a way that others who see our example will see something so good that they want to be a part of it.

In your prayer, reflect or journal on the following questions:

■ How connected do you feel to the Christian family?

■ What kind of support would you like to receive from other believers? What kind of support can you give?

▶ 1 Pt 2, 9–17

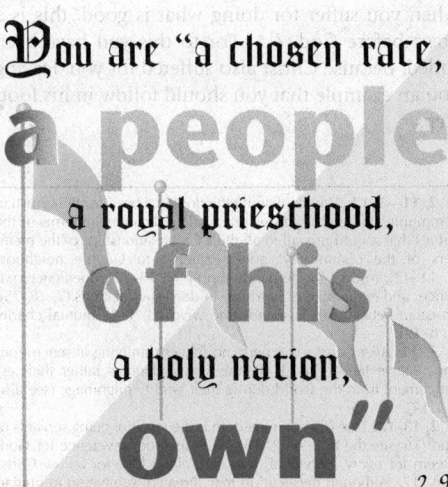

You are "a chosen race, a people of his a royal priesthood, a holy nation, own"

2, 9

1
P
T

---

† **2, 9–10:** The prerogatives of ancient Israel mentioned here are now more fully and fittingly applied to the Christian people: "a chosen race" (cf Is 43, 20–21) indicates their divine election (Eph 1, 4–6); "a royal priesthood" (cf Ex 19, 6) to serve and worship God in Christ, thus continuing the priestly functions of his life, passion, and resurrection; "a holy nation" (Ex 19, 6) reserved for God, a people he claims for his own (cf Mal 3, 17) in virtue of their baptism into his death and resurrection. This transcends all natural and national divisions and unites the people into one community to glorify the one who led them from the darkness of paganism to the light of faith in Christ. From being "no people" deprived of all mercy, they have become the very people of God, the chosen recipients of his mercy (cf Hos 1, 9; 2, 25).

*
2, 6: Is 28, 16.   2, 9: Ex 19, 6; Is 61, 6; Rv 1,
2, 7: Ps 118, 22; Mt 21, 42;   6; 20, 6.
    Lk 20, 17; Acts 4, 11.   2, 10: Hos 1, 9; 2, 25 / Hos
2, 8: Is 8, 14; Rom 9, 33.   1, 6.

III: The Christian in a Hostile World

Christian Examples

¹¹*† Beloved, I urge you as aliens and sojourners to keep away from worldly desires that wage war against the soul. ¹² Maintain good conduct among the Gentiles, so that if they speak of you as evildoers, they may observe your good works and glorify God on the day of visitation.

Christian Citizens

¹³*† Be subject to every human institution for the Lord's sake, whether it be to the king as supreme ¹⁴ or to governors as sent by him for the punishment of evildoers and the approval of those who do good. ¹⁵ For it is the will of God that by doing good you may silence the ignorance of foolish people. ¹⁶* Be free, yet without using freedom as a pretext for evil, but as slaves of God. ¹⁷* Give honor to all, love the community, fear God, honor the king.

Christian Slaves

¹⁸*† Slaves, be subject to your masters with all reverence, not only to those who are good and equitable but also to those who are perverse. ¹⁹ For whenever anyone bears the pain of unjust suffering because of consciousness of God, that is a grace. ²⁰ But what credit is there if you are patient when beaten for doing wrong? But if you are patient when you suffer for doing what is good, this is a grace before God. ²¹*† For to this you have been called, because Christ also suffered for you, leaving you an example that you should follow in his footsteps.

²²*† "He committed no sin,
 and no deceit was found in his mouth."

²³* When he was insulted, he returned no insult; when he suffered, he did not threaten; instead, he handed himself over to the one who judges justly. ²⁴* He himself bore our sins in his body upon the cross, so that, free from sin, we might live for righteousness. By his wounds you have been healed. ²⁵*† For you had gone astray like sheep, but you have now returned to the shepherd and guardian of your souls.

Christian Spouses

3 ¹† Likewise, you wives should be subordinate to your husbands so that, even if some disobey the word, they may be won over without a word by their wives' conduct ²* when they observe your reverent and chaste behavior. ³* Your adornment should not be an external one: braiding the hair, wearing gold jewelry, or dressing in fine clothes, ⁴ but rather the hidden character of the heart, expressed in the imperishable beauty of a gentle and calm disposition, which is precious in the sight of God. ⁵ For this is also how the holy women who hoped in God once used to adorn themselves and were subordinate to their husbands; ⁶ thus Sarah obeyed Abraham, calling him "lord." You are her children when you do what is good and fear no intimidation.

⁷*† Likewise, you husbands should live with your wives in understanding, showing honor to the weaker female sex, since we are joint heirs of the gift of life, so that your prayers may not be hindered.

---

†
2, 11—3, 12: After explaining the doctrinal basis for the Christian community, the author makes practical applications in terms of the virtues that should prevail in all the social relationships of the members of the community: good example to Gentile neighbors (2, 11–12); respect for human authority (2, 13–17); obedience, patience, and endurance of hardship in domestic relations (2, 18–25); Christian behavior of husbands and wives (3, 1–7); mutual charity (3, 8–12).

2, 11: *Aliens and sojourners:* no longer signifying absence from one's native land (Gn 23, 4), this image denotes rather their estrangement from the world during their earthly pilgrimage (see also 1, 1.17).

2, 13–17: True Christian freedom is the result of being servants of God (16; see the note on 2, 18–23). It includes reverence for God, esteem for every individual, and committed love for fellow Christians (17). Although persecution may threaten, subjection to human government is urged (13.17) and concern for the impact of Christians' conduct on those who are not Christians (12.15).

2, 18–21: Most of the labor in the commercial cities of first-century Asia Minor was performed by a working class of slaves. The sense of freedom contained in the gospel undoubtedly caused great tension among Christian slaves: witness the special advice given concerning them here and in 1 Cor 7, 21–24; Eph 6, 5–8; Col 3, 22–25; Philemon. The point made here does not have so much to do with the institution of slavery, which the author does not challenge, but with the nonviolent reaction (20) of slaves to unjust treatment. Their patient suffering is compared to that of Jesus (21), which won righteousness for all humanity.

2, 21: *Suffered:* some ancient manuscripts and versions read "died" (cf 3, 18).

2, 22–25: After the quotation of Is 53, 9b, the passage describes

Jesus' passion with phrases concerning the Suffering Servant from Is 53, 4–12, perhaps as employed in an early Christian confession of faith; cf 1, 18–21 and 3, 18–22.

2, 25: *The shepherd and guardian of your souls:* the familiar shepherd and flock figures express the care, vigilance, and love of God for his people in the Old Testament (Ps 23; Is 40, 11; Jer 23, 4–5; Ez 34, 11–16) and of Jesus for all humanity in the New Testament (Mt 18, 10–14; Lk 15, 4–7; Jn 10, 1–16; Heb 13, 20).

3, 1–6: The typical marital virtues of women of the ancient world, obedience, reverence, and chastity (1–2), are outlined here by the author, who gives them an entirely new motivation: Christian wives are to be virtuous so that they may be instrumental in the conversion of their husbands. In imitation of *holy women* in the past (5) they are to cultivate the interior life (4) instead of excessive concern with their appearance (3).

3, 7: Husbands who do not respect their wives will have as little success in prayer as those who, according to Paul, have no love: their prayers will be "a resounding gong or a clashing cymbal" (1 Cor 13, 1). Consideration for others is shown as a prerequisite for effective prayer also in Mt 5, 23–24; 1 Cor 11, 20–22; Jas 4, 3. After all, whatever the social position of women in the world and in the family, they are equal recipients of the gift of God's salvation. Paul is very clear on this point, too (see 1 Cor 11, 11–12; Gal 3, 28).

2, 11: Gal 5, 24.
2, 13: Rom 13, 1–7.
2, 16: Gal 5, 13.
2, 17: Prv 24, 21; Mt 22, 21.
2, 18: Eph 6, 5.
2, 21: Mt 16, 24.
2, 22: Is 53, 9.
2, 23: Mt 5, 39.

2, 24: Is 53, 4.12 / Is 53, 5.
2, 25: Is 53, 6.
3, 2: 1 Cor 7, 12–16; Eph 5, 22–24; Col 3, 18;
  1 Tm 2, 9–15.
3, 3: 1 Tm 2, 9–10.
3, 7: Eph 5, 25–33; Col 3, 19.

Christian Conduct

⁸† Finally, all of you, be of one mind, sympathetic, loving toward one another, compassionate, humble. ⁹* Do not return evil for evil, or insult for insult; but, on the contrary, a blessing, because to this you were called, that you might inherit a blessing. ¹⁰* For:

> "Whoever would love life
>   and see good days
> must keep the tongue from evil
>   and the lips from speaking deceit,
> ¹¹ must turn from evil and do good,
>   seek peace and follow after it.
> ¹² For the eyes of the Lord are on the righteous
>   and his ears turned to their prayer,
> but the face of the Lord is against evildoers."

Christian Suffering

¹³† Now who is going to harm you if you are enthusiastic for what is good? ¹⁴ But even if you should suffer because of righteousness, blessed are you. Do not be afraid or terrified with fear of them, ¹⁵* but sanctify Christ as Lord in your hearts. Always be ready to give an explanation to anyone who asks you for a reason for your hope, ¹⁶ but do it with gentleness and reverence, keeping your conscience clear, so that, when you are maligned, those who defame your good conduct in Christ may themselves be put to shame. ¹⁷ For it is better to suffer for doing good, if that be the will of God, than for doing evil.

¹⁸*† For Christ also suffered for sins once, the righteous for the sake of the unrighteous, that he

LIVING GOSPEL VALUES EVEN IF IT DEMANDS SUFFERING

Many Hispanic teenagers and young adults in the United States send money to parents in Latin America. Others work to sustain the education of younger brothers and sisters here. Many times, they are criticized because they are unable to continue their own studies and advance in society.

    Other young people, of any culture, also suffer for living the Gospel. Those who want to leave a gang are harassed by gang members. Young women and men who want to maintain their virginity are made fun of. Young people who start participating in church programs are not understood by their friends. The commitment of young leaders sometimes is misinterpreted by their parents as a way of escaping their duties at home.

    These behaviors cause suffering because Gospel values are conflicting with society's values. In today's First World, particularly in the United States, to blend into the surrounding society is pushed by the media and is almost an ideal set by society.

- How does a true Christian lifestyle cause conflict with mainstream society? How can young Hispanics keep their values of love, generosity, and solidarity with their family while continuing their own personal development?
- Think of Peter's advice to the early Christian communities. Remember Jesus' suffering, and offer yours together with his so that you and all young people may share Christ's new life.

▸ I Pt 3, 13–22

1
P
T

3, 8–12: For the proper ordering of Christian life in its various aspects as described in 2, 11—3, 9, there is promised the blessing expressed in Ps 34, 13–17. In the Old Testament this refers to longevity and prosperity; here, it also refers to eternal life.

3, 13–22: This exposition, centering on v 17, runs as follows: by his suffering and death Christ the righteous one saved the unrighteous (18); by his resurrection he received new life in the spirit, which he communicates to believers through the baptismal bath that cleanses their consciences from sin. As Noah's family was saved *through water*, so Christians are saved through the waters of baptism (19–22). Hence they need not share the fear of sinners; they should rather rejoice in suffering because of their hope in Christ. Thus their

innocence disappoints their accusers (13–16; cf Mt 10, 28; Rom 8, 35–39).

3, 18: *Suffered:* very many ancient manuscripts and versions read "died." *Put to death in the flesh:* affirms that Jesus truly died as a human being. *Brought to life in the spirit:* that is, in the new and transformed existence freed from the limitations and weaknesses of natural human life (cf 1 Cor 15, 45).

3, 9: Mt 5, 44; Lk 6, 28;   **3, 15:** Is 8, 12.
    Rom 12, 14.   **3, 18:** 1 Cor 15, 45.
3, 10–12: Ps 34, 13–17.

might lead you to God. Put to death in the flesh, he was brought to life in the spirit. [19]† In it he also went to preach to the spirits in prison, [20]* who had once been disobedient while God patiently waited in the days of Noah during the building of the ark, in which a few persons, eight in all, were saved through water. [21]*† This prefigured baptism, which saves you now. It is not a removal of dirt from the body but an appeal to God for a clear conscience, through the resurrection of Jesus Christ, [22]* who has gone into heaven and is at the right hand of God, with angels, authorities, and powers subject to him.

Christian Restraint

4 [1]† Therefore, since Christ suffered in the flesh, arm yourselves also with the same attitude (for whoever suffers in the flesh has broken with sin), [2] so as not to spend what remains of one's life in the flesh on human desires, but on the will of God. [3]* For the time that has passed is sufficient for doing what the Gentiles like to do: living in debauchery, evil desires, drunkenness, orgies, carousing, and wanton idolatry. [4] They are surprised that you do not plunge into the same swamp of profligacy, and they vilify you; [5]* but they will give an account to him who stands ready to judge the living and the dead. [6]† For this is why the gospel was preached even to the dead that, though condemned in the flesh in human estimation, they might live in the spirit in the estimation of God.

Christian Charity

[7]† The end of all things is at hand. Therefore, be serious and sober for prayers. [8]*† Above all, let your love for one another be intense, because love covers a multitude of sins. [9]* Be hospitable to one another without complaining. [10]* As each one has received a gift, use it to serve one another as good stewards of God's varied grace. [11]*† Whoever preaches, let it be with the words of God; whoever serves, let it be with the strength that God supplies, so that in all things God may be glorified through Jesus Christ, to whom belong glory and dominion forever and ever. Amen.

SHOUT FOR JOY!

No healthy person likes to suffer. Yet, when we suffer for something good—like being identified as a follower of Christ or defending someone who is under attack by others—First Peter calls us blessed. God notices when we are mocked or ridiculed for our faith. We are challenged to rejoice when we experience such treatment, rather than take it as a sign of failure. For didn't Christ suffer for doing good? And won't he be with us when we suffer for his name? The Gospel has a strange way of turning things upside down—it says that what would cause others sorrow should cause us joy!

The Bible has a lot of other things to say on the topic of suffering. You can use reading plan 7, "Why Do We Suffer?" to locate other passages.

▶ 1 Pt 4, 12–19

IV: Advice to the Persecuted

Trial of Persecution

[12]*† Beloved, do not be surprised that a trial by fire is occurring among you, as if something strange were happening to you. [13]* But rejoice to the extent

---

3, 19: *The spirits in prison:* it is not clear just who these spirits are. They may be the spirits of the sinners who died in the flood, or angelic powers, hostile to God, who have been overcome by Christ (cf 22; Gn 6, 4; Enoch 6–36, especially 21, 6; 2 Enoch 7, 1–5).

3, 21: *Appeal to God:* this could also be translated "pledge," that is, a promise on the part of Christians to live with a good conscience before God, or a pledge from God of forgiveness and therefore a good conscience for us.

4, 1–6: Willingness to suffer with Christ equips the Christian with the power to conquer sin (1). Christ is here portrayed as the judge to whom those guilty of pagan vices must render an account (5; cf Jn 5, 22–27; Acts 10, 42; 2 Tm 4, 1).

4, 6: *The dead:* these may be the sinners of the flood generation who are possibly referred to in 3, 19. But many scholars think that there is no connection between these two verses, and that *the dead* here are Christians who have died since hearing the preaching of the gospel.

4, 7–11: The inner life of the eschatological community is outlined as *the end* (the parousia of Christ) and the judgment draws near in terms of seriousness, sobriety, prayer, and love expressed through hospitality and the use of one's gifts for the glory of God and of Christ.

4, 8: *Love covers a multitude of sins:* a maxim based on Prv 10, 12; see also Ps 32, 1; Jas 5, 20.

4, 11: Some scholars feel that this doxology concludes the part of the homily addressed specifically to the newly baptized, begun in 1, 3; others that it concludes a baptismal liturgy. Such doxologies do occur within a New Testament letter, e.g., Rom 9, 5. Some propose that v 11 was an alternate ending, with 4, 12—5, 14 being read in places where persecution was more pressing. But such doxologies usually do not occur at the end of letters (the only examples are 2 Pt 3, 18, Jude 25, and Rom 16, 27, the last probably a liturgical insertion).

4, 12–19: The suffering to which the author has already frequently referred is presented in more severe terms. This has led some scholars to see these verses as referring to an actual persecution. Others see the heightening of the language as only a rhetorical device used at the end of the letter to emphasize the suffering motif.

3, 20: Gn 7, 7.17; 2 Pt 2, 5.
3, 21: Eph 5, 26; Heb 10, 22.
3, 22: Eph 1, 20–21.
4, 3: Eph 2, 2–3; 4, 17–19; Col 3, 7; Ti 3, 3.
4, 5: Acts 10, 42; 2 Tm 4, 1.
4, 8: Prv 10, 12; Jas 5, 20.
4, 9: Heb 13, 2.
4, 10: Rom 12, 6–8; 1 Cor 12, 4–11.
4, 11: 1 Cor 10, 31.
4, 12: 1 Pt 1, 6–7; 3, 14.17.
4, 13: Rom 5, 3–5; 8, 17; 2 Tm 2, 12.

that you share in the sufferings of Christ, so that when his glory is revealed you may also rejoice exultantly. 14* If you are insulted for the name of Christ, blessed are you, for the Spirit of glory and of God rests upon you. 15 But let no one among you be made to suffer as a murderer, a thief, an evildoer, or as an intriguer. 16 But whoever is made to suffer as a Christian should not be ashamed but glorify God because of the name. 17* For it is time for the judgment to begin with the household of God; if it begins with us, how will it end for those who fail to obey the gospel of God?

18* "And if the righteous one is barely saved,
    where will the godless and the
        sinner appear?"

19 As a result, those who suffer in accord with God's will hand their souls over to a faithful creator as they do good.

Advice to Presbyters†

5 1 So I exhort the presbyters among you, as a fellow presbyter† and witness to the sufferings of Christ and one who has a share in the glory to be revealed. 2* Tend the flock of God in your midst, [overseeing] not by constraint but willingly, as God would have it, not for shameful profit but eagerly. 3 Do not lord it over those assigned to you, but be examples to the flock. 4*† And when the chief Shepherd is revealed, you will receive the unfading crown of glory.

Advice to the Community†

5* Likewise, you younger members,† be subject to the presbyters. And all of you, clothe yourselves with humility in your dealings with one another, for:

"God opposes the proud
    but bestows favor on the humble."

6* So humble yourselves under the mighty hand of God, that he may exalt you in due time. 7* Cast all your worries upon him because he cares for you. 8* Be sober and vigilant. Your opponent the devil is prowling around like a roaring lion looking for [someone] to devour. 9 Resist him, steadfast in faith, knowing that your fellow believers throughout the world undergo the same sufferings. 10* The God of all grace who called you to his eternal glory through Christ [Jesus] will himself restore, confirm, strengthen, and establish you after you have suffered a little. 11 To him be dominion forever. Amen.

V: Conclusion

12† I write you this briefly through Silvanus, whom I consider a faithful brother, exhorting you and testifying that this is the true grace of God. Remain firm in it. 13† The chosen one at Babylon sends you greeting, as does Mark, my son. 14* Greet one another with a loving kiss. Peace to all of you who are in Christ.

5, 1–4: In imitation of Christ, the chief shepherd, those entrusted with a pastoral office are to tend the flock by their care and example.

5, 1: *Presbyters:* the officially appointed leaders and teachers of the Christian community (cf 1 Tm 5, 17–18; Ti 1, 5–8; Jas 5, 14).

5, 4: See the note on 2, 25.

5, 5–11: The community is to be subject to the presbyters and to show humility toward one another and trust in God's love and care (5–7). With sobriety, alertness, and steadfast faith they must resist the evil one; their sufferings are shared with Christians everywhere (8–9). They will be strengthened and called to eternal glory (10–11).

5, 5: *Younger members:* this may be a designation for office-holders of lesser rank.

5, 12: *Silvanus:* the companion of Paul (see 2 Cor 1, 19; 1 Thes 1, 1; 2 Thes 1, 1). Jews and Jewish Christians, like Paul, often had a Hebrew name (Saoul, Silas) and a Greek or Latin name (Paul, Silvanus). On Silvanus's possible role as amanuensis, see Introduction.

5, 13: *The chosen one:* feminine, referring to the Christian community *(ekklēsia)* at *Babylon,* the code name for Rome in Rv 14, 8; 17, 5; 18, 2. *Mark, my son:* traditionally a prominent disciple of Peter and co-worker at the church in Rome, perhaps the John Mark referred to in Acts 12, 12.25; 13, 5.13; and in 15, 37–39, a companion of Barnabas. Perhaps this is the same Mark mentioned as Barnabas's cousin in Col 4, 10, a co-worker with Paul in Phlm 24 (see also 2 Tm 4, 11).

4, 14: Acts 5, 41 / Is 11, 2.
4, 17: Lk 23, 31; 2 Thes 1, 8.
4, 18: Prv 11, 31 LXX.
5, 2: Acts 20, 28; Ti 1, 7.
5, 4: Wis 5, 15–16; 1 Cor 9, 25; 2 Tm 4, 8; Jas 1, 12.
5, 5: Prv 3, 34.
5, 6: Jb 22, 29; Jas 4, 10.
5, 7: Ps 55, 23; Mt 6, 25–33; Lk 12, 22–31; Phil 4, 6.
5, 8: 1 Thes 5, 6.
5, 10: Rom 8, 18; 2 Cor 4, 17.
5, 14: Rom 16, 16; 1 Cor 16, 20; 2 Cor 13, 12.

What happens to us when we die? What is heaven like? Does God even care what happens to us? Many people believe there is no heaven, no hell, and no God. Some say that when we die, our bodies simply decay and we no longer exist in any form. They say that there is no life after death, no punishment, and no reward. But the Bible tells us differently. Second Peter was written to reassure believers that God does indeed care, and that they will be rewarded for leading a faithful and virtuous life.

At a Glance

I. Address (1, 1–2).

II. Exhortation to Christian Virtue (1, 3–21).

III. Condemnation of the False Teachers (2, 1–22).

IV. The Delay of the Second Coming (3, 1–16).

V. Final Exhortation and Doxology (3, 17–18).

In-depth

Bible scholars have convincing evidence that 2 Peter is one of the latest books in the New Testament. The letter appears to have been written by someone who is appealing to the authority of the dead Apostle Peter (see "Introduction to the Letters and Revelation"). At the time of its writing—perhaps as much as one hundred years after Jesus' death and Resurrection—some Christians were starting to wonder if what they believed was true. People were even teaching that there would be no reward or punishment after death. So why not live any way you wanted to?

The author of the Second Letter of Peter is arguing against these false teachers. This writer uses famous examples from the Old Testament to remind readers how God has acted through history. And the author promises that those who have chosen to separate themselves from God in their lifetime will experience the fullness of separation from God in death—a separation that Christians call hell. Those who have stayed faithful to God's calling will enjoy eternal life in union with God—a life that Christians call heaven. Why? Because God is good and just.

Tied in to this argument is another concern. Many of the earliest Christians believed that Christ would return soon after his Resurrection, probably within their lifetime, to establish God's Reign once and for all (see "The Parousia," 2 Thes 1, 5—2, 17). When generations had passed and Christ had not yet returned, false teachers claimed that he would never return. The author of 2 Peter reminds readers that God's time is not our time—Christ is simply waiting so that more people have a chance to repent of their sins before he comes for judgment (2 Pt 3, 9).

Quick Facts

Author
an unknown person writing in Peter's name

Date Written
approximately A.D. 130

Audience
a community of both Jewish and Gentile (non-Jewish) Christians

2 Peter

We await new Heavens and a new earth
3, 13

I: Address

Greeting

1 ¹† Symeon Peter, a slave and apostle of Jesus Christ, to those who have received a faith of equal value to ours through the righteousness of our God and savior Jesus Christ: ²† may grace and peace be yours in abundance through knowledge of God and of Jesus our Lord.

II: Exhortation to Christian Virtue

The Power of God's Promise†

³*† His divine power has bestowed on us everything that makes for life and devotion, through the knowledge of him who called us by his own glory and power.† ⁴* Through these, he has bestowed on us the precious and very great promises, so that through them you may come to share in the divine nature, after escaping from the corruption that is in the world because of evil desire. ⁵*† For this very reason, make every effort to supplement your faith with virtue, virtue with knowledge, ⁶ knowledge with self-control, self-control with endurance, endurance with devotion, ⁷ devotion with mutual affection, mutual affection with love. ⁸ If these are yours and increase in abundance, they will keep you from being idle or unfruitful in the knowledge of our Lord Jesus Christ. ⁹* Anyone who lacks them is blind and shortsighted, forgetful of the cleansing of his past sins. ¹⁰† Therefore, brothers, be all the more eager to make your call and election firm, for, in doing so, you will never stumble. ¹¹ For, in this way, entry into the eternal kingdom

---

1, 1: *Symeon Peter:* on the authorship of 2 Peter, see Introduction; on the spelling here of the Hebrew name *Šim'ôn,* cf Acts 15, 14. The greeting is especially similar to those in 1 Peter and Jude. The words translated *our God and savior Jesus Christ* could also be rendered "our God and the savior Jesus Christ"; cf 11; 2, 20; 3, 2.18.
1, 2: *Knowledge:* a key term in the letter (3.8; 2, 20; 3, 18), perhaps used as a Christian emphasis against gnostic claims.
1, 3–4: Christian life in its fullness is a gift of divine power effecting a knowledge of Christ and the bestowal of divine promises (3, 4.9). *To share in the divine nature,* escaping from a corrupt world, is a thought found elsewhere in the Bible but expressed only here in such Hellenistic terms, since it is said to be accomplished through knowledge (3); cf 2; 2, 20; but see also Jn 15, 4; 17, 22–23; Rom 8, 14–17; Heb 3, 14; 1 Jn 1, 3; 3, 2.
1, 3: *By his own glory and power:* the most ancient papyrus and the best codex read "through glory and power."

1, 5–9: Note the climactic gradation of qualities (5–7), beginning with faith and leading to the fullness of Christian life, which is love; cf Rom 5, 3–4; Gal 5, 6.22 for a similar series of "virtues," though the program and sense here are different than in Paul. The fruit of these is knowledge of Christ (8) referred to in v 3; their absence is spiritual blindness (9).
1, 10–11: Perseverance in the Christian vocation is the best preventative against losing it and the safest provision for attaining its goal, the kingdom. *Kingdom of . . . Christ,* instead of "God," is unusual; cf Col 1, 13 and Mt 13, 41, as well as the *righteousness of . . . Christ* (1).

1, 3: 2 Cor 4, 6; 1 Pt 2, 9.	**1, 5–7:** Gal 5, 22–23.
1, 4: 2 Cor 7, 1; 1 Jn 2, 15.	**1, 9:** 1 Jn 2, 9.11.

of our Lord and savior Jesus Christ will be richly provided for you.

Apostolic Witness

¹²† Therefore, I will always remind you of these things, even though you already know them and are established in the truth you have. ¹³† I think it right, as long as I am in this "tent," to stir you up by a reminder, ¹⁴* since I know that I will soon have to put it aside, as indeed our Lord Jesus Christ has shown me. ¹⁵ I shall also make every effort to enable you always to remember these things after my departure.

¹⁶*† We did not follow cleverly devised myths when we made known to you the power and coming of our Lord Jesus Christ, but we had been eyewitnesses of his majesty. ¹⁷*† For he received honor and glory from God the Father when that unique declaration came to him from the majestic glory, "This is my Son, my beloved, with whom I am well pleased." ¹⁸† We ourselves heard this voice come from heaven while we were with him on the holy mountain. ¹⁹* Moreover, we possess the prophetic message that is altogether reliable. You will do well to be attentive to it, as to a lamp shining in a dark place, until day dawns and the morning star rises in your hearts. ²⁰† Know this first of all, that there is no prophecy of scripture that is a matter of personal interpretation, ²¹ for no prophecy ever came through human will; but rather human beings moved by the holy Spirit spoke under the influence of God.

III: Condemnation of the False Teachers

False Teachers

2 ¹*† There were also false prophets among the people, just as there will be false teachers among you, who will introduce destructive heresies and even deny the Master who ransomed them, bringing swift destruction on themselves. ²* Many will follow their licentious ways, and because of them the way of truth will be reviled. ³* In their greed they will exploit you with fabrications, but from of old their condemnation has not been idle and their destruction does not sleep.

?did you KNOW?
Identifying False Prophets

Many times throughout history, people have misled others in the name of God. Adolf Hitler is probably the best-known such leader in the twentieth century. Some of these leaders have even convinced their followers to commit mass suicide as part of their beliefs. These extreme examples show how people can be misguided by false prophets.

Second Peter 2, 1–3 gives guidelines for identifying false prophets. The author says false prophets use secrets, propose destructive opinions, deny God's teachings, twist the truth to their needs, and exploit their followers. Beware of any leader, religious or nonreligious, who uses these techniques. As 2 Peter says, they malign the way of truth.

▸ 2 Pt 2, 1–3

1, 12–19: The purpose in writing is to call to mind the apostle's witness to the truth, even as he faces the end of his life (12–15), his eyewitness testimony to Christ (16–18), and the true prophetic message (19) through the Spirit in scripture (20–21), in contrast to what false teachers are setting forth (ch 2).

1, 13: *Tent:* a biblical image for transitory human life (Is 38, 12), here combined with a verb that suggests not folding or packing up a tent but its being discarded in death (cf 2 Cor 5, 1–4).

1, 16: *Coming:* in Greek *parousia*, used at 3, 4.12 of the second coming of Christ. The word was used in the extrabiblical writings for the visitation of someone in authority; in Greek cult and Hellenistic Judaism it was used for the manifestation of the divine presence. What the apostles *made known* has been interpreted to refer to Jesus' transfiguration (17) or to his entire first coming or to his future coming in power (ch 3).

1, 17: The author assures the readers of the reliability of the apostolic message (including Jesus' power, glory, and coming; cf the note on 1, 16) by appeal to the transfiguration of Jesus in glory (cf Mt 17, 1–8 and parallels) and by appeal to the prophetic message (19; perhaps Nm 24, 17). Here, as elsewhere, the New Testament insists on continued reminders as necessary to preserve the historical facts about Jesus and the truths of the faith; cf 3, 1–2; 1 Cor 11, 2; 15, 1–3. *My Son, my beloved:* or, "my beloved Son."

1, 18: *We:* at Jesus' transfiguration, referring to Peter, James, and John (Mt 17, 1).

1, 20–21: Often cited, along with 2 Tm 3, 16, on the "inspiration" of scripture or against private interpretation, these verses in context are directed against the false teachers of ch 2 and clever tales (16). The prophetic word in scripture comes admittedly through *human beings* (21), but *moved by the holy Spirit,* not from their own interpretation, and is a matter of what the author and Spirit intended, not the *personal interpretation* of false teachers. Instead of *under the influence of God,* some manuscripts read "holy ones of God."

2, 1–3: The pattern of *false prophets* among the Old Testament people of God will recur through *false teachers* in the church. Such destructive opinions of heretical sects bring loss of faith in Christ, contempt for the way of salvation (cf 21), and immorality.

1, 14: Is 38, 12; Jn 21, 18–19.
1, 16: Lk 9, 28–36; Jn 1, 14.
1, 17: Ps 2, 7; Mt 17, 4–6.
1, 19: Lk 1, 78–79; Rv 2, 28.

2, 1: Mt 24, 11.24; 1 Tm 4, 1; Jude 4.
2, 2: Is 52, 5.
2, 3: Rom 16, 18.

Lessons from the Past

[4]*† For if God did not spare the angels when they sinned, but condemned them to the chains of Tartarus† and handed them over to be kept for judgment; [5]*† and if he did not spare the ancient world, even though he preserved Noah, a herald of righteousness, together with seven others, when he brought a flood upon the godless world; [6]* and if he condemned the cities of Sodom and Gomorrah [to destruction], reducing them to ashes, making them an example for the godless [people] of what is coming; [7] and if he rescued Lot, a righteous man oppressed by the licentious conduct of unprincipled people [8] (for day after day that righteous man living among them was tormented in his righteous soul at the lawless deeds that he saw and heard), [9]* then the Lord knows how to rescue the devout from trial and to keep the unrighteous under punishment for the day of judgment, [10]*† and especially those who follow the flesh with its depraved desire and show contempt for lordship.

False Teachers Denounced

Bold and arrogant, they are not afraid to revile glorious beings, [11]*† whereas angels, despite their superior strength and power, do not bring a reviling judgment against them from the Lord. [12]* But these people, like irrational animals born by nature for capture and destruction, revile things that they do not understand, and in their destruction they will also be destroyed, [13]*† suffering wrong as payment for wrongdoing. Thinking daytime revelry a delight, they are stains and defilements as they revel in their deceits while carousing with you. [14] Their eyes are full of adultery and insatiable for sin. They seduce unstable people, and their hearts are trained in greed. Accursed children! [15]*† Abandoning the straight road, they have gone astray, following the road of Balaam, the son of Bosor, who loved payment for wrongdoing, [16]* but he received a rebuke for his own crime: a mute beast spoke with a human voice and restrained the prophet's madness.

[17]* These people are waterless springs and mists driven by a gale; for them the gloom of darkness has been reserved. [18]*† For, talking empty bombast, they seduce with licentious desires of the flesh those who have barely escaped from people who live in error. [19]* They promise them freedom, though they themselves are slaves of corruption, for a person is a slave of whatever overcomes him. [20]* For if they, having escaped the defilements of the world through the knowledge of [our] Lord and savior Jesus Christ, again become entangled and overcome by them, their last condition is worse than their first. [21]*† For it would have been better for them not to have known the way of righteousness than after knowing it to turn back from the holy commandment handed down to them. [22]*† What is expressed in the true proverb has happened to them, "The dog returns to its own vomit," and "A bathed sow returns to wallowing in the mire."

IV: The Delay of the Second Coming

Denial of the Parousia

3 [1]† This is now, beloved, the second letter I am writing to you; through them by way of reminder I am trying to stir up your sincere disposition,

---

2, 4–6: The false teachers will be punished just as surely and as severely as were the fallen *angels* (4; cf Jude 6; Gn 6, 1–4), the sinners of Noah's day (5; Gn 7, 21–23), and the inhabitants of the cities of the Plain (6; Jude 7; Gn 19, 25). Whereas there are three examples in Jude 5–7 (Exodus and wilderness; rebellious angels; Sodom and Gomorrah), 2 Peter omitted the first of these, has inserted a new illustration about Noah (5) between Jude's second and third examples, and listed the resulting three examples in their Old Testament order (Gn 6; 7; 19).

2, 4: *Chains of Tartarus:* cf Jude 6; other manuscripts in 2 Peter read "pits of Tartarus." *Tartarus:* a term borrowed from Greek mythology to indicate the infernal regions.

2, 5–10a: Although God did not spare the sinful, he kept and saved the righteous, such as *Noah* (5) and *Lot* (7), and he *knows how to rescue the devout* (9), who are contrasted with the false teachers of the author's day. On Noah, cf Gn 5, 32—9, 29, especially 7, 1. On Lot, cf Gn 13 and 19.

2, 10b–22: Some take 10b and 11 with the preceding paragraph. Others begin the new paragraph with 10a, supplying from v 9 *The Lord knows how . . . to keep . . . under punishment,* with reference to God and probably specifically Christ (1). The conduct of the false teachers is described and condemned in language similar to that of Jude 8–16. This arrogance knows no bounds; animal-like, they are due to be caught and destroyed. They seduce even those who have knowledge of Christ (20).

2, 10b: *Glorious beings:* literally, "glories"; cf Jude 8. While some think that illustrious personages are meant or even political officials behind whom (fallen) angels stand, it is more likely that the reference is to glorious angelic beings (cf Jude 9).

2, 11: *From the Lord:* some manuscripts read "before the Lord"; cf Jude 9.

2, 13: *Suffering wrong:* some manuscripts read "receiving a reward." *In their deceits:* some manuscripts read "in their love feasts" (Jude 12).

2, 15: *Balaam, the son of Bosor:* in Nm 22, 5, Balaam is said to be the son of Beor, and it is this name that turns up in a few ancient Greek manuscripts by way of "correction" of the text. Balaam is not portrayed in such a bad light in Nm 22. His evil reputation and his *madness* (16), and possibly his surname Bosor, may have come from a Jewish tradition about him in the first/second century, of which we no longer have any knowledge.

2, 18: *Barely escaped:* some manuscripts read "really escaped."

2, 21: *Commandment handed down:* cf 3, 2 and Jude 3.

2, 22: The second proverb is of unknown origin, while the first appears in Prv 26, 11.

3, 1–4: The false teachers not only flout Christian morality (cf Jude 8–19); they also deny the second coming of Christ and the judgment (4; cf 7). They seek to justify their licentiousness by arguing that the promised return of Christ has not been realized and the world is the same, no better than it was before (3–4). The author wishes to strengthen the faithful against such errors by reminding them in this *second letter* of the instruction in 1 Peter and the teaching of the *prophets* and of Christ, conveyed through the *apostles* (1–2; cf Jude 17; cf 1 Pt 1, 10–12.16–21, especially 16–21; Eph 2, 20.

2, 4: Jude 6.	2, 15: Nm 31, 16; Jude 11.
2, 5: Gn 8, 15–19; Heb 11, 7.	2, 16: Nm 22, 28–33.
2, 6: Gn 19, 24–25; Jude 7.	2, 17: Jude 12–13.
2, 9: 1 Cor 10, 13; Rv 3, 10.	2, 18: Jude 16.
2, 10: Jude 8.	2, 19: Jn 8, 34; Rom 6, 16–17.
2, 11: Jude 9.	2, 20: Mt 12, 45.
2, 12: Ps 49, 13–15; Jude 10.	2, 21: Ez 3, 20.
2, 13: Jude 12.	2, 22: Prv 26, 11.

2* to recall the words previously spoken by the holy prophets and the commandment of the Lord and savior through your apostles. 3*† Know this first of all, that in the last days scoffers will come [to] scoff, living according to their own desires 4*† and saying, "Where is the promise of his coming? From the time when our ancestors fell asleep, everything has remained as it was from the beginning of creation." 5*† They deliberately ignore the fact that the heavens existed of old and earth was formed out of water and through water by the word of God; 6*† through these the world that then existed was destroyed, deluged with water. 7* The present heavens and earth have been reserved by the same word for fire, kept for the day of judgment and of destruction of the godless.

8*† But do not ignore this one fact, beloved, that with the Lord one day is like a thousand years and a thousand years like one day. 9* The Lord does not delay his promise, as some regard "delay," but he is patient with you, not wishing that any should perish but that all should come to repentance. 10*† But the day of the Lord will come like a thief, and then the heavens will pass away with a mighty roar and the elements will be dissolved by fire, and the earth and everything done on it will be found out.

Exhortation to Preparedness

11*† Since everything is to be dissolved in this way, what sort of persons ought [you] to be, conducting yourselves in holiness and devotion, 12*† waiting for and hastening the coming of the day of God, because of which the heavens will be dissolved in flames and the elements melted by

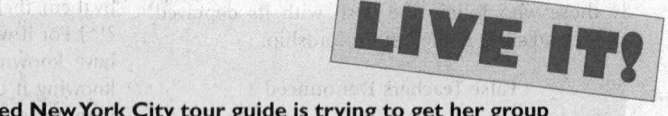

Where Is God?

A frustrated and frazzled New York City tour guide is trying to get her group through a maze of homeless people and panhandlers outside the great Saint Patrick's Cathedral. After the group has safely entered the cathedral, she exclaims, with arms outstretched, "God is definitely here!" A young girl whose gaze lingers on the people outside asks, with all seriousness, "Why won't they let him out?"

The early readers of 2 Peter were confused that Jesus Christ had not yet returned again (see "The Parousia," 2 Thes 1, 5—2, 17). They wondered, "Where is God?" The author reminds them not to apply human limits to God's response.

Sometimes, when we pray for something, it seems like God keeps us waiting for an eternity. We want something to happen quickly—but God is on a different schedule. You might say the only limits we have in seeing God's actions are the ones we establish. Where are you not seeing God these days?

▶ 2 Pt 3, 9

---

† **3, 3:** *Scoffers:* cf Jude 18, where, however, only the passions of the scoffers are mentioned, not a denial on their part of Jesus' parousia.

3, 4–7: The false teachers tried to justify their immorality by pointing out that the promised *coming (parousia)* of the Lord has not yet occurred, even though early Christians expected it in their day. They thus insinuate that God is not guiding the world's history anymore, since nothing has changed and the first generation of Christians, *our ancestors* (4) has all died by this time. The author replies that, just as God destroyed the earth by water in the flood (5–6, cf 2, 5), so he will destroy it along with the false teachers on judgment day (7). *The word of God,* which called the world into being (Gn 1; Ps 33, 6) and *destroyed* it by the waters of a flood, will destroy it again by fire on *the day of judgment* (5–7).

3, 5: *Formed out of water and through water:* Gn 1, 2.6–8 is reflected as well as Greek views that water was the basic element from which all is derived.

3, 6: *Destroyed, deluged with water:* cf 2, 5; Gn 7, 11—8, 2.

3, 8–10: The scoffers' objection (4) is refuted also by showing that delay of the Lord's second coming is not a failure to fulfill his word but rather a sign of his patience: God is giving time for repentance before the final judgment (cf Wis 11, 23–26; Ez 18, 23; 33, 11).

3, 8: Cf Ps 90, 4.

3, 10: *Like a thief:* Mt 24, 43; 1 Thes 5, 2; Rv 3, 3. *Will be found out:* cf 1 Cor 3, 13–15. Some few versions read, as the sense may demand, "will not be found out"; many manuscripts read "will be burned up"; there are further variants in other manuscripts, versions, and Fathers. Total destruction is assumed (11).

3, 11–16: The second coming of Christ and the judgment of the world are the doctrinal bases for the moral exhortation to readiness through vigilance and a virtuous life; cf Mt 24, 42.50–51; Lk 12, 40; 1 Thes 5, 1–11; Jude 20–21.

3, 12: *Flames . . . fire:* although this is the only New Testament passage about a final conflagration, the idea was common in apocalyptic and Greco-Roman thought. *Hastening:* eschatology is here used to motivate ethics (11), as elsewhere in the New Testament. Jewish sources and Acts 3, 19–20 assume that proper ethical conduct can help bring the promised day of the Lord; cf 9. Some render the phrase, however, "desiring it earnestly."

3, 2: Jude 17.
3, 3: 1 Tm 4, 1; 2 Tm 3, 1; Jude 18.
3, 4: Is 5, 19.
3, 5: Gn 1, 2.6.8; Ps 24, 2.
3, 6: Gn 7, 21.
3, 7: Is 51, 6; Mt 3, 12.

3, 8: Ps 90, 4.
3, 9: Ez 18, 23; 1 Tm 2, 4.
3, 10: Is 66, 15–16; Mt 24, 29.
3, 11: Acts 3, 19–21.
3, 12: Is 34, 4; Heb 10, 27.

fire. ¹³*† But according to his promise we await new heavens and a new earth in which righteousness dwells.

¹⁴ Therefore, beloved, since you await these things, be eager to be found without spot or blemish before him, at peace. ¹⁵* And consider the patience of our Lord as salvation, as our beloved brother Paul, according to the wisdom given to him, also wrote to you, ¹⁶† speaking of these things as he does in all his letters. In them there are some things hard to understand that the ignorant and unstable distort to their own destruction, just as they do the other scriptures.

V: Final Exhortation and Doxology

¹⁷*† Therefore, beloved, since you are forewarned, be on your guard not to be led into the error of the unprincipled and to fall from your own stability. ¹⁸* But grow in grace and in the knowledge of our Lord and savior Jesus Christ. To him be glory now and to the day of eternity. [Amen.]

3, 13: *New heavens and a new earth:* cf Is 65, 17; 66, 22. The divine promises will be fulfilled after the day of judgment will have passed. The universe will be transformed by the reign of God's *righteousness* or justice; cf Is 65, 17–18; Acts 3, 21; Rom 8, 18–25; Rv 21, 1.

3, 16: *These things:* the teachings of this letter find parallels in Paul, e.g., God's will to save (Rom 2, 4; 9, 22–23; 1 Cor 1, 7–8), the coming of Christ (1 Thes 4, 16–17; 1 Cor 15, 23–52), and preparedness for the judgment (Col 1, 22–23; Eph 1, 4–14; 4, 30; 5, 5–14). *Other scriptures:* used to guide the faith and life of the Christian community. The letters of Paul are thus here placed on the same level as books of the Old Testament. Possibly other New Testament writings could also be included.

3, 17–18: To avoid the dangers of *error* and loss of *stability,* Christians are *forewarned* to be *on your guard* and to *grow in grace and . . . knowledge* (1, 2) of Christ. The doxology (18) recalls 1 Pt 4, 11. Some manuscripts add *Amen.*

3, 13: Is 65, 17; 66, 22; Rom 8, 21; Rv 21, 1.27.
3, 15: Rom 8, 19; Jude 24.

3, 17: Mk 13, 5; Heb 2, 1.
3, 18: Rom 16, 27.

Betrayal is painful. Unfortunately, most of us have experienced it at one time or another. It often begins with a misunderstanding. Sometimes, harsh words are exchanged, and people part ways feeling sad and bitter. The community addressed by the three Letters of John had experienced sharp division and conflict. It is impossible to avoid the author's feeling of betrayal as you read these letters.

At a Glance

I. Prologue (1 Jn 1, 1–4).

II. God as Light (1 Jn 1, 5—3, 10).

III. Love for One Another (1 Jn 3, 11—5, 12).

IV. Epilogue (1 Jn 5, 13–21).

I. The Second Letter of John.

I. The Third Letter of John.

In-depth

All three Letters of John were probably written by the same person, the Presbyter referred to in the second and third letters. This writer had, perhaps a decade earlier, belonged to the community for which the Gospel of John was written. He saw himself and his community as being faithful to the true meaning of John's Gospel. Now, others who had once belonged to this community had abandoned it in its time of need. They too read the Gospel of John, but they interpreted it very differently. The disagreement between these two groups resulted in a bitter conflict.

The First Letter of John really isn't a letter at all but is more like a teaching homily. The second letter tells the community not to associate with the "deceivers" who have broken off from the group. The third letter asks the community to welcome a representative or missionary sent by the Presbyter.

Even after careful study of the first letter, it is difficult to determine exactly what the disagreement was about. One issue seems to have been the proper understanding of Jesus' humanity. Apparently, the deceivers did not fully believe in Jesus' humanity and its connection to salvation through Jesus' death and Resurrection. To emphasize Jesus' humanity, the author several times mentions that Jesus came "in the flesh" and comments on the saving power of the "blood of Jesus."

The author also challenges the deceivers' claims that they were free to do anything they wanted and still love God. If they truly loved God, they would also love their brothers and sisters and would not have abandoned the community.

Through this letter, God reminds today's Christians that believers can have profoundly different understandings about what they believe. Conflict and disagreement will occur even within the Christian community. Can Christians handle such discord with love and respect?

Quick Facts

Author
an unknown person associated with the community that produced the Gospel of John

Date Written
approximately A.D. 100

Audience
Christians who were suffering from a split in their community

1 John

Love one another

4, 7

I: Prologue

The Word of Life

1 ¹*† What was from the beginning,
what we have heard,
what we have seen with our eyes,
what we looked upon
and touched with our hands
concerns the Word of life—
²* for the life was made visible;
we have seen it and testify to it
and proclaim to you the eternal life
that was with the Father and was made visible
to us—
³* what we have seen and heard
we proclaim now to you,
so that you too may have fellowship
with us;
for our fellowship is with the Father
and with his Son, Jesus Christ.

⁴* We are writing this so that our joy may
be complete.

II: God As Light

God is Light

⁵† Now this is the message that we have heard from him and proclaim to you: God is light, and in him there is no darkness at all. ⁶* If we say, "We have fellowship with him," while we continue to walk in darkness, we lie and do not act in truth. ⁷* But if we walk in the light as he is in the light, then we have fellowship with one another, and the blood of his Son Jesus cleanses us from all sin. ⁸*† If we say, "We are without sin," we deceive ourselves, and the truth is not in us. ⁹* If we acknowledge our sins, he is faithful and just and will forgive our sins and cleanse us from every wrongdoing. ¹⁰* If we say, "We have not sinned," we make him a liar, and his word is not in us.

1, 1–4: There is a striking parallel to the prologue of the gospel of John (Jn 1, 1–18), but the emphasis here is not on the preexistent Word but rather on the apostles' witness to the incarnation of life by their experience of the historical Jesus. He is *the Word of life* (1; cf Jn 1, 4), *the eternal life that was with the Father and was made visible* (2; cf Jn 1, 14), and was *heard, seen, looked upon,* and *touched* by the apostles. The purpose of their teaching is to share that *life,* called *fellowship, . . . with the Father and with his Son, Jesus Christ,* with those who receive their witness (3; Jn 1, 14.16).

1, 5–7: *Light* is to be understood here as truth and goodness; *darkness* here is error and depravity (cf Jn 3, 19–21; 17, 17; Eph 5, 8). To *walk* in light or darkness is to live according to truth or error, not merely intellectual but moral as well. Fellowship with God and

with one another consists in a life according to the truth as found in God and in Christ.

1, 8–10: Denial of the condition of sin is self-deception and even contradictory of divine revelation; there is also the continual possibility of sin's recurrence. Forgiveness and deliverance from sin through Christ are assured through acknowledgment of them and repentance.

1, 1: 1 Jn 2, 13; Jn 1, 1.14; 20, 20.25.27.
1, 2: Jn 15, 27; 17, 5.
1, 3: Jn 17, 21; Acts 4, 20.
1, 4: Jn 15, 11; 2 Jn 12.
1, 6: Jn 12, 35.
1, 7: Mt 26, 28; Rom 3, 24–25; Heb 9, 14; 1 Pt 1, 19; Rv 1, 5.
1, 8: 2 Chr 6, 36; Prv 20, 9.
1, 9: Prv 28, 13; Jas 5, 16.
1, 10: 1 Jn 5, 10.

Live in the Light

Do you ever find it hard to decide whether something is right or wrong? Instead of the sharp distinction between light and darkness described in 1 John, you might see a lot of shades of gray. But be careful; you might simply be seeing what you want to see! Remember, "If we say, 'We are without sin,' we deceive ourselves" (1 Jn 1, 8). There are times when our choices aren't clear—but usually they are. Listen to your inner voice of honesty and integrity, and courageously choose to live in the light!

▸ 1 Jn 1, 5–10

Christ and His Commandments

2 ¹*† My children, I am writing this to you so that you may not commit sin. But if anyone does sin, we have an Advocate with the Father, Jesus Christ the righteous one. ²* He is expiation for our sins, and not for our sins only but for those of the whole world. ³*† The way we may be sure that we know him is to keep his commandments. ⁴* Whoever says, "I know him," but does not keep his commandments is a liar, and the truth is not in him. ⁵* But whoever keeps his word, the love of God is truly perfected in him. This is the way we may know that we are in union with him: ⁶ whoever claims to abide in him ought to live [just] as he lived.

The New Commandment

⁷*† Beloved, I am writing no new commandment to you but an old commandment that you had from the beginning. The old commandment is the word that you have heard. ⁸*† And yet I do write a new commandment to you, which holds true in him and among you, for the darkness is passing away, and the true light is already shining. ⁹* Whoever says he is in the light, yet hates his brother, is still in the darkness. ¹⁰* Whoever loves his brother remains in the light, and there is nothing in him to cause a fall.

¹¹ Whoever hates his brother is in darkness; he walks in darkness and does not know where he is going because the darkness has blinded his eyes.

Members of the Community

¹²*† I am writing to you, children, because your sins have been forgiven for his name's sake.†

¹³* I am writing to you, fathers, because you know him who is from the beginning.

I am writing to you, young men, because you have conquered the evil one.

¹⁴ I write to you, children, because you know the Father.

I write to you, fathers, because you know him who is from the beginning.

I write to you, young men, because you are strong and the word of God remains in you, and you have conquered the evil one.

¹⁵*† Do not love the world or the things of the world. If anyone loves the world, the love of the Father is not in him. ¹⁶† For all that is in the world, sensual lust, enticement for the eyes, and a pretentious life, is not from the Father but is from the world. ¹⁷* Yet the world and its enticement are passing away. But whoever does the will of God remains forever.

2, 1: *Children:* like the term "beloved," this is an expression of pastoral love (cf Jn 13, 33; 21, 5; 1 Cor 4, 14). *Advocate:* for the use of the term, see Jn 14, 16. Forgiveness of sin is assured through Christ's intercession and expiation or "offering"; the death of Christ effected the removal of sin.

2, 3–6: *The way we may be sure:* to those who claim, "I have known Christ and therefore I know him," our author insists on not mere intellectual knowledge but obedience to God's commandments in a life conformed to the example of Christ; this confirms our knowledge of him and is *the love of God . . . perfected.* Disparity between moral life and the commandments proves improper belief.

2, 7–11: The author expresses the continuity and freshness of mutual charity in Christian experience. Through Christ the commandment of love has become the *light* defeating the *darkness* of evil in a new age. All hatred as darkness is incompatible with the light and Christian life. Note also the characteristic Johannine polemic in which a positive assertion is emphasized by the negative statement of its opposite.

2, 8: *Which holds true in him and among you:* literally, "a thing that holds true in him and in you."

2, 12–17: The Christian community that has experienced the grace of God through forgiveness of sin and knowledge of Christ is armed against the evil one.

2, 12: *For his name's sake:* because of Christ our sins are forgiven.

2, 15: *The world:* all that is hostile toward God and alienated from him. Love of the *world* and love of God are thus mutually exclusive; cf Jas 4, 4.

2, 16: *Sensual lust:* literally, "the lust of the flesh," inordinate desire for physical gratification. *Enticement for the eyes:* literally, "the lust of the eyes," avarice or covetousness; the eyes are regarded as the windows of the soul. *Pretentious life:* literally, "pride of life," arrogance or ostentation in one's earthly style of life that reflects a willful independence from God and others.

2, 1: Jn 14, 16; Heb 7, 25.	**2, 9:** Jn 8, 12.
2, 2: 1 Jn 4, 10.	**2, 10:** Eccl 2, 14; Jn 11, 10.
2, 3: Jn 14, 15; 15, 10.	**2, 12:** 1 Cor 6, 11.
2, 4: 1 Jn 4, 20.	**2, 13:** 1 Jn 1, 1; Jn 1, 1.
2, 5: Jn 14, 23.	**2, 15:** Rom 8, 7–8; Jas 4, 4;
2, 7: 1 Jn 3, 11; Dt 6, 5; Mt	2 Pt 1, 4.
22, 37–40.	**2, 17:** Is 40, 8; Mt 7, 21;
2, 8: Jn 13, 34 / Jn 1, 5;	1 Cor 7, 31; 1 Pt 4, 2.
Rom 13, 12.	

BE RECONCILED

Sometimes, it's hardest to show your love to the people you are closest to. Maybe you get along great with all your friends but are always arguing with your brother or sister. Or in your youth group, you are always tense around that one person with whom you had angry words several months ago.

The author of 1 John tells us that we cannot ignore a relationship with a brother or sister in the Lord who has been upset. The Hmong culture has the same tradition. If you frighten or hurt or offend someone, you have created an imbalance of spirits. It is your responsibility to go back and seek to re-establish harmony. It is the Hmong custom to go to a shaman (an elder of the community, a holy person) for advice and to perform a ritual for reconciliation.

The Catholic Tradition has the sacrament of Reconciliation for the same purpose: to admit the imbalance in a relationship caused by sin, discuss ways to make things right, express sorrow, and celebrate God's forgiveness and love.

▶ 1 Jn 2, 7–11

Antichrists

18*† Children, it is the last hour; and just as you heard that the antichrist was coming, so now many antichrists have appeared. Thus we know this is the last hour. 19† They went out from us, but they were not really of our number; if they had been, they would have remained with us. Their desertion shows that none of them was of our number. 20*† But you have the anointing that comes from the holy one, and you all have knowledge. 21* I write to you not because you do not know the truth but because you do, and because every lie is alien to the truth. 22*† Who is the liar? Whoever denies that Jesus is the Christ. Whoever denies the Father and the Son, this is the antichrist. 23* No one who denies the Son has the Father, but whoever confesses the Son has the Father as well.

Life from God's Anointing

24*† Let what you heard from the beginning remain in you. If what you heard from the beginning remains in you, then you will remain in the Son and in the Father. 25* And this is the promise that he made us: eternal life. 26 I write you these things about those who would deceive you. 27 As for you, the anointing that you received from him remains in you, so that you do not need anyone to teach you. But his anointing teaches you about everything and is true and not false; just as it taught you, remain in him.

Children of God

28† And now, children, remain in him, so that when he appears we may have confidence and not be put to shame by him at his coming. 29 If you consider that he is righteous, you also know that everyone who acts in righteousness is begotten by him.

---

† **2, 18:** *It is the last hour:* literally, "a last hour," the period between the death and resurrection of Christ and his second coming. *The antichrist:* opponent or adversary of Christ; the term appears only in 1–2 John, but "pseudochrists" (translated "false messiahs") in Mt 24, 24 and Mk 13, 22, and Paul's "lawless one" in 2 Thes 2, 3, are similar figures. *Many antichrists:* Matthew, Mark, and Revelation seem to indicate a collectivity of persons, here related to the false teachers.

2, 19: *Not really of our number:* the apostate teachers only proved their lack of faith by leaving the community.

2, 20: *The anointing that comes from the holy one:* this anointing is in the Old Testament sense of receiving the Spirit of God. The *holy one* probably refers to Christ. True knowledge is the gift of the Spirit

(cf Is 11, 2), and the function of the Spirit is to lead Christians to the truth (Jn 14, 17.26; 16, 13).

2, 22–23: Certain gnostics denied that the earthly Jesus was the Christ; to deny knowledge of the Son is to deny the Father, since only through the Son has God been fully revealed (Jn 1, 18; 14, 8–9).

2, 24: Continuity with the apostolic witness as proclaimed in the prologue is the safeguard of right belief.

2, 28–29: Our confidence at his judgment is based on the daily assurance of salvation. Our actions reflect our true relation to him.

2, 18: 1 Tim 4, 1.
2, 20: Jn 14, 26.
2, 21: 1 Jn 3, 19; 2 Pt 1, 12.
2, 22: 2 Thes 2, 4.
2, 23: Jn 14, 7–9.
2, 24: Jn 14, 23.
2, 25: Jn 5, 24; 10, 28; 17, 2.

3 [1]*† See what love the Father has bestowed on us that we may be called the children of God. Yet so we are. The reason the world does not know us is that it did not know him. [2]*† Beloved, we are God's children now; what we shall be has not yet been revealed. We do know that when it is revealed we shall be like him, for we shall see him as he is. [3]* Everyone who has this hope based on him makes himself pure, as he is pure.

Avoiding Sin

[4]† Everyone who commits sin commits lawlessness, for sin is lawlessness. [5]* You know that he was revealed to take away sins, and in him there is no sin. [6] No one who remains in him sins; no one who sins has seen him or known him. [7] Children, let no one deceive you. The person who acts in righteousness is righteous, just as he is righteous. [8]* Whoever sins belongs to the devil, because the devil has sinned from the beginning. Indeed, the Son of God was revealed to destroy the works of the devil. [9]† No one who is begotten by God commits sin, because God's seed remains in him; he cannot sin because he is begotten by God. [10] In this way, the children of God and the children of the devil are made plain; no one who fails to act in righteousness belongs to God, nor anyone who does not love his brother.

III: Love for One Another

[11]*† For this is the message you have heard from the beginning: we should love one another, [12]* unlike Cain who belonged to the evil one and slaughtered his brother. Why did he slaughter him? Because his own works were evil, and those of his brother righteous. [13]* Do not be amazed, [then,] brothers, if the world hates you. [14]* We know that we have passed from death to life because we love our brothers. Whoever does not love

remains in death. [15]* Everyone who hates his brother is a murderer, and you know that no murderer has eternal life remaining in him. [16]* The way we came to know love was that he laid down his life for us; so we ought to lay down our lives for our brothers. [17]* If someone who has worldly means sees a brother in need and refuses him compassion, how can the love of God remain in him? [18]* Children, let us love not in word or speech but in deed and truth.

Confidence before God

[19]† [Now] this is how we shall know that we belong to the truth and reassure our hearts before him

Love in Action

Clear your mind of all thoughts and concerns. Help your body and mind relax with some deep breaths. Now, read 1 Jn 3, 18 several times until you can say it by heart. Reflect on its meaning. Think about how you have lived and acted during this past week. Have you shown love in truth and action? by word or speech?

Ask God to forgive you for any situations in which you failed to act lovingly. Pray for the gift of being able to put your love in action in your daily life. Throughout the remainder of this day, remind yourself of this prayer by calling to mind verse 18.

▶ 1 Jn 3, 18

---

†
3, 1–3: The greatest sign of God's love is the gift of his Son (Jn 3, 16) that has made Christians true children of God. This relationship is a present reality and also part of the life to come; true knowledge of God will ultimately be gained, and Christians prepare themselves now by virtuous lives in imitation of the Son.
3, 2: *When it is revealed:* or "when he is revealed" (the subject of the verb could be Christ).
3, 4: *Lawlessness:* a reference to the activity of the antichrist, so it is expressed as hostility toward God and a rejection of Christ. The author goes on to contrast the states of sin and righteousness. Christians do not escape sin but realize that when they sin they cease to have fellowship with God. Virtue and sin distinguish the children of God from the children of the devil.
3, 9: A habitual sinner is a child of the devil, while a child of God, who by definition is in fellowship with God, cannot sin. *Seed:* Christ or the Spirit who shares the nature of God with the Christian.
3, 11–18: Love, even to the point of self-sacrifice, is the point of the commandment. The story of Cain and Abel (12–15; Gn 4, 1–16) presents the rivalry of two brothers, in a contrast of evil and righteousness, where envy led to murder. For Christians, proof of deliverance is love toward others, after the example of Christ. This

includes concrete acts of charity, out of our material abundance.
3, 19–24: Living a life of faith in Jesus and of Christian love assures us of abiding in God no matter what our feelings may at times tell us. Our obedience gives us confidence in prayer and trust in God's judgment. This obedience includes our belief in Christ and love for one another.
3, 19b–20: This difficult passage may also be translated "we shall be at peace before him in whatever our hearts condemn, for . . ." or "and before God we shall convince our hearts, if our hearts condemn us, that God is greater than our hearts."

*
3, 1: Jn 1, 12; Eph 1, 5 / Jn 15, 21; 17, 25.
3, 2: Phil 3, 21.
3, 3: 1 Jn 2, 6.
3, 5: Is 53, 9; Jn 1, 29; 8, 46; 1 Pt 2, 22.
3, 8: Jn 8, 44; 12, 31–32.
3, 11: 1 Jn 2, 7; Jn 13, 34; 15, 12.17.
3, 12: Gn 4, 8; Jude 11.
3, 13: Mt 24, 9; Jn 15, 18; 17, 14.
3, 14: Lv 19, 17; Jn 5, 24.
3, 15: Jn 8, 44.
3, 16: Mt 20, 28; Jn 10, 11; 15, 13.
3, 17: Dt 15, 7.11; Jas 2, 15–16.
3, 18: Jas 1, 22.

Let us love not in word or speech but in deed and truth
3, 18

20 in whatever our hearts condemn, for God is greater than our hearts and knows everything. 21 Beloved, if [our] hearts do not condemn us, we have confidence in God 22* and receive from him whatever we ask, because we keep his commandments and do what pleases him. 23* And his commandment is this: we should believe in the name of his Son, Jesus Christ, and love one another just as he commanded us. 24* Those who keep his commandments remain in him, and he in them, and the way we know that he remains in us is from the Spirit that he gave us.

Testing the Spirits

4 1*† Beloved, do not trust every spirit but test the spirits to see whether they belong to God, because many false prophets have gone out into the world. 2* This is how you can know the Spirit of God: every spirit that acknowledges Jesus Christ come in the flesh belongs to God, 3*† and every spirit that does not acknowledge Jesus does not belong to God. This is the spirit of the antichrist that, as you heard, is to come, but in fact is already in the world. 4 You belong to God, children, and you have

Testing Spirits

The spirit is the primary essence of a person or a belief. The First Letter of John talks about two kinds of spirit: that which comes from God and that which does not come from God. This letter gives us two ways for testing whether our spirit comes from God: The first has to do with whether our actions reflect love for God and love for our brothers and sisters (3, 18). The second has to do with our beliefs about Jesus Christ. To understand this, let's look closer at the controversy that prompted the author of this letter to offer these two tests.

The controversy in the community addressed by 1 John seems to revolve around what Christians call the Incarnation—the belief that Jesus Christ is both fully God and fully human. The "false prophets" deny Christ's humanity, saying Jesus only appeared to be human. The author insists that the spirits who come from God will confess, "Jesus Christ come in the flesh" (4, 2)—that is, he is fully human. Believing in the Incarnation is the foundation for understanding "the Father sent his Son as savior of the world" (verse 14).

You can apply this letter's two tests to just about any spiritual idea or practice you come across, whether it has to do with different religious traditions, New Age spirituality, or magic or the occult. Ask yourself: Does this help me love God and other people? Does this support the Christian belief that Jesus Christ is fully God and fully human, and that faith in him is necessary for salvation? If you cannot answer yes to both these questions, stay away!

▸ 1 Jn 4, 1–21

---

† 4, 1–6: Deception is possible in spiritual phenomena and may be tested by its relation to Christian doctrine (cf 1 Cor 12, 3): those who fail to acknowledge Jesus Christ in the flesh are false prophets and belong to the antichrist. Even though these false prophets are well received in the world, the Christian who belongs to God has a greater power in the truth.

4, 3: *Does not acknowledge Jesus:* some ancient manuscripts add

"Christ" and/or "to have come in the flesh" (cf 2), and others read "every spirit that annuls (or severs) Jesus."

3, 22: 1 Jn 5, 15; Mt 7, 7–11;
    21, 22; Jn 14, 13–14.
3, 23: Jn 13, 34; 15, 17.
3, 24: 1 Jn 4, 13; Jn 14,
    21–23.
4, 1: 1 Jn 2, 18; Mt 24, 24.
4, 2: 1 Cor 12, 3; 1 Thes 5,
    21.
4, 3: 1 Jn 1, 22.

Understanding Love

Some of the most beautiful prose and poetry about love are contained in the Bible. First John 4, 7–21 is a particularly eloquent piece that captures the heart of the Good News: God has loved us in Christ Jesus, who came as the Savior of the world. Now, we have been given God and Jesus' spirit, and we are commanded to love others as we have been loved by God.

It is easy to say, "I love God." But 1 John tells us that our love for God is shown in our love for one another. Loving one another is much harder than simply saying, "I love God." What does this love for God look like? It is not the romantic love or sentimental affection the world usually presents to us. Read Mt 25, 31–36 or 1 Corinthians, chapter 13, for some ideas.

▸ 1 Jn 4, 7–21

conquered them, for the one who is in you is greater than the one who is in the world. 5* They belong to the world; accordingly, their teaching belongs to the world, and the world listens to them. 6* We belong to God, and anyone who knows God listens to us, while anyone who does not belong to God refuses to hear us. This is how we know the spirit of truth and the spirit of deceit.

God's Love and Christian Life

7† Beloved, let us love one another, because love is of God; everyone who loves is begotten by God and knows God. 8 Whoever is without love does not know God, for God is love. 9* In this way the love of God was revealed to us: God sent his only Son into the world so that we might have life through him. 10* In this is love: not that we have loved God, but that he loved us and sent his Son as expiation for our sins. 11 Beloved, if God so loved us, we also must love one another. 12* No one has ever seen God. Yet, if we love one another, God remains in us, and his love is brought to perfection in us.

13† This is how we know that we remain in him and he in us, that he has given us of his Spirit. 14 Moreover, we have seen and testify that the Father sent his Son as savior of the world. 15 Whoever acknowledges that Jesus is the Son of God, God remains in him and he in God. 16 We have come to know and to believe in the love God has for us.

God is love, and whoever remains in love remains in God and God in him. 17* In this is love brought to perfection among us, that we have confidence on the day of judgment because as he is, so are we in this world. 18 There is no fear in love, but perfect love drives out fear because fear has to do with punishment, and so one who fears is not yet perfect in love. 19 We love because he first loved us. 20*† If anyone says, "I love God," but hates his brother, he is a liar; for whoever does not love a brother whom he has seen cannot love God whom he has not seen. 21* This is the commandment we have from him: whoever loves God must also love his brother.

Faith is Victory over the World

5 1*† Everyone who believes that Jesus is the Christ is begotten by God, and everyone who loves the father loves [also] the one begotten by him. 2 In this way we know that we love the

---

†
4, 7–12: Love as we share in it testifies to the nature of God and to his presence in our lives. One who loves shows that one is a child of God and knows God, for God's very being is love; one without love is without love. The revelation of the nature of God's love is found in the free gift of his Son to us, so that we may share life with God and be delivered from our sins. The love we have for one another must be of the same sort: authentic, merciful; this unique Christian love is our proof that we know God and can "see" the invisible God.

4, 13–21: The testimony of the Spirit and that of faith join the testimony of love to confirm our knowledge of God. Our love is grounded in the confession of Jesus as the Son of God and the example of God's love for us. Christian life is founded on the knowledge of God as love and on his continuing presence that relieves us from fear of judgment (16–18). What Christ is gives us confidence, even as we live and love in this world. Yet Christian love is not abstract but lived in the concrete manner of love for one another.

4, 20: *Cannot love God:* some ancient manuscripts read "how can he love . . . ?"

5, 1–5: Children of God are identified not only by their love for others (4, 7–9) and for God (5, 1–2) but by their belief in the divine sonship of Jesus Christ. Faith, the acceptance of Jesus in his true character and the obedience in love to God's commands (3), is the source of the Christian's power in the world and conquers the world of evil (4–5), even as Christ overcame the world (Jn 16, 33).

4, 5: Jn 15, 19.
4, 6: Jn 8, 47; 10, 16.
4, 9: Jn 3, 16.
4, 10: Rom 5, 8.
4, 12: Jn 1, 18; 1 Tm 6, 16.
4, 17: 1 Jn 2, 28.
4, 20: 1 Jn 2, 4.
4, 21: Jn 13, 34; 14, 15.21; 15, 17.
5, 1: Jn 8, 42; 1 Pt 1, 23.

children of God when we love God and obey his commandments. 3* For the love of God is this, that we keep his commandments. And his commandments are not burdensome, 4* for whoever is begotten by God conquers the world. And the victory that conquers the world is our faith. 5* Who [indeed] is the victor over the world but the one who believes that Jesus is the Son of God?

6*† This is the one who came through water and blood, Jesus Christ, not by water alone, but by water and blood. The Spirit is the one that testifies, and the Spirit is truth. 7 So there are three that testify, 8* the Spirit, the water, and the blood, and the three are of one accord. 9* If we accept human testimony, the testimony of God is surely greater. Now the testimony of God is this, that he has testified on behalf of his Son. 10* Whoever believes in the Son of God has this testimony within himself. Whoever does not believe God has made him a liar by not believing the testimony God has given about his Son. 11* And this is the testimony: God gave us eternal life, and this life is in his Son. 12 Whoever possesses the Son has life; whoever does not possess the Son of God does not have life.

IV: Epilogue

Prayer for Sinners

13*† I write these things to you so that you may know that you have eternal life, you who believe in the name of the Son of God. 14* And we have this confidence in him, that if we ask anything according to his will, he hears us. 15 And if we know that he hears us in regard to whatever we ask, we know that what we have asked him for is ours. 16* If anyone sees his brother sinning, if the sin is not deadly, he should pray to God and he will give him life. This is only for those whose sin is not deadly. There is such a thing as deadly sin, about which I do not say that you should pray. 17 All wrongdoing is sin, but there is sin that is not deadly.

18 We know that no one begotten by God sins; but the one begotten by God he protects, and the evil one cannot touch him. 19 We know that we belong to God, and the whole world is under the power of the evil one. 20* We also know that the Son of God has come and has given us discernment to know the one who is true. And we are in the one who is true, in his Son Jesus Christ. He is the true God and eternal life. 21 Children, be on your guard against idols.

---

† **5, 6–12:** *Water and blood* (6) refers to Christ's baptism (Mt 3, 16–17) and to the shedding of his blood on the cross (Jn 19, 34). *The Spirit* was present at the baptism (Mt 3, 16; Mk 1, 10; Lk 3, 22; Jn 1, 32.34). *The testimony* to Christ as the Son of God is confirmed by divine witness (7–9), greater by far than the two legally required human witnesses (Dt 17, 6). To deny this is to deny God's truth; cf Jn 8, 17–18. The gist of the divine witness or *testimony* is that *eternal life* (11–12) is given in Christ and nowhere else. To *possess the Son* is not acceptance of a doctrine but of a person who lives now and provides life.

5, 13–21: As children of God we have confidence in prayer because of our intimate relationship with him (14–15). In love, we pray (16–17) for those who are in *sin*, but not in *deadly sin* (literally, "sin unto death"), probably referring to apostasy or activities brought on under the antichrist; cf Mk 3, 29; Heb 6, 4–6; 10, 26–31. Even in the latter case, however, prayer, while not enjoined, is not forbidden. The letter concludes with a summary of the themes of the letter (18–20). There is a sharp antithesis between the children of God and those belonging to the world and to the evil one. The Son reveals the God of truth; Christians dwell in the true God, *in his Son*, and have eternal life. The final verse (21) voices a perennial warning about *idols*, any type of rival to God.

---

*

5, 3: Jn 14, 15.	**5, 11:** 1 Jn 1, 2; Jn 1, 4; 5,
5, 4: Jn 16, 33.	21.26; 17, 3.
5, 5: 1 Cor 15, 57.	**5, 13:** Jn 1, 12; 20, 31.
5, 6: Jn 15, 26; 19, 34.	**5, 14:** 1 Jn 3, 21–22; Mt 7, 7;
5, 8: Jn 5, 32.36; 15, 26.	Jn 14, 13–14.
5, 9: Jn 5, 32.37.	**5, 16:** Mt 12, 31.
5, 10: 1 Jn 3, 33.	**5, 20:** Jer 24, 7; Jn 17, 3; Eph
	1, 17.

2 John

¹*† The Presbyter to the chosen Lady and to her children whom I love in truth—and not only I but also all who know the truth— ² because of the truth that dwells in us and will be with us forever. ³† Grace, mercy, and peace will be with us from God the Father and from Jesus Christ the Father's Son in truth and love.

⁴*† I rejoiced greatly to find some of your children walking in the truth just as we were commanded by the Father. ⁵* But now, Lady, I ask you, not as though I were writing a new commandment but the one we have had from the beginning: let us love one another. ⁶*† For this is love, that we walk according to his commandments; this is the commandment, as you heard from the beginning, in which you should walk.

⁷*† Many deceivers have gone out into the world, those who do not acknowledge Jesus Christ as coming in the flesh; such is the deceitful one and the antichrist. ⁸† Look to yourselves that you do not lose what we worked for but may receive a full recompense. ⁹*† Anyone who is so "progressive" as not to remain in the teaching of the Christ does not have God; whoever remains in the teaching has the Father and the Son. ¹⁰*† If anyone comes to you and does not bring this

---

† **1:** *The chosen Lady:* literally "elected"; this could also be translated "Kyria (a woman's name) chosen (by God)" or "the lady Electa" or "Electa Kyria." The adjective "chosen" is applied to all Christians at the beginning of other New Testament letters (1 Pt 1, 1; Ti 1, 1). The description is of a specific community with "children" who are its members. *The truth:* the affirmation of Jesus in the flesh and in contrast to false teaching (7).

3: *Grace, mercy, and peace:* like 1 and 2 Timothy this letter adds *mercy* to the terms used frequently in a salutation to describe Christian blessing; it appears only here in the Johannine writings. The author also puts the blessing in relation to *truth* and *love*, the watchwords of the Johannine teaching. *The Father's Son:* the title that affirms the close relationship of Christ to God; similar variations of this title occur elsewhere (Jn 1, 14; 3, 35), but the precise wording is not found elsewhere in the New Testament.

4: *Some of your children:* this refers to those whom the Presbyter has recently encountered, but it may also indicate the presence of false doctrine in the community: the Presbyter encourages those who have remained faithful. *Walking in the truth:* an expression used in the Johannine writings to describe a way of living in which the Christian faith is visibly expressed; cf 1 Jn 1, 6–7; 2, 6.11, 3 Jn 3.

6: *His commandments:* cf 1 Jn 3, 23; 2, 7–8; 4, 21; obedience to the commandment of faith and love includes all others.

7: *The antichrist:* see 1 Jn 2, 18–19.22; 4, 3.

8: *You* (plural): it is not certain whether this means the Christians addressed or includes the Presbyter, since some of the ancient Greek manuscripts and Greek Fathers have "we."

9: *Anyone who is so "progressive":* literally, "Anyone who goes ahead." Some gnostic groups held the doctrine of the Christ come in the flesh to be a first step in belief, which the more advanced and spiritual believer surpassed and abandoned in his knowledge of the spiritual Christ. The author affirms that fellowship with God may be gained only by holding to the complete doctrine of Jesus Christ (1 Jn 2, 22–23; 4, 2; 5, 5–6).

10–11: At this time false teachers were considered so dangerous and divisive as to be shunned completely. From this description they seem to be wandering preachers. We see here a natural suspicion of early Christians concerning such itinerants and can envisage the problems faced by missionaries such as those mentioned in 3 Jn 10.

1: Jn 8, 32; 3 Jn 1.
4: 3 Jn 3.
5: Jn 13, 34; 15, 12; 1 Jn 4, 7.
6: Jn 13, 34; 14, 15; 1 Jn 5, 3.

7: 1 Jn 2, 22; 4, 2.
9: Jn 8, 31; 1 Jn 2, 23; 4, 15.
10: Rom 16, 17; 2 Thes 3, 6.

Unwelcome Guests

The author of 2 John is warning a Christian community—called elect lady and dear lady—about the false message of some "deceivers" (see the introduction to 1, 2, and 3 John, before 1 John). The author cautions the community not to have anything to do with such people, not even to let them into their homes (verses 10–11). Although the words sound harsh, the reasoning is sound.

Every day, we could be letting people with false messages into our home "virtually" through television, books, music, the Internet, and even magazines. Their false messages promote values and behaviors that are contrary to a healthy and holy way of life. Can these "guests" affect our attitudes and choices? They sure can, especially if we welcome them blindly without thinking about the impact of their messages.

On a piece of paper or in your journal, identify the television shows, magazines, radio stations, and Internet sites that regularly visit your home. List the positive values and behaviors these guests display. Now, list the negative ones. How do the lists compare? How can you manage your media exposure wisely in order to resist its negative influence?

doctrine, do not receive him in your house or even greet him; [11] for whoever greets him shares in his evil works.

[12]*† Although I have much to write to you, I do not intend to use paper and ink. Instead, I hope to visit you and to speak face to face so that our joy may be complete. [13]† The children of your chosen sister send you greetings.

---

† **12:** *Our joy:* a number of other Greek manuscripts read "your joy."
13: *Chosen sister:* the community of which the Presbyter is now a part greets you (singular), the community of the Lady addressed.

* **12:** Jn 15, 11; 1 Jn 1, 4;
3 Jn 13.

3 John

For background on this letter, see the introduction to 1, 2, and 3 John, before 1 John.

¹*† The Presbyter to the beloved Gaius whom I love in truth.

² Beloved, I hope you are prospering in every respect and are in good health, just as your soul is prospering. ³*† I rejoiced greatly when some of the brothers came and testified to how truly you walk in the truth. ⁴* Nothing gives me greater joy than to hear that my children are walking in the truth.

⁵*† Beloved, you are faithful in all you do for the brothers, especially for strangers; ⁶*† they have

Supporting the Ministry of Others

Gaius was a man of faith who opened his home to missionaries who were passing through his city. Though Gaius did not personally know these missionaries, he provided hospitality for them because he knew that they were helping spread the Good News. In 3 John, the elder appeals to him to welcome his messenger, Demetrius, even when others refuse to do so.

Christians find many needs that they cannot respond to by themselves. The story of Gaius shows how you can become a co-missionary with Christians who are ministering in some way that you cannot. These may be ministers in your own parish or diocese, or a religious group that sends missionaries to other countries. You can offer them your hospitality, support them financially, or promote their work in your parish or community. Consider talking with your family about a specific ministry or missionary activity you can support together.

---

† **1:** *Beloved Gaius:* a frequent form of address for fellow Christians in New Testament epistolary literature.

3: *The brothers:* in this letter, the term may refer to Christians who have been missionaries and received hospitality from Gaius (5–6). *Walk in the truth:* the common Johannine term to describe Christian living; this description presents Gaius as following the teachings of the Presbyter in contrast to Diotrephes.

5: *You are faithful in all you do:* Gaius's aid to the missionaries is a manifestation of his true Christian faith.

6: *Help them . . . to continue their journey:* the Presbyter asks Gaius not only to continue to welcome the missionaries to his community but also to equip them for further travels.

*

1: 2 Jn 1.	**1:** 2 Jn 4.
3: 3 Jn 5; Gal 6, 10; 2 Jn 4.	**5:** Rom 12, 13; Gal 6, 10; Heb 13, 2.
4: 1 Thes 2, 11–12; 1 Tm 1, 2; 2 Tm 1, 2; 1 Jn 2,	**6:** Acts 15, 3; Col 1, 10; 1 Thes 2, 12.

testified to your love before the church. Please help them in a way worthy of God to continue their journey. ⁷† For they have set out for the sake of the Name and are accepting nothing from the pagans. ⁸ Therefore, we ought to support such persons, so that we may be co-workers in the truth.

⁹† I wrote to the church, but Diotrephes, who loves to dominate, does not acknowledge us. ¹⁰† Therefore, if I come, I will draw attention to what he is doing, spreading evil nonsense about us. And not content with that, he will not receive the brothers, hindering those who wish to do so and expelling them from the church. ¹¹*† Beloved, do not imitate evil but imitate good. Whoever does what is good is of God; whoever does what is evil has never seen God. ¹²*† Demetrius receives a good report from all, even from the truth itself. We give our testimonial as well, and you know our testimony is true.

¹³* I have much to write to you, but I do not wish to write with pen and ink. ¹⁴ Instead, I hope to see you soon, when we can talk face to face. ¹⁵*† Peace be with you. The friends greet you; greet the friends there each by name.

7: *The Name:* of Jesus Christ (cf Acts 5, 41; 1 Jn 2, 12; 3, 23; 5, 13). *Accepting nothing:* not expecting support from the pagans to whom they preach the gospel, so that they will not be considered as beggars; they required support from other Christians; cf Paul's complaints to the Corinthians (1 Cor 9, 3–12).

9: *Who loves to dominate:* the Presbyter does not deny Diotrephes' place as leader but indicates that his ambition may have caused him to disregard his letter and his influence.

10: *If I come:* the Presbyter may visit the community to challenge the actions of Diotrephes toward himself and the missionaries. *Will not receive the brothers:* Diotrephes may have been critical of the teachings of the Presbyter and sought to maintain doctrinal purity; cf 1 Jn 2, 19 and 2 Jn 10–11.

11: *Do not imitate evil:* Gaius should not be influenced by the behavior of Diotrephes.

12: *Demetrius:* because of the fear of false teachers, Demetrius, perhaps the bearer of the letter, is provided with a recommendation from the Presbyter; cf 2 Cor 3, 1; Rom 16, 1. *Even from the truth itself:* this refers probably to the manner of Demetrius's life that testifies to his true belief; cf Gaius above (v 3).

15: *Friends:* although a Johannine term for Christians (Jn 15, 15), the word here may refer to those in the community loyal to the Presbyter and to Gaius.

11: 1 Jn 2, 29; 3, 6.10.
12: Jn 19, 35; 21, 24; 1 Tm 3, 7.
13: 2 Jn 12.
15: Jn 20, 19.21.26; Eph 6, 23; 1 Pt 5, 14.

They pretend to be part of your group, but all they really do is cause trouble. They claim to have all the right answers, but they won't listen to other people's opinions. They flatter people to get what they want, but then they grumble and complain behind people's backs. They cause division wherever they go. Do you know people like this? Maybe you even find yourself acting like them sometimes. The Letter of Jude has some things to say about "these people."

At a Glance

I. Address and Greeting (verses 1–2).

II. Occasion for Writing, False Teachers, and Exhortations (verses 3–23).

III. Doxology (verses 24–25).

In-depth

The purpose of The Letter of Jude is to warn churches about false teachers who come into the Christian community with lies and tricks, making trouble wherever they go. The author recalls stories from the past in which God punished such people: stories about the Egyptians who opposed God's plan to bring the Hebrew people to the Promised Land; the immoral people of Sodom and Gomorrah; the angels who revolted against God; and Cain, who killed his brother. The author also encourages people to build themselves in the faith. Finally, the author cautions Christians to ignore ungodly people—unless those people truly want to change, in which case, Christians should be examples of the mercy of Jesus Christ.

Notice that this letter includes some words that are unfamiliar to modern Christians or that have different meanings today. For instance, the words *holy ones* refer to the members of the Christian community, and a *love feast* is a celebration of the Eucharist.

The message of The Letter of Jude is difficult to understand for many reasons. We know almost nothing about who wrote it, to whom it was written, when it was written, and what it is really addressing—except from hints in the letter itself. Tradition says that the author is Jude, the brother of James and Jesus (see Mk 6, 3; the name of Jude is a form of Judas).

Quick Facts

Author
unknown or possibly Jude, the brother of James

Date Written
maybe A.D. 80–90

Audience
unknown

The Letter of Jude

Jude

Address and Greeting

¹*† Jude, a slave of Jesus Christ and brother of James, to those who are called, beloved in God the Father and kept safe for Jesus Christ: ²* may mercy, peace, and love be yours in abundance.

Occasion for Writing

³*† Beloved, although I was making every effort to write to you about our common salvation, I now feel a need to write to encourage you to contend for the faith that was once for all handed down to the holy ones. ⁴* For there have been some intruders, who long ago were designated for this condemnation, godless persons, who pervert the grace of our God into licentiousness and who deny our only Master and Lord, Jesus Christ.

The False Teachers

⁵*† I wish to remind you, although you know all things, that [the] Lord who once saved a people from the land of Egypt later destroyed those who did not believe. ⁶*† The angels too, who did not keep to their own domain but deserted their proper dwelling, he has kept in eternal chains, in gloom, for the judgment of the great day. ⁷*† Likewise, Sodom, Gomorrah, and the surrounding towns, which, in the same manner as they, indulged in sexual promiscuity and practiced unnatural vice,

---

1: *Jude . . . brother of James:* for the identity of the author of this letter, see Introduction. *To those who are called:* the vocation to the Christian faith is God's free gift to those whom he loves and whom he safely protects in Christ until the Lord's second coming.

3–4: *Our common salvation:* the teachings of the Christian faith derived from the apostolic preaching and to be kept by the Christian community.

5: For this first example of divine punishment on those who had been saved but did not then keep faith, see Nm 14, 28–29 and the note there. Some manuscripts have the word "once" (*hapax* as at 3) after "you know"; some commentators have suggested that it means "knowing one thing" or "you know all things once for all." Instead of "[the] Lord" manuscripts vary, having "Jesus," "God," or no subject stated.

6: This second example draws on Gn 6, 1–4 as elaborated in the apocryphal Book of Enoch (cf 14): heavenly beings came to earth and had sexual intercourse with women. God punished them by casting them out of heaven into darkness and bondage.

7: *Practiced unnatural vice:* literally, "went after alien flesh." This example derives from Gn 19, 1–25, especially 4–11, when the townsmen of Sodom violated both hospitality and morality by demanding that Lot's two visitors (really messengers of Yahweh) be handed over to them so that they could abuse them sexually. *Unnatural vice:* this refers to the desire for intimacies by human beings with angels (the reverse of the example in 6). Sodom (whence "sodomy") and Gomorrah became proverbial as object lessons for God's punishment on sin (Is 1, 9; Jer 50, 40; Am 4, 11; Mt 10, 15; 2 Pt 2, 6).

1: Mt 13, 55; Mk 6, 3; Acts 12, 17; Rom 1, 7.
2: Gal 6, 16; 1 Tm 1, 2; 2 Pt 1, 2.
3: Jude 17.20; 1 Tm 6, 12.
4: Gal 2, 4; 2 Tm 3, 6; 2 Pt 2, 1.
5: Nm 14, 35; 1 Cor 10, 5; Heb 3, 16.17.
6: 2 Pt 2, 4.9.
7: Dt 29, 22–24; Mt 25, 41; 2 Thes 1, 8–9; 2 Pt 2, 6; 3, 7.

serve as an example by undergoing a punishment of eternal fire.

8† Similarly, these dreamers nevertheless also defile the flesh, scorn lordship, and revile glorious beings. 9*† Yet the archangel Michael, when he argued with the devil in a dispute over the body of Moses, did not venture to pronounce a reviling judgment upon him but said, "May the Lord rebuke you!" 10* But these people revile what they do not understand and are destroyed by what they know by nature like irrational animals. 11*† Woe to them! They followed the way of Cain, abandoned themselves to Balaam's error for the sake of gain, and perished in the rebellion of Korah. 12*† These are blemishes on your love feasts, as they carouse fearlessly and look after themselves. They are waterless clouds blown about by winds, fruitless trees in late autumn, twice dead and uprooted. 13 They are like wild waves of the sea, foaming up their shameless deeds, wandering stars for whom the gloom of darkness has been reserved forever.

14*† Enoch, of the seventh generation from Adam, prophesied also about them when he said, "Behold, the Lord has come with his countless holy ones 15 to execute judgment on all and to convict everyone for all the godless deeds that they committed and for all the harsh words godless sinners

have uttered against him." 16* These people are complainers, disgruntled ones who live by their desires; their mouths utter bombast as they fawn over people to gain advantage.

Exhortations

17* But you, beloved, remember the words spoken beforehand by the apostles of our Lord Jesus Christ, 18*† for they told you, "In [the] last time there will be scoffers who will live according to their own godless desires." 19* These are the ones who cause divisions; they live on the natural plane, devoid of the Spirit. 20* But you, beloved, build yourselves up in your most holy faith; pray in the holy Spirit. 21* Keep yourselves in the love of God and wait for the mercy of our Lord Jesus Christ that leads to eternal life. 22† On those who waver, have mercy; 23† save others by snatching them out of the fire; on others have mercy with fear, abhorring even the outer garment stained by the flesh.

Doxology

24*† To the one who is able to keep you from stumbling and to present you unblemished and exultant, in the presence of his glory, 25* to the only God, our savior, through Jesus Christ our Lord be glory, majesty, power, and authority from ages past, now, and for ages to come. Amen.

8: *Dreamers:* the writer returns to the false teachers of v 4, applying charges from the three examples in vv 5, 6, 7. This may apply to claims they make for revelations they have received by night (to the author, hallucinations). *Defile the flesh:* this may mean bodily pollutions from the erotic dreams of sexual license (7). *Lordship . . . glorious beings:* these may reflect the Lord (5; Jesus, 4) whom they spurn and the angels (6; cf the note on 2 Pt 2, 10, here, as there, literally, "glories").

9: *The archangel Michael . . . judgment:* a reference to an incident in the apocryphal Assumption of Moses. Dt 34, 6 had said of Moses, literally in Greek, "they buried him" or "he (God?) buried him" (taken to mean "he was buried"). The later account tells how Michael, who was sent to bury him, was challenged by the devil's interest in the body. Our author draws out the point that if an archangel refrained from reviling even the devil, how wrong it is for mere human beings to revile glorious beings (angels).

11: *Cain . . . Balaam . . . Korah:* examples of rebellious men and of the punishment their conduct incurred; cf Gn 4, 8–16; Nm 16, 1–35; 31, 16. See the note on 2 Pt 2, 15.

12: *Blemishes on your love feasts:* or "hidden rocks" or "submerged reefs" (cf 13). The opponents engaged in scandalous conduct in connection with community gatherings called *love feasts* (agape meals), which were associated with eucharistic celebrations at certain stages of early Christian practice; cf 1 Cor 11, 18–34 and the note on 2 Pt 2, 13.

14–15: Cited from the apocryphal Book of Enoch 1, 9.

18: This is the substance of much early Christian preaching rather than a direct quotation of any of the various New Testament passages on this theme (see Mk 13, 22; Acts 20, 30; 1 Tm 4, 1–3; 2 Pt 3, 3).

22: *Have mercy:* some manuscripts read "convince," "confute," or "reprove." Others have "even though you waver" or "doubt" instead of *who waver.*

23: *With fear:* some manuscripts connect the phrase "with fear" with the imperative "save" or with the participle "snatching." Other manuscripts omit the phrase "on others have mercy," so that only two groups are envisioned. Rescue others led astray and caution in the endeavor are both enjoined. *Outer garment stained by the flesh:* the imagery may come from Zec 3, 3–5, just as that of *snatching . . . out of the fire* comes from Zec 3, 2; the very garments of the godless are to be abhorred because of their contagion.

24–25: With this liturgical statement about the power of God to keep the faithful from stumbling, and praise to him through Jesus Christ, the letter reaches its conclusion by returning to the themes with which it began (1–2).

9: Dn 10, 21; 12, 1.
10: 2 Pt 2, 12.
11: Gn 4, 8–16; 1 Jn 3, 12 / Nm 31, 15–16; 2 Pt 2, 15; Rv 2, 14 / Nm 16, 19–35.
12: 2 Pt 2, 13.17.
14–15: Mt 16, 27; Heb 12, 22–23.
16: Jude 18; 1 Cor 10, 10; 2 Pt 2, 10.18.
17: Heb 2, 3; 2 Pt 3, 2.
18: 1 Tm 4, 1; 2 Tm 3, 1–5; 2 Pt 3, 3.
19: 1 Cor 2, 14; Jas 3, 15.
20: Jude 2; Eph 6, 18; Col 2, 7.
21: Ti 2, 13.
24: 2 Cor 4, 14; 1 Pt 4, 13.
25: Rom 11, 36; 1 Tm 1, 17.

What do you think about when someone mentions the Book of Revelation? Many people immediately think of its bizarre descriptions of monstrous beasts and its warnings about the terrible things that will happen at the end of the world. Some people believe it proves that the end of the world is about to take place very soon. In fact, the Book of Revelation does not predict when the world will end, but brings us hope in proclaiming God's ultimate triumph over evil in history.

In-depth

This book is unique in that the author—who calls himself John—received a series of visions from God that form most of the content. The recorded visions take the form of apocalyptic literature (see "Apocalyptic Literature," Daniel, chapters 7–10) and are full of symbols. These symbols are like the language of a secret club. You use it when you want to keep people who do not belong to your club from understanding what you are saying.

Why was it important that the meaning of the visions be known only to the Christian communities addressed by the letter? Because the Christians still remembered their persecution under the Roman emperor Nero Caesar (A.D. 54–68) and were suffering a new persecution under the Roman emperor Domitian (A.D. 81–96). This "coded language" allowed John to criticize the Roman emperor and empire without necessarily putting his readers at risk of persecution or even death. John himself was exiled to an island off Asia Minor for preaching the Gospel (Rv 1, 9).

Once the symbols are understood, it is clear that the Book of Revelation offers hope to a church under persecution. It expresses belief in God's justice and God's victory over evil—an evil that at John's time was embodied in the Roman Empire. But it also expresses the great Christian belief that God will ultimately be victorious, at the end of time, when Christ will come again in his full glory and power. It is a mistake for Christians to try to decipher Revelation as a prediction as to when and how that final coming will occur. But they can take great joy and hope in the promise of a new world where God will wipe away every tear, and suffering and death will be no more (21, 4).

At a Glance

I. Prologue (1, 1–3).

II. Letters to the Churches of Asia (1, 4—3, 22).

III. God and the Lamb in Heaven (4, 1—5, 14).

IV. The Seven Seals, Trumpets, and Plagues, with Interludes (6, 1—16, 21).

V. The Punishment of Babylon and the Destruction of Pagan Nations (17, 1—20, 15).

VI. The New Creation (21, 1—22, 5).

VII. Epilogue (22, 6–21).

Quick Facts

Author
a Jewish-Christian prophet named John

Date
probably A.D. 92–96

Audience
Christian churches in Asia Minor during a time of Roman persecution

The Revelation to John

Revelation

I: Prologue

1 [1]*† The revelation of Jesus Christ, which God gave to him, to show his servants what must happen soon. He made it known by sending his angel to his servant John, [2] who gives witness to the word of God and to the testimony of Jesus Christ by reporting what he saw. [3]*† Blessed is the one who reads aloud and blessed are those who listen to this prophetic message and heed what is written in it, for the appointed time is near.

II: Letters to the Churches of Asia

Greeting†

[4]* John, to the seven churches in Asia:† grace to you and peace from him who is and who was and who is to come, and from the seven spirits before his throne, [5]*† and from Jesus Christ, the faithful witness, the firstborn of the dead and ruler of the kings of the earth. To him who loves us and has freed us from our sins by his blood, [6]* who has made us into a kingdom, priests for his God and Father, to him be glory and power forever [and ever]. Amen.

[7]* Behold, he is coming amid the clouds,
    and every eye will see him,
    even those who pierced him.
All the peoples of the earth will
    lament him.
        Yes. Amen.

[8]*† "I am the Alpha and the Omega," says the Lord God, "the one who is and who was and who is to come, the almighty."

1, 1–3: This prologue describes the source, contents, and audience of the book and forms an inclusion with the epilogue (22, 6–21), with its similar themes and expressions.

1, 3: *Blessed is the one:* this is the first of seven beatitudes in this book; the others are in 14, 13; 16, 15; 19, 9; 20, 6; 22, 7.14. *This prophetic message:* literally, "the words of the prophecy"; so 22, 7.10.18.19 by inclusion. *The appointed time:* when Jesus will return in glory; cf 1, 7; 3, 11; 22, 7.10.12.20.

1, 4–8: Although Revelation begins and ends (22, 21) with Christian epistolary formulae, there is nothing between chs 4 and 22 resembling a letter. The author here employs the standard word order for greetings in Greek letter writing: "N. to N., greetings . . ."; see the note on Rom 1, 1.

1, 4: *Seven churches in Asia:* Asia refers to the Roman province of that name in western Asia Minor (modern Turkey); these representative churches are mentioned by name in v 11, and each is the recipient of a message (2, 1—3, 22). *Seven* is the biblical number

suggesting fullness and completeness; thus the seer is writing for the whole church.

1, 5: *Freed us:* the majority of Greek manuscripts and several early versions read "washed us"; but "freed us" is supported by the best manuscripts and fits well with Old Testament imagery, e.g., Is 40, 2.

1, 8: *The Alpha and the Omega:* the first and last letters of the Greek alphabet. In 22, 13 the same words occur together with the expressions "the First and the Last, the Beginning and the End"; cf 17; 2, 8; 21, 6; Is 41, 4; 44, 6.

1, 1: Rv 22, 6–8.20; Dn 2, 28 / Rv 19, 10.
1, 3: Rv 22, 7 / Lk 11, 28.
1, 4: Rv 1, 8; 4, 8; 11, 17; 16, 5; Ex 3, 14.
1, 5: Rv 3, 14; 1 Cor 15, 20; Col 1, 18 / Heb 9, 14;

1 Pt 1, 19; 1 Jn 1, 7.
1, 6: Ex 19, 6; 1 Pt 2, 9.
1, 7: Dn 7, 13 / Zec 12, 10; Mt 24, 30; Jn 19, 37.
1, 8: Rv 17; 21, 6; 22, 13; Is 41, 4; 44, 6; 48, 12.

The First Vision†

⁹ I, John, your brother, who share with you the distress, the kingdom, and the endurance we have in Jesus, found myself on the island called Patmos† because I proclaimed God's word and gave testimony to Jesus. ¹⁰† I was caught up in spirit on the Lord's day and heard behind me a voice as loud as a trumpet, ¹¹† which said, "Write on a scroll what you see and send it to the seven churches: to Ephesus, Smyrna, Pergamum, Thyatira, Sardis, Philadelphia, and Laodicea." ¹²† Then I turned to see whose voice it was that spoke to me, and when I turned, I saw seven gold lampstands ¹³*† and in the midst of the lampstands one like a son of man, wearing an ankle-length robe, with a gold sash around his chest. ¹⁴† The hair of his head was as white as white wool or as snow, and his eyes were like a fiery flame. ¹⁵† His feet were like polished brass refined in a furnace, and his voice was like the sound of rushing water. ¹⁶*† In his right hand he held seven stars. A sharp two-edged sword came out of his mouth, and his face shone like the sun at its brightest.

¹⁷*† When I caught sight of him, I fell down at his feet as though dead. He touched me with his right hand and said, "Do not be afraid. I am the first and the last, ¹⁸† the one who lives. Once I was dead, but now I am alive forever and ever. I hold the keys to death and the netherworld. ¹⁹† Write down, therefore, what you have seen, and what is happening, and what will happen afterwards. ²⁰† This is the secret meaning of the seven stars you saw in my

---

† **1, 9–20:** In this first vision, the seer is commanded to write what he sees to the seven churches (9–11). He sees Christ in glory, whom he depicts in stock apocalyptic imagery (12–16), and hears him describe himself in terms meant to encourage Christians by emphasizing his victory over death (17–20).

1, 9: *Island called Patmos:* one of the Sporades islands in the Aegean Sea, some fifty miles south of Ephesus, used by the Romans as a penal colony. *Because I proclaimed God's word:* literally, "on account of God's word."

1, 10: *The Lord's day:* Sunday. *As loud as a trumpet:* the imagery is derived from the theophany at Sinai (Ex 19, 16.19; cf Heb 12, 19 and the trumpet in other eschatological settings in Is 27, 13; Jl 2, 1; Mt 24, 31; 1 Cor 15, 52; 1 Thes 4, 16).

1, 11: *Scroll:* a papyrus roll.

1, 12–16: A symbolic description of Christ in glory. The metaphorical language is not to be understood literally; cf Introduction.

1, 13: *Son of man:* see the note on Mk 8, 31. *Ankle-length robe:* Christ is priest; cf Ex 28, 4; 29, 5; Wis 18, 24; Zec 3, 4. *Gold sash:* Christ is king; cf Ex 28, 4; 1 Mc 10, 89; 11, 58; Dn 10, 5.

1, 14: *Hair . . . as white as white wool or as snow:* Christ is eternal, clothed with the dignity that belonged to the "Ancient of Days"; cf 18; Dn 7, 9. *His eyes were like a fiery flame:* Christ is portrayed as all-knowing; cf 2, 23; Ps 7, 10; Jer 17, 10; and similar expressions in 2, 18; 19, 12; cf Dn 10, 6.

1, 15: *His feet . . . furnace:* Christ is depicted as unchangeable; cf Ez 1, 27; Dn 10, 6. The Greek word translated "refined" is unconnected grammatically with any other word in the sentence. *His voice . . . water:* Christ speaks with divine authority; cf Ez 1, 24.

1, 16: *Seven stars:* in the pagan world, Mithras and the Caesars were represented with seven stars in their right hand, symbolizing their universal dominion. *A sharp two-edged sword:* this refers to the word of God (cf Eph 6, 17; Heb 4, 12) that will destroy unrepentant sinners; cf 2, 16; 19, 15; Wis 18, 15; Is 11, 4; 49, 2. *His face . . . brightest:* this symbolizes the divine majesty of Christ; cf 10, 1; 21, 23; Jgs 5, 31; Is 60, 19; Mt 17, 2.

1, 17: It was an Old Testament belief that for sinful human beings to see God was to die; cf Ex 19, 21; 33, 20; Jgs 6, 22–23; Is 6, 5.

1, 18: *Netherworld:* Greek Hades, Hebrew Sheol, the abode of the dead; cf 20, 13–14; Nm 16, 33.

1, 19: *What you have seen, and what is happening, and what will happen afterwards:* the three parts of the Book of Revelation, the vision (10–20), the situation in the seven churches (chs 2–3), and the events of chs 6–22.

1, 20: *Secret meaning:* literally, "mystery." *Angels:* these are the presiding spirits of the seven churches. Angels were thought to be in charge of the physical world (cf 7, 1; 14, 18; 16, 5) and of nations (Dn 10, 13; 12, 1), communities (the seven churches), and individuals (Mt 18, 10; Acts 12, 15). Some have seen in the "angel" of each of the seven churches its pastor or a personification of the spirit of the congregation.

1, 13: Dn 7, 13; 10, 5.   **1, 17:** Dn 8, 18 / Rv 1, 8.
1, 16: Heb 4, 12.

The Alpha and the Omega

In the first chapter of Revelation, John introduces God's message to the seven churches in Asia. After explaining that he received the message through a vision and that an angel instructed him to communicate it to them, John describes a vision of Christ.

A vision is like a dream. It cannot be interpreted literally; we must seek its deep meaning and be open to its message. For example, in the vision of Rv 1, 12–16, a magnificently robed Jesus stands amid seven lampstands. The deeper meaning is that the resurrected Jesus in all his glory and power is watching over the seven churches. Here's another example: Rv 1, 8 has Jesus (or God) saying, "I am the Alpha and the Omega." In the Greek alphabet, *alpha* is the first letter, and *omega* is the last letter. This passage is telling us that God and Jesus are in control of all history, from its beginning to its end.

In your prayer, think of any current event that frightens you or harassments that you experience because of your faith or moral principles. See the image of the risen Christ described by John. Feel Jesus lovingly touching your head. Hear Jesus telling you that history is always in God's hands. Let God strengthen your faith and renew your hope with this wonderful revelation of God's love.

▶ Rv 1, 7–20

right hand, and of the seven gold lampstands: the seven stars are the angels of the seven churches, and the seven lampstands are the seven churches.

To Ephesus

2 ¹† "To the angel of the church† in Ephesus,† write this:

" 'The one who holds the seven stars in his right hand and walks in the midst of the seven gold lampstands says this: ²† "I know your works, your labor, and your endurance, and that you cannot tolerate the wicked; you have tested those who call themselves apostles but are not, and discovered that they are impostors. ³ Moreover, you have endurance and have suffered for my name, and you have not grown weary. ⁴ Yet I hold this against you: you have lost the love you had at first. ⁵ Realize how far you have fallen. Repent, and do the works you did at first. Otherwise, I will come to you and remove your lampstand from its place, unless you repent. ⁶† But you have this in your favor: you hate the works of the Nicolaitans, which I also hate.

⁷*† " ' "Whoever has ears ought to hear what the Spirit says to the churches. To the victor I will give the right to eat from the tree of life that is in the garden of God." '

To Smyrna†

⁸ "To the angel of the church in Smyrna,† write this:

" 'The first and the last, who once died but came to life, says this: ⁹*† "I know your tribulation and poverty, but you are rich. I know the slander of those who claim to be Jews and are not, but rather are members of the assembly of Satan. ¹⁰ Do not be afraid of anything that you are going to suffer. Indeed, the devil will throw some of you into prison,

that you may be tested, and you will face an ordeal for ten days. Remain faithful until death, and I will give you the crown of life.

¹¹*† " ' "Whoever has ears ought to hear what

---

† **2, 1—3, 22:** Each of the seven letters follows the same pattern: address; description of the exalted Christ; blame and/or praise for the church addressed; threat and/or admonition; final exhortation and promise to all Christians.

2, 1—7: The letter to Ephesus praises the members of the church there for their works and virtues, including discerning false teachers (2–3), but admonishes them to repent and return to their former devotion (4–5). It concludes with a reference to the Nicolaitans (see the note on 6) and a promise that the victor will have access to eternal life (7).

2, 1: *Ephesus:* this great ancient city had a population of ca. 250,000; it was the capital of the Roman province of Asia and the commercial, cultural, and religious center of Asia. The other six churches were located in the same province, situated roughly in a circle; they were selected for geographical reasons rather than for the size of their Christian communities. *Walks in the midst of the seven gold lampstands:* this signifies that Christ is always present in the church; see the note on 1, 4.

2, 2: *Who call themselves . . . impostors:* this refers to unauthorized and perverse missionaries; cf Acts 20, 29–30.

2, 6: *Nicolaitans:* these are perhaps the impostors of v 2; see the note on vv 14–15. There is little evidence for connecting this group with Nicolaus, the proselyte from Antioch, mentioned in Acts 6, 5.

2, 7: *Victor:* referring to any Christian individual who holds fast to the faith and does God's will in the face of persecution. *The tree of life that is in the garden of God:* this is a reference to the tree in

the primeval paradise (Gn 2, 9); cf 22, 2.14.19. The decree excluding humanity from the tree of life has been revoked by Christ.

2, 8—11: The letter to Smyrna encourages the Christians in this important commercial center by telling them that although they are impoverished, they are nevertheless rich, and calls those Jews who are slandering them members of the assembly of Satan (9). There is no admonition; rather, the Christians are told that they will suffer much, even death, but the time of tribulation will be short compared to their eternal reward (10), and they will thus escape final damnation (11).

2, 8: *Smyrna:* modern Izmir, ca. thirty miles north of Ephesus, and the chief city of Lydia, with a temple to the goddess Roma. It was renowned for its loyalty to Rome, and it also had a large Jewish community very hostile toward Christians.

2, 9—10: The church in Smyrna was materially poor but spiritually rich. Accusations made by Jewish brethren there occasioned the persecution of Christians; cf Acts 14, 2.19; 17, 5.13.

2, 11: *The second death:* this refers to the eternal death, when sinners will receive their final punishment; cf 20, 6.14–15; 21, 8.

2, 7: Rv 2, 11.17.29; 3, 6.13.22; 13, 9; Mt 11, 15.

2, 9: Jas 2, 5.
2, 11: Rv 20, 6.14; 21, 8.

the Spirit says to the churches. The victor shall not be harmed by the second death." '

To Pergamum†

12 "To the angel of the church in Pergamum,† write this:

" 'The one with the sharp two-edged sword says this: 13† "I know that you live where Satan's throne is, and yet you hold fast to my name and have not denied your faith in me, not even in the days of Antipas, my faithful witness, who was martyred among you, where Satan lives. 14*† Yet I have a few things against you. You have some people there who hold to the teaching of Balaam, who instructed Balak to put a stumbling block before the Israelites: to eat food sacrificed to idols and to play the harlot. 15 Likewise, you also have some people who hold to the teaching of [the] Nicolaitans. 16 Therefore, repent. Otherwise, I will come to you quickly and wage war against them with the sword of my mouth.

17*† " ' "Whoever has ears ought to hear what the Spirit says to the churches. To the victor I shall give some of the hidden manna; I shall also give a white amulet upon which is inscribed a new name, which no one knows except the one who receives it." '

To Thyatira†

18 "To the angel of the church in Thyatira,† write this:

" 'The Son of God, whose eyes are like a fiery flame and whose feet are like polished brass, says this: 19 "I know your works, your love, faith, service,

and endurance, and that your last works are greater than the first. 20† Yet I hold this against you, that you tolerate the woman Jezebel, who calls herself a prophetess, who teaches and misleads my servants to play the harlot and to eat food sacrificed to idols. 21 I have given her time to repent, but she refuses to repent of her harlotry. 22 So I will cast her on a sickbed and plunge those who commit adultery with her into intense suffering unless they repent of her works. 23*† I will also put her children to death. Thus shall all the churches come to know that I am the searcher of hearts and minds and that I will give each of you what your works deserve. 24† But I say to the rest of you in Thyatira, who do not uphold this teaching and know nothing of the so-called deep secrets of Satan: on you I will place no further burden, 25 except that you must hold fast to what you have until I come.

26*† " ' "To the victor, who keeps to my ways†
until the end,
I will give authority over the nations.
27   He will rule them with an iron rod.
Like clay vessels will they be smashed,

28 just as I received authority from my Father. And to him I will give the morning star.
29 " ' "Whoever has ears ought to hear what the Spirit says to the churches." '

To Sardis†

3 1 "To the angel of the church in Sardis,† write this:

2, 12–17: The letter to Pergamum praises the members of the church for persevering in their faith in Christ even in the midst of a pagan setting and in face of persecution and martyrdom (13). But it admonishes them about members who advocate an unprincipled morality (14; cf 2 Pt 2, 15; Jude 11) and others who follow the teaching of the Nicolaitans (15; see the note here). It urges them to repent (16) and promises them the hidden manna and Christ's amulet (17).

2, 12: *Pergamum:* modern Bergama, ca. forty-five miles northeast of Smyrna, a center for various kinds of pagan worship. It also had an outstanding library (the word *parchment* is derived from its name).

2, 13: *Satan's throne:* the reference is to emperor worship and other pagan practices that flourished in Pergamum, perhaps specifically to the white marble altar erected and dedicated to Zeus by Eumenes II (197–160 B.C.).

2, 14–15: Like Balaam, the biblical prototype of the religious compromiser (cf Nm 25, 1–3; 31, 16; 2 Pt 2, 15; Jude 11), the Nicolaitans in Pergamum and Ephesus (6) accommodated their Christian faith to paganism. They abused the principle of liberty enunciated by Paul (1 Cor 9, 19–23).

2, 17: *The hidden manna:* this is the food of life; cf Ps 78, 24–25. *White amulet:* literally, "white stone," on which was written a magical name, whose power could be tapped by one who knew the secret name. It is used here as a symbol of victory and joy; cf 3, 4–5. *New name:* this is a reference to the Christian's rebirth in Christ; cf 3, 12; 19, 12; Is 62, 2; 65, 15.

2, 18–29: The letter to Thyatira praises the progress in virtue of this small Christian community (19) but admonishes them for tolerating a false prophet who leads them astray (20). Her fate is sealed, but there is hope of repentance for her followers (21–22). Otherwise, they too shall die (23). They are warned against Satanic power or knowledge (24–25). Those who remain faithful will share in the mes-

sianic reign, having authority over nations (26–27), and will in fact possess Christ himself (28).

2, 18: *Thyatira:* modern Akhisar, ca. forty miles southeast of Pergamum, a frontier town famous for its workers' guilds (cf Acts 16, 14), membership in which may have involved festal meals in pagan temples.

2, 20: The scheming and treacherous Jezebel of old (cf 1 Kgs 19, 1–2; 21, 1–14; 2 Kgs 9, 22.30–34) introduced pagan customs into the religion of Israel; this new Jezebel was doing the same to Christianity.

2, 23: *Children:* spiritual descendants.

2, 24: *The so-called deep secrets of Satan:* literally, "the deep things of Satan," a scathing reference to the perverse teaching of the Nicolaitans (15).

2, 26–28: The Christian who perseveres in faith will share in Christ's messianic authority (cf Ps 2, 8–9) and resurrection victory over death, symbolized by the morning star; cf 22, 16.

2, 26: *Who keeps to my ways:* literally, "who keeps my works."

3, 1–6: The letter to Sardis does not praise the community but admonishes its members to watchfulness, mutual support, and repentance (2–3). The few who have remained pure and faithful will share Christ's victory and will be inscribed in the book of life (4–5).

3, 1: *Sardis:* this city, located ca. thirty miles southeast of Thyatira, was once the capital of Lydia, known for its wealth at the time of Croesus (6th century B.C.). Its citadel, reputed to be unassailable, was captured by surprise, first by Cyrus and later by Antiochus. The church is therefore warned to be on guard.

2, 14: Nm 22–24; 25, 1–3; 31,   **2, 23:** 1 Sm 16, 7; Jer 11, 20;
          16; 2 Pt 2, 15; Jude 11.   17, 10.
2, 17: Is 62, 2; 65, 15.   **2, 26:** Rv 12, 5; Ps 2, 8–9.

" 'The one who has the seven spirits of God and the seven stars says this: "I know your works, that you have the reputation of being alive, but you are dead. ² Be watchful and strengthen what is left, which is going to die, for I have not found your works complete in the sight of my God. ³* Remember then how you accepted and heard; keep it, and repent. If you are not watchful, I will come like a thief, and you will never know at what hour I will come upon you. ⁴* However, you have a few people in Sardis who have not soiled their garments; they will walk with me dressed in white, because they are worthy.

⁵*† " ' "The victor will thus be dressed in white, and I will never erase his name from the book of life but will acknowledge his name in the presence of my Father and of his angels.

⁶ " ' "Whoever has ears ought to hear what the Spirit says to the churches." '

To Philadelphia†

⁷* "To the angel of the church in Philadelphia,† write this:

" 'The holy one, the true,
  who holds the key of David,

who opens and no one shall close,
  who closes and no one shall open,

says this:

⁸† " ' "I know your works (behold, I have left an open door before you, which no one can close). You have limited strength, and yet you have kept my word and have not denied my name. ⁹* Behold, I will make those of the assembly of Satan who claim to be Jews and are not, but are lying, behold I will make them come and fall prostrate at your feet, and they will realize that I love you. ¹⁰† Because you have kept my message of endurance, I will keep you safe in the time of trial that is going to come to the whole world to test the inhabitants of the earth. ¹¹* I am coming quickly. Hold fast to what you have, so that no one may take your crown.

¹²*† " ' "The victor I will make into a pillar in the temple of my God, and he will never leave it again. On him I will inscribe the name of my God and the name of the city of my God, the new Jerusalem, which comes down out of heaven from my God, as well as my new name.

¹³ " ' "Whoever has ears ought to hear what the Spirit says to the churches." '

Opening the Door

The image in Rv 3, 20 inspired an artist to depict our relationship with Christ in a popular painting. The painting shows a door overgrown with vines. The door obviously has not been opened in a long time. As you examine it, you realize that it has no outside latch or knob—it can be opened only from the inside. At the door stands Jesus, knocking—not pounding, just knocking patiently.

What is your relationship with Christ like right now? Is the door of your life open to let Christ in? Or has it been closed for a while? Jesus will not force his way into your life. Jesus seeks a close friendship with you, and real friendship—real love—always involves a free choice. No one can choose to open the door but you.

▶ Rv 3, 14–22

3, 5: *In white:* white is a sign of victory and joy as well as resurrection; see the note on 2, 17. The *book of life:* the roll in which the names of the redeemed are kept; cf 13, 8; 17, 8; 20, 12.15; 21, 27; Phil 4, 3; Dn 12, 1. They will be acknowledged by Christ in heaven; cf Mt 10, 32.

3, 7–13: The letter to Philadelphia praises the Christians there for remaining faithful even with their limited strength (8). Members of the assembly of Satan are again singled out (9; see 2, 9 above). There is no admonition; rather, the letter promises that they will be kept safe at the great trial (10–11) and that the victors will become pillars of the heavenly temple, upon which three names will be inscribed: God, Jerusalem, and Christ (12).

3, 7: *Philadelphia:* modern Alasehir, ca. thirty miles southeast of Sardis, founded by Attalus II Philadelphus of Pergamum to be an "open door" (8) for Greek culture; it was destroyed by an earthquake in A.D. 17. Rebuilt by money from the Emperor Tiberius, the city was renamed Neo-Caesarea; this may explain the allusions to "name" in

v 12. *Key of David:* to the heavenly city of David (cf Is 22, 22), "the new Jerusalem" (12), over which Christ has supreme authority.

3, 8: *An open door:* opportunities for sharing and proclaiming the faith; cf Acts 14, 27; 1 Cor 16, 9; 2 Cor 2, 12.

3, 10: *My message of endurance:* this does not refer to a saying of Jesus about patience but to the example of Christ's patient endurance. *The inhabitants of the earth:* literally, "those who live on the earth." This expression, which also occurs in 6, 10; 8, 13; 11, 10; 13, 8.12.14; 17, 2.8, always refers to the pagan world.

3, 12: *Pillar:* this may be an allusion to the rebuilding of the city; see the note on v 7. *New Jerusalem:* it is described in 21, 10—22, 5.

3, 3: Mt 24, 42–44; Mk 13, 33; 1 Thes 5, 2; 2 Pt 3, 10.	**3, 7:** Is 22, 22; Mt 16, 19.
	3, 9: Rv 2, 9 / Is 45, 14; 60, 14.
3, 4: Rv 7, 13–14.	**3, 11:** Rv 2, 25; 22, 7.20.
3, 5: Ps 69, 29; Dn 12, 1 / Mt 10, 32.	**3, 12:** Rv 21, 2–3; Ez 48, 35 / Rv 19, 13.

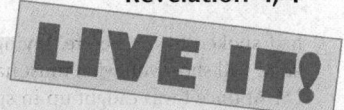

Jesus Christ Is the Lord of History

After the messages to the churches in Asia, John presents several visions that reveal God's action in history. Read Rv 4, 1–11. The vision of God's throne is the background of the whole Book of Revelation. It symbolizes God's authority over history. The vision is enhanced by a heavenly liturgy proclaiming and praising God's name:

"Holy, holy, holy is the Lord God almighty,
    who was, and who is, and who is to come."
                                                                        (4, 8)

Read 5, 1–14. The vision continues. Two symbols stand out: a sealed scroll and a lamb. God holds a scroll containing the history of Israel, whose meaning was hidden to the Christian communities in their persecution. A slain lamb appears. It's the risen Jesus, carrying in his body the signs of his Passion. He receives the scroll from God. He is the only one who can open the scroll and reveal the mystery of death and life.

Read both passages again and experience the honor, glory, and power of Christ. Let these visions reinforce your faith and renew your hope every time that you wonder about the meaning of an event you cannot make sense of.

▶ Revelation, chapters 4–5

To Laodicea†

14*† "To the angel of the church in Laodicea, write this:

" 'The Amen, the faithful and true witness, the source of God's creation, says this: 15† "I know your works; I know that you are neither cold nor hot. I wish you were either cold or hot. 16† So, because you are lukewarm, neither hot nor cold, I will spit you out of my mouth. 17*† For you say, 'I am rich and affluent and have no need of anything,' and yet do not realize that you are wretched, pitiable, poor, blind, and naked. 18† I advise you to buy from me gold refined by fire so that you may be rich, and white garments to put on so that your shameful nakedness may not be exposed, and buy ointment to smear on your eyes so that you may

see. 19* Those whom I love, I reprove and chastise. Be earnest, therefore, and repent.

20† " ' "Behold, I stand at the door and knock. If anyone hears my voice and opens the door, [then] I will enter his house and dine with him, and he with me. 21* I will give the victor the right to sit with me on my throne, as I myself first won the victory and sit with my Father on his throne.

22 " ' "Whoever has ears ought to hear what the Spirit says to the churches." ' "

III: God and the Lamb in Heaven

Vision of Heavenly Worship†

4 1 After this I had a vision of an open door† to heaven, and I heard the trumpetlike voice that

---

3, 14–22: The letter to Laodicea reprimands the community for being lukewarm (15–16), but no particular faults are singled out. Their material prosperity is contrasted with their spiritual poverty, the violet tunics that were the source of their wealth with the white robe of baptism, and their famous eye ointment with true spiritual perception (17–18). But Christ's chastisement is inspired by love and a desire to be allowed to share the messianic banquet with his followers in the heavenly kingdom (19–21).

3, 14: *Laodicea:* ca. forty miles southeast of Philadelphia and ca. eighty miles east of Ephesus, a wealthy industrial and commercial center, with a renowned medical school. It exported fine woolen garments and was famous for its eye salves. It was so wealthy that it was proudly rebuilt without outside aid after the devastating earthquake of A.D. 60/61. *The Amen:* this is a divine title (cf Hebrew text of Is 65, 16) applied to Christ; cf 2 Cor 1, 20. *Source of God's creation:* literally, "the beginning of God's creation," a concept found also in Jn 1, 3; Col 1, 16–17; Heb 1, 2; cf Prv 8, 22–31; Wis 9, 1–2.

3, 15–16: Halfhearted commitment to the faith is nauseating to Christ; cf Rom 12, 11.

3, 16: *Spit:* literally, "vomit." The image is that of a beverage that should be either hot or cold. Perhaps there is an allusion to the hot springs of Hierapolis across the Lycus river from Laodicea, which

would have been lukewarm by the time they reached Laodicea.

3, 17: Economic prosperity occasioned spiritual bankruptcy.

3, 18: *Gold . . . fire:* God's grace. *White garments:* symbol of an upright life; the city was noted for its violet/purple cloth. *Ointment . . . eyes:* to remove spiritual blindness; one of the city's exports was eye ointment (see the note on 3, 14).

3, 20: Christ invites all to the messianic banquet in heaven; cf Is 25, 6; Lk 14, 15; 22, 30.

4, 1–11: The seer now describes a vision of the heavenly court in worship of God enthroned. He reverently avoids naming or describing God but pictures twenty-four elders in priestly and regal attire (4) and God's throne and its surroundings made of precious gems and other symbols that traditionally express the majesty of God (5–6). Universal creation is represented by the four living creatures (6–7). Along with the twenty-four elders, they praise God unceasingly in humble adoration (8–11).

4, 1: The ancients viewed heaven as a solid vault, entered by way of actual doors.

3, 14: Rv 1, 5.	11, 32; Heb 12, 5–11.
3, 17: Prv 13, 7; Lk 12, 21.	**3, 21:** Lk 22, 28–30; Mt 19,
3, 19: Prv 3, 11–12; 1 Cor	28.

had spoken to me before, saying, "Come up here and I will show you what must happen afterwards." ²*† At once I was caught up in spirit. A throne was there in heaven, and on the throne sat ³ one whose appearance sparkled like jasper and carnelian. Around the throne was a halo as brilliant as an emerald. ⁴*† Surrounding the throne I saw twenty-four other thrones on which twenty-four elders sat, dressed in white garments and with gold crowns on their heads. ⁵† From the throne came flashes of lightning, rumblings, and peals of thunder. Seven flaming torches burned in front of the throne, which are the seven spirits of God. ⁶*† In front of the throne was something that resembled a sea of glass like crystal.

In the center and around the throne, there were four living creatures covered with eyes in front and in back. ⁷† The first creature resembled a lion, the second was like a calf, the third had a face like that of a human being, and the fourth looked like an eagle in flight. ⁸*† The four living creatures, each of them with six wings, were covered with eyes inside and out. Day and night they do not stop exclaiming:

"Holy, holy, holy is the Lord God almighty,
    who was, and who is, and who is
        to come."

⁹ Whenever the living creatures give glory and honor and thanks to the one who sits on the throne, who lives forever and ever, ¹⁰ the twenty-four elders fall down before the one who sits on the throne and worship him, who lives forever and ever. They throw down their crowns before the throne, exclaiming:

¹¹* "Worthy are you, Lord our God,
    to receive glory and honor and power,
    for you created all things;
        because of your will they came to be and
            were created."

Symbolic Numbers and Colors

To understand the Book of Revelation, we need to understand the symbolism of its numbers and colors. The numbers seven and twelve symbolize fullness or perfection. The number four symbolizes universalism (as in the four compass directions). The number one thousand symbolizes a multitude or a quantity too big to count. Thus, the twenty-four elders (4, 4) represent the perfection of the twelve tribes of Israel and the twelve Apostles. The Lamb with horns and eyes (5, 6) represents the risen Christ, who has the fullness of power (seven horns) and perfect knowledge (seven eyes). The 144,000 who will be saved (7, 4) represent a chosen multitude from the twelve tribes of Israel, because 144,000 equals 12 times 12 times 1,000.

The color white symbolizes victory, and red symbolizes bloodshed. Thus, the people who are slaughtered and given white robes (6, 9–11) are the martyrs, who gave up their life for their faith. They are victorious in martyrdom because God raised them to eternal life.

▸ Rv 4, 1—7, 17

The Scroll and the Lamb†

5 ¹* I saw a scroll† in the right hand of the one who sat on the throne. It had writing on both sides and was sealed with seven seals. ² Then I saw

---

† **4, 2–8:** Much of the imagery here is taken from Ez 1 and 10.
4, 4: *Twenty-four elders:* these represent the twelve tribes of Israel and the twelve apostles; cf 21, 12–14.
4, 5: *Flashes of lightning, rumblings, and peals of thunder:* as in other descriptions of God's appearance or activity; cf 8, 5; 11, 19; 16, 18; Ex 19, 16; Ez 1, 4.13. *The seven spirits of God:* the seven "angels of the presence" as in 8, 2 and Tb 12, 15.
4, 6: *A sea of glass like crystal:* an image adapted from Ez 1, 22–26. *Four living creatures:* these are symbols taken from Ez 1, 5–21; they are identified as cherubim in Ez 10, 20. *Covered with eyes:* these suggest God's knowledge and concern.
4, 7: *Lion . . . calf . . . human being . . . eagle:* these symbolize, respectively, what is noblest, strongest, wisest, and swiftest in creation. *Calf:* traditionally translated "ox," the Greek word refers to a heifer or young bull. Since the second century, these four creatures have been used as symbols of the evangelists Mark, Luke, Matthew, and John, respectively.
4, 8: *Six wings:* like the seraphim of Is 6, 2.
5, 1–14: The seer now describes a papyrus roll in God's right

hand (1) with seven seals indicating the importance of the message. A mighty angel asks who is worthy to open the scroll, i.e., who can accomplish God's salvific plan (2). There is despair at first when no one in creation can do it (3–4). But the seer is comforted by an elder who tells him that Christ, called the lion of the tribe of Judah, has won the right to open it (5). Christ then appears as a Lamb, coming to receive the scroll from God (6–7), for which he is acclaimed as at a coronation (8–10). This is followed by a doxology of the angels (11–12) and then finally by the heavenly church united with all of creation (13–14).
5, 1: *A scroll:* a papyrus roll possibly containing a list of afflictions for sinners (cf Ez 2, 9–10) or God's plan for the world. *Sealed with seven seals:* it is totally hidden from all but God. Only the Lamb (7–9) has the right to carry out the divine plan.

4, 2–3: Is 6, 1 / Ez 1, 26–28.
4, 4: Is 24, 23.
4, 6: Ex 24, 10.
4, 8: Is 6, 2–3 / Rv 1, 4.8;

11, 17; 16, 5.
4, 11: Rom 4, 17; 16, 27.
5, 1: Is 29, 11.

a mighty angel who proclaimed in a loud voice, "Who is worthy to open the scroll and break its seals?" 3 But no one in heaven or on earth or under the earth was able to open the scroll or to examine it. 4 I shed many tears because no one was found worthy to open the scroll or to examine it. 5*† One of the elders said to me, "Do not weep. The lion of the tribe of Judah, the root of David, has triumphed, enabling him to open the scroll with its seven seals."

6*† Then I saw standing in the midst of the throne and the four living creatures and the elders a Lamb that seemed to have been slain. He had seven horns and seven eyes; these are the [seven] spirits of God sent out into the whole world. 7 He came and received the scroll from the right hand of the one who sat on the throne. 8 When he took it, the four living creatures and the twenty-four elders fell down before the Lamb. Each of the elders held a harp and gold bowls filled with incense, which are the prayers of the holy ones. 9 They sang a new hymn:

> "Worthy are you to receive the scroll
>   and to break open its seals,
>   for you were slain and with your blood you
>   purchased for God
>   those from every tribe and tongue, people
>   and nation.
> 10* You made them a kingdom and priests for
>   our God,
>   and they will reign on earth."

11*† I looked again and heard the voices of many angels who surrounded the throne and the living creatures and the elders. They were countless in number, 12 and they cried out in a loud voice:

> "Worthy is the Lamb that was
>   slain
> to receive power and riches, wisdom
>   and strength,
> honor and glory and blessing."

13 Then I heard every creature in heaven and on earth and under the earth and in the sea, everything in the universe, cry out:

Enthusiastic Praise!

Over and over in John's vision of heaven, we find enthusiastic praise being offered to God, or to the Lamb of God, who is Christ Jesus. There are angels, incense, fantastic creatures, jewels, gold, elders, white-robed martyrs, and a crowd too great to number. The scenes of this vision inspire us to add our voice to theirs, to praise the majesty of God and the saving sacrifice of Jesus Christ.

In some Christian traditions, including some Catholic traditions, loud, spontaneous praise of God is common. However, most Catholics and many Christians from other denominations usually express their praise through softer types of songs and more solemn prayers. Whatever our expression, we should be enthusiastic with our praise!

How does the vision of the "countless in number, and they cried out in a loud voice" in Rv 5, 11–12 encourage you to be more bold in your praise of God? Can you sing out more loudly in Mass? Can you participate more from your heart in saying common prayers with others? In your private prayer, can you praise God without asking for anything or using memorized prayers?

▸ Rv 4, 1—5, 14

> "To the one who sits on the throne and to
>   the Lamb
>   be blessing and honor, glory and might,
>   forever and ever."

14 The four living creatures answered, "Amen," and the elders fell down and worshiped.

5, 5: *The lion of the tribe of Judah, the root of David:* these are the messianic titles applied to Christ to symbolize his victory; cf 22, 16; Gn 49, 9; Is 11, 1.10; Mt 1, 1.

5, 6: Christ is the Paschal Lamb without blemish, whose blood saved the new Israel from sin and death; cf Ex 12; Is 53, 7; Jn 1, 29.36; Acts 8, 32; 1 Pt 1, 18–19. This is the main title for Christ in Revelation, used twenty-eight times. *Seven horns and seven eyes:* Christ has the fullness (see the note on 1, 4) of power (horns) and knowledge (eyes); cf Zec 4, 10. *[Seven] spirits:* as in 1, 4; 3, 1; and 4, 5.

5, 11: *Countless:* literally, "100,000,000 plus 1,000,000," used by the author to express infinity.

5, 5: Is 11, 1.10; Rom 15, 12.	5, 10: Rv 1, 6; Ex 19, 6; Is 61, 6.
5, 6: Jn 1, 29.	5, 11: Dn 7, 10; Jude 14–15.

R
V

IV: The Seven Seals, Trumpets, and Plagues, with Interludes†

The First Six Seals†

6 ¹† Then I watched while the Lamb broke open the first of the seven seals, and I heard one of the four living creatures cry out in a voice like thunder, "Come forward." ²*† I looked, and there was a white horse, and its rider had a bow. He was given a crown, and he rode forth victorious to further his victories.

³ When he broke open the second seal, I heard the second living creature cry out, "Come forward." ⁴*† Another horse came out, a red one. Its rider was given power to take peace away from the earth, so that people would slaughter one another. And he was given a huge sword.

⁵† When he broke open the third seal, I heard the third living creature cry out, "Come forward." I looked, and there was a black horse, and its rider held a scale in his hand. ⁶*† I heard what seemed to be a voice in the midst of the four living creatures. It said, "A ration of wheat costs a day's pay, and three rations of barley cost a day's pay. But do not damage the olive oil or the wine."

⁷ When he broke open the fourth seal, I heard the voice of the fourth living creature cry out,

"Come forward." ⁸*† I looked, and there was a pale green horse. Its rider was named Death, and Hades accompanied him. They were given authority over a quarter of the earth, to kill with sword, famine, and plague, and by means of the beasts of the earth.

---

did you KNOW?

The Seven Seals and Seven Trumpets

The vision continues. In chapters 6–8 of Revelation, the Lamb opens the seven seals on the scroll and thus reveals the great forces in salvation history. The opening of the first four seals reveals the four horses of the apocalypse that bring conquest, strife, famine, and plagues. These are the things that throughout history have made people yearn for God's salvation.

The opening of the fifth seal reveals the souls of the martyrs, who demand justice. Their white robes indicate that they are already with the risen Christ. They are waiting for other martyrs, but this stage will end soon.

The opening of the sixth seal reveals the future. History will change, and all people, even the powerful, will suffer. The visions of the census and of the great crowd in 7, 1–17 reveal the destiny of Christians. As in the Exodus, 144,000 people from all the tribes of Israel will be saved. After this, a multitude that cannot be counted, from all nations, tribes, peoples, and languages, will experience God's salvation and sing of God's glory.

Finally, the Lamb opens the last seal. Seven more trumpets are revealed. When they are played by angels, a new series of plagues is released (8, 6—9, 21). One-third of the people are destroyed by these plagues so that those remaining might repent. But in spite of these warnings, many people do not change.

This vision tells us that no matter what evil besets us, God saves the faithful.

▸ **Revelation, chapters 6–9**

---

† **6, 1—16, 21:** A series of seven disasters now begins as each seal is broken (6, 1—8, 1), followed by a similar series as seven trumpets sound (8, 2—11, 19) and as seven angels pour bowls on the earth causing plagues (15, 1—16, 21). These gloomy sequences are interrupted by longer or shorter scenes suggesting the triumph of God and his witnesses (e.g., chs 7, 10, 11, 12, 13, 14).

6, 1–17: This chapter provides a symbolic description of the contents of the sealed scroll. The breaking of the first four seals reveals four riders. The first rider (of a white horse) is a conquering power (1–2), the second (red horse) a symbol of bloody war (3–4), the third (black horse) a symbol of famine (5–6), the fourth (pale green horse) a symbol of Death himself, accompanied by Hades (the netherworld) as his page (7–8). Verse 8b summarizes the role of all four riders. The breaking of the fifth seal reveals Christian martyrs in an attitude of sacrifice as blood poured out at the foot of an altar begging God for vindication, which will come only when their quota is filled; but they are given a white robe symbolic of victory (9–11). The breaking of the sixth seal reveals typical apocalyptic signs in the sky and the sheer terror of all people at the imminent divine judgment (12–17).

6, 1–8: The imagery is adapted from Zec 1, 8–10; 6, 1–8.

6, 2: *White horse . . . bow:* this may perhaps allude specifically to the Parthians on the eastern border of the Roman empire. Expert in the use of the bow, they constantly harassed the Romans and won a major victory in A.D. 62; see the note on 9, 13–21. But the Old Testament imagery typifies the history of oppression of God's people at all times.

6, 4: *Huge sword:* this is a symbol of war and violence; cf Ez 21, 14–17.

6, 5: *Black horse:* this is a symbol of famine, the usual accompaniment of war in antiquity; cf Lv 26, 26; Ez 4, 16–17. The *scale* is a symbol of shortage of food with a corresponding rise in price.

6, 6: *A day's pay:* literally, "a denarius," a Roman silver coin that constitutes a day's wage in Mt 20, 2. Because of the famine, food was rationed and sold at an exorbitant price. A liter of flour was considered a day's ration in the Greek historians Herodotus and Diogenes Laertius. *Barley:* food of the poor (Jn 6, 9.13; cf 2 Kgs 7, 1.16.18); it was also used to feed animals; cf 1 Kgs 5, 8. *Do not damage:* the olive and the vine are to be used more sparingly in time of famine.

6, 8: *Pale green:* symbol of death and decay; cf Ez 14, 21.

---

* 6, 2: Zec 1, 8–10; 6, 1–3.   6, 6: Lv 26, 26; Ez 4, 16–17.
6, 4: Ez 21, 14–16.   6, 8: Ez 14, 21.

9† When he broke open the fifth seal, I saw underneath the altar the souls of those who had been slaughtered because of the witness they bore to the word of God. 10† They cried out in a loud voice, "How long will it be, holy and true master, before you sit in judgment and avenge our blood on the inhabitants of the earth?" 11 Each of them was given a white robe, and they were told to be patient a little while longer until the number was filled of their fellow servants and brothers who were going to be killed as they had been.

12*† Then I watched while he broke open the sixth seal, and there was a great earthquake; the sun turned as black as dark sackcloth† and the whole moon became like blood. 13† The stars in the sky fell to the earth like unripe figs shaken loose from the tree in a strong wind. 14*† Then the sky was divided like a torn scroll curling up, and every mountain and island was moved from its place. 15† The kings of the earth, the nobles, the military officers, the rich, the powerful, and every slave and free person hid themselves in caves and among mountain crags. 16* They cried out to the mountains and the rocks, "Fall on us and hide us from the face of the one who sits on the throne and from the wrath of the Lamb, 17† because the great day of their wrath has come and who can withstand it?"

The 144,000 Sealed

7 1*† After this I saw four angels standing at the four corners of the earth,† holding back the four winds of the earth so that no wind could blow on land or sea or against any tree. 2† Then I saw another angel come up from the East, holding the seal of the living God. He cried out in a loud voice to the four angels who were given power to damage the land and the sea, 3* "Do not damage

the land or the sea or the trees until we put the seal on the foreheads of the servants of our God." 4*† I heard the number of those who had been marked with the seal, one hundred and forty-four thousand marked from every tribe of the Israelites: 5† twelve thousand were marked from the tribe of Judah, twelve thousand from the tribe of Reuben, twelve thousand from the tribe of Gad, 6 twelve thousand from the tribe of Asher, twelve thousand from the tribe of Naphtali, twelve thousand from the tribe of Manasseh, 7 twelve thousand from the tribe of Simeon, twelve thousand from the tribe of Levi, twelve thousand from the tribe of Issachar, 8 twelve thousand from the tribe of Zebulun, twelve thousand from the tribe of Joseph, and twelve thousand were marked from the tribe of Benjamin.

Triumph of the Elect

9† After this I had a vision of a great multitude, which no one could count, from every nation, race, people, and tongue. They stood before the throne and before the Lamb, wearing white robes and holding palm branches in their hands. 10† They cried out in a loud voice:

"Salvation comes from our God, who is seated
on the throne,
and from the Lamb."

11 All the angels stood around the throne and around the elders and the four living creatures. They prostrated themselves before the throne, worshiped God, 12 and exclaimed:

"Amen. Blessing and glory, wisdom
and thanksgiving,

6, 9: *The altar:* this altar corresponds to the altar of holocausts in the temple in Jerusalem; see also 11, 1. *Because of the witness . . . word of God:* literally, "because of the word of God and the witness they had borne."

6, 10: *Holy and true master:* Old Testament usage as well as the context indicates that this is addressed to God rather than to Christ.

6, 12–14: Symbolic rather than literal description of the cosmic upheavals attending the day of the Lord when the martyrs' prayer for vindication (10) would be answered; cf Am 8, 8–9; Is 34, 4; 50, 3; Jl 2, 10; 3, 3–4; Mt 24, 4–36; Mk 13, 5–37; Lk 21, 8–36.

6, 12: *Dark sackcloth:* for mourning, sackcloth was made from the skin of a black goat.

6, 13: *Unripe figs:* literally, "summer (or winter) fruit."

6, 14: *Was divided:* literally, "was split," like a broken papyrus roll torn in two, each half then curling up to form a roll on either side.

6, 15: *Nobles:* literally, "courtiers," "grandees." *Military officers:* literally, "commanders of 1,000 men," used in Josephus and other Greek authors as the equivalent of the Roman *tribunus militum*. The listing of various ranks of society represents the universality of terror at the impending doom.

6, 17: *Their:* this reading is attested in the best manuscripts, but the vast majority read "his" in reference to the wrath of the Lamb in the preceding verse.

7, 1–17: An interlude of two visions precedes the breaking of the seventh seal, just as two more will separate the sixth and seventh trumpets (ch 10). In the first vision (1–8), the elect receive the seal of the living God as protection against the coming cataclysm; cf 14, 1;

Ez 9, 4–6; 2 Cor 1, 22; Eph 1, 13; 4, 30. The second vision (9–17) portrays the faithful Christians before God's throne to encourage those on earth to persevere to the end, even to death.

7, 1: *The four corners of the earth:* the earth is seen as a table or rectangular surface.

7, 2: *East:* literally, "rising of the sun." The east was considered the source of light and the place of paradise (Gn 2, 8). *Seal:* whatever was marked by the impression of one's signet ring belonged to that person and was under his protection.

7, 4–9: *One hundred and forty-four thousand:* the square of twelve (the number of Israel's tribes) multiplied by a thousand, symbolic of the new Israel (cf 14, 1–5; Gal 6, 16; Jas 1, 1) that embraces people *from every nation, race, people, and tongue* (9).

7, 5–8: Judah is placed first because of Christ; cf "the Lion of the tribe of Judah" (5, 5). Dan is omitted because of a later tradition that the antichrist would arise from it.

7, 9: *White robes . . . palm branches:* symbols of joy and victory; see the note on 3, 5.

7, 10: *Salvation comes from:* literally, "(let) salvation (be ascribed) to." A similar hymn of praise is found at the fall of the dragon (12, 10) and of Babylon (19, 1).

6, 12: Jl 3, 4; Mt 24, 29.
6, 14: Is 34, 4 / Rv 16, 20.
6, 16: Is 2, 19; Hos 10, 8; Lk 23, 30.
7, 1: Jer 49, 36; Zec 6, 5.

7, 3: Ex 12, 7–14; Ez 9, 4; 2 Cor 1, 22; Eph 1, 13; 4, 30.
7, 4: Rv 14, 1.

honor, power, and might
be to our God forever and ever. Amen."

13 Then one of the elders spoke up and said to me, "Who are these wearing white robes, and where did they come from?" 14*† I said to him, "My lord, you are the one who knows." He said to me, "These are the ones who have survived the time of great distress; they have washed their robes and made them white in the blood of the Lamb.

15   "For this reason they stand before
      God's throne
and worship him day and night in his temple.
The one who sits on the throne will
      shelter them.
16* They will not hunger or thirst anymore,
nor will the sun or any heat strike them.
17*†For the Lamb who is in the center of the
      throne will shepherd them
and lead them to springs of life-
      giving water,
and God will wipe away every tear from
      their eyes."

The Seven Trumpets

8 1*† When he broke open the seventh seal, there was silence in heaven† for about half an hour. 2* And I saw that the seven angels who stood before God were given seven trumpets.

The Gold Censer

3*† Another angel came and stood at the altar, holding a gold censer. He was given a great quantity of incense to offer, along with the prayers of all the holy ones, on the gold altar that was before the throne. 4 The smoke of the incense along with the prayers of the holy ones went up before God from the hand of the angel. 5* Then the angel took the censer, filled it with burning coals from the altar, and hurled it down to the earth. There were peals of thunder, rumblings, flashes of lightning, and an earthquake.

Sing God's Glory

The Book of Revelation contains beautiful prayers of praise. Among them are the hymn to the Lamb (5, 9–14), the hymn of the multitude from every nation (7, 10–17), the song of the Lamb (15, 3–4), and the victory song (19, 1–8).

In your prayer, read these prayers slowly and carefully. Imagine the awe-inspiring scenes of God's glory they describe. Quietly reflect on how you have experienced the glory and power of God in your life. Look at the events you experience day to day; can you find the extraordinary in the ordinary? End your reflection by letting these songs inspire your own prayer of praise to God.

▸ Rv 7, 10–17

The First Four Trumpets

6* The seven angels who were holding the seven trumpets prepared to blow them.

7† When the first one blew his trumpet, there came hail and fire mixed with blood, which was hurled down to the earth. A third of the land was burned up, along with a third of the trees and all green grass.

8*† When the second angel blew his trumpet, something like a large burning mountain was hurled into the sea. A third of the sea turned to blood, 9† a third of the creatures living in the sea died, and a third of the ships were wrecked.

10* When the third angel blew his trumpet, a large star burning like a torch fell from the sky. It fell on a third of the rivers and on the springs of water. 11*† The star was called "Wormwood," and a

---

†   **7, 14:** *Time of great distress:* fierce persecution by the Romans; cf Introduction.
  7, 17: *Life-giving water:* literally, "the water of life," God's grace, which flows from Christ; cf 21, 6; 22, 1.17; Jn 4, 10.14.
  8, 1–13: The breaking of the seventh seal produces at first silence and then seven symbolic disasters, each announced by a trumpet blast, of which the first four form a unit as did the first four seals. A minor liturgy (3–5) is enclosed by a vision of seven angels (2.6). Then follow the first four trumpet blasts, each heralding catastrophes modeled on the plagues of Egypt affecting the traditional prophetic third (cf Ez 5, 12) of the earth, sea, fresh water, and stars (7–12). Finally, there is a vision of an eagle warning of the last three trumpet blasts (13).
  8, 1: *Silence in heaven:* as in Zep 1, 7, a prelude to the eschatological woes that are to follow; cf Introduction.
  8, 3: *Altar:* there seems to be only one altar in the heavenly temple, corresponding to the altar of holocausts in 6, 9, and here to

the altar of incense in Jerusalem; cf also 9, 13; 11, 1; 14, 18; 16, 7.
  8, 7: This woe resembles the seventh plague of Egypt (Ex 9, 23–24); cf Jl 3, 3.
  8, 8–11: The background of these two woes is the first plague of Egypt (Ex 7, 20–21).
  8, 9: *Creatures living in the sea:* literally, "creatures in the sea that had souls."
  8, 11: *Wormwood:* an extremely bitter and malignant plant symbolizing the punishment God inflicts on the ungodly; cf Jer 9, 12–14; 23, 15.

7, 14: Mt 24, 21.   8, 5: Ez 10, 2; Ps 11, 6 / Rv
7, 16: Is 49, 10.   4, 5; 11, 19; 16, 18.
7, 17: Rv 21, 4; Is 25, 8.   8, 6: Rv 16, 1–21.
8, 1: Hb 2, 20; Zep 1, 7; Zec   8, 8: Ex 7, 20.
    2, 17.   8, 10: Is 14, 12.
8, 2: Rv 4, 5; Tb 12, 15.   8, 11: Jer 9, 14.
8, 3: Ps 141, 2; Tb 12, 12.

third of all the water turned to wormwood. Many people died from this water, because it was made bitter.

12* When the fourth angel blew his trumpet, a third of the sun, a third of the moon, and a third of the stars were struck, so that a third of them became dark. The day lost its light for a third of the time, as did the night.

13† Then I looked again and heard an eagle flying high overhead cry out in a loud voice, "Woe! Woe! Woe to the inhabitants of the earth from the rest of the trumpet blasts that the three angels are about to blow!"

The Fifth Trumpet†

9 1*† Then the fifth angel blew his trumpet, and I saw a star that had fallen from the sky to the earth. It was given the key for the passage to the abyss. 2* It opened the passage to the abyss, and smoke came up out of the passage like smoke from a huge furnace. The sun and the air were darkened by the smoke from the passage. 3*† Locusts came out of the smoke onto the land, and they were given the same power as scorpions of the earth. 4 They were told not to harm the grass of the earth or any plant or any tree, but only those people who did not have the seal of God on their foreheads. 5† They were not allowed to kill them but only to torment them for five months; the torment they inflicted was like that of a scorpion when it stings a person. 6* During that time these people will seek death but will not find it, and they will long to die but death will escape them.

7*† The appearance of the locusts was like that of horses ready for battle. On their heads they wore what looked like crowns of gold; their faces were like human faces, 8* and they had hair like women's hair. Their teeth were like lions' teeth,

9 and they had chests like iron breastplates. The sound of their wings was like the sound of many horse-drawn chariots racing into battle. 10 They had tails like scorpions, with stingers; with their tails they had power to harm people for five months. 11† They had as their king the angel of the abyss, whose name in Hebrew is Abaddon and in Greek Apollyon.

12 The first woe has passed, but there are two more to come.

The Sixth Trumpet†

13* Then the sixth angel blew his trumpet, and I heard a voice coming from the [four]† horns of the gold altar before God, 14† telling the sixth angel who held the trumpet, "Release the four angels who are bound at the banks of the great river Euphrates." 15 So the four angels were released, who were prepared for this hour, day, month, and year to kill a third of the human race. 16 The number of cavalry troops was two hundred million; I heard their number. 17*† Now in my vision this is how I saw the horses and their riders. They wore red, blue, and yellow breastplates, and the horses' heads were like heads of lions, and out of their mouths came fire, smoke, and sulfur. 18 By these three plagues of fire, smoke, and sulfur that came out of their mouths a third of the human race was killed. 19 For the power of the horses is in their mouths and in their tails; for their tails are like snakes, with heads that inflict harm.

20*† The rest of the human race, who were not killed by these plagues, did not repent of the works of their hands, to give up the worship of demons and idols made from gold, silver, bronze, stone, and wood, which cannot see or hear or walk. 21 Nor did they repent of their murders, their magic potions, their unchastity, or their robberies.

8, 13: *Woe! Woe! Woe:* each of the three woes pronounced by the angel represents a separate disaster; cf 9, 12; 11, 14. The final woe, released by the seventh trumpet blast, includes the plagues of ch 16.

9, 1–12: The fifth trumpet heralds a woe containing elements from the eighth and ninth plagues of Egypt (Ex 10, 12–15.21–23) but specifically reminiscent of the invasion of locusts in Jl 1, 4—2, 10.

9, 1: *A star:* late Judaism represented fallen powers as stars (Is 14, 12–15; Lk 10, 18; Jude 13), but a comparison with 1, 20 and 20, 1 suggests that here it means an angel. *The passage to the abyss:* referring to Sheol, the netherworld, where Satan and the fallen angels are kept for a thousand years, to be cast afterwards into the pool of fire; cf 20, 7–10. The abyss was conceived of as a vast subterranean cavern full of fire. Its only link with the earth was a kind of passage or mine shaft, which was kept locked.

9, 3: *Scorpions:* their poisonous sting was proverbial; Ez 2, 6; Lk 11, 12.

9, 5: *For five months:* more or less corresponding to the life-span of locusts.

9, 7–10: Eight characteristics are listed to show the eschatological and diabolical nature of these locusts.

9, 11: *Abaddon:* Hebrew (more precisely, Aramaic) for destruction or ruin. *Apollyon:* Greek for the "Destroyer."

9, 13–21: The sixth trumpet heralds a woe representing another diabolical attack symbolized by an invasion by the Parthians living east of the Euphrates; see the note on 6, 2. At the appointed time (15), the frightful horses act as God's agents of judgment. The imaginative details are not to be taken literally; see Introduction and the note on 6, 12–14.

9, 13: *[Four]:* many Greek manuscripts and versions omit the word. The horns were situated at the four corners of the altar (Ex 27, 2; 30, 2–3); see the note on 8, 3.

9, 14–15: *The four angels:* they are symbolic of the destructive activity that will be extended throughout the universe.

9, 17: *Blue:* literally, "hyacinth-colored." *Yellow:* literally, "sulfurous."

9, 20: *The works of their hands:* i.e., the gods their hands had made.

8, 12: Ex 10, 21–23.	9, 7: Jl 2, 4.
9, 1: Rv 20, 1.	9, 8: Jl 1, 6.
9, 2: Gn 19, 28.	9, 13: Ex 30, 1–3.
9, 3: Ex 10, 12–15; Wis	9, 17: Jb 41, 10–13.
16, 9.	9, 20: Ps 135, 15–17; Is 17,
9, 6: Jb 3, 21.	8; Dn 5, 4.

The Angel with the Small Scroll

10 [1]† Then I saw another mighty angel come down from heaven wrapped in a cloud, with a halo around his head;† his face was like the sun and his feet were like pillars of fire. [2]† In his hand he held a small scroll that had been opened. He placed his right foot on the sea and his left foot on the land, [3]* and then he cried out in a loud voice as a lion roars. When he cried out, the seven thunders raised their voices, too. [4] When the seven thunders had spoken, I was about to write it down; but I heard a voice from heaven say, "Seal up what the seven thunders have spoken, but do not write it down." [5] Then the angel I saw standing on the sea and on the land raised his right hand to heaven [6]*† and swore by the one who lives forever and ever, who created heaven and earth and sea and all that is in them, "There shall be no more delay. [7]*† At the time when you hear the seventh angel blow his trumpet, the mysterious plan of God shall be fulfilled, as he promised to his servants the prophets."

[8] Then the voice that I had heard from heaven spoke to me again and said, "Go, take the scroll that lies open in the hand of the angel who is standing on the sea and on the land." [9]† So I went up to the angel and told him to give me the small scroll. He said to me, "Take and swallow it. It will turn your stomach sour, but in your mouth it will taste as sweet as honey." [10]* I took the small scroll from the angel's hand and swallowed it. In my mouth it was like sweet honey, but when I had eaten it, my stomach turned sour. [11]† Then someone said to me, "You must prophesy again about many peoples, nations, tongues, and kings."

The Two Witnesses

11 [1]*† Then I was given a measuring rod like a staff and I was told, "Come and measure the temple of God and the altar, and count those who are worshiping in it. [2]† But exclude the outer court of the temple; do not measure it, for it has been handed over to the Gentiles, who will trample the holy city for forty-two months. [3]† I will commission my two witnesses to prophesy for those twelve hundred and sixty days, wearing sackcloth." [4]*† These are the two olive trees and the two lampstands that stand before the Lord of the earth. [5]† If anyone wants to harm them, fire comes out of their mouths and devours their enemies. In this way, anyone wanting to harm them is sure to be slain. [6]* They have the power to close up the sky so that no rain can fall during the time of their prophesying. They also have power to turn water into blood and to afflict the earth with any plague as often as they wish.

[7]*† When they have finished their testimony, the beast that comes up from the abyss will wage war against them and conquer them and kill them. [8]† Their corpses will lie in the main street of the great city, which has the symbolic names "Sodom" and "Egypt," where indeed their Lord was crucified. [9]† Those from every people, tribe, tongue, and

---

10, 1—11, 14: An interlude in two scenes (10, 1–11 and 11, 1–14) precedes the sounding of the seventh trumpet; cf 7, 1–17. The first vision describes an angel astride sea and land like a colossus, with a small scroll open, the contents of which indicate that the end is imminent (ch 10). The second vision is of the measuring of the temple and of two witnesses, whose martyrdom means that the kingdom of God is about to be inaugurated.

10, 1–4: *The seven thunders:* God's voice announcing judgment and doom; cf Ps 29, 3–9, where thunder, as the voice of Yahweh, is praised seven times.

10, 2: *He placed . . . on the land:* this symbolizes the universality of the angel's message, as does the figure of the small scroll open to be read.

10, 6: *Heaven and earth and sea:* the three parts of the universe. *No more delay:* cf Dn 12, 7; Hb 2, 3.

10, 7: *The mysterious plan of God:* literally, "the mystery of God," the end of the present age when the forces of evil will be put down (17, 1—19, 4.11–21; 20, 7–10; cf 2 Thes 2, 6–12; Rom 16, 25–26), and the establishment of the reign of God when all creation will be made new (21, 1—22, 5).

10, 9–10: The small scroll was sweet because it predicted the final victory of God's people; it was sour because it also announced their sufferings. Cf Ez 3, 1–3.

10, 11: This further prophecy is contained in chs 12–22.

11, 1: The temple and altar symbolize the new Israel; see the note on 7, 4–9. The worshipers represent Christians. The measuring of the temple (cf Ez 40, 3—42, 20; 47, 1–12; Zec 2, 5–6) suggests that God will preserve the faithful remnant (cf Is 4, 2–3) who remain true to Christ (14, 1–5).

11, 2: *The outer court:* the Court of the Gentiles. *Trample . . . forty-two months:* the duration of the vicious persecution of the Jews by Antiochus IV Epiphanes (Dn 7, 25; 12, 7); this persecution of three and a half years (half of seven, counted as 1260 days in 3; 12, 6) became the prototype of periods of trial for God's people; cf Lk 4, 25; Jas 5, 17. The reference here is to the persecution by the Romans; cf Introduction.

11, 3: The two witnesses, wearing sackcloth symbolizing lamentation and repentance, cannot readily be identified. Do they represent Moses and Elijah, or the Law and the Prophets, or Peter and Paul? Most probably they refer to the universal church, especially the Christian martyrs, fulfilling the office of witness (two because of Dt 19, 15; cf Mk 6, 7; Jn 8, 17).

11, 4: *The two olive trees and the two lampstands:* the martyrs who stand in the presence of the Lord; the imagery is taken from Zec 4, 1–3.11–14, where the olive trees refer to Zerubbabel and Joshua.

11, 5–6: These details are derived from stories of Moses, who turned *water into blood* (Ex 7, 17–20), and of Elijah, who called down fire from heaven (1 Kgs 18, 36–40; 2 Kgs 1, 10) and closed up the sky for three years (1 Kgs 17, 1; cf 18, 1).

11, 7: *The beast . . . from the abyss:* the Roman emperor Nero, who symbolizes the forces of evil, or the antichrist (13, 1.8; 17, 8); cf Dn 7, 2–8.11–12.19–22 and Introduction.

11, 8: *The great city:* this expression is used constantly in Revelation for Babylon, i.e., Rome; cf 14, 8; 16, 19; 17, 18; 18, 2.10.21. *"Sodom" and "Egypt":* symbols of immorality (cf Is 1, 10) and oppression of God's people (cf Ex 1, 11–14). *Where indeed their Lord was crucified:* not the geographical but the symbolic Jerusalem that rejects God and his witnesses, i.e., Rome, called Babylon in chs 16–18; see the note on 17, 9 and Introduction.

11, 9–12: Over the martyrdom (7) of the two witnesses, now called prophets, the ungodly rejoice *for three and a half days,* a symbolic period of time; see the note on v 2. Afterwards they go in triumph to heaven, as did Elijah (2 Kgs 2, 11).

10, 3: Ps 29, 3–9; Jer 25, 30; Am 3, 8.
10, 6: Dn 32, 40; Dn 12, 7 / Ez 12, 28.
10, 7: Am 3, 7.
10, 10: Ez 3, 1–3.

11, 1: Ez 40, 3–5 / Zec 2, 5–9.
11, 4: Zec 4, 3.14.
11, 6: Ex 7, 17.
11, 7: Dn 7, 21.

nation will gaze on their corpses for three and a half days, and they will not allow their corpses to be buried. ¹⁰ The inhabitants of the earth will gloat over them and be glad and exchange gifts because these two prophets tormented the inhabitants of the earth. ¹¹* But after the three and a half days, a breath of life from God entered them. When they stood on their feet, great fear fell on those who saw them. ¹²* Then they heard a loud voice from heaven say to them, "Come up here." So they went up to heaven in a cloud as their enemies looked on. ¹³† At that moment there was a great earthquake, and a tenth of the city fell in ruins. Seven thousand people were killed during the earthquake; the rest were terrified and gave glory to the God of heaven.

¹⁴ The second woe has passed, but the third is coming soon.

The Seventh Trumpet

¹⁵† Then the seventh angel blew his trumpet. There were loud voices in heaven, saying, "The kingdom of the world now belongs to our Lord and to his Anointed, and he will reign forever and ever." ¹⁶ The twenty-four elders who sat on their thrones before God prostrated themselves and worshiped God ¹⁷ and said:

"We give thanks to you, Lord God almighty,
　who are and who were.
For you have assumed your great power
　and have established your reign.
¹⁸* The nations raged,
　but your wrath has come,
　and the time for the dead to be judged,
and to recompense your servants,
　the prophets,
　and the holy ones and those who fear
　　your name,
　the small and the great alike,
　and to destroy those who destroy the earth."

¹⁹ Then God's temple in heaven was opened, and the ark of his covenant could be seen in the temple. There were flashes of lightning, rumblings, and peals of thunder, an earthquake, and a violent hailstorm.

The Woman and the Dragon

12 ¹*† A great sign appeared in the sky, a woman† clothed with the sun, with the moon under her feet, and on her head a crown of twelve stars. ²† She was with child and wailed aloud

LIVE IT!

God in Control

The world is a wonderful place, full of life and hope. At the same time, it is full of pain and suffering, illness and death. It can seem frightening and out of control. Wars break out, a drought threatens the lives of millions, a friend dies in a senseless car accident, terrorists attack and kill innocent people; we can be left wondering why God allows such things.

The Book of Revelation was written to encourage the people of John's time that despite the evil that happens, God is in control. It can do the same for us too. The song in 11, 15–18 reminds us that there will come a time when the just will be rewarded and the wicked punished. And although God's Reign is not yet fully realized, as members of that Reign, we are called to be people of justice, peace, and hope to a world desperately seeking these things.

▸ Rv 11, 15–18

11, 13: *Seven thousand people:* a symbolic sum to represent all social classes (seven) and large numbers (thousands); cf Introduction.

11, 15–19: The seventh trumpet proclaims the coming of God's reign after the victory over diabolical powers; see the note on 10, 7.

12, 1–14, 20: This central section of Revelation portrays the power of evil, represented by a dragon, in opposition to God and his people. First, the dragon pursues the woman about to give birth, but her son is saved and "caught up to God and his throne" (12, 5). Then Michael and his angels cast the dragon and his angels out of heaven (12, 7–9). After this, the dragon tries to attack the boy indirectly by attacking members of his church (12, 13–18). A beast, symbolizing the Roman empire, then becomes the dragon's agent, mortally wounded but restored to life and worshiped by all the world (13, 1–10). A second beast arises from the land, symbolizing the antichrist, which leads people astray by its prodigies to idolize the first beast (13, 11–18). This is followed by a vision of the Lamb and his

faithful ones, and the proclamation of imminent judgment upon the world in terms of the wine of God's wrath (14, 1–20).

12, 1–6: The woman adorned with the sun, the moon, and the stars (images taken from Gn 37, 9–10) symbolizes God's people in the Old and New Testament. The Israel of old gave birth to the Messiah (5) and then became the new Israel, the church, which suffers persecution by the dragon (6.13–17); cf Is 50, 1; 66, 7; Jer 50, 12. This corresponds to a widespread myth throughout the ancient world that a goddess pregnant with a savior was pursued by a horrible monster; by miraculous intervention, she bore a son who then killed the monster.

12, 2: Because of Eve's sin, the woman gives birth in distress and pain (Gn 3, 16; cf Is 66, 7–14).

11, 11: Ez 37, 5.10.　　　　11, 18: Ps 2, 1.5 / Am 3, 7.
11, 12: 2 Kgs 2, 11.　　　　12, 1: Gn 37, 9.

in pain as she labored to give birth. ³*† Then another sign appeared in the sky; it was a huge red dragon, with seven heads and ten horns, and on its heads were seven diadems. ⁴* Its tail swept away a third of the stars in the sky and hurled them down to the earth. Then the dragon stood before the woman about to give birth, to devour her child when she gave birth. ⁵*† She gave birth to a son, a male child, destined to rule all the nations with an iron rod. Her child was caught up to God and his throne. ⁶† The woman herself fled into the desert where she had a place prepared by God, that there she might be taken care of for twelve hundred and sixty days.

⁷† Then war broke out in heaven; Michael† and his angels battled against the dragon. The dragon and its angels fought back, ⁸ but they did not prevail and there was no longer any place for them in heaven. ⁹*† The huge dragon, the ancient serpent, who is called the Devil and Satan, who deceived the whole world, was thrown down to earth, and its angels were thrown down with it.

¹⁰† Then I heard a loud voice in heaven say:

"Now have salvation and power come,
    and the kingdom of our God
    and the authority of his Anointed.
For the accuser of our brothers is cast out,
    who accuses them before our God day
        and night.
¹¹ They conquered him by the blood of
        the Lamb
    and by the word of their testimony;
    love for life did not deter them from death.
¹² Therefore, rejoice, you heavens,
    and you who dwell in them.
But woe to you, earth and sea,
    for the Devil has come down to you in
        great fury,
    for he knows he has but a short time."

¹³* When the dragon saw that it had been thrown down to the earth, it pursued the woman who had given birth to the male child. ¹⁴*† But the woman was given the two wings of the great eagle, so that she could fly to her place in the desert, where, far from the serpent, she was taken care of for a year, two years, and a half-year. ¹⁵† The serpent, however, spewed a torrent of water out of his mouth after the woman to sweep her away with the current. ¹⁶ But the earth helped the woman and opened its mouth and swallowed the flood that the dragon spewed out of its mouth. ¹⁷*† Then the dragon became angry with the woman and went off to wage war against the rest of her offspring, those who keep God's commandments and bear witness to Jesus. ¹⁸† It took its position on the sand of the sea.

The First Beast

13 ¹*† Then I saw a beast come out of the sea with ten horns and seven heads; on its horns were ten diadems, and on its heads

---

12, 3: *Huge red dragon:* the Devil or Satan (cf 9; 20, 2), symbol of the forces of evil, a mythical monster known also as Leviathan (Ps 74, 13–14) or Rahab (Jb 26, 12–13; Ps 89, 11). *Seven diadems:* these are symbolic of the fullness of the dragon's sovereignty over the kingdoms of this world; cf Christ with many diadems (19, 12).

12, 5: *Rule . . . iron rod:* fulfilled in 19, 15; cf Ps 2, 9. *Was caught up to God:* reference to Christ's ascension.

12, 6: God protects the persecuted church in the desert, the traditional Old Testament place of refuge for the afflicted, according to the typology of the Exodus; see the note on 11, 2.

12, 7–12: Michael, mentioned only here in Revelation, wins a victory over the dragon. A hymn of praise follows.

12, 7: *Michael:* the archangel, guardian and champion of Israel; cf Dn 10, 13.21; 12, 1; Jude 9. In Hebrew, the name Michael means "Who can compare with God?"; cf 13, 4.

12, 9: *The ancient serpent:* who seduced Eve (Gn 3, 1–6), mother of the human race; cf 20, 2; Eph 6, 11–12. *Was thrown down:* allusion to the expulsion of Satan from heaven; cf Lk 10, 18.

12, 10: *The accuser:* the meaning of the Hebrew word "Satan," found in v 9; Jb 1–2; Zec 3, 1; 1 Chr 21, 1; he continues to accuse Christ's disciples.

12, 14: *Great eagle:* symbol of the power and swiftness of divine help; cf Ex 19, 4; Dt 32, 11; Is 40, 31.

12, 15: The serpent is depicted as the sea monster; cf 13, 1; Is 27, 1; Ez 32, 2; Ps 74, 13–14.

12, 17: Although the church is protected by God's special providence (16), the individual Christian is to expect persecution and suffering.

12, 18: *It took its position:* many later manuscripts and versions read "I took my position," thus connecting the sentence to the following paragraph.

13, 1–10: This wild beast, combining features of the four beasts in Dn 7, 2–28, symbolizes the Roman empire; the seven heads represent the emperors; see the notes on 17, 10 and 17, 12–14. The blasphemous names are the divine titles assumed by the emperors.

12, 3: Dn 7, 7.	**12, 14:** Ex 19, 4; Dn 7, 25;
12, 4: Dn 8, 10.	12, 7.
12, 5: Is 66, 7 / Ps 2, 9.	**12, 17:** Gn 3, 15.
12, 9: Gn 3, 1–4 / Lk 10, 18.	**13, 1:** 2 Thes 2, 3–12.
12, 13: Gn 3, 15.	

did you KNOW?

The Woman and the Dragon

The vision in chapter 12 of Revelation symbolizes the great battle between Christ and Satan. In the opening scene, the pregnant woman represents Israel, from which the Messiah will come. The dragon waiting to devour her child is a symbol for Satan (verse 9). This child, who will rule all the nations, is the Messiah, Jesus Christ.

The conflict moves from heaven to earth when Satan fails to devour the child and is thrown down from his place in heaven. The dragon continues his pursuit of the woman on earth. The woman now represents the Christian churches, which the dragon angrily persecutes because he did not succeed in devouring her child. In this vision, John is telling the persecuted Christians of his time to have hope because in the end, Christ will totally and completely destroy Satan (see also 20, 1–10).

▶ Rv 12, 1–18

blasphemous name[s]. ²*† The beast I saw was like a leopard, but it had feet like a bear's, and its mouth was like the mouth of a lion. To it the dragon gave its own power and throne, along with great authority. ³† I saw that one of its heads seemed to have been mortally wounded, but this mortal wound was healed. Fascinated, the whole world followed after the beast. ⁴† They worshiped the dragon because it gave its authority to the beast; they also

worshiped the beast and said, "Who can compare with the beast or who can fight against it?"

⁵*† The beast was given a mouth uttering proud boasts and blasphemies, and it was given authority to act for forty-two months.† ⁶ It opened its mouth to utter blasphemies against God, blaspheming his name and his dwelling and those who dwell in heaven. ⁷* It was also allowed to wage war against the holy ones and conquer them, and it was granted authority over every tribe, people, tongue, and nation. ⁸* All the inhabitants of the earth will worship it, all whose names were not written from the foundation of the world in the book of life, which belongs to the Lamb who was slain.

⁹* Whoever has ears ought to hear these words.
¹⁰* Anyone destined for captivity goes
     into captivity.
Anyone destined to be slain by the sword
     shall be slain by the sword.

Such is the faithful endurance of the holy ones.

The Second Beast

¹¹† Then I saw another beast come up out of the earth; it had two horns like a lamb's but spoke like a dragon. ¹² It wielded all the authority of the first beast in its sight and made the earth and its inhabitants worship the first beast, whose mortal wound had been healed. ¹³* It performed great signs, even making fire come down from heaven to earth in the sight of everyone. ¹⁴ It deceived the inhabitants of the earth with the signs it was allowed to perform in the sight of the first beast, telling them to make an image for the beast who had been wounded by the sword and revived. ¹⁵* It was then permitted to breathe life into the beast's image, so that the beast's image could speak and [could] have anyone who did not worship it put to death. ¹⁶* It forced all the people, small and great, rich and poor, free and slave, to be given a stamped image on their right hands or their foreheads, ¹⁷ so that no one could buy or sell except one who had the stamped image of the beast's name or the number that stood for its name.

---

†
13, 2: Satan (12, 9), the prince of this world (Jn 12, 31), commissioned the beast to persecute the church (5–7).

13, 3: This may be a reference to the popular legend that Nero would come back to life and rule again after his death (which occurred in A.D. 68 from a self-inflicted stab wound in the throat); cf v 14; 17, 8. Domitian (A.D. 81–96) embodied all the cruelty and impiety of Nero. Cf Introduction.

13, 4: *Worshiped the beast:* allusion to emperor worship, which Domitian insisted upon and ruthlessly enforced. *Who can compare with the beast:* perhaps a deliberate parody of the name Michael; see the note on 12, 7.

13, 5–6: Domitian, like Antiochus IV Epiphanes (Dn 7, 8.11.25), demanded that he be called by divine titles such as "our lord and god" and "Jupiter." See the note on 11, 2.

13, 5: *Forty-two months:* this is the same duration as the profa-

nation of the holy city (11, 2), the prophetic mission of the two witnesses (11, 3), and the retreat of the woman into the desert (12, 6.14).

13, 11–18: The second beast is described in terms of the false prophets (cf 16, 13; 19, 20; 20, 10) who accompany the false messiahs (the first beast); cf Mt 24, 24; Mk 13, 22; 2 Thes 2, 9; cf also Dt 13, 2–4. Christians had either to worship the emperor and his image or to suffer martyrdom.

---

*

13, 2: Dn 7, 3–6.	**13, 10:** Jer 15, 2.
13, 5: Dn 7, 8.11.25; 8, 14;	**13, 13:** Dt 13, 2–4; Mt 24, 24;
9, 27; 11, 36; 12, 7.	2 Thes 2, 9–10.
13, 7: Dn 7, 21.	**13, 15:** Dn 3, 5–7.15.
13, 8: Rv 3, 5; 17, 8; 20, 12.	**13, 16:** Rv 14, 9; 16, 2; 19, 20;
13, 9: Mt 13, 9.	20, 4.

MARY HAS A VITAL MISSION IN SALVATION HISTORY

The New Testament links Mary's mission intimately to the mystery of Christ. In Lk 1, 38, Mary's yes to the angel Gabriel allows the Son of God to enter the world as a human being. At a wedding in Cana (Jn 2, 1–11), Mary is a model for the church as she intercedes before Jesus, has faith in him, points to him as the source of life, and leads others to follow his words. Jesus' words to Mary and the Beloved Disciple at the cross (Jn 19, 26–27) name Mary mother of the universal church, which is symbolized by the Beloved Disciple.

Over the centuries, some Catholics have seen in the unnamed woman mentioned in chapter 12 of Revelation representations of Mary and the church, who both share in Jesus' messianic mission. In the feast of the Assumption, this passage is one of the readings that celebrate Mary's entrance into heaven as the first disciple. Mary is a symbol of the triumphant church that awaits and intercedes for us, the pilgrim church.

Catholics of Latino origin have a long tradition of linking Mary to their history of salvation. She is their companion in their journey of faith and a very dear member of their community. Hispanic popular piety draws strength from Mary's example in daily life, in situations of need and suffering, and in times of celebration.

Reflect on the ways Mary teaches us to be servants of the Reign of God. Pray that we are as willing to fulfill our mission in salvation history as she is.

▸ **Revelation, chapter 12**

18*† Wisdom is needed here; one who understands can calculate the number of the beast, for it is a number that stands for a person. His number is six hundred and sixty-six.

The Lamb's Companions†

14 1* Then I looked and there was the Lamb standing on Mount Zion,† and with him a hundred and forty-four thousand who had his name and his Father's name written on their foreheads. 2 I heard a sound from heaven like the sound of rushing water or a loud peal of thunder. The sound I heard was like that of harpists playing their harps. 3* They were singing [what seemed to be] a new hymn before the throne, before the four living creatures and the elders. No one could learn this hymn except the hundred and forty-four thousand who had been ransomed from the earth. 4*† These are they who were not defiled with women; they are virgins and these are the ones who follow the Lamb wherever he goes. They have been ransomed as the firstfruits of the human race for God and the Lamb. 5*† On their lips no deceit has been found; they are unblemished.

The Three Angels†

6 Then I saw another angel flying high overhead, with everlasting good news† to announce to those

---

13, 18: Each of the letters of the alphabet in Hebrew as well as in Greek has a numerical value. Many possible combinations of letters will add up to 666, and many candidates have been nominated for this infamous number. The most likely is the emperor Caesar Nero (see the note on 13, 3), the Greek form of whose name in Hebrew letters gives the required sum. (The Latin form of this name equals 616, which is the reading of a few manuscripts.) Nero personifies the emperors who viciously persecuted the church. It has also been observed that "6" represents imperfection, falling short of the perfect number "7," and is represented here in a triple or superlative form.
14, 1–5: Now follows a tender and consoling vision of the Lamb and his companions.
14, 1: *Mount Zion:* in Jerusalem, the traditional place where the true remnant, the Israel of faith, is to be gathered in the messianic reign; cf 2 Kgs 19, 30–31; Jl 3, 5; Ob 17; Mi 4, 6–8; Zep 3, 12–20. *A hundred and forty-four thousand:* see the note on 7, 4–9. *His Father's name . . . foreheads:* in contrast to the pagans who were marked with the name or number of the beast (13, 16–17).

14, 4: *Virgins:* metaphorically, because they never indulged in any idolatrous practices, which are considered in the Old Testament to be adultery and fornication (2, 14–15.20–22; 17, 1–6; cf Ez 16, 1–58; 23, 1–49). The parallel passages (7, 3; 22, 4) indicate that the 144,000 whose foreheads are sealed represent all Christian people.
14, 5: *No deceit:* because they did not deny Christ or do homage to the beast. Lying is characteristic of the opponents of Christ (Jn 8, 44), but the Suffering Servant spoke no falsehood (Is 53, 9; 1 Pt 2, 22). *Unblemished:* a cultic term taken from the vocabulary of sacrificial ritual.
14, 6–13: Three angels proclaim imminent judgment on the pagan world, calling all peoples to worship God the creator. Babylon (Rome) will fall, and its supporters will be tormented forever.
14, 6: *Everlasting good news:* that God's eternal reign is about to begin; see the note on 10, 7.

13, 18: Rv 17, 9.   Is 42, 10.
14, 1: Jl 3, 5; Ob 17; Acts 2, 21.   **14, 4:** Jer 2, 2; Jas 1, 18.
14, 3: Pss 33, 3; 96, 1; 98, 1;   **14, 5:** Zep 3, 13.

did you KNOW?
The Number of the Beast

The vision of the two beasts in chapter 13 of Revelation is a continuation of the vision about the woman and the dragon in chapter 12. The beasts represent the Roman Empire and its emperor, which at the time threatened the true practice of Christianity. Roman leaders expected all citizens, including Christians, to offer sacrifices to the Roman gods and to worship the emperor as though he were a god. This may have been especially true in the cities in Asia Minor, which were trying to prove their loyalty to the Roman emperor.

In verse 18, we are told that the number of the second beast is 666. Most scholars believe that this stands for Nero Caesar, who was the emperor of Rome from A.D. 54 to 68. Their reasoning is that when you convert the Hebrew letters for Nero's name to Hebrew numbers, you get the number 666. Nero was responsible for some especially vicious attacks on Christians in Rome. The Book of Revelation was written after Nero committed suicide, but many people thought that he had not died and had come out of hiding in the East to lead this new wave of persecution against Christians (verse 3).

▸ Revelation, chapter 13

who dwell on earth, to every nation, tribe, tongue, and people. [7]* He said in a loud voice, "Fear God and give him glory, for his time has come to sit in judgment. Worship him who made heaven and earth and sea and springs of water."

[8]*† A second angel followed, saying:

"Fallen, fallen is Babylon the great,
    that made all the nations drink
    the wine of her licentious passion."

[9] A third angel followed them and said in a loud voice, "Anyone who worships the beast or its image, or accepts its mark on forehead or hand, [10]† will also drink the wine of God's fury, poured full strength into the cup of his wrath, and will be tormented in burning sulfur before the holy angels and before the Lamb. [11]* The smoke of the fire that torments them will rise forever and ever, and there will be no relief day or night for those who worship the beast or its image or accept the mark of its name." [12]*† Here is what sustains the holy ones who keep God's commandments and their faith in Jesus.

[13]*† I heard a voice from heaven say, "Write this: Blessed are the dead who die in the Lord from now on." "Yes," said the Spirit, "let them find rest from their labors, for their works accompany them."

The Harvest of the Earth

[14]*† Then I looked and there was a white cloud, and sitting on the cloud one who looked like a son of man, with a gold crown on his head and a sharp sickle in his hand. [15]* Another angel came out of the temple, crying out in a loud voice to the one sitting on the cloud, "Use your sickle and reap the harvest, for the time to reap has come, because the earth's harvest is fully ripe." [16] So the one who was sitting on the cloud swung his sickle over the earth, and the earth was harvested.

[17] Then another angel came out of the temple in heaven who also had a sharp sickle. [18]† Then another angel [came] from the altar, [who] was in charge of the fire, and cried out in a loud voice to the one who had the sharp sickle, "Use your sharp sickle and cut the clusters from the earth's vines, for its grapes are ripe." [19]* So the angel swung his sickle over the earth and cut the earth's vintage. He threw it into the great wine press of God's fury. [20]† The

R
V

---

† **14, 8:** This verse anticipates the lengthy dirge over Babylon (Rome) in 18, 1—19, 4. The oracle of Is 21, 9 to Babylon is applied here.

14, 10–11: *The wine of God's fury:* image taken from Is 51, 17; Jer 25, 15–16; 49, 12; 51, 7; Ez 23, 31–34. Eternal punishment in the fiery pool of burning sulfur (or "fire and brimstone"; cf Gn 19, 24) is also reserved for the Devil, the beast, and the false prophet (19, 20; 20, 10; 21, 8).

14, 12: In addition to *faith in Jesus,* the seer insists upon the necessity and value of works, as in 2, 23; 20, 12–13; 22, 12; cf Mt 16, 27; Rom 2, 6.

14, 13: See the note on 1, 3. According to Jewish thought, people's actions followed them as witnesses before the court of God.

14, 14–20: The reaping of the harvest symbolizes the gathering of the elect in the final judgment, while the reaping and treading of the grapes symbolizes the doom of the ungodly (cf Jl 4, 12–13; Is 63, 1–6) that will come in 19, 11–21.

14, 18: *Altar:* there was only one altar in the heavenly temple; see the notes above on 6, 9; 8, 3; 11, 1.

14, 20: *Two hundred miles:* literally sixteen hundred stades. The *stadion,* a Greek unit of measurement, was about 607 feet in length, approximately the length of a furlong.

14, 7: Rv 2, 10; Mt 10, 28.
14, 8: Rv 18, 2–3; Is 21, 9;
    Jer 51, 8 / Is 51, 17; Jer
    25, 15–17.
14, 11: Rv 19, 3.
14, 12: Rv 12, 17.

14, 13: Mt 11, 28–29; 2 Thes
    1, 7; Heb 4, 10.
14, 14: Rv 1, 7; Dn 7, 13.
14, 15: Jl 4, 13; Mt 13, 36–43.
14, 19: Rv 19, 15; Is 63, 1–6.

wine press was trodden outside the city and blood poured out of the wine press to the height of a horse's bridle for two hundred miles.

The Seven Last Plagues

15 ¹† Then I saw in heaven another sign,† great and awe-inspiring: seven angels with the seven last plagues, for through them God's fury is accomplished.

²*† Then I saw something like a sea of glass mingled with fire. On the sea of glass were standing those who had won the victory over the beast and its image and the number that signified its name. They were holding God's harps, ³*† and they sang the song of Moses, the servant of God, and the song of the Lamb:

"Great and wonderful are your works,
    Lord God almighty.
Just and true are your ways,
    O king of the nations.
⁴* Who will not fear you, Lord,
    or glorify your name?
For you alone are holy.
    All the nations will come
    and worship before you,
    for your righteous acts have been revealed."

⁵† After this I had another vision. The temple that is the heavenly tent of testimony† opened, ⁶* and the seven angels with the seven plagues came out of the temple. They were dressed in clean white linen, with a gold sash around their chests. ⁷ One of the four living creatures gave the seven angels seven gold bowls filled with the fury of God, who lives forever and ever. ⁸* Then the temple became so filled with the smoke from God's glory and might that no one could enter it until the seven plagues of the seven angels had been accomplished.

The Seven Bowls

16 ¹† I heard a loud voice speaking from the temple to the seven angels, "Go and pour out the seven bowls of God's fury upon the earth."

²† The first angel went and poured out his bowl on the earth. Festering and ugly sores broke out on those who had the mark of the beast or worshiped its image.

³† The second angel poured out his bowl on the sea. The sea turned to blood like that from a corpse; every creature living in the sea died.

⁴* The third angel poured out his bowl on the rivers and springs of water. These also turned to blood. ⁵* Then I heard the angel in charge of the waters say:

"You are just, O Holy One,
    who are and who were,
    in passing this sentence.
⁶* For they have shed the blood of the holy ones
    and the prophets,
    and you [have] given them blood to drink;
    it is what they deserve."

⁷* Then I heard the altar cry out,

"Yes, Lord God almighty,
    your judgments are true and just."

⁸ The fourth angel poured out his bowl on the sun. It was given the power to burn people with fire. ⁹* People were burned by the scorching heat and blasphemed the name of God who had power over these plagues, but they did not repent or give him glory.

¹⁰*† The fifth angel poured out his bowl on the throne of the beast. Its kingdom was plunged into darkness, and people bit their tongues in pain ¹¹* and blasphemed the God of heaven because of their pains and sores. But they did not repent of their works.

¹²† The sixth angel emptied his bowl on the great river Euphrates. Its water was dried up to prepare the way for the kings of the East. ¹³*† I saw three unclean spirits like frogs come from the mouth of

---

15, 1—16, 21: The seven bowls, the third and last group of seven after the seven seals and the seven trumpets, foreshadow the final cataclysm. Again, the series is introduced by a heavenly prelude, in which the victors over the beast sing the canticle of Moses (15, 2–4).

15, 1–4: A vision of the victorious martyrs precedes the vision of woe in 15, 5—16, 21; cf 7, 9–12.

15, 2: *Mingled with fire:* fire symbolizes the sanctity involved in facing God, reflected in the trials that have prepared the victorious Christians or in God's wrath.

15, 3: *The song of Moses:* the song that Moses and the Israelites sang after their escape from the oppression of Egypt (Ex 15, 1–18). The martyrs have escaped from the oppression of the Devil. *Nations:* many other Greek manuscripts and versions read "ages."

15, 5–8: Seven angels receive the bowls of God's wrath.

15, 5: *Tent of testimony:* the name of the meeting tent in the Greek text of Ex 40. Cf 2 Mc 2, 4–7.

16, 1–21: These seven bowls, like the seven seals (6, 1–17; 8, 1) and the seven trumpets (8, 2—9, 21; 11, 15–19), bring on a succession of disasters modeled in part on the plagues of Egypt (Ex 7–12).

See the note on 6, 12–14.

16, 2: Like the sixth Egyptian plague (Ex 9, 8–11).

16, 3–4: Like the first Egyptian plague (Ex 7, 20–21). The same woe followed the blowing of the second trumpet (8, 8–9).

16, 10: *The throne of the beast:* symbol of the forces of evil. *Darkness:* like the ninth Egyptian plague (Ex 10, 21–23); cf 9, 2.

16, 12: *The kings of the East:* Parthians; see the notes on 6, 2 and 17, 12–13. *East:* literally, "rising of the sun," as in 7, 2.

16, 13: *Frogs:* possibly an allusion to the second Egyptian plague (Ex 7, 26—8, 11). *The false prophet:* identified with the two-horned second beast (13, 11–18 and the note there).

15, 2: Rv 7, 9.14; 13, 15–18.
15, 3: Pss 92, 6; 98, 1 / Dt 32, 4; Ps 145, 17.
15, 4: Ps 86, 9–10; Jer 10, 7.
15, 6: Rv 19, 8.
15, 8: 1 Kgs 8, 10; Is 6, 4.
16, 4: Ex 7, 14–24.
16, 5: Rv 1, 4.
16, 6: Ez 35, 6; Mt 23, 34–35.
16, 7: Dn 3, 27; Tb 3, 2.
16, 9: Am 4, 6.
16, 10: Ex 10, 21–23.
16, 11: Ex 9, 8–11 / Jer 5, 3.
16, 13: Ex 8, 2–3.

the dragon, from the mouth of the beast, and from the mouth of the false prophet. 14* These were demonic spirits who performed signs. They went out to the kings of the whole world to assemble them for the battle on the great day of God the almighty. 15*† ("Behold, I am coming like a thief." Blessed is the one who watches and keeps his clothes ready, so that he may not go naked and people see him exposed.) 16† They then assembled the kings in the place that is named Armageddon in Hebrew.

17* The seventh angel poured out his bowl into the air. A loud voice came out of the temple from the throne, saying, "It is done." 18* Then there were lightning flashes, rumblings, and peals of thunder, and a great earthquake. It was such a violent earthquake that there has never been one like it since the human race began on earth. 19† The great city was split into three parts, and the gentile cities fell. But God remembered great Babylon, giving it the cup filled with the wine of his fury and wrath. 20† Every island fled, and mountains disappeared. 21* Large hailstones like huge weights came down from the sky on people, and they blasphemed God for the plague of hail because this plague was so severe.

V: The Punishment of Babylon and the Destruction of Pagan Nations

Babylon the Great

17 1*† Then one of the seven angels who were holding the seven bowls came and said to me, "Come here. I will show you the judgment on the great harlot† who lives near the many waters. 2*† The kings of the earth have had intercourse with her, and the inhabitants of the earth became drunk on the wine of her harlotry." 3*† Then he carried me away in spirit to a deserted place where I saw a woman seated on a scarlet beast that was covered with blasphemous names, with seven heads and ten horns. 4*† The woman was wearing

purple and scarlet and adorned with gold, precious stones, and pearls. She held in her hand a gold cup that was filled with the abominable and sordid deeds of her harlotry. 5 On her forehead was written a name, which is a mystery, "Babylon the great, the mother of harlots and of the abominations of the earth." 6† I saw that the woman was drunk on the blood of the holy ones and on the blood of the witnesses to Jesus.

Meaning of the Beast and Harlot

When I saw her I was greatly amazed. 7 The angel said to me, "Why are you amazed? I will explain to you the mystery of the woman and of the beast that carries her, the beast with the seven heads and the ten horns. 8*† The beast that you saw existed once but now exists no longer. It will come up from the abyss and is headed for destruction. The inhabitants of the earth whose names have not been written in the book of life from the foundation of the world shall be amazed when they see the beast, because it existed once but exists no longer, and yet it will come again. 9*† Here is a clue for one who has wisdom. The seven heads represent seven hills upon which the woman sits. They also represent seven kings: 10† five have already fallen, one still lives, and the last has not yet come, and when he comes he must remain only a short while. 11† The beast that existed once but exists no longer is an eighth king, but really belongs to the seven and is headed for destruction. 12*† The ten horns that you saw represent ten kings who have not yet been crowned; they will receive royal authority along with the beast for one hour. 13 They are of one mind and will give their power and authority to the beast. 14* They will fight with the Lamb, but the Lamb will conquer them, for he is Lord of lords and king of kings, and those with him are called, chosen, and faithful."

15 Then he said to me, "The waters that you saw where the harlot lives represent large numbers of

R
V

---

†

16, 15: *Like a thief:* as in 3, 3 (cf Mt 24, 42–44; 1 Thes 5, 2). *Blessed:* see the note on 1, 3.

16, 16: *Armageddon:* in Hebrew, this means "Mountain of Megiddo." Since Megiddo was the scene of many decisive battles in antiquity (Jgs 5, 19–20; 2 Kgs 9, 27; 2 Chr 35, 20–24), the town became the symbol of the final disastrous rout of the forces of evil.

16, 19: *The great city:* Rome and the empire.

16, 20–21: See the note on 6, 12–14. *Hailstones:* as in the seventh Egyptian plague (Ex 9, 23–24); cf 8, 7. *Like huge weights:* literally, "weighing a talent," about one hundred pounds.

17, 1—19, 10: The punishment of Babylon is now described as a past event and, metaphorically, under the image of the great harlot who leads people astray into idolatry.

17, 1–6: Babylon, the symbolic name (5) of Rome, is graphically described as "the great harlot."

17, 2: *Intercourse . . . harlotry:* see the note on 14, 4. The pagan kings subject to Rome adopted the cult of the emperor.

17, 3: *Scarlet beast:* see the note on 13, 1–10. *Blasphemous names:* divine titles assumed by the Roman emperors; see the note on 13, 5–6.

17, 4: Reference to the great wealth and idolatrous cults of Rome.

17, 6b–18: An interpretation of the vision is here given.

17, 8: Allusion to the belief that the dead Nero would return to power (11); see the note on 13, 3.

17, 9: *Here is a clue:* literally, "Here a mind that has wisdom." *Seven hills:* of Rome.

17, 10: There is little agreement as to the identity of the Roman emperors alluded to here. The number (9) suggests that all the emperors are meant; see the note on 1, 4.

17, 11: *The beast:* Nero; see the note on v 8.

17, 12–13: *Ten kings who have not yet been crowned:* perhaps Parthian satraps who are to accompany the revived Nero (the beast) in his march on Rome to regain power; see the note on 13, 3. In 19, 11–21, the Lamb and his companions will conquer them.

16, 14: 1 Cor 1, 8.	**17, 8:** Rv 13, 3–4 / Rv 3, 5;
16, 15: Mt 24, 42–44 / Rv 3, 17.	13, 8; 20, 12.
16, 17: Is 66, 6.	**17, 9:** Rv 13, 18.
16, 18: Mk 13, 19.	**17, 12:** Dn 7, 24.
16, 21: Ex 9, 22–26.	**17, 14:** Rv 19, 11–21; 2 Mc
17, 1: Jer 50, 38; 51, 13.	13, 4; 1 Tm 6, 15 /
17, 2: Jer 51, 7.	Rom 1, 6; 1 Pt 2, 9;
17, 3: Rv 13, 1.	Jude 1.
17, 4: Rv 18, 16.	

The Sins of Empires

In John's coded language, the whore called Babylon in chapter 17 is Rome, a city built on seven hills. She is dressed in colors that symbolize her royalty (purple) and her obscene and immoral behavior (scarlet). Her gold and pearls are signs of her wealth and excessive luxury. The blasphemous names on her forehead are the titles that should be given to God but are given to the emperor instead. By calling her Babylon, John is creating a tie with the capital of another evil empire from the Old Testament (see "The Fall of Jerusalem," 2 Kgs 25, 1–21).

The whore is drunk on the blood of the saints who have been killed for their faith. John indicates that her evil is caused by her unrestrained desire for wealth and luxury and her abuse of power (Rv 18, 3–19). He tells his Christian readers that they can be hopeful, even amid so much suffering, because in the end, the Lamb (Christ) will conquer the beast (17, 14).

Since Revelation was written, many other countries have abused their power, including the United States. Consider, for example, its treatment of Native Americans, practice of slavery, and lack of care for the environment.

Reflect for a moment. In what areas does your country need to take more responsibility to ensure justice for all people? Where has the desire for wealth and luxury gone too far? What can you do locally to take greater responsibility in these areas?

▶ Revelation, chapter 17

peoples, nations, and tongues. ¹⁶*† The ten horns that you saw and the beast will hate the harlot; they will leave her desolate and naked; they will eat her flesh and consume her with fire. ¹⁷ For God has put it into their minds to carry out his purpose and to make them come to an agreement to give their kingdom to the beast until the words of God are accomplished. ¹⁸ The woman whom you saw represents the great city that has sovereignty over the kings of the earth."

The Fall of Babylon

18 ¹*† After this I saw another angel coming down from heaven, having great authority, and the earth became illumined by his splendor. ²*† He cried out in a mighty voice:

"Fallen, fallen is Babylon the great.
   She has become a haunt for demons.
She is a cage for every unclean spirit,
   a cage for every unclean bird,
   [a cage for every unclean] and
      disgusting [beast].

³*† For all the nations have drunk
   the wine of her licentious passion.
The kings of the earth had intercourse
   with her,
   and the merchants of the earth grew rich
      from her drive for luxury."

⁴*† Then I heard another voice from heaven say:

"Depart from her, my people,
   so as not to take part in her sins
   and receive a share in her plagues,
⁵* for her sins are piled up to the sky,
   and God remembers her crimes.
⁶* Pay her back as she has paid others.
   Pay her back double for her deeds.
   Into her cup pour double what she
      poured.
⁷* To the measure of her boasting
      and wantonness
   repay her in torment and grief;
   for she said to herself,

† ——————————————
17, 16–18: *The ten horns:* the ten pagan kings (12) who unwittingly fulfill God's will against harlot Rome, the great city; cf Ez 16, 37.
18, 1—19, 4: A stirring dirge over the fall of Babylon-Rome. The perspective is prophetic, as if the fall of Rome had already taken place. The imagery here, as elsewhere in this book, is not to be taken literally. The vindictiveness of some of the language, borrowed from the scathing Old Testament prophecies against Babylon, Tyre, and Nineveh (Is 23; 24; 27; Jer 50–51; Ez 26–27), is meant to portray symbolically the inexorable demands of God's holiness and justice; cf Introduction. The section concludes with a joyous canticle on the future glory of heaven.

18, 2: Many Greek manuscripts and versions omit *a cage for every unclean . . . beast.*
18, 3–24: Rome is condemned for her immorality, symbol of idolatry (see the note on 14, 4), and for persecuting the church; cf 19, 2.
18, 4: *Depart from her:* not evacuation of the city but separation from sinners, as always in apocalyptic literature.

——————————————
17, 16: Ez 16, 37–41; 23,
   25–29.
18, 1: Ez 43, 2.
18, 2: Rv 14, 8; Is 21, 9; Jer
   50, 2–3; 51, 8.

18, 3: Rv 17, 2; Jer 51, 7.
18, 4: Is 48, 20; Jer 50, 8.
18, 5: Jer 51, 9.
18, 6: Jer 50, 15 / Jer 16, 18.
18, 7: Is 47, 8–9.

'I sit enthroned as queen;
    I am no widow,
    and I will never know grief.'
8   Therefore, her plagues will come in one day,
        pestilence, grief, and famine;
        she will be consumed by fire.
    For mighty is the Lord God who judges her."

9 The kings of the earth who had intercourse with
her in their wantonness will weep and mourn over
her when they see the smoke of her pyre. 10 They
will keep their distance for fear of the torment inflicted on her, and they will say:

    "Alas, alas, great city,
        Babylon, mighty city.
        In one hour your judgment has come."

11† The merchants of the earth will weep and
mourn for her, because there will be no more markets for their cargo: 12 their cargo of gold, silver, precious stones, and pearls; fine linen, purple silk, and
scarlet cloth; fragrant wood of every kind, all articles of ivory and all articles of the most expensive
wood, bronze, iron, and marble; 13† cinnamon,
spice, incense, myrrh, and frankincense; wine, olive
oil, fine flour, and wheat; cattle and sheep, horses
and chariots, and slaves, that is, human beings.
14*   "The fruit you craved
        has left you.
    All your luxury and splendor are gone,
        never again will one find them."

15 The merchants who deal in these goods, who
grew rich from her, will keep their distance for fear
of the torment inflicted on her. Weeping and
mourning, 16* they cry out:

    "Alas, alas, great city,
        wearing fine linen, purple and scarlet,
        adorned [in] gold, precious stones, and pearls.
17   In one hour this great wealth has been ruined."

Every captain of a ship, every traveler at sea, sailors,
and seafaring merchants stood at a distance 18 and
cried out when they saw the smoke of her pyre,
"What city could compare with the great city?"
19* They threw dust on their heads and cried out,
weeping and mourning:

"Alas, alas, great city,
    in which all who had ships at sea
    grew rich from her wealth.
In one hour she has been ruined.
20*   Rejoice over her, heaven,
        you holy ones, apostles, and prophets.
    For God has judged your case against her."

21* A mighty angel picked up a stone like a huge
millstone and threw it into the sea and said:

"With such force will Babylon the great city be
        thrown down,
    and will never be found again.
22*   No melodies of harpists and musicians,
        flutists and trumpeters,
        will ever be heard in you again.
    No craftsmen in any trade
        will ever be found in you again.
    No sound of the millstone
        will ever be heard in you again.
23*   No light from a lamp
        will ever be seen in you again.
    No voices of bride and groom
        will ever be heard in you again.
    Because your merchants were the great ones of
        the world,
        all nations were led astray by your
        magic potion.
24*   In her was found the blood of prophets and
        holy ones
        and all who have been slain on
        the earth."

19 1† After this I heard what sounded like
    the loud voice of a great multitude in
heaven, saying:

"Alleluia!
    Salvation, glory, and might belong to our God,
2*   for true and just are his judgments.
    He has condemned the great harlot
        who corrupted the earth with her harlotry.
    He has avenged on her the blood of
        his servants."

3* They said a second time:

"Alleluia! Smoke will rise from her forever
        and ever."

†
   18, 11: Ironically, the merchants weep not so much for Babylon-
Rome, but for their lost markets; cf Ez 27, 36.
   18, 13: *Spice:* an unidentified spice plant called in Greek
amōmon.
   19, 1.3.4.6: *Alleluia:* found only here in the New Testament, this
frequent exclamation of praise in the Hebrew psalms was important
in Jewish liturgy.

*
   18, 14: Hos 10, 5 / Am 6, 7.
   18, 16: Rv 17, 4.
   18, 19: Ez 27, 27–32.
   18, 20: Rv 19, 1–2; Dt 32, 43.
   18, 21: Jer 51, 63–64; Ez 26,
       21.
   18, 22: Is 24, 8; Ez 26, 13.
   18, 23: Jer 7, 34; 16, 9; 25, 10.
   18, 24: Rv 16, 6.
   19, 2: Dn 3, 27 / Jer 51, 48–49.
   19, 3: Rv 14, 11; Is 34, 10.

4 The twenty-four elders and the four living creatures fell down and worshiped God who sat on the throne, saying, "Amen. Alleluia."

The Victory Song

5*† A voice coming from the throne said:

"Praise our God, all you his servants,
[and] you who revere him, small and great."

6 Then I heard something like the sound of a great multitude or the sound of rushing water or mighty peals of thunder, as they said:

"Alleluia!
The Lord has established his reign,
[our] God, the almighty.
7*†Let us rejoice and be glad
and give him glory.
For the wedding day of the Lamb has come,
his bride has made herself ready.
8*†She was allowed to wear
a bright, clean linen garment."

(The linen represents the righteous deeds of the holy ones.)
9*† Then the angel said to me, "Write this: Blessed are those who have been called to the wedding feast of the Lamb." And he said to me, "These words are true; they come from God." 10*† I fell at his feet to worship him. But he said to me, "Don't! I am a fellow servant of yours and of your brothers who bear witness to Jesus. Worship God. Witness to Jesus is the spirit of prophecy."

The King of Kings

11*† Then I saw the heavens opened, and there was a white horse; its rider was [called] "Faithful and True." He judges and wages war in righteousness. 12*† His eyes were [like] a fiery flame, and on his head were many diadems. He had a name inscribed that no one knows except himself. 13*† He wore a cloak that had been dipped in blood, and his name was called the Word of God. 14* The armies of heaven followed him, mounted on white horses and wearing clean white linen. 15*† Out of his mouth came a sharp sword to strike the nations. He will rule them with an iron rod, and he himself will tread out in the wine press the wine of the fury and wrath of God the almighty. 16* He has a name written on his cloak and on his thigh, "King of kings and Lord of lords."

17† Then I saw an angel standing on the sun. He cried out [in] a loud voice to all the birds flying high overhead, "Come here. Gather for God's great feast, 18* to eat the flesh of kings, the flesh of military officers, and the flesh of warriors, the flesh of horses and of their riders, and the flesh of all, free and slave, small and great." 19 Then I saw the beast and the kings of the earth and their armies gathered to fight against the one riding the horse and against his army. 20*† The beast was caught and with it the false prophet who had performed in its sight the signs by which he led astray those who had accepted the mark of the beast and those who had worshiped its image. The two were thrown alive into the fiery pool burning with sulfur. 21 The rest were killed by the sword that came out of the mouth of the one riding the horse, and all the birds gorged themselves on their flesh.

The Thousand-year Reign

20 1*† Then I saw an angel come down from heaven, holding in his hand the key to the abyss† and a heavy chain. 2*† He seized the dragon, the ancient serpent, which is the Devil or

---

19, 5–10: A victory song follows, sung by the entire church, celebrating the marriage of the Lamb, the union of the Messiah with the community of the elect.

19, 7: *The wedding day of the Lamb:* symbol of God's reign about to begin (21, 1–22, 5); see the note on 10, 7. *His bride:* the church; cf 2 Cor 11, 2; Eph 5, 22–27. Marriage is one of the biblical metaphors used to describe the covenant relationship between God and his people; cf Hos 2, 16–22; Is 54, 5–6; 62, 5; Ez 16, 6–14. Hence, idolatry and apostasy are viewed as adultery and harlotry (Hos 2, 4–15; Ez 16, 15–63); see the note on 14, 4.

19, 8: See the note on 14, 12.

19, 9: *Blessed:* see the note on 1, 3.

19, 10: *The spirit of prophecy:* as the prophets were inspired to proclaim God's word, so the Christian is called to give witness to the Word of God (13) made flesh; cf 1, 2; 6, 9; 12, 17.

19, 11–16: Symbolic description of the exalted Christ (cf 1, 13–16) who together with the armies of heaven overcomes the beast and its followers; cf 17, 14.

19, 12: *A name:* in Semitic thought, the name conveyed the reality of the person; cf Mt 11, 27; Lk 10, 22.

19, 13: *Had been dipped in:* other Greek manuscripts and versions read "had been sprinkled with"; cf v 15. *The Word of God:* Christ is the revelation of the Father; cf Jn 1, 1.14; 1 Jn 2, 14.

19, 15: The treading of the wine press is a prophetic symbol used to describe the destruction of God's enemies; cf Is 63, 1–6; Jl 4, 13.

19, 17–21: The certainty of Christ's victory is proclaimed by an angel, followed by a reference to the mustering of enemy forces and a fearsome description of their annihilation. The gruesome imagery is borrowed from Ez 39, 4.17–20.

19, 20: *Beast . . . false prophet:* see the notes on ch 13. *The fiery pool . . . sulfur:* symbol of God's punishment (14, 10; 20, 10.14–15), different from the abyss; see the note on 9, 1.

20, 1–6: Like the other numerical values in this book, the thousand years are not to be taken literally; they symbolize the long period of time between the chaining up of Satan (a symbol for Christ's resurrection-victory over death and the forces of evil) and the end of the world. During this time God's people share in the glorious reign of God that is present to them by virtue of their baptismal victory over death and sin; cf Rom 6, 1–8; Jn 5, 24–25; 16, 33; 1 Jn 3, 14; Eph 2, 1.

20, 1: *Abyss:* see the note on 9, 1.

20, 2: *Dragon . . . serpent . . . Satan:* see the notes on 12, 3.9.10.15.

19, 5: Rv 11, 18; Ps 115, 13.
19, 7: Mt 22, 9; Eph 5, 27.
19, 8: Rv 15, 6; Is 61, 10; Mt 22, 11–12.
19, 9: Mt 8, 11; Lk 14, 15.
19, 11: Is 11, 4.
19, 12: Rv 1, 14–16; 2, 18 / Lk 10, 22.
19, 13: Is 63, 1 / Jn 1, 1.
19, 14: Rv 15, 6; 19, 8.
19, 15: Rv 14, 20; Is 63, 3.
19, 16: Rv 17, 14; 2 Mc 13, 4.
19, 18: Ez 39, 17–20.
20, 2: Gn 3, 1.
20, 20: Rv 14, 10.
20, 1: Rv 9, 1.

Satan, and tied it up for a thousand years ³ and threw it into the abyss, which he locked over it and sealed, so that it could no longer lead the nations astray until the thousand years are completed. After this, it is to be released for a short time.

20, 2

⁴*† Then I saw thrones; those who sat on them were entrusted with judgment. I also saw the souls of those who had been beheaded for their witness to Jesus and for the word of God, and who had not worshiped the beast or its image nor had accepted its mark on their foreheads or hands. They came to life and they reigned with Christ for a thousand years. ⁵ The rest of the dead did not come to life until the thousand years were over. This is the first resurrection. ⁶† Blessed and holy is the one who shares in the first resurrection. The second death has no power over these; they will be priests of God and of Christ, and they will reign with him for [the] thousand years.

⁷† When the thousand years are completed, Satan will be released from his prison. ⁸*† He will go out to deceive the nations at the four corners of the earth, Gog and Magog, to gather them for battle; their number is like the sand of the sea. ⁹*† They invaded the breadth of the earth and surrounded the camp of the holy ones and the beloved city. But fire came down from heaven and consumed them. ¹⁰ The Devil who had led them astray was thrown into the pool of fire and sulfur, where the beast and the false prophet were. There they will be tormented day and night forever and ever.

The Large White Throne

¹¹*† Next I saw a large white throne and the one who was sitting on it. The earth and the sky fled from his presence and there was no place for them. ¹²*† I saw the dead, the great and the lowly, standing before the throne, and scrolls were opened. Then another scroll was opened, the book of life. The dead were judged according to their deeds, by what was written in the scrolls. ¹³† The sea gave up its dead; then Death and Hades gave up their dead. All the dead were judged according to their deeds. ¹⁴*† Then Death and Hades were thrown into the pool of fire. (This pool of fire is the second death.) ¹⁵ Anyone whose name was not found written in the book of life was thrown into the pool of fire.

VI: The New Creation†

The New Heaven and the New Earth

21 ¹* Then I saw a new heaven and a new earth. The former heaven and the former earth had passed away, and the sea was no more.† ²*† I also saw the holy city, a new Jerusalem, coming down out of heaven from God, prepared as a bride adorned for her husband. ³* I heard a loud voice from the throne saying, "Behold, God's dwelling is with the human race. He will dwell with them and they will be his people† and God himself will always be with them [as their God].† ⁴* He will wipe every tear from their eyes, and there shall be no more death or mourning, wailing or pain, [for] the old order has passed away."

⁵*† The one who sat on the throne said, "Behold, I make all things new." Then he said, "Write these

† 20, 4: *Beast . . . mark:* see ch 13 and its notes.
  20, 6: *Blessed:* see the note on 1, 3. *Second death:* see the note on 2, 11. *Priests:* as in 1, 6; 5, 10; cf 1 Pt 2, 9.
  20, 7–10: A description of the symbolic battle to take place when Satan is released at the end of time, when the thousand years are over; see the note on vv 1–6.
  20, 8: *Gog and Magog:* symbols of all pagan nations; the names are taken from Ez 38, 1—39, 20.
  20, 9: *The breadth of the earth:* Palestine. *The beloved city:* Jerusalem; see the note on 14, 1.
  20, 11–15: A description of the final judgment. After the intermediate reign of Christ, all the dead are raised and judged, thus inaugurating the new age.
  20, 12: *The book of life:* see the note on 3, 5. *Judged . . . scrolls:* see the note on 14, 12.
  20, 13: *Hades:* the netherworld; see the note on 1, 18.
  20, 14: *Second death:* see the note on 2, 11.

21, 1—22, 5: A description of God's eternal kingdom in heaven under the symbols of a new heaven and a new earth; cf Is 65, 17–25; 66, 22; Mt 19, 28.
  21, 1: *Sea . . . no more:* because as home of the dragon it was doomed to disappear; cf Jb 7, 12.
  21, 2: *New Jerusalem . . . bride:* symbol of the church (Gal 4, 26); see the note on 19, 7.
  21, 3: *People:* other ancient manuscripts read a plural, "peoples."
  21, 3–4: Language taken from Ez 37, 27; Is 25, 8; 35, 10; cf 7, 17.
  21, 5: *The one . . . on the throne:* God himself; cf 4, 1–11.

20, 4: Mt 19, 28.
20, 8: Ez 38, 2.9.16.
20, 9: Ez 38, 22.
20, 11: 2 Pt 3, 7.10.12.
20, 12: Rom 2, 6.
20, 14: 1 Cor 15, 26.54–55.

21, 1: Is 65, 17; 66, 22; Rom 8, 19–23; 2 Pt 3, 13.
21, 2: Rv 19, 7–9.
21, 3: Ez 37, 27.
21, 4: Rv 7, 17; Is 25, 8; 35, 10.
21, 5: Is 43, 19; 2 Cor 5, 17.

R
V

words down, for they are trustworthy and true." [6]*† He said to me, "They are accomplished. I [am] the Alpha and the Omega, the beginning and the end. To the thirsty I will give a gift from the spring of life-giving water. [7]*† The victor will inherit these gifts, and I shall be his God, and he will be my son. [8]*† But as for cowards, the unfaithful, the depraved, murderers, the unchaste, sorcerers, idol-worshipers, and deceivers of every sort, their lot is in the burning pool of fire and sulfur, which is the second death."

The New Jerusalem†

[9] One of the seven angels who held the seven bowls filled with the seven last plagues came and said to me, "Come here. I will show you the bride, the wife of the Lamb."† [10]* He took me in spirit to a great, high mountain and showed me the holy city Jerusalem coming down out of heaven from God. [11]* It gleamed with the splendor of God. Its radiance was like that of a precious stone, like jasper, clear as crystal. [12] It had a massive, high wall, with twelve gates where twelve angels were stationed and on which names were inscribed, [the names] of the twelve tribes of the Israelites. [13]* There were three gates facing east, three north, three south, and three west. [14]*† The wall of the city had twelve courses of stones as its foundation, on which were inscribed the twelve names of the twelve apostles of the Lamb.

[15]† The one who spoke to me held a gold measuring rod to measure the city, its gates, and its wall. [16]† The city was square, its length the same as [also] its width. He measured the city with the rod and

The New Jerusalem   LIVE IT!

The last three chapters of Revelation contain John's visions of the Reign of God, the end of history, and eternal life. In chapter 20, Satan is alive but has limited power. This is symbolized by the dragon's thousand-year imprisonment, during which the martyrs reign with Christ. The thousand-year reign has been interpreted in many different ways over the centuries, but no one knows its true significance. At the end of the thousand years, Satan is defeated, and Christ sits in final judgment over all the dead.

In chapter 21, John describes a new heaven and a new earth. The Bible begins in Genesis with the story of the creation of a world in which everything is good. It ends in Revelation with a new creation where God's goodness again overflows. A holy city, the new Jerusalem, comes down out of heaven. The new Jerusalem is described as a beautiful bride who is preparing to marry Jesus Christ. John tells his Christian readers that they should look forward to the time of this new city with joy, because when it comes, God and Christ will live in their midst. The whole city will be God's temple. The sun will always shine, a river of living water will flow from God's throne, and the trees will produce fruit year-round. The new Jerusalem is a symbol for the new world that God will establish when evil is destroyed and suffering is banished.

These visions helped Christians at the end of the first century to maintain their hope by focusing on the glorious victory of God in history. They can also help us to renew our commitment to Christ and keep our hope alive, especially when we are misunderstood or harassed because of our faith.

▶ Rv 20, 1—22, 5

†
21, 6: *They are accomplished:* God's reign has already begun; see the note on 20, 1–6. *Alpha . . . Omega:* see the note on 1, 8. *Life-giving water:* see the note on 7, 17.

21, 7: *The victor:* over the forces of evil; see the conclusions of the seven letters (2, 7.11.17.26; 3, 5.12.21). *He will be my son:* the victorious Christian enjoys divine affiliation by adoption (Gal 4, 4–7; Rom 8, 14–17); see the note on 2, 26–28.

21, 8: *Cowards:* their conviction is so weak that they deny Christ in time of trial and become traitors. *Second death:* see the note on 2, 11.

21, 9—22, 5: Symbolic descriptions of the new Jerusalem, the church. Most of the images are borrowed from Ez 40–48.

21, 9: *The bride, the wife of the Lamb:* the church (2), the new Jerusalem (10); cf 2 Cor 11, 2.

21, 14: *Courses of stones . . . apostles:* literally, "twelve foundations"; cf Eph 2, 19–20.

21, 15–17: The city is shaped like a gigantic cube, a symbol of perfection (cf 1 Kgs 6, 19–20). The measurements of the city and its wall are multiples of the symbolic number twelve; see the note on 7, 4–9.

21, 16: *Fifteen hundred miles:* literally, twelve thousand stades, about 12,000 furlongs (see the note on 14, 20); the number is symbolic: twelve (the apostles as leaders of the new Israel) multiplied by 1,000 (the immensity of Christians); cf Introduction. *In length and width and height:* literally, "its length and width and height are the same."

*
21, 6: Rv 22, 17; Ps 36, 8–9; Is 55, 1.
21, 7: 2 Sm 7, 14.
21, 8: Rv 22, 15; Rom 1, 29–32.
21, 10: Ez 40, 2.
21, 11: Heb 11, 10.
21, 13: Ez 48, 31–35.
21, 14: Eph 2, 20.

found it fifteen hundred miles in length and width and height. [17]† He also measured its wall: one hundred and forty-four cubits according to the standard unit of measurement the angel used. [18]† The wall was constructed of jasper, while the city was pure gold, clear as glass. [19]* The foundations of the city wall were decorated with every precious stone; the first course of stones was jasper, the second sapphire, the third chalcedony, the fourth emerald, [20] the fifth sardonyx, the sixth carnelian, the seventh chrysolite, the eighth beryl, the ninth topaz, the tenth chrysoprase, the eleventh hyacinth, and the twelfth amethyst. [21] The twelve gates were twelve pearls, each of the gates made from a single pearl; and the street of the city was of pure gold, transparent as glass.

[22]*† I saw no temple in the city, for its temple is the Lord God almighty and the Lamb. [23]*† The city had no need of sun or moon to shine on it, for the glory of God gave it light, and its lamp was the Lamb. [24]*† The nations will walk by its light, and to it the kings of the earth will bring their treasure. [25] During the day its gates will never be shut, and there will be no night there. [26] The treasure and wealth of the nations will be brought there, [27]* but nothing unclean will enter it, nor any[one] who does abominable things or tells lies. Only those will enter whose names are written in the Lamb's book of life.

22 [1]*† Then the angel showed me the river of life-giving water, sparkling like crystal, flowing from the throne of God and of the Lamb [2]† down the middle of its street. On either side of the river grew the tree of life that produces fruit twelve times a year, once each month; the leaves of the trees serve as medicine for the nations. [3] Nothing accursed will be found there anymore. The throne of God and of the Lamb will be in it, and his servants will worship him. [4]† They will look upon his face, and his name will be on their foreheads. [5]* Night will be no more, nor will they need light from lamp or sun, for the Lord God shall give them light, and they shall reign forever and ever.

VII: Epilogue

[6]*† And he said to me, "These words are trustworthy and true, and the Lord, the God of prophetic spirits, sent his angel to show his servants what

Come, Lord Jesus!

Most young children want immediate gratification. Waiting for Christmas or a birthday is nearly impossible. Saving a piece of candy for after dinner is downright torture. And a long trip in a car produces the familiar and persistent question Are we there yet?

The Bible tells us that Jesus will return. In the creed, Christians proclaim, "He will come again in glory to judge the living and the dead, / and his kingdom will have no end" (Sacramentary, p. 368). When will this happen? Like impatient children, some people have tried to predict the Lord's Second Coming. "But of that day and hour no one knows, . . . but the Father alone" (Mt 24, 36).

Can we say, with John, "Amen! Come, Lord Jesus!" (Rv 22, 20) and really hope that Jesus will come today? We may hesitate, wanting to hang on to the life we know here and now. Yet, the coming of Christ will be the most glorious event imaginable for those who have put their trust in God. So keep preparing and praying for the return of Christ!

▶ **Rv 22, 7–21**

---

† **21, 17:** *One hundred and forty-four cubits:* the cubit was about eighteen inches in length. *Standard unit of measurement the angel used:* literally, "by a human measure, i.e., an angel's."

21, 18–21: The gold and precious gems symbolize the beauty and excellence of the church; cf Ex 28, 15–21; Tb 13, 16–17; Is 54, 11–12.

21, 22: Christ is present throughout the church; hence, no temple is needed as an earthly dwelling for God; cf Mt 18, 20; 28, 20; Jn 4, 21.

21, 23: *Lamp . . . Lamb:* cf Jn 8, 12.

21, 24–27: All men and women of good will are welcome in the church; cf Is 60, 1.3.5.11. *The . . . book of life:* see the note on 3, 5.

22, 1.17: *Life-giving water:* see the note on 7, 17.

22, 2: *The tree of life:* cf v 14; see the note on 2, 7. *Fruit . . . medicine:* cf Ez 47, 12.

22, 4: *Look upon his face:* cf Mt 5, 8; 1 Cor 13, 12; 1 Jn 3, 2.

22, 6–21: The book ends with an epilogue consisting of a series of warnings and exhortations and forming an inclusion with the prologue by resuming its themes and expressions; see the note on 1, 1–3.

21, 19: Is 54, 11–12.	**21, 27:** Is 35, 8; 52, 1; Zec 13,
21, 22: Jn 2, 19–20.	2 / Rv 3, 5; 20, 12.
21, 23: Is 60, 1–2.19–20.	**22, 1:** Ez 47, 1–12.
21, 24: Is 60, 11.	**22, 5:** Is 60, 20.
	22, 6: Rv 1, 1.

must happen soon." ⁷* "Behold, I am coming soon."† Blessed† is the one who keeps the prophetic message of this book.

⁸ It is I, John, who heard and saw these things, and when I heard and saw them I fell down to worship at the feet of the angel who showed them to me. ⁹* But he said to me, "Don't! I am a fellow servant of yours and of your brothers the prophets and of those who keep the message of this book. Worship God."

¹⁰† Then he said to me, "Do not seal up the prophetic words of this book, for the appointed time is near. ¹¹ Let the wicked still act wickedly, and the filthy still be filthy. The righteous must still do right, and the holy still be holy."

¹²* "Behold, I am coming soon. I bring with me the recompense I will give to each according to his deeds. ¹³*† I am the Alpha and the Omega, the first and the last, the beginning and the end."

¹⁴*† Blessed are they who wash their robes so as to have the right to the tree of life and enter the city through its gates. ¹⁵* Outside are the dogs, the sorcerers, the unchaste, the murderers, the idol-worshipers, and all who love and practice deceit.

¹⁶*† "I, Jesus, sent my angel to give you this testimony for the churches. I am the root and offspring of David, the bright morning star."

¹⁷*† The Spirit and the bride say, "Come." Let the hearer say, "Come." Let the one who thirsts come forward, and the one who wants it receive the gift of life-giving water.

¹⁸ I warn everyone who hears the prophetic words in this book: if anyone adds to them, God will add to him the plagues described in this book, ¹⁹* and if anyone takes away from the words in this prophetic book, God will take away his share in the tree of life

and in the holy city described in this book.

²⁰*† The one who gives this testimony says, "Yes, I am coming soon." Amen! Come, Lord Jesus!

²¹ The grace of the Lord Jesus be with all.

In Hebrew, *amen* means "so be it" or "yes, it is true." So saying "Amen" in your prayers is the same as saying, "Yes, I believe!" It is an appropriate way to conclude the last book of the Bible, and it should not be said lightly. Are you able to say "Amen" to all that you have read, prayed, and reflected on in this Bible? Have the stories and the poems, the teachings and the parables, the songs and the sayings led you to believe in a God who is with you every step of your journey, every minute of the day and night?

Each of us is invited to join the great Amen, to say: "Yes, I believe in a loving God who is father and mother to us all! Yes, I believe in God's Son, Jesus Christ, who is my Lord and Savior! Yes, I believe in the Holy Spirit, who will help me continue Jesus' mission of justice, reconciliation, and love!" But these words remain just words until people with courage and conviction take the risk to live them out in their own corner of the world. Take the risk; heaven awaits you! Amen!

▶ **Rv 22, 20**

---

†

22, 7.12.20: *I am coming soon:* Christ is the speaker; see the note on 1, 3.

22, 7.14: *Blessed:* see the note on 1, 3.
22, 10: *The appointed time:* see the note on 1, 3.
22, 13: Christ applies to himself words used by God in 1, 8.
22, 14: *The city:* heavenly Jerusalem; see the note on 21, 2.
22, 16: *The root . . . of David:* see the note on 5, 5. *Morning star:* see the note on 2, 26–28.
22, 17: *Bride:* the church; see the note on 21, 2.
22, 20: *Come, Lord Jesus:* a liturgical refrain, similar to the Aramaic expression *Marana tha*—"Our Lord, come!"—in 1 Cor 16, 22;

cf the note there. It was a prayer for the coming of Christ in glory at the parousia; see the note on 1, 3.

22, 7: Rv 22, 12.20 / Rv 1, 3.	**22, 16:** Rv 1, 1.11–12; 22, 6 / Rv 2, 28.
22, 9: Rv 19, 10.	**22, 17:** Rv 21, 6; Is 55, 1.
22, 12: Rv 22, 7.20 / Ps 62, 12; 2 Tm 4, 14.	**22, 19:** Dt 4, 2.
22, 13: Rv 1, 8; 21, 6; Is 41, 4; 44, 6.	**22, 20:** Rv 22, 7.12 / Acts 3, 20–21; 1 Cor 15, 23; 16, 22.
22, 14: Rv 7, 14–15; 22, 2.	
22, 15: Rv 21, 8; Rom 1, 29–32.	

Where Do I Find It?

EVENTS, PEOPLE, AND TEACHINGS

OLD TESTAMENT STORIES

These stories are listed in the order in which they first appear in the Bible.

Creation, *Gn, chs 1–2*
original sin and its punishment, *Gn, ch 3*
Cain and Abel, *Gn 4, 1–16*
Noah and the Great Flood, *Gn, chs 6–9*
God's covenant with Abraham,
   Gn 17, 1–18, 15
God's command to sacrifice Isaac,
   Gn 22, 1–19
Isaac's blessing of Jacob, *Gn 27, 1–29*
Jacob's dream, *Gn 28, 10–22*
Joseph and his brothers, *Gn, chs 37–46*
birth and youth of Moses, *Ex 2, 1–10*
Moses at the burning bush, *Ex 3, 1–12*
plagues on Egypt, *Ex, chs 7–12*
Passover and the Exodus, *Ex, chs 12–14*
Ten Commandments, *Ex 20, 1–17*
destruction of Jericho, *Jos 5, 13—6, 27*
Gideon and the sign of the fleece,
   Jgs 6, 36–40
Samson, *Jgs, chs 13–16*
Samuel's birth and calling, *1 Sm, chs 1–3*
David and Goliath, *1 Sm, ch 17*
David and Bathsheba, *2 Sm, ch 11*
Solomon's wisdom, *1 Kgs, ch 3*
Elijah's triumph over the priests of Baal,
   1 Kgs 18, 21–40
miracles of Elisha, *2 Kgs 4, 1—6, 23*
Return from exile, *Ezr, ch 1*
battles of Judas Maccabeus, *1 Mc, chs 3–5*
Ezekiel and the valley of dry bones,
   Ez 37, 1–14
Daniel, *Dn, chs 1–6*
Jonah and the Ninevites, *Jon, chs 1–3*

NEW TESTAMENT STORIES

These stories are listed in the order in which they first appear in the Bible.

birth of Jesus, *Mt 1, 18—2, 12; Lk, chs 1–2*
baptism of Jesus, *Mt 3, 13–17; Mk 1, 9–11;*
   Lk 3, 21–22
temptation of Jesus, *Mt 4, 1–11; Mk 1, 12–13;*
   Lk 4, 1–13
Peter's declaration about Jesus, *Mt 16, 13–20;*
   Mk 8, 27–30; Lk 9, 18–20
Transfiguration of Jesus, *Mt 17, 1–13;*
   Mk 9, 2–13; Lk 9, 28–36
Jesus' triumphal entry into Jerusalem,
   Mt 21, 1–11; Mk 11, 1–11; Lk 19, 28–40;
   Jn 12, 12–19
Jesus in the Temple, *Mt 21, 12–17;*
   Mk 11, 15–19; Lk 19, 45–48; Jn 2, 13–17
Judas's betrayal of Jesus, *Mt 26, 14–16.47–56;*
   Mk 14, 10–11.43–52; Lk 22, 1–53;
   Jn 13, 21–30; Jn 18, 1–5
Last Supper, *Mt 26, 17–30; Mk 14, 12–26;*
   Lk 22, 7–38; 1 Cor 11, 23–26
Jesus at Gethsemane, *Mt 26, 36–56;*
   Mk 14, 32–52; Lk 22, 39–53
Peter's denial of Christ, *Mt 26, 69–75;*
   Mk 14, 66–72; Lk 22, 54–62; Jn 18,
   15–18.25–27
Crucifixion, *Mt 27, 32–56; Mk 15, 21–41;*
   Lk 23, 26–49; Jn 19, 16–30
Resurrection and appearances, *Mt, ch 28;*
   Mk, ch 16; Lk, ch 24; Jn, chs 20–21;
   Acts 1, 1–11
Jesus washing his disciples' feet, *Jn 13, 1–17*
Holy Spirit at Pentecost, *Acts 2, 1–41*
stoning of Stephen, *Acts, chs 6–7*
conversion of Saul, *Acts 9, 1–30*
Peter's escape from prison, *Acts 12, 1–19*
Paul and Silas's escape from prison,
   Acts 16, 16–40
Paul's journey to Rome for his trial,
   Acts, chs 27–28

PEOPLE

Each person entry is followed by a page number or numbers that lead you to an "Introducing . . ." article or other articles in which the person is featured.

Abraham, *20, 25, 27, 28, 32, 35*
Barnabas, *1448*
Beloved Disciple, *1407*
David, *314, 315, 332, 340, 341*
Elijah, *381, 389*
Elisha, *381*
Ezekiel, *1050*
First Isaiah, *899*
Holy Family, *1214*
Jacob, *38, 39, 41, 42, 46, 47*
Jeremiah, *966, 980*
John the Baptist, *1217, 1325*
Joseph, *52*
Junia, *1501*
Lady Wisdom, *760, 817*
Lydia, *1456*
Mary, mother of Jesus, *225, 1317, 1319, 1419, 1698*
Mary Magdalene, *1420*
Moses, *72, 77, 92, 93, 108, 236*
Nicodemus, *1382*
Paul, *1441, 1444, 1450, 1458, 1464, 1469, 1470, 1475, 1532, 1553, 1575*
Peter, *1245, 1272, 1310, 1331, 1407, 1423*
Phoebe, *1501*
Priscilla, *1456*
Samson, *281, 284*
Sarah, *20, 27*
Satan, *612, 1291, 1697, 1706*
Solomon, *360, 363, 373, 446*
Stephen, *1438, 1439*

PRAYERS

These prayers are listed in the order in which they first appear in the Bible.

The Lord bless you and keep you, *Nm 6, 24–27*
Hannah's prayer, *1 Sm 2, 1–10*
Speak, Lord, for your servant is listening, *1 Sm 3, 9–10*
Blessed be the Lord, *1 Kgs 8, 56–61*
Tobit's thanksgiving, *Tb, ch 13*
Judith's hymn of praise, *Jdt 16, 1–17*

The Lord is my shepherd, *Ps 23*
Have mercy on me, O God, *Ps 51*
Lord, you have probed me, you know me, *Ps 139*
Holy, Holy, Holy (Hosanna), *Is 6, 3; Mt 21, 9; Mk 11, 9–10; Lk 19, 38; Jn 12, 13; Rv 4, 8*
Lord's Prayer, *Mt 6, 9–15; Lk 11, 2–4*
Lord, I am not worthy, *Mt 8, 8*
Jesus' prayer for deliverance, *Mt 26, 39; Mk 14, 36; Lk 22, 42*
Mary's song of praise, *Lk 1, 46–55*
Zechariah's prophecy, *Lk 1, 68–79*
Glory to God in the highest, *Lk 2, 14*
Simeon's prayer, *Lk 2, 29–32*
God, be merciful to me, a sinner!, *Lk 18, 13*
Lamb of God, *Jn 1, 29*
Jesus' prayer for his disciples, *Jn, ch 17*
Paul's prayer for the Ephesians, *Eph 3, 14–21*
Amen, *1 Pt 5, 11; Jude, v 25; Rv 1, 6–7; 3, 14*

MIRACLES OF JESUS

These miracle stories are listed in the order in which they first appear in the Bible.

Healing Individuals

leper, *Mt 8, 1–4; Mk 1, 40–45; Lk 5, 12–16*
centurion's servant, *Mt 8, 5–13; Lk 7, 1–10*
many at Peter's house, *Mt 8, 14–17; Mk 1, 29–34; Lk 4, 38–41*
Gadarene (Gerasene) demoniacs, *Mt 8, 28–34; Mk 5, 1–20; Lk 8, 26–39*
paralytic, *Mt 9, 1–8; Mk 2, 1–12; Lk 5, 17–26*
woman with bleeding, *Mt 9, 20–22; Mk 5, 25–34; Lk 8, 43–48*
two blind men, *Mt 9, 27–31*
mute man, *Mt 9, 32–34*
man with a withered hand, *Mt 12, 9–13; Mk 3, 1–5; Lk 6, 6–11*
blind, mute, and possessed man, *Mt 12, 22*
Canaanite woman's daughter, *Mt 15, 21–28; Mk 7, 24–30*
boy with a demon, *Mt 17, 14–21; Mk 9, 14–29; Lk 9, 37–43*
blind Bartimaeus, *Mt 20, 29–34; Mk 10, 46–52; Lk 18, 35–43*
man with an unclean spirit, *Mk 1, 21–28; Lk 4, 31–37*
deaf man, *Mk 7, 31–37*
blind man at Bethsaida, *Mk 8, 22–26*
crippled woman, *Lk 13, 11–13*

MIRACLES OF JESUS (continued)

man with dropsy, *Lk 14, 1–4*
ten lepers, *Lk 17, 11–19*
high priest's servant, *Lk 22, 50–51*
official's son, *Jn 4, 46–54*
man at the pool of Bethzatha, *Jn 5, 1–9*

Controlling Nature

stilling the storm, *Mt 8, 23–27; Mk 4, 35–41;*
   Lk 8, 22–25
feeding five thousand, *Mt 14, 13–21;*
   Mk 6, 30–44; Lk 9, 10–17; Jn 6, 1–14
walking on water, *Mt 14, 22–33; Mk 6, 45–52;*
   Jn 6, 16–21
feeding four thousand, *Mt 15, 32–39;*
   Mk 8, 1–10
fish with a coin, *Mt 17, 24–27*
fig tree withers, *Mt 21, 18–22;*
   Mk 11, 12–14.20–25
huge catch of fish, *Lk 5, 1–11; Jn 21, 1–11*
turning water into wine, *Jn 2, 1–11*

Raising the Dead

Jairus's daughter, *Mt 9, 18–19.23–26;*
   Mk 5, 21–24.35–43; Lk 8, 40–42.49–56
widow's son at Nain, *Lk 7, 11–17*
Lazarus, *Jn 11, 1–44*

PARABLES OF JESUS

These parables are listed in alphabetical order.

barren fig tree, *Lk 13, 6–9*
canceled debts, *Lk 7, 41–43*
cost of discipleship, *Lk 14, 25–33*
dishonest manager, *Lk 16, 1–8*
faithful or unfaithful slave, *Mt 24, 45–51;*
   Lk 12, 42–48
fig tree, *Mt 24, 32–35; Mk 13, 28–31;*
   Lk 21, 29–33
good Samaritan, *Lk 10, 30–37*
great dinner, *Lk 14, 16–24*
growing seed, *Mk 4, 26–29*
hidden treasure and pearl, *Mt 13, 44–46*
honor at a banquet, *Lk 14, 7–14*
laborers in the vineyard, *Mt 20, 1–16*
light of the world, *Mt 5, 14–16*
lost coin, *Lk 15, 8–10*
lost sheep, *Mt 18, 12–14; Lk 15, 3–7*
mustard seed, *Mt 13, 31–32; Mk 4, 30–32;*
   Lk 13, 18–19
net, *Mt 13, 47–50*

new wine in old wineskins, *Mt 9, 16–17;*
   Mk 2, 21–22; Lk 5, 36–39
persistent friend, *Lk 11, 5–8*
persistent widow, *Lk 18, 2–8*
Pharisee and the tax collector, *Lk 18, 10–14*
prodigal son, *Lk 15, 11–32*
rich fool, *Lk 12, 16–21*
rich man and Lazarus, *Lk 16, 19–31*
salt, *Mt 5, 13; Mk 9, 50; Lk 14, 34–35*
sheep and the goats, *Mt 25, 31–46*
sower, *Mt 13, 3–8.18–23; Mk 4, 3–9.14–20;*
   Lk 8, 5–8.11–15
talents, *Mt 25, 14–30*
ten virgins, *Mt 25, 1–13*
ten coins, *Lk 19, 11–27*
two sons, *Mt 21, 28–31*
unforgiving servant, *Mt 18, 23–35*
watchful slaves, *Lk 12, 35–40*
wedding banquet, *Mt 22, 1–14*
weeds among the wheat, *Mt 13, 24–30.36–43*
wicked tenants, *Mt 21, 33–44; Mk 12, 1–12;*
   Lk 20, 9–18
wise and foolish builders, *Mt 7, 24–27;*
   Lk 6, 47–49
worthless slaves, *Lk 17, 7–10*
yeast, *Mt 13, 33; Lk 13, 20–21*

TEACHINGS OF JESUS

These teachings are listed in alphabetical order.

Beatitudes, *Mt 5, 1–12; Lk 6, 20–26*
born from above, *Jn 3, 1–21*
bread of life, *Jn 6, 25–59*
children, *Mk 10, 13–16*
discipleship, *Lk 14, 25–33*
do not worry, *Mt 6, 19–21.25–34; Lk 12, 22–34*
golden rule, *Mt 7, 12; Lk 6, 31*
good shepherd, *Jn 10, 1–18*
greatest commandment, *Mt 22, 34–40;*
   Mk 12, 28–34; Lk 10, 25–28
living water, *Jn 4, 1–26*
Lord's Prayer, *Mt 6, 9–13; Lk 11, 2–4*
mission of the twelve Apostles, *Mt 10, 1–15*
paying taxes, *Mt 22, 15–22; Mk 12, 13–17;*
   Lk 20, 20–26
rich young man, *Mt 19, 16–30; Mk 10, 17–31;*
   Lk 18, 18–30
Sermon on the Mount, *Mt, chs 5–7*
Sermon on the Plain, *Lk 6, 17–49*
vine and branches, *Jn 15, 1–17*
"the way, the truth, and the life," *Jn 14, 1–14*
"where two or three are gathered," *Mt 18, 20*

SACRAMENT CONNECTIONS

These are some passages that can help us understand God's action in the sacraments. It is not meant to be a complete list of all the biblical connections for all seven sacraments.

BAPTISM

Isa 43, 1
Mt 3, 13–17; 28, 19–20
Mk 1, 9–11
Lk 3, 21–22
Jn 1, 29–34; 3, 5
Acts 2, 37–41
Rom 6, 3–4

CONFIRMATION

Is 11, 2; 61, 1
Mt 3, 13–17
Jn 1, 33–34; 14, 15–31;
    16, 5–15
Acts 2, 1–4; 8, 14–17
2 Cor 1, 21–22
Gal 5, 22–23

EUCHARIST

Gn 14, 17–20
Ex 12, 1–28; 24, 1–8
Mt 14, 13–21; 26, 17–29
Mk 6, 30–44; 14, 12–25
Lk 9, 10–17; 22, 7–20;
    24, 13–35
Jn 6, 1–13.25–59
1 Cor 11, 17–34

RECONCILIATION (PENANCE)

Gn 45, 1–15
Jl 2, 12–13
Mt 5, 21–26.38–48;
    18, 23–35
Mk 2, 1–12
Lk 15, 11–32
Jn 20, 19–22
Rom, ch 6

ANOINTING

Ps 23
Mk 6, 7–13
Lk 13, 10–13
2 Tm 2, 11–12
Jas 5, 14–16

HOLY ORDERS

Dt 18, 1–5
Ps 110, 1–4
Mt 10, 1–4
Mk 3, 14–19
Lk 6, 12–16
Jn 13, 1–14
Rom 12, 1–8
1 Tm 3, 1–13
Ti 1, 5–9
Heb 4, 14—5, 10

MARRIAGE

Gn 2, 18–25
Song 8, 6–7
Mt 19, 1–12
Mk 10, 2–12
Jn 2, 1–11
1 Cor, ch 13
Eph 5, 21–33
1 Jn 4, 7–16

LIFE AND FAITH ISSUES ❓

Here are some passages that can give you comfort or direction. There are many other passages in the Bible that also address these and other topics.

ANGER
Mt 5, 21–24
Jn 2, 13–17
Eph 4, 25–27.31–32
Jas 1, 19–21

CALL
Gn 12, 1–9
1 Sm, chs 1–3
Is 6, 1–8
Jer 1, 4–10
Mt 4, 18–22;
    28, 16–20
Mk 1, 16–20
Lk 5, 1–11

COMMITMENT
Nm 30, 2–3
Dt 6, 1–9; 11, 8–9
Jos 24, 14–15
Mk 8, 34–38

COURAGE
Jos 1, 9
1 Sm, ch 17
Ps 31

DISCIPLESHIP
Mk 8, 34–38
Lk 9, 1–6
Jn 4, 1–42

FAMILY
Gn 4, 9; 12, 10–20
Sir 3, 1–16
Eph 5, 21—6, 4

FEAR
Ps 27, 91
Zep 3, 14–20
Mt 14, 22–33
Mk 4, 35–41
Lk 22, 54–62

FORGIVENESS
Gn 33, 1–17
Ps 51
Mt 18, 21–35
Lk 6, 27–36; 23, 34
Jn 8, 2–11

FRIENDSHIP
Ru 1, 1–19
1 Sm, ch 20
Sir 6, 5–17
Jn 15, 12–17

FRIENDSHIP WITH GOD
Gn 28, 10–22
Mi 6, 8
Jn 15, 12–17

GIVING
2 Chr 31, 2–10
Ezr 1, 6–11
Mk 12, 41–44
Lk 21, 1–4

HAPPINESS
Sir 25, 1–11
Lk 12, 22–34
Phil 4, 4–9

HONESTY WITH GOD
Gn 18, 22–33
Jer 12
Mk 14, 32–42

HOPE
Eccl 3, 1–8
Lam 3, 22–26
Rom 8, 18–30

HYPOCRISY
Mt 6, 1–6; 23, 1–36
Lk 18, 9–14
Jas 1, 22—2, 4

IMAGES OF GOD
Gn 1, 26–27;
    32, 23–33
Ps 23
Jer 18, 1–11

JUDGMENT OF OTHERS
Mt 7, 1–5
Rom 14, 1–12
Gal 3, 26–28

LONELINESS AND ABANDONMENT
Ps 22, 1–12
Mk 15, 33–34
2 Tm 4, 9–18

LOVE
Song 8, 6–7
Mt 5, 43–48
Mk 12, 28–34
1 Cor, ch 13

PEACE
Is 11, 1–9
Mi 4, 1–5
Jn 14, 25–31

PERSISTENCE
Lk 11, 5–8; 18, 1–8

POPULARITY
Mk 9, 33–37
1 Cor 3, 1–9
Phil 2, 1–11

PRESENCE OF GOD
Gn 15, 7
Ex 3, 1–6; 33, 17–23
Mt 18, 20

PROMISES OF GOD
Ex 6, 1–9
Jer 29, 11
Lk 4, 14–30

REPENTANCE
1 Chr 21, 1–17
Jl 2, 12–18
Lk 15, 11–32

RESPONSIBILITY
Sir 15, 11–20
Ez, ch 18

SERVICE
Is 42, 1–7
Mt 20, 20–28;
    25, 31–46
Mk 10, 35–45
Jn 13, 1–17

SEXUALITY
Gn 1, 26–31
Tb 8, 4–9
Song
Eph 5, 1–14
1 Thes 4, 3–8

SUFFERING
Jb 1, 13–21
Ps 22
Mt 5, 1–12
1 Pt 3, 13–18

TEMPTATION
Gn, ch 3
Mt 4, 1–11
Mk 1, 12–13;
    7, 14–23
Lk 4, 1–13

TRUST IN GOD
Ps 62
Is 43, 1–5
Mt 11, 28–30
Mk 10, 46–52

VOCATION (*See* call; discipleship)

WISDOM
2 Chr 1, 7–13
Prv 8, 1–21
Wis, ch 7

ARTICLE SUBJECT INDEX

This subject index is not an index to the Bible itself (sometimes called a concordance). Rather, it is an index to the subjects covered in the various articles in The Catholic Youth Bible. But because most articles are based on a Bible passage, this index will also help you find Bible passages related to these topics.

A

abandonment
1313. See also despair; loneliness

abortion
71, 742, 1001, 1215

Abraham
20, 25, 27, 28, 32, 35

abuse
24, 30

acceptance
1254

addiction
1348, 1517

Advent
927

advertising
790

Advocate
1409

African American articles
87, 206, 208, 365, 530, 689, 693, 803, 1011, 1191, 1246, 1267, 1312, 1328, 1438, 1522, 1542, 1562, 1632

afterlife
797, 1114, 1528. See also Resurrection

agape
1524

aging
799

AIDS
702, 1479

alcohol
534, 868, 1572

altars
248

ancestors
25, 67, 146, 1438

angels
516, 1642

anger
612, 674, 715, 770, 1154, 1381

Anointing, sacrament of
1350

anxiety
798, 1008, 1344, 1349

apocalyptic literature
1108, 1681

apocryphal books
508

Apostles
1272, 1282, 1287, 1289, 1294

Apostles' Creed
1434

ark of the Covenant
114, 117, 1002

arrogance
588

Ash Wednesday
1135, 1222

Asian American articles
65, 73, 91, 117, 146, 443, 512, 593, 721, 792, 840, 953, 1129, 1249, 1335, 1371, 1384, 1406, 1408, 1521, 1535, 1568, 1669

Assyrian Empire
406, 1164

atheism
652

authority
268

awe
73, 656, 664, 772

B

baals
252, 381

Babylon
1026, 1702

Babylonian Exile
414

balance
791

Baptism, sacrament of
1217, 1383, 1485, 1654

Barnabas
1448

Beatitudes
1219, 1333

beauty
803, 1582

beliefs
1434

Beloved Disciple
1407

Benedictus
1320

Bethlehem
1160

betrayal
284, 681, 1310

Bible
vi–vii, xii–xv, 2–3, 215,
238–239, 393, 508, 542,
608–609, 1208–1209, 1327,
1376, 1474–1475, 1478,
1603, 1681. *See also* literary
devices and genres

bishops
See ministry in the church

blessing
161, 371

body of Christ
1496, 1522

boldness
530, 1267

bread and wine
22, 1226, 1390

breath
1084

brothers and sisters
11, 36, 653

C
....

call
900, 937, 965, 1050, 1051,
1199, 1282, 1360, 1639. *See
also* discipleship

Canaan
240, 252

canon
508

caretakers
8, 986

celebration
336, 537, 793, 840. *See also*
praise

childbirth
132

children
745, 840, 986, 1001, 1069,
1215

choices
142, 230, 686, 851, 1044,
1101, 1126, 1382, 1487, 1488,
1543, 1605, 1668, 1675

Christmas
903, 1213, 1321, 1322, 1384.
See also liturgical year

church
1423, 1571, 1589, 1697

circumcision
25, 1454, 1481, 1553

civil disobedience
71, 1257

commitment
188, 756, 1129, 1297, 1359,
1580

communion
See Eucharist, sacrament of

communion of saints
1594

community
1197, 1431, 1454, 1592

compassion of God
30, 702, 890–891, 944, 1394,
1488, 1629

complaining
90, 980

confession
See Reconciliation,
sacrament of

confidence
709, 1044

Confirmation, sacrament of
1217, 1429

conflict
19, 218, 261, 319, 1503, 1505

conscience
1605

consciousness raising
1053

consecration
1226, 1520

contentment
790

contrition
969. *See also* Reconciliation,
sacrament of

conversion
457, 477, 1044, 1105, 1222,
1225, 1360, 1378, 1442,
1444,

cooperation
1246, 1507

corruption
311, 1381

Council of Jerusalem
1441, 1454, 1556

courage
77, 242, 315, 569, 592, 593,
665, 1008, 1452, 1592

covenant
2–3, 8, 14, 16, 20, 23, 25, 38,
56, 1271. *See also* New
Covenant; Sinai Covenant

creation
6, 8, 638, 653, 747, 1582,
1706

creativity
1267

creeds
1434, 1527

crucifixion
1277, 1297, 1416, 1418

cults
1583, 1662

Cultural Connections articles
8, 65, 73, 74, 75, 87, 91, 117,
132, 146, 202, 204, 206, 208,
231, 365, 443, 484, 512, 530,
593, 653, 659, 665, 689, 693,
695, 706, 711, 721, 724, 741,
778, 792, 803, 804, 819, 823,
825, 839, 840, 901, 934, 953,
967, 986, 1011, 1019, 1082,
1117, 1129, 1136, 1178, 1185,
1191, 1213, 1240, 1243, 1246,
1249, 1267, 1277, 1283, 1288,
1305, 1312, 1319, 1322, 1328,
1335, 1361, 1371, 1372, 1384,
1395, 1396, 1406, 1408, 1412,
1419, 1422, 1438, 1447, 1470,
1518, 1521, 1522, 1527, 1535,
1542, 1545, 1562, 1568, 1570,
1571, 1582, 1595, 1596, 1619,
1632, 1653, 1657, 1669, 1698

culture
752, 1044, 1411, 1542, 1606,
1657

D
....

dancing
336

darkness
1153, 1372, 1396

daughters
825

David
314, 315, 332, 340, 341

Day of Atonement
186

deacons
See ministry in the church

death
350, 797, 1484. See also
crucifixion; suffering

death penalty
11

deception
42, 61

demons
1291

despair
658, 765, 1275, 1311, 1373,
1472, 1539

Diaspora
542

disappointment
1272

discernment
632, 754, 1671

disciples
1317, 1613. See also Apostles

discipleship
77, 725, 745, 768, 937, 1218,
1232, 1241, 1255, 1278, 1292,
1294, 1297, 1298, 1301, 1331,
1339, 1352, 1359, 1360, 1386,
1411, 1424, 1436, 1452, 1535,
1587, 1592, 1608, 1615, 1654,
1655, 1708

disobedience
9, 71, 1257

diversity
934, 1398, 1415, 1447, 1470

doubts
644, 965, 1254, 1299, 1324

dreams
56

E
....

Easter
1371, 1416. See also liturgical
year

eating disorders
1540

ecumenism
1498

elders
778, 799

Elijah
381, 389

Elisha
381

embarrassment
See humiliation

Emmanuel (Immanuel)
901, 903, 1213, 1374

encouragement
87, 1448, 1592

end time
1306, 1706

enemies, love of
1221

Epiphany
1213

equality
786, 879, 1559, 1621, 1623

Essenes
606

Eucharist, sacrament of
22, 91, 100, 1197, 1226, 1271,
1308, 1367, 1376, 1390, 1406,
1520, 1521, 1630

evangelization
1279, 1441, 1442, 1458,
1470, 1478, 1493, 1612

evil
14, 1291, 1675, 1695, 1697.
See also Satan

examination of conscience
856, 1480, 1551

Exile
See Babylonian Exile

Exodus
80, 831

Ezekiel
1050

Ezra
478

F

failure
943

faith
20, 32, 393, 494, 519, 612,
646, 652, 907, 1241, 1289,
1294, 1299, 1314, 1319,
1386, 1439, 1472, 1481,
1482, 1490, 1527, 1528,
1557, 1561, 1567, 1613,
1639, 1645, 1647

faith sharing
1432, 1465, 1541, 1613

false prophets
983, 1662

families
146, 721, 785, 839, 840,
1322, 1335, 1514, 1573, 1586

fasting
491

fatalism
1063

fear
204, 242, 772, 907, 943, 1008,
1289, 1311, 1472

festivals (feasts)
84, 112, 146, 186, 550, 560,
711, 1213, 1240, 1249, 1317,
1335, 1392, 1405, 1653. *See
also* individual names of

fidelity
957

fighting
770

fire
23

First Isaiah
899

flood
13, 14, 15

food
84, 91, 130, 512, 1422, 1518

forgiveness
47, 52, 278, 679, 715, 1122,
1221, 1251, 1335, 1353, 1370
See also Reconciliation,
sacrament of

fornication
1511, 1593

foundation, God as life's
353, 1508

freedom
1328, 1438

friendship
294, 319, 765, 843, 846,1009,
1122, 1272, 1284, 1310, 1414,
1463, 1577. *See also* God,
closeness with

fruits of the Spirit
1561, 1654

G

genealogies
67, 420, 1212

generosity
471, 480, 512, 724, 1304,
1305, 1545

genocide
543

Gentiles
1290, 1370, 1442, 1481, 1491

gifts
480, 759, 793, 1034, 1267,
1304, 1352, 1365, 1389,
1412, 1522, 1596

giving, sacrificial
471, 660, 1305, 1365, 1435,
1545

God
641, 642; closeness with, 30,
41, 110, 616, 807, 813, 901,
944, 1255, 1344, 1490; glory
of, 1048, 1692; help of, 30,
659, 734, 743, 835, 1189;
holiness of, 23; name of, 74,
443, 901, 1378; need for, 383;
power of, 656, 664, 1043;
struggling with, 46, 966; will
of, 39, 61, 77, 215, 754, 1154,
1687. *See also* compassion of
God; images of God; presence
of God; Reign of God; trust in
God

gods
14, 252, 381

golden calf
108

Good Friday
658, 1416

goodness
6, 8, 61, 519. *See also* right
living

Good News
1208–1209, 1292, 1442,
1478, 1493

good shepherd
659, 1081, 1399

good works
894, 1564, 1567, 1619, 1639

gospel, **meaning of term**
1209, 1478

gossip
763, 864, 1235, 1648

grace
835, 1484, 1567

gratitude
See thanksgiving

greatness, true
1255

greed
794, 1257, 1348

grief
350, 613, 1001, 1037, 1402,
1463

H

Hail Mary
225, 1317

Hanukkah
560

harassment
24

hard times
835, 1311

healing
350, 726, 873, 1037, 1243,
1284, 1286

heart
813, 1057

helping others
99, 480, 512, 516, 613, 659,
1011, 1268, 1288, 1356, 1676

heroes
569, 883, 1484

Hispanic articles
8, 75, 231, 659, 823, 825,
839, 901, 967, 1117, 1178,
1213, 1277, 1288, 1319, 1361,
1396, 1412, 1419, 1470, 1527,
1545, 1571, 1596, 1657, 1698

holiness
73, 120, 142

Holocaust
543, 1001

Holy Family
1214

Holy Orders, sacrament of
1287

holy places
369, 433, 1090

Holy Spirit
1082, 1084, 1136, 1409, 1412,
1428, 1429, 1430, 1442, 1536

Holy Thursday
1406, 1416

Holy Trinity
161, 1279, 1409, 1414

holy war
156

Holy Week
936, 1416. *See also* liturgical
year

homosexuality
1479

honesty
762, 980

hope
492, 519, 658, 890–891, 932,
951, 1034, 1373, 1539, 1571,
1632, 1695

hopelessness
See despair

hospitality
28, 1642, 1676

humiliation
674, 681

humility
531, 991, 1160, 1178, 1262,
1423, 1538, 1578

humor
27, 1151

hunger
495, 512, 1033

hypocrisy
894, 1144, 1243, 1257

I

idolatry
108, 381, 725, 828, 890–891,
1046, 1517

images of God
6, 8, 353, 535, 659, 664, 736,
808, 817, 820, 933, 944, 957,
959, 1081, 1128, 1166, 1402,
1524, 1585

immigrants
1214

imprisonment
1449

Incarnation
1362, 1629, 1671

injustice
30, 42, 545, 1157, 1257, 1358,
1363

integrity
662, 757, 782, 915, 1556. *See
also* honesty; right living

Islam
35

Israel (kingdom)
358, 375, 397, 406

Israel (people)
67

J

Jacob
38, 39, 41, 42, 46, 47

jealousy
24, 168

Jeremiah
966, 980

Jerusalem
358, 414, 737, 1706

Jesus Christ
84, 100, 1208–1209, 1280,
1331, 1374, 1378, 1394, 1396,
1585, 1626, 1637, 1683;
baptism of, 1217; childhood
of, 1324; death and Resurrection of, 1276, 1314, 1370,
1404, 1405, 1418; divinity of,
1370, 1388, 1417; as Em-
manuel (Immanuel), 901,
1213; family tree of, 1212;
humanity of, 1213, 1362,
1585, 1629; humility of,
1578; personal relationship
with, 1285, 1386, 1402, 1411,
1686; suffering of, 1311; trust
in, 1241, 1286; understanding, 1294, 1626. *See also*
Messiah; Second Coming

Pilate
1417, 1418

plagues
80

pleasure
793

politics
915

poor people
99, 179, 222, 293, 389, 495, 967, 1146, 1178, 1268, 1321, 1333, 1352, 1419, 1432, 1521, 1545. *See also* oppressed people; preferential option for the poor

pope
1245, 1327, 1423

pornography
805

positive attitude
87, 90

power
311, 664, 1702

praise
88, 338, 537, 644, 689, 747, 1689, 1692. *See also* celebration

prayer
92, 179, 203, 298, 300, 432, 468, 491, 510, 519, 531, 602, 616, 646, 739, 754, 768, 806, 835, 1083, 1111, 1115, 1222, 1223, 1276, 1299, 1303, 1333, 1345, 1358, 1650

preferential option
for the poor
922, 967, 1146, 1321, 1333, 1352, 1646

prejudice
243, 487, 543, 1343, 1382, 1398

preparedness
See readiness

presence of God
23, 41, 73, 110, 369, 383, 433, 516, 664, 697, 741, 1048, 1090, 1534, 1664

pride
19, 373, 1178, 1530

priests
See ministry in the church

priorities
1181, 1516

Priscilla
1456

prodigal son
1354

profanity
859

promiscuity
140

promises of God
78. *See also* covenant; New Covenant; Sinai Covenant

prophetic themes
1039, 1048, 1192, 1683

prophets
56, 72, 75, 179, 389, 462, 890–891, 892, 945, 1053, 1117, 1571, 1684

protection
1081, 1399

Purgatory
602

Purim, feast of
550

purity
122, 1082, 1199

R

race
293

Rachel
1001

racism
1343, 1438, 1632. *See also* prejudice

rainbow
16

rape
48

readiness
1199, 1265, 1266, 1512, 1516, 1600

reading plans
xviii–xxiii

Reconciliation, sacrament of
436, 1421, 1669

redeemer
123, 1277. *See* Jesus Christ; Messiah

reflection time
338, 697, 856, 1645

reforms, religious
411

Reign of God
906, 1225, 1227, 1239, 1352, 1695, 1706

remnant
1141, 1178

repentance
436, 1222, 1325. *See also* Reconciliation, sacrament of

respect
706, 772, 1498

responsibility
11, 93, 108, 138, 206, 341, 851, 991, 1048, 1063, 1069, 1126

Resurrection
1114, 1153, 1314, 1373, 1416, 1424, 1528

revenge
910, 1016, 1166, 1221

rice
91

ridicule
674

witnesses
1428, 1612, 1639

women
88, 270, 271, 298, 530, 537,
545, 879, 1385, 1420, 1456,
1501, 1526, 1606

work
206, 873, 1282, 1602

worship
369, 371, 660, 1144, 1526,
1689. *See also* Eucharist,
sacrament of; praise

Acknowledgments *(continued)*

Consultants: Barbara Allaire, Mary Lee Becker, Philip J. Calderone, Brian K. Johnson, Car Koch, Stephan Nagel, Pheme Perkins, and Kevin Schneider

The Catholic Youth Bible NRSV Publishing Team: Brian Singer-Towns, general editor; Carmen María Cervantes, Shirley Kelter, and Robert P. Stamschror, consulting editors; Lynn Riska Dahdal, production editor; Cheryl Drivdahl and Mary Duerson, copy editors; Hollace Storkel, article typesetter; Auto-Graphics, Scripture typesetters; Peachtree Editorial and Proofreading Service, Scripture proofreaders; Maurine R. Twait, art director; Stephan Nagel, art director and cover designer; Sue Campbell, Carol Evans-Smith, Kent Linder, and Cindi Ramm, designers; Alan S. Hanson, prepress specialist; Gary J. Boisvert and Alan S. Hanson, illustration colorizers; Michael O. McGrath, illustrator

The Catholic Youth Bible NAB Publishing team: Steven Roe development editor; Beverly DeGeorge, managing editor; Don Curtin, marketing coordinator; Bill Northam, printing coordinator; Stephan Nagel and Brian Singer-Towns, consulting editors; Cindi Ramm, consulting cover designer; Lynn Riska, consultant for typesetting and project management; Gabrielle Koenig and Brooke E. Saron, editorial assistance; Genevieve Nagel, photo and illustration acquisition editor; James Koenig and Alan S. Hanson, technical assistance; Cären Yang, contributing graphic designer; The Livingstone Corporation, article and Scripture typesetter, copy editor, cover design adaptation, and project management; Peachtree Editorial and Proofreading Service, Scripture and article proofreaders; Michael O. McGrath, illustrator

The Catholic Youth Bible, Revised, Publishing Team: Steven Roe and Brian Singer-Towns, development editors; Heather Sutton, marketing director; Bill Northam, printing coordinator; Jim Gurley and Cären Yang, production editors; Andy Palmer, designer; Lynn Riska, consultant for typesetting; Brooke E. Saron and Paul Grass, FSC, copy editors; Genevieve Nagel, photo and illustration acquisitions editor; James Koenig, technical consultant; Alan S. Hanson, prepress specialist; The Livingstone Corporation, article and Scripture typesetter and project management; Peachtree Editorial and Proofreading Service, Scripture and article proofreaders. We extend a special thank-you to our student article reviewers, for their time, enthusiasm, invaluable comments, and recommendations. The student article review team included Renea Carlson, Neal Frantzen, Joshua Hamann, Aubrey Hollnagel, William Jaspers, Benjamin Leist, Megan Leopold, Kendall Marsden, and Brenda Maurer.

A special thank-you to the members of the original *Catholic Youth Bible* focus group: Catherine Cory; Carole Goodwin; Maryann Hakowski; Shirley Kelter; Marilyn Kielbasa; Joseph A. Morris, CM; Daniel Ponsetto; Pat Rinker; Virginia Smith; Carleen Suttman; and especially Robert P. Stamschror for his work in starting this project.

Finally, we are very grateful for the many young people, youth leaders, and teachers who helped as reviewers and consultants through the duration of this project.

The prayer by Black Elk, "The Sun Dance," on page 1395 is from *The Sacred Pipe: Black Elk's Account of the Seven Rites of the Oglala Sioux,* by Joseph Espes Brown. Copyright © 1953 by the University of Oklahoma Press. Reprinted with permission.

The quotation on page 1419 is from *A Handbook on Guadalupe: Our Lady Patroness of the Americas* (Stockton, CA: Office of Religious Education, Department of Catechesis, 1974), pages 148 and 152. Copyright © 1974 by Franciscan Marytown Press, Kenosha, Wisconsin.

The Apostles' Creed on page 1434 is from the English translation *Catechism of the Catholic Church* for use in the United States of America. (*CCC*), pages 49-50. Copyright © 1994 by the United States Conference of Catholic Bishops (USCCB)—Libreria Editrice Vaticana. Used with permission.

The Native American meal blessing on page 1518 is from *One Hundred Graces,* selected by Marcia Kelly and Jack Kelly (New York: Bell Tower, 1992), page 85. Copyright © 1992 by Marcia Kelly and Jack Kelly. Used with permission of the Lama Foundation, New Mexico.

The quotation on page 1527 is from *Prophetic Voices: The Document on the Process of the III Encuentro Nacional Hispano de Pastoral,* by the Secretariat for Hispanic Affairs, pages 17–18. Copyright © 1986 by the USCCB, Washington, DC. Used by permission. All rights reserved.

The prayer from the Philippines on page 1568 is reprinted from *Your Will Be Done* (Hong Kong: Christian Conference of Asia, 1986). Copyright © 1986 CCA Youth, Christian Conference of Asia. Used with permission.

The Native American prayer on page 1570 is quoted from *Amen,* compiled by Suzanne Slesin and Emily Gwathmey.

The Peace Prayer on page 1574 is quoted from the *Catholic Source Book,* third edition, edited by the Reverend Peter Klein, page 25.

The line from Shakespeare's play *Hamlet* on page 1575 is quoted from *The Standard Book of Shakespeare Quotations,* compiled and arranged by Burton Stevenson (New York: Funk and Wagnalls Co., 1953), page 149. Copyright © 1953 by Funk and Wagnalls Co.

The Navaho prayer on page 1582 is quoted from *The Sacred Vision: Native American Religion and Its Practice Today,* by Michael F. Steltenkamp (New York: Paulist Press, 1982), page 82. Copyright © 1982 by Michael Steltenkamp. Used with permission.

Photo Credits

Bibliothèque Municipale, Rouen, Bridgeman Art Library, London, SuperStock: page 1811 (middle right)

Rachel at the Well, 1903, by Harry Mileham (1873–1957) Private Collection, courtesy of the Estate of Harry Mileham, Bridgeman Art Library: page 1810 (middle left)

The Covenant of Yahweh with Noah, a detail from Noah and the Flood Scroll, 1996 (acrylic on canvas), Laura James (Contemporary Artist), Private Collection: page 1810 (top left)

Cameraphoto Arte, Venice, Art Resource, NY: page 1813 (top left)

Dahlem Staatliche Gemaldegalerie, Berlin, A.K.G., Berlin, SuperStock: page 1810 (top right)

CM Dixon: page 1811 (bottom right)

Sonia Halliday Photographs: pages 1810 (bottom right), 1812 (center)

Collaborators on the Old Testament of the New American Bible

Bishops' Committee of the Confraternity of Christian Doctrine
Most Rev. Charles P. Greco, D.D., Chairman
Most Rev. Joseph T. McGucken, S.T.D.
Most Rev. Vincent S. Waters, D.D.
Most Rev. Romeo Blanchette, D.D.
Most Rev. Christopher J. Weldon, D.D.

Editors in Chief
Rev. Louis F. Hartman, C.SS.R., S.S.L., LING. OR. L., Chairman
Rev. Msgr. Patrick W. Skehan, S.T.D., LL.D., Vice-Chairman
Rev. Stephen J. Hartdegen, O.F.M., S.S.L., Secretary

Associate Editors and Translators

Rev. Edward P. Arbez, S.S., S.T.D.
Rev. Msgr. Edward J. Byrne, PH.D., S.T.D.
Rev. Edward A. Cerny, S.S., S.T.D.
Rev. James E. Coleran, S.J., S.T.L., S.S.L.
Rev. John J. Collins, S.J., M.A., S.S.L.
Sr. M. Emmanuel Collins, O.S.F., PH.D.
Prof. Frank M. Cross Jr., PH.D.
Rev. Patrick Cummins, O.S.B., S.T.D.
Rev. Antonine A. DeGuglielmo, O.F.M., S.T.D., S.S.L., S.S.LECT. GEN.
Rev. Alexander A. Di Lella, O.F.M., S.T.L., S.S.L., PH.D.
Most Rev. John J. Dougherty, S.T.L., S.S.D.
William A. Dowd, S.J., S.T.D., S.S.L.
Prof. David Noel Freedman, PH.D.
Rev. Michael J. Gruenthaner, S.J., S.T.D., S.S.D.
Rev. Msgr. Maurice A. Hofer, S.S.L.
Rev. Justin Krellner, O.S.B., S.T.D.
Rev. Joseph L. Lilly, C.M., S.T.D., S.S.L.
Rev. Roderick F. MacKenzie, S.J., M.A., S.S.D.
Rev. Edward A. Mangan, C.SS.R., S.S.L.

Rev. Daniel W. Martin, C.M., S.T.L., S.S.L.
Rev. William H. McClellan, S.J.
Rev. James McGlinchey, C.M., S.T.D.
Rev. Frederick Moriarty, S.J., S.S.L., S.T.D.
Rev. Richard T. Murphy, O.P., S.T.D., S.S.D.
Rev. Roland E. Murphy, O. CARM., M.A., S.T.D., S.S.L.
Rev. Msgr. William R. Newton, M.S., S.S.D.
Rev. Eberhard Olinger, O.S.B.
Rev. Charles H. Pickar, O.S.A., S.T.L., S.S.L.
Rev. Christopher Rehwinkel, O.F.M., S.T.D., S.S. LECT. GEN.
Rev. Msgr. John R. Rowan, S.T.D., S.S.L.
Prof. J. A. Sanders, PH.D.
Rev. Edward F. Siegman, C.PP.S., S.T.D., S.S.L.
Rev. Msgr. Matthew P. Stapleton, S.T.D., S.S.L.
Rev. Msgr. John E. Steinmueller, S.T.D., S.S.L.
Rev. John Ujlaki, O.S.B., LITT.D.
Rev. Bruce Vawter, C.M., S.T.L., S.S.D.
Rev. John B. Weisengoff, S.T.D., S.S.L.

Collaborators on the Revised Psalms of the New American Bible

Bishops' Ad Hoc Committee
Most Rev. Enrique San Pedro, S.J.
Most Rev. Richard Sklba, D.D.
Most Rev. Donald W. Trautman, S.T.D., S.S.L.
Most Rev. Emil A. Wcela
Most Rev. John F. Whealon, S.S.L., Chairman

Board of Editors
Rev. Richard Clifford, S.J.
Br. Aloysius Fitzgerald, F.S.C.
Rev. Joseph Jensen, O.S.B.

Rev. Roland Murphy, O. CARM.
Sr. Irene Nowell, O.S.B.
Dr. Judith Sanderson

Revisers
Prof. Gary Anderson
Rev. Michael L. Barré
Rev. Christopher T. Begg
Dr. Joseph Blenkinsopp
Rev. Anthony R. Ceresko, O.S.F.S.
Rev. Richard J. Clifford, S.J.
Rev. Aelred Cody, O.S.B.
Prof. Michael D. Coogan
Rev. Alexander A. Di Lella, O.F.M.
Dr. Robert A. Di Vito
Br. Aloysius Fitzgerald, F.S.C.
Rev. Michael D. Guinan, O.F.M.
Rev. William L. Holladay
Rev. William Irwin, C.S.B.
Rev. Joseph Jensen, O.S.B.

Rev. John S. Kselman
Rev. Leo Laberge, O.M.I.
Dr. Conrad E. L'Heureux
Dr. Paul G. Mosca
Rev. Dr. Roland E. Murphy, O.CARM.
Dr. Michael Patrick O'Connor
Rev. Brian J. Peckham, S.J.
Prof. Jimmy J. Roberts
Sr. Eileen M. Schuller, O.S.U.
Dr. Byron E. Shafer
Prof. Mark S. Smith
Prof. Matitiahu Tsevat
Dr. Eugene C. Ulrich
Prof. James C. VanderKam
Rev. Jerome T. Walsh

English Consultants
Dr. Catherine Dunn
Br. Daniel Burke, F.S.C.

Business Manager
Charles A. Buggé

Collaborators on the Revised New Testament of the New American Bible

Bishops' Ad Hoc Committee
Most Rev. Theodore E. McCarrick, D.D.
Most Rev. Richard J. Sklba, D.D.
Most Rev J. Francis Stafford, D.D.
Most Rev. John F. Whealon, D.D., Chairman

Board of Editors
Rev. Msgr. Myles M. Bourke
Rev. Francis T. Gignac, S.J., Chairman
Rev. Stephen J. Hartdegen, O.F.M., Secretary
Rev. Claude J. Peifer, O.S.B.
Rev. John H. Reumann

Revisers
Rev. Msrg. Myles M. Bourke
Rev. Frederick W. Danker
Rev. Alexander A. Di Lella, O.F.M.
Rev. Charles H. Giblin, S.J.
Rev. Francis T. Gignac, S.J.
Rev. Stephen J. Hartdegen, O.F.M.
Dr. Maurya P. Horgan
Rev. John R. Keating, S.J.
Rev. John Knox
Dr. Paul J. Kobelski
Dr. J. Rebecca Lyman
Br. Elliott C. Maloney, O.S.B.
Dr. Janet A. Timbie

Consultants
Rev. Joseph Jensen, O.S.B.
Rev. Aidan Kavanagh, O.S.B.
Dr. Marianne Sawicki

Business Manager
Charles A. Buggé

Word Processor
Suzanna Jordan

NOTES

Study Aids

Study Aids

ESSENTIAL CONCORDANCE

TO THE NAB: CATHOLIC EDITION

A

ABANDON (ED)
Dt 4,31 he will not a and destroy you
Jos 10, 6 "Do not a your servants.
2Sm 5,21 They a their gods there
2Mc 6, 1 force the Jews to a the
Lam 5,14 The old men have the gate
Lk 13,35 Behold, your house will be a.
Heb 13, 5 never forsake you or a you."

ABBA
Mk 14,36 A, Father, all things
Rom 8,15 we cry, "A, Father!"
Gal 4, 6 crying out, "A, Father!"

ABILITY (ABLE)
Ex 18,21 a and God-fearing men
1Mc 3,53 How shall we be a to resist
Acts 11,29 according to a, each should
Jude 24 To the one who is a

ABOLISH (ED)
1Mc 6,59 their laws, which we a
2Mc 2,22 were in danger of being a
Jl 1, 9 A are offering and libation from
Mt 5,17 that I have come to a the law

ABOMINATION (S) (ABOMINABLE)
Ex 8,22 sacrifices which are an a to
Dt 7,25 for it is an a to the Lord,
12,31 offered to their gods every a
Prv 12,28 but the a way leads to death.
Is 66, 3 taken pleasure in their own a
Dn 11,31 and setting up the horrible a.
12,11 and the horrible a is set up,
Mt 24,15 you see the desolating a
Mk 13,14 When you see the desolating a
Lk 16,15 human esteem is an a in

ABOUND (ING)
Gn 9, 7 a on earth and subdue it
Ps 4, 8 when grain and wine a.
16,11 a joy in your presence
Sir 44, 2 The a glory of the Most High's
Rom 6, 1 in sin that grace may a?
15,13 so that you may a in hope
2Cor 3, 9 righteousness will a
Phil 1,26 Christ Jesus may a
Col 2, 7 were taught, a in thanksgiving.
1Thes 3,12 increase and a in love

ABOVE
Gn 1, 7 separated the water a

27,39 the dew of the heavens a!
Ex 20, 4 of anything in the sky a
28,28 stay right a the embroidered
1Sm 9, 2 and shoulders a the people.
Neh 9, 5 exalted a all blessing and
12,37 a the house of David
Tb 1, 2 a and to the west of
4,12 and a all, marry a woman of
Jdt 13,18 a all the women on earth
2Mc 15, 2 exalted with holiness a all
Ps 7, 8 on your throne high a them,
27, 6 my head is held high a
50, 4 God summons the heavens a
Sir 15, 5 exalt him a his fellows;
40,11 what is from a returns above.
Jn 3, 7 You must be born from a.'
8,23 I belong to what is a.
19,11 been given to you from a.
Eph 1,21 far a every principality,
4,10 ascended far a all
Phil 2, 9 name that is a every name,
Col 3, 1 seek what is a, where Christ
Heb 1, 9 with the oil of gladness a
Jas 1,17 every perfect gift is from a,
3,17 wisdom from a

ABUNDANCE (ABUNDANTLY)
Gn 1,20 with an a of living creatures,
Gn 22,17 I will bless you a and make
Lv 25,19 you will have food in a,
26, 5 have food to eat in a,
Dt 15, 4 will bless you a in the land
28,47 gratitude for a of every kind,
33,19 the a of the seas and the
Ru 1,21 I went away with an a,
1Kgs 10,10 did anyone bring such an a
1Chr 22, 5 David laid up materials in a.
2Chr 11,23 sought an a of wives
18, 1 had wealth and glory in a;
20,25 they found an a of cattle
32, 4 come and find an a of water?"
Neh 5,18 all kinds of wine in a
9,25 and fruit trees in a.
Tb 4, 8 give alms out of your a;
12, 8 better than a with
Jdt 5, 9 gold, silver, and a great a
Ps 65,10 water it, make it a fertile.
Rom 5,17 who receive the a of grace
2Cor 9, 8 an a for every good work.
Phil 4,12 living in a
2Pt 1, 2 and peace be yours in a,
1, 8 increase in a, they will
Jude 2 and love be yours in a.

ABUSE (ABUSIVE)
Gn 16, 9 and submit to her a treatment.
Tb 3, 7 a, from one of her father's
Sir 22,24 a come before bloodshed.
23,15 who has the habit of a language
29, 6 with a instead of honor.
Am 4, 1 oppress the weak and a the
Acts 13,45 a contradicted what Paul
2Tm 3, 2 proud, haughty, a, disobedient
Heb 10,33 publicly exposed to a and

ACCEPT (ED) (ABLE)
Lv 1, 4 a to make atonement
1Sm 29, 9 you are a to me. But
29,10 as a to me as an angel
Neh 2, 6 a date that was a to him,
Est 3, 4 explanation was a, since
2Mc 11,18 that were a he has granted.
Prv 21, 3 a to the Lord than sacrifice
Wis 9,12 Thus my deeds will be a,
Lk 4,19 and to proclaim a year a
Acts 2,41 Those who a his message were
2Cor 6, 2 "In an a time I heard you
Phil 4,18 a sacrifice, pleasing to God.
2Tm 2,15 present yourself as a
1Pt 2, 5 spiritual sacrifices a to God

ACCESS
Jdt 4, 7 since these offered a to
2Mc 14, 3 regain a to the holy altar.
Prv 18,16 gains him a to great men.
Sir 38, 3 a to those in authority.
Is 58, 2 pleased to gain a to God
Zec 3, 7 I will give you a
Rom 5, 2 whom we have gained a
Eph 2,18 a in one Spirit to the Father
3,12 a through faith in him.

ACCOMPLISH (ED)
1Sm 9, 6 tell us how to a our errand."
12,16 the Lord is about to a
1Kgs 9,21 had been unable to a,
Tb 14, 4 God has spoken will be a.
Is 46,10 I a my every purpose.
Dn 3,99 God has a in my regard.
Jn 5,36 the Father gave me to a,
1Cor 15,29 a by having themselves
Eph 3,20 who is able to a far more
Heb 1, 3 When he had a purification

ACCOUNT (ABLE)
Gn 20,11 kill me on a of my wife.
Ex 38,21 The following is an a of the
Lv 21,21 on a of his defect he may
Dt 1,37 against me also on your a,

1739

3,26 angry with me on your a
9, 5 on a of their wickedness
1Sm 15, 9 was worthless and of no a.
20,34 he was grieved on David's a,
1Kgs 9,15 an an a of the forced labor
2Chr 9, 5 "The a I heard in my country
Neh 5, 7 to a, saying to them, "You are
9,32 take into a all the disasters
Jdt 14, 9 When she finished her a,
Est 10, 2 detailed a of the greatness
1Mc 1,28 on a of its inhabitants
2Mc 11, 4 not take God's power into a
Jb 9,19 who will call him to a?
40, 4 Behold, I am of little a;
Wis 10, 4 a the earth was flooded,
Jer 1,17 Be not crushed on their a,
9,24 I will demand an a of all
Ez 31,15 the land drooped on his a.
Dn 6, 3 these were a to three supervisors
Jon 1, 7 to find out on whose a
Mt 12,36 a for every careless word
Lk 16, 2 full a of your stewardship,
Rom 3,19 stand a to God

ACKNOWLEDGE
Jos 23,14 a with your whole heart
Jdt 8,20 since we a no other god
Sir 4,26 not ashamed to a your guilt,
Bar 4,13 did not a his statutes;
Mt 10,32 I will a before my
Lk 12, 8 a before the angels of God
Jn 12,42 the Pharisees they did not a
Rom 1,28 did not see fit to a God,
1Cor 14,38 If anyone does not a this,
2Thes 1, 8 those who do not a God
1Jn 1, 9 If we a our sins
4, 3 that does not a Jesus

ACT (S)
Gn 15, 6 as an a of righteousness.
Ex 1,16 "When you a as midwives
22,24 not a like an extortioner
Nm 5,29 of her husband and a impurely
Dt 17,10 you shall a, being careful
Jgs 6,31 let him a for himself!"
2Sm 5,24 a decisively, for the Lord
2Mc 3,29 due to an a of God's power,
Jb 34,12 God cannot a wickedly,
Ps 15, 5 Whoever a like this shall never
Ez 8,18 I in turn will a furiously
Mt 7,26 but does not a on them will
Lk 6,49 listens and does not a is like
8,21 the word of God and a on it."
Acts 17, 7 They all a in opposition to
Rom 5,18 through one righteous a
1Cor 16,14 a should be done with love.
2Cor 3,12 we a very boldly and not like
Heb 2, 4 signs, wonders, various a of

ADOPTION
Rom 8,15 you received a spirit of a,
8,23 as we wait for a,
9, 4 a, the glory, the covenants,
Gal 4, 5 so that we might receive a.
Eph 1, 5 he destined us for a to himself

ADORN (S) (MENT)
2Mc 9,16 a with the finest offerings
Ps 73, 6 Thus pride a them as a necklace
Prv 3,22 an a for your neck.
1Tm 2, 9 women should a themselves
Ti 2,10 so as to a the doctrine of God

ADULTERY (ADULTERESS) (ADULTERER) (ADULTERERS)
Ex 20,14 "You shall not commit a.

Lv 20,10 If a man commits a with his
Dt 5,18 'You shall not commit a.
Jb 24,15 The eye of the a watches for the
Wis 14,24 aggrieves him by a.
Sir 23,23 in her wanton a
Is 1,21 has she turned a, the faithful
Jer 5, 7 but they committed a;
9, 1 They are all a, a faithless band.
Ez 23,45 for they have committed a,
Hos 2, 4 her a from between her
4,14 daughters-in-law for their a?
Mt 5,28 a with her in his heart
Jn 8, 3 had been caught in a
Rom 2,22 You who forbid a
Jas 2,11 not commit a," also said,
2,11 if you do not commit a but
2Pt 2,14 Their eyes are full of a
Rv 2,22 plunge those who commit a

ADVOCATE
Jb 13, 8 you play a on behalf of God?
Jn 14,16 he will give you another a
14,26 The a, the holy Spirit
16, 7 the a will not come
1Jn 2, 1 we have an a with the Father,

AFFLICT (ED) (ION) (IONS)
Ex 9, 3 Lord will a all your livestock
Dt 7,15 he will not a you with
8,16 that he might a you and
28,60 He will again a you with
1Sm 6, 3 why he continues to a you."
6, 5 then he will cease to a you,
Ps 71,20 have sent me many bitter a, but
Is 58, 3 a ourselves, and you take no
Jer 51, 2 sides on the day of a.
Ez 22,29 they a the poor and the needy
Heb 11,37 or goats, needy, a, tormented.

AFRAID
Gn 3,10 I was a, because I was naked,
Ex 2,14 Then Moses became a
3, 6 he was a to look at God.
Nm 14, 9 You need not be a of the
14, 9 Therefore, do not be a
Dt 2, 4 Though they are a of you,
7,19 of whom you are now a
Jgs 7, 3 'If anyone is a or fearful,
8,20 he was a and did not draw his
20, 1 do not be a of them,
1Sm 7, 7 the Israelites became a of the
23, 3 "We are a here in Judah.
2Sm 1,14 you were not a to put forth
10,19 Arameans were a to give
1Kgs 17,13 "Do not be a," Elijah said
2Kgs 1,15 you need not be a of him."
25,24 not be a of the Chaldean
1Chr 13,12 David was now a of God,
2Chr 32, 7 do not be a or dismayed
Tb 6,15 I too am a of this demon.
Jdt 1,11 not a of him but regarded
1Mc 3,22 so do not be a of them."
4, 8 Do not be a of their numbers
2Mc 7,29 not be a of this executioner;
Jb 9,35 speak without being a of him.
Ps 27, 1 of whom am I a?
Sir 34,14 never alarmed, never a;
Mt 1,20 do not be a to take Mary
10,28 a of those who kill the soul
Mk 5,36 "Do not be a; just have faith."
Jn 14,27 your hearts be troubled or a.

AGGRESSIVE
1Tm 3, 3 not a drunkard, not a

Ti 1, 7 not a drunkard, not a

AGREE
Gn 34,22 men will a to live with us and
39,10 not a to lie beside her, or
Dt 1,14 'We a to do as you have
1Sm 30,24 Who could a with this
1Kgs 5,22 "I a to the proposal you sent
2Kgs 6, 3 "Please a to accompany
2Mc 11,24 Jews do not a
Mt 18,19 if two of you a on earth
Mk 14,56 their testimony did not a
Acts 5, 9 did you a to test the Spirit of
15,15 words of the prophets a with
1Cor 1,10 that all of you a in what you
2Cor 13,11 a with one another, live in
1Tm 6, 3 not a with the sound words of

ALIEN (S)
Gn 23, 4 I am a resident a among you,
Ex 22,20 molest or oppress an a,
Lv 17, 8 of Israel or of the a residing
Dt 10,19 you were once a yourselves
24,19 let it be for the a, the
2Chr 2,16 a census of all the a men
Est 3B, 5 divergent and a laws,
2Mc 6,24 gone over to an a religion.
Ps 81,10 must not worship an a god.
Prv 5,10 earnings go to an a's house;
Sir 10,21 tenant or wayfarer, a or
Is 33,19 To the people of a tongue
Bar 6, 4 not imitate their a example
Ez 14, 7 or any a resident in Israel
22, 7 extort from the resident a;
22,29 oppress the resident
Ob 11 on the day when a carried off
Zec 7,10 the a or the poor; do not
1Jn 2,21 every lie is a to the truth.

ALIVE
Gn 7, 3 a over all the earth.
Ex 22, 3 found a in his possession,
Lv 16,10 he shall set a before the Lord,
Nm 16,30 and swallows them a
Dt 4, 4 are all a today Therefore,
5, 3 all of us who are a here
20,16 not leave a single soul a.
1Sm 15, 8 took Agag, king of Amalek, a
2Sm 12,18 "When the child was a,
1Kgs 17,23 to her, "your son is a."
2Kgs 7,12 hoping to take us a and
Tb 5,10 a, I am among the dead
Jdt 10,19 leave one man of them a,
1Mc 2,13 Why are we still a?"
8, 7 They had taken him a
2Mc 9, 9 he was still a in hideous
Jb 33, 4 of the Almighty keeps me a
Ps 33,19 keeping them a in times of
Prv 1,12 a, in the prime of life
Eccl 4, 2 the living to be still a.
Sir 17,23 glorify the Lord who are a
Jer 49,11 keep them a; your widows,
Lam 3,53 struck me down a in the pit,
Ez 13,18 keep yourselves a?
13,19 not die and keeping a
37,10 came a and stood upright,
Dn 3,90 astonished at seeing them a
Mk 16,11 they heard that he was a
Acts 1, 3 presented himself a to them
Rom 8,10 spirit is a
Rv 1,18 I am a forever and ever.
3, 1 reputation of being a

ALMIGHTY
Gn 17, 1 "I am God the A.

Ex 6, 3 God the A I appeared
Jdt 16, 5 the LORD A thwarted them,
16,17 LORD A will requite them;
Nm 24, 4 sees what the A sees
Ru 1,20 the A has made it very bitter
Tb 3,16 glorious presence of A God.
Jdt 15,10 by the Lord A forever
Est 4C, 2 "O Lord God, a King,
2Mc 3,22 they were imploring the A
Jb 5,17 A's chastening
Ps 91, 1 in the shadow of the A,
Wis 7,25 the glory of the A;
Sir 42,21 Perennial is his a wisdom;
Jl 1,15 comes as ruin from the A.
Rv 4, 8 holy is the Lord God a,

ALMS
Tb 4,16 begrudge the a you give.
Sir 3,29 and a atone for sins.
Mt 6, 2 When you give a
Lk 12,33 belongings and give a.
11,41 give a, and behold,
12,33 give a. Provide money bags
Acts 3, 2 beg for a from the people

ALONE
Gn 2,18 not good for the man to be a.
Ex 18,18 you cannot do it a.
21, 3 If he comes into service a,
Nm 12, 2 Moses a that the Lord
Dt 1,12 But how can I a bear
8, 3 not by bread a does man live
Jgs 16,20 justice a shall be your aim,
2Chr 6,30 you a know the hearts
Ezr 4, 3 but we a must build it
Tb 8, 6 for the man to be a;
Jdt 3, 8 worship Nebuchadnezzar a
Est 1,16 has not wronged the king a,
4,14 Help me, who am a and
4,25 who am a and have no
2Mc 7,37 confess that he a is God.
Jb 36, 4 a has done great wonders,
Ps 148,13 for his name a is exalted,
Eccl 4,11 can one a keep warm?
Sir 18, 1 the LORD a is just.
Is 2,11 the LORD a will be exalted,
Am 3, 2 You a have I favored,
Mt 4, 4 does not live by bread a,
4,10 him a shall you serve.'"
Rom 3,29 God belong to Jews a?
Jas 2,24 and not by faith a.
1Jn 5, 6 not by water a,
Rv 15, 4 For you a are holy.

ALPHA
Rv 1, 8 the a and the Omega
21, 6 the a and the Omega
22,13 I am the a and the Omega

ALTAR (S)
Gn 8,20 Noah built an a to the LORD,
12, 7 Abram built an a there
13,18 built an a to the LORD.
22, 9 Abraham built an a there
26,25 a there and invoked
35, 1 Settle there and build an a
Ex 17,15 Moses also built an a there,
29,43 a, I will meet the Israelites
30, 1 make an a of acacia wood,
Dt 7, 5 Tear down their a, smash their
Jos 8,30 Joshua built an a to the LORD,
21, 4 the people built an a there
1Sm 7,17 built an a to the LORD.
14,35 Saul built an a to the LORD
2Sm 24,25 David built an a there
2Kgs 11,18 They shattered its a and images

1Mc 1,21 took away the golden a,
1,54 abomination upon the a
2,24 killed him upon the a.
2Mc 13, 8 many sins against the a
Is 17, 8 shall not look to the a,
Mt 5,24 leave your gift there at the a,
Jas 2,21 his son Isaac upon the a?
Rv 6, 9 underneath the a the souls
16, 7 the a cry out, "Yes, Lord

AMAZED (AMAZING)
Gn 29,25 In the morning Jacob was a,
Tb 11,16 they were a. Before them
Jdt 15, 1 still in their tents were a,
Ps 106,22 A deeds in the land of
Wis 5, 2 a at the unlooked-for salvation
Sir 43,26 a, all kinds of life
Hb 1, 5 and be utterly a! For
Mt 8,10 Jesus heard this, he was a
8,27 The men were a
9,33 The crowds were a
Mk 16, 6 "Do not be a! You seek Jesus
Lk 2,18 All who heard it were a
2,33 father and mother were a
Jn 9,30 This is what is so a
Acts 3,12 why are you a at this,
Gal 1, 6 I am a that you are so quickly
1Jn 3,13 Do not be a, [then,] brothers,

AMBASSADORS
2Sm 5,11 Hiram, king of Tyre, sent a
2Chr 32,31 to the a [princes] sent to
1Mc 10,51 Alexander sent a to Ptolemy
Is 18, 2 Sending a by sea,
2Cor 5,20 So we are a for Christ,

AMEN
Nm 5,22 the woman shall say, 'A, a!'
Dt 27,15 'A!"Cursed be he who
1Chr 16,36 Let all the people say, A!
Tb 14,15 Lord God forever and ever. A.
Jdt 13,20 "A! A!" Then Judith said
Ps 41,14 all eternity and forever. A
Prv 22,19 to you the words of A
Jer 11, 5 "A, Lord," I answered.
Mt 6, 5 that others may see them. A,
18, 3 in their midst, and said, "A,
Jn 3, 5 Jesus answered, "A, a,
13,20 believe that I AM. A,
1Cor 14,16 of the uninstructed say the "A"
2Cor 1,20 A from us also goes through
Gal 1, 5 be glory forever and ever. A
Phil 4,20 glory for every and ever. A.
1Tm 6,16 honor and eternal power. A
2Pt 3,18 to the day of eternity. [A.]
Jude ,25 and for ages to come. A.
Rv 5,14 "A," and the elders fell down

ANCESTORS
Gn 46,34 like our a, have been
Lv 25,41 to the property of his a.
Dt 10,22 Your a went down to Egypt
2Sm 7,12 and you rest with your a,
1Kgs 2,10 David rested with his a
2Kgs 9,28 tomb of his a in the
1Chr 6, 4 according to their a: of
2Chr 35,24 in the tombs of his a,
Neh 2, 3 where my a are buried lies
2, 5 to the city of my a' graves
Jdt 5, 8 abandoned the way of their a,
2Mc 4,15 their a had regarded as honors,
8,19 help had been given their a,
Sir 44, 1 praise those godly men, our a,
1Cor 10, 1 our a were all under the cloud

ANGEL (S)
Ex 23,20 I am sending an a before you,

Dt 32,43 glorify him, all you a of God
Jgs 6,22 I have seen the a of the LORD
13, 3 An a of the LORD appeared to
1Chr 21,12 destroying a in every part of
2Chr 32,21 LORD sent an a, who destroyed
Tb 5, 4 a Raphael standing before him,
1Mc 6,41 your a went out and killed
2Mc 11, 6 send a good a to save Israel.
Ps 34, 8 The a of the LORD,
Bar 6, 6 for my a is with you,
Hos 12, 5 with the a and triumphed,
Dn 3,49 the a of the LORD went down
Mt 4, 6 command his a concerning you
28, 2 an a of the LORD descended
Jn 12,29 "An a has spoken to him."
Acts 6,15 like the face of an a.
12, 7 the a of the Lord stood by
2Cor 11, 1 masquerades as an a
2Thes 1, 7 with his mighty a, in blazing

ANGER (ANGRY)
Gn 27,45 until your brother's a against
Ex 11, 8 Pharaoh's presence in hot a.
Nm 14,18 The LORD is slow to a
Dt 9,22 you provoked the Lord to a.
Jos 22,18 he will be a with the whole
2Kgs 22,13 the a of the LORD has been
Neh 9,17 slow to a and rich in mercy;
Jdt 8,14 do not a the LORD our God.
Jb 26,13 With his a breath he scatters
Ps 30, 6 a lasts but a moment;
78,38 again he turned back his a,
86,15 slow to a
90, 7 consumed by your a,
103, 8 slow to a
Prv 15, 1 a harsh word stirs up a.
29,11 fool gives vent to all his a;
30,33 a brings forth blood.
Wis 15, 1 slow to a, and governing all
Sir 5, 7 mercy and a alike
Bar 2,13 Let your a be withdrawn
Jn 7,23 are you a with me
Eph 4,26 the sun set on your a,

ANIMAL (S)
Gn 1,24 wild a of all kinds.
Ex 10,26 Not an a must be left behind.
Lv 1, 2 wishes to bring an a offering
Dt 14, 6 Any a that has hoofs you may
17, 1 an a with any serious defect;
2Kgs 14, 9 an a of Lebanon passed by
2Mc 5,11 Raging like a wild a
Ps 147, 9 Who gives a their food
Ez 32,13 will have all of her a perish
Lk 10,34 him up on his own a,
Heb 12,20 "If even an a touches the

ANOINT (ED)
Ex 30,26 a the meeting tent
Lv 8, 2 with the vestments, the a oil
Jgs 9, 8 the trees went to a a king
Ru 3, 3 So bathe and a yourself; then
1Sm 9,16 a as commander
15, 1 a you king over his people
2Kgs 9, 3 I a you king over Israel.'
Ps 23, 5 You a my head with oil;
Dn 10, 3 did not a myself at all until
Am 6, 6 a themselves with the best
Mt 6,17 when you fast, a your head
Mk 16, 1 go and a him. Very early
Lk 7,46 did not a my head with oil,
Heb 1, 9 God, your God, a you

ANSWER (ED)
Gn 24,52 servant heard their a, he
Ex 1,19 The midwives a Pharaoh

Lv 5,17 guilt for which he must a,
Nm 14,10 In a, the whole community
22, 8 I will give you whatever a
Dt 18,19 I myself will make him a for it.
27,15 And all the people shall a
1Chr 21,12 What a am I to give him
2Chr 2,10 wrote an a which he sent
7,22 will a: 'They forsook the Lord,
Ezr 4,17 The king sent this a
1Mc 2,19 But Mattathias a in a loud voice
Jb 9, 3 could not a him once
32, 1 men ceased to a Job,
Ps 13, 4 a me, LORD, my God!
65, 6 a us with awesome deeds
Prv 15, 1 A mild a calms wrath,
Sir 11, 8 Before hearing, a not,
Jer 3, 7 shall he a in that day: "I will
Bar 3,35 When he calls them, they a,
Ez 14, 7 will be his a in person.
33,25 a: Thus says the Lord God
Dn 9,23 mark the a and understand
Mi 3, 4 the Lord, he shall not a them;
3, 7 there is no a from God
Hb 2, 1 and what a he will give to my
2,11 woodwork shall a it! Woe to
Mt 4, 7 Jesus a him, "Again it is written
Jn 18,22 Is this the way you a the high
Acts 14, 6 They were unable to a his
1Cor 11,27 will have to a for the body

APOSTLE (S)
Lk 6,13 Twelve, whom he also named a
1Cor 1, 1 Paul, called to be an a
2Cor 8,23 they are a of the churches
1Tm 2, 7 appointed preacher and a
Heb 3, 1 Jesus, the a and high priest
1Pt 1, 1 Peter, an a of Jesus Christ
2Pt 3, 2 Lord and savior through your a.

APPEAR (ED) (ING) (S) (ANCE) (ANCES)
Gn 1, 9 that the dry land may a."
Ex 4, 1 'The Lord did not a to
Nm 14,10 the glory of the Lord a
Dt 16,16 every male among you shall a
19,17 parties in the dispute shall a
1Sm 16, 7 Do not judge from his a
2Sm 14, 2 with oil, that you may a to be
Neh 10, 1 document a the names of our
Tb 10, 1 and his son did not a,
Est 4C,27 when I a in public; abhor it
1Mc 9,27 the time prophets ceased to a
Jb 33,21 his bones, once invisible, a;
Ps 57, 6 God; may your glory a above
Eccl 3, 4 both a equally vain, in that
Song 2,12 The flowers a on the earth,
Wis 8,15 I should a noble, and in war
Sir 27, 4 sieve is shaken, the husks a;
Is 50, 8 let us a together. Who
Ez 16,51 made your sisters a just, with
Zec 9,14 The Lord shall a over them,
Mt 24,30 Son of Man shall a
Jn 7,24 Stop judging by a, but judge
Acts 1, 3 a to them during forty days
2Cor 13, 7 we may a to have passed
Col 3, 4 you too will a with him
1Thes 2, 5 did we ever a with flattering
1Tm 6,14 until the a of our Lord
2Tm 1,10 through the a of our savior
Heb 9,24 a before God on our behalf
9,28 will a a second time, not to
1Jn 2,28 when he a we may have

APPOINT (ED)
Gn 41,34 take action to a overseers,
Ezr 8,20 David and the princes a to serve

Dt 1,13 may a them as your leaders.'
16,18 on you. "You shall a and
1Sm 10,19 you must a a king over us.
1Chr 15,16 chiefs of the Levites to a
Ezr 7,25 a magistrates and judges
Est 2, 3 Let the king a commissaries
Sir 14,12 the grave's a time.
Is 60,17 I will a peace your governor,
Jer 23, 4 I will a shepherds for them
Ez 34,23 I will a one shepherd over
Mk 3,14 He a twelve whom he also
Acts 26,16 to a you as a servant and
Rom 6, 3 whom we shall a to this task,
Ti 1, 5 a presbyters in every town, as

ARGUE (ARGUEMENT) (ARGUMENTS)
Jb 15, 3 Should he a in speech
Mk 8,11 began to a with him,
Col 2, 4 may deceive you by specious a.
1Tm 2, 8 without anger or a.

ARISE
Nm 10,35 "A, O Lord, that your enemies
Jgs 5,12 a, Barak, make despoilers
7,15 "A, for the Lord has delivered
Neh 9, 5 "A, bless the Lord, your God
Jb 7, 4 I say, "When shall I a?"
Ps 12, 6 I will now a," says the LORD;
68, 2 God will a for battle;
Song 2,10 "A, my beloved, my beautiful
Is 23,12 daughter Sidon. A, pass
Ez 38,10 thoughts shall a in your mind,
Mi 6, 1 A, present your plea before
Hb 2,19 "A!" Can such a thing give
Zep 3, 8 the day when I a as accuser;
Mal 3,20 there will a the sun of justice
Mk 12,41 the men of Nineveh will a
Lk 7,14 Young man, I tell you, a!"
Eph 5,14 "Awake, O sleeper, and a
Heb 7,11 another priest to a according

ARK
Gn 6,14 "Make yourself an a
1Sm 3,17 the a of God has been captured
7, 2 the a came to rest in Kiriath
2Sm 6,17 The a of the LORD was brought
1Kgs 8, 9 the a but the two stone tablets
1Chr 13, 9 his hand to steady the a,
2Chr 35, 3 "Put the holy a in the house
2Mc 2, 4 the a should accompany him
Heb 9, 4 a of the covenant entirely
11, 7 built an a for the salvation of
Rv 11,19 the a of his covenant could be

ASCEND (ED) (ING)
2Chr 6,13 Having a it, Solomon knelt
Jdt 10,13 route by which he can a
Ps 139, 8 If I a to the heavens,
Is 14,14 I will a above the tops of the
Jn 1,51 and the angels of God a and

ASK (ED)
Dt 4, 6 When your children a you
2Kgs 1, 5 to Ahaziah, who a them
Neh 1, 2 I a them about the Jews
Mt 15,23 His disciples came and a him
Lk 11, 9 a and you will receive;
Jn 14,13 whatever you a in my name,
Jas 1, 5 he should a God who gives to
4, 2 because you do not a.
1Jn 3,22 whatever we a,
5,14 a anything according

ASSEMBLY (ASSEMBLE)
Nm 8, 9 where you shall a

Est 4,16 "Go and a all the Jews
Ps 149, 1 hymn in the a of the faithful.
Prv 26,26 will be revealed in the a.
Wis 8,15 in the a I should appear noble,
Mi 2,12 I will a all the remnant of Israel

ASSYRIA (ASSYRIANS)
Jdt 1, 1 Nebuchadnezzar, king of the A
Jer 38, 6 hand of the king of A;
Zec 10,11 pride of A shall be cast

ASTRAY
2Mc 2, 2 led a in their thoughts,
Ps 14, 3 All have gone a;
119,67 I was afflicted I went a,
Prv 10,17 disregards reproof goes a.
20, 1 who goes a for it is wise.
Rom 3,12 All have gone a;
1Pt 2,25 you had gone a like sheep,
Rv 19,20 signs by which he led a

ATONE (D) (MENT) (ATONING)
Ex 30,10 with the blood of the a sin
Lv 17,11 a may thereby be made
23,27 the Day of A,
Nm 31,50 make a for ourselves
2Mc 3,33 offering the sacrifice of a,
12,46 he made a for the dead
Sir 45,23 a for the children of Israel

AUTHORITY (AUTHORITIES)
1Mc 12, 4 addressed to the a in the various
Mt 9, 6 a on earth to forgive sins
Mk 2,10 a to forgive sins on earth
Jn 7,26 Could the a have realized
Rom 13, 1 no a except from God,
1Cor 11,10 a sign of a on her head,
Eph 3,10 and a in the heavens.
1Tm 2, 2 and for all in a,
2,12 to have a over a man.
Ti 2,15 and correct with all a.

AWAKE
Jb 8, 6 he will a for you and restore
Ps 17,15 I a, let me be filled with
57, 9 Awake, my soul; a,
Prv 23,35 I a to seek wine once again
Is 26,19 a and sing, you who lie
Dn 12, 2 dust of the earth shall a;
Hb 2, 7 who make you tremble a?
Mt 25,13 Therefore, stay a,
Lk 9,32 but becoming fully a,
Rom 13,11 for you to a from sleep.
Eph 5,14 "a, O sleeper, and arise
1Thes 5,10 are a or asleep we may live

AWE (SOME)
Dt 7,21 is a great and a God.
2Mc 1,24 God, creator of all things, a and
Ps 65, 6 with a deeds of justice,
66, 3 "How a your deeds!
89, 8 more a than all who sit
99, 3 great and a name
111, 9 holy and a is your name.
Dn 9, 4 Lord, great and a God
Lk 21,11 a sights and mighty signs

B

BAAL (S)
Gn 36,38 When Shaul died, B-hanan,
Ex 14, 2 camp in front of B-zephon,

Nm 22,41 took Balaam up on Bamoth-B,
Dt   4, 3 Lord did at B-peor: the Lord,
Jgs   2,11 the Lord by serving the **B**.
1Kgs 18,18 the Lord and following the **B**.
     18,25 said to the prophets of **B**,
2Kgs 10,28 rooted out the worship of **B**
Ps 106,28 joined in the rites of **B** of Peor,
Song 8,11 had a vineyard at B-hamon;
Jer   2,23 have not gone after the **B**"?
Hos   9,10 to B-peor and consecrated
Zep   1, 4 place the last vestige of **B**,
Rom 11, 4 who have not knelt to **B**."

BABYLON
Ps 137, 1 By the rivers of **B** we sat
Jer 29,10 years have elapsed for **B**
     51,58 walls of spacious **B**
Rv 14, 8 "Fallen, fallen is **B** the great,

BAPTISM (S)
Mt 21,25 Where was John's **b** from?
Mk   1, 4 proclaiming a **b** of repentance
     11,30 Was John's **b** of heavenly
Acts 13,24 proclaiming a **b** of repentance
     19, 4 with a **b** of repentance,
Rom 6, 4 buried with him through **b**
Eph 4, 5 one Lord, one faith, one **b**;
Heb 6, 2 instruction about **b** and laying
1Pt 3,21 prefigured **b**, which saves you

BAPTIZE (D) (BAPTIZING)
Mt   3,11 I am **b** you with water
Mk   1, 8 will **b** you with the holy Spirit
Lk   3, 7 who came out to be **b** by him
Jn   1,26 "I **b** with water;
     1,33 who will **b** with the holy Spirit.'
1Cor 1,17 send me to **b** but to preach

BARREN (NESS)
Gn 11,30 Sarai was **b**;
     29,31 while Rachel remained **b**.
1Sm 1, 5 the LORD had made her **b**.
Lk   1, 7 because Elizabeth was **b**
Jn   1,36 her who was called **b**;
Acts 23,29 will say, 'Blessed are the **b**,
Gal 4,27 Rejoice, you **b** one

BATTLE
1Sm 17,47 For the **b** is the LORD's,
2Chr 20,15 the **b** is not yours but God's.
2Mc 13,15 the **b** cry "God's Victory,"
Ps 24, 8 the LORD, mighty in **b**.
Eccl 9,11 nor the **b** by the valiant,
Wis 12, 9 vanquished in **b** by the just,
Sir 4,28 LORD your God will **b** for you.
Jl   2, 5 a mighty people arrayed for **b**.
2Cor 10, 4 weapons of our **b**
Rv 16,14 assemble them for the **b**

BEAR (S) (BORE)
Gn   4,13 punishment is too great to **b**.
Ex 21, 4 she **b** him sons or daughters
2Sm 17, 8 are as fierce as a **b** in the wild
Ru   4,12 whom Tamar **b** to Judah."
Dn   7, 5 The second was like a **b**;
Mt   1,21 She will **b** a son
     3,10 tree that does not **b** good fruit
     7,18 good tree cannot **b** bad fruit,
Jn 15, 4 branch cannot **b** fruit
1Cor 15,49 we shall also **b** the image
2Tm 1, 8 but **b** your share of hardship
Rv 13, 2 it had feet like a **b**'s,
     19,10 who **b** witness to Jesus.

BEAT (EN) (ING)
Ex   9,25 it **b** down every growing thing

Nm 22,23 Balaam had to **b** her to bring
Dt 28, 7 The Lord will **b** down before
Ru   2,17 **b** out what she had gleaned
1Sm 17, 9 but if I **b** him and kill him,
2Sm 20,19 seeking to **b** down a city
2Chr 10,11 father **b** you with whips, but I
Tb   3, 9 husbands. Why do you **b** us?
2Mc 9, 2 to **b** a shameful retreat.
Jb 39,13 wings of the ostrich **b** idly;
Prv 19,25 If you **b** an arrogant man, the
Wis 5,11 lashed by the **b** of pinions,
Is 27,12 The LORD shall **b** out the grain
Mi   4, 3 **b** their swords
Mt 21,35 they **b**, another they killed,
Lk 12,48 deserving of a severe **b** shall
Acts 18,17 and **b** him in full view of
1Pt 2,20 patient when **b** for doing

BEAUTIFUL (BEAUTY)
Gn   6, 2 how **b** the daughters
2Sm 11, 2 who was very **b**.
     13, 1 Absalom had a **b** sister
Jdt 10, 7 very much astounded at her **b**
Song 1, 8 O most **b** among women,
     7, 7 How **b** you are
Wis 8, 2 and was enamored of her **b**.
Jer 3,19 a heritage most **b**
Mt 23,27 appear **b** on the outside,
Acts 3, 2 the **B** Gate
Jas 1,11 the **b** of its appearance vanishes.

BEFORE
Dt   1,30 **b** you, will himself fight
1Sm 1,12 long at prayer **b** the LORD,
1Mc 1, 3 the earth fell silent **b** him,
Ps   5, 9 straight your way **b** me.
     7,11 shield **b** me is God
    26, 3 Your love is **b** my eyes;
    51, 5 my sin is always **b** me.
Prv 16,18 Pride goes **b** disaster,
Mt 10,33 denies me **b** others,
1Cor 1,29 might boast **b** God.
Eph 1, 4 **b** the foundation
Heb 12, 2 joy that lay **b** him

BEGGAR
Sir 4, 4 A **b** in distress do not reject
Acts 9, 8 seen him earlier as a **b**

BEGINNING
Gn   1, 1 In the **b**,
2Mc 7,23 shapes each man's **b**,
Ps 111,10 the **b** of wisdom;
Sir 1,12 The **b** of wisdom
     10,12 The **b** of pride
     18, 5 man ends he is only **b**,
     25,23 In woman was sin's **b**,
Lk   1, 2 eyewitnesses from the **b**
Jn   1, 1 In the **b** was the Word,
1Jn 1, 1 from the **b**, what we have heard,

BEHIND
Ex 14,19 took up its place **b** them,
Lv 14,38 the door of the house **b** him
Nm   3,23 camped **b** the Dwelling,
Dt   2, 8 we left **b** us the Arabah route,
     25,18 rear all those who lagged **b**.
1Sm 11, 5 in from the field, **b** his oxen.
2Sm 15,16 concubines whom he left **b**
1Kgs 14, 9 you have cast **b** your back.
2Kgs 3,25 was left **b** its stone walls,
1Chr 19,10 both in front of and **b** him,
2Chr 13,13 his ambush lay **b** them.
Neh 4, 7 **b** the wall, near the exposed
Tb   8, 4 and closed the door **b** them,

1Mc 2,28 leaving **b** in the city all their
2Mc 12,18 except to leave **b** in one place
Ps 50,17 you cast my words **b** you!
    85,14 good fortune will follow **b**.
Jl   2,14 leave **b** him a blessing,
Mt   9,20 **b** him and touched the tassel
    16,23 "Get **b** me, Satan!
Lk   2,43 Jesus remained **b**

BELIEVE (S) (D) (BELIEVING)
Ex   4, 1 they will not **b** me,
1Kgs 10, 7 I did not **b** the report
2Chr 9, 6 I did not **b** the report
Tb 14, 4 I **b** God's word
Ps 78,32 did not **b** in his wonders.
Wis 12, 2 their wickedness and **b**
Sir 34, 7 who **b** in them have perished.
Mt 18, 6 little ones who **b** in me
    27,42 and we will **b** in him.
Mk   1,15 Repent, and **b** in the gospel."
     9,24 "I do **b**, help my unbelief!"
    11,24 **b** that you will receive
    15,32 that we may see and **b**."
    16,16 does not **b**
    16,17 accompany those who **b**
Jn   1, 7 that all might **b** through him.
     3,18 not **b** has already
     4,42 **b** because of your word;
     5,38 because you do not **b**
     6,29 you **b** in the one he sent
     7, 5 his brothers did not **b** in him.
     9,35 "Do you **b** in the Son of Man
    12,11 turning away and **b** in Jesus
    12,37 they did not **b** in him,
    12,39 they could not **b**,
    17,21 world may **b** that you sent me.
    20,27 do not be unbelieving, but **b**."
    20,31 **b** that Jesus is the Messiah
Acts 16,31 "**b** in the Lord Jesus and
     19, 4 telling the people to **b**
    24,14 I **b** everything
    26,27 do you **b** the prophets?
Rom 1,16 the salvation of everyone who **b**
     4,11 all the uncircumcised who **b**,
    10, 9 and **b** in your heart that God
1Cor 14,22 who **b** but for unbelievers,
Gal 3,22 given to those who **b**.
Eph 1,19 his power for us who **b**,
Phil 1,29 not only to **b** in him but also to
1Thes 2,13 at work in you who **b**.
     4,14 we **b** that Jesus died and rose
1Tm 1,16 who would come to **b** in him
     4, 3 who **b** and know the truth.
Heb 11, 6 must **b** that he exists
Jas 2,19 demons **b** that and tremble.
1Pt 1, 8 not see him now yet **b** in him,

BELIEVER (S)
Acts 4,32 The community of **b**
2Cor 6,15 **b** in common
1Tm 5,16 If any woman **b** has widowed

BELOVED
Gn 22,12 from me your own **b** son."
Tb   3,10 'You had only one **b** daughter,
Jer 12, 7 The **b** of my soul I deliver
Bar 3,37 to Israel, his **b** son.
Hos 3, 1 to a woman **b** of a paramour,
Mt   3,17 "This is my **b** Son,
Mk   9, 7 "This is my **b** Son
Lk 20,13 I shall send my **b** son;
Eph 5, 1 as **b** children,
Jude   1 **b** in God the Father
        20 you, **b**, build yourselves up
Rv 20, 9 the holy ones and the **b** city.

BESIDES

Gn 14,16 **b** bringing back his kinsman
Dt 32,39 there is no god **b** me.
Jos 5, 7 not have other gods **b** me.
1Sm 16,18 **b** being an able speaker,
Wis 12,13 neither is there any god **b** you
Is 44, 8 or any Rock **b** me?
45, 5 there is no God **b** me.
56, 8 **b** those already gathered.
Dn 14,41 and there is no other **b** you!"
Mt 6,33 things will be given you **b**.

BETHLEHEM

Gn 35,19 Ephrath [that is, B].
Jgs 19, 2 for her father's house in B of
Ru 1,19 together till they reached B.
1Sm 16, 1 sending you to Jesse of B,
1Chr 2,51 the father of B, and Hareph,
2Chr 11, 6 He built up B, Etam, Tekoa,
Ezr 2,21 ninety-five; sons of B,
Jer 41,17 lplace of Chimham near B,
Mi 5, 2 But you, B-Ephrathah,
Mt 2, 1 Jesus was born in B
2, 6 'And you, B, land of Judah,
Jn 2,15 Let us go, then, to B

BETRAY (ED)

Jos 2,14 "If you do not **b** this errand
1Sm 27,11 they would **b** him by saying,
Ezr 10, 2 "We have indeed **b** our God
Ps 73,15 " I would have **b** your people.
Sir 27,17 if you **b** his confidence,
Jer 24,16 The traitors **b**: with treachery
Ob 14 **b** not his fugitives on the
Mt 26,23 the one who will **b** me.
Mk 3,19 Judas Iscariot who **b** him.
Lk 22,21 the one who is to **b** me
Jn 6,64 the one who would **b** him,
12, 4 and the one who would **b** him,

BETTER

Ex 14,12 Far **b** for us to be
1Sm 15,22 Obedience is **b** than sacrifice,
1Mc 3,59 It is **b** for us to die
13, 5 I am not **b** than my brothers.
Ps 63, 4 For your love is **b** than life;
84,11 **b** the threshold of the house
Prv 8,19 My fruit is **b** than gold,
Eccl 4, 9 Two are **b** than one
Wis 15,17 is **b** than the things he worships
Sir 7,16 yourself **b** than your fellows;
16, 3 one can be **b** than a thousand;
20, 2 much **b** to admonish than to
Dn 1,15 looked healthier and **b** fed
Jon 4, 3 it is **b** for me to die
Mt 5,29 It is **b** for you to lose one
Lk 10,42 Mary has chosen the **b** part
1Cor 7, 9 it is **b** to marry than to be
Heb 7,19 a **b** hope is introduced,
8, 6 he is mediator of a **b** covenant,
11,16 desire a **b** homeland,
11,40 foreseen something **b** for
1Pt 3,17 **b** to suffer for doing good

BEYOND

Ex 18,11 a deity great **b** any other;
Nm 11,23 "Is this the LORD's reach?
1Sm 20,22 the arrow is **b** you,'
1Chr 16,25 awesome is he, **b** all gods.
Jb 9,10 things **b** reckoning.
36,26 **b** our knowledge
Ps 139, 6 Such knowledge is **b** me,
145, 3 is **b** understanding.
Prv 31,10 her value is far **b** pearls.
Eccl 7,23 but it was **b** me.

Wis 7,24 mobile **b** all motion,
Jer 17, 9 human heart, **b** remedy;
Lk 12,26 things are **b** your control,
23,47 was innocent **b** doubt."
1Cor 10,13 be tried **b** your strength;

BIND (S)

Nm 30, 3 **b** himself under oath
Jgs 16,11 **b** me tight with new ropes
Jb 5,18 For he wounds, but he **b** up
Ps 147, 3 brokenhearted, **b** up their
Hos 5, 1 he will **b** our wounds.
Mk 16,19 **b** on earth shall be bound

BIRTH

Gn 17,17 Or can Sarah give **b** at ninety?"
Ex 28,10 in the order of their **b**.
Lv 12, 2 conceived and gives **b** to
Nm 11,12 it I who gave them **b**,
Dt 32,18 the God who gave you **b**.
Ru 2,11 and the land of your **b**,
1Kgs 3,18 third day after I gave **b**,
2Kgs 19, 3 are at the point of **b**,
2Mc 14,42 unworthy of his noble **b**.
Jb 3,11 did I not perish at **b**,
Ps 58, 4 corrupt since **b**;
71, 6 On you I depend since **b**;
Eccl 4,14 royalty he was poor at **b**.
Wis 7, 5 has any different origin or **b**,
Sir 11,16 sinners from their **b**,
Is 23, 4 been in labor, nor given **b**,
Ez 16, 3 By origin and **b** you are of
Hos 2, 3 on the day of her **b**;
Mi 5, 3 who is to give **b** has borne,
Mt 1,18 the **b** of Jesus Christ came
Mk 7,26 a Syrophoenician by **b**, o
Lk 1,14 many will rejoice at his **b**,
Jn 9, 1 saw a man blind from **b**.
16,21 she has given **b** to a child,
1Cor 1,26 not many were of noble **b**.
Heb 11,23 for three months after his **b**,
Jas 1,15 maturity it gives **b** to death.
1,18 give us **b** by the word of truth
1Pt 1, 3 new **b** to a living hope

BIRTHRIGHT

Gn 25,34 Esau cared little for his **b**.
Heb 12,16 sold his **b** for a single meal.

BISHOP

1Tm 3, 2 a **b** must be irreproachable,
Ti 1, 7 a **b** as God's steward

BITTER (NESS)

Ex 12, 8 bread and **b** herbs.
15,23 water, because it was too **b**.
2Sm 2,26 afterward there will be **b**?
Ps 71,20 many **b** afflictions,
Eccl 7,26 More **b** than death
Wis 8,16 with her involves no **b**
Lam 3,15 He has sated me with **b** food,
Acts 8,23 you are filled with **b** gall
Rom 3,14 mouths are full of **b** cursing.
Eph 4,31 All **b**, fury, anger, shouting

BLAMELESS

Gn 6, 9 Noah, a good man and **b**
1Mc 4,42 He chose **b** priests,
Jb 1, 1 **b** and upright man named Job
Ps 7, 9 I am **b**, free of any guilt.
19,14 Then shall I be **b**,
51, 6 **b** when you condemn.
118, 1 Happy those whose way is **b**,
Prv 28,10 **b** men will gain prosperity.]

Wis 10, 5 kept him before God,
10,15 holy people and **b** race—
Phil 1,10 **b** for the day of Christ
2,15 be **b** and innocent,
1Thes 3,13 be **b** in holiness
5,23 preserved **b** for the coming

BLASPHEME (D) (S)

Prv 14,31 He who oppresses the poor **b**
Is 37, 6 the king of Assyria have **b** me.
Acts 26,11 attempt to force them to **b**;
Jas 2, 7 **b** the noble name

BLESS (ED)

Gn 12, 2 and I will **b** you;
12, 3 I will **b** those who bless you
32,27 let you go until you **b** me."
Ex 20,24 come to you and **b** you.
Nm 22, 6 whoever you **b** is blessed
2Chr 2,11 "B be the Lord, the God
Tb 3,11 your works forever **b** you.
4,19 At all times **b** the Lord
Ps 29,11 **b** his people with peace!
34, 2 I will **b** the LORD at all times
62, 5 **b** with their mouths
63, 5 I will **b** you as long as I
100, 4 **b** his name;
103, 1 **b** the LORD, my soul;
Sir 39,14 **b** the LORD
Bar 4, 4 B are we, O Israel; for
Lk 1,42 "Most **b** are you among women
Heb 6,14 "I will indeed **b** you

BLESSING (S)

Gn 27, 4 my special **b** before I die."
Lv 25,21 I will bestow such **b** on you
Jos 8,34 the **b** and the curses
Sir 4,13 the Lord bestows **b**.
39,22 His **b** overflows
Mk 14,19 the **b**, broke the loaves,
Eph 1, 3 spiritual **b** in the heavens,

BLIND (ED) (NESS)

Ex 4,11 to one and makes another **b**?
Lv 19,14 block in front of the **b**,
Dt 15,21 a firstling is lame or **b** or
27,18 who misleads a **b** man on his
2Sm 5, 6 the **b** and the lame will drive
2Kgs 6,18 "Strike this people **b**, I
Tb 5,10 a **b** man who cannot see
Jb 17, 7 has grown **b** with anguish,
Ps 146, 8 Lord gives sight to the **b**.
Eccl 12, 3 through the windows grow **b**;
Wis 2,21 their wickedness **b** them
19,17 And they were struck with **b**
Zep 1,17 till they walk like the **b**,
Zec 11,17 his right eye be **b** forever!
Mal 1, 8 offer a **b** animal for sacrifice,
Mt 15,14 **b** person leads a **b** person
23,16 "Woe to you, **b** guides,
Jn 9,25 I was **b** and now I see."

BLOOD (SHED)

Gn 4,10 Your brother's **b** cries out
9, 6 sheds the **b** of man,
Ex 12,13 Seeing the **b**, I will pass
24, 8 the **b** of the covenant
Lv 17, 4 shall be judged guilty of **b**
Dt 12,23 do not partake of the **b**;
2Mc 1, 8 shedding innocent **b**.
8, 3 to the **b** that cried out
Ps 9,13 For the avenger of **b** remembers
Prv 6,17 hands that shed innocent **b**;
Wis 11, 6 troubled with impure **b**
Ez 5,17 Pestilence and **b** shall stalk

Mt   26,28 my **b** of the covenant,
      27,24 innocent of this man's **b**.
Lk   22,44 became like drops of **b**
Jn   6,53 and drink his **b**,
Rom 3,25 through faith, by his **b**,
      5, 9 justified by his **b**.
1Cor 11,25 new covenant in my **b**.
Eph   1, 7 redemption by his **b**,
      6,12 not with flesh and **b**
Col   1,20 peace by the **b** of his cross
Heb   9,20 'the **b** of the covenant
      9,22 without the shedding of **b**
    12,24 **b** that speaks
1Jn   1, 7 **b** of his Son Jesus
Rv   1, 5 from our sins by his **b**,
      5, 9 with your **b** you purchased
     7,14 white in the **b** of the Lamb.
    12,11 by the **b** of the Lamb

BOAST (ING)
Jdt   6,17 all the **b** threats of Holofernes
Rom 3,27 is there then for **b**?
2Cor 10,17 **b** in the Lord."
Gal   6,14 never **b** except in the cross
Phil   1,26 so that your **b** in Christ Jesus

BODY (BODIES)
Gn   1, 6 separate one **b** of water from
2Sm   1,22 from the **b** of the valiant
Jdt   9, 2 disgracefully violated her **b**.
2Mc   7,37 I offer up my **b** and my life
Ps   44,26 our **b** are pressed to the earth
Wis   8,20 I attained an unsullied **b**.
     9,15 corruptible **b** burdens the soul
Sir   10, 9 during life man's **b** decays;
Mt   10,28 **b** but cannot kill the soul
Rom 1,24 mutual degradation of their **b**.
1Cor 6,19 your **b** is a temple
    11,24 "This is my **b** that is for you.
    12,13 all baptized into one **b**,
    15,44 sown a natural **b**.
Eph   1,23 church, which is his **b**,
Phil   1,20 will be magnified in my **b**,
Col   1,24 his **b**, which is the church,

BOLD (NESS)
Jdt   16,10 appalled at her **b**.
Sir   12,15 he makes no **b** move;

BONE (S)
Gn   2,23 **b** of my **b** and flesh
Nm   19,16 touches a human **b** or a grave,
Jgs   9, 2 am your own flesh and **b**."
2Sm   5, 1 your **b** and your flesh.
1Chr 11, 1 same **b** and flesh as you.
Jb   2, 5 touch his **b** and his flesh,
Jer   8, 1 the **b** of the kings and princes
Zep   3, 3 that have had no **b** to gnaw

BOOK (S)
Ex   32,33 strike out of my **b**.
1Mc 12, 9 the sacred **b** that are in our
Eccl 12,12 the making of many **b**
Jn   21,25 contain the **b** that would be
Rv   3, 5 his name from the **b** of life
    20,12 the **b** of life.
    20,15 found written in the **b** of life
    21,27 written in the Lamb's **b** of life.

BORN
1Mc   2, 7 Why was I **b** to see the ruin
Eccl   3, 2 time to be **b**, and a time to die
Wis   2, 2 haphazard were we **b**,
     4, 6 children of lawless unions
Sir   14,18 one dies and another is **b**.
Is   9, 5 a child is **b** to us,

    66, 8 nation be **b**
Bar   3,26 In it were **b** the giants,
Lk   2, 11 a savior has been **b** for you
Jn   3, 3 being **b** from above."
     3, 4 be **b** again?
     3, 5 being **b** of water and Spirit.
     3, 7 'You must be **b** from above.'
     3, 8 everyone who is **b** of the Spirit
1Pt   1,23 You have been **b** anew,

BRANCH (ES)
Ex   25,33 one **b** there are to be three
Lv   23,40 **b** of palms and boughs of
Dt   32,32 They are a **b** of Sodom's
1Mc 13,37 and the palm **b** that you sent.
2Mc 14, 4 gold crown and a palm **b**,
Song 7, 9 will take hold of its **b**.
Is   4, 2 The **b** of the LORD will be
Ez   8,17 put the **b** to my nose?
    15, 2 That **b** among the trees of
Mal   3,19 neither root nor **b**, says
Mt   13,32 come and dwell in its **b**.
Jn   15, 2 every **b** in me that does not
    15, 4 **b** cannot bear fruit on its own
    15, 6 be thrown out like a **b**

BREAD
Ex   12, 8 **b** and bitter herbs.
    23,15 the feast of Unleavened **B**.
Dt   8, 3 not by **b** alone
Tb   4,17 lavish with your **b** and wine
Ps   78,24 **b** from heaven
Eccl 11, 1 **b** upon the waters;
Wis   16,20 **b** from heaven,
Sir   15, 3 the **b** of understanding,
Is   55, 2 money for what is not **b**;
Mt   4, 4 does not live by **b** alone,
     6, 11 Give us today our daily **b**;
Mk   14,22 he took **b**, said the blessing
Lk   4, 4 does not live by **b** alone
    11, 3 our daily **b**
Jn   6,35 "I am the **b** of life;
     6,41 **b** that came down
     6,51 I am the living **b**
1Cor 11,23 **b**, and, after he had given
    11,26 eat this **b** and drink the cup,

BREAK (ING) (BROKEN)
Jgs   2, 1 never **b** my covenant
Jdt   8,30 an oath that we cannot **b**.
Prv   25,15 a soft tongue will **b** a bone.
Sir   19,16 before you **b** with him;
Is   42, 3 bruised reed he shall not **b**,
Bar   6,15 As useless as one's **b** tools
Mk   4,37 waves were **b** over the boat
Acts 20, 7 gathered to **b** bread,
1Cor 10,16 The bread that we **b**,
Rv   5, 2 the scroll and **b** its seals

BREASTPLATE
1Kgs 22,34 between the joints of his **b**.
1Mc   3, 3 put on his **b** like a giant.
Wis   5,18 don justice for a **b**
Is   59,17 justice as his **b**,
Eph   6,14 righteousness as a **b**,
1Thes 5, 8 putting on the **b** of faith

BREATH
Gn   2, 7 into his nostrils the **b** of life,
2Mc   7,22 I who gave you the **b** of life,
Ps   39, 6 All mortals are but a **b**.
Prv   20,27 from the LORD is the **b** of man;
Wis   2, 2 the **b** in our nostrils is a
Lk   8,55 Her **b** returned
Rv   11,11 **b** of life from God entered

BRIDE
Sir   15, 2 young **b** she will embrace
Is   62, 5 bridegroom rejoices in his **b**
Rv   19, 7 **b** has made herself ready.
    21, 2 **b** adorned for her husband.
    22,17 Spirit and the **b** say

BRIDEGROOM
1Mc   1,27 **b** took up lamentation
Ps   19, 6 like a **b** from his chamber,
Bar   2,23 the voice of the **b**
Jl   2,16 Let the **b** quit his room,
Mt   25, 5 Since the **b** was long delayed,
Mk   2,19 guests fast while the **b** is
Jn   3,29 greatly at the **b**'s voice.

BRING (S) (ING)
Gn   1, 11 "Let the earth **b** forth
     1,24 earth **b** forth all kinds of living
     3,16 shall you **b** forth children
     3,18 thistles shall it **b** forth to you,
1Kgs 14,10 Therefore, I am **b** evil upon
Jdt   9,13 **b** wound and wale
Wis   17,13 the cause that **b** on torment.
Sir   1,27 fall and **b** upon you dishonor;
    23,25 branches will not **b** forth fruit.
Bar   2,34 I will **b** them back to the land
Jl   4, 2 **b** them down to the Valley
Mt   2, 8 **b** me word, that I too
1Cor 4, 5 **b** to light what is hidden
Eph   6, 4 but **b** them up with the training
Heb   9,28 **b** salvation to those

BROKENHEARTED
Ps   34,19 LORD is close to the **b**,
    147, 3 Heals the **b**,
Is   61, 1 heal the **b**,

BROTHER (S)
Gn   4, 9 Am I my **b**'s keeper?"
2Chr 5,12 their sons and **b**
1Mc   3, 2 All his **b** and all who
Mt   5,24 be reconciled with your **b**,
     7, 3 the splinter in your **b**'s eye,
    18,15 "If your **b** sins [against you],
Mk   3,35 my **b** and sister and mother."
Lk   17, 3 If your **b** sins, rebuke him;
Rom 14,21 causes your **b** to stumble.
1Cor 8,13 if food causes my **b** to sin,
2Thes 3, 6 shun any **b** who conducts
     3,15 admonish him as a **b**.
Phlm ,16 more than a slave, a **b**,
Jas   2,15 If a **b** or sister has nothing
     4, 11 speaks evil of a **b**
1Jn   2, 11 Whoever hates his **b**
     3,17 sees a **b** in need and refuses
     4,20 hates his **b**, he is a liar;
     4,21 must also love his **b**.
3Jn   3 when some of the **b** came

BUILD (S) (ER) (ERS) (BUILT)
2Sm   7, 5 **b** me a house to dwell in
1Kgs 6,38 seven years to **b** it.
1Mc 10,10 **b** and restore the city.
Prv   14, 1 Wisdom **b** her house, but Folly
Wis   9, 8 You have bid me **b** a temple
Sir   40,26 **b** up confidence,
Lk   4,29 their town had been **b**
    20,17 The stone which the **b** rejected
1Cor 3,10 like a wise master **b**
Jude   20 **b** yourselves up in your most

BUILDING
Gn   11, 8 they stopped **b** the city.
2Cor 5, 1 we have a **b** from God,

10, 8 for **b** you up
Eph   4,12 for **b** up the body of Christ

BURDEN (S)

Gn   49,15 bent his shoulder to the **b**
Ex   18,22 your **b** will be lightened,
Nm   11,11 you **b** me with all this people
Dt   1,12 I alone bear the crushing **b**
1Sm 25,31 this as a qualm or **b**
2Sm 13,25 go lest we be a **b** to you."
2Chr 35, 3 be a **b** on your shoulders.
Neh   5,15 laid a heavy **b** on the people,
Ps   73, 5 They are free of the **b** of life
Wis   9,15 For the corruptible body **b** the
Jer 17,21 not to carry **b** on the sabbath
Ez   12, 6 shoulder the **b** and set out
Hos   8,10 shortly succumb under the **b.**
Mal   1,13 You also say, "What a **b**!"
Mt   11,30 yoke is easy, and my **b** light
2Cor 11, 9 I did not **b** anyone,
Phil 3,11 is no **b** for me but is a
1Thes 2, 9 order not to **b** any of you,
2Thes 3, 8 so as not to **b** any of you.
Heb 12, 1 rid ourselves of every **b**

BURN (ED) (ING) (BURNT)

Ex   21,24 foot for foot, burn for **b,**
Lv   1, 9 **b** the whole offering
Nm   5,26 and **b** it on the altar.
Dt   13,16 you shall **b** the city with
Jos 11, 6 horses and **b** their chariots."
1Sm   2,28 to **b** incense, and to wear
1Kgs 9,25 and to **b** incense before the
2Kgs 8,12 You will **b** their fortresses,
2Chr 4,20 gold which were to **b**
Ezr 10,14 our God's **b** anger over this
Jdt 16,17 shall **b** and suffer forever."
1Mc   6,35 I will **b** this temple down."
Jb   31,12 should **b** down to the abyss
Ps   51,18 a **b** offering you would not
Sir 45,16 **b** sacrifices of sweet odor
Is   1,31 Both shall **b** together, and
Bar   6,62 to **b** up the mountains and
Ez   16,41 They shall **b** your apartments
Hos   4,13 on the hills they **b** incense,
1Cor 3,15 if someone's work is up **b**
Rv   16, 8 power to **b** people with fire.

C

CAESAR

Mt   22,21 repay to C what belongs
     22,17 census tax to C or not?"
Lk   2, 1 decree went out from C
Jn   19,12 are not a Friend of C.
Phil 4,22 those of C's household.

CALL (ED) (ING)

Jgs   1,10 Hebron, which was formerly **c**
      8, 1 not **c** us when you went to
Ps 116,13 **c** on the name of the
    145,18 near to all who **c** upon you,
Is   5,20 those who **c** evil good,
     55, 6 **c** him while he is near
     65,24 Before they **c**, I will answer;
Lam   3,21 I will **c** this to mind,
Jl   3, 5 whom the LORD shall **c.**
Zep   3, 9 may **c** upon the name
Zec 13, 9 shall **c** upon my name,
Mt   9,13 **c** the righteous but sinners
Acts 9,14 all who **c** upon your name."
Rom 10,12 enriching all who **c**
     11,29 **c** of God are irrevocable
1Cor 1, 2 who **c** upon the name
Eph   4, 1 worthy of the **c**

4, 4 the one hope of your **c**;
1Thes 4, 7 did not **c** us to impurity
2Tm   2,22 those who **c** on the Lord
Rv   2, 2 who **c** themselves apostles

CAPTIVE (CAPTIVITY)

Nm   21, 1 and took some of them **c.**
Dt   21,13 lay aside her **c**'s garb.
Jgs 18,30 until the time of the **c** of the
2Sm 21,16 was about to take him **c.**
1Kgs 8,48 who took them **c**, pray to
2Kgs 24,15 led **c** from Jerusalem
Neh   1, 2 remnant preserved after the **c**
1Chr 3,17 sons of Jeconiah the **c** were ,
2Chr 6,37 the land where they are **c**
Tb   1, 2 was taken **c** from Thisbe,
Jdt   4,12 their wives to be taken **c,**
1Mc   1,32 took **c** the women and
Jb   38,30 **c** the surface of the deep
Ps 106,46 from all who held them **c.**
Song 7, 5 a king is held **c** in its tresses.
Is   10, 4 Lest it sink beneath the **c**
Lam   1, 5 **c** before the foe. Gone from
Bar   4,24 lately saw you taken **c,**
Ez   5,12 the people **c** to Babylon.
     32, 9 peoples when I lead you **c**
Hos 10, 6 Ephraim shall be taken into **c**
Am   1, 6 they took **c** whole groups
Na   2, 9 Its mistress is led forth **c,**
Rom   7, 6 dead to what held us **c,**
2Cor 10, 5 take every thought **c**

CARE (S) (FUL) (CARING)

Jgs 13, 4 be **c** to take no wine
Est   2, 3 Under the **c** of the royal eunuch
Ps 118, 4 keep your precepts with **c.**
Wis   3, 9 his **c** is with his elect.
Ez   44, 8 Instead of **c** for the service
Mt   6, 1 **c** not to perform righteous
      6,34 tomorrow will take **c** of itself
     25,43 you did not **c** for me.'
Mk   4,24 "Take **c** what you hear.
      4,38 not **c** that we are perishing
1Thes 2, 7 nursing mother **c** for her
1Tm   3, 5 take **c** of the church of God

CAST

Gn   2,21 the LORD God **c** a deep sleep
Ex   15, 1 he has **c** into the sea.
Lv   16, 8 shall **c** lots to determine
Ps   22,19 for my clothing they **c** lots.
Prv 16,33 When the lot is **c** into the lap,
Sir 21,23 keeps his glance **c** down.
Jl   4, 3 they have **c** lots;
Jn   19,24 for my vesture they **c** lots."
     21, 6 "**c** the net over the right

CELEBRATE

Ex   5, 1 they may **c** a feast to me
     12,17 **c** this day
     12,48 **c** the Passover of the LORD
     23,14 **c** a pilgrim feast to me
Nm   36, 4 **c** the jubilee year,
Dt   16,13 **c** the feast of Booths
2Chr 30, 1 Jerusalem to **c** the Passover
     30,13 **c** the feast of Unleavened
Neh   7,12 **c** with great joy,
Ps 147, 1 to **c** our God in song;
Mt   26,18 I shall **c** the Passover
Lk   15,23 Then let us **c** with a feast,
     15,32 now we must **c** and rejoice,

CHAIN (CHAINED)

Gn   41,42 gold **c** about his neck.
Sir 21,21 Like a **c** of gold is learning to
Mk   5, 3 him any longer, even with a **c.**

2Tm   2, 9 word of God is not **c.**

CHANGE (D) (CHANGERS)

Nm   23,19 that he should **c** his mind.
Dt   30, 3 your God, will **c** your lot;
1Mc   1,49 might forget the law and **c**
2Mc   4,46 and persuaded him to **c**
Jb   17,12 Such men **c** the night into
Ps 102,27 Like clothing you **c** them
Wis 12,10 dispositions would never **c;**
Sir 43, 8 how wondrous in this **c!**
Is   5,20 who **c** darkness into light,
Bar   2,30 they shall have a **c** of heart;
Dn   7,25 thinking to **c** the feast days
Zep   3, 9 For then I will **c** and purify the
Mt   21,12 the tables of the money **c**
     21,29 afterwards he **c** his mind and
Acts 6,14 **c** the customs that Moses
Gal   4,20 to **c** my tone, for I am
Phil 3,21 He will **c** our lowly body
Heb   7,12 there is a **c** of priesthood,
Jas   1,17 shadow caused by **c.**

CHARGE

1Mc   6,14 in **c** of his whole kingdom.
     14,42 shall have **c** of the temple,
Mt   27,37 the written **c** against him
Lk   12,44 put him in **c** of all his property.
     19,17 take **c** of ten cities.'
Jn   7,46 Can any of you **c** me with sin?
     18,29 "What **c** do you bring
Rom   8,33 a **c** against God's chosen
1Cor 9,18 offer the gospel free of **c**
2Cor 11, 7 God to you without **c**
1Tm   5,21 I **c** you before God and Christ
2Tm   4, 1 I **c** you in the presence of
Phlm 18 owes you anything, **c** it to me.

CHARIOT (S)

Ex   15, 1 horse and **c** he has cast
Jos 11, 4 a multitude of horses and **c.**
Jgs   4,15 dismounted from his **c**
1Sm   8,11 they will run before his **c.**
2Sm   8, 4 hamstrung all the **c** horses,
1Kgs 4,19 horses and draft animals
2Kgs 2,11 flaming **c** and flaming horses
2Chr 1,14 he could station in the **c** cities
Jdt   1,13 entire cavalry and all his **c**
2Mc   9, 7 he hurtled from the dashing **c,**
Ps   77,19 thunder of your **c** wheels
    104, 3 You make the clouds your **c;**
Sir 48, 9 in a **c** with fiery horses.
     49, 8 different creatures of the **c;**
Hos 10,13 you have trusted in your **c**
Hb   3, 8 steeds of your victorious **c?**
Zec   6, 2 The first **c** had red horses,
Acts 8,28 in his **c**, he was reading

CHEERFUL

Prv 15,30 A **c** glance brings joy
2Cor 9, 7 God loves a **c** giver.

CHILD (REN)

1Sm   1,11 handmaid a male **c,**
2Kgs 2,24 tore forty-two of the **c** to pieces.
Sir 22, 3 An unruly **c** is a disgrace
     30, 9 Pamper your **c** and he will
Is   7,14 virgin shall be with **c,**
Mt   1,18 **c** through the holy Spirit.
      1,23 virgin shall be with **c**
      2, 9 the place where the **c** was
      2,14 took the **c** and his mother
     18, 4 humbles himself like this **c**
Mk   7,27 "Let the **c** be fed first.
     10,15 like a **c** will not enter it."
Rom   8,14 the Spirit of God are **c** of God.
Rv   12, 2 with **c** and wailed aloud

12, 4 devour her c

CHOOSE (S) (CHOSE) (CHOSEN)
Gn 28, 2 there a wife for yourself
Ex 20,24 In whatever place I c
Lv 1,14 he shall c a turtledove
Dt 10,15 attached to them as to c
30,19 c life, then, that you and
1Sm 2,35 I will c a faithful priest who
2Sm 17, 1 let me c twelve thousand
1Kgs 8,16 I c David to rule my people
1Chr 15, 2 for the Lord c them to carry
Jb 9,14 c out arguments
34,33 It is you who must c, not I;
Sir 15,17 whichever he c shall be given
Bar 3,27 Not these did God c,
Hg 2,23 for I have c you, says the Lord
Jn 6,70 "Did I not c you twelve?
Acts 15,22 to c representatives and
Phil 1,22 not know which I shall c.
Jas 2, 5 God c those who are poor

CHOSEN
Sir 24,11 in the c city he has given
32, 1 c to preside at dinner,
46, 1 savior of God's c ones,
47,22 posterity of his c one,
Is 41, 8 Jacob, whom I have c,
Mt 22,14 are invited, but few are c."
Lk 10,42 Mary has c the better part
23,35 if he is the c one,
Jn 15,19 c you out of the world
Rv 17,14 called, c, and faithful."

CHRIST
Mt 1, 1 genealogy of Jesus C,
Mk 1, 1 the gospel of Jesus C
Acts 9,34 Jesus C heals you.
11,17 believe in the Lord Jesus C,
Rom 1, 4 Jesus C our Lord.
3,22 through faith in Jesus C
5, 1 through our Lord Jesus C,
5, 6 C, while we were still
5, 8 still sinners C died for us.
5,11 through our Lord Jesus C,
5,17 the one person Jesus C.
5,21 eternal life through Jesus C
6, 4 C was raised from the dead
6, 8 we have died with C,
6, 9 C, raised from the dead,
6,23 eternal life in C Jesus
7, 4 through the body of C,
7,25 through Jesus C our Lord.
8, 1 those who are in C
8, 2 spirit of life in C
8, 9 C does not belong to him
8,10 But if C is in you,
8,17 joint heirs with C,
8,34 It is C [Jesus] who died,
8,35 us from the love of C?
10, 4 C is the end of the law
12, 5 one body in C
13,14 put on the Lord Jesus C,
14, 9 why C died and came to life
15, 3 C did not please himself; but
15, 5 in keeping with C Jesus,
15,29 come in the fullness of C
16,18 do not serve our Lord C
1Cor 1, 2 sanctified in C Jesus,
1, 7 revelation of our Lord Jesus C.
1,12 Is C divided?
1,17 For C did not send me to
1,23 we proclaim C crucified,
1,30 you are in C Jesus,
2, 2 Jesus C, and him crucified.
3,11 namely, Jesus C.

4,10 We are fools on C account
8, 6 one Lord, Jesus C,
8,12 you are sinning against C.
10, 4 the rock was the C.
11, 3 C is the head
12,27 you are C's body,
15, 3 C died for our sins
15,13 neither has C been raised.
15,22 in C shall all be brought to life
2Cor 1, 5 For as C sufferings overflow to
2,14 leads us in triumph in C
3, 3 letter of C administered by us,
3,14 through C it is taken away.
4, 4 gospel of the glory of C,
4, 5 ourselves but Jesus C
4, 6 the face of [Jesus] C.
5,10 before the judgment seat of C,
5,14 the love of C impels us,
5,17 in C is a new creation
6,15 What accord has C with Beliar
10, 1 and clemency of C,
11, 2 as a chaste virgin to C.
Gal 1, 7 to pervert the gospel of C.
2, 4 freedom that we have in C
2,16 justified by faith in C
2,17 is C then a minister of sin
2,19 I have been crucified with C;
2,21 then C died for nothing.
3,16 your descendant," who is C.
3,26 children of God in C Jesus.
4,19 until C be formed in you!
5, 1 For freedom C set us free;
5, 4 You are separated from C,
5,24 those who belong to C [Jesus]
Eph 1, 3 has blessed us in C
1,10 sum up all things in C,
1,20 which he worked in C,
2, 5 brought us to life with C
2,10 created in C Jesus
2,12 were at that time without C,
2,20 C Jesus himself
3, 8 the inscrutable riches of C,
3,17 C may dwell in your hearts
4, 7 the measure of C's gift.
4,13 the full stature of C,
4,15 him who is the head, C,
5, 2 live in love, as C loved us
5,21 out of reverence for C.
5,23 just as C is head of the church
5,25 even as C loved the church
Phil 1,18 C is being proclaimed?
1,21 For to me life is C,
1,27 worthy of the gospel of C,
1,29 for the sake of C,
2, 1 encouragement in C,
2,11 that Jesus C is Lord,
3, 7 a loss because of C.
3,18 enemies of the cross of C.
4,19 glorious riches in C Jesus.
Col 1, 4 your faith in C Jesus
1,27 it is C in you,
1,28 perfect in C.
2, 2 the mystery of God, C,
2,17 the reality belongs to C.
3, 1 you were raised with C,
3, 3 is hidden with C in God.
3,15 peace of C control
1Thes 4,16 the dead in C will rise first.
5, 9 through our Lord Jesus C
2Thes 2, 1 coming of our Lord Jesus C.
2,14 glory of our Lord Jesus C.
1Tm 1,15 C Jesus came
1,16 C Jesus might display
2, 5 C Jesus, himself human,
2Tm 1, 9 grace bestowed on us in C
1,10 appearance of our savior C

2, 1 grace that is in C Jesus.
2, 3 like a good soldier of C
2, 8 C, raised from the dead,
2,10 salvation that is in C Jesus,
3,12 live religiously in C Jesus
3,15 salvation through faith in C
4, 1 presence of God and of C
Ti 2,13 our savior Jesus C,
Heb 3, 6 but C was faithful as a son
3,14 partners of C
5, 5 not C who glorified himself
6, 1 basic teaching about C
9,11 when C came as high priest
9,14 the blood of C,
9,24 For C did not enter into
9,28 so also C, offered once
10,10 body of Jesus C once forall.
13, 8 Jesus C is the same
1Pt 1, 2 with the blood of Jesus C
1, 3 the resurrection of Jesus C
1,11 sufferings destined for C
1,19 precious blood of C
2,21 C also suffered for you,
3,15 sanctify C as Lord
3,18 C also suffered for sins
3,21 Jesus C, who has gone
4,13 share in the sufferings of C,
4,14 insulted for the name of C,
2Pt 1, 1 and apostle of Jesus C,
1,16 coming of our Lord Jesus C,
1Jn 2, 1 Jesus C the righteous one.
2,22 denies that Jesus is the C.
3,23 name of his Son, Jesus C,
4, 2 Jesus C come in the flesh
5, 1 Jesus is the C is begotten
5,20 in his Son Jesus C.
2Jn 9 the teaching of the C
Jude 4 Master and Lord, Jesus C.
Rv 1, 1 The revelation of Jesus C,
1, 5 Jesus C, the faithful witness
20, 4 reigned with C
20, 6 priests of God and of C,

CHRISTIAN (S)
Acts 11,26 the disciples were first called C.
1Pt 4,16 made to suffer as a C

CHURCH (ES)
Mt 16,18 rock I will build my c,
18,17 refuses to listen even to the c
Acts 15,41 bringing strength to the c.
1Cor 14, 4 prophesies builds up the c.
14,12 building up the c.
2Cor 8, 1 given to the c of Macedonia
Gal 1,13 I persecuted the c of God
Eph 5,23 Christ is head of the c,
Col 1,18 head of the body, the c.
1Thes 2,14 have become imitators of the c

CIRCUMCISE (D)
Dt 30, 6 will c your hearts
Rom 2,26 will he not be considered c?

CIRCUMCISION
Rom 2,25 c, to be sure, has value
2,29 c is of the heart,
Gal 5, 6 neither c nor uncircumcision

CLAY
Wis 15, 8 from the selfsame c;
Sir 33,10 all men are of c,
Is 45, 9 Dare the c say to its modeler,
64, 7 the c and you the potter
Jer 18, 6 like c in the hand of the
Dn 2,41 iron mixed with c tile,
Jn 9, 6 smeared the c on his eyes,
Rom 9,21 have a right over the c,

2Tm   2,20   of wood and c,

CLEAN (CLEANSED) (CLEANSING)
Gn   7, 2   c animal, take with you seven
Lv   4,12   a c place where the ashes
Nm   4,13   After c the altar of its ashes
Ps   24, 4   "The c of hand and pure of
    51,12   A c heart create for me, God
Prv   20, 9   I am c of my sin"?
Wis   15, 7   that serve for c purposes
Sir   34, 4   the unclean produce the c?
Mt   5, 8   Blessed are the c of heart,
    8, 2   you can make me c."
    12,44   swept c, and put in order.
Mk   7,19   Thus he declared all foods c
Jn   13,10   for he is c all over;
Acts   10,15   "What God has made c,
Rom   14,20   Everything is indeed c,
Ti   1,15   To the c all things are clean,
Heb   10,22   hearts sprinkled c

CLOTHE (S) (ED) (CLOTHING)
Gn   3,21   with which he c them.
Dt   8, 4   The c did not fall from you
Lk   2, 7   wrapped him in swaddling c
Rv   16,15   watches and keeps his c

CLOUD (S)
Ex   13,21   column of c
Dt   1,33   by day in the c,
1Kgs   18,44   c as small as a man's hand
2Mc   2, 8   will be seen in the c,
Ps   18,13   Before him scudded his c
Wis   19, 7   c overshadowed their camp;
Sir   24, 4   on a pillar of c.
    45, 5   led him into the c,
Ez   1,28   which appears in the c
Mt   24,30   coming upon the c of heaven
Heb   12, 1   so great a c of witnesses,
Rv   14,14   there was a white c,

COIN (S)
1Mc   15, 6   you to c your own money
Mk   12,42   put in two small c
Lk   15, 9   found the c that I lost.'

COME (S) (COMING)
Ex   3, 5   "C no nearer!
    7,25   When anguish c they shall seek
    34, 5   Having c down in a cloud,
Jgs   17,14   c into the land
2Kgs   1,10   fire c down from heaven
Tb   13,11   shall c to you from afar,
Jdt   5,19   c back from the Dispersion
1Mc   1, 11   many evils have c
2Mc   3,17   had c over the man
Ps   121, 1   From where will my help c?
Wis   2, 1   c back from the nether
Sir   22,24   abuse c before bloodshed.
Hos   3, 5   c trembling to the LORD
Mt   4,19   "C after me, and I will
    5,17   c to abolish the law
    6,10   your kingdom c,
    9,13   c to call the righteous
    10,34   c to bring not peace
    14,29   He said, "C."
    16,27   Son of Man will c
Mk   1,17   "C after me,
    8,34   "Whoever wishes to c
    10,14   "Let the children c to me;
    10,45   did not c to be served
    14,41   The hour has c.
Lk   19,10   c to seek and to save
    21, 8   many will c in my name,
    21, 11   signs will c from the sky.
Jn   1,32   Spirit c down like a dove

    4,16   call your husband and c
    7,37   c to me and drink.
    13,33   Where I go you cannot c,'
    14, 3   I will c back again
    17, 1   "Father, the hour has c.
1Cor   10,13   No trial has c to you
Gal   3,25   now that faith has c,
    4, 4   fullness of time had c,
Col   1, 6   gospel, that has c to you.
    2,17   shadows of things to c;
1Thes   1, 5   c to you in word alone
2Jn   7   acknowledge Jesus Christ as c
Rv   22,17   Spirit and the bride say, "C."
    22,17   Let the one who thirsts c
    22,20   Amen! C, Lord Jesus!

COMFORT
Ru   4,15   He will be your c
1Chr   19, 2   c him over the death
Jb   2, 11   sympathy and c.
    7,13   "My bed shall c me,
    21,34   you offer me vain c,
Ps   71,21   turn and c me,
    86,17   LORD, help and c me.
    119,50   This is my c in affliction,
Wis   3,18   nor c in the day of scrutiny
Sir   3, 6   brings c to his mother.
Is   40, 1   C, give c to my people,
    51, 3   LORD shall c Zion
    51,19   Who is there to c you?
    57,18   I will give full c to them
    61, 2   to c all who mourn;
    66,13   so will I c you;
Lam   2,13   your c, virgin daughter Zion?
Zec   1,17   LORD will again c Zion,
    10, 2   empty c they offer.
Jn   11,19   c them about their brother.
Col   4, 11   have been a c to me.

COMMAND (ED)
Ex   7, 2   tell him all that I c you.
Nm   24,13   contrary to the c of the LORD'?
Dt   4, 2   not add to what I c
1Sm   15,32   Afterward Samuel c, "Bring
Tb   3, 6   c my life breath
2Mc   7,30   I will not obey the king's c.
Sir   7,31   portion as you have been c
Jer   1, 7   I c you, you shall speak.
    1,17   tell them all that I c you.
    7,23   all the ways that I c you,
    11, 4   and do all that I c you.
    26, 2   whatever I c you, tell them,
Jon   2, 11   Then the Lord c the fish
Mt   4, 6   c his angels concerning you'
Lk   4,10   c his angels concerning you,
Jn   15,14   if you do what I c you.
    15,17   This I c you: love one another.

COMMANDMENT (S)
Dt   4, 2   In your observance of the c
1Mc   2,21   forsake the law and the c.
Eccl   8, 5   the c experiences no evil,
Mt   22,38   greatest and the first c.
Mk   12,31   c greater than these."
Jn   13,34   a new c: love one another.
    15,12   This is my c: love one another
Rom   7, 8   opportunity in the c,
    7, 9   c came, sin became alive;
    7,10   the c that was for life turned
    7, 11   an opportunity in the c,
    7,12   the c is holy and righteous
    7,13   measure through the c.
    13, 9   other c there may be,
Eph   6, 2   the first c with a promise,
1Tm   6,14   the c without stain or reproach
Heb   9,19   every c had been proclaimed

1Jn   2, 3   him is to keep his c.
2Jn   6   this is the c, as you heard

COMMIT (S)
Ex   20,14   "You shall not c adultery.
Lv   4, 2   a person inadvertently c a sin
Tb   14,10   c all sorts of wickedness
2Mc   2,25   c things to memory,
Mt   5,27   'You shall not c adultery.'
    5,32   a divorced woman c adultery.
    19,18   you shall not c adultery,
Mk   10,19   you shall not c adultery;
Lk   18,20   'You shall not c adultery;
Rom   2,22   do you c adultery?
1Cor   6,18   Every other sin a person c
Jas   2, 11   Even if you do not c adultery
1Jn   2, 1   so that you may not c sin.
Rv   2,22   those who c adultery

COMMON
Nm   16,29   the fate c to all mankind,
2Mc   8,29   made supplication in c,
    9, 4   Jerusalem the c graveyard
Prv   22, 2   have a c bond
    29,13   oppressor have a c bond
Wis   7, 3   inhaled the c air,
Acts   2,44   had all things in c;
2Cor   6,15   in c with an unbeliever?

COMPASSION
2Kgs   13,23   looked on them with c
1Mc   3,44   implore mercy and c.
2Mc   7, 6   he truly has c on us,
Ps   51, 3   in your abundant c
    77,10   in anger withheld c?"
    103, 4   you with love and c,
    103,13   has c on his children,
    103,13   LORD has c on the faithful.
    119,77   Show me c that I may live,
    119,156   Your c is great,
Hos   13,14   My eyes are closed to c.
    14, 4   in you the orphan finds c."
Mi   7,19   will again have c on us,
Hb   3, 2   in your wrath remember c!
Zec   7, 9   c toward each other.
Mal   3,17   I will have c on them,
Lk   15,20   was filled with c.
2Cor   1, 3   the Father of c
Phil   2, 1   c and mercy
Col   3,12   heartfelt c, kindness,
1Jn   3,17   in need and refuses him c,

CONDEMN (ATION) (ED)
2Mc   9, 4   Yet the c of Heaven rode with
Jb   34,17   c the supreme Just One,
    34,29   who then can c?
    40, 8   Would you c me that you
Ps   51, 6   blameless when you c.
    94,21   c the innocent to death?
Wis   2,20   Let us c him to a shameful
Mt   12,41   this generation and c it,
    12,42   this generation and c it,
    20,18   they will c him to death,
Mk   10,33   they will c him to death
Lk   6,37   and you will not be c.
    11,32   this generation and c it,
Jn   3,17   Son into the world to c the
    7,51   "Does our law c a person
    8, 11   "Neither do I c you.
    12,48   it will c him on the last day
Rom   14,22   the one who does not c
1Jn   3,20   in whatever our hearts c,
    3,21   if [our] hearts do not c us,

CONDUCT
Tb   4,14   yourself in all your c.
Jdt   8,19   for such c that our

Est   1,18 hear of the queen's c
2Mc   4,37 noble c of the deceased.
       14, 8 unreasonable c of the
Prv   1, 3 training in wise c,
       20,11 his c is innocent and right.
       21, 8 the c of the innocent is right
       31,27 watches the c of her
Eccl   6, 8 how to c himself in life?"
Sir   3,17 c your affairs with humility,
       37,17 The root of all c is the mind;
       42, 8 infirm answering for wanton c.
Jer   4,18 Your c, your misdeeds,
Ez   7, 3 judge you according to your c
Phil   1,27 c yourselves in a way worthy
1Tm   4,12 in speech, c, love, faith, and

CONFESS (ES)
Lv   5, 5 c the sin he has incurred
       16,21 he shall c over it
       26,40 c that they and their fathers
Nm   5, 7 he shall c the wrong he has
2Mc   7,37 c that he alone is God
Ps   32, 5 "I c my faults to the LORD
Prv   28,13 he who c and forsakes them
Rom   10,10 and one c with the mouth
Phil   2,11 every tongue c that Jesus
Heb   13,15 the fruit of lips that c his
1Jn   2,23 but whoever c the Son

CONFIDENCE (CONFIDENT)
2Kgs   18,19 do you base this c of yours?
2Chr   32, 8 people took c from the words
1Mc   10,71 If you have c in your forces,
2Mc   11, 4 felt exultant c in his myriads
Jb   6,20 though they were c
Prv   3,26 the Lord will be your c,
       11,13 trustworthy man keeps a c.
Sir   13, 5 smiles he will win your c;
       22,22 a c broken, or a treacherous
       40,26 Wealth and vigor build up c,
Is   36, 4 On what do you base this c
Rom   2,19 if you are c that you
2Cor   3, 4 Such c we have through
       7, 4 I have great c in you,
       7,16 I have c in you in every
       8,22 because of his great c in you.
Eph   3,12 c of access through faith
Phil   3, 3 do not put our c in flesh,
2Thes 3, 4 We are c of you in the Lord
Heb   3, 6 we hold fast to our c
       10,19 c of entrance into the
       10,35 do not throw away your c;
1Jn   2,28 he appears we may have c
       3,21 we have c in God
       4,17 we have c on the day of
       5,14 we have this c in him,

CONQUER (ED)
Nm   24,24 When they have c Asshur
1Mc   1, 4 strong army and c provinces
       8, 4 c the whole country,
       8,12 c kings both far and near
Jn   16,33 I have c the world."
Rom   12,21 Do not be c by evil
1Jn   2,13 you have c the evil one.

CONSCIENCE
1Sm   25,31 qualm or burden on your c,
Wis   17,11 because of a distressed c,
Sir   14, 2 the man whose c does not
       37,14 man's c can tell him his
Dn   13,56 lust has subverted your c.
Acts   23, 1 clear c before God to this
       24,16 keep my c clear before God
Rom   2,15 their c also bears witness
       9, 1 my c joins with the holy Spirit

       13, 5 also because of c.
1Cor   8, 7 their c, which is weak, is
       8,10 may not his c too, weak as
       10,25 questions on grounds of c,
       10,27 questions on grounds of c.
       10,28 on account of c;
       10,29 not your own c, but the
       10,29 someone else's c?
2Cor   1,12 testimony of our c
       4, 2 to everyone's c
1Tm   1, 5 good c, and a sincere faith.
       1,19 having faith and a good c.
       3, 9 faith with a clear c.
2Tm   1, 3 I worship with a clear c
Heb   9, 9 perfect the worshiper in c
       10,22 clean from an evil c
       13,18 we have a clear c,
1Pt   3,16 keeping your c clear,
       3,21 to God for a clear c,

CONSECRATE (D)
Ex   13, 2 "C to me every first-born
Dt   15,19 "You shall c to the LORD,
2Chr   2, 3 c it to him,
       13, 9 c himself with a young bull
Jn   17,19 I c myself for them,

CONSOLE
Gn   37,35 and daughters tried to c him,
2Sm   3,35 went to c David with food
Jer   15, 5 Jerusalem, who will c you?
       16, 7 to c them in their
       31, 9 I will c them and guide
       31,13 I will c and gladden them
Na   3, 7 can one find any to c her?"
1Thes 4,18 c one another with these

CONSUME (D) (CONSUMING)
Ex   15, 7 wrath to c them like stubble
       32,10 blaze up against them to c
Ps   21,10 LORD's anger will c them,
Eccl   10,12 but the fool's lips c him.
Wis   6,23 Neither shall I admit c jealousy
Is   33,11 spirit shall c you like fire.
       43, 2 the flames shall not c you.
Jer   17,27 c the palaces of Jerusalem.
Ez   22,31 my fiery wrath I have c them
Jn   2,17 Zeal for your house will c

CONTEMPT
1Mc   1,39 her honor to c.
2Mc   7,39 resented the boy's c.
       12,14 with c, insulting them
Ps   31,19 that attack the just in c
       55,13 foe had viewed me with c,
       71,13 Cover with c and scorn
Prv   18, 3 With wickedness comes c,
Wis   4,18 see, and hold him in c;
Sir   26,19 illustrious men held in c;
Ez   36, 5 wholehearted joy and utter c
Ob   2 you are held in dire c.
1Cor   11,22 c for the church of God
Gal   4,14 did not show disdain or c
1Tm   4,12 no one have c for your
Heb   6, 6 and holding him up to c.
       10,29 due the one who has c
2Pt   2,10 and show c for lordship.

CORNERSTONE
Jb   38, 6 who laid the c,
Is   28,16 precious c as a sure
Jer   51,26 not take from you a c,
Mt   21,42 has become the c
Mk   12,10 has become the c
Lk   20,17 has become the c
Acts   4,11 which has become the c

1Pt   2, 6 c, chosen and precious,
       2, 7 has become the c,"

CORRUPT (ION)
Gn   6,11 c and full of lawlessness.
1Mc   2,62 for his glory ends in c and
Ps   5,10 their hearts are c.
1Cor   15,50 nor does c inherit incorruption.

COUNSEL (OR) (ORS)
2Sm   15,12 the Gilonite, David's c, an
Tb   4,19 possesses good c,
Est   4C,22 but turn their own c against
1Mc   8,15 and twenty men took c
Jb   12,13 his are c and understanding
       18, 7 his own c casts him down.
Ps   1, 1 follow the c of the wicked,
       73,24 With your c you guide me,
       107,11 scorned the c of the Most High,
Prv   8,14 Mine are c and advice;
       15,22 fail when there is no c,
       19,20 Listen to c
       31,26 on her tongue is kindly c.
Wis   9,13 what man knows God's c,
       9,17 who ever knew your c,
Sir   8,17 Take no c with a fool,
       44, 3 Or c in their prudence
Is   11, 2 A spirit of c and of strength,
       28,29 wonderful is his c
Ez   7,26 and c to the elders, while
Dn   2,14 Daniel prudently took c with
Mi   4,12 nor understand his c,
1Cor   2,16 so as to c him?"

COURAGE
2Sm   2, 7 Take c, therefore,
       7,27 now finds the c
2Mc   6,31 a model of c
Jb   23,16 God has made my c fail;
Ps   23, 4 rod and staff give me c.
       27,14 take c; be stouthearted,
Sir   30,23 renew your c,
       34,13 Lively is the c of those
Mt   14,27 "Take c, it is I;
Mk   6,50 "Take c, it is I,
Acts   23,11 "Take c.
       27,22 keep up your c;
       27,25 keep up your c, men;
1Thes 2, 2 drew c through our God

COVENANT (S)
Gn   9, 9 establishing my c with you
       17, 2 I will establish my c,
Ex   19, 5 keep my c,
       24, 7 the book of the c,
Dt   4,13 proclaimed to you his c,
1Kgs   8,21 in which is the c of the LORD,
       8,23 you keep your c of kindness
2Kgs   23, 2 the book of the c
1Chr   16,15 remembers forever his c
2Chr   6,14 keep your c and show
       34,30 of the c that had been found
Neh   1, 5 preserve your c of mercy
Jdt   9,13 dire things against your c,
2Mc   8,15 for the sake of the c
Ps   105, 8 remembers forever his c,
Sir   17,10 everlasting c he has made
       24,22 book of the Most High's c,
       28, 7 the Most High's c,
Is   33, 8 C are broken, their terms are
       61, 8 a lasting c I will make
Jer   11, 3 observe the terms of this c,
       31,31 I will make a new c
       31,32 will not be like the c
       31,33 the c which I will make
Bar   2,35 as an eternal c,

Mal   3, 1 messenger of the c
Mt   26,28 my blood of the c,
Mk 14,24 my blood of the c,
Lk 22,20 new c in my blood,
1Cor 11,25 new c in my blood.
Gal 4,24 These women represent two c.
Heb 8, 6 mediator of a better c,
      8, 8 new c with the house of
      9,15 mediator of a new c
   12,24 mediator of a new c,

COVET
Ex 20,17 shall not c your neighbor's
   20,17 not c your neighbor's wife,
   34,24 no one to c your land
Dt   5,21 not c your neighbor's wife.
    7,25 Do not c the silver or gold
Mi   2, 2 They c fields
Rom 7, 7 "You shall not c."
   13, 9 you shall not c,"
Jas   4, 2 You c but do not possess.

CREATE (D)
Gn   1, 1 In the beginning, when God c
Is   4, 5 Then will the LORD c,
   45, 7 and c the darkness,
   45, 7 and c woe;
   65,17 about to c new heavens
Am 4,13 mountains, and c the wind
Eph 2,10 his handiwork, c in Christ Jesus

CREATION
Gn   2, 3 he had done in c.
Tb   8, 5 all your c praise you
Wis 2, 6 use the freshness of c
    5,17 arm c to requite the enemy;
Mk 10, 6 from the beginning of c,
Rom 1,20 since the c of the world,
    8,19 c awaits with eager
    8,20 c was made subject
    8,21 c itself would be set free
    8,22 all c is groaning in labor
2Cor 5,17 in Christ is a new c
Gal 6,15 only a new c.
Col 1,15 the firstborn of all c.
2Pt   3, 4 from the beginning of c."
Rv   3,14 the source of God's c,

CREATOR
Gn 14,19 c of heaven and earth;
   14,22 c of heaven and earth,
Jdt   9,12 c of the waters,
   13,18 c of heaven and earth,
2Mc 1,24 c of all things,
    7,23 c of the universe
   13,14 c of the world,
Eccl 12, 1 Remember your c
Sir   3,16 accursed of his c,
    4, 6 his c will hear his prayer.
Is 40,28 c of the ends of the earth
   43,15 c of Israel, your King.
Mt 19, 4 c 'made them male and
Rom 1,25 creature rather than the c,
Col 3,10 in the image of its c.
1Pt 4,19 over to a faithful c.

CREATURE
Jdt 16,14 Let your every c serve you;
Ps 145, 9 compassionate to every c.
Sir 31,13 No c is greedier than the eye
Mk 16,15 the gospel to every c.
Rom 1,25 the c rather than the creator,
    8,39 nor any other c will be able to
Heb 4,13 No c is concealed from him,
Rv   4, 7 first c resembled a lion,
    5,13 every c in heaven and on
    6, 3 second living c cry out,

    6, 5 third living c cry out,
    6, 7 fourth living c cry out,
   16, 3 every c living in the sea died.

CROOKED
Dt 32, 5 a perverse and c race!
2Sm 22,27 toward the c you are astute.
Ps 125, 5 turn aside to c ways
  139,24 See if my way is c,
Prv 2,15 Whose ways are c,
    8, 8 none of them is wily or c;
   10, 9 he whose ways are c
   28,18 he whose ways are c
Eccl 7,13 straight what he has made c?
Wis 16, 5 the bite of c serpents,
Is 59, 8 they have made c,
Lam 3,36 When he presses a c claim,
Phil 2,15 a c and perverse generation,

CROSS
Dt   4,21 I should not c the Jordan
1Mc 5,48 "We wish to c your territory
   16, 6 were afraid to c the stream,
Prv 4,15 c it not,
Mt   8,18 to c to the other side.
   10,38 take up his c and follow
   16,24 take up his c, and follow
Mk   8,34 take up his c, and follow
Lk   9,23 take up his c daily
   14,27 carry his own c and come
Jn 19,17 carrying the c himself he
1Cor 1,17 so that the c of Christ might
    1,18 message of the c is
Gal 5,11 stumbling block of the c
    6,12 persecuted for the c of
    6,14 never boast except in the c
Eph 2,16 one body, through the c,
Phil 2, 8 even death on a c.
    3,18 enemies of the c of Christ.
Col 1,20 by the blood of his c
    2,14 nailing it to the c;
Heb 12, 2 endured the c, despising its
1Pt 2,24 his body upon the c,

CROWN (ED)
Jdt 15,13 women c themselves with
Jb   2, 7 to the c of his head.
Prv 4, 9 a glorious c will she bestow
   12, 4 the c of her husband,
   16,31 Gray hair is a c of glory;
   17, 6 Grandchildren are the c of
Wis 4, 2 And forever it marches c in
    4, 9 is the hoary c for men,
Is 35,10 Zion singing, c with everlasting
Zec 9,16 jewels in a c raised aloft
Mt 27,29 Weaving a c out of thorns,
Mk 15,17 weaving a c of thorns,
Jn 19, 2 wove a c out of thorns
   19, 5 wearing the c of thorns
1Cor 9,25 to win a perishable c,
Phil 4, 1 my joy and c,
1Thes 2,19 our hope or joy or c
2Tm 2, 5 receive the winner's c
    4, 8 the c of righteousness
Jas 1,12 receive the c of life
1Pt 5, 4 the unfading c of glory.
Rv   2,10 I will give you the c of life. "
   14,14 with a gold c on his head

CRUCIFY (CRUCIFIED)
Mt 23,34 them you will kill and c,
   27,31 led him off to c him.
Mk 15,13 shouted again, "C him."
   15,14 shouted the louder, "C him."
   15,15 handed him over to be c.
Lk 23,21 "C him! Crucify him!"

Jn 19, 6 "C him, crucify him!"
   19, 6 yourselves and c him.
   19,10 I have power to c you?
   19,16 over to them to be c.
1Cor 1,13 Was Paul c for you?

CRUSH (ED)
Lv 22,24 bruised or c or torn
1Mc 3,22 He himself will c them
Jb   4,19 who are c more easily
    6, 9 God would decide to c me,
Ps 89,24 I will c his foes before him,
Jer 1,17 Be not c on their account
Rom 16,20 c Satan under your feet.

CRY (ING) (CRIED)
Gn 21,17 God heard the boy's c
Nm 11, 2 when the people c out to Moses
Neh 9, 4 who c out to the Lord
Ps   5, 3 Hear my c for help,
   34,16 ears for their c.
   40, 2 heard my c,
  130, 2 attentive to my c for mercy.
Prv 21,13 his ear to the c of the poor
Dn   3, 4 A herald c out, "Nations
Jon 1, 5 each one c to his god.
Jn   1,23 'the voice of one c out
Rom 8,15 we c, "Abba, Father!"

CUP
Ps 23, 5 my c overflows.
Is 51,22 the c of staggering;
Mt 10,42 gives only a c of cold water
   20,22 Can you drink the c that
   23,25 cleanse the outside of c
   23,26 first the inside of the c,
   26,27 he took a c, gave thanks,
   26,39 let this c pass from me;
Mk   9,41 gives you a c of water to drink
   10,38 you drink the c that I drink
   10,39 "The c that I drink,
   14,23 he took a c, gave thanks,
   14,36 Take this c away from me,
Lk 11,39 cleanse the outside of the c
   22,17 he took a c, gave thanks,
   22,20 the c after they had eaten,
   22,20 "This c is the new covenant
   22,42 take this c away from me;
Jn 18,11 Shall I not drink the c
1Cor 10,16 The c of blessing that we
   10,21 cannot drink the c of the Lord
   11,25 also the c, after supper,
   11,27 drinks the c of the Lord
Rv 14,10 into the c of his wrath,
   16,19 the c filled with the wine
   17, 4 a gold c that was filled
   18, 6 Into her c pour double

CURE (D)
2Kgs 5, 7 to me to be c of leprosy?
Wis 16,12 neither herb nor application c
Lk   9, 1 demons and to c diseases,
   14, 3 Is it lawful to c on the

CURSE
Gn   5,29 LORD has put under a c,
   12, 3 and c those who curse you.
2Sm 16, 9 dead dog c my lord the king?
Jb   2, 9 C God and die."
   31,30 uttering a c against his life—
Ps 109,28 Though they c, may you;
Prv 3,33 The c of the LORD is on
   24,24 men will c him,
Sir   3, 9 a mother's c uproots the
   41, 9 at death, you become a c.
Bar 1,20 the c which the LORD enjoined

Mal 2, 2 blessing I will make a c.
Mt 26,74 he began to c and to swear,
Lk 6,28 bless those who c you,
Rom 12,14 bless and do not c them.
Gal 3,10 under a c;
3,13 Christ ransomed us from the c
Jas 3, 9 with it we c human beings

D

DANCE (S)

1Sm 21,12 During their d do they not sing
Jdt 15,13 led the women in the d
Ps 149, 3 praise his name in festive d,
150, 4 with tambourines and d,
Eccl 3, 4 and a time to d.
Mt 11,17 but you did not d,
14, 6 performed a d before the

DARK (NESS)

Gn 1, 2 and d covered the abyss,
1, 4 separated the light from the d.
Ex 10,22 dense d throughout the land
2Sm 22,29 you brighten the d about me.
Tb 5,10 must remain in d,
14,10 into the everlasting d,
2Mc 3,27 enveloped in great d.
Ps 18,29 my God brightens the d
91, 6 pestilence that roams in d,
112, 4 shine through the d,
139,11 "Surely d shall hide me,
Prv 4,19 of the wicked is like d;
Wis 17, 2 shackled with d, fettered by
17,18 the one bond of d.
17,21 burdensome than the d.
Sir 11,16 Error and d were formed
23,18 d surrounds me,
Is 5,20 change d into light
42,16 I will turn d into light before
45, 7 and create the d,
Dn 2,22 knows what is in the d
Jl 2, 2 a day of d and of gloom,
3, 4 sun will be turned to d,
Mt 4,16 in d have seen a great light
6,23 the light in you is d,
Lk 11,34 your body is in d.
23,44 d came over the whole land
Jn 1, 5 the light shines in the d,
3,19 but people preferred the
Acts 2,20 sun shall be turned to d
1Cor 4, 5 what is hidden in d
2Cor 4, 6 Let light shine out of d,"
6,14 does light have with d?
Eph 5, 8 you were once d, but now
6,12 rulers of this present d,
1Pt 2, 9 called you out of d
2Pt 2,17 gloom of d has been
1Jn 1, 5 in him there is no d
2, 9 still in the d.
Jude 13 the gloom of d has been

DAUGHTER

Ex 2, 5 Pharaoh's d came down to
Jgs 11,40 mourn the d of Jephthah
Est 2, 7 taken her as his own d.
Ps 9,15 in the gates of d Zion.
Is 62,11 Say to d Zion, your savior
Zec 9, 9 Rejoice heartily, O d Zion,
Mk 5,34 "D, your faith has saved you
7,29 has gone out of your d."

DAY (S)

Gn 1, 5 God called the light "d,"
1, 8 the second d.

1,13 the third d.
1,19 the fourth d.
1,23 the fifth d.
1,31 the sixth d.
2, 2 he rested on the seventh d
8,22 d and night shall not cease
Ex 3,18 to go a three-d journey
20, 8 keep holy the sabbath d.
Lv 16,30 this d atonement is made
23,28 the D of Atonement,
Nu 14,14 you go before them by d
Jos 1, 8 Recite it by d and by night,
2Kgs 7, 9 This is a d of good news,
1Chr 16,23 his salvation, d after day.
Jdt 12,16 from the d he saw her.
12,20 on one single d in his life.
Ps 84,11 Better one d in your courts
96, 2 his salvation d after day.
118,24 the d the LORD has made;
Prv 3, 2 For many d, and years of life
Wis 3,18 comfort in the d of scrutiny;
Is 13, 9 Lo, the d of the LORD comes,
26, 1 On that d they will sing this
27, 1 On that d, The LORD will
Ez 30, 2 Cry, Oh, the d! for near is the
Jl 1,15 Alas, the d! for near is the
3, 4 the great and terrible d.
Am 3,14 On the d when I punish Israel
5,20 Will not the d of the LORD be
Ob ,15 near is the d of the LORD for all
Zep 1,14 the great d of the LORD,
Zec 14, 1 a d shall come for the LORD
14, 7 shall be one continuous d,
Mal 3,24 the great and terrible d.
Mt 24,38 d that Noah entered the ark
Lk 11, 3 each d our daily bread
Acts 5,42 And all d long,
Rom 14, 5 one d more important than
1Cor 5, 5 be saved on the d of the Lord.
2Cor 4,16 being renewed by day.
11,25 a night and a d on the deep;
Gal 1,18 remained with him for fifteen d.
1Thes 5, 2 the d of the Lord will come
5, 4 that d to overtake you
2Thes 2, 2 the d of the Lord is at
Heb 7,27 sacrifice d after day,
2Pt 3, 8 one d is like a thousand years
3,10 the d of the Lord will come
Rv 6,17 great d of their wrath has
16,14 great d of God the almighty.

DEAD

Dt 18,11 seeks oracles from the d.
Jdt 2, 8 choked with their d;
Sir 7,33 your kindness from the d.
Is 8,19 apply to the d on behalf
Bar 2,17 the d in the nether world,
3,10 Defiled with the d,
6,26 as beside the d.
Mt 8,22 let the d bury their dead."
Lk 15,24 son of mine was d,
24,46 from the d on the third day
Rom 6,11 d to sin and living for
1Cor 15,29 baptized for the d?
Eph 2, 1 d in your transgressions
1Thes 4,16 the d in Christ will rise
Jas 2,26 faith without works is d.
Rv 14,13 the d who die in the Lord
20,12 I saw the d,
20,12 d were judged according to
20,13 The sea gave up its d;
20,13 and Hades gave up their d.

DECEIT

1Mc 11, 1 by d to take Alexander's
Ps 32, 2 in whose spirit is no d.

50,19 harness your tongue to d.
Wis 1, 5 spirit of discipline flees d
4,11 or d beguile his soul;
Sir 37, 3 blanket the earth with d?"
Is 59, 3 your tongue utters d.
Dn 11,32 By his d he shall make some
Mk 7,22 greed, malice, d
Acts 13,10 full of every sort of d
1Pt 2, 1 all malice and all d,
2,22 no d was found in his mouth
Rv 14, 5 no d has been found;

DECEIVE (S)

2Sm 3,25 aware that Abner came to d
1Kgs 22,20 The Lord asked, 'Who will d
2Kgs 4,16 man of God; do not d your
Prv 26,19 Is the man who d his neighbor
Wis 15, 4 men's fancy d us,
Jer 9, 4 Each one d the other
Mt 24, 5 they will d many.
24,11 arise and d many;
24,24 so great as to d,
Mk 13, 5 "See that no one d you.
Rom 16,18 d the hearts of the innocent
1Cor 3,18 Let no one d himself.
Eph 5, 6 Let no one d you
Col 2, 4 that no one may d you
2Thes 2, 3 Let no one d you in any
1Jn 1, 8 we d ourselves, and the
Rv 20, 8 He will go out to d the

DEDICATED

Lv 21,12 he is d to his God,
Nm 6, 9 his d head becomes
6,18 shave his d head,
18, 6 d to the LORD
1Sm 1,28 he shall be d to the LORD."
1Kgs 8,63 d the temple of the LORD
Jdt 16,19 Judith d, as a votive
Sir 46,13 d from his mother's womb,
2Tm 2,21 d, beneficial to the master

DEED (S)

Ex 3,20 all kinds of wondrous d there.
2Mc 12, 5 barbarous d perpetrated
12,42 sinful d might be fully
Ps 40,10 I announced your d
40,11 Your d I did not hide
64,10 proclaim God's d,
106,31 for him as a righteous d
Prv 19,17 repay him for his good d.
Sir 3, 8 In word and d honor your
12, 6 every good d you do
Jer 32,10 written and sealed the d,
Lam 3,64 O Lord, according to their d
Jl 4, 4 return your d upon your
Col 3,17 in word or in d,
2Thes 2,17 them in every good d
2Pt 2, 8 the lawless d that he saw

DELIGHT

Dt 30, 9 take d in your prosperity,
1Sm 15,22 d in holocausts and
Jb 22,26 d in the Almighty
27,10 d in the Almighty
Ps 16, 3 all who d in them.
37, 4 Find your d in the LORD
40, 9 your will is my d;
43, 4 God, my joy, my d.
62, 5 They d in lies;
68,31 nations that d in war.
112, 1 d in God's commands.
119,16 In your laws I take d;
119,24 Your decrees are my d;
119,35 for that is my d.
119,47 I d in your commands,
119,70 your teaching is my d.

119,77   your teaching is my d.
119,92   your teaching not been my d,
119,143   your commands are my d.
119,174   your teaching is my d.
147,10   no d in the strength of horses
149,   4   the LORD takes d in his people,
Prv   2,14   Who d in doing evil,
    8,30   I was his d day by day,
    11,   1   a full weight is his d.
    11,20   walk blamelessly are his d.
    29,17   give d to your soul.
Song   2,   3   I d to rest in his shadow
    5,16   he is all d.
    7,   7   my love, my d!
Sir   1,24   loyal humility is his d.
    40,20   Wine and music d the soul,
    40,22   Charm and beauty d the eye,
Is   11,   3   his d shall be the fear of
    13,17   take no d in gold.
    55,   2   you shall d in rich fare.
    58,13   call the sabbath a d,
    62,   4   you shall be called "My d,"
    65,18   its people to be a d;
    66,11   you may nurse with d
Jer   31,20   the child in whom I d?
    32,41   d in doing good to them
    49,25   the town of d!
Ez   24,16   the d of your eyes,
    24,21   the d of your eyes,
    24,25   the d of their eyes,
Mt   12,18   my beloved in whom I d;
Mk   12,37   crowd heard this with d.
Rom   7,22   I take d in the law of God
Heb   10,   6   offerings you took no d in.

DELIVER
Dt   1,27   d us into the hands of
Jdt   2,   7   I will d them as spoils.
    2,11   but d them up to slaughter
Ps   22,   9   let him d you;
    79,   9   d us, pardon our sins
    120,   2   d me from lying lips,
    144,   7   d me from the many waters
    144,11   From the menacing sword d
Wis   2,18   defend him and d him
Sir   4,19   abandon him and d him into
Bar   2,14   d us for your own sake
    4,21   d you from oppression
Mt   6,13   d us from the evil one
Ti   2,14   d us from all lawlessness

DELIVERANCE
Gn   45,   7   an extraordinary d.
    49,18   "[I long for your d, O LORD!]
Tb   6,18   and grant you d.
1Mc   3,18   d by many or by few
    4,25   Israel had a great d that day.
Ps   14,   7   the d of Israel,
    40,11   your loyal d I have
    53,   7   the d of Israel,
Jon   2,10   d is from the LORD.

DEMONS
Dt   32,17   offered sacrifice to d,
Tb   6,   8   no d will ever return to him
Bar   4,   7   sacrifices to d,
    4,35   and d shall dwell in her
Mt   7,22   drive out d in your name?
    8,31   The d pleaded with him,
    9,34   drives out d by the prince of
    10,   8   cleanse lepers, drive out d.
    12,24   "This man drives out d
    12,24   Beelzebul, the prince of d."
    12,27   if I drive out d by Beelzebul,
    12,28   I drive out d,
Mk   1,34   he drove out many d,

    1,39   preaching and driving out d
    3,15   authority to drive out d
    3,22   prince of d he drives out
    6,13   They drove out many d,
    9,38   driving out d in your name,
    16,   9   driven seven d.
    16,17   drive out d,
Lk   4,41   d also came out from many
    8,   2   seven d had gone out,
    8,30   many d had entered him.
    8,33   d came out of the man
    8,35   the d had come out
    8,38   the d had come out
    9,   1   authority over all d
    9,49   casting out d in your name
    10,17   even the d are subject to us
    11,15   the prince of d,
    11,18   Beelzebul that I drive out d.
    11,20   I drive out d,
    13,32   cast out d and I perform
1Cor   10,20   [they sacrifice] to d,
    10,20   participants with d.
    10,21   and also the cup of d.
    10,21   and of the table of d.
Jas   2,19   the d believe that and
Rv   9,20   worship of d and idols
    18,   2   become a haunt for d.

DENY (DENIES)
Ex   23,   6   d one of your needy fellow
Lv   5,22   he d the fact and swears falsely
Prv   30,   7   d them not to me before
    30,   9   Lest, being full, I d you,
Sir   14,   4   What he d himself he collects
Dn   14,24   cannot d that this is a living
Mt   16,24   must d himself,
    26,34   will d me three times."
Mk   8,34   must d himself,
Lk   12,   9   But whoever d me before others
    22,34   you will d three times
Acts   4,16   we cannot d it.
2Tm   2,12   if we d him he will deny us
    2,13   for he cannot d himself.
    3,   5   but d its power.
Ti   1,16   by their deeds they d him.
Jude   4   who d our only Master

DESCENDANTS
Gn   5,   1   record for the d of Adam.
    6,   9   the d of Noah.
    13,16   make your d like the dust
    15,   5   he added, "shall your d be."
    15,18   "To your d I give this land,
    22,17   d as countless as the stars
    48,   4   give this land to your d
    48,19   d shall become a multitude
Dt   30,19   you and your d may live,
2Kgs   5,27   to you and your d forever."
Jdt   8,32   among the d of our race.
Ps   21,11   their d you will wipe out
    22,24   All d of Jacob, give honor;
    77,16   the d of Jacob and Joseph.
Sir   4,16   his d too will inherit her.
    44,21   in his d the nations would
Bar   2,15   his d bear your name.
Heb   2,16   the d of Abraham;
    7,   5   The d of Levi
    11,12   d as numerous as the stars
    11,18   d shall bear your name."

DESIRE (D) (S)
Gn   6,   5   no d that his heart conceived
Dt   5,21   shall not d your neighbor's
1Sm   9,20   Whom does Israel d
2Sm   23,   5   salvation and my every d?
1Chr   29,19   d to keep your

2Chr   15,15   sought him with complete d,
Tb   4,   5   suppress every d to sin
Jdt   12,16   burning with the d to possess
2Mc   4,16   whom they d to imitate
Ps   21,   3   granted him his heart's d;
    37,   4   give you your heart's d.
    40,15   those who d my ruin.
    51,18   you do not d sacrifice;
    145,19   the d of those who fear you
Prv   10,24   the d of the just will be
    11,23   The d of the just ends only
    24,   1   and d not to be with them
Eccl   6,   7   yet his d is not fulfilled.
Wis   4,12   d transforms the innocent
    6,20   the d for Wisdom leads up to
Sir   1,23   If you d wisdom,
    6,   4   contumacious d destroys its
Is   26,   8   the d of our souls,
    58,   2   and d to know my ways,
Ez   24,21   the d of your soul.
Hos   6,   6   it is love that I d,
Mal   3,   1   the covenant whom you d.
Mt   9,13   'I d mercy, not sacrifice.'
    12,   7   'I d mercy, not sacrifice,'
Rom   6,12   so that you obey their d.
1Cor   10,   6   that we might not d evil
2Cor   8,20   This we d to avoid,
Phil   2,13   both to d and to work.
1Tm   6,10   in their d for it have strayed
Heb   10,   5   offering you did not d,
Jas   1,14   enticed by his own d.
2Pt   2,10   with its depraved d

DESTROY (ED) (ING) (S)
Gn   6,17   to d everywhere all creatures
Dt   8,20   the nations which the Lord d
Tb   13,12   accursed are all who d you
Jdt   3,   8   commissioned to d all the
    6,   2   send his force and d them
2Mc   8,35   was eminently successful in d
Ps   5,   7   you d all who speak falsely.
    106,26   swore to d them in the desert,
Prv   6,32   he who would d himself does
Wis   12,   6   You willed to d by the hands
Sir   8,16   he will d you.
    22,27   that my tongue may not d
    28,13   they d the peace of many.
Mt   2,13   search for the child to d him."
    10,28   can d both soul and body
    26,61   'I can d the temple of God
    27,20   Barabbas but to d Jesus.
Mk   14,58   'I will d this temple
Lk   4,34   Have you come to d us?
Jn   10,10   slaughter and d;
Heb   7,16   a life that cannot be d.
Rv   11,18   d those who destroy the earth

DESTRUCTION
Dt   7,10   repays with d
Tb   14,15   the d of Nineveh
Jdt   2,   2   total d of those countries.
    8,19   great d before our enemies.
    11,15   handed over to you for d.
    11,22   to those who have
    14,13   to their utter d."
1Mc   4,32   tremble at their own d.
2Mc   13,   6   hurled down to d.
Jb   15,23   his d is imminent.
Ps   52,   4   All day long you plot d;
    92,   8   destined for eternal d;
Wis   1,12   nor draw to yourselves d
Sir   40,10   they who bring on d
    48,   6   You sent kings down to d,
Hos   8,   4   to their own d.
Mt   7,13   broad that leads to d,
Jn   17,12   except the son of d,

Rom 9,23 wrath made for d?
Phil 3,19 Their end is d.
1Tm 6, 9 them into ruin and d.
2Pt 2, 1 swift d on themselves.
　　　2, 3 their d does not sleep.
　　　3, 7 'd of the godless.
　　　3,16 distort to their own d,
Rv 17, 8 headed for d.
　　17,11 headed for d.

DEVIL
Wis 2,24 the envy of the d,
Mt 4, 1 tempted by the d.
　　4, 5 the d took him to the holy
　　4, 8 the d took him up to a
　　4,11 Then the d left him
　　13,39 who sows them is the d.
　　25,41 fire prepared for the d
Lk 4, 2 to be tempted by the d.
　　4, 3 The d said to him,
　　4, 6 The d said to him,
　　4,13 "When the d had finished
　　8,12 d comes and takes away
Jn 6,70 is not one of you a d?"
　　8,44 your father the d
　　13, 2 had already induced
Acts 10,38 oppressed by the d,
　　13,10 "You son of the d,
Eph 4,27 not leave room for the d.
　　6,11 against the tactics of the d.
1Tm 3, 6 incur the d's punishment.
　　3, 7 disgrace, the d's trap.
2Tm 2,26 out of the d's snare,
Heb 2,14 of death, that is, the d,
Jas 4, 7 Resist the d,
1Pt 5, 8 Your opponent the d
1Jn 3, 8 sins belongs to the d,
　　3, 8 destroy the works of the d.
　　3,10 children of the d
Jude 9 argued with the d
Rv 2,10 d will throw some of you
　　12, 9 serpent, who is called the d
　　12,12 d has come down to you
　　20, 2 serpent, which is the d
　　20,10 d who had led them astray

DIE (D) (DEAD)
Gn 2,17 surely doomed to d."
　　3, 3 even touch it, lest you d.'"
　　3, 4 "You certainly will not d!
Ex 11, 5 born in this land shall d,
Ru 1,17 Wherever you d I will die,
2Kgs 14, 6 one shall d for his own sin."
Tb 3, 6 better for me to d than to live,
　　10,13 Sarah before I d.
Jdt 6, 8 not d till you are destroyed
Est 4D,10 You shall not d
1Mc 1,63 they preferred to d
　　9,10 let us d bravely
2Mc 6,28 how to d willingly
Jb 2, 9 Curse God and d."
Ps 82, 7 mortal you shall d;
　　118,17 I shall not d but live
Prv 5,23 d from lack of discipline,
　　10,21 fools d for want of sense.
　　15,10 he who hates reproof will d.
　　23,13 the rod, he will not d.
Eccl 3, 2 born, and a time to d
Sir 14,17 All must d.
　　16, 3 rather d childless
　　25,23 because of her we all d.
Is 22,13 for tomorrow we d!"
Bar 4, 1 will d who forsake her.
Ez 3,18 shall d for his sin,
　　18,20 the one who sins shall d.
　　18,31 you d, O house of Israel?

33, 8 shall d for his guilt,
Mk 9,48 'their worm does not d,
Jn 8,21 you will d in your sin.
　　11,26 believes in me will never d.
Rom 5, 7 does one d for a just person,
　　14, 8 if we d, we die for the Lord
1Cor 15,22 in Adam all d,
2Cor 5,14 one d for all
Gal 1, 1 who raised him from the d

DISCIPLE (S)
Is 8,16 instruction kept among my d.
Mk 2,15 sat with Jesus and his d
Lk 14,26 cannot be my d.
Acts 9,26 believing that he was a d.

DISCIPLINE
Dt 4,36 his voice to d you;
　　11, 2 understand the d of the LORD,
Tb 4,14 d yourself in all your conduct
Ps 50,17 You hate d;
Prv 1, 2 appreciate wisdom and d,
　　3,11 The d of the LORD,
　　5,23 die from lack of d,
　　22,15 the rod of d
Wis 1, 5 holy spirit of d flees deceit
　　6,17 first step toward d
Sir 6,18 from your youth embrace d;
　　23, 2 the rod of d,
1Cor 9,25 Every athlete exercises d
Heb 12, 5 disdain the d of the Lord
　　12, 7 Endure your trials as "d";
　　12, 9 earthly fathers to d us,

DISDAIN
Gn 16, 5 looking on me with d.
Lv 26,11 and will not d you.
1Sm 2,17 offerings to the Lord with d.
Jdt 8,20 hope that he will not d
Est 1,17 with d upon their husbands
　　1,18 corresponding d and rancor.
2Mc 7,11 sake of his laws I d them;
Ps 123, 4 of d from the arrogant.
Prv 3,11 d not; spurn not his reproof
Gal 4,14 you did not show d
Heb 12, 5 not d the discipline of the Lord

DISEASE (S)
Ex 15,26 with any of the d with which
Mk 3,10 who had d were pressing
Lk 4,40 people sick with various d
　　9, 6 and curing d everywhere.

DISHONEST
Ex 18,21 men who hate d gain,
Dt 5,20 'You shall not bear d witness
　　25,16 Everyone who is d in any
Prv 4,24 Put away from you d talk,
Sir 19,21 shrewdness keen but d,
　　51, 6 from the arrows of d tongues.
Ez 33,31 desires are fixed on d gain.
Lk 16, 8 commended that d steward
　　16,10 d in very small matters
　　18,11 humanity—greedy, d, is

DISOBEY (DISOBEDIENT)
Jdt 2,13 Do not d a single one of the
Sir 2,15 d not his words;
Bar 1,19 we have been d to the Lord
Rom 10,21 to a d and contentious people.
1Pt 3, 1 if some d the word,

DISTRESS (ED)
Gn 21,11 Abraham was greatly d
　　35,16 labor and to suffer great d.
Nm 11,15 need no longer face this d."

Dt 4,30 your whole soul. In your d,
Jgs 2,15 till they were in great d.
2Sm 22, 7 In my d I called
2Chr 15, 4 in their d they turned
Jdt 4,13 regard for their d.
1Mc 1, 9 causing much d
2Mc 3,14 d throughout the city.
Jb 36,15 instructs them through d.
Ps 18, 7 In my d I called out
　　81, 8 In d you called
　　120, 1 when I called in my d
Sir 4, 4 beggar in d do not reject;
Is 8,23 where until now there was d.
Lam 1,20 Look, O Lord, upon my d
Dn 12, 1 a time unsurpassed in d
Ob 12 haughtily on the day of d!
　　14 fugitives on the day of d!
Jon 2, 3 Out of my d I called
Na 1, 7 refuge on the day of d;
Hb 3,16 I await the day of d
Zep 1,15 a day of anguish and d,
Mt 14, 9 The king was d
Acts 20,38 they were deeply d
Rom 8,35 or d, or persecution,
1Thes 3, 7 our every d and affliction,
1Tm 5,10 helped those in d,
Rv 7,14 the time of great d;

DIVORCE
Dt 22,19 may not d her
　　24, 1 writes out a bill of d
Is 50, 1 Where is the bill of d
Mal 2,16 I hate d, says the LORD,
Mt 1,19 decided to d her quietly.
　　5,31 give her a bill of d.'
　　19, 3 man to d his wife
　　19, 8 you to d your wives,
Mk 10, 2 lawful for a husband to d
1Cor 7,11 should not d his wife.

DOCTRINE
Prv 22,17 apply your heart to my d;
Mal 2, 6 True d was in his mouth,
2Tm 4, 3 not tolerate sound d
Ti 1, 9 exhort with sound d
　　2, 1 consistent with sound d,
　　2,10 adorn the d of God

DOMINION
Gn 1,26 d over the fish of the
Ps 145,13 your d for all generations.
Wis 16,13 d over life and death;
Sir 33,21 let no man have d
Is 9, 5 upon his shoulder d rests.
　　9, 6 His d is vast and forever
Bar 3,24 the scope of his d
Mi 4, 8 former d shall be restored,
Zec 9,10 d shall be from sea to
Eph 1,21 authority, power, and d,

DREAM (S) (ER)
Gn 37, 8 his talk about his d.
　　40, 5 had d on the same night,
　　41,25 "Both of Pharaoh's d
Dt 13, 2 a prophet or a d
Nm 12, 6 reveal myself to him, in d
Jb 7,14 you affright me with d
Wis 18,17 visions in horrible d
Sir 34, 1 borne aloft by d
Dn 1,17 of all visions and d.
　　5,16 d and solve difficulties;
Jl 3, 1 old men shall dream d,
Acts 2,17 old men shall dream d.

DRINK (DRANK)
Gn 24,45 Please let me have a d.'

Ex   17, 2   "Give us water to **d**."
    32,20   made the Israelites **d**.
Nm   6, 3   from wine and strong **d**;
Jgs   7, 5   who kneels down to **d**."
1Sm   1,18   ate and **d** with her husband
Tb   7,10   "Eat and **d** and be merry
1Mc   11,58   **d** from gold cups,
Ps   36, 9   stream you give us **d**.
    73,10   **d** deeply of their words.
    104,16   trees of the LORD **d** their fill,
Is   37,25   I dug wells and **d** water
Mt   6,25   what you will eat [or **d**],
    20,22   Can you **d** the cup
    26,27   "**D** from it, all of you
Lk   12,19   eat, **d**, be merry!"'
Jn   4,12   cistern and **d** from it himself
    18,11   Shall I not **d** the cup
1Cor   10, 4   drank the same spiritual **d**,
    10,31   whether you eat or **d**,
    12,13   given to **d** of one Spirit.
Rv   14,10   **d** the wine of God's fury,

DRUNK

Gn   9,21   and lay naked inside his
1Sm   1,13   Eli, thinking her **d**,
    25,36   because he was very **d**.
2Sm   11,13   David, who made him **d**.
1Mc   6,34   made the elephants **d**
2Mc   7,36   **d** of never-failing life,
Acts   2,15   These people are not **d**,
1Cor   11,21   hungry while another gets **d**.
Eph   5,18   do not get **d** on wine,

DUST

Gn   13,16   descendants like the **d**
    18,27   I am but **d** and ashes!
Ex   8,12   his staff and strike the **d**
    30,36   some of it into fine **d**
Nm   5,17   as well as some **d** that
    23,10   Who has ever counted the **d**
Dt   9,21   to powder as fine as **d**,
    28,24   will give your land powdery **d**
1Sm   2, 8   raises the needy from the **d**;
2Kgs   13, 7   and trampled them like **d**.
2Chr   1, 9   numerous as the **d** of the
Neh   3,34   from the heaps of **d**?" Tobiah
    9, 1   their heads covered with **d**.
Tb   3, 6   face of the earth into **d**.
Jdt   2,20   locusts or the **d** of the earth,
1Mc   2,63   has returned to his **d**,
Jb   42, 6   repent in **d** and ashes.
Ps   22,30   the **d** will kneel in homage.
    103,14   remembers that we are **d**.
Eccl   3,20   made from the **d**,
Sir   10, 9   Why are **d** and ashes proud?
Is   2,10   the rocks, hide in the **d**,
    47, 1   Come down, sit in the **d**,
Lam   2,10   They strew **d** on their heads
Bar   6,12   **d** which is thick upon them
Ez   24, 7   to be covered with **d**. To
Am   2, 7   of the weak into the **d**
Mi   1,10   Beth-leaphrah roll in the **d**.
    7,17   lick the **d** like the serpent,
Na   1, 3   clouds are the **d** at his feet;
Zep   1,17   shall be poured out like **d**,
Zec   9, 3   and heaped up silver like **d**,
Mt   10,14   shake the **d** from your feet.
Acts   13,51   shook the **d** from their feet

DWELL (S)

Ex   25, 8   I may **d** in their midst.
Lv   3,17   wherever they may
    25,18   for then you will **d** securely
Nm   13,29   **d** in the highlands,
Dt   12,10   crossed the Jordan and **d**
Jos   21, 2   cities be given us to **d** in,

2Sm   7, 5   build me a house to **d** in?
2Chr   6,18   God **d** with mankind on earth?
Tb   14, 7   in security shall they **d**
Jdt   11,23   shall **d** in the palace of King
Est   9,19   who **d** in villages, celebrate
Jb   4,19   those that **d** in houses of clay,
    30, 6   To **d** on the slopes of the
Ps   15, 1   **d** on your holy mountain?
    23, 6   **d** in the house of the LORD
    37, 3   may **d** in the land and live
    61, 5   ever **d** in your tent;
    69,37   God's name shall **d** there.
    84, 5   those who **d** in your house!
    140,14   will **d** in your presence.
Prv   21, 9   It is better to **d** in a corner
Eccl   5,19   For he will hardly **d** on the
Sir   23,27   who **d** on the earth shall know
    50,26   degenerate folk who **d** in.
Is   38,11   among those who **d** in the
Lam   3, 6   left me to **d** in the dark
    4,21   who **d** in the land of Uz
Bar   4,35   demons shall **d** in her
Ez   7, 7   for you who **d** in the land!
    17,23   Birds of every kind shall **d**
Hos   14, 8   they shall **d** in his shade
Jl   1, 2   all you who **d** in the land!
    2, 1   who **d** in the land tremble,
Am   3,12   Israelites who **d** in Samaria
Ob   3   you who **d** in the clefts
Mi   1,11   you who **d** in Shaphir!
Na   1, 5   the world and all who **d** in it.
Hb   2, 8   city and to all who **d** in it.
Zep   1,13   but shall not **d** in them,
Hg   1, 4   **d** in your own paneled
Zec   2,15   he will **d** among you,
Mt   12,45   and they move in and **d** there;
Lk   11,26   who move in and **d** there,
Acts   1,20   and may no one **d** in it.' And
    17,24   not **d** in sanctuaries made
2Cor   12, 9   of Christ may **d** with me
Eph   3,17   **d** in your hearts through
Col   3,16   word of Christ **d** in you
Jas   4, 5   he has made to **d** in us
Rv   12,12   and you who **d** in them.
    13, 6   and those who **d** in heaven.

DWELLING

Gn   27,39   fertile earth shall be your **d**;
Dt   12, 5   designates as his **d**
Ps   84, 2   How lovely your **d**,
Sir   24, 8   'In Jacob make your **d**,
Bar   2,16   down from your holy **d**
Mt   4,16   **d** in a land overshadowed
Jn   1,14   made his **d** among us,
    14, 2   there are many **d** places.
2Cor   5, 1   a **d** not made with hands,

E

EAGLE

Ex   19, 4   bore you up on **e** wings
Lv   11,13   not be eaten: the **e**,
Dt   28,49   swoops down like an **e**,
    32,11   As an **e** incites its nestlings
Jb   39,27   the **e** fly up at your command
Ps   103, 5   is renewed like the **e**'s.
Ez   1,10   had the face of an **e**.
    17, 3   The great **e**, with great wings,
Ob   4   go as high as the **e**, and
Mi   1,16   baldness be as the **e**'s,
Hb   1, 8   like the **e** hastening to devour;
Rv   4, 7   the fourth looked like an **e**

EAR (S)

Ex   21, 6   pierce his **e** with an awl,

Lv   14,25   the tip of the right **e**
Nm   23,18   give **e** to my testimony,
Dt   1,17   give **e** to the lowly and to
    1,45   your cry or give **e** to you.
    15,17   through his **e** into the door,
Ru   2, 2   go and glean **e** of grain
2Kgs   4,42   and fresh grain in the **e**.
Neh   6, 7   must reach the **e** of the king,
Jb   13, 1   eye has seen; my **e** has
Ps   17, 6   Turn your **e** to me;
    31, 3   incline your **e** to me;
Prv   5,13   my instructors incline my **e**!
    18,15   **e** of the wise seeks
Eccl   1, 8   the **e** filled with hearing.
Wis   1,10   jealous **e** hearkens to
Sir   3,28   attentive **e** is the wise
Is   8, 9   Give **e**, all you distant lands!
Jer   17,23   did not listen or give **e**,
Lam   3,56   "Let not your **e** be deaf to
Bar   2,31   give them hearts, and heedful **e**
Dn   9,18   Give **e**, O my God, and listen
Hos   5, 1   give **e**! It is you who are
    8, 7   grain that forms no **e**
Am   3,12   an **e** of his sheep,
Mt   26,51   cutting off his **e**.
Lk   22,51   the servant's **e** and healed
Rom   11, 8   **e** that should not hear
1Cor   12,16   Or if an **e** should say,

EARTH

Gn   1, 1   heavens and the **e**,
    7,23   wiped out from the **e**.
Ex   9,23   flashed toward the **e**,
    9,29   the **e** is the Lord's. But
Lv   17,13   blood and cover it with **e**.
Nm   12, 3   on the face of the **e**.
    14,21   glory that fills the whole **e**.
Dt   5, 8   in the waters beneath the **e**;
    7, 6   on the face of the **e**
    31,28   heaven and **e** to witness
    32, 1   **e** hearken to the words of
1Sm   2, 8   pillars of the **e** are the Lord's,
    28,13   rising from the **e**." "What does
2Sm   22, 8   "The **e** swayed and quaked;
1Kgs   8,27   dwells among men on **e**?
2Kgs   19,19   **e** may know that you alone
2Chr   36,23   All the kingdoms of the **e**
Ezr   5,11   the God of heaven and **e**,
Neh   9, 6   the **e** and all that is upon
Tb   10,14   Lord of heaven and **e**,
    14,10   went down alive into the **e**!
Jdt   9,12   Lord of heaven and **e**,
    11, 1   king of all the **e**. Nor
Est   A, 4   confusion upon the **e**
    A, 7   upon the **e**. The whole race
1Mc   9,13   **e** shook with the noise of
Jb   26, 7   suspends the **e** over
Ps   24, 1   The **e** is the LORD's
    102,26   you laid the **e**'s foundations
Prv   30,14   the needy from the **e**,
Eccl   11, 2   may come upon the **e**.
Song   2,12   flowers appear on the **e**,
Wis   7, 1   the first man formed of **e**.
Is   6, 3   the **e** is filled with his glory
    24,19   the **e** will be shaken apart,
    51, 6   **e** wears out like a garment
    65,17   new heavens and a new **e**;
    66, 1   the **e** is my footstool.
Jer   10,10   whose anger the **e** quakes,
Bar   2,15   the whole **e** may know
Mt   5,13   the salt of the **e**.
    6,10   on **e** as in heaven.
    6,19   treasures on **e**,
    16,19   Whatever you bind on **e**
    24,35   Heaven and **e** will pass away,
Lk   2,14   on **e** peace to those

Acts 7,49 the e is my footstool.
1Cor 10,26 "the e and its fullness are
Phil 2,10 and on e and under the earth,
Col 1,16 things in heaven and on e,
Heb 12,26 shake not only e but heaven."
2Pt 3,13 new heavens and a new e
Rv 8, 7 hurled down to the e.
21, 1 new heaven and a new e.

EAT (ER) (ING)
Gn 2,16 free to e from any of the trees
2,17 that tree you shall not e;
Ex 2,20 have something to e."
Dt 16, 7 You shall cook and e it
Jgs 14,14 "Out of the e came forth food
1Sm 14,34 Slaughter it here and then e,
2Sm 13,11 brought them to him to e,
1Kgs 17,15 able to e for a year,
2Kgs 4,43 'They shall e and there
Neh 9,25 They could e and have
Tb 7,11 Tobiah answered, "I will e
Jdt 12,11 care to come and to e
1Mc 1,62 not to e anything unclean;
Jb 5, 5 the hungry shall e up;
Ps 50,13 Do I e the flesh of bulls
127, 2 To e bread earned by hard
Prv 18,21 a friend shall e its fruit.
25,27 To e too much honey is not
Eccl 5,17 well for a man to e and drink
9, 7 Go, e your bread with joy
Song 5, 1 e, friends; drink! Drink
Sir 20,16 Those who e his bread have
Is 9,19 though they e on the left,
65,25 lion shall e hay like the ox
Lam 2,20 Must women e their offspring,
Bar 2, 3 should e the flesh of his son
Ez 3, 1 e what is before you;
18, 6 if he does not e
Hos 4,10 e but not be satisfied,
Jl 2,26 You shall e and be filled,
Am 6, 4 e lambs taken from the flock
Ob 7 Those who e your bread lay
Jon 3, 7 they shall not e, nor
Mi 7, 1 There is no cluster to e,
Zec 11,16 he will e the flesh of the fat
Mt 9,11 e with tax collectors and
Mk 14,14 e the Passover
Lk 12,19 e, drink, be merry!"'
12,22 life and what you will e,
Jn 4,32 food to e of which you do not
6,31 bread from heaven to e.' "
Rom 14,15 hurt by what you e,
14,21 to e meat or drink wine
1Cor 8, 4 So about the e of meat
10,31 whether you e or drink,
11,26 as often as you e this bread
Jas 2,16 keep warm, and e well,"
Rv 2, 7 to e from the tree of life

EGYPT
Gn 12,10 Abram went down to E
37,28 took him to E.
42, 3 supply of grain from E.
46, 6 descendants migrated to E.
Ex 3,11 lead the Israelites out of E?"
32, 1 out of the land of E,
Nm 11,18 well off we were in E!'
Bar 2,11 out of the land of E
Hos 11, 1 out of E I called my son.
Mt 2,15 "Out of E I called my son."
Heb 11,27 By faith he left E,

ELDER
1Sm 14,49 e, Merob, and the younger,
1Kgs 8, 1 the e of Israel and all the
Tb 5,13 Hananiah the e, one of your

Wis 8,10 and esteem from the e
Is 3, 2 fortune-teller and e,
3, 5 shall be bold toward the e,
9,15 The e and the noble are the
Ez 16,46 Your e sister was Samaria
23, 4 was the name of the e,
Mt 15, 2 break the tradition of the e?

ENCOURAGE (MENT)
Dt 1,38 e him, for he is to
3,28 e and strengthen him,
Jos 11,20 design of the Lord to e them
2Sm 11,25 the city and destroy it.' e him."
35, 2 e them in the service
2Chr 16, 9 to e those who are devoted
35, 2 e them in the service
1Mc 12, 9 we have for our e the sacred
Ps 11,17 you e them and hear their
Rom 15, 4 by the e of the scriptures
2Cor 2, 7 forgive and e him instead,
13,11 e one another, agree
Phil 1,14 having taken e in the Lord
1Thes 3, 2 e you in your faith,
2Tm 4, 2 e through all patience
Heb 10,25 but e one another,
Jude 3 need to write to e you

ENDURE (D) (S)
Ex 18, 8 e on their journey, and
Dt 33,25 may your strength e through
1Sm 13,14 your kingdom shall not e.
2Sm 7,16 your kingdom shall e
1Kgs 2,26 all the hardships my father e."
15, 4 permitting Jerusalem to e;
Tb 3, 6 than to e so much misery
2Mc 2,27 e these inconveniences,
Ps 72,17 may his name e.
Prv 12,19 Truthful lips e forever,
Eccl 3,14 God does will e forever;
Sir 44,13 all time their progeny will e,
50,24 goodness toward us e
Am 7,10 the country cannot e
Mi 7, 9 I will e because I have
Hb 1,13 misery you cannot e.
Mal 3, 2 e the day of his coming
Mk 9,19 How long will I e you?
Rom 12,12 e in affliction,
1Cor 4,12 when persecuted, we e;
2Cor 3,11 more will what e glorious.

ENEMY (ENEMIES)
Ex 15, 6 has shattered the e.
Lv 26,25 forced to surrender to the e.
Nm 10, 9 go to war against an e
Dt 33,27 He drove the e out
1Sm 10, 1 the grasp of their e roundabout.
2Kgs 21,14 deliver them into e hands,
2Chr 6,24 and are defeated by the e,
Jdt 15, 4 upon the e and destroy
Est 3,10 the e of the Jews.
1Mc 10,83 The e fled to Azotus
2Mc 8,25 they had pursued the e
Jb 31,29 the destruction of my e
Ps 9, 4 For my e turn back
Prv 24,17 not when your e falls,
Sir 12,16 an e speaks sweetly,
50, 4 his city against the e.
Lam 2,17 Letting the e gloat over you
Bar 4,21 from oppression at e hands.
Ez 36, 2 the e has said of you,
Hos 8, 3 the e shall pursue them.
Am 9, 4 led into captivity by their e
Mi 7,10 When my e sees this,
Na 1, 9 e shall not rise a second
Zec 8,10 no security from the e,

Mt 5,43 and hate your e.'
Rom 12,20 e is hungry, feed him;
1Cor 15,26 e to be destroyed is death
Gal 4,16 your e by telling you the truth
2Thes 3,15 not regard him as an e
Jas 4, 4 makes himself an e of God.

ENTER
Ps 95,11 shall never e my rest."
Jl 4, 2 And I will e into judgment
Mt 5,20 will not e into the kingdom
7,13 e through the narrow gate;
18, 8 better for you to e into life
19,23 rich to e the kingdom of
Mk 10,15 like a child will not e it."
Lk 13,24 e through the narrow gate,
Jn 3, 5 e the kingdom of God
Heb 3,11 shall not e into my rest
4,11 strive to e into that rest,

ENVY
1Mc 8,16 no e or jealousy among
Ps 37, 1 not e those who do wrong.
Wis 2,24 by the e of the devil,
Rom 1,29 full of e, murder, rivalry,
Phil 1,15 preach Christ from e
1Tm 6, 4 From these come e, rivalry,
Ti 3, 3 living in malice and e,
Jas 4, 2 e but you cannot obtain;

ESCAPE
Gn 19,20 near enough to e
Lv 26,37 as if to e a weapon,
Nm 32,23 not e the consequences
Jos 20, 9 flee to e death at
1Sm 19,12 made his e in safety.
Tb 13, 2 No one can e his hand.
Jdt 5, 5 no lie shall e your servant's
Est 4,13 of all the Jews will e.
1Mc 9,45 there is no way of e.
2Mc 10,20 a number of them to e.
Jb 11,20 e shall be cut off from
Ps 89,49 e the power of Sheol?
Prv 11, 9 the just make their e.
Eccl 7,26 pleasing to God will e her,
Wis 16,15 your hand none can e.
Sir 6,35 let no wise saying e you.
Jer 11,11 which they cannot e.
Lam 3, 7 hemmed me in with no e
Ez 7,16 Even those who e and
17,15 he who does such things e?
Jl 2, 3 from them there is no e.
Am 2,15 swift of foot shall not e,
Na 2, 9 e; "Stop! Stop!" but none
Hb 2, 9 e the reach of misfortune!
Zec 2,11 e to Zion! you who dwell
Mk 7,24 but he could not e notice.
Lk 21,21 Let those within the city e
21,36 you have the strength to e
Rom 2, 3 e the judgment of God?
Heb 2, 3 shall we e if we ignore
12,25 did not e when they refused

ETERNAL (ETERNITY)
1Chr 16,36 God of Israel, through all e!
Ps 41,14 God of Israel, from all e and
Wis 7,26 the refulgence of light,
Is 43,13 I am God, yes, from e I am He
Jer 10,10 living God, the e King,
Bar 2,35 an e covenant,
Mt 18, 8 thrown into e fire.
19,16 must I do to gain e life?"
25,41 e fire prepared for the devil
Lk 16, 9 welcomed into e dwellings.
Jn 3,16 not perish but might have e life.
4,14 welling up to e life."
6,47 whoever believes has e life.

	6,68	You have the words of e life.
	10,28	I give them e life,
	17, 3	Now this is e life,
Acts	13,48	who were destined for e life
Rom	5,21	justification for e life
	6,23	the gift of God is e life
2Cor	4,17	an e weight of glory
	4,18	but what is unseen is e.
Gal	6, 8	reap e life from the spirit.
Eph	3,11	e purpose that he
1Tm	6,12	Lay hold of e life,
Ti	3, 7	heirs in hope of e life.
Heb	5, 9	source of e salvation
	9,12	obtaining e redemption.
	9,15	the promised e inheritance.
	13,20	blood of the e covenant,
1Pt	5,10	called you to his e glory
2Pt	1,11	entry into the e kingdom
1Jn	1, 2	proclaim to you the e life
	5,11	God gave us e life,

EVERLASTING

Gn	9,16	recall the e covenant
Nm	25,13	pledge of an e priesthood,
Tb	3, 6	let me go to the e abode;
	14,10	went into the e darkness,
Jdt	13,20	redound to your e honor,
1Mc	2,51	great glory and an e name.
	2,54	covenant of an e priesthood.
Ps	78,66	e shame he dealt them.
	93, 2	you are from e, LORD.
	105,10	an e covenant for Israel
	106,48	from e to everlasting!
Is	35,10	crowned with e joy;
	55, 3	with you the e covenant,
	55,13	e imperishable sign.
	61, 7	e joy shall be theirs.
Jer	25, 9	ridicule, of e reproach.
Dn	7,14	dominion is an e dominion
	7,27	Whose kingdom shall be e
	12, 2	e horror and disgrace.
Mk	3,29	guilty of an e sin."
2Thes	2,16	e encouragement and good
1Tm	1,16	believe in him for e life.

EVERYTHING

Gn	1,31	God looked at e he had made,
	14,20	gave him a tenth of e.
Ex	4,30	Aaron told them e the LORD
1Mc	13,48	from it e that was impure,
Ps	89,12	founded the world and e in it.
	150, 6	Let e that has breath
Prv	16, 4	made e for his own ends,
Eccl	3, 1	an appointed time for e,
	3,11	e appropriate to its time,
Mt	19,27	given up e and followed you.
Mk	4,11	outside e comes in parables,
	4,34	he explained e in private.
	9,23	e is possible to one who
Lk	5,11	they left e and followed him.
	15,31	e I have is yours.
Jn	4,29	told me e I have done.
	17,10	e of mine is yours
Acts	4,32	they had e in common.
	22,10	e appointed for you to do
1Cor	2,10	the Spirit scrutinizes e,
	6,12	but not e is beneficial.
	13, 3	If I give away e I own,
Eph	5,13	e exposed by the light
Phil	2,14	e without grumbling or
	3, 8	consider e as a loss
	4, 6	in e, by prayer and petition,
Col	3,17	do e in the name of
	3,20	obey your parents in e,
1Thes	5,21	Test e; retain what is good.

EVIL

Gn	8,21	of man's heart are e
1Mc	13,32	much e on the land.
Jb	1, 1	feared God and avoided e.
	36,21	Take heed, turn not to e;
Ps	34,14	Keep your tongue from e,
	34,15	Turn from e and do good;
	51, 6	done such e in your sight
	97,10	loves those who hate e,
Prv	4,27	keep your foot far from e.
	24,20	the e man has no future,
Is	5,20	call e good, and good evil
	59, 7	Their feet run to e,
Jer	4,14	Cleanse your heart of e,
Am	5,13	for it is an e time.
Hb	2, 9	e gain for his household,
Mt	6,13	deliver us from the e one.
	12,35	an e person brings forth evil
	15,19	the heart come e thoughts,
Jn	3,19	their works were e.
Rom	7,19	but I do the e I do not want.
	12, 9	hate what is e, hold on to
	12,17	Do not repay anyone e
	12,21	Do not be conquered by e
1Cor	14,20	e be like infants,
Eph	5,16	because the days are e.
	6,16	flaming arrows of the e one.
1Thes	5,22	Refrain from every kind of e
2Thes	3, 3	guard you from the e one.
2Tm	4,18	me from every e threat
Heb	10,22	clean from an e conscience
Jas	3, 8	restless e, full of deadly
	4,11	Do not speak e of one
1Pt	3,10	keep the tongue from e
	3,11	turn from e and do good,
1Jn	5,18	the e one cannot touch him.
3Jn	11	not imitate e but imitate

EVILDOER (S)

Ps	14, 4	Will these e never learn?
Prv	24,25	those who convict the e
	29,27	The e is an abomination
Is	31, 2	and against those who help e.
Mal	2,17	"Every e is good in the sight
Lk	13,27	Depart from me, all you e!'

EXALT (ED)

Lv	21,10	"The most e of the priests
1Sm	1,10	e the horn of his anointed
1Kgs	1,37	and e his throne even more
	1,47	e his throne more than your
Tb	13, 4	e him before every living being
	13, 6	and e the King of the ages
	13, 7	I e my God, and my spirit
Jdt	16, 1	e and acclaim his name.
1Mc	14,35	he sought to e his people.
Prv	11,11	the city is e, but through
Sir	15, 5	will e him above his fellows;
Acts	2,33	E at the right hand of
1Pt	5, 6	he may e you in due time.

EXIST (S) (ED)

1Sm	26,15	does not e in Israel?
Jdt	8,18	nor does there e today,
Ps	10, 4	doesn't care, doesn't even e."
Eccl	7,24	What e is far-reaching
Is	59,15	that right did not e.
Jn	1,15	me because he e before me.
Rom	4,17	being what does not e.
	13, 1	and those that e have been
1Cor	8, 6	for whom we e,
	8, 6	through whom we e.
Heb	2,10	through whom all things e,

EXPIATE

1Sm	3,14	offering will ever e its crime."

Heb	2,17	to e the sins of the people

EYE (S)

2Kgs	4,34	his e upon the e
Jb	2,12	they lifted up their e
Ps	19, 9	enlightening the e.
	94, 9	who formed the e not see?
Mt	5,29	right e causes you to sin,
	5,38	'An e for an e
	6,22	If your e is sound
	9,29	Then he touched their e
	19,24	through the e of a needle
1Cor	2, 9	"What e has not seen,
	15,52	in the blink of an e,
Rv	1, 7	and every e will see him,

F

FACE

Gn	32,31	I have seen God f to f
Ex	3, 6	Moses hid his f
	33,11	speak to Moses f to f
	33,20	But my f you cannot see
	34,29	his f had become radiant
Nm	6,25	LORD let his f shine upon you
Dt	5, 4	LORD spoke with you f to f
	31,17	and hide my f from them
	34,10	whom the LORD knew f to f
Jgs	6,22	the angel of the LORD f to f
2Kgs	14, 8	Come, let us meet f to f
2Chr	25,17	meet each other f to f
Tb	3, 6	go from the f of the earth
	3,12	I turn my f and raise my eyes
Ps	4, 7	us the light of your f
	27, 8	seek God's f
	51,11	Turn away your f from my sins
	80, 4	Let your f shine upon us
	105, 4	constantly seek his f
Sir	12,18	and show his true f
	18,24	when he will hide his f
Is	50, 7	I have set my f like flint
	54, 8	I hid my f from you
Jer	32, 4	meet and speak f to f
	34, 3	speak to him f to f
Ez	1,10	four had the f of a man
	20,35	judgment with you f to f
Mt	17, 2	his f shone like the sun and
	18,10	the f of my heavenly Father
Lk	9,29	his f changed in appearance
1Cor	13,12	but then f to f
2Cor	3, 7	look intently at the f of Moses
	4, 6	on the f of [Jesus] Christ
	10, 1	when f to f with you
1Pt	3,12	but the f of the Lord is against
2Jn	12	to speak f to f so that our
3Jn	14	we can talk f to f
Rv	1,16	his f shone like the sun
	22, 4	They will look upon his f

FAIL

Dt	31, 6	never f you or forsake you
1Chr	28,20	He will not f you
Jdt	11, 6	f in any of his undertakings
Ps	73,26	flesh and my heart f
Prv	15,22	Plans f when there is no
Sir	24,21	serves me will never f
	34, 8	law is fulfilled without f
	42,17	God's holy ones must f
Lk	22,32	your own faith may not f
2Cor	13, 5	you f the test
1Pt	4,17	f to obey the gospel

FAITH

Gn	15, 6	Abram put his f in the LORD

Dt   32,51 broke f with me
1Mc   2,59 for their f, were saved
Sir   27,17 keep f with him
Is   7, 9 Unless your f is firm
      26, 2 one that keeps f. A nation
Hb   2, 4 because of his f, shall live
Mal   2,10 we break f with each other
       2,11 Judah has broken f
       2,15 not break f with the wife
Mt   6,30 you, O you of little f?
       8,10 Israel have I found such f
       9,22 Your f has saved you
      17,20 f the size of a mustard
      21,22 ask for in prayer with f
Mk   4,40 Do you not yet have f
       5,34 your f has saved you
      10,52 your f has saved you
      11,22 Have f in God.
Lk   7, 9 Israel have I found such f
       7,50 Your f has saved you
       8,25 Where is your f
      17, 6 f the size of a mustard
Acts   6, 5 Stephen, a man filled with f
       6, 7 becoming obedient to the f
      24,24 speak about f in Christ Jesus
      26,18 consecrated by f in me
Rom   1, 5 the obedience of f
       3,26 who has f in Jesus
       4, 9 f was credited to Abraham
       4,11 received through f
       9,32 they did it not by f
      10,17 f comes from what is heard
      14,23 whatever is not from f is sin
      16,26 of f, to the only wise God
1Cor   2, 5 your f might rest not on
      13, 2 all f so as to move
      15,17 your f is vain
      16,13 stand firm in the f
2Cor   4,13 have the same spirit of f
      10,15 hope is that, as your f increases
      13, 5 living in f. Test yourselves
Gal   1,23 f he once tried to destroy
       2,16 justified by f in Christ
       2,20 I live by f in the Son of God
       3,11 righteous by f will live
       3,14 of the Spirit through f
       3,22 that through f in Jesus Christ
       5, 6 only f working through love
Eph   1,15 hearing of your f
       2, 8 been saved through f
       3,17 in your hearts through f
       4, 5 one Lord, one f, one baptism
       6,16 hold f as a shield
Phil   1,27 f of the gospel
       2,17 sacrificial service of your f
       3, 9 comes through f in Christ
Col   1, 4 heard of your f in Christ
       1,23 persevere in the f
       2, 7 established in the f
       2,12 raised with him through f
1Thes 1, 3 work of f and labor of love
       1, 8 every place your f in God
       3, 2 encourage you in your f
       3, 7 and affliction, through your f
       3,10 the deficiencies of your f
       5, 8 the breastplate of f and love
2Thes 1, 3 your f flourishes ever more
       1, 4 and f in all your persecutions
       3, 2 for not all have f
1Tm   1, 2 Timothy, my true child in f
       1, 5 conscience, and a sincere f
       2,15 in f and love and holiness
       4, 1 turn away from the f
       6,10 strayed from the f
       6,11 devotion, f, love, patience
       6,12 Compete well for the f

2Tm   1, 5 I recall your sincere f
       2,18 upsetting the f of some
       3,15 salvation through f in Christ
       4, 7 I have kept the f
Ti   1, 1 sake of the f of God's chosen
       1, 4 true child in our common f
       2, 2 self- controlled, sound in f,
       2,10 exhibiting complete good f
Phlm   6 partnership in the f
Heb   3,19 not enter for lack of f
       6, 1 dead works and f in God
      10,38 just one shall live by f
      11, 3 By f we understand
      11, 7 By f Noah, warned
      11, 8 that comes through f. By f
      11,22 By f Joseph, near the end
      11,33 who by f conquered kingdoms
      13, 7 imitate their f
Jas   1, 3 testing of your f produces
       2, 5 be rich in f and heirs
       2,14 Can that f save him
       2,24 by works and not by f
       5,15 f will save the sick person
1Pt   1, 5 safeguarded through f
       1, 9 attain the goal of [your] f
       1,21 your f and hope are in God
       5, 9 steadfast in f
2Pt   1, 1 received a f of equal value
       1, 5 supplement your f with virtue
1Jn   5, 4 conquers the world is our f
Jude   3 contend for the f
       20 most holy f
Rv   2,13 denied your f in me
       2,19 your love, f, service

FAITHFUL (NESS)

Dt   7, 9 f God who keeps his merciful
      32, 4 f God, without deceit
1Sm   26,23 for his justice and f.
2Chr 31,20 upright and f before the LORD
Neh   9, 8 found his heart f in your sight
1Mc   2,52 Abraham found f in trial
Ps   18,26 Toward the f you are faithful
      25,10 paths of the LORD are f
      97,10 protects the lives of the f
     101, 6 I look to the f
     145,13 and f in every work
Wis   3, 9 the f shall abide with him
Sir   6,14 f friend is a sturdy shelter
Jer   7,28 F has disappeared
Mi   7,20 You will show f to Jacob
Mt   24,45 f and prudent servant
      25,21 my good and f servant
Lk   12,42 f and prudent steward
      19,17 f in this very small matter
1Cor   1, 9 Jesus [Christ.] God is f
      10,13 God is f and will not
2Cor   1,18 God is f, our word
1Thes 5,24 one who calls you is f
2Thes 3, 3 The Lord is f
2Tm   2,13 he remains f
Heb   2,17 merciful and f high priest
       3, 5 f in all his house
       3, 6 Christ was f as a son
1Pt   4,19 f creator
1Jn   1, 9 he is f and just
3Jn   5 you are f in all you do
Rv   1, 5 the f witness
       2,10 Remain f until death

FALL (S) (EN)

Nm   26,56 As the lot f shall each group
2Mc   7,38 the Almighty that has justly f
Ps   66, 4 f in worship before you
Prv   11,28 trusts in his riches will f
Sir   1,27 Exalt not yourself lest you f

      35,15 causes them to f
Is   40,30 stagger and f
Mt   5,45 causes rain to f
Lk   10,18 observed Satan f like lightning
1Cor 10,12 take care not to f
      15,51 We shall not all f asleep
Rv   4,10 twenty-four elders f down

FAMILY (FAMILIES)

Nm   16,32 swallowed them and their f
1Chr   9, 9 Their kindred of various f
Zec   12,14 all the rest of the f
Jn   7,42 David's f and come from
Acts 16,33 all his f were baptized
1Tm   5, 8 f members has denied the

FAMINE

Gn   12,10 There was f in the land
      26, 1 There was a f in the land
      41,30 seven years of f
Ru   1, 1 there was a f in the land
Jdt   5,10 f had gripped the whole land
1Mc   9,24 there was a very great f
Am   8,11 Not a f of bread
Rom   8,35 or f, or nakedness

FAST (ED)

Dt   10,20 hold f to him
1Sm   7, 6 and they f that day
Jdt   8, 6 She f all the days
Bar   1, 5 They wept and f and prayed
Eph   6,14 stand f with your loins girded
Ti   1, 9 holding f to the true message
Heb   4,14 let us hold f to our confession

FATHER

Gn   2,24 man leaves his f and mother
Ex   20,12 Honor your f and your mother
Lv   18, 7 not disgrace your f
Dt   5,16 Honor your f and your mother
2Sm   7,14 I will be a f to him, and he
1Chr 17,13 I will be a f to him
Ps   2, 7 son; today I am your f
      27,10 my f and mother forsake me
      89,27 You are my f, my God
Prv   10, 1 makes his f glad has no
Sir   3, 3 honors his f atones for sins
Is   9, 5 F-Forever, Prince of Peace
Jer   31, 9 I am a f to Israel
Ez   18,19 with the guilt of his f
Mal   2,10 we not all the one f
Mt   3, 9 We have Abraham as our f
       6, 9 Our F in heaven
      10,37 Whoever loves f or mother
      11,27 knows the F except the Son
Lk   9,59 go first and bury my f
      14,26 without hating his f and
      18,20 honor your f and your mother
Jn   3,35 The F loves the Son
       4,21 worship the F
       8,41 We have one F, God
      14, 9 seen me has seen the F
Rom   8,15 "Abba, F
1Cor   4,15 I became your f in Christ
2Cor   6,18 and I will be a f to you, and
Eph   5,31 shall leave [his] f and [his]
       6, 2 Honor your f and mother
Phil   2,11 the glory of God the fF
Heb   12, 7 whom his f does not discipline
1Jn   2,15 love of the F is not in him

FAVOR

Gn   4, 4 The LORD looked with f on Abel
Ex   33,12 'You have found f with me.'
Lv   26, 9 I will look with f upon you
Tb   1,13 granted me f and status

Ps   5,13 them with f like a shield.
     30, 6 divine f lasts a lifetime.
Prv 8,35 and wins f from the LORD;
Sir   3,18 and you will find f with God.
Is   61, 2 a year of f from the LORD
Zec 11, 7 one of which I called "F,"
Lk   1,30 for you have found f with God.
    2,52 f before God and man.
1Pt 5, 5 bestows f on the humble."

FEAR (S)

Dt   6,13 LORD, your God, shall you f;
Jos 24,14 f the LORD and serve him
1Sm 12,14 f the LORD and worship him
Ps   2,11 Serve the LORD with f;
    34, 5 delivered me from all my f.
Prv 1, 7 The f of the LORD is the
Eccl 12,13 f God and keep his
Sir   1,11 He who f the Lord will have
Is   11, 3 shall be the f of the LORD.
Jer 30,10 f not, says the LORD,
Mt 28, 4 guards were shaken with f
Lk   2, 9 were struck with great f.
Acts 10,35 in every nation whoever f him
Phil 2,12 with f and trembling.
1Jn 4,18 but perfect love drives out f
Rv 14, 7 "F God and give him glory

FEET

Ex   3, 5 the sandals from your f,
Ru   3, 8 a woman lying at his f.
Ps   8, 7 put all things at their f
  119,105 my f, a light for my path
Sir 37,15 set your f in the path
Is 52, 7 f of him who brings glad
Dn   2,33 f partly iron and partly tile
Mt 10,14 shake the dust from your f.
Rom 3,15 f are quick to shed blood
Eph 6,15 your f shod in readiness
Heb 12,13 straight paths for your f,

FIELD (S)

Gn 24,65 through the f toward us?
Song 7,12 go forth to the f
Mi   2, 2 They covet f, and seize them
Mt   6,30 clothes the grass of the f,
   13,44 treasure buried in a f,
Lk 14,18 'I have purchased a f
1Cor 3, 9 you are God's f,

FIGHT

Ex 14,14 The LORD himself will f for
Dt   3,22 LORD, your God, will f for you
Sir 4,28 Even to the death f for
1Cor 9,26 I do not f as if I were
1Tm 1,18 may you f a good fight

FILL (ED)

Gn 1,28 f the earth and subdue it
Ezr 6,22 the Lord had f them with joy
Bar 3,32 f it with four-footed beasts
Rom 15,13 May the God of hope f you

FIND

Dt   4,29 f him when you search
Ps 17, 3 but f no malice in me.
   94,22 the rock where I f refuge,
Prv 8,17 those who seek me f me.
Wis 13, 6 seek God and wish to f
Jer 6,16 you will f rest for your
Mt   7, 7 you; seek and you will f;
Lk 11, 9 receive; seek and you will f;
Heb 4,16 mercy and to f grace

FIRE

Ex   3, 2 LORD appeared to him in f

1Kgs 18,38 The LORD's f came down
2Kgs 1,10 And f came down from
Ps 17, 3 You have tried me by f,
Sir 2, 5 For in f gold is tested,
Is 30,27 tongue is like a consuming f
Jer 23,29 Is not my word like f,
Mal 3, 2 For he is like the refiner's f,
Mt   3,11 with the holy Spirit and f.
Mk 9,48 and the f is not quenched.
Lk   3,16 with the holy Spirit and f.
Acts 2, 3 to them tongues as of f,
1Cor 3,13 It will be revealed with f,
Jas   3, 6 The tongue is also a f.
Rv 20,14 thrown into the pool of f.

FIRST

Is 44, 6 I am the f and I am the last
Mt   5,24 go f and be reconciled with
   6,33 seek f the kingdom [of God]
  19,30 many who are f will be last,
  22,38 and the f commandment.
Mk 9,35 If anyone wishes to be f,
  13,10 gospel must f be preached
Jn   8, 7 f to throw a stone at
Eph 6, 2 f commandment with a
1Thes 4,16 dead in Christ will rise f.
1Tm 2,13 For Adam was formed f,
Heb 10, 9 takes away the f to establish
1Jn 4,19 love because he f loved us.
Rv 1,17 I am the f and the last,

FIRST-BORN

Ex 11, 5 Every f in this land shall die
Lv 27,26 "Note that a f animal,
Nm 1,20 the f of Israel, registered
Dt 12,17 of the f of your herd
  21,15 but the f is of her whom
2Sm 3, 2 his f, Amnon, of Ahinoam
  13,21 because he was his f.
1Kgs 16,34 He lost his f son, Abiram,
2Chr 21, 3 because he was the f.
Neh 10,37 the f of our children
Jb 15, 7 Are you indeed the f
  18,13 the f of death consumes
Prv 8,22 the f of his ways,
  31, 2 What, my son, my f!
Wis 18,13 at the destruction of the f
Sir 36,11 whom you named your f.
Jer 31, 9 Ephraim is my f.
Ez 20,26 immolation of every f,
Mi   6, 7 I give my f for my crime,
Heb 1, 6 he leads the f into the world,

FISH

Gn 1,28 Have dominion over the f
Ex   7,18 The f in the river shall die
   7,21 The f in the river died, and
Nm 11, 5 We remember the f
  11,22 If all the f of the sea
Dt   4,18 any f in the waters
2Chr 33,14 extending to the f Gate
Neh 3, 3 The f Gate was rebuilt
Tb   6, 3 a large f suddenly leaped
Jb 12, 8 and the f of the sea
  40,31 or his head with f spears?
Ps   8, 9 the f of the sea,
  105,29 blood and killed all their f.
Is 50, 2 Their f rot for lack of water
Ez 29, 4 make the f of your Niles
Jon 2, 1 the LORD sent a large f,
Mt   7,10 when he asks for a f?
  14,17 "Five loaves and two f
Lk   5, 6 caught a great number of f
Jn   6, 9 five barley loaves and two f;
  21,11 one hundred fifty-three large f.

FLESH

Gn 2,23 of my bones and f of my flesh;
Jb 19,26 from my f I shall see God;
Ps 38, 4 My f is afflicted because
Mt 19, 5 the two shall become one f?
Jn   1,14 And the Word became f
   6,51 my f for the life of the world
1Cor 6,16 "will become one f."
Gal 2,20 I now live in the f,
Eph 5,29 no one hates his own f
   6,12 our struggle is not with f
Phil 3, 3 not put our confidence in f,
1Pt 3,18 Put to death in the f,

FLOCK

Ps 77,21 led your people like a f
Sir 18,12 as a shepherd guides his f;
Is 40,11 a shepherd he feeds his f;
Jer 23, 1 who mislead and scatter the f
Mt 26,31 sheep of the f will be
Jn 10,16 and there will be one f,
1Pt 5, 2 the f of God in your midst

FLOOD

Gn 7, 7 the waters of the f.
Wis 19, 7 plain out of the mighty f.
Mt 24,38 In [those] days before the f,
2Pt 2, 5 when he brought a f upon

FOLLOW

Lv 18, 4 take care to f.
1Kgs 11, 6 did not f him unreservedly
Ps   1, 1 do not f the counsel
Mt 16,24 take up his cross, and f me.
   9,61 "I will f you, Lord, but first let
Jn 10,27 I know them, and they f me.
2Pt 1,16 not f cleverly devised myths
Rv 14, 4 f the Lamb wherever he

FOOD

Ps 69,22 they put gall in my f;
Prv 23, 3 they are deceitful f.
Dn   1, 8 with the king's f or wine;
Mt   3, 4 f was locusts and wild
Jn   4,32 I have f to eat of which you
   4,34 My f is to do the will
1Tm 6, 8 If we have f and clothing,
Heb 5,14 But solid f is for the mature,

FOOL

Prv 12,15 The way of the f seems right
Mt   7,26 be like a f who built his house
Lk 12,20 'You f, this night your life will
1Cor 3,18 become a f so as to become
2Cor 11,16 accept me as a f,

FOREVER

Gn 3,22 eat of it and live f.
Ex   3,15 This is my name f;
2Sm 7,26 Your name will be f great
1Chr 16,15 He remembers f his covenant
  16,34 for his kindness endures f;
2Chr 20,21 LORD, for his mercy endures f.
Ps   9, 8 The LORD rules f.
  136, 1 God's love endures f;
Wis 3, 8 LORD shall be their King f.
Sir 37,25 and his name endures f.
Is 25, 8 he will destroy death f
Jn   6,51 eats this bread will live f;
2Cor 9, 9 his righteousness endures f.
1Pt 1,25 word of the Lord remains f.
1Jn 2,17 the will of God remains f.

FORGIVE

1Sm 15,25 Now f my sin
Sir 5, 6 my many sins he will f
Jer 31,34 I will f their evildoing

Mt	6,12	and f us our debts
	18,21	how often must I f him?
Mk	2, 7	Who but God alone can f
	11,25	f anyone against whom you
Lk	23,34	Father, f them, they know not
2Cor	2, 7	f and encourage him instead
1Jn	1, 9	faithful and just and will f

FORGIVENESS

Ps	130, 4	But with you is f
Lk	1,77	through the f of their sins
Acts	10,43	f of sins through his name
Eph	1, 7	the f of transgressions,
Col	1,14	we have redemption, the f of

FORSAKE (N)

Dt	31, 6	will never fail you or f you
Jgs	10,10	we have f our God
Jdt	7,30	he will not utterly f us
Ps	68, 7	gives a home to the f
Dn	14,38	you have not f those
Heb	13, 5	I will never f you or abandon

FORTY

Gn	7, 4	for f days and forty nights
Ex	16,35	ate this manna for f years
Nm	14,33	children must wander for f
Mt	4, 2	He fasted for f days
Acts	1, 3	appearing to them during f

FOUNDATION

Ps	89,15	Justice and judgment are the f
Is	28,16	cornerstone as a sure f;
Rom	15,20	I do not build on another's f
1Cor	3,11	no one can lay a f
Eph	2,20	built upon the f of the
2Tm	2,19	God's solid f stands
Rv	17, 8	book of life from the f of the

FOUNTAIN

Ps	36,10	For with you is the f of life
Prv	14,27	of the LORD is a f of life
Bar	3,12	You have forsaken the f of
Zec	13, 1	a f to purify from sin

FREE

Gn	2,16	You are f to eat from any
Ps	118, 5	answered me and set me f.
Jn	8,32	the truth will set you f.
Gal	5, 1	For freedom Christ set us f
Heb	13, 5	your life be f from love of
1Pt	2,16	Be f, yet without using

FRIEND

Prv	18,24	but a true f is more loyal
Mt	11,19	a f of tax collectors and
Jas	2,23	and he was called "the f of

FRUIT

Gn	3, 6	she took some of its f and ate
Ps	92,15	They shall bear f even in old
Prv	11,30	The f of virtue is a tree
Sir	23,25	branches will not bring forth f.
Is	27, 6	covering all the world with f.
Jer	17, 8	to grow branches, bear f,
Mt	7,17	every good tree bears good f,
Lk	3, 9	that does not produce good f
Jn	15,16	you to go and bear f that will
Gal	5,22	In contrast, the f of the Spirit
Col	1,10	bearing f and growing in the
Jas	3,18	And the f of righteousness is

FULFILL

Ex	8, 8	implored the LORD to f the
Ps	22,26	my vows I will f before those
Jer	33,14	when I will f the promise

Mt	1,22	this took place to f
	5,17	not to abolish but to f.
Gal	6, 2	so you will f the law of Christ.
Col	4,17	f the ministry that you
Heb	13,17	that they may f their task with

FULL (NESS)

Ps	130, 7	with him is f redemption,
Wis	4,13	he reached the f of a long
Jl	4,13	for the wine press is f;
Lk	6,45	for from the f of the heart
Gal	4, 4	But when the f of time had
Phil	4,18	I have received f payment

FUTURE

Ex	40,15	throughout all f generations.
Ps	48,14	that you may tell f
Prv	23,18	you will surely have a f,
Wis	14, 6	left to the world a f for his
Sir	2, 3	thus will your f be great.
Jer	29,11	plans to give you a f full of
Rom	8,38	nor f things, nor powers, nor

G

GAIN

Gn	28, 4	g possession of the land
Prv	4, 1	that you may g
Wis	7,14	those who g this treasure win
Sir	31, 8	who turns not aside after g!
Mt	19,16	must I do to g eternal life?
1Tm	6, 6	with contentment is a great g.

GATE (S)

1Kgs	4,13	cities with g barred with bronze
Mal	1,10	you would shut the temple g
Jn	10, 7	I am the g for the sheep.

GATHER

Tb	13, 5	He will g you from all the
2Mc	2,18	have mercy on us and g us
Ps	106,47	g us from among the nations
Is	11,12	g the outcasts of Israel
Zec	14, 2	And I will g all the nations
Mk	13,27	send out the angels and g

GAVE

Gn	3, 6	she also g some to her
Ex	31,18	he g him the two tablets of
Dt	26, 9	he g us this land flowing with
Neh	9,15	Food from heaven you g them
Jb	1,21	The LORD g and the LORD has
Bar	2,21	the land I g your fathers
Mt	10, 1	g them authority over unclean
	27,50	in a loud voice, and g up his
Jn	1,12	who did accept him he g
	3,16	loved the world that he g his
Gal	1, 4	who g himself for our sins that
1Tm	2, 6	who g himself as ransom for

GENERATION (S)

Lv	6,11	perpetually throughout your g.
Jb	8, 8	you inquire of the former g
Ps	102,19	be written for the next g,
Jl	1, 3	their children to the next g.
Mt	12,39	"An evil and unfaithful g
Acts	2,40	yourselves from this corrupt g
Eph	3, 5	to human beings in other g

GENEROUS

Gn	33,11	God has been g toward me
1Kgs	8,56	unfulfilled of the entire g
Ps	37,21	the just are g in giving.

Ti	3, 4	g love of God our savior

GENTILE (S)

Lv	26,38	will be lost among the G
Gal	2,14	living like a G and not like a
Rom	1, 5	among all the G

GENTLE

Gal	6, 1	correct that one in a g spirit
1Thes	2, 7	Rather, we were g among
2Tm	2,24	but should be g with
1Pt	3, 4	beauty of a g and calm

GIFT

Ps	127, 3	Children too are a g from the
Sir	26, 3	good wife is a generous g
Jn	4,10	If you knew the g of God
Rom	6,23	but the g of God is eternal life
1Cor	1, 7	not lacking in any spiritual g
Eph	2, 8	it is the g of God
1Tm	4,14	Do not neglect the g you have
Jas	1,17	every perfect g is from above
1Pt	3, 7	joint heirs of the g of life

GLAD

1Chr	16,31	heavens be g and the earth
Ps	5,12	refuge in you will be g
	16, 9	my heart is g, my soul
	67, 5	May the nations be g and
Prv	10, 1	wise son makes his father g,
Is	25, 9	let us rejoice and be g
Zec	10, 7	shall see it and be g,
Mt	5,12	Rejoice and be g,
Acts	2,26	my heart has been g

GLORIFY (GLORIFIED)

Dt	32,43	g him, all you angels
Ps	86,12	g your name forever,
Sir	3,19	by the humble he is g.
Mt	5,16	g your heavenly Father.
Lk	5,26	seized them all and they g God
Jn	13,32	God will also g him in himself,
Rom	15, 6	g the God and Father of
Phil	3,21	to conform with his g body
1Pt	2,12	g God on the day of

GLORY (GLORIOUS)

Ex	14, 4	I will receive g through
Nm	14,21	the LORD's g that fills the
Dt	5,24	let us see his g and his
1Sm	4,21	"Gone is the g from Israel,"
Est	4, 7	he displayed the g riches
Ps	19, 2	The heavens declare the g of
	29, 1	give to the LORD g and might;
	149, 9	such is the g of all God's
Wis	7,25	effusion of the g of God
Is	11,10	for his dwelling shall be g.
	66,19	shall proclaim my g among
Ez	1,28	the likeness of the g of the
Mt	25,31	Man comes in his g,
Jn	1,14	and we saw his g,
Rom	1,23	fools and exchanged the g
	9,23	has prepared previously for g,
1Cor	10,31	do everything for the g of
Col	1, 11	in accord with his g might
2Thes	2,14	possess the g of our Lord
Heb	1, 3	is the refulgence of his g,
	2, 7	you crowned him with g and
1Pt	4, 11	g and dominion forever and

GODLY

Sir	6,35	Be eager to hear every g
Ez	28, 2	I occupy a g throne
Mal	2,15	one require but g offspring?
2Cor	7,10	For g sorrow produces

GODS

Ex   20, 3   You shall not have other g
1Chr 16,25   awesome is he, beyond all g
Ps   16, 3   Worthless are all the false g
Acts 19,26   made by hands are not g at

GOLD

Jb   22,25   himself shall be your g
Ps   119,127   more than the finest g.
Prv   3,14   better than g is her revenue;
Sir   2, 5   For in fire g is tested,
Mt   2,11   gifts of g, frankincense, and
Rv   3,18   buy from me g refined by fire

GOOD

Gn   1,31   and he found it very g.
     50,20   God meant it for g,
1Mc   4,24   for he is g, for his mercy
Ps   34, 9   Learn to savor how g the LORD
     84,12   LORD withholds no g thing
Prv   3,27   Refuse no one the g on which
     15,30   g news invigorates the bones.
     31,12   She brings him g, and not
Wis   15, 1   our God, are g and true,
Ez   34,14   In g pastures will I pasture
Mt   7,11   Father give g things to those
     25,21   'Well done, my g and faithful
Mk   10,18   Why do you call me g?
Jn   10,11   I am the g shepherd.
Rom   3,12   is not one who does g,
2Thes   1,11   bring to fulfillment every g
2Tm   3,17   equipped for every g work.
Hb   10,24   one another to love and g
1Pt   2, 3   tasted that the Lord is g.
3Jn   11   not imitate evil but imitate g.

GOSPEL

Mt   26,13   wherever this g is proclaimed
Rom   1,16   am not ashamed of the g
     15,20   I aspire to proclaim the g
1Cor   1,17   baptize but to preach the g,
2Cor   4, 4   see the light of the g
Eph   6,15   readiness for the g of peace.
Col   1,23   hope of the g that you heard,
1Thes   2, 4   to be entrusted with the g,
2Tm   1, 8   share of hardship for the g
1Pt   4, 6   the g was preached

GRACE

Ps   84,12   bestowing all g and glory.
Wis   3, 9   Because g and mercy
Mi   7,20   faithfulness to Jacob, and g to
Zec   12,10   spirit of g and petition;
Jn   1,14   full of g and truth.
Acts 15, 11   saved through the g of the
Rom   3,24   are justified freely by his g
2Cor   4,15   so that the g bestowed in
Gal   1,15   and called me through his g,
Eph   2, 7   immeasurable riches of his g
2Tm   2, 1   be strong in the g
Hb   4,16   approach the throne of g
1Pt   1,10   who prophesied about the g
2Pt   3,18   grow in g and in the

GRAPES

Jer   31,29   "The fathers ate unripe g,
Ez   18, 2   "Fathers have eaten green g,
Am   9,13   The juice of g shall drip down

GREAT (ER) (LY)

Gn   12, 2   will make of you a g nation,
1Chr 12,15   and the g over thousands.
Tb   8,16   with us according to your g
Ps   21, 2   your victory from g he rejoices!
Wis   6, 7   he himself made the g
Sir   17,24   How g the mercy of the LORD
Is   42,21   justice to make his law g and

Bar   2,11   with signs and wonders and g
Mt   20,26   whoever wishes to be g
Eph   2, 4   because of the g love he had
Heb   2, 3   if we ignore so g a salvation?

GREED (Y)

1Mc   4,17   "Do not be g for the plunder
Ps   10, 3   wicked even boast of their g;
Prv   19,22   From a man's g comes his
Jer   6,13   all are g for gain
Eph   5, 5   immoral or impure or g person
2Pt   2,14   their hearts are trained in g.

GREEK

2Mc   11,24   G customs but prefer their
Rom   1,16   for Jew first, and then G.
Gal   3,28   There is neither Jew nor G,

GUARD

Ps   91,11   commands the angels to g
Prv   4,23   With closest custody, g your
Sir   22,27   Who will set a g over my
Is   52,12   and your rear g is the God of
Lk   17, 3   Be on your g!
Phil   4, 7   all understanding will g
2Thes   3, 3   he will strengthen you and g

GUIDE

Ps   23, 3   You g me along the right path
    139,10   Even there your hand will g
Prv   5,22   wherever you turn, she will g
Wis   9, 11   and will g me discreetly in my
Jn   16,13   he will g you to all truth.

GUILT

Lv   5,15   to the LORD as his g offering
Sir   4,26   to acknowledge your g,
Ez   18,19   charged with the g of his

H

HAND

Gn   3,22   out his h to take fruit
Ex   4,17   Take this staff in your h;
Lv   14,17   the thumb of his right h,
Nm   35,17   death-dealing stone in his h
Dt   13,10   Your h shall be the first raised
Jos   8,18   the javelin in your h
Jgs   1,35   Joseph gained the upper h,
Ru   1,13   the LORD has extended his h
1Sm   17,46   deliver you into my h;
2Sm   23, 6   cannot be taken up by h.
1Kgs   8,15   by his h has brought it to
2Kgs 19,14   letter from the h of the
1Chr   6,24   Asaph stood at his right h.
2Chr 32,14   save his people from my h?
Ezr   7, 6   Because the h of the LORD,
Neh   1,10   might and your strong h.
Tb   11, 4   Have the gall in your h!"
Jdt   12, 4   LORD accomplishes by my h
Est   3,10   the signet ring from his h
1Mc   3,30   more liberal h than the
2Mc   7,34   raise your h against the
Jb   8,20   neither will he take the h of
Ps   39,11   by the touch of your h.
     36,12   the h of the wicked
     37,24   the Lord holds their h.
     44, 2   with your own h in days
     44, 4   It was your right h,
   123, 2   on the h of his master,
Prv   6, 1   given your h in pledge to
Eccl   9,10   Anything you can turn your h
Song   5, 4   My lover put his h through the
Wis   5,16   from the h of the LORD—

     13,10   work of an ancient h.
     14, 6   the guidance of your h.
Sir   12,12   not sit at your right h,
     51,19   My h opened her gate and I
Is   23, 11   His h he stretches out over
Jer   43, 3   to h us over to the Chaldeans
Lam   2, 4   his arrows in his right h
Bar   2,11   of Egypt with your mighty h,
Ez   21,16   to be put in the h of a slayer.
Dn   5, 5   the fingers of a human h
     14,30   the king was forced to h
Hos   2,12   deliver her out of my h.
Am   5,19   he were to rest his h against
Jon   4, 11   cannot distinguish their right h
Mi   5, 8   Your h shall be lifted above
Hb   2,16   cup from the LORD's right h,
Zep   1, 4   I will stretch out my h against
Hg   1, 11   all that is produced by h.
Zec   6,13   shall be at his right h,
Mal   2,13   it favorably from your h;
Mt   5,40   your tunic, h him your cloak
     14,31   Jesus stretched out his h
     20,19   h him over to the Gentiles
     24, 9   Then they will h you over
     26,16   opportunity to h him over.
Mk   5,41   by the h and said to her,
     16,19   his seat at the right h of God.
Lk   9,62   sets a h to the plow and looks
Jn   13, 2   of Simon the Iscariot, to h him
Acts 11,21   The h of the Lord was with
Rom   7,18   The willing is ready at h,
1Cor 12,15   Because I am not a h I do not
Gal   6, 11   to you in my own h!
Eph   1,20   at his right h in the heavens,
Col   2, 11   not administered by h,
     3, 1   at the right h of God.
     4,18   greeting is in my own h,
2Thes   2, 2   of the Lord is at h.
2Tm   4, 6   of my departure is at h.
Phlm   19   in my own h: I will pay.
Heb   1,13   my right h until I make your
Jas   5, 8   the Lord is at h. Do not
1Pt   3,22   and is at the right h of God,
Rv   10, 2   In his h he held a small scroll
     10, 5   his right h to heaven
     10,10   from the angel's h
     14,14   sickle in his h.
     20, 1   holding in his h the key

HAPPY

Dt   6,24   as prosperous and h a life as
1Kgs   8,66   rejoicing and h over all the
2Chr   9, 7   the stories I heard. H are your
Tb   8, 7   live together to a h old age."
     8,21   So be h, son!
     11,18   feast for seven h days, and
     13,14   and h those who rejoice in
Est   5, 9   That day Haman left h and in
1Mc   10,55   in these words: "H the day
2Mc   7,24   make him rich and h if he
Jb   5,17   h is the man whom God
Ps   34, 9   h are those who take refuge
     40, 5   h those whose trust is
     65, 5   h the chosen ones you
     84, 5   h are those who dwell in
     94,12   h those whom you guide,
   106, 3   h those who do what is
   126, 3   Oh, how h we were!
   144,15   h the people so blessed;
   146, 5   h those whose help is
Prv   20, 7   h are his children after him
     28,14   h the man who is always
     29,18   but h is he who keeps the
Sir   25, 8   h is he who dwells with
     25, 9   h is he who finds a
     28,19   h he who is sheltered from

50,28 h the man who meditates
Is 32,20 h are you who sow beside
Jer 30,19 of praise, the laughter of h
Jon 4, 6 Jonah was very h over the

HARLOT
Gn 38,15 he mistook her for a h,
Dt 23,18 no temple h among the
Jos 6,22 "Go into the h's house and
Jgs 11, 1 born to Gilead of a h.
Prv 23,27 For the h is a deep ditch,
Is 23,15 in the song about the h ,
Jer 3, 8 went off and played the h.
Ez 16,25 playing the h countless times.
Hos 3, 3 you shall not play the h
4,15 Though you play the h,
5, 3 has played the h, Israel is
9, 1 loving a h's hire upon
Jl 4, 3 gave a boy for a h,
Am 7,17 be made a h in the city,
Mi 1, 7 As the wages of a h
Na 3, 4 many debaucheries of the h,
Heb 11,31 By faith Rahab the h did not
Jas 2,25 was not Rahab the h also
Rv 2,14 idols and to play the h.
2,20 the h and to eat food
17, 1 judgment on the great h
17,15 that you saw where the h lives

HARM
Gn 31,29 to threaten Jacob with any h!'
Nm 35,23 enemy nor seeking to h him
Jos 9,19 so we cannot h them.
Jgs 15, 3 me if I h them." So Samson
Ru 2, 9 men to do you no h.
1Sm 25,26 seek to h my lord become as
2Sm 18,12 I would not h the king's son,
1Kgs 11,25 to the h done by Hadad,
1Chr 16,22 to my prophets do no h."
Ezr 4,13 only result in h to the throne.
Neh 6, 2 were planning to do me h.
Tb 6,15 he does not h her; but he
Jdt 11, 4 No one at all will h you.
Est 8, 3 the h done by Haman the
1Mc 5,48 no one will h you; we will only
6,18 continually trying to h them
15,19 that they are not to h them,
15,29 done great h to the land,
15,35 cities were doing great h
2Mc 8,32 done great h to the Jews.
Ps 37, 8 it brings only h.
57, 2 I seek shelter till h pass by.
105,15 to my prophets do no h."
121, 6 By day the sun cannot h you,
Prv 3,30 who has done you no h
Wis 14,29 idols, they expect no h
Sir 19,24 he will do h. One can
22,26 who brings h to his friend
27,27 Whoever does h will be
33, 1 No evil can h the man
38,21 but will do you h.
42,13 so h to women comes from
Is 11, 9 There shall be no h or ruin on
Jer 25, 7 handiwork to your own h. rd
Dn 3,50 or caused them pain or h.
Zec 1,15 they added to the h.
Mk 16,18 it will not h them.
Lk 10,19 nothing will h you.
Acts 16,28 "Do no h to yourself;
1Cor 11,17 meetings are doing more h
2Tm 4,14 a great deal of h; the Lord will
1Pt 3,13 going to h you if you are
Rv 9,19 with heads that inflict h.

HATE
Gn 26,27 seeing that you h me and

Ex 18,21 men who h dishonest gain,
Nm 10,35 those who h you may flee
Dt 32,41 foes and requite those who h
Jgs 14,16 "You must h me; you do not
2Sm 19, 7 by loving those who h you
1Kgs 22, 8 but I h him because he
2Chr 19, 2 love those who h the LORD?
Est 4C,26 You know that I h the glory of
Jb 8,22 They that h you shall be
Ps 25,19 see how fiercely they h me.
26, 5 I h the company of evildoers;
34,22 h the just are condemned.
44, 8 shamed those who h us.
50,17 You h discipline; you cast
69, 5 who h me without cause.
81,16 Those who h the Lord would
97,10 loves those who h evil,
105,25 turned their hearts to h his
119,128 every wrong way I h.
129, 5 all who h Zion. May they
139,22 With fierce hatred I h them,
Prv 8,36 all who h me love death."
9, 8 he h you; reprove a wise man
13,19 but fools h to turn from evil.
19, 7 poor man's brothers h him;
25,17 enough of you, and h you.
29,10 Bloodthirsty men h the honest
Eccl 3, 8 and a time to h; a time of war,
Sir 7,15 h not laborious tasks, nor
10, 7 oppression they both h.
17,21 h intensely what he loathes;
25, 2 Three kinds of men I h;
27,24 There is nothing that I h so
Is 61, 8 I h robbery and injustice;
Jer 44, 4 this horrible deed which I h,
Ez 23,28 over to those whom you h,
Am 5,21 I h, I spurn your feasts, I ₵
Mi 3, 2 you who h what is good,
Zec 8,17 For all these things I h,
Mal 2,16 For I h divorce, says the LORD,
Mt 6,24 He will either h one and love
Lk 6,22 are you when people h you,
Jn 7, 7 The world cannot h you,
Rom 12, 9 Let love be sincere; h what is
Rv 17,16 and the beast will h the harlot;

HEAD
Gn 4, 7 you can hold up your h;
28,11 he put it under his h
42,38 send my white h down
48,17 Ephraim's h to Manasseh's,
49,26 rest on the h of Joseph,
Ex 12, 2 stand at the h of your
Lv 3, 2 lay his hand on the h of his
Nm 6, 7 his h bears his dedication to
Dt 3,28 he shall cross at the h
10,11 at the h of your people,
19, 5 its h flies off the handle
21,12 she must shave her h and
28,13 LORD will make you the h, not
Jos 8,10 at its h, with the elders of
Jgs 9,53 down on Abimelech's h,
1Sm 31, 9 cut off Saul's h and stripped
2Sm 15,30 His h was covered, and he
1Kgs 1,52 hair shall fall from his h.
2Kgs 6,31 exclaimed, "if the h of Elisha,
1Chr 24, 4 each under its family h.
2Chr 20,27 with Jehoshaphat at their h,
31,10 priest Azariah, h of the house
Ezr 9, 3 plucked hair from my h and
Neh 12,36 the scribe was at their h.]
Jdt 9, 1 with ashes strewn upon her h,
13, 6 near the h of Holofernes, and
14, 6 saw the h of Holofernes in
14,11 daybreak they hung the h
15,13 At the h of all the people,

Est 6,12 hurried home, his h covered
1Mc 11,13 wore two crowns on his h,
2Mc 5,24 at the h of an army of twenty
7, 7 skin and hair of his h,
8, 9 the h of at least twenty
11, 8 appeared at their h,
15,32 the vile Nicanor's h
Jb 16, 4 or wag my h at you;
Ps 27, 6 Even now my h is held high
40,13 than the hairs of my h;
60, 9 is the helmet for my h,
108, 9 is the helmet for my h,
110, 7 and thus holds high his h.
133, 2 precious ointment on the h
Prv 10, 6 Blessings are for the h of the
11,26 blessings upon the h
25,22 you will heap on his h,
30,31 king at the h of his people.
Eccl 9, 8 not the perfume for your h.
Song 5,11 His h is pure gold; his locks
Wis 18,24 on the crown upon his h.
Sir 11,13 Lifts up his h and exalts him
12,18 Then he will nod his h
13, 7 and shake his h over you.
19,23 He bows his h and feigns
20,10 man can lift up his h. A
44,22 rested upon the h of Jacob.
Is 7,20 the king of Assyria] the h,
Jer 48,37 Every h has been made bald,
Lam 3,54 The waters flowed over my h,
Bar 5, 2 bear on your h the mitre that
Ez 13,18 veils for every size of h so as
Dn 7,20 the ten horns on its h, and
Hos 3, 2 appoint for themselves one h
Jl 2,11 raises his voice at the h of his
Am 8,10 sackcloth and make every h
Ob 15 come back upon your own h;
Jon 4, 8 sun beat upon Jonah's h till
Mi 2,13 the LORD at their h. And I said
Zec 2, 4 no man raised his h
3, 5 a clean miter on his h."
3, 5 a clean miter on his h
6,11 place it on the h of [Joshua,
Mt 5,36 Do not swear by your h,
8,20 has nowhere to rest his h."
13,52 of heaven is like the h
14,11 the prison. His h was brought
26, 7 and poured it on his h while
27,37 they placed over his h the
Mk 6,24 "The h of John the Baptist."
Lk 7,46 You did not anoint my h with
9,58 has nowhere to rest his h."
12, 7 Even the hairs of your h have
21,18 hair on your h will be
Jn 19,30 bowing his h, he handed over
Acts 27,34 Not a hair of the h of anyone
Rom 12,20 burning coals upon his h."
1Cor 11, 7 should not cover his h,
11,10 sign of authority on her h,
11,13 with her h unveiled?
12,21 again the h to the feet,
Eph 4,15 into him who is the h, Christ,
Col 2,19 to the h, from whom the whole
Rv 10, 1 halo around his h; his face
12, 1 and on her h a crown
14,14 a gold crown on his h
19,12 his h were many diadems.

HEAL (ED) (ING)
Nm 12,13 "Please, not this! Pray, h her!"
Dt 32,39 I who inflict wounds and h
2Kgs 5,10 flesh will h, and you will be
Tb 3,17 So Raphael was sent to h
Ps 30, 3 out to you and you h me.
Eccl 3, 3 a time to h; a time to tear
Wis 16,10 the antidote to h them.

Heal (continued)

Sir	38, 9	pray to God, who will h you
Is	19,22	he shall h them; they shall
	30,26	he will h the bruises left
	38, 5	I will h you: in three days
	57,18	but I will h them and lead
	57,19	and I will h them. But the
	61, 1	to h the brokenhearted,
Jer	33, 6	I will h them, and reveal to
Lam	2,13	who can h you? Your
Ez	34, 4	the weak nor h the sick
Hos	7, 1	people, when I would h Israel,
Mal	3,20	sun of justice with its h rays
Mt	13,15	and be converted, and I
Lk	9, 2	kingdom of God and to h [the
Jn	12,40	be converted, and I would h
Acts	28,27	and be converted, and I h

HEAR

Gn	21,26	nor did I ever h of it until now."
Ex	19, 9	when the people h me
	22,22	I will surely h their cry.
	22,26	I will h him; for I am
	32,18	sounds that I h are cries
Nm	14,13	"Are the Egyptians to h of
Dt	4,10	I will have them h my words,
	5,25	If we h the voice of the Lord
	6, 3	h then, Israel, and be careful
	9, 1	"H, O Israel! You are now
	18,16	'Let us not again h the voice
	20, 3	to the soldiers: 'H O Israel!
	29, 3	to see, or ears to h. 'I led you
	31,13	must h it and learn it, that
	32,44	song for the people to h.
Jos	6, 5	you h that signal, all the
Jgs	9, 7	"H me, citizens of Shechem,
1Sm	2,24	a good report that I h the
	13, 3	"Let the Hebrews h!"
	15,14	lowing of oxen that I h?"
	16, 2	Saul will h of it and kill me
2Sm	15,35	If you h anything from the
1Kgs	10,24	Solomon, to h from him the
2Kgs	19,16	see! h the words of
1Chr	14,15	When you h the sound of
2Chr	6,39	h their prayer and petitions,
	7,14	I will h them from heaven
	9,23	to h from him the wisdom
	15, 2	"H me, Asa and all Judah
	18,18	"Therefore h the word
Neh	9,27	and you would h them from
Tb	3, 6	and to h these insults!"
	3,10	no longer live to h such
	3,13	never again to h such insults.
	3,15	never again let me h these
	5,10	I can h a man's voice,
	10,12	let me h good reports
Jdt	9, 5	"O God, my God, h me also,
Est	1,18	ladies who h of the queen's
	4C,10	h my prayer; have pity
	4C,16	child I was wont to h
	4,30	h the voice of those in
Jb	3,18	and h not the voice of the
	13, 6	h now the rebuke I shall
	20, 3	puts me to shame I h,
	22,27	he will h you, and your
	26,14	faint is the word we h!
	31,35	I had one to h my case,
	33, 1	O Job, h my discourse,
	34, 2	H, O wise men, my discourse
	34, 2	have knowledge, h me!
	34,16	O Job, h this! Hearken to
	35,13	God does not h or that
	37, 2	To h his angry voice as it
Ps	4, 2	h my prayer. How long
	5, 2	h my words, O Lord; listen
	5, 3	h my cry for help, my
	5, 4	you will h my cry; at dawn I

	10,17	and h their prayers. You
	17, 1	h, Lord, my plea for justice
	17, 6	h my prayer. Show your
	27, 7	h my voice, Lord, when I
	28, 2	h the sound of my pleading
Prv	4,10	H, my son, and receive my
	19,27	a son ceases to h instruction,
	22,17	ear, and h my words,
	23,19	h, my son, and be wise
Eccl	7,21	lest you h your servant
Song	2,14	let me h your voice,
Wis	15,15	Nor ears to h, nor fingers on
Sir	4, 6	Creator will h his prayer.
	5,13	swift to h, but slow to
	6,35	Be eager to h every godly
	19, 9	Let anything you h die within
	41,23	Of repeating what you h, and
	43,25	h them we are thunderstruck;
	45, 5	permitted him to h his voice,
	47,16	their peoples came to h you;
Is	21, 3	I am too bewildered to h,
Jer	6,18	Therefore h, O nations, and
Lam	3,61	You h their insults, O LORD,
Bar	2,22	if you do not h the LORD's
	3, 2	h, O Lord, for you are
	3, 4	h the prayer of Israel's few,
	4, 9	"h, you neighbors of Zion!
Ez	3,10	that I speak to you; h them
Dn	3, 4	when you h the sound of the
Hos	5, 1	H this, O priests. Pay
Jl	1, 2	H this, you elders! Pay
Am	3, 1	H this word, O men of Israel
	3,13	H and bear witness against
	4, 1	H this word, women of the
	5, 1	H this word which I utter
	7,16	Now h the word of the Lord
	8, 4	H this, you who trample upon
Mi	6, 1	and let the hills h your voice!
Na	3,19	All who h this news of you
Hb	3,16	I h, and my body trembles; at
Zec	8, 9	who in these days h these
Mt	13,17	and to h what you hear but
	13,43	has ears ought to h.
	15,10	"H and understand.
	21,16	you h what they are saying?"
	21,33	"H another parable. There
	24, 6	You will h of wars and reports
	27,13	you not h how many
Mk	11,18	and the scribes came to h of it
Lk	9, 9	is this about whom I h such
Jn	3, 8	you can h the sound
	5,25	dead will h the voice
	5,25	and those who h will live.
	5,28	will h his voice and
	5,30	I judge as I h,
	8,43	cannot bear to h my word. o
	9,27	Why do you want to h it
Acts	15, 7	the Gentiles would h the word
Rom	2,13	those who h the law
	10,14	can they h without
	10,18	did they not h? Certainly they
	11, 8	and ears that should not h,
1Cor	11,18	First of all, I h that when you
Eph	4,29	impart grace to those who h.
Phil	1,27	I may h news of you, that you
2Thes	3,11	We h that some are
2Tm	4,17	and all the Gentiles might h it.
Phlm	5	as I h of the love
Heb	3, 7	that today you would h his
Jas	1,19	be quick to h, slow to speak,
1Jn	4, 6	belong to God refuses to h us.
3Jn	4	than to h that my children are
Rv	3, 6	ought to h what the Spirit says
	9,20	cannot see or h or walk.
	10, 7	h the seventh angel blow
	13, 9	ought to h these words.

HEART

Gn	34, 8	Shechem has his h set on
Ex	25, 2	contribution that his h prompts
	28,29	decision over his h
	28,30	h in the Lord's presence.
	35, 5	as his h prompts him,
	35,21	as his h suggested and
Lv	19,17	in your h. Though you may
Dt	1,21	Do not fear or lose h.'
	2,30	obstinate in h that he
	4,39	and fix in your h, that
	6, 6	Take to h these words
	7, 7	Lord set his h on you
	8,14	become haughty of h and
	9, 5	or the integrity of your h
	10,12	all your h and all your soul,
	11,16	lest your h be so lured away
	12,20	to your h's desire;
	13, 4	love him with all your h.
	15, 7	not harden your h nor
	17,17	lest his h be estranged,
	18, 6	as his h may desire,
	26,16	observe them with all your h
	28,67	your h must feel and the
	29,18	stubbornness of h,
	30, 2	all your h and all your soul,
	32,46	"Take to h all the warning
Jos	23,14	with your whole h and soul
Jgs	5,16	were the searchings of h!
Ru	3, 7	ate and drank to his h's
1Sm	12,20	him with your whole h.
	13,14	a man after his own h
	16, 7	the Lord looks into the h.
	28, 5	and lost h completely.
2Sm	6,16	she despised him in her h.
1Kgs	11, 4	gods, and his h was not
2Kgs	23,25	his whole h, his whole soul,
1Chr	15,29	she despised him in her h.
2Chr	20,17	Do not fear or lose h.
Ezr	7,10	Ezra had set his h on the
Neh	9, 8	When you had found his h
Tb	4,19	be erased from your h.
	6,17	take the fish's liver and h,
	6,18	and his h became set on her.
	8, 2	liver and h from the bag
	13, 6	to him with all your h,
Jdt	8,29	worthy dispositions of your h.
Est	4C,24	turn his h to hatred for our
1Mc	2,24	his h was moved and his
2Mc	3,16	priest was pierced to the h,
Jb	17,11	cherished purposes of my h.
	22,22	up his words in your h.
	23,12	I have treasured in my h.
	29,13	and the h of the widow
	31, 9	If my h has been enticed
	31,27	And had my h been secretly
	36, 5	God rejects the obstinate in h;
	36,13	in h lay up anger for
	37, 1	At this my h trembles
	38,36	puts wisdom in the h,
	41,15	His h is hard as stone
Ps	26, 2	search my h and mind.
	27, 3	my h does not fear; Though
	28, 7	in whom my h trusted and
	31,25	Be strong and take h, all
	32,11	all you upright of h. Rejoice,
	36, 2	Sin directs the h of the
	37, 4	will give you your h's desire.
	38, 9	I wail with anguish of h.
	40, 9	your law is in my h!"
	40,11	did not hide within my h;
	45, 2	My h is stirred by a noble
	49, 4	my h shall offer insight.
	51,19	spurn a broken, humbled h.
	57, 8	My h is steadfast, God, my
	62,11	do not set your h upon it.

69,21 Insult has broken my **h**, and
73,13 that I have kept my **h** clean,
73,26 my flesh and my **h** fail,
77, 7 night I meditate in my **h**;
78, 8 generation whose **h** was not
81,13 them over to hardness of **h**;
84, 3 My **h** and flesh cry out for
90,12 we may gain wisdom of **h**.
95,10 "This people's **h** goes astray;
97,11 for the honest of **h**.
101, 4 I shun the devious of **h**;
108, 2 My **h** is steadfast, God;
109,22 my **h** is pierced within me.
111, 1 the Lord with all my **h**
119,11 In my **h** I treasure your
119,69 your precepts with all my **h**.
119,145 I call with all my **h**,
125, 4 those who are upright of **h**.
131, 1 Lord, my **h** is not proud;
139,23 God, know my **h**; try me,
141, 4 not let my **h** incline to evil,
143, 4 my **h** is dismayed.
Prv 12,10 the **h** of the wicked is
12,25 Anxiety in a man's **h**
13,12 Hope deferred makes the **h**
14,13 laughter the **h** may be sad
15, 7 but the **h** of fools is perverted.
15,30 glance brings joy to the **h**;
16, 1 may make plans in his **h**,
17,22 A joyful **h** is the health
18,12 a man's **h** is haughty,
19,21 plans in a man's **h**,
20, 9 "I have made my **h** clean,
21, 4 eyes and a proud **h**—
22,17 apply your **h** to my doctrine;
23,26 give me your **h**, and let
24,17 let not your **h** exult,
25,20 gnaws at the human **h**.
26,25 abominations are in his **h**.
27,11 you will gladden my **h**,
28,14 hardens his **h** will fall into evil.
31,11 Her husband, entrusting his **h**
Eccl 2,10 but my **h** rejoiced in the fruit
2,22 the toil and anxiety of **h**
5, 1 not your **h** be quick to make a
7, 2 living should take it to **h**.
7, 7 and a bribe corrupts the **h**.
8,16 applied my **h** to know wisdom
9, 7 your wine with a merry **h**,
Song 5, 4 my **h** trembled within me, and
6,12 **h** had made me the blessed
8, 6 as a seal on your **h**,
Wis 1, 1 in integrity of **h**;
1, 6 the sure observer of his **h**
8,17 and reflecting in my **h**
8,21 said with all my **h**: God of my
Sir 1,10 warms the **h**, giving gladness d
2,13 Woe to the faint of **h** who
4,17 until his **h** is fully with her.
5, 2 the desires of your **h**.
7,27 whole **h** honor your father;
8,19 Open your **h** to no man,
9, 9 Lest your **h** be drawn to her
10,12 his **h** from his Maker;
12,16 **h** he schemes to plunge you
13,25 The sign of a good **h**
14,21 ponders her ways in his **h**,
Is 1, 5 the whole **h** faint.
13, 7 Every man's **h** melts in terror.
51, 7 who have my teaching at **h** ,
57, 1 no one takes it to **h**;
66,14 When you see this, your **h**
Jer 17,10 the mind and test the **h**, To
Lam 2,19 Pour out your **h** like water in
Bar 2,30 shall have a change of **h**;
Ez 11,19 replace it with a natural **h**,

14, 4 of his idols in his **h**
21,20 That every **h** may tremble;
27,27 Sank into the **h** of the sea
28, 2 you are haughty of **h**,
28,17 You became haughty of **h**
Dn 8,25 He shall be proud of **h** and
Hos 2,16 desert and speak to her **h**.
10, 2 Their **h** is false, now
11, 8 My **h** is overwhelmed,
13, 6 they became proud of **h** and
Jl 2,12 with your whole **h**, with
Ob 3 The pride of your **h** has
Jon 2, 4 into the **h** of the sea, and the
Zep 3,14 and exult with all your **h**,
Zec 8,17 evil against another in his **h**,
Mal 2, 2 do not lay it to **h**,
Mt 9,36 his **h** was moved with pity for
11,29 meek and humble of **h**;
12,34 from the fullness of the **h**
12,40 **h** of the earth three days
13,19 what was sown in his **h**.
14,14 his **h** was moved with pity
15,18 mouth come from the **h**,
22,37 your God, with all your **h**,
Mk 7,19 not the **h** but the stomach and
Lk 8,15 with a generous and good **h**,
Jn 12,40 eyes and hardened their **h**,
Acts 13,22 a man after my own **h**;
15, 8 God, who knows the **h**,
16,14 the Lord opened her **h** to
21,13 weeping and breaking my **h**?
28,27 Gross is the **h** of this people;
28,27 understand with their **h** and
Rom 2, 5 and impenitent **h**,
2,29 circumcision is of the **h**,
6,17 obedient from the **h** to
9, 2 and constant anguish in my **h**.
10, 6 Do not say in your **h**,
10, 9 believe in your **h** that
1Cor 14,25 secrets of his **h** will be
2Cor 2, 4 affliction and anguish of **h**
5,12 rather than of the **h**.
6,11 our **h** is open wide.
7,15 his **h** goes out to you all
8,16 into the **h** of Titus,
Eph 3,13 ask you not to lose **h**
4,18 of their hardness of **h**,
6, 5 in sincerity of **h**, as to Christ,
Phil 2, 2 united in **h**, thinking one thing.
Col 3,23 do from the **h**, as for the Lord
1Thes 2,17 in person, not in **h**, we were
1Tm 1, 5 love from a pure **h**, a good
2Tm 2,22 purity of **h**. Avoid foolish and
Phlm 20 Refresh my **h** in Christ.
Heb 4,12 and thoughts of the **h**.
10,22 with a sincere **h** and
12, 3 weary and lose **h**.
12, 5 lose **h** when reproved
Jas 1,26 his tongue but deceives his **h**,
1Pt 1,22 from a [pure] **h**. You have

HEAVEN
Gn 6, 2 the sons of **h** saw how
14,22 the creator of **h** and earth,
19,24 from the Lord out of **h**].
21,17 to Hagar from **h**
22,11 called to him from **h**,
Ex 16, 4 now rain down bread from **h**
Dt 26,15 then, from **h**, your holy abode,
Jos 2,11 your God, is God in **h** above
1Sm 2,10 The Most High in **h** thunders;
2Sm 18, 9 He hung between **h** and earth
1Kgs 22,19 the whole host of **h** standing
2Kgs 7, 2 windows in **h**, how could this
17,16 worshiped all the host of **h**,
21, 5 for the whole host of **h**,

23, 5 to the whole host of **h**.
1Chr 21,16 between earth and **h**, with a
2Chr 2,11 who made **h** and earth,
6,23 listen from **h**: take action
6,27 listen in **h** and forgive
7,13 If I close **h** so that there
18,18 with the whole host of **h**
20, 6 you not the God in **h**,
30,27 their prayer reached **h**,
33, 3 before the whole host of **h**
36,23 the God of **h**, has given to me,
Ezr 6,10 to the God of **h** and pray
Neh 1, 4 before the God of **h**.
2, 4 prayed to the God of **h**
9,13 spoke with them from **h**;
9,15 Food from **h** you gave them in
Tb 7,11 may the Lord of **h** prosper you
7,12 may the God of **h** grant
8,15 praised the God of **h**
10,14 he blessed the Lord of **h**
Jdt 5, 8 worship the God of **h**,
6,19 God of **h**, behold their
7,28 We adjure you by **h** and
9,12 LORD of **h** and earth, Creator
Est 4C, 3 You made **h** and earth and
1Mc 3,50 And they cried aloud to **h**
9,46 Cry out now to **h** for
12,15 with the help of **h** for
16, 3 by the mercy of **h**,
16, 3 and may the help of **h**
2Mc 3,15 loudly begged him in **h**
7,11 "It was from **h** that I
8,20 help they received from **h**.
9,20 for my hopes are in **h**. Now
Jb 38,37 tilts the water jars of **h** So that
Ps 2, 4 one enthroned in **h** laughs;
11, 4 the Lord's throne is in **h**.
14, 2 Lord looks down from **h**
18,14 Lord thundered from **h**;
33,13 From **h** the Lord looks down
36, 6 your love reaches to **h**;
57, 4 May God send help from **h**
71,19 the highest **h**. You have done
75, 6 raise your horns against **h**!
80,15 look down from **h** and see;
102,20 viewed the earth from **h**,
105,40 with bread from **h** he filled
113, 6 looking down on **h** and earth
115,15 who made **h** and earth.
123, 1 eyes, to you enthroned in **h**.
134, 3 the Lord who made **h** and
146, 6 The maker of **h** and earth,
150, 1 in the mighty dome of **h**.
Prv 30, 4 Who has gone up to **h** and
Eccl 5, 1 God is in **h** and you are on
Wis 9,16 but when things are in **h**,
13, 2 or the luminaries of **h**,
16,20 furnished them bread from **h**,
18,15 all-powerful word from **h**'s
18,16 he still reached to **h**, while he
Sir 16,15 hidden from God; in **h** who
17,27 the hosts of highest **h**,
24, 5 The vault of **h** I compassed
43, 1 like **h** itself, a vision of glory
46,17 Lord thundered forth from **h**,
Is 24, 4 both **h** and earth languish.
Jer 7,18 cakes for the queen of **h**,
8, 2 and the whole army of **h**,
10,11 did not make **h** and earth
19,13 to the whole host of **h** and
23,24 Do I not fill both **h** and earth?
32,17 you have made **h** and earth
Lam 3,50 Till the LORD made **h** looks
Bar 2, 2 done anywhere under **h**
Dn 2,18 mercy of the God of **h**
3,36 offspring like the stars of **h**,

4,22 bathed with the dew of h;
5,23 against the Lord of h.
6,28 signs and wonders in h
7,13 on the clouds of h; When
8,10 extended to the host of h,
9,12 has ever occurred under h.
12, 7 right and left hands to h,
13,35 tears she looked up to h,
14, 5 the living God who made h
Am 9, 6 I have built h, my upper
Jon 1, 9 the God of h, who made the
Zep 1, 5 adore the host of h on the
Zec 2,10 the four winds of h, says the
Mal 3,10 the floodgates of h, to pour
Mt 3, 2 the kingdom of h is at hand!"
5,12 reward will be great in h.
6,10 done, on earth as in h.
7,21 will enter the kingdom of h,
8,11 banquet in the kingdom of h,
11,11 least in the kingdom of h
13,24 "The kingdom of h
14,19 and looking up to h,
16,19 keys to the kingdom of h.
18, 3 not enter the kingdom of h.
20, 1 h is like a landowner
22, 2 kingdom of h may be likened
23, 9 but one Father in h.
24,30 of Man will appear in h,
25, 1 "Then the kingdom of h
26,64 coming on the clouds of h.'
28, 2 the Lord descended from h,
28,18 "All power in h and on earth
Mk 6,41 fish and looking up to h,
7,34 looked up to h and groaned,
8,11 a sign from h to test him.
10,21 you will have treasure in h;
12,25 are like the angels in h.
13,31 h and earth will pass away
13,32 neither the angels in h,
14,62 coming with the clouds of h.' "
Lk 2,15 went away from them to h,
3,21 h was opened and the holy
6,23 reward will be great in h.
9,54 from h to consume them?"
10,15 Will you be exalted to h?
11,16 him for a sign from h.
12,33 inexhaustible treasure in h
15,18 I have sinned against h and
16,17 It is easier for h and earth
18,13 even raise his eyes to h
18,22 will have a treasure in h. Then
Jn 3,13 one has gone up to h
6,32 who gave the bread from h;
6,41 that came down from h,"
12,28 Then a voice came from h,
17, 1 he raised his eyes to h
Acts 1,11 taken up from you into h
2, 5 from every nation under h
3,21 Jesus, whom h must receive
4,24 maker of h and earth and
7,42 to worship the host of h,
10,11 He saw h opened and
11, 9 a voice from h answered,
14,17 he gave you rains from h
17,24 the Lord of h and earth,
Rom 10, 6 Who will go up into h?' (that
1Cor 15,47 the second man, from h. As
2Cor 5, 1 made with hands, eternal in h.
Gal 1, 8 angel from h should preach
Eph 1,10 Christ, in h and on earth.
3,15 every family in h and on
6, 9 you have a Master in h
Phil 2,10 of those in h and on earth
Col 1, 5 hope reserved for you in h.
1,16 created all things in h and
1,20 on earth or those in h.

1,23 to every creature under h,
1Thes 1,10 to await his Son from h, whom
2Thes 1, 7 Lord Jesus from h with his
Heb 8, 1 throne of the Majesty in h,
9,24 of the true one, but h itself,
12,25 the one who warns from h.
12,26 shake not only earth but h."
Jas 5,12 not swear, either by h or by
1Pt 1, 4 unfading, kept in h for you
1,12 the holy Spirit sent from h,
3,22 who has gone into h and
2Pt 1,18 heard this voice come from h
Rv 3,12 comes down out of h from my
5, 3 But no one in h or on earth
8, 1 there was silence in h for
10, 8 that I had heard from h
11,15 There were loud voices in h,
12, 7 Then war broke out in h;
13, 6 and those who dwell in h.
14, 2 I heard a sound from h
15, 1 Then I saw in h another
16,11 blasphemed the God of h
18, 4 I heard another voice from h
19, 1 of a great multitude in h,
20, 1 an angel come down from h,
21, 1 a new h and a new earth. The

HELP

Gn 39,18 I screamed for h, he left his
Ex 21,19 walk around with the h of his
Lv 25, 6 for your hired h and the
Nm 31,26 "With the h of the priest
Dt 15, 9 you grudge h your needy
22,27 may have cried out for h,
32,38 I Rise up now and h you!
33, 7 be his h against his foes."
Jos 10,33 came up to h Lachish, but
Jgs 5,23 they came not to my h, as
1Sm 9,16 and accepted their cry for h."
2Sm 18, 3 we have you to h us
22,30 by the h of my God I leap
22,42 They cried for h—but no
2Kgs 6,26 "H my lord king!" "No," he
1Chr 19,12 come to my h; and if the
2Chr 14,10 none like you to h the
Ezr 6,22 he gave them h in their work
Neh 6,16 with our God's h that this work
Tb 8, 6 wife Eve to be his h and
Jdt 6,21 the God of Israel for h.
7,25 There is no h for us now!
7,31 without h coming to us,
8,17 us call upon him to h us,
Est 4C,25 us by your power, and h me,
1Mc 3,15 advanced with him to h him
3,53 resist them unless you h us?"
5,39 also hired Arabs to h them,
7,20 leaving troops to h him,
8,13 those whom they desired to h
10,74 brother joined him to h him.
12,15 with the h of Heaven for
14, 1 into Media to obtain h
16, 3 and may the h of Heaven be
2Mc 8,23 "The h of God," he himself
12,11 God's h, were victorious.
15, 7 he would receive h from the
Jb 19, 7 I cry for h, but there is no
26, 2 h you give to the powerless
29,12 poor who cried out for h,
30,24 to h a wretched man
35, 9 call for h because of the
36,13 they cry not for h when he
Ps 13, 6 my heart joy in your h,
18,30 with my God to h I can
20, 3 May God send you h from
22, 2 from my call for h, from my
40,14 Come quickly to h me, Lord!

57, 4 May God send h from heaven
60,14 triumph with the h of God,
69,14 with your constant h.
70, 2 Come quickly to h me, Lord!
86,17 Lord, h and comfort me.
94,17 the Lord were not my h,
106, 4 to me with your saving h,
115,11 who is their h and shield.
119,175 may your edicts give me h.
124, 8 Our h is the name of the
146, 5 Happy those whose h is
Prv 20,22 the LORD and he will h you.
Wis 13,16 knowing that it cannot h itself;
Sir 12,17 him at hand; feigning to h,
Is 10, 3 whom will you flee for h?
20, 6 We have fled here for h
22, 5 cry for h to the mountains.
30, 5 Neither h nor benefit,
37,21 prayer for h against
Jer 11,12 no h whatever when
Lam 3,26 in silence for the saving h of
Bar 6,57 and they cannot h
Ez 16,49 and they gave no h to the
Dn 11,45 his end with none to h him.
Hos 12, 7 You shall return by the h of
Jon 2, 3 nether world I cried for h,
Hb 1, 2 I cry for h but you do not listen
Mt 15,25 saying, "Lord, h me." He said
Mk 9,22 have compassion on us and h
9,24 "I do believe, h my unbelief!"
Lk 5, 7 other boat to come to h them.
10,40 Tell her to h me." The Lord
Acts 16, 9 over to Macedonia and h us."
20,35 we must h the weak,
21,28 "Fellow Israelites, h us.
26,22 But I have enjoyed God's h
Rom 16, 2 and h her in whatever she
2Cor 1, 11 as you h us with prayer, so
Phil 4, 3 to h them, for they have
1Tm 5,16 to h those who are truly
2Tm 1,14 with the h of the holy Spirit
Heb 2,16 Surely he did not h angels
2,18 he is able to h those
4,16 to find grace for timely h.
3Jn 6 Please h them in a way

HIDDEN

Dt 33,19 and the h treasures of the
Jos 6,25 Rahab the harlot had h
7,21 They are now h in the ground
Jgs 9, 5 escaped, for he was h.
2Sm 17, 9 now he lies h in one of the
1Kgs 10, 3 and there remained nothing h
2Kgs 11, 3 six years he remained h in the
2Chr 22,12 six years he remained h with
1Mc 16,15 he had his men h there. Then,
2Mc 1,20 priests who had h the fire
10,37 Timothy had h in a cistern,
12,41 light the things that are h.
Jb 28,11 and brings h things to light.
Ps 69, 6 my faults are not h from you.
89,47 Will you stay h forever?
90, 8 our h sins exposed to
139,15 bones were not h from you,
142, 4 they have h a trap for me.
Prv 27, 5 than a love that remains h.
Eccl 12,14 all its h qualities, whether
Wis 2,22 knew not the h counsels
7,21 as are h I learned,
10, 8 they could not even be h in
Sir 3,21 for what is h is not your
16,15 "I am h from God;
17,13 cannot be h from his eyes.
17,16 cannot be h from him;
20,29 h wisdom and unseen
23,19 peer into h corners. He

Is	48, 6	new things to you, h events of
Jer	16,17	they are not h from me, nor
Dn	13,18	that the elders were h inside.
Hos	5, 3	and Israel is not h from me;
Mt	11,25	for although you have h these
Mk	4,22	For there is nothing h except
Lk	19,42	but now it is h from your eyes.
Rom	2,16	God will judge people's h
1Cor	4, 5	bring to light what is h in
2Cor	4, 2	renounced shameful, h things;
Eph	3, 9	the mystery h from ages past
Col	1,26	the mystery h from ages
	2, 3	h all the treasures of wisdom
	3, 3	and your life is h with Christ in
1Tm	5,25	that are not cannot remain h.
Heb	11,23	By faith Moses was h by his
1Pt	3, 4	but rather the h character of
Rv	2,17	give some of the h manna;

HIGH

Gn	14,18	God Most H, he blessed
Ex	37,25	and two cubits h, having
Lv	26,30	I will demolish your h places,
Nm	21,28	the h places of the Arnon.
Dt	26,19	raise you h in praise and
Jos	8,20	the city was already sky-h.
Jgs	8,28	did they hold their heads h.
1Sm	9,25	came down from the h place
2Sm	22,17	He reached out from on h
1Kgs	6,26	was exactly ten cubits h.
2Kgs	21, 3	He rebuilt the h places which
1Chr	16,39	on the h place at Gibeon,
2Chr	34, 3	the h places, the sacred poles
Neh	8, 6	their hands raised h,
Tb	4,11	the sight of the Most H for all
Jdt	7, 4	Neither the h mountains nor
Est	7, 9	stands a gibbet fifty cubits h.
1Mc	12,36	for erecting a h barrier
2Mc	7,24	and entrust him with h office.
Jb	21,22	that he judges those on h?
Ps	10, 5	ignore your judgment on h;
Prv	22, 1	great riches, and h esteem,
Eccl	5, 7	for the h official has another
Wis	9,17	your holy spirit from on h?
Sir	50,21	the blessing of the Most H.
Is	2,12	all that is h, and it will be
Jer	31,37	If the heavens on h can be
Lam	1,13	"From on h he sent fire down
Bar	3,25	Vast and endless, h and
Ez	43,13	one cubit h and one cubit
Dn	5,18	Most H God gave your father
Hos	10, 8	The h places of Aven shall be
Am	7, 9	The h places of Isaac shall be
Ob	4	Though you go as h as the
Mi	6, 6	and bow before God most h?
Hb	2, 9	setting his nest on h to
Zep	1,16	against battlements on h.
Mt	17, 1	and led them up a h mountain
Lk	8,28	Jesus, son of the Most H
Acts	16,17	are slaves of the Most H God,
Eph	4, 8	"He ascended on h and took
Heb	7, 1	and priest of God Most H,"
Jas	1, 9	should take pride in his h
Rv	21,10	in spirit to a great, h mountain

HIGH PRIEST

Nm	35,25	death of the h who has been
Jos	20, 6	the death of the h who is in
2Kgs	22, 4	orders to go to the h Hilkiah
2Chr	19,11	See now, Amariah is h over
Ezr	7, 5	son of the h Aaron— this Ezra
Neh	13,28	Joiada, son of Eliashib the h,
Jdt	4,14	The h Joakim, and all the
1Mc	11,27	confirmed him in the hhood
2Mc	11, 3	and to put the hhood up for
Sir	45,24	should possess the hhood

Jer	52,24	also took Seraiah, the h,
Hg	2, 2	the h Joshua, son of
Zec	3, 1	he showed me Joshua the h
Mt	26,65	Then the h tore his robes and
Mk	2,26	of God when Abiathar was h
Lk	22,54	into the house of the h;
Jn	18,15	disciple known to the h,
Acts	7, 1	Then the h asked, "Is this
Heb	5,10	declared by God h according

HOLY

Gn	2, 3	seventh day and made it h,
Ex	3, 5	where you stand is h ground.
	15,13	to your h dwelling.
	19, 6	a h nation. That is what you
	20, 8	keep h the sabbath day.
	26,33	this veil which divides the h
Lv	11,44	keep yourselves h,
	11,45	be h, because I am holy.
	16,19	render it clean and h,
	19, 2	Be h, for I, the Lord, your
	19, 2	the Lord, your God, am h.
	20, 3	sanctuary and profaned my h
	21, 6	they must be h.
	22, 2	will profane my h name.
Nm	5,17	put some h water,
	15,40	and be h to your God.
	16, 7	LORD then chooses is the h
Dt	23,15	your camp must be h;
	26,15	your h abode,
	33, 3	h ones were in his hand
Jos	5,15	which you are standing is h."
	24,19	for he is a h God;
1Sm	6,20	presence of this h One?
	21, 5	only h bread;
	21, 7	So the priest gave him h,
1Kgs	6,16	the h of holies.
	8, 6	in the sanctuary, the h of
2Kgs	19,22	Against the H One of Israel!
1Chr	16,27	and joy are in his h place.
	16,35	thanks to your h name
	23,13	consecrated as most h,
	24, 5	officers of the h place,
	29, 3	stored up for the h house,
	29,16	honor of your h name
2Chr	5,11	priests came out of the h
Ezr	9, 2	have desecrated the h race
Neh	7,65	the most h foods
	8, 9	"Today is h to the Lord
	8,10	today is h to our Lord.
	8,11	"Hush, for today is h,
	9,14	Your h sabbath you made
	10,32	any other h day.
	10,34	for the h offerings,
	11, 1	Jerusalem, the h city,
	11,18	of the Levites in the h city
	13,22	sabbath day might be kept h.
Tb	3,11	honored is your h name;
	8,15	every h and pure blessing!
	11,14	blessed be all his h angels.
	13, 9	O Jerusalem, h city, he
Jdt	9,13	your h temple, Mount Zion,
1Mc	1,15	abandoned the h covenant;
	1,63	to profane the h covenant;
	2, 7	and the ruin of the h city,
	11,37	a conspicuous place on the h
2Mc	2,18	to his h Place,
	5,25	the h day of the sabbath;
	6,30	"The Lord in his h knowledge
	8,15	bore his h, glorious name.
	8,23	from the h book and
	9,14	he would set free the h city,
Jb	5, 1	To which of the h ones
	6,10	commands of the h One.
	15,15	in his h ones God places no
Ps	2, 6	my h mountain."

	5, 8	worship in your h temple
	15, 1	dwell on your h mountain?
	22, 4	enthroned as the H One;
	28, 2	toward your h place.
	30, 5	give thanks to God's h name.
	34,10	Fear the Lord, you h ones;
	46, 5	h dwelling of the Most High
	48, 2	The h mountain, fairest of
	65, 5	blessings of your h temple!
	68,18	Lord entered the h place.
	77,14	Your way, O God, is h;
	87, 1	founded on h mountains,
	96, 6	in his h place.
	102,20	from the h heights,
	114, 2	Judah became God's h place,
	138, 2	low toward your h temple;
	145,21	bless your h name forever.
	150, 1	God in his h sanctuary;
Prv	9,10	knowledge of the H One
	30, 3	I the knowledge of the H One.
Wis	9, 8	build a temple on your h
	10,10	knowledge of h things;
	11, 1	through the h prophet.
	12, 3	inhabitants of your h land,
	17, 2	to enslave the h nation,
	18, 9	your h ones should share
Sir	4,14	serve the H One;
	7,31	sacrifices and h offerings.
	17, 8	praise his h name.
	23, 9	familiar with the h Name.
	23,10	swears continually by the h
	24,10	In the h tent I ministered
Is	1, 4	spurned the H One of Israel,
	11, 9	or ruin on all my h mountain;
	27,13	h mountain, in Jerusalem.
	30,15	H One of Israel: By waiting
	35, 8	called the h way;
	40,25	says the H One.
	41,14	your redeemer is the H One of
	52, 1	O Jerusalem, h city.
	63,10	grieved his h spirit;
	66,20	Jerusalem, my h mountain,
Jer	17,22	but keep h the sabbath, ed
	23, 9	because of his h words.
	25,30	from his h dwelling
	31,23	h mountain, abode of justice!"
	51, 5	to be punished by the H One
Bar	4,37	By the word of the H One,
Ez	20,12	the Lord, who made them h.
	22, 8	h to me you have spurned
	28,14	you were on the h mountain
	36,22	for the sake of my h name,
	39, 7	the H One in Israel.
	39,25	will be jealous for my h name.
Dn	3,28	the h city of our fathers. By
	4, 5	is the spirit of the h God.
	5,11	is the spirit of the h God;
	7,18	the h ones of the Most High
	8,13	I heard a h one speaking,
	9,16	Jerusalem, your h mountain.
	12, 7	destroyer of the h people
	13,45	God stirred up the h spirit
Hos	11, 9	God and not man, the h One
	12, 1	against the h One, who
Jl	4,17	God, dwelling on Zion, my h;
Am	2, 7	profaning my h name.
Ob	16	you have drunk upon my h
	17	the mountain shall be h,
Jon	2, 8	prayer reached you in your h.
Mi	1, 2	you, the Lord from his h
Hb	1,12	O Lord, my h God,
	2,20	the Lord is in his h temple;
	3, 3	the h One from Mount Paran.
Zep	3,11	longer exalt yourself on my h.
Zec	2,16	his portion in the h land,
	2,17	from his h dwelling.

	8, 3	the **h** mountain.
	14, 5	and all his **h** ones with him.
Mt	4, 5	devil took him to the **h** city,
	7, 6	give what is **h** to dogs,
	12,32	against the **h** Spirit
	24,15	standing in the **h** place
	27,53	they entered the **h** city
	28,19	and of the **h** Spirit,
Mk	1, 8	baptize you with the **h** Spirit."
	1,24	the **H** One of God!"
	3,29	against the **h** Spirit will
	6,20	be a righteous and **h** man,
	8,38	in his Father's glory with the **h**
Lk	1,15	filled with the **h** Spirit
	3,22	the **h** Spirit descended
	9,26	and of the **h** angels.
	11,13	give the **h** Spirit to those
	12,10	against the **h** Spirit will given
	12,12	For the **h** Spirit will teach you
Jn	1,33	baptize with the **h** Spirit.
	6,69	you are the **h** One of God."
	14,26	The Advocate, the **h** Spirit
Acts	1, 2	through the **h** Spirit to
	2, 4	filled with the **h** Spirit
	3,14	denied the **h** and Righteous
	5,32	as is the **h** Spirit that God
	6,13	[this] **h** place and the law.
	7,55	filled with the **h** Spirit,
	8,15	that they might receive the **h**
	9,41	he had called the **h** ones
	10,47	received the **h** Spirit e
	13,52	joy and the **h** Spirit. red
	15, 8	granting them the **h** Spirit
	16, 6	prevented by the **h** Spirit
	19, 6	the **h** Spirit came upon them,
	20,23	the **h** Spirit has been warning
	21,11	"Thus says the **h** Spirit
	28,25	"Well did the **h** Spirit speak
Rom	1, 2	prophets in the **h** scriptures,
	5, 5	**h** Spirit that has been given
	7,12	So then the law is **h**,
	8,27	intercedes for the **h** ones
	9, 1	joins with the **h** Spirit
	11,16	If the firstfruits are **h**,
	12, 1	**h** and pleasing to God,
	14,17	and joy in the **h** Spirit;
	15,13	by the power of the **h** Spirit
	16, 2	a manner worthy of the **h**
	16,16	another with a **h** kiss.
1Cor	1, 2	called to be **h**,
	3,17	God, which you are, is **h**.
	6,19	temple of the **h** Spirit
	7,34	**h** in both body and spirit
	12, 3	except by the **h** Spirit.
	14,33	all the churches of the **h** ones,
2Cor	1, 1	**h** ones throughout Achaia
	6, 6	kindness, in a **h** spirit,
	8, 4	service to the **h** ones,
	13,12	Greet one another with a **h**
Eph	1,13	the promised **h** Spirit,
	3, 8	least of all the **h** ones,
	4,12	to equip the **h** ones for
	5, 3	fitting among **h** ones, no
	5,27	**h** and without blemish.
	6,18	supplication for all the **h**
Phil	1, 1	to all the **h** ones in Christ
	4,21	to every **h** one in Christ
	4,22	all the **h** ones send you their
Col	1,12	inheritance of the **h**
	1,22	**h**, without blemish.
	1,26	manifested to his **h** ones,
	3,12	as God's chosen ones, **h** and
1Thes	1, 6	joy from the **h** Spirit,
	3,13	Jesus with all his **h** ones.
	4, 8	God, who [also] gives his **h**
2Thes	1,10	to be glorified among his **h**

1Tm	2, 8	men should pray, lifting up **h**
	4, 5	for it is made **h** by
	5,10	washed the feet of the **h**
2Tm	1, 9	called us to a **h** life,
	1,14	help of the **h** Spirit that dwells
Ti	1, 8	just, **h**, and self-controlled,
	3, 5	rebirth and renewal by the **h**
Phlm	5	for all the **h** ones,
	7	the hearts of the **h** ones have
Heb	2, 4	gifts of the **h** Spirit
	3, 7	as the **h** Spirit says
	6,10	serve the **h** ones.
	7,26	**h**, innocent, undefiled,
	9, 8	In this way the **h** Spirit shows
1Pt	1,12	to you [through] the **h** Spirit
	1,15	he who called you is **h**,
	1,16	"Be **h** because I [am]
	2, 9	a **h** nation, a people of
	3, 5	**h** women who hoped in God
2Pt	1,18	on the **h** mountain.
	1,21	the **h** Spirit spoke
	2,21	the **h** commandment handed
	3, 2	spoken by the **h** prophets
1Jn	2,20	that comes from the **h** one,
Jude	3	all handed down to the **h**
Rv	3, 7	"The **h** one, the true,
	4, 8	"**h**, holy, holy is the Lord
	5, 8	are the prayers of the **h** ones.
	6,10	**h** and true master,
	8, 3	prayers of all the **h** ones,
	8, 4	the prayers of the **h** ones
	11, 2	trample the **h** city for
	11,18	and the **h** ones and those
	13, 7	to wage war against the **h**
	13,10	endurance of the **h**
	14,10	before the **h** angels
	14,12	sustains the **h** ones
	15, 4	you alone are **h**.
	16, 6	blood of the **h** ones
	19, 8	deeds of the **h** ones.)
	22,11	the **h** still be holy."

HOME (LESS)

Gn	18,33	and Abraham returned **h**.
Ex	18,23	all these people will go **h**
Nm	24,25	set out on his journey **h**;
Dt	6, 7	Speak of them at **h** and
Jos	20, 6	the killer may go back **h** to his
Jgs	19, 9	you can start your journey **h**."
Ru	3,16	Ruth went **h** to her mother-in-
1Sm	7,17	Ramah, for that was his **h**.
2Sm	14, 8	to the woman: "Go **h**. I will
1Kgs	14,12	So leave; go **h**! As you step
2Kgs	14,10	but stay at **h**! Why involve
1Chr	12,20	and sent him **h**, saying, "At
2Chr	11, 4	Let every man return **h**, for
Neh	5,13	God shake from his **h** and his
Tb	11,17	Welcome to your **h** with
Jdt	8, 4	years and four months at **h**,
Est	5,10	went **h**, where he summoned
1Mc	12,45	send the rest back **h**, and
2Mc	9,29	Philip brought the body **h**;
Jb	39, 6	made the wilderness his **h**
Ps	84, 4	My **h** is by your altars, LORD
Prv	27, 8	who is far from his **h**.
Eccl	12, 5	man goes to his lasting **h**,
Song	3, 4	bring him to the **h** of my
Sir	36,25	becomes a **h** wanderer.
Is	58, 7	the oppressed and the **h**
Jer	39,14	of Shaphan, to be brought **h**.
Lam	3,19	The thought of my **h** poverty
Bar	2, 9	and brought **h** to us;
Ez	38,15	come from your **h** in the
Dn	6,11	custom of going **h** to kneel in
Zep	3,20	time I will bring you **h**,
Hg	1, 9	and what you brought **h**, I

Mt	9, 6	up your stretcher, and go **h**."
Mk	2, 1	known that he was at **h**.
Lk	14, 1	went to dine at the **h** of one
Jn	20,10	Then the disciples returned **h**.
Acts	8,28	and was returning **h**.
1Cor	14,35	ask their husbands at **h**.
2Cor	5, 9	whether we are at **h** or away.
1Tm	5,14	children, and manage a **h**,

HONEY

Gn	43,11	some balm and **h**, gum and
Ex	33, 3	land flowing with milk and **h**.
Dt	11, 9	with milk and **h**. "For the land
Jgs	14, 8	bees and **h** in the lion's
1Sm	14,27	and dipped it into the **h**.
2Sm	17,29	grain, beans, lentils, **h**, butter
2Chr	31, 5	wine, oil and **h**, and all the
Jb	20,17	of oil, no torrents of **h** or milk.
Ps	119,103	your promise, sweeter than **h**
Prv	24,13	If you eat **h**, my son, because
Song	4,11	Your lips drip **h**, my bride,
Sir	24,19	me as sweeter than **h**,
Is	7,15	be living on curds and **h**
Jer	41, 8	wheat and barley, oil and **h**."
Bar	1,20	land flowing with milk and **h**,
Ez	16,13	Fine flour, **h**, and oil were
Mt	3, 4	food was locusts and wild **h**.
Mk	1, 6	fed on locusts and wild **h**.
Rv	10, 9	will taste as sweet as **h**."

HONOR

Gn	20,16	your **h** has been preserved
Ex	20,12	"**H** your father and your
Lv	21, 7	has lost her **h**, nor a woman
Nm	25,11	by his zeal for my **h** among;
Dt	16, 8	meeting in **h** of the LORD, your
Jos	7,19	glory and **h** by telling me
Jgs	9,19	in good faith and with **h**
1Sm	15,12	a trophy in his own **h**,
1Kgs	8,20	have built this temple to **h**
2Kgs	10,20	a solemn assembly in **h**
1Chr	19, 3	these consolers—to **h** your
2Chr	6,34	I have built to your **h**,
Tb	4, 3	**h** your mother, and
	10,14	"May I **h** you all the days of
	12, 6	Before all men, **h** and
	12, 7	Praise them with due **h**.
Jdt	13,20	redound to your everlasting **h**,
Est	A,17	who was in high **h** with the
	1,20	wives will **h** their
	2,18	feast in **h** of Esther
	4C, 7	place the **h** of man
	5, 8	and **h** my request,
1Mc	12,43	he received him with **h**,
2Mc	5,16	the glory, and the **h** of the
Ps	4, 3	will you people mock my **h**
	25,10	toward those who **h** the
	45,13	He is your lord; **h** him,
	50,23	sacrifice **h** me;
	63, 6	my mouth shall **h** you!
	73,24	receive me with **h**.
	86, 9	give **h** to your name.
	91,15	**h**. With length of days
	112, 9	horn shall be exalted in **h**.
Prv	3,16	her left are riches and **h**;
	8,18	With me are riches and **h**,
Eccl	6, 2	riches and property and **h**,
Wis	14,17	of him they wished to **h**,
Sir	7,27	With your whole heart **h** your
	29, 6	with abuse instead of **h**.
Is	43,23	nor **h** me with your sacrifices.
Jer	14, 7	O LORD, for the **h** of your
Dn	11,39	provide with abundant **h**;
Mi	2, 9	take away forever the **h** I gave
Mal	1, 6	where is the **h** due to me?
Mt	13,57	**h** except in his native

19,19 **h** your father and your
Mk 10,19 you shall not defraud; **h** your
Jn 8,49 I am not possessed; I **h** my
Acts 28,10 They paid us great **h** and
Rom 12,10 one another in showing **h**.
1Cor 4,10 you are held in **h**,
12,23 with greater **h**, and
12,24 body as to give greater **h** to a
Eph 6, 2 "**H** your father and mother."
1Thes 4, 4 in holiness and **h**, not in lustful
1Tm 5,17 well deserve double **h**.
Heb 5, 4 No one takes this **h** upon
1Pt 2,17 community, fear God, **h** the
2Pt 1,17 For he received **h** and glory
Rv 4,11 receive glory and **h**
5,12 wisdom and strength, **h**
7,12 wisdom and thanksgiving, **h**,

HOPE
Gn 32, 6 in the **h** of gaining your favor.'
2Sm 14, 7 will quench my remaining **h**
Ezr 10, 2 even now there remains a **h**
Tb 5,19 I **h** more money is not your
Jdt 6, 9 cherish the **h** that
8,20 **h** that he will not disdain
9,11 the savior of those without **h**.
1Mc 4,10 in the **h** that he will favor us
2Mc 7,14 God-given **h** of being restored
Jb 7, 6 come to an end without **h**.
Ps 9,19 will the **h** of the afflicted
31,25 you who **h** in the Lord.
33,18 those who **h** for his gracious
33,22 we have put our **h** in you.
39, 8 You are my only **h**.
62, 6 from whom comes my **h**.
Prv 19,18 for in this there is **h**;
Eccl 9, 4 among the living there is **h**;
Wis 12,19 good ground for **h** that you
Sir 14, 2 him, who has not lost **h**.
Is 51, 5 In me shall the coastlands **h**,
Jer 29,11 you a future full of **h**.
Lam 3,29 there may yet be **h**.
Ez 37,11 bones are dried up, our **h** is
Dn 13,60 God who saves those that **h**
Hos 2,17 Achor as a door of **h**.
Mi 1,12 inhabitants of Maroth **h** for
Zec 9, 5 Ekron, too, for her **h** shall
Mt 12,21 his name the Gentiles will **h**."
Jn 5,45 you have placed your **h**.
Acts 28,20 is on account of the **h** of Israel
Rom 12,12 Rejoice in **h**, endure in
1Cor 13,13 So faith, **h**, love remain, these
2Cor 3,12 since we have such **h**, we act
Gal 5, 5 we await the **h** of
Eph 4, 4 also called to the one **h** of
Phil 3,12 I continue my pursuit in **h** that
Col 1,27 is Christ in you, the **h** for
1Thes 2,19 For what is our **h** or joy
2Thes 2,16 encouragement and good **h**
1Tm 5, 5 has set her **h** on God and
Ti 3, 7 become heirs in **h** of eternal
Phlm 22 for I **h** to be granted to you
Heb 6,18 to hold fast to the **h** that lies
1Pt 3,15 for a reason for your **h**,
1Jn 3, 3 Everyone who has this **h**
2Jn 12 Instead, I **h** to visit you and to
3Jn 2 Beloved, I **h** you are

HORN (S)
Gn 22,13 a ram caught by its **h**
Jos 6,20 When they heard the signal **h**,
Jgs 6,34 he blew the **h** that summoned
1Sm 16, 1 Fill your **h** with oil, and be on
2Sm 15,10 hear the sound of the **h**,
Jdt 9, 8 the **h** of your altar.
Ps 132,17 make a **h** sprout for David's
Jer 17, 1 And the **h** of their altars

Ez 29,21 I will make a **h** sprout for
Dn 7,21 that **h** made war against the
Hos 5, 8 Blow the **h** in Gibeah, the
Mi 4,13 O daughter Zion; your **h** I will
Lk 1,69 He has raised up a **h** for our

HOSPITABLE
2Mc 6, 2 Mount Gerizim to Zeus the **h**,
1Tm 3, 2 self-controlled, decent, **h**, able
Ti 1, 8 greedy for sordid gain, but **h**,
1Pt 4, 9 Be **h** to one another without

HOUR
Gn 35, 3 answered me in my **h** of
Ex 9,18 tomorrow at this **h** I will rain
Jdt 13, 4 in this **h** look graciously on my
Est 10F, 8 lots were fulfilled in the **h**,
2Mc 8,26 by reason of the late **h**.
Ps 104,19 sun that knows the **h** of its
Sir 10, 4 it the man of the **h**;
Mt 24,43 the **h** of night when the thief
Mk 14,41 It is enough. The **h** has come.
Lk 1,10 at the **h** of the incense
Jn 4,23 But the **h** is coming, and is
Acts 16,33 took them in at that **h** of the
Rom 13,11 it is the **h** now for you to
1Cor 4,11 To this very **h** we go hungry
1Jn 2,18 know this is the last **h**.
Rv 3, 3 at what **h** I will come upon you

HOUSE
Gn 19, 4 closed in on the **h**. They
Ex 34,26 bring to the **h** of the LORD,
Lv 14,36 lest everything in the **h**
27,15 dedicated his **h** wishes to
Nm 20,29 thirty days the whole **h** of
Dt 24, 1 dismissing her from his **h**
Jos 9,23 drawers of water] for the **h** of
Jgs 11,31 the doors of my **h** to meet me
Ru 4,12 may your **h** become like the
1Sm 2,27 Egypt as slaves to the **h** of
2Sm 7,13 he who shall build a **h** for my
1Kgs 13,34 on the part of the **h** of
2Kgs 8, 3 to claim her **h** and her field.
1Chr 9,27 they lodged about the **h** of
2Chr 3, 4 the width of the **h** was also
Ezr 2,68 they arrived at the **h** of the
Neh 10,34 for every service of the **h** of
Tb 1, 4 from the **h** of David and from
Jdt 11, 7 and his whole **h**.
Est 8, 2 Mordecai in charge of the **h** of
1Mc 8,15 for themselves a senate **h**,
2Mc 8,33 taken refuge in a little **h**;
Jb 20,28 flood shall sweep away his **h**
Ps 118, 2 Let the **h** of Israel say
Prv 15,25 The LORD overturns the **h** of
Eccl 10,18 the **h** leaks. Bread and oil call
Song 1,17 the beams of our **h** are
Sir 29,12 almsgiving in your treasure **h**,
Is 66,20 their offering to the **h** of the
Jer 13,11 had I made the whole **h** of
Lam 2, 7 Who shout in the **h** of the LORD
Bar 6,12 their faces clean of the **h** dust
Ez 3,27 for they are a rebellious **h**.
17,12 say now to the rebellious **h**
Dn 13, 4 had a garden near his **h**,
Hos 5,14 a young lion to the **h** of Judah;
Jl 4,18 fountain shall issue from the **h**
Am 7, 9 I will attack the **h** of Jeroboam
Ob 18 none shall survive of the **h** of
Mi 4, 1 the mount of the LORD's **h**
Zep 2, 7 to the remnant of the **h** of
Hg 2, 7 And I will fill this **h** with glory,
Zec 14,21 be any merchant in the **h** of
Mal 3,10 may be food in my **h**,
Mt 12,29 enter a strong man's **h**

Mk 14,14 master of the **h**, 'The Teacher
Lk 8,49 the synagogue official's **h**
Jn 12, 3 the **h** was filled with the
Acts 16,32 everyone in his **h**. He took
Rom 16, 5 the church at their **h**. Greet
1Cor 16,19 church at their **h** send you
Col 4,15 to the church in her **h**.
1Tm 5,13 going about from **h** to house,
2Tm 2,21 to the master of the **h**,
Heb 3, 2 was "faithful in [all] his **h**."
1Pt 2, 5 spiritual **h** to be a holy
2Jn 10 not receive him in your **h**
Rv 3,20 I will enter his **h** and dine with

HUMAN (KIND)
Gn 32,29 contended with divine and **h**
Lv 27,28 whether it is a **h** being or an
Nm 23,19 should speak falsely, nor **h**,
1Sm 14,15 that the panic was beyond **h**
2Sm 7,14 rod of men and with **h**
1Kgs 13, 2 and he shall burn **h** bones
2Kgs 23,14 where they had been with **h**
2Chr 32,19 the earth, a work of **h** hands.
Tb 8, 6 and from these two the **h** race
Jdt 8,12 the place of God in **h** affairs?
2Mc 7,28 same way the **h** race came
Jb 31,33 Had I, out of **h** weakness,
Ps 144, 3 **h** beings, that you take
Prv 30, 2 have not even **h** intelligence;
Eccl 11, 5 fashions the **h** frame in the
Wis 13,10 gods things made by **h** hands
Sir 39,26 needs for **h** life are water and
Is 51,12 fear mortal man, who is **h**
Jer 17, 9 than all else is the **h** heart,
Bar 6,13 like the **h** ruler of a district;
Ez 10, 8 [Something like **h** hands
Dn 8,16 I heard a **h** voice that cried
Hos 11, 4 I drew them with **h** cords,
Mt 19,26 "For **h** beings this is
Mk 10,27 "For **h** beings it is impossible,
Lk 18,27 impossible for **h** beings is
Jn 5,34 not accept testimony from a **h**
Acts 14,11 come down to us in **h** form."
Rom 3, 4 though every **h** being is a liar,
1Cor 2,13 not with words taught by **h**,
2Cor 1,17 make my plans according to **h**
Gal 3,15 annul or amend even a **h** will
Eph 6, 5 Slaves, be obedient to your **h**
Phil 2, 7 coming in **h** likeness; and
Col 2, 8 according to **h** tradition,
1Thes 4, 8 disregards not a **h** being but
1Tm 6,16 whom no **h** being has seen or
Heb 8, 2 it is appointed that **h** beings
Jas 5,17 Elijah was a **h** being like us;
1Pt 2,13 Be subject to every **h**
2Pt 2,16 mute beast spoke with a **h**
1Jn 5, 9 If we accept **h** testimony, the
Rv 9,18 a third of the **h** race was

HUMBLE
2Chr 36,12 **h** himself before the prophet
Ezr 8,21 that we might **h** ourselves
Jb 22,29 but the man of **h** mien he
Ps 55,20 will hear me and **h** them.
Prv 16,19 It is better to be **h** with the
Sir 18,20 Before you have fallen, **h**
Is 13,11 insolence of tyrants I will **h**.
Dn 10,12 understanding and **h** yourself
Na 1,12 I will **h** you no more.
Zep 3,12 in your midst a people **h** and
Mt 11,29 for I am meek and **h** of heart;
2Cor 10, 1 I who am **h** when face to face
Phil 4,12 how to live in **h**
2Tm 2,20 for lofty and others for **h** use.
Jas 4, 6 but gives grace to the **h**."

1Pt   3, 8 another, compassionate, **h**.

HUNGER (HUNGRY)

Gn   41,55 When **h** came to be felt
Lv   26,26 enough food to still your **h**.
Dt   28,48 therefore in **h** and thirst, in
2Sm 17,29 people have been **h** and tired
Jdt   7,14 children will languish with **h**,
1Mc 13,49 they suffered greatly from **h**,
Jb   30, 3 In want and **h** was their lot,
Prv 13,25 the just man eats, his **h** is
Sir 24,20 who eats of me will **h** still,
Is   9,19 they are **h**; though they eat
Jer 42,16 the **h** you dread shall cling to
Lam   2,19 [Who faint from **h** at the
Bar   2,25 by **h** and the sword and
Ez   5,12 of pestilence and perish of **h**
Mt   5, 6 who **h** and thirst for
Lk   1,53 The **h** he has filled
Jn   6,35 comes to me will never **h**,
2Cor 11,27 through **h** and thirst, through
Rv   7,16 They will not **h** or thirst

HUSBAND (S)

Gn   3, 6 also gave some to her **h**,
Ex   21,22 much as the woman's **h**
Lv   21, 7 has been divorced by her **h**;
Nm   5,13 though her **h** has not sufficient
Dt   21,13 and you shall be her **h**
Jgs 13, 6 woman went and told her **h**,
Ru   1, 3 Elimelech, the **h** of Naomi,
1Sm   1, 8 Her **h** Elkanah used to ask
2Sm   3,15 took her away from her **h**
2Kgs 4, 1 Elisha: "My **h**, your servant, is.
Tb   3, 8 had been married to seven **h**
Prv 31,28 her **h**, too, extols her: "Many
Sir 42,10 sterile in that of her **h**.
Is   54, 5 he who has become your **h** is
Jer   6,11 Yes, all will be taken, **h** and
Ez   16,45 the mother who spurned her **h**
Dn   13,63 as did Joakim her **h** and all
Hos   2,18 "My **h**," and never again "My
Mt   1,19 Joseph her **h**, since he was a
Mk   10,12 if she divorces her **h** and
Lk   16,18 a woman divorced from her **h**
Jn   4,18 For you have had five **h**
Acts 5,10 and buried her beside her **h**.
Rom   9,10 conceived children by one **h**,
1Cor 11, 3 and a **h** the head of his wife
2Cor 11, 2 I betrothed you to one **h** to
Gal   4,27 of her who has a **h**." Now
Eph   5,22 to their **h** as to the Lord.
Rv   21, 2 a bride adorned for her **h**.

HYPOCRISY

Mt   23,28 you are filled with **h** and
Mk   12,15 Knowing their **h** he said
Lk   12, 1 the leaven—that is, the **h**—of
Gal   2,13 was carried away by their **h**.
1Tm   4, 2 through the **h** of liars

HYPOCRITE (S)

Ps   26, 4 nor with **h** do I mingle.
Sir   1,26 Play not the **h** before men;
Mt   6, 2 as the **h** do in the synagogues
Mk   7, 6 Isaiah prophesy about you **h**

I

IDOL (S)

Gn   31,33 he did not find the **i**. Leaving
Ex   20, 4 You shall not carve **i** for
Lv   19, 4 Do not turn aside to **i**,
Dt   5, 8 You shall not carve **i** for

Jgs   3,19 from where the **i** are
1Sm 12,21 Do not turn to meaningless **i**
1Kgs 15,12 removing all the **i** his father
2Kgs 17,12 and served **i**, although the
1Chr 10, 9 news to their **i** and their
2Chr 15, 8 the detestable **i** from the
Tb   14, 6 their **i** which have deceitfully
1Mc 13,47 houses in which there were **i**.
2Mc 12,40 found amulets sacred to the **i**
Ps   24, 4 who are not devoted to **i**
Wis 14,30 and devoted themselves to **i**,
Sir 49, 2 destroyed the abominable **i**.
Is   2, 8 Their land is full of **i**;
Jer 51,52 when I will punish her **i**,
Bar   6,72 just man who has no **i**
Ez   6, 4 your slain ones before your **i**;
Dn   14, 5 "Because I worship not **i**
Hos 13, 2 Silver **i** according to their
Jon   2, 9 Those who worship vain **i**
Mi   1, 7 All her **i** shall be broken to
Hb   2,18 and make dumb **i**? But the
Zec 13, 2 destroy the names of the **i**
Acts 14,15 turn from these **i** to the living
Rom   2,22 You who detest **i**, do you rob
1Cor 10,19 That meat sacrificed to **i** is
2Cor 6,16 the temple of God with **i**?
1Thes 1, 9 you turned to God from **i** to
1Jn   5,21 be on your guard against **i**.
Rv   9,20 the worship of demons and **i**

IMAGE

Gn   9, 6 For in the **i** of God has man
Tb   9, 6 I have seen the very **i** of my
Ps 106,20 their glorious God for the **i** of
Wis 17,21 an **i** of the darkness that next
Sir 17, 1 and in his own **i** he made him.
Is   48, 5 my molten **i** I commanded
Jer 44,19 in her **i** and poured out
Na   1,14 the carved and the molten **i**;
Hb   2,18 Or the molten **i** and lying
Mt   22,20 "Whose **i** is this and whose
Mk   12,16 "Whose **i** and inscription is
Lk   20,24 whose **i** and name does it
Acts 17,29 divinity is like an **i** fashioned
Rom   8,29 conformed to the **i** of his Son,
1Cor 15,49 we shall also bear the **i** of the
2Cor 4, 4 who is the **i** of God. For we
Col   3,10 for knowledge, in the **i** of its
Heb 10, 1 and not the very **i** of them,
Rv   15, 2 over the beast and its **i**

IMMANUEL (EMMANUEL)

Is   7,14 and shall name him **I**. He shall
Mt   1,23 and they shall name him **E**,"

IMMORALITY

Tb   4,12 against every form of **i**, and
Sir 41,15 and mother be ashamed of **i**,
1Cor 5, 1 widely reported that there is **i**
2Cor 12,21 not repented of the impurity, **i**,
Gal   5,19 are obvious: **i**, impurity,
Eph   5, 3 **i** or any impurity or greed
Col   3, 5 of you that are earthly: **i**,
1Thes 4, 3 that you refrain from **i**,

IMPOSSIBLE

Jos   8,20 Escape in any direction was **i**,
2Sm 13, 2 Amnon thought it **i** to carry out
1Mc   5,46 they found it **i** to encircle it
2Mc   4, 6 it would be **i** to have a
Jer 32,17 nothing is **i** to you.
Dn   6,19 Since sleep was **i** for him,
Zec   8, 6 Even if this should seem **i** in
Mt   17,20 Nothing will be **i** for you."
Mk   10,27 human beings it is **i**, but not
Lk   13,33 it is **i** that a prophet should die

Acts 4,20 It is **i** for us not to speak
Heb 10, 4 for it is **i** that the blood of bulls

IMPURE (IMPURITY)

Lv   15,19 be in a state of **i** for seven
Nm   5,13 so that her **i** remains
1Mc   1,48 defiled with every kind of **i** and,
Rom   6,19 bodies as slaves to **i** and to
2Cor 12,21 have not repented of the **i**
Gal   5,19 immorality, **i**, licentiousness,
Eph   5, 3 Immorality or any **i** or greed
Col   3, 5 immorality, **i**, passion, evil
1Thes 4, 7 did not call us to **i** but to

INHERIT (ANCE)

Jos 19,49 the land they were to **i**,
2Kgs 21,14 the survivors of my **i**
Tb   6,12 estate is rightfully yours to **i**.
Ps   2, 8 I will make your **i** the nations
Prv   3,35 but fools **i** shame. Be not
Sir 36,10 that they may **i** the land as of
Is   57,13 takes refuge in me shall **i** the
Jer 49, 2 destroyed by fire. Israel shall **i**
Mt   19,29 and will **i** eternal life. But
Mk   10,17 what must I do to **i** eternal
Rom   4,13 that he would **i** the world,
1Cor 15,50 flesh and blood cannot **i** the
Eph   1,14 the first installment of our **i**
Heb 12,17 when he wanted to **i** his
1Pt   3, 9 that you might **i** a blessing.
Rv   21, 7 The victor will **i** these gifts,

INNOCENT

Gn   18,25 to make the **i** die with the
Ex   23, 7 The **i** and the just you shall
Dt   21, 8 not the guilt of shedding **i**
1Sm 25,31 shed **i** blood or for having
2Sm   3,28 and my kingdom are forever **i**.
2Kgs 24, 4 especially because of the **i**
2Chr 6,23 but absolving the **i**
Tb   3,14 O Master, that I am **i** of any
1Mc   1,37 they shed **i** blood around the
2Mc   8, 4 criminal slaughter of **i** children
Jb   9,23 at the despair of the **i**.
Ps   64, 5 They shoot at the **i** from
Prv 20,11 whether his conduct is **i** and
Wis   4,12 whirl of desire transforms the **i**
Sir 51,13 I was young and, I sought
Is   59, 7 they are quick to shed **i** blood;
Jer 22,17 On shedding **i** blood, on
Dn   13,53 Lord says, 'The **i** and the just
Jl   4,19 because they shed **i** blood in
Jon   1,14 not charge us with shedding **i**
Mt   27, 4 I have sinned in betraying **i**
Lk   23,47 "This man was **i** beyond
Rom 16,18 deceive the hearts of the **i**.
2Cor 7,11 shown yourselves to be **i** in
Phil 2,15 blameless and **i**, children of
Heb   7,26 such a high priest: holy, **i**,

ISRAEL

Gn   33,20 "El, the God of **I**."
     34, 7 an outrage in **I**;
     35,22 When **I** heard of it,
     37, 3 **I** loved Joseph best of all
     42, 5 sons of **I** were among those
     43, 6 your brother is with you.' " **I**
Ex   5, 2 I would not let **I** go." They
      6,14 Reuben, the first-born of **I**,
     12,47 I must keep this feast.
     14,30 When **I** saw the Egyptians
     15,22 Then Moses led **I** forward
     17,11 **I** had the better of the
     18,12 with all the elders of **I**
     19, 2 While **I** was encamped
     24,10 they beheld the God of **I**.

	28,29	names of the sons of I	1Mc	2,46	found in the territory of I.	Wis	6,23	shall I admit consuming j

28,29 names of the sons of I
32,13 Abraham, Isaac and I,
39,14 names of the sons of I,
Lv 17, 8 house of I or of the aliens
20, 2 or an alien residing in I,
Nm 1, 3 men in I of twenty years
3,13 first-born in I sacred
7,84 princes of I on the
10,36 to the troops of I."
11,30 along with the elders of I.
18,21 assign all tithes in I
19,13 shall be cut off from I.
20,29 house of I mourned him.
21,17 Then it was that I sang this
Dt 1, 1 Moses spoke to all I
4, 1 "Now, I, hear the statutes
5, 1 "Hear, O I, the statutes and
10,12 now, I, what does the Lord,
11, 6 out of the midst of I,
13,12 And all I, hearing of it,
17,20 enjoy a long reign in I.
18, 6 anywhere in I in which
21,21 and all I, on hearing of it,
33,29 fortunate you are, O I!
34,10 arisen in I like Moses,
34,12 in the sight of all I.
Jos 3, 7 in the sight of all I,
3,12 each of the tribes of I.]
3,17 While all I crossed over
4,22 'I crossed the Jordan
6,25 midst of I to this day.
7,13 are under the ban, O I.
8,10 with the elders of I.
8,35 who had accompanied I.
9,16 and would be living in I.
11, 5 together to fight against I.
12, 7 apportioned to the tribes of I.
13,13 survive in the midst of I to this
Jgs 2,23 them into the power of I.
3,31 an oxgoad. He, too, rescued I.
4, 6 the God of I, commands,"
5, 7 the walls gone indeed from I.
5,11 that brought freedom to I.
6, 2 so that Midian held I subject.
6, 4 leaving no sustenance in I,
7, 2 lest I vaunt itself against me
8,35 good he had done for I.
10,16 grieved over the misery of I.
11, 4 the Ammonites warred on I.
21, 3 They said, "Lord, God of I,
21, 3 it come to pass in I that today
21,25 there was no king in I;
Ru 2,12 the God of I, under whose
4,14 become famous in I!
1Sm 1,17 may the God of I grant you
2Sm 24, 1 register the people of I.
1Kgs 16, 2 ruler of my people I, but you
2Kgs 19,15 "O LORD, God of I, enthroned
1Chr 11, 1 Then all I gathered about
2Chr 36,13 the LORD, the God of I.
Ezr 6,17 a sin-offering for all I,
7,13 to the people of I,
9,15 God of I, you are just;
10, 2 there remains a hope for I.
Neh 7, 7 census of the men of I
8, 1 Lord prescribed for I.
11,20 The rest of I, including priests
13, 3 they separated from I every
Tb 1, 5 Jeroboam, king of I, had
14, 5 back to the land of I. They
Jdt 6,17 against the house of I.
9,12 God of the heritage of I,
13,11 manifest his strength in I and
Est 4C, 6 the salvation of I.
4C,11 All I, too, cried out
10F,10 generations of his people I."

1Mc 2,46 found in the territory of I.
14,26 firm and repulsed I's enemies.
2Mc 1,25 and eternal, I's savior
11, 6 a good angel to save I.
Ps 14, 7 come the deliverance of I,
22, 4 you are the glory of I
41,14 the Lord, the God of I,
59, 6 hosts, are the God of I!
69, 7 who seek you, God of I,
72,18 God of I, who alone does
81,12 I did not obey me. So
98, 3 love toward the house of I.
105,23 Then I entered Egypt; Jacob
114, 1 I came forth from Egypt,
121, 4 the guardian of I never
130, 7 let I look for the Lord,
147, 2 the dispersed of I,
Prv 1, 1 son of David, king of I
Eccl 1,12 I, Qoheleth, was king over I in
Song 3, 7 of the valiant men of I: All of
Sir 17,14 Lord's own portion is I.
24, 8 in I your inheritance.'
36,11 I, whom you named
47,18 which was conferred upon I.
Is 44, 5 "The LORD's," and I shall be
Jer 14, 8 O Hope of I, O Lord,
51,33 the God of I: Daughter
Lam 2, 3 the horn that was I's whole
Bar 2,11 Lord, God of I,
3, 1 "Lord Almighty, God of I,
3,37 Jacob, his servant, to I, his
Ez 3, 1 speak to the house of I.
3, 4 now to the house of I,
6, 3 Mountains of I, hear
10,20 beneath the God of I
11,17 to you the land of I.
13, 5 wall about the house of I
18, 3 will repeat this proverb in I.
47,18 and the land of I on the other
Dn 3,35 and I your holy one,
9,20 sin of my people I,
13,48 condemn a woman of I
Hos 12, 3 has a grievance against I
Jl 4,16 stronghold to the men of I.
Am 9, 9 sift the house of I among all
Ob 20 the children of I shall occupy
Mi 4,14 the cheek the ruler of I.
Na 2, 3 of Jacob, the pride of I,
Zep 3,15 The King of I, the LORD, is in
Zec 2, 2 Judah and I and Jerusalem."
Mal 3,22 and ordinances for all I.
Mt 2, 6 shepherd my people I.' "
8,10 in I have I found such faith
10,23 the towns of I before the Son
15,24 sheep of the house of I."
Mk 15,32 the Messiah, the King of I,
Lk 24,21 be the one to redeem I;
Jn 3,10 You are the teacher of I and
Acts 28,20 hope of I that I wear these
Rom 11,25 a hardening has come upon I
1Cor 10,18 Look at I according to the
Gal 6,16 this rule and to the I of God.
Eph 2,12 from the community of I
Phil 3, 5 of the race of I, of the tribe of
Heb 8,10 establish with the house of I

J

JEALOUS (JEALOUSY)

Ex 20, 5 LORD, your God, am a j God,
Nm 11,29 answered him, "Are you j for
Dt 29,19 the Lord's wrath and j
Jos 24,19 he is a j God who will not
1Sm 18, 9 Saul was j of David.

Wis 6,23 shall I admit consuming j
Sir 30, 3 his son makes his enemy j,
Is 11,13 Ephraim shall not be j of
Ez 36, 6 With j fury I speak, because
Na 1, 2 A j and avenging God is the
Zec 8, 2 I am intensely j for Zion,
Acts 17, 5 But the Jews became j and
Rom 11,14 to make my race j and thus
1Cor 10,22 we provoking the Lord to j
2Cor 11, 2 jealous of you with the j of God

JERUSALEM

Jos 15, 8 of the Jebusites [that is, J], the
Jgs 1,21 the Jebusites who dwelt in J,
1Sm 17,54 Philistine and brought it to J;
2Sm 19,20 my lord the king left J.
1Kgs 11,36 a lamp before me in J,
2Kgs 23,20 Then he returned to J.
1Chr 14, 4 were born to him in J
2Chr 36,23 a house in J, which is in
Ezr 7,15 whose dwelling is in J, as well
Neh 13,19 the gates of J before the
Tb 13,17 The streets of J shall be paved
Jdt 13, 4 for the exaltation of J;
Est A, 3 had taken from J with
1Mc 3,45 J was uninhabited, like a
2Mc 11, 2 plan was to make J a Greek
Ps 137, 7 that day at J. They said: "Level
Eccl 2, 7 had been before me in J.
Song 5,16 O daughters of J.
Sir 24,11 given me rest, in J is my
Is 66,20 J, my holy mountain, says the
Jer 11, 6 in the streets of J: Hear the
Lam 2,13 you, O daughter J?
Bar 4,36 Look to the east, J! behold the
Ez 36,38 the sheep of J on its feast
Dn 6,11 the windows open toward J.
Jl 4,17 my holy mountain; J shall be
Am 1, 2 roar from Zion, and from J
Ob 11 gates and cast lots over J,
Mi 3,12 like a field, and J reduced to
Zep 3,14 O daughter J!
Zec 14,17 come up to J to worship the
Mal 2,11 Israel and in J. Judah has
Mt 21,10 And when he entered J the
Mk 11,11 entered J and went into the
Lk 21,20 "When you see J surrounded
Jn 12,12 Jesus was coming to J, they
Acts 1, 4 not to depart from J, but to
Rom 15,31 that my ministry for J may be
1Cor 16, 3 take your gracious gift to J.
Gal 2, 1 I again went up to J with
Heb 12,22 the living God, the heavenly J,
Rv 3,12 the new J, which comes down

JEW (S)

2Kgs 25,25 along with the J
Ezr 4,12 that the J who came up from
Neh 13,23 I saw J who had married
Tb 11,17 was joy for all the J who lived
Est 8, 5 for the destruction of the J
1Mc 4, 2 attack the camp of the J
2Mc 15,17 the J determined not to delay,
Jer 40,15 All the J who have now rallied
Dn 3, 8 came and accused the J
Mt 28,15 circulated among the J to the
Mk 15,18 "Hail, King of the J!" and kept
Lk 23,38 King of the J." Now one of
Jn 6,41 The J murmured about him
Acts 2, 5 Now there were devout J
Rom 3, 9 charge against J and Greeks
1Cor 12,13 one body, whether J or
2Cor 11,24 hands of the J I received forty
Gal 2,13 rest of the J [also] acted
1Thes 2,14 the J, who killed both the Lord
Rv 2, 9 those who claim to be J and

JOY (FUL)

Ex	32,25	to the scornful j of their foes,
Dt	24, 5	to bring j to the wife he has
1Sm	11,15	the occasion with great j.
2Sm	6,15	the LORD with shouts of j and
1Chr	15,28	covenant of the Lord with j
2Chr	30,23	With j, therefore, they
Ezr	3,13	the sound of the j shouting
Neh	8,12	and to celebrate with great j,
Tb	13,10	be rebuilt in you with j.
Jdt	12,14	This will be a j for me till the
Est	4C,10	and turn our sorrow into j
1Mc	4,59	be observed with j and
2Mc	3,30	was filled with j and gladness,
Jb	20, 5	wicked is short and the j of
Ps	132,16	its faithful shall shout for j.
Prv	15,30	A cheerful glance brings j to
Eccl	5,18	receives his lot and finds j in
Song	3,11	on the day of the j of his
Wis	8,16	but rather j and gladness.
Sir	30,16	no happiness, than a j heart!
Is	51,11	crowned with everlasting j.
Jer	25,10	song of j and the song of
Lam	5,15	The j of our hearts has
Bar	4,36	Jerusalem! behold the j that
Ez	36, 5	with wholehearted j and utter
Dn	6,24	This gave the king great j.
Hos	2,13	an end to all her j, her feasts,
Jl	1,12	Yes, j has withered away from
Zep	3,14	Shout for j, O daughter Zion!
Zec	8,19	shall become occasions of j
Mt	13,20	receives it at once with j.
Mk	4,16	receive it at once with j.
Lk	24,52	to Jerusalem with great j,
Jn	16,24	so that your j may be
Acts	2,28	you will fill me with j in your
Rom	15,32	may come to you with j by the
1Cor	12,26	all the parts share its j.
2Cor	8, 2	abundance of their j and their
Gal	5,22	of the Spirit is love, j, peace,
Phil	1, 4	praying always with j in my
Col	1,11	patience, with j giving thanks
1Thes	1, 6	with j from the holy Spirit, so
2Tm	1, 4	I may be filled with j, as I
Phlm	7	much j and encouragement
Heb	12, 2	the j that lay before him he
Jas	1, 2	Consider it all j, my brothers,
1Pt	1, 8	indescribable and glorious j,
1Jn	1, 4	so that our j may be complete.
2Jn	12	so that our j may be complete.
3Jn	4	Nothing gives me greater j

JUDEA

Tb	1,18	fugitive from J during the days
Jdt	1,12	Moab, Ammon, the whole of J,
1Mc	15,41	and patrol the roads of J.
2Mc	5, 11	he thought that J was in revolt.
Dn	14,33	In J there was a prophet,
Mt	2, 1	was born in Bethlehem of J,
Mk	13,14	then those in J must flee
Lk	23, 5	his teaching throughout all J,
Jn	11, 7	Let us go back to J." The
Acts	26,20	the whole country of J,
Rom	15,31	from the disobedient in J,
2Cor	1,16	me on my way to J.
Gal	1,22	churches of J that are in
1Thes	2,14	of God that are in J in Christ

JUDGE (D) (S)

Gn	18,25	Should not the j of all the
Ex	2,14	has appointed you ruler and j
Lv	13, 5	If he j that the sore
Dt	17, 9	to the j who is in office and
Jgs	2,18	he would be with the j and
1Sm	10, 7	do whatever you j feasible,
2Sm	12, 1	he said: "J this case for me!

1Kgs	3, 9	an understanding heart to j
1Chr	5,12	and Janai was j in Bashan.
2Chr	19, 8	heads of Israel to j in the
Tb	3, 2	you are the j of the world.
Jdt	7,24	"God j between you and us!
1Mc	2,55	became a j in Israel. Caleb,
2Mc	12,41	the just j who brings to light
Jb	22,13	Can he j through the thick
Ps	9,20	let the nations be j
Eccl	3,17	and the wicked God will j,
Wis	12,18	are master of might, you j with
Sir	38,33	They do not occupy the j's
Is	16, 5	A j upholding right and prompt
Jer	2,35	Behold, I will j you on that
Ez	35,11	known among you when I j
Am	2, 3	I will root out the j from her
Mi	4, 3	He shall j between many
Zec	3, 7	you shall j my house and
Mt	5,25	hand you over to the j,
Lk	12,14	who appointed me as your j
Jn	12,48	my words has something to j
Acts	18,15	not wish to be a j of such
Rom	14,10	Why then do you j your
1Cor	2,15	person, however, can j
2Tm	4, 1	Christ Jesus, who will j the
Heb	13, 4	for God will j the immoral and
Jas	4, 11	If you j the law, you are not
1Pt	4, 5	stands ready to j the living

JUDGMENT (S)

Gn	15,14	But I will bring j on the nation
Ex	6, 6	and with mighty acts of j.
Lv	19,15	dishonestly in rendering j.
Nm	35,29	you live, for rendering j.
Dt	1,17	alike, fearing no man, for j is
Jos	20, 6	Once he has stood j before
Jgs	4, 5	for j. She sent and summoned
1Sm	25,33	Blessed be your good j
2Sm	15, 6	came to the king for j.
1Kgs	10, 9	you king to carry out j and
1Chr	16,12	and the j he has uttered
Ezr	7,26	let strict j be executed upon
Tb	1,18	Judea during the days of j
Jdt	11,19	I will set up your j seat.
Est	10F, 8	and the day of j before God
2Mc	7,35	escaped the j of the almighty
Jb	14, 3	as to bring him into j before
Ps	9, 8	set up a throne for j.
Prv	24,23	To show partiality in j is not
Eccl	8, 6	is a time and a j for
Wis	17, 1	For great are your j
Sir	43,13	speeds the arrows of his j to
Jer	4, 2	LORD lives," in truth, in j, and in
Bar	6,63	They can neither execute j
Ez	7,27	according to their j I will judge
Dn	3,31	have done by a proper j.
Hos	6, 3	and his j shines forth like the
Jl	4,12	j upon all the neighboring
Am	7, 4	for a j by fire. It had devoured
Mi	3, 11	Her leaders render j for a
Hb	1,12	you have marked him for j,
Zep	3,15	The LORD has removed the j
Zec	7, 9	Render true j, and show
Mal	3, 5	draw near to you for j,
Mt	12,41	At the j, the men of Nineveh
Lk	11,42	you pay no attention to j and
Jn	9,39	came into this world for j,
Acts	24,25	self-restraint and the coming j,
Rom	13, 2	will bring j upon themselves.
1Cor	11,29	the body, eats and drinks j on
2Cor	5,10	appear before the j seat of
Col	2,16	Let no one, then, pass j on
2Thes	1, 5	evidence of the just j of God,
1Tm	5,24	preceding them to j; but other
Heb	6, 2	of the dead and eternal j.

Jas	2,13	For the j is merciless to one
1Pt	4,17	it is time for the j to begin
2Pt	3, 7	kept for the day of j
1Jn	4,17	confidence on the day of j
Jude	15	holy ones to execute j
Rv	17, 1	j on the great harlot who

JUST (ICE)

Gn	18,25	all the world act with j?"
Ex	23, 2	with the many in perverting j.
Dt	1,16	administer true j to both
1Sm	24,16	and grant me j beyond your
2Sm	8,15	judging and administering j to
1Kgs	3, 6	with j and an upright heart;
1Chr	18,14	over all Israel and dispensed j
2Chr	9, 8	king to administer right and j."
Ezr	7,25	and judges to administer j
Est	10F, 9	rendered j to his inheritance.
1Mc	14,35	the loyalty and j he had
2Mc	8,13	who lacked faith in God's j
Jb	31,13	Had I refused j to my
Ps	45, 5	truth and j may your right
Prv	17,23	to pervert the course of j.
Eccl	7,15	just man perishing in his j,
Wis	1, 1	Love j, you who judge the earth
Sir	40,17	never be cut off, and j
Is	60,17	your governor, and j your
Jer	4, 2	truth, in judgment, and in j;
Lam	3,59	I am wronged; do me j!
Bar	1,15	j is with the LORD, our
Ez	22,29	the resident alien without j.
Dn	12, 3	who lead the many to j shall
Hos	10,12	he come and rain down j upon
Jl	2,23	given you the teacher of j
Am	5,24	then let j surge like water, and
Mi	7, 9	I will see his j.
Zep	2, 3	Seek j, seek humility; perhaps
Zec	8, 8	with faithfulness and j. Thus
Mal	3,20	the sun of j with its healing
Mt	12,18	and he will proclaim j to the
Lk	18, 8	see to it that j is done
Acts	28, 4	j has not let him remain
Heb	1, 9	You loved j and hated

JUSTIFY (JUSTIFIED) (JUSTIFICATION)

Sir	1,19	One cannot j unjust anger;
Is	53,11	my servant shall j many, and
Lk	16,15	"You j yourselves in the sight
Acts	13,38	could not be j under the law
Rom	4,25	and was raised for our j.

K

KEEP (S) (ER)

Gn	38,23	"Let her k the things," Judah
Ex	13,10	Therefore, you shall k this
Lv	23,24	you shall k a sabbath rest,
Nm	16,26	"K away from the tents of
Dt	8, 2	your intention to k his
Jos	8, 6	They will k coming out after
Jgs	2,22	they would k to the way of the
1Sm	2,14	the priest would k. That is
2Sm	13,13	he will not k me from you."
1Kgs	1, 1	over him he could not k warm.
2Kgs	2, 3	I know it," he replied. "K still."
1Chr	29,18	k such thoughts in the hearts
2Chr	6,16	God of Israel, k the further
Ezr	4, 4	so as to k them from building.
Neh	6,14	k in mind as well Noadiah
Tb	12, 7	secret it is prudent to k,
Jdt	5,21	then your lordship should k
Est	3, 11	"The silver you may k," the
1Mc	2,20	my kinsmen will k to the
2Mc	12,42	to k themselves free from sin,

Jb	14,16	and not k watch for sin in me
Ps	19,15	k the thoughts of my heart
Prv	4,13	k her, for she is your
Eccl	4,17	they know not how to k from
Wis	6,10	For those who k the holy
Sir	23,14	k your father and mother in
Is	47,12	k up, now, your spells and
Jer	35, 4	son of Shallum, k of the
Ez	33,26	yet you would k possession of
Dn	13, 9	and did not k in mind just
Hos	13, 7	by the road I will k watch.
Am	2, 4	the LORD, and did not k his
Na	2, 2	guard the rampart, k watch on
Hb	1, 7	Shall he, then, k on
Zec	3, 7	shall judge my house and k
Mal	2, 7	of the priest are to k
Mt	26,43	for they could not k their eyes
Mk	14,37	Could you not k watch for one
Lk	19,40	if they k silent, the stones will
Jn	14,23	"Whoever loves me will k my
Acts	27,25	Therefore, k up your courage,
Rom	11,10	and k their backs bent
1Cor	14,28	the person should k silent in
2Cor	10,13	k to the limits God has
Phil	4, 9	K on doing what you have
1Tm	5,22	K yourself pure. Stop drinking
Heb	13,17	for they k watch over you
Jas	1,27	k oneself unstained by the
1Pt	2,11	k away from worldly desires
2Pt	1, 8	they will k you from being idle
1Jn	2, 5	But whoever k his word
Jude	21	K yourselves in the love of
Rv	14,12	the holy ones who k God's

KEY (S)

Jgs	3,25	they took the k and opened
Is	22,22	I will place the k of the House
Mt	16,19	I will give you the k
Rv	1,18	I hold the k to death

KILL (ED)

Gn	4,14	anyone may k me at sight."
Ex	1,16	if it is a boy, k him; but if it is
Nm	25, 5	"Each of you shall k those
Dt	13,10	spare or shield him, but k him.
Jgs	8,19	I should not k you."
1Sm	24,12	did not k you, see and be
2Sm	3,30	because he k their brother
1Kgs	3,26	living child—please do not k
2Kgs	11, 8	approach the cordon, k him;
2Chr	22,10	proceeded to k off all the royal
Neh	6,10	they are coming to come to k
Tb	14,10	for he had tried to k Ahiqar.
Jdt	11,12	they decided to k their
Est	8,11	to k, destroy, wipe out, along
1Mc	1,61	had circumcised them were k.
2Mc	5,24	with orders to k all the grown
Jb	24,14	to k the poor and needy.
Ps	59, 1	to watch his house and k him.
Eccl	3, 3	A time to k, and a time to heal
Sir	9,13	man who has power to k,
Is	14,30	But I will k your root with
Jer	40,15	"Let me go and k Ishmael,
Dn	5,19	Whomever he wished, he k
Mt	23,34	some of them you will k and
Mk	6,19	wanted to k him but was
Lk	11,49	they will k and persecute'
Jn	5,18	tried all the more to k him,
Acts	21,31	While they were trying to k
Rom	13, 9	adultery; you shall not k;
2Thes	2, 8	whom the Lord [Jesus] will k
1Tm	1, 9	those who k their fathers or
Jas	4, 2	You k and envy but you
Rv	6, 8	to k with sword, famine, and

KIND (NESS)

Gn	7,14	and every k of bird. Pairs of

Lv	22, 5	of whatever k it may be, is
Nm	13,18	and see what k of land it is.
Dt	24,10	make a loan of any k to your
Jgs	6,26	the proper k of altar to the
Ru	1, 8	May the LORD be k to you as
1Sm	15, 6	for you were k to the Israelites
2Sm	2, 5	Lord for having done this k
1Kgs	2, 7	"But be k to the sons of
2Kgs	9,11	"You know that k of man and
1Chr	28,21	skill in every k of
2Chr	15, 6	them by every k of adversity.
Neh	13,16	and every other k of
Tb	1,11	refrained from eating that k of
1Mc	1,48	defiled with every k of impurity
2Mc	15,11	by relating a dream, a k of
Ps	144,13	barns be full with every k of
Prv	3, 3	Let not k and fidelity leave you
Wis	12,19	who are just must be k;
Sir	13,15	is drawn to its own k;
Is	8,20	That k of thing they will surely
Jer	40,16	shall do nothing of the k;
Bar	5, 8	and every fragrant k of tree
Ez	47,12	fruit trees of every k shall
Jl	2,13	slow to anger, rich in k
Na	2,10	in precious things of every k!
Mt	13,47	which collects fish of every k.
Mk	9,29	"This k can only come out
Lk	6,35	for he himself is k to the
Jn	21,19	what k of death he would
Acts	7,49	What k of house can you build
Rom	7, 8	produced in me every k of
1Cor	15,41	of the sun is one k,
2Cor	6,13	As recompense in k
Eph	4,19	practice of every k of impurity
Phil	1, 9	knowledge and every k of
1Thes	5,22	Refrain from every k of evil.
Heb	13,16	pleased by sacrifices of that k.
Jas	1,18	we may be a k of firstfruits
Rv	18,12	fragrant wood of every k, all

KING (S) ('S)

Gn	14, 3	All the latter k joined forces
Ex	14, 5	reported to the k of Egypt
Nm	20,14	Moses sent men to the k of
Dt	1, 4	he had defeated Sihon, k of
Jos	10,28	Thus he did to the k of
Jgs	21,25	those days there was no k in
1Sm	2,10	he give strength to his k
2Sm	5, 3	they anointed him k of Israel.
1Kgs	1,23	the prophet entered the k's
2Kgs	25,30	granted him by the k
1Chr	18,11	These also K David
2Chr	1, 8	me to succeed him as k.
Ezr	5,17	And may the k pleasure
Neh	2,19	you rebelling against the k?"
Jdt	14,18	disgrace on the house of k
Est	1,16	Vashti has not wronged the k
1Mc	16,18	and sent it to the k,
2Mc	1,11	on our side against the k;
Jb	4,10	though the k of beasts cries
Ps	149, 2	of Zion rejoice in their k.
Prv	29, 4	By justice a k gives stability to
Eccl	10,20	not make light of the k,
Song	7, 6	a k is held captive in its
Wis	3, 8	the LORD shall be their K
Sir	7, 4	LORD authority, nor from the k
Is	57, 9	While you approached the k
Jer	36,20	entered the room where the k
Lam	2, 2	the ground in dishonor her k
Bar	6,58	better to be a k displaying his
Ez	29, 2	against Pharaoh, k of Egypt,
Dn	1, 1	of the reign of Jehoiakim, k of
Hos	13,11	I give you a k in my anger,
Am	7,13	the k's sanctuary and a royal
Jon	3, 6	When the news reached the k
Mi	2,13	Their k shall go through

Na	3,18	O k of Assyria, your nobles
Zep	1, 1	Josiah, the son of Amon, k of
Hg	1, 1	in the second year of K
Zec	14,16	after year to worship the k,
Mal	1,14	For a great k am I, says the
Mt	1, 6	the father of David the k.
Mk	6,14	K Herod heard about it,
Lk	23,38	"This is the K of the Jews."
Jn	19,15	"Shall I crucify your k?" The
Acts	26,27	K Agrippa, do you believe the
2Cor	11,32	the governor under K Aretas
1Tm	1,17	To the k of ages,
Heb	7, 1	This "Melchizedek, k of Salem
1Pt	2,13	whether it be to the k as
Rv	17,14	is Lord of lords and k of kings,

KINGDOM

Ex	19, 6	shall be to me a k of priests,
Dt	17,18	he is enthroned in his k,
1Sm	28,17	he has torn the k from your
2Sm	7,12	and I will make his k firm.
1Kgs	11,31	I will tear away the k from
1Chr	17,11	and I will establish his k.
Ps	105,13	from one k to another,
Wis	10,10	Showed him the k of God and
Jer	18, 7	destroy a nation or a k
Ez	17,14	so that the k would remain a
Dn	2,39	Another k shall take your
Mt	3, 2	"Repent, for the k of heaven is
	10, 7	'The k of heaven is at hand
	18,23	That is why the k of heaven
	26,29	with you new in the k of my
Mk	1,15	The k of God is at hand
	9,47	enter into the k of God with
	14,25	drink it new in the k of God."
Lk	1,33	of his k there will be no end
	14,15	who will dine in the k of God."
	23,51	awaiting the k of God. He
Jn	3, 3	no one can see the k of God
	3, 5	no one can enter the k of God
	18,36	But as it is, my k is not here."
Acts	1, 3	speaking about the k of God.
	28,31	he proclaimed the k of God
Rom	14,17	For the k of God is not a
1Cor	4,20	For the k of God is not a
	6, 9	unjust will not inherit the k
	15,50	blood cannot inherit the k of
Eph	5, 5	inheritance in the k of Christ
Col	1,13	the k of his beloved Son,
	4,11	my co-workers for the k of
1Thes	2,12	who calls you into his k and
2Tm	4,18	me safe to his heavenly k.
Heb	1, 8	is the scepter of your k.
Jas	2, 5	faith and heirs of the k
2Pt	1,11	entry into the eternal k of our
Rv	1, 6	has made us into a k, priests
	16,10	Its k was plunged into

KISS (ED)

Gn	27,26	"Come closer, son, and k me."
Ex	4,27	the mountain of God, Aaron k
2Sm	15, 5	his hand, hold him, and k him.
	20, 9	held Amasa's beard as if to k
Tb	5,17	Tobiah k his father and mother.
Ps	85,11	meet; justice and peace will k.
Prv	24,26	He gives a k on the lips who
Song	1, 2	Let him k me with kisses of
	8, 1	I would k you and none would
Mt	26,49	said, "Hail, Rabbi!" and he k
Lk	7,45	not give me a k, but she has
	22,47	went up to Jesus to k him.
	22,48	Son of Man with a k?"
Rom	16,16	one another with a holy k.
1Cor	16,20	one another with a holy k.
1Pt	5,14	with a loving k. Peace to all of

KNOW (ING) (KNEW)

Gn   15, 8 "how am I to k that I shall
      22,12 I k now how devoted you are
Ex   3,19 "Yet I k that the king of Egypt
     18,11 Now I k that the LORD is a
Nm 16,28 This is how you shall k that
Jos   3, 7 that they may k I am with
1Sm 17,28 I k your arrogance and your
1Kgs 8,39 You who alone k the hearts of
Jb   19,25 I k that my Vindicator lives,
     42, 3 for me, which I cannot k.
Ps 100, 3 k that the LORD is God
   139,23 Probe me, God, k my heart;
Prv 30, 4 is his son's name, if you k it?"
Eccl 8,16 I applied my heart to k
Is   44, 9 they neither see nor k
Jer 29,11 For I k well the plans I have
    31,34 shall k me, says the LORD, for
Ez   2, 5 they shall k that a prophet has
Mt   6, 3 left hand k what your right is
   26,74 "I do not k the man." And
Mk 12,24 you do not k the scriptures or
Lk 21,31 k that the kingdom of God
Jn   2, 9 without k where it came from
Acts 1, 7 not for you to k the times or
    1,24 "You, Lord, who k the hearts
Rom 6, 6 We k that our old self was
    8,28 We k that all things work for
1Cor 1,21 world did not come to k God
   13,12 At present I k partially;
2Cor 5,16 even if we once k Christ
Eph 3,19 and to k the love of Christ that
Phil 3,10 depending on faith to k him
Col   4, 6 so that you k how you should
1Thes 3, 3 For you yourselves k that we
2Thes 2, 6 And now you k what is
1Tm 3,15 you should k how to behave
2Tm 2,23 for you k that they breed
Ti   1,16 They claim to k God, but by
Heb 8,11 saying, 'K the Lord,' for all
Jas   1, 3 for you k that the testing of
    4, 4 Do you not k that to be a lover
2Pt 1,12 even though you already k
1Jn 2, 3 k him is to keep his
    5,18 We k that no one begotten by
2Jn   1 I but also all who k the truth—
Rv   2, 2 "I k your works, your labor,
    3,15 God's creation, says this: "I k

KNOWLEDGE

Gn   2, 9 tree of the k of good and bad.
2Chr 1,10 therefore, wisdom and k
Ps 73,11 the Most High have any k?"
   94,10 teaches humans not have k?
Prv 1, 4 to the young man k and
    1, 7 LORD is the beginning of k;
Eccl 1,18 who stores up k stores up
Sir 19,18 The k of wickedness is not
Is   11, 2 a spirit of k and of fear of the
Jer 16,21 I will give them k; this time
Dn   1,17 four young men God gave k
Hos 4, 6 people perish for want of k!
Hb   2,14 filled with the k of the LORD's
Mal 2, 7 the priest are to keep k,
Lk   1,77 to give his people k of
Rom 15,14 filled with all k, and able to
1Cor 8,11 Thus through your k, the
   13, 8 tongues, they will cease; if k,
2Cor 4, 6 bring to light the k of the glory
    8, 7 in faith, discourse, k, all
Eph 3,19 of Christ that surpasses k,
Phil 1, 9 in k and every kind of
Col   1,10 growing in the k of God,
    2, 3 treasures of wisdom and k.
1Tm 2, 4 saved and to come to k of the
Heb 10,26 after receiving k of the truth,

1Jn 2,20 and you all have k.

L

LABOR (ER)

Ex   1,11 to oppress them with forced l.
Lv 19,13 the wages of your day l.
Prv 16,26 The l's appetite labors for him
Sir   6,20 in cultivating her you will but
Is   54, 1 you who were not in l,
Mt 10,10 The l deserves his keep.
1Cor 3, 8 wages in proportion to his l.
Phil 2,16 not run in vain or l in vain.
1Thes 1, 3 l of love and endurance in

LAMB (S) ('S)

Ex 12, 5 The l must be a year-old
2Sm 12, 6 He shall restore the ewe l
Prv 27,26 The l will provide you
Is   11, 6 be a guest of the l,
Jer 12,19 like a trusting l led to
Mk 14,12 they sacrificed the Passover l,
Jn   1,29 "Behold, the L of God, who
Acts 8,32 and as a l before its shearer is
1Cor 5, 7 For our paschal l, Christ, has
1Pt 1,19 of a spotless unblemished l.
Rv 13,11 had two horns like a l
   21, 9 the wife of the L." He took me

LAMP (S)

1Sm 3, 3 The l of God was not yet
1Kgs 7,49 with their flowers, l, and tongs
2Kgs 8,19 leave him a l in the LORD's
Jdt 10,22 preceded by silver l
Prv 20,27 A l from the LORD is the
Sir 50,29 of the LORD is his l.
Mt   5,15 light a l and then put it under
Mk   4,21 "Is a l brought in to be placed
Lk 12,35 light your l and be like servants
Jn   5,35 was a burning and shining l,
Rv 22, 5 will they need light from l or

LAND

Gn 12, 1 to a l that I will show you
Ex   1, 7 the l was filled with them.
Nm 13, 2 Send men to reconnoiter the l
Dt 28,21 exterminated you from the l
Jos   1, 6 this people possession of the l
Jgs 1,26 went to the l of the Hittites,
Ru   1, 1 was a famine in the l;
2Sm 21,14 God granted relief to the l.
1Kgs 8,34 back to the l you gave their
2Kgs 25,21 was Judah exiled from her l.
2Chr 32,31 that had occurred in the l,
Ezr 9,11 as your possession is a l
Neh 9,36 and as for the l which you
Tb 14, 7 they dwell forever in the l of
1Mc 14,11 He brought peace to the l,
Ps 25,13 their descendants inherit the l.
Prv 2,21 upright will dwell in the l,
Sir 46, 8 the l flowing with milk and
Is   2, 8 Their l is full of idols;
   53, 8 was cut off from the l of the
Jer   2, 7 brought you into the garden l
Ez 39,28 gather them back on their l,
Mal 3,24 I come and strike the l with
Mk 15,33 came over the whole l
Heb 11, 9 he sojourned in the promised l
Rv 10, 2 his left foot on the l,

LAST

2Sm 23, 1 These are the l words of
1Chr 29,29 King David, first and l,
Sir 43,28 let the l word be, he is all

Is 41, 4 the first, and with the l I will
Mt 19,30 who are first will be l,
Mk 9,35 he shall be the l of all
Jn 11,24 in the resurrection on the l
Acts 2,17 come to pass in the l days,'
2Tm 3, 1 be terrifying times in the l
Heb 1, 2 in these l days, he spoke to
2Pt 2,20 their l condition is worse than
1Jn 2,18 Children, it is the l hour; and
Rv   1,17 the first and the l, the one who

LAUGH (INGSTOCK) (LAUGHTER)

Gn 18,13 "Why did Sarah l and say,
Jdt   5,21 we shall become the l
Prv 14,13 Even in l the heart may be sad
Lk   6,21 for you will l. Blessed are you

LAY (LAID)

Gn 22,12 "Do not l your hand on the
Ex   7, 4 Therefore I will l my hand on
Nm 17,22 Then Moses l the staffs down
Dt   9,25 I l prostrate before the LORD,
Jb 22,22 and l up his words in your
Lam 3,28 when it is l upon him.
Mt 28, 6 see the place where he l.
Jn 10,15 and I will l down my life for the
Acts 8,19 anyone upon whom I l my
1Cor 3,10 master builder I l a foundation
1Jn 3,16 so we ought to l down our

LAW (FUL)

Nm 5,29 "This, then, is the l for
Dt   1, 5 Moses began to explain the l
   31,26 Take this scroll of the l
Jos   1, 7 care to observe the entire l
2Kgs 22, 8 the book of the l in the temple
2Chr 6,16 to live according to my l,
   34,14 found the book of the l
Ezr 7, 6 well-versed in the l of Moses
Neh 8, 2 Ezra the priest brought the l
    8, 8 from the book of the l of God,
1Mc 1,56 Any scrolls of the l which they
   14,44 It shall not be l
Ps   1, 2 Rather, the l of the LORD is
   89,31 his descendants forsake my l,
Prv 28, 9 his ear from hearing the l,
Sir 2,16 him are filled with his l.
Jer   2, 8 Those who dealt with the l
Bar 4, 1 the l that endures forever;
Dn   9,11 Israel transgressed your l and
Hos 4, 6 Since you have ignored the l
Hb   1, 4 This is why the l is benumbed,
Mk   3, 4 "Is it l to do good
Lk   2,23 it is written in the l of the Lord,
   24,44 written about me in the l of
Jn   5,10 it is not l for you
Acts 6,13 holy place and the l.
   28,23 them about Jesus from the l
Rom 2,12 All who sin outside the l
    6,15 not under the l but under
1Cor 9, 9 It is written in the l of Moses,
   15,56 power of sin is the l.
Gal 2,19 For through the l I died to the
    5,23 Against such there is no l.
Eph 2,15 abolishing the l with its
Phil 3, 5 in observance of the l a
1Tm 1, 8 We know that the l is good,
Ti   3, 9 and quarrels about the l, for
Heb 7,12 is necessarily a change of l as
   10, 1 Since the l has only a shadow
Jas 1,25 peers into the perfect l of
    4,11 not a doer of the l but a judge.

LEAD (S) (ER) (ERS)

Ex 15,10 like l they sank in the mighty
Jdt   5, 3 king and the l of their army?

Sir 47,18 silver as though it were l;
Is 48,17 and l you on the way you
Jer 31,24 the farmers and those who l
Dn 12, 3 And those who l the many to
Mk 13,11 When they l you away and
Acts 3,17 just as your l did
Heb 1, 6 when he l the first-born

LEARN (ED) (ING)

Gn 24,21 silently waiting to l.
Dt 4,10 that they may l to fear me as
Ps 119,71 in order to l your laws.
Prv 19,25 the simple l a lesson; if you
Eccl 1,17 I l that this also is a
Is 1,17 cease doing evil; l to do good.
Mt 11,29 my yoke upon you and l from
Mk 13,28 L a lesson from the fig
Lk 23, 7 upon l that he was under
Ti 3,14 l to devote themselves to

LEFT (LEAVE)

Gn 7,23 in the ark were l. The waters
Nm 26,65 not one of them was l except
Dt 28,14 the right or to the l from any
Jos 1, 7 to the l, that you may succeed
1Chr 28, 8 this good land and afterward l it
Neh 6, 3 while I l it to come down
Sir 22, 9 for sense has l him.
Is 30,21 the right or to the l.
Mt 6, 3 do not let your l hand know
25,33 and the goats on his l.
Mk 5,17 to beg him to l their district.
10,40 my right or at my l is not mine
Lk 17,34 will be taken, the other l. And
1Thes 4,15 who are l until the coming
Rv 10, 2 and his l foot on the land,

LIAR (LYING)

Ru 3, 8 to find a woman l at his feet.
Prv 10,18 the lips of the l
19,22 a poor man than a l.
Sir 34, 4 can the l ever speak the truth?
Jer 48,30 his arrogance; l in boast, l
Jn 8,44 because he is a l and the
Rom 3, 4 every human being is a l,
1Jn 1,10 we make him a l, and his
2,22 Who is the l?
4,20 his brother, he is a l;
5,10 God has made him a l

LIE

Gn 19,32 father with wine and then l
Lv 18,22 You shall not l with a male as
Jos 9,22 "Why did you l to us and say
Ru 3, 4 and l down. He will tell you
Tb 10, 7 Stop it, and do not l to me!
Jdt 11, 5 I will tell no l to my lord this
Ps 4, 9 In peace I shall both l down
56, 7 they l in wait for my life
57, 5 I must l down in the midst
88, 6 slain who l in the grave.
102, 8 I l awake and moan,
119,25 I l prostrate in the dust;
132, 3 nor l on the couch
139, 8 if I l down in Sheol, you
Prv 3,24 When you l down, you need
5,22 When you l down
14, 5 witness does not l,
15,11 abyss l open before the
24,15 I not in wait against the
Eccl 11, 3 there shall it l. One who pays
Sir 7,13 Delight not in telling l after lie,
Is 11, 6 leopard shall l down with the
Ez 34,14 There they shall l down on
Jn 8,44 When he tells a l, he speaks
Rom 1,25 truth of God for a l and

2Thes 2,11 that they may believe the l,
Ti 1, 2 that God, who does not l,
Heb 6,18 was impossible for God to l,
Rv 11, 8 Their corpses will l in the main

LIFE (LIVE)

Gn 2, 7 his nostrils the breath of l,
Ex 21,23 you shall give l for life, eye for
Nm 35,31 indemnity in place of the l
Dt 12,23 not consume this seat of l
19,21 l for l, eye for eye
1Sm 19, 5 When he took his l in his
Neh 2, 3 "May the king l forever!
Tb 3, 6 command my l breath to
3, 6 so much misery in l,
10,14 all the days of my l!"
12, 9 alms shall enjoy a full l;
Jdt 13,20 because you risked your l
Jb 2, 6 your power; only spare his l."
Est 7, 3 I ask that my l be spared,
7, 7 Queen Esther for his l,
1Mc 6,44 he gave up his l to save
11,48 they saved the king's l.
2Mc 3,35 who had spared his l,
4,16 manner of l they emulated,
6,19 to a l of defilement,
Jb 7, 7 my l is like the wind;
9,21 I despise my l. It
12,10 l breath of all mankind.
13,14 take my l in my hand.
Ps 6, 5 Turn, Lord, save my l;
16,11 show me the path to l,
21, 5 He asked l of you; you
34,13 Who among you loves l, takes
40,15 who seek to take my l.
54, 5 the ruthless seek my l;
63, 4 your love is better than l;
74,19 the l of your afflicted.
90, 9 Our l ebbs away under
119,50 your promise that gives me l.
Prv 3,18 She is a tree of l to those who
4,22 For they are l to those
5, 6 before you the road to l,
9,11 years of your l increased."
10,27 fear of the Lord prolongs l,
13,14 wise is a fountain of l,
16,22 l to its possessor, but
21,21 justice and kindness will find l
29,10 show concern for his l.
31,12 all the days of her l.
Eccl 2,17 Therefore I loathed l, since for
Sir 30,22 the very l of man,
Is 53,10 If he gives his l as an offering
Lam 3,58 you redeemed my l. You see,
Ez 18,27 he shall preserve his l; since
Jon 2, 6 about me, threatening my l;
Mal 2, 5 one of l and peace; fear I put
Mt 6,25 do not worry about your l,
20,28 give his l as a ransom for
Mk 5,23 she may get well and l."
10,45 serve and to give his l as a
Lk 6, 9 to save l rather than to
12,25 add a moment to your l-span?
Jn 1, 4 to be through him was l,
5,40 come to me to have l.
17, 3 Now this is eternal l, that they
Acts 2,28 to me the paths of l;
Rom 1,17 is righteous by faith will l."
8,38 that neither death, nor l,
1Cor 3,22 or the world or l or death,
7,28 in their earthly l,
15,19 If for this l only we have
2Cor 2,16 the former an odor of l that
3, 6 but the Spirit gives l.
4,10 so that the l of Jesus
Gal 1,13 of my former way of l

3,21 been given that could bring l,
6, 8 the spirit will reap eternal l
Phil 1,20 in my body, whether by l or by
2,16 on to the word of l,
2,30 risking his l to make up se
Col 2,13 he brought you to l along
3, 3 and your l is hidden with
1Thes 4,11 aspire to live a tranquil l,
1Tm 1,16 in him for everlasting l.
4, 8 it holds a promise of l
6,12 Lay hold of eternal l,
2Tm 1,10 and brought l and immortality
2, 4 in the business affairs of l.
3,10 my teaching, way of l,
Ti 1, 2 in the hope of eternal l that
Heb 7,16 power of a l that cannot be
10,39 have faith and will possess l.
11,22 near the end of his l,
13, 5 Let your l be free from love
13, 7 outcome of their way of l
Jas 1,12 the crown of l that he
3,13 his works by a good l
4,14 have no idea what your l will
1Pt 3, 7 heirs of the gift of l, so that
3,10 "Whoever would love l
3,18 brought to l in the spirit.
4, 2 what remains of one's l
2Pt 1, 3 us everything that makes for l
1Jn 1, 1 concerns the Word of l—
2,16 the eyes, and a pretentious l,
3,14 have passed from death to l
3,16 that he laid down his l for us;
Jude 21 Christ that leads to eternal l.
Rv 2, 7 tree of l that is in the garden
3, 5 name from the book of l
7,17 springs of l-giving water,
11,11 a breath of l from God
12,11 love for l did not deter them
13, 8 l, which belongs to the Lamb
13,15 breathe l into the beast's
20, 4 They came to l and they
20,12 the book of l. The dead were

LIKE (NESS)

Gn 1,26 in our image, after our l.
Ex 15,11 Who is l to you among the
Nm 11, 7 Manna was l coriander seed
Dt 8,20 l the nations which the LORD
2Sm 7,22 Lord GOD! There is none l you
1Kgs 8,23 there is no God l you in
1Chr 17,21 "Is there, l your people Israel,
Jdt 11,19 You will drive them l sheep
Jb 1, 8 is no one on earth l him,
Ps 35,10 "O LORD, who is l you, Who
103,15 Our days are l the grass;
Prv 11,22 a golden ring in a
Eccl 12,11 sayings of the wise are l
Wis 14,19 labored over the l
Is 46, 9 God, there is none l me.
Jer 10, 6 No one is l you, O LORD,
Lam 1,12 there is any suffering l
Ez 1,26 something l a throne could be
Dn 7,13 I saw One l a son of man
Hos 6, 4 Your piety is l a morning
Mi 7,18 Who is there l you, the God
Na 1, 6 His fury is poured out l fire,
Zec 1, 4 Be not l your fathers whom
Mt 9,36 troubled and abandoned, l
Lk 6,48 That one is l a person building
Acts 3,22 Moses said: 'A prophet l me
Rom 5,15 But the gift is not l the
Heb 7,17 up after the l of Melchizedek
1Pt 1,24 "All flesh is l grass, and all its
2Pt 3, 8 a thousand years l one day.
Rv 13, 2 mouth was l the mouth of a

LION ('S) (S)

Gn	49, 9	like a l's whelp, you have
Dt	33,22	is a l whelp, that springs forth
1Sm	17,34	and whenever a l or bear
1Mc	2,60	delivered from the jaws of l.
Ps	91,13	trample the l and the dragon.
Prv	19,12	like the roaring of a l,
	20, 2	king is as when a l roars;
	22,13	"A l is outside; in the streets
	26,13	"There is a l in the street,
	28, 1	the just man, like a l,
	28,15	Like a roaring l or a ravenous
	30,30	The l, mightiest of beasts,
Eccl	9, 4	better off than a dead l.
Sir	27,28	wait for them like a l.
Is	11, 7	the l shall eat hay like the
	65,25	and the l shall eat hay like the
Jer	4, 7	Up comes the l from his lair,
Dn	7, 4	The first was like a l,
Hos	13, 7	I will be like a l to them,
1Pt	5, 8	around like a roaring l
Rv	5, 5	"Do not weep. The l of the
	10, 3	a loud voice as a l roars.
	13, 2	like the mouth of a l.

LIPS

Jb	33, 3	my l shall utter knowledge
Ps	12, 3	another speak with deceiving l
	17, 4	your l have instructed me,
	22, 8	they curl their l and jeer;
	34,14	your l from speaking lies.
	45, 3	speech has graced your l,
	51,17	Lord, open my l; my mouth
	63, 4	my l offer you worship!
	89,35	the promise of my l
	106,33	words crossed his l.
	119,171	my l pour forth your praise,
	141, 3	a gatekeeper at my l.
Prv	5, 3	The l of an adulteress drip
	6, 2	by the utterance of your l,
	7,21	with her smooth l she
	10,13	On the l of the intelligent
	12,13	l the evil man is ensnared
	13, 3	to open wide one's l brings
	14, 3	l of the wise preserve them
	15, 7	The l of the wise disseminate
	16,30	he who compresses his l
	17,28	if he closes his l, intelligent.
	18,20	with the yield of his l
	20,15	wise l are a precious
	22,18	all are ready on your l.
	23,16	when your l speak what
	26,23	smooth l with a wicked heart.
Eccl	10,12	win favor, but the fool's l
Song	4, 11	Your l drip honey, my bride,
Sir	20,23	it is constantly on the l of the
Is	29,13	and honors me with their l
Hos	8, 1	A trumpet to your l, You who
Mt	15, 8	people honors me with their l,
1Cor	14,21	strange tongues and by the l
Heb	13,15	the fruit of l that confess his
1Pt	3,10	tongue from evil and the l

LISTEN (S)

Ex	4, 1	will not believe me, nor l to my
	6,30	it be that Pharaoh will l to
2Kgs	17,40	They did not l, however, but
Ps	5, 2	l to my sighing. Hear my
	10,17	You l, Lord, to the needs of
	17, 1	l to my prayer spoken
	34,12	Come, children, l to me;
	39,13	l to my prayer, Lord,
	45,11	l, my daughter, and
	50, 7	"l, my people, I will speak
	54, 4	l to the words of my
	71, 2	l to me and save me

	81, 9	'L, my people, I give
Prv	5, 7	O children, l to me, go not
	5,13	Why did I not l to
	7,24	l to me, be attentive to
	12,15	but he who l to advice is wise.
	23,22	l to your father who
Sir	6,33	If you are willing to l, you will
Is	42,23	Who l and pays heed
Mt	18,16	If he does not l, take one or
Mk	9, 7	This is my beloved Son. L to
Lk	16,31	'If they will not l to Moses and
Jn	10, 8	but the sheep did not l to
1Cor	14, 2	for no one l; he utters mysteries
Rv	1, 3	blessed are those who l to

LITTLE

Ex	16,18	did not have too l. They so
1Kgs	17,12	in my jar and a l oil in my jug.
Ps	8, 6	made them l less than a god,
	37,10	Wait a l, and the wicked
Prv	6,10	A l sleep, a l slumber, a
	9,18	l he knows that the shades
	10,20	of the wicked is of l worth.
	13,11	but amassed l by little,
	15,16	a l with fear of the Lord
	23, 8	The l you have eaten
	24,33	A l sleep, a little slumber, a
Eccl	10, 1	wisdom or wealth is a l folly!
Sir	29,23	Be it l or much, be content
Is	11, 6	with a l child to guide them.
Mt	17,20	"Because of your l faith.
Lk	7,47	one to whom l is forgiven,
1Cor	5, 6	a l yeast leavens all the
2Cor	8,15	whoever had l did not have
Gal	5, 9	A l yeast leavens the whole
1Tm	5,23	but have a l wine for the sake
Heb	2, 7	made him for a l while lower
1Pt	5,10	after you have suffered a l.
Rv	6, 11	told to be patient a l while

LIVING

Gn	2, 7	and so man became a l being.
Dt	5,26	have, the voice of the l God
Jos	3,10	there is a l God in your midst,
1Sm	17,26	insult the armies of the l
2Kgs	19, 4	sent to taunt the l God, and
Ps	27,13	in the land of the l.
	36, 7	all l creatures you sustain,
	42, 3	the l God. When can I go
	49,19	When l, they congratulate
	52, 7	from the land of the l.
	56,14	in the light of the l.
	69,29	from the book of the l;
	84, 3	flesh cry out for the l God.
Prv	16,31	it is gained by virtuous l.
Eccl	4, 2	in death than are the l
	7, 2	and the l should take
	9, 4	among the l there is hope; a
Jer	10,10	he is the l God, the eternal
Lam	3,39	Why should any l man
Ez	1, 5	resembling four l creatures
Dn	6,27	"For he is the l God, enduring
Zec	14, 8	l waters shall flow from
Mt	16,16	Messiah, the Son of the l
	22,32	the dead but of the l."
Jn	4,10	he would have given you l
Rom	9,26	be called children of the l
2Cor	6,16	are the temple of the l God;
1Tm	4,10	set our hope on the l God,
2Tm	4, 1	who will judge the l and the
Heb	4,12	the word of God is l and
1Pt	1,23	through the l and abiding
Rv	4, 6	there were four l creatures

LOOK (ED) (S)

Gn	15, 5	and said, "L up at the sky and

Ex	3, 6	for he was afraid to l at God.
Dt	3,27	top of Pisgah and l out to the
1Sm	16,16	will l for a man skilled in
Jb	30,20	you stand off and l at me,
Ps	10, 11	never bothers to l.
	13, 4	l upon me, answer me,
	25,16	l upon me, have pity on
	34, 6	l to God that you may
	35,17	how long will you l on?
	37,10	l for them and they will
	54, 9	my eyes l down on my foes.
	80,15	Lord of hosts; l down from
Prv	4,25	Let your eyes l straight ahead
	7,13	with an impudent l says
	7,15	to l for you, and I have
	23,31	l not on the wine when
Is	3, 9	Their very l bears witness
Hb	1,13	pure are your eyes to l upon
Zec	12,10	and they shall l on him whom
Mt	6,26	more than clothing? L at the
Mk	13,21	'L, here is the Messiah! L
Lk	24,39	L at my hands and my
Jn	4,35	I tell you, l up and see the
1Pt	1,12	into which angels longed to l.

LOSE (LOSS) (LOST)

Is	41, 3	passing on without l
Jer	48, 11	and his scent was not l.
Jn	6,39	that I should not l anything of
Heb	12, 3	may not grow weary and l
2Jn	8	do not l what we worked for

LOVE (D) (S)

Gn	22, 2	your only one, whom you l,
	24,67	In his l for her Isaac found
	29,18	Jacob had fallen in l with
	34, 3	was really in l with the
	34,19	since he was deeply in l
Ex	20, 6	the children of those who l me
Lv	19,18	You shall l your neighbor as
Dt	4,37	For l of your fathers he chose
	5,10	those who l me and
	6, 5	you shall l the Lord,
	7, 8	It was because the Lord l you
	7,13	He will l and bless and
	10,12	to l and serve the Lord,
	10,15	Yet in his l for your
	11, 1	"l the Lord, your God,
	13, 4	really l him with all your heart
Jos	22, 5	l the Lord, your God; follow
Jgs	14,16	you do not l me, for you have
1Sm	18,22	and all his officers l you.
2Sm	13, 4	"I am in l with Tamar, my
1Kgs	11, 3	But Solomon fell in l with
2Chr	19, 2	you help the wicked and l
Neh	1, 5	mercy toward those who l you
Tb	4,13	Therefore, my son, l your
	6,18	he fell deeply in l with
	7, 11	now on you are her l,
	7,15	"My l, prepare the other
	8, 4	"My l, get up. Let us pray
	10, 6	not worry over him, my l.
	13,14	Happy are those who l
	14, 7	Those who sincerely l God
1Mc	4,33	the sword of those who l you,
2Mc	6,20	unlawful to taste even for l of
Ps	4, 3	mock my honor, l what
	5,12	those who l your name
	17, 7	Show your wonderful l,
	23, 6	Only goodness and l
	31, 8	and be glad in your l,
	44,27	Redeem us as your l
	52,10	trust in God's faithful l
	61, 8	may your l and fidelity
	77, 9	Has God's l ceased forever?
	89,34	I will not take my l from him,

90,14 daybreak with your l,
103, 4 surrounds you with l and
136,22 God's l endures forever. The
Prv 1,22 will you l inanity, how long
4, 6 l her, and she will safeguard
8,21 wealth to those who l me,
9, 8 wise man, and he will l you.
10,12 but l covers all offenses.
15,17 where l is than a fatted ox
Eccl 3, 8 A time to l, and a time
9, 1 l from hatred man cannot tell
9, 6 l and hatred and rivalry have
Song 2, 7 do not stir up l before
4,10 is your l than wine,
5, 8 that I am faint with l.
7, 7 how pleasing, my l,
7,13 will I give you my l.
8, 7 waters cannot quench l,
Wis 1, 1 l justice, you who judge
3, 9 shall abide with him in l
6,12 perceived by those who l her,
Sir 2,15 those who l him keep
4,14 who l her the Lord loves.
7,30 l your Creator, forsake not
11,15 l and virtuous paths are from
34,16 LORD are upon those who l
Is 61, 8 For I, the LORD, l what is right,
Jer 31, 3 With age-old l I have loved
Ez 16, 8 were now old enough for l.
Dn 9, 4 covenant toward those who l
Hos 11, 4 with bands of l;
Zec 8,17 nor l a false oath.
Mt 5,43 'You shall l your neighbor
6,24 will either hate one and l
22,37 "You shall l the Lord, your
Mk 12,33 'to l him with all your heart
Lk 10,27 "You shall l the Lord, your
Jn 5,42 you do not have the l of God
13,35 if you have l for one another."
14,21 my Father, and I will l him
15,10 remain in his l. "I
21,15 you know that I l you."
Rom 5, 5 because the l of God
8,39 separate us from the l
12,10 l one another with mutual n
13, 8 except to l one another;
13, 9 "You shall l your neighbor as
14,15 no longer in accord with l.
15,30 by the l of the Spirit,
1Cor 2, 9 prepared for those who l
4,21 or with l and a gentle spirit?
8, 3 But if one l God
13,13 So faith, hope, l remain, these
16,24 My l to all of you in
2Cor 2, 4 know the abundant l I have for
5,14 For the l of Christ impels
6, 6 in unfeigned l, in truthful
8,24 churches of your l and of
11,11 Because I do not l you?
12,15 If I l you more, am I to
13,13 and the l of God and
Gal 5,14 "You shall l your neighbor as
5,22 fruit of the Spirit is l,
Eph 1, 4 l he destined us for adoption
2, 4 because of the great l he had
3,19 and to know the l of Christ
4,16 and builds itself up in l.
5,28 husbands should l their wives
5,33 you should l his wife as
Phil 1, 9 that your l may increase
1,16 The latter act out of l,
2, 1 in Christ, any solace in l,
2, 2 with the same l, united in
Col 1, 8 also told us of your l
3,14 over all these put on l, that is,
1Thes 1, 3 of faith and labor of l

3, 6 news of your faith and l,
3,12 increase and abound in l
4, 9 taught by God to l one
5, 8 the breastplate of faith and l
2Thes 1, 3 and the l of every one of you
2,10 they have not accepted the l
3, 5 direct your hearts to the l
1Tm 1, 5 aim of this instruction is l
1,14 along with the faith and l
2,15 persevere in faith and l
4,12 in speech, conduct, l, faith,
6,10 For the l of money is the root
2Tm 1, 7 but rather of power and l
1,13 in the faith and l that are
2,22 pursue righteousness, faith, l,
3,10 faith, patience, l, endurance,
Ti 2, 2 sound in faith, l, and
2, 4 younger women to l their
3, 4 kindness and generous l
3,15 Greet those who l us in the
Heb 6,10 your work and the l
10,24 rouse one another to l
13, 1 Let mutual l continue.
13, 5 be free from l of money
Jas 1,12 he promised to those who l
2, 5 he promised to those who l
1Pt 1, 8 not seen him you l him;
1,22 for sincere mutual l,
2,17 honor to all, l the community,
3,10 "Whoever would l life and
4, 8 Above all, let your l for one
2Pt 1, 7 mutual affection with l.
1Jn 2, 5 the l of God is truly
2,15 Do not l the world
2,15 the l of the Father is not
3, 1 See what l the Father
3,10 does not l his brother.
3, 11 we should l one another,
3,18 Children, let us l not in word
4,12 Yet, if we l one another,
4,20 not l a brother whom he has
5, 2 that we l the children of God
5, 3 For the l of God is this, that
2Jn 3 Son in truth and l.
6 For this is l, that we walk
3Jn 6 testified to your l before
Jude 12 are blemishes on your l
21 Keep yourselves in the l
Rv 2, 4 you have lost the l
2,19 I know your works, your l,
3, 9 they will realize that I l you.
3,19 Those whom I l, I reprove and
12,11 l for life did not deter
22,15 and all who l and practice

LOW (ER) (LY)
Gn 23, 7 began to bow l before the
Lv 26, 7 lay them l with your sword.
Nm 32, 4 which the Lord has laid l
2Sm 9, 8 " Bowing l, he answered,
1Kgs 9,17 Solomon then rebuilt Gezer), L
Jdt 7,14 them they will be laid l
16, 6 nor did titans bring him l,
1Mc 6,40 some were on l ground,
2Mc 11,11 they laid l eleven
15,27 l at least thirty-five thousand
Jb 6, 5 Does the ox l over his
24,24 they are laid l and,
Ps 10,10 crushed, laid l; they fall
17,11 keeping l to the ground,
18,28 haughty eyes you bring l.
22,28 families of nations will bow l
22,30 earth will bow l before God;
75, 8 who brings some l and raises
78,31 laid l the youth of Israel.
79, 8 been brought very l.

138, 2 I bow l toward your holy
Eccl 12, 4 sound of the mill is l;
Sir 6,12 But if you are brought l,
33,12 he curses and brings l,
46,18 He brought l the rulers
Is 29,19 The l will ever find joy
Jer 5, 3 you laid them l, but
42, 1 high and l, approached
42, 8 high and l, and said to
44,12 High and l, they shall die
Bar 2, 5 We are brought l, not raised
5, 7 mountain be made l,
Ez 17, 6 dense and l-lying, Its
17,24 Bring l the high tree,
21,31 Up with the l and down
31,12 Its foliage was brought l in
Dn 3,37 brought l everywhere in
7,24 who shall lay l three kings.
11,12 he shall lay l tens of
Hb 3, 6 the age-old hills bow l
Lk 3, 5 and hill shall be made l.
Rom 2, 4 and patience in l esteem,

LUST (S)
Tb 8, 7 of mine not because of l,
Prv 6,25 l not in your heart after
13,19 l indulged starves the soul,
Wis 14,26 l, disorder in marriage,
Sir 18,30 Go not after your l
Ez 23,11 her l was more depraved than
Dn 13, 8 they began to l for her.
13,14 They admitted their l, and
13,56 "beauty has seduced you, l
Mt 5,28 looks at a woman with l has
Rom 1,24 through the l of their hearts

M

MADE
Gn 1, 7 God m the dome, and it
Ex 37,17 The lampstand was m of pure
Nm 21, 9 Moses accordingly m a
Dt 32, 6 Has he not m you and
Jos 24,25 So Joshua m a covenant with
Jgs 11,30 Jephthah m a vow to the LORD
1Sm 15,11 "I regret having m Saul king,
2Sm 23, 5 He has m an eternal covenant
1Kgs 12,28 the king m two calves of gold
2Kgs 23, 4 the objects that had been m
2Chr 4,19 had all these articles m
Neh 9, 6 you m the heavens, the
Tb 8, 6 You m Adam and you gave
Jb 33, 4 the spirit of God has m me,
Ps 96, 5 but the LORD m the heavens.
Prv 8,26 and the fields were not m,
Eccl 3, 11 He has m everything
Wis 14,10 and the thing m shall be
Sir 43,35 is the LORD who has m all
Is 45,12 It was I who m the earth and
Jer 51,15 He has sworn who m the
Dn 3, 1 had a golden statue m,
Am 5, 8 He who m the Pleiades and
Jon 1, 9 who m the sea and the dry
Mk 2,27 "The sabbath was m for man,
Lk 19,46 but you have m it a den of
Jn 9, 6 spat on the ground and m
Acts 10,15 "What God has m clean, you
1Cor 1,20 Has not God m the wisdom of
2Cor 5,21 For our sake he m him to be
Eph 2,14 he who m both one and
Heb 2, 7 You m him for a little while
Jas 3, 9 who are m in the likeness of
Rv 14, 7 Worship him who m heaven

MAJESTY (MAJESTIC)

Lv 23,40 shall gather foliage from m trees
Dt 5,24 see his glory and his m!
   9,26 heritage which your m
   11, 2 his m, his strong hand
1Chr 16,27 Splendor and m go before
Tb 13, 6 show his power and m to
   13, 8 all men speak of his m,
   14, 2 praising the divine m.
Est 4D,13 troubled with fear of your m.
   5, 4 please your m," Esther
2Mc 3,34 proclaim to all men the m
Jb 13,11 Surely will his m affright
   31,23 and his m will overpower me.
   37,22 God's awesome m!
Ps 21, 6 m and splendor you confer
   45, 4 In splendor and m ride
   68,35 whose m protects Israel,
   89,18 You are their m strength
   104, 1 clothed with m and glory,
   150, 2 praise him for his great m.
Sir 2,18 equal to his m is the mercy
   6,30 your throne of m; her bonds,
   10, 5 who imparts his m to the ruler.
   36,13 Fill Zion with your m, your
   43,15 In his m he gives the
   43,30 Awful indeed is the Lord's m,
   45, 7 and crowned him with lofty m;
   50,11 the glorious altar and lent m
Is 2,10 and the splendor of his m!
Dn 4,33 my m and my splendor
   5,18 great kingdom and glorious m.
Mi 5, 3 in the m name of the Lord
Hb 1, 7 derive his law and his m.
Lk 9,43 astonished by the m of God.
Heb 1, 3 the right hand of the M on
2Pt 1,16 been eyewitnesses of his m.
Jude 25 Christ our Lord be glory, m,

MAKE (R)

Gn 12, 2 "I will m of you a great nation
Ex 20,23 Do not m anything to rank
Nm 21, 8 "M a saraph and mount it
Dt 30, 5 and he will m you more
Jos 9, 7 can we m an alliance with
2Sm 7, 9 And I will m you famous
Jb 7,17 that you m much of him, or
Ps 110, 1 while I m your enemies your
Prv 14,31 the poor blasphemes his M
Eccl 5, 4 You had better not m a vow
Is 61, 8 I will m with them.
Bar 3,35 shining with joy for their M.
Ez 34,25 I will m a covenant of peace
Hb 2,18 that its m should carve it?
Mk 1,17 and I will m you fishers of
Jn 1,23 "M straight the way of the
Acts 2,35 until I m your enemies your
Rom 14, 4 the Lord is able to m him
Heb 1,13 until I m your enemies your
2Pt 1, 5 m every effort to supplement
1Jn 1,10 not sinned," we m him a liar,
Rv 17,17 m them come to an

MAN (MEN)

Gn 2,23 out of 'her m' this one has
Lv 20,13 If a m lies with a male as
Dt 1,17 fearing no m, for judgment
   4,16 form of a m or of a woman,
   5,24 found out today that a m can
   7,14 no m or woman among
   8, 3 by bread alone does m live,
   15,12 a Hebrew m or woman, sells
   17, 2 gives you, a m or a woman
   18,19 If any m will not listen to my
   19,16 takes the stand against a m
   22, 5 an article proper to a m,

Jgs 4,22 I will show you the m
   9, 2 or that one m rule over you?'
   13,11 When he reached the m,
   16,13 as weak as any other m."
   20,44 warriors to a m. The
   20,46 warriors to a m. But
Ru 1, 1 so a m from Bethlehem of
   3,18 for the m will not rest,
1Sm 13,14 LORD has sought out a m
Ezr 2, 1 each m in his own city
   6,11 If any m violates this edict,
Neh 7, 2 God-fearing m than most.
   12,36 David, the m of God.
Tb 4,18 counsel from every wise m,
   5,12 you looking for a hired m
   8, 1 They brought the young m out
   11, 6 and the m who traveled
Jdt 2,18 provisions for each m,
   6, 3 strike them down as one m,
   8,16 "God is not m that he should
Est 6, 7 "For the m whom the king
1Mc 7, 7 So now, send a m whom you
   10,35 Let no m have authority
   16, 3 have come to m's estate.
2Mc 3,17 come over the m clearly
   4, 2 the m who was a benefactor
   15,13 another m appeared,
Jb 40, 7 like a m. I will question you,
Ps 90, 1 A prayer of Moses, the m of
Prv 3,30 Quarrel not with a m without
   10,16 The just m's recompense
   12, 8 good sense a m is praised,
   14, 6 knowledge is easy to the m of
   20,24 then, can a m understand
   20,25 trap for a m, or to regret a vow
   30,19 and the way of a m with a
Eccl 2,16 the wise m dies as well
   4,10 Woe to the solitary m!
   8, 1 Who is like the wise m,
   10, 2 The wise m's understanding
   12,13 for this is m's all;
Wis 2, 1 any remedy for m's dying,
   4,16 of the wicked m grown old.
   9, 5 a m weak and short-lived
   15,16 For a m made them;
Sir 10,29 The poor m is honored
   13,14 every a m man like himself.
   16, 4 Through one wise m can a
   18,11 m may be merciful to his
   20, 4 One m is silent and is thought
   25, 7 The m who finds joy in his
Is 53, 3 a m of suffering, accustomed
Jer 31,22 must encompass the m with
Lam 1,15 me to crush my young m
Bar 6,63 nor benefit m. Know,
   6,72 The better for the just m
Mt 9, 6 the Son of M has authority on
   9, 9 he saw a man named Matthew
   10,23 the Son of M comes.
   10,35 m 'against his father,
   10,41 receives a righteous m
   10,41 a righteous m's reward.
   22,24 Moses said, 'If a m dies
   27,32 this m they pressed into
Mk 9,12 regarding the Son of M that
Lk 16,21 that fell from the rich m's table.
Jn 3,14 so must the Son of M be lifted
   5, 7 The sick m answered him,
   11,44 The dead m came out, tied
   18,14 it was better that one m
Acts 7,56 the Son of M standing at the
   12,22 a god, not of a m."
   23,17 "Take this young m to the
1Cor 11,14 if a m wears his hair long it
   15,47 first m was from the earth,
Eph 5,31 "For this reason a m shall

1Tm 2,12 to have authority over a m.
   6,11 you, m of God, avoid all this
Ti 1, 6 m be blameless, married
Phlm 9 I am, Paul, an old m,
   16 as a m and in the Lord. So
Heb 2, 6 "What is m that you are
   8, 2 not m, set up. Now every high
Jas 1, 8 since he is a m of two minds,
   2, 2 if a m with gold rings on his
2Pt 2, 7 a righteous m oppressed by
   2, 8 that righteous m living among
Rv 1,13 like a son of m, wearing an

MANNA

Ex 16,31 Israelites called this food m.
Nm 11, 6 nothing before us but this m."
Dt 8,16 m, a food unknown to your
Jos 5,12 the m ceased. No longer was
Ps 78,24 God rained m upon them for
Jn 6,49 Your ancestors ate the m in
Heb 9, 4 the gold jar containing the m,
Rv 2,17 give some of the hidden m;

MARRIAGE (MARRIED) (MARRIES)

Dt 22,16 daughter to this man in m,
Is 62, 5 As a young man m a virgin
Mt 22,30 marry nor are given in m
1Tm 3, 2 m only once, temperate,

MASTER (S)

Gn 4, 7 yet you can be his m."
Est 9, 1 had expected to become m of
Ps 123, 2 on the hand of his m,
Jer 27, 4 Tell your m, Thus says the Lord
Mt 10,24 no slave above his m.
Jn 13,16 slave is greater than his m nor
Eph 6, 9 you have a m in heaven
Col 3,22 Slaves, obey your human m in
2Pt 2, 1 even deny the m who
Jude 4 deny our only M and Lord,
Rv 6,10 true m, before you sit in

MATURE (MATURITY)

Lk 8,14 and they fail to produce m
1Cor 2, 6 wisdom to those who are m,
Phil 3,12 have already attained perfect m
Jas 1,15 when sin reaches m

MERCY (MERCIES) (MERCIFUL)

Ex 33,19 I who grant m to whom I will.
Dt 7, 2 them and show them no m.
Jos 11,20 and thus receive no m,
1Chr 21,13 whose m is very great,
Tb 3, 2 All your ways are m and truth;
Jdt 13,14 not withdrawn his m from the
1Mc 11,49 held the city at their m,
   16, 3 by the m of Heaven,
2Mc 1,24 awesome and strong, just and m
Jb 30,21 you turn upon me without m
Ps 30,11 Hear, O Lord, have m on me;
   51, 3 Have m on me, God, in your
   69,17 in your great m turn to me.
   102,14 again show m to Zion;
   109,21 in your great m rescue me.
   119,58 have m on me in accord with
   130, 2 attentive to my cry for m.
Prv 28,13 and forsakes them obtains m.
Wis 11,23 But you have m on all,
Sir 2, 7 wait for his m, turn not away
Is 47, 6 but you showed them no m,
Ez 5,11 you with pity nor have m.
Dn 2,18 implore the m of the God of
Zec 1,12 will you be without m for
Mt 5, 7 for they will be shown m.
   9,13 of the words, 'I desire m,
   12, 7 'I desire m, not sacrifice,'
Lk 10,37 one who treated him with m."

Rom 11,31 by virtue of the **m** shown to
    12, 1 brothers, by the **m** of God
    15, 9 might glorify God for his **m**.
1Cor 7,25 as one who by the Lord's **m** is
2Cor 4, 1 ministry through the **m** shown
Gal 6,16 a new creation. Peace and **m**
Eph 2, 4 God, who is rich in **m**,
Phil 2,27 but God had **m** on him,
1Tm 1, 2 grace, **m**, and peace from
2Tm 1,18 Lord grant him to find **m** from
Ti 3, 5 done but because of his **m**,
Heb 4,16 throne of grace to receive **m**
Jas 3,17 compliant, full of **m** and good
1Pt 2,10 but now you have received **m**.

MESSAGE (MESSENGER)

2Sm 11,19 the **m**, "When you have finished
Jb 1,14 a **m** came to Job and said
Lk 7,27 Behold, I am sending my **m**
1Cor 1,18 The **m** of the cross is
2Cor 5,19 and entrusting to us the **m** of
Ti 1, 9 holding fast to the true **m**
1Jn 1, 5 Now this is the **m** that we

MESSIAH

Mt 16,16 "You are the **M**,
Mk 13,21 'Look, here is the **M**!
Lk 2,11 born for you who is **M**
Jn 10,24 If you are the **M**, tell us
Acts 3,20 send you the **M** already
Rom 9, 5 is the **M**. God who is over all

MIGHTY

Gn 10, 9 "Like Nimrod, a **m** hunter
Lv 19,15 weak nor deference to the **m**
Dt 3,24 can perform deeds as **m** as
2Sm 22,18 He rescued me from my **m**
2Chr 6,32 your **m** power, and your
Neh 9,32 O our God, great, **m**, and
Jb 35, 9 of the power of the **m**, Saying,
Ps 24, 8 The LORD, a **m** warrior, the
Sir 15,18 he is **m** in power, and all-
Is 1,24 the Lord of hosts, the **M** One
Jer 32,19 great in counsel, **m** in deed,
Lam 1,15 "All the **m** ones in my midst
Bar 2,11 with your **m** hand, with signs
Ez 20,33 the Lord GOD, with a **m** hand
Mt 7,22 Did we not do **m** deeds
1Pt 5, 6 yourselves under the **m** hand
Rv 18, 8 For **m** is the Lord God who

MIND (FUL) (S)

Nm 23,19 that he should change his **m**.
Dt 29, 3 given you a **m** to understand,
1Chr 28, 9 understands all the **m**'s
Ps 8, 5 that you are **m** of them
Eccl 2, 3 though my **m** was concerned
Sir 21,14 A fool's **m** is like a broken jar
Jer 17,10 alone probe the **m** and test
Lam 3,21 I will call this to **m**, as my
Ez 28, 6 yourself to have the **m** of a
Mt 22,37 and with all your **m**.
Mk 3,21 He is out of his **m**."
Lk 10,27 and with all your **m**, and your
Rom 1,28 undiscerning **m** to do what is
1Cor 14,23 you are out of your **m**?
Phil 2, 2 by being of the same **m**,
1Thes 4,11 to **m** your own affairs,
2Tm 3, 8 of depraved **m**, unqualified in
Rv 17,13 They are of one **m** and will

MINISTRY

Ex 30,20 approach the altar in their **m**,
Dt 17,12 officiates there in the **m** of the
2Chr 8,14 their functions of praise and **m**
Neh 12,45 Levites who carried out the **m**

Lk 3,23 When Jesus began his **m** he
Acts 6, 4 to prayer and to the **m** of
Rom 12, 7 if **m**, in ministering; if one is
2Cor 4, 1 since we have this **m** through
Eph 4,12 ones for the work of **m**,
2Tm 4, 5 fulfill your **m**. For I am
Heb 8, 6 more excellent a **m** as he is

MONEY

Gn 43,12 Also take extra **m** along,
    47,18 with our **m** spent and our
Ex 22,24 "If you lend **m** to one of your
Lv 27, 2 at a fixed sum of **m**,
Dt 14,26 exchange the **m** for whatever
    23,20 on a loan of **m** or
Jos 24,32 for a hundred pieces of **m**.
Jgs 16,18 brought up the **m** with them.
1Kgs 21, 2 give you its value in **m**."
2Kgs 12, 5 personal redemption **m**, and
Ezr 7,17 to use this **m** to buy bulls
Neh 5, 4 borrowed **m** on our fields
    5,11 with the interest on the **m**,
Tb 5,19 I hope more **m** is not your
1Mc 3,29 exhausted the **m** in his treasury;
    10,43 because of he owes the king
    14,32 large sums of his own **m**
    15,31 more for the tribute of **m** of
2Mc 3, 6 that the total sum of **m**
    3,10 the **m** was a care fund
    10,20 **m** lovers let themselves be
Jb 42,11 a piece of **m** and a gold ring.
Ps 15, 5 lends no **m** at interest,
Eccl 5, 9 man is never satisfied with **m**,
    7,12 the protection of **m**; and the
    10,19 but **m** answers for everything.
Sir 7,18 Barter not a friend for **m**,
    21, 8 his house with another's **m**
    29,10 Spend your **m** for your brother
Is 55, 1 You who have no **m**, come,
Jer 32, 9 **m**, seventeen silver shekels.
    32,44 Fields shall be bought with **m**,
Bar 3,18 schemed anxiously for **m**,
Mi 3,11 her prophets divine for **m**,
Mt 25,27 have put my **m** in the bank
    26, 9 and the **m** given to the poor."
    28,12 gave a large sum of **m**
Mk 11,15 the tables of the **m**
    14, 5 days' wages and the **m**
Lk 9, 3 nor food, nor **m**, and let no
    19,15 whom he had given the **m**,
    19,23 not put my **m** in a bank?
    22,36 has a **m** bag should take it,
Jn 2,14 as well as the **m**-changers
Acts 8,20 "May your **m** perish with you,
1Tm 3, 3 contentious, not a lover of **m**.
2Tm 3, 2 self-centered and lovers of **m**,
Heb 13, 5 be free from love of **m** but be

MOON (S)

Gn 37, 9 the sun and the **m** and eleven
Dt 17, 3 worshiping the sun or the **m**
Jos 10,13 and the **m** stayed, while the
1Sm 20,18 "Tomorrow is the new **m**;
    20,24 the day of the new **m**,
2Kgs 4,23 It is neither the new **m** nor
1Chr 23,31 the Lord on sabbaths, new **m**
Neh 10,34 for the sabbaths, new **m**
1Mc 10,34 sabbaths, new **m** festivals,
Jb 31,26 or the **m** in the splendor of its
Ps 8, 4 the **m** and stars that you set
    74,16 set the **m** and sun in place.
    104,19 the **m** to mark the seasons,
    136, 9 The **m** and stars to rule the
    148, 3 Praise him, sun and **m**;
Prv 7,20 the full **m** he will return home."
Eccl 12, 2 and the **m**, and the stars,

Song 6,10 as beautiful as the **m**,
Sir 27,11 the godless man, like the **m**,
    43, 6 **m**, too, that marks
Is 1,14 Your new **m** and festivals I
    30,26 The light of the **m** will be
    60,20 or your **m** withdraw,
Jer 31,35 sun to light the day, **m** and
Bar 6,59 and **m** and stars are bright,
    6,66 nor shining like the **m**.
Ez 32, 7 and the **m** shall not give its
Dn 3,62 Sun and **m**, bless the Lord;
Hos 5, 7 Now shall the new **m** devour
Jl 2,10 sun and the **m** are darkened,
    3, 4 and **m** to blood,
    4,15 Sun and **m** are darkened,
Am 8, 5 "When will the new **m**
Hb 3,11 the **m** remains in its shelter,
Mt 24,29 and the **m** will not give its light
Acts 2,20 and the **m** to blood, before the
1Cor 15,41 the brightness of the **m**
Rv 8,12 a third of the **m**, and a third

MORNING

Gn 1, 5 Thus evening came, and **m**
    19,27 Early the next **m** Abraham
    20, 8 Early the next **m** Abimelech
    32, 1 Early the next **m**, Laban
    40, 6 came to them in the **m**,
    41, 8 Next **m** his spirit was agitated.
Ex 12,10 be kept beyond the next **m**;
    16, 7 in the **m** you will see
    18,13 from **m** until evening.
    27,21 From evening to **m** Aaron
    30, 7 **m** after morning, when he
    36, 3 Still, **m** after morning
Dt 16, 7 then in the **m** you may return
    28,67 'Would that it were **m**!'
Jos 7,16 **m** Joshua had Israel come
    8,10 the next **m** Joshua mustered
Jgs 6,38 next **m** he wrung the dew from
    9,33 at sunrise tomorrow **m**,
    16, 2 "Tomorrow **m** we will kill
    19, 5 they rose early in the **m**
Ru 2, 7 since she came this **m**
    3,13 Lie there until **m**."
    3,14 lay at his feet until **m**,
1Sm 3, 5 rose early the next **m**,
    19, 2 on your guard tomorrow **m**;
    29,11 men left early in the **m**
2Sm 23, 4 at sunrise on a cloudless **m**,
1Kgs 3,21 I rose in the **m** to nurse
    18,26 and called on Baal from **m**
2Kgs 3,20 In the **m**, at the time of the
    16,15 "burn the **m** holocaust
1Chr 23,30 must be present every **m**
2Chr 20,20 In the early **m** they hastened
Ezr 3, 3 the LORD on it, both **m** and
Tb 9, 6 following **m** they got
Est 2,14 return in the **m** to a
    5,14 and in the **m** ask the
1Mc 4,52 **m** on the twenty-fifth day
    9,13 raged from **m** until evening.
    12,29 what had happened until **m**.
Jb 38, 7 While the **m** stars sang in
Ps 73,14 chastised every **m**.
    88,14 in the **m** my prayer comes
    90, 6 It sprouts green in the **m**;
    92, 3 proclaim your love in the **m**,
Prv 7,18 let us feast on love
    27,14 loud voice in the early **m**,
Eccl 11, 6 In the **m** sow your seed, and
Wis 11,22 or a drop of **m** dew come
Sir 18,26 Between **m** and evening
Is 5,11 as they rise in the **m**,
    17,14 they spread terror, before **m**,
    33, 2 Be our strength every **m**,

50, 4 **m** after morning he opens
Lam 3,23 They are renewed each **m**,
Ez 24,19 spoke to the people that **m**,
    33,22 fugitive reached me in the **m**.
Dn 6,20 rose very early the next **m**
    14,12 when you return in the **m**,
Hos 13, 3 shall be like a **m** cloud or
Am 4, 4 Each **m** bring your sacrifices,
Jon 4, 7 But the next **m** at dawn
Mi 2, 1 In the **m** light they accomplish
Zep 3, 5 **m** after morning he renders
Mt 16, 3 sky is red'; and, in the **m**, '
    21,18 to the city in the **m**,
    27, 1 **m**, all the chief priests and
Mk 11,20 Early in the **m**, as they
    13,35 or in the **m**. May he
    15, 1 As soon as **m** came,
    15,25 It was nine o'clock in the **m**
Lk 21,38 would get up early each **m**
    24,22 the tomb early in the **m**
Acts 2,15 is only nine o'clock in the **m**.
    5,21 the temple early in the **m**
    28,23 From early **m** until evening,
2Pt 1,19 until day dawns and the **m**
Rv 2,28 him I will give the **m** star. "
    22,16 the bright **m** star."

MORTAL (S)

Gn 6,12 since all **m** led depraved lives
Ex 21,12 Whoever strikes a man a **m**
Dt 5,26 For what **m** has heard, as we
2Sm 1,15 youth struck him a **m** blow.
Est 4C,12 seized with **m** anguish,
2Mc 9,12 and not to think one's **m** self
Jb 10, 5 as the days of a **m**,
Ps 8, 5 are mindful of them, mere **m**
    82, 7 Yet like any **m** you shall
    89,49 What **m** can live and not see
Prv 30, 1 The pronouncement of **m** man
Wis 7, 1 I too am a **m** man, the
    15,17 being **m**, he makes a
Sir 36,23 lot is beyond that of **m** men.
Is 13,12 I will make **m** more rare
Jer 44,30 to his enemy and **m** foe,
Lam 3,39 living man complain, any **m**,
    3,58 defended me in **m** danger,
Na 3,19 your wound is **m**. All who
Rom 6,12 must not reign over your **m**
    7,24 deliver me from this **m** body?
    8,11 give life to your **m** bodies also,
1Cor 15,53 and that which is **m** must
2Cor 5, 4 so that what is **m** may be
Heb 7, 8 In the one case, **m** men
Rv 13, 3 wounded, but this **m** wound

MOTHER (S)

Gn 2,24 man leaves his father and **m**
Ex 20,12 Honor your father and your **m**,
Dt 22, 6 shall not take away the **m** bird
Jgs 5, 7 when I rose, a **m** in Israel,
Ru 2,18 showed to her **m**-in-law.
    2,19 So her **m**-in-law said to her
    4,15 his **m** is the daughter-in-law
1Sm 15,33 your **m** be childless among
    20,30 your **m**'s shame,
    22, 3 "Let my father and **m**
2Sm 20,19 a city that is a **m** in Israel.
1Kgs 19,20 me kiss my father and **m**
Tb 4, 3 Honor your **m**,
    14,10 The day you bury your **m**
Jdt 16,12 sons of rebel **m** cut them down
Est 1, 6 **m**-of-pearl, and colored
    2, 7 death of her father and **m**,
1Mc 13,28 for his father and his **m**
2Mc 7, 1 with their **m** were arrested and
    7,41 The **m** was last to die, after

Jb 1,21 forth from my **m**'s womb,
    17,14 "my **m**" and "my sister,"
    31,18 even from my **m**'s womb—
Ps 27,10 Even if my father and **m**
    51, 7 even as my **m** conceived me.
    69, 9 a stranger to my **m**'s children.
    71, 6 from my **m**'s womb you are
    109,14 fathers' guilt; his **m**'s sin not
    113, 9 the joyful **m** of children.
    131, 2 child on its **m**'s lap, so
    139,13 you knit me in my **m**'s womb.
Prv 20,20 one curses his father or **m**,
    28,24 He who defrauds father or **m**
    29,15 to his whims disgraces his **m**.
    30,11 father, and blesses not its **m**.
    30,17 father, or scorns an aged **m**,
Eccl 5,14 from his **m**'s womb,
    11, 5 in the **m**'s womb, So you
Song 6, 9 my perfect one, her **m**'s
Wis 7, 1 And in my **m**'s womb I
    7,12 she is the **m** of these.
Sir 3, 6 who brings comfort to his **m**.
    41,15 Before father and **m** be
    46,13 dedicated from his **m**'s womb,
    50,22 from their **m**'s womb,
Is 66, 9 Shall I bring a **m** to the point
Jer 6,24 like a **m** in childbirth.
Mi 7, 6 rises up against her **m**,
Mt 12,48 "Who is my **m**? Who are my
    19,19 honor your father and your **m**';
    27,56 and Mary the **m** of James
    27,56 **m** of the sons of Zebedee
Mk 7,10 'Whoever curses father or **m**
    10, 7 leave his father and **m**
    15,40 the **m** of the younger James
Lk 18,20 honor your father and your **m**.'
Jn 19,27 "Behold, your **m**." And
Acts 1,14 Mary the **m** of Jesus, and
    12,12 the **m** of John who is called
Rom 16,13 the Lord, and his **m** and mine.
Gal 1,15 who from my **m**'s womb had
    4,26 she is our **m**. For it is written
Eph 5,31 leave [his] father and [his] **m**
    6, 2 "Honor your father and **m**."
1Thes 2, 7 nursing **m** cares for her
2Tm 1, 5 Lois and in your **m** Eunice
Heb 7, 3 Without father, **m**, or ancestry
Rv 17, 5 "Babylon the great, the **m** of

MOUNT (AIN) (AINS)

Gn 7,20 higher than the submerged **m**.
    8, 5 the tops of the **m** appeared.
    14,10 the rest fled to the **m**.
Ex 32,12 might kill them in the **m**
Jos 18,12 up westward into the **m**,
Jgs 3,27 went down from the **m**
    6, 2 the fire signals on the **m**,
    11,37 **m** to mourn my virginity
1Sm 26,20 hunting partridge in the **m**."
2Sm 1,21 **m** of Gilboa, may there be
1Kgs 19,11 wind was rending the **m**
    22,17 Israel scattered on the **m**,
2Chr 2, 1 cut the stone in the **m**,
Tb 1, 5 sacrifice on all the **m** of Galilee
    5,10 crossed all its plains and **m**,
Jdt 1,15 he overtook in the **m** of Ragae,
    3, 9 main ridge of the Judean **m**;
    5, 3 this that dwells in the **m**?
    6, 4 and the **m** shall be drunk
    7,10 on the height of the **m**
    15, 7 towns and villages in the **m**
    16,15 The **m** to their bases, and
1Mc 4, 5 hunt for them in the **m**,
    10,70 power against us in the **m**?
2Mc 9,28 in the **m** of a foreign land.
    10, 6 animals in caves on the **m**.

Jb 9, 5 removes the **m** before
    40,20 For the produce of the **m**
Ps 36, 7 justice is like the highest **m**;
    46, 4 rage and foam and **m**
    65, 7 you set up the **m**
    68,17 You rugged **m**, why look
    75, 7 the desert or from the **m**,
    80,11 **m** were covered by its shadow
    90, 2 Before the **m** were born,
    104,18 The high **m** are for wild goats;
    114, 4 The **m** skipped like rams;
    121, 1 raise my eyes toward the **m**.
    125, 2 As **m** surround Jerusalem,
    133, 3 down upon the **m** of Zion.
    144, 5 touch the **m** and make them
    147, 8 makes grass sprout on the **m**,
    148, 9 You **m** and all hills,
Prv 8,25 Before the **m** were settled
Song 2, 8 springing across the **m**,
    4, 8 from the leopards' **m**.
    8,14 a young stag on the **m**
Sir 43,16 before his might the **m** quake.
Is 54,10 Though the **m** leave their
Jer 3,23 the thronging **m**;
    9, 9 Over the **m**, break out in
    18,14 fresh down the **m**?
    46,18 Like Tabor among the **m**
Lam 4,19 They harassed us on the **m**
Bar 6,38 are like stones from the **m**;
    6,62 burn up the **m** and the forests,
Ez 6, 2 turn toward the **m** of Israel,
    7,16 escape and flee to the **m**
    18,15 does not eat on the **m**,
    19, 9 heard on the **m** of Israel.
    22, 9 feast on the **m**; in
    31,12 and left it on the **m**.
    35,12 against the **m** of Israel
    39, 4 Upon the **m** of Israel you shall
Hos 10, 8 shall cry out to the **m**, "Cover
Jl 2, 2 dawn spreading over the **m**,
    4,18 the **m** shall drip new wine,
Am 3, 9 "Gather about the **m** of Samaria
    9,13 grapes shall drip down the **m**,
Jon 2, 7 to the roots of the **m**;
Hb 3, 6 The eternal **m** are shattered,
    3,10 at sight of you the **m** tremble.
Hg 1,11 the land and upon the **m**;
Zec 6, 1 out from between two **m**;
    14, 5 the valley of those two **m**
Mal 1, 3 I made his **m** a waste,
Mi 4, 1 established higher than the **m**;
Na 3,18 are scattered upon the **m**,
Mk 13,14 Judea must flee to the **m**,
Lk 23,30 people will say to the **m**,
1Cor 13, 2 faith so as to move **m**,
Rv 16,20 Every island fled, and **m**

MOURN (ING)

Gn 23, 2 the customary **m** rites.
    37,35 I will go down **m** to
    50, 4 When that period of **m** was
Ex 33, 4 they went into **m**
Dt 34, 8 **m** for Moses. Now Joshua,
1Sm 6,19 The people went into **m** at this
2Sm 14, 2 who has been long in **m**
    19, 2 weeping and **m** for Absalom;
1Kgs 14,18 was buried with all Israel **m**
Ezr 10, 6 for he was in **m** over
Neh 1, 4 to weep and continued **m**
Tb 2, 6 shall be turned into **m**,
Est 4, 3 the Jews went into deep **m**,
    9,22 from **m** into festivity.
1Mc 1,39 her feasts were turned into **m**,
    1,40 exaltation was turned into **m**.
    9,41 wedding was turned into **m**,

13,26 **m** over him for many days
Jb 30,31 My harp is turned to **m**,
Ps 30,12 You changed my **m** into
43, 2 Why must I go about **m**,
137, 1 we sat **m** and weeping
Eccl 7, 2 go to the house of **m** than
Wis 14,15 afflicted with untimely **m**,
18,10 piteous wail of **m**
19, 3 in funeral rites and were **m**
Sir 22,11 Seven days of **m** for the dead,
26, 6 wife is heartache and **m**
38,17 Weeping bitterly, **m** fully,
Is 61, 3 of gladness in place of **m**,
Jer 14, 2 Her people sink down in **m**,
16, 5 not into a house of **m**,
31,13 I will turn their **m** into joy,
Lam 5,15 our dance has turned into **m**;
Bar 4,23 With **m** and lament I sent you
5, 1 take off your robe of **m**
Ez 26,16 They shall be clothed in **m**
27,32 In their **m** they utter a lament
Jl 1, 9 In **m** are the priests,
2,12 fasting, and weeping, and **m**;
Am 8,10 turn your feasts into **m**
Mi 1, 8 and **m** like the ostriches
Zec 12,11 that day the **m** in Jerusalem
12,11 be as great as the **m**
Mk 16,10 who were **m** and weeping.
Lk 8,52 All were weeping and **m** for her
Jas 4, 9 your laughter be turned into **m**
Rv 18,19 weeping and **m**: "Alas, alas,
21, 4 be no more death or **m**,

MOUTH (S)

Ex 4,15 put the words in his **m**.
Nm 22,38 what God puts in my **m**."
Dt 18,18 put my words into his **m**;
Jos 10,27 over the **m** of the cave
15, 5 Sea as far as the **m**
Jgs 18,19 put your hand over your **m**.
1Sm 1,12 Eli watched her **m**,
14,26 raise a hand to his **m** from it,
17,35 the prey from its **m**
2Sm 22, 9 a devouring fire from his **m**;
1Kgs 8,15 who with his own **m**
17,24 truly from your **m**."
2Kgs 4,34 on the bed, placing his **m**
2Chr 6,15 your own **m** you spoke it,
35,22 came from the **m** of God,
Ezr 1, 1 by word of **m** and in writing
Est 4C,20 to close the **m** of those
1Mc 9,55 his **m** was closed and he was
2Mc 6,18 open his **m** to eat pork. But
Jb 3, 1 Job opened his **m** and cursed
8,21 he fill your **m** with laughter,
15, 6 Your own **m** condemns you,
20,13 keeps it still within his **m**,
22,22 instruction from his **m**,
41, 6 open the doors of his **m**,
41,11 of his **m** go forth firebrands;
41,13 a flame pours from his **m**.
42, 5 of you by word of **m**,
Ps 17, 3 My **m** has not transgressed
19,15 the words of my **m**
33, 6 by the breath of his **m**
49, 4 My **m** shall speak wisdom,
66,14 and my **m** spoke in distress.
71,15 My **m** shall proclaim your
94, 4 How long will they **m** haughty
119,103 sweeter than honey to my **m**!
Prv 2, 6 from his **m** come knowledge
8,13 and the perverse **m** I hate.
10,32 but the **m** of the wicked,
14, 3 In the **m** of the fool is a
18, 4 The words from a man's **m**
20,17 but afterward his **m** will

26, 7 A proverb in the **m** of a
30,20 she eats, wipes her **m**,
31,26 She opens her **m** in wisdom,
Eccl 6, 7 All man's toil is for his **m**,
Song 1, 2 me with kisses of his **m**!
Wis 1,11 and a lying **m** slays the soul.
Sir 23, 9 your **m** form the habit
26,12 traveler with eager **m**
28,24 set barred doors over your **m**;
34, 8 wisdom is found in the **m**
40,30 In the **m** of the shameless
Is 59,21 nor the **m** of your children
Jer 1, 9 his hand and touched my **m**,
Ez 3, 2 So I opened my **m** and he
Dn 7, 8 like a man, and a **m** that
Hos 6, 5 by the words of my **m**;
Mt 4, 4 that comes forth from the **m** of
Lk 6,45 fullness of the heart the **m**
Acts 8,32 so he opened not his **m**.
Eph 4,29 should come out of your **m**
Jas 3,10 From the same **m** come
1Pt 2,22 deceit was found in his **m**."
Rv 10,10 In my **m** it was like sweet

MURDER (S) (ERS)

Dt 22,26 against his neighbor and **m** him
2Mc 4,35 the unjust **m** of the man.
4,36 about the **m** of Onias.
Ps 10, 8 to **m** the innocent in secret.
94, 6 the fatherless they **m**.
Wis 14,25 confusion—blood and **m**,
Jer 7, 9 Are you to steal and **m**,
41, 4 day after the **m** of Gedaliah,
Hos 4, 2 False swearing, lying, **m**,
Mt 15,19 come evil thoughts, **m**,
Mk 7,21 thoughts, unchastity, theft, **m**,
Lk 23,25 for rebellion and **m**,
1Tm 1, 9 kill their fathers or mothers, **m**

MYSTERY

Dn 2,18 heaven in regard to this **m**,
Mk 4,11 "The **m** of the kingdom of God
Rom 11,25 to be unaware of this **m**,
1Cor 15,51 Behold, I tell you a **m**.
Eph 3, 4 insight into the **m** of Christ,
5,32 This is a great **m**,
6,19 with boldness the **m**
Col 1,27 this among the Gentiles;
2, 2 knowledge of the **m** of God,
4, 3 to speak of the **m** of Christ,
2Thes 2, 7 For the **m** of lawlessness is
1Tm 3, 9 holding fast to the **m** of the
Rv 17, 5 which is a **m**, "Babylon
17, 7 will explain to you the **m**

N

NAKED

Gn 2,25 and his wife were both **n**,
Ex 28,42 to cover their **n** flesh
1Sm 19,24 day and night he lay **n**.
1Chr 21,16 with a **n** sword in his hand
2Chr 28,15 who were **n** they clothed
Tb 1,17 and my clothing to the **n**.
4,16 the **n** some of your clothing.
Jb 1,21 "**N** I came forth from my
22, 6 left them stripped **n**
26, 6 **n** before him is the nether
Eccl 5,14 **n** as he came, having nothing
Is 58, 7 Clothing the **n** when you see
Lam 4,21 you shall become drunk and **n**.
Ez 16, 7 but you were still stark **n**.
16,37 all sides and expose you **n**

18,16 the hungry and clothes the **n**;
23,29 for and leaving you stark **n**,
Hos 2, 5 Or I will strip her **n**,
Am 2,16 warriors shall flee **n** on that
Mi 1, 8 I go barefoot and **n**;
Mt 25,36 **n** and you clothed me, ill
Mk 14,52 cloth behind and ran off **n**.
Acts 19,16 they fled **n** and wounded
2Cor 5, 3 we shall not be found **n**.
Heb 4,13 everything is **n** and exposed
Rv 3,17 pitiable, poor, blind, and **n**.
16,15 that he may not go **n**
17,16 will leave her desolate and **n**;

NAME

Gn 2,19 of them would be its **n**.
Ex 3,15 "This is my **n** forever;
Dt 12,11 the dwelling place for his **n**
Jos 7, 9 efface our **n** from the earth.
Jgs 13,17 "What is your **n**, that we
1Sm 25, 5 and greet him in my **n**.
2Chr 7,14 upon whom my **n** has been
Ezr 6,12 God who causes his **n** to
Neh 9,10 you made for yourself a **n**
Tb 11,14 May his holy **n** be praised
Jdt 16, 1 exalt and acclaim his **n**. For
Ps 9,11 honor your **n** trust in you;
18,50 sing the praises of your **n**.
23, 3 for the sake of your **n**.
33,21 in your holy **n** we trust.
45,18 I will make your **n** renowned
66, 4 sing of your **n**!" Selah
72,17 May his **n** be blessed
83, 5 Israel's **n** be mentioned
91,14 whoever knows my **n** I
102, 9 they make my **n** a curse.
106, 8 saved them for his **n's** sake
113, 1 praise the **n** of the Lord.
129, 8 in the **n** of the Lord!"
138, 2 exalted over all your **n** and
145, 1 I will bless your **n** forever.
148,13 praise the Lord's **n**,
Prv 10, 7 but the **n** of the wicked will
18,10 The **n** of the Lord is a
21,24 Arrogant is the **n** for the
22, 1 A good **n** is more desirable
Eccl 7, 1 A good **n** is better than good
Song 1, 3 Your **n** spoken is a
Sir 41,13 but a good **n**, for days
Is 50,10 Trusting in the **n** of the LORD
Jer 15,16 Because I bore your **n**, O
Ez 20,22 acting for my **n's** sake, lest
Dn 2,20 "Blessed be the **n** of God
Hos 12, 6 hosts, the LORD is his **n**!
Am 9,12 nations that shall bear my **n**,
Zep 3, 9 call upon the **n** of the LORD,
Mal 3,20 for you who fear my **n**,
Mt 18,20 are gathered together in my **n**,
Mk 11, 9 comes in the **n** of the Lord!
Lk 19,38 comes in the **n** of the Lord.
Jn 1,12 those who believe in his **n**,
Acts 3,16 his **n** has made strong,
Rom 10,13 calls on the **n** of the Lord
1Cor 6,11 you were justified in the **n**
Phil 2,10 that at the **n** of Jesus every
2Tm 2,19 who calls upon the **n** of the
Heb 13,15 of lips that confess his **n**.
Jas 5,14 with oil in the **n** of the Lord,
1Pt 4,16 glorify God because of the **n**.
1Jn 5,13 believe in the **n** of the Son
Rv 13,17 image of the beast's **n** or the

NATION (S)

Gn 17, 4 father of a host of **n**.
Ex 34,24 I will drive out the **n** before
Dt 7, 1 seven **n** more numerous

Jos 23, 3   for you against all these n
Jgs   3, 1   The following are the n which
1Sm 8,20   too must be like other n,
2Kgs 17,15   the surrounding n whom
Est   3, 8   "Dispersed among the n
Ps 33,10   Lord foils the plan of n,
Sir 44,21   his descendants the n would
Is   2, 2   All n shall stream toward it;
Jer 46,28   all the n to which I have
Lam 1, 1   she who was mistress over n;
Ez 22, 4   object of scorn to the n
Jl   2,17   with the n ruling over them!
Na   3, 4   Who enslaved n with her
Mt 24, 9   will be hated by all n because
Rom 4,18   "the father of many n,"
Gal   3, 8   you shall all the n be
Rv   2,26   will give authority over the n.

NEAR

Gen 39,10   or even stay in her.
     45,10   where you will be n me—
Dt 30,14   something very n to you,
Jos 10,34   encamping n it, they
     19,11   wadi that is n Jokneam.
Jgs   3,19   where the idols are, n Gilgal,
     4,11   which was n Kedesh.
   15,15   n him was the fresh jawbone
Ru   2,14   Then as she sat n the reapers,
     4, 8   So the n relative, in saying
1Sm 1, 9   on a chair n the doorpost
   19,22   "At the sheds n Ramah."
   24, 2   in the desert n Engedi.
   29, 1   at the spring of Harod n
2Sm 11,21   Why did you go n the wall?'
   20, 8   in its sheath n his thigh,
2Kgs 4,27   Gehazi came n to push her
   23,19   n the cities of Samaria which
   25, 5   in the desert n Jericho,
1Chr 23, 1   and was n the end of his days
2Chr 6,36   to another land, far or n,
   14, 9   n Mareshah. Asa called
Neh 4, 6   When the Jews who lived n
Tb   6,18   never again show himself n her.
   11, 1   When they were n Kaserin,
Jdt   2,21   next encamped n the mountains
    7, 3   spring in the valley n Bethulia,
   13, 6   to the bedpost n the head
Est 4D,11   Come n!" Raising the golden
   9,20   both n and far, in all the
1Mc 3,46   Mizpah n Jerusalem,
   4,18   n us on the mountain. But
   7,45   from Adasa to n Gazara,
   8,12   both far and n, and all who
  11,67   pitched their camp n the waters
2Mc 4,42   they slew n the treasury.
   7,14   When he was n death, he
  13,14   he pitched his camp n Modein.
Jb   9,11   Should he come n me, I
  33,22   His soul draws n to the pit,
Ps 22,12   for trouble is n, and there
  38,18   I am very n to falling; my
  59, 5   Come n and see my plight!
  73,28   to be n God is my good,
  85,10   n indeed is salvation for the
  88, 4   my life draws n to Sheol.
 119,150   Malicious persecutors draw n
  120, 5   I lived the tents of Kedar!
  148,14   the people n to their God.
Prv 7, 8   along the street n the corner,
  27,10   Better is a neighbor n at hand
Song 1, 8   young ones n the shepherds'
Sir 12,12   Let him not stand n you,
  14,24   Who encamps n her house,
  38,28   So with the smith standing n
Is 55, 6   call him while he is n.
Jer 48,16   n at hand is Moab's ruin,
  52, 8   in the desert n Jericho,

Lam 4,15   Away, away, do not draw n!"
   4,18   Our end drew n, and came;
Ez   7, 7   The time has come, n is the
Jl   1,15   Alas, the day! for n is the day
Zep 1,14   great day of the Lord, n and
Mal 3, 5   I will draw n to you for
Mt 24,32   you know that summer is n.
  26,18   "My appointed time draws n;
Mk 2, 4   Unable to get n Jesus
  11, 1   they drew n to Jerusalem,
  13,29   know that he is n,
Lk 18,40   and when he came n,
  21,30   know that summer is now n;
Jn   6, 4   Passover was n.
  11,18   Bethany was n Jerusalem,
  19,20   crucified was n the city;
Acts 7,31   he drew n to look at it,
  22, 6   as I drew n to Damascus,
Rom 10, 8   "The word is n you, in
Eph 2,13   become n by the blood
   2,17   peace to those who were n,
Phil 4, 5   The Lord is n. Have no
Heb 7,19   we draw n to God.
  10,25   see the day drawing n.
  11,22   Joseph, n the end of his
Jas 4, 8   God, and he will draw n to
Rv 1, 3   for the appointed time is n.
  17, 1   harlot who lives n the
  22,10   for the appointed time is n.

NEED (Y)

Gn 26,24   You have no n to fear, since I
Ex 23, 6   deny one of your n
Lv 26,26   ten women will n but one
Dt 15, 8   him enough to meet his n.
2Sm 3,29   or one in n of bread!"
Tb 5,12   "Why? Do you n a tribe and a
Ps 50, 9   I n no bullock from your
  68,11   to the poor in their n.
  91, 8   You n simply watch;
 109,22   sorely in n; my heart is
Prv 3,24   you n not be afraid,
  25,16   eat only what you n,
  30, 8   only with the food I n;]
Wis 2,10   Let us oppress the n just man
Sir 11,23   "What do I n? What
  29,27   brother's visit I n the room!"
Am 4, 1   the weak and abuse the n
Mt 3,14   "I n to be baptized by you
Mk 2,17   do not n a physician, but
Lk 15,14   he found himself in dire n.
Acts 4,35   to each according to n.
1Cor 12,21   the feet, "I do not n you."
Eph 4,28   to share with one in n.
Phil 4,19   fully supply whatever you n,
1Thes 5, 1   have no n for anything to be
Heb 7,27   He has no n, as did the high
1Jn 2,27   do not n anyone to teach you.
Rv 22, 5   nor will they n light from lamp

NEIGHBOR

Ex 3,22   Every woman shall ask her n
Dt 5,20   witness against your n.
Ru 4,17   And the n women gave him
1Sm 15,28   given it to a n of yours,
  28,16   you and is with your n?
  28,17   given it to your n David.
2Sm 12,11   will give them to your n.
1Kgs 8,31   a man sins against his n
2Chr 6,22   any man sins against his n
Jb 16,21   between a man and his n.
  31, 9   lain in wait at my n's door;
Ps 15, 3   Who does not slander a n,
Prv 3,29   Plot no evil against your n,
  6,24   from your n's wife,
  12,26   The just man surpasses his n,

  17,18   who becomes surety for his n.
  25, 8   your n puts you to shame?
  26,19   the man who deceives his n,
  29, 5   The man who flatters his n
Wis 14,24   either waylays and kills his n,
Sir 16,26   one should ever crowd its n,
  28, 2   Forgive your n's injustice;
  29,20   Go surety for your n
Is 3, 5   every man his n. The child
  9,18   devours the flesh of his n.
  19, 2   n against neighbor, city
Jer 7, 5   you deals justly with his n;
  22,13   Who works his n without pay,
Bar 6,43   she mocks her n who
Ez 18, 6   n's wife, nor have relations
  33,26   defiles his n's wife—yet
Dn 13,61   plotted to impose on their n
Zec 8,10   set every man against his n.
  14,13   raised against that of his n.
Mt 5,43   'You shall love your n and
Mk 12,31   'You shall love your n as
Lk 10,29   "And who is my n?" Jesus
Acts 7,27   who was harming his n
Rom 13, 9   "You shall love your n as
  13,10   does no evil to the n;
  15, 2   us please our n for the good,
1Cor 10,24   but that of his n. Eat anything
Gal 5,14   love your n as yourself."
Eph 4,25   truth, each one to his n,
Jas 2, 8   "You shall love your n as

NETHERWORLD

Dt 32,22   to the depths of the n,
Tb 13, 2   to the depths of the n,
Mt 16,18   and the gates of the n
Acts 2,31   abandoned to the n nor did
Rv 1,18   keys to death and the n.

NEVER

Gn 8,21   "N again will I doom the
Dt 32,17   their fathers had n stood in
2Kgs 25,16   was n calculated. Each of the
2Chr 7,18   'There shall n be lacking
Ps 16, 8   I shall n be shaken.
Prv 27,20   world and the abyss are n
Sir 4,25   n gainsay the truth, and
Is 51, 6   my justice shall n be
Jer 33,17   n shall David lack a successor
Mt 7,23   'I n knew you. Depart from
Mk 3,29   will n have forgiveness, but is
Jn 4,14   water I shall give will n thirst;
1Cor 13, 8   endures all things. Love n
Gal 6,14   But may I n boast except in
2Pt 1,10   you will n stumble. For, in this
Rv 18,14   n again will one find them

NEW

Ex 1, 8   Then a n king, who knew
Lv 14,42   and n mortar shall be made
  23,16   present the n cereal offering
  26,10   to make room for the n.
Nm 18,27   threshing floor or n wine from
  28,14   This is the n moon holocaust
Dt 22, 8   "When you build a n house,
Jos 9,13   which were n when we
Jgs 5, 8   n gods were their choice; then
Ezr 9, 9   Thus he has given us n life
Jdt 16, 1   Sing to him a n song,
1Mc 4,53   law on the n altar of
  10,88   he accorded n honors
2Mc 2,29   architect of a n house
  10, 3   they made a n altar
Jb 32,19   Like a n wineskin with
Ps 33, 3   Sing to God a n song;
  81, 4   trumpet at the n moon,

96, 1 Sing to the LORD a **n** song;
144, 9 O God, a **n** song I will
Eccl 1, 9 Nothing is **n** under the sun.
Wis 19,18 produce **n** melody, while
Sir 24,23 in the days of the **n** fruits.
36, 5 Give **n** signs and work
Is 42,10 Sing to the Lord a **n** song,
Jer 31,31 I will make a **n** covenant
Ez 18,31 a **n** heart and a new spirit
Hos 4,11 Old wine and **n** deprive
9, 2 the **n** wine shall fail them.
Jl 4,18 mountains shall drip **n** wine,
Am 8, 5 "When will the **n** moon be
Zep 1,10 a wail from the **n** Quarter,
Zec 9,17 and **n** wine, the maidens!
Mt 9,17 they pour **n** wine into fresh
Mk 1,27 A **n** teaching with authority.
Lk 22,20 "This cup is the **n** covenant in
Jn 13,34 I give you a **n** commandment
Acts 17,19 **n** teaching is that you speak
1Cor 11,25 "This cup is the **n** covenant in
2Cor 3, 6 ministers of a **n** covenant,
Gal 6,15 but only a **n** creation. Peace
Eph 4,24 and put on the **n** self, created
Col 3,10 and have put on the **n** self,
Heb 8, 8 I will conclude a **n** covenant
1Pt 1, 3 great mercy gave us a **n** birth
2Pt 3,13 we await **n** heavens and a
1Jn 2, 7 I am writing no **n**
Rv 2,17 upon which is inscribed a **n**

NIGHT

Gn 1, 5 the darkness he called "**n**."
Ex 13,21 at **n** by means of a column
Dt 28,66 in dread both day and **n**,
Jos 1, 8 it by day and by **n**,
Jgs 16, 2 at the city gate all **n** long.
20, 4 Gibeah of Benjamin for the **n**.
Ru 3, 8 In the middle of the **n**, however,
1Sm 14,36 pursuit of the Philistines by **n**,
15,11 out to the Lord all **n**.
19,24 all that day and **n** he lay naked.
28, 8 came to the woman by **n**,
31,12 marching throughout the **n**,
2Sm 2,29 marched all **n** long through
4, 7 on the Arabah road all **n** long.
12,16 retiring for the **n** to lie
21,10 and the wild animals by **n**.
1Kgs 8,29 eyes watch **n** and day
8,59 present to him day and **n**,
2Kgs 8,21 He arose by **n** and broke
19,35 That **n** the angel of the Lord
25, 4 soldiers left the city by **n**
1Chr 17, 3 But that same **n** the word
2Chr 7,12 Solomon during the **n** and
21, 9 He arose by **n** and broke
35,14 the fatty portions until **n**;
Ezr 10, 6 he spent the **n** neither
Neh 2,13 I rode out at **n** by the
4,16 serve as a guard by **n**
9,19 column of fire by **n** cease
13,21 Why do you spend the **n**
Tb 7,11 all died on the very **n** they
8, 9 went to bed for the **n**.
Jdt 11, 5 lie to my lord this **n**,
13,14 by my hand this very **n**."
Est 6, 1 That **n** the king, unable
A,11 tried in every way, until **n**,
1Mc 5,29 army from that place by **n**,
11, 6 and spent the **n** there.
13,22 heavy fall of snow that **n**,
16, 4 they spent the **n** at Modein,
2Mc 13,10 upon the Lord **n** and day,
13,15 he made a **n** attack on
Jb 3, 7 May that **n** be barren;
17,12 Such men change the **n**

24,15 In the **n** the thief roams
39,28 dwells and spends the **n**,
Ps 19, 3 one **n** to the next imparts that
42, 4 been my food day and **n**,
63, 7 the **n** watches I will recall
77, 7 In the **n** I meditate in my heart
91, 5 fear the terror of the **n**
119,55 Even at **n** I remember your
136, 9 and stars to rule the **n**,
Prv 31,18 at **n** her lamp is undimmed.
Eccl 2,23 even at **n** his mind is not at
Song 3, 1 On my bed at **n** I sought him
Wis 17, 5 in lighting up that gloomy **n**.
18,14 the **n** in its swift course was
Sir 38,27 laboring **n** and day,
40, 5 cares at **n** disturb his sleep.
Is 21,11 how much longer the **n**?"
Jer 33,20 day, and my covenant with **n**,
Mt 24,43 hour of **n** when the thief was
Lk 2, 8 the **n** watch over their flock.
Jn 3, 2 He came to Jesus at **n** and
1Cor 11,23 on the **n** he was handed over,
1Thes 5, 2 come like a thief at **n**.
2Thes 3, 8 **n** and day we worked, so
1Tm 5, 5 supplications and prayers **n**
2Tm 1, 3 **n** and day. I yearn to
Rv 8,12 as did the **n**. Then I looked
21,25 and there will be no **n** there.

NOTHING

Ex 12,20 **n** leavened may you eat;
Dt 29,22 its soil being **n** but sulphur
Jos 11,15 He left **n** undone that the Lord
Jgs 13, 7 eat **n** unclean. For the boy
19,30 "**n** like this has been done
1Sm 10,16 But he mentioned **n** to him of
25,21 so that he missed **n**.
30,19 **n** was missing, small or great
2Sm 15,11 knowing **n** of the plan.
24,24 holocausts that cost **n**."
1Kgs 17,12 "I have **n** baked; there is
2Kgs 20,13 there was **n** in his house or in
1Chr 21,24 holocausts that cost me **n**."
2Chr 9, 2 **n** hidden from Solomon
Neh 2,16 had disclosed **n** to the Jews,
5,12 exact **n** further from them.
8,17 Israelites had done **n** of
Tb 7,11 I will eat or drink **n** until you
10, 7 had taken, and she ate **n**.
Jdt 9, 1 wearing **n** over her sackcloth.
Est 6, 3 replied, "**n** was done for him."
1Mc 11, 5 done; but the king said **n**.
2Mc 4,25 with **n** that made him worthy
14,23 where he did **n** out of place.
Jb 2,10 Through all this, Job said **n**
26, 7 suspends the earth over **n** at
28,13 Man knows **n** to equal it,
Ps 96, 5 of the nations all do **n**,
Prv 13, 7 yet has **n**; another pretends to
Eccl 3,22 I saw that there is **n** better for
Is 44, 9 Idol makers all amount to **n**,
Mt 17,20 it will move. **N** will be
Lk 8,17 will not become visible, and **n**
Jn 15, 5 without me you can do **n**.
1Cor 13, 2 not have love, I am **n**.
Gal 2,21 law, then Christ died for **n**.
1Tm 6, 7 we brought **n** into the world,
Heb 7,19 for the law brought **n** to
1Jn 2,10 and there is in him to cause

NUMEROUS

Ex 1, 9 "Look how **n** and powerful the
Dt 28,62 Of you who were **n** as the
Ps 69, 5 More **n** than the hairs of my
Ez 17,17 with a great army and **n**
Mt 21,36 more **n** than the first ones,

Gal 4,27 for more **n** are the children

O

OBEY

Dt 11,28 curse if you do not **o** the
Jos 24,24 the LORD, our God, and **o** his
Jgs 3, 4 whether they would **o** the
1Sm 12,15 But if you do not **o** the LORD
Ezr 7,26 Whoever does not **o** the law
1Mc 2,22 We will not **o** the words of the
Jer 42, 6 we will **o** the command of the
Mt 8,27 the winds and the sea **o**?"
Acts 5,32 has given to those who **o**
Rom 6,16 slaves of the one you **o**,
Eph 6, 1 Children, **o** your parents [in
Col 3,22 Slaves, **o** your human
1Jn 5, 2 when we love God and **o** his

OFFER (ING) (INGS)

Gn 4, 3 Cain brought an **o** to the Lord
Ex 29,38 shall **o** on the altar: two
Dt 12,14 but **o** them up in the place
1Mc 2,23 the sight of all to **o** sacrifice
Ps 4, 6 **o** fitting sacrifice and trust in
Mt 5,24 then come and **o** your gift.
Heb 5, 3 must make sin **o** for himself

OIL

Gn 28,18 and poured **o** on top of it. He
Ex 29, 7 Then take the anointing **o** and
Dt 14,23 wine and **o**, as well as the
1Kgs 17,16 the jug of **o** run dry, as the
Ps 23, 5 You anoint my head with **o**;
Prv 5, 3 her mouth is smoother than **o**;
Is 61, 3 To give them **o** of gladness
Mt 25, 3 brought no **o** with them,
Heb 1, 9 anointed you with the **o** of
Jas 5,14 anoint [him] with **o** in the

OLD

Gn 17,12 when he is eight days **o**,
Dt 32, 7 back on the days of **o**,
Ps 74,12 are my king from of **o**, winning
Prv 22, 6 go; even when he is **o**,
Sir 9,10 Discard not an **o** friend,
Mi 5, 1 Whose origin is from of **o**,
Mk 2,22 one pours new wine into **o**
Jn 3, 4 person once grown **o** be born
Acts 2,17 your **o** men shall dream
Rom 4,19 almost a hundred years **o**)
1Cor 5, 7 Clear out the **o** yeast, so that
Eph 4,22 you should put away the **o**
1Jn 2, 7 but an **o** commandment that

ONE

Gn 2,24 the two of them become **o**
Jos 21,45 of Israel was broken; every **o**
Ps 14, 3 what is right, not even **o**. Will
Eccl 4, 9 Two are better than **o**: they
Sir 1, 6 There is but **o**, wise and truly
Ez 37,22 and there shall be **o** prince for
Zec 14, 9 and his name the only **o**.
Mal 2,10 Have we not all the **o** Father?
Mk 10,21 "You are lacking in **o** thing.
Lk 10,42 There is need of only **o** thing.
Jn 10,30 The Father and I are **o**."
Rom 5,15 For if by that **o** person's
1Cor 6,16 two," it says, "will become **o**
Eph 4, 5 **o** faith, one baptism; one God
1Tm 2, 5 For there is **o** God. There is
Heb 9, 2 the outer **o**, in which were the
2Pt 3, 8 But do not ignore this **o** fact,
2Jn 5 let us love **o** another. For this
Jude 24 To the **o** who is able to keep
Rv 1, 3 Blessed is the **o** who reads

ONLY

Gn	7,23	o Noah and those with him
Nm	22,20	yet o on the condition that you
1Kgs	18,22	"I am the o surviving prophet
Ps	37, 8	it brings o harm.
Mt	9,21	"If o I can touch his cloak
Mk	9,29	"This kind can o come out
Jn	1,14	the glory as of the Father's o
Rom	8,17	joint heirs with Christ, if o we
1Tm	1,17	incorruptible, invisible, the o
	3, 2	irreproachable, married o
Heb	6, 3	we shall do this, if o God
	11,17	was ready to offer his o son,
1Pt	2,18	not o to those who are good
1Jn	4, 9	God sent his o Son into the
Jude	25	to the o God, our savior,
Rv	17,10	he must remain o a short

OPEN (ED)

Dt	28,12	The LORD will o up for you his
Jgs	3,25	they took the key and o them.
Prv	27, 5	Better is an o rebuke than a
Song	5, 2	"O to me, my sister, my
Is	42, 7	To o the eyes of the blind
Lam	3,46	All our enemies have o their
Mt	13,35	"I will o my mouth in parables,
Eph	6,19	o my mouth, to make known
Heb	10,20	new and living way he o for us
Rv	4, 1	had a vision of an o door to

OPPRESS (ED)

Ex	1,12	Yet the more they were o
Jb	20,19	Because he has o the poor
Zec	7,10	Do not o the widow or the

ORPHAN

Ex	22,21	any widow or o. If ever you
Ps	146, 9	sustains the o and the widow,
Sir	35,14	to the wail of the o, nor
Is	1,17	hear the o's plea, defend the
Jer	7, 6	the o, and the widow; if you
Hos	14, 4	for in you the o finds

OTHER (S)

Gn	29,27	I will give you the o too,
Ex	23,13	the name of any o god;
Dt	4,35	God and there is no o.
Jgs	2,19	following o gods in service
1Sm	8,20	must be like o nations, with a
2Kgs	17, 7	venerated o gods. They
2Chr	2, 4	God is greater than all o gods.
Ps	20, 8	Some rely on chariots, o on
Sir	45,18	Men of o families were
Na	3, 9	Egypt, and o without end
Dn	3,37	O Lord, beyond any o nation,
Mt	6,24	to one and despise the o.
Lk	17,34	one will be taken, the o left.
Jn	20,30	Now Jesus did many o signs
Eph	4,11	some as apostles, o as prophets
2Pt	3,16	the o scriptures. Therefore,

OX

Ex	20,17	nor his o or ass, nor anything
Dt	22,10	shall not plow with an o and
Jos	7,22	his o, his ass and his sheep
Prv	7,22	like an o that is led to
Is	65,25	shall eat hay like the o
Ez	1,10	side the face of an o,
Lk	13,15	on the sabbath untie his o or
1Cor	9, 9	You shall not muzzle an o

P

PAIN

Gn	3,16	in p shall you bring forth

Jb	33,19	chastened on his bed by p
Ps	69,27	added to the p of the one you
Sir	27,29	and p will consume them
	38, 7	which the doctor eases p and
Is	26,18	conceived and writhed in p,
Jer	15,18	Why is my p continuous, my
Jn	16,21	no longer remembers the p
1Pt	2,19	bears the p of unjust suffering
Rv	21, 4	or mourning, wailing or p,

PARTIALITY

2Chr	19, 7	no injustice, no p, no bribe-
Jb	13,10	even in secret you show p.
Prv	24,23	To show p in judgment is not
Mal	2, 9	but show p in your decisions.
Lk	20,21	you show no p, but teach
Rom	2,11	There is no p with God. All
Gal	2, 6	shows no p)—those of repute
Eph	6, 9	with him there is no p.
Jas	2, 9	But if you show p, you commit

PASSOVER

Ex	12,11	It is the P of the LORD. For
Nm	9, 2	Israelites to celebrate the P
Dt	16, 1	of Abib by keeping the P of
Jos	5,11	On the day after the P they
2Kgs	23,21	observe the P of the LORD,
2Chr	30, 1	to celebrate the P in honor of
Ezr	6,19	The exiles kept the P on the
Mk	14,12	when they sacrificed the P
Lk	22, 8	for us to eat the P." They
Jn	6, 4	The Jewish feast of P was
Acts	12, 4	him before the people after P.
Heb	11,28	By faith he kept the P and

PATH

2Kgs	21,22	and did not follow the p of the
Tb	5,14	not stray from the right p;
Jdt	13,16	has protected me in the p
2Mc	2, 6	up intending to mark the p,
Jb	28, 7	the hawk's eye seen that p.
Ps	23, 3	guide me along the right p
Prv	4,26	Survey the p for your feet,
Sir	37,15	set your feet in the p of truth.
Mt	13,19	The seed sown on the p is the
Lk	1,79	guide our feet into the p of
Rom	4,12	follow the p of faith that our

PATIENT

Neh	9,30	You were p with them for
Jb	6,11	limit that I should be p?
Eccl	7, 8	better is the p spirit than the
Sir	1,20	A p man need stand firm but
Mt	18,29	'Be p with me, and I will
1Cor	13, 4	Love is p, love is kind. It is
1Thes	5,14	support the weak, be p with
Jas	5, 7	Be p, therefore, brothers, until
2Pt	3, 9	but he is p with you, not
Rv	6,11	they were told to be p a little

PAY

Ex	22, 2	he shall be sold to p for his
Dt	24,15	You shall p him each day's
1Mc	2,68	p back the Gentiles what they
Ps	45,11	understand; p me careful
Prv	6,31	be caught he must p back
Mt	22,17	Is it lawful to p the census tax
Rom	13, 7	to this very thing, P to all their
2Thes	1, 9	These will p the penalty of
Phlm	19	I will p. May I not tell you
Jas	2, 3	and you p attention to the one

PEACE

Lv	26, 6	I will establish p in the land,
Nm	6,26	you kindly and give you p!
Dt	20,10	first offer it terms of p.

Jos	11,19	no city made p with the
1Sm	1,17	Eli said, "Go in p, and may the
2Sm	10,19	then made p with the
1Chr	19,19	they made p with David and
1Mc	14,11	He brought p to the land, and
Jb	22,21	with him to be at p.
Ps	119,165	of your teaching have much p;
Prv	12,20	those who counsel p have joy.
Eccl	3, 8	war, and a time of p.
Wis	3, 3	But they are in p. For if
Sir	13,17	Can there be p between the
Is	26, 3	firm purpose you keep in p;
Jer	6,14	"P, p!" they say, though
Lam	3,17	My soul is deprived of p,
Bar	3,14	light of the eyes, and p.
Ez	37,26	with them a covenant of p;
Mi	5, 4	the earth; he shall be p.
Hg	2, 9	this place I will give p, says
Mt	10,34	I have come to bring p upon
Mk	9,50	you will have p with one
Lk	19,38	p in heaven and glory in
Jn	14,27	p I leave with you; my
Acts	10,36	he proclaimed p through
Rom	8, 6	the spirit is life and p. For
1Cor	7,15	God has called you to p.
2Cor	13,11	live in p, and the God of love
Gal	5,22	joy, p, patience, kindness,
Eph	2,17	He came and preached p to
Phil	4, 7	Then the p of God that
Col	3,15	the p into which you were also
1Thes	5,13	Be at p among yourselves.
2Thes	3,16	May the Lord of p himself give
2Tm	2,22	faith, love, and p,
Heb	12,14	Strive for p with everyone,
Jas	3,18	sown in p for those who
1Pt	3,11	seek p and follow after it. For
2Pt	3,14	or blemish before him, at p.
Rv	6, 4	power to take p away from the

PEOPLE

Gn	11, 6	while they are one p, all
Ex	3,10	to Pharaoh to lead my p, the
Nm	11,11	burden me with all this p?
	21, 7	Then the p came to Moses
Dt	31,16	and then this p will take to
Jos	24,25	made a covenant with the p
Jgs	2, 7	The p served the LORD during
Ru	1,16	your p shall be my people,
1Sm	10,24	like him among all the p!"
2Sm	7,10	fix a place for my p Israel;
1Kgs	18,39	Seeing this, all the p fell
2Kgs	25,11	exile the last of the p
1Chr	29,17	joy I have seen your p here
2Chr	36,16	of the LORD against his p was
Ezr	3, 1	the p gathered at Jerusalem
Neh	1,10	are your servants, your p,
Tb	3,10	"No! I would level this insult
Jdt	8, 9	the harsh words which the p,
Est	7, 3	spare the lives of my p.
1Mc	5, 4	and a stumblingblock to the p
2Mc	5,19	for the sake of the p.
Ps	81,12	But my p did not listen to my
Prv	14,34	but sin is a p's disgrace. The
	24,24	p will denounce him; But
Wis	16,20	you nourished your p with
Sir	36,11	Show mercy to the p called by
Is	9, 1	The p who walked in
Jer	7,16	do not intercede for this p;
Lam	4, 6	of the daughter of my p is
Bar	2,35	and they shall be my p; and
Ez	36,28	you shall be my p, and I will
	46,24	cook the sacrifices of the p."
Dn	10,14	to your p in the days to come
Hos	4,14	So must a p without
Jl	2,18	and took pity on his p.
Am	9,14	the restoration of my p Israel;

Ob 13 not the gate of my p on the
Jon 3, 5 when the p of Nineveh
Mi 6, 3 O my p, what have I done to
Na 3,18 Your p are scattered upon the
Hb 1, 6 that bitter and unruly p, That
Zec 8, 7 Lo, I will rescue my p from the
13, 9 "They are my p," and they
Mt 1,21 he will save his p from their
2, 6 who is to shepherd my p
4,16 the p who sit in darkness
Mk 7, 6 This p honors me with their
8,27 "Who do p say that I am?"
Lk 1,17 to prepare a p fit for the Lord."
2,10 will be for all the p.
7,31 what shall I compare the p of
Jn 11,50 should die instead of the p, so
17, 2 gave him authority over all p,
Acts 15,14 the Gentiles a p for his name.
Rom 15,10 O Gentiles, with his p."
16,18 For such p do not serve our
1Cor 10,15 am speaking as to sensible p;
16,16 be subordinate to such p and
2Cor 11,13 For such p are false apostles,
Gal 1,10 am I seeking to please p?
2,12 For, until some p came from
Phil 2,29 all joy and hold such p in
1Thes 1, 5 You know what sort of p we
5, 3 When p are saying, "Peace
2Thes 3, 2 from perverse and wicked p,
3,12 Such p we instruct and urge
1Tm 1, 6 Some p have deviated from
6, 5 p with corrupted minds, who
6,21 By professing it, some p have
2Tm 3, 2 p will be self-centered and
Ti 3,14 But let our p, too, learn to
Heb 2,17 expiate the sins of the p.
8,10 and they shall be my p.
Jas 2,12 speak and so act as p who
1Pt 2,10 you were "no p" but now you
2,15 the ignorance of foolish p.
2Pt 2, 1 false prophets among the p,
2, 7 conduct of unprincipled p
Jude 16 These p are complainers,
Rv 18, 4 "Depart from her, my p, so as
21, 3 and they will be his p and God

PERFECT
1Chr 28, 9 and serve him with a p heart
2Mc 3, 1 the holy city lived in p peace
9,15 he would put on p equality
Jb 36, 4 the one p in knowledge I set
37,16 work of him who is p in
Ps 19, 8 law of the LORD is p, refreshing
50, 2 From Zion God shines forth, p
Prv 4,18 that grows in brilliance till p
Song 6, 9 alone is my dove, my p one,
Wis 9, 6 Indeed, though one be p
Sir 21,11 he who is in fear of the LORD
Ez 16,14 your beauty, p as it was,
Mt 5,48 So be p, just as your heavenly
Acts 3,16 it has given him this p health,
Rom 12, 2 is good and pleasing and p.
1Cor 13,10 when the p comes, the partial
2Cor 7, 1 making holiness p in the fear
12, 9 for power is made p in
Phil 3,12 have already attained p
Col 1,28 may present everyone p in
4,12 so that you may be p and
1Tm 3, 4 under control with p dignity;
Heb 2,10 the leader to their salvation p
5, 9 and when he was made p, he
Jas 1, 4 so that you may be p and
1,25 one who peers into the p law
1Jn 4,18 but p love drives out fear
4,18 who fears is not yet p in love.

PERISH
Gn 6,17 everything on earth shall p.
Est 4,14 your father's house will p.
Ps 102,27 They p, but you remain;
Prv 11,10 wicked p, there is jubilation.
Wis 4,19 and their memory shall p.
Is 60,12 the people or kingdom shall p
Zec 11, 9 what is to p, let it perish,
Lk 13, 3 you will all p as they did!
Jn 3,16 believes in him might not p
Rom 2,12 outside the law will also p
Col 2,22 things destined to p with use;
Heb 1,11 They will p, but you remain;
2Pt 3, 9 not wishing that any should p

PERSECUTE (D)
2Mc 8,28 to the p and to widows
Jb 19,28 "How shall we p him,
Ps 119,86 Men p me without cause
Mt 5,11 when they insult you and p
Jn 15,20 they will also p you.
Acts 22, 4 I p this Way to death

PERSUADE
2Mc 11,14 promising to p the king also,
Acts 26,28 "You will soon p me to play
2Cor 5,11 we try to p others;

PHAROAH
Neh 9,10 wonders against P,

PHILISTINE (S)
Jgs 3,31 Anath, who slew six hundred P
2Chr 9,26 to the land of the P
Zec 9, 6 destroy the pride of the P

PILLAR
Gn 19,26 turned into a p of salt.
Dt 16,22 shall you erect a sacred p,
Rv 3,12 make into a p in the temple

PITY
Ex 2, 6 was moved with p for him
Dt 7,16 to look on them with p,
Jgs 2,18 p on their distressful cries
1Sm 24,11 but I took p on you instead
Tb 3,15 have p on me;
Jdt 6,19 Have p on the lowliness
Est 4C,10 have p on your inheritance
2Mc 4,37 deeply grieved and full of p;
Ps 72,13 He shows p to the needy
Prv 6,34 p on the day of vengeance
Lk 16,24 'Father Abraham, have p

PLAGUE
2Chr 6,28 whenever there is a p or
Ps 39,11 Take your p away from me;
Eccl 6, 2 is vanity and a dire p.
Wis 16, 3 the creatures sent to p them
Sir 40, 9 p and bloodshed,
Bar 2,25 hunger and the sword and p.
Ez 33,27 shall die by the p.
Hb 3, 5 and the p follows in his steps.
Rv 16,21 blasphemed God for the p

PLANT
Gn 1,11 p that bears seed
Lv 19,23 p any fruit tree there,
Dt 6,11 groves that you did not p;
2Sm 7,10 I will p them so that they may
2Kgs 19,29 p vineyards and eat their fruit
1Chr 17, 9 I will p them in it to dwell
Jb 30, 4 the roots of the broom p
Ps 44, 3 You rooted out nations to p
Eccl 3, 2 a time to p, and a time

Sir 3, 9 curse uproots the growing p.
Is 17,10 you p your pagan plants
Jer 1,10 demolish, to build and to p.
Ez 16, 7 grow like a p in the field.
Am 9,14 p vineyards and drink
Jon 4, 6 LORD God provided a gourd p,
Mi 1, 6 a place to p for vineyards;
Mt 15,13 p that my heavenly Father

PLEASE (D) (PLEASING)
Ps 69,32 My song will p the LORD more
Prv 2,10 knowledge will p your soul,
Sir 2,16 fear the LORD seek to p him,
Is 39, 2 Hezekiah was p at this
Jer 6,20 your sacrifices p me not.
Jon 4, 3 LORD, p take my life from me
Acts 12, 3 he saw that this was p
1Cor 7,32 how he may p the Lord.
2Cor 5, 9 Therefore, we aspire to p
Gal 1,10 Or am I seeking to p people?
1Thes 2, 4 not as trying to p human
Heb 11, 6 it is impossible to p him,

PLEASURE
1Chr 29,17 you take p in uprightness.
Jdt 8,17 if it is his good p.
Est 1, 8 the good p of everyone.
Jb 10, 3 Is it a p for you to oppress,
Ps 51,20 Zion prosper in your good p;
Prv 21,17 loves p will suffer want;
Is 1,11 I find no p.
Jer 14,10 The LORD has no p in them;
Ez 18,23 derive any p from the death
Heb 11,25 the fleeting p of sin.

POOR
Lv 19,10 for the p and the alien.
Dt 15,11 hand to your p and needy
Tb 2, 2 and try to find a p man
Jb 20,19 has oppressed the p,
Ps 14, 6 crush the hopes of the p,
Prv 13, 7 another pretends to be p,
Eccl 4,13 Better is a p but wise youth
Is 3,14 the loot wrested from the p
Jer 22,16 to the weak and the p,
Ez 16,49 no help to the p and needy.
Am 2, 6 and the p man for a pair
Zec 7,10 orphan, the alien or the p;
Mt 5, 3 "Blessed are the p in spirit,
Mk 12,42 A p widow also came
Lk 4,18 bring glad tidings to the p.
Jn 12, 8 have the p with you,
Rom 15,26 some contribution for the p
2Cor 8, 9 for your sake he became p
Gal 2,10 to be mindful of the p,
Jas 2, 2 a p person in shabby clothes

POUR
Ex 30, 9 you p out a libation upon it
Lv 2, 1 shall p oil on it
Dt 12,16 p it out on the ground
1Kgs 18,34 "and p it over the holocaust
Jb 10,10 Did you not p me out as milk,
Ps 62, 9 P out your hearts to God
Is 44, 3 p out water upon the thirsty
Mt 9,17 p new wine into fresh
Acts 2,17 'that I will p out a portion

POWER
Ex 18,11 the p of the Egyptians."
Dt 8,17 'It is my own p
1Sm 7, 3 the p of the Philistines."
1Chr 29,11 O LORD, are grandeur and p,
2Chr 20, 6 In your hand is p and might,
Tb 13, 6 and show his p and majesty
Jb 2, 6 "He is in your p; only spare

Power (continued)

Ps	10,10	fall into the **p** of the wicked,
Prv	3,27	it is in your **p** to do it for him
Is	10,13	"By my own **p** I have done it,
Jer	10, 5	neither is it in their **p**
Hos	13,14	the **p** of the nether world?
Na	1, 3	yet great in **p**,
Zec	11, 6	into the **p** of his neighbor,
Mt	22,29	scriptures or the **p** of God.
Lk	1,35	and the **p** of the Most High
Acts	1, 8	receive **p** when the holy Spirit
Rom	1,16	the **p** of God for the salvation
1Cor	2, 4	demonstration of spirit and **p**,
2Cor	4, 7	that the surpassing **p**
Gal	3,22	all things under the **p** of sin,
Eph	1,19	greatness of his **p**
Phil	3,10	the **p** of his resurrection
Col	1,11	strengthened with every **p**,
1Thes	1, 5	also in **p** and in the holy Spirit
2Thes	1, 9	from the glory of his **p**
Heb	2,14	who has the **p** of death,
1Pt	1, 5	the **p** of God are safeguarded
2Pt	1, 3	His divine **p** has bestowed
Jude	25	our Lord be glory, majesty, **p**,
Rv	4,11	glory and honor and **p**,

PRAISE

Ex	15, 2	He is my God, I **p** him;
Dt	26,19	then raise you high in **p**
2Sm	22,50	I will sing **p** to your name,
1Chr	16, 4	to celebrate, thank, and **p**
2Chr	6,24	they return and **p** your name,
Ezr	3,10	cymbals to **p** the LORD
Neh	9, 5	above all blessing and **p**."
2Mc	8,27	with fervent **p**
Ps	7,18	I **p** the justice of the LORD
Prv	27, 2	Let another **p** you
Is	25, 1	extol you and **p** your name;
Jer	33, 9	my joy, my **p**, my glory,
Dn	2,23	I give thanks and **p**,
Mt	6, 2	to win the **p** of others.
Lk	19,37	began to **p** God aloud
Jn	5,44	accept **p** from one another
Rom	2,29	his **p** is not from human
2Cor	6, 8	dishonor, insult and **p**.
Eph	1,12	for the **p** of his glory,
1Thes	2, 6	nor did we seek **p**
Heb	13,15	offer God a sacrifice of **p**,
Jas	5,13	He should sing **p**.
Rv	19, 5	"**P** our God, all you

PRAY

Ex	8, 5	**p** for you and your servants
1Sm	7, 5	that I may **p** to the LORD
1Kgs	8,35	repent of their sin, and **p**,
2Chr	7,14	humble themselves and **p**,
Ezr	6,10	God of heaven and **p**
Jb	42, 8	and let my servant Job **p**
Ps	5, 3	To you I **p**, O LORD;
Jer	29, 7	**p** for it to the LORD
Mt	5,44	**p** for those who persecute
Lk	6,28	**p** for those who mistreat you
Jn	17,20	"I **p** not only for them,
Rom	8,26	know how to **p** as we ought,
1Cor	14,15	I will **p** with the spirit,
Eph	6,18	**p** at every opportunity
Col	4, 3	at the same time, **p** for us,
1Thes	5,17	**P** without ceasing.
2Thes	1,11	we always **p** for you,
Jas	5,13	suffering? He should **p**.
Jude	20	**p** in the holy Spirit.

PRECEPT (S)

Ex	15,26	keep all his **p**
Ps	19, 9	The **p** of the Lord are right
Eccl	8, 2	Observe the **p** of the king,
Mk	7, 7	teaching as doctrines human **p**.'

PRECIOUS

Gn	30,20	God has brought me a **p** gift.
Ex	28,17	mount four rows of **p** stones
1Sm	26,21	have held my life **p** today.
1Kgs	10, 2	gold, and **p** stones.
2Chr	3, 6	decorated the building with **p**
Tb	13,16	your walls with **p** stones.
Jdt	10,21	emeralds and other **p** stones.
Est	4C,13	In place of her **p** ointments
1Mc	1,23	silver and the **p** vessels;
Ps	72,14	for **p** is their blood
Prv	1,13	All kinds of **p** wealth
Is	28,16	A **p** cornerstone as a sure
1Pt	1,19	but with the **p** blood of Christ
2Pt	1, 4	**p** and very great promises,

PRESENCE

Ex	8,26	Moses left Pharaoh's **p**,
Nm	4, 7	On the table of the **p** they
1Sm	6,20	Who can stand in the **p**?
2Kgs	13,23	cast them out from his **p**.
Ps	16,11	abounding joy in your **p**,
Is	26,17	so were we in your **p**, O LORD.
Jer	15,19	in my **p** you shall stand;
Bar	2,14	favor in the **p** of our captors,
Ez	16,50	abominable crimes in my **p**;
Hos	6, 2	to live in his **p**.
Acts	2,28	with joy in your **p**.'
1Thes	2,19	boast of in the **p** of our Lord
2Thes	1, 9	from the **p** of the Lord
Jude	24	in the **p** of his glory,

PRIDE

Dt	17,20	countrymen through **p**,
2Chr	32,26	humbled himself for his **p**—
Jdt	9, 9	See their **p**, and send forth
2Mc	5,21	carried away was he with **p**.
Jb	20, 6	Though his **p** mount up
Ps	73, 6	**p** adorns them as a necklace
Prv	11, 2	When **p** comes, disgrace
Is	25,11	He will bring low their **p**
Dn	4,34	those who walk in **p**
Am	8, 7	sworn by the **p** of Jacob
2Cor	7, 4	I have great **p** in you;
Jas	1, 9	circumstances should take **p**

PRIEST (HOOD)

Gn	14,18	being a **p** of God Most High,
Ex	29, 9	Thus shall the **p** be theirs
Lv	1,13	The **p** shall offer them up
Nm	5,10	become the property of the **p**
Ezr	2,62	they were degraded from the **p**
Ps	110, 4	you are a **p** forever."
Heb	7, 5	who receive the office of **p**

PRISON

Ps	142, 8	Lead me out of my **p**,
Mt	25,36	in **p** and you visited me.'
Heb	10,34	the sufferings of those in **p**
1Pt	3,19	preach to the spirits in **p**,
Rv	20, 7	will be released from his **p**

PROCLAIM (ED)

Lv	23,37	shall **p** a sacred assembly,
Dt	27,14	"The Levites shall **p** aloud
2Sm	22,50	will I **p** you, O LORD,
1Chr	16, 9	**p** all his wondrous deeds.
Tb	11,17	Before them all Tobit **p**
Ps	2, 7	I will **p** the decree of the LORD
Is	12, 4	**p** how exalted is his name
Jer	7, 2	and there **p** this message
Zec	9,10	and he shall **p** peace
Mt	11, 5	have the good news **p** to them.
Lk	4,18	He has sent me to **p** liberty
Acts	26,23	**p** light both to our people

Power (continued)

1Cor	11,26	you **p** the death of the Lord
Col	1,28	It is he whom we **p**,
1Pt	1,25	word that has been **p** to you.

PROMISE

Nm	30, 3	exactly the **p** he has uttered.
Jos	23,14	**p** has been fulfilled for you
2Sm	7,28	made this generous **p**
1Kgs	8,20	the LORD has fulfilled the **p**
Neh	5,13	who fails to keep this **p**,
1Mc	13,19	but Trypho broke his **p**
Ps	77, 9	Has the **p** failed for all ages?
Acts	2,39	For the **p** is made to you
Rom	4,13	the **p** was made to Abraham
Gal	3,14	receive the **p** of the Spirit
Eph	2,12	to the covenants of **p**,
1Tm	4, 8	since it holds a **p** of life
Heb	6,13	God made the **p** to Abraham,
2Pt	3, 9	Lord does not delay his **p**,

PROPHECY

2Sm	7,25	confirm for all time the **p** you
1Kgs	2,27	thus fulfilling the **p**
2Kgs	1,17	in fulfillment of the **p**
2Chr	10,15	ordained to fulfill the **p**
Neh	6,12	he voiced this **p**
Prv	29,18	Without **p** the people become
Sir	24,31	I pour out instruction like **p**
Ez	30, 2	Son of man, speak this **p**
Dn	9,24	vision and **p** ratified,
1Cor	12,10	deeds; to another **p**;
2Pt	1,20	there is no **p** of scripture
Rv	19,10	Jesus is the spirit of **p**."

PROPHESY

Jdt	6, 2	you, Achior, to **p** among us
Wis	14,28	with enjoyment, or **p** lies,
Ezr	5, 1	**p** to the Jews in Judah
Jer	12,21	"Do not **p** in the name
Ez	4, 7	with bared arm you shall **p**
Am	2,12	the prophets not to **p**.
Zec	13, 4	ashamed to **p** his vision,
Mt	7,22	did we not **p** in your name?
Acts	2,17	and your daughters shall **p**,
1Cor	13, 9	and we **p** partially,
Rv	10,11	"You must **p** again about

PROPHET

Ex	7, 1	brother shall act as your **p**.
Nm	12, 6	there be a **p** among you,
Dt	13, 2	there arises among you a **p**
1Sm	3,20	Samuel was an accredited **p**
1Kgs	1, 8	Nathan the **p**,
2Kgs	5, 8	there is a **p** in Israel."
2Chr	35,18	time of the **p** Samuel,
Ez	2, 5	know that a **p** has been
Hos	9, 7	"The **p** is a fool,
Am	7,14	"I was no **p**,
Hb	1, 1	Habakkuk the **p**
Hg	1, 1	came through the **p** Haggai
Zec	13, 4	On that day, every **p** shall be
Mal	3,23	will send you Elijah, the **p**,
Lk	1,76	called **p** of the Most High,
Jn	1,21	"Are you the **p**?"
Acts	8,28	he was reading the **p** Isaiah.
1Cor	14,37	thinks that he is a **p**
Rv	16,13	the mouth of the false **p**.

PROUD

1Mc	1, 3	became **p** and arrogant.
Ps	31,19	**p** lips that attack the just
Prv	16, 5	**p** man is an abomination
Is	2,12	all that is **p** and arrogant,
2Tm	3, 2	lovers of money, **p**, haughty,
Jas	4, 6	"God resists the **p**, but gives

PROVIDE

Gn   22, 8 "God himself will p the sheep
Is   25, 6 will p for all peoples
Ez   39,19 the slaughter which I will p
Dn   11,39 shall p with abundant honor;
Mt   6,30 not much more p for you,
Acts 23,24 p mounts for Paul to ride
1Cor 10,13 he will also p a way out,
1Tm   5, 8 does not p for relatives

PUNISH

Ex   32,34 is time for me to p,
Lv   26,16 p you with terrible woes—
2Sm 24,17 p me and my kindred."
1Kgs 8,32 Condemn the wicked and p
1Chr 21, 7 who began to p Israel.
Tb   3, 3 p me not for my sins
Is   13,11 I will p the world for its evil
Jer   2,19 your own infidelities p you.
Zep   1,12 I will p the men who thicken
Acts 4,21 finding no way to p them,

PURE

Jb   11, 4 you say: "My teaching is p,
Ps   19,10 fear of the LORD is p,
Prv 15,26 the p speak what is pleasing
Is   13,12 more rare than p gold,
Hb   1,13 Too p are your eyes to look
2Cor 11, 3 sincere [and p] commitment
Phil 4, 8 just, whatever is p,
1Tm   1, 5 love from a p heart,
Heb 10,22 bodies washed in p water.
Jas   1,27 Religion that is p and
1Jn   3, 3 makes himself p,

PURSUE

Ex   15, 9 The enemy boasted, "I will p
Dt   19, 6 his anger p the homicide
Jos   2, 5 p your enemies,
1Sm 26,18 "Why does my lord p his
2Sm 20, 6 servants and p him,
1Chr 14,14 "Do not try to p them, but
Jdt 14, 4 p them and strike them down
1Mc   9,48 but the enemy did not p them
Jb   13,25 or p a withered straw?
Ps   34,15 seek peace and p it.
Rom   9,30 who did not p righteousness,
1Tm   6,11 p righteousness, devotion,

Q

QUESTION

Ex   22, 8 q of dishonest appropriation,
Nm   5,15 for an appeal in a q of guilt.
Jgs   9, 2 "Put this q to all the citizens
Jb   38, 3 I will q you,
Mt   22,23 They put this q to him,
Mk   11,29 I shall ask you one q.

QUICK

Prv 14,29 q-tempered man displays
Eccl 5, 1 q to make a promise
Sir   8,16 quarrel with a q-tempered
Jas   1,19 be q to hear,

QUIET

Nm   13,30 q the people toward Moses,
Jgs 18,27 a q and trusting people;
2Kgs 11,20 rejoiced and the city was q,
1Chr 4,40 spacious, q, and peaceful.
1Mc   7,50 the land of Judah was q.
2Mc 14, 6 peace and q. For this reason,
Jb   20,20 has known no q in his greed,
Ps   35,20 but against the q in the land

Eccl 9,17 "The q words of the wise
Lk   4,35 "Be q! Come out of him!"
1Tm   2, 2 lead a q and tranquil life

R

RACE

2Mc   7,28 human r came into existence.
Eccl 9,11 the r is not won
Acts 4,12 given to the human r
1Cor 9,24 all run in the r, but only one
Gal   1,14 contemporaries among my r,
2Tm   4, 7 I have finished the r;
Heb 12, 1 persevere in running the r
1Pt   2, 9 "a chosen r, a royal
Rv   7, 9 nation, r, people, and tongue.

RAIN

Gn   7, 4 from now I will bring r down
Ex   9,18 I will r down such fierce hail
Lv   26, 4 give you r in due season,
Dt   11,11 drinks in r from the heavens,
1Sm 12,17 he will send thunder and r.
2Sm   1,21 neither dew nor r upon you,
1Kgs 17, 1 shall be no dew or r
Mt   5,45 causes r to fall on the just
Jas   5,17 earnestly that it might not r,

RAISE (D)

Dt   18,18 I will r up for them a prophet
1Sm 14,26 r a hand to his mouth
2Sm   7,12 I will r up your heir after you
1Kgs 14,14 will r up for himself a king
2Kgs 23,35 to r the amount Pharaoh
2Chr 5,13 and when they r the sound
Tb   3,12 I turn my face and r my eyes.
Jdt   1, 3 At the gates he r towers
2Mc   7, 9 will r us up to live again
Jb   30,22 You r me up and drive me
Ps   37,34 God will r you to possess
Prv   2, 3 understanding r your voice;
Sir 36, 2 R your hand against
Is   2, 4 nation shall not r the sword
Jer 23, 5 I will r up a righteous shoot
Bar   6,26 worshipers must r them up.
Ez   4, 2 R a siege against it: build
Hos   6, 2 the third day he will r us up,
Am   9,11 I will r up the fallen hut
Zec 11,16 For I will r up a shepherd
Mk   6,14 John the Baptist has been r
Lk   21,28 r your heads because your
Jn   6,39 I should r it [on] the last day
1Cor 15,15 whom he did not r

RANSOM

Ex   21,30 he must pay in r for his life
Lv   25,51 he shall pay back as r;
Tb   5,19 let it be a r for our son!
Is   50, 2 my hand too short to r?
Mt   20,28 give his life as a r for many."
1Tm   2, 6 who gave himself as r for all.

READ

Dt   17,19 r it all the days
Jos   8,34 r aloud all the words
2Kgs 23, 2 r out to them.
Neh   8, 8 Ezra r plainly from the book
Jer 36, 6 r publicly in the LORD's house
2Cor 3, 2 known and r by all,

REAP

Jb   4, 8 sow trouble, r the same.
Ps   126, 5 sow in tears will r with cries
Hos   8, 7 they shall r the whirlwind;
Jn   4,38 r what you have not worked

2Cor 9, 6 sparingly will also r sparingly,
Gal   6, 7 will r only what he sows,

REBEL

Nm   14, 9 But do not r against the LORD!
1Sm 12,14 r against the LORD's
Sir 46, 7 they opposed the r assembly,
Is   48, 8 a r you were called from birth
Jer   3,12 r Israel, says the LORD,

REBUKE

2Sm 22,16 At the r of the LORD,
2Kgs 19, 3 distress, of r, and of
Jb   26,11 stunned at his thunderous r;
Ps   141, 5 let them r me;
Prv 13, 1 senseless one heeds no r.
Eccl 7, 5 hearken to the wise man's r
Is   54, 9 angry with you, or to r you.
Jer 29,27 then, do you not r Jeremiah
Lk   17, 3 If your brother sins, r him;
1Tm   5, 1 Do not r an older man,

RECEIVE

Ex   14, 4 Then I will r glory through
Dt   32,11 he spread his wings to r them
Jos 11,20 and thus r no mercy,
Ru   2,12 May you r a full reward
Tb   4,14 you will r your reward.
Mt   10,41 r a righteous man's reward.
Mk   11,24 believe that you will r it
Jn   20,22 "R the holy Spirit.
Acts 1, 8 r power when the holy Spirit
1Cor 3, 8 r wages in proportion
2Cor 6,17 then I will r you
1Tm   2,11 A woman must r instruction
Jas   1, 7 not suppose that he will r
1Jn   3,22 have confidence in God and r
Rv   4,11 to r glory and honor and

RECONCILE

Acts 7,26 fighting and tried to r them
Eph   2,16 and might r both with God,
Col   1,20 through him to r all things

REDEEM (ER)

Ex   13,13 first-born son you must r.
Ps   19,15 Lord, my rock and my r.
Hos 13,14 shall I r them from death?

REFINE (S)

Is   1,25 r your dross in the furnace
Zec 13, 9 will r them as silver is refined

REFUGE

Nm   35, 6 where a homicide can take r,
Dt   19, 3 be able to find a r.
Ru   2,12 you have come for r."
2Sm 22, 3 my God, my rock of r!
Ps   2,11 Happy are all who take r
Prv 14,32 the just man finds a r
Na   1, 7 The LORD is good, a r

REIGN

Ex   15,18 LORD shall r forever and ever.
Ps   61, 8 May he r before God forever;
Wis   6,21 Wisdom, that you may r
Is   24,23 the LORD of hosts will r
Jer 23, 5 he shall r and govern wisely,
Lk   3, 1 fifteenth year of the r
Rom   6,12 r over your mortal bodies
1Cor 15,25 For he must r until
2Tm   2,12 we shall also r with him.
Rv   11,15 he will r forever and ever."

REJECT

Lv   26,15 you r my precepts

1Sm 8, 7 It is not you they r, they
2Kgs 23,27 I will r this city, Jerusalem,
2Mc 6,20 courage to r the food
Jb 5,17 chastening do not r.
Ps 77, 8 "Will the Lord r us forever,
Prv 1, 8 r not your mother's teaching;
Heb 12,25 do not r the one who speaks.

REJOICE

Dt 33,18 "R, O Zebulun, in your
1Chr 16,10 r, O hearts that seek
Ps 9, 3 I will delight and r in you;
Prv 23,15 my own heart also will r;
Is 14, 8 very cypresses r over you,
Jer 50,11 Yes, r and exult,
Zep 3,17 r over you with gladness,
Zec 9, 9 R heartily, O daughter Zion,
Lk 6,23 R and leap for joy
Rom 12,12 R in hope, endure in affliction
Phil 2,17 I r and share my joy
1Pt 4,13 you may also r exultantly.
Rv 19, 7 Let us r and be glad

RELY

Is 36, 5 On whom, then, do you r,
Ez 33,26 You r on your sword,
Dn 9,18 we r not on our just deeds
Rom 2,17 call yourself a Jew and r

REMAIN

Nm 33,55 whom you allow to r
Jdt 6, 4 shall not r unfulfilled.
Ps 102,27 They perish, but you r;
Jn 1,32 dove from the sky and r upon
Rom 11,22 provided you r in his
1Cor 13,13 So faith, hope, love r, these
2Tm 3,14 r faithful to what you have
Heb 1,11 They will perish, but you r;
1Jn 2,27 just as it taught you, r in him.

REMEMBER

Ex 20, 8 "R to keep holy the sabbath
Dt 5,15 For r that you too were once
Jb 7, 7 R that my life is like
Ps 25, 6 R your compassion and love,
Eccl 12, 1 R your Creator in the days
Is 46, 8 R this and be firm,
Jer 31,34 and r their sin no more.
Hb 3, 2 in your wrath r compassion!
Lk 17,32 R the wife of Lot.
2Tm 2, 8 R Jesus Christ, raised
Heb 8,12 and r their sins no more."

REMNANT

Ezr 9, 8 God, who left us a r
Is 11,11 reclaim the r of his people
Jer 23, 3 I myself will gather the r
Zec 8,12 I will have the r of the people
Rom 11, 5 there is a r, chosen by grace.

REPENT

1Kgs 8,35 and if then they r of their sin,
Jb 42, 6 and r in dust and ashes.
Sir 48,15 this the people did not r,
Jer 15,19 LORD answered me: If you r,
Mt 3, 2 "R, for the kingdom of heaven
Mk 1,15 R, and believe in the gospel
Lk 13, 3 if you do not r, you will all
Acts 2,38 "R and be baptized,
Rv 2, 5 R, and do the works

RESCUE (D) (S)

Gn 37,22 His purpose was to r him
Ex 3, 8 I have come down to r them
2Sm 22,49 the violent man you r me.
Jdt 8,33 the LORD will r Israel by my

1Mc 5,12 Come at once and r us from
Ps 31, 3 make haste to r me!
Dn 3,96 no other God who can r like
Gal 1, 4 that he might r us from the
2Pt 2, 9 knows how to r the devout

REST

Ex 31,15 is the sabbath of complete r,
Lv 25, 5 year of sabbath r for the land.
Dt 31,16 Soon you will be at r
Jos 10, 7 and the r of his soldiers.
1Kgs 8,56 the LORD who has given r
1Chr 11, 8 Joab restored the r of the
Jb 3,17 there the weary are at r.
Ps 95,11 They shall never enter my r."
Prv 6,10 folding of the arms to r—
Is 11, 2 LORD shall r upon him
Jer 6,16 thus you will find r
Mt 11,28 and I will give you r.
2Cor 12,13 you less privileged than the r
Heb 3,11 shall not enter into my r."'
Rv 14,13 "let them find r from their

RESTORE

Gn 37,22 r him to his father.
Ex 21,37 shall r five oxen for the one
Lv 5,16 r what he has sinfully
Nm 5, 7 r his ill-gotten goods in
2Sm 9, 7 I will r to you all the lands
1Kgs 12,21 r the kingdom to Rehoboam,
2Kgs 8, 6 "R all her property to her
2Chr 15, 8 and to r the altar of the LORD
1Mc 15, 3 I may r it to its former state
2Mc 9,16 r all the sacred vessels
Jb 8, 6 r your rightful domain;
Ps 51,14 R my joy in your salvation
Sir 43,23 The dripping clouds r them
Jer 15,19 repent, so that I r you,
Na 2, 3 r the vine of Jacob,
1Pt 5,10 Christ [Jesus] will himself r,

RESURRECTION

Mt 22,30 At the r they neither marry
Mk 12,18 who say there is no r,
Lk 14,14 at the r of the righteous."
Jn 11,24 he will rise, in the r on the
Acts 1,22 us a witness to his r."
Rom 6, 5 united with him in the r.
1Cor 15,12 say there is no r of the dead?
Phil 3,10 and the power of his r
Heb 6, 2 r of the dead and eternal
1Pt 1, 3 hope through the r of Jesus
Rv 20, 5 This is the first r.

RETURN

Gn 3,19 Until you r to the ground,
2Sm 12,23 but he will not r to me."
2Chr 30, 9 For when you r to the LORD,
Neh 1, 9 but should you r to me
Jb 16,22 from which I shall not r.
Ps 126, 6 Will r with cries of joy,
Is 10,21 A remnant will r,
Jer 24, 7 for they shall r to me
Lam 3,40 that we may r to the LORD!
Hos 6, 1 "Come, let us r to the LORD,
Jl 2,12 r to me with your whole
Zec 1, 3 R to me, says the LORD

REVEAL

Lv 9, 4 today the LORD will r himself
Est 2,10 Esther did not r her
Sir 1,28 the LORD will r your secrets
Is 26,21 will r the blood upon her,
Dn 2,47 able to r this mystery."
Mt 11,27 whom the Son wishes to r
Phil 3,15 this too God will r to you.

REVELATION (S)

2Sm 7,27 said in a r to your servant,
Dn 10, 1 a r was given to Daniel,
Lk 2,32 a light for r to the Gentiles,
Rom 16,25 to the r of the mystery
1Cor 14, 6 to you by way of r,
2Cor 12, 1 visions and r of the Lord.
12, 7 the abundance of the r.
Rv 1, 1 The r of Jesus Christ,

REVILE

Ex 22,27 "You shall not r God,
Ps 74,10 foe r your name forever?
Acts 23, 4 r God's high priest?"
Jude 10 But these people r what they

REWARD

Gn 15, 1 I will make your r very great."
1Sm 24,20 May the LORD r you
Ps 19,12 obeying them brings much r.
Prv 11,18 virtue has a sure r.
Is 40,10 Here is his r with him,
Jer 17,10 To r everyone according to
Mt 5,12 your r will be great in heaven
Lk 6,35 then your r will be great

RICH

Jb 34,19 the r more than the poor?
Ps 49,17 fear when others become r,
Prv 21,17 and perfume will not be r.
Eccl 5,11 the r man's abundance
Is 30,23 will be r and abundant.
Jer 5,27 grow powerful and r,
Mt 19,23 one who is r to enter
Lk 1,53 the r he has sent away empty
2Cor 8, 9 poor although he was r,
Eph 2, 4 But God, who is r in mercy,
1Tm 6, 9 Those who want to be r
Jas 1,10 the r one in his lowliness,
Rv 2, 9 but you are r.

RIGHT

Gn 18,19 by doing what is r and just,
Ex 15, 6 Your r hand, O LORD,
Dt 5,32 aside to the r or to the left,
Jos 1, 7 either to the r or to the left,
1Sm 12,23 teach you the good and r
1Kgs 3, 9 to distinguish r from wrong.
2Kgs 7, 9 "We are not doing r.
Neh 4,17 weapon at his r hand.
Ps 16, 8 with the Lord at my r,
Prv 1, 3 in what is r, just and honest;
Eccl 10, 2 turns him to his r;
Song 2, 6 and his r arm embraces me.
Is 1,18 set things r, says the LORD
Jer 23, 5 do what is just and r
Hos 12, 7 you remain loyal and do r
Mt 5,29 If your r eye causes you to
Jn 7, 6 the time is always r for you.
Rom 8,34 at the r hand of God,
1Cor 9, 4 Do we not have the r to eat
2Cor 6, 7 righteousness at the r
Eph 1,20 and seating him at his r hand
Phil 1, 7 It is r that I should think this
2Thes 3, 9 we do not have the r.
Heb 1, 3 took his seat at the r hand
Jas 4,17 who knows the r thing to do
Rv 2, 7 I will give the r to eat

RIGHTEOUS

Tb 3, 2 "You are r, O Lord,
Jb 4,17 "Can a man be r as against
Ps 55,23 never allow the r to stumble.
Prv 11,11 Through the blessing of the r
Jer 23, 5 raise up a r shoot to David;
Mt 1,19 since he was a r man,

Acts 24,15 of the r and the unrighteous.
Rom 1,17 who is r by faith will live."
1Tm 1, 9 is meant not for a r person
Ti 3, 5 not because of any r deeds
Heb 1, 8 and a r scepter
Jas 5,16 fervent prayer of a r person
1Pt 3,12 the Lord are on the r
1Jn 2, 1 Jesus Christ the r one.
Rv 19, 8 linen represents the r deeds

RISE (N)

Ezr 4,19 this city has r up against
Bar 3,19 others have r up in their stead.
Mi 2, 8 my people has r up
Mk 8,31 and r after three days.
Lk 18,33 the third day he will r."
Jn 20, 9 scripture that he had to r
Acts 17, 3 Messiah had to suffer and r
1Thes 4,16 the dead in Christ will r first.

RIVER (S)

Lv 11,10 the sea or in the r
Jer 46, 7 like r of billowing waters?
Ez 47,12 Along both banks of the r,
Rv 22, 1 showed me the r of life-giving

ROBE

Is 61,10 clothed me with a r of
Rv 6, 11 them was given a white r,

ROCK

Gn 49,24 Shepherd, the R of Israel,
Ex 17, 6 on the r in Horeb.
Nm 20, 8 order the r to yield its waters.
Dt 32, 4 The r—how faultless are his
2Sm 22, 2 "O LORD, my r, my fortress,
Ps 18,47 Blessed be my r!
Is 26, 4 the LORD is an eternal R
Mt 7,24 who built his house on r.
Rom 9,33 a r that will make them fall
1Cor 10, 4 they drank from a spiritual r
1Pt 2, 8 a r that will make them fall

ROD

2Sm 7,14 will correct him with the r
Ps 23, 4 your r and staff give me
Prv 13,24 He who spares his r hates
Is 11, 4 ruthless with the r of his

ROOT (ED)

2Kgs 10,28 Thus Jehu r out the worship
Sir 48,15 Until they were r out of their
Mt 3,10 ax lies at the r of the trees.
Eph 3,17 you, r and grounded in love
1Tm 6,10 love of money is the r of all
Rv 5, 5 r of David, has triumphed,

RULE

Jgs 8,23 "I will not r over you,
1Sm 12,12 but a king must r us,'
Ps 67, 3 So shall your r be known
Prv 17, 2 intelligent servant will r over
Is 28,10 r on r, r on r
Rom 15,12 raised up to r the Gentiles;
Gal 6,16 to all who follow this r
Rv 2,27 will r them with an iron rod

S

SABBATH

Ex 20, 8 Remember to keep holy the s
Lv 25, 2 keep a s for the LORD.
Dt 5,12 keep holy the s day as the
Is 56, 2 Who keeps the s free

Jer 17,21 to carry burdens on the s
Mt 12, 1 field of grain on the s.
Lk 13,10 in a synagogue on the s.
Col 2,16 festival or new moon or s.

SACRIFICE

Gn 31,54 He then offered a s
Ex 12,27 'This is the Passover s of the
1Sm 15,22 Obedience is better than s,
1Kgs 18,36 At the time for offering s,
1Chr 23,13 to offer s before the LORD,
Ps 50,14 Offer praise as your s to
Prv 15, 8 The s of the wicked
Dn 9,27 abolish s and oblation;
Hos 6, 6 love that I desire, not s,
Mt 9,13 'I desire mercy, not s.'
Rom 12, 1 your bodies as a living s,
Heb 9,26 take away sin by his s.

SADDUCEES

Mt 16, 6 of the Pharisees and S."
Mk 12,18 Some S, who say there is no
Acts 23, 8 the S say that there is no

SAKE

1Sm 12,22 s of his own great name
Ps 23, 3 for the s of your name.
Is 43,25 wipe out, for my own s,
Jer 14,21 For your name's s
Ez 20, 9 I acted for my name's s,
Dn 9,17 for your own s, O Lord,
Mt 10,39 loses his life for my s
1Cor 9,23 I do for the s of the gospel,
2Cor 12,10 for the s of Christ;
Phil 3, 8 For his s I have accepted
Heb 12, 2 For the s of the joy
1Pt 2,13 institution for the Lord's s,
3Jn 7 set out for the s of the Name

SALVATION

2Sm 22, 3 the horn of my s,
1Chr 16,23 announce his s,
2Chr 6,41 be clothed with s,
Ps 9,15 sing joyously of your s
Wis 5, 2 at the unlooked-for s.
Is 12, 3 water at the fountain of s,
Jer 3,23 alone is the s of Israel.
Lk 1,69 horn for our s
Jn 4,22 because s is from the Jews.
Acts 4,12 There is no s through anyone
Rom 1,16 for the s of everyone
2Cor 1, 6 your encouragement and s;
Eph 1,13 the gospel of your s,
Phil 2,12 work out your s with fear
1Thes 5, 8 helmet that is hope for s.
2Tm 2,10 s that is in Christ Jesus
Heb 1,14 who are to inherit s?
1Pt 1, 5 s that is ready
2Pt 3,15 patience of our Lord as s,
Jude 3 about our common s,
Rv 7,10 "S comes from our God,

SAMARITAN

Lk 10,33 But a S traveler who came
Jn 4, 9 he S woman said to him,

SANCTUARY

Ex 25, 8 "They shall make a s for me,
Lv 19,30 reverence my s.
Ps 63, 3 look to you in the s
Ez 37,26 put my s among them
Dn 9,26 come shall destroy the s.
Heb 8, 5 shadow of the heavenly s,

SATAN

Jb 1, 6 S also came among them.

Zec 3, 2 the LORD said to S
Mt 12,26 if S drives out S
Mk 4,15 S comes at once
Lk 10,18 I have observed S fall
Rom 16,20 quickly crush S under your
1Cor 5, 5 deliver this man to S
2Cor 11,14 S masquerades as an angel
1Tm 1,20 I have handed over to S
Rv 12, 9 is called the Devil and S

SAVE (D)

Gn 37,21 he tried to s him
2Sm 19, 6 "Though they s your life and
Jb 40,14 own right hand can s you.
Ps 6, 5 Turn, LORD, s my life;
Prv 23,14 you will s him from
Wis 14, 4 you can s from any danger,
Is 35, 4 he comes to s you.
Jer 17,14 s me, that I may be
Ez 3,19 but you shall s your life.
Dn 3,17 s us from the white-hot
Hos 1, 7 I will not s them by war,
Ob 17 there shall be a portion s
Zec 8,13 so will I s you
Mt 1,21 because he will s his people
Lk 19,10 come to seek and to s
Jn 12,27 'Father, s me from this hour'?
Rom 11,14 and thus s some of them.
2Cor 2,15 among those who are being s
1Tm 1,15 came into the world to s
Heb 7,25 he is always able to s
Jas 5,20 will s his soul from death
Jude 23 s others by snatching them

SAVIOR

2Sm 22, 3 my refuge, my s,
1Chr 16,35 O God, our s, gather us
Ps 18,47 Exalted be God, my s!
Is 17,10 forgotten God, your s,
Jer 14, 8 our s in time of need!
Hos 13, 4 there is no s but me.
Mi 7, 7 my trust in God my s;
Lk 1,47 rejoices in God my s.
Jn 4,42 truly the s of the world."
Acts 5,31 right hand as leader and s
Eph 5,23 he himself the s of the body.
Phil 3,20 it we also await a s,
1Tm 4,10 who is the s of all,
2Tm 1,10 appearance of our s Christ
Ti 1, 3 the command of God our s,
2Pt 1, 1 our God and s Jesus Christ
1Jn 4,14 Father sent his Son as s
Jude 25 to the only God, our s,

SCRIPTURE

Jn 2,22 they came to believe the s
Acts 8,32 This was the s passage
1Tm 5,18 the s says, "You shall not
2Pt 1,20 there is no prophecy of s

SEA

Ex 14,16 hand outstretched over the s,
Dt 30,13 it across the s,
1Kgs 7,23 The s was then cast;
Jb 11, 9 broader than the s.
Ps 93, 4 the breakers of the s,
Eccl 1, 7 All rivers go to the s,
Is 57,20 wicked are like the tossing s
Jon 1, 4 a violent wind upon the s,
Mi 7,19 into the depths of the s
Hb 2,14 as water covers the s.
3, 8 your rage against the s,
Zec 9,10 shall be from s to sea
Mt 18, 6 in the depths of the s.
1Cor 10, 1 and all passed through the s,
Jas 1, 6 like a wave of the s

Jude   13 like wild waves of the s,
Rv   10, 2 right foot on the s

SEAL

Song 8, 6 me as a s on your heart,
Dn   12, 4 s the book until the end
Jn   6,27 God, has set his s."
1Cor 9, 2 the s of my apostleship
2Cor 1,22 he has also put his s
Rv   6, 3 he broke open the second s,

SEARCH

Ps   26, 2 try me; s my heart
Prv   2, 4 like hidden treasures s
Jer   5, 1 S through her public places,
Ez   34, 6 look after them or to s
Lk   13, 6 when he came in s of fruit

SEAT (S)

1Mc 10,52 taken my s on the throne
Ps 113, 8 S them with princes
Lk   11,43 You love the s of honor
2Cor 5,10 appear before the judgment s

SEE

Gn   1,29 "S I give you every seed
Ex   1,16 s them giving birth,
Lv   13,12 far as the priest can s,
Jos   3, 3 "When you s the ark
2Kgs 2,10 "Still, if you s me taken up
Neh   2,17 "You s the evil plight
Ps   4, 7 "May we s better times!
Prv   5, 6 you s before you the road
Mt   5, 8 for they will s God.
Mk   1,44 "S that you tell no one
Lk   2,15 go, then, to Bethlehem to s
Jn   1,39 "Come, and you will s."
Acts 2,17 young men shall s visions,
Gal   6,11 s with what large letters
Heb   2, 8 at present we do not s
Rv   1, 7 every eye will s him,

SEED (S)

Gn   1,11 kind of plant that bears s
Wis   7, 2 from the s of man,
Is   55,10 Giving s to him who sows
Mt   13,32 smallest of all the s
Mk   4,31 smallest of all the s on the earth
1Cor 15,38 and to each of the s
2Cor 9,10 who supplies s to the sower
1Pt   1,23 from imperishable s,
1Jn   3, 9 God's s remains in him;

SEEK

Dt   4,29 too you shall s the LORD,
1Kgs 22, 5 "S the word of the LORD
1Chr 28, 9 If you s him, he will
2Chr 7,14 pray, and s my presence
Ps   34,15 s peace and pursue it.
Prv   8,17 those who s me find me.
Is   58, 2 They s me day after day,
Jer 29,13 you s me with all your heart
Hos 10,12 it is time to s the LORD,
Am   5, 4 s me, that you may live
Zep   2, 3 S the LORD, all you humble
Mt   6,33 s first the kingdom [of God
Lk   12,31 Instead, s his kingdom,
Jn   5,30 I do not s my own will but
Rom   2, 7 life to those who s glory
1Cor 7,27 Do not s a separation.
Heb 11, 6 he rewards those who s him.
1Pt   3,11 s peace and follow after it

SELF-CONTROL (LED)

Sir 37,30 lack of s many have died,

1Cor 7, 5 through your lack of s.
Gal   5,23 gentleness, s.
1Tm   3, 2 married only once, temperate, s
2Tm   1, 7 of power and love and s.
Ti   1, 8 temperate, just, holy, and s

SELFISH (NESS)

Gal   5,20 outbursts of fury, acts of s,
Phil 2, 3 Do nothing out of s
Jas   3,14 jealousy and s ambition

SEND

Ps   43, 3 S your light and fidelity,
Is   6, 8 "Whom shall I s?
Mal   3,23 I will s you Elijah
Mt   9,38 s out laborers for his harvest
Mk   3,14 s them forth to preach
Lk   20,13 I shall s my beloved son;
Jn   3,17 For God did not s his Son
1Cor 1,17 Christ did not s me

SERPENT

Gn   3, 1 s was the most cunning
Sir 21, 2 from sin as from a s
Is   27, 1 Leviathan the fleeing s,
Rv   12, 9 dragon, the ancient s,

SERVANT

Ex   14,31 in him and in his s Moses.
1Sm   3,10 "Speak, for your s is
2Sm   7,19 the house of your s
1Kgs 20,40 while your s was looking here
Jb   1, 8 "Have you noticed my s Job,
Ps   19,12 By them your s is instructed;
Prv 14,35 favors the intelligent s,
Is   41, 8 you, Israel, my s, Jacob,
Zec   3, 8 I will bring my s the Shoot.
Mal   1, 6 and a s fears his master;
Mt   8,13 very hour [his] s was healed.
Lk   16,13 No s can serve two masters.
Jn   12,26 there also will my s be.
Rom 13, 4 for it is a s of God

SERVE (D)

Dt   29,25 they went and s other gods
Jos 22, 5 s him with your whole heart
1Sm 17, 9 be our vassals and s us."
2Chr 10, 4 we will s you."
Jdt   4,14 the Lord who s his altar
Ps   2,11 S the LORD with fear;
Dn   3,17 our God, whom we s,
Mk   10,45 did not come to be s
Rom   9,12 older shall s the younger."
Gal   5,13 s one another through love.
1Tm   3,10 let them s as deacons.
Heb   1,14 ministering spirits sent to s,
1Pt   4,10 use it to s one another
Rv   22, 2 leaves of the trees s

SEVEN (SEVENTH)

Gn   7, 2 take with you s pairs,
Nm   6, 9 on the s day.
1Kgs 19,18 I will leave s thousand men
Ezr   3, 1 Now when the s month came
Is   4, 1 s women will take hold
Ez   20, 1 In the s year
Mt   18,21 As many as s times?"
Lk   11,26 brings back s other spirits
Rom 11, 4 left for myself s thousand
Rv   1, 4 John, to the s churches in

SEVENTY

Gn   5,12 When Kenan was s years
Ex   1, 5 descendants of Jacob was s.
1Sm   6,19 s of them were struck down
Jer 25,12 the s years have elapsed,
Mt   18,22 seven times but s-seven

SHAME

1Mc   1,28 Jacob was covered with s.
Ps   34, 6 faces may not blush for s.
Prv 13,18 Poverty and s befall the man
Jer   3,25 us lie down in our s,
Rom   9,33 shall not be put to s."
1Cor 1,27 foolish of the world to s
Heb 12, 2 despising its s,

SHARE

Gn   21,10 slave is going to s the
Lv   6,11 as their rightful s
Dt   10, 9 Levi has no s in the heritage
1Sm 30,24 Rather, the s of the one who
Mt   25,21 Come, s your master's joy.
Lk   3,11 has two cloaks should s
Rom   1,11 that I may s with you
2Cor 1, 7 you s in the sufferings,
Gal   4,30 woman shall not s
Eph   4,28 something to s with one in
Col   1,12 s in the inheritance
1Tm   5,22 do not s in another's sins.
2Tm   2, 6 ought to have the first s
Heb 12,10 that we may s his holiness.
Rv   22,19 God will take away his s

SHEEP

Nm   27,17 may not be like s
Dt   14, 4 may eat: the ox, the s,
1Sm 15,14 this bleating of s
Ps   44,23 considered only as s
Is   53, 6 had all gone astray like s,
Jer 50, 6 Lost s were my people,
Ez   34,11 look after and tend my s.
Zec 13, 7 that the s may be dispersed,
Mt   9,36 like s without a shepherd.
Jn   10, 2 is the shepherd of the s
1Pt   2,25 you had gone astray like s,

SHEPHERD

Gn   48,15 God who has been my s
Nm   27,17 like sheep without a s."
2Sm   5, 2 'You shall s my people Israel
1Kgs 22,17 like sheep without a s,
Jdt 11,19 like sheep that have no s,
Ps   23, 1 The LORD is my s;
Is   40,11 Like a s he feeds his flock;
Jer 31,10 guards them as a s his flock.
Ez   34, 5 scattered for lack of a s,
Zec 11,17 Woe to my foolish s
Mt   2, 6 who is to s my people Israel.'
Jn   10,11 I am the good s.
Heb 13,20 great s of the sheep
1Pt   5, 4 when the chief s is revealed,
Rv   7,17 center of the throne will s

SHINE

Nm   6,25 LORD let his face s upon you,
Jb   37,15 makes the light s forth
Ps   37, 6 make your integrity s like
Is   60,19 brightness of the moon s
Dn   12, 3 wise shall s brightly
Mt   5,16 light must s before others,
2Cor 4, 6 "Let light s out of darkness,"
Phil 2,15 you s like lights in the world

SHOW

Ex   33,19 'LORD'; I who s favors
2Sm   9, 1 to whom I may s kindness
Ps   17, 7 s your wonderful love,
Prv 24,23 To s partiality in judgment
Is   30,18 LORD is waiting to s you favor,
Ez   8,18 nor will I s mercy.
Zec   7, 9 s kindness and compassion
Acts 7, 3 land that I will s you.'

1Cor 12,31 But I shall s you a still
Eph   2, 7 he might s the immeasurable
Jas   2, 1 brothers, s no partiality

SICK

1Mc   6, 8 s with grief because his
Prv 13,12 deferred makes the heart s,
Ez   34, 4 nor heal the s
Mt   9,12 a physician, but the s do.
Jas   5,14 Is anyone among you s?

SIGHT

Gn   4,14 anyone may kill me at s."
Ex   3, 3 to look at this remarkable s,
Lv   10, 3 In the s of all the people
Nm 15,39 let the s of them remind you
Dt   6,18 good in the s of the LORD,
Jos   3, 7 exalt you in the s of all Israel,
1Sm   9,17 Samuel caught s of Saul,
2Sm 12, 9 and done evil in his s?
1Kgs 11, 6 Solomon did evil in the s of
2Kgs   3, 2 He did evil in the LORD's s,
1Chr   2, 3 wicked in the s of the Lord,
2Chr 20,32 was right in the LORD's s.
Neh   9, 8 his heart faithful in your s,
Tb   4,11 a worthy offering in the s of
Jdt   5,17 did not sin in the s of their
Est   4C,17 we have sinned in your s,
Ps   51, 6 done such evil in your s
Prv   3,21 these slip out of your s
Mt   11, 5 the blind regain their s,
Acts   4,19 it is right in the s of God
2Cor   5, 7 walk by faith, not by s.
1Pt   3, 4 precious in the s of God.

SIGN

Gn   9,12 "This is the s that I am giving
Is   7,14 himself will give you this s
Ez   20,12 s between me and them,
Mt   12,38 we wish to see a s
Lk   2,12 And this will be a s for you
Rom   4,11 the s of circumcision
1Cor 11,10 s of authority on her head
2Thes 3,17 This is the s in every letter;
Rv   12, 1 A great s appeared in the

SILENT

Est   4,14 if you now remain s,
Ps   32, 3 As long as I kept s, oaths
Prv 17,28 if he keeps s,
Eccl   3, 7 a time to be s,
Is   57,11 Was I to remain s
Acts   8,32 lamb before its shearer is s,
1Cor 14,34 women should keep s

SILVER

Ps   66,10 tried us as s tried by fire.
Prv   2, 4 If you seek her like s,
Is   48,10 have refined you like s,
Ez   22,18 dross from s have they become.
Dn   2,32 its chest and arms were s,
Hg   2, 8 Mine is the s
Zec   13, 9 I will refine them as s
Acts   3, 6 "I have neither s nor gold,
1Cor   3,12 with gold, s, precious stones,
1Pt   1,18 with perishable things like s

SIN (S) (SINNED)

Gn   4, 7 s is a demon lurking
Ex   32,32 would only forgive their s!
Nm 32,23 consequences of your s.
Dt   9,18 because of all the s
1Sm 12,23 to s against the LORD
1Kgs   8,46 "When they s against you
2Chr   6,25 forgive the s of your people

Jb   1,22 Job did not s,
Ps   4, 5 Tremble and do not s;
Prv   5,22 meshes of his own s
Is   3, 9 their s like Sodom they
Jer   3, 9 Eager to s, she polluted
Dn   3,28 all this because of our s
Am   4, 4 Come to Bethel and s,
Mi   6, 7 for the s of my soul?
Zec   13, 1 fountain to purify from s
Mt   18, 6 who believe in me to s,
Mk   3,29 guilty of an everlasting s."
Lk   15,18 "Father, I have s against heaven
Jn   1,29 who takes away the s
Rom   2,12 who s outside the law
1Cor   8,12 When you s in this way
2Cor   5,21 he made him to be s
Gal   3,22 things under the power of s,
1Tm   5,20 publicly those who do s,
Heb   4,15 yet without s.
Jas   1,15 conceives and brings forth s,
1Pt   2,22 "He committed no s,
1Jn   1, 7 Jesus cleanses us from all s.

SINAI

Ex   19,20 to the top of Mount S
Jdt   5,14 to S and Kadesh-barnea.
Ps   68,18 from S the Lord entered the

SLANDER

Lv   19,16 go about spreading s
Ps   15, 3 Who does not s a neighbor,
Prv   30,10 s not a servant
2Cor 12,20 fury, selfishness, s, gossip,
Ti   3, 2 They are to s no one,
1Pt   2, 1 insincerity, envy, and all s;

SLAUGHTER

Gn   22,10 took the knife to s his son.
Ex   12,21 s them as Passover victims.
Lv   16,15 s the people's sin-offering
Dt   12,15 s and eat to your heart's
Jgs   15, 8 he inflicted a great s on
1Kgs 11,24 David defeated them with s.
2Chr 28, 5 defeated him with great s.
Est   7, 4 destruction, s, and extinction.
Is   53, 7 a lamb led to the s
Jer   12, 3 like sheep for the s,
Acts   8,32 he was led to the s,

SLAVE (S) (SLAVERY)

Gn   21,10 "Drive out that s and her son!
Neh   5, 5 our sons and daughters to s
Jn   8,34 who commits sin is a s of sin.
Rom   1, 1 Paul, a s of Christ Jesus,
2Cor   4, 5 ourselves as your s
Phlm   16 no longer as a s but
2Pt   2,19 for a person is a s

SLEEP (ING)

Gn   2,21 God cast a deep s
1Sm   3, 3 Samuel was s in the temple
Prv   6, 9 will you rise from your s?
Wis   17,14 while all s the same sleep
Mk   13,36 come suddenly and find you s.

SLOW

Ex   34, 6 s to anger and rich
Nm 14,18 'The LORD is s to anger
Prv   19,11 man to be s to anger,
Lk   24,25 How s of heart
Jas   1,19 quick to hear, s to speak,

SON (S)

Gn   5, 4 he had other s and daughters.
Ex   4,23 Let my s go,
Dt   18,10 anyone who immolates his s

2Sm   7,14 and he shall be a s to me.
1Kgs   3,22 The living one is my s,
2Kgs   6,29 But she hid her s."
Jb   1, 2 Seven s and three daughters
Ps   2, 7 "You are my s;
Prv   3,12 he chastises the s he favors.
Is   7,14 bear a s, and shall name him
Jer   31,20 Ephraim not my favored s,
Hos   1, 1 Joel, the s of Pethuel.
Am   1, 1 Jeroboam, s of Joash,
Mal   1, 6 A s honors his father,
Mt   20,20 the mother of the s of Zebedee
Mk   1,11 "You are my beloved S;
Lk   1,32 called S of the Most High,
Jn   1,34 he is the S of God."
Acts   7,56 opened and the S of Man
Rom   1, 4 established as S of God
1Cor 15,28 then the S himself will
Col   1,13 kingdom of his beloved S,
1Thes 1,10 await his S from heaven,
Heb   1, 2 spoke to us through a s,
Jas   2,21 when he offered his s Isaac
2Pt   1,17 "This is my S, my beloved,
1Jn   1, 3 with his S, Jesus Christ.
Rv   1,13 lampstands one like a s

SONG (SING)

Ex   15, 1 Israelites sang this s
2Sm 22,50 I will s praise to your name,
Neh 12,24 stood opposite them to s
Is   5, 1 Let me now s of my friend
Rv   15, 3 the s of the Lamb

SOUL (S)

Dt   6, 5 and with all your s,
Jos   22, 5 your whole heart and s."
Jdt   7,27 children breathing out their s.
Ps   16, 9 my s rejoices,
Prv   13,19 Lust indulged starves the s,
Is   26, 8 the desire of our s,
Mi   6, 7 for the sin of my s?
Mt   10,28 but cannot kill the s;
Lk   1,46 "My s proclaims the
1Thes 5,23 spirit, s, and body,
Heb   4,12 penetrating even between s
Jas   1,21 able to save your s.
1Pt   2,11 wage war against the s.
3Jn   2 just as your s is prospering.

SOUND

Gn   3, 8 they heard the s of the LORD
Ex   32,18 "It does not s like cries
Dt   4,12 You heard the s of the words,
Ps   66, 8 loudly s his praise,
Prv   1, 5 man will gain s guidance,
Ez   1,24 I heard the s of their wings,
Jl   2, 1 s the alarm on my holy
Jn   3, 8 you can hear the s it makes,
Acts   2, 6 At this s, they gathered
1Cor 14, 8 bugle gives an indistinct s,
1Tm   1,10 opposed to s teaching,
2Tm   1,13 s words that you heard
Ti   1, 9 exhort with s doctrine
Rv   1,15 voice was like the s

SOW

Ex   23,10 For six years you may s
Jb   4, 8 s trouble, reap the same.
Ps   126, 5 Those who s in tears
Eccl   11, 6 In the morning s your seed,
Sir   7, 3 S not in the furrows
Hos   8, 7 When they s the wind,
Mt   6,26 they do not s or reap,
1Cor 15,36 What you s is not brought
2Pt   2,22 bathed s returns to wallowing

SPEAK

Gn   18,27 presuming to s to my Lord

Ex 33, 11 Lord used to s to Moses
Nm 12, 8 face to face I s to him,
Dt 18,20 presumes to s in my name
Jos 2, 4 men you s of came to me,
1Sm 3, 9 'S, Lord, for your servant
2Sm 7, 8 s thus to my servant David
1Kgs 2,18 "I will s to the king for you
2Kgs 18,26 s to your servants in Aramaic
2Chr 18,23 when he left me to s to you?"
Neh 13,24 knew how to s Jewish;
Tb 6,13 tonight we must s for the girl,
Jdt 8,30 they forced us to s to them
Est 4, 9 s to the king for us
Jb 13, 3 I would s with the Almighty;
Ps 49, 4 My mouth shall s wisdom,
Prv 8, 6 for noble things I s;
Eccl 3, 7 and a time to s.
Wis 7,15 God grant I s suitably
Sir 8, 4 lest he s ill of your forebears.
Is 28, 11 strange language he will s
Bar 6, 7 fraud, and cannot s.
Ez 3,18 do not warn him or s
Dn 7,25 shall s against the Most High
Ob 12 s not haughtily on the day
Mi 6,12 inhabitants s falsehood
Zec 8,16 s the truth to one another
Mt 9,32 demoniac who could not s
Mk 2, 7 "Why does this man s that
Jn 3,11 we s of what we know
Acts 2, 4 Spirit and began to s
Rom 9, 1 I s the truth in Christ,
1Cor 2, 6 Yet we do s a wisdom
2Cor 4,13 believe and therefore s,
Eph 4,25 s the truth,
Col 4, 3 s of the mystery of Christ
1Thes 2, 2 to you the gospel
Jas 1,19 slow to s, slow to wrath,

SPIRIT

Gn 41, 8 his s was agitated.
Ex 31, 3 filled him with a divine s
Jgs 3,10 The s of the Lord came upon
1Sm 10, 6 The s of the Lord will rush
2Sm 23, 2 s of the Lord spoke
1Kgs 18,12 s of the Lord will carry
2Kgs 2, 9 double portion of your s."
2Chr 18,20 until a s came forward
Neh 9,20 "Your good s you bestowed
Tb 3, 1 Grief-stricken in s, I groaned
Jdt 12,16 his s was shaken.
1Mc 13, 7 their s was rekindled.
2Mc 5,17 Puffed up in s, Antiochus
Ps 31, 6 your hands I commend my s;
Prv 1,23 pour out to you my s,
Wis 1, 6 For wisdom is a kindly s,
Sir 35, 7 In generous s pay homage
Is 11, 2 The s of the Lord shall rest
Bar 6,24 there is no s in them.
Dn 2, 1 dream which left his s no rest
Hos 4,12 the s of harlotry has led them
Jl 3, 1 I will pour out my s
Hg 1,14 Lord stirred up the s
Mt 1,18 with child through the holy S
Mk 1, 8 baptize you with the holy S.
Lk 1,17 go before him in the s
Jn 1,32 "I saw the S come down like
Acts 2,33 promise of the holy S
Rom 1, 4 power according to the s
1Cor 2, 4 demonstration of s and
2Cor 2,13 had no relief in my s
Eph 1,13 the promised holy S,
1Tm 3,16 vindicated in the s,
2Tm 1, 7 give us a s of cowardice
Ti 3, 5 renewal by the holy S
Jas 2,26 body without a s is dead,
Jude 19 devoid of the S.

Rv 1,10 I was caught up in s

SPURN

Lv 26,15 precepts and s my decrees,
Nm 14,11 How long will this people s
Ps 43, 2 Why then do you s me?
Prv 3, 11 s not his reproof;
Sir 8, 8 s not the discourse
Is 31, 7 you shall s his sinful idols
Am 5,21 I hate, I s your feasts,

STAFF

Gn 32, 11 here with nothing but my s,
Ex 4, 4 it became a s in his hand.
1Sm 14,27 out the end of the s
2Kgs 4,29 "take my s with you
1Chr 11,23 came against him with a s,
Tb 5,18 Is he not the s
Ps 23, 4 your rod and s give me
Sir 48, 2 Their s of bread he
Jer 48,17 How the strong s is broken,
Mi 7,14 people with your s,
Acts 10, 7 a devout soldier from his s,
Heb 9, 4 the s of Aaron that had

STAND (ING)

Ex 3, 5 where you s is holy ground.
Lv 19,32 s up in the presence of
Dt 7,24 man will be able to s up
Jgs 4,20 "S at the entrance
2Sm 1, 9 'S up to me, please,
1Kgs 13, 1 while Jeroboam was s at the
1Chr 11,14 made a s on the sown
Ezr 9,15 s in your presence."
Jdt 8,33 s at the gate tonight
1Mc 4,18 s firm against our enemies
2Mc 13,12 told them to s ready.
Ps 10, 1 Why, Lord, do you s at a
Prv 22,29 He will s in the presence of
Sir 1,20 A patient man need s firm
Is 48,13 they s forth at once.
Jer 7, 2 S at the gate
Bar 5, 5 s upon the heights;
Ez 40, 3 he was s in the gate
Hos 10, 9 There they took their s;
Ob 14 S not at the crossroads
Hb 2, 1 I will s at my guard post,
Mal 3, 2 who can s when he appears?
Mk 3,31 S outside they sent word
Lk 6, 8 "Come up and s before us."
Rom 3,19 whole world s accountable to
2Cor 1,24 s firm in the faith.
Gal 5, 1 so s firm and do not submit
Rv 3,20 I s at the door and knock

STAR (S)

Neh 4,15 from daybreak till the s came
Jer 31,35 moon and s to light
Mt 2, 2 We saw his s at its rising
1Cor 15,41 s differs from star in
Rv 2,28 I will give the morning s.

STONE (D) (S)

Gn 31,45 Jacob took a s and set it up
Ex 20,25 make an altar of s for me,
Lv 24,23 outside the camp and s him
Dt 4,13 wrote on two tablets of s.
1Kgs 6, 7 temple was built of s
1Chr 29, 2 other kind of precious s,
Neh 9, 11 s into the mighty waters.
1Mc 2,36 they neither threw s
Ps 91,12 strike your foot against a s.
Wis 11, 4 their thirst from the hard s.
Sir 22, 1 The sluggard is like a s
Is 8,14 stumbling s to both the
Lam 3,53 sealed me in with a s.

Am 5, 11 have built houses of hewn s,
Mt 7, 9 would hand his son a s
Mk 13, 2 There will not be one s left
Lk 4, 3 this s to become bread."
Jn 8, 7 first to throw a s at her."
Acts 4, 11 He is 'the s rejected by you,
1Pt 2, 4 Come to him, a living s,

STRAIGHT

Nm 20,17 will go s along the royal road
Tb 4,19 make all your paths s
Ps 5, 9 make s your way before me.
Prv 3, 6 he will make s your paths.
Wis 9,18 of those on earth made s,
Sir 2, 6 make s your ways
Mt 3, 3 make s his paths.' "
Lk 3, 5 roads shall be made s,
Jn 1,23 "Make s the way of the Lord

STRANGE (R)

Ex 2,22 "I am a s in a foreign land."
Jos 8,33 And all Israel, s and native
1Mc 1,38 a s to her own offspring,
Prv 27,13 for the sake of a s
Eccl 6, 2 but a s devours them.
Jer 14, 8 Why should you be a s
Hos 8,12 they are considered as a s's.
Mt 25,35 a s and you welcomed me,

STRENGTH (EN) (ENS) (STRONG)

Lv 26,20 your s will be spent in vain
Dt 3,28 encourage and s him
Jos 17,18 despite their s and iron
1Sm 2,10 may he give s to his king
2Sm 15,12 the conspiracy gained s,
Ezr 9,12 thus you will grow s
Tb 14, 9 sincerely and with all their s.
Jdt 4,15 all their s to look with favor
1Mc 6,47 saw the s of the royal army
2Mc 10,34 relying on the s of the place,
Ps 18, 2 I love you, Lord, my s,
Prv 31,25 clothed with s and dignity,
Wis 16,23 forgot even its proper s;
Sir 3,13 in the fullness of your s.
Is 11, 2 spirit of counsel and of s
Jer 49, 4 do you glory in your s,
Bar 1,12 the Lord may give us s,
Hos 7, 9 Strangers have sapped his s,
Am 2,14 man shall not retain his s;
Hb 1, 11 makes his own s his god!
Mk 12,33 with all your s,
Lk 21,36 pray that you have the s
Acts 9,19 he recovered his s.
1Cor 1,25 stronger than human s.
Phil 4,13 have the s for everything

STRIKE

Gn 3,15 He will s at your head,
Ex 8,12 s the dust of the earth
Nm 14,12 I will s them with pestilence
2Kgs 6,18 "S this people blind,
1Chr 14,15 s the army of the Philistines
Jdt 14, 4 s them down in their tracks
1Mc 4,32 S them with fear,
2Mc 14,43 he failed to s exactly.
Ps 9,21 S them with terror, Lord;
Wis 4,19 s them down speechless
Jer 21, 6 will s the inhabitants of this
Am 3,15 Then will I s the winter house
Mt 26,31 will s the shepherd,
Rv 19,15 sharp sword to s the nations.

STUMBLE (STUMBLING)

Lv 19,14 put a s block in front
Prv 4,12 you run, you will not s.
Sir 25,20 S not through woman's
Ez 3,20 when I place a s block

Jn 11, 9 he does not s, because he
Rom 14,21 that causes your brother to s.
2Cor 6, 3 cause no one to s in
Jude 24 able to keep you from s

SUFFER (ING) (INGS)

Gn 35,16 be in labor and to s
Nm 14,34 forty years shall you s for
Jdt 16,17 they shall burn and s
2Mc 7,18 We s these things on our
Prv 21,17 He who loves pleasure will s
Is 53, 3 a man of s, accustomed to
Mt 16,21 s greatly from the elders,
Mk 8,31 Son of Man must s greatly
Acts 2,27 nor will you s your holy one
Rom 8,17 if only we s with him so
2Cor 1, 5 For as Christ's s overflow to us
1Pt 2,20 you are patient when you s
Rv 2,10 that you are going to s.

SUN

Gn 15,12 As the s was about to set,
Ex 16,21 but when the s grew hot,
Dt 4,19 behold the s
Jgs 19,14 on their way till the s set
2Chr 18,34 He died as the s was setting.
Jdt 14, 2 the s rises on the earth,
1Mc 6,39 When the s shone on the
2Mc 1,22 the s, which had been
Ps 72, 5 live as long as the s endures,
Eccl 1, 9 Nothing is new under the s.
Song 1, 6 the s has burned me.
Wis 2, 4 mist pursued by the s's rays
Sir 17,26 anything brighter than the s?
Is 30,26 light of the s will be seven
Bar 6,59 The s and moon and stars
Ez 8,16 were bowing down to the s.
Jl 2,10 s and the moon are darkened
Am 8, 9 make the s set at midday
Hb 3,10 The s forgets to rise,
Zec 8, 7 land of the rising s,
Mt 5,45 makes his s rise on the bad
Mk 16, 2 early when the s had risen,
Acts 2,20 s shall be turned to darkness
Eph 4,26 let the s set on your anger,
Rv 1,16 his face shone like the s

SWEAR (SWORE) (SWORN)

Gn 14,22 "I have s to the Lord
Lv 19,12 You shall not s falsely
1Kgs 1,13 s to your handmaid
Jdt 13,16 I s that it was my face
Ps 63,12 all who s by the Lord
Ez 5,11 I s to cut you down.
Am 8,14 who s by the shameful idol
Mt 5,34 do not s at all;
Mk 6,23 He even s many things
Jas 5,12 do not s, either by heaven

SWEET (ER)

Gn 8,21 LORD smelled the s odor,
Jgs 14,18 "What is s than honey
Neh 8,10 rich foods and drink s drinks,
Jb 20,12 wickedness is s in his mouth,
Ps 19,11 S also than honey
Prv 20,17 bread of deceit is s to a man,
Eccl 5,11 Sleep is s to the laboring
Sir 24,19 remember me as s than honey
Is 5,20 who change bitter into s,
Ez 3, 3 it was as s as honey in my

SWORD (S)

Gn 3,24 fiery revolving s, to guard
Ex 15, 9 I will draw my s;
Nm 22,31 standing on the road with s
Jos 5,13 drawn s in hand. Joshua
Jgs 9,54 "Draw your s and dispatch

1Sm 13,19 the Hebrews will make s
2Sm 12, 9 with the s of the Ammonites.
2Kgs 11,15 let him die by the s."
1Chr 10, 4 Saul took his own s and fell
Jdt 2,27 all their youths to the s.
1Mc 4,33 Strike them down by the s
2Mc 12,23 putting the sinners to the s
Ps 37,14 The wicked draw their s
Prv 5, 4 sharp as a two-edged s.
Wis 5,20 his sudden anger for a s,
Sir 22,21 draw a s against a friend,
Is 1,20 s shall consume you
Jer 12,22 men shall die by the s;
Bar 2,25 by hunger and the s
Jl 4,10 Beat your plowshares into s
Na 2,14 s shall devour your young
Zep 2,12 shall be slain by the s
Mt 26,52 all who take the s will perish
Jn 18,10 Peter, who had a s, drew it,
Eph 6,17 s of the Spirit,
Heb 4,12 than any two-edged s,
Rv 1,16 two-edged s came out of his

SYNAGOGUE (S)

Mt 4,23 teaching in their s, proclaiming
Mk 1,39 So he went into their s
Lk 13,14 leader of the s, indignant
Acts 17,17 So he debated in the s

T

TABLET (S)

Ex 24,12 will give you the stone t
2Chr 5,10 in it but the two t which Moses
Ez 4, 1 take a clay t;
Lk 1,63 He asked for a t and wrote,

TAKE (N)

Gn 12,19 t her and be gone!"
Ex 8, 5 that the frogs may be t away
Lv 2, 8 priest, who shall t it to the
Nm 1, 2 "T a census of the whole
Dt 5,12 'T care to keep holy
Jos 1,11 t possession of the land
Ru 4, 5 Naomi, you must t also Ruth
1Sm 1,22 weaned, I will t him to appear
2Sm 2, 7 T courage, therefore, and
1Chr 7,21 gone down to t away their
Ezr 9,12 do not t their daughters
Neh 2, 6 how long my journey would t
Tb 4,13 refuse to t a wife for yourself
Jdt 8,35 to t vengeance upon our
Est 2,13 she was allowed to t
1Mc 2,10 What nation has not t
2Mc 3,14 he went in to t an inventory
Jb 1, 4 sons used to t turns giving
Ps 7, 2 my God, in you I t refuge;
Song 7, 9 I will t hold of its branches.
Wis 2,20 God will t care of him."
Sir 9,14 t your neighbors' measure,
Is 1,24 I will t vengeance on my foes
Jer 12,20 witness the vengeance you t
Bar 4,14 to t note of the captivity
Ez 16,39 t away your splendid
Hos 1, 2 t a harlot wife
Jl 4, 4 Would you t vengeance upon
Am 5,21 I t no pleasure
Ob 17 Jacob shall t possession
Zep 3,12 Who shall t refuge in the
Zec 3, 9 I will t away the guilt
Mt 1,20 do not t afraid to t Mary
Mk 8,34 deny himself, t up his cross,
Lk 2,15 see this thing that has t place
Jn 2, 8 t it to the headwaiter."

2Cor 3, 5 we are qualified to t credit
Gal 5,10 you will not t a different view,
2Thes 3,14 t note of this person not
Jas 1, 9 should t pride in his high

TASTE (D)

Ex 16,31 and it t like wafers
1Sm 14,24 So none of the people t food
Jb 6,30 cannot my t discern
Prv 24,13 honey is sweet to your t;
Wis 16,20 conforming to every t.
Sir 37,27 everything suited to every t.
Mt 5,13 But if salt loses its t,
Jn 2, 9 And when the headwaiter t the
Acts 23,14 t nothing until we have killed
Col 2,21 Do not t! Do not touch!"

TEACH

Lv 10,11 you must t the Israelites all
Dt 4, 9 t them to your children
Jgs 13, 8 return to us to t us
2Chr 6,27 But t them the right way
Jb 33,33 while I t you wisdom.
Ps 25, 4 t me your paths.
Song 8, 2 you would t me
Sir 45, 5 That he might t his precepts
Jer 5,31 priests t as they wish;
Mt 5, 2 He began to t them,
Mk 4, 1 he began to t by the sea.
Lk 11, 1 "Lord, t us to pray
Jn 14,26 he will t you everything
Col 3,16 you t and admonish one
1Tm 2,12 not permit a woman to t
Heb 5,12 you need to have someone t

TEMPLE

Jgs 4,21 drove the peg through his t
1Sm 3, 3 Samuel was sleeping in the t
1Kgs 5,19 I propose to build a t
2Kgs 11, 7 shall keep guard over the t
1Chr 6,17 Solomon built the t
2Chr 5, 7 holy of holies of the t.
Tb 14, 4 God's t there shall be burnt
Jdt 4, 3 t been purified from
1Mc 7,35 I will burn this t down."
2Mc 6, 4 Gentiles filled the t with
Ps 11, 4 LORD is in his holy t;
Wis 9, 8 have bid me build a t
Sir 49,12 They erected the holy t,
Is 38, 5 shall go up to the LORD's t;
Bar 1, 8 removed from the t,
Ez 40,47 stood in front of the t,
Dn 14,10 went with Daniel into the t
Jon 2, 5 look upon your holy t."
Hb 2,20 LORD is in his holy t;
Mal 1,10 shut the t gates
Mt 12, 6 something greater than the t
Mk 12,35 Jesus was teaching in the t
Lk 22, 4 t guards to discuss a plan
Jn 2,19 "Destroy this t and in three
Acts 3, 2 gate of the t called "the
1Cor 6,19 body is a t of the holy Spirit
2Thes 2, 4 seat himself in the t

TEMPT (ED) (TEMPTER)

Is 7,12 I will not t the LORD!"
Mt 4, 1 into the desert to be t
1Thes 3, 5 for fear that somehow the t

TEST (ED)

Gn 22, 1 God put Abraham to the t.
Ex 17, 7 quarreled there and t the Lord
Jgs 3, 4 to put Israel to the t,
1Kgs 10, 1 came to t him with subtle
2Chr 32,31 God forsook him to t him,
Tb 12,14 to put you to the t.
Jdt 8,25 for putting us to the t,

1Mc 10,71 let us t each other's strength
Ps   26, 2 t me, LORD, and try me
Wis   1, 2 those who t him not,
Sir   6, 7 first t him,
Jer   6,27 to search and t their way.
Ez   21,18 for the sword has been t
Mk   8,11 a sign from heaven to t him.
Lk 22,40 you may not undergo the t."
Jn   6, 6 He said this to t him,
1Cor 10, 9 Let us not t Christ
2Cor 13, 5 T yourselves.
Heb 2,18 Because he himself was t
Rv 3,10 to t the inhabitants of the

TESTIFY (TESTIFIED) (TESTIFIES) (TESTIMONY)

Gn 30,33 let my honesty t against me;
Ps 50, 7 I will t against you;
Dn 13,21 we will t against you
Jn 8,14 "Even if I do t on my own
2Cor 1,12 the t of our conscience
Heb 10,15 The holy Spirit also t to us
3Jn   3 the brothers came and t

THANK (S)

1Chr 16, 8 Give t to the Lord
2Chr 29,31 t offerings for the house
Tb 12, 6 "T God! Give him the praise
1Mc 14,25 "How can we t Simon
2Mc 9,20 I t God very much,
Ps 107,15 Let them t the LORD for such
Sir 51,12 For this reason I t him
Mk 8, 6 the seven loaves he gave t
Jn 11,41 "Father, I t you for hearing
1Cor 1, 4 I give t to my God

THIEF (THIEVES)

2Mc 4,42 The sacrilegious t himself
Jb 24,15 In the night the t roams
Prv 6,30 Men despise not the t
Sir 5,17 has been created for the t,
Jer 2,26 As the t is shamed
Ez 18,10 a son who is a t,
Jer 7,11 your eyes a den of t?
Hos 7, 1 They practice falsehood, t break
Lk 19,46 made it a den of t.' "
1Thes 5, 2 Lord will come like a t at
1Pt 4,15 suffer as a murderer, a t,
2Pt 3,10 Lord will come like a t,

THIRST (Y)

Jgs 4,19 water to drink. I am t."
2Sm 17,29 tired and t in the desert."
Jb 22, 7 To the t you have given no
Ps 107, 5 They were hungry and t
Prv 25,21 if he be t, give him to drink;
Sir 26,12 As a t traveler with eager
Is 29, 8 a t man dreams he is
Mt 25,35 I was t and you gave me drink
Jn 4,13 drinks this water will be t
Rom 12,20 if he is t, give him something
1Cor 4,11 we go hungry and t,
Rv 21, 6 To the t I will give a gift

THOUSAND (S)

Gn 24,60 may you grow into t of myriads
Dt 1,11 increase you a t times over,
Jos 4,13 forty t troops equipped for
Jgs 1, 4 they slew ten t of them
1Sm 13, 2 one t were with Jonathan
2Sm 8, 4 captured from him one t
1Chr 12,15 and the greater over t.
Est 3, 9 ten t silver talents for deposit
1Mc 3,39 he sent forty t men
2Mc 5, 5 Jason gathered fully a t men
Jb 1, 3 he had seven t sheep,
Ps 90, 4 A t years in your eyes

Eccl 6, 6 Should he live twice a t years
Wis 12,22 enemies with a t blows
Sir 41,12 than precious treasures in the t
Is 30,17 A t shall tremble at the threat
Dn 5, 1 banquet for a t of his lords,
Mt 16, 9 five loaves for the five t,
Jn 6,10 about five t in number.
Acts 2,41 three t persons were added
2Pt 3, 8 one day is like a t years
Rv 20, 6 reign with him for [the] t

THREE (THIRD)

Gn 1,13 morning followed—the t day.
Ex 2, 2 she hid him for t months.
Dt 17, 6 testimony of two or t
Jgs 16,15 t times already you have
1Sm 31, 8 found Saul and his t sons
2Sm 24,12 I offer you t alternatives;
Neh 2,11 I first rested there for t days.
Jdt 12, 7 she stayed in the camp t
1Mc 10,34 feast day, and the t days
2Mc 4,44 t men sent by the senate
Jb 42,14 the second Keziah, and the t
Prv 30,18 t things are too wonderful
Eccl 4,12 A t-ply cord is not easily
Sir 25, 1 With t things I am delighted,
Is 17, 6 Two or t olives remain
Dn 3,91 "Did we not cast t men bound
Hos 6, 2 on the t day he will raise us
Zec 11, 8 did away with the t
Mt 26,34 you will deny me t times."
Mk 8,31 rise after t days.
Lk 2,46 After t days they found him
Jn 2,19 in t days I will raise it
Acts 2,41 t thousand persons were
1Cor 13,13 these t; but the greatest of
2Cor 11,25 t times I was beaten
Gal 1,18 after t years I went up
Rv 8,13 t angels are about to blow

THRONE (S)

2Sm 3,10 establish the t of David
1Kgs 1,47 exalt his t more than your
1Chr 17,12 I will establish his t forever.
Jdt 1,12 swore by his t
Est 4D, 8 he sprang from his t,
1Mc 7, 4 Demetrius sat on the royal t.
Jb 36, 7 And with kings upon t he sets
Ps 11, 4 LORD's t is in heaven.
Prv 20, 8 king seated on the t of
Wis 6,21 pleasure in t and scepter,
Sir 10,14 The t of the arrogant God
Is 6, 1 on a high and lofty t,
Jer 17,25 kings who sit upon the t
Mt 5,34 for it is God's t;
Lk 1,52 down the rulers from their t
Acts 7,49 The heavens are my t,
Rv 3,21 sit with me on my t,

TIME (S)

Gn 4,26 At that t men began
Ex 1,10 in t of war they
Lv 4, 6 he shall sprinkle it seven t
Nm 32,10 At that t the wrath of the LORD
1Kgs 2,26 put you to death this t,
2Kgs 15,37 at that t that the LORD first
Tb 14, 4 take place in the t appointed
Jdt 8,15 to protect us at such t
Est 1, 5 At the end of this t
1Mc 9, 7 he had no t to gather them
2Mc 1,22 in t the sun,
Jb 8, 7 in t to come you will flourish
Ps 9, 6 you blotted out for all t,
Prv 24,16 the just man falls seven t
Eccl 3, 1 There is an appointed t for
Wis 2, 4 name will be forgotten in t,

Sir 1,20 stand firm but for a t,
Is 48,16 At the t it comes to pass,
Jer 14,19 for a t of healing,
Bar 1,19 From the t the LORD led
Ez 38,10 At that t thoughts shall arise
Dn 2,16 Daniel went and asked for t
Jl 4, 1 at that t, when I would
Am 5,13 man is silent at this t,
Zep 1,12 At that t I will explore
Hg 1, 2 now has the t come to rebuild
Mt 13,21 lasts only for a t.
Mk 1,15 This is the t of fulfillment.
Lk 1,20 be fulfilled at their proper t."
Jn 7, 6 "My t is not yet here,
Rom 5, 6 died at the appointed t
1Cor 7, 5 by mutual consent for a t,
2Cor 12,14 come to you this third t.
Gal 4, 4 fullness of t had come,
2Tm 1, 9 in Christ Jesus before t
Heb 1, 1 In t past, God spoke
1Pt 1, 5 be revealed in the final t.
Rv 1, 3 for the appointed t is near.

TONGUE (S)

Ex 4,10 am slow of speech and t."
Jgs 7, 5 a dog does with its t;
2Sm 23, 2 his word was on my t.
2Mc 7,10 He put out his t at once
Jb 20,12 he hides it under his t,
Ps 39, 2 lest I sin with my t;
Prv 6,17 Haughty eyes, a lying t,
Wis 1,11 from calumny withhold your t
Sir 5,16 use not your t for calumny;
Is 59, 3 your t utters deceit.
Bar 6, 7 Their t are smoothed by
Acts 2, 3 appeared to them t as of fire
Rom 14,11 every t shall give praise to
1Cor 14, 2 one who speaks in a t does
Phil 2,11 every t confess that Jesus
Jas 1,26 does not bridle his t
Rv 5, 9 those from every tribe and t,

TOUCH (ED)

Gn 3, 3 not eat it or even t it,
Nm 19,18 on him who t a bone
Dt 14, 8 dead bodies you shall not t.
Jgs 13, 5 no razor shall t his head,
1Chr 16,22 "T not my anointed,
Est 4D,12 Raising the golden scepter, he t
Ps 39,11 ravaged by the t of your
Wis 3, 1 no torment shall t them.
Is 52,11 t nothing unclean!
Am 9, 5 melt the earth with my t,
Mt 8, 3 He stretched out his hand, t
Mk 3,10 pressing upon him to t him.
Lk 6,19 crowd sought to t him
1Cor 7, 1 for a man not to t a woman,"
Col 2,21 Do not taste! Do not t!"
1Jn 5,18 evil one cannot t him.

TRANSFIGURED

Mt 17, 2 he was t before them;

TRANSGRESSION (S)

Lv 16,21 the sinful faults and t
Jb 33, 9 I am clean and without t;
Wis 3,13 knew not t of the marriage
Mk 11,25 in turn forgive you your t.
Rom 5,17 For if, by the t of one person,
Col 2,13 when you were dead in t

TREASURE (S) (D)

1Kgs 14,26 took everything, including the t
Jb 23,12 I have t in my heart.
Ps 119,11 t your promise,
Prv 2, 1 t my commands,

Wis 7,14 she is an unfailing t;
Sir 20,29 wisdom and unseen t—
Na 2,10 is no end to the t,
Mt 13,44 heaven is like a t
Mk 10,21 you will have t in heaven;
Lk 12,33 inexhaustible t in heaven
Jas 5, 3 You have stored up t
Rv 21,24 the earth will bring their t.

TREE (S)
Gn 1,11 and every kind of fruit t
Lv 19,23 plant any fruit t there,
Dt 21,22 his corpse hung on a t,
Jgs 9, 8 Once the t went to anoint
2Sm 18, 9 hair caught fast in the t.
1Kgs 19, 5 fell asleep under the broom t,
Neh 10,38 of the fruit of every t,
1Mc 14,12 his vine and his fig t,
Ps 74, 6 axes in a thicket of t.
Prv 13,12 a wish fulfilled is a t of life.
Wis 13,11 may saw out a suitable t
Sir 14,18 that grow on a vigorous t
Is 1,30 You shall become like a t
Bar 5, 8 every fragrant kind of t
Dn 4, 7 I saw a t of great height
Jl 1, 7 blighted my fig t;
Na 3,12 your fortresses are but fig t
Mt 3,10 every t that does not bear
Mk 11,13 from a distance a fig t in leaf,
Lk 6,43 "A good t does not bear
Jn 1,48 saw you under the fig t."
Acts 5,30 by hanging him on a t.
Gal 3,13 everyone who hangs on a t,"
Rv 2, 7 right to eat from the t of life

TRIBE (S)
Dt 1,23 one from each t.
Jos 3,12 from each of the t of Israel.
1Sm 9,21 clans of the t of Benjamin?
1Chr 6,50 from the t of the Judahites,
Tb 4,12 who is not of your father's t,
Jdt 3, 8 every people and t
Ps 74, 2 the t you redeemed
Sir 45, 6 Aaron, of the t of Levi.
Ez 37,19 and of the t of Israel
Heb 7,13 belonged to a different t,
Rv 5, 9 from every t and tongue,

TROUBLE (D)
Gn 34,30 "You have brought t upon me
1Sm 4,13 for he was t at heart
Jb 3,10 to shield my eyes from t!
Ps 9,10 a stronghold in times of t.
Sir 40, 2 and his t forebodings
Is 33, 2 our salvation in time of t!
Dn 5,10 Be not t in mind
Mt 26,10 "Why do you make t for the
Mk 5,35 why t the teacher any
Lk 7, 6 "Lord, do not t yourself,
Jn 16,33 you will have t,
Phil 1,17 cause me t in my

TRUE (TRUTH)
Gn 24,49 show t loyalty to my master,
Lv 19,36 You shall have a t scale
Jgs 13,12 that which you say comes t,
2Sm 7,28 God and your words are t
1Chr 11,10 in order to make him t king,
Tb 2,14 Your t character is finally
Jdt 11,10 for it is t.
1Mc 14,41 until a t prophet arises.
2Mc 3, 9 if these things were really t.
Ps 18,31 promise is tried and t;
Prv 18,24 a t friend is more loyal
Wis 2,17 see whether his words be t;
Sir 12,18 show his t face.

Dn 7,16 what all this meant in t
Lk 16,11 will trust you with t wealth?
Jn 15, 1 "I am the t vine,
1Thes 1, 9 to serve the living and t God
Ti 1, 1 the recognition of religious t
Heb 8, 2 t tabernacle that the Lord,
1Pt 5,12 this is the t grace of God
3Jn 12 you know our testimony is t.
Rv 15, 3 Just and t are your ways,

TRUMPET
Ex 19,19 t blast grew louder
Nm 29, 1 which you sound the t.
Neh 4,14 wherever you hear the t
1Mc 4,13 Judas blew the t.
Jb 39,24 at the sound of the t,
Is 27,13 On that day, A great t shall
Dn 3, 4 hear the sound of the t,
Jl 2, 1 Blow the t in Zion,
Zep 1,16 a day of t blasts and battle
Zec 9,14 Lord God shall sound the t,
Mt 6, 2 do not blow a t before you,
1Cor 15,52 at the last t.
Heb 12,19 t blast and a voice speaking
Rv 1,10 voice as loud as a t,

TRUST (TRUSTWORTHY)
Nm 12, 7 my house he bears my t
Dt 1,32 you would not t the Lord,
Jgs 9,26 put their t in him,
2Kgs 5,18 I t the Lord will forgive
1Chr 5,20 because they had put their t
Jdt 10,13 to give him a t report
1Mc 1,30 and won their t.
2Mc 2,18 We t in God,
Jb 4,18 he puts no t in his servants,
Ps 4, 6 fitting sacrifice and t in the
Wis 3, 9 Those who t in him
Sir 2, 8 who fear the Lord, t him,
Is 8,17 For I will t in the Lord,
Jer 7, 4 Put not your t in the deceitful
Bar 3,17 gold in which men t;
Mi 7, 5 Put no t in a friend,
1Cor 4, 2 stewards that they be found t.
Col 1, 7 who is a t minister of Christ
1Jn 4, 1 do not t every spirit

TURN (ED)
Gn 9,23 since their faces were t
Lv 19, 4 "Do not t aside to idols,
Jos 2,12 you in t will show kindness
1Sm 1,28 I, in t, give him to the Lord
1Kgs 2, 3 wherever you t,
2Kgs 12,12 They in t would give it
2Chr 7,14 t from their evil ways,
Tb 3,12 I t my face and raise
Jdt 11,19 I in t have been sent to tell
Est 2,12 Each girl went in t to visit
2Mc 7, 8 So he too in t suffered
Jb 30,23 know you will t me back
Ps 9, 4 For my enemies t back;
Prv 4,27 T neither to right nor
Song 6, 5 T your eyes from me,
Wis 16, 3 should be t from even the
Sir 2, 7 t not away lest you fall
Is 1,25 will t my hand against you,
Jer 4, 7 To t your land into
Bar 2,33 they shall t back
Ez 1, 9 they did not t when they
Dn 1,18 He shall t to the coastland
Hos 2,14 I will t them into rank growth
Zep 3,15 he has t away your enemies
Mal 3, 5 those who t aside the
Mt 5,39 t the other one to him
Acts 13, 8 attempt to t the proconsul
Rom 11,26 he will t away godlessness

2Tm 2,22 So t from youthful desires
Rv 10, 9 It will t your stomach sour,

TWELVE
Gn 42,32 There were t of us brothers,
Lv 24, 5 flour and bake it into t cakes,
Dt 1,23 I chose t men
Jgs 19,29 cut her into t pieces,
1Kgs 4, 7 Solomon had t commissaries
2Kgs 3, 1 he reigned for t years].
Tb 14, 1 age of a hundred and t,
Jdt 2, 5 t thousand cavalry,
Sir 44,23 division into t.
Dn 4,26 t months later,
Mt 9,20 suffering hemorrhages for t
Mk 3,14 He appointed t
Lk 2,42 when he was t years old,
Jn 6,13 filled t wicker baskets with
Rv 7, 5 t thousand were marked

TWO
Gn 1,16 God made the t great lights,
Dt 3, 8 we took from the t kings
Jos 2, 1 secretly sent out t spies
Jgs 3,16 Ehud made himself a t dagger
Ru 1, 3 she was left with her t sons,
1Sm 1, 2 He had t wives,
2Sm 23,20 was he who slew the t lions
1Kgs 3,25 Cut the living child in t,
2Kgs 5,22 'T young men have just come
2Chr 3,10 he made t cherubim
Neh 12,31 I arranged t great choirs.
Tb 1,21 assassinated by t of his sons,
Jdt 4, 7 wide enough for t abreast.
1Mc 9,57 Judah was quiet for t years.
2Mc 3,26 t other young men,
Jb 42, 7 with you and with your t
Ps 136,13 Who split in t the Red Sea
Prv 5, 4 as sharp as a t-edged sword.
Eccl 4,12 t together can resist.
Sir 21, 3 Every offense is a t sword
Jer 2,13 t evils have my people done
Ez 1, 11 Each had t wings
Hos 6, 2 revive us after t days;
Zec 4, 3 beside it are t olive trees,
Mt 4,18 he saw t brothers,
Mk 6, 7 send them out t by two
Lk 16,13 No servant can serve t
Jn 1,40 Peter, was one of the t
Acts 1,10 t men dressed in white
2Cor 13, 1 On the testimony of t
Eph 5,31 the t shall become one flesh."
1Tm 5,19 it is supported by t or three
Jas 1, 8 he is a man of t minds,
Rv 1,16 A sharp t sword came

U

UNBELIEF (UNBELIEVER)
(UNBELIEVERS)
Mk 9,24 I do believe, help my u!"
Rom 4,20 doubt God's promise in u;
2Cor 6,15 believer in common with an u?

UNCLEAN
Gn 7, 2 and of the u animals,
Lv 7,21 someone touches anything u,
Nm 5, 2 everyone who has become u
Dt 23,11 If one of you becomes u
Jgs 13, 4 drink and to eat nothing u.
2Chr 23,19 no one u in any respect
1Mc 1,47 sacrifice swine and u
Eccl 9, 2 for the clean and the u,
Sir 34, 4 Can the u produce the
Is 6, 5 I am a man of u lips,
Jer 2,33 have gone by ways u!

Hos 9, 3 they shall eat u food.
Am 7,17 yourself shall die in an u
Mt 10, 1 authority over u spirits
Mk 1,23 was a man with an u spirit;
Lk 8,29 ordered the u spirit to come
Acts 5,16 disturbed by u spirits,
Rom 14,14 Jesus that nothing is u in
1Cor 7,14 your children would be u,
Rv 16,13 I saw three u spirits

UNDERSTAND (ING)
Gn 11, 7 one will not u what another
Dt 28,49 whose tongue you do not u,
1Sm 12,17 you will see and u
Neh 8, 2 children old enough to u.
Jdt 8,13 will you never u anything?
Jb 8,10 and utter their words of u?
Ps 45,11 Listen, my daughter, and u;
Prv 2, 5 Then will you u the fear of
Eccl 10, 2 The wise man's u turns him
Wis 3, 9 shall u truth, and the faithful
Sir 23,19 He does not u that the eyes
Jer 5,15 whose speech you cannot u.
Bar 6,40 as though the man could u;
Ez 3, 6 words you cannot u.
Dn 9, 2 I, Daniel, tried to u
Hos 14,10 Let him who is wise u
Mt 13,13 but do not listen or u.'
Mk 7,18 even you likewise without u?
Lk 2,50 they did not u what he said to
Jn 8,43 Why do you not u what I am
Rom 10,19 I ask, did not Israel u?
1Cor 2,14 foolishness, and he cannot u
Heb 11, 3 By faith we u
Jude 10 revile what they do not u

UNRIGHTEOUS (NESS)
Acts 24,15 of the righteous and the u
1Pt 3,18 for the sake of the u,
2Pt 2, 9 keep the u under punishment

UPRIGHT
Gn 37, 7 my sheaf rose to an u
Dt 32, 4 how just and u he is!
1Kgs 3, 6 with justice and an u heart;
Tb 9, 6 u and charitable man,
Jb 1, 1 there was a blameless and u
Ps 11, 3 what can the u do?"
Prv 2,21 For the u will dwell in the
Sir 26,20 can hardly remain u,
Bar 6,26 if one sets them u,
Mi 7, 2 among men the u are no
Acts 8,21 for your heart is not u

USE (FUL)
Gn 43,18 they want to u it as a pretext
Nm 7, 5 things may be put to u
Dt 20,14 you may u this plunder
2Kgs 3,25 every u tree they felled.
2Mc 12,12 that they could indeed be u
Prv 17,16 Of what u in the fool's hand
Wis 13,11 something fit for daily u,
Sir 4,20 u your time well;
Mi 5,11 of divination from your u,
Zec 9,13 I will u you as a warrior's
Mk 4,30 or what parable can we u for
Jn 4, 9 For Jews u nothing in
1Cor 9,18 as not to make full u of my
Gal 5,13 do not u this freedom as
Col 2,22 destined to perish with u;
2Tm 2,14 This serves no u purpose

V

VAIN (VANITY)
Ex 20, 7 who takes his name in v.

Dt 32,21 and angered me with their v
2Kgs 17,15 The v they pursued
2Mc 7,18 "Have no v illusions.
Jb 9,29 then should I strive in v?
Eccl 1, 2 V of vanities, says Qoheleth
Wis 14,14 for by the v of men
Sir 20,12 their blandishments in v.
Is 30, 7 whose help is futile and v.
Mt 15, 9 in v do they worship me,
Rom 1,21 Instead, they became v in
1Cor 15,58 your labor is not in v.
Phil 2,16 I did not run in v or labor in

VENGEANCE
Nm 31, 3 execute the LORD's v on
Jos 10,13 while the nation took v on its
1Sm 18,25 that he may thus take v on
Ps 58,11 shall rejoice to see the v
Wis 11, 3 took v on their foes.
Sir 5, 9 at the time of v, you will be
Jer 5, 9 this shall I not take v?
Ez 24, 8 to excite my v,
Jl 4, 4 Would you take v upon me
Mi 5,14 I will wreak v in anger
Na 1, 2 The LORD brings v on his
Heb 10,30 "V is mine; I will repay

VICTORY
Ex 14,13 you will see the v the LORD
1Sm 14, 6 for the LORD to grant v
2Sm 8, 6 The LORD brought David v
1Chr 5,22 for v is from God;
Jdt 11,22 to bring v to our arms,
2Mc 5, 6 he was winning a v over his
Ps 20, 6 shout for joy at your v,
Prv 21,31 but v is the LORD's.
Is 42, 6 called you for the v of justice,
Mt 12,20 until he brings justice to v.
1Cor 15,54 Death is swallowed up in v.
Rv 3,21 I myself first won the v

VINE
Gn 40, 9 "I saw a v in front of me,
Dt 32,32 a branch of Sodom's v-stock,
1Kgs 5, 5 every man under his v
1Mc 14,12 Every man sat under his v
Jb 15,33 like a v that sheds its grapes
Ps 80, 9 You brought a v out of Egypt;
Sir 24,17 bud forth delights like the v,
Jer 2,21 a choice v of fully tested
Hos 10, 1 Israel is a luxuriant v
Jl 1, 7 He has laid waste my v,
Na 2, 3 The LORD will restore the v of
Zec 8,12 the v shall yield its fruit,
Mt 26,29 drink this fruit of the v until
Jn 15, 1 "I am the true v,

VIRGIN
1Kgs 1, 2 "Let a young v be sought to
2Kgs 19,21 the v daughter Zion!
Prv 24,13 if v honey is sweet
Sir 9, 5 no thoughts against a v,
Is 7,14 the v shall be with child,
Jl 1, 8 Lament like a v girt with
Mt 1,23 "Behold, the v shall be with
1Cor 7,34 An unmarried woman or a v
2Cor 11, 2 sent you as a chaste v to

VISION (S)
Gn 15, 1 came to Abram in a v: "Fear
Tb 12,19 you were seeing was a v.
Jb 4,13 In my thoughts during v
Wis 15,15 use of the eyes for v,
Is 28, 7 staggering in their v
Ez 1,28 Such was the v of the
Dn 2,19 revealed to Daniel in a v,

Am 1, 1 which he received in v
Ob 1 The v of Obadiah.
Mi 1, 1 the v he received concerning
Na 1, 1 The book of the v of Nahum
Mt 17, 9 "Do not tell the v to anyone
Lk 1,22 seen a v in the sanctuary.
2Cor 12, 1 I will go on to v and revelations
Rv 4, 1 I had a v of an open door

VOICE
Jos 10,14 when the LORD obeyed the v
Tb 5,10 I can hear a man's v,
Est 4C,30 hear the v of those in
1Mc 2,19 answered in a loud v
Jb 40, 9 can you thunder with a v like
Ps 142, 2 with full v I beseech the LORD.
Song 2,14 let me hear your v,
Sir 17,11 his glorious v their ears
Jer 3,13 would not listen to my v,
Bar 1,18 have neither heeded the v
Dn 4,28 a v spoke from heaven,
Mi 6, 1 let the hills hear your v!
Hg 1,12 the people listened to the v of
Mk 1, 3 A v of one crying out
Lk 23,46 cried out in a loud v, "Father,
Jn 5,25 the dead will hear the v of the

VOW (S)
Lv 27,28 which a man v as doomed
Dt 23,22 "When you make a v to the
Jb 22,27 and your v you shall fulfill.
Eccl 5, 3 When you make a v to God,
Sir 18,23 Before making a v have the
Jon 1,16 sacrifice and made v to him.
Acts 18,18 because he had taken a v.

W

WAIT (S)
Jdt 8,17 we w for the salvation that
2Mc 6,14 the Lord patiently w
Ps 25, 3 No one is disgraced who w for
Sir 2, 7 You who fear the LORD, w for
Is 33, 2 for you we w.
Dn 13,59 for the angel of God w
Zep 3, 8 Therefore, w for me, says the
Lk 12,37 Put on your apron and w on
Acts 1, 4 w for "the promise
Rom 8,23 as we w for adoption,
1Cor 1, 7 as you w for the revelation
Jude 21 and w for the mercy

WALK (S) (WALKING)
Dt 26,17 you are to w in his ways
Ps 23, 4 when I w through a dark
Prv 13,20 W with wise men
Wis 6, 4 nor w according to the will
Sir 10, 6 do not w the path of
Is 20, 2 This he did, w naked and .
Bar 4, 2 w by her light toward
Am 3, 3 Do two w together unless
Zec 3, 7 If you w in my ways
Mt 9, 5 'Rise and w'?
2Cor 5, 7 for we w by faith, not by sight
1Jn 2, 11 he w in darkness and does not
2Jn 6 that we w according to his
Rv 3, 4 they will w with me dressed

WANT (ING)
Ps 40, 7 and offering you do not w;
Prv 10,19 sin is not w; but he who
Wis 16, 4 inexorable w had to come;
Sir 18,25 poverty and w in the day of
Is 51,14 nor shall they w for bread.

Lam 2, 9 priestly instruction is w,
Mk 10,51 "What do you w me to do for
Lk 23, 8 he had been w to see him
2Tm 3,12 all who w to live religiously in

WAR (WARRIOR)

Lv 26, 6 and keep the sword of w
Nm 31, 5 thousand men armed for w.
Dt 4,34 by signs and wonders, by w,
Jos 11,18 Joshua waged w against all
1Sm 17,33 he has been a w from his
2Kgs 18,20 for strategy and might in w?
1Chr 5,10 Saul they waged w with the
Jdt 1, 5 Nebuchadnezzar waged w
Est A, 6 every nation prepared for w,
1Mc 1,18 to make w on Ptolemy,
2Mc 2,14 scattered because of the w,
Ps 24, 8 The Lord, a mighty w
Wis 5,20 And the universe shall w with
Is 3, 2 Hero and w, judge and prophet
Ez 7,14 no one shall go to w,
Dn 7,21 that horn made w against the
1Pt 2,11 wage w against the soul.
Rv 11, 7 will wage w against them

WASH (ED)

Lv 6,20 the stained part must be w
1Sm 25,41 w the feet of my lord's
2Kgs 5,10 "Go and w seven times
Jdt 10, 3 w her body with water
Ps 51, 9 w me, make me whiter than
Jn 9, 7 So he went and w, and came
Rv 22,14 Blessed are they who w their

WATER (S)

Gn 1, 6 to separate one body of w
Jos 2,10 the Lord dried up the w
1Chr 11,18 drew w from the cistern by
Jdt 2, 7 them to have earth and w
Est A, 9 a flood of w from a little
Ps 1, 3 planted near streams of w,
Song 5,12 are like doves beside running w
Wis 5,10 traversing the heaving w,
Sir 3,29 W quenches a flaming fire,
Is 1,22 your wine is mixed with w.
Jer 2,13 cisterns, that hold no w.
Lam 3,54 The w flowed over my head
Jl 1,20 For the streams of w are
Am 4, 8 w that did not quench their
Mi 1, 4 like w poured down a slope.
Na 3, 8 flood for her rampart and w
Hb 2,14 as w covers the sea.
Mk 1, 8 I have baptized you with w;
Lk 16,24 tip of his finger in w and cool
Jn 1,26 "I baptize with w;
Eph 5,26 bath of w with the word,
1Tm 5,23 Stop drinking only w,
Jas 3,11 both pure and brackish w?
1Pt 3,20 were saved through w.
2Pt 3, 5 earth was formed out of w
1Jn 5, 6 came through w and blood,
Rv 22,17 the gift of life-giving w.

WAY (S)

Gn 3,24 to guard the w to the tree of
Ex 13,21 cloud to show them the w,
2Chr 6,27 But teach them the right w to
Ezr 1, 6 gave them help in every w,
Neh 9,12 To light the w of their
Tb 3, 4 grieve her spirit in any w.
2Mc 12,41 praised the w of the Lord
Ps 1, 1 Nor go the w of sinners,
Prv 16,17 pays attention to his w
Wis 1,12 by your erring w of life,
Sir 8,15 he will go his own w straight,
Jer 2,33 pick your w when seeking

Lam 1,12 you who pass by the w,
Bar 3,13 Had you walked in the w of
Mi 4, 2 may instruct us in his w
Mal 2, 8 turned aside from the w,
Mt 3, 3 'Prepare the w of the Lord,
Lk 7,27 he will prepare your w before
Jn 14, 6 to him, "I am the w and the
Acts 9, 2 who belonged to the w,
Rom 1,10 may at last find my w clear to
2Cor 8,22 we often tested in many w
Eph 1,23 fills all things in every w.
Col 3, 7 when you lived in that w.
1Thes 3,11 our Lord Jesus direct our w
2Thes 2, 3 one deceive you in any w.
Ti 2,10 God our savior in every w.
Heb 2,17 like his brothers in every w,
2Pt 1,11 For, in this w, entry into the
Jude 11 They followed the w of Cain,

WEAK

Lv 19,15 neither partiality to the w!
Nm 13,18 strong or w, few or many?
Jgs 16, 7 "I shall be as w as any other
2Sm 3,39 I am w this day,
Jdt 9,11 the supporter of the w,
1Mc 3,17 Besides, we are w today
Wis 9, 5 a man w and short-lived
Sir 11,30 he will pick out the w spots.
Jer 22,16 he dispensed justice to the w
Ez 34, 4 You did not strengthen the w
Dn 8,27 w and ill for some days
Am 2, 7 trample the heads of the w
Mk 14,38 willing but the flesh is w."
Acts 20,35 we must help the w,
Rom 14, 1 Welcome anyone who is w in
1Cor 15,43 It is sown w; it is raised
2Cor 12,10 for when I am w, then I am
Gal 4, 9 w and destitute elemental
1Thes 5,14 support the w, be patient with

WEALTH

Dt 8,17 has obtained for me this w.'
Jos 22, 8 your own tents with great w,
1Sm 17,25 king would give him great w,
2Chr 17, 5 so that he enjoyed great w
Tb 4, 8 If you have great w, give
Est 1, 4 resplendent w of his royal
1Mc 6, 1 Elymais, famous for its w in
Prv 1,13 All kinds of precious w shall
Wis 5, 8 What have w and its
Sir 5, 1 Rely not on your w;
Hb 2, 4 w, too, is treacherous: the
Zec 9,17 For what w is theirs, and
Lk 16, 9 yourselves with dishonest w,
1Tm 6,17 so uncertain a thing as w
Jas 5, 2 Your w has rotted away,

WEEP (ING)

Tb 6,11 Then she stopped w.
Jdt 14,16 into a loud clamor of w,
Est 4, 3 mourning, with fasting, w,
2Mc 13,12 continuously with w and
Ps 6, 7 my couch is soaked with w.
Sir 38,17 W bitterly, mourning fully
Is 15, 3 sackcloth, lamenting and w;
Jer 3,21 the plaintive w of Israel's
Mt 2,18 Rachel w for her children
Lk 6,21 who are now w, for you will
Rv 18,15 W and mourning, they cry out

WHEAT

Gn 30,14 One day, during the w
Ex 9,32 But the w and the spelt were
Jgs 6,11 Gideon was beating out w
Ru 2,23 end of the barley and w

2Sm 4, 6 dozed off while sifting w,
1Chr 21,20 Ornan was threshing w, he
Jdt 2,27 at the time of the w harvest,
Ps 72,16 May w abound in the land,
Sir 39,26 The heart of the w, milk and
Jer 12,13 They have sown w and
Ez 4, 9 Again, take w and barley,
Hos 7,14 For w and wine they
Jl 1,11 Over the w and the barley,
Am 8, 5 that we may display the w?
Lk 3,17 gather the w into his barn,
Jn 12,24 unless a grain of w falls to
Acts 27,38 by throwing the w into the
1Cor 15,37 but a bare kernel of w,

WHITE (R)

Gn 49,12 his teeth are w than milk.
Nm 12,10 there was Miriam, a snow-w
2Kgs 5,27 Gehazi left Elisha, a leper w
2Mc 11, 8 clothed in w garments
Ps 51, 9 wash me, make me w than .
Wis 2,10 man for his hair grown w with
Is 1,18 they may become w as wool.
Lam 4, 7 were her princes, w than milk,
Lk 9,29 clothing became dazzling w.
Jn 20,12 and saw two angels in w
Acts 1,10 two men dressed in w
Rv 20,11 Next I saw a large w throne

WICKED (NESS)

Gn 13,13 of Sodom were very w
Ex 23, 1 Do not join the w
Nm 14,27 "How long will this w
1Kgs 2,44 requites you for your own w.
Tb 3, 8 but the w demon Asmodeus
Est 4,30 from the power of the w,
1Mc 1,36 and a w adversary to Israel
2Mc 1,17 has thus punished the w!
Jb 3,17 There the w cease from
Ps 1, 1 the counsel of the w,
Eccl 3,17 both the just and the w God
Wis 2,21 for their w blinded them,
Sir 5, 7 upon the w alights his wrath.
Jer 3, 2 defiled the land by your w
Ez 3,18 If I say to the w man,
Jon 1, 2 their w has come up before me
Zep 1, 3 I will overthrow the w
Mal 3,18 between the just and the w;
Mt 13,49 separate the w from the
Lk 22,37 was counted among the w';
Jn 3,20 who does w things hates the
Rv 2, 2 you cannot tolerate the w;

WIDOW (S)

Ex 22,23 your own wives will be w,
Dt 14,29 and the w who belong to your
1Kgs 17, 9 a w there to provide for you
Ps 146, 9 the orphan and the w,
Wis 2,10 let us neither spare the w
Sir 35,14 the orphan, nor to the w
Is 9,16 their orphans and w he does
Bar 4,12 gloat over me, a w, bereft of
Zec 7,10 Do not oppress the w or the
1Cor 7, 8 to the unmarried and to w I say

WIFE (WIVES)

Gn 2,24 mother and clings to his w,
Nm 5,12 If a man's w goes astray
Dt 5,21 not covet your neighbor's w.
1Sm 1, 2 He had two w
Est 1,20 all w will honor their husbands
Prv 5,18 And have joy of the w of your
Eccl 9, 9 Enjoy life with the w whom
Sir 7,19 Dismiss not a sensible w;
Jer 6,12 their fields and their w as well
Hos 1, 2 Go, take a harlot w

Jos	2, 4	The w had taken the two
Jgs	4, 9	into the power of a w."
Ru	1, 5	and the w was left with
1Sm	1,15	"I am an unhappy w.
2Sm	3, 8	with a crime involving a w!
1Kgs	3,17	One w said: "By your leave,
2Kgs	4, 1	A certain w, the widow of one
1Chr	2, 3	a Canaanite w.
2Chr	2,13	son of a Danite w
Tb	1, 9	I married Anna, a w of our
Jdt	8, 8	a very God-fearing w.
Est	4,11	any man or w who goes to
Jb	14, 1	Man born of w is short-lived
Ps	48, 7	anguish, like a w's labor,
Prv	6,26	the price of a loose w
Eccl	7,26	I find the w who is a hunter's
Sir	9, 2	Give no w power over you
Is	13, 8	like a w in labor they writhe;
Jer	3,20	But like a w faithless to her
Ez	8,14	I saw sitting there the w
Hos	3, 1	Give your love to a w
Mi	4, 9	seized with pains like a w in
Zec	5, 9	saw two w coming forth
Mal	2,11	has married an idolatrous w.
Mt	5,28	everyone who looks at a w
Mk	5,25	a w afflicted with
Lk	7,37	a sinful w in the city
Jn	2, 4	"W, how does your concern
Acts	16, 1	the son of a Jewish w
Rom	7, 2	a married w is bound by law
1Cor	7, 1	man not to touch a w,"
Gal	4, 4	born of a w, born under the
1Thes	5, 3	pains upon a pregnant w,
1Tm	2,11	A w must receive instruction
Rv	2,20	that you tolerate the w

WONDERFUL

2Chr	2, 8	must be lofty and w.
Jdt	16,13	w in power and
Est	4, 3	and every w thing under the
Jb	42, 3	things too w for me,
Ps	17, 7	Show your w love,
Prv	30,18	Three things are too w for
Sir	43, 2	what a w work of the Most
Is	25, 1	For you have fulfilled your w
Jer	21, 2	according to all his w works,
Mi	7,15	show us w signs.
Mk	12,11	and it is w in our eyes'?"
1Pt	2, 9	out of darkness into his w
Rv	15, 3	"Great and w are your

WONDERS

Ex	4,21	before Pharaoh all the w
Dt	4,34	by signs and w,
Jos	3, 5	the LORD will perform w
Est	10F, 6	worked signs and great w,
Jb	37, 5	w past our searching out.
Ps	4, 4	Know that the LORD works w
Wis	8, 8	signs and w she knows in
Sir	17, 8	the w of his deeds and praise
Bar	2,11	with signs and w and great
Mt	24,24	signs and w so great as to
Mk	13,22	perform signs and w
Jn	4,48	see signs and w, you will not
Acts	2,19	And I will work w in the
Rom	15,19	the power of signs and w,
2Cor	12,12	all endurance, signs and w,
2Thes	2, 9	and in signs and w that lie,
Heb	2, 4	his testimony by signs, w,

WONDROUS

Ex	3,20	doing all kinds of w deeds
Jgs	6,13	Where are his w deeds
1Chr	16, 9	proclaim all his w deeds.
Jb	37,14	Stand and consider the w
Ps	9, 2	I will declare all your w

Wis	10,17	Conducted them by a w road,
Sir	43, 8	how w in this change!

WORD (S)

Gn	15, 1	this w of the LORD came to
Ex	3,18	has sent us w.
Nm	15,31	Since he has despised the w
Dt	6,18	you may, according to his w,
Jos	6,10	outcry until he gave the w
Ru	1, 6	because w reached her
1Sm	3,19	not permitting any w of his to
1Kgs	5,21	When he had heard the w of
1Chr	11, 3	in accordance with the w of
2Chr	11, 2	However, the w of the LORD
Tb	13,12	all who speak a harsh w
Jdt	4, 4	So they sent w to the whole
Est	9,26	named Purim after the w pur.
1Mc	9,37	After this, w was brought to
2Mc	4,39	When w was spread that a
Jb	2,13	none of them spoke a w to
Ps	19, 4	There is no w or sound;
Prv	12,25	but a kindly w makes it glad.
Eccl	7,21	not give heed to every w
Wis	9, 1	made all things by your w
Sir	3, 8	In w and deed honor your
Is	1,10	Hear the w of the LORD,
Jer	1, 2	The w of the LORD first came
Bar	1, 1	these are the w of the scroll
Ez	1, 3	the w of the LORD came
Dn	9,25	From the utterance of the w
Jl	1, 1	The w of the LORD which
Am	1, 3	I will not revoke my w;
Mi	1, 1	The w of the LORD which
Zep	1, 1	The w of the LORD which
Hg	1, 1	the w of the LORD came
Zec	1, 1	the w of the LORD came to
Mal	1, 1	The w of the LORD to Israel
Mt	2, 8	bring me w, that I too may
Mk	2, 2	and he preached the w to
Lk	1, 2	ministers of the w have
Jn	1, 1	In the beginning was the w,
Acts	4, 4	those who heard the w came
Rom	9, 6	it is not that the w of God has
1Cor	14,36	Did the w of God go forth
Gal	6, 6	being instructed in the w
Eph	1,13	who have heard the w of
Phil	1,14	than ever to proclaim the w
Col	1, 5	heard through the w of truth,
1Thes	1, 5	not come to you in w alone,
2Thes	2,17	in every good deed and w.
1Tm	4,14	the prophetic w with the
2Tm	2, 9	But the w of God is not
Ti	1, 3	proper time revealed his w
Heb	1, 3	all things by his mighty w.
Jas	1,18	give us birth by the w of truth
1Pt	1,23	living and abiding w of God,
2Pt	3, 2	to recall the w previously
1Jn	1, 1	hands concerns the W of
Rv	1, 2	who gives witness to the w of

WORK (S)

Gn	2, 3	he rested from all the w he
Ex	1,14	hard w in mortar and brick
Lv	16,29	himself and shall do no w.
Nm	8,25	and w no longer.
Dt	5,13	and do all your w;
Jgs	2, 7	had seen all the great w
Ru	2,19	Where did you go to w?
1Sm	6, 7	So now set to w
2Sm	12,31	whom he assigned to w with
1Kgs	5,30	Solomon's prefects for the w,
2Kgs	19,32	nor cast up siege-w against it.
1Chr	9,13	valiant for the w of the
2Chr	2, 6	send me men skilled at w
Ezr	3, 8	to supervise the w on the
Neh	6,16	that this w had been

Tb	2, 11	the kind of w women do.
Est	10F, 1	"This is the w of God.
1Mc	2,47	and the w prospered in their
2Mc	5,25	the Jews refraining from w,
Jb	1, 3	and a great number of w
Ps	8, 4	the w of your fingers,
Eccl	12,14	bring to judgment every w,
Song	5,14	His body is a w of ivory
Wis	9,10	may be with me and w with
Sir	4,30	nor sly and suspicious at w.
Is	1,31	and his w shall become a
Jer	8,17	which no charm will w
Dn	3,57	Bless the Lord, all you w
Hos	8, 6	The w of an artisan,
Jl	3, 3	And I will w wonders in the
Mi	2, 1	and w out evil on their
Hg	1,14	and set to w on the house
Mt	6,28	They do not w or spin.
Mk	6,14	mighty powers are at w in
Lk	13,14	when w should be done.
Jn	4,34	and to finish his w.
Rom	4, 5	But when one does not w,
2Cor	1,24	rather, we w together for your
Gal	6, 4	must examine his own w,
Eph	2, 2	spirit that is now at w in the
Col	1,10	in every good w bearing fruit
1Thes	1, 3	calling to mind your w of faith
2Thes	2, 7	lawlessness is already at w.
1Tm	5,10	herself in every good w.
2Jn	11	shares in his evil w.

WORLD

Gn	10,25	in his time the w was divided;
Nm	16,30	alive down into the nether w,
Dt	30, 4	the farthest corner of the w,
1Kgs	10,24	And the whole w sought
1Chr	1,19	for in his time the w was
Neh	1, 9	the farthest corner of the w,
Tb	3, 2	are the judge of the w.
Jdt	2, 1	revenge on the whole w,
2Mc	2,22	possession of the w-famous
Ps	98, 9	To govern the w with justice
Prv	1,12	as the nether w does,
Song	8, 6	relentless as the nether w is
Sir	14,16	in the nether w there are no
Is	5,14	the nether w enlarges its
Jer	51,41	the glory of the whole w!
Lam	4,12	nor any of the w's
Bar	2,17	the dead in the nether w,
Ez	31,15	went down to the nether w
Am	9, 2	through to the nether w,
Jon	2, 3	the midst of the nether w I
Na	1, 5	the w and all who dwell in
Hb	2, 5	his throat like the nether w,
Mt	4, 8	kingdoms of the w in their
Rom	1, 8	is heralded throughout the w.
1Cor	7,33	about the things of the w,
2Cor	1,12	ourselves in the w,
Eph	1, 4	the foundation of the w,
Phil	2,15	shine like lights in the w,
Col	1, 6	in the whole w it is bearing
Heb	1, 6	the first-born into the w,
2Pt	1, 4	corruption that is in the w
1Jn	2, 2	for those of the whole w.
2Jn	7	have gone out into the w,

WORSHIP

Gn	22, 5	We will w and then come
Ex	3,12	you will w God on this very
Lv	17, 7	to render their wanton w.
Dt	5, 9	bow down before them or w
Jos	5,14	prostrate to the ground in w,
Jgs	2,12	and by their w of these gods
2Sm	15, 8	I will w him in Hebron.' "
1Kgs	9, 6	proceed to venerate and w
2Kgs	5,18	the temple of Rimmon to w

2Chr	7,19	proceed to venerate and w
Tb	5,14	where we would w together.
Jdt	3, 8	every nation might w
Ps	132, 7	let us w at God's footstool."
Wis	14,27	For the w of infamous idols
Is	2, 8	they w the works of their
Bar	5, 4	the glory of God's w.
Ez	20,40	without exception shall w me;
Dn	3, 5	and w the golden statue
Zec	14,16	up year after year to w the
Mt	4, 9	prostrate yourself and w me.
Lk	1,74	without fear we might w him
Jn	4,20	the place to w is in
Rom	9, 4	giving of the law, the w, and
Phil	3, 3	we who w through the Spirit
Col	2,18	and w of angels,
2Thes	2, 4	called god and object of w,
Heb	1, 6	all the angels of God w him."
Rv	4,10	sits on the throne and w him,

WORTHY

Ru	2,13	"May I prove w of your
1Kgs	1,52	"If he proves himself w,
Tb	4,11	Alms are a w offering in the
Jdt	8,29	corresponds to the w
Est	1,19	royal dignity to one more w
1Mc	10,19	and w to be our friend
2Mc	4,25	with nothing that made him w
Ps	145, 3	Great is the LORD and w of
Prv	12, 4	A w wife is the crown of
Wis	3, 5	and found them w of himself.
Sir	26, 2	A w wife brings joy to her
Mt	3,11	I am not w to carry his
Mk	1, 7	I am not w to stoop and
Lk	3,16	I am not w to loosen the
Jn	1,27	I am not w to untie."
Acts	5,41	found w to suffer dishonor
Rom	16, 2	in a manner w of the holy
Eph	4, 1	in a manner w of the call
Phil	1,27	w of the gospel of Christ
Col	1,10	to live in a manner w of the
1Thes	2, 4	judged w by God to be
2Thes	1, 5	considered w of the kingdom
1Tm	6, 1	regard their masters as w
Heb	3, 3	But he is w of more "glory"
3Jn	6	help them in a way w of God
Rv	3, 4	white, because they are w.

WRATH

Ex	15, 7	you loosed your w to
Nm	1,53	God's w will strike the
Dt	6,15	lest the w of the LORD, your God
Jos	22,20	did not w fall upon the entire
2Kgs	3,27	The w against Israel was so
2Chr	12, 7	and my w shall not be poured
Ezr	5,12	provoked the w of the God
Neh	13,18	add to the w against Israel
Jdt	2, 7	come against them in my w;
Est	1,12	At this the king's w flared up,
1Mc	2,44	and lawbreakers in their w,
2Mc	7,38	be an end to the w of the
Jb	4, 9	of his w they are consumed.
Eccl	5,16	vexation, sickness and w,
Wis	10, 3	through his fratricidal w.
Sir	5, 7	the wicked alights his w.
Is	66,15	wreak his w with burning
Jer	3, 5	"Will he keep his w forever,
Bar	1,13	and the w and anger of the
Ez	7,12	for w shall be upon all the
Hos	5,10	I will pour out my w like

Am	1, 11	and kept his w to the end
Na	1, 2	and lays up w for his
Hb	2,15	neighbors a flood of your w
Zep	1.15	A day of w is that day,
Zec	8, 2	stirred to jealous w for her.
Mt	3, 7	to flee from the coming w?
Jn	3,36	but the w of God remains
Eph	2, 3	were by nature children of w,
Col	3, 6	Because of these the w of
1Thes	1,10	us from the coming w.
Heb	3, 11	As I swore in my w,
Jas	1,19	slow to speak, slow to w,
Rv	6,16	and from the w of the Lamb,

WRITE (ING) (WRITTEN) (WROTE)

Ex	17,14	"W this down in a document
2Chr	9,29	Solomon, first and last, are w,
Neh	10, 1	which we are putting into w.
Est	8, 8	may w in the king's name
1Mc	10,24	I too will w them conciliatory
2Mc	2,32	nonsense to w a long preface
Jb	31,35	my accuser would w out his
Prv	7, 3	w them on the tablet of
Eccl	12,10	and to w down true sayings
Is	10, 1	who w oppressive decrees,
Jer	22,30	W this man down as one
Bar	2,28	ordered him to w down your
Ez	24, 2	Son of man, w down this
Hos	8,12	w for him my many
Hb	2, 2	W down the vision Clearly
Mk	10, 4	"Moses permitted him to w
Lk	1, 3	to w it down in an orderly
Jn	8, 6	began to w on the ground
Acts	25,26	nothing definite to w about
1Cor	5, 11	But I now w to you not to
2Cor	1,13	For we w you nothing but
1Thes	4, 9	no need for anyone to w you,
2Thes	3,17	this is how I w.
Phlm	19	I, Paul, w this in my own
Heb	8,10	I will w them upon their
2Pt	3,15	wisdom given to him, also w to
1Jn	2, 8	And yet I do w a new
2Jn	12	I have much to w to you,
3Jn	13	I have much to w to you,
Jude	3	was making every effort to w
Rv	1, 11	"W on a scroll what you

Y

YEAR (S)

Gn	17,21	you by this time next y."
Ex	23,14	"Three times a y you shall
Nm	14,34	one y for each day.
Dt	1, 3	In the fortieth y,
1Sm	1, 7	This went on y after year;
Ezr	3, 8	appointing the Levites twenty y
Tb	1, 7	And except for sabbatical y
Jdt	1, 1	It was the twelfth y of the
Est	A, 1	In the second y of the reign
1Mc	1,10	in the y one hundred and
2Mc	6,24	the ninety-y-old Eleazar had
Jb	3, 6	among the days of the y.
Ps	65,12	You adorn the y with your
Sir	47, 9	the seasons of each y
Is	6, 1	In the y king Uzziah died,
Jer	1, 2	in the thirteenth y of his
Bar	1, 2	in the fifth y
Ez	46,17	only until the y of release,

Dn	9, 2	in the first y of his reign I,
Mi	6, 6	with calves a y old?
Zec	1, 1	In the second y of Darius,
Lk	3, 1	In the fifteenth y of the reign
Jn	11,49	who was high priest that y,
Acts	11,26	For a whole y they met
Gal	1,18	Then after three y I went
Heb	9, 7	the inner one once a y,
Jas	4,13	spend a y there doing
Rv	9,15	and y to kill a third of

YOKE

Dt	28,48	put an iron y on your neck
1Kgs	12, 4	heavy y your father imposed
Mt	11,30	For my y is easy,
Gal	5, 1	again to the y of slavery.

YOUNG

Dt	22, 6	a bird's nest with y birds
Ru	2, 9	I have commanded the y
2Chr	10,14	to the advice of the y men
Ps	78,63	Fire consumed their y men;
Prv	7, 7	I observed among the y men,
Eccl	11, 9	Rejoice, O y man, while you
Dn	1, 4	y men without any defect,
Jl	3, 1	your y men shall see visions;
Mk	14,51	Now a y man followed him
Lk	2,24	pair of turtledoves or two y
Acts	2,17	your y men shall see visions,
1Jn	2,13	I am writing to you, y men,

YOUTH

1Sm	17,33	been a warrior from his y."
Ps	71, 5	my trust, God, from my y.
Prv	2,17	the companion of her y
Eccl	4,13	a poor but wise y
Is	65,20	He dies a mere y
Mal	2,14	and the wife of your y,

Z

ZEAL (OUS) (ZEALOT)

Nm	25, 11	his z for my honor among
2Kgs	10,16	"and see my z for the LORD."
Ps	69,10	z for your house consumes
Is	37,32	The z of the LORD of hosts
Lk	6,15	Simon who was called a Z
Acts	21,20	and they are all z observers
2Cor	7, 11	fear, and yearning, and z,
Phil	3, 6	in z I persecuted the church,

ZION

2Sm	5, 7	take the stronghold of Z
2Kgs	19,21	the virgin daughter Z!
Ps	2, 6	Z, my holy mountain."
Is	1,27	Z shall be redeemed by
Jer	50, 5	to their goal in Z they shall
Lam	2,13	virgin daughter Z?
Jl	2, 1	Blow the trumpet in Z,
Am	1, 2	The LORD will roar from Z,
Mi	3,12	Z shall be plowed like a field
Zec	1,17	the LORD will again comfort Z,
Mt	21, 5	"Say to daughter Z, 'Behold,
Rom	9,33	am laying a stone in Z
Heb	12,22	have approached Mount Z
1Pt	2, 6	am laying a stone in Z, a
Rv	14, 1	Lamb standing on Mount Z,

Map 1:
**THE WORLD OF
THE PATRIARCHS**

JAVAN Descendants of Japheth (Gn 10, 2–5)
PUT Descendants of Ham (Gn 10, 6–20)
LUD Descendants of Shem (Gn 10, 21–31)
(Egypt) Later biblical name
→ Abraham's route

Jacob meets
Leah and Rachel
(Gn, ch 29).

Abraham and Lot
first settle
(Gn 11, 31).

Abraham and Sarah's
original home
(Gn 11, 28)

Jacob wrestles
with God
(Gn 32, 23–33).

Abraham and
Sarah's burial site
(Gn 25, 9–10)

Joseph is sold into
slavery in Egypt
(Gn, ch 37).

GOMER

LUD
(Lydia)

JAVAN
(Greeks)

TOGARMAH

ASHKENAZ
(Scythians)

HITTITES

MADAI
(Medes)

ELAM
(Persia)

River Tigris

ASSHUR
(Assyria)

River Euphrates

Haran

Paddan-Aram

Mari

Babylon

Ur

ARPHAXAD

KITTIM
(Cyprus)

ARAM
(Syria)

Damascus

AMORITES

Penuel

Shechem

CANAAN

Hebron

Beersheba

PHILISTINES

Gaza

JOKTAN
(Arabia)

Zoan

On

MIZRAIM
(Egypt)

PUT

The Great Sea (Mediterranean Sea)

Red Sea

River Nile

Caspian Sea

Persian Gulf

200 miles
200 kilometers

© 2001 by Thomas Nelson, Inc.
and Saint Mary's Press

maps.com

1799

Map 2:
THE EXODUS FROM EGYPT

Moses' death (Dt, ch 34)

Desert wandering (Dt, ch 2)

God gives the Ten Commandments (Ex, ch 20).

Miracles of manna and quail (Ex, ch 16)

Legend:
- Route of the Exodus
- Alternate routes of Red Sea crossing
- Unsuccessful invasion of Canaan (Nm 14, 39–45)
- Trade routes
- ? Exact location questionable

75 miles

75 kilometers

**Labels:**

Ammon

Moab

River Arnon

Edom

Midian

Dead Sea (Salt Sea)

Zoar — Brook Zered

Punon

Hebron

Arad

Beersheba

Gaza

Wilderness of Zin

Kadesh Barnea

Arabah

Ezion Geber

Gulf of Aqaba

Wilderness of Paran

Way of the Philistines

Way of Shur

Route from Egypt to Arabia

The Great Sea (Mediterranean Sea)

Marah?

Elim?

Red Sea

SINAI HOREB

MT +

Avaris

Qantir

Pithom

Succoth

Baal Zephon

Land of Goshen

Memphis

River Nile

maps.com

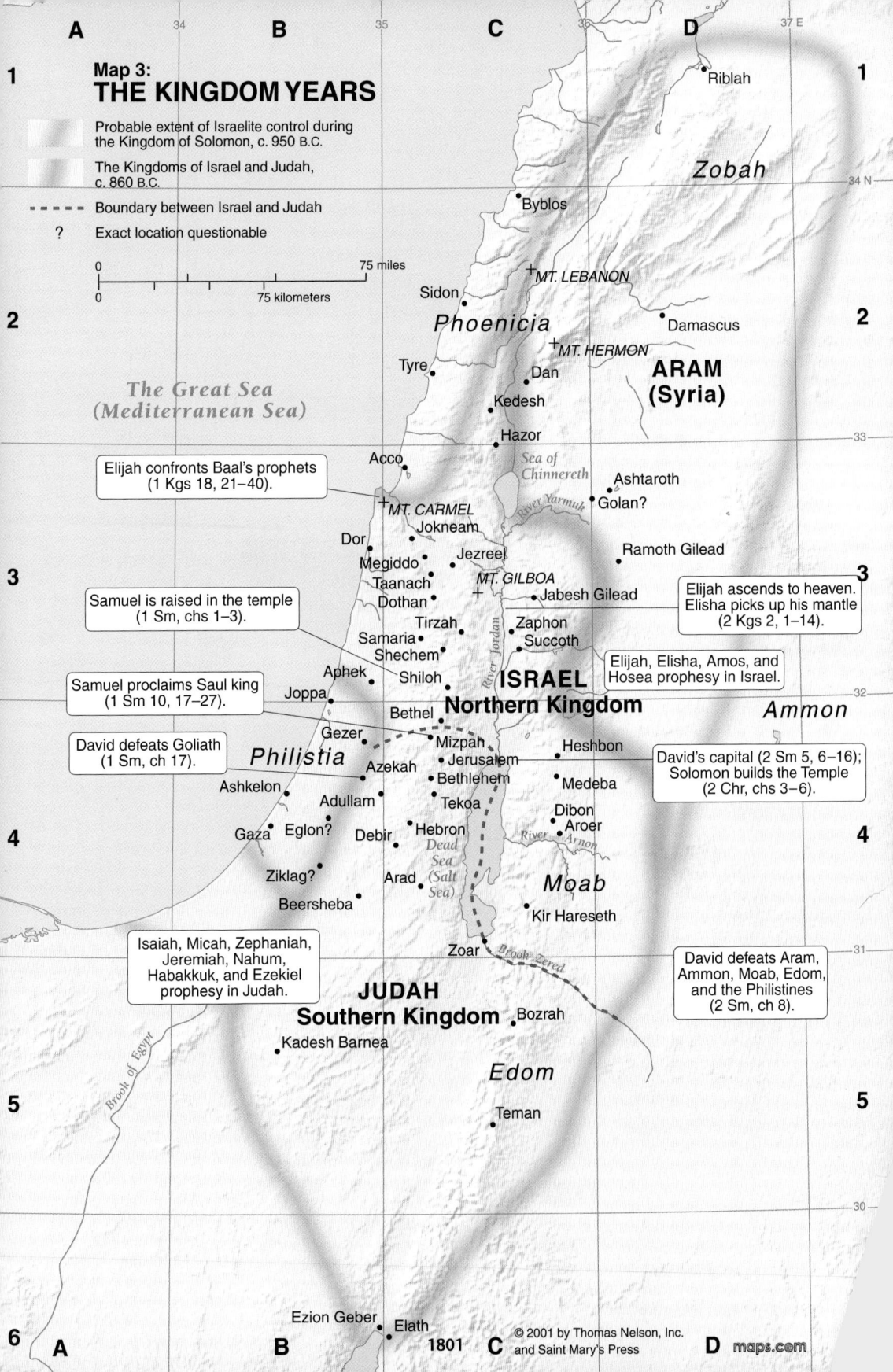

Map 3:
THE KINGDOM YEARS

Probable extent of Israelite control during the Kingdom of Solomon, c. 950 B.C.

The Kingdoms of Israel and Judah, c. 860 B.C.

- - - - Boundary between Israel and Judah

? Exact location questionable

0 —————— 75 miles
0 —————— 75 kilometers

The Great Sea
(Mediterranean Sea)

Elijah confronts Baal's prophets (1 Kgs 18, 21–40).

Samuel is raised in the temple (1 Sm, chs 1–3).

Samuel proclaims Saul king (1 Sm 10, 17–27).

David defeats Goliath (1 Sm, ch 17).

Isaiah, Micah, Zephaniah, Jeremiah, Nahum, Habakkuk, and Ezekiel prophesy in Judah.

Elijah ascends to heaven. Elisha picks up his mantle (2 Kgs 2, 1–14).

Elijah, Elisha, Amos, and Hosea prophesy in Israel.

David's capital (2 Sm 5, 6–16); Solomon builds the Temple (2 Chr, chs 3–6).

David defeats Aram, Ammon, Moab, Edom, and the Philistines (2 Sm, ch 8).

Riblah

Zobah

Byblos

+ MT. LEBANON

Sidon

Phoenicia

Damascus

+ MT. HERMON

Tyre

Dan

Kedesh

ARAM (Syria)

Hazor

Sea of Chinnereth

Acco

Ashtaroth

Golan?

+ MT. CARMEL

Jokneam

River Yarmuk

Ramoth Gilead

Dor

Megiddo

Jezreel

Taanach

+ MT. GILBOA

Dothan

Jabesh Gilead

Tirzah

Zaphon

Samaria

River Jordan

Succoth

Shechem

Aphek

Shiloh

ISRAEL
Northern Kingdom

Joppa

Ammon

Bethel

Gezer

Mizpah

Heshbon

Azekah

Jerusalem

Philistia

Bethlehem

Medeba

Ashkelon

Tekoa

Dibon

Adullam

Aroer

Gaza

Eglon?

Debir

Hebron

River Arnon

Ziklag?

Dead Sea (Salt Sea)

Moab

Arad

Beersheba

Kir Hareseth

Zoar

Brook Zered

JUDAH
Southern Kingdom

Bozrah

Kadesh Barnea

Edom

Teman

Brook of Egypt

Ezion Geber

Elath

1801

© 2001 by Thomas Nelson, Inc. and Saint Mary's Press

maps.com

Map 4:
THE ASSYRIAN EMPIRE
(C. 700 B.C.)

→ Exiles from Israel into Assyrian captivity (721 B.C.)

Map 5:
THE BABYLONIAN EMPIRE
(C. 600 B.C.)

→ Exiles from Israel into Babylonian captivity (605, 597, 587 B.C.)
→ Return of exiles under Shesbazzar and Zerubbabel (538 B.C.)
→ Return of exiles under Ezra and Nehemiah (445 B.C.)

1802

Map 6:
THE MINISTRY OF JESUS

(1,742) Elevation, in feet

? Exact location questionable

0 — 30 miles

0 — 30 kilometers

34 30'E   35 00'   35 30'   36 00'

33 30'N

Sidon

Damascus

Zarephath

MT. LEBANON (11,000) +

MT. HERMON (9,200) +

Iturea

Tyre

Phoenicia

Panias (Caesarea Philippi)

Trachonitis

33 00'

Galilee

Ptolemais

Chorazin

Bethsaida?

Feeds five thousand (Lk 9, 10–17)

Heals centurion's servant (Mt 8, 5–13) and a paralytic (Mt 9, 2–8), and raises Jairus's daughter (Mt 9, 18–26)

Capernaum

Magdala

Sea of Galilee

Gergesa

MT. CARMEL (1,742) +

Cana

Tiberias

Calms the storm (Mk 4, 35–41); walks on water (Mt 14, 22–33)

River Kishon

River Yarmuk

Performs wedding feast miracle (Jn 2, 1–11)

Nazareth

Nain

+ MT. TABOR (1,843)

Gadara?

Transfiguration? (Mt 17, 1–13)

Grows up in Nazareth (Lk 2, 39–40)

Esdraelon

River Jezreel

32 30'

Caesarea

Raises widow's son (Lk 7, 11–17)

Scythopolis

MT. GILBOA (1,696)

Decapolis

The Great Sea (Mediterranean Sea)

Samaria

Samaria

Gerasa

Talks to Samaritan woman (Jn 4, 4–42)

Sychar

River Jordan

River Jabbok

+ MT. GERIZIM (2,890)

Perea

Antipatris

32 00'

Joppa

Arimathea

Gadara?

Ephraim

Philadelphia

Lydda

Crucifixion and Resurrection

Heals Bartimaeus (Mk 10, 46–52); calls Zacchaeus (Lk 19, 9–10)

Appears to two disciples after Resurrection (Lk 24, 13–35)

Emmaus

Jericho

Kirjath Jearim

Jerusalem

Bethabara

Jesus' baptism? (Mk 1, 9–11)

Beth Haccerem

Bethany

Qumran

Azotus

Bethlehem

Raises Lazarus (Jn 11, 1–44)

Medeba

Ashkelon

Herodium

Jesus' birth (Lk 2, 1–7)

Judea

Hebron

Machaerus

Dead Sea (Salt Sea) (-1,300)

31 30'

River Arnon

Gaza

Idumea

Masada

Beersheba

maps.com

A   B   C   D

1   2   3   4   5

Map 7:
PAUL'S FIRST AND SECOND JOURNEYS
(ACTS 13–14; 15.39—18.22)

→ First missionary journey, with Barnabas and Mark
   (c. A.D. 46–48)
→ Second missionary journey, with Silas
   (c. A.D. 49–52)

© 2001 by Thomas Nelson, Inc.

maps.com

Illyricum
Italy
Adriatic Sea
Sicily
Macedonia
Thrace
Amphipolis
Philippi
Thessalonica
Neapolis
Berea
Apollonia
Troas
Achaia
Athens
Corinth
Ephesus
Phrygia
Antioch
Iconium
Lystra
Pisidia
Derbe
Attalia
Pamphylia
Tarsus
Lycia
Cilicia
Perga
Antioch
Seleucia
Syria
Patmos
Cyprus
Crete
Salamis
Paphos
Black Sea
Pontus
Bithynia
Galatia
Cappadocia
The Great Sea
(Mediterranean Sea)
Caesarea
Jerusalem
Palestine

Map 8:
PAUL'S THIRD AND FOURTH JOURNEYS
(ACTS 18.23—21.16; 27—28.16)

→ Third missionary journey (c. A.D. 53–57)
→ Fourth missionary journey (c. A.D. 59–62)

1804

© 2001 by Thomas Nelson, Inc.

maps.com

Illyricum
Italy
Rome
Three Inns
Appii Forum
Puteoli
Adriatic Sea
Rhegium
Sicily
Syracuse
Malta
Macedonia
Thrace
Amphipolis
Philippi
Thessalonica
Berea
Apollonia
Troas
Assos
Achaia
Mitylene
Colossae
Phrygia
Antioch
Chios
Ephesus
Pisidia
Iconium
Corinth
Athens
Lystra
Derbe
Samos
Miletus
Cos
Cnidus
Lycia
Pamphylia
Tarsus
Rhodes
Myra
Cilicia
Patara
Cyprus
Antioch
Crete
Syria
Fair Havens
The Great Sea
(Mediterranean Sea)
Tyre
Sidon
Ptolemais
Caesarea
Antipatris
Jerusalem
Palestine
Black Sea
Pontus
Bithynia
Galatia
Cappadocia

Map 9:
THE HOLY LAND IN MODERN TIMES

Area occupied by Israel since June, 1967

0 — 75 miles
0 — 75 kilometers

LEBANON

Tripoli

Beirut

BEKAA VALLEY

Sidon

LEBANON MOUNTAINS

ANTI-LEBANON MOUNTAINS

Damascus

SYRIA

Tyre
Dan
Qiryat Shemona
Quneitra

GOLAN HEIGHTS

Nahariyya

1973 Line
1967 Cease-Fire Line

Akko
Safad

Haifa
Tiberias

Sea of Galilee

Nazareth

Dera

Afula
Ramtha
Beth Shean

Hadera
Tulkarm
Netanya
Nablus
Jarash

Herzliyya
WEST BANK

Tel Aviv
Petah Tiqwa
Yafo

Rishon le Zion
Lod
Ramalah
Amman

Ramla
Jericho

Ashdod
Jerusalem

Ashqelon
Bethlehem
Madaba

Qiryat Gat
Hebron
Dhiban

Gaza
En Gedi

GAZA STRIP

Dead Sea (Salt Sea)

Beersheba

Karak

Al-Arish

ISRAEL

JORDAN

EGYPT

Negev   *Arabah*

Sinai

The Great Sea (Mediterranean Sea)

SAUDI ARABIA

Elat
Aqaba

© 2001 by Thomas Nelson, Inc

1805

maps.com

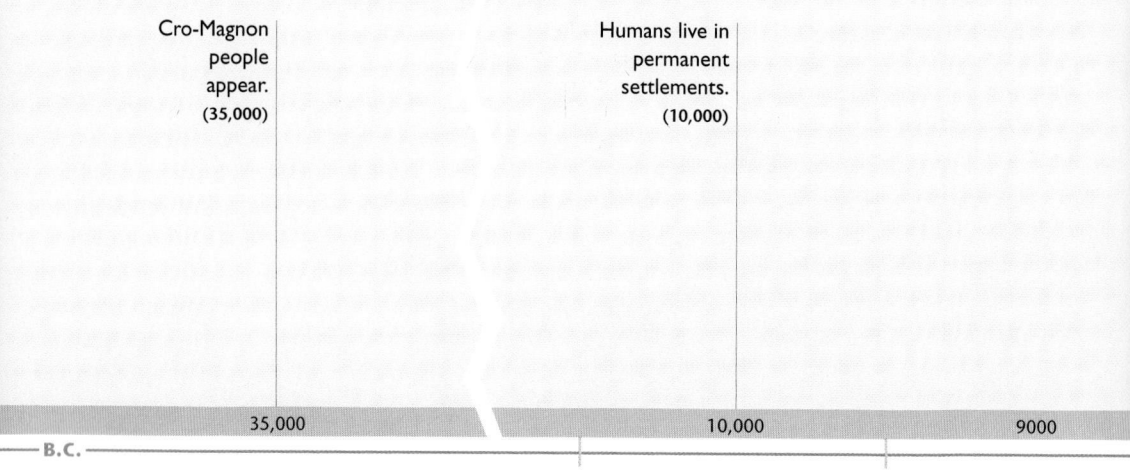

Timeline of Human History

	35,000		10,000	9000

Cro-Magnon people appear. (35,000)

Humans live in permanent settlements. (10,000)

Timeline of Biblical History

B.C.

PREHISTORY	2000	1900	1800	1700

Jacob's descendants settle in Egypt. (1750)

Abraham and Sarah arrive in Canaan. (1850)

BIBLICAL PREHISTORY

Important Biblical Figures
Adam and Eve
Cain and Abel
Noah

TIME OF THE PATRIARCHS AND MATRIARCHS

Important Biblical Figures
Abraham and Sarah
Isaac and Rebekah
Jacob, Leah, and Rachel
Joseph and Asenath

Last glacial
period ends.
(8200)

Farming villages form;
goats, sheep, and oxen
are domesticated.
(7000)

| 8000 | 7000 | 6000 | 5000 |

B.C.

Timeline of Human History

Timeline of Biblical History

B.C.

Judges lead Israelite
tribes in Canaan.
(1200)

Moses leads Exodus from Egypt.
(1290)

Joshua invades
Canaan.
(1250)

TIME IN EGYPT AND THE EXODUS

TIME OF THE JUDGES

Important Biblical Figures
Moses
Aaron
Miriam

Important Biblical Figures
Deborah
Gideon
Samson
Samuel

1807

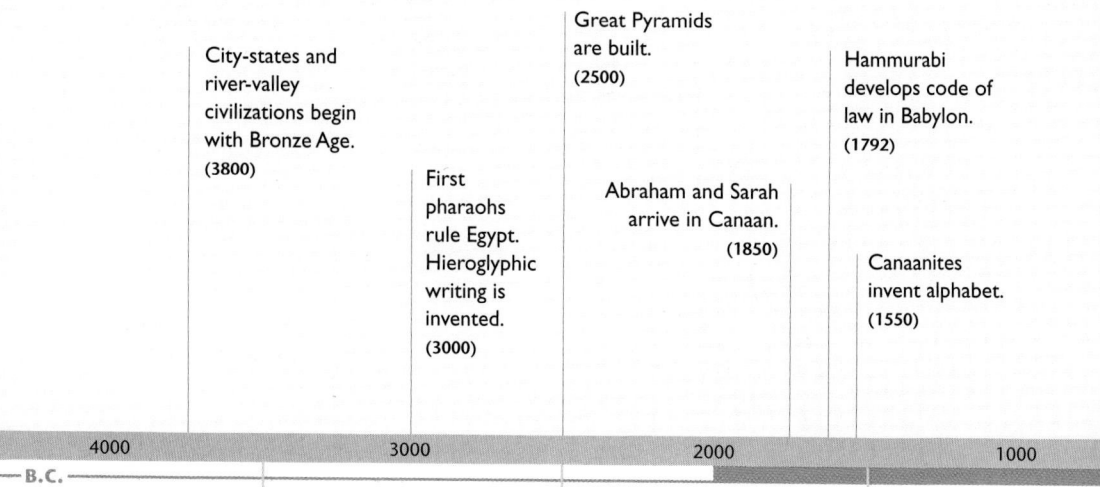

City-states and river-valley civilizations begin with Bronze Age. (3800)

First pharaohs rule Egypt. Hieroglyphic writing is invented. (3000)

Great Pyramids are built. (2500)

Abraham and Sarah arrive in Canaan. (1850)

Hammurabi develops code of law in Babylon. (1792)

Canaanites invent alphabet. (1550)

Timeline of Human History

Timeline of Biblical History   PROPHETS   Prominent Kings of Israel   Prominent Kings of Judah

B.C.
1000   900   800   700   600   500

Kingdom divides into Israel and Judah. (922)

Assyrians capture Samaria, ending the kingdom of Israel. (721)

ELIJAH (865)

Solomon rules kingdom, builds Temple. (961)

ELISHA (850)

AMOS (783)

Babylonians take Jerusalem. Exile of Judah begins. (587)

HOSEA (755)

David unites kingdom, takes Jerusalem as capital. (1000)

FIRST ISAIAH (740)

Cyrus of Persia frees Jews to return to Judah. (538)

MICAH (720)

NAHUM (663)

People of Judah rebuild Temple. (515)

Saul is named first king of Israel. (1020)

ZEPHANIAH (630)

JEREMIAH (626)

ZECHARIAH (520)

HABAKKUK (609)

HAGGAI (520)

EZEKIEL (593)

TIME OF THE KINGS AND PROPHETS

SECOND ISAIAH (540)

UNITED KINGDOM		DIVIDED KINGDOM			PERSIAN DOMINATION
	Jeroboam I (922)	Ahab (869)	Ahaziah (850)	Jeroboam II (786)	Hoshea (732)
avid Solomon	Rehoboam (922)	Ahaziah (842)	Jehoash (837)	Uzziah (783)	Hezekiah (715)	Josiah (640)	Jehoiachin (598)	Zedekiah (597)

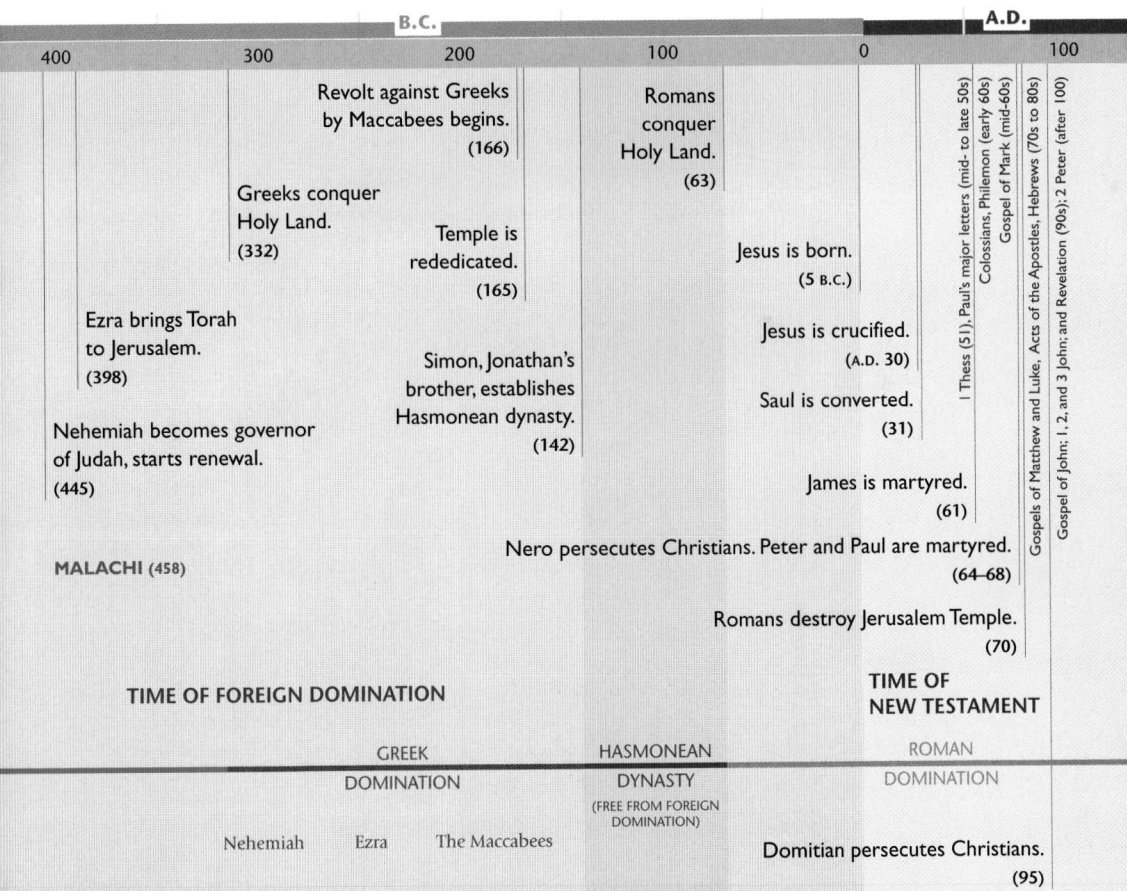

Buddha is born in India.
(563)

Confucius is born in China.
(551)

Greece has golden age.
(400)

Roman Empire is established.
(43 B.C.)

Jesus is crucified in Palestine.
(A.D. 30)

Roman Empire falls.
(476)

Muhammad founds Islam in Arabia.
(622)

Crusades begin.
(1096)

Gutenberg invents printing press.
(1450)

Columbus sails to America.
(1492)

Luther starts Protestant Reformation.
(1517)

Declaration of Independence is signed.
(1776)

Dominion of Canada is created.
(1867)

Personal computers become available.
(1972)

World War II begins.
(1939)

0   1000   2000

A.D.

Timeline of Human History

New Testament Books   **Timeline of Biblical History**

B.C.   A.D.

400   300   200   100   0   100

Revolt against Greeks by Maccabees begins.
(166)

Greeks conquer Holy Land.
(332)

Temple is rededicated.
(165)

Ezra brings Torah to Jerusalem.
(398)

Simon, Jonathan's brother, establishes Hasmonean dynasty.
(142)

Nehemiah becomes governor of Judah, starts renewal.
(445)

MALACHI (458)

Romans conquer Holy Land.
(63)

Jesus is born.
(5 B.C.)

Jesus is crucified.
(A.D. 30)

Saul is converted.
(31)

James is martyred.
(61)

Nero persecutes Christians. Peter and Paul are martyred.
(64–68)

Romans destroy Jerusalem Temple.
(70)

I Thess (51), Paul's major letters (mid- to late 50s)

Colossians, Philemon (early 60s)

Gospel of Mark (mid-60s)

Gospels of Matthew and Luke, Acts of the Apostles, Hebrews (70s to 80s)

Gospel of John; I, 2, and 3 John; and Revelation (90s); 2 Peter (after 100)

TIME OF FOREIGN DOMINATION

TIME OF NEW TESTAMENT

GREEK DOMINATION

HASMONEAN DYNASTY
(FREE FROM FOREIGN DOMINATION)

ROMAN DOMINATION

Nehemiah   Ezra   The Maccabees

Domitian persecutes Christians.
(95)

1809

Noah's Ark

(see Gn 5, 32—9, 28), by the contemporary American artist Laura James. The artist captures the energy of Noah's family as they load the ark with supplies. The Book of Genesis has many stories about families. When has your family worked together to accomplish an important goal?

Moses with the tablets of the law

(see Ex 20, 1–21; 32, 15–20), by the Dutch painter Rembrandt van Rijn, around 1660–69. The tablets always symbolize the Ten Commandments. Do you think images of the tablets should be allowed in public places?

The temptation and fall

(see Gn 3, 1–24), from the ceiling of the Sistine Chapel, in the Vatican, by Michelangelo, 1509–12. Notice how healthy and fit Adam and Eve look before they sin (on the left) and how worn and broken they look after being expelled from the Garden of Eden.

Rachel at the well

(see Gn 29, 1–30), by Harry Mileham, England, 1903. Jacob fell in love with Rachel at the well and served her father for fourteen years in order to marry her. Notice how young they look. What would you do for someone you loved?

Abraham's offering

(see Gn 22, 1–19), by the Dutch painter Jan Lievens, mid-1600s. God had asked Abraham to sacrifice Isaac but stopped him before he harmed Isaac. Abraham is shown rejoicing that Isaac has been spared. Notice that they are both turned toward God.

Joseph sending his brothers back to Jacob

(see Gn 44, 1–34), from a twelfth-century Byzantine manuscript. Joseph was trying to punish his brothers for selling him into slavery, but in the long run, he couldn't do it; he forgave them instead.

Jesus dies on the cross
(see Jn 19, 26–27), by the Bavarian painter
Martin Feuerstein, nineteenth century. Jesus
tells Mary that John is now her son and tells
John that Mary is now his mother. Imagine
the sorrow each must have been feeling.

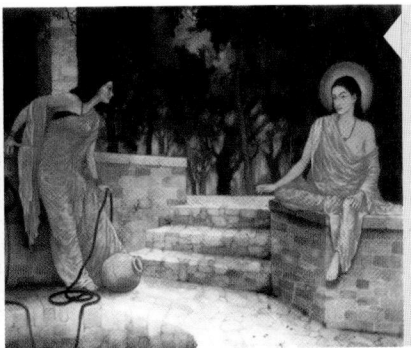

The woman at the well
(see Jn 4, 6–42), by Frank
Wesley, India, late twentieth
century. Jesus shocked
people, perhaps even the
woman herself, by talking to
her. It was improper to
speak with women or with
Samaritans. What kinds of
people do we classify as
improper to speak with
today? Is there a way we can
reach out to them safely?

Pentecost
(see Acts 2, 1–42), from a medieval,
Anglo-Saxon manuscript. The
illumination emphasizes the
tongues of flame, emanating from
the Holy Spirit in the form of a
dove, settling on these founders of
the Church. Notice that the dove
comes from the hand of God the
Father.

Lamentation of the dead Christ
(see Mt 27, 57–61; Mk 15, 42–47; Lk 23,
50–56; Jn 19, 38–42), by the early
Renaissance Italian painter Fra Angelico,
around 1436–40. The various disciples are
caring for the body of Jesus after it had
been removed from the cross. How would
you have reacted to Jesus' death?

Transfiguration
(see Mt 17, 1–13; Mk 9, 2–13; Lk 9,
28–36), by Theopan the Greek,
Pereslav, Russia, late 1300s. The icon
emphasizes the glory of Christ, the
elevated stature of Elijah and
Moses, and the humility of the
Apostles. An icon is a bridge
between the viewer and the reality
of the event depicted.

**Moone cross (detail of one
side of base),**
depicting the Flight into Egypt (see
Mt 2, 13–23) and the Five Loaves
and the Two Fish (see Mt 14,
13–21; Mk 6, 30–44; Lk 9, 10–17; Jn
6, 1–14), from County Kildare,
Ireland, ninth century. These
carvings symbolize the destiny of
Jesus and his saving actions. What
meaningful symbols would be
carved at the base of a cross
today?

Places of the Bible

The **Mount Sinai area** is where Moses received the Law (the Ten Commandments) from God (see Ex 20, 1–21). The people of Israel arrived at Mount Sinai three months after God led them out of slavery in Egypt (see Ex 19, 1–6). Can you imagine traveling by foot with hundreds of other people through country like this?

The **Second Temple** is presented here in a scale model as it would have appeared in Jerusalem at about the year A.D. 20. The Second Temple is where Mary and Joseph found the twelve-year-old Jesus conversing with the teachers (see Lk 2, 41–52) and where Jesus upset the trading of the money changers and the vendors (see Mt 21, 12–17; Mk 11, 15–19; Lk 19, 45–47; Jn 2, 12–25). It was built to replace Solomon's Temple when the people of Israel returned from exile.

A **fishing boat at sunrise on the Sea of Galilee** is a reminder of what Jesus might have seen when Simon and Andrew were casting their nets into the Sea of Galilee and Jesus invited them to follow him (see Mt 4, 18–22; Mk 1, 16–19; Lk 5, 1–11). Perhaps Simon and Andrew could see in Jesus something of the beauty or glory of God. What have you seen that motivates you to follow Jesus?

Jerusalem today is architecturally similar to the Jerusalem of Jesus' time in the arches, the kind of stone used, and the way the city is built into the hill. Jerusalem is a city that is holy to Christians, Jews, and Muslims. Nevertheless, it is a place that people have been fighting over since before the time of King David.

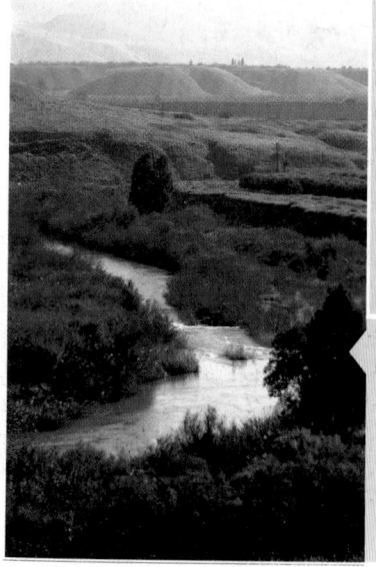

The **Jordan River** in the north as it leaves the Sea of Galilee. The people of Israel crossed the Jordan to finally reach the Promised Land (see Jos 3, 1–18). Jesus was baptized by John in the Jordan River (see Mt 3, 13–17; Mk 1, 9–11; Lk 3, 1–22).

The Mass of Saint Gregory, housed at the Museum of the Jacobins, AUCH, France, created by a school in Mexico City, 1539. Saint Gregory was saying Mass when Jesus appeared to him with all the implements of Jesus' suffering and death (see Mt 26, 47 —27, 31; Mk 14, 43—15, 20; Lk 22, 47—23, 25; Jn 18, 1—19, 6). The artists combined European imagery with Nahuatl pictographic style in this colorful mosaic of feathers.

The Last Supper (see Mt 26, 17–30; Mk 14, 12–25; Lk 22, 7–38; 1 Cor 11, 23–26), by the Venetian Jacopo Bassano, 1542. Bassano sees the Last Supper as a holiday gathering of good friends with only subtle indications of Jesus' divinity. What might the Apostles be talking about?

Resurrection of Lazarus (see Jn 11, 1–44), from the Catacomb of the Giordani, late third century. Jesus' raising Lazarus was an early-Church reminder of Jesus' own Resurrection. Another was the story of Jonah's being swallowed by the big fish and spit out again after three days. What reminders of Jesus' Resurrection do you see in churches today?

Nativity (see Mt 1, 18–25; Lk 2, 1–20), by the contemporary Chinese artist He Qi. The artist combines stories here: the shepherds are from Luke's Gospel, and the gifts of the magi, near where Mary and Jesus are sitting, we learn about in Matthew's Gospel.

Calming the storm (see Mt 8, 23–27; Mk 4, 35–41; Lk 8, 22–25), by the contemporary Malaysian artist Hanna Cheriyan Varghese. The artist reflects both the humanity of the Apostles and the divinity of Jesus. Imagine being on that boat.

Jesus prays in the Garden of Gethsemane (see Mt 26, 36–46; Mk 14, 32–42; Lk 22, 39–46), from the Mafa Life of Jesus series, late twentieth century. This painting reflects the West-African vision of a garden. Notice how rocky it is and how short the trees are. How do you envision the Garden of Gethsemane?

Alphabetical List of Bible Books and Abbreviations

Book	Abbreviation	Page	Book	Abbreviation	Page
Acts	Acts	1426	1 Kings	1 Kgs	358
Amos	Am	1138	2 Kings	2 Kgs	388
Baruch	Bar	1039	Lamentations	Lam	1029
1 Chronicles	1 Chr	416	Leviticus	Lv	120
2 Chronicles	2 Chr	445	Luke	Lk	1315
Colossians	Col	1583	1 Maccabees	1 Mc	552
1 Corinthians	1 Cor	1503	2 Maccabees	2 Mc	583
2 Corinthians	2 Cor	1532	Malachi	Mal	1195
Daniel	Dn	1097	Mark	Mk	1280
Deuteronomy	Dt	195	Matthew	Mt	1210
Ecclesiastes	Eccl	788	Micah	Mi	1156
Ephesians	Eph	1564	Nahum	Na	1164
Esther	Est	539	Nehemiah	Neh	490
Exodus	Ex	69	Numbers	Nm	153
Ezekiel	Ez	1048	Obadiah	Ob	1148
Ezra	Ezr	478	1 Peter	1 Pt	1651
Galatians	Gal	1553	2 Peter	2 Pt	1660
Genesis	Gn	4	Philemon	Phlm	1621
Habakkuk	Hb	1169	Philippians	Phil	1575
Haggai	Hg	1179	Proverbs	Prv	750
Hebrews	Heb	1624	Psalms	Ps(s)	644
Hosea	Hos	1119	Revelation	Rv	1681
Isaiah	Is	892	Romans	Rom	1476
James	Jas	1643	Ruth	Ru	290
Jeremiah	Jer	963	1 Samuel	1 Sm	296
Job	Jb	610	2 Samuel	2 Sm	330
Joel	Jl	1132	Sirach	Sir	836
1 John	1 Jn	1666	Song of Songs	Song	801
2 John	2 Jn	1674	1 Thessalonians	1 Thes	1590
3 John	3 Jn	1676	2 Thessalonians	2 Thes	1598
John	Jn	1376	1 Timothy	1 Tm	1603
Jonah	Jon	1151	2 Timothy	2 Tm	1611
Joshua	Jos	240	Titus	Ti	1617
Jude	Jude	1678	Tobit	Tb	506
Judges	Jgs	265	Wisdom	Wis	811
Judith	Jdt	523	Zechariah	Zec	1183
			Zephaniah	Zep	1174

All scripture is inspired by God and is useful for teaching, for refutation, for correction, and for training in righteousness, so that one who belongs to God may be competent, equipped for every good work.

(2 Tm 3, 16–17)